MARTINDALE-HUBBELL® LAW DIRECTORY

VOLUME 4

CONNECTICUT, DELAWARE
DISTRICT OF COLUMBIA
U.S. GOVERNMENT LAWYERS
LAW SCHOOLS

Martindale-Hubbell®
A Member of the LexisNexis Group

121 Chanlon Road, New Providence, NJ 07974 • Phone: 1-800-526-4902
Email: info@martindale.com • www.martindale.com • www.lawyers.com

Published by Martindale-Hubbell®, A Member of the LexisNexis™ Group

International Standard Book Number: 1-56160-491-7 (Set)

Printed and bound in the United States of America
by R.R. Donnelley & Sons Company
Chicago, Illinois and Willard, Ohio

ISBN 1-56160-491-7

9 781561 604913

IMPORTANT NOTICES

Martindale-Hubbell® has used its best efforts in collecting and preparing material for inclusion in the **Martindale-Hubbell Law Directory** but cannot warrant that the information herein is complete or accurate, and does not assume, and hereby disclaims, any liability to any person for any loss or damage caused by errors or omissions in the **Martindale-Hubbell Law Directory** whether such errors or omissions result from negligence, accident or any other cause.

Lawyers providing information regarding themselves and their law firms for inclusion in the **Martindale-Hubbell Law Directory** are responsible for both the accuracy of the information submitted and compliance with local law and bar regulations.

Some lawyers and law firms are omitted from the **Martindale-Hubbell Law Directory** by request while others are omitted because adequate information is not available.

The Martindale-Hubbell Ratings contained in this Directory are intended primarily for the use of lawyers and law firms in the practice of their profession. They may not be used in any advertisement or for any commercial, political or other purpose. Ratings may be referenced in printed lawyer-to-lawyer communications (such as law firm brochures), professional announcements, and legal directories targeted to lawyers and law firms. For more information on requirements for acknowledgements, please see Guidelines for Using Your Martindale-Hubbell Rating on page XVI, or visit www.martindale.com/ratings.

Omission of individual lawyer ratings should not be construed as unfavorable since Martindale-Hubbell does not undertake to develop ratings for every lawyer. In addition, certain lawyers have requested their ratings not be published while in other instances, definitive information has yet to be developed.

FOREWORD

We are pleased to present the 2002 edition of the **Martindale-Hubbell® Law Directory**, the world's leading guide to the legal profession.

This multi-volume reference is the only resource to include virtually every lawyer and law firm in the U.S. as well as extensive coverage of international lawyers and firms. It now contains more than one million lawyers and firms in 160 countries.

These print volumes are just one component of the Martindale-Hubbell Legal Network, a multimedia legal research and networking tool. Users who prefer the speed and flexibility of electronic searching can also access the **Law Directory** via the *Martindale-Hubbell Lawyer Locator* at *martindale.com*, on CD-ROM, and online through LexisNexis™.

Over the past year, we have taken advantage of technological developments to extend and improve our services. Last winter, we launched a new version of *martindale.com* — our Web site for the professional market — featuring improved navigation and search functionality as well as new content, including the *Dispute Resolution Directory* at *adr.martindale.com*. In addition, free online access to the **Martindale-Hubbell Law Digest** has been made available to our subscribers.

We have also created an extensive network of strategic alliance partners to increase the marketing reach of lawyers and firms represented in our database. Leading Web sites such as CNN.com, CNNfn.com and Vault.com now offer prominent access to *martindale.com*. And a new software application allows users of handheld devices including Palm VII or VIIx to search the database anywhere, at any time. It is, therefore, no surprise that *martindale.com* is the most frequently used Internet lawyer directory, with over 2.5 million searches a month.

Another major goal has been to enhance our penetration of the consumer market. *Lawyers.com*, Martindale-Hubbell's consumer Web site, is the basis for AOL's Legal Web Center and is accessible through the AOL Interactive Service, CompuServe.com and Netscape.com. Together, these alliances provide an audience of over 52 million visitors each month. *Lawyers.com* has also partnered with Respond.com to offer *Legal Services by Request*, an innovative lead-generation tool that matches lawyers and clients by email.

In addition to *Lawyer HomePages*, which are Web sites for small firms in the U.S., we offer *International Lawyer HomePages* and *Canadian Lawyer HomePages*. For larger law firms, we provide an entire menu of custom Web site design, development and redesign services.

I am excited by the opportunities that lie ahead. I look forward to building on Martindale-Hubbell's legacy of quality and technological innovation and providing new ways to link attorneys with those who need their services.

Carol D. Cooper
Senior Vice President and Publisher

TABLE OF CONTENTS

TABLE OF CONTENTS – *continued*

MARTINDALE-HUBBELL®/LexisNexis™ LEGAL ADVISORY BOARD

The Martindale-Hubbell/LexisNexis Legal Advisory Board was formed to ensure that Martindale-Hubbell and LexisNexis are responsive to the constantly changing needs of the legal profession. The following lawyers selected from the private, corporate and international sectors of the profession comprise the 2001-2002 Board.

MARTHA W. BARNETT of Holland & Knight, Tallahassee, Florida. Ms. Barnett is a former Chair of the House of Delegates of the American Bar Association, the first woman lawyer to be so honored, and has served on the ABA's Board of Governors. Currently, she is the President of the American Bar Association, to serve as such from July 2000 to August 2001.

BENJAMIN R. CIVILETTI of Venable, Baetjer, Howard & Civiletti, Washington, D.C. and Baltimore, Maryland. Mr. Civiletti is a former Attorney General of the United States under President Carter, 1979-1981. He is the former Chairman of the ABA Litigation Section and has been a member of the ABA House of Delegates since 1991. He also serves as the ABA Representative to the United Nations. He is the Chairman of Venable. Mr. Civiletti is a Fellow of the American College of Trial Lawyers and the American Law Institute.

THOMAS R. CURTIN of Graham, Curtin & Sheridan, A Professional Association, Morristown, New Jersey. Mr. Curtin is a Life Fellow of the American Bar Foundation. He is a past President of the Morris County Bar Association (1978-1979), the New Jersey State Bar Foundation (1986-1988), the New Jersey State Bar Association (1993-1994), and the Notre Dame Law Foundation (2000-2001). He is a former Chairman of the New Jersey Commission on Professionalism in the Law (1996-1998). He is a member of the American Bar Association House of Delegates, serving as the New Jersey State Delegate, and the Sports Lawyers Association. He is currently a member of the Notre Dame Law School Advisory Council.

THOMAS G. HEINTZMAN, O.C., Q.C., of McCarthy Tétrault, Toronto, Ontario, is a past President of the Canadian Bar Association (1994-1995). He is a member of the International Bar Association and the past Canadian member of the Council. Mr. Heintzman is a Fellow of the International Academy of Trial Lawyers, and the American College of Trial Lawyers and the past Chair of its Canadian Judiciary Committee. He is an Officer of the Order of Canada.

DOUGLAS B. HENDERSON is the Founding and Senior Partner of Finnegan, Henderson, Farabow, Garrett & Dunner, Washington, D.C. Mr. Henderson is a Member of the Advisory Council of the United States Court of Federal Claims, and a Member of the Board of the Federal Circuit Bar Association. He was formerly Chairman of the Patent Division and Member of Council of the Section of Intellectual Property Law of the American Bar Association. He was the Founder of the Federal Circuit Bar Association, a co-founder of the U.S. Court of Federal Claims Bar Association, and a co-founder of the ITC Trial Lawyers Association.

THOMAS J. KLITGAARD, formerly Senior Vice President and General Counsel of Sega of America, Inc., is now a partner with Dillingham & Murphy, San Francisco. He is a former Chairman of the California State Bar's Committee on the Maintenance of Professional Competence. He is a member of the panel of technology arbitrators of the American Arbitration Association in New York and a member of the Advisory Board of the Southwestern Legal Foundation in Dallas. He is currently the chairman of a graduate business management program in Shanghai, China.

RALPH I. LANCASTER, JR. of Pierce Atwood, Portland, Maine has served as Independent Counsel, In Re Herman, by appointment of the Special Division of the D.C. Court of Appeals. He previously served as Counsel for the United States before the International Court of Justice in a case concerning delimitation of the Maritime Boundary in the Gulf of Maine and as Special Master by appointment of the United States Supreme Court in State of New Jersey vs. State of Nebraska. Mr. Lancaster began his legal career as a law clerk to the Honorable Edward T. Gignoux. He is a Past-President of the Maine State Bar Association and a former member of the House of Delegates of the American Bar Association. He served as Chair of the Standing Committee on Federal Judiciary of the ABA. He is a Fellow of the American College of Trial Lawyers and served as its President, 1989-1990.

JUDY PERRY MARTINEZ of Simon, Peragine, Smith & Redfearn, L.L.P., New Orleans, Louisiana. Ms. Martinez has been on the Board of Directors of the American Judicature Society, (1991-1998) and the Elmo B. Hunter Center for Judicial Excellence, (1994-1997). She is a Lifetime Fellow of the Louisiana Bar Foundation and a Fellow of the American Bar Foundation. She is a Member of the New Orleans, Louisiana State (Chairperson of the Professionalism and Quality of Life Committee, 1992-1993) and American (Member of the Executive Committee, 1998-1999; Board of Governors, 1996-1999; Commission on Women in the Profession, 1991-1994; ABA Nominating Committee, 1993-1996; Chair: Young Lawyers Division, 1990-1991; Chair Commission on Domestic Violence, 1999—; Member: Executive Council, Young Lawyers Division, 1986-1996; Special Advisor, Standing Committee on the Federal Judiciary, 1994-1995; Division Delegate, 1991-1996 and Delegate-at-Large, 1999—, ABA House of Delegates; Young Lawyers Division Liason to the ABA Section of Litigation, 1991-1993); Bar Associations and also the Association for Women Attorneys.

JERALYN E. MERRITT, a sole practitioner from Denver, Colorado, is an author and frequent lecturer on criminal defense. She was selected by Chairman Bill McCollum, House Judiciary Committee, Subcommittee on Crime, to present oral and written congressional testimony on federal marijuana sentencing laws on behalf of the National Association of Criminal Defense Lawyers (NACDL) on March 6, 1996, in Washington, D.C. She served as Chair from 1995-1996 while a judicially appointed member of the Standing Committee on the Criminal Justice Act for the United States District Court for the District of Colorado from 1994-1996. Ms. Merritt is currently a member of the Board of Directors and Chair of the Advisory Board for the National Association of Criminal Defense Lawyers, the Director of the Cyberspace Bar Association and a member of the Board of Governors for the American Board of Criminal Lawyers.

WILLIAM G. PAUL of Crowe & Dunlevy, Oklahoma City, Oklahoma. Mr. Paul is the former Senior Vice President & General Counsel, Phillips Petroleum Company, Bartlesville, Oklahoma. In 1999, he was elected President of the American Bar Association, to serve as such from August 1999 to July 2000. He has served as President of the Oklahoma State Bar Association, President of the National Conference of Bar Presidents, a Member of the American Bar Association, House of Delegates 1975-1999 and is a Fellow in the American College of Trial Lawyers.

FERNANDO POMBO, Founder and Senior Partner of Gomez-Acebo & Pombo, Madrid, Spain, has contributed to and authored several publications in the field of international business law. Currently, he is the International Bar Association Chairman of SLP. Mr. Pombo has been a visiting professor at the Institute on International Legal Studies in Salzburg, Austria since 1985. He is also a former President of LES International and a member of the Spanish Arbitration Court. He is fluent in Spanish, English, French and German.

WM. REECE SMITH, JR. of Tampa, Florida, is the senior member of Carlton, Fields, Ward, Emmanuel, Smith & Cutler, P.A. A Rhodes Scholar at Oxford University, England, he was later President of The Florida Bar (1972-73), the American Bar Association (1980-81), and the International Bar Association (1988-90). He is a Fellow of the American College of Trial Lawyers and the International Academy of Trial Lawyers and serves on the Council of the American Law Institute. He received the American Bar Association's Gold Medal for "exceptionally distinguished service to the cause of American Jurisprudence."

STEVEN T. WALTHER of Walther, Key, Maupin, Oats, Cox & LeGoy of Reno, Nevada, is a Trustee of The National Judicial College, President of the Boalt Hall Alumni Association, University of California, Berkeley, Secretary of The Fellows of the American Bar Foundation, and a member of the Executive Board of the ABA Central and East European Law Initiative. Mr. Walther previously served as a member of the Board of Governors of the ABA, President of the State Bar of Nevada, Chair of the Board of Trustees of The Nevada Law Foundation, Chair of the ABA Standing Committee on World Order Under Law, and Chair of the ABA Section on International Activities. Mr. Walther has also served as the ABA representative to the United Nations. Mr. Walther has a degree in Russian and has lectured extensively on rule of law, international and human rights issues, both in the United States and Russia.

WALTER H. WHITE, JR. is a Partner of Bryan Cave L.L.P. in London, England. Mr. White previously has served as a Partner of Steptoe & Johnson L.L.P. in Washington, D.C. and as the Managing Director of its Moscow office. Mr. White is a former Commissioner of Securities for the State of Wisconsin 1988-1991. He has served as a member of the ABA House of Delegates, as the Chair of the Section of Individual Rights and Responsibilities and as chair of the Young Lawyers Division. Mr. White has also been a member of the State Bar of Wisconsin Board of Governors, on the Board of the Milwaukee Foundation and is currently a Board member of the Central-Asian-American Enterprise Fund by appointment of former President Clinton.

USER'S GUIDE

The **Martindale-Hubbell® Law Directory** now consists of:

- seventeen numbered U.S. volumes (burgundy spine accent). Each volume consists of three main sections, which have been separated for easy access: Practice Profiles on blue pages, Professional Biographies on white pages and Services, Suppliers, Consultants on white pages following the divider tab. Included in Volume 4 are Law School listings. In each Section, headings are provided at the top of each page to indicate the section being referenced and to provide a guide to the listings on that page.
- one volume containing listings for Corporate Law Departments and the American Corporate Counsel Association (burgundy spine accent).
- two volumes of the **Martindale-Hubbell International Law Directory** (blue spine accent), containing listings for lawyers and firms in over 160 countries (including sections for Canada and U.S. lawyers with international interests).
- two volumes of the **Martindale-Hubbell Law Digest** for the U.S. (black spine accent).
- one **Martindale-Hubbell International Law Digest** (black spine accent).

Guam, Puerto Rico, U.S. Pacific Territories and the Virgin Islands can be found both at the end of the U.S. volumes (Volume 17) and in the appropriate sections of the **Martindale-Hubbell International Law Directory** (see Table of Contents).

EXPLANATORY NOTES AND SYMBOLS

Dates following a name, i.e., "'31 '57," indicate the year of birth and the year of first admission to the Bar.

"C." or "L." followed by a numeral indicates the college or law school attended; first degree, if known, is shown following the number. See Index of Colleges, Universities and Law Schools in prefatory section.

Individual alphabetical listings, which are published without charge or other obligation, include lawyers admitted and located at a particular place, as well as others who are not admitted to the Bar of that jurisdiction. In the case of the latter, nonadmission is shown, as is the state of first admission. *It is always possible that a lawyer has been admitted subsequent to the insertion of a listing.* Confirmation of individual state admission can be obtained by writing the admitting authority of the jurisdiction or the lawyer.

"*" following the name of a place in the United States or Canada indicates a county seat. *Population* figures following the name of the place are the most recent available.

"[Lobe,B.&R.]" indicates a lawyer is in the primary firm management of Lobe, Bryant & Rogers; such as member, partner, managing partner, principal, shareholder, senior partner, marketing partner, hiring partner or director; or is an employee of an office operating as a legal professional association, company, corporation or other legal entity, unless otherwise disclosed.

"[🄰 Hane,M.&H.]" indicates a lawyer is employed as a junior partner, senior attorney, senior associate or similar position by the office shown.

"[🄲 Shipley&S.]" indicates a lawyer has the relationship of Counsel or Of Counsel, senior or special counsel with the office shown.

"[🅂 Snell,S.C.&B.]" indicates a lawyer is employed as a staff or contract attorney by the office shown.

"***PRACTICE AREAS***" appearing near the end of a lawyer's professional biography indicates the area(s) of practice to which he or she devotes a significant portion of professional time. In each case, the information has been supplied by the attorney and constitutes a "representation" by the lawyer and does not imply official approval or certification by any state authority.

All "officially recognized" specialties are indicated with language that identifies the approving or certifying authority. Such programs are now in existence in Arizona, Arkansas, California, Florida, Idaho, Louisiana, Minnesota, New Jersey, New Mexico, North Carolina, Ohio, South Carolina, Tennessee, Texas and Ontario, Canada.

Title of public office, company name, government agency, educational institution, etc., with which a lawyer is connected is shown in his or her listing.

Professional Companies, Corporations or Associations: Chartered, Associated, P.C., P.A., S.C., Inc., Ltd., etc. following the name of an individual lawyer or law firm means that such office is operating as a Professional Company, Corporation or Association under the laws of that jurisdiction.

"‡" indicates one who devotes all or the greater part of one's time to the affairs of a single client, or is retired, semi-retired or semi-active, or principally engaged in activities other than the practice of law.

"⊙" indicates a lawyer maintains law offices at more than one place.

"★" indicates a lawyer is with the Armed Forces.

"(Pat.)" indicates lawyers who are registered to practice before the U.S. Patent and Trademark Office and who devote a considerable portion of time or duties to Patent, Trademark and other related matters.

"Ⓣ" indicates the rating was established in an admitting jurisdiction other than where the attorney is currently listed.

"BR" indicates a subscriber to the **Martindale-Hubbell® Bar Register of Preeminent Lawyers™**.

SECTION DESCRIPTIONS

PRACTICE PROFILES (BLUE PAGES)

This section contains rosters for the Bars of the United States. Listings of United States Government Lawyers located in Washington, D.C. are grouped by departments, agencies and commissions, etc. and follow the regular listings for that city in Volume 4.

This Section is alphabetically arranged by state, by city or town, and then by name of attorney or law firm. Contact information for state bar associations appears on the first page of each state.

Listings for individual attorneys include the following information, when available: name, rating (if any), year of birth, first year of admission to the Bar, college attended, first degree received, law school attended, first degree received, and where the attorney practices.

A typical individual attorney listing follows:

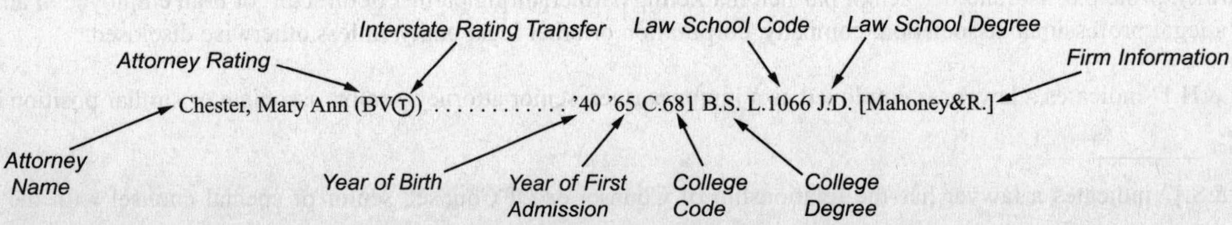

Law firm listings provide name, address and rating information, where available.

A typical law firm listing will appear as follows:

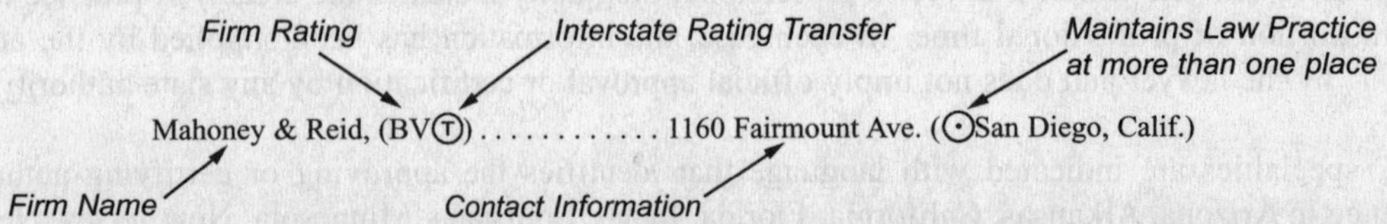

Practice Profiles listings for subscribing attorneys and law firms appear in boldface type and include name, rating (if available), address, firm personnel, statement of practice, representative clients, references, and language proficiency as well as other pertinent information.

USER'S GUIDE: SECTION DESCRIPTIONS — *continued*

Typical Subscriber Full Practice Profiles follow:

Firm Subscriber:

Firm Rating · Interstate Rating Transfer · Bar Register Listing Indicator · Firm Name · Contact Information · Statement of Practice · Clients · Biographical Listing Reference

Letterman & Lewis, (AV㊉) BR
713 Shady Lane, 94111⊙
Telephone: 415-555-1313
Email: lawinfo@lettlew.com URL: http://www.lettlew.com
Members of Firm: Michelle J. Letterman; Marvin Lewis;—Edgar Catello.
General Practice, Trials, Banking Estate Planning and Probate Law.
Representative Clients: California Home Security, Inc.; American Flight School, Inc.; West Coast Recycling Co.; American Fire Insurance Corp.
Reference: Pacific National Bank.
Berkeley, California Office: Suite 3500, Johnson Place. Telephone: 510-555-4563.

See Professional Biographies, SAN FRANCISCO, CALIFORNIA

Firm — members, associates, etc.:

Year of First Admission · College Degree · Attorney Rating · Year of Birth · College Code · Law School Code · Attorney Name · Number of Cases · Law School Degree · Firm Information

Bershad, Abe M., (AV) . . . . '35 '60 C.681 B.S. L.1066 J.D. [Davis&J.]
*PRACTICE AREAS: Insurance Law (68).

Individual subscriber:

Year of First Admission · College Degree · College Code · Attorney Rating · Law School Code · Year of Birth · Law School Degree · Attorney Name · Bar Register Indicator · Contact Information · Additional Firm Information · Biographical Listing Reference · Number of Cases

Schetlick, Robert M., (AV) '41 '65 C.816 B.S. L.705 J.D. BR
Suite 3500, Johnson Place, 07974⊙
Telephone: 908-555-4563 FAX: 908-555-4972
Email: schetlick@netadd.com URL: http://netadd.com/schetlick
(Also Of Counsel to Aiello & Smertick)
***PRACTICE AREAS: Insurance Law (125).**
Representative Client: East Coast Recycling Corp.
Approved Attorney For: SMAD Title Insurance Co.
Summit, New Jersey Office: 713 Shady Lane. Telephone: 908-555-1313.

See Professional Biographies, FLANDERS, NEW JERSEY

PATENT AND TRADEMARK PRACTICE PROFILES (BLUE PAGES)

This Section contains the names of subscribing lawyers registered to practice Patent Law and those who practice Trademark Law before the United States Patent and Trademark Office and who devote a considerable portion of their practice or duties to this field of law. It is arranged in the same manner as the Practice Profiles Section.

PROFESSIONAL BIOGRAPHIES (WHITE PAGES)

The Professional Biographies Section is arranged alphabetically by state, by city or town, and then by name of attorney or law firm. It provides substantial biographical information on individual attorneys within law firms. Entries in this section include the firm name, contact information, statement of practice, firm profile, individual biographical information, representative clients and references.

A typical entry appears as follows:

Firm Name
Firm Descriptor
Year Established
Formerly
Contact Information

LETTERMAN & LEWIS
A Partnership including A Professional Corporation
Established in 1990
Formerly Letterman and Rosta
731 SHADY LANE
SAN FRANCISCO, CALIFORNIA 94111
Telephone: 415-555-1313
FAX: 415-555-7351
Email: lawinfo@lettlew.com
URL: http://www.lettlew.com

Branch Office Information

Berkeley, California Office: Suite 3500, 110 Johnson Place. Telephone: 510-555-4563. Fax: 510-555-4972.

Statement of Practice

General Practice, Trials, Banking, Finance, Wills, Trusts, Estate Planning and Probate Law.

Firm Profile

FIRM PROFILE: Letterman & Lewis was founded in 1990. The firm encourages continuing professional development and all partners and associates participate in continuing legal education seminars, professional association activities and civic affairs.

Firm Associations

*LAW FIRM ALLIANCES/ASSOCIATIONS: **AmeriLaw:** Founded in 1981, AmeriLaw is an ever-expanding network of independent law firms organized to assist and support its firms in the development and improvement of their practices through a variety of programs so they can better serve their clients.*

MEMBERS OF FIRM

Individual Biographical Information
Military

MICHELLE J. LETTERMAN, (P.C.), born Summit, New Jersey, January 14, 1939; admitted to bar 1968, California. *Education:* United States Naval Academy (B.S., 1960); Harvard University (J.D., summa cum laude, 1968). Private Pilots License, 1960. *Member:* State Bar of California. [Lt., U.S. Navy, 1961-1964]. ***PRACTICE AREAS:*** Banking Law; Finance; Wills and Trusts. ***Email:*** mjletter@lettlew.com

Number of Cases

MARVIN LEWIS, born Jeanette, Pennsylvania, October 7, 1940; admitted to bar, 1965, California. *Education:* University of California at Berkeley (B.A., summa cum laude, 1962); Hastings College of the Law, University of California (J.D., summa cum laude, 1965). *Member:* State Bar of California. (Also Of Counsel, Rudy & Catello). ***LANGUAGES:*** Spanish and French. ***SPECIAL AGENCIES:*** Goodman Zoning Board. ***REPORTED CASES:*** Bilko Inc. v. Zotser Trucking Co. ***TRANSACTIONS:*** Aiello Packing merger with Alboum Paper Products. ***PRACTICE AREAS:*** Estate Planning Law (78); Probate Law. ***Email:*** mlewis@lettlew.com

Associate Indicator

Pending Admission Indicator
Individual Email Address

EDGAR CATELLO, born San Mateo, California, January 11, 1972; (admission pending). *Education:* Radcliffe College (B.S., cum laude, 1994); Boalt Hall School of Law, University of California (J.D. summa cum laude, 1998). ***Email:*** ecatello@lettlew.com

LEGAL SUPPORT PERSONNEL

KATHLEEN VEGA, born Summit, New Jersey, August 22, 1962. *Education:* Rutgers University (B.A., 1984). Certified Paralegal, New Jersey, 1984. *Member:* National Association of Paralegals. (Paralegal). ***PRACTICE AREAS:*** Estates.

Clients

REPRESENTATIVE CLIENTS: California Home Security, Inc.; American Flight School, Inc.; West Coast Recycling Co.; American Fire Insurance Corp.
REFERENCE: Pacific National Bank.

AMERICAN CORPORATE COUNSEL ASSOCIATION (WHITE PAGES)

The American Corporate Counsel Association Section is presented in the **Corporate Law Directory™**. This Section is divided into five segments which include the Description and Policy Statements, Index of Advertisers, Local Chapter Index, National Committee Index, and Member Company Index. The membership roster is included in the Corporate Practice Profiles Section.

CORPORATE LAW DEPARTMENTS (WHITE PAGES)

Corporate Law Department representations reside in the **Corporate Law Directory**. They are arranged alphabetically by name and present information about corporations and corporate attorneys. Typical information supplied includes name, company profile, office location(s) and type of business.

LAW SCHOOLS (WHITE PAGES)

The Law School Section, in Volume 4, profiles the academic programs, special course offerings and teaching staff of participating schools. Non-participating schools are also identified.

For each school, the data may include: school name, address, telephone and fax numbers; a substantial profile including ABA approval information, history, academic character, resources, special programs and activities of the institution; the names, titles and direct dial numbers of key contacts; and a roster of full-time faculty with biographical summary information. This Section is arranged alphabetically by law school name.

School Name → ***JOHN A. JAMES SCHOOL OF LAW***

Contact Information →

214 HOYT AVENUE
HONOLULU, HAWAII 98621
Telephone: (808) 555-9038
Fax: (808) 555-0983
Email: law@jaj.edu
URL: http://www.jaj.law.edu

ABA Approval Information → **ABA Approved Since 1994**

School Profile → The John A. James School of Law is a privately funded institution with a highly diversified student body, representing over 40 countries. Founded in 1988, it quickly achieved a reputation as one of the top universities specializing in the area of environmental law. With close connections to several firms on the North American and Asian continents, the School of Law provides its students with the opportunity to experience law as practiced on both sides of the Pacific. Sixty full-time faculty members represent 35 law schools across the globe; holding a total of 40 advanced degrees in law and 18 Ph.D. degrees.

Key Contacts →

Dean: John Posta (808) 555-5649
Admissions Officer: Tracey Hutchinson (808) 555-6218
Director of Library Services: Robert Berry (808) 555-6214
Placement Officer: Harriett Ko (808) 555-8281

FULL TIME FACULTY

Faculty Sketch → ***ARTHUR JAMES***, born Newark, New Jersey, June 30, 1957; admitted to bar 1982, New Jersey. Education: Drew University (B.A., 1978; M.A. 1984); Harvard University (J.D., 1982); Yale University (LL.M., 1985; J.S.D. 1989). Professor and a Director of the Environmental Law Center. *Courses:* Environmental Liability, Water Rights, Torts.

STATE BAR ASSOCIATION PROFILES

State Bar Association Profiles can now be found at *www.martindale.com*. These profiles include a bar profile, mission statements of the association, names of officers, directors, and key staff personnel, as well as membership and program information.

SERVICES, SUPPLIERS, CONSULTANTS (WHITE PAGES)

Services, Suppliers, Consultants provides information on businesses and professionals serving the legal community. This Section is arranged alphabetically by state, city or town, category of service provided, and company name. Typical information in the company listing includes contact information, company profile, office locations and services provided.

USER AIDS

In the front matter, sections are provided to aid in the use of the Directory. "Explanatory Notes and Symbols," found on page IX, provides a guide to the various symbols and notations which are utilized in the individual entries. The "Index of Colleges, Universities, and Law Schools," found on page XVII, provides a comprehensive guide to numeric codes which are used in Practice Profiles listings to indicate academic institutions and law schools attended by individual attorneys.

Page numbers in the 2002 **Martindale-Hubbell® Law Directory** are constructed in the format XXYYYZ, where XX is the state, province or international grouping, YYY is a consecutive page numbering, and Z is a code denoting section.

Pages listing attorneys under the U.S. Government use the abbreviation "GV", and the Law School Section uses the abbreviation "LS". For International Volumes, the following group abbreviations are used:

EU	Europe	NA	North America
AS	Asia	CB	The Caribbean
AU	Australasia	CS	Central & South America
AF	Middle East & Africa		

Z may be one of the following:

P	Practice Profiles	S	Services, Suppliers, Consultants
B	Professional Biographies		
T	Patent & Trademark		

For additional help or explanation, please call Martindale-Hubbell Customer Service at 1-800-526-4902, or in New Jersey at 908-464-6800.

MARTINDALE-HUBBELL℠ RATINGS

The first Martindale books were published in 1868, the principal one being *Martindale's United States Law Directory* and later *Martindale's American Law Directory*.

In 1930, the publishing rights to *Hubbell's Legal Directory* were purchased by the Martindale Company and ever since has been known as the **Martindale-Hubbell® Law Directory**.

Legal Ability and General Ethical Standards Ratings have appeared in the Directory for over 100 years. Martindale-Hubbell strives to publish fair and accurate ratings for as many lawyers as possible, subscribers and non-subscribers alike. While the vast majority of rating reviews are initiated by the Company, an inquiry will be undertaken upon request. When forwarding legal matters, lawyers in private practice and in corporate law departments rely with confidence on the accuracy of the ratings published.

Legal Ability Ratings are: "C" (from Good to High), "B" (from High to Very High), "A" (from Very High to Preeminent).

General Ethical Standards Rating is: "V" (Very High).

Unless a rating is established in both categories, no rating will be published.

Over 115,000 rating reviews are undertaken each year. Of those, approximately 80% are done at our own initiative. An additional 20% are conducted by request and through the efforts of our Field Staff.

Martindale-Hubbell develops its ratings for individual lawyers by soliciting confidential opinions from members of the Bar, including those who themselves have ratings and those who do not. In addition, members of the Judiciary are queried. We encourage all lawyers to participate in the process. Greater participation assures the continued accuracy of the system. Respondents to written questionnaires and personal interviews are asked to base their opinions on the following:

LEGAL ABILITY RATING

Based on the standard of ability for the area where the lawyer practices, it takes into consideration experience, nature of practice and qualifications relevant to the profession. Where a lawyer's practice is limited or specialized, rating opinions are made on the basis of performance in those Fields of Law. There are no minimum periods of time in practice required for any rating.

GENERAL ETHICAL STANDARDS RATING

Embraces faithful adherence to professional standards of conduct and ethics of the legal profession, professional reliability and diligence, and standards relevant to the attorney's discharge of his or her professional responsibilities.

Legal Ability and General Ethical Standards Ratings appearing in the Directory reflect strictly confidential opinions and responses to professionally developed surveys and adhere to meticulously monitored research principles and practices. Martindale-Hubbell does not make any independent evaluation of lawyers, depending exclusively upon the opinions expressed by its confidential sources.

FIRM RATING

Generally, a law firm will be accorded the rating of its highest-rated principal.

In some instances, lawyers may be asked to submit names of lawyers and judges with whom they have had professional experience. Inquiries are then directed to those sources in addition to sources developed by Martindale-Hubbell.

Field Representatives of Martindale-Hubbell visit tens of thousands of law offices on an annual basis. They make oral rating inquiries during these calls and submit written reports. However, a formal rating review must occur before any rating is established, advanced, lowered or withdrawn.

Martindale-Hubbell does not undertake developing ratings for every listed lawyer. The absence of a rating should not be construed as unfavorable since some lawyers have requested their ratings not be published while in other instances definitive information has not yet been completely developed.

MARTINDALE-HUBBELL℠ RATINGS —*continued*

Ratings are produced for lawyers in the United States, the U.S. Virgin Islands, Northern Mariana Islands and Canada.

No subscription or listing in the **Martindale-Hubbell® Law Directory** is ever solicited or accepted on the promise of publication of a particular rating. No preferential consideration is ever given to any lawyer or law firm.

As a general rule, ratings are transferable within state boundaries. Ratings may be transferred inter-state/inter-province, with the Ⓣ symbol indicating the rating was established in another jurisdiction.

It is our policy to conduct regular periodic reviews of all ratings to insure their accuracy. Where supporting opinions dictate, appropriate action (such as deleting, raising or lowering a rating) is taken.

There is never any payment made to lawyers and judges who participate in rating reviews. The process is a cooperative service to the Bar. It has always been Martindale-Hubbell policy to treat all phases of the rating review process as absolutely confidential. Sources contacted participate with that understanding, and under no circumstances will any review materials ever be released.

Guidelines for Using Your Martindale-Hubbell Rating

Ratings are intended primarily for the use of lawyers in the practice of their profession and not for the general public. You may reference your Martindale-Hubbell rating in printed lawyer-to-lawyer communications (such as law firm brochures), professional announcements, and legal directories targeted to lawyers and law firms. Listed below are the requirements for each type of communication.

- ***For printed lawyer-to-lawyer communications:***
  Include the following:
  "CV, BV and AV are registered certification marks of Reed Elsevier Properties Inc., used in accordance with the Martindale-Hubbell certification procedure standards and policies."

- ***For printed professional announcements:***
  Include the certification mark reference above AND the following explanation:
  "Martindale-Hubbell is the facilitator of a peer review process that rates lawyers. Ratings reflect the confidential opinions of members of the Bar and the Judiciary. MARTINDALE-HUBBELL℠ ratings fall into two categories – legal ability and general ethical standards.

  Legal Ability Ratings are:

  C – *Good to High*
  B – *High to Very High*
  A – *Very High to Preeminent*

  There is one general ethical standard rating – "V" or "very high." An attorney will not receive a Legal Ability Rating unless he or she has been endorsed for a "V." Only when both ratings are confirmed will an attorney receive a rating."

- ***For legal directories targeted to lawyers and law firms:***
  You must receive prior written consent from the Martindale-Hubbell Rating Department AND abide by the following policies:
  Print and CD-ROM based legal directories must include the certification mark reference and the rating explanation described above.
  Web-based legal directories targeted at lawyers and law firms must have a link to Martindale-Hubbell's Web site page (http://www.martindale.com/company/ratings.html) which includes the approved reference and explanation.

You may not use your Martindale-Hubbell rating in print, CD-ROM, or Web-based directories targeted in whole or in part to those other than lawyers and law firms, radio or television commercials, political advertisements or promotions, outdoor advertisements (billboards, buses, benches, etc.), newspaper or yellow page advertisements, law firm Web sites, Martindale-Hubbell Lawyer HomePages or Internet banner ads.

If you'd like to publish your rating in any other format not mentioned here, prior written consent from the Martindale-Hubbell Rating Department and adherence to specific guidelines are required. You may use the following email address to request permission: cdoscher@martindale.com.

Note: Please review Important Notices located on page III.

Index of Colleges, Universities and Law Schools

This list is a guide to the numeric school codes found in Practice Profiles Section entries. Institutions which no longer exist, junior colleges, correspondence schools or colleges with very small enrollments are not included. Such unlisted schools are indicated by the numeric code "999".

01. Acadia University
Wolfville, NS

02. Alberta, University of
Edmonton, AB

03. Bishop's University
Lennoxville, QU

04. British Columbia, Law Society of
Vancouver, BC

05. British Columbia, University of
Vancouver, BC

06. Dalhousie University
Halifax, NS

07. King's College, University of
Halifax, NS

08. Laval University
Quebec, QU

09. Concordia University
Formerly Loyola College
Montreal, QU

010. MacDonald College
Ste. A. de Bellevue, QU

011. Manitoba, University of
Winnipeg, MB

012. McGill University
Montreal, QU

013. McMaster University
Hamilton, ON

014. Montreal, University of
Montreal, QU

015. Mount Allison University
Sackville, NB

016. New Brunswick, University of
Fredericton, NB

017. Nova Scotia College of Agriculture
Truro, NS

018. Ottawa, University of
Ottawa, ON

019. Queen's University
Kingston, ON

020. St. Dunstan's University
Charlottetown, PE

021. St. Francis Xavier University
Antigonish, NS

022. St. Joseph's University
St. Joseph, NB

023. Ste. Marie, College of
Montreal, QU

024. Saskatchewan, University of
Saskatoon, SK

025. Toronto, University of
Toronto, ON

026. Upper Canada, Law Society of
Toronto, ON

027. Victoria University
Toronto, ON

028. Western Ontario, University of
London, ON

029. Osgoode Hall
Toronto, ON

030. Assumption University
Windsor, ON

031. Windsor, University of
Windsor, ON

032. Royal Military College
Kingston, ON

033. Wilfrid Laurier University
Formerly Waterloo Lutheran University
Waterloo, ON

034. Carleton University
Ottawa, ON

035. York University
Toronto, ON

036. Memorial University of Newfoundland
St. John's, NF

037. Calgary, University of
Calgary, AB

038. Waterloo, University of
Formerly Waterloo University
Waterloo, ON

039. Victoria, University of
Victoria, BC

040. Guelph, University of
Guelph, ON

041. Concordia University
Formerly (Sir) George Williams University
Montreal, QU

042. St. Marys University
Halifax, NS

043. Simon Fraser University
Burnaby, BC

044. Lethbridge, University of
Lethbridge, AB

045. Winnipeg, University of
Winnipeg, MB

046. Moncton, University of
Moncton, NB

047. St. Thomas University
Fredericton, NB

048. Regina, University of
Regina, SK

049. Brandon University
Brandon, MB

050. Cambridge University
Cambridge, England

051. Oxford University
Oxford, England

052. Heidelberg University
Baden, Germany

054. London, University of
London, England

055. Paris, University of
Formerly Sorbonne University
Paris, France

056. Rome, University of
Rome, Italy

057. Vienna, University of
Vienna, Austria

058. Trinity College, University of Dublin
Dublin, Ireland

059. Edinburgh University
Edinburgh, Scotland

060. Munich, University of
Munich, Germany

062. National University of Ireland, Dublin
Dublin, Ireland

063. Royal Military Academy
Sandhurst, England

064. Santo Thomas, University of
Manila, Philippines

065. Durham, University of
Durham, England

066. Manuel L. Quezon University
Manila, Philippines

067. Stockholm, University of
Stockholm, Sweden

068. Queen's University, The
Belfast, Northern Ireland

080. Lakehead University
Thunder Bay, ON

081. Brock University
St. Catharines, ON

082. Prince Edward Island, University of
Charlottetown, PE

083. Laurentian University of Sudbury
Sudbury, ON

084. Trent University
Peterborough, ON

085. Quebec, University of
Sainte Foy, Montreal, Trois-Rivieres, Chicoutimi, Hull and Rimouski, QU

086. Sherbrooke, University of
Sherbrooke, QU

087. Quebec Bar Law School
Montreal, QU

1. Abilene Christian University
Abilene, TX

2. Academy of the New Church
Bryn Athyn, PA

3. Adams State College
Alamosa, CO

4. Adelphi University
Garden City, NY

5. Adrian College
Adrian, MI

6. Agnes Scott College
Decatur, GA

7. Akron University Law School
Akron, OH

8. Akron, University of
Formerly Buchtel College
Akron, OH

9. Montevallo University
Formerly Alabama College
Montevallo, AL

10. Auburn University
Formerly Alabama Polytechnic Institute
Auburn and Montgomery, AL

11. North Alabama, University of
Formerly Alabama State Teachers College
Florence, AL

12. Jacksonville State University
Formerly Alabama State Teachers College
Jacksonville, AL

13. West Alabama, The University of
Formerly Livingston University
Livingston, AL

14. Alabama State University
Formerly Montgomery State College
Montgomery, AL

15. Troy State University
Formerly Alabama State Teachers College
Troy, AL

16. Alabama, University of
Birmingham, Huntsville and Tuscaloosa, AL

17. Alaska, University of
Fairbanks, Anchorage and Juneau, AK

18. Albany College
Portland, OR

19. Albertus Magnus College
New Haven, CT

20. Albion College
Albion, MI

21. Albright College
Reading, PA

22. Alcorn A. & M. College
Alcorn, MS

127. Catholic University of America
Formerly Catholic Sisters College
Washington, DC
See Also No. 128
128. Catholic University of America
Washington, DC
129. Cedar Crest College
Allentown, PA
130. Cedarville College
Cedarville, OH
131. Centenary College
Shreveport, LA
132. Central College
Pella, IA
133. Central Methodist College
Formerly Central College
Fayette, MO
134. Central Missouri State University
Formerly Missouri State University
Warrensburg, MO
135. Canterbury College
Formerly Central Normal College
Danville, IN
136. Central Michigan University
Mount Pleasant, MI
137. Central Y.M.C.A. College
Chicago, IL
138. Centre College of Kentucky
Danville, KY
139. Chapman College
Orange, CA
140. Charleston, College of
Charleston, SC
141. Charleston Educational Center
Charleston, WV
142. Chattanooga College of Law
Chattanooga, TN
143. Tennessee at Chattanooga, University of
Formerly Chattanooga, University of
Chattanooga, TN
144. Chicago Law School
Formerly Midland University
Chicago, IL
145. Chicago, University of
Chicago, IL
146. Chicago-Kent College of Law, Illinois
Institute of Technology
Chicago, IL
147. California State University, Chico
Formerly Chico State College
Chico, CA
148. Chicora College
Columbia, SC
149. Chowan College
Murfreesboro, NC
150. Cincinnati, University of
Cincinnati, OH
151. Cincinnati Y.M.C.A. Schools
Cincinnati, OH
152. Citadel, The
Charleston, SC
153. Claflin College
Orangeburg, SC
154. Claremont McKenna College
Claremont, CA
155. Clark Atlanta University
Atlanta, GA
156. Clark University
Worcester, MA
157. Clarke College
Dubuque, IA
158. Clarkson University
Formerly Clarkson College of Technology
Potsdam, NY
159. Cleary College
Ypsilanti, MI
160. Clemson University
Clemson, SC
161. Cleveland State University
Cleveland, OH
162. Coe College
Formerly Western College
Cedar Rapids, IA
163. Coker College
Hartsville, SC
164. Colby College
Waterville, ME
165. Colgate University
Hamilton, NY
166. Holy Names College
Formerly College of the Holy Names
Oakland, CA
167. College Misericordia
Dallas, PA
168. College of the Ozarks
Clarksville, AR
169. Pacific, University of the
Formerly College of the Pacific
Stockton, CA
See Also No. 464
170. Colorado College
Colorado Springs, CO
171. Colorado School of Mines
Golden, CO
172. Colorado State University
Formerly Colorado A. & M. College
Fort Collins, CO
173. Northern Colorado, University of
Formerly Colorado State College
Greeley, CO
174. Colorado at Boulder, University of
Boulder, CO
176. Columbia College
Columbia, SC
177. Loras College
Formerly Columbia College of Dubuque
Dubuque, IA
178. Columbia University
New York, NY
179. Capital University
Formerly Columbus College of Law
Columbus, OH
See Also No. 117
180. Columbus School of Law of The Catholic
University of America
Washington, DC
See Also No. 128
181. Concord College
Athens, WV
182. Concordia College
Moorehead, MN
183. Connecticut College
New London, CT
184. Connecticut, University of
Storrs and Hartford, CT
185. Converse College
Spartanburg, SC
186. Cooper Union
New York, NY
187. Cornell College
Mount Vernon, IA
188. Cornell University
Ithaca, NY
189. Cotner College
Lincoln, NE
190. Creighton University
Omaha, NE
191. Culver-Stockton College
Canton, MO
192. Cumberland School of Law of Samford
University
Formerly part of Cumberland University
(now Cumberland College of Tennessee, at
Lebanon, TN)
Birmingham, AL
193. Dakota Wesleyan University
Mitchell, SD
194. Dana College
Blair, NE
195. Daniel Baker College
Brownwood, TX
196. Daniel W. Voorhees Law School
Terre Haute, IN
197. Dartmouth College
Hanover, NH
198. Davidson College
Davidson, NC
199. Davis & Elkins College
Elkins, WV
200. Dayton Law School
Dayton, OH
201. Dayton, University of
Dayton, OH
202. Decorah College for Women
Decorah, IA
203. Defiance College
Defiance, OH
204. Delaware State College
Dover, DE
205. Delaware, University of
Newark, DE
206. Delta State College
Cleveland, MS
207. Denison University
Granville, OH
208. Denver, University of
Denver, CO
209. De Paul University
Chicago, IL
210. DePauw University
Greencastle, IN
211. Des Moines College of Law
Des Moines, IA
212. Wayne University
Formerly Detroit City Law School
Detroit, MI
213. Detroit College of Law at Michigan State
University
Detroit, MI
214. Detroit Institute of Technology
Detroit, MI
215. Detroit Mercy, University of
Formerly University of Detroit
Detroit, MI
216. Dickinson College
Carlisle, PA
217. Dillard University
New Orleans, LA
218. Doane College
Crete, NE
219. Dominican College of San Rafael
San Rafael, CA
220. St. Mary's Dominican College
Formerly Dominican College
New Orleans, LA
221. Drake University
Des Moines, IA
222. Drew University
Formerly Brothers College
Madison, NJ
223. Drexel University
Philadelphia, PA
224. Dropsie University
Philadelphia, PA
225. Drury College
Springfield, MO
226. Dubuque, University of
Dubuque, IA
227. Duchesne College
Omaha, NE
228. Duke University
Durham, NC
229. Duquesne University
Pittsburgh, PA
230. D'Youville College
Buffalo, NY
231. Earlham College
Richmond, IN
232. East Carolina University
Greenville, NC

233. Texas A&M University-Commerce
Formerly East Texas State University
Commerce, TX

234. Eastern Illinois University
Charleston, IL

235. Eastern Kentucky University
Formerly Kentucky Normal College
Richmond, KY

236. Eastern Nazarene College
Quincy, MA

237. Elizabethtown College
Elizabethtown, PA

238. Elmhurst College
Elmhurst, IL

239. Elmira College
Elmira, NY

240. Elon College
Elon College, NC

241. Emerson College
Boston, MA

242. Emmanuel College
Boston, MA

243. Andrews University
Formerly Emmanuel Missionary College
Berrien Springs, MI

244. Emory and Henry College
Emory, VA

245. Emory University School of Law
Formerly Lamar School of Law
Atlanta, GA

246. Emporia, College of
Emporia, KS

247. Erskine College
Due West, SC

248. Eureka College
Eureka, IL

249. Evansville, University of
Evansville, IN

250. Fairmont State College
Fairmont, WV

251. Cleveland State University
Formerly Fenn College
Cleveland, OH
See Also No. 161

252. Ferris State College
Big Rapids, MI

253. Findlay College
Findlay, OH

254. Fisk University
Nashville, TN

255. Fletcher School of Law & Diplomacy
Medford, MA

256. Flora Macdonald College
Red Springs, NC

257. Florida A. & M. University
Tallahassee, FL

258. Florida Southern College
Lakeland, FL

259. Florida State University
Tallahassee, FL

260. Florida, University of
Gainesville, FL

261. Fontbonne College
St. Louis, MO

262. Fordham University
New York, NY

263. Ft. Hays State University
Hays, KS

264. Franklin & Marshall College
Lancaster, PA

265. Franklin College of Indiana
Franklin, IN

266. Franklin University
Columbus, OH

267. California State University, Fresno
Formerly Fresno State College
Fresno, CA

268. Friends University
Wichita, KS

269. Furman University
Greenville, SC

270. Gallaudet College
Washington, DC

271. Geneva College
Beaver Falls, PA

272. George Peabody College for Teachers
Formerly University of Nashville
Nashville, TN

273. George Washington University
Washington, DC

274. George Williams College
Downer's Grove, IL

275. Georgetown College
Georgetown, KY

276. Georgetown University
Washington, DC

277. Georgia Institute of Technology
Atlanta, GA

278. Georgia College
Milledgeville, GA

280. Georgia, University of
Athens, GA

281. Georgian Court College
Lakewood, NJ

282. Gettysburg College
Gettysburg, PA

283. Glenville State College
Glenville, WV

284. Golden Gate University
San Francisco, CA

285. Gonzaga University
Spokane, WA

286. Good Counsel College
White Plains, NY

287. Gooding College
Wesleyan, ID

288. Goshen College
Goshen, IN

289. Goucher College
Towson, MD

290. Greensboro College
Greensboro, NC

291. Greenville College
Greenville, IL

292. Greenville Woman's College
Greenville, SC

293. Grinnell College
Grinnell, IA

294. Grove City College
Grove City, PA

295. Guadelupe College
Seguin, TX

296. Guilford College
Guilford College, NC

297. Gustavus Adolphus College
St. Peter, MN

298. H. Sophie Newcomb Memorial College
New Orleans, LA

299. Hamilton College
Clinton, NY

300. Hamline University
St. Paul, MN

301. Hampden-Sydney College
Hampden-Sydney, VA

302. Hampton University
Hampton, VA

303. Hanover College
Hanover, IN

304. Hardin-Simmons University
Abilene, TX

305. Harding University
Searcy, AR

306. Connecticut School of Law, University of
Formerly Hartford College of Law
Hartford, CT

307. Harris-Stowe State College
St. Louis, MO

308. Hartwick College
Oneonta, NY

309. Harvard University
Cambridge, MA

310. Hastings College
Hastings, NE

311. Haverford College
Haverford, PA

312. Hawaii, University of
Including William S. Richardson School of Law
Honolulu, Hilo and Manoa, HI

313. Heidelberg College
Tiffin, OH

314. Henderson State University
Arkadelphia, AR

315. Hendrix College
Conway, AR

316. High Point College
High Point, NC

317. Hillsdale College
Hillsdale, MI

318. Hiram College
Hiram, OH

319. Hobart and William Smith Colleges
Formerly Hobart College and William Smith College
Geneva, NY
Note: These are two separate schools operating under one name and sharing faculty and facilities.

320. Hollins College
Hollins, VA

321. Holy Cross, College of the
Worcester, MA

322. Hood College
Frederick, MD

323. Hope College
Holland, MI

324. Houghton College
Houghton, NY

325. Texas Southern University
Formerly Houston College
Houston, TX

326. Houston, University of
Including University of Houston Law Center
Houston, TX

327. Samford University
Formerly Howard College
Birmingham, AL

328. Howard Payne University
Brownwood, TX

329. Howard University
Washington, DC

330. Humboldt State University
Arcata, CA

331. Hunter College of the City University of New York
New York, NY

332. Huntingdon College
Montgomery, AL

333. Huntington College
Huntington, IN

334. Huron College
Huron, SD

335. Albertson College of Idaho
Caldwell, ID

336. Idaho, University of
Moscow, ID

337. Illinois College
Jacksonville, IL

338. Illinois State University
Normal, IL

339. Illinois, University of
Urbana-Champaign and Chicago, IL

340. Illinois Wesleyan University
Bloomington, IL

341. Immaculata College
Immaculata, PA

342. Immaculate Heart College
Hollywood, CA

343. Incarnate Word College
San Antonio, TX

344. Indianapolis, University of
Formerly Indiana Central University
Indianapolis, IN

345. Indiana University School of Law - Indianapolis
Indianapolis, IN

346. Indiana State University
Terre Haute, IN

347. Indiana University
Bloomington and Indianapolis, IN
(Also maintains campuses at Kokomo, South Bend, Gary and New Albany, IN, and jointly with Purdue University at Indianapolis and Ft. Wayne, IN)

348. Intermountain Union College
Great Falls, MT

349. Springfield College
Formerly International Y.M.C.A. College
Springfield, MA

350. Iowa State University
Formerly Iowa State College of A. & M. Arts
Ames, IA

351. Northern Iowa, University of
Formerly Iowa State Teachers College
Cedar Falls, IA

352. Iowa, University of
Formerly State University of Iowa
Iowa City, IA

353. Iowa Wesleyan College
Mt. Pleasant, IA

354. Ithaca College
Ithaca, NY

355. Jackson State University
Jackson, MS

356. Mississippi College School of Law
Formerly Jackson School of Law
Jackson and Clinton, MS

357. Millikin University
Formerly James Millikin University
Decatur, IL

358. Jamestown College
Jamestown, ND

360. Jefferson School of Law
Dallas, TX

361. John Brown University
Siloam Springs, AR

362. Stetson University
Formerly John B. Stetson University
De Land and St. Petersburg, FL

363. John Carroll University
Formerly St. Ignatius College
Cleveland, OH

364. Kletzing College
Formerly John Fletcher College
University Park, IA

365. John Marshall Law School
Chicago, IL

366. John Randolph Neal College of Law
Knoxville, TN

367. Johns Hopkins University
Baltimore, MD

368. Johnson Bible College
Kimberlin Heights, TN

369. Johnson C. Smith University
Formerly Biddle University
Charlotte, NC

370. Jones Law School
Montgomery, AL

371. Judson College
Marion, AL

372. Juniata College
Huntingdon, PA

373. Kalamazoo College
Kalamazoo, MI

374. Kansas City School of Law
Part of University of Missouri at Kansas City
Kansas City, MO

375. Kansas State University
Formerly Kansas State College of Agriculture and Applied Science
Manhattan, KS

376. Emporia State University
Formerly Kansas State College
Emporia, KS

377. Pittsburg State University
Formerly Kansas State College
Pittsburg, KS

378. Kansas, University of
Lawrence, KS

379. Kansas Wesleyan University
Salina, KS

380. Keene State College
Keene, NH

381. Kent State University
Kent, OH

382. Kentucky State University
Frankfort, KY

383. Kentucky, University of
Lexington, KY

384. Kentucky Wesleyan College
Owensboro, KY

385. Kenyon College
Gambier, OH

386. Keuka College
Keuka Park, NY

387. King College
Bristol, TN

388. Knox College
Galesburg, IL

389. Knoxville College
Knoxville, TN

390. Lafayette College
Easton, PA

391. LaGrange College
LaGrange, GA

392. Lake Erie College
Painesville, OH

393. Lake Forest College
Lake Forest, IL

394. Lambuth College
Jackson, TN

395. Lander College
Greenwood, SC

396. Lane College
Jackson, TN

397. LaSalle University
Philadelphia, PA

398. La Verne, University of
La Verne, CA

399. Lawrence University
Appleton, WI

400. Lebanon Valley College
Annville, PA

401. Lehigh University
Bethlehem, PA

402. Leland College
Baker, LA

403. Le Moyne-Owen College
Memphis, TN

404. Lenoir-Rhyne College
Hickory, NC

405. Illinois Institute of Technology
Formerly Lewis Institute
Chicago, IL
See Also No. 46

406. Limestone College
Gaffney, SC

407. Lincoln College of Indiana
Indianapolis, IN

408. Lincoln College of Law
Bakersfield, CA

409. Lincoln Memorial University
Harrogate, TN

410. Lincoln University
Jefferson City, MO

411. Lincoln University
Lincoln University, PA

412. Lindenwood Colleges, The
St. Charles, MO

413. Linfield College
McMinnville, OR

414. Livingstone College
Salisbury, NC

415. Long Island University, C.W. Post Campus of
Brookville, NY

416. Loretto Heights College
Denver, CO

417. Louisiana College
Pineville, LA

418. Louisiana Tech University
Formerly Louisiana Polytechnic Institute
Ruston, LA

419. Northwestern State University
Formerly Louisiana State Normal College
Natchitoches, LA

420. Louisiana State University
Baton Rouge, LA

421. Louisville, University of
Louisville, KY

422. Lowell Technological Institute
Part of University of Lowell
Lowell, MA

423. Loyola College
Baltimore, MD

424. Loyola University
Chicago, IL

425. Loyola University
New Orleans, LA

426. Loyola Marymount University
Los Angeles, CA

427. Luther College
Decorah, IA

428. Lynchburg College
Lynchburg, VA

429. Macalester College
St. Paul, MN

430. MacMurray College
Jacksonville, IL

431. Maine, University of
Orono, Farmington, Fort Kent, Machias and Presque Isle, ME

432. Manchester College
N. Manchester, IN

433. Manhattan College
Riverdale, NY

434. Marietta College
Marietta, OH

435. Marion College
Marion, IN

436. Marquette University
Milwaukee, WI

437. Marshall University
Huntington, WV

438. Mary Baldwin College
Staunton, VA

439. Mary Hardin-Baylor College
Belton, TX

440. Mary Manse College
Toledo, OH

441. Marygrove College
Detroit, MI

442. Maryland College for Women
Lutherville, MD

443. Frostburg State College
Formerly Maryland State Teachers College
Frostburg, MD

444. Salisbury State University
Formerly Maryland State Teachers College
Salisbury, MD

445. Towson State University
Formerly Maryland State Teachers College
Towson, MD

446. Maryland, University of
Baltimore and College Park, MD

447. Marylhurst College
Oswego, OR

448. Marymount College of Kansas
Salina, KS

449. Marymount College
Tarrytown, NY

450. Maryville College
St. Louis, MO

451. Maryville College
Maryville, TN

452. Marywood College
Scranton, PA

453. Massachusetts Institute of Technology
Cambridge, MA

454. Massachusetts, University of
Amherst and Boston, MA

455. Bridgewater State College
Formerly Massachusetts State College
Bridgewater, MA

456. Fitchburg State College
Formerly Massachusetts State College
Fitchburg, MA

457. Framingham State College
Formerly Massachusetts State College
Framingham, MA

458. Hyannis State College
Formerly Massachusetts State College
Hyannis, MA

459. Massachusetts Lowell, University of
Formerly Massachusetts State College
Lowell, MA

460. North Adams State College
Formerly Massachusetts State College
North Adams, MA

461. Salem State College
Formerly Massachusetts State College
Salem, MA

462. Westfield State College
Formerly Massachusetts State College
Westfield, MA

463. Worcester State College
Formerly Massachusetts State College
Worcester, MA

464. McGeorge School of Law
Part of University of the Pacific
Sacramento, CA

465. McKendree College
Lebanon, IL

466. McMurry College
Abilene, TX

467. McPherson College
McPherson, KS

468. Rutgers University
Formerly Mercer Beasley School of Law
Newark, NJ
See Also No. 705

469. Mercer University
Macon, GA

470. Mercyhurst College
Erie, PA

471. Meredith College
Raleigh, NC

472. Miami, University of
Coral Gables, FL

473. Miami University
Oxford, OH

474. Michigan Technological University
Houghton, MI

475. Michigan State University
East Lansing, MI

476. Eastern Michigan University
Formerly Michigan State Normal College
Ypsilanti, MI

477. Michigan, University of
Ann Arbor, Dearborn and Flint, MI

478. Middlebury College
Middlebury, VT

479. Middlesex University
Waltham, MA

480. Midland Lutheran College
Formerly Fremont College
Fremont, NE

481. Miles College
Birmingham, AL

482. Milligan College
Milligan College, TN

483. Mills College
Oakland, CA

484. Millsaps College
Jackson, MS

485. Milton College
Milton, WI

486. Milwaukee-Downer College
Milwaukee, WI

487. William Mitchell College of Law
Formerly Minnesota College of Law
Minneapolis, MN
See Also No. 1035

488. Bemidji State University
Bemidji, MN

489. Minnesota Duluth, University of
Duluth, MN

490. Mankato State University
Formerly Minnesota State Teachers College
Mankato, MN

491. Moorhead State University
Formerly Minnesota State Teachers College
Moorhead, MN

492. St. Cloud State University
Formerly Minnesota State Teachers College
St. Cloud, MN

493. Winona State University
Formerly Minnesota State Teachers College
Winona, MN

494. Minnesota, University of
Minneapolis and St. Paul, MN

495. Mission House College & Theological Seminary
Plymouth, WI

496. Mississippi College
Clinton, MS

497. Mississippi State University
State College, MS

498. Mississippi State University for Women
Columbus, MS

499. Mississippi, University of Southern
Hattiesburg, MS

500. Mississippi, University of
University, MS
(Also maintains branch campuses at Oxford, Jackson, Southaven and Tupelo, MS)

501. William Carey College
Formerly Mississippi Woman's College
Hattiesburg, MS

502. Missouri, University of
Columbia, Rolla, St. Louis and Kansas City, MO

503. Missouri Valley College
Marshall, MO

504. Monmouth College
Monmouth, IL

505. Montana College of Mineral Science and Technology
Butte, MT

506. Montana State University
Bozeman, MT

507. Western Montana College
Formerly Montana State Normal College
Dillon, MT

508. Montana, University of
Formerly Montana State University
Missoula, MT

509. Moravian College & Theological Seminary
Bethlehem, PA

510. Morehead State University
Morehead, KY

511. Morehouse College
Atlanta, GA

512. Morgan State University
Baltimore, MD

513. Morningside College
Formerly University of Northwest
Sioux City, IA

514. Morris Brown College
Atlanta, GA

515. Morris College
Sumter, SC

516. Charleston, University of
Formerly Morris Harvey College
Charleston, WV

517. Mount Angel Seminary
St. Benedict, OR

518. Mount Holyoke College
South Hadley, MA

519. Mount Mary College
Milwaukee, WI

520. Mount Mercy College
Grand Rapids, MI

521. Carlow College
Formerly Mount Mercy College
Pittsburgh, PA

522. Chestnut Hill College
Formerly Mount St. Joseph College
Chestnut Hill, PA

523. Mount St. Joseph-on the Ohio, College of
Mount St. Joseph, OH

524. Mount St. Mary's College
Emmitsburg, MD

525. Mount St. Mary's College
Los Angeles, CA

526. Mount St. Scholastica College
Atchison, KS

527. Mount St. Vincent, College of
Riverdale, NY

528. Mount Union College
Alliance, OH

529. Muhlenberg College
Allentown, PA

530. Mundelein College
Chicago, IL

531. Murray State University
Murray, KY

532. Muskingum College
New Concord, OH

533. Tennessee State University
Formerly Nashville Agricultural Normal Institute
Nashville, TN
See Also No. 1220

534. Nassau College
Hempstead, NY

535. Nasson College
Springvale, ME

536. National College of Education
Formerly Pestalozzi Froebel Teachers College
Evanston, IL

537. George Washington University
Formerly National University
Washington, DC
See Also No. 273

538. Nazareth College
Louisville, KY

539. Nazareth College
Nazareth, MI

540. Nazareth College of Rochester
Rochester, NY

541. Nebraska Central College
Central City, NE

542. Chadron State College
Formerly Nebraska State Teachers College
Chadron, NE

543. Nebraska at Kearny, University of
Formerly Nebraska State Teachers College
Kearney, NE

544. Peru State College
Formerly Nebraska State Teachers College
Peru, NE

545. Wayne State College
Formerly Nebraska State Teachers College
Wayne, NE

546. Nebraska at Lincoln, University of
Lincoln, NE

547. Nebraska Wesleyan University
Lincoln, NE

549. Nevada, University of
Reno and Las Vegas, NV

550. New Hampshire, University of
Durham, NH

551. Douglass College of Rutgers University
Formerly New Jersey College for Women
New Brunswick, NJ
See Also No. 705

552. Rutgers University
Formerly New Jersey Law School
Newark, NJ
See Also No. 705

553. Kean College of New Jersey
Formerly New Jersey State College
Union, NJ

555. Montclair State University
Formerly New Jersey State College
Upper Montclair, NJ

556. New Mexico State University
Formerly New Mexico College of A. & M. Arts
University Park, NM

557. New Mexico Highlands University
Las Vegas, NM

558. New Mexico Institute of Mining & Technology
Socorro, NM

559. Western New Mexico University
Formerly New Mexico Western College
Silver City, NM

560. New Mexico, University of
Albuquerque, NM

561. West Virginia Institute of Technology
Formerly New River State College
Montgomery, WV

562. New Rochelle, College of
New Rochelle, NY

563. New York, City College of the City University of
New York, NY

564. New York Law School
New York, NY

565. New York College of Environmental Science & Forestry, State University of
Formerly New York State College of Forestry
Syracuse, NY

566. New York State College for Teachers
Albany, NY

567. New York at Buffalo, State University of
Formerly New York State Teachers College
Buffalo, NY
See Also No. 107

568. New York Teachers College
New York, NY

569. New York University
New York, NY

570. New Jersey Institute of Technology
Formerly Newark College of Engineering
Newark, NJ

571. Rutgers University
Formerly Newark, University of
Newark, NJ
See Also No. 705

572. Newberry College
Newberry, SC

573. Niagara University
Niagara University, NY

574. North Carolina Central University
Durham, NC

575. North Carolina at Chapel Hill, University of
Chapel Hill, NC

576. North Carolina State University
Raleigh, NC

577. North Carolina, University of, Greensboro, N.C.
Greensboro, NC

578. North Central College
Naperville, IL

579. North Dakota State University
Formerly North Dakota Agricultural College
Fargo, ND

580. North Dakota State Normal & Industrial College
Part of University of North Dakota
Ellendale, ND

581. Dickinson State College
Formerly North Dakota State College
Dickinson, ND

582. Mayville State College
Formerly North Dakota State College
Mayville, ND

583. Valley City State University
Formerly North Dakota State College
Valley City, ND

584. Dakota Northwestern University
Formerly North Dakota State College
Minot, ND

585. North Dakota, University of
Grand Forks, ND

586. North Texas, University of
Formerly North Texas State University
Denton, TX

587. Northeast Missouri State University
Kirksville, MO

588. Northeastern University
Boston, MA

589. Northern Illinois University
DeKalb and Glen Ellyn, IL

590. Northern State College
Aberdeen, SD

591. Northern Michigan University
Marquette, MI

592. Northland College
Ashland, WI

593. Northwest Missouri State University
Maryville, MO

594. Northwest Nazarene College
Nampa, ID

595. Northwestern College
Watertown, WI

596. Northwestern School of Law
Formerly Northwestern College of Law
Portland, OR

597. Northwestern University
Evanston, IL

598. Norwich University
Northfield, VT

599. Notre Dame College
South Euclid, OH

600. Notre Dame of Maryland, College of
Baltimore, MD

601. Notre Dame College of Staten Island
Part of St. Johns University
Staten Island, NY
See Also No. 724

602. Notre Dame, University of
Notre Dame, IN

603. Oakland City College
Oakland City, IN

604. Oberlin College
Oberlin, OH

605. Occidental College
Los Angeles, CA

606. Oglethorpe University
Atlanta, GA

607. Ohio Northern University
Ada, OH

608. Ohio State University, The
Columbus, OH

609. Athenaeum of Ohio, The
Formerly Ohio Teachers College
Cincinnati, OH

610. Ohio University
Athens, OH

611. Ohio Wesleyan University
Delaware, OH

612. Oklahoma State University
Formerly Oklahoma A. & M. College
Stillwater, OK

613. Oklahoma Baptist University
Shawnee, OK

614. Central State University
Formerly Oklahoma Central State Teachers College
Edmond, OK
See Also No. 1147

615. Oklahoma City University School of Law
Formerly Oklahoma City College of Law
Oklahoma City, OK

616. Oklahoma City University
Formerly Epworth University
Oklahoma City, OK

617. Science and Arts of Oklahoma, University of
Formerly Oklahoma College of Liberal Arts
Chickasha, OK

618. East Central Oklahoma State University
Formerly Oklahoma East Central State College
Ada, OK

619. Northeastern Oklahoma State University
Tahlequah, OK

620. Northwestern Oklahoma State University
Formerly Oklahoma Northwestern State College
Alva, OK

621. Southeastern Oklahoma State University
Formerly Oklahoma Southeastern State College
Durant, OK

622. Southwestern Oklahoma State University
Formerly Oklahoma Southwestern Institute of Technology
Weatherford, OK

623. Oklahoma, University of
Norman, OK

624. Olivet Nazarene College
Kankakee, IL

625. Olivet College
Olivet, MI

626. Omaha Law School, Inc., University of
Omaha, NE

627. Nebraska at Omaha, University of
Formerly Omaha, Municipal University of
Omaha, NE

628. Oregon State University
Corvallis, OR

629. Oregon, University of
Eugene, OR

630. Ottawa University
Ottawa, KS

631. Otterbein College
Westerville, OH

632. Ouachita Baptist University
Arkadelphia, AR

633. Elms College
Formerly Our Lady of the Elms, College of
Chicopee, MA

634. Our Lady of the Lake University
San Antonio, TX

635. George Fox College
Formerly Pacific College
Newberg, OR

636. Pacific Union College
Angwin, CA

637. Pacific University
Forest Grove, OR

638. Paine College
Augusta, GA

639. Oklahoma Panhandle State University of Agriculture and Applied Sciences
Formerly Panhandle State College
Goodwell, OK

640. Park College
Parkville, MO

641. Parsons College
Fairfield, IA

642. Pasadena College
Pasadena, CA

643. Chatham College
Formerly Pennsylvania College for Women
Pittsburgh, PA

644. Widener University
Formerly Pennsylvania Military College
Chester, PA and Wilmington, DE
See Also No. 1338

645. Pennsylvania State University
University Park, PA

646. Bloomsburg University of Pennsylvania
Formerly Pennsylvania State Teachers College
Bloomsburg, PA

647. California University of Pennsylvania
Formerly Pennsylvania State Teachers College
California, PA

648. Clarion University of Pennsylvania
Formerly Pennsylvania State Teachers College
Clarion, PA

649. East Stroudsburg University
Formerly Pennsylvania State Teachers College
E. Stroudsburg, PA

650. Edinboro University of Pennsylvania
Formerly Pennsylvania State Teachers College
Edinboro, PA

651. Indiana University of Pennsylvania
Formerly Pennsylvania State Teachers College
Indiana, PA

652. Kutztown University
Formerly Pennsylvania State Teachers College
Kutztown, PA

653. Lock Haven University of Pennsylvania
Formerly Pennsylvania State Teachers College
Lock Haven, PA

654. Mansfield University
Formerly Pennsylvania State Teachers College
Mansfield, PA

655. Millersville University of Pennsylvania
Formerly Pennsylvania State Teachers College
Millersville, PA

656. Shippensburg University of Pennsylvania
Formerly Pennsylvania State Teachers College
Shippensburg, PA

657. Slippery Rock University
Formerly Pennsylvania State Teachers College
Slippery Rock, PA

658. West Chester University
Formerly Pennsylvania State Teachers College
West Chester, PA

659. Pennsylvania, University of
Philadelphia, PA

660. National College of Education
Formerly Pestalozzi Froebel Teachers College
Chicago, IL
See Also No. 536

661. Philander Smith College
Little Rock, AR

662. Philippines, University of
Manila, Philippines

663. Phillips University
Enid, OK

664. Piedmont College
Demorest, GA

665. Pittsburgh, University of
Bradford, Greensburg, Johnstown and Pittsburgh, PA

666. Plymouth State College
Plymouth, NH

667. Polytechnic Institute of New York
Formerly Polytechnic Institute of Brooklyn
Brooklyn, NY

668. Pomona College
Claremont, CA

669. New England School of Law
Formerly Portia Law School
Boston, MA
See Also No. 1202

670. Portland, University of
Portland, OR

671. Prairie View A & M University
Prairie View, TX

672. Pratt Institute
Brooklyn, NY

673. Presbyterian College
Clinton, SC

674. Princeton University
Princeton, NJ

675. Principia College, The
Elsah, IL

676. Providence College
Providence, RI

677. Puerto Rico, University of
Rio Piedras, PR

678. Puget Sound, University of
Tacoma, WA

679. Purdue University
Lafayette and Hammond, IN
(Also maintains joint campuses with Indiana University at Indianapolis and Ft. Wayne, IN)

680. Queens College
Charlotte, NC

681. Radcliffe College
Now Affiliated with Harvard University
Cambridge, MA

682. Randolph-Macon College
Ashland, VA

683. Randolph-Macon Woman's College
Lynchburg, VA

684. Redlands, University of
Redlands, CA

685. Reed College
Portland, OR

686. Regis College
Denver, CO

687. Regis College
Weston, MA

688. Rensselaer Polytechnic Institute
Troy, NY

689. Rhode Island College
Providence, RI

690. Rhode Island, University of
Kingston, RI

691. Rice University
Houston, TX

692. Richmond, University of
Richmond, VA

693. Rider University
Lawrenceville, NJ

694. Ripon College
Ripon, WI

695. Roanoke College
Salem, VA

696. Rochester, University of
Rochester, NY

697. Rockford College
Rockford, IL

698. Rockhurst College
Kansas City, MO

699. Rollins College
Winter Park, FL

700. Rosary College
River Forest, IL

701. Rose-Hulman Institute of Technology
Formerly Rose Polytechnic Institute
Terre Haute, IN

702. Rosemont College
Rosemont, PA

703. Russell Sage College
Troy, NY

704. Rust College
Holy Springs, MS

705. Rutgers University
Camden, Newark and New Brunswick, NJ
Note: There are two separate law schools, one at Newark, NJ (No. 705) and one at Camden, NJ (No. 1292)

706. Manhattanville College
Formerly Sacred Heart, Manhattanville College of the Purchase, NY

707. St. Ambrose College and Marycrest College
Formerly St. Ambrose College
Davenport, IA

708. St. Anselm College
Manchester, NH

709. St. Augustine's College
Raleigh, NC

710. St. Benedict, College of
St. Joseph, MN

711. St. Benedict's College
Atchison, KS

712. St. Bonaventure University
St. Bonaventure, NY

713. St. Catherine, College of
St. Paul, MN

714. St. Edward's University
Austin, TX

715. St. Elizabeth, College of
Convent Station, NJ

716. St. Francis College
Brooklyn, NY

717. St. Francis College
Loretto, PA

718. St. Francis College
Burlington, WI

719. St. Francis, College of
Joliet, IL

720. St. Xavier College
Formerly St. Francis Xavier College for Women
Chicago, IL

722. St. John's College
Annapolis, MD

723. St. John's University
Collegeville, MN

724. St. John's University
Jamaica, NY

725. St. Joseph College
W. Hartford, CT

726. St. Joseph's College
Emmitsburg, MD

727. St. Joseph's College
Princeton, NJ

728. St. Joseph's University
Philadelphia, PA

729. St. Joseph's College & Academy
Adrian, MI

730. St. Joseph's College
Standish, ME

731. St. Joseph's College
Formerly St. Joseph's College for Woman
Brooklyn, NY

732. St. Lawrence University
Canton, NY

733. St. Louis City College of Law
St. Louis, MO

734. St. Louis University
St. Louis, MO

735. St. Martin's College
Lacey, WA

736. St. Mary College
Leavenworth, KS

737. Ohio Dominican College
Formerly St. Mary of the Springs College
Columbus, OH

738. St. Mary-of-the-Wasatch, College of
Salt Lake City, UT

739. St. Mary-of-the-Woods College
St. Mary of the Woods, IN

740. St. Mary's College of California
Moraga, CA

741. St. Mary's College
Notre Dame, IN

742. St. Mary's University of Minnesota
Winona, MN

743. St. Mary's Seminary & University
Roland Park, MD

744. St. Mary's University of San Antonio
San Antonio, TX

745. St. Michael's College
Winooski, VT

746. St. Norbert College
West De Pere, WI

747. St. Olaf College
Northfield, MN

748. William Mitchell College of Law
Formerly St. Paul College of Law
St. Paul, MN
See Also No. 1035

749. St. Peter's College
Jersey City, NJ

750. Illinois Benedictine College
Formerly St. Procopius College
Lisle, IL

751. St. Rose, College of
Albany, NY

752. St. Scholastica, College of
Duluth, MN

753. St. Teresa, College of
Winona, MN

754. Scranton, University of
Formerly St. Thomas College
Scranton, PA

755. St. Thomas, College of
St. Paul, MN

756. St. Viator College
Bourbonnais, IL

757. St. Vincent College
Latrobe, PA

758. Salem College
Winston-Salem, NC

759. Salem College
Salem, WV

760. Sam Houston State University
Huntsville, TX

761. Huston-Tillotson College
Formerly Samuel Huston College
Austin, TX
See Also No. 1037

762. San Antonio Public School of Law
San Antonio, TX

763. San Diego State University
San Diego, CA

764. Lone Mountain College
Formerly San Francisco College for Women
San Francisco, CA

765. San Francisco Law School
San Francisco, CA

766. San Francisco State University
Formerly California State University
San Francisco, CA

767. San Francisco, University of
Formerly St. Ignatius College
San Francisco, CA

768. San Jose State University
San Jose, CA

769. California at Santa Barbara, University of
Formerly Santa Barbara State College
Santa Barbara, CA

770. Santa Clara University
Formerly Santa Clara, University of
Santa Clara, CA

771. Sarah Lawrence College
Bronxville, NY

772. Scarritt College for Christian Workers
Nashville, TN

773. Scripps College
Claremont, CA

774. Seattle Pacific University
Seattle, WA

775. Selma University
Selma, AL

776. Seton Hall University
South Orange & Newark, NJ

777. Seton Hill College
Greensburg, PA

778. Shaw University
Raleigh, NC

779. Shepherd College
Shepherdstown, WV

780. Shorter College
Formerly Shorter-Flipper-Curry College
N. Little Rock, AR

781. Shorter College
Rome, GA

782. Shurtleff College
Alton, IL

783. Simmons College
Boston, MA

784. Simpson College
Indianola, IA

785. Sioux Falls College
Sioux Falls, SD

786. Sisters' College of Cleveland
Cleveland, OH

787. Skidmore College
Saratoga Springs, NY

788. Smith College
Northampton, MA

789. South Carolina State College
Orangeburg, SC

790. South Carolina, University of
Columbia, SC

791. South Dakota State University
Brookings, SD

792. South Dakota School of Mines and Technology
Rapid City, SD

793. South Dakota, University of
Vermillion, SD

794. Georgia Teachers College
Formerly South Georgia Teachers College
Collegeboro, GA

795. Rutgers University
Formerly South Jersey, College of
Camden, NJ
See Also No. 1292

796. South Texas College of Law
Houston, TX

797. South, University of the
Sewanee, TN

798. Southeast Missouri State University
Cape Girardeau, MO

799. Southeastern University
Washington, DC

800. Southern California, University of
Los Angeles, CA

801. Southern Illinois University
Carbondale and Edwardsville, IL

802. Southern Methodist University
Dallas, TX

803. Southern University
Baton Rouge, LA

804. Southwest Missouri State University
Springfield, MO

805. Southwest Texas State University
San Marcos, TX

806. Rhodes College
Formerly Southwestern at Memphis
Memphis, TN

807. Southwestern College
Winfield, KS

808. Southwestern Louisiana, University of
Lafayette, LA

809. Southwestern University School of Law
Los Angeles, CA

810. Southwestern University
Georgetown, TX

811. Spelman College
Atlanta, GA

812. Spring Hill College
Spring Hill, AL

813. Stanford University
Palo Alto, CA

814. Stephen F. Austin State University
Nacogdoches, TX

815. Sterling College
Sterling, KS

816. Stevens Institute of Technology
Hoboken, NJ

817. Wisconsin-Stout, University of
Formerly Stout State College
Menomonie, WI

818. Suffolk University
Boston, MA

819. Sul Ross State University
Alpine, TX

820. Susquehanna University
Selinsgrove, PA

821. Swarthmore College
Swarthmore, PA

822. Sweet Briar College
Sweet Briar, VA

823. Syracuse University
Syracuse, NY

824. Talladega College
Talladega, AL

825. Tampa, University of
Tampa, FL

826. Tarkio College
Tarkio, MO

827. Taylor University
Upland, IN

828. Teachers College of the City of Boston
Boston, MA

829. Central Connecticut State College
Formerly Teachers College of Connecticut, The
New Britain, CT

830. Teachers College of Kansas City
Kansas City, MO

831. Temple University
Philadelphia, PA

832. Tennessee State University
Formerly Tennessee A. & I. State University
Nashville, TN

833. Tennessee College for Women
Murfreesboro, TN

834. Tennessee Technological University
Formerly Tennessee Polytechnic Institute
Cookeville, TN

835. East Tennessee State University
Formerly Tennessee State Teachers College
Johnson City, TN

836. Memphis, University of
Formerly Memphis State University
Memphis, TN
See Also No. 1015

837. Middle Tennessee State University
Formerly Tennessee State Teachers College
Murfreesboro, TN

838. Tennessee at Knoxville, University of
Knoxville, TN

839. Texas A & M University
College Station, TX

840. Texas Christian University
Fort Worth, TX

841. Texas College
Tyler, TX

842. Texas Arts & Industries University
Kingsville, TX

843. Texas at El Paso, University of
Formerly Texas, College of Mines & Metallurgy
El Paso, TX

844. Texas Woman's University
Formerly Texas State College for Women
Denton, TX

845. Texas Tech University
Lubbock, TX

846. Texas at Austin, University of
Austin, TX

847. Texas Wesleyan University
Fort Worth, TX

848. Thiel College
Greenville, PA

849. Huston-Tillotson College
Formerly Tillotson College
Austin, TX
See Also No. 1037

850. Toledo Teachers College
Toledo, OH

851. Toledo, University of
Toledo, OH

852. Tougaloo College
Tougaloo, MS

853. Transylvania University
Lexington, KY

854. Tri-State University
Angola, IN

855. Trinity College
Hartford, CT

856. Trinity College
Washington, DC

857. Trinity College
Sioux City, IA

858. Trinity College
Burlington, VT

859. Trinity University
San Antonio, TX

860. Tufts University
Medford, MA

861. Tulane University of Louisiana
New Orleans, LA

862. Tulsa, University of
Tulsa, OK

863. Tusculum College
Greeneville, TN

864. Tuskegee University
Tuskegee, AL

865. Union College
Barbourville, KY

866. Union College
Lincoln, NE

867. Union College
Schenectady, NY

868. Union University
Jackson, TN

869. United States Coast Guard Academy
New London, CT

870. United States Military Academy
West Point, NY

871. United States Naval Academy
Annapolis, MD

872. Upper Iowa University
Fayette, IA

873. Upsala College
East Orange, NJ

874. Ursinus College
Collegeville, PA

875. Ursuline College
New Orleans, LA

876. Ursuline College
Cleveland, OH

877. Utah State University
Formerly Utah State Agricultural College
Logan, UT

878. Utah, University of
Salt Lake City, UT

879. Valparaiso University
Formerly Northern Indiana Law School
Valparaiso, IN

880. Vanderbilt University
Nashville, TN

881. Vassar College
Poughkeepsie, NY

882. Vermont, University of
Burlington, VT

883. Villa Maria College
Erie, PA

884. Villanova University
Villanova, PA

885. Virginia Military Institute
Lexington, VA

886. Virginia Polytechnic Institute and State University
Blacksburg, VA

887. Virginia State University
Petersburg (Ettrick), VA

888. Radford University
Formerly Virginia State Teachers College
East Radford, VA

889. Longwood College
Formerly Virginia State Teachers College
Farmville, VA

890. Mary Washington College
Formerly Virginia State Teachers College
Fredericksburg, VA

892. Virginia Union University
Richmond, VA

893. Virginia, University of
Charlottesville, VA

894. Wabash College
Crawfordsville, IN

895. Wagner College
Staten Island, NY

896. Wake Forest University
Winston-Salem, NC

897. Walla Walla College
College Place, WA

898. Wartburg College
Waverly, IA

899. Wartburg Theological Seminary
Dubuque, IA

900. Washburn University of Topeka
Topeka, KS

901. Washington & Jefferson College
Washington, PA

902. Washington & Lee University
Lexington, VA

903. Washington College
Chestertown, MD

904. Washington College of Law
(of American University)
Washington, DC
See Also No. 30

905. Columbia Union College
Formerly Washington Missionary College
Takoma Park, DC

906. Washington State University
Pullman, WA

907. Western Washington University
Formerly Washington State Normal School
Bellingham, WA

908. Eastern Washington University
Formerly Washington State Normal School
Cheney, WA

909. Central Washington University
Formerly Washington State Normal School
Ellensburg, WA

910. Washington University
St. Louis, MO

911. Washington, University of
Seattle, WA

912. Wayne State University
Detroit, MI

913. Waynesburg College
Waynesburg, PA

914. Wellesley College
Wellesley, MA

915. Wells College
Aurora, NY

916. Wesley College
Grand Forks, ND

917. Wesleyan College
Macon, GA

918. Wesleyan University
Middletown, CT

919. West Baden College
West Baden, IN

920. West Liberty State College
W. Liberty, WV

921. West Texas State University
Canyon, TX

922. West Virginia State College
Institute, WV

923. West Virginia University
Morgantown, WV

924. West Virginia Wesleyan College
Buckhannon, WV

925. Western Carolina University
Cullowhee, NC

926. Western College
Oxford, OH

927. Western Illinois University
Macomb, IL

928. Western Maryland College
Westminster, MD

929. Western Kentucky University
Formerly Western Kentucky State College
Bowling Green, KY

930. Case Western Reserve University
Formerly Western Reserve University
Cleveland, OH

931. Western State College of Colorado
Gunnison, CO

932. Western Michigan University
Kalamazoo, MI

933. Westmar College
Formerly Western Union College
Le Mars, IA

934. Westminster College
Fulton, MO

935. Westminster College
New Wilmington, PA

937. Wheaton College
Wheaton, IL

938. Wheaton College
Norton, MA

939. Whitman College
Walla Walla, WA

940. Whittier College
Whittier, CA

941. Whitworth College
Spokane, WA

942. Wichita State University
Wichita, KS

943. Wilberforce University
Wilberforce, OH

944. Wiley College
Marshall, TX

945. William & Mary, College of
Williamsburg, VA

946. William Jennings Bryan College
Dayton, TN

947. William Jewell College
Liberty, MO

948. William McKinley School of Law
Canton, OH

949. William Penn College
Oskaloosa, IA

950. Willamette University
Salem, OR

951. Williams College
Williamstown, MA

952. Wilmington College
Wilmington, OH

953. North Carolina at Wilmington, University of
Formerly Wilmington College
Wilmington, NC

954. Wilson College
Chambersburg, PA

955. Winston-Salem State University
Winston-Salem, NC

956. Winthrop College
Rock Hill, SC

957. Wisconsin-Eau Claire, University of
Eau Claire, WI

958. Wisconsin-La Crosse, University of
La Crosse, WI

959. Wisconsin-Milwaukee, University of
Milwaukee, WI

960. Wisconsin-Oshkosh, University of
Oshkosh, WI

961. Wisconsin-Platteville, University of
Platteville, WI

962. Wisconsin-River Falls, University of
River Falls, WI

963. Wisconsin-Stevens Point, University of
Stevens Point, WI

964. Wisconsin-Superior, University of
Superior, WI

965. Wisconsin-Whitewater, University of
Whitewater, WI

966. Wisconsin-Madison, University of
Madison, WI

967. Wittenberg University
Springfield, OH

968. Wofford College
Spartanburg, SC

969. Woodrow Wilson College of Law
Formerly Kilbride Law School
Atlanta, GA

970. Wooster, College of
Wooster, OH

971. Worcester Polytechnic Institute
Worcester, MA

972. Wyoming, University of
Laramie, WY

973. Xavier University
Cincinnati, OH

974. Xavier University of Louisiana
New Orleans, LA

975. Y.M.C.A. Schools
Houston, TX

976. Yale University
New Haven, CT

977. Yankton College
Yankton, SD

978. Yeshiva University
New York, NY

979. York College
York, NE

980. Youngstown State University
Youngstown, OH

981. LaSalle Extension University
Chicago, IL

982. Albany Law School of Union University
Albany, NY

983. San Antonio, University of
San Antonio, TX

984. Blue Ridge College
New Windsor, MD

985. Briar Cliff College
Sioux City, IA

986. Missouri at Kansas City, University of
Formerly University of Kansas City
Kansas City, MO

987. Sulpician Seminary of the Northwest
Formerly St. Edward's Seminary
Seattle, WA

988. Seattle University
Seattle, WA

989. Cleveland-Marshall College of Law
Formerly John Marshall Law School
Cleveland, OH
See Also No. 1003

990. Pepperdine University
Los Angeles, Malibu, Anaheim and Santa Ana, CA

991. Barat College
Lake Forest, IL

992. Anderson College
Anderson, IN

993. St. Mary's College
Orchard Lake, MI

994. Queens College of the City University of New York
Flushing, NY

995. Alfred Holbrook College
Manchester, OH

996. Lincoln College of Law
Springfield, IL

997. Seton Hall University
Formerly John Marshall Law School
Jersey City, NJ
See Also No. 776

998. Houston Law School
Houston, TX

999. Unlisted colleges, etc., see prefatory notice

1000. John Marshall Law School
Atlanta, GA

1001. Pacific Coast University
Los Angeles, CA

1002. Baltimore School of Law, University of
Formerly Mt. Vernon School of Law
Baltimore, MD

1003. Cleveland-Marshall College of Law
Part of Cleveland State University
Cleveland, OH

1004. St. Mary of the Plains College
Dodge City, KS

1005. Southern Law University
Part of Memphis State University
Memphis, TN

1006. College of St. Francis Xavier
New York, NY

1007. American Extension School of Law
Chicago, IL

1008. Blackstone School of Law
Carrollton, TX

1009. Brooklyn Law School
Brooklyn, NY

1010. Alabama Agricultural & Mechanical University
Formerly State Agricultural and Mechanical Institute
Normal, AL

1011. Fayetteville State University
Fayetteville, NC

1012. Eastern New Mexico University
Portales, NM

1014. Robert H. Terrell Law School
Washington, DC

1015. Memphis State University
Memphis, TN

1016. Roosevelt University
Chicago, IL

1017. Dickinson School of Law of the Pennsylvania State University
Carlisle, PA

1018. William Mitchell College of Law
Formerly Minneapolis-Minnesota College of Law
Minneapolis, MN
See Also No. 1035

1019. Hofstra University
Hempstead, NY

1020. Portland University Law School
part of University of Maine
Portland, ME
See Also No. 431

1021. Siena College
Formerly St. Bernardine of Siena College
Loudonville, NY

1022. New England School of Law
Formerly Calvin Coolidge College
Boston, MA
See Also No. 1202

1023. Central State University
Wilberforce, OH

1024. St. Joseph's College
Rensselaer, IN

1025. Jersey City State College
Formerly New Jersey State College
Jersey City, NJ

1026. Lincoln University
San Francisco, San Jose and Sacramento, CA

1027. United States Merchant Marine Academy
Kings Point, NY

1028. Wilkes University
Wilkes-Barre, PA

1029. Bridgeport, University of
Bridgeport, CT

1030. Fairfield University
Fairfield, CT

1031. Le Moyne College
Syracuse, NY

1032. Idaho State University
Formerly Idaho State College
Pocatello, ID

1033. Hartford, University of
Formerly Hillyer College
Hartford, CT

1034. Christian Brothers College
Memphis, TN

1035. William Mitchell College of Law
St. Paul, MN

1036. Brandeis University
Waltham, MA

1037. Huston-Tillotson College
Austin, TX

1038. Jacksonville University
Jacksonville, FL

1039. North Georgia College
Dahlonega, GA

1040. Pace University
New York, Pleasantville and White Plains, NY

1041. Iona College
New Rochelle, NY

1042. California State University, Long Beach
Formerly Long Beach State University
Long Beach, CA

1043. California State University, Los Angeles
Formerly Los Angeles State College of Applied Arts and Sciences
Los Angeles, CA
See Also No. 1097

1044. New York at Albany, State University of
Albany, NY

1045. Nashville School of Law
Nashville, TN

1046. Fairleigh Dickinson University
Madison, Rutherford and Teaneck, NJ

1047. Lycoming College
Williamsport, PA

1048. Western New England College
Springfield, MA

1049. San Diego, University of
San Diego, CA

1050. Midwestern State University
Wichita Falls, TX

1051. Lewis and Clark College
Portland, OR

1052. Houston Baptist University
Houston, TX

1053. Messiah College
Grantham, PA

1054. Tennessee Wesleyan College
Athens, TN

1055. Southeastern Louisiana College
Hammond, LA

1056. Portland State University
Portland, OR

1057. Merrimack College
North Andover, MA

1058. Pacific Lutheran University
Tacoma, WA

1059. Georgia State University
Atlanta, GA

1060. California State University, Sacramento
Formerly Sacramento State College
Sacramento, CA

1061. Lamar University
Beaumont, TX

1062. Gannon University
Erie, PA

1063. Georgia Southern College
Statesboro, GA

1064. Lipscomb University
Formerly David Lipscomb College
Nashville, TN

1065. Hastings College of the Law, University of California
San Francisco, CA

1066. Boalt Hall School of Law, University of California
Berkeley, CA

1067. California School of Law, Davis, University of
Davis, CA

1068. California School of Law, Los Angeles, University of
Los Angeles, CA

1069. Chaminade University of Honolulu
Honolulu, HI

1070. United States Air Force Academy
Colorado Springs, CO

1071. Southern Oregon State College
Ashland, OR

1072. Alliance College
Cambridge Springs, PA

1073. California State University, Hayward
Hayward, CA

1074. California Polytechnic State University
San Luis Obispo, CA

1075. California State Polytechnic University
Pomona, CA

1076. Orange State College
Fullerton, CA

1077. California State University, Northridge
Formerly San Fernando Valley State College
Northridge, CA

1078. Sonoma State University
Rohnert Park, CA

1079. California State University, Stanislaus
Formerly Stanislaus State College
Turlock, CA

1080. Northeast Louisiana University
Monroe, LA

1081. Austin Peay State University
Clarksville, TN

1082. Quincy University
Quincy, IL

1083. Old Dominion University
Norfolk, VA

1084. Northern Montana College
Havre, MT

1085. Weber State College
Ogden, UT

1086. Florida Atlantic University
Boca Raton, FL

1087. Catholic University of Puerto Rico
Ponce, PR

1088. Inter-American University of Puerto Rico
San Juan, PR

1089. McNeese State University
Lake Charles, LA

1090. Virginia Commonwealth University
Formerly Richmond Professional Institute
Richmond, VA

1091. South Alabama, University of
Mobile, AL

1092. Princess Anne State College
Princess Anne, MD

1093. Utica College of Syracuse University
Utica, NY

1094. Southern Arkansas University
Formerly Southern State College
Magnolia, AR

1095. La Verne College of Law, University of
Formerly San Fernando Valley, University of
Sepulveda, CA

1096. Angelo State University
Formerly San Angelo State University
San Angelo, TX

1097. California State University, Los Angeles
Formerly Los Angeles State College
Los Angeles, CA

1098. Louisiana State University at Alexandria
Alexandria, LA

1099. New Orleans, University of
Formerly Louisiana State University of New Orleans
New Orleans, LA

1100. Shimer College
Waukegan, IL

1101. Blackburn College
Carlinville, IL

1102. Southern Connecticut State College
New Haven, CT

1103. Western Connecticut State University
Danbury, CT

1104. Eastern Oregon College
La Grande, OR

1105. Dallas, University of
Irving, TX

1106. North Park College
Chicago, IL

1107. Assumption College
Worcester, MA

1108. Monmouth University
West Long Branch, NJ

1109. California State University, Fullerton
Fullerton, CA

1110. California State University, San Bernardino
San Bernardino, CA

1111. South Florida, University of
Tampa, FL

1112. Urbana College
Urbana, OH

1113. King's College
Wilkes Barre, PA

1114. Van Norman University
Los Angeles, CA

1115. Wheeling Jesuit College
Formerly Wheeling College
Wheeling, WV

1116. Rowan University
Formerly Glassboro State College
Glassboro, NJ

1117. Pepperdine University School of Law
Formerly Orange University College of Law
Malibu, CA

1118. Thomas More College
Formerly Villa Madonna College
Covington, KY

1119. Indiana University School of Law - Bloomington
Bloomington, IN

1120. Westminster College
Salt Lake City, UT

1121. Aquinas College
Grand Rapids, MI

1122. St. John Fisher College
Rochester, NY

1123. Goddard College
Plainfield, VT

1124. Eastern Mennonite College
Harrisonburg, VA

1125. Arkansas Tech University
Formerly Arkansas Polytechnic University
Russellville, AR

1126. Belmont Abbey College
Belmont, NC

1127. California College of Law
Hollywood and West Covina, CA

1128. North Carolina at Charlotte, University of
Charlotte, NC

1129. Mars Hill College
Mars Hill, NC

1130. St. Andrews Presbyterian College
Laurinburg, NC

1131. California State University, Dominguez Hills
Dominguez Hills, CA

1132. Humphreys College
Stockton, CA

1133. New York Institute of Technology
New York, NY

1134. Bentley College
Waltham, MA

1135. Marymount-Manhattan College
New York, NY

1136. West Los Angeles, University of
Culver City, CA

1137. Western State University
Fullerton, CA

1138. Baruch College of the City University of New York
New York, NY

1139. John Jay College of Criminal Justice of the City University of New York
New York, NY

1140. College of Staten Island of the City University of New York
Formerly Richmond College of the City University of New York
Staten Island, NY

1141. York College of the City University of New York
Queens, NY

1142. Texas at Arlington, University of
Arlington, TX

1143. Albuquerque, University of
Albuquerque, NM

1144. Bethel College
St. Paul, MN

1145. Bryant College
Smithfield, RI

1146. Santa Fe, College of
Santa Fe, NM

1147. Central Oklahoma, University of
Formerly Central State University
Edmond, OK

1148. Whittier College School of Law
Formerly Beverly College of Law
Los Angeles, CA

1149. Boston State College
Boston, MA

1150. Bellarmine College
Formerly Bellarmine Ursuline College
Louisville, KY

1151. Lewis University
Lockport, IL

1152. South Bay University
Harbor City, CA

1153. John F. Kennedy University
Walnut Creek, CA

1154. Oakland University
Rochester, MI

1155. Babson College
Babson Park, MA

1156. New Haven, University of
West Haven, CT

1157. St. Joseph College
East Chicago, IN

1158. St. Thomas University
Formerly Biscayne College
Miami, FL

1159. Indiana Institute of Technology
Fort Wayne, IN

1160. Herbert H. Lehman College of the City
University of New York
Bronx, NY

1161. Northern Kentucky University
Highland Heights, KY

1162. Antioch School of Law
Washington, DC

1163. Loma Linda University
Formerly La Sierra College
Loma Linda, CA

1164. Colorado at Colorado Springs, University of
Colorado Springs, CO

1165. Colorado at Denver, University of
Denver, CO

1166. Nicholls State University
Thibodaux, LA

1167. Harvey Mudd College
Claremont, CA

1168. Pitzer College
Claremont, CA

1169. California at Santa Cruz, University of
Santa Cruz, CA

1170. Franklin Pierce College
Rindge, NH

1171. Wisconsin-Green Bay, University of
Green Bay, WI

1172. Wisconsin-Parkside, University of
Kenosha, WI

1173. Southeastern Massachusetts University
North Dartmouth, MA

1174. William Paterson College of New Jersey
Wayne, NJ

1175. Central Florida, University of
Formerly Florida Technological University
Orlando, FL

1176. West Florida, University of
Pensacola, FL

1177. Grambling State University
Grambling, LA

1178. City University of New York School of Law,
Queens College
Flushing, NY

1179. Northrop University
Inglewood, CA

1180. Bloomfield College
Bloomfield, NJ

1181. Western Oregon State College
Formerly Oregon College of Education
Monmouth, OR

1182. Benedictine College
Atchison, KS

1183. Northeastern Illinois University
Chicago, IL

1185. Southern College of Seventh-Day Adventists
Formerly Southern Missionary College
Collegedale, TN

1186. Ventura College of Law
Ventura, CA

1187. Thomas M. Cooley Law School
Lansing, MI

1188. United States International University
Formerly California Western University
San Diego, CA

1189. San Joaquin, College of Law
Fresno, CA

1190. Glendale University
Glendale, CA

1191. Chicago State University
Chicago, IL

1192. Dowling College
Oakdale, NY

1193. Boise State University
Boise, ID

1194. Vermont Law School
South Royalton, VT

1195. Covenant College
Lookout Mountain, TN

1196. Southern Colorado, University of
Pueblo, CO

1197. Armstrong College
Berkeley, CA

1198. Citrus Belt Law School
Riverside, CA

1199. Cabrini College
Radnor, PA

1200. Stonehill College
North Easton, MA

1201. Metropolitan State College
Denver, CO

1202. New England School of Law
Boston, MA

1203. St. Mary's College of Maryland
St. Mary's City, MD

1204. Tennessee at Martin, University of
Martin, TN

1205. Tennessee at Memphis, University of
Memphis, TN

1206. Nova Southeastern University
Formerly Nova University
Fort Lauderdale, FL

1207. Minnesota Morris, University of
Morris, MN

1208. Wright State University
Dayton, OH

1209. George Mason University School of Law
Formerly International School of Law
Arlington, VA

1210. Florida Institute of Technology
Melbourne, FL

1211. Sacred Heart University
Bridgeport, CT

1212. California State College, Bakersfield
Bakersfield, CA

1213. Rochester Institute of Technology
Rochester, NY

1214. Stockton State College
Pomona, NJ

1215. Simon's Rock of Bard College
Great Barrington, MA

1216. Marian College
Indianapolis, IN

1217. Lawrence Technological University
Southfield, MI

1218. Franklin Pierce Law Center
Formerly part of Franklin Pierce College
Concord, NH

1219. Pan American University
Edinburg, TX

1220. Tennessee at Nashville, University of
Formerly Nashville Agricultural Normal
Institute
Nashville, TN

1221. Woodland University
Van Nuys, CA

1222. Florida International University
Miami, FL

1223. West Georgia College
Carrollton, GA

1224. Valley University College of Law
North Hollywood, CA

1225. Irvine University
Irvine, CA

1226. Monterey College of Law
Monterey, CA

1227. Empire College School of Law
Santa Rosa, CA

1228. Campbell University
Buies Creek, NC

1229. General Motors Institute
Flint, MI

1230. New College of California
San Francisco, CA

1231. San Mateo Law School
San Mateo, CA

1232. Azusa Pacific University
Azusa, CA

1233. Briarcliff College
Briarcliff Manor, NY

1234. Potomac School of Law
Washington, DC

1235. Eastern Montana College
Billings, MT

1236. Eckerd College
St. Petersburg, FL

1237. Louisiana State University at Shreveport
Shreveport, LA

1238. Peoples College of Law
Los Angeles, CA

1239. Westmont College
Santa Barbara, CA

1240. American College of Law
Anaheim, CA

1241. National University
Formerly Cabrillo Pacific University
San Diego, CA

1242. United States Naval Postgraduate School
Monterey, CA

1243. Arkansas at Little Rock, University of
Formerly Little Rock University
Little Rock, AR

1244. St. Bernard College
St. Bernard, AL

1245. Phoenix, University of
Phoenix, AZ

1246. Woodbury University
Los Angeles, CA

1247. Sangamon State University
Springfield, IL

1248. Southern Maine, University of
Portland, ME

1249. Saginaw Valley College
University Center, MI

1250. California Maritime Academy
Vallejo, CA

1251. Los Angeles College of Law
Los Angeles, CA

1252. Quinnipiac College
Hamden, CT

1253. California Lutheran University
Formerly California Lutheran College
Thousand Oaks, CA

1254. Menlo College
Menlo Park, CA

1255. Black Hills State College
Spearfish, SD

1256. St. Patrick's College
Mountain View, CA

1364. District of Columbia School of Law
Washington, DC

1365. Emory University
Atlanta, GA

1366. California Southern Law School
Riverside, CA

1367. Siena Heights College
Adrian, MI

1369. James Madison University
Harrisonburg, VA

1370. Thomas Jefferson School of Law
San Diego, CA

1371. New York College at Cortland, State University of
Cortland, NY

1372. New York College at Geneseo, State University of
Geneseo, NY

1373. New York College at New Paltz, State University of
New Paltz, NY

1374. New York College at Oneonta, State University of
Oneonta, NY

1375. California, Berkeley, University of
Berkeley, CA

1376. College of New Jersey, The
Formerly Trenton State College
Trenton, NJ

1377. Valdosta State University
Valdosta, GA

1378. North Carolina Agricultural & Technical State University
Greensboro, NC

1379. Chapman University School of Law
Anaheim, CA

1380. New York College at Purchase, State University of
Purchase, NY

1381. New York College at Brockport, State University of
Brockport, NY

1382. Queensland, University of
Brisbane, Australia

1383. Madras, University of
Chennai, India

1384. National University of Ireland, Galway
Galway, Ireland

1385. New York College at Potsdam, State University of
Potsdam, NY

1386. Appalachian School of Law
Grundy, VA

1387. National Law School of India
Bangalore, India

1388. Virginia Wesleyan College
Norfolk, VA

1389. Massachusetts School of Law
Andover, MA

1390. Alfred Adler Institute of San Francisco
San Francisco, CA

1391. Francisan University of Steubenville
Steubenville, OH

1392. Francaise Alliance USA
Paris, France

1393. Thunderbird American Graduate School of International Management
Glendale, AZ

1394. American University in Cairo
Cairo, Egypt

1395. Anna Maria College
Paxton, MA

1396. Associated Mennonite Biblical Seminary
Elkhart, IN

1397. Bangalore University
Bangalore, India

1398. Benjamin N. Cardozo School of Law, Yeshiva University
New York, NY

1399. Cairo University
Cairo, Egypt

1400. Concordia University
Irvine, CA

1401. Canadian Mennonite University
Winnipeg, Manitoba

1402. Catholic University of Argentina
Buenos Aires, Argentina

1403. Central Bible College
Springfield, MO

1404. Chadwick University
Birmingham, AL

1405. City Colleges of Chicago
Chicago, IL

1406. City College of San Francisco
San Francisco, CA

1407. College for Financial Planning
Denver, CO

1408. College of Law, London, The
London, England

1409. College of Saint Mary
Omaha, NE

1410. Denver, College of Law, University of
Denver, CO

1411. Columbia Pacific University
Novato, CA

1412. Curtis Institute of Music, The
Philadelphia, PA

1413. Czech Technical University
Prague, Czechlovakia

1414. Daemen College
Amherst, NY

1415. Delft University of Technology
Delft, Netherlands

1416. Delhi, The University of
Delhi, India

1417. Finch University of Health Sciences/The Chicago Medical School

1418. Flagler College
St. Augustine, FL

1419. Francis Marion University
Florence, SC

1420. Freed-Hardeman University
Henderson, TN

1421. Fresno Pacific College
Fresno, CA

1422. Fuller Theological Seminary
Pasadena, CA

1423. Frankfurt, University of
Frankfurt, Germany

1424. Institute of Political Studies, Paris
Paris, France

1425. Institute for Advanced Studies
Geneva, Switzerland

1426. Sophia University
Tokyo, Japan

1427. Johannes Gutenberg University
Mainz, Germany

1428. Johnson State College
Westbury, VT

1429. Kemper Military School & College
Boonville, MO

1430. Kennesaw State University
Kennesaw, GA

1431. Kennedy-Western University
Cheyenne, WY

1432. Lehman College of the City University of New York
Bronx, NY

1433. Lesley College
Cambridge, MA

1434. Lourdes College
Sylvania, OH

1435. Catholic University of Louvain
Louvain, France

1436. Manhattan School of Music
New York, NY

1437. Massachusetts College of Pharmacy & Health Sciences
Boston, MA

1438. Mennonite Brethren Biblical Seminary
Fresno, CA

1439. Missouri at Columbia, School of Law, University of
Columbia, MO

1440. Molloy College
Rockville, NY

1441. National Chung Hsing University
Taiwan, China

1442. National Law Center for Inter-American Free Trade
Tucson, AZ

1443. National University of Mexico
Mexico City, Mexico

1444. National War College
Washington, DC

1445. New York Medical College
Valhalla, NY

1446. Pacific School of Religion
Berkeley, CA

1447. Parsons School of Design
New York, NY

1448. Polytechnic School of Engineering
Milan, Italy

1449. Rivier College
Nashua, NH

1450. Royal Academy of Arts
London, England

1451. Seoul National University
Seoul, Korea

1452. Shenandoah University
Winchester, VA

1453. Smith Institute
London, England

1454. Southwestern Michigan College
Dowagaic, MI

1455. Spring Garden College
Philadelphia, PA

1456. St. Petersburg State Institute of Technology
St. Petersburg, Russia

1457. State University of New York at Fredonia
Fredonia, NY

1458. State University of New York at Oswego
Oswego, NY

1459. State University of New York, Brooklyn College of Medicine
Brooklyn, NY

1460. State University of New York, Institute of Technology at Utica/Rome
Utica/Rome, NY

1461. Teheran, University of
Teheran, Iran

1462. National Judicial College, The
Reno, NV

1463. Texas Southern University, Thurgood Marshall School of Law
Houston, TX

1464. Defense Language Institute, The
Monterey, CA

1465. Union Theological Seminary
New York, NY

1466. Bordeaux, University of
Bordeaux, France

1467. Universidad Iberoamericana
La Cruz, Mexico

1468. Amsterdam, University of
Amsterdam, Netherlands

1469. Birmingham, University of
Birmingham, England

1470. Bristol, University of
Bristol, England

1471. Catholic University of Brussels
Brussels, Belgium

1472. Canterbury, University of
Canterbury, New Zealand

1473. Costa Rica, University of
Moravia, Costa Rica

1474. East Anglia, University of
East Anglia, England

1475. Exeter, University of
Exeter, England

1476. Geneva, University of
Geneva, Switzerland

1477. Grenoble, University of
Grenoble, France

1478. Hannover, University of
Hannover, Germany

1479. Keele, University of
Keele, England

1480. Kent at Canterbury, University of
Canterbury, England

1481. Manchester, University of
Manchester, England

1482. New South Wales, University of
New South Wales, Australia

1483. Newcastle-upon-Tyne, University of
Newcastle-upon-Tyne, England

1484. Northern California, University of
Petaluma, CA

1485. Panama, University of
Panama, Rep. of Panama

1486. San Carlos, University of
University City, Guatemala

1487. Santa Monica College
Santa Monica, CA

1488. Sheffield, University of
Sheffield, England

1489. National University of Singapore
Singapore, Singapore

1490. Sydney, University of
Sydney, Australia

1491. Vrije Universiteit
Amsterdam, Netherlands

1492. Valley Forge Military Academy and College
Wayne, PA

1493. Zurich, University of
Zurich, Switzerland

1494. California at Los Angeles, University of
Los Angeles, CA

1495. Henry W. Bloch School of Business & Public Administration, University of Missouri
Los Angeles, CA

1496. European University
Amsterdam, Netherlands

1497. Nevada Mackay School of Mines, University of
Reno, NV

1498. Havana, University of
Havana, Cuba

1499. Rio Grande University
Rio Grande, OH

1500. Rhode Island School of Design
Providence, RI

1502. Ryerson Polytechnic University
Toronto, Canada

1503. Paul H. Nitze School of Advanced International Studies
Washington, DC

1504. California at Sacramento, University of
Sacramento, CA

1505. State University of New York at Stony Brook
Stony Brook, NY

1506. Thayer School of Engineering at Darmouth College
Hanover, NH

1507. State University of New York at Brockport
Brockport, NY

1508. Denver, Graduate School of International Studies, University of
Denver, CO

1509. Richmond, T.C. Williams School of Law, University of
Richmond, VA

1510. Long Island University, Southampton College
Southampton, NY

1511. St. Paul's College
Lawrenceville, VA

1512. Strayer University
Washington, DC

1513. Hague Academy of International Law, The
The Hague, Netherlands

1514. Naval Justice School
Newport, RI

1515. Glasgow, University of
Glasgow, Scotland

1516. Madrid, University of
Madrid, Spain

1517. Americas, University of the
Mexico City, Mexico

1518. Witwatersrand, University of the
Johannesburg, South Africa

1519. Webb Institute
Glen Cove, NY

1520. Southern New England School of Law
North Dartmouth, MA

1521. Leicester, University of
Leicester, England

1522. Loyola Law School
Los Angeles, CA

1523. Katholieke Universiteit Leuven
Leuven, Belgium

1524. Belmont University
Nashville, TN

1525. Universidad Nacional de Mexico
Mexico City, Mexico

1526. Florida Coastal School of Law
Jacksonville, FL

1527. British-American University School of Law
Santa Ana, CA

1528. Florida Metropolitan University
Tampa, FL

1529. State University of New York College at Buffalo
Buffalo, NY

1530. Hebrew University of Jerusalem, The
Jerusalem, Israel

1531. Southern New Hampshire University
Manchester, NH

4210. Louis D. Brandeis School of Law, University of Louisville
Louisville, KY

PRACTICE PROFILES BAR ROSTER

CONNECTICUT, DELAWARE
DISTRICT OF COLUMBIA
U.S. GOVERNMENT LAWYERS

CONNECTICUT

CAPITAL: HARTFORD

Connecticut Bar Association
30 Bank Street
New Britain, Connecticut 06051
Telephone: 860-223-4400
Fax: 860-223-4488

Index of Towns and Cities Listed by County

*Indicates County Seat

Fairfield County
Bethel
* Bridgeport
Brookfield
Byram
Cos Cob
Danbury
Darien
Easton
Fairfield
Greens Farms
Greenwich
Huntington
Monroe
New Canaan
New Fairfield
Newtown
Norwalk
Old Greenwich
Redding
Ridgefield
Riverside
Rowayton
Sandy Hook
Shelton
Sherman
Southport
Stamford
Stratford
Trumbull
Weston
Westport
West Redding
Wilton

Hartford County
Avon
Berlin
Bloomfield
Bristol
Broad Brook
Burlington
Canton
Canton Center
Collinsville
East Glastonbury
East Granby
East Hartford
Enfield
Farmington
Glastonbury
Granby
* Hartford
Kensington
Manchester
Marlborough
New Britain
Newington
North Canton
Plainville
Plantsville
Rocky Hill
Simsbury
South Glastonbury
Southington
South Windsor
Suffield
Tariffville
Unionville
Warehouse Point
Weatogue

Hartford Co.—*Continued*
West Granby
West Hartford
West Simsbury
West Suffield
Wethersfield
Windsor
Windsor Locks

Litchfield County
Bethlehem
Bridgewater
Canaan
Colebrook
Falls Village
Goshen
Harwinton
Kent
Lakeville
* Litchfield
New Hartford
New Milford
New Preston
Norfolk
Northfield
Pleasant Valley
Roxbury
Salisbury
Sharon
South Kent
Terryville
Thomaston
Torrington
Warren
Washington
Washington Depot
Watertown
Winsted
Woodbury

Middlesex County
Chester
Clinton
Cromwell
Deep River
Durham
East Haddam
East Hampton
Essex
Fenwick
Haddam
Higganum
Ivoryton
Killingworth
Middlefield
* Middletown
Old Saybrook
Portland
Rockfall
Westbrook

New Haven County
Ansonia
Beacon Falls
Bethany
Branford
Cheshire
Derby
East Haven
Guilford
Hamden

New Haven Co.—*Continued*
Madison
Meriden
Middlebury
Milford
Naugatuck
* New Haven
North Branford
Northford
North Haven
Orange
Oxford
Prospect
Seymour
Southbury
Stony Creek
Wallingford
Waterbury
West Haven
Wolcott
Woodbridge

New London County
Bozrah
Colchester
East Lyme
Franklin
Gales Ferry
Groton
Hadlyme
Hanover
Jewett City
Lebanon
Ledyard
Lyme
Mystic
New London
Niantic
Noank
North Franklin
North Stonington
* Norwich
Oakdale
Old Lyme
Pawcatuck
Quaker Hill
Salem
Stonington
Uncasville
Waterford

Tolland County
Amston
Bolton
Columbia
Coventry
Ellington
Hebron
Mansfield Center
Rockville
Somers
Somersville
Stafford Springs
Staffordville
Storrs
Tolland
* Vernon

Windham County
Ashford
Brooklyn

Windham Co.—*Continued*
Canterbury
Danielson
Hampton
Moosup
Plainfield
Pomfret
Pomfret Center
* Putnam
Quinebaug
Scotland
Thompson
Willimantic
Windham
Woodstock

AMSTON, —, *Tolland Co.*

McKeon, Maria F. '56 '87
C&L.184 B.S.B.A., J.D. Gen. Coun., McKeon Professional Services

ANSONIA, 18,403, *New Haven Co.*

Altschuler, Milo J., (BV) .... '45 '70 C.264 A.B. L.184 J.D. 1 Kingston Dr.
Androski, Edward J., (BV) .... '47 '73 C.16 B.A. L.192 J.D. [Androski,A.&A.]
Androski, John F. .... '11 '40 L.16 LL.B. [Androski,A.&A.]
Androski, John F. X., (BV) .... '43 '69 C.573 B.A. L.1119 J.D. [Androski,A.&A.]
Androski, Androski & Androski, (BV) .... 156 Main St.
Bennett, John J., (BV) .... '44 '69 C.321 B.S. L.184 LL.B. [Bennett&W.]
Bennett & Walsh, (BV) .... 103 Main St.
Bruchal, Richard S., (CV) .... '37 '62 C.976 B.A. L.188 LL.B. 88 Main St.

Cohen & Thomas
(See Derby)

Condon, Kevin W., (BV) .... '54 '80 C.93 A.B. L.64 J.D. [Condon&S.]
Condon, Thomas J., (BV) .... '24 '55 C.976 B.A. L.902 LL.B. [Condon&S.]
Condon & Savitt, (BV) .... 400 Main St.
Dillon, Timothy P., (BV) .... '57 '83 C.676 B.A. L.1029 J.D. [Sheehy&D.]
Gallant, Gerald M., (BV) .... '58 '84 C.28 B.A. L.1029 J.D. [Lyons,T.&G.]
Goletz, Elena Castro .... '49 '81 C.724 B.A. L.425 J.D. 25 Main St.
Hoyle, Clifford D., (BV) .... '45 '70 C.262 B.S. L.184 J.D. Prob. J.
Korolyshun, Richard .... '51 '91 C.602 B.A. L.1029 J.D. 295 Main St.
Lafferty, Richard W., (BV) .... '41 '80 C.397 B.A. L.184 J.D. 60 Main St.
LeBas, Sean O. .... '55 '86 C.881 B.A. L.184 J.D. 20 West St.
Lyons, James C., (BV) .... '35 '62 C&L.184 B.A., LL.B. [Lyons,T.&G.]
Lyons, Tuccio & Gallant, (BV) .... 235 Wakelee Ave.
Mirabile, Lori Ann .... '61 '86 C.976 B.A. L.188 J.D. 11 Greenfield Ave.
Morris, Theodore C. '65 '91
C.999 B.M. L.184 J.D. V.P., Gen. Coun. & Secy., Farrel Corp.
Pepe, Pasquale, (BV) .... '24 '51 C&L.262 A.B., LL.B. 28 William St.
Savitt, Herbert S., (BV) .... '31 '59 C&L.228 B.A., LL.B. [Condon&S.]
Savitt, Richard P., (BV) .... '64 '90 C.867 B.A. L.818 J.D. [Condon&S.]
Sheehy, James E., (BV) .... '50 '75 C.1030 A.B. L.472 J.D. [Sheehy&D.]
Sheehy & Dillon, (BV) .... 303 Wakelee Ave.
Skuret, Daniel D. .... '42 '67 C.1030 B.A. L.184 LL.B. 215 Division St.
Spadaro, Joseph A. .... '65 '98 C.855 B.S. L.306 J.D. 38 William St.
Tuccio, William P., (BV) .... '42 '66 C.676 A.B. L.818 J.D. [Lyons,T.&G.]
Walsh, James W., (BV) .... '46 '77 C.1102 B.S. L.1048 J.D. [Bennett&W.]
Wilber, William J. .... '38 '64 C.1029 B.S. L.564 LL.B. 350 E. Main St.
Yuravich, Kenneth J. .... '50 '85 C.1102 B.S. L.1029 J.D. 21 Kathy Ln.‡

ASHFORD, 3,221, *Windham Co.*

Halvorsen, Kristin Jennie .... '59 '84 C.184 B.A. L.982 J.D. 155 Seckar Rd.
Halvorsen, Kristine J. .... '— '85 155 Seckar Rd.

AVON, 11,201, *Hartford Co.*

Anstey, Roger J. .... '49 '85 C.454 B.A. L.1048 J.D. 110 Hopmeadow St.
August, Robert B., (AV) .... '21 '50 C.977 B.A. L.276 J.D. [August&K.]
August & Kulick, (AV) .... 29 Old Avon Village
Barnes, Nan C. .... '69 '94 C.156 B.A. L.306 J.D. Claims Coun., Target Capital
Blackburn, Tegan .... '55 '90 C.1211 B.S. L.464 J.D. [T.Blackburn]
Blackburn, Tegan, LLC .... Old Avon Village, 29 East Main Street
Busemeyer, Gale K. '41 '89 C.436 B.A. L.184 J.D.
Counsel, Security-Connecticut Life Insurance Company
Carignan, Philip J., (BV) .... '57 '82 C.93 B.S. L.818 J.D. [Moran,S.C.&K.]
*PRACTICE AREAS: Probate; Estate Planning; Real Property; Land Use.
Case, Richard A., (BV) .... '36 '62 C.976 A.B. L.184 J.D. [R.A.Case]
Case, Richard A., P.C., (BV) .... 10 Tower Lane
Casella, Alfred R. .... '71 '96 C.857 B.S. L.184 J.D. [Ⓐ Drew&M.] (⊙Agawam, MA)
*PRACTICE AREAS: Estate Settlements; Estate Planning; Business Planning.
Cavo, Richard C., (AV) .... '57 '85 C.732 B.A. L.724 J.D. [Litchfield C.]
Chiniara, Ellen V. '58 '85 C.104 B.A. L.813 J.D.
Senior Vice President & General Counsel, Internet Health Care Group, LLC
Cohen, David J. '29 '67 C.94 A.B. L.184 LL.B.
Sr. V.P. & Gen. Coun., Security Conn. Life Ins. Co.
Corbett, David A. .... '71 '99 C.184 B.A. L.1048 J.D. [Ⓐ Litchfield C.]
Donoghue, Michael J., (BV) .... '45 '72 C.94 B.A. L.184 J.D. 111 Simsbury Rd.
Drake, E. Thayer '23 '49 C&L.309 A.B., LL.B.
(adm. in NY; not adm. in CT) 53 Old Wood Rd.‡
Drew, Christopher S. .... '67 '95 C.228 A.B. L.184 J.D. [Drew&M.]
*PRACTICE AREAS: Estate Planning; Business Planning; Corporate Law; Estate Settlement.
Drew, John E., (AV) .... '41 '67 C.165 A.B. L.880 J.D. [Drew&M.]
*PRACTICE AREAS: Estate Planning; Business Planning; Estate Settlement.

Drew & Mersereau, P.C., (AV)
47 West Main Street, 06001
Telephone: 860-677-1974 Fax: 860-677-9143
Email: dandmavon@aol.com URL: http://www.lawyers.com/drew&mersereau
John E. Drew; Paul E. Mersereau; Christopher S. Drew;—Alfred R. Casella; David C. Grimes.
Estate Planning, Business Planning, Estate Settlement, Estate and Gift Taxation and Corporate Law.
See Professional Biographies, AVON, CONNECTICUT

Edrich, Marc S., (BV) .... '64 '89 C.188 B.S. L.982 J.D. [Ⓐ Litchfield C.]
*PRACTICE AREAS: Insurance Coverage Defense; Commercial Litigation; Bankruptcy.
Fischer, Michael S., (BV) '60 '85 C.184 B.A. L.1019 J.D.
56 E. Main St. (⊙East Hartford)
Fitzgerald, Ronald J. .... '48 '83 C&L.1048 M.B.A., J.D. 17 Pioneer Dr.
Garfinkel, Harry .... '32 '77 C.401 B.S. L.184 J.D. 66 Country Club Rd.

Gasser, Edward W., (BV) '56 '88 C.1103 B.S. L.1048 J.D.
20 East Main Street, P.O. Box 984, 06001-0984
Telephone: 860-674-8342 Fax: 860-676-8912
Email: egasser@gasserlaw.com
***PRACTICE AREAS: Insurance Defense; Professional Liability Law; Real Estate Law; Insurance Law; Gaming Law.**
Insurance Law, Insurance Defense, Civil Litigation, Gaming Litigation.
See Professional Biographies, AVON, CONNECTICUT

Gillin, Peter G., (AV) .... '43 '69 C&L.276 B.A., J.D. 106 Fox Den Rd.
Glass, Norton .... '31 '78 C&L.184 B.A., J.D. Sr. V.P., Security Conn. Life Ins. Co.
Gollinger, Stuart H. .... '42 '66 C.164 B.A. L.818 J.D. Tax Atty., State Dept. of Rev. Servs.
Gonzalez, Lawrence A. '71 '00 C.260 B.S. L.184 J.D.
Claims Coun., Target Professional Associates
Grimes, David C. .... '74 '00 C.10 B.A. L.184 J.D. [Ⓐ Drew&M.]
*PRACTICE AREAS: Estate Planning; Business Planning; Corporate Law.
Ide, Henry C., (BV) .... '38 '68 C.860 B.A. L.339 J.D. 49 West Main Street
Jajliardo, Timothy S. .... '66 '99 C&L.184 B.A., J.D. [Ⓐ Litchfield C.]
Jaliardo, Timothy S. .... '66 '99 C.184 L.306 J.D. 40 Tower Lane
Jepson, John K. .... '37 '64 C.732 B.A. L.184 J.D. P.O. Box 457
Jones, W. Philip .... '49 '74 C.1059 B.S. L.280 J.D. [Jones&W.]
Jones & Wanchak, L.L.C. .... 22 Waterville Rd.
Jurczak, Richard J., (BV) .... '51 '78 C.690 B.A. L.1202 J.D. 101 Stagecoach Rd.
Kamins, David E. .... '38 '63 C&L.184 B.S., LL.B. P.O. Box 1463
Kantor, Dennis N., (BV) .... '46 '72 C.4 B.B.A. L.184 J.D. [Kantor,M.&M.] ⊙
Kantor, Mickelson and Meyers, P.C., (BV) .... 56 E. Main St. (⊙East Hartford)
Katz, Morton N., (BV) .... '19 '51 C&L.184 B.S., J.D. 77 Wellington Heights Rd.
Kihlmire-Caudil, Kelly '71 '00 L.1252 J.D.
Claims Coun., Target Professional Associates
Kittredge, Rachel L. ... '66 '90 C.860 B.A. L.94 J.D. Gen. Coun., Apple Health Care, Inc.
Knierim, Glenn E., Jr., (AV) .... '53 '78 C.321 A.B. L.128 J.D. [Moran,S.C.&K.]
*PRACTICE AREAS: Litigation.
Krass, Barrett L., (BV) .... '42 '66 C.665 B.A. L.306 J.D. 49 W. Main St.
Kulick, Michael S., (BV) .... '40 '65 C.478 B.A. L.178 LL.B. [August&K.]
Ladd, Edwin V., Jr. '25 '49 C.477 B.S.E. L.309 LL.B.
(adm. in OH; not adm. in CT) 51 Great Meadow Lane‡
Liberator, John D., (BV) .... '56 '81 C.184 B.A. L.990 J.D. P.O. Box 650

Litchfield Cavo, (AV)
40 Tower Lane, Suite 200, 06001 ⊙
Telephone: 860-255-5577 Telefax: 860-255-5566
Alan I. Becker (Resident, Chicago, Illinois Office); Tracy C. Beggs (Resident, Chicago, Illinois Office); Benjamin A. Blume (Resident, Chicago, Illinois Office); Richard C. Cavo; Robert L. Ciociola (Not admitted in CT; Resident, Lynnfield, Massachusetts Office); Thomas M. Crawford (Resident, Chicago, Illinois Office); Michael W. Donaubauer (Resident, Chicago, Illinois Office); Mitchell H. Frazen (Resident, Chicago, Illinois Office); Matthew J. Iverson (Resident, Chicago, Illinois Office); Eileen P. Kavanagh (Resident, Lynnfield, Massachusetts Office); Daniel G. Litchfield (Resident, Chicago, Illinois Office); Kathleen F. Munroe; Hope G. Nightingale (Resident, Chicago, Illinois Office); Mark W. Rattan; Patrick J. Sullivan (Resident, Chicago, Illinois Office); Charles E. Vermette, Jr. Associates: John J. Cavo (Resident, Chicago, Illinois Office); Kathleen J. Collins (Not admitted in CT; Resident, Chicago, Illinois Office); Gabriel Daniel Martin Ciociola (Not admitted in CT; Resident, Lynnfield, Massachusetts Office); David A. Corbett; Marc S. Edrich; Dawn M. Gonzalez (Resident, Chicago, Illinois Office); Timothy S. Jajliardo; John D. LaBarbera (Resident, Chicago, Illinois Office); Brian Peter Mularski (Resident, Shorewood, Wisconsin Office); Matthew D. Walker (Resident, Chicago, Illinois Office); Melicent B. Thompson; Stephanie Wing Tipton (Resident, Chicago, Illinois Office).
General Civil Practice in State and Federal Courts, Trials and Appeals. Arbitration and Mediation. Business Litigation, Insurance Coverage, Reinsurance, Insurance Litigation, Insurance Defense, Product Liability Defense, Professional Liability Defense, Employment Litigation, Technology Law and Litigation.
Chicago, Illinois Office: 303 West Madison Street, 60606. Telephone: 312-781-6677. Fax: 312-781-6630.
Boston, Massachusetts Area Office: 6 Kimball Lane, Suite 100, Lynnfield, Massachusetts, 01940-2682. Telephone: 781-246-0155. Fax: 781-246-0167.
Haddonfield, New Jersey Office: 3 South Haddon Avenue, 08033. Telephone: 856-428-6682. Fax: 856-354-1656.
Milwaukee, Wisconsin Area Office: 4447 North Oakland, Shorewood, Wisconsin, 53211. Telephone: 414-962-7240. Fax: 414-962-7243.
See Professional Biographies, AVON, CONNECTICUT

Livsey, Philip C. .... '59 '84 C.183 B.A. L.818 J.D. 239 Old Farms Rd.
Lowinger, Lloyd S., (BV) .... '58 '85 C.855 B.A. L.94 J.D. P.O. Box 564

Luria, Peter D., (BV) '53 '79 C.855 B.A. L.61 J.D.
32 East Main Street, P.O. Box 779, 06001
Telephone: 860-674-1411
Civil Litigation, Securities Litigation, Arbitration, Commercial Law, Commercial Litigation, Business Law, Real Estate, Trials in all courts, Arbitration.
See Professional Biographies, AVON, CONNECTICUT

Maher, Thomas F. .... '15 '41 C.602 B.C.S. L.309 LL.B. P.O. Box 1421
Manion, Francis V., (BV) .... '16 '40 C.855 B.S. L.306 LL.B. 1 Racebrook Lane
McMasters, Linda G., (BV) .... '49 '83 C.94 B.A. L.1029 J.D. 29 E. Main St.
Mersereau, Paul E., (AV) .... '39 '64 C.951 B.A. L.309 LL.B. [Drew&M.]
*PRACTICE AREAS: Estate Planning; Business Planning; Estate Settlement.

Meyer, Judith D., (BV) '49 '89 C.1090 B.S. L.184 J.D.
152 Simsbury Road, P.O. Box 451, 06001-0451
Mailing Address: P.O. Box 451, Avon, Connecticut 06001-0451
Telephone: 860-678-7711 Fax: 860-677-6832
Email: judithdmeyer@nela.org URL: http://www.lawyers.com/jdmlaw
Employment Law, Civil Litigation in all State and Federal Courts and Administrative Agencies, Professional Licensing.
See Professional Biographies, AVON, CONNECTICUT

Meyers, Linda B., (BV) .... '58 '84 C.588 B.S. L.93 J.D. [Kantor,M.&M.] ⊙
Mickelson, Jeffrey D., (BV) .... '54 '82 C.260 B.A. L.1206 J.D. [Kantor,M.&M.] ⊙
Moran, Robert R., Jr., (BV) .... '46 '71 C.823 B.A. L.818 J.D. [Moran,S.C.&K.]
*PRACTICE AREAS: Real Property; Probate; Estate Planning.

Moran, Shuster, Carignan & Knierim, LLP, (AV)
111 Simsbury Road, 06001
Telephone: 860-678-0450 Fax: 860-676-2507
URL: http://www.lawyers.com/msc&k
Carl H. Shuster; Robert R. Moran, Jr.; Philip J. Carignan; Glenn E. Knierim, Jr.
Real Estate, Land Use, Probate, Estate Planning, Small Business Representation, Personal Injury, Civil and Criminal Litigation.
See Professional Biographies, AVON, CONNECTICUT

Munroe, Kathleen F., (CV) .... '49 '88 C.95 B.A. L.184 J.D. [Litchfield C.] (⊙Chgo., IL)

O'Connor, F. William, (CV) '48 '79 C.855 M.A. L.184 J.D.
20 East Main Street, 06001-1224
Telephone: 860-677-2254 Fax: 860-676-8912
Email: fwoc@aol.com URL: http://www.lawyers.com/oconnorfw
***PRACTICE AREAS: Estate Planning; Tax Law; Real Estate; Corporate Law.**
Estate Planning, Tax Law, Real Estate, Corporate Law, Probate.
See Professional Biographies, AVON, CONNECTICUT

Peters, John C., (AV) .... '31 '59 C.56 B.A. L.477 J.D. [J.C.Peters]

Peters, John C., P.C., (AV) BR
30 Avon Meadow Lane, P.O. Box 797, 06001-0797
Telephone: 860-676-1608 Fax: 860-676-2250
Email: Pete68may@aol.com
John C. Peters.
General Corporate, Finance, Banking and Securities Law. Litigation, Probate, Elder Law.
See Professional Biographies, AVON, CONNECTICUT

Powell, Kathleen Lynch '49 '77
C.527 B.A. L.446 J.D. V.P. & Coun., Berwind Property Grp., Inc.
Rossetti, Christopher J., (BV) .... '53 '80 C.1036 B.A. L.184 J.D. 2 Arrowhead Ct.
Sanderford, David M. '43 '69 C.418 B.S. L.744 J.D.
(adm. in TX; not adm. in CT) 32 Hastings Turn‡
Sellman, Richard I., (BV) .... '50 '74 C.401 B.S. L.184 J.D. [Kantor,M.&M.] ⊙
Shuster, Carl H., (AV) .... '36 '62 C.855 B.A. L.145 J.D. [Moran,S.C.&K.]
*PRACTICE AREAS: Real Property; Estate Planning.
Spalla, Joseph R. .... '25 '56 C.184 B.S.E.E. L.276 J.D. 17 Oxbow Dr.‡

Thompson, Melicent B. .... '67 '96 C.276 B.S. L.306 J.D. [Ⓐ Litchfield C.] (⊙Chgo., IL)
Vayos, Daphne R. .... '62 '87 C.518 B.A. L.94 J.D. 69 Rosewood Rd.
Vermette, Charles E., Jr. ...... '64 '89 C.273 B.A. L.95 J.D. [Litchfield C.] (⊙Chgo., IL)
Voight, Robert J. '49 '80
C.321 B.A. L.184 J.D. V.P. & Treas., Security Conn. Life Ins. Co.
Wanchak, Wendy W. .... '57 '87 C.972 B.A. L.1292 J.D. [Jones&W.]
Widing, Carol, (BV) '41 '81
C.914 B.A. L.1338 J.D. 33 East Main Street, Suite 4 (⊙Hartford)

BEACON FALLS, 3,995, *New Haven Co.*

Woodward, James W. '28 '77 C.870 B.S. L.64 J.D.
(adm. in VA; not adm. in CT) 11 Wolfe Ave.‡

BERLIN, 15,121, *Hartford Co.*

Bourne, Robert J. .... '58 '85 C.918 B.A. L.184 J.D. Sr. Coun., N.E. Utilities
*RESPONSIBILITIES: Commercial Law; Real Estate Law; Liability Law.
Butler, Gregory B. '57 '89 C.1350 B.A. L.982 J.D.
(adm. in NY; not adm. in CT) V.P., Gen. Coun. & Sec., Northeast Utilities
*RESPONSIBILITIES: General Corporate.
Carlson, James L. .... '56 '96 C.546 B.S. L.1048 J.D. [Ⓐ Scibilia&M.]
*PRACTICE AREAS: Construction Law; Zoning, Planning and Land Use; Corporate Law; Securities; Real Estate.
Crown, Jeffrey L., (AV) .... '44 '73 C.1033 B.A. L.184 J.D. 129 Mill St.
Cugno, Jeffrey P. .... '50 '87 C.184 B.S. L.1029 J.D. [Ⓒ Scibilia&M.]
*PRACTICE AREAS: Real Estate; Land Use; Commercial; Corporate Law.
Davenport, Alicia B., (BV) .... '62 '90 C&L.577 B.A., J.D. Sr. Coun., Northeast Utilities
*RESPONSIBILITIES: Labor and Employment Litigation.
Eagle, Kenneth H. .... '51 '88 C.401 B.A. L.1066 J.D. Sr. Coun., Northeast Utilities
Early, Richard M., (BV) .... '53 '81 C.453 S.B. L.569 J.D. Sr. Coun., Northeast Utilities
Gilbane, Donna M. .... '56 '90 C.454 B.A. L.184 J.D. Sr. Coun., Northeast Utilities
Kellogg, Thomas O., (BV) .... '47 '72 C.732 B.A. L.188 J.D. 1263 Wilbur Cross Hwy.
Klein, Frederic Lee '53 '79
C.588 B.S.E.E. L.93 J.D. Asst. Gen. Coun., Northeast Utilities
Lemell, Phyllis E. .... '55 '79 C&L.823 B.A., J.D. Sr. Coun., Northeast Utilities
MacKay, Duncan R., (AV) '62 '88 C.454 B.A. L.818 J.D.
Sr. Coun., Northeast Utilities
Maldonado, Elizabeth A., (BVⓉ) '60 '87
C.1252 B.A. L.184 J.D. Sr. Coun., Northeast Utilities
McCuin, J. Scott, (CV) .... '65 '89 C&L.184 B.A., J.D. [Scibilia&M.]
*PRACTICE AREAS: Real Estate; Land Use; Commercial Transactions; Corporate; Securities Law.
Michalski, Carrie Damico .... '56 '89 C.999 B.S.N. L.978 J.D. 198 Lamentation Dr.
Miller, Jeffrey C., (AV) '43 '70 C.976 B.A. L.188 J.D.
(adm. in NY; not adm. in CT) Asst. Gen. Coun., Northeast Utilities
Murphy, Laura M. ..... '66 '92 C.855 B.A. L.1048 J.D. [Ⓐ Scibilia&M.] (⊙Seattle, WA)
*PRACTICE AREAS: Real Estate; Commercial Transactions; Corporate Law; Commercial Litigation; Wills.
Olson, Edward, Jr. .... '21 '50 C.918 B.A. L.309 LL.B. 826 Worthington Rdg.
Quinlan, William J. '60 '93
C.884 B.S.M.E. L.184 J.D. Dep. Gen. Coun., Northeast Utilities
Rodriguez, Leonard .... '62 '94 C.1107 B.A. L.184 J.D. Coun., Northeast Utilities
Rowtham-Kennedy, Monique '66 '91
C.103 A.B. L.228 J.D. Sr. Coun., Northeast Utilities
Scibilia, Suzanne M., (BV) .... '56 '83 C.1033 B.A. L.724 J.D. [Scibilia&M.]
*PRACTICE AREAS: Commercial Transactions; Real Estate; General Corporate; Business Law; Securities.

Scibilia & McCuin, P.C., (BV)
Worthington Professional Park, 1263 Wilbur Cross Highway, 06037
Telephone: 860-828-8884 Fax: 860-829-0410
Suzanne M. Scibilia; J. Scott McCuin;—Laura M. Murphy; James L. Carlson. Of Counsel: Jeffrey P. Cugno.
Commercial Transactions, Corporate, Business and Securities, Real Estate and Litigation.
See Professional Biographies, BERLIN, CONNECTICUT

Seidl, Jane P. .... '58 '85 C.93 B.A. L.184 J.D. Sr. Coun., Northeast Utilities
Venora, Daniel P. '59 '84 C.262 B.A. L.724 J.D.
Assoc. Gen. Coun., Northeast Utilities
Walker, Cristi C. .... '69 '95 C.112 B.A. L.329 J.D. Coun., N.E. Utilities
*RESPONSIBILITIES: Public Utility Regulation.

BETHANY, 1,170, *New Haven Co.*

Brinton, Robert Harrison .... '66 '97 C.184 B.S.C.E. L.306 J.D. 562 Amity Rd.
Bronson, Rice & Simon, (AV) .... 649 Amity Rd.
Cohen, Louis B. .... '47 '77 C&L.184 B.S., J.D. 50 Bethridge Rd.
Eisner, Lawrence B. .... '51 '76 C.867 B.A. L.276 J.D. 49 Valley Rd.‡
Hirschoff, Mary-Michelle Upson .... '42 '70 C.813 A.B. L.976 J.D. 392 Sperry Rd.
Jennes, Jeffrey Andrew .... '65 '90 C.390 B.A. L.659 J.D. 59 Bethany Farms Rd.

Knott, John K., Jr.
(See Cheshire)

Latimer, Arthur H. .... '40 '67 C.197 A.B. L.309 LL.B. Ret. U.S. Mag. J.
Rice, Cleaveland J., Jr., (AV) .... '24 '51 C.976 B.S. L.477 J.D. [Bronson,R.&S.]
Simon, Martin .... '48 '74 C&L.184 B.A., J.D. 361 Amity Rd.‡
Simon, W. Peter, Jr., (BV) .... '61 '86 C.282 B.A. L.818 J.D. [Bronson,R.&S.]
Simon, William P., (AV) .... '32 '59 C.103 A.B. L.178 LL.B. [Bronson,R.&S.]

BETHEL, 16,004, *Fairfield Co.*

Anderson, John W., II .... '60 '88 C.184 B.A. L.1029 J.D. 235 Greenwood Ave.
Aquilio, Mark '56 '84 C&L.262 B.S., J.D.
(adm. in NY; not adm. in CT) 138 Codfish Hill Rd.
Bower, Kathy S., (BV) ...... '63 '88 C.1044 B.A. L.1019 J.D. [Gager&P.] (⊙Southbury)
*PRACTICE AREAS: Personal Injury Litigation.
Chamberlain, Scott B. .... '54 '85 C&L.420 B.S., J.D. [S.B.Chamberlain]
*PRACTICE AREAS: Family Law; Divorce; Criminal Law; Personal Injury.

Chamberlain, Scott B., P.C., The Law Office of
275 Greenwood Avenue, 06801
Telephone: 203-798-2877 Fax: 203-798-6359
Email: mx5madness@aol.com URL: http://www.lawyers.com/chamberlainlaw
Scott B. Chamberlain.
Family Law, Divorce, Bankruptcy, Criminal Law, Personal Injury.
See Professional Biographies, BETHEL, CONNECTICUT

Dipentima, Christian Lawrence '71 '97
C.93 B.A. L.1252 J.D. [Ⓐ Gager&P.] (⊙Southbury)
*PRACTICE AREAS: Insurance Defense (45%); Plaintiffs Personal Injury (45%); Workers Compensation (5%); Family Law (3%); Labor and Employment (2%).
Driscoll, James C., III, (BV) .... '51 '76 C.321 B.A. L.262 J.D. [Driscoll,T.F.O.&D.]
Driscoll, Talarico, Frizzell, Olivo & Driscoll, (AV)
235 Greenwood Avenue (⊙Danbury, Southbury)
Emerson, Richard L., (BV) .... '46 '73 C.918 B.A. L.273 J.D. [Gager&P.]
*PRACTICE AREAS: Corporate Law; Banking Law; Trusts and Estates.

Evans, Kenneth M., (BV) .... '44 '75 C.184 B.A. L.669 J.D. 93 Greenwood Ave.
Frizzell, Thomas A., (BV) '40 '68
C&L.724 B.B.A., LL.B. [Driscoll,T.F.O.&D.] (⊙Danbury)

Gager & Peterson, LLP, (AV)
2 Stony Hill Road, 06801 ⊙
Telephone: 203-207-5400 Telecopier: 203-207-5407
Richard L. Emerson; Thomas J. McHale; Thomas M. Rickart; Kathy S. Bower; Frank J. Scinto. Associate: Peter A. Scalzo; Christian Lawrence Dipentima.
General Practice. Corporate Law, Banks and Banking, Securities, Administrative Law, Litigation, Insurance, Trusts and Estates, Probate, Real Estate, Taxation, Patents, Trademarks, Copyrights, Zoning, Planning and Land Use, Consumer Law, Environmental Law, Computers and Software, Information Technology, Labor and Employment Law, Personal Injury.
Waterbury, Connecticut Office: One Exchange Place, P.O. Box 2480. Telephone: 203-597-5100. Telecopier: 203-757-7888.
Litchfield, Connecticut Office: 782 Bantam Road. Telephone: 860-567-0828. Telecopier: 860-567-5844.
Sharon, Connecticut Office: 25 West Main Street, P.O. Box 158. Telephone: 860-364-5531. Telecopier: 860-364-5805.
Southbury, Connecticut Office: 325 Main Street South. Telephone: 203-262-6600. Telecopier: 203-262-6780.
See Professional Biographies, BETHEL, CONNECTICUT

Gallagher, Edward J., (BV) .... '34 '60 C.1030 B.S. L.276 LL.B. 8 School Street
Kennedy, Timothy P. .... '69 '98 C.999 B.A. L.1252 J.D. [Ⓐ Mihaly&K.] ⊙

Kulawitz, Harvey J., LLC
(See Ridgefield)

Lawlor, Martin J., Jr., (BV) .... '53 '78 C.1102 B.A. L.1048 J.D. 99 Greenwood Ave.
Mannion, James M., (BV) .... '45 '71 C.524 B.A. L.724 J.D. 225 Greenwood Ave.
Mayer, Jerome A., (BV) .... '56 '81 C.184 B.A. L.128 J.D. [Driscoll,T.F.O.&D.]
McHale, Thomas J., (AV) ..... '41 '67 C.745 B.A. L.128 J.D. [Gager&P.] (⊙Waterbury)
*PRACTICE AREAS: Banking Law; Consumer Credit Law; Computer Law; Employment Law.
Medvecky, Thomas E., (BV) .... '37 '62 C.95 A.B. L.724 LL.B. 99 Greenwood Ave.
Mihaly & Kascak, (BV) .... 93 Greenwood Ave. (⊙Trumbull)
Mummert, Catherine C. .... '59 '84 C.914 B.A. L.575 J.D. 10 Grand St.
Murray, Gwen E. .... '— '96 C.1103 B.B.A. L.1252 J.D. 153 Greenwood Ave.
Olivo, Steven M., (BV) ... '48 '75 C.197 A.B. L.94 J.D. [Driscoll,T.F.O.&D.] (⊙Danbury)
Rasamny, Robert .... '49 '76 C.184 B.A. L.262 J.D. 165 Grassy Plain
Rickart, Thomas M., (BV) ...... '53 '81 C.976 B.A. L.93 J.D. [Gager&P.] (⊙Southbury)
*PRACTICE AREAS: Real Estate Law; Environmental Law; Commercial Lending.
Riordan, Denis J. .... '36 '61 C.529 L.724 J.D. 17 Linda Lane
Scalzo, Peter A. .... '62 '95 C.1053 B.S. L.1339 J.D. [Ⓐ Gager&P.]
*PRACTICE AREAS: Real Estate; Landlord and Tenant Law; Zoning, Planning and Land Use; Wills, Trusts and Estates; Business Law.
Scinto, Frank J., (BV) .... '53 '83 C.276 B.S. L.93 J.D. [Gager&P.] (⊙Waterbury)
*PRACTICE AREAS: Business Law; Intellectual Property; Commercial Litigation; Employment Law.
Spain, John F., (BV) .... '39 '64 C.321 A.B. L.569 LL.B. 9 Chestnut St.
Talarico, Robert N., (BV) '42 '65 C&L.184 B.A., LL.B.
[Driscoll,T.F.O.&D.] (⊙Danbury)
Winokur, Richard M. .... '33 '59 C&L.976 B.A., LL.B. 5 Second Lane

BETHLEHEM, 2,573, *Litchfield Co.*

Bardelli, John F. .... '44 '81 C.1156 A.S. L.184 J.D. 17 Arrowhead Ln.

Jackson, O'Keefe and Phelan, (AV)
423 Munger Lane, 06751 ⊙
Telephone: 203-266-5255 Fax: 203-266-5255
Andrew J. O'Keefe; Matthew J. O'Keefe.
General Practice including Civil Trial and Appellate Practice in all Courts, Governmental Law and Relations, Personal Injury, Medical Malpractice, Construction Litigation, Products Liability, Probate and Estate Planning, Residential and Commercial Real Estate, Corporation, Insurance, Banking, Legislative Practice, Mediation and Arbitration.
Hartford, Connecticut Office: 36-40 Russ Street. Telephone: 860-278-4040. Fax: 860-527-2500.
See Professional Biographies, BETHLEHEM, CONNECTICUT

Matarese, A. L. .... '33 '58 C&L.184 B.A., J.D. 273 Flanders Rd.
O'Keefe, Andrew J., (AV) .... '31 '56 C.321 B.S. L.184 J.D. [Jackson,O.&P.] ⊙
O'Keefe, Matthew J., (BV) .... '57 '82 C.321 B.A. L.818 J.D. [Jackson,O.&P.] ⊙
*PRACTICE AREAS: Estate Planning and Administration; Real Estate; Family Law; Divorce; Child Custody.
Rush, Thomas P., (AV) .... '53 '78 C.588 B.A. L.309 J.D. 519 Carmel Hill Rd. North

BLOOMFIELD, 18,608, *Hartford Co.*

Albrecht & Zelman, (BV) .... 116 Cottage Grove Rd.
Anderson, Buist M., (AV) .... '04 '28 C.893 B.S. L.976 J.D. 24 Alice Dr.‡
Anderson, Lisa K., (BV) .... '57 '83 C.19 B.A. L.1048 J.D. [Ⓐ Nair&L.]
*PRACTICE AREAS: Bankruptcy; Collection Law; Real Estate Law.
Arnold, Jane A. H. .... '40 '80 C.477 B.A. L.184 J.D. 7 Cliffmount Dr.
Barall, Stanley M., (BV) .... '26 '58 C&L.184 B.A., J.D. 34 Jerome Ave.
Baram, David A., (BV) .... '53 '78 C.184 B.A. L.744 J.D. Mayor [Clayman,M.T.&B.]
*PRACTICE AREAS: Family Law; Business Law; Commercial Transactions; Real Estate; Zoning and Municipal Law.
Barry, Anne D. .... '59 '01 C.184 B.S. L.306 J.D. [Ⓐ Cantor C.]
Beck, Alan L., (BV) .... '35 '62 C.184 B.A. L.94 LL.B. 21 Maple Edge Drive
Bedingfield, Herbert M. ..... '72 '99 C.228 B.A. L.184 J.D. [Ⓐ Cantor C.] (See Pat. Sect.)
*PRACTICE AREAS: Patent Law; Trademark Law; Copyright Law.
Beutel, Karen .... '71 '01 C&L.424 B.S., J.D. [Ⓐ Cantor C.]
*PRACTICE AREAS: Patents.
Bongiovi, Lisa A. '66 '94 C.184 B.S. L.1048 J.D.
(adm. in PA; not adm. in CT) [Ⓐ Cantor C.]
Brandwein, David I., (BV) '49 '74 C.119 B.S. L.184 J.D.
Principal & Environmental Counsel, Environmental Risk Ltd.
Bruso, Daniel E. '67 '96 C.971 B.S. L.1048 J.D.
(adm. in MA; not adm. in CT) [Ⓐ Cantor C.]
*PRACTICE AREAS: Commercial Law; Bankruptcy; Creditors Rights; Commercial Litigation; Intellectual Property.
Bunker, Roger E. .... '41 '94 C.309 B.A. L.306 J.D. 28 Old Village Rd.
Burke, Solomon T. .... '20 '44 C.28 B.A. L.184 LL.B. P.O. Box 11241
Cabral Caruk, Anna-Cristina ... '66 '92 C.1103 B.A. L.184 J.D. [Ⓐ S.S.Chinitz&Assoc.]
*PRACTICE AREAS: Collections; Personal Injury; Divorce.
Cantor, Michael, (BV) '58 '84
C&L.184 B.S., J.D. [Cantor C.] (See Pat. Sect.) (⊙Norwalk)
*PRACTICE AREAS: Patent Law; Trademark and Copyright Law; Unfair Competition; Intellectual Property Law.

Cantor Colburn LLP, (BV)
55 Griffin Road South, 06002-1355 ⊙
Telephone: 860-286-2929 Fax: 860-286-0115
Email: iplaw@cantorcolburn.com URL: http://www.cantorcolburn.com
Members of Firm: Michael Cantor; Philmore H. Colburn, II; Keith J. Murphy; Leah M. Reimer; David A. Fox; William J. Cass; Michael J. Rye; Pamela J. Curbelo. Associates: Andrew C. Ryan; Wayne R. Grohs; Timothy J. Olson; Herbert M. Bedingfield; Steven M. Coyle; Charles F. O'Brien; George A. Pelletier, Jr.; Troy LaMontagne; Deborah B. Crenshaw (Not admitted in CT); Leonard E.

(This Listing Continued)

Cantor Colburn LLP (Continued)

Heyman; Daniel F. Drexler; George J. Lyman; James J. Merrick; Sean F. Sullivan; Pamela S. Chestek; Daniel E. Bruso (Not admitted in CT); Lisa A. Bongiovi (Not admitted in CT); Peter R. Hagerty (Not admitted in CT); Marisa J. Dubuc; Michael J. Chang; Anne D. Barry; Karen Beutel; Jennifer A. D'Errico (Not admitted in CT).
Patent, Trademark and Copyright Law, Unfair Competition, Computer and Related Intellectual Property Law including Litigation in all Courts.
Norwalk, Connecticut Office: 101 Merritt 7, 06853. Telephone: 203-849-8266. Fax: 203-849-8292.
See Professional Biographies, BLOOMFIELD, CONNECTICUT

Carlson, Susan J. . . . '56 '81 C&L.184 B.S., J.D. [Ⓐ Clayman,M.T.&B.]
*PRACTICE AREAS: Business Law; Real Estate; Trademarks.
Cass, William J., (BVⓉ) '62 '88 C.971 B.S. L.1048 J.D. [Cantor C.] (See Pat. Sect.) (⊙Springfield, MA)
*PRACTICE AREAS: Intellectual Property; Litigation.
Chang, Michael J. . . . '74 '01 [Ⓐ Cantor C.]
Chestek, Pamela S. . . . '55 '01 C.645 B.F.A. L.1048 J.D. [Ⓐ Cantor C.]
*PRACTICE AREAS: Trademarks; Copyrights; Intellectual Property Litigation.

Chinitz, Stephen S., & Associates, (BV) '53 '79 C.184 B.A. L.365 J.D.
800 Cottage Grove Road, Suite 421, 06002
Telephone: 860-769-6999 Fax: 860-769-6998
Email: ssc@home.com URL: http://www.lawyers.com/stephenschinitz
***PRACTICE AREAS: Commercial Law; Litigation; Bankruptcy Law; Creditor's Rights; Collections.**
Associate: Anna-Cristina Cabral Caruk.
Collections, Creditor's Rights, Personal Injury, Insurance, Subrogation, Bankruptcy Court Litigation (Creditors), Legal Malpractice, Domestic Relations and Real Estate, Trials in all Courts.
See Professional Biographies, BLOOMFIELD, CONNECTICUT

Clark, Candace A., (BV) '55 '80 C.855 B.A. L.184 J.D. Sr. V.P. Chf. Legal Offr. & Secy., Kaman Corp.
*RESPONSIBILITIES: Corporate Law.
Clark, Robert F. . . . '59 '89 C.1145 M.B.A. L.184 J.D. V.P., CIGNA Invest., Inc.
Clayman, Martin A., (BV) . . . '36 '62 C.976 B.A. L.184 J.D. [Clayman,M.T.&B.]
*PRACTICE AREAS: Franchise Law; Business Law; Commercial Litigation; Commercial Real Estate; Trademark Law.

Clayman, Markowitz, Tapper and Baram, L.L.C., (BV)
3 Regency Dr., 06002-2331
Telephone: 860-242-2221 Telecopier: 860-286-0185
Email: office@ctattys.com URL: http://www.ctattys.com
Members of Firm: Martin A. Clayman; David J. Markowitz; Paul Litman; Joseph M. Tapper; Francis J. Farrelly; Jason Y. Gans; David A. Baram; Kent D. Mawhinney;—Susan J. Carlson.
Business Law, Commercial, Condominium, Corporate, Criminal Law, Elder Law, Employment Law, Entertainment Law, Estate Planning, Family, Franchise Law, General Practice. Immigration, Municipal Law, Nationality, Negligence, Personal Injury, Planning and Zoning, Probate, Real Estate, Trademarks, Trials in all Courts.
See Professional Biographies, BLOOMFIELD, CONNECTICUT

Clifford, Thomas D. . . . '33 '62 C.262 A.B. L.276 J.D. Supr. Ct. J.
Colburn, Philmore H., II, (BV) '59 '91 C.588 B.S.E.E. L.1048 J.D. [Cantor C.] (See Pat. Sect.) ⊙
*PRACTICE AREAS: Patent Law; Trademark and Copyright Law; Unfair Competition; Intellectual Property Law.
Collins, Atwood, II, (AV) . . . '17 '42 C&L.976 A.B., J.D. 20 Loeffler Rd.‡
Coyle, Steven M., (BVⓉ) . . . '68 '93 C.855 B.A. L.1048 J.D. [Ⓐ Cantor C.]
*PRACTICE AREAS: Intellectual Property Litigation.
Crane, Newton D. . . . '10 '35 C&L.976 B.A., LL.B. 60 Loeffler Rd.‡
Crenshaw, Deborah B. '59 '94 C.326 B.S.E.E. L.845 J.D. (adm. in TX; not adm. in CT; See Pat. Sect.) [Ⓐ Cantor C.]
*PRACTICE AREAS: Intellectual Property.
Curbelo, Pamela J. . . . '66 '91 C.971 B.S. L.1048 J.D. [Cantor C.] (See Pat. Sect.)
*PRACTICE AREAS: Intellectual Property Law.
Daly, John F., III, (BV) . . . '42 '83 C.676 B.A. L.1029 J.D. 140 Park Ave.
Daly, John G. . . . '36 '61 C.604 A.B. L.930 J.D. Sr. V.P. & Chf. Coun., CIGNA Corp.
Dayner, Judith C. . . . '55 '93 C.184 B.S. L.306 J.D. 14 Walts Hill
D'Errico, Jennifer A. '74 '00 C.823 B.A. L.1398 J.D. (adm. in NY; not adm. in CT) [Ⓐ Cantor C.]
*PRACTICE AREAS: Intellectual Property.
DiCorleto, Dominic A., (AV) '15 '41 C.855 B.A. L.306 LL.B. Clk. of Supr. Ct & Supr. Ct.‡
Dominianni, Paul A., (BV) . . . '56 '81 C.823 B.A. L.94 J.D. Sr. Coun., CIGNA Corp.
Drexler, Daniel F. . . . '72 '00 C.1292 B.S. L.1040 J.D. [Ⓐ Cantor C.]
*PRACTICE AREAS: Patent; Intellectual Property; Trademark.
Dubuc, Marisa J. . . . '60 '01 C.462 B.S. L.1048 J.D. [Ⓐ Cantor C.]
*PRACTICE AREAS: Patent Prosecution.
Famely, Max '17 '76 C.102 B.A. L.1148 J.D. (adm. in CA; not adm. in CT) 18 Bear Ridge Dr.‡
Farrelly, Francis J., (BV) . . . '41 '66 C.93 B.S. L.184 LL.B. [Clayman,M.T.&B.]
*PRACTICE AREAS: Probate Law; Estate Planning Law; Elder Law; Real Estate Law.
Fox, David A. . . . '67 '95 C.688 B.S.E.E. L.128 J.D. [Cantor C.] (See Pat. Sect.)
*PRACTICE AREAS: Patent Law; Trademark Law; Copyright Law; Unfair Competition; Intellectual Property.
Freeman, Gregory C. . . . '49 '75 C.105 B.S. L.904 J.D. Conn. Gen. Life Ins. Co.
Gans, Jason Y., (BV) . . . '43 '68 C.477 B.A. L.94 LL.B. [Clayman,M.T.&B.]
*PRACTICE AREAS: Immigration and Nationality Practice.
George, Elizabeth . . . '56 '82 C.788 B.A. L.184 J.D. Coun., CIGNA Corp.
Ginsberg, Elliot A., (BV) . . . '47 '73 C.264 B.A. L.184 J.D. 22 Stuart Dr.
Goldman, Jacob J. . . . '27 '54 C.1029 B.A. L.569 LL.B. 3 Candlewood Dr.
Goldstein, Lawrence P. '36 '60 C.264 B.A. L.446 LL.B. (adm. in MD; not adm. in CT) Conn. Gen. Life Ins. Co.
Greenberg, Gary S. . . . '50 '75 C.823 B.A. L.809 J.D. V.P., Birken Mfg. Co.
Greenberg, Sidney . . . '24 '51 C.16 B.S. L.184 LL.B. 3 Old Windsor Rd.‡
Grohs, Wayne R. . . . '64 '99 C.1156 B.S. L.1252 J.D. [Ⓐ Cantor C.]
*PRACTICE AREAS: Patent Law; Trademark Law.
Hagerty, Peter R. '61 '94 C.454 B.S.Chem. L.1202 J.D. (adm. in MA; not adm. in CT; See Pat. Sect.) [Ⓐ Cantor C.]
*PRACTICE AREAS: Intellectual Property; Patents; Trademarks; Copyrights.
Helms, James R. . . . '58 '84 C.354 B.A. L.184 J.D. 8 Basswood Ct.
Heyman, Leonard E. . . . '67 '00 C.1083 B.S.M.E. L.107 J.D. [Ⓐ Cantor C.]
*PRACTICE AREAS: Intellectual Property.
Hubbard, David R. . . . '16 '48 C.976 A.B. L.188 LL.B. 40 Locefller Rd., #316P‡
Hussain, Sabeena . . . '69 '94 C&L.705 B.A., J.D. Coun., CIGNA
Jamgochian, Hagop H. . . . '22 '53 C.156 B.B.A. L.273 J.D. 750 Cottage Grove Rd.
Johnson, Chester N. . . . '18 '49 C.918 B.A. L.309 LL.B. 25 Walker Lane
Karlin, Rhonda Michelle '60 '85 C.188 B.A. L.94 J.D. Sr. Cnsl., Cigna Corporation (Legal Department)
Keir, Diana J. . . . '63 '89 C.184 B.A. L.1029 J.D. [Ⓐ Nair&L.]
*PRACTICE AREAS: Collection Law; Commercial Litigation; Creditors Rights; Labor Law.
Kelly, John M., (CV) . . . '64 '91 C.1030 B.A. L.1048 J.D. [Ⓐ M.N.Needelman]
*PRACTICE AREAS: General Litigation; Personal Injury; Real Estate; Municipal; Landlord/Tenant.
Kent, Cynthia J. . . . '57 '84 C.347 B.A. L.879 J.D. 510 Cottage Grove Rd.

Knierim, Glenn E., (AV) '30 '60 C.188 B.S. L.184 J.D. 693 Bloomfield Ave. (⊙Hartford)
LaMontagne, Troy . . . '62 '98 C.1213 B.S.E.E. L.1048 J.D. [Ⓐ Cantor C.]
*PRACTICE AREAS: Intellectual Property.
Levin, Robert M., (BV) . . . '50 '75 C.94 B.S. L.472 J.D. [Nair&L.]
*PRACTICE AREAS: Collection Law; Personal Injury; Real Estate; Creditors Rights; Bankruptcy.
Levine, Mitchell J., (BV) . . . '65 '90 C.1019 B.A. L.1048 J.D. [Ⓐ Nair&L.]
*PRACTICE AREAS: Bankruptcy; Foreclosure; Commercial Litigation; Personal Injury; Creditors' Rights.
Lewin, Richard H. . . . '44 '73 C.93 B.S. L.184 J.D. 14 Wild Rose Ct.
Lichtenberger, Paul H., (BV) . . . '52 '81 C.433 B.C.E. L.184 J.D. 1 Bestor Ln.
Litman, Paul, (BV) . . . '39 '64 C.28 B.S. L.94 LL.B. [Clayman,M.T.&B.]
*PRACTICE AREAS: Family Law; Personal Injury; Criminal Law; Arbitration; Mediation.
Lyman, George J. . . . '52 '00 C.1033 B.S. L.1048 J.D. [Ⓐ Cantor C.]
*PRACTICE AREAS: Patent Prosecution.
Maglieri, Charles A., (BV) . . . '54 '81 C.829 B.A. L.1048 J.D. 34 Jerome Ave.
Markowitz, David J., (BV) . . . '48 '74 C.156 B.A. L.184 J.D. [Clayman,M.T.&B.]
*PRACTICE AREAS: Business Law; Real Estate Law; Planning Law; Zoning Law; Condominium Law.
Mawhinney, Kent D. . . . '65 '90 C.1155 B.S. L.1048 J.D. [Clayman,M.T.&B.]
*PRACTICE AREAS: Civil Litigation; Immigration Law.
McClure, Ann, (BV) . . . '50 '78 C.915 B.A. L.229 J.D. [McClure&W.]
McClure & Weatherby, LLC, (BV) . . . 2 Croydon Dr.
McNeill, Thomas C., Jr., (BV) . . . '52 '79 C.478 B.S. L.597 J.D. [McNeill&Assoc.]
McNeill & Associates, (BV) . . . 816 Park Ave.
Meeker, Lori B. . . . '64 '91 C.937 B.A. L.1048 J.D. [Ⓐ Nair&L.]
*PRACTICE AREAS: Collection Law; Real Estate; Personal Injury; Commercial Law; Probate Administration.
Merrick, James J. . . . '61 '97 C.999 B.S. L.1048 J.D. [Ⓐ Cantor C.] (See Pat. Sect.)
*PRACTICE AREAS: Litigation; Trial Practice; Intellectual Property Litigation; Investigations; Personal Injury.
Messemer, Glenn M., (BV) '47 '72 C.276 B.S.B.A. L.306 J.D. Gen. Coun., Kaman Corp.
*RESPONSIBILITIES: Corporate Law.
Murphy, Keith J. . . . '65 '94 C.308 B.A. L.724 J.D. [Cantor C.] (See Pat. Sect.)
*PRACTICE AREAS: Intellectual Property; Patent Law; Trademark; Copyright.

Nair & Levin, P.C., (BV)
510 Cottage Grove Road, 06002
Telephone: 860-242-7585 Facsimile: 860-242-2980
Robert M. Levin;—Lisa K. Anderson; Diana J. Keir; Mitchell J. Levine; Lori B. Meeker; Catherine A. Wilowski; Peter J. Sterling; Melissa E. Schwalbach.
Commercial Litigation, Collections, General Practice, Bankruptcy, Personal Injury, Creditors' Rights, Real Estate.
Representative Clients: Hartford Hospital, Inc.; St. Francis Hospital and Medical Center; Ford Motor Credit Co.; General Motors Acceptance Corp.; Chrysler Credit Corp.; East Hartford Aircraft Federal Credit Union.
See Professional Biographies, BLOOMFIELD, CONNECTICUT

Nassau, Arthur M., (BV) . . . '35 '60 C&L.976 B.A., LL.B. 11 Mountain Ave.
Neal, Patricia '46 '74 C&L.352 B.A., J.D. (adm. in IA; not adm. in CT) Conn. Gen. Life Ins. Co.

Needelman, Marc N., Law Offices of, (BV) '52 '77 C.273 B.A. L.1048 J.D.
Suite 313 800 Cottage Grove Road, 06002-2343
Telephone: 860-242-7174 Telecopier: 860-242-8291
***PRACTICE AREAS: Civil; Real Estate; Corporate; Commercial; Personal Injury.**
Associate: John M. Kelly.
General Practice. Trials in all Courts. Real Estate, Corporate and Commercial, Personal Injury, Criminal, Municipal, Workers Compensation, Zoning, Domestic and Family, Landlord and Tenant.
Representative Clients: Town of Bloomfield; Bernie's Audio Video T.V. Appliance Co., Inc.; Merchants Insurance Group; Countrywide Home Mortgage Corp.; Connecticut Electric Railway Association, Inc.
References: Connecticut Attorneys Title Insurance Co.
See Professional Biographies, BLOOMFIELD, CONNECTICUT

O'Brien, Charles F. . . . '70 '97 C.588 B.S.M.E. L.1048 J.D. [Ⓐ Cantor C.]
*PRACTICE AREAS: Intellectual Property Litigation.
Olson, Timothy J. . . . '65 '99 C.1027 B.S. L.306 [Ⓐ Cantor C.] (See Pat. Sect.)
*PRACTICE AREAS: Patent Law; Trademark Law; Copyright Law; Intellectual Property Law.
Pelletier, George A., Jr. . . . '70 '97 C.65 B.A. L.1048 J.D. [Ⓐ Cantor C.]
*PRACTICE AREAS: Trademark Law.
Reimer, Leah M. . . . '60 '95 C.69 B.Sc. L.184 J.D. [Cantor C.] (See Pat. Sect.)
*PRACTICE AREAS: Patent Law; Trademark Law; Copyright Law; Unfair Competition; Intellectual Property.
Riege, John H., (AV) . . . '22 '48 C.918 B.A. L.976 LL.B. 10 Biltmore Park‡
Ryan, Andrew C. . . . '68 '97 C.999 B.S. L.1048 J.D. [Ⓐ Cantor C.]
*PRACTICE AREAS: Patent Law; Trademark Law; Intellectual Property Litigation.
Rye, Michael J., (BVⓉ) '62 '90 C.494 B.A. L.823 J.D. [Cantor C.] (See Pat. Sect.) (⊙Springfield, MA)
*PRACTICE AREAS: Intellectual Property Litigation.
Schatz, Arthur H., (AV) . . . '18 '42 C&L.188 A.B., LL.B. 33 Juniper Rd.
Schwalbach, Melissa E. . . . '68 '93 C.184 B.A. L.1048 J.D. [Ⓐ Nair&L.]
*PRACTICE AREAS: Commercial Litigation; Civil Litigation; Personal Injury; Creditors' Rights.
Silver, Charles S., (BV) . . . '52 '78 C.401 B.S. L.851 J.D. 11 Mountain Ave.
Sollima, Francesca M. . . . '66 '92 C.1211 B.S. L.1029 J.D. Primax Recoveries, Inc.
Soycher, Mark D., (BV) . . . '51 '80 C.705 B.A. L.564 J.D. [Soycher&W.]
Soycher & Winslow, LLC, (BV) . . . 120 Mountain Avenue, Suite 320
Sterling, Peter J. . . . '46 '74 C.128 B.A. L.276 J.D. [Ⓐ Nair&L.]
*PRACTICE AREAS: Creditors' Rights; Personal Injury; Real Estate; Zoning Law; Environmental Law.
Sullivan, Sean F. . . . '— '93 C.184 BSEE L.1048 J.D. [Ⓐ Cantor C.]
*PRACTICE AREAS: Patent.
Tager, Jeff S. . . . '— '83 C.94 B.A. L.184 J.D. 29 Wintonbury Ave.
Tapper, Joseph M., (BV) . . . '41 '66 C.264 A.B. L.184 LL.B. [Clayman,M.T.&B.]
*PRACTICE AREAS: Immigration and Nationality Law.
Taylor, Alvin E. . . . '40 '74 C.966 B.S. L.309 J.D. 816 Park Ave.
Taylor, William A., (AV) '48 '73 C.478 B.A. L.184 J.D. Coun., Conn. Gen. Life Ins. Co.
Upchurch, Nancy C. . . . '52 '78 C.1044 B.A. L.184 J.D. Conn. Gen. Life Ins. Co.
Vicente, Rebecca M. . . . '69 '94 C.676 B.A. L.184 J.D. [Ⓐ Soycher&W.]
Walker, Earle H. '40 '76 C.831 B.S. L.494 (adm. in PA; not adm. in CT) 8 Willow Ln.‡
Weatherby, Henry C. . . . '50 '93 C.1044 B.S. L.184 J.D. [Soycher&W.]
Weed, Dwight D., (BV) . . . '45 '76 C&L.184 B.S., J.D. 1 Bestor Lane
Wilowski, Catherine A. . . . '56 '85 C.184 B.A. L.596 J.D. [Ⓐ Nair&L.]
*PRACTICE AREAS: Personal Injury; Commercial Litigation; Probate Administration; Real Estate; Collection Law.
Winslow, Mark S., (BV) . . . '58 '89 C.1155 B.S. L.1048 J.D. [Soycher&W.]
Witt, Otto P., (CV) . . . '42 '77 C.475 B.A. L.930 J.D. 9 Northcliff St.
Zelman, Steven M., (BV) . . . '47 '73 C.184 B.A. L.818 J.D. [Albrecht&Z.]

BOLTON, 3,951, *Tolland Co.*

Cabrera, Pamela J. . . . '59 '94 C.1145 B.S. L.1048 J.D. 84 Brookfield Rd.
Ramirez, Jose R., (BV) . . . '41 '75 C.1156 B.A. L.184 J.D. Corp. Coun.
Rudalevige, Suzanne '43 '83 C.051 B.A. L.588 J.D. (adm. in MA; not adm. in CT) P.O. Box 9405

Shankman, Leonard I., (BV) '36 '61 C&L.184 B.S., J.D. 18 Sunset Lane
Teller, Samuel H. '34 '64 C.563 B.S. L.184 LL.B. Supr. Ct. J.

BOZRAH, 2,135, *New London Co.*

Kofkoff, Robert A. '50 '75 C.1365 B.A. L.245 J.D. P.O. Box 187

BRANFORD, 23,363, *New Haven Co.*

Amore, Frederick P., (BV) '49 '74 C.93 A.B. L.184 J.D. 420 E. Main St.
Angelo, Charles B., (BV) '48 '73 C.1030 A.B. L.262 J.D. [Antollino,A.&S.]
Antollino, Frank, (BV) '42 '69 [Antollino,A.&S.]
Antollino, Angelo & Scalesse, (BV) 500 E. Main St.
Antonio & Coppola Law Firm, (BV) 500 E. Main St., Ste. 326
Apicella, Anthony G., (BV) '31 '59 C&L.184 B.S., LL.B. [A.G.Apicella]
Apicella, Douglas J., (CV) '63 '88 C.93 B.S. L.1048 J.D. [A.G.Apicella]
Apicella, Anthony G., P.C., (BV) P.O. Box 613
Bainer, Todd R., (BV) '59 '85 C.694 B.A. L.823 J.D. P.O. Box 1092
Beebe, Michael G., (BV) '59 '85 C.1102 B.S. L.1029 J.D. 150 W. Main St.
Black, Peter L. '59 '94 C.976 B.A. L.306 J.D. 7 Stone St.
Bonenberger, Gregory H., (BV) '48 '86 C.976 B.A. L.184 J.D. 80 Mill Plain Rd.
Bowman, Bruce W. '54 '80 C&L.8 B.S., J.D.
(adm. in OH; not adm. in CT) V.P., Delker Corp.
Brencher, George, III, (BV) '42 '67 C.1030 B.A. L.184 LL.B. [Patterson&B.]
Bruno, Alice A., (BV) '55 '81 C.860 B.A. L.184 J.D. [Edmonds&B.]
*PRACTICE AREAS: Litigation; Mediation; Family Law; Personal Injury; Workers Compensation.
Campbell, Andrew J. '66 '91 C.918 B.A. L.902 J.D. 1052 Main St.
Cannatelli, Frank P., (BV) '54 '88 C.184 B.A. L.1029 J.D. P.O. Box 954
Carroll, James J., (BV) '29 '65 C&L.184 B.A., J.D. [McGrail,C.&F.]
Casale, Robert M., (AV) '50 '78 C.1102 B.A. L.365 J.D. 250 W. Main St.
Chello, Paul L., (BV) '42 '85 C.367 B.A. L.1029 J.D. 500 E. Main St.
Chotiner, Renee D. '49 '74 C.681 A.B. L.309 J.D. 2 Summit Pl.

Church and Church
(See New Haven)

Cioffi, Gregory J. '56 '82 C.184 B.S. L.228 J.D. 105 Stannard Ave.
Clark, John Phelps, (AV) '32 '59 C&L.976 B.A., LL.B. 12 Pine Orchard Rd.
Coppola, Joseph T., (BV) '65 '91 C.1211 B.A. L.1029 J.D. [Antonio&C.]
Donegan, John E., (AV) '42 '66 C.321 B.S. L.184 LL.B. [Gibson&D.]
Drazen, James A. '38 '63 C.659 B.S. L.976 LL.B. 127 Highland Ave.
Dumark, Frank J., (AV) '28 '59 C.184 B.A. L.659 J.D. [Dumark&L.]
Dumark & Lindsay, (AV) 197 Montowese Street
Edmonds, Christian P., (AV) '52 '78 C.676 B.A. L.184 J.D. [Edmonds&B.]
*PRACTICE AREAS: Estate Planning; Probate; Real Estate; Taxation; Corporate Law.

Edmonds & Bruno, P.C., (AV)
52 Harrison Avenue, P.O. Box 807, 06405
Telephone: 203-488-1000 Telecopier: 203-488-1200
Christian P. Edmonds; Alice A. Bruno.
Estate Planning, Probate, Taxation, Corporation and Real Estate Law, Mediation, Family, Litigation, Workers Compensation, Personal Injury.
See Professional Biographies, BRANFORD, CONNECTICUT

Faris, Lisa M. '62 '92 C.1252 B.S. L.1029 J.D. [McGrail,C.&F.]
Florentine, Richard T., (BV) '59 '84 C.860 B.A. L.1029 J.D. 2 Summit Pl.
Forgione, Frank J., (BV) '57 '84 C.31 B.A. L.184 J.D. 226 E. Main St.
Foster, Randall J., (CV) '50 '88 C.999 B.S. L.1029 J.D. 100 Double Beach Rd.
Ghiroli, Al, (CV) '43 '88 C.1033 B.A. L.1029 J.D. 150 W. Main St.
Gibson, David A., (BV) '42 '68 C.945 B.A. L.184 J.D. [Gibson&D.]
Gibson & Donegan, (AV) 420 E. Main St.
Greenblatt, Morton H. '16 '41 C.976 B.A. L.309 LL.B. 50 Turtle Bay Dr.‡
Hanchuruck, Stephen P., (BV) '55 '82 C.999 B.A. L.607 J.D. 5 Summit Pl.
Harrington, Robert T., III, (BV) '52 '79 C.431 B.S. L.818 J.D. 226 E. Main St.
Hart, Philip Matthew, (CV) '47 '79 C.94 B.A. L.472 J.D. 101 W. Main St.
Kass, Frederic C. '48 '74 C.188 B.A. L.569 J.D.
(adm. in NY; not adm. in CT) 60 Yowego Ave.‡
Kennedy, Bernard T., (BV) '32 '85 C.1252 B.S. L.1187 J.D. 44 Sunset Hill Rd.
Killelea, James K. '40 '66 C.976 B.A. L.569 LL.B. 10 Halstead Lane
Killion, Susan Westrick '48 '83 C.249 B.S.N. L.1029 J.D. 22 Pepperwood Ln.
Lindsay, John H., (BV) '40 '67 C.1030 B.S.S. L.893 J.D. [Dumark&L.]
Loeb, Rhoda Leshine '21 '44 C.477 A.B. L.976 LL.B. 130 Johnsons Point Rd.
Lyons, Michele Olsen '69 '95 C.1044 B.A. L.1048 J.D. [[A] McGrail,C.&F.]
Marotta, Sharon Zak '72 '98 C.1292 B.S. L.1009 J.D. 136 Watch Hill Rd.
McGrail, John R., (AV) '35 '64 C.860 B.A. L.184 J.D. [McGrail,C.&F.]
McGrail, Carroll & Faris, P.C., A Professional Corporation, (AV) 388 E. Main St.
McMahon, Elizabeth Lorion, (BV) '56 '87
C&L.276 B.A., J.D. 202 S. Montowese St., Suite 5
Miessau, James A., (BV) '52 '77 C.309 B.A. L.818 J.D. 500 E. Main St.
Milano & Wanat, LLC, (BV) 471 East Main Street (⊙New Haven)
Morrison, Thomas R. '28 '76 C.367 B.S.E.E. L.446 J.D.
(adm. in NY; not adm. in CT; Pat.) [Morrison] ⊙
Morrison Law Firm 225 Montowese Street (Pat.) (⊙Mount Vernon, NY)
Motti, Peter K., (BV) '48 '73 C.776 B.A. L.945 J.D. 270 E. Main St.

Naizby, John F. '66 '93 C.308 B.A. L.1252 J.D.
10 Middle Street, 06601
Telephone: 203-315-1000
***PRACTICE AREAS: Personal Injury.**
Personal Injury.
See Professional Biographies, BRANFORD, CONNECTICUT

Olgin, Jeffrey '51 '75 C.94 B.A. L.421 J.D. 74 Rose Hill Rd.
Pantaleo, Carl V., (CV) '51 '77 C.93 B.S. L.472 J.D. 470 E Main St 2nd Fl
Patterson, Richard D., (BV) '33 '64 C.184 B.A. L.1066 LL.B. [Patterson&B.]
Patterson and Brencher, (BV) 730 Main St.
Reynolds, Edward L., (BV) '23 '52 C.262 B.S. L.588 LL.B. 20 Yowago Ave.‡
Richheimer, David E., (AV) '46 '73 C.696 B.A. L.477 J.D. 2 Summit Pl.
Rozen, Lynne '— '87 C.659 B.A. L.1252 J.D. 150 W. Main St.
Ryan, Gerald P., (BV) '46 '73 C.860 B.A. L.818 J.D. 270 E. Main St.
Sachs, Gregory J., (CV) '64 '91 C.94 B.S.B.A. L.904 J.D. 420 E. Main St.
Sandler, Robin Bruce, (BV) '54 '84 C.1102 B.A. L.1029 J.D. [R.B.Sandler]
Sandler, Robin Bruce, P.C., (BV) 175 Montowese St.
Scalesse, Charles P., (BV) '48 '73 C.1030 A.B. L.93 J.D. [Antollino,A.&S.]
Scharf, Roy H., (BV) '28 '53 C.184 B.A. L.309 LL.B. 127 Cedar St.
Schneider, Andrew J. '65 '95 C.385 B.A. L.902 J.D. [[A] McGrail,C.&F.]
Shea, James O'Connor, (AV) '20 '47 C&L.976 B.A., LL.B. 1052 Main St.‡
Smith, Richard J., Jr., (BV) '35 '62 C.262 B.S. L.184 J.D. [R.J.Smith Jr.]
Smith, Richard J., Jr., P.C., (BV) 175 N. Main St.
Stevens, Donald E., (BV) '28 '56 C.156 B.A. L.184 LL.B. 698 Main St.
Sullivan, Roger M., Law Offices of, (AV) '30 '68
C.1266 B.A. L.178 LL.B. 7 South Main Street

Twohill, Frank B., (CV) '57 '85 C.999 B.A. L.1194 J.D. 107 Montowese St.
Wanat, Christopher F., (BV) '62 '87 C.184 B.S. L.1017 J.D. [Milano&W.] ⊙
Ward, Robert M., (BV) '52 '78 C.184 B.A. L.150 J.D. State Rep.
Whalen, Michael J., (BV) '44 '69 C.276 A.B. L.184 J.D. 175 Montowese St.
Wieler, Martha Anne '64 '92 C.183 B.A. L.1194 J.D. 500 E. Main St.
Wilson, Francis P. '41 '68 C.976 B.A. L.880 J.D. Pres., Image Processing

BRIDGEPORT, * 141,686, *Fairfield Co.*

Aceto, Leslie Paier, (BV) '62 '88 C.93 B.A. L.184 J.D. [Zeldes,N.&C.]
*PRACTICE AREAS: Real Estate; Commercial; Corporate.
Adams, Taggart D. '41 '71 C.299 A.B. L.309 LL.B. Supr. Ct. J.
Adelman, Robert B., (AV) '52 '78 C.732 B.A. L.188 J.D. [Adelman H.&N.]
*PRACTICE AREAS: Personal Injury; Medical Malpractice; Products Liability; Legal Malpractice.

Adelman Hirsch & Newman, LLP, (AV)
1000 Lafayette Boulevard, 06604
Telephone: 203-331-8888 Fax: 203-333-4650 URL: http://www.ahnlaw.com
Email: ahnlaw@hotmail.com URL: http://www.lawyers.com/injurylawct
Members of Firm: Robert B. Adelman; Joram Hirsch; Richard L. Newman; Neil W. Sutton; Mary Ann Connors; Michael F. Ewing.
Plaintiff's Personal Injury, Medical Malpractice, Products Liability, Wrongful Death, Automobile Accidents, Truck Accidents and Legal Malpractice.
See Professional Biographies, BRIDGEPORT, CONNECTICUT

Afonso, Louis A., (BV) '64 '89 C.1102 B.S. L.184 J.D. 3324 Main St.
Albert, Martin J., (AV) '45 '70
C.659 B.S. L.94 J.D. [Cohen&W.] (⊙Stamford, Westport)
*PRACTICE AREAS: Taxation; Estate Planning; Probate.
Albrecht, Richard L., (AV) '38 '62
C.105 B.S. L.188 J.D. [Cohen&W.] (⊙Stamford, Westport)
*PRACTICE AREAS: Litigation.
Albrecht, W. Kenneth, (BV) '57 '84
C.951 B.A. L.352 J.D. Gen. Coun., D'Addario Industries
Altieri, Maria R., (BV) '57 '84 C.1030 B.S. L.809 J.D. 1836 Noble Avenue
Ambrose, Joseph P. '43 '67 C.1030 A.B. L.184 LL.B. Int. Rev. Serv.

Amendola & Amendola
(See Fairfield)

Anastasi, Mark T., (BV) '52 '77 C.321 B.A. L.94 J.D. City Atty.
Anderson, Dennis P., (BV) '46 '72 C.31 B.A. L.184 J.D. [Zeisler&Z.]
*PRACTICE AREAS: Commercial Real Estate; Commercial Litigation.
Antignani, N. Edwin, (BV) '23 '51 C&L.184 B.A., LL.B. 275 Congress St.
Arcobello, Daniel M., (BV) '49 '82 C&L.1029 B.A., J.D. 1087 Broad St., 2nd Fl.
Arons, Mark D., (BV) '58 '83 C.880 B.A. L.930 J.D. [Willinger,W.&B.]
*PRACTICE AREAS: Personal Injury; Medical Malpractice; Governmental Liability; Wrongful Death; Products Liability.
Ashkins, Robert J., (AV) '28 '58 C.1029 B.A. L.976 LL.B. [[C] Cohen&W.]
*PRACTICE AREAS: Business; Labor; Health Care.
Atkins, David P., (AV) '56 '82 C.178 B.A. L.976 J.D. [Zeldes,N.&C.]
*PRACTICE AREAS: Criminal and Commercial Litigation; Appeals; Professional Licensing and Discipline; Legal Ethics.
Austin, Elizabeth J., (BV) '57 '83 C&L.546 B.A., J.D.
[Pullman&C.] (⊙Hartford, New Haven, Stamford)
*PRACTICE AREAS: Insolvency Law; Bankruptcy Litigation; Commercial Litigation.
Avery, Robert W., (BV) '27 '54 C.1029 B.A. L.823 J.D. 3715 Main St.
Babycos, Frank Edward, (P.C.), (BV) '29 '63 C.1030 B.S.S. L.262 J.D.
734 Clinton Ave.

Bai, Pollock, Blueweiss & Mulcahey, P.C., (AV) [BB]
Park City Plaza, 10 Middle Street, P.O. Box 1978, 06604
Telephone: 203-366-7991 Fax: 203-366-4723
Arnold J. Bai (1931-1992); Paul E. Pollock; Jeffrey A. Blueweiss; Garie J. Mulcahey; Raymond J. Plouffe, Jr.; Madonna A. Sacco; Michael S. Lynch; David J. Robertson; Gaileen A. Kaufman;—Heidi Marie Cilano; Keith M. Blumenstock; Mark S. Leso; Linda D. D'Albis; Jeffrey R. Owens; Joshua A. Yahwak; Catherine L. Creager; MaryAnne Evan; Jeffrey N. Gaull.
Insurance Defense, Civil Trial Practice. Negligence, Professional Liability, Products Liability, Toxic Substances, Real Estate and Commercial Loans.
See Professional Biographies, BRIDGEPORT, CONNECTICUT

Bailey, Frank A., (BV) '61 '87 C.188 A.B. L.184 J.D. [Tremont&S.]
*PRACTICE AREAS: Personal Injury; Commercial Litigation; Workers Compensation; Civil Rights; Appellate Practice.
Baldwin, Raymond E., Jr., (BV) '27 '56
C.951 B.A. L.976 LL.B. [Pullman&C.] (⊙Southport)
*PRACTICE AREAS: Public Finance; Bond Finance; Trusts and Estates; Real Estate.
Ball, David A. '66 '91 C.1036 B.A. L.659 J.D. [Cohen&W.]
*PRACTICE AREAS: Commercial Litigation; Securities Litigation; Corporate.
Ballen, Myron R. '29 '54 C.823 B.A. L.184 LL.B. Supr. Ct. J.
Bargar, Hillary Markman, (AV) '55 '81 C.184 B.A. L.190 J.D. Juv. Pros.
Baron, Collin P., (BV) '47 '73 C.893 B.A. L.273 J.D. [Pullman&C.]
*PRACTICE AREAS: Health Care Law; Banking Law; Corporate Law.

Barr & LaCava
(See Stamford)

Bartlett, Keeler & Cohn, (AV) 955 Main St.
Bassick, Edgar W., III '27 '55 C.976 A.B. L.309 J.D. Supr. Ct. J.
Batt, Charles M., (CV) '50 '81 C.183 B.A. L.1029 J.D. 1087 Broad St.
Bauchner, Lawrence '47 '71 C.264 A.B. L.94 J.D. 900 Madison Ave.
Bear, Stuart, (AV) '44 '68 C&L.309 A.B., LL.B. [Zeldes,N.&C.]
*PRACTICE AREAS: Commercial Law and Litigation; Bankruptcy Law; Business Reorganization Law; Matrimonial Law.
Beatman, Matthew K., (BV) '65 '90 C.184 B.S. L.306 J.D. [Zeisler&Z.]
*PRACTICE AREAS: Bankruptcy; Commercial Litigation.
Beck, Jeffrey, (BV) '62 '88 C.264 B.A. L.1048 J.D. 251 North Ave.
Becker, Janine M. '66 '91 C.1349 B.A. L.1040 J.D. 3296 Main St.

Belinkie, Alfred R., & Associates, (AV) '24 '49 C.197 A.B. L.976 LL.B.
1087 Broad Street, 06604-4379
Telephone: 203-368-4201 Fax: 203-368-3075
Email: blink19@aol.com URL: http://www.lawyers.com/belinkielaw
***PRACTICE AREAS: Family Law; Divorce; Child Custody; Child Support; Juvenile Law.**
Associates: Donald J. Bowers; Diane Belinkie; Holly A. Heslin.
Family Law, Real Estate, Probate, Personal Injury, Elder Law, Bankruptcy, Divorce, Criminal, Estates, Wills, Workers Compensation.
See Professional Biographies, BRIDGEPORT, CONNECTICUT

Belinkie, Diane, (CV) '54 '97 C.156 B.A. L.1252 J.D. [[A] A.R.Belinkie&Assoc.]
*PRACTICE AREAS: Family Law; Elder Law; Criminal Law; Juvenile Law; Childrens Rights.
Belinkie, Milton H. '12 '36 C.976 B.A. L.178 LL.B. State Trial Ref.‡
Beltz, Christian G. '69 '95 C&L.262 B.S., J.D. [[A] Pullman&C.]
*PRACTICE AREAS: Municipal Law; Real Estate.
Bepko, Richard P., (CV) '31 '56 C.1030 B.S.S. L.93 LL.B. 3334 Main St.
Berman, James, (AV) '55 '81 C.976 B.A. L.184 J.D. [Zeisler&Z.]
*PRACTICE AREAS: Bankruptcy; Commercial Law.
Bernacki, Barbara '55 '82 C.881 B.A. L.184 J.D. Gen. Coun., D'Addario Industries

Bernard, Christopher D., (AV) '54 '79
C.472 B.B.A. L.260 J.D. [Koskoff,K.&B.] (⊙Stamford)
*PRACTICE AREAS: Medical Malpractice; Personal Injury.
Bernhard, G. Kenneth, (BV) ...'44 '69 C.976 B.A. L.569 J.D. [Cohen&W.] (⊙Westport)
*PRACTICE AREAS: Civil Litigation; Municipal; Domestic; Criminal; Zoning Appeals.
Bernier, Carrie L. .... '70 '00 C.93 B.A. L.1040 J.D. [Ⓐ Pullman&C.]
*PRACTICE AREAS: Litigation; Employment Law.
Bieder, Richard A., (AV) ....'40 '65 C.659 B.S. L.569 LL.B. [Koskoff,K.&B.]
*PRACTICE AREAS: Aviation Liability; Mass Torts; Commercial Litigation; Personal Injury.
Biggs, G. Whitney, (BV) ....'38 '64 C.976 B.A. L.893 LL.B. 850 Main St.
Bingham, James F. .... '25 '51 C&L.262 B.S., LL.B. Supr. Ct. J.
Blank, John B., (BV) ....'49 '74 C.867 B.A. L.982 J.D. 853 Fairfield Ave.
Blank, Lester E. .... '27 '53 C&L.184 B.A., LL.B. [Blank&B.]
Blank, Raymond E. ....'20 '46 C.401 L.184 LL.B. [Blank&B.]
Blank & Blank .... 853 Fairfield Ave.
Blawie, John F., (AV) ....'57 '83 C.321 A.B. L.184 J.D. Asst. States Atty.
Blueweiss, Jeffrey A., (BV) .... '56 '81 C.910 B.S.B.A. L.945 J.D. [Bai,P.B.&M.]
*PRACTICE AREAS: Civil Litigation; Construction Law; State Liability; Municipal Liability; Business Litigation.
Blumenstock, Keith M. .... '69 '99 C.688 B.S. L.1252 J.D. [Ⓐ Bai,P.B.&M.]
*PRACTICE AREAS: Professional Liability; Litigation.
Bochanis, John T., (BV) ....'58 '84 C.790 B.A. L.190 J.D. [Daly,W.&B.]
*PRACTICE AREAS: Trials and Appeals.
Bodell, Gerald E., (AV) '33 '58 C.321 A.B. L.262 LL.B.
177 State Street Suite 401 (⊙New York, NY)
Bodine, David ....'52 '76 C.855 B.A. L.94 J.D. Pres., Bodine Corp.
Bono, Bette L. .... '50 '85 C.339 B.A. L.309 J.D. 1000 Lafayette Blvd.
Bowen, Patrick H. .... '39 '65 C.434 A.B. L.228 J.D. 139 Grovers Ave.
Bowers, Donald J., (BV) ..... '61 '89 C.1349 B.A. L.1029 J.D. [Ⓐ A.R.Belinkie&Assoc.]
*PRACTICE AREAS: Civil Litigation; Commercial Litigation; Collections; Family Law; Foreclosures.
Bowman, Jonathan S., (AV) '42 '66
C.347 A.B. L.184 J.D. [Cohen&W.] (⊙Stamford, Westport)
*PRACTICE AREAS: Real Estate; Condominium; Property Tax Appeals; Bankruptcy; Title Insurance.

Bowman, Andrew B.
(See Westport)

Brandner & Ponzini
(See Stamford)

Braunstein & Todisco, LLC
(See Fairfield)

Brazzel-Massaro, Barbara, (BV) ....'52 '81 C.555 B.A. L.1048 J.D. Assoc. City Atty.
Breck, Deborah S., (BV) '53 '83
C.1102 B.A. L.184 J.D. [Pullman&C.] (⊙Southport, Stamford)
*PRACTICE AREAS: Estates and Trusts; Elder Law; Trust and Probate Litigation.
Brienes, Harold ....'35 '83 C.563 B.A. L.1029 J.D. 1566 Park Avenue

Brody, Wilkinson and Ober, P.C.
(See Southport)

Brooks, Lucia B. .... '45 '83 C.273 A.B. L.1029 J.D. Law Clk., U.S. Dist. Ct.
Browne, Donald A., (AV) ....'33 '58 C.1030 B.S.S. L.184 LL.B. [Browne&B.]
Browne, William T., (BV) ....'31 '58 C.1030 B.S.S. L.184 LL.B. [Browne&B.]
Browne & Browne, (AV) ....144 Golden Hill St. (⊙Beaumont, TX)
Brozdowski, Paul L., (CV) '59 '86 C.860 B.S. L.1040 J.D.
1087 Broad St., Ste. 403 (⊙Cortlandt Manor, NY)
Bryk, John R., (BV) .... '50 '74 C.1029 B.A. L.184 J.D. [Ⓒ Zeldes,N.&C.]
*PRACTICE AREAS: Business Law; Commercial Litigation; Commercial Real Estate; Residential Real Estate; Municipal Taxation.
Bucci, Thomas W., (AV) .... '48 '73 C.1211 B.A. L.184 J.D. [Willinger,W.&B.]
*PRACTICE AREAS: Trial and Appellate Practice; Loan Restructures; Employment Law; Foreclosures; Bankruptcy.
Bucci, Thomas W., Jr. .... '69 '95 C.184 B.A. L.724 J.D. [Ⓐ Willinger,W.&B.]
*PRACTICE AREAS: Land Use; Civil Litigation; Commercial Litigation; Labor and Employment Law; Municipal Law.
Budnick, Leo T., Jr., (BV) ....'49 '86 C.1030 B.A. L.1029 J.D. Asst. Atty. Gen.
Butler, James E. ....'— '94 C.436 B.A. L.1252 J.D. 1087 Broad St.
Cahill, Maria A. ....'64 '00 C.999 B.A. L.1252 J.D. [Ⓐ Murphy&K.]
*PRACTICE AREAS: Insurance Defense; Litigation.
Caldwell, J. Edward, (BV) ....'27 '54 C.1030 B.A. L.184 LL.B. [Caldwell,E.K.&L.]
Caldwell, Ehrsam, Kennedy & Lavery, (BV) .... 773 Huntington Tpke
Casper, Marie A., (BV) ....'48 '90 C.112 B.A. L.976 J.D. [Zeldes,N.&C.]
*PRACTICE AREAS: Commercial Litigation.

Casper & de Toledo LLC
(See Stamford)

Castro, Carmen Iris ....'49 '89 C&L.184 B.A., J.D. 419 Mill Hill Ave.
Caulfield, Katherine E. .... '66 '91 C.93 B.S. L.306 J.D. [Ⓐ Pullman&C.]
*PRACTICE AREAS: Estate and Gift Planning; Estate and Trust Administration; Elder Law.
Cava, Gregory J., (BV) ....'58 '83 C&L.94 B.A., J.D. [Zeldes,N.&C.]
*PRACTICE AREAS: Real Estate Transactions, Financing and Development; Land Use; Condominium Law; Condominium Development; Community Association Law.
Cavanaugh, Robert L., Jr. ....'67 '93 C.588 B.S. L.818 J.D. [Goldstein&P.] ⊙
*PRACTICE AREAS: Personal Injury; Insurance Defense; Civil Litigation.

Cerrato, Richard A., (BV) '49 '83 C.184 B.A. L.1048 J.D.
Suite 2A, 3180 Main Street, 06606
Telephone: 203-374-4600 Fax: 203-372-0824
URL: http://www.lawyers.com/cerratolaw
General Civil Practice before State and Federal Courts. Family, Personal Injury, Probate, Real Estate, Education, Labor, Bankruptcy and Workers Compensation Law. Trials and Appeals.
Representative Clients: Northeastern Pennsylvania Educational Television Association (WVIA); Southwestern Connecticut Agency on Aging, Inc.
References: Chase-Connecticut; People's Bank.
See Professional Biographies, BRIDGEPORT, CONNECTICUT

Charles, Barry A. ....'44 '73 C.184 B.A. L.190 J.D. 3715 Main St.
Cilano, Heidi Marie ....'71 '96 C.128 B.A. L.1252 J.D. [Ⓐ Bai,P.B.&M.]
*PRACTICE AREAS: Professional Liability; Civil Litigation; Domestic Relations.
Citronberg, David L., (BV) ....'27 '57 C.659 B.A. L.94 LL.B. 1000 Lafayette Blvd.

Clear, Michael Gene, Law Offices of
(See Stamford)

Cleary, Edward L., Jr., (BV) ....'46 '73 C.321 B.A. L.184 J.D. [Ferrante&C.]
Cleary, Frank B., (BV) ....'47 '73 C.674 B.A. L.262 J.D. [Pullman&C.]
*PRACTICE AREAS: Taxation; Public Finance; Commercial Law; State and Local Government Law.
Cocco, Leonard M. ....'33 '58 C.1029 B.A. L.94 LL.B. Supr. Ct. J.
Cohen, Adam J. ....'73 '98 C.881 B.A. L.188 J.D. [Ⓐ Pullman&C.]
*PRACTICE AREAS: Litigation.
Cohen, Loris L. ....'41 '80 C.145 B.A. L.472 J.D. Conn. Legal Servs., Inc.
Cohen, Robert P., (BV) ....'44 '70 C.1029 B.A. L.818 J.D. 1000 LaFayette Blvd.

Cohen and Wolf, P.C., (AV)
1115 Broad Street, 06604 ⊙
Telephone: 203-368-0211 Facsimile: 203-394-9901
URL: http://www.cohenandwolf.com

(This Listing Continued)

Cohen and Wolf, P.C. (Continued)
Herbert L. Cohen (1905-1983); Austin K. Wolf; Richard L. Albrecht; Jonathan S. Bowman; Irving J. Kern; Martin J. Albert; Stewart I. Edelstein; Neil R. Marcus (Resident at Danbury Office); G. Kenneth Bernhard; David L. Grogins (Resident at Danbury Office); Greta E. Solomon; Robin A. Kahn (Resident at Danbury Office); Richard G. Kent; Richard Slavin; Daniel S. Nagel; Richard J. Di Marco; David B. Zabel; Mark A. Kirsch; David M. Levine; Joseph G. Walsh (Resident at Danbury Office); David A. Ball; Jocelyn B. Hurwitz; Stuart M. Katz; Monte E. Frank (See Danbury listing for Biography);—Patricia C. Sullivan; Vincent M. Marino; Ann B. Mulcahy; Marnie J. Rubin (See Danbury listing for Biography); Ari J. Hoffman; Barbara M. Schellenberg; Frederic B. Eisman. Of Counsel: Martin F. Wolf; Robert J. Ashkins; Stuart A. Epstein; Jack E. McGregor.
General Practice. Business Transactions, Commercial Litigation, Employment and Labor, Family and Matrimonial, Land Use, Municipal, Personal Injury, Physicians Practice, Real Estate, Securities, Tax, Trusts and Estates. Litigation in all Courts.
Danbury, Connecticut Office: 158 Deer Hill Avenue. Telephone: 203-792-2771. Facsimile: 203-791-8149.
Stamford, Connecticut Office: 112 Prospect Street. Telephone: 203-964-9907. Facsimile: 203-576-8504.
Westport, Connecticut Office: 190 Main Street. Telephone: 203-222-1034.
See Professional Biographies, BRIDGEPORT, CONNECTICUT

Cohn, Milton L., (AV) ....'15 '39 C&L.976 B.A., LL.B. [Bartlett,K.&C.]
Cole, Erwin J. ....'23 '51 C.831 L.94 LL.B. 239 Golden Hill St.
Coleman, Henry D., (AVⓉ) '54 '85 C.1044 B.S. L.966 J.D.
(adm. in WI; not adm. in CT; See Pat. Sect.) [Coleman S.S.] ⊙
Coleman Sudol Sapone, P.C., (AVⓉ)
714 Colorado Avenue (See Pat. Sect.) (⊙Mamaroneck, NY)

Coles, O'Connell, Dolan & McDonald, P.C.
(See O'Donnell, McDonald and Cregeen, L.L.C.)

Collins, Hannafin, Garamella, Jaber & Tuozzolo, Professional Corporation
(See Danbury)

Comley, Frederick L., (AV) .... '16 '40 C&L.976 A.B., LL.B. 850 Main St.
Connelly, Michael .... '71 '96 C&L.128 B.A., J.D. [Ⓐ Murphy&K.]
*PRACTICE AREAS: Insurance Defense; Litigation.
Connors, Mary Ann, (BV) ....'62 '87 C&L.184 B.A., J.D. [Adelman H.&N.]
*PRACTICE AREAS: Personal Injury; Medical Malpractice; Products Liability; Legal Malpractice.

Conte, Gregory M., (BV) '47 '80 C.1211 B.A. L.1029 J.D.
4083 Main Street, Suite 2B-F, 06606
Telephone: 203-371-8137 Fax: 203-371-2304
Email: gmjc123@cs.com URL: http://www.lawyers.com/gregoryconte
***PRACTICE AREAS: Personal Injury (40%); Real Estate (30%); Family Law (10%); General Practice.**
Family Law, Divorce, Child Custody, Real Estate, Zoning Law, Personal Injury.
See Professional Biographies, BRIDGEPORT, CONNECTICUT

Conway, Douglas E. ....'57 '84 C.184 B.A. L.1029 J.D. Grant Mfg. Co.
Cook, William J., III ....'59 '86 C.184 B.A. L.1048 J.D. Asst. Clk., Supr. Ct.
Cooper, Robert S., (AV) ....'38 '63 C.197 A.B. L.976 LL.B. [Zeldes,N.&C.]
*PRACTICE AREAS: Business Law; Financial Law; Commercial Planning; Transactions; Dispute Resolution.
Copertino, Anthony P., Jr., (BV) .... '35 '60 C.1030 B.S.S. L.262 LL.B. 4270 Main St.
Cortese-Costa, Loraine, (BV) ....'60 '86 C.1044 B.A. L.982 J.D. [Durant,N.H.H.&C.]

Cousins, Johnson & Desrosiers, P.C.
(See Stratford)

Creager, Catherine L. ....'61 '00 C.929 B.A. L.1252 J.D. [Ⓐ Bai,P.B.&M.]
*PRACTICE AREAS: Civil Litigation; Professional Liability.
Curran, Hugh C. ....'24 '51 C.321 L.93 LL.B. Supr. Ct. J.
Curtis, Ronald E., (BV) ....'49 '75 C.415 B.A. L.818 J.D. Asst. Pub. Def.
Czepiga, Edward F., II, (BV) ....'54 '81 C.208 B.A. L.1029 J.D. [DePiano G.C.&S.]
D'Albis, Linda D. ....'57 '84 C.951 B.A. L.128 J.D. [Ⓐ Bai,P.B.&M.]
*PRACTICE AREAS: Professional Liability; Insurance Defense.
D'Alesio, Joseph D. ....'49 '76 C.1030 B.A. L.365 J.D. Law Clk., Supr. Ct.

Daly, Weihing & Bochanis, (BV)
Suite 710, Security Building, 1115 Main Street, 06604
Telephone: 203-333-8500 Fax: 203-334-0305
Email: lawdwb@aol.com
Members of Firm: James J. A. Daly (1914-1982); Thomas J. Weihing; John T. Bochanis.
General Trial, Administrative and Appellate Practice including Arbitration, Transportation, Estate Planning, Probate, Corporation, Torts, Workers Compensation, Real Estate, Domestic Relations, Labor and Legislative Law.
See Professional Biographies, BRIDGEPORT, CONNECTICUT

D'Amico, George P., (BV) ....'59 '85 C&L.1029 B.A., J.D. [Miller,R.&D.]
D'Amore, Alfred A., (BV) .... '30 '55 C&L.276 A.B., J.D. [D'Amore&S.]
D'Amore & Shamiss, (BV) .... 181 Middle St.
DeFusco, Leopold P., (BV) ....'57 '81 C.1030 A.B. L.818 J.D. [DeFusco&L.]
DeFusco & Lyman-Askew, (BV) ....4920 Main St.
DelPercio, Fred, (BV) ....'39 '71 C.1156 B.S. L.724 J.D. 239 Golden Hill St.
DeLuca, Regina M., (BV) .... '57 '85 C.705 B.S.N. L.184 J.D. [Ⓐ Koskoff,K.&B.]
*PRACTICE AREAS: Medical Malpractice.
De Lucia, Joseph J. ....'62 '90 C.164 B.A. L.910 J.D. [Ⓐ Miller,R.&D.]
Denton, Sheila Anne ....'65 '92 C.1211 B.S. L.1048 J.D. [Pullman&C.]
*PRACTICE AREAS: Litigation; Bankruptcy.
DePalma, Michael G. .... '43 '67 C.1030 A.B. L.184 LL.B. Int. Rev. Serv.

DePanfilis & Vallerie, LLC
(See Norwalk)

De Piano, Salvatore C., (AV) ....'27 '55 C.184 B.A. L.724 J.D. [DePiano G.C.&S.]
DePiano Gentile Czepiga & Soares, (AV) ....56 Lyon Terrace
Dequaine, Lester J. '30 '59 C.966 B.S. L.262 LL.B.
(adm. in NY; not adm. in CT) 155 Brewster St.
D'Eramo, Loretta Lynn .... '46 '80 C&L.1029 B.A., J.D. 4150 Park Ave.
De Siena, Charles L., (BV) .... '33 '57 C.1030 B.S. L.262 LL.B. 239 Golden Hill St.
DeSilva, Lionel A. ....'62 '88 C.184 B.A. L.1029 J.D. 34 Fayerweather Ter.
Dillon, John M. ....'18 '51 C.573 B.S. L.823 J.D. 3030 Park Ave.
Di Marco, Richard J., (BV) '55 '84
C.1044 B.A. L.1009 J.D. [Cohen&W.] (⊙Stamford, Westport)
*PRACTICE AREAS: Taxation; Estate Planning; Corporate.
Dinan, Althea, II ....'53 '86 C.788 B.A. L.1202 J.D. [Dinan&D.]
Dinan, Althea S. ....'27 '52 C.1029 B.A. L.94 J.D. [Dinan&D.]
Dinan & Dinan, P.C. ....1776 North Ave.
Di Natale, Natale V. ....'68 '94 C.860 B.A. L.245 J.D. [Ⓐ Durant,N.H.H.&C.]
Dinegar, Wilbur Ward, (BV) ....'26 '73 C.871 B.S. L.273 J.D. Asst. Atty. Gen.‡

Diserio Martin O'Connor & Castiglioni LLP
(See Stamford)

Docters, Robert G ....'57 '82 C.813 A.B. L.945 J.D. 3030 Park Avenue Apt. 10E6‡
Doherty, John R. '31 '59
C.816 M.E. L.1003 LL.B. 4380 Main Street (Pat.) (⊙New Haven)

Donlon, Rosalie L. '53 '80 C.1030 B.A. L.851 J.D.
(adm. in NY; not adm. in CT) 161 Nancy Dr.‡
D'Onofrio, Michael A. .... '69 '95 C.1102 B.S. L.1252 J.D. P.O. Box 491
Dowling, James G., Jr., (AV) '52 '78 C.860 B.A. L.818 J.D.
[Pullman&C.] (⊙Hartford)
*PRACTICE AREAS: Real Estate Law; Commercial Transactions.
Driscoll, Margaret Connors .... '15 '38 C.914 B.A. L.976 LL.B. State Trial Ref.
Durant, E. Terry, (AV) .... '32 '59 C.165 B.A. L.893 LL.B. [Durant,N.H.H.&C.]
Durant, Nichols, Houston, Hodgson & Cortese-Costa, P.C., (AV) .... 1057 Broad Street
Dworken, Martin A., (BV) .... '31 '55 C.860 B.S. L.94 LL.B. 10 Middle St.
Dworski, David H., (BV) .... '61 '88 C.611 B.A. L.1029 J.D. 387 Clinton Ave.
Dzurik, John G., (AV) .... '50 '75 C&L.276 B.S.F.S., J.D. [Goldstein&P.] ⊙
*PRACTICE AREAS: Leases and Leasing; Real Estate Finance; Commercial Real Estate.
Eaton, Gary M. .... '58 '85 C.262 B.A. L.93 J.D. 2704 Fairfield Ave.
Eckhardt, Cheryl E., (BV) .... '45 '85 C.241 B.S. L.1029 J.D. 370 Brooklawn Ave.
Edelstein, Stewart I., (AV) '48 '73
C.604 B.A. L.188 J.D. [Cohen&W.] (⊙Stamford, Westport)
*PRACTICE AREAS: Commercial Litigation; High Technology.
Eginton, Warren W. .... '24 '52 C.674 A.B. L.976 LL.B. Sr. U.S. Dist. J.
Ehrsam, Frederick F., Jr., (BV) .... '37 '66 C.276 B.A. L.880 LL.B. [Caldwell,E.K.&L.]
Eielson, Rodney S. .... '24 '51 C.1029 B.A. L.184 LL.B. Supr. Ct. J.
Eisenman, Gerard P., (BV) .... '49 '80 C.1266 B.A. L.1029 J.D. 1061 Main St.
Eisman, Frederic B. .... '65 '92 C.867 B.A. L.910 J.D. [Ⓐ Cohen&W.]
*PRACTICE AREAS: Corporate Law; Business Law; Trusts and Estates; Real Estate.
Elstein, Bruce L., (BV) .... '61 '86 C.787 B.S. L.1019 J.D. [Elstein&E.]
*PRACTICE AREAS: Personal Injury; Defamation; Commercial Law and Litigation; Real Estate; Mechanics Lien.
Elstein, Henry, (AV) .... '34 '59 C&L.976 B.A., LL.B. [Elstein&E.]
*PRACTICE AREAS: Financing; Real Estate; Real Estate Acquisition; Debt Restructuring; Mechanics Liens.

Elstein and Elstein, P.C., (AV) BR
Suite 400 1087 Broad Street, 06604-4260
Telephone: 203-367-4421 Telecopier: 203-366-8615
Email: belstein@snet.net URL: http://www.lawyers.com/elsteinandelstein
Henry Elstein; Bruce L. Elstein.
Trials and Appeals emphasizing Personal Injury and Commercial Law, Real Estate Acquisition, Negotiation and Financing, Domestic Relations, Corporate and Business Planning.
See Professional Biographies, BRIDGEPORT, CONNECTICUT

Epstein, Stuart A., (BV) ....'38 '62 C.945 B.A. L.976 LL.B. [Ⓖ Cohen&W.] (⊙Stamford)
*PRACTICE AREAS: Real Estate; Private Syndications of Real Estate Transactions.
Etkind, Hyman G., (BV) ....'27 '52 C&L.188 A.B., LL.B. 10 Middle St.
Evan, MaryAnne .... '74 '00 C.999 B.A. L.982 J.D. [Ⓐ Bai,P.B.&M.]
*PRACTICE AREAS: Medical Malpractice; Professional Liability.
Ewing, Michael F. .... '61 '91 C.602 B.A. L.569 J.D. [Adelman H.&N.]
*PRACTICE AREAS: Personal Injury; Medical Malpractice; Products Liability; Legal Malpractice.
Farcus, Joan I., (BV) .... '44 '72 C.1029 B.A. L.818 J.D. 56 Lyon Ter.
Fawcett, Frederick W., (BV) .... '45 '69 C&L.184 A.B., J.D. Sr. Asst. States Atty.
Faxon, Joel Thomas .... '68 '94 C.222 B.A. L.1194 J.D. [Ⓐ Koskoff,K.&B.]
*PRACTICE AREAS: Securities; Civil Rights; Personal Injury; Products Liability; Aviation Law.

Feliu, David N., (BV) '57 '83 C.181 B.A. L.276 J.D.
44 Lyon Terrace, 06604
Telephone: 203-335-2650 Fax: 203-367-8493
Personal Injury, Collections, Real Estate, Divorce, and Workers Compensation.

Feola-Guerrieri, Nathalie .... '69 '96 C.1030 B.A. L.1252 J.D. [Ⓐ Willinger,W.&B.]
*PRACTICE AREAS: Land Use Law; Litigation; Bankruptcy Law.
Ferrante, Victor M., (BV) .... '46 '72 C.884 B.A. L.94 J.D. [Ferrante&C.]
Ferrante & Cleary, (BV) .... 2970 Main St.
Filan, James K., Jr. .... '62 '92 C.967 B.A. L.1029 J.D. 1000 Lafayette Blvd.
Fink, Susan B. .... '56 '87 C.1029 B.S.N. L.994 J.D. 350 Fairfield Ave.

Finn Dixon & Herling LLP
(See Stamford)

Finnie, Anne Stoddard, (BV) .... '32 '82 C.881 B.A. L.1029 J.D. [Rubenstein&F.]
Fitzsimmons, Holly B. .... '50 '76 C.788 A.B. L.893 J.D. U.S. Mag. J.
Fleisher, Roslyn, (BV) .... '51 '75 C.1138 B.B.A. L.1009 J.D. Sr. Asst. State's Atty.
Flynn, Walter A., Jr., (BV) .... '43 '68 C.93 B.S. L.276 J.D. [Goldstein&P.] ⊙
*PRACTICE AREAS: Wills; Trusts and Estates; Probate; Taxation; Eminent Domain.

Fogarty Cohen Selby & Nemiroff LLC
(See Greenwich)

Forbes, John A., Jr., (BV) ...... '44 '68 C.1200 A.B. L.184 J.D. Asst. Pub. Def., Supr. Ct.
Ford, G. Sarsfield .... '33 '59 C.602 B.A. L.276 LL.B. Admin. Law J., Supr. Ct.
Forrence, Jennifer L. .... '61 '89 C.367 B.A. L.976 J.D. 1000 Lafayette Blvd.
Fray, William T. .... '63 '88 C.1030 B.A. L.896 J.D. [Ⓐ Tellalian&T.]
*PRACTICE AREAS: Probate; Real Estate; Wills; Trusts.
Friedman, David P., (AV) .... '57 '84 C.813 B.A. L.569 J.D. [Zeldes,N.&C.]
*PRACTICE AREAS: Civil Litigation; Commercial Litigation; Legal Malpractice Litigation.
Frost, Robert M., Jr. .... '73 '98 C.321 B.A. L.306 J.D. [Ⓐ Zeldes,N.&C.]
*PRACTICE AREAS: Civil Litigation; State and Federal Criminal Litigation.
Furkiotis, George C., (BV) .... '32 '58 C.152 A.B. L.276 J.D. 635 Fairfield Ave.
Ganim, George W., Jr., (BV) .... '60 '85 C.1211 B.S. L.1029 J.D. [Ganim,G.&G.]
Ganim, George W., Sr., (BV) ....'27 '51 C.1029 B.A. L.94 LL.B. [Ganim,G.&G.]
Ganim, Joseph P., (BV) ....'59 '84 C.184 B.S. L.1029 J.D. [Ganim,G.&G.]
Ganim, Paul J. .... '63 '92 C.1030 B.A. L.1029 J.D. [Ganim,G.&G.]
Ganim, Raymond W., II, (BV) .... '62 '88 C.1211 B.S. L.1029 J.D. [Ganim,G.&G.]
Ganim, Thomas G. .... '66 '92 C.1030 B.S. L.1029 J.D. [Ganim,G.&G.]
Ganim, Ganim & Ganim, P.C., (BV) .... 4666 Main Street
Gans, Myrna E., (BV) ....'39 '80 C&L.1029 B.A., J.D. [Gans&R.]
Gans & Reynolds, (BV) ....1335 Wood Avenue
Garfinkel, William I. .... '56 '82 C&L.976 B.A., J.D. U.S. Mag.

Gaston, James O., Law Offices of, (BV) '59 '83 C.401 B.S. L.229 J.D.
239 Golden Hill Street, 06604
Telephone: 203-334-1656 Fax: 203-333-4532
***PRACTICE AREAS: Personal Injury Law; Products Liability Law; Workers Compensation; Commercial Law.**
Personal Injury, Products Liability, Workers Compensation, Medical Malpractice, Commercial Law.
See Professional Biographies, BRIDGEPORT, CONNECTICUT

Gaull, Jeffrey N. .... '70 '01 C.882 B.A. L.1194 J.D. [Ⓐ Bai,P.B.&M.]
*PRACTICE AREAS: Civil Litigation; Medical Malpractice.
Gavin, Edward J., (BV) .... '61 '90 C.1044 B.S. L.1029 J.D. [Meehan,M.&G.]
*PRACTICE AREAS: Criminal Law; Felonies; Drug Crimes; Driving While Intoxicated; Personal Injury.
Gelineau, Toni Marie, (BV) .... '55 '80 C.1030 B.A. L.184 J.D. [Ⓐ Willinger,W.&B.]
*PRACTICE AREAS: Real Estate and Zoning; Probate; Domestic Relations; General Practice.
Gentile, Bryon A., (BV) .... '48 '75 C.184 B.A. L.1009 J.D. [DePiano G.C.&S.]

Genuario & Conover
(See Norwalk)

George, Eric J. .... '73 '00 C.184 B.A. L.306 J.D. [Ⓐ Pullman&C.]
*PRACTICE AREAS: Corporate Law; Taxation; Limited Liability Company Law; Nonprofit Organizations Law.
Gergely, Ernest '28 '70 C.569 B.E.E. L.564 J.D.
(adm. in NY; not adm. in CT; Pat.) Pat. Coun., Assigned Components, Gen. Elec. Co.
Gerstl, Arthur J. .... '08 '33 C&L.976 Asst. Clk., Supr. Ct.‡
Gill, Susann E. .... '57 '82 C.201 B.S. L.893 J.D. Asst. State's Atty.
Glasser, James I. '60 '85 C.550 B.A. L.1009 J.D.
(adm. in NY; not adm. in CT) U.S. Atty's. Off.
Goldberger, Robert R., (BV) .... '08 '33 C&L.976 B.A., LL.B. 955 Main St.
Goldman, Irve J., (AV) .... '58 '85 C.831 B.B.A. L.1048 J.D. [Pullman&C.]
*PRACTICE AREAS: Commercial Bankruptcy; Personal Bankruptcy; Bankruptcy Litigation; Commercial Litigation.

Goldstein and Peck, P.C., (AV)
1087 Broad Street, P.O. Box 1538, 06601 ⊙
Telephone: 203-334-9421 Telefax: 203-334-6949
Email: info@goldsteinandpeck.com URL: http://www.lawyers.com/goldsteinpeck
David Goldstein (1898-1992); William J. Kupinse, Jr.; Walter A. Flynn, Jr.; John G. Dzurik; Dennis M. Laccavole; Robert L. Cavanaugh, Jr.; Tiziana M. Scaccia; Christopher M. Harrington. Of Counsel: Peter B. O'Connell.
General Practice, including Litigation (State and Federal Courts; Trials and Appeals) and Transactional Representation (Banking, Corporate, Real Estate). Arbitration, Domestic Relations, Estate Planning, Insurance, Municipal Law, Personal Injury, Probate, Product Liability, Zoning.
Representative Clients: Bee Publishing Co., Inc.; The Chase Manhattan Bank; Great American Insurance Companies; Physicians Health Services, Inc.; Town of Westport; Greenwich Board of Education; Newtown Savings Bank; People's Bank.
See Professional Biographies, BRIDGEPORT, CONNECTICUT

Goodspeed, Norwick R. G., (AV) '22 '45
C&L.976 A.B., LL.B. Chmn. of the Bd., People's Mutual Holdings
Gordon, A. Reynolds, (AV) .... '33 '58 C.674 A.B. L.976 LL.B. [Gordon&H.]
Gordon, Abraham I., (BV) .... '30 '54 C.1029 B.A. L.228 J.D. [Gordon&S.]
Gordon, Bruce S. .... '57 '96 C.184 B.S. L.1252 J.D. [Ⓐ Gordon&S.]
Gordon and Hiller, (AV) .... 1087 Broad St.
Gordon & Scalo, (BV) .... 140 John St.
Gorton, Karen E. .... '63 '91 C.354 B.S. L.1029 J.D. Atty., People's Bank
Gouveia, Bill L., (BV) .... '56 '81 C.1030 B.A. L.831 J.D. 44 Lyon Terr.
Graham, Kenneth A. .... '48 '77 C.1029 B.A. L.818 J.D. Asst. Atty. Gen.
Grasso, Lisa M. .... '63 '88 C.676 B.A. L.276 J.D. [Ⓐ Durant,N.H.H.&C.]
Green, Barbara F., (CV) .... '54 '86 C.183 B.A. L.184 J.D. [Green&G.]
Green, Bernard, (AV) .... '26 '52 C.976 B.S. L.178 LL.B. [Green&G.]
Green, Joel Z., (BV) .... '57 '82 C.156 A.B. L.930 J.D. [Green&G.]

Green and Gross, P.C., (AV)
Suite 401, 1087 Broad Street, 06604-4231
Telephone: 203-335-5141 Fax: 203-367-9964
URL: http://www.lawyers.com/green&grosspc
Bernard Green; Eric M. Gross; Samuel T. Rost; Joel Z. Green; Barbara F. Green;—Jeffrey W. Keim. Of Counsel: Paul A. Sobel.
Bankruptcy Law, Commercial and Construction Claims.
See Professional Biographies, BRIDGEPORT, CONNECTICUT

Greenwood, Christopher T., (BV) .... '56 '81 C.745 B.A. L.1029 J.D. 3233 Main St.
Gross, Eric M., (BV) .... '47 '73 C.478 B.A. L.184 J.D. [Green&G.]
Grossberg, Suzan .... '54 '82 C.415 B.A. L.1029 J.D. 1061 Main St.
Grossman, Lawrence S. .... '60 '94 C.165 A.B. L.262 J.D [Ⓐ Zeisler&Z.]
*PRACTICE AREAS: Commercial Litigation; Bankruptcy Litigation.
Gulash, John R., Jr., (AV) .... '50 '76 C.401 B.A. L.362 J.D. [J.R.Gulash,Jr.&E.J.R.]
*PRACTICE AREAS: Criminal Defense Law; Trial Practice; Appellate Practice.

Gulash, John R., Jr. & Eugene J. Riccio, Law Offices of, (AV)
Suite 703, 350 Fairfield Avenue, P.O. Box 9118, 06601
Telephone: 203-367-7440 Fax: 203-336-8379
Email: gulashandriccio@aol.com
Members of Firm: John R. Gulash, Jr.; Eugene J. Riccio. Associate: C. Christian Young.
General Civil and Criminal Trial and Appellate Practice before State and Federal Courts. Civil and Criminal Litigation. Personal Injury and Products Liability Law, Professional Grievance and Disciplinary Proceedings.
See Professional Biographies, BRIDGEPORT, CONNECTICUT

Guman, John D., Jr., (BV) .... '32 '64 C.1030 B.S.S. L.184 LL.B. Asst. City Atty.
Gusmano, Paul C., (BV) .... '64 '90 C.705 B.A. L.1029 J.D. 3301 Main St.
Haase, Todd D. .... '61 '91 C.846 B.A. L.564 J.D. 1720 Noble Ave.
Hager, Barbara G. .... '57 '96 C.25 B.A. L.306 J.D. [Ⓐ Zeldes,N.&C.]
*PRACTICE AREAS: Condominium Law; Business Law; Foreclosures; Municipal Law.
Hall, Janet C. .... '48 '73 C.518 A.B. L.569 J.D. U.S. Dist. J.
Hallas, Charles C., (CV) .... '52 '77 C.1030 B.A. L.823 J.D. 36 Harmony St.
Hancock, Nancy A. D., (BV) .... '— '84 C.674 A.B. L.188 J.D. [Pullman&C.]
*PRACTICE AREAS: Venture Capital; Finance; Corporate Law; Securities Law; International Business Law.

Harlow, Adams & Friedman, P.C.
(See Milford)

Harrington, Christopher M. .... '61 '95 C.1373 B.A. L.1048 J.D. [Goldstein&P.] ⊙
*PRACTICE AREAS: Insurance Defense; Commercial Litigation; Personal Injury; Environmental Litigation; Family Law.
Harris, Robert A., (AV) .... '56 '82 C.311 B.A. L.893 J.D. [Zeldes,N.&C.]
*PRACTICE AREAS: Commercial Litigation; Arbitration; Mediation.
Harry, Joseph James .... '57 '89 C.1156 B.S. L.1029 J.D. Asst. States Atty.
Hatch, Roberta A. .... '41 '87 C.938 B.A. L.1029 J.D. V.P., Chase Manhattan Bk.
Hausman, Matthew M., (AV) .... '59 '90 C.156 B.A. L.273 J.D. [Ⓐ Pullman&C.]
*PRACTICE AREAS: Commercial Litigation; Administrative and Zoning Law; Municipal Litigation; Property Valuation and Tax Appeals; ERISA Litigation.

Heagney, Lennon & Slane LLP
(See Greenwich)

Heche, Raymond G., (BV) .... '38 '64 C.1030 B.B.A. L.262 LL.B. 4920 Main St.
Hellman, Jeffrey, (BV) .... '61 '86 C.228 A.B. L.309 J.D. [Zeisler&Z.]
*PRACTICE AREAS: Commercial Litigation; Bankruptcy; Criminal Law.
Hennessey, William John .... '49 '89 C.1102 B.A. L.1029 J.D. 49 Cannon St.
Henry, Patrick K., (BV) .... '49 '76 C.1030 B.A. L.1202 J.D. 1293 Wood Ave.
Herman, Milton J. .... '12 '38 L.564 LL.B. Supr. Ct. J.
Hernandez, Anthony .... '49 '92 C.1211 B.S. L.1029 J.D. 2600 Main St.
Heslin, Holly A. .... '66 '96 C.184 B.A. L.1003 J.D. [Ⓐ A.R.Belinkie&Assoc.]
*PRACTICE AREAS: Divorce; Real Estate; Wills; Probate; Personal Injury.

Hill Rivkins & Hayden LLP, (AV⊤)
1115 Broad Street, 06601-1821 ⊙
Telephone: 203-367-5535 Telecopier: 203-367-5536
Email: hillrivkinsct@snet.net
Resident Partner: Richard H. Webber.
Admiralty, Transportation, Insurance and Reinsurance, International and Commercial Law, including Trial and Appellate Practice and Arbitration.

(This Listing Continued)

Hill Rivkins & Hayden LLP (Continued)

New York, New York Office: c/o Kirlin, Campbell & Keating, 5 Hanover Square, Suite 1400. Telephone: 212-669-0600. Telecopier: 212-669-0698-0699.
Houston, Texas Office: 712 Main Street, Suite 1515. Telephone: 713-222-1515. Telecopier: 713-222-1359.
Hoboken, New Jersey Office: 96 Hudson Street. Telephone: 201-222-5180. Telecopier: 201-222-5182.
See Professional Biographies, BRIDGEPORT, CONNECTICUT

Hiller, Arthur A., (BV) .... '43 '68 C.156 A.B. L.306 J.D. [Gordon&H.]
Hirsch, Joram, (AV) .... '54 '79 C.918 B.A. L.276 J.D. [Adelman H.&N.]
*PRACTICE AREAS: Personal Injury; Medical Malpractice; Products Liability; Legal Malpractice.
Hirsch, Matthew S. .... '69 '95 C.401 B.A. L.982 J.D. [🄰 Zeldes,N.&C.]
*PRACTICE AREAS: Medical Malpractice; Appellate Practice; Professional Liability; Products Liability; Business Litigation.
Hodgson, Christopher M., (BV) .... '59 '85 C.882 B.A. L.692 J.D. [Durant,N.H.H.&C.]
Hoffman, Ari J. .... '74 '00 C.1036 B.A. L.93 J.D. [🄰 Cohen&W.]
*PRACTICE AREAS: Commercial Litigation.
Hoffman, Laurence K., (BV) .... '48 '73 C&L.94 B.A., J.D. 10 Middle St.

Holahan, Gumpper & Dowling
(See Fairfield)

Holland Kaufmann & Bartels, LLC
(See Greenwich)

Hornstein, Diane G., (BV) .... '42 '85 C.102 B.A. L.1029 J.D. 44 Lyon Ter.
Horwitt, Jed, (AV) .... '59 '88 C.354 B.S. L.188 J.D. [Zeisler&Z.]
*PRACTICE AREAS: Bankruptcy; Creditors Rights; Securities Investor Protection Act; Litigation.
Horwitz, James D., (AV) .... '57 '84 C.165 B.A. L.978 J.D. [Koskoff,K.&B.]
*PRACTICE AREAS: Medical Malpractice.
Houston, Donald F., (AV) .... '46 '73 C.976 B.A. L.893 J.D. [Durant,N.H.H.&C.]
Howe, Linda N. .... '48 '81 C.732 B.A. L.184 J.D. Asst. State's Atty.
Hurlie-Dunn, Coleen .... '— '86 C.354 B.A. L.659 J.D. [Zeisler&Z.]
*PRACTICE AREAS: Commercial Law; Commercial Leasing; Real Property; Corporate Law; Debtor and Creditor Reorganization.
Hurwitz, Jocelyn B. ..... '67 '92 C&L.188 B.S., J.D. [Cohen&W.] (⊙Stamford, Westport)
*PRACTICE AREAS: Family Law; Commercial Litigation; Divorce Mediation.
Hutchison, Joseph C. .... '56 '83 C.299 B.A. L.569 J.D. [Zeldes,N.&C.]
*PRACTICE AREAS: Complex Commercial Litigation; White Collar Crime; Health Care Litigation; Environmental Litigation.
Ignal, Howard Evan, (BV) .... '47 '72 C.184 B.A. L.188 J.D. [Weinstein,W.I.N.&S.]
*PRACTICE AREAS: Banking; Commercial Law; Workers Compensation.
Inman, Nicole L. '72 '99 C.172 B.A. L.724 J.D.
(adm. in IL; not adm. in CT) [🄰 Zeisler&Z.]
*PRACTICE AREAS: Bankruptcy; Commercial Litigation.

Ivey, Barnum & O'Mara, LLC
(See Greenwich)

Jackson, David O., (AV) .... '36 '62 C.821 A.B. L.309 LL.B. [Pullman&C.]
*PRACTICE AREAS: Real Estate Law.

Jacobs Partners LLC
(See Norwalk)

Janczewski, Janet L. '44 '86 C.1211 B.S. L.1029 J.D.
Senior Corporate Counsel & Secretary, Southern Conn. Gas Co., The
Janello, Kenneth A., (BV) .... '33 '58 C.860 A.B. L.228 LL.B. 285 Congress St.
Japha, Ronald D., (BV) .... '54 '79 C.893 B.A. L.1017 J.D. [Gordon&S.]
Jennings, Alfred J., Jr., (AV) .... '39 '64 C.321 B.A. L.976 LL.B. [Zeldes,N.&C.]
*PRACTICE AREAS: Transactions; Business Law; Dispute Resolution; Real Estate Law; Health Care Law.
Johnson, Kathy Anita .... '54 '80 C.1350 B.A. L.61 J.D. Sr. Coun., People's Bk.
Johnson, Richard A. .... '47 '74 C.207 B.A. L.823 J.D. 1 Lafayette Circle Sq.

Kanasky, Thomas L., Jr., (BV) '46 '79 C.1029 B.S. L.1040 J.D.
180 Fairfield Avenue, P.O. Box 9281, 06604-9281
Telephone: 203-366-3156 Fax: 203-331-1802
General Civil Practice. Commercial, Collections, Bankruptcy and Real Estate Law. Litigation.
Reference: First Fidelity.
See Professional Biographies, BRIDGEPORT, CONNECTICUT

Karpie, Karen L., (BV) .... '52 '77 C&L.184 B.A., J.D. [Murphy&K.]
*PRACTICE AREAS: Litigation; Insurance Defense Law; Medical Malpractice; Employment; Appellate Practice.
Kasper, George J. .... '59 '87 C.1260 B.A. L.607 J.D. [Pullman&C.]
*PRACTICE AREAS: Employee Benefits; Tax; Corporate.
Katz, Stuart M. .... '67 '92 C.1036 B.A. L.94 J.D. [Cohen&W.]
*PRACTICE AREAS: Commercial and Criminal Litigation; Employment Law.
Kaufman, Gaileen A., (CV) .... '65 '90 C.1030 B.A. L.306 J.D. [Bai,P.B.&M.]
*PRACTICE AREAS: Professional Liability Law; General Litigation.
Keim, Jeffrey W. .... '75 '00 C.240 B.A. L.184 J.D. [🄰 Green&G.]
*PRACTICE AREAS: Civil Litigation; Criminal Defense.
Kelly, Cornelius P., (BV) .... '58 '88 C.349 B.S. L.1029 J.D. P.O. Box 491
Kelly, David J. .... '63 '98 C.1102 B.S. L.306 J.D. [🄰 Durant,N.H.H.&C.]
Kelly, Kevin C. .... '59 '97 C.1107 B.A. L.184 J.D. [🄰 Zeldes,N.&C.]
*PRACTICE AREAS: Trusts and Estates; Estate Planning; Probate; Elder Law; Municipal Law.
Kennedy, E. Stanton, (BV) .... '28 '52 C.321 A.B. L.184 LL.B. [Caldwell,E.K.&L.]
Kent, Richard G., (AV) '51 '75
C.705 B.A. L.93 J.D. [Cohen&W.] (⊙Stamford, Westport)
*PRACTICE AREAS: Family; Civil; Criminal Litigation.
Kern, Irving J., (AV) .... '46 '71 C.184 B.S. L.893 J.D. [Cohen&W.] (⊙Stamford)
*PRACTICE AREAS: Real Estate; Commercial; Corporate; Estate Planning; Health Care.
Kiaunis, Gertrude A. .... '53 '85 C.93 B.S.N. L.184 J.D. [🄰 Koskoff,K.&B.]
*PRACTICE AREAS: Medical Malpractice; Products Liability.
Kindseth, Stephen M. .... '68 '94 C.262 B.A. L.184 J.D. [🄰 Zeisler&Z.]
*PRACTICE AREAS: Bankruptcy; Bankruptcy Litigation; Liquidations; Commercial Litigation.
King, Arthur M. '32 '63 C.262 B.S.Ch. L.776 LL.B.
(adm. in NJ; not adm. in CT; Pat.) 1285 Boston Ave.
Kirsch, Mark A., (BV) .... '60 '85 C.1044 B.S. L.94 J.D. [Cohen&W.]
*PRACTICE AREAS: Real Estate.
Kisliak, John .... '34 '60 C&L.184 B.A., LL.B. 92 Sage Ave.‡
Klein, John A. .... '49 '77 C&L.184 B.A., J.D. Exec. V.P., People's Bk.

Klein, Jonathan J., (BV) '55 '81 C.978 B.A. L.262 J.D.
1445 Capitol Avenue, 06604-1619
Telephone: 203-330-1900 Telecopier: 203-330-1526
Email: jjkesq@hotmail.com URL: http://www.lawyers.com/jjklaw
Commercial, Civil, Tax and Securities Litigation and Appeals in all State and Federal Courts, White Collar Criminal Defense, Corporate Law, Labor and Employment Law, Administrative Law, Military Law.
Representative Clients: D'Addario Industries; A-P-A Transport Corp.; G.O.D., Inc.; Phoenix Security Corporation; Industrial Wrecking, Inc.; Pulmonary & Internal Medicine Associates, P.C.; Custom Air Systems, Inc.
See Professional Biographies, BRIDGEPORT, CONNECTICUT

Klein, Monte S., (CV) .... '39 '64 C.258 B.A. L.362 LL.B. 4083 Main St.
Koskoff, Joshua D. .... '66 '94 C.823 B.A. L.818 J.D. [🄰 Koskoff,K.&B.]
*PRACTICE AREAS: Medical Malpractice; Personal Injury.
Koskoff, Michael P., (AV) .... '42 '66 C.1029 B.A. L.184 J.D. [Koskoff,K.&B.]
*PRACTICE AREAS: Medical Malpractice; Products Liability; Class Actions; Personal Injury; Civil Rights.
Koskoff, Rosalind J., (BV) .... '41 '82 C.103 B.A. L.1029 J.D. [Koskoff,K.&B.]
*PRACTICE AREAS: Personal Injury; Products Liability; Appellate Practice.

Koskoff, Koskoff & Bieder, P.C., (AV) [BB]
350 Fairfield Avenue, 06604 ⊙
Telephone: 203-336-4421 Fax: 203-368-3244
Email: KKB@KOSKOFF.com URL: http://www.koskoff.com
Theodore I. Koskoff (1913-1989); Richard A. Fuchs (1945-1995); Michael P. Koskoff; Richard A. Bieder; Joel H. Lichtenstein; John D. Jessep; Christopher D. Bernard; Carey B. Reilly; James D. Horwitz; Vincent M. Musto; Michael A. Stratton; Rosalind J. Koskoff;—Regina M. DeLuca; Gertrude A. Kiaunis; Joshua D. Koskoff; Joel Thomas Faxon; Antonio Ponvert III. Of Counsel: James Wu.
Litigation in all State and Federal Courts. Medical Malpractice, Equal Opportunity, Negligence, Products Liability, Civil Rights, and Class Actions.
Stamford, Connecticut Office: 1172 Bedford Street. Telephone: 203-325-3686.
Danbury, Connecticut Office: 1 Moss Avenue. Telephone: 203-792-7100.
See Professional Biographies, BRIDGEPORT, CONNECTICUT

Kosturko, William T. '49 '74
C.976 B.A. L.659 J.D. Exec. V.P. & Gen. Coun., People's Bank
Koteas, George R., (CV) .... '47 '81 C.280 B.A. L.1029 J.D. 1198 Main St.
Krasnow, Edward .... '36 '63 C.277 B.I.E. L.94 LL.B. 35 Cannon St.
Krasnow, Eileen Kramer, (CV) .... '38 '84 C.1102 B.S. L.1029 J.D. 35 Cannon St.
Krasnow, Jennifer S., (CV) .... '65 '90 C.454 B.A. L.1029 J.D. 35 Cannon St.
Krasnow, Marc A., (CV) .... '66 '91 C.94 B.S.B.A. L.1029 J.D. 35 Cannon St.
Kupinse, William J., Jr., (AV) .... '39 '64 C.197 A.B. L.188 LL.B. [Goldstein&P.] ⊙
*PRACTICE AREAS: General Practice; Litigation; Trusts and Estates; Commercial Law; Family Law.
Kurs, Michael A., (BV) ...... '55 '80 C.976 B.A. L.1162 J.D. [Pullman&C.] (⊙Hartford)
*PRACTICE AREAS: Health Care Law; Litigation and Administrative Law; Education Law; Antitrust Law.
Kusnitz, H. Norman .... '11 '37 C.569 B.A. L.245 LL.B. 1543 North Ave.
Laccavole, Dennis M., (BV) .... '53 '78 C.1030 B.S. L.724 J.D. [Goldstein&P.] ⊙
*PRACTICE AREAS: Insurance; Personal Injury; Premises Liability; Products Liability; Professional Liability.
Lapera, Nancy DeFonce, (BV) .... '52 '82 C.915 B.A. L.823 J.D. [Pullman&C.]
*PRACTICE AREAS: Employee Benefits Law.
Larracuente, Jerome J. .... '67 '92 C.884 B.S. L.1029 J.D. 3301 Main St.

Laske, Arthur C., III
(See Trumbull)

LaVelle, Michael N., (AV) .... '46 '75 C.309 A.B. L.94 J.D. [Pullman&C.]
*PRACTICE AREAS: Labor Law; Zoning Law; Municipal Law.
Lavery, Hugh J., (BV) .... '40 '65 [Caldwell,E.K.&L.]
Lazinger, Samuel J., (BV) .... '50 '74 C.1029 B.A. L.1202 J.D. 295 Congress St.
Leso, Mark S. .... '69 '95 C.1102 B.S. L.1049 J.D. [🄰 Bai,P.B.&M.]
*PRACTICE AREAS: Professional Liability; Municipal Liability; Directors and Officers Liability; Civil Litigation; Real Estate Law.
Lesser, Robert K., (AV) .... '24 '49 C.951 B.A. L.309 LL.B. [Lesser&L.]
Lesser, Stanton H., (BV) .... '51 '76 C.860 B.S.E.E. L.1048 J.D. [Lesser&L.]
Lesser & Lieberthal, P.C., (AV) .... 1000 Lafayette Boulevard
Lessler, Stanley M., (BV) .... '37 '62 C.860 B.A. L.184 LL.B. 940 White Plains Rd.

Lev & Berlin, P.C.
(See Norwalk)

LeVan, Molly S., (BV) .... '50 '85 C.895 B.A. L.1029 J.D. 350 Fairfield Ave.
Levine, David M., (BV) .... '61 '86 C.1036 A.B. L.94 J.D. [Cohen&W.] (⊙Westport)
*PRACTICE AREAS: Corporate; Commercial; Health Care; Real Estate.
Levy, Sharon L. Bulbin '64 '89 C.260 B.S.B.A. L.472 J.D.
360 Fairfield Ave., Suite 302
Lichtenstein, Joel H., (AV) .... '38 '64 C&L.94 B.A., LL.B. [Koskoff,K.&B.]
*PRACTICE AREAS: Medical Malpractice; Hospital Liability; Health Maintenance Organizations; Health Care.
Lieberthal, Neil A., (BV) .... '50 '76 C.390 A.B. L.1202 J.D. [Lesser&L.]
Lifland, Craig I., (AV) .... '56 '83 C.823 B.S. L.1206 J.D. [Zeisler&Z.]
*PRACTICE AREAS: Bankruptcy; Commercial Law.

Lipson, Jack S.
(See Westport)

Liskov, Andrew S., (BV) .... '44 '68 C.434 B.A. L.184 LL.B. Pub. Def.Offc.
Lopez, Carmen L. .... '51 '76 C.1211 B.S. L.818 J.D. Supr. Ct. J.
Lopez, Joseph E. .... '63 '97 L.1048 J.D. Off. of Pub. Def.
Luckart, Bernard J. .... '36 '64 C.1030 B.S.S. L.724 LL.B. Trial Ct. Admr.
Lundy, Matthew P. .... '67 '94 C.262 B.A. L.896 J.D. [🄰 Pullman&C.]
*PRACTICE AREAS: Litigation; Construction Law; Intellectual Property.
Lustig, Jordan R., (BV) .... '32 '58 C.184 B.A. L.472 J.D. 881 Lafayette Blvd.
Lyddy, Raymond C. .... '24 '51 C.321 A.B. L.276 J.D. Prob. J.
Lyman-Askew, Brian, (BV) .... '54 '81 C.1030 B.A. L.818 J.D. [DeFusco&L.]
Lynch, Michael S. .... '62 '87 C&L.184 B.A., J.D. [Bai,P.B.&M.]
*PRACTICE AREAS: Civil Litigation; Real Estate Law; Professional Liability Law; Probate.
Lyons, Jay C. .... '50 '82 C.1030 A.B. L.564 J.D. 848 Colorado Ave.

Maher & Murtha, LLC, (BV)
528 Clinton Avenue, P.O. Box 901, 06601
Telephone: 203-367-2700 Fax: 203-335-0589
Email: maherandmurtha@snet.net
James J. Maher (1931-1998); Thomas M. Murtha; Geoffrey L. Squitiero; Edward V. Walsh; John C. Turner, Jr.; Mark A. Perkins.
General Insurance Defense Practice including Negligence, Malpractice, Products liability, Errors and Omissions, Worker's Compensation, Municipal Liability, Law Enforcement Liability and Subrogation Law, Trials and Appeals, State and Federal.
Reference: U.S.T. Bank Connecticut.
See Professional Biographies, BRIDGEPORT, CONNECTICUT

Maher and Williams
(See Fairfield)

Mahoney, Douglas P. .... '67 '92 C.321 A.B. L.184 J.D. [Tremont&S.]
*PRACTICE AREAS: Personal Injury; Sexual Abuse; Premises Security.
Maiocco, John P., Jr. .... '32 '57 C.276 B.S.S. L.184 LL.B. Supr. Ct. J.
Mandulak, Norma R. .... '70 '99 C.1102 B.S. L.1252 J.D. [🄰 Pullman&C.]
*PRACTICE AREAS: Corporate.
Mangines, Brian A., (BV) .... '63 '90 C.188 B.S. L.184 J.D. [Mangines&M.]
Mangines, Thomas E. .... '25 '62 C.1029 L.588 LL.D. [Mangines&M.]
Mangines and Mangines, (BV) .... 1115 Main St.
Marcus, Jan Arthur .... '55 '80 C.994 B.A. L.564 J.D. 1000 Lafayette Blvd.
Maresca, Robert A., (BV) .... '50 '76 C.1113 A.B. L.1338 J.D. 275 Congress St.
Maresca, Salvatore A., Jr., (BV) .... '57 '82 C.94 B.A. L.184 J.D. 275 Congress St.
Marino, Vincent M. .... '71 '96 C.1349 B.A. L.1252 J.D. [🄰 Cohen&W.]
*PRACTICE AREAS: Commercial Litigation; Employment Law; Construction Law; Real Estate; Bankruptcy.

Maronich, Michael G., (BV) '55 '80 C.93 B.A. L.1194 J.D.
180 Fairfield Avenue, 06604
Telephone: 203-336-1595 Fax: 203-331-1802
Email: mgmaronich@aol.com

(This Listing Continued)

Maronich, Michael G. (Continued)
Civil Litigation, Negligence and Personal Injury, Land Title Consulting & Litigation, Probate and Business Law.
See Professional Biographies, BRIDGEPORT, CONNECTICUT

Martin, Lucas & Chioffi, LLP
(See Stamford)

Marzik, Robert K., P.C., Law Offices of
(See Stratford)

Massaro, Carl A., Jr., (BV) .... '55 '80 C.676 B.S. L.1048 J.D. 180 Fairfield Ave.‡
Mastronardi, Gary A., (BV) .... '52 '82 C.840 B.B.A. L.262 J.D. 2112 North Ave.
Mauzaka, Judith A., (AV) .... '51 '82 C.1033 B.A. L.184 J.D. [Weinstein,W.I.N.&S.]
*PRACTICE AREAS: Employment Law; Civil Rights; Personal Injury; Family Law; Divorce.
Maxwell, Thomas F., Jr., (BV) .... '41 '66 C.602 B.A. L.16 J.D. [Pullman&C.]
*PRACTICE AREAS: Civil Litigation; Criminal Litigation; Administrative Law; Arbitration; Personal Injury.
McCann, Martin L., (BV) .... '58 '92 C.1030 B.S. L.1252 J.D. [Zeldes,N.&C.]
*PRACTICE AREAS: Business Law; Commercial Law; Bankruptcy; Taxation.
McCreery, Edward P., III, (AV) .... '54 '79 C.882 B.A. L.1048 J.D. [Pullman&C.]
*PRACTICE AREAS: Commercial Litigation; Construction; Insurance Coverage; Product Liability; Admiralty.
McCrory, Anne O'Connor '62 '89 C&L.93 B.A., J.D.
Coun., Southern Conn. Gas Co., The
McEnery, Gerard, (BV) .... '56 '83 C.724 B.S. L.1029 J.D. P.O. Box 5660
McGee, Heidi C. .... '65 '92 C.165 B.A. L.184 J.D. [Ⓐ Willinger,W.&B.]
*PRACTICE AREAS: Mortgage Foreclosure; Municipal Taxation; Commercial Litigation.

McGovern & Associates
(See Greenwich)

McGrath, William J. .... '29 '59 C.1029 B.A. L.262 LL.B. Supr. Ct. J.
McGregor, Jack E. .... '34 '63 C.976 B.S. L.665 LL.B. [Ⓒ Cohen&W.] (⊙Stamford)
*PRACTICE AREAS: Corporate; Finance; Real Estate Development.
McGuinness, John J., Jr. .... '20 '50 C.475 B.A. L.184 LL.B. Com. Pleas J.
McIntosh, Erskine D., (BV) .... '51 '79 C.302 B.S. L.128 J.D. Asst. Pub. Def.
Medina, Maximino, Jr., (BV) .... '58 '84 C.309 B.A. L.569 J.D. [Zeldes,N.&C.]
*PRACTICE AREAS: Commercial Litigation; Bankruptcy Law; Personal Injury Litigation.
Meehan, Michael T. .... '71 '96 C.1033 B.S. L.1252 J.D. [Ⓐ Meehan,M.&G.]
Meehan, Richard T., Jr., (AV) .... '49 '74 C.602 B.A. L.184 J.D. [Meehan,M.&G.]
*PRACTICE AREAS: Criminal Law; Drug Crimes; Felonies; White Collar Crime; Personal Injury Law.
Meehan, Richard T., Sr., (AV) ...... '23 '60 C.1029 B.A. L.184 LL.B. [Meehan,M.&G.]
*PRACTICE AREAS: Criminal Law; Personal Injury; Labor Law.

Meehan, Meehan & Gavin, (AV)
76 Lyon Terrace, 06604
Telephone: 203-333-1888 Fax: 203-331-0107
Email: thefirm@meehanlaw.com URL: http://www.meehanlaw.com
Richard T. Meehan, Sr.; Richard T. Meehan, Jr.; Edward J. Gavin. Associates: Michael T. Meehan; Rosemarie Talio Weber.
Criminal Law, Personal Injury, Medical Malpractice, Dental Malpractice, Legal Malpractice, Wrongful Death, Labor Law, Commercial Litigation, Appellate.
See Professional Biographies, BRIDGEPORT, CONNECTICUT

Melville, L. Scott .... '33 '62 C.569 A.B. L.329 LL.B. Supr. Ct. J.

Merly, Lawrence J., (AV) '39 '64 C.1030 B.S.S. L.184 J.D. BR
76 Lyon Terrace, 06604-4022
Telephone: 203-333-1353 Fax: 203-332-7984
Email: lawrencemerly@yahoo.com
***PRACTICE AREAS: Personal Injury Law; Medical Malpractice; Civil Litigation; Trials and Appeals Law.**
General Civil Practice before State Courts. Personal Injury, Medical Malpractice and Workers Compensation Law. Trials and Appeals.
Reference: Hudson United Bank; First Union Securities.
See Professional Biographies, BRIDGEPORT, CONNECTICUT

Meuser, Joseph E., (BV) .... '31 '57 C&L.184 B.S., J.D. 387 Clinton Ave.
Meyer, Jonas J., III, (BV) .... '29 '54 C.1030 B.S. L.93 J.D. [Sedensky&M.]
Meyer, R.C. .... '61 '87 C.1103 B.A. L.1029 J.D. 3223 Main St.
Miller, Rosnick & D'Amico, P.C., (BV) .... 1087 Broad St.
Mills, John W., (BV) .... '64 '90 C.184 B.A. L.1040 J.D. [Murphy&K.]
*PRACTICE AREAS: Litigation; Insurance Defense; Toxic Torts; Appellate Practice.
Minchella, Anthony R. .... '67 '97 C.712 B.A. L.1252 J.D. [Ⓐ Zeldes,N.&C.]
*PRACTICE AREAS: Commercial Litigation; Product Liability Litigation; Real Property Litigation; Personal Injury; Family Law.
Mirsky, Joseph .... '27 '52 C.1029 B.A. L.94 LL.B. 1115 Main St.
Mitchell, Robert B., (AV) .... '53 '79 C.611 B.A. L.861 J.D. [Pullman&C.] (⊙Stamford)
*PRACTICE AREAS: General Civil Litigation; Trial Practice; Labor Law; Employment Law; Civil Rights Law.
Moorin, Herbert H., (AV) .... '38 '62 C.855 B.A. L.309 LL.B. [Pullman&C.]
*PRACTICE AREAS: Trusts and Estates; Pension and Profit-Sharing Law; Corporate Law.
Morris, D. Robert, (AV) .... '50 '75 C&L.188 B.A., J.D. [Pullman&C.] (⊙Stamford)
*PRACTICE AREAS: Taxation Law; Corporate Law; Employee Benefits Law; Estate Planning; Computer Law.
Mulcahey, Garic J., (AV) .... '43 '81 C.184 B.A. L.1040 J.D. [Bai,P.B.&M.]
*PRACTICE AREAS: General Litigation; Professional Liability Law.
Mulcahy, Ann B. .... '73 '99 C.855 B.A. L.188 J.D. [Ⓐ Cohen&W.]
*PRACTICE AREAS: Employment Law; Commercial Litigation.
Munich, C. David, (BV) .... '17 '40 C.1029 L.306 J.D. 213 Thorme St.
Murphy, Kevin R., (BV) .... '49 '77 C.197 A.B. L.184 J.D. [Murphy&K.]
*PRACTICE AREAS: Personal Injury Law; Litigation; Products Liability Law; Insurance Defense Law; Medical Malpractice.

Murphy and Karpie, LLC, (BV)
350 Fairfield Avenue, Suite 408, 06604
Telephone: 203-333-0177 Fax: 203-333-8475
Email: murphykarpie@aol.com
Kevin R. Murphy; Karen L. Karpie; John W. Mills;—Michael Connelly; Maria A. Cahill.
General Civil Practice before State and Federal Courts. Insurance Defense, Personal Injury, Negligence, Products Liability, Medical Malpractice, Professional Liability, Employment Litigation, Commercial and Civil Rights Law, Appellate Practice, Toxic Torts.
See Professional Biographies, BRIDGEPORT, CONNECTICUT

Murtha, Thomas M., (BV) .... '55 '81 C.1030 B.A. L.1029 J.D. [Maher&M.]
*PRACTICE AREAS: Defense Litigation; Errors and Omissions; Construction Litigation; Municipal Liability.
Musto, Vincent M., (BV) .... '50 '86 C.477 B.S.C.E. L.563 J.D. [Koskoff,K.&B.]
*PRACTICE AREAS: Products Liability; Toxic Substances; Motor Vehicle Accidents and Injuries; Premises Liability.
Nadeau, Thomas L., (AV) .... '40 '69 C.184 B.A. L.276 J.D. 1061 Main St.
Nagel, Daniel S., (BV) .... '59 '84 C&L.188 B.S., J.D. [Cohen&W.]
*PRACTICE AREAS: Real Estate; Commercial; Environmental.
Napolitano, Roberta, (BV) .... '58 '82 C.104 A.B. L.184 J.D. [Weinstein,W.I.N.&S.]
*PRACTICE AREAS: Commercial Litigation; Bankruptcy; Foreclosures.
Neary, William J. .... '69 '95 C.823 B.A. L.1252 J.D. 3354 Main St.
Needle, Charles M., (AV) .... '38 '63 C.309 B.A. L.976 LL.B. [Zeldes,N.&C.]
*PRACTICE AREAS: Commercial Law and Litigation; Bankruptcy Law; Business Reorganization; Real Estate Law.
Nelson, Geoffrey W., (AV) .... '32 '60 C&L.976 B.A., LL.B. Corp. Coun.
Nevas, Alan H. .... '28 '51 C.823 A.B. L.569 LL.B. U.S. Sr. Dist. J.
Newman, Matthew D. .... '57 '85 C.183 B.A. L.1252 J.D. 855 Main Street, Suite 5
Newman, Richard L., (BV) .... '55 '79 C.1044 B.A. L.966 J.D. [Adelman H.&N.]
*PRACTICE AREAS: Personal Injury; Medical Malpractice; Products Liability; Legal Malpractice.
Nichols, George N. .... '40 '65 C.31 B.A. L.309 LL.B. [Durant,N.H.H.&C.]
Nickowitz, Arlen D., (BV) .... '29 '54 C.184 B.S. L.94 LL.B. 285 Congress St.
Nolan, Thomas M. .... '70 '95 C.93 B.A. L.184 J.D. 1000 Lafayette Blvd.
O'Brien, Johnpatrick .... '67 '95 C.1211 B.S. L.1187 J.D. [Ⓐ Zeisler&Z.]
*PRACTICE AREAS: Personal Injury; Criminal Law; Workers Compensation; Appellate Practice.
O'Connell, Peter B., (BV) .... '44 '70 C.276 B.A. L.262 LL.B. [Ⓒ Goldstein&P.] ⊙
*PRACTICE AREAS: Probate Law; Real Estate Law.

O'Donnell, McDonald and Cregeen, L.L.C.
(See Fairfield)

O'Hara, Charles D., Jr. '69 '94 C.1030 B.A. L.1252 J.D.
2145 North Avenue, 06604-2412
Telephone: 203-333-3434; 203- 929-8831 Fax: 203-368-1055
Email: coharajr@msn.com
***PRACTICE AREAS: Personal Injury; Real Estate; Wills; Probate; Divorce.**
Personal Injury, Real Estate, Wills, Probate, Divorce, Bankruptcy.
See Professional Biographies, BRIDGEPORT, CONNECTICUT

Oleyer, George R., (BV) .... '46 '71 C.860 A.B. L.94 J.D. Supv. Asst. Pub. Def.
Olson, Peter S. .... '70 '95 C.67 B.A. L.184 J.D. [Ⓐ Pullman&C.]
*PRACTICE AREAS: Municipal Law; Litigation.
Orleans, Jonathan B., (AV) .... '54 '85 C.1307 B.A. L.569 J.D. [Zeldes,N.&C.]
*PRACTICE AREAS: Civil Litigation; Employment Law.
Owens, Jeffrey R. .... '72 '00 C.855 B.A. L.1252 J.D. [Ⓐ Bai,P.B.&M.]
*PRACTICE AREAS: Civil Litigation; Insurance; Real Estate; Probate.
Pacacha, Ronald J., (BV) .... '46 '81 C.563 B.A. L.1019 J.D. Assoc. City Atty.
Pacelli, Robert A., Jr. .... '72 '97 C.1036 B.A. L.94 J.D. [Ⓐ Zeldes,N.&C.]
*PRACTICE AREAS: Business Law; Commercial Real Estate; Residential Real Estate; Community Association Law.
Paoletti, Frederick D., Jr., (BV) .... '55 '82 C.184 B.A. L.61 J.D. 3301 Main St.
Parnoff, Laurence V. .... '42 '70 C.1030 B.A. L.724 J.D. [L.V.Parnoff]
Parnoff, Laurence V., P.C. .... 1566 Park Ave.
Patterson, Adele V., (BV) .... '59 '89 C.103 A.B. L.184 J.D. 1000 Lafayette Blvd.
Payne, Cynthia Howard .... '52 '77 C.183 B.A. L.128 J.D. Atty., People's Bank

Pearl Professional Corporation
(See Westport)

Pepe & Hazard LLP
(See Southport)

Perkins, Mark A. .... '63 '98 C.550 B.S. L.1252 J.D. [Maher&M.]
*PRACTICE AREAS: Insurance Defense.
Phillips, Jane, (BV) .... '54 '79 C.1211 B.S. L.724 J.D. 56 Lyon Terr.

Piazza & Pickel
(See Stamford)

Pinheiro, John A., (CV) .... '58 '88 C.1102 B.S. L.1029 J.D. 2112 N. Ave.
Piquette, Edward L., Jr. .... '56 '88 C.1030 B.S. L.306 J.D. 1057 Broad St.
Plouffe, Raymond J., Jr., (BV) .... '59 '84 C.1030 B.A. L.884 J.D. [Bai,P.B.&M.]
*PRACTICE AREAS: General Litigation.
Plude, Donald A. .... '53 '79 C.1030 B.S. L.838 J.D. 636 Burnsford Ave.★
Pollack, Elliott B., (AV) '43 '65
C&L.178 A.B., LL.B. [Pullman&C.] (⊙Hartford, Stamford)
*PRACTICE AREAS: Health Care; Tax Appeal and Condemnation Law; Commercial Litigation.
Pollock, Paul E., (AV) .... '41 '70 C&L.602 B.S., J.D. [Bai,P.B.&M.]
*PRACTICE AREAS: Litigation; Professional Liability.
Ponvert, Antonio, III, (AV) .... '62 '90 C.690 B.S. L.659 J.D. [Ⓐ Koskoff,K.&B.]
*PRACTICE AREAS: Civil Rights; Class Actions; Criminal Appeals.
Poston, Sarah W. .... '65 '94 C.103 A.B. L.569 J.D. [Ⓐ Zeldes,N.&C.]
*PRACTICE AREAS: Civil Litigation; Criminal Law.
Proctor, Michael G., (AV) .... '57 '83 C.183 B.A. L.93 J.D. [Pullman&C.]
*PRACTICE AREAS: Real Estate Law; Commercial Lending Law; Creditors' Rights Law.

Pullman & Comley, L.L.C., (AV)
(Formerly Pullman, Comley, Bradley & Reeves)
850 Main Street, P.O. Box 7006, 06601-7006 ⊙
Telephone: 203-330-2000 Telecopier: 203-576-8888
URL: http://www.pullcom.com
John S. Pullman (1871-1943); Arthur M. Comley (1883-1969); J. Kenneth Bradley (1903-1969); William Reeves (1906-1967). Members of Firm: Elizabeth J. Austin; Raymond E. Baldwin, Jr.; Collin P. Baron; Deborah S. Breck; Charles K. Campbell, Jr. (Resident at Stamford Office); Frank B. Cleary; Sheila Anne Denton; James G. Dowling, Jr.; Lawrence J. Golden (Resident at Hartford Office); Irve J. Goldman; Nancy A. D. Hancock; David O. Jackson; George J. Kasper; Michael A. Kurs; Nancy DeFonce Lapera; Michael N. LaVelle; Joseph M. Lodato (Resident at Stamford Office); Thomas F. Maxwell, Jr.; Edward P. McCreery III; Andrew J. McDonald (Resident in Stamford Office); Robert B. Mitchell; Herbert H. Moorin; D. Robert Morris; Marie V. Phelan (Resident at Hartford Office); Elliott B. Pollack; Michael G. Proctor; Thomas A. Rouse; Alan I. Scheer (At Hartford Office); Gregory F. Servodidio; Ronald Case Sharp; Margaret M. Sheahan; James T. Shearin; H. William Shure; Christopher J. Smith; John F. Stafstrom, Jr.; James B. Stewart; Grove W. Stoddard; Marshall J. Touponse; John R. Ward (Resident at New Haven Office); William J. Wenzel; James P. White, Jr.; Marjorie S. Wilder (Resident at Hartford Office). Associates: Christian G. Beltz; Carrie L. Bernier; Katherine E. Caulfield; Adam J. Cohen; Richard S. DiPreta; Eric J. George; Matthew M. Hausman; Matthew P. Lundy; Norma R. Mandulak; Jennifer T. McGrath (Resident at Southport Office); Julie A. Morgan (Resident at Hartford Office); Peter S. Olson; Mary Beth K. Rapice; Brian C. Roche; Patricia Squires; Lori L. Underberger; Aimee J. Wood.
General Practice including Administrative, Antitrust, Banking, Bankruptcy and Creditors Rights, Bonds, Business and Commercial, Corporate, Education, Employee Benefits, Environmental, Hospital and Health Care, Labor and Employment, Municipal Finance, Real Estate, Securities, Tax, Trusts and Estates, and Zoning. Energy and Utilities, Litigation in all Courts.
Hartford, Connecticut Office: 90 State House Square. Telephone: 860-424-4300. Telecopier: 860-424-4370.
New Haven, Connecticut Office: One Century Tower, 265 Church Street. Telephone: 203-773-3006. Telecopier: 203-776-7075.
Simsbury, Connecticut Office: 720 Hopmeadow Street. Telephone: 860-651-9348. Fax: 860-651-1431.
Southport, Connecticut Office: 200 Pequot Avenue, P.O. Box 510. Telephone: 203-254-5000. Telecopier: 203-254-5070.
Stamford, Connecticut Office: 350 Bedford Street. Telephone: 203-324-5000. Telecopier: 203-363-8659.
See Professional Biographies, BRIDGEPORT, CONNECTICUT

Quatrella & Rizio, LLC
(See Fairfield)

Radano, Pamela Coyne .... '54 '00 C.1211 B.S. L.1252 J.D. [Ⓐ Durant,N.H.H.&C.]
Rapice, Mary Beth K., (BV) .... '59 '85 C.741 B.A. L.1252 J.D. [Ⓐ Pullman&C.]
*PRACTICE AREAS: Real Estate Law.

Reath, Patricia C., (BV) '41 '87 C.967 B.A. L.1029 J.D.
The Legal Center, 1087 Broad Street, Fourth Floor, 06604
Telephone: 203-331-1206 Fax: 203-331-1337
Email: attyreath@aol.com

(This Listing Continued)

Reath, Patricia C. (Continued)
Family Law, Domestic Relations, Custody, Children and Mediation.
See Professional Biographies, BRIDGEPORT, CONNECTICUT

Reich, Veronica E., (BV) . . . . '55 '80 C.66 B.A. L.1292 J.D. 295 Congress St.
Reilly, Carey B., (BV) . . . . '57 '82 C&L.184 B.A., J.D. [Koskoff,K.&B.]
*PRACTICE AREAS: Medical Malpractice; Products Liability; Negligence.

Reisman, Glenn M.
(See Shelton)

Reynolds, Karen, (BV) . . . . '51 '81 C.1029 B.A. L.1194 J.D. [Gans&R.]
Reynolds, Stephen B. . . . . '71 '97 C.299 B.A. L.188 J.D. Law Clk.
Ricci, Frances, (BV) . . . . '52 '79 C.703 B.A. L.184 J.D. Mgn. Coun., People's Bank
Riccio, Eugene J., (BV) . . . . '51 '76 C.436 B.A. L.564 J.D. [J.R.Gulash,Jr.&E.J.R.]
*PRACTICE AREAS: Civil Litigation; Criminal Defense.
Riccio, Frank J., (BV) . . . . '42 '68 C.1030 A.B. L.564 J.D. 923 E. Main St.
Riccio-Ryan, Jeanmarie A., (CV) . . . . '56 '90 C.829 B.S. L.1029 J.D. 1057 Broad St.
Robbins, Bradd S., (BV) . . . . '63 '88 C.1036 B.A. L.94 J.D. [Willinger,W.&B.]
*PRACTICE AREAS: Real Estate Development; Commercial Lending; Workouts; Commercial and Residential Leasing and related Transactions; Corporate Law.

Roberts, Rose & Bates, P.C.
(See Stamford)

Robertson, David J., (CV) . . . . '63 '88 C.1030 B.A. L.276 J.D. [Bai,P.B.&M.]
*PRACTICE AREAS: Civil Litigation; Professional Liability; Products Liability; Municipal Liability.
Robinson, Cindy Lori, (AV) . . . . '61 '86 C.918 B.A. L.184 J.D. [Tremont&S.]
*PRACTICE AREAS: Medical Malpractice; Personal Injury; Sexual Abuse.
Roche, Brian C. . . . . '70 '95 C.1030 B.A. L.588 J.D. [Ⓐ Pullman&C.]
*PRACTICE AREAS: Litigation.
Rodriguez, Cheryl Ann, Law Offices of, (BV) '51 '76
C.645 B.A. L.831 J.D. 118 Brooklawn Ave.
Rodriguez, Eddie, Jr. . . . . '49 '76 C.1030 B.A. L.831 J.D. Supr. Ct. J.
Rodriguez, Jennifer S. . . . . '69 '01 C.690 B.A. L.1252 J.D. [Ⓐ Tremont&S.]
*PRACTICE AREAS: Personal Injury.
Rogers, Elizabeth Ann . . . . '54 '91 C.1030 B.A. L.1029 J.D. 1000 Lafayette Blvd.

Rome McGuigan Sabanosh, P.C., (AV)
1000 Lafayette Boulevard, 06604 ⊙
Telephone: 203-382-8000 Telecopier: 203-382-8005
John A. Sabanosh.
Labor and Employment, Education, Administrative Law, Alternative Dispute Resolution, Bankruptcy, Benefits Planning/ERISA, Business Planning, Commercial Finance, Construction, Corporate, Creditor's Rights, Environmental, Estate Planning and Administration, Government Relations, Insurance, Intellectual Property, Investigations, Land Use, Litigation, Municipal, Personal Injury, Product Liability, Real Estate, Tax, Tax and Valuation Appeal, Tribal Gaming, White-Collar Crime. Hartford, Connecticut Office: One State Street. Telephone: 203-549-1000. Telecopier: 203-724-3921.
See Professional Biographies, BRIDGEPORT, CONNECTICUT

Rosander, Sheryl J., (BV) . . . . '51 '77 C.937 B.A. L.1035 J.D. [Ⓒ Zeldes,N.&C.]
Rosenblum, Jerome J., (BV) . . . . '34 '59 C.103 B.A. L.569 J.D. 285 Congress St.

Rosenstein & Barnes
(See Fairfield)

Rosnick, Harold L., (BV) . . . . '47 '72 C&L.184 B.A., J.D. [Miller,R.&D.]
Ross, Richard G. . . . . '40 '65 C.401 B.A. L.94 LL.B. Int. Rev. Serv.
Rost, Samuel T., (BV) . . . . '43 '69 C.95 A.B. L.94 J.D. [Green&G.]
Rouse, Thomas A., (BV) . . . . . . '50 '75 C.855 B.A. L.184 J.D. [Pullman&C.] (⊙Hartford)
*PRACTICE AREAS: Electronic Commerce; Environmental Litigation; Telecommunications Law; Electric Power; Technology Startups.
Ruane, James J., (AV) . . . . '49 '77 C.1030 B.A. L.184 J.D. [Ruane L.]
Ruane, James O. . . . . '72 '98 C.754 B.A. L.184 J.D. [Ruane L.]
*PRACTICE AREAS: DWI Defense; Criminal Defense; Appellate Practice; Civil Torts; Personal Injury.

Ruane Attorneys At Law, (AV)
10 Middle Street, 06604
Telephone: 203-382-0394 URL: http://www.ctdwi.com; URL: http://www.connecticutcriminaldefense.com
Members of Firm: James J. Ruane; James O. Ruane.
Criminal Defense, Personal Injury, Appellate, DWI, Drug Crimes, Felonies, White Collar Crime, Automobile Accidents, Medical Malpractice, Wrongful Death.
See Professional Biographies, BRIDGEPORT, CONNECTICUT

Rubenstein, Keith A., (BV) . . . . '50 '75 C&L.184 B.A., J.D. [Rubenstein&F.]
Rubenstein & Finnie, (BV) . . . . Suite 200, One Lafayette Square

Rubenstein, Green & Bass, LLC
(See Westport)

Rush, William B., (AV) . . . . '34 '59 C.918 B.A. L.184 LL.B. 850 Main St.
Russell, Edward W. '10 '35 C.611 B.A. L.309
(adm. in OH; not adm. in CT) Chmn. of the Bd., Crown Foundations
Rutigliano, Dominick J., (BV) . . . . '52 '77 C.1030 B.A. L.262 J.D. 3321 Main St.
Sabanosh, John A., (AV) . . . . '38 '63 C&L.893 B.A., LL.B. [Rome M.S.]
*PRACTICE AREAS: Management Labor and Employment Law; Education Law; Public Education; Private Education.
Sacco, Madonna A., (BV) . . . . '55 '85 C.1030 B.A. L.1029 J.D. [Bai,P.B.&M.]
*PRACTICE AREAS: Professional Liability Litigation.
Saden, George A. . . . . '10 '34 C.976 B.A. L.309 LL.B. Ret. Supr. Ct. J.
Sadin, Shelley R., (AV) . . . . '57 '84 C.976 B.A. L.276 J.D. [Zeldes,N.&C.]
*PRACTICE AREAS: Criminal Investigations, Trials and Appeals; Civil Litigation and Appeals.
Salerno, Francis H. '22 '65 C.623 J.D. L.51 LL.B.
(adm. in GA; not adm. in CT) Exec. Dir., Astra Associates
Samowitz, Lee A. . . . . '53 '78 C.696 B.A. L.221 J.D. State Rep.

Sandak Friedman Hennessey & Greco, LLP
(See Stamford)

Sapone, William J., (BVⓉ) '54 '84 C.459 B.S. L.1040 J.D.
[Coleman S.S.] (See Pat. Sect.) (⊙New York, NY)
Scaccia, Tiziana M. . . . . '64 '90 C.1030 B.S. L.184 J.D. [Goldstein&P.] ⊙
*PRACTICE AREAS: Civil and Commercial Litigation; Personal Injury; Family Law; Real Estate; Probate.
Scalo, Richard S., (BV) . . . . '34 '63 C.94 B.A. L.306 J.D. [Gordon&S.]
Schellenberg, Barbara M. . . . . '59 '86 C.188 B.S. L.659 J.D. [Ⓐ Cohen&W.]
*PRACTICE AREAS: Commercial Litigation; Appellate Practice.
Schiller, Gregory B. . . . . '58 '99 C.1103 B.A. L.1048 J.D. [Ⓐ Zeisler&Z.]
*PRACTICE AREAS: Bankruptcy; Commercial Law; Corporate Law; Bankruptcy Litigation.
Schmitt, Duncan M. . . . . '59 '89 C.976 B.A. L.184 J.D. 1000 Lafayette Blvd.

Schoonmaker, George & Colin, P.C.
(See Greenwich)

Schopick, Daniel F., (BV) . . . . '48 '74 C.1036 B.A. L.564 J.D. [Steiber&S.]
Schul, Eduard . . . . '31 '79 C.976 B.A. L.262 J.D. P.O. Box 6355
Schwartz, Roberta S., (BV) . . . . '59 '87 C.1036 B.A. L.1029 J.D. 4920 Main Street
Scofield, Edward R., (BV) . . . . '61 '85 C.976 B.A. L.184 J.D. [Zeldes,N.&C.]
*PRACTICE AREAS: Civil Litigation; Intellectual Property Litigation.
Sedensky, Stephen J., III, (BV) . . . . '58 '83 C.666 B.S. L.818 J.D. Sr. Asst. States Atty.
Sedensky, Stephen J., Jr., (BV) '30 '54
C.1030 B.S. L.93 J.D. Asst. City Atty. [Sedensky&M.]
Sedensky & Meyer, (BV) . . . . 1612 Capitol Ave.
Servodidio, Gregory F. . . . . '61 '86 C&L.276 A.B., J.D. [Pullman&C.] (⊙Hartford)
*PRACTICE AREAS: Property Taxation; Condemnation and Relocation; Land Use; Litigation.
Shapiro, Richard J., (BV) . . . . '54 '78 C.679 B.A. L.813 J.D. [Weinstein,W.I.N.&S.]
*PRACTICE AREAS: Real Estate; Commercial Law.
Sharnick, Wayne R., (BV) . . . . '60 '86 C.1030 B.A. L.276 J.D. 295 Congress St.
Sharp, Ronald Case, (AV) . . . . '— '64 C.976 B.A. L.184 LL.B. [Pullman&C.]
*PRACTICE AREAS: Corporate and Partnership Law; Health Care Law; Commercial Transactions; Banking Law; Tax Law.
Sheahan, Margaret M., (AV) '54 '80 C.262 B.A. L.569 J.D.
[Pullman&C.] (⊙Stamford)
*PRACTICE AREAS: Labor Law; Employment Law; Civil Litigation.
Shearin, James T., (AV) '61 '86
C&L.184 B.A., J.D. [Pullman&C.] (⊙Hartford, Stamford)
*PRACTICE AREAS: Litigation; Intellectual Property; Admiralty; Securities.
Sheiman, Stuart M. . . . . '42 '69 C.477 B.B.A. L.1119 J.D. 4697 Main St.
Sheldon, Robert R., (AV) . . . . '49 '74 C.321 B.A. L.184 J.D. [Tremont&S.]
*PRACTICE AREAS: Personal Injury; Legal Malpractice; Workers Compensation.
Shiff, Alan H. W. . . . . '34 '60 C.976 B.A. L.893 LL.B. U.S. Bkrptcy. J.

Shumway & Spencer, LLC
(See Fairfield)

Shupik, Rudolph A. '18 '51 C&L.45 B.S., LL.B.
(adm. in AR; not adm. in CT) 355 Frenchtown Rd.‡
Shure, H. William, (AV) '40 '64 C.197 A.B. L.893 LL.B.
[Pullman&C.] (⊙New Haven)
*PRACTICE AREAS: Commercial Law; Banking Law; Bankruptcy Law; Government Law.
Silva, Joseph J. . . . . '28 '57 C.1030 B.S.S. L.262 LL.B. 1720 Noble Ave.

Silver, Golub & Teitell LLP
(See Stamford)

Silvestri, Frank J., Jr., (AV) . . . . '46 '74 C.276 A.B. L.976 J.D. [Zeldes,N.&C.]
*PRACTICE AREAS: Commercial Litigation; Arbitration.
Simko, V. Michael, Jr., (BV) . . . . '56 '88 C.676 B.A. L.1029 J.D. [Simko]
*PRACTICE AREAS: Employment Litigation; Workers Compensation; Construction Litigation; Domestic Relations; Divorce.
Simko, Vincent M., (AV) . . . . '26 '53 C.262 B.S.II L.184 LL.B. [Simko]
*PRACTICE AREAS: Construction Law; Construction Litigation; Litigation; Probate; Real Estate.

Simko Law Firm, The, L.L.C., (AV)
1087 Broad Street, Suite 201, 06604-4231
Telephone: 203-367-2220 Fax: 203-367-3552
URL: http://www.lawyers.com/simkolaw
Vincent M. Simko; V. Michael Simko, Jr.
Construction Litigation, Mechanics Liens, Workers Compensation, Probate, Personal Injury, Medical Collections, Trials and Appeals.
Representative Clients: Wright Investors Service; Pace Construction, Inc.
References: UST Bank/Connecticut; Lafayette American Bank and Trust Company.
Approved Attorneys For: Chicago Title Insurance Company; Connecticut Attorneys Title Insurance Company. Lawyers Title Insurance Company.
See Professional Biographies, BRIDGEPORT, CONNECTICUT

Skyers, Eroll V. . . . . '62 '92 C.902 B.S. L.574 J.D. [Skyers&S.]
Skyers, Sharon A. . . . . '68 '93 C.228 B.A. L.574 J.D [Skyers&S.]
Skyers & Skyers, P.C. . . . . 622 Clinton Ave.
Slavin, Richard, (BV) '47 '77 C.930 B.A. L.8 J.D.
[Cohen&W.] (⊙Stamford, Westport)
*PRACTICE AREAS: Securities Regulation; Banking Regulation; Securities, Banking and Corporate Litigation; Arbitrations.

Slavitt, Connery & Vardamis
(See Norwalk)

Smith, Christopher J., (BV) . . . . '58 '83 C.676 B.A. L.184 J.D. [Pullman&C.]
*PRACTICE AREAS: Zoning; Planning; Wetlands; Environmental; Real Estate Litigation.
Smith, Donald R., (BV) . . . . '24 '53 C&L.184 B.S., LL.B. 180 Fairfield Ave.
Smriga, John C., (BV) . . . . '53 '80 C.659 B.A. L.724 J.D. Asst. States Atty.
Soares, Guy P., (BV) . . . . '59 '87 C.1211 B.S L.1029 J.D. [DePiano G.C.&S.]
Sobel, Paul A., (BV) . . . . '54 '79 C.688 B.S. L.1048 J.D. [Ⓒ Green&G.] (Pat.)
*PRACTICE AREAS: Real Estate; Construction Law.
Sohon, Michael C., (BV) . . . . '52 '81 C.276 B.A. L.425 J.D. 800 Clinton Ave.
Solomon, Greta E., (AV) . . . . '51 '76 C.788 A.B. L.184 J.D. [Cohen&W.] (⊙Westport)
*PRACTICE AREAS: Taxation; Estate Planning; Trusts and Estates; Elder Law; Retirement Planning.
Spain, Darius J. . . . . '27 '62 C.188 A.B. L.262 LL.B. Workers Comp. Comr.
Spear, E. Eugene . . . . '38 '63 C&L.184 B.A., LL.B. Supr. Ct. J.
Squires, Patricia . . . . '57 '94 C.1029 B.S.N. L.1252 J.D. [Ⓐ Pullman&C.]
*PRACTICE AREAS: Health Law; Administrative Law; Corporate Law.
Squitiero, Geoffrey L., (BV) . . . . '60 '85 C.861 B.S.M. L.851 J.D. [Maher&M.]
*PRACTICE AREAS: Litigation; Subrogation; Products Liability; Municipal Liability; Law Enforcement Liability.
Stafstrom, John F., Jr., (AV) '56 '81 C.321 B.A. L.184 J.D.
[Pullman&C.] (⊙Hartford)
*PRACTICE AREAS: Public Finance; Corporate Law; Banking Law; Commercial Law.
Stanley, Susan D., (BV) . . . . '56 '82 C.858 B.A. L.184 J.D. Corp. Coun., People's Bank
Steiber, Richard I., (AV) . . . . '17 '41 C.976 B.A. L.477 J.D. [Steiber&S.]
Steiber & Schopick, (AV) . . . . 4270 Main Street
Stewart, James B., (AV) . . . . . . '43 '68 C.918 B.A. L.880 J.D. [Pullman&C.] (⊙Southport)
*PRACTICE AREAS: Estates and Trusts; Real Estate.
Stoddard, Grove W., (AV) . . . . '41 '66 C.509 B.A. L.1017 J.D. [Pullman&C.]
*PRACTICE AREAS: Banking Law.
Stodolink, Edw. F. . . . . '28 '53 C.976 B.S. L.178 LL.B. Supr. Ct. J.
Stone, Huntley, (AV) . . . . . '20 '44 C.674 A.B. L.823 LL.B. 850 Main St. (⊙Boulder, CO)
Stovall, Marcy Tench . . . . '56 '93 C.813 B.A. L.184 J.D. [Ⓐ Zeldes,N.&C.]
*PRACTICE AREAS: Civil Litigation; Professional Licensing; Legal Ethics; Family Law.
Stracka, Daniel '47 '90 C.1046 B.A. L.1252 J.D.
Dir., Immig., Intl. Institute of Conn., Inc.
Stratton, Michael A., (BV) . . . . '65 '90 C.165 B.A. L.94 J.D. [Koskoff,K.&B.]
*PRACTICE AREAS: Brain Injury; Toxic Torts; Motor Vehicle Accidents and Injuries; Product Liability; Securities.
Sudol, R. Neil, (BVⓉ) '51 '84 C.401 B.A.,B.S. L.569 J.D.
(adm. in NY; not adm. in CT; See Pat. Sect.) [Coleman S.S.]
Sullivan, Patricia C., (BV) . . . . . . '59 '89 C&L.262 B.A., J.D. [Ⓐ Cohen&W.] (⊙Westport)
Sutton, Neil W., (BV) . . . . '58 '84 C.659 B.A. L.93 J.D. [Adelman H.&N.]
*PRACTICE AREAS: Personal Injury; Medical Malpractice; Products Liability; Legal Malpractice; Automobile Accidents and Injuries.
Teitell, Catherine E., (BV) . . . . '51 '85 C.1030 B.A. L.1252 J.D. Off. of Pub. Def.
Tellalian, Aram H., Jr., (AV) . . . . '13 '36 C&L.976 B.A., LL.B. Prob. J. [Tellalian&T.]
*PRACTICE AREAS: Probate; Wills; Trust.
Tellalian, Robert S., (AV) . . . . '21 '49 C.976 B.A. L.184 LL.B. [Tellalian&T.]
*PRACTICE AREAS: Probate; Real Estate; Wills; Trust Law.

Tellalian & Tellalian, (AV)
Court Exchange Building, 211 State Street, 06604
Telephone: 203-333-5566 Fax: 203-330-1379

(This Listing Continued)

Tellalian & Tellalian (Continued)

Members of Firm: Aram H. Tellalian, Jr.; Robert S. Tellalian. Associate: William T. Fray.
General Practice, Probate, Corporation and Real Estate Law.
Representative Clients: People's Bank; Chase-Manhattan; Fleet Bank.
See Professional Biographies, BRIDGEPORT, CONNECTICUT

Tenenbaum, Richard L., (CV) '50 '75
C.550 B.A. L.273 J.D. Task Force Dir., Conn. Legal Servs., Inc.
Testo, Robt. J. .... '20 '49 C&L.262 B.S., LL.B. Supr. Ct. J.
Thomas, Paul F., (AV) .... '51 '82 C.918 B.A. L.184 J.D. 1000 Lafayette Blvd.
Tornillo, Daniel A. .... '28 '55 C.1029 B.A. L.976 LL.B. 2160 Main St.‡
Touponse, Marshall J. .... '60 '85 C.976 B.A. L.184 J.D. [Pullman&C.]
*PRACTICE AREAS: E-Commerce Law; Corporate Law; Intellectual Property Law; Banking Law; Health Care.
Trachtenburg, Lisa R. '63 '90
C.1349 B.A. L.1029 J.D. Consolidated Asset Recovery Corp.
Trautmann, Robert E. .... '53 '85 C&L.910 A.B., J.D. Mng. Coun., People's Bank
Treco, Arnold .... '73 '99 C.724 B.S. L.1252 J.D. 622 Clinton Ave.
Tremont, Jason E. .... '67 '92 C.216 B.A. L.64 J.D. [Tremont&S.]
*PRACTICE AREAS: Medical Malpractice; Personal Injury; Products Liability.

Tremont & Sheldon, P.C., (AV)
64 Lyon Terrace, 06604
Telephone: 203-335-5145 Fax: 203-366-8503
Email: lawfirm@tremont-sheldon.com URL: http://www.tremont-sheldon.com
T. Paul Tremont (1933-1999); Robert R. Sheldon; Cindy Lori Robinson; Frank A. Bailey; Jason E. Tremont; Douglas P. Mahoney;—Jennifer S. Rodriguez.
Civil Litigation in Federal and State Courts. Personal Injury and Commercial Law.
See Professional Biographies, BRIDGEPORT, CONNECTICUT

Turner, John C., Jr. .... '62 '99 C.1093 B.A. L.1252 J.D. [Maher&M.]
*PRACTICE AREAS: Defense Litigation; Subrogation.
Underberger, Lori L. .... '61 '85 C.1036 B.A. L.273 J.D. [Ⓐ Pullman&C.]
*PRACTICE AREAS: Employee Benefits.
Vaccaro, Enrico, (BV) .... '51 '76 C.976 B.A. L.184 J.D. 56 Boston Ave., 2nd Fl.
Varga, Douglas J., (BV) .... '63 '89 C.1030 B.A. L.880 J.D. [Zeldes,N.&C.]
*PRACTICE AREAS: Commercial Litigation; Employment Litigation.
Varone, Anthony T., (BV) .... '27 '54 C.1030 B.S. L.93 J.D. 1087 Broad St.
Vatti, S. Dave, (BV) .... '68 '93 C.178 B.A. L.184 J.D. [Zeldes,N.&C.]
*PRACTICE AREAS: Business Litigation; Personal Injury; Civil Rights; Employment Law; Campaign Finance Law.
Venditti, Jason M. .... '73 '00 C.586 B.A. L.1252 J.D. [Ⓐ Zeisler&Z.]
*PRACTICE AREAS: Commercial Litigation.
Verrilli, Frank J. .... '22 '48 L.94 LL.B. 1115 Main St.
Verrillo, James G., (BV) .... '51 '76 C.276 A.B. L.184 J.D. [Zeisler&Z.]
*PRACTICE AREAS: Bankruptcy; Commercial Law.
Vioni, Edward W. .... '55 '82 C.575 B.A. L.1029 J.D. Law Clk., Supr. Ct.
Vogel, Alan Garson, (BV) .... '48 '75 C.475 B.A. L.184 J.D. 350 Fairfield Ave.‡

Wake, See, Dimes & Bryniczka
(See Westport)

Wallace, John F., (BV) '48 '85
C.282 B.A. L.184 J.D. Councel-Legal Department, People's Bank
Walsh, Edward V., (BV) .... '55 '81 C.1030 B.A. L.1029 J.D. [Maher&M.]
*PRACTICE AREAS: Litigation; Federal Litigation; Subrogation.

Ware, Fressola, Van Der Sluys & Adolphson, LLP
(See Monroe)

Warren, Elliot R.
(See Westport)

Webber, Richard H., (AVⓉ) .... '39 '68 C.976 B.A. L.178 LL.B. [Hill R.&H.]
Weber, Rosemarie Talio .... '69 '99 C.659 B.A. L.1252 J.D. [Ⓐ Meehan,M.&G.]
Weihing, Thomas J., (BV) .... '43 '70 C.999 B.S. L.669 J.D. [Daly,W.&B.]
*PRACTICE AREAS: Arbitration Law; Transportation Law; Labor Law; Legislative Law; Trials and Appeals.
Weiner, Gerald T., (AV) .... '43 '68 C&L.184 B.A., J.D. [Weinstein,W.I.N.&S.]
*PRACTICE AREAS: Family Law; Divorce; Child Custody; Commercial Law; Bankruptcy.
Weinstein, Albert L. .... '29 '60 C.1029 B.S. L.184 LL.B. 4920 Main St.
Weinstein, Burton M., (AV) .... '29 '59 C.823 A.B. L.976 J.D. [Weinstein,W.I.N.&S.]
*PRACTICE AREAS: Litigation; Criminal Defense; Civil Rights; Labor Law; Medical Malpractice.

Weinstein, Weiner, Ignal, Napolitano & Shapiro, P.C., (AV) BB
350 Fairfield Avenue, P.O. Box 9177, 06601
Telephone: 203-333-1177 Cable Address: "Moot" Fax: 203-384-9832
URL: http://www.lawyers.com/wwin
Howard Evan Ignal; Gerald T. Weiner; Burton M. Weinstein; Roberta Napolitano; Richard J. Shapiro; Judith A. Mauzaka.
General Practice including Personal Injury, Negligence, Commercial, Reorganization, Bankruptcy, Foreclosures, Criminal, Civil Rights, Employee Rights and Benefits, Employment Discrimination, Family, Workers Compensation, Real Estate. Trial and Appellate Practice in all State and Federal Courts and Administrative Agencies.
See Professional Biographies, BRIDGEPORT, CONNECTICUT

Weisman, Michael J., (BV) .... '42 '69 C&L.184 B.A., J.D. [M.J.Weisman]
Weisman, Michael J., (BV) .... 1115 Main St.
Wenzel, William J., (BV) .... '51 '78 C.165 B.A. L.862 J.D. [Pullman&C.]
*PRACTICE AREAS: Litigation.
White, James P., Jr., (BV) .... '42 '67 C.1030 A.B. L.262 LL.B. [Pullman&C.]
*PRACTICE AREAS: Real Estate, Environmental and Land Use Law; Municipal Law; Business Enterprises.

Williams, Cooney & Sheehy
(See Trumbull)

Willinger, Ann Marie Kent, (BV) ... '54 '81 C.1030 B.A. L.1029 J.D. [Willinger,W.&B.]
*PRACTICE AREAS: Land Use Planning; Civil Litigation; Commercial Litigation.
Willinger, Charles J., Jr., (AV) ...... '49 '73 C.1030 A.B. L.472 J.D. [Willinger,W.&B.]
*PRACTICE AREAS: Land Use; Real Estate; Financing Transactions; Loan Restructures; Corporate Law.

Willinger, Willinger & Bucci, P.C., (AV)
855 Main Street, 06604
Telephone: 203-366-3939 Telecopier: 203-337-4588
Charles J. Willinger, Jr.; Thomas W. Bucci; Ann Marie Kent Willinger; Bradd S. Robbins; Mark D. Arons;—Toni Marie Gelineau; Heidi C. McGee; Thomas W. Bucci, Jr.; Nathalie Feola-Guerrieri.
General Practice. Real Estate, Corporate, Commercial, Foreclosure, Bankruptcy, Secured Financing, Zoning, Labor, Probate, Condemnation, Workers Compensation, Financial, Banking, Personal Injury and Criminal Law. Trials in all Courts.
See Professional Biographies, BRIDGEPORT, CONNECTICUT

Wisser, Ellen B., (CV) .... '30 '83 C.102 B.A. L.1029 J.D. 4920 Main St., Ste. 303
Wolf, Austin K., (AV) .... '23 '51 C.976 B.A. L.309 LL.B. [Cohen&W.]
*PRACTICE AREAS: Land Use; Real Estate.
Wolf, Martin F., (AV) .... '29 '55 C.184 A.B. L.309 LL.B. [Ⓒ Cohen&W.]
*PRACTICE AREAS: Real Estate; Corporate; Education.
Woltch, Saml. H., (BV) .... '12 '37 L.569 LL.B. 169 Woodside Ave.

Wood, Aimee J. .... '72 '97 C.902 B.A. L.184 J.D. [Ⓐ Pullman&C.]
*PRACTICE AREAS: Litigation.
Woodstock, Donna-Marie J. .... '67 '93 C&L.188 B.A., J.D. 915 Lafayette Blvd.
Woolen, Michael John, (CV) .... '59 '89 C.999 B.A. L.1029 J.D. 49 Cannon St.
Wu, James, (AV) .... '49 '75 C.855 B.A. L.184 J.D. [Ⓒ Koskoff,K.&B.]
*PRACTICE AREAS: Personal Injury; Family Law; Tax Appeals; Condemnations.

Yaffie, Burton S.
(See Trumbull)

Yahwak, Joshua A. .... '75 '00 C.264 B.A. L.902 J.D. [Ⓐ Bai,P.B.&M.]
*PRACTICE AREAS: Insurance Defense; Litigation; Real Estate.
Young, C. Christian .... '70 '98 C.114 B.A. L.1252 J.D. [Ⓐ J.R.Gulash,Jr.&E.J.R.]
*PRACTICE AREAS: Criminal Defense; Civil Litigation.

Yuditski, Thomas M., (AV) '46 '71 C.1030 B.S. L.724 J.D.
105 Brooklawn Place, 06604
Telephone: 203-335-5996 Fax: 203-336-5438
***PRACTICE AREAS: Personal Injury Law; Medical Malpractice; Workers Compensation; Automobile Accidents; Arbitration.**
Personal Injury, Automobile Accidents, Medical Malpractice, Workers Compensation, Arbitration.
See Professional Biographies, BRIDGEPORT, CONNECTICUT

Zabel, David B., (AV) '57 '82
C.103 A.B. L.893 J.D. [Cohen&W.] (⊙Stamford, Westport)
*PRACTICE AREAS: Employment; Civil Litigation; Bankruptcy.
Zackrison, Mary K., (BV) .... '58 '83 C.855 B.A. L.734 J.D. 105 Brooklawn Place
Zeisler, Richard D., (AV) .... '37 '63 C.659 A.B. L.184 LL.B. [Zeisler&Z.]
*PRACTICE AREAS: Bankruptcy; Commercial Law.
Zeisler, Robert M., (AV) .... '32 '57 C.184 B.A. L.94 LL.B. [Ⓒ Zeisler&Z.]
*PRACTICE AREAS: Civil Practice; Personal Injury; Arbitration.

Zeisler & Zeisler, P.C., (AV) BB
558 Clinton Avenue, P.O. Box 3186, 06605-0186
Telephone: 203-368-4234 Fax: 203-367-9678
Email: info@zeislaw.com URL: http://www.zeislaw.com
Richard D. Zeisler; James G. Verrillo; James Berman; Craig I. Lifland; Jed Horwitt; Matthew K. Beatman; Jeffrey Hellman; Coleen Hurlie-Dunn; Dennis P. Anderson;—Lawrence S. Grossman; Stephen M. Kindseth; Johnpatrick O'Brien; Gregory B. Schiller; Nicole L. Inman (Not admitted in CT); Jason M. Venditti. Of Counsel: Robert M. Zeisler.
General Civil Practice. Bankruptcy, Corporate Reorganization, Securities Investor Protection Act Litigation, Real Estate, Probate, Corporation, Family, Personal Injury, Negligence and Commercial Law. Trials.
See Professional Biographies, BRIDGEPORT, CONNECTICUT

Zeldes, Jacob D., (AV) .... '29 '57 C.966 B.S. L.976 LL.B. [Zeldes,N.&C.]
*PRACTICE AREAS: Civil and Criminal Litigation.

Zeldes, Needle & Cooper, A Professional Corporation, (AV) BB
1000 Lafayette Boulevard, P.O. Box 1740, 06601-1740
Telephone: 203-333-9441 Telecopiers: 203-333-1489; 579-2933
Email: znclaw.com URL: http://www.znclaw.com
Jacob D. Zeldes; Charles M. Needle; Robert S. Cooper; Alfred J. Jennings, Jr.; Stuart Bear; Frank J. Silvestri, Jr.; Robert A. Harris; Gregory J. Cava; David P. Atkins; Maximino Medina, Jr.; Jonathan B. Orleans; Shelley R. Sadin; Edward R. Scofield; David P. Friedman; Leslie Paier Aceto; Martin L. McCann; S. Dave Vatti; Douglas J. Varga; Marie A. Casper; Joseph C. Hutchison;—Marcy Tench Stovall; Sarah W. Poston; Matthew S. Hirsch; Anthony R. Minchella; Barbara G. Hager; Kevin C. Kelly; Robert M. Frost, Jr.; Robert A. Pacelli, Jr. Of Counsel: John R. Bryk; Sheryl J. Rosander.
Litigation in all Courts. Corporate, Probate, Real Estate, Bankruptcy, Family, Condemnation, Criminal, Administrative and Environmental Law.
Representative Clients: Jeneric/Pentron, Inc.; Pace Motor Lines, Inc.; C.W. Pond Contractors, Inc.
See Professional Biographies, BRIDGEPORT, CONNECTICUT

Zoppo, Joseph P. .... '63 '89 C.588 B.S.B.A. L.94 J.D. 1000 Lafayette Blvd.
Zowine, Louis C., (BV) .... '40 '66 C.1030 A.B. L.262 LL.B. 1087 Broad St.

BRIDGEWATER, 1,563, *Litchfield Co.*

Carvalko, Joseph R., Jr., (BV) '42 '80
C.1030 B.S.E.E. L.1252 J.D. 188 Iron Ore Hill Rd. (Pat.) (⊙Southbury)
Hoeniger, Berthold H., (AVⓉ) .... '28 '50 C&L.178 B.A., J.D. [B.H.Hoeniger] ⊙
Hoeniger, Berthold H., P.C., (AVⓉ) .... P.O. Box 460 (⊙New York, NY)
Horwitz, Philip H., (AVⓉ) '38 '63 C.659 S.B.Econ. L.309 LL.B.
(adm. in NY; not adm. in CT) 245 Christian St.
Schramm, Harold B. .... '43 '74 C.321 A.B. L.184 J.D. P.O. Box 155‡

BRISTOL, 60,640, *Hartford Co.*

Alden, Richard H., (AV) .... '36 '61 C&L.184 B.A., J.D. [Anderson,A.H.Z.&S.]
Allaire, Stephen O., (BV) .... '45 '75 C.870 B.S. L.276 J.D. [Ruggiero,Z.&A.]
*PRACTICE AREAS: Trusts and Estates; Elder Law; Probate.
Anderson, Sherwood L., III, (AV) '34 '58
C.976 A.B. L.178 J.D. [Ⓒ Anderson,A.H.Z.&S.] ‡
Anderson, Alden, Hayes, Ziogas & Storm, L.L.C., (AV) .... 106 North St.
Armata, Barry F., (BV) .... '59 '84 C.93 B.A. L.823 J.D. [Hammack&A.]
Baldwin, Ann T., (BV) .... '51 '76 C.518 A.B. L.184 J.D. Asst. Corp. Coun.
Barnes, Wallace ...... '26 '52 C.951 B.A. L.976 LL.B. Chmn. of the Bd., Barnes Grp. Inc.
Chadwick, Libbey & Stone, (BV) .... 131 Summer St. (⊙East Hartford)
Chang, Alan '67 '93 C.569 B.A. L.94 J.D.
(adm. in NY; not adm. in CT) Assist. Gen. Coun., ESPN
Chiasson, Roger E., II, (BV) .... '61 '87 C.1048 B.A. L.1218 J.D. 160 Farmington Ave.
Clark, Nancy M. '47 '92 C.36 B.S. L.659 J.D.
(adm. in NY; not adm. in CT) Sr. Corp. Coun. & Asst. Secy., Barnes Grp., Inc.
*RESPONSIBILITIES: Corporate; Mergers and Acquisitions; Financing.
Clift, Wyland Dale .... '53 '84 C.645 B.A. L.184 J.D. Asst. Corp. Coun.
Cohen, Robert F. .... '51 '77 C.94 B.A. L.982 J.D. 580 Broad St.
Conlin, Thomas W. .... '60 '93 C.751 B.A. L.1048 J.D. [Hamzy&C.]
*PRACTICE AREAS: Real Estate; Family Law; Bankruptcy; General Practice.
Constant, Gary D., (CV) .... '49 '75 C.156 A.B. L.184 J.D. 301 W. St.
Creed, Kevin E. .... '51 '97 C.1164 B.A. L.209 J.D. [Newman C.&Assoc.] ⊙
*PRACTICE AREAS: Personal Injury; Product Liability; Employment Law; Aviation Law.
Daly, Michael C., (BV) .... '57 '82 C.855 B.A. L.1048 J.D. [Furey,D.T.&D.]
*PRACTICE AREAS: Criminal Law; Negligence Law; Civil Litigation.
DeAngelo, Vincent M., (BV) .... '52 '77 C.025 B.A. L.276 J.D. 1001 Farmington Ave.
Donovan, James D., (BV) .... '55 '85 C.829 B.A. L.1048 J.D. [Furey,D.T.&D.]
*PRACTICE AREAS: Personal Injury; Criminal Law; Family Law.
Dorval, Andre D., (BV) .... '51 '76 C.1030 B.A. L.184 J.D. [Krawiecki&D.]
Durso, Edwin M. '— '78 C.309 B.A. L.273 J.D.
(adm. in DC; not adm. in CT) Exec. V.P., Admin., ESPN
Dutkiewicz, Edward P. .... '51 '89 C.273 B.S. L.1048 J.D. 200 Summer St.
Ferraro, Mark J., (BV) .... '60 '86 C.827 B.A. L.362 J.D. [Lewis,L.&F.] ⊙
Furey, Timothy W., (BV) .... '59 '84 C.321 B.A. L.818 J.D. [Furey,D.T.&D.]
*PRACTICE AREAS: Family Law; Land Use Law; Business Law; Elder Law; Bankruptcy.

Furey, Donovan, Tracy & Daly, P.C., (BV)
43 Bellevue Avenue, 06011
Telephone: 860-589-4343 Fax: 860-583-8674
William J. Tracy, Jr.; Michael C. Daly; Timothy W. Furey; F. Patrick O'Sullivan; James D. Donovan; Christopher M. Reeves.

(This Listing Continued)

Furey, Donovan, Tracy & Daly, P.C. (Continued)

General Practice. Probate, Corporation, Real Estate, Land Use, Criminal and Negligence Law. Trials in all Courts. Family Law.
Reference: Eagle Financial Corporation.

See Professional Biographies, BRISTOL, CONNECTICUT

Gaffen, Marilyn M. .... '45 '96 C.914 B.A. L.1048 J.D. Pub. Def. Off.
Gates, Signe S. '49 '81 C.820 B.A. L.477 J.D.
Sr. V.P., Gen. Coun. & Corp. Secy., Barnes Group Inc.
*RESPONSIBILITIES: Mergers and Acquisitions; Commercial Law; General Corporate.
Grabowski, Bernard F., (BV) .... '23 '53 C&L.184 B.S., J.D. [Hanrahan,G.&H.]
Hammack, Timothy L. .... '59 '84 C.628 B.S. L.823 J.D. [Hammack&A.]
Hammack & Armata, (BV) ....747 Stafford Ave.
Hamzy, William A. .... '66 '93 C.184 B.A. L.1170 J.D. [Hamzy&C.]
*PRACTICE AREAS: Bankruptcy; Real Estate; Small Business Corporations.

Hamzy & Conlin
140 Farmington Avenue, 06010
Telephone: 860-589-6525 Fax: 860-589-7370
Member of the Firm: William A. Hamzy; Thomas W. Conlin.
Bankruptcy, Real Estate, Small Business Incorporations, Family Law, General Practice.

See Professional Biographies, BRISTOL, CONNECTICUT

Hanrahan, Louis F., (BV) .... '18 '46 C.128 B.A. L.184 LL.B. [Hanrahan,G.&H.] ‡
Hanrahan, Grabowski & Hayes, P.C., (BV) ....683 Farmington Avenue
Hayes, James E., (BV) ....'35 '64 C.276 B.S.S. L.184 LL.B. [Hanrahan,G.&H.]
Hayes, Margaret M., (BV) ....'57 '82 C.860 B.A. L.184 J.D. [Anderson,A.H.Z.&S.]
Jazlowiecki, Edward A. .... '48 '74 C.688 B.S. L.94 J.D. 11 Lincoln Ave.

Johnson, James C., (BV) '53 '78 C.884 B.A. L.982 J.D.
10 Riverside Avenue, P.O. Box 256, 06011-0256
Telephone: 860-584-0551 Fax: 860-583-4453
Email: jcjohnsonesq@aol.com
***PRACTICE AREAS: Real Estate; Zoning; Wills; Trusts; Probate.**
Real Estate, Zoning, Wills, Trusts, Probate, Criminal Law, Driving While Intoxicated.

See Professional Biographies, BRISTOL, CONNECTICUT

Jurkiewicz, Thomas W., (BV) ....'54 '82 200 Summer St.
Kemmler, Eric L. ....'47 '73 C.976 B.A. L.145 J.D. V.P., Assoc. Gen. Coun., ESPN
Kilbourne, Dean B. ....'62 '88 C.699 B.A. L.94 J.D. 120 Laurel St.
Krawiecki, Edward C., (BV) ...... '19 '47 C.823 A.B. L.976 LL.B. City Asst. Corp. Coun.
Krawiecki, Edward C., Jr., (BV) ....'52 '80 C.1030 L.1202 State Rep. [Krawiecki&D.]
Krawiecki & Dorval, (BV) ....25 N. St.
Lacey, Richard E., (BV) ....'50 '76 C.184 B.A. L.564 J.D. 22 Pine Street, Suite 300
Lewis, Lewis & Ferraro, L.L.C., (BV) .... 5 Maple St. (⊙West Hartford)
Libbey, Morton H., Jr., (BV) .... '60 '85 C.321 B.A. L.818 J.D. [Chadwick,L.&S.] ⊙
Lodge, Timothy M. ....'73 '99 C.829 B.A. L.1252 J.D. [Ⓐ Krawiecki&D.]
Marko, Allen A. ....'55 '80 C&L.184 B.A., J.D. 25 North St.
Maynard, Robert R., (BV) ....'25 '55 C.918 B.A. L.893 J.D. 45 Brightwood Rd.‡
McGinley, R. Patrick, (BV) .... '34 '66 C.208 B.S.B.A. L.184 LL.B. Asst. State's Atty.
Morrocco, Alfred F., Jr. ....'47 '75 C.816 B.E. L.669 J.D. [A.F.Morrocco&Assoc.]
Morrocco, Alfred F., Jr. & Associates, Law Offices of .... 200 Summer St.
Morse, Diane M. '63 '90 C.763 B.S. L.228 J.D.
(adm. in CA; not adm. in CT) Assist. Gen. Coun., ESPN
Nawrocki, Mary-Lynn ....'65 '91 C.1139 B.A. L.945 J.D. 200 Summer St.
Newman, Bruce E. ....'64 '90 C.165 B.A. L.982 J.D. [Newman C.&Assoc.] ⊙
*PRACTICE AREAS: Personal Injury; Labor and Employment Law; Product Liability; Civil Litigation.

Newman Creed & Associates
99 North Street, Route 6, P.O. Box 575, 06010 ⊙
Telephone: 860-583-5200 Telecopier: 860-582-0012
Email: bnewman@newmancreedlaw.com URL: http://www.lawyers.com/newmancreed
Bruce E. Newman; Kevin E. Creed.
Civil Litigation, Personal Injury, Employment Law, Product Liability, Commercial Law, Medical Malpractice, Wrongful Death, Aviation Law.
Deep River, Connecticut Office: One High Street, 06417. Telephone: 860-526-8003.

See Professional Biographies, BRISTOL, CONNECTICUT

Noel, James B. '52 '79 C.629 B.S. L.16 J.D.
(adm. in AL; not adm. in CT) Asst. Gen. Coun., ESPN
Orcutt, Timothy J. '62 '87 C.746 B.B.A. L.966 J.D.
(adm. in WI; not adm. in CT) ESPN Inc.
O'Sullivan, F. Patrick, (BV) .... '48 '74 C.94 B.A. L.818 J.D. [Furey,D.T.&D.]
*PRACTICE AREAS: Personal Injury (Plaintiff and Defendant) Law.
Pahl, David R. .... '53 '80 C.72 B.A. L.477 J.D. Sr. V.P. & Gen. Coun., ESPN
Papa, John S., Jr., (BV) ....'37 '62 C.31 B.A. L.893 LL.B. Supvr. Asst. Pub. Def.
Petosa, Ronald, (BV) ....'59 '84 C.1030 B.S. L.1040 J.D. 735 Farmington Ave.
Pierce, Michael J. '55 '90 C.280 A.B.J. L.178 J.D.
(adm. in NY; not adm. in CT) Assist. Gen. Coun., ESPN
Preleski, David J. ....'56 '89 C.829 B.S. L.1048 J.D. Bristol Savings Bank
Preleski, Stephen G., (BV) '52 '78 C.128 B.A. L.796 J.D.
Supervisory Asst. State's Atty.
Reeves, Christopher M., (BV) .... '56 '82 C.855 B.A. L.184 J.D. [Furey,D.T.&D.]
*PRACTICE AREAS: Personal Injury; Business Litigation.

Ruggiero, Ziogas & Allaire, (BV)
271 Farmington Avenue, 06010
Telephone: 860-584-2384 Fax: 860-589-8213
URL: http://www.lawyers.com/rza
Members of Firm: James Ziogas, Jr.; Stephen O. Allaire.
General Practice. Probate, Real Estate, Corporate, Negligence, Criminal, Elder Law, Family Law and Litigation.
Reference: Connecticut Bank & Trust Co.

See Professional Biographies, BRISTOL, CONNECTICUT

Schnipper, Michael '47 '74 C&L.178 B.A., J.D.
(adm. in NY; not adm. in CT) Asst. Gen. Coun., ESPN
Schwartz, Irving ....'30 '57 C.976 B.A. L.569 LL.B. Clk., Supr. Ct.
Smith, Edward H., Jr., (BV) .... '52 '84 C.93 B.A. L.184 J.D. 40 High St.
Steeg, Howard R., (BV) .... '23 '52 C.569 B.S. L.262 LL.B. 124 Main St.
Storm, Christopher D., (BV) ....'58 '83 C.855 B.A. L.818 J.D. [Anderson,A.H.Z.&S.]
Storm, Matthew, (BV) ....'29 '56 C.659 B.S.E. L.569 LL.B. [Storm&S.]
Storm & Storm, P.C., (BV) ....242 Center St.
Tokay, Alan R. ....'49 '76 C.881 B.A. L.976 J.D. 137 Rhoda Lane
Tracy, James E., (BV) ....'36 '64 C.321 B.S. L.93 LL.B. 10 Riverside Ave.
Tracy, William J., Jr., (BV) ....'54 '79 C.478 A.B. L.1051 J.D. [Furey,D.T.&D.]
*PRACTICE AREAS: Appellate Law; Civil Litigation; Land Use Law; Estate Planning; Probate.
Verde, Michael A. ....'56 '92 C.1044 B.S. L.1048 J.D. [M.A.Verde]
Verde, Michael A., P.C. .... 761 Middle St.
Vitrano, Salvatore V., (BV) ....'49 '77 C.690 B.S. L.184 J.D. 135 West St.
Watstein, David Michael ....'65 '95 C.696 A.B. L.564 J.D. 155 Redstone Hill Rd., #10
Watstein, Herbert, (BV) ....'25 '50 C.184 B.A. L.976 J.D. [Watstein&W.] ⊙
Watstein, Julius, (CV) ....'34 '63 C.1029 B.A. L.184 J.D. [Watstein&W.] ⊙
Watstein & Watstein, P.C., (BV) .... 685 Middle St. (⊙Cheshire)
Wurz, Theodore J. ....'51 '80 C.1044 B.S. L.1029 J.D. 200 Summer St.
Wynne, Robert K., (BV) ....'56 '81 C.93 B.A. L.184 J.D. 135 West St.
Ziogas, James, Jr., (BV) ....'52 '77 C.349 B.S. L.1048 J.D. [Ruggiero,Z.&A.]
*PRACTICE AREAS: Zoning, Planning and Land Use; Real Estate; Family Law; Criminal Law; Personal Injury.
Ziogas, Mark, (BV) ....'57 '82 C.349 B.A. L.1048 J.D. [Anderson,A.H.Z.&S.]

BROAD BROOK, 1,548, *Hartford Co.*

Regina, Alfred E. '42 '77 C.1033 B.S.B.A. L.1048 J.D.
(adm. in MA; not adm. in CT) 12 Petticoat Ln.

BROOKFIELD, 12,872, *Fairfield Co.*

Bogie, Robert Reid ....'52 '78 C.94 B.A. L.1202 J.D. 33 Junction Rd.
Buscemi, Peter P., (CV) ....'42 '71 C.262 B.A. L.184 LL.B. 846 Federal Rd.
Eder, James A. '45 '77 C.415 B.S. L.1048 J.D.
Vice President, Secretary & General Counsel, Photronics Inc
Grossman, David S. .... '32 '62 C.178 B.S. L.1009 LL.B. 304 Federal Rd.
Kulawitz, Harvey J., LLC
(See Ridgefield)
Lindberg, Charles S. '29 '54 C&L.378 A.B., LL.B.
(adm. in KS; not adm. in CT) 44 Indian Trail
Martinez, Jose V. ....'46 '94 C.677 B.A. L.1088 J.D. 60 Old New Milford Rd.
McGonigle, Helen L., (BV) '61 '86 C.1030 B.S. L.425 J.D.
24 Meadowview, P.O. Box 540, 06804-0540
Telephone: 203-740-0074 Fax: 203-740-1171
Email: attymcg@aol.com URL: http://www.lawyers.com/hmcgoniglelaw
***PRACTICE AREAS: Litigation; Appellate Law; Insurance Law; Probate; Wills.**
Litigation, Victims Rights, Real Estate, Land Use, Appellate Law, Insurance Law, Personal Injury Law, Probate, Estate Planning, Wills and Equine Law.

See Professional Biographies, BROOKFIELD, CONNECTICUT

Moonan, Jeffrey P. '56 '82 C.1044 B.A. L.569 J.D.
General Counsel, Sr. Vice President & Secretary, Photronics, Inc.
Nohe, David L., (CV) .... '45 '76 C.390 A.B. L.94 J.D. Old State Rd.
Norton, Bruce .... '41 '67 C.860 B.A. L.564 LL.B. P.O. Box 5202
O'Connor, Denise, (BVⓉ) '61 '87 C.610 B.S. L.1040 J.D.
(adm. in NJ; not adm. in CT)
[O'Connor,R.G.&S.] (⊙Hackensack, NJ; White Plains, NY)
O'Connor, Steven M., (AVⓉ) '58 '86 C.597 B.A. L.1040 J.D.
[O'Connor,R.G.&S.] (⊙Stamford, CT; White Plains, NY)
O'Connor, Redd, Gollihue & Sklarin, LLP, (AVⓉ)
304 Federal Rd., Ste. 310 (⊙Stamford, CT; Hackensack, NJ; New York, White Plains, NY)
Ruvolo, Peter H., III, (CV) ....'57 '83 C.602 B.A. L.1029 J.D. 14 Hollis Dr.
Secola, Joseph P., (CV) ....'59 '84 C.1030 B.A. L.1288 J.D. [Secola]
Secola Law Offices, LLC, (CV) .... 67 Federal Rd., Bldg. A
Wamer, Gary L. ....'51 '78 C.381 B.S. L.851 J.D. Chief Patent Counsel, FBC (Pat.)

BROOKLYN, 5,691, *Windham Co.*

Egan, Thomas J., (BV) .... '49 '83 C.1033 B.A. L.1029 J.D. 13 Canterbury Rd.
Harris, Tamsen H., (BV) ....'39 '64 C.954 A.B. L.184 J.D. 51 Canterbury Rd.

BURLINGTON, 400, *Hartford Co.*

Pardo, Jeffrey J., (AVⓉ) '55 '79 C.228 B.A. L.472 J.D.
(adm. in FL; not adm. in CT) 10 N. Ridge

BYRAM, —, *Fairfield Co.*

Brodsky, Irving '— '28 C.569 L.732
(adm. in NY; not adm. in CT) 245 Byram Shore Rd.‡
Tamm, Rudra, (Mr.) ....'46 '73 C.585 B.A. L.184 J.D. 5 James St. W.

CANAAN, 1,002, *Litchfield Co.*

Capecelatro, Mark J., (BV) .... '48 '73 C.165 B.A. L.184 J.D. [Capecelatro&N.]
Capecelatro & Nelligan, (BV) .... 117 Main St.
Drury, Geoffrey ....'45 '70 C.31 A.B. L.976 LL.B. [Nania&D.]
Nania, Anthony J. ....'45 '81 C.31 B.A. L.184 J.D. [Nania&D.]
Nania & Drury .... 7 Church St.
Nelligan, Kevin F., (BV) ....'59 '84 C&L.184 B.A., J.D. [Capecelatro&N.]
Patz, Linda M. ....'62 '92 C.67 B.A. L.818 J.D. [Nania&D.]
Roche, Pamela Weidman, (BV) ...... '64 '89 C.882 B.A. L.1048 J.D. [Ⓐ Capecelatro&N.]
Roraback, Catherine G., (AV) ....'20 '48 C.518 B.A. L.976 LL.B. 115 Main St.‡

CANTERBURY, 3,426, *Windham Co.*

Anderson, Lloyd, (BV) ....'42 '77 C&L.184 B.A., J.D. 132 Westminster Rd.
Cooke, William .... '43 '74 C.184 B.A. L.818 J.D. Route 14‡

CANTON, 7,635, *Hartford Co.*

Bahre, Jared H. ....'46 '76 C.184 B.S. L.818 P.O. Box 547
Bochinski, Julianne Blair ....'66 '92 C.829 B.S. L.1048 J.D. 50 Albany Turnpike
Donald L. Mackie & Associates, Inc., (BV) ....141 Dowd Ave.
Duncan, Susan R. ....'44 '69 C.914 B.A. L.178 J.D. 67 Washburn Rd.
Eaglin, Patrick G. ....'43 '85 C.629 B.A. L.976 J.D. 150 E. Hill Rd.
Hampton, Walter R., Jr., (BV) ....'57 '84 C.1033 B.A. L.188 J.D. [Hampton]
*PRACTICE AREAS: Civil Litigation; Criminal Litigation; Appellate Practice; Corporate; Business.

Hampton Law Offices, LLC, (BV)
185 Albany Turnpike, P.O. Box 1008, 06019
Telephone: 860-693-8800 Fax: 860-693-8609
URL: http://www.lawyers.com/hamptonlaw
Walter R. Hampton, Jr.; Laura A. Klein.
Civil and Criminal Litigation, Appellate Practice, Personal Injury, Motor Vehicle, Corporate, Business, Commercial, Family, Real Estate, Probate and Estate.

See Professional Biographies, CANTON, CONNECTICUT

Hauser, Peter V. ....'56 '90 C.103 A.B. L.262 J.D. 130 E. Mountain Rd.
Kilburn, Ralph M., (BV) ....'21 '50 C.882 B.S. L.184 J.D. 21 Trailsend Dr.‡
Klein, Laura A. ....'70 '96 C.184 B.A. L.306 J.D. [Hampton]
*PRACTICE AREAS: Civil Litigation; Personal Injury; Sexual Abuse; Commercial Litigation; Appellate Practice.
Lovejoy, Maureen M. ....'53 '84 C.242 A.B. L.1048 J.D. 26 Center Street
Lowell, Mark E., (BV) ....'55 '81 C.823 B.A. L.1048 J.D. 171-173 Albany Tpke.
MacKie, Donald L., (BV) ....'48 '73 C.434 B.A. L.276 J.D. [D.L.Mackie&Assoc.]
McDonough, Helen L., (BV) ....'14 '46 C.562 B.A. L.976 LL.B. 98 Morgan Rd.
Myers, Helene Sfikas ....'57 '87 C.165 A.B. L.1048 J.D. 26 N. Mountain Rd.
Potanka, Paul E., (BV) ....'50 '75 C.31 B.A. L.831 J.D. P.O. Box 215
Sanger, Richard C., (BV) .... '30 '61 C.855 B.A. L.184 LL.B. P.O. Box 332

CANTON CENTER, —, *Hartford Co.*

Francis, Bernard E. .... '20 '51 C.67 A.B. L.94 LL.B. [Francis&F.]
Francis, Robert T., (CV) ....'49 '80 C.598 B.A. L.1029 J.D. [Francis&F.]

Francis & Francis, P.C., (CV) .... 512 Cherry Brook Rd. (⊙Stanford, KY)

CHESHIRE, 21,788, *New Haven Co.*

Adams, Allisan Lee, (BV) .... '63 '89 C.914 B.A. L.184 J.D. 411 W. Main St.
Armenia, Katy J. .... '68 '96 C.282 B.A. L.1252 J.D. [[A] Fazzone B.R.&S.L.]
*PRACTICE AREAS: Real Estate; Bankruptcy.
Baillie, Donald S., (BV) .... '49 '74 C.103 A.B. L.818 J.D. [Fazzone B.R.&S.L.]
*PRACTICE AREAS: Corporate; General Practice; Probate; Real Property; Trusts and Estates.
Begemann, Paul H. '62 '90 C.184 B.A. L.273 J.D.
Assoc. Gen. Coun., DeGeorge Financial Corp.
Branciforte, Amber .... '— '99 C.562 B.A. L.1252 J.D. [[A] Nuzzo&R.]
Burgdorff, Mary-Margaret Dalton, (BV) '59 '85 C.741 B.A. L.285 J.D.
[Dodd,L.R.&D.]
*PRACTICE AREAS: Personal Injury Law; Products Liability Law; Litigation; Workers Compensation Law.
Camerota, Michele C. .... '— '98 C.820 B.A. L.306 J.D. [[A] Nuzzo&R.]
Camilleri, Mary Ann .... '56 '86 C&L.184 B.S., J.D. 70 Philson Ct.
Cannata, Lisa M. .... '— '99 C.184 B.A. L.306 J.D. [[A] Nuzzo&R.]
Cappalli, Lisa J., (BV) '58 '84
C.401 B.A. L.188 J.D. 673 S. Main St. (⊙Cheshire, Hartford)

Cappalli, Lisa J., (BV) '58 '84 C.401 B.A. L.188 J.D.
673 South Main Street, 06410 ⊙
Telephone: 203-271-3888 Fax: 203-271-3850
Email: lcappalli@abanet.org URL: http://www.lawyers.com/cappalli
Matrimonial Law and Mediation.
Hartford, Connecticut Office: 43 Woodland Street. 06105-2336. Telephone: 860-251-6792.
See Professional Biographies, CHESHIRE, CONNECTICUT

Carlozzi, Jane M. .... '— '98 C.918 B.A. L.184 J.D. [[A] Nuzzo&R.]
Cavalier, Jennifer J. .... '— '99 C.1145 B.S. L.1252 J.D. [[A] Nuzzo&R.]
Chomiak, Robert J., Jr. .... '— '96 C.94 B.A. L.1202 J.D. [[A] Nuzzo&R.]
*PRACTICE AREAS: Civil Litigation.
Cipriano, Anthony P., Jr., (BV) .... '52 '79 C.150 B.A. L.1003 J.D. P.O. Box 1089
Cohen, Carla L. '51 '82 C.1275 B.A. L.569 J.D.
(adm. in NY; not adm. in CT) 551 Maple Ave.‡
Coleman, Andrew D., (BV) .... '49 '74 C.321 B.A. L.880 J.D. 1120 S. Main St.
Dabekis, Nicole C. .... '— '97 C.676 B.S. L.1252 J.D. [[A] Nuzzo&R.]
Daly, Kevin R. .... '57 '90 C.829 B.S. L.1048 J.D. V.P. and Gen. Coun., Bozzuto's, Inc.
Deganis, Sergio C., (BV) .... '55 '81 C.107 B.A. L.818 J.D. [Deganis&G.]
Deganis & Gallagher, LLC, (BV) .... 100 Hinman Street
DePaolo, Anthony R. .... '70 '95 C.390 A.B. L.93 J.D. [[A] Winters&F.]
Dice, Richard A., (AV) .... '26 '55 C.352 B.A. L.976 J.D. 20 Promontory Dr.
Dinnan, Maureen Sullivan, (BV) .... '59 '84 C.788 A.B. L.184 J.D. [[C] Hitt,S.&M.]
*PRACTICE AREAS: Medical Malpractice.
Dodd, Edward T., Jr., (AV) .... '44 '69 C.446 B.S. L.904 J.D. [Dodd,L.R.&D.]
*PRACTICE AREAS: Personal Injury Law; Workers Compensation Law.
Dodd, Jonathan H. .... '74 '00 C.880 B.S. L.273 J.D. [[A] Dodd,L.R.&D.]
*PRACTICE AREAS: Personal Injury; Workers Compensation.

Dodd, Lessack, Ranando & Dalton, L.L.C., (AV)
700 West Johnson Avenue, Suite 305, 06410
Telephone: 203-272-1883 Fax: 203-272-2077
Email: doddlrd@aol.com
Members of Firm: Edward T. Dodd, Jr.; Ross T. Lessack; Paul S. Ranando; Mary-Margaret Dalton Burgdorff; Charles F. Senich;—Jonathan H. Dodd.
Trials in all State and Federal Courts. Personal Injury, Products Liability, Social Security Disability, Workers Compensation and Negligence. Appellate Practice.
See Professional Biographies, CHESHIRE, CONNECTICUT

Dodge, Jonathan K., (AVⓉ) '49 '78 C.309 B.A. L.276 J.D.
(adm. in NY; not adm. in CT) V.P., Secy. & Gen. Coun., DeGeorge Fin. Corp.
Esty, Elizabeth Henderson '59 '85 C.309 A.B. L.976 J.D.
(adm. in MA; not adm. in CT) 213 Preston Ter.‡
Fazzone, Anthony J., (AV) .... '43 '68 C.276 B.A. L.184 J.D. [Fazzone B.R.&S.L.]
*PRACTICE AREAS: Real Property; Corporation Law; Zoning and Land Use; Probate; Trusts and Estates.

Fazzone Baillie Ryan & Seadale LLC, (AV)
One Town Center, P.O. Box 785, 06410
Telephone: 203-250-2222 Fax: 203-250-7388
Email: info@fazzonebaillielaw.com URL: http://www.fazzonebaillielaw.com
Anthony J. Fazzone; Donald S. Baillie; Joanne M. Ryan; Vincent G. Seadale;—David S. Veleber; Katy J. Armenia. Of Counsel: E. Ernest Oberst.
General Practice. Real Estate, Bankruptcy, Labor, Corporate, Commercial, Landlord-Tenant, Tax and Estate Planning, Probate, Zoning, Litigation.

Florian, Jan Pennito .... '57 '94 C.184 B.G.S. L.306 J.D. 1 Town Ctr.
Foley, Michael P., Jr., (BV) .... '54 '79 C.184 B.A. L.818 J.D. 1120 S. Main St.
Forte, Michael C., (BV) .... '53 '79 C.1102 B.S. L.1048 J.D. [Winters&F.]
Gallagher, Karen J. .... '63 '88 C.879 B.A. L.306 J.D. [Deganis&G.]
Garber, Angus G., Jr. '32 '58 C.951 A.B. L.309 LL.B.
(adm. in MA; not adm. in CT) 473 Buckland Dr.‡
Gerber, Karen T. .... '— '92 C.184 B.A. L.188 J.D. [Nuzzo&R.]
*PRACTICE AREAS: Insurance Defense; Appellate Practice.
Griffin, Maureen C. .... '54 '80 C.829 B.S. L.184 J.D. 600 Wood Pond Rd.
Hackett, Thomas P., (BV) .... '27 '53 C&L.976 B.A., J.D. 1030 S. Main St.
Hally, Paul F., (AV) .... '50 '76 C.321 B.A. L.276 J.D. Grp. Gen. Coun., SPX Corp.
Hardy, Karen S. .... '61 '87 C.690 B.A. L.1202 J.D. 399 Mt. Sanford Rd.
Hecht, Kevin J., (BV) .... '53 '85 C.829 B.S. L.184 J.D. [K.J.Hecht]
Hecht, Kevin J., P.C., Law Offices of, (BV) .... 220 S. Main St.
Hershman, Jay N. .... '76 '01 C.1145 B.A. L.1252 J.D. [[A] Hitt,S.&M.]
*PRACTICE AREAS: General Practice; Business Law; Civil Litigation; Real Estate; Trusts and Estates.
Hitt, Fred A., (AV) .... '31 '58 C.197 B.A. L.184 LL.B. [[C] Hitt,S.&M.]

Hitt, Sachner & Miele, (AV)
673 South Main Street, P.O. Box 724, 06410
Telephone: 203-272-0371 Fax: 203-272-9854
Email: admin@hittsachnermiele.com URL: http://www.hittsachnermiele.com
Members of Firm: Stephen P. Sachner; James M. Miele. Associates: Christine A. Robinson; Scott R. Parulski; Jay N. Hershman. Of Counsel: Fred A. Hitt; Maureen Sullivan Dinnan.
General Practice. Real Estate, Corporate, Business Acquisitions Law, Probate, Estate Planning, Personal Injury, Medical Malpractice, Family, Insurance and Zoning Law. Trials in all Courts.
Representative Clients: Connecticut Medical Insurance Co.; Lafayette American Bank & Trust; Liberty Mutual Insurance Co.; Middlesex Hospital; Ravenswood Development Corp.; Harte Nissan, Inc.; Dowling Ford, Inc.; Doug Calcagni Associates, Inc.; Diversified Builders, Inc.; Dalton Enterprises, Inc.
See Professional Biographies, CHESHIRE, CONNECTICUT

Holley, Jeffrey J., (BV) .... '63 '88 C.1030 B.A. L.184 J.D. [K.J.Hecht]
Jackson, Thomas M., (BV) .... '41 '66 C.93 A.B. L.276 J.D. [Jackson&R.]
Jackson and Reed, (BV) .... 163 S. Main St.
Jacques, Stephen L., (BV) .... '47 '83 C.1077 B.A. L.426 J.D. [Moore,O.J.&Y.]
*PRACTICE AREAS: Personal Injury; Medical Malpractice Law.
Janis, Christine A., (BV) .... '60 '87 C.546 B.A. L.1029 J.D. [K.J.Hecht]
Johnson, Robert J. .... '— '99 C.829 B.A. L.1252 J.D. [[A] Nuzzo&R.]

Knott, John K., Jr., (AV) '38 '64 C.152 B.A. L.94 J.D.
325 South Main Street, 06410
Telephone: 203-271-3031 Fax: 203-272-5388
Email: jknottjr@freewwweb.com
***PRACTICE AREAS: Municipal Law; Land Use Law; Administrative; Probate Law; Trusts and Estates.**
Associate: Priscilla C. Mulvaney.
General Civil Practice, Municipal and Administrative Law, Land Use Law, Probate and Estate, Real Estate, Selected Civil Trials and Appeals, Education and Special Education.
See Professional Biographies, CHESHIRE, CONNECTICUT

Leight, Peter '51 '78 C&L.309 B.A., J.D.
(adm. in NY; not adm. in CT) 755 S. Brooksvale Rd.‡
Lessack, Ross T., (BV) .... '55 '80 C.588 B.S. L.260 J.D. [Dodd,L.R.&D.]
*PRACTICE AREAS: Personal Injury Law; Appellate Law; Workers Compensation Law.
Lien, Katherine M. .... '35 '83 C.1102 B.S. L.184 J.D. 189 Shagbark Ct.
Lipsky, Jason M. .... '— '97 C.676 B.A. L.184 J.D. [[A] Nuzzo&R.]
Maloney, Robert E., Jr. '64 '89 C.611 B.A. L.896 J.D.
(adm. in MA; not adm. in CT) 29 Applewood Dr.‡
Meenan, James F. .... '27 '58 C&L.184 A.B., LL.B. 2 Quarry Vil.‡
Miele, James M., (BV) .... '64 '89 C&L.184 B.A.P.A., J.D. [Hitt,S.&M.]
*PRACTICE AREAS: General Practice; Business Law; Civil Litigation; Real Estate; Family Law.
Moore, Garrett M., (AV) .... '52 '81 C.184 B.S. L.276 J.D. [Moore,O.J.&Y.]
*PRACTICE AREAS: Medical Malpractice Law; Products Liability Law; Personal Injury.

Moore, O'Brien, Jacques & Yelenak, (AV) BB
700 West Johnson Avenue Suite 207, 06410
Telephone: 203-272-5881 Fax: 203-272-9273
Members of Firm: Garrett M. Moore; Gregory E. O'Brien; Stephen L. Jacques; William P. Yelenak.
Civil, Trial and Appellate Practice in State and Federal Courts. Negligence, Products Liability, Aviation and Medical Malpractice.
See Professional Biographies, CHESHIRE, CONNECTICUT

Morley, Michele H. .... '66 '91 C&L.184 B.A., J.D. 358 Talmadge Rd.
Morrison, Joseph W. '15 '41 C&L.262 B.A., LL.B.
(adm. in NY; not adm. in CT) 1681 Orchard Hill Rd.‡
Moser, Margaret Broderick .... '39 '77 C.331 B.A. L.184 J.D. P.O. Box 302
Mulvaney, Priscilla C., (BV) .... '58 '84 C.1044 B.A. L.567 J.D. [[A] J.K.Knott,Jr.]
*PRACTICE AREAS: Real Estate Law; Municipal and Administrative Law; Civil Trials and Appeals; Education Law; Special Education Law.
Murolo, Frederick L., (BV) .... '— '86 C.183 B.A. L.184 J.D. [Nuzzo&R.]
*PRACTICE AREAS: Insurance Coverage; Insurance Defense; Uninsured Motorist; Appellate Practice.
Nemeth, Deborah L., (BV) .... '54 '81 C.763 B.A. L.1188 J.D. 195 S. Main St.
Nuzzo, Anthony, Jr., (AV) .... '— '68 C&L.184 B.A., J.D. [Nuzzo&R.]
*PRACTICE AREAS: Legal Malpractice; Insurance Defense; Insurance Coverage; Insurance Bad Faith.

Nuzzo & Roberts, L.L.C., (AV) BB
One Town Center, P.O. Box 747, 06410
Telephone: 203-250-2000 Fax: 203-250-3131
Anthony Nuzzo, Jr.; Richard A. Roberts; Frederick L. Murolo; David J. Weil; Karen T. Gerber;—Jane E. Stoddard; Marc J. Ubaldi; Robert J. Chomiak, Jr.; Jason M. Lipsky; Nicole C. Dabekis; Michele C. Camerota; Olga E. Zargos; Jane M. Carlozzi; Jennifer J. Cavalier; Robert J. Johnson; Amber Branciforte; Lisa M. Cannata; Nadine Pare.
Civil Trial Practice in all State and Federal Courts, Insurance Law and Insurance Defense, Coverage and Bad Faith Litigation, Products Liability, Personal Injury, Professional Liability, Directors and Officers Liability, Legal Malpractice, Employment Litigation, School Liability, Appellate Practice and Workers Compensation.
See Professional Biographies, CHESHIRE, CONNECTICUT

Oberst, E. Ernest, (BV) .... '18 '48 C.67 A.B. L.976 J.D. [[C] Fazzone B.R.&S.L.]
O'Brien, Gregory E., (BV) .... '61 '87 C.676 B.A. L.1029 J.D. [Moore,O.J.&Y.]
*PRACTICE AREAS: Personal Injury; Products Liability.
Ottaviano, John, Jr. .... '17 '41 C.976 A.B. L.309 LL.B. 47 Lynwood Dr.‡
Ouellette, Steven A. .... '49 '90 C.1330 B.S. L.1048 J.D. 143 Main Street
Pare, Nadine .... '— '00 C.184 B.A. L.1252 J.D. [[A] Nuzzo&R.]
Parulski, Scott R. .... '— '99 C.1030 B.A. L.1252 J.D. [[A] Hitt,S.&M.]
*PRACTICE AREAS: General Practice; Civil Litigation; Real Estate; Business Law.
Ranando, Paul S., (CV) .... '56 '81 C&L.184 B.A., J.D. [Dodd,L.R.&D.]
*PRACTICE AREAS: Personal Injury Law; Products Liability Law; Real Property Law; Workers Compensation Law; Social Security Disability.
Reed, Philip C., (BV) .... '46 '75 C.1252 B.S. L.352 J.D. [Jackson&R.]
Rimer, Alec A. .... '65 '90 C.884 B.A. L.1029 J.D. 315 S. Main St.
Roberts, Richard A., (AV) .... '— '84 C.1044 B.A. L.107 J.D. [Nuzzo&R.]
*PRACTICE AREAS: Insurance Defense; Personal Injury; Employment Litigation; Commercial Litigation; Professional Liability.
Robinson, Christine A. .... '65 '97 C.569 B.A. L.1252 J.D. [[A] Hitt,S.&M.]
*PRACTICE AREAS: Medical Malpractice Defense; General Practice; Business Law.
Robitalle, Vincent C., (BV) .... '62 '88 C.745 B.A. L.1048 J.D. 420 Highland Ave.
Ruszczyk, Paul .... '54 '86 C.1044 B.A. L.188 J.D. 418 Highland Ave.
Ryan, Joanne M., (BV) .... '54 '82 C.1033 B.F.A. L.1029 J.D. [Fazzone B.R.&S.L.]
*PRACTICE AREAS: Probate; Trusts and Estates; Real Property Law; General Practice.
Sachner, Stephen P., (AV) .... '39 '64 C.674 A.B. L.569 LL.B. [Hitt,S.&M.]
*PRACTICE AREAS: Medical Malpractice; Personal Injury Law; General Defense Law.
Saundry, Susan L. .... '57 '85 C.911 B.A. L.678 J.D. P.O. Box 26
Savage, John J., Jr. '32 '57 C&L.93 B.S., J.D.
(adm. in MA; not adm. in CT) 38 Royalwood Ct.‡
Seadale, Vincent G., (BV) .... '60 '88 C.165 B.A. L.184 J.D. [Fazzone B.R.&S.L.]
*PRACTICE AREAS: Commercial Law; Corporate Law; Real Estate; Wills; Trusts.
Senich, Charles F., (BV) .... '61 '89 C&L.1029 B.S., J.D. [Dodd,L.R.&D.]
*PRACTICE AREAS: Personal Injury Law; Workers Compensation; Social Security Disability; ERISA.
Slocum, Shaun M., (BV) .... '51 '81 C.1030 B.A. L.1029 J.D. [S.M.Slocum]
Slocum, Shaun M., LLC, Law Offices of, (BV) .... 776 Bethany Mountain Road
Stoddard, Jane E. .... '— '94 C.95 B.A. L.184 J.D. [[A] Nuzzo&R.]
Turney, William C., (BV) .... '45 '83 C.1030 A.B. L.93 J.D. [W.C.Turney]
Turney, William C., Law Offices of, LLC, (BV) .... 677 S. Main St.
Ubaldi, Marc J. .... '— '96 C.1033 B.A. L.306 J.D. [[A] Nuzzo&R.]
Veleber, David S. .... '70 '96 C.401 B.A. L.184 J.D. [[A] Fazzone B.R.&S.L.]
*PRACTICE AREAS: Residential Real Estate; Bankruptcy.
Voelker, Raymond F., (AV) .... '45 '70 C.434 B.A. L.930 J.D. 100 Hinman Street
Ward, William J., (CV) .... '64 '91 C.1170 B.A. L.128 J.D. [Deganis&G.]
Watstein, Herbert, (BV) .... '25 '50 C.184 B.A. L.976 J.D. [Watstein&W.] ⊙
Watstein, Julius, (CV) .... '34 '63 C.1029 B.A. L.184 J.D. [Watstein&W.] ⊙
Watstein & Watstein, P.C., (BV) .... 114 S. Main St. (⊙Bristol)
Weil, David J., (BV) .... '— '88 C.264 B.A. L.273 J.D. [Nuzzo&R.]
*PRACTICE AREAS: Workers' Compensation.
Winters, David Wayne, (AV) .... '43 '69 C.164 A.B. L.93 J.D. [Winters&F.]
Winters & Forte, (AV) .... 315 Highland Avenue, Suite 102
Yelenak, William P., (AV) .... '53 '78 C.855 B.A. L.930 J.D. [Moore,O.J.&Y.]
*PRACTICE AREAS: Personal Injury.
Yerkes, David John .... '52 '78 C.855 B.A. L.184 J.D. 396 Mountain Rd.‡
Zargos, Olga E. .... '— '99 C.1030 B.A. L.124 J.D. [[A] Nuzzo&R.]
Zarkades, Karen L. .... '55 '89 C.1033 B.A. L.1202 J.D. 860 Maribou Ct.
Zullo, Laura Naclerio, (CV) .... '62 '88 C.706 B.A. L.818 J.D. 350 S. Main St.

CHESTER, 3,068, *Middlesex Co.*

Chorches, Samuel H., (BV) '42 '66 C&L.94 B.S.B.A., LL.B. P.O. Box 658
Delaney, Edmund T. '14 '36 C.674 A.B. L.309 J.D. P.O. Box 359‡
DiFazio, Lucien P., Jr. '43 '73 C.855 B.A. L.94 J.D. P.O. Box 418
Klomp, Robert P., (CV) '45 '73 C.867 B.A. L.184 J.D. 324 Goose Hill Rd.
Sweeney, Anna Shubik '52 '83 C.788 A.B. L.705 J.D. 20 Maple Street

CLINTON, 11,195, *Middlesex Co.*

Burnham, Ernest C., Jr., (BV) '27 '53 C.184 B.A. L.94 LL.B. 130 E. Main St.
Donahue, Dennis J., Jr., (BV) '35 '60 C&L.184 B.A., J.D. [Donahue,V.&D.] ⊙
Donahue, Votto & DeGennaro, P.C., (AV) 63 W. Main St. (⊙West Haven)

Hoyt, Jonathan, (BV) '48 '74 C.513 B.A. L.802 J.D.
10 Bluff Avenue, 06413-2255
Telephone: 860-669-0182 Fax: 860-669-7893
Email: hoytlaw@aol.com URL: http://www.lawyers.com/hoytlaw
***PRACTICE AREAS: Elder Law; Covenants Not To Compete; Restrictive Covenants; Lender Law; Loan Workouts.**
Real Estate both Residential and Commercial, Probate, Estate Planning, Business and Corporate Law, Commercial Transactions.

See Professional Biographies, CLINTON, CONNECTICUT

Johnson, Adrian L., (BV) '54 '82 C.30 B.S. L.831 J.D. 34 Long Hill Rd.
Labbadia, Pat, III '56 '80 C.1036 B.A. L.229 J.D. 63 W. Main St.
McDonough, Kevin C. '54 '81 C&L.767 B.A., J.D. 19 Commerce St.
Quinn, Raymond J., Jr., (AV) '21 '48 C.321 L.262 LL.B. 3 Hoop Rd.‡
Schubert, Arthur C., (BV) '28 '56 C.184 B.A. L.93 LL.B. 130 E. Main St.
Shulman, Irwin '27 '70 C.569 B.S. L.1009 LL.B. 17 Bargate Rd.
Sipples, Peter M., (BV) '42 '75 C.918 B.A. L.362 J.D. 11 Commerce St.
Strittmatter, Jacqueline B. '58 '86 C.783 B.A. L.1202 J.D. 26 Pleasant Valley Rd.
Votto, Louis Smith, (AV) '35 '61 C.262 B.S. L.184 J.D. [Donahue,V.&D.] ⊙

COLCHESTER, 3,212, *New London Co.*

Broder, Joseph A., (BV) '39 '63 C.855 A.B. L.309 J.D. [Broder&B.]
Broder & Butts, LLP, (BV) 188 Norwich Ave.
Butts, John W., (BV) '52 '77 C.945 A.B. L.884 J.D. [Broder&B.]
Goldstein, Ronald A. '67 '92 C.1036 A.B. L.309 J.D. 151 Broadway
Gregory, Robert F. '29 '59 C&L.184 B.A., LL.B. 79 Norwich Ave.
Kaback, Gilbert P., (CV) '63 '91 C.1033 B.A. L.1194 J.D. [G.P.Kaback]
Kaback, Gilbert P., P.C., Law Offices of, (CV) 100 Linwood Ave.
Kanabis & Houle, P.C., (BV) 15 Norwich Avenue (⊙New London)
Kennedy, Kevin, (CV) '59 '86 C.999 B.A. L.1048 J.D. 163 Bway.
Mende, Susan L. V. '51 '79 C.478 B.A. L.184 J.D. 39 Jaffe Ter.
Miller, James E. '66 '91 C.188 B.S. L.659 J.D. 108 Norwich Ave.
Preisner, Peter J., (BV) '32 '62 C.188 B.A. L.976 LL.B. [■ Broder&B.]
St. Clair, James E. '30 '66 C&L.184 B.S., LL.B. 79 Norwich Ave.
Schober, George C., (CV) '59 '94 C.475 B.A. L.184 J.D. [G.C.Schober]
Schober, George C., P.C., (CV) 48 Main St.
Scott, David R. '64 '89 C.732 B.A. L.831 J.D.
(adm. in PA; not adm. in CT) 53A Hayward Ave.
Scott, Melvin, (BV) '27 '57 C.184 B.S. L.383 LL.B. [Kanabis&H.] (⊙New London)
Stawicki, Jean M., (CV) '51 '81 C.184 B.S. L.1029 J.D. [Stawicki&S.]
Stawicki, John L., (BV) '44 '80 C.184 B.A. L.1029 J.D. [Stawicki&S.]
Stawicki and Stawicki, (BV) 100 Amston Rd.

COLEBROOK, 1,020, *Litchfield Co.*

Cords, Manuel, (AV) '48 '74 C.178 A.B. L.309 J.D.
(adm. in NY; not adm. in CT) Mng. Dir., Secy. & Treas., The Thetford Mgmt. Co.
White, Thomas C., (AV) '35 '62 C&L.309 B.A., LL.B. Eight Shantry Rd.‡

COLLINSVILLE, 2,897, *Hartford Co.*

Becker, Thomas S., (BV) '59 '90 C.156 B.A. L.1029 J.D. 101 River Rd.
Boyko, Gregory A. '51 '79 C.184 B.S. L.306 J.D. 100 Bartourtown Rd.
Casale, Douglas A. '69 '96 C.94 B.A. L.1252 J.D. [[A] Heffernan&H.]
Fullwood, Stanley G. '36 '66 C.385 A.B. L.146 J.D. 37 West Rd.‡

Hampton, Maria L., (BV) '60 '86 C.788 B.A. L.1048 J.D.
33 Maple Avenue, 06019
Telephone: 860-693-1100 Fax: 860-693-1100
Email: attymariahampton@snet.net
***PRACTICE AREAS: Real Estate; Collections; Business Law; Employment Law; Litigation.**
Real Estate, Collections, Business Law, Employment Law, Litigation.

See Professional Biographies, COLLINSVILLE, CONNECTICUT

Heffernan & Heffernan, (BV) 101 River Road
Hourihan, Joseph A., (BV) '44 '69 C.855 B.A. L.184 J.D. 101 River Rd.
Janssen, Lizanne M. '59 '85 C.754 B.S. L.884 J.D. 147 Robin Dr.
Keating-McKeon, Joan B. '54 '91 C.563 B.A. L.184 J.D. [[A] Heffernan&H.]
Roche, Vincent E., (BV) '45 '80 C.276 B.A. L.1029 J.D. [Heffernan&H.]
Sherlock, Ronald P., (BV) '51 '80 C.184 B.A. L.1048 J.D. [Heffernan&H.]
Shettle, Gregory R., (BV) '65 '90 C.184 B.S. L.692 J.D. 101 River Rd.

COLUMBIA, 3,386, *Tolland Co.*

Cianci, Donald P., (BV) '46 '74 C&L.184 B.A., LL.B. P.O. Box 210
Hutchins, Elizabeth Dennis '14 '39 C&L.184 B.A., LL.B. P.O. Box 145‡
Mrosek, Elaine W. '26 '49 C&L.184 LL.B. 16 Erdoni Rd.
Prignano, Pascal A., (BV) '38 '65 C&L.724 B.A., LL.B. 56 Erdoni Rd. (⊙Manchester)

COS COB, —, *Fairfield Co.*

Abate, Alfred M. '51 '77 C.262 B.A. L.724 J.D. 18 Patricia Lane
Carlson, Curtis W. '26 '54 C&L.966 B.S., J.D.
(adm. in WI; not adm. in CT; Pat.) 277 Cognewaugh Rd.‡
Caruso, Frank L., (BV) '36 '64 C&L.94 B.S.B.A., LL.B. 450 E. Putnam Ave.
Caruso, Mary M. '45 '91 C.739 B.A. L.1040 J.D. 533 E. Putnam Ave.
Charles, Marianne J. '65 '90 C.1046 B.A. L.1019 J.D. P.O. Box 213
Connor, Haldan E., Jr., (CV) '49 '82 C.415 B.A. L.1029 J.D. 8 Sinoway Rd.
Driscoll, Lois R. '31 '62 C.102 B.A. L.564 LL.B.
(adm. in NY; not adm. in CT) Indian Mill Rd.
Fisk, George W. '19 '48 C.165 A.B. L.178 LL.B.
(adm. in NY; not adm. in CT) 500 River Rd.‡
Gruendel, Clare M. '54 '84 C.569 B.A. L.262 J.D.
(adm. in NY; not adm. in CT) 28 Licata Ter.‡
Kaplan, Lori B. '67 '92 C.867 B.A. L.1019 J.D. Protective Alarms, Inc.
Long, Leslie Rankin '36 '72 C.367 B.S. L.818 J.D. 44 E. Putnam Ave.
Newton, John F. '34 '64 C&L.262 B.S., LL.B. 399 Post Rd.
Strong, Thomas J. '45 '75 C&L.724 B.A., J.D. P.O. Box 213
Trotta, Frank P., Jr., (AV) '55 '79 C.1044 B.A. L.982 J.D. [Trotta] ⊙
Trotta Law Firm, (AV) 4 Shelter Dr. (⊙Greenwich, CT; New Rochelle, NY)
Wilson, Mary Patricia '36 '92 C.1211 B.S. L.1187 J.D. 20 Meadow Dr

COVENTRY, 8,895, *Tolland Co.*

Kobetitsch, John Frederick '52 '93 C.415 B.S. L.1048 J.D. 149 Cornwall Dr.‡
Lavine, Stuart A. '49 '83 C.012 B.A. L.1048 J.D. Conn. Gen. Life Ins. Co.
Meacham, Michael R. '53 '83 C.942 B.A. L.378 J.D.
(adm. in KS; not adm. in CT) 764 Goose Lane
Rappe, David C., (BV) '39 '64 C.349 B.S. L.184 LL.B. 2181 Boston Tpke.

CROMWELL, 10,265, *Middlesex Co.*

Barber, Stephen M., (CV) '53 '80 C.184 B.A. L.1194 J.D. 332 Main St.
Becker, Andrew E., (BV) '46 '74 C.67 B.A. L.276 J.D. 162 West St.
Caron, Denis R., (AV) '46 '74
C.708 A.B. L.184 J.D. Connecticut Coun., Lawyers Title Ins. Corp.
*RESPONSIBILITIES: Real Estate Title Insurance; Like-Kind Deferred, Reverse and Build-to-Suit Exchanges; Escrow Law.
Cholewa, Matthew J., (BV) '63 '92 C.184 B.S. L.893 J.D.
Coun., Lawyers Title Ins. Co.
*RESPONSIBILITIES: Real Estate Title Insurance; Like Kind Exchanges; Escrow Law.
Donen, Steven R. '57 '91 C.184 B.A. L.306 J.D. Pres., S. D. Associates
Donovan, John R., (AV) '53 '79 C.893 B.A. L.184 J.D. [Donovan&M.] ⊙
*PRACTICE AREAS: Criminal Defense; Driving While Intoxicated; Homicide; Sex Crimes; Drugs and Narcotics.

Donovan & Morello, LLP, (AV)
Cromwell West Office Park, 154 West Street, 06416 ⊙
Telephone: 860-635-7373 Fax: 860-635-6734 Email: jrd@donmorlaw.com
Email: pam@donmorlaw.com URL: http://www.donmorlaw.con
Members of Firm: John R. Donovan; Paul A. Morello, Jr.
General Civil and Criminal Practice before State and Federal Courts. Personal Injury, Product Liability, Workers Compensation Law, Trials, Arbitration, Mediation, Uninsured and Underinsured Motorists, Medical Malpractice.
Reference: Citizens Bank.
Meriden, Connecticut Office: 816 Broad Street. Telephone: 203-635-7373.

See Professional Biographies, CROMWELL, CONNECTICUT

Frazer, Robert H. '46 '71 C.97 B.S. L.184 J.D. 25 Iron Gate Ln.
Hagel, Harry, (BV) '25 '53 C.184 B.S. L.228 J.D. 62 Evergreen Rd.
Herbst, John C., III '46 '83 C.28 B.A. L.1048 J.D. 10 Winthrop Blvd.
Lawler, George V. '31 '71 C&L.184 B.A., J.D. 75 Berlin Rd.
Love, Thomas J., Jr., (AV) '57 '84 C.659 B.S.Econ. L.184 J.D. 5 Upper Heatherwood
Morello, Paul A., Jr., (BV) '54 '79 C.321 B.A. L.982 J.D. [Donovan&M.] ⊙
*PRACTICE AREAS: Personal Injury Law; Medical Malpractice; Bicycle Accidents; Head and Spinal Injury; Uninsured and Underinsured Motorists.
Nguyen, Cat-Tuong T. '69 '96 C.1036 B.A. L.306 J.D. 119 Skyview Dr.

DANBURY, 65,585, *Fairfield Co.*

Abrams, Belle-Ann '52 '84 C.289 B.A. L.569 J.D.
(adm. in NY; not adm. in CT) Opers. Coun., Vendor Fin. Servs., GE Capital Corp.
Adams, Daniel L. '66 '98 C.94 B.S. L.1252 J.D. [[A] A.Barry&Assoc.]

Adelman Hirsch & Newman, LLP
(See Bridgeport)

Allen, Helen L., (BV) '54 '78 C&L.260 B.S., J.D. 36 Mill Plain Rd., Ste. 102
Andersen, Dianne M., (AV) '33 '57 C.1029 B.A. L.94 LL.B. [Andersen&F.]
Andersen & Ferlazzo, P.C., (AV) 72 North St.
Arconti, Richard D., (BV) '52 '77 C.602 B.A. L.184 J.D. [Pinney,P.V.B.W.&D.]
*PRACTICE AREAS: Civil Litigation; Personal Injury Law; Criminal Law.
Backer, Ted D., (BV) '52 '78 C&L.273 B.A., J.D. [Pinney,P.V.B.W.&D.]
*PRACTICE AREAS: Administrative Law; Real Estate Law; Environmental Law.
Badanes, Peter L. '44 '69 C.611 B.A. L.276 J.D.
(adm. in NY; not adm. in CT) Sr. Coun., Praxair, Inc.
Baker, Fred L., (BV) '43 '69 C&L.184 B.A., J.D. [Baker] ⊙
*PRACTICE AREAS: Taxation; Estate Planning; Probate; Corporate Law; Business Law.
Baker, Wayne A., (BV) '36 '64 C.165 A.B. L.188 LL.B. 7 Short Lane

Baker Law Firm, P.C., (BV)
24 Delay Street, 06810 ⊙
Telephone: 203-792-8765 Fax: 203-791-1892
Email: Fred@Baker-Law.com URL: http://www.lawyers.com/bakerlawfirm
Fred L. Baker; Hillel Goldman.
Taxation, Estate Planning, Probate, Business and Corporate, Real Estate.
New Milford Office: Baker Fields, 4 Mine Hill Road. Telephone: 860-354-9100.

See Professional Biographies, DANBURY, CONNECTICUT

Ball, David P., (BV) '49 '74 C.321 A.B. L.818 J.D. 36 Mill Plain Rd.
Ballard, David P. '50 '76 C&L.309 A.B., J.D. Columbia House
Balmer, Norman L. '46 '71 C.645 B.S. L.273 J.D.
(adm. in VA; not adm. in CT; Pat.) Chf. Pat. Coun., Union Carbide Corp.
Banks, Pamela A. '64 '92 C.1031 B.S. L.1040 J.D.
Legal Coun., Corp. Real Estate Div., Ethan Allen Inc.
Barry, Alan, & Associates '51 '76 C.184 B.A. L.1048 J.D. 64 North Street
Bassett, Robert A. '46 '91 C.870 B.S. L.1029 J.D. Asst. Corp. Secy., Praxair, Inc.
Bay, Walter D. '63 '92 C.970 B.A. L.276 J.D.
Oper. Coun., General Electric Capital Corp.
Beecher, Thomas W., (BV) '58 '83 C.165 B.A. L.818 J.D. [Collins,H.G.J.&T.]
*PRACTICE AREAS: Civil Litigation; Criminal Litigation; Land Use Law; Appellate Practice.
Belkin, Harvey '47 '72 C.102 B.A. L.1009 J.D. Asst. Gen. Coun., Praxair, Inc.

Bennett, David F., Law Offices of '52 '77 C.860 B.A. L.273 J.D.
72 North Street, Suite 103, 06810
Telephone: 203-797-9888 Telecopier: 203-743-4672
Email: BULLDOG799@AOL.COM URL: http://www.lawyers.com/dfblaw
***PRACTICE AREAS: Civil Litigation; Personal Injury; Wrongful Death; Commercial; Real Estate.**
Civil Litigation, Personal Injury, Wrongful Death, Commercial, Real Estate, Trusts and Estates Law. Aviation.
Representative Clients available upon request.
Reference: Fleet Bank, Danbury.

See Professional Biographies, DANBURY, CONNECTICUT

Biederman, Blake T. '62 '88 C.474 B.S. L.1035 J.D.
(adm. in MI; not adm. in CT) Sr. Pat. Coun., Praxair, Inc.
Bochino, Harold A., (BV) '38 '64 C.321 A.B. L.276 J.D. 57 North St.
Bollo, Paul L., (BV) '37 '68 C.321 A.B. L.724 LL.B. 57 North St. (Pat.)
Booth-Barton, Elisabeth '46 '93 C.183 B.A. L.678 J.D. 36 Mill Plain Rd.
Borger, John E. '52 '82 C.216 B.A. L.262 J.D.
Sr. V.P. & Gen. Coun, Cendant Mobility Servs. Corp.
Borofsky, Marvin, (BV) '48 '73 C.30 B.A. L.818 J.D. [Jones,D.K.B.&D.]
*PRACTICE AREAS: Family Law; Civil Litigation; Real Estate.
Brauneisen, Gregg A. '68 '97 C.790 B.S. L.692 J.D. [[A] Collins,H.G.J.&T.]
*PRACTICE AREAS: Estate Planning; Real Estate; Corporate Law.
Bresch, Saul R. '28 '56 C.659 A.B. L.569 LL.B.
(adm. in NY; not adm. in CT; Pat.) Sr. Pat. Coun., Union Carbide Corp.
Brown, Robert C. '28 '59 C.685 B.A. L.800 J.D. 31 Tanglewood Dr. (Pat.)
Brunetti, Robert C., (BV) '51 '80 C.745 B.A. L.1029 J.D. Sr. Asst. States Atty.

Burke, David P., (AV) .... '53 '78 C.473 B.A. L.273 J.D. [Cramer&A.]
*PRACTICE AREAS: Commercial Litigation; Civil Law; Personal Injury Law; Family Law.
Burrell, Hugh A., (AV) ....'39 '64 C&L.893 B.S., LL.B. [Pinney,P.V.B.W.&D.]
*PRACTICE AREAS: Real Estate Law; Estate Law; Probate Law; Banking Law.
Butler, Robert A. '37 '64 C.674 A.B. L.477 J.D.
Chief Litigation Counsel, Union Carbide Corp.
Buzaid, Norman A. .... '23 '50 C&L.262 B.S., LL.B. Chf. Family Support Mag.
Buzzi, Andrew J., Jr. .... '64 '89 C.1030 B.A. L.94 J.D. 64 Lake Ave.
Carter, Willard R. .... '33 '58 C.1029 B.A. L.564 LL.B. 6 Crosby St.
Casagrande, Daniel E., (BV) .....'54 '80 C.1030 B.A. L.262 J.D. [Pinney,P.V.B.W.&D.]
*PRACTICE AREAS: Civil Litigation; Commercial Litigation; Municipal Law; Land Use Law.
Casden, Mary H., (CV) .... '46 '86 C.339 B.S. L.184 J.D. 158 Deer Hill Ave.
Castillo, Martha ....'49 '81 C.262 B.S. L.966 J.D. Bus. Grp., Praxair, Inc.‡
Chaifetz, David '42 '68 C.156 B.S.B.A. L.93 LL.B.
(adm. in MI; not adm. in CT) Vice President, General Counsel & Secretary, Praxair, Inc.
Chan, Jackie, (BV) ....'48 '74 C.165 B.A. L.724 J.D. [Pinney,P.V.B.W.&D.]
*PRACTICE AREAS: Criminal and Civil Litigation; Personal Injury; Commercial Law.
Chipman, David R., (AV) ....'33 '59 C.118 B.A. L.228 LL.B. [Chipman,M.L.&P.]
*PRACTICE AREAS: Business Law; Corporate Law; Taxation; Trusts and Estates; Mergers and Acquisitions.

Chipman, Mazzucco, Land & Pennarola, LLC, (AV)
30 Main Street, Suite 204, 06810-3043
Telephone: 203-744-1929 FAX: 203-790-5954
URL: http://www.danburylaw.com
David R. Chipman; Richard S. Land; Ward J. Mazzucco; Francis G. Pennarola;—Elizabeth Lachterman; Ryan J. Morley.
Business Law, Litigation, Real Estate, Trusts and Estates, Taxation, Zoning Law, Computer Law.
See Professional Biographies, DANBURY, CONNECTICUT

Cistulli, Joseph P. ....'65 '89 C&L.93 B.A., J.D. Oper. Coun., Vendor Fin. Servs.

Cohen and Wolf, P.C., (AV)
158 Deer Hill Avenue, 06810 ⊙
Telephone: 203-792-2771 Facsimile: 203-791-8149
Email: c&w@cohenandwolf.com URL: http://www.cohenandwolf.com
Neil R. Marcus; David L. Grogins; Robin A. Kahn; Joseph G. Walsh; Monte E. Frank;—Marnie J. Rubin.
General Practice. Business Transactions, Commercial Litigation, Employment and Labor, Family and Matrimonial, Land Use, Municipal, Personal Injury, Physicians Practice, Real Estate, Securities, Tax, Trusts and Estates. Litigation in all Courts.
Bridgeport, Connecticut Office: 1115 Broad Street. Telephone: 203-368-0211. Facsimile: 203-394-9901.
Stamford, Connecticut Office: 112 Prospect Street. Telephone: 203-964-9907. Facsimile: 203-576-8504.
Westport, Connecticut Office: 190 Main Street. Telephone: 203-222-1034.
See Professional Biographies, DANBURY, CONNECTICUT

Collins, Francis J., (AV) .... '33 '62 C.473 B.S. L.184 LL.B. [Collins,H.G.J.&T.]
*PRACTICE AREAS: Real Estate Law; Land Use Law; Commercial Law; Administrative Law; Worker's Compensation.

Collins, Hannafin, Garamella, Jaber & Tuozzolo, Professional Corporation, (AV)
148 Deer Hill Avenue, P.O. Box 440, 06810 ⊙
Telephone: 203-744-2150 Telecopier: 203-791-1126
URL: http://www.chgjtlaw.com
Francis J. Collins; Edward J. Hannafin; Jack D. Garamella; Paul N. Jaber; Robert M. Opotzner; E. O'Malley Smith; Thomas W. Beecher; Eva M. DeFranco; Christopher K. Leonard;—Laura A. Goldstein; Gregg A. Brauneisen; Gail H. Matthews. Of Counsel: John J. Tuozzolo.
General Practice. Real Estate, Estate Planning, Probate, Zoning and Land Use, Tax, Corporation, Commercial, Banking, Family Law, Criminal Law, Negligence, and Civil Trials in all Courts.
Ridgefield, Connecticut Office: 24 Bailey Avenue, 06877. Telephone: 203-438-7403. Fax: 203-438-7425.
See Professional Biographies, DANBURY, CONNECTICUT

Corleto, Anthony B. .... '59 '89 C.999 B.B.A. L.1040 J.D. [Corleto&Assoc.]
*PRACTICE AREAS: Insurance Defense; Insurance Bad Faith; Insurance Coverage; Environmental Law; Corporate Litigation.

Corleto & Associates, P.C.
107 Mill Plain Road, Suite 200, 06811
Telephone: 203-790-7540 Fax: 203-790-7536
URL: http://www.corletofirm.com
Anthony B. Corleto;—Lori A. Eaton; Dharman P. Niles; Hugh J. Donnelly. Of Counsel: Kenneth L. Robinson (Not admitted in CT).
Insurance Defense, Coverage Dispute and Bad Faith Litigation, Environmental Law, Municipal Liability, Corporate Litigation, Corporate Governance, Intellectual Property, Employment Practices Liability.
See Professional Biographies, DANBURY, CONNECTICUT

Coté, Andrew C., P.C.
(See Sharon)

Cotter, Brian E. .... '46 '71 C.276 A.B. L.94 J.D. 82 Deer Hill Ave.‡
Courtney, Michael K., (BV) ....'51 '83 C&L.262 B.A., J.D. Asst. Pub. Def.
Coury, Elie S., (BV) ....'32 '60 C.1030 B.S.S. L.818 LL.B. 182 White St.
Cowin, Jeffrey A. '50 '76 C.602 B.A. L.734 J.D.
(adm. in MO; not adm. in CT) General Electric Capital Corp.

Cramer & Anderson LLP, (AV)
68 North Street, 06810 ⊙
Telephone: 203-790-7747 Fax: 203-790-9538
Email: danbury@crameranderson.com URL: http://www.cramer-anderson.com
Joseph A. Saffi; David P. Burke.
General Practice. Probate, Estate Planning, Municipal, Family and Real Estate. Trials. Planning and Zoning, Corporate, Banking, Securities.
Litchfield, Connecticut Office: 46 West Street. P.O. Box 278. Telephone: 860-567-8718. Email: litchfield@cramer-anderson.com
Kent, Connecticut Office: Kent Green, P.O. Box 333. Telephone: 860-927-3568. Email: gnelson@cramer-anderson.com
New Milford, Connecticut Office: 51 Main Street. Telephone: 860-355-2631. Email: newmilford@crameranderson.com
Washington Depot, Connecticut Office: 2 Green Hill Road, P.O. Box, 321. Telephone: 860-868-0527. Email: wfairbairn@cramer-anderson.com
See Professional Biographies, DANBURY, CONNECTICUT

Crawford, Robert L. '43 '68 C.976 A.B. L.178 LL.B.
Group Counsel, Union Carbide Corp.
Crisorio, Lory A., (Mr.), (CV) ....'30 '76 C.46 B.S. L.776 J.D. 57 North St.
Crossen, Kevin J. '51 '88 C.971 B.S. L.64 J.D.
(adm. in MD; not adm. in CT) Amer. Cyanamid Co.
Crowell, Donald R., II, (AV) '47 '74 C.573 B.S. L.262 J.D.
Labor Coun., Chem. & Plastics Law Dept., Union Carbide Corp.
Currier, Allen A., (CV) ....'38 '84 C.1019 B.B.A. L.564 J.D. 7 National Pl.
Daly, Gerald J., (BV) .... '40 '72 C.184 B.S. L.262 J.D. [Gemza&D.]
Damia, A. Peter, (AV) .... '33 '58 C.184 B.A. L.309 LL.B. [Jones,D.K.B.&D.]
*PRACTICE AREAS: Real Estate Law; Probate Law; Banking Law.
DaSilva, Joseph, Jr. .... '70 '99 C.1103 B.A. L.1252 J.D. [A Pinney,P.V.B.W.&D.]
*PRACTICE AREAS: General Litigation.

Day, John ... '51 '77 C.597 B.A. L.188 J.D. Chief Human Resources Counsel, Praxair, Inc.
DeFranco, Eva M., (BV) ....'61 '86 C.1102 B.S. L.184 J.D. [Collins,H.G.J.&T.]
*PRACTICE AREAS: Civil Litigation; Family Law; Collections; Personal Injury Law.
DeLuca, Paul P., (BV) .... '46 '73 C.188 B.S. L.184 J.D. 52 Main St.
DePaul, Guy L., (BV) ....'58 '84 C.1021 B.A. L.1029 J.D. [Jones,D.K.B.&D.]
*PRACTICE AREAS: Workers Compensation; Personal Injury.
Dillman, John M., (BV) .... '39 '65 C.401 B.S. L.184 LL.B. [Pinney,P.V.B.W.&D.]
*PRACTICE AREAS: Estate Planning and Settlement; Trust Law.
Dimyan, Joseph, (BV) ....'53 '79 C.1030 B.A. L.262 J.D. [Pinney,P.V.B.W.&D.]
*PRACTICE AREAS: Personal Injury Law; Criminal and Civil Litigation.
DiPerrio, Anthony J., II, (BV) .... '52 '77 C.1103 B.A. L.818 J.D. 57 North St.
Donnelly, Hugh J. ....'57 '84 C.724 B.S. L.1325 J.D. [A Corleto&Assoc.]
*PRACTICE AREAS: Litigation.
Donohue, Christopher T., (BV) ....'57 '82 C&L.184 B.A., J.D. [Riefberg,S.D.&N.]

Dornfeld, Sharon Wicks, (BV) '52 '82 C&L.477 B.A., J.D.
70 North Street, Suite 104, 06810
Telephone: 203-748-3363 Fax: 203-748-3104
Civil Trial Practice, Child Advocacy, Guardianship, Adoptions, Conservatorships, Real Estate, Municipal Law, Appellate Practice.

Driscoll, Talarico, Frizzell, Olivo & Driscoll, (AV)
142 Deer Hill Avenue, 06810-7727 ⊙
Telephone: 203-792-8333 Facsimile: 203-778-9570
Email: attystfo@snet.net
Julius J. Bielizna (1914-1988); Herbert B. Wanderer (1902-1979); Robert N. Talarico; Thomas A. Frizzell; Steven M. Olivo; Thomas A. Frizzell, Jr.; Richard W. Hanna; George S. Papazoglou.
General Practice in all Courts. Trials, Real Estate, Probate, Corporation and Foreclosure Law, Commercial Litigation.
See Professional Biographies, DANBURY, CONNECTICUT

Dudnick, Carol Lee '46 '73 C.696 B.A. L.569 J.D.
Envir. Coun., Chem. & Plastics Law Dept., Union Carbide Corp.
Durkin, Joseph J. .... '49 '76 C.1103 B.A. L.818 J.D. 100 Wooster Heights Rd.
Duvall, Mark N. '52 '78 C.31 B.A. L.893 J.D.
Coun., Health & Safety, Chem. & Plastics, Union Carbide Corp.
Eaton, Lori A. .... '64 '97 C.1103 B.A. L.1252 J.D. [A Corleto&Assoc.]
*PRACTICE AREAS: Insurance Defense; Municipal Liability; Environmental Law; Employment Practices Liability.
Eberhard, Robert V., (BV) .... '51 '76 C.1030 B.A. L.128 J.D. 24 Shelter Rock Road
Ellis, Christine M., (BV) .... '50 '80 C.475 B.A. L.823 J.D. [Ellis&T.]
Ellis & Trattner, P.C., (BV) ....27 Mill Plain Road
Erickson, John R. '59 '91 C.105 B.S. L.705 J.D.
(adm. in NJ; not adm. in CT) Envir. Coun., Union Carbide Corp.
Erwin, Clyde V., Jr. '27 '53 C.578 B.A. L.273 J.D.
(adm. in DC; not adm. in CT) 39 Old Ridgebury Rd.‡
Exner, Cynthia R., (BV) ....'51 '80 C.859 B.A. L.1040 J.D. 270 Main Street
Ferlazzo, Jean S., (BV) ....'43 '77 C.860 B.A. L.823 J.D. [Andersen&F.]
Ferrara, John J. ....'42 '69 C.724 B.B.A. L.564 J.D. Sr. Grp. Coun., Praxair, Inc.
Field, Robert F., (BV) ....'48 '72 C.994 B.A. L.184 J.D. Pub. Def.
Fiscella, Robert A. ....'50 '76 C.1030 B.S. L.893 J.D. Tax Coun., Union Carbide Corp.
Fitzgerald, Bruce D. '39 '69 C.569 A.B. L.309 LL.B.
(adm. in NY; not adm. in CT) V.P., General Counsel & Secretary, Union Carbide Corp.
Flanagan, Barbara E., (BV) .... '51 '76 C.855 B.A. L.184 J.D. [Flanagan&P.]
Flanagan, Walter D., (BV) ....'38 '63 C.93 B.S. L.184 LL.B. Asst. State's Atty.
Flanagan & Peat, (BV) ....57 North St.
Florio, Roger '57 '86 C.205 B.S. L.128 J.D.
(adm. in SC; not adm. in CT)
Envir. Coun., Chem. & Plastics Law Dept., Union Carbide Corp.

Fogarty Cohen Selby & Nemiroff LLC
(See Greenwich)

Follett, Robert J. '66 '96 C.95 B.A. L.273 J.D.
(adm. in MA; not adm. in CT) Sr. Coun., Intell. Prop. & E-Commerce, Praxair, Inc.
Fox, Karen, (CV) .... '48 '84 C.725 B.A. L.1040 J.D. 75 West Street
Frank, Monte E. ....'68 '93 C&L.188 B.A., J.D. [Cohen&W.]
*PRACTICE AREAS: Commercial Litigation; Employment.
Friar, Martha J., (AV) ....'52 '78 C.93 A.B. L.184 J.D. Sr. Lit. Coun., Praxair, Inc.
Fritschler, Alvin H. '29 '61 C.688 B.S.Ch.E. L.982 LL.B.
(adm. in NY; not adm. in CT; Pat.) 39 Old Ridgebury Rd.‡
Frizzell, Thomas A., (BV) '40 '68
C&L.724 B.B.A., LL.B. [Driscoll,T.F.O.&D.] (⊙Bethel)
*PRACTICE AREAS: Real Estate Law; Estates; Wills; Probate; Commercial Law.
Frizzell, Thomas A., Jr. ....'69 '97 C.1103 B.S. L.724 J.D. [Driscoll,T.F.O.&D.]
*PRACTICE AREAS: Personal Injury Litigation; Wrongful Death Litigation; Products Liability; Aviation Law; International Aviation Law.
Fusaro, Robert F. X. .... '41 '67 C.321 B.S. L.276 J.D. Director, Praxair, Inc.

Gallagher, Stephen C., (BV) '42 '67 C.1030 B.A. L.569 J.D.
57 North Street Suite 114, 06810
Telephone: 203-792-0525 Fax: 203-792-8182
Email: scgatt@msn.com URL: http://www.lawyers.com/gallagher&gallagher
***PRACTICE AREAS: Municipal Law; Zoning Law; Workers Compensation; Criminal Law; Personal Injury.**
General Practice, Real Estate, Municipal, Zoning, Condominium, Probate, Personal Injury, Negligence, Criminal and Family Law, Trials in all Courts.
Approved Attorneys for: First American Title Insurance Co.; Lawyers Title Insurance Co.; Chicago Title Insurance Co.; Connecticut Attorneys Title Insurance Co.;
References: Connecticut Bank & Trust Co.; Union Trust Co.
See Professional Biographies, DANBURY, CONNECTICUT

Garamella, Jack D., (AV) ....'45 '69 C.197 A.B. L.597 J.D. [Collins,H.G.J.&T.]
*PRACTICE AREAS: Civil Litigation; Personal Injury Law; Health Care Law.
Gaudiosi, Monica Marie '62 '88 C&L.659 B.A., J.D.
(adm. in GA; not adm. in CT) Gen. Coun., Vendor Fin. Servs.
Geen, Patricia A. ....'29 '52 C.19 L.831 LL.B. Supr. Ct. J.
Gemza, Theodore A., (AV) .... '26 '50 C&L.273 A.A., LL.B. [⊡ Gemza&D.]
Gemza & Daly, (BV) .... 30 Main St., Suite 502
Geoghan, Joseph E. '37 '64 C.724 B.B.A. L.262 J.D.
(adm. in NY; not adm. in CT) 39 Old Ridgebury Rd.‡
George, Ronald J., (BV) .... '35 '66 C.184 B.A. L.1009 LL.B. 57 North St.

Gill Law Practice
(See Ridgefield)

Glynn, Liam Davis, (CV) '64 '90 C.354 B.S. L.1029 J.D.
74 West Street, 06810
Telephone: 203-744-5434 Fax: 203-744-1446
Email: liamglynn@gte.net
Real Estate, Personal Injury, Criminal, Commercial Collections.
See Professional Biographies, DANBURY, CONNECTICUT

Godfrey, Robert D. .... '48 '85 C.262 B.A. L.306 J.D. 13 Stillman Ave.
Goldberg, Judith M. .... '— '86 C.1373 B.S. L.1040 J.D. 100 Mill Plain Road

Goldman, Hillel, (BV) ....'59 '89 C.881 A.B. L.1325 J.D. [Baker]
*PRACTICE AREAS: Business Organizations; Corporate Law; Business Law; Commercial Transactions; Finance.
Goldstein, Irving J. .... '54 '79 C.390 B.A. L.818 J.D. V.P., Berkshire Bdcstg. Co.
Goldstein, Laura A. ....'69 '94 C.860 B.A. L.184 J.D. [Ⓐ Collins,H.G.J.&T.]
*PRACTICE AREAS: Civil Litigation.
Gottschalk, Eric L., (BV) ....'51 '76 C&L.94 A.B., J.D. Asst. Corp. Coun.
Grauel, Melissa A., (CV) ....'57 '82 C.184 B.A. L.1048 J.D. [Ⓐ Andersen&F.]
Gregory, James P. .... '34 '62 C.103 A.B. L.273 J.D. Danbury Health Systems, Inc.
Grispin, Wendy A. .... '66 '93 C.1103 B.B.A. L.1040 J.D. [Pinney,P.V.B.W.&D.]
*PRACTICE AREAS: Criminal and Civil Litigation; Personal Injury; Domestic Relations Law.
Grogins, David L., (BV) ....'45 '71 C.867 A.B. L.94 J.D. [Cohen&W.]
*PRACTICE AREAS: Corporate; Commercial Real Estate; Planning and Zoning; Municipal.
Grover, Deborah L., (BV) ....'54 '79 C.1103 B.A. L.1048 J.D. 42 Main Street
Hagan, William J., (BV) ....'57 '83 C.855 B.A. L.1019 J.D. 26 Mill Plain Road

Hall & Savarese, P.C.
(See Newtown)

Hampilos, Gus Theodore '53 '81 C.688 B.S.M.Eng. L.128 J.D.
(adm. in VA; not adm. in CT; Pat.) Mng. Pat. Coun., Union Carbide Corp.
Hanna, Richard W., (AV) .... '30 '53 C&L.184 B.A., LL.B. [Driscoll,T.F.O.&D.]
*PRACTICE AREAS: Banking Law; Estate Planning; Land Use Law; Landlord and Tenant Law; Probate Law.
Hannafin, Edward J., (BV) ....'36 '65 C.103 A.B. L.184 J.D. [Collins,H.G.J.&T.]
*PRACTICE AREAS: Commercial Law; Corporate Law; Real Estate Law.
Hecht, Gerald ....'52 '78 C.94 B.S. L.1048 J.D. 30 Main St.
Heneghan, Laura A. '69 '95 C.1349 B.A. L.1040 J.D.
Contract Counsel, Cendant Mobility Services Corporation
Hibbard, Crystelle M., (CV) .... '52 '85 C.788 A.B. L.184 J.D. 72 North St.
Holmes, William B., Jr. .... '47 '74 C.1266 B.A. L.421 J.D. 13 Farview Ave.
Holzbach, David M., (BV) ....'59 '85 C.885 B.A. L.1029 J.D. Asst. States Atty.
Hunt, Peter C., (BV) .... '50 '76 C.494 A.B. L.184 J.D. 85 North St.
Hutchinson, Vicki H. ....'50 '82 C.112 B.A. L.1029 J.D. 270 Main St.
Jaber, Paul N., (BV) .... '42 '68 C.524 B.S. L.184 LL.B. [Collins,H.G.J.&T.]
*PRACTICE AREAS: Real Estate Law; Land Use Law; Commercial Law.
Jackson, Lynne D. .... '59 '89 C&L.184 B.A., J.D. [Ⓐ Andersen&F.]
Jackson, Robert A. .... '60 '86 C.184 B.A. L.345 J.D. Asst. Clk., Supr. Ct.
Jessep, John D., (AV) .... '44 '72 C&L.879 B.A., J.D. [Koskoff,K.&B.]
*PRACTICE AREAS: Personal Injury.
Jones, William R., (AV) ....'20 '48 C.732 B.S. L.184 LL.B. [Ⓒ Jones,D.K.B.&D.]
*PRACTICE AREAS: Workers Compensation; Personal Injury.

Jones, Damia, Kaufman, Borofsky & DePaul, LLC, (AV)
301 Main Street, 3rd Floor, P.O. Box 157, 06813-0157
Telephone: 203-744-1313 Fax: 203-797-8403
Email: info@danburyattorneys.com URL: http://www.danburyattorneys.com
Members of Firm: A. Peter Damia; Sanford D. Kaufman; Marvin Borofsky; Guy L. DePaul; Michael R. Kaufman. Of Counsel: William R. Jones; Charles F. Stelljes.
General Civil and Criminal Practice Including Trials in all Courts, Personal Injury, Workers' Compensation, Family Law/Divorce, Employment and Discrimination Law, Corporate, Wills and Probate, Zoning, Real Estate, Banking and Finance, Foreclosures and Collections.
Representative Clients: People's Bank; Albany Savings Bank; Sears Mtg. Corp.; Fairfield Processing Co.; Berkshire Broadcasting Co., Inc.; Fleet Bank; New Milford Bank & Trust Co.
See Professional Biographies, DANBURY, CONNECTICUT

Jowdy, James J., Jr., (BV) ....'51 '76 C.896 B.S. L.93 J.D. [Jowdy&J.]
Jowdy, Jeffrey J. ....'68 '94 C.896 B.A. L.1040 J.D. [Jowdy&J.]
Jowdy, John, (BV) ....'53 '79 C.93 B.S. L.1202 J.D. [Jowdy&J.]
Jowdy & Jowdy, (BV) .... 67 West St.
Kabak, Edward M. '44 '70 C&L.178 A.B., J.D.
(adm. in NY; not adm. in CT) V.P., Gen. Coun. & Secy., Grolier, Inc.
Kahn, Robin A., (BV) ....'55 '80 C.855 B.A. L.184 J.D. [Cohen&W.]
*PRACTICE AREAS: Real Estate; Planning and Zoning; Condominium Association Representation.
Kastriner, Lawrence G. '30 '63 C.178 B.A. L.273 J.D.
Chf. Pat. Coun., Praxair, Inc. (Pat.)
Kaufman, Michael R., (BV) .... '63 '88 C.390 A.B. L.564 J.D. [Jones,D.K.B.&D.]
*PRACTICE AREAS: Civil Litigation; Personal Injury; Employment Law; Banking Law; Commercial Law.
Kaufman, Sanford D., (BV) '33 '59
C.994 B.A. L.564 LL.B. [Jones,D.K.B.&D.] (⊙Brewster, NY)
*PRACTICE AREAS: Corporate Law; Banking Law; Negligence Law; Employment Law.
Khazarian, Roxanne '55 '80
C.976 B.A. L.659 J.D. V.P., Gen. Coun. & Secy., Ethan Allen Inc.
*RESPONSIBILITIES: Corporate Law.
Kilcullen, Richard J., (BV) .... '53 '80 C.423 B.A. L.64 J.D. 57 North St.
Kim, Jean Young ....'73 '01 C.976 B.A. L.1019 J.D. [Ⓐ Pinney,P.V.B.W.&D.]
*PRACTICE AREAS: Civil Litigation; Commercial Litigation; Land Use; Toxic Torts; Administrative Law.
Klein, Amy L. A., (CV) ....'63 '88 C.787 B.A. L.184 J.D. Fed. Rd.
Klein, Gregory P., (CV) ....'62 '87 C.1036 B.A. L.94 J.D. [Ⓐ A.Barry&Assoc.]
Klein, Ira Paul '45 '71 C.994 B.A. L.94 J.D.
(adm. in NY; not adm. in CT) Sr. Tax Coun., Union Carbide Corp.
Korotash, Mark W., (BV) .... '48 '73 C.197 A.B. L.945 J.D. [Mulvey&K.]
*PRACTICE AREAS: Real Estate; Probate; Wills; Estate Planning; Civil Litigation.
Kortlandt, Catherine E. M. ....'63 '89 C.976 B.A. L.178 J.D. Sr. Coun., Praxair, Inc.

Koskoff, Koskoff & Bieder, P.C., (AV)
1 Moss Avenue, 06810 ⊙
Telephone: 203-792-7100
URL: http://www.koskoff.com
John D. Jessep (Resident).
Litigation in all State and Federal Courts. Medical Malpractice, Equal Opportunity, Negligence, Products Liability, Civil Rights, Criminal Law and Class Actions.
Bridgeport, Connecticut Office: 350 Fairfield Avenue. Telephone: 203-336-4421.
Stamford, Connecticut Office: 1172 Bedford Street. Telephone: 203-325-3686.
See Professional Biographies, DANBURY, CONNECTICUT

Ktorides, Stanley '49 '78 C.454 B.S.Ch.E. L.1048 J.D.
Sr. Pat. Coun., Praxair, Inc. (Pat.)
Lachterman, Elizabeth, (BV) ....'59 '85 C.860 B.S. L.273 J.D. [Ⓐ Chipman,M.L.&P.]
*PRACTICE AREAS: Litigation; Real Estate; Business Law.
La Forge, Thomas J. '45 '71 C.893 B.A. L.145 J.D.
(adm. in NY; not adm. in CT)
Group Coun., Chem. & Plastics Law Dept., Union Carbide Corp.

Lamontagne, James Mark '65 '92 C.1103 B.S. L.1040 J.D.
68 Main Street, 06810
Telephone: 203-778-1422
***PRACTICE AREAS: Real Estate; Criminal Law; Civil Law.**
General Practice.
See Professional Biographies, DANBURY, CONNECTICUT

Land, Richard S. .... '48 '75 C.197 B.A. L.245 J.D. [Chipman,M.L.&P.]
*PRACTICE AREAS: Estate Planning; Estate Administration; Elder Law; Taxation; Nonprofit and Charitable Organizations.
Lane, D. Joseph, Jr., (BV) .... '22 '49 C&L.602 B.S., LL.B. 142 Deer Hill Avenue
Lau, Bernard '63 '91 C.951 B.A. L.602 J.D.
(adm. in PA; not adm. in CT; Pat.) Sr. Pat. Coun., Praxair, Inc.
Leaphart, Jerry V. .... '46 '72 C.912 B.A. L.569 J.D. [J.V.Leaphart&Assoc.] ⊙
Leaphart, Jerry V., & Associates, P.C. ....155 Main Street, Suite 201 (⊙Red Bank, NJ)
Leheny, Sandra Vilardi .... '38 '79 C.19 B.A. L.184 J.D. Supr. Ct. J.
Leonard, Christopher K., (BV) ... '63 '89 C.690 B.S. L.1202 J.D. [Collins,H.G.J.&T.] ⊙
*PRACTICE AREAS: Civil Litigation; Real Estate Law; Land Use Law; Probate; Bankruptcy Law.
Levitan, Jonathan M. ....'70 '96 C.205 B.A. L.1202 J.D. [Matz&L.]
Lombardi, Bonnell M. '36 '64
C.674 B.A. L.976 LL.B. Assoc. Gen. Coun., First Brands Corp.
Maier, Raymond G. '53 '78 C.165 A.B. L.339 J.D.
Group Counsel, Union Carbide Corp.
Mancino, Peter B. '43 '68 C&L.724 B.A., J.D.
V.P., Gen. Coun. & Secy., UCAR Intl. Inc.
Manetti, Mary G. '32 '70 C.242 A.B. L.309 J.D.
(adm. in NY; not adm. in CT) 39 Old Ridgebury Rd.‡
Marcus, Neil R., (BV) ....'47 '73 C.659 B.A. L.569 J.D. [Cohen&W.]
*PRACTICE AREAS: Planning and Zoning; Commercial Real Estate; Corporate.
Markosky, Edward J., Jr., (CV) .... '41 '66 C&L.184 B.A., J.D. [Spiro&M.]
Matthews, Gail H. .... '58 '84 C.665 B.A. L.1187 J.D. [Ⓐ Collins,H.G.J.&T.]
*PRACTICE AREAS: Estate and Trusts.
Matz, Jay B., (CV) ....'59 '87 C.102 B.A. L.1029 J.D. [Matz&L.]
Matz & Levitan, LLC, (CV) .... 100 Mill Plain Rd.
Mazzucco, Ward J., (BV) .... '53 '78 C.103 A.B. L.188 J.D. [Chipman,M.L.&P.]
*PRACTICE AREAS: Litigation; Business Law; Zoning, Planning and Land Use; Health Law; Construction Law.
McCarthy, Audrey Hilda ... '68 '95 C.518 B.A. L.306 J.D. Assoc. Tax Coun., Praxair, Inc.
McClure, William F., Jr. ....'46 '74 C.848 B.A. L.659 J.D. Asst. Gen. Coun., Praxair, Inc.
McGetrick, Michael S., (CV) ....'60 '90 C.588 L.1029 153 White St.

McGonigle, Helen L.
(See Brookfield)

McGovern, Philip F. '45 '72 C.1041 B.A. L.602 J.D.
(adm. in NJ; not adm. in CT) V.P., Union Carbide Corp.
McMahon, Paul J., (P.C.) '47 '72 C.821 B.A. L.659 J.D.
(adm. in PA; not adm. in CT) 51 Sugar Hollow Rd.‡
McNamara, William J., Jr., (BV) .... '41 '66 C.676 A.B. L.184 J.D. 57 North St.
Meehan, Michael A. '47 '73 C.728 A.B. L.276 J.D.
(adm. in PA; not adm. in CT) Coun., Coml. Equip. Fin., GE Capital Corp.
Mevs, Peggy ....'57 '84 C.156 B.A. L.276 J.D. 44 Old Ridgebury Rd.
Michael, Gary R. ....'50 '77 C.201 B.A. L.1194 J.D. 70 West St.‡
Mihalakos, Socrates H. ....'33 '62 C.103 A.B. L.184 LL.B. Supr. Ct. J.
Miller, Josephine S. '53 '80 C.811 B.A. L.245 J.D.
(adm. in MI; not adm. in CT) Sr. Human Resources & Litig. Coun., Praxair, Inc.
Mitchell, Donald A., (BV) .... '44 '71 C.884 B.S. L.208 J.D. 10 Harmony St.

Mix, Lawrence J., (CV) '57 '81 C.188 B.S. L.94 J.D.
57 North Street, Suite 214, 06810-5660
Telephone: 203-744-0220
***PRACTICE AREAS: Business Law; Real Estate; Litigation; Labor and Employment; Alternative Dispute Resolution.**
Business Law, Real Estate, Litigation, Labor and Employment, Alternative Dispute Resolution, General Practice.
See Professional Biographies, DANBURY, CONNECTICUT

Moore, Stephen M. .... '59 '84 C&L.276 A.B., J.D. Oper. Coun., Vendor Fin. Servs.

Moots, Pellegrini, Mannion, Martindale & Dratch, P.C.
(See New Milford)

Moraghan, Howard J. ....'30 '57 C.321 B.S. L.93 J.D. Supr. Ct. J.
Morley, Ryan J. .... '76 '01 C.473 B.A. L.1252 J.D. [Ⓐ Chipman,M.L.&P.]
*PRACTICE AREAS: Litigation; Business Law; Land Use.
Morris, Julia B. ....'69 '94 C.401 B.A. L.93 J.D. [O'Connell,F.&A.] (⊙Hartford)
Morrison, Robert I. '60 '88 C.084 B.A. L.019
(adm. in ON; not adm. in CT) Sr. Coun., Praxair, Inc.
Moy, Henry H., (BV) .... '51 '77 C.165 A.B. L.1009 J.D. 57 North St.
Mullaney, Charles P. '42 '68
C.676 B.A. L.818 LL.B. Prof. of Law, Western Conn. State Univ.
Mulvey, James Ryan, (BV) .... '47 '72 C.197 A.B. L.262 J.D. [Mulvey&K.]
*PRACTICE AREAS: Civil and Criminal Litigation; Domestic Relations; Divorce; Real Estate.

Mulvey & Korotash, (BV)
The West Street Building, 31 West Street, P.O. Box 751, 06813
Telephone: 203-792-5900 Telecopier: 203-798-2057
Members of Firm: James Ryan Mulvey; Mark W. Korotash.
General Civil and Criminal Trial Practice. Real Estate, Probate, Corporate, Negligence, Workers Compensation, Commercial and Family Law.
Approved Attorneys for: Chicago Title Insurance Co.; Connecticut Attorneys Title Insurance Co.; First American Title Insurance Co.
See Professional Biographies, DANBURY, CONNECTICUT

Murphy and Karpie, LLC
(See Bridgeport)

NeJame, Karin A., (BV) ....'55 '81 C.1103 B.A. L.1048 J.D. [Riefberg,S.D.&N.]
Niles, Dharman P. ....'69 '95 C.1256 B.A. L.30 J.D. [Ⓐ Corleto&Assoc.]
*PRACTICE AREAS: Corporate Law; Intellectual Property; Contracts; Insurance Defense.
Nolan, Kim E., (BV) ....'49 '77 C.598 B.A. L.1194 J.D. [Pinney,P.V.B.W.&D.]
*PRACTICE AREAS: Personal Injury; Civil Litigation; Real Estate Law; Commercial Law; Landlord/Tenant Law.
O'Brien, Cornelius F. ......'36 '67 C.563 B.E.E. L.564 J.D. 39 Old Ridgebury Rd. (Pat.)‡
O'Connell, Flaherty & Attmore, L.L.C., (AV)
50 Newtown Rd (⊙Hartford, Moosup, Old Saybrook, West Hartford, CT; Springfield, MA)
Olivo, Steven M., (BV) .....'48 '75 C.197 A.B. L.94 J.D. [Driscoll,T.F.O.&D.] (⊙Bethel)
*PRACTICE AREAS: Civil Practice; Personal Injury Law; Negligence Law; Landlord and Tenant Law.
Opotzner, Robert M., (BV) ....'53 '78 C.976 B.A. L.228 J.D. [Collins,H.G.J.&T.] ⊙
*PRACTICE AREAS: Civil Litigation; Commercial Litigation; Labor Law; Matrimonial Law.
Ortega, Michael A., Jr. ....'55 '87 C&L.1040 B.B.A., J.D. 4 Apple Orchard Dr.
Pace, Louis A., Jr., (CV) ....'55 '81 C.999 B.A. L.1003 J.D. Clk. of the Supr. Ct.
Papazoglou, George S., (AV) ....'19 '51 C.1029 L.588 LL.B. [Driscoll,T.F.O.&D.]
Payne, Bobby S., (AV) .... '33 '60 C.575 B.A. L.893 LL.B. [Ⓒ Pinney,P.V.B.W.&D.]
*PRACTICE AREAS: Real Estate Law; Land Use Law.
Peat, Robert L., (BV) ....'53 '80 C&L.16 B.A., J.D. [Flanagan&P.]
Pennarola, Francis G., (BV) ....'51 '76 C.918 B.A. L.184 J.D. [Chipman,M.L.&P.]
*PRACTICE AREAS: Litigation; Elder Law; Probate; Computer Law; Workouts.
Perlman, Bruce M., (CV) '57 '82 C.1036 A.B. L.94 J.D.
V.P. & Assoc. Gen. Coun., Cendant Mobility Services Corp.
Pflederer, Gail '56 '87 C.966 B.S. L.1066 J.D.
Coun.-Bus. Devlopment, GE Capital Corp.

Piazza & Pickel
(See Stamford)

Pinney, A. Searle, (AV) .... '20 '48 C.860 A.B. L.309 LL.B. [Ⓒ Pinney,P.V.B.W.&D.]
*PRACTICE AREAS: Estate Planning and Administration.

Pinney, Payne, Van Lenten, Burrell, Wolfe & Dillman, P.C., (AV)
Lee Farm Corporate Park, 83 Wooster Heights, P.O. Box 3499, 06813-3499
Telephone: 203-743-2721 Fax: 203-792-4759
Email: ppv@ntplx.com
Thomas W. Van Lenten; Hugh A. Burrell; Robert J. Wolfe; John M. Dillman; Martin A. Rader, Jr.; William S. Steele, Jr.; Sheldon A. Rosenbaum; Jackie Chan; Richard D. Arconti; Ted D. Backer; Joseph Dimyan; Daniel E. Casagrande; Kim E. Nolan; Wendy A. Grispin;—John H. Van Lenten; Joseph DaSilva, Jr.; Jean Young Kim. Of Counsel: A. Searle Pinney; Bobby S. Payne.
General Practice. Civil and Criminal Litigation in all State and Federal Courts, State and Federal Appeals, Real Estate, Planning, Zoning and Land Use, Estate Planning and Administration, Corporate, Business, Commercial, Banking, Personal Injury, Domestic Relations, Medical Malpractice, Administrative Law, Tax, Native American Law, Corporate Mergers and Acquisitions.
Representative Clients: Savings Bank of Danbury.
See Professional Biographies, DANBURY, CONNECTICUT

Pinter, Laszlo L., (BV) .... '53 '84 C.262 B.A. L.1029 J.D. Asst. Corp. Coun.
Poll, Susan J., (CV) .... '50 '75 C.659 B.A. L.94 J.D. [Ellis&T.]
Popper, Richard H. .... '48 '74 C.94 B.A. L.724 J.D. [Ⓒ J.V.Leaphart&Assoc.]
Quinn, Valerie .... '60 '88 C&L.276 B.S.L.A., J.D. Dep. Asst. Pub. Def.
Quitmeyer, John M., (AVⓉ) '50 '80 C.1154 B.A. L.477 J.D.
(adm. in NY; not adm. in CT) Gen. Coun.- Consum. Prod. Grp., AlliedSignal, Inc.
Rachlin, Mark '56 '85 C.165 A.B. L.564 J.D.
(adm. in NY; not adm. in CT) Sr. Litig. Coun., Union Carbide Corp.
Rader, Martin A., Jr., (BV) ....'45 '70 C.976 B.A. L.184 J.D. [Pinney,P.V.B.W.&D.]
*PRACTICE AREAS: Real Estate Law; Personal Injury Litigation; Commercial Litigation; Probate Law.
Rapp, David M. '37 '62 C.823 B.A. L.188 LL.B.
(adm. in NY; not adm. in CT)
Vice President, Associate General Counsel, Cendant Mobility Services Corporation
Reidy, Gerald P. '40 '68 C.433 B.S. L.569 J.D.
(adm. in NY; not adm. in CT) Asst. Gen. Coun., Praxair, Inc.
Reinisch, Morris N. '49 '75 C.667 B.S.Ch.E. L.1009 J.D.
(adm. in DC; not adm. in CT; Pat.) UNIPOL Lic. Coun., Union Carbide Corp.
Riefberg, Lawrence M., (BV) ....'58 '82 C.860 B.A. L.184 J.D. [Riefberg,S.D.&N.]
Riefberg, Morton I. .... '27 '55 C.1035 B.S. L.569 J.D. Sr. Supr. Ct. J.
Riefberg, Smart, Donohue & NeJame, P.C., (BV) ....17 Downs Street
Roberts, Gloria J. '60 '87 C.1236 B.A. L.659 J.D.
(adm. in NY; not adm. in CT) 44 Old Ridgebury Rd.
Robinson, Jerry L. '39 '66 C.347 B.A. L.1119 J.D.
(adm. in IN; not adm. in CT) Gen. Tax Coun., Union Carbide Corp.
Robinson, Kenneth L. '53 '79 C.33 B.S. L.588 J.D.
(adm. in NY; not adm. in CT) [Ⓒ Corleto&Assoc.]
*PRACTICE AREAS: Environmental Law; Insurance; Land Use; Real Estate; Litigation.
Ronan, Michael P., (CV) .... '56 '85 C.184 B.S. L.1040 J.D. 30 Main St.
Rooney, Gerard P. '36 '63 C.433 B.S. L.276 J.D.
(adm. in VA; not adm. in CT; Pat.) Consulting Pat. Coun., Union Carbide Corporation
Rosenbaum, Sheldon A., (BV) ....'48 '74 C.705 B.A. L.1292 J.D. [Pinney,P.V.B.W.&D.]
*PRACTICE AREAS: Domestic Relations Law; Personal Injury Law; Real Estate Law.
Rubin, Marnie J. ....'71 '99 C.881 B.A. L.880 J.D. [Ⓐ Cohen&W.]
*PRACTICE AREAS: Commercial Litigation; Family Law; Municipal Law.
Ryan, Thomas J., (CV) .... '49 '79 C.1041 B.A. L.1095 J.D. 57 North St.
Sachs, Terry L., (BV) ....'51 '76 C.273 B.A. L.184 J.D. 27 Mill Plain Rd.
Saffi, Joseph A., (BV) .... '49 '77 C.184 B.A. L.1202 J.D. [Cramer&A.]
*PRACTICE AREAS: Residential Real Estate Law; Commercial Real Estate Law; Estate Planning Law; Corporate Law.
Sakellares, George S., (CV) .... '36 '63 C.184 B.A. L.564 LL.B. 13 Harmony St.
Savage, Phyllis '45 '77 C.563 B.A. L.262 J.D.
Assistant General Counsel, Union Carbide Corp.
Scire, Grace M. .... '56 '88 C.102 B.A. L.1009 J.D. 10 Filmore Ave.
Searing, Richelle E. '— '89
C.1103 B.A. L.1029 J.D. Asst. Venture's Coun., Union Carbide Corp.
Servas, Therese A. '51 '76 C.776 B.A. L.734 J.D.
Trial Ct. Admin. & Chief Clk., Supr. Ct.
Setaro, Christopher C., (BV) ....'65 '90 C.184 B.A. L.128 J.D. 52 Fed. Rd.
Shelton, George L. '31 '62 C.569 B.A.
(adm. in NY; not adm. in CT) 3 Cedar Rd.‡
Sibley, John J. ....'45 '72 C.602 A.B. L.188 J.D. Sr. Coun., Praxair, Inc.

Silver, Golub & Teitell LLP
(See Stamford)

Silvert, Corinne G., Esq., (CV) .... '— '83 C.011 B.A. L.1029 J.D. 113 Deer Hill Ave.
Sjovall, John P., (BV) ....'34 '60 C&L.184 B.A., LL.B. 57 North St.
Smart, Steven R., (BV) ....'58 '83 C.893 B.A. L.904 J.D. [Riefberg,S.D.&N.]
Smith, E. O'Malley, (BV) .... '48 '74 C.602 B.A. L.1292 J.D. [Collins,H.G.J.&T.]
*PRACTICE AREAS: Residential Real Estate; Commercial Real Estate; Trusts and Estate Planning; Probate; Corporate Law.
Smith, Robin J. .... '56 '84 C.184 B.S. L.818 J.D. Dep. Chf. Clk., Supr. Ct.‡
Spiro & Markosky, (CV) ....64 Lake Ave.
Steele, William S., Jr. ....'45 '70 C.976 B.A. L.569 J.D. [Pinney,P.V.B.W.&D.]
*PRACTICE AREAS: Real Estate Law; Land Use Law.
Stelljes, Charles F., (BV) .... '28 '52 C.667 L.564 LL.B. [Ⓒ Jones,D.K.B.&D.]
*PRACTICE AREAS: Negligence Litigation; Domestic Litigation; Commercial Litigation.
Suhr, Paul H. ....'45 '72 C.893 B.S. L.178 J.D. Asst. Gen. Coun., Union Carbide Corp.
Sullivan, Ronald M. ....'40 '72 C.262 B.A. L.184 J.D. Fam. Support Mag.
Sullivan, William W., (P.C.), (BV) .....'31 '56 C&L.976 B.A., LL.B. 24 Shelter Rock Rd.
Swenson, Paul E., (BV) ....'58 '86 C.829 B.S. L.464 J.D. 17 Downs St.
Talarico, Robert N., (BV) '42 '65 C&L.184 B.A., LL.B.
[Driscoll,T.F.O.&D.] (☉Bethel)
*PRACTICE AREAS: Banking Law; Estate Planning; Land Use Law; Landlord and Tenant Law; Probate Law.
Tisch, Richard '48 '74 C.165 B.A. L.982 J.D.
(adm. in NY; not adm. in CT) Senior Group Counsel, Praxair, Inc.
Trattner, Jeffrey B., (BV) .... '42 '66 C.102 B.A. L.1009 LL.B. [Ellis&T.]
Trinker, Steven T. '53 '79 C.597 B.A. L.273 J.D.
(adm. in VA; not adm. in CT; Pat.) 39 Old Ridgebury Rd.
Tuozzolo, John J., (BV) ....'48 '73 C.201 B.A. L.945 J.D. [Ⓒ Collins,H.G.J.&T.]
*PRACTICE AREAS: Probate Law; Federal Tax Law; Estate Planning.
Uva, Dominick M, (BV) .... '62 '88 C.1030 B.S. L.1019 J.D. 17 Downs St.
Van Lenten, John H. .... '62 '96 C.1103 B.B.A. L.1252 J.D. [Ⓐ Pinney,P.V.B.W.&D.]
*PRACTICE AREAS: Commercial Law; Real Estate; Appellate Practice; Construction Law; Land Use.
Van Lenten, Thomas W., (AV) '34 '62 C.1029 B.S. L.184 LL.B.
[Pinney,P.V.B.W.&D.]
*PRACTICE AREAS: Commercial Law; Litigation; Banking Law; Construction Law; Probate Law.
Ventura, Americo S., (BV) ....'27 '57 C.276 B.S. L.94 LL.B. 52 Federal St.
Volles, Warren K. '58 '88 C.184 B.S. L.1040 J.D.
(adm. in RI; not adm. in CT; Pat.) Pat. Coun., Union Carbide Corp.
Von Ancken, Linda '63 '88 C.569 B.A. L.724 J.D.
Asst. Secy. & Corp. Coun., Grolier Inc.
Vournazos, C. Anthony, (CV) ......'60 '85 C.184 B.A. L.128 J.D. 53 Lake Ave. Extension
Walsh, Joseph G., (BV) .... '57 '84 C.433 B.S. L.93 J.D. [Cohen&W.]
*PRACTICE AREAS: Personal Injury; Civil and Criminal Litigation.

Ware, Fressola, Van Der Sluys & Adolphson, LLP
(See Monroe)

Weir, Christopher H., P.C. ....'48 '95 C.597 B.A. L.999 J.D. 185 Lake Place South
Wellman, Eric N., (BV) ....'40 '69 C.1103 B.S. L.184 J.D. 1001 Crows Nest Lane
Wessler, Stuart G. '56 '79 C.1044 B.S. L.273 J.D.
(adm. in DC; not adm. in CT) Tax Coun., GE Capital Corp.
West, Thomas G. .... '34 '69 C.1103 B.A. L.184 J.D. Supr. Ct. J.
Whitcombe, Nathaniel B. .... '57 '97 C.478 A.B. L.184 J.D. [N.B.Whitcombe]
Whitcombe, Nathaniel B., LLC, Law Office of .... 70 North Street, Suite 204
White, Betty-Lynn '51 '77 C.282 B.A. L.569 J.D.
Senior Litigation Counsel, Union Carbide Corp.
White, Gary J. ....'53 '79 C.321 A.B. L.309 J.D. Danbury Sup. Ct.
Willcox, Susan, (CV) .... '— '89 C.1103 B.S. L.1029 J.D. 57 North St.
Williams, Joanne '50 '89 C.522 B.S. L.1009 J.D.
(adm. in NY; not adm. in CT) Litig. Coun., Union Carbide Corp.
Winans, Christopher G., (BV) ....'61 '87 C.1010 B.A. L.1292 J.D. [C.G.Winans]
*PRACTICE AREAS: Collections; Commercial Law; Construction Litigation; Foreclosures; Landlord and Tenant Law.

Winans, Christopher G., P.C., (BV)
d/b/a Sullivan, Biraglia, Winans and Eberhard
24 Shelter Rock Road, 06810
Telephone: 203-798-1000 Fax: 203-797-0000
Email: CGWinans@aol.com URL: http://www.lawyers.com/winans
Christopher G. Winans.
Collections, Commercial Litigation, Civil Litigation and Personal Injury.
See Professional Biographies, DANBURY, CONNECTICUT

Winslow, Heidi G., (BV) .... '48 '76 C.914 B.A. L.184 J.D. 57 North St.
Wolfe, Robert J., (BV) .... '36 '60 C.882 B.S. L.893 LL.B. [Pinney,P.V.B.W.&D.]
*PRACTICE AREAS: Commercial Law; Corporations and Other Businesses; Estate Planning; Estate Settlement; Probate Law.
Wunsch, Alan V. .... '63 '89 C.223 B.S. L.930 J.D. 98 Mill Plain Rd.
Yamin, Dianne E., (BV) ....'61 '86 C.401 B.A. L.469 J.D. [Yamin&Y.]
Yamin, Raymond P., (BV) ....'55 '80 C.1103 B.B.A. L.347 J.D. [Yamin&Y.]
Yamin, Robert J., (BV) ....'49 '82 C.1103 A.B. L.309 J.D. [Yamin&Y.]
Yamin & Yamin, (BV) .... Four Moss Ave.
Zitzmann, Oliver A. '67 '94 C.688 B.S. L.1009 J.D.
(adm. in NY; not adm. in CT; Pat.) Chief Patent Counsel, ATMI

DANIELSON, 4,441, *Windham Co.*

Adams, Doris M. '— '73 C.94 B.S. L.262 J.D.
(adm. in MO; not adm. in CT) Exec. Dir., Windham Area Community Action Prog., Inc.
Arters, Harry M., (BV) ....'38 '69 C&L.184 B.S., J.D. 219 Broad St.
Brigham, Carol A., (BV) ....'60 '85 C.184 B.A. L.1048 J.D. 100 Broad St.
Burlingame, Stephen J., (BV) .... '43 '69 C.67 A.B. L.184 J.D. [Jackson H.B.&H.]
*PRACTICE AREAS: Probate; Planning; Zoning; Corporate; Municipal.
Caridad, Roger R. .... '61 '86 C&L.184 B.A., J.D. Asst. State Atty.
Chabot, Raymond J., (AV) .... '21 '52 C.550 L.94 LL.B. P.O. Box 487
Dupont, Thomas E., (BV) .... '35 '61 C.676 A.B. L.93 LL.B. 35 Academy St.
Ferland, Charles P. .... '47 '73 C.184 B.S. L.446 J.D. P.O. Box 330
Griffiths, Eldon L. ....'51 '78 C.184 B.A. L.383 J.D. 685 S. Frontage Rd.
Harris, John K., Jr., (BV) ....'37 '66 C.454 B.S. L.184 LL.B. [Jackson H.B.&H.]
*PRACTICE AREAS: Civil Litigation; Criminal Defense; Bankruptcy; Elder Law.
Hubert, David M., (BV) .... '51 '79 C&L.184 B.A., J.D. [Jackson H.B.&H.]
*PRACTICE AREAS: Real Estate; Personal Injury; Municipal; Landlord/Tenant; Automobile Accidents and Injuries.
Jackson, George H., III, (AV) .... '39 '64 C.197 A.B. L.659 J.D. [Jackson H.B.&H.]
*PRACTICE AREAS: Real Estate.

Jackson Harris Burlingame & Hubert, LLC, (AV)
245 Main Street, 06239
Telephone: 860-774-9627 Fax: 860-774-5784
Email: jhbhlaw@snet.net
Members of Firm: George H. Jackson, III; John K. Harris, Jr.; Stephen J. Burlingame; David M. Hubert.
General Civil Practice. Criminal, Family, Probate, Estate Planning, Corporate, Real Estate, Municipal and Bankruptcy Law. Litigation.
Representative Client: Cargill Bank.
See Professional Biographies, DANIELSON, CONNECTICUT

Kelley, James K., (BV) .... '50 '76 C.1107 A.B. L.1048 J.D. Prob. J.
Leotsakos, Anastasios M., (BV) ....'61 '88 C.184 B.A. L.1048 J.D. 219 Broad St.
Parlato, Raymond F., (BV) .... '51 '77 C&L.184 B.A., J.D. 107 Broad St.
Rooke-Norman, Gail J., (CV) .... '51 '93 C.184 B.A. L.818 J.D. 31 Academy St.
Sarantopoulos, Nicholas G., (BV) ....'23 '59 C.150 B.A. L.184 LL.B. 8 Center St.
Scheibeler, James N., (BV) ....'34 '62 C&L.184 B.A., LL.B. P.O. Box 711
Tsakonas, Basil T., (AV) .... '25 '54 C&L.184 B.A., LL.B. 181 Main St.
Veilleux, Paul E., (BV) .... '37 '66 C.676 A.B. L.276 J.D. 42 L'Homme St.

DARIEN, 18,892, *Fairfield Co.*

Akoury, Sandra J. ....'60 '98 C&L.184 B.S., B.S. [Ⓐ Rucci,B.C.&E.]
*PRACTICE AREAS: Construction Arbitration; Mechanics Liens; Civil Litigation; Zoning Planning and Land Use; Construction Law.
Altman, Richard C. '63 '89 C.273 B.A. L.1040 J.D.
V.P. &Gen. Coun., The Americas, Danzas AEI Inc.
*RESPONSIBILITIES: Labor and Employment; Corporate; International.
Ambrette, L. Conrad, (BV) ....'47 '72 C.478 B.A. L.188 J.D. [Ⓒ Gleason&H.] (☉Darien)
*PRACTICE AREAS: Probate and Estates; Elder Law; Wills; Trusts.
Ambrette, L. Conrad, (BV) .... '47 '72 C.478 B.A. L.188 J.D. [Millar&A.] (☉Darien)
*PRACTICE AREAS: Probate and Estates; Elder Law; Real Estate; Wills; Trusts.
Avery, Lori L. .... '71 '97 C.184 B.A. L.1048 J.D. 1 Thorndale Cir.
Basham, Marianne '58 '91 C.1016 B.A. L.209 J.D.
(adm. in IL; not adm. in CT) [Danzas A.]
*RESPONSIBILITIES: U.S Customs.; Transportation; Contracts; Employment Law; Immigration Law.
Beach, Stephen Holbrook .... '15 '41 C.373 B.A. L.215 LL.B. 52 Brushy Hill Rd.
Bell, M. Ramsay, (BV) .... '55 '80 C.855 B.A. L.446 J.D. 473 Hollow Tree Ridge Rd.
Bieluch, William C., Jr. ....'45 '73 C.103 A.B. L.724 J.D. 989 Post Rd.
Blumenstock, Hyman '23 '56 C.569 B.E.E. L.564 LL.B.
(adm. in NY; not adm. in CT; Pat.) P.O. Box 1106
Bowen, Joanna F. .... '54 '95 C.623 B.S. L.1040 J.D. [Ⓐ Tibbetts K.&B.]
*PRACTICE AREAS: Trusts and Estates; General; Real Estate.
Boyd, Jennifer N., (AV) ... '52 '78 C.860 B.A. L.184 J.D. [Ⓒ Gleason&H.] (☉Greenwich)
*PRACTICE AREAS: Corporate Finance; Corporate Law; Mergers and Acquisitions; Partnership Law; Limited Liability Company Law.

Brainard, Hayden R. .... '73 '99 C.823 L.982 J.D. [🄰 Rucci,B.C.&E.]
*PRACTICE AREAS: Corporate Law; Internet Law; Business Law; Intellectual Property.
Breen, Joseph B. .... '30 '58 C.321 A.B. L.262 LL.B. [Breen&B.]
Breen & Bartlett, P.C. .... 9 Old Kings Hwy. S.
Brown, Heather M., (BV) .... '59 '84 C.339 B.A. L.1040 J.D. [H.M.Brown]
*PRACTICE AREAS: Real Estate; Probate; Civil Litigation; Family Law.

Brown, Heather M., LLC, Law Office of, (BV)
1051 Post Road, Suite 2, P.O. Box 37, 06820-0537
Telephone: 203-655-1900 Fax: 203-655-2210
Email: darienlaw@snet.net URL: http://www.lawyers.com/hmbrown
Heather M. Brown.
Civil Litigation, Family Law, Divorce, Child Custody, Child Support, Land Use, Real Estate, Real Estate Finance, Probate Administration.
See Professional Biographies, DARIEN, CONNECTICUT

Burnham, Paul H., (BV) .... '54 '80 C.976 B.A. L.184 J.D. [Rucci,B.C.&E.]
*PRACTICE AREAS: Estate Planning; Estate Administration; Individual Taxation; Corporate Tax Planning.
Butler, Timothy F. .... '65 '92 C.569 B.A. L.262 J.D. [Tibbetts K.&B.] ⊙
*PRACTICE AREAS: Litigation; Corporate; Criminal.
Canevari, Thomas M., (AVⓉ) '59 '89
C.1027 B.S. L.1029 J.D. [Freehill H.&M.] (⊙New York, NY)
Carello, William M. .... '62 '89 C&L.184 B.S., J.D. [Rucci,B.C.&E.]
*PRACTICE AREAS: Corporate Law; Business Law; Commercial Law; Mergers and Acquisitions; Real Estate.
Carta, Mark R., (BV) .... '50 '78 C.659 B.A. L.184 J.D. [Rucci,B.C.&E.]
*PRACTICE AREAS: Commercial Litigation; Employment Discrimination; Fiduciary; Construction Litigation; Civil Appeals.
Catanzaro, Michael E., Jr. '35 '62 C.602 A.B. L.64 LL.B.
(adm. in MD; not adm. in CT) 21 Nickerson Lane
Chesley, Roger D., (AVⓉ) ...... '43 '72 C.659 B.S.Econ. L.309 LL.B. 2 Pine Brook Lane
Cirillo, Marianne Christopher .... '61 '86 C.1044 B.A. L.1040 J.D. 46 Herman Ave.
Colbert, Christina M. .... '67 '92 C&L.724 B.A., J.D. [🄰 P.J.Damanti] ⊙
Costello, Jan A. .... '51 '94 C.331 B.A. L.1178 J.D. [🄰 Pierson]
Crawford, Ian R. '43 '70 C.103 B.A. L.823 J.D.
[⊡ Rucci,B.C.&E.] (⊙New York, NY)
*PRACTICE AREAS: Employee Benefits; Deferred Compensation; ERISA; COBRA; Individual Taxation.
Crowe, Martin A. '31 '60 C.573 B.S. L.724 J.D.
(adm. in NY; not adm. in CT) V.P. Security, Brink's, Inc.

Curtis, Brinckerhoff & Barrett, P.C.
(See Stamford)

Daly, Robert P., (BV) .... '55 '80 C&L.276 A.B., J.D. P.O. Box 62

Damanti, Patrick J., (AVⓉ) '47 '73 C.321 A.B. L.724 J.D.
777 Post Road, P.O. Box 134, 06820-0634 ⊙
Telephone: 203-655-7104 Fax: 203-655-6417
Email: patdamanti@snet.net
Associate: Christina M. Colbert.
Real Estate, Foreclosure, Workouts, Creditors Rights, Bankruptcy, Banking, Probate, Trusts and Estates.
New York, New York Office: 36 West 44th Street, Suite 900, 10036. Telephone:212-764-6206. Fax: 212-997-7686.
See Professional Biographies, DARIEN, CONNECTICUT

Dempsey, James C. .... '37 '62 C&L.262 B.A., LL.B. [⊡ Rucci,B.C.&E.]
*PRACTICE AREAS: Corporate Law; Securities; Commercial Law; Estate Planning; Estate Administration.
DeVito, Anthony M., III .... '53 '79 C.184 B.A. L.93 J.D. 46 Greenwood Ave.
Doukas, Patricia A. '49 '75 C.999 B.A. L.724 J.D.
(adm. in NY; not adm. in CT) 51 Old Farm Rd.‡
Driscoll, Daryl A., (BVⓉ) .... '53 '80 C.184 B.A. L.1040 J.D. 144 Holmes Ave.
Eisenberg, Mitchell S. '63 '90
C.184 B.S. L.569 J.D. General Coun., internet.com Corporation
Finke, Robert W. .... '66 '95 C.911 B.S. L.1252 J.D. 14 Henry St.
Flanagan, Mari Jo F. .... '48 '77 C.705 A.B. L.575 J.D. Asst. Gen Coun., Brink's Inc.
Flanagan, William K., Jr. '26 '52 C.103 A.B. L.705 LL.B.
(adm. in NJ; not adm. in CT) Retired‡

Freehill Hogan & Mahar LLP, (AVⓉ)
23 Old Kings Highway South, 06820 ⊙
Telephone: 203-921-1913 Facsimile: 203-358-8377
Email: reception@freehill.com URL: http://www.freehill.com
Thomas M. Canevari.
Admiralty and Maritime Law, Administrative Law, Charter Parties, Contracts, Marine Pollution and Environmental Law, Ship Finance, Marine Insurance, Personal Injury, General Commercial Litigation, Occupational Disease Defense, Maritime and Environmental Criminal Law, Criminal Law. All aspects of Litigation and Arbitration, including Trials and Appeals in Federal and State Courts.
See Professional Biographies, DARIEN, CONNECTICUT

Giarratana, Salvatore A. .... '22 '53 C&L.128 B.A., J.D. 4 Short Lane (Pat.)‡
Gilliam, Carole Currin '55 '81 C.575 A.B. L.500 J.D.
(adm. in MS; not adm. in CT) 27 Beach Dr.
Gleason, Wilder G., (BV) .... '50 '77 C.951 B.A. L.184 J.D. [Gleason&H.]
*PRACTICE AREAS: Zoning, Planning and Land Use; Real Estate; Leases and Leasing; Environmental.

Gleason & Hill, LLC, (BV)
23 Old Kings Highway South, P.O. Box 1636, 06820
Telephone: 203-655-9696 Fax: 203-656-2055
Email: attorneys@gleasonlaw.com
Wilder G. Gleason; D.B. Hill;—Kathryn L. Pasternak. Of Counsel: Jennifer N. Boyd; L. Conrad Ambrette (Also Member, Millar & Ambrette, Darien, CT).
Land Use, Commercial and Residential Real Estate, Business, Environmental, Litigation, Family, Personal Injury.
See Professional Biographies, DARIEN, CONNECTICUT

Green, Robert G. '38 '64 C.674 B.A. L.276 J.D.
(adm. in NY; not adm. in CT) Pres., Conn. Minerals & Metals Inc.
Gross, Patricia Moreland, (BV) .... '36 '85 C.184 B.G.S. L.1040 J.D. [🄰 Millar&A.]
*PRACTICE AREAS: General Practice; Real Estate.
Hall, John R., II .... '61 '89 C&L.184 B.A., J.D. [🄰 Tibbetts K.&B.]
*PRACTICE AREAS: Litigation; Real Estate; Corporate.

Heagney, Lennon & Slane LLP
(See Greenwich)

Hill, D.B. .... '56 '87 C.30 B.S. L.1029 J.D. [Gleason&H.]
*PRACTICE AREAS: Administrative Appeals; Zoning, Planning and Land Use; Litigation.
Hohler, Barbara A. '59 '86 C.966 B.A. L.846 J.D.
(adm. in NY; not adm. in CT) 362 Hollow Tree Ridge‡

Horner, Stephen P., Law Office of, (AV) '46 '74 C.216 B.A. L.831 J.D.
2183 Boston Post Road, 06820
Telephone: 203-655-7905 Facsimile: 203-656-1075 URL: http://www.hornerlaw.com
Email: shorner@sphorner.com URL: http://www.lawyers.com/hornerlaw
***PRACTICE AREAS: Employment Law; Labor Law.**
Labor and Employment Practice before State and Federal Courts.
See Professional Biographies, DARIEN, CONNECTICUT

Hrusa, Thomas H. .... '57 '87 C.1211 B.S. L.1029 J.D. 62 Sedgewick Ave.

Humes, Botzow, Wagner & Miller
(See Davidson, Dawson & Clark LLP)

Iori, Max E. .... '72 '97 C.1107 B.S. L.1252 J.D. Coun., internet.com Corporation
Jamar, Jessie E. '57 '82 C&L.012 B.C.L., LL.B.
(adm. in NY; not adm. in CT) 29 Raiders Ln.
Johnson, Charles A. .... '67 '94 C.1030 B.A. L.823 J.D. [🄰 Rucci,B.C.&E.]
*PRACTICE AREAS: Commercial Litigation; Maritime Admiralty Litigation.
Kaynor, Sanford B., (AV) .... '26 '53 C.976 B.S. L.178 J.D. 14 East Trail‡
Keating, Mary P., (BV) .... '58 '86 C.706 B.A. L.976 J.D. [Tibbetts K.&B.]
*PRACTICE AREAS: Computer Law; Contract Law; Real Estate Law; Estate Planning; Corporate Law.
Kelleher, Patricia A. .... '51 '84 C.1044 B.A. L.1040 J.D. Corp. Atty., Brink's, Inc.
Kraig, Thomas L. '16 '43 C.569 B.A. L.262 J.D.
(adm. in NY; not adm. in CT) 3 Stephanie Lane, S.
Larossa, Sonia T. .... '74 '99 C.105 B.A. L.884 J.D. [🄰 Rucci,B.C.&E.]
*PRACTICE AREAS: Civil Litigation.
Larson, Katherine B. .... '59 '85 C.602 B.A. L.424 J.D. 38 Briar Brae Road
Love, James Hogan, (BV) .... '60 '85 C.1030 B.A. L.245 J.D. 43 Corbin Dr.
Luedecker, Margaret Ann .... '50 '80 C.112 A.B. L.569 J.D. 63 Dubois St.
Luedecker, Margaret R. .... '50 '80 C.1375 A.B. L.569 J.D. 63 DuBois Street
Mann, Joel E. '32 '58 C.867 A.B. L.309 LL.B.
(adm. in NY; not adm. in CT) 15 Hillsley Rd.
Marlow, Tracy A. .... '42 '85 C.569 B.S. L.1009 J.D. 600 Hollow Tree Ridge Rd.
Maslan, Robert F., Jr., (BV) .... '51 '90 C.1030 B.S. L.262 J.D. [Rucci,B.C.&E.]
*PRACTICE AREAS: Commercial Litigation; Federal Civil Practice; Real Estate; Zoning, Planning and Land Use.
McCauley, Daniel J. '34 '58 C.1019 B.B.A. L.724 LL.B.
(adm. in NY; not adm. in CT) [Danzas A.]

McClancy, Christopher P. '61 '87 C.884 B.A. L.564 J.D.
1051 Post Road Suite 3, P.O. Box 1124, 06820-1124 ⊙
Telephone: 203-656-4700 Fax: 203-656-4800
Email: CPMcClancy@msn.com URL: http://www.lawyers.com/cpmcclancy
***PRACTICE AREAS: General Practice; Probate; Trusts and Estates; Civil Litigation; Business Formation.**
General Practice, Trusts and Estates, Civil Litigation, Property Tax Assessments, Business Formation, Commercial Law, Legal Ethics and Professional Responsibility.
See Professional Biographies, DARIEN, CONNECTICUT

McClancy, Christopher P. '61 '87 C.884 B.A. L.564 J.D.
[⊡ Tibbetts K.&B.] (⊙Darien)
*PRACTICE AREAS: General Practice; Probate; Trusts and Estates; Civil Litigation; Business Formation.
Millar, Samuel D. B., Jr., (AV) .... '31 '57 C.918 B.A. L.705 LL.B. [Millar&A.]
*PRACTICE AREAS: Real Estate; Probate and Estates.

Millar & Ambrette, (AV) BB
23 Old King's Highway South, 06820-1267
Telephone: 203-655-7931 FAX: 203-656-2055
URL: http://www.lawyers.com/millar&ambrette
Members of Firm: Samuel D. B. Millar, Jr.; L. Conrad Ambrette (Also Of Counsel, Gleason & Hill, LLC, Darien, CT). Associate: Patricia Moreland Gross.
Real Estate, Probate and Estate Planning, Elder Law, Corporation, and General Practice.
See Professional Biographies, DARIEN, CONNECTICUT

Morehouse, Philip A. .... '18 '48 C&L.184 B.A., LL.B. Ret. Prob. J.
Moris, Alberto N. '66 '91 C.472 B.A. L.245 J.D.
(adm. in FL; not adm. in CT) [⊡ Rucci,B.C.&E.]
*PRACTICE AREAS: Corporate Law; Commercial Law; Commercial Litigation; Corporate Banking Law; Aviation Law.
Morris, Lawrence B., Jr. '17 '48 C.674 A.B. L.309 LL.B.
(adm. in NY; not adm. in CT) 13 Greenleaf Ave.‡
Murphy, Natalie Anne '50 '77 C.913 B.A. L.245 J.D.
(adm. in GA; not adm. in CT) 18 Libby Ln.‡
Murray, Emmet V. '26 '51 C.103 B.A. L.893 LL.B.
(adm. in NY; not adm. in CT) 14 Dorchester Rd.‡
Nanos, Nicholas P. .... '12 '37 C.197 B.A. L.309 LL.B. 23 Butlers Island‡
Neafsey, Mara T. '66 '92 C.188 A.B. L.309 J.D.
(adm. in NY; not adm. in CT) 28 Scofield Farms Rd.
Newton, Blake T., III, (AVⓉ) '42 '70 C.945 A.B. L.893 LL.B.
(adm. in NY; not adm. in CT)
Executive Vice President & General Counsel, Swisher International
O'Grady, Daniel W. .... '54 '85 C.829 B.S. L.1029 J.D. 120 Tokeneke Rd.
Ogren, Lawrence S. .... '55 '99 C.205 B.S. L.724 J.D. 278 West Avenue
Ottenstein, David L. '31 '58 C.446 B.S. L.276 LL.B.
(adm. in DC; not adm. in CT) 22 Country Club Rd.‡
Parsons, Thomas, III '19 '48 C.976 A.B. L.262 J.D.
(adm. in NY; not adm. in CT) 171 Pear Tree Point Rd.‡
Pasternak, Kathryn L. .... '51 '97 C.822 B.A. L.1040 J.D. [🄰 Gleason&H.]
*PRACTICE AREAS: Real Estate; Zoning, Planning and Land Use.
Peña, Carlos E. .... '58 '84 C.994 B.A. L.228 J.D. Asst. Gen. Coun., Brink's, Inc.
Pierson, Stephen, (BV) .... '31 '58 C.165 B.A. L.178 LL.B. [Pierson]
Pierson Law Firm, (BV) .... 777 Post Road
Rankin, Lucy W. .... '41 '93 C.788 B.A. L.1252 J.D. P.O. Box 2300
Rearden, John B., Jr., (AV) .... '42 '67 C.103 A.B. L.569 LL.B. Prob. J.
Reilly, George A., (BV) .... '54 '84 C.867 B.A. L.262 J.D. [Reilly&R.]
*PRACTICE AREAS: Family Law; Divorce; Post Divorce; Litigation; Residential Real Estate.
Reilly, Lawrence H., (AVⓉ) .... '22 '50 C.262 A.B. L.178 LL.B. [⊡ Reilly&R.]
*PRACTICE AREAS: Elder Law; Trusts and Estates.

Reilly & Reilly, (BV)
800 Post Road, P.O. Box 1072, 06820-1072
Telephone: 203-655-6785 Fax: 203-655-7462 URL: http://www.reillylaw.com
Email: lawyers@reillylaw.com URL: http://www.lawyers.com/georgereilly
George A. Reilly. Of Counsel: Lawrence H. Reilly.
Family Law, Litigation, Trusts and Estates Planning and Administration, Residential Real Estate.
See Professional Biographies, DARIEN, CONNECTICUT

Richards, Benjamin T., Jr. '27 '54 C&L.309 A.B., LL.B.
(adm. in NY; not adm. in CT) 2 Valley Forge Rd.‡
Roux, Peter Robert '43 '86 C.339 B.A. L.262 J.D.
(adm. in DC; not adm. in CT) 28 Fairmead Road
Rucci, Joseph J., Jr., (AV) '41 '66 C.1030 A.B. L.884 J.D.
[Rucci,B.C.&E.] (⊙Stamford)
*PRACTICE AREAS: Information Technology; Banking; Business Law; Commercial Law.

Rucci, Burnham, Carta & Edelberg, LLP, (AV) BB
800 Post Road, P.O. Box 1107, 06820 ⊙
Telephone: 203-655-7695 Facsimile: 203-655-4302
URL: http://www.rbce.com
Members of Firm: Joseph J. Rucci, Jr.; Paul H. Burnham; Mark R. Carta; Paul B. Edelberg (Resident, Stamford Office); William M. Carello; Robert F. Maslan, Jr.; Colette C. Symon. Associates: David J. Rucci (Resident, New Canaan Office); Sandra J. Akoury; Hayden R. Brainard; Sonia T. Larossa; Theresa Anne Twigg; Charles A. Johnson. Of Counsel: Ian R. Crawford; James C. Dempsey; Alberto N. Moris (Not admitted in CT); James F. Sullivan (Resident, New Canaan Office).

(This Listing Continued)

Rucci, Burnham, Carta & Edelberg, LLP (Continued)

Commercial and Residential Real Estate, Trusts and Estates, Estate Planning, Civil Trial Practice including Fiduciary Disputes, Employment, Commercial, Construction and Personal Injury Litigation, Corporate, Commercial, Information Technology, Banking, Workouts and Bankruptcy, Business Law, Environmental Law, Pre-Nuptial Agreements, State, Local and Federal Taxation, Zoning, Pensions, ERISA Matters and Charitable Organizations.
New Canaan, Connecticut Office: 71 Elm Street, P.O. Box 1680. Telephone: 203-966-6500.
Stamford, Connecticut Office: 6 Landmark Square, Suite 470. Telephone: 203-359-5637.

See Professional Biographies, DARIEN, CONNECTICUT

Ryan, Peter M., (BV) '37 '63 C.776 B.S. L.659 J.D.
777 Post Road, 06820
Telephone: 203-655-8921 Fax: 203-656-0019
Email: pryanlex@aol.com
***PRACTICE AREAS: Civil Litigation; Probate Litigation; Criminal Litigation; Appellate Practice; Administrative Law.**
Civil Litigation, Criminal Litigation, Appellate Practice, Administrative Law, Personal Injury.

See Professional Biographies, DARIEN, CONNECTICUT

Ryan, Thomas J., III, (CV) .... '49 '73 C.676 B.S. L.724 J.D. 20 Fairfield Ave.
Ryan-Boyle, Lisa Margaret '64 '93 C.103 B.A. L.276 J.D.
(adm. in MD; not adm. in CT) 150 Goodwives River Rd.
Salvia, Margherita ....'48 '74 C.706 B.A. L.262 J.D. 1 Thornal Cir.

Schoonmaker, George & Colin, P.C.
(See Greenwich)

Seeberger, George J. '60 '87 C.178 A.B. L.309 J.D.
(adm. in NY; not adm. in CT) Portfolio Information Corp.
Silbersack, John W. ....'36 '60 C&L.976 B.A., LL.B. 65 Bridle Trail
Smith, Edward P. '15 '40 C.433 B.A. L.724 J.D.
(adm. in NY; not adm. in CT) 2 1/2 Peach Hill Rd.‡
Soderman, Kenneth J. ....'51 '75 C.156 A.B. L.184 J.D. 59 Relihan Rd.
Spain, Joseph H., (AVⓉ) '39 '64 C.433 B.E.E. L.93 LL.B.
(adm. in NY; not adm. in CT) 126 Leroy Ave.
Spielberger, John R. '56 '83 C.524 B.A. L.64 J.D.
(adm. in MD; not adm. in CT) General Counsel, Danzas AEI Inc.
Sprole, Frank A. ....'18 '49 C.976 A.B. L.178 LL.B. 394 Mansfield Ave.‡
Sweeney, Anthony E. ....'— '79 C.1029 B.S. L.724 J.D. 15 Archer Lane

Swiggart, Carolyn C. '58 '83 C.914 A.B. L.184 J.D.
777 Post Road, P.O. Box 941, 06820
Telephone: 203-655-8921 Fax: 203-656-0019
Email: cswiggart@aol.com URL: http://www.lawyers.com/swiggartfamilylaw
***PRACTICE AREAS: Family Law; General Practice.**
Of Counsel: Pierson Law Firm, Darien, Connecticut.
Family Law, Divorce, Child Custody, Domestic Relations.

See Professional Biographies, DARIEN, CONNECTICUT

Symon, Colette C., (BV) .... '64 '91 C.860 B.A. L.184 J.D. [Rucci,B.C.&E.]
*PRACTICE AREAS: Residential Real Estate; Zoning; General Business Law.
Thomas, Ronald J. ....'42 '67 C.1044 B.A. L.107 J.D. 26 Red Rose Circle
Tibbetts, Alfred P., (BV) ....'56 '84 C.675 B.A. L.902 J.D. [Tibbetts K.&B.]
*PRACTICE AREAS: Real Estate; Trusts and Estates.

Tibbetts Keating & Butler, LLC, (BV)
43 Corbin Drive, P.O. Box 5, 06820 ⊙
Telephone: 203-656-1066 Fax: 203-656-2573 http://www.tkblaw.com
URL: http://www.lawyers.com/tibbettskeating&butler
Alfred P. Tibbetts; Mary P. Keating; Timothy F. Butler. Associates: John R. Hall, II; Joanna F. Bowen. Of Counsel: Christopher P. McClancy.
General Practice. Residential Real Estate, Civil Litigation, State and Federal, Bankruptcy Chapter 7, Bankruptcy Litigation, Civil Appeals, Estate Planning, Estate Administration, Family Trusts, Living Trusts, Personal Injury, Commercial Real Estate, Corporate Law, Computer Law, Criminal Law.
A list of Representative Clients will be furnished upon request.
References: Bank of Darien; People's Bank.
New York City Office: 1155 Avenue of the Americas, 28th Floor, 10036. Telephone: 212-398-9509. Fax: 212-398-9788.

See Professional Biographies, DARIEN, CONNECTICUT

Twigg, Theresa Anne .... '55 '82 C.659 A.B. L.184 J.D. [Ⓐ Rucci,B.C.&E.]
*PRACTICE AREAS: Corporate; Land Use; Employment Law.
von Schmidt, Georgia C., (BV) ....'50 '78 C.912 B.A. L.564 J.D. 777 Boston Post Rd.

Wake, See, Dimes & Bryniczka
(See Westport)

Waldau, William G., (BV) ....'40 '70 C.103 A.B. L.884 J.D. 745 Post Road
Washburn Boe, Christine .....'65 '91 C.608 B.S./B.A. L.117 J.D. 249 Old Kings Hwy., S.
Williamson, Laurie E. .... '49 '80 C.228 B.A. L.262 J.D. Tinywood Rd.
Wiswell, Peter S., (BVⓉ) '51 '80 C.478 B.A. L.861 J.D.
(adm. in NY; not adm. in CT) TBS Adjusting Inc.
Womer, Martin C. .... '53 '97 C.164 A.B. L.1294 J.D. [Womer]
*PRACTICE AREAS: Trusts and Estates; Probate; Nonprofit and Charitable Organizations; Conservation Easements; Zoning, Planning and Land Use.

Womer Law Firm, LLC
777 Post Road, 06820
Telephone: 203-656-0753 Fax: 203-656-0019
Email: martinwomer@cs.com URL: http://www.nnepa.com/WomerLaw
Martin C. Womer.
Trusts and Estates, Wills, Non Profit and Charitable Organizations, Conservation Easements, Zoning, Planning and Land Use, Real Estate.

See Professional Biographies, DARIEN, CONNECTICUT

DEEP RIVER, 3,994, *Middlesex Co.*

Bouregy, William L., (BV) ....'54 '89 C.262 B.A. L.564 J.D. [Marsh&B.]
Creed, Kevin E. ....'51 '97 C.1164 B.A. L.209 J.D. [B.E.Newman] ⊙
Marsh, Jane R., (BV) ....'51 '80 C.320 B.A. L.184 J.D. [Marsh&B.]
Marsh & Bouregy, LLC, (BV) .... 6 Elm St.
Newman, Bruce E. ....'64 '90 C.165 B.A. L.982 J.D. [B.E.Newman] ⊙
Newman, Bruce E., L.L.C., Law Offices of ....One High St. (⊙Bristol)
Tucker, William Gareth ....'51 '80 C.902 B.A. L.184 J.D. 5 Elm St.

DERBY, 12,199, *New Haven Co.*

Berns, Edward J., (BV) '49 '74 C.1202 B.A. L.669 J.D.
VP Legal Affrs., Griffin Hospital
Carr, Gayle C. .... '61 '90 C.94 B.A. L.884 J.D. [Ⓐ Cohen&T.] ⊙
*PRACTICE AREAS: Family Law; Civil Litigation; Personal Injury; Negligence; Medical Malpractice.
Cohen, James E., (BV) ....'46 '71 C.659 B.A. L.184 J.D. [Cohen&T.]
*PRACTICE AREAS: Real Estate and Mortgage Financing; Probate; Wills and Trusts; Zoning, Planning and Land Use; Municipal Law.

Cohen & Thomas, (BV)
315 Main Street, P.O. Box 313, 06418 ⊙
Telephone: 203-735-9521 Fax: 203-732-8129
Email: cohen.and.thomas@att.net URL: http://www.lawyers.com/cohen-and-thomas-attys

(This Listing Continued)

Cohen & Thomas (Continued)

Members of Firm: David B. Cohen (1913-1991); James E. Cohen; Dominick J. Thomas, Jr. Associates: Ian A. Cole; Christine L. Curtiss; Gayle C. Carr (Resident, Litchfield Office); Gregory M. Thomas.
General Civil and Criminal Practice. Trials in all Courts. Personal Injury, Negligence and Medical Malpractice Litigation, Real Estate Purchase, Sale, Financing, Zoning and Development, Domestic Law and Divorce, Probate, Wills and Trusts, Banking, Foreclosure and Workouts, Commercial Litigation and Collections, Municipal, Elder Law, Worker's Compensation.
Representative Clients: Great Country Bank; Housatonic Bank & Trust Co.; Derby Savings Bank; Ansonia Derby Water Co.; Griffin Hospital.
Lichtfield, Connecticut Office: 15 Meadow Street, 06759. Telephone: 860-567-3754. Fax: 860-567-3894.

See Professional Biographies, DERBY, CONNECTICUT

Cole, Ian A. .... '54 '80 C.184 B.A. L.1048 J.D. [Ⓐ Cohen&T.]
*PRACTICE AREAS: Commercial Litigation; Bankruptcy; Civil Rights; Appellate Law; Workers Compensation.
Curtiss, Christine L., (CV) .... '64 '89 C.1156 B.A. L.306 J.D. [Ⓐ Cohen&T.]
*PRACTICE AREAS: Civil Rights; Consumer Collections; Commercial Collections; Civil Litigation; Elder Law.
De Gennaro, Barbara L., (BV) .... '62 '88 33 Elizabeth St.
Donahue, Eileen A., (BV) .... '53 '78 C.562 B.A. L.93 J.D. 33 Elizabeth St.
Donahue, Laura J., (BV) .... '48 '73 C.788 A.B. L.184 J.D. [Donahue&A.]
Donahue & Allen, (BV) ....2nd New Haven Bk. Bldg.
Esposito, Gerard F., (BV) .... '52 '78 C.94 B.A. L.818 J.D. Asst. State's Atty.
Jalowiec, Matthew J. .... '74 '00 C.1156 B.A. L.1252 J.D. [Jalowiec&Z.]
Jalowiec & Zeck, LLC .... 90 Sodom Ln.
McEvoy, Sharlene A. ....'50 '75 C.19 B.A. L.184 J.D. 198 Emmett Ave.
McQuade, Francis J., (BV) ...... '40 '65 C.1030 B.S.S. L.184 LL.B. Sr. Asst. States Atty.
Micci, Eugene D. .... '45 '70 C.1030 B.A. L.94 J.D. 6 Elizabeth St.
Mongillo, Carmen J., (CV) .... '26 '53 C&L.184 B.A., LL.B. 8 Lombardi Dr.
Sabetta, Andrew, Jr., (CV) ....'54 '85 C.1156 B.S. L.1187 J.D. [Sabetta&S.]
Sabetta, Andrew D., (BV) .... '23 '50 C&L.976 B.A., J.D. [Sabetta&S.]
Sabetta & Sabetta, (BV) .... 111 New Haven Ave.
Sadek, William '52 '77
C.415 B.A. L.1048 J.D. Dir., Lower Naugatuck Valley Legal Servs.
Skowronski, Eugene A., (BV) ....'44 '75 C.309 A.B. L.93 J.D. [Skowronski&S.]
Skowronski, Theodore E., (BV) ....'47 '76 C.309 A.B. L.184 J.D. [Skowronski&S.]
Skowronski & Skowronski, (BV) ....7 Pershing Dr.
Smirnoff, Irving .... '25 '52 C&L.184 B.A., LL.B. 106 Elizabeth St.‡
Sylvester, Joseph H. .... '29 '53 C.588 L.93 J.D. Supr. Ct. J.
Thomas, Dominick J., Jr., (BV) ....'46 '71 C.321 B.A. L.893 J.D. [Cohen&T.]
*PRACTICE AREAS: Personal Injury; Medical Malpractice; Criminal Law; Domestic; Appellate Practice.
Thomas, Gregory M. .... '72 '99 C.1030 B.A. L.884 J.D. [Ⓐ Cohen&T.]
*PRACTICE AREAS: Criminal Law; Commercial Collections; Personal Injury; Juvenile Law; Civil Rights.
Vitello, Paul J. ....'54 '81 C.183 B.A. L.818 J.D. 273 Olivia St.
Volo, Richard A., (BV) .... '53 '78 C.976 B.A. L.94 J.D. 17 Elizabeth St.
Zeck, Mark R. .... '72 '00 C.1266 B.A. L.1252 J.D. [Jalowiec&Z.]

DURHAM, 5,143, *Middlesex Co.*

Bush, Milton W., Jr., (BV) .... '43 '69 C.477 B.A. L.213 J.D. 205 Tri-Mountain Rd.
Dahlmeyer, Fred D., (BV) ....'35 '65 C&L.472 B.B.A., LL.B. P.O. Box 52
Field, Howard B., III .... '36 '65 C.976 B.A. L.184 LL.B. 23R Carriage Dr.
Horn, Robert Seemann ....'45 '83 C.1102 M.L.S. L.1029 J.D. Rte. 9, Madison Rd.
Lucashu, Pamela M., (BV) ....'56 '84 C.972 B.A. L.1048 J.D. 72 Anna Trail

EAST GLASTONBURY, 24,327, *Hartford Co.*

Klock, Peter A. ....'43 '85 C.453 B.S. L.184 J.D. P.O. Box 36

EAST GRANBY, 4,102, *Hartford Co.*

Bickford, George B., (AV) .... '51 '78 C.309 B.A. L.184 J.D. 12 Church Rd.
Kraner, Neil W. .... '59 '95 C.165 B.A. L.306 J.D. 12 Church Rd.
Rainville, Peter J. '57 '96 C.326 B.S. L.818 J.D.
(adm. in MA; not adm. in CT; Pat.) Coun.
Ridgeway, Paul A., (BV) .... '41 '82 C&L.1048 B.M.E., J.D. 84 Old Country Rd.
Roznoy, Richard T. .... '44 '94 C.477 B.Mus. L.184 J.D. 59 Rainbow Rd.

EAST HADDAM, 4,621, *Middlesex Co.*

D'Addeo, Antonio M. .... '64 '95 C.184 B.S. L.1048 J.D. 72 Millington Rd.
Milardo, Terrence J., (BV) .... '41 '90 C.829 B.A. L.1252 J.D. 110 Boardman Rd.

EAST HAMPTON, 8,572, *Middlesex Co.*

Berkenstock, Jennifer L. .... '61 '89 C.67 B.A. L.184 J.D. 13 Viola Dr.
Brown, Paindiris & Scott, LLP, (AV)
42 East High Street (⊙Glastonbury, Hartford, Hebron, Stamford)
Grady, William D., (BV) ....'48 '79 C.608 B.S. L.1003 J.D. 8 W. High St.
LeMaire, Phyllis B. ....'41 '88 C.771 B.A. L.184 J.D. East Hampton Schools
Maxwell, John D., (BV) '52 '79
C.873 A.B. L.1035 J.D. [Brown,P.&S.] (⊙Glastonbury, Hartford)
Smith, Robert A. .... '39 '65 C.659 B.S. L.976 LL.B. 71 Bay St.‡

EAST HARTFORD, 52,563, *Hartford Co.*

Adams, Theodore M. ....'60 '95 C.454 B.B.A. L.184 J.D. Asst. Coun., Pratt & Whitney
Alair, Elise Frost ....'51 '83 C.165 B.A. L.1048 J.D. Dist. Coun., I.R.S.
Aletta, John ....'61 '87 C&L.184 B.A., J.D. I.R.S.

Alexander, Ralph J., (BV) '46 '73 C.882 B.A. L.1202 J.D.
330 Roberts Street, Suite 400, 06108-3694
Telephone: 860-289-5477 Fax: 860-291-9282
Email: bwa@snet.net
***PRACTICE AREAS: Administrative Law; Business Law; Commercial Law; Domestic Relations; Estates and Probate.**
General Trial Practice in all Courts, Real Estate, Trusts, Probate, Estate Planning, Business Law, Workers Compensation, Social Security Disability Claims, Municipal, Personal Injury, Family Law, Labor Relations Public Sector, Public Housing, Public Housing Law.

See Professional Biographies, EAST HARTFORD, CONNECTICUT

Arcari, Michael A., (CV) ....'34 '64 C&L.472 B.B.A., LL.B. 927 Burnside Ave.
Argazzi, Robert A., (AV) ....'38 '63 C.197 A.B. L.976 J.D. 400 Main Street‡
Austin, Thomas C., Jr., (BV) ....'53 '80 C.745 B.A. L.1029 J.D. [Gilman&M.]
*PRACTICE AREAS: Foreclosures Law; Litigation; Commercial Law; Criminal Law; Driving While Intoxicated.
Barall, Douglas T. .... '57 '88 C.1033 B.A. L.1048 J.D. [Leone,T.T.&N.]
*PRACTICE AREAS: Family Law; Personal Injury; Civil Litigation; Criminal Law; Divorce.
Barnsley, Kerry Duncan '60 '87 C.1049 B.B.A. L.1149 J.D.
(adm. in NH; not adm. in CT) [Ⓐ H.L.Schiff] (⊙Concord, NH)★
Barron, Stephen C., (BV) ....'42 '69 C.67 A.B. L.94 LL.B. 5 Central Ave.
Bashaw, Catherine F. '55 '82 C.1044 B.M. Ed. L.1040 J.D.
Assoc. Coun., Pratt & Whitney
Beach, Chester Paul, Jr. '54 '80 C.880 B.A. L.145 J.D.
(adm. in IL; not adm. in CT) V.P. and Gen. Coun., Pratt & Whitney

Behrens, Theresa A. ... '— '90 C.36 B.A. L.1029 J.D. 330 Roberts St.
Berek, Martha S. ... '67 '94 C.309 B.A. L.94 J.D. Asst. Coun., United Technologies Corp.
Best, Stephen C. ... '54 '82 C.102 B.A. L.184 J.D. I.R.S.
Blair, Cynthia A., (BV) ... '59 '85 C.321 B.A. L.184 J.D. Asst. Law Clk., Prob. Ct.
Boulton, Amy Fernand '72 '97 C.184 B.A. L.306 J.D.
Asst. Coun., United Technologies Research Ctr.
Bozek, Margaret M. ... '54 '99 C.19 B.A. L.184 J.D. [Kantor,M.&M.]
Bradrick, Roy B., (BV) ... '53 '84 C.184 B.A. L.1048 J.D. [H.L.Schiff]
*PRACTICE AREAS: Collection Law; Commercial Law; Subrogation.
Brennan, John D., III, (BV) ... '50 '84 C.1033 B.A. L.1048 J.D. 59 Burnside Ave.
Brennan, Kathleen M. ... '61 '87 C.1044 B.A. L.1194 J.D. 55 Hartland St.
Brennan, Peter L., (BV) ... '52 '85 C.183 B.A. L.1048 J.D. 59 Burnside Ave.
Breton, Michael P. ... '57 '83 C.184 B.S. L.588 J.D. U.S. Treasury Dept.
Brockett, Thomas M. ... '47 '92 C.918 B.A. L.306 J.D. 333 E. River Dr.
Bromson, Lois V. ... '25 '56 C.103 A.B. L.184 LL.B. 1291 Burnside Ave.‡
Bufford, Patrick H. ... '67 '92 C&L.215 B.S., J.D. Bentana Technologies
Byron, Robert E., Jr. ... '48 '90 C.15 B.S. L.184 J.D. F.D.I.C.
Carey, Robert S., Jr., (AV) ... '49 '76 C&L.184 B.A., J.D. [Gilman&M.]
*PRACTICE AREAS: Commercial Real Estate; Residential Real Estate; Title Matters; Mortgages.
Cavallari, Augustus I., Jr. ... '49 '74 C.676 B.A. L.818 J.D. 101 E. River Dr.
Ceccherini, Andrew R., Jr. ... '50 '79 C.184 B.S. L.1202 J.D. Sr. Tax Atty., I.R.S.
Chadwick, Scott R., (CV) ... '62 '87 C.1048 B.A. L.184 J.D. [Chadwick,L.&S.]
Chadwick, Libbey & Stone, (BV) ... 111 Founders Plaza, Suite 1403 (⊙Bristol)
Chavey, Mark E. ... '65 '92 C.197 A.B. L.94 J.D. United Technologies Corp.
Cheverie, Robert M., (BV) ... '50 '80 C.455 B.A. L.818 J.D. 333 E. River Dr.
Clifford, John F. ... '12 '53 C&L.184 LL.B. 17 Adams St.‡
Collins, Elizabeth F., (BV) '53 '79 C.855 B.A. L.184 J.D.
Asst. Bar Coun., Statewide Grievance Comm.
Collotta, Michael A. '53 '79 C.309 B.A. L.93 J.D.
(adm. in MA; not adm. in CT) Coun., Fed. Deposit Ins. Corp.
Cundall, Cheryl L. ... '62 '90 C.188 B.S. L.823 J.D. Assoc. Gen. Coun., Pratt & Whitney
Dorman, Erin A. ... '58 '84 C.829 B.A. L.705 J.D. Conn. Bk. & Tr. Co.
Dorman, Ira S. ... '38 '67 C.645 B.S.Ch.E. L.831 J.D. 330 Roberts St. (Pat.)
Doyle, Kevin M., (BV) '53 '84
C.184 B.S.E. L.93 J.D. Assoc. Gen. Coun., Pratt & Whitney
Duggan, Timothy J., (AVⓉ) ... '60 '85 C.676 B.A. L.588 J.D. [Duggan&C.] ⊙
Duggan & Caccavaro, (AVⓉ)
Suite 1403 111 Founders Plza. (⊙Boston, Norwood, MA; Providence, RI)
Engin, Mutahare Saritabak ... '61 '88 C.184 B.A. L.1029 J.D. IAE Intl. Aero Engines AG
Ertman, David F., (BV) ... '42 '74 C.1033 B.A. L.184 J.D. [Ⓐ H.L.Schiff]
*PRACTICE AREAS: Alternative Dispute Resolution; Civil Litigation; Children's Rights Law; Health Law.
Every, Judy R. ... '63 '92 C.882 B.A. L.1325 J.D. F.D.I.C.
Fatone, Toni M. ... '61 '87 C.184 B.A. L.362 J.D. 99 E. River Dr.
Fischer, Michael S., (BV) ... '60 '85 C.184 B.A. L.1019 J.D. 330 Roberts St. (⊙Avon)
Fizzarotti, Ronald V. '53 '88 C.1138 B.A. L.1009 J.D.
(adm. in NY; not adm. in CT) Fed. Deposit Ins. Corp.
Fleischhauer, Gene D. '42 '76 C.598 B.S.M.E. L.184 J.D.
Asst. Pat. Coun., United Technologies Corp. (Pat.)
Frattallone, Susan Ann ... '65 '90 C.1030 B.S. L.1048 J.D. F.D.I.C.
Fussell, John T. ... '53 '96 C.999 B.A. L.306 J.D. 333 E. River Dr.
Garner, Gregory J. '51 '76 C.499 B.S. L.500 J.D.
Dep. Coun., United Technologies Research Ctr.
Gately, Noelle ... '69 '97 C.128 B.A. L.818 J.D. 1406 Main St.

Gilman & Marks, (AV)
Two Riverview Square, 99 East Riverview Drive, 06108
Telephone: 860-282-0301 Fax: 860-289-3198
Email: gmatty@msn.com
Members of Firm: Robert S. Carey, Jr.; Thomas C. Austin, Jr.; Robert W. Heagney; J. Mark Silhavy.
General Practice. Real Estate, Tax and Probate Law, Trials, Corporation, Estate Planning, Zoning and Land Use, Employment Law, Criminal, Banking, Mortgage, Litigation, Mortgage Foreclosures, DUI, Civil Rights, Discrimination, Wrongful Termination, Sexual Harassment, Family and Medical Leave Act, Americans with Disabilities.
Reference: The Connecticut Bank & Trust Co.
See Professional Biographies, EAST HARTFORD, CONNECTICUT

Gindlin, Herbert M. '30 '59 C.563 B.B.A. L.309 LL.B.
(adm. in NY; not adm. in CT) V.P. & Coun., Home Life Ins. Co.
Goldschmidt, Daniel Jack '55 '82 C.178 B.A. L.569 J.D.
(adm. in NY; not adm. in CT) Sr. Atty., Fed. Deposit Ins. Corp.
Goodberg, George Barry, (CV) ... '51 '81 C.105 B.A. L.184 J.D. 440 Main St.
Graber-Lipperman, Peter J. '63 '91 C.188 B.S. L.569 J.D.
(adm. in NY; not adm. in CT)
Assistant Counsel, United Technologies Corp., Pratt & Whitney
Green, Randall W. '51 '81 C.502 B.S.B.A. L.309 J.D.
(adm. in WA; not adm. in CT) Asst. Gen. Coun., Pratt & Whitney
Gustafson, Steven R. '46 '70 C.350 B.A. L.352 J.D.
(adm. in IA; not adm. in CT) Chf. Pat. Coun., United Technologies Corp.
Heagney, Robert W., (BV) ... '53 '80 C.708 B.A. L.1029 J.D. [Gilman&M.]
*PRACTICE AREAS: Employment Law; Estates; Zoning, Planning and Land Use; Civil Litigation; Driving While Intoxicated.
Healy, John M. ... '54 '85 C.178 A.B. L.184 J.D. Chf. Legal Offr., Pratt & Whitney
Henn, Stephen K. '63 '94 C.145 B.A. L.184 J.D.
V.P. & CFO, Accent Color Sciences, Inc.
Herrick, Daniel P., (BV) '47 '73
C.732 B.A. L.188 J.D. Coun., United Technologies Research Ctr.
Holland, Peter M. ... '66 '94 C.1030 B.A. L.184 J.D. Asst. Coun., Pratt & Whitney
Horwitch, Daniel B., (BV) '53 '81 C.184 B.A. L.818 J.D.
Statewide Bar Coun., Statewide Grievance Committee
Intravia, Joseph ... '22 '50 32 Godar Terr.‡
Intravia, Sebastian A. ... '12 '36 C.264 B.A. L.94 LL.B. 32 Godar Terr.‡
Jacobs, Ira A., (BV) ... '— '91 C.1349 B.A. L.823 J.D. [Kantor,M.&M.]
Jacobs, Peter C. '60 '86 C.197 A.B. L.1068 J.D.
(adm. in PA; not adm. in CT) Fed. Deposit Ins. Corp.
Johnson, Bradford A. '46 '75 C.971 B.S.M.E. L.7 J.D.
(adm. in OH; not adm. in CT) Asst. Dist. Coun., I.R.S.
Johnson, Robert E., Jr., (BV) '59 '84
C.690 B.A. L.1029 J.D. [H.L.Schiff] (⊙Providence, RI)
*PRACTICE AREAS: Collection Law; Foreclosure; Negligence; Real Estate.
Kantor, Dennis N., (BV) ... '46 '72 C.4 B.B.A. L.184 J.D. [Kantor,M.&M.] ⊙
Kantor, Mickelson and Meyers, P.C., (BV) ... 330 Roberts Street, Suite 100 (⊙Avon)
Karlson, Roy V., (BV) ... '32 '57 C&L.184 B.A., LL.B. [Karlson&K.]
Karlson, Steven M. ... '70 '97 [Karlson&K.]
Karlson & Karlson, (BV) ... 28 Connecticut Blvd.
Kennedy, Patrick L., (BV) ... '61 '86 C.183 B.A. L.184 J.D. 5 Central Ave.
Kerrigan, Vanessa Griffith '61 '92
C&L.945 B.A., J.D. Asst. Coun., United Technologies Corp.
Kim, Ginny ... '68 '96 C.309 A.B. L.276 J.D. Asst. Coun., Pratt & Whitney
King, Hugh M. ... '39 '64 C.118 B.A. L.976 LL.B. Coun., F.D.I.C.
Klock, Susan Hallock ... '45 '76 C.914 B.A. L.184 J.D. 53 Connecticut Blvd.‡
Krasinski, Monica G. ... '64 '97 C.855 B.S. L.306 J.D. Pratt & Whitney Aircraft
Lapierre, Leon, (BV) ... '56 '83 C.550 B.S. L.184 J.D. F.D.I.C.
LaRocca, Paul J. ... '41 '65 C.855 A.B. L.188 LL.B. 82 Whiting Rd.
Laschever, Richard B., (CV) ... '29 '55 C.184 B.S. L.188 LL.B. 440 Main St.
Latino, Joseph P. ... '52 '87 C.454 B.A. L.1252 J.D. [Ⓐ H.L.Schiff]
*PRACTICE AREAS: Collections (80%); Landlord and Tenant Law (15%); Probate (5%).
Leone, Frank A., (BV) ... '49 '75 C.918 B.A. L.818 J.D. [Leone,T.T.&N.]
*PRACTICE AREAS: Civil and Criminal Litigation; Real Estate; Probate; Estate Planning; Business Law.
Leone, Valerie ... '75 '00 C.390 B.A. L.818 J.D. [Leone,T.T.&N.]
*PRACTICE AREAS: Civil Litigation; Criminal Litigation; Personal Injury; Real Estate; Estate Planning.
Leone, William A., (BV) ... '43 '69 C.918 B.A. L.184 J.D. [Leone,T.T.&N.]
*PRACTICE AREAS: Civil and Criminal Litigation; Real Estate; Estate Planning and Probate; Personal Injury; Business Law.

Leone, Throwe, Teller & Nagle, (BV)
33 Connecticut Boulevard, 06108
Telephone: 860-528-2145 Fax: 860-282-1539
Email: lttn@snet.net URL: http://www.lawyers.com/lttnlaw
Alvin C. Leone (1910-1986); John F. Nagle (1925-1997). Members of Firm: William A. Leone; Frank A. Leone; Adam J. Teller; Douglas T. Barall; Valerie Leone. Of Counsel: James H. Throwe.
General Trial Practice in all Courts. Real Estate, Trusts, Probate, Estate Planning, Workers Compensation, Municipal, Personal Injury, Family Law and Criminal Law, Divorce, Child Custody, Child Support, Juvenile Law, Business Law, Landlord/Tenant, Drunk Driving Defense.
Representative Clients: Holland Machine Co.; Safeco Insurance Companies.
See Professional Biographies, EAST HARTFORD, CONNECTICUT

Libbey, Morton H., Jr., (BV) ... '60 '85 C.321 B.A. L.818 J.D. [Chadwick,L.&S.] ⊙
Link, Leslie Ann ... '49 '98 C.1505 B.A. L.184 J.D. [Kantor,M.&M.]
Lockard, Frank P., (CV) ... '19 '55 C.597 B.S. L.184 J.D. 209 High St.
Long, Joseph F., III, (BV) ... '53 '78 C.184 B.A. L.45 J.D. Spec. Asst. U.S. Atty.
MacKinnon, Stephen J. ... '62 '92 C.184 B.A. L.1029 J.D. 991 Main St.
Marino, John W., Jr., (BV) ... '39 '64 C.67 B.A. L.188 LL.B. 1011 Main St.
Marum, Robert E. '40 '72 C.455 B.S. L.94 J.D.
(adm. in MA; not adm. in CT) I.R.S.
McCusker, Karen C. '64 '91
C.550 B.A. L.276 J.D. Asst. Coun., United Technologies Corp.
McFadden, Kathleen M. ... '53 '93 C.966 B.S. L.184 J.D. Coun., Pratt & Whitney
Meyers, Linda B., (BV) ... '58 '84 C.588 B.S. L.93 J.D. [Kantor,M.&M.] ⊙
Meyers, Robert M. ... '46 '71 C.976 B.S. L.306 J.D. [Kantor,M.&M.]
Mickelson, Jeffrey D., (BV) ... '54 '82 C.260 B.A. L.1206 J.D. [Kantor,M.&M.] ⊙
Morrison, F. Tyler, III ... '66 '91 C.228 B.S.E. L.184 J.D. United Tech. Corp.
Moylan, Christopher T. ... '59 '90 C.67 B.A. L.1048 J.D. [H.L.Schiff]
*PRACTICE AREAS: Bankruptcy; Collection Law; Commercial Law; Creditors' Rights; Negligence.
Nelson, Andréa Laurena '70 '96 C&L.94 B.A., J.D.
(adm. in MA; not adm. in CT) Asst. Coun., Pratt & Whitney
Ngobeni, Paul Mpande ... '60 '89 C.299 B.A. L.569 J.D. 914 Main St.
Novotny, Norman E. '38 '66 C.363 B.S.B.A. L.1003 J.D.
V.P. & Gen. Coun., Travel Insured International, Inc.
Oestreicher, Karen ... '59 '84 C.188 B.A. L.184 J.D. United Technologies Corp.
Olshan, Adam J. ... '66 '91 C.976 B.A. L.93 J.D. [H.L.Schiff]
*PRACTICE AREAS: Collection Law; Commercial Law; Creditors Rights; Health Care Collections; Workers Compensation Law.
Oulundsen, Donald C. ... '46 '74 C&L.184 B.A., J.D. Assoc. Coun., Pratt & Whitney
Piscitelli, Robert J. ... '64 '89 C&L.184 B.A., J.D. [Kantor,M.&M.]
Ramsey, Virginia L., (BV) ... '54 '82 C&L.184 B.S., J.D. 212 Naubuc Ave.
Revis, Stephen E. '43 '72 C.860 B.S.M.E. L.184 J.D.
Intell. Prop. Coun., United Technologies Research Ctr. (Pat.)
Rhodes, Judith D. '64 '95 C.201 B.A. L.200 J.D.
(adm. in NE; not adm. in CT) Cigna Healthcare
Romanik, George J. '59 '90
C.401 B.S.Ch.E. L.184 J.D. Asst. Pat. Coun., Pratt & Whitney (Pat.)
Sanders, Karen J. ... '63 '88 C.879 B.A. L.184 J.D. [Serignese,P.&Z.]
Santos, Joseph A. '59 '86 C.321 B.A. L.93 J.D.
(adm. in MA; not adm. in CT)
Associate General Counsel, United Technologies Corporation
Schiff, Howard Lee, (BV) ... '33 '58 C.918 B.A. L.188 J.D. [Ⓒ H.L.Schiff]
*PRACTICE AREAS: Collection Law; Commercial Law; Creditors' Rights; Negligence; Subrogation.

Schiff, Howard Lee, P.C., Law Offices, (BV)
510 Tolland Street, P.O. Box 280245, 06128-0245 ⊙
Telephone: 860-528-9991, Toll Free: 800-ATTY-HLS Fax: 860-528-7602
Email: newclaim@hlschiffpc.com URL: http://www.hlschiffpc.com
Roy B. Bradrick; Robert E. Johnson, Jr. (Also Member of Providence, Rhode Island Office); Christopher T. Moylan; Adam J. Olshan;—Stephen A. Wiener; David F. Ertman; Douglas F. Jennings; Harry Joseph Theodoss; Joseph P. Latino; Carl Brugnoli (Not admitted in CT; Resident, Worcester, Massachusetts Office); Jessica Ellicott; Kerry Duncan Barnsley (Not admitted in CT). Of Counsel: Howard Lee Schiff.
Collection Law (Retail and Commercial), Commercial Law, Creditor's Rights, Creditor Bankruptcy, Enforcement of Judgement, Foreclosures, Subrogation in the entire New England region.
Representative Clients: Chase Manhattan Bank; AT&T Universal Card Services; Sears Roebuck & Co.; General Electric Capital Corp; Connecticut State Employees Credit Union; Connecticut Student Loan Foundation; Aetna Life & Casualty; Yankee Gas; University of Connecticut Health Center-John Dempsey Hospital.
Reference: Connecticut National Bank.
Worcester, Massachusetts Office: 340 Main Street, Suite 959. Telephone: 508-753-9991. Fax: 508-753-0260.
Providence, Rhode Island Office: 10 Dorrance Street, Suite 515. Telephone: 401-861-9991. Fax: 401-861-0246.
Augusta, Maine Office: 150 State Street, 04330. Telephone: 207-621-9991. Fax: 207-621-1819.
Concord, New Hampshire Office: 36 Warren Street, Suite 1, P.O. Box 2372, 03302. Telephone: 603-228-4444. Fax: 603-228-6644.
Rutland, Vermont Office: 1 Scale Avenue, Suite 112, 05071. Telephone: 802-775-3988. Fax: 802-773-9990.
See Professional Biographies, EAST HARTFORD, CONNECTICUT

Schneeberger, Stephen A. '38 '67 C.260 B.E.E. L.446 LL.B.
Asst. Intell. Prop. Coun., United Technologies Research Ctr. (Pat.)
Sellman, Richard I., (BV) ... '50 '74 C.401 B.S. L.184 J.D. [Kantor,M.&M.] ⊙
Serignese, Nicholas F., (BV) ... '43 '74 C.708 B.A. L.184 J.D. [Serignese,P.&Z.]
Serignese, Petrone & Zipfel, (BV) ... 59 Burnside Ave.
Sessa, Daniel M. ... '64 '89 C.1349 B.A. L.1019 J.D. United Technologies Corp.
Severni, William J., (BV) ... '52 '78 C.31 B.A. L.184 J.D. [Kantor,M.&M.]
Silhavy, J. Mark ... '55 '81 C.319 B.A. L.1029 J.D. [Gilman&M.]
*PRACTICE AREAS: Commercial Real Estate; Residential Real Estate; Probate; Estate Planning; Corporate Law.
Silver, Meryl '50 '75 C.696 B.A. L.982 J.D.
(adm. in NY; not adm. in CT) I.R.S.
Smith, Murdo T. ... '70 '95 C.1030 B.A. L.1048 J.D. [Ⓐ Chadwick,L.&S.]
Stolp, Loren P. '47 '79 C.645 B.S. L.184 J.D.
V.P. and Dep. Gen. Coun., Pratt & Whitney

Stone, Raymond E., Jr. '42 '78 C.871 B.S. L.184 J.D.
Group. Dep. Coun., Pratt & Whitney
Straceski, Laura M. . . . .'60 '86 C.918 B.A. L.184 J.D. 31 Eleanor Rd.
Sward, James R. . . . . '46 '83 C.184 B.A. L.1048 J.D. 59 Burnside Ave.
Swiatocha, John '50 '77
C.688 B.S.M.E. L.276 J.D. Intell. Prop. Coun., Pratt & Whitney (Pat.)
Swigert, Stephen B. '49 '74 C.31 A.B. L.309 J.D.
(adm. in NY; not adm. in CT) Coun., Pratt & Whitney
Teller, Adam J., (BV) . . . . '63 '87 C&L.309 A.B., J.D. [Leone,T.T.&N.]
*PRACTICE AREAS: Civil and Criminal Litigation; Personal Injury; Drunk Driving Defense; Family Law; Divorce.
Thompson, David L., (BV) . . . . '52 '77 C.608 B.A. L.1048 J.D. 135 Burnside Ave.
Thorpe, Gerald A. '45 '76 C&L.378 B.S., J.D.
(adm. in KS; not adm. in CT) Dist. Coun.
Throwe, James H., (AV) . . . .'30 '57 C&L.184 B.A., LL.B. [Leone,T.T.&N.]
*PRACTICE AREAS: Civil and Criminal Litigation; Family Law; Divorce; Child Custody.
Valencia, Melinda S. . . . .'52 '78 C.299 B.A. L.569 J.D. 400 Main St.
Vartelas, John J. . . . . '56 '81 C.184 B.A. L.818 J.D. F.D.I.C.
Vignati, Francis C., (BV) . . . . '27 '53 C.855 B.A. L.184 J.D. [Vignati&V.]
Vignati, Francis C., Jr., (BV) . . . . '53 '80 C.1030 B.A. L.1029 J.D. [Vignati&V.]
Vignati & Vignati, P.C., (BV) . . . . 621 Burnside Ave.

Whelton, Michael J., (BV) '47 '75 C.1155 B.S.B.A. L.818 J.D.
111 Founders Plaza Seventeenth Floor, 06108
Telephone: 860-289-9358 Fax: 860-289-6210
Email: attorneymwelton@snet.net
General Practice. Trials in all State and Federal Courts. Personal Injury, Criminal, Municipal, Zoning, Family, Divorce, Probate, Wills, and Real Estate Law.
See Professional Biographies, EAST HARTFORD, CONNECTICUT

Whiston, Richard M., (AV) . . . . '44 '68 C.659 B.S. L.309 J.D. 400 Main Street‡
Wiener, Stephen A., (BV) . . . . '47 '79 C.103 A.B. L.184 J.D. [H.L.Schiff]
*PRACTICE AREAS: Bankruptcy; Collection Law; Commercial Law; Creditor's Rights; Mortgage Law.
Wilson, F. Scott '56 '81 C.970 B.A. L.161 J.D.
(adm. in OH; not adm. in CT) Assoc. Coun., Pratt & Whitney
Winkler, Steven H. '46 '71 C.867 B.A. L.477 J.D.
Senior Vice President, Fidelity National Title Insurance Co.
Witter, Dwayne A. '43 '76 C.197 A.B. L.1035 J.D.
(adm. in MN; not adm. in CT)
Assoc. Coun. & Dir., Export/Import Compl., Pratt & Whitney
Woolf, Brian J. . . . .'47 '77 C.999 B.A. L.184 J.D. [B.J.Woolf]

Woolf, Brian J., LLC, The Law Offices of
50 Founders Plaza, 06108-3209
Telephone: 860-290-8690 Fax: 860-290-8697
Email: woolflaw@rcn.com URL: http://www.lawyers.com/woolf
Brian J. Woolf.
Criminal Defense, State and Federal, (including White Collar), Motor Vehicle and DUI's, Civil Litigation including Major Personal Injury and Negligence Matter, Family Law, Divorce, Child Custody, Banking (New Charters Only), Real Estate and Commercial Loan Workouts.
See Professional Biographies, EAST HARTFORD, CONNECTICUT

Zachary, Stephen '55 '80 C&L.838 B.S., J.D.
(adm. in TN; not adm. in CT) FDIC
Zipfel, David A., (BV) . . . .'51 '77 C&L.184 B.A., J.D. [Serignese,P.&Z.]

EAST HAVEN, 25,028, *New Haven Co.*

Acampora, John A., (BV) . . . . '44 '69 C.1252 B.S. L.818 J.D. [Cohen&A.] ⊙
*PRACTICE AREAS: General Civil and Criminal Litigation; Personal Injury Law; Products Liability Law; Environmental Law; Real Estate Law.
Albis, Michael A., (BV) . . . .'53 '78 C.976 B.A. L.184 J.D. Town Atty.
Amendola, Andrew M., (BV) . . . . '50 '76 C&L.184 B.A., J.D. 591 Thompson Ave.
Cohen, Edward W., (AV) . . . . '12 '37 C&L.976 B.S., LL.B. [Cohen&A.]
*PRACTICE AREAS: General Practice.
Cohen, Linda D. '41 '83 C.04 B.A. L.1040 J.D.
(adm. in NY; not adm. in CT) 72 Cosey Beach Ave.

Cohen and Acampora, (BV)
8 Frontage Road, P.O. Box 190, 06512 ⊙
Telephone: 203-467-7337 Telecopier: 203-468-7865
Members of Firm: John A. Acampora; Gary W. Stegina; David L. Weiss; Frank S. Marcucci. Of Counsel: Edward W. Cohen.
General Civil and Criminal Practice before State and Federal Courts. Personal Injury, Litigation, Products Liability, Environmental, Real Estate, Zoning, Acquisitions and Development, Probate, Estate Planning, Workers Compensation, Domestic Relations, Foreclosure, Bankruptcy, Insolvency, Maritime Law, Real Estate, Tax Appeals, Business, Commercial and Corporation Law.
New Haven, Connecticut Office: 109 Church Street. Telephone: 203-624-4126.
See Professional Biographies, EAST HAVEN, CONNECTICUT

Cote, William W., (BV) . . . . '57 '86 C.1156 B.A. L.1252 J.D. 305 South End Road
Couto, Tracey Pascale . . . . '70 '96 C.690 B.A. L.1252 J.D. [A.J.Zullo]
Crisci, Louis A., Jr. . . . .'64 '91 C.262 B.A. L.1029 J.D. [Kolb&C.]
Crow, David E., Jr. . . . .'69 '94 C.184 B.A. L.1029 J.D. [Kolb&C.]
De Mayo, Anthony V. . . . .'24 '51 C.976 B.A. L.184 J.D. Supr. J.
Flanagan, Robert C. . . . .'30 '63 C.184 B.S. L.564 LL.B. Ret. Supr. Ct. J.
Gallagher, Charles P. . . . . '26 '52 C&L.276 B.S., J.D. 204 Maple St.
Giaimo, Thomas J., (BV) . . . .'37 '62 C.321 B.S. L.184 LL.B. 9 Thomas Ct.‡
Grillo, John T., (BV) . . . .'48 '76 C.385 B.A. L.1170 J.D. 845 Foxon Rd.
Jacks, Kenneth M., (BV) . . . .'40 '65 C&L.184 B.S., LL.B. [Sohcot&J.]
Kamerling, Joanne M. '47 '81 C.446 B.A. L.724 J.D.
(adm. in NY; not adm. in CT) 173 Russo Ave.‡
Kolb, Frank J., Jr., (BV) . . . .'47 '81 C.1252 B.A. L.1029 J.D. [Kolb&C.]
Kolb & Crisci, P.C., (BV) . . . . 49 High St.
Marcucci, Frank S., (BV) . . . . '57 '82 C.1156 B.S. L.1048 J.D. [Cohen&A.]
*PRACTICE AREAS: Civil Trial Litigation; Domestic Relations; Personal Injury Litigation.
Nuzzo, Raymond A. . . . .'60 '92 C.1030 B.A. L.1029 J.D. 65 Osmond St.
Riccio, Arthur R., Jr., (BV) . . . .'49 '75 C.867 B.A. L.472 J.D. 310 Main St.
Sohcot and Jacks, (BV) . . . . 422 Main St.
Stegina, Gary W., (BV) . . . .'55 '80 C.1156 B.S. L.161 J.D. [Cohen&A.]
*PRACTICE AREAS: Commercial and Residential Real Estate Law; Business and Corporate Law; Mergers and Acquisitions Law; General Practice.
Weiss, David L., (BV) . . . . '63 '88 C.145 B.A. L.910 J.D. [Cohen&A.]
*PRACTICE AREAS: Real Estate; Civil Litigation; Commercial Litigation; Condemnation; Tax Appeals.
Zullo, Alfred J., (BV) . . . .'57 '84 C.1156 B.S. L.1048 J.D. [A.J.Zullo]
Zullo, Alfred J., & Associates, LLC, Law Offices of, (BV) . . . . 83 Main St.

EAST LYME, 13,870, *New London Co.*

Mattern, James E., (BV) . . . . '51 '76 C.321 A.B. L.184 J.D. 22 Village Dr.
Santoro, Anne R. . . . .'56 '83 C.813 B.A. L.184 J.D. 11 Rose Lane‡

Stevens, Harris & Guernsey, P.C.
(See Niantic)

EASTON, 5,962, *Fairfield Co.*

Herzog, Barbara N. . . . . '54 '80 C.273 B.A. L.1009 J.D. P.O. Box 434
Kivell, Britta K., (BV) . . . .'57 '83 C.1044 B.A. L.990 J.D. 15 High Ridge Rd.
Lieb, Charles H. . . . .'07 '31 C.659 B.S. L.262 LL.B. 65 Redding Rd.‡
Luckhardt, Philip G. . . . .'30 '76 C.273 B.S. L.178 J.D. 20 Ridgeway St.‡
Michelson, Herman A. . . . . . '30 '57 C.569 B.I.E. L.184 LL.B. 12 Princess Pine Ln. (Pat.)‡
Salemme-Riccio, Cynthia M. . . . .'65 '92 C.1156 B.A. L.1029 J.D. 125 Maple Rd.
Stone, Huntley J. . . . .'50 '76 C.674 A.B. L.94 J.D. 895 Sport Hill Rd.‡

ELLINGTON, 9,711, *Tolland Co.*

Allen, Steven M. . . . .'59 '87 C.183 B.A. L.818 J.D. Maple St.
Best-Parris, Karen . . . . '65 '92 C.66 B.A. L.306 J.D. 185 W. Rd.
Draghi, Brenda A., (BV) . . . . '39 '70 C&L.184 B.S., J.D. 18 Main St.
Fader, Bruce P., (BV) . . . .'53 '86 C.705 B.A. L.46 J.D. 11 Woodmar Circle
Kumiega, Bonnie Drumm . . . .'63 '91 C.184 B.A. L.1048 J.D. [Robertson&K.]
Richert, Cara S., (BV) . . . . '60 '86 C.588 B.S. L.184 J.D. 159 Crystal Lake Rd.
Robertson & Kumiega, LLC . . . . .185 West Rd.
Sandberg, Kevin C. . . . .'69 '94 185 W. Rd.
Sherman, James W., (BV) . . . . '28 '59 C.860 A.B. L.30 LL.B. 185 W. Rd.
Thiesing, Robert A. . . . .'45 '79 C.021 B.S. L.1048 J.D. 67 Kibbe Rd.

ENFIELD, 42,695, *Hartford Co.*

Adams, John D., (BV) . . . . '33 '59 C.976 B.A. L.184 LL.B. [Adams&E.]
*PRACTICE AREAS: Real Property; Municipal Law; Zoning Law; Family and Matrimonial; Commercial Law.

Adams & Eliason
69 High Street, 06082-3509
Telephone: 860-745-1659
Members of Firm: Deborah W. A. Eliason. Of Counsel: John D. Adams.
General Practice. Family Law, Children, Civil Litigation, Commercial Law, Real Estate, Wills, Trusts & Estates, Bankruptcy, Municipal Law, Zoning Law.
See Professional Biographies, ENFIELD, CONNECTICUT

Alaimo, Charles B., (BV) . . . . '28 '53 C.229 B.A. L.94 J.D. 707 Enfield St.
Alaimo, James J., Jr., (BV) . . . .'42 '67 C.184 B.A. L.818 J.D. P.O. Box 1120
Angelica, Santa C., (BV) . . . .'56 '81 C.676 B.A. L.184 J.D. 64 Palomba Dr.
Arakas, Peter, (AV) '49 '84 C.107 B.A. L.184 J.D.
General Counsel Americas, Lego Systems Inc.
Arvantely, Thomas P., (BV) . . . .'39 '67 C.855 B.S. L.1292 LL.B. 64 Palomba Dr.
Barbieri, T. Mark, (BV) . . . .'43 '76 C.644 B.A. L.1048 J.D. [Fallon,B.&K.]
Bergamini, Mary T., (BV) . . . . '60 '91 C.1048 B.A. L.1202 J.D. [Berger&S.]
Berger, Robert B., (AV) . . . . '24 '52 C.276 B.S.F.S. L.184 J.D. [Berger&S.]
Berger & Santy, P.C., (AV) . . . . 709 Enfield St.
Blaney, Michael C., (BV) . . . . '44 '69 C&L.184 B.A., J.D. 74 Palomba Dr.
Cerrato, John, (BV) . . . . '37 '77 C.28 B.S. L.1048 J.D. 5300 Bigelow Commons
Cohen, Rudolph . . . .'42 '82 C.999 B.S. L.184 J.D. 6 The Hamlet
DeBell, Richard S. . . . . '27 '88 C.453 S.B. L.1048 J.D. 4 Crescent Beach Dr.‡
Demers, Ronald F., (BV) . . . .'47 '84 C.588 B.S. L.1048 J.D. 308 Enfield St.
DuBoff, Keith B., (BV) . . . .'52 '78 C.228 A.B. L.1003 J.D. Asst. States Atty.
Eliason, Deborah W. A. . . . . '56 '83 C.860 B.A. L.184 J.D. [Adams&E.]
*PRACTICE AREAS: Family Law; Children; Civil Litigation; Commercial Law; Real Estate.
Faille, Christopher C. '58 '82 C.1266 B.A. L.1048 J.D. 25 Aloha Dr.
Fallon, Joseph E., (BV) . . . . '46 '73 C.262 B.A. L.184 J.D. [Fallon,B.&K.]
Fallon, Barbieri & Kissel, P.C., (BV) . . . . 308 Enfield St.
Felicetti, Elinor '36 '87 C.66 B.A. L.1048 J.D.
(adm. in MA; not adm. in CT) 94 The Laurels‡
Feola, Eugene David '48 '74 C.563 B.A. L.472 J.D.
(adm. in FL; not adm. in CT) V.P. & Gen. Coun., Casual Corner Grp., Inc.
Fukuda, Tsuyoshi . . . .'71 '01 C.321 B.A. L.184 J.D. 3107 Bigelow Commons
Kissel, John A., (BV) . . . . '59 '84 C.184 B.S.Ed. L.1048 J.D. [Fallon,B.&K.]
Locario, Elizabeth J., (BV) . . . . '51 '86 C.184 B.S. L.1048 J.D. [Tyler&T.]
Loconsolo, John M., Jr. . . . .'46 '87 C.454 B.A. L.1252 J.D. 146 High St.
Malone, John H., (BV) . . . . . .'43 '74 C.708 B.A. L.184 J.D. Supervisary Asst. State's Atty.
McDonald, William F. . . . . '29 '66 C.1033 B.S. L.184 LL.B. 1052 Enfield St.
Ovian, Douglas A., (BV) . . . .'60 '89 C.321 A.B. L.1048 J.D. Asst. Pub. Def.
Paperny, Alan K. . . . . .'60 '87 C.164 B.A. L.94 J.D. Corp. Coun., Casual Corner Grp., Inc.
Parakilas, Charles M., (BV) . . . . '27 '57 C.184 B.A. L.94 LL.B. 341 Hazard Ave.
Poitras, Alison Faltersack '65 '91
C.966 B.A. L.365 J.D. Corp. Coun., Casual Corner Grp., Inc.
Rokosz, Roseann . . . .'62 '97 C.1374 B.A. L.94 J.D. Corp. Coun., Casual Corner Grp., Inc.
Santy, Frank G., (BV) . . . . '42 '75 C.93 A.B. L.1048 J.D. [Berger&S.]
Schober, Leroy E. . . . . '24 '57 C.659 B.S. L.184 J.D. 6 Hillcrest Rd.‡

Skoler, Abbott & Presser, P.C.
(See Springfield, Massachusetts)

Stavropoulos, Maria N. . . . .'58 '83 C.999 B.A. L.1048 J.D. 820 Enfield St.
Tatoian, Richard M., (BV) . . . .'46 '76 C.1033 B.A. L.184 J.D. 1106 Enfield St.
Tyler, Russell J., (BV) . . . .'50 '74 C.103 A.B. L.184 J.D. [Tyler&T.]
Tyler, Thomas J., (BV) . . . .'46 '73 C.321 B.A. L.184 J.D. [Tyler&T.]
Tyler & Tyler, (BV) . . . . 92 High St.
Warner, Susan L. . . . .'53 '83 C.231 B.A. L.1048 J.D. 20 Tyler Rd.

ESSEX, 5,078, *Middlesex Co.*

Beccaro, William P. . . . .'57 '90 C.184 B.A. L.602 J.D. 12 New City St.
Bennet, Helen B. . . . .'53 '85 C.951 B.A. L.184 J.D. [Gould,L.B.W.&M.]
*PRACTICE AREAS: Estate Planning Law; Probate Law.
Bennet, John S., (BV) . . . . '51 '77 C.30 B.A. L.1170 J.D. [Gould,L.B.W.&M.]
*PRACTICE AREAS: Civil Law; Commercial Litigation; Banking Law; Municipal Law; Planning and Zoning Law.

Carlisle, Jonathan D., (BV) '42 '68 C.976 B.A. L.184 LL.B.
67 Main Street, Center Brook, P.O. Box 800, 06426 ⊙
Telephone: 203-629-9600
Wills and Estate Planning, Taxation, Trust and Estate Administration, Contested Probate Matters, Residential and Investment Real Estate, Land Use and Zoning Law.
Greenwich Office: 125 Mason Street, 06830. Telephone: 203-629-9600. Fax: 203-629-9072.
See Professional Biographies, ESSEX, CONNECTICUT

Carr, H. Judson, (BV) . . . .'34 '64 C.105 B.S. L.1017 J.D. 145 Dennison Road
Carta, John J., Jr., (BV) . . . . '44 '69 C.918 B.A. L.306 J.D. 11 N. Main St.
Charbonnier, Peter H. . . . .'61 '91 C.197 B.A. L.184 J.D. A is A, Ltd.
Cline, Stephen R., (CV) . . . . '63 '88 C.105 B.A. L.1017 J.D. 145 Dennison Road
Douglas, Linda Trombly, (BV) . . . . '62 '87 C.550 B.A. L.1048 J.D. 145 Dennison Road
Galiette, Robert J. . . . .'50 '81 C.1200 B.S. L.184 J.D. 3 Teal Lane

Gould, Larson, Bennet, Wells & McDonnell, P.C., (AV)
Essex Savings Bank Building, 35 Plains Road, P.O. Box 959, 06426
Telephone: 860-767-9055 Fax: 860-767-2742 URL: http://www.gould-larson.com
URL: http://www.lawyers.com/glbw&m

(This Listing Continued)

Gould, Larson, Bennet, Wells & McDonnell, P.C. (Continued)

James H. Gould (1911-1985); John E. Larson; John S. Bennet; Michael J. Wells; Kenneth J. McDonnell; Helen B. Bennet.
General Practice in all Courts. Real Estate, Zoning, Family, Bankruptcy, Banking, Probate, Corporation Law, Estate Planning and Taxation, and Personal Injury Law, Trials, Appeals, Domestic Relations, Municipal Law and Land Use Law, Insurance Defense, Elder Law, Arbitration and Mediation.
Representative Clients: Town of Clinton; Essex Savings Bank.
See Professional Biographies, ESSEX, CONNECTICUT

Hudson, W. Campbell, III, (BV) .... '51 '76 C&L.861 B.A., J.D. [Hudson&K.]
*PRACTICE AREAS: Real Property; Estate Planning; Probate; Municipal Law; Land Use Law.

Hudson and Kilby, (BV)
78 Main Street, Centerbrook Village, P.O. Box 398, 06426
Telephone: 860-767-0195 Fax: 860-767-7077
Email: hudson.kilby@snet.net URL: http://www.lawyers.com/hudsonandkilby
Members of Firm: W. Campbell Hudson, III; Marianne B. Kilby; Suzanna Urban; Cynthia M. Offredi.
General Practice. Probate, Estate Planning, Real Estate, Zoning and Land Use, Taxation, Business Organizations, and Municipal.
Reference: Fleet Bank.
See Professional Biographies, ESSEX, CONNECTICUT

Kilby, Marianne B., (BV) .... '35 '79 C.66 B.A. L.184 J.D. [Hudson&K.]
*PRACTICE AREAS: Estate Planning; Probate; Real Property; Taxation; Elder Law.
Larson, John E., (AV) .... '24 '53 C.31 A.B. L.309 LL.B. [Gould,L.B.W.&M.]
*PRACTICE AREAS: Estate Planning Law; Probate Law; Real Estate Law.
Larson, Robert J., (BV) .... '55 '82 C.882 B.A. L.818 J.D. 35 Plains Rd.
McDonnell, Kenneth J., (BV) .... '58 '83 C.93 B.A. L.184 J.D. [Gould,L.B.W.&M.]
*PRACTICE AREAS: Personal Injury Law; Civil Litigation Law; Domestic Relations; Environmental Law.
Morano, Christopher L. .... '55 '81 C.184 B.A. L.1202 J.D. P.O. Box 84
Offredi, Cynthia M. .... '70 '97 C.25 L.1040 J.D. [Hudson&K.]
*PRACTICE AREAS: Estate Planning; Probate; Land Use; Real Estate.
Phillips, Laurel Gilbert '51 '87 C.112 B.A. L.809 J.D.
(adm. in CA; not adm. in CT) 10 Meigs Ln.
Rafal, John W. .... '49 '75 C.184 B.A. L.831 J.D. Pres., John W. Rafal & Assoc., Inc.
Rieder, Richard E., (BV) .... '37 '61 C.477 A.B. L.893 LL.B. [Senning&R.]
*PRACTICE AREAS: Corporate; Probate/Estate Planning.
Scala, James R. '48 '75 C.276 A.B. L.178 J.D.
(adm. in NY; not adm. in CT) P.O. Box 636‡
Senning, John L., (BV) .... '43 '70 C.882 B.A. L.1294 J.D. [Senning&R.]
*PRACTICE AREAS: Admiralty; Marine Law; Corporate; Probate/Estate Planning; Administration.

Senning & Rieder, (BV)
16 Saybrook Road, 06426
Telephone: 860-767-2618 Fax: 860-767-2740
Email: jlssealaw@aol.com URL: http://www.lawyers.com/senningriederlaw
Members of Firm: John L. Senning; Richard E. Rieder.
General Practice. Trial and Appellate Practice in all State and Federal Courts, Admiralty, Litigation, Corporate, Estate Planning and Administration, Real Estate and Business Law.
See Professional Biographies, ESSEX, CONNECTICUT

Sheehan, Judith Marie ... '— '95 C.540 B.S. L.1252 J.D. Pres., Legal & Health Issues, Inc.

Stichter, John A., (AVⓉ) '34 '61 C.597 B.S. L.477 LL.B.
15 Nott Lane, P.O. Box 412, 06426 ⊙
Telephone: 860-767-9173 Telecopier: 860-767-8584
Email: jstichter@excelonline.com URL: http://www.lawyers.com/jastichterlaw
***PRACTICE AREAS: Estate Planning; Estate Administration; Real Estate; Corporate Law; Civil Litigation.**
General Practice, Civil Trials and Appeals in State and Federal Courts. Litigation, Arbitration, Trust, Estate, Probate, Estate Planning, Real Estate and Corporation Law.
New York, New York Office: 641 Lexington Avenue, 18th Floor. Telephone: 212-751-3488. Telecopier: 212-486-1600.
See Professional Biographies, ESSEX, CONNECTICUT

Stremlau, William M. .... '12 '40 C.184 L.306 LL.B. P.O. Box 402‡
Tredwell, Constance C. .... '29 '80 C.999 B.M. L.184 J.D. B-3 Heritage Cove
Urban, Suzanna .... '70 '96 C.910 A.B. L.831 J.D. [Hudson&K.]
*PRACTICE AREAS: Real Property; Land Use; Corporate Law; Probate.
Wells, Michael J., (BV) .... '56 '81 C.1048 B.A. L.1019 J.D. [Gould,L.B.W.&M.]
*PRACTICE AREAS: Real Estate Law; Probate Law; Planning and Zoning Law; Corporation Law; Municipal Law.

FAIRFIELD, 54,849, *Fairfield Co.*

Absher, Cecilia T. '62 '88 C.425 B.B.A. L.861 J.D.
(adm. in LA; not adm. in CT) Coun., Transactions & Fin., General Electric Company
*RESPONSIBILITIES: Mergers and Acquisitions; Corporate.
Adler, Bruce R. '53 '80 C.273 B.A. L.564 J.D.
Sr. EHS Coun., Envir. Opers., General Electric Comp.
Aiello, Sally A. .... '58 '86 C.66 A.B. L.262 J.D. 1119 Fairfield Beach Rd.
Aker, David '51 '82 C.186 B.S. L.724 J.D.
(adm. in NY; not adm. in CT; See Pat. Sect.) [Ⓐ Perman&G.]
*PRACTICE AREAS: Intellectual Property Matters.

Albert, Ward & Johnson, P.C.
(See Greenwich)

Ambrose, Peter, (BV) .... '44 '70 C.882 B.S. L.184 J.D. [Ambrose&C.]
Ambrose & Cohane, (BV) .... 1100 Kings Hwy. E.
Amendola, Bonnie L. .... '66 '92 C.659 B.A. L.184 J.D. [Amendola&A.]
*PRACTICE AREAS: Litigation; Matrimonial.
Amendola, Elaine S., (AV) .... '35 '62 C.914 B.A. L.976 LL.B. [Amendola&A.]
*PRACTICE AREAS: Matrimonial Law.

Amendola & Amendola, (AV)
A Limited Liability Co.
1248 Post Road, P.O. Box 237, 06430-0237
Telephone: 203-319-1143 Fax: 203-319-1196
Email: amrndolalaw@freewweb.com URL: http://www.lawyers.com/amendola&amendola
Members of Firm: Elaine S. Amendola; Bonnie L. Amendola.
Matrimonial Law, Family, Divorce, Child Custody, Domestic Relations and Litigation.
See Professional Biographies, FAIRFIELD, CONNECTICUT

Axiotis, Ares Demetrius '56 '96 C.309 B.A. L.564 J.D.
937 Post Rd. (⊙New York, NY)
Barnes, Peter A. '51 '81 C.575 A.B. L.976 J.D.
(adm. in DC; not adm. in CT) Tax Coun., Intl., General Electric Company
Barnes, William B., (BV) .... '52 '79 C.293 B.A. L.184 J.D. [Rosenstein&B.]
*PRACTICE AREAS: Employment; Litigation; Civil Litigation; Covenants Not To Compete Litigation; Appeals.
Bartiromo, Margaret A. .... '63 '92 C.331 B.A. L.178 J.D. [Ⓐ Jeffers&I.]
Beams, Mark '55 '83 C.197 A.B. L.276 J.D.
(adm. in DC; not adm. in CT) Tax Coun., Intl., General Electric Company
Bellitto, Rick R., (BV) .... '53 '79 C.1030 B.A. L.1202 J.D. 1210 Post Rd.
Bellitto, Robert B., (BV) .... '41 '67 C.1029 B.A. L.1009 J.D. 1495 Black Rock Tpke.
Beninati, John F. '64 '94
C.667 B.S.E.E. L.823 J.D. Patent Coun., General Electric Co. (Pat.)
Berkowitz, David S., (BV) .... '51 '76 C.823 B.S. L.472 J.D. 171 Bailey Rd.
Berkowitz, Robert J. '55 '80 C.94 B.S. L.813 J.D.
(adm. in CA; not adm. in CT) 171 Bailey Rd.‡
Bernardo, Manuel A. .... '45 '70 C&L.262 B.A., J.D. 3740 Black Rock Turnpike
Berrier, Erwin F., Jr. '38 '66 C.679 B.S.M.E. L.345 J.D.
(adm. in IN; not adm. in CT; Pat.) 3135 Easton Tpke.
Bien, Sherwood .... '42 '88 C.184 B.S. L.1040 J.D. 70 Brion Dr.
Blanchfield, James P. .... '68 '96 C.184 B.A. L.1252 J.D. [Ⓐ Quatrella&R.]
*PRACTICE AREAS: Litigation.
Boggs, Larry A. '45 '73 C.181 B.A. L.276 J.D.
(adm. in WV; not adm. in CT)
Coun., Envir. Leg. & Reg. Affairs, General Electric Company
Bologna, Michael T., (BV) .... '56 '81 C.321 B.A. L.184 J.D. [Fitzpatrick,F.&B.]
*PRACTICE AREAS: Personal Injury; Wetlands; Zoning; Real Estate; Wills.
Boyd, William H. .... '48 '82 C&L.184 B.A., J.D. 3197 North St.
Braunstein, Samuel L., (AV) .... '41 '69 C.838 B.S.B.A. L.744 J.D. [Braunstein&T.]
*PRACTICE AREAS: Taxation; Trusts and Estates; Estate Planning; Nonprofit and Charitable Organizations; Business Law.

Braunstein & Todisco, LLC, (AV) BR
One Eliot Place, 06430 ⊙
Telephone: 203-254-1118 Telecopier: 203-254-2453
URL: http://www.btlawfirm.com
Samuel L. Braunstein; Amy E. Todisco. Of Counsel: Roger L. Stavis (Not admitted in CT; Resident, New York, NY Office); Randy M. Kornfeld (Not admitted in CT; Resident, New York, NY Office); Frederick E. Schmidt (Resident, New York, NY Office).
Taxation, Business Law, Estate Planning, Elder Law, Trusts, Probate Administration and Probate Proceedings, Commercial Transactions and Real Estate.
Reference: People's Bank.
New York, New York Office: 820 Second Avenue, 4th Floor, 10017. Telephone: 212-557-6767. Telecopy: 212-557-3760.
See Professional Biographies, FAIRFIELD, CONNECTICUT

Breiner, Alexander, (BV) .... '48 '73 C.367 B.S. L.446 J.D. [Meyers B.&N.]
Brennan, Robert J., Jr., (BV) .... '43 '70 C.1030 B.A. L.1017 J.D. [Brennan,M.&B.] ⊙
Brennan, McNamara & Baldwin, P.C., (BV) .... 1243 Post Road (⊙Trumbull)

Brody, Wilkinson and Ober, P.C.
(See Southport)

Brown, Gary S. .... '58 '83 C.569 B.S. L.823 J.D. 1700 Post Rd.
Bruce, James '19 '47 C.178 B.A. L.309 LL.B.
(adm. in NY; not adm. in CT) 2680 Congress St.‡
Burke, Dominick F. .... '37 '64 C.156 B.A. L.276 LL.B. 1432 Post Rd.
Burwell, Jane E. Hugo .... '58 '87 C.184 B.A. L.1029 J.D. [Jontos&L.]
*PRACTICE AREAS: Insurance Defense; Municipal Law; Trial Practice; Appellate Practice.
Cantor, Brian S. .... '62 '87 C.454 B.S. L.1048 J.D. 1220 Post Rd.
Carolan, Cheryl Ann, (BV) .... '63 '89 C.829 B.S. L.1029 J.D. [Friedman,M.&N.]
Carstanjen, William C. '68 '95 C.112 B.A. L.178 J.D.
(adm. in NY; not adm. in CT)
Coun., Transactions & Finance, General Electric Company
Cartier, Susan G. .... '59 '95 C.823 B.S. L.1252 J.D. [Cartier&D.]
Cartier & DeMatteo, LLC .... 1100 Kings Hwy. E., Ste. 2B
Caruso, Daniel F., (BV) .... '57 '83 C.184 B.A. L.1194 J.D. [Owens,S.&N.] ⊙
*PRACTICE AREAS: Trusts and Estates; Real Estate; Small Business Law; General Practice.
Cassidy, Kieran S. '60 '86 C.433 B.A. L.1029 J.D.
Managing Attorney, Cassidy, Miolene & Mazza
Caulfield, Donald C. .... '42 '68 C.321 B.S. L.93 J.D. [Ⓒ Perman&G.] (See Pat. Sect.)
*PRACTICE AREAS: Patent, Trademark, Copyright.
Ceruzzi, Louis L., Jr., (BV) .... '53 '80 C.276 B.A. L.564 J.D. 1720 Post Rd.
Charmoy, Ira B., (BV) .... '41 '66 C&L.184 B.A., J.D. [I.B.Charmoy]
*PRACTICE AREAS: Debtor and Creditor; Bankruptcy; Civil Litigation; Business Litigation; Commercial Litigation.
Charmoy, Scott M. .... '70 '95 C.228 A.B. L.910 J.D. [Ⓐ I.B.Charmoy]
*PRACTICE AREAS: Debtor and Creditor; Civil Litigation; Business Litigation; Commercial Litigation; Commercial Real Estate.

Charmoy, Ira B., L.L.C., The Law Offices of, (BV)
1700 Post Road, Suite D-3, P.O. Box 745, 06430-0745
Telephone: 203-254-9393 Fax: 203-254-9797
Email: charmoy@snet.net URL: http://www.lawyers.com/charmoy
Ira B. Charmoy; Scott M. Charmoy.
Consumer and Business Bankruptcy, Commercial and General Civil Litigation, Entity Formation, Wills and Trusts, Probate, and Residential and Commercial Real Estate.
Reference: Webster Bank.
See Professional Biographies, FAIRFIELD, CONNECTICUT

Chaskin, Jay L. '37 '66 C.569 B.A. L.30 J.D.
(adm. in NY; not adm. in CT; Pat.) Assoc. Intl. Pat. Coun., General Electric Company
Chiota, John P., (BV) .... '43 '68 C.321 B.S. L.262 J.D. 1700 Post Rd.
Claydon, John M., Jr. .... '49 '77 C.93 B.S. L.262 J.D. 1216 Post Rd.
Clomiro, Richard T. .... '63 '90 C.999 B.S. L.1029 J.D. 1261 Post Rd.
Cohane, John K., (BV) .... '56 '83 C.1057 B.S.B.A. L.1029 J.D. [Ambrose&C.]
Coles, Kevin A., (BV) .... '47 '74 C.276 B.S.B.A. L.326 J.D. 1261 Post Rd.
Collimore, Donal C., (BV) .... '38 '62 C.321 A.B. L.184 LL.B. [Collimore&C.]
Collimore and Collimore, (BV) .... 1150 Post Road
Condon, Ann E. .... '56 '82 C.184 B.A. L.273 J.D. [General E.]
Connor, Colleen H. '60 '85 C.475 B.A. L.1194 J.D.
(adm. in NY; not adm. in CT)
Mgr. & Coun., Envir. Protec. Transactions, General Electric Company
*RESPONSIBILITIES: Environmental Law.
Correll, Kevin P. '56 '99 C.1033 B.S.E.E. L.1360 J.D.
(adm. in MA; not adm. in CT) [Ⓐ Harrington&S.]
*PRACTICE AREAS: Patent, Trademark, Copyright.
Cotter, Daniel H., (BV) .... '52 '82 C.276 B.A. L.1029 J.D. 457 Castle Avenue
Cotter, William L., (BV) .... '57 '85 C.276 B.S.B.A. L.1029 J.D. 457 Castle Ave

Cousins, Johnson & Desrosiers, P.C.
(See Stratford)

Crandall, Nancy .... '65 '91 C.1350 B.A. L.1029 J.D. 1 Post Road, Suite 100‡
Cregeen, Sharon A., (BV) .... '60 '85 C.25 B.A. L.273 J.D. [O'Donnell,M.&C.]
*PRACTICE AREAS: Trusts and Estates; Probate; General Practice; Litigation; Land Use Law.
Crego, Sue Anne .... '57 '86 C.562 B.A. L.861 J.D. 1846 Mill Plain Rd.
Curran, John E. .... '55 '97 C.280 B.A. L.1059 J.D. 79 S. Benson Rd.
Curran, John R., (AV) .... '25 '51 C.705 B.A. L.976 LL.B. 79 South Benson Rd.
Daley, Pamela '— '79 C.674 A.B. L.659 J.D.
(adm. in PA; not adm. in CT) V.P. & Sr. Coun., Trans., General Electric Company
Darcy, John J., (BV) .... '24 '51 C.112 L.569 LL.B. 79 S. Benson Rd.
DeMatteo, Ronald F. .... '48 '95 C.188 B.S. L.1252 J.D. [Cartier&D.]
Denniston, Brackett B., III, (AVⓉ) '47 '74 C.385 A.B. L.309 J.D.
V.P., Sr. Coun., Litig. & Legal Policy, General Electric Company

Dowd, Thomas P., (AVⓉ) '33 '63 C&L.262 B.S., LL.B.
(adm. in NY; not adm. in CT; See Pat. Sect.) [🄰 Perman&G.]
*PRACTICE AREAS: Patent, Trademark, Copyright.
Dowling, Michael A., (BV) . . . . '53 '79 C.745 B.A. L.1048 J.D. [Holahan,G.&D.]
*PRACTICE AREAS: Civil Litigation; Products Liability; Premises Liability; Insurance; Arbitration.
Driscoll, Maureen E., (BV) . . . . '65 '90 C.184 B.A. L.1048 J.D. [Maher&W.]
*PRACTICE AREAS: Workers Compensation.
Eisenstadt, Amy '57 '82 C.494 B.A. L.300 J.D.
(adm. in MN; not adm. in CT) State Tax Coun., General Electric Company
*RESPONSIBILITIES: State and Local Tax.
Eliovson, Linda L. '45 '93 C.1211 B.A. L.1252 J.D.
1817 Black Rock Turnpike, Suite 102
Ervin, Roy H., (BV) . . . . '31 '57 C.1030 B.S.S. L.94 LL.B. [Ervin&E.]
Ervin, Roy H., Jr., (BV) . . . . '60 '85 C.855 B.S. L.982 J.D. [Ervin&E.]
Ervin & Ervin, (BV) . . . . 1177 Post Rd.
Fallon, John F., (AV) . . . . '50 '76 C.1030 B.A. L.262 J.D. [🄲 Owens,S.&N.] ⊙
*PRACTICE AREAS: Litigation; Zoning Law; Administrative Law.
Farnsworth, Effa G. '59 '89 C.101 B.A. L.276 J.D.
Coun., Environmental Torts, General Electric Company
*RESPONSIBILITIES: Environmental Law; Toxic Torts; Health Care; Products Liability.
Fatse, J. Brian, (BV) . . . . '58 '88 C.264 B.A. L.1048 J.D. [🄲 Owens,S.&N.] ⊙
*PRACTICE AREAS: Corporate Law; Bankruptcy; Real Estate.
Felsen, Marvin Jerome . . . . '40 '95 C.563 B.S. L.1252 J.D. 407 Lockwood Rd.
Ferrara, Victoria T. . . . . '56 '85 C.1030 B.A. L.724 J.D. [Murphy,M.F.&N.] ⊙
Ficarra, Francis J., (BV) . . . . '57 '87 C.67 B.A. L.1029 J.D. 1375 Kings Hwy.

Finn Dixon & Herling LLP
(See Stamford)

Fitzgerald, Kevin J. F. '62 '88 C&L.309 A.B., J.D.
Health Care Coun., General Electric Company
*RESPONSIBILITIES: Health Care Law; Labor and Employment Law.
Fitzpatrick, William J., III, (BV) . . . . . '49 '75 C.276 A.B. L.184 J.D. [Fitzpatrick,F.&B.]
*PRACTICE AREAS: Zoning and Land Use; Wetland/Conservation Approvals and Appeals; Residential and Commercial Real Estate Closings.

Fitzpatrick, Fray & Bologna LLC, (BV)
1238 Post Road, P.O. Box 278, 06430
Telephone: 203-255-3581 Fax: 203-254-7745
John T. Fitzpatrick (1925-1989); William J. Fitzpatrick, III; Michael T. Bologna. Of Counsel: John P. Fray.
General Practice. Wetlands, Zoning and Land Use Litigation and Municipal Board Approvals and Appeals; Personal Injury, Trials in all Courts, Wills and Probate, Real Estate Law.
See Professional Biographies, FAIRFIELD, CONNECTICUT

Fodeman, Alan B. . . . . '38 '62 C.184 B.A. L.94 LL.B. [Fodeman&F.]
Fodeman, Leslie J. . . . . '40 '75 C.367 B.A. L.184 J.D. [Fodeman&F.]
Fodeman & Fodeman . . . . 783 Kings Hwy.

Fogarty Cohen Selby & Nemiroff LLC
(See Greenwich)

Fong, Ivan K. '61 '87 C.453 S.B. L.813 J.D.
(adm. in CA; not adm. in CT)
Sr. Coun. E-Com. & Info. Tech., General Electric Company
Fraser, Eliza W. '54 '81 C.951 B.A. L.94 J.D.
(adm. in NY; not adm. in CT) Assoc. Corp. Coun., General Electric Company
Fray, John P., (BV) . . . . '30 '55 C.1030 B.A. L.976 LL.B. [🄲 Fitzpatrick,F.&B.]
Friedman, Arthur D., (AV) . . . . '32 '58 C.860 A.B. L.569 J.D. [Friedman,M.&N.]
Friedman, Irwin E., (BV) . . . . '10 '34 C&L.94 J.D. 140 Sherman St.
Friedman, Mellitz & Newman, P.C., (AV) . . . . One Eliot Place
Gadbaw, R. Michael, (AVⓉ) '47 '74 C.262 B.A. L.477 J.D.
(adm. in MI; not adm. in CT) V.P. & Sr. Coun., General Electric Company
Gardner, Jane W. '53 '85
C.597 B.S. L.174 J.D. Mgr. & Coun., General Electric Company
Garofalo, Albert A., (BV) . . . . '12 '38 C.262 B.A. L.309 LL.B. [Garofalo&G.]
Garofalo & Garofalo, (BV) . . . . 53 Unquowa Pl.
Garrell, Stanley B., (AV) . . . . '32 '59 C.188 B.A. L.569 LL.B. 1700 Post Rd.
Garson, Andrew Emery, (BV) . . . . '45 '72 C.604 B.A. L.569 J.D. [Garson&S.]
*PRACTICE AREAS: Real Estate; Estate Planning; Settlement; Family Law.

Garson & Slepian, (BV)
72 Ruane Street, 06430
Telephone: 203-255-3483 Fax: 203-254-8339
Email: garsnlaw@javanet.com URL: http://www.lawyers.com/garson&slepian
Andrew Emery Garson; David Craig Slepian.
General Civil Practice. Trusts, Estate Planning, Probate, Estate and Gift Tax, Real Estate, Family, Corporate and Commercial Law.
References: Shawmut Bank; Peoples Bank.
See Professional Biographies, FAIRFIELD, CONNECTICUT

Gelderman, Peter V., (BV) . . . . '54 '79 C.184 B.A. L.365 J.D. [🄰 Quatrella&R.]
Gelling, Ralph D. '41 '70 C.971 B.S.E.E. L.724 J.D.
(adm. in NY; not adm. in CT; See Pat. Sect.) [🄰 Perman&G.]
*PRACTICE AREAS: Patent, Trademark, Copyright.
Gentile, James J., (BV) . . . . '32 '57 C.197 B.A. L.184 J.D. [Gentile&C.]
Gentile & Chiota, (BV) . . . . 1700 Post Rd.
Gerety, Peter L., (BV) . . . . '42 '74 C.1029 B.A. L.851 J.D. 72 Ruane Street
Gilbert, E. Scott '55 '81 C&L.309 A.B., J.D.
(adm. in NY; not adm. in CT) Coun., Litig. & Legal Policy, General Electric Company
Gilinsky, Armand . . . . '18 '49 C&L.309 A.B., J.D. 72 Ruane St. (⊙New York, NY)
Giordano, Vincent J. '57 '83 C.184 B.S. L.273 J.D.
(adm. in DC; not adm. in CT)
Compliance Coun., Corp. Environ. Prog., General Electric Company
Glass, Susan R. . . . . '28 '81 C.184 B.A. L.1029 J.D. 1463 Black Rock Tpke.‡
Golger, Robert G., (BV) . . . . '61 '87 C.588 B.A. L.818 J.D. [🄰 Quatrella&R.]
*PRACTICE AREAS: Civil Litigation; Criminal Law; Appellate Practice.
Goodspeed, George S., Jr., (BV) . . . . '20 '49 C.871 B.S. L.472 LL.B. 575 Hillside Rd.
Goodwin, John J. '32 '60 C.433 B.S.E.E. L.724 J.D.
(adm. in NY; not adm. in CT; See Pat. Sect.) [🄰 Perman&G.]
*PRACTICE AREAS: Patent, Trademark, Copyright.
Green, Clarence A., (AV) '38 '66
C.454 B.S.M.E. L.94 J.D. [Perman&G.] (See Pat. Sect.)
*PRACTICE AREAS: Patent, Trademark, Copyright.

Green, Robert W.
(See Stamford)

Grogins, Auden, (BV) . . . . '62 '89 C.1044 B.S. L.1029 J.D. [Grogins&G.]
*PRACTICE AREAS: Criminal Law; Personal Injury Law; Foreclosure Law.
Grogins, Jack L., (BV) . . . . '31 '55 C&L.184 B.A., LL.B. 400 Stillson Rd.

Grogins & Grogins, (BV)
400 Stillson Road, 06430
Telephone: 203-335-2112
URL: http://www.lawyers.com/grogins&grogins

(This Listing Continued)

Grogins & Grogins (Continued)

Auden Grogins.
Criminal Defense, DWI, Personal Injury Litigation, Automobile Accidents, Slip and Fall Accidents, Family Law, Divorce and Juvenile Law. Civil Litigation.
See Professional Biographies, FAIRFIELD, CONNECTICUT

Gumpper, Kevin J., (BV) . . . . '50 '75 C.976 B.A. L.184 J.D. [Holahan,G.&D.]
*PRACTICE AREAS: Real Estate; Land Use; Probate; Estate Planning; Appellate Practice.
Gumpper, William P., (AV) . . . . . '17 '43 C.712 B.A. L.184 LL.B. [🄰 Holahan,G.&D.] ‡

Hall, Donald D. '51 '81 C.205 B.S. L.184 J.D.
3366 Congress Street, 06430-2030
Telephone: 203-256-9468
URL: http://www.lawyers.com/hallsavarese
General Practice.
See Professional Biographies, FAIRFIELD, CONNECTICUT

Harrington, John H. . . . . '66 '95 C.802 B.A. L.252 J.D. [J.H.Harrington]
*PRACTICE AREAS: International Commercial Arbitration; Real Estate; Land Use; Immigration Law; Probate.
Harrington, Mark F. . . . . '60 '85 C.885 B.S. L.1040 J.D. [Harrington&S.] (See Pat. Sect.)
*PRACTICE AREAS: Patent, Trademark, Copyright.

Harrington, John H., Esq., LLC, Law Office of
527 Tunxis Hill Road, 06432
Telephone: 203-331-1881 Fax: 203-330-9252
Email: JHH@johnharrington.net URL: http://www.johnharrington.net
John H. Harrington.
International Commercial Arbitration; Real Estate, Land Use, Immigration, Probate.
See Professional Biographies, FAIRFIELD, CONNECTICUT

Harrington & Smith, LLP . . . . 1809 Black Rock Turnpike (See Pat. Sect.)
Hawkins, Suzanne E. '56 '81 C&L.276 B.A., J.D.
(adm. in NY; not adm. in CT) Sr. Coun., Legal Operations, General Electric Company

Heagney, Lennon & Slane LLP
(See Greenwich)

Healing, Robert E. '43 '72 C.321 B.S. L.188 J.D.
Corp. Coun., General Electric Company
Heimann, Fritz F. '27 '51 C&L.145 A.B., J.D.
(adm. in DC; not adm. in CT) 3135 Easton Tpke.
Heineman, Benjamin W., Jr., (AV) '44 '73 C.309 B.A. L.976 J.D.
(adm. in DC; not adm. in CT) Sr. V.P., Gen. Coun. & Secy., General Electric Company
Herndon, Gayle W. '54 '82 C&L.383 B.S., J.D.
(adm. in NY; not adm. in CT) Tax Coun., General Electric Company
Higgins, Richard E. '49 '76 C.178 B.A. L.776 J.D.
(adm. in NJ; not adm. in CT) 75 Hillside Rd.
Hilburger, Albert W. '37 '62
C.477 B.S.M.E. L.276 LL.B. [🄰 Perman&G.] (See Pat. Sect.)
*PRACTICE AREAS: Patent, Trademark, Copyright.
Hilgendorff, Robert F., (BV) . . . . '55 '81 C.855 B.A. L.665 J.D. [🄰 Ambrose&C.]
Hill, Thomas H., (AV) '56 '83 C.912 B.S. L.213 J.D.
(adm. in MI; not adm. in CT)
Sr. Coun., Envir. Torts/Ins. Litig., General Electric Company
Hirsch, Harry, (BV) . . . . '50 '75 C.1030 B.S. L.184 J.D. 6 Woody Lane
Hirsch, Ivan A., (BV) . . . . '31 '56 C.976 B.A. L.309 LL.B. 46 Northwood Rd.
Holahan, Edward J., Jr., (AV) . . . . '36 '67 C.976 B.A. L.276 J.D. [Holahan,G.&D.]
*PRACTICE AREAS: Civil Litigation; Products Liability; Insurance; Uninsured and Underinsured Motorists; Arbitration.

Holahan, Gumpper & Dowling, (AV)
1375 Kings Highway East, P.O. Box 320177, 06432-0177
Telephone: 203-384-1385 Fax: 203-335-3594
Email: hgd.law@hganddlaw.com
Members of Firm: Edward J. Holahan, Jr.; Kevin J. Gumpper; Michael A. Dowling. Associates: John M. Rowan; William P. Gumpper (Retired).
General Practice. Real Estate, Land Use, Corporation, Estate Planning and Probate Law. Civil Trials in all Courts. Product Liability, Insurance Law, Environmental Law and Arbitration.
See Professional Biographies, FAIRFIELD, CONNECTICUT

Holland Kaufmann & Bartels, LLC
(See Greenwich)

Holms, Richard L., Jr. . . . . '42 '78 C.573 B.B.A. L.724 J.D. 131 Lamplighter Ln.
Homa, James A., (CV) . . . . '30 '58 C.1030 B.S. L.262 LL.B. [Murren&H.]

Hopper & Hopper
(See Greenwich)

Howell, John G., III . . . . '65 '92 C.692 B.A. L.1029 J.D. P.O. Box 572
Ireland, Pamela T., (BV) . . . . '53 '87 C.999 B.S. L.1065 J.D. [Jeffers&I.]
*PRACTICE AREAS: Business; Corporate; Employment; E-Commerce; Marketing.
Ivanko, Kathleen . . . . '58 '84 C.893 B.A. L.1029 J.D. FKI Indus., Inc.
Jacobs, Adele R. . . . . '58 '84 C.788 B.A. L.978 J.D. 1375 Kings Hwy., E.

Jacobs Partners LLC
(See Norwalk)

Jankovsky, Charles S., (BV) '42 '72 C.1029 B.A. L.184 J.D.
134 Round Hill Rd., 3rd Fl.
Jeffers, Karen A. . . . . '54 '79 C.855 B.A. L.178 J.D. [Jeffers&I.]
*PRACTICE AREAS: Corporate; Business; Advertising and Marketing; Health Care; Employment.

Jeffers & Ireland, Professional Corporation, (BV)
1248 Post Road, 06430
Telephone: 203-259-7900 Fax: 203-259-1070
Email: firm@jeffire.com URL: http://www.jeffire.com
Karen A. Jeffers; Pamela T. Ireland;—Margaret A. Bartiromo; Tina Passalaris.
General Corporate and Business. Health Care. Employment. Entertainment. Marketing, Advertising and Sales Promotion. E-Commerce. Copyright and Trademark. Commercial Real Estate.
See Professional Biographies, FAIRFIELD, CONNECTICUT

Jeffrey, Peter '35 '61 C.608 B.S. L.273 J.D.
(adm. in VA; not adm. in CT) 3135 Easton Tpke.‡
Johnson, Frank A., (CV) . . . . '59 '88 C.1029 B.S. L.607 J.D. 3375 Morehouse Hwy.
Johnson, Stephen M. '43 '69 C.597 A.B. L.861 J.D.
(adm. in IN; not adm. in CT) 420 Greenfield Hill Rd.‡
Johnston, Donald F., Jr. '31 '62 C.128 A.B. L.309 LL.B.
(adm. in NY; not adm. in CT) 1422 Melville Ave‡

Jontos & Lotty, (AV)
1212 Post Road, P.O. Box 218, 06430
Telephone: 203-259-7009 Fax: 203-254-7780
Email: lottyesq@aol.com
Members of Firm: Richard A. Jontos (1935-1995); Robert W. Lotty; Jane E. Hugo Burwell.
General Litigation, Insurance Defense, Legal, Medical, Dental and Accountant Malpractice, Uninsured Motorist Arbitration, Claims.
See Professional Biographies, FAIRFIELD, CONNECTICUT

Josovitz, Robert M., (BV) ....'49 '73 C.28 B.S. L.669 J.D. 195 Tunxis Hill Rd.
Joyce, Arthur E. '42 '67 C.103 A.B. L.94 J.D.
(adm. in MA; not adm. in CT)
Sr. Coun., Labor & Employ. Law, General Electric Company
Kaelin, William G. .... '29 '55 C&L.228 A.B., J.D. 495 Old Academy Rd.
Kanner, Sheri ....'62 '88 C&L.276 B.S.N., J.D. 41 Wynn Wood Dr.
Kanter, Joel E., (BV) '33 '58
C.998 B.S. L.94 J.D. 1859 Fairfield Beach Road (⊙Santa Fe, NM)
Kantrowitz, Jonathan D., (BV) .... '45 '69 C.103 B.A. L.309 J.D. 877 Burr St.
Katz, Lucy V., (BV) ....'43 '68 C.788 B.A. L.569 J.D. Fairfield Univ.
Kelly, Raymond J., (BV) ....'53 '81 C.1030 B.A. L.1252 J.D. [Kelly&M.]
*PRACTICE AREAS: Civil Litigation; Criminal Litigation; Personal Injury; Insurance Defense; Uninsured Motorist Arbitration.

Kelly and Mooney, (BV)
2452 Black Rock Turnpike, 06432
Telephone: 203-373-7780 Fax: 203-373-6860
Raymond J. Kelly; James P. Mooney.
Criminal and Civil Litigation including Personal Injury, Insurance Defense and Uninsured Motorist Arbitration.
See Professional Biographies, FAIRFIELD, CONNECTICUT

Kleban & Samor, P.C.
(See Southport)

Klee, Maurice M. '45 '77 C.339 B.S. L.273 J.D.
(adm. in NY; not adm. in CT) 1951 Burr St.
Koch, Victoria Jane '47 '93 C.331 B.A. L.1029 J.D.
(adm. in FL; not adm. in CT) [V.J.Koch]
Koch, Victoria J., P.C., Law Offices of ....3939 Park Ave.
Kornfeld, Randy M. '54 '80 C.102 B.A. L.1009 J.D.
(adm. in NY; not adm. in CT) [Braunstein&T.] (⊙New York, NY)
*PRACTICE AREAS: Bankruptcy; Commercial Litigation.
Kosakowski, Aaron E. ....'56 '81 C.93 A.B. L.94 J.D. V.P., Ceruzzi Props., Inc.
Kreitlow, Saramae .... '69 '98 C&L.1252 B.A., J.D. [Quatrella&R.]
*PRACTICE AREAS: Civil Litigation.
Kulikowski, John F., III .... '55 '80 C.1029 B.S. L.831 J.D. 108 New England Ave.
LaFollette, Ernest C., (BV) ....'34 '59 C.24 B.A. L.823 J.D. 1432 Post Rd.
Lax, Sandra P., (BV) ....'51 '88 C.102 B.S. L.1029 J.D. [Lax&T.]
*PRACTICE AREAS: Elder Law; Real Estate; Domestic Relations; Matrimonial Law; Family Law.

Lax & Truax, LLC, (BV)
The Brick Walk, 1275 Post Road, Suite 200 C, P.O. Box 336, 06430
Telephone: 203-254-9877 Fax: 203-255-6991
Email: slaxax@aol.com
Sandra P. Lax; Louise T. Truax;—Daniel J. Roberts.
General Practice.
See Professional Biographies, FAIRFIELD, CONNECTICUT

Lee, James H., (BV) '47 '75 C.31 A.B. L.823 J.D.
140 Sherman Street, 06430
Telephone: 203-259-4665
Appellate Practice, Civil Practice, General Practice.
See Professional Biographies, FAIRFIELD, CONNECTICUT

Lee, Thomas E., (BV) ....'45 '77 C.188 A.B. L.94 J.D. 765 Post Rd.
Levin-Weiss, Pamela H ....'62 '93 2000 Post Road Lower Level, 2nd Floor
Levitsky, Paul A. '57 '91 C.1041 B.B.A. L.1252 J.D.
Assoc. Gen. Cnsl, Competitive Technologies, Inc. (Pat.)
Levy, Arthur, Jr., (BV) ....'20 '47 C.569 A.B. L.309 LL.B. [Friedman,M.&N.]
Levy, Steven A., (BV) .... '52 '77 C.976 B.A. L.569 J.D. [Friedman,M.&N.]
Loh, Robert Daniel, Jr. ....'51 '76 C.882 B.A. L.184 J.D. 133 Lawrence Rd.
Lotty, Robert W., (AV) ......'46 '74 C.184 B.A. L.966 J.D. [Jontos&L.] (⊙New Haven)
*PRACTICE AREAS: Litigation; Legal Malpractice; Medical Malpractice; Dental Malpractice; Accountants Malpractice.
Lyons, Henry, III, (BV) ....'44 '69 C.93 B.S. L.818 J.D. 34 Sherman Ct.
Macol, Katherine M. ....'68 '93 C.183 B.A. L.1252 J.D. [Quatrella&R.]
Maggiola, Stephen P., (BV) .... '51 '80 C.94 B.S. L.184 J.D. 2465 Black Rock Tpke.
Maher, Kevin J., (BV) .... '39 '64 C.524 B.S. L.896 J.D. [Maher&W.]
*PRACTICE AREAS: Workers Compensation.

Maher and Williams, (BV)
268 Post Road, P.O. Box 550, 06430
Telephone: 203-255-7777 Fax: 203-254-6611
URL: http://www.lawyers.com/maher&williams
Members of Firm: Kevin J. Maher; Scott Wilson Williams; Maureen E. Driscoll; James L. Sullivan; James D. Moran, Jr.
General and Federal Practice. Workers Compensation, Probate, Insurance, Subrogation, Estate Planning and Administrative Law. Trials.
Counsel for: Zurich-American Insurance Group; Fireman's Fund Insurance Co.; Liberty Mutual Insurance Co.
See Professional Biographies, FAIRFIELD, CONNECTICUT

Maniscalco, Robert A., (BV) ....'50 '76 C.184 B.S. L.188 J.D. [Reid&M.]
Marcovici, Janik .... '63 '97 C.667 B.S.A.E. L.1252 J.D. [Perman&G.]
*PRACTICE AREAS: Patent, Trademark, Copyright.
Markley, George J., (AV) ....'45 '70 C.164 B.A. L.569 J.D. 1700 Post Rd.
Martin, C. Wesley .... '60 '88 C.164 A.B. L.1029 J.D. [Martin&R.]
Martin and Rome, LLC, (BV) .... 23 Morehouse Dr.
Mason, Kevin M. ....'66 '93 C.433 B.E.E.E. L.724 J.D. [Ryan,M.&L.] (Pat.) ⊙
Mathews, Jeanne M. '59 '85 C.1044 B.A. L.94 J.D.
(adm. in MA; not adm. in CT) Coun., Employ. Law, General Electric Company
*RESPONSIBILITIES: Employment Law.
Mauri, Robert J. '64 '99 C.36 B.S.E.E. L.37 J.D.
(adm. in AZ; not adm. in CT; Pat.) [Ryan,M.&L.] ⊙
Maya, Joseph C. ....'62 '90 C.569 B.A. L.477 J.D. 183 Sherman Street
McCarthy, John P., (BV) ....'44 '82 C.1139 B.S. L.724 J.D. 1150 Post Rd.
McCarthy, Richard, (BV) ....'47 '71 C.976 B.A. L.477 J.D. 140 Sherman St.
McCormack, Karen A. ....'66 '95 C.1030 B.S. L.1252 J.D. 2000 Post Rd.
McDonald, David J., (BV) ....'59 '85 C.321 B.A. L.184 J.D. [O'Donnell,M.&C.]
*PRACTICE AREAS: Civil Trials; General Practice; Real Estate; Probate.

McHugh, David M., (BV) '39 '66 C.1030 B.S.S. L.306 J.D.
1261 Post Road, 06430
Telephone: 203-319-1970 Facsimile: 203-319-0199
Email: d.mchugh@snet.net URL: http://www.lawyers.com/mchughlaw
Real Estate, Estate Planning, Probate, Trusts and Estates, Personal Injury, Business Law.
See Professional Biographies, FAIRFIELD, CONNECTICUT

Meeks & Sheppard .... 1735 Post Rd., Ste. 4 (⊙Newport Beach, CA; New York, NY)
Mellitz, Jacob, (AV) ....'17 '41 C.976 B.A. L.569 J.D. 281 Ferncliff Rd.‡
Meyer, Lee '— '89 C.668 B.A. L.976 J.D.
Tax Coun., Employ. Benefits, General Electric Company
*RESPONSIBILITIES: Employee Benefits; Tax.
Meyers, Michael A., (AV) ....'44 '69 C.184 B.A. L.94 J.D. [Meyers B.&N.]

Meyers Breiner & Neufeld, L.L.P., (AV)
55 Walls Drive, Suite 204, 06430
Telephone: 203-255-9410 Fax: 203-254-1388
Email: mbnllp@worldnet.att.net
Michael A. Meyers; Alexander Breiner; Michael A. Neufeld.
Family, Corporate, Estate Planning, Real Estate, Negligence and Taxation Law.
Reference: People's Bank.
See Professional Biographies, FAIRFIELD, CONNECTICUT

Miller, James A., Jr., (BV) ....'42 '67 C.367 B.A. L.188 J.D. 1700 Post Rd.
Miller, Robert M. ......'48 '73 C.823 B.A. L.276 J.D. V.P., Law & Secy., FKI Indus., Inc.
Mitchell, James W. '— '67 C.433 B.S.C.E. L.724 J.D.
(adm. in NY; not adm. in CT) Pat. Coun., General Electric Company
Mooney, James P., (BV) .... '56 '83 C.94 B.S. L.1048 J.D. [Kelly&M.]
*PRACTICE AREAS: Insurance Defense Work; Uninsured Motorist Arbitration; Plaintiff Personal Injury.
Moran, James D., Jr. ....'66 '92 C.188 B.A. L.861 J.D. [Maher&W.]
Morehouse, W. Bradley, (AV) ..... '23 '51 C.197 B.A. L.976 LL.B. [Morehouse,H.&W.]
*PRACTICE AREAS: Zoning Law; Civil Litigation; Real Estate; Probate; Estate Planning.

Morehouse, Harlow & Weldy, (AV)
1735 Post Road, P.O. Box 827, 06430-0827
Telephone: 203-255-5981 Telecopier: 203-259-0130
Email: MHWlawfirm@aol.com
Members of Firm: Albert L. Harlow (1928-1995); W. Bradley Morehouse; Thomas P. Weldy. Of Counsel: Gregory C. Willis.
General Practice. Corporation, Estate Planning, Probate, Taxation, Real Estate, Environmental and Zoning Law, Foreclosure. Trials in all Courts.
Representative Clients: The Connecticut Audubon Society; Harvey Hubbell, Inc.; People's Bank; Fairfield Board of Realtors, Inc.; Domestic Kitchens, Inc.; Entertainment Publications, Inc.

Morrell, Linwood A., (AVⓉ) '30 '61 C.95 A.B. L.178 J.D.
(adm. in NY; not adm. in CT) 111 Sturges Rd.‡
Morris, William H. '62 '90 C.999 B.A. L.893 LL.M.
(adm. in NY; not adm. in CT) Tax Coun. Intl., G.E. Co.
Murphy, Helen D., (AV) .... '51 '86 C.341 B.A. L.1252 J.D. [Murphy,M.F.&N.] ⊙
Murphy, Maureen M., (AV) .... '50 '86 C.741 B.A. L.1029 J.D. [Murphy,M.F.&N.] ⊙
Murphy, Murphy, Ferrara & Nugent, LLC, (AV) .... 53 Unquowa Place (⊙New Haven)
Murren & Homa, (CV) .... 1583 Post Rd.
Muskus, John F. ....'54 '79 C.262 B.S. L.184 J.D. 111 Beach Rd.
Myrick, Ronald E., (AVⓉ) '— '74 C.421 B.S.E.E. L.424 J.D.
(adm. in IL; not adm. in CT; Pat.) Gen. Pat. Coun., General Electric Company
*RESPONSIBILITIES: Intellectual Property; Patents; Trade Secrets; Computer and Software Law; Litigation.
Neufeld, Michael A., (AV) ....'49 '77 C.659 B.A. L.472 J.D. [Meyers B.&N.]
Newman, Noel R., (AV) ....'32 '56 C.976 A.B. L.309 LL.B. [Friedman,M.&N.]
Nordstrom, Mark A. '51 '83 C.165 B.A. L.982 J.D.
(adm. in NY; not adm. in CT) Coun., Labor Law, General Electric Company
Novack, Michael R. '68 '93
C.867 B.S. L.1218 J.D. Gen. Coun., Competitive Technologies, Inc.
Nugent, Susan E. .... '61 '90 C.262 B.A. L.128 J.D. [Murphy,M.F.&N.] ⊙
O'Brien, Stephen J. ....'15 '40 C.918 B.A. L.976 LL.B. 1434 Melville Ave.
O'Donnell, Carol Befanis ....'56 '82 C.787 B.S. L.978 J.D. 540 Joan Dr.
O'Donnell, James E., (BV) ....'52 '78 C.178 B.A. L.93 J.D. [O'Donnell,M.&C.]
*PRACTICE AREAS: Civil Trials; Real Estate; Probate; General Practice.
O'Donnell, Maura, (BV) ....'53 '78 C.999 B.A. L.93 J.D. [O'Donnell,M.&C.]
*PRACTICE AREAS: General Practice; Probate.

O'Donnell, McDonald and Cregeen, L.L.C., (BV)
Successor to Coles, O'Connell, Dolan & McDonald, P.C.
2452 Black Rock Turnpike, Suite 2, 06432
Telephone: 203-374-9700 Fax: 203-374-9772
James E. O'Donnell; Maura O'Donnell; David J. McDonald; Sharon A. Cregeen.
General Practice. Trials in all Courts. Probate, Real Estate, Zoning and Administrative Law, Environmental.
Representative Clients: Chevron U.S.A., Inc.; The Bridgeport Roman Catholic Diocesan Corp.; United Illuminating Co.; Allstate Insurance Co.; Savings Bank of Ansonia; Steiner, Inc.
See Professional Biographies, FAIRFIELD, CONNECTICUT

O'Malley, Joseph S. '35 '63 C.321 A.B. L.262 LL.B.
(adm. in NY; not adm. in CT) V.P., The Chase Manhattan Bk., N.A.
O'Reilly, Francis Lee ....'62 '00 C.1507 B.S. L.1252 J.D. 2 Sherman Ct.

Owens, Schine & Nicola, P.C., (AV)
53 Sherman Street, 06430 ⊙
Telephone: 203-259-6612 Fax: 203-256-8796
Daniel F. Caruso. Of Counsel: J. Brian Fatse; John F. Fallon.
General Trial Practice in all Courts. Real Estate, Corporate, Probate, Personal Injury, Criminal, Family, Workers Compensation, University, Labor Law, Commercial and Bankruptcy. Administrative Agency Proceedings and Appeals, Environmental, Construction Law, Arbitration and Land Use. Trumbull, Connecticut Office: 799 Silver Lane, P.O. Box 753. Telephone:203-375-0600. Fax: 203-375-5003.
See Professional Biographies, FAIRFIELD, CONNECTICUT

Park, Kathryn Barrett '58 '85 C.103 A.B. L.178 J.D.
(adm. in NY; not adm. in CT) General Electric Company
Passalaris, Tina .... '68 '95 C&L.178 B.A., J.D. [Jeffers&I.]
Pavarini, George Francis, III ....'68 '94 C.1365 B.A. L.1040 J.D. 1820 Stratfield Rd.

Perman & Green, LLP, (AV)
425 Post Road, 06430-6232
Telephone: 203-259-1800 Facsimile: 203-255-5170
Email: pgpatent@aol.com URL: http://www.pgpatent.com
Members of Firm: Martey R. Perman (1939-1993). Managing Partner: Clarence A. Green. Associates: David M. Warren (Not admitted in CT); Albert W. Hilburger; Thomas L. Tully; Michael J. Tully (Not admitted in CT); John J. Goodwin (Not admitted in CT); Ralph D. Gelling (Not admitted in CT); Thomas P. Dowd (Not admitted in CT); Janik Marcovici; David Aker (Not admitted in CT); Geza C. Ziegler, Jr.; Henry I. Steckler (Not admitted in CT). Of Counsel: Donald C. Caulfield; Paul Weinstein. Patent, Trademark, Copyright and Related Matters.
See Professional Biographies, FAIRFIELD, CONNECTICUT

Petersen, E. Frederick, III ....'60 '85 C.910 B.A. L.734 J.D. 445 Valley Rd.
Petroccio, William M., (BV) .... '60 '85 C.1102 B.S. L.1029 J.D. [Quatrella&R.]
*PRACTICE AREAS: Business Law; Corporate Law; Real Estate; Commercial Law; Banking Law.
Piels, Barry Y. .... '46 '73 C.102 B.A. L.1009 J.D. 208 S. Benson Rd.
Policinski, Henry J. '43 '70 C.602 B.A. L.215 J.D.
(adm. in MI; not adm. in CT; Pat.)
Assoc. Gen. Pat. Coun. & Trademark Coun., General Electric Company
*RESPONSIBILITIES: Patent Law; Trademark Law; Copyright Law.
Primps, Deborah A. ....'64 '93 C.184 B.A. L.1040 J.D. [Friedman,M.&N.]
Quatrella, David L., (BV) ....'55 '80 C.1030 B.A. L.884 J.D. [Quatrella&R.]
*PRACTICE AREAS: Real Estate Law; Business Organizations Law; Banking Law.

Quatrella & Rizio, LLC, (BV)
One Post Road, P.O. Box 320019, 06432
Telephone: 203-335-2222; 203-255-9928 Fax: 203-255-6618
Members of Firm: David L. Quatrella; Raymond Rizio. Associates: James P. Blanchfield; Peter V. Gelderman; Robert G. Golger; Saramae Kreitlow; Katherine M. Macol; William M. Petroccio.

(This Listing Continued)

Quatrella & Rizio, LLC (Continued)

General Civil Practice, Real Estate, Commercial, Corporate, Probate, Commercial and Residential Landlord and Tenant, Financial, Partnership and Negligence Law.
Approved Attorneys For: Lawyers Title Insurance Co.
References: Robert D. Russo M.D. & Associates Radiology, P.C.; PNC Mortgage Corp.; Lawyers Title Insurance Corp.; Peoples Bank; The Home Depot, Inc.; International Developers; United Properties; Anthony Julian Railroad Construction Co., Inc.

See Professional Biographies, FAIRFIELD, CONNECTICUT

Rabbitt, Donna J. . . . . '15 '54 C.966 B.S. L.1033 J.D. 134 Rolling Ridge Rd.
Ramsey, Stephen D., (AV) '47 '72 C.674 A.B. L.846 J.D.
(adm. in TX; not adm. in CT) V.P., Corp. Envir. Progs., General Electric Company
Rebay, Alexandra . . . . '60 '85 C.66 B.A. L.178 J.D. General Electric Company
*RESPONSIBILITIES: Litigation; Criminal Law; Compliance.
Reid, Tanis M. . . . . '52 '78 C.188 A.B. L.107 J.D. [Reid&M.]
Reid & Maniscalco, (BV) . . . . 425 Kings Hwy. E.
Reilly, Francis L.O. . . . . '62 '96 C.1044 B.S. L.1252 J.D. 87 Ruane St.
Rhame, Harold Ellis, Jr. . . . . '26 '91 C.674 A.B. L.1029 J.D. 501 Mine Hill Road
Riccio, Joyce A., (BV) . . . . '52 '81 C&L.1029 B.S., J.D. 1224 Post Rd.
Rizio, Raymond, (BV) . . . . '60 '85 C.264 B.A. L.1029 J.D. [Quatrella&R.]
Roberts, Daniel J. . . . . '74 '00 C.184 B.A. L.1252 J.D. [🄰 Lax&T.]
*PRACTICE AREAS: Domestic Relations; Family Law; Matrimonial Law.
Rome, Michael D., (BV) . . . . '54 '88 C.420 B.A. L.1029 J.D. [Martin&R.]
Rosenstein, Sheila K., (BV) . . . . '46 '81 C.66 A.B. L.178 J.D. [Rosenstein&B.]
*PRACTICE AREAS: Family Law; Domestic Relations; Child Custody; Civil Litigation; Appeals.

Rosenstein & Barnes, (BV)
1100 Kings Highway East, P.O. Box 687, 06432-5466
Telephone: 203-367-7922 Fax: 203-367-8110 URL: http://www.rosenbar.com
Email: srosenstein@rosenbar.com URL: http://www.lawyers.com/rosenbar
Members of Firm: Sheila K. Rosenstein; William B. Barnes.
General Civil and Criminal Practice before State and Federal Courts. Civil Litigation, Employment Litigation, Commercial Litigation and Family Law. Domestic Relations and Child Custody Law, Covenants Not to Compete Litigation, Trials and Appeals.
Reference: Chase Connecticut.

See Professional Biographies, FAIRFIELD, CONNECTICUT

Rosten, Marjorie Worman, (BV) . . . . '48 '83 C.347 B.A. L.1029 J.D. 253 Shelter Rock Rd.
Rosten, Michael S., (AV) . . . . '53 '78 C.951 B.A. L.188 J.D. 1700 Post Rd.
Rowan, John M. . . . . '71 '96 C.1349 B.A. L.262 J.D. [🄰 Holahan,G.&D.]
*PRACTICE AREAS: Civil Litigation; Insurance Defense; Premises Liability; Products Liability; Personal Injury.

Ruchandani, Nandita P. '68 '94 C.66 B.A. L.273 J.D.
161 Kings Highway East, Suite 212-214, 06432-4837
Telephone: 203-576-9211 Fax: 203-576-9158
Email: attynpr@aol.com URL: http://www.members.aol.com/attynpr/index/html
***PRACTICE AREAS: Immigration Law; International Business Law; International Corporate Law; Leases and Leasing; Landlord and Tenant Law.**
Immigration Law, International Business Law, International Corporate Law, Leases and Leasing, Landlord and Tenant Law.

See Professional Biographies, FAIRFIELD, CONNECTICUT

Ryan, Mason & Lewis, LLP
1300 Post Road, Suite 205, 06430 ⊙
Telephone: 203-255-6560 Fax: 203-255-6570
Email: iplaw@rml-law.com
Kevin M. Mason. Associate: Robert J. Mauri (Not admitted in CT).
Intellectual Property Law, including Patent, Trademark, Copyright, Trade Secret, Unfair Competition, Licensing and Related Matters.
Locust Valley, New York Office: 90 Forest Avenue. Telephone: 516-759-2772. Fax: 516-759-9512.

See Professional Biographies, FAIRFIELD, CONNECTICUT

Sak, Andrew H. '65 '90 C&L.569 B.A., J.D.
(adm. in CA; not adm. in CT) 52 Adams Rd.
Samuels, John M. '44 '69 C.880 B.A. L.145 J.D.
(adm. in FL; not adm. in CT) V.P. & Sr. Tax Coun., General Electric Company

Sandak Friedman Hennessey & Greco, LLP
(See Stamford)

Saracco, Louis A., Jr. . . . . '30 '55 C&L.262 B.S., LL.B. 317 Edward St.
Schmidt, Erik A. '65 '91 C.197 B.A. L.188 J.D.
(adm. in NY; not adm. in CT) Coun., General Electric Company
*RESPONSIBILITIES: Insurance Litigation; Toxic Tort Litigation.
Schmidt, Frederick E. '68 '95
C.184 B.S. L.1009 J.D. [🄲 Braunstein&T.] (⊙New York, NY)
*PRACTICE AREAS: Bankruptcy; Criminal; Commercial Litigation; Appellate Practice.
Seymour, Jeffrey C. . . . . '57 '82 C.951 B.A. L.564 J.D. 91 Quincy St.
Shannon, John H. . . . . '28 '53 C.276 A.B. L.184 LL.B. Prob. J.
Sheehan, Joanne Patricia, (BV) . . . . '57 '87 C&L.1040 B.S.N., J.D. [Friedman,M.&N.]
Shen, Leonard H. '61 '85 C&L.309 B.A., J.D.
(adm. in MA; not adm. in CT)
Coun., Envir. Remediation & Compliance, General Electric Company
*RESPONSIBILITIES: Governmental; Litigation.
Sheppard, Ralph H. '50 '82 C.882 B.A. L.904 J.D.
(adm. in NY; not adm. in CT) [Meeks&S.] (⊙New York, NY)
Shereda, Cynthia L. '60 '93 C.569 B.S. L.846 J.D.
(adm. in NY; not adm. in CT) Trans. & Fin. Coun., General Electric Company
Shumway, Susan H., (AV) . . . . '50 '75 C.966 B.A. L.94 J.D. [Shumway&S.]
*PRACTICE AREAS: Environmental Law.

Shumway & Spencer, LLC, (AV)
1 Post Road, 06430
Telephone: 203-255-7444 Facsimile: 203-255-0365
Members of Firm: Susan H. Shumway; William C. Spencer.
Environmental and Corporate Law.
Representative Clients: Uniroyal Chemical Co., Inc.; Clayton, Dubilier & Rice.

See Professional Biographies, FAIRFIELD, CONNECTICUT

Silver, Golub & Teitell LLP
(See Stamford)

Sinclair, Jeanne Morrison . . . . '59 '90 C.527 B.S.N. L.262 J.D. 56 Dogwood Ln.
Slepian, David Craig, (BV) . . . . '56 '82 C.103 A.B. L.94 J.D. [Garson&S.]
*PRACTICE AREAS: Tax and Estate Planning; Medicaid Planning; Foreclosure and Litigation.
Smith, Harry F. . . . . . . '49 '86 C.999 B.S.E.E. L.1029 J.D. [Harrington&S.] (See Pat. Sect.)
*PRACTICE AREAS: Patent, Trademark, Copyright Law.
Snitkoff, Adam L. . . . . '65 '92 C.1349 B.A. L.1029 J.D. 53 Edgewood Pl.
Snyder, Bernard '40 '64 C.667 B.Ch.E. L.569 J.D.
(adm. in NY; not adm. in CT) Sr. Pat. Coun., General Electric Company
Sohon, Julian A., Jr. '23 '62 C.184 B.S. L.262 LL.B. 105 Patrick Dr.‡
Spencer, William C. . . . . '49 '75 C.874 B.A. L.724 J.D. [Shumway&S.]
*PRACTICE AREAS: Environmental Law; Corporate Law; Health Care Law.
Stavis, Roger L., (AVⓉ) '58 '83 C.994 B.A. L.273 J.D.
(adm. in NY; not adm. in CT) [🄲 Braunstein&T.] (⊙New York, NY)
*PRACTICE AREAS: Criminal; Civil Litigation; Appellate Practice.

Steckler, Henry I. '42 '67 C.688 B.S.E.E. L.1009 J.D.
(adm. in NY; not adm. in CT; See Pat. Sect.) [🄰 Perman&G.]
*PRACTICE AREAS: Patent, Trademark, Copyright.
Stelben, Brian T. . . . . '68 '93 C.477 B.A. L.1252 J.D. [🄰 Ambrose&C.]
Stuckal, Elizabeth . . . . '— '81 C.477 B.A. L.1029 J.D. 83 Flower House Dr.
Sullivan, David J., Jr., (AV) . . . . '31 '58 C.262 B.S.S. L.276 LL.B. 39 Sherman Ct.
Sullivan, Gayle Hacker . . . . '58 '84 C.184 B.S. L.1292 J.D. Quality Assurance Assocs., Inc.
Sullivan, James L. . . . . '64 '93 C.478 B.A. L.1194 J.D. [Maher&W.]
*PRACTICE AREAS: Workers' Compensation.
Sullivan, Robert P., (BV) . . . . '52 '78 C&L.184 B.A., J.D. 555 Tunxix Hill Rd
Sweeney, Elizabeth M. '56 '84 C.103 A.B. L.569 J.D.
(adm. in NY; not adm. in CT) 35 Norcliff Ln.

Sweeney, Joseph H. '36 '94 C.116 B.B.A. L.1040 J.D.
1305 Post Road, Suite 206A, 06430-0454
Telephone: 203-256-1299
***PRACTICE AREAS: Taxation; Aged and Aging; Trusts and Estates; Real Estate.**
Taxation, Estate Planning, Trusts, Real Estate, IRS Disputes.

See Professional Biographies, FAIRFIELD, CONNECTICUT

Tabackman, Bruce . . . . '44 '73 C.823 B.A. L.818 J.D. 960 N. Benson Rd.
Tanzer, Matthew O. '60 '88 C.188 A.B. L.309 J.D.
Coun., Environ. Affairs, General Electric Company
Tedesco, Frank J., (CV) . . . . '33 '59 C.184 B.S. L.94 LL.B. 1375 Kings Hwy. E.
Tennant, William H., Jr., (BVⓉ) '52 '77 C.397 B.A. L.744 J.D.
(adm. in TX; not adm. in CT) 135 Ridge Common
Thomas, Andrew J., Jr. '61 '86 C.197 A.B. L.276 J.D.
(adm. in MO; not adm. in CT)
Coun., Envir. Matters, Corp. Envir. Prog., General Electric Company
Todisco, Amy E., (BV) . . . . '59 '84 C.787 B.A. L.1029 J.D. [Braunstein&T.]
*PRACTICE AREAS: Elder Law; Probate; Trusts and Estates; Real Estate.
Tooher & Wocl, L.L.C., (BV) . . . . 1375 Kings Hwy., Ste. 425 (⊙Stamford)
Truax, Louise T. . . . . '62 '93 C.882 B.A. L.1040 J.D. [Lax&T.]
*PRACTICE AREAS: Domestic Relations Law; Family Law; Matrimonial Law.
Tsimbidaros, Peter . . . . '69 '95 C.1030 B.A. L.184 J.D. P.O. Box 320482
Tully, Michael J. '39 '70 C.588 B.S. L.128 J.D.
(adm. in VA; not adm. in CT; See Pat. Sect.) [🄰 Perman&G.]
*PRACTICE AREAS: Patent, Trademark, Copyright.
Tully, Thomas L. . . . . '33 '60 C.93 B.S. L.276 J.D. [🄰 Perman&G.] (See Pat. Sect.)
*PRACTICE AREAS: Patent, Trademark, Copyright.
VanDenburgh, Howard F. '35 '62 C.339 B.S. L.260 J.D.
(adm. in FL; not adm. in CT; Pat.) 3135 Easton Tpke.‡
Villarreal, Elpidio '60 '86 C.178 B.A. L.976 J.D.
(adm. in IL; not adm. in CT) Coun., Litig. & Legal Pol., General Electric Company
*RESPONSIBILITIES: Litigation; Alternative Dispute Resolution.

Wake, See, Dimes & Bryniczka
(See Westport)

Wald, Jerry '58 '83 C.339 B.S. L.145 J.D.
(adm. in IL; not adm. in CT) Pension Coun., General Electric Company
*RESPONSIBILITIES: Employee Benefits Law.
Waniak, Donna M. '60 '85 C.914 B.A. L.273 J.D.
Coun., Environ. Tort Lit., General Electric Company
*RESPONSIBILITIES: Toxic Tort Litigation; Environmental Law; Products Liability.
Warren, David M. '35 '71 C.453 B.S.E.E. L.818 J.D.
(adm. in MA; not adm. in CT; See Pat. Sect.) [🄰 Perman&G.]
*PRACTICE AREAS: Patent, Trademark, Copyright.
Watson, Felicia B. . . . . '58 '83 C.712 B.A. L.607 J.D. 1506 Post Rd.
Weber, David F. . . . . '61 '86 C.1030 B.A. L.276 J.D. 394 Rowland Rd.
Weinstein, Paul . . . . '40 '70 C.667 B.M.E. L.276 J.D. [🄲 Perman&G.] (See Pat. Sect.)
Weiss, Scott A. . . . . '60 '86 C.1044 B.A. L.365 J.D. 2000 Post Rd., LL106
Welch, Karin L. '59 '90 C.776 B.A. L.1029 J.D. [🄲 Friedman,M.&N.]
Weldy, Thomas P., (BV) . . . . '47 '72 C.197 A.B. L.477 J.D. [Morehouse,H.&W.]
*PRACTICE AREAS: Litigation; Real Estate; Probate; Estate Planning; Foreclosure.
Wells, Galen W. . . . . '43 '75 C.300 B.A. L.1035 J.D. [Wilcox&W.]
Wilcox, Eileen K., (BV) . . . . '52 '76 C.66 B.A. L.178 J.D. [Wilcox&W.]
Wilcox & Wells, (BV) . . . . P.O. Box 1025
Williams, Scott Wilson, (BV) . . . . '58 '84 C&L.896 B.A., J.D. [Maher&W.]
*PRACTICE AREAS: Workers Compensation.
Willis, Gregory C., (AV) . . . . '19 '47 C.918 B.A. L.976 LL.B. [🄲 Morehouse,H.&W.]
Winter, Catherine J. '63 '91
C.347 B.S. L.910 J.D. Pat. Coun., General Electric Company (Pat.)
*RESPONSIBILITIES: Patent.
Winter, Richard L., (BV) . . . . '29 '54 C&L.184 B.A., J.D. 220 Fairmount Terr.

Wittstein, James Richard '62 '94 C.1211 B.S.N. L.1040 J.D.
341 Melville Avenue, 06432
Telephone: 203-334-4552 Fax: 203-330-0369
Email: jrwlaw@cshore.com
***PRACTICE AREAS: Nursing Law; Medical Law; Real Estate.**
Nursing Law, Medical Law, Real Estate.

See Professional Biographies, FAIRFIELD, CONNECTICUT

Wocl, Nicholas E., (BV) . . . . '59 '84 C.676 B.A. L.1029 J.D. [Tooher&W.] ⊙
Zalucki, Robert J. '61 '85 C.453 S.B. L.813 J.D.
(adm. in CA; not adm. in CT) Tax Coun., General Electric Company
Ziegler, Geza C., Jr. '61 '94 C.1029 B.S.E.E. L.1252 J.D.
[🄰 Perman&G.] (See Pat. Sect.)
*PRACTICE AREAS: Patent, Trademark, Copyright.
Zwecker, Samuel W. . . . . '06 '35 C.569 B.S. L.1009 LL.B. 451 Lockwood Rd.‡

FALLS VILLAGE, 650, *Litchfield Co.*

Coolidge, Thomas R. '34 '63 C&L.309 A.B., LL.B.
(adm. in NY; not adm. in CT) Pres., Coolidge & Co.

FARMINGTON, 16,407, *Hartford Co.*

Andrews, Jomarie T., (AV) . . . . '54 '79 C.165 B.A. L.184 J.D. [Levy&D.]
*PRACTICE AREAS: Commercial Real Estate Law; Real Estate Development Law; Conveyancing Law; Financing Law; Leasing Law.
Appletree, Steven R. . . . . '46 '72 C.1033 B.A. L.818 J.D. 270 Farmington Ave
Bailey, Samuel, Jr., (AV) . . . . '40 '69 C.855 A.B. L.184 J.D. 2 Bridgewater Rd.
Baker, George A., (BV) . . . . '64 '89 C.999 B.S. L.1048 J.D. [🄰 Levy&D.]
*PRACTICE AREAS: Estate Planning; Estate Administration; Business Planning.
Bassett, Jack M., (BV) . . . . '52 '79 C.165 B.A. L.896 J.D. 3 Melrose Dr.
Bendett, Adam L., (BV) . . . . '59 '85 C.659 B.A. L.184 J.D. 160 Farmington Ave.
Bernis, Susan R. . . . . '62 '88 C.1044 B.A. L.107 J.D. Transition Unit Mgr., Orion Specialty
Bertini, M. Katherine, (BV) '65 '90 C.276 A.B. L.184 J.D.
Asst. Coun., Otis Elevator Co.
Bickle, Gregory L. '51 '77 C&L.585 B.S., J.D.
(adm. in ND; not adm. in CT) Pres., Berkley Administrators of Connecticut, Inc.
Bissonnette, Marsha O. . . . . '48 '80 C&L.184 B.A., J.D. 9 Farm Springs Dr.

Bogossian, Gail, (AV) '55 '85 C.855 B.A. L.184 J.D.
Associate General Counsel, Connecticare, Inc.
Boisture, J. Bruce, (BV) ... '50 '80 C.674 A.B. L.976 J.D. 49 High St.
Bonassar, Joseph M. '59 '87 C.401 B.S.Ch.E. L.184 J.D.
Asst. Gen. Coun., Carvel Corp.
*RESPONSIBILITIES: General Corporate Counseling; Litigation; Corporate Finance and Governance; Contracts; Franchise Law.
Boyle, Elaine I. ... '56 '87 C.602 B.A. L.93 J.D. 17 Whitehall Pl.
Breetz, William R., (AV) ... '41 '68 C.197 B.A. L.893 LL.B. [🄲 Levy&D.]
*PRACTICE AREAS: Real Estate Law; Finance Law; Energy Law.
Brogan, Christopher J. '54 '79 C.276 A.B. L.94 J.D.
Deputy General Counsel, Carrier World Headquarters
Bruce, William C. '52 '77 C.1156 B.A. L.976 J.D.
Vice Pres., Indust. and Employee Relations, Carrier Corp.‡
Bryant, Susan E., (AV) ... '48 '76 C.914 B.A. L.623 J.D. [S.E.Bryant]
*PRACTICE AREAS: Securities; Corporate; Broker-Dealer; Investment Adviser; Business Law.

Bryant, Susan E., P.C., (AV)
Six Forest Park Drive, P.O. Box 444, 06032
Telephone: 860-674-0111 Fax: 860-674-0011
Email: sebry@aol.com
Susan E. Bryant;—Lois L. McGuire.
Practice includes Securities, Corporate, Commercial Law.
See Professional Biographies, FARMINGTON, CONNECTICUT

Byrne, Steven, (BV) ... '64 '91 C.829 B.A. L.1029 J.D. [Byrne&B.]
Byrne, Thomas P., (AV) ... '30 '55 C.1030 B.B.A. L.93 LL.B. [Byrne&B.]
Byrne & Byrne, (AV) ... 790 Farmington Ave.
Cardinez, Benjamin F. ... '40 '85 L.184 J.D. 65 Woodruff Rd.
Cawley, Donald K., (AV) '52 '78 C.103 A.B. L.976 J.D.
Dep. Gen. Coun., Carrier World Headquarters
Clark, Gregory E. ... '62 '88 C.176 B.A. L.184 J.D. TransAmerica Business Credit
Cohen, Jason W. ... '70 '95 C.67 B.A. L.818 J.D. [🄰 Levy&D.]
*PRACTICE AREAS: Civil Litigation; Labor and Employment Law; Municipal Law; Workers' Compensation; Unemployment Compensation.
Cohen, Richard D., (BV) ... '47 '73 C.659 B.A. L.184 J.D. [🄲 Cohen,W.&M.]
*PRACTICE AREAS: Commercial Real Estate Law; Shopping Center Development; Real Estate Finance.
Cohen, Robert B., (BV) ... '33 '57 C.216 A.B. L.659 LL.B. [🄲 Levy&D.]
*PRACTICE AREAS: Environmental Law; Litigation.

Cohen, Wakim & Merlin, P.C., (AV)
16 Munson Road, 06032
Mailing Address: P.O. Box 4055, Farmington, Connecticut 06034-4055
Telephone: 860-284-7107 Telecopy: 860-284-1176
James E. Wakim; Lawrence E. Merlin;—Anthony Crosby; Robert A. Randich; James P. Juliano. Of Counsel: Richard D. Cohen.
Commercial Real Estate Acquisition, Disposition, Development, Leasing, Finance and Litigation.
Reference: Fleet National Bank, N.A.

Crosby, Anthony ... '58 '86 C.855 B.A. L.184 J.D. [🄰 Cohen,W.&M.]
*PRACTICE AREAS: Commercial Real Estate Law; Shopping Center Development; Real Estate Finance.
Cullina, Karen M. ... '60 '94 C.1155 B.S. L.306 J.D. Connecticare, Inc.
Daraskevich, Heidi J., (BV) ... '64 '91 C.855 B.A. L.306 J.D. [🄰 M.N.Perlstein]
*PRACTICE AREAS: Condominium Association Law; Common Interest Community Law; Commercial Litigation; Civil Litigation; Creditors Rights.
Dreilinger, Gwen B., (BV) ... '54 '82 C.597 B.A. L.184 J.D. 10 Melrose Dr.
Droney, John F., Jr., (AV) ... '46 '73 C.321 A.B. L.184 J.D. [Levy&D.]
*PRACTICE AREAS: Litigation.
Dunn, Robert G. ... '66 '92 C.378 B.S. L.818 J.D. Coun., Konover Construction Corp.
Duprey, Michelle M. ... '66 '94 C.1145 B.S.B.A. L.184 J.D. 321 Main St.
Engstrom, Elizabeth L. ... '44 '73 C.696 A.B. L.184 J.D. 173 Garden St.
Evans, David Cyril ... '59 '85 C.411 B.S. L.260 J.D. P.O. Box 887
Evans, Peter V., (BV) '45 '71 C.107 B.A. L.724 J.D.
Sr. V.P., Chf. Admin. Offr., & Gen. Coun., Sec., Familymeds, Inc.
Evans, Ross S., (BV) '47 '74 C.67 B.A. L.184 J.D.
V.P. & Gen. Coun., Otis Elevator Co.
Fahey, John P., (BV) ... '62 '86 C.93 A.B. L.1029 J.D. [🄰 Witherspoon]
Feldman, Michael, (BV) ... '54 '81 C.1044 B.A. L.978 J.D. [Feldman&H.]

Feldman & Hickey, LLC, (BV)
10 Waterside Drive, Suite 303, 06032
Telephone: 860-677-0551
Email: michaelfeldman@feldmanhickey.com
Michael Feldman; Charles E. Ned Hickey; Kristen Schultze Greene.
See Professional Biographies, FARMINGTON, CONNECTICUT

Fingold, Ross G., (AV) ... '56 '81 C.659 B.A. L.823 J.D. [Levy&D.]
*PRACTICE AREAS: Commercial and Financial Litigation; Commercial Finance; Asset Based Finance; Real Estate Litigation; Loan Workouts and Restructuring.
Fischman, Bruce A., (BV) ... '47 '74 C.415 B.S. L.1009 J.D. 231 Farmington Ave.
Fisher, Jeffrey L., (BV) '63 '88
C.945 B.A. L.276 J.D. Asst. V.P., Discover Reinsurance Co
Flynn, Daniel F. ... '35 '62 C.321 B.S. L.184 LL.B. Mng. Dir., Resources Mgmt. Grp.
Foley, John C. ... '53 '78 C&L.184 B.S., J.D. Asst. Gen. Coun., Carrier Corp.
Galli, Robert E. ... '45 '76 C.93 A.B. L.184 J.D. V.P., Gen Coun. & Secy., Carrier Corp.
Green, Louis F., (AV) ... '42 '68 C&L.184 B.A., LL.B. [Green&L.]
*PRACTICE AREAS: Entrepreneurial Business Law; Corporate Law; Commercial Real Estate; Real Estate Development; Real Estate Acquisitions.

Green & Levine LLP, (AV)
231 Farmington Avenue, 06032
Telephone: 860-677-7004 Facsimile: 860-677-7005
URL: http://www.lawyers.com/g&llaw
Louis F. Green; Tamara Kagan Levine. Of Counsel: Eugene M. Kagan.
Commercial and Residential Real Estate, Zoning, Development, Finance, Corporate Workouts and Foreclosures, Commercial Leasing, Business Law.
See Professional Biographies, FARMINGTON, CONNECTICUT

Greene, Kristen Schultze ... '71 '96 C.550 B.A. L.1048 J.D. [Feldman&H.]
Groberg, Neil '53 '80 C.659 B.S. L.1019 J.D.
Asst. V.P., Asst. Secy. & Asst. Gen. Coun., Orion Capital Cos.
Gross, Howard I., (AV) ... '23 '51 C&L.184 B.A., J.D. [🄲 Levy&D.]
*PRACTICE AREAS: Business Planning; Estate Planning; Asset Protection.
Gurrola, Edward M., (CVⓉ) '56 '81 C&L.813 A.B., J.D.
(adm. in CA; not adm. in CT) 28 Cedar Ridge Dr.‡
Halloran, R. Bartley, (AV) ... '50 '75 C.276 B.A. L.184 J.D. [🄲 Levy&D.]
*PRACTICE AREAS: Malpractice; Negligence; Class Actions; Commercial Litigation; Securities Litigation.
Hannon, Robert J. ... '51 '91 C.910 B.A. L.184 J.D. P.O. Box 67
Hartstone, Joel Martin, (AV) '45 '70 C.454 B.B.A. L.188 J.D.
Chmn. of the Bd., Hartstone & Dickstein Inc.
Harvey, Elton Bartlett, III ... '46 '86 C.1156 L.1048 J.D. 3 Melrose Dr.
Hickey, Charles E. Ned ... '53 '90 C.1057 B.A. L.184 J.D. [Feldman&H.]
Hogan, Carolyn M. ... '— '92 C.262 B.A. L.1202 J.D. [🄰 Witherspoon]
Hyland, Robert E., (AV) ... '44 '74 C&L.184 B.S., J.D. Traveler Spec. Liability Grp.
Isaacson, Herbert G., (AV) ... '36 '63 C.197 A.B. L.309 LL.B. [🄲 Levy&D.]
*PRACTICE AREAS: Real Estate Law; Conveyancing Law; Condominium Law; Foreclosure Law.
Johnson, Amy K. ... '61 '87 C.885 B.A. L.228 J.D. Carrington Lane
Jones, David M. '72 '97 C.855 B.A. L.276 J.D.
Asst. V.P. & Sr. Corp. Coun., Familymeds, Inc.
Jones, William W. '34 '68 C.549 B.S. L.276 J.D.
(adm. in DC; not adm. in CT; Pat.) 10 Farm Springs‡
Josephson, Donald A., (AV) ... '54 '79 C.951 B.A. L.188 J.D. 1484 New Britain Ave.
Juliano, James P. ... '64 '90 C.884 B.A. L.184 J.D. [🄰 Cohen,W.&M.]
*PRACTICE AREAS: Commercial Real Estate Law; Shopping Center Development; Real Estate Finance.
Kagan, Eugene M., (AV) ... '30 '56 C&L.184 B.A., LL.B. [🄲 Green&L.]
*PRACTICE AREAS: Commercial Real Estate; Real Estate Development.
Kane, Edmund J. '16 '42 C&L.262 A.B., J.D.
(adm. in NY; not adm. in CT) 42 Tunxis Vil.‡
Keen, Ralph S., III, (BV) ... '57 '83 C.92 B.A. L.589 J.D. 406 Farmington Ave.
Kelley, Robert J. ... '48 '78 C.971 B.S.E.E. L.184 J.D. 1810 New Britain Ave.
Keppelman, Richard T., (AV) ... '43 '72 C.976 B.A. L.178 J.D. [Levy&D.]
*PRACTICE AREAS: Corporate Law; Securities Law; Commercial Finance Law; Mergers and Acquisitions; Health Care Law.
Kern, Scott C. ... '58 '84 C.976 B.A. L.893 J.D. Gen. Coun., Carvel Corp.
*RESPONSIBILITIES: General Corporate Counseling; Corporate Finance and Governance; Mergers and Acquisitions.
Kiel, Lawrence J., (BV) ... '57 '83 C&L.184 B.A., J.D. [Murphy,L.&K.] ⊙
*PRACTICE AREAS: Corporate; Real Estate; Commercial Lending; Contracts; Bankruptcy.
King, Edgar A. ... '23 '54 C.340 Ph.B. L.184 LL.B. [🄲 Levy&D.]
*PRACTICE AREAS: Estate Planning; Probate Administration.
Kleinman, Daniel E., (AV) ... '44 '69 C.309 A.B. L.94 J.D. [Levy&D.]
*PRACTICE AREAS: Land Use Law; Real Estate Law; Banking Law; Finance Law; Sports Law.
Kleinman, William N., (AV) ... '48 '74 C.309 B.A. L.94 J.D. Asst. Atty. Gen.
Kostin, Dane R., (BV) ... '47 '72 C.659 B.S. L.94 J.D. [Levy&D.]
*PRACTICE AREAS: Securities Law; Business Planning Law; Franchise Law; Corporate Law; Commercial Law.
Lapuk, Marvin H., (AV) ... '31 '60 C&L.184 B.S., J.D. [Levy&D.]
*PRACTICE AREAS: Estate Planning Law; Business Planning Law; Estate Administration Law.
Laudati, John L., (BV) ... '55 '81 C&L.184 B.A., J.D. [Murphy,L.&K.] ⊙
*PRACTICE AREAS: Commercial Litigation; Criminal Law; Personal Injury; Family Law.
Lemaire, Leon L. ... '30 '59 C&L.184 B.A., LL.B. P.O. Box 1067
Lemire, Daniel J., (AV) '56 '85 C.184 B.A. L.818 J.D.
Vice President & General Counsel, Center Capital Corporation
Levine, Kenneth J., (BV) ... '65 '90 C.867 B.S. L.245 J.D. [Levy&D.]
*PRACTICE AREAS: Civil Litigation; Criminal Litigation; Personal Injury; Workers Compensation; Family Law.
Levine, Robert B., (BV) ... '60 '85 C.183 B.A. L.818 J.D. [Levy&D.]
*PRACTICE AREAS: Estate Planning; Estate Administration; Business Reorganization; Succession Planning.
Levine, Tamara Kagan, (BV) ... '56 '81 C.183 B.A. L.184 J.D. [Green&L.]
*PRACTICE AREAS: Commercial Real Estate; Real Estate Development; Real Estate Finance; Commercial Leasing; Affordable Housing.
Levy, Coleman B., (AV) ... '39 '66 C&L.184 B.A., LL.B. [Levy&D.]
*PRACTICE AREAS: Real Estate; Corporation; Business; Finance; Mergers and Acquisitions.

Levy & Droney, P.C., (AV)
Pond View Corporate Center, 74 Batterson Park Road, P.O. Box 887, 06034-0887
Telephone: 860-676-3000 Telecopier Ext: 860-676-3200
Email: ldlaw.com URL: http://www.ldlaw.com
Coleman B. Levy; John F. Droney, Jr.; Joel Mandell; Dane R. Kostin; Marvin H. Lapuk; John Rose, Jr.; Daniel E. Kleinman; Jomarie T. Andrews; Jeffrey J. Mirman; Robin Messier Pearson; Joseph A. Vitale; Richard T. Keppelman; William C. Stokesbury; Robert B. Levine; David M. Sheridan; Ross G. Fingold; Lawrence J. Marks; Kenneth J. Levine; C. Robert Zelinger;—Lisa A. Zaccardelli; Joseph B. Sappington; George A. Baker; Jason W. Cohen. Counsel: William R. Breetz; Robert B. Cohen; Howard I. Gross; R. Bartley Halloran; Herbert G. Isaacson; Edgar A. King; Peter J. Tyrrell; Louis Wang; George M. Hyman (1904-1985); Harry H. Kleinman (1933-1981); John P. Pavia, III.
Administrative Law, Banking, Business Law, Civil and Criminal Litigation in State and Federal Courts, Condominiums, Construction, Corporate, Environmental Law, Estate Planning, Family Law, Foreclosures, Health Care, Labor and Employment, Mergers and Acquisitions, Municipal, Personal Injury and Insurance Defense Law, Practice Before Federal and State Agencies and Commissions, Probate, Public Finance, Real Estate, Secured and Unsecured Commercial Transactions, Securities, Taxation, Title Insurance Litigation, Zoning.
See Professional Biographies, FARMINGTON, CONNECTICUT

Lovell, Peter H. ... '58 '85 C.902 B.A. L.1202 J.D. 9 Farm Springs Dr.
Mallery, Nancy B., (BV) ... '58 '86 C.103 A.B. L.1009 J.D. Counsel, Travelers Ins.
Mamrosh, Ronald G. ... '61 '90 C.1349 B.S. L.184 J.D. 2 Bridgewater Rd.
Mandell, Joel, (AV) ... '39 '66 C&L.184 B.A., J.D. [Levy&D.]
*PRACTICE AREAS: Commercial Real Estate Law; Conveyancing Law; Finance Law; Title Insurance Law.
Mangs, Gail K., (BV) ... '52 '85 C.156 B.A. L.184 J.D. 270 Farmington Ave.
Marks, Lawrence J., (BV) ... '65 '90 C.855 B.A. L.569 J.D. [Levy&D.]
*PRACTICE AREAS: Federal and State Taxation; Pension, Profit Sharing and Employee Benefits Law; Municipal and Public Finance Law; Limited Liability Company Law.
Martin, Leah A. '65 '90 C.1019 B.A. L.184 J.D.
Dir. Tech. Servs., United Systems Integrators Corp.
Matney, Scott H. ... '70 '96 C.999 B.A. L.306 J.D. 406 Farmington Ave.
Mayer, Dennis M. '48 '80 C.688 B.S. L.184 J.D.
Vice President - Counsel, United Technologies Corporation
McCormack, Marcia, (BV) ... '43 '91 C.725 B.A. L.1048 J.D. P.O. Box 125
McGuire, Lois L. ... '57 '83 C.1175 B.A. L.184 J.D. [🄰 S.E.Bryant]
*PRACTICE AREAS: Securities; Corporate Law; Broker-Dealer Arbitration; Investment Management; Business Law.
McHugh, Randall S., (BV) ... '62 '88 C.390 B.S. L.216 J.D. 160 Farmington Ave.
Merlin, Lawrence E., (BV) ... '59 '87 C.659 B.S.B.A. L.94 J.D. [Cohen,W.&M.]
*PRACTICE AREAS: Commercial Real Estate Law; Shopping Center Development; Real Estate Finance.
Michaud, Lucy ... '53 '96 C.1330 B.A. L.1252 J.D. 14 Ridgeview Dr.
Mirman, Jeffrey J., (BV) ... '53 '78 C.367 B.A. L.273 J.D. [Levy&D.]
*PRACTICE AREAS: Litigation.
Moore, John W., Jr. ... '26 '62 C.976 B.A. L.184 LL.B. 23 Waterville Rd.
Morris, Julius D. ... '23 '53 C&L.790 LL.B. 58 Forest Hills Dr.‡
Morrissey, J. David, Jr., (BV) ... '48 '81 C.478 B.A. L.1048 J.D. 200 Main St.
Murphy, Neil F., Jr., (BV) ... '45 '70 C.93 A.B. L.184 J.D. [Murphy,L.&K.] ⊙
*PRACTICE AREAS: Personal Injury Litigation; Criminal Law; Civil Rights; Real Property Litigation.

Murphy, Laudati & Kiel, P.C., (BV)
The Exchange, Suite 360 270 Farmington Avenue, 06032 ⊙
Telephone: 860-674-8296 Fax: 860-674-0850
URL: http://www.lawyers.com/mlklaw
Neil F. Murphy, Jr.; John L. Laudati; Lawrence J. Kiel;—Margaret Fogerty Rattigan.
General Civil and Criminal Practice before State and Federal Courts.
Litchfield County Office: Plaza Park North, 249 Winsted Road, Torrington, 06790. Telephone: 860-482-3478. Fax: 860-674-0850.
See Professional Biographies, FARMINGTON, CONNECTICUT

Nevius, Garrett W. ... '14 '41 C.674 A.B. L.178 LL.B. 45 Diamond Glen Rd.‡
O'Connell, Brian Michael ... '60 '88 C.855 B.A. L.184 J.D. 6 Farm Dr.
O'Reilly, John A., Jr., (BV) ... '41 '66 C.1030 B.S. L.184 LL.B. 161 Tunxis Vil.

Pavia, John P., III, (CV) ....'63 '90 C.229 B.A. L.29 J.D. [ⓒLevy&D.]
*PRACTICE AREAS: Commercial Litigation; Corporate Transactions; Intellectual Property; Government Relations; Municipal and Public Finance.
Pearson, Robin Messier, (AV) ....'51 '80 C.855 B.A. L.184 J.D. [Levy&D.]
*PRACTICE AREAS: Land Use and Environmental Law.

Perlstein, Matthew N., Law Office of, (AV) '46 '73 C.65 A.B. L.94 J.D.
10 Waterside Drive, Suite 303, 06032
Telephone: 860-677-2177 Telecopier: 860-677-1147
Email: mnp@ctcondolaw.com URL: http://www.ctcondolaw.com
***PRACTICE AREAS: Condominium Law; Community Association Law.**
—Julia Duchow Thompson; Heidi J. Daraskevich.
Condominium and Community Association Law.
See Professional Biographies, FARMINGTON, CONNECTICUT

Pew, Douglas J. '42 '67 C&L.910 A.B., J.D.
Associate General Counsel, United Technologies Corporation
Randich, Robert A., (BV) ....'61 '86 C&L.184 B.A., J.D. [ⒶCohen,W.&M.]
*PRACTICE AREAS: Commercial Law; Real Estate Litigation.
Rattigan, Margaret Fogerty .... '60 '91 C.184 B.A. L.306 J.D. [ⒶMurphy,L.&K.]
Reiner, Michael D., (BV) .... '59 '84 C.855 B.A. L.184 J.D. 160 Farmington Ave.
Rockwell, Bryan D. .... '64 '92 C.184 B.S.M.E. L.705 J.D. Sr. Pat. Atty., Carrier Corp.
Rome, David A. ....'62 '88 C.575 B.A. L.184 J.D. Gen. Coun., BerkleyCare
Rose, John, Jr., (AV) ....'40 '66 C.197 A.B. L.976 LL.B. [Levy&D.]
*PRACTICE AREAS: Commercial Law; Construction Litigation; Employment Litigation.
Rosenfeld, Robert M., (AV) .... '35 '60 C.855 B.A. L.184 LL.B. P.O. Box 1345

Rosenfield, Howard M. '53 '80 C.1331 B.A. L.61 J.D.
10 Waterside Drive, Suite 303, 06032
Telephone: 860-677-4334 Fax: 860-677-1147 Email: howard@stockbrokerproblems.com
Email: howisu4u@aol.com
***PRACTICE AREAS: Securities Arbitration; Mediation; Securities Consumer Arbitration; Shareholder Disputes; Investment Fraud.**
Securities Arbitration, Arbitration and Mediation, Securities Consumer Arbitration, Shareholders Disputes, Investment Fraud.
See Professional Biographies, FARMINGTON, CONNECTICUT

Rubin, Jack .... '13 '39 C.197 B.A. L.976 LL.B. 74 Batterson Pk., Rd.
Sappington, Joseph B. .... '72 '99 C.423 B.A. L.1194 J.D. [ⒶLevy&D.]
*PRACTICE AREAS: Environmental Law; Civil Litigation.
Scholl, Glenn L. ....'47 '74 C.67 B.A. L.184 J.D. Mgr., Mun. Remediation Servs., LLC
Schwartz, Scott M., (BV) '58 '83
C.188 B.A. L.245 J.D. 406 Farmington Avenue Suite 1002
Scinto, Michael L. ....'58 '84 C.855 B.A. L.184 J.D. 18 Wakefield Ln.
Sensale, Michele D. .... '64 '92 C.855 B.A. L.1040 J.D. [ⒶWitherspoon]
Sha'afi, Sheryl J., (BV) .... '43 '79 C.339 A.B. L.1048 J.D. 11 Skyline Dr.
Sheridan, David M., (BV) .... '55 '85 C.37 B.S. L.184 J.D. [Levy&D.]
*PRACTICE AREAS: Litigation.
Snyder, Troxell K. '53 '82 C.688 B.S. L.184 J.D.
Dep. Intell. Prop. Coun., Otis Elevator Co. (Pat.)
Stokesbury, William C., (BV) ....'59 '84 C.976 B.A. L.94 J.D. [Levy&D.]
*PRACTICE AREAS: Real Estate Law; Conveyancing Law; Financing Law; Leasing Law.
Szydlowski, George S. .... '47 '72 C&L.184 B.A., J.D. Asst. Atty. Gen.
Tarlow, Jules S., (AV) ....'24 '50 C.184 L.94 LL.B. 74 Batterson Pk. Rd.
Thompson, Julia Duchow .... '68 '96 C.473 B.S.ED. L.588 J.D. [ⒶM.N.Perlstein]
*PRACTICE AREAS: Condominium Law; Community Association Law.
Tyrrell, Peter J. ....'44 '69 C.884 B.S. L.93 J.D. [ⓒLevy&D.]
*PRACTICE AREAS: Telecommunications.
Vitale, Joseph A., (BV) ....'56 '81 C.93 A.B. L.276 J.D. [Levy&D.]
*PRACTICE AREAS: Health Care Law; Municipal and Public Finance Law.
Wakim, James E., (AV) ....'57 '82 C&L.184 B.A., J.D. [Cohen,W.&M.]
*PRACTICE AREAS: Commercial Real Estate Law; Shopping Center Development; Real Estate; Finance.
Walker, Philip N. .... '48 '86 C.103 A.B. L.1048 J.D. 270 Farmington Ave., Ste. 360
Wang, Louis ....'50 '94 C.860 B.S. L.184 J.D. [ⓒLevy&D.]
Webbe, Peggy J. '52 '93 C.101 B.A. L.184 J.D.
Asst. Coun., United Technologies Corp./Otis Elevator Co.
Whiton, Molly T., (BV) .... '51 '87 C.1030 B.A. L.184 J.D. [ⒶWitherspoon]
Williams, Nancy R. .... '50 '86 C.829 B.A. L.184 J.D. Univ. of Conn. Health Ctr.
Wilson, Scott A. .... '45 '72 C&L.184 B.A., J.D. 195 Farmington Ave.‡
Winslow, Thomas H., (BV) ....'55 '83 C&L.607 B.S., J.D. [T.H.Winslow]

Winslow, Thomas H., LLC, The Law Office of, (BV)
321 Main Street, 06032-2976
Telephone: 860-678-4425 Fax: 860-678-4427
Email: thomaswins@aol.com
Thomas H. Winslow.
Insurance, Insurance Defense, Products Liability, Vehicle Rental, Municipal Defense, Health Insurance, ERISA, Litigation, Pharmacists Liability.
See Professional Biographies, FARMINGTON, CONNECTICUT

Witherspoon, Thomas W., Jr., (BV) .... '46 '73 C.188 B.A. L.184 J.D. [Witherspoon]
Witherspoon Law Offices, The, (BV) ....790 Farmington Avenue
Wollenberg, William L. ....'32 '67 C.478 B.A. L.184 LL.B. Supr. Ct. J.
Wu, Michael '55 '83 C.1101 B.A. L.1048 J.D.
Associate Counsel, United Technologies Corporation
Zaccardelli, Lisa A., (BV) ....'65 '90 C.93 B.A. L.1263 J.D. [ⒶLevy&D.]
*PRACTICE AREAS: Litigation.
Zelinger, C. Robert, (BV) ....'55 '86 C.855 B.A. L.184 J.D. [Levy&D.]
*PRACTICE AREAS: Business Law; Mergers and Acquisitions; Information Technology.
Zemetis, Joseph C., (AV) .....'50 '80 C&L.184 B.A., J.D. Assoc. Coun., Otis Elevator Co.

FENWICK, 89, *Middlesex Co.*

Graham, James T. ....'42 '69 C.524 B.S. L.262 LL.B. 2 Mohegan Ave.‡

FRANKLIN, 1,592, *New London Co.*

Fisher, William W., Jr. .... '32 '61 C.95 B.A. L.477 J.D. 243 Route 32

GALES FERRY, —, *New London Co.*

Lubin, Harold M., (BV) ....'48 '75 C.390 A.B. L.184 J.D. 1527 Rt. 12

GLASTONBURY, 24,327, *Hartford Co.*

Aiken, Richard L., Jr., (BV) ....'56 '85 C.1156 B.S. L.1048 J.D. [Pomeranz,D.&S.]
*PRACTICE AREAS: Workers Compensation Law.
Alter, Peter Jay, (BV) ....'46 '73 C.309 A.B. L.184 J.D. [Alter&S.]
*PRACTICE AREAS: Real Estate Development Law.

Alter and Sherwood, LLC, (BV)
701 Hebron Avenue, P.O. Box 1420, 06033
Telephone: 860-652-4020 Telecopier: 860-652-4022
Members of Firm: Peter Jay Alter; David F. Sherwood;—Ryan K. McKain.
General Civil Practice before State and Federal Courts. Real Estate, Zoning, Land Use and Administrative Practice, Corporation, Environmental Law and Real Estate Development.
See Professional Biographies, GLASTONBURY, CONNECTICUT

Arnold, Steven E., (BV) '50 '77
C.820 B.A. L.1048 J.D. [Howard,K.S.&F.] (⊙West Hartford)
Auchter, Donald F. ....'20 '52 C.31 B.A. L.184 LL.B. Ret. Probate J.
Ayars, Patricia A., (BV) ....'50 '83 C&L.184 B.A., J.D. [Ayars&Assoc.]
*PRACTICE AREAS: Condominium Law; Real Estate Law.

Ayars & Associates, LLC, (BV)
131 New London Turnpike, Suite 318, 06033
Telephone: 860-652-7070 Fax: 860-652-7073
Email: pattylaw50@aol.com
Patricia A. Ayars.
Real Estate, Condominium Law, Cooperative Housing Law, Cooperative Housing Association Law, Real Estate Development, Water Rights, Riparian Rights, Family Law, ADR, Mortgage Financing, Consumer Credit and Finance.
See Professional Biographies, GLASTONBURY, CONNECTICUT

Basine, Robert B., (BV) .... '32 '60 C.94 B.S.B.A. L.184 LL.B. [Trowbridge&B.]
Boatman, Patrick W., (AV) ....'51 '79 C.1075 B.A. L.94 J.D. [Boatman,B.G.&T.]
*PRACTICE AREAS: Commercial Law; Bankruptcy; General Litigation; Personal Injury.

Boatman, Boscarino, Grasso & Twachtman, (AV)
628 Hebron Avenue, Building 3, P.O. Box 650, 06033-0650
Telephone: 860-659-5657 Telecopier: 860-657-4549
Members of Firm: Patrick W. Boatman; Thomas C. Boscarino; John H. Grasso; Walter A. Twachtman, Jr.
Commercial, Debtor and Creditor Rights, Bankruptcy, Litigation, Real Estate and Real Estate Development, Estate Planning, Personal Injury, Representation before IRS, Litigation in all Courts. Approved Attorney and Agent For: Lawyers Title Insurance Corp.; Connecticut Attorneys Title Insurance Co.; Chicago Title Insurance Co.
See Professional Biographies, GLASTONBURY, CONNECTICUT

Boscarino, Thomas C., (AV) ....'52 '77 C.184 B.A. L.192 J.D. [Boatman,B.G.&T.]
*PRACTICE AREAS: Bankruptcy; Debtor and Creditor Rights; Tax Collection; Commercial Law; Commercial Litigation.
Branse, Mark K., (BV) .... '47 '79 C.228 B.A. L.184 J.D. [Branse&W.]
Branse & Willis, LLC, (BV) .... 41 C New London Turnpike
Briggs, Carole Williams, & Associates, (BV) '60 '85
C.494 B.A. L.273 J.D. 45 Glastonbury Boulevard
Brown, Richard R., (AV) ...... '45 '71 C.454 B.A. L.184 J.D. [Brown,P.&S.] (⊙Hartford)
Brown, Paindiris & Scott, LLP ....
Brown, Paindiris & Scott, LLP, (AV)
2252 Main Street (⊙East Hampton, Hartford, Hebron, Stamford)
Brunstad, Sheryl Kim .... '62 '87 C.228 A.B. L.477 J.D. 96 Strickland St.
Buonopane, Michael M. ....'71 '96 C.184 B.A. L.1202 J.D. [ⒶMontstream&M.]
*PRACTICE AREAS: Workers' Compensation; Civil Litigation; Insurance Defense.
Burmeister, Richard R. ....'47 '75 C.823 B.A. L.421 J.D. 200 Glastonbury Blvd.
Burnham, Anne .... '66 '95 C.184 B.A. L.306 J.D. [ⒶJaconetta&Assoc.]
*PRACTICE AREAS: Estate Planning; Estate Administration; Real Estate; Probate.
Canivan, James T., (BV) ....'37 '62 C.855 B.A. L.145 J.D. 124 Hebron Ave.
Chalé, M. Edward '45 '74 C.569 B.S. L.1099 J.D.
(adm. in NY; not adm. in CT) USI Consulting Group, Inc.
Clarke, Timothy A. '55 '81 C.732 B.A. L.1048 J.D.
(adm. in MA; not adm. in CT) Sr. V.P., Gen. Coun. & Secy., Fleet Capital Corporation
*RESPONSIBILITIES: Corporate Law; Commercial Law; Finance Law; Secured Transactions.
Clemens, David R., (BV) ....'56 '83 C.184 B.A. L.831 J.D. 41 New London Tpke.
Clinton, Michael H. .... '63 '88 C.1360 B.A. L.1029 J.D. 2510 Main St.
Collins, Marshall R. ....'49 '74 C.1033 B.A. L.790 J.D. 117 New London Tpke.
Collins, Paul W., (BV) ....'57 '85 C.264 B.A. L.1202 J.D. [Collins&D.]
*PRACTICE AREAS: Corporate Law; Buying and Selling of Businesses; Commercial and Residential Lending and Closings; Estate Planning and Settlement Law.

Collins & Deans, LLC, (AV)
212 New London Turnpike, Suite D, 06033
Telephone: 860-659-4488 Telefax: 860-659-4486
Paul W. Collins; John E. Deans.
Real Estate, Business Law, Corporate.

Constantine, Constantine, (BV) '40 '68 C.895 B.A. L.184 LL.B.
117 New London Tpke.
Convicer, Richard G., (AV) ....'48 '81 C.94 B.A. L.93 J.D. [R.G.Convicer]

Convicer, Richard G., LLC, (AV)
41 Hebron Avenue, 06033
Telephone: 860-657-9040 Fax: 860-657-9039
Email: RConvi3589@aol.com
Richard G. Convicer.
Civil and Criminal Tax Representation, Business and Tax Planning, IRS Tax Disputes, Estate Planning, Probate.
See Professional Biographies, GLASTONBURY, CONNECTICUT

Cromwell, Cynthia .... '57 '82 C.918 B.A. L.184 J.D. 43 Riverview Rd.
Deans, John E., (AV) ....'46 '74 C.732 B.A. L.823 J.D. [Collins&D.]
DiLorenzo, Theodore J., (BV) '24 '53
C.855 B.A. L.273 J.D. [ⓒBrown,P.&S.] (⊙Hartford)
Dodge, Jason M., (BV) ....'58 '83 C&L.184 B.A., J.D. [Pomeranz,D.&S.]
*PRACTICE AREAS: Workers Compensation Law; Longshore and Harborworkers Compensation Act.
Doody, James J., III '49 '78 C.659 B.A. L.184 J.D.
Sr. Advsr., Legal/Coml. Affrs., Parallax Grp. Intl., LLC
Drayton, Douglas L., (AV) .... '44 '69 C&L.184 B.S., J.D. [Pomeranz,D.&S.]
*PRACTICE AREAS: Workers Compensation Law.
DuBorg, George J., (BV) .... '38 '71 C.768 B.A. L.1065 J.D. [G.J.Duborg]

DuBorg, George J., Law Offices of, (BV)
200 Glastonbury Boulevard, Suite 301, 06033
Telephone: 860-633-4797 Fax: 860-633-0694
Staff Counsel American International Companies: Managing Attorney: George J. DuBorg. Senior Trial Attorneys: Julie A. Harris; Thomas F. Kelsey. Trial Attorneys: Donald P. Guerrini; Carla Ottaviano; Brian J. Farrell, Jr.
Professional Liability, Products Liability, General Liability and Construction.
See Professional Biographies, GLASTONBURY, CONNECTICUT

Duhamel, Diane D., (BV) ....'60 '87 C.745 A.B. L.1218 J.D. [Duhamel&S.]
*PRACTICE AREAS: Insurance Defense; Workers Compensation; Personal Injury.

Duhamel & Schoolcraft LLC, (BV)
131 New London Turnpike, 06033
Telephone: 860-652-0072 Fax: 860-652-8412
Email: duhamel.schoolcraft@snet.net
Diane D. Duhamel; David W. Schoolcraft.
General Litigation, Insurance Defense, Workers Compensation, Personal Injury and Commercial Litigation.
See Professional Biographies, GLASTONBURY, CONNECTICUT

Dwyer, J. Patrick, (BV) .... '45 '70 C.918 B.A. L.184 J.D. [Dwyer&S.]
Dwyer, Kathleen A. .... '66 '98 C.829 B.S. L.1048 J.D. 2 Firethorn Dr.
Dwyer & Sheridan, (BV) ....100 Sycamore St.
Eisenberg, Deborah R. ....'54 '94 C.184 B.A. L.273 J.D. [Frauenglass&E.]
*PRACTICE AREAS: Divorce; Child Custody Law; Family Law.

Ewalt, Andrew W. .... '72 '99 C.645 B.A. L.1338 J.D. 381 Hubbard St.
Farrell, Brian J., Jr. .... '68 '96 C.745 B.A. L.1252 J.D. [G.J.Duborg]
Ferguson, Gordon S., (AV) .... '28 '60 C.477 A.B. L.309 J.D. 90 Hollister Way S.
Finn, Michael J. .... '61 '89 C.524 B.S. L.1048 J.D. [Montstream&M.]
*PRACTICE AREAS: Insurance Defense; Workers Compensation.
Fitzgerald, Timothy J., (BV) .... '54 '82 C.860 B.A. L.184 J.D. 100 Sycamore St.

Franckling, John E., (BV) '47 '83 C.349 B.S. L.1048 J.D.
41-A New London Turnpike, 06033
Telephone: 860-633-8461 Fax: 860-633-4545
Criminal Law, Family Law, Personal Injury.
See Professional Biographies, GLASTONBURY, CONNECTICUT

Frauenglass, Lloyd, (BV) .... '37 '66 C.855 B.S. L.184 J.D. [Frauenglass&E.]
*PRACTICE AREAS: Divorce; Child Custody Law; Family Law; Divorce Mediation.

Frauenglass & Eisenberg, (BV)
206 New London Turnpike, 06033-0357
Telephone: 860-633-0300 Fax: 860-657-4096
Email: FrauenglassEisenberg@SNET.Net
Lloyd Frauenglass; Deborah R. Eisenberg.
Visitation, Property Division, Alimony, Child Support, Post-Judgment Modifications, Prenuptial Agreements, Mediation, Practice limited to Divorce and Custody Law.
See Professional Biographies, GLASTONBURY, CONNECTICUT

Frazier, Kristen L. .... '74 '99 C.184 B.S. L.306 J.D. [Ⓐ Pomeranz,D.&S.]
*PRACTICE AREAS: Workers Compensation.
Gallo-Hall, Marie E. .... '62 '01 C&L.184 B.A., J.D. [Ⓐ Montstream&M.]
*PRACTICE AREAS: Workers Compensation; Personal Injury; Social Security Disability.
Goodstein, Gregory .... '67 '95 C.896 B.A. L.1048 J.D. 655 Winding Brook Dr.
Grant, Robert E., (CV) .... '54 '83 C.604 B.A. L.851 J.D. 200 Glastonbury Blvd.
Grasso, John H. .... '56 '82 C.184 B.A. L.245 J.D. [Boatman,B.G.&T.]
*PRACTICE AREAS: General Litigation; Debtor and Creditor Rights; Commercial Law; Estate Planning; Personal Injury.
Greer, Mark Charles, (BV) .... '56 '81 C.184 B.S. L.426 J.D. 15 Concord St.
Guerrini, Donald P., (BV) .... '45 '81 C.184 B.A. L.1029 J.D. [G.J.Duborg]
Haakonsen, Kate W., (BV) '53 '78
C.874 B.A. L.184 J.D. [Brown,P.&S.] (⊙Hartford, Hebron)
Hadaway, Deborah L. .... '52 '84 C.829 B.S. L.284 J.D. 119 Hebron Ave.
Hamer, Donald L., (BV) .... '50 '77 C&L.276 A.B., J.D. [Brown,P.&S.] (⊙Hartford)
Han, Su Lin '63 '91 C.999 B.A. L.1066 J.D.
(adm. in CA; not adm. in CT) 92 Heritage Dr.‡
Harris, Julie A., (BV) .... '56 '81 C.1033 B.A. L.184 J.D. [G.J.Duborg]
Hartley, Richard H., III, (BV) .... '49 '74 C&L.184 B.A., J.D. [Kane,H.&K.]
Haskell, April, (BV) .... '50 '76 C.112 B.A. L.426 J.D. [Montstream&M.]
*PRACTICE AREAS: Civil Litigation; Insurance Defense; Medical Malpractice; Products Liability.
Higgins, Thomas E. '30 '60 C.823 B.A. L.564 LL.B.
(adm. in NY; not adm. in CT) 18 Littel Acres Rd.‡
Hook, Keith B. .... '17 '41 C&L.477 A.B., J.D. 56 Surrey Lane‡
Howard, Kohn, Sprague & FitzGerald, (AV)
41 Hebron Avenue (⊙Hartford, Manchester)
Isaac, Charles D. '32 '56
C.188 B.S. L.976 LL.B. J. G. Furniture Systems, Burlington Indus.
Jaconetta, Joseph P., (BV) .... '61 '87 C.690 B.A. L.904 J.D. [Jaconetta&Assoc.]
*PRACTICE AREAS: Taxation; Trusts and Estates; Business Planning; Elder Law; Probate.

Jaconetta & Associates, (BV)
2934 Main Street, 06033
Telephone: 860-657-8805 FAX: 860-657-8617
Joseph P. Jaconetta;—David P. Wimer; Anne Burnham.
Taxation, Corporations, Limited Liability Companies, Partnerships, Estate Planning, Probate, Estate Administration, Trusts, Elder Law, Federal and State Tax Controversies.
See Professional Biographies, GLASTONBURY, CONNECTICUT

Kaeser, Steven D. '62 '85 C.174 B.A. L.801 J.D.
V.P. & Gen. Coun., HSBC Equator (U.S.A.) Incorporated
Kane, Thomas P., (BV) .... '42 '67 C.745 B.A. L.184 LL.B. [Kane,H.&K.]
Kane, Hartley & Katz, P.C., (BV) .... 972 New London Tpke.
Katz, Harvey A., (BV) .... '27 '49 C.855 B.A. L.188 J.D. [Kane,H.&K.]
Kelley, Kenneth T., (BV) '39 '81
C.1033 B.S. L.1048 J.D. [Brown,P.&S.] (⊙Hartford, Stamford)
Kelly, David A., (BV) .... '52 '77 C.30 B.S. L.818 J.D. [Montstream&M.]
*PRACTICE AREAS: Insurance Defense; Workers Compensation.
Kelsey, Thomas F., (BV) .... '43 '74 C.1033 B.S. L.117 J.D. [G.J.Duborg]
Klineberg, Heather .... '75 '00 C.823 B.S. L.1252 J.D. [Ⓐ Pomeranz,D.&S.]
*PRACTICE AREAS: Civil Litigation; Workers Compensation.
Knapp, Eric .... '65 '91 C.821 B.A. L.184 J.D. [Ⓐ Branse&W.]
Lebo, Simon J. .... '74 '99 C.216 B.A. L.1017 J.D. [Ⓐ Brown,P.&S.] (⊙Hartford)
Lemoine, Richard G. '46 '77 C.1107 B.A. L.818 J.D.
(adm. in MA; not adm. in CT) 21 Peachtree Rd.‡
Locke, Philip .... '20 '53 C.197 B.A. L.184 LL.B. 361 Chestnut Hill Rd.‡
Lucheme, Roberto Tschudin, (CV) .... '51 '76 C.33 B.A. L.1162 J.D. 41 Hebron Avenue
Lynch, David R., (BV) .... '42 '67 C.93 B.A. L.184 LL.B. [D.R.Lynch&Assoc.]
Lynch, David R., & Associates, LLC, Law Offices, (BV) .... 2510 Main Street
Mabe, Joseph M. .... '75 '01 C.629 B.S. L.306 J.D. [Ⓐ Montstream&M.]
Mather, Walter S. .... '28 '56 C.95 A.B. L.309 LL.B. 219 Carriage Dr.
Maxwell, John D., (BV) '52 '79
C.873 A.B. L.1035 J.D. [Brown,P.&S.] (⊙East Hampton, Hartford)
May, Frank A., (AV) .... '48 '75 C.690 B.S.E.E. L.184 J.D. [Montstream&M.]
*PRACTICE AREAS: Civil Litigation; Insurance Defense; Workers Compensation.

Mayo, Gilligan & Zito, LLP
(See Wethersfield)

McAuliffe, Michael J., (BV) .... '61 '86 C.273 B.A. L.1048 J.D. [Pomeranz,D.&S.]
*PRACTICE AREAS: Workers Compensation Law.
McCarthy, Christopher J., (BV) '64 '89
C.184 B.A. L.1202 J.D. [Brown,P.&S.] (⊙Hartford)
McGill, Samuel W. P., Jr. .... '23 '54 C.855 B.A. L.184 J.D. 150 Three Mile Rd.
McGrail, Margaret E. .... '61 '96 C.1030 B.A. L.1048 J.D. [Ⓐ Montstream&M.]
*PRACTICE AREAS: Workers Compensation Law.
McKain, Ryan K. .... '74 '00 C.645 B.S. L.184 J.D. [Ⓐ Alter&S.]
Mcnevin, Valerie J. '53 '82 C.1288 B.S. L.285 J.D.
(adm. in CO; not adm. in CT) 97 Stanley Drive‡
Mendoza, Lynette .... '72 '98 C.725 B.A. L.184 J.D. [Ⓐ Brown,P.&S.]
Moher, James M., (BV) .... '47 '72 C.676 B.A. L.184 J.D. [Howard,K.S.&F.] (⊙Hartford)
Molloy, Jean D., (BV) .... '60 '88 C.93 B.A. L.1048 J.D. [Montstream&M.]
*PRACTICE AREAS: Insurance Defense; Workers Compensation.
Montstream, Robert G. .... '31 '64 C.918 B.A. L.184 LL.B. [Montstream&M.] ‡
*PRACTICE AREAS: WOrker's Compensation Law.

Montstream & May, L.L.P., (AV)
Salmon Brook Corporate Park, 655 Winding Brook Drive, P.O. Box 1087, 06033-6087
Telephone: 860-659-1341 Fax: 860-657-8519
Email: email@montmaylaw.com
Robert G. Montstream (Retired); Frank A. May; April Haskell; David A. Kelly; Michael J. Finn; Jean D. Molloy; Dominick C. Statile. Associates: Joseph J. Passaretti, Jr.; Michael M. Buonopane; Margaret E. McGrail; Karen A. Wright; Joseph M. Mabe; Marie E. Gallo-Hall; Melissa A. Murello.
Workers' Compensation, Civil Litigation, Insurance Defense, Products Liability, Medical Malpractice, Legal Malpractice.
See Professional Biographies, GLASTONBURY, CONNECTICUT

Mulholland, James C., (BV) .... '52 '80 C.1156 B.S. L.1048 J.D. 377 Hubbard St.
Mullaney, Thomas P., III, (BV) .... '53 '79 C.276 B.A. L.184 J.D. 43 Western Blvd.
Munn, Richard A. '48 '91 C.966 B.A. L.1048 J.D.
Assistant Counsel, HSBC Equator USA Incorporated
Murello, Melissa A. .... '76 '01 C.119 B.S. L.665 J.D. [Ⓐ Montstream&M.]
Nettleton, Ronald E., (CV) .... '44 '79 C.97 M.B.A. L.184 J.D. 41-B New London Tpke.
Oliver, Vernon D. .... '71 '97 C&L.184 B.A., J.D. 655 Winding Brook Drive
Ottaviano, Carla, (BV) .... '52 '85 C.788 A.B. L.1218 J.D. [G.J.Duborg]
Paindiris, Nicholas, (BV) .... '46 '73 C.976 B.A. L.184 J.D. [Brown,P.&S.] (⊙Hartford)
Passaretti, Joseph J., Jr. .... '68 '94 C.705 B.A. L.1252 J.D. [Ⓐ Montstream&M.]
*PRACTICE AREAS: Insurance Defense; Workers Compensation.
Paulding, T. R., Jr., (BV) .... '55 '81 C.602 B.A. L.184 J.D. 118 Shallowbrook La.
Peoples, Sean M. .... '60 '89 C.183 B.A. L.1218 J.D. [Brown,P.&S.] (⊙Hartford)
Pomeranz, James L., (AV) .... '46 '72 C.976 B.A. L.276 J.D. [Pomeranz,D.&S.]
*PRACTICE AREAS: Workers Compensation Law; Longshore and Harborworkers Compensation Act.

Pomeranz, Drayton & Stabnick, (AV) BB
95 Glastonbury Boulevard, 06033-4412
Telephone: 860-657-8000; 800-246-5541 Fax: 860-657-9838
Email: pdslaw@pdslaw.coom
Douglas L. Drayton; James L. Pomeranz; Richard T. Stabnick; Lucas D. Strunk; Jason M. Dodge; Anne Kelly Zovas; Richard L. Aiken, Jr.; Michael J. McAuliffe. Associate: Kristen L. Frazier; Heather Klineberg.
Workers Compensation Law, Federal Longshore and Harborworkers Act.
See Professional Biographies, GLASTONBURY, CONNECTICUT

Pontillo, Clement J., Jr., (BV) .... '31 '58 C&L.184 B.S., LL.B. [Wynne,P.&L.]
Quinlan, Richard M., (CV) .... '55 '81 C.012 B.A. L.1119 J.D. 124 Hebron Ave.‡
Ramsay, Sharon, (BV) .... '63 '91 C.184 B.S. L.1029 J.D. 200 Glastonbury Blvd.
Randall, Gerald J. '31 '57 C&L.966 B.B.A., J.D.
(adm. in WI; not adm. in CT) 178 Tall Timbers Rd.
Rimmer, Robert T. .... '70 '96 C.976 B.A. L.184 J.D. [Ⓐ Brown,P.&S.] (⊙Hartford)
Rintoul, David S. .... '61 '86 C.367 B.A. L.184 J.D. [Brown,P.&S.]
Roberto, William A., (BV) .... '46 '71 C.184 B.S. L.7 J.D. [W.A.Roberto]

Roberto, William A., LLC, (BV)
381 Hubbard Street, 06033
Telephone: 860-657-3300 Fax: 860-657-2900
William A. Roberto.
Civil Litigation, Criminal Litigation, Personal Injury, Family Law, Probate.
See Professional Biographies, GLASTONBURY, CONNECTICUT

Ruddell, J. Preston, (BV) .... '49 '75 C&L.575 B.A., J.D. 89 Chestnut Hill Rd.
Sassi, William A., Jr. .... '61 '91 C.690 B.A. L.1048 J.D. 200 Glastonbury Blvd.
Schoolcraft, David W., (BV) .... '56 '85 C.184 B.A. L.1048 J.D. [Duhamel&S.]
*PRACTICE AREAS: Insurance Defense; Workers Compensation; Personal Injury.
Scott, Ronald T., (BV) .... '52 '78 C.24 B.A. L.184 J.D. [Brown,P.&S.] (⊙Hartford)
Shaulys, Gail S., Law Offices of, (BV) '41 '83 C.1102 B.A. L.1048 J.D.
15 Concord Street
Sheridan, Thomas P., (BV) .... '49 '78 C.31 B.A. L.818 J.D. [Dwyer&S.]
Sherwood, David F., (BV) .... '55 '87 C.659 B.A. L.184 J.D. [Alter&S.]

Shluger, Kenneth L., (BV) '55 '80 C.184 B.A. L.306 J.D.
119 Hebron Avenue, 06033
Telephone: 860-633-4767 Fax: 860-652-8145
Email: shluger@aol.com URL: http://www.lawyers.com/shlugerlaw
Civil and Criminal Litigation, Personal Injury, Medical Malpractice, Products Liability, Divorce, Bankruptcy, Driving While Intoxicated; Slip and Fall, Automobile Accidents.
Hartford, Connecticut Office: 216 Main Street, 06106. Telephone: 860-247-8681.
Hebron, Connecticut Office: 17 Main Street, 06248. Telephone: 860-228-1242.
See Professional Biographies, GLASTONBURY, CONNECTICUT

Shluger, Robert J. .... '56 '81 C.174 B.S. L.1048 J.D. 2389 Main St.
Smith, Allen W. .... '31 '60 C&L.184 B.A., J.D. Supr. Ct. J.
Stabnick, Richard T., (AV) .... '44 '70 C.918 B.A. L.184 J.D. [Pomeranz,D.&S.]
*PRACTICE AREAS: Workers Compensation Law; Longshore and Harborworkers Compensation Act.
Statile, Dominick C. .... '66 '91 C.884 B.A. L.306 J.D. [Montstream&M.]
*PRACTICE AREAS: Workers' Compensation; Insurance Defense.
Strunk, Lucas D., (BV) .... '56 '82 C.321 B.A. L.184 J.D. [Pomeranz,D.&S.]
*PRACTICE AREAS: Workers Compensation Law; Longshore and Harborworkers Compensation Act.
Thomas, Nancy L., (CV) .... '57 '84 C.732 B.A. L.930 J.D. 3 Arrowhead Dr.
Thompson, Scott Alexander .... '— '00 C.860 B.A. L.228 J.D. Clk., Ct. of Appeals
Tillinghast, George E., Jr., (BV) .... '40 '70 C&L.184 B.S., J.D. 41-A New London Tpk.
Tougas, Jeffrey G., (BV) '60 '90 C.999 B.S.B.A. L.1048 J.D.
V.P., Sr. Coun. & Asst. Secy., Fleet Capital Corp.
*RESPONSIBILITIES: Corporate Law; Commercial Law; Finance Law; Secured Transactions.
Trowbridge, Robert L., (AV) .... '34 '64 C.165 A.B. L.178 LL.B. [Trowbridge&B.]
Trowbridge & Basine, P.C., (AV) .... 45 Glastonbury Boulevard
Twachtman, Walter A., Jr., (BV) .... '39 '67 C&L.184 B.A., LL.B. [Boatman,B.G.&T.]
*PRACTICE AREAS: Zoning, Planning and Land Use; Real Estate; Appellate Practice.
Urbaniak, Irena J. .... '61 '86 C.829 B.A. L.1019 J.D. 200 Glastongury Blvd.
Varney, Steven W., (BV) .... '59 '85 C&L.184 B.A., J.D. [Brown,P.&S.] (⊙Hartford)
Vehslage, Royce L. .... '55 '85 C.788 B.A. L.1218 J.D. 200 Glastonbury Blvd.
Volgenau, Peter .... '57 '84 C.197 A.B. L.930 J.D. 140 Glastonbury Blvd.
Watts, Cynthia A. .... '61 '91 C.597 B.A. L.1029 J.D. 43 Western Blvd.
Willis, Matthew J. .... '63 '88 C.454 B.A. L.184 J.D. [Branse&W.]
Wimer, David P. .... '63 '95 C.645 B.S. L.184 J.D. [Ⓐ Jaconetta&Assoc.]
*PRACTICE AREAS: Estate Planning; Probate; Real Estate; Elder Law.
Wright, Karen A. .... '72 '00 C&L.1252 B.A., J.D. [Ⓐ Montstream&M.]
*PRACTICE AREAS: Workers Compensation; Personal Injury.
Wynne, Edward C., (BV) .... '23 '50 C.976 B.A. L.94 LL.B. [Wynne,P.&L.]
Wynne, Pontillo & Lynch, (BV) .... 2510 Main St.
Zovas, Anne Kelly, (BV) .... '61 '86 C.93 B.A. L.184 J.D. [Pomeranz,D.&S.]
*PRACTICE AREAS: Workers Compensation Law; Civil Litigation; Subrogation.

GOSHEN, 1,706, *Litchfield Co.*

Shore, Martin H., (AV) .... '26 '60 C.563 B.B.A. L.1009 J.D. 174 Hyerdale Drive E.‡

GRANBY, 7,956, *Hartford Co.*

Gracey, Jerome B., (AV) .... '33 '60 C.95 B.A. L.309 LL.B. 4 E. Granby Rd.‡
Hale, Robert J. .... '52 '82 C.184 B.A. L.1048 J.D. 33 Hartford Ave.
Kevorkian, Gary R., (BV) .... '53 '81 C.855 B.A. L.94 J.D. Spec. Mas., State Tax Ct.

King, Sally S., (BV) ....'50 '78 C.918 B.A. L.1048 J.D. 168 Day St.
Lareau, Margaret A. ....'50 '83 C.454 B.A. L.184 J.D. Field Atty., Natl. Labor Rel. Bd.
May, Peter J. ....'16 '41 C.855 B.A. L.184 LL.B. 7 Fawn Dr.‡
Mooney, Arline R., (BV) ....'22 '50 C.725 A.B. L.178 LL.B. 32 E. Granby R.
Sorensen, Robin G. ....'52 '90 C.703 B.S. L.184 J.D. 16 Windcrest Dr.

GREENS FARMS, —, *Fairfield Co.*

O'Neill, Bracken C. ....'46 '77 C.867 B.A. L.477 J.D. P.O. Box 415
Vail, Richard G. '34 '59 C.674 A.B. L.893 LL.B.
(adm. in VA; not adm. in CT) Hay Assocs.

GREENWICH, 59,578, *Fairfield Co.*

Aberasturi, Mark G. '64 '89 C.1044 B.S. L.1048 J.D.
(adm. in NY; not adm. in CT) [McGovern&Assoc.]
*PRACTICE AREAS: Taxation; Mergers and Acquisitions; Bankruptcy; Trusts and Estates.
Adams, Daniel D. '42 '65 C.188 B.A. L.569 LL.B.
(adm. in NY; not adm. in CT) Chmn. of the Bd. & CEO, AlleRx Inc.
Adams, Jennifer L. '59 '85 C.674 B.A. L.813 J.D.
(adm. in NY; not adm. in CT)
Vice Chmn., Chf. Legal Admin. Offr., World Color Press, Inc.
Adler, Anne '48 '74 C.938 B.A. L.93 J.D.
(adm. in NY; not adm. in CT) 938 Lake Ave.‡
Ahmad, Aamina ....'70 '94 C.999 B.A. L.1040 J.D. Asst. Town Atty.
Albert, David, (AV) ....'28 '54 C.610 A.B. L.976 LL.B. [▣ Albert,W.&J.]
*PRACTICE AREAS: Zoning; Civil Litigation; Family Law.

Albert, Ward & Johnson, P.C., (AV) BB
125 Mason Street, P.O. Box 1668, 06836
Telephone: 203-661-8600 Telecopier: 203-661-8051
URL: http://www.lawyers.com/awj
Tom S. Ward, Jr.; Scott R. Johnson; Jane D. Hogeman; Howard R. Wolfe; Christopher A. Kristoff; Vicki K. Comberiati. Associate: Albert T. Strazza. Of Counsel: David Albert; C. Robton Perelli-Minetti.
General Practice. Real Estate, Zoning, Corporation, Litigation, Probate, Taxation, Construction, Environmental and Family Law.
See Professional Biographies, GREENWICH, CONNECTICUT

Allen, Michael J., (BV) ....'60 '85 C&L.188 B.S., J.D. [Ivey,B.&O.]
*PRACTICE AREAS: Corporate Law; Commercial Law; Commercial Real Estate.
Amron, Arthur H., (AVⓉ) '56 '83 C.165 B.A. L.309 J.D.
(adm. in DC; not adm. in CT) Sr. V.P. & Gen. Coun., Wexford Management Corp.
Anderson, J. Eric, (BVⓉ) ....'38 '67 C.197 A.B. L.1065 J.D. 43 Arch St.

Anner, John Lloyd, III, (AV) '37 '64 C&L.262 B.S., LL.B.
125 Mason Street, 06830
Telephone: 203-862-9237 New York: 212-645-0779; New York Fax: 212-645-3229 FAX: 203-629-8462
Arbitration, Corporate, Commercial, International, Labor and Benefits Law, Litigation in all Courts, Real Estate, Trusts and Estates.
See Professional Biographies, GREENWICH, CONNECTICUT

Anthony, Nicholas A. '47 '77 C.93 B.S. L.128 J.D.
(adm. in NY; not adm. in CT) V.P., Tax, Witco Corp.
Aranha, Jean Mills ....'55 '89 C.976 B.A. L.262 J.D. [Holland K.&B.]
*PRACTICE AREAS: Estate Planning; Probate; Administration of Trusts and Estates; Administrative Law.
Ashenfelter, Mark J. '59 '86 C.309 B.A. L.564 J.D.
(adm. in NY; not adm. in CT) V.P., The Haebler Co.
Attura, Clare J. ....'53 '80 C&L.724 B.S., J.D. General Counsel, Helm Capital Group, Inc.
Avellino, John T. '47 '74 C.415 B.A. L.1009 J.D.
[Zeichner E.&K.] (⊙New York, NY)
Babson, David F., (AV) ....'23 '50 C.309 A.B. L.477 J.D. [Bentley,M.B.&L.]
*PRACTICE AREAS: Estates and Trusts; Estate Planning; Personal Taxation.
Badger, Daniel B., (AV) ....'15 '41 C&L.976 B.A., LL.B. 235 N. Maple Ave.‡
Baity, Patricia A. ....'46 '79 C.881 A.B. L.188 J.D. 44 Maher Ave.
Bam, Foster, (AV) ....'27 '54 C&L.976 B.A., LL.B. [Cummings&L.]
Barber, Charles F. '17 '42 C.597 B.S. L.309 LL.B.
(adm. in DC; not adm. in CT) 66 Glenwood Dr.‡
Barnes, Mortimer P., (BV) ....'21 '55 C.103 A.B. L.976 LL.B. 100 Field Point Rd.‡
Barnett, Charles E. ....'39 '65 C&L.477 B.A., J.D. [Barnett&Assoc.] (⊙Greenwich)
*PRACTICE AREAS: Legal Consulting; Securities; Mergers and Acquisitions; Venture Capital; Corporate.
Barnett, Charles E. ....'39 '65 C&L.477 B.A., J.D. [McGovern&Assoc.] (⊙Greenwich)
*PRACTICE AREAS: Legal Consulting; Securities; Mergers and Acquisitions; Venture Capital; Corporate.

Barnett & Associates
One Lafayette Place, 3rd Floor, 06830
Telephone: 203-622-0350 Fax: 203-622-0375
Email: cblegal@aol.com URL: http://www.lawyers.com/cbarnett
Charles E. Barnett.
Legal Consulting, Securities, Mergers and Acquisitions, Venture Capital, General Corporate, Business Law, Contracts.
See Professional Biographies, GREENWICH, CONNECTICUT

Barnum, Robert C., Jr., (AV) ....'21 '48 C.197 A.B. L.188 LL.B. [Ivey,B.&O.]
*PRACTICE AREAS: Trusts and Estates; Tax Planning; Real Estate.
Bartels, Philip H., (BV) ....'49 '74 C.188 B.A. L.145 J.D. [Holland K.&B.]
*PRACTICE AREAS: Matrimonial Law; Litigation; Exempt Organizations.
Batlan, Felice J. '65 '91 C.788 B.A. L.309 J.D.
(adm. in NY; not adm. in CT) Assoc. Gen. Coun., Grennwich Capital Markets, Inc.
Battista, Leo F. '23 '55 C.651 B.S. L.229 LL.B.
(adm. in PA; not adm. in CT) State Natl. Bk. of Conn.
Baum, Jonathan N. '54 '79 C.860 B.A. L.569 J.D.
(adm. in NY; not adm. in CT) Integrated Resources Inc.
Beach, R. Scott ....'68 '93 C.1365 B.A. L.273 J.D. [Day,B.&H.]
*PRACTICE AREAS: Emerging Companies; Mergers and Acquisitions; Strategic Joint Ventures; Private Equity Funds; Finance and Investments.
Becker, Beth S. ....'62 '87 C.183 B.A. L.904 J.D. [🄰 Ivey,B.&O.]
*PRACTICE AREAS: Real Estate; Land Use; Zoning Law.
Belknap, A. Dudley ....'46 '95 C.1165 B.A. L.1040 J.D. [🄰 Whitman B.A.&M.]
*PRACTICE AREAS: Estate Administration; Estate Taxation; Estate Planning.
Belletsky, Marc R. ....'61 '86 C.184 B.A. L.1202 J.D. Conn. Bk. & Tr. Co.
Bendfeldt, Sandra K. ....'37 '81 C.178 B.S. L.1040 J.D. 15 E. Putnam Ave.
Bentley, Peter, (AV) ....'15 '42 C.674 A.B. L.976 J.D. [▣ Bentley,M.B.&L.]

Bentley, Mosher, Babson & Lambert, P.C., (AV)
321 Railroad Avenue, P.O. Box 788, 06836-0788
Telephone: 203-629-2424 Telecopier: 203-629-2545
Email: attysbmbl@aol.com
David F. Babson; John F. Lambert; M. Dean Montgomery; Charles E. Mosher; Richard J. Slagle. Counsel: Peter Bentley; Catherine P. Whelan. Retired: Edwin M. Jones.
General Practice. Estates and Trusts, Corporate, Tax, Real Estate, Mortgage and Banking, Consumer Lending. State and Federal Litigation including Domestic Relations.
See Professional Biographies, GREENWICH, CONNECTICUT

Berkouits, Markus I. '56 '82 C.966 B.S. L.107 J.D.
(adm. in NY; not adm. in CT) V.P., Sea Crest Trading of CT., Inc.

Berkowitz, Malowitz & Mullin
(See Stamford)

Berman, Valerie Juster '59 '86 C.867 B.A. L.978 J.D.
(adm. in NY; not adm. in CT) Bankers Trust Co.
Bickford, G. Thomas ....'63 '95 C.1156 B.S. L.1040 J.D. [🄰 Giacomo,G.F.&N.] ⊙
Bird, Susan Willett '40 '74 C.436 B.A. L.813 J.D.
(adm. in CA; not adm. in CT) American Med. Council, LLC
Bishop, Tracy R., (BVⓉ) '62 '87 C.1365 B.A. L.425 J.D.
(adm. in LA; not adm. in CT) 1 Halsey Drive
Bisset, Andrew W., (AV) ....'19 '48 C.390 A.B. L.976 LL.B. [Bisset&A.] ⊙
Bisset & Atkins, (AV) ....777 North Street (⊙New York, NY)

Bleakley Platt & Schmidt LLP, (BV)
Sixty-Six Field Point Road, 06830 ⊙
Telephone: 203-661-5222 Telecopier: 203-661-1197
Email: info@bpslaw.com URL: http://www.bpslaw.com
Resident Partners: John J. Ferguson; John E. Meerbergen; Steven Paul DeRicco. Resident Counsel: J. Lincoln Hallowell.
General Civil and Trial Practice. Corporation, Securities, Litigation (including Tax Certiorari), Banking, Probate, Trust, Estate Planning, Life Insurance, Municipal, Zoning, Utility, Real Estate Law, Employment and Environmental Law.
White Plains, New York Office: One North Lexington Avenue. Telephone: 914-949-2700. Telecopier: 914-683-6956.
See Professional Biographies, GREENWICH, CONNECTICUT

Blomberg, Jill Heitler ....'72 '97 C.659 B.A. L.262 J.D. [Schoonmaker,G.&C.]
*PRACTICE AREAS: Family Law; Matrimonial Law.
Bloom, Edward C. '30 '55 C&L.309 A.B., LL.B.
(adm. in MA; not adm. in CT) 92 Maple Ave.‡
Boak, Jeffrey L. '52 '78 C.188 A.B. L.178 J.D.
(adm. in NY; not adm. in CT) Business Unit Counsel, Howmet Corporation

Boeggeman, George, Hodges & Corde, P.C.
(See White Plains)

Boer, Ellen S., (BV) ....'41 '78 C.518 B.A. L.796 J.D. 325 Taconic Rd.
Bolger, Thomas J '59 '85 C.399 B.A. L.221 J.D.
(adm. in WI; not adm. in CT) 100 W Putnam Ave.
Bologna, John V., (BV) ....'63 '88 C.93 A.B. L.276 J.D. P.O. Box 4168
Boyd, Jennifer N., (AV) '52 '78 C.860 B.A. L.184 J.D.
[▣ Fogarty C.S.&N.] (⊙Darien)
*PRACTICE AREAS: Corporate Finance; Corporate Law; Mergers and Acquisitions; Partnership and Limited Liability Companies.
Bradford, Charles S. ....'17 '41 C.951 B.A. L.976 LL.B. 42 Alpine Rd.
Brandt, Bernard B. '10 '34 C.823 L.732
(adm. in NY; not adm. in CT) 1 W. Elm St.‡
Brandt, Gary '53 '78 C.860 B.A. L.178 J.D.
(adm. in NY; not adm. in CT) 1 W. Elm St.‡
Brandt, James '49 '75 C.597 B.A. L.178 J.D.
(adm. in NY; not adm. in CT) Robert Brandt Consulting
Braxton, Meredith C. ....'60 '90 C.823 B.S. L.262 J.D. [🄰 Tranfo&T.]
Breed, Rebecca S. ....'37 '92 C.706 B.A. L.1040 J.D. State Jud. Dept.
Brown, Kenneth Douglas ....'60 '88 C.472 B.B.A. L.1029 J.D. P.O. Box 81
Brown, Rex D., Jr. ....'44 '83 C.823 A.B. L.1029 J.D. 17 Prospect St.
Burke, Harold R., (BV) ....'59 '88 C.1102 B.S. L.1040 J.D. [Holland K.&B.]
*PRACTICE AREAS: Litigation; Employment Law; Personal Injury Law; Business Litigation; Matrimonial Law.

Cacace, Tusch & Santagata
(See Stamford)

Cahill, Thomas J., (AVⓉ) '31 '60 C.1041 A.B. L.276 LL.B.
(adm. in NY; not adm. in CT) [T.J.Cahill]
Cahill, William T. ....'21 '50 C.976 A.B. L.93 LL.B. 100 Field Point Rd.‡
Cahill, Thomas J., P.C., (AVⓉ) ....420 Davis Ave.
Caldwell, Christopher W. ....'67 '92 C.645 B.A. L.365 J.D. [🄰 P.Russell]
*PRACTICE AREAS: Commercial Litigation; Criminal Law.
Cantor, Samuel C. '19 '43 C.563 B.S. L.178 J.D.
(adm. in NY; not adm. in CT) 10 Audubon Lane‡

Cantore, J. Michael, Jr.
(See Stamford)

Cantwell, Robert ....'31 '56 C&L.188 B.A., J.D. 5 Meadow Dr.

Carlisle, Jonathan D., (BV) '42 '68 C.976 B.A. L.184 LL.B.
125 Mason Street, 06830 ⊙
Telephone: 203-629-9600 Fax: 203-629-9072
Email: jdcarlisleassoc@aol.com URL: http://www.lawyers.com/jonathandcarlisle
Wills and Estate Planning, Taxation, Trust and Estate Administration, Contested Probate Matters, Residential and Investment Real Estate, Land Use and Zoning Law.
Essex Office: 67 Main Street Center Brook, P.O. Box 800, 06426.
See Professional Biographies, GREENWICH, CONNECTICUT

Carr, Daniel ....'63 '92 C.550 B.A. L.818 J.D. Asst. Gen. Coun., Stolt-Nielsen Inc.
*RESPONSIBILITIES: Admiralty and Transportation; Commercial Law.
Casey, Lawrence W. '49 '76 C.24 B.A. L.724 J.D.
(adm. in NY; not adm. in CT) [▣ McGovern&Assoc.]
*PRACTICE AREAS: Legislation Regulation; Washington Practice.

Casper & de Toledo LLC
(See Stamford)

Cerussi, Thomas F. ....'63 '89 C.433 B.A. L.1019 J.D. [Cerussi&S.]

Cerussi & Spring, A Professional Corporation
66 Field Point Road, 06830-6473 ⊙
Telephone: 203-661-4000 Facsimile: 203-661-1197
Thomas F. Cerussi.
Litigation. Trials and Appeals in all State and Federal Courts. Insurance, Products Liability, Construction, Commercial, Environmental, Toxic Tort and Employment Law.
White Plains, New York Office: One North Lexington Avenue. Telephone: 914-948-1200. Facsimile: 914-948-1579.
See Professional Biographies, GREENWICH, CONNECTICUT

Chadwick, Peter, (AV) ....'63 '90 C.976 B.A. L.813 J.D. [🄰 Day,B.&H.]
*PRACTICE AREAS: Estate Planning; Estate Administration; Tax Exempt Organizations; Family Business Law.
Chaffee, John E. ....'70 '97 C&L.884 B.S., J.D. [🄰 Ivey,B.&O.]
*PRACTICE AREAS: Business Law; Corporate Law; Commercial Law; Real Estate.
Chaikin, Lee D. '73 '99 C.659 B.S. L.178 J.D.
(adm. in NY; not adm. in CT) MMC Capital
Chapin, James W. '29 '59 C.976 B.A. L.893 LL.B.
(adm. in NY; not adm. in CT) Of Coun., UST Inc.

Chase, John B. '41 '71 C.976 B.A. L.178 J.D.
(adm. in NY; not adm. in CT) 295 Taconic Rd.‡

Clear, Michael Gene, Law Offices of
(See Stamford)

Close, Peter D. .... '51 '83 C.231 B.A. L.564 J.D. 1 Pine Ridge Rd.

Coates, Charles E., III, (AV) .... '48 '74 C&L.309 B.A., J.D. [Whitman B.A.&M.]
*PRACTICE AREAS: Estate Planning and Administration; Land Use Law; Estate and Gift Taxation Law; Probate Law; Trust Administration.

Cohen, Bruce F., (AV) .... '35 '59 C.569 B.A. L.976 LL.B. [Fogarty C.S.&N.]
*PRACTICE AREAS: Land Use Law; Real Estate Law; Real Estate Finance Law.

Cohen, Gary I., (AV) '43 '67 C.976 B.A. L.893 LL.B. BB
781 North Street, 06831
Telephone: 203-622-8787 Facsimile: 203-622-8798
Email: GICLAW@AOL.COM URL: http://www.lawyers.com/giclaw
***PRACTICE AREAS: Family Law; Matrimonial Law.**
Associate: Marci E. Finkelstein.
Practice Limited to Family and Matrimonial Law.
See Professional Biographies, GREENWICH, CONNECTICUT

Cohen, Jennifer Paul .... '64 '92 C.103 B.A. L.723 J.D. 10 Larkspur Ln.

Colin, Thomas D. .... '67 '92 C.415 B.S. L.724 J.D. [Schoonmaker,G.&C.]
*PRACTICE AREAS: Matrimonial Law; Family Law.

Collins, Carolyn Alexander, (BV) .... '63 '88 C.188 B.A. L.184 J.D. [[A] Fogarty C.S.&N.]
*PRACTICE AREAS: Appellate Practice; Medical Malpractice; Commercial Litigation; Personal Injury; Business Torts.

Comberiati, Vicki K. .... '54 '95 C.1110 B.A. L.1040 J.D. [Albert,W.&J.]
*PRACTICE AREAS: Real Estate; Corporate.

Conboy, Margaret E. .... '68 '94 C.569 B.A. L.1040 J.D. [[A] Whitman B.A.&M.]
*PRACTICE AREAS: Residential and Commercial Real Estate; Planning and Zoning; Land Use.

Condon, April F. .... '70 '96 C&L.276 B.A., J.D. [[A] Cummings&L.]
*PRACTICE AREAS: Commercial Real Estate; Residential Real Estate.

Connors, Joseph P. '49 '90 C.367 B.A. L.569 J.D.
(adm. in NY; not adm. in CT) [[C] McGovern&Assoc.]
*PRACTICE AREAS: Banking Law; Securities; Corporate Law.

Conway, John B., (AVⓉ) '46 '75 C.436 B.A. L.262 J.D.
[Nourse&B.] (⊙New York, NY)

Coomaraswamy, Bernadette M., (BV) .... '26 '60 C.94 B.S. L.262 LL.B. Mag.

Cosden, Edward D., Jr., (BV) .... '45 '71 C.934 B.A. L.862 J.D. [Ivey,B.&O.]
*PRACTICE AREAS: Trusts and Estates; Tax Planning.

Cotter, William D. '45 '70 C.93 A.B. L.893 J.D.
V.P., Gen. Coun. & Secy., American Optical Corp.

Cowin, Andrew Josephs .... '58 '86 C.860 B.A. L.564 J.D. 43 Sawmill Lane

Coyle, Frank J., (AV) .... '19 '45 C.674 B.A. L.976 LL.B. [Cummings&L.]
*PRACTICE AREAS: Trusts Law; Estates Law; Real Estate.

Crooks, Robert M. '12 '38 C.831 B.S. L.659 LL.B.
(adm. in PA; not adm. in CT) 132 Zaccheus Mead Lane‡

Crystal, David, II .... '38 '65 C.732 B.A. L.94 J.D. [Gilbride,T.L.&S.] ⊙
*PRACTICE AREAS: Securities Regulation; Arbitration; Litigation.

Cuminale, James W., (AV) .... '53 '78 C.855 B.A. L.880 J.D. Panamsat

Cummings & Lockwood, (AV)
Two Greenwich Plaza, P.O. Box 2505, 06836 ⊙
Telephone: (203) 869-1200 Telecopier: (203) 869-3120
Email: info@cl-law.com URL: http://www.cl-law.com
Partners: Foster Bam; Frank J. Coyle; B. Cort Delany; Philip M. Drake; John R. French; Jessie A. Gilbert; Robert T. Gilhuly; Robert F. Grele; William R. Lynch; Jonathan B. Mills; Douglas H. Olin; Edward F. Rodenbach. Resident Associates: April F. Condon; Rani Newman Mathura; Eugénie D. Verrillo.
General Practice. National and Regional Litigation Counsel, Corporate Law, Patent and Intellectual Property, Trusts and Estates, Labor and Employment, Mergers and Acquisitions, Partnerships and Joint Ventures, Commercial Lending, Corporate Finance, Creditors' Rights, Bankruptcy and Workouts, Securities Regulation and Litigation, Tax, Arbitration, Insurance, Banking and Financial Services, Leasing, Commercial and Residential Real Estate, Construction, Environmental, Toxic Torts, Health Law, Products Liability Litigation, Probate Litigation, Family Law and International Business.
Stamford, Connecticut Office: Four Stamford Plaza, P.O. Box 120, 06904-0120. Telephone: (203) 327-1700. Telecopier: (203) 351-4535.
Hartford, Connecticut Office: CityPlace I, 185 Asylum Street, 36th Floor, 06103-3495. Telephone: (860) 275-6700. Telecopier: (860) 724-3397.
New Haven, Connecticut Office: 700 State Street, P.O. Box 1960. 06509-1960. Telephone: (203) 782-3000. Telecopier: (203) 777-3347.
West Hartford, Connecticut Office: Town Center, 29 South Main Street, Suite 208, 06107. Telephone: (860) 275-6700. Telecopier: (860) 313-0293.
Bonita Springs, Florida Office: 24311 Walden Center, Suite 201, 34134. Telephone: (941) 947-8811. Telecopier: (941) 947-8025.
Naples, Florida Office: 3001 Tamiami Trail North, P.O. Box 413032, 34101-3032. Telephone: (941) 262-8311. Telecopier: (941) 263-0703.
See Professional Biographies, GREENWICH, CONNECTICUT

Curtis, Brinckerhoff & Barrett, P.C.
(See Stamford)

Czajkowski, Frank H. .... '36 '60 C&L.724 B.A., J.D. 33 Benedict Pl.‡

Day, Berry & Howard LLP, (AV)
One East Putnam Avenue, 06830 ⊙
Telephone: 203-862-7800 Fax: 203-862-7801
Email: postmaster@dbh.com URL: http://www.dbh.com
Members of Firm in Greenwich: R. Scott Beach; Ronald Osburn Dederick; Forrest Lee Griffith III; Amy K. Wilfert. Associates of the firm in Greenwich: Peter Chadwick; Shawn T. Wooden. Counsel in Greenwich: Lesley I. B. Schless (Not admitted in CT).
Antitrust, Banking, Bank Lending, Bankruptcy, Bankruptcy Counseling, Benefits and Executive Compensation, Business Succession Planning, Business Transactions and Counseling, Closely Held Businesses, Credit Tenant Lease Financing, Commercial Litigation, Commercial Leasing, Construction, Direct Liability and Casualty Insurance, Disability, Emerging Companies, Energy, Environmental and Land Use, Equipment Finance and Leasing, Employment Law and Litigation, Environmental Law and Litigation, Executive Planning, Family Law, Finance and Investments, First Party Insurance, Franchise and Distributorship Litigation, Government Investigations, Health Care, Insurance Regulation and Proceedings, Insurance Litigation, International Tax, International Transactions, Life Insurance and Annuities, Low Income Housing Tax Credits, Medical and Professional Malpractice, Mergers and Acquisitions, Multi-Property Transactions, Municipal Finance, Negligence Defense, Planning for Entrepreneurs, Private Equity Funds, Product Liability, Real Estate Development, Real Estate Equity Investors, Real Estate Finance, Real Estate Workouts and Restructuring, Regulatory Insurance Proceedings and Litigation, Reinsurance, Securities Law, Securities Litigation, Strategic Joint Ventures, Structured Finance, Tax, Tax Litigation Group, Tax Exempt and Charity Giving, Tax Exempt Organizations, Technology and Intellectual Property Business and Litigation, Torts Litigation, Telecommunications, Trusts and Estates Administration, Trusts and Estates Litigation, Water Companies.
Hartford, Connecticut Office: CityPlace I. Telephone: 860-275-0100. Telecopier: 860-275-0343.
Stamford, Connecticut Office: One Canterbury Green. Telephone: 203-977-7300. Telecopier: 203-977-7301.
Boston, Massachusetts Office: 260 Franklin Street. Telephone: 617-345-4600. Telecopier: 617-439-4453.
See Professional Biographies, GREENWICH, CONNECTICUT

Dean, Harold H. .... '29 '57 C.732 B.S. L.1009 LL.B. [[C] P.Russell]
*PRACTICE AREAS: Litigation; Civil Litigation; Arbitration.

de Arango, Fernando F., (BV) .... '51 '78 C.321 B.A. L.276 J.D. Law Dept. of Greenwich

Dederick, Ronald Osburn, (AV) .... '35 '63 C&L.893 B.A., J.D. [Day,B.&H.]
*PRACTICE AREAS: Estate Planning; Tax-Exempt Organizations and Charitable Giving; Trust and Estate Administration; Trust and Estate Litigation.

Deegan, Martha E.H., (BV) .... '49 '77 C.97 B.A. L.607 J.D. [M.E.H.Deegan]

Deegan, Martha E.H., LLC, (BV) .... 100 Brookside Drive (⊙Rockville Centre, NY)

De Forest & Duer
Two Sound View Drive, Suite 100 (⊙Hackensack, NJ; New York, NY)

Delany, B. Cort, (BV) .... '55 '82 C.197 A.B. L.262 J.D. [Cummings&L.]
*PRACTICE AREAS: Real Estate; Will Contests; Taxation; Probate Law; Estate Planning.

DeRicco, Steven Paul .... '— '87 C.716 B.S. L.262 J.D. [Bleakley P.&S.]
*PRACTICE AREAS: Estate Planning; Trusts and Estates; Surrogates Court Practice; Litigation; Tax Law.

De Stefano, Nicholas E. E. '36 '62 C.563 B.B.A. L.1009 LL.B.
(adm. in NY; not adm. in CT) 17 Copper Beech Rd.‡

DeStefano, Philip F., Jr. .... '43 '70 C.976 B.A. L.262 J.D. Calhoun Dr.‡

Diserio Martin O'Connor & Castiglioni LLP
(See Stamford)

Donohue, James P., Jr. '50 '76 C&L.262 B.A., J.D.
(adm. in NY; not adm. in CT) [Gilbride,T.L.&S.] ⊙
*PRACTICE AREAS: Litigation; Securities Arbitration.

Dougherty, James Bruce, (BV) .... '58 '83 C.1041 B.B.A. L.184 J.D. [Dougherty,D.&V.]
*PRACTICE AREAS: Estate Planning; Probate; Real Estate; Land Use; Elder Law.

Dougherty, Dougherty & Vecchiolla, (BV)
28 Sound View Drive, P.O. Box 4239, 06830
Telephone: 203-869-0290; 869-3085 FAX: 203-869-3159
URL: http://www.lawyers.com/dd&vlaw
James A. Dougherty (1902-1992); Hugh Bruce Dougherty (1931-1999). Members of Firm: John L. Vecchiolla; James Bruce Dougherty.
General Practice. Estate Planning and Probate Law. Real Estate, Taxation and Corporate Law, Business Law, Trusts and Estates.
References: Fleet Bank, N.A.; Putnam Trust Co.
See Professional Biographies, GREENWICH, CONNECTICUT

Douvas Orme, Maria '63 '89 C&L.228 B.A., J.D.
(adm. in NY; not adm. in CT) Asst. Gen. Coun., AIG Trading Grp., Inc.

Drake, Philip M., (AV) .... '25 '52 C.976 B.A. L.893 J.D. [Cummings&L.]

Duel, Arthur B., III, (BV) .... '37 '65 C.216 B.A. L.893 LL.B. 125 Mason St.

Duncan, John Bruce, (AV) ..... '23 '50 C.31 L.309 J.D. [More P.&D.] (⊙New Canaan)‡

Effron, Wayne D., (AV) .... '50 '77 C&L.184 B.A., J.D. [W.D.Effron]
*PRACTICE AREAS: Family Law; Civil Litigation; Personal Injury.

Effron, Wayne D., P.C., (AV) BB
165 West Putnam Avenue, P.O. Box 499, 06836
Telephone: 203-622-1160 Fax: 203-622-4004
Email: effronlaw@effronlaw.com URL: http://www.effronlaw.com
Wayne D. Effron; Allen Gary Palmer. Of Counsel: Joel M. Kaye.
Matrimonial Law and Civil Litigation including Personal Injury and Commercial Law at the Trial and Appellate Levels.
See Professional Biographies, GREENWICH, CONNECTICUT

Ekberg, John P., III, (BV) .... '47 '90 C.970 B.A. L.1040 J.D. [Schoonmaker,G.&C.]
*PRACTICE AREAS: Matrimonial Law; Family Law.

Epstein, Louis '15 '84 C.724 B.B.A. L.978 J.D.
(adm. in NY; not adm. in CT) 76 Thunder Mountain Rd.‡

Epstein, Robert A., (AV) .... '29 '54 C.945 B.A. L.976 LL.B. [[C] Fogarty C.S.&N.]
*PRACTICE AREAS: Matrimonial Law.

Epstein Fogarty Cohen Selby
(See Fogarty Cohen Selby & Nemiroff LLC)

Esposito, James M. '66 '91 C.276 B.A. L.262 J.D.
(adm. in NY; not adm. in CT)
Assoc. Gen. Coun. & Sr. V.P., Greenwich Capital Markets, Inc.

Farley, Deirdre M. '53 '84 C.264 B.A. L.1051 J.D.
(adm. in OR; not adm. in CT) Assistant General Counsel, Quebecor World USA Inc.

Feinstein, Steven D., (BVⓉ) '60 '86 C.575 B.A. L.607 J.D.
(adm. in NY; not adm. in CT) [Giacomo,G.F.&N.] ⊙

Ferguson, John J., (BV) .... '39 '66 C.321 B.S. L.262 LL.B. [Bleakley P.&S.]

Ferguson, John T., II '46 '76 C&L.893 B.A., J.D.
(adm. in PA; not adm. in CT) Sr. V.P. & Gen. Coun., Crompton Corp.

Finkelstein, Marci E. .... '72 '98 C.260 B.A. L.1325 J.D. [[A] G.I.Cohen]
*PRACTICE AREAS: Family Law; Matrimonial Law.

Finkelstein, Steven .... '62 '87 C.705 B.A. L.276 J.D. [Rinaldi,F.&F.]
*PRACTICE AREAS: Corporate Law.

Finn Dixon & Herling LLP
(See Stamford)

Fisher, Everett, (AV) .... '20 '48 C&L.976 B.A., LL.B. [[C] Fogarty C.S.&N.]
*PRACTICE AREAS: Probate Law; Estate and Gift Taxation.

Fleisher, Cary L., (BV) .... '44 '69 C.95 B.A. L.1294 J.D. 41 W. Putnam Ave.

Fletcher, Raymond R., Jr. '29 '56 C.688 B.Ch.E. L.309 J.D.
(adm. in NY; not adm. in CT) [[C] Gilbride,T.L.&S.] ⊙

Flinn, Michael deV. .... '41 '68 C.976 A.B. L.309 LL.B. 295 Round Hill Rd.

Fogarty, James R., (AV) .... '43 '67 C&L.262 B.A., LL.B. [Fogarty C.S.&N.]
*PRACTICE AREAS: Appellate Practice; Business Torts; Complex Litigation; Personal Injury Law; Malpractice.

Fogarty Cohen Selby & Nemiroff LLC, (AV) BB
88 Field Point Road, P.O. Box 2508, 06836-2508
Telephone: 203-661-1000 Telefax: 203-629-7300
URL: http://www.lawyers.com/fcs&n
Members of Firm: James R. Fogarty; Bruce F. Cohen; Leland C. Selby; Andrew P. Nemiroff; Steven W. Russo. Counsel: Robert A. Epstein; Everett Fisher; Jennifer N. Boyd. Associates: William Bradford Smith, Jr.; Carolyn Alexander Collins; Lawrence F. Reilly; Anne M. Piedade; Eric R. Posmantier.
Litigation in all Courts, Real Estate and Land Use, Estate Planning and Probate, Corporate, Matrimonial, Administrative and Environmental, Appellate Practice, Business, Civil Trial, Commercial Litigation, Construction, Family, Labor and Employment, Medical Malpractice, Trust and Product Liability.
See Professional Biographies, GREENWICH, CONNECTICUT

Foley, Brian T. .... '59 '85 C.706 B.A. L.564 J.D. [McGovern&Assoc.]
*PRACTICE AREAS: Commercial Litigation; Patent Enforcement Litigation.

Ford, F. Richards, III '28 '53
C.674 A.B. L.893 LL.B. Chmn. of the Bd., Genesis Aviation Ltd.

Forrow, Brian D. .... '27 '50 C.674 A.B. L.309 LL.B. 704 Lake Ave.‡

Fraleigh, Andrea M. '68 '93 C.477 B.B.A. L.309 J.D.
(adm. in IL; not adm. in CT) [[A] Whitman B.A.&M.]
*PRACTICE AREAS: Estate Planning; Estate Administration.

Francis, Theodore E. '64 '89 C.688 B.S. L.178 J.D.
(adm. in NY; not adm. in CT)
V.P. & Coun., Creditanstalt-Bankverein (⊙New York, NY)

Franklin, Eric W. .... '66 '93 C.861 B.A. L.1187 J.D. [Rinaldi,F.&F.]
*PRACTICE AREAS: Real Estate; Corporate Law.

Fraser, P. Benedict, (AV) .... '33 '62 C.1041 B.A. L.262 LL.B. 28 Lafayette Pl.

Fredericks, Frank O. '19 '48 C.569 B.S. L.178 LL.B.
(adm. in NY; not adm. in CT) 14 Dewart Rd.‡

French, John R., (AV) ....'41 '66 C&L.309 A.B., LL.B. [Cummings&L.]
*PRACTICE AREAS: Estate Settlement Law; Trust Administration Law; Taxation Law.

Friedman, Morton '37 '70 C.563 B.S. L.1009 J.D.
(adm. in NY; not adm. in CT; Pat.) Witco Corp.

Fuller, Robert F. ....'29 '56 C&L.309 A.B., J.D. 4 Sound Shore Dr.‡

Fuller, Theodore '18 '48 C.674 B.A. L.178 LL.B.
(adm. in NY; not adm. in CT) 3 Mercia Lane‡

Fullerton, Arthur C. '51 '76 C.705 B.A. L.1292 J.D.
Asst. Gen. Coun., Crompton Corp.
*RESPONSIBILITIES: Corporate Law; Finance; International Mergers and Acquisitions.

Fulton, James A., (BV) ....'52 '77 C.184 B.A. L.188 J.D. [Whitman B.A.&M.]
*PRACTICE AREAS: Litigation; Personal Injury Litigation; Products Liability Litigation; Landlord-Tenant Litigation.

Fuqua, James B. '67 '92 C.309 A.B. L.569 J.D.
(adm. in NY; not adm. in CT) Asst. Gen. Coun., Greenwich Capital Markets, Inc.

Fusco, John C. ....'61 '93 C.676 B.A. L.1029 J.D. [Holland K.&B.]
*PRACTICE AREAS: Litigation; Employment Law; Business Litigation; Real Estate; Small Business Law.

Gabler, Kathryn '45 '71 C.112 A.B. L.1066 J.D.
(adm. in CA; not adm. in CT) 106 Parsonage Rd.‡

Gaccione, Samuel G. ....'64 '89 C.676 B.S. L.724 J.D. NAC Reinsurance Corp.

Gallo, David G., (AVⓉ) '49 '79 C.1040 B.B.A. L.107 J.D.
(adm. in NY; not adm. in CT) [Giacomo,G.F.&N.] ⊙

Gammill, Kenneth M., (AV) ....'— '69 C.228 B.A. L.94 LL.B. [Robinson&C.]
*PRACTICE AREAS: Trusts and Estates.

Gammill, Kenneth M., Jr. ....'68 '95 C.299 A.B. L.1194 J.D. [Ⓐ Gilbride,T.L.&S.] ⊙
*PRACTICE AREAS: Real Estate; Land Use; Environmental Law.

Gangei, Gitty D. Samrad ....'59 '86 C&L.607 B.A., J.D. 12 Old Forge Rd.

Garnett, Hugh A. '26 '52 C.339 A.B. L.477 J.D.
(adm. in DC; not adm. in CT) 75 Dearfield Dr.‡

Gaughan, James D. '51 '81 C.326 B.A. L.796 J.D.
(adm. in TX; not adm. in CT) Sr. Corp. Coun. & Asst. Secy., Tenneco

Gaulin, Patricia B. '52 '79 C.823 B.A. L.564 J.D.
(adm. in NY; not adm. in CT) Win Properties, Inc.

Gelfand, Murray '29 '57 C.623 B.A. L.188 LL.B.
(adm. in NY; not adm. in CT) 10 Brookside Dr.‡

Geller, Frank W., (AVⓉ) '39 '66 C&L.823 A.B., LL.B.
(adm. in NY; not adm. in CT) Integrated Res., Inc.

George, Cynthia Coulter, (AV) .... '53 '78 C.188 B.A. L.425 J.D. [Schoonmaker,G.&C.]
*PRACTICE AREAS: Matrimonial Law; Family Law.

Gerrish, Haden P. ....'57 '84 C.674 A.B. L.262 J.D. Law Dept. of Greenwich

Giacomo, M. Theresa, (BVⓉ) ....'53 '82 C.706 B.A. L.1040 J.D. 21 W. Ln.

Giacomo, William J., (BV) ....'50 '84 C.93 B.S. L.1040 J.D. [Giacomo,G.F.&N.] ⊙

Giacomo, Gallo, Feinstein & Naishtut, LLP, (AVⓉ)
28 Soundview Ave. (⊙Rye Brook, NY)

Gil, Patrick R., (BV) ....'42 '71 C.321 B.S. L.262 J.D. [Orlovitz&G.]

Gilbert, Jessie A., (BV) ....'60 '86 C.299 A.B. L.930 J.D. [Cummings&L.] (⊙Greenwich)
*PRACTICE AREAS: Trusts and Estates; Estate Planning; Estate Administration; Taxation; Family Business Law.

Gilbride, Frank J., II, (AV) .... '41 '68 C.884 B.S. L.262 J.D. [Gilbride,T.L.&S.] ⊙
*PRACTICE AREAS: Trusts and Estates Law; Real Estate Law; Admiralty Law; Family Law.

Gilbride, Tusa, Last & Spellane, LLC, (AV)
31 Brookside Drive, P.O. Box 658, 06836 ⊙
Telephone: 203-622-9360 Facsimile: 203-622-9392
Members of Firm: Frank J. Gilbride, II; Charles S. Tusa; Bennett H. Last (Not admitted in CT); Thomas P. Spellane; John P. Tesei; Eric H. Seltzer; David Crystal, II; James P. Donohue, Jr. (Not admitted in CT); Frederic P. Rickles (Not admitted in CT); Sarah J. Otis;—Kenneth M. Gammill Jr.; Glen J. Moore; Thomas W. Littman (Not admitted in CT). Of Counsel: Raymond R. Fletcher, Jr. (Not admitted in CT); Robert N. Littman (Not admitted in CT).
General Practice. Real Estate, Corporation, Securities, Federal and State Courts, Litigation, Franchise Law, Taxation, Admiralty, International, Trademark, Probate, Zoning, Land Use, Family Law and Aviation.
New York, New York Office: The Graybar Building, 420 Lexington Avenue. Telephone: 212-692-9666. Facsimile: 212-661-6328.
See Professional Biographies, GREENWICH, CONNECTICUT

Gilhuly, Robert T., (AV) ....'30 '54 C.321 B.A. L.976 LL.B. [Cummings&L.]
*PRACTICE AREAS: Estate Settlement and Trust Administration; Estate Planning; Real Estate Law.

Gladstone, Richard H. ....'63 '89 C.228 A.B. L.309 J.D. Coun., Gladstone Develop. Corp.

Goldfarb, Sheldon I., (AVⓉ) '51 '78 C.1044 B.A. L.823 J.D.
(adm. in NY; not adm. in CT) Gen. Coun., Greenwich Capital Markets, Inc.

Gordon, Allan S. '41 '64 C.569 B.S. L.309 LL.B.
(adm. in NY; not adm. in CT) 50 N. Stanwich Rd.‡

Grant, Elizabeth M., (BV) ....'— '89 C.788 A.B. L.262 J.D. [Ⓒ Robinson&C.]
*PRACTICE AREAS: Trusts and Estates; Wills; Probate.

Graubard, Myra L.
(See Stamford)

Grayson, Eric D., (BV) ....'57 '83 C.732 B.A. L.861 J.D. [E.D.Grayson] (⊙Stamford)

Grayson, Eric D., Law Offices of, (BV) ....124 West Putnam Ave., Second Floor

Green, Robert W.
(See Stamford)

Gregory, Alison M. '64 '93 C.893 B.A. L.813 J.D.
(adm. in NY; not adm. in CT) Long-Term Cap. Mgmt. Lp

Grele, Robert F., (AV) ....'39 '64 C.282 A.B. L.188 LL.B. [Cummings&L.]
*PRACTICE AREAS: Estate Settlement Law; Trust Administration Law; Real Estate Law.

Griffith, Forrest Lee, III, (AV) ....'47 '72 C.951 B.A. L.94 J.D. [Day,B.&H.]
*PRACTICE AREAS: Emerging Companies; Mergers and Acquisitions; Strategic Joint Ventures; Finance and Investments; International Transactions.

Grimes & Battersby L.L.P.
(See Stamford)

Gromulat, Martin A. '66 '92 C.1350 B.A. L.823 J.D.
(adm. in NY; not adm. in CT) [Ⓐ Rinaldi,F.&F.]
*PRACTICE AREAS: Negligence; Insurance Coverage; Municipal Liability.

Gwydir, Raymond J. '45 '73 C.262 B.S. L.724 J.D.
(adm. in NY; not adm. in CT) Howmet Corp.

Hack, Robert A., (AV) ....'22 '50 C.674 A.B. L.178 LL.B. [Ⓒ Jackson&N.] ⊙

Hallowell, J. Lincoln ....'39 '72 C.884 A.B. L.724 J.D. [Ⓒ Bleakley P.&S.] ⊙

Halprin, Joseph R. '64 '91 C&L.659 B.S., J.D.
(adm. in CA; not adm. in CT)
Director, Law & Government Affairs, The New Power Company

Hansson, Beth K., (BV) ....'61 '86 C.692 B.A. L.904 J.D. [Ⓒ Holland K.&B.]
*PRACTICE AREAS: Corporate Law; Business Law; Small Business Law; Real Estate.

Harris, Wilmot L., Jr., (AV) ....'41 '67 C.902 B.S. L.659 LL.B. [Ivey,B.&O.]
*PRACTICE AREAS: Trusts and Estates; Tax Planning; Real Estate; Corporate Law.

Hartch, Thomas F., (BV) ....'41 '67 C.976 B.A. L.178 J.D. [Whitman B.A.&M.]
*PRACTICE AREAS: Real Estate; Trusts and Estates; Land Use.

Haslun, William I., II, (BV) ....'58 '87 C.299 B.A. L.184 J.D. [Ivey,B.&O.]
*PRACTICE AREAS: Civil Litigation; Family Law; Land Use; Zoning Law.

Heagney, Thomas J., (BV) ....'53 '80 C.222 B.A. L.564 J.D. [Heagney,L.&S.]
*PRACTICE AREAS: General Practice; Corporate; Business; Probate Law; Estate Planning.

Heagney, Lennon & Slane LLP, (BV)
248 Greenwich Avenue, P.O. Box 7910, 06836
Telephone: 203-661-8400 Fax: 203-661-7496
Email: slane@prodigy.net URL: http://www.lawyers.com/hlslaw
Members of Firm: John G. Heagney (1925-1982); Francis X. Lennon, Jr. (1928-1999); John F. Slane, Jr.; Thomas J. Heagney.
General Practice, Real Estate, Trusts and Estates, Probate, Corporation and Business Law, Civil and Criminal Litigation, Zoning and Family Law.
See Professional Biographies, GREENWICH, CONNECTICUT

Hegarty, William E. ....'26 '51 C.674 A.B. L.976 LL.B. 511 Indian Field Rd.‡

Heim, Juerg A., (BV) ....'62 '90 C.183 B.A. L.564 J.D. [Ivey,B.&O.]
*PRACTICE AREAS: Corporate Law; Commercial Law; Business Law.

Hennessey, Jevera Kaye, (AV) ....'60 '84 C.276 B.A. L.94 J.D. [Kaye&H.]
*PRACTICE AREAS: Estate Planning; Probate Law; Trust Law.

Hlavaty, Marie D. '63 '91 C.696 B.A. L.262 J.D.
(adm. in NY; not adm. in CT) V.P., Dep. Gen. Coun., World Color Press Inc.

Hoffman, Kevin T. '56 '82 C.197 A.B. L.262 J.D.
289 Greenwich Avenue, Second Floor, 06830
Telephone: 203-869-8744 Fax: 203-869-8648
Email: KTH9@aol.com URL: http://www.lawyers.com/kthoffman
***PRACTICE AREAS: Securities Arbitration; NASD Arbitration; New York Stock Exchange Arbitration; SEC Enforcement; Securities Litigation.**
Commercial Litigation. Securities Arbitration, Employment and Litigation.
See Professional Biographies, GREENWICH, CONNECTICUT

Hoffman, Marianne ....'68 '94 C.914 A.B. L.659 J.D. [Ⓐ Ivey,B.&O.]
*PRACTICE AREAS: Litigation.

Hogan, Kathleen A., (BVⓉ) '52 '77 C.1146 B.A. L.838 J.D.
[Ⓒ Rutkin&O.] (⊙Denver, CO; Westport, CT)

Hogeman, Jane D., (BV) ....'50 '77 C&L.477 B.A., J.D. [Albert,W.&J.]
*PRACTICE AREAS: Real Estate and Zoning Law.

Holland, Alexander J., (AV) .... '31 '56 C.1019 B.A. L.309 LL.B. [Holland K.&B.]
*PRACTICE AREAS: Estate Planning Law; Probate Law; Trust Law; Taxation; Family Law.

Holland Kaufmann & Bartels, LLC, (AV) BR
289 Greenwich Avenue, 06830-6595
Telephone: 203-869-5600 Fax: 203-869-4648
Alexander J. Holland; Charles B. Kaufmann, III; Philip H. Bartels; Harold R. Burke; Jean Mills Aranha; Lori E. Romano; John C. Fusco. Of Counsel: Beth K. Hansson.
General Practice. Business and Corporate Law, Employment Law, Estate Planning and Probate Law, Family and Matrimonial Law, Litigation, Residential and Commercial Real Estate and Taxation.
See Professional Biographies, GREENWICH, CONNECTICUT

Hopper, Cameron F., (AV) .... '33 '59 C.855 B.A. L.976 J.D. [Hopper&H.]
*PRACTICE AREAS: Probate; Estate Planning; Wills; Trusts and Estates; Real Estate.

Hopper, David W., (BV) .... '65 '91 C.692 B.A. L.1029 J.D. [Hopper&H.]
*PRACTICE AREAS: Land Use; Land Development; Real Estate; Probate; Estate Planning.

Hopper & Hopper, (AV)
170 Mason Street, 06830
Telephone: 203-629-1100 Facsimile: 203-629-1104
Email: hopperandhopper@aol.com URL: http://www.lawyers.com/hopperandhopper
Members of Firm: Cameron F. Hopper; David W. Hopper; Veronica C. Staplefield. Of Counsel: Pamela D. Bochinski.
Probate and Estate Planning, Wills, Trusts and Real Estate Law.
See Professional Biographies, GREENWICH, CONNECTICUT

Hull, Lloyd N. ....'22 '52 C.659 B.S. L.564 J.D. [Sullivan&D.]

Ingber, Clifford J. '54 '78 C&L.1019 B.A., J.D.
(adm. in NY; not adm. in CT) [Ingber&I.]

Ingber, Victoria M. ....'54 '84 C.188 B.A. L.724 J.D. [Ingber&I.]

Ingber & Ingber ....335 Greenwich Ave., 2nd Fl.

Ivey, Barnum & O'Mara, LLC, (AV) BR
170 Mason Street, P.O. Box 1689, 06830
Telephone: 203-661-6000 Telecopier: 203-661-9462
Email: general@ibolaw.com URL: http://www.ibolaw.com
Members of Firm: Michael J. Allen; Robert C. Barnum, Jr.; Edward D. Cosden, Jr.; Wilmot L. Harris, Jr.; William I. Haslun II; Juerg A. Heim; Michael J. Jones; Edward T. Krumeich, Jr.; Donat C. Marchand; Miles F. McDonald, Jr.; Edwin J. O'Mara, Jr.; Jennifer D. Port; Karla Pankratz Ray; Gregory A. Saum; Lorraine Slavin; Steven B. Steinmetz. Associates: Beth S. Becker; John E. Chaffee; Marianne Hoffman; Jennifer B. Kallenbach; Kurt David Koehler; Cynthia L. Singer. Of Counsel: Deirdre A Martini; Melissa Townsend Klauberg; Paul M. O'Connor, Jr.
General Practice. E-Commerce, Litigation in all Courts. Corporate, Commercial, Finance, Taxation, Trusts, Probate, Estate Planning, Family Law, Zoning, Environmental, Real Estate, Employment Law and Elder Law.
See Professional Biographies, GREENWICH, CONNECTICUT

Jackson, Susan '50 '76 C.914 B.A. L.145 J.D.
Asst. Senior Associate Counsel, Quebecor World USA Inc.

Jackson & Nash ....12 Ivanhoe Lane (⊙New York, NY)

Jacobowitz, Bradford L. '59 '87
C&L.1040 B.B.A., J.D. Assoc. Gen. Coun., Timber Hill Grp., The

Jacques, Emile W., (BV) .... '29 '58 C&L.976 B.A., LL.B. [Jacques&M.]
*PRACTICE AREAS: Wealth Transfer; Estate Planning; Estate Administration; Estate Settlement; Trust Planning.

Jacques & Moger, P.C., (BV)
530 Old Post Road #3, 06830
Telephone: 203-629-4434 FAX: 203-629-4865
Email: jacmogpc@aol.com URL: http://www.lawyers.com/jacques&moger
Emile W. Jacques; Daniel W. Moger, Jr.
Litigation in all Courts. Wealth Transfer Planning, Probate, Taxation, Real Estate, Family, Banking and Closely Held Corporate Law.
Representative Clients: Cornerstone Bank; Douglas Elliman-Pickering Associates, Inc.; Harrison Management Co.; Weeks Automobile Corp.; Fuel Tech, Inc.
Approved Attorneys For: Most Institutions Active in the Local Mortgage Market.
See Professional Biographies, GREENWICH, CONNECTICUT

Jamieson, Jean Marie ....'63 '90 C.676 B.A. L.724 J.D. 556 Riversville Rd.

Johnson, Scott R., (BV) ....'52 '80 C.188 B.A. L.1194 J.D. [Albert,W.&J.]
*PRACTICE AREAS: Real Estate; Environmental; Construction Law.

Jones, Charles L., II '21 '45 C.674 A.B. L.976 LL.B.
(adm. in NY; not adm. in CT) 43 Hunting Ridge Rd.‡

Jones, Edwin M. ....'16 '43 C.976 B.A. L.569 LL.B. [Ⓒ Bentley,M.B.&L.] ‡
*PRACTICE AREAS: ERISA Employee Benefits; General Corporate.

Jones, Gerard E. .... '37 '66 C&L.976 B.A., LL.B [Ⓒ Shipman&G.]
*PRACTICE AREAS: Corporate Law; Securities Law.

Jones, Michael J., (BV) ....'58 '83 C.165 B.A. L.93 J.D. [Ivey,B.&O.]
*PRACTICE AREAS: General Practice; Residential Real Estate; Commercial Real Estate; Commercial Law; Litigation.

Josephs, Laurie R., (AVⓉ) '57 '82 C.881 B.A. L.309 J.D.
(adm. in NY; not adm. in CT) 615 Round Hill Rd.‡

Juan, Peter D. '56 '83 C.699 B.A. L.050
(adm. in NY; not adm. in CT) 14 Lafayette Ct.

Kallenbach, Jennifer B. ....'67 '95 C.276 B.A. L.861 J.D. [🄰 Ivey,B.&O.]
*PRACTICE AREAS: Real Estate; Land Use; Zoning Law.

Kallman, Irwin ....'28 '56 C.563 B.S.S. L.564 LL.B. 66 Field Point Rd.

Kambas, James W., (AV) ....'31 '64 C.829 B.S. L.188 LL.B. 365 Taconic Rd.

Kanowitz, Edward, (CV) ....'51 '76 C.868 A.B. L.569 J.D. [McGovern&Assoc.]
*PRACTICE AREAS: Taxation; Civil Litigation; Corporate Law.

Kaplan, Andrew R. '58 '84 C.860 B.A. L.188 J.D.
(adm. in NY; not adm. in CT) Sr. Gen. Coun., AIG Trading Grp., Inc.

Kaufmann, Charles B., III, (AV) .... '44 '69 C.976 B.A. L.178 J.D. [Holland K.&B.]
*PRACTICE AREAS: Corporate Law; Business Law; Buying and Selling of Businesses; Small Business Law; Real Estate.

Kaye, Jeremy E., (AV) ....'55 '80 C.30 B.A. L.184 J.D. [Kaye&H.]
*PRACTICE AREAS: Real Estate Law; Probate Law.

Kaye, Joel M. ....'53 '77 C.30 B.A. L.184 J.D. [🄲 W.D.Effron] (⊙Greenwich)
*PRACTICE AREAS: Real Estate; Commercial Law; Probate.

Kaye, Joel M., (BV) '53 '77 C.30 B.A. L.184 J.D.
165 West Putnam Avenue, 06830 ⊙
Telephone: 203-622-4500 Fax: 203-622-1797
Email: KAYESONGS@AOL.com
***PRACTICE AREAS: Real Estate; Commercial Law; Probate.**
General Practice, Real Estate, Probate, Business Law.
See Professional Biographies, GREENWICH, CONNECTICUT

Kaye, Joseph Mitchell, (AV) ....'20 '53 C.563 B.B.A. L.976 J.D. 100 Field Point Rd.‡

Kaye and Hennessey, LLC, (AV)
71 Lewis Street, P.O. Box 768, 06836
Telephone: 203-625-5300 Fax: 203-625-3161
Email: kayehenlaw.com URL: http://www.kayehenlaw.com
Jeremy E. Kaye; Jevera Kaye Hennessey.
Real Estate, Probate, Estate Planning.
See Professional Biographies, GREENWICH, CONNECTICUT

Kearney, John F. '39 '71 C.94 A.B. L.818 J.D.
(adm. in MA; not adm. in CT) Gen. Coun., Aotec LLC, American Optical Corp.

Keats, Ellen, (BV) '57 '82 C.299 B.A. L.245 J.D.
Senior Vice President & General Counsel, Fine Host Corporation

Kelly, Wendy A. .... '56 '81 C.966 B.A. L.128 J.D. 48 Indian Field Rd.★

Kiefer, Donald R., (BV) '36 '62 C.165 B.A. L.178 LL.B.
Outdoor Trader Building, 79 East Putnam Avenue, 06830
Telephone: 203-869-5511 Telecopier: 203-869-6855
Email: Ctlawyr@aol.com URL: http://www.lawyers.com/donladkiefer
General Civil and Taxation, Practice with emphasis in Litigation, Family, Divorce, Domestic Relations, Real Estate, Commercial, Corporate, International, Admiralty; Probate Law & Litigation.
Reference: People's Bank.
See Professional Biographies, GREENWICH, CONNECTICUT

Klann, Reigh F. '29 '54 C&L.976 B.A., LL.B.
(adm. in WI; not adm. in CT) 7 Ridgebrook Rd.‡

Klauberg, Melissa Townsend, (BV) ....'56 '82 C.696 B.A. L.982 J.D. [🄲 Ivey,B.&O.]
*PRACTICE AREAS: Real Estate; Land Use; Zoning Law.

Klug, Sarah Scova '56 '96
C.999 B.S. L.1040 J.D. Assoc. Gen. Coun., Blyth Industries, Inc.

Knight, Haven A. '29 '58 C.855 B.A. L.893 LL.B.
Sr. V.P., Tr., The Putnam Tr. Co. of Greenwich

Koehler, Kurt David ....'67 '94 C.174 B.A. L.1252 J.D. [🄰 Ivey,B.&O.]
*PRACTICE AREAS: Trusts and Estates; Tax Planning; Probate; Estate Litigation.

Kolakowski, Pierre-Yves '67 '93
C.1030 B.A. L.1252 J.D. [🄰 Zeichner E.&K.] (⊙New York, NY)

Koomey, Richard A. '32 '62 C.178 A.B. L.569 LL.B.
(adm. in NY; not adm. in CT) Dep. Gen. Coun., Pechiney Corp.

Koskoff, Koskoff & Bieder, P.C.
(See Bridgeport)

Krause, Robert G., (BV) ....'31 '58 C.184 B.A. L.94 LL.B. [🄲 Whitman B.A.&M.]
*PRACTICE AREAS: Trusts and Estates; Real Estate.

Kreiger, Bruce D. '43 '72 C.563 B.A. L.1065 J.D.
(adm. in CA; not adm. in CT) V.P. & Gen. Coun., Blyth Industries, Inc.

Kristoff, Christopher A., (BV) ....'55 '85 C.24 B.A. L.1187 J.D. [Albert,W.&J.]
*PRACTICE AREAS: Probate Administration; Civil Litigation.

Krumeich, Edward T., Jr., (BV) ....'50 '75 C.299 A.B. L.930 J.D. [Ivey,B.&O.]
*PRACTICE AREAS: Litigation; Construction Law; Employment Law; Residential Real Estate.

Kurtz, Melvin H. '36 '63 C.563 B.Ch.E. L.262 J.D.
(adm. in NY; not adm. in CT; Pat.)
Vice President - Law, Unilever Home & Personal Care

Lambert, John F., (AV) ....'30 '56 C.602 A.B. L.178 LL.B. [Bentley,M.B.&L.]
*PRACTICE AREAS: State and Federal Litigation; Domestic Relations.

Lane, Robert M., (BV) '28 '54 C.734 B.S. L.178 LL.B.
530 Old Post Road No. 3, 06830
Telephone: 203-869-3700 Telecopier: 203-869-6019
Email: RMLANE530@aol.com
***PRACTICE AREAS: Estate Planning; Real Estate; Taxation; Corporate Law.**
General Practice. Probate, Taxation, Real Estate, Estate Planning.
See Professional Biographies, GREENWICH, CONNECTICUT

Larsen, Lance D. '70 '97 C.878 B.S. L.945 J.D.
(adm. in NY; not adm. in CT) Legal Coun., Kenmar Corp.

Larson, Lawrence E., (BV) '32 '60 C.165 A.B. L.188 LL.B.
153 Mason Street, 06830-6608
Telephone: 203-661-2300 FAX: 203-661-2350
Trusts, Estates, Taxation, Real Estate and Corporate Law, Business Transactions, Elder Law.
See Professional Biographies, GREENWICH, CONNECTICUT

Last, Bennett H. '44 '69 C.994 B.A. L.178 LL.B.
(adm. in NY; not adm. in CT) [Gilbride,T.L.&S.] ⊙
*PRACTICE AREAS: Commercial Litigation.

Lauricella, Anthony G., (CV) .... '28 '53 C.262 B.S. L.184 LL.B. 319 Greenwich Ave.

Lauricella, Thomas J. ....'13 '38 C.262 B.S. L.306 LL.B. 3 Benedict Ct.‡

Lederman, Ira S. '53 '80 C.994 B.A. L.1019 J.D.
(adm. in NY; not adm. in CT) Sr. V.P., Gen. Coun. & Asst. Secy., W.R. Berkley Corp.
*RESPONSIBILITIES: Corporate Law; Insurance Regulation; International.

Leff, Meredith Ann '— '98 C.188 B.S. L.1019 J.D.
(adm. in NY; not adm. in CT) [🄰 Robinson&C.]
*PRACTICE AREAS: Real Estate; Trusts and Estates.

Levine, L. Andrew '45 '73 C.569 B.A. L.564 J.D.
(adm. in NY; not adm. in CT) P.O. Box 1627

Levine, Seymour '26 '77 C.339 B.S.E.E. L.1009 J.D.
(adm. in NY; not adm. in CT; Pat.) 243 Weaver St.

Lieberson, Rhona S. Derrin ....'43 '85 C&L.1029 B.S., J.D. Arnold Foods Co., Inc.

Littman, Robert N. '32 '61 C.401 B.S. L.1009 LL.B.
(adm. in NY; not adm. in CT) [🄲 Gilbride,T.L.&S.] ⊙
*PRACTICE AREAS: Taxation; Trusts and Estates; Probate.

Littman, Thomas W. '70 '99 C.401 B.A. L.861 J.D.
(adm. in NY; not adm. in CT) [🄰 Gilbride,T.L.&S.] ⊙
*PRACTICE AREAS: Civil Litigation; Real Estate.

Loeser, Constance Tilden '45 '82 C.788 B.A. L.878 J.D.
(adm. in NY; not adm. in CT) [McGovern&Assoc.]
*PRACTICE AREAS: Securities Law; Corporate Law; Mergers and Acquisitions Law.

Loforese, John T., (BV) ....'59 '84 C.433 B.A. L.724 J.D. [J.T.Loforese] ⊙
*PRACTICE AREAS: Litigation; Real Estate; General Practice.

Loforese, John T., LLC, Law Offices of, (BV)
25 Lewis Street, Suite 304, 06830 ⊙
Telephone: 203-625-5594 Fax: 203-625-0154
URL: http://www.lawyers.com/loforese
John T. Loforese.
Civil Litigation, Real Estate, Wills and Probate, Personal Injury, Family Law, Collections.
White Plains, New York Office: 81 Main Street, 10601. Telephone: 914-328-8800.
See Professional Biographies, GREENWICH, CONNECTICUT

Lois, Dale J., (BV) .... '60 '90 C.1021 B.A. L.564 J.D. [Whitman B.A.&M.]
*PRACTICE AREAS: Commercial Real Estate; Corporate Law; Electronic Commerce.

Lorenzo, Michael E. '29 '53 C&L.262 B.S., J.D.
(adm. in NY; not adm. in CT) 14 Ivanhoe Lane‡

Loughran, Thomas D. '61 '89 C.999 B.B.S. L.724 J.D.
(adm. in NJ; not adm. in CT) 111 Overlook Dr.

Lowin, Maida Meyers '54 '84 C.831 B.M. L.564 J.D.
(adm. in NY; not adm. in CT) 21 Fox Run Lane

Lutz, Carol Lombard ....'31 '76 C.724 B.A. L.262 J.D. 112 Patterson Ave.‡

Lydon, Patricia '46 '71 C&L.494 B.A., J.D.
(adm. in MN; not adm. in CT) V.P., Sherman Fairchild Found.

Lynch, Jacob R., (BV) .... '17 '48 C.197 A.B. L.309 LL.B. 100 Field Point Road‡

Lynch, William R., (AV) ....'28 '59 C.976 B.A. L.178 LL.B. [Cummings&L.]
*PRACTICE AREAS: Trusts and Estates Law; Real Estate Law; Business Law.

MacCracken, Alan M., (AV) ....'07 '36 C.674 A.B. L.569 J.D. 100 Field Point Rd.‡

Macleod, Anthony M., (AV) ....'47 '72 C.602 A.B. L.893 J.D. [Whitman B.A.&M.]
*PRACTICE AREAS: Corporation Law; Public Utility Law; Real Estate Law.

Madden, Michael K. '51 '78 C.228 B.A. L.273 J.D.
(adm. in NY; not adm. in CT) [🄲 Whitman B.A.&M.]
*PRACTICE AREAS: Litigation; Complex Commercial Litigation; Insurance Coverage; Products Liability; Drug and Medical Device Defense.

Maddy, Elmer C., (AVⓉ) ....'25 '49 C.611 B.A. L.178 J.D. 16 Round Hill Rd.

Maher and Williams
(See Fairfield)

Mahone, William L. '51 '84 C.813 B.A. L.309 J.D.
(adm. in NY; not adm. in CT) V.P. & Gen. Coun., Interlaken Capital, Inc.

Malawer, Steven J. ....'70 '96 C.477 B.A. L.1019 J.D. Atty., W. R. Berkley Corp.
*RESPONSIBILITIES: Corporate Law; Insurance Regulation; International.

Maloney, Patrick C. '24 '49 C.674 A.B. L.309 J.D.
(adm. in NY; not adm. in CT) 41 Putnam Park‡

Mancuso, Richard E., (BV) ....'61 '88 C.273 B.A. L.93 J.D. [Whitman B.A.&M.]
*PRACTICE AREAS: Intellectual Property; Unfair Competition; Corporate Law; Employment Law; Mergers, Acquisitions and Divestitures.

Manero, Richard P., (BV) .... '39 '66 C.197 B.A. L.976 LL.B. 270 Greenwich Ave.

Marchand, Donat C., (AV) ....'34 '58 C.184 B.S. L.309 LL.B. [Ivey,B.&O.]
*PRACTICE AREAS: Trusts and Estates; Tax Planning; Real Estate; Taxation; Land Use.

Marchisotto, Alan L. '49 '75 C.855 B.A. L.880 J.D.
(adm. in NY; not adm. in CT) Secy. & Gen. Coun., Moran Towing Corp.
*RESPONSIBILITIES: Corporate; Maritime; Labor; Litigation.

Margenot, Richard J. '57 '85 C.855 B.A. L.1040 J.D.
537 Steamboat Road, 06830
Telephone: 203-869-7888 Fax: 203-869-0458
URL: http://www.lawyers.com/rjmargenot
Real Estate, Business Law, Wills, Trusts, Probate and Estate Planning Settlement, Conservationships, Fraud.
See Professional Biographies, GREENWICH, CONNECTICUT

Marren, Elizabeth T. '55 '81 C.741 B.B.A. L.262 J.D.
(adm. in NY; not adm. in CT) Sr. Corp. Coun., UST Inc.

Martin, Lucas & Chioffi, LLP
(See Stamford)

Martini, Deirdre A .... '60 '87 C.569 B.A. L.1029 J.D. [🄲 Ivey,B.&O.]
*PRACTICE AREAS: Bankruptcy; Commercial Law; Federal Litigation; Alternate Dispute Resolution.

Mathews, Claire Anne .... '44 '78 C.184 B.A. L.818 J.D. 3 Putnam Park

Mathura, Rani Newman ....'71 '95 [🄰 Cummings&L.]

Maze, Valerie E. ....'59 '93 C.103 A.B. L.184 J.D. Law Dept. of Greenwich

McDonald, Miles F., Jr., (BV) .... '38 '64 C&L.178 A.B., LL.B. [Ivey,B.&O.]
*PRACTICE AREAS: Litigation; Probate Litigation.

Mcdonald, Paul K. '32 '56 C&L.309 A.B., J.D.
(adm. in MA; not adm. in CT) 128 Cutler Rd.

McGovern, Kevin M., (BV) '48 '75
C.188 B.A. L.724 J.D. [McGovern&Assoc.] & [🄲 E.D.Grayson]

McGovern & Associates, (BV)
One Lafayette Place, 06830 ⊙
Telephone: 203-622-1101 Telecopier: 203-622-9192 URL: http://www.lawyers.com/mcgovernassociates
Email: kmcgovern@mcgovernlaw.com URL: http://www.mcgovernlaw.com
Kevin M. McGovern; Constance Tilden Loeser (Not admitted in CT); Brian T. Foley; Charles E. Barnett; Mark G. Aberasturi (Not admitted in CT); Edward Kanowitz; David R. Westra (Not admitted in CT). Of Counsel: Lawrence W. Casey (Not admitted in CT); Joseph P. Connors (Not admitted in CT); James J. Quinn (Not admitted in CT; Resident at New York, N.Y. Office).
General Commercial Practice. Corporate (Foreign and Domestic), Mergers and Acquisitions, Securities, Venture Capital, Taxation, Litigation in all Courts. International, Joint Ventures, Admiralty, Sports, Commercial and Residential Real Estate Law. Estates and Trusts.
New York, N.Y. Office: Trump Tower, 721 5th Avenue, Suite 52-D, 10022. Telephone: 212-697-0955.
See Professional Biographies, GREENWICH, CONNECTICUT

McIntyre, Marie J. .... '60 '85 C.93 B.S. L.724 J.D. 66 Field Point Rd.

McKee, Thomas J., (AV) ....'— '61 C.743 A.B. L.276 J.D. [🄲 Robinson&C.]
*PRACTICE AREAS: Probate Law; Estate and Gift Taxation; Estate Planning and Administration.

McKeithen, Lee S. ....'13 '34 C&L.228 A.B., J.D. 2 Greenwich Plz.‡

McLaughlin, Eugene F., Jr., (BV) '50 '76 C.93 B.A. L.184 J.D.
Law Dept. of Greenwich

McLaughlin, Michael J. '51 '85 C.433 B.S. L.1040 J.D.
(adm. in NY; not adm. in CT) 600 Steamboat Road

Meerbergen, John E., (BV) ....'43 '72 C.1033 B.A. L.365 J.D. [Bleakley P.&S.]

Melnyk, Michael .... '47 '74 C.705 B.S. L.1292 J.D. Sr. Corp. Coun., UST Inc.
Meyers, M. Richard .... '38 '64 C.154 B.A. L.188 LL.B. Henry-Richards Co., Inc.
Milan, Douglas I. .... '46 '71 C.259 B.S. L.597 J.D. 16 N. Water St.
Miller, Alfred E. .... '21 '49 C.184 B.S. L.569 LL.B. 150 Mason St. (Pat.)
Miller, Hilary B., (AV) .... '51 '82 C.197 A.B. L.262 J.D. [H.B.Miller]
*PRACTICE AREAS: Litigation; Corporate Law; Intellectual Property; Family Law.

Miller, Hilary B., (AV) BR
112 Parsonage Road, 06830-3942
Telephone: 203-861-6262 Facsimile: 203-622-6264
Email: hilary@miller.net URL: http://www.lawyers.com/hilarymiller
Hilary B. Miller.
Litigation and Corporate Law. Family Law.
See Professional Biographies, GREENWICH, CONNECTICUT

Mills, Jonathan B., (AV) ....'59 '85 C.674 A.B. L.184 J.D. [Cummings&L.]
*PRACTICE AREAS: Real Estate Law; Leasing; Financing.
Moger, Daniel W., Jr., (BV) .... '41 '66 C.976 B.A. L.659 LL.B. [Jacques&M.]
*PRACTICE AREAS: Real Estate; Civil Litigation; Family Law.
Montgomery, M. Dean, (BV) .... '42 '67 C.478 B.A. L.208 J.D. [Bentley,M.B.&L.]
*PRACTICE AREAS: Real Estate; Mortgage Banking; Consumer Lending; Property Related Litigation and Appeals.
Moore, Glen J. ....'72 '97 C.276 B.A, L.1040 J.D [Ⓐ Gilbride,T.L.&S.] ⊙
*PRACTICE AREAS: Trusts and Estates; Real Estate.
More, Douglas M., (AV) .... '26 '50 C.309 A.B. L.178 LL.B. [More P.&D.] ‡

More Phillips & Duncan, P.C., (AV) BR
95 East Putnam Avenue, 06830
Telephone: 203-629-2611 Fax: 203-629-2375
Email: morphildunc@mindspring.com
William A. Phillips; Douglas M. More (Retired); John Bruce Duncan (Retired).
General Civil Practice, Trials and Appeals in Federal and State Courts, Corporate, Probate.
See Professional Biographies, GREENWICH, CONNECTICUT

Morgen, Barbara J. '51 '78 C.103 A.B. L.1065 J.D.
(adm. in CA; not adm. in CT) AIG Trading Group, Inc.
Morra, Maria G. .... '61 '86 C.569 B.S. L.1019 J.D. 66 Field Point Rd.
Morrison, David R. '57 '90 C.624 B.S. L.705 J.D.
(adm. in NY; not adm. in CT) 33 Benedict Pl.
Mosher, Charles E., (AV) .... '31 '59 C.569 B.S. L.893 LL.B. [Bentley,M.B.&L.]
*PRACTICE AREAS: Estate Planning; Probate; Real Estate; Corporate.
Mozer, Gary N. .... '74 '99 C.1349 B.A. L.306 J.D. [Ⓐ Whitman B.A.&M.]
*PRACTICE AREAS: Corporate Law; Mergers and Acquisitions; Divestitures; Electronic Commerce; Venture Capital.
Murray, John V. A., (BV) '52 '77
C.103 A.B. L.184 J.D. 530 Old Post Road #3 (⊙Stamford)
Muskus, Thomas B. .... '49 '76 C.276 A.B. L.421 J.D. 1 Hunt Terr.
Nachimson, Steven G., (BVⓉ) '60 '86 C.881 A.B. L.107 J.D.
(adm. in NY; not adm. in CT) Corporate Counsel, Fine Host Corporation
Naishtut, Norman B., (BVⓉ) '55 '81 C.156 B.A. L.1019 J.D.
(adm. in NY; not adm. in CT) [Giacomo,G.F.&N.] ⊙
Nelson, Jonathan P. .... '45 '72 C.569 B.A. L.823 J.D. Retired
Nemiroff, Andrew P., (AV) .... '51 '79 C.829 B.S. L.365 J.D. [Fogarty C.S.&N.]
*PRACTICE AREAS: Matrimonial Law; Accident and Personal Injury Law; Complex Litigation.
Ness, Peter S. '39 '64 C.976 B.S. L.178 LL.B.
(adm. in NY; not adm. in CT) Ctr. Develop. Invests., Inc.
Nickerson, William H. .... '39 '64 C.309 A.B. L.178 LL.B. 35 Quail Rd.
Nielsen, J. Susanne .... '46 '81 C.339 B.A. L.1029 J.D. 71 Indian Harbor Dr.
Nortz, James A. '60 '86 C.1213 B.S. L.1017 J.D.
(adm. in PA; not adm. in CT) Sr. Envir. Coun., Crompton Corp.
*RESPONSIBILITIES: Environmental Law; Health Law; Toxic Torts; Litigation.
Nourse & Bowles, LLP, (AVⓉ) ....115 Mason St. (⊙Millburn, NJ; New York, NY)
O'Brien, Paul E. '58 '83 C.228 B.A. L.276 J.D.
(adm. in LA; not adm. in CT) Sr. V.P. & Gen. Coun., Stolt-Nielsen Trans. Grp. Ltd.
*RESPONSIBILITIES: Admiralty and Transportation; Commercial Law; Projects and Capital Investments.
O'Connor, Paul M., Jr., (AV) .... '33 '61 C.188 A.B. L.276 J.D. [Ⓒ Ivey,B.&O.] ‡
*PRACTICE AREAS: General Practice; Real Estate; Civil Litigation; Construction Law; Land Use.
O'Donnell, William J. .... '45 '72 C&L.262 B.S., J.D. Asst. Gen. Coun., UST Inc.

Ohlandt, Greeley, Ruggiero & Perle
(See Stamford)

Oldham, Sarah S., (BV) .... '51 '88 C.918 B.S. L.184 J.D. [Rutkin&O.] ⊙
Olin, Douglas H. .... '68 '94 C.1365 B.B.A. L.569 J.D. [Cummings&L.]
*PRACTICE AREAS: Estate Planning; Tax Planning; Estate Administration; Trust Administration.
O'Mara, Edwin J., Jr., (AV) .... '20 '50 C&L.309 A.B., LL.B. [Ivey,B.&O.]
*PRACTICE AREAS: Real Estate; Trusts and Estates; Tax Planning.
Orlovitz, Arnold, (BV) .... '30 '54 C&L.823 B.A., LL.B. [Orlovitz&G.]
Orlovitz & Gil, (BV) ....239 Glenville Rd.
Otis, Sarah J. .... '67 '93 C.197 A.B. L.978 J.D. [Gilbride,T.L.&S.] ⊙
*PRACTICE AREAS: Trust and Estates.
Paine, C. Lawrence, (BV) .... '41 '66 C.31 A.B. L.178 J.D. [C.L.Paine]

Paine, C. Lawrence, LLC, (BV)
153 Mason Street, 06830
Telephone: 203-661-4488 Fax: 203-661-2350
C. Lawrence Paine.
Practice limited to Residential and Commercial Real Estate, Land Use and Zoning, Condominiums, Elder Law, Wills and Estate Planning, Trust and Estate Administration.

Palmer, Allen Gary, (BV) .... '63 '88 C.184 B.A. L.978 J.D. [W.D.Effron]
*PRACTICE AREAS: Family Law; Civil Litigation; Personal Injury Law.
Parson, Diane Amado .... '62 '88 C.1044 B.A. L.188 J.D. One American Lane
Pascarella, Henry W., (AV) .... '33 '58 C.659 B.S. L.976 LL.B. [Ⓒ Tyler C.&A.]
*PRACTICE AREAS: Trusts and Estates; Real Estate; Environmental and Land Use Regulation; Litigation.
Pastore, James J. .... '72 '98 C.1266 B.S. L.994 J.D. [Ⓐ P.Russell]
*PRACTICE AREAS: Criminal Litigation; Civil Litigation.
Pastore, Richard S., (BV) .... '32 '60 C.31 A.B. L.178 LL.B. [R.S.Pastore]
*PRACTICE AREAS: General and Commercial Practice; Taxation; Estate Planning and Estate Administration.

Pastore, Richard S., P.C., (BV)
125 Mason Street, 06830
Telephone: 203-661-8988 Fax: 203-661-8051
Richard S. Pastore.
General and Commercial Practice. Taxation, Estate Planning and Estate Administration, Probate and Real Estate Law.
Approved Attorney For: First American Title Insurance Co.
Reference: Putnam Trust Co.
See Professional Biographies, GREENWICH, CONNECTICUT

Peden, Harry E., III, (BV) .... '45 '75 C.103 B.A. L.724 J.D. [Whitman B.A.&M.]
*PRACTICE AREAS: Corporate Law; Mergers, Acquisitions and Divestitures, Securities.
Peden, Harry E., Jr., (AV) .... '23 '48 C.103 A.B. L.724 LL.B. [Whitman B.A.&M.]
*PRACTICE AREAS: Real Estate; Planning, Zoning and Land Use.
Pedersen, Peer T. '24 '50 C.197 B.A. L.564 LL.B.
(adm. in NY; not adm. in CT) 2 Greenwich Plaza
Perelli-Minetti, C. Robton .... '48 '83 C&L.112 B.A., J.D. [Ⓒ Albert,W.&J.]
*PRACTICE AREAS: Corporate; Mergers and Acquisitions; Tax.
Peterfreund, Joshua '13 '38 C.800 B.A. L.309 LL.B.
(adm. in NY; not adm. in CT) Weaver Hill Apts.‡
Phillips, Stephen G. '50 '79 C.112 B.A. L.809 J.D.
Corp. Gen. Legal Coun., Watson Enterprises Inc.
Phillips, William A., (AV) .... '25 '54 C.103 A.B. L.184 LL.B. [More P.&D.]
*PRACTICE AREAS: Litigation; Corporate; Probate.
Piatkowski, Maciej A. .... '71 '97 C.276 B.A. L.306 J.D. [Ⓐ Whitman B.A.&M.]
*PRACTICE AREAS: Litigation; Civil Litigation; Commercial Litigation; Landlord and Tenant Law; Breach of Contract.

Piazza & Pickel
(See Stamford)

Piedade, Anne M. .... '67 '96 C.184 B.A. L.306 J.D. [Ⓐ Fogarty C.S.&N.]
*PRACTICE AREAS: Estate Planning; Estate Administration; Trust Law; Estate and Gift Taxation; Charitable Organizations.
Pieterse, Charles W., (BV) .... '60 '86 C.454 B.A. L.262 J.D. [Whitman B.A.&M.]
*PRACTICE AREAS: Civil Litigation; Complex Commercial Litigation; Products Liability; Drug and Medical Device Defense; Creditors Rights.
Pintoff, Craig A. '69 '97 C.156 B.A. L.178 J.D.
(adm. in NY; not adm. in CT) [Crompton]
*RESPONSIBILITIES: Labor and Employment; Company Benefits.
Pittocco, Louis P., (BV) .... '42 '67 C.1029 B.S. L.724 J.D. 90 Greenwich Ave.
Pohorille, Cecilia '69 '95 C.918 B.A. L.569 J.D.
(adm. in NY; not adm. in CT) Sr. Coun., PanAmSat Corp.
Pollack, Mindy '55 '80 C.184 B.A. L.273 J.D.
(adm. in NJ; not adm. in CT) Mgr., Risk Capital Reins. Co.
Port, Jennifer D. .... '55 '84 C.867 B.A. L.978 J.D. [Ivey,B.&O.]
*PRACTICE AREAS: Trusts and Estates; Tax Planning; Probate; Estate Litigation; Charitable Trusts and Foundations.
Posmantier, Eric R. .... '71 '97 C.1044 B.A. L.795 J.D. [Ⓐ Fogarty C.S.&N.]
*PRACTICE AREAS: Family Law; Civil Litigation.

Potash, Robert B., (BV) '48 '74 C.94 B.S. L.818 J.D.
31 Brookside Drive, 06830
Telephone: 203-661-7580 Telecopier: 203-661-7623
***PRACTICE AREAS: Real Estate Law; Residential Real Estate; Commercial Real Estate.**
General Practice, Real Estate, Probate and Estate Planning.
References: Union Trust Co.; Putnam Trust Co.
See Professional Biographies, GREENWICH, CONNECTICUT

Quinn, James J. '45 '75 C.263 B.A. L.724 J.D.
(adm. in NJ; not adm. in CT) [Ⓒ McGovern&Assoc.] ⊙
*PRACTICE AREAS: Taxation; Corporate Law; International Law.
Raimondi, Josephine A. '57 '88 C.276 B.S.B.A. L.477 J.D.
(adm. in NY; not adm. in CT) V.P.-Sr. Coun., W. R. Berkley Corp.
*RESPONSIBILITIES: Insurance Regulation; Corporate Law; Employment Law.
Ramer, Jeffrey S., (BV) .... '44 '70 C.264 A.B. L.262 J.D. [Ramer&R.]
*PRACTICE AREAS: General Practice; Real Estate; Business Law; Zoning; Wills.
Ramer, Nancy N., (BV) .... '46 '74 C.37 B.A. L.724 J.D. [Ramer&R.]
*PRACTICE AREAS: Family Law; Divorce; Child Custody; Visitation Rights; Property Rights.

Ramer & Ramer, (BV)
21 Benedict Place, 06830
Telephone: 203-629-1600 Fax: 203-629-1844
Members of Firm: Jeffrey S. Ramer; Nancy N. Ramer.
General Practice, Family Law, Real Estate, Business Law, Litigation, Zoning, Wills and Estates.
See Professional Biographies, GREENWICH, CONNECTICUT

Ray, Karla Pankratz .... '66 '91 C.966 B.A. L.486 J.D. [Ivey,B.&O.]
*PRACTICE AREAS: Residential Real Estate; Commercial Real Estate; Commercial Finance; Franchise Law.
Raymond, Richard C., (AVⓉ) '52 '81 C.367 B.A. L.276 J.D.
(adm. in NY; not adm. in CT) [Riemer&R.] ⊙
Reilly, Lawrence F., (BV) .... '63 '89 C.1044 B.A. L.564 J.D. [Ⓐ Fogarty C.S.&N.]
*PRACTICE AREAS: Litigation; Constitutional Law.
Rhee, Andrew D. .... '65 '91 C.918 B.A. L.569 J.D. Aquila Capital
Ribak, Pamela B. .... '61 '86 C.1365 B.A. L.1019 J.D. 7 Londonderry Dr.
Ricci, Michael A. '66 '93
(adm. in NY; not adm. in CT) Folksamerica Reinsurance Co.
Rickles, Frederic P. '65 '92 C.893 B.A. L.273 J.D.
(adm. in NY; not adm. in CT) [Gilbride,T.L.&S.] ⊙
*PRACTICE AREAS: Commercial Litigation; Real Estate Law; Trusts and Estates Law.
Riemer, Joseph G., III, (AVⓉ) '48 '75 C&L.262 B.A., J.D.
(adm. in NY; not adm. in CT) [Riemer&R.] ⊙
Riemer & Raymond, L.L.P., (AVⓉ) ....9 Benedict Place (⊙New York, NY)
Riley, James C., (BV) .... '60 '85 C&L.276 B.A., J.D. [Whitman B.A.&M.]
*PRACTICE AREAS: Commercial Litigation; Employment Litigation.
Rinaldi, Ellis F. .... '62 '87 C.454 B.B.A. L.273 J.D. [Rinaldi,F.&F.]
*PRACTICE AREAS: Real Estate; Corporate Law.
Rinaldi, Rose A. .... '65 '90 C.724 B.S. L.262 J.D. [Ⓐ Rinaldi,F.&F.]
*PRACTICE AREAS: Real Estate; Corporate Law.

Rinaldi, Finkelstein & Franklin, LLC
591 West Putnam Avenue, 06830
Telephone: 203-422-7770 FAX: 203-422-7782
Email: rinaldi@starwood.com
Ellis F. Rinaldi; Steven Finkelstein; Eric W. Franklin. Associates: Rose A. Rinaldi; Martin A. Gromulat (Not admitted in CT).
Real Estate and Corporate Law.
Representative Clients: Starwood Capital Group; Starwood Hotels and Resorts Worldwide, Inc.

Roberts, Rose & Bates, P.C.
(See Stamford)

Robinson & Cole LLP, (AV)
80 Field Point Road, 06836-1538 ⊙
Telephone: 203-862-4100 Fax: 203-862-4199
Email: gren.rc.com URL: http://www.rc.com
Partners: Kenneth M. Gammill; George L. Smith (Resident). Of Counsel: Thomas J. McKee (Resident); Clark Whittemore, Jr. Counsel: Elizabeth M. Grant (Resident). Associate: Meredith Ann Leff (Not admitted in CT).
General Practice including Admiralty, Antitrust and Trade Regulation, Appellate, Banking and Institutional Finance, Bankruptcy and Creditors' Rights, Business Litigation, Business Workouts, Construction, Corporate and Closely Held Business, Criminal Litigation, E-Commerce and Intellectual Property, Employee Benefits and ERISA Litigation, Employment Litigation and Counseling, Environmental, Estate Planning and Probate, Government Relations, Healthcare, Immigration, Insurance, International, Labor Relations and Collective Bargaining, Land Use and Zoning, Personal Injury, Product Liability, Professional Liability, Public Finance, Real Estate Finance, Development and Leasing, Securities, Tax-Exempt Organizations, Tax Planning and Representation, Utilities and Telecommunications.
Other Offices: Hartford, CT, Stamford, CT, New London, CT, Boston, MA, New York, NY and Manchester, NH.
See Professional Biographies, GREENWICH, CONNECTICUT

Rodenbach, Edward F., (AV) ....'51 '76 C.390 A.B. L.188 J.D. [Cummings&L.]
*PRACTICE AREAS: Estate Settlement Law; Trust Administration Law; Estate Law; Tax Planning Law; Executive Tax Planning Law.
Romano, Lori E. ....'67 '92 C.1030 B.A. L.1029 J.D. [Holland K.&B.]
*PRACTICE AREAS: Estate Planning Law; Probate Law; Trust Law.
Rose, Kathy Lynne Herbert '59 '84 C.1036 B.A. L.178 J.D.
Sr. V.P. & Gen. Coun., Creditanstalt-Bankverein (⊙New York, NY)
Rose, Mark H. '65 '91 C.1349 B.A. L.228 J.D.
Asst. Gen. Coun., Greenwich Capital Markets, Inc.
Rosen, Barbara ....'52 '78 C.102 B.A. L.564 J.D. 361 Stanwich Rd.
Rosenbaum, Helaine S. '67 '95 C.112 B.A. L.309 J.D.
(adm. in NY; not adm. in CT) Long-Term Capital Mgmt, L.P.
Rubin, Thai Edan '66 '94 C.966 B.S. L.329 J.D.
(adm. in MD; not adm. in CT) Sr. Coun., PanAmSat Corp.
Russell, Philip D., (AV) ....'58 '85 C.1044 B.A. L.1009 J.D. [P.Russell]
*PRACTICE AREAS: Civil Litigation; Criminal Litigation.

Russell, Philip, P.C., (AV)
71 Lewis Street, P.O. Box 1437, 06836
Telephone: 203-661-4200 Fax: 203-661-3666
URL: http://www.lawyers.com/philiprussell
Philip D. Russell;—Roy S. Ward; James J. Pastore; Christopher W. Caldwell. Of Counsel: Harold H. Dean.
Civil and Criminal Litigation in all State and Federal Courts. Traffic, Automobile Accidents, DWI, DUI, White Collar Crimes.
See Professional Biographies, GREENWICH, CONNECTICUT

Russo, Steven W., (BV) ....'56 '81 C.184 B.S. L.273 J.D. [Fogarty C.S.&N.]
*PRACTICE AREAS: Commercial Real Estate; Banking Law; Real Estate; Real Estate Finance; Land Use.
Rutkin, Arnold H., (AV) ....'39 '65 C.659 B.S. L.94 LL.B. [Rutkin&O.] ⊙
Rutkin and Oldham, L.L.C., (AV) ....125 Mason St. (⊙Westport)
Saba, William M. '21 '55 C.563 B.B.A. L.569 J.D.
(adm. in NY; not adm. in CT) 13 Perryridge Rd.‡
St. John, Orson L., (AV) ....'05 '33 C.951 B.A. L.178 LL.B. [St. John,P.&S.] ‡

St. John, Park & Scott, (BV)
P.O. Box 697, 06836-0697
Telephone: 203-637-2518 Fax: 203-637-8005
George W. Scott, Jr.;—Orson L. St. John (Retired); Halford W. Park (1918-1997).
General Practice. Wills and Estate Planning, Probate and Taxation, Trust and Estate Administration, Real Estate, Corporate, Family and Zoning Law. Civil Litigation.
See Professional Biographies, GREENWICH, CONNECTICUT

Sandak Friedman Hennessey & Greco, LLP
(See Stamford)

Sanders, David A. '42 '68 C.659 B.A. L.178 LL.B.
(adm. in IL; not adm. in CT) 100 Putnam Green
Sanislow, James R. '64 '94
C.1308 B.S. L.1187 J.D. Corporate Attorney, Moran Services Corp.
Saum, Gregory A., (BV) ....'54 '79 C.197 A.B. L.94 J.D. [Ivey,B.&O.]
*PRACTICE AREAS: Trusts and Estates; Tax Planning; Probate; Real Estate.
Schectman, Herbert A. '30 '59 C.823 A.B. L.178 LL.B.
(adm. in NY; not adm. in CT) 2 Greenwich Plaza, Suite 100
Schless, Lesley I. B. '54 '80 C.881 A.B. L.902 J.D.
(adm. in PA; not adm. in CT) [ⓒ Day,B.&H.]
Schoonmaker, Samuel V., III, (AV) '35 '61 C&L.976 B.A., J.D.
[Schoonmaker,G.&C.]
*PRACTICE AREAS: Matrimonial Law; Family Law.
Schoonmaker, Samuel V., IV ......'67 '94 C.976 B.A. L.178 J.D. [Schoonmaker,G.&C.]
*PRACTICE AREAS: Matrimonial Law; Family Law.

Schoonmaker, George & Colin, P.C., (AV) BB
81 Holly Hill Lane, P.O. Box 5059, 06831-5059
Telephone: 203-862-5000 Fax: 203-862-5099
Email: schoon@sgcfamlaw.com URL: http://www.sgcfamlaw.com
Samuel V. Schoonmaker, III; Cynthia Coulter George; Thomas D. Colin; Samuel V. Schoonmaker IV; John P. Ekberg, III; Jill Heitler Blomberg.
Matrimonial and Family Law.
See Professional Biographies, GREENWICH, CONNECTICUT

Scott, George W., Jr., (BV) ....'41 '66 C.197 A.B. L.976 LL.B. [St. John,P.&S.]
Scova, Sarah ....'— '96 C.999 B.S. L.1040 J.D. One East Weaver St
Season, Randi L. '48 '74 C.188 A.B. L.178 J.D.
(adm. in NY; not adm. in CT) 117 Stanwich Rd.‡

Segore-Freshman, Nancy
(See Westport)

Selby, Leland C., (AV) ....'44 '69 C.692 B.A. L.893 LL.B. [Fogarty C.S.&N.]
*PRACTICE AREAS: Estate Planning and Administration; Trust Law; Estate and Gift Taxation Law; Charitable Organizations.

Selsberg, William
(See Stamford)

Seltzer, Eric H. ....'59 '85 C.174 B.A. L.1009 J.D. [Gilbride,T.L.&S.] ⊙
*PRACTICE AREAS: Commercial Litigation; Real Estate Law; Public Finance.
Shabecoff, Deborah Frank '66 '92 C.976 B.A. L.309 J.D.
(adm. in NY; not adm. in CT) 153 Riversville Rd.
Shainman, Barry J. '43 '68 C.1349 B.A. L.1009 J.D.
(adm. in NY; not adm. in CT) Secy. & Asst. Gen. Coun., Crompton Corp.
*RESPONSIBILITIES: Corporate Law; Securities Law.

Shanley, Thomas M., Law Office of, (AV) '54 '79 C.1030 B.A. L.564 J.D. BB
37 Arch Street, 06830
Telephone: 203-622-9004 FAX: 203-622-3086
Email: tmshanley@snet.net URL: http://www.lawyers.com/shanley
***PRACTICE AREAS: Divorce; Matrimonial Law; Family and Domestic Relations Law.**
Matrimonial, Family, Divorce, Paternity, Custody, Appeals and all areas of Domestic Relations Law.
See Professional Biographies, GREENWICH, CONNECTICUT

Shaughnessy, Thomas J. '58 '84 C.107 B.S. L.16 J.D.
(adm. in CO; not adm. in CT)
V.P., Chief Credit Off., FMAC/Imperial Credit Industries, Inc.
Shedlin, Randy P. '54 '80 C.860 B.A. L.1009 J.D.
(adm. in NY; not adm. in CT) Coun., Control Data Corp.

Shipman & Goodwin LLP, (AV)
43 Arch Street, 06830 ⊙
Telephone: 203-869-6222 Telecopier: 203-869-6565
Email: www@goodwin.com URL: http://shipman-goodwin.com
Of Counsel: Gerard E. Jones.
General Practice. Banking, Corporation, Tax, Antitrust, Commercial Finance, Securities, Venture Capital, Labor and Employment, Health Care, Environmental, Pension and Employee Benefits, Estate Planning, Estate Settlement, Trust Administration, Real Estate, Municipal Law, Franchise, Dealer and Distributor Litigation. Trials in all Courts.
Representative Clients: Aetna Casualty & Surety Co.; Agri-Mark, Inc.; Anthem Blue Cross & Blue Shield of Connecticut.; City of Hartford; Hartford Hospital; Stanadyne, Inc.; United Technologies Corp.; Yankee Energy System, Inc.

(This Listing Continued)

Shipman & Goodwin LLP (Continued)
Hartford, Connecticut Office: One American Row. Telephone: 203-251-5000.
Lakeville, Connecticut Office: 12 Porter Street, P.O. Box 1809. Telephone: 203-435-2539.
Stamford, Connecticut Office: One Landmark Square. Telephone: 203-324-8100.
See Professional Biographies, GREENWICH, CONNECTICUT

Siddons, Charles L. ....'41 '93 C.453 B.S. L.1252 J.D. 49 Greenwich Avenue Suite 2

Silver, Golub & Teitell LLP
(See Stamford)

Simeonidis, Nicholas '61 '87 C.674 A.B. L.602 J.D.
(adm. in NY; not adm. in CT) Sr. Corp Coun., UST, Inc.
Simms, Lorna R. ....'64 '90 C.94 B.A. L.569 J.D. Blyth Industries, Inc.
Simon, Judith G. '55 '82 C.1044 B.S.W. L.982 J.D.
(adm. in NY; not adm. in CT) Belle Haven Investments
Singer, Cynthia L. ....'61 '92 C.546 B.S. L.424 J.D. [Ⓐ Ivey,B.&O.]
*PRACTICE AREAS: Estate Planning; Probate.

Singer, David M., (BV) '45 '69 C.659 B.A. L.94 J.D.
125 Mason Street, 06830
Telephone: 203-629-2700 Facsimile: 203-629-8462
Email: d.m.singer@worldnet.att.net URL: http://www.lawyers.com/dmsinger
***PRACTICE AREAS: General Civil Practice; Corporation: Mergers and Acquisitions; Real Estate; Wills, Estates and Trusts.**
General Civil Practice. Business Law, Real Estate, Probate and Estate Planning, Corporate and Mergers and Acquisitions.
Approved Attorney for: Fleet Bank of Connecticut; People's Bank; First Union; Putnam Trust Co.; Sound Beach Financial Co.; Connecticut Attorneys Title Insurance Co.; First American Title Insurance Company.
See Professional Biographies, GREENWICH, CONNECTICUT

Singer, Gregory S. '70 '96 C.112 B.A. L.809 J.D.
(adm. in CA; not adm. in CT) Panamsat
Slagle, Richard J., (BV) ....'48 '78 C.184 B.A. L.823 J.D. [Bentley,M.B.&L.]
*PRACTICE AREAS: Estate Planning; Probate; Real Estate.
Slane, John F., Jr., (BV) ....'49 '74 C.745 B.A. L.1294 J.D. [Heagney,L.&S.]
*PRACTICE AREAS: General Practice; Family Law; Real Estate Litigation; Construction Litigation; Civil Litigation.
Slavin, Lorraine, (BV) ....'53 '85 C.449 B.A. L.262 J.D. [Ivey,B.&O.]
*PRACTICE AREAS: Real Estate; Land Use; Zoning Law.
Smith, Cyd L. ....'58 '88 C.1183 B.A. L.1040 J.D. [Whitman B.A.&M.]
*PRACTICE AREAS: Commercial Real Estate; Leasing; Finance; Acquisitions and Divestitures; Residential Real Estate.
Smith, George L., (AV) ....'— '82 C.855 B.A. L.724 J.D. [Robinson&C.]
*PRACTICE AREAS: Trusts and Estates; Wills; Probates.
Smith, Richard Joyce ....'03 '27 C.128 A.B. L.976 LL.B. 100 Field Point Rd.‡
Smith, William Bradford, Jr., (BV) ...'51 '85 C&L.1040 B.S., J.D. [Ⓐ Fogarty C.S.&N.]
*PRACTICE AREAS: Estate Planning and Administration; Trust Law; Estate and Gift Taxation; Charitable Organizations.
Snyder, Frank V. '22 '49 C.309 B.S. L.893 LL.B.
(adm. in NY; not adm. in CT) 640 Round Hill Rd.‡
Spellane, Thomas P. ....'50 '76 C.298 B.A. L.823 J.D. [Gilbride,T.L.&S.] ⊙
*PRACTICE AREAS: Taxation Law; Trusts and Estates Law; Real Estate Law.
Spring, Andrew L. '68 '95 C.659 B.S. L.188 J.D.
(adm. in NJ; not adm. in CT) Assoc. Coun., World Color Press, Inc.
Staplefield, Veronica C. ....'56 '89 C.1211 B.S. L.1040 J.D. [Hopper&H.]
*PRACTICE AREAS: Trusts and Estates; Real Estate.
Steinmetz, Richard B., Jr., (AVⓉ) '29 '55 C.976 B.A. L.309 J.D.
(adm. in NY; not adm. in CT) 78 Zaccheus Mead Lane‡
Steinmetz, Steven B., (BV) ....'62 '85 C&L.978 B.A., J.D. [Ivey,B.&O.]
*PRACTICE AREAS: Commercial Real Estate; Commercial Leasing; Franchise Law; Commercial Finance; Secured Lending.
Stern, Rachel R. '65 '94 C.976 B.A. L.659 J.D.
(adm. in NY; not adm. in CT) V.P. & Gen. Coun., Factset Research Systems Inc.
Stevelman, Paul D. '63 '88 C.178 B.A. L.569 J.D.
(adm. in NY; not adm. in CT) Assoc. Gen. Coun., Greenwich Capital Markets, Inc.
Stewart, Karl A. '43 '68 C.1142 B.A. L.796 J.D.
(adm. in TX; not adm. in CT) V.P. & Corp. Secy., Tenneco
Stokke, Alice Kraus ....'62 '89 C.183 B.A. L.893 J.D. Win Properties, Inc.
Strazza, Albert T............................'70 '01 C.1102 B.S. L.1040 J.D. [Ⓐ Albert,W.&J.]
*PRACTICE AREAS: Real Estate; Business Law; Construction Law; Commercial Real estate.
Sullivan & Donovan, LLP
21 Benedict Place (⊙Flemington, NJ; East Meadow, New York, NY)
Sutherland, Anne '59 '84 C&L.477 B.A., J.D.
(adm. in NY; not adm. in CT) Intl. Tax Coun., Howmet Corp.‡
Sutton, S. Guy ....'51 '76 C.37 B.A. L.472 J.D. 87 Greenwich Avenue
Sutton, Stanford H. ....'17 '44 C.24 A.B. L.262 87 Greenwich Ave, Ste 8
Tanzi, C. William .....'56 '83 C.188 B.A. L.215 J.D. [De Forest&D.] (⊙New York, NY)
Tesei, John P., (BV) ....'48 '75 C.602 B.S. L.262 J.D. [Gilbride,T.L.&S.] ⊙
*PRACTICE AREAS: Environmental Law; Land Use; Commercial Real Estate; Aviation Law.
Thomas, Frederick A. ....'63 '88 C.855 B.S. L.896 J.D. Greenwich Hospital

Tierney, Zullo, Flaherty & Murphy, P.C.
(See Norwalk)

Tirino, Kristin M. ....'70 '95 C.706 B.A. L.1040 J.D. [Ⓐ Tranfo&T.]
Tobin, David R., (AV) ....'42 '67 C.602 B.B.A. L.569 J.D. 530 Old Post Rd.
Towe, Rolf H. '38 '65 C.228 B.S. L.976 J.D.
(adm. in NY; not adm. in CT) Exec. Partner Ltd.
Tranfo, Joseph A. ....'63 '89 C.659 B.A. L.262 J.D. [Tranfo&T.] ⊙
Tranfo, Joseph C. '31 '59 C&L.724 B.B.A., LL.B.
(adm. in NY; not adm. in CT) [ⓒ Tranfo&T.]
Tranfo & Tranfo, LLC ....19 Benedict Place (⊙Jericho, NY)
Treacy, Patrick T. ....'63 '90 C.390 B.A. L.724 J.D. TradeSource, Inc.
Trotta, Frank P., Jr., (AV) ....'55 '79 C.1044 B.A. L.982 J.D. [Trotta] ⊙
Trotta Law Firm, (AV) ....1 Fawcett Pl. (⊙Cos Cob, CT; New Rochelle, NY)

Trow & Sank, P.C.
(See Stamford)

Turner, Stephen M. '39 '64 C.947 B.A. L.352 J.D.
(adm. in IA; not adm. in CT) 67 Londonberry Dr.‡
Tusa, Charles S. ....'44 '70 C.165 B.A. L.564 J.D. [Gilbride,T.L.&S.] ⊙
*PRACTICE AREAS: Corporation Law; Commercial Law; Securities Law; Franchise Law.
Tuttle, David P., (BV) ....'60 '85 C.674 B.A. L.228 J.D. [ⓒ Whitman B.A.&M.]
*PRACTICE AREAS: Finance; Mergers and Acquisitions; Venture Capital; Securities; Real Estate.

Tyler Cooper & Alcorn, LLP, (AV)
675 Steamboat Road, 06830-7140 ⊙
Telephone: 203-869-2000 Telecopier: 203-869-2001
URL: http://www.tylercooper.com
Senior Counsel: Henry W. Pascarella.
Administrative Law, Alternative Dispute Resolution, Antitrust and Trade Regulation, Banking, Bankruptcy and Reorganization, Business Crimes, Business Organizations and Securities Law, Computer Law, Domestic Relations, Environmental Law, Financial Services, Franchising, Health Care,

(This Listing Continued)

Tyler Cooper & Alcorn, LLP (Continued)

Immigration, Insurance Defense and Insurance Coverage Defense, Intellectual Property, Labor and Employment, Legislative Lawyering, Litigation, Media Law, Medical Malpractice Defense, Pension and Employee Benefits, Public Utilities, Real Estate, Taxation, Trusts and Estates and Workers' Compensation.
Hartford, Connecticut Office: CityPlace. Telephone: 860-725-6200. Telecopier: 860-278-3802.
New Haven, Connecticut Office: 205 Church Street. Telephone: 203-784-8200. Telecopier: 203-789-2133.
Stamford, Connecticut Office: One Landmark Square. Telephone: 203-348-5555. Telecopier: 203-348-3875.
Madison, Connecticut Office: 23 Woodland Road. Telephone: 203-318-3600. Telecopier: 203-318-3609.

See Professional Biographies, GREENWICH, CONNECTICUT

Urstadt, Charles J. '28 '54 C.197 A.B. L.188 LL.B.
(adm. in NY; not adm. in CT) Urstadt Biddle Prop.
Valeri, Gina '71 '98 C.705 B.A. L.1040 J.D.
Director of Legislative Affairs & General Counsel, American Pet Products Manufacturers Association, Inc.
van Essche, Sandra '60 '89 C.788 B.A. L.564 J.D.
(adm. in NY; not adm. in CT) Sr. Coun., Panamsat Corp.
Vecchiolla, John L., (BV) .... '42 '71 C.478 A.B. L.94 J.D. [Dougherty,D.&V.]
*PRACTICE AREAS: Probate; Real Estate; General Practice; Taxation; Estate Planning.
Velarde, Stacy Lynn .... '65 '90 C.298 B.A. L.563 J.D. Putnam Tr.
Verheij, Richard H. '58 '83 C&L.930 B.A., J.D.
(adm. in OH; not adm. in CT) Gen. Coun. & Exec. V.P., UST Inc.
Verrillo, Eugénie D., (BV) .... '53 '78 C.228 B.A. L.184 J.D. [A Cummings&L.]
*PRACTICE AREAS: Commercial Real Estate Law; Residential Real Estate Law; Zoning.
Vosper, Paul A. '66 '93 C.276 B.S.F.S. L.228 J.D.
(adm. in NY; not adm. in CT) Asst. Gen. Coun., Greenwich Capital Markets, Inc.
Waiter, Joseph J. '51 '77 C.1113 B.A. L.1209 J.D.
(adm. in VA; not adm. in CT) One American Lane
Waldman, Stephen N. .... '64 '93 C.659 B.S. L.178 J.D. 1275 King St.

Wall, Peter V. '42 '68 C.197 A.B. L.188 J.D.
95 East Putnam Avenue, 06830 ⊙
Telephone: 203-629-2122 Telecopier: 203-629-3822
URL: http://www.lawyers.com/peterwall
***PRACTICE AREAS: Estate Planning and Probate Law; Real Estate Law; Small Business Law; Taxation Law.**
Tax Law. Probate and Estate Planning, Small Business and Real Estate.
New York, NY Office: 305 Madison Avenue, Suite 1146, 10165.

See Professional Biographies, GREENWICH, CONNECTICUT

Wallace, Stratford C., (AVⓉ) '37 '62 C.276 A.B. L.262 J.D.
(adm. in NY; not adm. in CT) 68 Mayo Avenue
Walsh, Kevin A., (AV) .... '50 '78 C.861 B.A. L.724 J.D. [Whitman B.A.&M.]
*PRACTICE AREAS: Taxation; Trusts and Estates; Corporate Law; Municipal Finance.
Ward, Roy S. .... '59 '92 C.393 B.A. L.1029 J.D. [A P.Russell]
*PRACTICE AREAS: Civil Litigation; Criminal Litigation.
Ward, Tom S., Jr., (AV) .... '44 '69 C.299 B.A. L.262 J.D. [Albert,W.&J.]
*PRACTICE AREAS: Commercial and Residential Real Estate; Financing.

Warren, Elliot R.
(See Westport)

Weir, Michael B. '25 '51 C.976 B.A. L.659 LL.B.
(adm. in NY; not adm. in CT) [C Whitman B.A.&M.]
*PRACTICE AREAS: Antitrust; Trade Regulation; Non Profit Organization.
Weiser, Bruce I. '62 '88
C.910 B.S.B.A. L.1009 J.D. Asst. V.P.-Coun., W.R. Berkley Corp.
*RESPONSIBILITIES: Corporate Law; Insurance Regulation; Securities Law.
Weiss, Martha J. '57 '85 C.690 B.S. L.930 J.D.
(adm. in NY; not adm. in CT) Sr. Corp. Coun., UST Inc.
Weiss, Richard D. '47 '73 C.659 B.A. L.178 J.D.
(adm. in NY; not adm. in CT) Asst. Gen. Coun., Osi & Crop Protection, Crompton Corp.
*RESPONSIBILITIES: Mergers and Acquisitions Finance (60%); Corporate Law (40%).
Werner, Christine L. '56 '82 C.705 B.A. L.94 J.D.
(adm. in NY; not adm. in CT) Sr. Corp. Coun., AmBase Corp.
Westra, David R. '65 '99 C.1269 B.S. L.1040 J.D.
(adm. in NY; not adm. in CT) [McGovern&Assoc.]
*PRACTICE AREAS: Internet Law; Technology Law; Year 2000 Computer Conversion; Intellectual Property; Corporate Law.
Wetmore, John K., (BV) '58 '83
C.1041 B.A. L.1029 J.D. Town Atty., Law Dept. of Greenwich
Whelan, Catherine P., (BV) .... '60 '85 C.184 B.A. L.1029 J.D. [C Bentley,M.B.&L.]
*PRACTICE AREAS: Litigation; Personal Injury; Divorce.
Whelan, Frederick J., Jr., (BV) .... '37 '63 C.321 B.S. L.184 LL.B. 7 Benedict Pl.
Whelan, Mary Jo L., (BV) .... '62 '89 C.787 B.A. L.1029 J.D. 7 Benedict Pl.
Whidden, Paul W. .... '— '92 C.1111 B.A. L.306 J.D. 20 Church St.

Whitman Breed Abbott & Morgan, (AV)
100 Field Point Road, 06830
Telephone: 203-869-3800 Telecopier: 203-869-1951
Members of Firm: Charles E. Coates, III; James A. Fulton; Thomas F. Hartch; Dale J. Lois; Anthony M. Macleod; Richard E. Mancuso; Harry E. Peden, Jr.; Harry E. Peden, III; Charles W. Pieterse; James C. Riley; Cyd L. Smith; Kevin A. Walsh. Associates: A. Dudley Belknap; Margaret E. Conboy; Andrea M. Fraleigh (Not admitted in CT); Maciej A. Piatkowski; Gary N. Mozer. Of Counsel: Robert G. Krause; Michael K. Madden (Not admitted in CT); David P. Tuttle; Michael B. Weir (Not admitted in CT).
Corporate Law, Litigation, Real Estate, Trusts and Estates.

See Professional Biographies, GREENWICH, CONNECTICUT

Whittemore, Clark, Jr., (AV) '23 '50
C.309 A.B. L.893 LL.B. [C Robinson&C.] (⊙Hartford)
Wilfert, Amy K., (AV) .... '57 '84 C.31 B.A. L.262 J.D. [Day,B.&H.]
*PRACTICE AREAS: Estate Planning; Entrepreneurs Trust and Estate Administration; Tax-Exempt Organizations.
Williams, George R. D. '23 '52 C&L.893 B.S.C., LL.B.
(adm. in NY; not adm. in CT) 133 Otter Rock Dr.‡

Williams, Thomas J. '55 '82 C.999 B.S. L.1029 J.D.
99 Indian Field Road, 06830
Telephone: 203-661-7404 Fax: 203-622-6718
Email: tjwmslaw@aol.com URL: http://www.lawyers.com/thomasjwilliams
***PRACTICE AREAS: General Practice; Civil Practice; Criminal Law.**
General Practice, Civil, Criminal, Domestic Relations, Family, Divorce.

See Professional Biographies, GREENWICH, CONNECTICUT

Willinger, Willinger & Bucci, P.C.
(See Bridgeport)

Winokur, Marshall E., (Ltd.) '28 '52 C.145 Ph.B. L.597 J.D.
(adm. in IL; not adm. in CT) 35 Edgewater Dr.
Winsor, Alan B., (AV) '47 '73 C.118 B.A. L.178 J.D.
Sr. V.P. & Gen. Coun., Stolt Parcel Tankers Inc.

Wolansky, Paul S. '56 '82 C.31 B.A. L.309 J.D.
(adm. in NY; not adm. in CT) Mng. Dir., Paloma Partners
Wolfe, Howard R., (BV) .... '60 '84 C.597 B.A. L.94 J.D. [Albert,W.&J.]
*PRACTICE AREAS: Civil Litigation; Commercial Litigation; Foreclosures; Landlord/Tenant.
Wooden, Shawn T. .... '69 '97 C.855 B.A. L.569 J.D. [A Day,B.&H.]
*PRACTICE AREAS: Institutional Finance; Business Law.
Yates, Kathryn J. .... '53 '88 C.602 B.A. L.262 J.D. Amer. Natl. Can Co.

Zeichner Ellman & Krause LLP
35 Mason Street, 06830 ⊙
Telephone: 203-622-0900 Fax: 203-862-9889
Email: zek@zeklaw.com
John T. Avellino. Associate: Pierre-Yves Kolakowski.
General Civil Practice. Banking, Corporate, Real Estate, Litigation, Creditor's Rights and Bankruptcy Law.
New York, N.Y. Office: 575 Lexington Avenue. Telephone: 212-223-0400. Fax: 212-753-0396.
Newark, New Jersey Office: One Gateway Center. Telephone: 973-624-8600. Fax: 973-624-8585.

See Professional Biographies, GREENWICH, CONNECTICUT

Ziegler, Alan S. ....'40 '72 C.1046 B.A. L.976 J.D. Gen. Coun. & Secy., Intelligroup, Inc.

GROTON, 9,837, *New London Co.*

Albin, Thomas, (BV) .... '52 '84 C.478 M.A. L.477 J.D. P.O. Box 1409
Antipas, Constantine G., (CV) ...... '62 '91 C.184 B.S.E. L.1040 J.D. One Fort Hill Road
Arnold, Lester "L.J.", III, (BV) '58 '94 C.197 A.B. L.184 J.D.
[O'Brien,S.S.K.&M.] ⊙
*PRACTICE AREAS: Commercial Litigation; Foreclosure; Bankruptcy; Construction Law; Real Estate Law.
Bartinik, Lori Nader .... '67 '92 C.741 B.A. L.128 J.D. [Bartinik,G.B.B.&G.]
*PRACTICE AREAS: Family Law; Domestic Law; Estate Planning; Civil Litigation.
Bartinik, Peter J., Jr., (CV) .... '67 '92 C.676 B.A. L.128 J.D. [Bartinik,G.B.B.&G.]
*PRACTICE AREAS: Personal Injury Litigation; Criminal Defense; Commercial Litigation; Real Estate; Estate Planning.
Bartinik, Peter J., Sr., (AV) .... '42 '67 C&L.184 B.S., J.D. [Bartinik,G.B.B.&G.]
*PRACTICE AREAS: Trials; Civil Litigation; Personal Injury Law; Insurance Law; Commercial Litigation.

Bartinik, Gianacoplos, Bartinik, Bartinik & Grater, P.C., (AV)
100 Fort Hill Road, P.O. Box 942, 06340
Telephone: 860-445-8521 Fax: 860-445-5873
Peter J. Bartinik, Sr.; Peter S. Gianacoplos; Ellen C. Brown; Mark O. Grater; Peter J. Bartinik, Jr.; Lori Nader Bartinik. Of Counsel: Shelley M. Weiss.
Personal Injury, Workers Compensation, Commercial Litigation, Business Law, Family/Domestic Law, Medical Malpractice, Products Liability, Municipal Law, Real Estate, Bankruptcy, Wills and Estates, Zoning, Planning and Land Use, General Civil Trial and Appeals.
References: Chelsea Groton Bank; Fleet Bank; Connecticut Attorneys Title Insurance Co.; USI Inc.; City of Groton; Town of Griswold.

Barton, Arthur M. .... '31 '62 C.436 B.S.M.E. L.276 J.D. General Dynamics Corp.
Benson, Gregg C. ..... '53 '81 C&L.184 B.A., J.D. Asst. Gen. Pat. Coun., Pfizer Inc. (Pat.)
Brokke, Mervin '32 '85 C.950 B.A. L.1040 J.D. Pat. Coun., Pfizer Inc.
Brown, Ellen C., (BV) .... '55 '81 C.611 B.A. L.1048 J.D. [Bartinik,G.B.B.&G.]
*PRACTICE AREAS: Family/Domestic; Real Estate; Wills; Estates.
Chesler, Lawrence C. .... '44 '71 C.97 B.S. L.818 J.D. Pres., Spicer Fuel Co.
Coleman, Kathleen M., (CV) ...... '57 '88 C.708 B.S.N. L.1187 J.D. 118 Poguannock Rd.
Collier, Thomas F. .... '61 '99 C.184 B.A. L.1048 J.D. [A O'Brien,S.S.K.&M.]
*PRACTICE AREAS: Land Use; Elder Law; Estate Planning; Construction Law; Contracts.
Cravinho, Lynn T. .... '68 '93 C.676 B.A. L.1048 J.D. [O'Brien,S.S.K.&M.]
*PRACTICE AREAS: Estate Planning; Probate Administration; Elder Law.
Della Porta, Mark P. '53 '81 C.884 B.A. L.1338 J.D.
(adm. in PA; not adm. in CT) Grp. Dir. R&D Oper., Pfizer Inc.
Dempski, Katherine M. .... '64 '95 C.759 B.S.N. L.1252 J.D. 475 Bridge St.,
Embry, Stephen C., (BV) .... '49 '75 C.30 B.A. L.184 J.D. [Embry&N.]
Embry and Neusner, (BV) .... 118 Poquonnock Rd.
Eppinger, Frank N., (AV) .... '43 '73 C.645 B.A. L.904 J.D. [O'Brien,S.S.K.&M.]
*PRACTICE AREAS: Municipal Law; Civil and Probate Litigation; Appellate Litigation; Real Estate Law; Estate Planning Law.
Falvey, David F. .... '44 '81 C.676 B.A. L.818 J.D. 258 Rt. 12
Gianacoplos, Peter S., (BV) .... '48 '75 C.882 B.A. L.669 J.D. [Bartinik,G.B.B.&G.]
*PRACTICE AREAS: Commercial Law; Zoning; Real Estate; Banking.
Gifford, Charles H. ..... '33 '66 C.205 B.S.Mech.E. L.184 LL.B. General Dynamics Corp.
Gill, George E. '31 '55
C.103 A.B. L.94 LL.B. Asst. Gen. Coun., Electric Boat Corporation
Grater, Mark O., (BV) .... '48 '75 C.94 B.S. L.1202 J.D. [Bartinik,G.B.B.&G.]
*PRACTICE AREAS: Personal Injury; Criminal; Bankruptcy; Real Estate; Municipal.
Hall, James .... '— '97 C.174 B.A. L.564 J.D. [A O'Brien,S.S.K.&M.]
*PRACTICE AREAS: Personal Injury; Workers Compensation; Unfair Insurance Practices Act; Products Liability.
Hansen, Marcelle F. '59 '84 C.273 B.A. L.945 J.D.
(adm. in VA; not adm. in CT) Atty. Advsr., U.S. Navy
Hirschberg, Stuart M., Jr. '26 '51 C.976 L.188 LL.B.
(adm. in NY; not adm. in CT) General Dynamics Corp.
Hurley, Steven Paul .... '50 '91 C.94 B.A. L.564 J.D. 403 Long Hill Rd.
Janney, Eric M., (BV) .... '66 '91 C.276 B.S. L.184 J.D. [O'Brien,S.S.K.&M.]
*PRACTICE AREAS: Real Estate; Municipal Law; Business Organization.
Jay, W. Walton .... '43 '68 C.1365 B.A. L.145 J.D. Electric Boat Corporation
Johnson, Bonde Erik, (BVⓉ) '63 '89
C.94 B.A. L.879 J.D. Asst. State Atty. [O'Brien,S.S.K.&M.]
*PRACTICE AREAS: Personal Injury Law; Negligence; Product Liability.
Johnson, Douglas C., (CV) .... '47 '75 C.354 B.S. L.983 J.D. 100 Fort Hill Rd.‡
Jones, James Thomas '48 '82 C.446 B.Sc. L.273 J.D.
(adm. in DC; not adm. in CT; Pat.) Pat. Coun., Pfizer Inc.
Kalkstein, Joshua A. '43 '68 C.103 A.B. L.659 J.D.
(adm. in NY; not adm. in CT) Sr. Corp. Coun., Resch., Pfizer Inc.
Kehoe, Thomas J. .... '49 '75 C.321 B.A. L.1019 J.D. 75 Eastern Point Rd.
Kelly, Carolyn P., (BV) .... '37 '71 C.823 B.A. L.629 J.D. [O'Brien,S.S.K.&M.]
*PRACTICE AREAS: Workers Compensation Law; Civil Litigation; Non-Profit Organizations Law; Employment Law.
Langhammer, Lloyd L. .... '61 '86 C.478 B.A. L.61 J.D. [O'Brien,S.S.K.&M.] ⊙
*PRACTICE AREAS: Commercial Litigation; Bankruptcy.
Lehr, Rodger W., Jr. .... '54 '82 C.299 B.A. L.184 J.D. 75 Eastern Point Rd.
Lumb, J. Trevor '41 '91 C.999 B.S. L.262 J.D.
(adm. in NY; not adm. in CT) Asst. Gen. Pat. Coun., Pfizer Inc.
McBride, Rosemary L. '54 '82
C.676 B.A. L.1048 J.D. Assoc. Gen. Coun, Electric Boat Corporation
McIntosh, Frank J. .... '22 '49 C.705 A.B. L.569 J.D. 402 Long Hill Rd.‡
Monaghan, Douglas J., (BV) .... '50 '80 C.390 A.B. L.1338 J.D. 216 Thames St.
Morris, Granville R., (AV) .... '46 '74 C.264 A.B. L.94 J.D. [O'Brien,S.S.K.&M.]
*PRACTICE AREAS: Estate Planning Law; Probate Administration; Real Estate Law.
Moukawsher, Edward E., (BV) .... '52 '78 C.321 B.A. L.818 J.D. 85 Thames St.
Moukawsher, Joseph E., (AV) ....'20 '49 C.918 B.A. L.309 LL.B. [Moukawsher&W.] ⊙
*PRACTICE AREAS: Real Estate; Probate; Estate Planning; Civil Litigation.
Moukawsher, Thomas G., (BV) .... '62 '86 C.152 B.A. L.184 J.D. [Moukawsher&W.] ⊙
*PRACTICE AREAS: ERISA; Commercial Litigation; Employment Law.

Moukawsher & Walsh LLC, (AV)
328 Mitchell Street, P.O. Box 966, 06340 ⊙
Telephone: 860-445-1809 Fax: 860-446-8161 URL: http://www.benefitlawyers.com
Email: moukwals@snet.net URL: http://www.lawyers.com/moukawsher&walshllc
Joseph E. Moukawsher; Michael J. Walsh; Thomas G. Moukawsher;—Jeffrey M. Sklarz.
Civil Litigation, ERISA Law, Benefits Law, Estates, Negligence, Personal Injury, Wrongful Death, Medical Malpractice, Products Liability, Commercial Litigation, Employment Law, Trials and Appeals.
Reference: Fleet Bank.
Hartford, Connecticut Office: 21 Oak Street. Telephone: 860-549-8440. Fax: 860-549-8443.
See Professional Biographies, GROTON, CONNECTICUT

Neusner, David N., (BV) '55 '80 C.103 A.B. L.94 J.D. [Embry&N.]
O'Brien, John C., (AV) '33 '62 C.184 B.A. L.276 J.D. [O'Brien,S.S.K.&M.]
*PRACTICE AREAS: Real Estate Law; Probate Law; Corporations Law.

O'Brien, Shafner, Stuart, Kelly & Morris, P.C., (AV) BR
475 Bridge Street, P.O. Drawer 929, 06340-3723 ⊙
Telephone: 860-445-2463 Fax: 860-445-4539
Email: osskm@snet.net URL: http://www.obrienshafner.com
John C. O'Brien; Matthew Shafner; Peter F. Stuart; Carolyn P. Kelly; Granville R. Morris; Frank N. Eppinger; Mark E. Block (Resident at Norwich Office); Lloyd L. Langhammer (Resident Norwich Office); Nathan J. Shafner; Richard J. Pascal (Resident Norwich Office); Eric M. Janney; Bonde Erik Johnson; Lynn T. Cravinho; Lester "L.J." Arnold, III (Resident Norwich Office);—James Hall; Thomas F. Collier.
Trials in all Courts. Personal Injury, Products Liability, Workers Compensation, Medical Malpractice, Corporations, Estate Planning, Probate, Trust Law, Real Estate, General Practice, Administrative and Admiralty Law.
Norwich, Connecticut Office: 138 Main Street. Telephone: 860-889-3855. Fax: 860-886-6352.
See Professional Biographies, GROTON, CONNECTICUT

Olson, A. Dean '55 '83 C&L.184 B.A., J.D. Sr. Pat. Coun., Pfizer Inc. (Pat.)
Pascal, Richard J. '59 '88 C.659 B.S. L.273 J.D. [O'Brien,S.S.K.&M.] ⊙
*PRACTICE AREAS: Commercial and General Litigation; Corporate Law; Employment Law; Tax Law.
Peachey, Douglas M. '50 '81
C.763 B.A. L.1049 J.D. Asst. Gen. Coun., Electric Boat Corporation
Roberts, Scott N., (CV) '54 '83 C.184 B.A. L.1029 J.D. 349 Mitchell St.
Schwarz, Peter C. '59 '87 C.1044 B.A. L.823 J.D.
(adm. in NY; not adm. in CT) Asst. Gen. Coun., Electric Boat Corp.
Shafner, Matthew, (AV) '35 '59 C&L.184 B.A., J.D. [O'Brien,S.S.K.&M.]
*PRACTICE AREAS: Personal Injury Law; Workers Compensation; Admiralty; Asbestos Litigation.
Shafner, Nathan J., (CV) '60 '88 C.454 B.A. L.1019 J.D. [O'Brien,S.S.K.&M.]
*PRACTICE AREAS: Workers Compensation Law; Employment Law; Insurance Disputes.
Sheets, Paulann Hosler '41 '73 C.347 A.B. L.178 J.D. 87 Neptune Dr.‡
Sklarz, Jeffrey M. '74 '99 C.164 B.A. L.184 J.D. [A Moukawsher&W.] ⊙
*PRACTICE AREAS: ERISA; Personal Injury; Employment Law; Civil Litigation; Taxation.
Stuart, Peter F., (BV) '39 '70 C.197 A.B. L.1017 J.D. [O'Brien,S.S.K.&M.]
*PRACTICE AREAS: Corporations Law; Business Organizations Law; Elder Law; Estate Planning; Probate Law.

Suisman, Shapiro, Wool, Brennan, Gray & Greenberg, P.C.
(See New London)

Vogel, William D. '39 '72 C.184 A.B. L.588 J.D.
(adm. in MA; not adm. in CT) 65 Riverview Ave.‡
Walsh, Michael J., (BV) '62 '87 C.1200 B.S. L.184 J.D. [Moukawsher&W.] ⊙
*PRACTICE AREAS: Civil Litigation; Personal Injury; Medical Malpractice.
Weiss, Shelley M., (CV) '57 '83 C.188 B.A. L.575 J.D. [C Bartinik,G.B.B.&G.]
*PRACTICE AREAS: Personal Injury Litigation; Civil Litigation.

GUILFORD, 17,375, *New Haven Co.*

Allen, Renée B. '64 '89 C.1349 B.A. L.94 J.D. 5 Adirondack Lane
Beatty, Richard J., (AV) '38 '66 C.321 B.S. L.184 LL.B. 25 Boston St.
Burkle, Kurt E. '58 '90 C.349 B.S. L.1029 J.D. 32 Jefferson Dr.‡
Burkle, Margot Kenefick '61 '88 C.938 B.A. L.1029 J.D. [C J.A.Ravel]
*PRACTICE AREAS: Family Law; Civil Litigation; Real Estate.
Carter, Arthur F., (BV) '36 '61 C&L.184 B.S., J.D. 116 Whitfield St.
Cleaver, Kathleen Neal '45 '90 C&L.976 B.A., J.D.
(adm. in NY; not adm. in CT) P.O. Box 461
Costanzo, Charles P., (BV) '43 '71 C&L.184 B.A., J.D. 1110 Boston Post Rd.
Cox, Barry H., (BV) '33 '66 C.197 B.A. L.184 LL.B. 25 Boston St.
Crosby, Thomas E., (BV) '55 '81 C.1044 B.A. L.30 J.D. 35 State St.
Daddio, Deborah L., (BV) '54 '79 C.184 B.A. L.30 J.D. 35 Water St.

Delaney, Zemetis, Donahue, Durham & Noonan, P.C., (AV)
741 Boston Post Road, 06437 ⊙
Telephone: 203-458-9168 Fax: 203-458-4424
Michael G. Durham; Patrick M. Noonan.
Practice Primarily Limited to Professional Malpractice, Products Liability, Insurance Defense, Personal Injury, Employment and Commercial Litigation in all Courts.
Wallingford, Connecticut Office: 111 South Main Street, P.O. Box 747, 06492. Telephone: 203-269-1441. Fax: 203-284-9428. Email: dzddn@worldnet.att.net
See Professional Biographies, GUILFORD, CONNECTICUT

Dillon, John T., (BV) '37 '81 C.321 B.S. L.184 J.D.
64 Boston Street, 06437
Telephone: 203-453-9190; 203-453-1234 Fax: 203-453-9889
*PRACTICE AREAS: Real Estate; Zoning; Trusts; Estates; Probate.
General Civil Practice. Real Estate, Zoning, Trusts, Estates, Probate and Corporation Law.
References: Connecticut National Bank; Guilford Savings Bank.
See Professional Biographies, GUILFORD, CONNECTICUT

Dudley, Marshall N., (BV) '26 '54 C.855 A.B. L.184 LL.B. 35 Water St.
Duncan, Basil R., (BV) '43 '69 C.105 A.B. L.178 LL.B. 20 Water Street
Durham, Michael G., (BV) '57 '82 C.197 B.A. L.184 J.D. [Delaney,Z.D.D.&N.]
*PRACTICE AREAS: Negligence Law; Products Liability Law; Arbitration Law; Insurance Coverage; Health Care Law.
Emanuelson, Eric I. '60 '87 C.282 B.A. L.1048 J.D. 1575 Boston Post Road, Ste. C
Feleppa, Edward E., Jr., (BVⓉ) '32 '73 C.103 A.B. L.705 J.D.
(adm. in NJ; not adm. in CT) 14 Long Hill Farm

Franchi, Richard M., (CV) '58 '89 C.184 B.S.E. L.1029 J.D.
206 Church Street, 06437-2439
Telephone: 203-495-1000 Fax: 203-786-4750
Email: richard.franchi@erols.com URL: http://www.lawyers.com/rfranchilaw
*PRACTICE AREAS: Products Liability; Personal Injury; Medical Malpractice; Construction Law; Contractor Performance Bonds.
Products Liability, Personal Injury, Medical Malpractice, Construction Law, Intellectual Property, Copyright Infringement, Copyright Litigation.
See Professional Biographies, GUILFORD, CONNECTICUT

Jawitz, Larry E. '42 '83 C.184 B.S.E.E. L.1029 J.D. 11 Elizabeth St.
Kenefick, James G., Jr. '34 '67 C.855 B.A. L.184 LL.B. Supr. Ct. J.
Killiam, Theodore R., (CV) '51 '80 C.309 B.A. L.184 J.D. 185 Denison Dr.

Kotowski, Gail S., (BV) '50 '80 C.999 A.B. L.1048 J.D.
397 Church Street, P.O. Box 37, 06437-0037
Telephone: 203-453-6030 FAX: 203-458-6981
Email: atty.kotowski@cshore.com URL: http://www.ct-attorney.com

(This Listing Continued)

Kotowski, Gail S. (Continued)
General Civil and Criminal Practice before State and Federal Courts, Administrative, Corporation, Domestic Relations, Criminal, Personal Injury, Real Estate, Copyright, Trademark, Sports, Trials and Appeals, Social Security, Immigration.
Licensed Agent for: Chicago Title Insurance.
See Professional Biographies, GUILFORD, CONNECTICUT

Leffingwell, John V., (AV) '30 '58 C&L.184 B.A., LL.B.
36 State Street, 06437
Telephone: 203-453-2408; Fax: 203-453-6612
Real Estate, Estate Planning, Probate Law.
References: Guilford Savings Bank; Fleet Bank Connecticut; New Haven Savings Bank.

Lund, Robin '56 '80 C.787 B.A. L.809 J.D. 4775 Durham Rd
Mack, Kathryn S., (BV) '59 '86 C.188 B.A. L.976 J.D.
(adm. in PA; not adm. in CT) 200 Whitfield St.
Mack, William M., (BV) '33 '58 C.696 B.A. L.976 LL.B. 382 Old Whitfield St.
Millham, Anne K. '67 '93 C.67 B.A. L.306 J.D. [A J.A.Ravel]
*PRACTICE AREAS: Labor and Employment Law; Civil Litigation; Family.
Moalli, Thomas E. '59 '84 C.676 B.A. L.823 J.D. 16 Fox Ridge
Noonan, Patrick M., (AV) '52 '77 C.976 B.A. L.893 J.D. [Delaney,Z.D.D.&N.]
*PRACTICE AREAS: Civil Litigation; Aviation Law; Medical Malpractice; Products Liability; Professional Liability.
O'Leary, Eugene C. '41 '73 C.299 B.A. L.228 J.D. Conn. Law Book Co.

Ravel, Judith A., (BV) '38 '84 C.397 A.B. L.184 J.D.
246 Goose Lane Suite 201, 06437-2186
Telephone: 203-458-2300 Telecopier: 203-458-8822
Email: J.Ravel@worldnet.att.net URL: http://www.lawyers.com/ravelaw
*PRACTICE AREAS: Labor and Employment Law; Civil Litigation; Family; Municipal.
Associate: Anne K. Millham. Of Counsel: Margot Kenefick Burkle.
Civil Litigation, Family, Municipal, Labor and Employment.
See Professional Biographies, GUILFORD, CONNECTICUT

Small, Theodore D. '39 '66 C.178 A.B. L.976 LL.B.
(adm. in DC; not adm. in CT) 55 Church St.‡

Sullivan, Paul K., Jr. '65 '91 C.321 B.A. L.184 J.D.
Lighthouse Square, 705 Boston Post Road, P.O. Drawer 327, 06437
Telephone: 203-453-1490 Fax: 203-453-2639
URL: http://www.lawyers.com/sullivan
*PRACTICE AREAS: Trust and Estates; Estate Administration; Estate Planning; Probate; Ancillary Probate.
Of Counsel: Jeann R. Terrazzano.
Estate Planning, Estate Administration, Trusts and Probate Law, Conservatorships.
See Professional Biographies, GUILFORD, CONNECTICUT

Terrazzano, Jeann R., (BV) '45 '76 C.1252 B.S. L.184 J.D. [C P.K.Sullivan,Jr.]
*PRACTICE AREAS: Trusts and Estates; Estate Administration; Estate Planning; Probate; Ancillary Probate.
Tietjen, Riefe, (BV) '49 '79 C.207 B.A. L.800 J.D. 135 Church St.
Vavra, Nancy J. '61 '87 C.33 B.A. L.776 J.D. 33 Church St.
Wagner, Leslie Simon '61 '88 C.112 B.A. L.1049 J.D. Connecticut Law Book Co.
Willis, Carroll T. '37 '73 C.611 A.B. L.574 J.D.
(adm. in NC; not adm. in CT) 124 New Quarry Rd.‡
Wortmann, Frank A. '19 '48 C&L.569 B.S., LL.B.
(adm. in NY; not adm. in CT) 103 Russo Dr.‡

HADDAM, 6,383, *Middlesex Co.*

Epright, Michael W. '65 '90 C.676 B.S. L.1048 J.D. P.O. Box 248
Ierardi, Pasquale R. '05 '34 C.128 A.B. L.94 LL.B. 280 Walkley Hill Rd.

HADLYME, —, *New London Co.*

Augusciak, Joseph S. '42 '71 C.309 A.B. L.659 J.D. P.O. Box 112
Lightfoot, Richard '37 '63 C.976 B.A. L.309 J.D. 430 Joshuatown Rd.

HAMDEN, 51,071, *New Haven Co.*

Abbott, Melanie Beth '51 '84 C.67 B.A. L.1029 J.D. 275 Mt. Carmel Ave.
Aho, Ellen S. '61 '87 C.276 B.S.F.S. L.184 J.D. Quinnipiac College
Amato, Michael Dean, (BV) '55 '83 C&L.184 B.S., J.D. [Parrett,P.P.&C.]
Amento, Carl J., (BV) '50 '77 C.976 B.A. L.93 J.D. 273 Highland Ave.
Anderson, Lisa J., (BV) '53 '82 C.918 B.A. L.184 J.D. [Bender&A.]
Aranci, Arnold A. '60 '86 C.1030 B.A. L.184 J.D. 360 Hume Dr.
Atwater, Russell H., (AV) '09 '32 C&L.976 B.A., LL.B. 200 Leeder Hill Dr.‡
Bender, Ronald M., (BV) '49 '76 C.28 B.A. L.1202 J.D. [Bender&A.]
Bender and Anderson, P.C., (BV) 3190 Whitney Ave.
Bershtein, Herman S., (BV) '25 '53 C.976 B.A. L.790 LL.B. [Bershtein,B.&B.]
Bershtein, Jan '62 '89 C.454 B.A. L.978 J.D. [Bershtein,B.&B.]
Bershtein, Joy A. '57 '81 C.156 B.A. L.94 J.D. [Bershtein,B.&B.]
Bershtein, Richard A. '58 '83 C.976 B.A. L.178 J.D. [Bershtein,B.&B.]
Bershtein, Bershtein & Bershtein, Professional Corporation, (BV) 1188 Dixwell Ave.
Biller, Jon D., (BV) '60 '86 C.156 B.A. L.1040 J.D. [Biller,S.R.&B.]
Biller, Sachs, Raio & Bonadies, (BV) 2750 Whitney Avenue
Bix, Brian '62 '94 C.910 B.A. L.309 J.D. Prof. of Law, Quinnipiac Law Sch.
Blair, Edward T. '30 '57 C.197 B.A. L.178 LL.B. 43 Dessa Dr.‡
Bonadies, Anthony S., (BV) '62 '87 C.105 B.S. L.184 J.D. [Sette B.]
Bonadies, Doreen J. '59 '92 C.776 B.S. L.184 J.D. [Biller,S.R.&B.]
Botwick, Edward J. '45 '73 C.971 B.S.Ch.E. L.184 J.D. [Botwick&K.]
Botwick & Kurzawa, (BV) 1 Evergreen Ave.
Boutaugh, Ben '69 '00 C.829 B.S. L.1252 J.D. [A Biller,S.R.&B.]
Brown, Douglas S. '66 '91
C.823 B.S. L.904 J.D. Corp. Coun., USCO Logistics Services, Inc.
Brown, Jennifer Gerarda '60 '85 C.104 B.A. L.339 J.D.
(adm. in IL; not adm. in CT) 275 Mt. Carmel Ave.
Bruno, Alfred P. '70 '97 C.67 B.A. L.1252 J.D. [A Saxe D.&V.] (⊙New Haven)
*PRACTICE AREAS: Complex Commercial Litigation; Insurance Coverage Litigation; Environmental Litigation; Employment Law; Bankruptcy.
Burt, Edward C., Jr., (BV) '55 '81 C.1030 B.A. L.1048 J.D. 2583 Whitney Ave.
Cahill, David A. '57 '87 C.945 B.A. L.262 J.D.
(adm. in NY; not adm. in CT) Gen. Coun., USCO Logistics Services, Inc.
Callahan, Richard W. '67 '95 C.588 B.S.B.A. L.472 J.D. 68 Cassella Dr.
Carbonella, Anthony M., III, (BV) '57 '83 C.1156 B.S. L.61 J.D. [Carbonella&W.]
Carbonella & Walsh, (BV) 2572 Whitney Ave.
Carlson, Tracy L. '69 '95 C.354 B.S. L.1252 J.D. 1188 Dixwell Ave.
Carlucci, Victor, Jr., (BV) '44 '75 C.1252 B.S. L.221 J.D. 2838 Whitney Ave.
Cavallaro, Joseph J. '65 '90 C.884 B.S.A. L.1029 J.D. Ernst & Young
Chabot, Philip Vernon, (BV) '50 '76 C.216 B.A. L.94 J.D.
Sr. Mng. Atty., St. Paul Fire & Marine Ins. Co.
Choate, Edward L., (CVⓉ) '51 '75 C.801 B.A. L.602 J.D. 68 Nutmeg Hill Rd.
Ciardiello, Steven P., (BV) '58 '83 C.1030 B.S. L.724 J.D. 2840 Whitney Ave.
Cipriano, Francis P., (BV) '54 '81 C.918 B.A. L.1206 1220 Whitney Ave
Cipriano, John L., Jr., (BV) '48 '74 C.184 B.S. L.421 J.D. [Nathanson&C.]

Cogan, Neil H. '44 '69 C&L.659 B.A., LL.B. (adm. in PA; not adm. in CT) Dean, Quinnipiac Coll. Sch. of Law
Colwell, William S., (BV) .... '50 '76 C.165 A.B. L.1202 J.D. [Parrett,P.P.&C.]
Crane, Neil R., (BV) .... '57 '83 C.245 B.A. L.184 J.D. 2702 Whitney Avenue
DeMarco, Christopher P., (BV) .... '60 '88 C.829 B.A. L.1029 J.D. [Farver&D.]
DeMartino, Karen, (BV) .... '63 '89 C.1156 B.S. L.1029 J.D. 60 Washington Ave.
Diglio, Salvatore L. .... '43 '72 C.676 B.A. L.184 J.D. Prob. J.
Doernberger, Edwin L., (BV) .... '44 '76 C.178 A.B. L.312 J.D. [Saxe D.&V.]
*PRACTICE AREAS: Commercial; Bankruptcy; Insurance; Environmental Litigation; Construction.
Doherty, Francis J., (AV) .... '46 '74 C.93 A.B. L.184 J.D. 3190 Whitney Ave.
Doherty, James T., (BV) .... '35 '62 C.1030 B.S. L.30 LL.B. 35 Worth Ave.
Dunlap, William V. '44 '82 C.1313 B.A. L.976 J.D. (adm. in NY; not adm. in CT) 275 Mt. Carmel Ave.‡
Edeen, Lars O. .... '58 '96 C.1102 B.S. L.1252 J.D. 2840 Whitney Ave.
Emanuel, Richard .... '47 '70 C.184 B.A. L.273 J.D. 275 Mt. Carmel Ave.
Esposito, David V., (BV) .... '50 '77 C.93 B.S. L.1202 J.D. 1240 Whitney Ave.
Fadus, Michael J. '59 '88 C.94 B.A. L.846 J.D. (adm. in CA; not adm. in CT) Gen. Coun. & Secy., American Payment Systems, Inc.
Farrell, Robert C. .... '51 '77 C.855 B.A. L.309 J.D. 275 Mt. Carmel Ave.
Farver, Thomas E., (BV) .... '54 '80 C.1044 B.A. L.575 J.D. [Farver&D.]
Farver & De Marco, (BV) .... 2842 Old Dixwell Ave.
Federici, Louis M., (BV) .... '60 '87 C.223 B.S. L.884 J.D. [Parrett,P.P.&C.]
Feigenson, Neal R. '56 '80 C.446 B.A. L.309 J.D. (adm. in MA; not adm. in CT) 275 Mt. Carmel Ave.
Ferrari, Mary .... '52 '77 C.602 B.A. L.188 J.D. 275 Mt. Carmel Ave.
Finney, Valerie A., (BV) .... '57 '83 C.184 B.A. L.1048 J.D. 2324 Whitney Ave.
Foley, Christopher J. .... '63 '88 C&L.184 B.S., J.D. 3000 Whitney Ave.
Frazier, Patrick W., Jr., (BV) .... '61 '87 C.1252 B.S. L.1029 J.D. 2558 Whitney Rd.
Gamm, Morris, (AV) .... '08 '33 C.659 A.B. L.309 LL.B. Washington Ave.
Gesmonde, John M., (BV) .... '46 '73 C.178 B.A. L.184 J.D. [Gesmonde P.S.&P.]
Gesmonde Pietrosimone Sgrignari & Pinkus LLC, (BV) .... 3127-3129 Whitney Ave.
Gilles, Stephen G. '55 '86 C.722 B.A. L.145 J.D. (adm. in IL; not adm. in CT) 275 Mt. Carmel Ave.
Giovanni, Michael J. .... '58 '87 C.1102 B.S. L.1252 J.D. 280 Hillfield Rd.
Glynn, Francis M., (BV) .... '47 '73 C.1102 B.A. L.184 J.D. 3217 Whitney Ave.
Goldblatt, Richard L., (BV) .... '34 '61 C.1029 B.S. L.94 LL.B. [Goldblatt,G.&R.]
Goldblatt, Greenstein & Rashba, P.C., (AV) .... 60 Washington St.
Goldman, David W., (BV) .... '26 '53 C.823 B.S. L.184 LL.B. 2764 Whitney Ave.
Gordon, Angus N., Jr., (AV) .... '19 '48 C&L.976 B.A., LL.B. 206 Armory St.‡
Greenstein, George, (BV) .... '28 '54 C.184 B.S. in B.A. L.94 LL.B. [Goldblatt,G.&R.]
Hadden, Arthur C., (BV) .... '51 '76 C&L.93 B.A., J.D. 3190 Whitney Ave.
Heckman, Charles A. '38 '65 C.103 A.B. L.145 J.D. (adm. in CA; not adm. in CT) 275 Mt. Carmel Ave.
Huggins, Sandra G. .... '61 '91 C.1102 B.S. L.1048 J.D. 130 Fernwood Rd.
Kaas, Carolyn Wilkes '55 '83 C.188 B.A. L.184 J.D. Assoc. Prof. of Law, Quinnipiac Coll.
Karajanis, Tony .... '68 '95 C.918 B.A. L.1252 J.D. 1905 State St.
Kernan, John D. .... '11 '37 C.309 A.B. L.178 LL.B. 222 Blake Rd.‡
Ketaineck, Stuart M., (BV) '50 '75 C.156 B.A. L.472 J.D. Staff Atty., St. Paul Fire & Marine Ins. Co.
Kinsella, Gregory P., (BV) .... '57 '82 C.951 B.A. L.472 J.D. [Parrett,P.P.&C.]
Kittredge, Ronald E., (BV) .... '45 '71 C.588 B.A. L.184 J.D. 2676 Whitney Ave.
Krauss, Stanton D. '53 '78 C.976 B.A. L.477 J.D. (adm. in IL; not adm. in CT) 275 Mt. Carmel Ave.
Krick, John H., (AV) .... '28 '53 C.197 A.B. L.178 LL.B. [Parrett,P.P.&C.]
Kurzawa, David J., (BV) .... '47 '78 C.1102 B.A. L.1202 J.D. [Botwick&K.]
Lamboley, Francis E., (BV) .... '40 '66 C.602 A.B. L.184 J.D. [Lamboley]
Lamboley, Harold J., III .... '66 '91 C.262 B.A. L.896 J.D. [Lamboley]
Lamboley Law Firm, The, (BV) .... 2827 Old Dixwell Ave.
Lettick, Sharon P. .... '58 '90 C.999 B.S. L.1029 J.D. [Lettick&L.]
Lettick, Steven M., (BV) .... '47 '72 C.184 B.S. L.818 J.D. [Lettick&L.]
Lettick & Lettick, P.C., (BV) .... 2494 Whitney Ave.
Lev, Bruce L., (AV) '43 '68 C.918 B.A. L.893 J.D. Chmn., USCO Logistics Services, Inc.
Levy, Eileen C. '— '85 C.914 B.A. L.188 J.D. (adm. in NY; not adm. in CT) 50 Hawley Rd.‡
Litvin, Richard E. .... '44 '76 C.216 B.A. L.831 J.D. 275 Mt. Carmel Ave.
Long, Leonard J. '51 '88 C.46 B.S. L.145 J.D. (adm. in IL; not adm. in CT) Prof. of Law, Quinnipiac Coll. Sch. of Law
Loughlin, Edward P., (BV) .... '36 '62 C.976 B.A. L.184 LL.B. [Loughlin F.] ⊙
Loughlin FitzGerald, (BV) .... 1960 Whitney Avenue (⊙Wallingford)
Mahale, Raj R. .... '70 '97 C.846 B.A. L.1252 J.D. 9 Washington Ave.
Margulies, Martin B. .... '40 '68 C.178 A.B. L.309 LL.B. 275 Mt. Carmel Ave.
Marsh, Elizabeth Phillips .... '52 '78 C.309 A.B. L.569 J.D. Prof. of Law, Quinnipiac Coll.
McGlinchey, Kevin M. .... '67 '95 C.976 B.A. L.128 J.D. IBM Corp.
McKiernan, James J., Jr. .... '24 '57 C.659 B.S. L.184 LL.B. 140 Central Ave.
McLaren, John R. '16 '44 C.94 L.818 LL.B. (adm. in MA; not adm. in CT) V.P. & Coun., J & S Hydraulics, Inc.
McVerry, Joseph F., (BV) .... '31 '63 C&L.184 B.S., LL.B. P.O. Box 5424
Meiklejohn, Alexander M. '44 '76 C.31 B.A. L.145 J.D. (adm. in VT; not adm. in CT) 275 Mt. Carmel Ave.
Meyer, Linda R. '62 '87 C.378 B.A. L.1375 J.D. (adm. in CA; not adm. in CT) Prof. of Law, Quinnipiac Sch. of Law
Miller, Sid M., (AV) .... '28 '54 C.102 A.B. L.976 J.D. 2764 Whitney Avenue
Morgan, John T. .... '45 '69 C.804 B.A. L.910 J.D. 275 Mt. Carmel Ave.
Musco, Joseph M., (BV) .... '60 '85 C.676 B.S. L.1029 J.D. 9 Washington Ave., Ste. 3A
Nathanson, William S., (BV) .... '46 '71 C.94 B.A. L.276 J.D. [Nathanson&C.]
Nathanson & Cipriano, P.C., (BV) .... 60 Washington Ave.
Nuzzolo, Mark J. '56 '89 C.999 B.A. L.1029 J.D. Pres., Mountain Run Development Corporation
O'Brien, Henry W., (AV) .... '29 '62 C&L.184 B.S., LL.B. P.O. Box 185583
Parese, John A., (BV) .... '48 '73 C.884 B.A. L.724 J.D. [Parrett,P.P.&C.]
Parnoff, David V. .... '68 '99 C.690 B.S. L.1252 J.D. 2324 Whitney Ave.
Parrett, Richard J., (BV) .... '32 '61 C.184 B.A. L.276 J.D. [Parrett,P.P.&C.]

Parrett, Porto, Parese & Colwell, P.C., (AV)
One Hamden Center, 2319 Whitney Avenue, 06518
Telephone: 203-281-2700 Fax: 203-281-0700
Email: info@pppclaw.com URL: http://www.pppclaw.com
Richard J. Parrett; Carl M. Porto; John A. Parese; William S. Colwell; Gregory P. Kinsella; Michael Dean Amato; Louis M. Federici; Anthony M. Solomine; Carl M. Porto II; Joseph M. Porto; John P. Pfannenbecker; William M. Raccio. Of Counsel: John H. Krick.
Bankruptcy, Commercial, Construction Litigation, Corporate, Criminal, Elder and Administrative Law, Estate Administration, Estate Planning, Family, Foreclosures, General Civil Practice, Insurance Law, Intellectual Property, Labor and Employment, Medical Malpractice, Municipal, Personal Injury, Products Liability, Real Estate, Taxation, Trials and Appeals in all State and Federal Courts, State Workers Compensation, Zoning.

(This Listing Continued)

Parrett, Porto, Parese & Colwell, P.C. (Continued)
Reference: Citizens Bank.
North Haven, Connecticut Office: 13 Peck Street, 06473. Telephone: 203-239-1111.
See Professional Biographies, HAMDEN, CONNECTICUT

Peterson, George E., Jr. .... '31 '59 C.976 B.A. L.893 LL.B. 225 Blue Trail‡
Pfannenbecker, John P. .... '72 '99 C.696 B.A. L.1252 J.D. [Parrett,P.P.&C.]
*PRACTICE AREAS: Corporate Law; Commercial Litigation; Commercial Transactions; Taxation; Internet Law.
Pietrosimone, Frank W., Jr., (BV) .... '54 '79 C.94 B.A. L.665 J.D. [Gesmonde P.S.&P.]
Pinkus, Barry C., (BV) .... '51 '76 C.184 B.A. L.472 J.D. [Gesmonde P.S.&P.]
Poirier, Brian W., (BV) .... '40 '71 C&L.184 B.A., J.D. 107 Middle Rd.
Porto, Carl M., (AV) .... '42 '67 C.94 B.A. L.184 J.D. [Parrett,P.P.&C.]
Porto, Carl M., II .... '67 '93 C.94 B.A. L.1252 J.D. [Parrett,P.P.&C.]
Porto, Joseph M. .... '70 '96 C.855 B.A. L.1252 J.D. [Parrett,P.P.&C.]
Raccio, William M. .... '56 '98 C.884 B.S.B.A. L.1252 J.D. [Parrett,P.P.&C.]
Rademacher, Mark, (BV) .... '53 '82 C.1307 B.A. L.184 LL.B. 1188 Dixwell Ave.
Raio, Frank J. .... '60 '91 C.1036 B.A. L.1029 J.D. [Biller,S.R.&B.]
Ranciato, Jennifer M. .... '71 '01 C.308 B.A. L.1252 J.D. [Saxe D.&V.]
*PRACTICE AREAS: Complex Commercial Litigation; Construction Litigation; Insurance Coverage Litigation; Labor and Employment Law; Civil Rights Law.
Rashba, Malcolm L., (AV) .... '31 '56 C&L.184 B.S., J.D. [Goldblatt,G.&R.]
Raucher, Steven A. .... '50 '93 C.994 B.A. L.1029 J.D. 1890 Dixwell Ave.
Raynor, Gordon R., (BV) .... '24 '54 C.477 B.A. L.893 LL.B. 2508 Whitney Ave.
Reger, Robert S., (BV) .... '48 '74 C.184 B.A. L.1292 J.D. [Rolnick&R.]
Reynolds, John N. .... '19 '50 C.676 B.S. L.276 J.D. State Trial Ref., Jud. Dept.‡
Ricciardi, Peter E., (BV) .... '44 '74 C.1252 B.A. L.365 J.D. 3217 Whitney Ave.
Robinson, Toni '— '77 C.771 B.A. L.178 J.D. (adm. in NY; not adm. in CT) Prof. of Law & Dir., Quinnipiac Coll. Sch. of Law
Rolnick, Steven R., (BV) .... '46 '71 C.156 A.B. L.178 J.D. [Rolnick&R.]
Rolnick & Reger, (BV) .... 2832A Whitney Ave.
Romania, George H., (BV) .... '59 '86 C.676 B.S. L.1029 J.D. 2862 Whitney Ave.
Sachs, Jeffrey M., (BV) .... '57 '82 C.164 B.A. L.245 J.D. [Biller,S.R.&B.]
Saxe, Tracy Alan, (BV) .... '58 '83 C.823 B.A. L.276 J.D. [Saxe D.&V.]
*PRACTICE AREAS: Complex Commercial Litigation; Insurance Coverage; Employment Law; Bankruptcy; Environmental Litigation.

Saxe Doernberger & Vita P.C., (BV)
1952 Whitney Avenue, 06517
Telephone: 203-287-8890 Fax: 203-287-8847
URL: http://www.lawyers.com/sevlaw
Tracy Alan Saxe; Jeffrey J. Vita; Edwin L. Doernberger; Maria A. VanDerLaan. Associates: Alfred P. Bruno; Jennifer M. Ranciato.
Complex Commercial Litigation, Insurance Coverage Litigation, Environmental Litigation, Employment, Bankruptcy, Real Estate and Zoning, Construction Litigation.
See Professional Biographies, HAMDEN, CONNECTICUT

Schairer, Mary Beattie .... '58 '84 C.676 B.A. L.1029 J.D. 275 Mt. Carmel Ave.
Schroeder, Mark E. .... '64 '92 C.951 B.A. L.184 J.D. 275 Mt. Carmel Ave.
Sette, Fred David, (BV) .... '39 '64 C.676 B.A. L.184 J.D. [Sette B.]
Sette Bonadies, P.C., (BV) .... 2324 Whitney Ave.
Sgrignari, Lawrence C., (BV) .... '58 '84 C.1156 B.A. L.831 J.D. [Gesmonde P.S.&P.]
Shedd, Lea Nordlicht, (AV) .... '51 '78 C.569 B.A. L.184 J.D. 2508 Whitney Ave.
Singer, Robert M. .... '62 '88 C.1145 B.S. L.1048 J.D. [R.M.Singer]
*PRACTICE AREAS: Bankruptcy; Business Law; Debtor and Creditor; Collections; Insurance.

Singer, Robert M., L.L.C., Law Offices of
2377 Whitney Avenue, 06518-3225
Telephone: 203-248-8278; Toll Free: 888-218-7772 Fax: 203-407-0602
Email: SingerLawLLC@aol.com URL: http://www.lawyers.com/rmsinger
Robert M. Singer.
General Civil Practice. Business Law, Commercial Litigation, Bankruptcy, Collections, Insurance, Tax Delinquencies, Tax Appeals and Audits, and Tax Planning.
See Professional Biographies, HAMDEN, CONNECTICUT

Slane, Cindy R. .... '51 '92 C.705 B.A. L.976 J.D. Quinnipiac College Sch. of Law
Sledziona, Frank W. .... '26 '54 C.1029 B.A. L.1009 LL.B. 117 Ridge Rd.
Smith, Kevin W., (BV) .... '55 '80 C.259 B.S. L.904 J.D. 2911 Dixwell Ave.
Solomine, Anthony M., (BV) .... '63 '88 C.93 B.A. L.818 J.D. [Parrett,P.P.&C.]
Speziale, Marcia Jean .... '52 '77 C.855 A.B. L.183 J.D. 275 Mt. Carmel Ave.‡
Spinner, David M., (BV) .... '48 '76 C&L.184 B.A., J.D. 2702 Whitnery Avenue
Stankewich, Paul J. '68 '93 C&L.184 B.A., J.D. Corp. Coun., USCO Logistics Services, Inc.
Starr, Carolyn M. .... '49 '90 C.1375 B.A. L.846 J.D. 120 High Ridge Rd.
Stern, Gail S. .... '50 '91 C.94 B.A. L.1029 J.D. 275 Mt. Carmel Ave.
Switko, Shari J. .... '63 '90 C.454 B.A. L.564 J.D. 3000 Dixwell Ave.
Terrace, Thomas O., (BV) .... '49 '77 C.676 B.A. L.989 J.D. 60 Washington Avenue
Thomas, W. John .... '55 '82 C&L.37 B.A., J.D. 275 Mt. Carmel Ave.
Tomlin, Mary-Elise .... '65 '96 C.829 B.S. L.1252 J.D. 33 Sandquist Cir.
VanDerLaan, Maria A. .... '66 '92 C.938 B.A. L.1029 J.D. [Saxe D.&V.]
*PRACTICE AREAS: Complex Commercial Litigation; Insurance Coverage; Construction Litigation; Bankruptcy; Professional Malpractice Defense.
Vita, Jeffrey J., (BV) .... '65 '90 C.184 B.A. L.1029 J.D. [Saxe D.&V.]
*PRACTICE AREAS: Complex Commercial Litigation; Insurance Coverage Litigation; Construction Litigation; Bankruptcy; Real Estate.
Waldron, George A., (BV) .... '49 '80 C.1156 B.S.B.A. L.1029 J.D. Wkrs. Comp. Comm.
Walsh, Steven, (BV) .... '60 '85 C.1030 B.A. L.564 J.D. [Carbonella&W.]
Wasserman, Elga Ruth, (AV) .... '24 '76 C.788 B.A. L.976 J.D. 1153 Whitney Ave.‡
Wenig, Mary Moers, (AV) '26 '52 C.881 B.A. L.178 J.D. Prof. of Law, Quinnipiac Coll. Sch. of Law
White, Andrew S., (BV) .... '64 '89 C.659 B.S.Econ. L.184 J.D. 3190 Whitney Ave.
Wilcox, Jamison V. V. '46 '74 C.31 A.B. L.178 J.D. (adm. in NY; not adm. in CT) Assoc. Prof. of Law, Quinnipiac Coll. Sch. of Law
Williams, Gary G., (BV) .... '51 '76 C.184 B.A. L.607 J.D. 31 Norwood Ave.
Wolak, Michael A., III .... '50 '75 C.976 B.A. L.665 J.D. 1884 Whitney Avenue
Zehalla, Stephen J., (BV) .... '54 '79 C.712 B.A. L.1048 J.D. 1030 Mix Ave.
Zeoli, Michael D. .... '71 '97 C.19 B.A. L.818 J.D. 724 Pine Rock Ave.

HAMPTON, 1,322, *Windham Co.*

Case, Stuart .... '41 '91 C.178 B.A. L.1048 J.D. 71 W. Old Route 6

HANOVER, —, *New London Co.*

Foley, Francis J., III .... '41 '68 C.93 B.S. L.94 LL.B. Supr. Ct. J.

HARTFORD, * 139,739, *Hartford Co.*

Abate, Ernest N., (AV) .... '43 '69 C.884 B.S. L.602 J.D. [Updike,K.&S.] (⊙Stamford)
*PRACTICE AREAS: Business; Trusts and Estates; Wills; Real Estate; Zoning.
Ackley, Maria T. .... '— '96 C.682 B.A. L.1048 J.D. [Robinson&C.]
Acosta, Ruben E. .... '52 '84 C&L.184 B.A., J.D. Corp. Coun.
Acquaviva, Charlotte M. '39 '63 C.681 A.B. L.309 LL.B. Coun., Bank of New England Corp.

Adams, Susan M. ...... '61 '88 C.165 B.A. L.659 J.D. Senior Counsel, CIGNA Corporation
Adamy, Jennifer L. .... '65 '95 C.1349 B.A. L.1019 J.D. [Ⓐ Shipman&G.]
*PRACTICE AREAS: Commercial Litigation; Bankruptcy Law.
Adler, Gregg D., (AV) .... '56 '82 C.103 B.A. L.588 J.D. [Livingston,A.P.&M.]
Adler, Lawrence H., (BV) .... '60 '85 C.184 B.S. L.1048 J.D. [O'Connell,F.&A.]
*PRACTICE AREAS: Civil Litigation; Insurance Defense; Product Liability Law.

Advocates Law Firm, LLC
(See New Britian)

Agress, Benjamin Y. .... '72 '00 C.860 B.A. L.184 J.D. [Ⓐ Alix,Y.&R.]
*PRACTICE AREAS: Trademarks; Unfair Competition; Copyright Licensing; Noncompetition and Non-Solicitation Agreements.
Ahearn, Donald P. .... '29 '54 C.93 B.S.B.A. L.276 J.D. 179 Allyn St.‡
Ahearn, John E. .... '46 '71 C.309 B.A. L.184 J.D. Coun., AETNA Inc.
*RESPONSIBILITIES: Compliance; Litigation.
Albanese, Christopher J. .... '— '01 C.1044 B.A. L.184 J.D. [Ⓐ O'Connell,F.&A.]
*PRACTICE AREAS: Litigation; Real Property; Bankruptcy; Indian Law.
Albano, Michael G. .... '53 '96 C.1044 B.S. L.1009 J.D. [Ⓐ Sabia&H.]
*PRACTICE AREAS: Commercial Litigation; Torts.
Albert, Harold W. ...... '49 '74 C.951 B.A. L.309 J.D. Chf. Coun., Invests., CIGNA Corp.
Alderman, Linda Wiesenthal, (BV) ...... '63 '87 C.597 B.A. L.823 J.D. [Alderman&A.]
*PRACTICE AREAS: Land Use and Environmental Law.
Alderman, Myles H., Jr., (BV) .... '59 '86 C.385 A.B. L.823 J.D. [Alderman&A.]
*PRACTICE AREAS: Commercial Law; Insolvency and Creditors' Rights.

Alderman & Alderman, (BV)
One Corporate Center, 06103
Telephone: 860-249-0090 Telecopier: 860-249-0117
Email: lawyers@alderman.com URL: http://www.alderman.com
Members of Firm: Myles H. Alderman, Jr.; Linda Wiesenthal Alderman. Of Counsel: Francis J. Browne.
General Practice, Commercial Law and Bankruptcy, Creditors' Rights, Environmental Law and Land Use, Business and eBusiness, Arbitration, Mediation and Civil Litigation.
See Professional Biographies, HARTFORD, CONNECTICUT

Aldrich, William C. '32 '56 C&L.309 A.B., LL.B.
(adm. in MA; not adm. in CT) V.P., ITT Hartford Ins. Grp.
Alexander, John M. .... '12 '39 C.976 B.A. L.306 LL.B. Ret. Supr. Ct. J.
Alexander, Mark D. .... '67 '93 C.347 B.A. L.188 J.D. [Ⓐ Axinn,V.&H.]
*PRACTICE AREAS: Litigation; Antitrust and Trade Regulation; Intellectual Property.

Alexander, Ralph J.
(See East Hartford)

Alfano & Flynn, LLC
(See Suffield)

Alissi, Amy E. .... '67 '92 C.855 B.A. L.128 J.D. [Updike,K.&S.]
*PRACTICE AREAS: Commercial Finance; Real Estate.
Alissi, James A. .... '67 '94 C.183 B.A. L.1280 J.D. [Cramer,A.&F.]
*PRACTICE AREAS: Civil Litigation; Professional Liability; Premises Liability.
Alissi, John J. .... '70 '98 C.951 B.A. L.184 J.D. [Ⓐ Updike,K.&S.]
*PRACTICE AREAS: Business Law; Commercial Lending; Real Estate.
Alix, James E., (AV) ..... '33 '62 C.321 B.S. L.276 LL.B. [Ⓒ Alix,Y.&R.] (See Pat. Sect.)
Alix, Kristin T. .... '71 '98 C&L.128 B.A., J.D. [Ⓐ Halloran&S.]
*PRACTICE AREAS: Trucking Law; Transportation.

Alix, Yale & Ristas, LLP, (BV)
(Formerly Chilton, Alix & Van Kirk)
750 Main Street, 06103-2703
Telephone: 860-527-9211 Facsimile: 860-527-5029
Email: ayrllp@pctlaw.com
Members of Firm: Guy D. Yale; L. James Ristas; Richard H. Berneike; Clifford P. Kelly. Associates: James E. Piotrowski; Thomas J. Menard; Benjamin Y. Agress; Robert S. Smith. Of Counsel: James E. Alix; Ralph H. Chilton; Roger A. Van Kirk.
Patent, Trademark, Computer, Copyright and Unfair Competition Law and Related Licensing and Litigation.
See Professional Biographies, HARTFORD, CONNECTICUT

Allen, Brian T. .... '56 '83 C.918 B.A. L.184 J.D. Caucus Dir., Sen. Republican Offc.
Allen, Frances .... '24 '62 C.938 B.A. L.178 LL.B. 95 Wash. St.
Allen, Richard W., III .... '54 '80 C.415 B.A. L.1029 J.D. The Connecticut Surety Co.
Alquist, Elizabeth A. .... '69 '94 C.524 B.A. L.184 J.D. [Ⓐ Day,B.&H.]
*PRACTICE AREAS: Employment Litigation; Employment Defense.
Alter, Jonathan B., (BV) .... '64 '89 C.264 B.A. L.1009 J.D. [Bingham D.]
*PRACTICE AREAS: Commercial Litigation; Financial Law; Loan Workouts; Loan Restructuring; Bankruptcy.
Altermatt, Mark T., (BV) .... '60 '88 C.902 B.A. L.823 J.D. [Halloran&S.]
*PRACTICE AREAS: Civil Litigation.
Amata, Doreen West .... '67 '92 C.676 B.S. L.1048 J.D. [Ⓐ Gordon,M.&F.]
*PRACTICE AREAS: Insurance Defense; Premises Liability; Medical Malpractice Defense; Legal Malpractice Defense.
Ambrogio, Mary J. .... '66 '92 C.855 B.A. L.184 J.D. [Morrison,M.&M.]
*PRACTICE AREAS: Professional Liability; Employment Liability; Appellate Advocacy.
Amodeo, Pasquale .... '68 '97 C.165 B.A. L.276 J.D. [Ⓐ Halloran&S.]
*PRACTICE AREAS: Taxation; Corporate; Venture Capital Financings; Securities.
Anastasi, William J. .... '51 '82 C.653 B.A. L.831 J.D. 18 Elm St.
Anderson, Ann K. .... '65 '94 C.105 B.A. L.184 J.D. [Ⓢ Day,B.&H.]
Anderson, Calum B. .... '51 '77 C.282 A.B. L.93 J.D. [Danaher,T.L.&N.]
Anderson, Jacqueline Smith .... '70 '98 C.309 B.A. L.818 J.D. One State Street
Anderson, Jan Rosker .... '57 '82 C.867 B.A. L.818 J.D. Coun., Travelers Ins. Co.
Anderson, Lisa M. .... '68 '93 C.1134 B.S. L.1048 J.D. [Ⓐ Rogin,N.C.L.&H.]
*PRACTICE AREAS: Construction Law; Surety Law; Commercial Litigation; Litigation.
Anderson, Mark P. .... '59 '84 C.918 B.A. L.184 J.D. The Travelers Corp.
Anderson, Maureen J. .... '— '92 C.184 B.A. L.306 J.D. [Ⓒ Shipman&G.]
*PRACTICE AREAS: Health Law; Corporate Law; Insurance Law.
Anderson, Patricia D., (BV) .... '65 '90 C.19 B.A. L.1048 J.D. [Cranmore,F.&M.]
Anderson, Thomas O., (AV) .... '59 '84 C.882 B.A. L.862 J.D. [Danaher,T.L.&N.]
*PRACTICE AREAS: Civil Litigation; Insurance Defense; Medical Malpractice Defense; Professional Liability Defense; Products Liability.
Andreana, Michael J. .... '62 '87 C.659 B.S. L.228 J.D. 1 American Row
Andreini, John M., (BV) .... '49 '79 C.870 B.S. L.306 J.D. [Dubay&A.]
Andrews, Edward C., II .... '73 '94 C.319 B.A L.930 J.D. [Ⓐ Updike,K.&S.]
*PRACTICE AREAS: Litigation.
Andrews, Elizabeth K. .... '73 '99 C.107 B.S. L.930 J.D. [Ⓐ Tyler C.&A.]
Andrews, Joan M. .... '67 '93 C.276 B.A. L.273 J.D. State Elections Enforce. Comm.
Andrews, Mary Jo Blain .... '55 '89 C.855 A.B. L.309 J.D. [Ⓒ Shipman&G.]
*PRACTICE AREAS: Real Estate; Zoning, Planning and Land Use; Municipal Corporation Law.
Andrews, Raymond S., Jr., (AV) .... '— '68 C.870 B.S. L.309 J.D. [Ⓒ Robinson&C.]
*PRACTICE AREAS: Business; Health Care; Non-Profit Organizations.
Andros, Carl W., (AV) .... '49 '77 C.197 A.B. L.1048 J.D. [Andros,F.&M.]
Andros, Floyd & Miller, P.C., (AV) .... 864 Wethersfield Avenue
Anker, Nicole J. .... '72 '98 C.976 B.A. L.306 J.D. [Ⓐ Bingham D.]
*PRACTICE AREAS: Litigation.
Antanaitis, Cynthia E. .... '54 '83 C.1103 B.S. L.107 J.D. State Dept. of Banking

Anthony, J. Danford, Jr., (AV) .... '35 '61 C.918 A.B. L.309 LL.B. [Day,B.&H.]
*PRACTICE AREAS: Tax; Tax-Exempt Organizations; Municipal Finance.
Anthony, Robert J. .... '— '92 C.93 B.A. L.184 J.D. [Brown,R.F.&G.]
*PRACTICE AREAS: Health Care; Business.
Anthony, Tennyson S. .... '66 '95 C.1033 B.A. L.1218 J.D. [Byrne&S.]
*PRACTICE AREAS: Residential Real Estate; Commercial Real Estate; Corporate Law; Estate Planning; Probate.
Anthony, William J. .... '63 '89 C.299 B.A. L.94 J.D. [Jackson L.S.&K.]
Antonacci, Sherida '51 '86 C.184 B.A. L.1048 J.D.
Clk. of the Centralized Infractions Bur.
Aparo, Paul J., (BV) .... '49 '76 C.1030 B.S. L.184 J.D. [O'Connell,F.&A.]
*PRACTICE AREAS: Real Estate; Probate; Zoning; Corporations; Business Law.
Aponte, Alexander, (BV) .... '55 '80 C.321 B.A. L.178 J.D. [Ⓐ Perakos&Z.]
Apostolidis, Helen .... '56 '84 C.829 B.A. L.184 J.D. Asst. Corp. Coun.
Appicelli, Frank A., (AV) .... '64 '89 C.1030 B.A. L.276 J.D. [Bingham D.]
*PRACTICE AREAS: Commercial Finance; Real Estate; Corporate Law.
Appleton, Amie S. .... '68 '94 C.1365 B.A. L.1048 J.D. 100 Pearl St.
Appleton, Morton W., (BV) .... '29 '55 C.184 B.S. L.94 LL.B. [Appleton&A.]
*PRACTICE AREAS: Civil Litigation; Personal Injury; Medical Malpractice; Commercial Litigation; Administrative Law.
Appleton, Peter M., (BV) .... '62 '88 C.855 B.A. L.94 J.D. [Appleton&A.]
*PRACTICE AREAS: Civil Litigation; Personal Injury; Medical Malpractice; Product Liability; Employment Litigation.

Appleton & Appleton, LLC, (BV)
100 Pearl Street, Suite 1210, 06103-4500
Telephone: 860-246-5481 Facsimile: 860-246-5554
URL: http://www.appleton-law.com
Members of Firm: Morton W. Appleton; Peter M. Appleton. Associates: Linda A. Kesten; Peter T. Evans.
Civil Litigation, Litigation, Personal Injury, Medical Malpractice. Commercial Litigation, Employment Litigation, Real Estate, Family, Probate, Appellate Practice.
See Professional Biographies, HARTFORD, CONNECTICUT

Arcaro, Melissa Rotenberg .... '69 '95 C.289 B.S. L.1048 J.D. [Ⓐ Halloran&S.]
*PRACTICE AREAS: Trucking and Transportation.
Archer, Kenneth D. '40 '66 C.339 B.S. L.309 J.D.
(adm. in NY; not adm. in CT) One American Row
Armentano, James A., (BV) .... '49 '75 C.856 B.A. L.94 J.D. [Katz&S.]
*PRACTICE AREAS: Civil Litigation; Insurance Defense.
Armour, Norman E. .... '28 '57 C.478 B.A. L.184 LL.B. Exec. V.P., Tr. Co. of Conn.‡
Armstrong, Jack D. .... '53 '78 C.123 B.A. L.425 J.D. Coun., Travelers Ins. Co.
Armstrong, Thomas M., (BV) .... '46 '73 C.935 B.A. L.184 J.D. [Reid&R.]
*PRACTICE AREAS: Environmental Law; Occupational Safety and Health; Land Use.
Arnold, Rudolph P., (BV) .... '48 '75 C.329 B.S. L.184 J.D. [Arnold&Assoc.]
*PRACTICE AREAS: Civil Litigation; Landlord and Tenant Law; Housing Law; Public Housing.

Arnold & Associates, (BV)
80 Cedar Street, 06106
Telephone: 860-728-0037 Fax: 860-524-8357
Email: rarnold@ursa.hartnet.org
Rudolph P. Arnold;—Raul A. Rodriguez; LeAnne Baggetta.
Civil Litigation, Housing, Landlord Tenant, Public Finance, Securities and Commercial Transactions, Small Business Law and Probate.
See Professional Biographies, HARTFORD, CONNECTICUT

Aronson, Stephen W., (BV) .... '— '87 C.860 B.A. L.184 J.D. [Ⓒ Robinson&C.]
*PRACTICE AREAS: Litigation; Labor and Employment.
Arsenault, Jon E. .... '57 '82 C.1030 B.S. L.884 J.D. Coun., State Ins. Dept.
Arvidson, R. Regner, (AV) .... '— '54 C.210 B.A. L.309 LL.B. [Ⓒ Robinson&C.]
*PRACTICE AREAS: Federal Tax Law; Tax Planning for U.S. Activities of Foreign Taxpayers and Resident Aliens.
Askinas, David M., (BV) .... '51 '77 C.910 A.B. L.184 J.D. 97 Elm St.
Asklof, Laurann, (BV) .... '60 '86 C.276 B.A. L.982 J.D. Off. of Atty. Gen.
Asmar, Mark A., (AV) .... '— '70 C.347 A.B. L.184 J.D. [Brown,R.F.&G.]
*PRACTICE AREAS: Commercial Real Estate Development; Financing, Leasing and Conveyancing; Loan Workouts; Land Use and Zoning.
Aspell, James F., (BV) .... '61 '86 C.611 B.A. L.1048 J.D. [Furniss&Q.]
Atkinson, Gary R. .... '53 '85 C.94 B.A. L.184 J.D. [Ⓐ A.J.Palermino]
Attmore, Gary G., (BV) .... '46 '74 C.588 B.S. L.818 J.D. [O'Connell,F.&A.]
*PRACTICE AREAS: Taxation; Estate Planning; Closely-held Business Planning.
Auburn, Travers T. ..... '46 '72 C.951 B.A. L.184 [Reid&R.] (⊙Lakeville, West Hartford)
*PRACTICE AREAS: Probate; Real Estate; Trusts and Estates.
Augur, Carolyn E. .... '68 '96 C.103 B.A. L.306 J.D. 225 Asylum Street, 13th Floor
Augustinos, Theodore P., (BV) .... '60 '85 C.732 B.A. L.94 J.D. [Edwards&A.]
*PRACTICE AREAS: Banking Regulation; General Corporate Law; Mergers and Acquisitions; Insurance Regulation.
Austin, Elizabeth J., (BV) '57 '83 C&L.546 B.A., J.D.
[Pullman&C.] (⊙Bridgeport, New Haven, Stamford)
*PRACTICE AREAS: Insolvency Law; Bankruptcy Litigation; Commercial Litigation.

Axinn, Veltrop & Harkrider LLP, (AV)
90 State House Square, 11th Floor, 06103 ⊙
Telephone: 860-275-8100 Facsimile: 860-275-8101
URL: http://www.avhlaw.com
Members of Firm: Stephen M. Axinn (Resident, New York, NY Office); James D. Veltrop; John D. Harkrider (Resident, New York, NY Office); William M. Rubenstein; Lauren S. Albert (Resident, New York, NY Office). Associates: Mark D. Alexander; Eric D. Beal; Michael L. Keeley (Resident, New York, NY Office); Sivan R. Korn (Resident, New York, NY Office); Chad A. Landmon; Sonja A. Larson (Resident, New York, NY Office); Mary Elizabeth LaRuffa (Resident, New York, NY Office); Charles Loesner (Resident, New York, NY Office); Eric L. Palmquist (Not admitted in CT); Michelle H. Seagull.
Antitrust and Trade Regulation, Intellectual Property, Litigation, and International.
New York, New York Office: 1370 Avenue of the Americas, 19th Floor. Telephone: 212-728-2200. Facsimile: 212-728-2201.
Washington, DC Office: 1801 K Street, N.W., Suite 411. Telephone: 202-912-4700. Facsimile: 202-912-4701.
See Professional Biographies, HARTFORD, CONNECTICUT

Ayars & Associates, LLC
(See Glastonbury)

Ayers, Rosemary G., (BV) .... '58 '88 C.855 B.A. L.184 J.D. [Ⓒ Day,B.&H.]
*PRACTICE AREAS: Commercial Real Estate; Construction Law; Housing Law.
Azano, Warren B. .... '46 '75 C.401 B.A. L.309 J.D. V.P., Govt. Affairs, The Hartford
Baatz, Catherine P. .... '— '96 C.518 A.B. L.309 J.D. [Ⓐ Wiggin&D.]
Babbitt, Bradford S. .... '— '93 C.855 B.A. L.93 J.D. [Robinson&C.]
*PRACTICE AREAS: Business Litigation.
Babcock, Reginald L. '51 '77 C&L.30 B.A., J.D.
V.P., Gen. Coun. & Secy., Conn. Nat. Gas Corp.
Backmender, Harvey L., (BV) .... '40 '72 C.563 B.S. L.94 J.D. 10 Grand St.
Badillo-Rodriguez, Roxanna '55 '86 C&L.677 B.A., J.D.
Staff Atty., State Comm. on Human Rights and Opp.
Baggetta, LeAnne .... '74 '00 C.1030 B.A. L.1048 J.D. [Ⓐ Arnold&Assoc.]
*PRACTICE AREAS: Civil Litigation; Landlord and Tenant Law; Foreclosures; Public Housing.
Baily, Christine A. .... '67 '99 C.705 B.A. L.1048 J.D. [Ⓐ Day,B.&H.]
*PRACTICE AREAS: Administrative Law; Regulatory Law.

Baird, Archibald W. .... '12 '47 C.867 A.B. L.184 LL.B. 19 Scarsdale Rd.
Baker, Sandra R. .... '69 '94 C.918 B.A. L.184 J.D. [A Regnier,T.C.&E.]
*PRACTICE AREAS: General Practice; Trial Practice; Insurance; Toxic Torts; Products Liability.

Baker O'Sullivan & Bliss PC
(See Wethersfield)

Balavender, Paul Thomas .... '58 '89 C.1252 B.S. L.273 J.D. Dept. of Envir. Protec.
Baldini, Laura Flynn .... '70 '97 C.976 B.A. L.776 J.D. [A Updike,K.&S.]
*PRACTICE AREAS: Insurance Defense Litigation; Personal Injury; Commercial Litigation.
Baldwin, Eileen P., (BV) ....'— '86 C.477 B.B.A. L.94 J.D. [C Robinson&C.]
*PRACTICE AREAS: Finance; Banking Law.
Baldwin, Kenneth C. .... '— '94 C.1044 B.A. L.1048 J.D. [Robinson&C.]
*PRACTICE AREAS: Energy; Zoning, Planning and Land Use; Real Estate.
Baldwin, Lucian E., (AV) ....'— '50 C.918 A.B. L.976 LL.B. [C Robinson&C.]
Baldwin, Mark S., (BV) ....'— '86 C.477 A.B. L.94 J.D. [Brown,R.F.&G.]
*PRACTICE AREAS: Complex Commercial, Corporate and Employment Litigation.
Ballman, Donald R. .... '56 '98 C.201 B.A. L.184 J.D. [A Brown R.M.F.&S.]
*PRACTICE AREAS: Corporate; Computer Law; E-Commerce; Internet Law; Intellectual Property.
Banbury, Richard F., (AV) ....'38 '64 C&L.976 B.A., J.D. [Rome M.S.]
*PRACTICE AREAS: Litigation; Professional Liability; Alternative Dispute Resolution.
Banks, Morris W., (AV) ....'39 '64 C.197 A.B. L.178 LL.B. [Pullman&C.]
*PRACTICE AREAS: Corporate Law; Corporate Securities; Taxation; Mergers and Acquisitions; Succession Planning for Closely-Held Business.
Barall, Herbert .... '32 '56 C.569 B.S. L.309 LL.B. Supr. Ct. J.
Barber, Steven J. ....'72 '97 C.1200 B.A. L.1048 J.D. [A Howard,K.S.&F.]
*PRACTICE AREAS: Insurance Defense; Personal Injury; Civil Litigation; Domestic Relations; Criminal Law.
Barclay, John Williams, (AV) ....'13 '39 C.976 B.A. L.309 LL.B. 185 Asylum St.
Bard, Robert L. '31 '60 C.477 B.A. L.976 LL.B.
(adm. in NY; not adm. in CT) Prof. of Law, Univ. of Conn.
Barger, Richard L., (AV) ....'44 '69 C&L.184 B.S., J.D. [Michelson,K.R.&B.]
*PRACTICE AREAS: Public Utilities; Administrative Law; Municipal Law; Construction Law; Civil Litigation.
Barlow, Boce W., Jr., (BV) ....'15 '49 C.329 A.B. L.309 LL.B. [Barlow&L.]
Barlow & Lewis, (BV) .... 1229 Albany Ave.
Barnes, Christopher G ......'69 '98 C.174 B.A. L.1252 J.D. 225 Asylum Street, 13th Floor
Baronas, Mark W., (BV) .... '54 '81 C.31 B.A. L.184 J.D. [Gould,K.&W.]
*PRACTICE AREAS: Personal Injury; Insurance Defense; Medical Malpractice; Employment Law.
Barr, Catherine '— '87 C.914 B.A. L.309 J.D.
(adm. in MA; and limited adm. in CT) [Brown,R.F.&G.]
*PRACTICE AREAS: Commercial and Real Estate Finance; Commercial Lending; Loan Workouts; Bankruptcy.
Barrack, Robert M. ....'57 '90 C.881 B.A. L.1292 J.D. [Halloran&S.]
*PRACTICE AREAS: Commercial Litigation; Construction Litigation; Breach of Contract; Business Torts; Creditors Rights.
Barrett, Campbell Duggan .... '70 '95 C.855 B.A. L.30 J.D. 89 Oak Street
Barrow, Mary L. ....'58 '84 C.103 B.A. L.659 J.D. [C Halloran&S.]
*PRACTICE AREAS: Estate Planning; Family Wealth Transfer; Trust Planning.
Barry, David M. ....'30 '55 C.855 B.A. L.94 LL.B. Supr. Ct. J.
Barry, Ryan P. ....'72 '00 C.184 B.A. L.306 J.D. [A Sabia&H.]
*PRACTICE AREAS: Commercial Litigation.
Bartels, Millard, (AV) ....'05 '30 C&L.188 B.A., LL.B. 185 Asylum St.‡
Bartelstone, Steven D., (AV) .... '47 '72 C&L.184 B.A., J.D. [Rogin,N.C.L.&H.]
*PRACTICE AREAS: Commercial Law; Corporate Law; Real Estate.
Barth, Bruce B., (BV) ....'— '81 C.184 B.S. L.273 J.D. [Robinson&C.]
*PRACTICE AREAS: Employee Benefits; Labor and Employment; Taxation.
Bartholic, Mary E. R. ....'62 '93 C.633 B.A. L.665 J.D. [A Cohn B.&S.]
*PRACTICE AREAS: Commercial Litigation; Employment Law; Land Use Law.
Bartol, William E. .... '58 '91 C.688 B.S. L.184 J.D. State Dept. of Bkg.
Bartolini, James D., (AV) ....'46 '75 C.855 B.A. L.184 J.D. [RisCassi&D.]
*PRACTICE AREAS: Medical Malpractice; Negligence; Products Liability.
Barton, Elizabeth C., (BV) ....'52 '77 C.860 B.A. L.184 J.D. [Day,B.&H.]
*PRACTICE AREAS: Administrative Law; Environmental; Utility Law; Legislative Representation.
Bartschi, Kenneth J. ....'65 '96 C.1044 B.M. L.184 J.D. [Horton,S.&C.]
*PRACTICE AREAS: Civil Litigation; Appellate Practice; Civil Rights; Constitutional Law; Wills.
Baskin, Sarah C. ....'65 '93 C.478 B.A. L.94 J.D. [S Day,B.&H.]
Baskin, William C., III ....'62 '90 C.951 B.A. L.976 J.D. Coun., Aetna Inc.
*RESPONSIBILITIES: Mergers and Acquisitions; Securities Law; Corporate Law.
Bassock, Irene E. ....'68 '95 C.282 B.A. L.94 J.D. [A Updike,K.&S.]
*PRACTICE AREAS: Commercial Litigation; Employment Based Immigration Law; Labor and Employment Law.
Bates, Cynthia J. ....'— '85 C.918 B.A. L.184 J.D. Coun., Aetna Inc.
Batts, Bruce J. ....'50 '80 C.293 A.B. L.976 J.D. Legal Aid Soc. of Hartford Co. Inc.
Bauer, Jon '60 '85 C.188 B.A. L.976 J.D.
Clinical Prof. of Law, Univ. of Conn. Law Sch.
Baughns, Dana Rene ....'68 '98 C.329 B.A. L.184 J.D. [A Updike,K.&S.]
*PRACTICE AREAS: Employment Litigation; ERISA Litigation; Collective Bargaining.
Baumert, William A. ....'45 '73 C.602 B.B.A. L.184 J.D. Pres., Baumert Sales Co.
Baummer, Nicole M. ....'74 '00 C.184 B.A. L.306 J.D. [A Pepe&H.]
Baxter, Richard J. ....'45 '75 C.105 B.A. L.228 J.D. 151 Farmington Avenue
Bayer, Aaron Seth ....'55 '80 C.976 B.A. L.309 J.D. Dep. Atty. Gen.
Bayonne, Michel ......'76 '01 C.1030 B.A. L.306 J.D. [A Updike,K.&S.] (⊙New Haven)
*PRACTICE AREAS: Business Law.
Beach, Morrison H. '17 '54 C.951 B.A. L.184 LL.B.
Chmn. of the Bd. & CEO, The Travelers Corp.
Beach, Robert E., Jr. ....'47 '72 C.976 B.A. L.893 J.D. Supr. Ct. J.
Beal, Eric D. ....'70 '00 C.454 B.A. L.306 J.D. [A Axinn,V.&H.]
*PRACTICE AREAS: Antitrust and Trade Regulation; Commercial Litigation.
Beaudoin, Gerald ....'60 '90 C&L.259 B.S., J.D. [A Hunt L.C.&J.]
Beck, Bruce S., (BV) ....'46 '73 C.446 B.S. L.128 J.D. [Beck&E.] ⊙
*PRACTICE AREAS: Commercial Litigation; Domestic Relations; Bankruptcy.
Beck, Henry M., Jr., (AV) ....'51 '77 C.228 B.S. L.309 J.D. [Halloran&S.]
*PRACTICE AREAS: Business Planning; Closely Held Business Law; Business Reorganization; Securities Law; Private Placement.
Beck, John W., (AV) ....'54 '79 C.197 B.A. L.184 J.D. [Siegel,O.S.&Z.]
*PRACTICE AREAS: Real Estate Law; Business Law; Taxation Law; Low Income Tax Credits; Affordable Housing.

Beck & Eldergill, P.C., (AV)
97 Oak Street, 06109 ⊙
Telephone: 860-646-5606 FAX: 860-646-0054
Email: firm@beckeldergill.com URL: http://www.beckeldergill.com
Bruce S. Beck.
General Civil and Criminal Litigation before all State and Federal Trial and Appellate Courts with a concentration on Employment, Civil Rights, Personal Injury, Car Accidents and Divorce.
See Professional Biographies, HARTFORD, CONNECTICUT

Becker, Brian S., (BV) '61 '87 C.659 B.A. L.94 J.D.
Asst. Gen. Coun., Hartford Life, Inc.
Becker, Matthew J. ....'66 '91 C&L.347 B.S., J.D. [Day,B.&H.] (Pat.)
*PRACTICE AREAS: Commercial Litigation; Technology & Intellectual Property - Litigation; Technology & Intellectual Property - Business.
Beckett, Suzann L., (BV) ....'61 '87 C.1033 B.A. L.184 J.D. [Beckett]
Beckett Law Group, LLC, (BV) ....543 Prospect Avenue
Beers, John H., (AV) '54 '81 C.674 A.B. L.724 J.D.
Vice President & Associate General Counsel, Phoenix Home Life Mutual Insurance Company
Begemann, Jill B. ....'64 '90 C.112 B.A. L.273 J.D. Clk., Supr. Crt.
Beizer, Arnold L. ....'45 '80 C.94 A.B. L.1029 J.D. 429 Capitol Ave.
Belbruno, Diana Rousseau, (BV) '52 '78 C&L.184 B.A., J.D.
Asst. Gen. Coun., Hartford Financial Services Group, Inc.
Belgrade, Neale Susan ....'49 '81 C&L.184 B.A., J.D. State Dept. of Consumer Protection
Bell, Jamey, (BV) '58 '82 C.477 B.A. L.588 J.D.
Staff Atty., Legal Aid Soc. of Hartford Co., Inc.
Bellantoni, Diane C. ....'60 '95 C.1214 B.S. L.1350 J.D. [A Murtha C.]
Bellis, Marvin P. ....'62 '98 C.1102 B.S. L.306 J.D. [A Murtha C.]
Bellizzi, Jerry J. .... '63 '99 C.184 B.S. L.1048 J.D. Coun., AETNA Inc.
Bellobuono, Michael C., (BV) '41 '67
C.1155 B.S.B.A. L.818 LL.B. [McVane,B.K.W.&B.]
Bellotti, Laura A. '72 '98 C.1021 B.A. L.1048 J.D.
(adm. in MA; not adm. in CT) Fin. Analyst, Arthur Andersen LLP
Belval, Paul N. ....'62 '89 C.454 B.A. L.1040 J.D. [Day,B.&H.]
*PRACTICE AREAS: Energy; Telecommunications.
Bemben, Brenda J., (BV) '40 '80 C.454 B.A. L.1048 J.D.
Associate Counsel, Connecticut Natural Gas Corporation
Bendza, Shirley A. ....'69 '94 C.976 B.A. L.659 J.D. United Tech. Corp.
Bengston, Eric J., (BV) .....'54 '79 C&L.184 B.A., J.D. Asst. Pub. Def., Personnel Admin.
Benner, Peter W., (AV) .... '50 '76 C.674 A.B. L.276 J.D. [Shipman&G.]
*PRACTICE AREAS: Commercial Litigation; Bankruptcy Litigation; Health Care Litigation.
Bennett, N. Kane ....'72 '97 C.184 B.A. L.818 J.D. [A Halloran&S.]
*PRACTICE AREAS: Insurance Defense; Products Liability; Litigation.
Benoit, David B. ....'72 '00 C.184 B.A. L.306 J.D. [A Brown R.M.F.&S.]
Benson, Charles H. ....'47 '89 C.829 B.S. L.184 J.D. Asst. Atty. Gen.
Berall, Frank S., (AV) ....'29 '55 C&L.976 B.S., J.D. [Copp&B.]
*PRACTICE AREAS: Probate; Federal and State Taxation; Estate Planning; Trust Administration; Tax Litigation.

Berchem, Moses & Devlin, A Professional Corporation
(See Milford)

Berdon, Robert I. ....'29 '57 C&L.184 B.S., LL.B. Supr. Ct. J.
Bergenn, James W., (AV) ....'54 '79 C.128 B.A. L.178 J.D. [Shipman&G.]
*PRACTICE AREAS: Trial Practice; White Collar Litigation; Criminal Litigation; Antitrust Litigation; Health Care Litigation.
Berger, Marjorie J. ....'52 '84 C.94 B.A. L.184 J.D. Coun., Travelers Ins. Co.
Bergeron, Brenda M. ....'59 '83 C&L.184 B.A., J.D. Staff Atty., State Ethics Comm.‡
Bergman, Bruce E., (BV) .... '43 '70 C.306 B.A. L.818 J.D. 63 Imlay St.
Berk, Jon Stephen, (AV) ....'50 '75 C.918 B.A. L.94 J.D. [Gordon,M.&F.]
*PRACTICE AREAS: Automobile Liability; Commercial Liability; Insurance Coverage; Product Liability; Municipal Liability.
Berman, Harvey P. ....'39 '64 C&L.184 B.A., J.D. Aetna Inc.
Berman, Michael P., (AV) ....'39 '69 C.119 B.S. L.184 J.D. [Berman&S.]
*PRACTICE AREAS: Commercial Litigation; Litigation on Behalf of Financial Institutions; Defense of Lender Liability Claims; Creditors Rights; Bankruptcy Litigation.
Berman, Paul Schiff '66 '96 C.674 A.B. L.569 J.D.
(adm. in NY; not adm. in CT) [S Day,B.&H.]
*PRACTICE AREAS: Internet Law; Copyrights.

Berman, Bourns, Aaron & Dembo, LLC
(See West Hartford)

Berman and Sable, (AV)
100 Pearl Street, 06103 ⊙
Telephone: 860-527-9699 Telecopier: 860-527-9077
Email: info@bermansable.com URL: http://www.bermansable.com
Members of Firm: Michael P. Berman; Joel N. Sable; Steven A. Berman (Resident Partner, New Haven Office); James W. Oliver; Maria K. Tougas. Associates: Robert J. Caffrey; James J. Brault (Resident, New Haven Office); Alena C. Gfeller; Andrew R. Sherriff, Jr.; David R. Levesque; Suzanne LaPlante; Jacqueline Forgione. Of Counsel: I. Milton Widem (1923-2000).
Commercial Litigation, Commercial and Corporate Finance Transactions, Real Estate, Corporate Law, Acquisitions, Mergers and Divestitures, Problem Loan Workouts, Loan Restructure and Recoveries, Mortgage and Foreclosure, Creditor's Rights, Defense of Lender Liability Claims, Creditor Bankruptcy Rights, Reorganizations, Tax Appeals, Construction Litigation, Probate and Trials and Appeals in all Courts. FDIC/RTC Approved Counsel.
New Haven, Connecticut Office: 195 Church Street. Telephone: 203-495-6200. Fax: 203-495-6220.
See Professional Biographies, HARTFORD, CONNECTICUT

Berneike, Richard H. '32 '64 C.679 B.S.Ch.E. L.273 LL.B.
[Alix,Y.&R.] (See Pat. Sect.)
Bernier, Marcel J., (AV) ....'58 '82 C.259 B.A. L.184 J.D. [Murtha C.]
*PRACTICE AREAS: Business Law; Limited Liability Company Law; Mergers and Acquisitions Law; Business Successions; Tax Law.
Bernstein, Sara L., (BV) ....'50 '80 C.999 B.A. L.1048 J.D. Asst. Pub. Def.
Berry, Christel Ford ....'54 '79 C.66 B.A. L.659 J.D. 169 Whitney St.
Bertrand, Donald E. '46 '73 C.31 B.A. L.976 J.D.
V.P. & Ins. & Invest. Products Coun., Phoenix Home Life Mutual Ins. Co.
*RESPONSIBILITIES: Insurance; Securities.
Betts, James T., (AV) ....'43 '68 C&L.976 B.A., LL.B. [Shipman&G.]
*PRACTICE AREAS: Estate Planning and Settlement Law; Probate Matters; Financial Planning and Trust Administration Law.
Bevacqua, Renee L. ....'60 '85 C.1030 B.A. L.734 J.D. Dep. of Pub. Safety
Bezz, Gregory J. ....'55 '80 C.688 B.S. L.184 J.D. [Siegel,O.S.&Z.]
*PRACTICE AREAS: Business Law; Tax Law; Commercial Law.
Bibbins, Deborah M. ....'65 '99 C.184 B.S.B.A. L.306 J.D. [A Bingham D.]
*PRACTICE AREAS: Insurance; Reinsurance; Bankruptcy.
Bibisi, Joseph W., (BV) ....'51 '90 C.183 B.A. L.184 J.D. [McVane,B.K.W.&B.]
Bieluch, William C. ....'18 '42 C.103 A.B. L.976 J.D. Ret. Appl. Ct. J.
Bieringer, Leonard M., (BV) '54 '81 C.910 B.A. L.734 J.D.
Coun., The Travelers Ins. Co.
Biklen, David D. ...'43 '68 C.504 B.A. L.893 J.D. Exec. Dir., State Law Revision Comm.
Bingham, Robert Kim '42 '69 C.976 B.A. L.94 LL.B.
(adm. in MA; not adm. in CT) Spec. Coun., Immig. & Nat. Serv.

Bingham Dana LLP, (AV) BB
One State Street, 06103 ⊙
Telephone: 860-240-2700 Telefax: 860-240-2800
Email: info@bingham.com URL: http://www.bingham.com
Partners: Jonathan B. Alter; Frank A. Appicelli; Robert M. Borden; G. Eric Brunstad, Jr.; Robert M. Dombroff; Scott A. Falk; Chester L. Fisher III; Evan D. Flaschen; Deborah Samuels Freeman; F. Mark Fucci; James Greenfield; Harold S. Horwich; William E. Kelly; Ben M. Krowicki; Gregory W. Nye; Thomas F. O'Connor; Mark Oland; Thomas J. O'Shea; Daniel I. Papermaster; Michael J. Reilly; James Scott Rollins; Stuart D. Rosen; James G. Scantling; Bruce C. Silvers; R. Jeffrey Smith. Resident Of Counsel: Gary H. Collins (Not admitted in CT); Edwin Gordon Hebb, Jr.; Peter H. Levine; Ann M. Siczewicz. Resident Associates: Nicole J. Anker; Deborah M. Bibbins; Patti Lynn Boss; Michael H.M. Brown; Elizabeth A. Calvert; Lisa M. Ciottone; Alexia E. Cruz; Renée M. Dailey; Dawn E. Duncan; John P. Dyro, Sr.; Celia Eggert; William F. Govier; Brent L. Hoffman; Edward B. Karns; Susan Kim; Alan H. Kosberg; Christopher E. Lawrence; Marc R. Leduc; Stewart E. Newman; Christine C. Peaslee; Richard A. Rochlin; Trevor T. Sanford; Rupal S. Shah; Margaret J. Sheehan;

(This Listing Continued)

Bingham Dana LLP (Continued)

Vi R. Smalley; Anthony J. Smits; Christopher S. Snow; Marialta Z. Sparagna; Susannah M. Stapleton; Frank J. Taboada; Patrick J. Trostle; Tanya Tymchenko; Michael P. Ungaro; Oscar Urizar; Lisa Valentovish; Mary L. Weil; Steven S. Wheeler; Scott A. Wood; Jeffrey B. Zeman.
Corporate and Securities Law, Banking and Financial Services, Financial Restructuring, Project/Structured Finance, Technology, Private Equity, Investment Management, Commercial and Criminal Litigation, Corporate Acquisitions, Real Estate, Entrepreneurial Services, Intellectual Property, Tax, Estate Planning, Securities Litigation, Business Regulation and White Collar Defense, Product Liability, Antitrust, Distribution and Franchising, Employment Law, Environmental Law, Sports, Media, Entertainment, International Transactions including International Trade, European, Japanese and Latin American Practices and Alternative Dispute Resolution.
Boston, Massachusetts Office: 150 Federal Street. Telephone: 617-951-8000. Telecopy: 617-951-8736.
New York, New York Office: 399 Park Avenue. Telephone: 212-318-7700. Fax: 212-752-5378.
Washington, D.C. Office: 1120 20th Street, N.W. Telephone: 202-778-6150. Fax: 202-778-6155.
Los Angeles, California Office: 444 South Flower Street, Suite 4500. Telephone: 213-817-3700. Fax: 213-817-3701.
London, England Office: 39 Victoria Street, SWIH 0EE. Telephone: 011-44-71-799-2646. Telecopy: 011-44-71-799-2654.
Singapore Office: Level 15 Prudential Tower, 30 Cecil Street, 049712. Telephone: 011.65.232.2768. Fax: 011.65.232.2888.

See Professional Biographies, HARTFORD, CONNECTICUT

Birmingham, Alan, (AV) '43 '69 C.860 B.A. L.276 J.D. [Reid&R.] (⊙West Hartford, Woodbury)
*PRACTICE AREAS: Probate; Real Estate; Trusts and Estates.
Birnbaum, Robert J., (AV) .... '30 '57 C.105 B.A. L.309 LL.B. [Ⓒ Cohn B.&S.]
*PRACTICE AREAS: Commercial Real Estate; Commercial Real Estate Acquisitions; Commercial Real Estate Development; Commercial Real Estate Finance; Leasing.
Birney, Patrick M. ....'65 '98 C.201 B.A. L.1218 J.D. [Ⓐ Halloran&S.]
*PRACTICE AREAS: Creditors Rights; Creditor Bankruptcy; Intellectual Property.
Bizar, David M. .... '— '94 C.588 B.S. L.472 J.D. [Ⓐ Day,B.&H.]
*PRACTICE AREAS: Commercial Litigation; Technology; Intellectual Property.
Blackall, Brewster, (BV) .... '33 '61 C.197 B.A. L.208 LL.B. Asst. Atty. Gen.
Blackwell, Lynn C. '53 '87 C.829 B.A. L.306 J.D. Asst. Secy. & Coun., Conn. Nat. Gas Corp.
Blair, Courtney R. ....'76 '01 C.183 B.A L.1252 J.D. [Ⓐ Updike,K.&S.]
*PRACTICE AREAS: Government Relations; Legislative Representation.
Blair, Russell J. ....'46 '71 C.184 B.S. L.306 J.D. Gen. Coun., Cambridge Realty Partners
Blake, Jonathan J. ....'61 '00 C.184 B.A. L.818 J.D. [Ⓐ Rome M.S.]
*PRACTICE AREAS: Labor and Employment; Indian Law; Litigation.
Blake, Julie D. ....'75 '99 C.893 B.A. L.818 J.D. [Ⓐ Rome M.S.]
*PRACTICE AREAS: Litigation; Internet Law; E-Commerce; Appellate Practice.
Blakeman, Mark E. ....'51 '84 C.197 A.B. L.1048 J.D. [Michelson,K.R.&B.]
*PRACTICE AREAS: Civil Litigation; Construction Law; Workers Compensation Law.
Blank, Judith A. ....'57 '85 C.867 B.A. L.982 J.D. [Ⓒ Day,B.&H.]
*PRACTICE AREAS: Municipal Bonds; Municipal Bonds Taxation; Municipal Finance; Municipal Leasing; Tax Exempt Bonds.
Blinderman, Harold M., (BV) ....'57 '87 C.156 B.A. L.823 J.D. [Day,B.&H.]
*PRACTICE AREAS: Environmental Law; Administrative Law; Utilities Law.
Blinn, C. Duane, (AV) ....'27 '51 C&L.976 B.A., LL.B. [Ⓒ Day,B.&H.]
*PRACTICE AREAS: Corporate Law; Public Utility Regulation and Finance.
Block, Philip M., (CV) .... '40 '80 C.612 B.Sc. L.1029 J.D. 254 Prospect Ave.
Blodgett, Verne E. ....'37 '71 C.976 B.A. L.184 J.D. CIGNA Corp.
Bloom, Marvin S., (BV) .... '29 '54 C.910 A.B. L.94 J.D. [Ⓒ T.P.Willcutts&Assoc.]
Blum, Peter R., (BV) ....'37 '64 C.860 B.A. L.93 J.D. 1 Linden Pl.
Blumenfeld, Louis B., (AV) ....'45 '70 C.882 B.A. L.93 J.D. [Cooney,S.&D.]
*PRACTICE AREAS: Legal Malpractice; Insurance Coverage; Environmental Law; Appellate Practice.

Boatman, Boscarino, Grasso & Twachtman
(See Glastonbury)

Bobryk, Michal L. '49 '78 C.563 B.A. L.1009 J.D. (adm. in DC; not adm. in CT) One American Row
Boccaccio, Christopher J. ....'70 '95 C.93 B.A. L.884 J.D. [Ⓐ Day,B.&H.]
*PRACTICE AREAS: Business Law; Emerging Growth Companies.
Bocchini, Suzanne S., (AV) '47 '73 C.128 B.A. L.734 J.D. [Reid&R.] (⊙West Hartford)
*PRACTICE AREAS: Probate; Trusts and Estates.
Boe, Rodger C., (BV) ....'46 '77 C.385 A.B. L.880 J.D. [Byrne&S.]
*PRACTICE AREAS: Civil Litigation.
Bogdanski, John J., (AV) ....'53 '79 C.860 B.A. L.1048 J.D. [Howd&L.]
*PRACTICE AREAS: Product Liability Litigation; Insurance Defense Litigation; Toxic Tort.
Bolgard, Robert D. .... '36 '84 C.674 A.B. L.184 J.D. V.P., Fleet Bk., N.A.
Boltryk, Izabela E. .... '67 '99 C.999 M.A. L.184 J.D. [Ⓐ Dechert]
*PRACTICE AREAS: Real Estate Finance.
Bondi, Steven A. ....'68 '94 C.945 B.S. L.309 J.D. One American Row
Bonee, John L., (AV) ....'21 '50 C.855 B.S. L.976 LL.B. [Bonee]
*PRACTICE AREAS: Elder Law; Estate Planning; Wills; Trust Law; Probate Administration.
Bonee, John L., III, (BV) ....'47 '74 C.855 B.A. L.818 J.D. [Bonee]
*PRACTICE AREAS: Civil Litigation; Personal Injury; Family Law; Divorce; Estates and Probate.

Bonee Law Offices, LLP, (AV)
One State Street, Suite 1510, 06103
Telephone: 860-522-7161 Fax: 860-522-6049
Email: boneelaw@aol.com URL: http://www.lawyers.com/boneelaw
Members of Firm: John L. Bonee; John L. Bonee III; Eric H. Rothauser.
General Civil, Trial and Appellate Practice in State and Federal Courts, Estate Planning and Probate, Real Estate, Negligence, Wills and Trusts.

See Professional Biographies, HARTFORD, CONNECTICUT

Bonner Kiernan Trebach & Crociata
44 Capitol Avenue Suite 402, 06106 ⊙
Telephone: 860-249-9900 FAX: 860-246-3727
URL: http://www.bktc.net
Of Counsel: Michael J. Smith; Hugh R. Curran.
General Civil Defense, Appellate and Trial Practice, Civil Mediation and Arbitrations, Product Liability, Malpractice, Property, Casualty, Insurance Law, Construction Litigation, Toxic and Environmental Litigation, Insurance Coverage Disputes, Railroad and Airline Litigation, Employment Law, Commercial Litigation and Counseling, Alternative Dispute Resolutions, Aviation, Computer Law, Technology Law, Consumer Fraud, White Collar Crime.
Washington, D.C. Office: 1250 Eye Street, N.W. Telephone: 202-712-7000. Fax: 202-712-7100,
Rockville, Maryland Office: 51 Monroe Street. Telephone: 301-340-9155. Fax: 301-340-1310.
Fairfax, Virginia Office: 10511 Judicial Drive. Telephone: 703-691-0500. Fax: 703-591-5082.
Boston, Massachusetts Office: One Liberty Square. Telephone: 617-426-3900. Fax: 617-426-0380.
New York, New York Office: Empire State Building, Suite 3304. Telephone: 212-268-7535. Fax: 212-268-4965.
Providence, Rhode Island Office: 55 Pine Street. Telephone: 401-273-0100. Fax: 401-273-0101.

See Professional Biographies, HARTFORD, CONNECTICUT

Bonuomo, Nancy H. '55 '86 C.129 B.A. L.1029 J.D. Chf. Law Clk., Wrkrs. Comp. Comm.
Booher, Martin T. ....'— '98 C.105 B.A. L.1040 J.D. [Ⓐ Robinson&C.]
Booth, Kevin E. ....'42 '67 C.321 A.B. L.128 J.D. Supr. Ct. J.
Boots, Holly J Gower ....'43 '98 C.164 B.A. L.1040 J.D. 95 Washington St.
Borchert, William P., (AV) ....'50 '74 C.855 B.A. L.228 J.D. [Halloran&S.]
*PRACTICE AREAS: Business Law; Corporate Law; Mergers, Acquisitions and Divestitures.
Borden, David M. ....'37 '62 C.31 B.A. L.309 LL.B. Supm. Ct. J.
Borden, Richard M., (BV) .... '65 '90 C.31 B.A. L.569 J.D. [Ⓒ Brown R.M.F.&S.]
*PRACTICE AREAS: Information Technology; Corporate; Mergers and Acquisitions; Securities.
Borden, Robert M. .... '55 '87 C.1044 B.M. L.1009 J.D. [Bingham D.]
*PRACTICE AREAS: Corporate Trust; Lease and Asset-Based Financing; Trademark Law; Copyright Law; Computer Law.
Borea, Morris R., (BV) .... '57 '82 C.855 B.S. L.184 J.D. [Rome M.S.]
*PRACTICE AREAS: Civil Litigation; Complex Commercial Litigation; Personal Injury; Medical Malpractice; Products Liability.
Borelli, Mario R. .... '71 '98 C.602 B.S. L.347 J.D. [Ⓐ Day,B.&H.]
*PRACTICE AREAS: Commercial Litigation; Federal Civil Practice; Media and First Amendment.
Borges, Saundra A. Kee, (BV) ....'59 '84 C.855 B.S. L.184 J.D. City Mgr.
Bornhorst, Kathleen F., (BV) ....'41 '84 C.201 A.B. L.851 J.D. [Pepe&H.]
*PRACTICE AREAS: Business Estate Planning; Charitable Trusts and Foundations; Probate; Estate and Gift Taxation; Trusts and Estates.
Borod, Donald L. ....'47 '73 C.477 B.A. L.178 J.D. [Cummings&L.]
*PRACTICE AREAS: International Business; Distribution and Development Agreements; Joint Ventures; Corporate; Emerging Technologies.
Bortolan, Eleanor N., (BV) .... '65 '90 C.94 B.A. L.128 J.D. [Ⓐ Levin,F.&P.]
*PRACTICE AREAS: Commercial Real Estate; Finance.
Bosco, Dana M. '66 '92 C.184 B.S. L.1048 J.D. Regional Trademark Coun., Intl. Distillers & Vintners Ltd.
Boss, Patti Lynn ....'67 '93 C.788 B.A. L.93 J.D. [Ⓐ Bingham D.]
Botelho, Michael P. ....'66 '91 C.95 A.B. L.276 J.D. [Ⓒ Updike,K.&S.]
*PRACTICE AREAS: Public Finance/Public Law; Administrative Law; Commercial Lending; Real Estate.
Boucher, Peter G., (BV) ....'45 '72 C&L.184 B.S., J.D. [Halloran&S.]
*PRACTICE AREAS: Administrative Hearings and Appeals; Administrative Litigation; Judicial Review; Professional Regulation; Telecommunications Law.
Boudreau, Lawrence J. ....'57 '85 C&L.93 B.S., J.D. [Ⓒ Day,B.&H.]
*PRACTICE AREAS: Commercial Leasing; Corporate Law; Real Estate.
Boulton, Wayne T. ....'70 '97 C.165 B.S. L.306 J.D. [Ⓐ Schatz&N.]
*PRACTICE AREAS: Securities Litigation; Commercial Litigation.
Bourdeau, Paul L., (AV) ....'55 '80 C.976 B.A. L.94 J.D. [Cummings&L.]
*PRACTICE AREAS: Estate Planning; Estate Administration; Charitable Giving.
Bourque, William Michael '60 '93 C.1041 B.A. L.1252 J.D. Assistant General Counsel, Conning & Company
Bouton, William W., III, (AV) ....'53 '80 C.611 B.A. L.184 J.D. [Tyler C.&A.]
*PRACTICE AREAS: Banking, Corporate, Securities.
Bowen, Kim .... '52 '79 Assoc. Coun., Hartford Financial Services Group, Inc.

Bowman, Andrew B.
(See Westport)

Boyce, Timothy J., (BV) ....'54 '79 C.276 B.S.F.S. L.659 J.D. [Dechert]
*PRACTICE AREAS: Commercial Real Estate; Commercial Leasing; Lease Finance; Real Estate Finance; Leasing.
Boyle, Lisa M., (BV) ....'64 '89 C.242 B.A. L.776 J.D. [Cummings&L.]
*PRACTICE AREAS: Health Care; Public Finance; Corporate Finance.
Bradley, John W., Jr., (BV) ....'48 '76 C.321 B.A. L.678 J.D. [Rome M.S.]
*PRACTICE AREAS: Litigation; Administrative Law.
Brady, Francis J., (AV) ....'45 '74 C.971 B.S. L.309 J.D. [Murtha C.]
*PRACTICE AREAS: Insurance Litigation For Policyholders; Securities Litigation; Environmental Litigation.
Brady, Timothy Patrick ....'59 '90 C.1030 B.A. L.93 J.D. 1 American Row
Brand, Karen L., (BV) ....'61 '86 C.260 B.A. L.228 [Ⓐ Reid&R.]
*PRACTICE AREAS: Business Law; Corporate Law; Labor and Employment; Mergers and Acquisitions.
Brandi, Michael J. ....'71 '96 C.321 B.A. L.184 J.D. [Ⓐ Updike,K.&S.]
*PRACTICE AREAS: Business Law; Real Estate; Commercial Lending; Municipal Law.
Branson, Maxwell ....'72 '98 C.184 L.431 [Ⓐ Day,B.&H.]
*PRACTICE AREAS: Insurance Coverage Defense; Products Liability Defense.
Brantlinger-Angus, Elizabeth G. '65 '90 C.732 B.A. L.184 J.D. Staff Atty., State Elections Enforce. Comm.
Brawley, James L. .... '65 '90 C.865 B.A. L.818 J.D. [Morrison,M.&M.]
*PRACTICE AREAS: General Liability; Products Liability; Employment; Business Law.
Bray, Andrew W., (BV) ....'59 '91 C&L.184 B.A., J.D. [Ⓐ Regnier,T.C.&E.]
*PRACTICE AREAS: General Practice; Trial Practice; Insurance; Toxic Torts; Products Liability.
Bray, Holly Jean ....'56 '85 C.183 B.A. L.184 J.D. Asst. Atty. Gen.
Braz, Antonio B. '60 '88 C.690 B.A. L.228 J.D. Assistant General Counsel, United Technologies Corporation
Brennan, Joseph F. ....'54 '84 C.321 B.A. L.1202 J.D. Conn. Bus. & Indus. Assn.
Brennan, Terrance M. ....'74 '99 C.184 B.A. L.1048 J.D. [Ⓐ Kenny,B.M.&M.]
*PRACTICE AREAS: Insurance Defense; Personal Injury; Real Estate.
Brenneman, Russell L. .... '28 '53 C.608 B.A. L.309 LL.B. [Ⓒ Murtha C.]
*PRACTICE AREAS: Environmental Law.

Brenner, Saltzman & Wallman LLP
(See New Haven)

Briggs, Sandra S. '47 '78 C.473 B.A. L.616 J.D. (adm. in OK; not adm. in CT) Coun., Hartford Financial Services Group, Inc.
Brigham, Christopher L. '62 '92 C.478 B.A. L.1194 J.D. [Updike,K.&S.] (⊙New Haven)
*PRACTICE AREAS: Labor and Employment; Professional Defense.
Bright, Jane M. .... '53 '79 C.788 B.A. L.184 J.D. Atty., United Tech. Corp.
Bright, William H., Jr., (AV) ....'62 '87 C.216 B.A. L.145 J.D. [Cummings&L.]
*PRACTICE AREAS: Civil Litigation; Franchise Disputes, Antitrust; Intellectual Property.
Brimmer, Leslie R., (AV) .... '29 '57 C.1030 B.S. L.93 J.D. [Ⓒ Kenny,B.M.&M.]
*PRACTICE AREAS: Alternative Dispute Resolution; Insurance Defense; Personal Injury.
Briones, Annmarie P. .... '66 '95 C.1030 B.A. L.1040 J.D. [Ⓐ Halloran&S.]
*PRACTICE AREAS: Civil Litigation.
Bristol, Patrick S. ....'71 '96 C.550 B.A. L.184 J.D. [Ⓐ Santos&S.]
*PRACTICE AREAS: Criminal Defense; Civil Litigation; White Collar Crime.
Britt, John R., (BV) '48 '73 C.321 A.B. L.309 J.D. (adm. in MA; not adm. in CT) Coun., Travelers Ins. Co.
Britt, Robert J. T., (BV) .... '59 '84 C.1030 B.A. L.1202 J.D. [Rome M.S.]
*PRACTICE AREAS: DUI Defense; Criminal Litigation.
Brittain, John C. .... '44 '69 C&L.329 B.A., J.D. Prof. of Law, Univ. of Conn.
Broadus, Charlsa D. '68 '92 C.197 B.A. L.94 J.D. (adm. in DC; not adm. in CT) [Ⓒ Day,B.&H.]
*PRACTICE AREAS: Commercial Litigation; Insurance; Torts.
Brodeur, Margaret R. ....'61 '86 C.855 B.A. L.982 J.D. ITT Hartford Ins. Grp.
Broer, Stephen H. ....'66 '99 C.184 B.S. L.1048 J.D. [Ⓐ Halloran&S.]
*PRACTICE AREAS: Appellate Practice; Litigation; Insurance Coverage; Insurance Bad Faith.
Bromberg, Louis J., (BV) ....'59 '84 C.855 B.S. L.184 J.D. 999 Asylum Ave.
Brooks, Donna L., (BV) .... '60 '85 C.945 B.A. L.893 J.D. [Shipman&G.]
*PRACTICE AREAS: Venture Capital; Emerging Growth Companies; Business Law; Commercial Finance; Mergers and Acquisitions.
Brooks, Janet Pauline, (BV) ....'54 '81 C.918 B.A. L.588 J.D. Asst. Atty. Gen.
Brooks, Kara L. ....'— '94 C.1044 B.S. L.94 J.D. [Ⓐ Brown,R.F.&G.]
*PRACTICE AREAS: Complex Commercial Litigation; Intellectual Property Litigation.
Brooks, Robert A., (AV) ....'53 '81 C.67 B.A. L.184 J.D. [Day,B.&H.]
*PRACTICE AREAS: Technology & Intellectual Property - Litigation; Commercial Litigation.
Brooks, Robert S. '47 '75 C.94 B.S. L.818 J.D. Asst. Gen. Coun., Hartford Financial Services Group, Inc.
Brown, Avry L. ....'63 '90 C.105 B.A. L.893 J.D. Asst. Atty. Gen.

Brown, Daniel P., Jr., (AV) . . . . '43 '68 C.951 B.A. L.976 LL.B. [Shipman&G.]
*PRACTICE AREAS: Corporate Law; Business Law; Corporate Finance; Corporate Trust Law.
Brown, Dennis O., (BVⓉ) . . . . '54 '89 C.475 B.A. L.184 J.D. [Ⓒ LeBoeuf,L.G.&M.]
*PRACTICE AREAS: Commercial Litigation; Employment Law; Business Law.
Brown, Frank J. . . . . '34 '60 C.184 B.S. L.94 LL.B. 57 Pratt St.
Brown, Iris June, (AV) . . . . '48 '77 C.174 B.A. L.184 J.D. [Rogin,N.C.L.&H.]
*PRACTICE AREAS: Tax Law; Business Law.
Brown, James E. . . . . '50 '74 C.321 B.A. L.184 J.D. Reg. Gen. Coun., Aetna Inc.
Brown, Judith A. . . . . '50 '89 C.188 B.S. L.184 J.D. Asst. Atty. Gen.
Brown, Michael H.M. . . . . '67 '96 C.604 B.A. L.588 J.D. [Ⓐ Bingham D.]
Brown, Nathaniel G. '55 '92 C&L.855 B.A., J.D. 646 Prospect Ave.
Brown, Paul F. . . . . '47 '73 C&L.184 B.A., J.D. Chief Bail Comm.
Brown, Peter J., (BV) . . . .'60 '90 C.1030 B.A. L.1048 J.D. [Ⓐ Noble,Y.&O.]
*PRACTICE AREAS: Insurance Defense; Personal Injury; Products Liability.
Brown, Richard R., (AV) '45 '71 C.454 B.A. L.184 J.D.
[Brown,P.&S.] (⊙Glastonbury)
*PRACTICE AREAS: Criminal Law; Civil Litigation; Administrative Law.

Brown, Paindiris & Scott, LLP, (AV)
100 Pearl Street, 06103-4506 ⊙
Telephone: 860-522-3343 Telecopier: 860-522-2490
URL: http://www.bpslawyers.com
Members of Firm: Richard R. Brown; Nicholas Paindiris; Ronald T. Scott; John D. Maxwell; Kenneth T. Kelley; Donald L. Hamer; Kate W. Haakonsen; Steven W. Varney; Christopher J. McCarthy; Sean M. Peoples; David S. Rintoul. Associates: Robert T. Rimmer; Simon J. Lebo; Courtney P. Staron. Of Counsel: Theodore J. DiLorenzo.
General Practice. Administrative, Bankruptcy, Commercial, Communications, Corporate, Criminal, Education, Employment, Estate Planning, Family, Immigration, Insurance, Landlord and Tenant, Municipal, Personal Injury, Probate, Real Estate. Trials and Appeals in all Courts.
Glastonbury, Connecticut Office: The Old Town Hall, 2252 Main Street, 06033. Telephone: 860-659-0700. Fax: 860-659-8292.
Stamford, Connecticut Office: 6 Landmark Square, Suite 400. Telephone: 203-359-5772.
East Hampton, Connecticut Office: 42 East High Street, 06424. Telephone: 860-267-2044.
Hebron, Connecticut Office: 10 Main Street, 06248. Telephone: 860-228-3506.
See Professional Biographies, HARTFORD, CONNECTICUT

Brown Raysman Millstein Felder & Steiner LLP, (AV)
CityPlace II, 185 Asylum Street, 10th Floor, 06103 ⊙
Telephone: 860-275-6400 Fax: 860-275-6410
URL: http://www.brownraysman.com
Members of Firm: Norman H. Roos; Beverly W. Garofalo; Robert D. Gilbert. Counsel: H. David Leventhal; Bruce H. Leshine (Not admitted in CT); Richard M. Borden. Resident Associates: Samuel L. Molinari; James R. Kinyon; Candace M. Cunningham; Joseph M. Pastore, III; Diane Duhaime; Mitchell L. Fishberg; Catherine L. Moreton; Nathaniel Selleck; Douglas D. Sheehan; Karen Baldwin Kravetz; Donald R. Ballman; Frederik F. Erikson (Not admitted in CT); David B. Benoit.
General Practice. Computer, Corporate, Securities, Real Estate, Internet, High Technology, Commercial Finance, Employment, Insurance, Patent, Copyright, Trademarks, Bankruptcy, Equipment Leasing and Tax. Trial and Appellate Practice.
New York, New York Office: 900 Third Avenue. Telephone: 212-895-2000. Fax: 212-895-2900.
Los Angeles, California Office: 1880 Century Park East, Suite 711. Telephone: 310-712-8300. Fax: 310-712-8383.
Morristown, New Jersey Office: 55 Madison Avenue, Suite 70. Telephone: 973-285-3222. Fax: 973-285-3262.
Uniondale, New York Office: EAB Plaza, West Tower, 6th Floor, 11556-0615 (Long Island). Telephone: 516-522-2731. Fax: 516-522-2731.
Toronto, Ontario, Canada Office: 2407-40 King Street West, M5H 3 Y2. Telephone: 416-657-4470. Facsimile: 416-657-4475.
See Professional Biographies, HARTFORD, CONNECTICUT

Brown, Rudnick, Freed & Gesmer, (AV)
A Partnership of Professional Corporations
Cityplace I, 185 Asylum Street, 06103-3402 ⊙
Telephone: 860-509-6500 Fax: 860-509-6501
URL: http://www.brownrudnick.com
Members of Firm: Robert J. Anthony (Resident); Mark A. Asmar (Resident); Mark S. Baldwin (Resident); Catherine Barr (Resident); Lawrence F. Cafero, Jr. (Resident); Douglas A. Cohen (Resident); Scott P. Consoli (Resident); Brian C. Courtney (Resident); Franca L. DeRosa (Resident); J. Hanson Guest (Resident); Harvey Hoberman (Resident); Thomas D. Ritter (Resident); Howard L. Siegel (Resident); Philip M. Small (Resident);—Kara L. Brooks (Resident); Michael J. Camilleri (Resident); Sandra K. Davis (Resident); David E. Golden (Resident); Michael E. Kozlik (Resident); Veronica J. Lee (Resident); Jonathan M. Lewis (Resident); Thomas J. Regan (Resident).
Banking, Bankruptcy, Civil Litigation, Corporate, Employment, Environmental, ERISA, Family, Government Relations, Health Care, High Technology, Insurance Coverage, Intellectual Property, International, Media, Patents, Public and Structured Finance, Real Estate, Secured Lending, Securities, Taxation.
Boston, Massachusetts Office: One Financial Center. Telephone: 617-856-8200. Fax: 617-856-8201.
Providence, Rhode Island Office: One Providence Washington Plaza. Telephone: 401-276-2600. Fax: 401-276-2601.
London, England Office: 8 Clifford Street. Telephone: +44-20-7851-6000. Fax: +44-20-7851-6100.
See Professional Biographies, HARTFORD, CONNECTICUT

Browne, Francis J., (BV) . . . '59 '84 C.602 B.A. L.94 J.D. [Ⓒ Alderman&A.] (⊙Stamford)
*PRACTICE AREAS: Business Organizations.
Brunjes, John A. . . . . '62 '89 C.165 A.B. L.188 J.D. 225 Asylum Street, 13th Floor
Brunstad, G. Eric, Jr., (AV) . . . . '61 '86 C.183 B.A. L.477 J.D. [Bingham D.]
*PRACTICE AREAS: Appellate; Bankruptcy.
Bucci, Michael A., (BV) . . . . '62 '91 C.823 B.S. L.1065 J.D. [Day,B.&H.]
*PRACTICE AREAS: Technology and Intellectual Property - Litigation; Commercial Litigation.
Buck, Bradford H., (AV) '52 '77
C.184 B.A. L.94 J.D. Coun., Phoenix Home Life Mut. Ins. Co.
*RESPONSIBILITIES: Real Estate; Bankruptcy; Environmental Law.
Buck, Gurdon H., (AV) . . . .'— '65 C.401 B.A. L.659 J.D. [Robinson&C.]
*PRACTICE AREAS: Real Estate; Zoning, Planning and Land Use; Common Interest Communities; Condominiums; Urban Villages.
Buckingham, Harold C., Jr., (AV) . . . .'30 '57 C.918 B.A. L.893 J.D. [Ⓒ Day,B.&H.]
*PRACTICE AREAS: Estate Administration; Trust Administration; Estate Planning; Small Business Law; Nonprofit Corporations.
Buckley, John F., Jr., (BV) . . . . '59 '84 C.478 B.S. L.184 J.D. [Buckley&W.] ⊙
Buckley & Wynne, (BV) . . . . .10 Columbus Blvd. (⊙New Haven)
Bucknam, Andrew G. '63 '91 C.478 B.A. L.184 J.D.
Coun. Select Lit., Hartford Financial Services Group, Inc.
Bucknam, Heather Wilson . . . . '69 '96 C.105 B.A. L.184 J.D. [Ⓐ Updike,K.&S.]
*PRACTICE AREAS: Business Law; Commercial Lending; Real Estate.
Budlong, C. Michael, (BV) . . . .'44 '69 C.184 B.A. L.421 J.D. 89 Oak St.
Budlong, Jonathan P. . . . .'72 '00 C.421 B.A. L.1048 J.D. 89 Oak St.
Budzik, Matthew J. . . . .'65 '98 C.29 B.A. L.276 J.D. [Ⓐ Murtha C.]
Bufford, Alexandria L. . . . . '73 '99 C.477 B.A. L.184 J.D. [Howd&L.]
*PRACTICE AREAS: Municipal Litigation; Insurance Defense Litigation; Employment Law.
Bukowski, Chester J., Jr. . . . .'52 '77 C.855 B.A. L.178 J.D. [Ⓒ Michelson,K.R.&B.]
*PRACTICE AREAS: Construction Law; Design Professional Liability; Appellate Practice.
Bunge, Kenneth E. '46 '72 C.107 B.A. L.724 J.D.
Mng. Atty., United Techologies Corp.
*RESPONSIBILITIES: Corporate Law.
Burke, Barbara T. . . . . '56 '99 C.823 B.S. L.1048 J.D. [Ⓐ Day,B.&H.]
*PRACTICE AREAS: Insurance Litigation; Torts Litigation.
Burkley, Zisca . . . . '74 '00 C.1507 B.A. L.1019 J.D. [Ⓐ Rome M.S.]
Burns, Eban D., (CV) . . . . '55 '85 C&L.184 B.A., J.D. 19 Cumberland St.

Burns, Joseph B., (BV) . . . .'60 '85 C.94 B.A. L.1048 J.D. [Rome M.S.]
*PRACTICE AREAS: Litigation.
Burns, Peter M. '45 '77 C.712 B.A. L.1048 J.D.
(adm. in MA; not adm. in CT) Coun., Travelers Ins. Co.
Burns, Thomas J. '48 '79
C.321 B.A. L.184 J.D. Coun., Phoenix Home Life Mut. Ins. Co.
*RESPONSIBILITIES: ERISA; Employee Benefits; Pension Plans.
Burrick, Todd S. . . . . '64 '96 C.1349 B.A. L.306 J.D. Actuarial Assoc., HartRe
Burroughs, Katherine A., (BV) . . . . '63 '88 C.188 B.S. L.945 J.D. [Ⓐ Dechert]
*PRACTICE AREAS: Real Estate Finance; Securitization; Bankruptcy.
Busby, Susan . . . . '61 '93 C.012 B.A. L.184 J.D. [Louden]
Busher, Joseph M., Jr. . . . .'70 '96 C.321 A.B. L.184 J.D. [Jackson,O.&P.]
*PRACTICE AREAS: Civil Trial Practice; Insurance Defense; Appellate Practice.
Butler, Barry A., (BV) . . . .'57 '84 C.184 B.A. L.1029 J.D. Chf. Pub. Def. Off.
Butler, Jolyan A. '45 '72 C.1108 B.A. L.184 J.D.
Coun., Connecticut Mutual Life Insurance Company
Butler Norris & Gold, (BV) . . . . 254 Prospect Ave.
Buttner, Indrek H. . . . . '51 '81 C.184 B.A. L.823 J.D. [Ⓐ Reid&R.]
*PRACTICE AREAS: Real Estate; Real Estate Finance; Real Estate Acquisitions; Real Estate Sales; Commercial Leasing.
Bye, Gareth D. . . . . '63 '88 C.262 B.A. L.823 J.D. Legal Off., Dept. of Pub. Health
Byrne, James F., (AV) . . . . '40 '66 C.415 B.A. L.262 J.D. [Byrne&S.]
*PRACTICE AREAS: Commercial Real Estate; Corporate Law; Commercial Financing; Workouts; Restructuring.
Byrne, James R. . . . .'69 '94 C.94 B.A. L.184 J.D. [Ⓐ Tyler C.&A.]
*PRACTICE AREAS: Commercial Litigation.
Byrne, Thomas P. '61 '91
C.1030 B.S. L.1252 J.D. Asst. Gen. Coun., The Advest Grp., Inc.
*RESPONSIBILITIES: Securities Law; Litigation; Corporate Law.

Byrne & Storm, P.C., (AV)
330 Main Street, P.O. Box 231315, 06123-1315
Telephone: 860-525-3700 Telecopy: 860-525-0287
Email: info@byrnestorm.com URL: http://www.byrnestorm.com
James F. Byrne; Christina M. Storm; Rodger C. Boe; Robert L. Iamonaco; Tennyson S. Anthony.
General Practice, Commercial, Real Estate, Transactions, Foreclosures and Work Outs, Zoning, Corporate, Domestic and Commercial Litigation, Employment Discrimination Defense, Federal and State Court, Trial and Appellate.
See Professional Biographies, HARTFORD, CONNECTICUT

Bysiewicz, Susan . . . .'61 '86 C.976 B.A. L.228 J.D. Secy. of State
Bystrowski, Robert S., (BV) . . . . '66 '91 C.222 B.A. L.184 J.D. [Morrison,M.&M.]
*PRACTICE AREAS: Workers Compensation; Insurance Defense Litigation; Products Liability; Employment.
Cafero, Lawrence F., Jr., (BV) . . . .'— '82 C.184 B.A. L.1048 J.D. [Brown,R.F.&G.]
*PRACTICE AREAS: Real Estate; Administrative Law.
Caffrey, Robert J. . . . . '59 '84 C.602 B.A. L.930 J.D. [Ⓐ Berman&S.]
*PRACTICE AREAS: Commercial Litigation; Construction Litigation; Business Litigation; Products Liability Defense; Insurance.
Cahill, Laura Anne . . . . '59 '84 C.93 B.A. L.184 J.D. Off. of U.S. Sen.
Cain, George H., (AV) . . . . '20 '48 C.276 B.S.S. L.309 J.D. [Ⓒ Day,B.&H.]
*PRACTICE AREAS: Corporate Finance; Mergers and Acquisitions; Corporate Control Disputes.
Calafiore, Frances Z., (BV) . . . . '53 '85 C.951 B.A. L.306 J.D. 55 Airport Rd.
Caldwell, Donald B., (AV) '30 '54
C.367 A.B. L.184 LL.B. Exec. Dir., Conn. Jud. Rev. Coun.
Calhoun, Jose M., (AV) . . . . '28 '53 C.976 B.A. L.309 J.D. 1 Constitution Plaza‡
Calibey, Kathryn, (BV) . . . . '53 '82 C.184 B.A. L.1048 J.D. [RisCassi&D.]
*PRACTICE AREAS: Negligence; Medical Malpractice; Appellate Practice.
Caligiuri, Sam S.F. . . . .'66 '94 C.93 B.A. L.128 J.D. [Ⓐ Day,B.&H.]
Calio, Christopher T. . . . .'73 '00 C.855 B.A. L.184 J.D. [Ⓐ Cummings&L.]
Call, David M., (AV) . . . . '43 '68 C.184 B.A. L.178 LL.B. [Rogin,N.C.L.&H.]
*PRACTICE AREAS: Business Law; Securities Regulation; Taxation; Estate Planning.
Callahan, Albert J., (BV) . . . . '28 '54 C.676 A.B. L.94 LL.B. 21 Oak St.
Callahan, Katherine C., (BV) . . . . '59 '84 C.93 B.A. L.184 J.D. [Updike,K.&S.]
*PRACTICE AREAS: Professional Defense; Appellate Law; Commercial Litigation.
Callahan, Kerry R., (BV) . . . . '61 '89 C.478 B.A. L.184 J.D. [Updike,K.&S.]
*PRACTICE AREAS: Civil Litigation; Professional Malpractice and Insurance Defense; Personal Injury Law; Insurance Coverage; Construction Litigation.
Callas, George N. '26 '50 L.669 LL.B.
(adm. in MA; not adm. in CT) 133 Mountain St.‡
Calloway, Deborah A. '49 '80 C.478 B.A. L.276 J.D.
(adm. in DC; not adm. in CT) Prof. of Law, Univ. of Conn.
Calvert, Elizabeth A. . . . .'77 '01 C.999 B.A. L.188 J.D. [Ⓐ Bingham D.]
*PRACTICE AREAS: Litigation.
Calvocoressi, John L., (BV) . . . . '17 '56 C.309 A.B. L.184 LL.B. [Ⓒ Gale&K.] ‡
*PRACTICE AREAS: Liquor Licensing; Administrative Law; Property Tax Appeals.
Camilleri, Michael J. . . . . '— '00 C.855 B.A. L.184 J.D [Ⓐ Brown,R.F.&G.]
*PRACTICE AREAS: Commercial Real Estate.
Campane, Lawrence J., (BV) . . . . '45 '72 C.776 B.A. L.184 J.D. [Sullivan,S.C.&C.]
Campbell, Andrew B. . . . . '19 '54 C.823 L.184 LL.B. Secy., The Travelers Ins. Co.
Campbell, James M., (AVⓉ) '58 '83 C.93 B.A. L.893 J.D.
(adm. in MA; not adm. in CT)
[Campbell C.E.&C.] (⊙Boston, MA; Port., ME; Concord, NH; Providence, RI)

Campbell Campbell Edwards & Conroy, Professional Corporation, (AVⓉ)
Two Riverview Square, 06108 ⊙
Telephone: 860-291-8419 Fax: 860-291-8428
Email: info@campbell-trial-lawyers.com URL: http://www.campbell-trial-lawyers.com
James M. Campbell (Not admitted in CT);—Holly M. Polglase.
Complex Litigation and Business Counseling, Multi-District Litigation, Class Actions, Products Liability, Business Law, Toxic Torts, Environmental Law, Employment Law and Professional Liability.
Portland, Maine Office: 50 Monument Square, 04101. Telephone: 207-780-1190. Fax: 207-780-1194.
Boston, Massachusetts Office: One Constitution Plaza, Third Floor, 02129. Telephone: 617-241-3000. Fax: 617-241-5115.
Concord, New Hampshire Office: 14 South Street, 03301. Telephone: 603-226-4111. Fax: 603-226-4111.
Turnersville, New Jersey Office: Washington Professional Campus II, 901 Route 168, Suite 201, 08012. Telephone: 856-374-8300. Fax: 856-374-8301.
Wayne, Pennsylvania Office: Three Glenhardie Corporate Center, 1265 Drummers Lane, Suite 2000, 19087. Telephone: 610-964-1900. Fax: 610-964-1981.
Providence, Rhode Island Office: 123 Dyer Street, 02903. Telephone: 401-421-5123. Fax: 401-421-5136.
See Professional Biographies, HARTFORD, CONNECTICUT

Campion, Carrie J. . . . . '74 '00 C.1349 B.A. L.93 J.D. [Ⓐ Updike,K.&S.]
*PRACTICE AREAS: Labor and Employment; Municipal Law.
Canavan, Daniel R. . . . . '75 '00 C.999 B.S. L.1252 J.D. [Ⓐ Updike,K.&S.]
*PRACTICE AREAS: Insurance Defense; Appellate; Litigation.
Canino, Cheryl Ann . . . .'60 '97 C.306 B.A. L.184 J.D. 1229 Albany Ave., 4th Fl.
Cantin, Raynald B., (BV) . . . .'43 '70 C.712 B.A. L.184 J.D. 97 Elm St.
Cantor, Donald J., (AV) . . . . '31 '59 C&L.309 A.B., J.D. [Hyman,C.&K.]

Cantor Colburn LLP
(See Bloomfield)

Caplan, Jerome E., (AV) ....'27 '51 C.659 B.S. L.976 LL.B. [Rogin,N.C.L.&H.]
*PRACTICE AREAS: Bankruptcy Litigation; Corporate Law; Partnership Law; Commercial Law.
Cappalli, Lisa J., (BV) ... '58 '84 C.401 B.A. L.188 J.D. 43 Woodland Street (⊙Cheshire)
Carberry, Glenn T., (BV) ....'55 '79 C.282 B.A. L.659 J.D. [Tobin,C.O.R.&S.] ⊙
*PRACTICE AREAS: Banking Law; Corporate Law; Land Use; Administrative Law; Telecommunications Law.
Cardwell, M. Donald, (BV) ....'33 '63 C.855 B.A. L.93 LL.B. [Cardwell,C.&S.]
Cardwell, Nicholas P., (BV) ....'34 '64 C.1033 B.A. L.184 LL.B. [Cardwell,C.&S.]
Cardwell, Cardwell & Smoragiewicz, (BV) .... 108 Oak St.
Carey, Austin, Jr., (AV) ....'43 '68 C.976 B.A. L.608 J.D. [A.Carey,Jr.]
*PRACTICE AREAS: Environmental Law; Environmental Insurance Claims; Litigation.

Carey, Austin, Jr., P.C., (AV)
Gothic Park, Suite 200, 43 Woodland Street, 06105-2340
Telephone: 860-724-0012 Fax: 860-724-1211
Email: acarey@careyfirm.com
Austin Carey, Jr.
Environmental Law, Environmental Insurance Claims, Litigation.
See Professional Biographies, HARTFORD, CONNECTICUT

Carlow, Donald N., (CV) ....'54 '81 C.30 B.A. L.184 J.D. 999 Asylum Ave.
Carlson, Herbert E., Jr., (BV) '42 '69 C.197 A.B. L.184 J.D.
Supervisory Sr. Asst. State's Atty., Div. Crim. Jus.
Carpenter, Christine A. '— '91 C.1044 B.A. L.1029 J.D.
Assoc. Coun., Travelers Ins. Co.
Carr, David Brian ....'58 '85 C.1021 B.A. L.1048 J.D. 99B Hamner St.
Carr, Kevin J. '54 '81 C.1033 B.A. L.221 J.D.
Coun., Hartford Financial Services Group, Inc.
Carroll, James J. .... '72 '98 C&L.184 B.A., J.D. [Shipman&G.]
*PRACTICE AREAS: Federal Taxation; State and Local Tax; Tax Exempt Organizations; Partnership Taxation.
Carvlin, Stephanie M. .... '57 '85 C.1307 B.A. L.184 J.D. State. Judicial Dept.
Casazza, William J., (AV) '55 '85 C.860 B.A. L.188 J.D.
V.P., Dep. Gen. Coun. & Corp. Secy., Aetna Inc.
*RESPONSIBILITIES: Mergers and Acquisitions; Securities Law; Corporate Law; Governance.
Case, Edward W. ....'58 '87 C.829 B.A. L.1048 J.D. 21 Oak St.
Case, Gary M. ....'66 '91 C.1030 B.S. L.184 J.D. [Wolf,H.E.&C.]
*PRACTICE AREAS: Civil Litigation; Insurance Defense; Fidelity and Surety; Toxic Torts.
Casella, Raymond J. .... '66 '99 C.1134 B.S. L.1048 J.D. [Shipman&G.]
*PRACTICE AREAS: Tax.
Casey, Coleman H., (AV) .... '47 '73 C.31 B.A. L.976 J.D. [Shipman&G.]
*PRACTICE AREAS: Real Estate Law; Public Finance; Commercial Finance; Independent Schools Law.
Casey, Joel B. ....'70 '98 [Cummings&L.]
Casey, Karen Jansen, (BV) ....'55 '81 C.882 B.A. L.184 J.D. [Cooney,S.&D.]
Casey, Peter J., (BV) ....'64 '90 C.94 B.S. L.1029 J.D. [Regnier,T.C.&E.]
*PRACTICE AREAS: General Practice; Trial Practice; Insurance; Toxic Torts; Products Liability.
Cashman, Stephen F., (BV) .... '56 '82 C.184 B.A. L.831 J.D. 179 Allyn St.
Caspar, George J. '33 '57
C.608 B.S. L.477 LL.B. Coun. & Corp. Secy., The Travelers Corp.
Cass, David M. ....'53 '85 C.858 B.A. L.184 J.D. CIGNA Corp.
Cassetta, Frank N. ....'63 '97 C.184 B.F.A. L.1009 J.D. [Pepe&H.]
Cassidy, Joseph J., (BV) ....'58 '84 C.184 B.A. L.1019 J.D. [Rome M.S.]
*PRACTICE AREAS: Commercial and Tax Litigation; Intellectual Property Litigation; General Civil Litigation; Appellate Practice.
Cassot, Robert William ....'63 '96 C.338 B.S. L.1358 J.D. [Morrison,M.&M.]
*PRACTICE AREAS: General Litigation; Insurance Defense; Medical Malpractice.
Cathcart, Frank H., (BV) .... '56 '82 C.321 A.B. L.184 J.D. 43 Woodland St.
Cathcart, Robert J., (AV) .... '35 '62 C.309 B.A. L.930 LL.B. [Shipman&G.]
*PRACTICE AREAS: Civil Litigation; Insurance Coverage and Defense; ERISA Litigation; Personal Injury Law.
Catino, Ann M., (BV) ....'60 '87 C.708 A.B. L.383 J.D. [Halloran&S.]
*PRACTICE AREAS: Environmental Law; Environmental Litigation; Land Use; Administrative Law.
Cavanaugh, Dennis C., (BV) ....'56 '81 C.184 B.A. L.472 J.D. [Halloran&S.]
*PRACTICE AREAS: Construction Law; Fidelity and Surety Law; Business Litigation.
Cavanaugh, Susan J., (AV) '57 '82 C.588 B.S. L.1048 J.D.
Coun., Hartford Financial Services Group, Inc.
Cavicke, David L. .... '61 '89 C.178 A.B. L.813 J.D. Supr. Ct.
Cavilia, John W. ....'50 '84 C.740 B.A. L.276 J.D. Coun., The Travelers Corp.
Celentano, James M. ....'69 '96 C.184 B.A. L.306 J.D. [Cramer,A.&F.]
*PRACTICE AREAS: Insurance Law; Personal Injury; Bad Faith Litigation.
Cella, Thomas P., (BV) '57 '83
C.184 B.A. L.1048 J.D. [Howard,K.S.&F.] (⊙Manchester)
*PRACTICE AREAS: Civil Litigation.
Chabot, David A., (BV) ....'58 '86 C.93 B.S. L.273 J.D. Hartford Plaza
Chaclas, George .... '65 '99 C.454 B.S. L.306 J.D. [Cummings&L.]
Chambers, Theodore D. ....'31 '57 C.184 B.A. L.976 LL.B. 1 Financial Plz.
Chambers-Ford, Jeanette T. .... '53 '79 C.103 B.A. L.597 J.D. 57 Pratt St.
Champlin, William H., III, (AV) ....'46 '72 C.276 B.S. L.184 J.D. [Tyler C.&A.]
*PRACTICE AREAS: Litigation, Alternative Dispute Resolution.
Chapple, Wayne E. ....'50 '90 C.745 B.A. L.1048 J.D. [Globman,M.&C.]
Charron, Mary Anne Alicia, (BV) ....'61 '86 C.321 A.B. L.128 J.D. [Gordon,M.&F.]
*PRACTICE AREAS: Construction; Surety/Fidelity; Social Security Disability; Probate.
Chase, Cheryl A. '53 '79
C.860 B.A. L.184 J.D. Exec. V.P. & Gen. Coun., Chase Enterprises
Chatigny, Robert N. .... '51 '78 C.103 A.B. L.276 J.D. U.S. Dist. J.
Chatinover, Leah Cohen, (BV) ....'57 '85 C.66 B.A. L.976 J.D. [Reid&R.]
*PRACTICE AREAS: Business Law; Corporate Law; Nonprofit Organizations Law; Intellectual Property.
Chavey, Victoria Woodin ....'66 '92 C.197 B.A. L.94 J.D. [Day,B.&H.]
*PRACTICE AREAS: Employment Litigation; Employment Law.
Chen, Carlton S. '51 '83 C.178 B.A. L.569 J.D.
Vice President, General Counsel & Secretary, Colt's Manufacturing Company, Inc.
Chester, Samuel D., (AV) ....'49 '74 C.966 B.A. L.61 J.D. [Hunt L.C.&J.]
*PRACTICE AREAS: Foreclosure; Commercial Litigation; Collection.
Chill, Paul .... '56 '85 C.918 B.A. L.184 J.D. Clinical Prof. of Law, Univ. of Conn.
Chilton, Ralph H., (AV) '30 '61
C.679 B.S.M.E. L.273 J.D. [Alix,Y.&R.] (See Pat. Sect.)
Chin, Ralph, (BV) .... '53 '85 C.1044 B.A. L.569 J.D. Coun., The Travelers Ins. Co.

Chinitz, Stephen S., & Associates
(See Bloomfield)

Chinni, Christine L. ....'62 '91 C.477 B.A. L.1048 J.D. [Shipman&G.]
*PRACTICE AREAS: Management Labor Law; Public School Law; School Board Defense; School Equal Protection.
Chioffi, Joseph, (BV) '61 '87 C&L.184 B.A., J.D.
Assoc. Coun., Hartford Financial Services Group, Inc.
Chipman, Christine L. ....'58 '87 C.118 B.A. L.306 J.D. [Gordon,M.&F.]
*PRACTICE AREAS: Corporate Law; Limited Liability Company Law; Real Estate; Commercial Finance.

Cho, Douglas A., (BV) .... '62 '91 C.918 B.A. L.184 J.D. [T.P.Willcutts&Assoc.]
*PRACTICE AREAS: Securities Litigation; Securities Arbitration; Commercial Litigation; Legal Malpractice; Professional Malpractice.
Chorches, Ronald I. ....'64 '91 C.787 B.A. L.1048 J.D. 1010 Wethersfield Ave.

Chorches & Novak, P.C.
(See Wethersfield)

Chotkowski, Alexander J. ....'70 '96 C.901 B.A. L.1218 J.D. [Rome M.S.]
*PRACTICE AREAS: Commercial Litigation; Insurance Defense; Products Liability Defense.
Christensen, M. Jane, (BV) ....'34 '76 C.932 B.A. L.184 J.D. 73 Russ St.
Christensen, Ronald M., (BV) .... '57 '85 C.676 B.A. L.1048 J.D. 1792 Main St.
Christianson, Dennis P. '42 '68 C&L.546 B.S., J.D.
(adm. in NE; not adm. in CT) Aetna Inc.
Chudwick, Bruce A. .... '57 '88 C.1145 B.S. L.184 J.D. [Shipman&G.]
*PRACTICE AREAS: Municipal Law; Public Finance.
Churchill, Sharon P. .... '53 '92 C&L.184 B.A., J.D. [Cohn B.&S.]
*PRACTICE AREAS: Business Law; Corporate Law; Asset Based Finance; Securities.
Cicchiello, Angelo ....'49 '81 C.184 B.A. L.1029 J.D. 364 Franklin Ave.
Cioffi, Nicholas A. .... '39 '64 C.745 B.A. L.184 J.D. Comr., Dept. of Pub. Safety
Ciottone, Lisa M. ....'70 '00 C.309 A.B. L.262 J.D. [Bingham D.]
*PRACTICE AREAS: Real Estate.
Cipparone, Joseph A., (BV) ....'57 '83 C&L.477 B.A., J.D. [Reid&R.]
*PRACTICE AREAS: Trusts and Estates; Probate; Business Law.
Claflin, Mark J., (BV) .... '59 '84 C.676 B.S. L.184 J.D. [Howd&L.]
*PRACTICE AREAS: Products Liability Litigation; Insurance Defense Litigation; General Trial and Appellate Practice.
Clark, Frederick P. '53 '78 C.855 B.A. L.184 J.D.
Tax Atty., State Dept. of Rev. Servs.‡
Clark, Karen Keefe .... '65 '90 C.321 A.B. L.184 J.D. [Updike,K.&S.]
*PRACTICE AREAS: Appellate; Product Liability; Professional Defense; Commercial Litigation.
Clark, Lori R. ....'64 '98 C.184 B.A. L.1048 [Wiggin&D.]
Clark, Thomas C., (AV) ....'42 '69 C.197 B.A. L.188 J.D. [Tyler C.&A.]
*PRACTICE AREAS: Insurance Coverage Litigation; Civil Litigation; Bad Faith; E-Commerce; Franchise Law.
Clarke, Wm. J. .... '19 '49 C.918 B.A. L.184 LL.B. Asst. Atty. Gen.

Clayman, Markowitz, Tapper and Baram, L.L.C.
(See Bloomfield)

Clayton, Dale M. ....'61 '94 C.28 B.S. L.464 J.D. [Polivy&T.]
*PRACTICE AREAS: Commercial Litigation; Bankruptcy; Real Estate; Secured and Unsecured Lending.
Clemente, Robert G., (BV) ....'63 '88 C.93 B.A. L.184 J.D. [Cooney,S.&D.]
Clemow, Brian, (AV) ....'44 '69 C.309 B.A. L.659 LL.B. [Shipman&G.]
*PRACTICE AREAS: Labor Relations; Employment Law; Education Law.
Clifford, Brian C. ....'67 '98 C.871 B.S. L.306 J.D. [Halloran&S.]
*PRACTICE AREAS: Professional Liability; Admiralty Law.
Clifford, John P., Jr., (BV) ....'54 '80 C.855 B.S. L.472 J.D. [Gersten&C.]
*PRACTICE AREAS: Personal Injury Litigation; Domestic Relations; Family Law; Workers Compensation Law; Divorce Law.
Cloherty, Thomas M., (AV) ....'40 '73 C.93 A.B. L.229 J.D. [Murtha C.]
*PRACTICE AREAS: Labor Law; Employment Law.
Coassin, Lawrence P., (BV) ....'— '83 C.1155 B.S. L.472 J.D. [Robinson&C.]
*PRACTICE AREAS: Mergers and Acquisitions; Corporate Law; Business Law; Finance.
Coatsworth, Karen T. ....'47 '72 350 Church St.
Cobb, Christopher C. ....'65 '91 C.262 B.A. L.818 J.D. 142 Jefferson St.
Cocchiola, Gina '72 '98 C.184 B.A. L.1048 J.D.
(adm. in MA; not adm. in CT) 21 Oak St.
Codeanne, Sharon L. ....'67 '94 C.855 B.A. L.1040 J.D. [Murtha C.]
Cody, Richard .... '58 '86 C&L.184 B.A., J.D. 93 Oak St.
Cody, Thomas P., (BV) ....'— '91 C.105 B.A. L.945 J.D. [Robinson&C.]
*PRACTICE AREAS: Zoning, Planning and Land Use; Environmental Law.
Coe, Glenn E., (AV) ....'44 '74 C.243 B.A. L.184 J.D. [Rome M.S.]
*PRACTICE AREAS: Commercial Litigation; Intellectual Property Litigation; Corporate Investigations and Litigation; Government Investigations; White Collar Crime.
Coffey, Robert D. .... '50 '77 C.705 A.B. L.184 J.D. Conn. Jud. Dept.
Cohen, Alan Curtis, (BV) '45 '81 C.472 B.S. L.1048 J.D.
(adm. in MA; not adm. in CT; Pat.) Assistant Patent Counsel, United Tech. Corp.
Cohen, Burton B., (BV) ....'51 '84 C.855 B.A. L.1048 J.D. [Murtha C.]
*PRACTICE AREAS: Communications Law and Litigation; Cable Television Law; Administrative Law; State Tax.
Cohen, Douglas A., (AV) ....'— '81 C.107 B.A. L.273 J.D. [Brown,R.F.&G.]
*PRACTICE AREAS: Environmental; Energy; Administrative Law.
Cohen, Jonathan G. ....'65 '94 C.855 B.S. L.1019 J.D. 2 Congress St.
Cohen, Mitchell A., (BV) ....'48 '76 C.156 A.B. L.1048 J.D. 43 Woodland St.
Cohen, Richard I., (AV) ....'58 '84 C.918 B.A. L.188 J.D. [Shipman&G.]
*PRACTICE AREAS: ERISA; Pension and Profit Sharing Plans; Employee Benefits.
Cohen, Simon S. ....'09 '31 C.823 L.94 J.D. Ret. Supr. Ct. J.
Cohen, Stanley, (BV) ....'36 '63 C.1033 B.A. L.184 LL.B. 39 Grand St.
Cohn, Henry S., (AV) ....'45 '70 C.367 B.A. L.184 J.D. 75 Elm St.
Cohn, Jean A. '60 '88 C.788 B.A. L.184 J.D.
Coun., Hartford Steam Boiler Inspection & Ins. Co.
Cohn, Linda A. .... '49 '75 C.855 B.A. L.184 J.D. Asst. Clk., Supr. Ct. J.
Cohn, Robert E., (AV) ....'24 '51 C.31 A.B. L.178 LL.B. [Cohn B.&S.] ‡

Cohn Birnbaum & Shea P.C., (AV)
100 Pearl Street, 06103-4500 ⊙
Telephone: 860-493-2200 Fax: 860-727-0361
Robert E. Cohn (Retired); Leslie Inrig Olear; Richard J. Shea, Jr.; Michael F. Mulpeter; Thomas W. Witherington; Scott D. Rosen; Melvin A. Simon; Sharon P. Churchill;—Mary E. R. Bartholic; Douglas S. Pelham; Matthew Feigenbaum (Resident, Westport Office; Also Of Counsel, New York, NY Office); Robert H. Feigenbaum (Resident, Westport Office); Matthew C. McGrath; Stephen D. Oppenheim. Of Counsel: Robert J. Birnbaum.
Banking, Bankruptcy, Business, Commercial, Communications, Condominium, Construction, Contracting, Corporation, Creditors Rights, Employment, Environmental, Finance, Health Care Administrative, Joint Ventures, Land Use, Media, Municipal, Professional Liability Defense, Real Estate, Securities, Shopping Center, Taxation, Technology, Litigation in all State and Federal Courts.
Westport, Connecticut Office: 830 Post Road East, 2nd. Floor. Telephone: 203-341-9595. Fax: 203-341-9696.
New York, New York Office: 67 Wall Street, Suite 2411, 10005. Telephone: 212-949-9555. Fax: 212-949-7997.
See Professional Biographies, HARTFORD, CONNECTICUT

Cole, Charles J., (AV) ....'— '47 C.976 B.A. L.309 LL.B. [Robinson&C.]
Cole, Michael E. ....'59 '92 C.354 B.S. L.1252 J.D. 1 American Row
Cole, Morton E. .... '02 '26 L.94 LL.B. [Cole&C.]
Cole, William K., (AV) ....'— '39 C&L.976 B.A., LL.B. [Robinson&C.]
Cole & Cole ....1 Constitution Plaza
Colla, Raymond A., Jr. .... '68 '97 C&L.184 B.S., J.D. [Day,B.&H.]
*PRACTICE AREAS: Trusts and Estates; Estate Planning; Estate Administration; Trust Law; Estate and Gift Taxation.
Collier, William A. ....'51 '84 C.1030 B.S. L.1029 J.D. State's Atty. Off
Collins, Barbara J., (BV) .... '53 '78 C&L.184 B.A., J.D. 44 Capitol Avenue Suite 402
Collins, Gary H. '65 '92 C.107 B.A. L.880 J.D.
(adm. in IL; not adm. in CT) [Bingham D.]

Collins, Gerard S. '67 '97
C.93 B.A. L.1048 J.D. [Ⓐ O'Connell,F.&A.] (⊙Springfield, MA)
*PRACTICE AREAS: Insurance Defense; Civil Litigation; Commercial Collections; Real Estate; Federal Criminal Law.

Collins, James F. ... '19 '49 C.855 B.S. L.309 LL.B. Supr. Ct. J.

Colosky, Douglas S. ... '69 '97 C.690 B.A. L.1252 J.D. V.P., Travelers Prop. Cas.

Comerford, Brian J., (BV) ... '53 '77 C.1030 B.A. L.818 J.D. Asst. Atty. Gen.

Concepcion, Rick ... '62 '94 C.1134 B.S. L.306 J.D. N.L.R.B.

Condon, Thomas J. ... '46 '76 C.602 B.A. L.184 J.D. 285 Broad St.‡

Cone, H. Maria, (BV) ... '51 '77 C.706 B.A. L.184 J.D. Dep. Corp. Coun.

Connell, Thomas H., (BV) ... '34 '66 C.918 B.A. L.184 J.D. [Ⓒ Michelson,K.R.&B.]
*PRACTICE AREAS: Civil Litigation; Construction Law; Corporate Law; Labor Law.

Connelli, Lawrence L., (BV) ... '58 '83 C&L.184 B.A., J.D. [Regnier,T.C.&E.]
*PRACTICE AREAS: General Practice; Trial Practice; Insurance; Toxic Torts; Products Liability.

Connolly, Mark V., (BV) ... '57 '82 C&L.184 B.A., J.D. [Tyler C.&A.]
*PRACTICE AREAS: Litigation.

Connon, William R. ... '51 '76 C.184 B.A. L.823 J.D. [Sullivan,S.C.&C.]

Connor, James M., (BV) ... '56 '80 C.309 A.B. L.276 J.D. [Updike,K.&S.]
*PRACTICE AREAS: Business Law; Commercial Lending; Real Estate.

Consoli, Scott P. ... '— '86 C.454 B.A. L.93 J.D. [Brown,R.F.&G.]
*PRACTICE AREAS: Real Estate Development; Commercial Leasing; Commercial Lending; Loan Workouts.

Conway, Karen P. ... '54 '96 C.788 A.B. L.1048 J.D. [Ⓐ Cummings&L.]
*PRACTICE AREAS: Corporate; Health.

Conway, Matthew G., (BV) ... '66 '91 C.93 B.A. L.818 J.D. [Danaher,T.L.&N.]
*PRACTICE AREAS: Products Liability; Personal Injury.

Coombes, Kevin W., (BV) ... '47 '76 C.381 B.A. L.1048 J.D. [McCarthy,S.&C.]

Coon, Lorinda S., (BV) ... '57 '84 C.1044 B.S. L.982 J.D. [Ⓐ Cooney,S.&D.]

Cooney, David W., (AV) ... '53 '78 C.705 B.A. L.184 J.D. [RisCassi&D.]
*PRACTICE AREAS: Insurance Litigation; Professional Liability; Medical Malpractice; Negligence.

Cooney, Eugene A., (AV) ... '50 '77 C.745 B.A. L.184 J.D. [Cooney,S.&D.]
*PRACTICE AREAS: Medical Malpractice; Insurance Coverage; Administrative Law.

Cooney, Scully and Dowling, (AV)
Hartford Square North, Ten Columbus Boulevard, 06106
Telephone: 860-527-1141 Fax: 860-247-5215
Members of Firm: Joseph P. Cooney (1906-1984); Henry Cooney (1951-1991); Richard A. Ferris (1956-2001); Vincent J. Dowling; Patrick J. Flaherty; Louis B. Blumenfeld; John W. Sitarz; Eugene A. Cooney; John T. Scully; Karen Jansen Casey; Jeffrey C. Pingpank; Paul T. Nowosadko; Herbert J. Shepardson; David A. Haught; James T. Scully; William J. Scully; Robert G. Clemente. Of Counsel: John F. Scully. Associates: Lorinda S. Coon; Rebecca L. Pidlak; Paul A. Croce, II; Jessica D. Meerbergen.
General Practice. Insurance, Corporation, Probate, Construction and Railroad Law. Trials in all Courts.
Reference: Fleet Bank.
See Professional Biographies, HARTFORD, CONNECTICUT

Cooper, Gary G., (AVⓉ) '43 '72 C.1261 L.329 J.D.
(adm. in NY; not adm. in CT) [Moniz,C.&M.] (⊙Elmsford, New York, NY)

Cooper, Isaiah D. ... '55 '91 C.107 B.F.A. L.569 J.D. [Ⓐ Pepe&H.]

Cooper, Susan L. ... '63 '90 C.188 B.A. L.273 J.D. Counsel, CIGNA Corp.

Copp, Belton A., (AV) ... '20 '47 C&L.976 B.A., LL.B. [Ⓒ Copp&B.]

Copp & Berall, LLP, (AV) BB
864 Wethersfield Avenue, 06114
Telephone: 860-249-5261 Fax: 860-249-4111
Email: frank_berall@coppberall.com
Members of Firm: Frank S. Berall. Of Counsel: Belton A. Copp; Mark H. Neikrie.
Taxation, Probate, Wills, Trusts and Estate.
Reference: Fleet Bank, N.A.
See Professional Biographies, HARTFORD, CONNECTICUT

Coppage, Jeffrey B., (BV) ... '52 '79 C.174 B.A. L.184 J.D. Phoenix Life Mut. Ins. Co.

Cordiano, Dean M., (AV) ... '52 '76 C.1044 B.A. L.228 J.D. [Day,B.&H.]
*PRACTICE AREAS: Environmental; Land Use.

Corey, Timothy T., (BV) ... '57 '84 C.047 B.A. L.016 LL.B. [Pepe&H.]
*PRACTICE AREAS: Construction and Surety; Litigation.

Cormier, Susan M., (BV) ... '54 '82 C.676 B.A. L.184 J.D. [Ⓒ Horton,S.&C.]
*PRACTICE AREAS: Civil Litigation; Appellate Practice; Insurance Litigation.

Corrigan, Thomas H. ... '27 '52 C.321 A.B. L.93 LL.B. Supr. Ct. J.

Corrigan, William F., (BV) ... '59 '87 C.1030 B.A. L.1048 J.D. [Howd&L.]
*PRACTICE AREAS: Products Liability Litigation; Insurance Defense; Commercial Litigation; Municipal Litigation.

Corriveau, Christine E. ... '67 '99 C.823 B.S. L.306 J.D. [Ⓐ Miniter&Assoc.]
*PRACTICE AREAS: Civil Rights; Employment Law; Insurance Law.

Coscia, Thomas P. '70 '98 C.1103 B.A. L.1252 J.D.
(adm. in MA; not adm. in CT) [Andros,F.&M.]

Cosgrove, Emmet L. ... '48 '74 C&L.276 B.S.F.S., J.D. Supr. Ct. J.

Cosgrove, Richd. M., (AV) ... '25 '50 C.976 B.A. L.93 LL.B. Sr. Dep. Corp. Coun.

Costas, Peter L., (AV) ... '31 '54 C&L.823 B.S.Chem., J.D. [Pepe&H.]
*PRACTICE AREAS: Antitrust and Trade Regulation; Intellectual Property; International Trade; Civil Litigation.

Costle, Douglas M. '39 '65 C.309 B.A. L.145 J.D.
(adm. in DC; not adm. in CT) [Ⓒ Updike,K.&S.]

Coté, Andrew C., P.C.
(See Sharon)

Coughlan, Joseph D., Jr. ... '34 '64 C.674 A.B. L.276 J.D. 1 Financial Plz.

Coulom, Frank F., Jr., (AV) ... '— '82 C.708 B.A. L.724 J.D. [Robinson&C.]
*PRACTICE AREAS: Litigation; Reinsurance; Insurance.

Courtney, Brian C., (BV) ... '— '87 C&L.93 B.A., J.D. [Brown,R.F.&G.]
*PRACTICE AREAS: Banking Law; Finance; Commercial Lending; Creditors Rights in Bankruptcy.

Couture, Richard T., (AV) ... '47 '74 C.550 B.A. L.184 J.D. Asst. Atty. Gen.

Covello, Alfred V. ... '33 '60 C.309 A.B. L.184 LL.B. U.S. Dist. J.

Cowdery, James T., (AV) ... '53 '80 C.855 B.A. L.184 J.D. [Cowdery,E.&M.]
*PRACTICE AREAS: White Collar Criminal Defense; Commercial Litigation; Professional Discipline.

Cowdery, Ecker & Murphy, L.L.C., (AV)
750 Main Street, 06103-2703
Telephone: 860-278-5555 Facsimile: 860-249-0012
Email: lawyers@cemlaw.com
Members of Firm: James T. Cowdery; Steven D. Ecker; Thomas J. Murphy; James R. Smart.
White Collar Criminal Defense, Commercial Litigation, Personal Injury. Appellate Practice, Professional Discipline.
See Professional Biographies, HARTFORD, CONNECTICUT

Cox, Berkeley, Jr. ... '30 '61 C.976 B.A. L.902 LL.B. 146 Fern St.

Cox, Lawrence A. ... '48 '77 C.339 B.S. L.184 J.D. Sr. Coun., CIGNA Corp. (Pat.)

Cox, Robert B., (BV) ... '54 '80 C.94 B.A. L.184 J.D. [Halloran&S.]
*PRACTICE AREAS: Finance; Bankruptcy; Corporate Law; Real Estate; Energy.

Cox, Thomas R., (BV) ... '54 '80 C.276 B.A. L.184 J.D. Gen. Couns.

Coyle, Michael L., (AV) ... '44 '72 C&L.823 B.S., J.D. [Reid&R.]
*PRACTICE AREAS: Taxation.

Coyne, Shawn P. ... '70 '98 C.550 B.A. L.1048 J.D. [Ⓐ Siegel,O.S.&Z.]
*PRACTICE AREAS: Labor Law; Employment Law; Municipal; Education; Immigration.

Cramer, Christopher B. ... '72 '00 C.745 B.A. L.1252 J.D. [Ⓐ Pepe&H.]

Cramer, Mark R. ... '59 '86 C.918 B.A. L.1048 J.D. [Cramer,A.&F.]
*PRACTICE AREAS: Civil Litigation; Professional Liability; Premises Liability; Insurance; Real Estate Agents and Brokers Errors and Omissions.

Cramer, Alissi & Fontaine, P.C., (BV)
750 Main Street, 16 Floor, Suite 1600, 06103
Telephone: 860-548-1122 Fax: 860-548-1223 URL: http://www.cafpc.com
URL: http://www.lawyers.com/crameralissi
Mark R. Cramer; James A. Alissi; Craig A. Fontaine; Michael J. Dugan;—James M. Celentano; Christopher J. Sochacki; Richard A. Lord, Jr.; Steven B. Ryan.
Civil Litigation, Insurance Defense, Insurance Coverage, Professional Liability, Professional Malpractice, Common Carrier Liability, Personal Injury, Motor Vehicle and Truck Accidents, Liquor Liability, Premises and Product Liability, Trials and Appeals in all courts.
See Professional Biographies, HARTFORD, CONNECTICUT

Cramer & Anderson LLP
(See Litchfield)

Cranmore, J. J., (AV) ... '55 '79 C.67 B.A. L.128 J.D. [Cranmore,F.&M.]

Cranmore, FitzGerald & Meaney, (AV) BB
49 Wethersfield Avenue, 06114-1102
Telephone: 860-522-9100 Telecopier: 860-522-3379
Members of Firm: J. J. Cranmore; John C. FitzGerald, Jr.; Joseph V. Meaney, Jr.; John P. McHugh; Patricia D. Anderson; Michael P. McGoldrick. Associate: Jennifer A. Levack.
Banking, Financial Services, Litigation, Real Estate, Corporate, Bankruptcy, Administrative Law and General Practice.
See Professional Biographies, HARTFORD, CONNECTICUT

Crawford, Beth A. ... '65 '92 C.1107 A.B. L.128 J.D. Asst. Atty. Gen.

Cristofaro, Elizabeth M., (BV) ... '— '84 C.914 B.A. L.184 J.D. [Morrison,M.&M.]
*PRACTICE AREAS: Professional Liability; Defense Litigation.

Croce, Paul A., II ... '70 '99 C.308 B.A. L.306 J.D. [Ⓐ Cooney,S.&D.]

Crosky, Morris, (BV) ... '19 '49 C.472 L.184 LL.B. 59 Hungerford St.

Crosswhite, Ilona T. '45 '83 C.289 B.A. L.306 J.D.
Coun., Hartford Financial Services Group, Inc.

Crowley, Donald F., (BV) ... '30 '59 C&L.184 A.B., J.D. 59 Hungerford St.

Cruz, Alexia E. ... '72 '97 C.309 A.B. L.1117 J.D. [Ⓐ Bingham D.]
*PRACTICE AREAS: Commercial Litigation.

Cuatto, Raymond R., Jr., (BV) ... '49 '81 C.276 B.S.B.A. L.1048 J.D. Dep. Asst. Pub. Def.

Cuddy, William H., (AV) ... '35 '61 C&L.976 B.A., LL.B. [Ⓒ Day,B.&H.]
*PRACTICE AREAS: Mergers, Acquisitions and Divestitures; Corporate Law; Securities Regulation.

Cullina, William M., (AV) ... '21 '48 C.128 A.B. L.976 LL.B. [Ⓒ Murtha C.]
*PRACTICE AREAS: Labor and Employment Law; Health Care Law.

Cullison, Alan D. '36 '62 C.145 B.S. L.352 J.D.
(adm. in IA; not adm. in CT) Prof. of Law, Univ. of Conn.

Cummings, Rochelle S. ... '47 '87 C.477 B.A. L.976 Coun., CIGNA Corp.

Cummings, William F., (BV) ... '63 '88 C&L.107 B.S., J.D. [Tyler C.&A.]
*PRACTICE AREAS: Corporate; Banking; Securities; Investments.

Cummings & Lockwood, (AV)
CityPlace I, 185 Asylum Street, 36th Floor, 06103-3495 ⊙
Telephone: (860) 275-6700 Telecopier: (860) 724-3397
Email: info@cl-law.com URL: http://www.cl-law.com
Partners: Donald L. Borod; Paul L. Bourdeau; Lisa M. Boyle; William H. Bright, Jr.; Timothy S. Fisher; Mark D. Giarratana; Robert B. Katz; Wendi J. Kemp; Gina S. Linstone (Resident, West Hartford, Connecticut Office); James I. Lotstein; John R. Mallin; William H. Narwold (Firm Managing Partner) (Also at Stamford, Connecticut Office); Gregory B. Nokes; Kevin D. O'Leary; Charles D. Ray; Richard R. Rendeiro; Richard Voigt; Jane Kimball Warren; Eric Watt Wiechmann; Holly J. Winger. Counsel: Lauren R. Greenspoon; Margaret M. Murphy. Senior Attorney: Robert B. Fawber (Resident, West Hartford, Connecticut Office). Resident Associates: Christopher T. Calio; Joel B. Casey; George Chaclas; Karen P. Conway; Patrick J. Day; Alfred A. DiVincentis, Jr.; Robert J. Gallo; Fiona M. Greaves; Eric E. Grondahl; Kristina M. Hendrickson; Peter W. Hull; David M. Mack; W. Joseph Nielsen; Moyahoena N. Ogilvie; Heather J. Rhoades; Robert L. Rispoli; Vanessa D. Roberts; Steven D. Shaffer; Alexandra B. Stevens; Evelyn V. Williams; Allison A. Wood.
General Practice. National and Regional Litigation Counsel, Corporate Law, Patent and Intellectual Property, Trusts and Estates, Labor and Employment Law, Mergers and Acquisitions, Partnerships and Joint Ventures, Commercial Lending, Corporate Finance, Creditors' Rights, Bankruptcy and Workouts, Securities Regulation and Litigation, Tax, Insurance, Banking and Financial Services, Leasing, Commercial and Residential Real Estate, Construction, Environmental, Toxic Torts, Health Law, Products Liability Litigation, Probate Litigation, Family Law and International business.
Stamford, Connecticut Office: Four Stamford Plaza, P.O. Box 120, 06904-0120. Telephone: (203) 327-1700. Telecopier: (203) 351-4535.
Greenwich, Connecticut Office: Two Greenwich Plaza, P.O. Box 2505, 06836. Telephone: (203) 869-1200. Telecopier: (203) 869-3120.
New Haven, Connecticut Office: 700 State Street, P.O. Box 1960. 06509-1960. Telephone: (203) 782-3000. Telecopier: (203) 777-3347.
West Hartford, Connecticut Office: Town Center, 29 South Main Street, Suite 208, 06107. Telephone: (860) 275-6700. Telecopier: (860) 313-0293.
Bonita Springs, Florida Office: 24311 Walden Center, Suite 201, 34134. Telephone: (941) 947-8811. Telecopier: (941) 947-8025.
Naples, Florida Office: 3001 Tamiami Trail North, P.O. Box 413032, 34101-3032. Telephone: (941) 262-8311. Telecopier: (941) 263-0703.
See Professional Biographies, HARTFORD, CONNECTICUT

Cunningham, Candace M. ... '60 '87 C.93 B.A. L.940 J.D. [Ⓐ Brown R.M.F.&S.]
*PRACTICE AREAS: Commercial Real Estate; Commercial Finance.

Cunningham, Glenn M. ... '66 '91 C&L.884 B.A., J.D. [Shipman&G.]
*PRACTICE AREAS: Intellectual Property Litigation; Business Litigation; Business Torts Litigation.

Cunningham, Kathryn M. ... '63 '95 C.101 B.A. L.184 J.D. [Jackson,O.&P.]
*PRACTICE AREAS: Civil Trial Practice; Insurance Defense Law; Appellate Practice.

Cunningham, Marina F. '64 '93
C.178 B.S. L.184 J.D. [McCormick,P.&H.] (See Pat. Sect.)
*PRACTICE AREAS: Intellectual Property; Patents; Trademarks; Copyrights; E-Commerce.

Curran, Edmund T., (AV) ... '37 '62 C&L.976 B.A., LL.B. [Regnier,T.C.&E.]
*PRACTICE AREAS: General Practice; Trial Practice; Insurance; Toxic Torts; Products Liability.

Curran, Hugh R., (AVⓉ) '62 '88
C.321 B.A. L.818 J.D. [Ⓒ Bonner K.T.&C.] (⊙Boston, MA)
*PRACTICE AREAS: Trial and Appellate Practice; General Liability; Insurance.

Curry, David A. ... '60 '89 C.31 B.A. L.184 J.D. 102 Oak St.

Curto, Alan P. ... '56 '98 C&L.184 B.S., J.D. [Ⓐ Halloran&S.]
*PRACTICE AREAS: Business; Corporate; Health Care; Telecommunications; Financial Transactions.

Cusano, Todd E. ... '72 '00 C.184 B.A. L.306 J.D. [Ⓐ Updike,K.&S.]
*PRACTICE AREAS: Commercial Litigation; Insurance Defense; Professional Defense.

Cvarch, John A. ... '56 '82 C.103 A.B. L.477 J.D. Coun., The Travelers Ins. Co.

Dacey, Anne E. K. ... '69 '95 C.967 B.A. L.588 J.D. [Ⓐ Shipman&G.]
*PRACTICE AREAS: Health Care Law; Corporate.

Dagon, George A., Jr., (BV) ... '54 '79 C.976 B.A. L.893 J.D. [Murtha C.]
*PRACTICE AREAS: Product Liability; Tort Litigation; Probate Litigation; Trust Litigation; Insurance Litigation for Policyholders.

D'Agostino, John B., (AV) ... '46 '72 C&L.184 B.A., J.D. [Edwards&A.]

Dailey, Renée M. ... '73 '99 C.184 B.A. L.306 J.D. [Ⓐ Bingham D.]
*PRACTICE AREAS: Business; Restructured Finance.

Dalley, Karla A. ... '60 '89 C.1108 B.A. L.306 J.D. 10 Trumbull St.

Dalton, Robert B. ... '43 '67 C.860 B.S. L.94 J.D. V.P., Conn. Mut. Life Ins. Co.

Daly, Edward J., Jr., (AV) ... '29 '57 C.188 B.A. L.184 LL.B. [Silvester&D.]

Daly, Evelyn Mukjian '56 '84
C.938 B.A. L.1048 J.D. The CT. LOB-House DEMS, Capitol Ave.
Daly, John J. . . . . '23 '50 C.855 B.A. L.184 J.D. Trial Ref. J.
Daly, Kenna Irene '50 '84 C.788 A.B. L.107 J.D.
Coun., Hartford Financial Services Group, Inc.
Dames, Jeanine . . . . '75 '00 C.188 B.A. L.262 J.D. 225 Asylum Street, 13th Floor
D'Amico, John E., (BV) . . . . '52 '76 C.860 B.S. L.184 J.D. [Reid&R.]
*PRACTICE AREAS: Bankruptcy; Business Law; Commercial Law; Commercial Real Estate and Finance; Corporate Law.
Danaher, R. Cornelius, Jr., (AV) '47 '73
C&L.276 B.A., J.D. [Danaher,T.L.&N.] (⊙Westport)
Danaher, Robert C., (AV) . . . . '22 '49 C&L.276 A.B., J.D. [Danaher,T.L.&N.]

Danaher, Tedford, Lagnese & Neal, P.C., (AV)
Capitol Place, 21 Oak Street, 06106 ⊙
Telephone: 860-247-3666 Telecopier: 860-547-1321
Email: dtln@dtln.com
R. Cornelius Danaher, Jr.; Frederick B. Tedford; Joyce A. Lagnese; Kenneth R. Neal; Frank H. Santoro; Calum B. Anderson; Matthew G. Conway; Paul T. Edwards; Robert E. Kiley; Thomas O. Anderson;—Stacey L. De Rosa; Nancy A. DeRose; Brian P. Henry; M. Karen Noble; Andrew S. Wildstein. Of Counsel: Robert C. Danaher.
Litigation in State and Federal Courts, Toxic Tort, Insurance Coverage, Insurance Defense, Product Liability, Personal Injury, Criminal, Corporate, Securities, Commercial, Bankruptcy, Real Estate, Land Use, Environmental, Probate, Estate and Tax Law. Medical, Legal, Accountant, Architect and Engineer Professional Malpractice, Fire and Arson Litigation.
Westport Office: 3 Sylvan Road South. Telephone: 203-226-3646.
See Professional Biographies, HARTFORD, CONNECTICUT

Danforth, Brian D. . . . . '72 '97 C.93 B.A. L.306 J.D. 2 Congress St.
Daniells, Thomas M., (BV) . . . . '54 '82 C.197 A.B. L.818 J.D. [Murtha C.]
*PRACTICE AREAS: Real Estate; Corporate; Financing.
Daniels, Eric D., (AV) . . . . '— '86 C.103 B.A. L.93 J.D. [Robinson&C.]
*PRACTICE AREAS: Litigation; Products Liability.
Danker, Albert G., Jr. . . . . '55 '92 C.918 B.A. L.184 J.D. [O'Brien,T.&Y.]
*PRACTICE AREAS: Litigation; Medical Malpractice Defense; Workers Compensation.
D'Antonio, Albert . . . . '54 '79 C.602 B.A. L.184 J.D. 999 Asylum Ave.
D'Auria, Gregory Thomas, (AV) . . . . '63 '88 C&L.184 B.A., J.D. Asst. Atty. Gen.
Davenport, Leslie L., (BV) . . . . '56 '87 C.1030 B.A. L.184 J.D. [Shipman&G.]
*PRACTICE AREAS: Corporate Finance; Securities Regulation.
Davidson, C. Simon . . . . '71 '99 C&L.893 [Day,B.&H.]
Davies, Wendy J., (CV) . . . . '65 '90 C.1033 B.A. L.1048 J.D. [Gersten&C.]
*PRACTICE AREAS: Personal Injury Law; Domestic Law; Criminal Law; Civil Litigation; Divorce Law.
Davis, Andrew N., (BV) . . . . '59 '90 C.855 B.S. L.273 J.D. [LeBoeuf,L.G.&M.]
*PRACTICE AREAS: Environmental Law; Land Use Law; Health and Safety Law.
Davis, Florence K. S. . . . . '68 '97 C.945 B.S. L.276 J.D. [Day,B.&H.]
Davis, Kimberly '64 '91 C.184 B.A. L.306 J.D.
Staff Atty., Legal Aid Soc. of Hartford Co. Inc.
Davis, Rachel O. . . . . '58 '85 C.478 A.B. L.904 J.D. Asst. Atty. Gen.
Davis, Sandra K. . . . . '— '98 C.184 B.A. L.94 J.D. [Brown,R.F.&G.]
*PRACTICE AREAS: Litigation; Employment Law; Zoning Law; Land Use.
Davis, William R., (AV) . . . . '30 '55 C.676 B.A. L.184 LL.B. [RisCassi&D.]
*PRACTICE AREAS: Medical Malpractice; Products Liability; Negligence.
Day, Patrick J. . . . . '69 '98 C.676 B.A. L.1338 J.D. [Cummings&L.]

Day, Berry & Howard LLP, (AV)
CityPlace I, 06103-3499 ⊙
Telephone: 860-275-0100 Telecopier: 860-275-0343
Email: postmaster@dbh.com URL: http://www.dbh.com
Members of Firm in Hartford: J. Danforth Anthony, Jr.; Elizabeth C. Barton; Matthew J. Becker; Paul N. Belval; Harold M. Blinderman; Robert A. Brooks; Michael A. Bucci; Victoria Woodin Chavey; Dean M. Cordiano; David T. Doot; Glenn W. Dowd; David J. Elliott; Michael W. Elsass; Steven M. Fast; Diane M. Fitzgerald; Daniel L. FitzMaurice; Charles W. Fortune; Gerald Garfield; Steven M. Greenspan; Thomas J. Groark, Jr.; Jeffrey G. Grody; Michael F. Halloran; J. Roger Hanlon; Mitchell R. Harris; Richard D. Harris; Thomas F. Harrison; Tricia A. Haught; Paula Lacey Herman; Robert P. Knickerbocker, Jr.; Charles H. Lenore; Timothy R. Lyman; Daniel S. Matos; Ernest J. Mattei; Paul F. McAlenney; James A. McGraw; Kathleen Dondero Monnes; Francis H. Morrison III; John B. Nolan; James H. Rotondo; Edmund M. See; James Sicilian; Robert G. Siegel; Felix J. Springer; James J. Tancredi; Allan B. Taylor; Robert M. Taylor III; Lyn Gammill Walker; Philip S. Walker; Richard J. Wasserman; Thomas R. Wildman; Paul D. Williams; Martin Wolman; Albert Zakarian. Associates of Firm in Hartford: Elizabeth A. Alquist; Christine A. Baily; David M. Bizar; Christopher J. Boccaccio; Mario R. Borelli; Maxwell Branson; Barbara T. Burke; Sam S.F. Caligiuri; Raymond A. Colla, Jr.; C. Simon Davidson; Florence K. S. Davis; Meredith G. Diette; Debra J. Dreibelbis; B. Dane Dudley; William H. Erickson; Alex G. Filotto; Sean M. Fisher; Suzanne Garrow; Patrick M. Gerity; Valicia D. Harmon; Marie C. Kuban; Jonathan M. Levine; Robert J. Lewton; Ronald E. Lyles; Donald J. Marchesseault; Kurosh L. Marjani; Carolyn B. Martino; Kelly G. Miley; Jessica J. Mitchell; Ann Grunbeck Monaghan; Karen A. Moreno; Tracey A. Morgan; Samuel T. D. Neves, Jr.; Leigh A. Newman; Clifford E. Nichols; Vincent P. Pace; Donna Poresky; Samantha A. Pravecek; Deborah S. Russo; Daniel A. Schwartz; James D. Scrimgeour; Sharon M. Seligman; Namita Tripathi Shah; Kathleen A. Shea; Michael P. Shea; Edward S. Shelton; Steven Steinmetz; Erin S. Stephen; Eric L. Sussman; Michelle I. Turner (Not admitted in CT); Keith S. Varian; Andrew R. Wallace; Darren M. Wallace; Lane T. Watson; Peter Wilson. Of Counsel: C. Duane Blinn; Harold C. Buckingham, Jr.; George H. Cain; William H. Cuddy; John C. Glezen; Raymond B. Green; Richard C. MacKenzie; James R. McIntosh; Richard M. Reynolds. Counsel: Rosemary G. Ayers; Charlsa D. Broadus (Not admitted in CT); Douglas E. Fiske; Laurence P. Fleming; David H. Flynn; Douglas W. Gillette; Joseph L. Hammer; Michael P. Hammond, Jr.; Elin Swanson Katz; Edward F. Krzanowski; Barbara B. Lindsay; Priya S. Morganstern; Scott P. Myers; Kevin J. O'Connor; J. James Perkins (Not admitted in CT). Special Counsel: Judith A. Blank; Stephen B. Middlebrook. Independent Contractor: Ann K. Anderson; Sarah C. Baskin; Paul Schiff Berman (Not admitted in CT); Lawrence J. Boudreau. Resident Partners in Boston Office: David B. Broughel; Daniel J. Carragher; Jeffrey A. Clopeck; Nancy M. Cullen; George L. Cushing; Stephen G. Howard; William A. Hunter; J. Charles Mokriski; Francis H. Morrison III; Richard S. Novak; William Shields; H. Lawrence Tafe III; Kenneth E. Werner. Partners in Stamford Office: Jerome Berkman; Martin L. Budd; Michael P. Byrne; Patricia A. Carpenter; Michael G. Considine; Kenneth W. Gage; Andrew P. Gaillard; Thomas D. Goldberg; Gregory A. Hayes; Robert J. Miller; Kenneth W. Ritt; Sabino Rodriguez III; Bonnie J. Roe (Not admitted in CT); Daniel L. Schwartz; James F. Stapleton; David A. Swerdloff; Stanley A. Twardy, Jr. Partners in Greenwich Office: R. Scott Beach; Ronald Osburn Dederick; Forrest Lee Griffith III; Amy K. Wilfert. Resident Counsel in Greenwich Office: Lesley I. B. Schless. Resident Counsel in Boston Office: Eric K. Runge. Resident Of Counsel in Boston Office: Charles Donelan. Of Counsel in Stamford Office: Emil H. Frankel. Resident Counsel in Stamford Office: Stacey B. Babson-Smith; Patricia M. Canavan; Derek Gilman; Benedicta S. McGrath; Roland A. Paul; Jonathan B. Tropp; Kathleen D. Warner; Paulette Wunsch. Staff Attorney in Boston Office: Bonny E. Lambert. Resident Associatse in Greenwich Office: Peter Chadwick; Shawn T. Wooden. Resident Associates in Boston Office: John G. Balboni; Kathleen A. Bergin; Viktoria K. Cech-Vinhais; Patricia A. DeJuneas; Tricia F. Deraska; Jonathan I. Handler; Louise A. Handler; Edgar B. Hatrick, IV; Paul J. Keenan, Jr.; Kathleen A. Lind; Shannon A. McAuliffe; John P. McLafferty; Brian T. Moore; Kimberly K. Ryan; Andrea P. Testa. Associates in Stamford Office: Tricia S. Begg; Melissa L. Bellavia; Ann Lisa Braun; Rob Roy Buckingham, Jr.; David Y. Choi; Richard P. Colbert; Elizabeth Corwin; Jamal M. Dawkins; Sarah Moore Fass; Kelly E. P. Flatt; Deborah S. Gordon; Joli Lyn Gross; Lorey Rives Leddy; Natasha M. Lipcan; Margaret A. McComish; Catherine Dugan O'Connor; Thomas J. O'Neill; Brian D. Porch, Jr.; Allen J. Roberts, III; Mark B. Robinson; Jennifer L. Sachs; Fritz Strohmeyer; Ray A. Wynter.
Antitrust, Banking, Bank Lending, Bankruptcy, Bankruptcy Counseling, Benefits and Executive Compensation, Business Succession Planning, Business Transactions and Counseling, Closely Held Businesses, Credit Tenant Lease Financing, Commercial Litigation, Commercial Leasing, Construction, Direct Liability and Casualty Insurance, Disability, Emerging Companies, Energy, Environmental and Land Use, Equipment Finance and Leasing, Employment Law and Litigation, Environmental Law and Litigation, Executive Planning, Family Law, Finance and Investments, First Party Insurance, Franchise and Distributorship Litigation, Government Investigations, Health Care, Insurance Regulation and Proceedings, Insurance Litigation, International Tax, International Transactions, Life Insurance and Annuities, Low Income Housing Tax Credits, Medical and Professional

(This Listing Continued)

Day, Berry & Howard LLP (Continued)
Malpractice, Mergers and Acquisitions, Multi-Property Transactions, Municipal Finance, Negligence Defense, Planning for Entrepreneurs, Private Equity Funds, Product Liability, Real Estate Development, Real Estate Equity Investors, Real Estate Finance, Real Estate Workouts and Restructuring, Regulatory Insurance Proceedings and Litigation, Reinsurance, Securities Law, Securities Litigation, Strategic Joint Ventures, Structured Finance, Tax, Tax Litigation Group, Tax Exempt and Charity Giving, Tax Exempt Organizations, Technology and Intellectual Property Business and Litigation, Torts Litigation, Telecommunications, Trusts and Estates Administration, Trusts and Estates Litigation, Water Companies.
Greenwich, Connecticut Office: One East Putnam Avenue. Telephone: 203-862-7800.
Stamford, Connecticut Office: One Canterbury Green. Telephone: 203-977-7300. Telecopier: 203-977-7301.
Boston, Massachusetts Office: 260 Franklin Street. Telephone: 617-345-4600. Telecopier: 617-345-4745.
See Professional Biographies, HARTFORD, CONNECTICUT

Dean, Mark H., (BV) . . . . '58 '86 C&L.184 B.A., J.D. [M.H.Dean]

Dean, Martha A., Law Offices of, (BV) '59 '86 C.914 B.A. L.184 J.D.
77 Buckingham Street, 06106
Telephone: 860-278-6009 Fax: 860-727-4107
Email: mdean@mdeanlaw.com
***PRACTICE AREAS: Environmental.**
Associate: David R. Purvis.
Environmental Law: Representation of Industrial, Financial, and Commercial Establishments, and Select Citizen Plaintiffs, Litigation in State and Federal Courts.
See Professional Biographies, HARTFORD, CONNECTICUT

Dean, Mark H., P.C., (BV)
241 Main Street, 06106
Telephone: 860-541-6699 Fax: 860-241-7744
Mark H. Dean.
Civil Trial Practice. Commercial and Business Litigation, Personal Injury, Employment Law and Administrative Proceedings.
See Professional Biographies, HARTFORD, CONNECTICUT

DeBarge, Michelle Wilcox . . . . '65 '93 C.951 B.A. L.184 J.D. [Wiggin&D.]
DeCaprio, M. Fred, (BV) . . . . '47 '73 C&L.184 B.A., J.D. Pub. Def.

Dechert, (AV)
90 State House Square, 06103-3702 ⊙
Telephone: 860.524.3999 Fax: 860.524.3930
URL: http://www.dechert.com
Partners: Timothy J. Boyce; John J. Gillies Jr. Associates: Izabela E. Boltryk; Katherine A. Burroughs; Robert E. Grady; Steven Kapiloff; Andrea J. Levine; Miriam Berlin Schneider; Nadine Kline Young.
Antitrust, Banking, Bankruptcy and Reorganization, Business and Technology, Commercial Litigation, Complex Litigation, Copyrights, Corporate Finance, Competition, Construction, Customs and Excise, Criminal and Civil Fraud, Defamation, Domestic Taxation, Employee Benefits and Executive Compensation, Employment, Environmental, Estate Planning, EU Legislation, Financial Services, First Amendment, Government Affairs, Health Care, Immigration, Insurance, Intellectual Property, Internet and e-Commerce, Information Technology, International Business, International Taxation, International Trade, Investment Management, Labor, Latin America, Life Sciences, Mass Torts, Media, Mergers and Acquisitions, Patent Law and Litigation, Privacy, Private Equity, Products Liability, Property Planning, Real Estate and Mortgage Finance, Retail, Securities Litigation and Enforcement, Securitization, State and Local Taxation, Tax-Exempt Organizations, Trademarks, Venture Capital.
Philadelphia, Pennsylvania: 4000 Bell Atlantic Tower, 1717 Arch Street, 19103-2793. Telephone: 215.994.4000.
New York, New York: 30 Rockefeller Plaza, 10112. Telephone: 212.698.3500.
Washington, D.C.: 1775 Eye Street, N.W., 20006-2401. Telephone: 202.261.3300.
Boston, Massachusetts: Ten Post Office Square South, 02109-4603. Telephone: 617.728.7100.
Princeton, New Jersey: Princeton Pike Corporate Center, P.O. Box 5218, 08543-5218. Telephone: 609.620.3200.
Harrisburg, Pennsylvania: Thirty North Third Street, 17101-1603. Telephone: 717.237.2000.
Newport Beach, California: 4675 MacArthur Court, Suite 1400, 92660-8842. Telephone: 949.442.6000.
London, England: 2 Serjeants' Inn, EC4Y 1LT. Telephone: +44.20.7583.5353.
Brussels, Belgium: 65 Avenue Louise 1050. Telephone: +32.2.535.5411.
Paris, France: 55, avenue Kléber, 75116. Telephone: +33.1.53.65.05.00.
Luxembourg: Brucher & Seimetz in association with Dechert, Avocats a la Cour, 10 rue de Vianden, B.P. 709, L-2017. Telephone: +352.45.62.62.
See Professional Biographies, HARTFORD, CONNECTICUT

Decko, Kenneth O., (AV) '44 '70 C.228 B.A. L.184 J.D.
Pres., Conn. Bus. & Indus. Assn.
DeCrescenzo, Robert M., (BV) . . . . '57 '88 C&L.184 B.A., J.D. [Updike,K.&S.]
*PRACTICE AREAS: Municipal; Litigation; Public Policy; Land Use; Land Development.
Decrosta, Anthony E. . . . . '63 '89 C.158 B.S. L.1029 J.D. 50 Russ St.
DeDominicis, Felicia . . . . '— '90 C.103 A.B. L.306 J.D. [Robinson&C.]
*PRACTICE AREAS: Health Care; Business Law; Mergers and Acquisitions.
Dee, David A., (CV) . . . . '58 '84 C.184 B.A. L.1029 J.D. 67 Russ St.
DeFilippo, Joseph N., (BV) . . . . '62 '91 C.676 B.A. L.192 J.D. [Morrison,M.&M.]
*PRACTICE AREAS: Civil Litigation; Products Liability.
DeFrino, Robert A., (BV) . . . . '49 '78 C.93 B.A. L.1202 J.D. [O'Connell,F.&A.]
*PRACTICE AREAS: Business Law; Commercial Law; Bankruptcy Law; Real Estate Law.
DeGraffenreidt, Ann-Marie . . . . '59 '86 C.976 B.A. L.569 J.D. 1 American Row
Delaney, John F., (BV) . . . . '10 '49 C.321 B.A. L.184 J.D. 72 Russ St.
Delbarba, Deborah J. Dunham . . . . '64 '96 C.94 B.A. L.306 J.D. [Spinella&J.]
DelCastilloSalamanca, Jose L. . . . . '59 '92 C.569 B.S. L.306 J.D. 255 Main St., 1st Fl.
Dellasandro, Nicole Louise . . . . '75 '01 C.659 B.A. L.1048 J.D. 95 Washington St.
Delman, David A. '62 '87 C.30 B.A. L.276 J.D.
(adm. in IN; not adm. in CT) [Pepe&H.]
*PRACTICE AREAS: Construction Litigation; Insurance; Environmental Law; Commercial Law.
Del Negro, John T., (AV) . . . . '48 '75 C.273 B.A. L.188 J.D. [Del Negro,F.&V.]
*PRACTICE AREAS: Health Care Law; Corporate.

Del Negro, Feldman & Volpe, LLC, (AV)
Goodwin Square, 225 Asylum Street, 06103-1516
Telephone: 860-241-4141 Facsimile: 860-241-4150
John T. Del Negro; Barry Feldman; Michele M. Volpe.
Health Care Law, Hospital Law, Managed Care Law.
See Professional Biographies, HARTFORD, CONNECTICUT

Del Piano, Gerald A., (BV) . . . . '51 '76 C.184 B.A. L.767 J.D. [Francis,O.&D.]
DeMeo, Raymond T. '58 '86
C.951 B.A. L.184 J.D. Mng. Coun., The Travelers Indemnity Co.
DeMerchant, Daniel C. . . . . '70 '97 C.362 B.B.A. L.1252 J.D. [Howd&L.]
*PRACTICE AREAS: Products Liability; Insurance Defense; Municipal; General Trial and Appellate Practice.
DeMille, Thomas W., (AV) . . . . '38 '69 C.588 B.S. L.184 J.D. [Updike,K.&S.]
*PRACTICE AREAS: Real Estate.
DeMore, William G. . . . . '58 '86 C&L.184 B.S., J.D. V.P., Fleet Bk., N.A.
DeMoura, Ana Isabel . . . . '70 '98 C.1030 B.A. L.1048 J.D. [Siegel,O.S.&Z.]
*PRACTICE AREAS: Employment Law; Litigation; Labor Law; Education Law.
Dempsey, Edward J., (BV) '43 '70 C.93 A.B. L.128 J.D.
Labor Coun., United Tech. Corp.

Dempsey, John J., (AVⓉ) '24 '57 C.871 B.S. L.446 LL.B.
(adm. in MD; not adm. in CT; See Pat. Sect.) [◙ McCormick,P.&H.] ⊙
*PRACTICE AREAS: Patents; Trademarks; Copyrights.
Denne, R. Gregory .... '14 '39 C&L.893 LL.B. 31 Woodland St.
Dennis, Anthony J. .... '63 '88 C.860 B.A. L.597 J.D. Coun., Aetna Inc.
*RESPONSIBILITIES: Antitrust; Corporate Law; Compliance; Government Relations; Mergers and Acquisitions.
Dennis, Maureen D. ....'52 '80 C&L.184 B.A., J.D. Supr. Ct. J.
Den Ouden, Matthew W. .... '65 '92 C.1033 B.A. L.184 J.D. [O'Connell,F.&A.]
*PRACTICE AREAS: Indian Law; Products Liability Defense; Computer Law; Risk Management; Insurance Defense.
D'Ercole, S. Frank, (AV) '— '68
C.164 A.B. L.188 J.D. [Robinson&C.] (⊙Manchester, NH)
*PRACTICE AREAS: Finance; Securities; Government.
DeRosa, Franca L., (BV) ....'— '90 C.855 B.A. L.30 J.D. [Brown,R.F.&G.]
*PRACTICE AREAS: Environmental; Energy; Administrative Law.
De Rosa, Stacey L. .... '76 '01 C.446 B.A. L.1252 J.D. [Ⓐ Danaher,T.L.&N.]
*PRACTICE AREAS: Litigation.
DeRose, Nancy A. ....'68 '93 C.1030 B.A. L.1048 J.D. [Ⓐ Danaher,T.L.&N.]
*PRACTICE AREAS: Medical Malpractice; Personal Injury.
Derrig, Ellen N. .... '62 '90 C.1044 B.S. L.1048 J.D. Assoc. Coun., The Travelers Ins. Co.
Desautel, Doris Ellen .... '74 '99 C.164 B.A. L.818 J.D. [Ⓐ Edwards&A.]
*PRACTICE AREAS: Insurance; Reinsurance; Litigation.
Desjardins, Garry, (BV) ....'53 '78 C.197 B.A. L.184 J.D. Asst. Atty. Gen.
DeTora, Alice E. ....'— '84 C.475 B.A. L.1194 J.D. [Robinson&C.]
*PRACTICE AREAS: Labor and Employment; Immigration.
Devaney, Deirdre A. ....'— '98 C.569 B.A. L.184 J.D. [Ⓐ Robinson&C.]
Devine, Michael J. .... '68 '95 C.184 B.A. L.190 J.D. [Ⓐ Wiggin&D.]
Devokaitis, Gerald F., (BV) .... '43 '71 C.676 A.B. L.94 LL.B. 21 Oak St.
Devonshire, Linda B. .... '42 '68 C&L.184 B.S., J.D. Coun., Conn. Mut. Life Ins. Co.
DiBella, Lori D. ....'70 '96 C.518 B.A. L.1048 J.D. [Ⓐ Halloran&S.]
*PRACTICE AREAS: Environmental Law; Land Use Planning; Administrative Law; Utility Law; Telecommunications.
Dickinson, Craig Thoms .... '63 '94 C.1030 B.A. L.1040 J.D. [Ⓐ Madsen,P.&P.]
*PRACTICE AREAS: Labor and Employment; Civil Rights.
Dieso, Joseph, (BV) '56 '84 C.1044 B.A. L.184 J.D.
Asst. Gen. Cnsl, Colt's Manufacturing Company, Inc.
Diette, Meredith G. .... '72 '00 C.446 B.A. L.93 J.D. [Ⓐ Day,B.&H.]
*PRACTICE AREAS: Employment Law; Employee Benefits.
Dighello, Richard M., Jr. .... '69 '96 C.1252 B.A. L.94 J.D. [Ⓐ Updike,K.&S.]
*PRACTICE AREAS: Professional Defense; Construction and Design Litigation; Insurance Litigation.
DiLorenzo, Theodore J., (BV) '24 '53
C.855 B.A. L.273 J.D. [◙ Brown,P.&S.] (⊙Glastonbury)
*PRACTICE AREAS: Personal Injury; Small Business Law; Business Law; Residential Real Estate; Commercial Real Estate.
Dion, Faye A. .... '52 '89 C.103 A.B. L.184 J.D. Coun., Aetna Inc.
*RESPONSIBILITIES: Computer Law; Intellectual Property.
Dirks, Marilyn K., (BV) .... '50 '79 C.546 B.A. L.846 J.D. 208 Kenyon St.
DiVincentis, Alfred A., Jr. ....'63 '00 C.829 B.S. L.306 J.D. [Ⓐ Cummings&L.]
Divine, Thomas M., (AV) .... '47 '78 C.178 B.A. L.976 J.D. [Rogin,N.C.L.&H.]
*PRACTICE AREAS: Taxation; Trusts and Estates.
Divins, Phyllis M. ....'73 '98 C.994 B.A. L.1325 J.D. [Ⓐ Kern&W.] (⊙L.A., CA)
DiVirgilio, James M. '60 '85 C.645 B.S. L.884 J.D.
(adm. in PA; not adm. in CT) Dep. Gen. Coun., Travelers Property Casualty Co.
Dixon, Jennifer Lian ....'64 '94 C.477 A.B. L.1202 J.D. [Kainen,E.&M.]
*PRACTICE AREAS: Employment Law; Litigation; Labor Law.
Doeg, Donald W. ....'60 '91 C.228 B.S.C.E. L.184 J.D. [Updike,K.&S.]
*PRACTICE AREAS: Construction and Design Litigation; Professional Defense; Insurance Defense; Civil Litigation.
Dolan, William J., (BV) ... '49 '74 C.708 A.B. L.602 J.D. Legal Coun., Conn. Educ. Assn.
Dombroff, Robert M., (AV) '47 '71
C&L.184 B.A., J.D. [Bingham D.] (⊙New York, NY)
*PRACTICE AREAS: Commercial and Financial Litigation; Reinsurance; Loan Workouts and Restructuring; Bankruptcy and Insolvency; Lender Liability Defense.
Dombrosky, Joseph P. ....'54 '85 C.93 B.A. L.836 J.D. Coun., Industrial Risk Insurers
Don Francisco, Jay Thomas ....'73 '99 C.183 B.A. L.1194 J.D. [Howd&L.]
*PRACTICE AREAS: Insurance Defense; Litigation; Municipal Law.
Donaghue, Ethel F., (Miss) ....'— '23 L.569 S.J.D. 1 Constitution Plz.‡
Donahue, John M., (AV) .... '— '51 C&L.976 B.A., LL.B. [◙ Robinson&C.]
*PRACTICE AREAS: Estate Law; Tax Planning; Exempt Organizations; Exempt Organizations Law.
Donegan, Michael P. '64 '89 C.93 B.A. L.1202 J.D.
(adm. in MA; not adm. in CT) The Travelers Ins. Co.
Donnell, Brian J., (BV) ....'55 '80 C.855 B.A. L.93 J.D. [Halloran&S.]
*PRACTICE AREAS: Construction Litigation; Construction and Design Law; Corporate Contracts; Business Litigation; Class Actions.
Donnelly, Justin J., Sr. ....'41 '70 C.1030 B.S. L.306 J.D. [◙ Spinella&J.]
Donnelly, Michael J., (BV) ....'63 '90 C.321 B.A. L.184 J.D. [◙ Murtha C.]
*PRACTICE AREAS: Litigation; Environmental Litigation.
Donofrio, Louis J. ....'67 '92 C.273 B.A. L.128 J.D. [Reid&R.]
*PRACTICE AREAS: Commercial Real Estate and Finance; Real Estate; Leasing.
Donohue, Thomas J., Jr., (BV) .... '51 '76 C.321 B.A. L.184 J.D. [Killian,D.&J.] ⊙
*PRACTICE AREAS: Real Estate; Zoning and Planning; Banking; Corporate and Utility; Governmental Relations.
Donovan, Arthur S. '56 '85 C.1033 B.A. L.93 J.D.
Sr. Legis. Atty., Conn. Gen. Assembly
Doot, David T., (BV) .... '57 '85 C.188 B.S. L.692 J.D. [Day,B.&H.]
*PRACTICE AREAS: Energy.
Dos Santos, Antonio E. .... '75 '00 C.93 B.A. L.306 J.D. [Ⓐ Updike,K.&S.]
*PRACTICE AREAS: Business Law.
Douglas, Bruce A. '51 '77 C.197 A.B. L.188 J.D.
(adm. in MA; not adm. in CT) CIGNA Corp.
Dowd, Glenn W., (BV) .... '61 '89 C.829 B.S. L.184 J.D. [Day,B.&H.]
*PRACTICE AREAS: Employment Law; Employment Litigation.
Dowd, Karen L. ....'67 '91 C.893 B.A. L.183 J.D. [Horton,S.&C.]
*PRACTICE AREAS: Civil Litigation; Appellate Practice; Insurance Defense; Personal Injury; Product Liability.
Dowd, Kevin M. '61 '87 C.1030 B.A. L.273 J.D.
Gen. Coun. and V.P., Developers Realty, Inc.

Dowley, Michael F.
(See Middletown)

Dowling, James G., Jr., (AV) '52 '78
C.860 B.A. L.818 J.D. [Pullman&C.] (⊙Bridgeport)
*PRACTICE AREAS: Real Estate Law; Commercial Transactions.
Dowling, Vincent J., (AV) .... '27 '57 C.401 B.S. L.184 J.D. [Cooney,S.&D.]
*PRACTICE AREAS: Construction Liability; Litigation; Professional Liability; Mediation.
Dreibelbis, Debra J. .... '73 '01 C.645 B.S. L.1048 J.D. [Ⓐ Day,B.&H.]
Dressler, Jeffrey P. ....'49 '78 C.184 B.A. L.1088 J.D. 84 Cedar St.
Driscoll, Donald J. '59 '85 C.879 B.A. L.339 J.D.
(adm. in IL; not adm. in CT) Dir., The Travelers Ins. Co.
Droney, Christopher F. .... '54 '79 C.321 A.B. L.184 J.D. U.S. Dist. J.

Drumm, Francis J., Jr. .... '46 '81 C.829 B.S. L.184 J.D. Chf. Clk., Supm. Ct.
Drummey, Charles E., (AV) ....'33 '74 C.976 B.A. L.184 J.D. [◙ Murtha C.]
*PRACTICE AREAS: Estate Planning Law; Estate and Trust Administration Law.
DuBay, Keith Edward, Jr., (BV) .... '53 '85 C.1307 B.A. L.1048 J.D. 101 Oak St.
Dubay, Kevin G., (BV) .... '54 '79 C.860 B.A. L.184 J.D. [Dubay&A.]
Dubay & Andreini, (BV) .... 101 Oak St.
Dudley, B. Dane ....'67 '92 C.951 B.A. L.93 J.D. [Ⓐ Day,B.&H.]
*PRACTICE AREAS: Probate; Estate and Gift Taxation; Generation Skipping Tax; Trusts and Estates; Wills.
Duell, Kim L., (BV) .... '58 '84 C.184 B.A. L.1048 J.D. 81 Wethersfield Ave.
Duffy, Mary C. '61 '89 C.103 A.B. L.128 J.D.
Assoc. Coun., Travelers Property Casualty Corp.
Dugan, Michael J. ....'63 '90 C.311 B.A. L.831 J.D. [Cramer,A.&F.]
*PRACTICE AREAS: Civil Litigation; Personal Injury; Insurance Defense; Products Liability; Professional Malpractice.
Duhaime, Diane ....'57 '92 C&L.184 B.A., J.D. [Ⓐ Brown R.M.F.&S.]
*PRACTICE AREAS: Technology Law; Trademarks; Copyrights; Unfair Competition; Trade Secrets.

Duhamel & Schoolcraft LLC
(See Glastonbury)

Duhl, Glenn A. .... '61 '86 C.918 B.A. L.861 J.D. [Siegel,O.S.&Z.]
*PRACTICE AREAS: Labor Law; Employment Law; Litigation; NASD Arbitration.
Dukes, Philip ... '69 '94 C.184 B.A. L.7 J.D. Sr. Secs. Pros., Connecticut Dept. of Banking
Dully, Bertram J. .... '24 '66 C.602 B.A. L.184 LL.B. The Travelers Ins. Co.
Dumont, Jeanine M., (BV) ....'58 '84 C.112 B.A. L.426 J.D. [Pepe&H.]
*PRACTICE AREAS: Commercial Litigation; Debtor and Creditor; Collections; Civil Fraud; Litigation.
Duncan, Dawn E. ....'63 '01 C&L.925 B.S.Ed., J.D. [Ⓐ Bingham D.]
*PRACTICE AREAS: Business.
Duncan, William M. ...... '44 '69 C.674 A.B. L.178 J.D. Asst. Gen. Coun., CIGNA Corp.
Dunham, John M. .... '41 '69 C.103 B.A. L.184 J.D. State Dept. of Rev. Servs.
Dunn, Philip R., Jr., (BV) ....'63 '88 C.1030 B.A. L.184 J.D. [Jackson,O.&P.]
*PRACTICE AREAS: Civil Trial Practice; Insurance Defense Law; Personal Injury Law.
Dunne, Kerrie C. .... '55 '87 C.1044 B.A. L.563 J.D. 55 Farmington Ave.
Dunnell, Christina G. .... '44 '75 C.744 B.A. L.184 J.D. Supr. Ct. J.
Dupont, Antoinette L. .... '29 '55 C.103 A.B. L.309 J.D. Chf. Appl. Ct. J.
Dusyn, Kenneth F. .....'42 '70 C.201 B.Ch.E. L.184 J.D. 330 Main Street, 3rd Floor (Pat.)
Dvorin, Lawrence A., (BV) ....'61 '89 C.472 B.M. L.818 J.D. [Levin,F.&P.]
*PRACTICE AREAS: Commercial Litigation; Commercial Workouts; Commercial Finance; Corporate Transactions.
Dwyer, Gerald P., Jr. ....'66 '95 C.165 A.B. L.285 J.D. [Ⓐ Robinson&C.]
Dwyer, Reneé W., (BV) ....'66 '91 C.676 B.S. L.128 J.D. [Gordon,M.&F.]
*PRACTICE AREAS: Insurance Defense; Civil Litigation; Retail Liability; Premises Liability.
Dyro, John P., Sr. .... '65 '01 C.1222 B.S. L.602 J.D. [Ⓐ Bingham D.]
Eagan, F. Owen ....'30 '56 C&L.276 B.S., J.D. U.S. Mag. J.
Earle, Eleanor M. '20 '65 C.575 A.B. L.1035 LL.B.
(adm. in MN; not adm. in CT) 31 Woodland St.‡
Eberle, Mary U. .... '49 '76 C.734 B.A. L.477 J.D. Coun., CIGNA Corp.
Ecker, Steven D., (AV) .... '61 '88 C.976 B.A. L.309 J.D. [Cowdery,E.&M.]
*PRACTICE AREAS: Commercial Litigation; Appellate Practice; Personal Injury; White Collar Criminal Defense.
Eckert, Brenda A., (AV) ....'45 '73 C.771 B.A. L.184 J.D. [Shipman&G.]
*PRACTICE AREAS: Civil Litigation; Employment Litigation; Immigration Law.
Eddy, Paul H. '55 '80 C.611 B.A. L.184 J.D.
Coun. & Asst. Corp. Secy., The Travelers Ins. Co.
Eddy, Ralph G., (AV) ....'47 '72 C.95 A.B. L.184 J.D. [Regnier,T.C.&E.]
*PRACTICE AREAS: General Practice; Trial Practice; Insurance; Toxic Torts; Products Liability.
Eddy, Robert L., Jr. .....'44 '69 C.264 B.A. L.1294 J.D. Sr. Tax Atty., State Dept. of Rev.
Edgington, Thomas W. ....'75 '00 C.712 B.A. L.982 J.D. [Ⓐ Updike,K.&S.]
*PRACTICE AREAS: Commercial Litigation.
Edwards, Paul T., (BV) ....'66 '91 C.945 B.A. L.1029 J.D. [Danaher,T.L.&N.]
*PRACTICE AREAS: Civil Litigation; Medical Malpractice; Products Liability; Toxic Tort; Professional Liability.
Edwards, Warren E. '35 '67 C.103 A.B. L.818 LL.B.
(adm. in MA; not adm. in CT) 2nd V.P., General Reins. Corp.

Edwards & Angell, LLP, (AV)
A Partnership including Professional Corporations
90 State House Square, 06103-2715 ⊙
Telephone: 860-525-5065 Telecopy: 860-527-4198
Email: postmaster@ealaw.com URL: http://www.ealaw.com
Members of Firm: Theodore P. Augustinos; John B. D'Agostino; Donald E. Frechette; Alan J. Levin; John H. Reid III; Mark B. Seiger. Counsel: Janet M. Helmke-Elmore; Thomas F. X. Hodson. Associates: Doris Ellen Desautel; John N. Emmanuel; Ann Elizabeth Favale; Michael T. Griffin; Cathleen Tobin Heath; Matthew J. Hoberman; Tamara S. LaPointe; Jeffrey Joseph Medeiros; Joshua L. Milrad.
General Practice.
Providence, Rhode Island Office: 2800 Financial Plaza. Telephone: 401-274-9200. Cable Address: "Edwangle Providence." Telex: 952001 "E A PVD" Telecopier: 401-276-6611.
Newport, Rhode Island Office: 130 Bellevue Avenue. Telephone: 401-849-7800.
New York, New York Office: 750 Lexington Avenue. Telephone: 212- 308-4411.
West Palm Beach, Florida Office: One North Clematis Street, Suite 400. Telephone: 561-833-7700.
Boston, Massachusetts Office: 101 Federal Street. Telephone: 617-439-4444.
Short Hills, New Jersey Office: 51 John F. Kennedy Parkway. Telephone: 973-376-7700.
Fort Lauderdale, Florida Office: 600 Corporate Drive, Suite 514. Telephone: 954-491-8050.
Revisers of the Rhode Island Law Digest for this Directory.
See Professional Biographies, HARTFORD, CONNECTICUT

Egan, William J., (BV) ....'65 '90 C.309 A.B. L.184 J.D. [Levin,F.&P.]
*PRACTICE AREAS: Commercial Litigation; Bankruptcy; Creditors Rights and Collections; E-Commerce; Commercial Leasing.
Eggert, Celia .... '61 '00 C.184 B.S. L.1048 J.D. [Ⓐ Bingham D.]
*PRACTICE AREAS: Litigation.
Ehle, Gary J., (BV) '52 '80 C.829 B.A. L.184 J.D.
Senior Vice President & General Counsel, Advest Bank & Trust Company
Eichner, John C. .... '52 '83 C.222 B.A. L.184 J.D. Sr. Proj. Mgr., City of Hartford
Eisele, Michael J. .... '58 '87 C.1027 B.S. L.276 J.D. The Travelers Ins. Co.

Eisenberg, Anderson, Michalik & Lynch LLP
(See New Britain)

Ekern, Stephen G. .... '63 '92 C.165 B.A. L.184 J.D. Hartford Ins. Grp.

Elder, Joseph S. '56 '85 C&L.184 B.A., J.D.
661 Wethersfield Avenue, 06114-1928
Telephone: 860-296-3247 Fax: 860-296-9131
Email: jselderesq@aol.com URL: http://www.lawyers.com/jelder
***PRACTICE AREAS: Civil Litigation; Criminal Law; Felonies; Misdemeanors; Driving While Intoxicated.**
Civil and Criminal Litigation, Felonies, Misdemeanors, Driving While Intoxicated, Personal Injury, Automobile Accidents.
See Professional Biographies, HARTFORD, CONNECTICUT

Elgo, Nina F. ....'62 '90 C.183 B.A. L.276 J.D. Asst. Atty. Gen.
Elikann, Peter T. '53 '81 C.94 B.S. L.1048 J.D.
(adm. in MA; not adm. in CT) Asst. Reporter of Jud. Decisions, Supm. Ct.

Elliot, Ralph Gregory, (AV) .... '36 '61 C&L.976 B.A., LL.B. [Tyler C.&A.]
*PRACTICE AREAS: Litigation; Constitutional Law; Media Law; Municipal; Legal Ethics.
Elliott, David J., (AV) ....'53 '78 C.184 B.A. L.818 J.D. [Day,B.&H.]
*PRACTICE AREAS: Securities Litigation; Commercial Litigation.
Elliott, Jessica G. ....'70 '95 C.188 B.S. L.93 J.D. 1 American Row
Ellis, Joel M., (AV) ....'36 '62 C.184 B.A. L.976 LL.B. [Ⓐ Butler N.&G.]
Elsass, Michael W., (BV) ....'52 '82 C.910 B.A. L.911 J.D. [Day,B.&H.]
*PRACTICE AREAS: Trusts and Estates Administration; Trusts and Estates Litigation; Estate Planning.
Elsner, Morton A., (AV) ....'13 '39 C&L.976 B.A., LL.B. 31 Woodland St.‡
Emmanuel, John N. ....'69 '94 C.184 B.S. L.94 J.D. [Ⓐ Edwards&A.]
*PRACTICE AREAS: Insurance; General Corporate; Banking.
Emminger, Michael M., (AVⓉ) '51 '77 C.116 B.A. L.982 J.D.
(adm. in NY; not adm. in CT) AVP & Director of Counsel, The Hartford
Engel, Benjamin ....'54 '87 C.674 A.B. L.184 J.D. [Rogin,N.C.L.&H.]
*PRACTICE AREAS: Corporate Law; Commercial Law.
Engstrom, Robert C., (BV) ....'41 '66 C.659 B.A. L.93 J.D. [Ⓒ Halloran&S.]
*PRACTICE AREAS: ERISA; Tax Law; Trusts and Estates Law; Corporate Law.
Enright, Michael R., (BV) ....'— '81 C.339 B.A. L.424 J.D. [Robinson&C.]
*PRACTICE AREAS: Creditors' Rights; Bankruptcy; Workouts.
Ensign, Jonathon L., (BV) ....'45 '73 C&L.184 B.A., J.D. Asst. Atty. Gen.
Epstein, Constance L., (BV) '43 '79
C.338 B.A. L.184 J.D. [Howard,K.S.&F.] (⊙Manchester)
*PRACTICE AREAS: Civil Litigation; Arbitration; Appeals.
Erickson, Paul ....'65 '94 C.1048 B.A. L.260 J.D. [Howd&L.]
*PRACTICE AREAS: Insurance Defense Litigation; Municipal Liability; Medical Malpractice; Products Liability.
Erickson, William H. ....'70 '96 C.1031 B.S. L.602 J.D. [Ⓐ Day,B.&H.]
*PRACTICE AREAS: Commercial Litigation.
Erikson, Frederik F. '72 '00 C.1044 B.A. L.982 J.D.
(adm. in NY; not adm. in CT) [Ⓐ Brown R.M.F.&S.]
Escalera, Miguel A., Jr. ....'55 '81 C.276 B.S. L.904 J.D. [Kainen,E.&M.]
*PRACTICE AREAS: Employment Law; Litigation; Labor Law.
Esoian, Mitchell, (BV) ....'24 '53 C.598 B.A. L.184 J.D. 100 Pearl St.
Esposito, Catherine M. .... '75 '01 C.184 B.S. L.1252 J.D. [Ⓐ Shipman&G.]
Etlinger, Deborah ....'57 '87 C.454 B.A. L.1048 J.D. [Wolf,H.E.&C.]
*PRACTICE AREAS: Civil Litigation; Insurance Defense; Employment Defense; Health Insurance; ERISA.
Evans, David J. D. ....'44 '69 C.1030 B.A. L.213 J.D. 100 Pearl St.
Evans, Peter T. ....'59 '89 C.855 B.A. L.184 J.D. [Ⓐ Appleton&A.]
*PRACTICE AREAS: Personal Injury; Insurance Law; Commercial Litigation; Employment Litigation; Appellate Practice.
Everett, Timothy H. '51 '84
C.156 B.A. L.184 J.D. Prof. of Law, Univ. of Conn.School of Law
Eyges, Debra Susan, (BV) ....'56 '85 C.156 B.A. L.184 J.D. [Krevolin,F.G.E.&H.]
Facey, Kim ....'72 '00 C.93 B.S. L.818 J.D. 78 Bretton Rd.
Fahey, John F. ....'68 '93 C.1030 B.A. L.1048 J.D. Dep. Asst. State's Atty.
Fahey, Patrick ....'68 '93 C.321 A.B. L.184 J.D. [Ⓐ Shipman&G.]
Fain, Joel M., (BV) ....'53 '78 C.976 B.A. L.184 J.D. [Morrison,M.&M.]
*PRACTICE AREAS: Property; Insurance Coverage; Professional Liability.
Falk, Scott A. ....'64 '89 C.575 B.S. L.228 J.D. [Bingham D.]
*PRACTICE AREAS: Corporate Finance.
Falker, Michael J. ....'46 '71 C.705 B.A. L.184 J.D. Cambridge Realty Partners
Fanning, Philip J., (BV) '54 '78
C.676 B.A. L.229 J.D. Assoc. Reg. Coun., Chicago Title Ins. Co.
Faraguna, Joseph R. '49 '75
C.870 B.S. L.569 J.D. Admin. Law J., Off. of Hearings & App.
Farina, Doreen J. ....'50 '98 C.184 B.A. L.1048 J.D. [Ⓐ Reid&R.]
*PRACTICE AREAS: Employee Benefits.
Farley, John B., (AV) ....'58 '87 C.276 A.B. L.184 J.D. [Halloran&S.]
*PRACTICE AREAS: Appellate Practice; Commercial Litigation; Insurance Litigation; Insurance Regulation; Legal Malpractice.
Farley, Melissa A. ....'65 '92 C.855 B.A. L.306 J.D. 231 Capitol Ave.
Farr, Robert, (BV) ....'43 '69 C&L.184 B.S., J.D. [Heffernan&F.]
*PRACTICE AREAS: Real Estate; Corporate Law; Family Law; Divorce.
Farrell, Rod W., (CV) ....'58 '85 C.976 B.A. L.184 J.D. [Ⓐ Pullman&C.]
*PRACTICE AREAS: Bankruptcy; Litigation; Business Financing.
Farrell, Thomas J., (BV) ....'54 '85 C.690 B.A. L.184 J.D. [Ⓐ Hunt L.C.&J.]
Fasi, Joseph P., (BV) ....'54 '79 C&L.184 B.A., J.D. [Murtha C.]
*PRACTICE AREAS: Public and Corporate Finance; Securities; Municipal.
Fast, Steven M., (AV) ....'47 '71 C.197 B.A. L.178 J.D. [Day,B.&H.]
*PRACTICE AREAS: Trusts and Estate Administration; Trust and Estate Litigation; Estate Planning.
Faulise, S. V., (BV) ....'34 '61 C.184 B.A. L.94 J.D. 363 Main St.
Faulkner, Gregory R., (BV) ....'66 '91 C.676 B.S. L.128 J.D. [Halloran&S.]
*PRACTICE AREAS: Construction Litigation; Surety and Fidelity; Creditor's Rights; Bankruptcy.
Favale, Ann Elizabeth ....'75 '00 C&L.184 B.A., J.D. [Ⓐ Edwards&A.]
*PRACTICE AREAS: Litigation; Arbitration.
Fay, Julie C. '69 '01 C.951 B.A. L.306 J.D.
(adm. in MA; not adm. in CT) [Ⓐ Shipman&G.]
*PRACTICE AREAS: Education; Labor and Employment.
Feder, Daniel E. ....'63 '87 C.454 B.A. L.94 J.D. CIGNA Corp.
Feigenbaum, Barry S., (AV) ....'57 '81 C.273 B.B.A. L.184 J.D. [Rogin,N.C.L.&H.]
*PRACTICE AREAS: Bankruptcy; Corporate Law; Commercial Law.
Feigin, Arnold B., (BV) ....'45 '70 C.696 B.A. L.184 J.D. Asst. Atty. Gen.
Feiner, Robert A., (BV) .... '58 '85 C.184 B.S. L.188 J.D. [Feiner W.]
*PRACTICE AREAS: Mergers and Acquisitions; Franchise Law; Corporate Law; Limited Liability Company; Commercial Transactions.

Feiner Wolfson LLC, (BV)
100 Constitution Plaza, Suite 600, 06103
Telephone: 860-713-8900 Fax: 860-713-8905
Robert A. Feiner; John M. Wolfson;—Andrea A. Hewitt.
Corporate, Commercial, Franchise, Business Law, Complex Business Litigation, Employment Law and Professional Liability.
See Professional Biographies, HARTFORD, CONNECTICUT

Feinstein, Arthur W., (BV) ....'20 '43 C.918 L.184 LL.B. [Krevolin,F.G.E.&H.]
Feldman, Barry, (AV) ....'50 '75 C.674 A.B. L.309 J.D. [Del Negro,F.&V.]
*PRACTICE AREAS: Hospital Law; Health Care Law.
Feldman, Joan W., (BV) ....'56 '86 C.1044 B.S.N. L.184 J.D. [Shipman&G.]
*PRACTICE AREAS: Business Law; Health Care Law.
Felson, Ethan J. '65 '96 C.401 B.A. L.184 J.D.
Dir., Jewish Federation Community Rel. Council
Feltman, Art ....'58 '87 C.918 B.A. L.184 J.D. 221 Main St.
Ferguson, Robert, Jr., (AV) ....'16 '48 C.976 B.A. L.184 LL.B. One American Row
Ferko, George ....'54 '87 C.959 B.A. L.966 J.D. Asst. State's Atty.
Fernino, Kenneth D., (BV) ....'35 '65 C.262 B.S. L.184 LL.B. 1 Lewis St.
Fernow, Todd D. ....'54 '83 C.188 B.A. L.306 J.D. Univ. of Conn. Sch. of Law
Ferrante, John J. '55 '83 C.93 B.A. L.1002 J.D.
(adm. in MA; not adm. in CT) I.R.S.
Ferrigno, Kevin G., (BV) ....'62 '89 C.867 B.S. L.184 J.D. [Tyler C.&A.]
*PRACTICE AREAS: Corporate Law; Real Estate; Environmental Law; Commercial Law; Mergers and Acquisitions.
Ferrucci, Danielle P. ....'73 '99 C&L.184 B.A., J.D. [Ⓐ Shipman&G.]
*PRACTICE AREAS: Trusts and Estates.
Ferry, Kevin C. ....'65 '91 C.184 B.S. L.1252 J.D. 286 Farmington Ave.
Ficeto, Anna Carbonaro, (BV) '64 '90
C.518 B.A. L.184 J.D. Mng. Atty., State Dept. of Consumer Protec.
Ficks, Carl R., Jr., (BV) ....'63 '88 C.676 B.A. L.128 J.D. [Halloran&S.]
*PRACTICE AREAS: Construction Litigation; Litigation; Civil Rights; Insurance Defense; General Practice.
Fiedler, Susan Birke ....'65 '89 C.66 B.A. L.978 J.D. Coun., Ward-Burns & Grainger
Field, Gerald A., (BV) ....'42 '70 C&L.184 B.S., J.D. 11 Asylum St.
Fil, Richard M. ....'— '94 C.688 B.S. L.184 J.D. [Ⓐ Robinson&C.]
*PRACTICE AREAS: Environmental Law; Zoning, Planning and Land Use.
Filotto, Alex G. ....'73 '98 C.976 B.A. L.184 J.D. [Ⓐ Day,B.&H.]
*PRACTICE AREAS: Administrative Law; Regulatory Law.
Fineberg, David L. ....'31 '56 C.165 B.A. L.178 LL.B. Supr. Ct. J.

Fink & Highmark
(See West Hartford)

Finn, Thomas J. ....'67 '92 C.1044 B.S. L.823 J.D. [Ⓐ Halloran&S.]
*PRACTICE AREAS: Commercial Litigation; Federal Litigation; White Collar Crime; Admiralty and Maritime Law; Creditors Rights in Bankruptcy.
Finn, Vaughan ....'51 '77 C.681 B.A. L.309 J.D. [Shipman&G.]
*PRACTICE AREAS: Employment Law; Litigation.

Finn Dixon & Herling LLP
(See Stamford)

Firger, Robert A., (AV) '47 '77
C.1036 B.A. L.184 J.D. Sr. V.P. & Assoc. Coun., Society for Svgs.
Fischer, James L. ....'45 '92 C.674 B.A. L.273 J.D. 225 Asylum Street, 13th Floor
Fish, Lawrence R. ....'42 '67 C&L.145 A.B., J.D. ITT Hartford Ins. Grp.
Fish, William S., Jr., (BV) ....'58 '83 C.1044 B.A. L.893 J.D. [Tyler C.&A.]
*PRACTICE AREAS: Bankruptcy and Creditors' Rights; Commercial Litigation.
Fishberg, Mitchell L. ....'67 '93 C.390 A.B. L.273 J.D. [Ⓐ Brown R.M.F.&S.]
*PRACTICE AREAS: Labor and Employment; Executive Compensation.
Fisher, Chester L., III, (AV) ....'50 '76 C.674 A.B. L.178 J.D. [Bingham D.]
Fisher, Dina Schwarz ....'— '94 C.103 A.B. L.184 J.D. [Ⓒ Robinson&C.]
*PRACTICE AREAS: Products Liability; Litigation; Intellectual Property.
Fisher, Roger J. '30 '53 C&L.94 LL.B.
(adm. in MA; not adm. in CT) V.P., The Travelers Ins. Co.
Fisher, Sean M. ....'74 '00 C.299 B.A. L.1252 J.D. [Ⓐ Day,B.&H.]
Fisher, Stephen P. ....'62 '88 C.188 B.S. L.309 J.D. Coun., Aetna Inc.
*RESPONSIBILITIES: Corporate; Insurance Regulation; Health Insurance.
Fisher, Timothy S., (AV) ....'53 '78 C.976 B.A. L.178 J.D. [Cummings&L.]
*PRACTICE AREAS: Construction Disputes; Alternate Dispute Resolution; Check Fraud Law; Probate and Trust Litigation.
Fishman, Mark I., (AV) ....'45 '70 C&L.309 A.B., J.D. [Pepe&H.] ⊙
*PRACTICE AREAS: Bankruptcy Law; Commercial Litigation.
Fishman, Neil G., (BV) ....'56 '82 C.273 B.A. L.184 J.D. Off. of Atty. Gen.
Fiske, Douglas E., (BV) ....'59 '85 C.918 B.A. L.178 J.D. [Ⓒ Day,B.&H.]
*PRACTICE AREAS: Business Law.
Fitzgerald, Diane M. ....'55 '82 C.276 A.B. L.184 J.D. [Day,B.&H.]
*PRACTICE AREAS: Benefits and Executive Compensation; Mergers and Acquisitions.
FitzGerald, John C., Jr., (AV) .... '55 '80 C.1307 B.A. L.184 J.D. [Cranmore,F.&M.]
FitzGerald, John R., (AV) '27 '53 C&L.184 B.A., J.D.
[Howard,K.S.&F.] (⊙Manchester)
*PRACTICE AREAS: Trial Practice.
Fitzhugh, Michael A., (AVⓉ) '52 '81 C.951 B.A. L.309 J.D.
(adm. in MA; not adm. in CT) [Fitzhugh&Assoc.] ⊙
*PRACTICE AREAS: Products Liability; Employment and Insurance Law.

Fitzhugh & Associates, (AVⓉ)
100 Constitution Plaza, Suite 600, 06106 ⊙
Telephone: 860-549-6803 Fax: 860-728-0546
Michael A. Fitzhugh (Not admitted in CT).
General Civil Practice before State and Federal Courts. Insurance Defense, Negligence and Products Liability Defense. Bankruptcy, Environmental and Employment Law.
Boston, Massachusetts Office: 155 Federal Street, Suite 1700, 02110-1727. Telephone: 617-695-2330. Fax: 617-695-2335.
Cranston, Rhode Island Office: 571 Pontiac Avenue. Telephone: 401-941-3220. Facsimile: 401-941-3055.
See Professional Biographies, HARTFORD, CONNECTICUT

FitzMaurice, Daniel L., (AV) ....'54 '79 C.183 B.S. L.477 J.D. [Day,B.&H.]
*PRACTICE AREAS: Commercial Litigation; Insurance Litigation; Direct Liability and Casualty; Disability Insurance; Life Insurance and Annuities.
FitzMaurice, Maurice T., (AV) ....'44 '71 C.184 B.A. L.602 J.D. [Reid&R.]
*PRACTICE AREAS: Litigation.
Fitzpatrick, Elizabeth O'N. '56 '86
C.706 B.A. L.1029 J.D. Sr. Coun., Fleet Financial Grp.
Fitzsimmons, Elizabeth A. ....'69 '95 C.529 B.A. L.273 J.D. [Ⓐ Halloran&S.]
*PRACTICE AREAS: Insurance Coverage; Insurance Bad Faith; Appellate Advocacy; Insurance Defense.
Flaherty, James T., (BV) .... '46 '77 C.860 B.A. L.107 J.D. [O'Connell,F.&A.]
*PRACTICE AREAS: Civil Litigation; Domestic Relations.
Flaherty, Patrick J., (AV) ....'33 '58 C.321 A.B. L.976 LL.B. [Cooney,S.&D.]
*PRACTICE AREAS: Railroad Liability; Transportation Liability; Food, Drug and Cosmetic Liability; Products Liability; Professional Liability.
Flanagan, Sheila B. '40 '68
C.856 B.A. L.128 LL.B. Assoc. Coun., Conn. Mut. Life Ins. Co.
Flanagan, Thomas M., (AV) .... '49 '81 C.188 B.A. L.823 J.D. [T.M.Flanagan]
*PRACTICE AREAS: Wills; Trusts and Estates; Probate; Estate Planning; Business Planning.

Flanagan, Thomas M., P.C., (AV)
1010 Wethersfield Avenue Suite 202, 06114-3149
Telephone: 860-296-1144 Fax: 860-296-7823
Email: tmfpc@snet.net URL: http://www.lawyers.com/fpc
Thomas M. Flanagan.
Estate Planning, Trust Administration, Estate Administration, Wills and Probate.
See Professional Biographies, HARTFORD, CONNECTICUT

Flanders, Susan Brooks, (BV) ....'58 '83 C.882 B.A. L.184 J.D. Asst. Atty. Gen.
Flannery, Sharon M. '64 '89 C.788 B.A. L.273 J.D.
(adm. in MD; not adm. in CT) Assoc. Coun., The Travelers Ins. Co.
Flaschen, Evan D., (BV) ....'57 '82 C.918 B.A. L.184 J.D. [Bingham D.]
Fleischmann, Eric ....'61 '87 C.976 B.A. L.893 J.D. [Leete&K.]
*PRACTICE AREAS: Immigration Law; Business Immigration.
Fleischmann, Karl, (AV) ....'37 '60 C.178 A.B. L.309 LL.B. [K.Fleischmann]

Fleischmann, Karl, P.C., (AV)
Capitol Place, 21 Oak Street Suite 210, 06106-8002
Telephone: 860-278-5500 Fax: 860-278-5503
Email: kfleischmann@snet.net
Karl Fleischmann.

(This Listing Continued)

Fleischmann, Karl, P.C. (Continued)
Real Estate Investment, Real Estate Finance and Real Estate Litigation.
See Professional Biographies, HARTFORD, CONNECTICUT

Fleming, Laurence P., (AV) . . . . '41 '66 C&L.184 B.A., J.D. [© Day,B.&H.]
*PRACTICE AREAS: Real Estate (100%).
Flinn, Horace G., Jr. . . . . '38 '87 C.586 B.S. L.184 J.D. [© Rome M.S.]
*PRACTICE AREAS: Estate Planning.
Flint, Kelly . . . . '— '92 C.602 B.A. L.209 J.D. 55 Elm St.
Flores, John R., (BV) '56 '81 C&L.178 B.A., J.D.
V.P., Litig. & Employ. Coun., Phoenix Home Life Mutual Ins. Co.
*RESPONSIBILITIES: Litigation; Department Head; Employment.
Flowers, Tammi Tuve '71 '96 C&L.93 B.A., J.D.
(adm. in MA; not adm. in CT) [Ⓐ Shipman&G.]
Floyd, Timothy J., (AV) . . . . '46 '78 C.575 B.S. L.280 J.D. [© Andros,F.&M.]
Flynn, Brendan T., (BV) . . . . '64 '89 C.821 B.A. L.184 J.D. [Ⓐ Rogin,N.C.L.&H.]
*PRACTICE AREAS: Appellate Practice; Administrative Law; Litigation; Commercial Litigation.
Flynn, David H., (BV) . . . . '53 '79 C.575 B.A. L.184 J.D. [© Day,B.&H.]
*PRACTICE AREAS: Asset Based Lending; Bankruptcy.
Flynn, Ellen Coward, (BV) '48 '78 C.914 A.B. L.184 J.D.
Asst. Gen. Coun., CIGNA Corp.
Flynn, Garrett S. . . . . '68 '93 C.321 B.A. L.273 J.D. 225 Asylum Street, 13th Floor
Flynn, Joseph P. . . . . '40 '65 C.1030 B.A. L.276 J.D. Supr. Ct. J.
Flynn, Thomas P. . . . . '64 '89 C&L.184 B.A., J.D. [Shipman&G.]
*PRACTICE AREAS: Corporate Law; Business Law; Corporate Finance Law; Corporate Trust Law; Emerging Growth and High Tech Companies.
Foden, Maria Luisa de C. . . . . '47 '80 C.705 B.A. L.184 J.D. 107 Oak St.

Fogarty Cohen Selby & Nemiroff LLC
(See Greenwich)

Foley, Jackson W., Jr. '43 '72
C.951 B.A. L.184 J.D. Coun., Conn. Community College Sys.
Foley, Michael E., (BV) . . . . . '61 '87 C.454 B.A. L.1048 J.D. [Pepe&H.] (◯Boston, MA)
*PRACTICE AREAS: Management Labor Law; Unfair Labor Practice; Collective Bargaining; Municipal Labor Law; School Board Defense.
Foltz, Laura J. '64 '90 C&L.184 B.A., J.D.
Coun., Hartford Financial Services Group, Inc.
Fontaine, Craig A., (BV) . . . . '55 '83 C.1156 B.S. L.900 J.D. [Cramer,A.&F.]
Foran, David M. . . . . '58 '86 C.829 B.A. L.945 J.D. 38 Woodland St.
Foran, Terrence J. . . . . '53 '80 C.1030 B.A. L.776 J.D. The Travelers Ins. Co.
Ford, Marilyn J. Ward . . . . '— '73 C.801 B.A. L.705 J.D. [© Moniz,C.&M.]
Ford, Paul W., (AV) . . . . '50 '78 C.94 B.A. L.1294 J.D. [Levin,F.&P.]
*PRACTICE AREAS: Commercial Real Estate; Real Estate; Finance; Leases and Leasing; Securities.
Ford, T. Mitchell . . . . '21 '48 C.309 A.B. L.976 J.D. One American Row
Forgione, Jacqueline . . . . '64 '00 C&L.1252 B.A., J.D. [Ⓐ Berman&S.]
*PRACTICE AREAS: Commercial Litigation; Business Litigation; Corporate Transactions.
Forman, Ina A. . . . . '56 '84 C.454 B.A. L.1048 J.D. Coun., House of Rep.
Fornaciari, Salvatore N. . . . . '68 '00 C.829 B.A. L.1252 J.D. [Ⓐ Halloran&S.]
Forsyth, Duncan J., (BV) . . . . '51 '77 C.901 B.A. L.896 J.D. [Halloran&S.]
*PRACTICE AREAS: Civil Litigation; Commercial Litigation; Land Use; Administrative; Environmental.
Fortier, Joseph K., (BV) . . . . '58 '84 C.184 B.A.B.S. L.188 J.D. [Reid&R.]
*PRACTICE AREAS: Commercial Real Estate; Commercial Leasing.
Fortier, Richard A. '45 '75 C.454 B.S. L.1048 J.D.
(adm. in MA; not adm. in CT) Coun., The Travelers Ins. Co.‡
Fortner, Joseph G., Jr., (BV) . . . . '56 '83 C.228 A.B. L.880 J.D. [Halloran&S.]
*PRACTICE AREAS: Civil Litigation; Complex Litigation; Federal Litigation; Commercial Litigation; Torts.
Fortune, Charles W., (BV) . . . . '57 '89 C.696 B.A. L.184 J.D. [Day,B.&H.]
*PRACTICE AREAS: Insurance Litigation; Commercial Litigation; Direct Liability and Casualty; Reinsurance.

Forzani, Carlo, (BV) '48 '76 C.855 B.A. L.184 J.D.
43 Woodland Street, Suite 500, 06105
Telephone: 860-482-4701 Fax: 860-251-6790
URL: http://www.lawyers.com/forzanilaw
Family Law and Mediation.
See Professional Biographies, HARTFORD, CONNECTICUT

Foss, Charles M. . . . . '48 '75 C.855 B.A. L.339 J.D. Coun., The Travelers Ins. Co.
Fountain, Shirley A. . . . . '47 '87 C.259 B.A. L.306 J.D. The Travelers Ins. Co.
Fournier, Stephen E. D., (BV) . . . . '45 '78 C&L.184 B.A., J.D. 74 Tremont St.
Fox, Christi Leigh '59 '85 C.798 B.S. L.862 J.D.
(adm. in MO; not adm. in CT) The Travelers Ins. Co.
Foy, Eric J. . . . . '71 '96 C.976 B.A. L.309 J.D. [Ⓐ Morrison,M.&M.]
*PRACTICE AREAS: Labor and Employment Law.
Francia, Rosina . . . . '63 '89 C&L.276 B.S., J.D. Office of State's Atty.
Francis, Nicholas Ward . . . . '63 '89 C.829 B.S. L.1048 J.D. 182 Collins Street
Francis, O'Neil & Del Piano, (AV) . . . . 255 Main St.
Francklyn, Reginald Endicott, (AV) '— '55 C.976 B.A. L.893 LL.B.
[© Robinson&C.]
Frankl, Jesse M., (BV) '38 '66 C&L.184 B.A., LL.B.
Chmn., State Wkrs. Comp. Comm.

Fransson, Karl A., (BV) '48 '75 C&L.184 B.A., J.D.
100 Wells Street, 06103
Telephone: 860-728-0259 Facsimile: 860-728-0231
Email: karl.a.fransson@SNET.NET URL: http://www.lawyers.com/kfransson
Bankruptcy, Collections; Foreclosure, Probate, Wills, Trust and Estates, Elder Law, Commercial, Business Law, Real Estate, General Practice, Living Wills, Powers of Attorney, Health Care, Commercial Bankruptcy, Consumer Bankruptcy, Contested Wills, Guardianship, Conservatorship.
See Professional Biographies, HARTFORD, CONNECTICUT

Frauenglass & Eisenberg
(See Glastonbury)

Frazzini, Stephen F. '47 '76
C&L.976 B.A., J.D. Exec. Dir., Greater Hartford Legal Asst., Inc
Frechette, Donald E. . . . . '58 '81 C.550 B.A. L.564 J.D. [Edwards&A.]
*PRACTICE AREAS: Complex Commercial Litigation; Products Liability; Reinsurance Arbitration; Reinsurance Litigation.
Frederick, Barbara A. . . . . '49 '97 C.449 B.A. L.184 J.D. [Ⓐ Updike,K.&S.]
*PRACTICE AREAS: Appellate Law; Litigation.
Freed, Samuel . . . . '27 '51 C.598 B.A. L.309 LL.B. Supr. Ct. J.
Freedman, Frederick A. . . . . '29 '54 C.184 B.A. L.976 LL.B. Sr. App. Ct. J.
Freedman, Susan C., (AV) . . . . '49 '89 C.184 B.A. L.273 J.D. [Shipman&G.]
*PRACTICE AREAS: College and University Law; Independent School Law; School Board Defense; Special Education Litigation.
Freeman, Brian C. S. . . . . '— '91 C.276 B.A. L.893 J.D. [Ⓐ Robinson&C.]
*PRACTICE AREAS: Environmental; Zoning, Planning and Land Use.
Freeman, Deborah Samuels, (BV) . . . . '51 '76 C.910 B.A. L.276 J.D. [Bingham D.]
Freeman, Donald E., (BV) . . . . '47 '76 C.511 B.A. L.184 J.D. 21 Oak St.
Freitag, William C. . . . . '51 '87 C.282 B.A. L.262 J.D. Compl. Offr., Advest, Inc.

Frey, Sara J. '56 '82 C&L.184 B.A., J.D.
Dir., Grants Legal & Admin. Affs., Rice Heights Health Ctr., Inc.
Fried, Robert B., (BV) . . . . '47 '72 C&L.184 B.A., J.D. 2 Congress St.
Fried, Samuel C., (AV) . . . . '47 '73 C.1044 B.A. L.107 J.D. 999 Asylum Ave.
Friedland, Allan S. . . . . '55 '82 C.659 B.S. L.1338 J.D. [© Jackson L.S.&K.]
Friedman, Matthew L. . . . . '58 '84 C.145 B.A. L.228 J.D. Coun., The Travelers Ins. Co.
Frisone, Deborah Smith . . . . '51 '87 C&L.184 B.A., J.D. [Shipman&G.]
*PRACTICE AREAS: Business Law; Computer and Technology Law; Electronic Commerce; Commercial Finance; Corporate Trust Law.
Fucci, F. Mark, (AV) . . . . '50 '77 C.390 A.B. L.184 J.D. [Bingham D.]
*PRACTICE AREAS: Commercial Finance; Corporate Finance; Loan Workouts and Restructuring; Creditors' Rights; Aviation Law.
Fulco, Dominic, III, (AV) . . . . '59 '84 C.309 B.A. L.831 J.D. [Reid&R.]
*PRACTICE AREAS: Alternative Dispute Resolution; Bankruptcy; Litigation.
Fung, Jean C. . . . . '69 '95 C.813 A.B./B.S. L.1066 J.D. [Ⓐ Murtha C.]
Furie, David J. . . . . '54 '80 C&L.184 B.A., J.D. U.S. Dept. HUD
Furniss, C. Thomas, (BV) . . . . '43 '72 C.31 B.A. L.893 J.D. [Furniss&Q.]
Furniss & Quinn, P.C., (AV) . . . . 248 Hudson St.
Fusco, August John, II, (BV) . . . . '54 '81 C.229 B.A. L.1029 J.D. [Fusco&G.]
Fusco, Michael A. . . . . '72 '97 C.93 B.A. L.1252 J.D. [Ⓐ Pepe&H.]
Fusco & Giuliano, (BV) . . . . 39 Russ St.
Gadarowski, James J., (BV) '43 '67
C&L.184 B.A., J.D. Coun., Phoenix Home Life Mut. Ins. Co.
*RESPONSIBILITIES: Distribution Systems; Litigation and Conflict Management; Broker-Dealer Arbitration.
Gaetano, Susan L. . . . . '70 '00 C.688 B.S. L.184 J.D. [Ⓐ Murtha C.]
Gaffney, Bernard F. . . . . '66 '93 C.708 B.A. L.818 J.D. [Ⓐ Rome M.S.]
*PRACTICE AREAS: Civil and Commercial Litigation; Products Liability Defense.
Galasyn, Peter C., Jr. . . . . '57 '83 C.184 B.A. L.1202 J.D. Mgr., The Travelers Ins. Co.
Gale, John Q., (BV) . . . . '51 '77 C.659 B.S. L.184 J.D. [Gale&K.]
*PRACTICE AREAS: Personal Injury Law; Estate Planning; Bankruptcy Law; Collections.

Gale & Kowalyshyn, LLC, (BV)
(Successor to Calvocoressi & Gale)
363 Main Street, 06106
Telephone: 860-522-8296 Fax: 860-522-8298
John Q. Gale; Kathleen J. Kowalyshyn; John L. Calvocoressi (Retired from firm 12/31/99).
General Practice. Trials and Appellate Practice in all Courts. Personal Injury, Real Estate, Estate Planning, Family, Administrative, Liquor Licensing and Disciplinary Proceedings, Collections.
Representative Clients: Zurich Insurance Co.; United Artist Communications and All Lending Institutions; Vinifera Imports; Monarch Wine; Laboratory Corp. of America.
Approved Attorney For: Connecticut Attorneys Title Insurance Co.
See Professional Biographies, HARTFORD, CONNECTICUT

Galiette, John V. . . . . '54 '79 C.309 B.A. L.93 J.D. [Reid&R.]
*PRACTICE AREAS: Employee Benefits; Pension Plans; Executive Compensation; Securities.

Gallagher & Calistro
(See New Haven)

Gallent, Amy '60 '86 C.188 B.S. L.262 J.D.
(adm. in NY; not adm. in CT)
Asst. Gen. Coun. & Corp. Secy., Hartford Financial Services Group, Inc.
Gallitto, William J. . . . . '50 '76 C.918 B.A. L.93 J.D. [Gordon,M.&F.]
*PRACTICE AREAS: Personal Injury Law; Medical Malpractice; Product Liability.
Gallo, Robert J. . . . . '73 '98 C.1030 B.A. L.184 J.D. [Ⓐ Cummings&L.]
*PRACTICE AREAS: Labor and Employment Law; Litigation.
Gamache, Paul H. . . . . '70 '95 C.860 B.S. L.184 J.D. [Ⓐ Siegel,O.S.&Z.]
*PRACTICE AREAS: Employment Litigation; Civil Rights Litigation; Commercial Litigation.
Gara, Elizabeth E. '60 '90 C.184 B.A. L.1029 J.D.
Asst. Coun., Conn. Bus. & Indus. Assn.
Garber, Ross H. . . . . '67 '92 C&L.184 B.A., J.D. [Ⓐ Shipman&G.]
*PRACTICE AREAS: Civil Fraud; Criminal Fraud; Criminal Defense; Health Care Fraud.
Gardner, Bruce D. '51 '81 C.184 B.A. L.724 J.D.
(adm. in NY; not adm. in CT) Hartford Plz.
Garfield, Diana, (AV) . . . . '44 '75 C.696 A.B. L.184 J.D. [Kainen,E.&M.]
*PRACTICE AREAS: Employment Law; Litigation; Labor Law.
Garfield, Gerald, (AV) . . . . '46 '71 C&L.477 B.A., J.D. [Day,B.&H.]
*PRACTICE AREAS: Energy.
Garger, Walter F. '65 '90 C.1030 B.A. L.1040 J.D.
Coun., Hartford Financial Services Group, Inc.
Garlick, Gerald L., (AV) . . . . '54 '79 C.1044 B.A. L.276 J.D. [Krasow,G.&H.]
Garofalo, Beverly W., (BV) . . . . '63 '91 C.170 B.A. L.184 J.D. [Brown R.M.F.&S.]
*PRACTICE AREAS: Employment Law; Executive Compensation.
Garrow, Suzanne . . . . '62 '97 C.788 L.588 [Ⓐ Day,B.&H.]
*PRACTICE AREAS: Employment; Employee Benefits; Litigation.
Gaston, Erich Henry . . . . '63 '98 C.829 B.S. L.1252 J.D. [Ⓐ Morrison,M.&M.]
*PRACTICE AREAS: Insurance Coverage; Insurance Defense.
Gates, Wendell S., (BV) . . . . '28 '58 C&L.94 B.S., LL.B. Asst. Atty. Gen.
Gaudreau, Donald G., (BV) . . . . '53 '82 C.1107 B.A. L.1048 J.D. 241 Main St.
Geanuracos, James G., (BV) . . . . '54 '83 C.178 B.A. L.184 J.D. [Skelley R.]
*PRACTICE AREAS: Personal Injury Law; Insurance Defense; Products Liability Law; Professional Liability; Workers Compensation Law.
Geathers, Tammy . . . . '62 '89 C.329 B.A. L.184 J.D. Asst. Atty. Gen.
Geetter, Melissa B. . . . . '72 '97 C.1044 B.S. L.306 J.D. [Ⓐ Gordon,M.&F.]
*PRACTICE AREAS: Employment Litigation; Labor Law; Insurance Defense; Product Liability; Civil Litigation.
Geissler, Stephen J. '62 '87 C.187 B.A. L.309 J.D. 1 American Row
Gellman, Stephen K., (AV) . . . . '63 '89 C.855 B.A. L.659 J.D. [Shipman&G.]
*PRACTICE AREAS: Estate Planning; Probate Matters; Trusts Administration.
Gelston, Bruce J. . . . . '69 '97 C.907 B.A. L.1252 J.D. [Howd&L.]
*PRACTICE AREAS: Insurance Defense; Products Liability; Municipal Law.
Generas, George P., Jr . . . . '43 '92 C.754 B.S. L.184 J.D. [© Rome M.S.]
*PRACTICE AREAS: General.
Gentile, Joan M. . . . . '59 '84 Coun., Hartford Financial Services Group, Inc.
Gentile, Richard P., (BV) . . . . '59 '85 C.178 A.B. L.262 J.D. 21 Oak St.
Geon, Tracy H. '66 '99 C.446 B.A. L.1243 J.D.
(adm. in NC; not adm. in CT) Claims Coun., Travelers Property Casualty
George, Louis N. . . . . '61 '87 C.867 B.A. L.1029 J.D. [Hassett&G.]
*PRACTICE AREAS: Civil Litigation; Commercial Litigation; Personal Injury; Worker's Compensation; Internet Law.
Georgetti, Michael A., (BV) . . . . '49 '80 C.1349 B.A. L.1048 J.D. 67 Russ St.
Gerace, William T., (AV) . . . . '54 '80 C&L.184 B.A., J.D. 21 Oak St.
Gerarde, Thomas R., (BV) . . . . '56 '81 C.1030 B.S. L.818 J.D. [Howd&L.]
*PRACTICE AREAS: Municipal Litigation; Product Liability Litigation; Insurance Defense Litigation; Employment Litigation; Appellate Practice.
Gerity, Patrick M. . . . . '65 '92 C&L.276 B.S.F.S., J.D. [Ⓐ Day,B.&H.]
*PRACTICE AREAS: Electric Utilities; Emerging Growth Companies; Corporate Contracts.
Gerson, Elliot F., (AV) . . . . '52 '81 C.309 A.B. L.976 J.D. Sr. V.P., The Travelers Corp.
Gersten, Aaron L., (AV) . . . . '26 '54 C&L.184 B.S., LL.B. [Gersten&G.]
Gersten, Charles D., (AV) . . . . '22 '49 C.273 B.A. L.309 LL.B. [© Gersten&C.]
Gersten, Eliot B., (BV) . . . . '52 '79 C.273 B.A. L.472 J.D. [Gersten&C.]
*PRACTICE AREAS: Business Litigation; Securities; White Collar Fraud.

Gersten, Joseph Z. . . . . '— '98 C.273 M.F.S. L.1252 J.D. [Ⓐ O'Connell,F.&A.]
Gersten, Karen S., (BV) . . . . '65 '90 C.156 B.A. L.818 J.D. [Ⓐ Gersten&G.]
*PRACTICE AREAS: Family Law.
Gersten, Maurice R., (AV) . . . . '— '41 C&L.273 A.B., LL.B. [Gersten&G.]

Gersten & Clifford, (BV)
214 Main Street, 06106-1892
Telephone: 860-527-7044 Fax: 860-527-4968
Members of Firm: Eliot B. Gersten; John P. Clifford, Jr.; Allan W. Koerner. Associates: Wendy J. Davies; John Joseph Robacynski. Of Counsel: Charles D. Gersten.
General Practice, Trials in all Courts. Negligence, White Collar Fraud, Securities Litigation, Professional Malpractice, Attorney Malpractice, Family, Real Estate and Probate.
See Professional Biographies, HARTFORD, CONNECTICUT

Gersten & Gersten, (AV)
234 Pearl Street, 06103
Telephone: 860-522-0173 URL: http://gerstenandgersten.com
Email: legal@gerstenandgersten.com URL: http://www.lawyers.com/gersten&gersten
Members of Firm: Maurice R. Gersten; Aaron L. Gersten. Associates: Philip K. Meister; Thomas D. Jacobs; Karen S. Gersten.
Trial Practice in State and Federal Courts, including plaintiffs in all types of Personal Injury, Malpractice, Workers Compensation, Probate, Real Estate, Matrimonial and Domestic Relations. Bankruptcy, Small Business, Professional Misconduct, Employee Discrimination, and Wrongful Termination.
See Professional Biographies, HARTFORD, CONNECTICUT

Getz, Janette R. . . . . '59 '86 C.1033 B.A. L.1048 J.D. [Ⓐ Trantolo&T.]
Getz, Richard D. '62 '92
C.184 B.S.M.E. L.1048 J.D. [Ⓐ McCormick,P.&H.] (See Pat. Sect.)
*PRACTICE AREAS: Intellectual Property Transactions; Licensing; Patents; Trademarks; Copyrights.
Gfeller, Alena C. . . . . '69 '95 C.36 B.A. L.1338 J.D. [Ⓐ Berman&S.]
*PRACTICE AREAS: Commercial Law and Litigation; Bankruptcy; Creditor's Rights; Construction Law; Litigation.
Gfeller, Charles F. . . . . '70 '95 C.264 B.A. L.1338 J.D. 225 Asylum Street, 13th Floor
Giantonio, Brian A. '55 '83
C.745 B.A. L.300 J.D. Coun., Phoenix Home Life Mut. Ins. Co.
*RESPONSIBILITIES: Taxation (100%).
Giarratana, Mark D. . . . . '60 '87 C.128 B.S.M.E. L.306 J.D. [Cummings&L.] (Pat.)
*PRACTICE AREAS: Patents; Trademarks; Copyrights; Antitrust; Unfair Competition.
Gibbons, Thomas R. . . . . '51 '80 C.264 B.A. L.64 J.D. [Jackson L.S.&K.]
Gibbs, J. David, (AVⓉ) '54 '79 C.692 B.A. L.245 J.D.
(adm. in GA; not adm. in CT)
Exec. V.P., Claims Servs., Travelers/Aetna Property Casualty Corp.
Gifford, Nancy V. . . . . '69 '95 C.550 B.A. L.94 J.D. 1 American Row
Gilbert, Robert D. . . . . '55 '82 C.674 A.B. L.976 J.D. [Brown R.M.F.&S.]
*PRACTICE AREAS: Complex Civil Litigation; Intellectual Property Litigation; Internet Litigation; Finance Litigation; Franchise Litigation.
Gilcreast, Mark S., (BV) . . . . '56 '86 C.93 A.B. L.1048 J.D. 21 Oak St.
Gillette, Douglas W. . . . . '53 '81 C.311 B.A. L.94 J.D. [Ⓒ Day,B.&H.]
*PRACTICE AREAS: Municipal Bonds; Municipal Finance; Municipal Securities; Municipal Corporation Law.
Gillies, John J., Jr., (AV) . . . . '46 '72 C.276 A.B. L.93 J.D. [Dechert]
*PRACTICE AREAS: Investment Management; Investments; Institutional Investment Law; Investment Partnerships; Debt and Equity Finance.

Gilman & Marks
(See East Hartford)

Gilmore, Douglas E. . . . . '66 '91 C.787 B.A. L.1202 J.D. [Ⓐ Regnier,T.C.&E.]
*PRACTICE AREAS: General Practice; Trial Practice; Insurance; Toxic Torts; Products Liability.
Gilmore, Paul N., (BV) . . . . '63 '88 C.259 B.S. L.575 J.D. [Ⓐ Updike,K.&S.]
*PRACTICE AREAS: Commercial Litigation; Appellate Law; Creditors' Rights; Bankruptcy; Loan Workouts.
Ginnetti, John P. . . . . '45 '71 C&L.184 B.A., J.D. Hartford Plz.‡
Giordanella, Frank . . . . '59 '85 C.276 B.S.F.S. L.309 J.D. [Murtha C.]
*PRACTICE AREAS: Finance Law; Municipal Bond Law; Resource Recovery Law.
Girolamo, Sandi Beth . . . . '71 '01 C.184 B.A. L.1252 J.D. [Ⓐ O'Connell,F.&A.]
*PRACTICE AREAS: Ciovil Litigation; Family Law.
Giuliani, Mark R. . . . . '60 '92 C.1103 B.S. L.1029 J.D. [Ⓐ Halloran&S.]
*PRACTICE AREAS: Premises Liability; Homeowners Liability.
Giuliano, Carmine J. . . . . '47 '81 C.793 B.A. L.1029 J.D. [Fusco&G.]
Giunta, Robert V., Jr., (BV) . . . . '49 '77 C.30 B.A. L.184 J.D. [Murtha C.]
*PRACTICE AREAS: Bond Finance Law; Real Estate and Housing Law.
Gladke, Lisa Denise . . . . '— '98 C.183 B.A. L.93 J.D. [Ⓐ Shipman&G.]
*PRACTICE AREAS: Public Finance; Real Estate.
Gladstone, Steven J. '58 '86 C.1365 B.A. L.990 J.D.
Sr. Vice Pres., Executive Liability Underwriters
Glaser, Claude E., Jr. '19 '41 L.262 LL.B.
(adm. in NY; not adm. in CT) Sr. V.P., ITT Hartford Ins. Grp.
Glassman, Andrew C., (BV) '60 '85 C.188 B.S. L.184 J.D.
[Pullman&C.] (☉Simsbury)
*PRACTICE AREAS: Corporate Law; Mergers and Acquisitions; Employment Law; Commercial Transactions.
Glezen, John C., (AV) . . . . '36 '61 C.299 B.A. L.976 LL.B. [Ⓒ Day,B.&H.]
*PRACTICE AREAS: Real Estate Law; Real Estate Finance and Development.
Glissman, David R., (AV) . . . . '57 '84 C.763 B.S. L.464 J.D. [MacDermid,R.&G.]
*PRACTICE AREAS: Real Property; Conveyancing; Leasing; Workouts; Finance.
Globman, Marcus & Chapple, P.C. . . . . .44 Capitol Ave.
Gnocchi, Thadd A. . . . . '50 '75 C.321 B.A. L.184 J.D. Asst. Atty. Gen.
Goddard, Stephen B., (BV) . . . . '41 '72 C.67 B.A. L.184 J.D. 330 Main St.
Goetz, Matthew D. . . . . '65 '91 C.1044 B.A. L.823 J.D. Ct. Clk.
Gold, Lee Andrew . . . . '72 '97 C.401 B.A. L.306 J.D. [Ⓐ Butler N.&G.]
Gold, Martin P., (BV) . . . . '45 '71 C.184 B.A. L.306 J.D. [Butler N.&G.]
Gold, Ronald, (AV) . . . . '45 '71 C.477 A.B. L.1009 J.D. Sr. Asst. Pub. Def.
Goldberg, Gerald B. . . . . '66 '90 C.1349 B.A. L.273 J.D. Prudential Securities, Inc.
Golden, Andrew S. . . . . '— '96 C.184 B.A. L.1048 J.D. [Ⓐ Robinson&C.]
*PRACTICE AREAS: Labor and Employment; Litigation.
Golden, David E. . . . . '— '94 C.1036 B.A. L.569 J.D. [Ⓐ Brown,R.F.&G.]
*PRACTICE AREAS: Corporate.
Golden, Lawrence J., (BV) . . . . '47 '73 C&L.893 B.A., J.D. [Pullman&C.]
*PRACTICE AREAS: Energy; Environmental; Public Utility; Land Use; Litigation.
Goldman, Ira H., (AV) . . . . '47 '72 C.188 B.A. L.976 J.D. [Shipman&G.]
*PRACTICE AREAS: Bankruptcy and Reorganization Law; Pension, Compensation and Employee Benefit Planning Law.
Goldman, Stephen E., (AV) . . . . '— '80 C.918 B.A. L.569 J.D. [Robinson&C.]
*PRACTICE AREAS: Litigation; Insurance.
Goldstein, Evan S. . . . . '73 '00 C.882 B.A L.1398 J.D. [Ⓐ Reid&R.]
*PRACTICE AREAS: Bankruptcy.
Goldstein, Richard H., (BV) . . . . '49 '76 C.67 B.S. L.30 J.D. [Sandler,G.&M.]
*PRACTICE AREAS: Municipal and Public Agency.
Goldstein, Samuel S. . . . . '25 '51 C.855 B.A. L.976 LL.B. Sr. Trial Ref. J.
Good, Joan R. . . . . '46 '71 C.431 B.A. L.1294 J.D. The Travelers Ins. Co.
Goodman, Harriet J., (BV) . . . .'41 '81 C.914 B.A. L.184 J.D. Coun., The Travelers Ins. Co.
Goodman, Marcia B. '44 '75
C.1044 B.A. L.184 J.D. Dir., State Gen. Assembly, Legis. Comr. Off.

Goodman, Rosenthal & McKenna, P.C.
(See West Hartford)

Goodrich, John H., Jr. . . . . '43 '68 C.454 B.A. L.945 J.D. [Gordon,M.&F.]
*PRACTICE AREAS: Real Estate; Probate; Elder Law; Estate Planning.
Goodstein, Gregory C. . . . . '67 '94 C.896 B.A. L.1048 J.D. [Ⓐ Morrison,M.&M.]
*PRACTICE AREAS: Workers Compensation.
Goodusky, Amy F. . . . . '— '96 C.1307 B.A. L.184 J.D. [Ⓐ O'Brien,T.&Y.]
*PRACTICE AREAS: Litigation; Medical Malpractice Defense; Workers Compensation.
Googins, Robert R. . . . . '37 '61 C&L.184 B.S., LL.B. Comr. of Ins.
Gordon, Matthew Dallas, (BV) . . . . '56 '87 C.65 B.A. L.184 J.D. [Skelley R.]
*PRACTICE AREAS: Insurance Defense Law; Commercial Litigation; Professional Liability; Municipal Liability.

Gordon, Muir and Foley, LLP, (AV)
Hartford Square North, Ten Columbus Boulevard, 06106-5123
Telephone: 860-525-5361 Telecopier: 860-525-4849
Email: admin@gmflaw.com URL: http://www.gmflaw.com
Members of Firm: William S. Gordon, Jr. (1946-1956); George Muir (1939-1976); Edward J. Foley (1955-1983); John J. Reid; John H. Goodrich, Jr.; R. Bradley Wolfe; Jon Stephen Berk; William J. Gallitto; Gerald R. Swirsky; Robert J. O'Brien; Philip J. O'Connor; Kenneth G. Williams; Mary Anne Alicia Charron; Andrew James Hern; Reneé W. Dwyer; Patty G. Swan; Erik E. Roberts. Associates: Doreen West Amata; Durwin P. Jones; Melissa B. Geetter; Christine L. Chipman; William P. Mastrogiovanni, Jr. Of Counsel: Peter C. Schwartz.
General Practice. Trials in all Courts. Insurance, Construction, Fidelity, Surety, Product Liability, Toxic Substances, Personal Injury, Professional Malpractice, Commercial, Real Estate, Probate, Corporation and Administrative Law.
Reference: People's Bank.
See Professional Biographies, HARTFORD, CONNECTICUT

Gore, Gerald B. . . . . '61 '89 C.976 B.A. L.1048 J.D. 363 Main St.
Gorman, Robert J., Jr., (AV) . . . . '53 '78 C.321 B.A. L.184 J.D. [Krevolin,F.G.E.&H.]
Gorna, Susan L. . . . . '54 '96 C.665 B.S.W. L.1048 J.D. Coun., Litig., Aetna Inc.
*RESPONSIBILITIES: ERISA and New ERISA Group Disability Litigation; ERISA and New ERISA Group Life Litigation.
Gorra, Nicholas J., II, (CV) '63 '92
C.156 B.A. L.1202 J.D. [Ⓐ O'Connell,F.&A.] (☉Old Saybrook)
*PRACTICE AREAS: Commercial Transactions; Commercial Litigation; Real Estate; Estate Planning; Civil Litigation.
Goss, Kenneth A. . . . . '74 '00 C.1046 B.A. L.1252 J.D. [Ⓐ Krasow,G.&H.]
*PRACTICE AREAS: Commercial Real Estate; Banking Law; Finance; Corporate Law; Bankruptcy.
Gostyla, Jeffrey F. . . . . '68 '94 C.884 B.A. L.1252 J.D. [Ⓐ Halloran&S.]
*PRACTICE AREAS: Litigation; Criminal Law; Labor and Employment Law; Probate Law; Insurance Defense.
Gottehrer, Gail L. '67 '92 C.1349 B.A. L.659 J.D.
(adm. in NJ; not adm. in CT) 225 Asylum Street, 13th Floor
Gottesman, Gary F., (BV) . . . . '51 '78 C.1033 B.A. L.1048 J.D. 179 Allyn St.

Gould, Jonathan, (AV) '51 '76 C.858 A.B. L.184 J.D.
214 Main Street, 06106-1817
Telephone: 860-278-9115 Fax: 860-278-9124
Email: jgould@nela.org
***PRACTICE AREAS: Labor Law; Workers Compensation Law.**
All aspects of Labor and Employment Law, Employee Benefits, Workplace and Other Injuries.
See Professional Biographies, HARTFORD, CONNECTICUT

Gould, Martin A., (AV) . . . . '40 '65 C&L.94 B.A., LL.B. [Gould,K.&W.]
*PRACTICE AREAS: Estate Planning; Probate; Commercial Real Estate; Residential Real Estate; Civil Litigation.
Gould, Nancy E. . . . . '66 '91 C.867 B.S. L.94 J.D. [Gould,K.&W.]
*PRACTICE AREAS: Employment Law; Real Estate; Family Law; Civil Litigation; Divorce.

Gould, Killian & Wynne, (AV) BB
280 Trumbull Street, 25th Floor, 06103-3595
Telephone: 860-278-1270 Telecopier: 860-244-9290
Members of Firm: Samuel Gould (1905-1994); Robert K. Killian; Francis J. Wynne; Martin A. Gould; Mark W. Baronas; Nancy E. Gould; Robert O. Wynne.
General Practice. Real Estate, Probate, Corporation, Estate Planning, Family, Education, Personal Injury, Divorce and Child Custody, Trials and Appeals in all Courts.
See Professional Biographies, HARTFORD, CONNECTICUT

Goumas, Gregg P. . . . . '70 '97 C.951 B.A. L.1048 J.D. [Ⓐ Shipman&G.]
*PRACTICE AREAS: Employment Litigation.
Govier, William F. . . . . '68 '99 C.800 B.M. L.306 J.D. [Ⓐ Bingham D.]
*PRACTICE AREAS: Restructured Finance; Institutional Finance; Structured Finance.
Gowanlock, William B. '52 '95
C.477 B.S.E. L.128 J.D. [Ⓐ McCormick,P.&H.] (See Pat. Sect.)
*PRACTICE AREAS: Intellectual Property; Patent Prosecution; Government Contracts.
Grady, Christine S., (BV) . . . . '51 '83 C.216 B.A. L.184 J.D. Coun., Aetna Life & Cas. Co.
Grady, Robert E. . . . . '— '99 C.454 B.A. L.184 J.D. [Ⓐ Dechert]
*PRACTICE AREAS: Real Estate Finance.
Graham, Drew S. . . . . '67 '95 C.860 B.A. L.184 J.D. [Ⓐ Updike,K.&S.]
*PRACTICE AREAS: Insurance Defense; Personal Injury; Municipal Law.
Graham, James C., (AV) . . . . '55 '80 C.976 B.A. L.893 J.D. [Pepe&H.] (☉Southport)
*PRACTICE AREAS: Bankruptcy; Litigation; Commercial Law; Legal Ethics and Professional Responsibility; Debtor and Creditor.
Graham, Kimberly Anne . . . . '61 '87 C.329 B.A. L.472 J.D. Asst. States Atty.
Graves, Suzanne E. . . . . '76 '01 C.264 B.A. L.306 J.D. [Ⓐ Updike,K.&S.]
*PRACTICE AREAS: Commercial Litigation; Personal Law.
Greaves, Fiona M. . . . . '— '93 C.881 A.B. L.178 J.D. [Ⓐ Cummings&L.]
*PRACTICE AREAS: Litigation.
Green, James G., Jr., (BV) . . . . '55 '80 C.93 B.A. L.893 J.D. [Pepe&H.]
*PRACTICE AREAS: Business Litigation; Contract Litigation; Accountants' Liability; Corporate Litigation; Civil Appeals.
Green, Raymond B., (AV) . . . . '29 '54 C&L.976 A.B., LL.B. [Ⓒ Day,B.&H.]
*PRACTICE AREAS: Products Liability Defense; Legal Ethics; Commercial Litigation.
Green, Robert B. . . . . '41 '66 C.976 B.A. L.178 LL.B. Sr. V.P., The Travelers Corp.

Green and Gross, P.C.
(See Bridgeport)

Green & Levine LLP
(See Farmington)

Greenberg, Richard K., (BV) . . . . '45 '70 C.659 B.S. L.94 J.D. Asst. Atty. Gen.
Greene, Barry D., (AV) . . . . '34 '59 C.103 A.B. L.184 LL.B. [Pullman&C.]
*PRACTICE AREAS: Real Estate; Corporate Law; Business Law.
Greene, David R. . . . . '63 '94 C.171 B.S. L.1040 J.D. 225 Asylum Street, 13th Floor
Greene, Gary, (BV) . . . . '58 '82 C.994 B.A. L.229 J.D. 39 Grand St.
Greene, Kevin J. . . . . '70 '95 C.262 B.A. L.1048 J.D. [Ⓐ Halloran&S.]
*PRACTICE AREAS: Insurance Defense; Commercial Litigation; Subrogation; Motor Vehicle Tort; Premises Liability.
Greenfield, James, (AV) . . . . '47 '74 C.103 A.B. L.178 J.D. [Bingham D.]
Greenslade, Maria Marena . . . . '59 '85 C.184 B.A. L.809 J.D. Mng. Atty., Secy. of State
Greenspan, Steven M., (AV) . . . . '60 '85 C.659 B.A. L.184 J.D. [Day,B.&H.]
*PRACTICE AREAS: Franchise and Distributorship Litigation; Commercial Litigation.
Greenspoon, Lauren R. . . . . '64 '89 C&L.659 B.A., J.D. [Ⓒ Cummings&L.]
*PRACTICE AREAS: Securities Litigation; Commercial Litigation; Insurance Coverage; Bad Faith Litigation.

Grello, Nicholas J., Jr. ....'63 '89 C&L.94 B.A., J.D. [Siegel,O.S.&Z.]
*PRACTICE AREAS: Labor Relations; Privacy Law; Public Sector Labor Relations; Employment Law; Education Law.
Grey, Julie Fairchild ....'62 '88 C.938 B.A. L.818 J.D. [Ⓒ Murtha C.]
*PRACTICE AREAS: Commercial Real Estate; Transactional.
Griffin, Colette S. ....'58 '87 C.112 B.A. L.1252 J.D. [Howd&L.]
*PRACTICE AREAS: Insurance Defense; Workers Compensation.
Griffin, Michael T. ....'69 '98 C.184 B.A. L.306 J.D. [Ⓐ Edwards&A.]
*PRACTICE AREAS: Insurance; Reinsurance; Corporate Law.
Griffith, Wm. Tucker '73 '98
C.971 B.S. L.306 J.D. [Ⓐ McCormick,P.&H.] (See Pat. Sect.)
*PRACTICE AREAS: Intellectual Property; Litigation; Patents; Trademarks; Copyrights.
Grinnell, Christopher M. '63 '91 C.860 B.A. L.184 J.D.
Assoc. Coun., Hartford Life, Inc.
Groark, Thomas J., Jr., (AV) ....'37 '65 C.321 A.B. L.184 LL.B. [Day,B.&H.]
*PRACTICE AREAS: Securities Litigation; Direct Liability and Casualty; Commercial Litigation; Insurance Litigation; Regulatory Insurance Proceedings and Litigation.
Grob, Bettina Cavanagh ....'66 '91 C.702 B.S. L.1252 J.D. [Ⓐ Morrison,M.&M.]
*PRACTICE AREAS: Insurance Defense; Environmental; Employment Discrimination; Personal Injury.
Grody, Jeffrey G., (AV) ....'55 '80 C.674 A.B. L.178 J.D. [Day,B.&H.]
*PRACTICE AREAS: Closely Held Businesses; Bankruptcy; Finance and Investments; Emerging Companies; Bankruptcy Counseling.
Groher, Andrew S., (AV) ....'52 '78 C.893 B.A. L.184 J.D. [RisCassi&D.]
*PRACTICE AREAS: Medical Malpractice; Negligence; Products Liability.
Grondahl, Eric E. ....'59 '91 C.860 B.S. L.184 J.D. [Ⓐ Cummings&L.]
Groves, Jennifer L. ......'73 '98 C.976 B.A. L.93 J.D. [Ⓐ Updike,K.&S.] (⊙New Haven)
*PRACTICE AREAS: Professional Liability Defense; Insurance Defense; Human Services.
Grzybowski, Donald Michael '69 '95 C.588 B.S. L.1040 J.D.
Travelers Property Casualty
Guest, J. Hanson, (BV) ....'— '82 C.145 B.A. L.976 J.D. [Brown,R.F.&G.]
*PRACTICE AREAS: International Corporate Finance; Corporate Finance; Banking Law; Public Finance; Economic Development.
Guggina, Paul ....'65 '01 C.801 B.S. L.93 J.D. [Ⓐ Tyler C.&A.]
Gugliotti, Thomas A., (AV) ....'49 '75 C.1030 A.B. L.818 J.D. [Updike,K.&S.]
*PRACTICE AREAS: Bankruptcy, Loan Workouts, Creditors' Rights; Commercial Foreclosures and Related Litigation; Real Estate and Title Litigation.
Guido, Amy LaVelle ....'64 '89 C.1252 B.A. L.94 J.D. Asst. Atty. Gen.
Guolee, Terrence '65 '91 C.966 B.A. L.209 J.D.
(adm. in IL; not adm. in CT) Asst. Dir., Ouside Coun., Hartford Ins.
Gurevitz, Mark S., (AV) '54 '79 C.645 B.S. L.831 J.D.
V.P. & Assoc. Gen. Coun., Hartford Financial Services Group, Inc.
Guss, Debra F. .... '65 '91 C.918 B.A. L.911 J.D. Coun., United Technologies Corp.
*RESPONSIBILITIES: Finance.
Gutermann, Peter A., (BV) '59 '86 C.855 B.A. L.930 J.D.
Assoc. Gen. Coun., United Technologies Corp.
*RESPONSIBILITIES: Corporate Law; Litigation.
Gutowski, Julie Larson '65 '90 C.645 B.B.A. L.588 J.D.
(adm. in MA; not adm. in CT) Assoc. Envir. Coun., ITT Hartford Ins. Grp.
Haakonsen, Kate W., (BV) '53 '78
C.874 B.A. L.184 J.D. [Brown,P.&S.] (⊙Glastonbury, Hebron)
*PRACTICE AREAS: Domestic Relations; Mediation; Civil Litigation; Medical Malpractice; Employment Mediation.
Haddad, Christopher Markham ....'69 '95 C.893 B.A. L.184 J.D. [Ⓐ Tyler C.&A.]
Haddad, Jennifer W. ....'72 '97 C.1030 B.S. L.184 J.D. [Ⓐ Pepe&H.]
Hadden, J. C. David, (AV) ....'— '80 C.309 A.B. L.893 J.D. [Robinson&C.]
*PRACTICE AREAS: Trusts and Estates; Wills; Probate; Tax Exempt Organizations.
Hadley, Linda Clifford, (BV) ....'59 '84 C.164 B.A. L.93 J.D. [Krasow,G.&H.]
Haerter, Ursula L. ....'62 '93 C.188 B.S. L.184 J.D. [Pepe&H.]
*PRACTICE AREAS: Labor and Employment; Employment Defense; Management Labor Law.
Haesche, Frederick J. '24 '66
C&L.184 B.S., J.D. [Ⓒ McCormick,P.&H.] (See Pat. Sect.) ⊙
*PRACTICE AREAS: Intellectual Property; Patents; Trademarks; Copyrights.

Haese, LLC
100 Pearl Street, 14th Floor, 06103 ⊙
Telephone: 860-249-7194 Facsimile: 860-249-7195
URL: http://www.haese.com
Glenn H. Haese (Not admitted in CT).
Construction and Design Law, Insurance, Fidelity and Surety, Environmental Law, Government Contract Law, Commercial, OSHA Laws and Regulations, Real Property and Finance, Banking and Trial and Appellate Practice in all State and Federal Courts.
Boston, Massachusetts Office: 70 Franklin Street, 9th Floor. Telephone: 617-428-0266. Facsimile: 617-428-0276. URL: http://www.haese.com.
See Professional Biographies, HARTFORD, CONNECTICUT

Haese, Glenn H. '57 '83 C.37 B.S.C.E. L.208 J.D.
(adm. in CO; not adm. in CT) [Haese] ⊙
*PRACTICE AREAS: Construction Law; Engineering Law; Environmental Law; Government Contract Law; Hazardous Waste.
Hagarty, Thomas J., Jr., (BV) ....'52 '77 C.321 B.A. L.184 J.D. [Halloran&S.]
*PRACTICE AREAS: Professional Liability; Insurance Defense; Workers Compensation Law.
Hager, Karen Halpern ......'46 '89 C.1029 B.S. L.1048 J.D. Legal Resch. Clk., Jud. Dept.
Haines, John G., (BV) ....'47 '72 C.415 B.A. L.884 J.D. Asst. Atty. Gen.
Hajost, Theresa W. '54 '85 C.1105 B.A. L.273 J.D.
(adm. in MD; not adm. in CT) [Halloran&S.]
*PRACTICE AREAS: Litigation; Arbitration; Insurance; Reinsurance; Commercial Litigation.
Hale, Darryl ....'61 '87 C.188 B.S. L.309 J.D. Natl. Labor Rel. Bd.
Hall, Laurie A. ....'57 '93 C.183 B.A. L.184 J.D. [Ⓐ Hawkins,D.&W.]
Hall, Matthew S. ....'66 '93 C.67 B.A. L.93 J.D. 864 Wethers Field Avenue
Hallas, Louise L. ....'47 '83 C.1318 A.B. L.1048 J.D. Staff Atty., Supm. & App. Cts.
Hallisey, John P. '64 '93 C.321 A.B. L.1048 J.D.
Hartford Financial Services Group, Inc.
Halloran, Michael F., (AV) .... '40 '65 C&L.976 B.A., LL.B. [Day,B.&H.]
*PRACTICE AREAS: Water Companies; Energy.

Halloran, R. Bartley, Law Offices of
(See Levy and Droney, P.C. in Farmington)

Halloran & Sage LLP, (AV) BR
One Goodwin Square, 225 Asylum Street, 06103 ⊙
Telephone: 860-522-6103 Fax: 860-548-0006
URL: http://www.halloran-sage.com
Members of Firm: Joseph G. Lynch; Joseph T. Sweeney; George Royster; Arthur P. McGowan, Jr.; John W. Lemega; Vincent M. Marino (Resident, Middletown Office); Richard C. Tynan; William P. Borchert; Thomas J. Hagarty, Jr.; Paul V. Knopf; Brian J. Donnell; James J. Szerejko; William J. McGrath, Jr.; Dennis C. Cavanaugh; Christopher J. Lynch; Paul D. Meade; Joseph G. Fortner, Jr.; Stephen P. Fogerty (Resident, Westport Office); Peter G. Boucher; Steven H. Malitz; John B. Farley; David B. Losee; Mark T. Altermatt; Henry M. Beck, Jr.; Susan O'Donnell; Bruce H. Raymond; Kevin M. Roche; David G. Hill; Daniel P. Scapellati; James M. Sconzo; Robert B. Cox; Thomas P. O'Dea, Jr. (Resident, Westport Office); Gregory R. Faulkner; Dan E. LaBelle (Resident, Westport Office); Duncan J. Forsyth; Ann M. Catino; James P. Maher; Carl R. Ficks, Jr.; Robert M. Barrack; John W. Dietz (Resident, Westport Office); Brian P. Leaming; James C. Stearns (Not admitted in CT); Theresa W. Hajost (Not admitted in CT). Associates: Richard P. Roberts; John S. Rosania; Mark T. Livesay; Thomas P. Lambert (Resident, Westport Office); Robert A. Rhodes (Resident, Westport Office); Laura A. Zaino; Reed A. Slatas; Thomas J. Finn; Janice D. Lai; Melissa Rotenberg Arcaro; Ralph W.

(This Listing Continued)

Halloran & Sage LLP (Continued)

Johnson, III; Martin A. Onorato; Jeffrey F. Gostyla; Elizabeth A. Fitzsimmons; Pasquale Amodeo; Brett M. Szczesny (Resident, Westport Office); Alan P. Curto; Kevin J. Greene; Mark R. Giuliani; Brian C. Clifford; N. Kane Bennett; Kristin T. Alix; Lori D. DiBella; John C. Huggins; Patrick M. Birney; Stephanie J. Sweeney; Gregory K. Holness; Stephen H. Broer; Peter E. Strniste, Jr.; Erik J. Ness; Andrew D. Moore; Salvatore N. Fornaciari; Amy Sargeant Lang; Annmarie P. Briones; Kristie E. Mackin. Of Counsel: Irwin J. Mittleman (Not admitted in CT); Robert C. Engstrom; Alan S. Rubenstein (Resident, Westport Office); Mary L. Barrow; Gina L. Schaecher (Not admitted in CT); Lisa M. Kowtko (Resident, Westport Office).
Administrative Law, Administrative Hearings and Appeals, Alternative Dispute Resolution, Appellate Practice, Aviation Products Liability, Bad Faith Litigation, Banking Law, Bankruptcy, Breach of Contract, Business Disputes, Business Law, Business Litigation, Business Planning, Casualty Insurance Litigation, Civil Appeals, Civil Litigation, Civil Rights Litigation, Class Action, Commercial Litigation, Complex Civil Litigation, Construction and Design Law, Construction Litigation, Corporate Contracts, Corporate Law, Criminal Litigation, Drug and Medical Device Litigation, Employment Law, Energy and Health Law, Environmental Law, Excess Insurance, Family Business Succession, Fidelity and Surety Law, Finance, Education Law, Employment Law, Environmental, Environmental Insurance Coverage, ERISA, ERISA Litigation, Estate Administration, Estate and Gift Taxation, Estates Law, Excess Insurance, General Corporate Law, General Liability, Government Contracts, Government Finance, Government Relations, Health and Life Insurance Litigation, Insurance Bad Faith Litigation, Insurance Coverage, Institutional Liability Law, Insurance Litigation, Insurance Regulation, Intellectual Property Litigation, International Law, Judicial Review, Labor and Employment, Land Use Planning Law, Lead Paint Litigation, Legislative Practice, Liquor Liability, Lobbying, Marine Insurance Defense, Medical Malpractice, Mergers and Acquisitions and Divestitures, Municipal Law, Municipal Liability, Probate Law, Products Liability Litigation, Professional Liability Litigation, Professional Regulation, Premises Liability, Property Insurance, Psychological Injury Claims, Public Utilities Law, Public Utility Regulation, Real Estate Transactions, Reinsurance Law, Risk Management Consulting, Secured Lending, Securities Law, Subrogation, Taxation Law, Telecommunications Law, Torts, Trade Association, Trucking Transportation Litigation, Trust Law, Unfair Trade, Uninsured and Underinsured Motorists, University Law, Workers Compensation Law, Zoning, Planning and Land Use.
Middletown, Connecticut Office: 300 Plaza Middlesex, 06457. Telephone: 860-346-8641. Fax: 860-344-1641.
Westport, Connecticut Office: 315 Post Road West, 06880-4739. Telephone: 203-227-2855. Fax: 203-227-6992.
Washington, D.C. Office: 1627 I Street, N.W., Suite 610, 20006. Telephone: 202-496-9270. Fax: 202-496-9279.
See Professional Biographies, HARTFORD, CONNECTICUT

Halperin, Jeffrey P. '67 '92
C.477 B.A. L.184 J.D. Sr. Admin. Atty., State Dept. of Banking
Halperin, Susan E. ....'47 '73 C&L.184 B.A., J.D. Mag.
Halpern, Kenneth S., (BV) ....'33 '58 C&L.184 B.S., J.D. 1 Corporate Ctr.
Hamer, Donald L., (BV) .... '50 '77 C&L.276 A.B., J.D. [Brown,P.&S.] (⊙Glastonbury)
*PRACTICE AREAS: Estate Planning; Probate; Commercial Real Estate; Residential Real Estate; Business Law.
Hammer, Joseph L., (BV) ....'60 '85 C.478 A.B. L.184 J.D. [Ⓒ Day,B.&H.]
*PRACTICE AREAS: Environmental Litigation; Land Use Permitting; Land Use Litigation; Real Estate Tax Appeals; Condemnation.
Hammersmith, Gary S. .... '60 '86 C.945 A.B. L.893 J.D. [Shipman&G.]
*PRACTICE AREAS: Business Law; Venture and Intellectual Property; Mergers and Acquisitions; Corporate Transactions; Commercial Law.
Hammond, Douglas W., (BV) .... '60 '88 C.976 B.A. L.184 J.D. [RisCassi&D.]
*PRACTICE AREAS: Personal Injury; Products Liability; Negligence.
Hammond, Michael P., Jr. .... '— '91 C&L.184 B.A., J.D. [Ⓒ Day,B.&H.]
*PRACTICE AREAS: Technology; Intellectual Property.
Hanks, John H., (BV) ....'59 '87 C.674 A.B. L.184 J.D. [Ⓐ Noble,Y.&O.]
*PRACTICE AREAS: Insurance Defense.
Hanlon, J. Roger, (AV) ....'38 '64 C.197 B.A. L.188 LL.B. [Day,B.&H.]
*PRACTICE AREAS: Real Estate Finance; Commercial Leasing; Real Estate Development; Real Estate Workouts and Restructuring.
Hannon, Kathleen M., (BV) '58 '83 C.999 B.A. L.128 J.D.
Coun., The Travelers Ins. Co.
Hard, Eric C., (BV) ....'60 '87 C.881 B.A. L.477 J.D. 39 Grand St.
Harleston, Patricia Lilly, (BV) ....'48 '74 C.329 B.M.E. L.184 J.D. Asst. Atty. Gen.
Harmon, Bryon W. ....'67 '97 C.184 B.A L.1048 J.D. [Ⓐ Shipman&G.]
*PRACTICE AREAS: Trusts and Estates.
Harmon, Valicia D. ....'65 '99 C.914 B.A. L.306 J.D. [Ⓐ Day,B.&H.]
*PRACTICE AREAS: Insurance Defense; Products Liability; Negligence Defense; Torts; Commercial Litigation.
Harper, Albert B., (BV) ....'50 '90 C.846 B.A. L.184 J.D. [Harper&H.]
Harper, Monica Lafferty, (BV) ....'42 '78 C.522 B.A. L.184 J.D. [Harper&H.]
Harper and Harper, (BV) .... 21 Oak St.
Harrington, Michael C. .... '69 '95 C.012 B.Comm. L.823 J.D. [Ⓐ Murtha C.]
Harris, John T., (AV) ....'42 '67 C.674 B.S.E. L.966 J.D. [Shipman&G.]
*PRACTICE AREAS: Civil Litigation; Insurance Coverage and Defense Law; Fidelity and Surety Law; Construction Law.
Harris, Judah J. ....'34 '63 C.978 B.A. L.564 LL.B. Asst. Atty. Gen.
Harris, Mitchell R., (BV) ....'64 '90 C.855 B.A. L.276 J.D. [Day,B.&H.]
*PRACTICE AREAS: Commercial Litigation; Insurance Litigation.
Harris, Richard D., (BV) .... '61 '90 C.659 B.S.E. L.184 J.D. [Day,B.&H.]
*PRACTICE AREAS: Technology and Intellectual Property - Business; Emerging Companies; International Transactions; Strategic Joint Ventures.
Harris, Stephen B., (BV) .... '61 '87 C.1036 B.A. L.1019 J.D. [Wiggin&D.]
*PRACTICE AREAS: Employment Litigation; Wrongful Termination Defense; Employer Rights; Sexual Harassment; Wage and Hour Law.
Harrison, Thomas F., (AV) ....'42 '67 C.321 A.B. L.262 J.D. [Day,B.&H.]
*PRACTICE AREAS: Environmental and Land Use.
Hartley, Jill, (BV) .... '64 '89 C.846 B.A. L.326 J.D. [Sabia&H.]
*PRACTICE AREAS: Employment Law; Commercial Litigation; Tort Litigation.
Hartley, Sharon M. ....'59 '89 C.923 B.A. L.1029 J.D. Asst. Atty. Gen.
Hassett, Neil A. '— '72
C.645 B.S.M.E. L.184 J.D. Asst. Gen. Coun., United Techologies Corp.
*RESPONSIBILITIES: General Corporate.
Hassett, Raymond M. .... '62 '87 C.128 B.A. L.1029 J.D. [Hassett&G.]
*PRACTICE AREAS: Criminal Law; Driving While Intoxicated; Divorce; Separation Agreements; Labor and Employment.

Hassett & George, P.C.
555 Franklin Avenue, 06114
Telephone: 860-296-2111 Fax: 860-296-8494
Email: info@hgesq.com URL: http://www.hgesq.com
Raymond M. Hassett; Louis N. George;—John S. Rubrich.
Civil Litigation, Commercial Law, Real Estate, Commercial Real Estate, Internet Law, PACA Litigation, Family Law, Criminal Law, Appellate Practice.
See Professional Biographies, HARTFORD, CONNECTICUT

Hastings, George C., (AV) .... '— '56 C&L.976 B.A., LL.B. [Ⓒ Robinson&C.]
*PRACTICE AREAS: Trial Practice; Legislative Drafting; Lobbying; Appellate Practice.
Hatch, Jonathan D., (BV) ....'56 '82 C.674 A.B. L.94 J.D. CIGNA Corp.
Haught, David A., (BV) ....'60 '86 C.31 B.A. L.818 J.D. [Cooney,S.&D.]
Haught, Tricia A. ....'61 '89 C.31 B.A. L.184 J.D. [Day,B.&H.]
*PRACTICE AREAS: Environmental and Land Use.
Hausman, Irwin J., (AV) .... '43 '68 C&L.184 B.A., J.D. [Murtha C.]
*PRACTICE AREAS: Real Estate Law; Commercial Lending Law; Commercial Litigation.

Hawkins, Delafield & Wood, (AV)
City Place, 185 Asylum Street, 06103 ⊙
Telephone: 860-275-6260 Fax: 860-527-5786
Members of Firm: Michela Daliana (Resident, New York Office); C. Steven Donovan (Resident, New York Office); Ronald C. Grosser (Resident, New York Office); Kenneth B. Roberts (Resident, New York Office); Richard L. Sigal (Resident, New York Office); Jean E. Winn (Resident); Kam Wong (Resident, New York Office). Associate: Laurie A. Hall.
General Practice. Probate, Tax, Domestic and International Corporate and Banking, Federal Securities, Real Estate and Litigation. Law of State, Municipal and Public Authority Financing.
New York, N.Y. Office: 67 Wall Street. Telephone: 212-820-9300. Fax: 212-514-8425.
Newark, New Jersey Office: One Gateway Center. Telephone: 973-642-8584. Fax: 973-642-6773.
Los Angeles, California Office: 633 West Fifth Street, Suite 3550. Telephone: 213-236-9050. Fax: 213-236-9060.
Washington, D.C. Office: 601 13th Street., N.W., Suite 800 South. Telephone: 202-682-1480. Fax: 202-682-1497.
San Francisco, California Office: One Embarcadero, Suite 1040. Telephone: 415-486-4200. Fax: 415-397-1513.
See Professional Biographies, HARTFORD, CONNECTICUT

Hawks-Ladds, Joshua A., (BV) .... '65 '91 C.184 B.A. L.1048 J.D. [Pullman&C.]
*PRACTICE AREAS: Civil Litigation; Labor and Employment Law; Municipal Law; Workers' Compensation.
Hayes, Randall M., (BV) .... '56 '83 C.319 B.A. L.1048 J.D. [Skelley R.]
*PRACTICE AREAS: Insurance Defense; Professional Liability; Municipal Liability.
Haymond, David .... '05 '30 C.659 B.S. L.309 LL.B. 999 Asylum Ave.
Haymond, John, Law Firm of .... '47 '75 C.184 B.A. L.818 J.D. 999 Asylum Ave.
Haynes, Dan A. .... '50 '77 C.30 B.S. L.273 J.D. [Pepe&H.]
*PRACTICE AREAS: Construction and Design Law; Construction Contracts; International Construction Law; Public Construction Law; Government Procurement.
Hays, Susan A., (AV) .... '59 '84 C.95 A.B. L.93 J.D. [Updike,K.&S.]
*PRACTICE AREAS: Business Law; Real Estate.
Hayter, Robert P. '48 '74 C.107 B.S.M.E. L.823 J.D.
Assoc. Gen. Coun. and Chf. Intell. Prop. Coun., United Technologies Corp. (Pat.)
*RESPONSIBILITIES: Intellectual Property.
Hazard, Stephen B., (AV) .....'45 '73 C.103 B.A. L.911 J.D. [Pepe&H.] (⊙Boston, MA)
*PRACTICE AREAS: Corporate Law; Mergers, Acquisitions and Divestitures; Venture Capital; Technology Transfer; Emerging Growth Companies.
Hazelwood, Joshua A. .... '58 '87 C.1044 B.S. L.1019 J.D. [Ⓒ Andros,F.&M.]
Healey, James T., (AV) '29 '54
C&L.976 B.A., LL.B. Asst. Gen. Coun., United Technologies Corp.
Healey, Richard P., (BV) .... '51 '77 C&L.93 A.B., J.D. [Rome M.S.]
*PRACTICE AREAS: Commercial Real Estate Finance and Development; Litigation; Employment Law.
Heath, Cathleen Tobin .... '73 '99 C.1372 B.A. L.602 J.D. [Ⓐ Edwards&A.]
*PRACTICE AREAS: Insurance Regulation.
Heath, Edward J. .... '— '99 C.1086 B.A. L.602 J.D. [Ⓐ Robinson&C.]
Heath, Honor S., (BV) '— '84
C.178 A.B. L.1252 J.D. Sr. Coun., Fleet Boston Financial Corp.
Hebb, Edwin Gordon, Jr., (AV) .... '28 '59 C.882 B.S. L.276 J.D. [Ⓒ Bingham D.]
Heffernan, John Connery, (BV) .... '44 '73 C.1030 B.A. L.128 J.D. [Heffernan&F.]
*PRACTICE AREAS: Probate; Real Estate; Family Law; Divorce; Child Support.

Heffernan & Farr, L.L.P., (BV)
650 Farmington Avenue, 06105
Telephone: 860-233-6336 Fax: 860-523-0419
Email: heffernan-farr@lawyers.com
Members of Firm: John Connery Heffernan; Robert Farr.
General Practice. Probate, Real Estate, Construction Arbitration, Corporation, Workers Compensation, Personal Injury Law, Development, Family, Elder Law, Commercial Collections. Trials in all Courts.
See Professional Biographies, HARTFORD, CONNECTICUT

Heinlein, David J., (AV) .... '51 '76 C.855 B.A. L.1049 J.D. [Rogin,N.C.L.&H.]
*PRACTICE AREAS: Personal Injury; Workers Compensation; Bankruptcy Litigation; Commercial Litigation.
Helmke-Elmore, Janet M. .... '62 '88 C&L.823 B.A., J.D. [Ⓒ Edwards&A.]
*PRACTICE AREAS: Commercial Litigation; Products Liability; Personal Injury Defense.
Hemond, David L. .... '50 '76 C&L.184 B.A., J.D. Chf. Atty., State Law Revision Comm.
Hempstead, Robert B., (BV) .... '39 '64 C.860 B.A. L.976 LL.B. 100 Pearl Street
Hendrickson, Kristina M. .... '73 '99 C.156 B.A. L.1040 J.D. [Ⓐ Cummings&L.]
Hendrickson, Michael P. ....'61 '88 C.1044 B.A. L.997 J.D. [Ⓐ Regnier,T.C.&E.]
*PRACTICE AREAS: General Practice; Trial Practice; Insurance; Toxic Torts; Products Liability.
Henfey, Edward M. .... '54 '79 C&L.776 B.A., J.D. 55 Farmington Ave.
Henneberger, John A .... '64 '98 C.184 B.G.S. L.1252 J.D. 34 Sequassen St.
Hennessey, Edward F., (AV) .... '— '62 C.197 A.B. L.93 J.D. [Robinson&C.]
*PRACTICE AREAS: Litigation.
Hennessy, Francis X. .... '30 '61 C.262 B.S. L.184 J.D. Appl. Ct. J.
Henry, Brian P. .... '74 '99 C.314 B.A. L.45 J.D. [Ⓐ Danaher,T.L.&N.]
*PRACTICE AREAS: Insurance Defense; Civil Litigation.
Henzy, Eric A., (AV) .... '62 '89 C&L.184 B.A., J.D. [Reid&R.]
*PRACTICE AREAS: Bankruptcy; Commercial Law; Litigation.
Herman, Paula Lacey, (AV) .... '48 '78 C.900 B.A. L.976 J.D. [Day,B.&H.]
*PRACTICE AREAS: Mergers and Acquisitions; Emerging Companies; Private Equity Funds; Finance and Investments; Securities Law.
Hern, Andrew James, (BV) .... '62 '89 C.855 B.A. L.184 J.D. [Gordon,M.&F.]
*PRACTICE AREAS: Insurance Defense; Workers Compensation; Bad Faith Insurance Claims.
Herrmann, David H., (AV) .... '53 '79 C.321 B.A. L.184 J.D. [Krevolin,F.G.E.&H.]
Hersh, Dennis G., (BV) .... '46 '72 C.1033 B.A. L.184 J.D. [Hersh&R.]
Hersh & Ritson, (BV) .... 21 Oak St.
Hershman, Linda D. .... '47 '70 C.665 B.A. L.184 J.D. Southern New Eng. Tele. Co.
Heslin, Thomas P., (AV) .... '26 '55 C&L.184 B.A., LL.B. 40 Russ Street
Hess, Catherine Ann '53 '89 C.518 B.A. L.665 J.D.
Dept. Pub. Health & Addict In Sevrs.
Hess, Peter L., (BV) .... '42 '73 C.205 B.A. L.184 J.D. 225 Asylum St., 13th Fl.
Hewitt, Andrea A., (BV) .... '55 '90 C.999 B.S. L.184 J.D. [Ⓐ Feiner W.]
*PRACTICE AREAS: Business Litigation; Commercial Litigation; Employment Litigation.
Hickey, Brandon J., (AV) .... '30 '57 C&L.976 B.A., LL.B. [Ⓒ Murtha C.]
Hicks, Robert .... '74 '01 C.183 B.A. L.306 J.D. [Ⓐ Updike,K.&S.]
*PRACTICE AREAS: Business Law.
Higgins, Charles B. .... '56 '81 C.184 B.A. L.94 J.D. CIGNA Corp.
Hildebrand, Charles F. '54 '80 C.112 A.B. L.188 J.D.
Assoc. Gen. Coun. & Asst. Secy., United Techologies Corp.
*RESPONSIBILITIES: Securities; General Corporate.
Hill, David A., Jr. .... '66 '92 C.918 B.A. L.184 J.D. [Levin,F.&P.]
*PRACTICE AREAS: Commercial Litigation; Civil Litigation; Commercial Foreclosure; Commercial Workouts; Creditor Bankruptcy.
Hill, David G. .... '62 '88 C.855 B.A. L.184 J.D. [Halloran&S.]
*PRACTICE AREAS: Litigation; Professional Liability; Personal Injury Law; Product Liability Law; Construction Law.
Hill, Edward S., (AV) .... '— '72 C.855 B.A. L.184 J.D. [Robinson&C.]
*PRACTICE AREAS: Real Estate; Finance; Bankruptcy; Litigation; Zoning, Planning and Land Use.
Hilton, John C., (BV) '31 '62 C.453 B.S. L.184 J.D.
[McCormick,P.&H.] (See Pat. Sect.)
*PRACTICE AREAS: Trademarks; Patents.

Hincks, John W., (AV) .... '— '59 C&L.976 B.A., LL.B. [Ⓒ Robinson&C.]
*PRACTICE AREAS: Estate Settlement; Trust Administration; Estate; Tax Planning; Exempt Organizations.
Hirtle, Robert L., (AV) .... '37 '62 C.1030 B.S. L.893 J.D. [Rogin,N.C.L.&H.]
*PRACTICE AREAS: Litigation; Appellate Practice; Administrative Law; Health Care.
Hobbs, Carol S. .... '60 '91 C.788 A.B. L.184 J.D. Coun., Aetna Inc.‡
*RESPONSIBILITIES: Health Care; Corporate.
Hoberman, Harvey, (AV) .... '— '60 C&L.184 B.A., LL.B. [Brown,R.F.&G.]
*PRACTICE AREAS: Commercial Finance; Workouts and Financing; Real Estate Workouts and Financing; Corporate Restructures and Turn-Arounds.
Hoberman, Matthew J. .... '71 '98 C.390 A.B. L.472 J.D. [Ⓐ Edwards&A.]
*PRACTICE AREAS: Corporate Law; Business Law; Mergers and Acquisitions; Insurance; Securities.
Hochberg, Robert A. .... '48 '74 C.401 B.A. L.818 J.D. 999 Asylum Ave.
Hodgdon, Sally .... '53 '88 C.184 B.A. L.1048 J.D. The Communities Law Ctr.
Hodgman, Jill Cutler .... '73 '99 C.188 B.A. L.306 J.D. [Ⓐ Shipman&G.]
*PRACTICE AREAS: Education Law; School Law; Labor and Employment.
Hodson, Thomas F. X. .... '59 '88 C.745 B.A. L.128 J.D. [Ⓒ Edwards&A.]
Hoffman, Brent L. .... '71 '96 C.282 B.A. L.1017 J.D. [Ⓐ Bingham D.]
*PRACTICE AREAS: Commercial Litigation; Securities Litigation; Insurance Litigation; Business Torts; Products Liability.
Hoffman, Lee D. .... '69 '94 C.861 B.A. L.276 J.D. 225 Asylum Street, 13th Floor
Hoffnagle, Susan B., (AV) .... '47 '73 C.881 B.A. L.184 J.D. Sr. Coun., CIGNA Corp.
Hollister, Timothy S., (AV) .... '57 '82 C.918 B.A. L.94 J.D. [Shipman&G.]
*PRACTICE AREAS: Land Use Law; Environmental Law and Litigation.
Holness, Gregory K. .... '70 '00 C.184 B.S. L.1252 J.D. [Ⓐ Halloran&S.]
*PRACTICE AREAS: Construction Law; Fidelity and Surety.
Holtman, Donald R., (BV) .... '36 '58 C&L.879 B.A., LL.B. [Katz&S.]
*PRACTICE AREAS: Civil Litigation; Insurance Defense.
Homelson, Rochelle, (BV) .... '54 '82 C.855 B.A. L.184 J.D. 234 Pearl St.
Hooker, Richard, (AV) .... '11 '38 C.951 B.A. L.976 J.D. 185 Asylum St.
Hootsmans, Alice M. S. .... '63 '89 C&L.309 B.A., J.D. [Ⓐ Murtha C.]
Horak, John M., (AV) .... '54 '80 C.197 B.A. L.602 J.D. [Reid&R.]
*PRACTICE AREAS: Corporate Law; Nonprofit and Charitable Organizations; Taxation; Trade and Professional Associations.
Horan, Brien P. .... '— '79 C.31 B.A. L.184 J.D. [Robinson&C.]
*PRACTICE AREAS: Products Liability; Litigation.
Horan, Maura Hughes .... '62 '88 C.112 B.A. L.184 J.D. [Ⓒ Ruben,J.&M.]
*PRACTICE AREAS: Litigation; Real Estate.
Horan, William Patrick, Jr. .... '65 '92 C.184 B.A. L.1292 J.D. 28 Grand St.
Horowitz, Barry D. .... '59 '85 C.75 B.A. L.184 J.D. [Nirenstein,H.&Assoc.]
Horowitz, David A., (AV) '56 '83
C.999 B.A. L.178 J.D. Asst. Gen. Coun., The Advest Grp., Inc.
*RESPONSIBILITIES: Corporate Law; Securities Law.
Horowitz, Matthew M., (BV) .... '52 '76 C.860 B.A. L.569 J.D. [Wolf,H.E.&C.]
*PRACTICE AREAS: Fidelity and Surety; Construction.
Horrigan, Christine S. .... '53 '81 C.518 B.A. L.184 J.D. 1 American Row‡
Horton, Wesley W., (AV) .... '42 '70 C.309 A.B. L.184 J.D. [Horton,S.&C.]
*PRACTICE AREAS: State and Federal Appellate Litigation; Constitutional Law; Insurance Law; Professional Grievance.

Horton, Shields & Cormier, P.C., (AV)
90 Gillett Street, 06105
Telephone: 860-522-8338 Fax: 860-728-0401
Email: hsclaw@hsclaw.com
Wesley W. Horton; Robert M. Shields, Jr.; Kimberly A. Knox; Karen L. Dowd; Michael S. Taylor; Kenneth J. Bartschi;—Daniel Jonah Krisch. Of Counsel: Susan M. Cormier.
Trial and Appellate Practice in all State and Federal Courts. Personal Injury, Insurance Defense, Insurance Coverage, Commercial, Business Organization, Professional Grievance, Workers Compensation, Products Liability and Real Estate Law.
See Professional Biographies, HARTFORD, CONNECTICUT

Horwich, Harold S., (AV) .... '53 '78 C.103 A.B. L.94 J.D. [Bingham D.]
Hotaling, Elizabeth I. .... '66 '91 C.966 B.A. L.184 J.D. D.E.P.
Hotaling, Michael E. '61 '87 C.454 B.A. L.982 J.D.
Assoc. Coun., The Travelers Ins. Co.
Houlding, Andrew L. .... '45 '92 C.94 B.A. L.184 J.D. [Rome M.S.]
*PRACTICE AREAS: Labor and Employment; Litigation; Indian Law.
Houlihan, John J., Jr., (AV) .... '55 '80 C.676 B.A. L.724 J.D. [RisCassi&D.]
*PRACTICE AREAS: Negligence; Products Liability; Medical Malpractice.
Howard, Antoria D. ..... '59 '84 C.518 B.A. L.184 J.D. Staff Atty., Dept. of Health Servcs.
Howard, Charles L., (AV) .... '50 '75 C.674 A.B. L.893 J.D. [Shipman&G.]
*PRACTICE AREAS: Civil Litigation; Intellectual Property Litigation; ERISA Litigation; Municipal Litigation; Representation of Corporate Ombudsman.

Howard, Kohn, Sprague & FitzGerald, (AV)
Practice established by Enoch Perkins in 1786.
237 Buckingham Street, P.O. Box 261798, 06126-1798 ⊙
Telephone: 860-525-3101 Telecopier: 860-247-4201
Email: atty@hksflaw.com URL: http://www.hksflaw.com
Members of Firm: John R. FitzGerald; John Stephen Papa; James M. Moher; Robert P. Volpe; Constance L. Epstein; Thomas P. Cella; Jack G. Steigelfest; James F. Sullivan. Associates: Todd W. Whitford; Steven J. Barber; Kevin Ladieu; Joseph E. Mascaro.
General Practice. Corporation, Probate, Insurance, Aviation, Medical-Legal Law, Real Estate, Environmental Law, Family Law, Admiralty, Medical Malpractice, Longshoremen's, Harborworker's Compensation Act and Worker's Compensation Law. Trials in all Courts.
Manchester, Connecticut Office: 99 East Center Street, 06040. Telephone: 203-646-8075.
Glastonbury, Connecticut Office: 41B New London Turnpike, 06033. Telephone: 203-633-3373.
See Professional Biographies, HARTFORD, CONNECTICUT

Howat, Andrew J., (AV) .... '46 '71 C.184 B.A. L.188 J.D. [Reid&R.]
*PRACTICE AREAS: Commercial Law; Corporate Law; Labor and Employment; Mergers and Acquisitions; Securities.

Howd & Ludorf, (AV) BR
65 Wethersfield Avenue, 06114
Telephone: 860-249-1361 Fax: 860-249-7665
URL: http://www.hl-law.com
Members of Firm: John R. Lilliendahl, III; John J. Bogdanski; Philip T. Newbury, Jr.; Thomas R. Gerarde; Mark J. Claflin; Christopher M. Vossler; William F. Corrigan; David S. Monastersky; Michael J. Rose; Colette S. Griffin; Melinda A. Powell; Keith E. Marquis; Paul Erickson; Daniel C. DeMerchant; Bruce J. Gelston; Lisa K. Titus; Alexandria L. Bufford; Beatrice D. Sukhdeo; Jay Thomas Don Francisco; John J. Radshaw; Deann K. Seymour. Retired: Edward S. Ludorf.
Products Liability Litigation, Insurance Defense Litigation, Commercial Litigation, Toxic Tort, Municipal Litigation, Medical Malpractice, General Trial and Appellate Practice.
Representative Clients: CIGNA; Reliance; Daimler Chrysler; Toyota; Harsco; Ladder Management; Baxter International; Black & Decker; Texaco.
See Professional Biographies, HARTFORD, CONNECTICUT

Howson, Hubert F. '31 '61 C.454 B.A. L.273 J.D.
(adm. in DC; not adm. in CT; Pat.) Dept. of Veterans Affrs.
Hoyt, Anne R., (BV) .... '55 '80 C.183 B.A. L.184 J.D. [Ⓐ O'Connell,F.&A.] (⊙Moosup)
*PRACTICE AREAS: Residential Real Estate Law; Domestic Relations Law; Commercial Law; Civil Litigation; Workers Compensation.
Hryniewicz, Stephen M. .... '73 '99 C.602 B.A. L.184 J.D. [Ⓐ Rogin,N.C.L.&H.]
*PRACTICE AREAS: Bankruptcy Litigation; Civil Litigation; Commercial Litigation.

Huber, Donald K., (AV) '30 '58
C&L.597 B.S.M.E., J.D. [Ⓒ McCormick,P.&H.] (See Pat. Sect.) ⊙
*PRACTICE AREAS: Intellectual Property; Patents; Trademarks; Copyrights.
Huck, Christopher W. .... '68 '94 C.67 B.A. L.184 J.D. [Michelson,K.R.&B.]
*PRACTICE AREAS: Construction Law; Surety Law; Estate Planning; Employment Law; Commercial Litigation.
Huddleston, Megan A., (AV) '54 '81
C.732 B.A. L.982 J.D. Coun., Phoenix Home Life Mut. Ins. Co.
*RESPONSIBILITIES: Investment; General Corporate.
Huddleston, Sheila A., (BV) .... '53 '90 C&L.976 B.A., J.D. [Shipman&G.]
*PRACTICE AREAS: Civil Appeals; Complex Litigation; Antitrust; Medical Antitrust; Criminal Appeals.
Hudner, H. Kennedy, (AV) .... '50 '78 C.588 B.A. L.976 J.D. [Murtha C.]
*PRACTICE AREAS: Business Litigation; Health Care Litigation; Antitrust; Intellectual Property; Computer Law.
Hudzikiewicz, Kathleen A. .... '74 '00 C.462 B.A. L.1048 J.D. [Ⓐ Updike,K.&S.]
*PRACTICE AREAS: Tax Law; Trusts and Estates.
Hug, Christopher J., (BV) .... '— '89 C.103 A.B. L.1048 J.D. [Robinson&C.]
*PRACTICE AREAS: Litigation; Bankruptcy; Construction Law.
Huget, Kirby G., (BV) .... '60 '85 C.152 B.A. L.1048 J.D. [Skelley R.]
*PRACTICE AREAS: Insurance Defense; Insurance Fraud; Liquor Liability Law; Products Liability Law; Wrongful Death Law.
Huggins, John C. .... '63 '98 C.329 B.B.A. L.306 J.D. [Ⓐ Halloran&S.]
Hull, Peter W. .... '57 '87 C.1236 B.A. L.902 J.D. [Ⓐ Cummings&L.]
Hulton, Patrick T., (BV) .... '55 '84 C.347 B.A. L.184 J.D. 81 Weathersfield Ave.
Hume, Carlton L. .... '59 '93 C.1033 B.Sc. L.306 J.D. 125 Hungerford St.
Humes, Stephen J. .... '64 '94 C.1030 B.S. L.1252 J.D. 225 Asylum Street, 13th Floor
Humphrey, Steven R., (AV) '— '66 C.918 B.A. L.880 J.D.
[Robinson&C.] (⊙Stamford)
*PRACTICE AREAS: Litigation; Administrative Law; Energy; Telecommunications.
Hunt, Charles E. '50 '77 C&L.262 B.A., J.D.
(adm. in NY; not adm. in CT) P.O. Box 2999
Hunt, Kimball Haines, (BV) .... '48 '74 C.550 B.A. L.574 J.D. [Hunt L.C.&J.]
*PRACTICE AREAS: Personal Injury; Criminal; Litigation; Commercial; Driving While Intoxicated.
Hunt, Laurie J., (BV) '55 '83
C.918 B.A. L.184 J.D. Gen. Coun., Independent Energy Corp.
Hunt, Robert C., Jr., (AV) .... '25 '54 C.197 B.A. L.184 LL.B. [Ⓒ Pepe&H.]
*PRACTICE AREAS: Fidelity and Surety; Municipal Law.

Hunt Leibert Chester & Jacobson, P.C., (AV)
94 Hungerford Street, 06106-4626
Telephone: 860-808-0606 Fax: 860-549-0163; 524-5602; 522-4815
URL: http://www.hlcj.com
Kimball Haines Hunt; Richard M. Leibert; Samuel D. Chester; Richard C. Jacobson;—Gerald Beaudoin; Thomas J. Farrell; Geoffrey Kent Milne; Kathryn R. Sylvester; Sean E. Sweeney.
Foreclosure, Bankruptcy, Real Estate, Personal Injury, Criminal.
See Professional Biographies, HARTFORD, CONNECTICUT

Huntington, Jay F., (BV) .... '55 '81 C.588 B.S. L.770 J.D. [Ⓐ Regnier,T.C.&E.]
*PRACTICE AREAS: General Practice; Trial Practice; Insurance; Toxic Torts; Products Liability.
Huntsman, Peter R., (AV) .... '52 '79 C.309 A.B. L.94 J.D. Asst. Atty. Gen.

Hurvitz, Henry B.
(See West Hartford)

Hussey, Jeffrey W. .... '63 '98 C.431 B.S. L.1048 J.D. [Ⓐ Shipman&G.]
*PRACTICE AREAS: Corporate; Mergers and Acquisitions; Venture Capital; Finance Law; Corporate Trust.
Hutton, Deborah L. .... '71 '00 C.184 B.A. L.306 J.D. [Ⓐ Updike,K.&S.]
*PRACTICE AREAS: Government Relations; Legislative Representation.
Hyde, John R., (BV) .... '55 '80 C.829 B.A. L.1048 J.D. 250 Main St.
Hyman, Cantor & Klau, P.C., (AV) .... 21 Oak St.
Iaia, Brian P. .... '67 '99 C.1031 B.S. L.982 J.D. 225 Asylum Street, 13th Floor
Iamonaco, Robert L., (BV) .... '59 '88 C.676 B.S. L.1048 J.D. [Byrne&S.]
*PRACTICE AREAS: Commercial Financing; Commercial Real Estate; Residential Real Estate; Corporate Law; Estate Planning.
Iannaccone, Paul M. .... '61 '94 C.184 B.A. L.1048 J.D. [RisCassi&D.]
*PRACTICE AREAS: Personal Injury; Products Liability; Medical Malpractice; Civil Litigation.
Ikari, Carolyn A. .... '65 '93 C.659 B.S.E. L.893 J.D. One American Row
Im, Harry .... '67 '94 C.918 B.A. L.184 J.D. Sr. Mngr., Arthur Andersen
Ingle, Nicole A. F. .... '72 '98 C&L.893 B.A., J.D. [Ⓐ Murtha C.]
Inglis, Ernest A., Jr., (AV) .... '26 '52 C.918 B.A. L.893 J.D. Cityplace
Ingram, Vincent J. .... '72 '01 C&L.329 B.A., J.D. [Ⓐ Pepe&H.]
Intravia, Catherine Franklin .... '— '99 C.184 B.S. L.1048 J.D. [Ⓐ Shipman&G.]
*PRACTICE AREAS: Real Estate; Intellectual Property; Computer Law; E-Business; Corporate Law.
Ioannou, Angeline N. .... '69 '96 C.1211 B.S. L.1338 J.D. [Ⓐ Morrison,M.&M.]
*PRACTICE AREAS: General Liability; Products Liability.
Iodice, Frank P. .... '24 '53 C&L.184 B.S., LL.B. State Tax Div.
Isbell, Cecily A. '41 '79 C.210 B.A. L.184 J.D.
Coun., Hartford Financial Services Group, Inc.
Ivimey, John R. .... '63 '91 C.165 B.A. L.184 J.D. [Reid&R.] (⊙West Hartford)
*PRACTICE AREAS: Probate; Trusts and Estates.
Izard, Robert Andrews, Jr., (AV) .... '— '83 C.976 B.A. L.245 J.D. [Schatz&N.]
*PRACTICE AREAS: Complex Commercial Litigation; Securities Litigation.
Jacewicz, John Steven .... '48 '81 C&L.1048 B.S., J.D. Conn. State Pol. Dept.
Jachimowicz, Lucien J. .... '27 '55 C.184 B.A. L.94 LL.B. Chief Clk., Supr. Ct.
Jackson, Daniel W. .... '52 '78 C.976 B.A. L.477 J.D. Coun., The Travelers Ins. Co.
Jackson, Gianna S. '66 '92 C&L.276 B.S.L.A., J.D.
(adm. in VA; not adm. in CT) [Ⓒ]
Jackson, Jay W., (AV) '30 '58 C&L.902 B.A., LL.B.
[Jackson,O.&P.] (⊙West Hartford)
*PRACTICE AREAS: Governmental Law; Government Relations; Legislative Practice; Administrative Law; Estate Planning.

Jackson Lewis Schnitzler & Krupman, (AV)
55 Farmington Avenue, 06105 ⊙
Telephone: 860-522-0404 Facsimile: 860-247-1330
Email: hartford@jacksonlewis.com URL: http://www.jacksonlewis.com
Members of Firm: William J. Anthony; Thomas R. Gibbons; Susan K. Krell; Margaret J. Strange. Of Counsel: Allan S. Friedland; Edward M. Richters. Associates: Tasos C. Paindiris; Michael G. Petrie; James F. Shea; Jennifer Tindall.
Labor Relations, Employment Discrimination, Wrongful Discharge and Other Employment-Related Litigation, Employee Benefits and Pension Law, Wage and Hour, OSHA, Immigration Law, Public Sector and State Labor Relations Law, On Behalf of Management.
Other offices located in: Atlanta, Georgia; Boston, Massachusetts; Chicago, Illinois; Dallas, Texas; Greenville, South Carolina; Long Island, New York; Los Angeles, California; Miami, Florida; Minneapolis, Minnesota; Morristown, New Jersey; New York, New York; Orlando, Florida; Pittsburgh, Pennsylvania; Sacramento, California; San Francisco, California; Seattle, Washington; Stamford, Connecticut; Washington, D.C.; White Plains, New York.
See Professional Biographies, HARTFORD, CONNECTICUT

Jackson, O'Keefe and Phelan, (AV) BB
36-40 Russ Street, 06106-1571 ⊙
Telephone: 860-278-4040 Fax: 860-527-2500
URL: http://www.joplaw.com

(This Listing Continued)

Jackson, O'Keefe and Phelan (Continued)
Members of Firm: Jay W. Jackson; Andrew J. O'Keefe; Denise Martino Phelan; Michael E. Riley; Matthew J. O'Keefe; Peter K. O'Keefe; Philip R. Dunn, Jr.; Kathryn M. Cunningham; Joseph M. Busher, Jr.; James M. Joseph.
General Practice including Civil Trial and Appellate Practice in all Courts, Governmental Law and Relations, Personal Injury, Medical Malpractice, Construction Litigation, Products Liability, Probate and Estate Planning, Residential and Commercial Real Estate, Corporation, Insurance, Banking, Legislative Practice, Mediation and Arbitration.
Representative Clients: Travelers Property Casualty Co.; ITT Hartford; Liberty Mutual Insurance Co.; Connecticut Medical Insurance Co.
Bethlehem, Connecticut Office: 423 Munger Lane. Telephone/Fax: 203-266-5255.
See Professional Biographies, HARTFORD, CONNECTICUT

Jacobs, Donald A., (BV) .... '52 '77 C&L.184 B.A., J.D. [Webber,J.&M.]
Jacobs, Thomas D. .... '53 '78 C.184 B.A. L.436 J.D. [Ⓐ Gersten&G.]

Jacobs Partners LLC
(See Norwalk)

Jacobs, Walker, Rice & Basche, P.C.
(See Manchester)

Jacobson, John J., (AV) .... '51 '76 C.95 A.B. L.275 J.D. [Reid&R.]
*PRACTICE AREAS: Employee Benefits; Pension Plans; Executive Compensation.
Jacobson, Richard C., (BV) .... '52 '77 C&L.184 B.A., J.D. [Hunt L.C.&J.]
*PRACTICE AREAS: Real Estate Law; Corporate Law; Commercial Litigation; Foreclosure.
Jacques, Bernard E., (BV) .... '46 '86 C.1266 B.A. L.724 J.D. [Updike,K.&S.]
*PRACTICE AREAS: Employment Litigation; Labor and Employment Law.
Jaff, Jennifer C. .... '57 '85 C.994 B.A. L.276 J.D. [Ⓒ Killian,D.&J.]
*PRACTICE AREAS: Health Care; Health Care Fraud; Civil RICO; Civil Rights; Complex Litigation.
Jaffe, David K., (BV) .... '55 '80 C.659 B.S. L.184 J.D. [Spinella&J.]
Jainchill, Michael C., (AV) .... '53 '78 C&L.184 B.A., J.D. [RisCassi&D.]
*PRACTICE AREAS: Products Liability; Negligence; Medical Malpractice; Uninsured and Underinsured Motorists.
Janelle, Jennifer D. .... '72 '97 C&L.94 B.A., J.D. [Ⓐ Murtha C.]
Janis, Mark Weston '47 '78 C.674 A.B. L.309 J.D.
Prof. of Law, Univ. of Conn. Law Sch.
Janus, Peter A., (AV) .... '46 '70 C.188 A.B. L.94 J.D. [Siegel,O.S.&Z.]
*PRACTICE AREAS: Labor Law; Employment Law; Litigation; Education Law.

Januszewski, McQuillan and DeNigris
(See New Britain)

Jimenez, David R. '66 '91 C.846 B.A. L.1019 J.D.
(adm. in TX; not adm. in CT) Assoc. Coun., Hartford Financial Services Group, Inc.
Jiran, Gabriel J. '71 '96 C.473 B.S. L.150 J.D.
(adm. in OH; not adm. in CT) [Ⓐ Shipman&G.]
*PRACTICE AREAS: Labor and Employment.
Johnson, David Allen .... '64 '92 C.529 B.A. L.1048 J.D. Acct. Underwriter
Johnson, Derek M., (BV) .... '57 '85 C.910 B.A. L.245 J.D. [Ruben,J.&M.]
*PRACTICE AREAS: Bankruptcy; Corporate Litigation.
Johnson, Dwight A., (AV) .... '45 '75 C.674 B.A. L.976 J.D. [Murtha C.]
*PRACTICE AREAS: Communications Law; Public Utilities Law; Energy Law; Corporate Law; Municipal Law.
Johnson, Kurt W. .... '41 '72 C&L.184 B.A., J.D. [Ⓒ Tyler C.&A.]
*PRACTICE AREAS: Independent Power Production and Cogeneration; Corporate; Environmental Law; International Law; Real Estate Law.
Johnson, Melvin E. .... '39 '71 C.208 B.A. L.569 J.D. Pres., G.R. Phelps & Co., Inc.
Johnson, Ralph W., III .... '68 '93 C.1041 B.A. L.262 J.D. [Ⓐ Halloran&S.]
*PRACTICE AREAS: Appellate Practice; Insurance Law; Litigation.
Jones, Durwin P. .... '68 '93 C.705 B.A. L.831 J.D. [Ⓐ Gordon,M.&F.]
*PRACTICE AREAS: Commercial Litigation; Construction Litigation; Federal Practice; Creditor's Rights; Lender Liability Defense.
Jones, Judith H. .... '61 '86 C.676 B.S. L.1048 J.D. Coun., Aetna Inc.
*RESPONSIBILITIES: Employee Benefits/ERISA; Corporate Law; Securities; Executive Compensation.
Jones, Stuart L. '56 '89 C.184 B.A. L.1048 J.D.
Assoc. Coun., Hartford Financial Services Group, Inc.
Jordan, William J. .... '60 '85 C&L.276 A.B., J.D. Sen. Coun., CIGNA Corp.
Joseph, James M. .... '75 '00 C.321 B.A. L.818 J.D. [Jackson,O.&P.]
*PRACTICE AREAS: Estate Planning; Estate Administration; Real Estate; Family Law; Divorce.
Joyce, Thomas A. '43 '68 C&L.585 Ph.B., J.D.
(adm. in ND; not adm. in CT) Asst. Secy., ITT Hartford Ins. Grp.
Joyce, Thomas J. .... '59 '84 C.309 B.A. L.184 J.D. The Travelers Ins. Co.
Judy, William R., (AV) .... '31 '59 C.250 B.S. L.273 J.D. 1 State St.
Jungk, G. Warren '33 '59 C&L.378 B.S., LL.B.
(adm. in KS; not adm. in CT) ITT Hartford Ins. Grp.
Jurenka, David P. '57 '86 C.184 B.A. L.1029 J.D.
Supvr. Contract Specialist, Army Natl. Guard★
Kaas, Glenn .... '48 '88 C.1102 B.S. L.184 J.D. Ass't. State's Atty.
Kaatz, Leon M., (BV) .... '42 '76 C.453 B.S. L.184 J.D. [Kaatz&P.]
Kaatz & Peikes, (BV) .... 111 Oak St.
Kabakoff, Randy P. .... '73 '99 C&L.184 B.S., J.D. [Ⓐ Rogin,N.C.L.&H.]
*PRACTICE AREAS: Real Estate; Corporate Law.
Kaelin, Robert E. .... '65 '92 C.473 B.A. L.228 J.D. [Murtha C.]
*PRACTICE AREAS: Bankruptcy; Creditors Rights; Commercial Litigation.
Kahn, Maria Araujo .... '64 '89 C.569 B.A. L.262 J.D. 60-B Weston St
Kainen, Burton, (AV) .... '42 '71 C.732 B.A. L.184 J.D. [Kainen,E.&M.]
*PRACTICE AREAS: Employment Law; Litigation; Labor Law.

Kainen, Escalera & McHale, P.C., (AV) BB
21 Oak Street, 06106
Telephone: 860-493-0870 Facsimile: 860-493-0871
Email: kemlaw@kemlaw.com URL: http://www.lawyers.com/kemlaw
Burton Kainen; Miguel A. Escalera, Jr.; Patrick J. McHale; Diana Garfield; Sheldon D. Myers; Jennifer Lian Dixon; Joseph W. McQuade.
Management Representation in Employment and Labor Law and Related Litigation.
See Professional Biographies, HARTFORD, CONNECTICUT

Kaliff, William W. .... '63 '88 C&L.93 B.A., J.D. [Rome M.S.]
*PRACTICE AREAS: Civil and Commercial Litigation; Intellectual Property Litigation.
Kallet, Mitchel E., (BV) .... '48 '73 C.273 B.B.A. L.184 J.D. [Ⓒ Kern&W.]
Kapiloff, Steven .... '61 '88 C.94 B.A. L.800 J.D. [Ⓐ Dechert]
*PRACTICE AREAS: Commercial Real Estate.
Kaplan, Richard M., (AV) '49 '75
C.696 A.B. L.184 J.D. Asst. Gen. Coun., United Technologies Corp.
*RESPONSIBILITIES: Labor and Employment Law.
Kaplan, Steven B. .... '53 '82 C.178 B.A. L.184 J.D. [Michelson,K.R.&B.]
*PRACTICE AREAS: Civil Litigation; Construction Law; Fidelity and Surety.
Kappes, Robert F. .... '68 '93 C.708 B.A. L.1202 J.D. [Silvester&D.]
Karam, Solomon J. '25 '57 C.569 A.B. L.94 LL.B.
Dir. of Legal, Dept. of Revenue Servs.
Karns, Edward B. .... '73 '01 C.273 B.A. L.184 J.D. [Ⓐ Bingham D.]
*PRACTICE AREAS: Business.
Karpe, Brian S., (BV) .... '60 '85 C.431 B.S. L.221 J.D. 81 Wethersfield Ave.

Kasper, Thomas R. ... '64 '95 C.184 B.A. L.1048 J.D. [🄰 Reid&R.]
*PRACTICE AREAS: Commercial Real Estate and Finance; Real Estate.
Katz, Charles D. '59 '85 C.982 B.A. L.262 J.D.
(adm. in NY; not adm. in CT) [🄲 Soeder&Assoc.]
*PRACTICE AREAS: Municipal Finance; Tax; Business Development.
Katz, Elin Swanson ... '65 '90 C.188 B.S. L.94 J.D. [🄲 Day,B.&H.]
*PRACTICE AREAS: Environmental Law; Land Use Law; Insurance Law.
Katz, Henry '37 '61 C&L.569 A.B., LL.B.
(adm. in NY; not adm. in CT) ITT Hartford Ins. Grp.
Katz, Lester, (BV) ... '24 '50 C&L.309 A.B., LL.B. [Katz&S.]
*PRACTICE AREAS: Civil Litigation; Insurance Defense.
Katz, Melvin S., (AV) ... '15 '40 C&L.976 B.A., LL.B. [🄲 Schatz&S.R.&K.]
Katz, Robert B., (BV) ... '47 '83 C.1029 B.S. L.1048 J.D. [Cummings&L.]
*PRACTICE AREAS: Family Law (100%).
Katz, Steven L. ... '65 '91 C.1365 B.A. L.94 J.D. [🄰 Butler N.&G.]

Katz and Seligman, (AV) BR
130 Washington Street, 06106
Telephone: 860-547-1857 Fax: 860-241-9127
Email: katzandseligman@aol.com
Lester Katz; Steven L. Seligman; James A. Armentano; Donald R. Holtman.
Insurance Defense and Coverage Issues, Professional Licensure Representation (Lawyers and Doctors), Legal Estate; Lawyers Discipline; Plaintiffs Medical Malpractice, Personal Injury, Criminal Defense: State and Federal Courts, Municipal Law.
See Professional Biographies, HARTFORD, CONNECTICUT

Kaufman, Kenneth B. ... '47 '72 C.30 B.A. L.659 J.D. Asst. Corp. Coun.
Kaye, Johanna L. ... '65 '91 C.605 A.B. L.1029 J.D. 75 Elm St.
Keane, John B. '46 '72 C.103 A.B. L.309 J.D.
(adm. in MA; not adm. in CT) P.O. Box 270‡
Keating, James A., (BVⓉ) '52 '77 C.610 A.B. L.851 J.D.
(adm. in OH; not adm. in CT) Asst. Gen. Atty., ITT Hartford Ins. Grp.
Keegan, Marcia Kenny ... '58 '89 C.867 B.A. L.188 J.D. [🄲 Wiggin&D.]
*PRACTICE AREAS: Employment Law.
Keenan, William J., Jr., (AV) ... '51 '76 C.31 B.A. L.893 J.D. [Murtha C.]
*PRACTICE AREAS: Employee Benefits Law.
Keeney, Timothy R. ... '48 '76 C.659 B.S. L.184 J.D. Northeast Utilities Service Co.
Keepnews, Robert L., (BV) ... '47 '75 C.276 B.S. L.262 J.D. [Pepe&H.]
*PRACTICE AREAS: Commercial Litigation; Employment Litigation; Alternative Dispute Resolution.

Keily, Paul A.
(See West Hartford)

Keith, Harold F., (AV) ... '22 '48 C&L.588 LL.B. [O'Connell,F.&A.]
*PRACTICE AREAS: Real Estate; Probate; Zoning; Corporations; Business Law.
Keithline, W. Wilson, (BV) ... '38 '70 C.976 B.S. L.184 J.D. 100 Constitution Plz.
Kelleher, Brian E., (BV) '59 '85
C.184 B.A. L.569 J.D. Asst. Gen. Coun., United Technologies Corp.
*RESPONSIBILITIES: Mergers and Acquisitions; Corporate Law.
Keller, Christine E. ... '52 '77 C.788 B.A. L.184 J.D. Supr. Ct. J.
Kelley, John J. '46 '72 C.93 B.A. L.184 J.D.
Sr. V.P., Hartford Steam Boiler Inspection & Ins. Co.
Kelley, Kenneth T., (BV) '39 '81
C.1033 B.S. L.1048 J.D. [Brown,P.&S.] (⊙Glastonbury, Stamford)
*PRACTICE AREAS: Estate Planning; Estate Settlements; Trusts and Estates; Tax Planning; Real Estate.
Kelly, Clifford P., (BV) ... '50 '93 C.871 B.S. L.184 J.D. [Alix,Y.&R.] (See Pat. Sect.)
Kelly, Linda J., (BV) '49 '76 C.575 B.A. L.184 J.D.
Sr. V.P. & Gen. Coun., Shawmut Bk. Conn., N.A.
Kelly, Peter G., (AV) '37 '62 C.276 B.S. L.976 J.D.
[Updike,K.&S.] (⊙Alexandria, VA)
*PRACTICE AREAS: Business Law; Design/Construction; Legislative Representation; Professional Defense.
Kelly, William E., (AV) ... '47 '73 C&L.178 B.A., J.D. [Bingham D.]
Kemp, Helen M. ... '— '94 C.31 B.A. L.94 J.D. [🄰 Robinson&C.]
Kemp, Wendi J., (BV) ... '64 '89 C.597 B.S. L.184 J.D. [Cummings&L.]
*PRACTICE AREAS: Labor Law; Employment Law; Education Law.
Kendellen, Lindsey E. ... '— '97 C.860 B.A. L.705 J.D. Natl. Labor Rel. Bd.
Kennedy, Jack S., (AV) ... '— '72 C.309 B.A. L.893 J.D. [Robinson&C.]
*PRACTICE AREAS: Mergers and Acquisitions; Corporate Law; Business Law; Closely-Held Business Planning.
Kennedy, Kenneth H., Jr ... '65 '92 C.502 B.A. L.383 J.D. Asst. Atty. Gen.
Kennelly, John B. ... '69 '96 C.918 B.A. L.184 J.D. [🄰 Updike,K.&S.]
*PRACTICE AREAS: Construction and Design Law; Real Estate Law.
Kenney, John R. '27 '53 C&L.976 A.B., LL.B.
Assoc. Gen. Coun. & Corp. Secy., The Travelers Ins. Co.
Kenny, Kevin B., (BV) ... '22 '49 C.197 A.B. L.184 J.D. 5 Grand St.
Kenny, Richard J., (AV) ... '50 '75 C.321 B.A. L.184 J.D. [Rome M.S.]
*PRACTICE AREAS: Civil Litigation; Commercial Litigation; Products Liability; Medical Malpractice.

Kenny, Brimmer, Melley & Mahoney, (AV) BR
5 Grand Street, 06106
Telephone: 860-527-4226 FAX: 860-527-0214
URL: http://www.lawyers.com/kbmmlaw
Joseph P. Kenny (1920-1993). Members of Firm: William J. Melley, III; Richard C. Mahoney; Anita M. Varunes; Dennis F. McCarthy. Associates: Shannon K. McCarthy; Nicholas C. Varunes; Terrance M. Brennan. Of Counsel: Leslie R. Brimmer.
General Practice. Personal Injury, Litigation, Products Liability, Medical Malpractice, Insurance, Corporation, and Administrative Law. Trials in all Courts.
Representative Clients: Allstate Insurance Co.; Peerless Insurance Co.; Berkshire Mutual Fire Insurance Co.; Dorchester Mutual Fire Insurance Co.; Abington Mutual Fire Insurance Co.
See Professional Biographies, HARTFORD, CONNECTICUT

Keough, Richard D. ... '59 '92 C&L.1048 B.S., J.D. City Law Dept.
Keppelman, Judith M., (AV) ... '— '79 C.881 A.B. L.262 J.D. [Robinson&C.]
*PRACTICE AREAS: Trusts and Estates; Wills; Probate.
Kern and Wooley LLP, (BV)
280 Trumbull Street (⊙L.A., CA; Kennesaw, GA; Irving, TX)
Kerns, Robert M. ... '44 '74 C.575 B.S. L.790 J.D. Asst. V.P., CIGNA Corp.
Kerrigan, Dennis F., Jr., (BV) ... '65 '91 C.321 B.A. L.945 J.D. [🄲 LeBoeuf,L.G.&M.]
*PRACTICE AREAS: Litigation.
Kesten, Linda A. ... '61 '89 C.860 B.A. L.184 J.D. [🄰 Appleton&A.]
*PRACTICE AREAS: Civil Litigation; Personal Injury; Family Law; Real Estate; Probate.
Kestenband, Jeffrey C. ... '— '97 C.918 B.A. L.184 J.D. [🄰 Robinson&C.]
Kiefer, Louis, (BV) ... '36 '61 C.882 B.A. L.823 J.D. 21 Oak St.
Kiley, Robert E., (BV) ... '62 '87 C.183 B.A. L.184 J.D. [Danaher,T.L.&N.]
*PRACTICE AREAS: Medical Malpractice Defense; Civil Trial Practice; Insurance Defense.
Killian, Robert K., (AV) ... '19 '48 C.867 A.B. L.184 LL.B. [Gould,K.&W.]
Killian, Robert K., Jr., (AV) ... '47 '72 C.867 B.A. L.276 J.D. [Killian,D.&J.] ⊙
*PRACTICE AREAS: Government Relations; Municipal; Land Use; Administrative Law; Arbitration.

Killian, Donohue & Jaff, LLC, (AV) BR
363 Main Street, 06106-1885 ⊙
Telephone: 860-560-1977 Telecopier: 860-249-6638
Robert K. Killian, Jr.; Thomas J. Donohue, Jr.; Jennifer C. Jaff.
General Practice. Litigation, Administrative, Banking, Municipal, Public Utility, Insurance, Real Estate and Regulatory, Government Relations and Health Care.

(This Listing Continued)

Killian, Donohue & Jaff, LLC (Continued)
Simsbury, Connecticut Office: 141 West Street. Telephone: 860-658-0436. Telecopier: 860-249-6638.
See Professional Biographies, HARTFORD, CONNECTICUT

Kim, Susan ... '72 '98 C.860 B.A. L.823 J.D. [🄰 Bingham D.]
*PRACTICE AREAS: Commercial Litigation; Bankruptcy; Appellate Practice.
Kindall, Clare E. ... '61 '89 C.914 B.A. L.893 J.D. 55 Elm St.
Kindl, John J., (BV) ... '51 '77 C.855 B.A. L.306 J.D. [Pullman&C.]
*PRACTICE AREAS: Real Estate Law.
King, John C., (AV) ... '46 '73 C&L.276 B.S.F.S., J.D. [Updike,K.&S.]
*PRACTICE AREAS: Labor and Employment; Litigation; Legislative Representation; Utilities Law.
Kinney, Shea S. ... '74 '99 C.518 B.A. L.184 J.D. [🄰 Updike,K.&S.]
*PRACTICE AREAS: Personal Injury Law; Product Liability; Insurance Defense Law.
Kinsella, James H. ... '24 '52 C.855 A.B. L.546 LL.B. 97 Elm St.‡
Kinyon, James R. ... '60 '87 C.823 B.A. L.107 J.D. [🄰 Brown R.M.F.&S.]
*PRACTICE AREAS: Real Estate; Banking; Consumer Protection; Finance; General Practice.
Kirschbaum, Amy R. ... '71 '97 C.276 B.A. L.184 J.D. [🄰 Shipman&G.]
*PRACTICE AREAS: Pension Plans; Employee Benefits.
Kitt, Doniel ... '49 '81 C.188 B.A. L.329 J.D. State Dept. of Banking
Klau, Arnold H., (BV) ... '32 '57 C&L.309 A.B., J.D. [Hyman,C.&K.]
Klau, Daniel J., (BV) ... '61 '91 C.112 B.A. L.94 J.D. [Wiggin&D.]
Klee, Thomas A., (BV) ... '44 '69 C&L.188 B.S., J.D. [🄲 Shipman&G.]
*PRACTICE AREAS: Securities; Corporate Law; Corporate Finance.
Klein, Gerald M., (BV) ... '45 '75 C.260 B.S. L.64 J.D. 21 Oak St.
Kleinman, Stewart F., (BV) ... '40 '66 C.569 B.S. L.1009 LL.B. [Kleinman&Assoc.] ⊙
*PRACTICE AREAS: Commercial Real Estate Development and Finance Law; Loan Workouts Law; Corporate Law; Commercial Leasing Law; Contracts.

Kleinman & Associates, P.C., (BV)
2 Congress Street, 06114-1024 ⊙
Telephone: 860-525-2930
Email: stewart.kleinman@snet.net URL: http://www.lawyers.com/kleinmanlaw
Stewart F. Kleinman.
Business Law, Commercial Real Estate, Leases and Leasing, Mortgages, Loan Workouts, Corporate Finance, Contracts, Corporation, Commercial, Collections, Banking, Bankruptcy, Probate, Estate Planning, Real Estate, Construction Contracts, Family Law, Mortgage Foreclosures, Landlord and Tenant, Zoning, Personal Injury, Consumer Law, Partnership Law, Property Law.
New London, Connecticut Office: 22 Masonic Street. Telephone: 860-437-2342. Facsimile: 860-437-2346.
See Professional Biographies, HARTFORD, CONNECTICUT

Klingman, Patrick A. ... '65 '91 C.884 B.A. L.823 J.D. [🄰 Schatz&N.]
*PRACTICE AREAS: Securities Litigation; Commercial Litigation.
Klippel, Charles H. ... '52 '81 C&L.309 A.B., J.D. Sr. V.P. & Gen. Coun., Aetna Inc.
*RESPONSIBILITIES: International Law; Health Care Law.
Knickerbocker, Robert P., Jr., (AV) ... '44 '69 C.188 B.A. L.184 J.D. [Day,B.&H.]
*PRACTICE AREAS: Energy; Telecommunications.
Knierim, Glenn E., (AV) ... '30 '60 C.188 B.S. L.184 J.D. 1 State St. (⊙Bloomfield)
Knight, Douglas K. ... '66 '92 C.454 B.B.A. L.823 J.D. [Reid&R.]
*PRACTICE AREAS: Employee Benefits; Pension Plans; Taft-Hartley Plans.
Knight, Peter R. ... '66 '96 C.918 B.A. L.306 J.D. 225 Asylum Street, 13th Floor
Knishkowy, David S. ... '52 '81 C.216 B.A. L.184 J.D. Dept. of Envir. Protec.
Knopf, Paul V., (BV) ... '47 '77 C.31 B.A. L.880 J.D. [Halloran&S.]
*PRACTICE AREAS: Banking Law; Real Estate Law; Secured Lending; Government Finance.
Knox, Kimberly A., (BV) ... '60 '86 C.183 B.A. L.184 J.D. [Horton,S.&C.]
*PRACTICE AREAS: Professional Grievance; Civil Litigation; Insurance Defense; Insurance Coverage; Personal Injury.
Koch, Priscilla F. ... '54 '80 C.66 B.A. L.1194 J.D. The Travelers Ins. Co.
Kochenburger, Peter Ralph '59 '86
C.976 B.A. L.309 J.D. The Travelers Insurance Company
Koerner, Allan W., (BV) ... '55 '82 C.164 B.A. L.184 J.D. [Gersten&C.]
*PRACTICE AREAS: Real Estate Law; Corporate Law; Estate Planning Law; Probate Law; Wills.
Koff, Marvin S. ... '38 '94 C.874 B.S. L.184 J.D. 660 Prospect Ave.
Kogut, Michael T., (BVⓉ) '55 '81 C.349 B.A. L.1048 J.D.
(adm. in MA; not adm. in CT) [🄲 Murtha C.] (⊙Boston, MA)
*PRACTICE AREAS: Health Care Regulation; Health Care Litigation; Long Term Care Facilities; Health Care Fraud; Abuse Counseling.
Kohler, Mark F. ... '60 '87 C.755 B.A. L.184 J.D. Office of State's Atty.
Koniuta, Ronald John ... '55 '95 C.184 B.A. L.1048 J.D. [🄰 Reid&R.]
*PRACTICE AREAS: Employee Benefits; Pension Plans; Executive Compensation; Taxation; Trusts and Estates.
Koontz, Roger E., (AV) ... '40 '65 C.339 B.S. L.976 LL.B. [🄲 Tyler C.&A.]
*PRACTICE AREAS: Public Utility; Administrative Law; Energy Law.
Kopp, David C. ... '45 '70 C.589 B.S. L.339 J.D. Asst. Gen. Coun., CIGNA Corp.
Korber, Mark F., (AV) ... '47 '78 C.446 B.A. L.184 J.D. [Murtha C.]
*PRACTICE AREAS: Corporate Law; Health Care Law; Estate Planning Law; Estate and Trust Administration Law; Resources Recovery Law.
Kornbrath, Brian J. ... '59 '87 C.93 B.A. L.184 J.D. Univ. of Conn. Law School

Korzenik, Armand A., (AV) '27 '51 C&L.309 A.B., J.D.
436 Farmington Avenue, 06105
Telephone: 860-236-1665 Fax: 860-231-7035
Email: armkor@ntplx.net
General Practice, including Personal Injury, Workers Compensation, Real Estate, Wills and Probate, Divorce, Motor Vehicle, Municipal and Administrative Law, Collection, Civil and Criminal Litigation.
See Professional Biographies, HARTFORD, CONNECTICUT

Kosberg, Alan H. ... '64 '91 C.659 B.A. L.94 J.D. [🄰 Bingham D.]
*PRACTICE AREAS: Commercial Law; Business Law; Commercial Litigation.
Koschwitz, Scott N. ... '67 '95 C.184 B.A. L.1040 J.D. [🄰 Updike,K.&S.]
*PRACTICE AREAS: Environmental Law; Commercial Litigation.
Kosior, Dana L. ... '70 '95 C.93 B.S. L.306 J.D. Arthur Andersen LLP

Koskoff, Koskoff & Bieder, P.C.
(See Bridgeport)

Kosloff & Harding
(See West Hartford)

Kostin, Michele G., (AV) ... '48 '72 C&L.94 B.A., J.D. V.P. & Coun., Aetna Inc.
*RESPONSIBILITIES: Executive Compensation; Employee Benefits; Employment Counseling and Litigation; Mergers and Acquisitions; Real Estate Investment/Private Equity Investments.
Kosto, Gale S., (BV) ... '37 '79 C.788 B.A. L.184 J.D. [Leete&K.]
*PRACTICE AREAS: Immigration and Naturalization; Visas; Business Immigration.
Kotkin, David, (AV) ... '13 '40 C&L.976 B.A., LL.B. [🄲 Schatz&S.R.&K.]
Kotsaftis, Kate F. ... '76 '01 C.184 B.A. L.306 J.D. [🄰 Updike,K.&S.]
*PRACTICE AREAS: Commercial Litigation.
Kowalski, Bill ... '59 '85 C.293 B.A. L.306 J.D. Sr. Coun., Natl. Accts., Aetna Inc.
Kowalyshyn, Kathleen J., (BV) ... '57 '90 C&L.184 B.A., J.D. [Gale&K.]
*PRACTICE AREAS: Family Law; Real Estate; Probate.
Koziol, Sharon Sloan ... '69 '96 C.184 B.S. L.982 J.D. [🄰 Shipman&G.]
*PRACTICE AREAS: Commercial Litigation; Collections and Foreclosures; Healthcare Fraud.
Kozlik, Michael E. ... '— '00 C.602 B.S. L.184 J.D. [🄰 Brown,R.F.&G.]
*PRACTICE AREAS: Environmental Law; Energy Law.
Kraczkowsky, Mark P. '55 '82
C.184 B.A. L.818 J.D. Asst. Reporter of Jud. Decisions Supm. Ct.

Krasow, Herbert A., (AV) ....'38 '64 C.184 B.A. L.831 LL.B. [Krasow,G.&H.]

Krasow, Garlick & Hadley, LLC, (AV)
One State Street, 06103
Telephone: 860-549-7100 Facsimile: 860-728-1651
Email: mail@krasowgarlick.com URL: http://www.krasowgarlick.com
Herbert A. Krasow; Gerald L. Garlick; Linda Clifford Hadley. Associate: Kenneth M. Rozich; Kenneth A. Goss.
General Practice including Real Estate, Commercial Litigation, Finance, Common Interest Communities, Banking, Corporate, Real Estate Development, Land Use, Shopping Centers, Insurance Defense, Family, Creditor's Rights.
See Professional Biographies, HARTFORD, CONNECTICUT

Kravetz, Karen Baldwin ....'72 '98 C.188 B.S. L.1019 J.D. [Ⓐ Brown R.M.F.&S.]
*PRACTICE AREAS: Civil Litigation.
Krechevsky, Robert L. .... '22 '48 C.976 B.A. L.184 LL.B. U.S. Bkrptcy. J.
Kreisberg, Jonathan B. .... '53 '77 C.188 B.S. L.30 J.D. Reg. Atty., NLRB
Kreitler, John E., (AV) ....'46 '74 C.918 B.A. L.966 J.D. [Shipman&G.]
*PRACTICE AREAS: Corporate Law; Computer Law; Mergers and Acquisitions Law; Health Insurance Law; Venture Capital Finance Law.
Krell, Susan K., (AV) ....'41 '75 C.994 B.A. L.184 J.D. [Jackson L.S.&K.]
Krevolin, Milton, (AV) ....'20 '46 C.676 L.306 J.D. [Krevolin,F.G.E.&H.]
Krevolin, Feinstein, Gorman, Eyges & Herrmann, P.C., (AV) ....21 Woodland St.

Krevolin, Roth & Connors LLC
(See West Hartford)

Krisch, Daniel Jonah ....'73 '99 C.178 B.A. L.184 J.D. [Ⓐ Horton,S.&C.]
*PRACTICE AREAS: Appellate Litigation; Civil Litigation; Criminal Law.

Kroll, McNamara & Evans, LLP
(See West Hartford)

Krowicki, Ben M., (BV) ....'53 '81 C.569 B.A. L.1194 J.D. [Bingham D.]
*PRACTICE AREAS: Commercial Litigation.
Krusz, Keith E. .... '60 '89 C.385 A.B. L.945 J.D. One American Row
Krzanowski, Edward F., (BV) .... '60 '85 C.184 B.S. L.1048 J.D. [Ⓒ Day,B.&H.]
*PRACTICE AREAS: Estate Planning; Estate Administration; Estate and Gift Taxation.
Kuban, Marie C. ....'75 '00 C.611 B.A. L.1048 J.D. [Ⓐ Day,B.&H.]
Kuckro, Lee G., (AV) ... '41 '68 C.93 A.B. L.276 J.D. Gen. Coun., The Advest Grp., Inc.
*RESPONSIBILITIES: Corporate Law; Securities Law; Litigation.
Kulak, Gregory W. ....'69 '96 C.184 B.A. L.306 J.D. 225 Asylum Street, 13th Floor
Kulawiz, JoAnne Kiely ....'35 '59 C.19 A.B. L.273 J.D. App. Ct. J.
Kulle, David A., (BV) ....'— '85 C.299 B.A. L.184 J.D. [Robinson&C.]
*PRACTICE AREAS: Labor and Employment; Litigation.
Kurs, Michael A., (BV) .... '55 '80 C.976 B.A. L.1162 J.D. [Pullman&C.] (⊙Bridgeport)
*PRACTICE AREAS: Health Care Law; Litigation and Administrative Law; Employment Law; Education Law; Antitrust Law.
Kuselias, Jason ....'— '98 C.855 B.A. L.94 J.D. [Ⓐ Robinson&C.]
Kuzmak, Richard P., (BV) .... '41 '66 C&L.184 B.A., J.D. [McVane,B.K.W.&B.]
Ladieu, Kevin ....'— '96 C.184 B.A. L.1252 J.D. [Ⓐ Howard,K.S.&F.]
*PRACTICE AREAS: Litigation; Personal Injury; Medical Malpractice; Criminal Law; Products Liability.
La Fontaine, Mark R., (BV) .... '64 '89 C.1036 B.A. L.94 J.D. [Andros,F.&M.]
Lagnese, Joyce A., (BV) .... '55 '80 C.1044 B.S. L.1019 J.D. [Danaher,T.L.&N.]
Lahey, Judith A. .... '43 '68 C.706 B.A. L.184 J.D. Asst. Rept. of Jud. Decisions‡
Lai, Janice D. ....'66 '91 C.802 B.B.A. L.221 J.D. [Ⓐ Halloran&S.]
*PRACTICE AREAS: Products Liability; Complex Civil Litigation; Insurance Defense.
Lallier, Gregg J. .... '72 '98 C.93 B.S. L.245 J.D. [Ⓐ Updike,K.&S.] (⊙New Haven)
*PRACTICE AREAS: Business Law; Intellectual Property; Electronic Commerce Law.
LaManna, Kathleen M. .... '70 '95 C.93 B.A. L.184 J.D. [Ⓐ Shipman&G.]
*PRACTICE AREAS: Litigation; Commercial Litigation; Creditors Rights; Bankruptcy; Workouts.
Lambert, Katherine J., (BV) .... '50 '81 C.299 B.A. L.818 J.D. [Shipman&G.]
*PRACTICE AREAS: Real Estate; Finance; Leases and Leasing; Zoning, Planning and Land Use.
Lambert, Thomas P. ....'67 '92 C.659 B.A. L.94 J.D. [Ⓐ Halloran&S.] (⊙Westport)
*PRACTICE AREAS: Insurance Defense Law; Civil Trial Law; Professional Liability.
Landau, Sidney S. .... '35 '60 C.24 B.A. L.569 LL.B. Appl. Ct. J.
Landino, Michael T., (CV) .... '58 '83 C.184 B.A. L.1048 J.D. [Ⓐ Miniter&Assoc.]
*PRACTICE AREAS: Construction Litigation; Corporate Law; Land Use; Technology Law; Employment Law.
Landmon, Chad A. ....'75 '99 C.184 B.A. L.306 J.D. [Ⓐ Axinn,V.&H.]
*PRACTICE AREAS: Commercial Litigation; Antitrust and Trade Regulation.
Lane, Elliot J., (BV) ....'50 '77 C.415 B.A. L.1048 J.D. 360 Main St.
Lane, Peter A. .... '26 '67 C.178 A.B. L.184 LL.B. 55 Elizabeth St.‡
Lang, Amy Sargeant ....'66 '93 C.1030 B.S. L.184 J.D. [Ⓐ Halloran&S.]
*PRACTICE AREAS: Family Law; Civil Litigation.
Lang, Richard David '63 '89 C.436 B.A. L.184 J.D.
Gen. Coun., CitiInsurance International Holdings, Inc.
Langer, Robert M., (AV) .... '48 '73 C.264 A.B. L.184 J.D. [Wiggin&D.]
*PRACTICE AREAS: Antitrust and Trade Regulation; Administrative Law; Consumer Law; Medical Antitrust.
Lanoue, Michael J. .... '46 '74 C&L.184 B.S., J.D. Asst. Atty. Gen.
Lanza, Michael H. .... '61 '86 C&L.184 B.A., J.D. Asst. Gen. Coun., CIGNA Corp.
LaPlante, Suzanne .... '66 '97 L.823 J.D. [Ⓐ Berman&S.]
*PRACTICE AREAS: Commercial Litigation.
LaPointe, Tamara S. ....'— '99 C.347 B.A. L.818 J.D. [Ⓐ Edwards&A.]
*PRACTICE AREAS: Corporate Law.
Largay, Timothy L., (AV) ....'43 '69 C&L.273 A.B., J.D. [Murtha C.]
*PRACTICE AREAS: Securities Law; Corporate Law; Mergers and Acquisitions Law.
Larson, Fred A. .... '40 '69 C&L.184 B.S., J.D. Sr. V.P., Hartford Natl. Bk.
LaSaracina, Christopher R. .... '74 '99 C.184 B.S. L.1252 J.D. [Ⓐ Shipman&G.]
*PRACTICE AREAS: Litigation; Labor Law.
Lassman, Edwin A., (AV) .... '28 '53 C.184 B.A. L.188 LL.B. [Ⓒ Rogin,N.C.L.&H.]
*PRACTICE AREAS: Construction Litigation; Health Care Litigation; Long Term Care; Commercial Real Estate; Corporate Law.
Lassman, Mark J., (BV) ....'54 '82 C.184 B.A. L.1048 J.D. [Ⓐ Rogin,N.C.L.&H.]
*PRACTICE AREAS: Criminal Law; Construction Litigation.
Lauretti, David G., (BV) '46 '76 C.855 B.A. L.893 J.D.
V.P. & Dir., Mtge. & Real Estate, Conn. Mut. Life Ins. Co.
Lavelle-Lafleur, Caitlin '69 '97 C.454 B.A. L.1048 J.D.
(adm. in IN; not adm. in CT) Supr. Ct.
Lavette, Dennis R., (BV) .... '54 '81 C.880 B.A. L.209 J.D. [O'Connell,F.&A.]
*PRACTICE AREAS: Residential Real Estate Law; Probate Law; Family Law.
Laviana, Robert ....'59 '89 C.1033 M.S. L.1048 J.D. 72 Cedar St.
Lavitt, Robert G. ....'62 '87 C.145 B.A. L.94 J.D. Bond Coun., Travelers Insurance
Law, Timothy E. .... '56 '85 C.184 B.A. L.1029 J.D. 94 Hungerford St.
Lawes, Charles O., III '59 '88 C.170 B.A. L.184 J.D.
Assoc. Coun., Hartford Financial Services Group, Inc.
Lawrence, Christopher E. ....'72 '99 C.645 B.A. L.262 J.D. [Ⓐ Bingham D.]
*PRACTICE AREAS: Corporate Law; Mergers and Acquisitions; Securities; Venture Capital.
Lawrence, John H., Jr., (AV) ....'46 '75 C.902 B.S. L.893 J.D. [Shipman&G.]
*PRACTICE AREAS: Health Care Law; Corporate Law; Business Law; Insurance Law; Federal and State Taxation Law.
Leach, Clifford G. '56 '82 C.309 B.A. L.184 J.D.
The Hartford Financial Services Group

Leaming, Brian P. ....'65 '91 C.676 B.A. L.128 J.D. [Halloran&S.]
*PRACTICE AREAS: Municipal Law; Governmental Liability; Constitutional Law; Professional Liability; Premises Liability.
Lear, Carol L., (BV) .... '49 '87 C.886 B.S. L.326 J.D. 225 Asylum St., 13th Fl.
Lebo, Simon J. ....'74 '99 C.216 B.A. L.1017 J.D. [Ⓐ Brown,P.&S.] (⊙Glastonbury)
*PRACTICE AREAS: Estate Planning; Probate Administration; Commercial Law; Real Estate.

LeBoeuf, Lamb, Greene & MacRae, L.L.P., (AV)
A Limited Liability Partnership including Professional Corporations
Formerly LeBoeuf, Lamb, Leiby & MacRae
Goodwin Square, 225 Asylum Street, 13th Floor, 06103 ⊙
Telephone: 860-293-3500 Facsimile: 860-293-3555
URL: http://www.llgm.com
Partners: Andrew N. Davis; Thomas G. Rohback; James A. Thompson, Jr.; Charles R. Welsh; Diane Woodfield Whitney; Ronald W. Zdrojeski. Of Counsel: Robert P. Wax. Special Counsel: Dennis O. Brown; Dennis F. Kerrigan, Jr.; Catherine K. Lin.
General Practice including Administrative, Corporate, Securities, Venture Capital Financing, Banking, Environmental, Insurance, Litigation, Municipal Bonds, Copyrights, Trademarks and Patents.
Eastern United States:
New York, N.Y. Office: 125 West 55th Street. Telephone: 212-424-8000. Facsimile: 212-424-8500. Telex: 423416 or 1561363.
Washington, D.C. Office: 1875 Connecticut Avenue, N.W. Telephone: 202-986-8000. Facsimile: 202-986-8102. Telex: 440274.
Albany, New York Office: One Commerce Plaza, 99 Washington Avenue, Suite 2020. Telephone: 518-626-9000. Facsimile: 518-626-9010.
Boston, Massachusetts Office: 260 Franklin Street. Telephone: 617-439-9500. Facsimile: 617-439-0341; 439-0342.
Harrisburg, Pennsylvania Office: 200 North Third Street, Suite 300, P.O. Box 12105. Telephone: 717-232-8199. Facsimile: 717-232-8720.
Newark, New Jersey Office: The Legal Center, One Riverfront Plaza. Telephone: 973-643-8000. Facsimile: 973-643-6111.
Pittsburgh, Pennsylvania Office: One Gateway Center, Fort Duquesne Boulevard, Suite 1600. Telephone: 412-594-2300. Facsimile: 412-594-5237.
Western United States:
Denver, Colorado Office: 633 17th Street, Suite 2000. Telephone: 303-291-2600. Facsimile: 303-297-0422.
Los Angeles, California Office: 725 South Figueroa Street, Suite 3100. Telephone: 213-955-7300. Facsimile: 213-955-7399. Telex: 678982.
Salt Lake City, Utah Office: 1000 Kearns Building, 136 South Main Street. Telephone: 801-320-6700. Facsimile: 801-359-8256.
San Francisco, California Office: One Embarcadero Center, Suite 400. Telephone: 415-951-1100. Facsimile: 415-951-1180; 951-1181. Telex: 470167.
Southern United States:
Houston, Texas Office: 1000 Louisiana Avenue. Telephone: 713-287-2000. Facsimile: 713-287-2100.
Jacksonville, Florida Office: 50 North Laura Street, Suite 2800. Telephone: 904-354-8000. Facsimile: 904-353-1673.
European Offices:
Brussels, Belgium Office: Kunstlaan/Avenue des Arts, 19H, B-1000 Brussels, Belgium. Telephone: 011-32-2-227-0900. Facsimile: 011-32-2-227-0909.
London, England Office: LeBoeuf, Lamb, Greene & MacRae (A London Based Multinational Partnership); One Minster Court, Mincing Lane, 6th Floor, London EC3R 7AA England. Telephone: 011-44-20-7-459-5000. Facsimile: 011-44-20-7-459-5099.
Moscow, Russian Federation Office: Nikitsky Pereulok, 5 (formerly Ulitsa Belinskogo) 103473 Moscow, Russian Federation. Telephone: 011-7-095-737-5000. Facsimile: 011-7-095-737-5050.
Paris, France Office: 130, rue du Faubourg Saint-Honoreé75008 Paris, France. Telephone: 011-33-1-53-93-77-00. Facsimile: 011-33-1-42-56-08-06.
Asian Offices:
Almaty, Kazakhstan Office: Prospect Seyfullin, 531, 5th Floor, 480083, Almaty, Republic of Kazakhstan. Telephone: 011-7-3272-50-7575. Facsimile: 011-7-3272-50-7576.
Bishkek, Kyrgyz Office: Ulitsa Panfilova, 205 Bishkek, Kyrgyz Republic. Telephone: 011-996-3312-22-2994. Facsimile: 011-996-3312-66-2233.
Tashkent, Uzbekistan Office: Ulitsa Turab Tula, 1 700003 Tashkent Republic of Uzbekistan. Telephone: 011-7-3712-40-6050. Facsimile: 011-7-3712-40-6052.
African Office:
Johannesburg, South Africa Office: 11 Alice Lane, 2nd Floor, West Wing, Standard Bank Building, Sandton 2196 Johannesburg, South Africa. Telephone: 27-011-784-0233. Fax: 27-011-784-2855.
See Professional Biographies, HARTFORD, CONNECTICUT

Lebovitz, Emily J. ....'48 '74 C&L.184 B.A., J.D. Rept. of Jud. Decisions
Lebovitz, Gilbert ... '30 '53 C&L.588 LL.B. Reg. Coun. & V.P., First Amer. Title Ins. Co.
Lederer, Amy B., (BV) .... '60 '85 C.197 B.A. L.184 J.D. Asst. U.S. Atty.
Leduc, Marc R. ....'— '00 C.93 B.A. L.602 J.D. [Ⓐ Bingham D.]
*PRACTICE AREAS: Business Law.
Lee, Veronica J. ....'— '99 C.725 B.A. L.184 J.D. [Ⓐ Brown,R.F.&G.]
*PRACTICE AREAS: Commercial Real Estate.
Leete, Elizabeth B., (AV) .... '33 '76 C.914 B.A. L.184 J.D. [Leete&K.]
*PRACTICE AREAS: Immigration and Naturalization; Visas; Business Immigration.

Leete & Kosto, LLP, (AV)
21 Oak Street Suite 309, 06106-8002
Telephone: 860-249-8100 Fax: 860-727-9184
Email: lk@visacounsel.com URL: http://www.visacounsel.com
Members of Firm: Elizabeth B. Leete; Gale S. Kosto; Andrew L. Wizner; Eric Fleischmann.
Limited to Immigration and Naturalization Law, including Visas, Employment Visas, Business Immigration and Citizenship.
References: Connecticut National Bank; Connecticut Attorneys Title Insurance Co.
See Professional Biographies, HARTFORD, CONNECTICUT

Lefevre, Matthew J., (AV) .... '62 '87 C.1234 B.A. L.184 J.D. [M.J.Lefevre] ⊙
*PRACTICE AREAS: Estate Planning Law; Elder Law; Estate Administration Law; Trust Administration Law; Tax Law.
Lefevre, Regina Wexler, (CV) ....'62 '87 C.855 B.A. L.184 J.D. [Ⓒ M.J.Lefevre] ⊙

Lefevre, Matthew J., Esq., P.C., The Law Offices of, (AV)
241 Asylum Street, 3rd Floor, 06103 ⊙
Telephone: 860-522-6288 Fax: 860-522-7585
Email: mjlesqpc@snet.net URL: http://www.lawyers.com/lefevrelaw
Matthew J. Lefevre. Of Counsel: Regina Wexler Lefevre.
Tax Law, Estate Planning and Administration, Trust, Elder Law, Business Planning, Corporate, Partnership, Limited Liability Company, Commercial Law and Financing.
Torrington, Connecticut Office: 94 Church Street, 06790. Telephone: 860-626-8590. Fax: 860-489-4316.
See Professional Biographies, HARTFORD, CONNECTICUT

Leff, David K. ....'55 '78 C.454 B.A. L.184 J.D. Asst. Comr.
Leffard, Gregory W. '59 '98 C.1091 B.S. L.1048 J.D.
(adm. in AL; not adm. in CT) Vice Pres., Prof. Liab., Gulf Insur. Grp.
Legenhausen, Thomas R. .... '55 '81 C.188 B.A. L.569 J.D. Asst. V.P., The Hartford
Leibert, Richard M., (BV) ....'51 '79 C.415 B.A. L.184 J.D. [Hunt L.C.&J.]
*PRACTICE AREAS: Foreclosure; Bankruptcy; Commercial Litigation; Real Estate.
Leibowitz, Alan I. '47 '72 C.260 B.S. L.276 J.D.
(adm. in DC; not adm. in CT) Kidder, Peabody & Co., Inc.
Leikin, William F. '48 '73
C&L.184 B.A., J.D. Asst. Gen. Coun., United Technologies Corp.
Leil, Hisham A. .... '68 '97 C.184 B.A. L.1218 J.D. 179 Allyn St.
Lembo, Joseph A. '48 '73
C.1030 B.A. L.724 J.D. Dir., Legal Div., Dept. of Consumer Protec.
Lemega, John W., (AV) .... '43 '68 C.855 B.A. L.93 LL.B. [Halloran&S.]
*PRACTICE AREAS: Insurance Coverage; Insurance Bad Faith Defense; Insurance Litigation; Fire Insurance Defense; Property Insurance.

Lena, Glory Martyn, (BV) ....'66 '91 C.197 B.A. L.94 J.D. [Tyler C.&A.]
*PRACTICE AREAS: Civil Litigation; Products Liability; Medical Malpractice Defense; Appellate Practice.

Lenehan, Robert ....'45 '72 C.276 B.A. L.174 J.D. 350 Church St.

Lengyel, Thomas J. ....'73 '99 C.665 B.A. L.1252 J.D. [Ⓐ Rome M.S.]
*PRACTICE AREAS: Commercial Litigation; Civil Litigation; Securities Regulation; Ad Valorem Tax; Business Consultation.

Lennon, Kathleen A. .... '60 '85 C.1030 A.B. L.930 J.D. Coun., The Travelers Ins. Co.

Lenore, Charles H., (AV) ....'53 '78 C.184 B.A. L.823 J.D. [Day,B.&H.]
*PRACTICE AREAS: Emerging Companies; Technology and Intellectual Property - Business; Closely Held Businesses; Tax.

Leone, Throwe, Teller & Nagle
(See East Hartford)

Leonhardt, Mary Alice, (BV) '56 '85 C.276 B.S.N. L.818 J.D.
102 Oak Street, 06106
Telephone: 860-727-8874 Fax: 860-525-2194
Email: maleonhardt@email.msn.com URL: http://www.lawyers.com/bsn-jd
Health Care, Administrative Law, Corporate Law, Employment Law, Personal Injury, Medical Malpractice.
See Professional Biographies, HARTFORD, CONNECTICUT

Leshine, Bruce H. '60 '92 C.688 B.S.I.E. L.276 J.D.
(adm. in VA; not adm. in CT) [© Brown R.M.F.&S.]

Lessne, Scott A., (BV) '58 '83
C.855 B.A. L.1048 J.D. Group Sr. Coun., Fleet Financial Grp., Inc.

Leuba, Robert C. ....'32 '60 C.690 B.S. L.184 LL.B. Supr. Ct. J.

Levack, Jennifer A. ....'74 '00 C.184 B.S. L.1048 J.D. [Ⓐ Cranmore,F.&M.]

Leventhal, H. David, (AV) ....'29 '56 C.976 A.B. L.309 LL.B. [© Brown R.M.F.&S.]
*PRACTICE AREAS: Real Estate; Litigation; Corporate; Information Technology.

Levesque, Alan T., (BV) '58 '89 C.870 B.S. L.178 J.D.
Executive Assistant to the Chairman, United Technologies Corporation

Levesque, David R. .... '72 '97 C.478 A.B. L.1048 J.D. [Ⓐ Berman&S.]
*PRACTICE AREAS: Commercial Litigation; Business Litigation.

Levin, Alan J. .... '60 '86 C.156 B.A. L.1009 J.D. [Edwards&A.]
*PRACTICE AREAS: Insurance; General Corporate.

Levin, Daniel W. ....'66 '92 C.691 B.A. L.145 J.D. [Ⓐ Schatz&S.R.&K.]

Levin, Leslie C. ... '55 '81 C.597 B.S.J. L.178 J.D. Assoc. Prof., Univ. of CT Sch. of Law

Levin, Michael R., (AV) ....'39 '69 C.860 A.B. L.477 J.D. [© Levin,F.&P.]
*PRACTICE AREAS: Real Estate; Corporate Finance; Business Law; Securities.

Levin, Ford & Paulekas, LLP, (AV)
One State Street, 06103
Telephone: 860-527-0400 Telecopier: 860-249-7500
Email: info@lfpllp.com URL: http://www.lfpllp.com
Members of Firm: Paul W. Ford; Walter E. Paulekas; William J. Egan; David A. Hill, Jr.; Lawrence A. Dvorin. Associates: Matthew H. Youmans; Eleanor N. Bortolan. Of Counsel: Michael R. Levin; Peter Menting (Not admitted in CT).
Commercial Finance, Real Estate Finance, Investment and Development, Business and Corporate Finance, Creditors Rights and Bankruptcy, Environmental and Land Use, International Business Practice, and Litigation in all State and Federal Courts.
See Professional Biographies, HARTFORD, CONNECTICUT

Levine, Andrea J. ....'66 '92 C.103 B.A. L.188 J.D. [Ⓐ Dechert]
*PRACTICE AREAS: Commercial Real Estate Acquisitions; Commercial Real Estate Finance; Commercial Leasing; Office Leasing.

Levine, Ellen S. ....'48 '73 C&L.188 A.B., J.D. Webster Bk.

Levine, Eric Marc ....'68 '94 C.472 B.S. L.982 J.D. 231 Capitol Avenue

Levine, I. Oscar, (AV) ....'06 '30 C&L.976 B.A., J.D. [© Schatz&S.R.&K.]

Levine, Jonathan M. ....'71 '99 C.860 L.184 [Ⓐ Day,B.&H.]
*PRACTICE AREAS: Business Law; Electric Utility Regulation; Utility Finance; Utility Mergers; Utility Rates.

Levine, Kenneth L. ....'53 '78 C.319 B.A. L.930 J.D. [Murtha C.]
*PRACTICE AREAS: Tax Law; Tax Planning; Exempt Organizations Tax; Partnership Taxation.

Levine, Mark M., (AVⓉ) .... '49 '75 C.665 B.A. L.229 J.D. The Travelers Ins. Co.

Levine, Peter H., (AV) ....'49 '72 C.563 B.A. L.188 J.D. [© Bingham D.]
*PRACTICE AREAS: Commercial Finance; Corporate and Securities Law; Mergers and Acquisitions.

Levison, Barbara S. ....'60 '85 C.855 B.A. L.93 J.D. P.O. Box 340890

Levy, Andrea F. .... '53 '79 C&L.184 B.A., J.D. Coun., CIGNA Corp.

Levy, Harold M. '46 '70 C&L.184 B.A., J.D.
Assoc. Gen. Coun. & Dir., Prop.-Cas. Litig., Hartford Financial Services Group, Inc.

Levy, Joel G., (BV) ....'47 '73 C.1036 B.A. L.184 J.D. [Ⓐ Trantolo&T.]

Levy, Michael W., (BV) ....'50 '77 C.319 B.A. L.1009 J.D. 21 Oak St.

Levy & Droney, P.C.
(See Farmington)

Lewis, Jacques C. ....'49 '75 C&L.494 B.A., J.D. V.P., Shawmut Bk. Conn., N.A.

Lewis, Jennifer Hamilton ....'72 '97 C.37 B.A. L.184 J.D. [Ⓐ Pepe&H.]

Lewis, John C., III ....'68 '93 C.93 B.S. L.1048 J.D. 73 Wadsworth St.

Lewis, Jonathan M. ....'— '98 C.67 B.A. L.184 J.D. [Ⓐ Brown,R.F.&G.]

Lewis, Paul, (BV) ....'34 '61 C.94 B.S. L.184 LL.B. [Barlow&L.]

Lewis, Lewis & Ferraro, L.L.C.
(See West Hartford)

Lewton, Robert J. .... '71 '96 C.882 B.S. L.982 J.D. [Ⓐ Day,B.&H.]
*PRACTICE AREAS: Secured Lending; Structured Finance.

Li, Xin '69 '00 L.999 LL.B.
(adm. in NY; not adm. in CT) United Tech. Corp.

Libassi, Frank Peter S. .... '30 '55 C.165 B.A. L.976 LL.B. The Travelers Ins. Co.

Libbin, Martin R. ....'53 '78 C.184 B.S. L.306 J.D. 100 Washington St.‡

Libby, Frank A., Jr. ....'52 '82 CityPlace I

Libby, Joan G. ....'44 '81 C.1036 B.A. L.184 J.D. V.P. & Assoc. Coun., Society for Svgs.

Libert & Associates
(See Simsbury)

Librizzi, Thomas G., (BV) ....'59 '84 C.282 B.A. L.365 J.D. [Pepe&H.]
*PRACTICE AREAS: Alternative Dispute Resolution; Construction Law; Contracts; Government Contracts; Insurance.

Lieberman, Alan E., (AV) .... '56 '82 C.976 B.A. L.477 J.D. [Shipman&G.]
*PRACTICE AREAS: Federal and State Taxation; Business Law.

Liegeot, Adam .... '72 '00 C.976 B.A. L.184 J.D. 210 Capitol Ave., Ste. 208

Lifshitz, Harris T. ....'46 '71 C.94 A.B. L.184 J.D. Fam. Support Mag.

Lilliendahl, John R., III, (AV) ....'45 '70 C.478 A.B. L.184 LL.B. [Howd&L.]
*PRACTICE AREAS: Product Liability Litigation; Insurance Defense Litigation; General Trial and Appellate Practice; Toxic Tort; Commercial Litigation.

Lin, Catherine K. .... '54 '91 C.914 B.A. L.976 J.D. [© LeBoeuf,L.G.&M.]
*PRACTICE AREAS: Environmental Law; International Environmental Law.

Linderman, John C. '38 '70 C.453 B.S. L.184 J.D.
[McCormick,P.&H.] (See Pat. Sect.)
*PRACTICE AREAS: Intellectual Property; Patents; Trademarks; Copyrights.

Lindgren, Christian L. '51 '76 C.855 B.A. L.184 J.D.
Coun., Bank of New England Corp.

Lindlauf, Ronald Wayne, Jr. .... '64 '90 C.692 B.A. L.61 J.D. 55 Farmington Ave.

Lindsay, Barbara B. ...... '50 '83 C.681 A.B. L.178 J.D. [© Day,B.&H.] (⊙New Haven)

Lines, Mimi M., (AV) ....'— '80 C.976 B.A. L.184 J.D. [© Robinson&C.]
*PRACTICE AREAS: Real Estate.

Linker, Robin S. .... '50 '89 C.102 B.S. L.184 J.D. The Hartford Spec. Litigation Unit

Lissitzyn, Lawrence H., (AV) .... '44 '74 C.178 B.A. L.880 J.D. [Reid&R.]
*PRACTICE AREAS: Litigation.

Littlefield, Anne H. .... '67 '95 C.93 A.B. L.893 J.D. [Ⓐ Shipman&G.]
*PRACTICE AREAS: Labor and Employment Law; Education Law.

Litwinka, Michael '44 '73 C.705 B.S. L.724 J.D.
(adm. in NY; not adm. in CT) V.P., Workplus.com, Inc.

Livesay, Mark T. ....'69 '94 C.228 A.B. L.823 J.D. [Ⓐ Halloran&S.]
*PRACTICE AREAS: ERISA; Intellectual Property.

Livesay, Viviana L. ....'68 '94 C.276 B.S. L.823 J.D. Coun., Legal Services

Livingston, Daniel E., (BV) .... '55 '82 C.1307 B.A. L.976 J.D. [Livingston,A.P.&M.]

Livingston, Adler, Pulda & Meiklejohn, (AV) .... 557 Prospect Ave.

Lloyd, Alex, (AV) .... '42 '67 C.164 B.A. L.976 LL.B. [Shipman&G.]
*PRACTICE AREAS: Health Care Law; Corporate Law; Business Law; Federal Taxation; State Taxation.

Lloyd, James H., III, (AV) '43 '73 C.674 A.B. L.184 J.D.
[Updike,K.&S.] (⊙Stamford)
*PRACTICE AREAS: Public Finance; Public Law; Commercial Law; Utilities Law.

Lobo, Jason M. .... '67 '94 C.197 A.B. L.306 J.D. Off. of Atty. Gen.

Localio, Jan Maria ....'67 '01 C.951 B.A. L.184 J.D. [Wolf,H.E.&C.]
*PRACTICE AREAS: Insurance Defense; Toxic Torts; Fidelity and Surety; Construction Law.

Logie, Donald J., Jr. .... '46 '74 C.918 B.A. L.228 J.D. Counsel, CIGNA Corporation

Loiselle, Alva P. ....'10 '43 C&L.184 State Ref.

Lombardo, Thomas E. '49 '79 C.676 B.A. L.1048 J.D.
Dir., Mktg., The Travelers Ins. Co.

Lomeli, Patricia Ann Futter '56 '80 C.976 B.A. L.94 J.D.
Corp. Secy. & Coun., Conn. Mut. Life Ins. Co.

London, Marjorie A. '48 '82
C.518 A.B. L.262 J.D. Mgr. & Asst. Coun., Community-Tech. Coll.

Longley, Donald M., (BV) ....'45 '73 C.882 B.A. L.184 J.D. Asst. Atty. Gen.

Longo, Santo ....'63 '94 C.31 B.A. L.184 J.D. 225 Asylum Street, 13th Floor

Loomis, Carol L. ....'54 '97 C.518 B.A. L.184 J.D. [Ⓐ Tyler C.&A.]

Looney, John M., Jr., (BV) ....'50 '76 C.93 B.A. L.1048 J.D. Asst. Atty. Gen.

Lord, Andrew W. ....'61 '96 C.431 B.S. L.184 J.D. [Ⓐ Murtha C.]

Lord, Richard A., Jr. ....'74 '00 C.184 B.A. L.1252 J.D. [Ⓐ Cramer,A.&F.]
*PRACTICE AREAS: Insurance Defense.

Lorenzo, Joseph A., (BV) .... '26 '52 C.855 B.S. L.184 LL.B. 74 Bloomfield Ave.

Losee, David B., (BV) ....'45 '71 C.918 B.A. L.184 J.D. [Halloran&S.]
*PRACTICE AREAS: Environmental; Zoning, Planning and Land Use; Real Estate Law; Real Estate Development.

Lotstein, James I., (AV) ....'44 '69 C.597 B.S. L.184 J.D. [Cummings&L.]
*PRACTICE AREAS: Corporate Law; Securities Law; Finance; Banking Law.

Louden, Shannon O. ....'63 '93 C.821 B.A. L.659 J.D. [Louden]

Louden, Wm. Bruce, (AV) ....'38 '63 C&L.260 B.A., J.D. [Louden]

Louden Legal Group LLC, (AV)
638 Prospect Avenue, 06105
Telephone: 860-231-7150 Fax: 860-231-7425
Email: info@loudenlegalgroup.com URL: http://www.loudenlegalgroup.com
Wm. Bruce Louden; Shannon O. Louden; Susan Busby.
Divorce, Divorce Mediation, Matrimonial Law, Premarital Agreements.
See Professional Biographies, HARTFORD, CONNECTICUT

Louis, Frank W. ....'47 '73 C.951 B.A. L.893 J.D. [© Andros,F.&M.]

Lowe, Moira C. '70 '97 C.823 B.S. L.1048 J.D.
Dir., Phoenix Home Life Mutual Ins. Co.

Lubinsky, Theodore A., (BV) ....'31 '60 C.184 B.S. L.94 LL.B. 621 Farmington Ave.

Lucarelli, Jennifer R. ....'73 '99 C.976 B.A. L.602 J.D. [Ⓐ Reid&R.]
*PRACTICE AREAS: Litigation.

Ludgin, Robert F., (BV) '40 '66 C.674 A.B. L.477 J.D.
33 Linden Place, P.O. Box 261775, 06126-1775
Telephone: 860-549-3920 Fax: 860-524-8238
Civil and Criminal Litigation, Motor Vehicle, D.W.I., Personal Injury, Commercial, Collections, Estates, Family Law, Real Estate, Landlord and Tenant.
See Professional Biographies, HARTFORD, CONNECTICUT

Ludorf, Edward S., (AV) .... '28 '58 C.855 B.A. L.94 LL.B. [Howd&L.] ‡

Ludovico, Anthony B. ....'43 '68 C.103 A.B. L.184 J.D. [Rome M.S.]
*PRACTICE AREAS: Trusts and Estates.

Lugli, Richard H. ....'— '90 C.31 A.B. L.306 J.D. [Ⓐ Wiggin&D.]

Lukacs, Andrew Z. .... '47 '72 C&L.184 B.A., J.D. The Travelers Ins. Co.

Lukingbeal, Eric, (AV) ....'— '74 C.951 B.A. L.893 J.D. [Robinson&C.]
*PRACTICE AREAS: Environmental Law; Zoning, Planning and Land Use; Litigation; Toxic Torts.

Lutsk, Bruce M., (AV) .... '42 '74 C.95 B.A. L.184 J.D. [Reid&R.]
*PRACTICE AREAS: Commercial Law; Commercial Real Estate and Financing; Health Care; Real Estate; Zoning, Planning and Land Use.

Lyles, Ronald E. .... '66 '95 C.188 B.S. L.1252 J.D. [Ⓐ Day,B.&H.]
*PRACTICE AREAS: Commercial Litigation; Creditors Rights; Truth in Lending.

Lyman, Timothy R. ....'57 '87 C.309 B.A. L.569 J.D. [Day,B.&H.]
*PRACTICE AREAS: Finance and Investment; Tax Exempt Organizations; International Transactions.

Lynch, Ann E. .... '65 '90 C.1044 B.A. L.184 J.D. 110 Sherman St.

Lynch, Christopher J., (BV) ....'58 '84 C.918 B.A. L.184 J.D. [Halloran&S.]
*PRACTICE AREAS: Products Liability Litigation; Drug and Medical Device Litigation; Complex Civil Litigation.

Lynch, J. Shannon '54 '81 C.138 A.B. L.421 J.D.
(adm. in KY; not adm. in CT) The Travelers Ins. Co.

Lynch, John B., Jr., (AV) ....'— '84 C.321 B.A. L.893 J.D. [Robinson&C.]
*PRACTICE AREAS: Mergers and Acquisitions; Finance; Corporate Law; Banking Law.

Lynch, Joseph G., (AV) ....'24 '51 C.918 A.B. L.309 LL.B. [Halloran&S.]
*PRACTICE AREAS: Civil Litigation; Insurance Litigation; Educational Law.

Lynch, Matthew H. '57 '85
C.309 A.B. L.94 J.D. Gen. Coun., Allegis Realty Investors LLC

Lynch, Richard J., (BV) ....'45 '73 C.93 A.B. L.184 J.D. Asst. Atty. Gen.

Lynch, Timothy P. ....'66 '96 C.184 B.A. L.262 J.D. 225 Asylum Street, 13th Floor

Lynch, Traub, Keefe and Errante, A Professional Corporation
(See New Haven)

Lyon, James B., (AV) .... '30 '55 C.31 B.A. L.976 LL.B. [© Murtha C.]
*PRACTICE AREAS: Tax Exempt Organizations Law; Corporate Income Tax Law; State and Local Tax Law.

Lyons, Charles M. '38 '67 C.103 A.B. L.818 J.D.
Coun., Hartford Steam Boiler Inspection & Ins. Co.

Lyons, Timothy F. ....'46 '73 C.367 B.A. L.184 J.D. Coun., The Travelers Ins. Co.

Ma, Shirley S. .....'69 '96 C.1044 B.S. L.201 J.D. [Ⓐ McCormick,P.&H.] (See Pat. Sect.)
*PRACTICE AREAS: Intellectual Property.

MacDermid, Bruce G., (AV) ....'47 '75 C.95 A.B. L.94 J.D. [MacDermid,R.&G.]
*PRACTICE AREAS: Civil Litigation; Real Estate Litigation; Personal Injury; Family Law; Corporate Litigation.

MacDermid, Reynolds & Glissman, P.C., (AV)
86 Farmington Avenue, 06105
Telephone: 860-278-1900 Telecopier: 860-547-1191
URL: http://www.lawyers.com/mrglaw
Paul W. Orth; Bruce G. MacDermid; Peter R. Reynolds; David R. Glissman; Jeanne S. Roberts; Michael S. Stiebel.
Civil Litigation; Commercial and Residential Real Estate Litigation; Real Estate, Conveyancing, Leasing, Workout and Finance; Environmental and Land Use Law; Real Estate Brokerage; Communications; Construction Law; Surety; Probate and Estate Law; Employment Law, Alternative Dispute Resolution and Family Law.
See Professional Biographies, HARTFORD, CONNECTICUT

Macdonald, Cynthia P. '52 '89
C.94 B.L.S. L.818 J.D. Counsel, The Travelers Insurance Company
MacDonald, Donald J. '60 '99 C.1154 B.S. L.1389 J.D.
(adm. in MA; not adm. in CT; See Pat. Sect.) [Ⓐ McCormick,P.&H.]
*PRACTICE AREAS: Intellectual Property Litigation; Patent Prosecution.
MacDonald, Jeffrey S. .....'73 '98 C.216 B.A. L.1009 J.D. 225 Asylum Street, 13th Floor
Macdonald, Scott D., (BV) .... '60 '87 C&L.575 B.A., J.D. 1 American Row
MacGrady, Glenn J. ....'— '75 C.178 A.B. L.259 J.D. [Ⓒ Pepe&H.]
*PRACTICE AREAS: Tax Law; Employee Benefits; Corporate Law; Estate Planning; Computer Law.
Mack, David M. ....'70 '00 [Ⓐ Cummings&L.]
Mack, Diane ....'50 '80 C.70 B.A. L.831 J.D. Compl. Offr., Conn. Mut. Life Ins. Co.
Mack, Kevin A. '57 '84 C.477 B.A. L.201 J.D.
(adm. in OH; not adm. in CT) Natl. Dir., The Travelers Ins. Co.
Mackas, Daniel G. '61 '97 C&L.184 B.S.E., J.D.
[Ⓐ McCormick,P.&H.] (See Pat. Sect.)
*PRACTICE AREAS: Patents; Trademarks; Copyrights.
MacKenzie, Richard C., (AV) ....'39 '71 C.103 B.A. L.94 J.D. [Ⓒ Day,B.&H.]
*PRACTICE AREAS: Debt and Equity Finance; Closely Held Business Law; Municipal Finance.
Mackin, Kristie E. ....'73 '00 C&L.184 B.A., J.D. [Ⓐ Halloran&S.]
*PRACTICE AREAS: Labor and Employment.
MacKinnon, Dana, (BV) '62 '90 C&L.184 B.A., J.D.
Assoc. Coun., Hartford Financial Services Group, Inc.
MacPherson, Diana, (AV) ....'— '78 C.773 B.A. L.184 J.D. [Robinson&C.]
*PRACTICE AREAS: Real Estate; Finance; Leasing; Construction Law.
Madin, Everett Howard, Jr. .... '51 '92 C.823 B.F.A. L.184 J.D. [RisCassi&D.]
*PRACTICE AREAS: Personal Injury; Products Liability; Medical Malpractice.
Madsen, William G., (BV) .... '59 '90 C.454 B.A. L.1194 J.D. [Madsen,P.&P.] ⊙
*PRACTICE AREAS: Labor and Employment Law; Civil Rights Law; Age Discrimination Law; Sexual Harassment Law; Employment Disability Law.

Madsen, Prestley & Parenteau, LLC, (BV)
44 Capitol Avenue Suite 201, 06106 ⊙
Telephone: 860-246-2466 Facsimile: 860-246-1794
Email: mppjustice.com URL: http://www.lawyers.com/mppllc
William G. Madsen; Peter B. Prestley; Jacques J. Parenteau. Associate: Craig Thoms Dickinson.
Employment, Benefits Law and Related Litigation. Employment Contracts; Age, Race, Sex and Disability Discrimination; Civil Rights, Section 1983. Wage and Hour Law, Class Actions and Qui Tam Actions, Negotiations, Mediations, Arbitrations, Trials.
New London Office: 111 Huntington Street, P.O. Box 1631. Telephone: 860-442-2466. Facsimile: 860-447-9206.
See Professional Biographies, HARTFORD, CONNECTICUT

Maglio, Michael F., (BV) ....'— '82 C.184 B.A. L.818 J.D. [Robinson&C.]
*PRACTICE AREAS: Debtor and Creditor; Commercial Law.
Magliochetti, Lisa A. .... '61 '87 C.1252 B.S. L.93 J.D. [Pullman&C.]
*PRACTICE AREAS: Litigation; Family Law.
Maguire, Jeffrey G. .... '— '81 C.184 B.A. L.976 J.D. UBS Realty Investors, LLC
Maher, James P. ....'61 '87 C.1030 A.B. L.184 J.D. [Halloran&S.]
*PRACTICE AREAS: Real Estate; Financial Transactions; Internet and E-Business Law; Business Organization; Creditors Rights.
Mahoney, John W. .... '64 '89 C.321 B.A. L.184 J.D. 1 American Row
Mahoney, Mary Ellen Shea '64 '90 C.103 A.B. L.93 J.D.
Asst. Gen. Cnsl, Colt's Manufacturing Company, Inc.
Mahoney, Richard C., (AV) ....'53 '79 C.951 B.A. L.184 J.D. [Kenny,B.M.&M.]
*PRACTICE AREAS: Personal Injury; Real Estate; Insurance Defense.
Mailly, Jennifer Brown ....'60 '87 C.103 A.B. L.608 J.D. [Ⓒ Shipman&G.]
*PRACTICE AREAS: Labor and Employment.
Majeski, Stephen L. '50 '77 C.103 A.B. L.184 J.D.
Asst. Gen. Coun., Hartford Financial Services Group, Inc.
Majewski, Kevin E. ....'— '94 C.918 B.A. L.184 J.D. [Ⓐ Robinson&C.]
Malchodi, Eric A. ....'60 '90 C&L.184 B.A., J.D. Shawmut Bk. Conn., N.A.
Malech, Steven P. .... '66 '95 C.846 B.A. L.184 J.D. [Ⓐ Wiggin&D.]
Maley, Edwin J., Jr. ....'53 '78 C&L.184 B.A., J.D. Chf. of Staff
Malitz, Steven H., (BV) ....'61 '86 C.156 B.A. L.982 J.D. [Halloran&S.]
*PRACTICE AREAS: Insurance Defense Litigation; Trucking Transportation Litigation; Products Liability Litigation; Aviation Products Liability.
Malliet, Susan E., (BV) ....'54 '79 C.881 A.B. L.184 J.D. [Ⓒ Skelley R.]
*PRACTICE AREAS: Insurance Defense Litigation; Personal Injury; Professional Liability.
Mallin, John R., (BV) ....'50 '75 C.676 A.B. L.309 J.D. [Cummings&L.]
*PRACTICE AREAS: Commercial Real Estate; Leasing Law; Finance Law; Construction Law; Land Use Regulations.
Manke, Hugh I., (BV) .... '42 '76 C.674 A.B. L.107 J.D. [Updike,K.&S.] (⊙New Haven)
*PRACTICE AREAS: Administrative Law; Business Law; Public Finance/Public Law; Real Estate.
Mann, Janet '59 '87 C.303 B.A. L.347 J.D.
(adm. in IN; not adm. in CT) Head Coun., Legis. Analysis Unit, Aetna Inc.
Manning, Julie A. .... '61 '88 C.1030 B.A. L.818 J.D. [Shipman&G.]
*PRACTICE AREAS: Bankruptcy Litigation; Bankruptcy Reorganization; Commercial Law; Creditors Rights; Foreclosures.
Manning, Stephen V. ....'56 '82 C.321 B.A. L.818 J.D. [Ⓒ O'Brien,T.&Y.] ‡
*PRACTICE AREAS: Civil Litigation; Appellate Practice; White Collar Criminal Defense.
Mantak, Ruth H., (BV) ....'31 '57 C.787 B.A. L.184 J.D. 73 Russ St.
Manternach, Bruce W., (AV) ....'— '40 C.197 A.B. L.976 LL.B. [Ⓒ Robinson&C.]
Manzo, Marion B. ....'— '99 C.1030 B.A. L.184 J.D. [Ⓐ Robinson&C.]
Mara, Daniel N., (BV) ....'60 '85 C.299 A.B. L.184 J.D. [Sandler,G.&M.]
*PRACTICE AREAS: Trial Practice; Commercial Law; Litigation; Employment Litigation; Real Estate.
Marchesseault, Donald J. ....'68 '00 C.184 B.A. L.1048 J.D. [Ⓐ Day,B.&H.]
Marchetti, Josephine, (BV) '43 '78
C.103 A.B. L.184 J.D. V.P. & Chf. Coun., CIGNA Corp.
Marcionese, Michael A. ....'54 '79 C.72 B.A. L.188 J.D. NLRB
Marcus, Daniel E. ....'59 '85 C.867 B.A. L.818 J.D. [Globman,M.&C.]
Marcus, Henry D. ....'32 '57 C&L.976 B.A., LL.B. 621 Farmington Ave.
Margolis, P. Michael ....'63 '88 C.823 B.S. L.273 J.D. [Butler N.&G.]
Margulies, Beth Z., (BV) ....'54 '83 C.012 B.A. L.1029 J.D. Asst. Atty. Gen.
Marjani, Kurosh L. ....'76 '00 C.321 B.A. L.184 J.D. [Ⓐ Day,B.&H.]
*PRACTICE AREAS: Employment Law; Employee Benefits; Litigation.
Marks, Eileen M., (AV) ....'50 '79 C.706 A.B. L.184 J.D. [Reid&R.]
*PRACTICE AREAS: Employee Benefits; Pension and Health Plans; Taft-Hartley Plans.
Marone, Richard A., (AV) ....'56 '81 C.1030 B.A. L.945 J.D. [Murtha C.]
*PRACTICE AREAS: Trusts and Estates; Probate; Taxation; Business Law; Corporate Law.
Marquis, Keith E. ....'65 '97 C.1102 B.S. L.1252 J.D. [Howd&L.]
*PRACTICE AREAS: Insurance Defense; Workers Compensation.

Marrion, Thomas S., (AV) ....'60 '85 C.321 A.B. L.184 J.D. [Tyler C.&A.]
*PRACTICE AREAS: Corporate Law; Commercial Finance; Creditors Rights in Bankruptcy; Municipal Law; Health Care.
Martin, Jeffrey R., (BV) .... '53 '79 C.855 B.A. L.184 J.D. [Ⓐ O'Connell,F.&A.]
*PRACTICE AREAS: Litigation; Personal Injury.
Martin, Melissa M. ....'— '00 C.93 B.A. L.184 J.D. [Ⓐ Robinson&C.]
Martino, Carolyn B., (BV) ....'61 '86 C.197 A.B. L.184 J.D. [Ⓐ Day,B.&H.]
*PRACTICE AREAS: Estate Planning; Living Trusts; Estate Planning for Parents of Handicapped Children.
Martino, Robert J., (BV) .... '60 '85 C.367 B.A. L.184 J.D. [Updike,K.&S.]
*PRACTICE AREAS: Commercial Lending; Banking Law; Real Estate; Real Estate Finance.
Mascaro, Joseph E. ....'67 '92 C.262 B.A. L.306 J.D. [Ⓐ Howard,K.S.&F.]
*PRACTICE AREAS: Civil Litigation; Insurance Defense; Immigration and Naturalization; Criminal Law.
Masters, Carole A. '48 '75 C.788 B.A. L.945 J.D.
V.P. and Coun., Phoenix Home Life Mut. Ins. Co.
*RESPONSIBILITIES: General Corporate Law (10%); Mergers, Acquisitions & Divestitures (70%); Securities (20%).
Mastrogiovanni, William P., Jr. ..... '68 '93 C.1030 B.A. L.306 J.D. [Ⓐ Gordon,M.&F.]
*PRACTICE AREAS: Litigation.
Mathieu, Joseph B. ....'68 '94 C.676 B.A. L.306 J.D. [Michelson,K.R.&B.]
*PRACTICE AREAS: Civil Litigation; Surety Law; Bankruptcy; Construction Law.
Mathieu, Robert J. ....'42 '67 C.676 B.A. L.184 LL.B. ITT Hartford Ins. Grp.
Mathis, David J., (BV) ....'59 '88 C.823 B.A. L.1202 J.D. 55 Farmington Ave.
Matos, Daniel S., (AV) ....'50 '76 C.184 B.A. L.831 J.D. [Day,B.&H.]
*PRACTICE AREAS: Real Estate Developments; Real Estate Workouts and Restructuring; Commercial Leasing; Real Estate Finance.
Mattei, Ernest J., (AV) ....'48 '75 C.855 B.A. L.276 J.D. [Day,B.&H.]
*PRACTICE AREAS: Insurance Litigation; Commercial Litigation; Family Law; First Party Insurance.
Mattiello, Donna M. ....'66 '92 C.976 B.A. L.184 J.D. 1 American Row
Maxwell, John D., (BV) '52 '79 C.873 A.B. L.1035 J.D.
[Brown,P.&S.] (⊙East Hampton, Glastonbury)
*PRACTICE AREAS: Personal Injury; Workers Compensation; Criminal Defense; Civil Litigation.

Mayo, Gilligan & Zito, LLP
(See Wethersfield)

Mazadoorian, Harry N., (AV) '38 '63
C&L.976 B.A., LL.B. Asst. Gen. Coun. / Ins. Law, CIGNA Corp.
McAlenney, Paul F., (AV) .... '42 '67 C&L.976 B.A., LL.B. [Day,B.&H.]
*PRACTICE AREAS: Closely Held Businesses; Mergers and Acquisitions; Benefits and Executive Compensation; Banking; Insurance Regulation and Proceedings.
McCabe, Keith S., (BV) ....'66 '91 C.855 B.A. L.1029 J.D. [Ⓐ Regnier,T.C.&E.]
*PRACTICE AREAS: General Practice; Trial Practice; Insurance; Toxic Torts; Products Liability.
McCallum, Leslie D., (BV) .... '43 '74 C.259 B.S. L.818 J.D. Asst. Atty. Gen.
McCann, Kevin, (AV) ....'54 '83 C.269 B.A. L.945 J.D. [Tyler C.&A.]
*PRACTICE AREAS: Estate Planning; Trusts and Estates; Elder Law; Retirement Planning.
McCann, Marie L., (AVⓉ) '31 '54 C.562 B.A. L.724 LL.B.
(adm. in NY; not adm. in CT) [Moniz,C.&M.] (⊙Elmsford, NY)

McCarter & English, LLP
One Financial Plaza, 755 Main Street, 06103 ⊙
Telephone: 860-493-3900
URL: http://www.mccarter.com
Member of Firm: Catherine Ann Mohan. Associates: John J. Robinson; Christine S. Synodi.
Administrative Law, Alternative Dispute Resolution, Antitrust and Trade Regulation, Appellate Practice, Aviation and Aerospace, Bankruptcy, Banks and Banking, Business Law, Civil Practice, Class Actions, Commercial Law, Commercial Real Estate, Communications and Media, Complex and Multi-District Litigation, Computers and Software, Contracts, Copyrights, Corporate Law, Debtor and Creditor, Education Law, Eminent Domain, Employee Benefits, Environmental Law, Equipment Finance and Leasing, Finance, General Practice, Health Care, Insurance, Insurance Coverage, Intellectual Property, International Law, Investments, Labor and Employment, Leases and Leasing, Litigation, Mergers, Acquisitions and Divestitures, Natural Resources, Nonprofit and Charitable Organizations, Patents, Probate, Products Liability, Professional Liability, Public Finance, Real Estate, Taxation, Torts, Toxic Torts, Trade Secrets, Trademarks, Transportation, Trusts and Estates, Unfair Competition, White Collar Crime, Wills, Zoning, Planning and Land Use.
Newark, New Jersey Office: Four Gateway Center, 100 Mulberry Street. P.O. Box 652. Telephone: 973-622-4444. Telecopier: 973-624-7070.
Cherry Hill, New Jersey Office: 1820 Chapel Avenue West, Suite 380. Telephone: 609-662-8444. Telecopier: 609-662-6203.
New York, New York Office: 300 Park Avenue, 18th Floor. Telephone: 212-466-9018. Telecopier: 212-432-6568.
Wilmington, Delaware Office: Mellon Bank Center, 919 Market Street. Telephone: 302-654-8010. Telecopier: 302-654-0795.
Philadelphia, Pennsylvania Office: One Commerce Square, 2005 Market Street, Suite 3600. Telephone: 215-557-7700. Telecopier: 215-557-6544.
Baltimore, Maryland Office: 201 North Charles Street. Telephone: 410-385-1088.
See Professional Biographies, HARTFORD, CONNECTICUT

McCarthy, Christopher J., (BV) '64 '89
C.184 B.A. L.1202 J.D. [Brown,P.&S.] (⊙Glastonbury)
*PRACTICE AREAS: Criminal Law; Juvenile Law; School Law; Education Law; Civil Litigation.
McCarthy, Dennis F., (BV) ....'63 '89 C.308 B.A. L.904 J.D. [Kenny,B.M.&M.]
*PRACTICE AREAS: Insurance Defense; Personal Injury; Civil Litigation.

McCarthy, Donald J., Jr., (BV) '50 '80 C.184 B.A. L.1029 J.D.
107 Oak Street, 06106
Telephone: 860-560-0468 Fax: 860-560-0763
General Civil Litigation, Personal Injury, Product Liability, Medical Malpractice, Criminal Trials and Family Law.
See Professional Biographies, HARTFORD, CONNECTICUT

McCarthy, Shannon K. ....'72 '98 C.676 B.A. L.1048 J.D. [Ⓐ Kenny,B.M.&M.]
*PRACTICE AREAS: Insurance Defense; Personal Injury; Real Estate; Litigation.
McCarthy, Schuman & Coombes, (BV) .... 107 Oak St.
McCarthy Small & Associates, P.C. .... 10 Columbus Blvd. (⊙New York, NY)
McCary, Paul R., (AV) ....'52 '79 C.184 B.A. L.1048 J.D. [Murtha C.]
*PRACTICE AREAS: Public Utilities Law; Energy Law.
McCleary, Charles A. ....'52 '79 C.860 B.A. L.184 J.D. Kidder, Peabody & Co., Inc.
McCormack, Michael T. ....'67 '93 C.676 B.S. L.128 J.D. [Ⓐ Tyler C.&A.]
McCormick, Paul L., (AV) ....'40 '65 C.103 A.B. L.309 J.D. [Updike,K.&S.]
*PRACTICE AREAS: Business Law; Taxation; Trusts and Estates; Probate.

McCormick, Paulding & Huber, LLP, (BV)
CityPlace II, 185 Asylum Street, 06103-4102 ⊙
Telephone: 860-549-5290 Fax: 860-527-0464
Email: MPH@IP-Lawyers.com URL: http://www.IP-lawyers.com
Members of Firm: John C. Hilton; John C. Linderman; J. Kevin Grogan (Resident, Springfield, Massachusetts Office); Arthur F. Dionne (Resident, Springfield, Massachusetts Office); Richard R. Michaud; Marina F. Cunningham. Associates: Daniel G. Mackas; Susan C. Oygard (Resident, Springfield, Massachusetts Office); Nicholas J. Tuccillo (Resident, Springfield, Massachusetts Office); Wm. Tucker Griffith; Stephen P. Scuderi (Resident, Springfield, Massachusetts Office); Mary-Jacq Holroyd (Resident, Springfield, Massachusetts Office); Richard D. Getz; William B. Gowanlock; Donald J. MacDonald (Not admitted in CT); Shirley S. Ma. Of Counsel: Theodore R. Paulding; Donald K. Huber; Frederick J. Haesche; John J. Dempsey (Not admitted in CT); Charles E. Sohl.
Patent, Trademark, Copyright, Unfair Competition, Franchise, Computer and Related Intellectual Property Law including Litigation in all Courts.
Springfield, Massachusetts Office: 1350 Main Street, 5th Floor. Telephone: 413-736-5401. Fax: 413-733-4543.
See Professional Biographies, HARTFORD, CONNECTICUT

McCracken, Gregory W. ....'— '93 C.112 B.A. L.464 J.D. [Ⓐ Robinson&C.]

McCullough, William J., (BV) ....'47 '73 C.550 B.A. L.184 J.D. Asst. Atty. Gen.
McDonnell, Michael L., (BV) ....'53 '88 C.999 B.S. L.1202 J.D. [A Trantolo&T.]
McDonough, Michael E. ....'63 '97 C&L.184 B.A., J.D. [A Murtha C.]
McDowell, Linda J., (AV) ....'— '86 C.216 B.A. L.945 J.D. [Robinson&C.]
*PRACTICE AREAS: Trusts and Estates; Wills; Probates.
McEleney, Stephen F., (BV) ....'48 '74 C.93 B.S. L.184 J.D. [McEleney&M.]
McEleney & McGrail, (BV) .... 363 Main St.
McEvoy, Patricia A. '56 '82 C.184 B.A. L.818 J.D.
(adm. in MA; not adm. in CT) The Travelers Ins. Co.
McGaughey, James D. '50 '84 C&L.184 B.A., J.D.
Off. of Protec. & Advoc. for Persons with Disab.
McGee, Hugh P., Jr., (AV) ....'43 '72 C.197 A.B. L.184 J.D. [Murtha C.]
*PRACTICE AREAS: Corporate Law; Non-Stock Corporations; Commercial Law.
McGee, Palmer S., Jr., (AV) ....'21 '55 C.216 B.A. L.976 LL.B. Cityplace I
McGoldrick, Michael P., (BV) ...... '59 '91 C.602 B.B.A. L.184 J.D. [Cranmore,F.&M.]
McGovern, Bernard F., Jr., (AV) ....'43 '67 C.93 A.B. L.184 J.D. Asst. Atty. Gen.
McGovern, Stephen J., (BV) ....'47 '74 C.659 B.S. L.184 J.D. Asst. Atty. Gen.

McGovern & Associates
(See Greenwich)

McGowan, Arthur P., Jr., (AV) ....'36 '68 C.971 B.S. L.180 J.D. [Halloran&S.]
*PRACTICE AREAS: Estate Planning; Trust Law; Estates Law; Estate Administration; General Corporate Law.
McGrail, Albert J., (BV) ....'48 '74 C.367 A.B. L.184 J.D. [McEleney&M.]
McGrath, James ....'57 '97 C.768 B.A. L.329 J.D. 1 American Row
McGrath, Matthew C. ....'67 '95 C.433 B.A. L.262 J.D. [A Cohn B.&S.]
*PRACTICE AREAS: Business Law; Corporate Law.
McGrath, William J., Jr., (AV) ....'58 '83 C.1031 B.A. L.188 J.D. [Halloran&S.]
*PRACTICE AREAS: Civil Litigation; Personal Injury Law; Insurance Litigation.
McGraw, James A., (AV) ....'50 '75 C.197 A.B. L.94 J.D. [Day,B.&H.]
*PRACTICE AREAS: Real Estate Equity Investors; Real Estate Finance; Real Estate Development; Real Estate Workouts; Real Estate Restructuring.
McGregor, Lauren L. '64 '90 C.659 B.A. L.145 J.D.
(adm. in CA; not adm. in CT) Coun., United Techologies Corp.
*RESPONSIBILITIES: Commercial.
McGuigan, Austin J., (AV) ....'43 '72 C.1057 B.A. L.94 J.D. [Rome M.S.]
*PRACTICE AREAS: Theft of Trade Secrets; Corporate Investigations; Government Investigations; Commercial Litigation; White Collar Criminal Defense.
McGuire, Tedra Weisbrod ....'46 '76 C.188 A.B. L.184 J.D. Coun., The Travelers Ins. Co.
McGuire, Thomas J. '63 '88 C.1044 B.A. L.569 J.D.
Assoc. Coun., The Travelers Ins. Co.
McHale, Patrick J., (BV) ....'64 '91 C.1030 B.A. L.1048 J.D. [Kainen,E.&M.]
*PRACTICE AREAS: Employment Law; Labor Law.
McHugh, Alexandra M. ....'65 '00 C.309 B.A. L.184 J.D. [A Shipman&G.]
*PRACTICE AREAS: Commercial Litigation.
McHugh, John P., (BV) .... '60 '86 C.321 A.B. L.724 J.D. [Cranmore,F.&M.]
McIntosh, James R., (AV) ....'30 '55 C.674 B.A. L.309 J.D. [C Day,B.&H.]
*PRACTICE AREAS: Public Utility Regulation; Finance.
McKenna, Michael F. ....'55 '81 C.321 B.A. L.734 J.D. Atty. Gen. Off.
McKeon, Michael Peter ....'56 '87 C.550 B.A. L.184 J.D. 646 Prospect Ave.
McKernan, Mary Borden ....'66 '91 C.184 B.A. L.306 J.D. Asst. Atty.Gen.
McLaughlin, Elizabeth K., (BV) .... '60 '85 C.93 B.A. L.823 J.D. The Travelers Corp.
McLaughlin, Patricia O'Leary ....'56 '82 C.788 A.B. L.128 J.D. 1 American Row, 11th Fl.
McLean, Lauchlin H., (AV) ......'21 '48 C.608 B.A. L.309 LL.B. 93 Pioneer Drive West
McMahon, Earl F., (AV) ....'60 '85 C.197 B.A. L.276 J.D. [Reid&R.]
*PRACTICE AREAS: Commercial Real Estate and Finance; Health Care; Real Estate.
McMurtry, Vanda B. '49 '85 C.112 B.A. L.276 J.D.
(adm. in DC; not adm. in CT) Sr. V.P., Aetna Inc.
*RESPONSIBILITIES: Federal Government Relations.
McNamara, F. Timothy, (AV) ....'26 '55 C&L.184 B.A., J.D. [F.T.McNamara]
McNamara, Glenn F. ....'49 '78 C.184 B.A. L.262 J.D. Coun., The Travelers Ins. Co.

McNamara, F. Timothy, P.C., (AV)
102 Oak Street, 06106
Telephone: 860-249-8458 Fax: 860-249-8850
Email: ftimothymcnamara@aol.com URL: http://www.lawyers.com/timothy_mcnamara
F. Timothy McNamara.
Insurance, Corporate and Administrative Law. Criminal Law, Appellate Practice, Eminent Domain, Aviation. Practice restricted to Litigation.
See Professional Biographies, HARTFORD, CONNECTICUT

McQuade, Joseph W. ....'67 '92 C.976 B.A. L.306 J.D. [Kainen,E.&M.]
*PRACTICE AREAS: Litigation; Employment Law; Civil Rights Litigation; Labor Law.
McVane, M. Patricia, (BV) .... '49 '74 C.856 B.A. L.128 J.D. [McVane,B.K.W.&B.]
McVane, Bellobuono, Kuzmak, Wiezalis & Bibisi, LLP, (BV) .... 801 Maple Ave.
McWilliams, Jeremiah F. '24 '60 C.665 B.S. L.229 LL.B.
(adm. in PA; not adm. in CT) The Travelers Ins. Co.
Meade, Paul D., (BV) ....'59 '85 C.164 B.A. L.228 J.D. [Halloran&S.]
*PRACTICE AREAS: Insurance Defense; Insurance Litigation; Products Liability; Marine Insurance Defense; Insurance Coverage.
Meaney, Joseph V., Jr., (AV) .... '55 '80 C.188 B.A. L.184 J.D. [Cranmore,F.&M.]
Medeiros, Jeffrey Joseph .... '66 '94 C.1048 B.S.B.A. L.851 J.D. [A Edwards&A.]
*PRACTICE AREAS: Litigation; Insurance; Reinsurance; Professional Liability Defense; Products Liability.
Meerbergen, Jessica D. .... '74 '99 C.67 B.S. L.184 J.D. [A Cooney,S.&D.]
Mehta, Lisa Banatoski .... '73 '98 C.273 B.A. L.659 J.D. [A Shipman&G.]
*PRACTICE AREAS: Public Sector Labor Relations Law; Labor and Employment Law; Privacy and Publicity Law; Employment Law.
Meiklejohn, Thomas W. ....'51 '77 C.976 B.A. L.659 J.D. [Livingston,A.P.&M.]
Meister, Philip K., (BV) ....'55 '79 C.855 B.A. L.184 J.D. [A Gersten&G.]
Melillo, Lisa .....'69 '94 C.184 B.A. L.1048 J.D. Atty., Travelers Indemnity Co. of Amer.
Melley, William J., III, (AV) ....'53 '79 C.321 B.A. L.1048 J.D. [Kenny,B.M.&M.]
*PRACTICE AREAS: Personal Injury; Medical Malpractice; Insurance Defense; Products Liability.
Mellitz, Jonathan A., (AV) ......'52 '77 C.94 B.A. L.818 J.D. David T. Chase Enterprises
Melly, Patricia J. '70 '96 C.1030 B.A. L.184 J.D.
Coun., Exec. Liability Underwriters, XL Capital Group
Melvin, Robert S. ....'— '91 C&L.184 B.S., J.D. [Robinson&C.]
*PRACTICE AREAS: Environmental Law; Litigation.
Menard, Thomas J. ....'65 '98 C.829 B.S. L.306 J.D. [A Alix,Y.&R.]
*PRACTICE AREAS: Patents.
Ment, Jeffrey L. ....'67 '92 C.184 B.S. L.472 J.D. [Rome M.S.]
*PRACTICE AREAS: Civil Liability; Commercial Litigation; Products Liability; Professional Liability.
Menting, Peter '44 '73 C&L.273 B.A., J.D.
(adm. in DC; not adm. in CT) [C Levin,F.&P.]
*PRACTICE AREAS: International & European Community Law; Immigration & Trade.
Meo, Steven F., (BV) ....'55 '83 C.184 B.A. L.1048 J.D. 21 Oak St.
Meotti, Michael P., (BV) .... '53 '78 C&L.276 B.S.F.S., J.D. 179 Allyn St.

Mercado-Espinoza, Ramona, (BV) '57 '86 C.829 B.A. L.184 J.D.
250 Main Street, 06106-1867
Telephone: 860-560-8188 Fax: 860-560-8189

(This Listing Continued)

Mercado-Espinoza, Ramona (Continued)

Civil and Criminal Litigation, Personal Injury, Family Law and Real Estate.
See Professional Biographies, HARTFORD, CONNECTICUT

Mercier, Beth .... '69 '95 C&L.184 B.A., J.D. [A Michelson,K.R.&B.]
*PRACTICE AREAS: Civil Litigation; Construction Law; Personal Injury; Workers' Compensation.
Merriam, Dwight H., (AV) ....'— '78 C.454 B.A. L.976 J.D. [Robinson&C.]
*PRACTICE AREAS: Zoning, Planning and Land Use; Environmental Law; Real Estate; Retail Development.
Merrill, Judith ....'46 '71 C.691 B.A. L.184 J.D. Asst. Atty. Gen.
Meshako, Katherine Elizabeth, (BV) ....'61 '86 C.93 B.A. L.184 J.D. 999 Asylum Ave.
Messina, Natale A., (BV) .... '52 '81 C&L.184 B.S., J.D. [Murtha C.]
*PRACTICE AREAS: Business Law; Corporate Law; Federal Tax Controversies; Limited Liability Company Law; Partnership Law.
Metzger, David L., (BV) .... '48 '85 C&L.184 B.A., J.D. [Metzger&Assoc.]

Metzger & Associates, (BV)
25 Capitol Avenue, 06106-1867
Telephone: 860-549-5026 Fax: 860-549-5224
Email: dmetzger@snet.net
David L. Metzger.
Labor and Employment.
See Professional Biographies, HARTFORD, CONNECTICUT

Metzler, Robert J., II, (AV) ....'48 '74 C.674 A.B. L.184 J.D. [Tyler C.&A.]
*PRACTICE AREAS: Corporate, Public Utilities, Business Finance.
Meuser, Craig S. .... '64 '97 C.197 B.A. L.1252 J.D. [A Shipman&G.]
*PRACTICE AREAS: Education; Labor; Employment.
Meyer, Harry E. .... '36 '61 C&L.309 A.B., LL.B. Coun., The Travelers Ins. Co.

Meyer, Judith D.
(See Avon)

Miano, Thomas P., (BV) .... '44 '71 C.676 B.A. L.273 J.D. Asst. State's Atty.
Michaud, Richard R. '63 '96
C.1029 B.S.M.E. L.1252 J.D. [McCormick,P.&H.] (See Pat. Sect.)
*PRACTICE AREAS: Patents; Trademarks; Copyrights; Intellectual Property; Litigation.

Michelson, Kane, Royster & Barger, P.C., (AV)
93 Oak Street, 06106
Telephone: 860-522-1243 Fax: 860-548-0194
Email: mkrb@snet.net
Richard L. Barger; Steven B. Kaplan; Mark E. Blakeman; Joseph B. Mathieu; Christopher W. Huck; Paul S. Tagatac. Associates: Justine R. Tobis; Beth Mercier. Of Counsel: James N. Royster; Thomas H. Connell; Chester J. Bukowski, Jr.
Construction Law, Civil Litigation, Surety Law, Labor & Employment Law, Public Utilities, Commercial Law, Personal Injury and Workers Compensation.
See Professional Biographies, HARTFORD, CONNECTICUT

Michener, James M. ....'52 '77 C.93 A.B. L.276 J.D. Coun., The Travelers Ins. Co.
Mickelson-Dera, Frances M. '59 '98
C.1176 B.A. L.1048 J.D. Corp. Coun., David T. Chase Enterprises
Middlebrook, Stephen B., (AV) .... '37 '61 C&L.976 B.A., LL.B. [C Day,B.&H.]
*PRACTICE AREAS: Insurance Regulation; Regulatory Agency Practice; Unfair Insurance Practices.
Mikolowsky, Edmund A., (AV) .... '52 '79 C.321 B.A. L.976 J.D. [Reid&R.]
*PRACTICE AREAS: Business Law; Corporate Law; Labor and Employment; Mergers and Acquisitions.
Miles, Michael S. .... '— '64 C.823 B.A. L.184 LL.B. State Wkrs. Comp. Comr.
Miley, Kelly G. ....'70 '97 C.321 B.A. L.94 J.D. [A Day,B.&H.]
*PRACTICE AREAS: Commercial Real Estate Finance; Structured Finance; Commercial Loans.
Miller, Charles I., (BV) ....'64 '90 C&L.184 B.A., J.D. [A O'Connell,F.&A.]
*PRACTICE AREAS: Commercial Law; Commercial Litigation; Foreclosures; Collections.
Miller, Elliott C. ....'34 '62 C.309 A.B. L.477 LL.B. Pres., Society for Svgs.
Miller, Jack D., (BV) ....'52 '79 C.930 B.A. L.1003 J.D. [Regnier,T.C.&E.]
*PRACTICE AREAS: General Practice; Trial Practice; Insurance; Toxic Torts; Products Liability.
Miller, Richard A., Sr. .... '31 '79 C.645 B.A. L.477 LL.B. The Travelers Ins. Co.
Miller, Stephen J., (AV) ....'50 '79 C.999 B.S.B.A. L.1048 J.D. [Andros,F.&M.]
Miller, Susan J. ....'51 '79 C.787 B.A. L.184 J.D. Legal Research Systems, Inc.
Miller, Susan L., (BV) ....'48 '83 C.184 B.S. L.1048 J.D. [Skelley R.]
*PRACTICE AREAS: Insurance Defense Law; Products Liability Law; Plaintiff Personal Injury; Underinsured/Uninsured Motorist; Toxic Torts.
Miller, Tuck, Jr., (AV) ....'47 '72 C.197 A.B. L.276 J.D. [Reid&R.]
*PRACTICE AREAS: Health Care.
Milliken, Charles B., (AV) .... '31 '57 C.976 B.A. L.309 J.D. [C Shipman&G.]
Mills, Richard A., Jr., (CV) .... '60 '86 C&L.893 B.A., J.D. [Shipman&G.]
*PRACTICE AREAS: Public and Private Sector Labor Relations and Employment Law; Education Law.
Milne, Geoffrey Kent, (BV) ....'65 '90 C.1266 B.A. L.884 J.D. [A Hunt L.C.&J.]
*PRACTICE AREAS: Commercial Litigation; Personal Injury Litigation.
Milrad, Joshua L. ....'68 '96 C.588 B.S. L.818 J.D. [A Edwards&A.]
*PRACTICE AREAS: Civil Litigation.
Miniter, Francis A., (BV) ....'48 '78 C.855 B.A. L.025 LL.B. [Miniter&Assoc.]
*PRACTICE AREAS: Corporate Transactions; Commercial Transactions; International Sales; Bankruptcy; Real Estate.

Miniter and Associates, (BV)
147 Charter Oak Avenue, 06106
Telephone: 860-560-2590 Telefax: 860-560-3238
Email: miniter@attglobal.net
Francis A. Miniter. Associates: Daniel C. Spineti; Christine E. Corriveau; Michael T. Landino; George C. Springer, Jr.
Corporate, Commercial, Bankruptcy, General Litigation, Commercial and Construction Litigation, Environmental, Real Estate and Zoning Law. Commercial, Employment, Estate Planning and Administrative Law, International Sales, Immigration, Family Law, ERISA, Health Care.
See Professional Biographies, HARTFORD, CONNECTICUT

Miranda, Joey Lee .... '— '98 C.1019 B.B.A. L.1252 J.D. [A Robinson&C.]
Mirer, Joshua S. .... '— '00 C.1432 B.A. L.1048 J.D. [A Robinson&C.]
Mitchell, Jessica J. ....'71 '97 C.914 B.A. L.861 J.D. [A Day,B.&H.]
*PRACTICE AREAS: Commercial Litigation; Insurance Defense; Medical Malpractice; Products Liability; Torts.
Mitchell, Thomas B., (AV) .....'56 '81 C.31 B.A. L.880 J.D. [Pepe&H.] (⊙Boston, MA)
*PRACTICE AREAS: Banks and Banking; Commercial Real Estate; Capital Markets; Leases and Leasing; Mortgages.
Mittleman, Irwin J. '53 '85 C.273 M.B.A. L.564 J.D.
(adm. in NJ; not adm. in CT) [C Halloran&S.]
*PRACTICE AREAS: Taxation (State) Law (100%, 10).
Moalli, Mary-Ann Bono '59 '86 C.855 B.A. L.1048 J.D.
(adm. in MA; not adm. in CT) Asst. Reporter of Jud. Decisions
Mobley, Kathryn A. ....'47 '76 C.1071 B.A. L.208 J.D. Asst. Atty. Gen.
Mochnick, Thomas W., (BV) '44 '80 C.347 B.A. L.1048 J.D.
V.P. & Litig. Coun., Hartford Steam Boiler Inspection & Ins. Co.
Mogel, Greg C. ....'64 '90 C.800 B.S. L.184 J.D. 107 Oak St.
Mohan, Catherine Ann ....'58 '85 C.938 B.A. L.276 J.D. [McCarter&E.]
*PRACTICE AREAS: Litigation; Mass Torts.
Moher, James M., (BV) '47 '72
C.676 B.A. L.184 J.D. [Howard,K.S.&F.] (⊙Glastonbury)
*PRACTICE AREAS: Civil Litigation.

Mokriski, Diane C. .... '70 '98 C.165 B.A. L.306 J.D. [Ⓐ O'Connell,F.&A.]
*PRACTICE AREAS: Labor and Employment; Products Liability; Insurance Defense; Civil Litigation; Indian Law.
Molinari, Laurie K. ....'64 '94 C.518 B.A. L.184 J.D. [Ⓐ Murtha C.]
Molinari, Samuel L., (BV) ....'47 '77 C&L.262 B.A., J.D. [Ⓐ Brown R.M.F.&S.]
*PRACTICE AREAS: Commercial Finance; Real Estate Development; Commercial Leasing; Commercial Real Estate.
Molitor, Karen Ann .... '53 '90 C&L.45 B.Sc., J.D. One American Row
Moller, William R., (AV) .... '25 '49 C.918 B.A. L.184 LL.B. [Ⓒ Moller,P.&O.]
Moller, Peck and O'Brien, LLC, (BV) ....1010 Wethersfield Avenue
Monaghan, Ann Grunbeck ....'66 '94 C.855 B.A. L.306 J.D. [Ⓐ Day,B.&H.]
*PRACTICE AREAS: Class Action Defense; Insurance Defense; Litigation; Personal Injury; Products Liability.
Monahan, Patrick J., II, (BV) .... '58 '83 C.1200 B.A. L.93 J.D. [Wiggin&D.]
*PRACTICE AREAS: Litigation.
Monastersky, David S. ....'68 '93 C.860 B.A. L.93 J.D. [Howd&L.]
*PRACTICE AREAS: Insurance Defense; Municipal Litigation; Products Liability; Toxic Tort; General Trial and Appellate Practice.
Mondell, Denise ....'64 '89 C.93 B.A. L.1019 J.D. Atty. Gen. Off.
Mondschein, Brad N. .... '68 '93 C.867 B.A. L.1048 J.D. [Ⓐ Updike,K.&S.]
*PRACTICE AREAS: Utility Law; Franchise Law; Litigation.
Moniz, Joseph A., (AV) .... '47 '75 C.353 B.A. L.569 J.D. [Moniz,C.&M.]
Moniz, Cooper & McCann, LLP, (AV) ....100 Allyn Street
Monnes, Kathleen Dondero ....'66 '92 C.183 B.A. L.273 J.D. [Day,B.&H.]
*PRACTICE AREAS: Insurance Litigation; Commercial Litigation; Direct Liability and Casualty; First Party Insurance; Disability Insurance.
Monson, Melinda S. .... '59 '90 C.589 B.S.N. L.1029 J.D. [Ⓒ O'Brien,T.&Y.]
*PRACTICE AREAS: Medical Malpractice Defense; Civil Trial Practice; Health Law.
Montovani, Tara C. '72 '00
C.1030 B.S. L.184 J.D. Sr. Tax Consultant, Ernst & Young LLP

Montstream & May, L.L.P.
(See Glastonbury)

Monz, David J., (AV) .....'58 '89 C.264 B.S. L.184 J.D. [Updike,K.&S.] (⊙New Haven)
*PRACTICE AREAS: Environmental Law; Administrative Law; Criminal Law.
Mooney, Thomas B., (AV) .... '51 '76 C.976 B.A. L.309 J.D. [Shipman&G.]
*PRACTICE AREAS: Education Law; Public Sector Labor Relations; Labor and Employment Law.
Moore, Andrew D. ....'76 '00 C&L.188 B.S., J.D. [Ⓐ Halloran&S.]
*PRACTICE AREAS: Commercial Litigation.
Moore, Daphne G. ....'63 '95 C.518 B.A. L.1048 J.D. 1 American Row
Moran, Elizabeth Doyle .... '58 '87 C.276 B.S.F.S. State Ethics Comm.
Morelli, Edward, (BV) ....'55 '83 C.184 B.A. L.1048 J.D. [Roggi,M.&M.]
Morelli, Joseph C., (BV) ...'56 '81 C.1030 B.A. L.1048 J.D. 461 Farmington Ave., 1st Fl.
Morelli, Stephen M. ....'60 '87 C&L.184 B.A., J.D. [Roggi,M.&M.]
Morelli-Wolfe, Maria Nicole '70 '97
C.976 B.S. L.30 J.D. Greater Hartford Legal Assistance
Moreno, Karen A. ....'75 '00 C.1021 B.A. L.982 J.D. [Ⓐ Day,B.&H.]
*PRACTICE AREAS: Technology; Intellectual Property.
Moreshead, Elizabeth A. ....'65 '93 C.183 B.A. L.1252 J.D. [Ⓐ Noble,Y.&O.]
*PRACTICE AREAS: Insurance Defense; Personal Injury; Products Liability.
Moreton, Catherine L. .... '61 '97 C.296 B.A. L.184 J.D. [Ⓐ Brown R.M.F.&S.]
*PRACTICE AREAS: Labor and Employment; Mediation.
Morgan, Glen D., (BV) ....'54 '79 C&L.184 B.A., J.D. 999 Asylum Ave.
Morgan, Julie A. ....'69 '98 C.184 B.A. L.1252 J.D. [Ⓐ Pullman&C.]
*PRACTICE AREAS: Litigation; Property Taxation; Real Estate and Personal Property Valuation; Land Use.
Morgan, Lisa Kelly, (BV) ....'62 '87 C.884 B.A. L.184 J.D. [Ruben,J.&M.]
*PRACTICE AREAS: Litigation; Real Estate.
Morgan, Robert Andrew .... '73 '99 C.770 B.S. L.1202 J.D. [Ⓐ Updike,K.&S.]
*PRACTICE AREAS: Commercial Litigation.
Morgan, Tracey A. ....'74 '99 C.1145 B.S.B.A. L.1202 J.D. [Ⓐ Day,B.&H.]
*PRACTICE AREAS: Employee Benefits; Pension Plans; Taft-Hartley Plans.
Morganstern, Priya S. ....'56 '87 C.1044 B.S. L.94 J.D. [Ⓒ Day,B.&H.]
*PRACTICE AREAS: Health Care Corporate Law; Integrated Health Care Delivery Systems; Certificates of Need.
Morisse, Carl F. '15 '38 C&L.910 B.A., J.D.
(adm. in MO; not adm. in CT) The Travelers Ins. Co.
Morkan, Linda L., (AV) ....'— '87 C.1103 B.S. L.184 J.D. [Ⓒ Robinson&C.]
*PRACTICE AREAS: Appellate Practice; Indians and Native Populations; Litigation.
Morris, John F., (BV) ....'60 '89 C.184 B.A. L.1029 J.D. 97 Elm St.
Morris, Julia B. ....'69 '94 C.401 B.A. L.93 J.D. [O'Connell,F.&A.] (⊙Danbury)
*PRACTICE AREAS: Business Law; Construction Law; Commercial Litigation; Commercial Transactions; Appellate Practice.
Morris, Susan F. ....'67 '98 C.999 B.S. L.1252 J.D. CIGNA Corp.
Morrison, Francis H., III, (AV) ....'47 '75 C.321 A.B. L.228 J.D. [Day,B.&H.]
*PRACTICE AREAS: Commercial Litigation; Trust and Estate Litigation; Disability Insurance; Negligence Defense; Product Liability.

Morrison, Mahoney & Miller, LLP, (BV)
One Constitution Plaza, 10th Floor, 06103 ⊙
Telephone: 860-616-4441 Facsimile: 860-244-3800
Email: info@mail.mm-m.com URL: http://www.mm-m.com
Resident Partners: Mary J. Ambrogio; James L. Brawley; Robert S. Bystrowski; Elizabeth M. Cristofaro; Joel M. Fain; Lloyd D. Pedersen. Resident Associates: Robert William Cassot; Joseph N. DeFilippo; Eric J. Foy; Erich Henry Gaston; Gregory C. Goodstein; Bettina Cavanagh Grob; Angeline N. Ioannou; Jonathan Newman; Darren E. Sinofsky; Catherine A. Stewart; Patricia A. Tisdall.
The firm represents its clients in a broad range of Civil matters, including: Property and Liability Insurance Coverage Claims and Issues, Appellate Reinsurance, Environmental and Pollution Defense and Coverage, Arson, and other Insurance Fraud, Professional Liability including Medical, Legal, Accounting, Directors and Officers, Architects and Engineers, Insurance Agents and Brokers, Fidelity and Surety Bond Claims, Insurance Regulatory and Governmental Affairs, Subrogation, Regulatory, General and Corporate Representation of Insurers, Agents and Brokers, Life, Accident, Health, including Sports, Employee Benefits and ERISA, Health Law, Employment Law, Products Liability including Pharmaceutical and Medical Devices, General Liability, Construction Law, Emerging Businesses Consulting, Commercial/Business Litigation Energy, Premises Liability, Retail Premises Liability, Lead Paint, Transportation, Marine and Inland Marine, Workers Compensation for Insurers and Self-Insureds, and General Litigation in State and Federal Courts in numerous jurisdictions throughout the country.
Boston, Massachusetts Office: 250 Summer Street, 02210. Telephone: 617-439-7500. Facsimile: 617-439-7590.
Fall River, Massachusetts Office: 10 North Main Street, 02722. Telephone: 508-677-3100. Facsimile: 508-672-3840.
London, England Office: 60 Lombard Street, EC3V 9EA. Telephone: 011-44-0207-464-8499. Facsimile: 011-44-0207-509-7238.
New York, N.Y. Office: 100 Maiden Lane, 22nd Floor, 10038-4892. Telephone: 212-825-1212. Facsimile: 212-825-1313.
Providence, Rhode Island Office: One Providence Washington Plaza, 02903. Telephone: 401-331-4660. Facsimile: 401-351-4420.
Springfield, Massachusetts Office: Tower Square, 1500 Main Street, Suite 2400, 01115. Telephone: 413-737-4373. Facsimile: 413-739-3125.
Worcester, Massachusetts Office: One Chestnut Place, 10 Chestnut Street, Suite 470, 01608. Telephone: 508-757-7777. Facsimile: 508-752-6224.
See Professional Biographies, HARTFORD, CONNECTICUT

Moskey, Eileen C. ....'64 '95 C.184 B.A. L.1048 J.D. [Ⓐ Sabia&H.]
*PRACTICE AREAS: Commercial Transactions; Real Estate; Uniform Commercial Code; Commercial Foreclosures; Commercial Collections.
Moukawsher, Joseph E., (AV) ....'20 '49 C.918 B.A. L.309 LL.B. [Moukawsher&W.] ⊙
*PRACTICE AREAS: Real Estate; Probate; Estate Planning; Civil Litigation.
Moukawsher, Thomas G., (BV) .... '62 '86 C.152 B.A. L.184 J.D. [Moukawsher&W.] ⊙
*PRACTICE AREAS: ERISA; Commercial Litigation; Employment Law.

Moukawsher & Walsh LLC, (AV)
21 Oak Street, 06106 ⊙
Telephone: 860-549-8440 Fax: 860-549-8443
URL: http://www.lawyers.com/moukawsher&walshllc
Joseph E. Moukawsher; Michael J. Walsh; Thomas G. Moukawsher;—Jeffrey M. Sklarz.
Civil Litigation, ERISA Law, Benefits Law, Estates, Negligence, Personal Injury, Wrongful Death, Medical Malpractice, Products Liability, Commercial Litigation, Employment Law, Trials and Appeals.
Reference: Fleet Bank.
Groton, Connecticut Office: 328 Mitchell Street, P.O. Box 966. Telephone: 860-445-1809. Fax: 860-446-8161. Internet E-Mail: moukwals@snet.net
See Professional Biographies, HARTFORD, CONNECTICUT

Mowbray, Elinor H. '45 '82 C.247 B.A. L.969 J.D.
(adm. in GA; not adm. in CT) The Travelers Ins. Co.
Mowell, Lawrence V., Jr. '47 '76 C.813 B.A. L.184 J.D.
Assoc. Gen. Coun., United Techologies Corp.
*RESPONSIBILITIES: Corporate; Finance; Mergers and Acquisitions; Litigation.
Moylan, Sean P. '64 '92 C&L.228 A.B., J.D.
(adm. in NC; not adm. in CT) United Tech. Corp.
Muhlanger, Gilda O. ....'51 '81 C.918 B.A. L.306 J.D. Aetna Inc.
Mulcahy, John F., Jr. ....'34 '59 C.478 A.B. L.188 LL.B. Supr. Ct. J.
Mulé, Robert M., (BV) ....'55 '81 C.309 A.B. L.94 J.D. [Reid&R.]
*PRACTICE AREAS: Bankruptcy; Business Law; Commercial Law; Commercial Real Estate and Finance; Corporate Law.
Mullen, Frederick J., Jr., (AV) '51 '77
C.976 B.A. L.893 J.D. [Reid&R.] (⊙West Hartford)
*PRACTICE AREAS: Probate; Trusts and Estates.
Mulligan, David A. .... '50 '83 C.188 B.A. L.184 J.D. State Dept. of Soc. Servs.
Mulpeter, Michael F., (BV) ....'58 '84 C.867 B.A. L.184 J.D. [Cohn B.&S.]
*PRACTICE AREAS: Corporate Law; Business Law; Securities; Communications Law.
Mulrain, John T., (AV) '49 '74 C.321 A.B. L.976 J.D.
V.P. & Coun., Phoenix Home Life Mut. Ins. Co.
*RESPONSIBILITIES: Investments; Bankruptcy; Securities; Corporate Finance.
Murley, Joanne K. ....'63 '88 C.156 B.A. L.306 J.D. State Jud. Branch
Murphy, Albert G., (BV) ....'31 '58 C.197 A.B. L.184 LL.B. [Webber,J.&M.]
Murphy, Donna P., (BV) ....'47 '71 C.94 B.S. L.208 J.D. [Ossen&M.]
Murphy, J. Read, (AV) ....'20 '49 C.976 B.A. L.188 LL.B. 185 Asylum St.
Murphy, James R. ....'46 '75 C.757 B.A. L.1003 J.D. The Travelers Ins. Co.
Murphy, James T. ....'66 '00 C.861 B.Arch. L.1048 J.D. [Ⓐ Pepe&H.]
Murphy, John F., The Law Office of, (AV) '36 '67 C.197 B.A. L.93 LL.B.
1324 Asylum Avenue, 06105-6011
Telephone: 860-233-9946 Fax: 860-523-5065
Email: jmurphy@Internet-95.com URL: http://www.lawyers.com/connecticutaccidentlawyer
***PRACTICE AREAS: Personal Injury; Medical Malpractice; False Claims Act; Products Liability; Government.**
Personal Injury, Medical Malpractice, Federal False Claims, Products Liability.
See Professional Biographies, HARTFORD, CONNECTICUT
Murphy, John J. '17 '42 C.602 B.A. L.597 J.D.
(adm. in IL; not adm. in CT) 777 Main St.‡
Murphy, Kevin J. ....'57 '82 C.276 B.A. L.128 J.D. Asst. States Atty.
Murphy, Margaret M. ....'61 '88 C.518 B.A. L.184 J.D. [Ⓒ Cummings&L.]
*PRACTICE AREAS: Estate Planning (60%); Probate (30%); Tax Law (10%).
Murphy, Robert J. .... '55 '81 C.861 B.A. L.184 J.D. [Sullivan,S.C.&C.]
Murphy, Robert W., (BV) '38 '69 C.676 B.A. L.184 J.D.
(adm. in FL; not adm. in CT) Asst. Atty. Gen.
Murphy, Scott L., (AV) .... '47 '73 C.951 B.A. L.178 J.D. [Shipman&G.]
*PRACTICE AREAS: Corporate Law; Securities Law; Public Finance; Corporate Finance and Corporate Trust Law.
Murphy, Thomas J., (BV) ....'59 '86 C.276 A.B. L.724 J.D. [Cowdery,E.&M.]
*PRACTICE AREAS: White Collar Criminal Defense; Commercial Litigation; Appellate Practice; Personal Injury.

Murphy, Laudati & Kiel, P.C.
(See Farmington)

Murray, Hugh F., III, (AV) ....'65 '90 C.309 A.B. L.93 J.D. [Murtha C.]
*PRACTICE AREAS: Labor Law; Employment Litigation.
Murray, Saranne P., (AV) ....'47 '83 C.242 B.A. L.184 J.D. [Shipman&G.]
*PRACTICE AREAS: Public and Private Sector Labor Relations and Employment Law.
Murray, Thomas A. '31 '61 C.363 B.B.S. L.161 LL.B.
(adm. in OH; not adm. in CT) The Travelers Ins. Co.
Murray, William C. '47 '77 C.676 A.B. L.818 J.D.
(adm. in MA; not adm. in CT) Asst. Gen. Coun., Hartford Financial Services Group, Inc.
Murray, William E. ....'72 '98 C.321 B.A. L.184 J.D. 225 Asylum Street, 13th Floor
Murtha, John S., (AV) ....'13 '38 C&L.976 B.A., LL.B. [Ⓒ Murtha C.]

Murtha Cullina LLP, (AV)
CityPlace I, 185 Asylum Street, 06103-3469 ⊙
Telephone: 860-240-6000 Facsimile: 860-240-6150
Email: firm@murthalaw.com URL: http://www.murthalaw.com
Members of Firm: Marcel J. Bernier; Francis J. Brady; Thomas M. Cloherty; Burton B. Cohen; George A. Dagon, Jr.; Thomas M. Daniells; Joseph P. Fasi; Frank Giordanella; Robert V. Giunta, Jr.; Irwin J. Hausman; H. Kennedy Hudner; Dwight A. Johnson; Robert E. Kaelin; William J. Keenan, Jr.; Mark F. Korber; Timothy L. Largay; Kenneth L. Levine; Richard A. Marone; Paul R. McCary; Hugh P. McGee, Jr.; Martha E. Meng (Resident, New Haven Office); Natale A. Messina; Hugh F. Murray, III; Everett E. Newton; Lissa J. Paris; Willard F. Pinney, Jr.; David Platt; R. William Reinsmith; Stephen E. Ronai (Resident, New Haven Office); Frank J. Saccomandi, III; Barbara A. Sarrantonio; Gregory A. Sharp; James H. Shulman; Alfred E. Smith, Jr. (Resident, New Haven Office); Richard S. Smith, Jr.; Sara R. Stadler (Resident, New Haven Office); Elizabeth J. Stewart (Resident, New Haven Office); Mark R. Sussman; Louis B. Todisco (Resident, New Haven Office); Barry J. Waters (Resident, New Haven Office); Robert A. White; John C. Yavis, Jr.; Michael A. Zizka. Counsel: Russell L. Brenneman; William M. Cullina; Michael J. Donnelly; Charles E. Drummey; Julie Fairchild Grey; Brandon J. Hickey; Michael T. Kogut (Not admitted in CT); James B. Lyon; John S. Murtha; Donald P. Richter; Michael Sudarsky; Robert W. Sullivan; Philip J. Tellerine. Associates: Diane C. Bellantoni; Marvin P. Bellis; Matthew J. Budzik; Sharon L. Codeanne; Jennifer Morgan DelMonico (Resident, New Haven Office); Jean C. Fung; Susan L. Gaetano; Michael C. Harrington; Alice M. S. Hootsmans; Nicole A. F. Ingle; Jennifer D. Janelle; Rachel Snow Kindseth (Resident, New Haven Office); Andrew W. Lord; Michael E. McDonough; Laurie K. Molinari; Kari L. Olson; Aaron Sarra; Robert L. Scanlon; Edward B. Whittemore; Seth M. Wilson.
General Practice. Administrative, Antitrust, Banking, Bankruptcy, Cable Television, Commercial, Communications, Construction, Copyright, Corporation, Criminal, Employee Benefits, Energy, Environmental, Estate Planning and Administration, Exempt Organizations, Government Contracts, Health Care, Hospital, Insurance Litigation for Policyholders, Labor, Limited Liability Company Law, Litigation, Mergers and Acquisitions, Municipal Law and Finance, Patents, Probate, Product Liability, Public Utility, Real Estate, Securities, Taxation and Trademark.
Representative Clients: Colts Manufacturing, Co., Inc.; Connecticut Natural Gas Corp.; Kaman Corp.
New Haven, Connecticut Office: Whitney Grove Square, 2 Whitney Avenue, P.O. Box 704-A, 06503-0704. Telephone: 203-772-7700. Facsimile: 203-772-7723.

(This Listing Continued)

Murtha Cullina LLP (Continued)

Boston, Massachusetts Office: Murtha Cullina Roche Carens & DeGiacomo. 99 High Street. Telephone: 617-457-4000. Facsimile: 617-482-3868.
Woburn, Massachusetts Office: 600 Unicorn Park Drive. Telephone; 781-933-5505. Facsimile: 781-933-1530.

See Professional Biographies, HARTFORD, CONNECTICUT

Myers, Scott P. . . . . . '58 '90 C.855 B.A. L.184 J.D. [Ⓒ Day,B.&H.]
*PRACTICE AREAS: Administrative Hearing and Appeals; Federal Energy Regulation; Insurance Coverage.
Myers, Sheldon D. . . . . . '67 '93 C.1036 B.A. L.184 J.D. [Kainen,E.&M.]
*PRACTICE AREAS: Employment Law; Litigation; Labor Law.
Nagy, Robert A., (BV) . . . . . '47 '73 C.184 B.A. L.1294 J.D. Asst. Atty. Gen.
Nahas, Elisa Anastasio '54 '81 C.184 B.A. L.588 J.D.
Admin. Hearings Atty. 2, Dept. of Consumer Protec.

Nair & Levin, P.C.
(See Bloomfield)

Namnoum, Kenneth P., Jr., (BV) . . . . . '59 '84 C.93 A.B. L.128 J.D. 279 Farmington Ave.
Narus, Edward R. . . . . . '56 '81 C.184 B.S. L.1048 J.D. Sr. Asst. States Atty.
Narwold, William H., (AV) '52 '79 C.164 B.A. L.184 J.D.
[Cummings&L.] (◎Stamford)
*PRACTICE AREAS: Appellate; Products and Professional Liability; Environmental Litigation.
Natale, Anthony J. . . . . . '64 '90 C.676 B.A. L.818 J.D. [Pepe&H.]
*PRACTICE AREAS: Civil Litigation.
Naughton, Megan R. . . . . . '— '98 C.823 B.A. L.184 J.D. [Ⓐ Robinson&C.]
Neal, Kenneth R. . . . . . '42 '69 C.103 B.A. L.93 J.D. [Danaher,T.L.&N.]
Neale, Charles C. . . . . . '56 '85 C.976 B.A. L.982 J.D. ITT Hartford Ins. Grp.
Nealon, John R. . . . . . '55 '86 C.674 A.B. L.569 J.D. Coun., The Travelers Ins. Co.

Needelman, Marc N., Law Offices of
(See Bloomfield)

Neikrie, Mark H., (AV) . . . . . '59 '84 C.319 B.S. L.930 J.D. [Ⓒ Copp&B.]
*PRACTICE AREAS: Taxation; Probate; Trust; Business; Estate Planning.
Nelson, Duane R., (BV) . . . . . '54 '80 C.976 B.A. L.276 J.D. Coun., The Travelers Ins. Co.
Nelson, Hilary Fisher, (BV) . . . . . '55 '86 C.321 B.S. L.184 J.D. [O'Brien,T.&Y.]
*PRACTICE AREAS: Medical Malpractice Defense; Product Liability; Health Law.
Nelson, Sherwin M. '48 '74 C.994 B.A. L.184 J.D.
Atty., Off. of Dist. Coun., Vet. Admn.

Nerenberg, Eliot J., Law Offices of
(See West Hartford)

Ness, Erik J. . . . . . '66 '99 C.690 B.S. L.1048 J.D. [Ⓐ Halloran&S.]
*PRACTICE AREAS: Insurance; Appellate Practice.
Neuberg, Susan E. . . . . . '58 '84 C.1349 B.A. L.978 J.D. [Ⓒ Pepe&H.]
*PRACTICE AREAS: Real Estate Finance; Real Estate Development; Leasing; Asset Management and Recovery; Workouts.
Neves, Samuel T. D., Jr. . . . . . '71 '00 C.689 B.A. L.966 J.D. [Ⓐ Day,B.&H.]
*PRACTICE AREAS: Commercial Litigation.
Nevins, Albert E., Jr., (BV) . . . . . '38 '62 C.321 B.S. L.93 J.D. [Nevins&N.]
Nevins, Richard P., (BV) . . . . . '46 '72 C.321 A.B. L.184 J.D. [Nevins&N.]
Nevins & Nevins, (BV) . . . . . 1 Webster St.
Newbury, Philip T., Jr., (BV) . . . . . '55 '81 C.184 B.S. L.818 J.D. [Howd&L.]
*PRACTICE AREAS: Products Liability Litigation; Insurance Defense Litigation; Toxic Tort; Municipal Litigation; General Trial and Appellate Practice.
Newman, John D., (BV) . . . . . '59 '84 C&L.228 A.B., J.D. [Reid&R.]
*PRACTICE AREAS: Corporate Law; Health Law; Administrative Law.
Newman, Jon O. . . . . . '32 '56 C.674 A.B. L.976 LL.B. Sr. U.S. Ct. of App. J.
Newman, Jonathan . . . . . '— '96 C.645 B.S. L.1252 J.D. [Ⓐ Morrison,M.&M.]
*PRACTICE AREAS: Workers Compensation.
Newman, Leigh A. . . . . . '56 '95 C.674 A.B. L.184 J.D. [Ⓐ Day,B.&H.]
*PRACTICE AREAS: White Collar Criminal Defense; Commercial Litigation; Personal Injury; Appellate Practice.
Newman, Stewart E. . . . . . '72 '97 C.976 B.A. L.93 J.D. [Ⓐ Bingham D.]
*PRACTICE AREAS: Litigation.
Newton, Everett E., (BV) . . . . . '48 '86 C.1033 B.S. L.184 J.D. [Murtha C.]
*PRACTICE AREAS: Litigation; Appeals.
Newton, Jon P., (BV) . . . . . '62 '88 C.103 A.B. L.184 J.D. [Reid&R.]
*PRACTICE AREAS: Bankruptcy; Commercial Law; Commercial Real Estate and Finance; Litigation.
Newton, Linda E. . . . . . '49 '78 C.112 B.A. L.284 J.D. Aetna Life Ins. Co.
Nichols, Clifford E. . . . . . '71 '01 C.1033 B.A. L.472 J.D. [Ⓐ Day,B.&H.]
Nicholson, Alpha O., III . . . . . '52 '77 C.674 A.B. L.976 J.D. CIGNA Corp.
Nicholson, Richard D., (AV) . . . . . '48 '73 C.321 A.B. L.184 J.D. [Shipman&G.]
*PRACTICE AREAS: State Taxation (100%); Local Taxation; Taxation; State Legislative Practice.
Nicol, Charles J., (BV) . . . . . '56 '83 C.690 B.S. L.976 J.D. [Updike,K.&S.]
*PRACTICE AREAS: Administrative Law; Environmental Litigation; Utilities Law.
Nielsen, W. Joseph . . . . . '71 '98 C.184 B.A. L.776 J.D. [Ⓐ Cummings&L.]
*PRACTICE AREAS: Litigation.
Nirenstein, Jeffrey A., (BV) . . . . . '52 '78 C.156 B.A. L.564 J.D. [Nirenstein,H.&Assoc.]
Nirenstein, Horowitz & Associates, (BV) . . . . . 43 Woodland St.
Nissel, Stanley N. . . . . . '30 '54 C.569 B.S. L.309 J.D. 1 Financial Plz.

Nixon Peabody LLP, (AVⓉ)
City Place, 185 Asylum Street, 06103 ⊙
Telephone: 860-275-6820 FAX: 860-275-6821
Email: nixonpeabody@nixonpeabody.com URL: http://www.nixonpeabody.com
Partner: Alphonso E. Tindall, Jr.
General Practice with an emphasis on Public Finance.
Rochester, New York Office: Clinton Square. Telephone: 716-263-1000. Fax: 716-263-1600.
New York, N.Y. Office: 437 Madison Avenue. Telephone: 212-940-3000. Fax: 212-940-3111.
Washington, D.C. Office: 401 9th Street, N.W., Suite 900. Telephone: 202-585-8000. Fax: 202-585-8080.
Garden City, New York Office: 990 Stewart Avenue. Telephone: 516-832-7500. Fax: 516-832-7555.
Buffalo, New York Office: 1600 Main Place Tower. Telephone: 716-853-8100. Fax: 716-853-8109.
Boston, Massachusetts Office: 101 Federal Street. Telephone: 617-345-1000. Fax: 617-345-1300.
Manchester, New Hampshire Office: 889 Elm Street. Telephone: 603-628-4000. Fax: 603-628-4040.
Providence, Rhode Island Office: One Citizens Plaza. Telephone: 401-454-1000. Fax: 401-454-1030.
McLean, Virginia Office: 8180 Greensboro Drive, Suite 800. Telephone: 703-790-9110. Telecopier: 703-883-0370.
Costa Mesa, California Office: 600 Anton Boulevard, Suite 1600, 92626. Telephone: 714-241-0101. Fax: 714-241-0105.
San Francisco, California Office: Two Embarcadero Center, Suite 2700, 94111-3996. Telephone: 415-984-8200. Fax: 415-984-8300.

See Professional Biographies, HARTFORD, CONNECTICUT

Nobel, Jeffrey S., (BV) . . . . . '64 '89 C.184 B.A. L.982 J.D. [Schatz&N.]
*PRACTICE AREAS: Securities Litigation; Commercial Litigation; Professional Liability; Business Litigation; Employment Litigation.
Noble, Cesar A., (BV) . . . . . '58 '83 C.918 B.A. L.184 J.D. [Noble,Y.&O.]
*PRACTICE AREAS: Insurance Defense; Products Liability; Medical Malpractice.
Noble, M. Karen . . . . . '68 '93 C&L.93 B.A., J.D. [Ⓐ Danaher,T.L.&N.]
*PRACTICE AREAS: Medical Malpractice Defense; Litigation.

Noble, Young & O'Connor, P.C., (BV)
1 Congress Street, 06114-1067
Telephone: 860-525-9975 Fax: 860-525-9985
URL: http://www.nyolaw.com
Cesar A. Noble; Robert E. Young; Dennis P. O'Connor, II;—John H. Hanks; Peter J. Brown; Amelia Nord; Elizabeth A. Moreshead; Stephanie P. Tibbetts.
Practice concentrating in the defense and trial of motor vehicle, premises liability, product liability, medical device and malpractice actions.

See Professional Biographies, HARTFORD, CONNECTICUT

Noga, Andrew L. '57 '83 C.1048 B.A. L.1029 J.D.
Coun., Hartford Financial Services Group, Inc.
Nokes, Gregory B., (AV) . . . . '51 '80 C.882 B.S. L.184 J.D. [Cummings&L.] (◎Stamford)
*PRACTICE AREAS: Labor Law; Employment Law; Civil Litigation.
Nolan, John B., (AV) . . . . . '43 '68 C.103 A.B. L.276 J.D. [Day,B.&H.]
*PRACTICE AREAS: Bankruptcy; Commercial Litigation.
Nolan, Lucy P. . . . . . '57 '91 C.611 B.A. L.306 J.D. Asst. Clk., Jud. Ct.
Nome, Janis S. . . . . . '60 '86 C&L.184 B.A., J.D. Dept. of Admin. Servs.
Nord, Amelia . . . . . '70 '97 C.1042 B.A. L.209 J.D. [Ⓐ Noble,Y.&O.]
*PRACTICE AREAS: Insurance Defense.
Norko, Raymond R. . . . . . '42 '71 C.184 B.S. L.851 J.D. Supr. Ct. J.

Norris, M. Hatcher, (AV) '49 '74 C.705 B.A. L.184 J.D.
254 Prospect Avenue, 06106-2041
Telephone: 860-236-6951 Fax: 860-236-5263
Email: rnorris@bnglaw.com
General Civil, Criminal, Trials and Appellate Practice in all State and Federal Courts. Personal Injury Law.

See Professional Biographies, HARTFORD, CONNECTICUT

Nowosadko, Paul T., (BV) . . . . . '57 '83 C.197 B.A. L.184 J.D. [Cooney,S.&D.]
Nye, Gregory W., (AV) . . . . . '55 '81 C.575 A.B. L.893 J.D. [Bingham D.]
O'Brien, Donald W., (AV) . . . . . '25 '51 C.128 A.B. L.276 J.D. [Ⓒ O'Brien,T.&Y.]
*PRACTICE AREAS: Admiralty; Health Care Law; Civil Litigation.
O'Brien, Erin K. . . . . . '— '97 C.321 B.A. L.178 J.D. [Ⓐ Robinson&C.]
O'Brien, Frederick M. . . . . . '46 '90 C.112 A.B. L.184 J.D. [Ⓐ Regnier,T.C.&E.]
*PRACTICE AREAS: General Practice; Trial Practice; Insurance; Toxic Torts; Products Liability.
O'Brien, John J., Jr., (BV) . . . . . '63 '88 C.1030 B.A. L.94 J.D. [Moller,P.&O.]
O'Brien, Robert J. . . . . . '54 '79 C.31 B.A. L.930 J.D. [Gordon,M.&F.]
O'Brien, Roberta A. '55 '80 C&L.184 B.A., J.D.
V.P. & Dep. Gen. Coun., Hartford Steam Boiler Inspection & Ins. Co.

O'Brien, Shafner, Stuart, Kelly & Morris, P.C.
(See Groton)

O'Brien, Tanski & Young, (AV) BR
CityPlace II, 06103
Telephone: 860-525-2700 Telefax: 860-247-7861
Members of Firm: James M. Tanski; Roland F. Young, III; Robert D. Silva; Hilary Fisher Nelson; Donna R. Zito; Albert G. Danker, Jr.; Richard A. O'Connor. Counsel: Stephen V. Manning; Melinda S. Monson. Associate: Amy F. Goodusky. Of Counsel: Donald W. O'Brien.
Civil Trial and Appellate Practice. Healthcare Law and Professional Medical Liability. Negligence, Products Liability, Workers Compensation, Admiralty, Maritime. Trials in all Courts.
References: Shawmut National Bank; New England Bank.

See Professional Biographies, HARTFORD, CONNECTICUT

O'Connell, John J. . . . . . '70 '98 C.1030 B.A. L.306 J.D. [Ⓐ Siegel,O.S.&Z.]
*PRACTICE AREAS: Employment; Labor; Litigation; Education; Business.
O'Connell, Michael D., (AV) '45 '72
C.602 B.A. L.184 J.D. [O'Connell,F.&A.] (◎Moosup)
*PRACTICE AREAS: Employment Law; Product Liability; Commercial Law; Commercial Litigation; Civil Litigation.

O'Connell, Flaherty & Attmore, L.L.C., (AV)
280 Trumbull Street, 06103-3598 ⊙
Telephone: 860-548-1300 Facsimile: 860-548-0023; Telecopier: 860-548-0023
Email: mac@ofalaw.com
Members of Firm: Michael D. O'Connell; James T. Flaherty; Gary G. Attmore; Stephen H. Solomson; Robert A. DeFrino; Lawrence H. Adler; Paul J. Aparo; Harold F. Keith; Alan J. Sobol; Stephen J. Sinatro; John Adam Cvejanovich (Resident, Springfield, Massachusetts Office); Matthew W. Den Ouden; Dennis R. Lavette; Claudia M. Sklar; Julia B. Morris;—Anne R. Hoyt; Charles I. Miller; Laura Waltman; Diane C. Mokriski; Mary Ann Santacroce; Gerard S. Collins; Jeffrey R. Martin; Joseph Z. Gersten; Nicholas J. Gorra, II; Sandi Beth Girolamo; Christopher J. Albanese.
Trials, State and Federal Courts. Family, Probate, Estate Planning, Taxation, Corporation, Real Estate, Insurance, Commercial, Criminal, Environmental, Labor, Zoning, Hazardous and Toxic Substances, Wetlands and Land Use, Health and Administrative Law, Indian Law.
Springfield, Massachusetts Office: 1350 Main Street. Telephone: 413-747-1773. Telecopier: 413-746-1529.
Moosup, Connecticut Office: 22 Main Street, 06354. Telephone: 860-564-4064. Telecopier: 860-564-1536.
Danbury, Connecticut Office: 50 Newtown Road, 06810. Telephone: 203-748-6632. Telecopier: 203-743-8823.
West Hartford, Connecticut Office: 993 Farmington Avenue, 06107. Telephone: 860-570-1004.
Old Saybrook, Connecticut Office: 163 Saybrook Road, 06457. Telephone: 860-388-6173. Telecopier: 860-388-6865.

See Professional Biographies, HARTFORD, CONNECTICUT

O'Connor, David E. . . . . . '45 '80 C.454 B.A. L.818 J.D. Sr. Atty., State Gen. Assembly
O'Connor, Dennis P., II, (BV) . . . . . '55 '84 C&L.276 B.A., J.D. [Noble,Y.&O.]
*PRACTICE AREAS: Insurance Defense; Products Liability.
O'Connor, Kevin J. . . . . . '67 '92 C.602 B.A. L.184 J.D. [Ⓒ Day,B.&H.]
*PRACTICE AREAS: Complex and Multi-District Litigation; County Government Law; Government Investigations; SEC Enforcement; Securities Class Actions.
O'Connor, Mary B. . . . . . '53 '87 C&L.184 B.S., J.D. Supr. Ct.
O'Connor, Philip J. . . . . . '49 '76 C.367 B.A. L.184 J.D. [Gordon,M.&F.]
*PRACTICE AREAS: Litigation; Products Liability; Insurance Coverage; Toxic Torts; Negligence Defense.
O'Connor, Richard A., (BV) . . . . . '60 '85 C.1031 B.S. L.128 J.D. [O'Brien,T.&Y.]
*PRACTICE AREAS: Medical Malpractice Defense; Civil Trial Practice.
O'Connor, Richard D., (AV) . . . . . '37 '64 C.321 B.S. L.276 LL.B. [Siegel,O.S.&Z.]
*PRACTICE AREAS: Labor Law; Litigation; Employment Law; Education Law.
O'Connor, Thomas F., (BV) . . . . . '58 '90 C.861 B.A. L.502 J.D. [Bingham D.]

O'Connor, F. William
(See Avon)

Odlum, Peter F., (BV) . . . . . '45 '72 C.1030 B.A. L.818 J.D. 250 Main St.
O'Donnell, Brian . . . . . '58 '95 C.918 B.A. L.477 J.D. 225 Asylum Street, 13th Floor
O'Donnell, Edward F., Jr. . . . . . '50 '77 C.708 B.A. L.184 J.D. [Siegel,O.S.&Z.]
*PRACTICE AREAS: Labor Law; Employment Law; Litigation.
O'Donnell, Susan, (BV) . . . . . '64 '89 C.1211 B.S. L.818 J.D. [Halloran&S.]
*PRACTICE AREAS: Civil Litigation; Civil Practice; University Law; Personal Injury; Insurance Defense.
Ogilvie, Moyahoena N. . . . . . '68 '96 C.95 B.A. L.94 J.D. [Ⓐ Cummings&L.]
O'Halloran, C. Michael '47 '72
Senior Vice President & Dir. of Corporate Law, Hartford Financial Services Group, Inc.
O'Halloran, Charles M. '47 '72 C.728 B.S. L.184 J.D.
Sr. Assoc. Gen. Coun. & Dir., ITT Hartford Ins. Grp.

Ohlandt, Greeley, Ruggiero & Perle
(See Stamford)

O'Keefe, Andrew J., (AV) . . . . '31 '56 C.321 B.S. L.184 J.D. [Jackson,O.&P.] ⊙
*PRACTICE AREAS: Medical Malpractice; Insurance Defense; Civil Practice; Appellate Practice; Civil Trial Practice.

O'Keefe, John W. . . . . '46 '75 C.1030 B.A. L.818 J.D. Coun., The Travelers Ins. Co.

O'Keefe, Matthew J., (BV) . . . . '57 '82 C.321 B.A. L.818 J.D. [Jackson,O.&P.] ⊙
*PRACTICE AREAS: Estate Planning and Administration; Real Estate; Family Law; Divorce; Child Custody.

O'Keefe, Peter K., (BV) . . . . '60 '85 C.321 B.A. L.818 J.D. [Jackson,O.&P.]
*PRACTICE AREAS: Civil Trial Practice; Insurance Defense; Personal Injury Law; Medical Malpractice Law.

O'Keefe, Timothy L. . . . . '67 '92 C.321 B.A. L.1048 J.D. [A Updike,K.&S.]
*PRACTICE AREAS: Personal Injury; Product Liability; Worker's Compensation; Domestic Relations.

Oland, Mark, (AV) . . . . '47 '72 C.882 B.A. L.178 J.D. [Bingham D.]
*PRACTICE AREAS: Commercial Real Estate Law and Finance; Real Estate Loan Workouts; Mortgage Law.

Olear, Leslie Inrig, (AV) . . . . '55 '81 C.829 B.A. L.1048 J.D. [Cohn B.&S.]
*PRACTICE AREAS: Commercial Real Estate Finance; Commercial Real Estate Leasing; Business Law; Communications Law.

O'Leary, Anne . . . . '51 '83 C.309 A.B. L.184 J.D. Asst. Atty. Gen.

O'Leary, Kevin D. . . . . '63 '90 C.860 B.A. L.184 J.D. [Cummings&L.]
*PRACTICE AREAS: Labor Law; Employment Law; Workers' Compensation.

Oliver, James W., (BV) . . . . '59 '87 C.165 B.A. L.93 J.D. [Berman&S.]
*PRACTICE AREAS: Commercial and Complex Litigation; Environmental Law.

Olson, Christine A., (BV) . . . '63 '91 C.184 B.S. L.818 J.D. 225 Asylum Street, 13th Floor

Olson, Kari L. . . . . '63 '98 C.184 B.S. L.306 J.D. [A Murtha C.]

Ondrush, Laura, (BV) . . . . '56 '89 C.282 B.S. L.1048 J.D. [A Skelley R.]
*PRACTICE AREAS: Insurance Defense Litigation; Personal Injury; Products Liability.

O'Neil, John J., Jr., (BV) . . . . '42 '68 C.1107 A.B. L.184 J.D. [Francis,O.&D.]

O'Neil, Patricia A., (BV) . . . . '60 '85 C&L.128 B.A., J.D. [O'Neil&Assoc.]
*PRACTICE AREAS: Personal Injury Law; Real Estate Law; Domestic Relations Law; DUI; DWI.

O'Neil & Associates, P.C., (BV)
38 Hungerford Street, Suite 300, 06106
Telephone: 860-522-5188 Fax: 860-247-3468
Patricia A. O'Neil;—J. Lawrence Price.
Civil Litigation, Personal Injury, DUI, DWI, Slip and Fall, Dog Bites, Automobile Accidents, Product Liability, Family, Real Estate.
See Professional Biographies, HARTFORD, CONNECTICUT

O'Neill, Megan, (BV) . . . . '51 '79 C.855 B.A. L.184 J.D. Asst. Atty. Gen.

O'Neill, Norris L. . . . . '26 '52 C.103 L.705 LL.B. Trial Ref. J.

O'Neill, Thomas J., III, (BV) . . . . '64 '90 C.676 B.S. L.184 J.D. [Andros,F.&M.]

Onken, Nancy C. '62 '86 C.788 A.B. L.1048 J.D.
Asst. Coun., Hartford Steam Boiler Inspection & Ins. Co.

Onorato, Martin A. . . . . '67 '96 C.602 B.Arch. L.823 J.D. [A Halloran&S.]
*PRACTICE AREAS: Design Professionals Liability; Construction Law; Commercial Litigation; Fidelity and Surety; Construction and Design Law.

Oppenheim, Stephen D. . . . . '67 '92 C.477 B.A. L.904 J.D. [A Cohn B.&S.]
*PRACTICE AREAS: Commercial Law; Real Estate; Commercial Lending; Creditors Rights.

Order, Richard S., (BV) . . . . '56 '82 C.918 B.A. L.178 J.D. [Updike,K.&S.]
*PRACTICE AREAS: Commercial Litigation; Franchise Law; Human Service.

Orenstein, Scott S. . . . . '67 '01 C.454 B.S.C.E. L.1252 J.D. [A Updike,K.&S.]
*PRACTICE AREAS: Construction and Design Litigation; Professional Defense.

Orland, Leonard '36 '63 C.705 B.A. L.659 LL.B.
(adm. in NY; not adm. in CT) Prof. of Law, Univ. of Conn.

Orr, Susan M., (BV) . . . . '56 '80 C.165 B.A. L.94 J.D. [Pepe&H.]
*PRACTICE AREAS: Commercial Real Estate Finance; Real Estate Leasing; Real Estate Transfers; Real Estate Workouts.

Orth, Paul W., (AV) . . . . '30 '54 C.197 A.B. L.309 J.D. [MacDermid,R.&G.]
*PRACTICE AREAS: Civil Litigation; Employment Litigation; Alternative Dispute Resolution.

Osborne, Lorraine W. '33 '80 C.550 B.A. L.184 J.D.
Staff Atty., Hearings Ofc., Dept. of Health Servs.

O'Shea, Thomas J. . . . . '62 '92 C.1033 B.S. L.276 J.D. [Bingham D.]
*PRACTICE AREAS: Real Estate; Finance.

Osowiecki, Jennifer A. . . . . '62 '94 C&L.184 B.S., J.D. [A Pepe&H.]

Ossen, Neal, (BV) . . . . '41 '68 C.164 B.A. L.184 J.D. [Ossen&M.]

Ossen & Murphy, (BV) . . . . 21 Oak St.

Ostrowski, Mark K., (BV) . . . . '63 '88 C&L.184 B.A., J.D. [Shipman&G.]
*PRACTICE AREAS: Civil Litigation; Insurance; Health Care; Business; Torts.

Overend, Charles A., (BV) . . . . '42 '74 C&L.184 B.S., J.D. Asst. Atty. Gen.

Owens, Ann H. '40 '86 C.838 B.S. L.884 J.D.
(adm. in MA; not adm. in CT) Asst. Gen. Coun., Hartford Financial Services Group, Inc.

Pac, Patricia, (BV) . . . . '48 '73 C.94 B.A. L.818 J.D. Asst. Atty. Gen.

Pace, Vincent P. . . . . '72 '98 C.1030 B.A. L.306 J.D. [A Day,B.&H.]
*PRACTICE AREAS: Administrative Law; Regulatory Law; Utility Law.

Page, Thompson Gould . . . . '59 '92 C.1033 B.A. L.982 J.D. [T.G.Page]

Page, Thompson Gould, Law Offices of, LLC . . . . 942 Main Street, Suite 300

Paige, Reginald R., Sr. '62 '89 C.367 B.A. L.569 J.D.
Assistant Counsel, United Technologies Corporation

Paindiris, Nicholas, (BV) '46 '73 C.976 B.A. L.184 J.D.
[Brown,P.&S.] (⊙Glastonbury)
*PRACTICE AREAS: Corporate Law; Real Estate Law; Commercial Law; Municipal Law; Estate Planning.

Paindiris, Tasos C. . . . . '70 '95 C.918 B.A. L.184 J.D. [A Jackson L.S.&K.]

Palermino, Anthony J., (BV) . . . . '50 '75 C.321 A.B. L.184 J.D. [A.J.Palermino]

Palermino, Anthony J., LLC, Law Office of, (BV)
945 Wethersfield Avenue, 06114
Telephone: 860-296-0035 FAX: 860-296-9468
Email: a.palermino.atty@snet.net URL: http://www.lawyers.com/apalermino
Anthony J. Palermino;—Gary R. Atkinson.
Labor and Employment Law, Labor Relations (Private and Public Sector), Civil Rights, Administrative Law, Workers Compensation, Personal Injury, Real Estate, Business Law, Probate Law, Legislative Practice, Community Action Law, Litigation in all Courts.
See Professional Biographies, HARTFORD, CONNECTICUT

Palmer, Richard N. . . . . '50 '77 C.855 B.A. L.184 J.D. Supm. Ct. Jus.

Palmquist, Eric L. '66 '00 C.95 A.B. L.188 J.D.
(adm. in NY; not adm. in CT) [A Axinn,V.&H.]
*PRACTICE AREAS: Antitrust and Trade Regulation; Intellectual Property.

Palmunen, Arthur A. . . . . '46 '77 C.103 B.A. L.184 J.D. Coun., Aetna Inc.
*RESPONSIBILITIES: Litigation; ERISA; Health Care; Disability Insurance; Life Insurance.

Palten, Paul M., (BV) . . . . '11 '39 C.103 B.A. L.309 J.D. 10 Grand St.

Panico, David M. . . . . '— '89 C.1030 B.S. L.184 J.D. [Robinson&C.]
*PRACTICE AREAS: Indians and Native Populations.

Papa, John Stephen, (BV) '42 '67 C&L.262 A.B., J.D.
[Howard,K.S.&F.] (⊙Manchester)
*PRACTICE AREAS: Litigation; Real Estate Development.

Papermaster, Daniel I., (BV) . . . . '64 '89 C.477 B.A. L.846 J.D. [Bingham D.]

Parenteau, Jacques J., (BV) . . . . '57 '82 C.454 B.A. L.30 J.D. [Madsen,P.&P.] ⊙
*PRACTICE AREAS: Employment Law; Academic Employment; Commercial Litigation; Personal Injury; Products Liability.

Paris, Lissa J., (BV) . . . . '50 '78 C.145 B.A. L.976 J.D. [Murtha C.]
*PRACTICE AREAS: Employment and ERISA Litigation.

Parker, Alan S., (BV) . . . . '55 '80 C.1044 B.A. L.851 J.D. [Pullman&C.] (⊙Simsbury)
*PRACTICE AREAS: Probate and Estate Planning; Tax Law.

Parker, Cammie Joan '60 '86 C.199 B.A. L.276 J.D.
Comm. on Human Rights & Oppts.

Parrent, Ann '58 '84 C&L.477 B.A., J.D.
Staff Atty., Conn. Civil Liberties Union Found.

Parrott, R. Dial, (BV) . . . . '43 '80 C.674 A.B. L.893 J.D. [Updike,K.&S.]
*PRACTICE AREAS: Public Finance; Public Law; Solid Waste.

Parskey, Leo . . . . '15 '40 C&L.309 A.B., LL.B. State Trial Ref.

Pastore, Joseph M., III . . . . '66 '91 C.108 B.A. L.1040 J.D. [A Brown R.M.F.&S.]
*PRACTICE AREAS: Litigation; Telecommunications; Electronic Commerce.

Paul, Jeremy R. '56 '82 C.674 A.B. L.309 J.D.
(adm. in NY; not adm. in CT) Univ. of Conn., Sch. of Law

Paulding, Theodore R., (AV) '30 '57
C.602 B.S. L.184 J.D. [A McCormick,P.&H.] (See Pat. Sect.) ⊙
*PRACTICE AREAS: Intellectual Property.

Paulekas, Walter E., (BV) . . . . '56 '86 C.870 B.S. L.1048 J.D. [Levin,F.&P.]
*PRACTICE AREAS: Commercial Litigation; Bankruptcy; Corporate and Business Law; Creditors Rights; Environmental.

Pavano, John Jay . . . . '64 '94 C.184 B.A. L.1252 J.D. [A T.P.Willcutts&Assoc.]
*PRACTICE AREAS: Securities Litigation; Securities Arbitration; Commercial Litigation; Legal Malpractice; Professional Malpractice.

Payne, Rachel J. . . . . '73 '98 C&L.259 B.A., J.D. 254 Prospect Avenue

Payton, Jeffrey L. . . . . '50 '75 C.31 B.A. L.184 J.D. Coun., The Travelers Ins. Co.

Pearlman, Mitchell W. . . . . . .'45 '70 C.665 B.A. L.306 J.D. State Freedom of Info. Comm.

Pease, Michael A., (BV) . . . . '59 '85 C.93 B.S. L.184 J.D. 150 Trumbull St.

Peaslee, Christine C. . . . . '65 '98 C.478 B.A. L.1048 J.D. [A Bingham D.]

Pech, Raymond Parker '48 '81
C.855 B.A. L.1048 J.D. Mng. Dir., Comm. on Human Rights

Peck, A. Susan . . . . '46 '76 C.454 B.A. L.184 J.D. Supr. Ct. J.

Peck, Michael Ruben, (BV) . . . . '47 '75 C.886 B.A. L.215 J.D. [Moller,P.&O.]

Pedersen, Lloyd D., (BV) . . . . '59 '85 C.207 B.A. L.184 J.D. [Morrison,M.&M.]
*PRACTICE AREAS: Insurance; General Liability.

Peikes, Ronald D., (BV) . . . . '58 '83 C.881 B.A. L.184 J.D. [Kaatz&P.]

Pelham, Douglas S. . . . . '64 '98 C.390 B.S. L.1252 J.D. [A Cohn B.&S.]
*PRACTICE AREAS: Commercial Real Estate Finance; Real Estate Leasing; Land Use Law; Environmental Law.

Pellegrino, Joseph H. . . . . '36 '63 C.602 B.A. L.93 J.D. Appl. Ct. J.

Penn, Timothy Harold '58 '89
C.326 B.B.A. L.69 J.D. Dir., Travelers Property Casualty Co.

Pennito, Jan . . . . '57 '94 C&L.184 B.A., J.D. 300 Windsor St.

Peoples, Sean M. . . . . '60 '89 C.183 B.A. L.1218 J.D. [Brown,P.&S.] (⊙Glastonbury)
*PRACTICE AREAS: Civil Litigation; Probate; Residential Real Estate; Immigration Law.

Pepe, Louis R., (AV) . . . . '43 '70 C.688 B.S. L.188 J.D. [Pepe&H.]
*PRACTICE AREAS: Construction Law; Commercial Litigation; Alternative Dispute Resolution; Appellate Practice; Complex Litigation.

Pepe & Hazard LLP, (AV)
Goodwin Square, 06103-4302 ⊙
Telephone: 860-522-5175 FAX: 860-522-2796
URL: http://www.pepehazard.com
Members of Firm: Kathleen F. Bornhorst; Timothy T. Corey; Peter L. Costas; Jeanine M. Dumont; Mark I. Fishman; Michael E. Foley; James C. Graham; James G. Green, Jr.; Ursula L. Haerter; Dan A. Haynes; Stephen B. Hazard; Robert L. Keepnews; Thomas G. Librizzi; Thomas B. Mitchell; Anthony J. Natale; Susan M. Orr; Louis R. Pepe; Thomas J. Rechen; David E. Rosengren; Reed D. Rubinstein; Walter W. Simmers; Alfred A. Turco; Anne Noble Walker; Richard F. Wareing; Edward C. White; Adam F. Zweifler. Of Counsel: David A. Delman (Not admitted in CT); Robert C. Hunt, Jr.; Glenn J. MacGrady; Susan E. Neuberg. Associates: Nicole M. Baummer; Frank N. Cassetta; Isaiah D. Cooper; Christopher B. Cramer; James J. Flaherty, Jr. (Southport Office); Michael A. Fusco; Jennifer W. Haddad; Vincent J. Ingram; Jennifer Hamilton Lewis; James T. Murphy; Jennifer A. Osowiecki; Douglas M. Poulin; A. Rachel Rothman; Shellie D. Rosan; Gary F. Sheldon; Wendy Kennedy Venoit; Kenneth S. Weinstock; Brian L. Wolinetz; David Andre Woodard. Resident Partners in Boston Office: Thomas H. Brantley; Bret A. Cohen; Michael C. Gilleran; Sean W. Gilligan; Timothy Mark Hughes; David M. McGlone; David S. Mortensen. Partners in Southport Office: Suzanne E. Baldasare; Joseph W. Martini (Not admitted in CT); Harold James Pickerstein. Of Counsel in Boston Office: Jane L. King; Richard S. Rosenstein; Sari Ann Strasburg. Resident Associates in Boston Office: Katharine P. Costello (Not admitted in CT); Brendan J. Faulkner; Paul O. Mulroney; Neal F. Splaine. Associates in Southport Office: Stephan B. Grozinger; Kristin B. Mayhew. Counsel in Southport: Jennifer L. Cox.
Commercial, Construction, Corporations, Taxation, Finance and Real Estate, Commercial and Asset-Based Finance, Environmental/Health/Safety, Fidelity and Surety, Securities, Labor/Employment and Education, Municipal, Administrative, Health Care, Intellectual Property, Patent, International Trade, Estate Planning, Probate, White Collar Crime, and Bankruptcy. Trials in all Courts.
Southport, Connecticut Office: 30 Jelliff Lane, 06490-1436. Telephone: 203-319-4000. Fax: 203-259-0251.
Boston, Massachusetts Office: 150 Federal Street, 02110-1745. Telephone: 617-695-9090. Fax: 617-695-9255.
See Professional Biographies, HARTFORD, CONNECTICUT

Pepper, Anthony M. '61 '86 C.273 B.A. L.818 J.D.
Assoc. Coun., Hartford Financial Services Group, Inc.

Perakos, Peter G., II, (BV) . . . . '47 '72 C&L.94 B.S.B.A., J.D. [Perakos&Z.]

Perakos & Zitser, P.C., (BV) . . . . 44 Capitol Avenue Suite 302

Percy, Robert J. . . . . '45 '73 C.688 B.M.E. L.184 J.D. [Siegel,O.S.&Z.]
*PRACTICE AREAS: Taxation Law; Employee Benefit Law; Business Law; Criminal Tax Defense.

Perkins, J. James '42 '75 C.347 A.B. L.146 J.D.
(adm. in NJ; not adm. in CT; Pat.) [A Day,B.&H.]

Perkins, Patricia B., (BV) . . . . '46 '78 C.67 B.A. L.184 J.D. Sr. Coun., CIGNA Corp.

Perlstein, John R., (BV) . . . . '52 '77 C.867 B.A. L.569 J.D. Gen. Coun., CIGNA Corp.

Perlstein, Matthew N., Law Office of
(See Farmington)

Pernerewski, Paul K., Jr. . . . . '61 '86 C.184 B.S. L.276 J.D. Asst. Atty. Gen.

Perpenia, Victor R. . . . . '51 '85 C.309 A.B. L.184 J.D. State Freedom of Info. Comm.

Perra, Craig Lyle . . . . '71 '97 C&L.184 B.A., J.D. [A Updike,K.&S.]
*PRACTICE AREAS: Commercial Litigation; Creditors Rights; Bankruptcy.

Perrotti, Janet A. . . . . '52 '78 C.19 B.A. L.607 J.D. Pub. Defender

Perry, Karen A. . . . . '— '94 C.867 B.A. L.184 J.D. [A Robinson&C.]

Perry, Maya N. . . . . '75 '00 C.183 B.A. L.276 J.D. [A Shipman&G.]

Perry, Putnam H. . . . . '59 '93 C.94 B.A. L.893 J.D. [Rome M.S.]
*PRACTICE AREAS: Litigation.

Pershan, Richard H., Jr. '57 '87 C&L.976 B.A., J.D. P.O. Box 270

Peters, Ellen A. . . . . '30 '57 C.821 B.A. L.976 LL.B. Sr. Jus., Supm. Ct.

Peters, John C., P.C.
(See Avon)

Petrie, Michael G. . . . . '71 '00 C&L.184 B.A., J.D. [A Jackson L.S.&K.]
*PRACTICE AREAS: Employment Law.

Phelan, Denise Martino, (BV) . . . . '54 '80 C.93 B.A. L.184 J.D. [Jackson,O.&P.]
*PRACTICE AREAS: Civil Trial Practice; Medical Malpractice Law; Insurance Defense Law.

Phelan, Marie V. . . . . '47 '89 C.918 B.A. L.184 J.D. [Pullman&C.]
*PRACTICE AREAS: Public Finance; Public Law; Commercial Lending.

Phelon, FitzGerald & Wood, P.C.
(See Manchester)

Phillips, Earl W., Jr., (AV) ....'— '80 C.918 B.A. L.128 J.D. [Robinson&C.]
*PRACTICE AREAS: Environmental Law.

Piazza & Pickel
(See Stamford)

Pidlak, Rebecca L. .... '73 '98 C.184 B.S. L.356 J.D. [🄰 Cooney,S.&D.]
Pier, John T. ....'41 '74 C.201 B.A. L.184 J.D. CIGNA Corp.
Pierce, Howard L. ....'48 '91 C.107 B.S. L.1252 J.D. [Shipman&G.]
*PRACTICE AREAS: Health Care Fraud and Abuse Litigation; Insurance Fraud; Criminal Fraud; Civil Rights Litigation.
Pieszak, Temmy Ann .... '58 '83 C.881 A.B. L.184 J.D. Chf. Pub. Def. Off.
Pilo, Marvin, (BV) '46 '83 C&L.178 B.A., J.D.
Asst. Gen. Coun., Hartford Financial Services Group, Inc.
Pilver, Joan E., (AV) ....'48 '72 C.994 B.A. L.184 J.D. Asst. Atty. Gen.
Pingpank, Jeffrey C., (BV) ....'50 '75 C.367 B.A. L.184 J.D. [Cooney,S.&D.]
Pinkes, Andrew J., (AV) '62 '87 C.183 B.A. L.1048 J.D.
V.P., The Travelers Prop. Cas. Speciality Liability Grp.
Pinney, Willard F., Jr., (AV) ....'43 '68 C.976 B.A. L.477 J.D. [Murtha C.]
*PRACTICE AREAS: Corporate Law; Securities Law.
Piotrowski, James E. ...... '58 '98 C.184 B.S. L.1252 J.D. [🄰 Alix,Y.&R.] (See Pat. Sect.)
Pirina, John, Jr. ....'48 '77 C.188 A.B. L.930 J.D. Coun., Bank of New England Corp.
Pitt, Harold T., (BV) '26 '53 C.276 A.B. L.262 J.D.
Dist. Coun., U.S. Small Bus. Admn.
Platt, David, (BV) ....'61 '87 C.882 B.S. L.107 J.D. [Murtha C.]
*PRACTICE AREAS: Environmental Law; Litigation; Land Use Law; Land Conservation Law.
Plofsky, Alan S. '49 '79 C.188 B.A. L.1048 J.D.
(adm. in MA; not adm. in CT) Exec. Dir. & Gen Coun., State Ethics Comm.
Podorowsky, Leon .... '14 '40 C.855 L.309 LL.B. 99 Pratt St.
Polglase, Holly M. '62 '88 C.1107 B.A. L.818 J.D.
[🄰 Campbell C.E.&C.] (⊙Boston, MA; Port., ME; Concord, NH)
Polidoro, Monique R. ....'70 '97 C.184 B.A. L.306 J.D. [🄰 Rogin,N.C.L.&H.]
*PRACTICE AREAS: Trusts and Estates; Taxation; Corporate Law; Securities Regulation.

Poliner, Poliner, Antin & Cienava Rocco, P.C.
(See Middletown)

Polinsky, Eric A., (CV) .... '66 '91 C.1036 B.A. L.1202 J.D. [Polinsky,S.S.&P.]
*PRACTICE AREAS: Personal Injury; Estate Planning; Wills; Trust Law; Real Estate.
Polinsky, Jeffrey, (BV) ....'56 '82 C.94 B.A. L.1170 J.D. [Polinsky,S.S.&P.]
*PRACTICE AREAS: Civil Litigation; Personal Injury; Workers Compensation; Head Injury; Insurance.

Polinsky, Santos, Siegel & Polinsky, LLC, (BV)
890 West Boulevard, 06105-4139
Telephone: 860-232-9959 Fax: 860-236-8337
Email: eapolinsky@mindspring.com URL: http://www.lawyers.com/psplaw
Jeffrey Polinsky; Eric A. Polinsky; Carlos M. Santos; David H. Siegel.
Civil Litigation, Personal Injury, Workers Compensation, Negligence, Criminal Law, Real Estate, Wills, Divorce, Employment Law.
See Professional Biographies, HARTFORD, CONNECTICUT

Polivy, Richard B., (AV) ....'46 '71 C.930 B.A. L.93 J.D. [Polivy&T.]
*PRACTICE AREAS: Bankruptcy; Secured, Asset-Based and Unsecured Commercial Loan Documentation; Real Estate; Creditor's Rights; Workouts.

Polivy & Taschner, LLC, (AV)
Six Central Row, 06103
Mailing Address: P.O. Box 230294, Hartford, Connecticut 06123-0294
Telephone: 860-560-1180 Telecopier: 860-560-1354
Email: RPolivy@AOL.COM
Members of Firm: Richard B. Polivy; Craig S. Taschner. Associate: Dale M. Clayton.
Corporate, Financial Transactions, Real Estate Transactions, State and Federal Court Commercial Litigation, Workouts, Bankruptcy and Collections.
See Professional Biographies, HARTFORD, CONNECTICUT

Pollack, Elliott B., (AV) '43 '65
C&L.178 A.B., LL.B. [Pullman&C.] (⊙Bridgeport, Stamford)
*PRACTICE AREAS: Health Care; Tax Appeal and Condemnation Law; Commercial Litigation.
Pollard, Bryan K. ....'63 '88 C.184 B.A. L.976 J.D. United Tech. Corp.
Pomp, Richard D. '46 '72 C.477 B.S. L.309 J.D.
(adm. in MA; not adm. in CT) Prof. of Law, Univ. of Conn.
Pond, Robert K. '34 '77 C.184 B.S. L.1048 J.D.
(adm. in MA; not adm. in CT) 140 Garden St.
Pontacoloni, Edward J., (BV) ....'50 '79 C.436 B.A. L.1048 J.D. [Updike,K.&S.]
*PRACTICE AREAS: Commercial Lending; Secured Transactions; Commercial Litigation; Creditors Rights; Banking.
Pool, Franz L. .... '51 '78 C.697 B.S. L.910 J.D. 2nd V.P., The Travelers Corp.
Poresky, Donna ....'64 '91 C&L.184 B.S., J.D. [🄰 Day,B.&H.]
*PRACTICE AREAS: Administrative Law; Regulatory Law.
Poriss, Emily J. '51 '76 C.475 B.A. L.861 J.D.
Coun., Phoenix Home Life Mut. Ins. Co.
*RESPONSIBILITIES: Life Insurance; Annuities; Privacy.
Porter, Jamie Lynn ....'61 '85 C&L.184 B.A., J.D. Staff Atty., Supm. Ct.
Post, Russell L., Jr., (AV) ....'37 '61 C&L.976 B.A., LL.B. 185 Asylum St., 36th Fl.
Potanka, Edward P. ....'48 '74 C.31 B.A. L.188 J.D. Asst. Gen. Coun., CIGNA Corp.
Poulin, Douglas M. ....'65 '91 C.473 B.A. L.1066 J.D. [🄰 Pepe&H.]
Powell, Melinda A. ....'71 '96 C.1086 B.P.A. L.1194 J.D. [Howd&L.]
*PRACTICE AREAS: Insurance Defense Law; Personal Injury Law; Litigation; Trial Practice; Products Liability.
Pravecek, Samantha A. ....'74 '99 C.999 B.A. L.285 J.D. [🄰 Day,B.&H.]
Prensky, William J., (BV) ....'47 '74 C.264 B.A. L.184 J.D. Asst. Atty. Gen.
Prestley, Linda Pearce, (BV) ....'56 '86 C.322 B.A. L.184 J.D. Asst. Atty. Gen.
Prestley, Peter B., (BV) ....'45 '72 C.918 B.A. L.184 J.D. [Madsen,P.&P.] ⊙
*PRACTICE AREAS: Employment Law; Benefits Law; Class Actions; Age Discrimination; False Claims Act.
Price, J. Lawrence, (BV) .... '51 '86 C.679 B.A. L.180 J.D. [🄰 O'Neil&Assoc.]
*PRACTICE AREAS: Litigation; Commercial Litigation; Employment Litigation.
Price, Jason M. ....'71 '96 C.473 B.A. L.1048 J.D. [🄰 Shipman&G.]
*PRACTICE AREAS: Litigation; Insurance; Torts; Products Liability; ERISA.
Pripstein, Shirley M., (BV) '47 '79 C.831 B.S. L.184 J.D.
Coun., Greater Hartford Legal Assistance, Inc.
Psarakis, Emanuel N., (BV) ....'— '59 C.184 A.B. L.94 LL.B. [Robinson&C.]
*PRACTICE AREAS: Civil Rights; Labor and Employment; Discrimination Law; Litigation.
Pulda, Ruth L., (BV) ....'55 '83 C.183 B.A. L.569 J.D. [Livingston,A.P.&M.]

Pullman & Comley, L.L.C., (AV)
(Formerly Pullman, Comley, Bradley & Reeves)
90 State House Square, 06103-3702 ⊙
Telephone: 860-424-4300 Telecopier: 860-424-4370
URL: http://www.pullcom.com
John S. Pullman (1871-1943); Arthur M. Comley (1883-1969); J. Kenneth Bradley (1903-1969); William Reeves (1906-1967). Members of the Firm: Elizabeth J. Austin; Morris W. Banks; James G. Dowling, Jr.; Andrew C. Glassman; Lawrence J. Golden; Barry D. Greene; Joshua A. Hawks-Ladds; John J. Kindl; Michael A. Kurs; Lisa A. Magliochetti; Alan S. Parker; Marie V. Phelan; Elliott B.

(This Listing Continued)

Pullman & Comley, L.L.C. (Continued)
Pollack; Lewis Rabinovitz; Richard C. Robinson; Thomas A. Rouse; Alan I. Scheer; Gregory F. Servodidio; James T. Shearin; John F. Stafstrom, Jr.; Barrie K. Wetstone; Marjorie S. Wilder. Associate: Rod W. Farrell; Julie A. Morgan; Jonathan M. Shapiro; Gwen P. Weisberg.
General Practice including Administrative, Antitrust, Banking, Bankruptcy and Creditors Rights, Bonds, Business and Commercial, Corporate, Education, Employee Benefits, Environmental, Hospital and Health Care, Labor and Employment, Municipal Finance, Real Estate, Securities, Tax, Trusts and Estates, and Zoning. Energy and Utilities, Litigation in all Courts.
Bridgeport, Connecticut Office: 850 Main Street. Telephone: 203-330-2000. Telecopier: 203-576-8888.
New Haven, Connecticut Office: One Century Tower, 265 Church Street. Telephone: 203-773-3006. Telecopier: 203-776-7075.
Simsbury, Connecticut Office: 720 Hopmeadow Street. Telephone: 860-651-9348. Fax: 860-651-1431.
Southport, Connecticut Office: 200 Pequot Avenue, P.O. Box 510. Telephone: 203-254-5000. Telecopier: 203-254-5070.
Stamford, Connecticut Office: 350 Bedford Street. Telephone: 203-324-5000. Telecopier: 203-363-8659.
See Professional Biographies, HARTFORD, CONNECTICUT

Purvis, David R. ....'61 '86 C.264 B.A. L.184 J.D. [🄰 M.A.Dean]
*PRACTICE AREAS: Environmental Law.
Pustilnik, David D., (AV) '31 '58
C&L.569 B.S., J.D. Assoc. Gen. Coun., The Travelers Ins. Co.
Quigley, Brian M. ....'51 '76 C.321 B.A. L.184 J.D. Coun., The Travelers Ins. Co.
Quigley, Thomas E. ....'59 '89 C.1369 B.S. L.128 J.D. N.L.R.B.
Quinn, James M., (BV) ....'55 '83 C.321 B.A. L.184 J.D. [Furniss&Q.]
Quinn, John J., (BV) ....'51 '76 C.321 B.A. L.184 J.D. [Furniss&Q.]
Quinn, Joseph P., Jr., (AV) ....'49 '81 C.321 B.A. L.184 J.D. [Furniss&Q.]
Raabe, Craig A., (BV) ....'— '88 C.879 B.A. L.1048 J.D. [Robinson&C.]
*PRACTICE AREAS: Criminal Law.
Rabinovitz, Lewis, (BV) ....'35 '60 C.976 B.A. L.309 LL.B. [Pullman&C.]
*PRACTICE AREAS: Corporate Law; Tax Law; Family Law; Litigation.
Rachlin, Joseph S., (BV) ....'32 '60 C&L.569 B.A., J.D. 100 Constitution Plz.
Radner, Samuel Marc ....'67 '94 C.860 B.A. L.472 J.D. 999 Asylum Ave.
Radshaw, John J. ....'71 '98 C.890 B.A. L.1252 J.D. [Howd&L.]
*PRACTICE AREAS: Municipal Law; Insurance Defense Litigation; Civil Litigation.
Ramirez, Vanessa L. .... '73 '01 C&L.659 B.A., J.D. [🄰 Updike,K.&S.]
*PRACTICE AREAS: Business Law.
Randall, Karen B. .... '57 '81 C.901 B.A. L.229 J.D. The Travelers Ins. Co.
Ranelli, Gian-Matthew ....'65 '94 C.210 B.A. L.1194 J.D. [🄰 Shipman&G.]
*PRACTICE AREAS: Environmental Law; Land Use Law.
Rapo, Paul S. ... '48 '75 C.588 B.S.B.A. L.1202 J.D. Head Govt. Progs. Coun., Aetna Inc.
Rasch, Kevin S. ....'— '98 C.19 B.A. L.945 J.D. [🄰 Robinson&C.]
Rathgeber, John R. '50 '76 C.165 A.B. L.818 J.D.
Exec. V.P. & Secy., Conn. Bus. & Indus. Assn.
Ray, Charles D. ....'54 '89 C.654 B.A. L.184 J.D. [Cummings&L.]
*PRACTICE AREAS: Education Law (90%); Criminal Law (10%, 3).
Ray, James P. .... '— '92 C&L.184 B.S., J.D. [Robinson&C.]
*PRACTICE AREAS: Environmental Law; Litigation.
Raymond, Bruce H., (BV) ....'64 '89 C.184 B.A. L.1202 J.D. [Halloran&S.]
*PRACTICE AREAS: Litigation; Products Liability Law; Toxic Tort; Business Disputes; Risk Management.
Reade, Steven C., (BV) ....'56 '86 C.999 B.A. L.1048 J.D. 81 Wethersfield Ave.
Reardon, James J., Jr. ....'68 '93 C.454 B.A. L.93 J.D. 225 Asylum Street, 13th Floor
Rechen, Thomas J., (BV) ....'63 '88 C.1044 B.A. L.94 J.D. [Pepe&H.]
*PRACTICE AREAS: Business Litigation; Business Tort; Complex Litigation; Premises Liability Defense; Professional Liability.
Regan, Thomas J. ....'— '95 C.855 B.A. L.184 J.D. [🄰 Brown,R.F.&G.]
*PRACTICE AREAS: Real Estate; Zoning Law; Land Use; Finance; Telecommunications.

Regnier, Taylor, Curran & Eddy, (AV)
CityPlace, 06103-4402
Telephone: 860-249-9121 FAX: 860-527-4343
Email: RTCE@SNET.NET
Members of Firm: J. Ronald Regnier (1906-1987); Robert F. Taylor (1930-1994); Edmund T. Curran; Ralph G. Eddy; Jack D. Miller; Lawrence L. Connelli. Associates: Jay F. Huntington; Frederick M. O'Brien; Keith S. McCabe; Douglas E. Gilmore; Peter J. Casey; Andrew W. Bray; Sandra R. Baker; Michael P. Hendrickson; M. Paula Silva.
General Practice. Trials in all Courts. Probate, Insurance, Corporations and Real Estate Law. Family and Municipal Law, Professional Malpractice, Municipal Litigation, Professional Malpractice, Municipal Litigation.
Representative Clients: Atlantic Mutual Insurance Co.; Government Employees Insurance Co.; Hartford Accident & Indemnity Co.; Hartford Fire Insurance Co.; Pioneer Co-operative Fire; United Services Automobile Assn.; Vermont Mutual Insurance Co.
See Professional Biographies, HARTFORD, CONNECTICUT

Regula, Maureen Duggan ....'60 '87 C.367 B.A. L.1048 J.D. Atty. Gen's. Off.‡
Rehm, Angela R. ....'69 '98 C.911 B.A. L.188 J.D. Legis. Atty.
Reichert, Robert C., (BV) ....'52 '82 C&L.508 B.A., J.D. [🄰 Reid&R.]
*PRACTICE AREAS: Alternative Dispute Resolution; Bankruptcy; Litigation.
Reid, John H., III, (AVⓉ) ....'44 '69 C.976 B.A. L.893 LL.B. [Edwards&A.]
*PRACTICE AREAS: Taxation Law; Employee Benefits Law; Professional Organizations Law; Health Law.
Reid, John J. ....'43 '68 C.156 A.B. L.93 J.D. [Gordon,M.&F.]
*PRACTICE AREAS: Construction Law; Fidelity and Surety Law; Alternate Dispute Resolution; Civil Litigation; Commercial Litigation.
Reid, Sylvia D. ....'60 '94 C.289 B.A. L.184 J.D. 434 Franklin Ave.

Reid and Riege, P.C., (AV) BR
One State Street, 06103 ⊙
Telephone: 860-278-1150 FAX: 860-240-1002
URL: http://www.reidriege.com
Andrew J. Howat; Travers T. Auburn; Maurice T. FitzMaurice; Bruce M. Lutsk; Tuck Miller, Jr.; Michael L. Coyle; Suzanne S. Bocchini; John J. Jacobson; John E. D'Amico; Lawrence H. Lissitzyn; Frederick J. Mullen, Jr.; Edmund A. Mikolowsky; Robert U. Sattin; John M. Horak; Edward F. Spinella; Craig L. Sylvester; Robert M. Mulé; Eileen M. Marks; Earl F. McMahon; Jon P. Newton; Mark X. Ryan; John D. Newman; Joseph K. Fortier; Thomas M. Armstrong; Eric A. Henzy; Alan Birmingham; John V. Galiette; Dominic Fulco, III; Douglas K. Knight; John R. Ivimey; Louis J. Donofrio. Senior Attorneys: Karen L. Brand; Robert C. Reichert; Leah Cohen Chatinover;—Michael T. Wade; Ames B. Shea; Thomas R. Kasper; Barbara A. Taylor; Ronald John Koniuta; Joseph A. Cipparone; Indrek H. Buttner; Jennifer R. Lucarelli; Doreen J. Farina; Evan S. Goldstein.
Alternative Dispute Resolution. Antitrust & Trade Regulation. Bankruptcy. Business Law. Commercial Law. Commercial Real Estate/Finance. Corporate Law. Employee Benefits/Pension Plans. Employee Benefits/Taft-Hartley Plans. Environmental Law. Health Care. Labor and Employment. Litigation. Mergers and Acquisitions. Nonprofit and Charitable Organizations. Occupational Safety & Health. Probate. Real Estate. Securities. Taxation. Trade and Professional Associations. Trusts & Estates. Zoning, Planning and Land Use.
West Hartford, Connecticut Office: 65 LaSalle Road. Telephone: 860-232-6565. FAX: 860-232-6066.
Lakeville, Connecticut Office: 322 Main Street. Telephone: 860-435-9894. FAX: 860-240-1002.
Woodbury, Connecticut Office: 47 Sherman Hill Road. Telephone: 203-267-6680. FAX: 860-240-1002.
See Professional Biographies, HARTFORD, CONNECTICUT

Reilly, Michael J., (AV) ....'51 '76 C&L.184 B.A., J.D. [Bingham D.]
Reinsmith, R. William, (AV) .... '36 '61 C.792 B.S.M.E. L.976 LL.B. [Murtha C.] (Pat.)
*PRACTICE AREAS: Intellectual Property; Copyrights; Patent and Trademark; Foreign Patents and Trademarks.
Reisner, Alan K., (BV) ....'53 '79 C&L.184 B.A., J.D. [Butler N.&G.]
Rendeiro, Jill J. .... '60 '92 C.1044 B.A. L.184 J.D. One American Row

Rendeiro, Richard R., (BV) .... '56 '84 C.966 B.S. L.30 J.D. [Cummings&L.]
*PRACTICE AREAS: Commercial Real Estate; Commercial Finance; Bankruptcy Law.
Retallick, Cynthia C. .... '62 '97 C.788 A.B. L.184 J.D. 225 Asylum Street, 13th Floor
Reutenauer, Jeri E. .... '70 '00 C&L.1252 B.A., J.D. [Ⓐ Shipman&G.]
Reveruzzi, John A. '40 '75 C.28 B.A. L.1048 LL.B.
(adm. in MA; not adm. in CT) Pres., CBT Realty Corp.
Reynolds, Cathryn A. ....'— '99 C.164 B.A. L.184 J.D. [Ⓐ Robinson&C.]
Reynolds, Edward F., Jr. ....'44 '69 C.262 A.B. L.184 J.D. Asst. Atty. Gen.
Reynolds, Kevin N. .... '62 '91 C.385 A.B. L.893 J.D. [Updike,K.&S.]
*PRACTICE AREAS: Administrative Law; Legislative Representation; Litigation.
Reynolds, Peter R., (AV) ....'56 '84 C.309 A.B. L.306 J.D. [MacDermid,R.&G.]
*PRACTICE AREAS: Litigation; Fidelity and Surety; Construction Law; Commercial Law; Insurance.
Reynolds, Richard M., (AV) .... '37 '62 C&L.976 B.A., LL.B. [Ⓒ Day,B.&H.]
*PRACTICE AREAS: Antitrust and Trade Regulation; Reinsurance Litigation; Corporate Control Contests.
Reynolds, Roger F. ....'65 '93 C.429 B.A. L.569 J.D. Asst. Atty. Gen.
Reynolds, Sharon M. '49 '86 C.1044 B.A. L.184 J.D.
Assoc. Coun., The Travelers Ins. Co.
Rezner, Barbara A. .... '55 '80 C.282 B.A. L.902 J.D. The Travelers Ins. Co.
Rhoades, Heather J. ....'74 '99 C&L.184 B.A., J.D. [Ⓐ Cummings&L.]
Rich, Charles B. ....'53 '78 C.390 B.A. L.345 J.D. One Commercial Plz., 24th Fl.
Rich, Tracy L. '52 '78 C.867 B.A. L.569 J.D.
Sr. V.P. & Gen. Coun., Phoenix Home Life Mut. Ins. Co.
*RESPONSIBILITIES: Tax; Insurance; Corporate; Litigation.
Richter, Donald P., (AV) .... '24 '51 C.67 B.A. L.976 LL.B. [Ⓒ Murtha C.]
*PRACTICE AREAS: Corporate Law; Estate Planning Law; Taxation Law.
Richters, Edward M. ....'52 '81 C.184 B.A. L.128 J.D. [Ⓒ Jackson L.S.&K.]
*PRACTICE AREAS: Labor and Employment; Arbitration; Mediation.
Rickard, Linda, (AV) '47 '78
C.914 B.A. L.184 J.D. Coun., Aetna Life & Cas. Co. (⊙Hartford)
Rickard, Linda, (AV) ......'47 '78 C.914 B.A. L.184 J.D. Coun., Aetna Inc. (⊙Hartford).
Ridenour, Michael D. ....'49 '85 C&L.259 B.A., J.D. 1 American Row
Rieger, Donald F., Jr. .... '46 '75 C.976 B.A. L.188 J.D. CIGNA Corp., S-307
Riihimaki, Arthur A., Jr. '43 '76 C.236 B.A. L.184 J.D.
Assoc. Coun., Hartford Financial Services Group, Inc.
Riley, Michael E., (AV) ....'50 '79 C.184 B.A. L.1048 J.D. [Jackson,O.&P.]
*PRACTICE AREAS: Civil Trial Practice; Insurance Defense Law; Personal Injury Law.
Rimmer, Robert T. ..... '70 '96 C.976 B.A. L.184 J.D. [Ⓐ Brown,P.&S.] (⊙Glastonbury)
*PRACTICE AREAS: Civil Litigation; Criminal Law; Administrative Law; Employment Litigation.

RisCassi and Davis, P.C., (AV)
131 Oak Street, P.O. Box 261557, 06126-1557
Telephone: 860-522-1196 Fax: 860-246-5847
URL: http://www.riscassi-davis.com
Leon RisCassi (1908-1986); William R. Davis; James D. Bartolini; Andrew S. Groher; Michael C. Jainchill; John J. Houlihan, Jr.; David W. Cooney; Eugene K. Swain; Kathryn Calibey; Douglas W. Hammond; Everett Howard Madin, Jr.; Paul M. Iannaccone.
Civil, Trial and Appellate Practice in State and Federal Courts. Negligence, Products Liability, Aviation and Medical Malpractice.
See Professional Biographies, HARTFORD, CONNECTICUT

Rispoli, Robert L. ....'65 '99 C&L.184 B.S.M.E., J.D. [Ⓐ Cummings&L.]
*PRACTICE AREAS: Intellectual Property; Litigation.
Ristas, L. James .... '49 '78 C.188 B.S. L.184 J.D. [Alix,Y.&R.] (See Pat. Sect.)
Ritson, John D., (BV) .... '59 '85 C.184 B.S. L.1048 J.D. [Hersh&R.]
Ritter, George J. '20 '47
C.705 B.A. L.976 LL.B. Chmn. of the Bd., Independent Energy Corp.
Ritter, Thomas D., (BV) ....'— '78 C.31 B.A. L.184 J.D. [Brown,R.F.&G.]
*PRACTICE AREAS: Government Relations (30%); Municipal (20%); Utility (20%); Banking (10%); Environmental (10%).
Riviere, Russell F.A. .... '74 '00 C.260 B.A. L.276 J.D. [Ⓐ Updike,K.&S.]
*PRACTICE AREAS: Labor and Employment; Litigation.
Robacynski, John Joseph .... '55 '81 C.1030 A.B. L.607 J.D. [Ⓐ Gersten&C.]
*PRACTICE AREAS: Corporate Law; Business Litigation; Mergers and Acquisitions; Environmental Law.
Robb, David R. '47 '73 C.97 B.A. L.273 J.D.
(adm. in DC; not adm. in CT) V.P., ITT Hartford Ins. Grp.
Robbin, Elizabeth J. ....'69 '94 C.197 B.A. L.184 J.D. [Ⓐ Rogin,N.C.L.&H.]
*PRACTICE AREAS: Civil Litigation; Commercial Litigation.
Roberge, Kristi Stapf '55 '81 C.1038 B.A. L.1019 J.D.
Dir., Hartford Steam Boiler Inspection & Ins. Co.
Robert, Paul L. '— '80 C.321 A.B. L.262 J.D.
(adm. in MA; not adm. in CT)
Assoc. Gen. Coun. & Due Contracts & Compl., United Techologies Corp.
*RESPONSIBILITIES: Government Contracts; Government Relations; Compliance.
Roberts, Erik E. ....'64 '95 C.896 B.A. L.306 J.D. [Gordon,M.&F.]
*PRACTICE AREAS: Insurance Defense; Civil Litigation; Workers Compensation.
Roberts, Jeanne S. ....'65 '90 C.477 B.A. L.818 J.D. [MacDermid,R.&G.]
*PRACTICE AREAS: Real Property; Conveyancing; Leasing; Finance; Land Use.
Roberts, Jo Ann, (BV) '55 '81 C.980 B.A. L.436 J.D.
State Capitol Building, Room 509A
Roberts, Richard P., (BV) ....'61 '86 C.197 A.B. L.893 J.D. [Ⓐ Halloran&S.]
*PRACTICE AREAS: Commercial Lending; Loan Workouts and Restructuring; Banking; Financial Transactions; Real Estate.
Roberts, Vanessa D. ....'74 '99 C.976 B.A. L.276 J.D. [Ⓐ Cummings&L.]
Robinson, Barclay, Jr., (AV) .... '— '64 C&L.976 B.A., LL.B. [Ⓒ Robinson&C.]
*PRACTICE AREAS: Labor and Employment; Family; Education; Nonprofit Organizations.
Robinson, John J. .... '65 '94 C&L.128 B.S., J.D. [Ⓐ McCarter&E.]
*PRACTICE AREAS: Products Liability; Nursing Home Litigation; Tort Litigation.
Robinson, Lewis J., Jr. '43 '74
C&L.329 B.A., J.D. Gen. Coun., Travelers Prop. Casualty Corp.
Robinson, Richard C., (AV) ....'45 '71 C.659 B.A. L.306 J.D. [Pullman&C.]
*PRACTICE AREAS: Litigation; Employment Law.

Robinson & Cole LLP, (AV)
280 Trumbull Street, 06103-3597 ⊙
Telephone: 860-275-8200 Fax: 860-275-8299
Email: rc.com URL: http://www.rc.com
Partners: Bradford S. Babbitt; Kenneth C. Baldwin; Bruce B. Barth; Gurdon H. Buck; Lawrence P. Coassin; Thomas P. Cody; Frank F. Coulom, Jr.; Eric D. Daniels; S. Frank D'Ercole; Alice E. DeTora; Michael R. Enright; Stephen E. Goldman; J. C. David Hadden; Edward F. Hennessey; Edward S. Hill; Brien P. Horan; Christopher J. Hug; Steven R. Humphrey; Jack S. Kennedy; Judith M. Keppelman; David A. Kulle; Eric Lukingbeal; John B. Lynch, Jr.; Diana MacPherson; Michael F. Maglio; Linda J. McDowell; Robert S. Melvin; Dwight H. Merriam; David M. Panico; Earl W. Phillips, Jr.; Emanuel N. Psarakis; Craig A. Raabe; James P. Ray; David Thomas Ryan; Edward J. Samorajczyk, Jr.; Glenn A. Santoro; Edward P. Scherer; William T. Sellay; Brian R. Smith; Robert H. Smith, Jr.; W. Richard Smith, Jr.; Alan R. Spier; Daniel F. Sullivan; John O. Tannenbaum; Richard W. Tomeo; Theodore J. Tucci; James A. Wade. Of Counsel: Raymond S. Andrews, Jr.; R. Regner Arvidson; Lucian E. Baldwin; Charles J. Cole; William K. Cole; John M. Donahue; Reginald Endicott Francklyn; George C. Hastings; John W. Hincks; Bruce W. Manternach; Barclay Robinson, Jr.; Clark Whittemore, Jr. Counsel: Stephen W. Aronson; Eileen P. Baldwin; Felicia DeDominicis; Dina Schwarz Fisher; Mimi M. Lines; Linda L. Morkan; Rafael A. Santiago; John R. Shaughnessy, Jr.; Kevin C. Sullivan; Rhonda J. Tobin; Richard F. Vitarelli; Amy Span Wergeles. Associates: Maria T. Ackley; Martin T. Booher; Deirdre A. Devaney; Gerald P. Dwyer Jr.; Richard M. Fil; Brian C. S. Freeman; Andrew S. Golden; Edward J. Heath; Helen M. Kemp; Jeffrey C. Kestenband; Jason Kuselias; Kevin E. Majewski; Marion B. Manzo; Melissa M. Martin; Gregory W. McCracken; Joey Lee Miranda; Joshua S. Mirer;

(This Listing Continued)

Robinson & Cole LLP (Continued)
Megan R. Naughton; Erin K. O'Brien; Karen A. Perry; Kevin S. Rasch; Cathryn A. Reynolds; Glenn G. Rybacki; Jacqueline Pennino Scheib; John A. Schuster; Jeanmarie B. Shea; Carol A. Shubinski; Robert J. Sitkowski; Jeffrey M. Thomen; Dawn N. Zammitti; Jennifer Croteau Zettergren.
General Practice including Admiralty, Antitrust and Trade Regulation, Appellate, Banking and Institutional Finance, Bankruptcy and Creditors' Rights, Business Litigation, Business Workouts, Construction, Corporate and Closely Held Business, Criminal Litigation, E-Commerce and Intellectual Property, Employee Benefits and ERISA Litigation, Employment Litigation and Counseling, Environmental, Estate Planning and Probate, Government Relations, Healthcare, Immigration, Insurance, International, Labor Relations and Collective Bargaining, Land Use and Zoning, Personal Injury, Product Liability, Professional Liability, Public Finance, Real Estate Finance, Development and Leasing, Securities, Tax-Exempt Organizations, Tax Planning and Representation, Utilities and Telecommunications.
Stamford, Connecticut Office: Financial Centre, P.O. Box 10305, 695 East Main Street. Telephone: 203-462-7500. Fax: 203-462-7599.
Greenwich, Connecticut Office: 80 Field Point Road. Telephone: 203-862-4100. Fax: 203-862-4199.
New London, Connecticut Office: 75 Eugene O'Neill Drive. Telephone: 860-437-5000. Fax: 860-437-5099.
Boston, Massachusetts Office: One Boston Place. Telephone: 617-557-5900. Fax: 617-557-5999.
New York, N.Y. Office: 4th Floor, 780 Third Avenue. Telephone: 212-451-2900. Fax: 212-451-2999.
Manchester, New Hampshire Office: Robinson & Cole & Craig, 84 Bay Street. Telephone: 603-641-2500. Fax: 603-669-1310.
See Professional Biographies, HARTFORD, CONNECTICUT

Roche, Kevin M. .... '61 '87 C.1021 B.A. L.1048 J.D. [Halloran&S.]
*PRACTICE AREAS: Breach of Contract; General Liability; Insurance Contracts; Insurance Coverage; Insurance Litigation.
Rochlin, Richard A. .... '75 '00 C.30 B.A. L.184 J.D. [Ⓐ Bingham D.]
*PRACTICE AREAS: Corporate Law; Structured Finance.
Rock, William G., (BV) .... '59 '84 C.884 B.A. L.893 J.D. [Shipman&G.]
*PRACTICE AREAS: Real Estate Law; Commercial Finance Law; Corporate Trust Law.
Rodia, John M. .... '63 '98 C.1156 B.S. L.178 J.D. 1 American Row
Rodriguez, Raul A., (BV) ....'61 '86 C.188 B.A. L.107 J.D. [Ⓐ Arnold&Assoc.]
*PRACTICE AREAS: Civil Litigation; Landlord and Tenant Law; Foreclosure; Housing Law; Public Housing.
Rodriguez-Schack, Y., (BV) ....'62 '88 C.472 B.A. L.1035 J.D. Asst. Pub. Def.
Rogers, William S., (AV) .... '32 '60 C.94 B.S. L.184 J.D. [Ⓒ Tyler C.&A.]
*PRACTICE AREAS: Securities Law, Litigation and Regulation; Municipal Law and Litigation; Administrative Law and Litigation; Appellate Practice.
Roggi, Curtis H., (BV) .... '52 '80 C.999 B.A. L.1194 J.D. [Roggi,M.&M.]
Roggi, Morelli & Morelli, LLP, (BV) ....221 Main Street, Suite 400
Rogin, A. Ned, (BV) ....'42 '69 C.659 A.B. L.94 LL.B. 185 Asylum St., 22nd Fl.

Rogin, Nassau, Caplan, Lassman & Hirtle, LLC, (AV)
CityPlace I, 22nd Floor, 185 Asylum Street, 06103-3460
Telephone: 860-278-7480 Fax: 860-278-2179
Members of Firm: Edward S. Rogin (1908-2000); Louis E. Nassau (1908-1999); Robert L. Hirtle; Steven D. Bartelstone; David M. Call; Paul B. Zolan; David J. Heinlein; Lewis K. Wise; Mark A. Rosenblum; Barry S. Feigenbaum; Peter S. Sorokin; Iris June Brown; Benjamin Engel; Thomas M. Divine; Lawrence G. Rosenthal. Associates: Mark J. Lassman; Brendan T. Flynn; Lisa M. Anderson; Elizabeth J. Robbin; Jonathan M. Starble; Monique R. Polidoro; Stephen M. Hryniewicz; Randy P. Kabakoff. Of Counsel: Jerome E. Caplan; Edwin A. Lassman.
General Practice, including Administrative, Antitrust and Trade Regulation, Banking, Bankruptcy, Civil Rights, Commercial, Commercial Leasing Law, Condominium and Other Common Interest Communities; Construction Law, Corporate, Corporate Reorganization, Eminent Domain, Employment, Environmental, Estate Planning and Administration, Family, Franchise Regulation, Health Care, Internet Law, Legislative Practice, Pension and Profit Sharing, Personal Injury, Land Use, Probate, Real Estate, Securities, Surety, Tax Law and Workers Compensation Law. Trials and Appeals in all Courts.
See Professional Biographies, HARTFORD, CONNECTICUT

Rohback, Thomas G., (AVⓉ) .... '51 '79 C.867 B.A. L.178 J.D. [LeBoeuf,L.G.&M.]
*PRACTICE AREAS: Litigation.
Rojas, Jose M .... '72 '97 C.1134 B.S. L.1252 J.D. [Ⓐ Shipman&G.]
*PRACTICE AREAS: Litigation; Criminal Law.
Rollins, James Scott, (BV) ....'62 '89 C.674 A.B. L.893 J.D. [Bingham D.]
*PRACTICE AREAS: Commercial Litigation; Labor and Employment Law; Media Law.
Romanelli, Irene Pysariw ....'— '88 C.690 B.A. L.1048 J.D. [Romanelli]

Romanelli Law Offices, The
255 Main Street, Suite 303, 06106
Telephone: 860-560-0611 Facsimile: 860-724-6002
Email: iromanelli@yahoo.com URL: http://www.lawyers.com/romanellilaw
Irene Pysariw Romanelli.
Real Estate, Foreclosures, Collections, contracts, Business Law, Immigration, Wills and Probate, U.S. Law for International Clients, Probate Litigation.
See Professional Biographies, HARTFORD, CONNECTICUT

Romanik, Donald V., (BV) '54 '79
C.855 B.A. L.94 J.D. Gen. Coun., Conn. Inst. for the Blind
Rome, Alan J., (BV) .... '64 '89 C.184 B.S. L.1048 J.D. [Butler N.&G.]
Rome, Lewis B., (AV) .... '33 '57 C&L.184 B.A., LL.B. [Rome M.S.]
Rome, Thomas S., (BV) ....'56 '83 C.976 B.A. L.273 J.D. [Ⓐ Butler N.&G.]

Rome McGuigan Sabanosh, P.C., (AV)
One State Street, 06103 ⊙
Telephone: 860-549-1000 Telecopier: 860-724-3921
URL: http://www.rms-law.com
Lewis B. Rome; Austin J. McGuigan; John A. Sabanosh; Richard F. Banbury; Morris R. Borea; John W. Bradley, Jr.; Robert J. T. Britt; Joseph B. Burns; Joseph J. Cassidy; Glenn E. Coe; Richard P. Healey; Andrew L. Houlding; William W. Kaliff; Richard J. Kenny; Anthony B. Ludovico; Jeffrey L. Ment; Putnam H. Perry; Debra C. Ruel; Helga Mayer Woods;—Jonathan J. Blake; Julie D. Blake; Zisca Burkley; Alexander J. Chotkowski; Bernard F. Gaffney; Thomas J. Lengyel; Jayme E. Stamper; Jacqueline A. Wilson. Counsel: Horace G. Flinn, Jr.; George P. Generas, Jr; John F. Strother.
Litigation, Investigations, Intellectual Property, Tax and Valuation Appeal, Tribal Gaming, Administrative Law, Alternative Dispute Resolution, Bankruptcy, Benefits Planning/ERISA, Business Planning, Commercial Finance, Construction, Corporate, Creditor's Rights, Criminal Defense, Education, Environmental, Estate Planning and Administration, Government Relations, Insurance, Labor and Employment, Land Use, Matrimonial Law, Municipal, Personal Injury, Product Liability, Real Estate, Tax, White-Collar Crime.
Bridgeport, Connecticut Office: 1000 Lafayette Boulevard. Telephone: 203-382-8000. Telecopier: 203-382-8005.
See Professional Biographies, HARTFORD, CONNECTICUT

Romeo, Frank J., III .... '68 '96 C.93 B.A. L.1360 J.D. [Ⓐ McVane,B.K.W.&B.]
Ronalter, William J. ....'66 '92 C.787 B.A. L.884 J.D. [Ⓐ Trantolo&T.]
Roos, Norman H., (AV) ....'48 '73 C.659 B.S. L.477 J.D. [Brown R.M.F.&S.]
*PRACTICE AREAS: Financial Transactions; Electronic Commerce; Banking Law; Financial Services Law; Regulatory Law.
Rosan, Shellie D. ....'63 '96 C.659 B.A. L.978 J.D. [Ⓐ Pepe&H.]
Rosania, John S. ....'59 '85 C.31 B.A. L.262 J.D. [Ⓐ Halloran&S.]
*PRACTICE AREAS: Insurance Coverage Litigation; Insurance Defense Litigation; General Civil Litigation; Motor Vehicle Torts; Premises Liability.
Rose, Michael J. ....'66 '94 C.550 B.A. L.1218 J.D. [Howd&L.]
*PRACTICE AREAS: Civil Rights; Employment Law; Municipal; Insurance Defense.
Rosen, Scott D. .... '57 '86 C.1030 B.A. L.94 J.D. [Cohn B.&S.]
*PRACTICE AREAS: Creditors Rights; Bankruptcy Reorganization; Real Estate; Commercial Workouts; Commercial Litigation.

Rosen, Stuart D., (BV) .... '56 '82 C.184 B.A. L.128 J.D. [Bingham D.]
*PRACTICE AREAS: Commercial Litigation; Insurance and Reinsurance Litigation; Business Torts; Real Estate Litigation.

Rosenberg, Sanford L., (AV) .... '34 '58 C&L.188 B.A., LL.B. 1 Corporate Ctr.

Rosenblum, Mark A., (BV) .... '53 '79 C.309 A.B. L.245 J.D. [Rogin,N.C.L.&H.]
*PRACTICE AREAS: Commercial Litigation; Construction Litigation.

Rosengren, David E., (BV) .... '51 '81 C.683 B.A. L.893 J.D. [Pepe&H.]
*PRACTICE AREAS: Construction Litigation; Complex Commercial Litigation; Environmental Litigation.

Rosensweig, Robert L., (AV) .... '28 '52 C.976 B.A. L.262 LL.B. [▣ Shipman&G.]

Rosenthal, Edward M. .... '68 '92 C.94 B.S.B.A. L.472 J.D. [Ⓐ Sabia&H.]
*PRACTICE AREAS: Commercial Litigation; Civil Litigation; Personal Injury.

Rosenthal, Joseph A. ... '69 '96 C.1349 B.A. L.93 J.D. [Ⓐ Updike,K.&S.] (⊙New Haven)
*PRACTICE AREAS: Environmental; Administrative Law; Utilities Law.

Rosenthal, Lawrence G. .... '56 '82 C.846 B.A. L.326 J.D. [Rogin,N.C.L.&H.]
*PRACTICE AREAS: Construction Law; Surety and Fidelity Law; Insurance Defense Law; Maritime Law; Litigation.

Rosenthal, Mark A. .... '30 '56 C.184 B.S. L.94 LL.B. 21 Oak St.

Rosenthal, Robert S. '60 '85
C.1036 B.A. L.184 J.D. Compl. Offr., Conn. Mut. Life Ins. Co.

Ross, Malcolm A. M. .... '47 '73 C.178 B.A. L.184 J.D. Pres., Ernest Peterson, Inc.

Rostocki, Alexander, Jr. '54 '83
C.184 B.A. L.1029 J.D. Sr. Coun., Fleet Financial Grp., Inc.

Rothauser, Eric H. .... '69 '94 C.184 B.A. L.645 J.D. [Bonee]
*PRACTICE AREAS: Civil Litigation; Workers Compensation; Criminal Law; Real Estate; Probate.

Rothman, A. Rachel .... '75 '00 C.659 B.A. L.188 J.D. [Ⓐ Pepe&H.]

Rothstein, Scott H. .... '65 '94 C.659 B.A. L.184 J.D. 151 Farmington Avenue

Rotondo, James H., (BV) .... '56 '81 C.855 B.A. L.94 J.D. [Day,B.&H.]
*PRACTICE AREAS: Product Liability; Negligence Defense; Direct Liability and Casualty; Torts Litigation; Insurance Litigation.

Rottner, Joel J., (AV) .... '44 '73 C.918 B.A. L.184 J.D. [Skelley R.]
*PRACTICE AREAS: Products Liability and Toxic Torts; Property Insurance; Arson and Insurance Fraud; Insurance Coverage.

Rouse, Thomas A., (BV) .... '50 '75 C.855 B.A. L.184 J.D. [Pullman&C.] (⊙Bridgeport)
*PRACTICE AREAS: Electronic Commerce; Environmental Litigation; Telecommunications Law; Electric Power; Technology Startups.

Rowlenson, Richard C. '49 '75 C&L.276 B.S., J.D.
(adm. in DC; not adm. in CT) Vice President & General Counsel, Gemini Networks, Inc.

Royster, George, (AV) .... '41 '66 C.390 A.B. L.910 J.D. [Halloran&S.]
*PRACTICE AREAS: Commercial Litigation; Products Liability; Torts.

Royster, James N., (AV) .... '44 '71 C.303 B.A. L.184 J.D. [▣ Michelson,K.R.&B.]

Rozich, Kenneth M. .... '73 '98 C.573 B.A. L.1048 J.D. [Ⓐ Krasow,G.&H.]

Rua, Christine E. .... '66 '91 C.867 B.S. L.893 J.D. Attorney, United Tech. Corp.

Ruben, Marshall S., (BV) .... '60 '85 C.976 B.A. L.178 J.D. [Ruben,J.&M.]
*PRACTICE AREAS: Real Estate; Real Estate Finance; Corporate; Taxation.

Ruben, Johnson & Morgan, P.C., (BV)
Cityplace II, 185 Asylum Street, 06103
Telephone: 860-275-6888 Telecopier: 860-275-6884
Marshall S. Ruben; Derek M. Johnson; Lisa Kelly Morgan. Of Counsel: Maura Hughes Horan.
Real Estate, Corporate, Bankruptcy, Litigation.
See Professional Biographies, HARTFORD, CONNECTICUT

Rubenstein, William M., (BV) .... '51 '81 C.555 B.A. L.1048 J.D. [Axinn,V.&H.]
*PRACTICE AREAS: Antitrust and Trade Regulation; Litigation.

Rubenstein, Green & Bass, LLC
(See Westport)

Rubin, Joseph, (AV) .... '49 '75 C.976 B.A. L.309 J.D. Assoc. Atty. Gen.

Rubin, Richard P., (BV) .... '55 '80 C.659 B.S. L.94 J.D. The Travelers Ins. Co.

Rubinow, Nicola E. .... '50 '77 C.66 B.A. L.184 J.D. Supr. Ct. J.

Rubinstein, Reed D., (BV) .... '60 '85 C&L.477 A.B., J.D. [Pepe&H.] (⊙Southport)
*PRACTICE AREAS: Environmental Liability; Real Estate Finance; Land Use and Zoning.

Rubrich, John S. .... '66 '92 C.602 B.A. L.1029 J.D. [Ⓐ Hassett&G.]
*PRACTICE AREAS: Civil Litigation; Trial Practice; Computer Law; Corporate Law; Estate Planning.

Rudewicz, Frank E. '56 '92 C.829 B.S. L.306 J.D.
Managing Director & Counsel, DSFX International, LLC

Rueckert, Morgan P. .... '70 '98 C&L.184 B.A., J.D. [Ⓐ Shipman&G.]
*PRACTICE AREAS: Litigation.

Ruel, Debra C., (BV) .... '53 '84 C.562 B.A. L.184 J.D. [Rome M.S.]
*PRACTICE AREAS: Matrimonial Law.

Ruffee, Richard E. '64 '90 C.93 A.B. L.884 J.D.
(adm. in PA; not adm. in CT)
V.P., Professional Liability Claims, Travelers Prop. Casualty‡

Rugland, Amelia M., (BV) .... '38 '79 C.879 B.A. L.46 J.D. 1 Corporate Center

Ruhe, Barbara J.
(See Wethersfield)

Rummel, Cynthia J. .... '58 '88 C&L.184 B.S., J.D. The Hartford Spec. Litigation Unit

Russo, Deborah S. .... '52 '81 C.550 B.A. L.94 J.D. [Ⓐ Day,B.&H.]
*PRACTICE AREAS: Tort Defense; Products Liability; Insurance Defense; Labor and Employment.

Russo, Linda A, (BV) .... '54 '88 C.787 B.A. L.1029 J.D. Asst. Atty. Gen.

Rutstein, Steven M., (AV) .... '50 '76 C.4 B.A. L.1048 J.D. Asst. Atty. Gen.

Rutt, Ellen Keane .... '55 '90 C.602 B.A. L.184 J.D. Univ. of Conn. Sch. of Law

Ruzek, Peter R. '41 '79 C.186 M.S.M.E. L.724 J.D.
(adm. in NY; not adm. in CT; Pat.) 1 Financial Plz.

Ruzzier, Antoinette Leone .... '52 '76 C.855 B.A. L.184 J.D. 886 Maple Ave.

Ryan, David Thomas, (AV) .... '— '66 C.446 B.S. L.276 LL.B. [Robinson&C.]
*PRACTICE AREAS: Personal Injury; Medical Malpractice; Litigation; Trusts and Estates.

Ryan, Mark X. .... '63 '88 C.276 A.B. L.602 J.D. [Reid&R.]
*PRACTICE AREAS: Antitrust; Trade Regulation; Business Law; Corporate Law; Mergers and Acquisitions.

Ryan, Michael C. .... '65 '90 C.264 B.A. L.602 J.D. Hartford Ins. Co.

Ryan, Steven B. .... '74 '00 C.125 B.A. L.1202 J.D. [Ⓐ Cramer,A.&F.]
*PRACTICE AREAS: Insurance Defense; Civil Rights Defense; Workers Compensation Defense; General Liability Defense.

Rybacki, Glenn G. .... '62 '98 C.676 B.S. L.1252 J.D. [Ⓐ Robinson&C.]

Sabatini and Associates, LLC
(See Newington)

Sabia, Randall J., (BV) .... '57 '85 C.478 B.A. L.184 J.D. [Sabia&H.]
*PRACTICE AREAS: Commercial Transactions; Uniform Commercial Code; Commercial Foreclosures; Commercial Collections; Bankruptcy.

Sabia & Hartley, LLC, (BV)
190 Trumbull Street Suite 202, 06103-2205
Telephone: 860-541-2077 Facsimile: 860-713-8944
URL: http://www.sabiahart.com
Randall J. Sabia; Jill Hartley; Edward C. Taiman, Jr.;—Eileen C. Moskey; Michael G. Albano; Edward M. Rosenthal; Ryan P. Barry.
Commercial Law and Transactions, Employment Law, Civil Litigation, Commercial Litigation, Tort Litigation, Corporate Transactions, Real Estate and Banking.
See Professional Biographies, HARTFORD, CONNECTICUT

Sable, Joel N., (AV) .... '44 '71 C&L.184 B.A., J.D. [Berman&S.]
*PRACTICE AREAS: Real Estate and Commercial Finance Transactions and Workouts; Corporate Law; Foreclosures; Creditors Rights; Bankruptcy.

Saccomandi, Frank J., III, (BV) .... '55 '80 C.831 B.A. L.659 J.D. [Murtha C.]
*PRACTICE AREAS: Commercial; Real Estate Law; Commercial Finance Law.

Sacks, Howard R. '21 '48 C.494 B.A. L.976 LL.B.
(adm. in MN; not adm. in CT) Prof., Univ. of Conn. Sch. of Law

St. Onge, Kathleen A. .... '66 '94 C.914 B.A. L.184 J.D. 225 Asylum Street, 13th Floor

Salve, Patrick J. '36 '62 C&L.659 B.S., J.D.
(adm. in PA; not adm. in CT)
Sr. V.P. & Dir., Prop.-Cas. Opers., Hartford Financial Services Group, Inc.

Samorajczyk, Edward J., Jr., (BV) .... '— '80 C.309 A.B. L.184 J.D. [Robinson&C.]
*PRACTICE AREAS: Corporate Law; Securities; Finance; Insurance.

Samuel, Denise L. .... '69 '97 C.454 B.A. L.329 J.D. 1 American Row

Samuels, Robert C. .... '38 '74 C.1145 B.S. L.184 J.D. The Travelers Ins. Co.

Sanchez-Figueroa, Norma I. .... '62 '93 C.1036 B.A. L.93 J.D. 77 Buckingham Street

Sandak Friedman Hennessey & Greco, LLP
(See Stamford)

Sandler, James P., (BV) .... '36 '62 C.674 A.B. L.309 J.D. [Sandler,G.&M.]
*PRACTICE AREAS: Municipal; Public Agency; Public Employment; Energy; Corporate Law.

Sandler, Goldstein & Mara, P.C., (BV)
One Hartford Square West Suite 302, 06106
Telephone: 860-241-7700 Fax: 860-241-7701
James P. Sandler; Richard H. Goldstein; Daniel N. Mara.
General Commercial Practice including Litigation, Corporations, Administrative, Real Estate, Public Utilities, Communications, Zoning, Energy, Environmental, Labor Relations, Municipal and Public Agency, Public Finance and Entertainment Law, Personal Injury.
See Professional Biographies, HARTFORD, CONNECTICUT

Sanford, Trevor T. .... '70 '99 C.696 L.30 J.D. [Ⓐ Bingham D.]
*PRACTICE AREAS: Finance; Corporate Law.

Sanson, Paul D., (AV) .... '49 '77 C.674 A.B. L.276 J.D. [Shipman&G.]
*PRACTICE AREAS: Business Litigation; Franchise Litigation; Distribution Litigation; Antitrust Litigation; Environmental Litigation.

Santacroce, Mary Ann, (BV) .... '61 '86 C.93 B.A. L.184 J.D. [Ⓐ O'Connell,F.&A.]
*PRACTICE AREAS: Business; Corporate; Commercial; Real Estate; Commercial Transaction.

Santaniello, Carmino J., Jr. .... '57 '86 C.454 B.S. L.1048 J.D. I.R.S.

Santiago, Rafael A., (AV) .... '— '83 C.860 B.S.E.E. L.184 J.D. [▣ Robinson&C.]
*PRACTICE AREAS: Business Law; International Law.

Santiello, Carmino J. .... '57 '86 C.454 B.S. L.1048 J.D. IRS

Santoro, Frank H., (BV) .... '42 '68 C&L.276 A.B., J.D. [Danaher,T.L.&N.]

Santoro, Glenn A., (AV) .... '— '89 C.93 B.S. L.184 J.D. [Robinson&C.]
*PRACTICE AREAS: Mergers and Acquisitions; Corporate; Municipal Law; Government; Finance.

Santos, Carlos M., (BV) .... '64 '89 C.855 B.A. L.306 J.D. [Polinsky,S.S.&P.]
*PRACTICE AREAS: Civil Litigation; Criminal Litigation; Personal Injury; Workers Compensation; Administrative Law.

Santos, Hubert J., (AV) .... '44 '69 C.1033 B.A. L.184 J.D. [Santos&S.]
*PRACTICE AREAS: Criminal Defense; Commercial Law; Business Litigation; Personal Injury; Appellate Practice.

Santos & Seeley, P.C., (AV)
51 Russ Street, 06106
Telephone: 860-249-6548 Fax: 860-724-5533
Hubert J. Santos; Hope C. Seeley;—Patrick S. Bristol.
Trial and Appellate Practice in State and Federal Courts, Criminal Law, White Collar Crime, Employment, Personal Injury, Commercial Litigation, Civil Rights.
See Professional Biographies, HARTFORD, CONNECTICUT

Sarra, Aaron .... '71 '01 C.999 B.S. L.201 J.D. [Ⓐ Murtha C.]

Sarrantonio, Barbara A., (AV) .... '47 '85 C.1033 B.A. L.184 J.D. [Murtha C.]
*PRACTICE AREAS: Commercial Real Estate Law; Commercial Finance Law.

Satter, Robert .... '19 '47 C.705 B.A. L.178 LL.B. Sr. Ref., Supr. Ct.

Sattin, Robert U., (AV) .... '48 '74 C.696 A.B. L.184 J.D. [Reid&R.]
*PRACTICE AREAS: Alternative Dispute Resolution; Bankruptcy; Business Law; Commercial; Commercial Real Estate and Finance.

Savage, John S. '56 '85 C.197 A.B. L.569 J.D.
151 New Park Avenue (⊙Hartsdale, NY)

Savage, Joseph F., III '40 '68 C.976 B.A. L.893 LL.B.
(adm. in NY; not adm. in CT) Shawmut Bank Connecticut

Savill, Nirja N. .... '— '83 C.999 B.A. L.1067 J.D. Dept. of Banking

Sayler, Linda C. '48 '82 C.336 B.A. L.767 J.D.
Coun., The Hartford Financial Service Grp., Inc.

Scanlon, Cornelius J. '25 '56 C&L.93 A.B., LL.B.
(adm. in MA; not adm. in CT) Prof. of Law, Emeritus, Univ. of Conn.

Scanlon, Katherine A. .... '70 '96 C&L.184 B.A., J.D. 225 Asylum Street, 13th Floor

Scanlon, Robert L. .... '67 '99 C.184 B.A. L.306 J.D. [Ⓐ Murtha C.]

Scantling, James G., (AV) .... '49 '74 C.94 B.S. L.345 J.D. [Bingham D.]
*PRACTICE AREAS: Leveraged Leasing; Asset-Based Lending; Project Financing; Mergers and Acquisitions; Lease Finance.

Scapellati, Daniel P. .... '57 '82 C.884 B.S. L.1029 J.D. [Halloran&S.]
*PRACTICE AREAS: Civil Appeals; Civil Litigation; Arson and Insurance Fraud; First Party Insurance Defense; Insurance Bad Faith Defense.

Schaecher, Gina L. '65 '94 C.627 B.S.B.A. L.546 J.D.
(adm. in NE; not adm. in CT) [▣ Halloran&S.]
*PRACTICE AREAS: Commercial Litigation; Construction Law; Government Contracts.

Schaefer, Daniel R., (BV) .... '39 '64 C.976 A.B. L.184 LL.B. Asst. Atty. Gen.

Schaller, Barry R. .... '38 '63 C&L.976 B.A., J.D. Appl. Ct. J.

Schatz, Andrew M. .... '51 '76 C.188 B.A. L.309 J.D. [Schatz&N.]
*PRACTICE AREAS: Securities Litigation; Business Litigation; Professional Liability; Antitrust.

Schatz, Louis B., (AV) .... '54 '81 C&L.188 B.A., J.D. [Shipman&G.]
*PRACTICE AREAS: Tax Law; Limited Liability Company Law; State Taxation; Partnership Taxation; Partnership Law.

Schatz, S. Michael, (AV) .... '21 '46 C&L.188 A.B., LL.B. [▣ Schatz&S.R.&K.]

Schatz & Nobel, P.C., (AV)
330 Main Street, 06106
Telephone: 860-493-6292 Telecopier: 860-493-6290
Email: SN06106@aol.com URL: http://www.snlaw.net
Andrew M. Schatz; Jeffrey S. Nobel; Robert Andrews Izard, Jr.;—Patrick A. Klingman; Wayne T. Boulton.
General Business Litigation in all Federal and State Courts. Securities Litigation, including class and derivative actions and licensing proceedings. Antitrust Litigation, Employment Litigation, Professional Liability Litigation.
See Professional Biographies, HARTFORD, CONNECTICUT

Schatz & Schatz, Ribicoff & Kotkin .... 90 State House Square (⊙Stamford)

Schatzki, George '33 '58 C&L.309 A.B., LL.B.
(adm. in MA; not adm. in CT) Prof. of Law, Univ. of Conn. School of Law

Scheer, Alan I., (AV) .... '42 '67 C.569 B.S. L.1009 J.D. [Pullman&C.]
*PRACTICE AREAS: Labor and Employment Law; Litigation; Health Care; Antitrust.

Scheffey, Thomas B. '50 '80 C.685 B.A. L.1340 J.D.
(adm. in PA; not adm. in CT) American Lawyer Media

Scheib, Jacqueline Pennino .... '— '96 C.264 B.A. L.184 J.D. [Ⓐ Robinson&C.]

Schenker, Michael S., (AV) ... '46 '74 C&L.188 B.Ch.E., J.D. [Francis,O.&D.]
Scherer, Edward P., (AV) ... '— '71 C.164 B.A. L.424 J.D. [Robinson&C.]
*PRACTICE AREAS: Real Estate; Real Estate Leasing; Government.
Schiaffo, Thomas C. ... '49 '75 C.823 A.B. L.1292 J.D. Coun., CIGNA Corp.
Schiessl, Carl J., (BV) '59 '84
C.855 B.A. L.184 J.D. Coun., Phoenix Home Life Mutual Ins. Co.
*RESPONSIBILITIES: General Corporate; Real Estate; Intellectual Property; Ethics; Government Affairs.

Schiff, Howard Lee, P.C., Law Offices
(See East Hartford)

Schmeisser, Christopher W. ... '62 '89 C.976 B.A. L.309 J.D. 750 Main St.
Schmidt, Edmund F., (BV) ... '49 '75 C.1103 B.A. L.912 J.D. Sr. Coun., House of Rep.
Schneider, Miriam Berlin ... '72 '98 C.659 B.A. L.569 J.D. [Ⓐ Dechert]
*PRACTICE AREAS: Real Estate Finance.
Schneider, Stacy M. ... '67 '93 C.188 B.S. L.260 J.D. 254 Prospect Ave.
Schoen, Victor, (AV) ... '44 '71 C.855 B.A. L.184 J.D. [Sullivan,S.C.&C.]
Scholl, Jane S., (AV) ... '50 '75 C&L.184 B.A., J.D. Assoc. Atty. Gen.
Schulwolf, James C., (AV) ... '56 '80 C.31 B.A. L.569 J.D. [Shipman&G.]
*PRACTICE AREAS: Asset Based Lending; Commercial Lending; Mergers and Acquisitions; Electronic Commerce; Equipment Leasing.
Schuman, Alan L., (BV) ... '45 '80 C.184 B.A. L.1029 J.D. [McCarthy,S.&C.]
Schuster, John A. ... '71 '00 C.867 B.A. L.588 J.D. [Ⓐ Robinson&C.]
Schwane, Steven J. '50 '75 C.502 B.S. L.228 J.D.
Adm. Hearings Atty., Dept. of Consumer Protection
Schwartz, Daniel A. ... '70 '95 C.659 B.A. L.904 J.D. [Ⓐ Day,B.&H.]
*PRACTICE AREAS: Labor and Employment; Litigation; Employee Benefits.
Schwartz, Peter, (BV) ... '58 '84 C&L.184 B.A., J.D. The Travelers Corp.
Schwartz, Peter C., (AV) ... '38 '65 C.197 A.B. L.659 LL.B. [Ⓒ Gordon,M.&F.]
*PRACTICE AREAS: Products Liability; Legal Malpractice; Accountants Malpractice.

Scibilia & McCuin, P.C.
(See Berlin)

Scimonelli, Paul M. ... '53 '78 C.1021 B.A. L.982 J.D. Asst. Atty. Gen.
Sconzo, James M., (BV) ... '63 '89 C.184 B.A. L.823 J.D. [Halloran&S.]
*PRACTICE AREAS: Labor and Employment; Litigation; Professional Liability; Torts; Alternative Dispute Resolution.
Scott, Christy ... '68 '93 C.788 B.A. L.184 J.D. 90 Gillett St.
Scott, Frazier G., (BV) '49 '75 C.855 B.A. L.734 J.D.
Sr. V.P. & Reg. Fiduciary Offr., Fleet National Bank, Private Clients Group
Scott, Robert C. ... '68 '98 C.222 B.A. L.184 J.D. [Ⓐ Shipman&G.]
*PRACTICE AREAS: Business Law; Public Finance; Banking Law; Corporate; Government Relations.
Scott, Ronald T., (BV) ... '52 '78 C.24 B.A. L.184 J.D. [Brown,P.&S.] (⊙Glastonbury)
*PRACTICE AREAS: Personal Injury Law; Family Law.
Scrimgeour, James D. ... '69 '99 C.31 B.A. L.184 J.D. [Ⓐ Day,B.&H.]
*PRACTICE AREAS: Business Law.
Scudder, Daniel ... '60 '85 C.860 B.A. L.184 J.D. Coun., The Travelers Ins. Co.
Scully, James T., (BV) ... '61 '88 C.999 B.A. L.1048 J.D. [Cooney,S.&D.]
Scully, John F., (AV) ... '25 '54 C.855 A.B. L.184 LL.B. [Ⓒ Cooney,S.&D.]
Scully, John T., (AV) ... '54 '80 C.1033 B.A. L.184 J.D. [Cooney,S.&D.]
*PRACTICE AREAS: Personal Injury; Criminal Defense; Workers Compensation; Insurance Defense Subrogation.
Scully, William J., (BV) ... '62 '87 C.183 B.A. L.1048 J.D. [Cooney,S.&D.]
Seagull, Michelle H. ... '75 '00 C.910 B.A. L.309 J.D. [Ⓐ Axinn,V.&H.]
*PRACTICE AREAS: Antitrust and Trade Regulation; Commercial Litigation.
Sedor, Stephen M. ... '69 '95 C.158 B.S. L.1252 J.D. [Ⓐ Shipman&G.]
*PRACTICE AREAS: Employment Litigation; Litigation.
See, Edmund M., (AV) ... '43 '71 C.918 B.A. L.309 J.D. [Day,B.&H.]
*PRACTICE AREAS: Municipal Finance; Finance and Investments; Tax Exempt Organizations.
Seeley, Hope C., (AV) ... '64 '89 C&L.184 B.A., J.D. [Santos&S.]
*PRACTICE AREAS: Criminal Defense; White Collar Crime; Civil Litigation; Appellate Litigation.
Segal, Lewis, (AV) ... '35 '60 C.178 A.B. L.976 LL.B. [Tyler C.&A.]
*PRACTICE AREAS: Business Law; Corporate Finance; Commercial Finance; Mergers and Acquisitions.
Seifel, Donald R., Jr., (BV) ... '57 '83 C.477 B.A. L.94 J.D. [Updike,K.&S.]
*PRACTICE AREAS: Business Law; Trusts and Estates; Probate; Taxation.
Seiger, Mark B. ... '55 '81 C.1033 B.A. L.930 J.D. [Edwards&A.]
*PRACTICE AREAS: Products Liability (30%); Risk Management (30%); Complex Civil Litigation (20%); Employment Litigation (10%); Insurance Coverage (10%).
Seiling, Valerie A., (BV) ... '57 '82 C&L.188 B.S., J.D. [Wiggin&D.]
*PRACTICE AREAS: Corporate Finance; Secured Transactions; Mergers and Acquisitions; Commercial Mortgages; Real Estate Finance.
Seligman, Sharon M. ... '75 '00 C.183 B.A. L.184 J.D. [Ⓐ Day,B.&H.]
*PRACTICE AREAS: Environmental Law; Land Use.
Seligman, Steven L., (AV) ... '52 '79 C.976 B.A. L.184 J.D. [Katz&S.]
*PRACTICE AREAS: Civil Litigation; Professional Licensing Regulation; Legal Ethics and Professional Responsibility; Criminal Litigation; Insurance Defense.
Selinger, Joseph J., Jr., (BV) ... '52 '78 C.31 B.A. L.184 J.D. [Tobin,C.O.R.&S.] ⊙
*PRACTICE AREAS: Corporate Finance; Securities Law; Health Care Law; Public Finance.
Sellay, William T., (AV) '— '71
C.475 B.S. L.477 J.D. [Robinson&C.] (⊙New York, NY)
*PRACTICE AREAS: Business Law; Mergers and Acquisitions; Antitrust and Trade Regulation; Intellectual Property; Technology and Science.
Selleck, Nathaniel ... '57 '97 C.184 B.A. L.1252 J.D. [Ⓐ Brown R.M.F.&S.]
*PRACTICE AREAS: Litigation; Commercial Litigation; Employment Litigation.
Senter, Caren A. ... '59 '86 C.31 B.A. L.228 J.D. Assoc. Coun., The Travelers Ins. Co.
Servodidio, Gregory F. ... '61 '86 C&L.276 A.B., J.D. [Pullman&C.] (⊙Bridgeport)
*PRACTICE AREAS: Property Taxation; Condemnation and Relocation; Land Use; Litigation.
Seymour, Deann K. ... '64 '01 C.999 B.S. L.1048 J.D. [Howd&L.]
*PRACTICE AREAS: Workers Compensation; Insurance Defense; Municipal Law.
Shaffer, Steven D. ... '66 '98 C.1145 B.S.B.A. L.823 J.D. [Ⓐ Cummings&L.]
*PRACTICE AREAS: Corporate Law; Health Care; Real Estate.
Shah, Namita Tripathi ... '71 '96 C.184 B.S. L.94 J.D. [Ⓐ Day,B.&H.]
*PRACTICE AREAS: Private Finance; Structured Finance; Bond Finance.
Shah, Rupal S. ... '73 '99 C.321 B.A. L.276 J.D. [Ⓐ Bingham D.]
*PRACTICE AREAS: Corporate; Bankruptcy.
Shaiken, David M. S., (AV) ... '60 '87 C.821 B.A. L.184 J.D. [D.M.S.Shaiken]

Shaiken, David M. S., P.C., (AV)
330 Main Street, 06106
Telephone: 860-244-0720 Facsimile: 860-244-0725
Email: david.shaiken@snet.net URL: http://www.shaiken.com
David M. S. Shaiken.
Bankruptcy, Insolvency, Creditor's Rights, Commercial Law, Commercial Litigation, Commercial Finance, Commercial Arbitration and Mediation, Family Law, Alternative Dispute Resolution.
See Professional Biographies, HARTFORD, CONNECTICUT

Shapera, Paul N., (BV) ... '54 '79 C.184 B.A. L.851 J.D. 179 Alley St.
Shapiro, Jonathan M. ... '76 '01 C.93 B.A. L.184 J.D. [Ⓐ Pullman&C.]
*PRACTICE AREAS: Health Care; Litigation.
Shapiro, Peter D. ... '43 '71 C.262 B.A. L.245 J.D. 555 Asylum St.
Shapiro, Robert B., (BV) ... '48 '74 C.604 A.B. L.178 J.D. 100 Pearl St.
Sharaf, Robert M., (AV) ... '32 '57 C.67 A.B. L.976 J.D. One Corporate Ctr.

Sharp, Gregory A., (AV) ... '44 '78 C.197 B.A. L.184 J.D. [Murtha C.]
*PRACTICE AREAS: Environmental Law; Site Remediation; Environmental Enforcement; Water Resource and Wetlands Regulation.
Shaughnessy, John R., Jr. ... '— '68 C.321 A.B. L.93 J.D. [Ⓒ Robinson&C.]
*PRACTICE AREAS: Taxation.
Shaughnessy, William M. ... '29 '60 C.855 B.S. L.184 LL.B. Supr. Ct. J.
Shaw, David C., (BV) ... '44 '73 C.867 B.S. L.184 J.D. 179 Allyn St.
Shaw, John A. ... '51 '77 C.659 B.A. L.184 J.D. CIGNA Corp.
Shaw, L. Edward, Jr., (AV⊤) '44 '69 C.276 A.B. L.976 LL.D.
(adm. in NY; not adm. in CT) Gen. Coun., Aetna Inc.
*RESPONSIBILITIES: Executive Compensation.
Shea, Ames B. ... '68 '93 C.207 B.A. L.902 J.D. [Ⓐ Reid&R.]
*PRACTICE AREAS: Corporate Law; Mergers and Acquisitions; Nonprofit and Charitable Organizations.
Shea, David M. ... '22 '48 C.918 B.A. L.976 LL.B. Trial Ref. J.‡
Shea, James F. ... '70 '96 C.321 B.A. L.602 J.D. [Ⓐ Jackson L.S.&K.]
Shea, Jeanmarie B., (AV) ... '— '85 C.976 B.A. L.184 J.D. [Ⓐ Robinson&C.]
*PRACTICE AREAS: Trusts and Estates; Corporate Law.
Shea, Kathleen A. ... '67 '97 C.184 B.S. L.1048 J.D. [Ⓐ Day,B.&H.]
*PRACTICE AREAS: Administrative Law; Regulatory Law; Business Transactions.
Shea, Michael P. ... '67 '93 C.31 B.A. L.976 J.D. [Ⓐ Day,B.&H.]
*PRACTICE AREAS: White Collar Crime; Commercial Litigation.
Shea, Richard J., Jr., (AV) '57 '82
C.976 B.A. L.184 J.D. [Cohn B.&S.] (⊙New York, NY)
*PRACTICE AREAS: Business Law; Commercial Real Estate; Securities; Technology Law.
Shea, William J., (BV) ... '60 '89 C.708 B.S. L.1048 J.D. 44 Capitol Ave., Ste 402
Shearin, James T., (AV) '61 '86
C&L.184 B.A., J.D. [Pullman&C.] (⊙Bridgeport, Stamford)
*PRACTICE AREAS: Litigation; Intellectual Property; Admiralty; Securities.
Sheehan, Douglas D. ... '70 '99 C&L.1252 B.S., J.D. [Ⓐ Brown R.M.F.&S.]
*PRACTICE AREAS: Banking; Consumer Finance; Financial Services Law; Commercial Real Estate.
Sheehan, Margaret J. ... '70 '01 C.183 B.A. L.124 J.D. [Ⓐ Bingham D.]
*PRACTICE AREAS: Corporate Finance.
Sheldon, Gary F. ... '65 '94 C.158 B.S.M.E. L.184 J.D. [Ⓐ Pepe&H.]
Shelton, Edward S. ... '58 '96 C.241 B.S.S.P. L.1048 J.D. [Ⓐ Day,B.&H.]
*PRACTICE AREAS: Business Law; Commercial Real Estate; Corporate Law; Emerging Markets; Venture Capital.
Shepardson, Herbert J., (BV) ... '56 '82 C.454 B.A. L.1048 J.D. [Cooney,S.&D.]
*PRACTICE AREAS: Medical Malpractice; Civil Litigation.
Sheppard, Rachel ... '55 '84 C.184 B.S. L.818 State Ethics Comm.
Sheridan, Richard M., (BV) ... '43 '68 C.1030 A.B. L.184 LL.B. Asst. Atty. Gen.
Sherman, Douglas B. ... '49 '75 C.197 A.B. L.184 J.D. Asst. Atty. Gen.
Sherman, George J., (BV) ... '09 '37 C.228 L.94 LL.B. 40 Grand St.
Sherman, Wendelyne A. ... '63 '95 C.858 B.S. L.184 J.D. 77 Buckingham St.

Sherman, Ralph D.
(See West Hartford)

Sherriff, Andrew R., Jr. ... '72 '98 C.262 B.A. L.1009 J.D. [Ⓐ Berman&S.] (⊙Westport)
*PRACTICE AREAS: Corporate Law; Real Estate; Commercial Loans; Corporate Finance; Mergers and Acquisitions.
Shields, Robert M., Jr., (BV) ... '51 '78 C.321 B.A. L.184 J.D. [Horton,S.&C.]
*PRACTICE AREAS: Civil Litigation; Appellate Litigation; Insurance Law; Corporate Law; Real Estate.
Shimelman, Arnold K., (BV) ... '45 '71 C.882 B.S. L.818 J.D. [Ⓒ Shipman&G.]
*PRACTICE AREAS: Real Estate Law; Transportation Law; Land Use Law.
Shimkus, Charles J., Jr., (BV) ... '60 '85 C.93 A.B. L.276 J.D. 382 New Britain Ave.
Shipman, Lawrence S., (BV) ... '65 '90 C.385 B.A. L.818 J.D. 363 Main Street
Shipman, Mark S., (AV) ... '37 '62 C&L.184 B.A., LL.B. 363 Main Street

Shipman & Goodwin LLP, (AV) BR
One American Row, 06103-2819 ⊙
Telephone: 860-251-5000 Telecopier: 860-251-5099
Email: www@goodwin.com URL: http://shipman-goodwin.com
Members of Firm: Stuyvesant K. Bearns (Lakeville Office); Peter W. Benner; James W. Bergenn; James T. Betts; Donna L. Brooks; Daniel P. Brown, Jr.; Coleman H. Casey; Robert J. Cathcart; Christine L. Chinni; Bruce A. Chudwick; Brian Clemow; Richard I. Cohen; Glenn M. Cunningham; Leslie L. Davenport; Brenda A. Eckert; Joan W. Feldman; Vaughan Finn; Thomas P. Flynn; Susan C. Freedman; Deborah Smith Frisone; Stephen K. Gellman; Ira H. Goldman; Gary S. Hammersmith; John T. Harris; Barry C. Hawkins (Stamford Office); Timothy S. Hollister; Charles L. Howard; Sheila A. Huddleston; John E. Kreitler; Katherine J. Lambert; John H. Lawrence, Jr.; Alan E. Lieberman; Alex Lloyd; Julie A. Manning; Richard A. Mills, Jr.; Thomas B. Mooney; Scott L. Murphy; Saranne P. Murray; Richard D. Nicholson; Mark K. Ostrowski; Howard L. Pierce; William G. Rock; Paul D. Sanson; Louis B. Schatz; James C. Schulwolf; Theodore M. Space; Gary S. Starr; Janet S. Stulting; Thomas F. Tresselt; Natalie W. Welsh; John E. Wertam; Marcus D. Wilkinson; Joseph P. Williams; Robert L. Wyld; Linda L. Yoder. Counsel: Maureen J. Anderson; Mary Jo Blain Andrews; Thomas A. Klee; Jennifer Brown Mailly; Arnold K. Shimelman; Gerald P. Stergio. Associates: Jennifer L. Adamy; Catherine M. Brennan (Stamford Office); James J. Carroll; Raymond J. Casella; Anne E. K. Dacey; Catherine M. Esposito; Patrick Fahey; Julie C. Fay (Not admitted in CT); Danielle P. Ferrucci; Tammi Tuve Flowers (Not admitted in CT); Ross H. Garber; Lisa Denise Gladke; Gregg P. Goumas; Bryon W. Harmon; Jill Cutler Hodgman; Jeffrey W. Hussey; Catherine Franklin Intravia; Gabriel J. Jiran (Not admitted in CT); Amy R. Kirschbaum; Sharon Sloan Koziol; Kathleen M. LaManna; Christopher R. LaSaracina; Anne H. Littlefield; Alexandra M. McHugh; Lisa Banatoski Mehta; Craig S. Meuser; Maya N. Perry; Jason M. Price; Gian-Matthew Ranelli; Jeri E. Reutenauer; Jose M Rojas; Morgan P. Rueckert; Robert C. Scott; Stephen M. Sedor; Amy E. Souchuns; Karen Therese Staib; Kara Lawson Van Ausdall; Jennifer C. Vickery; Marianne Monti Wallace; Henry J. Zaccardi. Of Counsel: George C. Jepsen (Stamford Office); Charles B. Milliken; Robert L. Rosensweig.
General Practice. Banking, Corporation, Tax, Antitrust, Commercial Finance, Securities, Venture Capital, Labor and Employment, Health Care, Environmental, Pension and Employee Benefits, Estate Planning, Estate Settlement, Trust Administration, Real Estate, Municipal Law, Franchise, Dealer and Distributor Litigation. Trials in all Courts.
Representative Clients: Aetna Casualty & Surety Co.; Agri-Mark, Inc.; Anthem Blue Cross & Blue Shield of Connecticut.; City of Hartford; Hartford Hospital; Stanadyne, Inc.; United Technologies Corp.; Yankee Energy System, Inc.
Greenwich, Connecticut Office: 43 Arch Street. Telephone: 203-869-6222.
Lakeville, Connecticut Office: 12 Porter Street, P.O. Box 1809. Telephone: 203-435-2539.
Stamford, Connecticut Office: One Landmark Square. Telephone: 203-324-8100.
See Professional Biographies, HARTFORD, CONNECTICUT

Shubinski, Carol A. ... '— '95 C.228 A.B. L.910 J.D. [Ⓐ Robinson&C.]
Shulansky, Ralph M., (AV) '29 '52 C.299 A.B. L.188 LL.B.
Sr. V.P., Conn. Bk. & Tr. Co.
Shulman, James H., (AV) ... '46 '71 C&L.273 B.A., J.D. [Murtha C.] (⊙Boston, MA)
*PRACTICE AREAS: Commercial Real Estate Law; Zoning and Land Planning.
Shweky, Evan Y. ... '64 '90 C.860 B.A. L.184 J.D. 94 Hungerford St.
Sicilian, James, (AV) ... '56 '81 C.105 B.A. L.184 J.D. [Day,B.&H.]
*PRACTICE AREAS: Antitrust; Commercial Litigation; Technology and Intellectual Property - Litigation.
Sicklick, Jay E. ... '— '95 282 Washington Street
Siczewicz, Ann M., (BV) ... '55 '80 C&L.184 B.A., J.D. [Ⓒ Bingham D.]
Siegel, David H. ... '59 '87 C.588 B.S. L.990 J.D. [Polinsky,S.S.&P.]
*PRACTICE AREAS: Aviation Accidents; International Aviation; Personal Injury; Wrongful Death; Catastrophic Injury.
Siegel, Howard L., (AV) ... '— '74 C.453 B.S. L.94 J.D. [Brown,R.F.&G.]
*PRACTICE AREAS: Banking Law; Finance; Commercial Lending; Creditors Rights in Bankruptcy.
Siegel, Jay S., (AV) ... '29 '55 C&L.569 A.B., J.D. [Ⓒ Siegel,O.S.&Z.]
Siegel, Robert G., (AV) ... '50 '76 C.918 B.A. L.188 J.D. [Day,B.&H.]
*PRACTICE AREAS: Health Care; Tax; Mergers and Acquisitions; Closely Held Businesses.

Siegel, O'Connor, Schiff & Zangari, P.C., (AV)
150 Trumbull Street, 06103 ⊙
Telephone: 860-727-8900 Telecopier: 860-527-5131
Email: first initial last name @soszlaw.com URL: http://www.soszlaw.com
Christine A. Barker (Resident, New Haven, Connecticut Office); John W. Beck (Resident); Gregory J. Bezz (Resident); Robert F. Cohn (Resident, New Haven, Connecticut Office); Hugh W. Cuthbertson (Resident, New Haven, Connecticut Office); Frederick L. Dorsey (Resident, New Haven, Connecticut Office); Glenn A. Duhl (Resident); Nicholas J. Grello, Jr. (Resident); Peter D. Hershman (Resident, New Haven, Connecticut Office); Peter A. Janus (Resident); George J. Kelly, Jr. (Resident, New Haven, Connecticut Office); Richard D. O'Connor (Resident); Edward F. O'Donnell, Jr. (Resident); Robert J. Percy (Resident); Donald W. Strickland (Resident); Mario J. Zangari (Resident, New Haven, Connecticut Office). Of Counsel: Robert W. Blythe (Resident, New Haven, Connecticut Office); Jay S. Siegel (Resident);—Jody Pagano Benbow (Resident, New Haven, Connecticut Office); Shawn P. Coyne (Resident); Ana Isabel DeMoura (Resident); Kevin J. Diadamo (Resident, New Haven, Connecticut Office); Paul H. Gamache (Resident); Daniel P. Murphy (Resident, New Haven, Connecticut Office); John J. O'Connell.
Labor Relations and Employment Law representing management in the private and public sectors, including related Litigation in Federal and State Courts, Tax Law, Education Law, Municipal Law, Commercial Law, Corporate Law, Estate Planning and Estate Administration Matters.
New Haven, Connecticut Office: 171 Orange Street, P.O. Drawer 906. Telephone: 203-789-0001. Telecopier: 203-782-2766.
See Professional Biographies, HARTFORD, CONNECTICUT

Silliman, John E., (AV) ....'34 '59 C.976 B.A. L.178 LL.B. 185 Asylum St.
Silva, M. Paula ....'72 '00 C.1033 B.S. L.1048 J.D. [[A] Regnier,T.C.&E.]
*PRACTICE AREAS: General Practice; Trial Practice; Insurance; Toxic Torts; Products Liability.
Silva, Robert D., (BV) ....'64 '90 C.184 B.S. L.1029 J.D [O'Brien,T.&Y.]
*PRACTICE AREAS: Civil Litigation; Medical Malpractice Defense; Products Liability Defense.

Silver, Alan B., LLC, Law Offices of
(See Wethersfield)

Silver, Golub & Teitell LLP
(See Stamford)

Silvers, Bruce C., (BV) ....'61 '86 C.855 B.A. L.245 J.D. [Bingham D.]
*PRACTICE AREAS: Banking; Finance and Debt Restructuring; Corporate and Securities Law; Public Finance; Project Finance.
Silverstone, David, (AV) ....'46 '76 C.401 B.A. L.178 J.D. [Silverstone&K.]
Silverstone & Koontz, P.C., (AV) .... 1 Cityplace, 35th Fl.
Silvester, George A. ....'23 '52 C&L.184 B.A., LL.B. 72 Russ St.‡

Silvester & Daly, (AV)
72 Russ Street, 06106
Telephone: Telephone: 860-278-2650 Fax: 860-727-9243
Edward J. Daly, Jr.; Robert F. Kappes. Of Counsel: Frank J. Szilagyi.
General Insurance Defense, Fire, Arson and Fraud Matters, Automobile Liability, Medical and Legal Malpractice Defense, Workers' Compensation, Construction Litigation, Labor Law and Relations, Personal Injury, Residential and Commercial Real Estate, Civil and Criminal Trials in all Courts.
See Professional Biographies, HARTFORD, CONNECTICUT

Simard, Joanne M. '60 '86 C.1044 B.A. L.184 J.D.
Assoc. Coun., The Travelers Ins. Co.
Simmers, Walter W., (BV) ....'48 '79 C.659 B.S.M.E. L.893 J.D. [Pepe&H.]
*PRACTICE AREAS: Corporate; Corporate Finance; Securities.
Simon, Melvin A., (BV) ....'56 '83 C.829 B.A. L.978 J.D. [Cohn B.&S.]
*PRACTICE AREAS: Commercial Litigation; Bankruptcy; Construction Litigation; Lender Liability Defense; Workouts.
Simpson, Douglas K. '48 '75 C.197 A.B. L.184 J.D.
Coun., Hartford Financial Services Group, Inc.
Simpson, Robert R. ....'68 '93 C.94 B.A. L.930 J.D. [Updike,K.&S.]
*PRACTICE AREAS: Complex Litigation; Professional Liability Defense; Employment Litigation.
Sinatro, Stephen J., (BV) '64 '89
C.184 B.A. L.1048 J.D. [O'Connell,F.&A.] (⊙West Hartford)
*PRACTICE AREAS: Commercial Litigation; Domestic Law.
Singer, Lewis A. '43 '69 C&L.184 B.S.Pharm., J.D.
Vice President, Office of Corporate Compliance, Phoenix Home Life Mutual Insurance Company
Sinofsky, Darren E. ....'— '95 C.94 B.A. L.1048 J.D. [[A] Morrison,M.&M.]
Sistare, Janet P., (BV) ....'63 '88 C.454 B.A. L.1048 J.D. [Moller,P.&O.]
Sitarz, John W., (AV) ....'47 '72 C.918 B.A. L.1294 J.D. [Cooney,S.&D.]
Sitkowski, Robert J. ....'— '95 C.339 B.Arch. L.665 J.D. [[A] Robinson&C.]

Skelley Rottner P.C., (AV) [BB]
P.O. Box 340890, 06134-0890
Telephone: 860-561-7077 Telecopier: 860-561-7088
Email: postmaster@skelleyrottner.com URL: http://www.skelleyrottner.com
Joseph F. Skelley, Jr. (1927-1995); Joel J. Rottner; Susan L. Miller; James G. Geanuracos; Randall M. Hayes; Kirby G. Huget; Matthew Dallas Gordon; Carl F. Yeich;—Laura Ondrush. Of Counsel: Susan E. Malliet.
Trials in all Courts. Casualty Insurance, Fire and Property Insurance, Insurance Fraud, Bad Faith and Unfair Insurance Practice Claims, Insurance Coverage, Plaintiff's Personal Injury Litigation, Professional Liability, Environmental Law, Liquor Liability, Products Liability and Toxic Tort Litigation, Subrogation and Recovery, Commercial Litigation.
References: Fleet Bank; Liberty Bank.
See Professional Biographies, HARTFORD, CONNECTICUT

Sklar, Claudia M., (BV) ....'52 '77 C.4 B.A. L.184 J.D. [O'Connell,F.&A.]
*PRACTICE AREAS: Civil Litigation; Commercial Litigation; Real Estate; Bankruptcy; Foreclosure Law.
Sklarz, Jeffrey M. .... '74 '99 C.164 B.A. L.184 J.D. [[A] Moukawsher&W.] ⊙
*PRACTICE AREAS: ERISA; Personal Injury; Employment Law; Civil Litigation; Taxation.
Slatas, Reed A. ....'66 '91 C.597 B.S. L.823 J.D. [[A] Halloran&S.]
*PRACTICE AREAS: Contract Law; Collection Law; Foreclosures; Premises Liability; Homeowners Liability.
Slater, Deborah R., (BV) ....'57 '85 C.860 B.A. L.818 J.D. Asst. U.S. Atty.
Slifka, R. Scott .... '74 '99 C&L.273 B.A., J.D. [[A] Updike,K.&S.]
*PRACTICE AREAS: Design/Construction; Professional Defense Law.
Slitt, Wayne L. .... '47 '72 C.918 B.A. L.184 J.D. Coun., Aetna Inc.
*RESPONSIBILITIES: Employment Law and Litigation.
Small, Andrew B. ....'59 '87 C.860 B.S. L.436 J.D. [McCarthy S.&Assoc.] ⊙
Small, Philip M., (AV) ....'— '78 C.659 A.B. L.273 J.D. [Brown,R.F.&G.]
*PRACTICE AREAS: Environmental; Energy; Public Utilities; Administrative Law.
Smalley, Vi R. ....'68 '94 C.788 A.B. L.306 J.D. [[A] Bingham D.]
Smart, James R. ....'67 '97 C.647 A.B. L.309 J.D. [Cowdery,E.&M.]
*PRACTICE AREAS: Commercial Litigation; White Collar Defense; Personal Injury; Appellate Practice.
Smiley, Michael S. ....'53 '77 C.1036 B.A. L.569 J.D. The Travelers Ins. Co.
Smith, Brian R., (BV) ....'— '85 C.165 B.A. L.188 J.D. [Robinson&C.]
*PRACTICE AREAS: Zoning, Planning and Land Use; Real Estate; Litigation.
Smith, Elizabeth M. ....'60 '98 C.497 B.S. L.184 J.D. [[A] Tyler C.&A.]
Smith, Marianne DuVal ......'54 '79 C&L.184 B.A., J.D. Staff Atty., State Ethics Comm.
Smith, Michael J. '67 '92 C.676 B.A. L.1252 J.D.
[[C] Bonner K.T.&C.] (⊙Boston, MA; Providence, RI)
Smith, R. Jeffrey, (AV) ....'53 '78 C.228 B.A. L.276 J.D. [Bingham D.]
*PRACTICE AREAS: Real Estate Finance; Commercial Finance; Workouts.
Smith, Richard S., Jr., (AV) ....'59 '84 C&L.228 A.B., J.D. [Murtha C.]
*PRACTICE AREAS: Corporate Law; Securities Law; Mergers and Acquisitions; Divestitures.
Smith, Robert H., Jr., (AV) ....'— '69 C.309 B.A. L.94 LL.B. [Robinson&C.]
*PRACTICE AREAS: Wills; Probate; Trusts and Estates; Taxation.
Smith, Robert S. ......'33 '67 C.454 B.S.M.E. L.569 J.D. [[A] Alix,Y.&R.] (See Pat. Sect.)
*PRACTICE AREAS: Patent Law; Trademark Law; Copyright Law; Trade Secrets Law; Computer Law.
Smith, Thomas G. ......'56 '82 C.1021 B.A. L.1048 J.D. Asst. Reporter of Jud. Decisions
Smith, W. Richard, Jr., (BV) ....'— '83 C.1102 B.S. L.823 J.D. [Robinson&C.]
*PRACTICE AREAS: Environmental Law; Aquaculture and Coastal Development Projects.
Smits, Anthony J. ....'67 '94 C&L.999 B.Comm, LL.B. [[A] Bingham D.]
*PRACTICE AREAS: Insolvency; Bankruptcy; Workouts.
Smoragiewicz, Edward R., (BV) ....'37 '63 C&L.184 B.A., LL.B. [Cardwell,C.&S.]
Smyth, Gerard A., (AV) ....'45 '75 C.1030 B.A. L.184 J.D. Chf. Pub. Def.
Snow, Christopher S. ....'71 '98 C.690 B.S. L.1252 J.D. [[A] Bingham D.]
*PRACTICE AREAS: Insolvency; Restructured Finance; Corporate Finance; Bankruptcy.
Sobol, Alan J., (BV) ....'48 '74 C.446 B.A. L.7 J.D. [O'Connell,F.&A.]
*PRACTICE AREAS: Litigation; Construction Law; Criminal Law.
Sochacki, Christopher J. ....'71 '98 C.93 B.A. L.1252 J.D. [[A] Cramer,A.&F.]
*PRACTICE AREAS: Insurance Defense; Products Liability; Medical Malpractice; Civil Litigation.
Soeder, Lisa P., (AV) ....'58 '84 C.1044 B.A. L.602 J.D. [Soeder&Assoc.]
*PRACTICE AREAS: Municipal Finance; Tax; Business Development.

Soeder & Associates, L.L.C., (AV)
241 Asylum Street Suite 700, 06103
Telephone: 860-246-1600 Fax: 860-246-1700
Email: lsoeder@soeder-associates.com URL: http://www.soeder-associates.com
Lisa P. Soeder. Of Counsel: Charles D. Katz (Not admitted in CT).
Municipal Finance, Business Development, Federal Tax Law.
See Professional Biographies, HARTFORD, CONNECTICUT

Sohl, Charles E. '45 '76
C.223 B.S.M.E. L.184 J.D. [[C] McCormick,P.&H.] (See Pat. Sect.) ⊙
*PRACTICE AREAS: Intellectual Property Law; Business Law.
Solomson, Stephen H., (BV) ....'48 '74 C.676 B.A. L.184 J.D. [O'Connell,F.&A.]
*PRACTICE AREAS: Insurance Litigation; Commercial Litigation; Securities Law; Criminal Defense.
Sommaruga, Mark J. ....'66 '91 C.855 B.A. L.306 J.D. 646 Prospect Ave.
Sorokin, Peter S., (BV) ....'51 '76 C.696 B.A. L.94 J.D. [Rogin,N.C.L.&H.]
*PRACTICE AREAS: Real Estate; Commercial Leasing.
Souchuns, Amy E. ....'74 '99 C.321 B.A. L.180 J.D. [[A] Shipman&G.]
*PRACTICE AREAS: Land Use; Environmental Law.
Souliotis, George ....'58 '89 C.184 B.A. L.1048 J.D. Assoc. Coun., The Travelers Ins. Co.
Soulsby, Peter W., (BV) ....'54 '81 C&L.184 B.A., J.D. [[A] Butler N.&G.]
Space, Theodore M., (AV) ....'38 '66 C.309 A.B. L.976 LL.B. [Shipman&G.]
*PRACTICE AREAS: Administrative Law; Complex Litigation; Health Care Law; Real Estate Law; Copyright Law.
Spada, Arthur L. ....'32 '57 C.918 B.A. L.184 95 Washington
Spadoni, Charles B., (AV) '48 '77 C.821 B.A. L.893 J.D.
V.P. & Gen. Coun., Triumph Capital Grp., Inc
Spagnoli, Michael D. '48 '77 C.28 B.S. L.1048 J.D.
Admin. Hearings Atty., Dept. of Consumer Protec.
Spalding, Maria S. .....'55 '87 C.703 B.S.N. L.1029 J.D. [Updike,K.&S.] (⊙New Haven)
*PRACTICE AREAS: Product Liability; Professional Defense.
Sparagna, Marialta Z. ....'60 '00 C.918 B.A. L.1048 J.D. [[A] Bingham D.]
*PRACTICE AREAS: Real Estate; Corporate Finance; Insolvency.
Spaulding-Ruddell, Janet A., (BV) ....'— '84 C.860 B.A. L.94 J.D. Asst. Atty. Gen.
Spear, H. Dyke N., Jr., (BV) ....'35 '60 C.855 B.A. L.184 J.D. 10 Trumbull St.
Spearman, Elicia Pegues ....'— '91 C.914 B.A. L.930 J.D. Coun., Aetna Inc.
*RESPONSIBILITIES: Labor and Employment Litigation; Health Care Law.
Spegele, Janet C. ....'42 '84 C.339 B.A. L.184 J.D. V.P., Conn. Bus. & Indus. Assn.
Spellacy, Bourke G., (AV) ....'37 '61 C.674 A.B. L.976 J.D. [Updike,K.&S.]
*PRACTICE AREAS: Administrative Law; Appellate Law; Business Law; Commercial Litigation; Legislative Representation.
Sperber, Jerome M. '34 '61 C.563 B.B.A. L.569 LL.B.
(adm. in NY; not adm. in CT) One American Row
Spier, Alan R., (AV) ....'— '64 C&L.309 A.B., J.D. [Robinson&C.]
*PRACTICE AREAS: Corporate Law; Securities; Banking Law; Business Law.
Spinella, A. Paul, (BV) ....'51 '78 C.855 B.S. L.184 J.D. [Spinella&J.]
Spinella, Edward F., (AV) ....'52 '78 C.321 B.A. L.184 J.D. [Reid&R.]
*PRACTICE AREAS: Criminal Law; Civil Litigation; Health Care.
Spinella & Jaffe, P.C., (BV) ....City Place II 185 Asylum Street
Spineti, Daniel C. ....'64 '92 C.184 B.A. L.1048 J.D. [[A] Miniter&Assoc.]
*PRACTICE AREAS: Real Estate; Litigation; Family Law; Corporate Law; Criminal Law.
Sponzo, Maurice J. ....'14 '40 C.321 A.B. L.306 LL.B. Supr. Ct. J.
Sponzo, Richard T., (BV) ....'46 '73 C.321 A.B. L.276 J.D. Asst. Atty. Gen.
Springer, Felix J., (AV) ....'46 '79 C.31 B.A. L.184 LL.B. [Day,B.&H.]
*PRACTICE AREAS: Employment Law; Employment Litigation.
Springer, George C., Jr., (CV) ....'63 '88 C&L.184 B.A., J.D. [[A] Miniter&Assoc.]
*PRACTICE AREAS: Civil Rights; Employment; Wrongful Termination; Domestic Relations; Workers Compensation.
Sprouls, Joseph W. '50 '76 C.276 B.A. L.776 J.D.
(adm. in NJ; not adm. in CT) Coun., The Travelers Ins. Co.
Squatrito, Dominic J. ....'39 '66 C.918 B.A. L.976 LL.B. U.S. Dist. J.
Stackhouse, Martin E. '43 '68 C.197 A.B. L.94 LL.B.
(adm. in MA; not adm. in CT) Govt. Rels. Offr., Conn. Mut. Life Ins. Co.
Stafstrom, John F., Jr., (AV) '56 '81 C.321 B.A. L.184 J.D.
[Pullman&C.] (⊙Bridgeport)
*PRACTICE AREAS: Public Finance; Corporate Law; Banking Law; Commercial Law.
Staib, Karen Therese ....'72 '98 C.197 B.A. L.306 J.D. [[A] Shipman&G.]
*PRACTICE AREAS: Intellectual Property.
Staley, Edmund J. '43 '70 C.321 A.B. L.262 J.D.
(adm. in NY; not adm. in CT) V.P., Fleet Bk., N.A.
Stamm, R. David '50 '75
C.855 A.B. L.902 J.D. Admin. Dir., Conn. Bar Examining Comm.
Stamper, Jayme E. ....'65 '00 C.1033 B.A L.184 J.D. [[A] Rome M.S.]
*PRACTICE AREAS: Civil Litigation; Family Law; Municipal Law.
Stapleton, Mark A. ....'52 '77 Chf., Off. of Leg. & Govt. Affrs., Dept. of Ed.‡
Stapleton, Susannah M. ....'72 '98 C.184 B.A. L.306 J.D. [[A] Bingham D.]
*PRACTICE AREAS: Commercial Real Estate; Finance.
Starble, Jonathan M. ....'70 '95 C.184 B.A. L.306 J.D. [[A] Rogin,N.C.L.&H.]
*PRACTICE AREAS: Commercial Litigation; Construction Litigation.
Staron, Courtney P. ....'75 '00 C.184 B.A. L.306 J.D. [[A] Brown,P.&S.]
*PRACTICE AREAS: Family Law; Special Education; Litigation.
Starr, Gary S., (BV) ....'50 '75 C.867 B.A. L.184 J.D. [Shipman&G.]
*PRACTICE AREAS: Employment Law; Litigation; Labor Law.
Steadman, R. Webb ....'59 '91 C.31 B.A. L.94 J.D. One American Row
Stearns, James C. '50 '77 C.197 A.B. L.276 J.D.
(adm. in DC; not adm. in CT) [Halloran&S.]
*PRACTICE AREAS: Administrative; Government Contracts; International Trade.
Steele, Philip L., (BV) ....'44 '81 C.31 B.A. L.184 J.D. 5 Linden Pl.
Steenburg, Thomas N., (BV) '49 '78 C.309 A.B. L.184 J.D.
V.P. & Coun., Phoenix Investment Partners, LTD.
Steigelfest, Jack G., (BV) ....'60 '84 C.401 B.S. L.184 J.D. [Howard,K.S.&F.]
*PRACTICE AREAS: Civil Litigation; Appeals; Insurance Coverage.
Steinberg, Joseph L. ....'28 '54 C.102 A.B. L.178 LL.B. Supr. Ct. J.

Steinmetz, Steven ....'65 '94 C.273 B.A. L.1338 J.D. [🄰 Day,B.&H.]
*PRACTICE AREAS: Energy Regulation; Electric Power; Powerpooling Contracts; Telecommunications Regulation; Gas Utility Regulation.

Stephan, George P. '33 '58 C&L.966 B.S., LL.B.
(adm. in WI; not adm. in CT) 185 Asylum St.

Stephen, Erin S. ....'72 '97 C.1021 B.S. L.982 J.D. [🄰 Day,B.&H.]
*PRACTICE AREAS: Intellectual Property; Computers and Software; Internet Law; Corporate Law; Technology and Science.

Stergio, Gerald P. ....'53 '93 C&L.184 B.A., J.D. [🄲 Shipman&G.]

Stevens, Alexandra B. ....'73 '99 C.299 A.B. L.306 J.D. [🄰 Cummings&L.]
*PRACTICE AREAS: Intellectual Property Litigation; Commercial Litigation; Probate Litigation.

Stevenson, John F. ....'55 '80 C.105 B.A. L.184 J.D. The Travelers Ins. Co.

Steverman, Benjamin W., Jr. .....'51 '76 C.645 B.A. L.665 J.D. Travelers Prop. Cas. Corp.

Stewart, Bonnie D., (BV) '62 '89
C.184 B.S. L.1218 J.D. Asso. Coun., Conn. Bus. & Indus. Assn.

Stewart, Catherine A. ....'50 '94 C.751 B.A. L.1252 J.D. [🄰 Morrison,M.&M.]
*PRACTICE AREAS: Insurance Defense; Appellate Practice; Employment Discrimination; Products Liability.

Stiebel, Michael S., (BV) ....'49 '75 C.1090 B.A. L.744 J.D. [MacDermid,R.&G.]
*PRACTICE AREAS: Real Property; Conveyancing; Leasing; Workouts; Communications.

Stillman, Robert J., (AV) ....'56 '82 C.976 B.A. L.309 J.D. Coun., Aetna Inc.
*RESPONSIBILITIES: Litigation; Business Counseling; Mergers and Acquisitions.

Stober, Fillis W. ....'49 '79 C&L.184 B.A., J.D. [Tyler C.&A.]
*PRACTICE AREAS: Bank Regulation; E-Commerce; ATM Networks; Bank Collections; Bank Fraud.

Stone, David C. ....'48 '81 C.93 A.B. L.184 J.D. St. Francis Hosp. & Med. Ctr.

Stone, Martha ....'48 '74 C.938 B.A. L.276 J.D. 65 Elizabeth St. Hartford

Storm, Christina M., (BV) ....'52 '78 C.706 B.A. L.564 J.D. [Byrne&S.]
*PRACTICE AREAS: Conflicts Resolution; Human Rights; International Law.

Stoughton, George D. ....'19 '50 C.855 B.S. L.06 LL.B. Trial Ref. J.

Stoughton, Paul H. D., (BV) '59 '86 C.732 B.A. L.1065 J.D.
241 Main Street 5th Floor, 06106
Telephone: 860-525-5529 Fax: 860-241-7744
Trials and Appeals. General Business Litigation, Negligence and Personal Injury, Probate Litigation, Labor and Employment Law.
See Professional Biographies, HARTFORD, CONNECTICUT

Strange, Margaret J., (BV) ....'63 '90 C.1303 B.A. L.818 J.D. [Jackson L.S.&K.]

Strapp, Christopher E. '64 '95 C.999 B.A. L.1048 J.D.
Atty., Travelers Insurance Company

Strasser, Kurt A. ....'47 '72 C&L.880 B.A., J.D. Univ. of Conn. Law Sch.

Streim, Eliot R., (BV) .....'57 '83 C.311 B.A. L.818 J.D. Coun., First Amer. Title Ins. Co.

Stretton, John G. ....'73 '98 C.93 B.A. L.94 J.D. [🄰 Updike,K.&S.] (⊙New Haven)
*PRACTICE AREAS: Civil Litigation; Professional Liability Defense; Employment Litigation; Personal Injury Defense; Insurance Coverage Defense.

Strickland, Donald W., (AV) ....'45 '73 C.434 B.A. L.184 J.D. [Siegel,O.S.&Z.]
*PRACTICE AREAS: Labor Law; Employment Law; Education Law; Municipal Law.

Strickland, Gary, (BV) ....'53 '86 C.1030 B.A. L.184 J.D. [🄰 Trantolo&T.]

Strniste, Peter E., Jr. ....'73 '99 C.1083 B.S. L.665 J.D. [🄰 Halloran&S.]
*PRACTICE AREAS: Construction Law; Fidelity and Surety; Commercial Litigation.

Strohmenger, Thomas C. '47 '72 C.262 B.A. L.724 J.D.
Coun., AETNA Inc. (⊙Hartford)

Strohmenger, Thomas C. '47 '72
C.262 B.A. L.724 J.D. V.P. & Coun., Aetna Inc. (⊙Hartford)
*RESPONSIBILITIES: Regulatory Affairs; Litigation.

Strom, Steven R., (BV) ....'50 '86 C.976 B.A. L.184 J.D. Asst. Atty. Gen.

Strother, John F. ....'42 '70 C.674 A.B. L.976 LL.B. [🄲 Rome M.S.]
*PRACTICE AREAS: Employee Benefits Law; ERISA; General Practice.

Stulting, Janet S., (AV) ....'48 '80 C&L.184 B.A., J.D. [Shipman&G.]
*PRACTICE AREAS: Trusts and Estates; Adoption; Assisted Reproduction Technology.

Sturgess, David E., (AV) ....'56 '81 C.184 B.S. L.228 J.D. [Updike,K.&S.]
*PRACTICE AREAS: Business Law; Commercial Lending; Human Service; Real Estate Leasing; Finance.

Stutman, Robert A. '63 '88 C.529 A.B. L.831 J.D.
(adm. in PA; not adm. in CT) [R.A.Stutman] ⊙

Stutman, Robert A., P.C., Law Offices of
1010 Weathersfield Avenue (⊙Cranbury, NJ; New York, NY; Fort Wash., PA)

Sucoll, Michael, (BV) ....'46 '71 C.222 B.A. L.184 J.D. 67 Russ St.

Sudarsky, Joseph S., (AV) ....'18 '42 C.197 A.B. L.976 LL.B. [Sudarsky&S.]

Sudarsky, Michael, (AV) ....'24 '50 C.976 B.A. L.178 LL.B. [🄲 Murtha C.]
*PRACTICE AREAS: Corporate Law; Mergers and Acquisitions Law; Estate and Trust Administration Law.

Sudarsky and Sudarsky, (AV) ....100 Constitution Plz.

Sukhdeo, Beatrice D. ....'74 '99 C.724 B.S. L.184 J.D. [Howd&L.]
*PRACTICE AREAS: Insurance Defense Litigation; Municipal Litigation.

Sullivan, Daniel F. ....'— '87 C&L.273 B.A., J.D. [Robinson&C.]
*PRACTICE AREAS: Insurance; Litigation.

Sullivan, James F. ....'63 '92 C.93 B.A. L.184 J.D. [Howard,K.S.&F.]
*PRACTICE AREAS: Products Liability; Personal Injury; Premises Liability; Professional Malpractice; Construction.

Sullivan, Kevin C. ....'— '93 C.1044 B.S. L.1019 J.D. [🄲 Robinson&C.]

Sullivan, Robert W., (BV) ....'44 '69 C.976 B.A. L.184 J.D. [🄲 Murtha C.]
*PRACTICE AREAS: Real Estate; Land Use; Construction; Financing.

Sullivan, Thomas C. '49 '75 C.93 B.A. L.128 J.D.
(adm. in DC; not adm. in CT) Sr. Coun., Advanced Sales, Conn. Mut. Life Ins. Co.

Sullivan, Thomas N., (AV) ....'44 '72 C.1030 B.A. L.184 J.D. [Sullivan,S.C.&C.]

Sullivan, Schoen, Campane & Connon, L.L.C., (AV) ....646 Prospect Ave.

Summa & Ryan, P.C.
(See Waterbury)

Sussman, Eric L. ....'73 '98 C.299 B.A. L.188 J.D. [🄰 Day,B.&H.]
*PRACTICE AREAS: Employment Law; Employment Litigation; Commercial Litigation.

Sussman, Mark R., (BV) ....'52 '77 C.860 B.S. L.659 J.D. [Murtha C.]
*PRACTICE AREAS: Environmental Law.

Sussman, Nancy Rubin, (BV) ....'54 '90 C.273 B.A. L.184 J.D. Asst. Atty. Gen.

Swain, Eugene K., (AV) ....'47 '77 C.446 B.A. L.280 J.D. [RisCassi&D.]
*PRACTICE AREAS: Personal Injury; Products Liability; Professional Malpractice.

Swan, Patty G. ....'69 '94 C.184 B.A. L.1048 J.D. [Gordon,M.&F.]
*PRACTICE AREAS: Insurance Defense; Litigation; Civil Litigation; Insurance Coverage Litigation; Employment Law.

Sweeney, John J. '57 '83 C.36 B.S. L.1040 J.D.
(adm. in NY; not adm. in CT) Actna Intl. Inc.

Sweeney, Joseph T., (AV) ....'37 '62 C.321 A.B. L.276 J.D. [Halloran&S.]
*PRACTICE AREAS: Professional Liability Litigation; Clergy Malpractice; Clergy Sexual Misconduct; Insurance Litigation.

Sweeney, Sean E., (BV) ....'58 '83 C.1200 B.A. L.1048 J.D. [🄰 Hunt L.C.&J.]

Sweeney, Stephanie J. ....'74 '99 C.966 B.S. L.1252 J.D. [🄰 Halloran&S.]
*PRACTICE AREAS: Motor Vehicle Torts; Premises Liability.

Swirsky, Gerald R., (AV) ....'41 '66 C.976 B.A. L.184 LL.B. [Gordon,M.&F.]
*PRACTICE AREAS: Civil Litigation; Insurance Law; Legal Malpractice Defense; Medical Malpractice Defense; Dental Malpractice Defense.

Sylvester, Craig L., (AV) ....'51 '81 C.30 A.B. L.184 J.D. [Reid&R.]
*PRACTICE AREAS: Business Law; Corporate Law; Mergers and Acquisitions; Securities.

Sylvester, Kathryn R. ....'68 '96 C.702 B.A. L.882 J.D. [🄰 Hunt L.C.&J.]
*PRACTICE AREAS: Real Estate; General Practice; Environmental Law.

Synodi, Christine S. ....'— '96 C.183 B.A. L.184 J.D. [🄰 McCarter&E.]
*PRACTICE AREAS: Products Liability; Toxic Torts; Civil Litigation.

Szerejko, James J., (AV) ....'48 '74 C.184 B.A. L.818 J.D. [Halloran&S.]
*PRACTICE AREAS: Insurance Litigation; Municipal Law; Civil Rights Litigation; Trade Associations.

Szilagyi, Frank J., (BV) ....'59 '90 C.184 B.S. L.1048 J.D. [🄲 Silvester&D.]

Taboada, Frank J. ....'63 '96 C.871 B.S. L.597 J.D. [🄰 Bingham D.]
*PRACTICE AREAS: Corporate; Mergers and Acquisitions; Finance.

Tagatac, Paul S. ....'65 '90 C&L.184 B.A., B.A. [Michelson,K.R.&B.]
*PRACTICE AREAS: Labor and Employment.

Taiman, Edward C., Jr., (BV) ....'56 '86 C.184 B.S. L.990 J.D. [Sabia&H.]
*PRACTICE AREAS: Bankruptcy Law; State and Federal Litigation.

Tait, Colin C. ....'32 '59 C.188 B.A. L.976 LL.B. Prof., Univ. of Conn. Sch. of Law

Tallaksen, James J. ....'57 '93 C.1103 B.B.A. L.285 J.D. One American Row

Tallberg, James N. ....'65 '96 C.1102 B.S. L.184 J.D. [🄰 Updike,K.&S.]
*PRACTICE AREAS: Civil Litigation; Municipal Liability Defense; Professional Liability Defense; Insurance Coverage Defense.

Tancredi, James J., (AV) ....'54 '79 C.321 B.A. L.184 J.D. [Day,B.&H.]
*PRACTICE AREAS: Bankruptcy; Commercial Litigation; Bankruptcy Counseling.

Tannenbaum, John O., (AV) ....'— '72 C.645 B.A. L.1009 J.D. [Robinson&C.]
*PRACTICE AREAS: Taxation.

Tanski, James M., (AV) ....'46 '76 C.870 B.S. L.184 J.D. [O'Brien,T.&Y.]
*PRACTICE AREAS: Medical Malpractice Defense; Health Care Law; Product Liability Defense; Civil Trial Practice; Insurance Defense Law.

Tapogna, Anthony M., (BV) ....'10 '34 C&L.276 J.D. 550 Main St.

Taschner, Craig S., (BV) ....'62 '87 C.999 B.S. L.564 J.D. [Polivy&T.]
*PRACTICE AREAS: Commercial Law; Commercial Litigation; Creditors Rights; Bankruptcy; Workouts.

Taylor, Alexander C. ....'39 '70 C.223 B.S. L.1292 J.D. Sr. Atty., Aetna Life Ins. Co.

Taylor, Allan B., (AV) ....'48 '75 C&L.309 A.B., J.D. [Day,B.&H.]
*PRACTICE AREAS: Commercial Litigation; Insurance Litigation; Direct Liability and Casualty; Life Insurance and Annuities.

Taylor, Barbara A. ....'72 '99 C.401 B.S. L.184 J.D. [🄰 Reid&R.]
*PRACTICE AREAS: Probate; Trusts and Estates.

Taylor, Carl E., (BV) ....'56 '81 C.918 B.A. L.184 J.D. Sr. Asst. States Atty.

Taylor, Michael S. ....'68 '94 C&L.184 B.A., J.D. [Horton,S.&C.]
*PRACTICE AREAS: State and Federal Appellate Litigation; Insurance Law; Insurance Defense; Civil Litigation; Product Liability.

Taylor, Robert M., III, (AV) ....'54 '80 C.184 B.S. L.1048 J.D. [Day,B.&H.]
*PRACTICE AREAS: Banking; Insurance Regulation and Proceedings; Securities Law.

Taylor, Susan E. ....'71 '99 C.431 B.S. L.1252 J.D. [🄰 Tyler C.&A.] (⊙New Haven)

Tedford, Frederick B., (BV) '47 '72
C.184 B.A. L.818 J.D. [Danaher,T.L.&N.] (⊙Westport)

Tedford, Kenneth N., (BV) ....'43 '68 C.872 B.A. L.184 LL.B. Asst. Atty. Gen.

Tedone, Joseph, (BV) '55 '80
C.708 B.A. L.184 J.D. Coun., Phoenix Home Life Mut. Ins. Co.
*RESPONSIBILITIES: Litigation.

Teed, David M., (AV) ....'54 '79 C&L.184 B.A., J.D. Asst. Atty. Gen.

Teeuwissen, Peter A. ....'49 '85 C.477 B.A. L.184 J.D. State Dept. of Rev. Servs.

Tegeler, Philip Dean ....'55 '84 C.309 B.A. L.178 J.D. 32 Grand St.

Teitelman, Robert B., (BV) ....'59 '84 C.976 B.A. L.94 J.D. Asst. Atty. Gen.

Tellerine, Philip J. ....'56 '82 C.1350 B.A. L.809 J.D. [🄲 Murtha C.]
*PRACTICE AREAS: Trusts and Estates; Closely Held Business Law; Federal Taxation.

Temkin, Bruce G., (BV) ....'52 '76 C.860 B.A. L.245 J.D. 100 Pearl St., 14th Fl.

Terry, Linda M. ....'49 '79 C.1033 B.S. L.184 J.D. Sr. Coun., CIGNA Corp.

Testone, Michael G. '59 '85
C.1156 B.S. L.831 J.D. V.P., The Hartford Financial Servs. Grp.

Thacher, Alexander C. ....'75 '00 C.93 B.A. L.306 Arthur Andersen, LLP

Thomas, Calvert '16 '40
C.902 B.S. L.446 LL.B. Chmn. of the Bd., Thomas Cadillac, Inc.‡

Thomas, Douglas M. '52 '77
C&L.902 B.A., J.D. V.P. & Gen. Mgr., Thomas Cadillac, Inc.

Thomas, James E., (BV) ....'52 '77 C.829 B.A. L.1048 J.D. Off. of State's Atty.

Thomen, Jeffrey M. ....'— '98 C.1030 B.A. L.776 J.D. [🄰 Robinson&C.]

Thompson, Alvin W. ....'53 '79 C.674 B.A. L.976 J.D. U.S. Dist. J.

Thompson, Catherine M. ....'44 '76 C.999 B.A. L.912 J.D. [Sullivan,S.C.&C.]

Thompson, James A., Jr., (AV) ......'45 '74 C.659 B.A. L.273 J.D. [LeBoeuf,L.G.&M.]
*PRACTICE AREAS: Environmental; Health and Safety Law.

Thompson, Mark G. ....'66 '95 C.174 B.A. L.306 J.D. 1 American Row

Tibbetts, Stephanie P. ....'70 '97 C.128 B.A. L.990 J.D. [🄰 Noble,Y.&O.]
*PRACTICE AREAS: Insurance Defense.

Tichy, Karen ....'53 '84 C.1029 B.A. L.831 J.D. Sr. Legis. Atty., Gen. Assembly

Tindall, Alphonso E., Jr., (AVⓉ) '55 '85
C.747 B.A. L.184 J.D. [Nixon P.] (⊙New York, NY)

Tindall, Jennifer ....'71 '97 C.518 B.A. L.259 J.D. [🄰 Jackson L.S.&K.]
*PRACTICE AREAS: Employment Law.

Tinley, Nastri, Renehan & Dost, LLP
(See Waterbury)

Tisdall, Patricia A. ....'— '93 C.696 B.A. L.767 J.D. [🄰 Morrison,M.&M.]
*PRACTICE AREAS: Civil Litigation Defense.

Titus, Lisa K. ....'71 '96 C.105 B.A. L.306 J.D. [Howd&L.]
*PRACTICE AREAS: Insurance Defense; Municipal Litigation.

Tobin, Rhonda J., (BV) ....'— '90 C&L.228 B.A., J.D. [🄲 Robinson&C.]
*PRACTICE AREAS: Professional Liability; Insurance; Litigation.

Tobin, Robert D., (AV) ....'42 '68 C&L.93 B.A., J.D. [Tobin,C.O'R.&S.] ⊙
*PRACTICE AREAS: Commercial Law; Litigation; Real Estate; Zoning; Administrative Law.

Tobin, Carberry, O'Malley, Riley & Selinger, P.C., (AV)
3rd Floor, 330 Main Street, 06106 ⊙
Telephone: 860-541-6438 Fax: 860-541-6484
Email: govrelations@tcors.com
Robert D. Tobin; Glenn T. Carberry; Joseph J. Selinger, Jr.
Government Relations, General Civil and Criminal Practice, Trials and Appeals in all Courts, Administrative Law, Banking and Commercial Law, Commercial Real Estate, Contract Law, Employment Law, Public Finance, Health Care Law, Land Use Law, Personal Injury, Product Liability, Estate Planning and Probate, Real Estate Law, Sports Law, Federal, State and Local Tax Law.
New London, Connecticut Office: 43 Broad Street, P.O. Box 58, 06320. Telephone: 860-447-0335. Fax: 860-442-3469.
See Professional Biographies, HARTFORD, CONNECTICUT

Tobis, Justine R. ....'51 '92 C.829 B.F.A. L.1048 J.D. [🄰 Michelson,K.R.&B.]
*PRACTICE AREAS: Corporate Law; Real Estate; Workers' Compensation; Personal Injury.

Todoroff, Christopher M. ....'62 '88 C.705 B.A. L.188 J.D. Coun., Aetna Inc.
*RESPONSIBILITIES: Corporate; Finance; Mergers and Acquisitions; General Securities and Corporate.

Tomeo, Richard W., (AV) ....'— '66 C&L.184 B.A., J.D. [Robinson&C.]
*PRACTICE AREAS: Taxation.

Tondro, Helle S. ....'41 '81 C.112 A.B. L.184 J.D. Coun., ITT Hartford Ins. Grp.

Tondro, Terry J. .....'38 '68 C.188 A.B. L.569 LL.B. Prof., Univ. of Conn. School of Law

Topodas, Jonathan M. ....'46 '74 C.903 B.A. L.802 J.D. V.P. & Coun., Aetna Inc.
*RESPONSIBILITIES: Federal Government Relations.

Toro, Amalia M., (BV) ....'20 '44 C.184 B.A. L.976 J.D. 234 Pearl St.

Tougas, Maria K., (BV) .... '63 '89 C.95 A.B. L.1048 J.D. [Berman&S.]
*PRACTICE AREAS: Bankruptcy; Commercial Litigation; Creditors Rights.
Towbin, Rachel Reich .... '52 '81 C.188 B.S. L.184 J.D. Dept. of Envir. Protection
Trachsel, William H., (AV) '43 '71 C.260 B.S. L.184 J.D.
Senior Vice President, Secretary & Gen. Coun., United Technologies Corp.
Trantolo & Trantolo, P.C. ....50 Russ St.
Tresselt, Thomas F., (AV) .... '43 '68 C.976 B.A. L.477 J.D. [Shipman&G.]
*PRACTICE AREAS: Antitrust and Trade Regulation Law; Corporate Law; Business Law; Corporate Trust Law.
Triggs, Claudia J. ......'62 '88 C.597 B.A. L.306 J.D. Assoc. Coun., Conn. Nat. Gas Corp.
Trostle, Patrick J. .... '66 '92 C.855 B.A. L.1194 J.D. [A Bingham D.]
*PRACTICE AREAS: Insolvency.
Troy, John F. .... '36 '64 C&L.184 A.B., LL.B. V.P., The Travelers Ins. Co.
Tucci, Theodore J., (BV) ....'— '82 C.951 B.A. L.930 J.D. [Robinson&C.]
*PRACTICE AREAS: Litigation; Health; Insurance.
Tucker, John Essex ....'63 '89 C.918 B.A. L.910 J.D. Asst. Atty. Gen.
Turco, Alfred A. ....'45 '69 C.262 B.A. L.184 J.D. [Pepe&H.]
*PRACTICE AREAS: ERISA; Insurance.
Turekian, Karla A. .... '66 '96 C.976 B.A. L.184 J.D. 1 American Row
Turner, Elvin D. '55 '81 C.976 B.A. L.309 J.D.
Mktg. Resch. Analyst, Conn. Mut. Life Ins. Co.
Turner, Eric V. '52 '81 C.1044 B.A. L.107 J.D.
(adm. in MA; not adm. in CT) Aetna Life Ins. Co.
Turner, Michelle I. '74 '00 C.30 B.A. L.880 J.D.
(adm. in CA; not adm. in CT) [A Day,B.&H.]
Tuttle, Seale W. '42 '73 C&L.188 B.S., J.D.
V.P., Gen. Coun. & Secy., Industrial Risk Insurers

Tyler Cooper & Alcorn, LLP, (AV) BR
CityPlace, 06103-3488 ⊙
Telephone: 860-725-6200 Telecopier: 860-278-3802
URL: http://www.tylercooper.com
Members of Firm: Ralph Gregory Elliot; Lewis Segal; William H. Champlin III; Robert J. Metzler II; William W. Bouton III; Thomas C. Clark; Mark V. Connolly; William S. Fish, Jr.; Kevin McCann; David J. Wiese; Fillis W. Stober; Thomas S. Marrion; Kevin G. Ferrigno; William F. Cummings; Glory Martyn Lena. Of Counsel: William S. Rogers; Roger E. Koontz. Counsel: Kurt W. Johnson; Barry M. Winnick. Resident Associates: James R. Byrne; Christopher Markham Haddad; Michael T. McCormack; Carol L. Loomis; Elizabeth M. Smith; Susan E. Taylor; Elizabeth K. Andrews; Paul Guggina.
Administrative Law, Alternative Dispute Resolution, Antitrust and Trade Regulation, Banking, Bankruptcy and Reorganization, Business Crimes, Business Organizations and Securities Law, Computer Law, Domestic Relations, Environmental Law, Financial Services, Franchising, Health Care, Immigration, Insurance Defense and Insurance Coverage Defense, Intellectual Property, Labor and Employment, Legislative Lawyering, Litigation, Media Law, Medical Malpractice Defense, Pension and Employee Benefits, Public Utilities, Real Estate, Taxation, Trusts and Estates and Workers' Compensation.
Representative Clients: Purolator Courier Corp.; American Society of Composers, Authors and Publishers (ASCAP); The Hartford Courant Co.; Sears, Roebuck & Co.; Shearson Lehman Brothers; Prudential Securities Inc.; Aetna Life and Casualty Co.; The Travelers Companies.
New Haven, Connecticut Office: 205 Church Street. Telephone: 203-784-8200. Telecopier: 203-789-2133.
Stamford, Connecticut Office: One Landmark Square. Telephone: 203-348-5555. Telecopier: 203-348-3875.
Greenwich, Connecticut Office: 675 Steamboat Road. Telephone: 203-869-2000. Telecopier: 203-869-2001.
Madison, Connecticut Office: 23 Woodland Road. Telephone: 203-318-3600. Telecopier: 203-218-3609.

See Professional Biographies, HARTFORD, CONNECTICUT

Tymann, Deirdre M. ....'65 '94 C.971 B.S.E.E. L.818 J.D. 1 American Row
Tymchenko, Tanya ....'— '00 C.1349 B.A. L.184 J.D. [A Bingham D.]
*PRACTICE AREAS: Litigation.
Tynan, Richard C., (AV) ....'47 '72 C.573 B.A. L.188 J.D. [Halloran&S.]
*PRACTICE AREAS: Medical Malpractice; Professional Liability; Civil Litigation; Alternative Dispute Resolution.
Tyrrell, Michael A. '46 '73 C.602 B.A. L.477 J.D.
Reg. Staff Coun., Travelers Property Casualty Co.
Ungaro, Michael P. ....'65 '98 C.184 B.A. L.306 J.D. [A Bingham D.]
*PRACTICE AREAS: Litigation; Insurance.

Updike, Kelly & Spellacy, P.C., (AV)
One State Street, P.O. Box 231277, 06123-1277 ⊙
Telephone: 860-548-2600 Cable Address: "Ukslaw." Fax: 860-548-2680
Email: Info@uks.com URL: http://www.uks.com
Stuart N. Updike (1904-1983); Peter G. Kelly; Bourke G. Spellacy; Thomas J. Shortell (1942-1997); Thomas W. DeMille; Paul L. McCormick; James H. Lloyd, III; John C. King; James M. Connor; R. Dial Parrott; David E. Sturgess; Mark J. Zimmermann; Charles J. Nicol; Richard S. Order; Hugh I. Manke; Katherine C. Callahan; Susan A. Hays; Robert J. Martino; John F. Wolter; Frank G. Usseglio; David J. Monz; Thomas A. Gugliotti (Certified in Commercial Bankruptcy Law by the American Board of Certification).; Edward J. Pontacoloni; Kerry R. Callahan; Donald W. Doeg; Maria S. Spalding; Kevin N. Reynolds; Robert M. DeCrescenzo; Bernard E. Jacques; Christopher L. Brigham; Donald R. Seifel, Jr.; Robert R. Simpson; Amy E. Alissi; R. Alisha Verdone; Rolan J. Young. Of Counsel: Ernest N. Abate; Douglas M. Costle (Not admitted in CT). Counsel: Michael P. Botelho; Karen Keefe Clark;—John J. Alissi; Edward C. Andrews, II; Laura Flynn Baldini; Irene E. Bassock; Dana Rene Baughns; Michel Bayonne; Courtney R. Blair; Michael J. Brandi; Heather Wilson Bucknam; Carrie J. Campion; Daniel R. Canavan; Todd E. Cusano; Richard M. Dighello, Jr.; Antonio E. Dos Santos; Thomas W. Edgington; Barbara A. Frederick; Paul N. Gilmore; Drew S. Graham; Suzanne E. Graves; Jennifer L. Groves; Robert Hicks; Kathleen A. Hudzikiewicz; Deborah L. Hutton; John B. Kennelly; Shea S. Kinney; Scott N. Koschwitz; Kate F. Kotsaftis; Gregg J. Lallier; Brad N. Mondschein; Robert Andrew Morgan; Timothy L. O'Keefe; Scott S. Orenstein; Craig Lyle Perra; Vanessa L. Ramirez; Russell F.A. Riviere; Joseph A. Rosenthal; R. Scott Slifka; John G. Stretton; James N. Tallberg; Amy L. Van Dyke; Corinna M. Warhurst.
Administrative Law, Appellate Law, Brownfields Redevelopment, Business Law, Commercial Lending and Banking, Commercial Litigation, Complex Litigation, Creditors' Rights and Bankruptcy, Criminal, Design/Construction Law, Electronic Commerce Law, Employment Based Immigration Law, Environmental Law, Franchise Law, Human Service Law, Insurance Coverage Defense, Insurance Defense Law, Labor and Employment Law, Legislative Representation, Personal Law, Probate Law, Product Liability Law, Professional Defense Law, Public Finance/Public Law, Real Estate Law, Taxation, Trusts and Estates and Utilities Law.
Representative Clients: Shawmut Bank; Design Professionals Insurance Corp.; The Travelers Insurance Co.; Westinghouse Electric Corp.; J. C. Penney Co.; State of Connecticut; Northeast Utilities (Public Utility); Dexter Corp.; United Technologies Corp.; Homart Development Co.
New Haven, Connecticut Office: 265 Church Street, 10th Floor. Telephone: 860-786-8300. Fax: 203-772-2037.
Stamford, Connecticut Office: 6 Landmark Square, Fourth Floor. Telephone: 203-359-5749. Fax: 203-359-5858.

See Professional Biographies, HARTFORD, CONNECTICUT

Urizar, Oscar ....'58 '96 C.112 B.A. L.306 J.D. [A Bingham D.]
Usseglio, Frank G., (BV) .... '61 '86 C.321 B.A. L.982 J.D. [Updike,K.&S.]
*PRACTICE AREAS: Product Liability; Design/Construction; Insurance Defense; Professional Defense; Personal Law.
Vacchelli, Robert F., (BV) ....'51 '77 C.321 A.B. L.818 J.D. Asst. Atty. Gen.
Valentovish, Lisa ....'67 '00 C.976 B.A. L.1252 J.D. [A Bingham D.]
*PRACTICE AREAS: Banking Law; Finance; Corporate Law.
Van Ausdall, Kara Lawson .... '73 '00 C.676 B.A. L.93 J.D. [A Shipman&G.]
*PRACTICE AREAS: Litigation.

Van Dyke, Amy L. .... '72 '99 C.529 B.A. L.1338 J.D. [A Updike,K.&S.]
*PRACTICE AREAS: Commercial Litigation; Professional Defense; Products Liability.
Van Kirk, Roger A., (AV) '32 '62
C.882 B.S.E.E. L.273 J.D. [⊡ Alix,Y.&R.] (See Pat. Sect.)
VanTassel, Janet L. '48 '77 C.349 B.S. L.818 J.D.
Exec. Dir., Legal Assistance Resource Ctr. of Conn., Inc.
Van Winkle, Dale .... '27 '56 C.823 A.B. L.477 J.D. 1 Financial Plz.
Varga, Mary Ann K. .... '55 '83 C.829 B.A. L.184 J.D. Coun., Aetna Inc.
Varian, Keith S. ....'76 '01 C.676 B.A. L.930 J.D. [A Day,B.&H.]
Varney, Steven W., (BV) .... '59 '85 C&L.184 B.A., J.D. [Brown,P.&S.] (⊙Glastonbury)
*PRACTICE AREAS: Litigation; Bankruptcy Law; Criminal Law; Appellate Practice.
Varunes, Anita M., (BV) ....'63 '89 C.518 B.A. L.1048 J.D. [Kenny,B.M.&M.]
*PRACTICE AREAS: Personal Injury; Workers' Compensation; Employment Law.
Varunes, Nicholas C. ....'65 '97 C.696 B.A. L.1048 J.D. [A Kenny,B.M.&M.]
*PRACTICE AREAS: Insurance Defense; Personal Injury; Real Estate.
Vasta, Philip A. .... '43 '69 C.276 A.B. L.309 J.D. ITT Hartford Ins. Grp.
Veley, Charles ....'43 '85 C.165 B.A. L.1029 J.D. 222 N. Beacon St.
Velez, Rafael, (CV) ....'50 '80 C&L.677 B.A., J.D. 255 Main St.
Veltri, Victoria Lynn ....'64 '95 C.184 B.S. L.1048 J.D. Greater Hartford Legal Assistance
Veltrop, James D., (AV) .... '58 '86 C.502 A.B. L.309 J.D. [Axinn,V.&H.] (Pat.)
*PRACTICE AREAS: Intellectual Property; Antitrust and Trade Regulation; Litigation.
Venoit, Wendy Kennedy ....'71 '97 C.321 B.A. L.1040 J.D. [A Pepe&H.]
Ventre, Thomas R., (BV) ....'49 '75 C.884 A.B. L.93 J.D. Asst. Atty. Gen.
Verdone, R. Alisha ....'62 '90 C.184 B.A. L.1029 J.D. [Updike,K.&S.]
*PRACTICE AREAS: Business Law; Commercial Lending; Real Estate; Creditor's Rights.
Vickery, Jennifer C. ....'64 '00 C.1307 B.A. L.1048 J.D. [A Shipman&G.]
*PRACTICE AREAS: Intellectual Property; Business Law.
Vinkels, Valdis, (BV) ....'39 '68 C&L.184 B.A., LL.B. 214 Main St.
Vitale, Laureen J. ....'64 '89 C.019 B.A. L.1194 J.D. P.O. Box 2138
Vitarelli, Richard F. ....'— '94 C.93 B.A. L.818 J.D. [⊡ Robinson&C.]
Vitelli, James T. ....'62 '87 C.976 B.A. L.945 J.D. Assoc. Coun., The Travelers Ins. Co.
Vitelli, Kristine Hughes ....'63 '88 C&L.208 B.A., J.D. Hartford Plaza
Vodola, Peter Joseph ..... '64 '96 C.94 B.A.B.S. L.184 J.D. 225 Asylum Street, 13th Floor
Voigt, Richard ....'46 '74 C.918 B.A. L.893 J.D. [Cummings&L.]
*PRACTICE AREAS: Labor Law; Employment Law; Litigation; Occupational Safety and Health Law.
Volpe, Michele M., (BV) .... '66 '91 C.93 A.B. L.184 J.D. [Del Negro,F.&V.]
*PRACTICE AREAS: Health Care Law; Managed Care Law.
Volpe, Robert P., (BV) ....'34 '59 C.309 B.A. L.477 J.D. [Howard,K.S.&F.]
*PRACTICE AREAS: Civil Litigation; Estate Planning and Settlement.
Vossler, Christopher M., (BV) ....'60 '85 C.93 B.A. L.1029 J.D. [Howd&L.]
*PRACTICE AREAS: Products Liability Litigation; Commercial; Premises Liability Litigation; Environmental Insurance Claims; General Trial and Appellate Practice.
Wade, Helene H. ....'38 '69 C.188 B.A. L.893 LL.B. Coun., The Travelers Ins. Co.
Wade, James A., (AV) ....'— '62 C.976 B.A. L.893 LL.B. [Robinson&C.]
*PRACTICE AREAS: Litigation; Criminal Law.
Wade, Michael T. ....'65 '92 C.976 B.A. L.184 J.D. [A Reid&R.]
*PRACTICE AREAS: Litigation.
Wagner, Barbara C., (BV) ....'50 '84 C.446 B.A. L.184 J.D. P.O. Box 231277
Wagner, Jerry ....'26 '49 C.976 B.S. L.309 LL.B. Ref., Supr. Ct.
Wagner, Michael S. ....'61 '86 C.184 B.A. L.1029 J.D. 101 Lafayette St.
Walkama, Mary Ellen G. .... '51 '84 C&L.184 B.A., J.D. Riggs & Assoc., LLP
Walker, Anne Noble ....'63 '92 C.188 B.S. L.107 J.D. [Pepe&H.]
*PRACTICE AREAS: Disabilities; Employee Benefits; Labor and Employment.
Walker, Daniel A. ....'50 '78 C.976 B.A. L.893 J.D. CIGNA Corp.
Walker, Lyn Gammill, (AV) ....'50 '78 C.914 B.A. L.893 J.D. [Day,B.&H.]
*PRACTICE AREAS: Planning for Entrepreneurs; Trusts and Estates Administration; Tax Exempt Organizations; Estate Planning.
Walker, Philip S., (AV) .... '33 '60 C.602 B.A. L.976 LL.B. [Day,B.&H.]
*PRACTICE AREAS: Products Liability; Commercial Litigation; Torts Litigation.
Walker, Robert C. '43 '74 C.869 B.S. L.184 J.D.
Sr. V.P. & Gen. Coun., Hartford Steam Boiler Inspection & Ins. Co. (Pat.)
Wallace, Andrew R. ....'71 '97 C.184 B.A. L.94 J.D. [A Day,B.&H.]
*PRACTICE AREAS: Real Estate; Commercial Real Estate; Leases and Leasing.
Wallace, Darren M. ....'72 '97 C.165 B.A. L.184 J.D. [A Day,B.&H.]
*PRACTICE AREAS: Trusts and Estates; Estate Planning; Probate; Taxation.
Wallace, Marianne Monti ....'72 '97 C.1030 B.A. L.184 J.D. [A Shipman&G.]
*PRACTICE AREAS: General Litigation; Commercial Litigation; Insurance Defense; Bankruptcy.
Wallace, Shelley L '51 '78 C.103 B.A. L.1019 J.D.
Executive Vice President & General Counsel, TyMetrix, Inc.

Waller, Smith & Palmer, P.C.
(See New London)

Walsh, Catherine B. .... '64 '90 C&L.309 B.A., J.D. Aetna Inc.
Walsh, Michael J., (BV) ....'62 '87 C.1200 B.S. L.184 J.D. [Moukawsher&W.] ⊙
*PRACTICE AREAS: Civil Litigation; Personal Injury; Medical Malpractice.
Walter, Robert E. '30 '58 C.563 B.B.A. L.569 LL.B.
(adm. in NY; not adm. in CT) The Travelers Ins. Co.
Waltman, Laura ....'73 '98 C&L.184 B.A., J.D. [A O'Connell,F.&A.]
*PRACTICE AREAS: Civil Litigation; Commercial Litigation.
Ward, Lawson L. .... '41 '66 C.691 A.B. L.846 LL.B. ITT Hartford Ins. Grp.
Ward, Terence S., (BV) .... '57 '82 C.228 A.B. L.184 J.D. Asst. Fed. Pub. Def.
Wareing, Richard F. ....'68 '93 C.321 A.B. L.309 J.D. [Pepe&H.]
*PRACTICE AREAS: Civil Appeals; Construction Litigation; Civil Litigation.
Warhurst, Corinna M. ....'74 '00 C.105 B.A. L.930 J.D. [A Updike,K.&S.]
*PRACTICE AREAS: Construction and Design Law; Professional Defense.
Warren, Jane Kimball, (AV) ....'61 '86 C.95 B.A. L.184 J.D. [Cummings&L.]
*PRACTICE AREAS: Environmental Law.
Wasik, Donald E., (BV) .... '32 '60 C.602 B.S. L.184 LL.B. Asst. Atty. Gen.
Wasserman, Richard J., (BV) ....'56 '81 C.184 B.A. L.94 J.D. [Day,B.&H.]
*PRACTICE AREAS: Finance and Investments; Structured Finance; Energy.
Watkins, Stephanie A., (AV) '65 '90 C.462 B.S. L.1048 J.D.
Coun., Hartford Steam Boiler Inspection & Ins. Co.
Watson, John W., (BV) .... '45 '79 C.880 B.A. L.184 J.D. Sr. Asst. Pub. Def.
Watson, Lane T. ....'67 '97 C.37 B.A. L.1065 J.D. [A Day,B.&H.]
Wax, Robert P., (AV) .... '48 '74 C.860 B.A. L.893 J.D. [⊡ LeBoeuf,L.G.&M.]
*PRACTICE AREAS: Utility; Energy.
Webb, Julia D. .... '46 '84 C.999 B.A. L.1048 J.D. Asst. Clk., Supr. Ct.
Webb, Richard F., (AV) ....'45 '73 C.694 A.B. L.184 J.D. Asst. Atty. Gen.
Webb, Wm. A. '20 '48 C.301 B.A. L.893 LL.B.
(adm. in VA; not adm. in CT) Travelers Indemnity Co. of Amer.
Webber, M. Jackson, (BV) ....'40 '65 C&L.94 B.A., LL.B. 661 Wethersfield Ave.
Webber, Morton M., (BV) ....'32 '57 C.855 B.A. L.178 LL.B. [Webber,J.&M.]
Webber, Jacobs & Murphy, LLP, (BV) .... 28 Grand St.
Weil, Mary L. ....'— '01 L.184 J.D. [A Bingham D.]
*PRACTICE AREAS: Business.
Weinberger, Steven '53 '78 C.1349 B.A. L.472 J.D.
Dir., Ret. & Benefit Servs., State Comptr. Off.
Weinstein, Robert H., (BV) .... '52 '78 L.902 J.D. [Weinstein&Assoc.]
Weinstein and Associates, (BV) .... 1 Hartford Square W.

Weinstock, Kenneth S. .... '68 '93 C&L.94 B.A., J.D. [Ⓐ Pepe&H.]
Weir, Robert F. '41 '84 C.871 B.S. L.818 J.D.
(adm. in MA; not adm. in CT) 1 State St.
Weisberg, Gwen P. .... '58 '86 C.454 B.S. L.831 J.D. [Ⓐ Pullman&C.]
*PRACTICE AREAS: Litigation; Civil Litigation; Commercial Law; Construction Law; Real Estate Law.
Weisburst, Marsha J. ......'48 '81 C.860 B.A. L.184 J.D. Coun., AETNA Inc. (⊙Hartford)
Weisburst, Marsha J. ...... '48 '81 C.860 B.A. L.184 J.D. Coun., Aetna, Inc. (⊙Hartford)
*RESPONSIBILITIES: Investment Law; Insurance Law.
Weisman, Donald E., (BV) .... '36 '69 C.184 B.A. L.564 J.D. 59 Hungerford St.
Wellman, Philip S., (AV) '64 '91
C.855 B.A. L.184 J.D. Asst. Gen. Coun., The Advest Grp., Inc.
*RESPONSIBILITIES: Antitrust and Trade Regulation; Theft of Trade Secrets; Noncompetition and Non-Solicitation Agreements; Securities Fraud Class Actions.
Welsh, Charles R. .... '60 '88 C.855 B.A. L.184 J.D. [LeBoeuf,L.G.&M.]
*PRACTICE AREAS: Insurance; Business Law; Mergers and Acquisitions; Venture Capital.
Welsh, John H., (BV) .... '58 '90 C.93 B.A. L.184 J.D. 2 Wethersfield Ave.
Welsh, Natalie W. .... '64 '94 C.893 B.A. L.306 J.D. [Shipman&G.]
*PRACTICE AREAS: Employee Benefits; Pension and Profit Sharing Plans; Public Pension Plans.
Welsh, Walter C. .... '47 '72 C.860 B.S.M.E. L.184 J.D. Harford Plz.

Wenc Law Offices
(See Windsor Locks)

Wendzel, Peter M. .... '67 '92 C.273 B.A. L.893 J.D. [Wiggin&D.]
Wergeles, Amy Span ....'— '87 C.705 B.A. L.893 J.D. [Ⓒ Robinson&C.]
*PRACTICE AREAS: Intellectual Property; Technology and Science.
Werner, Frederic P. .... '32 '58 C.31 B.A. L.178 LL.B. Sr. Coun., Conn. Bk. & Tr. Co.
Werner, Suzanne Heggie .... '60 '86 C.518 B.A. L.569 J.D. 1 American Row
Wertam, John E., (BV) ....'57 '86 C.431 B.S. L.184 J.D. [Shipman&G.]
*PRACTICE AREAS: Environmental Law; Land Use Law.
West, Arnold B. ....'63 '90 C.103 A.B. L.893 J.D. 151 Farmington Ave.
West, Marilyn T. '55 '80 C.93 B.S. L.276 J.D.
V.P. & Assoc. Gen. Coun., Hartford Financial Services Group, Inc.
Westbrook, Melinda .... '54 '92 C.431 B.A. L.184 J.D. Compl. Mgr., Aetna Inc.
Wetstone, Barrie K., (AV) .... '38 '63 C.309 B.A. L.178 LL.B. [Pullman&C.]
*PRACTICE AREAS: Tax Law; Pension and Profit Sharing Law; Estate Planning Law.
Wheeler, Steven S. ....'70 '98 C.1060 B.A. L.184 J.D. [Ⓐ Bingham D.]
Whelan, John R., (BV) ....'52 '77 C.1102 B.A. L.8 J.D. Asst. Atty. Gen.
White, Edward C. .... '58 '90 C.690 B.S. L.464 J.D. [Pepe&H.]
*PRACTICE AREAS: Securities Regulation; Mergers and Acquisitions; Emerging Growth Companies.
White, Robert A., (AV) ....'48 '76 C.860 B.A. L.569 J.D. [Murtha C.]
*PRACTICE AREAS: Bankruptcy; Creditors' Rights and Commercial Litigation; Alternative Dispute Resolution.

Whitehead, Christine M., (AV) '50 '75 C.788 B.A. L.184 J.D.
241 Main Street, 06106
Telephone: 860-241-7797 Fax: 860-241-7744
***PRACTICE AREAS: Family Law (80%, 50); Personal Injury Law (20%, 3).**
Matrimonial, Custody, Mediation.
See Professional Biographies, HARTFORD, CONNECTICUT

Whitehead, Robert A., Jr., (BV) ....'49 '75 C.855 A.B. L.184 J.D. Asst. Atty. Gen.
Whitford, Todd W. ....'70 '95 C.21 B.A. L.184 J.D. [Ⓐ Howard,K.S.&F.]
*PRACTICE AREAS: Civil Litigation; Personal Injury; Insurance Defense; Land Use; Domestic Relations.
Whitman, Robert .... '36 '59 C.563 B.B.A. L.178 LL.B. Prof. of Law, Univ. of Conn.
Whitney, Diane Woodfield, (BV) .... '45 '85 C.319 B.A. L.184 J.D. [LeBoeuf,L.G.&M.]
*PRACTICE AREAS: Environmental; Land Use; Civil Litigation; Appeals; Juvenile.
Whittemore, Clark, Jr., (AV) '— '50
C.309 A.B. L.893 LL.B. [Ⓒ Robinson&C.] (⊙Greenwich)
Whittemore, Edward B. ....'68 '95 C.197 B.A. L.273 J.D. [Ⓐ Murtha C.]
Widem, Lawrence G., (BV) ....'58 '85 C.1033 B.A. L.823 J.D. Asst. Atty. Gen.
Widing, Carol, (BV) ....'41 '81 C.914 B.A. L.1338 J.D. 100 Pearl St., Ste. 1400 (⊙Avon)
Wiechmann, Eric Watt, (AV) ....'48 '74 C.299 B.A. L.188 J.D. [Cummings&L.]
*PRACTICE AREAS: Civil Litigation; Products Liability; Toxic Tort Litigation; Antitrust Law.
Wieleba, Joanie .... '55 '89 C.112 A.B. L.184 J.D. Asst. Gen. Coun., Hartford Life, Inc.
Wiese, David J., (BV) ....'58 '84 C.93 B.S. L.823 J.D. [Tyler C.&A.]
*PRACTICE AREAS: Banking; Regulatory Compliance; Corporate.
Wiese, Peter Emmett .... '52 '78 C.1156 B.S. L.1218 J.D. Supr. Ct. J.
Wiezalis, Raymond J., (BV) .....'47 '75 C.884 B.S.C.E. L.184 J.D. [McVane,B.K.W.&B.]

Wiggin & Dana LLP, (AV) BB
One CityPlace, 06103-3402 ⊙
Telephone: 860-297-3700 Telefax: 860-525-9380
URL: http://www.wiggin.com
Members of Firm: Valerie A. Seiling (Resident); Patrick J. Monahan, II (Resident); Robert M. Langer (Resident); Stephen B. Harris (Resident); Daniel J. Klau (Resident); Peter M. Wendzel (Resident). Resident Counsel: Sharyn B. Zuch; Marcia Kenny Keegan. Resident Associates: Catherine P. Baatz; Lori R. Clark; Michelle Wilcox DeBarge; Michael J. Devine; Richard H. Lugli; Steven P. Malech (Resident); Gayle Carol Wintjen.
Antitrust and Trade Regulation, Appellate, Automotive Industry Law, Banking and Financial Services, Bankruptcy Law, Biotechnology Law, Civil Litigation, Closely Held Business, Cogeneration, Construction Law, Employee Benefits and ERISA Law, Environmental Law, Estate Planning and Settlement Law, Franchise Law, Governmental Affairs, Health Care, Hospital Law, Institutional Finance, Insurance Coverage Litigation, Intellectual Property, Internal Corporate Investigations and White Collar Criminal Defense Law, International Transactions, Labor Law, Litigation, Long Term Care Facilities and Financing, Mental Health Law, Mergers and Acquisitions, National and Regional Litigation Counsel, Partnerships and Joint Ventures, Patent Prosecution and Litigation, Professional Malpractice Litigation, Public Finance, Public Utilities, Real Estate Leasing, Development and Finance, Secured Transactions, Securities Regulation, State and Federal Tax Law, Tax Exempt Organizations, Technology Licensing, Telecommunications, Trademarks and Copyright, Trust and Estates Administration, Venture Capital and Zoning.
New Haven, Connecticut Office: One Century Tower, P.O. Box 1832. Telephone: 203-498-4400. Telefax: 203-782-2889.
Stamford, Connecticut Office: 400 Atlantic Street, P.O. Box 110325. Telephone: 203-363-7600. Telefax: 203-363-7676.
Berwyn, Pennsylvania Office: 1055 Westlake Drive. Telephone: 610-727-4153. Telefax: 610-727-4085.
Cherry Hill, New Jersey Office: 402 Park Boulevard North, 08802. Telephone: 856-662-3331. Telefax: 856-662-1783.
See Professional Biographies, HARTFORD, CONNECTICUT

Wigmore, W. Mark, (BV) ....'61 '86 C.967 B.A. L.273 J.D. Coun., The Travelers Ins. Co.
Wilcox, William D. '64 '90 C.184 B.A. L.818 J.D.
Coun., Connecticut Mutual Life Insurance Company
Wilder, Marjorie S., (BV) ....'43 '72 C.788 A.B. L.184 J.D. [Pullman&C.]
*PRACTICE AREAS: Administrative Law; Condemnation Law; Real and Personal Property Taxation; Litigation; Zoning, Planning and Land Use.
Wilder, Michael S., (AV) '41 '66 C.976 B.A. L.309 LL.B.
Group Sr. V.P. & Gen. Coun., Hartford Financial Services Group, Inc.
Wildman, Thomas R., (AV) .... '46 '71 C&L.966 B.A., J.D. [Day,B.&H.]
*PRACTICE AREAS: Finance and Investments; Structured Finance; Equipment Finance/Leasing; Private Equity Funds.
Wildstein, Andrew S. .... '71 '96 C.183 B.A. L.1019 J.D. [Ⓐ Danaher,T.L.&N.]
*PRACTICE AREAS: Medical Malpractice Defense; Civil Litigation.
Wilkinson, George B., III '66 '92 C&L.184 B.S., J.D.
Assoc. Coun., Hartford Financial Services Group, Inc.

Wilkinson, Marcus D. .... '62 '88 C.311 B.A. L.178 J.D. [Shipman&G.]
*PRACTICE AREAS: Mergers and Acquisitions; Corporate Law; Securities; Finance; Venture Capital.

Willcutts, Thomas P., & Associates, (BV) '59 '84 C.691 B.A. L.910 J.D.
Capitol Place, 21 Oak Street Suite 602, 06106-8002
Telephone: 860-524-6800 Fax: 860-524-7766
Email: tpw@ntplx.net URL: http://www.lawyers.com/willcuttslaw
***PRACTICE AREAS: Securities Litigation; Securities Arbitration; Commercial Litigation; Legal Malpractice; Professional Malpractice.**
Associates: John Jay Pavano; Douglas A. Cho. Of Counsel: Marvin S. Bloom.
Securities Litigation and Arbitration, Commercial Litigation, Legal Malpractice, Professional Malpractice, Products Liability, Personal Injury and General Civil Litigation in Federal and State Courts.
See Professional Biographies, HARTFORD, CONNECTICUT

Williams, Andrew C., (AV) '58 '85 C.112 B.A. L.831 J.D.
Mng. Coun., Cornerstone Real Estate Advisors, Inc.
Williams, Evelyn V. ....'74 '99 C.811 B.A. L.588 J.D. [Ⓐ Cummings&L.]
Williams, Jeffrey L., (AV) ....'47 '72 C.321 B.A. L.184 J.D. 90 State House Square
Williams, Joseph P. .... '68 '94 C.29 B.A. L.276 J.D. [Shipman&G.]
*PRACTICE AREAS: Environmental Law; Land Use Law.
Williams, Kenneth G. ....'56 '82 C&L.184 B.A., J.D. [Gordon,M.&F.]
*PRACTICE AREAS: Tort Liability; Products Liability; Toxic Torts; Environmental Law; Employment Law.
Williams, Melvin P. .... '30 '61 C.688 B.E.E. L.273 J.D. 1 Financial Plz. (Pat.)
Williams, Paul D., (BV) ....'53 '84 C.563 B.A. L.1009 J.D. [Day,B.&H.]
*PRACTICE AREAS: Torts Litigation; Medical And Professional Malpractice Defense; Franchise And Distributorship Litigation; Commercial Litigation; Product Liability.

Willinger, Willinger & Bucci, P.C.
(See Bridgeport)

Willnamer, Carolyn K. .... '64 '89 C.375 B.S. L.502 J.D. Jud. Clk., Supr. Ct.
Wilmot, Donald P. ....'45 '70 C.165 B.A. L.982 J.D. Society for Svgs.
Wilson, Holly J. ....'56 '81 C.473 B.A. L.1003 J.D. State Dept. of Rev.
Wilson, Jacqueline A. ....'51 '86 C.708 B.S. L.1048 J.D. [Ⓐ Rome M.S.]
*PRACTICE AREAS: Family Law; Juvenile Law; Civil Litigation.
Wilson, Peter ....'73 '01 C.823 B.A. L.184 J.D. [Ⓐ Day,B.&H.]
Wilson, Seth M. .... '71 '98 C.945 B.S. L.1048 J.D. [Ⓐ Murtha C.] (Pat.)
Wilson-Coker, Patricia .... '50 '81 C&L.184 B.A., J.D. Reg. Admr., Dept. of Social Servs.
Winger, Holly J., (BV) ....'56 '81 C.228 B.A. L.880 J.D. [Cummings&L.]
*PRACTICE AREAS: Products Liability Law; Toxic Tort Defense Law; Commercial Litigation.

Winiarski, Henry C., Jr., (BV) '53 '78 C.829 B.A. L.184 J.D.
941 Wethersfield Avenue, 06114-3137
Telephone: 860-296-2127 Fax: 860-296-2131
Email: hcwjr53@msn.com
General Practice, Real Estate, Probate and Conservatorship Law, Wills, Trusts, Zoning, Title Insurance, Civil Litigation and Commercial Law.
See Professional Biographies, HARTFORD, CONNECTICUT

Winn, Jean E., (AV) '55 '89 C.23 B.S. L.1029 J.D.
[Hawkins,D.&W.] (⊙New York, NY)
Winnick, Barry M., (BV) ....'62 '87 C.860 B.A. L.823 J.D. [Ⓒ Tyler C.&A.]
*PRACTICE AREAS: Commercial Litigation; Collections; Foreclosures; Municipal Law.
Winslow, James A. ....'45 '81 C.184 B.A. L.1048 J.D. Asst. Pub. Def.
Winter, Matthew E. '57 '85 C.477 B.S. L.982 J.D.
V.P. & Chf. Ethics & Corp. Compl. Offr., Conn. Mut. Life Ins. Co.
Winterson, Howard M., Jr. '55 '81
C.611 B.A. L.184 J.D. Asst. V.P., Conn. Nat. Gas Corp.
Wintjen, Gayle Carol .... '64 '90 C.454 B.B.A. L.1202 J.D. [Ⓐ Wiggin&D.]
Wirth, Richard J., (BV) '58 '83
C.1349 B.A. L.978 J.D. Coun., Phoenix Home Life Mut. Ins. Co.
*RESPONSIBILITIES: Investments; Intellectual Property.
Wise, Lewis K., (AV) ....'47 '74 C.178 B.A. L.184 J.D. [Rogin,N.C.L.&H.]
*PRACTICE AREAS: Litigation; Administrative Law; Land Use; Employment Law.
Witherington, Thomas W., (BV) ....'56 '82 C.976 B.A. L.306 J.D. [Cohn B.&S.]
*PRACTICE AREAS: Commercial Litigation; Lender Liability; Environmental Litigation.
Wizner, Andrew L., (BV) ....'62 '89 C.276 B.S. L.880 J.D. [Leete&K.]
*PRACTICE AREAS: Immigration Law; Visas; Employment Visas.
Wolf, Penrose, (BV) .... '25 '67 C.645 B.S. L.184 J.D. [Wolf,H.E.&C.]
*PRACTICE AREAS: Fidelity; Surety; Construction; Subdivisions.

Wolf, Horowitz, Etlinger & Case, L.L.C., (BV)
241 Main Street, 06106-1817
Telephone: 860-724-6667 Facsimile: 860-293-1979
Penrose Wolf; Matthew M. Horowitz; Deborah Etlinger; Gary M. Case; Jan Maria Localio.
Litigation in all Courts. Insurance Defense, Fidelity, Surety, Construction Law, Professional Malpractice, Insurance Coverage, Toxic Torts, Products Liability, Commercial Litigation and Subrogation.
See Professional Biographies, HARTFORD, CONNECTICUT

Wolfe, R. Bradley, (BV) ....'48 '74 C.311 B.A. L.184 J.D. [Gordon,M.&F.]
*PRACTICE AREAS: Construction Law; Surety Law; Commercial Litigation.
Wolfson, John M., (BV) .... '58 '83 C.222 B.A. L.184 J.D. [Feiner W.]
*PRACTICE AREAS: Business and Financial Litigation; Commercial Litigation; Employment Litigation; Tax Controversies; Professional Liability.
Wolfson, Nicholas '32 '56 C.178 B.A. L.309 LL.B.
(adm. in NY; not adm. in CT) Prof. of Law, Univ. of Conn.
Wolinetz, Brian L. .... '72 '98 C&L.260 B.A., J.D. [Ⓐ Pepe&H.]
Wolman, Martin, (AV) ....'37 '64 C.103 A.B. L.1066 LL.B. [Day,B.&H.]
*PRACTICE AREAS: Trusts and Estates Administration; Estate Planning; Tax Exempt Organization.
Wolter, John F., (BV) .... '61 '86 C.708 B.A. L.276 J.D. [Updike,K.&S.] (⊙New Haven)
*PRACTICE AREAS: Business Law; Commercial Lending; Human Service; Franchise Law; Utilities Law.
Wood, Allison A. ....'74 '99 C&L.184 B.A., J.D. [Ⓐ Cummings&L.]
Wood, Sandra B. ...'52 '82 C.976 B.A. L.184 J.D. Hartford Foundation For Public Giving
Wood, Scott A. ....'70 '01 C.999 M.B.A. [Ⓐ Bingham D.]
*PRACTICE AREAS: Business.
Wood, William H., Jr., (AV) .... '21 '49 C.976 B.S. L.477 J.D. 1 American Row
Woodard, David Andre ....'74 '00 C.325 B.S. L.329 J.D. [Ⓐ Pepe&H.]
Woodbridge, Timothy F., (BV) .... '38 '64 C.31 B.A. L.976 LL.B. 350 Church St.
Woods, Glenn A. .... '52 '91 C.855 B.S. L.1162 J.D. Off. of Atty. Gen.
Woods, Helga Mayer, (BV) ....'57 '83 C.659 B.A. L.884 J.D. [Rome M.S.]
*PRACTICE AREAS: Commercial Finance; Commercial Real Estate Finance; Commercial Real Estate Development.

Woolf, Brian J., LLC, The Law Offices of
(See East Hartford)

Woollams, Richard C., Jr. '54 '79 C.381 B.A. L.1003 J.D.
(adm. in OH; not adm. in CT) The Travelers Ins. Co.
Wright, Douglass B. ....'12 '37 C.976 A.B. L.306 LL.B. Supr. Ct. J.
Wright, Ernest J. .... '40 '65 C.93 B.S. L.94 LL.B. Coun., The Travelers Ins. Co.
Wright, Kathleen H. .... '50 '80 C.433 B.A. L.184 J.D. Ofc. of the Legis. Comm.
Wright, Robert E. '55 '82
C&L.184 B.A., J.D. Exec. V.P., Conn. Resources Recovery Auth.
Wrinn, David H., (CV) ....'61 '84 C.216 A.B. L.184 J.D. Asst. Atty. Gen.

Wyld, Robert L., (AV) .... '51 '76 C.882 B.A. L.276 J.D. [Shipman&G.]
*PRACTICE AREAS: Civil Litigation; Business Litigation; Securities Litigation; Intra-Corporate Disputes; Health Care Litigation.
Wynne, Francis J., (BV) .... '23 '60 C&L.184 B.S., LL.B. [Gould,K.&W.]
*PRACTICE AREAS: Personal Injury; Insurance Defense; Medical Malpractice.
Wynne, Robert O., (BV) ....'59 '91 C.184 B.S. L.1202 J.D. [Gould,K.&W.]
*PRACTICE AREAS: Personal Injury; Insurance Defense; Civil Litigation; Divorce.
Yale, Guy D. .... '45 '76 C.608 B.S. L.184 J.D. [Alix,Y.&R.] (See Pat. Sect.)
Yandow, Joanne Vonasek .... '59 '88 C.184 B.A. L.1048 J.D. Asst. Comm. Coun. II
Yasensky, Thomas, (BV) .... '33 '74 C.321 B.S. L.855 J.D. Asst. Atty. Gen.
Yass, Robert K. .... '51 '78 C.1349 B.A. L.564 J.D. 2nd V.P., The Travelers Corp.
Yavis, John C., Jr., (AV) .... '36 '61 C.184 B.A. L.976 LL.B. [Murtha C.]
*PRACTICE AREAS: Litigation; Government Contracts Law; Construction Law.
Yeich, Carl F., (BV) ....'56 '82 C.367 B.A. L.188 J.D. [Skelley R.]
*PRACTICE AREAS: Property Insurance Law; Subrogation; Insurance Recovery; Casualty Defense; Arson and Insurance Fraud.
Yetzer, Jody L. '72 '97 C.867 B.A. L.976 J.D.
Staff Atty., Conn. Civil Liberties Union Found.
Yoder, Linda L. .... '57 '81 C.294 B.A. L.276 J.D. [Shipman&G.]
*PRACTICE AREAS: Civil Litigation; ERISA Litigation; Employment and Education Law.
Youmans, Matthew H., (BV) .... '65 '91 C.860 B.A. L.184 J.D. [Ⓐ Levin,F.&P.]
*PRACTICE AREAS: Labor and Employment Litigation; Commercial Litigation; Corporate Transactions.
Young, Dona Davis Gagliano, (AV) '54 '80
C.222 B.A. L.184 J.D. Pres., Phoenix Home Life Mut. Ins. Co.
Young, Mary S. ....'43 '73 C.725 B.A. L.184 J.D. Off. of the Secy of State (Elections)
Young, Nadine Kline, (BV) ....'51 '77 C.112 B.A. L.188 J.D. [Ⓐ Dechert]
*PRACTICE AREAS: Commercial Real Estate Finance; Commercial Leasing; Securitization; Construction Finance; Construction Contracts.
Young, Robert E., (BV) ....'58 '84 C.1103 B.A. L.1048 J.D. [Noble,Y.&O.]
*PRACTICE AREAS: Insurance Defense; Products Liability; Medical Malpractice; Municipal Law; Law Enforcement.
Young, Rolan J. .... '60 '93 C.197 A.B. L.904 J.D. [Updike,K.&S.] (⊙New Haven)
*PRACTICE AREAS: Business Law; Commercial Lending; Public Finance/Public Law; Real Estate; Affordable Housing.
Young, Roland F., III, (AV) .... '54 '79 C.188 B.A. L.184 J.D. [O'Brien,T.&Y.]
*PRACTICE AREAS: Health Care Law; Civil Litigation; Medical Malpractice Defense; Insurance Defense; Personal Injury.
Young, Thomas A. .... '57 '82 C.674 A.B. L.228 J.D. Chf. Privacy Offr., Aetna Inc.
*RESPONSIBILITIES: Privacy; Health Care Compliance.
Yules, Robert B., (BV) .... '52 '78 C.611 B.A. L.851 J.D. [Yules&Y.] ⊙
*PRACTICE AREAS: Drugs and Medical Devices; Insurance Law; Products Liability; Professional Malpractice; Transportation.

Yules & Yules, LLC, (BV)
P.O. Box 230278, 06123-0278 ⊙
Telephone: 860-724-5815
Robert B. Yules.
Trial Practice, Automobile, Mobile Carrier, Bad Faith, Corporate Business Torts, Drug and Medical Device Litigation, Fraud, Insurance, Products Liability, Professional Malpractice, Transportation, Workers' Compensation Law, Securities Arbitration and Financial Institutions Litigation.
Representative Clients: Aetna Casualty and Surety Co.; Allstate Insurance Co.; Nationwide Insurance Co.; Transamerica Insurance Group; Zurich-American Insurance Cos.
New Haven, Connecticut Office: 195 Church Street, Seventeenth Floor. 06510. Telephone: 203-789-1000. Fax: 203-789-6320.
Stamford, Connecticut Office: P.O. Box 522. 06904-0522. Telephone: 203-327-9200.
New York, N.Y. Office: Grand Central Station, P.O. Box 4419. 10163-4419. Telephone: 203-327-9200.
See Professional Biographies, HARTFORD, CONNECTICUT

Zaccardi, Henry J., (BV) .... '56 '89 C.860 B.A. L.818 J.D. [Ⓐ Shipman&G.]
*PRACTICE AREAS: Labor and Employment.
Zachs, Eric M. .... '59 '85 C.860 B.A. L.178 J.D. Pres. & COO, Message Ctr. Beepers
Zaino, Laura A. ....'69 '96 C.938 B.A. L.306 J.D. [Ⓐ Halloran&S.]
*PRACTICE AREAS: Motor Vehicle Torts; Premises Liability; Homeowners Liability; Dram Shop Liability.
Zakarian, Albert, (AV) .... '40 '65 C.855 B.A. L.178 LL.B. [Day,B.&H.]
*PRACTICE AREAS: Employment Litigation; Employment Law; Commercial Litigation.
Zamlowski, Robert J. '56 '91 C.1102 B.A. L.184 J.D.
Asst. Comm. Coun., Comm. on Human Rights
Zammitti, Dawn N. .... '— '89 C.585 B.S. L.184 J.D. [Ⓐ Robinson&C.]
*PRACTICE AREAS: Labor and Employment; Trusts and Estates.
Zayas, Richard L., (CV) ....'54 '90 C.454 B.A. L.184 J.D. 83 Oak St.
Zdrojeski, Ronald W., (BV) ....'60 '83 C&L.273 B.A., J.D. [LeBoeuf,L.G.&M.]
*PRACTICE AREAS: Environmental; Litigation.
Zeilman, Timothy J. '70 '95 C.197 A.B. L.273 J.D.
Coun., Hartford Steam Boiler Inspection & Ins. Co.
Zeman, Jeffrey B. .... '69 '95 C.95 A.B. L.93 J.D. [Ⓐ Bingham D.]
Zeman, William S., (AV) '13 '41 C.309 B.A. L.184 LL.B.
44 Capitol Avenue, Suite 402
Zettergren, Jennifer Croteau ....'— '98 C.184 B.A. L.1252 J.D. [Ⓐ Robinson&C.]
Zimberlin, Winona, (BV) .... '54 '80 C.611 B.A. L.1048 J.D. 2 Congress St.
Zimmermann, Mark J., (BV) .... '56 '81 C.276 B.S.B.A. L.861 J.D. [Updike,K.&S.]
*PRACTICE AREAS: Environmental; Administrative Law.
Zito, Donna R. .... '— '80 C.855 B.A. L.184 J.D. [O'Brien,T.&Y.]
*PRACTICE AREAS: Medical Malpractice Defense; Civil Trial Practice.
Zitomer, Alan .... '60 '85 C.881 A.B. L.94 J.D. 999 Asylum St.
Zitser, Barry S., (BV) .... '48 '73 C.156 B.A. L.184 J.D. [Perakos&Z.]
Zitzkat, W. David .... '43 '81 C.659 B.A. L.184 J.D. 999 Asylum Ave.
Zizka, Michael A., (BV) .... '54 '82 C.688 B.S. L.184 J.D. [Murtha C.]
*PRACTICE AREAS: Environmental; Land Use Law; Municipal Law; Litigation.
Zolan, Paul B., (AV) ....'51 '77 C.855 B.A. L.184 J.D. [Rogin,N.C.L.&H.]
*PRACTICE AREAS: Commercial Law; Corporate Law; Commercial Litigation; Real Estate.
Zuch, Sharyn B. ....'56 '81 C.188 B.S. L.145 J.D. [Ⓒ Wiggin&D.]
*PRACTICE AREAS: Antitrust; Bankruptcy.
Zweifler, Adam F. ....'60 '86 C.1044 B.A. L.1066 J.D. [Pepe&H.]
*PRACTICE AREAS: Real Estate; Real Estate Finance; Estate Planning; Probate.

HARWINTON, 4,889, *Litchfield Co.*

Wall, Patrick J. .... '52 '80 C.884 B.A. L.1048 J.D. P.O. Box 265

HEBRON, 5,453, *Tolland Co.*

Aissis, John S. .... '66 '91 C.321 B.A. L.184 J.D. 21 Pendleton Dr.
Borst, William V., (BV) .... '47 '73 C.300 B.A. L.184 J.D. [Kalom&B.]
Brown, Paindiris & Scott, LLP, (AV)
10 Main Street (⊙East Hampton, Glastonbury, Hartford, Stamford)
Dee, Debra S., (BV) .... '59 '85 C.745 B.A. L.1048 J.D. 400 Martin Rd.
Haakonsen, Kate W., (BV) '53 '78
C.874 B.A. L.184 J.D. [Brown,P.&S.] (⊙Glastonbury, Hartford)
Kalom, Bruce, (BV) .... '38 '62 C.197 B.A. L.477 J.D. [Kalom&B.]
Kalom & Borst, (BV) .... 107 Main St.
Villani, Francesca J. '60 '87 C.262 B.S. L.564 J.D.
(adm. in NY; not adm. in CT) 110 Hoadly Rd.‡
Yeterian, Joanne Steinkamp ....'61 '86 C.970 B.A. L.1040 J.D. 9 Charles Lane

HIGGANUM, 650, *Middlesex Co.*

Barone, Bonye W. .... '57 '91 C.67 B.A. L.1048 J.D. 107 McTigh Rd.
Clary, Joseph P. .... '59 '90 C.1105 B.A. L.602 J.D. 171 W. Shore Dr.

HUNTINGTON, —, *Fairfield Co.*

Falco, Justin K. ....'68 '94 C.36 B.S. L.597 J.D. [R.G.Fashjian]
Fashjian, Robert G., (CV) .... '51 '90 C.829 B.S. L.1029 J.D. [R.G.Fashjian]
Fashjian, Robert G., P.C., (CV) .... 66 Huntington Street
Goldstein, Jerome N. ....'58 '88 C.1116 B.A. L.1029 J.D. 45 Huntington Plz.
Pierson, Virginia Orr ....'55 '83 C.184 B.A. L.1194 J.D. 31 Redwood Cir.
Schneider, Daniel H. ....'66 '93 C.184 B.A. L.1048 J.D. 66 Old Shelton Rd.

IVORYTON, —, *Middlesex Co.*

Trendowski, Jan C. .... '57 '83 C.184 B.A. L.1048 J.D. P.O. Box 488
Watts, John D. .... '60 '91 C&L.930 B.S., J.D. 39 Mares Hill Road

JEWETT CITY, 3,349, *New London Co.*

Duda, Mary Beth, (CV) ....'69 '94 C.999 B.A. L.128 J.D. [Ⓐ R.J.Duda]
Duda, Richard J., (BV) ....'35 '60 C.184 B.A. L.276 J.D. [R.J.Duda]
Duda, Richard J., P.C., (BV) .... 110 Main St.
Kennedy, George L., Jr. ....'51 '80 C.354 B.A. L.1194 J.D. Prob. J.
Norman, Stuart R., Jr., (CV) .... '49 '74 C.95 A.B. L.184 J.D. 10 School St.
Young, Robert B., (CV) .... '54 '89 C.1033 B.A. L.1048 J.D. [Ⓐ R.J.Duda]

KENSINGTON, —, *Hartford Co.*

Beatman, Lillian E. P. ....'31 '59 C.725 B.S. L.184 LL.B. 261 Kensington Rd.
Denuzze, Andrew P. .... '20 '50 C.608 B.S. L.150 J.D. 42 Stockings Brouf Rd.‡
Legenza, Lawrence J., (BV) .... '55 '80 C.184 B.S. L.831 J.D. P.O. Box 127
Leib, David ....'19 '50 C.184 B.S. L.659 LL.B. 75 Windsor Rd.‡
London, Russell, (BV) ....'63 '89 C.67 B.A. L.902 J.D. [London&L.]
London & London, (BV) .... 300 New Britain Rd.
Meskill, John B, (BV) .... '61 '88 C.708 B.S. L.262 J.D. 84 Randecker Lane
Pease, Allen H., (BV) ....'25 '54 C.145 A.B. L.893 LL.B. [Pease&S.]
*PRACTICE AREAS: Taxation (20%); Estate Planning (20%); Estate Administration; Trust Administration; Corporate Law.

Pease & Shortz, P.C., (BV)
52 Chamberlain Highway, 06037
Telephone: 860-828-4879 Fax: 860-828-9432
Email: pease-shortz@erols.com
Allen H. Pease; Frederick M. Shortz.
Taxation and Estate Planning, Probate, Estate and Trust Administration, Business Planning, Business Mediation.
See Professional Biographies, KENSINGTON, CONNECTICUT

Pentore, Richard H., (BV) ....'52 '77 C.184 B.S. L.1202 J.D. 9 High Rd.
Schulz, Robert F., (CV) ....'48 '86 C.188 B.S. L.1029 J.D. 52 Chamberlain Hwy.
Shortz, Frederick M., (BV) .... '55 '85 C.860 B.A. L.1065 J.D. [Pease&S.]
*PRACTICE AREAS: Taxation (10%); Estate Planning (40%); Estate Administration; Trust Administration; Closely Held Corporations (10%).

KENT, 2,505, *Litchfield Co.*

Andrea, Lawrence W. .... '64 '89 C.602 B.S. L.1009 J.D. 127 Kent Hollow Rd.

Cramer & Anderson LLP, (AV)
Kent Green, P.O. Box 333, 06757 ⊙
Telephone: 860-927-3568 Fax: 860-927-4194
Email: gnelson@cramer-anderson.com URL: http://www.cramer-anderson.com
Resident Partner: Grant J. Nelson.
General Practice. Probate, Estate Planning, Municipal, Family and Real Estate Law. Trials. Planning and Zoning, Corporate, Banking, Securities.
Danbury, Connecticut Office: 68 North Street. Telephone: 203-790-7747. Email: danbury@crameranderson.com
Litchfield, Connecticut Office: 46 West Street. P.O. Box 278. Telephone: 860-567-8718. Email: litchfield@cramer-anderson.com
New Milford, Connecticut Office: 51 Main Street. Telephone: 860-355-2631. Email: newmilford@crameranderson.com
Washington Depot, Connecticut Office: 2 Green Hill Road, P.O. Box 321. Telephone: 860-868-0527. Email: wfairbairn@cramer-anderson.com
See Professional Biographies, KENT, CONNECTICUT

D'Alton, Theresa Benedict, (CV) .....'55 '81 C.1030 B.A. L.818 J.D. [Sienkiewicz&M.]
*PRACTICE AREAS: Business Law; Real Estate; Commercial Law; Zoning, Planning and Land Use.
DiPentima, Alexandra Davis, (AV) .... '53 '79 C.674 A.B. L.184 J.D. Supr. Ct. J.
DiPentima, Anthony F., (BV) .... '51 '80 C.303 B.A. L.1029 J.D. [A.F.DiPentima]
DiPentima, Anthony F., LLC, (BV) ....31 North Main Street
Manasse, William J., (BV) .... '50 '80 C.184 B.A. L.1048 J.D. [Manasse,S.&L.]
Manasse, Slaiby & Leard, LLP, (BV) ....31 N. Main St. (⊙Torrington)
McKenna, Michael S., (BV) .... '57 '82 C.184 B.A. L.884 J.D. [Sienkiewicz&M.] ⊙
*PRACTICE AREAS: Litigation; Civil Practice; Personal Injury; Administrative Law; Employment Law.
Nelson, Grant J., (BV) ....'35 '64 C.221 B.A. L.976 LL.B. [Cramer&A.]
*PRACTICE AREAS: Estate Planning Law; Probate Administration Law; Real Estate Law.
Schiesel, Dolores R. .... '51 '92 C.1044 B.A. L.184 J.D. Mayor
Sienkiewicz, Jeffrey B., (BV) .... '48 '72 C.367 B.A. L.823 J.D. [Sienkiewicz&M.] ⊙
*PRACTICE AREAS: Municipal Law; Personal Injury; Medical Malpractice; Zoning, Planning and Land Use; Products Liability.
Sienkiewicz, Nancy ....'50 '77 C.823 B.S. L.184 J.D. [Sienkiewicz&M.] ⊙
*PRACTICE AREAS: Real Estate Law; Divorce Mediation; Trusts and Estates; Wills; Commercial Law.

Sienkiewicz & McKenna, P.C., (BV)
25 North Main Street, Suite 13A, 06757 ⊙
Telephone: 860-927-4640 Fax: 860-927-1909
URL: http://www.lawyers.com/smlaw
Nancy Sienkiewicz; Jeffrey B. Sienkiewicz; Michael S. McKenna; Theresa Benedict D'Alton (Resident).
Civil Practice. Personal Injury, Medical Malpractice, Product Liability, Real Estate, Commercial Law, Administrative Law, Family Law, Mediation, Trusts and Estates, Zoning, Planning and Land Use, Contracts, Appellate Practice.
New Milford, Connecticut Office: 9 South Main Street, P.O. Box 786. Telephone: 860-354-1583. Fax: 860-355-4439.
See Professional Biographies, KENT, CONNECTICUT

KILLINGWORTH, 3,976, *Middlesex Co.*

Baran, Howard A., (BV) .... '32 '62 C.604 A.B. L.94 LL.B. 21 Robin Lane
Barnum, Evelyn A. .... '52 '84 C.1307 B.A. L.184 J.D. 11 Burr Hill Rd.
Cousineau, Sue A. ....'56 '87 C.184 B.A. L.306 J.D. 206 Rte. 80
Davidson, Robert T. H., (AV) .... '25 '56 C&L.976 B.A., LL.B. 65 Parker Hill Rd.
Forsythe, David W. ....'59 '97 C.999 B.A. L.306 J.D. Admr., Lake Grove Schools

Hoyt, Jonathan
(See Clinton)

LeVasseur, W. David, (BV) .... '54 '79 C.184 B.A. L.1048 J.D. 3 Firetower Rd.
Mininberg, Mark, (BV) .... '59 '84 C.918 B.A. L.184 J.D. 50 Bethke Rd.

Weiss, Kimberly F. '64 '91 C.880 B.S.N. L.280 J.D.
(adm. in GA; not adm. in CT) 5 Bethke Rd.

LAKEVILLE, —, *Litchfield Co.*

Aller, Rodney G., (BV) . . . . . '16 '42 C.674 A.B. L.976 LL.B. [Aller&R.]
Aller & Rout, (BV) . . . . . 3 Farnam Rd.
Auburn, Travers T. . . . . '46 '72 C.951 B.A. L.184 [Reid&R.] (⊙Hartford, West Hartford)
*PRACTICE AREAS: Probate; Real Estate; Trusts and Estates.
Bearns, Stuyvesant K., (AV) . . . . . '37 '65 C.976 B.A. L.893 LL.B. [Shipman&G.]
*PRACTICE AREAS: Estate Planning and Settlement Law; Probate Matters; Trust Administration Law; Land Preservation Law.
Blum, John R. H., (AVⓉ) . . . . . '29 '56 C.976 A.B. L.309 LL.B. 322 Main St.
Ceppi, Dario . . . . . '38 '77 C.999 L.569 LL.M. P.O. Box 553
D'Andrea, Robert A. . . . . . '55 '80 C.1033 B.A. L.818 J.D. [Guendelsberger&T.]
Dooley, Francis M., (AV) . . . . . '29 '62 C.608 B.S. L.184 J.D. [Guendelsberger&T.]
Fitzgerald, Richard T., (BV) . . . . . '37 '66 C.454 B.B.A. L.276 J.D. 29 Bissell St.
Foley, Eamonn F. . . . . . '62 '94 C.918 B.A. L.262 J.D. [Layton B.&H.] (⊙New York, NY)
Guendelsberger and Taylor, (AV) . . . . . 12 Porter Street (⊙New Milford)
Layton Brooks & Hecht LLP
37 Old Asylum Rd. (⊙New York, White Plains, NY; Tokyo, Japan)
Meyerhoff, Barton '41 '84 C.184 B.A. L.978 J.D.
(adm. in NY; not adm. in CT) Natl. Regulatory Servs.
Miller, Martha Ann '43 '81 C.641 B.S. L.597 J.D.
(adm. in NY; not adm. in CT) Pomroy Mgmt. Co. Inc.
Morrill, William F. . . . . . '38 '67 C.188 A.B. L.178 J.D. 29 Bissell St.
Nolan, J. Keith, (BV) . . . . . '35 '63 C.197 A.B. L.309 LL.B. [J.K.Nolan]

Nolan, J. Keith, P.C., (BV)
346 Main Street, P.O. Box 687, 06039
Telephone: 860-435-2567 Fax: 860-435-2797
Email: jknolan@snet.net
J. Keith Nolan.
Federal and State Taxation, Private Foundations, Corporations, Partnerships, Real Estate and Zoning, Estate Planning and Probate Law.
Representative Clients: Mobil Foundation, Inc.; Anglo-American Foundation; Between the Lakes Group; Burton Wholesale Materials, LLC; Clocktower Realty, Inc.; Indian Mountain Management Corp.; Lakeville Automotive, LLC; Mill River Textiles, Inc.; Las Pastures Textiles S.A. de C.V.; Salisbury Kitchens & Building Supplies, LLC.

Reid and Riege, P.C., (AV)
322 Main Street, 06039 ⊙
Telephone: 860-435-9894 FAX: 860-240-1002
URL: http://www.reidriege.com
Travers T. Auburn.
Alternative Dispute Resolution. Antitrust & Trade Regulation. Bankruptcy. Business Law. Commercial Law. Commercial Real Estate/Finance. Corporate Law. Employee Benefits/Pension Plans. Employee Benefits/Taft-Hartley Plans. Environmental Law. Health Care. Labor and Employment. Litigation. Mergers and Acquisitions. Nonprofit and Charitable Organizations. Occupational Safety & Health. Probate. Real Estate. Securities. Taxation. Trade and Professional Associations. Trusts & Estates. Zoning, Planning and Land Use.
Hartford, Connecticut Office: One State Street. Telephone: 860-278-1150. FAX: 860-240-1002.
West Hartford, Connecticut Office: 65 LaSalle Road. Telephone: 860-232-6565. FAX: 860-232-6066.
Woodbury, Connecticut Office: 47 Sherman Hill Road. Telephone: 203-267-6680. FAX: 860-240-1002.
See Professional Biographies, LAKEVILLE, CONNECTICUT

Roberts, Howard A. . . . . . '37 '62 C.309 B.A. L.188 LL.B. Salisbury Bk. & Tr. Co.
Rout, Robert H. . . . . . '27 '53 C.966 A.B. L.309 J.D. [Aller&R.]

Shipman & Goodwin LLP, (AV) BR
12 Porter Street, P.O. Box 1809, 06039 ⊙
Telephone: 860-435-2539 Telecopier: 860-435-0011
Email: www@goodwin.com URL: http://shipman-goodwin.com
Partner: Stuyvesant K. Bearns.
General Practice. Banking, Corporation, Tax, Antitrust, Trade Regulation, Finance and Securities, Venture Capital, Labor and Employment, Health Care, Environmental, Professional Liability, Pension and Profit Sharing, Estate Planning, Probate, Trust Administration and Financial Management, Real Estate, Municipal Law. Trials in all Courts.
Representative Clients: Salisbury Bank & Trust Co.
Greenwich, Connecticut Office: 43 Arch Street. Telephone: 203-869-6222.
Hartford, Connecticut Office: One American Row. Telephone: 203-251-5000.
Stamford, Connecticut Office: One Landmark Square. Telephone: 203-324-8100.
See Professional Biographies, LAKEVILLE, CONNECTICUT

Yoakum, Alice B. . . . . . '31 '75 C.681 B.A. L.184 J.D. 322 Main Street

LEBANON, 350, *New London Co.*

Bancroft, Mark W., (BV) . . . . . '48 '81 C&L.184 B.S., J.D. P.O. Box 127
Cusano, John N. . . . . . '49 '88 C.861 B.A. L.184 J.D. Gated Rd.
Wentworth, Rene T. . . . . . '61 '87 C.829 B.S. L.306 J.D. 122 Seabury Rd.

LEDYARD, 13,735, *New London Co.*

Sockbeson, Henry J. . . . . . '50 '77 C.164 B.A. L.309 J.D. Mashantucket Pequot Tribe

LITCHFIELD, * 1,378, *Litchfield Co.*

Ackerly, Mary M., (AV) . . . . . '47 '77 C.66 B.A. L.976 J.D. [Gager&P.]
*PRACTICE AREAS: Estate Planning; Probate; Estate and Trust Administration; Elder Law; Real Estate.
Blick, Clayton L., (AV) . . . . . '17 '41 C&L.569 A.B., J.D. [Cramer&A.]
*PRACTICE AREAS: Real Estate Law; Probate Administration Law; Estate Planning Law.
Booth, John T. '29 '57
C.31 B.A. L.309 LL.B. Chmn., Coleman Swenson Hoffman & Booth
Brakeman, Jill B., (BV) . . . . . '64 '90 C.184 B.A. L.1048 J.D. 174 West St.
Bristol, David C. . . . . . '41 '66 C&L.184 B.A., LL.B. Clk., Supr. Ct.
Carr, Gayle C. . . . . . '61 '90 C.94 B.A. L.884 J.D. [Ⓐ Cohen&T.] ⊙
*PRACTICE AREAS: Family Law; Civil Litigation; Personal Injury; Negligence; Medical Malpractice.
Cloutier, Denise M., (BV) . . . . . '61 '91 C.197 B.A. L.178 J.D. [Ⓐ Cramer&A.]
*PRACTICE AREAS: Civil Litigation; Family Law.

Cohen & Thomas, (BV)
15 Meadow Street, 06759 ⊙
Telephone: 860-567-3754 Fax: 860-567-3894
Email: cohen.and.thomas@att.net URL: http://www.lawyers.com/cohen-and-thomas-attys
Associate: Gayle C. Carr.
General Civil and Criminal Practice. Trials in all Courts. Personal Injury, Negligence and Medical Malpractice Litigation, Real Estate Purchase, Sale, Financing, Zoning and Development, Domestic Law and Divorce, Probate, Wills and Trusts, Banking, Foreclosure and Workouts, Commercial Litigation and Collections, Municipal, Elder Law, Worker's Compensation.
Representative Clients: Great Country Bank; Housatonic Bank & Trust Co.; Derby Savings Bank; Ansonia Derby Water Co.; Griffin Hospital.
Derby, Connecticut Office: 315 Main Street, P.O. Box 313, 06418. Telephone: 203-735-9521. Fax: 203-732-8129.
See Professional Biographies, LITCHFIELD, CONNECTICUT

Cosgrove, Christopher M., (AV) . . . . . '46 '85 C&L.184 B.A., J.D. Pub. Def.

Cramer & Anderson LLP, (AV)
46 West Street, P.O. Box 278, 06759-0278 ⊙
Telephone: 860-567-8718 Fax: 860-567-4531
Email: litchfield@cramer-anderson.com URL: http://www.cramer-anderson.com

(This Listing Continued)

Cramer & Anderson LLP (Continued)
Members of Firm: David Cramer (1902-1981); Clayton L. Blick; Perley H. Grimes, Jr.; Robert L. Fisher, Jr.; William C. Franklin; Barry S. Moller; James D. Hirschfield; Grant J. Nelson (Resident, Kent Office); Reginald William H. Fairbairn (Resident, Washington Depot Office); Randall J. Breeckner (Resident, New Milford Office); Arthur C. Weinshank (Resident, New Milford Office); David P. Burke (Resident, Danbury Office); Joseph A. Saffi (Resident, Danbury Office); D. Randall DiBella (Resident, New Milford Office); Mitchell J. Melnick (Resident, New Milford Office); John D. Tower (Resident, New Milford Office); Lisa L. Buzaid (Resident, New Milford Office). Associates: Denise M. Cloutier; Rosemary B. Jones. Of Counsel: Robert M. FitzGerald; Stephen N. Hume (Resident, New Milford Office); Henry B. Anderson (Resident, New Milford Office); Paul B. Altermatt (Resident, New Milford Office).
General Practice. Probate, Estate Planning, Taxation, Municipal, Family, Real Estate, Negligence and Bankruptcy Law. Civil and Criminal Trials. Planning and Zoning, Corporate, Banking, Securities.
Counsel for: Town of Cornwall; First National Bank of Litchfield; Marriott Corp.; Neeltran, Inc.; New Milford Hospital, Inc.; NMBT (formerly known as The New Milford Bank & Trust); Canterbury School; New Milford Savings Bank; South Kent School; Marvelwood School.
Danbury, Connecticut Office: 68 North Street. Telephone: 203-790-7747. Email: danbury@crameranderson.com
Kent, Connecticut Office: Kent Green, P.O. Box 333. Telephone: 860-927-3568. Email: gnelson@cramer-anderson.com
New Milford, Connecticut Office: 51 Main Street. Telephone: 860-355-2631. Email: newmilford@crameranderson.com
Washington Depot, Connecticut Office: 2 Green Hill Road, P.O. Box 321. Telephone: 860-868-0527.Email: wfairbairn@cramer-anderson.com
See Professional Biographies, LITCHFIELD, CONNECTICUT

Dranginis, Anne C. . . . . . '48 '73 C.706 A.B. L.184 J.D. Supr. Ct. J.
Fisher, Robert L., Jr., (BV) . . . . . '46 '76 C.674 A.B. L.184 J.D. [Cramer&A.]
*PRACTICE AREAS: Real Estate Law; Planning and Zoning Law; Civil Litigation; Elder Law.
FitzGerald, Robert M., (AV) . . . . . '26 '50 C.976 B.A. L.569 LL.B. [◙ Cramer&A.]
Franklin, William C., (BV) . . . . . '53 '78 C.67 B.A. L.1292 J.D. [Cramer&A.]
*PRACTICE AREAS: Commercial Litigation; General Civil Litigation; Personal Injury Litigation; Civil Appeals.
Friday, Jo E., (BV) . . . . . '50 '81 C&L.259 B.A., J.D. [Gager&P.] (⊙Sharon)
*PRACTICE AREAS: Real Estate Law; Litigation; Family Law; Probate Law.

Gager & Peterson, LLP, (AV)
782 Bantam Road, 06759 ⊙
Mailing Address: 782 Bantam Road, P.O. Box 815, Bantam, CT 06750-0815
Telephone: 860-567-0828 Telecopier: 860-567-5844
Mary M. Ackerly (Resident); J. Michael Sconyers; Donna D. Vincenti; Jo E. Friday.
General Practice. Corporate Law, Banks and Banking, Securities, Administrative Law, Litigation in all Courts, Insurance, Trusts and Estates, Probate, Health Care, Real Estate, Commercial Real Estate, Commercial Law, Taxation, Patents, Trademarks, Copyrights, Consumer Law, Computers and Software, Family Law, Environmental Law, Employment Law.
Waterbury, Connecticut Office: One Exchange Place, P.O. Box 2480. Telephone: 203-597-5100. Telecopier: 203-757-7888.
Bethel, Connecticut Office: 2 Stony Hill Road. Telephone: 203-207-5400. Telecopier: 203-207-5407.
Sharon, Connecticut Office: 25 West Main Street, P.O. Box 158. Telephone: 860-364-5531. Telecopier: 860-364-5805.
Southbury, Connecticut Office: 325 Main Street South. Telephone: 203-262-6600. Telecopier: 203-262-6780.
See Professional Biographies, LITCHFIELD, CONNECTICUT

Gill, Charles D. . . . . . '38 '64 C.1102 B.S. L.128 LL.B. Supr. Ct. J.
Grimes, Perley H., Jr., (BV) . . . . . '44 '69 C.197 B.A. L.276 J.D. [Cramer&A.]
*PRACTICE AREAS: Estate Planning; Probate Administration; Real Estate; Zoning, Planning and Land Use.
Guion, Stevens & Rybak, (AV) . . . . . 93 West St.

Herbst, Peter C., Law Offices of
(See Torrington)

Hirschfield, James D., (BV) . . . . . '57 '85 C.829 B.A. L.1029 J.D. [Cramer&A.]
*PRACTICE AREAS: Family Law; Divorce; Custody and Visitation; Support; Paternity.
Hogan, Thomas F., (BV) . . . . . '45 '74 C.321 A.B. L.184 J.D. [Guion,S.&R.]
Hoopes, Dallett, (AV) . . . . . '29 '57 C.311 B.S. L.273 J.D. P.O. Box 205 (Pat.)
Kleeman, John A., P.C. . . . . . '47 '81 C.813 B.A. L.659 J.D. 209 Beach St.
Litwin, Peter A., (BV) . . . . . '47 '72 C&L.184 B.A., J.D. [P.A.Litwin]
Litwin, Peter A., P.C., (BV) . . . . . 782 Bantam Rd.
Luzzi, Margherita A., (BV) . . . . . '64 '90 C.575 B.S. L.446 J.D. 65 E. Chestnut Hill Rd.
Maco, Frank S., (BV) . . . . . '46 '71 C.1030 B.A. L.472 J.D. State's Atty.
Magary, Susan B. . . . . . '— '84 C.771 B.A. L.146 J.D. P.O. Box 1329‡
Melnick, Kim . . . . . '62 '87 C.861 B.A. L.260 J.D. Litchfield Supr. Ct.
Meter, James J. . . . . . '35 '69 C.967 B.A. L.879 J.D. [Meter&M.]
Meter, Jonathan J. . . . . . '72 '98 C.354 B.S. L.184 J.D. [Meter&M.]
Meter & Meter, LLC . . . . . 457 Bantam Rd.
Moller, Barry S. . . . . . '56 '87 C.535 B.A. L.1029 J.D. [Cramer&A.]
*PRACTICE AREAS: Personal Injury; Workers Compensation Law.
Pickett, Walter M., Jr. . . . . . '26 '52 C.976 B.A. L.184 LL.B. Adm. J., Jud. Dept.
Pulos, Theodore . . . . . '54 '85 C.184 B.S. L.1029 J.D. Corporate Counsel, B/E Aerospace
Rybak, Michael D., (BV) . . . . . '51 '76 C&L.276 A.B., J.D. [Guion,S.&R.]
Sconyers, J. Michael, (BV) . . . . . '46 '76 C.1059 A.B. L.273 J.D. [Gager&P.] (⊙Sharon)
*PRACTICE AREAS: Civil Litigation; Real Property Law; Family Law; Planning and Zoning Law.
Stevens, E. Seward, (AV) . . . . . '10 '37 C.976 B.A. L.1009 LL.B. [Guion,S.&R.]
Van Winkle, Wm. Mitchell, Jr. '13 '41 C.309 L.178 LL.B.
(adm. in NY; not adm. in CT) 293 N. Lake St.‡
Vincenti, Donna D., (AV) . . . . . '56 '83 C.164 B.A. L.1294 J.D. [Gager&P.]
*PRACTICE AREAS: Estate Administration; Trust Administration; Probate; Estate Planning; Elder Law.
Walzer, Roy S. . . . . . '47 '74 C.861 B.A. L.904 J.D. Litchfield Partners
Wolf, Guy W., III, (BV) . . . . . '43 '71 C.1027 B.S. L.184 J.D. Sr. Asst. States Atty.

LYME, 1,822, *New London Co.*

Koch, William T., Jr. . . . . . '53 '79 C.178 B.A. L.1194 J.D. 151 Brush Hill Rd.

MADISON, 14,031, *New Haven Co.*

Armstrong, Robert F. '13 '39 C.433 A.B. L.262 LL.B.
(adm. in NY; not adm. in CT) 20 Downing Way
Atticks, John K., III, (BV) . . . . . '38 '72 C&L.184 B.A., J.D. [Snow,A.&H.]
*PRACTICE AREAS: Real Estate; Foreclosures; Workouts; Commercial Litigation; Probate.
Austin, Hadley W. . . . . . '26 '58 C&L.184 B.A., LL.B. Supr. Ct. J.
Bilcheck, William B., Jr. . . . . . '58 '89 C.184 B.S. L.724 J.D. 107D Bradley Rd.
Brady, Margaret Fox . . . . . '47 '79 C.183 B.A. L.184 J.D. 14 Juniper Ln.
Brady, Robert L. . . . . . '46 '79 C.602 B.A. L.184 J.D. Pres., Business & Legal Reports, Inc.
Burdick, Stanley H., (BV) . . . . . '32 '56 C&L.184 A.B., LL.B. [Burdick&P.]
Burdick & Piombino, (BV) . . . . . 26 Durham Road
Burns, Edward T., (AV) . . . . . '18 '51 C.524 B.S. L.178 LL.B. 42 Strathmore Lane‡
Byrne, Elizabeth N. . . . . . '57 '85 C.1021 B.A. L.1040 J.D. 86 Winding Road
Campbell, Bruce H., (BV) . . . . . '43 '68 C.901 B.A. L.880 J.D. 145 Durham Rd.
Cassidy, Susan O. . . . . . '53 '94 C.446 B.S. L.306 J.D. 10 Sheffield Lane

Clendenen, William H., Jr., A Professional Corporation
(See New Haven)

Costello, Philip N., Jr., (BV) . . . . . '30 '55 C.976 B.A. L.309 LL.B. 16 Wall St.
Cronan, Thomas E., (CV) . . . . . '48 '81 C.197 A.B. L.184 J.D. 71 Bradley Rd.

Dib, Albert '23 '51 C.102 B.A. L.724 LL.B.
(adm. in NY; not adm. in CT) 63 Copse Rd.‡
Dickinson, Elizabeth Morison ....'55 '86 C.309 A.B. L.184 J.D. 945 Boston Post Rd.
Edelberg, Harry W. ....'16 '43 C.918 B.A. L.262 LL.B. Ret. Supr. Ct. J.
Ellis, Sandra K. '51 '92 C.953 B.A. L.574 J.D.
(adm. in NC; not adm. in CT) Bus. & Legal Reports, Inc.
Emanuelson, Herbert L., Jr., (AV) '29 '54 C.976 B.A. L.184 LL.B.
129 Samson Rock Dr.
Fretel, Theodore G., (BV) .... '41 '69 C.602 B.A. L.262 J.D. 26 Durham Rd.

Gibson, Marshal D., Professional Corporation
(See New Haven)

Griffin, John V., Jr., (BV) ....'49 '76 C.433 B.S. L.724 J.D. 25 Willow La.
Grundman, Frank R., (BV) .... '36 '68 C.869 B.S. L.1003 J.D. [Hill,H.&G.]
Hill, Christopher, (BV) ....'48 '74 C.696 B.A. L.818 J.D. [Hill,H.&G.]
Hill, Joseph A., (BV) ....'39 '70 C.93 A.B. L.1202 J.D. [Hill,H.&G.]
Hill, Hill & Grundman, (BV) .... 121 Samson Rock Dr.
Hollo, Leslie S. ....'63 '88 C&L.178 B.A., J.D. [Snow,A.&H.]
*PRACTICE AREAS: Litigation; Negligence; Personal Injury Law; Criminal Defense; Family Law.
Joyce, James R. .... '40 '77 C.994 B.A. L.184 J.D. 149 Durham Rd.
Kinsley, George J., (AV) .... '34 '59 C.676 B.A. L.184 J.D. [G.J.Kinsley]
Kinsley, George J., P.C., (BV) .... Meigswood
Leckerling, Jon P., (AV) ....'48 '78 C.870 B.S. L.902 J.D. [Tyler C.&A.]
Lilburn, Verna B. ....'— '91 C.724 B.S. L.1029 J.D. 101 Laurel Crest Rd.
McManus, George G., Jr., (BV) ....'33 '58 C.321 B.S. L.1202 LL.B. Prob. J.
Metz, Peter A., (BV) .... '37 '62 C.197 A.B. L.893 LL.B. State Rep.
Montgomery, Robert H., (AV) .... '28 '60 C&L.273 B.E.E., J.D. [R.H.Montgomery] (Pat.)
Montgomery, Robert H., P.C., (AV) .... 36 Sportsman Hills Rd. (Pat.)
Patterson, Stephanie Kinsley, (CV) .... '60 '87 C.94 B.A. L.1218 J.D. [G.J.Kinsley]
Piombino, Ronald J., (BV) .... '59 '84 C.184 B.A. L.1048 J.D. [Burdick&P.]
Rubano, Matthew F., Law Office of '55 '97 C.971 B.S.C.E. L.1252 J.D.
41 Cottage Road
Scheffler, Richard J., (BVⓣ) '45 '73 C&L.502 A.B., J.D.
(adm. in MO; not adm. in CT) 12 Richborough Rd.
Schiraldi, Benedict A. .... '29 '63 C.1353 B.S. L.1009 LL.B. 11 Hampshire Rd.
Schloss, Irving S., (AV) ... '45 '72 C.309 A.B. L.976 LL.B. [Tyler C.&A.] (⊙New Haven)
Sellers, Holly Taylor .... '57 '83 C.1044 B.A. L.982 J.D. 24 Carmel Ct.‡
Shanley, James A., Jr. .... '36 '63 C.976 B.A. L.276 J.D. 724 Boston Post Rd.
Singewald, Dean R., (BV) .... '36 '63 C.602 B.S. L.93 J.D. 12 Apple Way (⊙New Haven)
Snow, Donald F., Jr., (AV) .... '47 '72 C.598 B.A. L.945 J.D. [Snow,A.&H.]
*PRACTICE AREAS: Real Estate; Corporate; Banking; Financing.

Snow, Atticks & Hollo, LLC, (AV)
69 Wall Street, P.O. Box 247, 06443
Telephone: 203-245-4800 Facsimile: 203-245-4495 Toll Free: 888-9-THE-LAW
Email: sahattys@aol.com URL: http://www.lawyers.com/sahattys
Donald F. Snow, Jr.; John K. Atticks, III; Leslie S. Hollo.
General Practice including Real Estate, Financing, Banking, Business Law, Probate, Wills, Tax, Trusts and Estates, Personal Injury and Civil and Criminal Litigation, Family Law, Trials in all State and Federal Courts.
See Professional Biographies, MADISON, CONNECTICUT

Spellman, Michael J. '35 '61 C&L.262 B.S., LL.B.
(adm. in NY; not adm. in CT) 15 Esterly Farms Rd.‡
Sweeney, Michael J. .... '68 '98 C.281 B.A. L.1252 J.D. [Ⓐ Burdick&P.]
Tocchi, William P. '55 '82 C.708 B.S. L.1218 J.D.
(adm. in NH; not adm. in CT) Structured Settlement
Tyler Cooper & Alcorn, LLP, (AV)
23 Woodland Rd. (⊙Greenwich, Hartford, New Haven, Stamford)
Weaver, Nancy Zacher '60 '86 C.105 B.A. L.982 J.D.
(adm. in NY; not adm. in CT) 53 Beach Avenue
Willenkin, Roberta G. '39 '79 C.184 B.S. L.284 J.D.
(adm. in PA; not adm. in CT) 255 Neck Rd.
Willig, Peter F. '31 '60 C.453 M.S.C.E. L.569 J.D.
(adm. in NY; not adm. in CT) 22 Wilshire Rd.‡

MANCHESTER, 49,761, *Hartford Co.*

Adkins, Allan B., (AVⓣ) '34 '58 C&L.846 B.A., LL.B.
(adm. in TX; not adm. in CT) 150 Pine St.
Amato, Thomas A. ....'56 '82 C&L.184 B.S., J.D. 357 E. Center St.
Bagley, Roger B. '10 '35 L.107 LL.B.
(adm. in NY; not adm. in CT) 66 Dale Rd.‡
Balskus-Kelly, Caryl E. .... '70 '95 C.184 B.A. L.306 J.D. [Diana,C.&T.]
*PRACTICE AREAS: Family; Corporate; Real Estate.
Barlow, Malcolm F., (BV) ....'43 '78 C&L.184 B.A., J.D. [Barlow,M.&L.]
*PRACTICE AREAS: Real Estate; Probate; Elder Law.

Barlow, Murphy & Lavigne, LLP, (BV)
172 East Center Street, 06040-5252
Telephone: 860-646-4081 Fax: 860-645-1608
Email: info@barlow-murphy.com URL: http://www.lawyers.com/barlowmurphy
Members of Firm: Malcolm F. Barlow; Brian J. Murphy; Gary D. Lavigne.
General Civil Practice before State and Federal Courts. Personal Injury, Real Estate, Estate Planning, Elder Law and Probate Administration, Trials and Appeals, Probate, Elder Law, Business Law, Foreclosure, Bankruptcy.
References: Connecticut Attorney's Title Insurance Co.; Connecticut National Bank; Manchester State Bank; Savings Bank of Manchester.
See Professional Biographies, MANCHESTER, CONNECTICUT

Barry, David M., Jr. .... '63 '92 C.855 B.A. L.184 J.D. [Ⓐ Jacobs,W.R.&B.]
*PRACTICE AREAS: Zoning; Commercial Transactions; Secured Transactions; Commercial Real Estate; Residential Real Estate.
Basche, Steven M., (BV) .... '61 '86 C&L.184 B.A., J.D. [Jacobs,W.R.&B.]
*PRACTICE AREAS: Civil Litigation; Commercial Litigation; Construction Litigation; Intellectual Property Litigation; Commercial Real Estate.
Beck, Bruce S., (BV) ....'46 '73 C.446 B.S. L.128 J.D. [Beck&E.] ⊙
*PRACTICE AREAS: Commercial Litigation; Domestic Relations; Bankruptcy.

Beck & Eldergill, P.C., (AV)
447 Center Street, 06040 ⊙
Telephone: 860-646-5606 FAX: 860-646-0054
Email: firm@beckeldergill.com URL: http://www.beckeldergill.com
Bruce S. Beck; Kathleen Eldergill; Kenneth I. Friedman; Marc P. Mercier; Fatima T. Lobo; David R. Kritzman; Matthew R. Potter;—Derek V. Oatis; Maria C. Monick.
General Civil and Criminal Litigation before all State and Federal Trial and Appellate Courts with a concentration on Employment, Civil Rights, Personal Injury, Car Accidents and Divorce.
Hartford, Connecticut Office: 97 Oak Street. 06109. Telephone: 860-522-5606.
See Professional Biographies, MANCHESTER, CONNECTICUT

Bennett, Charles P. '20 '42 C.415 B.A. L.732 LL.B.
(adm. in NY; not adm. in CT) 403 W. Center St.‡
Botticello, Barry W., (BV) ....'50 '75 C.184 B.A. L.306 J.D. [Penny,B.O.&H.]
Bradley, Donald F. ....'32 '63 C.717 B.S. L.184 J.D. 65 Ludlow Rd. (Pat.)
Broneill, William M., (BV) .... '40 '66 C&L.184 B.A., J.D. 178 E. Center St.

Camposeo, Elaine N., (BV) '47 '89 C.999 B.S. L.1048 J.D.
445 Center Street, P.O. Box 741, 06045-0741
Telephone: 860-643-8330 Telefax: 860-646-0054
Email: ENCamposeo@aol.com
Probate, Wills and Estate Planning, Real Estate, Parental Rights, Landlord & Tenant Law, Mortgages.
See Professional Biographies, MANCHESTER, CONNECTICUT

Carlson, Jeffrey M. .....'55 '82 C.1030 B.A. L.809 J.D. Gen. Coun., First Hartford Corp.
*RESPONSIBILITIES: Commercial Real Estate; Commercial Litigation; Construction Litigation; Corporate Law.
Cella, Thomas P., (BV) ... '57 '83 C.184 B.A. L.1048 J.D. [Howard,K.S.&F.] (⊙Hartford)
Collins, William B., (BV) .... '28 '59 C&L.184 B.S., J.D. [Collins]
Collins Law Firm, P.C., (BV) .... 357 E. Center St.
Comollo, Bruce J., (BV) .... '62 '87 C.156 B.A. L.1048 J.D. 519 Center St.
Conti, Richard S., (BV) .... '53 '79 C.321 B.A. L.184 J.D. [Diana,C.&T.]
*PRACTICE AREAS: Civil and Criminal Litigation; Municipal Law; Personal Injury; Real Estate; Zoning Law.
Cooney, John W., (BV) ....'42 '78 C.1033 B.A. L.184 J.D. 561 E. Center St.
Corbeil, Stephen R. .... '57 '85 C.588 B.S. L.607 J.D. 64 Irving St.
Darby, Michael M., (BV) '57 '82
C.1033 B.A. L.228 J.D. [Phelon,F.&W.] & [Ⓒ Litchfield C.]
*PRACTICE AREAS: Real Estate; Probate Administration; Estate Planning; Elder Law; Zoning.
Darren, Marc .... '68 '00 C.645 B.S. L.1017 J.D. [Ⓐ Diana,C.&T.]
*PRACTICE AREAS: General Corporate; Business Planning; Business Formation; Tax Law; Bankruptcy.
Deichmann, Petra F. .....'— '82 C.296 B.A. L.575 J.D. Gen. Coun., First Hartford Corp.
*RESPONSIBILITIES: Real Estate; Corpoorate Law; SEC Filings.
Diana, Leo V., (BV) .... '61 '88 C.184 B.A. L.1048 J.D. [Diana,C.&T.]
*PRACTICE AREAS: Domestic; Family Law; Criminal Litigation; Probate; Real Estate.
Diana, Vincent L., (AV) .... '30 '55 C.855 B.A. L.145 J.D. [Ⓒ Diana,C.&T.]
*PRACTICE AREAS: Probate; Domestic; Real Estate; Criminal Litigation.

Diana, Conti & Tunila, LLP, (BV)
1091 Main Street, 06040
Telephone: 860-643-2181 Fax: 860-647-7950
Email: rconti@dcaudt.com
Members of Firm: Harold W. Garrity (Deceased); Jerome I. Walsh (Deceased); Richard S. Conti; John G. Tunila; Leo V. Diana; Caryl E. Balskus-Kelly. Of Counsel: Vincent L. Diana. Associates: James J. Walker; Marc Darren.
Civil and Criminal Litigation. Corporations, Partnerships, Business Law, Tax Law, Commercial Law, Real Estate, Bankruptcy, Estate Planning, Probate, Zoning, Municipal Law, Family Law, Negligence. Trials in all Courts.
References: Savings Bank of Rockville; Savings Bank of Manchester, Connecticut; Attorneys Title Insurance Company; Webster Bank.

Di Loreto, Mario ....'68 '95 C.867 B.A. L.982 J.D. 117 Meadowbrook Dr.
Dyer, Richard W., (AV) ....'50 '77 C.321 B.A. L.184 J.D. 773 Main St.
Eldergill, Kathleen, (AV) .... '53 '81 C&L.184 B.A., J.D. [Beck&E.]
*PRACTICE AREAS: Employment; Civil Rights; Civil Litigation; Consumer Law; Environmental Law.
Epstein, Constance L., (BV) '43 '79 C.338 B.A. L.184 J.D.
[Howard,K.S.&F.] (⊙Hartford)
Falkenstein, Stanley, (BV) .... '44 '71 C.188 A.B. L.569 J.D. [Marte,K.F.M.&P.]
Fiano, Lawrence A. ....'51 '77 C.1029 B.S. L.796 J.D. Pres., LandTech Props., Inc
Fiorentino, Thomas S., (BV) '57 '82
C.67 B.A. L.184 J.D. [Phelon,F.&W.] & [Ⓒ Litchfield C.]
*PRACTICE AREAS: Family and Juvenile Law; Real Estate; Personal Injury; Probate and Estate Planning; Criminal.
FitzGerald, John R., (AV) .... '27 '53 C&L.184 B.A., J.D. [Howard,K.S.&F.] (⊙Hartford)
FitzGerald, Thomas P., (AV) '44 '69
C.712 B.B.A. L.823 J.D. [Phelon,F.&W.] & [Ⓒ Litchfield C.]
*PRACTICE AREAS: Personal Injury; Commercial Litigation; Civil Litigation.
FitzGerald, William E. .... '24 '53 C&L.184 B.A., LL.B. 140 Richmond Dr.
Friedman, Kenneth I., (BV) ....'62 '88 C.188 A.B. L.880 J.D. [Beck&E.]
*PRACTICE AREAS: Employment; Personal Injury; Civil Litigation; Civil Rights.
Frolich, Evelyn G., (BV) .... '54 '79 C.1107 B.A. L.1338 J.D. [Gryk,F.&F.]
Frolich, Terrance J., (BV) ....'53 '79 C.1107 B.A. L.1338 J.D. [Gryk,F.&F.]
Fuger, Stanley T., Jr. ....'50 '78 C.869 B.S. L.273 J.D. Supr. Ct. J.
Gaines, Robert M. ....'31 '56 C&L.184 A.B., J.D. 441-63 S. Main St.
Gardner, Barbara E. ....'55 '86 C.705 B.A. L.1202 J.D. 843 Main Street
Golas, David A., (BV) ....'38 '65 C.855 A.B. L.184 J.D. [Golas&G.]
Golas, David A., II ....'70 '96 C.855 B.A. L.1202 J.D. [Golas&G.]
Golas & Golas, P.C., (BV) .... 945 Main St.
Groobert, Paul B., (BV) .... '24 '52 C.184 B.S. L.178 LL.B. 257 E. Center St.
Gryk, Anthony J., Jr., (CV) .... '59 '86 C.1107 B.A. L.1338 J.D. [Gryk,F.&F.]
Gryk, Wesley C. .... '17 '43 C.860 B.S. L.94 LL.B. 470 Main St.
Gryk, Frolich & Frolich, (BV) .... 333 E. Center St.
Handler, Michael H., (BV) ....'46 '72 C.184 B.A. L.818 J.D. Supv. Asst. Pub. Def.
Hauschild, Vernon F. ....'21 '51 C.869 B.S. L.184 J.D. 93 Constance Dr. (Pat.)
Higgins, James M., Jr., (BV) ....'55 '80 C.321 A.B. L.306 J.D. [Penny,B.O.&H.]
Horvath, Leonard M., (BV) ....'49 '76 C.397 B.A. L.1048 J.D. [LaBelle,L.N.&H.]
Horwitz, Melvin .... '26 '86 C.178 B.A. L.976 J.D. Pres., Helapol Assocs.‡
Howard, James H., (BV) '63 '88
C.319 B.A. L.184 J.D. [Phelon,F.&W.] & [Ⓒ Litchfield C.]
*PRACTICE AREAS: Civil Litigation; Real Estate.
Howard, Kohn, Sprague & FitzGerald, (AV)
99 East Center Street (⊙Glastonbury, Hartford)
Jacobs, Leonard, (AV) ....'43 '68 C&L.184 B.S., LL.B. [Jacobs,W.R.&B.]
*PRACTICE AREAS: Zoning; Commercial Real Estate; Commercial Transactions; Secured Transactions; Banking.
Jacobs, Ronald, (AV) .... '27 '52 C.855 B.A. L.184 LL.B. [Jacobs,W.R.&B.]
*PRACTICE AREAS: Corporation; Taxation; Probate; Estate Planning and Administration; Commercial Transactions.

Jacobs, Walker, Rice & Basche, P.C., (AV)
146 Main Street, P.O. Box 480, 06045-0480
Telephone: 860-646-0121 Fax: 860-645-6229
Email: jwrblaw@hotmail.com
Ronald Jacobs; Leonard Jacobs; Jean T. Walker; Michael J. Rice; Steven M. Basche;—David M. Barry, Jr.; Catherine J. Kulak.
General Practice. Banking, Probate and Estate Planning, Commercial Transactions, Secured Transactions, Commercial and Residential Real Estate, Zoning, Corporation and Taxation Law, Civil and Commercial Litigation, Creditors Rights.
See Professional Biographies, MANCHESTER, CONNECTICUT

Jacobson, Margaret J., (BV) ....'51 '84 C.788 B.A. L.184 J.D. [Thomas,S.J.&R.]
Janenda, Joel E., (BV) ....'42 '66 C&L.184 B.A., LL.B. 249 E. Ctr. St.
Johnson, Nancy Jeanne, (BV) '57 '83
C.281 B.A. L.1048 J.D. [Ⓐ Phelon,F.&W.] & [Ⓒ Litchfield C.]
*PRACTICE AREAS: Probate Administration; Estate Planning; Elder Law.
Keith, W. David, (BV) .... '21 '49 C.918 B.A. L.306 J.D. [Marte,K.F.M.&P.]
Kibler, Frank N. ....'47 '93 C.550 B.A. L.184 J.D. 257 E. Center St.
Kritzman, David R., (BV) .... '58 '84 C&L.184 B.A., J.D. [Beck&E.]
*PRACTICE AREAS: Criminal; Personal Injury; Family Litigation.

Kulak, Catherine J. .... '71 '00 C.551 B.A. L.184 J.D. [Ⓐ Jacobs,W.R.&B.]
*PRACTICE AREAS: Residential Real Estate; Civil Litigation; Commercial Litigation.
LaBelle, John D., (AV) ....'15 '46 C.165 A.B. L.273 LL.B. [LaBelle,L.N.&H.]
LaBelle, John D., Jr., (BV) ....'49 '75 C.165 A.B. L.94 J.D. [LaBelle,L.N.&H.]
LaBelle, LaBelle, Naab & Horvath, P.C., (AV) ....295 East Center Street
Lavigne, Gary D., (BV) ....'53 '80 C.184 B.A. L.1048 J.D. [Barlow,M.&L.]
*PRACTICE AREAS: Residential Real Estate; Commercial Real Estate; Corporate Law; Business Law; Foreclosures.
Lehmann, Linda Carole ....'53 '97 C.793 B.A. L.1048 J.D. P.O. Box 1812
Lobo, Fatima T., (BV) ....'66 '91 C.184 B.A. L.306 J.D. [Beck&E.]
*PRACTICE AREAS: Domestic Relations; Probate; Real Estate; Bankruptcy and Credit Problems.
Lopiano, George M. ....'39 '83 C.1030 B.A. L.306 J.D. 147 Bentley Dr.
Mabbett, Deborah ....'— '96 C.1278 B.P.S. L.1252 J.D. 410 Center St.
Macht, Elliot G., (BV) ....'52 '79 C.472 B.B.A. L.285 J.D. [Woodhouse,R.&M.]
Marlow, George H. ....'14 '42 C.309 S.B. L.184 LL.B. 51 Blue Ridge Dr.‡
Marquez, Ernest R. '48 '81 C.184 B.A. L.1048 J.D.
Asst. V.P. for Pers., Conn. State Univ.
Marte, Paul R., (AV) ....'27 '53 C.855 B.S. L.94 J.D. [Marte,K.F.M.&P.]
Marte, Keith, Falkenstein, Meggers & Paul, P.C., (AV) ....113 E. Center St.
McKeon, John P., (BV) .... '27 '57 C&L.276 A.B., LL.B. 46C Esquire Dr.
McMahon, Dennis P., (BV) ....'56 '81 C.708 B.A. L.607 J.D. 128 E. Center St.
Mercier, Marc P. ....'65 '91 C&L.184 B.A., J.D. [Beck&E.]
*PRACTICE AREAS: Civil Litigation; Employment; Civil Rights; School and Education Law.
Monick, Maria C. ....'65 '96 C.1145 B.S. L.1048 J.D. [Ⓐ Beck&E.]
*PRACTICE AREAS: Criminal Law; Foreclosures; Probate; Real Estate; Bankruptcy.
Moriarty, Thomas P., (BV) ....'54 '88 C.93 B.A. L.1048 J.D. 295 E. Center St.
Moses, Victor I., (BV) ....'38 '64 C.184 B.S. L.94 LL.B. 357 E. Center St.
Murdock-Meggers, Robin S., (BV) ....'57 '83 C.93 B.S. L.818 J.D. [Marte,K.F.M.&P.]
Murphy, Brian J. ....'58 '96 C.999 B.S. L.184 J.D. [Barlow,M.&L.]
*PRACTICE AREAS: Real Estate; General Practice; Construction Law.
Naab, Geoffrey, (AV) ....'38 '72 C&L.813 A.B., J.D. [LaBelle,L.N.&H.]
Oatis, Derek V. ....'66 '98 C.1102 B.A. L.306 J.D. [Ⓐ Beck&E.]
*PRACTICE AREAS: Employment; Environmental Law; Criminal Litigation; Zoning Law.
O'Brien, Kevin M., (BV) ....'49 '75 C.708 B.A. L.818 J.D. [Penny,B.O.&H.]
O'Connell, David L. ....'46 '74 C.93 B.S. L.184 J.D. Twenty Tolland Tpke.
O'Marra, Thomas R. ....'42 '67 C.1030 A.B. L.184 LL.B. 20 Schaller Rd.‡
O'Neil, Timothy P., (BV) ....'51 '82 C.184 B.A. L.1048 J.D. [T.P.O'Neil]
O'Neil, Timothy P., P.C., (BV) ....202 E. Center St.
Onore, Eric, (BV) ....'52 '81 C.550 B.S. L.184 J.D. [Pagano&Z.]
Pagano, Anthony F., (BV) ....'48 '73 C.776 B.A. L.128 J.D. [Pagano&Z.]
Pagano & Zuboff, (BV) ....344 Center Street
Papa, John Stephen, (BV) .... '42 '67 C&L.262 A.B., J.D. [Howard,K.S.&F.] (⊙Hartford)
Paul, Julia Morris, (CV) ....'52 '79 C.308 B.A. L.982 J.D. [Marte,K.F.M.&P.]
Penny, Stephen T., (BV) ....'48 '73 C.611 B.A. L.306 J.D. [Penny,B.O.&H.]
Penny, Botticello, O'Brien & Higgins, P.C., (BV) ....202 W. Center St.
Peterson, Donna M. ....'59 '98 C.404 B.A. L.1048 J.D. Asst. Coun., Lydall, Inc.
Petrone, Peter J., (BV) ....'54 '82 C.1033 B.A. L.744 J.D. [Ⓐ Phelon,F.&W.]
*PRACTICE AREAS: Real Estate; General Practice.

Phelon, FitzGerald & Wood, P.C., (AV)
773 Main Street, 06040
Telephone: 860-643-1136 Fax: 860-643-5773
Email: PFW_LAWFIRM@COMPUSERV.COM
Herbert A. Phelon, Jr. (1925-2000); Thomas P. FitzGerald; Howard M. Wood, III; Michael M. Darby; Thomas S. Fiorentino; James H. Howard; James J. Sullivan;—Nancy Jeanne Johnson; Peter J. Petrone.
General Civil and Criminal Litigation before all State and Federal Courts. Commercial Litigation, Corporation, Workers' Compensation, Zoning, Wills and Probate, Personal Injury, Medical Malpractice.
Representative Clients: Dean Machine Products, Inc.; Citizens Mortgage Corp.; Liberty Bank; Shawmut Bank FNA Connecticut National Bank; Town of Manchester; Town of South Windsor; Natchaug Hospital; Reliable Refuse.
Reference: First Federal Savings & Loan Association.
See Professional Biographies, MANCHESTER, CONNECTICUT

Plepler, Sanford J., (BV) ....'29 '56 C.184 B.A. L.94 LL.B. 113 E. Center St.
Potter, Matthew R. ....'69 '94 C.910 B.A. L.1048 J.D. [Beck&E.]
*PRACTICE AREAS: Personal Injury; Domestic Relations; Criminal Litigation; Bankruptcy and Credit Problems.
Prignano, Pascal A., (BV) ..... '38 '65 C&L.724 B.A., LL.B. 519 Center St. (⊙Columbia)
Prindle, Brian E., (BV) ....'52 '76 C.188 B.A. L.184 J.D. 72 Bissell St.
Reese, M. Frances ....'57 '83 C.562 B.A. L.184 J.D. P.O. Box 1203
Rice, Michael J., (BV) ....'61 '86 C.187 B.S. L.1194 J.D. [Jacobs,W.R.&B.]
*PRACTICE AREAS: Corporation; Taxation; Probate; Estate Planning and Administration; Commercial Transactions.
Robinson, Thomas A. ....'68 '96 C.855 B.A. L.861 J.D. [Ⓐ Woodhouse,R.&M.]
Rossettie, Mary Ann ....'54 '79 C.188 B.A. L.94 J.D. 280 Main St.
Rubinow, Jay E. ....'12 '38 C&L.309 A.B., LL.B. 49 Pitkin St.‡
Rubinow, Laurence P., (BV) ....'44 '69 C.930 B.A. L.184 J.D. [Woodhouse,R.&M.]
Shea, Cornelius J., (BV) ....'36 '62 C.745 B.A. L.184 LL.B. Asst. States Atty.
Shea, Francis Courtney, (BV) ....'26 '54 C.128 A.B. L.276 LL.B. 237 E. Center St.
Shea, William J. ....'32 '59 C.321 B.S. L.184 LL.B. Asst. Town Atty.
Simon, Jorge A., (BV) ....'51 '82 C.201 B.S. L.184 J.D. Asst. State's Atty.
Soranno, Richard S., (BV) ....'44 '74 C&L.184 B.S., J.D. [Thomas,S.J.&R.]
Starkweather, Van A., (BV) ....'51 '78 C.184 B.A. L.1202 J.D. 257 E. Center St.
Sullivan, James J., (BV) ....'48 '73 C.676 B.A. L.818 J.D. [Phelon,F.&W.]
*PRACTICE AREAS: Family Law; Real Estate; Probate; Criminal Law; Zoning Law.
Summers, L. T. Archer ....'59 '97 C&L.276 A.B., J.D. Sr. Min.
Tanguay, Raymond J., (BV) ....'36 '79 C.431 B.A. L.1048 J.D. 333 E. Center St.
Taylor, Marshall C. ....'39 '65 C.976 B.A. L.477 J.D. 102 Lakewood Cir., S.
Terenzio, Lisa ....'60 '92 C.771 B.A. L.1029 J.D. 843 Main St.
Thomas, Allan D., (BV) ....'32 '57 C&L.184 B.A., J.D. [Thomas,S.J.&R.]
Thomas, Soranno, Jacobson & Radke, (BV) ....945 Main St.
Tomaro, Anthony A., (BV) ....'22 '51 C&L.16 B.S., LL.B. 70 Middle Turnpike E.‡
Tremblay, Mary Adamowicz '60 '85
C.1030 B.A. L.569 J.D. Gen. Coun. & Secy., Lydall, Inc.
Tunila, John G., (BV) ....'58 '84 C&L.184 B.A., J.D. [Diana,C.&T.]
*PRACTICE AREAS: Corporations; Partnerships; Business Law; Tax Law; Commercial Law.
Walker, James J. ....'65 '97 C.184 B.A. L.1003 J.D. [Ⓐ Diana,C.&T.]
*PRACTICE AREAS: Personal Injury; Bankruptcy; Civil Litigation.
Walker, Jean T., (BV) ....'43 '85 C.183 B.A. L.184 J.D. [Jacobs,W.R.&B.]
*PRACTICE AREAS: Commercial and Residential Real Estate.
Wallace, Karen D. ....'54 '85 C.676 B.A. L.306 J.D. 45 Boulder Rd.
Walsh, Jeffrey T., (BV) ....'58 '83 C.1200 B.A. L.1048 J.D. 210 Main St.
Walsh, Milton I., (BV) ....'66 '90 C.1030 B.A. L.184 J.D. Pub. Def.
Wichman, David C., (BV) ....'37 '65 C.188 B.A. L.184 LL.B. 21 Middle Tpke E
Wood, Howard M., III, (BV) '40 '65
C.1033 B.S. L.69 LL.B. [Phelon,F.&W.] & [◎ Litchfield C.]
*PRACTICE AREAS: Civil Litigation; Construction Law; Church and Non-Profit Law; Commercial Law.
Woodhouse, Richard C., (BV) ....'34 '60 C.197 A.B. L.309 J.D. [Woodhouse,R.&M.]
Woodhouse, Rubinow & Macht, P.C., (BV) ....555 Main St.
Zuboff, Steven D., (BV) ....'56 '84 C.93 B.A. L.940 J.D. [Pagano&Z.]

MANSFIELD CENTER, 20,634, *Tolland Co.*

Huffmire, Madelyn M. ....'38 '80 C.518 B.A. L.1294 J.D. 79 Mulberry Rd.
Ossen, Jeffrey P., (BV) ....'40 '67 C.184 B.A. L.309 LL.B. 236 Stafford Rd.

MARLBOROUGH, 4,746, *Hartford Co.*

Elliott, Robert M. ....'45 '71 C.708 B.A. L.818 J.D. 7A S. Main St.
Farrell, Joseph D. ....'59 '85 C.800 A.B. L.990 J.D. 25 S. Stonybrook Dr.
Goode, Peter H. ....'46 '68 C.184 B.A. L.1029 J.D. 23 Gina Lane
Guzman, William D. ....'45 '82 C.724 B.B.A. L.184 J.D. 11 Virginia Rail Dr.
O'Connell, John J., Jr. '39 '65 C&L.276 A.B., J.D.
(adm. in MA; not adm. in CT) 54 N. Main St.‡
Parker, Jann M. ....'57 '83 C.1044 B.A. L.184 J.D. 62 So Stony Brook Dr
Phelps, Carol B. ....'56 '85 C.67 B.A. L.184 J.D. 11 Williamsburg Rd.‡
Reisine, Gary R. ....'51 '86 C.1044 B.A. L.184 J.D. 445 Jones Hollow Rd.
Ruggiero, Louis J. ....'46 '77 C.184 B.S. L.306 J.D. 29 Sherwood Lane

MERIDEN, 59,479, *New Haven Co.*

Abrams, Arnold B., (CV) ....'43 '77 C.454 B.A. L.818 J.D. One Barristers Ct.
Adelman, Gerard I., (BV) ....'46 '82 C.608 B.A. L.184 J.D. [Weigand,M.&A.]
*PRACTICE AREAS: Divorce Mediation; Family; Social Security; Landlord and Tenant Law; General Practice.
Axelrod, Robert M., (AV) ....'45 '70 C.732 B.A. L.184 J.D. 204 East Main Street
Brown, David, (AV) ....'30 '62 C&L.184 B.S., LL.B. [◎ Brown&W.]
*PRACTICE AREAS: Commercial Law; Uniform Commercial Code; Bankruptcy; Probate.

Brown & Welsh, P.C., (AV)
Meriden Executive Park, 530 Preston Avenue, 2nd Floor, P.O. Box 183, 06450-0183
Telephone: 203-235-1651 Telecopier: 203-235-9600 http://www.brownwelsh.com
URL: http://www.brown&welsh@brownwelsh.com
Thomas J. Welsh; Houston Putnam Lowry. Of Counsel: David Brown.
Domestic and International Business Law and related Litigation, including Contracts, Uniform Commercial Code, Bankruptcy, Arbitration, Corporate Law, Computer Law, Real Property and Probate.
See Professional Biographies, MERIDEN, CONNECTICUT

Cadden, Thomas P., (BV) ....'51 '78 C.184 B.S. L.1048 J.D. [Cadden,I.&I.]
Cadden, Ivers & Ivers, (BV) ....107 E. Main St.
Chapman, David D., (BV) ....'57 '85 C.178 B.A. L.1048 J.D. 639 Resch. Pkwy.
Cheerman, Leonard H., (BV) ....'45 '72 C.264 A.B. L.94 J.D. 12 Curtis St.
Cruickshank, Jay S. ....'54 '99 C.971 B.S. L.1252 J.D. 965 East Main St
D'Astous, Paul, (BV) ....'48 '73 C&L.184 B.A., J.D. 17 Brian Ct.
DeFrances, Guy, Jr., (BV) ....'61 '86 C.183 B.A. L.184 J.D. 405 Broad St.
DeFrances, Guy R., (BV) ....'34 '59 C.918 A.B. L.184 J.D. [Luby,O.M.G.&D.]
Donovan, John R., (AV) ....'53 '79 C.893 B.A. L.184 J.D. [Donovan&M.] ⊙
*PRACTICE AREAS: Criminal Defense; Driving While Intoxicated; Homicide; Sex Crimes; Drugs and Narcotics.

Donovan & Morello, LLP, (AV)
816 Broad Street, 06450 ⊙
Telephone: 860-635-7373
URL: http://www.donmorlaw.com
Members of Firm: John R. Donovan; Paul A. Morello, Jr.
General Civil and Criminal Practice before State and Federal Courts. Personal Injury, Product Liability, Workers Compensation Law, Trials, Arbitration, Mediation, Uninsured and Underinsured Motorists, Medical Malpractice.
Cromwell, Connecticut Office: Cromwell West Office Park, 154 West Street. Telephone: 860-635-7373. Fax: 860-635-6734.
See Professional Biographies, MERIDEN, CONNECTICUT

Eppler-Epstein, Steven D. ....'58 '83 C&L.976 B.A., J.D. Connecticut Legal Servs.
Fontanella, Bruce A., (BV) ....'49 '81 C.216 B.A. L.184 J.D. [Luby,O.M.G.&D.]
Fordiani, Alfred L., Jr., (BV) ....'31 '60 C.712 A.B. L.94 LL.B. Asst. Corp. Coun.
Fordiani, Martha L., (BV) '37 '78 C.94 A.B. L.184 J.D.
Exec. V.P. & Gen. Coun., Veterans Memorial Med. Ctr.
Friedman, Judi E. '60 '87 C.1046 B.A. L.564 J.D.
(adm. in NJ; not adm. in CT) 200 Pratt ST.
Gaffney, Dennis F., (BV) ....'39 '65 C.321 B.S. L.184 LL.B. [Luby,O.M.G.&D.]

Gerber, Sandra K., (BV) '48 '83 C&L.1029 B.S., J.D.
636 Broad Street, P.O. Box 2420, 06450
Telephone: 203-238-1010 Fax: 203-630-1930
URL: http://www.lawyers.com/sgerber,atty
***PRACTICE AREAS: Family Law; Personal Injury; Workers Compensation; General Practice; Civil Litigation.**
Family, Real Estate, Negligence, Civil Litigation, Workers Compensation, Products Liability, Medical Liability and Professional Malpractice Law.
See Professional Biographies, MERIDEN, CONNECTICUT

Gooley, Charles E. ....'53 '78 C.855 B.A. L.184 J.D. Yankee Gas
Graham, Colin R. '67 '96 C.388 B.A. L.1218 J.D.
Assoc. Coun., Information Management Associates, Inc.
Healey, Mary Joy '51 '77 C.518 A.B. L.93 J.D.
Vice President, General Counsel & Secretary, Yankee Gas Services Co.
Hector, Rivera ....'— '96 C.1102 B.S. L.896 J.D. [H.Rivera]
Hillman, Lawrence S. ....'56 '81 C.319 B.A. L.818 J.D. [Ⓐ Solomon,K.W.&G.]
Ivers, Cornelius J., (BV) ....'49 '78 C.1103 B.A. L.365 J.D. [Cadden,I.&I.]
Ivers, John D., Jr. ....'66 '92 C.690 B.S. L.692 J.D. [Cadden,I.&I.]
Jacobs, Barry, (BV) ....'52 '81 C.472 B.A. L.1029 J.D. [Jacobs&J.]
*PRACTICE AREAS: Personal Injury; Real Estate Law; Domestic Relations Law; Criminal Law; Probate.
Jacobs, Stephen D., (BV) ....'46 '72 C.276 B.A. L.473 J.D. [Jacobs&J.]
*PRACTICE AREAS: Personal Injury Law; Criminal Law; Domestic Relations Law; Workers Compensation Law; Real Estate Law.

Jacobs & Jacobs, P.C., (BV)
71 Catlin Street, P.O. Box 193, 06450-0193 ⊙
Telephone: 203-235-5787 Fax: 203-235-0447
Email: jacobs.jacobs@snet.net URL: http://www.lawyers.com/jacobs&jacobs
Stephen D. Jacobs; Barry Jacobs.
Litigation, Civil Trial, Real Estate, Construction, Personal Injury, Workers Compensation, Criminal Defense, Domestic Relations, Real Estate and Social Security Disability Law.
Reference: Center Bank.
See Professional Biographies, MERIDEN, CONNECTICUT

Johnson, Jeanette A.A. ....'58 '86 C.184 B.S. L.1202 J.D. P.O. Box 5008
Johnson, Walter G., Jr., (BV) ....'49 '74 C.103 A.B. L.188 J.D. [Larsen,S.&J.]
Keegan, Kristina F. ....'71 '96 C.945 B.A. L.597 J.D. 800 Research Pkwy.
Kendzior, Lawrence J., (BV) ....'50 '75 C.569 B.A. L.94 J.D. [Tonkonow&K.]
Koblish, Vincent A., (BV) ....'38 '69 89 E. Main St.
Kobrin, Robyn R. ....'64 '89 C.1029 B.S. L.1048 J.D. 290 Pratt St.
Krupnikoff, Jeffrey M., (BV) ....'50 '79 C.696 B.A. L.184 J.D. [Solomon,K.W.&G.]
LaMontagne, Louise C., (BV) ....'43 '79 C.788 B.A. L.184 J.D. 639 Resch. Pkway.

Lanzoni, Dennis C., (BV) .... '52 '77 C.105 B.A. L.184 J.D. [D.C.Lanzoni]
Lanzoni, Dennis C., P.C., (BV) .... 834 Broad St.
Larsen, St. John & Johnson, P.C., (BV) .... 3 Colony St., 2nd Fl.
Lewis, Larry H., (BV) '49 '80 C.546 B.A. L.1029 J.D.
Administrative Trial Attorney, Nationwide Mutual Insurance Company
Lonardo, Thomas T., (BV) .... '48 '73 C&L.93 A.B., J.D. [T.T.Lonardo]
Lonardo, Thomas T., P.C., (BV) .... 290 Pratt St.
Lowry, Houston Putnam, (AV) .... '55 '80 C.1168 B.A. L.285 J.D. [Brown&W.]
*PRACTICE AREAS: Business Law; Civil Litigation; Arbitration; International; Appellate Practice.
Luby, Robert M., (AV) .... '14 '39 C&L.976 A.B., LL.B. [Ⓒ Luby,O.M.G.&D.]
Luby, Thomas S., (BV) .... '52 '77 C.976 B.A. L.184 J.D. [Luby,O.M.G.&D.]
Luby, Olson, Mango, Gaffney and DeFrances, P.C., (BV) ....405 Broad Street
Mack, Janice N., (CV) .... '62 '87 C.329 B.A. L.893 J.D. [J.N.Mack]
Mack, Janice N., P.C., (CV) .... 29 W. Main St., Suite 201
Mahon, Brian T., (AV) .... '48 '73 C.321 A.B. L.880 J.D. [Weigand,M.&A.]
*PRACTICE AREAS: Plaintiff's Negligence; Workers' Compensation; Labor Law; Civil Trials.
Mango, Kenneth W., (BV) .... '39 '65 C&L.184 B.S., LL.B. [Luby,O.M.G.&D.]
Mark, William I., (CV) .... '28 '60 C&L.569 A.B., LL.B. 272 W. Main St.
McGroarty, Michael P. '60 '87 C.276 B.S.B.A. L.884 J.D.
COO, General Counsel & Secretary, Information Management Associates, Inc.
Melien, Peter E., (BV) .... '51 '76 C.321 B.A. L.184 J.D. [Tobin&M.] ⊙
Moore, Kieren M. .... '57 '92 C.1102 B.A. L.1048 J.D. 19 Coe Ave.
Morasutti, Bruno R., (BV) .... '53 '83 C.569 B.A. L.1202 J.D. [Luby,O.M.G.&D.]
Morello, Paul A., Jr., (BV) .... '54 '79 C.321 B.A. L.982 J.D. [Donovan&M.] ⊙
*PRACTICE AREAS: Personal Injury Law; Medical Malpractice; Bicycle Accidents; Head and Spinal Injury; Uninsured and Underinsured Motorists.
Noonan, Thomas F. .... '46 '76 C.184 B.S. L.724 J.D. 827 Broad St.
O'Brien, D. T. .... '17 '41 C&L.976 B.A., LL.B. Station A-Box 2082
O'Brien, Francis J. .... '19 '48 C.262 A.B. L.184 LL.B. State Trial Ref.
Olson, Gary O., (AV) .... '29 '56 C.1033 B.S. L.184 LL.B. [Ⓒ Luby,O.M.G.&D.]
Palmbach, Timothy Mark .... '60 '98 C.1156 B.S. L.184 J.D. 278 Colony St.
Papandrea, John F. .... '34 '59 C.1030 B.S. L.306 J.D. 66 Orchard Hill Rd.
Patrucco, Jon, (CV) .... '64 '90 C.475 B.A. L.1187 J.D. 39 Butler St.
Powers, Leonard J., (BV) '26 '58 C.676 B.A. L.93 J.D.
(adm. in MA; not adm. in CT) 827 Broad St.
Quinn, Michael D. .... '68 '97 C.28 B.S. L.1187 J.D. [Ⓐ Weigand,M.&A.]
*PRACTICE AREAS: Personal Injury; Workers' Compensation; Criminal Law.
Rivera, Hector, L.L.C. .... 816 Broad Street
Roccapriore, Marie C. .... '71 '97 C.19 B.A. L.982 J.D. 69 Hillcrest Ave.
Russo, Charlene M. .... '57 '85 C.184 B.S. L.1048 J.D. 538 Preston Ave.
St. John, Frank W., (BV) .... '42 '70 C.1031 B.B.A. L.184 J.D. [Larsen,S.&J.]
Sargalski, Dianne .... '59 '97 C.184 B.G.S. L.1048 J.D. 35 Pleasant St.
Shorr, E. Jack, (BV) .... '49 '74 C&L.184 B.A., J.D. 97 E. Main St.
Sokolowski, Robert J., (BV) .... '47 '76 C.976 B.A. L.184 J.D. One Barrister's Ct.
Solomon, Alan M., (BV) .... '33 '56 C&L.472 B.B.A., LL.B. [Solomon,K.W.&G.]
Solomon, Krupnikoff, Wyskiel & Gerber, P.C., (BV) .... 35 Pleasant St.
Somers, A. Jeffrey, (BV) .... '57 '84 C.902 B.A. L.1048 J.D. 639 Research Pkwy.
Somers, Jeffrey D. '53 '77 C&L.692 B.S., J.D.
(adm. in VA; not adm. in CT) 639 Research Pkwy.
Stanton, John F., (BV) .... '47 '75 C.321 B.A. L.184 J.D. [Ⓒ Weigand,M.&A.]
*PRACTICE AREAS: Commercial Law; Real Property Law; Probate Law.
Stapleton, Richard D. '36 '61 C.401 B.A. L.184 J.D.
Exec. V.P., Secy. & Gen. Coun., The Lane Construction Corp.
Stempien, Ronald J. .... '42 '90 C.951 B.A. L.1252 J.D. 1 Barristers Ct.

Teague, Norman B., Law Offices of, (BV) '46 '82 C&L.1029 B.S., J.D.
204 East Main Street, P.O. Box 2404, 06450
Telephone: 203-238-4242 Fax: 203-630-1133
Email: nbt425@hotmail.com URL: http://www.lawyers.com/teague
***PRACTICE AREAS: Criminal Law; DWI/DUI/OUI; Drivers License Suspension Law; Family Law; Automobile Accident.**
Criminal Trial Practice in all State Courts including DWI/DUI/OUI Law, Department of Motor Vehicles License Suspension Hearing Practice in all Connecticut locations including Administrative Per Se Law, Commercial Driver's License Law, Work Permit Law, Medical Unit Law and Traffic Law, Criminal Appeals, Family Law, Automobile Accident and Personal Injury Law.
See Professional Biographies, MERIDEN, CONNECTICUT

Tobin & Melien, (BV) .... 721 Broad St. (⊙New Haven)
Tomich, John A. '57 '83 C.980 B.E. L.7 J.D.
(adm. in OH; not adm. in CT; Pat.) Coun. & Secy., CUNO Inc.
Tonkonow, Sherman M., (BV) .... '19 '46 C&L.309 A.B., LL.B. [Tonkonow&K.]
Tonkonow and Kendzior, (BV) .... 3 Colony St.
Triplett, Martha S., (AV) '60 '86 C&L.880 B.A., J.D.
Trial Attorney, Nationwide Mutual Insurance Company
Weaver, Thomas A., (BV) .... '51 '76 C&L.184 B.A., J.D. 721 Broad St.
Weigand, Joseph F., Jr., (BV) .... '36 '66 C&L.184 B.S., LL.B. [Weigand,M.&A.]
*PRACTICE AREAS: Commercial Real Estate; Residential Real Estate; Probate; Estate Planning; Commercial Law.

Weigand, Mahon and Adelman, Attorneys At Law, P.C., (AV)
636 Broad Street, P.O. Box 2420, 06450
Telephone: 203-238-1010 Fax: 203-630-1930 URL: http://www.lawyers.com/wma
Email: info@wmalawyer.com URL: http://www.wmalawyer.com
Joseph F. Weigand, Jr.; Brian T. Mahon; Gerard I. Adelman;—Michael D. Quinn. Of Counsel: John F. Stanton.
General Civil Practice before State and Federal Courts. Personal Injury, Products Liability, Medical Malpractice, Tort, Workers Compensation, Labor, Real Estate, Estate Planning, Probate, Commercial, Domestic Relations Law, and Social Security Law.
General Counsel For: William Dubinsky & Sons, Inc.; Meriden Public Health and Visiting Nurses; Meriden-Wallingford Physicians Center, P.C.
References: Meriden Trust and Safety Deposit Co.; Dime Savings Bank of Wallingford; Fleet Real Estate Funding Corp.
See Professional Biographies, MERIDEN, CONNECTICUT

Weiss, Michael D. .... '55 '84 C.999 B.A. L.564 J.D. Robert S. Weiss & Co.
Welsh, Thomas J., (AV) .... '53 '80 C&L.184 B.S., J.D. [Brown&W.]
*PRACTICE AREAS: Commercial Law; Uniform Commercial Code; Real Property; Bankruptcy.
White, Carter H. .... '16 '42 C&L.309 B.A., LL.B. Chmn., The Meriden Record Co.
Williams, Elton R., (BV) '55 '83 C.696 B.A. L.1051 J.D.
290 Pratt St. (⊙Springfield, MA)
Wyskiel, David E., (BV) .... '56 '81 C.478 B.A. L.94 J.D. [Solomon,K.W.&G.]
Zito, Jennifer L., (BV) .... '62 '88 C.788 B.A. L.184 J.D. 204 E. Main St.

MIDDLEBURY, 5,995, *New Haven Co.*

Angelo, Dana D. .... '67 '89 C.676 B.A. L.818 J.D. 459 Middlebury Rd.
Barnes, Brian A., (BV) .... '41 '67 C.712 B.A. L.1294 LL.B. 190 Green Hill Rd.
Barnes, Gregory, (BV) .... '47 '82 C.1102 B.S. L.329 J.D. 190 Green Hill Rd.
Brooke, P. Cynthia '— '81 C.867 B.S. L.744 J.D.
(adm. in TX; not adm. in CT) P.O. Box 165
Davis, Joanne Fatse '56 '82 C.94 B.S. L.1029 J.D.
Asst. Gen. Coun., Fin. & Admn., Crompton Corp.
Dilworth, Michael P. '67 '93 C.724 B.S. L.982 J.D.
Sr. Pat. Coun., Crompton Corp. (Pat.)
Fluckiger, G. Markell '59 '87 C.101 B.S. L.1066 J.D.
(adm. in CA; not adm. in CT) Tax Coun. & Dir., Taxes, Timex Corp.
Galaro, Bruce L. '50 '90
C.1156 B.S. L.1029 J.D. V.P., Legal Affs., General DataComm, Inc.
Griffin, Gregory .... '47 '73 C.999 B.A. L.818 J.D. 170 Algin Dr.
Harkins, Robert Wm., (BV) .... '35 '83 C.812 B.S. L.184 J.D. 415 Middlebury Rd.
Judge, Frank T., III, (AV) '56 '84 C.321 A.B. L.477 J.D.
Asst. Gen. Coun. & Asst. Secy., Timex Corp.
Missal, Pamela I. S. ......'62 '88 C.183 B.A. L.904 J.D. Sr. Envir. Coun., Crompton Corp.
Reitenbach, Daniel '49 '83 C.895 B.S. L.818 J.D.
Chf. Pat. Coun., Crompton Corp. (Pat.)
Shaffer, Lewis A. '50 '75 C.1044 B.A. L.347 J.D.
(adm. in IN; not adm. in CT) Asst. Gen. Coun., Crompton Corp.
Shea, Paul J., (BV) .... '43 '74 C.884 A.B. L.184 J.D. 390 Middlebury Rd.
Sherer, Frank A., Jr., (AV) '47 '73 C.976 B.A. L.94 J.D.
(adm. in NY; not adm. in CT) V.P., Gen. Coun. & Secy., Timex Corp.
*RESPONSIBILITIES: Tax Law; Intellectual Property; Licensing.
Smith, James R., (BV) .... '44 '79 C.1156 B.S. L.184 J.D. 459 Middlebury Rd.
Smith, Robert W., (BV) .... '54 '82 C.184 B.A. L.1048 J.D. 459 Middlebury Rd.
Sperry, Leavenworth P., Jr. .... '25 '51 C.976 B.A. L.309 LL.B. 346 South St.‡
Thompson, Raymond D. .... '50 '80 C.679 B.S.CHE L.776 J.D. Benson Road (Pat.)
Tzepos, George C., (BV) .... '60 '85 C.184 B.S. L.209 J.D. 444 Middlebury Rd.

MIDDLEFIELD, 3,796, *Middlesex Co.*

Corona, John A., P.C., (BV) .... '58 '85 C.1033 B.A. L.1048 J.D. 470 Main St.
Gold, David P. .... '55 '80 C.390 A.B. L.184 J.D. 26 Sylvan Dr.
Lang, Edward G., (BV) .... '48 '73 C.659 B.S. L.184 J.D. 470 Main St.
Partin, Mark S. '60 '85 C.1142 B.A. L.846 J.D.
(adm. in TX; not adm. in CT) 80 Toad Ridge Rd.
Willis, Annette V., (CV) .... '63 '88 C.1030 B.A. L.184 J.D. 6 Way Rd.

MIDDLETOWN, * 42,762, *Middlesex Co.*

Acker, Keith W. .... '46 '78 C.299 B.A. L.184 J.D. 46 Washington St.
Adams, Richard G., (BV) .... '41 '67 C.674 A.B. L.976 LL.B. [R.G.Adams&Assoc.]
*PRACTICE AREAS: Environmental Law; Land Use Regulation; Legislative Lobbying.

Adams, Richard G., & Associates, LLC, (BV)
Jacob Frederick Huber House, 163 College Street, 06457
Telephone: 860-347-4696 Fax: 860-347-0295
Email: richardgadams@snet.net URL: http://www.lawyers.com/richardgadams
Members of Firm: Richard G. Adams.
General Trial, Appellate and Administrative Practice before all Courts. Litigation. Environmental Law, Health and Safety, Health Care, Real Estate, Land Use, Corporate, Commercial, Taxation, Estate Planning, and Legislative Lobbying and Mediation.
See Professional Biographies, MIDDLETOWN, CONNECTICUT

Adelstein, Richard P. .... '47 '78 C.453 B.S. L.659 J.D. Wesleyan Univ.
Antin, Kenneth H., (BV) .... '43 '76 C.103 B.A. L.184 J.D. [Poliner,P.A.&C.R.]
Antognini-O'Neill, Jennifer .... '66 '93 C.706 B.A. L.306 J.D. 679 Ridge Rd.
Aucaigne, Trina A. Solecki, (BV) .... '55 '82 C.1102 B.A. L.1029 J.D. City Atty.
Bakanas, Lisa G. .... '62 '90 C.855 B.A. L.659 J.D. 3 Timothy Dr.
Balaban, Mark A., (BV) .... '62 '91 C.1134 B.S. L.1252 J.D. 425 Main St., 4th Fl.
Bengtson, David A., (BV) .... '44 '68 C.694 A.B. L.184 LL.B. 363 Main St.
Bernazani, Jennifer A. .... '75 '00 C.321 B.A. L.184 J.D. [Ⓐ M.F.Dowley]
Boccalatte, John L., (BV) .... '54 '79 C.239 B.A. L.184 J.D. [Farrell,G.&B.]
Borkowski, Joseph S., (BV) .... '47 '73 C.1030 B.A. L.93 J.D. [Fortuna&C.]
Briggs, Walter D., (CV) .... '24 '51 C&L.94 A.B., LL.B. P.O. Box 831‡
Brigsted, Annette .... '58 '97 C.999 B.A. L.184 J.D. 200 Court St.
Brown, Audrey A. '50 '91 C.588 B.A. L.508 J.D.
(adm. in AK; not adm. in CT) 179 Butternut St.
Budney, Walter R. .... '25 '55 C.1029 B.A. L.94 LL.B. Supr. J.

Buhl, Paul D., (BV) '60 '85 C.742 B.A. L.602 J.D.
The Caleb Fuller House, 49 Main Street, 06457
Telephone: 860-347-0879 Fax: 860-344-8876
Civil Trials and Appeals in all Courts. General Commercial Practice, Business Organizations Law, Real Estate, Securities, Zoning, Land Use, Construction, Environment, Banking, Employment, Estate Planning and Probate Law.
See Professional Biographies, MIDDLETOWN, CONNECTICUT

Cannata, Linda J. .... '61 '89 C.183 B.A. L.1017 J.D. [Ⓐ Jozus,M.&T.]
*PRACTICE AREAS: Civil Litigation; Personal Injury.
Carella, Richard D. .... '66 '92 C.1030 B.S. L.1252 J.D. 203 Main St.
Carta, Scott A. .... '73 '99 C.184 B.A. L.306 J.D. [Ⓐ Dzialo,P.&A.]
*PRACTICE AREAS: Litigation; Personal Injury.
Cartelli, Salvatore J., (BV) .... '37 '63 C&L.184 B.A., LL.B. [Fortuna&C.]
Cartelli, Thomas, (BV) .... '64 '89 C.184 B.S. L.1029 J.D. 134 Washington St.
Conaway-Raczka, Nancy .... '53 '80 C.346 B.S. L.678 J.D. [Raczka&R.]
Connors, Susan A. .... '66 '91 C&L.184 B.S., J.D. [Krevolin,R.&C.L.] ⊙
Cosham, David E., (CV) .... '46 '73 C.829 B.A. L.184 J.D. 547 Main St.
Crawford, Julé A., (BV) .... '47 '84 C.918 B.A. L.184 J.D. 154 College St.
Crean, Gerald P., III '62 '88 C.390 B.A. L.184 J.D.
CEO & Pres., Xerographic Supplies & Equipment Co.
Curzan, Robert L., (BV) .... '52 '81 C.959 B.S. L.285 J.D. 134 Washington St.
D'Aquila, Jean M., (BV) .... '59 '84 C&L.184 B.A., J.D. [Howard,M.&D.]
*PRACTICE AREAS: Municipal Law; Government; Real Estate; Zoning Law; Land Use.
DeMaso, Jeffrey A. '64 '89 C&L.93 B.S., J.D.
Assoc. Coun., Mortgage Lenders Network USA, Inc.
Donlan, Sean E. .... '65 '97 C.1155 B.A. L.818 J.D. [Ⓐ Dzialo,P.&A.]
*PRACTICE AREAS: Real Estate; Litigation; Personal Injury.
Dorsey, Christine Schunmann, (CV) .... '65 '90 C.745 B.A. L.1029 J.D. [Faccadio&D.]

Dowley, Michael F., (BV) '43 '68 C.676 A.B. L.884 J.D.
116 Washington Street, P.O. Box 1235, 06457
Telephone: 860-347-9987 Fax: 860-347-3597
URL: http://www.dowleyandassociates.com
***PRACTICE AREAS: Civil Litigation; Environmental Law; Real Estate Development; Regulatory Law.**
Associates: Jennifer A. Bernazani.
Administrative Law, Alcoholic Beverages, Alternative Dispute Resolution, Banks and Banking, Business Law, Commercial Law, Commercial Real Estate, Computers and Software, Contracts, Copyrights, Corporate Law, Eminent Domain, Environmental Law, Guardianship and Conservatorship, Health Care, Intellectual Property, Leases and Leasing, Litigation, Media Law, Medical Malpractice, Mortgages, Negligence, Nonprofit and Charitable Organizations, Partnership Law, Personal Injury, Premises Liability, Probate, Professional Liability, Real Estate, Resorts and Leisure, Sports Law, Torts, Trademarks, Trusts and Estates, Unfair Competition, Wills, Zoning, Planning and Land Use.
References: Centerbank; Farmers & Mechanics Bank.
See Professional Biographies, MIDDLETOWN, CONNECTICUT

Drewniany, Jeffrey J. .... '58 '84 C.95 B.A. L.184 J.D. 484 Main St.

Dutcher, Robert P., (BV) . . . . '50 '75 C.918 B.A. L.276 J.D. [Dzialo,P.&A.]
*PRACTICE AREAS: Litigation; Plaintiffs Personal Injury.

Dzialo, Pickett & Allen, P.C., (AV)
200 Court Street, P.O. Box 661, 06457 ⊙
Telephone: 860-638-5400 Fax: 860-638-5410
Email: welcome@dpapc.com URL: http://www.lawyers.com/dpapc
David M. Royston; Philip F. Karpel; Robert P. Dutcher; Gregory M. Harris; D. Jeanne Messick; John N. Montalbano;—Sean E. Donlan; Scott A. Carta.
General Practice. Litigation in all Courts, Residential Real Estate, Commercial Real Estate, Zoning and Land Use, Corporate, Estate Planning, Elder Law, Probate Law, Personal Injury Litigation, Municipal Law.
Representative Clients: Liberty Bank; Connecticut National Bank; The Middletown Press Publishing Co.; Town of Essex.
Old Saybrook, Connecticut Office: 15 Elm Street, P.O. Box 779. Telephone: 203-395-6340. Fax: 203-388-9399. Email: welcome@dpapc.com.
See Professional Biographies, MIDDLETOWN, CONNECTICUT

Faccadio, Lisa A., (BV) . . . . '52 '77 C.449 B.A. L.1048 J.D. [Faccadio&D.]
Faccadio & Dorsey, P.C., (BV) . . . . 547 Main St.
Farrell, Patricia C., (BV) . . . . '53 '78 C.788 B.A. L.184 J.D. [Farrell,G.&B.]
Farrell, Guarino & Boccalatte, P.C., (BV) . . . . 141 Broad St.
Felix, Nancy . . . . '60 '97 C.725 B.A. L.306 J.D. Statewide Legal Sevices of Conn., Inc.
Field, Jonathan W. . . . . '51 '83 C.276 B.S. L.1048 J.D. Dep. Chf. Clk., Supr. Ct.
Fortuna, Carl P., (BV) . . . . '28 '54 C&L.94 A.B., LL.B. [Fortuna&C.]
Fortuna & Cartelli, P.C., (BV) . . . . 134 Washington St.
Fox, Alaric J. . . . . '64 '90 C.1156 B.S. L.1048 J.D. State Police
Geenty, Susan Perrin, (BV) . . . . '58 '86 C.1349 B.A. L.1040 J.D. [Farrell,G.&B.]
Gionfriddo, Stephen T., (CV) . . . . '50 '75 C.550 B.A. L.1017 J.D. 62 Washington St.
Giuliano, Sebastian N., (CV) . . . . '52 '78 C.93 B.A. L.128 J.D. P.O. Box 820

Gould, Larson, Bennet, Wells & McDonnell, P.C.
(See Essex)

Grady, William G., (BV) . . . . '38 '83 C.28 A.B. L.1048 J.D. 154 College St.
Halloran & Sage LLP, (AV)
300 Plaza Middlesex (⊙Hartford, Westport, CT; Wash., DC)
Halpin, Charles J. '31 '60 C.672 B.M.E. L.446 LL.B.
(adm. in MD; not adm. in CT) Raymond Engr. Inc.‡
Hanna, Jefferson, III, (BV) . . . . '55 '83 C.696 B.A. L.1048 J.D. 484 Main St.
Harris, Gregory M., (BV) . . . . '51 '76 C.976 B.S. L.184 J.D. [Dzialo,P.&A.]
*PRACTICE AREAS: Real Estate Litigation; Consumer Litigation; Commercial Litigation; Foreclosures; Property Rights.
Holzberg, Maria M. . . . . '55 '83 C.518 A.B. L.306 J.D. 55 Clover St.
Howard, William, (AV) . . . . '38 '67 C.184 B.A. L.309 J.D. [Howard,M.&D.]
*PRACTICE AREAS: Real Estate Law; Business Law; Litigation; Taxation Law; Municipal Law.

Howard, McMillan & D'Aquila, (AV)
386 Main Street, 06457
Telephone: 860-346-1377 Fax: 860-346-5121
Email: hmd@snet.net
William Howard; Jane S. McMillan; Jean M. D'Aquila.
General Trial, Appellate and Administrative Practice before all Courts. Municipal, Real Estate, Environmental, Zoning, Corporate, Commercial, Tax, Probate and Estate Planning Law.
See Professional Biographies, MIDDLETOWN, CONNECTICUT

Iannucci, Gena M. . . . . '67 '92 C.938 A.B. L.1048 J.D. Clk., Supr. Ct.
Janes, Norman K. . . . . '43 '68 C.231 B.A. L.184 LL.B. Exec. Dir., Conn. Legal Servs.
Jozus, Ivar A., (BV) . . . . '38 '70 C.197 A.B. L.184 J.D. [Jozus,M.&T.]
*PRACTICE AREAS: Corporate Law; Real Estate Law; Estate Planning Law; Probate Law.

Jozus, Milardo & Thomasson, (BV)
The William Southmayd House, 73 Main Street, 06457
Telephone: 860-347-4686 Telecopier: 860-347-2283
Email: jmtlaw@snet.net URL: http://www.lawyers.com/jmtlaw
Members of Firm: Ivar A. Jozus; Joseph E. Milardo, Jr.; Dean A. Thomasson. Associate: Linda J. Cannata.
Trial and Appellate Practice in all Courts. Corporate and Commercial Law, Domestic Relations, Estate Planning and Probate, Municipal Law, Personal Injury and Products Liability Law, Residential and Commercial Real Estate, Land Use, Zoning and Development.
References: Fleet Bank, N.A.; Liberty Bank.
See Professional Biographies, MIDDLETOWN, CONNECTICUT

Karpel, Philip F., (BV) . . . . '42 '67 C.321 B.S. L.184 LL.B. [Dzialo,P.&A.]
*PRACTICE AREAS: Commercial Real Estate; Residential Real Estate; Corporate Law; Land Use Regulation; Environmental Law.
Krevolin, Andrew W., (AV) . . . . '55 '80 C.183 B.A. L.184 J.D. [Krevolin,R.&C.L.] ⊙
Krevolin, Roth & Connors LLC, (AV) . . . . . . .100 Main Street, Suite 201 (⊙West Hartford)
Levin, Bruce L. . . . . '51 '76 C.156 B.A. L.276 J.D. Supr. Ct. J.
Loman, Mark S. . . . . '55 '96 C.829 B.A. L.1048 J.D. 21 Overlook Ave.
Marino, Vincent M., (BV) . . . . '44 '71 C.1029 B.S. L.184 J.D. [Halloran&S.]
Marlowe, Dennis H., (BV) . . . . '42 '68 C.184 B.A. L.976 LL.B. 134 Washington Street

Mayo, Gilligan & Zito, LLP
(See Wethersfield)

McGovern, Janet G. . . . . '53 '87 C.999 B.A. L.1162 J.D. 1 Court Street
McKay, Antonina . . . . '55 '96 C.918 B.A. L.306 J.D. 85 Broad St.
McMillan, Jane S., (BV) . . . . '37 '75 C.659 B.A. L.107 J.D. [Howard,M.&D.]
*PRACTICE AREAS: Estate Planning Law; Business Law; Taxation Law.
Messick, D. Jeanne, (BV) . . . . '53 '81 C.183 B.S. L.184 J.D. [Dzialo,P.&A.] ⊙
*PRACTICE AREAS: Estate Planning; Probate Law; Elder Law; Planned Residential Communities; Condominium Law.
Milardo, Joseph E., Jr., (BV) . . . . '48 '74 C.262 B.A. L.818 J.D. [Jozus,M.&T.]
*PRACTICE AREAS: Civil Law; Criminal Litigation; Probate Law; Workers Compensation Law; Family Law.
Montalbano, John N., (BV) . . . . '54 '80 C&L.93 B.S., J.D. [Dzialo,P.&A.]
*PRACTICE AREAS: Litigation; Plaintiffs Personal Injury.
Moore, David M. . . . . '62 '88 C.273 B.A. L.1029 J.D. 90 Court Street, 2nd Floor
Olearcek, Steven F. '71 '96 C&L.1048 B.A., J.D.
(adm. in MA; not adm. in CT) Corp. Coun., Mortgage Lenders Network USA, Inc.
Palmer, Robert S. . . . . '26 '51 C.184 B.A. L.188 LL.B. 173 S. Main St.
Palmer, Russell, (BV) . . . . '60 '86 C.884 B.A. L.896 J.D. 90 Court St.
Poliner, Bernard, (BV) . . . . '31 '58 C.184 B.A. L.94 LL.B. [Poliner,P.A.&C.R.]
Poliner, Myron J., (AV) . . . . '33 '57 C.918 B.A. L.893 LL.B. [Poliner,P.A.&C.R.]
Poliner, Robert S., (BV) . . . . '43 '67 C.105 A.B. L.94 LL.B. [Poliner,P.A.&C.R.]

Poliner, Poliner, Antin & Cienava Rocco, P.C., (AV)
Poliner Building, 516 Main Street, 06457-2810
Telephone: 860-346-8691 Fax: 860-346-3643
Email: lawyers@poliner.com URL: http://www.poliner.com
Israel Poliner (1898-1980); Myron J. Poliner; Robert S. Poliner; Kenneth H. Antin; Bernard Poliner; AnnMarie Cienava Rocco.
General Civil Practice. Estate Planning, Probate, Corporate Law, Real Estate, Eminent Domain, Municipal, Personal Injury, Workers Compensation and Family Law. Trials and Appeals in all Courts.

Quattro, Mark H., (BV) . . . . '55 '81 C.184 B.A. L.276 J.D. [M.H.Quattro]
Quattro, Mark H., P.C., (BV) . . . . .520 Saybrook Rd.
Quinn, Barbara M. . . . . '43 '77 C.104 A.B. L.245 J.D. Supr. Ct. J.
Quinn, Patricia S. . . . . '69 '94 C.164 B.A. L.436 J.D. Middlesex Convalescent Ctr.
Raczka, Theodore J., (BV) . . . . '17 '41 C.918 B.A. L.976 LL.B. [Raczka&R.] ‡
Raczka, Theodore V., (BV) . . . . '51 '79 C.349 B.S. L.678 J.D. [Raczka&R.]
Raczka & Raczka, (BV) . . . . 363 Main St.
Radler, Monte P., (BV) . . . . '52 '79 C.597 B.A. L.184 J.D. Supervisory Asst. Pub. Def.
Rafala, Nella R. . . . . '67 '94 C.999 B.A. L.1218 J.D. 484 Main St.
Redway, John T., (AV) . . . . '37 '62 C.1030 B.B.A. L.262 LL.B. State's Atty.
Reich, David J. . . . . '60 '94 C.787 B.A. L.1048 J.D. 116 Front St.
Rocco, AnnMarie Cienava, (BV) . . . . '61 '88 C&L.818 B.A., J.D. [Poliner,P.A.&C.R.]
*PRACTICE AREAS: Probate; Domestic Relations; Real Estate; Estate Planning; Elder Law.
Roth, Stuart M., (BV) . . . . '45 '71 C&L.184 B.S., J.D. [Krevolin,R.&C.L.] ⊙
Royston, David M., (AV) . . . . '39 '64 C.1030 B.S L.276 J.D. [Dzialo,P.&A.]
*PRACTICE AREAS: Real Estate; Municipal Law; Land Use Regulation.
Ryan, Daniel B., (BV) . . . . '41 '69 C.321 B.A. L.184 J.D. [Ryan&R.]
Ryan, Helen F., (BV) . . . . '46 '71 C.706 B.A. L.184 J.D. [Ryan&R.]
Ryan and Ryan, P.C., (BV) . . . . 46 Washington St.
Schatz, Walter B., (BV) . . . . '22 '49 C&L.188 A.B., LL.B. [Krevolin,R.&C.L.] ⊙
Shainess, Joseph J., (CV) . . . . '48 '76 C.1029 B.A. L.669 J.D. 547 Main St.
Shapiro, Daniel Z., (BV) . . . . '49 '74 C.415 B.A. L.945 J.D. 72 Court St.
Shapiro, Deborah Dickson, (BV) . . . . '49 '76 C.183 B.A. L.184 J.D. 72 Court St.
Shaw, John F., (BV) . . . . '44 '72 C.604 B.A. L.184 J.D. 363 Main St.
Snow, Charles W., Jr., (CV) . . . . '23 '50 C.918 B.A. L.94 LL.B. 547 Main St., Rm. 3
Sprecher, Averum J., (BV) . . . . '41 '69 C.94 B.A. L.796 J.D. 90 Court St.
Steele, Alan . . . . '28 '59 C.569 B.M.E. L.184 LL.B. Mag. (Fam. Div.)
Szewczyk, Phrances L. . . . . '68 '93 C.788 A.B. L.1048 J.D. 519 Coleman Rd.
Thomasson, Dean A., (BV) . . . . '48 '81 C.46 B.S.C.E. L.1048 J.D. [Jozus,M.&T.]
*PRACTICE AREAS: Planning and Zoning Law; Land Use Law; Real Estate Development Law.
Thornton, Domenique S., (CV) . . . . '49 '89 C.1044 B.A. L.1048 J.D. 168 Timber Ridge Rd.
Tomc, Richard W., (AV) . . . . '45 '71 C.363 A.B. L.309 J.D. [R.W.Tomc&Assoc.]

Tomc, Richard W., & Associates, P.C., (AV)
Caleb Fuller House, 49 Main Street, 06457
Telephone: 860-347-4415 Fax: 860-347-1930
Email: RiTom@aol.com
Richard W. Tomc.
Business Organizations, Commercial Loan Transactions, Trusts and Estates.
Reference: Citizens Bank.
See Professional Biographies, MIDDLETOWN, CONNECTICUT

Trick, Penny L. '52 '88 C.645 B.A. L.1048 J.D.
Mng. Atty., Statewide Legal Servs. of Conn., Inc.
Vargas, Amado J., (BV) . . . . '61 '88 C.4 B.B.A. L.831 J.D. Wrkrs. Comp. J.
Waldron, Meg A. . . . . '54 '93 C.184 B.S. L.1048 J.D. 116 Washington St.

MILFORD, 48,168, *New Haven Co.*

Adams, George W., III, (AV) . . . . '49 '75 C.976 B.A. L.94 J.D. [Harlow,A.&F.]
*PRACTICE AREAS: Real Estate; Zoning Law; Probate.
Alexiades, Elias A., (BV) . . . . '59 '88 C.276 B.S. L.1252 J.D. [Hurwitz&S.]
Apicella, Andrew, (BV) . . . . '50 '75 C.184 B.A. L.1292 J.D. 291 Seaside Avenue
Avallone, Anthony V., (BV) . . . . '47 '74 C.184 B.A. L.818 J.D. 75 Broad St.
Barba, Ronald J. . . . . '61 '94 C.184 B.A. L.1252 J.D. [Kapusta&O.]
Barnes, Joseph B., (CV) '52 '79
C.321 B.A. L.472 J.D. Chmn., Milford Planning and Zoning Bd.
Bartek, Mark J. . . . . '59 '86 C.1102 B.A. L.1029 J.D. 75 Broad St.
Becker, Lucille J. . . . . '32 '57 C.999 A.B. L.262 LL.B. [Dimenstein&C.]
Benedosso, Anthony N., (BV) . . . . '49 '74 C.884 B.S. L.262 LL.B. 51 Cherry St.
Berchem, Jonathan David . . . . '69 '95 C.1030 B.A. L.823 J.D. [Berchem,M.&D.]
*PRACTICE AREAS: Litigation; Insurance Defense; Labor and Employment.
Berchem, Robert L., (AV) . . . . '41 '65 C.1030 A.B. L.884 J.D. [Berchem,M.&D.]
*PRACTICE AREAS: Commercial Law; Real Estate; Land Use Planning; Energy Law; Utility Law.

Berchem, Moses & Devlin, A Professional Corporation, (AV)
75 Broad Street, 06460-3363
Telephone: 203-783-1200 Facsimile: 203-878-2235; 203-877-8422
URL: http://www.bmd-law.com
Robert L. Berchem; Marsha Belman Moses; Michael P. Devlin; Stephen W. Studer; Richard J. Buturla; Floyd J. Dugas; Kenneth R. Plumb; Lawrence B. Pellegrino;—Brian A. Lema; Warren L. Holcomb; Michelle C. Laubin; Jonathan David Berchem; Dean R. Singewald; Michael V. Vocalina; Bryan L. LeClerc; Brian W. Smith; Carolyn Mazanec Dugas. Of Counsel: Thomas Galvin Cotter; Mark J. Rosen.
Commercial, Corporate Law, Labor and Employment Law, Litigation, Real Estate, Education, Land Use Planning, Estate Planning, Energy and Utility Law, Environmental, Probate. Partnership Law and Taxation Law. Trials and Appeals in State and Federal Courts.
See Professional Biographies, MILFORD, CONNECTICUT

Bogdan, Francis G. . . . . '58 '84 C.1156 B.S. L.1029 J.D. 22 Roller Terr.
Bonsangue, Louis J. . . . . '68 '93 C.262 B.S. L.1019 J.D. [Jacobi,K.&C.]
*PRACTICE AREAS: Civil Litigation; Personal Injury Litigation; Environmental Law.
Bottinick, Andrew . . . . '59 '93 C.1027 B.S. L.1252 J.D. [Perkins&M.]
Boynton, Michael S., (BV) . . . . '60 '86 C.1200 B.A. L.1029 J.D. [Lynch,T.M.&B.]
*PRACTICE AREAS: Civil Litigation; Personal Injury; Criminal Defense; Drug Crimes; Driving While Intoxicated.
Boynton, Robert H., (BV) . . . . '39 '72 C.229 B.S. L.1202 J.D. [R.H.Boynton]
Boynton, Robert H., P.C., (BV) . . . . .41 Cherry St.

Broughel, Andrew J., (BV) '38 '64 C.1030 B.S.S. L.276 J.D.
243 Broad Street, P.O. Box 45, 06460
Telephone: 203-874-6166 Fax: 203-878-1681
***PRACTICE AREAS: Real Estate; Zoning; Probate; Family Law; Trials in all Courts.**
General Civil Practice. Real Estate, Probate, Family.
See Professional Biographies, MILFORD, CONNECTICUT

Burkhart, Steven A., (AV) '63 '89 C.911 B.A. L.128 J.D.
(adm. in MD; not adm. in CT) Asst. Gen. Coun., BIC Corp.
*RESPONSIBILITIES: Products Liability; Employment Law; Labor Law; Intellectual Property Litigation; Commercial Litigation.
Buturla, Richard J., (BV) . . . . '57 '82 C.1102 B.S. L.884 J.D. [Berchem,M.&D.]
*PRACTICE AREAS: Litigation; Insurance Defense.
Canty, Brendan T., (BV) . . . . '58 '87 C.588 B.S. L.1029 J.D. [Kerin&C.]
Capozziello, Edward, (BV) . . . . '66 '91 C.1211 B.S. L.1048 J.D. 415 Boston Post Rd.
Carroll, Leo P., (BV) . . . . '44 '69 C.884 A.B. L.93 J.D. [Stevens,C.&C.]
*PRACTICE AREAS: Planning and Zoning Law; Commercial and Residential Real Estate Law; Estates and Trusts.
Carveth, Christopher B., (BV) . . . . '50 '75 C.1029 B.A. L.128 J.D. [Stevens,C.&C.]
*PRACTICE AREAS: Civil Litigation-Plaintiff Law; Criminal Defense Law; Workers Compensation Law.
Case, Max S., (BV) . . . . '47 '74 C.659 B.A. L.831 J.D. [Jacobi,K.&C.]
*PRACTICE AREAS: Real Estate; Land Use; Tax Appeals; Civil Litigation.
Cashin, Julie M. . . . . '67 '95 C.1211 B.S. L.1252 J.D. 147 N. Broad St.
Castignoli, Vito A., (AV) . . . . '51 '76 C.178 B.A. L.184 J.D. [Castignoli,S.&L.]
Castignoli, Skudlarek & Leo, (AV) . . . . 185 Broad St.
Celentano, Michele R., (BV) . . . . '59 '83 C.976 B.A. L.724 J.D. [Dimenstein&C.]
Cody, Christopher M., (BV) . . . . '57 '83 C.690 B.A. L.184 J.D. [Cody&G.]

Cody & Gonillo, LLP, (BV) ....185 North Broad Street
Collier, Edmund Q., (BV) '58 '83
C.705 B.A. L.1029 J.D. 771 Boston Post Rd. (⊙Norwalk)
Conroy, John W. '50 '80 C.602 B.A. L.93 J.D.
Chmn. of the Bd., McMillan-Conroy Machinery Co. Inc.
Coppeto, Barbara A. ....'33 '58 C.856 A.B. L.893 LL.B. Supr. Ct. J.
Costantini, Lawrence J., (BV) ....'43 '70 C.30 A.B. L.818 J.D. 64 Cherry St.
Cotter, John J., (AV) ....'24 '49 C&L.276 B.S.S., LL.B. 500 Boston Post Road
Cotter, Thomas Galvin, (BV) ....'56 '84 C.999 B.S. L.1029 J.D. [Ⓒ Berchem,M.&D.]
*PRACTICE AREAS: Workers Compensation; Bad Faith Litigation; Professional Liability; General Litigation; Personal Injury Litigation.
Coughlin, John J., (BV) ....'41 '66 C.676 A.B. L.128 J.D. [Coughlin&M.]
Coughlin & Malone, (BV) ....92 Cherry St.
Creane, John M., (BV) ....'41 '70 C.103 A.B. L.276 J.D. 92 Cherry St.
Curseaden, Kevin J. ....'69 '97 C.93 B.A. L.1252 J.D. [Ⓐ Stevens,C.&C.]
*PRACTICE AREAS: Litigation; Real Estate.
Darrin, William A., Jr. ....'45 '73 C.299 B.A. L.823 J.D. Subway World Hdqrs.
DeRosa, Kara Kelly ....'71 '98 C.1145 B.S.B.A. L.1252 J.D. Staff Atty., BIC Corp.
*RESPONSIBILITIES: Corporate Law; ERISA; Contracts; Employee Benefits; Advertising and Labeling.
Devlin, Michael P. ....'50 '76 C.93 B.A. L.178 J.D. [Berchem,M.&D.]
*PRACTICE AREAS: Labor and Employment.
Dey, Joseph S., (BV) ....'56 '85 C.184 B.S. L.1029 J.D. [Dey,S.&Assoc.]
Dey, Smith & Associates, (BV) ....771 Boston Post Rd.
Dickson, Kimberly Roy ....'71 '96 C.676 B.A. L.1048 J.D. Staff Atty., Bic Corp.
*RESPONSIBILITIES: Contracts; Trademarks and Licensing; Labeling and Advertising Law; Acquisitions; Other Commercial Transactions.
Dimenstein, Morton J., (BV) ....'33 '57 C&L.94 A.B., J.D. [Dimenstein&C.]
Dimenstein & Celentano, (BV) ....99 Cherry St.
Donahue, Michael E. ....'67 '95 C.93 A.B. L.818 J.D. Subway Real Estate Corp.
Drazen, Franklin A., (BV) ....'53 '77 C.1155 B.S. L.1202 J.D. 245 Cherry St.
Dubin, Nellie J. ....'52 '77 C.1030 B.A. L.184 J.D. Chief Clk., Jud. Dept.
DuBois, Cheryl A. '63 '89
C.690 B.A. L.1048 J.D. Asst. Gen. Coun. & Asst. Secy., BIC Corp.
*RESPONSIBILITIES: Intellectual Property; Customs and Trade; Employment and Labor Law; Marketing, Labeling and Advertising Law; Contracts and Other Commercial Transactions.
Dugas, Carolyn Mazanec ....'62 '87 C&L.831 B.A., J.D. [Ⓐ Berchem,M.&D.]
*PRACTICE AREAS: Education Law.
Dugas, Floyd J., (BV) ....'59 '86 C.184 B.S. L.831 J.D. [Berchem,M.&D.]
*PRACTICE AREAS: Labor and Employment; Corporate Law; Education.
Duhl, Lisa D. ....'64 '94 C.184 B.A. L.1029 J.D. 81 Barbara Dr.
Eagan, James E. '41 '66 C.1040 L.564 LL.B.
(adm. in NY; not adm. in CT) 99 Timber Trail‡
Eckenrode, Howard C., (BV) ....'41 '69 C.1029 B.S. L.184 J.D. [Meuser,E.&H.]
Egan, David F., (AV) ....'42 '72 C.454 B.A. L.284 J.D. Pub. Def.
Einbinder, Hillard, (BV) ....'56 '82 C.867 L.245 J.D. 50 Cherry St
Ferencek, Paul J. ....'60 '87 C.262 B.A. L.1029 J.D. Asst. State's Atty.
Fitzmaurice, Karen A. ....'60 '84 C.415 B.S. L.976 J.D. 53 Pelham St.

Fogler, Linda M., (BV) '57 '83 C.184 B.S. L.1029 J.D.
51 Cherry Street, 06460
Telephone: 203-876-2525 FAX: 203-878-9607
***PRACTICE AREAS: Real Estate; Bankruptcy; Foreclosures; Collections; Banking Law. Condominium Law, Loan Workouts, Civil Litigation, Commercial Law, Personal Injury, Probate Administration.**

Foley, Kristin Dorney, (BV) ....'62 '86 C.478 B.A. L.93 J.D. [Ⓐ Stevens,C.&C.]
*PRACTICE AREAS: Workers' Compensation Law; General Practice; Real Estate Law; Estates and Trusts.
Friedman, Dana Eric, (AV) ....'46 '71 C.477 B.A. L.273 J.D. [Harlow,A.&F.]
*PRACTICE AREAS: Real Estate Acquisitions; Real Estate Development; Real Estate Finance; Probate; Estate Settlements.
Galvin, Mary M., (AV) ....'49 '74 C.1102 B.A. L.128 J.D. Off. of States Atty.
Gaynor, Eric R., (BV) ....'62 '87 C.1365 B.A. L.184 J.D. [Harlow,A.&F.]
*PRACTICE AREAS: Commercial Litigation; Collections; Bankruptcy; Landlord and Tenant Law; Personal Injury.
Geib, Julia Byrne ....'60 '85 C.19 B.A. L.262 J.D. 21 Beacon Hill Lane‡
Gonillo, Christine M., (BV) ....'60 '86 C.321 A.B. L.128 J.D. [Cody&G.]
Graham, John J., (BV) ....'38 '70 C.184 B.S. L.838 J.D. 28 1/2 Crowley Ave.
Grossman, Jed S., (BV) ....'48 '73 C.401 B.A. L.1202 J.D. 61 Cherry St.
Haering, Margaret E. ....'47 '75 C.705 B.A. L.273 J.D. 147 N. Broad St.

Harlow, Adams & Friedman, P.C., (AV) BR
300 Bic Drive, 06460
Telephone: 203-878-0661 Fax: 203-878-9568
Email: attorney@quidproquo.com URL: http://www.harlowadamsfriedman.com
William D. Harlow (1921-1988); George W. Adams, III; Dana Eric Friedman; Theodore H. Shumaker; Stephen P. Wright (Board Certified Civil Law Specialist, Tax Board of Legal Specialization, 1986-1991); James M. Nugent; Michael P. A. Williams; Eric R. Gaynor; Joseph A. Kubic; James R. Winkel.
General Civil Practice, General Civil Litigation in State and Federal Courts, Real Estate Conveyancing, Financing and Development, Zoning, Probate, Personal Injury, Commercial Litigation, Construction Law, Bankruptcy, Business Formations, Landlord and Tenant, Title Opinions, Trials and Appeals.
See Professional Biographies, MILFORD, CONNECTICUT

Haselkamp, H. James, Jr. ....'58 '86 C.184 B.S. L.1048 J.D. 45 Paschal Dr.
Hayes, Michael J., (BV) ....'59 '84 C.1102 B.S. L.1048 J.D. [Meuser,E.&H.]
Healey, William F., Jr., (BV) ....'25 '50 C.976 B.A. L.184 LL.B. 85 Viscount Dr.
Holcomb, Warren L. ....'50 '77 C.184 B.A. L.809 J.D. [Ⓐ Berchem,M.&D.]
*PRACTICE AREAS: Labor and Employment; Entertainment Law.
Holler, Jane T. ....'49 '84 L.1029 J.D. 203 North St.
Hurley, L. Mark ....'60 '85 C.1102 B.S. L.1029 J.D. Asst. State's Atty.
Hurwitz, Lewis A., (AV) ....'35 '61 C.165 A.B. L.94 J.D. [Hurwitz&S.]
Hurwitz & Sagarin, LLC, (AV) ....147 N. Broad St.
Jacobi, Paul, (BV) ....'50 '76 C&L.1019 B.A., J.D. [Jacobi,K.&C.]
*PRACTICE AREAS: Environmental Law.

Jacobi, Kappel & Case, P.C., (BV)
300 Bic Drive, 06460
Telephone: 203-874-7110 Fax: 203-874-6469
Email: info@jkc-law.com
Paul Jacobi; Robert Kappel; Max S. Case; Louis J. Bonsangue;—David Speranzini.
Environmental, Real Estate, Planning and Zoning, Motor Vehicle Accidents, Personal Injury, Estate Planning and Administration, Business Law. Litigation in all Courts.
Representative Clients: Satin American Corp.; Remtech Inc.; TPA Design Group; North American Bank; Environmental Assurance Inc.; Environmental Resource Management Northeast Inc.; Environmental Digital Systems Inc.; Roux Associates.
Reference: North American Bank.
See Professional Biographies, MILFORD, CONNECTICUT

Jaser, George J., (BV) ....'30 '59 C.1030 B.S. L.724 LL.B. 69 Broad St.
Johnson, Joyce E. ....'58 '90 C.1044 B.S. L.1040 J.D. Claricom, Inc.
Joy, Bernard F., (BV) ....'32 '58 C.1030 B.S. L.724 J.D. 243 Broad St.
Kappel, Robert, (BV) ....'50 '77 C.994 B.A. L.1019 J.D. [Jacobi,K.&C.]
*PRACTICE AREAS: Environmental Law; Civil Litigation; Commercial Transactions; Personal Injury Litigation.
Kapusta, Robert, (BV) ....'31 '58 C.184 B.A. L.276 LL.B. [Kapusta&O.]
Kapusta & Otzel, (BV) ....250 Broad St.
Karp, Joel C., (AV) ....'40 '64 C.103 B.A. L.184 J.D. [Karp&L.]
*PRACTICE AREAS: Tax; Business; Estate Planning; Probate.

Karp & Langerman, P.C., (AV)
Milford Place Corporate Center, 185 Plains Road, 06460
Telephone: 203-876-0606 Westport: 203-866-5892 Fax: 203-876-0768
Joel C. Karp; Lawrence Langerman.
Corporation, Probate, Estate Planning, Taxation, Pension and Profit Sharing, Commercial, Real Estate.
Reference: Fleet Bank.
See Professional Biographies, MILFORD, CONNECTICUT

Kelleher, Thomas M. '53 '83 C.262 B.A. L.1040 J.D.
(adm. in NY; not adm. in CT) Sr. V.P.-Admn. Gen. Coun. & Secy., BIC Corp.
Kerin, Michael R., (BV) ....'58 '88 C.881 B.A. L.1029 J.D. [Kerin&C.]
*PRACTICE AREAS: Personal Injury; Workers' Compensation.

Kerin & Canty, P.C., (BV)
120 Broad Street, 06460
Telephone: 203-876-9831 Fax: 203-876-0100
Email: blackfin34@aol.com URL: http://www.lawyers.com/kcjlaw
Brendan T. Canty; Michael R. Kerin.
Personal Injury, Workers' Compensation.
See Professional Biographies, MILFORD, CONNECTICUT

Kierstead, Nancy L. ....'45 '88 C.380 B.S. L.1048 J.D. Trial Ct. Admr.
Klinger, Roger M., (BV) ....'43 '86 C&L.1029 B.S., J.D. 244 Bridgeport Ave.
Knuff, John W. ....'59 '95 C.363 B.A. L.1252 J.D. 147 N. Broad St.
Kruger, Andrew C. ....'65 '94 C.273 B.S.M.E. L.1252 J.D. 147 N. Broad St.
Kubic, Joseph A. ....'61 '92 C.184 B.A. L.1029 J.D. [Harlow,A.&F.]
*PRACTICE AREAS: Construction Law; Real Estate; Personal Injury.
Langerman, Lawrence, (AV) ....'51 '76 C.882 B.A. L.128 J.D. [Karp&L.]
*PRACTICE AREAS: Corporate; Tax; Estate Planning; Business; Pension and Profit Sharing.
Langewisch, Stacy Lynne ....'72 '97 C.1156 B.A. L.1252 J.D. [Ⓐ Kapusta&O.]
Laubin, Michelle C. ....'71 '96 C.915 B.A. L.588 J.D. [Ⓐ Berchem,M.&D.]
*PRACTICE AREAS: Education Law.
LeClerc, Bryan L. ....'62 '87 C.1030 B.A. L.184 J.D. [Ⓐ Berchem,M.&D.]
*PRACTICE AREAS: Litigation; Probate.
Lema, Brian A. ....'65 '90 C&L.276 B.A., J.D. [Ⓐ Berchem,M.&D.]
*PRACTICE AREAS: Litigation; Land Use; Commercial Law.
Leo, Steven J., (BV) ....'52 '77 C.1102 B.A. L.1009 J.D. [Castignoli,S.&L.]
Levin, Juliana B. ....'30 '84 C.731 B.A. L.1029 J.D. 200 Milford Pt. Rd.‡
Levin, Martin ....'36 '86 C.184 B.S. L.1029 J.D. 200 Milford Pt. Rd.
Lipton, Marilyn J. '50 '84 C.823 B.A. L.362 J.D.
(adm. in FL; not adm. in CT) 147 Sandpiper Cr
Lisko, Rita C. ....'49 '85 C.1103 B.S. L.184 J.D. 92 Cherry St.
Luysterborghs, Robert E. ....'67 '94 C.645 B.S. L.184 J.D. [Perkins&M.]
Lynch, Thomas B., (BV) ....'55 '80 C.93 B.A. L.184 J.D. [Lynch,T.M.&B.]
*PRACTICE AREAS: Commercial Real Estate; Residential Real Estate; Residential Development; Zoning, Planning and Land Use; Estate Planning.

Lynch, Trembicki, Martelon and Boynton, (BV)
63 Cherry Street, P.O. Box 453, 06460 ⊙
Telephone: 203-878-4669 Fax: 203-876-0644
URL: http://www.lawyers.com/llmtblaw
Members of Firm: Richard H. Lynch (1912-1991); Thomas B. Lynch; George F. Martelon, Jr.; Alexander J. Trembicki (Resident, Westport Office); Michael S. Boynton.
General Practice. Probate, Real Estate, Zoning, Negligence, Workers' Compensation and Labor Relations, Domestic Relations and Municipal Law. Trials in all Courts.
Westport, Connecticut Office: 225 Main Street, Suite 103. Telephone: 203-227-6808. Fax: 203-226-6215.
See Professional Biographies, MILFORD, CONNECTICUT

Mager, John J., (BV) ....'65 '90 C.1030 B.A. L.1252 J.D. [Mager&M.]
Mager, Joseph J., (BV) ....'26 '55 C.197 A.B. L.976 LL.B. [Mager&M.]
Mager, Joseph J., Jr., (BV) ....'54 '81 C.1030 B.A. L.1029 J.D. [Mager&M.]
Mager & Mager, (BV) ....87 River St.
Magyar, Jennifer A. ....'60 '85 C.184 B.A. L.1048 J.D. Doctor's Associates, Inc.
Malone, Robert J., (BV) ....'45 '75 C.895 B.A. L.1202 J.D. [Coughlin&M.]
Mario, Carter E., (BV) ....'57 '86 C.575 B.S. L.362 J.D. [Perkins&M.]
Martelon, George F., Jr., (BV) ....'49 '74 C.93 A.B. L.902 J.D. [Lynch,T.M.&B.]
*PRACTICE AREAS: Probate Law; Real Estate; Labor and Employment; Civil Litigation; Family Law.
McCabe, Michael J., (BV) ....'57 '80 C.1211 B.A. L.1048 J.D. 5 Higgins Dr.
McKeever, Martin L. ....'31 '57 C.184 A.B. L.93 LL.B. Supr. Ct. J.
Mead, Robert J. ....'56 '83 C.164 B.A. L.1029 J.D. 1567 New Haven Ave.
Meuser, William J., (BV) ....'27 '65 C&L.262 B.S., LL.B. [Ⓒ Meuser,E.&H.]
Meuser, Eckenrode & Hayes, (BV) ....86 Cherry Street
Minter, Rachel J. ....'53 '79 C.156 A.B. L.1162 J.D. 92 Cherry St.
Moran, John W. ....'35 '64 C&L.184 B.S., J.D. Supr. Ct. J.
Moses, Marsha Belman, (AV) ....'48 '76 C.473 B.A. L.912 J.D. [Berchem,M.&D.]
*PRACTICE AREAS: Education Law; Labor and Employment.
Nugent, James M., (BV) ....'55 '80 C.184 B.A. L.1029 J.D. [Harlow,A.&F.]
*PRACTICE AREAS: Bankruptcy; Commercial Litigation; Real Estate; Civil Litigation; Commercial Law.
Olejarczyk, Pamela A. ....'69 '94 C.262 B.A. L.306 J.D. 245 Cherry St.
O'Sullivan, Thomas J. ....'14 '38 C&L.976 B.A., LL.B. State Trial Ref.
Otzel, Paul Lewis, (BV) ....'54 '79 C.1030 B.A. L.818 J.D. [Kapusta&O.]
Paperno, Pearl R. ....'08 '38 L.669 LL.B. 93 Hilltop Circle‡
Passero, Michael E. ....'56 '92 C.183 B.A. L.306 J.D. 92 Cherry St.
Pellegrino, Lawrence B., (BV) ....'66 '91 C.183 B.A. L.893 J.D. [Berchem,M.&D.]
*PRACTICE AREAS: Public Finance; Commercial Law; Real Estate; Bankruptcy.
Perkins, Jonathan N., (BV) ....'61 '87 C.1040 B.A. L.569 J.D. [Perkins&M.]
Perkins & Mario, P.C., (BV) ....54 Broad St.
Peterson, John L. ....'51 '75 C.291 B.A. L.879 J.D. 18 Alden Pl. (Pat.)
Piechota, David M. ....'67 '93 C.1019 B.B.A. L.1252 J.D. [Ⓐ Dey,S.&Assoc.]
Plumb, Kenneth R., (AV) ....'57 '84 C.867 B.A. L.1048 J.D. [Berchem,M.&D.]
*PRACTICE AREAS: Employer-Employee Relations; Employment Discrimination; Labor (Management); Workers Compensation.
Quigley, Sean W. ....'58 '93 C.616 B.S. L.1252 J.D. 771 Boston Post Rd.
Rogers, Steven F. ....'45 '75 C.67 A.B. L.831 J.D. 51 Cherry St.
Rosen, Mark J., (BV) ....'46 '75 C.477 B.A. L.184 J.D. [Ⓒ Berchem,M.&D.]
*PRACTICE AREAS: Domestic Law; Childrens Rights; Foreclosures; Collections.
Ross, Michael F. ....'50 '79 C.976 B.A. L.184 J.D. Supr. Ct. Mag.
Sagarin, J. Daniel, (AV) ....'41 '65 C.401 B.A. L.976 J.D. [Hurwitz&S.]
Shingara, Valerie A. ....'54 '79 C.829 B.A. L.1048 J.D. Dep. Chf. Clk., Supr. Ct.
Shumaker, Theodore H., (BV) ....'55 '81 C.184 B.S. L.472 J.D. [Harlow,A.&F.]
*PRACTICE AREAS: Real Estate; Zoning Law; Probate; Estate Planning.
Singewald, Dean R., (CV) ....'64 '90 C.103 B.A. L.1202 J.D. [Ⓐ Berchem,M.&D.]
*PRACTICE AREAS: Labor and Employment; Education.
Skudlarek, Stephen J. (Jack), Jr., (BV) '51 '83 C.1030 B.A. L.1029 J.D.
[Castignoli,S.&L.]
Slossberg, David A. ....'63 '89 C.178 B.A. L.569 J.D. [Hurwitz&S.]

Smith, Brian W., (BV) ....'57 '81 C.107 B.A. L.228 J.D. [Ⓐ Berchem,M.&D.]
*PRACTICE AREAS: Litigation; Insurance.
Smith, Richard B. ....'46 '71 C.94 B.S. L.472 J.D. 550 New Haven Ave.
Smith, Winthrop S., Jr., (BV) ....'58 '84 C.37 B.A. L.564 J.D. [Dey,S.&Assoc.]
Speranzini, David ....'65 '97 C&L.184 B.S., J.D. [Ⓐ Jacobi,K.&C.]
*PRACTICE AREAS: Environmental Law.
Staar, William A. ....'72 '97 C.93 B.A. L.1019 J.D. 147 N. Broad St.
Stark, Peter R., (BV) ....'58 '86 C.1030 B.A. L.724 J.D. [Ⓖ Winget,S.&S.]
Steenson, Anita Flannigan ....'63 '90 C.19 B.S. L.1029 J.D. [Ⓐ Dey,S.&Assoc.]

Stevens, Carroll & Carveth, (BV)
26 Cherry Street, P.O. Box 432, 06460
Telephone: 203-877-5471 Fax: 203-877-3970
Email: email@stevenscarrollcarveth.com
Members of Firm: Gerald F. Stevens (1938-1990); Leo P. Carroll; Christopher B. Carveth. Associate: Kristin Dorney Foley; Kevin J. Curseaden.
Real Estate, Zoning, Condominium, Family, Civil Litigation, Criminal Litigation, Corporate Law, Business Law, Appeals in all Courts, Workers Compensation, Estate Planning, Wills, Probate.
See Professional Biographies, MILFORD, CONNECTICUT

Stoltz, Melvin I., (AV) '43 '69 C&L.184 B.S.Ch. E., J.D. BB
51 Cherry Street, 06460
Telephone: 203-874-8183 Facsimile: 203-878-9607
Email: patlaw@snet.net
Patent, Trademark, Copyright and Unfair Competition. Foreign Patent and Trademark Law and Related Litigation.
See Professional Biographies, MILFORD, CONNECTICUT

Streit-Kefalas, Beverly K., (BV) ....'64 '90 C.788 A.B. L.184 J.D. 62 W. Main St.
Studer, Stephen W., (BV) ....'50 '77 C.1200 B.A. L.818 J.D. [Berchem,M.&D.]
*PRACTICE AREAS: Land Use; Environmental Law; Estate Planning; Family Law; Trusts.
Telker, Ellen M., (BV) ....'51 '76 C.518 B.A. L.982 J.D. 564 Boston Post Rd.
Tracey, William J. '32 '57
C.1029 B.A. L.276 J.D. V.P., Secy. & Gen. Coun., Dorr-Oliver Inc.
Vocalina, Michael V. ....'64 '93 C.999 B.S. L.1187 J.D. [Ⓐ Berchem,M.&D.]
*PRACTICE AREAS: Workers Compensation; Personal Injury; General Litigation.
Weishaupt, T. Christopher ....'62 '92 C.708 B.A. L.1029 J.D. 75 Broad St.
Whitsett, Peter A. ....'48 '74 C.966 B.A. L.184 J.D. Asst. Clk., Supr. Ct.
Williams, Michael P. A., (BV) ....'45 '74 C.94 A.B. L.192 J.D. [Harlow,A.&F.]
*PRACTICE AREAS: Real Estate; Freedom of Information.
Winget, Spadafora & Schwartzberg, LLP
183 N. Broad Street (⊙Newark, NJ; New York, NY)
Winkel, James R. ....'63 '96 C.1145 B.S. L.306 J.D. [Harlow,A.&F.]
*PRACTICE AREAS: Commercial Law; Civil Litigation; Personal Injury.
Wright, Stephen P., (BV) ....'54 '81 C.259 B.S. L.1048 J.D. [Harlow,A.&F.]
*PRACTICE AREAS: Civil Litigation; Debtor and Creditor Rights; Debtor and Creditor Bankruptcy.

MONROE, 14,010, *Fairfield Co.*

Adolphson, K. Bradford '56 '83 C.184 B.S. L.273 J.D.
[Ware,F.V.S.&A.] (See Pat. Sect.)
Agatston, Roger C., (CV) ....'50 '81 C.563 B.A. L.1029 J.D. 324 Elm St.
Baghdady, David G. ....'68 '93 C.1029 B.S. L.1252 J.D. [D.G.Baghdady]
Baghdady, David G., LLC ....345 Monroe Turnpike
Barber, William J. ....'59 '86 C.1350 B.S. L.1009 J.D. [Ware,F.V.S.&A.] (See Pat. Sect.)
*PRACTICE AREAS: Patents; Copyrights; Trademarks.
Bellenot, Ronald K. ....'59 '90 C.1290 B.A. L.1252 J.D. 501 Main St.
Berg, Peter Van Dyk, Jr. ....'49 '79 C.1028 B.A. L.896 J.D. 262 Main St.
Boufford, Kathy C. ....'70 '95 C.708 B.A. L.1252 J.D. 501 Main St.
Carvis, Thaddius J. '43 '71
C.966 B.S.Ch.E. L.128 J.D. [Ware,F.V.S.&A.] (See Pat. Sect.)
*PRACTICE AREAS: Patent Law; Trademark Law; Copyright Law; Antitrust Law; Unfair Competition Law.
Catalano, Victor, (BV) ....'41 '83 C.184 B.S. L.1029 J.D. 324 Elm St.
Chittick, David O., (BV) ....'40 '67 C.970 B.A. L.184 LL.B. 518 Monroe Tpke.
Dalaker, Lawrence, (BV) ....'56 '81 C.874 B.A. L.1029 J.D. 450 Monroe Tpke.
Delaney, Dennis J., (BV) ....'36 '71 C.563 B.M.E. L.184 J.D. 324 Elm St.
Fracassini, John P., (BV) ....'44 '70 C.1030 B.A. L.276 J.D. 188 Main St.
Frederick, James R., (AV) '44 '69 C&L.477 B.S., J.D.
[Ware,F.V.S.&A.] (See Pat. Sect.)
Fressola, Alfred A., (AV) '46 '73
C&L.184 B.S.E., J.D. [Ware,F.V.S.&A.] (See Pat. Sect.)
Gaynor, Gerald M. ....'51 '84 C&L.1029 B.S., J.D. 31 Nelson Brook Rd.
Hunsberger, Daniel P. ....'49 '96 C.1029 B.S. L.1252 J.D. 35 Glen Hollow Dr.
Hyman, Andrew T. ....'62 '96 C.454 B.S. L.1051 J.D. [Ware,F.V.S.&A.] (See Pat. Sect.)
*PRACTICE AREAS: Patents; Trademarks; Copyrights; Intellectual Property.
Kollmann, David A., (BV) ....'48 '81 C.546 B.A. L.1029 J.D. 33 Colonia Dr.
Lipsitz, Barry R. ....'53 '80 C.119 B.S.E.E. L.1040 J.D. 755 Main St. (Pat.)
Maguire, Francis J., Jr. '47 '83
C.690 B.S.E.E. L.306 J.D. [Ware,F.V.S.&A.] (See Pat. Sect.)
Martin, Frederick J., (BV) ....'52 '77 C.128 B.A. L.1202 J.D. 450 Monroe Tpke.
Morley, Edward B. ....'51 '78 C.165 B.A. L.990 J.D. 135 Hillside Lane
Oliver, Milton M., (AVⓉ) '51 '75 C.309 B.A. L.284 J.D.
(adm. in MA; not adm. in CT; See Pat. Sect.) [Ware,F.V.S.&A.]
*PRACTICE AREAS: International Patent Law; Trademarks; Copyrights; Computer Law; Litigation.
Oppenheimer, Mark V., (CV) ....'49 '75 C.208 B.A. L.1068 J.D. 8 Rosewood Circle
Pasquale, Jack M. '43 '81 C.570 B.S.E.E. L.1048 J.D.
[Ware,F.V.S.&A.] (See Pat. Sect.)
*PRACTICE AREAS: Patents; Trademarks; Copyrights; Intellectual Property.
Retter, James A. ....'51 '00 C.228 B.A. L.184 J.D. [Ware,F.V.S.&A.] (See Pat. Sect.)
Shear, Stephen B. '43 '74 C.861 B.S. L.273 J.D.
(adm. in VA; not adm. in CT; See Pat. Sect.) [Ware,F.V.S.&A.]
Treschitta, Nora ....'62 '87 C.184 B.A. L.1029 J.D. 28 Oak Ridge Rd.
Walkley, John T., (BV) ....'53 '80 C.745 A.B. L.1048 J.D. 450 Monroe Tpke.
Ware, Robert H., (AV) '27 '51
C.477 B.S.M.E. L.309 LL.B. [Ware,F.V.S.&A.] (See Pat. Sect.)

Ware, Fressola, Van Der Sluys & Adolphson, LLP, (AV)
Bradford Green, Building Five, 755 Main Street, P.O. Box 224, 06468
Telephone: 203-261-1234 Fax: 203-261-5676
Email: mail@wfva.net
Robert H. Ware; Alfred A. Fressola; Peter C. Van Der Sluys (1939-1991); K. Bradford Adolphson; Francis J. Maguire, Jr.; William J. Barber; James R. Frederick; Thaddius J. Carvis; Stephen B. Shear (Not admitted in CT); Milton M. Oliver (Not admitted in CT); Jack M. Pasquale; James A. Retter; Andrew T. Hyman.
Patent, Trademark, Copyright, Computer, Antitrust, Unfair Competition, Foreign Patent Law, Litigation and Federal Practice.
See Professional Biographies, MONROE, CONNECTICUT

Weeks, Robert W., Jr., (BV) ....'45 '70 C.705 B.A. L.184 J.D. [Weeks]
*PRACTICE AREAS: Civil Litigation; Real Estate.

Weeks Law Firm, (BV)
337 Monroe Turnpike, 06468
Telephone: 203-261-6052 Telecopier: 203-452-7563
Email: weekslaw@aol.com URL: http://www.lawyers.com/weekslawfirm
Robert W. Weeks, Jr.
Civil Litigation, Real Estate.
See Professional Biographies, MONROE, CONNECTICUT

Williams, Wallace R., III ....'44 '85 C.1252 B.S. L.1029 J.D. 501 Main St.

MOOSUP, 3,376, *Windham Co.*

Hoyt, Anne R., (BV) ....'55 '80 C.183 B.A. L.184 J.D. [O'Connell,F.&A.] (⊙Hartford)
O'Connell, Michael D., (AV) '45 '72
C.602 B.A. L.184 J.D. [O'Connell,F.&A.] (⊙Hartford)
O'Connell, Flaherty & Attmore, L.L.C., (AV)
22 Main St. (⊙Danbury, Hartford, Old Saybrook, West Hartford, CT; Springfield, MA)

MYSTIC, 2,568, *New London Co.*

Bobruff, Neal M., (BV) ....'58 '83 C.881 B.A. L.184 J.D. 49 Whitehall Ave.
Conway, Kevin W., (AV) ....'32 '57 C.321 B.A. L.184 LL.B. [Conway&L.] ⊙
Conway & Londregan, P.C., (AV) .... Masons Island Rd. (⊙New London)
Copp, Webster T. ....'29 '69 C.184 B.S. L.818 LL.B. 4 Money Point Rd.
Deasy, Michael P., (BV) ....'50 '77 C.829 B.A. L.1048 J.D. 86 Denison Avenue
Everett, William C. ....'35 '61 C.976 B.S. L.309 J.D. 1 Prospect St. (Pat.)
Feinstein, Andrew A., (BV) ....'50 '80 C.918 B.A. L.569 J.D. 12 Roosevelt Ave.
Gianni, Michelle M., (BV) ....'54 '80 C.745 B.A. L.602 J.D. [Tedford,G.J.&L.]
Jensen, Wade D., (BV) ....'50 '83 C.172 B.S. L.1068 J.D. [Tedford,G.J.&L.]
Laffey, Myles J., (AV) ....'38 '68 C.229 B.A. L.184 J.D. [Tedford,G.J.&L.]
Lamb, Virginia A. '49 '76 C.276 B.S.F.S. L.30 J.D.
(adm. in MD; not adm. in CT) 4 Hickory Ledge‡
Laskey, Norman P. ....'50 '75 C&L.260 B.A., J.D. 31 Water St.
McClelland, Roger '52 '77 C.30 B.S. L.904 J.D.
(adm. in FL; not adm. in CT) 44 Pearl St.‡
Morgan, Roger P., (AV) ....'32 '58 C.31 B.A. L.976 LL.B. P.O. Box 588
Pochal, Susan B., (BV) ....'60 '85 C.1103 B.S. L.1048 J.D. [Conway&L.] ⊙
Sergeant, Russell E. ....'56 '86 C.688 B.S.M.A. L.659 J.D. 3B Rowland St.
Tedford, Deborah J., (AV) ....'50 '76 C.976 B.A. L.94 J.D. [Tedford,G.J.&L.]
Tedford, Gianni, Jensen & Laffey, (AV) .... 12 Roosevelt Avenue

NAUGATUCK, 30,625, *New Haven Co.*

Bradley, Edward F. ....'17 '49 C.676 L.184 LL.B. Worker's Comp. Comr.
Caine, M. Leonard, III, (BV) ....'57 '83 C.884 B.A. L.329 J.D. [Caine&C.]
Caine, Maureen S., (BV) ....'58 '83 C.783 B.A. L.1202 J.D. [Caine&C.]
Caine & Caine, (BV) ....35 Porter Ave.
Casella, Charles L., (CV) ....'65 '91 C.787 B.S. L.1029 J.D. [Casella&C.]
Casella and Casella, P.C., (CV) .... 16 Hillside Ave.
Clark, Millard W. '32 '61 C&L.425 B.B.A., J.D.
(adm. in LA; not adm. in CT) 99 Ridge Rd., 9‡
Cremins, William T. '47 '73 C&L.184 B.S., J.D.
Exec. V.P., Secy. & Gen. Coun., The Naugatuck Glass Co.
D'Angelo, Robert V., Jr., (BV) '55 '81
C.390 A.B. L.184 J.D. Assoc. Gen. Coun., Uniroyal Holding, Inc.
Dlugokecki, Frederick '56 '81 C.184 B.S. L.128 J.D.
(adm. in PA; not adm. in CT) 175 Church St.
Eschuk, Paul D. ....'53 '78 C.321 B.A. L.184 J.D. 290 Park Ave.★
Hanlon, Neal B., (BV) ....'45 '70 C.262 B.A. L.184 J.D. 83 Meadow St.
Harris, Sylvia ....'48 '94 C.588 B.S. L.1202 J.D. 102 Water St.
Hess, Newman W., III, (BV) ....'48 '73 C.94 B.S. L.767 J.D. 42 Terrace Ave.
Jennings, William L., (BVⓉ) ....'49 '83 C.1290 B.A. L.469 J.D. 174 Cliff Street
Kelly, Christpher J. ....'62 '89 C&L.1029 B.S., J.D. 15 Raykwich Dr.
Labriola, David K., (BV) ....'60 '86 C.976 B.A. L.306 J.D. [Labriola&L.]
Labriola, Gerald, Jr., (BV) ....'57 '83 C.282 B.A. L.128 J.D. [Labriola&L.]
Labriola & Labriola, LLC, (BV) .... 175 Church Street
Makowsky, Dorold A. ....'34 '81 C.184 B.A. L.1029 J.D. 53 Conrad St. Apt 2E
Mariano, Peter E., (BV) ....'60 '85 C.829 B.S. L.1202 J.D. 500 Hillside Ave.
Marlor, Henry S., Jr., (BV) ....'17 '49 C.197 A.B. L.910 LL.B. 185 Meadow St.
McGuire, James M. '51 '86 C.165 B.A. L.564 J.D.
(adm. in NY; not adm. in CT) V.P., USCO Distribution Servs. Inc.
McVerry, Michael J., (BV) ....'48 '73 C.1030 B.A. L.724 J.D. 35 Porter Ave.
Morrissey, David J., (BV) ....'53 '79 C.390 A.B. L.184 J.D. [D.J.Morrissey]
Morrissey, LLC, David J., Law Offices of, (BV) .... 203 Church St.
Mulhall, James A., Jr., (BV) ....'60 '85 C.184 B.A. L.425 J.D. [Nixon&M.]
Nixon, Kevin T., Sr., (BV) ....'33 '58 C.184 B.S. L.262 J.D. [Nixon&M.]
Nixon & Mulhall, (BV) ....35 Porter Ave.
Noonan, Gerald M., (BV) ....'45 '75 C.1266 B.A. L.724 J.D. 13 Rockwell Ave.
O'Boyle, David J. '24 '51 C.659 A.B. L.309 LL.B.
(adm. in NY; not adm. in CT) 70 Great Hill Rd.
Rotatori, Peter, III, (BV) ....'63 '88 C.930 B.A. L.896 J.D. [Rotatori] ⊙
Rotatori, Peter, Jr., (BV) ....'35 '62 C.1030 B.S. L.262 LL.B. [Rotatori] ⊙
Rotatori Law Firm, The, (BV) ....226 Meadow Street (⊙Southbury)
Rozanski, Donald H. ....'59 '98 C.1102 B.S. L.1040 J.D. 45 Parkman Place
Santos, Carlos A. ....'71 '96 C.184 B.S. L.1252 J.D. 203 Church St.
Sheedy, Barbara J. ....'42 '80 C&L.184 B.A., J.D. Supr. J.
Tuohy, Cornelius F. ....'42 '72 C&L.184 B.A., J.D. 53 Genl. Dalton Dr.
Zehnder, Donald J., (BV) ....'26 '53 C.602 B.A. L.976 LL.B. [Zehnder&Z.]
Zehnder, Donald J., Jr., (BV) ....'59 '85 C.602 B.A. L.128 J.D. [Zehnder&Z.]
Zehnder & Zehnder, (BV) .... 305 Church St.

NEW BRITAIN, 75,491, *Hartford Co.*

Advocates Law Firm, LLC, (AV)
11 Franklin Square, 06051
Telephone: 860-348-1900 Facsimile: 860-348-1942
URL: http://www.advocateslawfirm.com
Ron Murphy;—Francis D. Paola, Jr.; Michael G. Rigg; Janis K. Malec.
Criminal Defense, White Collar Criminal Defense, Personal Injury, Medical Malpractice, Legal Malpractice, Legal Ethics and Professional Responsibility, Attorney Discipline. Trials and Appeals in all Courts and Administrative Agencies.
Reference: First Bank of West Hartford.
See Professional Biographies, NEW BRITAIN, CONNECTICUT

Anderson, Stephen J., (AV) ....'36 '61 C&L.184 B.A., LL.B. [Eisenberg,A.M.&L.]
*PRACTICE AREAS: Commercial Law; Real Estate Law; Planning and Zoning Law.
Anderson, Steven D., (BV) ....'54 '84 C.870 B.S. L.184 J.D. [Januszewski,M.&D.]
*PRACTICE AREAS: Personal Injury Law; Criminal Law; Family Law; Workers Compensation Law; Probate Law.
Aronson, Arnold W. ....'26 '54 C&L.184 B.A., J.D. Sr. Trial Ref. J.
Aurigemma, Julia L. ....'53 '78 C.188 B.A. L.184 J.D. Supr. J.
Badorek-Welch, Stacy, (BV) ....'61 '88 C.184 B.A. L.1029 J.D. 66 Franklin Sq.

Barbieri, John A. ....'39 '64 C.1030 B.S.S. L.306 J.D. 18 Cedar St.
Bauer, Charles W., (BV) .... '43 '71 C.299 A.B. L.184 J.D. [Eisenberg,A.M.&L.]
*PRACTICE AREAS: Municipal Law; Elder Law; Estate Planning; Construction Law; Land Use.
Beatt, Bruce H. '52 '78
C.881 A.B. L.831 J.D. V.P., Gen. Cnsl and Sec., The Stanley Works
Belkin, Howard H., (BV) .... '38 '63 C&L.184 B.A., LL.B. 1 Prospect St.
Berger, Marshall K., Jr. .... '47 '73 C.882 B.A. L.273 J.D. Supr. Ct. J.
Butler, Anita L., (BV) ....'62 '87 C.197 A.B. L.94 J.D. City Atty.
Camp, Williams & Richardson, (BV) ....130 W. Main St.
Carabillo, Antonia .... '56 '87 C.184 B.S. L.1029 J.D. Asst. State's Atty.
Carey, Brian C., (BV) ....'48 '73 C.829 B.A. L.184 J.D. P.O. Box 1868
Carifa, Kenneth J., (BV) ....'57 '82 C.184 B.A. L.818 J.D. [Camp,W.&R.]
Carrier, Michael A., (BV) .... '60 '86 C.1156 B.S. L.1048 J.D. [Weber]
Centrilla-Silvia, JoAnn, (CV) ...... '60 '89 C.262 B.A. L.1029 J.D. [Eisenberg,A.M.&L.]
*PRACTICE AREAS: Commercial Collections; Consumer Collections; Bankruptcy Law.
Ciccarillo, Dennis G., (BV) .... '53 '79 C.103 A.B. L.184 J.D. [Eisenberg,A.M.&L.]
*PRACTICE AREAS: Labor and Employment Law; Social Security; Disability.
Clancy, Cynthia J., (BV) ....'61 '90 C.19 B.A. L.1252 J.D. Asst. Pub. Def.
Clebowicz, Walter A., (BV) ....'51 '76 C.264 B.A. L.184 J.D. Prob. J.
Cobb, Anita D., (BV) ....'42 '74 C.242 A.B. L.184 J.D. Asst. Corp. Coun.
Coppage, Robert B. ....'23 '54 C.473 B.S. L.1003 LL.B. 24 Cedar St.‡
Cosgrove, David J., (BV) ....'55 '81 C&L.184 B.A., J.D. Asst. Pub. Def.
Delaney, Stephen B. ....'50 '80 C.184 B.A. L.1202 J.D. Wrkrs. Comp. J.
DeNigris, Laurie G., (BV) .... '59 '84 C.787 B.A. L.607 J.D. [Eisenberg,A.M.&L.]
*PRACTICE AREAS: Family Law; Childrens Rights; Social Security; Litigation.
DeNigris, Nicholas E., (BV) ...... '35 '60 C.156 B.A. L.184 LL.B. [Januszewski,M.&D.]
*PRACTICE AREAS: Real Estate Law; Domestic Relations Law; Criminal Law; Personal Injury; Corporate Law.
DeVivo, Donald A. ....'62 '88 C.1033 B.A. L.184 J.D. V.P., Dattco, Inc.
Dickson, Lawrence H., (BV) ....'61 '88 C&L.477 B.A., J.D. [Weber]
Dilzer, Daniel ....'66 '92 C.829 B.A. L.1029 J.D. 1232 Corbin Ave.
Dorsey, Christopher J. ....'65 '92 C.184 B.A. L.1187 J.D. [Sledzik&M.]
Dunn, Philip R. ....'30 '56 C.321 B.S. L.276 J.D. Supr. Ct. J.
Dworski, William V., (BV) .... '26 '53 C&L.184 B.S., J.D. [W.V.Dworski]
Dworski, William V., P.C., (BV) ....65 S. High St.

Eisenberg, Anderson, Michalik & Lynch LLP, (AV) [BR]
136 West Main Street, P.O. Box 2950, 06050-2950
Telephone: 860-229-4855; 225-8403 Fax: 860-223-4026
URL: http://www.eaml.com
Harold J. Eisenberg (1906-1995). Members of Firm: Stephen J. Anderson; Robert A. Michalik; Edward T. Lynch, Jr.; Charles W. Bauer; Dennis G. Ciccarillo; Pamela Reardon Reynolds; JoAnn Centrilla-Silvia; Kenneth R. Slater, Jr.; Peter N. Upton; Gregory J. Spuches; Laurie G. DeNigris. Associates: David G. Jordan; Bruce A. Zawodniak.
Construction Law, Employment Law, Elder Law, Estate Planning, Taxation Law, Family Law, Federal and State Litigation and Appeals, Municipal, Real Estate, Zoning, Corporate Law, Commercial Law.
Representative Clients: Apple Health Care; Berlin Steel Construction Co.; CIGNA; Connecticut Employees Union "Independent"; Fleet Bank, N.A.; Magson Uniform Corp.; TILCON Connecticut Inc.
See Professional Biographies, NEW BRITAIN, CONNECTICUT

Ericson, Scalise, Mangan & Zembko, P.C., (BV) .... 35 Pearl St.
Fagan, Lawrence J., (BV) ....'30 '56 C.1030 B.S. L.93 LL.B. [Rosenzweig,F.&S.]
Flynn, Michael J. ....'47 '74 C&L.1033 B.A., J.D. Clk., Supr. Ct. Housing Session
Forbes, William J., (BV) ....'52 '79 C.454 B.A. L.1048 J.D. 17 Lenox Pl.
Friedle, Gary A., (BV) ....'39 '64 C.165 B.A. L.184 J.D. 25 Court St.
Gaffney, Bernard D. ....'30 '58 C.976 B.A. L.184 LL.B. Supr. Ct. J.
Gaffney, J. Brian, (AV) .... '33 '60 C.602 B.A. L.262 LL.B. [Gaffney K.]
Gaffney Kane P.C., (AV) .... One Liberty Square
Gardner, Mitchell, (BV) ....'30 '60 C.105 B.S. L.184 LL.B. 208 S. Mountain St.
Geragosian, Harold J., (BV) ....'27 '53 C.184 B.A. L.94 LL.B. 380 W. Main St.
Goff, Linda E. '50 '96 C.1201 B.S. L.284 J.D.
(adm. in CA; not adm. in CT) 183 Hartford Rd., Suite B10
Goldberg, Joseph H. ....'26 '51 C.976 B.S. L.309 LL.B. Sr. Supr. Ct. J.
Graham, James T. ....'51 '76 C&L.477 A.B., J.D. Supr. J.
Griffen, Thomas P., (BV) .... '51 '80 C&L.184 B.A., J.D. [Sweeney&G.]
Hartshorn, David B., (BV) .... '54 '86 C.478 B.A. L.184 J.D. 55 Lexington St.
Jackaway, Harry N. ....'25 '51 C&L.184 B.A., LL.B. Supr. Ct. J.

Januszewski, McQuillan and DeNigris, (AV) [BR]
165 West Main Street, P.O. Box 150, 06050-0150
Telephone: 860-225-7667 Fax: 860-826-1814
Email: JMDNBCT@WORLDNET.ATT.NET
Members of Firm: Edward Januszewski (1921-1999); Paul J. McQuillan; Nicholas E. DeNigris; John C. Matulis, Jr.; Steven D. Anderson; Martin McQuillan.
General Practice, Civil and Criminal Litigation, Real Estate, Family Law, Administrative Agency Proceedings, Workers Compensation, Personal Injury, Products Liability, Professional Malpractice, Probate, Representation to Professional Responsibilities, Trials in State and Federal Courts.
Representative Clients: The Peoples Savings Bank of New Britain, Inc.; Tilcon, Inc.; Acmat, Inc.
See Professional Biographies, NEW BRITAIN, CONNECTICUT

Jordan, David G. .... '74 '99 C.1030 B.A. L.184 J.D. [[A] Eisenberg,A.M.&L.]
*PRACTICE AREAS: Litigation.
Judd, William H., Jr. ....'12 '38 C.197 A.B. L.309 LL.B. 85 Brookside Rd.‡
Kane, James F., (BV) ....'46 '82 C.724 B.A. L.1048 J.D. [Gaffney K.]
Karanian, Charles G., (BV) ....'25 '53 C.472 B.B.A. L.184 LL.B. 66 Franklin Sq.
Karanian, Robert M., (BV) .... '52 '80 C.184 B.A. L.464 J.D. 41 Lexington St.
Kern, Dennis L., (BV) ....'45 '75 C.602 B.A. L.306 J.D. [Pignatella&K.]
Kosinski, Richard H. .... '41 '66 C.184 B.A. L.724 J.D. 106 Farmington Ave.
Kozloski, Walter B., (BV) ....'25 '54 C.454 B.A. L.184 J.D. 35 Pearl St.
Kremski, Julius J. ....'19 '55 C&L.184 B.A., LL.B. Ref. & Supr. Ct. J.‡
Laczewski, John M. .... '69 '95 C&L.472 B.B.A., J.D. 35 Pearl St.
Langer, Sharon D., (BV) ....'52 '84 C.783 B.A. L.184 J.D. Conn. Legal Servs. Inc.
Levesque, Larry P., (BV) ....'55 '82 C.37 B.A. L.184 J.D. 103 Elbridge Rd.
Levine, Harvey L., (BV) ....'43 '80 C.184 B.A. L.1029 J.D. 754 W. Main St.
Lewis, Joanne, (BV) '50 '75
C.914 B.A. L.94 J.D. Mng. Atty., Connecticut Legal Servs., Inc.
Luba, Louis John, Jr. .... '67 '93 C.1213 B.S. L.823 J.D. State Div. of Crim. Jus.
Ludwikow, Steven J., (BV) ....'55 '82 C.829 B.A. L.818 J.D. 111 Lexington St.
Lynch, Edward T., Jr., (BV) .... '45 '70 C.276 A.B. L.184 J.D. [Eisenberg,A.M.&L.]
*PRACTICE AREAS: Corporate Litigation; Business Litigation; Labor and Employment Litigation; Construction Litigation; Arbitration.
Madorin, A. Raymond, (BV) ....'46 '72 C.855 B.A. L.184 J.D. 25 Court St.
Malec, Janis K. ....'58 '96 C.184 B.S. L.1048 J.D. [[A] Advocates]
*PRACTICE AREAS: Medical Malpractice; Personal Injury; Criminal Defense.
Mangan, John J. ....'18 '46 C&L.902 LL.B. 35 Pearl St.‡
Mangan, Stephen L., (BV) ....'57 '83 C.902 B.A. L.192 J.D. [Ericson,S.M.&Z.]
Mantell, Rodd J. ....'60 '90 C.1044 B.A. L.306 J.D. SAFECO Prop. & Cas. Ins. Co.
Marinelli, James M., (BV) .... '41 '67 C&L.184 B.A., J.D. [Marinelli&S.]
Marinelli & Sauer, P.C., (BV) ....55 Lexington St.
Matulis, John C., Jr., (BV) ....'50 '76 C.855 A.B. L.184 J.D. [Januszewski,M.&D.]
*PRACTICE AREAS: Civil Litigation; Professional Malpractice; Domestic Relations Law.
McCarthy, Francis J., (AV) ....'18 '47 C.918 A.B. L.976 J.D. [[G] Gaffney K.]
McCormack, James F. '60 '86 C.1030 B.A. L.1048 J.D.
Corporate Counsel, Connecticut Lottery Corporation
McGuire, Mark P., (BV) ....'51 '76 C.1030 B.A. L.790 J.D. [Sledzik&M.]
Mckinstry, Ryan R. '71 '99 C.878 B.S. L.273 J.D.
(adm. in UT; not adm. in CT) Law Clk, Supr. Ct.
McQuillan, Martin, (BV) ....'62 '90 C.276 B.A. L.1048 J.D. [Januszewski,M.&D.]
*PRACTICE AREAS: Personal Injury Law; Workers Compensation Law; Criminal Law.
McQuillan, Paul J., (AV) .... '28 '57 C&L.276 B.S., J.D. [Januszewski,M.&D.]
*PRACTICE AREAS: Personal Injury Law; Criminal Law; Malpractice; Professional Ethics.
Meskill, Thomas J. ....'28 '56 C.855 B.S. L.184 LL.B. U.S. Ct. App. J.
Michalik, Robert A., (BV) .... '41 '66 C&L.184 B.A., J.D. [Eisenberg,A.M.&L.]
*PRACTICE AREAS: Municipal Law; Banking Law; Family Law.
Mills, Timothy F., (BV) ....'52 '88 C.607 B.A. L.1218 J.D. 122 Main St.
Mindera, Lisabeth B. ....'57 '82 C.184 B.A. L.128 J.D. 19 Bassett St.
Mlynarczyk, Peter C., (BV) ....'57 '88 C.1156 B.S. L.1048 J.D. 1 Prospect St.
Monterosso, Anthony J. .... '19 '44 C.145 B.A. L.228 LL.B. 19 Bassett St.
Moran, Antonia C. '42 '88 C.966 B.S. L.184 J.D.
Assoc. Prof., Central Conn. State Univ.
Murphy, Ron, (AV) ....'58 '83 C.349 B.S. L.184 J.D. [Advocates]
*PRACTICE AREAS: Criminal Defense; White Collar Criminal Defense; Personal Injury; Medical Malpractice; Legal Malpractice.
Palmieri, Catherine T. '63 '89 C&L.184 B.A., J.D.
Atty., SAFECO Prop. & Cas. Ins. Co.
Paola, Francis D., Jr., (BV) .... '49 '80 C.884 A.B. L.1252 J.D. [[A] Advocates]
Partridge, Kathryn, (AV) '63 '90
C.309 A.B. L.188 J.D. Sr. Corp. Cnsl., The Stanley Works
Pearl, Helen Z., (BV) ....'38 '78 C.881 B.A. L.184 J.D. [Weber]
Pearl, Jason E. ....'32 '56 C&L.188 A.B., LL.B. 19 S. High St.
Pignatella, Ralph C., (BV) ....'44 '69 C.184 B.A. L.306 J.D. [Pignatella&K.]
Pignatella and Kern, (BV) ....28 Park Pl.
Piskorski, David A., (BV) ....'41 '67 C.1030 B.S. L.128 LL.B. 450 Main St.
Platt, Lewis M., (BV) ....'45 '70 C.184 B.A. L.818 J.D. P.O. Box 1868
Pollowitz, David I., (BV) ....'23 '59 C.569 B.S. L.184 LL.B. 35 Pearl St.
Proulx, Albert P., (BV) ....'42 '68 C.014 B.A. L.184 LL.B. 450 Main St.
Reicher, Max H. .... '07 '30 L.94 J.D. State Trial Ref., Supr. Ct.
Reynolds, Pamela Reardon, (BV) '52 '85 C.1102 B.S. L.184 J.D.
[Eisenberg,A.M.&L.]
*PRACTICE AREAS: Corporate Law; Commercial Law; Trust and Estate Planning; Mergers and Acquisitions Law; Franchise Law.
Reynolds, Robert N., Jr. .... '53 '81 C.999 B.S. L.1029 J.D. [Gaffney K.]
Rigg, Michael G. .... '70 '96 C.237 B.A. L.1252 J.D. [[A] Advocates]
*PRACTICE AREAS: Criminal Defense; Personal Injury.
Rosenzweig, Israel, (BV) ....'16 '46 C&L.184 B.S., J.D. [Rosenzweig,F.&S.]
Rosenzweig, Fagan & Sheehan, (BV) .... 35 Pearl St.
Sauer, David A., (BV) ....'57 '82 C.732 B.A. L.184 J.D. [Marinelli&S.]
Scalise, Joseph R., (BV) .... '66 '91 C.1048 B.A. L.1187 J.D. [Ericson,S.M.&Z.]
Scalise, Robert A., (BV) ....'64 '89 C.067 B.A. L.1048 J.D. [Ericson,S.M.&Z.]
Scalise, Robert A., (BV) ....'37 '62 C.184 B.A. L.94 LL.B. [Ericson,S.M.&Z.]
Schlaff, Elizabeth, (BV) ....'55 '82 C.103 B.A. L.94 J.D. New Gen. Hosp.
Schultz, James J. ....'52 '88 C.659 B.A. L.1065 J.D. 164 Belridge Rd.
Sheary, Albert E. ....'28 '54 C.855 B.A. L.184 LL.B. [Ericson,S.M.&Z.]
Sheehan, Timothy, (BV) ....'40 '72 C&L.184 B.A., J.D. [Rosenzweig,F.&S.]
Shevchuk, Donald E. ....'56 '83 C&L.184 B.S., J.D. 35 Pearl St.
Silver, Daniel A., (BV) ....'45 '70 C.434 B.A. L.161 J.D. 1 Liberty Sq.
Simon, Kenneth W., (BV) ....'51 '81 C.1077 B.A. L.1048 J.D. Pub. Def.
Slater, Kenneth R., Jr., (BV) .... '66 '91 C.696 B.A. L.184 J.D. [Eisenberg,A.M.&L.]
*PRACTICE AREAS: Environmental Law; Land Use Law; Litigation; Arbitration.
Sledzik, Chester S., (BV) ....'27 '56 C.477 B.B.A. L.608 J.D. [Sledzik&M.]
Sledzik & McGuire, (BV) .... 52 Main Street
Speyer, Kenneth J. ....'50 '75 C.178 B.A. L.306 J.D. 13 Audubon St.
Spuches, Gregory J. .... '60 '88 C.1044 B.P.S. L.1029 J.D. [Eisenberg,A.M.&L.]
*PRACTICE AREAS: Taxation; Estate Planning; Probate; Estate Administration; Elder Law.
Sullivan, E. Timothy, Jr., (BV) ....'59 '84 C.1048 B.S.B.A. L.862 J.D. [Gaffney K.]
Sussman, J. Bruce ....'47 '72 C.4 B.A. L.851 J.D. 2086 Stanley St.
Sweeney, William J., Jr., (AV) ....'47 '75 C.1030 B.A. L.818 J.D. [Sweeney&G.]
Sweeney & Griffen, (AV) .... Old Post Office Plaza
Tabellione, Thomas P., (P.C.), (BV) ....'47 '75 C.184 B.A. L.818 J.D. 35 Pearl St.
Traceski, Stanley J., Jr., (BV) ....'29 '54 C.976 B.S. L.184 LL.B. 28 Park Place
Upton, Peter N., (BV) .... '44 '73 C.674 B.A. L.94 J.D. [Eisenberg,A.M.&L.]
*PRACTICE AREAS: Litigation.
Ustach, Lynne A., (BV) .... '56 '82 C.321 A.B. L.823 J.D. 25 Court St.
Vayer, Paul S., (CV) ....'46 '84 C.829 B.A. L.1048 J.D. 50 Hillcrest Ave.
Vollmer, Thomas E. .... '42 '66 C.602 B.A. L.309 LL.B. [Gaffney K.]
Walsh, Brian T., (BV) ....'52 '77 C&L.884 B.S., J.D. 16 Russell St.
Webb, D. J. Harry, (AV) ....'29 '56 C&L.184 B.A., J.D. 1 Liberty Sq.
Weber, Robert F., Jr., (BV) ....'59 '84 C&L.184 B.A., J.D. [Weber]
Weber, William W., (BV) ....'39 '64 C.855 B.A. L.188 LL.B. [Weber]
Weber Law Firm, (BV) ....24 Cedar St.
Williams, Charles North, (BV) ....'33 '62 C.197 A.B. L.188 LL.B. [Camp,W.&R.]
Winakor, David S. '68 '96
C.608 B.A. L.184 J.D. Corp. Cnsl & Asst. Sec., The Stanley Works
Woodfield, Gary J. ....'57 '82 C.184 B.S. L.818 J.D. 41 Lexington St.
Yukna, Paula Jean, (BV) ....'53 '78 C.184 B.A. L.744 J.D. 16 Russell St.
Zawodniak, Bruce A., (BV) ...... '61 '88 C.855 B.A. L.184 J.D. [[A] Eisenberg,A.M.&L.]
*PRACTICE AREAS: Real Estate Law; Real Estate Foreclosures; Condominium Law; Landlord/Tenant Law; Commercial Law.
Zembko, Elizabeth A., (BV) ....'60 '87 [Ericson,S.M.&Z.]
Zeolla, Anthony V. ....'72 '97 C.262 B.A. L.1048 J.D. [[A] Gaffney K.]
Zultowsky, Heidi '58 '87 C&L.184 B.S., J.D.
Mng. Atty., SAFECO Prop. & Cas. Ins. Co.

NEW CANAAN, 17,931, *Fairfield Co.*

Ackerly, Dana C., (AV) ....'20 '48 C.951 B.A. L.976 LL.B. [[G] Hawthorne,A.&D.]
*PRACTICE AREAS: Estate and Trust Administration; Taxation.

Albert, Ward & Johnson, P.C.
(See Greenwich)

Amarilios, John A. ....'58 '87 C.401 B.S. L.1029 J.D. P.O. Box 28
Ambler, Beth S. ....'58 '84 C.105 B.S. L.262 J.D. 585 Weed St.
Baker, George W., (BV) ....'48 '73 C&L.178 B.A., J.D. [Hawthorne,A.&D.]
*PRACTICE AREAS: General Litigation; Employment Law.
Bakes, George D. .... '60 '87 C.1102 B.S. L.1029 J.D. 256 Lukes Wood Rd.
Barocas, Morris L. ....'68 '96 C.273 B.B.A. L.1252 J.D. [[A] Franco&Assoc.]
*PRACTICE AREAS: Residential Real Estate; Commercial Real Estate; Banking Law; Corporate Law; Trusts and Estates.

Bazata, Christine M. .... '67 '92 C.1030 B.A. L.1048 J.D. [Ⓐ T.H.Lampert]
Behan, Thomas R .... '27 '53 136 South Ave‡
Bell, Robert C., Jr. '12 '36 C.494 A.B. L.309 LL.B.
(adm. in MN; not adm. in CT) 528 Main St.‡
Bennett, James H., (BV) .... '37 '63 C.674 A.B. L.813 LL.B. 137 Old Kings Hwy
Bradley, Andrew G. '56 '82 C.184 B.A. L.188 J.D.
V.P./Envir. Affs. & Asst. Gen. Coun., Unimin Corporation
Buckley, Patrick J. '64 '97 C.886 B.S.E.E. L.724 J.D.
(adm. in NY; not adm. in CT) [Buckley,M.&T.]
Buckley, Maschoff & Talwalker, LLC .... 111 Elm St.
Burke, Richard E., (BV) .... '46 '74 C.436 B.A. L.861 J.D. Prob. J.
Burnett, Jane '29 '55 C.813 A.B. L.976 LL.B.
(adm. in CA; not adm. in CT) 112 S. Balo Hill Rd.‡
Campbell Priveterre, Joyce D. .... '64 '98 C.569 B.A. L.93 J.D. [Gogick,B.&O.]
*PRACTICE AREAS: Professional Liability; Construction Law; Environmental Law; Surety; Litigation.
Christopher, William S. .... '42 '69 C.112 B.A. L.426 J.D. 327 West Rd.
Clark, Robert D. .... '38 '66 C.569 B.S. L.564 LL.B. [Finch,M.V.&C.]
Cleary, John J. .... '30 '60 C&L.884 B.S., J.D. Parade Road Hill
Collins, Audrey W. '57 '83 C.705 B.A. L.276 J.D.
(adm. in DC; not adm. in CT) 68 Fitch Ln.
Coughlin, Francis R., (CV) '27 '89
C.976 M.D. L.1029 J.D. V. Chmn., State Comm. Med-Legal Invest.

Curtis, Brinckerhoff & Barrett, P.C.
(See Stamford)

Dale, Charline V. .... '25 '49 C&L.150 B.A., LL.B. [O'Rourke&Assoc.]
*PRACTICE AREAS: Taxation; Trusts and Estates; Probate.
Daniels, Martin P., (BV) '63 '90
C.787 B.A. L.823 J.D. [Ⓐ Davidson,D.&C.] (⊙New York, NY)
*PRACTICE AREAS: Estate Planning; Wills and Trusts; Probate; Real Estate and Zoning.

Davidson, Dawson & Clark LLP, (AV)
36 Grove Street, 06840 ⊙
Telephone: 203-966-8759 Telecopier: 203-966-7894
Members of Firm: Berkeley D. Johnson, Jr. (Resident Partner); Alan P. Donaldson (Resident Partner). Of Counsel: William M. Throop, Jr. Associates: Martin P. Daniels (Resident); Thomas M. Sheehan (Resident).
General Civil Practice. Trust and Estate Planning and Administration, Probate, Taxation, Corporate, Real Estate and Non-Profit Organizations.
New York, New York Office: 330 Madison Avenue. Telephone: 212-557-7700. Telecopier: 212-286-8513.
See Professional Biographies, NEW CANAAN, CONNECTICUT

De Cew, Sperry A., (BV) '46 '75 C.188 B.A. L.184 J.D.
22 East Avenue, P.O. Box 1056, 06840
Telephone: 203-966-6019 Facsimile: 203-972-3780
Email: dqlaw@snet.net
***PRACTICE AREAS: Civil Litigation; Personal Injury; Real Estate; Family Law.**
General Civil and Criminal Practice. Trials and Appeals in State and Federal Courts. Domestic Relations, Personal Injury, Commercial Litigation, Business, Real Estate and Probate Law.
References: New Canaan Bank & Trust Co.; Connecticut Attorney's Title Insurance Co.; Lawyers Title Insurance Co.
See Professional Biographies, NEW CANAAN, CONNECTICUT

Diamond, James D., (BV) .... '59 '88 C.1044 B.A. L.1009 J.D. [Reese,H.D.&S.] ⊙
Donaldson, Alan P., (AV) .... '47 '73 C.674 A.B. L.597 J.D. [Davidson,D.&C.]
*PRACTICE AREAS: Estate Planning; Wills and Trusts; Probate; Federal Income, Estate and Gift Taxation.
Dudzik, Chester John, Jr. '56 '82 C.93 B.A. L.884 J.D.
(adm. in MA; not adm. in CT) P.O. Box 274
Duncan, John Bruce, (AV) .... '23 '50 C.31 L.309 J.D. 106 Elm Pl. (⊙Greenwich)
Dweck, Jack S., (AVⓉ) .... '38 '61 C.563 B.B.A. L.569 J.D. [Dweck] ⊙
Dweck Law Firm LLP, The, (AVⓉ)
Gravel Island Road (⊙New York, White Plains, NY)
Eldridge, Dolores D. '51 '83 C.1133 B.S. L.724 J.D.
(adm. in NY; not adm. in CT) 447 Cheese Spring Rd.
Evans, James H. .... '27 '50 C.602 B.S.Chem. L.734 LL.B. 81 Evergreen Rd.‡
Ferro, Gaetano, (AV) .... '52 '78 C.103 B.A. L.184 J.D. [Marvin&F.]
Finch, E. C. Kip, (BV) .... '11 '40 C.178 A.B. L.309 J.D. [Finch,M.V.&C.]
Finch, Makepeace, Van Dyke & Clark, (BV) .... 76 Elm St.

Finn Dixon & Herling LLP
(See Stamford)

Ford, Jill H., (BV) .... '50 '85 C.477 B.B.A. L.1029 J.D. 22 E. St.
Foster, Michael J. '53 '79 C&L.188 B.S., J.D.
(adm. in NY; not adm. in CT) RFE Invests. Partners
Fowler, Patricia L.R. .... '59 '90 C.103 B.A. L.306 J.D. 40 Dans Hwy.
Franciscovich, George '54 '80 C.823 B.S. L.982 J.D.
(adm. in NY; not adm. in CT) Century Communication Corp.
Franco, Michael J., (BV) .... '59 '85 C.1057 B.A. L.1194 J.D. [Franco&Assoc.]
*PRACTICE AREAS: Real Estate; Real Estate Development; Zoning, Planning and Land Use; Corporate Law; Commercial Law.

Franco & Associates, (BV)
125 Elm Street, 06840
Telephone: 203-972-7339 Fax: 203-972-7321
Email: mfranco@francolaw.com URL: http://www.lawyers.com/francolaw
Member of Firm: Michael J. Franco. Associate: Morris L. Barocas.
Real Estate, Real Estate Development, Zoning, Planning and Land Use, Corporate Law, Commercial Law, Partnership Law, Securities Law, Trusts and Estates.
See Professional Biographies, NEW CANAAN, CONNECTICUT

Gaw, Mary Ellen '47 '84 C.856 B.A. L.262 J.D.
(adm. in NY; not adm. in CT) 13 Brookwood Lane‡
Gaynor, Paul B. '39 '73 C.871 B.S. L.262 J.D.
(adm. in NY; not adm. in CT) 208 Silvermine Road

Gogick, Byrne & O'Neill, LLP
280 Elm Street, 06840-5313 ⊙
Telephone: 203-327-7561 Fax: 203-966-1431
Joyce D. Campbell Priveterre.
Professional Liability, Construction, Environmental, Surety and General Litigation, Mediation, Arbitration and Employment Discrimination.
New York, New York Office: 26 Broadway. Telephone: 212-422-9424. Facsimile: 212-422-9429.
West Orange, New Jersey Office: 80 Main Street. Telephone: 973-778-7074. Facsimile: 973-731-9319.
See Professional Biographies, NEW CANAAN, CONNECTICUT

Goldstein, Henry L., (BV) '41 '66 C.188 A.B. L.659 J.D.
46 Main Street, 06840-4523
Telephone: 203-356-9511 Fax: 203-357-1445
URL: http://www.lawyers.com/henrygoldstein
Estate Planning, Probate, Real Estate and Corporate Law.
Reference: First Union Bank.
See Professional Biographies, NEW CANAAN, CONNECTICUT

Groher, Julius, (BV) .... '15 '42 C.184 B.A. L.569 LL.B. [Groher&S.]
Groher & Sullivan, (BV) .... 43 Pine St.
Gruss, Marvin I., (AV) .... '24 '62 C.156 A.B. L.976 LL.B. [ⓒ Hawthorne,A.&D.]
*PRACTICE AREAS: Trust Administration; Estate Administration; Real Estate; Taxation; Closely Held Corporations.

Hawthorne, Ackerly & Dorrance, LLC, (BV)
25 South Avenue, P.O. Box 937, 06840
Telephone: 203-966-9583 Fax: 203-966-1296
Jeremiah S. Miller; Michelle R. Hubbard; Lawrence S. Mannix; George W. Baker;—Michael Nedder. Of Counsel: Dana C. Ackerly; Marvin I. Gruss; Louis S. Pryor.
General Practice. Probate, Estate Planning, Business Planning, Real Estate, Taxation, Family, Litigation, Employment and Elder Law.
References: First Union Bank; Fleet Bank; U.S. Trust Co. of Connecticut.
See Professional Biographies, NEW CANAAN, CONNECTICUT

Healey, Thomas C., (BV) .... '54 '88 C.1102 B.S. L.1029 J.D. [Reese,H.D.&S.] ⊙
Hicks, Ira E., (BV) .... '10 '38 C&L.976 B.A., J.D. 191 Main St.
Hirsch, Lawrence, (BV) .... '37 '63 C.1019 B.A. L.477 J.D. [Reese,H.D.&S.] ⊙
Howard, Cynthia Theresa .... '52 '77 C.183 B.A. L.128 J.D. 131 W. Cross Rd.‡
Hubbard, Michelle R., (BV) .... '47 '85 C.706 B.A. L.564 J.D. [Hawthorne,A.&D.]
*PRACTICE AREAS: Estate Planning; Probate; Trust Administration; Real Estate.

Jacobs Partners LLC
(See Norwalk)

Jaffe, Alan H. .... '47 '73 C&L.184 B.S., J.D. [Jaffe&J.]
Jaffe, Sari B., (BV) .... '48 '84 C.184 B.A. L.1040 J.D. [Jaffe&J.]
Jaffe & Jaffe, (BV) .... 140 Elm St.
Jerge, Edward C. '32 '64 C.102 B.S. L.724 LL.B.
(adm. in NY; not adm. in CT) 310 Talmadge Hill Rd.‡
Jex, Kay Parker, (AV) .... '28 '74 C.611 B.A. L.724 J.D. 106 Main Street
Johnson, Berkeley D., Jr., (AV) ...... '31 '60 C.309 A.B. L.184 LL.B. [Davidson,D.&C.]
*PRACTICE AREAS: Estate Planning; Wills and Trusts; Probate; Zoning Law.
Kabot, Byron E. '18 '43 C&L.145 B.A., J.D.
(adm. in NY; not adm. in CT) 109 Evergreen Rd.‡
Kalapos, George J., Jr. '51 '76 C.1029 B.A. L.184 J.D.
Assistant General Counsel, Unimin Corporation
Kelley, John D. '10 '37 L.998 LL.B.
(adm. in TX; not adm. in CT) 92C-East Ave.‡
Kimes, Russell A., Jr., (CV) .... '42 '67 C.853 A.B. L.945 J.D. 22 East Ave.
Knight, Craig F. '55 '84 C.125 B.A. L.051 J.D.
(adm. in NY; not adm. in CT) 119 Proprietors Crossing

Koskoff, Koskoff & Bieder, P.C.
(See Bridgeport)

Lake, Michael '51 '75 C&L.659 B.S., J.D.
(adm. in PA; not adm. in CT) 44 Hickok Rd.‡
Lampert, Todd H., Law Offices of, (CV) ... '63 '90 C.174 B.S. L.1029 J.D. 46 Main Street
LaRocco, Joseph B., (BV) '58 '83 C.1040 B.B.A. L.809 J.D.
49 Locust Avenue, Suite 107
Layton, Robert P. .... '25 '53 C.976 B.A. L.309 LL.B. [Wise&L.]
Lee, Marlene W., (CV) .... '35 '83 C.309 A.B. L.1029 J.D. 207 Weed St.
Love, John P. .... '43 '74 C.1041 B.A. L.262 J.D. 44 Hickok Rd.
Macauda, Marlene E., (BV) .... '55 '81 C.676 B.A. L.1029 J.D. [ⓒ Mellick&S.]
*PRACTICE AREAS: Real Estate; Zoning.
MacCracken, Constable '13 '39 C.309 B.S. L.178 LL.B.
(adm. in NY; not adm. in CT) 630 Oenoke Ridge St.‡
Mannix, Lawrence S. .... '62 '87 C.321 B.A. L.128 J.D. [Hawthorne,A.&D.]
*PRACTICE AREAS: Taxation; Estate Planning and Administration; Business Planning and Administration.
Marvin, Morton E., (AV) .... '36 '61 C.184 B.A. L.94 J.D. [Marvin&F.]
Marvin and Ferro, (AV) .... 34 Elm St.
Maschoff, Kurt M. '63 '93 C.556 B.S.E.E. L.629 J.D.
(adm. in WA; not adm. in CT) [Buckley,M.&T.]
McCormick, Jeffrey M. .... '72 '98 C.423 B.A. L.1338 J.D. [O'Rourke&Assoc.]
*PRACTICE AREAS: Commercial Litigation; Corporation Law; Sports Law; Entertainment Law.
McDaniel, Morey W. .... '39 '66 C.918 B.A. L.813 LL.B. 183 Brushy Ridge Rd.
McLanahan, Bruce '35 '61 C.976 B.A. L.309 LL.B.
(adm. in NY; not adm. in CT) 81 Woodway Ridge Ln.‡
Mead, Penfield C., (AV) .... '20 '48 C&L.976 B.A., LL.B. 284 Park St.‡
Mellick, Edward G., (AV) .... '45 '70 C.197 B.A. L.30 J.D. [Mellick&S.]

Mellick & Sexton, P.C., (AV)
70 Pine Street, 06840
Telephone: 203-972-0200 Fax: 203-972-0708
Email: emellick@aol.com
Edward G. Mellick. Of Counsel: Marlene E. Macauda.
Real Estate and Zoning Law.
See Professional Biographies, NEW CANAAN, CONNECTICUT

Melzer, Franklin, (BV) .... '34 '61 C.184 B.A. L.564 J.D. 49 Locust Ave. (⊙Stamford)
Melzer, Harvey, (BV) .... '43 '75 C.1102 B.S. L.64 J.D. 49 Locust Ave.
Miller, Jeremiah S., (BV) .... '45 '73 C.385 B.A. L.902 J.D. [Hawthorne,A.&D.]
*PRACTICE AREAS: Estate Settlements; Trust Administration; Conservatorships; Elder Law; Real Estate.
Morgan, Patrick J. .... '35 '61 C&L.262 A.B., LL.D. 760 Valley Rd.
Moylan, Robert J. '30 '59 C.321 A.B. L.569 J.D.
(adm. in NY; not adm. in CT) 15 Lockwood Ave.
Murray, Paul B. '23 '49 C.276 B.S.S. L.262 LL.B.
(adm. in NY; not adm. in CT) 87 Lone Tree Farm Rd.‡
Nedder, Michael .... '73 '99 C.1030 B.S. L.262 J.D. [Ⓐ Hawthorne,A.&D.]
*PRACTICE AREAS: Estate Planning; Business Planning; Real Estate; Taxation.
O'Rourke, Brendan J., (BV) .... '58 '85 C&L.893 B.A., J.D. [O'Rourke&Assoc.]
*PRACTICE AREAS: Commercial Litigation; Commercial Arbitration; Corporate Law; Real Estate.

O'Rourke & Associates, LLC, (BV)
27 Pine Street, 06840
Telephone: 203-966-6664 Fax: 203-966-5710
Email: obrendan@aol.com
Brendan J. O'Rourke; Jeffrey M. McCormick; Charline V. Dale.
Commercial and Securities Litigation, Corporate and Real Estate Law, Entertainment Law.
See Professional Biographies, NEW CANAAN, CONNECTICUT

Palizza, Donna G. '54 '84 C.339 B.A. L.424 J.D.
(adm. in IL; not adm. in CT) 160 Ferris Hill Rd.
Perlmutter, Sharon R. .... '59 '88 C.994 B.A. L.1029 J.D. 39 River Wind Rd.
Phillips, Dudley C. .... '22 '49 C&L.623 B.S., LL.B. 871 Weed St.

Piazza & Pickel
(See Stamford)

Pierson, William C. '36 '60 C&L.352 B.A., J.D.
(adm. in IA; not adm. in CT) 53 Journeys End Rd.‡
Piscitello, John S. '30 '57 C.262 B.S. L.564 LL.B.
(adm. in NY; not adm. in CT; Pat.) Sr. Pat. Coun., Union Carbide Corp.

Pryor, Louis S., (BV) . . . . '34 '60 C&L.976 B.A., LL.B. [🄲 Hawthorne,A.&D.]
*PRACTICE AREAS: Estate Planning; Trust Administration.
Reese, John R., (BV) . . . . '40 '65 C.197 B.A. L.976 LL.B. [Reese,H.D.&S.] ⊙
Reese, Hirsch, Diamond & Shoults, (BV) . . . . .51 Locust Ave. (⊙Ridgefield)

Rucci, Burnham, Carta & Edelberg, LLP, (AV)
71 Elm Street, P.O. Box 1680, 06840 ⊙
Telephone: 203-966-6500
URL: http://www.rbce.com
Associates: David J. Rucci. Of Counsel: James F. Sullivan.
Commercial and Residential Real Estate, Trusts and Estates, Estate Planning, Civil Trial Practice including Fiduciary Disputes, Employment, Commercial, Construction and Personal Injury Litigation, Corporate, Commercial, Information Technology, Banking, Workouts and Bankruptcy, Business Law, Environmental Law, Pre-Nuptial Agreements, State, Local and Federal Taxation, Zoning, Pensions, ERISA Matters and Charitable Organizations.
Darien, Connecticut Office: 800 Post Road, P.O. Box 1107. Telephone: 203-655-7695.
Stamford, Connecticut Office: 6 Landmark Square, Suite 470. Telephone: 203-359-5637.
See Professional Biographies, NEW CANAAN, CONNECTICUT

Runnette, Charles W. '35 '68 C.976 B.S. L.178 LL.B.
(adm. in CA; not adm. in CT) 49 St. John Pl.

Sandak Friedman Hennessey & Greco, LLP
(See Stamford)

Scannell, David G. '39 '65 C.276 A.B. L.178 J.D.
(adm. in NY; not adm. in CT) 574 Cascade Rd.

Schoonmaker, George & Colin, P.C.
(See Greenwich)

Seelert, John E. . . . .'68 '94 C.197 B.A. L.902 J.D. 444 Oenoke Ride Rd.
Shapiro, Joseph C. '51 '78 C.910 A.B. L.569 J.D.
Sr. V.P./Legal & Regulatory Affs. & Secy., Unimin Corporation
Sheehan, Thomas M. . . . .'71 '97 C.676 B.A. L.1360 J.D. [🄰 Davidson,D.&C.]
*PRACTICE AREAS: Trusts and Estates; Estate Planning; Estate Administration; Tax Law.
Shoults, Tamsin A.S. . . . .'66 '94 C.67 B.A. L.184 J.D. [Reese,H.D.&S.] ⊙
Siegel, Charles A. . . . . '52 '92 C.178 L.999 J.D. 193 Parish Rd., S.

Silver, Golub & Teitell LLP
(See Stamford)

Silverberg, Jeroll R., (AV) . . . .'24 '46 C.105 A.B. L.228 LL.B. 140 Elm St.‡
Stebbins, Edward C. '30 '54 C.951 B.A. L.309 LL.B.
(adm. in NY; not adm. in CT) 124 Hickok Rd.
Stevens, Allen L. '43 '69 C.477 B.S.I.E. L.309 J.D.
(adm. in MI; not adm. in CT) Pres., Stevens Industries, Inc.

Stewart, Richard C., Law Offices of, (BV) '43 '72 C.72 B.A. L.184 J.D.
237 Elm Street, 06840
Telephone: 203-966-5949 Facsimile: 203-972-0784
Email: rcstewart@aol.com
General Civil and Criminal Practice. Trials and Appeals in all State and Federal Courts. Domestic Relations, Personal Injury, Commercial Litigation, Business, Real Estate and Probate Law.
See Professional Biographies, NEW CANAAN, CONNECTICUT

Strumpf, Linda . . . .'49 '76 C.823 B.A. L.262 J.D. 244 Colonial Rd.
Sullivan, Gerald J., (BV) . . . . '37 '61 C&L.184 B.A., J.D. [Groher&S.]
Sullivan, James F., (BV) . . . .'50 '76 C.93 A.B. L.734 J.D. [🄲 Rucci,B.C.&E.]
Talwalkar, Nandu A. '70 '95 C.339 B.S.E.E. L.800 J.D.
(adm. in CA; not adm. in CT; Pat.) [Buckley,M.&T.]
Thacher, Thomas, (AVⓉ) '16 '42 C&L.976 B.A., LL.B.
(adm. in NY; not adm. in CT) 125 West Rd.‡
Throckmorton, Timothy H., (CV) . . . .'59 '89 C.208 B.S.B.A. L.564 J.D. 36 Grove St.
Throop, William M., Jr., (AV) '24 '51 C.674 A.B. L.976 LL.B.
[🄲 Davidson,D.&C.] ⊙
*PRACTICE AREAS: Estate Planning; Wills and Trusts; Probate; Not-for-Profit Organizations.
Tobiason, Pamela Messmore '46 '88 C&L.262 B.A., J.D.
(adm. in NY; not adm. in CT) General Counsel, Messmore Group, LLC
Trebing, Al P., (AV) . . . .'51 '80 C.693 B.S. L.1040 J.D. [A.P.Trebing&Assoc.] ⊙

Trebing, Al P., & Associates, P.C., (AV)
106 Main Street, 06840 ⊙
Telephone: 203-972-5856 Fax: 203-972-6307
Email: alptrebing@aol.com URL: http://www.lawyers.com/alptreb
Al P. Trebing.
Corporations, Partnerships and Limited Liability Companies, Small Businesses, Taxation, Contracts and Commercial Transactions, Estate and Trust Planning, Probate.
Ridgefield, Connecticut Office: 54 Danbury Road, Suite 266. Telephone: 203-798-8851. Fax: 203-730-0061.
See Professional Biographies, NEW CANAAN, CONNECTICUT

Tucker, Diane Reese, (BVⓉ) '50 '74 C.645 B.A. L.838 J.D.
(adm. in PA; not adm. in CT) 135 Jonathan Rd.‡
van Dyke, Henry, (CV) . . . .'27 '53 C.976 B.A. L.178 LL.B. [Finch,M.V.&C.]
Von Oehsen, Gina M., (BV) . . . .'69 '94 C.93 B.A. L.262 J.D. 280 Elm Street

Wake, See, Dimes & Bryniczka
(See Westport)

Walker, Richard H. . . . .'22 '57 C.871 B.S. L.831 LL.B. 1137 Smith Ridge Rd.
Wallace, Kenneth D., (AV) . . . . '18 '47 C.906 A.B. L.178 LL.B. 947 Smith Ridge Rd.‡
Williams, Gregory J. '61 '92 C.112 B.A. L.1029 J.D. [🄰 T.H.Lampert]
Williams, Robert E. . . . .'39 '82 C.178 B.A. L.1029 J.D. 137 Bowery Rd.
Wise, Stephen A., (AV) . . . .'25 '54 C.309 A.B. L.178 LL.B. [Wise&L.]
Wise & Layton, (AV) . . . . 52 Turtle Back Rd.
Wolff, Sanford I. '15 '40 C.388 L.365 J.D.
(adm. in IL; not adm. in CT) 312 Elm St.

NEW FAIRFIELD, 11,260, *Fairfield Co.*

Coleman, David W. '53 '80 C.668 B.A. L.608 J.D.
(adm. in OH; not adm. in CT) 8 Cold Spring Rd.
Dangelo, Michael D. '48 '84 C.999 B.B.A. L.564 J.D.
(adm. in NY; not adm. in CT) [Dangelo&Assoc.]
Dangelo & Associates . . . . 60 Ball Pond Road East
Day, Margaret Ranft . . . . '56 '81 C.573 B.S. L.724 J.D. 24 Pheasant Dr.
Flanagan, Paula, (CV) . . . .'55 '80 C.277 B.S. L.1040 J.D. 26 Sail Harbour Dr.
Keating, John F., Jr.(A Professional Corporation) '54 '82
C.188 A.B. L.861 J.D. 2 Whipstick Rd. (⊙New York, NY)
Lubus, Raymond C., (CV) . . . .'57 '83 C.1103 B.A. L.1048 J.D. 22 Brush Hill Rd.
Lucking, John T., (BV) . . . .'53 '79 C&L.93 A.B., J.D. 26 Sail Harbour Drive
Morrison, Marguerite E.H. . . . . '56 '83 C.367 B.A. L.446 J.D. 20 Woods Rd.
Pancrazio, Mark D. . . . . '64 '92 C.829 B.A. L.184 J.D. 25 Old Rte. 37
Redecha, Tina '48 '84 C.331 B.A. L.564 J.D.
(adm. in NY; not adm. in CT) 105 Shortwoods Rd.
Smith, Richard A., (BV) . . . .'58 '83 C.1156 B.A. L.1029 J.D. 25 Old Rte. 37
Vannucci, Peter S., (CV) . . . .'57 '82 C.1036 B.A. L.306 J.D. 22 Inglenook Dr.

Warton, John F., Jr. . . . . '50 '81 C&L.608 B.A., J.D. [J.F.Warton]
Warton, John F., P.C. . . . . 8 Indian Hill Lane

NEW HARTFORD, 4,884, *Litchfield Co.*

Cianciolo, Lawrence J. . . . .'43 '76 C.184 B.A. L.306 J.D. 47 Hemlock Dr.
Falco, Eugene P. . . . .'45 '92 C.860 A.B. L.184 J.D. P.O. Box 625
Gerner, William L. . . . .'42 '72 C.1029 B.S. L.724 J.D. P.O. Box 209
Hart, Thomas M. . . . . '48 '78 C.198 A.B. L.184 J.D. Bruning Rd.
Hatch, Dorothy . . . . '55 '81 C.97 B.A. L.161 J.D. 571 Main Street
Rogers, Norman E., Jr., (BV) . . . .'51 '79 C.308 B.A. L.1048 J.D. [Rogers]
*PRACTICE AREAS: Commercial Law; Real Estate; Estate Planning.

Rogers Law Firm LLC, (BV)
7 Church Street North, P.O. Box 1020, 06057
Telephone: 860-379-9600 Facsimile: 860-379-8560 URL: http://www.lawyers.com/kwlaw
Email: attorneyrogers@aol.com URL: http://www.rogerslawfirm.com
Norman E. Rogers, Jr.
Commercial, Real Estate, Estate Planning, Corporate, Business Law.
See Professional Biographies, NEW HARTFORD, CONNECTICUT

NEW HAVEN, * 130,474, *New Haven Co.*

Aaronson, Lester H. . . . .'16 '41 C.918 B.A. L.309 LL.B. Supr. Ct. J.
Acampora, John A., (BV) . . . . '44 '69 C.1252 B.S. L.818 J.D. [Cohen&A.] ⊙
Aceto, Joseph A. . . . . '62 '87 C.976 B.A. L.93 J.D. 205 Church St.
Ackerman, Bruce A. '43 '70 C.309 B.A. L.976 LL.B.
(adm. in PA; not adm. in CT) Prof. of Law, Yale Law School
Acquarulo, Adam F. . . . .'65 '92 C.184 B.S. L.446 J.D. [🄰 Milano&W.]
*PRACTICE AREAS: Commercial Litigation; Insurance Defense.
Adelman, Daniel W., (BV) . . . .'55 '84 C.184 B.A. L.1029 J.D. [Adelman&G.]
Adelman & Gallant, (BV) . . . . 129 Church St.
Agsten, Melinda A., (AV) . . . . '50 '75 C.228 A.B. L.880 J.D. [Wiggin&D.]
*PRACTICE AREAS: Health Care Law; Hospital Law; Tax Exempt Organizations Law; Nonprofit Corporations; Charitable Organizations Law.
Ahern, Leo E., (BV) . . . .'50 '83 C.1252 B.A. L.1029 J.D. 12 Trumbull St.
Ainsworth, Keith R., (BV) . . . .'65 '90 C.830 B.S. L.472 J.D. [🄰 Evans,F.&B.]
*PRACTICE AREAS: Environmental Law; Civil Litigation; Commercial Litigation.
Airone, Thomas J. . . . . '66 '96 C.67 B.A. L.1252 J.D. [Gallagher&C.]
*PRACTICE AREAS: Trials; Appeals.
Ajello, Michael J. . . . .'67 '96 C.588 B.S. L.1187 J.D. [🄰 Bershtein,L.B.&M.]
*PRACTICE AREAS: Commercial Litigation; Civil Litigation; Real Estate; Landlord and Tenant; Foreclosures.
Albinger, William John . . . .'67 '97 C.1156 B.S. L.1252 J.D. [🄰 Wiggin&D.]
Alexander, Lori B. . . . .'56 '90 C.197 B.A. L.184 J.D. [Tyler C.&A.]
*PRACTICE AREAS: Employment Law; Personal Injury Defense; Immigration Law.
Alexy, Christopher . . . .'62 '87 C&L.831 B.A., J.D. Asst. States Atty.
Allen, Noble F., (BV) . . . .'59 '91 C.598 B.A. L.30 J.D. [Tyler C.&A.]
*PRACTICE AREAS: Litigation; Commercial Landlord and Tenant Law; Landlord and Tenant Law; Immigration Law.
Allen, Robert W., (AV) . . . .'48 '73 C.918 B.A. L.184 J.D. [Tyler C.&A.]
*PRACTICE AREAS: Litigation; Environmental Law; Consumer Credit; Insurance.
Allentuch, Simon I. . . . . '68 '94 C.145 B.A. L.569 J.D. [🄰 Neubert,P.&M.]
*PRACTICE AREAS: Civil Litigation; Federal Civil Litigation; Employment Litigation; Employment Law; Physicians Licensing.
Alter, Burton Z. . . . .'40 '67 C.674 A.B. L.178 J.D. [Carmody&T.]
*PRACTICE AREAS: Corporate Law; Mergers and Acquisitions; International Mergers and Acquisitions.
Amarante, Erika L. . . . . '73 '98 C.188 B.A. L.569 J.D. [🄰 Wiggin&D.]
Ambrose, Neil J. . . . .'63 '89 C.860 B.A. L.184 J.D. [Letizia,A.C.]
Ambroziak, Jeffrey Russell . . . . '66 '98 C.674 B.S.E. L.945 J.D. [🄰 Wiggin&D.]
Anderson, Donald W., (P.C.) . . . .'44 '73 C.884 B.A. L.178 J.D. [Brenner,S.&W.]
*PRACTICE AREAS: Trusts and Estates.
Anderson, Paula M. '61 '86 C.976 B.A. L.228 J.D.
Sr. Coun. & Asst. Secy., Southern New England Telecom. Corp.
Andres, Charles R., (BV) . . . .'55 '84 C.478 B.A. L.184 J.D. [🄲 Tyler C.&A.]
*PRACTICE AREAS: Land Use; Litigation.
Annunziata, Albert R., (BV) . . . . '30 '56 C.1030 B.S.B.A. L.93 J.D. 109 Church St.
Anthopolos, Penny Harkleroad '70 '98
C.150 B.Mus. L.823 J.D. Connecticut Fund for the Environment
Appleby, Bethany L. . . . . '67 '97 C.976 B.A. L.184 J.D. [🄰 Wiggin&D.]
Apter, Ronald S. . . . . '61 '89 C.860 B.A. L.976 J.D. Asst. U.S. Atty.
Arterton, Janet Bond, (AV) . . . . '44 '77 C.518 B.A. L.588 J.D. U.S. Dist. J.
Asard, Karen E. . . . . '62 '95 C.1102 B.S. L.1364 J.D. Soc. Sec. Admn.
Atkinson, Leonard K., Jr. . . . . '66 '91 C.184 B.A. L.1029 J.D. [🄰 Silverstein&O.]
*PRACTICE AREAS: Tax; Estate Planning; Pensions.
Auerbach, Hillel J., (AV) . . . . '36 '62 C.453 B.S. L.976 LL.B. [H.J.Auerbach]
Auerbach, Hillel J., P.C., (AV) . . . . 555 Long Whart Dr., 12th Fl.
Austin, Elizabeth J., (BV) '57 '83 C&L.546 B.A., J.D.
[Pullman&C.] (⊙Bridgeport, Hartford, Stamford)
*PRACTICE AREAS: Insolvency Law; Bankruptcy Litigation; Commercial Litigation.
Avigdor, David, (BV) . . . .'53 '83 C.999 B.A. L.1029 J.D. 395 Orange St.
Ayres, Ian '59 '87 C&L.976 B.A., J.D.
(adm. in IL; not adm. in CT) Prof. of Law, Yale Univ.
Babbin, Jeffrey R. . . . .'60 '84 C.659 B.S.Econ. L.813 J.D. [Wiggin&D.]
*PRACTICE AREAS: Appellate Practice; Civil Appeals; Administrative; U.S. Supreme Court Litigation; Personal Injury.
Bachman, Robert H. '33 '58 C.184 B.A. L.569 LL.B.
(adm. in NY; not adm. in CT; See Pat. Sect.) [Bachman&L.]
*PRACTICE AREAS: Patents; Trademarks; Copyrights; Unfair Competition; Licensing Law.
Bachman, Staci H. . . . .'66 '91 C.914 B.A. L.273 J.D. [Bershtein,L.B.&M.]
*PRACTICE AREAS: Real Estate; Leasing; Finance; Business Law.

Bachman & LaPointe, P.C., (AV) 🄱🄱
900 Chapel Street, Suite 1201, 06510
Telephone: 203-777-6628 Fax: 203-865-0297
Email: iplaw@bachlap.com
Robert H. Bachman (Not admitted in CT); Gregory P. LaPointe; Barry L. Kelmachter; George A. Coury.
Intellectual Property Law including U.S. and International practice in Patent, Trademark, Copyright, International Trade, Unfair Competition, Antitrust and Licensing Law. Trials and Appeals in all Federal Courts and Administrative Agencies.
See Professional Biographies, NEW HAVEN, CONNECTICUT

Bader, Paul L. . . . .'— '94 C.228 B.A. L.469 J.D. [🄰 Tyler C.&A.]
*PRACTICE AREAS: Labor and Employment.
Bagnell, Jeffrey S. . . . .'66 '92 C.321 B.A. L.93 J.D. [🄰 Garrison L.C.&R.]
*PRACTICE AREAS: Civil Litigation; Employment Law.
Bailey Jongbloed, Barbara, (BV) '59 '84 C.399 B.A. L.569 J.D.
Dep. Chf., Criminal Div.
Baker, Dean W., (BV) . . . .'56 '83 C&L.228 B.A., J.D. [🄲 Bohonnon]
*PRACTICE AREAS: Bankruptcy; Commercial Transactions; Commercial Litigation; Contract Law.
Ball, Philip W., (BV) . . . .'49 '80 C.867 B.A. L.184 J.D. 51 Elm St.
Ballard, Diana C. . . . .'45 '86 C.1156 M.B.A. L.1040 J.D. [🄲 Susman,D.&S.]
*PRACTICE AREAS: Healthcare Law; Mediation.

Ballou, Jessica A. .... '75 '00 C.695 B.A. L.1252 J.D. [Ⓐ Wiggin&D.]
Baran, Mary Elizabeth, (CV) ....'57 '84 C.241 B.A. L.705 J.D. Sr. Asst. States Atty.
Barbara, Tara M ....'75 '99 C.690 B.A. L.1252 J.D. 45 Court St.
Barberio, Francis P., (BV) .... '24 '53 C.262 B.S. L.184 LL.B. [Barberio,S.&M.]
Barberio, Staley & Moquet, (AV) ....60 Trumbull St.
Barker, Christine A. ....'59 '87 C.1102 B.S. L.475 J.D. [Siegel,O.S.&Z.]
*PRACTICE AREAS: Business Law; Computer Law; Taxation Law.
Barnett, Jerrold H. ....'29 '54 C.823 A.B. L.184 J.D. Supr. Ct. J.
Barnett, John W., (AV) ....'27 '53 C.604 A.B. L.309 LL.B. [Wiggin&D.]
*PRACTICE AREAS: Estate Planning; Trusts and Estates; Estate Litigation; Property Tax Appeals.
Barnston, Jack D., (AV) .... '21 '43 C&L.846 B.A., LL.B. 2 Lincoln St.

Barr & LaCava
(See Stamford)

Barringer, Greg R., (BV) ....'57 '88 C.508 B.A. L.178 J.D. [Tyler C.&A.]
*PRACTICE AREAS: Estate Planning; Probate; Elder Law; Real Estate.
Bartholomew, Susan H., (BV) .... '44 '78 C.608 B.A. L.117 J.D. [Bartholomew&P.]
*PRACTICE AREAS: Personal Injury Litigation; Medical Malpractice Litigation; Business Litigation; Employment Litigation.

Bartholomew & Price, (BV)
104 Linden Street, 06511
Telephone: 203-777-4505 Fax: 203-777-5330
Email: bartholomew@bartholomewandprice URL: http://www.lawyers.com/bartholomew&price
Susan H. Bartholomew; Charles B. Price, Jr.
Medical Malpractice, Personal Injury, Employment Litigation.
See Professional Biographies, NEW HAVEN, CONNECTICUT

Bartlett, Kenneth G., (BV) .... '54 '81 C.882 B.A. L.1252 J.D. [Bartlett]
*PRACTICE AREAS: Personal Injury Law; Medical Malpractice Law; Workers Compensation; Bankruptcy.

Bartlett Law Offices, P.C., (BV)
742 Chapel Street, 06510
Telephone: 203-772-4844 Fax: 203-772-2773
Email: bartlettlaw@yahoo.com URL: http://www.lawyers.com/bartlettpc
Kenneth G. Bartlett;—Charles A. Eggert, Jr.
Plaintiff Personal Injury, Wrongful Death, Plaintiff Medical Malpractice, Personal Bankruptcy, Probate, Criminal.
Reference: Fleet Bank.
See Professional Biographies, NEW HAVEN, CONNECTICUT

Bashaw, John R. .... '60 '87 C.882 B.S. L.1194 J.D. [Brenner,S.&W.]
*PRACTICE AREAS: Environmental Regulation; Environmental Litigation.
Baskin, William C., Jr., (AV) ....'31 '58 C&L.976 B.A., LL.B. [Wiggin&D.]
*PRACTICE AREAS: Corporation Law; Public Utility Law; Securities Law.
Baum, Kenneth F. .... '— '01 C.1375 B.A. L.976 J.D. [Ⓐ Wiggin&D.]
Bayonne, Michel .... '76 '01 C.1030 B.A. L.306 J.D. [Ⓐ Updike,K.&S.] (⊙Hartford)
*PRACTICE AREAS: Business Law.
Beamon, Tina Clark .... '72 '97 C.184 B.A. L.902 J.D. [Ⓐ Neubert,P.&M.]
*PRACTICE AREAS: Health Law; Medical Malpractice; Civil Litigation; Charitable Organizations Law.
Beardsley, Ellen Jean .... '— '99 C.124 B.A. L.1252 J.D. [Ⓐ Tyler C.&A.]
Beatty, Jonathan A. .... '72 '99 C.93 B.A. L.306 J.D. [Ⓐ Esty&B.]
*PRACTICE AREAS: Insurance Defense; Civil Practice.
Beatty, Nancy A. ....'62 '93 C.276 B.A. L.188 J.D. One Century Twr.
Beauregard, Patricia R. .... '60 '98 C.1030 B.A. L.1252 J.D. [Ⓐ Wiggin&D.]
Becker, Eileen Reynolds .... '67 '92 C.823 A.B. L.1292 J.D. [Ⓐ Wiggin&D.]
Behling, Paul L., (AV) ....'48 '73 C.1033 B.S. L.184 J.D. [Bergman,H.&R.]
*PRACTICE AREAS: Business; Employee Benefits; Taxation.
Beletsky, Barry P., (BV) ....'53 '79 C.165 A.B. L.184 J.D. [Sperandeo&D.]
Belford, Richard, (BV) ....'27 '52 C.705 B.S. L.569 LL.B. 9 Trumbull St.
Bell, Aileen ....'64 '89 C.184 B.A. L.276 J.D. Asst. Corp. Coun.
Bell, Richard G., (AV) ....'32 '60 C.976 B.A. L.309 LL.B. [Ⓒ Tyler C.&A.]
*PRACTICE AREAS: Banking, Corporate, Cable Television.
Bellamy, Penelope L., (BV) .... '47 '84 C.821 B.A. L.184 J.D. [Ⓐ Wiggin&D.]
Beller, Eric I. B., (BV) .... '50 '79 C.309 A.B. L.976 J.D. [Neubert,P.&M.]
*PRACTICE AREAS: Health Law; Managed Care; Physicians Contracts; Physicians Licensing; Environmental Law.
Bellis, Barbara N., (BV) ....'61 '86 C.93 B.A. L.128 J.D. [Mulvey,O.&G.]
*PRACTICE AREAS: Trials; Negligence; Civil Litigation; Commercial Litigation; Criminal Litigation.
Bellis, Stephen R., (BV) ....'59 '84 C.94 B.A. L.128 J.D. [Pellegrino]
Belt, David L., (AV) ....'44 '70 C&L.976 B.A., LL.B. [Jacobs,G.B.&D.]
*PRACTICE AREAS: Business Litigation; Antitrust; Business Torts Litigation; Employment Litigation; Appellate Practice.
Benbow, Jody Pagano .... '70 '96 [Ⓐ Siegel,O.S.&Z.]
*PRACTICE AREAS: Labor Law; Employment Law; Education Law; Special Education Law.

Berchem, Moses & Devlin, A Professional Corporation
(See Milford)

Berdon, Peter A, (BV) .... '66 '91 C.228 B.A. L.184 J.D. [Berdon,Y.&M.]
*PRACTICE AREAS: Business Law; Alcoholic Beverage Law; Government Relations; Litigation; Trusts and Estates.

Berdon, Young & Margolis, P.C., (BV)
132 Temple Street, 06510
Telephone: 203-772-3740 Fax: 203-492-4444
Email: yberdon@snet.net URL: http://www.lawyers.com/berdonyoung&margolis
Pasquale Young; Stuart A. Margolis; Peter A Berdon;—Paul E. Barrett, Jr. (1955-1995); David D. Berdon (1925-1998).
Automobile Accidents, Bankruptcy, Business Law, Child Custody, Child Support, Construction Law, Consumer Law, Contracts, Criminal Law, Debtor and Creditor, Discrimination, Divorce, Driving While Intoxicated, Eminent Domain, Employment Law, Estate Planning, Family Law, General Practice, Landlord and Tenant, Legal Malpractice, Personal Injury, Products Liability, Real Estate, Sexual Harassment, Social Security, Traffic Violations, Trust and Estates, Wills and Probate, Worker's Compensation, Zoning and Land Use.
See Professional Biographies, NEW HAVEN, CONNECTICUT

Bergamo, Mark L., (CV) ....'58 '84 C.1102 B.A. L.1029 J.D. [Ⓐ Marcus]
*PRACTICE AREAS: Bankruptcy; Foreclosure; Real Estate; Secured Transaction; Litigation.
Berglass, Steven ....'53 '78 C&L.976 B.A., J.D. [Seeley&B.]
*PRACTICE AREAS: Insurance Coverage; Commercial Litigation.
Bergman, Stanley N., (AV) ....'33 '59 C.197 A.B. L.477 J.D. [Bergman,H.&R.] ⊙
*PRACTICE AREAS: Business; ERISA; Estate Planning; Taxation (Local, Personal Property, State, Federal or International Law).

Bergman, Horowitz & Reynolds, P.C., (AV)
157 Church Street, 19th Floor, P.O. Box 426, 06502-0426 ⊙
Telephone: 203-789-1320 Fax: 203-785-8127
Email: bhr@taxlawyers.com URL: http://www.taxlawyers.com
Stanley N. Bergman; David L. Reynolds; Melvin Ditman; William C. G. Swift, Jr.; Paul L. Behling; Richard J. Klein; James Russell Brockway; Bruce I. Judelson; David A. Ringold; David L. Dubrow; Paul M. Roy; Jeremy A. Mellitz; Louis R. Piscatelli; Edward A. Renn; Elizabeth A. Whalen. Of Counsel: Kenneth N. Musen;—Patricia A. Campana; Raquel S. Colby (Not admitted in CT); Richard A. Fava (Not admitted in CT); Bryan P. Galat; Jaclyn S. Kim; Mitchell R. Kops; Jay F. Krause; Stephen Liss; Hunter N. Norton; Jeffrey H. Roberts; Jay H. Rubinstein; Jason S. Rudnick; Von E. Sanborn; Deborah K. Snyder; Karen E. Yates.
Practice restricted to Federal, State and Foreign Taxation. Estate Planning, Probate, Corporation, Financing, Employee Benefits, Pension and Profit Sharing Law. Real Estate, Commercial.

(This Listing Continued)

Bergman, Horowitz & Reynolds, P.C. (Continued)
New York, N.Y. Office: 499 Park Avenue, 26th Floor. Telephone: 212-688-4150 Fax: 212-688-4236.
See Professional Biographies, NEW HAVEN, CONNECTICUT

Berke, Robert .... '66 '92 C.1044 B.A. L.1252 J.D. [Ⓐ Williams&P.]
*PRACTICE AREAS: Criminal Law; Civil Rights; Employment Discrimination.
Berke, Robyn H. .... '68 '94 C.1044 B.A. L.1019 J.D. [Moss&C.]
Berkowitz, Morris, (BV) .... '17 '60 C.976 A.B. L.184 J.D. 50 Alden Ave.
Berman, Sheri L. ....'— '98 C&L.1252 B.A., J.D. [Ⓐ Kahn&S.]
*PRACTICE AREAS: Family Law.
Berman, Steven A., (AV) ....'47 '77 C.119 B.S. L.184 J.D. [Berman&S.]
*PRACTICE AREAS: Commercial Loan Documentation; Corporate Transactions; Banking Law; Corporate Finance; Corporate Acquisitions, Divestitures and Restructures.

Berman and Sable, (AV)
195 Church Street, 06510 ⊙
Telephone: 203-495-6200 FAX: 203-495-6220
Email: info@bermansable.com
Steven A. Berman. Associates: James J. Brault.
Commercial Litigation, Commercial and Corporate Finance Transactions, Real Estate, Corporate Law, Acquisitions, Mergers and Divestitures, Problem Loan Workouts, Loan Restructure and Recoveries, Mortgage and Foreclosure, Creditor's Rights, Defense of Lender Liability Claims, Creditor Bankruptcy Rights, Reorganizations, Tax Appeals, Construction Litigation, Probate and Trials and Appeals in all Courts. FDIC/RTC Approved Counsel.
Hartford, Connecticut Office: 100 Pearl Street. Telephone: 203-527-9699. Telecopier: 203-527-9077.
See Professional Biographies, NEW HAVEN, CONNECTICUT

Bernblum, Bennett J., (BV) .... '47 '82 C.976 B.A. L.569 J.D. [Wiggin&D.]
*PRACTICE AREAS: Business Law; Corporate Law; Corporate Health Care Law; Mergers and Acquisitions Law; State Taxation Law.
Bernblum, Milton A., (AV) ....'24 '49 C.976 B.A. L.184 LL.B. [Bernblum&G.] ‡
Bernblum & Greenberg, (AV) ....One Whitney Ave.
Berner, Cecilia R. .... '42 '82 C&L.1029 B.S., J.D. 159 Fairfield St.
Bershtein, Raymond C., (BV) ......'58 '83 C.1365 B.A. L.273 J.D. [Bershtein,L.B.&M.]
*PRACTICE AREAS: Real Estate; Municipal Tax Liens; Finance; Business Law.

Bershtein, Lippman, Bachman & McKeon, P.C., (BV)
59 Elm Street, 06510-2047
Telephone: 203-777-5800 Fax: 203-777-5806
Email: blbm@reallawyers.com URL: http://www.lawyers.com/blbm
Raymond C. Bershtein; Neil A. Lippman; Staci H. Bachman; Christopher M. McKeon;—Michael J. Ajello. Of Counsel: Leslie A. Zackin; Thomas P. McKeon.
General Practice including Real Estate, Federal and State Court Litigation, Public and Private Finance, Banking, Leasing, Business, Municipal Tax Law, Health Care, Creditors and Debtors Rights including Workouts, Collections and Foreclosures, Landlord and Tenant, Estate Planning, Probate and Personal Injury.
Westport, Connecticut Office: 735 Post Road East. Telephone: 203-222-7048. Fax: 203-777-5806.
See Professional Biographies, NEW HAVEN, CONNECTICUT

Berthold, Margaret J., (BV) '39 '77 C.473 B.A. L.306 J.D.
110 Whitney Avenue, 3rd Floor
Bettencourt, Jessica M. '— '96 C.178 B.A. L.276 J.D.
(adm. in VA; not adm. in CT) 157 Church Street
Bingham, Timothy W., (AV) ....'45 '71 C&L.976 B.A., J.D. [Tyler C.&A.]
*PRACTICE AREAS: Banking, Consumer Credit, Computer Law.
Birdwhistell, Nan Mead, (BV) ....'54 '79 C.1365 B.A. L.309 J.D. [Ⓒ Murtha C.]
*PRACTICE AREAS: Municipal Law; Health Care Law.
Birnbaum, Irwin M., (AVⓉ) '35 '62 C.103 B.S. L.569 J.D.
Yale Univ. Sch. of Medicine
Bittker, Boris I. '16 '42 C.188 A.B. L.976 LL.B.
(adm. in NY; not adm. in CT) Prof. of Law, Yale Law Sch.
Bjorkman, Ian E. .... '58 '87 C.569 B.A. L.1009 J.D. [Wiggin&D.]
*PRACTICE AREAS: Litigation.
Black, Charles L., Jr. '15 '46 C.846 B.A. L.976 LL.B.
(adm. in NY; not adm. in CT) Prof., Yale Law Sch.
Blasini, Peter B., (BV) ....'47 '78 C.976 B.A. L.306 J.D. 31 Whitney Ave.
Block, Julie Thalen, (BV) ....'53 '78 C.867 B.A. L.1019 J.D. Amity Station
Bloss, William M., (AV) .... '57 '84 C.896 B.A. L.30 J.D. [Jacobs,G.B.&D.]
*PRACTICE AREAS: Criminal Defense; Civil Rights Litigation; Business Litigation; Appellate Practice.
Blue, Jon C. '48 '74 C.118 B.A. L.813 J.D.
(adm. in CA; not adm. in CT) Supr. Ct. J.
Blythe, Robert W., (BV) .... '55 '80 C.184 B.A.B.S. L.831 J.D. [Ⓒ Siegel,O.S.&Z.]
*PRACTICE AREAS: Real Estate Law; Commercial Law.
Bochenek, Malgorzata J. ....'72 '99 C.999 B.A. L.306 J.D. [Ⓐ Tyler C.&A.]
Bogdanski, Joseph W. ....'11 '40 C.165 B.A. L.306 LL.B. Trial Ref., Jud. Dept.
Bohonnon, David M., (AV) ....'56 '82 C.183 B.A. L.1029 J.D. [Bohonnon]
*PRACTICE AREAS: Admiralty and Maritime Law; Aviation Law; State and Federal Taxation; Corporate Law; Venture Capital.
Bohonnon, K. Wynne, (AV) ....'52 '82 C.918 B.A. L.1029 J.D. [Bohonnon]
*PRACTICE AREAS: Admiralty and Maritime Law; Family Law; Personal Injury; Civil Litigation; Computer Law.
Bohonnon, R. William, (AV) ....'21 '44 C.918 L.732 LL.B. [Ⓒ Bohonnon]
*PRACTICE AREAS: Admiralty and Maritime Law; State and Federal Taxation; Probate; Trust Administration; Contract.

Bohonnon Law Firm, The, LLC, (AV)
205 Church Street, 06510
Telephone: 203-787-2151 Fax: 203-773-1427
Email: bohonnon.com URL: http://www.lawyers.com/bohonnonlaw
Members of Firm: K. Wynne Bohonnon; David M. Bohonnon. Of Counsel: R. William Bohonnon; Dean W. Baker.
General Practice. Admiralty, Corporation, Insurance, Probate, Estate Planning, Real Estate, Zoning, Family, Administrative and Taxation Law. Trials, Aviation, Bankruptcy and Environmental.
See Professional Biographies, NEW HAVEN, CONNECTICUT

Bolden, Victor Allen ....'65 '90 C.178 L.309 [Ⓐ Wiggin&D.]
Bollinger, Maura Cantrill '64 '92 C.518 B.A. L.276 J.D.
(adm. in MD; not adm. in CT) Counsel, Southern New England Telecom. Corp.
Bonds, Alison L. .... '60 '87 C&L.575 B.A., J.D. 3 Austin Dr. Ext.
Bonini, John E. .... '68 '98 C.918 B.A. L.818 J.D. 157 Church Street
Bourque, Denise M. ....'65 '90 C.562 B.A. L.184 J.D. One Century Twr.
Bowerman, Richard W., (AV) ....'46 '75 C.282 B.A. L.184 J.D. [Tyler C.&A.]
*PRACTICE AREAS: Personal Injury; Employment Law; Entertainment Law; Commercial Litigation.
Bowlby, Samuel W., (AV) ....'38 '66 C.197 A.B. L.976 LL.B. [Ⓒ Tyler C.&A.]
*PRACTICE AREAS: Corporate Law; Public Utility Law; Securities.
Boyce-Iassogna, Patricia, (BV) ....'56 '91 C.1044 B.A. L.1029 J.D. 683 State St.
Boyer, Phoebe Bennet, (BV) .... '40 [Evans,F.&B.] ‡
Bozek, Joan L., (BV) .... '57 '82 C.188 B.A. L.276 J.D. Sr. V.P., Fleet Natl. Bank‡
Bradley, Charles H. D., II, (BV) .... '38 '64 C.103 A.B. L.893 LL.B. 102 Audobon St.
Brault, James J. ....'65 '91 C.93 B.S. L.1048 J.D. [Ⓐ Berman&S.]
*PRACTICE AREAS: Commercial Loan Documentation; Real Estate Transactions; Corporate Transactions; Corporate Finance; Mergers and Acquisitions.
Braun, Kevin P. ....'— '98 C&L.184 B.S., J.D. 157 Church Street
Brencher, George, IV .... '66 '92 C&L.659 B.A., J.D. [Brenner,S.&W.]
*PRACTICE AREAS: Internet Law; Business Start-Ups; Corporate; Securities.

Brenner, Newton D., (P.C.), (AV) ......'34 '58 C.659 B.S. L.976 LL.B. [Brenner,S.&W.]
*PRACTICE AREAS: Taxation; Acquisitions and Mergers; Corporate Reorganization; Estate Planning.

Brenner, Saltzman & Wallman LLP, (AV)
A Limited Liability Partnership including Professional Corporations
271 Whitney Avenue, P.O. Box 1746, 06507-1746
Telephone: 203-772-2600 Facsimile: 203-562-2098
Email: postmaster@bswlaw.com
Newton D. Brenner (P.C.); Stephen L. Saltzman (P.C.); Marc A. Wallman (P.C.); David R. Schaefer (P.C.); Stuart Jay Mandel (P.C.); Donald W. Anderson (P.C.); Samuel M. Hurwitz; Wayne A. Martino (P.C.); John R. Bashaw; Mitchell S. Jaffe (P.C.); Alice J. Mick (P.C.); Kenneth Rosenthal; Carolyn W. Kone; Brian P. Daniels; George Brencher IV;—Jennifer Dowd Deakin; Michelle Goglia; Rowena A. Moffett; Saraab A. Saleh. Of Counsel: Sharon Kowal Freilich (Also of Counsel to Brenner Satlzman & Wallman LLP); Stephen M. Pincus.
Corporate, Securities, Federal Income, Estate and Gift Taxation, Real Estate, Estate Planning and Probate, Pension and Profit Sharing, Employee Benefit, Environmental, Health Care Law, Trial Practice and Administrative Law.
See Professional Biographies, NEW HAVEN, CONNECTICUT

Brigham, Christopher L. ... '62 '92 C.478 B.A. L.1194 J.D. [Updike,K.&S.] (⊙Hartford)
*PRACTICE AREAS: Labor and Employment; Professional Defense.
Brochin, James P., (BV) .... '53 '87 C.103 A.B. L.184 J.D. [Ⓐ Evans,F.&B.]
*PRACTICE AREAS: Commercial Law; Litigation; Bankruptcy.
Brockway, James Russell .... '52 '76 C.197 A.B. L.228 J.D. [Bergman,H.&R.]
*PRACTICE AREAS: Business; Estate Planning; State Taxation; Federal Taxation; International Taxation.
Brodhead, Cynthia .... '46 '82 C.823 B.A. L.184 J.D. [Ⓖ Wiggin&D.]
*PRACTICE AREAS: Utility Law; Regulated Industries.
Brouillard, Adam M. .... '71 '97 C.478 B.S. L.306 J.D. 545 Orange St.
Brown, Carol A., (BV) .... '47 '86 C.19 B.A. L.184 J.D. 412 Orange St.
Brown, Ralph S. '13 '41 C&L.976 B.A., LL.B.
(adm. in NY; not adm. in CT) Prof. of Law, Emeritus, Yale Univ.
Brown, Stephen P. '70 '97 C.1044 B.A. L.1398 J.D.
[Ⓐ Gibson&B.] (⊙Burlington, MA; New York, NY)
Brown, Theresa A. .... '55 '80 C.321 B.A. L.184 J.D. Counsel, SNET
Brown, Thomas F., (BV) .... '31 '64 C.676 A.B. L.276 J.D. 205 Church St.
Brownstein, James S., (BV) ....'48 '74 C.156 B.A. L.184 J.D. [Kantrovitz&B.]
Brunetti, Alfred J. '51 '77 C.855 B.A. L.813 J.D.
Assistant General Counsel, Southern New England Telecom. Corp.
Bruno, Alfred P. ....'70 '97 C.67 B.A. L.1252 J.D. [Ⓐ Del Sole&D.] (⊙Hamden)
*PRACTICE AREAS: Insurance Defense Litigation; Personal Injury Law.
Brunswick, Max F., (BV) .... '41 '67 C.28 B.A. L.273 LL.B. 129 Church St.
Bryant, Stearns J., Jr., (BV) ....'43 '68 C.1033 B.A. L.1294 LL.B. 129 Church St.
Bryne, James R. ....'69 '94 C.94 B.A. L.184 J.D. [Ⓐ Tyler C.&A.]
*PRACTICE AREAS: Commercial Litigation.
Bryson, Susan J., (AV) .... '48 '77 C.813 B.A. L.184 J.D. [Wiggin&D.]
*PRACTICE AREAS: Commercial Real Estate; Development; Downtown Development; Corporate Real Estate; Zoning, Planning and Land Use.
Bucar, Jacqueline DeAndrus, (AV) .... '44 '86 C&L.184 B.S., J.D. [Tyler C.&A.]
*PRACTICE AREAS: Labor and Employment; Immigration; Commercial Litigation.
Buckley, John F., Jr., (BV) ....'59 '84 C.478 B.S. L.184 J.D. [Buckley&W.] ⊙
*PRACTICE AREAS: Personal Injury Litigation; Product Liability; Medical Malpractice; Legal Malpractice.
Buckley, John J., (BV) ....'26 '52 C.976 B.A. L.184 LL.B. [Buckley&B.]
Buckley, Melissa A., (BV) ....'54 '80 C.976 B.A. L.184 J.D. [Buckley&B.]
Buckley & Buckley, (BV) .... 250 Church St. (⊙Tifton, GA)

Buckley & Wynne, (BV)
685 State Street, 06511 ⊙
Telephone: 203-776-2278 Fax: 203-495-6020
Email: buckley.and.wynne@snet.net
Members of Firm: John F. Wynne; John F. Buckley, Jr.; John F. Wynne, Jr.
General Civil and Criminal Practice before State and Federal Courts. Personal Injury, Medical and Legal Malpractice, Product Liability, Probate, Workers Compensation Law. Trials and Appeals.
Reference: Centerbank.
Hartford, Connecticut Office: 10 Columbus Boulevard. Telephone: 203-560-2278.
See Professional Biographies, NEW HAVEN, CONNECTICUT

Buckmir, Elizabeth M., (BV) .... '63 '88 C.184 B.A. L.306 J.D. [Esty&B.]
*PRACTICE AREAS: Insurance Defense; Civil Practice.
Budge, Kevin S. .... '71 '96 C.184 B.A. L.1048 J.D. [Ⓐ Wiggin&D.]
Burns, Ellen B. ....'23 '47 C.19 B.A. L.976 LL.B. Sr. U.S. Dist. J.
Burns, Maureen E., (BV) ....'58 '83 C.19 B.A. L.1048 J.D. [McNerney,T.&B.]
Burt, Michael E., (BV) ....'59 '84 C.165 B.A. L.128 J.D. [Walsh,B.&W.]
Burt, Robert A. '39 '66 C.674 B.A. L.976 LL.B.
(adm. in DC; not adm. in CT) Yale Law Sch.
Busca, Morris J. ....'47 '98 C.184 B.A. L.999 J.D. [Ⓐ Garrison L.C.&R.]
*PRACTICE AREAS: Labor; Employment; Workers Compensation; Civil Litigation.
Bush, Richard A. ....'43 '69 C.165 A.B. L.184 LL.B. Int. Rev. Serv.
Bye, Dori N. '— '91 C.75 B.A. L.94 J.D.
Sr. Coun., Southern New England Telecom. Corp.
Byrne, Kathleen M., (AV) ....'62 '87 C.1044 B.A. L.262 J.D. [Letizia,A.C.]
Cabranes, Jose A. .... '40 '68 C.178 A.B. L.976 J.D. U.S. Cir. J.
Cahill, George J., Jr., (AV) ....'50 '77 C.1102 B.A. L.1202 J.D. [Cahill,G.&D.]
Cahill, Goetsch & DiPersia, P.C., (AV) ....43 Trumbull St.
Calabresi, Guido ....'32 '58 C&L.976 B.A., LL.B. U.S. Cir. J.
Calistro, Eugene R, Jr. ....'58 '89 C.1156 B.A. L.469 J.D. Asst. State's Atty.
Calistro, Roger B., (AV) .... '54 '79 C.188 B.A. L.228 J.D. [Gallagher&C.]
*PRACTICE AREAS: Trials; Appeals.
Calsyn, Dylan S. .... '71 '00 C.597 B.A. L.976 J.D. [Ⓐ Wiggin&D.]
Campana, Patricia A. .... '59 '85 C.145 B.A. L.146 J.D. [Ⓐ Bergman,H.&R.]
*PRACTICE AREAS: Corporate Law; Commercial Law; Real Estate; Investments; Securities.
Candrick, Thomas R., Jr., (AV) .... '47 '75 C.188 A.B. L.659 J.D. [Carmody&T.]
*PRACTICE AREAS: Corporate Law; Commercial Law; Bankruptcy; Banking.
Caplan, Milton I., (AV) .... '33 '58 C.976 B.A. L.184 J.D. [Virshup,C.&H.]
Cappel, Andrew J. ....'56 '92 C&L.976 B.A., J.D. One Century Twr.
Carangelo, Robert W., (BV) ....'28 '55 C.103 A.B. L.276 LL.B. Prob. J.
Carlson, Dale L. .... '46 '76 C.567 B.S. L.823 J.D. [Wiggin&D.] (Pat.)
*PRACTICE AREAS: Intellectual Property; Chemical Patents; Technology and Science; Trade Secrets; Patent Licensing.

Carmody & Torrance LLP, (AV) BB
195 Church Street, P.O. Box 1950, 06509-1950 ⊙
Telephone: 203-777-5501 Facsimile: 203-784-3199
Email: contactus@carmodylaw.com URL: http://www.carmodylaw.com
Partners: Anthony M. Fitzgerald; Burton Z. Alter; Charles F. Corcoran, III; Thomas R. Candrick, Jr.; Susan Seidler Chambers; Ann Harris Rubin; Thomas J. Sansone; Ann Hedges Zucker; Christopher Rooney; Howard K. Levine. Associates: David S. Hardy; Anne D. Peterson; William G. Lewis; Lucy M. Romeo.
General Practice including Administrative, Alternative Dispute Resolution, Antitrust and Trade Regulation, Arbitration, Banking, Bankruptcy, Bond Finance, Closely Held Business, Commercial Real Estate, Commercial Litigation, Complex Litigation, Construction, Contracts, Corporate, Creditors' Rights, Employment Benefits, Employer Defense, Energy, Environmental, ERISA, Estate Planning, Family Business Successions, Finance, Freedom of Information, Government (State and Municipal Contracts), Health Care, Insurance, Intellectual Property, Patents and Trademarks, Labor and Employment, Land Use, Management Counseling, Medical Malpractice Defense, Municipal,

(This Listing Continued)

Carmody & Torrance LLP (Continued)
Nonprofit Organizations, Pension, Privatization, Probate, Products Liability, Professional Liability Defense, Profit Sharing, Public-Private Finance, Public Utility, Securities, Tax, Toxic Torts, Zoning Law. General Civil, Criminal and Appellate Practice in all Courts.
Representative Clients: Algonquin Gas Transmission Co.; Anthem Blue Cross & Blue Shield of Connecticut, Inc.; Fleet Boston Financial Co.; MacDermid, Inc.; Northeast Utilities; Timex Corp.; Verizon Wireless; Waterbury Hospital.
Trial Counsel for: Aetna Life and Casualty; St. Paul Fire & Marine Insurance.
Waterbury, Connecticut Office: 50 Leavenworth Street. P.O. Box 1110, 06721-1110. Telephone: 203-573-1200. Facsimile: 203-575-2600.
Southbury, Connecticut Office: 900 Main Street South. P.O. Box 410, 06488-0410. Telephone: 203-264-7882. Facsimile: 203-264-7847.
See Professional Biographies, NEW HAVEN, CONNECTICUT

Carocci, Albert, (CV) ....'64 '89 C.676 B.S. L.1029 J.D. 169 Olive St.
Carolan, James M., (AV) ... '59 '89 C.188 A.B. L.184 J.D. Assoc. Gen. Coun., Yale Univ.
Carr, Cynthia '53 '85 C.59 B.A. L.309 J.D.
(adm. in NY; not adm. in CT) Yale University
Carroll, Richard B. '47 '73
C.93 A.B. L.659 J.D. Assoc. Gen. Coun., Knights of Columbus
*RESPONSIBILITIES: Insurance Operations.
Carter, Julie Behm .... '62 '89 C.575 B.A. L.893 J.D. Assoc. Gen. Coun., Yale Univ.
Carter, Stephen L. '54 '81 C.813 B.A. L.976 J.D.
(adm. in DC; not adm. in CT) Prof. of Law, Yale Law School

Carter & Civitello
(See Woodbridge)

Carty, Paul V., Law Offices of, (BV) '54 '85 C.918 B.A. L.184 J.D.
506 Whalley Avenue, P.O. Box 3192, 06515-0292
Telephone: 203-387-5400 Fax: 203-387-5402
Email: pvcartyesq@aol.com URL: http://www.lawyers.com/pvcartyesq
***PRACTICE AREAS: Criminal Defense; Personal Injury; Workers Compensation; Family Law; Landlord and Tenant Law.**
Criminal Defense, Personal Injury, Civil Litigation, Workers Compensation, Family Law, Landlord and Tenant Law, Driving While Intoxicated, Civil Litigation.
See Professional Biographies, NEW HAVEN, CONNECTICUT

Cashman, William H., (BV) .... '45 '72 C.28 B.A. L.818 J.D. 91 William St.
Cavanagh, Robert F., (AV) ....'36 '59 C&L.976 B.A., LL.B. [Wiggin&D.]
*PRACTICE AREAS: Corporation Law; College Law; Health Care Law; Hospital Law.
Celotto, Donald W. ....'23 '54 C.976 B.A. L.184 LL.B. Supr. Ct. J.
Celotto, Donald W., Jr., (BV) ....'52 '77 C.276 B.A. L.421 J.D. 12 Trumbull St.
Chambers, Susan Seidler, (AV) .... '55 '80 C.188 B.A. L.184 J.D. [Carmody&T.]
*PRACTICE AREAS: Construction; Contract Litigation; Insurance Litigation; Employer Defense.
Chambers, Wick R., (BV) ....'48 '79 C.976 B.A. L.1194 J.D. [Winnick,R.C.E.&H.]
*PRACTICE AREAS: Legal Ethics; Software Licensing; Computer Law; Technology Law; Estate Planning.
Chapman, Avery S. .... '66 '91 C.855 B.A. L.978 J.D. 7 Elm Street
Chapnick, Randall B., (CV) ....'49 '77 C.299 B.A. L.724 J.D. 129 Church St.
Chase, James M. ....'39 '85 C.1252 B.A. L.184 J.D. Off. of Pub. Def.
Chaucer, Bradford J. .... '49 '88 C.563 B.E.E. L.1029 J.D. [Chaucer&R.] (Pat.)
Chaucer and Rosado .... 139 Orange St.
Chimes, Lewis H., (BV) ....'60 '85 C.860 B.A. L.178 J.D. [Garrison L.C.&R.]
*PRACTICE AREAS: Criminal and Civil Litigation; Employment Law; Personal Injury.
Christianson, Bernard C., (BV) .... '44 '87 C.1030 B.A. L.184 J.D. [Jacobs,G.B.&D.]
*PRACTICE AREAS: Matrimonial and Family Law.
Church, Margaret Kezer, (BV) ....'53 '80 C.938 B.A. L.1202 J.D. [Church&C.]
*PRACTICE AREAS: Probate Law; Estate Planning Law; Real Estate Law; Elder Law.
Church, Norbert W., Jr., (BV) ....'52 '79 C.105 B.S.B.A. L.1202 J.D. [Church&C.]
*PRACTICE AREAS: Municipal Law; Planning and Zoning Law; Real Estate; Condominium Law; Probate.

Church and Church, (AV)
35 Elm Street, P.O. Box 78, 06501-0078
Telephone: 203-562-0300 Fax: 203-624-5134
Email: nwchurch@gateway.net URL: http://www.lawyers.com/churchandchurch
Members of Firm: Norbert W. Church, Jr.; Margaret Kezer Church; David T. Totman.
General Civil and Criminal Practice before State and Federal Courts, Municipal Law, Real Estate, Zoning, Land Use, Corporation, Probate, Estate Planning, Elder Law, Commercial, Condominium and Collections, Trials and Appeals.
Reference: Shawmut Bank.
See Professional Biographies, NEW HAVEN, CONNECTICUT

Cicchetti & Tansley
(See Waterbury)

Cimmino, Nicholas J. .... '40 '66 C.976 B.A. L.276 J.D. Trial Ct. Admr.
Cirello, John A. ....'70 '00 C.1145 B.S. L.1252 J.D. 35-37 Audubon St
Cirillo, Frank L., (BV) .... '49 '75 C.184 B.A. L.192 J.D. [Moss&C.]
Cirillo, James F., Jr., (BV) ....'47 '73 C.93 B.A. L.818 J.D. 142 Temple St.

Ciulla & Donofrio, LLP
(See North Haven)

Claiborn, Holley L. ....'69 '96 C.95 B.A. L.823 J.D. [Ⓐ Cummings&L.]
*PRACTICE AREAS: Litigation.
Clark, Elias ....'21 '48 C&L.976 B.A., LL.B. Prof., Yale Law School‡
Clark, James G. ....'50 '82 C.976 B.A. L.1065 J.D. Asst. State's Atty.
Clark, Joseph B. .... '32 '57 C.602 B.A. L.184 J.D. Supr. Ct. J.
Clark, Peter A., (AV) ....'40 '66 C.184 B.A. L.705 J.D. Asst. U.S. Atty.
Clendenen, William H., Jr., (AV) ....'42 '67 C.676 B.A. L.128 J.D. [W.H.Clendenen,Jr.]
*PRACTICE AREAS: Litigation; Personal Injury Law; Estates; Probate Law; Civil Rights Law.

Clendenen, William H., Jr., A Professional Corporation, (AV) BB
400 Orange Street, P.O. Box 301, 06502-0301
Telephone: 203-787-1183 Fax: 203-787-2847
William H. Clendenen, Jr.;—James E. Clifford; Nancy L. Walker; Thomas C. Pellegrino; Kevin C. Shea.
General Civil and Appellate Practice. Banking, Civil Rights, Employment, Construction, Consumer, Commercial Litigation, Estates and Probate, Real Estate, Personal Injury. General Litigation in all Courts.
See Professional Biographies, NEW HAVEN, CONNECTICUT

Clifford, James E., (BV) .... '59 '85 C.276 B.A. L.180 J.D. [Ⓐ W.H.Clendenen,Jr.]
*PRACTICE AREAS: Litigation; Personal Injury Law; Real Estate Law; Commercial Law.
Clifford, Patrick J. .... '50 '75 C.676 B.A. L.818 J.D. Supr. Ct. J.
Clune, Jonathan E. ....'52 '80 C&L.976 B.A., J.D. Assoc. Gen. Coun., Yale Univ.
Clute, Karen L. .... '56 '86 C.1044 B.A. L.569 J.D. [Wiggin&D.]
*PRACTICE AREAS: Employee Benefits; Executive Compensation; Estate Planning; Tax Exempt Organizations; Trusts and Estates.
Coan, Richard M., (AV) .... '48 '74 C.696 A.B. L.976 J.D. [Coan,L.G.&M.]
*PRACTICE AREAS: Real Estate Law; Bankruptcy Law; Commercial Law.

Coan, Lewendon, Gulliver & Miltenberger, LLC, (AV) BB
495 Orange Street, 06511
Telephone: 203-624-4756 Fax: 203-865-3673
URL: http://www.lawyers.com/clrglawoffices
Members of Firm: Richard M. Coan; Whitney M. Lewendon; Carl T. Gulliver; Timothy D. Miltenberger. Of Counsel: E. Huntington Deming.

(This Listing Continued)

Coan, Lewendon, Gulliver & Miltenberger, LLC (Continued)

General Civil Practice. Bankruptcy, Commercial, Banking, Personal Injury, Real Estate, Corporation, Probate, and Estate Planning Law, Elder Law, Trials and Appeals before all Courts.
Reference: Peoples Bank.

See Professional Biographies, NEW HAVEN, CONNECTICUT

Cobey, Donald E., (AV) .... '08 '32 C&L.976 B.A., LL.B. 21 Bradley Rd.St.‡
Cochran, Frank B., (BV) .... '44 '70 C.821 B.A. L.976 LL.B. [Cooper,W.C.&F.]
Cohen, Andrew A. .... '58 '87 C.1044 B.A. L.276 J.D. [Letizia,A.C.]
Cohen, Gerald H., (AV) .... '41 '66 C.1252 B.S. L.818 LL.B. [G.H.Cohen]
Cohen, Joshua W. .... '68 '94 C.659 B.A. L.978 J.D. [🄰 Cummings&L.]
*PRACTICE AREAS: Litigation.
Cohen, Morris L. '27 '51 C.145 B.A. L.178 J.D.
(adm. in NY; not adm. in CT) Prof. Emeritus, Yale Univ.
Cohen, Ronald J., (AV) .... '50 '75 C.855 B.A. L.569 J.D. [Tyler C.&A.]
*PRACTICE AREAS: Commercial Litigation; Commercial Landlord and Tenant Law; Antitrust and Trade Regulation; Health Care.

Cohen and Acampora, (BV)
109 Church Street, 06510 ⊙
Telephone: 203-624-4126
John A. Acampora.
General Civil and Criminal Practice before State and Federal Courts. Personal Injury, Litigation, Products Liability, Environmental, Real Estate, Zoning, Acquisitions and Development, Probate, Estate Planning, Workers Compensation, Domestic Relations, Foreclosure, Bankruptcy, Insolvency, Maritime Law, Real Estate, Tax Appeals, Business, Commercial and Corporation Law.
East Haven, Connecticut Office: 8 Frontage Road, P.O. Box 190. Telephone: 203-467-7337. Telecopier: 203-468-7865.

See Professional Biographies, NEW HAVEN, CONNECTICUT

Cohen, Gerald H., A Professional Corporation, (AV) .... 12 Trumbull St.

Cohen & Thomas
(See Derby)

Cohn, Robert F. .... '54 '79 C.1044 B.S. L.910 J.D. [Siegel,O.S.&Z.]
*PRACTICE AREAS: Estate Planning Law; Trust Law; Elder Law; Taxation Law; Corporate Law.
Colby, Raquel S. '66 '91 C.690 B.S. L.776 J.D.
(adm. in NJ; not adm. in CT) [🄰 Bergman,H.&R.]
*PRACTICE AREAS: Tax Law; Business Planning for Individuals; Partnerships and Corporations; State Taxation; Estate Planning.
Colleran, John W., (AV) .... '30 '55 C&L.976 B.A., LL.B. [J.W.Colleran]
*PRACTICE AREAS: Real Estate Law; Administrative Law; Hazardous Waste Law; Personal Injury Law.

Colleran, John W., P.C., Law Offices of, (AV)
19 Whitney Avenue, 06510
Telephone: 203-865-2899 Fax: 203-777-4587
Email: colleran@iconn.net URL: http://www.lawyers.com/jwcolleranatty
John W. Colleran.
General Practice in all Courts. Corporation, Negligence, Probate, Environmental, Zoning, Real Estate and Administrative Law, Personal Injury. Trials.
References: The Bank of New Haven; New Haven Savings Bank.

See Professional Biographies, NEW HAVEN, CONNECTICUT

Comstock, Roland W. '30 '57 C.490 B.A. L.494 J.D.
(adm. in MN; not adm. in CT) Sr. V.P., Corp. Affs., United Illuminating
Cone, Neal .... '48 '88 C.94 B.S. L.184 J.D. Asst. Pub. Def.
Connors, Sean C. .... '66 '92 C.676 B.A. L.1029 J.D. [Milano&W.]
*PRACTICE AREAS: Products Liability; Insurance Defense Litigation; Municipal Litigation; General Trial and Appellate Practice.
Conroy, Michael C., (CV) .... '— '95 C.197 A.B. L.1194 J.D. [🄰 Susman,D.&S.]
*PRACTICE AREAS: Civil Litigation; Insurance Defense; Insurance Coverage; Professional Malpractice Defense.
Conway, Bernadette, (BV) .... '58 '85 C.588 B.S.N. L.1029 J.D. 239 Whalley Ave.
Conway, Glenn M. .... '62 '97 C&L.184 B.S., J.D. 7-9 Elm St.
Conway, Kathleen M. .... '40 '87 C.209 B.S.N. L.184 J.D. 385 Orange Street
Coonley, Ann P., (BV) .... '41 '82 C.185 B.A. L.1029 J.D. 27 Elm St.
Cooper, Gary G., (BV) .... '51 '77 C.273 B.A. L.7 J.D. [Greenberg,H.C.&S.]
Cooper, Gerald H., (AV) .... '44 '69 C.349 B.A. L.818 J.D. 265 Church St.
Cooper, Peter B., (AV) .... '39 '64 C&L.976 B.A., LL.B. [Cooper,W.C.&F.]
Cooper, Whitney, Cochran & Francois, (AV) .... 51 Elm St.
Corcoran, Charles F., III, (AV) .... '45 '71 C&L.976 A.B., J.D. [Carmody&T.]
*PRACTICE AREAS: Trials and Appeals; Environmental Law; Professional Malpractice Law; Labor and Employment; Commercial and Contract Law.
Cornell, Monika Dorota .... '64 '00 C.477 A.B. L.94 [🄰 Wiggin&D.]
Costa, Giacinto G., (BV) .... '39 '64 C.676 B.A. L.184 LL.B. [Greenberg&C.]
Costa, Keith N. .... '58 '85 C.184 B.A. L.904 J.D. [🄲 Cummings&L.]
*PRACTICE AREAS: Corporate Law; Creditors Rights; Bankruptcy; Debtor and Creditor.
Costello, Ellen M. .... '47 '88 C.730 B.S. L.818 J.D. [🄰 Del Sole&D.]
*PRACTICE AREAS: Medical and Dental Malpractice; General Litigation.
Costello, John K. '53 '81 C.309 B.A. L.818 J.D.
Sr. Coun., Southern New England Telecom. Corp.
Cotta, David '72 '99 C.855 B.A. L.188 J.D.
(adm. in NY; not adm. in CT) [🄰 Wiggin&D.]
Courtney, Stephen J. .... '52 '92 C.321 B.A. L.184 J.D. 171 Orange St.
Coury, George A. .... '63 '90 C.645 B.S. L.1040 J.D. [Bachman&L.] (See Pat. Sect.)
*PRACTICE AREAS: Patents; Trademarks; Copyrights; Unfair Competition; Licensing Law.

Cousins, Johnson & Desrosiers, P.C.
(See Stratford)

Cox, Barbara L., (BV) .... '51 '82 C.645 B.A. L.184 J.D. [Gallagher&C.]
*PRACTICE AREAS: Trials; Appeals.
Craig, William E., (AV) .... '42 '67 C.197 B.A. L.976 LL.B. [🄲 Wiggin&D.]
*PRACTICE AREAS: Real Property Law; Mortgage Law; Municipal Law.
Cramer, Richard B., (BV) .... '37 '64 C.477 A.B. L.273 LL.B. [Land&C.]
Craven, James O. .... '68 '94 C.216 B.A. L.930 J.D. [🄰 Wiggin&D.]
Cretella, Albert W., Jr. .... '25 '50 C.870 B.S. L.184 LL.B. Appl. Ct. J.
Crislip, Heather M. .... '73 '00 C.890 B.A. L.184 J.D. 900 Chapel Street, Suite 620
Crotta, David J., Jr., (BV) .... '60 '88 C.1030 A.B. L.184 J.D. [Mulvey,O.&G.]
*PRACTICE AREAS: Trials; Negligence and Commercial Litigation; Civil Litigation; Appeals; Probate Appeals.
Crowley, Timothy W. .... '58 '97 C.324 B.A. L.823 J.D. [🄰 Cummings&L.]

Cummings & Lockwood, (AV)
700 State Street, P.O. Box 1960, 06509-1960 ⊙
Telephone: (203) 782-3000 Telecopier: (203) 777-3347
Email: info@cl-law.com URL: http://www.cl-law.com
Members of Firm: Michael N. Delgass; Charles J. Filardi, Jr.; Jamie Johnson Fitzgerald; Keith Bradoc Gallant; David W. Kesner; David A. Reif; Mark G. Sklarz; Charles M. Tatelbaum (See Biography at Naples, Florida Office). Counsel: Keith N. Costa. Associates: Holley L. Claiborn; Joshua W. Cohen; Timothy W. Crowley; Thomas J. Dufour; Sean P. Merrill; Graceann A. Pisano.
General Practice. National and Regional Litigation Counsel, Corporate Law, Patent and Intellectual Property, Trusts and Estates, Labor and Employment, Mergers and Acquisitions, Partnerships and Joint Ventures, Commercial Lending, Corporate Finance, Creditors' Rights, Bankruptcy and Workouts, Securities Regulation and Litigation, Tax, Insurance, Banking and Financial Services, Leasing, Commercial and Residential Real Estate, Construction, Environmental, Toxic Torts, Health Law, Products Liability Litigation, Probate Litigation, Family Law and International Business.

(This Listing Continued)

Cummings & Lockwood (Continued)

Stamford, Connecticut Office: Four Stamford Plaza, P.O. Box 120, 06904-0120. Telephone: (203) 327-1700. Telecopier: (2^3) 351-4535.
Greenwich, Connecticut Office: Two Greenwich Plaza, P.O. Box 2505, 06836. Telephone: (203) 869-1200. Telecopier: (203) 869-3120.
Hartford, Connecticut Office: CityPlace I, 185 Asylum Street, 36th Floor, 06103-3495. Telephone: (860) 275-6700. Telecopier: (860) 724-3397.
West Hartford, Connecticut Office: Town Center, 29 South Main Street, Suite 208, 06107. Telephone: (860) 275-6700. Telecopier: (860) 313-0293.
Bonita Springs, Florida Office: 24311 Walden Center, Suite 201, 34134. Telephone: (941) 947-8811. Telecopier: (941) 947-8025.
Naples, Florida Office: 3001 Tamiami Trail North, P.O. Box 413032, 34101-3032. Telephone: (941) 262-8311. Telecopier: (941) 263-0703.

See Professional Biographies, NEW HAVEN, CONNECTICUT

Curcio, Robert .... '58 '97 C.882 B.A. L.1358 J.D. [🄰 DeLio&P.]
*PRACTICE AREAS: Intellectual Property Litigation; Patents; Trademarks; Copyrights; Unfair Competition.
Curtin, Daniel D. .... '64 '90 C.156 B.A. L.1202 J.D. Spec. Agent, FBI
Curtin, James B., (AV) .... '29 '58 C.855 B.S. L.184 LL.B. 205 Church St.
Cusanelli, Gabriel H., (BV) .... '61 '87 C.93 B.A. L.818 J.D. 181 Edwards St.
Cuthbertson, Hugh W., (BV) .... '46 '73 C.930 B.A. L.93 J.D. [Siegel,O.S.&Z.]
*PRACTICE AREAS: Labor Law; Employment Law; Litigation.
Dabrowski, Albert S., (BV) .... '44 '71 C.184 B.S. L.818 J.D. U.S. Bkrptcy. J.
D'Agostino, Michael C. .... '71 '96 C&L.893 B.A., J.D. [🄰 Tyler C.&A.]
Daine, Kimberly A. '64 '91 C&L.472 B.A., J.D.
(adm. in NY; not adm. in CT) One Century Twr.‡
Dalton, Harlon L. '47 '74 C.309 A.B. L.976 J.D.
(adm. in NY; not adm. in CT) Yale Law Sch.
Daniels, Brian P. .... '66 '92 C.111 B.S. L.309 J.D. [Brenner,S.&W.]
*PRACTICE AREAS: Federal Litigation; Commercial Litigation; Environmental; Contracts; Insurance Coverage.
Daniels, Douglas R., (BV) .... '36 '65 C&L.976 B.A., J.D. 234 Church St.
Davis, Lisa N. .... '60 '90 C&L.976 B.A., J.D. [🄰 Tyler C.&A.]
*PRACTICE AREAS: Estate Planning; Administration; Probate Law; Disabilities Law; Nonprofit Organizations.
Deakin, Jennifer Dowd .... '68 '93 C&L.93 B.A., J.D. [🄰 Brenner,S.&W.]
*PRACTICE AREAS: Corporate Law; Commercial Law.
Dean, Eric T., Jr. .... '50 '78 C.821 B.A. L.1119 J.D. [🄰 Marcus]
Dean, Kevin Paul .... '66 '98 C.1030 B.S. L.306 J.D. [🄰 Wiggin&D.]
Dearington, Michael, (AV) .... '42 '67 C.855 B.A. L.904 J.D. States Atty.
De Barbieri, Roy L., (BV) .... '47 '73 C.524 B.S. L.161 J.D. 677 State St.
DeChello, Anthony R., (BV) .... '60 '85 C.1200 B.S. L.602 J.D. [Pellegrino]
DeFrank, Steven J., (BV) .... '58 '88 C.1269 B.A. L.1029 J.D. [Jacobs,G.B.&D.]
*PRACTICE AREAS: Personal Injury Litigation; Product Liability Litigation.

Delaney, Zemetis, Donahue, Durham & Noonan, P.C.
(See Wallingford)

Delgass, Michael N. .... '69 '95 C.347 B.S.B.A. L.145 J.D. [Cummings&L.] (⊙Stamford)
*PRACTICE AREAS: Trusts and Estates.
Delia, Anselmo M., (BV) .... '55 '82 C.446 B.S. L.564 J.D. 45 Court St.
D'Elia, John J., (BV) .... '61 '86 C.855 B.A. L.184 J.D. [Kennedy,J.D.&G.]
*PRACTICE AREAS: Personal Injury Law; Workers Compensation.
DeLio, Anthony P., (AV) ...... '28 '57 C.667 B.S. L.273 J.D. [DeLio&P.] (See Pat. Sect.)
*PRACTICE AREAS: Patents; Trademarks; Copyrights; Unfair Competition; Intellectual Property Licensing.

DeLio & Peterson, LLC, (AV)
121 Whitney Avenue, 06510-1241
Telephone: 203-787-0595 FAX: 203-787-5818
Email: delpet@delpet.com URL: http://www.lawyers.com/delio
Anthony P. DeLio; Peter W. Peterson;—John J. Tomaszewski (Not admitted in CT); Robert Curcio; Kelly Reynolds Nowak; Michael A. Petrocelli.
United States and International Patent, Trademark, Copyright and Unfair Competition Law. Licensing, Franchising and Technology - Litigation.

See Professional Biographies, NEW HAVEN, CONNECTICUT

DelMonico, Jennifer Morgan .... '73 '97 C.597 B.M. L.893 J.D. [🄰 Murtha C.]
DelMonico, W. Bruce .... '69 '97 C.103 B.A. L.893 J.D. [🄰 Wiggin&D.] (⊙Stamford)
Del Sole, Dominic P., (AV) .... '26 '62 C.602 B.S. L.184 LL.B. [🄲 Del Sole&D.]
*PRACTICE AREAS: Litigation; Insurance Law.
Del Sole, Michael P., (BV) .... '53 '79 C.93 B.A. L.184 J.D. [Del Sole&D.]
*PRACTICE AREAS: Litigation; Insurance Law; Appellate Practice.
Del Sole, Stephen P., (AV) .... '52 '77 C.93 B.A. L.1009 J.D. [Del Sole&D.]
*PRACTICE AREAS: Litigation; Insurance Law.

Del Sole & Del Sole, L.L.P., (AV) BR
27 Elm Street, 06510 ⊙
Mailing Address: 46 South Whittlesey Avenue, Wallingford, Connecticut 06492
Telephone: 203-785-8500 Fax: 203-777-4485
Email: delsole@delsoledelsole.com URL: http://www.lawyers.com/delsoledelsole
Members of Firm: Stephen P. Del Sole; Michael P. Del Sole; Denise Del Sole-Kennedy. Associates: Ellen M. Costello; Rene Gerard Martineau; Edward F. Piazza; Alfred P. Bruno. Of Counsel: Dominic P. Del Sole.
Trials and Appeals in all Courts. General, Tort and Malpractice, Litigation, Probate, Workers Compensation, Corporate, Real Estate Law and Insurance Law.
Wallingford, Connecticut Office: 46 South Whittlesey Avenue, 06492. Telephone: 203-284-8000. Fax: 203-284-9800.

See Professional Biographies, NEW HAVEN, CONNECTICUT

Del Sole-Kennedy, Denise .... '57 '90 [Del Sole&D.]
*PRACTICE AREAS: Litigation; Real Estate Law.
DeLuca, Mary S. .... '65 '94 C.475 B.A. L.776 J.D. Dep. Clk., Supr. Ct.
DeMaio, Pat, Jr. .... '65 '88 C.884 B.A. L.1019 J.D. 169 Olive St.
DeMatteo, Madelyn M. '48 '73 C.183 B.A. L.184 J.D.
V.P., Gen. Coun. & Secy., Southern New England Telecom. Corp.
Deming, E. Huntington, (BV) .... '50 '77 C.813 B.A. L.30 J.D. [🄲 Coan,L.G.&M.]
*PRACTICE AREAS: Civil Law; Commercial Litigation.
Dennis, Daniel H., Jr., (AV) .... '21 '48 C.676 Ph.B. L.184 LL.B. [Dennis&N.]
Dennis & North, (AV) .... 129 Church St.
De Palma, Christopher D. .... '74 '99 C.1030 B.A. L.1252 J.D. [🄰 Kennedy,J.D.&G.]
*PRACTICE AREAS: Personal Injury; Workers Compensation.
DeSanto, Elizabeth C. .... '63 '99 C.19 B.A. L.1252 J.D. [🄰 Trotta,T.&T.]
Deutsch, Barbara W. .... '33 '61 C.914 B.A. L.976 LL.B. Yale Law Sch.
Deutsch, Jan G. '35 '63 C&L.976 B.A., LL.B.
(adm. in DC; not adm. in CT) Yale Law Sch.
DeVane, Milton P., (AV) .... '29 '58 C&L.976 B.A., LL.B. [🄲 Tyler C.&A.]
*PRACTICE AREAS: Estate Planning, Probate and Trust Administration, Corporate.
Devlin, Robert J., Jr. .... '50 '75 C.1102 B.A. L.184 J.D. Supr. Ct. J.
Diadamo, Kevin J. .... '73 '98 C.321 B.A. L.1252 J.D. [🄰 Siegel,O.S.&Z.]
*PRACTICE AREAS: Estate Planning; Corporate; Tax.
Diaz, Inez M. .... '70 '95 C.999 B.A. L.184 J.D. 1 Century Twr.
DiBiccaro, Robert A. '46 '71 C.665 B.A. L.145 J.D.
Admin. Law J., U.S. Soc. Sec. Admn.

Diemand, Timothy A. . . . . '67 '92 C.156 B.A. L.273 J.D. [🄰 Wiggin&D.]
DiGioia, Anita C. . . . . '71 '97 C.1021 B.A. L.861 J.D. [🄰 Wiggin&D.]
Dignam, Brett . . . . '51 '83 C.518 B.A. L.800 J.D. Prof. of Law, Yale Law Sch.
Dineen, Francis X., (AV) '35 '61
C.197 A.B. L.976 LL.B. New Haven Legal Assistance Assn., Inc.
DiPersia, John G., (BV) . . . . '52 '77 C.454 B.A. L.1202 J.D. [Cahill,G.&D.]
DiPietro, Andrew M., Jr., (AV) '32 '61
C.732 B.A. L.188 LL.B. 205 Church Street, 3rd Floor
DiSesa, Victoria M., (BV) . . . . '52 '79 C.659 B.A. L.276 J.D. [DiSesa&D.]
*PRACTICE AREAS: Real Estate; Trusts and Estates; Small Business.

DiSesa & DiSesa, (BV)
385 Orange Street, 06511
Telephone: 203-781-0870 Telefax: 203-781-0861
Email: v.disesa@snet.net
Joseph D. DiSesa (1944-1983); Victoria M. DiSesa.
General Practice. Real Estate, Trusts and Estates, Small Business.
Reference: Fleet Bank.
See Professional Biographies, NEW HAVEN, CONNECTICUT

Ditman, Melvin, (AV) . . . . '46 '71 C.184 B.A. L.188 J.D. [Bergman,H.&R.]
*PRACTICE AREAS: Bankruptcy; Business; Commercial; Litigation; Real Estate.
Dobris, Roger S. . . . . '57 '84 C.1030 A.B. L.184 J.D. Sr. Asst. State's Atty.‡
Dobrowolski, Jos. S., (BV) . . . . '23 '53 C&L.588 LL.B. 51 Elm St., 2nd Fl.
Dodd, Martin H. . . . . '53 '83 C.855 B.S. L.184 J.D. [🄲 Wiggin&D.]
*PRACTICE AREAS: Environmental; Corporate Law.
Doherty, Adam Paul . . . . '74 '01 C.976 B.A. L.945 J.D. [🄰 Wiggin&D.]
Doherty, John R. . . .'31 '59 C.816 M.E. L.1003 LL.B. 5 Science Park (Pat.) (⊙Bridgeport)
Doherty, Meghan E. . . . . '74 '01 C.184 B.A. L.1252 J.D. [🄰 Wiggin&D.]
Dolan, Edward J., (AV) . . . . '44 '69 C.93 A.B. L.184 J.D. [Rosen&D.]
*PRACTICE AREAS: Family Law; Divorce Law; Child Custody Law; Criminal Defense.
Dolan, Michael . . . . '67 '96 C.870 B.S. L.1252 J.D. 683 State St.
Dombroski, Stan R., (BV) . . . . '65 '90 C.184 B.A. L.1202 J.D. [Dombroski,K.&H.]
Dombroski, Knapsack & Hillis, LLC, (BV) . . . . 205 Whitney Ave.
Dominick, Sherry L. . . . . '56 '81 C.976 B.A. L.569 J.D. [Wiggin&D.]
*PRACTICE AREAS: Employee Benefits Law; Executive Compensation Law.
Donato, Charles J., (BV) . . . . '45 '72 C.1030 B.A. L.184 J.D. [Krevolin&D.]
*PRACTICE AREAS: Real Estate; Probate; Corporation; Tax Law.
Donegan, Harold C., (AV) . . . . '37 '62 C.976 B.A. L.309 J.D. [Sperandeo&D.]
Dorflinger, Laura Lee A. . . . . '69 '96 C.1102 B.S. L.1252 J.D. [🄰 W.M.Philpot,Jr.]
*PRACTICE AREAS: Litigation; Employment Discrimination; Torts; Family Law; Bankruptcy.
Dorney, Michael J., (AV) . . . . '38 '63 C&L.93 B.A., LL.B. [Tyler C.&A.]
*PRACTICE AREAS: Litigation, Labor and Employment Law, Municipal.
Dorsey, Frederick L., (BV) . . . . '53 '84 C.437 B.A. L.1048 J.D. [Siegel,O.S.&Z.]
*PRACTICE AREAS: Labor Law; Employment Law; Litigation; Education Law; Special Education of Disabled Children Law.
Dorsey, Peter C. . . . . '31 '59 C.976 B.A. L.309 LL.B. Chf. U.S. Dist. J.
Douthat, Charles R., (BV) . . . . '50 '82 C.813 B.A. L.1065 J.D. [Jacobs&J.]
*PRACTICE AREAS: Personal Injury Law; Products Liability Law; Medical Malpractice; Civil Trial Practice.
Dow, William F., III, (AV) . . . . '41 '68 C.976 B.A. L.659 LL.B. [Jacobs,G.B.&D.]
*PRACTICE AREAS: Criminal Defense; Personal Injury.
Downey, John T. . . . . '30 '76 C.976 B.A. L.309 J.D. Supr. Ct. J.
Doyle, David S., (BV) . . . . '56 '85 C.893 B.A. L.184 J.D. [🄰 Marcus]
*PRACTICE AREAS: Personal Injury; Collections; Workers Compensation.
Doyle, William J., (AV) . . . . '36 '62 C.1030 B.B.A. L.724 LL.B. [Wiggin&D.]
*PRACTICE AREAS: Business Litigation; Complex Litigation; Civil Litigation; Commercial Litigation; Health Care Litigation.
Dressler, Lawrence S. . . . . '66 '92 C.1030 B.A. L.1252 J.D. [H.A.Lawrence]
Driscoll, Dennis W. . . . . '60 '91 C.690 B.S. L.1029 J.D. 234 Church St.
Dubrow, David L., (BV Ⓣ) . . . . '57 '83 C.881 A.B. L.569 J.D. [Bergman,H.&R.]
*PRACTICE AREAS: Tax Law; Business Planning; Personal Planning; Non-Profit Organizations; Partnership Planning.
Duffin, Francis J. . . . . '62 '88 C.829 B.A. L.1029 J.D. [Wiggin&D.]
*PRACTICE AREAS: Trademarks; Copyrights; Intellectual Property; Unfair Competition; Computers and Software.
Dufour, Thomas J. . . . . '59 '85 C.103 A.B. L.94 J.D. [🄰 Cummings&L.]
*PRACTICE AREAS: Real Estate; Banking; Environmental; Contracts.
Duke, Steven B. '34 '59 C.36 B.S. L.37 J.D.
(adm. in AZ; not adm. in CT) Prof. of Law, Yale Law Sch.
Dunham, Edward Wood, (AV) . . . . '53 '78 C.855 B.A. L.569 J.D. [Wiggin&D.]
*PRACTICE AREAS: Franchise Litigation; Litigation; Complex Litigation; Corporate Litigation; Franchises and Franchising.

Dwyer, Gerald P., (AV) '36 '64 C&L.184 B.A., J.D.
377 Orange Street, P.O. Box 1975, 06511
Telephone: 203-865-2392 Fax: 203-785-1749
***PRACTICE AREAS: Negligence Law; Municipal Law; Insurance Law; Arbitration Law.**
General Practice, Negligence, Personal Injury, Municipal, Insurance and Arbitration Law. Trials in all Courts.
See Professional Biographies, NEW HAVEN, CONNECTICUT

Early, Ethan . . . . '72 '99 C.674 B.A. L.184 J.D. [🄰 Early,L.&S.] (⊙New York, NY)
Early, James F., (AV) . . . . '46 '71 C.309 A.B. L.94 J.D. [Early,L.&S.] (⊙New York, NY)
*PRACTICE AREAS: Toxic Torts; Asbestos Disease; Lead Paint and Personal Injury Litigation; Trials.

Early, Ludwick & Sweeney, L.L.C., (AV) BR
One Century Tower, 11th Floor, 265 Church Street, P.O. Box 1866, 06508-1866
Telephone: 203-777-7799 Fax: 203-785-1671
Email: INFO@ELSLAW.COM URL: http://www.lawyers.com/elslaw
James F. Early; Lindalea P. Ludwick; Robert J. Sweeney; Brian C. Fournier;—Christopher Meisenkothen; Ethan Early; Michael J. Luzzi.
Plaintiffs' Toxic Tort Litigation, Products Liability, Personal Injury and Industrial Accidents, Workers' Compensation, Lead Paint Litigation, Asbestos Disease Litigation, Fen-Phen Litigation, FELA and Railroad Litigation, Criminal Law, Wrongful Termination, Malpractice, and Trials and Appeals.
See Professional Biographies, NEW HAVEN, CONNECTICUT

Echter, Martin S. . . . . '42 '71 C.197 B.A. L.273 J.D. Dep. Corp. Coun.
Edgington, Todd Andrew . . . . '51 '88 C.502 B.A. L.1048 J.D. Asst. Pub. Def.
Edwards, Mark C., (BV) . . . . '46 '74 C.1252 B.S. L.818 J.D. 174 Bradley St.
Egan, William J., (AV) . . . . '39 '64 C.309 B.A. L.184 LL.B. One Century Twr.
Eggert, Charles A., Jr. . . . . '48 '81 C.184 B.A. L.365 J.D. [🄰 Bartlett]
*PRACTICE AREAS: Bankruptcy; Family Law; Social Security Disability; Probate; Real Estate.
Einhorn, Jonathan J., (AV) . . . . '48 '74 C.31 B.A. L.184 J.D. 412 Orange Street
Eisner, J. Michael, (AV) . . . . '— '71 C.930 A.B. L.976 J.D. [Wiggin&D.]
*PRACTICE AREAS: Health Care Law; Hospital Law; Medical Staff Law; Election Law; Campaign Law.
Eldrich, Sarah D., (AV) . . . . '51 '83 C&L.1252 B.A., J.D. [Rubin&E.]
*PRACTICE AREAS: Family Law; Matrimonial Law; Divorce; Child Custody; Alimony.
Ely, John I., (AV) . . . . '13 '39 C&L.976 B.A., LL.B. One Century Twr.‡
Enders, Michael B. '48 '76 C.347 A.B. L.146 J.D.
(adm. in IL; not adm. in CT) Off. of Hearings & App., Soc. Sec. Admn.
Engelman, Robert J., (AV) . . . . '32 '59 C&L.976 B.A., LL.B. [Engelman&W.]
*PRACTICE AREAS: Probate Law; Estate Planning Law; Corporate Law; Family Law; Litigation.

Engelman & Welch-Rubin, L.L.P., (AV)
(Formerly Schwartz & Knight; Schwartz & Engelman)
278 Orange Street, 06510
Telephone: 203-787-4249 Fax: 203-785-8378
Members of Firm: Robert J. Engelman; Lori A. Welch-Rubin; David Welch-Rubin; Max H. Schwartz (Retired); J. Stephen Knight (1912-1961).
General Practice. Probate, Estate Planning, Corporate, Litigation, Family, Personal Injury and Appellate Practice.
Reference: Bank of Boston, Connecticut.
See Professional Biographies, NEW HAVEN, CONNECTICUT

Engstrom, Katrena . . . . '47 '75 C.881 B.A. L.94 J.D. [🄰 Williams&P.]
*PRACTICE AREAS: Criminal Law; Civil Practice; Civil Rights; Appellate Practice.
Enright, Brian G., (BV) . . . . '60 '87 C.1102 B.S. L.205 J.D. [Gorman&E.]
Epler, Palmer Y., (BV) . . . . '57 '82 C.105 B.A. L.184 J.D. Asst. Corp. Coun.‡
Eppler-Epstein, Amy, (BV) '60 '86 C.103 B.A. L.976 J.D.
Staff Atty., New Haven Legal Assistance Assn., Inc.
Errante, Steven J., (AV) . . . . '53 '79 C.1019 B.A. L.107 J.D. [Lynch,T.K.&E.]
*PRACTICE AREAS: Medical Malpractice; Negligence; Products Liability; Commercial Litigation; Sports Law.
Erskine, G. Randolph . . . . '12 '37 C.478 B.S. L.976 LL.B. Asst. Clk., Supr. Ct.
Esposito, John J., Jr., (BV) . . . . '61 '87 C.93 B.A. L.818 J.D. 373 Humphrey St.
Esposito, John J., (P.C.), (AV) . . . . '36 '61 C.184 B.A. L.477 LL.B. 373 Humphrey St.
Esterman, Marc R., (BV) '64 '90 C.855 B.A. L.184 J.D.
Assoc. Gen. Coun., DSL.net, Inc.
Estes, Frank W., (AV) '40 '66 C.976 B.A. L.813 LL.B.
Dir. of Planned Giving, Yale-New Haven Hosp.
Esty, Miles N., (BV) . . . . '62 '89 C.855 B.A. L.564 J.D. [Esty&B.]
*PRACTICE AREAS: Insurance Defense; Civil Practice.

Esty & Buckmir, LLC, (BV)
714 State Street, 06511
Telephone: 203-495-9999 Fax: 203-495-9662
Email: estyandbuckmir@aol.com
Miles N. Esty; Elizabeth M. Buckmir. Associate: Marla L. Seligson; Jonathan A. Beatty.
General Insurance Defense. Motor Vehicle, Premises Liability, Product Liability, Professional, Medical and Legal Malpractice, Construction Litigation, Commercial Litigation, Worker's Compensation and Miscellaneous Personal Injury Litigation.
See Professional Biographies, NEW HAVEN, CONNECTICUT

Evans, Gordon Alan, (AV) . . . . '29 '54 C.453 B.S. L.188 J.D. [G.A.Evans&Assoc.]
Evans, Jack H., (AV) . . . . '15 '37 C.184 L.94 J.D. [Evans,F.&B.]
*PRACTICE AREAS: Real Property Law; Probate Law; Trust Law; Corporation Law; Insurance Law.
Evans, Robert S., (AV) '36 '60
C&L.188 B.A., J.D. [Winnick,R.C.E.&H.] (⊙Brattleboro, VT)
*PRACTICE AREAS: Creditors Rights; Business Bankruptcy; Business Reorganization; Workouts; Business Litigation.

Evans, Feldman & Boyer, L.L.C., (AV)
261 Bradley Street, P.O. Box 1694, 06507-1694
Telephone: 203-772-4900 Telecopier: 203-782-1356
Email: Judgment@1conn.net
Phoebe Bennet Boyer (Retired); Jack H. Evans; Richard C. Feldman; Keith R. Ainsworth; James P. Brochin.
General Practice. Transactions and Litigation involving Commercial, Banking, Equipment Leasing, Corporation, Taxation, Estate Planning, Probate, Environmental, Real Estate, Condemnation, Negligence and Personal Injury and Employment Law. Trials in State and Federal Courts. Appeals, Administrative, Bankruptcy.
See Professional Biographies, NEW HAVEN, CONNECTICUT

Evans, Gordon Alan, & Associates, P.C., (AV) . . . . 31 Whitney Ave.
Fagelson, Marilyn B., (CV) . . . . '56 '84 C.918 B.A. L.1019 J.D. [🄲 Murtha C.]
*PRACTICE AREAS: Commercial Litigation; Insurance Coverage; Appellate Practice.
Fagnani, Louis P., Jr. . . . . '52 '77 C&L.184 B.A., J.D. Clk., Supr. Ct.
Fain, Gordon Y., (BV) . . . . '48 '73 C.918 B.A. L.976 J.D. Soc. Sec. Admin.
Falls, Kristen Sotnik . . . . '69 '94 C.676 B.A. L.306 J.D. [Letizia,A.C.]
Farrell, Sloan W. . . . . '65 '99 C.902 B.A. L.1252 J.D. [Seeley&B.]
*PRACTICE AREAS: Commercial Litigation; Insurance Coverage; Employment Law.
Farren, Paul E., Jr., (BV) . . . . '45 '69 C.976 B.A. L.184 J.D. [Farren&K.]
*PRACTICE AREAS: Personal Injury; Workers' Compensation; Domestic Relations; Real Estate; Trusts and Estates.

Farren and King, (AV)
94 Prospect Street, P.O. Box 1989, 06521-1989
Telephone: 203-562-9813 Fax: 203-562-3248
Email: administrator@farrenkinglaw.com URL: http://www.lawyers.com/farrenandking
Members of Firm: Paul E. Farren (1915-1992); Jackson T. King; Paul E. Farren, Jr.; Susan King Shaw.
General Practice including Personal Injury, Workers Compensation, Domestic Relations, Real Estate, Criminal, Probate, Corporations, Labor Relations and Zoning. Trials and Appeals in State and Federal Courts. Municipal, State and Federal Administrative Practice.
See Professional Biographies, NEW HAVEN, CONNECTICUT

Fasanella, George M. . . . . '47 '74 C.93 B.A. L.273 J.D. Dep. Chf. Clk., Supr. Ct.
Fasano, Christopher D. . . . . '75 '00 C.884 B.A. L.823 J.D. [🄰 Wiggin&D.]
Fasano, Leonard A., (BV) . . . . '58 '84 C.976 B.A. L.1029 J.D. 388 Orange St.
Fasano, Roland D. . . . . '48 '74 C.659 B.A. L.1202 J.D. Supr. Ct. J.
Faughnan, Joseph E., (BV) . . . . '50 '76 C.262 B.A. L.184 J.D. [Susman,D.&S.]
*PRACTICE AREAS: Civil Litigation; Commercial Law; Construction Law.
Faulkner, Joanne S. . . . . '38 '63 C.540 B.A. L.188 LL.B. 123 Avon St.
Fava, Richard A. '74 '00 C.659 B.S. L.30 J.D.
(adm. in NY; not adm. in CT) [🄰 Bergman,H.&R.]
Favale, Beth L. . . . . '72 '97 C.706 B.A. L.1252 J.D. [🄰 M.W.Mackniak]
Fay, Peter T., (BV) . . . . '65 '90 C.1030 B.A. L.945 J.D. [Neubert,P.&M.]
*PRACTICE AREAS: Commercial Litigation; Professional Malpractice Defense; Products Liability; Personal Injury.
Feldman, Richard C., (BV) . . . . '43 '68 C.705 B.A. L.184 J.D. [Evans,F.&B.]
*PRACTICE AREAS: Commercial Litigation; Banking Law; Leasing Law; Commercial Finance Law; Real Property.
Feliciano, Tanya . . . . '68 '94 C.183 B.A. L.306 J.D. 2 Whitney Ave.
Ferland, Niclas A. . . . . '67 '92 C.385 B.A. L.184 J.D. [Tyler C.&A.]
*PRACTICE AREAS: Bankruptcy; Commercial Finance.

Ferranti, John A., (BV) '63 '89 C.884 B.A. L.1029 J.D.
45 Court Street, 06511
Telephone: 203-562-1354 Fax: 203-498-2692
URL: http://www.lawyers.com/jaferrantilaw
***PRACTICE AREAS: Real Estate Law; Personal Injury Law; Landlord and Tenant Law; Collections; Criminal Law.**
Real Estate, Personal Injury, Landlord and Tenant Law, Collections, Criminal Law.
See Professional Biographies, NEW HAVEN, CONNECTICUT

Ferrara, Victoria T. . . . . '56 '85 C.1030 B.A. L.724 J.D. [Murphy,M.F.&N.] ⊙
Ferraro, V. James, (BV) . . . . '48 '74 C.1102 B.S. L.30 J.D. 234 Church St., Ste. 902
Filardi, Charles J., Jr. . . . . '56 '91 C.390 A.B. L.1029 J.D. [Cummings&L.] (⊙Stamford)
*PRACTICE AREAS: Bankruptcy; Debtor and Creditor; Commercial Litigation; Creditors Rights.

Fineberg, Norman, (AV) . . . . '41 '71 C.971 B.S. L.94 J.D. [Wiggin&D.]
*PRACTICE AREAS: Real Property Law; Real Estate Development; Real Estate Leasing; Condominium Law; Land Use Law.

Finn Dixon & Herling LLP
(See Stamford)

Fiss, Owen M. '38 '65 C.197 B.A. L.309 LL.B.
(adm. in NY; not adm. in CT) Yale Law Sch.

Fitzgerald, Anthony M., (AV) . . . . . . '44 '69 C.976 A.B. L.178 J.D. [Carmody&T.]
*PRACTICE AREAS: Civil Litigation; Business Torts; Public Utilities.

Fitzgerald, Edward J. '53 '82 C.276 B.S. L.472 J.D.
Senior Counsel, Southern New England Telephone Co.

Fitzgerald, Jamie Johnson . . . . . . '47 '72 C.478 A.B. L.145 J.D. [Cummings&L.]
*PRACTICE AREAS: Trademarks; Copyrights; Intellectual Property.

Fitzgerald, Stephen J. . . . . . . '63 '89 C.93 B.A. L.262 J.D. [A Garrison L.C.&R.]
*PRACTICE AREAS: Litigation.

Flamm, Brett C., (BV) . . . . . . '46 '77 C.178 B.A. L.472 J.D. 9 Trumball St.

Flanagan, John C. . . . . . . '21 '49 C.262 B.S. L.976 LL.B. Supr. Ct. J.

Fleming, Norman J. . . . . . . '53 '79 C&L.309 B.A., J.D. [Wiggin&D.]
*PRACTICE AREAS: Corporation Law; Mergers and Acquisitions Law; Securities Law; Debt and Equity Finance; Bond Finance.

Flynn, Robert B. . . . . . . '63 '91 C.602 B.A. L.276 J.D. [Tyler C.&A.]

Flynn, W. Paul, (AV) . . . . . . '26 '54 C.228 B.A. L.276 J.D. 1 Trumbull St.

Fornes, Kirk A., (BV) . . . . . . '59 '86 C.1031 B.A. L.1048 J.D. 59 Elm St.

Forte, Laura . . . . . . '63 '87 C.93 B.A. L.184 J.D. One Century Twr.

Fournier, Brian C. . . . . . . '69 '95 C.93 B.A. L.128 J.D. [Early,L.&S.]
*PRACTICE AREAS: Toxic Torts; Lead Poisoning; Civil Litigation; Criminal Defense; Personal Injury.

Fournier, Nicole M. . . . . . . '71 '97 C.689 B.A. L.1252 J.D. [A Lynch,T.K.&E.]
*PRACTICE AREAS: Civil Litigation; Appellate Practice; Criminal Defense.

Fracasse, Ronald J. . . . . . . '32 '57 C.976 B.A. L.93 LL.B. Supr. Ct. J.

Franchi, Richard M.
(See Guilford)

Francois, Linda P., (BV) . . . . . . '57 '82 C&L.184 B.A., J.D. [Cooper,W.C.&F.]

Fraser, Cecile Monique . . . . . . '65 '00 C.262 B.A. L.1292 J.D. [A Wiggin&D.]

Frechette, Matthew E., (BV) . . . . . . '62 '87 C.319 B.A. L.216 J.D. [Frechette&F.]

Frechette, Roger J., (AV) . . . . . . '28 '58 C.197 B.A. L.724 J.D. [Frechette&F.]

Frechette & Frechette, (AV) . . . . . . 12 Trumbull St.

Frederick, Mary Beth . . . . . . '55 '82 C.276 B.S.F.S. L.128 J.D. P.O. Box 1936

Freed, Daniel J. '27 '52 C&L.976 B.S., LL.B.
(adm. in NY; not adm. in CT) Clinical Prof. of Law, Yale Univ.‡

Freeman, Richard M. . . . . . . '47 '76 C&L.184 B.A., J.D. 129 Church St.

Freilich, Sharon Kowal . . . . . . '56 '80 C&L.273 B.A., J.D. [C Brenner,S.&W.]
*PRACTICE AREAS: Intellectual Property; Corporate Law; Securities Law; Pension Law; Employee Benefits Law.

Freiman, Jonathan Marc '64 '99 C.604 B.A. L.976 J.D.
(adm. in PA; not adm. in CT) 112 Bishop St.‡

Frey, Douglas A. . . . . . . '— '95 C.971 B.S.C.E. L.184 J.D. [A Garcia&M.]
*PRACTICE AREAS: Construction Litigation; Arbitration.

Friedler, Stephen G., (AV) . . . . . . '37 '63 C.645 B.S. L.446 LL.B. 142 Temple St.

Friedman, Roberta S., (BV) . . . . . . '45 '84 C.705 B.A. L.184 J.D. 383 Orange St.

Frontis, Constance E. '49 '83
C.19 B.A. L.1048 J.D. New Haven Legal Assistance Assn., Inc.

Fusco, Ellen M. . . . . . . '62 '92 C.690 B.S. L.1252 J.D. 205 Church St.‡

Galat, Bryan P. . . . . . . '76 '01 C.197 B.A. L.184 J.D. [A Bergman,H.&R.]

Galbo, Tara Justine . . . . . . '74 '00 C.708 B.A. L.1252 J.D. [A Votre&Assoc.]
*PRACTICE AREAS: Commercial Law; Personal Injury; Tax Law; International Business Law; Corporate Law.

Gallagher, William F., (AV) . . . . . . '37 '63 C.1030 B.S.S. L.184 LL.B. [Gallagher&C.]
*PRACTICE AREAS: Civil Litigation; Trials; Appeals; Personal Injury Litigation.

Gallagher & Calistro, (AV) BR
1377 Boulevard, P.O. Box 1925, 06509
Telephone: 203-624-4165 Fax: 203-865-5598 URL: http://www.gallagher-calistro.com
Email: lawoffices@gallagher-calistro.com URL: http://www.lawyers.com/gallagher-calistro
William F. Gallagher; Roger B. Calistro; Barbara L. Cox; Thomas J. Airone; Hugh D. Hughes.
General Civil Litigation and Appellate Practice in all Courts. Personal Injury Litigation, Business Litigation, Commercial Litigation.
See Professional Biographies, NEW HAVEN, CONNECTICUT

Gallant, Anne C. . . . . . . '53 '80 C.681 B.A. L.564 J.D. 700 State St.

Gallant, Edward, (BV) . . . . . . '21 '56 C.174 B.A. L.184 J.D. 700 State St.

Gallant, Keith Bradoc, (AV) . . . . . . '52 '78 C.050 B.A. L.184 J.D. [Cummings&L.]
*PRACTICE AREAS: Estate Planning and Administration; Probate Litigation; Elder Law; Disabilities Law; Fiduciary Litigation.

Garabedian, Todd E. . . . . . . '62 '94 C.112 B.S. L.1202 J.D. [C Wiggin&D.] (Pat.)
*PRACTICE AREAS: Intellectual Property; Biochemical Technology; Pharmaceutical Intellectual Property; Biotechnology Licensing; Trademarks.

Garcia, Raymond A., (BV) . . . . . . '50 '79 C.1102 B.A. L.365 J.D. [Garcia&M.]
*PRACTICE AREAS: Construction Litigation; Franchise Litigation.

Garcia & Milas, A Professional Corporation, (BV)
44 Trumbull Street, 06510-1001
Telephone: 203-773-3824 Facsimile: 203-782-2312
URL: http://www.lawyers.com/garciamilaslaw
Raymond A. Garcia; Jane I. Milas;—William S. Wilson, II; Douglas A. Frey; Warren F. Sasso, Jr.; Lori A. Petruzzelli; Frederick E. Hedberg; Steven R. Kolodziej.
Construction Litigation, Real Estate, Arbitration, Mediation, Commercial Litigation, Franchise Litigation.
See Professional Biographies, NEW HAVEN, CONNECTICUT

Garrett, Elizabeth Mary . . . . . . '68 '99 C.1102 B.S. L.184 J.D. [A Wiggin&D.]

Garrison, Joseph D., (AV) . . . . . . '43 '68 C.918 B.A. L.188 J.D. [Garrison L.C.&R.]
*PRACTICE AREAS: Employment Law; Personal Injury Law.

Garrison Levin-Epstein Chimes & Richardson, P.C., (AV)
405 Orange Street, 06511
Telephone: 203-777-4425 Fax: 203-776-3965
URL: http://www.garrisonlaw.com
Joseph D. Garrison; Ethan A. Levin-Epstein; Lewis H. Chimes; Robert A. Richardson; Jeffrey S. Bagnell;—Stephen J. Fitzgerald; Morris J. "Mickey" Busca.
General Civil and Criminal Practice before State and Federal Courts. Labor, Employee Rights and Benefits, Personal Injury, Product Liability, Professional Negligence, Civil Rights, Professional Licensure and Discipline, Workers Compensation Law. Trials and Appeals.
Reference: Bank of New Haven.
See Professional Biographies, NEW HAVEN, CONNECTICUT

Garrity-Rokous, Frances . . . . . . '61 '94 C.788 A.B. L.976 J.D. 1960 Chapel St.

Garrity-Rokous, Gates . . . . . . '63 '93 C.858 B.A. L.976 J.D. [C Wiggin&D.]
*PRACTICE AREAS: Litigation; White Collar Criminal Defense; Corporate Law; Criminal Law; Civil Litigation.

Geisler, Thomas M., Jr., (AV Ⓣ) '43 '68 C&L.309 B.A., J.D.
205 Church Street, Suite 508, 06510
Telephone: 203-787-0077 Fax: 203-773-1427
Email: T1827@aol.com URL: http://www.lawyers.com/tmgeisler
(This Listing Continued)

Geisler, Thomas M., Jr. (Continued)
General Civil Practice and Litigation in State and Federal Courts, Corporate, Commercial and Business Law, Appellate Practice and Arbitrations.
See Professional Biographies, NEW HAVEN, CONNECTICUT

Geller, Roberta . . . . . . '— '92 C.1102 B.S. L.1029 J.D. [Scheirer&G.]

Gemeiner, Howard I., (AV) . . . . . . '45 '69 C.563 B.A. L.184 J.D. 132 Temple St.

George, Helen W. . . . . . . '— '88 C.823 A.B. L.724 J.D. One Century Twr.

Gerety, Miles S., (BV) . . . . . . '50 '78 C.918 B.A. L.1162 J.D. Asst. Pub. Def.

Gerroir, Michele B. . . . . . . '70 '96 C.823 B.A. L.930 J.D. [A Wiggin&D.]

Gershon, Colin M., (BV) '46 '71 C.165 A.B. L.902 J.D.
1 Century Tower, 5th Floor, 265 Church Street, 06510
Telephone: 203-782-7798 Fax: 203-776-7075
***PRACTICE AREAS: Employee Benefits Law; Estates and Trusts.**
Employee Benefits Law, Estates and Trusts.
See Professional Biographies, NEW HAVEN, CONNECTICUT

Gewirtz, Paul '47 '73 C.178 B.A. L.976 J.D.
(adm. in DC; not adm. in CT) Prof. of Law, Yale Law Sch.

Giaimo, Gerald T. . . . . . . '69 '94 C.321 B.A. L.184 J.D. [A Tyler C.&A.]
*PRACTICE AREAS: Bodily Injury Litigation; Criminal Defense; Employment Law.

Gibson, Marshal D., (AV) . . . . . . '44 '70 C.156 A.B. L.1009 J.D. [M.D.Gibson]
*PRACTICE AREAS: Estate Planning; Pension; Federal Income Taxation; Corporate; Probate.

Gibson and Behman, P.C.
18 Trumbull Street (⊙Boston, Burlington, MA; Manchester, NH; New York, NY; Providence, RI)

Gibson, Marshal D., Professional Corporation, (AV)
2 Whitney Avenue, 06510
Telephone: 203-562-8080 Fax: 203-624-3388
Email: mgibtax@aol.com URL: http://www.lawyers.com/mgibson-tax-atty
Marshal D. Gibson (Board Certified Taxation Lawyer, Florida Bar Board of Legal Specialization and Education).
Federal Income Taxation, Estate Planning, Corporate, Pension, Probate Law and Tax Litigation.
Reference: New Haven Savings Bank.
See Professional Biographies, NEW HAVEN, CONNECTICUT

Gildea, Brian M., (BV) . . . . . . '39 '70 C.676 B.A. L.818 J.D. 512 Blake St.

Gillis, Edward M. . . . . . . '65 '92 C.174 B.A. L.882 J.D. [Gillis&G.]
*PRACTICE AREAS: Personal Injury; Worker's Compensation; Family Law; Criminal Law; Business Law.

Gillis, Howard T., (BV) . . . . . . '35 '60 C.976 B.A. L.184 LL.B. [Gillis&G.]
*PRACTICE AREAS: Personal Injury; Worker's Compensation; Family Law; Business Law; Probate.

Gillis, Joseph L. . . . . . . '63 '91 C.174 B.A. L.1194 J.D. [Gillis&G.]
*PRACTICE AREAS: Personal Injury; Workers Compensation; Family Law; Criminal Law; Business Law.

Gillis & Gillis, P.C., (BV)
Two Whitney Avenue, Suite 502, 06510
Telephone: 203-562-5104 Telefax: 203-495-6476
Email: gillislawct@snet.net URL: http://www.lawyers.com/gillis&gillis
Howard T. Gillis; Joseph L. Gillis; Edward M. Gillis; Lisa M. Kolb;—Enzo A. Pellegrino.
General Practice including Litigation, Personal Injury including Automobile, Fall Down and Work Related Injuries, Business, Family, Real Estate, Probate, Trust and Wills, Estate and Tax Planning, Criminal, Employment, Social Security Disability and Transportation Law. Trials in all State Courts, Federal Courts and Administrative Agencies.
Approved Attorney For: Commonwealth Land Title Insurance, Co.; Stewart Title Guaranty Company; Lawyers Title Insurance.
References: The Lafayette American Bank & Trust Company; Shawmut Bank; Centerbank; New Haven Savings Bank.
See Professional Biographies, NEW HAVEN, CONNECTICUT

Gillooly, Dennis W., (BV) . . . . . . '60 '86 C.855 B.A. L.184 J.D. [Kennedy,J.D.&G.]
*PRACTICE AREAS: Personal Injury Law; Products Liability Law; Workers Compensation; Professional Malpractice; Insurance Disputes.

Gilson, Elizabeth P., (BV) . . . . . . '48 '87 C.1056 B.A. L.184 J.D. 383 Orange St.

Gimple, Sidney, (BV) . . . . . . '26 '55 C.184 B.S. L.94 LL.B. 129 Church St., Suite 400

Giovanniello, Earle, (BV) '59 '85 C.309 B.A. L.477 J.D.
59 Elm Street Suite 215, 06510
Telephone: 203-777-4003 Fax: 203-777-3993
Email: egiovanniello@erols.com URL: http://www.lawyers.com/giovanniellolaw
***PRACTICE AREAS: Foreclosures; Bankruptcy; Civil Litigation; Commercial Litigation; Appellate Practice.**
Commercial Litigation, Criminal, Appellate Practice, Foreclosures, Class Actions, Civil Rights and Bankruptcy.
See Professional Biographies, NEW HAVEN, CONNECTICUT

Girard, Margaret F. '52 '79 C.999 B.A. L.184 J.D.
Sr. Coun., Southern New England Telecom. Corp.

Glass, Joseph, (BV) . . . . . . '25 '56 C.184 B.S. L.260 LL.B. 267 Orange St.

Glassman, Richard A. '49 '74 C.860 B.S.E. L.184 J.D.
Chf. Admin. Offr., Worltek Travel

Glenn, Marc L. . . . . . . '70 '99 C.831 B.A. L.1252 J.D. [A W.M.Philpot,Jr.]

Glynn, Elisabeth, (BV) . . . . . . '— '84 C.1102 B.S. L.306 J.D. [Levine&G.]

Godbout, Kevin M. . . . . . . '68 '94 C.165 B.A. L.1252 J.D. [A Neubert,P.&M.]
*PRACTICE AREAS: Commercial Litigation; Construction Litigation; Premises Liability; Products Liability.

Goetsch, Charles C., (AV) . . . . . . '50 '78 C.103 A.B. L.184 J.D. [Cahill,G.&D.]

Goglia, Michelle . . . . . . '75 '00 C.165 B.A. L.306 J.D. [A Brenner,S.&W.]
*PRACTICE AREAS: Commercial Litigation; Corporate Law; Environmental.

Goldfield, Carl, (BV) . . . . . . '50 '75 C.597 B.A. L.107 J.D. [Meneo&G.]

Goldman, Renée . . . . . . '66 '92 C.401 B.A. L.1338 J.D. 235 Church St.

Goldstein, Abraham S. '25 '49 C.563 B.B.A. L.976 LL.B.
(adm. in DC; not adm. in CT) Yale Law Sch.

Goldstein, Joseph '23 '54 C.197 A.B. L.976 LL.B.
(adm. in VA; not adm. in CT) Yale Law Sch.

Goldstein, Sonja, (BV) . . . . . . '26 '52 C.054 B.S. L.976 LL.B. [A Neubert,P.&M.]
*PRACTICE AREAS: Health Law; Managed Care; Physicians Contracts.

Gollaher, Merton G. . . . . . . '62 '91 C.31 B.A. L.184 J.D. [Wiggin&D.]
*PRACTICE AREAS: Corporate Law; Health Care; Biotechnology; Business Law; Mergers, Acquisitions and Divestitures.

Goodbody, Katharine S. . . . . . . '51 '79 C.659 B.A. L.128 J.D. 261 Bradley Street

Goodman, Mark L., (BV) . . . . . . '50 '83 C.705 B.A. L.1202 J.D. [McNamara&G.]

Gordon, Elaine . . . . . . '49 '76 C.597 B.S. L.184 J.D. Supr. Ct. J.

Goren, Barbara . . . . . . '55 '83 C&L.976 B.A., J.D. 15 Edgehill Rd.

Gorman, John R., (AV) . . . . . . '34 '60 C.197 A.B. L.184 J.D. [Gorman&E.]

Gorman & Enright, P.C., (AV) . . . . . . 59 Elm Street

Goss, Victoria A. . . . . . . '52 '83 C.228 B.A. L.469 J.D. 934 Grand Ave.

Gould, Carolyn P., (AV) . . . . . . '37 '71 C.914 A.B. L.184 J.D. [Mulvey,O.&G.]
*PRACTICE AREAS: Insurance Law; Estate Administration; Estate Planning.

Granquist, Frances B. . . . . . . '62 '87 C.1030 B.S. L.469 J.D. [Pellegrino]

Grant, Richard L. . . . . . . '65 '96 C.473 B.A. L.930 J.D. [A Lippman&O.]

Grazioso, Frank M., (BV) . . . . . . '39 '64 C.976 A.B. L.145 J.D. [Grazioso&H.]

Grazioso & Hosen, (BV) . . . . . . 746 Chapel St.

Green, Eric L. . . . . . . '70 '99 C.1019 B.B.A. L.1202 J.D. Centerprise Advisors

Greenberg, David B., (AV) . . . . '20 '49 C&L.184 B.S., LL.B. [Greenberg,H.C.&S.]
Greenberg, Frederick L., (BV) . . . . '26 '53 C.999 B.A. L.596 LL.B. [Greenberg&C.]
Greenberg, Lawrence J., (BV) . . . . '47 '72 C.264 A.B. L.1292 J.D. [Bernblum&G.]
Greenberg & Costa, P.C., (BV) . . . . 934 Grand Ave.
Greenberg, Hurwitz, Cooper & Silverman, P.C., (AV) . . . . 667 State St.
Greenfield, James R., (AV) . . . . '26 '50 C.67 B.S. L.976 LL.B. [Ⓒ Tyler C.&A.]
*PRACTICE AREAS: Trial Law; Family Law; Matrimonial Law; Divorce.
Greer, Daniel, (BV) . . . . '40 '64 C.674 A.B. L.976 LL.B. 278 Orange St.
Grigsby, David C. . . . . '67 '96 C.976 B.A. L.477 J.D. [Ⓐ Wiggin&D.]
Grodski, Alexander J. . . . . '70 '00 C.776 B.A L.184 J.D. [Ⓐ Wiggin&D.]
Groob, Ressler & Mulqueen, A Professional Corporation, (BV) . . . . 123 York St.
Groves, Jennifer L. . . . . '73 '98 C.976 B.A. L.93 J.D. [Ⓐ Updike,K.&S.] (⊙Hartford)
*PRACTICE AREAS: Professional Liability Defense; Insurance Defense; Human Services.
Grudberg, David T., (BV) . . . . '60 '86 C.976 B.A. L.575 J.D. [Jacobs,G.B.&D.]
*PRACTICE AREAS: Criminal Defense; Personal Injury Litigation; Business Litigation; Appellate Practice.
Grudberg, Ira B., (AV) . . . . '33 '60 C&L.976 B.A., LL.B. [Jacobs,G.B.&D.]
*PRACTICE AREAS: Criminal Defense; Personal Injury Litigation; Business Litigation; Appellate Practice.
Gruen, Peter H., (AV) . . . . '54 '79 C.184 B.A. L.94 J.D. [Wiggin&D.]
*PRACTICE AREAS: International and Federal Taxation Law; Low Income Housing Tax Credits; Connecticut Taxation Law.

Gruenbaum, Jerry, Law Offices of '55 '79 C.102 B.S. L.1048 J.D.
205 Church Street, Third Floor, 06510
Telephone: 203-498-6080 Fax: 203-498-6022
Email: jerry@seclawyer.org URL: http://www.lawyers.com/gruenbaum
***PRACTICE AREAS: Securities Law; Corporate Law; Taxation; Franchise Law; Trust and Estate Law.**
Corporate Law, Securities, Business Law, Business Tax, Mergers and Acquisitions, Trusts and Estates, International Law.
See Professional Biographies, NEW HAVEN, CONNECTICUT

Gruszkiewicz, Marjorie R. . . . . '62 '90 C.184 B.A. L.1048 J.D. [Ⓐ Marcus]
*PRACTICE AREAS: Bankruptcy; Foreclosure; Litigation.
Gulliver, Carl T., (AV) . . . . '51 '80 C.611 B.A. L.273 J.D. [Coan,L.G.&M.]
*PRACTICE AREAS: Bankruptcy Law; Creditors Rights Law; Commercial Law.
Hadden, Wm. L., Jr. . . . . '25 '53 C&L.184 B.A., LL.B. Supr. Ct. J.
Hall, H. Gordon, (BV) '54 '80 C.309 A.B. L.184 J.D.
Asst. U.S. Atty., U.S. Dept. of Jus.
Hambleton, David P., (AV) . . . . '39 '64 C.197 A.B. L.178 LL.B. [Ⓒ Susman,D.&S.]
*PRACTICE AREAS: Corporation Law; Business Law.
Hancock, J. Vance, (BV) '59 '84 C.976 B.A. L.188 J.D.
Sr. Coun., Southern New England Telecom. Corp.
Hanf, Noel E., (AV) . . . . '40 '65 C.976 A.B. L.309 LL.B. [Wiggin&D.]
*PRACTICE AREAS: Public Utility Law; Tax Exempt Organizations Law.
Haray, Jonathan W. . . . . '69 '95 C.1044 B.A. L.823 J.D. [Ⓐ Wiggin&D.]★
Hardy, David S. . . . . '73 '99 C.165 A.B. L.184 J.D. [Ⓐ Carmody&T.]
*PRACTICE AREAS: Civil Litigation.

Harlow, Adams & Friedman, P.C.
(See Milford)

Harmon, Gerald Lewis . . . . '60 '93 C.201 B.S. L.93 J.D. One Century Twr.
Harrison, Jane C. . . . . '72 '97 C.321 B.A. L.184 J.D. 157 Church Street
Harrison, Robert D. . . . . '47 '85 C.31 B.A. L.976 J.D. 127 Wall Street
Hartmere, Michael . . . . '43 '73 C.03 B.A. L.669 J.D. Supr. Ct. J.
Hawkins, Terence S., (BV) . . . . '56 '82 C.976 B.A. L.966 J.D. 129 Church St.
Hayman, Margaret . . . . '47 '75 C.604 B.A. L.588 J.D. Asst. Pub. Def.
Healey, Arthur H. . . . . '20 '48 C.855 B.A. L.309 LL.B. Trial Ref. J.
Heaphy, Mark W. . . . . '69 '96 C.945 B.A. L.893 J.D. [Ⓐ Wiggin&D.]
Heath, Kenneth Decatur . . . . '70 '99 C.893 B.A. L.976 J.D. [Ⓐ Wiggin&D.]
Hecht, Geoffrey A., (BV) . . . . '46 '70 C.264 B.A. L.472 J.D. [Virshup,C.&H.]
Hedberg, Frederick E. . . . . '66 '98 C.184 B.S.E. L.1252 J.D. [Ⓐ Garcia&M.]
*PRACTICE AREAS: Construction Law; Commercial Litigation.
Hendel, Caroline Grace, (BV) '61 '86
C.976 B.A. L.309 J.D. Assoc. Gen. Coun., Yale Univ.
Hershman, Peter D., (BV) . . . . '47 '72 C.665 B.A. L.184 J.D. [Siegel,O.S.&Z.]
*PRACTICE AREAS: Corporate Law; Estate Planning Law; Employee Benefit Plans Law.
Heslin, Lisa Page . . . . '66 '91 C.976 B.A. L.276 J.D. [Wiggin&D.]
Hibson, Emmet P., Jr. . . . . '64 '00 C.1083 B.S.B.A. L.1252 J.D. [Ⓐ Licari&W.]
*PRACTICE AREAS: Labor and Employment; Civil Litigation; Workers' Compensation.
Hilcoff, Stephan L., (P.C.), (BV) . . . '34 '59 C.184 B.S. L.94 LL.B. 209 Orange St., 4th Fl.
Hill, William E. . . . . '50 '75 C.1030 B.A. L.184 J.D. Asst. Clk., Supr. Ct.
Hillis, Michael S. . . . . '61 '91 [Dombroski,K.&H.]
Hinton, Robert C. . . . . '62 '95 C.870 B.S. L.184 J.D. [Ⓐ Tyler C.&A.]
Hirschoff, Jon T., (AV) . . . . '41 '67 C.813 A.B. L.976 LL.B. [Tyler C.&A.]
*PRACTICE AREAS: Corporate, Mergers and Acquisitions, Securities.
Hoffnung, Daniel N., (BV) . . . . '50 '87 C.1252 B.A. L.184 J.D. [Winnick,R.C.E.&H.]
*PRACTICE AREAS: Commercial Law; Finance; Real Property; Business Organization; Licensing.
Hogan, John W., Jr., (AV) . . . . '39 '64 C.321 A.B. L.184 LL.B. [Hogan&R.]
*PRACTICE AREAS: Commercial Banking; Mergers and Acquisitions; Corporate Planning; Commercial Real Estate; Commercial Contracts.

Hogan & Rini, P.C., (AV)
234 Church Street, Suite 803, 06510-1804
Telephone: 203-787-4191 Telecopier: 203-777-4032
URL: http://www.lawyers.com/hogan&rini
John W. Hogan, Jr.; Joseph L. Rini.
Business Formation, Commercial Banking, Civil Rights Section 1983, Public Construction Law, International Commercial Contracts, Executive Compensation, Medical Staff Contracts, Real Estate Development, Probate Administration, Land Use Regulation, Limited Liability Corporations, Contested Trusts and Estates, Municipal Redevelopment, Mergers and Acquisitions, Civil Litigation, Commercial Real Estate Finance, Economic Development, Taxation, Banking Regulation, Business Development, Commercial Real Estate Development, Shopping Center Development, Corporate Law, Corporate Finance, Corporate Governance, Nonprofit Organizations Law, Nonprofit Corporations, Employee Benefits, Employer Rights, Estate Planning, Local Government Civil Rights, Municipal Law, Municipal Civil Rights, Municipal Redevelopment, Appellate Practice, Civil Appeals.
See Professional Biographies, NEW HAVEN, CONNECTICUT

Holder, Angela Roddey . . . . '38 '60 C.298 B.A. L.861 J.D. Yale Univ. Sch. of Med.
Holt, Philetus H., IV . . . . '36 '62 C&L.976 B.A., LL.B. 900 Chapel St.‡
Hornkohl, Romey K. . . . . '73 '99 C.1252 B.A. L.184 J.D [Ⓐ Neubert,P.&M.]
*PRACTICE AREAS: Health Care Law; Commercial Litigation; Bankruptcy.
Hornkohl, Roomey K . . . . '73 '99 C.1252 B.A. L.306 J.D. 195 Church St. 13th Fl
Horowitz, Robert H., (AV) '37 '65 C.575 A.B. L.976 J.D.
157 Church Street, 19th Floor (⊙New York, NY)‡
Hosen, Sheldon D., (BV) . . . . '39 '64 C.976 A.B. L.145 J.D. [Grazioso&H.]
Hoskins, Nancy I., (BV) . . . . '34 '81 C.914 B.A. L.184 J.D. 227 Everit St.

Hudson Cook, LLP, (AV)
Building One, Unit 7, 3rd Floor, 85 Willow Street, 06511 ⊙
Telephone: 203-776-1911 Fax: 203-776-1922
Email: contact@hudco.com URL: http://www.hudco.com
Elizabeth C. Yen.

(This Listing Continued)

Hudson Cook, LLP (Continued)
Consumer Financial Services.
Linthicum, Maryland Office: 971 Corporate Boulevard, Suite 301, 21909-2232. Telephone: 410-684-3200. Fax: 410-684-2001.
Gardena, California Office: 1515 West 190th Street, Suite 410, 90248. Telephone: 310-851-5522. Fax: 310-851-5526.
Charlottesville, Virginia Office: 301 E. Market Street, 22902. Telephone: 804-220-9310. Fax: 804-220-9311.
Clifton Park, New York Office: 632 Plank Road, Suite 201, 12065. Telephone: 518-383-9440. Fax: 518-383-9401.
See Professional Biographies, NEW HAVEN, CONNECTICUT

Hughes, Hugh D. . . . . '70 '97 C.674 A.B. L.184 J.D. [Gallagher&C.]
*PRACTICE AREAS: Appeals.
Hughes, John B., (BV) . . . . '52 '78 C.1030 B.A. L.724 J.D. Asst. U.S. Atty.
Hughes, Paul A. . . . . '63 '93 C.184 B.A. L.306 J.D. [Mintz,L.C.F.G.&P.]
*PRACTICE AREAS: Venture Capital; Emerging Growth Companies; Mergers and Acquisitions; Public Offerings; Joint Ventures.
Hurwitz, Norman E., (AV) . . . . '32 '57 C&L.976 A.B., LL.B. [Greenberg,H.C.&S.]
Hurwitz, Samuel M., (BV) . . . . '53 '83 C.178 B.A. L.813 J.D. [Brenner,S.&W.]
*PRACTICE AREAS: Taxation; Estate Planning; Business.
Hurwitz, Scott A. . . . . '66 '91 C.477 A.B. L.188 J.D. 667 State St.
Hyland, James M., (BV) . . . . '62 '90 C.93 A.B. L.1009 J.D. [Ⓐ Mulvey,O.&G.]
*PRACTICE AREAS: Trials; Civil Litigation.
Hyman, Herbert G., (BV) . . . . '33 '60 C.976 B.A. L.893 LL.B. 900 Chapel St.
Hyman, Thomas S. . . . . '64 '90 C&L.884 B.A., J.D. [Kantrovitz&B.]
Iacurci, Michael P. . . . . '70 '97 C.30 B.A. L.1252 J.D. [Letizia,A.C.]
Iannotti, Frank A., (AV) . . . . '54 '81 683 State St.
Inkster, Elizabeth M., (BV) . . . . '51 '82 C&L.184 B.A., J.D. Asst. Pub. Def.
Insler, Bernard, (BV) . . . . '17 '46 C&L.569 A.B., LL.B. [Mongillo&I.]
Ippolito, Alphonse, (BV) . . . . '57 '82 C.309 A.B. L.94 J.D. 388 Orange St.
Irwin, Craig D. . . . . '58 '83 C.882 B.A. L.818 J.D. Merrill Lynch

Jacobi, Kappel & Case, P.C.
(See Milford)

Jacobs, Bruce D., (BV) . . . . '51 '77 C&L.910 B.A., J.D. [Jacobs&J.]
*PRACTICE AREAS: Personal Injury Law; Medical Malpractice; Products Liability Law; Civil Trial Practice.
Jacobs, Howard A., (AV) . . . . '24 '47 C&L.477 A.B., J.D. [Jacobs,G.B.&D.]
*PRACTICE AREAS: Personal Injury Litigation; Domestic Relations Litigation.
Jacobs, Irene Prosky, (BV) . . . . '51 '86 C.1044 B.A. L.184 J.D. [Jacobs&J.]
*PRACTICE AREAS: Personal Injury Law; Medical Malpractice; Products Liability Law; Civil Trial Practice.
Jacobs, Richard L., (AV) . . . . '30 '57 C&L.976 B.A., LL.B. [Jacobs,J.&S.]
*PRACTICE AREAS: Personal Injury; Medical Malpractice; Products Liability; Workers Compensation; Federal Employers Liability Act.
Jacobs, Stanley A., (AV) . . . . '26 '50 C.871 B.S. L.976 LL.B. [Jacobs&J.]
*PRACTICE AREAS: Personal Injury Law; Medical Malpractice; Products Liability Law; Civil Law.
Jacobs, Steven D., (BV) . . . . '58 '85 C.855 B.A. L.665 J.D. [Jacobs,J.&S.]
*PRACTICE AREAS: Personal Injury; Medical Malpractice; Product Liability; Federal Employers Liability Act; Civil Litigation.
Jacobs, Susan Laura . . . . '53 '79 C.112 B.A. L.809 J.D. P.O. Box 5002

Jacobs, Grudberg, Belt & Dow, P.C., (AV) BB
350 Orange Street, P.O. Box 606, 06503
Telephone: 203-772-3100 Fax: 203-772-1691 URL: http://www.lawyers.com/jgb&d
Email: jacobslaw@jacobslaw.com URL: http://www.jacobslaw.com
Israel J. Jacobs (1918-1963); Howard A. Jacobs; Ira B. Grudberg; David L. Belt; William F. Dow, III; Jonathan Katz; William M. Bloss; David T. Grudberg; Steven J. DeFrank; Bernard C. Christianson;—Joseph J. Packtor; Rosemarie Paine; Alinor C. Sterling; Trisha Morris Porto.
General Trial and Appellate Practice in all Courts. Personal Injury, Medical Malpractice, Product Liability, Insurance, Criminal, Constitutional, Civil Rights, Unfair Competition, Antitrust, Securities, Business Torts, Employment, Environmental, Real Estate, Construction and Family Law Litigation.
See Professional Biographies, NEW HAVEN, CONNECTICUT

Jacobs & Jacobs, (AV) BB
Granite Square, 700 State Street, 3rd Floor, 06511
Telephone: 203-777-2300 Fax: 203-787-5628
Email: info@jacobs-jacobs.com URL: http://www.jacobs-jacobs.com
Members of Firm: Israel J. Jacobs (1918-1963); Stanley A. Jacobs; Bruce D. Jacobs; Irene Prosky Jacobs; Charles R. Douthat;—Kevin Ryder.
Practice Limited to Personal Injury, Medical Malpractice and Products Liability Law.
Reference: BankBoston.
See Professional Biographies, NEW HAVEN, CONNECTICUT

Jacobs, Jacobs & Shannon, P.C., (AV)
265 Orange Street, 06510
Telephone: 203-562-6111 Fax: 203-624-8752
Email: jjslaw@msn.com
Israel J. Jacobs (1918-1963); Richard L. Jacobs; Steven D. Jacobs; John M. Shannon.
General Trial Practice in all Courts. Tort, Personal Injury, Malpractice, Products Liability, Federal Employers Liability Act, Employment Discrimination, Criminal, Workers Compensation, Family, Eminent Domain, Appellate Practice.
Reference: New Haven Savings Bank
See Professional Biographies, NEW HAVEN, CONNECTICUT

Jacobs Partners LLC
(See Norwalk)

Jaffe, Mitchell S., (P.C.), (BV) . . . . '55 '79 C.1044 B.A. L.569 J.D. [Brenner,S.&W.]
*PRACTICE AREAS: Commercial Real Estate; Commercial Leasing; Real Estate Finance; Condominium Law; Loan Workouts.

Januszewski, McQuillan and DeNigris
(See New Britain)

Jeffress, Bart Duncan . . . . '71 '99 C.367 B.A. L.976 J.D. [Ⓐ Wiggin&D.]
Jelley, S. Robert, (AV) . . . . '30 '61 C.197 A.B. L.309 LL.B. [Ⓒ Wiggin&D.]
*PRACTICE AREAS: Litigation; Environmental Law.
Jensen, Timothy P. . . . . '67 '97 C.858 B.A. L.1252 J.D. [Ⓐ Tyler C.&A.]
Johnson, David H., (AV) . . . . '50 '76 C.339 B.S. L.146 J.D. [Kennedy,J.D.&G.]
*PRACTICE AREAS: Personal Injury Law; Medical Malpractice Law; Products Liability Law.
Johnson, Kenneth A. '59 '87 C.188 B.A. L.107 J.D.
(adm. in NY; not adm. in CT) One Century Twr.‡
Johnson, Stuart C. . . . . '63 '95 C.164 B.A. L.588 J.D. [Ⓐ Wiggin&D.]
Jolles, Joel M., (BV) . . . . '62 '87 C&L.1029 B.S., J.D. 27 Elm St., 3rd Fl.
Jones, Clarance J. . . . . '43 '70 C.864 B.A. L.329 J.D. Supr. Ct. J.
Jones, D. Terence, (AV) . . . . '46 '74 C.696 B.A. L.976 J.D. [Wiggin&D.]
*PRACTICE AREAS: Corporation Law; Mergers and Acquisitions Law; Securities Law.
Jones, Durrick O. K. . . . . '30 '67 C.512 B.A. L.329 LL.B. 71 Vista Terr.
Jones, Mary A. '69 '95 C.45 B.A. L.1243 J.D.
(adm. in AR; not adm. in CT) 652 Prospect St.
Jones, Scott M. . . . . '66 '92 C&L.184 B.S., J.D. Off. of Pub. Def.
Jones, Sonia M. . . . . '74 '00 C.184 B.A. L.1360 J.D. [Ⓐ Lynch,T.K.&E.]
*PRACTICE AREAS: Civil Litigation; Criminal Defense.
Jongbloed, Peter S., (AV) . . . . '58 '85 C.855 B.A. L.1252 J.D. Asst. U.S. Atty.

Judelson, Bruce I. ... '52 '77 C.453 B.S. L.309 J.D. [Bergman,H.&R.]
*PRACTICE AREAS: Business; Estate Planning; Taxation (Local, Personal Property, State, Federal or International Law).
Kahn, Gerald H., (AV) ... '44 '70 C.976 B.A. L.477 J.D. [Kahn&S.]
*PRACTICE AREAS: Family Law; Divorce; Custody; Alimony; Child Support.

Kahn and Stark, LLC, (AV)
110 Whitney Avenue, 06510
Telephone: 203-777-0506 Facsimile: 203-777-9971 URL: http://www.mediator.com/divorceresources
URL: http://www.lawyers.com/kahnandstark
Gerald H. Kahn; Barbara Kahn Stark;—Sheri L. Berman.
Family Law.
See Professional Biographies, NEW HAVEN, CONNECTICUT

Kaisen, Gary C. ... '66 '95 C.855 B.A. L.93 J.D. [Ⓐ Milano&W.]
*PRACTICE AREAS: Litigation; Commercial Litigation; General Practice.
Kakalik, Mary A. ... '44 '91 C.475 B.A. L.1029 J.D. Off. of Hearings & App., S.S.A.
Kantrovitz, Howard E., (BV) ... '40 '69 C&L.184 B.A., J.D. [Kantrovitz&B.]
Kantrovitz & Brownstein, P.C., (BV) ... 1764 Litchfield Turnpike
Kaplan, Anthony E., (BV) ... '57 '85 C.881 A.B. L.1019 J.D. Asst. U.S. Atty.
Kaplan, Burton A., (BV) ... '46 '71 C.184 B.S. L.1009 J.D. Supvr. Asst. State's Atty.
Kaplan, Paul M., (BV) ... '59 '84 C.94 B.A. L.982 J.D. 1948 Chapel St. (⊙Orange)
Katon, Thomas E., (BV) ... '59 '86 C.659 B.A. L.1029 J.D. [Susman,D.&S.]
*PRACTICE AREAS: Civil Litigation; Insurance Defense; Employment Law; Criminal Law.
Katz, Barbara Hadley, (AV) ... '53 '78 C.183 B.A. L.588 J.D. 57 Trumbull Street
Katz, Ivan M., (BV) ... '53 '78 C&L.276 B.A., J.D. 57 Trumbull St.
Katz, Jonathan, (BV) ... '53 '79 C.184 B.A. L.588 J.D. [Jacobs,G.B.&D.]
*PRACTICE AREAS: Personal Injury Litigation; Environmental Litigation.
Katz, Susan L. ... '48 '86 C.771 B.A. L.184 J.D. Yale Univ. Sch. of Medicine
Keefe, Hugh F., (AV) ... '43 '67 C.1252 B.S. L.184 J.D. [Lynch,T.K.&E.]
*PRACTICE AREAS: Civil Litigation; Criminal Litigation; Matrimonial Law.
Keefe, John J., Jr., (AV) ... '47 '80 C.1156 B.S. L.184 J.D. [Lynch,T.K.&E.]
*PRACTICE AREAS: Criminal Law; Domestic Relations; Workers Compensation.
Kelland, Christopher A. ... '71 '99 C.184 B.A. L.306 J.D. [Ⓐ Tyler C.&A.]
Kelly, George J., Jr. ... '47 '74 [Siegel,O.S.&Z.]
*PRACTICE AREAS: Commercial Litigation; Labor and Employment Litigation.
Kelly, Peter A., (BV) ... '41 '72 C.870 B.S. L.477 J.D. 385 Orange St.
Kelly, Stacie A. ... '75 '00 C.472 B.A. L.309 J.D. [Ⓐ Wiggin&D.]
Kelmachter, Barry L. ... '46 '79 C.823 B.S. L.30 J.D. [Bachman&L.] (See Pat. Sect.)
*PRACTICE AREAS: Patents; Trademarks; Copyrights; Unfair Competition; Licensing Law.
Kennedy, Jeffrey W. ... '67 '94 C.184 B.A. L.1048 J.D. [Ⓐ Milano&W.]
*PRACTICE AREAS: Insurance Defense; Workers Compensation; Products Liability; Appellate Practice.
Kennedy, John J., Jr., (AV) ... '53 '78 C.976 B.A. L.184 J.D. [Kennedy,J.D.&G.]
*PRACTICE AREAS: Personal Injury Law; Medical Malpractice Law; Products Liability Law.
Kennedy, Kevin M. ... '66 '91 C.183 B.A. L.184 J.D. [Wiggin&D.]
*PRACTICE AREAS: Litigation; Arbitration; Franchise Litigation; Franchise Arbitration; Business Litigation.

Kennedy, Johnson, D'Elia & Gillooly L.L.C., (AV)
Long Wharf Maritime Center, 545 Long Wharf Drive, 06511
Telephone: 203-865-8430 Fax: 203-865-5345 URL: http://www.kennedyjohnson.com
URL: http://www.lawyers.com/kjdglaw
Members of Firm: David H. Johnson; John J. Kennedy, Jr.; John J. D'Elia; Dennis W. Gillooly; Robert L. Schwab. Associates: Stephanie Z. Roberge; Christopher D. De Palma.
General Civil Practice. Personal Injury, Medical Malpractice, Professional Malpractice, Products Liability, Workers Compensation, Family Law, Real Estate and Probate Law. Trials before all State and Federal Courts.
Reference: Bank of Boston - Connecticut.
See Professional Biographies, NEW HAVEN, CONNECTICUT

Kesner, David W. ... '55 '92 C.1133 B.S. L.564 [Cummings&L.]
*PRACTICE AREAS: Trusts and Estates; Estate Planning.
Kessler, Robert M., (BV) ... '61 '88 C.1030 B.A. L.1029 J.D. 35-37 Audubon St.
Keyes, Thos. F., Jr., (AV) ... '15 '40 C&L.976 B.A., LL.B. 215 Church St.
Killeen, Denis ... '37 '74 C.178 Ph.D. L.184 J.D. Coun., Knights of Columbus
*RESPONSIBILITIES: Investment; Mortgage; Insurance.
Killion, Bruce M., (BV) ... '48 '76 C.602 B.A. L.607 J.D. [Ⓒ Lippman&O.]
Kim, Jaclyn S. ... '73 '01 C.188 B.S. L.262 J.D. [Ⓐ Bergman,H.&R.]
Kindseth, Rachel Snow ... '71 '96 C.67 B.A. L.184 J.D. [Ⓐ Murtha C.]
King, Amy E. ... '62 '93 C.145 B.A. L.184 J.D. 44 Trumbull St.
King, Jackson T., (AV) ... '29 '60 C.165 A.B. L.178 LL.B. [Farren&K.]
*PRACTICE AREAS: Personal Injury Law; Domestic Relations; Probate Law; Workers' Compensation; Criminal Law.
Kingsley, Charles C., (AV) ... '37 '62 C.976 A.B. L.309 J.D. [Wiggin&D.]
*PRACTICE AREAS: Estate Planning; Trust and Estates; Tax Exempt Organizations; Taxation; Closely Held Business Law.
Kinney, David C., (BV) ... '59 '85 C.676 B.A. L.1029 J.D. 685 State St.
Kinney, Michael K. ... '63 '96 C.184 B.S. L.1252 J.D. [Ⓐ Wiggin&D.] (Pat.)
Kinsella, Nancy L. Bohan ... '65 '91 C.999 B.S. L.262 J.D. [Neubert,P.&M.]
*PRACTICE AREAS: Corporate Law; Commercial Litigation; Bankruptcy.
Klaskin, Seth C. ... '68 '97 C.665 B.A. L.1325 J.D. 514 Foxon Blvd.
Klein, Linda Booz '47 '75 C.432 B.S. L.884 J.D.
Mgr., Intell. Prop. and Contracts, Yale Univ. Press
Klein, Richard J., (BV) ... '46 '77 C.453 S.B. L.262 J.D. [Bergman,H.&R.] ⊙
*PRACTICE AREAS: Business; Estate Planning; Estate Administration; Taxation (Local, State, Federal Law).
Kliger, Mark S., (CV) ... '49 '87 C.184 B.A. L.1029 J.D. 109 Howe St.
Kline, Lisa W. ... '60 '85 C.184 B.A. L.1048 J.D. New Haven Legal Assistance Assn., Inc.
Knapsack, Terri-Ann ... '65 '90 C.588 B.S. L.1202 J.D. [Dombroski,K.&H.]
Knight, Tara L., (BV) ... '65 '90 C.1030 B.A. L.818 J.D. 7-9 Elm St.
Knobelsdorff, Kerry E. ... '65 '93 C.855 B.A. L.306 J.D. [Ⓐ Neubert,P.&M.]
*PRACTICE AREAS: Insurance Defense; Commercial Litigation.
Koenigsberg, Michael L., (BV) ... '40 '80 C.94 B.A. L.1049 J.D. Dep. City Corp. Coun.
Koh, Harold H. ... '54 '81 C&L.309 B.A., J.D. Yale Univ.
Koizim, Harvey L. '27 '51 C.164 A.B. L.976 J.D.
Comr., New Haven Redevelop. Agency‡
Kolb, Lisa M. ... '72 '99 C.689 B.A. L.1360 J.D. [Gillis&G.]
*PRACTICE AREAS: Personal Injury; Workers' Compensation; Real Estate; Wills; Trust and Estates.
Koleci, Fatos ... '69 '97 C.1102 B.S. L.564 J.D. 746 Chapel Street, Suite 204
Kolodziej, Steven R. ... '64 '00 C.184 B.A. L.1252 J.D. [Ⓐ Garcia&M.]
*PRACTICE AREAS: Construction Law.
Kone, Carolyn W., (AV) ... '50 '75 C.66 B.A. L.94 J.D. [Brenner,S.&W.]
*PRACTICE AREAS: Federal Litigation; Commercial Litigation; Municipal Law; Foreclosures; Real Estate Contracts.
Koosa, Robert E. ... '76 '01 C.1057 B.A. L.1252 J.D. [Ⓐ Wiggin&D.]
Kops, Mitchell R. ... '68 '95 C.893 B.A. L.262 J.D. [Ⓐ Bergman,H.&R.]
*PRACTICE AREAS: Estate Planning; Federal Taxation; State Taxation; Local Taxation.
Kornacki, Anthony, Jr. ... '75 '01 C.93 B.A. L.1252 J.D. 121 Elm St.

Koskoff, Koskoff & Bieder, P.C.
(See Bridgeport)

Kowalczyk, Robert P., (CV) ... '53 '80 C.184 B.A. L.818 J.D. 395 Orange St.
Kramer, Audrey C. ... '58 '93 C.1156 B.S. L.1252 J.D. Off. of the Corp. Coun.

Kraus, Regina Duchin ... '47 '91 C.273 B.A. L.184 J.D. [Ⓒ Tyler C.&A.]
*PRACTICE AREAS: Commercial Litigation; General Civil Litigation; Professional Liability Defense.
Krause, Jay F. ... '66 '91 C.276 B.S.B.A. L.659 J.D. [Ⓐ Bergman,H.&R.]
*PRACTICE AREAS: Business; Estate Planning; Personal Taxation; Corporate Taxation; Partnership Taxation.
Kravitz, Mark R., (AV) ... '50 '75 C.918 B.A. L.276 J.D. [Wiggin&D.]
*PRACTICE AREAS: Appellate Practice; Civil Appeals; Media Law; First Amendment; Libel and Slander.
Krevolin, Sherman H., (AV) ... '29 '54 C&L.976 B.A., LL.B. [Krevolin&D.]
*PRACTICE AREAS: Probate; Estate Planning; Profit Sharing; Corporation; Elder Law.

Krevolin & Donato, P.C., (AV)
59 Elm Street, P.O. Box 612, 06503
Telephone: 203-624-3191 Fax: 203-624-4187
Email: krevolin.donato.pc@snet.net URL: http://www.lawyers.com/krevolinanddonatoattys
Sherman H. Krevolin; Charles J. Donato.
General Civil Practice. Probate, Estate Planning, Elder Law, Asset Protection, Pension and Profit Sharing, Corporation, Real Estate, Gift Estate, Taxation, Personal Injury, Family and Workers Compensation Law. Trials.
See Professional Biographies, NEW HAVEN, CONNECTICUT

Krinsky, Mary M. ... '46 '77 C.350 B.S. L.508 J.D. [St. Onge S.J.&R.] ⊙
Kruzynski, Peter G. ... '66 '93 C.276 B.S. L.823 J.D. [Ⓐ Susman,D.&S.]
*PRACTICE AREAS: Litigation; Banks and Banking; Collections; Commercial Law; Bankruptcy.
Kun, Sigrid E. ... '66 '98 C.354 B.S. L.1252 J.D. [Ⓐ Wiggin&D.]
Lable, Stephen Jared ... '— '99 C.1036 B.A. L.1398 J.D. [Ⓐ Wiggin&D.]
Lager, Linda K. ... '51 '75 C.107 B.A. L.94 J.D. Supr. Ct. J.
Lahiri, Monika Niva Marie ... '71 '95 C.676 B.A. L.976 J.D. [Ⓐ Wiggin&D.]
Lahr, Jeffrey F. ... '53 '87 C.563 B.A. L.184 J.D. [Lippman&O.]
Lallier, Gregg J. ... '72 '98 C.93 B.S. L.245 J.D. [Ⓐ Updike,K.&S.] (⊙Hartford)
*PRACTICE AREAS: Business Law; Intellectual Property; Electronic Commerce Law.
LaMarr, Catherine E. ... '60 '85 C.188 B.A. L.329 J.D. 1654 Ella Grasse Blvd.
Lancaster, Robert E. ... '66 '93 C.484 B.A. L.861 J.D. P.O. Box 209090
Land, Wilbur J., (BV) ... '30 '57 C.1029 B.A. L.976 LL.B. [Land&C.]
Land & Cramer, (BV) ... 88 Prospect St.
Lane, Courtney ... '67 '01 C.787 B.A. L.306 J.D. [Ⓐ Tyler C.&A.]
Langbein, John H. '41 '68 C.178 A.B. L.309 LL.B.
(adm. in DC; not adm. in CT) Prof. of Law, Yale Univ.
LaPointe, Gregory P., (AV) '46 '78 C.880 B.E. L.30 J.D.
[Bachman&L.] (See Pat. Sect.)
*PRACTICE AREAS: Patents; Trademarks; Copyrights; Unfair Competition; Licensing Law.
Lara, Yamil ... '42 '80 C.112 B.A. L.976 J.D. P.O. Box 1423
Lasala, Anthony J., (AV) ... '40 '66 C.316 A.B. L.902 LL.B. [Lasala,W.&W.]
Lasala, Walsh & Wicklow, (AV) ... 168 Bradley St.
Lasser, Mitchel D. '64 '91 C.976 B.A. L.309 J.D.
(adm. in NY; not adm. in CT) Yale Univ.
Lattanzi, Gregory T. ... '66 '94 C.787 B.A. L.607 J.D. [Ⓐ Tobin&M.]
Lawrence, Howard Alan, (BV) ... '49 '83 C.373 A.B. L.1029 J.D. [H.A.Lawrence]
Lawrence, Howard A., P.C., Law Offices of, (BV) ... 1 Trumbull St.

Leaf, Frederick P., (BV) '46 '71 C.573 B.B.A. L.93 J.D.
234 Church Street, Suite 401, P.O. Box 2044, 06521-2044
Telephone: 203-776-9368 Fax: 203-498-1505
Email: frederick.p.leaf@snet.net
General Civil and Criminal Practice before State and Federal Courts. Personal Injury, Products Liability, Family, Business, Corporation, Real Estate, Probate, Workers Compensation and Immigration Law. Trials.
Approved Attorney for: Chicago Title Insurance Co.; Commonwealth Land Title Insurance Co.; First American Title Insurance Co.
Reference: Fleet Bank.

LeDonne, James J. ... '69 '94 C.1033 B.S.B.A. L.1188 J.D. [Ⓐ Pellegrino]

Lee, John E., (AV) '44 '69 C.276 A.B. L.184 J.D.
205 Church Street, Suite 406, 06510-1805
Telephone: 203-865-6499 Fax: 203-865-0236
Email: johnelee@iconn.net URL: http://www.lawyers.com/jeleeatty
***PRACTICE AREAS: Real Estate; Business Law; Personal Injury; Family Law; Corporate Law.**
General Civil Practice before State and Federal Courts. Real Estate, Business Law, Personal Injury, Family Law, Corporate Law, Construction Law, Trusts and Estates, Commercial Real Estate, Contracts, Leases and Leasing, Litigation, Mortgage, Probate, Products Liability, Torts, Wills, Zoning, Planning and Land Use, Trials and Appeals.
Reference: Centerbank.
See Professional Biographies, NEW HAVEN, CONNECTICUT

Lee, Joseph C., (AV) ... '39 '67 C.276 A.B. L.184 J.D. [Tyler C.&A.]
*PRACTICE AREAS: Energy; Public Utility Law; Secured Transactions; Cogeneration; Real Estate.
Lefeber, Peter J., (AV) ... '55 '80 C.745 A.B. L.184 J.D. [Wiggin&D.]
*PRACTICE AREAS: Labor Law; Employment Law.
Leff, David A., (BV) ... '63 '88 C.184 B.A. L.228 J.D. [Levy,L.&T.]
*PRACTICE AREAS: Personal Injury; Business Litigation; Appellate Practice.
Leitze, Robert C., (BV) ... '47 '79 C.430 B.A. L.146 J.D. 555 Long Wharf Dr.
Lemley, Raymond J., (BV) ... '61 '87 C.184 B.A. L.1048 J.D. 345 Whitney Ave.
Lenes, James A. ... '64 '91 C.401 B.S. L.306 J.D. [Ⓐ Neubert,P.&M.]
*PRACTICE AREAS: Civil Litigation; Commercial Law; Bankruptcy; Immigration Law.
Letizia, John M., (BV) ... '61 '86 C.724 B.A. L.276 J.D. [Letizia,A.C.]
Letizia, Ambrose Cohen, (AV) ... 1 Church Street
Levenstein, David A. ... '63 '01 C.311 B.A. L.1048 J.D. [Ⓐ Wiggin&D.]
Levin-Epstein, Ethan A., (AV) ... '47 '72 C&L.823 B.A., J.D. [Garrison L.C.&R.]
*PRACTICE AREAS: Litigation; Criminal Law; Civil Law.
Levin-Tavares, Jennifer ... '62 '88 C.347 B.A. L.904 J.D. APT Found. Financial Servs.
Levine, Donna R., (BV) ... '48 '89 C.569 B.A. L.184 J.D. 830 Elm St.
Levine, Howard K. ... '64 '90 C.184 B.S. L.1029 J.D. [Carmody&T.]
*PRACTICE AREAS: Civil Litigation; Labor and Employment.
LeVine, Richard S., (AVⓉ) '61 '86 C.597 B.A. L.309 J.D.
157 Church Street, 19th Floor
Levine, Robert C., (BV) ... '42 '67 C.665 B.S. L.306 J.D. [Levine&G.]
Levine & Glynn, LLC, (BV) ... 770 Orange St.
Levinson, Lawrence A. ... '61 '87 C.94 B.A. L.1029 J.D. 181 Edwards St.
Levy, Leonard L. ... '22 '48 C&L.976 B.A., LL.B. [Levy,L.&T.]
*PRACTICE AREAS: Personal Injury; Negligence; Divorce; Real Estate.

Levy, Leff & Toole, (BV)
129 Church Street, 06510-2026
Telephone: 203-777-6887 Fax: 203-776-9448
Leonard L. Levy; David A. Leff; Elizabeth Toole.
Business Litigation, Appellate Practice and Personal Injury.
See Professional Biographies, NEW HAVEN, CONNECTICUT

Lewellyn, Bruce, (AV) ... '38 '67 C.378 B.S. L.813 LL.B. [Tyler C.&A.]
*PRACTICE AREAS: Pension and Employee Benefits; Real Estate; Banking.
Lewendon, Whitney M., (AV) ... '48 '73 C.178 B.A. L.588 J.D. [Coan,L.G.&M.]
*PRACTICE AREAS: Elder Law; Probate Law; Estate Planning Law.
Lewis, William G. ... '64 '98 C.354 B.A. L.184 J.D. [Ⓐ Carmody&T.]
*PRACTICE AREAS: Corporate Law; Commercial Law; Intellectual Property.
Licari, Christopher M. ... '67 '92 C.860 B.A. L.1029 J.D. [Licari&W.]
*PRACTICE AREAS: Civil Litigation; Personal Injury; Real Estate.

Licari & Walsh LLC
105 Court Street, 06511
Telephone: 203-752-1450 Fax: 203-752-1401
Christopher M. Licari; John M. Walsh, Jr.;—Emmet P. Hibson, Jr.
General Practice, including Civil Litigation, Labor and Employment Law, Workers' Compensation, Real Estate.
See Professional Biographies, NEW HAVEN, CONNECTICUT

Lilly, Douglas Gerard .... '69 '96 C.321 A.B. L.978 J.D. 419 Whalley Ave.
Lindsay, Barbara B. .... '50 '83 C.681 A.B. L.178 J.D. [Stein&L.] (⊙Hartford)
Lippman, Ira H., (BV) .... '45 '70 C.184 B.S. L.818 J.D. [Lippman&O.]
Lippman, Neil A. .... '65 '90 C.410 A.B. L.472 J.D. [Bershtein,L.B.&M.]
*PRACTICE AREAS: Commercial Litigation; Foreclosures; Collections; Creditors Rights.
Lippman & Ouellette, L.L.C., (BV) .... One Whitney Avenue
Lipson, Leon '21 '51 C&L.309 A.B., LL.B.
(adm. in NY; not adm. in CT) Yale Law Sch.
Liss, Stephen .... '75 '01 C.881 B.A. L.276 J.D. [Ⓐ Bergman,H.&R.]
*PRACTICE AREAS: Estate Planning; Trusts and Estates; Partnership Taxation.
Logue, Frank .... '24 '51 C&L.976 B.A., LL.B. 173 Livingston St.‡
Lombard, Sarah .... '75 '01 C.321 B.A. L.818 J.D. [Ⓐ Tyler C.&A.]
Looney, Martin M., (BV) .... '48 '85 C.1030 B.A. L.184 J.D. 201 Orange St.
LoRicco, Richard A., Jr., (BV) .... '61 '86 C.262 B.S. L.1029 J.D. [LoRicco&L.]
LoRicco, Ronald Joseph, (CV) .... '64 '89 C.1030 B.A. L.1029 J.D. 216 Crowe St.
LoRicco & LoRicco, (BV) .... 216 Crown St.
Lotty, Robert W., (AV) ..... '46 '74 C.184 B.A. L.966 J.D. [Ⓒ Lippman&O.] (⊙Fairfield)
Lubin, Andrew R., (AV) .... '54 '79 C.156 B.A. L.365 J.D. [Susman,D.&S.]
*PRACTICE AREAS: Real Estate Law; Real Estate Finance; Commercial and Finance Law; Leasing Law; Common Interest Community (Condominium) Law.
Lubin-Szafranski, J. C., (BV) '55 '80 C.93 B.A. L.184 J.D.
V.P. & Gen. Coun., St. Raphael Health Care Sys.
Lucht, Carroll L. '42 '73 C&L.546 B.A., J.D.
(adm. in NE; not adm. in CT) Clinical Prof. of Law, Yale Univ.
Ludwick, Lindalea P., (BV) '45 '83
C.966 B.S. L.184 J.D. [Early,L.&S.] (⊙New York, NY)
*PRACTICE AREAS: Trials; Workers Compensation Law; Asbestos Disease; Toxic Torts.
Lutz, Kelly P. .... '74 '00 C.273 B.A. L.306 J.D. [Ⓐ Tyler C.&A.]
Luzzi, Michael J. .... '62 '91 C.976 B.A. L.201 J.D. [Ⓐ Early,L.&S.]
*PRACTICE AREAS: Tort Defense; Asbestos Defense.
Lynch, Richard W., (BV) .... '60 '87 C.1210 B.S. L.1029 J.D. [Lynch,T.K.&E.]
*PRACTICE AREAS: Domestic Relations; Workers Compensation; Criminal Law; Forfeiture Defense; Administrative Law.
Lynch, Robert W., (BV) .... '49 '83 C.103 Sc.B. L.64 J.D. [Lynch,T.K.&E.]
*PRACTICE AREAS: Real Estate; Business Law; Consumer Law; Probate; Estate Planning.
Lynch, William C., (AV) .... '24 '50 C&L.273 LL.B. [Ⓒ Lynch,T.K.&E.] ‡
*PRACTICE AREAS: Labor Law.

Lynch, Traub, Keefe and Errante, A Professional Corporation, (AV)
52 Trumbull Street, P.O. Box 1612, 06506-1612
Telephone: 203-787-0275 Fax: 203-782-0278 URL: http://www.lawyers.com/ltke
Email: lawyers@ltke.com URL: http://www.ltke.com
Hugh F. Keefe; Steven J. Errante; John J. Keefe, Jr.; Donn A. Swift; Charles E. Tiernan, III; Robert W. Lynch; Richard W. Lynch; Timothy P. Pothin; Eric P. Smith;—Lee Kennedy Tiernan; Nicole M. Fournier; Louis Mark Rubano; Sonia M. Jones. Of Counsel: Stephen I. Traub; William C. Lynch (Retired).
General Practice. Corporation, Employment Law, Computer Law, Transportation, OSHA, Tax, Probate, Real Estate, Social Security, Criminal, Negligence, Medical Malpractice and Products Liability Law. Trials and Appeals in all Civil, Administrative and Criminal Courts, Federal and State. Family Law, Workers Compensation, Bankruptcy Law.
Local Counsel for: Transport Insurance Co., Dallas, Texas; American Trucking Associations; Roadway Express, Inc., Akron, Ohio; A.R.A. Philadelphia, Penn.; Consolidated Freightways, Menlo Park, California; Ogden Corp.
Labor Counsel: Coca-Cola, U.S.A., Atlanta, Georgia (Private Truck Operation); The Dow Chemical Co.; Cincinnati Milacron.
See Professional Biographies, NEW HAVEN, CONNECTICUT

Lyons, Lauragene .... '53 '83 C.706 A.B. L.184 J.D. 700 State St.
Mackler, Harvey K. '16 '40 C.102 B.S. L.1009 LL.B.
(adm. in NY; not adm. in CT) 41 Bydron Place‡
Mackniak, Michael W. .... '69 '94 C.354 B.A. L.1252 J.D. 869 Whalley Avenue
Maher, Kathleen A. .... '56 '84 C.502 B.A. L.910 J.D. [Ⓒ Tyler C.&A.]
*PRACTICE AREAS: Corporate; Finance; Securities; Business Law; Mergers and Acquisitions.
Malafronte, Richard W. .... '60 '88 C.156 B.A. L.1029 J.D. 55 Trumbull St.
Mancini, Philip E., Jr. .... '21 '48 C&L.724 LL.B. Supr. Ct. J.
Mandanici, Francis T. .... '46 '74 C.1030 A.B. L.818 J.D. Asst. Pub. Def.
Mandel, Stuart Jay, (P.C.) .... '49 '74 C.1044 B.A. L.309 J.D. [Brenner,S.&W.]
*PRACTICE AREAS: Business; Corporate; Securities.
Manke, Hugh I., (BV) .... '42 '76 C.674 A.B. L.107 J.D. [Updike,K.&S.] (⊙Hartford)
*PRACTICE AREAS: Administrative Law; Business Law; Public Finance/Public Law; Real Estate.
Manko, Peter K. .... '52 '84 C.30 B.S.B.A. L.1029 J.D. Corp. Coun., F. J. Dahill Co.
Mantell, Charles A., (AV) .... '42 '68 C.401 B.S. L.724 J.D. 59 Elm St.
Marco, Frank J., (AV) .... '47 '73 C.732 B.S. L.262 J.D. [Mintz,L.C.F.G.&P.]
*PRACTICE AREAS: Venture Capital; Emerging Growth Companies; Mergers and Acquisitions; Public Offerings; High Technology.
Marcus, Edward L., (AV) .... '27 '50 C&L.976 B.A., LL.B. [Marcus]
*PRACTICE AREAS: Banking; Construction; Real Estate Law and Litigation related thereto.
Marcus, Shelley A. .... '51 '77 C.19 B.A. L.184 J.D. [Marcus]

Marcus Law Firm, The, (AV)
111 Whitney Avenue, 06510
Telephone: 203-787-5885 FAX: 203-789-8705
Members of Firm: Edward L. Marcus; Shelley A. Marcus;—Mark L. Bergamo; David S. Doyle; Marjorie R. Gruszkiewicz; Eric T. Dean, Jr.
General Civil Practice before State and Federal Courts. Real Estate, Construction, Commercial Banking, Foreclosure and Bankruptcy Law, Zoning and Planning, Eminent Domain, Condominium, Trials and Appeals.
References: People's Bank; New Haven Savings Bank; Breen Capital Corp.; Fleet Bank; Superior Savings Bank; Co-Lex Services LLC; Greentree Corp.; Ocwen Federal Bank; FSB.

Margolis, Joan Glazer .... '53 '78 C.1036 B.A. L.184 J.D. U.S. Mag.
Margolis, Stuart A., (BV) .... '53 '78 C.1036 B.A. L.184 J.D. [Berdon,Y.&M.]
*PRACTICE AREAS: Corporate Law; Administrative Law; Commercial Law; Bankruptcy; Personal Injury.
Markle, Peter D., (AV) .... '55 '80 C.156 B.A. L.184 J.D. Asst. U.S. Atty.
Marlow, Lee, (AV) .... '55 '82 C.1102 B.A. L.1029 J.D. 181 Edwards St.
Marshall, Burke '22 '52 C&L.976 B.A., LL.B.
(adm. in DC; not adm. in CT) Prof. of Law, Yale Univ.‡
Martineau, Rene Gerard, (BV) .... '61 '87 C.459 B.S. L.1048 J.D. [Ⓐ Del Sole&D.]
*PRACTICE AREAS: Civil Litigation.
Martino, Wayne A., (P.C.), (BV) .... '59 '84 C.30 B.A. L.184 J.D. [Brenner,S.&W.]
*PRACTICE AREAS: Internet Law; Business Start-Ups; Corporate; Securities.
Maser, Scott M., (BV) .... '56 '83 C.183 B.A. L.184 J.D. [Sirois&M.]
Mashaw, Jerry L. '41 '64 C&L.861 B.A., LL.B.
(adm. in LA; not adm. in CT) Prof. of Law, Yale Univ.
Mason, Margaret P., (AV) .... '44 '78 C.289 B.A. L.976 J.D. [Tyler C.&A.]
*PRACTICE AREAS: Civil Litigation; Employment Law; Medical Malpractice Defense.

Mastroni, Kenneth J. .... '64 '89 C.1030 B.A. L.1048 J.D. [Ⓐ Milano&W.]
*PRACTICE AREAS: Municipal and Governmental Litigation; Commercial Insurance Defense; Employment Litigation; Federal Practice; Civil Rights Defense.
Mather, Richard W. .... '58 '90 C&L.184 B.A., J.D. [Ⓐ Yules&Y.]
*PRACTICE AREAS: Insurance; Products Liability; Workers Compensation; Medical Negligence.
Matthews, Rebecca A. .... '69 '94 C.273 B.A. L.94 J.D. 157 Church Street
McCarthy, Eugene B. '40 '66 C.884 B.S. L.262 LL.B.
(adm. in NY; not adm. in CT) F.B.I.
McCormack, Christopher P. .... '57 '87 C.976 B.A. L.262 J.D. [Tyler C.&A.]
*PRACTICE AREAS: Commercial Litigation; Environmental Law; Environmental Insurance Coverage Law.

McCormick, Paulding & Huber, LLP
(See Hartford)

McDermott, Bruce L. .... '64 '89 C.390 B.A. L.930 J.D. [Ⓐ Wiggin&D.]
McDevitt, John K. .... '41 '67 C.321 B.S. L.93 J.D. Knights of Columbus
*RESPONSIBILITIES: Insurance Claims; Fraternal Matters; Employee Agent Matters.
McKeon, Christopher M. .... '66 '91 C.1030 B.A. L.1029 J.D. [Bershtein,L.B.&M.]
*PRACTICE AREAS: Commercial Litigation; Landlord and Tenant; Foreclosures; Collections; Real Estate.
McKeon, Thomas P., (BV) .... '38 '63 C.676 A.B. L.94 J.D. [Ⓒ Bershtein,L.B.&M.] ‡
*PRACTICE AREAS: Real Estate Transactions; Probate; Estate Planning; Planning and Zoning.
McNamara, Thomas M., (BV) .... '53 '86 C.1102 B.A. L.245 J.D. [McNamara&G.]
McNamara & Goodman, (BV) .... 142 Temple St.
McNerney, Tiernan & Burns, (AV) .... 59 Elm Street
Meadow, Frank S. .... '22 '51 C.860 B.S. L.472 LL.B. Supr. Ct. J.

Mednick, Steven G., (BV) '52 '79 C.1030 B.A L.184 J.D.
195 Church Street, P.O. Box 1747, 06507
Telephone: 203-784-3116 Fax: 203-784-3119 URL: http://www.mednicklaw.com
Email: smednick@snet.net URL: http://www.lawyers.com/smednick
***PRACTICE AREAS: Government Relations; Legislative Practice; Labor and Employment; Technology Contracts; State Government Law.**
Government Relations and Legislative Practice, Labor and Employment, Technology Contracts, State, County and Local Government Law, Contracts and Procurement, and Zoning, Planning and Land Use.
See Professional Biographies, NEW HAVEN, CONNECTICUT

Meisenkothen, Christopher .... '74 '99 C&L.184 B.A., J.D. [Ⓐ Early,L.&S.]
*PRACTICE AREAS: Products Liability; Personal Injury; Toxic Torts; Workers' Compensation.
Melien, Peter E., (BV) .... '51 '76 C.321 B.A. L.184 J.D. [Tobin&M.] ⊙
Mellitz, Jeremy A., (BV) .... '55 '81 C.94 B.A. L.245 J.D. [Bergman,H.&R.]
*PRACTICE AREAS: Business; Commercial Litigation; Labor and Employment; Real Estate Finance; Real Estate Property Law.
Mendel, Nancy K. .... '54 '92 C.976 BLS L.184 J.D. 20 Trumbull St.
Meneo, Ronald Michael, (BV) .... '53 '79 C.1030 B.A. L.1048 J.D. [Meneo&G.]
Meneo & Goldfield, L.L.C., (BV) .... 234 Church St.
Meng, Martha E. .... '43 '85 C.788 B.A. L.184 J.D. [Murtha C.]
*PRACTICE AREAS: Health Care Law; Long Term Care; Retirement Housing and Assisted Living.
Mengwall, Erik L. .... '74 '01 C.976 B.A. L.273 J.D. [Ⓐ Wiggin&D.]
Menna, James J. .... '— '99 C.1349 L.1202 J.D. [Ⓐ Wiggin&D.]
Meredith, Susan R. .... '44 '74 C.880 B.A. L.588 J.D. 19 Foster St.
Merriam, Martin M., (AV) .... '04 '35 C&L.976 B.S., LL.B. [Ⓒ Virshup,C.&H.]
Merrill, Sean P. .... '68 '01 C.588 B.S. L.1252 J.D. [Ⓐ Cummings&L.]
*PRACTICE AREAS: Intellectual Property; Trademarks; Internet Law.
Messey, Robert Charles .... '57 '94 C.999 M.D. L.1252 142 Temple St.
Messinger, Sheldon A., (BV) .... '41 '66 C.184 B.A. L.94 J.D. 2 Lincoln St.
Meyer, Jeffrey A. .... '63 '89 C&L.976 B.A., J.D. Asst. U.S. Atty.
Mick, Alice J., (P.C.), (BV) .... '44 '89 C.813 B.A. L.976 J.D. [Brenner,S.&W.]
*PRACTICE AREAS: Corporate Law; Health Law; Employment Law.
Milano, Mark A., (BV) .... '60 '85 C.93 B.A. L.184 J.D. [Milano&W.]
*PRACTICE AREAS: Insurance Defense; Premises Liability; Product Liability; Appellate Practice; Environmental Law.

Milano & Wanat, LLC, (BV)
205 Church Street, Third Floor, 06510 ⊙
Telephone: 203-315-7000; 203-498-6061 Fax: 203-315-7007
Christopher F. Wanat; Mark A. Milano; Sean C. Connors; Stephen G. Murphy, Jr. Associates: Adam F. Acquarulo; Gary C. Kaisen; Jeffrey W. Kennedy; Lawrence D. Paelet; Kenneth J. Mastroni; Jack S. Taylor; Indeg M. Raimundo; Anthony J. Saraco; Naureen R. Weissman; Karen L. Zielinski; Joseph G. Rinaldi.
Trial Counsel for Commercial Insurance, Construction, Employment, Products Liability, Trade Secrets, Medical Malpractice Defense and Professional Malpractice Defense.
Branford, Connecticut Office: 471 East Main Street, 06405. Telephone: 203-315-7000. Fax: 203-315-7007.
See Professional Biographies, NEW HAVEN, CONNECTICUT

Milas, Jane I. .... '54 '86 C.104 A.B. L.184 J.D. [Garcia&M.]
*PRACTICE AREAS: Construction Litigation; Contracts; Commercial Litigation; Real Estate.
Miller, Justine FitzGerald .... '41 '90 C.881 A.B. L.1029 J.D. 258 Church St.
Miller, Kenneth R. .... '49 '79 C.976 B.A. L.309 J.D. Assoc. Gen. Coun., Yale Univ.
Miller, Roswitha .... '64 '95 C.37 B.A. L.1252 J.D. [Seeley&B.]
*PRACTICE AREAS: Litigation.
Millman, Pamela P. .... '57 '84 C.228 A.B. L.245 J.D. [Ⓐ Wiggin&D.]
Miltenberger, Timothy D. .... '64 '90 C.910 A.B. L.94 J.D. [Coan,L.G.&M.]
*PRACTICE AREAS: Bankruptcy Law; Commercial Litigation; Creditors Rights.

Mintz, Levin, Cohn, Ferris, Glovsky and Popeo, P.C., (AV)
157 Church Street, 06510 ⊙
Telephone: 203-777-8200 Fax: 203-777-7111 Internet: Each Attorney's Internet Address takes the following form: first initial, last name @mintz.com (e.g., rmintz@mintz.com)
URL: http://www.mintz.com
Frank J. Marco; Paul A. Hughes.
Administrative Law, Business Law, Commercial Finance, Commercial Litigation, Commercial Real Estate Finance, Corporate, Emerging Growth Companies, Employment Law, Employment Litigation, Executive Severance Contracts, High Technology, Medicare Fraud and Abuse, Nonprofit Organizations Law, Personnel Policies, Public Finance, Public Law, Public Offerings, Tax, Venture Capital.
Boston, Massachusetts Office: One Financial Center. Telephone: 617-542-6000. Fax: 617-542-2241.
New York, N.Y. Office: Chrysler Center, 666 Third Avenue. Telephone: 212-935-3000. Fax: 212-983-3115.
Washington, D.C. Office: 701 Pennsylvania Avenue, N.W. Telephone: 202-434-7300. Fax: 202-434-7400.
Reston, Virginia Office: One Fountain Square, 11911 Freedom Drive. Telephone: 703-464-4800. Fax: 703-464-4895.
See Professional Biographies, NEW HAVEN, CONNECTICUT

Mirrione, Joseph R., (AV) .... '52 '79 C.1266 B.A. L.1194 J.D. 27 Elm Street
Moffett, Rowena A. .... '67 '98 C.575 B.A. L.306 J.D. [Ⓐ Brenner,S.&W.]
*PRACTICE AREAS: Federal Litigation; Commercial Litigation; Employment Litigation; Civil Rights Litigation; Administrative Law.
Monahan, John M. .... '54 '84 C.178 B.A. L.724 J.D. [Ⓒ Murtha C.]
*PRACTICE AREAS: Trusts and Estates.
Mongillo, Frank J., Jr., (BV) .... '35 '63 C.976 B.A. L.184 J.D. [Mongillo&I.]
Mongillo, James A. .... '68 '95 C.855 B.A. L.1252 J.D. [Ⓐ Sperandeo&D.]
Mongillo & Insler, (BV) .... 26 Elm St.
Monz, David J., (AV) .... '58 '89 C.264 B.S. L.184 J.D. [Updike,K.&S.] (⊙Hartford)
*PRACTICE AREAS: Environmental Law; Administrative Law; Criminal Law.

Moquet, Albert R., (AV) . . . . '23 '48 C.184 B.A. L.94 J.D. [Barberio,S.&M.]
Moran, Stephen V. . . . . '57 '82 C.976 B.A. L.184 J.D. Asst. Pub. Def.
Morgan, Christine Owens . . . . '65 '90 C.183 B.A. L.184 J.D. [⊡ Wiggin&D.]
*PRACTICE AREAS: Commercial Real Estate Finance; Commercial Real Estate Development; Commercial Real Estate Acquisitions; Real Estate Finance; Real Estate Secured Lending.
Morgillo, Frank M., (BV) . . . . '40 '66 C.165 B.A. L.184 LL.B. [Pellegrino]
Morris, Donna Decker, (BV) . . . . '50 '79 C.860 B.S. L.976 J.D. 240 Colony Rd.
Moss, Benedict S., (BV) . . . . '16 '43 C.659 B.A. L.309 LL.B. 37 Audubon St.
Moss, Frederick S., (BV) . . . . '25 '53 C.659 B.A. L.184 J.D. Prob. J. [Moss&C.]
Moss, Michael B. . . . . '53 '81 C.699 B.A. L.192 J.D. 35-37 Audubon St.
Moss and Cirillo, (BV) . . . . 35-37 Audubon St.
Motsko, Donald R. '35 '61 C.645 B.S. L.273 J.D.
(adm. in VA; not adm. in CT) U.S. Repeating Arms Co.
Mulqueen, John P., Jr., (BV) . . . . '52 '76 C.676 B.A. L.1202 J.D. [Groob,R.&M.]
Mulvey, Harold M. . . . . '14 '42 C&L.262 B.S., LL.B. Supr. Ct. J.
Mulvey, Kenneth J., Jr., (AV) . . . . '50 '75 C.93 B.S. L.262 J.D. [Mulvey,O.&G.]
*PRACTICE AREAS: Insurance Law; Commercial Litigation; Civil Litigation.

Mulvey, Oliver & Gould, (AV)
83 Trumbull Street, 06511
Telephone: 203-624-5111 Telecopier: 203-789-8371
Email: mog@moglaw.com URL: http://www.lawyers.com/moglaw
Members of Firm: Kenneth J. Mulvey, Jr.; Robert G. Oliver; Carolyn P. Gould; Barbara N. Bellis; David J. Crotta, Jr. Associates: James M. Hyland; Brian J. Rieger.
Insurance, Workers Compensation and Negligence Law. General Trial and Appellate Practice in all Courts. Real Estate, Corporation and Probate Practice.
See Professional Biographies, NEW HAVEN, CONNECTICUT

Munro, Lynda B. . . . . '54 '79 C.183 B.A. L.930 J.D. Supr. Ct. J.
Murphy, Brian J., (BV) . . . . '44 '69 C.276 A.B. L.184 J.D. 30 McKinley Ave.
Murphy, Daniel P. . . . . '68 '94 C.390 A.B. L.776 J.D. [⊡ Siegel,O.S.&Z.]
*PRACTICE AREAS: Employment Law; Labor Law; Education Law; Immigration Law.
Murphy, Helen D., (AV) . . . . '51 '86 C.341 B.A. L.1252 J.D. [Murphy,M.F.&N.] ⊙
Murphy, Maureen M., (AV) . . . . '50 '86 C.741 B.A. L.1029 J.D. [Murphy,M.F.&N.] ⊙
Murphy, Shari A. . . . . '67 '92 C.1102 B.S. L.1029 J.D. 201 Orange Street, 2nd Floor
Murphy, Stephen G., Jr., (BV) . . . . '53 '87 C.951 B.A. L.184 J.D. [Milano&W.]
*PRACTICE AREAS: Insurance Defense; Commercial Litigation; Products Liability; ERISA; Appellate Practice.
Murphy, William R., (AV) . . . . '27 '53 C&L.976 B.A., LL.B. [⊡ Tyler C.&A.]
*PRACTICE AREAS: Litigation, Antitrust and Trade Regulation.
Murphy, Murphy, Ferrara & Nugent, LLC, (AV) . . . . 234 Church Street (⊙Fairfield)

Murray, Martha, (BV) '49 '83 C.478 B.A. L.184 J.D.
383 Orange Street, 06511
Telephone: 203-772-3444 Telefax: 203-787-3259
Email: marthamurray@worldnet.att.net
Professional Licensure and Discipline, Health Law, Nursing Law, Probate, Real Estate.
Approved Attorney for: Connecticut Attorneys Title Insurance Co.
Representative Client: Connecticut Association of Nurse Anesthetists; Connecticut Psychiatric Society, The APT Foundation, Inc.
Reference: New Haven Savings Bank.

Murtha Cullina LLP, (AV)
A Limited Liability Partnership
Whitney Grove Square, 2 Whitney Avenue, P.O. Box 704-A, 06503-0704 ⊙
Telephone: 203-772-7700 Facsimile: 203-772-7723
Email: mcrp@mcrp.com URL: http://www.murthalaw.com
Resident Members of Firm: Burton B. Cohen (Resident, Hartford Office); Martha E. Meng; Stephen E. Ronai; Alfred E. Smith, Jr.; Sara R. Stadler; Elizabeth J. Stewart; Louis B. Todisco; Barry J. Waters. Counsel: Nan Mead Birdwhistell; Marilyn B. Fagelson; John M. Monahan; Laura K. Norden; Robert N. Schmalz. Resident Associates: Jennifer Morgan DelMonico; Rachel Snow Kindseth; Heather Lynn Overholser.
General Practice. Administrative, Antitrust, Banking, Bankruptcy, Cable Television, Commercial, Communications, Construction, Copyright, Corporation, Employee Benefits, Energy, Environmental, Estate Planning and Administration, Exempt Organizations, Government Contracts, Health Care, Hospital, Insurance Litigation for Policyholders, Intellectual Property, Labor, Litigation, Mergers and Acquisitions, Probate, Product Liability, Public Utility, Real Estate, Securities, Taxation and Trademark.
Hartford, Connecticut Office: CityPlace I, 185 Asylum Street, 06103-3469. Telephone: 860-240-6000. Facsimile: 860-240-6150.
Boston, Massachusetts Office: Murtha Cullina Roche Carens & DeGiacomo. 99 High Street. Telephone: 617-457-4000. Facsimile: 617-482-3868.
Woburn, Massachusetts Office: 600 Unicorn Park Drive. Telephone; 781-933-5505. Facsimile: 781-933-1530.
See Professional Biographies, NEW HAVEN, CONNECTICUT

Musen, Kenneth N., (AV) . . . . '50 '75 C.453 B.S. L.309 J.D. [⊡ Bergman,H.&R.] ⊙
*PRACTICE AREAS: Business; Estate Planning; Taxation; State and Federal Tax; International Tax Law.
Mysogland, Ernest C. . . . . '65 '90 C.602 B.A. L.178 J.D. 157 Church Street
Nace, Richard F., Jr. . . . . '62 '92 C.732 A.B. L.880 J.D. 1 Century Tower
Nadel, Laurence P., (BV) . . . . '49 '77 C.145 B.A. L.184 J.D. [L.P.Nadel]
Nadel, Laurence P., A Professional Corporation, (BV) . . . . 261 Bradley St.
Nash, G. Douglas, (BV) '50 '76
C.860 B.A. L.184 J.D. Chf.of Legal Servcs., Pub. Def. Offc.
Neubert, Deborah Monteith, (BV) . . . . . . '55 '80 C.951 B.A. L.184 J.D. [Neubert,P.&M.]
*PRACTICE AREAS: Design Professional Liability; Construction; Employment Law; Commercial Litigation.
Neubert, Michael D., (AV) . . . . '52 '78 C.602 B.A. L.184 J.D. [Neubert,P.&M.]
*PRACTICE AREAS: Hospital Liability; Commercial Litigation; Professional Malpractice Defense; Products Liability Defense; Health Care Law.

Neubert, Pepe & Monteith, P.C., (AV)
195 Church Street 13th Floor, 06510 ⊙
Telephone: 203-821-2000 Facsimile: 203-821-2009
Email: thm@npmlaw.com URL: http://www.lawyers.com/npmpclaw
Michael D. Neubert; Gregory J. Pepe; Deborah Monteith Neubert; Douglas S. Skalka; Judy K. Weinstein; Peter T. Fay; Eric I. B. Beller; Nancy L. Bohan Kinsella; Eric J. Stockman;—Simon I. Allentuch; Sonja Goldstein; Cameron C. Staples; James A. Lenes; Kevin M. Godbout; Kerry E. Knobelsdorff; Tina Clark Beamon; Romey K. Hornkohl.
General Civil and Appellate Practice before State and Federal Courts, Commercial and Banking Litigation, Product Liability, Hospital Liability, Medical Malpractice, Lawyer Malpractice, Design Professional Malpractice, Employment Discrimination and Wrongful Discharge, Health Care Law, Managed Care, Physicians Contract, Physicians Licensing, Bankruptcy, Creditors's Rights, Real Estate, Corporations, Business, Banking, Environmental Law, Trials and Appeals.
Southport, Connecticut Office: 30 Jelliff Lane, 06490. Telephone: 203-254-9332. Facsimile: 203-254-9239.
See Professional Biographies, NEW HAVEN, CONNECTICUT

Newman, Claire Bette . . . . '44 '93 C.1102 B.S. L.1252 J.D. 31 McKinley Ave.
Newman, David J. . . . . '46 '76 C.308 B.A. L.1048 J.D. Supvr. Asst. State's Atty.
Nikkel, Henry A. '19 '48 C&L.477 B.A., LL.B.
(adm. in CO; not adm. in CT) P.O. Box 9077‡
Norden, Laura K. . . . . '65 '90 C.477 B.A. L.692 J.D. [⊡ Murtha C.]
*PRACTICE AREAS: Communications Law; Utility Law; Commercial Litigation.
Norris, Mary R. . . . . '55 '84 C.150 B.S. L.276 J.D. [Wiggin&D.]
*PRACTICE AREAS: Information Technology Contracts; Publishing Contracts; New Media Law; Intellectual Property Licensing; Copyright Protection.
North, Paul R., Jr., (AV) . . . . '27 '53 C.976 A.B. L.184 LL.B. [Dennis&N.]

Norton, Hunter N. . . . . '67 '93 C.184 B.S. L.831 J.D. [⊡ Bergman,H.&R.]
*PRACTICE AREAS: Federal Taxation; International Taxation; State and Local Taxation; Estate Planning; Business Law.
Nugent, Susan E. . . . . '61 '90 C.262 B.A. L.128 J.D. [Murphy,M.F.&N.] ⊙
Nulsen, William J., (BV) . . . . '47 '74 C.253 B.A. L.607 J.D. 174 Bradley St.

Nuzzo & Roberts, L.L.C.
(See Cheshire)

O'Brien, George E., Jr., (AV) . . . . '47 '75 C.674 A.B. L.184 J.D. [Tyler C.&A.]
*PRACTICE AREAS: Litigation; Labor and Employment; Management Labor Law; Collective Bargaining; Labor Arbitration.
O'Brien, Robert J. . . . . '47 '73 C.745 B.A. L.184 J.D. Asst. State's Atty.
O'Connor, Martin J. . . . . '46 '81 C.1156 B.A. L.184 J.D. New Haven Fire Dept.
O'Connor, Maureen . . . . '75 '00 C.602 B.A. L.184 J.D. [⊡ Wiggin&D.]
O'Donnell, Jack, (BV) . . . . '54 '81 C.918 B.A. L.1048 J.D. 683 State St.
Oechsle, Linda C. '65 '90 C.112 B.A. L.976 J.D.
New Haven Legal Assistance Assn., Inc.
Oliver, Robert G., (AV) . . . . '40 '65 C&L.976 B.A., LL.B. [Mulvey,O.&G.]
*PRACTICE AREAS: Trials; Federal Practice; Civil Litigation; Appeals.
Olmer, Morris I., (BV) . . . . '28 '53 C.569 B.A. L.421 LL.B. 152 Temple St.
O'Neill, Andrew J., (BV) . . . . '57 '84 C.1102 B.A. L.128 J.D. [Walsh&O.]
Onorato, Alfred J., (BV) . . . . '39 '66 C.316 B.A. L.896 J.D. 445 Orange Street
Osach, Ronald C., (AV) . . . . '48 '75 C.105 B.A. L.1022 J.D. [Silverstein&O.]
*PRACTICE AREAS: Tax Law; Tax Litigation; Estate Planning; Corporate Pension.
O'Sullivan, Shawn L., (AV) . . . . '53 '80 C.676 B.A. L.1048 J.D. [⊡ Tyler C.&A.]
*PRACTICE AREAS: Estate Planning; Probate Administration; Trust Administration; Taxation.
Ouellette, Lawrence A., Jr., (BV) . . . . '55 '81 C.184 B.A. L.1194 J.D. [Lippman&O.]
Overholser, Heather Lynn . . . . '69 '95 C.112 B.A. L.94 J.D. [⊡ Murtha C.]
Owens, Howard T., Jr. . . . . '34 '60 C.321 B.S. L.880 LL.B. Supr. J.
Packtor, Joseph J. . . . . '63 '91 C.1175 B.A. L.228 J.D. [⊡ Jacobs,G.B.&D.]
*PRACTICE AREAS: Personal Injury Litigation; Business Litigation; Employment Litigation; Medical Malpractice; Products Liability Litigation.
Paelet, Lawrence D. . . . . '65 '92 C.1102 B.A. L.184 J.D. [⊡ Milano&W.]
*PRACTICE AREAS: Insurance Defense; Workers Compensation.
Paine, Rosemarie . . . . '66 '92 C.1102 B.S. L.184 J.D. [⊡ Jacobs,G.B.&D.]
*PRACTICE AREAS: Personal Injury Litigation; Criminal Defense; Civil Rights Litigation.
Palmieri, William S. . . . . '63 '94 C.19 B.A. L.1194 J.D. [⊡ Williams&P.]
*PRACTICE AREAS: Criminal Law; Civil Practice; Civil Rights; Appellate Practice.
Pantani, Edmund L. . . . . '39 '67 C.184 B.S. L.884 LL.B. 216 Crown St.
Papa, Kenneth J., (BV) . . . . '60 '85 C.855 B.A. L.184 J.D. 357 Whitney Ave.
Papantones, Melissa J. '59 '85 C.881 A.B. L.245 J.D. 265 Church St.
Papastavros-Corbo, Angelica N. . . . . '69 '96 C.1029 B.A. L.1252 J.D. [⊡ Williams&P.]
*PRACTICE AREAS: Criminal Law; Civil Practice; Civil Rights; Appellate Practice.
Pari, Phyllis M., (BV) . . . . '65 '90 C&L.94 B.S., J.D. [Wiggin&D.]
*PRACTICE AREAS: Litigation.
Parietti, Theresa M. . . . . '68 '98 C.705 B.A. L.306 J.D. [⊡ Wiggin&D.]
Parks, Philip M., (CV) . . . . '57 '88 C.380 B.Sc. L.1048 J.D. 22 Trumbull St.
Parley, Louis I., (AV) . . . . '45 '69 C.563 B.A. L.273 J.D. 27 Elm Street
Patten, Bonnie Lynne . . . . '66 '92 C.659 B.A. L.94 J.D. [⊡ Wiggin&D.]
Pattis, Norman A. . . . . '55 '93 C.679 B.A. L.306 J.D. [Williams&P.]
*PRACTICE AREAS: Criminal Law; Civil Practice; Civil Rights; Appellate Practice.
Peabody, Bruce R., (BV) . . . . '56 '81 C.976 B.A. L.893 J.D. 110 Whitney Ave.
Pearson, Mark H. . . . . '55 '85 C.689 B.A. L.285 J.D. 60 Trumbull St.
Peck, Christine B., (BV) . . . . '58 '88 C.855 B.A. L.1029 J.D. 33 Whitney Ave.
Peck, John H., Jr., (BV) . . . . '53 '79 C.31 B.A. L.1202 J.D. 33 Whitney Ave.
Peck, John H., Sr., (AV) . . . . '21 '49 C.31 B.A. L.893 LL.B. 33 Whitney Ave.
Peckham, Dean E. . . . . '43 '68 C.309 B.A. L.94 LL.B. 45 Richmond Ave.
Pellegrino, Bernard, (BV) . . . . '63 '88 C.602 B.A. L.93 J.D. [⊡ Pellegrino]
Pellegrino, Bernard A., (AV) . . . . '36 '61 C.602 B.A. L.184 J.D. [Pellegrino]
Pellegrino, Enzo A. . . . . '70 '97 C.1102 B.S. L.1252 J.D. [⊡ Gillis&G.]
*PRACTICE AREAS: Personal Injury; Workers Compensation; Criminal Law; Divorce.
Pellegrino, Robert L. '57 '82 C.95 B.A. L.1294 J.D. 209 Orange St.
Pellegrino, Thomas C. . . . . '68 '93 C.1030 B.A. L.823 J.D. [⊡ W.H.Clendenen,Jr.]
*PRACTICE AREAS: Litigation; Commercial Law; Real Estate; Family Law.
Pellegrino Law Firm, The, A Professional Corporation, (AV) . . . . 475 Whitney Avenue
Pepe, Gregory J., (BV) . . . . '55 '82 C.299 B.A. L.1029 J.D. [Neubert,P.&M.]
*PRACTICE AREAS: Health Care; Real Estate; Banking-Workout; Lender Representation.

Pepe & Hazard LLP
(See Hartford)

Pepper, Michael A. . . . . '56 '83 C.93 B.A. L.1048 J.D. Sr. Asst. States Atty.
Perito, James J., (BV) . . . . '56 '83 C.390 B.S. L.184 J.D. [Susman,D.&S.]
*PRACTICE AREAS: Zoning Law; Environmental Law; Commercial Law; Real Estate Law; Civil Litigation.
Perlmutter, Irving H., (AV) . . . . '29 '54 C.178 B.S. L.976 LL.B. [Ullman,P.&S.]
Perlroth, Wm. S. . . . . '— '35 30 Pine Rock Rd.
Perry, Christopher R. . . . . '74 '01 C.30 B.A. L.184 J.D. [⊡ Wiggin&D.]
Perzin, Michael, (AV) . . . . '55 '81 C.705 B.A. L.976 J.D. [Yolen&P.]
*PRACTICE AREAS: Family Law; Negligence; Medical Malpractice; Education Law.
Peterson, Anne D. . . . . '69 '98 C.67 B.A. L.306 J.D. [⊡ Carmody&T.]
*PRACTICE AREAS: Civil Litigation; Commercial Real Estate; Construction Law.
Peterson, Peter W., (AV) . . . . '54 '82 C&L.184 B.S., J.D. [DeLio&P.] (See Pat. Sect.)
*PRACTICE AREAS: Patents; Trademarks; Copyrights; Unfair Competition; Intellectual Property Licensing.
Petrocelli, Michael A. . . . . '60 '99 C.1133 BSME L.564 J.D. [⊡ DeLio&P.]
*PRACTICE AREAS: Patents; Trademarks; Copyrights; Intellectual Property Litigation.
Petroni, Romeo G. . . . . '29 '53 C.823 A.B. L.262 LL.B. Prob. J.
Petruzzelli, Lori A. . . . . '70 '95 C.1030 B.A. L.945 J.D. [⊡ Garcia&M.]
*PRACTICE AREAS: Construction Litigation; Franchise Litigation.
Petshaft, David Bryan . . . . '59 '89 C.829 B.S. L.978 J.D. Coopers & Lybrand
Philpot, W. Martyn, Jr., (BV) . . . . '56 '82 C.188 B.S. L.276 J.D. [W.M.Philpot,Jr.]
*PRACTICE AREAS: Litigation; Employment; Civil Rights; Personal Injury; Medical Malpractice.

Philpot, W. Martyn, Jr., L.L.C., Law Office of, (BV)
409 Orange Street, 06511
Telephone: 203-624-4666 Fax: 203-624-5050
Email: philpot.law@snet.net URL: http://www.lawyers.com/wmphilpot
W. Martyn Philpot, Jr.;—Laura Lee A. Dorflinger; Marc L. Glenn.
General Trial Practice before State and Federal Courts, Civil Litigation, Employment, Civil Rights, Personal Injury and Medical Malpractice Law, Trials and Appeals, Workers' Compensation, Criminal Defense, Family Law, Education Law, Landlord/Tenant Law, Product Liability, Probate and Administrative Law.
See Professional Biographies, NEW HAVEN, CONNECTICUT

Piazza, Edward F., (BV) . . . . '41 '66 C.262 B.S. L.93 J.D. [⊡ Del Sole&D.]
*PRACTICE AREAS: Trials; Workers Compensation; Probate; Real Estate.
Pilgrim, Caleb M., Law Offices of . . . . . . '52 '91 C.860 B.A. L.976 J.D. 1404 Whalley Ave.
Pillsbury, Charles A., (AV) '47 '75
C.976 B.A. L.94 J.D. Exec. Dir., Community Mediation, Inc.
Pinciaro, David, (BV) . . . . '58 '84 C.1211 B.S. L.1029 J.D. 22 Trumbull St.

Pincus, Stephen M. .... '67 '93 C.477 A.B. L.446 J.D. [Ⓒ Brenner,S.&W.]
*PRACTICE AREAS: Federal Litigation; Commercial Litigation; Employment Litigation; Civil Rights; Employment Law.
Pinsky, Irving J., (BV) .... '52 '81 C.184 B.A. L.1029 J.D. 109 Harlow St.
Pisano, Graceann A. .... '— '01 L.1252 J.D. [Ⓐ Cummings&L.]
Piscatelli, Louis R. .... '60 '89 C.164 B.A. L.184 J.D. [Bergman,H.&R.]
*PRACTICE AREAS: Business; ERISA; Estate Planning; Taxation (Local, Personal Property, State, Federal or International Law).
Pite, David C., (CV) .... '62 '88 C.860 B.A. L.184 J.D. 27 Elm St., 3rd Fl.
Polan, Diane, (BV) .... '51 '80 C&L.976 B.A., J.D. 129 Church Street, Suite 802
Porto, Trisha Morris .... '69 '95 C&L.588 B.A., J.D. [Ⓐ Jacobs,G.B.&D.]
*PRACTICE AREAS: Business Litigation; Personal Injury Litigation.
Pothin, Margaret A., (BV) .... '59 '89 C.823 B.A. L.1029 J.D. 265 Church St.
Pothin, Timothy P., (BV) .... '58 '85 C.260 B.A. L.1252 J.D. [Lynch,T.K.&E.]
*PRACTICE AREAS: Negligence; Products Liability; Professional Malpractice; Criminal Defense; Business Litigation.
Pottenger, John L., Jr. .... '50 '76 C.674 A.B. L.976 J.D. Yale Univ.
Price, Charles B., Jr., (BV) .... '58 '83 C.588 B.S. L.831 J.D. [Bartholomew&P.]
*PRACTICE AREAS: Personal Injury Litigation; Medical Malpractice Litigation; Employment Litigation; Insurance Litigation.
Priest, Kathy K., (BV) .... '48 '80 C.881 B.A. L.107 J.D. 129 Church St.
Prout, William H., Jr., (AV) .... '45 '73 C.976 B.A. L.94 J.D. [Wiggin&D.]
*PRACTICE AREAS: Litigation; Construction Law; Professional Responsibility.

Pullman and Comley, L.L.C., (AV)
(Formerly Pullman, Comley, Bradley & Reeves)
One Century Tower, 265 Church Street, 06510-7000 ⊙
Telephone: 203-773-3006 Telecopier: 203-776-7075
URL: http//www.pullcom.com
John S. Pullman (1871-1943); Arthur M. Comley (1883-1969); J. Kenneth Bradley (1903-1969); William Reeves (1906-1967). Members of Firm: Elizabeth J. Austin; H. William Shure; John R. Ward.
General Practice including Administrative, Antitrust, Banking, Bankruptcy and Creditors Rights, Bonds, Business and Commercial, Corporate, Education, Employee Benefits, Environmental, Hospital and Health Care, Labor and Employment, Municipal Finance, Real Estate, Securities, Tax, Trusts and Estates, and Zoning. Energy and Utilities, Litigation in all Courts.
Bridgeport, Connecticut Office: 850 Main Street, P.O. Box 7006, Telephone: 203-330-2000. Telecopier: 203-576-8888.
Hartford, Connecticut Office: 90 State House Square. Telephone: 860-424-4300. Telecopier: 860-424-4370.
Simsbury, Connecticut Office: 720 Hopmeadow Street. Telephone: 860-651-9348. Fax: 860-651-1431.
Southport, Connecticut Office: 200 Pequot Avenue, P.O. Box 510. Telephone: 203-254-5000. Telecopier: 203-254-5070.
Stamford, Connecticut Office: 350 Bedford Street. Telephone: 203-324-5000. Telecopier: 203-363-8659.
See Professional Biographies, NEW HAVEN, CONNECTICUT

Quinn, John M. .... '44 '69 C.602 A.B. L.902 LL.B. F.B.I.
Radziunas, John A. .... '53 '97 C.1102 B.S. L.1187 J.D. 26 Elm St.
Raimundo, Indeg M. .... '73 '99 C.529 B.A. L.1252 J.D. [Ⓐ Milano&W.]
*PRACTICE AREAS: Commercial Litigation; Insurance Defense.
Randell, Linda L., (AV) .... '50 '74 C.477 A.B. L.976 J.D. [Wiggin&D.]
*PRACTICE AREAS: Public Utility Law; Regulatory Law; Antitrust Law.

Ravel, Judith A.
(See Branford)

Reed, Renee M. .... '67 '92 C.1030 B.A. L.930 J.D. [Ⓐ Tyler C.&A.]
*PRACTICE AREAS: Insurance Defense; Medical Malpractice Defense; Plaintiffs Personal Injury; Workers Compensation.
Reeve, Richard A. .... '51 '78 C.867 B.A. L.276 J.D. 105 Court St.
Regula, Steven M. .... '58 '88 C.829 B.A. L.1048 J.D. [Lasala,W.&W.]
Reif, David A., (AV) .... '46 '71 C.390 A.B. L.309 J.D. [Cummings&L.]
*PRACTICE AREAS: Civil Trials; Personal Injury Trials; Products and Professional Liability Litigation; Franchise Law; Bankruptcy.
Reilly, Patricia E., (BV) .... '60 '91 C.918 B.A. L.1066 J.D. [Tyler C.&A.]
*PRACTICE AREAS: Civil Litigation; Employment Law; Employment Discrimination; Sexual Harassment.
Reilly, Peter B., (BV) .... '55 '80 C.823 B.S. L.1202 J.D. [Reilly&R.]
Reilly and Reilly, P.C., (BV) .... Suite 202, 129 Church Street
Reisman, William M. .... '39 '64 C.367 B.A. L.999 LL.B. Yale Univ.
Reizfeld, Leonard C. .... '61 '86 C&L.94 B.S., J.D. 139 Orange St.
Renn, Edward A. .... '58 '88 C.823 A.B. L.184 J.D. [Bergman,H.&R.]
*PRACTICE AREAS: Employee Benefits; Business Planning; Estate Planning; Taxation (Federal, State and International).
Resnik, John J., (AV) .... '35 '60 C&L.976 B.A., J.D. [Resnik&R.] ⊙
Resnik Conn, Emily, (BV) .... '63 '88 C.385 A.B. L.245 J.D. [Resnik&R.] ⊙
Resnik and Resnik, P.C., (AV) .... 56 Whitney Ave. (⊙Woodbridge)
Ressler, Peter L., (BV) .... '47 '73 C.264 A.B. L.273 J.D. [Groob,R.&M.]
Reynolds, David L., (AV) .... '41 '66 C&L.976 B.A., LL.B. [Bergman,H.&R.]
*PRACTICE AREAS: Business; ERISA; Estate Planning and Administration; Taxation (Local Personal Property, State, Federal or International Law); Corporate Law.
Reynolds Nowak, Kelly .... '68 '00 C.1102 B.S. L.1252 J.D. [Ⓐ DeLio&P.]
*PRACTICE AREAS: Patents; Trademarks; Copyrights; Intellectual Property; Litigation.
Rhieu, David M. '54 '80 C.463 B.A. L.818 J.D.
(adm. in MA; not adm. in CT) F.B.I., Chief Coun.
Rhodeen, Penn, (BV) .... '43 '71 C.282 A.B. L.966 J.D. 278 Orange St.
Richardson, Aimee N. '67 '93 C.945 B.A. L.896 J.D.
(adm. in VA; not adm. in CT) 150 Court St., 5th Fl.
Richardson, Robert A. .... '66 '91 C.645 B.A. L.608 J.D. [Garrison L.C.&R.]
*PRACTICE AREAS: Employment Law; Criminal Defense.
Ridinger, Willa J. .... '62 '89 C.197 B.A. L.184 J.D. 545 Long Warf Dr.
Rieger, Brian J. .... '72 '99 C.608 B.A. L.306 J.D. [Ⓐ Mulvey,O.&G.]
*PRACTICE AREAS: Trial Practice; Negligence; Civil Litigation.
Rigler, Lionel .... '55 '86 C.188 B.S. L.107 J.D. 176 Willard St.
Riley, John F., Jr. .... '63 '92 C.184 B.A. L.1029 J.D. 683 State St.
Rinaldi, Joseph G. .... '72 '00 C.025 B.S. L.1252 J.D. [Ⓐ Milano&W.]
*PRACTICE AREAS: Insurance Defense; Commercial Litigation.
Ringold, David A., (BV) .... '56 '80 C.276 B.A. L.976 J.D. [Bergman,H.&R.]
*PRACTICE AREAS: Business; ERISA; Estate Planning; Taxation (Local, Personal Property, State, Federal or International Law).
Rini, Joseph L., (BV) .... '49 '75 C.94 A.B. L.569 J.D. [Hogan&R.]
*PRACTICE AREAS: Civil Litigation; Land Use Regulation; Local Government Law; Public Construction Law; Municipal Contracts.
Rioux, Denise M. .... '52 '80 C.454 B.A. L.1029 J.D. P.O. Box 396
Rizzuti, Edward T. '70 '99 C.705 B.S. L.569 J.D.
(adm. in NY; not adm. in CT) 157 Church Street
Robaina, Antonio, (AV) .... '27 '72 C.999 B.A. L.184 J.D. [Robaina&R.]
Robaina, Antonio C., (AV) .... '54 '79 C&L.184 B.A., J.D. [Robaina&R.]
Robaina & Robaina, (AV) .... 943 Grand Ave.
Roberge, Stephanie Z. .... '65 '90 C.690 B.S. L.1252 J.D. [Ⓐ Kennedy,J.D.&G.]
*PRACTICE AREAS: Medical Malpractice; Personal Injury; Commercial Litigation; Products Liability.
Roberts, Jeffrey H. .... '73 '01 C.882 B.A. L.276 J.D. [Ⓐ Bergman,H.&R.]
*PRACTICE AREAS: Taxation; Estate Planning.
Robinson, Dorothy K., (AV) '51 '75
C.821 B.A. L.1066 J.D. V.P. & Gen. Coun., Yale Univ.
Robinson, Elizabeth K. .... '64 '90 C&L.846 B.A., J.D. 131 Eagle Street
Robinson, Katharine H. '35 '83
C.788 B.A. L.184 J.D. Sr. Staff Atty., Conn. Fund for the Envir.
Roddy, Virginia D., (AV) '51 '78
C.280 A.B. L.893 J.D. Dir., Legal Affs., Yale-New Haven Med. Ctr.
Romanow, John M. .... '48 '75 C.188 B.S. L.564 J.D. 869 Orange St.
Romeo, Lucy M. .... '73 '98 C.976 B.A. L.306 J.D. [Ⓐ Carmody&T.]
*PRACTICE AREAS: Civil Litigation; Products Liability Defense; Insurance Defense.
Ronai, Stephen E., (AV) .... '36 '60 C.178 A.B. L.976 LL.B. [Murtha C.]
*PRACTICE AREAS: Health Care Law; Health Care Networks; Physician Practice Regulation; Administrative Law.
Ronan, John J. .... '32 '63 C.1030 B.S. L.184 J.D. Chief Admin. J, Supr. Ct.
Rooney, Christopher, (AV) .... '55 '84 C.893 B.A. L.184 J.D. [Carmody&T.]
*PRACTICE AREAS: Commercial Litigation; Land Use; Environmental Law; Criminal Law; Antitrust.
Rosado, Justino .... '43 '89 C.1211 B.S. L.1029 J.D. [Chaucer&R.]
Roscoe, Edwin A. .... '27 '61 C.94 B.A. L.184 J.D. 111 Whitney Ave.
Rosen, Beth L. .... '57 '85 C.1044 B.A. L.1162 J.D. 36 Elmwood Rd.
Rosen, David N., (AV) .... '44 '69 C.309 B.A. L.976 LL.B. [Rosen&D.]
*PRACTICE AREAS: Appellate Practice; Employment; Personal Injury; Civil Rights.

Rosen & Dolan, P.C., (AV) BR
400 Orange Street, 06511
Telephone: 203-787-3513 Fax: 203-789-1605
Email: david.rosen@rosendolan.com URL: http://www.lawyers.com/rosen&dolan
David N. Rosen; Edward J. Dolan.
Trial and Appellate Practice before State and Federal Courts. Plaintiffs' Personal Injury, Civil Rights, Employment Discrimination, Class Actions, Divorce, Family and Criminal Defense Law.
Reference: Peoples Bank.
See Professional Biographies, NEW HAVEN, CONNECTICUT

Rosenblatt, Gregory S. .... '55 '84 C.188 B.S. L.564 J.D. [Wiggin&D.]
*PRACTICE AREAS: Metallurgical Patents; Patent Prosecution; Patent Litigation; International Patents; Mechanical Patents.
Rosenthal, Joseph A. ...... '69 '96 C.1349 B.A. L.93 J.D. [Ⓐ Updike,K.&S.] (⊙Hartford)
*PRACTICE AREAS: Environmental; Administrative Law; Utilities Law.
Rosenthal, Kenneth, (AV) .... '44 '78 C.976 B.A. L.184 J.D. [Brenner,S.&W.]
*PRACTICE AREAS: Federal Litigation; Commercial Litigation; Business Disputes; Real Estate; Construction.
Rothschild-Rippe, Judith H. .... '60 '85 C.184 B.A. L.1029 J.D. Asst. States Atty.
Rowe, Joan Allen .... '61 '88 C.882 B.A. L.94 J.D. [Ⓐ Wiggin&D.]
Roy, Paul M. .... '58 '83 C.659 B.S.B.A. L.276 J.D. [Bergman,H.&R.]
*PRACTICE AREAS: Business; Estate Planning; Taxation (Local, Personal Property, State, Federal or International Law); Nonprofit and Charitable Organizations.

Royle, Mary Anne, (BV) '52 '90 C.950 B.A. L.959 J.D.
27 Elm Street, 06510
Telephone: 203-624-7752 Fax: 203-785-0778
Email: mroylelaw@msn.com
***PRACTICE AREAS: Veterans Appeals; Appellate Practice; Administrative Law; General Practice. General Practice.**
See Professional Biographies, NEW HAVEN, CONNECTICUT

Royston, Christopher M., (BV) ...... '50 '76 C.659 B.A. L.94 J.D. 280 McKinley Avenue
Rozen, Jeffrey A., (BV) .... '46 '73 C.241 B.A. L.1009 LL.B. 50 Elm Street
Rubano, Louis Mark .... '70 '98 C.93 B.A. L.818 J.D. [Ⓐ Lynch,T.K.&E.]
*PRACTICE AREAS: Personal Injury; Civil Litigation; Products Liability; Negligence.
Ruben, Diane Daskal, (AV) .... '46 '73 C.145 B.A. L.273 J.D. [Winnick,R.C.E.&H.]
*PRACTICE AREAS: Commercial; Real Estate; Medical Corporations; Professional Corporations; Litigation.
Rubenstein, Allan B., (BV) .... '48 '75 C.569 B.A. L.276 J.D. 261 Bradley Street
Rubin, Ann Harris, (BV) .... '57 '83 C.188 B.A. L.184 J.D. [Carmody&T.]
*PRACTICE AREAS: Civil Litigation; Business Litigation; Insurance Law; Banking; Creditors Rights Law.
Rubin, Jennifer B. .... '63 '89 C&L.184 B.A., J.D. 157 Church Street
Rubin, Kenneth B., (AV) .... '48 '77 C.102 B.A. L.64 J.D. [Rubin&E.]
*PRACTICE AREAS: Family Law; Matrimonial Law; Child Custody; Marital Property Distribution.

Rubin & Eldrich, P.C., (AV)
59 Elm Street, P.O. Box 1422, 06506-1422
Telephone: 203-821-3023 Fax: 203-821-3026
URL: http://www.lawyers.com/rubin&eldridge
Kenneth B. Rubin; Sarah D. Eldrich.
Practice Limited to All Areas of Family and Matrimonial Law including Divorce, Custody, Property Distribution and Support Issues.
See Professional Biographies, NEW HAVEN, CONNECTICUT

Rubinstein, Jay H. .... '60 '89 C.823 B.S. L.588 J.D. [Ⓐ Bergman,H.&R.]
*PRACTICE AREAS: Federal Taxation; International Taxation; State and Local Taxation; Estate Planning; Business Law.
Rudnick, Jason S. .... '75 '00 C.367 B.A. L.306 J.D. [Ⓐ Bergman,H.&R.]
*PRACTICE AREAS: Tax; Litigation; Commercial.
Ruggiero, Robert C., Jr., (BV) .... '46 '82 C&L.184 B.A., J.D. 746 Chapel St., 4th Fl.
Runowicz, Michael E. .... '51 '81 C.184 B.A. L.724 J.D. Asst. U.S. Atty.
Russo, Daniel P. .... '51 '79 C.855 B.A. L.818 J.D. Coun., Knights of Columbus
*RESPONSIBILITIES: Tax Exempt Organizations; Tax Compliance; Insurance Taxation; Corporate Compliance.
Rutherford, Margaret A. .... '65 '01 C.918 B.A. L.276 J.D. [Ⓐ Wiggin&D.]
Rutter, Neil K. .... '47 '80 C.031 LL.B. L.569 LL.M. [Ⓒ Votre&Assoc.]
*PRACTICE AREAS: International Commercial Arbitration; International Commercial Law; International Commercial Contracts; Corporate Law; Immigration and Naturalization.
Ryder, Kevin .... '49 '93 C.1156 B.S. L.184 J.D. [Ⓐ Jacobs&J.]
*PRACTICE AREAS: Personal Injury; Medical Malpractice; Products Liability.
Sabetta, Paul M., (CV) .... '49 '74 C.676 B.A. L.588 J.D. 216 Crown Street, 5th Floor
Sachner, S. Peter .... '65 '92 C.674 A.B. L.184 J.D. [Ⓐ Tyler C.&A.]
*PRACTICE AREAS: Litigation; Medical Malpractice Defense Law; Personal Injury Law.
Sachs, Kalman A., (AV) .... '29 '57 C.184 B.A. L.94 LL.B. 388 Orange St.
Sacks, Katharine B. .... '55 '87 C.976 B.A. L.880 J.D. [K.Sacks]
Sacks, Katharine, Attorney at Law, LLC .... 165 Bishop St.
Saffer, Michael D., (AV) .... '40 '65 C.659 B.S.E. L.669 LL.B. [Pellegrino]
St. Onge Steward Johnston & Reens, LLC, (AV) .... 88 Prospect Street (⊙Stamford)
Saleh, Saraab A. .... '71 '96 C.732 B.S. L.902 J.D. [Ⓐ Brenner,S.&W.]
*PRACTICE AREAS: Internet Law; Corporate Law; Securities.
Saltzman, Stephen L., (P.C.), (AV) ...... '37 '63 C.659 B.S. L.94 LL.B. [Brenner,S.&W.]
Sammarco, Cynthia K. '63 '93 C.705 B.A. L.1252 J.D.
195 Church Street - Eighth Floor
Sanborn, Von E. .... '68 '97 C.94 B.A. L.982 J.D. [Ⓐ Bergman,H.&R.]
*PRACTICE AREAS: International Tax Planning; Corporate Tax Planning; Multi-State Tax Planning; Tax Litigation; Business.
SanFilippo, Joseph A. .... '66 '93 C.676 B.A. L.564 J.D. [Ⓐ Wiggin&D.]
Sansone, Thomas J., (BV) .... '60 '85 C&L.94 B.A., J.D. [Carmody&T.]
*PRACTICE AREAS: Civil Litigation; Creditors Rights Law; Bankruptcy.
Sappern, Yale W. .... '36 '65 C.184 B.S. L.262 LL.B. Dep. Ct. Admn., Supr. Ct.
Saraco, Anthony J. .... '72 '99 C.184 B.S. L.1252 J.D. [Ⓐ Milano&W.]
*PRACTICE AREAS: Commercial Litigation; Insurance Defense.
Sasso, Warren F., Jr. .... '70 '97 C.262 B.A. L.306 J.D. [Ⓐ Garcia&M.]
*PRACTICE AREAS: Civil Litigation; Commercial Litigation.

Scanlon, John R., (BV) . . . . '62 '87 C.1030 B.A. L.823 J.D. [Virshup,C.&H.]
Scarpellino, Philip A., (BV) . . . . '47 '86 C.184 B.A. L.1206 J.D. Asst. State's Atty.
Schaefer, David R., (P.C.), (AV) . . . . '48 '73 C.966 B.A. L.569 J.D. [Brenner,S.&W.]
*PRACTICE AREAS: Federal Litigation; Commercial Litigation including Employment; Environmental; Real Estate; Banking.
Schancupp, David E., (BV) . . . . '41 '64 C.184 B.A. L.178 LL.B. [Shiff&S.]
Schancupp, Jennifer L. . . . . '61 '92 C.385 A.B. L.184 J.D. [Ⓐ Susman,D.&S.]
*PRACTICE AREAS: Civil Litigation; Commercial Litigation; Creditors Rights; Employment Law; Bankruptcy.
Scheirer, Alexander . . . . '52 '87 C.1156 B.S. L.1029 J.D. [Scheirer&G.]
Scheirer & Geller . . . . 445 Orange St.
Schenck, Charles N., III, (AV) . . . . '23 '48 C.976 A.B. L.178 LL.B. [Ⓒ Wiggin&D.]
*PRACTICE AREAS: Estate Planning; Trusts and Estates; Business Venture Law; Taxation; Closely Held Business.
Scherban, Ronald M., (BV) . . . . '46 '73 C.94 B.A. L.184 J.D. [R.M.Scherban]
Scherban, Ronald M., P.C., (BV) . . . . 395 Orange St., 1st Fl.
Schloss, Irving S., (AV) . . . . . '45 '72 C.309 A.B. L.976 LL.B. [Tyler C.&A.] (⊙Madison)
*PRACTICE AREAS: Estate and Gift Taxation; Federal Tax Controversies; Trusts and Estates Taxation; Tax Litigation; Retirement Planning.
Schmalz, Robert N., (AV) . . . . '32 '59 C.674 A.B. L.309 LL.B. [Ⓒ Murtha C.]
*PRACTICE AREAS: Estate Planning Law; Estate and Trust Administration Law.
Schneider, David W., (AV) . . . . '42 '71 C.282 B.A. L.976 J.D. [Tyler C.&A.]
*PRACTICE AREAS: Probate Litigation; Commercial Litigation.
Scholder, Paul A., (AV) . . . . '33 '58 C.860 B.S. L.569 LL.B. [P.A.Scholder]
*PRACTICE AREAS: Insurance Law; Product Liability Law; Negligence Law; Civil Litigation.

Scholder, Paul A., Attorney At Law, P.C., (AV)
2 Whitney Avenue, P.O. Box 1722, 06507
Telephone: 203-777-7218 Fax: 203-772-2672
Email: PaulA.Scholder,P.C.102261.2673@CompuServe.com URL: http://www.lawyers.com/paulascholderlaw
Paul A. Scholder.
General Civil Practice before State and Federal Courts. Civil Litigation, Personal Injury, Products Liability, Workers Compensation Insurance, Family and Probate Law, Environmental Law. Trials and Appeals.
References: Peoples Bank; Nocson United Bank.
See Professional Biographies, NEW HAVEN, CONNECTICUT

Schreiber, Jeanette Carpenter, (BV) . . . . . . '55 '82 C.1365 B.A. L.309 J.D. [Wiggin&D.]
*PRACTICE AREAS: Health Care; Managed Care; Mental Health; Hospital Law; Medical Staff.
Schwab, Robert L., (BV) . . . . '59 '90 C.31 B.A. L.1029 J.D. [Kennedy,J.D.&G.]
*PRACTICE AREAS: Personal Injury; Workers' Compensation; Products Liability; Criminal Law.
Schwartz, Alan '40 '65 C.67 B.S. L.976 LL.B.
(adm. in NY; not adm. in CT) Yale Law Sch.
Schwartz, Alan G., (BV) . . . . '56 '81 C.659 B.A. L.569 J.D. [Wiggin&D.]
*PRACTICE AREAS: Civil Litigation; Utility Law; Environmental Litigation; Construction Law; Real Estate Litigation.
Schwartz, Max H., (AV) . . . . '10 '35 C.390 B.A. L.976 LL.B. [Engelman&W.] ‡
*PRACTICE AREAS: Probate Law; Estates Law; Family Law.
Schweikert, G. Adam, III . . . . '— '99 C.602 B.A. L.306 J.D. [Ⓐ Wiggin&D.]
Sciarrino, Christine L. . . . . '61 '88 C.1030 B.A. L.1029 J.D. Asst. U.S. Atty.
Seaman, Penny Quinn, (AV) . . . . '51 '80 C.945 B.A. L.205 J.D. [Ⓒ Wiggin&D.]
*PRACTICE AREAS: Litigation.
Secola, Carl A., Jr., (BV) . . . . '60 '85 C.1030 B.A. L.1029 J.D. 685 State St.

Seeley & Berglass, (AV)
121 Whitney Avenue, 06510 ⊙
Telephone: 203-562-5888 Fax: 203-562-9365
Email: wps3695@aol.com
W. Parker Seeley, Jr. (Resident, Southport Office); Steven Berglass; Roswitha Miller; Sloan W. Farrell; John W. Sullivan.
Commercial Litigation, Insurance Claims Litigation, Personal Injury, and Appeals in all Courts, Arbitration and Employment Law, General Practice of Corporate and Commercial Law.
Representative Clients: Advance Machinery Co., Inc.; Bill Wheeler Real Estate, Inc.; Bridgeport Machines, Inc.; Connecticut Business Credit; First National Bank of Hartford; Florian Fine Jewelers; Gale Research, Inc.; General Electric Credit Corp.; Gerosa, Inc.; Kelly Enterprises.
See Professional Biographies, NEW HAVEN, CONNECTICUT

Segaloff, James H., (AV) . . . . '43 '69 C.823 A.B. L.184 LL.B. [Susman,D.&S.]
*PRACTICE AREAS: Commercial Law; Real Estate Law; Corporate Law.
Seligson, Marla L. . . . . '72 '98 C.1102 B.S. L.823 J.D. [Ⓐ Esty&B.]
*PRACTICE AREAS: Insurance Defense; Civil Practice.
Selmont, George Austin . . . . '67 '99 C.65 B.A. L.588 J.D. [Ⓐ Wiggin&D.]
Sensale, Joseph J., (AV) . . . . '38 '62 C.676 B.A. L.94 LL.B. [Sensale&S.]
Sensale, Robert N. . . . . '66 '91 C.676 B.A. L.1029 J.D. [Sensale&S.]
Sensale & Sensale, (AV) . . . . 667 State St.
Shannon, John M., (BV) . . . . '62 '88 C.259 B.S. L.260 J.D. [Jacobs,J.&S.]
*PRACTICE AREAS: Personal Injury; Medical Malpractice; Products Liability; Employment Discrimination; Workers Compensation.
Shansky, Marjorie F., (BV) . . . . '48 '85 C.597 B.M.E. L.184 J.D. 61 E. Grand Ave.
Shaw, David A. . . . . '59 '85 C.882 B.A. L.184 J.D. 94 Prospect Street
Shaw, Susan King, (BV) . . . . '59 '85 C.165 B.A. L.184 J.D. [Farren&K.]
*PRACTICE AREAS: Trials; Personal Injury Law; Workers' Compensation; Domestic Relations; Employment Law.
Shea, Kevin C. . . . . '66 '93 C&L.184 B.S., J.D. [Ⓐ W.H.Clendenen,Jr.]
*PRACTICE AREAS: Civil Litigation; Medical Malpractice; Professional Liability; Products Liability; Labor and Employment.
Sheedy, John J., (BV) . . . . '56 '86 C.1086 B.A. L.1048 J.D. 265 Church St.
Sheehan, Michael O., (BV) . . . . '47 '77 C.321 B.A. L.94 J.D. 105 Court St.
Sherwood, Charles A., (BV) . . . . '29 '56 C&L.184 B.A., J.D. [C.A.Sherwood&Assoc.]
Sherwood, Charles A., & Associates, (BV) . . . . 55 Trumbull St.
Shiff, Philip Robert, (AV) . . . . '05 '29 C&L.976 Ph.B., LL.B. [Shiff&S.]
Shiff and Schancupp, (AV) . . . . 900 Chapel St.
Shtivelband, Inna '72 '97 C.1349 B.S. L.94 J.D.
(adm. in NJ; not adm. in CT; Pat.) Genaissance Pharmaceuticals
Shure, H. William, (AV) '40 '64 C.197 A.B. L.893 LL.B.
[Pullman&C.] (⊙Bridgeport)
*PRACTICE AREAS: Commercial Law; Banking Law; Bankruptcy Law; Government Law.

Siegel, O'Connor, Schiff & Zangari, P.C., (AV)
171 Orange Street P.O. Drawer 906, 06510 ⊙
Telephone: 203-789-0001 Telecopier: 203-782-2766
Email: first initial last name @soszlaw.com URL: http://www.soszlaw.com
Christine A. Barker (Resident); John W. Beck (Resident, Hartford, Connecticut Office); Gregory J. Bezz (Resident, Hartford, Connecticut Office); Robert F. Cohn (Resident); Hugh W. Cuthbertson (Resident); Frederick L. Dorsey (Resident); Glenn A. Duhl (Resident, Hartford, Connecticut Office); Nicholas J. Grello, Jr. (Resident, Hartford, Connecticut Office); Peter D. Hershman (Resident); Peter A. Janus (Resident, Hartford, Connecticut Office); George J. Kelly, Jr.; Richard D. O'Connor (Resident, Hartford, Connecticut Office); Edward F. O'Donnell, Jr. (Resident, Hartford, Connecticut Office); Robert J. Percy (Resident, Hartford, Connecticut Office); Donald W. Strickland (Resident, Hartford, Connecticut Office); Mario J. Zangari (Resident). Of Counsel: Robert W. Blythe (Resident); Jay S. Siegel (Resident, Hartford, Connecticut Office);—Jody Pagano Benbow (Resident); Shawn P. Coyne (Resident, Hartford, Connecticut Office); Ana Isabel DeMoura (Resident, Hartford, Connecticut, Office); Kevin J. Diadamo (Resident); Paul H. Gamache (Resident, Hartford, Connecticut Office); Daniel P. Murphy (Resident); John J. O'Connell (Resident, Hartford, Connecticut Office).

(This Listing Continued)

Siegel, O'Connor, Schiff & Zangari, P.C. (Continued)

Labor Relations and Employment Law representing management in the private and public sectors, including related Litigation in Federal and State Courts, Tax Law, Education Law, Municipal Law, Commercial Law, Corporate Law, Estate Planning and Estate Administration Matters.
Hartford, Connecticut Office: 150 Trumbull Street. Telephone: 860-727-8900. Telecopier: 860-527-5131.
See Professional Biographies, NEW HAVEN, CONNECTICUT

Silbert, Jonathan E. . . . . '43 '68 C.197 A.B. L.309 J.D. Supr. Ct. J.
Silver, Alan E., (P.C.) . . . . '37 '63 C&L.184 B.A., LL.B. 275 Orange St.

Silver, Golub & Teitell LLP
(See Stamford)

Silverman, Henry N., (BV) . . . . '40 '65 C.164 B.A. L.178 LL.B. [Greenberg,H.C.&S.]
Silverman, Ina L. . . . . '58 '86 C.976 B.S. L.184 J.D. 187 Willard St.
Silverstein, Nathan M., (AV) . . . . '24 '50 C.184 L.94 LL.B. [Silverstein&O.]
*PRACTICE AREAS: Tax Law; Litigation; Estate Planning Law.
Silverstein, Richard P., (BV) . . . . '57 '86 50 Elm St.

Silverstein & Osach, P.C., (AV)
Suite 903, 234 Church Street, P.O. Box 1727, 06507
Telephone: 203-865-0121 Fax: 203-865-0255
Email: taxlawyer@worldnet.att.net
Nathan M. Silverstein; Ronald C. Osach; Kurt F. Zimmermann;—Leonard K. Atkinson, Jr.
General Tax Practice. Federal and State Tax Litigation. Estate Planning, Probate, Corporation, Pension and Profit Sharing Law.
See Professional Biographies, NEW HAVEN, CONNECTICUT

Simons, William A. . . . . '46 '73 C.475 B.S. L.276 J.D. [Wiggin&D.] (Pat.)
*PRACTICE AREAS: Chemical Patents; Intellectual Property Infringement; Intellectual Property; Portfolio Management; International Intellectual Property.

Singer, Robert M., L.L.C., Law Offices of
(See Hamden)

Singewald, Dean R., (BV) . . . . . . '36 '63 C.602 B.S. L.93 J.D. 34 Trumbull St. (⊙Madison)
Sirois, David R., (BV) . . . . '56 '82 C.712 B.A. L.823 J.D. [Sirois&M.]
Sirois & Maser, P.C., (BV) . . . . 1948 Chapel St.
Sitar, Raymond . . . . '43 '72 C.1102 B.S. L.574 J.D. 392 Edgewood Ave
Sizensky, Jill M. . . . . '64 '89 C.184 B.S. L.1048 J.D. 275 Orange St.
Skalka, Douglas S., (BV) . . . . '60 '85 C.188 A.B. L.94 J.D. [Neubert,P.&M.]
*PRACTICE AREAS: Bankruptcy; Commercial Litigation; Corporate Finance; Real Estate.
Sklarz, Mark G., (AV) . . . . '45 '70 C.264 B.A. L.184 J.D. [Cummings&L.]
*PRACTICE AREAS: Taxation; Business and Corporate; Trust and Estates; Licensing.
Sklaver, Gary P., (BV) . . . . '50 '75 C.31 B.A. L.930 J.D. [Ullman,P.&S.]
Sklaver, Laura M., (BV) . . . . '50 '81 C.914 B.A. L.184 J.D. [Susman,D.&S.]
*PRACTICE AREAS: Business Law; Closely Held Corporations; Limited Liability Company; Partnership Law; Real Estate Financing Law.
Skolnick, David J. . . . . '47 '71 C.390 A.B. L.184 J.D. 62 Trumbull St.
Slate, William B. . . . . '66 '92 C.111 B.S. L.1068 J.D. [Ⓐ Wiggin&D.] (Pat.)
Slye, Ronald C. . . . . '62 '90 C.178 B.A. L.976 J.D. Yale Law Sch.
Smith, Alfred E., Jr., (BV) . . . . '56 '86 C.276 B.A. L.184 J.D. [Murtha C.]
*PRACTICE AREAS: Environmental Law; Health Care Law.
Smith, Eric P. . . . . '71 '95 C.1156 B.S. L.1252 J.D. [Lynch,T.K.&E.]
*PRACTICE AREAS: Medical Malpractice; Personal Injury; Civil Litigation; Appellate Practice.
Snaider, Benson A., P.C., (BV) . . . . '37 '62 C.882 B.A. L.893 LL.B. [B.A.Snaider]
*PRACTICE AREAS: Condemnation; Eminent Domain; Zoning Law; Divorce.

Snaider, Benson A., P.C., (BV)
389 Orange Street, 06511
Telephone: 203-777-6426 Fax: 203-782-0366
Email: bslaw@snet.net URL: http://www.lawyers.com/bslaw
Benson A. Snaider.
Condemnation, Zoning, Real Estate Development, Land Use.
Representative Clients: Bank of New Haven; Timberland Development Corp.
Approved Attorneys for: Connecticut Attorneys Title Insurance Co (Issuing Agent); Lawyers Title Insurance Co.
References: Union Trust Co.; The Bank of New Haven.
See Professional Biographies, NEW HAVEN, CONNECTICUT

Snow, Atticks & Hollo, LLC
(See Madison)

Snyder, Deborah K. . . . . '67 '92 C.367 B.A. L.309 J.D. [Ⓐ Bergman,H.&R.]
*PRACTICE AREAS: Taxation; Estate Planning.
Snyder, Richard K., (AV) . . . . '35 '64 C&L.477 A.B., J.D. [Ⓒ Tyler C.&A.]
*PRACTICE AREAS: Estate Planning; Estate Administration; Estate Litigation; Real Estate.
Sokol, Matthew A. . . . . '72 '99 C.1372 B.A. L.1040 J.D. [Ⓐ Tyler C.&A.]
Solnit, Ben A., (AV) . . . . '57 '84 C.918 B.A. L.976 J.D. [Tyler C.&A.]
*PRACTICE AREAS: Commercial Litigation; Appellate Practice.
Solomon, Paul R., (BV) . . . . '38 '64 C.4 B.A. L.93 LL.B. 62 Trumbull St.
Solomon, Robert A., (AV) . . . . '47 '72 C.705 B.A. L.273 J.D. Yale Law Sch.
Soloway, Alan M. . . . . '55 '81 C.1044 B.A. L.978 J.D. U.S. Atty. Off.
Sosensky, Steven C. . . . . '63 '88 C.184 B.A. L.1048 J.D. 9 Trumbull St.
Sosnoff, Sandra S., (BV) . . . . '44 '76 C.547 B.A. L.569 J.D. 111 Whitney Avenue
Souza, Karen E., (BV) . . . . '60 '85 C.689 B.A. L.831 J.D. 275 Orange St.
Spalding, Maria S. . . . . '55 '87 C.703 B.S.N. L.1029 J.D. [Updike,K.&S.] (⊙Hartford)
*PRACTICE AREAS: Product Liability; Professional Defense.
Sparks, Marilyn . . . . '— '90 C.4 B.A. L.1019 J.D. P.O. Box 377
Sperandeo, Richard P., (AV) . . . . '27 '54 C&L.184 B.A., J.D. [Sperandeo&D.]
Sperandeo & Donegan, (AV) . . . . 59 Elm Street
Stadler, Sara R., (AV) . . . . '43 '79 C.546 B.A. L.184 J.D. [Murtha C.]
*PRACTICE AREAS: Estate Planning Law; Estate and Trust Administration Law; Tax Exempt Corporations Law.
Staley, Thomas J., (BV) . . . . '33 '60 C.1030 B.B.A. L.184 LL.B. [Barberio,S.&M.]
Staples, Cameron C. . . . . '58 '89 C.918 B.A. L.184 J.D. [Ⓐ Neubert,P.&M.]
*PRACTICE AREAS: Health Care; Corporate Law.
Stark, Barbara Kahn, (AVⓉ) . . . . '50 '76 C.446 B.A. L.208 J.D. [Kahn&S.]
*PRACTICE AREAS: Divorce Mediation; Divorce Collaboration; Divorce Financial Planning.
Steele, John-Henry M. . . . . '62 '91 C.855 B.A. L.1048 J.D. [Ⓐ Votre&Assoc.]
*PRACTICE AREAS: Commercial Litigation; Toxic Torts; Lead Poisoning; Litigation; Personal Injury.
Stein & Lindsay, LLC, (AV) . . . . 234 Church Street, Suite 803 (⊙Stamford)
Stempel, William D., (BV) . . . . . '54 '79 C&L.976 B.A., J.D. Dep. Gen. Coun., Yale Univ.
Stephanie, Baier S. . . . . '71 '01 C.999 B.S. L.306 J.D. [Ⓐ Susman,D.&S.]
*PRACTICE AREAS: Commercial Law; Business Law; Family Law.
Sterling, Alinor C. . . . . '67 '96 C.674 B.A. L.112 J.D. [Ⓐ Jacobs,G.B.&D.]
*PRACTICE AREAS: Litigation.
Stevens, Carroll D. '49 '76 C.275 B.A. L.383 J.D.
(adm. in KY; not adm. in CT) Assoc. Dean, Yale Univ. Law Sch.

Stevens, Carroll & Carveth
(See Milford)

Stewart, Elizabeth J., (AV) . . . . '61 '86 C&L.893 B.A., J.D. [Murtha C.]
*PRACTICE AREAS: Corporate and Securities Litigation; Antitrust Litigation; Insurance Coverage Litigation.

Stockman, Eric J. .... '67 '94 C&L.184 B.A., J.D. [Neubert,P.&M.]
*PRACTICE AREAS: Professional Liability; Toxic Torts; Products Liability; Personal Injury.
Stoloff, Sonia S. .... '44 '75 C.102 B.A. L.1009 J.D. Asst. Atty. Gen.
Stretton, John G. .... '73 '98 C.93 B.A. L.94 J.D. [Ⓐ Updike,K.&S.] (⊙Hartford)
*PRACTICE AREAS: Civil Litigation; Professional Liability Defense; Employment Litigation; Personal Injury Defense; Insurance Coverage Defense.
Strickland, Michele L. .... '60 '92 C.1099 B.A. L.1252 J.D. 234 Church St., Ste. 300
Strosberg, Gail E. .... '55 '81 C.477 B.S. L.1066 J.D. Yale Univ.
Subbloie, Linda A. .... '57 '90 C&L.1206 B.S., J.D. 105 Court St.
Sugarmann, Richard A., (BV) .... '37 '62 C&L.184 B.A., J.D. [Sugarmann&S.]
Sugarmann, Steven A .... '63 '88 C.1365 B.A. L.94 J.D. [Sugarmann&S.]
Sugarmann and Sugarmann, (BV) .... One Bradley Rd., Suite 105, Woodbridge
Sullivan, John W. .... '70 '99 C.37 B.S. L.1252 J.D. [Seeley&B.]
*PRACTICE AREAS: Commercial Litigation.
Sullivan, Lauren A. .... '62 '95 C&L.1338 B.S., J.D. [Ⓐ Wiggin&D.]
Sullivan, Margaret E. .... '56 '88 C.454 B.A. L.1029 J.D. 685 State St.
Sullivan, Shaun S., (AV) .... '40 '67 C.1030 B.S. L.262 LL.B. [Wiggin&D.]
*PRACTICE AREAS: Litigation.

Sulzbach, J. Michael, (BV) '47 '72 C&L.659 B.A., J.D.
385 Orange Street, 06511
Telephone: 203-781-0880 Fax: 203-781-0861
***PRACTICE AREAS: Trials and Appeals in State and Federal Courts; Insurance; Real Estate; Products Liability; Probate Law.**
Trials and Appeals in State and Federal Courts. Insurance, Real Estate, Products Liability and Probate Law.
See Professional Biographies, NEW HAVEN, CONNECTICUT

Summa & Ryan, P.C.
(See Waterbury)

Susman, Matthew C., (BV) .... '57 '84 C.178 A.B. L.262 J.D. [Susman,D.&S.]
*PRACTICE AREAS: Commercial Law; Corporate Law; Real Estate Law; Municipal Finance.
Susman, Michael, (AV) .... '31 '55 C&L.184 B.A., LL.B. [Susman,D.&S.]
*PRACTICE AREAS: Real Estate Development Law; Real Estate Leasing; Municipal Law; Commercial Law.

Susman, Duffy & Segaloff, P.C., (AV) BB
55 Whitney Avenue, 06510-1300
Mailing Address: P.O. Box 1684, New Haven, Connecticut 06507-1684
Telephone: 203-624-9830 Fax: 203-562-8430
URL: http://www.lawyers.com/susmanduffy
Allen H. Duffy (1931-1986); Michael Susman; James H. Segaloff; Joseph E. Faughnan; Susan W. Wolfson; Laura M. Sklaver; Andrew R. Lubin; James J. Perito; Matthew C. Susman; Thomas E. Katon;—Jennifer L. Schancupp; Peter G. Kruzynski; Michael C. Conroy; Baier S. Stephanie. Of Counsel: Diana C. Ballard; David P. Hambleton.
Administrative, Appellate, Banking, Bankruptcy, Business, Civil Trial, Commercial Litigation, Corporate, Construction, Creditors Rights, Criminal Trial, Employment Law, Eminent Domain, Environmental, Family, Franchise, Governmental Relations Law, Healthcare, Housing, Insurance Defense, Land Use, Legal Malpractice Defense, Medical Malpractice Defense, Municipal Bond Public Authority Financing, Non Profit and Tax Exempt Organizations Municipal, Personal Injury, Product Liability, Probate, Professional Liability Defense, Real Estate, Trial Practice in all State and Federal Courts, Trusts and Estates, Wills and Probate, Urban Development, Zoning.
See Professional Biographies, NEW HAVEN, CONNECTICUT

Swaine, James E., (AV) .... '48 '76 C.867 B.A. L.184 J.D. 234 Church St., Ste. 300
Sweeney, Robert J., (BV) .... '52 '77 C.676 B.A. L.184 J.D. [Early,L.&S.]
*PRACTICE AREAS: Trials; Personal Injury Litigation; Civil Litigation; Criminal Litigation.
Swift, Donn A., (BV) .... '56 '81 C.1107 B.A. L.767 J.D. [Lynch,T.K.&E.]
*PRACTICE AREAS: Products Liability; Negligence; Personal Injury.
Swift, William C. G., Jr. .... '48 '73 C.659 B.S. L.184 J.D. [Bergman,H.&R.] ⊙
*PRACTICE AREAS: Business; Estate Planning; Taxation (Local, Personal Property, State, Federal or International Law).
Taylor, Jack S. .... '71 '97 C.183 B.A. L.352 J.D. [Ⓐ Milano&W.]
*PRACTICE AREAS: Insurance Defense; Commercial Litigation.
Taylor, Susan .... '71 '99 [Ⓐ Tyler C.&A.] (⊙Hartford)
Teixeira, Christine P. .... '75 '00 C.884 B.S. L.184 J.D. [Ⓐ Wiggin&D.]
Thomas, James A. '39 '64 C.918 B.A. L.976 LL.B.
(adm. in IA; not adm. in CT) Assoc. Dean, Yale Law Sch.
Thompson, Bruce W. .... '43 '67 C.93 B.S. L.184 LL.B. Supr. Ct. J.
Thompson, Mike Kevin '55 '91 C.397 B.A. L.276 J.D.
(adm. in PA; not adm. in CT) Asst. Dean, Yale Univ. Law Sch.
Thorne, Robert E. .... '34 '62 C&L.477 B.B.A., J.D. Admn. Law J.
Tiernan, Charles E., III, (BV) .... '58 '83 C.855 B.A. L.221 J.D. [Lynch,T.K.&E.]
*PRACTICE AREAS: Criminal Law; Workers Compensation; Matrimonial Law.
Tiernan, Lee Kennedy, (BV) .... '61 '91 C.156 B.A. L.818 J.D. [Ⓐ Lynch,T.K.&E.]
*PRACTICE AREAS: Negligence; Personal Injury; Social Security; Landlord and Tenant Law; Labor and Employment.
Tiernan, Shawn G., (CV) .... '59 '86 C.1307 B.A. L.184 J.D. Asst. Pub. Def.
Tiernan, William F., Jr., (AV) .... '39 '64 C&L.184 B.S., LL.B. [McNerney,T.&B.]
Tilson, John Q., (AV) .... '11 '36 C&L.976 B.A., LL.B. [Wiggin&D.]
*PRACTICE AREAS: Health Care Law; Hospital Law; Tax Exempt Organizations Law; Estate Planning; Estate Settlements.

Tinley, Nastri, Renehan & Dost, LLP
(See Waterbury)

Titus, Lee S., (BV) .... '41 '64 C.976 B.A. L.184 J.D. 139 Orange St.
Tobin, Joseph M., (BV) .... '44 '69 C.884 B.S. L.262 J.D. [Tobin&M.]
Tobin & Melien, (BV) .... 45 Court St. (⊙Meriden)
Todd, Erica W. .... '67 '92 C.1029 B.A. L.1252 J.D. [Trotta,T.&T.]
Todisco, Louis B., (BV) .... '49 '77 C.184 B.A. L.472 J.D. [Murtha C.]
*PRACTICE AREAS: Health Care Law; Labor and Employment Law.
Tomaszewski, John J. '40 '71 C.569 B.Ch.E. L.724 J.D.
(adm. in NY; not adm. in CT; See Pat. Sect.) [Ⓐ DeLio&P.]
*PRACTICE AREAS: Patents; Trademarks; Copyrights; Intellectual Property Licensing; Unfair Competition.
Toole, Elizabeth .... '67 '94 C.311 B.A. L.1202 J.D. [Levy,L.&T.]
Toro, Frank, Jr., (BV) .... '41 '66 C.676 A.B. L.818 LL.B. 22 Trumbull St.
Torre, Karen Lee, (BV) .... '58 '85 C.1102 B.S. L.1029 J.D. 61 Elm St.
Totman, David T., (AV) .... '38 '66 C&L.976 B.A., LL.B. [Church&C.]
*PRACTICE AREAS: Corporations; Family Law; Estate Planning; Probate; Real Estate.
Toubman, Sheldon V. '57 '83
C.184 B.S. L.659 J.D. New Haven Legal Assistance Assn., Inc.
Traub, Stephen I., (AV) .... '30 '60 C.184 B.A. L.893 J.D. [Ⓒ Lynch,T.K.&E.]
*PRACTICE AREAS: Professional Malpractice; Negligence; Commercial Litigation; Airplane Crash Litigation.
Treffers, Peter A., (BV) .... '41 '70 C.918 B.A. L.347 J.D. 129 Church St.
Tristine, Joseph R. .... '71 '97 C.309 A.B. L.1068 J.D. [Ⓐ Wiggin&D.]
Trotta, Frederick J., (BV) '61 '87
C.1048 A.B. L.1029 J.D. 195 Church Street - Eighth Floor
Trotta, Joseph F., (BV) .... '32 '57 C&L.184 A.B., LL.B. [Trotta,T.&T.]
Trotta, Trotta & Trotta, (BV) .... 195 Church Street, Eighth Floor
Turbak, Stephen Albin '56 '82 C.339 B.A. L.884 J.D.
(adm. in PA; not adm. in CT) Intel. Prop. Coun., Annco., Inc.
Turret, Andrew S. .... '64 '90 C.1044 B.S. L.982 J.D. 265 Church St.

Tyler Cooper & Alcorn, LLP, (AV) BB
205 Church Street, P.O. Box 1936, 06509-1910 ⊙
Telephone: 203-784-8200 Telecopier: 203-789-2133
URL: http://www.tylercooper.com
Members of Firm: Ralph Gregory Elliot (Resident at Hartford Office); Michael J. Dorney; Bruce Lewellyn; Joseph C. Lee (Managing Partner of the Firm); Lewis Segal (Resident at Hartford Office); Irving S. Schloss; Jon T. Hirschoff; William H. Champlin III (Resident at Hartford Office); Timothy W. Bingham; David W. Schneider; Robert W. Allen; Richard W. Bowerman; George E. O'Brien, Jr.; Robert J. Metzler II (Resident at Hartford Office); Ronald J. Cohen; Margaret P. Mason; William W. Bouton III (Resident at Hartford Office); Thomas C. Clark (Resident at Hartford Office); Mark V. Connolly (Resident at Hartford Office); William S. Fish, Jr. (Resident at Hartford Office); Kevin McCann (Resident at Hartford Office); David J. Wiese (Resident at Hartford Office); Emmett E. Brown III (Resident at Stamford Office); Jon P. Leckerling (Resident at Madison Office); Ben A. Solnit; Jacqueline DeAndrus Bucar; Fillis W. Stober (Resident at Hartford Office); Thomas S. Marrion (Resident at Hartford Office); Christopher P. McCormack; Christopher L. Ulrich (Resident at Stamford Office); Kevin G. Ferrigno (Resident at Hartford Office); Lori B. Alexander; Greg R. Barringer; William F. Cummings (Resident at Hartford Office); Patricia E. Reilly; Noble F. Allen; Glory Martyn Lena (Resident at Hartford Office); Robert B. Flynn; Niclas A. Ferland. Of Counsel: Richard G. Bell; Milton P. DeVane; William S. Rogers (Resident at Hartford Office); James R. Greenfield; William R. Murphy; Roger E. Koontz (Resident at Hartford Office); Richard K. Snyder; Samuel W. Bowlby. Senior Counsel: Henry W. Pascarella (Resident at Greenwich Office). Counsel: Kurt W. Johnson (Resident at Hartford Office); Nan Budde Chequer (Resident at Stamford Office); Kathleen A. Maher; Charles R. Andres; Barry M. Winnick (Resident at Hartford Office); Deborah D. Cannavino (Resident at Stamford Office); Regina Duchin Kraus; Shawn L. O'Sullivan. Associates: Renee M. Reed; Lisa N. Davis; James R. Bryne; S. Peter Sachner; Robert C. Hinton; Michael C. D'Agostino; Paul L. Bader; Christopher Markham Haddad (Resident at Hartford Office); Michael T. McCormack (Resident at Hartford Office); Timothy P. Jensen; Gerald T. Giaimo; Carol L. Loomis (Resident at Hartford Office); Elizabeth M. Smith (Resident at Hartford Office); Stuart Weichsel (Not admitted in CT); Malgorzata J. Bochenek; Susan Taylor (Resident at Hartford Office); Matthew A. Sokol; Elizabeth K. Andrews (Resident at Hartford Office); Ellen Jean Beardsley; Christopher A. Kelland; W. Joe Wilson; Kelly P. Lutz; Tricia White; Courtney Lane; Sarah Lombard; Paul Guggina (Resident at Hartford Office).
Administrative Law, Alternative Dispute Resolution, Antitrust and Trade Regulation, Banking, Bankruptcy and Reorganization, Business Crimes, Business Organizations and Securities Law, Computer Law, Domestic Relations, Environmental Law, Financial Services, Franchising, Health Care, Immigration, Insurance Defense and Insurance Coverage Defense, Intellectual Property, Labor and Employment, Legislative Lawyering, Litigation, Media Law, Medical Malpractice Defense, Pension and Employee Benefits, Public Utilities, Real Estate, Taxation, Trusts and Estates and Workers' Compensation.
Counsel for: Hospital of St. Raphael; The Stanley Works; The Southern Connecticut Gas Co.; Southern New England Telephone Co.; Science Park Development Corp.; Connecticut American Water Co.; General Electric Co.
Hartford, Connecticut Office: CityPlace. Telephone: 860-725-6200. Telecopier: 860-278-3802.
Stamford, Connecticut Office: One Landmark Square. Telephone: 203-348-5555. Telecopier: 203-348-3875.
Greenwich, Connecticut Office: 675 Steamboat Road. Telephone: 203-869-2000. Telecopier: 203-869-2001.
Madison, Connecticut Office: 23 Woodland Road. Telephone: 203-318-3600. Telecopier: 203-318-3609.
See Professional Biographies, NEW HAVEN, CONNECTICUT

Tyma, James J. .... '63 '88 C.93 B.S. L.184 J.D. [Ⓒ Lippman&O.]
Ullman, Andrew M., (AV) .... '39 '64 C&L.976 B.A., LL.B. [Ullman,P.&S.]
Ullman, Perlmutter & Sklaver, (AV) .... 47 Trumbull St.
Ullmann, Thomas J., (AV) .... '50 '80 C.1252 B.S. L.184 J.D. Pub. Def.

Updike, Kelly & Spellacy, P.C., (AV)
265 Church Street, Tenth Floor, 06510-7002 ⊙
Telephone: 203-786-8300 Fax: 203-772-2037
Email: Info@uks.com URL: http://www.uks.com
Hugh I. Manke; John F. Wolter; David J. Monz; Maria S. Spalding; Christopher L. Brigham; Rolan J. Young;—Michel Bayonne; Jennifer L. Groves; Gregg J. Lallier; Joseph A. Rosenthal; John G. Stretton.
Administrative Law, Appellate Law, Business Law, Commercial Lending and Banking, Commercial Litigation, Creditors' Rights, Design/Construction Law, Employment Law, Environmental Law, Franchise Law, Human Service Law, Legislative Representation, Personal Law, Product Liability Law, Professional Defense Law, Public Finance/Public Law, Real Estate Law, Taxation, Financial and Estate Planning and Pensions, and Probate Law, Venture Capital.
Hartford, Connecticut Office: One State Street, P.O. Box: 231277. Telephone: 860-548-2600. Cable Address: "Ukslaw." Fax: 860-548-2680.
Stamford, Connecticut Office: 6 Landmark Square, Fourth Floor. Telephone: 203-359-5749. Fax: 203-359-5858.
See Professional Biographies, NEW HAVEN, CONNECTICUT

Velardi, Frank B., Jr., (BV) .... '57 '83 C.93 B.A. L.724 J.D. [Lasala,W.&W.]
Virgulto, Thomas A. .... '67 '92 C.976 B.A. L.1048 J.D. [Ⓐ Mongillo&I.]
Virshup, Caplan & Hecht, (AV) .... 20 Trumbull St.
Vishno, Jeremy G., (CV) .... '64 '90 C.454 B.A. L.472 J.D. 142 Temple St.
Votre, Kenneth A., (AV) .... '60 '84 C&L.1029 B.E.S., J.D. [Votre&Assoc.]
*PRACTICE AREAS: Commercial Litigation; Taxation; Tax Litigation; International Business Litigation; Health Care Regulation.

Votre & Associates, P.C., (AV) BB
105 Court Street, Suite 405, 06511-6957
Telephone: 203-498-0065 Fax: 203-821-3595
Email: kvotre@aol.com URL: http://www.lawyers.com/votre&associates
Kenneth A. Votre;—John-Henry M. Steele; Tara Justine Galbo. Of Counsel: Neil K. Rutter.
Commercial Litigation, Taxation, Tax Litigation, International Business Litigation, Health Care Regulation, Health Care Finance, Intellectual Property, Personal Injury, Corporate Law.
See Professional Biographies, NEW HAVEN, CONNECTICUT

Wagoner, Walter D., Jr., (BV) .... '42 '71 C&L.976 B.A., LL.B. 840 Elm St.
Walker, Nancy L., (BV) .... '53 '83 C.112 B.A. L.1065 J.D. [Ⓐ W.H.Clendenen,Jr.]
*PRACTICE AREAS: Litigation; Appellate Practice; Commercial Law.
Wallace, Anthony A., (BV) .... '61 '90 C.1303 B.A. L.1218 J.D. 419 Whalley Ave.
Wallman, Marc A., (P.C.), (AV) ...... '42 '66 C.994 B.A. L.976 LL.B. [Brenner,S.&W.]
*PRACTICE AREAS: Corporate; Real Estate; Commercial Law; Health Care Law.
Walsh, Donald G., (AV) .... '34 '58 C.745 B.A. L.276 J.D. [Walsh,B.&W.]
Walsh, Donald G., Jr., (BV) .... '57 '87 C.745 B.A. L.1048 J.D. [Walsh,B.&W.]
Walsh, Edward L., (BV) .... '51 '76 C.602 B.A. L.306 J.D. [Walsh&O.]
Walsh, James O., (BV) .... '47 '73 C.321 A.B. L.818 J.D. [Lasala,W.&W.]
Walsh, John F. .... '30 '58 C.573 B.S. L.276 J.D. 52 Trumbull St.
Walsh, John M., Jr. .... '64 '90 C.93 B.A. L.128 J.D. [Licari&W.]
*PRACTICE AREAS: Labor and Employment; Workers' Compensation; Civil Litigation.
Walsh, Burt & Walsh, (AV) .... 169 Olive St.
Walsh & O'Neill, (BV) .... 51 Elm St.
Wanat, Christopher F., (BV) .... '62 '87 C.184 B.S. L.1017 J.D. [Milano&W.] ⊙
*PRACTICE AREAS: Commercial Litigation; Construction Litigation; Employment Litigation; Insurance Defense; Trade Secrets.
Ward, John R., (AV) .... '62 '90 C.999 LL.B. L.184 J.D. [Pullman&C.]
*PRACTICE AREAS: Real Estate Law; Commercial Law; Municipal Law.
Warrecker, Janis Lynn .... '66 '92 C.112 B.S. L.1066 J.D. One Century Twr.
Waters, Barry J., (AV) .... '52 '81 C.276 A.B. L.273 J.D. [Murtha C.]
*PRACTICE AREAS: Employment; Litigation; Noncompetition; Trade Secrets.
Weaver, Maureen, (BV) .... '55 '86 C.228 A.B. L.1068 J.D. [Wiggin&D.]
*PRACTICE AREAS: Health Law; Long Term Care; Health Care Compliance; Hospital Law; Administrative Law.
Webb, Sharon Cohen .... '62 '89 C.867 B.A. L.1029 J.D. [Ⓐ Virshup,C.&H.]

Weichsel, Stuart '65 '94 C.860 B.A. L.276 J.D.
(adm. in NY; not adm. in CT) [Ⓐ Tyler C.&A.]
Weinstein, Judy K. .... '55 '80 C.914 B.A. L.184 J.D. [Neubert,P.&M.] ⊙
*PRACTICE AREAS: Health Law; Commercial Finance; Commercial Real Estate; Banking Law; Workouts.

Weinstein, Weiner, Ignal, Napolitano & Shapiro, P.C.
(See Bridgeport)

Weisfeld, Lauren M., (BV) .... '52 '77 C.33 B.A. L.910 J.D. Pub. Def.
Weisselberg, Susan E. '54 '82 C.855 B.A. L.184 J.D.
Dir. of Legis & Proj., Ofc. of the Chief Admin.
Weissman, Naureen R. .... '70 '95 C&L.846 B.A., J.D. [Ⓐ Milano&W.]
*PRACTICE AREAS: Insurance Defense; Commercial Litigation; Administrative Law.
Welch-Rubin, David .... '54 '84 C.976 B.A. L.178 J.D. [Engelman&W.]
*PRACTICE AREAS: Litigation; Family Law; Personal Injury; Divorce.
Welch-Rubin, Lori A., (BV) .... '59 '91 C.309 B.A. L.976 J.D. [Engelman&W.]
*PRACTICE AREAS: Litigation; Family Law; Appellate Practice; Divorce.

Welty, Jean L., (AV) '49 '75 C.187 B.A. L.976 J.D. BR
385 Orange Street, P.O. Box 1662, 06507
Telephone: 203-781-0877 Fax: 203-781-0899
URL: http://www.lawyers.com/jlwelty
***PRACTICE AREAS: Matrimonial and Family Law.**
Matrimonial and Family Law, Child Custody, Child Support, Paternity.
Reference: People's Bank.
See Professional Biographies, NEW HAVEN, CONNECTICUT

Westbrook, Dawne .... '70 '99 C.254 B.A. L.880 J.D. [Ⓐ Williams&P.]
*PRACTICE AREAS: Employment Discrimination; Police Misconduct; Civil Rights; Criminal Law.
Wexler, Harry J., (AV) .... '35 '62 C.309 B.A. L.976 LL.B. 900 Chapel St.
Whalen, Elizabeth A. .... '57 '90 C.102 B.S. L.178 J.D. [Bergman,H.&R.]
*PRACTICE AREAS: Partnership Law; Real Estate; International Taxation; Financial Investments.
White, Shelley A. '52 '77 C.893 B.A. L.93 J.D.
Litigation Dir., New Haven Legal Asst. Assoc.
White, Tricia .... '69 '01 C.1103 B.S. L.1252 J.D. [Ⓐ Tyler C.&A.]
Whitney, James C., (AV) .... '42 '68 C&L.976 B.A., J.D. [Cooper,W.C.&F.]
Wicklow, Joseph M., III, (BV) .... '47 '81 C.1156 B.S. L.1048 J.D. [Lasala,W.&W.]
Wiederhold, Cecilia B. .... '53 '85 C.1102 B.A. L.184 J.D. Asst. State's Atty.

Wiggin & Dana LLP, (AV) BR
One Century Tower, P.O. Box 1832, 06508-1832 ⊙
Telephone: 203-498-4400 Telefax: 203-782-2889
URL: http://www.wiggin.com
Members of Firm: Frederick H. Wiggin (1882-1963); J. Dwight Dana (1889-1951); John Q. Tilson; John W. Barnett; William C. Baskin, Jr.; Robert F. Cavanagh; Charles C. Kingsley; William J. Doyle; Noel E. Hanf; Shaun S. Sullivan; Jeremy G. Zimmermann; J. Michael Eisner; Norman Fineberg; William H. Prout, Jr.; Linda L. Randell; D. Terence Jones; Mark R. Kravitz; Melinda A. Agsten; Edward Wood Dunham; Norman J. Fleming; Peter J. Lefeber; John G. Zandy; Sherry L. Dominick; Alan G. Schwartz; Valerie A. Seiling (Resident, Hartford Office); Bennett J. Bernblum; Susan J. Bryson; Jeanette Carpenter Schreiber; Patrick J. Monahan, II (Resident, Hartford Office); Peter H. Gruen; Mary R. Norris; Maureen Weaver; Robert M. Langer (Resident, Hartford Office); James F. Farrington, Jr. (Resident, Stamford Office); Karen L. Clute; Leonard Leader (Resident, Stamford Office); Jeffrey R. Babbin; Ian E. Bjorkman; Dale L. Carlson; William A. Simons; David B. Fein (Resident, Stamford Office); William A. Perrone (Resident, Stamford Office); Merton G. Gollaher; Stephen B. Harris (Resident, Hartford Office); Phyllis M. Pari; Gregory S. Rosenblatt; Francis J. Duffin; Kevin M. Kennedy; Michael Grundei (Resident, Stamford Office); Patricia Kavee Melick (Resident, Stamford Office); William J. Speranza (Resident, Stamford Office); Lisa Page Heslin; Mark E. Haranzo (Resident, Stamford Office); Lawrence Peikes (Resident, Stamford Office); James H. Bicks (Resident, Stamford Office); Daniel J. Klau (Resident, Hartford Office); Peter M. Wendzel (Resident, Hartford Office); Joseph Schumacher (Resident, Berwyn, Pennsylvania Office and Cherry Hill, New Jersey). Senior Counsel: William E. Craig; S. Robert Jelley; Robert M. McAnerney (Resident, Stamford Office); Charles N. Schenck, III. Counsel: Penny Quinn Seaman; Sharyn B. Zuch (Resident, Hartford Office); Marcia Kenny Keegan (Resident, Hartford Office); Cynthia Brodhead; Martin H. Dodd; Christine Owens Morgan; Todd E. Garabedian; Gates Garrity-Rokous. Associates: William John Albinger; Erika L. Amarante; Jeffrey Russell Ambroziak; Bethany L. Appleby; Catherine P. Baatz (Resident, Hartford Office); Jessica A. Ballou; Kenneth F. Baum; Patricia R. Beauregard; Eileen Reynolds Becker; Penelope I. Bellamy; Elizabeth Anne Bloomfield (Resident, Stamford Office); Victor Allen Bolden; Kevin S. Budge; Dylan S. Calsyn; Julie Min Chayet (Resident, Stamford Office); Lori R. Clark (Resident, Hartford Office); Monika Dorota Cornell; David Cotta (Not admitted in CT); James O. Craven; Jeffrey John Danile (Resident, Stamford Office); Kevin Paul Dean; Michelle Wilcox DeBarge (Resident, Hartford Office); W. Bruce DelMonico (Resident, Stamford Office); Jody L. DeStefanis (Resident, Stamford Office); Michael J. Devine (Resident, Hartford Office); Timothy A. Diemand; Anita C. DiGioia; Adam Paul Doherty; Meghan E. Doherty; Christopher D. Fasano; Cecile Monique Fraser; Jesse M. Furman (Not admitted in CT; Resident, Stamford Office); Elizabeth Mary Garrett; Michele B. Gerroir; Sara A. Goldberg (Not admitted in CT; Resident, Stamford Office); Nicole H. Gollaher; Naomi B. Graubard (Resident, Stamford Office); David C. Grigsby; Alexander J. Grodski; Jonathan W. Haray; Mark W. Heaphy; Kenneth Decatur Heath; Bart Duncan Jeffress; Stuart C. Johnson; Russell G. Kauff (Resident, Stamford Office); William James Kelleher, III (Resident, Stamford Office); Stacie A. Kelly; Michael K. Kinney; Robert E. Koosa; Sigrid E. Kun; Stephen Jared Lable; Monika Niva Marie Lahiri; David A. Levenstein; Richard H. Lugli (Resident, Hartford Office); Steven P. Malech (Resident, Hartford Office); Bruce L. McDermott; Erik L. Mengwall; James J. Menna; Pamela P. Millman; Clement J. Naples (Resident, Stamford Office); Maureen O'Connor; Theresa M. Parietti; Bonnie Lynne Patten; Christopher R. Perry; Christina Kam Peterson (Resident, Berwyn, Pennsylvania Office and Cherry Hill, New Jersey); Joan Allen Rowe; Margaret A. Rutherford; Joseph A. SanFilippo; G. Adam Schweikert, III; George Austin Selmont; William B. Slate; Lauren A. Sullivan; Christine P. Teixeira; Kimberly S. Toomey (Resident, Berwyn, Pennsylvania Office and Cherry Hill, New Jersey); Janie L. Treanor (Resident, Stamford Office); Joseph R. Tristine; Suzanne E. Wachsstock (Resident, Stamford Office); Jennifer Neyan Willcox; Amy Ghory Winnick; Gayle Carol Wintjen (Resident, Hartford Office).
Antitrust and Trade Regulation, Appellate, Automotive Industry Law, Banking and Financial Services, Bankruptcy Law, Biotechnology Law, Civil Litigation, Closely Held Business, Cogeneration, Construction Law, Employee Benefits and ERISA Law, Environmental Law, Estate Planning and Settlement Law, Franchise Law, Governmental Affairs, Health Care, Hospital Law, Institutional Finance, Insurance Coverage Litigation, Intellectual Property, Internal Corporate Investigations and White Collar Criminal Defense Law, International Transactions, Labor Law, Litigation, Long Term Care Facilities and Financing, Mental Health Law, Mergers and Acquisitions, National and Regional Litigation Counsel, Partnerships and Joint Ventures, Patent Prosecution and Litigation, Professional Malpractice Litigation, Public Finance, Public Utilities, Real Estate Leasing, Development and Finance, Secured Transactions, Securities Regulation, State and Federal Tax Law, Tax Exempt Organizations, Technology Licensing, Telecommunications, Trademarks and Copyright, Trust and Estates Administration, Venture Capital and Zoning.
Hartford, Connecticut Office: One CityPlace. Telephone: 860-297-3700. Telefax: 860-525-9380.
Stamford, Connecticut Office: 400 Atlantic Street, P.O. Box 110325. Telephone: 203-363-7600. Telefax: 203-363-7676.
Berwyn, Pennsylvania Office: 1055 Westlake Drive. Telephone: 610-727-4153. Telefax: 610-727-4085.
Cherry Hill, New Jersey Office: 402 Park Boulevard North, 08802. Telephone: 856-662-3331. Telefax: 856-662-1783.
See Professional Biographies, NEW HAVEN, CONNECTICUT

Wilcox, Cheryl Jane '43 '90
C.222 B.A. L.1029 J.D. Asst. Clk., Housing Session, Supr. Ct.
Wilder, Carole F. '47 '86 C.112 B.A. L.1040 J.D.
Senior Counsel, Southern New England Telephone Co.
Willard, Sherwood S., (BV) '41 '69 C.893 B.A. L.273 J.D.
V.P., Gen. Coun. & Secy., Pirelli Armstrong Tire Corp.
Willcox, Jennifer Neyan .... '69 '98 C.976 B.A. L.588 J.D. [Ⓐ Wiggin&D.]
Williams, Earl I. .... '29 '57 C.329 B.A. L.94 LL.B. 129 Church St.
Williams, John R., (AV) .... '41 '68 C.309 A.B. L.276 J.D. [Williams&P.]
*PRACTICE AREAS: Criminal Law; Civil Practice; Civil Rights; Appellate Practice.

Williams and Pattis, LLC, (AV) BR
51 Elm Street, 06510
Telephone: 203-562-9931 Fax: 203-776-9494
Email: jrw@johnrwilliams.com
John R. Williams; Norman A. Pattis;—Katrena Engstrom; William S. Palmieri; Angelica N. Papastavros-Corbo; Dawne Westbrook; Robert Berke.
Criminal and Civil Trial Practice before all State and Federal Courts. Civil Rights Law. Appellate Practice.
References: Webster Bank; Citizens Bank.
See Professional Biographies, NEW HAVEN, CONNECTICUT

Wilson, W. Joe .... '47 '99 C.802 B.A. L.306 J.D. [Ⓐ Tyler C.&A.]
Wilson, William S., II .... '66 '96 C.550 B.S.C.E. L.1048 J.D. [Ⓐ Garcia&M.]
*PRACTICE AREAS: Construction Law; Contracts; Commercial Law.
Winer, Louis Marshall .... '30 '61 C.821 B.A. L.309 LL.B. 315 Peck St.
Winnick, Amy Ghory .... '57 '83 C.188 B.A. L.276 J.D. [Ⓐ Wiggin&D.]
Winnick, Edward B., (AV) .... '33 '59 C.197 A.B. L.976 LL.B. [Winnick,R.C.E.&H.]
*PRACTICE AREAS: Commercial Law; Litigation; Property Tax Appeals; Business Litigation.
Winnick, Joshua A., (BV) .... '56 '86 C.309 B.A. L.30 J.D. [Winnick,R.C.E.&H.]
*PRACTICE AREAS: Civil Litigation; Real Estate; Commercial Litigation; Personal Injury; Domestic Relations.

Winnick, Ruben, Chambers, Evans and Hoffnung, LLC, (AV)
110 Whitney Avenue, 06510-1238
Telephone: 203-772-4400 Fax: 203-772-2763
Alexander Winnick (1903-1989); Gilbert H. Winnick (1928-1999); Edward B. Winnick; Diane Daskal Ruben; Wick R. Chambers; Joshua A. Winnick; Robert S. Evans; Daniel N. Hoffnung.
Corporate, Commercial, Real Estate, Litigation, Personal Injury, Family, Probate, Taxation, Estate Planning and Estate Administration, Commercial Lending, Creditors' Rights, Business Bankruptcy.
See Professional Biographies, NEW HAVEN, CONNECTICUT

Wizner, Stephen .... '38 '64 C.197 A.B. L.145 J.D. Prof. of Law, Yale Law Sch.
Wiznia, Carolann K. .... '50 '75 C.98 B.A. L.93 J.D. 850 Howard Ave.
Wolfert-Marino, Debra B. .... '70 '95 C.94 B.A. L.1252 J.D. 265 Church St.
Wolfson, Susan W., (AV) .... '38 '76 C.66 B.A. L.184 J.D. [Susman,D.&S.]
*PRACTICE AREAS: Family Law; Civil Litigation.
Wolter, John F., (BV) .... '61 '86 C.708 B.A. L.276 J.D. [Updike,K.&S.] (⊙Hartford)
*PRACTICE AREAS: Business Law; Commercial Lending; Human Service; Franchise Law; Utilities Law.
Wynne, John F., (BV) .... '20 '51 C.197 B.A. L.724 J.D. [Buckley&W.]
*PRACTICE AREAS: Probate Law.
Wynne, John F., Jr., (BV) .... '58 '84 C&L.184 B.A., J.D. [Buckley&W.]
*PRACTICE AREAS: Personal Injury Litigation; Product Liability; Medical Malpractice; Legal Malpractice.
Xixis, George A. '66 '94 C.453 S.B. L.1009 J.D.
(adm. in NY; not adm. in CT; Pat.) Intellectual Property Counsel, CuraGen Corporation
Yandle, Stephen T. .... '47 '72 C&L.893 B.A., J.D. Assoc. Dean, Yale Law Sch.
Yates, Karen E. .... '71 '96 C.30 B.A. L.188 J.D. [Ⓐ Bergman,H.&R.]
*PRACTICE AREAS: Estate Planning; Estate Administration; Tax.
Yen, Elizabeth C., (AV) .... '57 '80 C.976 B.A. L.477 J.D. [Hudson C.]
*PRACTICE AREAS: Banking Law; Consumer Law; Financial Services Law.
Yokow, William M. .... '53 '89 C.1033 B.A. L.1252 J.D. U.S. Treas. Dept.
Yolen, Timothy B., (AV) .... '49 '80 C.319 B.A. L.1048 J.D. [Yolen&P.]
*PRACTICE AREAS: Business Law; Commercial Litigation; Commercial Real Estate; Residential Real Estate; Zoning, Planning and Land Use.

Yolen and Perzin, LLC, (AV)
5 Trumbull Street, P.O. Box 1990, 06521
Telephone: 203-562-5100 Fax: 203-562-5211
URL: http://www.lawyers.com/yolen&perzin
Timothy B. Yolen; Michael Perzin.
General and Trial Practice in State and Federal Courts. Negligence, Malpractice, Commercial Litigation, Family and Special Education Law, Real Estate, Zoning. Trials in all Civil, Administrative and Criminal Courts.
References: Union Trust Co.
See Professional Biographies, NEW HAVEN, CONNECTICUT

Young, Pasquale, (BV) .... '36 '63 C.1027 B.S. L.976 LL.B. [Berdon,Y.&M.]
*PRACTICE AREAS: Real Estate; Zoning and Land Use; Litigation; Family Law; Criminal Law.
Young, Rolan J. .... '60 '93 C.197 A.B. L.904 J.D. [Updike,K.&S.] (⊙Hartford)
*PRACTICE AREAS: Business Law; Commercial Lending; Public Finance/Public Law; Real Estate; Affordable Housing.
Yules, Robert B., (BV) .... '52 '78 C.611 B.A. L.851 J.D. [Yules&Y.] ⊙
*PRACTICE AREAS: Drugs and Medical Devices; Insurance; Products Liability; Professional Malpractice; Transportation.

Yules & Yules, LLC, (BV)
195 Church Street, Seventeenth Floor, 06510 ⊙
Telephone: 203-789-1000 Fax: 203-789-6320
Email: yuleslaw@yuleslaw.com URL: http://www.lawyers.com/yules&yules
Herman Yules (1910-1999); Robert B. Yules. Associate: Richard W. Mather.
Trial Practice, Automobile, Mobile Carrier, Bad Faith, Corporate Business Torts, Drug and Medical Device Litigation, Fraud, Insurance, Products Liability, Professional Malpractice, Transportation, Workers' Compensation Law, Securities Arbitration and Financial Institutions Litigation.
Representative Clients: Aetna Casualty and Surety Co.; Allstate Insurance Co.; Nationwide Insurance Co.; Transamerica Insurance Group; Zurich-American Insurance Cos.
Hartford, Connecticut Office: P.O. Box 230278, 06123-0278. Telephone: 860-724-5815.
Stamford, Connecticut Office: P.O. Box 522. 06904-0522. Telephone: 203-327-9200.
New York, N.Y. Office: Grand Central Station, P.O. Box 4419. 10163-4419. Telephone: 203-327-9200.
See Professional Biographies, NEW HAVEN, CONNECTICUT

Zackin, Leslie A. .... '64 '90 C.860 B.A. L.262 J.D. [Ⓒ Bershtein,L.B.&M.]
*PRACTICE AREAS: Estate Planning; Probate; Business Law.
Zampano, Robert C. .... '29 '54 C&L.976 B.A., LL.B. Sta-Fed ADR, Inc.
Zandy, John G., (AV) .... '48 '75 C.473 B.A. L.879 J.D. [Wiggin&D.]
*PRACTICE AREAS: Labor Law; Employment Law.
Zangari, Mario J., (AV) .... '40 '69 C.1145 B.S. L.818 J.D. [Siegel,O.S.&Z.]
*PRACTICE AREAS: Business Law; Taxation Law; Estate Planning Law.

Zeldes, Needle & Cooper, A Professional Corporation
(See Bridgeport)

Ziehl, Joseph P. .... '52 '92 C.165 B.A. L.1029 J.D. 47 Trumbull St.
Zielinski, Karen L. .... '74 '00 C.184 B.A. L.306 J.D. [Ⓐ Milano&W.]
*PRACTICE AREAS: Insurance Defense; Commercial Litigation.
Zimmermann, Jeremy G., (AV) .... '41 '66 C.103 A.B. L.276 J.D. [Wiggin&D.]
*PRACTICE AREAS: Litigation; Insurance Defense Law; Product Liability Defense Law; Professional Liability Defense Law.
Zimmermann, Kurt F., (BV) .... '47 '77 C.184 B.A. L.1202 J.D. [Silverstein&O.]
*PRACTICE AREAS: Tax Law; Litigation.
Zito, Louise R., (BV) .... '50 '86 C.1102 B.A. L.564 J.D. 33 Whitney Ave.
Zoarski, Howard F. .... '26 '54 C.446 B.S. L.273 LL.B. Sr. Supr. Ct. J.
Zucker, Ann Hedges, (BV) .... '59 '85 C.976 B.A. L.262 J.D. [Carmody&T.]
*PRACTICE AREAS: Banking; Public Finance; Health Care; Corporate Law; Commercial Real Estate.

NEWINGTON, 28,841, *Hartford Co.*

Antoinetti, Amelia M., (BV) .... '54 '80 C.918 B.A. L.184 J.D. [Nassau,B.&F.]
Boorman, Peter J., (BV) .... '53 '85 C.184 B.A. L.1048 J.D. [Nassau,B.&F.]
Borowy, Frank R., (BV) .... '48 '73 C.282 B.A. L.184 J.D. [Nassau,B.&F.]

Budney, Alan F., (BV) ....'48 '74 C.184 B.A. L.94 J.D. 1150 Main St.
Cantin, Eileen J. ....'51 '84 C&L.184 B.S., J.D. Div. of Spec. Rev.
Cramer, Paul M. ....'67 '92 C.184 B.A. L.1048 J.D. 1 Market Sq.
Doyle, Thomas H. .... '61 '95 C.829 B.A. L.1048 J.D. State Dept. of Transp.
Early, Francine Davis ....'52 '87 C.681 B.A. L.588 J.D. [Ⓐ Scoler,G.S.&G.]
Ferris, Eileen G. ....'44 '80 C.1077 B.A. L.184 J.D. 148 Hunters Ln.
French, William C., (BV) .... '38 '70 C.478 B.A. L.184 J.D. [Nassau,B.&F.]
Galligan, William C., (BV) .... '24 '54 C.676 B.A. L.93 LL.B. [Ⓒ Scoler,G.S.&G.]
Goodgion, Gilbert ....'43 '74 C.339 A.B. L.1119 J.D. 30 Sequin St.
Griffith, David L., (BV) ....'49 '79 C.165 B.A. L.184 J.D. [Scoler,G.S.&G.]
Hojnowski, Claudia Rich ....'43 '90 C.829 B.A. L.128 J.D. One Market Square
Kablik, Richard A., (P.C.), (BV) ....'47 '72 C.321 A.B. L.184 J.D. 171 Market Sq.
Kelly, Frank A., Jr. ....'19 '49 C.855 B.A. L.309 LL.B. 21 Forest Dr.‡
Klein, Robert L., (BV) ....'46 '73 C&L.184 B.A., J.D. Asst. Atty. Gen.
Kosowicz, Francis G., Jr. ....'57 '85 C.184 B.S. L.1048 J.D. 107 Maple Hill Ave.
Lanza, William A. ....'64 '91 C.918 B.A. L.569 J.D. 36 Ralph Ave.
Lovesky, Jerome, (AV) .... '30 '56 C.102 B.A. L.976 LL.B. 14 Birchlawn Terr.‡
Lucisano, Dana M. ....'58 '93 C.145 B.A. L.306 J.D. 41 Garvan St.
Mason, Kevin L., (BV) ....'57 '85 C&L.184 B.A., J.D. 47 E. Cedar St.

Mayo, Gilligan & Zito, LLP
(See Wethersfield)

Nassau, Steven M., (BV) ....'39 '65 C.976 B.A. L.188 LL.B. [Nassau,B.&F.]
Nassau, Borowy & French, (BV) ....66 Cedar St.
Reney, Donald P., Jr. ....'55 '84 C.184 B.A. L.1029 J.D. 142 Market Sq.
Rosenblatt, Sidney L., (BV) ....'28 '62 C&L.184 B.A., LL.B. 66 Lamplighter Lane
Sabatini, James V. ....'71 '98 C.299 B.A. L.930 J.D. [Ⓐ Sabatini&Assoc.]
*PRACTICE AREAS: Civil Litigation.
Sabatini, Vincent F., (BV) ....'42 '69 C.690 B.S. L.818 J.D. [Sabatini&Assoc.]
*PRACTICE AREAS: Land Use; Civil Litigation.

Sabatini and Associates, LLC, (BV)
One Market Square, 06111
Telephone: 860-667-0839 Fax: 860-667-0867
Email: LAWNEW@aol.com
Vincent F. Sabatini. Associate: James V. Sabatini.
General Civil Practice. Trials in all State and Federal Courts. Litigation, Probate, Corporate, Personal Injury, Commercial, Zoning.
Representative Clients: Pizza Hut of America, Inc.; Midas Muffler; Piper Brook Associates; Farmers and Mechanics Bank; Keeney Manufacturing; Crest Mazda; Town of Wethersfield; RD Management: Webster Bank; Eastco Development.
Reference: Webster Bank.
See Professional Biographies, NEWINGTON, CONNECTICUT

Scheinberg, Barry, (BV) ....'48 '72 C.509 B.A. L.1009 J.D. 705 N. Mountain Rd.
Schless, Michael, (BV) ....'37 '62 C&L.184 A.B., J.D. [Scoler,G.S.&G.]
Schwartz, Kove J. ....'38 '78 C.829 B.A. L.184 J.D. 1247 Main St.
Scoler, Jerome A., (BV) ....'21 '46 C.692 L.94 LL.B. 505 Willard Ave.‡
Scoler, Galligan, Schless & Griffith, L.L.C., (BV) .... 505 Willard Ave.
Spadaccini, Louis A. ....'72 '97 C.1030 B.A. L.184 J.D. 66 Cedar St.
Willin, Joan K. ....'— '76 C.788 A.B. L.184 J.D. 21 Mountain View Dr.

NEW LONDON, 28,540, *New London Co.*

Anderson, Charles C. ....'64 '92 C.604 B.A. L.184 J.D [Waller,S.&P.]
*PRACTICE AREAS: Estate Planning; Real Estate; Probate.
Anderson, Robert P., Jr., (BV) ....'35 '60 C&L.976 B.A., LL.B. [Waller,S.&P.]
*PRACTICE AREAS: Trust Law; Estate Planning; Estate Administration; Real Estate.
Andrews, Lois G., (BV) ....'47 '73 C.112 B.A. L.1068 J.D. [Andrews,Y.&G.]
*PRACTICE AREAS: Estate Planning; Probate; Elder Law; Real Estate; Business Law.

Andrews, Young & Geraghty, P.C., (BV)
216 Broad Street, P.O. Box 751, 06320-0751
Telephone: 860-444-2101 Fax: 860-440-2615 URL: http://www.lawyers.com/andrewscosgrove&young
URL: http://www.newlondonlegal.com
Lois G. Andrews; James L. Young, Jr.; Paul M. Geraghty. Associate: Barbara Arnold; Ryan M. Suerth.
General Civil Practice. Real Estate, Estate Planning, Probate, Elder Law, Corporations, Business Law, Commercial and Financial Transactions, Creditors' Rights, Bankruptcy, Collections, Personal Injury, Trials and Appeals, Municipal Law, Foreclosure, Land Use and Development, Zoning.
See Professional Biographies, NEW LONDON, CONNECTICUT

Ansell, Denise ....'52 '90 C.999 B.S. L.184 J.D. 94 Broad St.
Arnold, Barbara ....'71 '98 C.1320 B.A. L.446 J.D. [Ⓐ Andrews,Y.&G.]
*PRACTICE AREAS: Litigation; Commercial Law; Municipal Law; Real Property; Personal Injury.
Auger, Matthew E., (BV) ....'58 '84 C.276 B.A. L.107 J.D. [Suisman,S.W.B.G.&G.]
*PRACTICE AREAS: Personal Injury; Arbitration; Mediation; Commercial Litigation; Breach of Contract.
Baribeault, Raymond L., Jr., (BV) '64 '89 C.184 B.S. L.1194 J.D. [Suisman,S.W.B.G.&G.]
*PRACTICE AREAS: Contracts Law; Corporate Law; Business Law; Commercial Transactions; Bankruptcy.
Basilica, Anthony R., (CV) ....'56 '82 C.918 B.A. L.1048 J.D. 37 Granite St.
Bates, Timothy D., (BV) ....'— '73 C.976 B.A. L.178 J.D. [Ⓒ Robinson&C.]
*PRACTICE AREAS: Zoning, Planning and Land Use.

Beebe and O'Neil
(See Norwich)

Berger, Matthew G., (BV) ....'67 '95 C.787 B.A. L.588 J.D. [Ⓐ Kanabis&H.]
Berryman, James P. ....'57 '83 C.602 B.A. L.180 J.D. [Suisman,S.W.B.G.&G.]
*PRACTICE AREAS: Workers Compensation Law; Social Security and Disability.
Bevza, Denise, (CV) ....'59 '85 C.184 B.S. L.1029 J.D. 24 Channing St.
Blanchard, Michael A., (BV) '57 '82 C.1107 B.A. L.1048 J.D. [Suisman,S.W.B.G.&G.]
*PRACTICE AREAS: Family Law; Criminal Law; Personal Injury.
Boyce, Thomas W., Jr., (AV) ....'51 '76 C.676 B.A. L.1009 J.D. [Faulkner&B.]
*PRACTICE AREAS: Personal Injury; Medical Malpractice Defense; Products Liability Defense; Insurance Litigation.
Brand, Andrew, (BV) ....'41 '66 C&L.659 B.S., LL.B. [Suisman,S.W.B.G.&G.]
*PRACTICE AREAS: Civil Litigation.
Brennan, James F., (AV) ......'30 '55 C.321 A.B. L.184 LL.B. [Suisman,S.W.B.G.&G.]
*PRACTICE AREAS: Civil Litigation; Municipal Law.
Brotherton, Carolyn Ogden, (BV) ....'29 '84 C.66 B.A. L.446 J.D. 83 Broad St.

Brown Jacobson P.C.
(See Norwich)

Burlingham, Nicholas W. ....'62 '94 C.183 B.A. L.184 J.D. 470 Bank St.
Cable, Jane, (CV) ....'42 '85 C.273 A.B. L.184 J.D. 71 Granite St.
Calmar, Harry E., (AV) ....'58 '85 C.860 B.A. L.982 J.D. [Suisman,S.W.B.G.&G.]
*PRACTICE AREAS: Labor and Employment; Administrative; Municipal; School Law; Civil Rights.
Camassar, Garon, (BV) ....'43 '68 C.184 B.A. L.818 J.D. [Irving,D.&C.]
Camassar, Scott D., (CV) ....'70 '95 C.184 B.A. L.1048 J.D. [Reardon]
*PRACTICE AREAS: Personal Injury; Wrongful Death; Products Liability; Appellate Practice.

Carberry, Glenn T., (BV) ....'55 '79 C.282 B.A. L.659 J.D. [Tobin,C.O.R.&S.] ⊙
*PRACTICE AREAS: Banking Law; Corporate Law; Land Use; Administrative Law; Telecommunications Law.
Carey, John T. P. ....'57 '88 C.1033 B.A. L.184 J.D. 71 Granite St.
Carey, Michael P., (BV) .... '55 '80 C.696 B.A. L.184 J.D. [Suisman,S.W.B.G.&G.]
*PRACTICE AREAS: Civil Litigation; Workers Compensation; Zoning and Planning; Land Use; Municipal Law.
Cartier, Michael J., (CV) ....'59 '85 C.708 A.B. L.1218 J.D. [Ⓐ Mariani&R.]
*PRACTICE AREAS: Personal Injury; Criminal Law; Negligence Law; Employment Discrimination; Military Law.
Cary, Robert J., Jr., (BV) ....'53 '86 C.454 B.A. L.184 J.D. 216 Broad Street
Casey, John Patrick ....'68 '97 C.184 B.A. L.904 J.D. [Ⓐ Faulkner&B.]★
*PRACTICE AREAS: Personal Injury; Premises Liability.
Chamberlain, Bruce A. ....'59 '84 C.184 B.A. L.1292 J.D. 400 Bayonet St.
Cocheo, John F., (BV) ....'44 '74 C.1252 B.A. L.669 J.D. 5 Shaws Cove, Suite 200
Cole-Chu, Leeland J., (BV) .... '48 '78 C.309 B.A. L.767 J.D. 261 Williams Street
Cole-Chu, Ruth A. ....'50 '83 C.937 B.A. L.284 J.D. 261 Williams St.‡
Collins, John A., III, (BV) .... '56 '81 C.321 A.B. L.930 J.D. [Suisman,S.W.B.G.&G.]
*PRACTICE AREAS: Personal Injury Law; Criminal Law.
Collins, Tracy M., (CV) ....'60 '87 C.1200 B.A. L.1202 J.D. [Waller,S.&P.]
*PRACTICE AREAS: Personal Injury; Commercial Litigation; Real Estate Litigation; Family Law; Litigation.
Condon, David P., (BV) ....'63 '91 C.184 B.A. L.306 J.D. [Waller,S.&P.]
*PRACTICE AREAS: Litigation; Commercial Litigation; Real Estate Litigation; Municipal Law; Family Law.
Connolly, Susan M., (BV) ...... '59 '85 C.184 B.A. L.1029 J.D. 190 Gov. Winthrop Blvd.
Conway, Kevin W., (AV) ....'32 '57 C.321 B.A. L.184 LL.B. [Conway&L.] ⊙
*PRACTICE AREAS: Estate Planning; Probate; Real Estate; Business Law; Municipal Law.

Conway & Londregan, P.C., (AV)
38 Huntington Street, 06320-6170 ⊙
Telephone: 860-447-3171 Fax: 860-444-6103
Email: conway.londregan@snet.net URL: http://www.lawyers.com/clpc
Kevin W. Conway; Francis T. Londregan; Thomas J. Londregan; Michael W. Sheehan; Ralph J. Monaco; Susan B. Pochal; Brian K. Estep; Jeffrey T. Londregan.
General Practice in all Courts. Municipal Law, Administrative, Real Estate, Commercial Loans, Personal Injury, Probate, Zoning and Real Estate Law, Corporation, Estate Planning, Civil and Commercial Litigation.
Mystic, Connecticut Office: Masons Island Road, P.O. Box 396, 06355-0396. Telephone: 203-536-4991.
See Professional Biographies, NEW LONDON, CONNECTICUT

Coric, Drzislav (Dado), (BV) ....'58 '87 C.228 A.B. L.910 J.D. 45 Channing St.
Cushman, Eugene C. ....'44 '75 C.184 B.A. L.803 J.D. 671 Broad St.
Dalcher, Bruce P. '57 '94 C.260 B.A. L.861 J.D. (adm. in PA; not adm. in CT) 15 Mohegan Ave.
Dean, Harold B. ....'10 '38 C.264 B.S. L.94 LL.B. 28 Worthington Rd.‡
Desmond, Cynthia L. .... '67 '93 C.93 B.A. L.1048 J.D. [Suisman,S.W.B.G.&G.]
*PRACTICE AREAS: Marital.
Dixon, Richard D., (CV) ....'48 '84 C.430 B.A. L.184 J.D. 58 Huntington St.
Donohue, Patricia A. ....'26 '53 C.725 B.S. L.184 LL.B. 197 Ledyard St.‡
Dostie, Jeanette M., (BV) ....'64 '95 C.103 B.A. L.184 J.D. [Suisman,S.W.B.G.&G.]
*PRACTICE AREAS: Medicaid Planning; Wills, Trusts and Probate; Real Estate.
Dubicki, Narcy Z., (BV) ....'45 '72 C&L.184 B.S., J.D. [Irving,D.&C.]
Dubois, Mark A., (BV) ....'50 '78 C.321 A.B. L.184 J.D. [Ⓒ Reardon]
*PRACTICE AREAS: Personal Injury; Wrongful Death; Medical Malpractice; Products Liability.
Duggan, Eileen C. ....'68 '93 C.976 B.A. L.893 J.D. [Suisman,S.W.B.G.&G.]
*PRACTICE AREAS: Labor and Employment Law; Litigation.
Dupont, Ralph P., (AV) ....'29 '56 C.103 A.B. L.309 J.D. [Dupont&R.]
*PRACTICE AREAS: Litigation; Probate; Business Organization.

Dupont and Radlauer, L.L.P., (AV) BR
Captain's Walk, 165 State Street, Suite 502, P.O. Box 710, 06320-0710
Telephone: 860-447-0090 Fax: 860-437-7442
Email: radlaw@snet.net URL: http://www.lawyers.com/dupontandradlauer
Members of Firm: Ralph P. Dupont; Barbara J. Radlauer.
Litigation, Probate, Business Organization.
See Professional Biographies, NEW LONDON, CONNECTICUT

Emerson, Kevin B. F. ....'70 '95 C.1305 B.A. L.276 J.D. [Ⓐ Mariani&R.]
*PRACTICE AREAS: Divorce; Family Law.
Estep, Brian K., (CV) ....'60 '86 C.25 B.A. L.1017 J.D. [Conway&L.]
*PRACTICE AREAS: Litigation; Worker Compensation; Municipal.
Fairlie, Chester W., (BV) .... '44 '72 C.674 B.A. L.184 J.D. [Holth,K.F.&G.]
Faulkner, Dale Patrick, (AV) ....'38 '63 C.676 A.B. L.184 LL.B. [Faulkner&B.]
*PRACTICE AREAS: Personal Injury; Premises Liability; Wrongful Death; Professional Liability.

Faulkner & Boyce, P.C., (AV)
216 Broad Street, P.O. Box 391, 06320
Telephone: 860-442-9900 Fax: 860-443-6428
Email: law@faulknerandboyce.com URL: http://www.faulknerandboyce.com
Dale Patrick Faulkner; Thomas W. Boyce, Jr.; Humbert J. Polito, Jr.;—Shelley L. Graves; John Patrick Casey.
Reference: Fleet National Bank of Connecticut.
See Professional Biographies, NEW LONDON, CONNECTICUT

Francisconi, JoAnn ....'52 '85 C.184 B.S. L.1048 J.D. 46 Niles Hill Rd.‡
Gahagan, Frederick B., (BV) ....'52 '80 C.385 B.A. L.184 J.D. [Waller,S.&P.] ⊙
*PRACTICE AREAS: Corporate Law; Business Organization; Land Conservation; Zoning, Planning and Land Use; Real Estate.
Gardner-Frum, Miriam .... '47 '87 C&L.184 B.A., J.D. 190 Governor Winthrop Blvd.
Geraghty, Paul M., (BV) .... '57 '84 C.431 B.A. L.1029 J.D. [Andrews,Y.&G.]
*PRACTICE AREAS: Commercial Transactions; Commercial Litigation; Business Law; Municipal Law.
Gildea, Tammie L., (CV) ....'65 '90 C&L.184 B.A., J.D. 363 Glenwood Ave.
Glassman, Sanford ....'23 '62 C&L.184 B.S., LL.B. 216 Broad St.
Golembeski, Dean J., (CV) ....'49 '87 C.184 B.A. L.1029 J.D. [Holth,K.F.&G.]
Graves, Shelley L., (CV) ....'68 '94 C&L.184 B.A., J.D. [Ⓐ Faulkner&B.]
*PRACTICE AREAS: Personal Injury; Premises Liability.
Gray, Louis Patrick, III ....'16 '49 C.871 B.S. L.273 J.D. [Ⓒ Suisman,S.W.B.G.&G.]
Greenberg, Lawrence J., (AV) ... '30 '55 C.976 B.A. L.309 J.D. [Suisman,S.W.B.G.&G.]
*PRACTICE AREAS: Corporate Law; Commercial Transactions; Business and Estate Planning.
Griffis, Hughes, (AV) ....'44 '72 C.976 B.A. L.188 J.D. [Waller,S.&P.]
*PRACTICE AREAS: Real Estate; Banking Law; Commercial Law.
Gruskin, Richard E. ....'33 '64 C.472 B.A. L.669 LL.B. 56 Huntington St.
Guinan, Kathryn D., (BV) ....'52 '81 C&L.184 B.A., J.D. 56 Huntington St.
Handy, Susan B. ....'49 '80 C.454 B.A. L.184 J.D. Supr. Ct. J.
Hardman, Tracey E. ....'70 '00 C.164 B.A. L.306 J.D. [Reardon]
*PRACTICE AREAS: Personal Injury; Wrongful Death; Products Liability; Medical Malpractice; Appellate Practice.
Harkins, Kathleen M., (CV) ....'55 '80 C.156 B.A. L.1202 J.D. 90 Broad St.
Hasse, Michael R., (CV) ....'57 '91 C.183 B.A. L.1187 J.D. 89 Hempstead St.
Haviland, James T., II, (BV) ....'31 '64 C.478 B.A. L.184 J.D. 71 Granite
Haviland, Richard D. ....'60 '88 C.550 B.S. L.1048 J.D. 71 Granite St.
Hendel, Seymour L. ....'31 '56 C.178 A.B. L.309 LL.B. Sr. Supm. Ct. J.
Hill, Jeffrey W., (BV) ....'55 '83 C.309 B.A. L.184 J.D. [Suisman,S.W.B.G.&G.]
*PRACTICE AREAS: Family Law; Marital Law.

Holth, Fredrik D., (BV) .... '40 '67 C.676 A.B. L.262 J.D. [Holth,K.F.&G.]
Holth, Kollman, Fairlie & Golembeski, (BV) .... 58 Huntington Street
Horgan, Daniel J. .... '62 '89 C.1044 B.A. L.1048 J.D. 5 Shaws Cove

Horvitz & Caisse
(See Norwich)

Houle, Renee Marie, (CV) ....'61 '86 C.1236 B.A. L.362 J.D. [Kanabis&H.]
Hurley, D. Michael ....'26 '59 C.433 B.A. L.569 LL.B. Supr. Ct. J.
Irving, Charles J., (BV) .... '46 '72 C.276 B.A. L.184 J.D. [Irving,D.&C.]
Irving, Dubicki & Camassar, (BV) .... 181 Broad St.
Johnstone, Philip M., (BV) .... '61 '86 C.228 B.A. L.659 J.D. [Waller,S.&P.]
*PRACTICE AREAS: Estate Planning; Probate; Real Estate; Corporate Law; Commercial Transactions.
Kanabis, C. George, (BV) .... '35 '64 C.659 B.S. L.184 LL.B. [Kanabis&H.]
Kanabis & Houle, P.C., (BV) ....5 Shaw's Cove, Suite 202 (⊙Colchester)
Kane, Kevin T., (AV) ....'43 '68 C.436 A.B. L.184 J.D. States Atty.
Keramidas, Thomas J., (BV) ....'54 '84 C.184 B.A. L.767 J.D. 45 Channing St.
Keville, Robert B., (BV) .... '58 '90 C.349 B.S. L.1029 J.D. [Suisman,S.W.B.G.&G.]
*PRACTICE AREAS: Workers Compensation Law; Personal Injury; Civil Litigation.
Kimmel, Hinda K., (CV) .... '49 '94 C.485 B.A. L.1202 J.D. [Suisman,S.W.B.G.&G.]
*PRACTICE AREAS: Labor and Employment; Civil Rights; Special Education of Handicapped Law.
Kleinman, Stewart F., (BV) .... '40 '66 C.569 B.S. L.1009 LL.B. [Kleinman&Assoc.] ⊙
*PRACTICE AREAS: Commercial Real Estate Development and Finance Law; Loan Workouts Law; Corporate Law; Commercial Leasing Law; Contracts.

Kleinman & Associates, P.C., (BV)
22 Masonic Street, 06320-6404 ⊙
Telephone: 860-437-2342 Facsimile: 860-437-2346
Email: stewart.kleinman@snet.net URL: http://www.lawyers.com/kleinmanlaw
Stewart F. Kleinman; Meredith E. Russell.
Business Law, Commercial Real Estate, Leases and Leasing, Mortgages, Loan Workouts, Corporate Finance, Contracts, Corporation, Commercial, Collections, Banking, Bankruptcy, Probate, Estate Planning, Real Estate, Construction Contracts, Family Law, Mortgage Foreclosures, Landlord and Tenant, Zoning, Personal Injury, Consumer Law, Partnership Law, Property Law.
Hartford, Connecticut Office: 2 Congress Street. Telephone: 860-525-2930.
See Professional Biographies, NEW LONDON, CONNECTICUT

Koletsky, Joseph Q. ....'38 '62 C&L.976 B.A., J.D. Supr. Ct. J.
Kollman, William C., II ....'48 '75 C.94 B.S.B.A. L.424 J.D. [Holth,K.F.&G.]
Laben, Ansell ....'61 '90 L.184 J.D. 94 Broad St.
Lang, Jeffrey A. .... '63 '89 C.184 B.S. L.823 J.D. Suite 203, Three Shaws Cove
Lasky, Ronald E. .... '49 '75 C.1033 B.S. L.93 J.D. 5 Shaws, Suite 204
Leary, Kenneth A., (CV) ....'41 '70 C.187 B.A. L.145 J.D. 165 State St.
LeClair, Brian A. ....'62 '88 C.882 B.A. L.1194 J.D. 83 Broad St.
Liberty, Frank J., (BV) ....'58 '90 C.145 B.A. L.1009 J.D. [Suisman,S.W.B.G.&G.]
*PRACTICE AREAS: Intellectual Property; Personal Injury; Civil Trial Law; Commercial Litigation; Business Arbitration.
Londregan, Francis T., (AV) ....'35 '60 C.321 B.S. L.184 LL.B. [Conway&L.]
*PRACTICE AREAS: Commercial Law; Corporate Law; Banking; Secured Transactions; Real Estate.
Londregan, Jeffrey T. ....'71 '98 C.1030 B.A. L.1252 J.D. [Conway&L.]
Londregan, Thomas J., (BV) ....'44 '69 C.1030 A.B. L.184 J.D. [Conway&L.]
*PRACTICE AREAS: Municipal Law; Estate Planning; Probate; Business Law and Zoning; Commercial Litigation.
Madsen, William G., (BV) .... '59 '90 C.454 B.A. L.1194 J.D. [Madsen,P.&P.] ⊙
*PRACTICE AREAS: Labor and Employment Law; Civil Rights Law; Age Discrimination Law; Sexual Harassment Law; Employment Disability Law.

Madsen, Prestley & Parenteau, LLC, (BV)
111 Huntington Street, P.O. Box 1631, 06320 ⊙
Telephone: 860-442-2466 Facsimile: 860-447-9206
William G. Madsen; Peter B. Prestley; Jacques J. Parenteau.
Employment, Benefits Law and Related Litigation. Employment Contracts; Age, Race, Sex and Disability Discrimination; Civil Rights, Section 1983. Wage and Hour Law, Class Actions and Qui Tam Actions, Negotiations, Mediations, Arbitrations, Trials.
Hartford Office: 44 Capitol Avenue, Suite 201. Telephone: 860-246-2466. Facsimile: 860-246-1794.
See Professional Biographies, NEW LONDON, CONNECTICUT

Mariani, Linda L., (BV) ....'52 '77 C.188 B.A. L.818 J.D. [Mariani&R.]
*PRACTICE AREAS: Matrimonial Law; Personal Injury; Family Mediation; Mediation.

Mariani & Reck, LLC, (BV)
83 Broad Street, 06320-1630
Telephone: 860-443-5023 Fax: 860-443-8897
Email: info@marianireck.com
Linda L. Mariani; Stephen E. Reck;—Michael J. Cartier; Kevin B. F. Emerson; Rachel M. Proulx.
General Civil and Criminal Practice before State and Federal Courts. Personal Injury, Product Liability, Medical Malpractice, Domestic Relations, Child Custody, Labor and Employment, Municipal, Real Estate, Landlord and Tenant Law, Probate and Corporate Law. Trials and Appeals. Mediation.
See Professional Biographies, NEW LONDON, CONNECTICUT

Marion, Geoffrey E. ....'52 '86 C.184 B.A. L.724 J.D. Asst. State's Atty.
Marrion, Robert W., (AV) ....'31 '58 C.321 A.B. L.309 LL.B. [Waller,S.&P.] ⊙
*PRACTICE AREAS: Corporate Law; Business Organization; Commercial Real Estate; Estate Planning; Estate Administration.
Martin, Robert A. ....'47 '79 C.1123 B.A. L.1048 J.D. Supr. Ct.J.
McGarry, Thomas F., (BV) .... '39 '64 C.676 A.B. L.184 LL.B. [McGarry,P.M.]

McGarry, Prince, McGarry, P.C., (BV)
58 Huntington Street, 06320
Telephone: 860-443-1818 Fax: 860-443-1810
Email: tfmcal@aol.com URL: http://www.lawyers.com/mcgarryprincemcgarry.law
S. Victor Prince (1892-1991); John J. McGarry (1900-1973); Thomas F. McGarry.
General Practice. Probate, Estate Planning, Real Estate, Corporation, Municipal, Banking and Commercial Law, Zoning and Condominium Law. Trials in all Courts.
See Professional Biographies, NEW LONDON, CONNECTICUT

McGuire, James C., (AV) ....'47 '73 C.976 B.A. L.659 J.D. [McGuire&M.]

McGuire & McGuire, (AV)
68 Federal Street, P.O. Box 270, 06320
Telephone: 860-443-4357 Fax: 860-440-3817
Email: mcguire@ctol.net URL: http://www.lawyers.com/mcguire&mcguire
Francis F. McGuire (1910-1982); Frank L. McGuire (1940-1990); James C. McGuire.
General Civil Practice. Corporate, Probate, Estate Planning, Real Estate, Business, Land Use.
Representative Clients: Connecticut College; Day Publishing Co.; Lawrence and Memorial Hospital; Analysis & Technology, Inc.; Whaling City Dredge & Dock Corp.; Fleet Bank.
Approved Attorneys For: Chicago Title Insurance Co.; Connecticut Attorneys Title Insurance Co.; First American Title Insurance Co.
Reference: Fleet Bank.
See Professional Biographies, NEW LONDON, CONNECTICUT

McIntyre, Bruce B., (CV) ....'45 '84 C.1156 B.A. L.184 J.D. 5 Shaw's Cove
McNamara, Kathleen A. .... '62 '88 C.93 A.B. L.823 J.D. [Tobin,C.O.R.&S.]
*PRACTICE AREAS: Estate Planning Law; Probate; Administrative Law; Liquor Licensing; Real Estate Law.
Mendoza, Santa .... '57 '84 C.1030 B.A. L.184 J.D. [Suisman,S.W.B.G.&G.]
*PRACTICE AREAS: Taxation; Business Transactions; Commercial Transactions; Real Estate.

Mercurio, Lucia M., (BV) .... '62 '89 C.1030 B.A. L.306 J.D. [L.M.Mercurio]
*PRACTICE AREAS: Automobile Accidents and Injuries; Wrongful Death; Personal Injury; Employment Law; Discrimination.

Mercurio, Lucia M., LLC, (BV)
470 Bank Street, Second Floor, 06320
Telephone: 860-447-9942 Fax: 860-447-8157
Email: lmm@lmercuriolaw.com URL: http://www.lawyers.com/mercurio
Lucia M. Mercurio.
Automobile Accidents, Wrongful Death, Personal Injury, Employment Law, Discrimination, Premises Liability.
See Professional Biographies, NEW LONDON, CONNECTICUT

Messier, Alan R., (BV) .... '60 '85 C.855 B.A. L.1048 J.D. 21 Huntington St.
Mikolitch, M. Paul, (CV) .... '27 '60 C.221 B.A. L.184 LL.B. P.O. Box 1966
Miller, Warren .... '41 '66 C.454 B.A. L.309 J.D. 1 Union Plz., 2nd Fl.
Miner, William W., (AV) .... '30 '57 C.976 B.A. L.893 LL.B. [Waller,S.&P.]
*PRACTICE AREAS: Estate Planning; Estate Administration; Real Estate.
Modzelewski, Patricia H., (BV) .... '58 '84 C.184 B.A. L.1029 J.D. [Peck&T.] ⊙
*PRACTICE AREAS: Commercial Law; Litigation; Landlord and Tenant Law; Foreclosure Law; Family Law.
Monaco, Ralph J. ....'67 '93 C.262 B.A. L.1252 J.D. [Conway&L.]
*PRACTICE AREAS: Civil Litigation; Commercial Litigation; Product Liability; Personal Injury; Municipal Litigation.
Murphy, Edward J., Jr., (AVⓉ) '33 '68 C.550 A.B. L.818 J.D.
(adm. in MA; not adm. in CT) [Murphy&B.] ⊙
Murphy and Beane, (AVⓉ) ....Two Union Plaza (⊙Culver City, CA; Boston, MA)
Murray, Paul E., (BV) ....'46 '75 C&L.184 B.S., J.D. Supvr. Asst. States Atty.
Nagardeolekar, Lily S. .... '70 '95 C.93 B.A. L.184 J.D. 160 Hempstead St.
Nasser, Nathan P., (CV) ....'— '85 C.184 L.659 J.D. 45 Channing St.
Nazzaro, John J., (BV) .... '58 '84 C.1102 B.S.J. L.1029 J.D. 164 Hempstead St.

O'Brien, Shafner, Stuart, Kelly & Morris, P.C.
(See Groton)

O'Connell, Edward B., (BV) .... '43 '68 C.321 B.S. L.184 J.D. [Waller,S.&P.]
*PRACTICE AREAS: Commercial Transactions; Commercial Litigation; Real Estate Litigation; Municipal Law; Zoning, Planning and Land Use Law.
O'Malley, F. Jerome, (BV) .... '52 '78 C.321 B.A. L.184 J.D. [Tobin,C.O.R.&S.]
*PRACTICE AREAS: Personal Injury Law; Criminal Defense Law; Civil Litigation; Workers Compensation; Municipal Labor Law.
Palmer, Birdsey G., (AV) ....'15 '41 C.184 B.A. L.94 LL.B. [Waller,S.&P.] ‡
Papp, Robert J., (CV) ....'32 '78 C.1156 B.S. L.184 J.D. 71 Granite St.
Parenteau, Jacques J., (BV) ....'57 '82 C.454 B.A. L.30 J.D. [Madsen,P.&P.] ⊙
*PRACTICE AREAS: Employment Law; Academic Employment; Commercial Litigation; Personal Injury; Products Liability.
Pavetti, Francis J., Law Offices of, (AV) '31 '59
C.184 B.S. L.93 J.D. 83 Huntington Street
Peck, Jonathan A., (BV) ....'59 '85 C.156 B.A. L.818 J.D. [Peck&T.]
*PRACTICE AREAS: Commercial Law; Lender Representation Law; Loan Workouts Law; Collections; Litigation.

Peck & Tuneski, P.C., (BV)
10 Pearl Street, P.O. Box 37, 06320 ⊙
Telephone: 860-447-3370 Telefax: 860-447-3150 http://www.peck-tuneski.com
URL: http://www.lawyers.com/peck&tuneski
Robert D. Peck (1935-2000); Patricia H. Modzelewski; Jonathan A. Peck. Of Counsel: Robert S. Tuneski (Retired).
Lender Representation in Loan Workouts and Bankruptcy, Commercial Collections, Real Estate and Foreclosure, both residential and commercial, Land Use and Zoning, Probate, Estate and Tax Planning, Business and Corporate Law, Employment and Labor Law, Family Law, Personal Injury, Wrongful Death, Leasing, Zoning and Litigation in all Courts.
Representative Clients: Shawmut Bank, N.A.; The Bank of Southeastern Connecticut; Commonwealth United Mortgage Co., Inc.; Navy Federal Credit Union; Boston Five Mortgage Co.; Citicorp Leasing Co.; Citicorp Mortgage Co.; Baybank of Connecticut; Levine Distributing Co.; First Eastern Mortgage Corp.
Old Saybrook Office: 6 Business Park Road 06475. Telephone: 860-395-1811. Fax: 860-395-1812. Url: http://www.peck-tuneski.com.
See Professional Biographies, NEW LONDON, CONNECTICUT

Phillips, Susan Mara, (CV) ..... '68 '95 C.1307 B.A. L.184 J.D. [Suisman,S.W.B.G.&G.]
*PRACTICE AREAS: Labor and Employment; Municipal; Appellate.
Piacenza, Dominic S., (CV) .... '47 '79 C.184 B.A. L.1218 J.D. 164 Hempstead St.
Pochal, Susan B., (BV) ....'60 '85 C.1103 B.S. L.1048 J.D. [Conway&L.] ⊙
*PRACTICE AREAS: Probate Law; Estate Planning; Trusts and Estates Taxation.
Polito, Humbert J., Jr., (BV) .... '56 '86 C.321 B.A. L.184 J.D. [Faulkner&B.]
*PRACTICE AREAS: Personal Injury; Product Liability; Medical Malpractice; Premises Liability; Wrongful Death.
Prestley, Peter B., (BV) ....'45 '72 C.918 B.A. L.184 J.D. [Madsen,P.&P.] ⊙
*PRACTICE AREAS: Labor and Employment Law.
Proulx, Rachel M. ....'71 '99 C.1350 B.A. L.1252 J.D. [🄰 Mariani&R.]
*PRACTICE AREAS: Family Law; Probate.
Provatas, Rita ....'61 '88 C.67 B.A. L.1029 J.D. [Tobin,C.O.R.&S.]
*PRACTICE AREAS: Civil Litigation; Immigration Law; Negligence; Personal Injury.
Purtill, Joseph J. ....'27 '53 C.745 A.B. L.184 LL.B. Supr. Ct. J.
Radlauer, Barbara J. ....'61 '95 C.1044 B.S.N. L.1252 J.D. [Dupont&R.]
*PRACTICE AREAS: Civil Litigation; Personal Injury.
Rakosky, Michael A., (BV) .... '38 '64 C.1027 B.S. L.1009 LL.B. 71 Granite St.
Reardon, Robert I., Jr., (AV) ....'45 '70 C.93 B.S. L.262 J.D. [Reardon]
*PRACTICE AREAS: Personal Injury; Wrongful Death; Medical Malpractice; Products Liability; Aviation.

Reardon Law Firm, The, P.C., (AV) BB
160 Hempstead Street, Drawer 1430, 06320
Telephone: 860-442-0444 Telecopier: 860-444-6445
Email: reardonlaw@aol.com URL: http://www.reardonlaw.com
Robert I. Reardon, Jr.; Scott D. Camassar; Tracey E. Hardman. Of Counsel: Mark A. Dubois.
Civil Trial Practice limited to Personal Injury, Wrongful Death, Medical Malpractice, Product Liability, Aviation Accidents, Admiralty Claims, Military, and Governmental Liability.
See Professional Biographies, NEW LONDON, CONNECTICUT

Reck, Stephen E. ....'65 '90 C.184 B.A. L.1048 J.D. [Mariani&R.]
*PRACTICE AREAS: Family Law; Personal Injury; Criminal Law; Real Estate; Probate.
Regan, Joseph F. ....'21 '49 C.745 Ph.B. L.724 LL.B. 52 Mott Ave.‡
Regan, Michael L., (BV) ....'54 '82 C.184 B.A. L.724 J.D. Asst. States Atty.
Riley, Thomas J., (AV) ....'53 '77 C.321 B.A. L.184 J.D. [Tobin,C.O.R.&S.]
*PRACTICE AREAS: Litigation; Employment Law; Waterfront Development.
Robinson, William A., (AV) ....'19 '51 C.976 B.A. L.893 J.D. 2 Union Plaza‡

Robinson & Cole LLP, (AV)
75 Eugene O'Neill Drive, 06320-6306 ⊙
Telephone: 860-437-5000 Fax: 860-437-5099
Email: rc.com URL: http://www.rc.com
Resident Attorney: Timothy D. Bates.
General Practice including Admiralty, Antitrust and Trade Regulation, Appellate, Banking and Institutional Finance, Bankruptcy and Creditors' Rights, Business Litigation, Business Workouts, Construction, Corporate and Closely Held Business, Criminal Litigation, E-Commerce and Intellectual Property, Employee Benefits and ERISA Litigation, Employment Litigation and Counseling, Environmental, Estate Planning and Probate, Government Relations, Healthcare, Immigration, Insurance, International, Labor Relations and Collective Bargaining, Land Use and Zoning, Personal

(This Listing Continued)

Robinson & Cole LLP (Continued)

Injury, Product Liability, Professional Liability, Public Finance, Real Estate Finance, Development and Leasing, Securities, Tax-Exempt Organizations, Tax Planning and Representation, Utilities and Telecommunications.
Other Offices: Hartford, CT, Stamford, CT, Greenwich, CT, New York, NY, Boston, MA and Manchester, NH.

See Professional Biographies, NEW LONDON, CONNECTICUT

Rotella, Peter W., (BV) .... '47 '73 C.184 B.S. L.362 J.D. [Rotella&S.]
Rotella & Segal, (BV) .... 190 Broad St.
Russell, Meredith E., (CV) .... '49 '89 C.94 B.A. L.1029 J.D. [Kleinman&Assoc.]
*PRACTICE AREAS: Foreclosures; Bankruptcy; Evictions; Real Estate; Family Law.
Sabilia, Elizabeth A. .... '— '98 L.818 J.D. 53 Eugene O'Neill Dr.
Santaniello, Angelo G. .... '24 '50 C.321 B.A. L.276 J.D. Ret. Assoc. Supm. Ct. Jus.
Satti, C. Robert, Sr., (AV) .... '28 '51 C.602 A.B. L.262 LL.B. 517 Alewife Pkwy.
Schatz, Richard A., (AV) ...... '29 '54 C.31 B.A. L.976 LL.B. [Suisman,S.W.B.G.&G.]
*PRACTICE AREAS: Personal Injury; Insurance Defense; Civil Litigation; Criminal.
Schimelman, Stuart M. .... '42 '67 C&L.184 B.A., LL.B. Supr. Ct. J.
Schoepfer, Martin W. .... '48 '97 C.94 B.S. L.1252 J.D. [Suisman,S.W.B.G.&G.]
*PRACTICE AREAS: Family; Criminal.
Scott, Melvin, (BV) .... '27 '57 C.184 B.S. L.383 LL.B. 20 Channing St. (⊙Colchester)
Segal, Joseph F., (BV) .... '40 '66 C&L.184 B.A., LL.B. [Rotella&S.]
Selinger, Joseph J., Jr., (BV) .... '52 '78 C.31 B.A. L.184 J.D. [Tobin,C.O.R.&S.] ⊙
*PRACTICE AREAS: Corporate Finance; Public Finance; Health Care Law.
Shapiro, Michael D., (BV) .... '40 '65 C.103 A.B. L.93 J.D. [M.D.Shapiro]
Shapiro, Michael D., P.C., (BV) .... 39 Bristol St
Shasha, Gilbert, (BV) .... '39 '67 C.31 B.A. L.184 LL.B. 81 Granite St.
Sheehan, Michael W., (BV) .... '60 '89 C.321 B.A. L.184 J.D. [Conway&L.]
*PRACTICE AREAS: Banking Law; Commercial Law; Real Estate Law; Probate Law; Estate Planning.

Sherb, J. Michael, (BV) '36 '63 C.197 A.B. L.184 J.D.
228 Captain's Walk (State Street), P.O. Box 921, 06320
Telephone: 860-447-1442 Telecopier: 860-442-6096
Email: jsherb8517@aol.com
Family Law, Debt Collection/Commercial Law, Probate and Real Estate, Personal Injury, Workers Compensation, Landlord/Tenant Law, Criminal, Motor Vehicle Defense, Civil Litigation.
Reference: Fleet Bank.

Simonson, Richard S. .... '57 '95 C.659 B.A. L.184 J.D. 181 Broad St.
Sobieraj, Ronald E. .... '58 '88 C.262 B.A. L.607 J.D. 37 Granite St.
Solomon, Elliot N. .... '49 '74 C.282 B.A. L.831 J.D. Supr. Ct. J.
Spallone, James F. .... '65 '92 C.951 B.A. L.184 J.D. [Waller,S.&P.]
*PRACTICE AREAS: Civil Litigation; Municipal Law; Criminal Law; Appellate Practice.
Speziali, Albert, (CV) .... '57 '83 C.184 B.A. L.306 J.D. 5 Shaw's Cove
Sprecace, George A. .... '33 '84 C.569 B.A. L.306 J.D. 248 Montauk Ave.
Statchen, Robert R. .... '68 '93 C.156 B.A. L.146 J.D. [Tobin,C.O.R.&S.]
*PRACTICE AREAS: Corporate Law; Business Law; Public Finance; Federal Taxation; State Taxation.

Stevens, Harris & Guernsey, P.C.
(See Niantic)

Stewart, G. Russell .... '59 '86 C.184 B.A. L.93 J.D. 37 Granite St.
Strafaci, M. John, (CV) .... '60 '85 C.273 B.A. L.823 J.D. 191 Hempstead St.
Suerth, Ryan M. .... '74 '00 C.1117 B.A. L.809 J.D. [Andrews,Y.&G.]
*PRACTICE AREAS: Commercial Law; Business Law; Debtor and Creditor; Estate Planning.
Suisman, Charles, (AV) ..... '06 '30 C.94 B.B.A. L.976 LL.B. [Suisman,S.W.B.G.&G.]
Suisman, S. Joel, (BV) .... '35 '60 C.1155 B.S. L.569 LL.B. [Suisman,S.W.B.G.&G.]
*PRACTICE AREAS: Asset Protection; Business Law; Banking; Finance; Corporate.

Suisman, Shapiro, Wool, Brennan, Gray & Greenberg, P.C., (AV)
Suite 200 The Courtney Building, 2 Union Plaza, P.O. Box 1591, 06320
Telephone: 860-442-4416 Fax: 860-442-0495
Email: sswbgg@aol.com URL: http://www.sswbgg.com
James F. Brennan; S. Joel Suisman; Lawrence J. Greenberg; Thomas B. Wilson; Andrew Brand; John A. Collins, III; Jeffrey W. Hill; James P. Berryman; Harry E. Calmar; Matthew E. Auger; Raymond L. Baribeault, Jr.; Robert B. Keville; Frank J. Liberty; Eileen C. Duggan; Hinda K. Kimmel; Susan Mara Phillips; Jeanette M. Dostie; Martin W. Schoepfer; Robert G. Tukey; Cynthia L. Desmond; Michael P. Carey; Michael A. Blanchard; Santa Mendoza. Of Counsel: Charles Suisman; Marilynne Graboys Wool; Louis Patrick Gray, III; Richard A. Schatz.
Administrative Law, Aged and Aging, Appellate Practice, Asset Protection, Business Law, Civil Practice, Civil Rights, Commercial Law, Commercial Real Estate, Constitutional Law, Contracts, Corporate Law, Criminal Law, Debtor and Creditor, Family Law, Finance, Health Care, Indians and Native Populations, Insurance, Intellectual Property, Labor and Employment, Leases and Leasing, Litigation, Medical Malpractice, Municipal Law, Partnership Law, Personal Injury, Probate, Products Liability, Property Law, Real Estate, Regulatory Law, Social Security, Taxation, Torts, Trusts and Estates, Workers Compensation, Zoning, Planning and Land Use.
Representative Clients: First New London Savings & Loan Assn., Inc.; Mitchell College; The Connecticut Bricklayers International Pension Fund; New London Flying Service, Inc.
Local Counsel for: Avis Rent-A-Car Systems, Inc.; Kemper Insurance Co.

See Professional Biographies, NEW LONDON, CONNECTICUT

Sullivan, Linda J. .... '52 '79 C&L.184 B.A., J.D. Suite 203, Three Shaw's Cove
Sulmasy, Glenn M. '66 '98 C.869 B.S. L.1002 J.D.
(adm. in MD; not adm. in CT) Staff Atty., U.S. Coast Guard Academy
Tedeschi, John P., (BV) .... '32 '61 C&L.184 B.A., LL.B. 164 Hempstead St.
Tobin, Robert D., (AV) .... '42 '68 C&L.93 B.A., J.D. [Tobin,C.O.R.&S.] ⊙
*PRACTICE AREAS: Commercial Law; Litigation; Real Estate; Zoning; Administrative Law.

Tobin, Carberry, O'Malley, Riley & Selinger, P.C., (AV)
43 Broad Street, P.O. Box 58, 06320 ⊙
Telephone: 860-447-0335 Fax: 860-442-3469
Email: attorneys@tcors.com URL: http://www.tcors.com
Robert D. Tobin; Glenn T. Carberry; F. Jerome O'Malley; Thomas J. Riley; Joseph J. Selinger, Jr.; Kathleen A. McNamara; Rita Provatas;—Robert R. Statchen.
General Civil and Criminal Practice, Trials and Appeals in all Courts, Administrative Law, Banking and Commercial Law, Commercial Real Estate, Contract Law, Corporate Law, Business Law, Employment Law, Government Relations, Public Finance, Public Utility Law, Health Care Law, Land Use Law, Personal Injury, Product Liability, Estate Planning and Probate, Elder Law, Immigration, Federal, State and Local Tax Law.
Reference: Shawmut Bank, New London, Connecticut.
Hartford, Connecticut Office: 3rd Floor, 330 Main Street, 06106. Telephone: 860-541-6438. Fax: 860-541-6484.

See Professional Biographies, NEW LONDON, CONNECTICUT

Traystman, Gary B., (BV) .... '54 '81 C.62 B.A. L.1187 LL.B. 45 Channing St.
Traystman, Harry R., (BV) .... '35 '60 C.882 B.A. L.184 LL.B. 45 Channing St.
Tukey, Robert G. .... '71 '96 C.1030 B.A. L.1048 J.D. [Suisman,S.W.B.G.&G.]
*PRACTICE AREAS: Civil Litigation; Personal Injury Law.
Tuneski, Robert S., (BV) .... '35 '81 C.869 B.S. L.1048 J.D. [Peck&T.]
Valentin, Elisa .... '71 '98 C.1145 B.S. L.306 J.D. [Waller,S.&P.]
*PRACTICE AREAS: Real Estate; Civil Litigation.
Vile, Russell E., (CV) .... '49 '78 C.918 B.A. L.678 J.D. 71 Granite St.
Votto, Valerie Ann .... '61 '87 C.401 B.A. L.128 J.D. [Waller,S.&P.] ⊙
*PRACTICE AREAS: Real Estate; Land Use Law; Municipal Law.
Wagman, Gregg W. .... '59 '92 C.1373 B.A. L.1252 J.D. 5 Shaw's Cove
Walker, C. Michael .... '61 '89 C.676 B.A. L.776 J.D. 111 Huntington Street

Waller, Smith & Palmer, P.C., (AV)
52 Eugene O'Neill Drive, P.O. Box 88, 06320 ⊙
Telephone: 860-442-0367 Telecopier: 860-447-9915
Email: wspmain@snet.net URL: http://www.snetyp.com/wallersmithpalmer
Tracy Waller (1862-1947); J. Rodney Smith (1906-1979); Birdsey G. Palmer (Retired); William W. Miner; Robert P. Anderson, Jr.; Robert W. Marrion; Hughes Griffis; Edward B. O'Connell; Frederick B. Gahagan; Tracy M. Collins; Philip M. Johnstone; David P. Condon; Valerie Ann Votto; Charles C. Anderson;—James F. Spallone; Elisa Valentin.
General Practice. Corporation, Commercial, Estate Planning, Probate, Real Estate, Personal Injury, Municipal, Banking and Trials in all Courts.
General Counsel For: Town of East Lyme.
Counsel For: Citizens Bank of Connecticut; Soneco/Northeastern, Inc.; The Nature Conservancy; Fleet Bank.
Local Counsel For: McCue Mortgage Co.; Citicorp Mortgage; U.S. Department of Housing and Urban Development.
Old Lyme Office: 103 Halls Road. Telephone: 860-434-8063. Telecopier: 860-434-9452. Email: wspol@snet.net

See Professional Biographies, NEW LONDON, CONNECTICUT

Ward, Barry J. .... '51 '78 C.264 B.A. L.93 J.D. 245 Williams St.
Willetts, William J., Jr., (BV) .... '34 '59 C.478 B.A. L.184 J.D. 125 Shaw St.
Wilson, Thomas B., (AV) .... '39 '67 C.855 B.A. L.184 J.D. [Suisman,S.W.B.G.&G.]
*PRACTICE AREAS: Municipal Law; Land Use and Planning Law; Indian Law.
Wool, Louis C., (BV) .... '11 '33 C.823 L.94 LL.B. 2 Union Plaza
Wool, Marilynne Graboys .... '26 '50 C.732 L.262 LL.B. [Suisman,S.W.B.G.&G.]
Young, James L., Jr., (BV) .... '51 '81 C.1102 B.A. L.1051 J.D. [Andrews,Y.&G.]
*PRACTICE AREAS: Debtor and Creditor; Commercial Law; Business Law; Zoning; Real Estate.

NEW MILFORD, 19,420, *Litchfield Co.*

Allingham, Thomas J., (BV) .... '65 '91 C.94 B.S./B.A. L.1029 J.D. [Allingham&S.]
*PRACTICE AREAS: Criminal Litigation; Personal Injury Litigation; Civil Litigation; Workers Compensation Law; Real Estate.

Allingham & Spillane, (BV)
11 South Main Street, 06776
Telephone: 860-350-5454 Fax: 860-350-5457
Members of the Firm: Thomas J. Allingham; Philip F. Spillane.
Criminal Litigation, Personal Injury, Workers Compensation, Real Estate, Civil Litigation.

See Professional Biographies, NEW MILFORD, CONNECTICUT

Altermatt, Paul B., (AV) .... '30 '56 C.918 B.A. L.276 LL.B. [Cramer&A.]
American Center For Law and Justice, The
8 S. Main (⊙Mobile, AL; Scottsdale, AZ; Wash., DC; New Hope, KY; Virginia Beach, VA; Strasbourg, France)
Anderson, Henry B., (AV) .... '18 '47 C.918 B.A. L.184 LL.B. [Cramer&A.]
Arnold, Lynda Lee .... '63 '96 C.1103 B.A. L.1040 J.D. [Moots,P.M.M.&D.]
*PRACTICE AREAS: Family Law.
Baker, Fred L., (BV) .... '43 '69 C&L.184 B.A., J.D. [Baker] ⊙
*PRACTICE AREAS: Taxation; Estate Planning; Probate; Corporate Law; Business Law.

Baker Law Firm, P.C., (BV)
Baker Fields, 4 Mine Hill Road, 06776 ⊙
Telephone: 860-354-9100
Email: Fred@Baker-Law.com URL: http://www.lawyers.com/blaw
Fred L. Baker.
Taxation, Estate Planning, Probate, Business and Corporate, Real Estate.
Danbury Office: 24 Delay Street. Telephone: 203-792-8765. Fax: 203-791-1892.

See Professional Biographies, NEW MILFORD, CONNECTICUT

Beck, Thomas A. '34 '66 C.347 B.A. L.128 LL.B.
(adm. in DC; not adm. in CT) 26 Rockledge Lane

Bennett, David F., Law Offices of
(See Danbury)

Bliss, T. Stevens, (BV) .... '43 '69 C.367 A.B. L.831 J.D. 11 S Main St.
Breeckner, Randall J., (BV) .... '48 '73 C.696 B.A. L.184 J.D. [Cramer&A.]
*PRACTICE AREAS: Real Estate Law; Criminal Law; Motor Vehicle Defense Law; Business Law; Family Law.
Buck-Taylor, Cecilia, (CV) .... '53 '91 C.1044 B.A. L.262 J.D. [C.Buck-Taylor]

Buck-Taylor, Cecilia, P.C., Law Office of, (CV)
6 Main Street, P.O. Box 1121, 06776
Telephone: 860-355-9191 Fax: 860-355-3061
Cecilia Buck-Taylor.
Family Law, Divorce, Adoption, Guardianship, Probate, Estates & Wills, Juvenile Law, Criminal Law, Real Estate.

See Professional Biographies, NEW MILFORD, CONNECTICUT

Buzaid, Lisa L. .... '59 '88 C.1103 B.A. L.1029 J.D. [Cramer&A.]
*PRACTICE AREAS: Commercial and Residential Real Estate; Landlord and Tenant Law.
Cohen, Harry .... '20 '46 C.164 B.A. L.94 LL.B. [Cohen&K.]
Cohen & Kessler .... 62 Bridge St.
Collins, Jennifer H. .... '72 '98 C.1030 B.A. L.180 J.D. [Guendelsberger&T.]

Cramer & Anderson LLP, (AV)
51 Main Street, 06776 ⊙
Telephone: 860-355-2631 Fax: 860-355-9460
Email: newmilford@crameranderson.com URL: http://www.cramer-anderson.com
Members of Firm: David Cramer (1902-1981); Randall J. Breeckner (Resident); Arthur C. Weinshank (Resident); D. Randall DiBella (Resident); Mitchell J. Melnick (Resident); John D. Tower (Resident); Lisa L. Buzaid (Resident); Clayton L. Blick (Resident, Litchfield Office); Grant J. Nelson (Resident, Kent Office); Perley H. Grimes, Jr. (Resident, Litchfield Office); Robert L. Fisher, Jr. (Resident, Litchfield Office); Reginald William H. Fairbairn (Resident, Washington Depot Office); William C. Franklin (Resident, Litchfield Office); David P. Burke (Resident, Danbury Office); Joseph A. Saffi (Resident, Danbury Office); Barry S. Moller (Resident, Litchfield Office); James D. Hirschfield (Resident, Litchfield Office). Associates: Denise M. Cloutier (Resident, Litchfield Office); Rosemary B. Jones (Resident). Of Counsel: Henry B. Anderson; Stephen N. Hume; Paul B. Altermatt (Resident); Robert M. FitzGerald (Resident, Litchfield Office).
General Practice. Probate, Estate Planning, Taxation, Municipal, Family, Real Estate, Negligence and Bankruptcy Law. Civil and Criminal Trials. Planning and Zoning, Corporate, Banking, Securities.
Danbury, Connecticut Office: 68 North Street. Telephone: 203-790-7747. Email: danbury@crameranderson.com
Litchfield, Connecticut Office: 46 West Street. P.O. Box 278. Telephone: 860-567-8718. Email: litchfield@cramer-anderson.com
Kent, Connecticut Office: Kent Green, P.O. Box 333. Telephone: 860-927-3568. Email: gnelson@cramer-anderson.com
Washington Depot, Connecticut Office: 2 Green Hill Road, P.O. Box 321. Telephone: 860-868-0527. Email: wfairbairn@cramer-anderson.com

See Professional Biographies, NEW MILFORD, CONNECTICUT

Diamond, Jeffrey A. .... '57 '87 C.103 B.A. L.978 J.D. 72 Diamond Ln.
DiBella, D. Randall, (AV) .... '53 '80 C.1103 B.A. L.1209 J.D. [Cramer&A.]
*PRACTICE AREAS: Personal Injury Law; Civil Litigation; Uninsured Motorist; Underinsured Motorist Arbitration; Mediation.
Dratch, Barbara McMahon, (CV) '42 '91 C.999 B.A. L.1029 J.D.
[Moots,P.M.M.&D.]
*PRACTICE AREAS: Family Law; Civil Litigation; Personal Injury Law; Real Estate; Probate.
Dunham, Carl M., Jr. .... '43 '67 C&L.184 B.A., LL.B. P.O. Box 418
Fisher, Ann E., (BV) .... '53 '79 C.478 B.A. L.184 J.D. 459 Danbury Rd

Garlasco, Paul James ....'57 '85 C.1102 B.S. L.1029 J.D. 35 Park Ln.
Gradowski, Richard C., (BV) ....'40 '67 C.184 B.A. L.94 LL.B. 50 Park Lane
Guendelsberger, Robert J., (BV) .....'50 '76 C.24 B.A. L.607 J.D. [Guendelsberger&T.]

Guendelsberger and Taylor, (AV)
28 Park Lane, 06776 ⊙
Telephone: 860-354-4444 Fax: 860-210-2128
URL: http://www.G-T-law.com
Members of Firm: Robert J. Guendelsberger; Kenneth E. Taylor; Scott R. McCarthy; Bernard Pitterman; Francis M. Dooley. Associates: Jennifer H. Collins; Robert A. D'Andrea.
General Civil Practice. Civil Litigation. Personal Injury, Negligence, Real Estate, Matrimonial, Commercial, Bankruptcy, Workers Compensation, Social Security Disability, Probate, Estate Planning and Wills.

Hume, Stephen N., (AV) ....'25 '51 C.321 B.N.S. L.178 LL.B. [Ⓒ Cramer&A.]
Jones, Rosemary B. ....'65 '92 C.145 B.A. L.184 J.D. [Ⓐ Cramer&A.]
*PRACTICE AREAS: Elder Law; Real Estate; Environmental Law.
Kessler, Murray J. ....'41 '74 C.158 B.S.E.E. L.184 J.D. [Cohen&K.]
Kuss, Rudolf L. ....'42 '81 C.1133 B.S. L.724 J.D. 56 Danbury Rd.
Larson, Paul T. ....'47 '74 C.339 B.S. L.1049 J.D. 99 Great Brook Rd.
Lohr, Ann-Louise ....'56 '81 C.338 B.S. L.365 J.D. [American L.&J.]
Mannion, Michael J., (BV) ....'45 '74 C.93 B.A. L.724 J.D. [Moots,P.M.M.&D.]
*PRACTICE AREAS: Civil Litigation; Criminal Litigation; Domestic Relations Law; Zoning, Planning and Land Use.
Marchak, Claudia Jackson, (CV) ....'41 '84 C.339 B.A. L.1040 J.D. 56 Danbury Rd.
Martindale, Ann ....'47 '88 C.477 B.A. L.184 J.D. [Moots,P.M.M.&D.]
*PRACTICE AREAS: Real Estate; Commercial Lending; Environmental Law; Business Law; Estates.
McCarthy, Scott R., (BV) ....'66 '91 C.884 B.S. L.93 J.D. [Guendelsberger&T.]
*PRACTICE AREAS: Civil Litigation; Criminal Litigation; Worker's Compensation.
McCarthy, Vincent Patrick ....'47 '73 C.728 B.S. L.262 J.D. [American L.&J.]
McKenna, Michael S., (BV) ....'57 '82 C.184 B.A. L.884 J.D. [Sienkiewicz&M.] ⊙
*PRACTICE AREAS: Litigation; Civil Practice; Personal Injury; Administrative Law; Employment Law.
Melnick, Mitchell J. ....'59 '84 C.696 B.A. L.472 J.D. [Cramer&A.]
*PRACTICE AREAS: Corporate Law; Banking Law; Health Care Law; Securities Law.
Moots, Roland F., Jr., (BV) ....'44 '69 C.472 A.B. L.94 J.D. [Moots,P.M.M.&D.]
*PRACTICE AREAS: Family Law; Criminal Law; Litigation; Personal Injury.

Moots, Pellegrini, Mannion, Martindale & Dratch, P.C., (BV)
Forty Six Main Street, 06776
Mailing Address: P.O. Box 1319, New Milford, Connecticut 06776
Telephone: 860-355-4191 Fax: 860-355-8487
URL: http://www.mpsmlaw.com
Roland F. Moots, Jr.; Terry C. Pellegrini; Michael J. Mannion; Ann Martindale; Barbara McMahon Dratch;—Lynda Lee Arnold.
Estate Planning, Probate, Business and Corporate, Real Estate, Domestic Relations, Personal Injury, Workers Compensation, Criminal and Civil Litigation. Planning Zoning and Land Use.
See Professional Biographies, NEW MILFORD, CONNECTICUT

Nevel, Ann Ariel '48 '81 C.1214 B.A. L.884 J.D.
(adm. in PA; not adm. in CT) 161 Paper Mill Rd.‡
Peitler, Arthur J. ....'48 '83 C.724 B.S. L.184 J.D. P.O. Box 567
Pellegrini, Terry C., (BV) ....'43 '69 C.999 A.B. L.884 J.D. [Moots,P.M.M.&D.]
*PRACTICE AREAS: Real Estate Law; Zoning, Planning and Land Use.
Pitterman, Bernard, (BV) ....'45 '85 C.696 B.A. L.1029 J.D. [Guendelsberger&T.]
*PRACTICE AREAS: Personal Injury; Social Security Disability; Worker's Compensation; Insurance Law; Litigation.
Pomerantz, Richard M., (BV) .....'57 '84 C.882 B.A. L.1009 J.D. [Webster-O'Keefe&P.]
Reynolds, Barbara W. ....'47 '93 C.97 B.S. L.184 J.D. [B.W.Reynolds]
Reynolds, Barbara W., L.L.C. ....15 South Main Street
Rosen, Robert J., (CV) ...'42 '85 C.1156 B.S. L.1048 J.D. 147 Candlewood Mountain Rd.
Sienkiewicz, Jeffrey B., (BV) ....'48 '72 C.367 B.A. L.823 J.D. [Sienkiewicz&M.] ⊙
*PRACTICE AREAS: Municipal Law; Personal Injury; Medical Malpractice; Zoning, Planning and Land Use; Products Liability.
Sienkiewicz, Nancy ....'50 '77 C.823 B.S. L.184 J.D. [Sienkiewicz&M.] ⊙
*PRACTICE AREAS: Real Estate Law; Divorce Mediation; Trusts and Estates; Wills; Commercial Law.

Sienkiewicz & McKenna, P.C., (BV)
9 South Main Street, P.O. Box 786, 06776 ⊙
Telephone: 860-354-1583 Fax: 860-355-4439
URL: http://www.lawyers.com/smlaw
Members of Firm: Nancy Sienkiewicz; Jeffrey B. Sienkiewicz; Michael S. McKenna; Theresa Benedict D'Alton (Resident, Kent).
Civil Practice. Personal Injury, Medical Malpractice, Product Liability, Real Estate, Commercial Law, Administrative Law, Family Law, Mediation, Trusts and Estates, Wills and Probate, Zoning, Planning and Land Use, Contracts, Appellate Practice.
Kent, Connecticut Office: 25 North Main Street, Suite 13A. Telephone: 860-927-4640. Fax: 860-927-1909.
See Professional Biographies, NEW MILFORD, CONNECTICUT

Spillane, Philip F. ....'52 '78 C.184 B.A. L.1048 J.D. [Allingham&S.]
*PRACTICE AREAS: Personal Injury Law; Workers Compensation Law.
Taylor, Kenneth E., (BV) ....'60 '85 C.1102 B.S. L.1029 J.D. [Guendelsberger&T.]
*PRACTICE AREAS: Matrimonial Law; Personal Injury; Litigation.
Tower, John D. ....'63 '89 C.188 B.A. L.477 J.D. [Cramer&A.]
*PRACTICE AREAS: Civil Litigation.
Ward, Eva A. Bilodeau '47 '76 C.999 B.A. L.724 J.D.
(adm. in MA; not adm. in CT) 70 Lanesville Rd.‡
Webber, Arthur L. '12 '38 C.674 A.B. L.309 LL.B.
(adm. in NY; not adm. in CT) 4 Mountain View Lane‡
Webster-O'Keefe, M. Katherine, (CV) ......'53 '83 C&L.923 B.A. [Webster-O'Keefe&P.]
Webster-O'Keefe & Pomerantz, (BV) ....72 Park Lane Rd.
Weinshank, Arthur C. ....'50 '75 C.1040 B.B.A. L.472 J.D. [Cramer&A.]
*PRACTICE AREAS: Taxation Law; Trust Planning; Estate Planning; Probate; Administrative Law.
Wellman, William J. ....'43 '68 C&L.188 B.A., J.D. 147 Pumpkin Hill Rd.
Wharton, Donald L., II, (CV) ....'61 '86 C.184 B.A. L.1048 J.D. 227 Danbury Rd.
Wittstein, Andrew M., (BV) ....'47 '72 C.94 A.B. L.184 J.D. Asst. States Atty.
Zitzmann, Kelly C. '68 '94 C.188 A.B. L.1009 J.D.
(adm. in NY; not adm. in CT) Zitzmann Consulting, LLC

NEW PRESTON, —, *Litchfield Co.*

Hubbard, David N. ....'46 '71 C.478 B.A. L.178 J.D. P.O. Box 385
Mclean, Sarah H. '08 '33 C.881 L.178 LL.B.
(adm. in NY; not adm. in CT) 145 Kinney Hill Rd.

NEWTOWN, 1,800, *Fairfield Co.*

Buckley, Moira F. ....'54 '85 C.918 B.A. L.184 J.D. 208 Hattertown Rd.
Darling, Peter S. ....'37 '67 C.924 B.A. L.94 LL.B. 12 Brookwood Dr.
Denlinger, Sutherland W. G., (BV) ....'38 '68 C.184 B.A. L.306 LL.B. [Denlinger&P.]
Denlinger and Previdi, (BV) ....33 Church Hill Road
Dougherty, John H. '15 '39 L.180 LL.B.
(adm. in DC; not adm. in CT) 17 Beaver Dam Rd.‡
Dougherty, Katharine E. '47 '81 C.608 B.S. L.128 J.D.
(adm. in VA; not adm. in CT) Beaver Dam Rd., Rt. 4‡
Emmett, Kathryn, (AV) ....'44 '70 C.681 B.A. L.976 J.D. [Emmett&G.] ⊙
Emmett & Glander, (AV) ....17 Pond Brook Road (⊙Stamford)
Gersten, Martin J. '42 '66 C.273 B.A. L.178 J.D.
90 Birch Hill Road, 06470-1740
Telephone: 203-364-0290 Fax: 203-364-0292
Email: MJGLAW@aol.com URL: http://www.lawyers.com/gerstenlaw
***PRACTICE AREAS: Corporate Law (70%); Securities (10%); Finance (10%); Taxation (10%).**
Corporate Law, Securities, Finance, Taxation.
See Professional Biographies, NEWTOWN, CONNECTICUT
Glander, Jane W., (BV) ....'54 '89 C.1030 B.A. L.724 J.D. [Emmett&G.] ⊙
Goldstein, William N. ....'34 '62 C.102 B.A. L.178 LL.B. 10 Queen St.
Hall, Robert H., (AV) ....'39 '64 C.976 B.A. L.309 LL.B. [Hall&S.]
*PRACTICE AREAS: Civil and Commercial Litigation; Zoning and Land Use; Estate Planning.

Hall & Savarese, P.C., (AV)
43 Main Street, P.O. Box 395, 06470
Telephone: 203-426-8177; Waterbury: 203-575-9768 Fax: 203-426-6529
Robert H. Hall; Stephen L. Savarese.
General Practice. Trials in all State and Federal Courts. Zoning and Land Use, Real Estate, Probate and Estate Planning, Personal Injury, Workers Compensation.
See Professional Biographies, NEWTOWN, CONNECTICUT

Hamilton, Scott J., (CV) '56 '83 C&L.1048 B.A., J.D.
(adm. in MA; not adm. in CT) P.O. Box 119

Jacobs Partners LLC
(See Norwalk)

Keane, Lawrence G., (AVⓉ) '62 '89 C&L.262 B.A., J.D.
(adm. in NY; not adm. in CT) General Counsel, National Shooting Sports Foundation
Koehler, Robert A. '29 '54 C&L.724 B.A., J.D.
(adm. in NY; not adm. in CT) 24 Appleblossom Lane‡

Kulawitz, Harvey J., LLC
(See Ridgefield)

Lux, Paul S. ....'50 '74 C.228 A.B. L.184 J.D. [Lux&T.]
Lux & Timmel ....30 Church Hill Rd.
Murphy, Michele F., (CV) ....'60 '88 C.659 B.S. L.1040 J.D. [Murphy&M.]
*PRACTICE AREAS: Elder Law; Probate; Real Estate; Medicare and Medicaid.
Murphy, Thomas E. ....'60 '96 C.659 B.S. L.1040 J.D. [Murphy&M.]
*PRACTICE AREAS: Elder Law; Probate; Real Estate; Medicare and Medicaid.

Murphy & Murphy LLP, (CV)
38 Church Hill Road, 06470
Telephone: 203-270-0805 Facsimile: 203-270-8239
URL: http://www.lawyers.com/murphy&murphy
Michele F. Murphy; Thomas E. Murphy.
Elder Law, Probate, Estate Planning, Conservatorships, Medicare and Medicaid and Nursing Home Regulation.
See Professional Biographies, NEWTOWN, CONNECTICUT

Nahoum, Michael B., (BV) ....'44 '73 C.1029 B.A. L.818 J.D. 103 S. Main St.
Nickse, Judith S., (CV) ....'55 '89 C.184 B.A. L.1029 J.D. 33 Main St.
Persky, Arnold ....'33 '59 C.855 B.A. L.94 LL.B. 38 Taunton Lake Rd.
Plasil, Ellen, (CV) ....'50 '86 C.1111 B.A. L.705 J.D. 5 Smoke Rise Ridge
Previdi, Helen Joy, (BV) ....'42 '83 C.829 B.S. L.1029 J.D. [Denlinger&P.]
Ragusa, Anne M. ....'57 '91 C.184 B.A. L.911 J.D. 103 S. Main St.
Rodgers, William F. L., (AV) '60 '85 C.659 B.A. L.94 J.D.
Sugarbrook Law Center, 4 Hi Barlow Road, 06470
Telephone: 203-270-8879 FAX: 203-270-3415; URL: http://www.sugarbrooklaw.com
Email: wflr@sugarbrooklaw.com URL: http://www.lawyers.com/sugarbrooklaw
General Practice, Probate, Wills, Trusts and Estate Planning, Matrimonial and Family Law, Elder Law, Corporate Law, Personal Injury, Trials.
See Professional Biographies, NEWTOWN, CONNECTICUT
Savarese, Stephen L., (BV) ....'60 '86 C.602 B.A. L.904 J.D. [Hall&S.]
*PRACTICE AREAS: Real Estate; Personal Injury; Workers Compensation.
Schwartz, C. Harold, (AV) ....'28 '53 C.362 B.A. L.569 LL.B. 20 Rock Ridge Rd
Timmel, William C. ....'47 '75 C.884 B.S. L.724 J.D. [Lux&T.]
Wakelee, George N., (BV) ....'25 '53 C.1019 A.B. L.188 LL.B. [Wakelee&I.]
Wakelee & Isaac, (BV) ....10 Queen St.
Winokur, Theodore D. ....'60 '85 C.659 B.A. L.94 J.D. P.O. Box 355
Wippermann, Stephen D. ....'47 '75 C.93 A.B. L.184 J.D. 103 South Main Street

NIANTIC, 3,422, *New London Co.*

Bodenhofer, Paul J. '47 '75 C.869 B.S. L.472 J.D.
(adm. in FL; not adm. in CT) 110 N. Bridebrook Rd.★
Cunningham, Daniel R., (BV) ....'54 '90 C.184 B.S. L.1048 J.D. 90 Penn. Ave.
Ewers, Stephen D. ....'54 '90 C.871 B.S. L.1029 J.D. 156 Old Black Point Rd.
Guernsey, Paul M., (BV) ....'50 '75 C.602 B.A. L.184 J.D. [Stevens,H.&G.]
*PRACTICE AREAS: Civil and Criminal Litigation; Personal Injury; Wrongful Death; Motor Vehicle Accidents and Injuries.
Harkins, James A. ....'23 '66 C.178 B.S. L.184 J.D. 97 W. Main St.
Harris, Theodore A., (BV) ....'49 '75 C.223 B.S. L.184 J.D. [Stevens,H.&G.]
*PRACTICE AREAS: Planning and Zoning Law; Real Estate Law; Commercial Law.
Hubby, Frank W., 3rd '07 '34 C.976 B.A. L.309 LL.B.
(adm. in NY; not adm. in CT) 249 Old Black Point Rd.‡
McKeever, Kenneth M., (P.C.), (BV) ....'43 '74 C.1033 B.S. L.184 J.D. P.O. Box 514
McNamara, Jeffrey A., (BV) ....'59 '85 C.1030 B.A. L.1048 J.D. [McNamara&M.]
McNamara, Leo J., (AV) ....'29 '59 C.184 B.A. L.262 LL.B. [McNamara&M.]
McNamara & McNamara, P.C., (AV) ....94 Pennsylvania Ave.
Ostrow, Robert W. ....'26 '53 C.569 B.A. L.564 LL.B. 5 Apple Blossom Lane
Quilliam, Paige Stevens ....'73 '99 C.745 B.A. L.1252 J.D. [Ⓐ Stevens,H.&G.]
*PRACTICE AREAS: Family Law; Probate Law.
Stevens, Ronald F., (BV) ....'45 '72 C.276 B.S.B.A. L.94 J.D. [Stevens,H.&G.]
*PRACTICE AREAS: Criminal Law; Civil Litigation.

Stevens, Harris & Guernsey, P.C., (BV)
351 Main Street, P.O. Box P.O.Drawer 660, 06357
Telephone: 860-739-6906 Fax: 860-739-2997
Email: SHG@CTOL.net URL: http://www.lawyers.com/stevensharrisguernseylaw
Ronald F. Stevens; Theodore A. Harris; Paul M. Guernsey;—Paige Stevens Quilliam.
General Civil and Criminal Practice before State and Federal Courts. Personal Injury, Wrongful Death, Real Estate, Probate, Corporation, Domestic Relations, Environmental and Workers Compensation Law. Trials and Appeals.
Approved Attorneys for: Chicago Title Insurance Co.; First American Title Insurance Co.; Lawyers Title Insurance Co; Connecticut Attorneys Title Insurance Co.
Representative Client: Chucks Steak House.
References: Connecticut National Bank; New London Federal Savings & Loan Assn.
See Professional Biographies, NIANTIC, CONNECTICUT

Turner, Ira M. ....'62 '00 C.422 B.S. L.1252 J.D. P.O. Box 538
Waller, Robin W., (Mr.) ....'34 '67 C.31 B.A. L.184 LL.B. Workers Comp. Comm.

NOANK, 1,371, *New London Co.*

Cheney, Thomas L., (BV) ....'17 '48 C&L.976 B.A., LL.B. 5 Morgan Point‡
Viering, Russell W. ....'15 '39 C.976 B.A. L.309 LL.B. P.O. Box 296

Wright, Elissa T., (BV) ....'46 '79 C.183 B.A. L.184 J.D. 51 Pearl St.

NORFOLK, 2,060, *Litchfield Co.*

Tracey, Martin J., III .... '39 '68 C&L.262 A.B., J.D. 88 Doolittle Dr.

NORTH BRANFORD, 11,554, *New Haven Co.*

Caporale, Michael R., Jr. ....'24 '61 C.94 B.S. L.276 J.D. 288 Notch Hill Rd.
Gordon, Eugene H., (AV(T)) '14 '39 C.569 B.A. L.976 J.D.
(adm. in NY; not adm. in CT) Evergreen Woods, 88 Notch Hill Rd.‡
Haas, Frederick P. '11 '39 C&L.976 B.A., LL.B.
(adm. in NY; not adm. in CT) 88 Notch Hill Rd.‡
Hannan, William J. '18 '50 C.602 L.564 LL.B.
(adm. in PA; not adm. in CT) 88 Notch Hill Rd.‡
Oestreicher, John B., (BV) ....'64 '90 C.529 B.A. L.692 J.D. 275 Branford Rd.
Shea, James W., (BV) ....'53 '79 C.999 B.A. L.365 J.D. 275 Branford Rd.
Sprunger, Powell L., (AV) '39 '68 C.679 B.S. L.800 J.D.
(adm. in CA; not adm. in CT; Pat.) 82 Linsley Lake Rd.
Warne, Frederick P. '14 '41 C.197 A.B. L.309 J.D.
(adm. in VA; not adm. in CT) 88 Notch Hill Rd.‡

NORTH CANTON, 1,680, *Hartford Co.*

Trionfini, Sandra A., (BV) .... '55 '80 C.823 B.A. L.1048 J.D. 14 Case St.

NORTHFIELD, —, *Litchfield Co.*

Olmstead, Donald L. .... '46 '75 C&L.184 B.S., J.D. Newton Rd.

NORTHFORD, —, *New Haven Co.*

Buddington, Perry C. .... '57 '83 C.1156 B.S. L.184 J.D. 30 Mansfield Dr.
Dubin, Lawrence A. .... '48 '75 C.30 B.A. L.184 J.D. P.O. Box 69
Guertin, George P. .... '45 '90 C.1156 B.S. L.306 J.D. 26 Jackson Ln.
Sawyer, Clarence E., Jr., (BV) .... '46 '82 C.745 B.A. L.1029 J.D. 1038 Middletown Ave.

NORTH FRANKLIN, 150, *New London Co.*

Auwood, James W., (CV) ....'56 '82 C.184 B.A. L.190 J.D. 27 Southgate Cir.

NORTH HAVEN, 22,080, *New Haven Co.*

Bassick, Gayle T. '54 '80 C.860 B.A. L.930 J.D.
Assoc. Gen. Coun., Anthem Blue Cross and Blue Shield
*RESPONSIBILITIES: Health Care (60%); General Corporate (40%).
Bourke, Robert M., (CV) ....'46 '72 C.1033 B.A. L.208 J.D. Marlin Firearms Co.
Bown, Robert T. ....'41 '67 C.1030 B.S.S. L.880 J.D. 370 Bassett Rd.
Boyle, Michael J. ....'57 '93 C.976 B.A. L.184 J.D. [M.J.Boyle]
Boyle, Michael J., Law Offices of ....169 Montowese Ave.
Buemi, Sally J., (BV) ....'56 '83 C.184 B.A. L.1048 J.D. 26 St. John St.
Carrano, Frank, (BV) .... '57 '82 C.1102 B.A. L.900 J.D. 270 Quinnipiac Ave.
Cella, Carl E., (AV) ....'41 '66 C.276 A.B. L.184 J.D. [Cella,M.&W.]
*PRACTICE AREAS: Medical Malpractice; Personal Injury; Arbitration; Mediation; Automobile Liability.

Cella, McKeon & Williams, P.C., (AV) [BB]
Suite A, 21 Washington Avenue, P.O. Box 221, 06473
Telephone: 203-239-5851 Fax: 203-234-2974
Email: carlc@cmwlawyers.com
Carl E. Cella; James G. Williams; Kevin P. Walsh; Michael F. O'Connor; Lisa D. Galati; Robert J. Flanagan, Jr.; Robert J. Weber, III.
General Practice. Trials in all Courts. Personal Injury, Products Liability, Medical Malpractice, Insurance, Workers Compensation, Real Estate, Municipal, Zoning, Family Law, Estates and Probate.
See Professional Biographies, NORTH HAVEN, CONNECTICUT

Ciulla, Robert K., (AV) ....'41 '67 C.951 B.A. L.976 LL.B. [Ciulla&D.]
*PRACTICE AREAS: Civil Litigation; Commercial Litigation; Product Liability; Personal Injury; Municipal Law.

Ciulla & Donofrio, LLP, (AV) [BB]
127 Washington Avenue, 06473
Telephone: 203-239-9828 Fax: 203-234-0379
Robert K. Ciulla; Jeffrey M. Donofrio;—Jennifer N. Coppola; Glenn L. Formica. Of Counsel: Richard F. Connors; Paul E. Monaghan, Jr.
Civil Litigation in all State and Federal Courts, Commercial Litigation, Business Law, Municipal and Governmental Law, Construction and Surety Law, Product Liability, Personal Injury, Employment Law, Insurance Litigation, Tax and Zoning Appeals, Antitrust, Securities, Tax and Corporate Law.
See Professional Biographies, NORTH HAVEN, CONNECTICUT

Connors, Richard F., (AV) ....'42 '67 C.884 A.B. L.178 LL.B. [R.F.Connors]
Connors, Richard F., P.C., (AV) ....127 Washington Avenue
Coppola, Jennifer N. ....'70 '96 C.855 B.A. L.1194 J.D. [A Ciulla&D.]
*PRACTICE AREAS: Personal Injury; Collection Litigation; Commercial Litigation; Contracts; Zoning Law.
Corso, David J., Jr., (BV) ....'49 '77 C.1252 B.A. L.564 J.D. 1081 Hartford Tpke.
Daly, Thomas J. ....'59 '85 C.1030 B.A. L.982 J.D. 84 Washington Ave.
Dauster, Marjorie Allen, (BV) .... '54 '83 C.918 B.A. L.184 J.D. 1699 Ridge Rd.
DeSarbo, D. Richard, (AV) ....'40 '71 C.184 B.S. L.800 J.D. [DeSarbo,R.&G.]
DeSarbo, Reichert & Gradoville, P.C., (AV) .... 250 State St.
Donofrio, Jeffrey M., (AV) ....'65 '90 C.93 B.A. L.128 J.D. [Ciulla&D.]
*PRACTICE AREAS: Commercial Litigation; Construction Law; Municipal; Tax Appeals; Insurance Litigation.
Elia, Anthony J., Jr., (BV) ....'55 '79 C.1156 B.S. L.1206 J.D. 270 Quinnipiac Ave.
Engstrom, David L. '44 '69 C.184 B.S. L.818 J.D.
(adm. in MA; not adm. in CT) 9 Koczak Ct.★
Falaro, Judith L. ....'49 '93 C.1102 B.S. L.1048 J.D. 98 Millbrook Rd.
Falsey, Edward T., Jr., (AV) ....'22 '50 C.188 B.A. L.184 LL.B. Prob. J.
Flanagan, Robert J., Jr. .... '69 '94 C&L.602 B.A., J.D. [Cella,M.&W.]
*PRACTICE AREAS: Litigation; Workers' Compensation.
Formica, Glenn L. ....'69 '97 C.94 B.A. L.128 J.D. [A Ciulla&D.]
*PRACTICE AREAS: Commercial Litigation; Employment Litigation; Construction Litigation.
Fresher, Brian L., (BV) ....'55 '81 C.690 B.S. L.1048 J.D. 370 Bassett Road
Galati, Lisa D., (BV) ....'66 '91 C.867 B.A. L.1029 J.D. [Cella,M.&W.]
*PRACTICE AREAS: Divorce; Real Estate; Wills; Probate; Zoning.
Gillooly, Robert J., (AV) ....'32 '57 C.855 A.B. L.976 J.D. 16 Crestview Dr.‡
Giulietti, James J., (BV) .... '54 '81 C.184 B.A. L.1202 J.D. [Giulietti&M.]
Giulietti & Morytko, L.L.C., (BV) ....22 Broadway
Gormley, Kevin T., (AV) ....'30 '56 C.178 B.A. L.184 J.D. 28 Crestview Dr.
Gradoville, Robert T., (AV) ....'46 '75 C.177 B.A. L.228 J.D. [DeSarbo,R.&G.]
Hendel, Donald S., (BV) ....'56 '83 C.696 B.A. L.184 J.D. [D.S.Hendel]

Hendel, Donald S., LLC, (BV)
116 Washington Avenue, 4th Floor, 06473-1723
Telephone: 203-234-6321 Facsimile: 203-234-6322
Email: taxlawyer@prodigy.net URL: http://www.lawyers.com/dhendel
Donald S. Hendel.
Tax, Business and Estate Planning.
See Professional Biographies, NORTH HAVEN, CONNECTICUT

Jarvis, Alfred R. '56 '84 C.860 B.A. L.659 J.D.
Assoc. Gen. Coun. & Asst. Secy., Anthem Blue Cross and Blue Shield
*RESPONSIBILITIES: Mergers, Acquisitions, Joint Ventures, Corporations and Partnerships; Regulatory Matters; General Contract Development-Health Care, Insurance, Alternate Funding Arrangements; Intellectual Property; Insurance/Health Care Law-Corporate.
Kennedy, William J., Jr. .... '24 '51 L.588 J.D. 36 Monroe St.‡
Kopetz, Kevin J., (BV) ....'54 '82 C.165 B.A. L.184 J.D. 140 Washington Ave.
Krassner, David M., (BV) .... '57 '82 C.1312 B.A. L.1218 J.D. 96 Pond Mill Rd.
McDermott, Leonard A. .... '51 '97 C.999 B.S. L.1252 J.D. 336 State St.
Mendelsohn, Herbert I., (BV) ....'49 '82 C.264 B.A. L.1029 J.D. 110 Washington Ave.
Mercer-Falkoff, Robert D., (BV) ....'49 '81 C.870 B.S. L.602 J.D. [DeSarbo,R.&G.]
Merk, Howard S. ....'41 '66 C.152 B.A. L.976 LL.B. Pres., Petro. Distributors, Inc.
Monaghan, Paul E., Jr. ....'71 '96 C.1044 B.A. L.976 J.D. [© Ciulla&D.]
*PRACTICE AREAS: Mergers and Acquisitions; Securities; Tax Planning; Tax Controversies; Contracts.
Morytko, Jeremiah J., (BV) ....'55 '81 C.184 B.A. L.1202 J.D. [Giulietti&M.]
Nichols, Georgia L. '36 '84 C.693 B.S. L.1252 J.D.
General Counsel, O. F. Mossberg & Sons Inc.
Nutile, John F., Jr., (BV) ....'32 '60 C.745 B.A. L.94 LL.B. 75 Washington Ave.
O'Connor, Michael F., (BV) ....'64 '90 C.884 B.A. L.1029 J.D. [Cella,M.&W.]
*PRACTICE AREAS: Products Liability; Personal Injury; Criminal Law.
Patterson, R. Scott, (BV) ....'58 '86 C.1134 B.S. L.1218 J.D. Coun., J. E. Robert Cos.
Pearce, Barbara L. ....'54 '80 C.681 A.B. L.309 J.D. H. Pearce Co.
Proto, Paul E., (BV) ....'63 '88 C.676 B.S. L.1048 J.D. [Sachs,B.&P.]
Ravitz, Amy L. '57 '84 C.477 B.A. L.184 J.D.
Assoc. Gen. Coun., Anthem Blue Cross and Blue Shield
*RESPONSIBILITIES: Litigation (50%); Employment (30%); Fraud (20%).
Reichert, Teresa ....'59 '84 C.602 B.A. L.228 J.D. [DeSarbo,R.&G.]
Roll, Donald L. '44 '73 C.679 B.S. L.345 J.D.
Assoc. Gen. Coun., Anthem Blue Cross and Blue Shield
*RESPONSIBILITIES: Government Relations (80%); General Insurance Law (20%).
Russo, John M. '51 '85 C.178 B.A. L.910 J.D.
Assoc. Gen. Coun., Anthem Blue Cross and Blue Shield
*RESPONSIBILITIES: Health Care (40%, 5); Litigation-Insurance/Health Care (30%); Health Care Law-Corporate (30%).
Sachs, Arthur S., (AV) ....'27 '52 C&L.976 A.B., LL.B [© Sachs,B.&P.]
Sachs, Brown & Proto, LLC, (BV) .... 112 Washington Ave.
Schettino, Joseph E., Jr., (BV) ....'50 '79 C.1102 B.A. L.724 J.D. 250 State St.
Varrone, James A. ....'11 '36 C.976 B.A. L.309 LL.B. 1645 Hartford Tpke‡
Walsh, Kevin P., (BV) ....'61 '86 C.676 B.A. L.818 J.D. [Cella,M.&W.]
*PRACTICE AREAS: Medical Malpractice; Products Liability; Commercial Litigation; Personal Injury.
Walsh, Robert K., (BV) .... '38 '63 C.976 B.A. L.276 LL.B. 193 State St.
Weber, Robert J., III ....'66 '97 C.1102 B.S. L.1252 J.D. [Cella,M.&W.]
*PRACTICE AREAS: Personal Injury; Medical Malpractice; Products Liability.
Williams, James G., (BV) ....'61 '86 C.676 B.A. L.1252 J.D. [Cella,M.&W.]
*PRACTICE AREAS: Personal Injury; Products Liability; Medical Malpractice; Municipal Law; Public School Law.
Zabin, Jonathan D. ....'59 '90 C.1036 B.A. L.1029 J.D. 59 Winchester Dr.
Zudekoff, Shimen B. .... '35 '62 C&L.976 B.A., LL.B. V.P., The City Printing Co.
Zullo, John M., (BV) ....'57 '87 C.1156 B.S. L.1048 J.D. 489 Quinnipiac Ave.

NORTH STONINGTON, 4,219, *New London Co.*

Hescock, William H., (BV) ....'52 '81 C&L.184 B.A., J.D. Corner Main St. & Rt. 2

NORWALK, 78,331, *Fairfield Co.*

Albert, Ward & Johnson, P.C.
(See Greenwich)

Allen, William D., (BV) ....'32 '59 C.401 B.S. L.184 J.D. 16 River St.
Anderson, Barbara C. '52 '79 C.478 B.A. L.569 J.D.
Vice President, General Counsel & Secretary, Executone Information Systems Inc.
Andres, John C., (BV) '58 '84 C.401 B.A. L.1040 J.D.
V.P., Chief Pat. Coun., Asst. Secy., Priceline.com, Inc. (Pat.)
Audet, Paul R. '39 '70 C.1036 B.A. L.93 J.D.
Sr. Patent & Trademark Coun., U.S. Surgical (Pat.)
Barbarula, Michael Jon, (BV) .... '56 '84 C.1211 B.S. L.221 J.D. 267 Newtown Ave.
Barbour, David M. ... '59 '87 C.1103 B.B.A. L.117 J.D. Daimler Chrysler Capital Services

Barr & LaCava
(See Stamford)

Bartlett, Richard J. '47 '79 C.871 B.S. L.770 J.D.
(adm. in CA; not adm. in CT; Pat.) Corporate Attorney, PE Corporation
Beltz-Jacobson, Diane P., (CV) .... '60 '85 C.855 B.A. L.1009 J.D. Asst. Corp. Coun.
Berger, John J., (CV) .... '42 '68 C&L.734 B.S., J.D. 4 Berkeley St.
Berlin, Duane L., (BV) .... '58 '84 C.1036 B.A. L.472 J.D. [Lev&B.] ⊙
*PRACTICE AREAS: Corporate Finance and Securities; Real Estate; General Corporate.
Bermas, Stephen '25 '50 C&L.188 B.S., J.D.
(adm. in NY; not adm. in CT) Exec. V.P. & Gen. Coun., Continental Can Co., Inc.
Bernstein, Kimberly Grillo, (BV) ....'59 '86 C.829 B.S. L.904 J.D. 150 Glover Ave.
Beyman, Susan E. Bleckman ....'58 '84 C.188 B.S. L.262 J.D. 1 Singing Woods Ct.‡
Block, Andrew T. '63 '92 C.881 B.A. L.178 J.D.
(adm. in CA; not adm. in CT)
Asst. Gen. Coun. Intell. Prop., Kodak Polychrome Graphics, LLC
Boehm, Christopher C. .... '65 '96 C.690 B.S. L.1252 J.D. [A Cantor C.] (See Pat. Sect.)
*PRACTICE AREAS: Intellectual Property.
Bosze, Francis M., (BV) .... '40 '65 C.1030 B.S.S. L.923 LL.B. 618 W. Ave.‡
Boucher, Edward M., Jr. ....'46 '80 C.1072 B.A. L.1029 J.D. 25 Grand St.
Bove, John J., (BV) .... '52 '80 C.1211 B.S. L.724 J.D. [Bove,J.&J.]
Bove, Josem & Josem, (BV) .... 111 East Ave.

Bowman, Andrew B.
(See Westport)

Boyd, Jeffery H., (BV) '56 '82 C.732 B.A. L.188 J.D.
Exec. V.P., Gen. Coun., Secy., Priceline.com, Inc.
Bremer, Thomas R. '53 '80 C.1044 B.S. L.107 J.D.
(adm. in NY; not adm. in CT; Pat.) 150 Glover Ave.
Brett, John P. '42 '72
C.1033 B.S. L.184 J.D. V.P. & Chf. Coun., Asea Brown Boveri Inc.

Brody, Wilkinson and Ober, P.C.
(See Southport)

Browning, William E. S. '32 '62 C.674 A.B. L.309 J.D.
(adm. in NY; not adm. in CT) Counsel, Cronus Partners, Inc.

Brucker, Andrew G., (AV) '43 '67 C.696 A.B. L.976 LL.B.
11 Belden Avenue, 2nd Floor, 06850 ⊙
Telephone: 203-840-1133 Fax: 203-846-3551
Email: AGBESQ@AOL.COM URL: http://www.lawyers.com/bruckerlaw
Corporate, Real Estate, Probate, and Non-Profit Charitable Law.
See Professional Biographies, NORWALK, CONNECTICUT

Brunner, Donald A. ....'29 '54 C.184 B.S. L.1009 LL.B. Beiersdorf, Inc.

Burkhart, Alfred W., (AV) . . . . '23 '51 C&L.188 A.B., LL.B. [Keogh,B.&V.]
*PRACTICE AREAS: Litigation; Probate Law; Elder Law; Real Estate Law.
Burt, Richard M. '44 '70 C.282 B.A. L.1017 J.D.
(adm. in NY; not adm. in CT) V.P., Gen. Coun. & Secy., Asea Brown Boveri Inc. & Combustion Engg., Inc. (⊙Windsor)
Busek, Charles T., (BV) . . . . '49 '75 C.1030 B.A. L.184 J.D. [C.T.Busek]
Busek, Charles T., P.C., (BV) . . . . 85 East Ave.
Cammaker, Sheldon I., (AVⓉ) '39 '65 C.1036 B.A. L.309 LL.B.
(adm. in NY; not adm. in CT) Exec. V.P. & Gen. Coun., Emcor Group
*RESPONSIBILITIES: Corporate Law (50%); Securities (25%); Commercial Law (25%).
Cannella, Lisa . . . . '62 '90 C.184 B.A. L.262 J.D. 12 Green Hill Rd.
Cantor, Michael, (BV) '58 '84
C&L.184 B.S., J.D. [Cantor C.] (See Pat. Sect.) (⊙Bloomfield)
*PRACTICE AREAS: Patent Law; Trademark and Copyright Law; Unfair Competition; Intellectual Property Law.
Cantor Colburn LLP, (BV)
101 Merritt 7 (See Pat. Sect.) (⊙Bloomfield, CT; Springfield, MA)
Caputo, Matthew A., (BV) . . . .'53 '78 C.33 B.A. L.1218 J.D. 6 Larkspur Lane
Carlton, Alan R. . . . . . . '52 '83 C.4 B.A. L.1292 J.D. Sr. Corp. Coun., U.S. Surgical Corp.
Carroll, George F., Jr., (AV) . . . . '25 '50 C.197 A.B. L.309 J.D. [Carroll&L.]
Carroll & Lane, (AV) . . . . 4 Berkeley St.

Casper & de Toledo LLC
(See Stamford)

Chapman, Warren N. '53 '85 C.682 B.A. L.1209 J.D.
Corporate Counsel, Mercedes-Benz Credit Corporaton
Christie, Frederick W. '45 '74 C.976 B.A. L.276 J.D.
Coun., Consumer Prod. Div., Georgia-Pacific Corp.
Christie, Ross J. . . . .'72 '97 C.294 B.S. L.201 J.D. [Ⓐ Cantor C.]
*PRACTICE AREAS: Intellectual Property.
Church, Lawrence D., (BV) . . . . '52 '77 C.385 A.B. L.184 J.D. [Pirro,C.&C.]
Ciccarello, Louis S., (BV) . . . .'38 '65 C.918 B.A. L.813 LL.B. [Lovejoy&R.]
*PRACTICE AREAS: Personal Injury; Municipal Law; Zoning Law; Litigation.
Clements, Ann Carol . . . .'62 '88 C.886 B.A. L.893 J.D. 148 Newtown Ave.
Cohen, Randy L., (BV) . . . .'57 '82 C.184 B.A. L.818 J.D. [Corsello&C.]
Colangelo, Carolyn Gentile . . . . '69 '94 C.1102 B.A. L.1252 J.D. [Ⓐ DePanfilis&V.]
*PRACTICE AREAS: Civil Litigation; Workers Compensation; Criminal Law; Personal Injury.
Colangelo, Louis J., Jr., (BV) . . . .'45 '70 C.201 B.A. L.184 J.D. [Mintz&C.]
Colburn, Philmore H., II, (BV) '59 '91
C.588 B.S.E.E. L.1048 J.D. [Cantor C.] (See Pat. Sect.) ⊙
*PRACTICE AREAS: Patent Law; Trademark and Copyright Law; Unfair Competition; Intellectual Property Law.
Coll, Lynne A. . . . .'55 '81 C.205 B.A. L.569 J.D. 46 Prospect St.
Collier, Edmund Q., (BV) . . . .'58 '83 C.705 B.A. L.1029 J.D. 21 Isaac St. (⊙Milford)
Conover, Stephen J., (BV) . . . .'56 '82 C.602 B.A. L.724 J.D. [Genuario&C.]
*PRACTICE AREAS: Civil Litigation.
Cook, Cheryl Brienza, (BV) . . . . '63 '88 C.602 B.A. L.1029 J.D. [Pirro,C.&C.]
Cooper, Mark L. . . . . '65 '01 C.1347 B.S. L.326 J.D. [Ⓐ Cantor C.]
Corsello, Michael R., (BV) . . . .'57 '82 C.184 B.A. L.818 J.D. [Corsello&C.]
Corsello & Cohen, LLC, (BV) . . . . 10 Byington Place
Coughlan, Barbara, (BV) . . . .'59 '84 C&L.93 B.A., J.D. [Tierney,Z.F.&M.]
*PRACTICE AREAS: Civil Litigation; Zoning, Planning and Land Use; Employment Law.

Cousins, Johnson & Desrosiers, P.C.
(See Stratford)

Cozart, Richard M. '51 '76 C.381 B.A. L.1003 J.D.
(adm. in OH; not adm. in CT) Gen. Coun., Chrysler Capital Co., L.L.C.
Cruz, Lawrence '65 '93 C.801 B.S.M.E. L.273 J.D.
Patent Counsel, Tyco Healthcare Group LP (Pat.) (⊙Hamilton, Bermuda)

Cuddy & Feder & Worby LLP
One Marshall Street, Suite 201, 06854 ⊙
Telephone: 203-853-8001 Telecopier: 203-831-8250
URL: http://www.cfwlaw.com
Of Counsel: Andrew A. Glickson.
General Practice. Corporate, Real Estate, Zoning, Environmental, Historic Preservation, Housing and Urban Development, Condominium, Municipal, Trusts, Estates, Probate, Estate Planning and Taxation, Elder, Commercial Litigation, Industrial Development Bond Financing and Secured Lending Law.
White Plains, New York Office: 90 Maple Avenue. Telephone: 914-761-1300. Telecopier: 914-761-5372.
New York, N.Y. Office: 500 Fifth Avenue, Suite 2900. Telephone: 212-944-2841. Telecopier: 212-944-2843.
Hudson Valley Office: Westage Business Center, 300 South Lake Drive, Fishkill, NY, 12524. Telephone: 845-896-2229. Telecopier: 845-896-3672.
Stamford, Connecticut Office: 733 Summer Street. Telephone: 203-348-4780.
See Professional Biographies, NORWALK, CONNECTICUT

Cullen, Thomas J., (CV) . . . .'45 '82 C.870 B.S. L.262 J.D. [Cullen&J.]
Cullen & Jacobson, (CV) . . . . .7 Sawmill Rd.

Curtis, Brinckerhoff & Barrett, P.C.
(See Stamford)

Davidson, Marilyn F. . . . . '63 '91 C.1111 B.A. L.1029 J.D. [Ⓐ DePanfilis&V.]
*PRACTICE AREAS: Personal Injury; Real Estate.
Davidson, Robert M., (BV) . . . .'35 '61 C.321 A.B. L.262 J.D. [Davidson&N.]
Davidson & Naylor, (BV) . . . . .70 New Canaan Ave.
Dennin, Lawrence P., Jr., (BV) . . . .'39 '64 C.321 A.B. L.184 LL.B. [Lovejoy&R.]
*PRACTICE AREAS: Commercial Law; Corporate Law; Real Estate.
DePanfilis, Anthony J., (AV) . . . .'49 '74 C.1030 B.A. L.276 J.D. [DePanfilis&V.]
*PRACTICE AREAS: Criminal Law; Real Estate; Personal Injury Law; Litigation; Probate.

DePanfilis & Vallerie, LLC, (AV)
25 Belden Avenue, P.O. Box 699, 06852-0699
Telephone: 203-846-9585 FAX: 203-847-2849
Anthony J. DePanfilis; John E. Vallerie, Jr. (1930-1997); David W. Stergas; Deborah J. Lindstrom; Marc J. Grenier;—Carolyn Gentile Colangelo; John P. Thygerson; Marilyn F. Davidson; Neal P. Rogan.
General Civil and Criminal Litigation Practice in all Courts. Negligence, Medical Malpractice, Taxation, Corporation, Estate Planning, Probate, Real Estate, Workers Compensation, Family and Landlord and Tenant Law.
Reference: Northwestern Mutual Life Insurance Co.
See Professional Biographies, NORWALK, CONNECTICUT

Devitt, Sonja M. . . . . '37 '89 C.94 B.S.Ed L.1029 J.D. Dir., City Human Rel. & Fair Rent .
DeWitt, Patricia A. . . . . '48 '88 C&L.262 B.A., J.D. 77 Clinton Ave. (⊙White Plains, NY)
DiScala, Francis J., Jr., (BV) . . . . '61 '89 C.184 B.A. L.1202 J.D. 49 Wall St.
DiScala, Francis J., Law Offices of . . . .'28 '54 C.1030 B.S. L.262 LL.B. 49 Wall St.

Diserio Martin O'Connor & Castiglioni LLP
(See Stamford)

Dittmar, Dawn M., (CV) '55 '85 C.563 B.A. L.1029 J.D.
Spec. Accts. Rep., Mercedes Benz Credit Corp.
Donovan, Sharon E., (BV) . . . .'52 '80 C.201 B.S. L.564 J.D. [Hapke&D.]
Dottori, Jodi P. '64 '90 C.207 B.A. L.128 J.D.
V.P., Asst. Gen. Coun., Priceline.com, Inc.

Dougherty, Dougherty & Vecchiolla
(See Greenwich)

Drakos, Peter G., (AVⓉ) '56 '84 C.882 B.A. L.285 J.D.
[Healy&B.] (⊙New York, NY)
*PRACTICE AREAS: Maritime Law; Maritime Arbitration; Commercial Law; Corporate Law.
Dulberg, Jay M., (BV) . . . . '42 '71 C.103 B.A. L.208 J.D. [Hohn&D.]
*PRACTICE AREAS: General Practice.
Ephraim, Edward H. . . . . '37 '74 C.197 A.B. L.976 LL.B. 32 Woodlawn Ave.
Eren, Günter '66 '91 C&L.999 B.A., M.L.
Asst. Gen. Coun.-Europe, Kodak Polychrome Graphics LLC
Erensen, George B. . . . .'44 '69 C&L.724 B.B.A., J.D. Olin Corp.
Farrell, James J. . . . .'45 '74 C.184 B.A. L.724 J.D. 8 Elm St.
Fay and Garfunkel, (BV) . . . . Five Union Avenue
Feinstein, Norton P. . . . .'29 '54 C&L.569 B.S., LL.B. [Feinstein&H.]
Feinstein, Stephen M., (BV) . . . .'59 '84 C.184 B.A. L.1029 J.D. [Feinstein&H.]
Feinstein & Hermann, (BV) . . . . .5 Myrtle St.

Ferraro, Carl A., Jr. '64 '90 C.1292 B.A. L.1029 J.D.
21 Isaacs Street, 06850
Telephone: 203-866-6503 Fax: 203-866-6002 URL: http://www.connecticutattorney.cc
Email: ferrarocar@aol.com URL: http://www.lawyers.com/caferraro
***PRACTICE AREAS: Personal Injury; Divorce; Family Law; Real Estate; Probate.**
Family Law, Residential Real Estate, Commercial Real Estate, Personal Injury, Criminal Law, Domestic Relations.
See Professional Biographies, NORWALK, CONNECTICUT

File, Joseph C. '45 '74 C.188 B.S. L.659 J.D.
General Counsel, Pepperidge Farm, Incorporated

Finn Dixon & Herling LLP
(See Stamford)

Fiore, Charles A., (BV) . . . .'52 '77 C&L.128 A.B., J.D. [Fiore&F.]
Fiore, John R., (BV) . . . .'46 '72 C&L.128 A.B., J.D. [Fiore&F.]
Fiore & Fiore, P.C., (BV) . . . . 2 Lovatt St.
Fisher, David '11 '36 C&L.262 B.A., LL.B.
(adm. in NY; not adm. in CT) U.S. Surgical Corp.
Flaherty, Regina M., (AV) . . . .'61 '88 C.573 B.S. L.724 J.D. 9 Mott Ave.
Flaherty, Thomas A., (AV) . . . .'29 '56 C.1030 A.B. L.178 LL.B. [Tierney,Z.F.&M.]
*PRACTICE AREAS: Health Care; Corporate Law; Administrative Law.
Flaherty, Vincent D., (AV) . . . . '20 '48 C.573 B.S. Econ. L.724 LL.B. 9 Mott Ave.
Fleischer, Robert M. . . . . '62 '92 C.588 B.S. L.1040 J.D. [Ⓐ Jacobs]
*PRACTICE AREAS: Litigation; Bankruptcy.

Fogarty Cohen Selby & Nemiroff LLC
(See Greenwich)

Gallagher, Nancy D., (CV) . . . . '— '91 C.313 B.A. L.1029 J.D. [Ⓐ J.J.Ryan]
Gallogly, Vincent . . . .'38 '68 C.563 B.C.E. L.569 J.D. [Ⓒ Tierney,Z.F.&M.]
*PRACTICE AREAS: Environmental Law; Real Estate.
Garfunkel, Kenneth, (BV) . . . . '31 '55 C&L.569 A.B., J.D. [Fay&G.]
Garni, Joseph C. '46 '74 C&L.262 B.A., J.D.
Chief Counsel & Director of Risk Mngmt., Arch Chemicals
Garrigan, John P. '30 '55 C.776 L.724 LL.B.
Asst. Gen. Coun., Continental Can Co., Inc.
Geller, Lawrence A. . . . . '64 '89 C.999 B.S. L.1202 J.D. 49 Wall St.
Genuario, Robert L., (BV) . . . . '52 '77 C&L.884 B.A., J.D. [Genuario&C.]
*PRACTICE AREAS: Planning and Zoning Law; Land Use Law; Real Estate Law; Civil Litigation.

Genuario & Conover, (BV)
94 East Avenue, P.O. Box 2044, 06852
Telephone: 203-849-9292 Fax: 203-855-0370
URL: http://www.lawyers.com/genuario&conover
Robert L. Genuario; Stephen J. Conover. Associate: Amy J. LiVolsi. Of Counsel: Sherwin A. Rodin.
General Civil Practice. Trials in all State and Federal Courts. Real Estate, Probate, Employment, Construction, Personal Injury, Foreclosures, Commercial and Zoning Law.
See Professional Biographies, NORWALK, CONNECTICUT

Ghouralal, Mark J. '56 '82 C.453 B.S. L.930 J.D.
(adm. in NY; not adm. in CT) 4 Rockridge Dr.
Gillis, Richard '34 '80 C.385 B.A. L.569 J.D.
(adm. in NY; not adm. in CT) 35 Splitrock Rd.‡
Glickson, Andrew A., (BV) '49 '75
C.309 A.B. L.94 J.D. One Marshall Street (⊙Stamford)
Goldblatt, Arthur Jacob, (BV) . . . .'34 '59 C.309 A.B. L.976 LL.B. 83 East Ave.‡
Goldman, Michael L., (BV) . . . .'61 '86 C&L.659 B.S.Ec., J.D. [Goldman G.W.&M.]
Goldman Gruder Woods & Miller, LLC, (BV) . . . . 200 Connecticut Ave.
Gordon, Lelieth L. . . . . '62 '91 C.188 B.S. L.809 J.D. 52 Myrtle St., East Norwalk
Graf, Diane L. '64 '90 C.867 B.A. L.982 J.D.
(adm. in NY; not adm. in CT) [D.L.Graf]
Graf, Diane L., P.A. . . . . .6 Creeping Hemlock Dr.

Green, Robert W.
(See Stamford)

Grenier, Marc J., (BV) . . . . '66 '91 C.676 B.S. L.1202 J.D. [DePanfilis&V.]
*PRACTICE AREAS: Civil Litigation; Real Estate; Matrimonial; Zoning.
Griffin, Timothy G. '59 '85 C.602 B.A. L.724 J.D.
(adm. in NY; not adm. in CT) 150 Glover Ave.

Grimes & Battersby L.L.P.
(See Stamford)

Gruder, Kenneth M., (BV) . . . .'63 '88 C.273 B.A. L.94 J.D. [Goldman G.W.&M.]
Habetz, Stephen A., (BV) . . . .'38 '64 C.1030 B.A. L.276 LL.B. [Slavitt,C.&V.]
*PRACTICE AREAS: Estate Planning Law; Probate Law; Real Estate Law.
Hall, Robert G., Jr., (BV) . . . .'49 '74 C.276 B.S.B.A. L.184 J.D. Sr. Asst. States Atty.
Halmagean, Marcela '63 '97 C.326 B.S. L.796 J.D.
(adm. in TX; not adm. in CT) Assoc. Gen. Coun., ABB Energy Ventures, Inc.
*RESPONSIBILITIES: Finance; Corporate Law; International Law.
Handal, Anthony H. . . . . '48 '73 C.667 B.S.E.E. L.276 J.D. [Handal&M.] (Pat.)
Handal & Morofsky . . . . .80 Washington St. (Pat.)
Hapke, Kenneth A., (BV) . . . . '52 '79 C.918 B.A. L.1009 J.D. [Hapke&D.]
Hapke & Donovan, (BV) . . . . Three Morgan Avenue
Harris, Arthur B., (BV) . . . . '26 '52 C.860 B.S.,B.A. L.976 LL.B. [Harris&H.]
*PRACTICE AREAS: Estate Law (50%); Criminal Law (25%); Litigation (10%); Business Law (15%).
Harris, Charles S. . . . .'62 '90 C.1307 B.A. L.30 J.D. [Harris&H.]
*PRACTICE AREAS: Civil Litigation; Family Law; Personal Injury; Workers Compensation; Commercial Litigation.

Harris & Harris, (BV)
A Professional Limited Liability Company
11 Belden Avenue, Second Floor, 06850
Telephone: 203-838-7111 Fax: 203-845-0772 URL: http://www.lawyers.com/harris&harris
URL: http://www.harrisharris.com

(This Listing Continued)

Harris & Harris (Continued)
Arthur B. Harris; Charles S. Harris;—Suzanne D'Orsi Koetsch; Aunemetta Schmid.
General Practice, Trials in all State and Federal Courts and Agencies, Civil Litigation, Family Law, Probate, Administrative Law, Estate Planning, Special Education, Representation of Minors before Juvenile Court, Real Estate.
See Professional Biographies, NORWALK, CONNECTICUT

Hauser, Lawrence L. .... '42 '67 C.276 A.B. L.273 J.D. Supr. Ct. J.

Healy & Baillie, LLP, (AVⓉ)
The Lock Building, 20 Marshall Street, Suite 104 (South Norwalk), 06854-2282 ⊙
Telephone: 203-354-1360 Fax: 203-354-1363
Email: mmarion@healy.com URL: http://www.healy.com
Resident Partners: Matthew A. Marion; Peter G. Drakos.
Admiralty, Corporate, Insurance, Reinsurance and General Practice.
New York, New York Office: 29 Broadway, 10006-3293. Telephone: 212-943-3980. Fax: 212-425-0131. Email: reception@healy.com. Telex: 422089. Cable "Mainbrace New York".
Hong Kong Office: Healy & Baillie, Suite 1303, Dina House, Ruttonjee Centre, 11 Duddell Street, Central. Telephone: 852-2537-8628. Fax: 852-2521-9072. Email: recpt@healy.com.hk.
Millburn, New Jersey Office: Healy & Baillie, 374 Millburn Avenue, P.O. Box 599, 07041-0599. Telephone: 973-912-8955. Fax: 973-912-9767. Email: llambert@healy.com.
See Professional Biographies, NORWALK, CONNECTICUT

Hegermiller, Kimberly L. '58 '87 C.276 B.S. L.724 J.D.
(adm. in NY; not adm. in CT) 4 Oakledge Cir.
Heinzer, Charles J. '53 '78 C.390 B.A. L.884 J.D.
Senior Corporate Attorney, The Perkin-Elmer Corp.
Hermann, Leonard S. .... '26 '50 C.103 A.B. L.569 LL.B. [Feinstein&H.] ‡
Hoe, Richard L. '47 '74 C.415 B.A. L.724 J.D.
(adm. in NY; not adm. in CT) 180 W. Rocks Rd.‡

Hohn and Dulberg, (BV)
11 Isaac Street, P.O. Box 127, 06852-0127
Telephone: 203-866-4457
URL: http://www.lawyers.com/hohnanddulberg
Jay M. Dulberg.
General Practice. Probate, Negligence, Real Estate, Criminal and Family Law. Trials in all Courts.
References: Merchants Bank and Trust Co.; Fairfield County Savings Bank; Union Trust Co.
See Professional Biographies, NORWALK, CONNECTICUT

Imhoff, John W., Jr. ....'46 '77 C.1156 B.S. L.1003 J.D. 9 Mott Ave.
Ivey, Robert F. '35 '65 C.260 B.A. L.893 LL.B.
VP, General Counsel, & Secretary, Reeves Brothers, Inc.

Ivey, Barnum & O'Mara, LLC
(See Greenwich)

Jackson, Johnnie M., Jr., (AV) '45 '74
C.896 B.A. L.893 J.D. V.P., Gen. Coun., & Secy., Olin Corp.
*RESPONSIBILITIES: Chief Legal Officer; Law Department Management; Risk Management; Business Ethics and Integrity.
Jackson, Thomas K., (BV) ....'51 '76 C&L.900 B.A., J.D. Norwalk Comm. Tech. Coll.
Jacobs, Mark R., (BVⓉ) ....'53 '83 C.976 B.A. L.569 J.D. [Jacobs]
*PRACTICE AREAS: Bankruptcy; Insolvency; Commercial Law.

Jacobs Partners LLC, (BVⓉ)
383 Main Avenue, 06851
Telephone: 203-846-6622 Fax: 203-846-6621
Members of Firm: Mark R. Jacobs. Associates: Robert M. Fleischer.
Business and Personal Bankruptcy, Workouts, Debtor Creditor's Rights, Commercial Litigation, Contracts and Business Disputes.
See Professional Biographies, NORWALK, CONNECTICUT

Jacobson, Jill A. ....'45 '76 C.914 B.A. L.262 J.D. [Cullen&J.]
Jarboe, Christopher J., (BV) ....'64 '89 C&L.184 B.A., J.D. [Lovejoy&R.]
*PRACTICE AREAS: Personal Injury; Collections; Litigation; Landlord and Tenant Law; Real Estate.
Jonas, Ruth Waltuch, Law Offices of, (BV) '31 '80 C.309 B.A. L.1040 J.D.
9 Mott Ave.
Jones, Laurence C., Jr. '17 '51 C.511 A.B. L.564 LL.B.
(adm. in MS; not adm. in CT) 36 Winding Lane‡
Josem, Ernest L., (BV) ....'11 '36 C.918 B.A. L.309 LL.B. 96 East Ave.‡
Josem, Milton B., (BV) ....'19 '48 C.309 B.A. L.569 LL.B. [Bove,J.&J.]
Karol, Sheon '57 '86 C.978 B.A. L.976 J.D.
(adm. in NY; not adm. in CT) Asst. Gen. Coun., Caldor Corporation, The
Karpel, Kenneth N. ....'42 '69 C.994 B.A. L.705 J.D. 157 Silvermine Avenue
Kealey, Warren D., (BV) ....'22 '51 C.197 B.A. L.184 LL.B. 91 East Ave.
Keating, Thomas A., Jr. ....'15 '39 C&L.976 B.A., LL.B. [Ⓒ Tierney,Z.F.&M.]
*PRACTICE AREAS: Real Estate.
Kelly, Michael J. ....'43 '76 C.1046 B.S. L.776 J.D. [Cantor C.] (See Pat. Sect.)
*PRACTICE AREAS: Intellectual Property Law.
Keogh, Stephen B., (BV) ....'60 '85 C.976 B.A. L.178 J.D. [Keogh,B.&V.]
*PRACTICE AREAS: Elder Law; Probate Law; Litigation.

Keogh, Burkhart & Vetter, (AV)
34 Wall Street, P.O. Box 126, 06852
Telephone: 203-866-2535, 866-2536 Fax: 203-855-9016
Members of Firm: John Keogh (1871-1960); John Keogh, Jr. (1910-1992); Alfred W. Burkhart; Thomas J. Vetter; Stephen B. Keogh.
General Practice. Insurance, Real Estate, Probate, Corporation and Commercial Law, Elder Law. Trials in all Courts.
Local Counsel for: Metropolitan Life Insurance Co.
See Professional Biographies, NORWALK, CONNECTICUT

Keyes, Robert B. ....'63 '95 C.1211 B.S. L.1252 J.D. [Ⓐ Corsello&C.]
Khachian, Gary R. ....'61 '88 C.103 B.A. L.818 J.D. [Goldman G.W.&M.]
Khachian, Richard ....'33 '58 C.103 A.B. L.309 LL.B. Pres., Ritar Ford Sales, Inc.
Kimmel, Eugene M., (BV) ....'40 '67 C.1029 B.A. L.724 LL.B. 9 Morgan Ave.
Kimmel, Gregory S. ....'69 '97 C.690 B.A. L.1360 J.D. 9 Morgan Ave.
Knopp, Alex A., (CV) ....'47 '81 C.918 B.A. L.273 J.D. 35 5th St.
Koetsch, Suzanne D'Orsi ....'64 '98 C.1102 B.S. L.1252 J.D. [Ⓐ Harris&H.]
*PRACTICE AREAS: Juvenile Law; Special Education; Family Law; Real Estate Transactions.
Kolb, Albert J. J., Jr. '51 '80 C.222 B.A. L.569 J.D.
(adm. in NY; not adm. in CT) Asst. Gen. Coun., Phoenixcor, Inc.
Koleszar, Miklos P., (BV) ....'48 '76 C.800 B.S. L.809 J.D. 9 Mott Ave.
Kordas, Andrew F., (BV) ....'53 '79 C&L.1040 B.S., J.D. [Tierney,Z.F.&M.]
*PRACTICE AREAS: Corporate Law; Tax Law; Real Estate.

Koskoff, Koskoff & Bieder, P.C.
(See Bridgeport)

Krieger, Beverly Moskowitz, (BV) .... '46 '84 C.1019 B.A. L.1040 J.D. [Lepofsky,L.&L.]
Kuller, Alan S. '27 '49 C&L.178 A.B., LL.B.
(adm. in NY; not adm. in CT) The Caldor Corp.
Lacerenza, Joseph P. '55 '80
C.276 B.S. L.309 J.D. Deputy General Counsel, Arch Chemicals
Lane, John D. ....'21 '48 C&L.276 B.S., J.D. 4 Berkeley St. (⊙Wash., DC)
Lane, William D., (BV) ....'28 '57 C.712 A.B. L.262 LL.B. [Carroll&L.]

Lang, Jules, (AV) ....'38 '63 C.184 B.A. L.477 J.D. [Lepofsky,L.&L.]
Lattarulo, Donna M., (BV) ....'62 '86 C.93 A.B. L.1040 J.D. [Ⓐ Lev&B.] ⊙
*PRACTICE AREAS: Civil Litigation; Landlord/Tenant Law; Personal Injury Litigation; Bankruptcy; Real Estate.
Lepofsky, Lepofsky and Lang, (AV) ....7-9 Isaac St.
Lesser, Laurence M. '19 '42 C.193 L.793 LL.B.
(adm. in SD; not adm. in CT) 14 Esquire Rd.‡
Lessler, Robert H. ....'56 '81 C.867 B.A. L.30 J.D. Law Clk., Juv. Ct.

Lev & Berlin, P.C., (BV)
535 Connecticut Avenue, 06854 ⊙
Telephone: 203-838-8500 Telecopier: 203-854-1652 URL: http://www.lawyers.com/levberlin
Email: dberlin@levberlin.com URL: http://www.levberlin.com
Duane L. Berlin;—Donna M. Lattarulo; Stephen J. Velie. Of Counsel: Bruce L. Lev; Donald M. Kleban (Resident, New York Office).
Corporation, Securities, Commercial and Investment Banking, Tax, Real Estate, Estate Planning, Intellectual Property and Civil Litigation in all State and Federal Courts.
References: NSS Bank; Chicago Title Insurance Co.
New York Office: 420 Lexington Avenue, Suite 300, 10170. Telephone: 212-297-6166. Telecopier: 212-986-1952.
See Professional Biographies, NORWALK, CONNECTICUT

Levine, Ruth M. '51 '76 C.597 B.A. L.273 J.D.
(adm. in PA; not adm. in CT) 3 Oakwood Ave., #A8‡
Levy, Sloane '— '89 C.156 B.A. L.273 J.D.
Vice President, General Counsel & Corp. Secretary, Modem Media Poppe Tyson
Lewis, Richard S. '33 '61 C.866 B.A. L.823 LL.B.
(adm. in NY; not adm. in CT) Tax Coun., Kiewit Holdings Grp., Inc.
Lindstrom, Deborah J., (BV) ....'47 '81 C.339 B.S. L.1029 J.D. [DePanfilis&V.]
*PRACTICE AREAS: Domestic Litigation; Family Law; Employment Law.
Livingston, Thomas P. ....'57 '86 C.299 B.A. L.188 J.D. Secretary, PE Corporation
LiVolsi, Amy J. ....'69 '94 C.93 B.A. L.1338 J.D. [Ⓐ Genuario&C.]
*PRACTICE AREAS: Real Estate Law; Civil Litigation.
Ljungquist, Carol S. ....'44 '89 C.184 B.A. L.1029 J.D. 2 Reynolds St.
Lorusso, Gary, (BV) ....'48 '75 C.321 A.B. L.724 J.D. [Tierney,Z.F.&M.]
*PRACTICE AREAS: Real Estate.
Loughlin, Nancy ....'66 '91 C.602 B.A. L.306 J.D. Phoenixcor, Inc.
Lovejoy, Jonathan, (AV) ....'31 '56 C.918 B.A. L.976 LL.B. [Ⓒ Lovejoy&R.]
*PRACTICE AREAS: Estate Planning; Real Estate; Trust Law.

Lovejoy and Rimer, P.C., (AV)
65 East Avenue, P.O. Box 390, 06852-0390 ⊙
Telephone: 203-853-4400 Fax: 203-866-3386
URL: http://www.lovejoyrimer.com
Lawrence P. Dennin, Jr.; Louis S. Ciccarello; William R. Pascucci; Christopher J. Jarboe; Steven Daniel Smith;—Neil P. Phillips. Of Counsel: Jonathan Lovejoy.
General Practice. Real Estate, Probate, Estate and Tax Planning, Corporate, Municipal, Planning and Zoning, Wetlands, Family, Condominium, Collection, Litigation and Health and Hospital Law.
General Counsel for: Norwalk Hospital; Town of New Canaan.
Local Counsel for: The Wilton Bank.
See Professional Biographies, NORWALK, CONNECTICUT

Lyon, E. Barry '46 '77 C.116 B.A. L.262 J.D.
(adm. in NY; not adm. in CT) Asst. Gen. Coun., Asea Brown Boveri, Inc.
Lyons, Michael W., (BV) '55 '82
C.1030 B.A. L.93 J.D. Sr. Corp. Coun., U.S. Surgical Corp.
Mack, Alice C. ....'67 '94 C.24 B.S. L.1252 J.D. 191 East Ave.
Madara, Eugene E. '48 '74 C.708 B.A. L.184 J.D.
V.P. & Gen. Coun. & Secy., ABB Automation Inc.
Mahoney, Jeffrey P. '61 '88 C.477 B.B.A. L.575 J.D.
(adm. in NC; not adm. in CT) 401 Merritt 7
Marcus, Jeremy ....'14 '42 C&L.724 LL.B. Dep. Clk., Supr. Ct.
Marcus, Walter, (BV) ....'47 '72 C&L.184 B.A., J.D. 10 Wall St.
Marion, Matthew A. ....'57 '88 C.178 B.A. L.904 J.D. [Healy&B.]
*PRACTICE AREAS: Maritime Law; Environmental Law; Insurance Law; Commercial Law; International Practice.

Martin, Lucas & Chioffi, LLP
(See Stamford)

Martinez, Paul H. ....'43 '84 C.1027 B.S.M.E. L.1040 J.D. 20 Linden St.
McCauley, John E. '46 '82 C.433 B.B.A. L.1040 J.D.
Sr. V.P., Tax, Sotheby's Serv. Corp.

McGovern & Associates
(See Greenwich)

McMahon, Ned '69 '97 C.884 B.S. L.64 J.D.
(adm. in MD; not adm. in CT) [Ⓐ Cantor C.]
*PRACTICE AREAS: Patent Law (90%); Trademarks (10%).
Merck, Robert M. '50 '75 C.911 B.A. L.596 J.D.
(adm. in OR; not adm. in CT) V.P., Gen. Coun. & Secy., Mercedes-Benz Credit Corp.
Midler, Laurence H. '64 '90 C.893 B.A. L.569 J.D.
(adm. in NY; not adm. in CT) Asst. Gen. Coun., Micro Warehouse, Inc.
*RESPONSIBILITIES: Corporate and Regulatory Matters; Contracts; Employment Law.
Midler, Reuben S., (BV) ....'49 '73 C.1029 B.A. L.1292 J.D. [Tierney,Z.F.&M.]
*PRACTICE AREAS: Civil Litigation; Criminal Law; Domestic Relations.
Milici, John A., (BV) ....'43 '67 C.860 B.A. L.94 J.D. 96 East Ave.
Millones, Peter J., Jr. '69 '96 C.881 B.A. L.93 J.D.
(adm. in NY; not adm. in CT) V.P., Assoc. Gen. Coun., Priceline.com, Inc.
Miniccucci, Jill Hanau ....'55 '81 C.692 B.A. L.770 J.D. 7 Hilltop Rd.‡
Mintz, Richard L., (BV) ....'46 '71 C.477 B.A. L.273 J.D. [Mintz&C.]
Mintz and Colangelo, (BV) ....16 River St.
Modugno, Frank, (CV) ....'65 '90 C.273 B.B.A. L.306 J.D. 30 Westport Ave.
Moran, Patricia C. ....'48 '74 C.562 B.A. L.724 J.D. [Ⓐ G.Oberst]
*PRACTICE AREAS: Labor Law; Employment Law.
Morofsky, Paul B. '26 '52 C.563 B.S.S. L.178 J.D.
(adm. in NY; not adm. in CT) [Handal&M.]
Morton, S. Antoinette, (BV) ....'47 '83 C&L.378 B.S., J.D. [Ⓐ Slavitt,C.&V.]
*PRACTICE AREAS: Probate; Real Estate Law; Family Law; Litigation.

Moss, Roy W., (BV) '54 '81 C.659 A.B. L.184 J.D.
102 Highland Avenue, 06852
Telephone: 203-852-1907 Fax: 203-852-9174
Email: roywmoss@prodigy.net URL: http://www.lawyers.com/roymosslaw
***PRACTICE AREAS: Bankruptcy Law.**
Bankruptcy.
See Professional Biographies, NORWALK, CONNECTICUT

Mott, Barbara K. '51 '82 C.562 B.S. L.1040 J.D.
(adm. in NY; not adm. in CT) 55 Glen Ave.
Mulvey, Joseph F., (CV) ....'58 '86 C.1030 B.A. L.1029 J.D. 11 Isaac St., 2nd Fl.
Murphy, Frank W., (AV) ....'37 '62 C.390 A.B. L.659 LL.B. [Tierney,Z.F.&M.]
*PRACTICE AREAS: Civil Litigation; Employment Law; Municipal Law; Health Law.
Murphy, Kara A.T. ....'70 '96 C.390 B.A. L.306 J.D. [Tierney,Z.F.&M.]
*PRACTICE AREAS: Civil Litigation.

Musicant, Robert, (CV) .... '51 '83 C.178 A.B. L.1068 J.D. 9 Mott Ave.
Naylor, Howard B., Jr., (BV) .... '46 '78 C.569 B.A. L.1218 J.D. [Davidson&N.]
Nemeth, Lynda L. ....'42 '91 C&L.1029 B.S.N., J.D. 11 Buckthorn Rd.
Nemore, L. Richard .... '15 '39 C.563 L.262 LL.B. [Nemore&N.]
Nemore & Nemore .... 111 East Ave.
Newbould, Mary Z. '50 '78 C.679 B.A. L.589 J.D.
(adm. in IL; not adm. in CT) 7 Lancaster Dr.‡
Oberst, Gary, (CV) .... '41 '90 C.645 B.S. L.1029 J.D. [G.Oberst]
Oberst, Sharon T. ....'64 '92 C.184 B.A. L.1051 J.D. [Ⓐ G.Oberst]
*PRACTICE AREAS: Family; Real Estate; Probate; Wills.

Oberst, Gary, P.C., Law Offices of, (CV)
111 East Avenue, 06851
Telephone: 203-866-4646 Fax: 203-852-1574
Gary Oberst;—Sharon T. Oberst; Patricia C. Moran.
General Practice with Concentration in Computer Law. Family Law, Personal Injury, Real Estate, Copyright, Business, Intellectual Property, Civil Litigation, Trusts and Estates, Wills and Probate.

O'Connor, Sarah Ann '59 '86 C.178 B.S. L.262 J.D.
(adm. in NY; not adm. in CT) Vice President, Arch Chemicals
Oehley, Gregory A. '72 '99 C.1044 B.A. L.608 J.D.
(adm. in NY; not adm. in CT)
Asst. Gen. Coun.-Americas, Kodak Polychrome Graphics LLC
*RESPONSIBILITIES: Commercial Law; Antitrust; Trade Regulation; Contracts; Corporate Law.
Paige, Sheri B. .... '60 '88 C.1041 B.S. L.1040 J.D. Wall Street Legal Servs.
Palestro, Christopher J., Jr. ....'— '01 C&L.262 B.S., J.D. [Ⓐ Cantor C.]
*PRACTICE AREAS: :Patents; Copyrights; Trademarks.
Paris, Michael E ....'48 '87 C.102 B.A. L.1029 J.D. 3 Hadik Parkway
Pascucci, William R., (BV) .... '39 '65 C.1030 B.A. L.276 LL.B. [Lovejoy&R.]
*PRACTICE AREAS: Probate; Federal Income Tax; Federal Estate and Gift Taxation; Estate Planning.
Pasetsky, Alan E. ....'64 '88 C.659 B.A. L.724 J.D. Counsel, Nestle Holdings, Inc.
Pelletreau, William A., (BV) .... '51 '80 C.550 B.A. L.1029 J.D. [W.A.Pelletreau]
*PRACTICE AREAS: Criminal Law; Divorce; Personal Injury; Real Estate; General Practice.

Pelletreau, William A., L.L.C., (BV)
5 Mott Avenue, P.O. Box 270, 06850-0270
Telephone: 203-838-0529 Fax: 203-831-8285
Email: WPelleLLC@aol.com URL: http://www.lawyers.com/pelletreau
William A. Pelletreau.
Criminal, Divorce, Personal Injury, Real Estate and General Practice.
See Professional Biographies, NORWALK, CONNECTICUT

Phillips, Neil P. ....'67 '96 C.529 B.A. L.823 J.D. [Ⓐ Lovejoy&R.]
*PRACTICE AREAS: Estate Planning; Probate; Real Estate; Elder Law.

Piazza & Pickel
(See Stamford)

Pinto, Tricia L. ....'70 '97 C.1040 B.S. L.1252 J.D. [Ⓐ Slavitt,C.&V.]
*PRACTICE AREAS: General Practice.
Pirro, Charles A., III, (BV) .... '43 '68 C.976 B.A. L.188 J.D. [Pirro,C.&C.]
Pirro, Church & Cook, L.L.C., (BV) .... 120 East Ave.
Popkin, Dean E. ....'67 '93 C.319 B.A. L.1252 J.D. 9 Morgan Ave.
Pugliese, Mathew A., (CV) .... '39 '64 C.1030 B.S.S. L.262 LL.B. 15 Belden Ave.
Rath, Deborah R. ....'54 '80 C.881 B.A. L.276 J.D. 4 Berkeley St.
Reid, Donald F., (BV) ....'41 '66 C&L.724 B.A., J.D. [Reid,C.&C.]
Reid, Cafero & Corsello, (BV) .... 191 East Ave.

Roberts, Rose & Bates, P.C.
(See Stamford)

Robinson, Marnia L. '54 '79 C.103 B.A. L.976 J.D.
(adm. in GA; not adm. in CT) 595 Westport Ave.‡
Rodin, Sherwin A. ....'23 '48 C&L.178 B.A., LL.B. [Ⓒ Genuario&C.] ‡
*PRACTICE AREAS: Probate; Trust Administration; Estate Planning.
Rogan, Neal P. ....'58 '93 C.999 B.S. L.1029 J.D. [Ⓐ DePanfilis&V.]
*PRACTICE AREAS: Civil Litigation; Criminal Law; Commercial Real Estate.
Rollings, Jeffrey M. '63 '88 C.188 A.B. L.347 J.D.
(adm. in CA; not adm. in CT) 18 Juhasz Rd.
Rose, Nancy Ileen .... '54 '93 C.1102 B.S. L.1252 J.D. Atty., Debis Financial Services
Rosenfeld, Mitchell J. ....'51 '90 C&L.1029 B.E.S., J.D. 2 Reynolds St.
Ross, Carol Motyka '64 '90
C.184 B.S. L.705 J.D. Asst. Gen. Coun., Micro Warehouse, Inc.
*RESPONSIBILITIES: Intellectual Property Matters; Licensing; Regulatory Matters; Contracts; Various Corporate and Employment Matters.
Roth, Stuart N. '49 '77 C.186 B.E. L.724 J.D.
V.P. Reg. Audit, Dep. Gen. Coun., Olin Corp.
*RESPONSIBILITIES: General Corporate; Litigation; Antitrust; Environmental Law; Commercial Law.

Rubenstein, Green & Bass, LLC
(See Westport)

Ryan, John J., Law Offices of, (BV) .... '51 '76 C.602 B.A. L.93 J.D. 71 East Avenue

Sandak Friedman Hennessey & Greco, LLP
(See Stamford)

Santaniello, Alfred T., (AV) .... '13 '40 C.262 B.S. L.306 J.D. Prob. J.
Sawch, William B. '54 '80 C.674 B.S.E. L.276 J.D.
Senior Vice President, General Counsel & Secretary, Perkin-Elmer Corp., The

Schaffer, Stephen N., (BV) '37 '62 C.401 B.S. L.94 J.D.
9 Mott Avenue, Suite 208, 06850
Telephone: 203-853-7711 Fax: 203-853-0448
URL: http://www.lawyers.com/stephenschaffer
General Civil Practice, Family Law, Divorce, Child Custody, Child Support, Real Estate, Personal Injury, Auto Accidents, Corporate, Business, Commercial and Litigation in all Courts.
See Professional Biographies, NORWALK, CONNECTICUT

Schmid, Aunemetta ....'67 '01 C.1102 B.S. L.1252 J.D. [Ⓐ Harris&H.]
*PRACTICE AREAS: Family Law; Tax Law; Civil Litigation; Criminal Defense.

Schoonmaker, George & Colin, P.C.
(See Greenwich)

Schwartz, Anthony E., (BV) ....'63 '88 C.855 B.A. L.1029 J.D. 17 Washington St.
Senie, Kathryn C., (BV) .... '58 '83 C.184 B.A. L.1029 J.D. City Clk.
Shipp, Nathaniel W. ....'59 '93 C.184 B.A. L.1252 J.D. [N.W.Shipp]
Shipp, Nathaniel W., LLC, Law Office of .... 71 East Avenue, Suite D

Silver, Golub & Teitell LLP
(See Stamford)

Sinha, Jessica ....'42 '82 C.339 B.A. L.978 J.D. 11 Belden Avenue
Slavitt, Robert A., (AV) ....'28 '52 C.164 B.A. L.569 LL.B. [Slavitt,C.&V.]
*PRACTICE AREAS: Eminent Domain Law; Real Estate Law; Civil Litigation; Business Law; Construction Law.

Slavitt, Connery & Vardamis, (AV)
618 West Avenue, P.O. Box 2129, 06852-2129
Telephone: 203-838-7555 Telecopier: 203-866-9724

(This Listing Continued)

Slavitt, Connery & Vardamis (Continued)

Members of Firm: Abraham D. Slavitt (1900-1994); Paul R. Connery (l897-1953); Robert A. Slavitt; George A. Vardamis; Stephen A. Habetz; Michael P. Sweeney. Associates: S. Antoinette Morton; Tricia L. Pinto; Kenneth R. Sosnoski, Jr. Of Counsel: Harry M. Lessin (1909-1990); R. E. Van Norstrand (1937-1995).
General Practice. Commercial Law, Condemnation, Real Estate, Estate Planning, Probate, Family and Personal Injury Law. Civil and Criminal Trial Practice in all Courts. Agency and Distributorships, Alternative Dispute Resolution, Bankruptcy, Banks and Banking, Business Law, Civil Practice, Debtor and Creditor, Eminent Domain, Inverse Condemnation, Land Annexation, Commercial Real Estate, Construction Law, Contracts, Corporate Law, Equipment Finance and Leasing, Family Law, Finance, Franchises and Franchising, Fire Insurance Subrogation, Uninsured and Underinsured Motorists, Uninsured and Underinsured Motorists Arbitration, Commercial Leasing, Evictions, Landlord and Tenant Law, Lease Finance, Leasing, Office Leasing, Retail Leasing, Shopping Center Leasing, Legal Malpractice, Civil Litigation, Business Acquisitions, Business Divestitures, Mortgages, Negligence, Negligence Defense, Partnership Law, Torts, Civil Liability, Tort Liability, Trusts and Estates, Wills, Workers' Compensation, Zoning, Planning and Land Use.
See Professional Biographies, NORWALK, CONNECTICUT

Smith, Steven Daniel ....'66 '92 C&L.692 B.S.B.A., J.D. [Lovejoy&R.]
*PRACTICE AREAS: Probate; Real Estate; Estate Administration; Trust Administration; Elder Law.
Snyder, John, Jr. '48 '74 C.577 B.Mus.Ed. L.575 J.D.
(adm. in NY; not adm. in CT) 34 Homer St.
Sosnoski, Kenneth R., Jr. ....'— '95 C.645 B.S. L.1002 J.D. [Ⓐ Slavitt,C.&V.]
*PRACTICE AREAS: Commercial Litigation; Civil Litigation; Real Estate.
Soutar, Douglas L. ....'43 '76 C.813 A.B. L.966 J.D. 9-11 Park Street
Spahr, M. Jeffry, (BV) .... '56 '83 C.321 B.A. L.818 J.D. Asst. Corp. Coun.
Steckler, Judith J. .....'54 '78 C.1044 B.A. L.724 J.D. Asst. Gen. Coun., The Caldor Corp.
Stergas, David W., (BV) ....'47 '76 C.497 B.S. L.500 J.D. [DePanfilis&V.]
*PRACTICE AREAS: Commercial Law; Corporate; Estate Planning; Real Estate; Probate.
Stone, Norman L ....'30 '55 C.659 B.S. L.309 LL.B. 15 Oakwood Ave.
Strassberger, Peter J., (CV) ....'45 '73 C.197 A.B. L.94 J.D. 16 River St.
Suchy, Elizabeth A.B. ....'62 '92 C.93 A.B. L.262 J.D. [Tierney,Z.F.&M.]
*PRACTICE AREAS: Zoning.
Suib, Margaret K., (BV) .... '58 '84 C.401 B.A. L.861 J.D. 16 Donna Dr.
Sumberg, Simon, (BV) ....'45 '72 C.264 A.B. L.1009 J.D. 96 East Ave.
Sweeney, Michael P., (BV) ....'58 '83 C.1030 A.B. Econ. L.818 J.D. [Slavitt,C.&V.]
*PRACTICE AREAS: Real Estate Law; Land Use Law; Corporate Law.
Teich, Katherine M. Blakeley '54 '80 C.831 B.A. L.178 J.D.
(adm. in NY; not adm. in CT) ABB Inc.
Theiss, John C. ....'66 '92 C.478 B.A. L.209 J.D. 333 Silvermine Ave.
Thygerson, John P. ....'66 '96 C.1030 B.A. L.978 J.D. [Ⓐ DePanfilis&V.]
*PRACTICE AREAS: Criminal Defense; Criminal Appeals; Workers Compensation; Civil Litigation; Personal Injury.
Tierney, Thomas, (AV) .... '30 '56 C.1030 A.B. L.262 J.D. [Tierney,Z.F.&M.]
*PRACTICE AREAS: Probate; Real Estate; Estate Planning.

Tierney, Zullo, Flaherty & Murphy, P.C., (AV) BB
134 East Avenue, P.O. Box 2028-Belden Station, 06852
Telephone: 203-853-7000 Fax: 203-838-4829
Email: tierneyzulloflaherty@snet.net
Thomas Tierney; Frank N. Zullo; Thomas A. Flaherty; Frank W. Murphy; Reuben S. Midler; Gary Lorusso; Andrew F. Kordas; Barbara Coughlan; Elizabeth A.B. Suchy; Kara A.T. Murphy. Of Counsel: Thomas A. Keating, Jr.; Vincent Gallogly.
General Practice. Real Estate, Probate, Administrative, Condemnation, Employment, Healthcare, Municipal, Land Use, Planning, Zoning and Family Law. Civil Litigation, State and Federal Courts.
References: First Union Bank of Connecticut; Fleet Bank; Summit Bank.
See Professional Biographies, NORWALK, CONNECTICUT

Tubbs, Robert James '47 '72 C.321 A.B. L.276 J.D.
(adm. in MD; not adm. in CT)
V.P., Gen. Coun. & Secy., Kodak Polychrome Graphics LLC
*RESPONSIBILITIES: Antitrust; Environmental; Corporate.
Unger, Steven F. '46 '76 C.188 M.C.E. L.285 J.D.
Joint STARS Contracts Mgr., Westinghouse Norden Systems, Inc.
Vallerie, Margaret M. ....'33 '58 C.562 A.B. L.276 J.D. 36 Dairy Farm Rd.
Vallerie-Zingaro, Colleen ....'67 '93 C.433 B.A. L.1029 J.D. 25 Belden Ave.
Vardamis, George A., (AV) ....'23 '52 C.431 B.A. L.309 LL.B. [Slavitt,C.&V.]
*PRACTICE AREAS: Real Estate Law; Corporate Law; Business Organization Law.
Velie, Stephen J. ....'67 '98 C.605 A.B. L.1194 J.D. [Ⓐ Lev&B.] ⊙
*PRACTICE AREAS: Securities; Corporate Law.
Ventricelli, Joseph C., (CV) ....'58 '86 C.94 B.A. L.724 J.D. 191 East Ave.
Vetter, Thomas J., (BV) .... '54 '79 C.535 B.A. L.1048 J.D. [Keogh,B.&V.]
*PRACTICE AREAS: Real Estate Law; Probate Law; Litigation.
Vigilante, John A. .... '31 '62 C.1041 B.A. L.724 LL.B. P.O. Box 2010

Wake, See, Dimes & Bryniczka
(See Westport)

Warren, Steven M., (BV) '52 '80
C.165 B.A. L.564 J.D. General Counsel, Albert D. Phelps, Inc.

Warren, Elliot R.
(See Westport)

Waters, David Fite, (BV) .... '56 '81 C.645 B.A. L.184 J.D. [Lepofsky,L.&L.]
Weiner, Lawrence S. '50 '76 C.966 B.A. L.724 J.D.
(adm. in NY; not adm. in CT) Sr. Coun., Executone Information Systems, Inc.
Wells, Stuart W., III '42 '66 C.31 B.A. L.494 LL.B.
(adm. in MN; not adm. in CT) 224 W. Norwalk Rd.‡
Wieneke, Daniel L. '45 '71 C.742 B.A. L.1035 J.D.
Sr. V.P., Gen. Coun. & Secy., Phoenixcor, Inc.

Willinger, Willinger & Bucci, P.C.
(See Bridgeport)

Winkelman, Barbara Gaines ....'— '88 C.659 B.A. L.978 J.D. 10 Top Sail Rd.
Wise, Carl L. '48 '82 C.454 B.A. L.564 J.D.
V.P. & Grp. Coun., Chrysler Capital Co., L.L.C.
Woodman, Catherine L. '49 '85
C.207 B.A. L.705 J.D. General Counsel, R. T. Vanderbilt Company
Woods, Matthew B., (BV) .... '51 '78 C.184 B.A. L.94 J.D. [Goldman G.W.&M.]
Zamm, Edward J., (BV) ....'26 '55 C.184 B.S. L.178 LL.B. 9 Mott Ave.
Zullo, Frank N., (AV) .... '32 '57 C&L.262 B.S.S., J.D. [Tierney,Z.F.&M.]
*PRACTICE AREAS: Zoning, Planning and Land Use; Health Law; Real Estate.

NORWICH, * 37,391, *New London Co.*

Anderson, Carl D., (BV) .... '42 '67 C&L.184 B.A., LL.B. [Anderson&F.]
Anderson, Christopher P., (BV) ....'68 '95 C.999 B.A. L.1194 J.D. [Anderson&F.]
Anderson, Peter A., (BV) ....'42 '69 C.976 B.A. L.188 J.D. [Anderson&F.]
Anderson & Ferdon, P.C., (BV) .... 82 Chelsea Harbor Drive
Archambault, John C., (BV) .... '44 '69 C.164 A.B. L.94 J.D. 208 Otrobando Ave.
Arnold, Lester "L.J.", III, (BV) '58 '94 C.197 A.B. L.184 J.D.
[O'Brien,S.S.K.&M.] ⊙
*PRACTICE AREAS: Commercial Litigation; Foreclosure; Bankruptcy; Construction Law; Real Estate Law.
Axelrod, Sidney ....'31 '61 C.221 B.A. L.184 LL.B. Supr. Ct. J.

Baker, Kent Steven, (BV) . . . . '45 '73 C.659 B.S. L.184 J.D. 161 Water St.
Bataille-Ferry, Valerie G. . . . .'61 '88 C.183 B.A. L.1029 J.D. 22 Courthouse Sq.
Beebe, Donald R., (BV) . . . .'50 '75 C.309 B.A. L.893 J.D. [Beebe&O.]
*PRACTICE AREAS: Personal Injury; Medical Malpractice; Criminal Law; Civil Litigation; Commercial Litigation.

Beebe and O'Neil, (BV)
335 Washington Street, 06360
Telephone: 860-889-5266 Fax: 860-887-1378
URL: http://www.lawyers.com/beebeandoneil
Donald R. Beebe; Nancy M. O'Neil. Of Counsel: Janis M. Small.
General Civil and Criminal Practice before State and Federal Courts. Corporation, Personal Injury, Medical Malpractice, Family Law, Commercial, Workers Compensation, Real Estate, Zoning, Wills, Probate, Bankruptcy, Collections and Taxation Law. Trials and Appeals. Banking, Lender Liability, FDIC, Governmental Bank Acquisitions.
Reference: Chelsea-Groton Savings Bank.
See Professional Biographies, NORWICH, CONNECTICUT

Benson, Deborah H., (BV) . . . .'54 '79 C.788 A.B. L.184 J.D. 199 W. Town St.
Berberick, Frederick C., Jr., (BV) . . . .'33 '63 C.712 B.S. L.184 J.D. [Berberick,M.D.&W.]
Berberick, Murphy, Devine & Whitty, P.C., (BV) . . . . 82 Chelsea Harbor Dr.
Bessette, Dana M. . . . .'72 '99 C.690 B.A. L.1202 J.D. [A Brown J.]
*PRACTICE AREAS: Civil Litigation; Personal Injury; Insurance Defense.
Block, Mark E., (BV) . . . . '48 '73 C.354 B.A. L.1009 J.D. [O'Brien,S.S.K.&M.]
*PRACTICE AREAS: Real Estate; Commercial Law; Bankruptcy; Construction Law.
Brouillet, Nancy A. . . . .'58 '87 C&L.184 B.S., J.D. Wrkrs. Comp. Comr.
Brown, Allyn L., Jr., (AV) . . . .'15 '40 C.103 A.B. L.976 LL.B. [⊡ Brown J.]

Brown Jacobson P.C., (AV)
Uncas-Merchants National Bank Building, 22 Courthouse Square, 06360
Telephone: 860-889-3321 Fax: 860-886-0673
Email: bjtlk@snet.net URL: http://www.brownjacobson.com
Milton L. Jacobson; Wayne G. Tillinghast; Michael E. Driscoll; David S. Williams; John C. Wirzbicki; Michael D. Colonese; Karl-Erik Sternlof; Jeffrey R. Godley; John F. Duggan; Jeffrey F. Buebendorf;—Dana M. Bessette. Of Counsel: Allyn L. Brown, Jr.; Vincent A. Laudone; James J. Dutton, Jr.
General Practice in all Courts. Trials, Probate, Insurance, Real Estate, Corporate, Commercial and Administrative Law.
Representative Clients: Nationwide Insurance Co.; Aetna Casualty & Surety Co.; Chelsea-Groton Savings Bank; Norwich Community Development Corp.
See Professional Biographies, NORWICH, CONNECTICUT

Buebendorf, Jeffrey F., (CV) . . . .'61 '94 C.299 B.A. L.184 J.D. [Brown J.]
*PRACTICE AREAS: Civil Litigation; Personal Injury; Products Liability; Employment Law.
Caisse, Kenneth E., (CV) . . . .'66 '91 C.1030 B.A. L.1048 J.D. [Horvitz&C.]
Castle, Thomas R. '52 '78 C.674 A.B. L.569 J.D.
(adm. in NY; not adm. in CT) Lehigh Oil Co.
Chinigo, Paul F., (BV) . . . . '47 '75 C.1107 B.A. L.818 J.D. [Fitzgerald,G.C.&L.]
Clark, Robert W., (CV) . . . .'58 '85 C.184 B.A. L.1202 J.D. [Costa&C.]
Coit, Stephen R. . . . .'42 '67 C.197 B.A. L.976 LL.B. 83 Town St.
Colonese, Michael D., (BV) . . . .'59 '85 C&L.184 B.A., J.D. [Brown J.]
*PRACTICE AREAS: Civil Litigation; Personal Injury; Workers Compensation.
Comforti, Lori M. . . . . '63 '88 C.690 B.A. L.1202 J.D. 12 Case Street, Suite 316
Costa, Paul T., (BV) . . . .'59 '85 C.183 B.A. L.607 J.D. [Costa&C.]
Costa & Clark, (BV) . . . . 1 Thames Pl.
Cotter, John A. . . . .'43 '68 C.588 A.B. L.94 J.D. [Cotter,G.M.&L.]
Cotter, Greenfield, Manfredi & Lenes, P.C., (BV) . . . . 223 W. Town St.
Couture, Jorene Michele . . . .'56 '81 C.184 B.A. L.1048 J.D. Chf. Law Clk., Supr. Ct.
Cramer, Eli L. . . . . '09 '40 C.309 A.B. L.306 LL.B. Ret. Supr. Ct. J.
Czaczkes, Edward, (BV) . . . .'50 '76 C.30 B.A. L.64 J.D. [Czaczkes&C.]
Czaczkes, Morris, (BV) . . . .'55 '81 C.178 B.A. L.597 J.D. [Czaczkes&C.]
Czaczkes & Czaczkes, (BV) . . . . .482 W. Main St.
Devine, James J., (BV) . . . .'48 '73 C&L.184 B.A., J.D. [Berberick,M.D.&W.]
DiFrancesca, Donald J., (BV) . . . . '45 '69 C.676 A.B. L.884 J.D. [DiFrancesca&S.]
*PRACTICE AREAS: Real Estate Law; Family Law; Probate; Elder Law; Bankruptcy.

DiFrancesca & Steele, P.C., (BV)
811 Boswell Avenue, P.O. Box 548, 06360
Telephone: 860-889-3871 Fax: 860-889-7156
Email: difrancescasteele.pc@snet.net URL: http://www.lawyers.com/difrancescasteele
Donald J. DiFrancesca; Beth A. Steele.
General Civil and Criminal Practice, Real Estate, Probate, Negligence, Domestic Relations and Corporation Law, Trials and Workers Compensation, Bankruptcy.
Reference: Shawmut Bank Connecticut, N.A.
See Professional Biographies, NORWICH, CONNECTICUT

Doherty, Barbara J . . . .'49 '87 C.184 B.A. L.306 J.D. 111 Hansen Rd.
Driscoll, John C., (BV) . . . .'50 '79 C.276 A.B. L.184 J.D. Supr. Ct. J.
Driscoll, Mary E., (BV) . . . . '47 '80 C.97 B.S.Ed. L.184 J.D. 1 Courthouse Sq.
Driscoll, Michael E., (BV) . . . . '48 '73 C&L.276 B.S., J.D. [Brown J.]
*PRACTICE AREAS: Civil Litigation; Medical Malpractice Defense; Personal Injury.
Duggan, John F., (BV) . . . .'64 '90 C.855 B.A. L.990 J.D. [Brown J.]
*PRACTICE AREAS: Estate Planning; Probate; Taxation; Elder Law.
Dutton, James J., Jr., (BV) . . . . '14 '42 C.602 B.C.S. L.306 LL.B. [⊡ Brown J.]
*PRACTICE AREAS: Estate Planning; Probate; Taxation.
Eckert, Lorraine D. . . . .'51 '79 C.222 B.A. L.1048 J.D. 101 Water St.
Ferdon, Dennis A., (BV) . . . .'53 '85 C.1030 B.A. L.184 J.D. [Anderson&F.]
FitzGerald, John R., (BV) . . . .'32 '62 C.184 B.S. L.93 LL.B. [Fitzgerald,G.C.&L.]
FitzGerald, Gordon, Chinigo and Leone, P.C., (BV) . . . . .141 Broadway
Godley, Jeffrey R., (BV) . . . .'62 '87 C.184 B.A. L.1048 J.D. [Brown J.]
*PRACTICE AREAS: Commercial Transactions; Real Estate Law; Indian Law and Gaming.
Gordon, Glenn M., (BV) . . . .'46 '74 C.611 B.A. L.831 J.D. [Fitzgerald,G.C.&L.]
Gorin, Tracy Ann . . . . '62 '88 C.1048 B.A. L.1206 J.D. 82 Weber Farm Rd.
Greenfield, Stuart B., (BV) . . . .'45 '71 C.184 B.S. L.818 J.D. [Cotter,G.M.&L.]
Gruber, Alan R. '42 '67 C.197 A.B. L.188 J.D.
Prof. of Bus. Law, Three Rivers Community-Tech. Coll.
Gwiazdowski, Leo M., (BV) . . . .'18 '54 C.918 A.B. L.184 LL.B. 209 McKinley Ave.
Horvitz, Sheila S., (BV) . . . . '44 '77 C.994 B.A. L.184 J.D. [Horvitz&C.]

Horvitz & Caisse, (BV)
208 Otrobando Avenue, 06360
Telephone: 860-889-5529 Fax: 860-889-1319 Email: sshesq@99main.com
Email: kcesq@99main.com
Members of Firm: Sheila S. Horvitz; Kenneth E. Caisse.
Practice Limited to Matrimonial Law.
References: People's Bank; Dime Savings Bank.
See Professional Biographies, NORWICH, CONNECTICUT

Horwitz, Marvin M., (BV) . . . .'30 '54 C.184 B.A. L.94 J.D. [Horwitz&M.]
Horwitz & Maruzo, P.C., (BV) . . . . .141 Broadway
Jacobson, Milton L., (AV) . . . . '20 '49 C&L.477 B.S., J.D. [Brown J.]
*PRACTICE AREAS: Corporate Law; Real Estate.
Kennedy, Michael E., (CV) . . . .'52 '88 C.903 B.A. L.1202 J.D. 22 Courthouse Sq.
Kirker, James M., (BV) . . . . '45 '70 C.712 B.A. L.602 J.D. [J.M.Kirker]
Kirker, James M., P.C., (BV) . . . . .290 Salem Tpke.

Lamb, Karen K. . . . .'55 '80 C.860 B.A. L.976 J.D. 22 Courthouse Sq.
Langhammer, Lloyd L. . . . .'61 '86 C.478 B.A. L.61 J.D. [O'Brien,S.S.K.&M.] ⊙
*PRACTICE AREAS: Commercial Litigation; Bankruptcy.
Laudone, Vincent A., (AV) . . . . '18 '49 C.918 A.B. L.94 LL.B. [⊡ Brown J.]
*PRACTICE AREAS: Criminal Law; Motor Vehicle Accidents and Injuries.
Lenes, Timothy P., (CV) . . . .'55 '83 C.588 B.S. L.818 J.D. [Cotter,G.M.&L.]
Leone, Donald E., Jr., (BV) . . . .'58 '84 C.184 B.A. L.990 J.D. [Fitzgerald,G.C.&L.]
Low, Jeffrey N., (CV) . . . . '63 '88 C.1030 B.A. L.1029 J.D. [Fitzgerald,G.C.&L.]
Lucas, Stanley Maxim, (BV) . . . .'45 '73 C.454 B.S. L.910 J.D. [S.M.Lucas]
Lucas, Stanley Maxim, P.C., (BV) . . . . .116 Sachem St.
Mahler, Frederick . . . .'25 '57 C.865 A.B. L.184 LL.B. Clk., Supr. Ct.
Mandell, David E. . . . .'55 '79 C.882 B.A. L.1048 J.D. Supr. Ct. Mag.
Mandell, Marc S. . . . . '55 '79 C.30 B.A. L.930 J.D. Asst. Corp. Coun.
Manfredi, Frank A., (BV) . . . .'51 '76 C.1030 B.S. L.1048 J.D. [Cotter,G.M.&L.]
Maruzo, Lewis C., (BV) . . . . '42 '67 C&L.184 B.A., LL.B. [Horwitz&M.]
Masters, Barbara J., (CV) . . . .'33 '76 C.478 B.A. L.184 J.D. 199 W. Town St.
Mazzotta, Salvatore A. '32 '61 C.128 B.A. L.276 J.D.
Asst. Chanc., Diocese of Norwich
McCoy, Robert C. . . . .'47 '82 C.152 B.A. L.1029 J.D. P.O. Box 824
McPherson, Michael Earl . . . .'73 '00 C.184 B.S. L.1252 J.D. 22 Court House Sq.
Morell, Konstant W. . . . .'30 '67 C&L.184 B.A., J.D. Corp. Coun.
Murphy, James J., Jr., (BV) . . . .'36 '64 C&L.184 B.A., J.D. [Berberick,M.D.&W.]
Norris, Charles K., (CV) . . . .'64 '94 C&L.184 B.A., J.D. 141 Broadway

O'Brien, Shafner, Stuart, Kelly & Morris, P.C., (AV)
138 Main Street, P.O. Box 310, 06360 ⊙
Telephone: 860-889-3855 Fax: 860-886-6352
Email: osskm@snet.net URL: http://www.obrienshafner.com
Mark E. Block (Resident); Lloyd L. Langhammer (Resident); Richard J. Pascal (Resident); Lester "L.J." Arnold, III (Resident).
Trials in all Courts. Personal Injury, Products Liability, Workers Compensation, Medical Malpractice, Corporations, Estate Planning, Probate, Trust Law, Real Estate, General Practice, Family and Labor Law, Administrative and Admiralty Law.
Groton, Connecticut Office: 475 Bridge Street. Telephone: 860-445-2463. Fax: 860-445-4539.
See Professional Biographies, NORWICH, CONNECTICUT

Ochsner, Ronald F. . . . .'42 '67 C&L.966 B.S.C.E., J.D. 82 Chelsea Harbor Dr.
O'Neil, Nancy M., (BV) . . . .'51 '76 C.999 B.A. L.893 J.D. [Beebe&O.]
*PRACTICE AREAS: Personal Injury; Family Law; Commercial Litigation; Medical Malpractice; Civil Litigation.
Paniagua, Keri E. '72 '98 C.210 B.A. L.560 J.D.
(adm. in NM; not adm. in CT) 36 Avery St.
Pascal, Richard J. . . . .'59 '88 C.659 B.S. L.273 J.D. [O'Brien,S.S.K.&M.] ⊙
*PRACTICE AREAS: Commercial and General Litigation; Corporate Law; Employment Law.
Perrone, Michael J. . . . .'49 '74 C.602 B.A. L.184 Brickyard Rd.★
Perry, Richard J., (CV) . . . .'49 '82 C.184 B.S. L.1048 J.D. 185 Broadway
Phillips, Theodore N., II, (BV) . . . .'56 '81 C.860 A.B. L.184 J.D. 12 Case St.

Reardon Law Firm, The, P.C.
(See New London)

Rothstein, Richard I. . . . . '43 '68 C&L.184 B.A., LL.B. 121 Bway.
Rutchik, Martin M., (BV) . . . .'30 '59 C.184 B.A. L.976 LL.B. 126 Broadway
Sayet, Bart A. . . . .'58 '83 C.273 B.A. L.184 J.D. [Sayet&S.]
*PRACTICE AREAS: Personal Injury; Workers Compensation; Criminal; Probate; Landlord/Tenant.

Sayet & Seder, (CV)
126 Main Street, P.O. Box 128, 06360-5738
Telephone: 860-889-2369 Fax: 860-889-4386
Email: sayetandseder.com
Bart A. Sayet; Laura B. Seder.
General Civil and Criminal Practice before State and Federal Courts. Personal Injury, Workers Compensation, Domestic Relations, Commercial, Criminal, Real Estate, Corporation, Probate, and Landlord-Tenant Law.
Approved Attorneys for: Connecticut Attorneys Title Insurance Co.
References: Peoples Bank; Dime Savings Bank.

Seder, Laura B., (CV) . . . .'61 '87 C.289 B.A. L.472 J.D. [Sayet&S.]
*PRACTICE AREAS: Domestic Relations; Criminal; Real Estate; Corporate.
Skaats, Donna Richer, (CV) . . . .'57 '82 C.918 B.A. L.94 J.D. 60 Chelsea Harbor Dr.
Small, Janis M. . . . .'58 '83 C.1156 B.A. L.1040 J.D. [⊡ Beebe&O.]
Smith, Gerald M., Jr. . . . . '66 '93 C.367 B.A. L.184 J.D. 141 Broadway
Soloff, Harold A. '31 '57 C.143 B.A. L.838 J.D.
(adm. in TN; not adm. in CT) 20 Cherry Hill Rd.‡
Steele, Beth A., (CV) . . . .'69 '94 C.676 B.A. L.884 J.D. [DiFrancesca&S.]
*PRACTICE AREAS: Personal Injury; Workers Compensation; Criminal Defense; Zoning Law; Land Use.
Sternlof, Karl-Erik . . . .'58 '83 C.855 B.A. L.184 J.D. [Brown J.]
*PRACTICE AREAS: Commercial Real Estate; Commercial Transactions; Banking Law; Indian Law.

Suisman, Shapiro, Wool, Brennan, Gray & Greenberg, P.C.
(See New London)

Tamborra, Sabino P. . . . .'26 '54 C&L.184 B.A., J.D. Supr. Ct. J.
Terry, Lee Ellen . . . .'40 '86 C&L.184 B.A., J.D. Employment Security Appls. Referee
Tillinghast, Wayne G., (AV) . . . .'35 '60 C&L.184 B.S., LL.B. [Brown J.]
*PRACTICE AREAS: Civil Litigation; Medical Malpractice Defense; Personal Injury.

Tobin, Carberry, O'Malley, Riley & Selinger, P.C.
(See New London)

Vasington, Paul M. . . . . '24 '52 C&L.184 B.S., LL.B. Supr. Ct. J.
Whitty, Charles C. . . . .'44 '72 C.712 B.A. L.884 LL.B. [Berberick,M.D.&W.]
Williams, David S., (BV) . . . .'51 '78 C.112 B.A. L.169 J.D. [Brown J.]
*PRACTICE AREAS: Civil Litigation; Defense Litigation; Personal Injury.
Wirzbicki, John C., (BV) . . . .'50 '75 C.95 A.B. L.184 J.D. [Brown J.]
*PRACTICE AREAS: Civil Litigation; Social Security Disability; Indian Law.

OAKDALE, —, *New London Co.*

Kowalewski, John P. . . . .'42 '90 C.1156 B.S. L.884 J.D. 27 Turner Rd.
Traystman, Ellen S. . . . .'61 '87 C&L.184 B.A., J.D. 237 Black Ash Swamp Rd.

OLD GREENWICH, —, *Fairfield Co.*

Alley, William J. '29 '54 C&L.623 B.B.A., S.J.D.
(adm. in OK; not adm. in CT) Chmn. of the Bd. & CEO, Amer. Brands, Inc.
Angiolillo, Carol '52 '77 C.569 B.F.A. L.178 J.D.
(adm. in NY; not adm. in CT) 77 Shore Rd.
Barnaby, Michael J., (BVⓉ) '63 '94
C.401 B.A. L.1040 J.D. [Welby,B.&G.] (⊙White Plains, NY)
*PRACTICE AREAS: Construction Law; Mechanics Liens; Environmental Law; Arbitration.
Borman, Wendelin K. . . . .'61 '87 C.825 B.A. L.1040 J.D. 8 Shorehame Club Rd.
Butler, Stephen B. '48 '78 C.397 B.A. L.569 J.D.
(adm. in MD; not adm. in CT) Collins Enterp., LLC‡
Carroll, William Nathaniel, (BVⓉ) '41 '72 C.188 B.S. L.724 J.D.
200 Sound Beach Ave.
Cassidy, John F.K. . . . .'32 '59 C.433 B.B.A. L.188 LL.B. [⊡ Craig&E.] (⊙New York, NY)
Craig & Ells, (AV) . . . . .3 West End Ave., Ste. 201 (⊙New York, White Plains, NY)

DiCarlo, Gregory G. '66 '96
C.588 B.S.E.E. L.724 J.D. [Ⓐ Welby,B.&G.] (⊙White Plains, NY)
*PRACTICE AREAS: Construction and Design Law; Mechanics Liens; Surety Law.
Ells, Theodore F., (AV) ....'39 '64 C.31 B.A. L.893 LL.B. [Craig&E.] (⊙New York, NY)
Fignar, Eugene M. ....'46 '72 C.1113 B.S. L.229 J.D. 21 West End Ave.
Filler, Garret I. '68 '94 C&L.188 B.S., J.D.
(adm. in NY; not adm. in CT) General Counsel, Ellington Management Group, L.L.C.
Greenblatt, Michael E., (BVⓉ) ....'63 '91 C.1044 B.A. L.724 J.D. [Welby,B.&G.] ⊙
*PRACTICE AREAS: Construction Contracts; Mechanics Liens.
Griffin, Joseph J. '32 '70 C&L.262 B.S., J.D.
(adm. in NY; not adm. in CT) V.P. & Controller, Amer. Brands, Inc.
Harper, James, Jr. '19 '43 C&L.178 A.B., LL.B.
(adm. in NY; not adm. in CT) 178 Shore Rd.‡
Henson, Arnold, (AV) '31 '60 C.165 A.B. L.477 J.D.
(adm. in NY; not adm. in CT) Amer. Brands, Inc.
Hicks, Lawrence E. ....'34 '64 C.674 A.B. L.309 J.D. 19 Benjamin St.
Kaufman, Herman '42 '68 C.659 B.A. L.477 J.D.
(adm. in MI; not adm. in CT) 310 Hycliff Terrace
Kent, John F., Jr. ....'42 '71 C.210 A.B. L.1119 J.D. 20 Forest Ave.
McClave, Wilkes, III '47 '77 C.976 B.A. L.208 J.D.
(adm. in CO; not adm. in CT)
Senior Vice President & General Counsel, Tosco Corporation
Mendenhall, Steven C. '48 '72 C.347 B.S. L.1119 J.D.
(adm. in IN; not adm. in CT) V.P., Human Res., Amer. Brands, Inc.
Munkenbeck, Alfred H., Jr. '19 '48 C.674 A.B. L.178 LL.B.
(adm. in NY; not adm. in CT) V.P. & Treas., Perkin-Elmer Corp.
Netter, Arthur B., (AV) '27 '51 C&L.188 A.B., LL.B.
(adm. in NY; not adm. in CT) 13 Esther Pl.‡
Porricelli, Gerald J. ...'48 '75 C&L.262 B.S., J.D. Corp. Coun. & C.O.O., Food Mart, Inc.
Raby, Harold J. '14 '40 C.31 A.B. L.262 LL.B.
(adm. in NY; not adm. in CT) 21 Watch Tower Lane‡
Thalheim, Peter A., (CV) ....'60 '85 C.478 B.A. L.228 J.D. 146 Sound Beach Ave.
Valentine, Regis '33 '58 C.528 A.B. L.477 LL.B.
(adm. in OH; not adm. in CT) 12 Middle Way‡
Welby, Thomas H., (AVⓉ) '49 '86
C.433 B.E. L.1040 J.D. [Welby,B.&G.] (⊙White Plains, NY)
*PRACTICE AREAS: Construction Law; Arbitration; Mediation; Contract Disputes; Public Bidding.

Welby, Brady & Greenblatt, LLP, (AVⓉ)
200 Sound Beach Avenue, P.O. Box 622, 06870 ⊙
Telephone: 203-637-1044
URL: http://www.wbgllp.com
Thomas H. Welby; Michael E. Greenblatt; Michael J. Barnaby. Associate: Gregory G. DiCarlo.
Construction Law and Litigation, Public and Private Construction Contracts, Construction Claims, Mechanics Liens, Surety Law, Arbitration, Mediation, Architect and Engineers Liability, Environmental Law.
White Plains, New York Office: Westchester Financial Center, 50 Main Street. Telephone: 914-428-2100. Fax: 914-428-2172.
Cranford, New Jersey Office: 123 North Union Avenue, Suite 103. Telephone: 908-272-7870. Fax: 908-272-7901.
See Professional Biographies, OLD GREENWICH, CONNECTICUT

OLD LYME, 6,159, *New London Co.*

Christopher, Rita G. ....'41 '97 C.881 B.A. L.184 J.D. P.O. Box 842
Clarke, Marylin C., (BV) ....'42 '72 C.706 B.A. L.912 J.D. Halls Rd., Ste 224
Etherington, Edwin D. '24 '53 C.918 B.A. L.976 LL.B.
(adm. in DC; not adm. in CT) P.O. Box 100‡
Gahagan, Frederick B., (BV) ....'52 '80 C.385 B.A. L.184 J.D. [Waller,S.&P.] ⊙
*PRACTICE AREAS: Corporate Law; Business Organization; Land Conservation; Zoning, Planning and Land Use.
Hogan, Beth A. ....'— '87 C.94 B.A. L.1029 J.D. Halls Rd., Old Mrktpl.
Kenny, Daniel E. ....'30 '61 C.659 B.S.E. L.184 LL.B. Prob. J.
Kitchings, Suzanne Donnelly, (BV) ....'46 '75 C.813 B.A. L.276 J.D. [Kitchings&P.]

Kitchings & Potter, LLC, (BV)
7 Halls Road, P.O. Box 187, 06371
Telephone: 860-434-5333 Fax: 860-434-5447
Email: kitchpot@ctol.net
Suzanne Donnelly Kitchings; Edward B. Potter.
Trusts and Estates, Wills, Probate and Real Estate.
See Professional Biographies, OLD LYME, CONNECTICUT

Marrion, Robert W., (AV) ....'31 '58 C.321 A.B. L.309 LL.B. [Waller,S.&P.] ⊙
*PRACTICE AREAS: Corporate Law; Business Organization; Commercial Real Estate; Estate Planning; Administration Law.

McGarry, Prince, McGarry, P.C.
(See New London)

Obstler, Harold, (AV) '25 '53 C.178 B.A. L.976 LL.B.
(adm. in NY; not adm. in CT) 1 Mill Pond Lane‡
Obstler, Mimi '29 '53 C.183 B.A. L.976 LL.B.
(adm. in NY; not adm. in CT) 1 Mill Pond Lane‡
Patch, Kathryn V. Woodward '25 '61 C.914 B.A. L.276 J.D.
(adm. in DC; not adm. in CT) 25 McCurdy Rd.‡
Pierson, Roger G., Jr. ....'25 '54 C.860 A.B. L.790 LL.B. Sill Lane‡
Potter, Edward B. ....'58 '83 C.688 B.S. L.178 J.D. [Kitchings&P.]
Quinn, Michael J., (AV) ....'51 '87 C.446 B.A. L.184 J.D. 100 Halls Rd.
Rintoul, William Mallory '30 '61 C.184 B.A. L.569 LL.B.
(adm. in NY; not adm. in CT) 4 Candlewick Lane
Rodgers, Thomas J. ....'46 '79 C.855 M.A. L.564 J.D. 34 Johnny Cake Hill Rd.
Rodriguez, Edward J. ....'46 '72 C.103 A.B. L.184 J.D. 8 Davis Rd. W.
Seifert, Conrad Ost, (BV) ....'— '81 C.855 B.A. L.117 J.D. Halls Rd., Old Lyme Mrktpl.
Smith, Elting H. ....'17 '48 C.674 A.B. L.976 LL.B. 307 Ferry Rd.‡
Votto, Valerie Ann ....'61 '87 C.401 B.A. L.128 J.D. [Waller,S.&P.] ⊙
*PRACTICE AREAS: Real Estate; Land Use Law; Municipal Law.

Waller, Smith & Palmer, P.C., (AV) 🅱🅡
103 Halls Road, 06371 ⊙
Telephone: 860-434-8063 Telecopier: 860-434-9452
Email: wspol@snet.net URL: http://www.snetyp.com/wallersmithpalmer
Robert W. Marrion; Frederick B. Gahagan; Valerie Ann Votto.
General Practice. Corporation, Commercial, Estate Planning, Probate, Real Estate, Personal Injury, Municipal, Banking and Trials in all Courts.
New London Office: 52 Eugene O'Neill Drive. Telephone: 860-442-0367. Telecopier: 860-447-9915.
Email: wspmain@snet.net
See Professional Biographies, OLD LYME, CONNECTICUT

OLD SAYBROOK, 9,287, *Middlesex Co.*

Carol, David J. '55 '81 C.31 B.A. L.893 J.D.
(adm. in DC; not adm. in CT) V.P., High-Speed Rail, AMTRAK

Childress, William A., (AV) '45 '69 C.674 A.B. L.477 J.D.
147 Main Street, 06475
Telephone: 860-388-4464 Fax: 860-388-6052
***PRACTICE AREAS: Real Estate Law; Estate Planning Law; Probate Law; Zoning Law.**
References: Essex Savings Bank; Liberty Bank; Maritime Bank & Trust Co.

Cloutier, Thomas A., (BV) ....'46 '73 C.676 A.B. L.94 J.D. [Cloutier&E.]
*PRACTICE AREAS: Personal Injury; Wrongful Death; Negligence Law; Zoning.

Cloutier & Eddy, (BV)
29 Elm Street, P.O. Box 831, 06475-1101
Telephone: 860-388-3456 Fax: 860-388-6374
Email: c-e@celaw.org URL: http://www.lawyers.com/cloutier&eddy
Members of Firm: Thomas A. Cloutier; Jeffrey C. Eddy. Associate: Richard R. Hanratty, Jr.
Personal Injury and Negligence Law, Criminal and Civil Trials in all Courts. Domestic Relations, Probate, Real Estate, Commercial, Corporation, Zoning Law, Business Transactions, Estate Planning and Elder Law.
Representative Clients: Town of Old Saybrook; Essex Island Marina, Inc.
Reference: The Connecticut Bank & Trust Co., N.A.
See Professional Biographies, OLD SAYBROOK, CONNECTICUT

Croman, Charlotte ....'— '90 C.331 M.A. L.564 J.D. 251 Main St.

Cronin, Michael E., Jr., (BV) '37 '64 C.197 B.A. L.184 LL.B.
201 Main Street, P.O. Box 454, 06475
Telephone: 860-388-5728 Fax: 860-388-4981
***PRACTICE AREAS: Municipal Law; Zoning, Planning and Land Use; Personal Injury Law; Real Estate Law; Probate.**
General Civil Practice before State and Federal Courts. Municipal, Personal Injury, Domestic Relations, Real Estate, Zoning, Estate Planning and Probate, Corporation, Workmen's Compensation and Environmental Law. Trials and Appeals. General Litigation.
References: Connecticut National Bank.; Essex Savings Bank.
See Professional Biographies, OLD SAYBROOK, CONNECTICUT

Domnarski, Edward S., (BV) ....'49 '75 C.829 B.S. L.669 J.D. 29 Elm Street
Donovan, Jeremiah, (BV) ....'48 '78 C.309 B.A. L.976 J.D. 123 Elm St.
Donovan, Terry S. ....'48 '73 C.873 B.A. L.184 J.D. 123 Elm St.
Dzialo, Pickett & Allen, P.C., (AV) ....15 Elm St. (⊙Middletown)
Eddy, Jeffrey C., (BV) ....'56 '81 C&L.184 B.A., J.D. [Cloutier&E.]
*PRACTICE AREAS: Elder Law; Business Transactions; Corporate Law; Probate; Trusts and Estates.
Farrell, Edward J., Jr. ....'46 '76 C&L.1048 B.S., J.D. Phoenix Mut. Life Ins. Co.
Gaboury, Mario Thomas ....'57 '87 C.184 B.A. L.276 J.D. 105 Elm St. (⊙Ft Laud., FL)
Gillin, Patricia J., (BV) ....'56 '86 C.184 B.S. L.1029 J.D. [Gould&G.]
Gorra, Nicholas J., II, (CV) '63 '92
C.156 B.A. L.1202 J.D. [Ⓐ O'Connell,F.&A.] (⊙Hartford)
Gould, Howard M., (BV) ....'51 '76 C.103 A.B. L.94 J.D. [Gould&G.]
Gould & Gillin, P.C., (BV) ....222 Old Boston Post Road

Gould, Larson, Bennet, Wells & McDonnell, P.C.
(See Essex)

Gozzi, Paul, (CV) ....'57 '82 C.1252 B.S. L.831 J.D. 929 Boston Post Rd.
Hanratty, Richard R., Jr. ....'65 '96 C.690 B.A. L.1338 J.D. [Ⓐ Cloutier&E.]
*PRACTICE AREAS: Business Law; Civil Litigation; Real Estate; Commercial Transactions.
Howley, J. Waide, (BV) ....'34 '61 C.423 B.S. L.262 LL.B. 2 Neponset Ave.
Ingellis, Patricia, (CV) ....'64 '91 C.184 B.S. L.1048 J.D. 46 Maple Ave.
Lee, Marina, (CV) ....'56 '90 C.862 B.S. L.1040 J.D. 10 Springbrook Rd.
Long, Susan E. ....'66 '91 C.867 B.A. L.273 J.D. 141 Mill Rock Rd., E.
Lord, John J., Jr. '30 '58 C.262 B.A. L.724 LL.B.
(adm. in NY; not adm. in CT) P.O. Box 547‡
Messick, D. Jeanne, (BV) ....'53 '81 C.183 B.A. L.306 J.D. [Dzialo,P.&A.] ⊙
Modzelewski, Patricia H., (BV) ....'58 '84 C.184 B.A. L.1029 J.D. [Peck&T.] ⊙
Moore, Douglas S. '18 '43 C&L.188 B.A., LL.B.
(adm. in NY; not adm. in CT) P.O. Box 85‡
O'Connell, Richard T. ....'28 '54 C.882 B.A. L.472 LL.B. Supr. Ct. J.
O'Connell, Flaherty & Attmore, L.L.C., (AV)
163 Springbrook Rd (⊙Danbury, Hartford, Moosup, West Hartford, CT; Springfield, MA)
Paladino, Richard, (BV) ....'52 '79 C.1252 B.A. L.1048 J.D. 929 Boston Post Rd.
Peck & Tuneski, P.C., (BV) ....6 Business Park Road (⊙New London)
Rice, Michael Downey, (AV) ....'38 '70 C.674 B.S.E. L.831 J.D. 515 Main St. (Pat.)
Sablone, Francis R., Jr. ....'49 '74 C.321 B.A. L.184 J.D. 140 Ferry Rd.
Sheehan, Bernard F. '36 '63 C.435 A.B. L.276 J.D.
(adm. in IN; not adm. in CT) 40 Bridge St.‡
Spargo, Alan D. ....'33 '85 C.999 B.S. L.1029 J.D. P.O. Box 1023
Stern, Michael R. '60 '86 C.659 B.A. L.94 J.D.
Assoc. Gen. Coun., NECIP, Natl. Railroad Passenger Corp. (AMTRAK)
Stone, Christiaan Mark '72 '99 C.454 B.A. L.1048 J.D.
(adm. in MA; not adm. in CT) Bus. & Legal Reports
Tighe, Alexander W., (BV) ....'59 '86 C.183 B.A. L.734 J.D. 12 Old Boston Post Rd.
Wicker, Howard J. ....'45 '78 C.475 B.A. L.966 J.D. P.O. Box 391

ORANGE, 13,237, *New Haven Co.*

Aiardo, Anthony P. ....'49 '85 C.1102 B.S. L.1029 J.D. 35 Old Tavern Rd.
Albom & Braffman, (BV) ....378 Boston Post Rd.
Amendola, Vincent N., Jr. ....'53 '89 C.1102 B.S. L.1029 J.D. [Cantor,F.G.K.A.&S.]
Antonucci, Francis J., (AV) ....'47 '74 C.93 B.S. L.851 J.D. [Schine,J.&A.] ⊙
*PRACTICE AREAS: Taxation Law; Estate Planning Law; Corporate Law; Probate Law; Employee Benefits Law.
Arnold, Ernest M. ....'16 '46 C.128 B.S. L.184 LL.B. 28 Tyler City Rd.‡
Barton, John H. ....'40 '66 C&L.37 B.S., LL.B. 380 Boston Post Rd.
Barton, John M., III ....'64 '92 C.855 B.A. L.494 J.D. [Ⓐ Cantor,F.G.K.A.&S.]
Becque, Motier, (BV) ....'24 '59 C.367 B.S. L.184 LL.B. 162 Christian Circle
Benedict, Jonathan C. ....'46 '74 C.390 B.A. L.724 J.D. 296 Meeting House Lane
Benevides, Diane ....'71 '96 C.689 B.S. L.1252 J.D. [Ⓐ Cantor,F.G.K.A.&S.]
Bozelko, Ronald F., (BV) ....'37 '64 C.745 B.A. L.276 J.D. [R.F.Bozelko]
Bozelko, Ronald F., P.C., (BV) ....236 Boston Post Road
Braffman, Elaine Albom, (BV) ....'45 '75 C.788 B.A. L.184 J.D. [Albom&B.]
Braffman, Gerald H., (BV) ....'37 '62 C.659 B.A. L.184 LL.B. [Albom&B.]
Cahill, Elena L. ....'65 '91 C&L.1029 B.S., J.D. 749 Racebrok Rd.
Cantor, Floman, Gross, Kelly, Amendola & Sacramone, P.C., (AV) ....378 Boston Post Rd.
Celentano, Jeffrey ....'60 '86 C.1030 B.A. L.564 J.D. 167 Old Tavern Rd.‡
Davies, Richard W. '46 '71 C.461 B.A. L.94 J.D.
Vice President, General Coun. & Secy., Hubbell Incorporated
Dichele, Ernest Michael, (BV) ....'49 '78 C.1156 B.S. L.93 J.D. 315 Meetinghouse Ln.
Floman, Steven P., (BV) ....'42 '67 C.976 B.A. L.659 LL.B. [Cantor,F.G.K.A.&S.]
Flynn, Charles L., (AV) ....'21 '50 C.676 Ph.B. L.276 J.D. 311 Hotchkiss Rd.‡
Friedman, Bernard L. '30 '53 C&L.569 B.S., LL.B.
(adm. in NY; not adm. in CT) Gen. Coun. & Pres., Contractors Problem Solvers, Inc.
Ginsburg, Robert A., (BV) ....'42 '67 C.197 B.A. L.184 LL.B. [R.A.Ginsburg]
Ginsburg, Robert A., P.C., (BV) ....254 Bull Hill Lane
Greco, David, (CV) ....'55 '82 C.184 B.S. L.1029 J.D. 284A Racebrook Rd.

Gross, Richard L. .... '42 '75 C.994 B.A. L.1019 J.D. [Cantor,F.G.K.A.&S.]
Julianelle, Robert L., (AV) .... '40 '64 C.1030 B.S. L.276 J.D. [Schine,J.&A.] ⊙
*PRACTICE AREAS: Litigation; Estate Planning; Wills, Trusts and Probate Law; Business Law; Real Estate.
Kanaga, Lawrence W., (AV) '40 '65
C.951 A.B. L.309 LL.B. [▣ Schine,J.&A.] (⊙Westport)
Kaplan, Paul M., (BV) .... '59 '84 C.94 B.A. L.982 J.D. 254 Bull Hill Ln. (⊙New Haven)
Kelly, John J., (AV) .... '41 '67 C.676 B.A. L.184 LL.B. [Cantor,F.G.K.A.&S.]
Leginsky, Ned M., (BV) .... '55 '80 C.696 B.A. L.1049 J.D. 10 Williamsburg Dr.
Lenz, Kenneth E., (BV) .... '49 '77 C.28 B.A. L.1048 J.D. [Lenz]
Lenz Law Firm, L.L.C., (BV) .... 35 Old Tavern Rd., Ste. 1-2
Lupoli, Geraldine A. .... '41 '66 C.19 B.A. L.306 J.D. [G.A.Lupoli]
Lupoli, Geraldine A., P.C. .... 325 Boston Post Rd.
Marquette, Richard Charles .... '57 '89 C.569 B.S. L.893 J.D. 284 Racebrook Rd.
McManus, Brian P. .... '67 '93 C.676 B.A. L.1252 J.D. [Ⓐ Cantor,F.G.K.A.&S.]
Mezzanotte, John J. .... '13 '38 C&L.976 B.S., LL.B. 262 Old Tavern Rd.‡
Moore, Joy Topazian .... '62 '88 C.273 B.A. L.306 J.D. 644 S. Greenbrier Dr.
Mulvihill, John F. '52 '80 C.93 B.A. L.1202 J.D.
Asst. Gen. Coun., Hubbell Incorporated
Nugent, James A., (BV) .... '38 '67 C.1102 B.S. L.128 J.D. 236 Boston Post Road
Nugent, James J., (BV) .... '63 '89 C&L.128 B.A., J.D. 236 Boston Post Rd.
Quigley, Thomas A. .... '57 '85 C.855 B.A. L.1202 J.D. 340 Hotchkiss Rd.
Ruggiero, Robt. C. .... '21 '56 C.976 B.A. L.184 LL.B. 967 Green Circle
Sacramone, Frank, Jr., (BV) .... '57 '83 C.349 B.S. L.1194 J.D. [Cantor,F.G.K.A.&S.]

Schine, Julianelle & Antonucci, P.C., (AV)
35 Old Tavern Road, P.O. Box 905, 06477-0905 ⊙
Telephone: 203-795-3563 Fax: 203-799-9655
Email: sjalaw1@snet.net
Leonard A. Schine (1917-1982); Robert L. Julianelle; Francis J. Antonucci. Of Counsel: Lawrence W. Kanaga.
General Civil and Trial Practice. Corporate, Commercial and Business Law, Probate, Personal Injury, Administrative, Estate Planning, Commercial and Residential Real Estate, Higher Education Law.
Representative Client: Sacred Heart University.
Westport, Connecticut Office: Suite 100, 830 Post Road East. Telephone: 203-226-6861. Fax: 203-226-6866.
See Professional Biographies, ORANGE, CONNECTICUT

Shay, Edward N., (AV) .... '29 '58 C.976 B.A. L.184 LL.B. 259 Karen Dr.‡
Sobocinski, Nancy L., (BV) .... '53 '79 C.706 B.A. L.930 J.D. 378 Boston Post Rd.
Walters, Lawrence S., Jr. '56 '82 C.183 B.A. L.1194 J.D.
General Counsel-Business Development, KX Industries, Inc.
Weinstein, Josef A., (AV) .... '27 '54 C.976 B.A. L.184 J.D. 233 Hemlock Hill Rd.‡

OXFORD, 6,634, *New Haven Co.*

Stern, Carey E. '66 '97 C.679 B.S.M.E L.1338 J.D.
(adm. in MA; not adm. in CT) 581 Oxford Rd.

PAWCATUCK, 5,255, *New London Co.*

Avena, Robert A., (BV) .... '55 '80 C&L.184 B.A., J.D. 20 S. Anguilla Rd.
Crouch, Howard E., (BV) .... '09 '45 C.690 B.S. L.178 LL.B. 31 W. Broad St.
Fiore, Samuel J., (BV) .... '31 '56 C.676 B.A. L.276 J.D. 149 Liberty St.
Kepple, Nicholas F., (BV) .... '51 '89 C.1107 B.A. L.1029 J.D. 20 S. Anguilla Rd.

Ladwig, Theodore M., (BV) '43 '71 C.184 B.A. L.94 J.D.
HTP Building, 185 South Broad Street, 06379
Telephone: 860-599-1165 FAX: 860-599-1172
Email: email/atty.tedladwig@worldnet.att.net
General Civil Practice. Residential and Commercial Real Estate and Zoning Family, Estate Planning, Probate, Corporation, Municipal, Personal Injury, Family and Equine Law. Trials and Appeals.
See Professional Biographies, PAWCATUCK, CONNECTICUT

Reck, Stephen M., (BV) .... '64 '91 C.882 B.A. L.1029 J.D. [Trebisacci&R.]
Scorziello, Melody Leavenworth, (CV) '62 '89 C.323 B.A. L.215 J.D.
[Ⓐ Trebisacci&R.]
Smith, Roy L., (BV) .... '33 '58 C.184 B.A. L.94 LL.B. 38 S. Broad St.
Trebisacci, Raymond T., (BV) .... '57 '82 C.276 B.S.F.S. L.776 J.D. [Trebisacci&R.]
Trebisacci & Reck, L.L.C., (BV) .... 398 Liberty Street
Wildes, Nancy E., (CV) .... '58 '86 C.156 B.A. L.209 J.D. 20 S. Anguilla Rd.

PLAINFIELD, 12,774, *Windham Co.*

Brennan, James F., III, (BV) .... '59 '84 C.321 B.A. L.818 J.D. [Kaplan&B.]
Carbonneau, John L., Jr. .... '55 '80 C.184 B.A. L.128 J.D. 643 Norwich Rd.
Friar, Marguerite T., (BV) .... '57 '87 C.436 B.A. L.659 J.D. 643 Norwich Rd.
Kaplan, B. Paul, (BV) .... '53 '81 C.184 B.A. L.1029 J.D. [Kaplan&B.]
Kaplan and Brennan, (BV) .... 643 Norwich Rd.
Scola, Nicholas R., (CV) .... '59 '84 C.93 B.A. L.94 J.D. 643 Norwich Rd.

PLAINVILLE, 16,401, *Hartford Co.*

Anderson, Edmund P. '57 '85 C.474 B.S. L.1035 J.D.
(adm. in MN; not adm. in CT) 41 Woodford Ave.
Anderson, William C. '58 '84 C.903 B.A. L.823 J.D.
(adm. in FL; not adm. in CT) EHS, Mgr. & Sr. Coun., GE Industrial Systems
Baldini, Matthew ..... '70 '96 C.1040 B.A. L.776 J.D. General Electric Industrial Systems
Bernkopf, Walter C. .... '26 '57 C.208 B.S.E.E. L.273 J.D. 41 Woodford Ave. (Pat.)
Billingsley, James R., Jr. '62 '88 C.95 B.A. L.893 J.D.
Sr. Coun., Transactions, GE Industrial Systems
Colabella, Mark R. '63 '92 C&L.1019 B.B.A., J.D.
(adm. in NY; not adm. in CT) Sr. Tax Coun., Gen. Electric Ind. Systems
Famiglietti, Anthony O., (BV) .... '45 '76 C&L.184 B.A., J.D. 145 W. Main St.
Famiglietti, Jason S. .... '71 '97 C.184 B.S. L.1048 J.D. [Famiglietti,T.&V.]
Famiglietti, Thompson & Vollono, LLC, (BV) .... 49 Broad St.
Flynn, James P. .... '45 '72 C&L.262 B.A., J.D. Sr. Coun., GE Industrial Systems
Galske, William, III, (BV) .... '61 '86 C.184 B.S. L.1029 J.D. [Zagorsky,Z.&G.]
Han, Grace H., (BVⓉ) '58 '85 C.347 B.G.S. L.345 J.D.
(adm. in IN; not adm. in CT) Sr. Coun., GE Industrial Systems
Herman, Mona E., (BV) .... '53 '79 C.910 B.A. L.623 J.D. Hearing Offr.
Horton, Carl B. '64 '92 C.878 B.S. L.273 J.D.
(adm. in VA; not adm. in CT) Sr. Coun., Intell. Prop., GE Industrial Systems
Koskoff, David E., (BV) .... '39 '65 C&L.976 B.A., LL.B. 144 W. Main St.
Koskoff, Milton M. .... '07 '31 C&L.976 B.A., LL.B. 33 Williams St.‡
LaFrance, Thomas P. '62 '87 C.93 B.A. L.276 J.D.
(adm. in MA; not adm. in CT) Sr. Lit. Coun., GE Industrial Systems
Laska, Kenneth John, (BV) .... '44 '69 C.264 B.A. L.818 J.D. [Segal&L.]
Mastrianni, Michael W., (BV) .... '58 '84 C.1102 B.S. L.1029 J.D. [Mastrianni&S.]
Mastrianni & Seguljic, LLC, (BV) .... 73 E. Main St.
Matteo, Carole L., (CV) .... '46 '80 C.1046 B.A. L.1048 J.D. 159 Unionville Ave.
Michaud & Solari, LLC .... 98 West Main Street
Poulos, Theodore, (BV) .... '30 '56 C&L.184 B.A., LL.B. 73 E. Main St.
Ross, Donald A. '37 '74 C.569 B.A. L.982 J.D.
(adm. in NY; not adm. in CT) 41 Woodford Ave.
Saglio, Joan L., (BV) .... '44 '72 C.643 A.B. L.184 J.D. State Pros.
Segal, Allen J., (BV) .... '29 '55 C.569 B.S. L.184 LL.B. [Segal&L.]
Segal & Laska, LLC, (BV) .... 63 East Main Street
Seguljic, Richard M., (BV) .... '55 '79 C.688 B.S. L.982 J.D. [Mastrianni&S.]
Sloan, Robert D. '47 '73 C.477 B.A. L.309 J.D.
(adm. in DC; not adm. in CT) V.P. & Gen. Coun., GE Industrial Systems
Solari, Lisa C. .... '64 '93 C.184 B.S. L.306 J.D. [Michaud&S.]
Thompson, Barry L., (BV) .... '50 '75 C.276 B.A. L.184 J.D. [Famiglietti,T.&V.]
Vallen, Marc W., (BV) .... '61 '90 C.588 L.1252 J.D. 96 W. Main St.
Wasserbauer, Damian G. '63 '90
C.973 B.S. L.930 J.D. Intell. Prop. Coun., GE Indus. Systems (Pat.)
Zagorsky, Paul E., (BV) .... '58 '84 C.184 B.A. L.823 J.D. [Zagorsky,Z.&G.]
Zagorsky, Peter J., (BV) .... '50 '75 C.1019 B.A. L.276 J.D. [Zagorsky,Z.&G.]
Zagorsky, Zagorsky & Galske, (BV) .... 73 E. Main St.
Ziegler, Robert, (CV) .... '53 '80 C.93 B.S. L.1029 J.D. 100 E. Main St.

PLANTSVILLE, 6,800, *Hartford Co.*

Bailey, Richard M., (BV) .... '53 '82 C.184 B.A. L.1048 J.D. P.O. Box 593
DePaolo, Joseph F., Jr. .... '64 '89 C.860 B.A. L.1048 J.D. 16 Cornerstone Ct.
Galick, Thomas J., (BV) .... '22 '52 C&L.94 LL.B. 48 Parkview Dr.
Klikna, John J. .... '38 '86 C.178 B.A. L.184 J.D. P.O. Box 162
Morelli, Barbara J., (CV) .... '61 '90 C.829 B.A. L.1048 J.D. 1006 S. Main St.
Ryan, Mary B. .... '55 '81 C.1103 B.S. L.588 J.D. F&F Concrete Corp.
Theriault, Stephen M. '— '94 C.184 B.A. L.1048 J.D.
(adm. in FL; not adm. in CT) 424 Prospect St.

PLEASANT VALLEY, —, *Litchfield Co.*

Eddy, Nicholas B., (BV) .... '26 '50 C.188 B.S.C.E. L.184 LL.B. P.O. Box 166

POMFRET, 2,775, *Windham Co.*

Garvais, William B. '55 '81 C.184 B.A. L.69 J.D.
(adm. in TX; not adm. in CT) Rte 97‡

POMFRET CENTER, 350, *Windham Co.*

Cerrone, Kathleen M. .... '71 '00 C.602 B.A. L.1040 J.D. 5 Sanda Cir.
Kulig, Stephen T., (CV) .... '55 '86 C.184 B.A. L.1048 J.D. 30 Longmeadow Dr.

PORTLAND, 8,383, *Middlesex Co.*

Barry, Jane E., (CV) .... '51 '92 C.184 B.A. L.1059 J.D. 64 Riverview St.
Ertel, Peter .... '51 '91 C.829 B.A. L.184 J.D. 2 Riverview St. Ext.
Guliani, Richard J., (BV) .... '52 '77 C.93 B.A. L.734 J.D. Prob. J.
Hibino, Don Y. .... '19 '71 C.112 B.S. L.184 J.D. 19 Scenic Dr.‡
Law, George A., (BV) .... '60 '87 C.1145 B.S. L.796 J.D. 130 Marlborough St.
Marino, Joseph D., (BV) .... '55 '80 C.363 B.A. L.127 J.D. Prob. J.
Oppenheim, Mary E. .... '64 '91 C.966 B.A. L.306 J.D. 135 Apple Tree Lane
Peters, Edward J., Jr., (BV) .... '34 '67 C&L.184 B.A., LL.B. 595 Main St.
Phillips, Dean E. '32 '62 C&L.352 B.S.C.E., LL.B.
(adm. in IA; not adm. in CT) Pres., Surveco, Inc.
White, A. Thomas, Jr. .... '41 '66 C.884 B.S. L.724 LL.B. Wrkrs. Comp. J.

PROSPECT, 6,543, *New Haven Co.*

Fertig, John W., Jr. .... '45 '70 C.874 B.A. L.838 J.D. Prob. J.

PUTNAM, * 8,580, *Windham Co.*

Bachand, Longo & Higgins, (AV)
168 Main Street, P.O. Box 528, 06260-0528
Telephone: 860-928-6549 Fax: 860-928-1684
Email: ehiggins@baclh.com
Members of Firm: Jean M. Bachand (1935-1969); Nicholas A. Longo; Edwin C. Higgins, III.
General Civil Practice. Real Estate, Probate, Corporation Law and Civil Litigation.
Representative Clients: Citizens National Bank; Putnam Savings Bank; Webster Five Cents Savings Bank; Webster First Federal Credit Union; Southbridge Savings Bank; Citizens Mortgage Corp.; New London Trust Co.; Day Kimball Hospital.
Reference: Citizens National Bank.
See Professional Biographies, PUTNAM, CONNECTICUT

Boland, John D., (BV) .... '48 '77 C.184 B.A. L.276 J.D. [Boland,S.&B.]
*PRACTICE AREAS: Civil Litigation; Municipal Law; Real Estate Law; Mediation; Family Law.

Boland, St. Onge & Brouillard, (BV)
50 Route 171 (Woodstock), 06260
Mailing Address: P.O. Box 550, Putnam, Connecticut 06260
Telephone: 860-928-0481 Telecopier: 860-928-9950
Email: bsb.law@snet.net URL: http://www.lawyers.com/boblaw
Members of Firm: John D. Boland; William H. St. Onge; Mark R. Brouillard. Associates: Douglas J. Williams; Colleen Creevy Cording.
General Civil and Criminal Practice before all Courts. Corporation, Banking, Leasing, Real Estate, Divorce, Custody, Mediation, Municipal, Personal Injury, Workers Compensation and Estate Planning, Probate Law. Trials and Appeals.
References: Shawmut Bank; Putnam Savings Bank.
See Professional Biographies, PUTNAM, CONNECTICUT

Borner, Thomas A., (BV) .... '54 '79 C&L.184 B.S., J.D. 155 Providence St.
Boyd, David B., (BV) .... '39 '64 C.95 B.A. L.184 LL.B. [Wheaton,B.&H.]
Brouillard, Mark R., (BV) .... '53 '79 C.676 B.A. L.425 J.D. [Boland,S.&B.]
*PRACTICE AREAS: Family Law; Workers Compensation Law; Personal Injury; Civil and Criminal Trials.

Brown Jacobson P.C.
(See Norwich)

Cording, Colleen Creevy, (CV) .... '56 '86 C.321 B.A. L.93 J.D. [Ⓐ Boland,S.&B.]
*PRACTICE AREAS: Litigation; Administrative Law; Education Law.
Cotnoir, Ernest J., (BV) .... '61 '86 C&L.184 B.A., J.D. [Maher&C.]
*PRACTICE AREAS: Litigation; Real Estate; Probate and Estate Planning; Zoning, Planning and Land Use; Appellate Practice.
Herman, Alan S., (BV) .... '52 '82 C.184 B.S. L.1048 J.D. 16 S. Main St., Box 663
Higgins, Edwin C., III, (BV) .... '54 '79 C.598 B.A. L.1048 J.D. [Bachand,L.&H.]
*PRACTICE AREAS: Real Estate; Land Use and Zoning; Probate and Estate Planning; Commercial Law.
Horne, John S., (CV) .... '42 '74 C.363 A.B. L.146 J.D. [Wheaton,B.&H.]

Horvitz & Caisse
(See Norwich)

Kennedy, Brian J., (CV) .... '43 '80 C.184 B.S.C.E. L.326 J.D. 544 Liberty Hwy.
Longo, Nicholas A., (AV) .... '35 '59 C.156 B.A. L.477 J.D. [Bachand,L.&H.]
*PRACTICE AREAS: Real Estate (65%, 500); Probate and Estate Planning (25%, 100); Banking and Corporation Law (10%, 50).
Maher, John J., (BV) .... '34 '60 C.321 A.B. L.184 J.D. [Maher&C.]
*PRACTICE AREAS: Real Estate; Probate; Estate Planning.

Maher and Cotnoir, (BV)
163 Providence Street, P.O. Box 187, 06260
Telephone: 860-928-9694 Fax: 860-928-9459
Email: maher.and.cotnoir@snet.net

(This Listing Continued)

Maher and Cotnoir (Continued)
John J. Maher; Ernest J. Cotnoir.
General Practice, Real Estate, Probate, Estate Planning, Civil Litigation.
See Professional Biographies, PUTNAM, CONNECTICUT

Orszulak, Francis A. .... '51 '77 C.1200 B.A. L.362 J.D. Chf. Law Clk., Supr. Ct.
St. Onge, William H., (BV) .... '47 '74 C.276 A.B. L.184 J.D. [Boland,S.&B.]
*PRACTICE AREAS: Wills Law; Estates Law; Municipal Law; Real Estate Law.
Wheaton, Boyd & Horne, (BV) .... 162 Main St.
Williams, Douglas J., (CV) .... '63 '88 C.855 B.A. L.902 J.D. [Ⓐ Boland,S.&B.]
*PRACTICE AREAS: Real Estate; Criminal Law; Workers Compensation.

QUAKER HILL, —, *New London Co.*

Deedy-Sincali, Elaine .... '55 '82 C.184 B.A. L.818 J.D. 113 Old Colchester Rd.‡

QUINEBAUG, —, *Windham Co.*

Mead, Brian S., (CV) .... '47 '80 C.1172 B.S. L.1048 J.D. Rte. 197

REDDING, 7,272, *Fairfield Co.*

Ambler, Tracy B. '49 '74 C.367 B.A. L.184 J.D.
9 Church Hill Road, 06896
Telephone: 203-938-4000 Telecopier: 203-938-4008
Email: tbambler@msn.com
***PRACTICE AREAS: General Business; Advertising and Sales Promotion.**
Business Formation, Buying and Selling of Businesses, Closely Held Business Law, Marketing Law.
Representative Clients: Reach Marketing; Datacomm Management Sciences, Inc.; Vision Rx.com Inc., Intersect LLC.
See Professional Biographies, REDDING, CONNECTICUT

Bacon, James E. '31 '59 C&L.309 B.A., LL.B.
(adm. in DC; not adm. in CT) 89 Cross Hwy.‡
Kaufmann, Anthony S. .... '42 '71 C.197 B.A. L.659 J.D. [A.S.Kaufmann]
Kaufmann, Anthony S., P.C. .... 38 Meeker Hill Rd.

Kulawitz, Harvey J., LLC
(See Ridgefield)

LeMoult, John E., (AV) .... '39 '65 C.973 A.B. L.262 LL.B. 23 Beeholm Rd.
Torchio, Daniel S. '57 '88 C.188 B.S. L.564 J.D.
(adm. in NY; not adm. in CT) 173 Black Rock Tpke.

RIDGEFIELD, 20,120, *Fairfield Co.*

Adams, Richard N. .... '44 '77 C.178 A.B. L.245 J.D. 52 Nod Hill Road
Allan, Mark D., (BV) .... '56 '81 C.134 B.S. L.1029 J.D. [Hastings&A.]
Andreoli, Brian E. '51 '82 C.264 B.A. L.262 J.D.
Tax Coun., Boehringer Ingelheim Pharm. Inc.
Banks, Bruce J. '47 '73 C.1044 B.A. L.1009 J.D.
(adm. in NY; not adm. in CT)
Assoc. Gen. Coun. Pharmaceuticals, Boehringer Ingelheim Corp.
*RESPONSIBILITIES: Food and Drug Regulation; Commercial Law; Antitrust; Government Contracts.
Bartels, Ursula B. '57 '83 C.104 A.B. L.893 J.D.
(adm. in PA; not adm. in CT) VP, Gen. Coun. & Secy., Boehringer Ingelheim Corp.
*RESPONSIBILITIES: Health Care; Commercial Law.
Batzer, William B. '58 '91 C.932 B.S. L.477 J.D.
(adm. in MI; not adm. in CT; Pat.) Intel. Prop. Law Coun., Schlumberger-Doll Research
Bello, Robert S., (AV) .... '37 '61 C.1030 B.S.S. L.724 LL.B. [Bello,L.&C.] ⊙
Bello, Lapine & Cassone, L.L.P., (AV) .... 369 N. St. (⊙Stamford)
Belote, Jane W., (BV) .... '40 '79 C.586 B.A. L.1040 J.D. [Belote&B.]
Belote, Thomas H., (BV) .... '47 '73 C.156 B.A. L.184 J.D. [Belote&B.]
Belote & Belote, (BV) .... 24 Bailey Ave., Suite 3
Bottino, Anthony P. '58 '95 C.569 B.A. L.436 J.D.
(adm. in NY; not adm. in CT; Pat.) Patent Atty., Boehringer Ingelheim Corp.
*RESPONSIBILITIES: Patent; Trademark.
Bracken, Nanette B., (BV) .... '50 '76 C.881 B.A. L.64 J.D. 22 Green Lane
Camp, Herbert V., Jr. .... '35 '61 C.918 B.A. L.178 J.D. 409 Main‡
Caputo, Lawrence '49 '76 C.1040 B.B.A. L.1338 J.D.
(adm. in NY; not adm. in CT)
Gen. Coun., V.P., & Corp. Secy., World Duty Free Americas, Inc.
Carnam, Allyn Myles '44 '68 C.434 B.A. L.94 LL.B.
Sr. Div. Coun., Boeh. Omge;. Cheml., Inc., Boehringer Ingelheim Corp.
Cassone, Thomas M., (BV) .... '56 '81 C.401 B.A. L.1048 J.D. [Bello,L.&C.] ⊙
Chan, Eva Yulan '51 '79 C.339 B.A. L.1066 J.D.
(adm. in NY; not adm. in CT) 35 High Ridge Ave.

Collins, Hannafin, Garamella, Jaber & Tuozzolo, Professioinal Corporation, (AV)
24 Bailey Avenue, 06877 ⊙
Telephone: 203-438-7403 Fax: 203-438-7425
URL: http://www.chgjtlaw.com
Robert M. Opotzner; Christopher K. Leonard.
General Practice. Real Estate, Estate Planning, Probate, Zoning and Land Use, Tax, Corporation, Commercial, Banking, Family Law, Criminal Law, Negligence, and Civil Trials in all Courts.
Danbury, Connecticut Office: 148 Deer Hill Avenue, P.O. Box 440, 06810. Telephone: 203-744-2150; Fax: 203-791-1126.
See Professional Biographies, RIDGEFIELD, CONNECTICUT

Corrie, Pamela B. .... '58 '87 C.813 B.S. L.1068 J.D. 400 Old Sib Rd.
Crehan, Patrick J., (BV) .... '36 '64 C.1030 B.A. L.564 LL.B. 181 Main St.
Crowe, Bernard F. .... '21 '63 C.262 B.S. L.564 LL.B. 17 Langstroth Dr. (Pat.)‡
Cummings, James W. .... '62 '87 C.699 B.A. L.464 J.D. 177 Holmes Rd.
Datlow, Philip Israel '65 '97 C.446 B.S. L.1209 J.D.
(adm. in MD; not adm. in CT; Pat.) Pat. Atty., Boehringer Ingelheim Corp.
*RESPONSIBILITIES: Patent Law.
Davis, Alan C. '30 '60 C.197 A.B. L.309 LL.B.
(adm. in PA; not adm. in CT) Sr. Coun. Corp., Boehringer Ingelheim Corp.
*RESPONSIBILITIES: Corporate Law; Computer Law; Contract Law; Antitrust Law.
Devlin, Mary-Ellen M., (AV) '51 '77 C.706 B.A. L.262 J.D.
Sr. Pat. Atty., Boehringer Ingelheim Corp. (Pat.)
*RESPONSIBILITIES: Patent Law; Trademark Law; Copyright Law; Food and Drug Law; Antitrust Law.
Diamond, James D., (BV) .... '59 '88 C.1044 B.A. L.1009 J.D. [Reese,H.D.&S.] ⊙
*PRACTICE AREAS: Criminal Law; Personal Injury; Civil Litigation.
DiMattia, A.J. .... '46 '72 C.107 B.A. L.930 J.D. 195 Old Branchville Rd.
Donnelly, McNamara & Gustafson, P.C., (BV) .... 150 Danbury Rd.
Dwyer, Rosetta '23 '74 C.331 A.B. L.724 J.D.
(adm. in NY; not adm. in CT) 61 Sleepy Hollow Rd.‡
Flynn, Anne M. '— '82 C.1044 B.A. L.262 J.D.
(adm. in NY; not adm. in CT) 22 Manor Rd.
Foster, Julie I., (CV) .... '55 '82 C.829 B.S. L.1048 J.D. 805 N. Salem Rd.
Franks, Philip J. '36 '63 C.610 B.S. L.608 J.D.
(adm. in OH; not adm. in CT) 900 Ridgebury Rd.
Fricke, Richard J., (BV) .... '45 '70 C&L.188 B.A., J.D. 440 Main St.
Gelfman, Mary H. B. .... '35 '79 C.821 B.A. L.184 J.D. 374 N. Salem Rd.

Gill, Harry .... '45 '77 C.999 B.A. L.861 LL.M. [Gill]
*PRACTICE AREAS: Family Law; Real Estate; Business Law; Civil Litigation; Divorce.

Gill Law Practice
38-B Grove Street, 06877
Telephone: 203-438-4449 Fax: 203-431-7839 URL: http://www.gillpractice.com
Email: gill1law@aol.com URL: http://www.lawyers.com/gillaw
Harry Gill.
Family Law, Real Estate, Business Law, Litigation, Divorce, Child Support, Child Custody.
See Professional Biographies, RIDGEFIELD, CONNECTICUT

Grayson, Valerie Levy .... '55 '91 C.1350 B.A. L.1040 J.D. 309 Florida Hill Rd.
Gustafson, Rex, (BV) .... '49 '76 C.184 B.A. L.1048 J.D. [Donnelly,M.&G.]
Guzzo, Susan M. '53 '91 C.665 B.S. L.472 J.D.
(adm. in FL; not adm. in CT) Coun., Boehringer Ingelheim Corp.
*RESPONSIBILITIES: Health Care; Fraud; Contracts; Advertising Law; Food and Drug Regulation.
Hastings, Richard P., (BV) .... '56 '84 C.184 B.S. L.262 J.D. [Hastings&A.]
Hastings & Allan, (BV) .... 440 Main St.
Healey, Thomas C., (BV) .... '54 '88 C.1102 B.S. L.1029 J.D. [Reese,H.D.&S.] ⊙
*PRACTICE AREAS: Real Property.
Hirsch, Lawrence, (BV) .... '37 '63 C.1019 B.A. L.477 J.D. [Reese,H.D.&S.] ⊙
*PRACTICE AREAS: Real Property.
Hoddinott, Alfred H., Jr. .. '38 '64 C.276 A.B. L.569 LL.B. 85 Lincoln Lane (⊙Stamford)
Jewell, Robert R. .... '66 '96 C.1102 B.S. L.1202 J.D. [Ⓐ Donnelly,M.&G.]
Kennedy, Susan Patricia .... '61 '89 C.705 B.A. L.262 J.D. 102 Rising Ridge Road
Killea, John L., (BVⓉ) .... '55 '81 C.390 B.A. L.262 J.D. 32 Circle Drive
Kresic, Mladen Don .... '59 '86 C.1044 B.A. L.262 J.D. 7 Big Shop Ln.
Kulawitz, Harvey J., (BV) .... '53 '79 C.823 B.S. L.831 J.D. [H.J.Kulawitz]
*PRACTICE AREAS: Personal Injury; Automobile Accidents and Injuries; Aircraft & Boating Accidents; Slip and Fall; Dog Bites.

Kulawitz, Harvey J., LLC, (BV)
402 Main Street, 06877
Telephone: 203-438-9663 Ext. 2 FAX: 203-431-6178
URL: http://www.lawyers.com/HarveyKulawitz
Members of Firm: Harvey J. Kulawitz.
All Personal Injury Cases, including Car Accident cases, Aircraft & Boating accidents, Slip & Fall accidents, Dog Bite attacks, and Wrongful Death accidents & claims.
See Professional Biographies, RIDGEFIELD, CONNECTICUT

Lampasso, Victor M., (CV) .... '57 '85 C.1041 B.A. L.1029 J.D. 11 Harding Drive
Lapine, Lawrence M., (AV) .... '44 '69 C.103 B.A. L.184 J.D. [Bello,L.&C.] ⊙
Laviano, William M. .... '41 '82 C.929 L.1029 J.D. 632 Danbury Rd.
LaVoie, Charlene, (CV) .... '54 '85 C&L.1029 B.S., J.D. [LaVoie&H.]
LaVoie & Hyde, LLC, (CV) .... 57 Main St.
Leonard, Christopher K., (BV) ... '63 '89 C.690 B.S. L.1202 J.D. [Collins,H.G.J.&T.] ⊙
*PRACTICE AREAS: Civil Litigation; Real Estate Law; Land Use Law; Probate; Bankruptcy Law.

Mandel, Laura K. '67 '93 C.477 B.A. L.1009 J.D.
11 Evergreen Place, 06877-1129
Telephone: 203-778-9662
(Not admitted in CT).
General Practice.
See Professional Biographies, RIDGEFIELD, CONNECTICUT

Marhoffer, Susan B. .... '57 '88 C.1164 B.A. L.978 J.D. 100 Danbury Rd.
Maurer, Elisabeth Ann Seieroe .... '53 '88 C.339 B.S. L.209 J.D. 46 Nod Hill Rd.
McNamara, Paul S., (BV) .... '43 '69 C.30 B.S. L.1294 J.D. [◎ Donnelly,M.&G.]
Miller, Edward '64 '92 C.674 A.B. L.705 J.D.
(adm. in NY; not adm. in CT) Sr. Litig. & Compl. Coun., Boehringer Ingelheim Corp.
*RESPONSIBILITIES: Litigation; Compliance; Food and Drug Law.
Molyneaux, Christopher J., (CV) .... '65 '91 C.1103 B.A. L.1029 J.D. [Ⓐ N.J.Voog]
Murphy, Joseph F. .... '29 '86 C.93 B.S. L.1040 J.D. 89 Blackman Rd.
Neafsey, William A. '11 '37 C.188 L.732 LL.B.
(adm. in NY; not adm. in CT) 2 Lookout Point‡
Newman, Kenneth .... '67 '93 C.183 B.A. L.1252 J.D. 900 Ridgebury Rd.
O'Brien, Melanie P., (BV) .... '55 '85 C.787 B.A. L.818 J.D. 386 Main St.
O'Connor, Jill H., (BV) .... '60 '87 C.1211 B.S. L.1252 J.D. 470 Main St.
Opotzner, Robert M., (BV) .... '53 '78 C.976 B.A. L.228 J.D. [Collins,H.G.J.&T.] ⊙
*PRACTICE AREAS: Civil Litigation; Commercial Litigation; Labor Law; Matrimonial Law.
Pedersen, C. Richard .... '23 '51 C.508 B.A. L.309 LL.B. 2 Peaceable Hill Rd.‡
Peel, Edward B. '38 '73 C.869 B.S. L.836 J.D.
Sr. Coun., Corp., Boehringer Ingelheim Corp.
*RESPONSIBILITIES: Commercial Law.
Pocchiari, Susan K. '61 '98 C.1349 B.A. L.107 J.D.
(adm. in NY; not adm. in CT) Pat. Atty., Boehringer Ingelheim Corp.
*RESPONSIBILITIES: Patent Law.
Pomer, Frank A. '58 '88 C.1030 B.S. L.1040 J.D.
Boehringer Ingelheim Pharmaceuticals
Provenzale, Anthony Leonard '72 '99 C.262 B.A. L.1187 J.D.
19-48 Prospect Ridge Road
Raymond, Robert P., (AV) '39 '69 C.705 B.S. L.276 J.D.
Assoc. Gen. Coun., Intell. Prop., Boehringer Ingelheim Corp. (Pat.)
*RESPONSIBILITIES: Patent Law; Trademark Law; Copyright Law; Food and Drug Law; Antitrust Law.
Reese, John R., (BV) .... '40 '65 C.197 B.A. L.976 LL.B. [Reese,H.D.&S.] ⊙
*PRACTICE AREAS: Estate and Trust Planning; Real Property; Business Law.

Reese, Hirsch, Diamond & Shoults, (BV)
470 Main Street, P.O. Box 1048, 06877 ⊙
Telephone: 203-431-2302 Telecopier: 203-438-1576
Email: general@rhdslaw.com URL: http://www.lawyers.com/rhds
John R. Reese; Lawrence Hirsch; James D. Diamond; Tamsin A.S. Shoults; Thomas C. Healey.
Probate, Trust and Estate Planning, Real Property, Business Law, Criminal Law, Civil Litigation.
New Canaan, Connecticut Office: 51 Locust Avenue. P.O. Box 1147. 06840. Telephone: 203-966-1618. Telecopier: 203-972-5192.
See Professional Biographies, RIDGEFIELD, CONNECTICUT

Reynolds, Susan Sheridan, (BV) .... '50 '81 C.563 B.A. L.1040 J.D. 470 Main St.
Rosenberg, Herbert F., (BV) .... '42 '70 C&L.184 B.A., J.D. 80 Grove St.
Ryba, Walter G., Jr. '41 '76 C.197 A.B. L.184 J.D.
Prof. of Law & Dean, Fairfield Univ.
Shea, Francis X. .... '29 '64 C&L.262 A.B., J.D. 415 Main St.
Sherman, Harold .... '21 '87 C.102 A.B. L.1040 J.D. 24 Webster Rd.
Shoults, Tamsin A.S. .... '66 '94 C.67 B.A. L.184 J.D. [Reese,H.D.&S.] ⊙
*PRACTICE AREAS: Probate; Trusts and Estates; Real Property.
Smith, Mary Mann '52 '77 C.945 B.S. L.880 J.D.
(adm. in GA; not adm. in CT) Law Clk., U.S. Dist. J.
Stella, Paul J. '47 '74 C.884 B.A. L.564 J.D.
(adm. in NY; not adm. in CT) 22 Grove St.
Stempel, Alan R. '52 '78 C.264 B.A. L.1202 J.D.
Sr. Pat. Atty., Boehringer Ingelheim Corp. (Pat.)
Terrillion, Scott M. '62 '91 C.999 B.S. L.982 J.D.
(adm. in NY; not adm. in CT) Sr. Coun., Boehringer Ingelheim Corp.
*RESPONSIBILITIES: Contract Law; Fraud and Abuse; Food and Drug Law; Government Contracts.

Trebing, Al P., (AV) ....'51 '80 C.693 B.S. L.1040 J.D. [A.P.Trebing&Assoc.] ⊙
Trebing, Al P., & Associates, P.C., (AV) .... 54 Danbury Road, Suite 266 (⊙New Canaan)
Vanmoffaert, Glenn J. '60 '96 C.145 B.A. L.1040 J.D.
Boehringer Ingelheim Pharm., Inc.
Voog, Norman J., (BV) ....'41 '67 C&L.184 B.A., J.D. [N.J.Voog]
Voog, Norman J., P.C., The Law Offices of, (BV) .... 90 Grove St.
Whittemore, William C., III ....'46 '72 C.884 B.A. L.273 J.D. 7 Big Shop Lane
Witkowski, Timothy X. '67 '96 C.433 B.A. L.1009 J.D.
(adm. in NY; not adm. in CT; Pat.) Pat. Atty., Boehringer Ingelheim Corp.
*RESPONSIBILITIES: Patent Law; Intellectual Property Law; Antitrust Law.
Zakreski, Randall J. '61 '86 C.93 A.B. L.884 J.D.
(adm. in PA; not adm. in CT)
Sr. Coun., Employ. Law & Consumer Healthcare, Boehringer Ingelheim Corp.
*RESPONSIBILITIES: Employee Counseling Issues and Employment Law; Human Resources Issues; All Legal Operations regarding Consumer Healthcare, including Self Medication/OTC Product Issues; General Contracts; Regulatory Matters.

RIVERSIDE, —, *Fairfield Co.*

Barolak, Robert R. '53 '79 C.216 B.A. L.659 J.D.
(adm. in PA; not adm. in CT) 44 Wesskum Wood Rd.‡
Castronovo, Donna M., (BV) ....'61 '86 C&L.1040 B.S., J.D. [D.M.Castronovo]
Castronovo, Donna M., P.C., (BV) ....1081 East Putnam Ave.
Cosgrove, Jody L. '55 '82 C.918 B.A. L.262 J.D.
(adm. in NY; not adm. in CT) 80 Old Orchard Rd.
Donahue, Kara S. ....'63 '91 C.860 B.A. L.262 J.D. 146 Lockwood Rd.
Hall, George E. ....'25 '52 C.923 A.B. L.309 LL.B. 57 Gilliam Ln.
Hellendale, Robert '17 '47 C.918 A.B. L.309 LL.B.
(adm. in NY; not adm. in CT) 21 Shoal Pt. Ln.‡
Lewis, William B. .... '30 '58 Supr. Ct. J.
Murphy, Pamela J. '53 '79 C.1123 B.A. L.659 J.D.
(adm. in PA; not adm. in CT) 26 Jones Park Dr.‡
Perna, Rocco R. P. ....'16 '42 C&L.188 B.A., LL.B. 4 Somerset Lane
Pipitone, Marie '56 '83 C.112 B.A. L.284 J.D.
(adm. in CA; not adm. in CT) 59 Indian Head Rd.‡
Reynolds, Clinton A. '20 '47 C.197 A.B. L.309 J.D.
(adm. in MA; not adm. in CT) 4 Carriglea Dr.‡
Rogers, David Anthony ....'69 '97 C.706 B.A. L.1252 J.D. 1205 E. Putnam Ave.
Romaine, Carol Grey ....'50 '75 C.914 A.B. L.912 J.D. P.O. Box 404
Shields, David Stuart, II, (BV) ....'49 '84 C.588 B.S. L.1040 J.D. 46 Thornhill Rd.
Sparks, Jonathan W. '62 '88 C.222 B.A. L.1017 J.D.
(adm. in NY; not adm. in CT) 90 Lockwood Rd.
Wellington, Elizabeth P. ....'39 '63 C.562 A.B. L.188 J.D. 1 Winthrop Dr.
Worthington, Kathy Ann ....'53 '79 C.264 B.A. L.1019 J.D. 10 Glen Avon Dr.

ROCKFALL, —, *Middlesex Co.*

Cahill, Agnes M. ....'58 '84 C.732 B.A. L.982 J.D. 76 Cider Mill Rd.

ROCKVILLE, 13,500, *Tolland Co.*

Drapeau, Francis X. ....'60 '91 C.1030 B.A. L.1048 J.D. [Leighton&K.]
Emond, Howard Earl, Jr. ....'47 '85 C.1030 B.A. L.1048 J.D. Trial Ct. Admr.

Flaherty, Meisler & Courtney, LLC
(See Vernon)

Gedansky, Matthew C., (BV) ....'65 '90 C.184 B.S. L.208 J.D. Asst. States Atty.
George, Margaret R. ....'52 '88 C.1044 B.A. L.1048 J.D. Asst. Law Clk., Supr. Ct.
Grover, Kathleen M. ....'53 '93 C.988 B.A. L.184 J.D. [🄰 Leighton&K.]
Kaplan, Jonathan J. ....'46 '71 C.1145 B.S. L.184 J.D. Supr. Ct. J.
Katz, James L., (BV) ....'50 '81 C.454 B.A. L.184 J.D. [Leighton&K.]
Klaczak, Lawrence C. ....'32 '66 C&L.184 B.A., LL.B. Supr. Ct. J.
Leighton, Mark D., (BV) ....'55 '80 C.462 B.A. L.1048 J.D. [Leighton&K.]
Leighton & Katz, (BV) ....20 E. Main St.
McKone, Frederick W. ....'16 '69 C.829 B.S. L.184 J.D. 54 Windsor Ave.‡
O'Brien, John F., (BV) ....'53 '86 C.184 B.A. L.1048 J.D. [J.F.O'Brien]
O'Brien, John F., Law Office of, (BV) .... 15 Park Street
Sullivan, L. Paul ....'33 '60 C&L.184 B.A., LL.B. Supr. Ct. J.
Sullivan, Terence A. ....'38 '71 C&L.184 B.A., J.D. Supr. Ct. J.
Swords, Patricia A., (BV) ....'50 '78 C&L.184 B.A., J.D. States Atty.
Zarella, Peter T. ....'49 '75 C.588 B.S.Ch.E. L.818 J.D. Supr. Ct. J.

ROCKY HILL, 14,559, *Hartford Co.*

Allen, Gordon T., (BV) ....'46 '70 C.178 B.A. L.184 J.D. [Heneghan,P.K.&A.]
Antoinetti, John Jude, (BV) ....'56 '84 C.860 B.A. L.1029 J.D. 1 Danforth Ln.
Baio, Claudia A., (BV) ....'64 '89 C.855 B.A. L.184 J.D. [Baio&Assoc.]
*PRACTICE AREAS: Civil Litigation; Insurance Coverage Liability.

Baio & Associates, P.C., (BV)
15 Elm Street, 06067
Telephone: 860-571-8880 Facsimile: 860-571-8853
Claudia A. Baio. Associate: Andrew M. Dewey.
Insurance Defense and Coverage, Liability Defense Including Municipalities and Workers' Compensation Defense.
See Professional Biographies, ROCKY HILL, CONNECTICUT

Barlow, Cynthia M. ....'68 '92 C.184 B.A. L.306 J.D. Dep. Asst. Pub. Def.
Battey, Wendella Ault, (CV) ..... '61 '90 C.1019 B.A. L.1009 J.D. 2139 Silas Deane Hwy
Bauman, Steven C. '62 '91
C.454 B.S. L.1040 J.D. Intell. Prop. Coun., Loctite Corp. (Pat.)
Blinn, Daniel S., (BV) ....'61 '87 C.97 B.A. L.569 J.D. P.O. Box 1039
Bohan, L. Stewart, (AV) '29 '54
C.976 B.A. L.569 J.D. Bd. Chmn., Conn. Attys. Title Ins. Co.
Buckley, George A., Jr. '58 '84 C.967 B.A. L.424 J.D.
(adm. in IL; not adm. in CT) Asst. Exec. Dir., Conn. Bar. Assn.
Carroll, Kevin ....'56 '91 C.184 B.A. L.1338 J.D. 41 New Britain Ave.
Chabot, Kelly Anne ....'62 '91 C&L.184 B.A., J.D. P.O. Box 129
Charamut, William C. '57 '91
C.184 B.A. L.1048 J.D. V.P. & Gen. Coun., Conn. Radio, Inc.
Colello, John J. ....'51 '80 C.1033 B.S. L.1048 J.D. 140 Silo Dr
Corr, Richard M. '40 '73 C.262 B.S. L.184 J.D.
Dir., Develop., Conn. Attys. Title Ins. Co.
Cronin, Michael T., (BV) '52 '78
C.882 B.A. L.285 J.D. Connecticut Laborers' Legal Servs.
D'Attelo, Anne Marie '56 '85 C.689 B.S. L.1029 J.D.
Managing Attorney, Zurich Financial Services Group
Dewey, Andrew M., (CV) ....'64 '89 C.184 B.A. L.306 J.D. [🄰 Baio&Assoc.]
*PRACTICE AREAS: Workers Compensation Defense; General Liability; Personal Injury Defense.
DiCara, Phyllis M., (BV) ....'57 '82 C.1024 B.S. L.823 J.D. 750 Old Main St.
Doyle, Brian A., (BV) ....'50 '87 C.999 B.A. L.1048 J.D. [Ferguson&D.]
Farrell, Robert J., Jr., (BV) ....'46 '76 C.976 B.A. L.184 J.D. 11 Riverview Rd.
Ferguson, James C., (BV) ....'46 '76 C.1102 B.S. L.1048 J.D. [Ferguson&D.]
Ferguson & Doyle, (BV) .... 35 Marshall Rd.
Gallivan, John E. ....'12 '39 C.262 B.S. L.184 LL.B. 20 Little Oak Lane‡
Glass, Marc Jerome, (BV) ....'45 '70 C&L.309 B.A., J.D. [Glass,L.&K.]
Glass, Lebovitz & Kasheta, LLC, (BV) ....P.O. Box 129
Godialis, Christopher T. ....'57 '92 C.1133 B.S. L.1029 J.D. Asst. States Atty.
Heneghan, Michael H., (BV) ....'40 '66 [Heneghan,P.K.&A.]
Heneghan, Pikor, Kennedy & Allen, (BV) .... 21 New Britain Ave.
Holland, Daniel E., Jr., (BV) ....'24 '53 C.165 A.B. L.188 LL.B. 750 Old Main St.
Johnson, Richard S., (BV) ....'48 '79 C.299 B.A. L.184 J.D. 8 Matteson Ave.
Kasheta, Kelly Anne, (CV) ....'62 '91 [Glass,L.&K.]
Kennedy, Daniel H., Jr., (BV) ....'47 '73 C.676 A.B. L.818 J.D. [Heneghan,P.K.&A.]
Kinney, Francis L. ....'32 '63 C.321 B.S. L.184 LL.B. 265 Whitewood Dr.
Kotchen, William J., (BV) ....'42 '67 C.659 B.A. L.94 LL.B. [Kotchen&R.]
Kotchen & Ripper, P.C., (BV) .... 21 New Britain Ave., Suite 201
LeFoll, Raymond G., (BV) ....'40 '69 C.94 B.S. L.184 J.D. [LeFoll&L.]
LeFoll, Tammy ....'66 '92 C.94 B.A. L.184 J.D. [LeFoll&L.]
LeFoll & LeFoll, (BV) .... 2301 Silas Deane Highway
Lifshitz, Miriam L. ....'49 '85 C.184 B.S.E. L.1048 J.D. Trinty Ridge
Lindroos, David W., (BV) ....'51 '76 C&L.184 B.A., J.D. 89 Sunset Rdg.
Lissy, David H. '43 '69 C&L.659 B.A., LL.B.
(adm. in PA; not adm. in CT)
Sr. V.P., Gen. Coun. & Corp. Secy., Ames Dept. Stores Inc.
Mason, A. Richard ....'70 '97 C.1030 B.S. L.1252 J.D. 805 Brook St.
Massameno, John M., (BV) ....'52 '78 C.184 B.A. L.823 J.D. Sr. Asst. States Atty.

Mayo, Gilligan & Zito, LLP
(See Wethersfield)

Mullarkey, Edward J. ....'46 '71 C.855 B.A. L.309 J.D. Supr. Ct. J.
Patterson, Richard J., (AV) '50 '75
C.29 B.A. L.1292 J.D. Pres., Conn. Attys. Title Ins. Co.
Petty, Mark W., (BV) '53 '87
C.502 B.J. L.184 J.D. Title Coun., Conn. Attys. Title Ins. Co.
Pickett, James M. ....'61 '87 C&L.184 B.S., J.D. 805 Brook St.
Pikor, Richard E., (BV) ....'42 '67 C.602 B.A. L.93 J.D. [Heneghan,P.K.&A.]
Pilcher, Lawrence C. ....'46 '75 C.951 B.A. L.262 J.D. State Housing Fin. Auth.
Pirretti, James J. ....'42 '66 C&L.569 B.S., J.D. V.P., Ames Department Stores, Inc.
Porcello, Clara A., (BV) ....'54 '79 C&L.184 B.S., J.D. 37 Waters Avenue
Preysner, John P., Jr. '55 '81 C.976 B.A. L.184 J.D.
Assoc. Gen. Coun. & Asst. Secy., Loctite Corp.
*RESPONSIBILITIES: Mergers and Acquisitions (20%); General Corporate (40%); Employment (20%); Litigation (20%).
Ralls, James M. ....'57 '85 C.112 B.A. L.276 J.D. Asst. State's Atty.‡
Reck, J. Rodney ....'38 '64 C&L.150 Ch.E., J.D. V.P., Loctite Corp. (Pat.)
Ripper, James F., (BV) ....'45 '72 C.205 B.A. L.184 J.D. [Kotchen&R.]
Rodosevich, Denise ....'54 '92 C.174 B.A. L.184 J.D. 805 Brook St.
Romano, Michael F., (BV) .... '54 '83 C.1297 B.A. L.1029 J.D. 41 New Britain Ave.
Rosen, Leo, (AV) ....'25 '50 C.855 B.S. L.184 LL.B. 336 Old Main St.
Rosow, Mark B. ....'47 '72 C.598 B.S. L.930 J.D. Spec. Dep. Asst. States Atty.
Salzarulo, Anthony J., (CV) ....'54 '85 C.1033 B.S. L.1048 J.D. 750 Old Main St.
Seidman, David S., (BV) ....'56 '86 C.184 B.S. L.659 J.D. 1080 Elm St.
Sellers, Steven M. ....'56 '82 C.1145 B.S. L.982 J.D. Off. of Chf. State's Atty.
Sheehan, Christopher C., (BV) ....'61 '86 C.95 B.A. L.184 J.D. 3195 Main St.
Short, John T., Jr., (BV) ....'54 '79 C.264 B.A. L.184 J.D. P.O. Box 782
Speed, William G., IV, (BV) ....'50 '76 C.855 B.A. L.276 J.D. 35 Marshall Rd.
Stillman, Martin S. ....'45 '70 C.569 B.A. L.94 J.D. 750 Old Main St., Ste. 303A
Thompson, Christy E. '70 '95
C.354 B.A. L.1048 J.D. Assoc. Cnsl, Ames Department Stores, Inc.

ROWAYTON, —, *Fairfield Co.*

Allen, J. Philip '52 '83 C.575 B.A. L.309 J.D.
(adm. in NY; not adm. in CT) 40 Highland Ave.
Burnett, Marjorie Ann '53 '79 C.588 B.A. L.188 J.D.
(adm. in MA; not adm. in CT) 40 Highland Ave.
Butterworth, Thomas C. '44 '78 C.502 B.A. L.724 J.D.
(adm. in NY; not adm. in CT) 40 Highland Ave.
Grin, S. Spencer ....'28 '52 C.569 B.A. L.1009 LL.B. 7 Plant Ct.
Hirsch, Gary D. '— '89 C.197 B.A. L.569 J.D.
(adm. in NY; not adm. in CT) Director of Legal Affairs, Currenex, Inc.
Lazaroff, Joseph L. ....'40 '65 C.477 B.S.E. L.309 J.D. 16 Yarmouth Rd. (Pat.)
Long, Jerry E. '40 '64 C&L.846 B.A., LL.B.
(adm. in TX; not adm. in CT) 40 Highland Ave.
McColpin, Andrew K., (AV) '29 '52 C&L.846 B.A., LL.B.
(adm. in TX; not adm. in CT) 61 Bluff Ave.‡
Meehan, Kevin L. '45 '76 C.321 B.A. L.724 J.D.
(adm. in NY; not adm. in CT) 40 Highland Ave.
Newman, Dorothy G. ....'17 '58 C.783 B.S. L.262 LL.B. [Newman&N.]
Newman & Newman .... 75 Witch Lane (⊙Cleve., OH)
Pillon, Charles G. ....'23 '48 C&L.893 LL.B. 2 St. James Pl.
Planicka, Dale M. '51 '77 C&L.602 B.B.A., J.D.
(adm. in OH; not adm. in CT) 15 Old Field Pl.‡
Sullivan, Alicia L. ....'67 '95 C.882 B.A. L.1040 J.D. 10 Topsail Rd.
Zernike, Barbara B. '31 '82 C.025 B.A. L.1040 J.D.
(adm. in NY; not adm. in CT) 19 Rowayton Ave.‡

ROXBURY, 1,468, *Litchfield Co.*

Goldstein, Barrie L., (AV) ....'49 '75 C.823 B.A. L.273 J.D. 1024 Washington Road
Johnson, Haynes N., (AV) ....'25 '50 C.674 A.B. L.976 LL.B. 28 Old Lane (Pat.)
Sperry, Richard D. ....'42 '71 C.390 A.B. L.966 J.D. 41 Chalybes Rd.
Weppler, Lawrence G. ....'45 '69 C&L.424 B.S. Retired‡

SALEM, 2,335, *New London Co.*

Steadman, Bernard W., (BV) ....'40 '78 C.1156 B.S. L.184 J.D. P.O. Box 2036

SALISBURY, 3,896, *Litchfield Co.*

Dakin, Christopher M., (BV) ....'39 '68 C.164 A.B. L.184 J.D. 11 Hammertown Rd.
Deavers, Karl A. '34 '59 C&L.923 B.S., LL.B.
(adm. in NY; not adm. in CT) P.O. Box 315‡
Dubin, M. R. ....'15 '42 C&L.893 B.S., LL.B. Village Green
Fitzpatrick, John C. '31 '62 C.262 B.S. L.276 J.D.
(adm. in NY; not adm. in CT) 215 Factory St.‡
Galos, Jodie-Beth H. ....'51 '77 C.66 B.A. L.94 J.D. 77 Selleck Hill Rd.
Haab, Michele W. ....'46 '76 C.1019 B.A. L.262 J.D. 254 Twin Lakes Rd.
Warner, Scott, (CV) ....'42 '72 C.178 B.S. L.184 J.D. 70 Selleck Hill Rd.

SANDY HOOK, —, *Fairfield Co.*

Dewhirst, Linda N., (CV) ....'54 '88 C.184 B.S. L.1040 J.D. 75 Glen Rd.
Gustilo, Lillian C. ....'63 '91 C.103 B.A. L.494 J.D. 35 Yoganada St.‡
Mihalko, Virginia P., (CV) ....'55 '81 C.184 B.A. L.1194 J.D. 75 Glen Rd.

SCOTLAND, 1,072, *Windham Co.*

Fichter, Angela Hawkins, (CV) ....'47 '81 C.611 B.A. L.184 J.D. Rte. 14
Taalman, Juri Eino, (BV) ....'40 '69 C.145 B.S. L.184 J.D. P.O. Box 289

SEYMOUR, 13,434, *New Haven Co.*

Barton, Scott A., (BV) ....'63 '89 C.1156 B.S. L.464 J.D. 14 Amber Dr.
Behuniak, Thomas E. ....'43 '69 C.823 A.B. L.818 J.D. 40 Church St.★
Beyer, Dana J. ....'60 '89 C.273 B.A. L.1029 J.D. 7 Wakeley St.
Ginzberg, Jeffrey D., (BV) ....'55 '80 C.1036 B.A. L.93 J.D. [Perelmutter,P.&G.]
*PRACTICE AREAS: Personal Injury; Family Law; Divorce; Child Custody; Retail Collections.
Kulas, Steven P., (BV) ....'60 '85 C&L.184 B.A., J.D. [May&S.]
May, Prescott W. ....'42 '67 C.103 B.S. L.184 J.D. [May&S.]
May & Stanek, P.C., (BV) .... 12 Bank Street

Perelmutter, Potash & Ginzberg, P.C., (BV)
11 Bank Street, 06483
Telephone: 203-888-2501 Fax: 203-888-7928
URL: http://www.lawyers.com/perelmutterpotash&ginzber
Joseph N. Perelmutter (1909-1982); Arnold M. Potash; Jeffrey D. Ginzberg; Kenneth Potash.
Family Law, Personal Injury Litigation, Criminal Litigation, Jury Trials, Consumer Law, Negligence Law, Products Liability, Automobile Dealership Liability, Unfair Trade Practice Litigation, Probate, Real Estate, General Practice. Trials in all Courts, Appellate Practice.
Reference: Shawmut National Bank.
See Professional Biographies, SEYMOUR, CONNECTICUT

Potash, Arnold M., (BV) ....'36 '61 C&L.188 A.B., LL.B. [Perelmutter,P.&G.]
*PRACTICE AREAS: Family Law; Personal Injury; Criminal Litigation; General Practice; Appellate Practice.
Potash, Kenneth ....'70 '96 C&L.188 B.A., J.D. [Perelmutter,P.&G.]
*PRACTICE AREAS: Personal Injury; Family Law; Criminal Law; Real Estate; General Practice.
Sakal, Joseph E., (BV) ....'38 '70 C&L.469 B.A., J.D. [J.E.Sakal]
Sakal, Joseph E., P.C., (BV) .... 246 Bank St.
Sous, Ramon S. ....'47 '71 C.321 A.B. L.884 J.D. 159 Main St.
Stanek, Frederick D. ....'54 '79 C.184 B.S. L.823 J.D. [May&S.]
Tamis, Donald H., (BV) ....'45 '70 C.860 B.A. L.273 J.D. 246 Bank St.
Wolf, George, (BV) ....'29 '57 C.184 B.A. L.94 LL.B. 276 Bank St. (⊙Trumbull)

SHARON, 2,623, *Litchfield Co.*

Brown, Louise F., (BV) ....'43 '72 C.309 B.A. L.94 J.D. [Gager&P.]
*PRACTICE AREAS: Real Estate Law; Estate Planning; Estate Administration; Probate Law.
Coté, Andrew C. ....'47 '80 C.156 B.A. L.184 J.D. [A.C.Coté]
*PRACTICE AREAS: Securities Litigation, Arbitration and Mediation; Business Litigation; Arbitration and Mediation; Broker-Dealer Regulation; Securities Regulation.

Coté, Andrew C., P.C.
11 Gay Street, P.O. Box 1294, 06069
Telephone: 860-435-4721 Fax: 860-364-0496
Email: acclegal@aol.com URL: http://www.lawyers.com/andrewcotelaw
Andrew C. Coté .
See Professional Biographies, SHARON, CONNECTICUT

Friday, Jo E., (BV) ....'50 '81 C&L.259 B.A., J.D. [Gager&P.] (⊙Litchfield)
*PRACTICE AREAS: Real Estate Law; Family Law; Probate Law; Estate Planning; Family Mediation.

Gager & Peterson, LLP, (AV)
25 West Main Street, P.O. Box 158, 06069-0158 ⊙
Telephone: 860-364-5531 Telecopier: 860-364-5805
Louise F. Brown (Resident); Jo E. Friday; J. Michael Sconyers.
General Practice. Corporate Law, Banks and Banking, Securities, Administrative Law, Litigation, Insurance, Estate Planning, Probate, Real Estate, Family Law, Taxation, Patents, Trademarks, Copyrights, Consumer Law, Environmental, Computers and Software, Labor and Employment Law.
Representative Clients: The Sharon Hospital; Salisbury Bank & Trust Co.
Waterbury, Connecticut Office: One Exchange Place, P. O. Box 2480. Telephone: 203-597-5100. Telecopier: 203-757-7888.
Bethel, Connecticut Office: 2 Stony Hill Road. Telephone: 203-207-5400. Telecopier: 203-207-5407.
Litchfield, Connecticut Office: 782 Bantam Road. Telephone: 860-567-0828. Telecopier: 860-567-5844.
Southbury, Connecticut Office: 325 Main Street South. Telephone: 203-262-6600. Telecopier: 203-262-6780.
See Professional Biographies, SHARON, CONNECTICUT

Sconyers, J. Michael, (BV) ....'46 '76 C.1059 A.B. L.273 J.D. [Gager&P.] (⊙Litchfield)
*PRACTICE AREAS: Civil Litigation; Real Property Law; Family Law; Planning and Zoning Law.

SHELTON, 35,418, *Fairfield Co.*

Asija, S. Pal ....'42 '74 C.415 B.S. L.1340 J.D. [O.P.Asija] (Pat.)
Barbara, Jacqueline F. ....'66 '92 C.1349 B.A. L.1252 J.D. [Schlesinger&B.]
Bracnaro, James W. ....'22 '52 C.976 A.B. L.818 LL.B. 161 Summerfield Gardens
Briones, Brian E. ....'65 '90 C.1030 B.A. L.1019 J.D. [Ⓐ McNamara&K.]
Bruner, Jeffrey A. '59 '84 C&L.208 B.S.B.A., J.D.
V.P. & Gen. Coun., Iroquois Gas Transmission Sys.
Buddenhagen, Scott J. ....'57 '83 C.884 B.S.A. L.472 J.D. Gen. Coun., bbc Corp.
Buffam, David J. '44 '76 C.937 A.B. L.477 J.D.
(adm. in NY; not adm. in CT) Pres., New Castle Hotel Corp.
Cahill, Gary P., (BV) '52 '83 C.1102 B.A. L.1029 J.D.
525 Bridgeport Avenue Suite 201
Camper, Stephen P. .... '63 '91 C.1494 B.A. L.734 J.D. Physicians Health Servs., Inc.
Capelli, Christopher J. '66 '94 C.273 B.S.E.E. L.564 J.D.
(adm. in NJ; not adm. in CT; Pat.) Sr. Corp. Coun., Pitney Bowes, Inc.
*RESPONSIBILITIES: Intellectual Property; Commercial Transactions; Corporate Law; Exports.
Carlton, Dennis E. '47 '73 C.112 B.A. L.1065 J.D.
(adm. in CA; not adm. in CT) Gen. Coun.
Chaclas, Angelo N. '63 '96
C.860 B.S.M.E. L.1040 J.D. Sr. Corp. Coun., Pitney Bowes, Inc. (Pat.)
*RESPONSIBILITIES: Patents; Trademarks; EPO Opposition Activity; Contracts; General Practice.
Chase, Norman K. ....'52 '82 C.36 B.A. L.1029 J.D. 2 Corporate Dr.
Clark, Peter D., (BV) ....'47 '72 C.855 B.A. L.823 J.D. 525 Bridgeport Ave.
Cummings, Michael J. .....'68 '98 C.971 B.S. L.94 J.D. Corp. Coun., Pitney Bowes Inc.
*RESPONSIBILITIES: Intellectual Property; Technology Law.
Deagan, Diane M. '48 '79 C.643 B.A. L.724 J.D.
Corporate Counsel, Capital Services Division, Pitney Bowes Credit Corporation
Deakin, Michael Cuff ....'63 '93 C.354 B.A. L.1017 J.D. 525 Bridgeport Avenue
Del Mastro, Annacarina ....'65 '91 C.19 B.A. L.818 J.D. 375 Bridgeport Ave.
Deutsch, Barry E. '41 '69 C.1027 B.S. L.1009 J.D.
(adm. in NY; not adm. in CT; Pat.) Black & Decker, Inc.
De Vivo, Ann Marie ....'73 '99 C.1266 L.1252 J.D. [Ⓐ McNamara&K.]
Diehl, Paul W. '54 '79 C.665 B.S. L.276 J.D.
(adm. in PA; not adm. in CT) Sr. Atty., Iroquois Gas Transmission Sys.
Dragan, William P. ....'66 '91 C.354 B.S. L.823 J.D Centrix, Inc.
Englis, James G., (BV) ....'34 '60 C.976 B.A. L.178 LL.B. 375 Bridgeport Ave.
FitzSimons, James Michael, (AVⓉ) '26 '52
C.724 L.1009 LL.B. [J.M.Fitzsimons] (⊙New York, NY)
FitzSimons, James Michael, P.C., (AVⓉ) ....917A Bridgeport Ave.
Fray, Jennifer H. ....'64 '90 C.860 B.A. L.818 J.D. Senior Attorney, Tetley USA Inc.
Geiss, J. Suzanne '36 '61 C.174 B.Mus. L.846 LL.B.
(adm. in TX; not adm. in CT) Counsel, Rhodia Inc.
Giacci, Edward R., (BV) ....'45 '74 C.598 B.A. L.823 J.D. [E.R.Giacci]

Giacci, Edward R., P.C., (BV)
375 Bridgeport Avenue, 06484
Telephone: 203-925-0442 Facsimile: 203-925-3003
URL: http://www.lawyers.com/gizcci
Edward R. Giacci.
General Practice.
See Professional Biographies, SHELTON, CONNECTICUT

Golger, J. Kevin, (BV) ....'57 '83 C.860 B.A. L.734 J.D. [McNamara&K.]
Green, Stacey M. '63 '88 C&L.569 B.F.A., J.D.
Corporate Counsel, Pitney Bowes Credit Corporation
Hart, William D., III ....'55 '85 C.105 B.A. L.564 J.D. Allstate Ins. Co.
Hellauer, Gretchen A. ....'— '92 C.184 B.A. L.1048 J.D. 17 Frank Dr.
Hine, Zeena Young ....'50 '75 C.477 B.A. L.912 J.D. Pitney Bowes Credit Corp.
Holmes, George L., Jr., (AV) ....'47 '73 C.1030 B.A. L.184 J.D. [McNamara&K.]
Hughes, Christian D. '55 '80 C.10 B.A. L.16 J.D.
(adm. in GA; not adm. in CT) V.P., Secy. & Gen. Coun., Pitney Bowes Credit Corp.
Hughes, James M., (BV) ....'51 '82 C.676 B.A. L.1029 J.D. [Ⓐ McNamara&K.]
Keegan, Frank Joseph '46 '83
C.184 B.S. L.326 J.D. Coun., Philips Med. Systems N. Amer. Co.
Kempf, Joseph J., Jr. ....'49 '80 C.676 B.A. L.1048 J.D. Physicians Health Servs.
Kirincich, Joseph C. '67 '93 C.433 B.S.E.E. L.564 J.D.
(adm. in NJ; not adm. in CT; Pat.) Asst. Dep. Gen. Coun., Pitney Bowes Inc.
*RESPONSIBILITIES: Intellectual Property.
Koether, Rosamond A. ......'64 '91 C.72 B.A. L.1048 J.D. Pres.-Corp. Coun., Kelsey Co.
Lapera, Patrick J. .....'54 '81 C.754 B.S. L.823 J.D. [McKinnis&L.] (⊙New York, NY)
*PRACTICE AREAS: Corporate Law; Business Law; Municipal Finance; Commercial Law; Finance.
Leitz, Rosemary Keating '62 '98
C.184 B.S. L.1252 J.D. Atty., Iroquois Gas Transmission Sys.
Lemm, Brian A. '66 '98 C.105 B.S.E.E. L.724 J.D.
(adm. in NY; not adm. in CT; Pat.) Corp. Coun., Pitney Bowes Inc.
*RESPONSIBILITIES: Intellectual Property.
Lynch, Gregory P., (BV) ....'46 '72 C.1029 B.A. L.724 J.D. [McNamara&K.]
Macdonald, Edward P. '67 '94 C.754 B.A. L.180 J.D.
(adm. in PA; not adm. in CT) American Skandia Investment Holding Corp.
Macdonald, Marcy F. ....'60 '86 C.1044 B.A. L.1029 J.D. 27 Waterview Dr.
Malandra, Charles R., Jr. '49 '80 C.602 B.S.E.E. L.446 J.D.
(adm. in MD; not adm. in CT; Pat.) Sr. Corp. Coun., Pitney Bowes Inc.
*RESPONSIBILITIES: Intellectual Property; Contracts.
Marcello, Joseph D. ....'46 '79 C.184 B.A. L.1202 J.D. Asst. Clk., Supr. Ct.
McGuinness, Peter J., (BV) ....'57 '87 C.676 B.A. L.1029 J.D. [Olayos&M.]
McKinnis, George C., (AVⓉ) ....'37 '65 C.623 B.A. L.477 J.D. [McKinnis&L.] ⊙
*PRACTICE AREAS: Emerging Growth Companies; Entrepreneurial Business Law; International Business Law; Telecommunications Contracts; Telecommunications Licensing.

McKinnis & Lapera, (AVⓉ)
1077 Bridgeport Ave, 06484 ⊙
Telephone: 203-925-8799 Fax: 203-925-8780 Email: lapera@mlawtek.com
Email: mckinnis@mlawtech.com URL: http://www.mlawtek.com
Patrick J. Lapera; George C. McKinnis.
Emerging Growth Companies including Telecommunications and Electronics, Information Systems and Semiconductor Industries, Entrepreneurial Business Law, International Business Law, Capital Formation, Telecommunications Contracts and Licensing, Computer Contracts, International Commercial Contracts, Corporate Commercial Law, Strategic Associations, Semiconductor Technology, Business Startups, Technology Finance and Licensing.
New York, N.Y. Office: 445 Park Avenue, 10022. Telephone: 212-371-5400. Fax: 212-688-8036.
Westchester County Office: 40 Oriole Avenue, Bronxville, N.Y. 10708. Telephone: 914-793-9215. Fax: 914-793-9433.
See Professional Biographies, SHELTON, CONNECTICUT

McNamara and Kenney, (AV)
375 Bridgeport Avenue, 06484-3844
Telephone: 203-366-5661 Fax: 203-366-5335
James F. Kenney (1921-1997); Thomas A. Mulligan, Jr.; Gregory P. Lynch; George L. Holmes, Jr.; J. Kevin Golger. Associate: James M. Hughes; Thomas R. Rowe; Brian E. Briones; Ann Marie De Vivo.
General and Trial Practice in all State and Federal Courts. Real Estate, Probate, Corporation, Family, Insurance, Medical and Legal Malpractice, Negligence, Products Liability, Workers Compensation and Zoning.
Representative Clients: American International Co.; The Atlantic Companies; General Accident Group; Government Employees Insurance Co.; National Car Rental Claim Services; Prudential Property & Casualty Insurance Co.; Royal Insurance; Safeco Insurance Companies; Yellow Freight Systems, Inc.
See Professional Biographies, SHELTON, CONNECTICUT

Melton, Michael E. '58 '84 C&L.502 B.S.E.E., J.D.
(adm. in MO; not adm. in CT; Pat.) Dep. Gen. Coun., Pitney Bowes Inc.
*RESPONSIBILITIES: Management Labor Law; Intellectual Property; Technology and Science; Alternative Dispute Resolution; Antitrust and Trade Regulation.
Mintz, Stacey M. '63 '88 C&L.569 B.F.A., J.D.
Senior Division Counsel & Assistant Secretary, Pitney Bowes Financial Services
Mitola, Thomas F. ....'61 '87 C.1156 B.A. L.607 J.D. 38 Rolling Ridge Rd.
Mortimer, Stanley '42 '69 C.309 A.B. L.893 J.D.
(adm. in NY; not adm. in CT) Exec. V.P., The Forschner Grp.
Mulligan, Thomas A., Jr., (BV) ....'45 '70 C.1030 A.B. L.128 J.D. [McNamara&K.]
Noonan, Martin F. '66 '97 C.433 B.E. L.884 J.D.
(adm. in NY; not adm. in CT; Pat.) Sr. Corp. Coun., Pitney Bowes Inc.
*RESPONSIBILITIES: Intellectual Property.
Olayos, James N., (BV) ....'58 '83 C.1030 B.A. L.1029 J.D. [Olayos&M.]
Olayos & McGuinness, (BV) .... 1077 Bridgeport Ave.
O'Leary, Mary Ellen '60 '86 C.602 B.S. L.339 J.D.
Special Counsel, American Skandia Life Insurance Corp.
Our Pal Asija .... 7 Woonsocket Avenue
Parisi, Donald '56 '82 C.705 B.A. L.1292 J.D.
(adm. in NJ; not adm. in CT) Physicians Health Servs., Inc.
Parks, Charles G., Jr. '50 '77 C&L.665 B.S., J.D.
(adm. in PA; not adm. in CT; Pat.) 35 Waterview Dr.
Pignatelia, Michael A. '69 '95 C.184 B.A. L.93 J.D.
Staff Coun., American Skandia Investment Holding Corp.

Pitchenik, David E. '40 '66 C.893 B.E.E. L.273 J.D.
Assoc. Dep. Gen. Coun., Pitney Bowes Inc. (Pat.)
*RESPONSIBILITIES: Capital Asset Management Group; Intellectual Property Licensing; Business / Technical Strategic Alliances; Intellectual Property Competitive Analysis; Intellectual Property Portfolio Management.
Porter, Scott Douglas '59 '85 C.293 B.A. L.930 J.D.
(adm. in NY; not adm. in CT) General Counsel, OCI Chemical Corporation
Praino, Ingrid E. ....'54 '96 C.680 B.A. L.1009 J.D. Atty., Physicians Health Servs., Inc.
Presson, Thomas F. '67 '95
C.880 B.E. L.1252 J.D. Sr. Corp. Coun., Pitney Bowes Inc. (Pat.)
*RESPONSIBILITIES: Intellectual Property.
Reichman, Ronald '46 '73 C.415 B.S. L.1009 J.D.
(adm. in NY; not adm. in CT; Pat.) Sr. Corp. Coun., Pitney Bowes Inc.
*RESPONSIBILITIES: Patents; Licensing; Corporate Law; Exports.
Reisman, Andrew E. '50 '75 C.188 B.S. L.569 J.D.
(adm. in NY; not adm. in CT) Div. Coun., GE Supply

Reisman, Glenn M., (AV) '50 '76 C.299 A.B. L.982 J.D. BB
Two Corporate Drive, Suite 650, P.O. Box 861, 06484-0861
Telephone: 203-944-3040 Fax: 203-944-3044 URL: http://www.ReismanLaw.com URL: http://www.CreditCollectionLaw.com
Email: Glenn.Reisman@corporate.ge.com URL: http://www.lawyers.com/reisman
***PRACTICE AREAS: Creditors' Rights Law; Bankruptcy Law; Workouts Law.**
—J. Michelle Reisman (Not admitted in CT).
Creditors' Rights, Bankruptcy, Risk Management, Workouts.
See Professional Biographies, SHELTON, CONNECTICUT

Reisman, J. Michelle '51 '77 C.94 B.A. L.982 J.D.
(adm. in NY; not adm. in CT) [Ⓐ G.M.Reisman]
*PRACTICE AREAS: Creditor's Rights Law; Bankruptcy; Workouts.
Rigoglioso, Joseph P. .... '62 '91 C.454 B.A. L.1029 J.D. 215 Corum Ave.
Ripley, George W., II .... '26 '55 C&L.184 A.B., LL.B. Supr. Ct. J.
Rondos, A. Wm. .... '26 '53 C.208 B.S. L.184 LL.B. 258 Schoolside Ln.‡
Rowe, Thomas R. .... '69 '95 C.128 B.A. L.1252 J.D. [Ⓐ McNamara&K.]
Rubinson, Elaine .... '50 '90 C.331 B.A. L.1029 J.D. [Ⓐ G.P.Cahill]
Ryan, Richard R. .... '53 '80 C.31 B.A. L.724 J.D. 231 Coram Avenue
Ryan, William J., Jr., (BV) .... '51 '77 C.1030 B.A. L.184 J.D. [Ryan&T.]
Ryan & Tyma, (BV) .... 231 Coram Ave.
Scanlon, Elaine M., (BV) .... '56 '83 C.884 B.A. L.1029 J.D. 215 Coram Ave.
Schlesinger, Alan R. .... '58 '95 C.659 B.S. L.184 J.D. [Schlesinger&B.]
Schlesinger & Barbara, LLC .... 375 Coram Avenue
Schoenberger, Lincoln F .... '49 '87 C.397 B.S. L.1029 J.D. OEM Control, Inc.
Scully, Douglas E. '63 '93 C.184 B.A. L.1003 J.D.
Counsel, American Skandia Investment Holding Corp.
Shapiro, Steven J. '55 '90 C.1350 B.S.M.E. L.446 J.D.
(adm. in VA; not adm. in CT; Pat.) Sr. Corp. Coun., Pitney Bowes Inc.
*RESPONSIBILITIES: Intellectual Property; Commercial Transactions; International Law.

Silver, Golub & Teitell LLP
(See Stamford)

Sklar, Lawrence E. '43 '69 C.705 B.S. L.776 J.D.
(adm. in NJ; not adm. in CT; Pat.) 35 Waterview Dr.
Smarz, Thomas R. .... '37 '67 C.1030 B.S.S. L.128 J.D. 120 Cliff St.
Teodosio, Francis A., (BV) .... '58 '84 C.1030 B.A. L.184 J.D. [Winnick,V.W.&T.]
Torrito, Richard '47 '76 C.271 B.S. L.64 J.D.
(adm. in PA; not adm. in CT) HSE Coun., Rhodia, Inc.
Tyma, Alan J., (BV) .... '51 '76 C.1030 B.A. L.184 J.D. [Ryan&T.]
Urso, Kelly Marie .... '65 '92 C.150 B.B.A. L.1187 J.D. General Electric Co.
Vine, Leo, (BV) .... '30 '55 C.103 A.B. L.309 J.D. [Winnick,V.W.&T.]
Vitale, Alberta A. '65 '95 C.1033 B,S.E.E. L.502 J.D.
Sr. Atty., Pitney Bowes, Inc. (Pat.)
*RESPONSIBILITIES: Intellectual Property; Intellectual Property Licensing; Copyrights; Contracts.
Volman, David Gregg, (CV) .... '62 '87 C.454 B.A. L.692 J.D. 215 Coram Ave.
Walsh, Christopher J. .... '61 '87 C.999 B.S. L.607 J.D. 165-B Center St.
Welch, John H., Jr., (AV) .... '31 '58 C.1030 B.S.S. L.184 LL.B. [Winnick,V.W.&T.]
Welch, Thomas J., (BV) .... '65 '90 C.321 B.A. L.306 J.D. [Winnick,V.W.&T.]
Williamson, Keith H. '52 '78 C.103 B.A. L.309 J.D.
(adm. in DC; not adm. in CT)
VP, Secretary & General Counsel-PBFS, Pitney Bowes Credit Corporation
Winnick, Bronislaw, (AV) .... '23 '51 C&L.184 B.A., J.D. [Winnick,V.W.&T.]
Winnick, Vine, Welch & Teodosio, LLC, (AV) .... 375 Bridgeport Avenue
Young, Foster M., (BV) .... '44 '69 C.477 B.A. L.1119 J.D. [Yudkin&Y.]
Young, LeGrande L. '36 '63
C.101 B.S. L.878 J.D. V.P., Secy. & Gen. Coun., Raytech Corp.
Yudkin, Harold B. .... '12 '37 C.67 B.S. L.692 LL.B. [Yudkin&Y.]
Yudkin & Young, (BV) .... Coram Ave.
Zein, Monica C. '70 '96 C&L.790 B.A., J.D.
Director of Operations, Caps Business Recovery Services

SHERMAN, —, *Fairfield Co.*

Jones, William R., Jr. .... '57 '87 C.349 B.S. L.607 J.D. 1 Memory Ln.
O'Connor, Andrea B. .... '45 '96 C.188 B.S.N. L.184 J.D. 9 Pepper Pine Road

SIMSBURY, 21,161, *Hartford Co.*

Alden, Melinda Ann .... '74 '01 C.633 B.A. L.1048 J.D. [Ⓐ Libert&Assoc.]
*PRACTICE AREAS: Patents; Trademarks; Copyrights.
Altobelli, Nancy L. .... '73 '00 C.454 B.B.A. L.1048 J.D. 82 Hopmeadow St.
Bartell, Thomas E. .... '64 '94 C&L.188 B.S., J.D. 200 Hopmeadow St.
Beers, Lewis F., III ... '52 '77 C.867 B.A. L.184 J.D. Asst. Gen. Coun., Hartford Life, Inc.
Benneche, Thomas G., (BV) .... '62 '87 C.93 B.A. L.818 J.D. 885 Hopmeadow Street
Biondolillo, Jimmy B., (BV) '58 '92 C.999 B.M. L.306 J.D.
Clms. Atty., Executive Risk
Blakeslee, H. James .... '59 '88 C.183 B.A. L.184 J.D. 200 Hopmeadow St.
Blessis, Lisa Billy .... '57 '92 C.573 B.S. L.823 J.D. Clms. Atty., Executive Risk
Boyd, Philip C. .... '22 '53 C.103 A.B. L.188 LL.B. 5 Minister Brook Dr.
Brady, Matthew J. .... '52 '81 C.454 B.A. L.184 J.D. [Wieselman&B.]
Brodzinski, Carrie A., (BV) ..... '63 '88 C&L.184 B.S., J.D. Prod. Mgr., EPLI, Exec. Risk
Buchman, Steven E. .... '40 '65 C.659 B.S.in Ec. L.184 LL.B. 45 Berkshire Way‡
Burrell, Susan Brown .... '68 '96 C.645 B.A. L.1252 J.D. Clms. Atty., Executive Risk
Canning, Kimberly M. .... '67 '92 C.29 B.A. L.184 J.D. [Ⓐ Wieselman&B.]
Casey, Michael J., (BV) .... '54 '82 C.1019 B.A. L.945 J.D. 200 Hopmeadow St.
Cicchetti, Anthony N., (AV) '59 '84 C.976 B.A. L.569 J.D.
Sr. Corp. Atty., Ensign-Bickford Industries, Inc.
*RESPONSIBILITIES: Corporate Law; Antitrust; Product Distribution; Mergers and Acquisitions; Transnational Transactions.
Clark, Thomas S. .... '66 '93 C.184 B.S. L.420 J.D. Hartford Life Ins. Co.
Coburn, Raymond E. .... '24 '60 C.976 B.A. L.306 LL.B. 25 Clifdon Dr.
Coran, Kimberly Dean '63 '88 C.373 B.A. L.477 J.D.
Clms. Atty. & Mgr., Executive Risk
Cosgrove, Martha A. Shaw .... '61 '91 C.94 B.A. L.30 J.D. Executive Risk
Covello, Timothy J., (BV) '61 '88
C.309 B.A. L.228 J.D. Underwriting Mgr., Executive Risk
Crimmins, Kevin M. .... '64 '94 C.1134 B.S. L.365 J.D. 32 Walker Dr.
Curry, Timothy J., (BV) '51 '77
C.1349 B.A. L.228 J.D. Asst. V.P. & Coun., Chubb Executive Risk
Daly, Kelly '62 '93 C.882 B.A. L.184 J.D.
Sr. Atty., Chubb Executive Risk Inc. (Legal Department)
Delehanty, Jeanne Mazur, (BV) '53 '79 C.1033 B.A. L.1048 J.D.
Corporate Attorney, Ensign-Bickford Industries, Inc.
DiBartolo, Annamarie, (CV) ... '61 '86 C.1030 A.B. L.93 J.D. Clms. Atty., Executive Risk
Dickins, Oliver B., Jr., (BV) .... '41 '69 C.806 B.S. L.893 J.D. One Phelps Lane
Dodell, Leib '63 '88 C.446 B.A. L.273 J.D.
(adm. in MD; not adm. in CT) Underwriting Mgr., Executive Risk
Doherty, Kelly L. .... '71 '97 C.321 B.A. L.306 J.D. Clms. Atty., Exec. Risk
Donohue, Thomas J., Jr., (BV) .... '51 '76 C.321 B.A. L.184 J.D. [Killian D.&J.] ⊙
Dowling, Victor J., (BV) .... '23 '52 C.309 B.S. L.184 LL.B. [Dowling&D.]
Dowling, Victor J., Jr., (BV) .... '57 '85 C.93 B.A. L.1048 J.D. [Dowling&D.]
Dowling and Dowling, (BV) .... 987 Hopmeadow Street
Dropick, Dorothy K., (AV) .... '47 '74 C.242 B.A. L.184 J.D. 5 School House Ln.
Eisenmann, Carl D., (BV) '28 '51
C&L.276 A.B., J.D. Chmn., State Pub. Def. Servs. Comm.
Eisenstein, Roger M., (BV) .... '47 '73 C&L.184 B.A., J.D. P.O. Box 186
Erlichson, Frances .... '52 '87 C.1044 B.A. L.1048 J.D. Clms. Atty., Executive Risk
Ettman, Philip, (BV) .... '48 '72 C.107 B.A. L.94 J.D. 237 Hopmeadow St.
Fagan, Christopher J. .... '66 '91 C.93 B.A. L.184 J.D. Atty., Chubb Executive Risk
Falcigno, Richard J. .... '63 '90 C.882 B.A. L.1040 J.D. Chubb Exec. Risk
Fish, Michelle A. .... '72 '98 C.105 B.S.B.A. L.1040 J.D. Atty., Chubb Executive Risk
Fitzpatrick, Sean M. .... '59 '85 C.31 B.A. L.309 J.D. V.P., Executive Risk
Fortgang, Robert M., (BV) .... '50 '80 C.4 B.A. L.1029 J.D. [R.Fortgang]
Fortgang, Robert, Associates, (BV) .... 573 Hopmeadow Street
Frangie, Frederick Paul .... '66 '96 C.676 B.S. L.1218 J.D. 573 Hopmeadow St.
Freedman, Jonathan R. ..... '49 '79 C.94 B.S. L.809 J.D. Assoc. Coun., Hartford Life, Inc.
Gallo, Catherine .... '55 '83 C.705 B.S. L.823 J.D. Loss Prevention Coun., Executive Risk
Glassman, Andrew C., (BV) ... '60 '85 C.188 B.S. L.184 J.D. [Pullman&C.] (⊙Hartford)
*PRACTICE AREAS: Corporate Law; Mergers and Acquisitions; Employment Law; Commercial Transactions.
Godkin, Lynda .... '54 '82 C.518 A.B. L.1048 J.D. Gen. Coun., Hartford Life, Inc.
Goldfarb, Katrin Doane .... '72 '97 C.228 B.A. L.184 J.D. Corp. Atty., Executive Risk
Goldstein, Kenneth T. .... '71 '97 C.999 B.A. L.1048 J.D. Clms. Atty., Executive Risk
Gorski, Janet Weinberg .... '51 '77 C.788 A.B. L.306 J.D. 200 Hopmeadow St.
Graves, Robert G., (BVⓉ) '53 '85 C.884 B.A. L.1325 J.D.
(adm. in XX; not adm. in CT) Chubb Insurance Co.
Greenlaw, Dawn S. .... '69 '96 C.882 B.A. L.184 J.D. Sr. Atty., Executive Risk
Hamborg, Robert C. '21 '49 C&L.352 B.A., J.D.
(adm. in IA; not adm. in CT) 1 Tower Dr.‡
Hammett, Dorothy T. '— '87 C.651 B.S. L.229 J.D.
Corp. Atty. & Dir. of Risk Mgmt. Systems, Ensign-Bickford Industries, Inc.
*RESPONSIBILITIES: Environmental Law; Corporate Law; Labor Law; Products Liability; Regulatory Compliance.
Hampson, Debra A. .... '63 '93 C&L.184 B.A., J.D. Assoc. Coun., Hartford Life, Inc.
Hams, Thomas P. '65 '92 C.477 B.A. L.30 J.D.
(adm. in PA; not adm. in CT) Claims Atty., Executive Risk, Inc.
Hannan, Raymond T., Jr. .... '67 '94 C.855 B.A. L.29 J.D. Corp. Atty., Executive Risk

Hassett & George, P.C.
(See Hartford)

Holly, Powell W., Jr. '23 '61 C.511 A.B. L.1009 J.D.
(adm. in NY; not adm. in CT) Western New England Coll. Sch. of Law‡

Houlihan, Charles D., Jr., (AVⓉ) '53 '79 C.454 B.A. L.823 J.D.
1276 Hopmeadow Street, 06070-0582
Telephone: 860-658-9668 Facsimile: 860-658-1339
Email: CDHatty@aol.com URL: http://www.lawyers.com/houlihanlaw
(Board Certified, Civil Trial Law, Texas Board of Legal Specialization).
General Civil Trials and Appellate Practice in all State and Federal Courts. Business Litigation, Construction, Mediation. Employment Law.
See Professional Biographies, SIMSBURY, CONNECTICUT

Huntington, Susan R. '55 '91 C.966 B.S. L.276 J.D.
Dir. Health Care Risk Mngt. & Underwriting Coun., Executive Risk
Julian, Laurie Crown .... '61 '91 C.1252 B.A. L.306 J.D. Clms. Atty., Executive Risk
Killian, Robert K., Jr., (AV) .... '47 '72 C.867 B.A. L.276 J.D. [Killian D.&J.] ⊙
Killian Donohue & Jaff, LLC, (AV) .... 927 Hopmeadow St. (⊙Hartford)
Klenk, Jeffrey P. '69 '93 C.259 B.S. L.273 J.D.
(adm. in PA; not adm. in CT) Dir., Prod. Mgmt., Executive Risk
Kurien, Ruth A., (BV) .... '47 '88 C.184 B.S. L.976 J.D. 200 Hopmeadow St.
Lamberson, Kevin J. .... '63 '90 C.178 B.A. L.724 J.D. 4 Elliot Dr.
Laroche, Bruce E. '64 '91 L.831 J.D.
Tax Liability/ Fin. Trans. Dept., Chubb Specialty Insurance
LaRock, Jacqueline Trojnar .... '64 '90 C.299 B.A. L.245 J.D. Corp. Atty., Executive Risk
Lawshe, Susan J. '65 '90 C.289 B.A. L.276 J.D.
Sr. Underwriter & Risk Mgmt. Coun., Executive Risk
Lawson, Douglas A. .... '58 '92 C.473 B.S. L.1048 J.D. 200 Hopmeadow St.
Leedham, Sophie van Til .... '64 '89 C.999 J.D. L.184 J.D. Corp. Atty., Executive Risk
Lennon, John M. '29 '56 C.363 B.S. L.930 LL.B.
(adm. in OH; not adm. in CT) The Travelers Ins. Co.
Lenz, Frederick S., Jr. .... '43 '67 C.676 A.B. L.93 J.D. 55 Winterset Lane
Lenzi, Danielle E. .... '75 '00 C.475 B.S./B.A. L.184 J.D. Legal Dept., Exec. Risk
Libert, Victor E., (AV) '36 '69
C.667 B.Ch.E. L.1009 J.D. [Libert&Assoc.] (See Pat. Sect.)
*PRACTICE AREAS: Intellectual Property; Patents; Trademarks; Copyrights; Trade Secrets.

Libert & Associates, (AV)
3 Mill Pond Lane Powder Forest Business Park, P.O. Box 538, 06070-0538
Telephone: 860-651-9321 Fax: 860-651-5735
Email: libert.i.p.law@snet.net
Victor E. Libert. Associates: Frederick A. Spaeth; Melinda Ann Alden.
Patent, Trademark, Copyright, Intellectual Property and Related Matters.
See Professional Biographies, SIMSBURY, CONNECTICUT

Liegeot, Lisa M., (BV) .... '59 '84 C&L.184 B.A., J.D. 237 Hopmeadow St.
Lipponen, Tarja Marketta ..... '60 '95 C.1086 B.B.A. L.184 J.D. 24 Berkshire Way‡
Long, Michael T., (BV) '42 '67 C.602 B.B.A. L.184 LL.B.
V.P. & Gen. Coun., Ensign-Bickford Industries, Inc.
*RESPONSIBILITIES: Corporate Law; Products Liability.
Main, Philip D., (BV) .... '36 '62 C.67 B.A. L.273 LL.B. [Pease&M.]
Melanson, Andrea M. .... '67 '92 C.321 B.A. L.306 J.D. 110 Hopmeadow St.
Moloney, Kelley '68 '93 C.454 B.A. L.1048 J.D.
(adm. in MA; not adm. in CT) Clms. Atty., Executive Risk

Moroney, John J. '64 '90 C.276 A.B. L.184 J.D.
Mgr., Professional Firms E&O, Executive Risk
O'Brien, Jonathan B. .... '38 '64 C.951 B.A. L.178 LL.B. Westminister Sch.
O'Doherty, Marianne '58 '88 C.770 B.S. L.276 J.D.
(adm. in VA; not adm. in CT) Coun., Hartford Life, Inc.
Pameijer, Huguet .... '46 '95 L.306 J.D. 10 Highwood
Parker, Alan S., (BV) .... '55 '80 C.1044 B.A. L.851 J.D. [Pullman&C.] (⊙Hartford)
*PRACTICE AREAS: Probate and Estate Planning; Tax Law.
Parker, Diane M. ....'64 '91 C&L.846 B.A., J.D. Clms. Atty. & Mgr., Executive Risk
Pease, William, (AV) .... '26 '53 C.311 B.A. L.184 LL.B. [Pease&M.]
Pease & Main, LLC, (AV) .... Mall Way
Penna, Thomas F. .... '71 '96 C.262 B.A. L.306 J.D. Clms. Atty., Executive Risk
Pernerewski, Colleen B. ....'69 '96 C&L.184 B.S., J.D. Atty., Hartford Life, Inc.
Peters, Kelly A. '62 '93 C.882 B.A. L.184 J.D.
Underwriter, Lawyers Professional Liability, Executive Risk
Pexa, E. Joseph, Jr. '45 '69 C.755 B.A. L.436 J.D.
(adm. in MN; not adm. in CT) 200 Hopmeadow St.‡
Phelps, Michele J. .... '70 '95 C.L.1048 B.A., J.D. Clms. Atty., Executive Risk
Piccoli, Marie A. '52 '86 C.184 B.S. L.831 J.D.
Asst. V.P. & Regulatory Affs. Coun., Executive Risk
Pickett, David S. .... '53 '79 C.454 B.A. L.184 J.D. Coun., Hartford Life, Inc.
Pudenz, Brian L. '60 '85 C.190 B.A. L.802 J.D.
(adm. in TX; not adm. in CT) Unit Mgr. - Employment Claims, Chubb Executive Risk

Pullman & Comley, L.L.C., (AV)
(Formerly Pullman, Comley, Bradley & Reeves)
720 Hopmeadow Street, 06070-2225 ⊙
Telephone: 860-651-9348 Fax: 860-651-1431
URL: http://www.pullcom.com
Members of the Firm: Andrew C. Glassman; Alan S. Parker.
General Practice including Administrative, Antitrust, Banking, Bankruptcy and Creditors Rights, Bonds, Business and Commercial, Corporate, Education, Employee Benefits, Environmental, Hospital and Health Care, Labor and Employment, Municipal Finance, Real Estate, Securities, Tax, Trusts and Estates, and Zoning. Energy and Utilities, Litigation in all Courts.
Bridgeport, Connecticut Office: 850 Main Street, P.O. Box 7006, Telephone: 203-330-2000. Telecopier: 203-576-8888.
Hartford, Connecticut Office: 90 State House Square. Telephone: 860-424-4300. Telecopier: 860-424-4370.
New Haven, Connecticut Office: One Century Tower, 265 Church Street. Telephone: 203-773-3006. Telecopier: 203-776-7075.
Southport, Connecticut Office: 200 Pequot Avenue, P.O. Box 510. Telephone: 203-254-5000. Telecopier: 203-254-5070.
Stamford, Connecticut Office: 350 Bedford Street. Telephone: 203-324-5000. Telecopier: 203-363-8659.
See Professional Biographies, SIMSBURY, CONNECTICUT

Querfeld, Kathleen '66 '98 C.788 A.B. L.184 J.D.
Assoc. Coun. Regulatory Affs., Chubb Executive Risk Inc. (Legal Department)
Repasy, Christine Hayer '56 '85
C.197 B.A L.184 J.D. Assoc. Gen. Coun., Hartford Life, Inc.
Ricciuti, Louis A., Jr. '67 '93
C.93 B.A. L.184 J.D. Asst. Coun., Chubb Executive Risk Inc.
Richardson, Scott K. .... '66 '93 C.184 B.A. L.93 J.D. 200 Hopmeadow St.
Robinson, David C. .... '65 '93 C.918 B.A. L.188 J.D. V.P. & Coun., Executive Risk
Rosen, Mark I. '51 '77 C&L.188 B.A., J.D.
(adm. in NY; not adm. in CT) Chf. Legal Offr. & Sr. V.P., Clms., Executive Risk
Roy, William A. .... '66 '94 C.184 B.A. L.306 J.D. Clms. Atty., Executive Risk
Sablak, Laurie J. '68 '95 C.95 A.B. L.306 J.D.
Underwriter, Professional Firm Liab. Coverages, Executive Risk
Salerni, Lisa M. .... '73 '98 C.93 B.A. L.306 J.D. Clms. Atty., Exec. Risk
Schaffrick, Susan B. .... '58 '91 C.93 B.A. L.1048 J.D. Asst. Coun., Hartford Life, Inc.
Scheinfeldt, Jerry K. .... '50 '78 C.31 B.A. L.184 J.D. Coun., Hartford Life, Inc.
Seidenberg, Frederick S. ....'49 '77 C.696 B.A. L.1202 J.D. 412 Bushy Hill Rd.
Sharaf, Adam D. '59 '87 C.67 B.A. L.564 J.D.
Atty., Mgr., Intl. LPL & Sr. Underwriter, Executive Risk
Sholovitz, Arnold C., (BV) .... '48 '73 C&L.184 B.A., J.D. 10 Hampshire Ln.
Singer, Meredith L. ....'72 '97 C.865 B.A. L.306 J.D. Underwriter, Executive Risk
Smith, Patrick C. ....'52 '78 C.184 B.A. L.1048 J.D. Hartford Life Ins. Co.
Snaden, Sandra L. .... '71 '96 C.477 A.B. L.184 J.D. [⊠ Wieselman&B.]
Socha, Mark M. ....'67 '93 C.31 A.B. L.178 J.D. Assoc. Coun., Hartford Life, Inc.
Soler, Leslie T. .... '71 '96 C.855 B.S. L.306 J.D. Asst. Coun., Hartford Life, Inc.
Spaeth, Frederick A. '59 '86 C.184 B.S. L.1029 J.D.
[⊠ Libert&Assoc.] (See Pat. Sect.)
*PRACTICE AREAS: Patents; Trademarks; Copyrights; Intellectual Property.
Spiro, Ellen L. .... '62 '87 C.228 B.A. L.569 J.D. 14 Lincoln Lane‡
Splain, Julianne, (BV) '55 '82 C.454 B.A. L.1358 J.D.
Asst. V.P., Loss Prevention Coun., Executive Risk
Stein, Joshua O. '60 '89 C.976 B.A. L.184 J.D.
Corp. Coun. & Dir., Reins., Executive Risk
Strimaitis, Jonas V. ....'39 '79 C.178 A.B. L.1048 J.D. Combustion Engg., Inc.
Sukert, David A. '65 '91 C.1349 B.A. L.276 J.D.
(adm. in NY; not adm. in CT) 82 Hopmeadow St.
Taft, Diana G. .... '64 '97 C.1033 B.S./B.A. L.1048 J.D. Atty., Hartford Life, Inc.
Tefft, Traci .... '58 '89 C.260 B.S. L.184 J.D. 200 Hopmeadow St.
Terrell, Beth N. .... '62 '87 C&L.184 B.A., J.D. 86 Hopmeadow St.
Thompson, Nichole A. .... '72 '97 C.273 B.A. L.982 J.D. Clms. Atty., Executive Risk
Townsend, Joel Scott '63 '87 C.813 A.B. L.893 J.D.
(adm. in VA; not adm. in CT) Underwriting Mgr., Executive Risk
Tuttle, Heidi J. .... '61 '89 C.518 B.A. L.1048 J.D. 548 Hopmeadow St.
Van Dyck, Louise, (AV) ...... '57 '91 C.951 B.A. L.184 J.D. Clms. Atty., Executive Risk
Vogt, Henry T., (BV) ....'54 '84 C.31 B.A. L.884 J. D. 75 Hickory Hill Rd.
Vumback, Lisa '73 '98 C.93 B.A. L.184 J.D.
Atty., Chubb Executive Risk Inc. (Legal Department)
Walsh, Kevin J. .... '62 '96 C.1030 B.S. L.128 J.D. Clms. Atty., Executive Risk
Welk, Robert F., (BV) .... '45 '71 C&L.184 B.A., J.D. 141 West St.
Wieselman, Jacob, (BV) .... '52 '77 C.477 B.A. L.276 J.D. [Wieselman&B.]
Wieselman & Brady, LLP, (BV) .... 690 Hopmeadow St.
Wise, Robert J. .... '32 '60 C.884 B.S. L.1068 J.D. 3 Vincent Dr.
Wood, Natalie A. .... '67 '98 C.676 B.A. L.1048 J.D. Corp. Atty., Executive Risk
Young, Karen E. .... '56 '83 C.95 A.B. L.228 J.D. 16 Hampden Circle

SOMERS, 8,473, *Tolland Co.*

Davis, Glenn T., (BV) ....'47 '79 C.829 B.S. L.1048 J.D. 11 South Rd.
Devlin, Michael J., (BV) ....'46 '71 C&L.184 B.A., J.D. [Devlin&P.]
Devlin and Peters, (BV) .... 11 South Rd.
Fahey, John B. .... '24 '58 C.871 B.S. L.184 LL.B. 114 Colton Rd.
Johnson, David E., (BV) .... '51 '81 C.321 B.A. L.1048 J.D. 19 Gracie Dr.
Lussier, Robert G. ....'28 '50 C&L.424 LL.B. 36 South Rd.
O'Grady, Thomas S. .... '58 '88 C&L.1048 B.A., J.D. P.O. Box 871

Parks, John H., (BV) ....'54 '80 36 South Rd.
Peters, Robert F., (BV) .... '41 '68 C.94 B.S. L.184 J.D. [Devlin&P.]
Schwebel, Abbot B., (BV) .... '40 '64 C.197 B.S. L.94 J.D. [Schwebel&T.]
Schwebel & Tarpey, P.C., (BV) .... P.O. Box 400
Shannon, J. Donald, (BV) ....'22 '53 C.473 A.B. L.902 LL.B. 48 South Rd.
Tarpey, Kerry A. ....'65 '92 C.321 A.B. L.1048 J.D. [Schwebel&T.]
Tyler, Bruce D., Sr., (BV) ....'43 '72 C.602 B.B.A. L.724 J.D. 48 South Rd.

SOMERSVILLE, —, *Tolland Co.*

Grant, Olin Harold ....'70 '99 C.1236 B.A. L.1048 J.D. P.O. Box 521

SOUTHBURY, 14,156, *New Haven Co.*

Barrett, Beth A. ....'54 '80 C.703 B.A. L.262 J.D. 348 Main St. N.‡
Barry, Robert J., (BV) .... '41 '66 C.264 A.B. L.94 LL.B. [Sturges&M.]
Bower, Kathy S., (BV) .... '63 '88 C.1044 B.A. L.1019 J.D. [Gager&P.] (⊙Bethel)
*PRACTICE AREAS: Personal Injury; Family Law; Litigation.
Brown, Gordon R. '20 '52 C.674 A.B. L.262 LL.B.
(adm. in NY; not adm. in CT) 698B Heritage Village‡
Burkard, Peter H. ....'40 '68 C.309 A.B. L.477 J.D. 9 Union Sq.

Carmody & Torrance LLP, (AV)
900 Main Street South, P.O. Box 410, 06488-0410 ⊙
Telephone: 203-264-7882 Facsimile: 203-264-7847
Email: contactus@carmodylaw.com URL: http://www.carmodylaw.com
Partners: Michael J. Reardon (Also at Waterbury Office); David L. Sfara.
General Practice including Administrative, Alternative Dispute Resolution, Antitrust and Trade Regulation, Arbitration, Banking, Bankruptcy, Bond Finance, Closely Held Business, Commercial Real Estate, Commercial Litigation, Complex Litigation, Construction, Contracts, Corporate, Creditors' Rights, Employment Benefits, Employer Defense, Energy, Environmental, ERISA, Estate Planning, Family Business Successions, Finance, Freedom of Information, Government (State and Municipal Contracts), Health Care, Insurance, Intellectual Property, Patents and Trademarks, Labor and Employment, Land Use, Management Counseling, Medical Malpractice Defense, Municipal, Nonprofit Organizations, Pension, Privatization, Probate, Products Liability, Professional Liability Defense, Profit Sharing, Public-Private Finance, Public Utility, Securities, Tax, Toxic Torts, Zoning Law. General Civil, Criminal and Appellate Practice in all Courts.
Waterbury, Connecticut Office: 50 Leavenworth Street. P.O. Box 1110, 06721-1110. Telephone: 203-573-1200. Facsimile: 203-575-2600.
New Haven, Connecticut Office: 195 Church Street, P.O. Box 1950, 06509-1950. Telephone: 203-777-5501. Facsimile: 203-784-3199.
See Professional Biographies, SOUTHBURY, CONNECTICUT

Cartoceti, Robert J., (BV) .... '57 '82 C.184 B.A. L.1029 J.D. 2 Pomperaug Off. Park
Carvalko, Joseph R., Jr., (BV) '42 '80
C.1030 B.S.E.E. L.1252 J.D. 10 Main Street, South (Pat.) (⊙Bridgewater)
Caulfield, Michele A., (CV) ....'62 '87 C.93 A.B. L.184 J.D. [Thornton&C.]
Clough, David A., (BV) ....'55 '80 C.401 B.A. L.285 J.D. 304 Pomperaug Off. Park
Coulon, Jos. R. ....'21 '53 C.569 B.S. L.262 LL.B. 702A Heritage Village
Dipentima, Christian Lawrence '71 '97 C.93 B.A. L.1252 J.D.
[⊠ Gager&P.] (⊙Bethel)
*PRACTICE AREAS: Insurance Defense (45%); Plaintiffs Personal Injury (45%); Workers Compensation (5%); Family Law (3%); Labor and Employment (2%).
Driscoll, James C., Jr., (BV) ....'21 '49 C.321 A.B. L.262 LL.B. [Driscoll,T.F.O.&D.]
Driscoll, Talarico, Frizzell, Olivo & Driscoll, (AV)
Three Pomperaug Office Park, Suite 203 (⊙Bethel, Danbury)
Engelman, Lawrence H., (AV) .... '54 '80 C.228 B.A. L.472 J.D. [Engelman&E.]
*PRACTICE AREAS: Estate Planning; Wills; Trust Law; Probate; Title XIX.

Engelman & Engelman, (AV)
800 Main Street South Suite 122, 06488
Telephone: 203-264-1441 Fax: 203-264-1443
URL: http://www.lawyers.com/engelman&engelman
Morton H. Engelman (1924-1998); Lawrence H. Engelman; Michael R. Pohl.
Elder Law, Estate Planning, Probate, Taxation, Wills, Trusts, Title XIX and Medicaid Hearings.
See Professional Biographies, SOUTHBURY, CONNECTICUT

Federer, Wendy R. ....'55 '92 C.273 B.A. L.1029 J.D. [Kernan&H.] ⊙

Gager & Peterson, LLP, (AV)
325 Main Street South, 06488 ⊙
Telephone: 203-262-6600 Telecopier: 203-262-6780
Kathy S. Bower; Thomas M. Rickart;—Christian Lawrence Dipentima.
General Practice. Corporate Law, Banks and Banking, Securities, Administrative, Litigation in all Courts, Insurance, Estate Planning, Probate, Real Estate, Commercial Transactions, Taxation, Patents, Trademarks, Copyrights, Consumer, Computers and Software, Family Law, Environmental Law, Employment Law, Personal Injury.
Waterbury, Connecticut Office: One Exchange Place, P.O. Box 2480. Telephone: 203-597-5100. Telecopier: 203-757-7888.
Bethel, Connecticut Office: 2 Stony Hill Road. Telephone: 203-207-5400. Telecopier: 203-207-5407.
Litchfield, Connecticut Office: 782 Bantam Road. Telephone: 860-567-0828. Telecopier: 860-567-5844.
Sharon, Connecticut Office: 25 West Main Street, P.O. Box 158. Telephone: 860-364-5531. Telecopier: 860-364-5805.
See Professional Biographies, SOUTHBURY, CONNECTICUT

Giardina, Michael A. ....'71 '97 C.555 B.S. L.1252 J.D. [⊠ Kernan&H.]
Guttman, Lou .... '38 '88 C.999 B.S. L.1029 J.D. 157 Laurelwood Ln.
Hager, Lawrence '43 '74 C.1133 B.S. L.1009 J.D.
(adm. in NY; not adm. in CT; Pat.) Surrey Lane
Healey, James R., (AV) .... '29 '55 C.597 B.S. L.188 J.D. [Secor,C.&M.]
*PRACTICE AREAS: Real Estate; Estate Planning; Estate Administration.
Heitler, George '15 '38 C&L.178 B.S., J.D.
(adm. in NY; not adm. in CT) 851A Heritage Village‡
Henry, Charles W., (AV) .... '49 '75 C.393 B.A. L.818 J.D. [Kernan&H.] ⊙
Kernan & Henry, (AV) ....9 Heritage Road (⊙Waterbury)
Liedlich, Nancy C., (BV) .... '35 '76 C.604 B.A. L.184 J.D. Two Pomperaug Off. Park
Longstreth, Carolyn K. ....'48 '84 C.813 B.A. L.184 J.D. 846 Southford Rd.
McGann, Curtis, (BV) ....'33 '60 C&L.188 A.B., J.D. [Sturges&M.]
O'Neill, Arthur J. ....'52 '78 C.184 B.A. L.1292 J.D. State Repr.
Pohl, Michael R. .... '42 '86 C.1323 B.A. L.692 J.D. [Engelman&E.]
*PRACTICE AREAS: Estate Planning; Wills; Trust Law; Probate; Title XIX.
Reardon, Michael J., (BV) '56 '84 C.183 B.A. L.1029 J.D.
[Carmody&T.] (⊙Waterbury)
*PRACTICE AREAS: Estate Planning; Business Succession; Trust Administration; Taxation; Probate.
Reinhardt, Steven .... '55 '91 C.865 B.S.E.E. L.184 J.D. 160 Woods Way Dr.
Rickart, Thomas M., (BV) .... '53 '81 C.976 B.A. L.93 J.D. [Gager&P.] (⊙Bethel)
*PRACTICE AREAS: Real Estate Law; Environmental Law; Commercial Lending.
Rink, Harold H. '16 '53 C&L.724 B.B.A., LL.B.
(adm. in NY; not adm. in CT) 18B Heritage Village‡
Rotatori, Peter, III, (BV) .... '63 '88 C.930 B.A. L.896 J.D. [Rotatori] ⊙
Rotatori, Peter, Jr., (BV) ....'35 '62 C.1030 B.S. L.262 LL.B. [Rotatori] ⊙
Rotatori Law Firm, The, (BV) .... 2 Pomperaug Office Park, Suite 107 (⊙Naugatuck)
Rothstein, Nathaniel '11 '34 C&L.569 J.D.
(adm. in NY; not adm. in CT) 754 A Heritage Village‡

Secor, Cassidy & McPartland, P.C., (AV) BB
Successors to Bronson, Lewis, Upson & Secor; Lewis, Hart, Upson & Secor; Upson, Secor, Greene & Cassidy and Upson, Secor, Cassidy & McPartland, P.C.
900 Main Street South, 06488 ⊙
Telephone: 203-264-8223 Fax: 203-264-6730
Email: scm@ctlawyers.com URL: http://www.ctlawyers.com
James R. Healey (Resident).
General Practice. Probate, Corporation, Negligence, Real Estate, Land Use, Banking, Municipal, Commercial and Taxation Law. Criminal and Civil Trials in all Courts.
Attorneys for: The Mattatuck Museum; American Republican, Inc.; Hubbard-Hall, Inc.; The Siemon Co.; Engineered Sinterings and Plastics, Inc.; Boutin Industries; County Line Buick-Nissan, Inc.; Taft School.
Waterbury, Connecticut Office: 41 Church Street, P.O. Box 2818. Telephone: 203-757-9261. Fax: 203-756-5762.
See Professional Biographies, SOUTHBURY, CONNECTICUT

Sfara, David L., (AV) ...... '52 '77 C.674 A.B. L.893 J.D. [Carmody&T.] (⊙Waterbury)
*PRACTICE AREAS: Estate Planning; Trust Administration; Probate; Elder Law.
Smith, George E. R. '12 '39 C.401 B.S. L.1009 LL.B.
(adm. in NY; not adm. in CT) 166A Heritage Village‡
Sturges & Mathes, (BV) .... Heritage Office Bldg. (⊙Woodbury)
Swaniger, Peri H. .... '56 '84 C.1156 B.A. L.1029 J.D. 256 Beecher Dr.
Thornton, Kevin P., (BV) .... '50 '79 C.128 B.A. L.184 J.D. [Thornton&C.]
Thornton & Caulfield, (BV) .... 88 Main St.
Uskevich, Robert J., (BV) ......'43 '67 C.861 B.B.A. L.94 J.D. Two Pomperaug Off. Park
Welch, Sheila J. .... '— '77 C.33 B.A. L.588 J.D. 555-B Heritage Village
Whitehead, Lewis R., Jr., (BV) '40 '65 C.31 B.A. L.184 LL.B.
Two Pomperaug Off. Park

SOUTH GLASTONBURY, —, *Hartford Co.*

Croce, R. Richard, (BV) ....'62 '90 C.25 B.A. L.201 J.D. [Ⓐ Purtill,P.&P.]
Pfeffer, Kathleen Purtill, (BV) .... '59 '86 C.945 B.A. L.1029 J.D. [Purtill,P.&P.]
Purtill, George Morrow, (BV) ....'52 '84 C.945 B.B.A. L.184 J.D. [Purtill,P.&P.]
Purtill, Sharon Holland, (BV) ....'58 '83 C.105 B.A. L.184 J.D. [Purtill,P.&P.]
Purtill, Purtill & Pfeffer, (BV) ....P.O. Box 50
Schroth, Peter W. '46 '69 C.1100 A.B. L.145 J.D.
Vice President & General Counsel, Equator U.S.A. Incorporated
Shettle, Kenneth B. ....'53 '79 C.184 B.A. L.192 J.D. 28 Copley Road
Summit, Steven C. ....'50 '76 C.145 B.A. L.285 J.D. 269 Hopewell Rd.

SOUTHINGTON, 36,879, *Hartford Co.*

Bornstein, Shari D., (BV) ....'62 '88 C.818 B.S. L.1048 J.D. [Maccariello&B.]
Coburn, Hayward H., (AVⓉ) '07 '39 C.95 A.B.
(adm. in PA; not adm. in CT) 26 Village Rd.‡
Crispino, Joseph R., (BV) ....'49 '74 C.276 A.B. L.128 J.D. [Kelley,C.&K.]
Dunham, John J., (BV) ....'39 '66 C.454 B.A. L.306 J.D. 97 N. Main St.
Elliott, Stanek, Mazzaccaro & Sciota, (BV) .... 98 Main St.
Forgione, Henry E., II, (BV) .... '36 '62 C.262 B.S. L.128 J.D. [Foti&F.]
Foti, Joseph D., Jr., (BV) .... '60 '85 C.184 B.S. L.1048 J.D. [Foti&F.]
Foti & Forgione, P.C., (BV) ....P.O. Box 935
Frank, Ira L. '51 '78 C.994 B.A. L.724 J.D.
(adm. in NY; not adm. in CT) 81 Tallwood Dr.
Gallagher, Bridget ....'69 '94 L.818 J.D. 133 Main St.
Garbacik, Roman F., (BV) ....'46 '73 C&L.184 B.A., J.D. P.O. Box 62
Garver, Scott A., (CV) .... '50 '75 C.103 B.A. L.276 J.D. 315 Little Fawn Rd.
Gworek, Gary M., (BV) .... '57 '82 C.999 B.A. L.1048 J.D. [Sokolowski&G.]
Izzo, Robert A., (BV) ....'52 '77 C.951 B.A. L.93 J.D. [Izzo&M.]
Izzo & McLaughlin, L.L.C., (BV) .... 168 Main St.
Kania, John F., (BV) ....'53 '80 C.184 B.A. L.818 J.D. [Kelley,C.&K.]
Kelley, David P., (BV) ....'41 '66 C.860 B.A. L.184 J.D. [Kelley,C.&K.]
Kelley, Crispino & Kania, (BV) ....25 Berlin Ave.
Krezel, Richard M., (BV) ....'44 '69 C.855 B.S. L.818 J.D. 100 Queen St.
Maccariello & Bornstein, (BV) .... 37 N. Main St.
Mazzaccaro, Joseph A., (BV) ....'54 '79 C.184 B.A. L.1202 J.D. [Elliott,S.M.&S.]
Meccariello, Bryan F., (BV) ....'63 '89 C.999 B.S. L.1048 J.D. [Maccariello&B.]
Murray, William P. ....'35 '68 C.999 A.B. L.184 LL.B. Supr. Ct. J.
Nugent, John T. ....'46 '81 C.321 A.B. L.602 J.D. U.S. Mag.
Pellett, Marilyn Clark .... '54 '83 C.1029 B.S. L.990 J.D. 197 E. Mt. Dr.
Rosenblatt, Edward M., (BV) ....'52 '81 C.1044 B.A. L.184 J.D. [Rosenblatt&S.]
*PRACTICE AREAS: Real Estate; Commercial Lending; Asset Recovery Law; Family Law.

Rosenblatt & Sheffy, L.L.P., (BV)
35 North Main Street, 06489
Telephone: 860-620-9460 Fax: 860-620-9348
Email: ed@randslaw.com URL: http://www.randslaw.com
Edward M. Rosenblatt; A. Alan Sheffy.
General Practice, Real Estate, Insurance Defense, Municipal Law, Personal Injury, Litigation, Commercial Lending, Asset Recovery Law, Construction Law, Family law, Employment Law, Estate Planning, Trials in State and Federal Courts.
See Professional Biographies, SOUTHINGTON, CONNECTICUT

Sciota, Mark J., (BV) ....'63 '88 C.446 B.S.Ed. L.1029 J.D. [Elliott,S.M.&S.]
Sheffy, A. Alan, (BV) ....'63 '88 C.400 B.S. L.1048 J.D. [Rosenblatt&S.]
*PRACTICE AREAS: Insurance Defense; Personal Injury; Construction Law; Trials in State and Federal Courts.
Sokolowski, Carl J., (BV) ....'29 '63 C&L.976 B.A., LL.B. [Sokolowski&G.]
Sokolowski & Gworek, (BV) .... 132 Main St.
Stanek, Robert S., (BV) .... '48 '73 C.884 B.S. L.893 J.D. [Elliott,S.M.&S.]

SOUTH KENT, —, *Litchfield Co.*

Crawford-Kelly, Diane M. '58 '89 C.629 B.S. L.94 J.D.
(adm. in MA; not adm. in CT) 40 Bull's Bridge Rd.

SOUTHPORT, —, *Fairfield Co.*

Anderson, Derby Ferris, (BV) '42 '89 C.901 B.A. L.1029 J.D.
75 Station Street, P.O. Box 484, 06490
Telephone: 203-259-4043 Fax: 203-259-2691
Personal Injury, Estates, Trusts, Real Estate, General Civil Trial Practice in all State and Federal Courts.

Baldasare, Suzanne E., (AV) ....'56 '81 C.1030 B.A. L.818 J.D. [Pepe&H.]
*PRACTICE AREAS: Real Estate Finance; Loan Workouts; Asset Based Lending.
Baldwin, Raymond E., Jr., (BV) '27 '56
C.951 B.A. L.976 LL.B. [Pullman&C.] (⊙Bridgeport)
*PRACTICE AREAS: Public Finance Law; Bond Finance; Estates and Trusts; Real Estate.
Basciano, Jennifer A. ....'75 '00 C.401 B.A. L.306 J.D. [Brody,W.&O.]
*PRACTICE AREAS: Trusts and Estates.
Bisset, Sandra W. ....'53 '79 C.188 B.S. L.178 J.D. 411 Pequot Ave.
Blum, Leonard C., (AV) .... '41 '66 C.659 B.S. L.184 J.D. [Ⓒ Kleban&S.]
*PRACTICE AREAS: Real Estate Law; Zoning Law; Land Use; Condominium Law.

Breck, Deborah S., (BV) '53 '83
C.1102 B.A. L.184 J.D. [Pullman&C.] (⊙Bridgeport, Stamford)
*PRACTICE AREAS: Estates and Trusts; Elder Law; Trust and Probate Litigation.
Britt, William J., (AV) .... '48 '73 C.1030 B.A. L.180 J.D. [Brody,W.&O.]
*PRACTICE AREAS: Corporate Law; Mergers and Acquisitions; Estate Planning; Trusts and Estates; Real Estate.
Brody, Seth O. L., (AV) ....'27 '55 C&L.976 B.A., LL.B. [Brody,W.&O.]
*PRACTICE AREAS: Corporate Law; Mergers and Acquisitions; Estate Planning; Trusts and Estates; Entertainment Law.

Brody, Wilkinson and Ober, P.C., (AV) BB
2507 Post Road, 06490
Telephone: 203-319-7100 Fax: 203-254-1772
URL: http://www.brodywilk.com
Seth O. L. Brody; Peter Wilkinson; Frank Fritz Ober; S. Giles Payne; James E. Rice; William J. Britt; Barbara S. Miller; Ronald B. Noren; Robert L. Teicher; Peter T. Mott; Thomas J. Walsh, Jr.; Diane F. Martucci; Seth L. Cooper; Douglas R. Brown; William A. Harrison; Jennifer A. Basciano; Charles S. Brody (1894-1976). Of Counsel: Bruce E. Dillingham; Roy W. Moore, III.
General Civil Practice, Corporation, Probate, Estate Planning, Trusts and Estates, Real Estate, Employment, Commercial, Environmental, Creditors Rights, Tax, Pension, Profit Sharing, Entertainment Law, Banking, General Business, Municipal, Freedom of Information Matters, Telecommunications, Public Utilities, Commercial Litigation.
See Professional Biographies, SOUTHPORT, CONNECTICUT

Brown, Douglas R. .... '65 '94 C.228 B.A. L.904 J.D. [Brody,W.&O.]
*PRACTICE AREAS: Probate; Trusts and Estates; Probate Litigation; Trust Litigation; Zoning.
Brucker, Andrew G., (AV) '43 '67 C.696 A.B. L.976 LL.B.
416 Westford Dr. (⊙Norwalk)
Carey, Mark P. ....'67 '97 C.823 B.A. L.201 J.D. 71 Old Post Road, Suite 1
Carles, JennyAnn ....'69 '97 C.569 B.A. L.564 J.D. [Ⓐ Kleban&S.]
*PRACTICE AREAS: Corporate Law; Bankruptcy; Debtor and Creditor Rights.
Caulfield, Katherine E. .... '66 '91 C.93 B.S. L.306 J.D. [Ⓐ Pullman&C.]
*PRACTICE AREAS: Estate and Gift Planning; Estate and Trust Administration; Elder Law.
Cifelli, Armand, (AV) ....'24 '51 C.277 L.273 J.D. 181 Old Post Road (Pat.)
Cobb, Jeffrey B., (AVⓉ) '45 '69 C.309 A.B. L.569 J.D.
(adm. in NY; not adm. in CT) [Cobb&E.]
*PRACTICE AREAS: Securities; Corporate Law; Venture Capital; Public Offerings; Investments.

Cobb & Eisenberg LLC, (AVⓉ)
2600 Post Road, 06490
Telephone: 203-254-0000 Fax: 203-254-6060 URL: http://www.cobbeisenberg.com
Email: info@cobbeisenberg.com URL: http://www.lawyers.com/cobbeisenberg
Jeffrey B. Cobb (Not admitted in CT); Matthew S. Eisenberg.
Securities, Corporate Law, Venture Capital, Public Offerings, Domestic and Offshore Hedge Funds and other investment vehicles, Investment Adviser Regulation; Broker-Dealer Regulation.
See Professional Biographies, SOUTHPORT, CONNECTICUT

Cooper, Seth L., (BV) .... '62 '91 C.692 B.A. L.1202 J.D. [Brody,W.&O.]
*PRACTICE AREAS: Commercial Law; Business Law; Debtor and Creditor; Real Estate.
Cox, Jennifer L. ....'68 '93 C&L.184 B.A., J.D. [Ⓒ Pepe&H.]
Curran, Patricia Ann ....'67 '96 C.788 B.A. L.1252 J.D. 126 Arbor Ter.
Daly, Deirdre M., (AVⓉ) .... '59 '85 C.197 B.A. L.276 J.D. [Daly&P.]
*PRACTICE AREAS: Civil Litigation; Criminal Litigation.

Daly & Pavlis, LLC, (AV)
107 John Street, 06490
Telephone: 203-255-6700 Fax: 203-255-1953
Email: info@dalypavlis.com URL: http://www.dalypavlis.com
Alfred U. Pavlis; Deirdre M. Daly.
Civil and Criminal Litigation, Corporate, Internal Investigations and Monitoring.
See Professional Biographies, SOUTHPORT, CONNECTICUT

Danaher, Robert L., (BV) '46 '81 C.911 B.A. L.1065 J.D.
Asst. Gen. Coun., Sturm, Ruger & Company, Inc.
Dardani, Thomas E., (BV) ....'43 '68 C.918 B.A. L.880 J.D. [Kleban&S.]
*PRACTICE AREAS: Commercial Law; Corporation Law; Personal Injury Law.
Dawson, Jonathan T. '44 '75 C.674 A.B. L.262 J.D.
Chmn. of the Bd., Dawson-Samberg Capital Mgmt.
Dewan, Maureen, (BV) ....'47 '73 C.705 B.A. L.818 J.D. [Ⓐ Kleban&S.]
*PRACTICE AREAS: Medical Malpractice.
Dillingham, Bruce E., (AV) ....'25 '57 C.165 A.B. L.976 LL.B. [Ⓒ Brody,W.&O.]
DiPreta, Richard S. ....'68 '98 C.855 B.A. L.184 J.D. [Ⓐ Pullman&C.]
*PRACTICE AREAS: Estate Administration; Estate Planning; Probate.
Donahue, Stephen F., (BV) ....'45 '73 C.321 A.B. L.187 J.D. [Kleban&S.]
*PRACTICE AREAS: Civil; Personal Injury; Health Service Law; Commercial Litigation.
Eisenberg, Matthew S. .... '65 '90 C.1349 B.A. L.569 J.D. [Cobb&E.]
*PRACTICE AREAS: Securities; Corporate Law; Venture Capital; Public Offerings; Investments.
Elliot, Jonathan D., (BV) ....'55 '80 C.976 B.A. L.477 J.D. [Kleban&S.]
*PRACTICE AREAS: Civil Litigation; Family Law; Consumer Law; Collections.
Fattibene, Arthur T. .... '23 '52 C.610 B.S. L.276 J.D. [Fattibene&F.] (See Pat. Sect.)
*PRACTICE AREAS: Intellectual Property; Patent; Trademark; Copyright.
Fattibene, Paul A. ....'57 '83 C.882 B.S. L.1029 J.D. [Fattibene&F.] (See Pat. Sect.)
*PRACTICE AREAS: Patent; Trademark; Copyright; Intellectual Property.

Fattibene & Fattibene
2480 Post Road, 06490
Telephone: 203-255-4400 Fax: 203-259-0033
URL: http://www.fattibene.com
Arthur T. Fattibene; Paul A. Fattibene.
Patent, Trademark, Copyright and other Intellectual Property Law.
See Professional Biographies, SOUTHPORT, CONNECTICUT

Fiano, Sabato P. ....'72 '97 C.1030 B.A. L.306 J.D. [Ⓐ Kleban&S.]
*PRACTICE AREAS: Civil Litigation.
Fishman, Mark I., (AV) ....'45 '70 C&L.309 A.B., J.D. [Pepe&H.] ⊙
*PRACTICE AREAS: Bankruptcy Law; Commercial Litigation.
Fitzmaurice, Therese A. ....'61 '89 C.562 B.A. L.1029 J.D. [Ⓒ Kleban&S.]
*PRACTICE AREAS: Employment Law; Employment and Business Litigation.
Flaherty, James J., Jr. ....'60 '95 C.1030 B.S. L.184 J.D. [Ⓐ Pepe&H.]
Galuppo, Christopher J. ....'67 '93 C&L.472 B.B.A., J.D. [Ⓐ Kleban&S.]
*PRACTICE AREAS: Federal Taxation; Estate Planning; State and Local Taxation; Business.
Gladstone, Schwartz, Blum, Woods, L.L.C. .... 1087 Broad St.
Graham, James C., (AV) ....'55 '80 C.976 B.A. L.893 J.D. [Pepe&H.] (⊙Hartford)
*PRACTICE AREAS: Bankruptcy; Litigation; Commercial Law; Legal Ethics and Professional Responsibility; Debtor and Creditor.
Grozinger, Stephan B. ....'69 '95 C.025 B.A. L.184 J.D. [Ⓐ Pepe&H.]
Hamlin, Julie Meck '50 '77 C.309 B.A. L.94 J.D.
(adm. in MA; not adm. in CT) P.O. Box 506‡
Harrison, William A. ....'68 '95 C.893 B.A. L.184 J.D. [Brody,W.&O.]
*PRACTICE AREAS: Real Estate; Corporate Law; Commercial Lending; Entertainment Law.
Hawley, James M., (BV) ....'41 '67 C.103 A.B. L.276 J.D. 2507 Post Rd.
Kleban, Albert J., (AV) ....'31 '56 C&L.184 B.A., J.D. [Kleban&S.]
*PRACTICE AREAS: Public Utilities Law; Commercial Real Estate Law; Corporation Law.

Kleban & Samor, P.C., (AV)
2425 Post Road, P.O. Box 763, 06490
Telephone: 203-255-4646 Fax: 203-259-9617
Email: info@kleban-samor.com URL: http://www.kleban-samor.com
(This Listing Continued)

Kleban & Samor, P.C. (Continued)

Jerome Goldman (1936-1991); Albert J. Kleban; Allan J. Rosen; Alexander W. Samor; Thomas E. Minogue, Jr.; Henry A. Perles; Thomas E. Dardani; Stephen J. Saft; Brian T. Silvestro; Stephen F. Donahue; Jonathan D. Elliot; Theodore R. Tyma; David M. Lehn. Of Counsel: Elliot I. Miller; Leonard C. Blum; Therese A. Fitzmaurice; John J. Novak, Jr.;—Sabato P. Fiano; JennyAnn Carles; Maureen Dewan; Janice M. McGrath; Christopher J. Galuppo.
General Practice. Corporation, Federal, State and Foreign Taxation, Relocation, Residential and Commercial Real Estate, Civil Litigation in Federal and State Courts. Negligence, Estate Planning, Probate, Pension and Profit Sharing, Foreclosure, Banking, Regulatory and Financing, Securities, Zoning, Workers Compensation and Public Utilities Law.
Reference: People's Bank.
New York, New York Office: 900 Third Avenue, 13th Floor, 10022. Telephone: 212-826-6755. Fax: 212-371-1084.

See Professional Biographies, SOUTHPORT, CONNECTICUT

Lehn, David M., (BV) .... '56 '82 C.1030 B.S. L.276 J.D. [Kleban&S.]
*PRACTICE AREAS: Taxation; Estates and Trusts; Probate; Business and Estate Planning.
Lennon, Kevin J. '70 '97 C.658 B.A. L.982 J.D.
(adm. in NY; not adm. in CT) [🄰 Tisdale&L.] ⊙
Lennon, Patrick F. .... '65 '92 C.658 B.S. L.1029 J.D. [Tisdale&L.] ⊙
Lennon, Tracy Wheeler .... '63 '92 C.95 B.A. L.1029 J.D. [🄰 Pullman&C.]
*PRACTICE AREAS: Estate Planning; Estate Administration; Nonprofit Organizations Law.
Lovejoy, Frederick A. .... '53 '84 C.1030 B.A. L.879 J.D. [Lovejoy&Assoc.]
Lovejoy & Associates .... 3695 Post Rd.
Lunin, Arthur A. .... '08 '33 L.1009 LL.B. [🄲 Gladstone,S.B.W.]
Maclay, David S., (AV) .... '20 '48 C.951 B.A. L.976 LL.B. 2507 Post Rd.
Martini, Joseph W. '60 '86 C.282 B.A. L.1009 J.D.
(adm. in NY; not adm. in CT) [Pepe&H.]
*PRACTICE AREAS: Complex Civil Litigation; White Collar Crime.
Martucci, Diane F. .... '51 '84 C.696 B.A. L.262 J.D. [Brody,W.&O.]
*PRACTICE AREAS: Employee Benefits; ERISA; Taxation; Trusts and Estates.
Mayhew, Kristin B. .... '70 '95 C.390 B.A. L.1017 J.D. [🄰 Pepe&H.]
McGrath, Janice M. .... '57 '83 C.1030 B.S. L.276 J.D. [🄰 Kleban&S.]
*PRACTICE AREAS: Taxation; Estate Planning; Trusts and Estates.
McGrath, Jennifer T. .... '71 '98 C.184 B.A. L.306 J.D. [🄰 Pullman&C.]
*PRACTICE AREAS: Estate and Gift Planning; Estate and Trust Administration.
McNamara, Richard J. .... '22 '50 C&L.309 A.B., LL.B. P.O. Box 1027‡
Miller, Barbara S., (BV) .... '50 '77 C.976 B.A. L.184 J.D. [Brody,W.&O.]
*PRACTICE AREAS: Environmental Law; Employment Law; Commercial Litigation; Probate Litigation.
Miller, Elliot I. .... '34 '58 C.860 B.A. L.178 LL.B. [🄲 Kleban&S.]
*PRACTICE AREAS: Tax Law; Business Related Transactions; Work-outs; Complex Litigation.
Minahan, Daniel F. .... '29 '64 C.602 A.B. L.306 J.D. P.O. Box 173
Minogue, Thomas E., Jr., (BV) .... '39 '66 C.276 B.A. L.184 LL.B. [Kleban&S.]
*PRACTICE AREAS: Civil Litigation; Criminal Litigation.
Moore, Roy W., III, (BV) .... '41 '66 C.309 B.A. L.228 LL.B. [🄲 Brody,W.&O.]
Mott, Peter T., (AV) .... '56 '83 C.855 B.A. L.184 J.D. [Brody,W.&O.]
*PRACTICE AREAS: Probate Law; Trusts; Tax Law.
Murphy, Charles E. .... '71 '97 C.207 B.A. L.823 J.D. [🄰 Tisdale&L.] ⊙
Nagy, Andre L., (BV) .... '31 '58 C.276 B.S. L.262 J.D. P.O. Box 576

Neubert, Pepe & Monteith, P.C., (AV)
30 Jelliff Lane, 06490 ⊙
Telephone: 203-254-9332
Judy K. Weinstein.
General Civil and Appellate Practice before State and Federal Courts. Commercial and Banking Litigation, Product Liability, Hospital Liability, Medical Malpractice, Lawyer Malpractice, Design Professional Malpractice, Employment Discrimination and Wrongful Discharge, Health Care Law, Bankruptcy, Creditor's Rights, Real Estate, Corporations, Business, Banking, Trials and Appeals.
New Haven, Connecticut Office: 195 Church Street, 13th Floor, 06510-2026. Telephone: 203-821-2009. Fax: 821-203-821-2009.

See Professional Biographies, SOUTHPORT, CONNECTICUT

Noren, Ronald B., (AV) .... '53 '78 C.860 B.A. L.818 J.D. [Brody,W.&O.]
*PRACTICE AREAS: Probate; Trust Law; Estate Planning.
Novak, John J., Jr. ....'47 '72 C.1030 B.A. L.178 J.D. [🄲 Kleban&S.]
*PRACTICE AREAS: Corporate; Securities; Mergers and Acquisitions; Commercial Law.
Ober, Frank Fritz, (AV) .... '37 '62 C.976 A.B. L.145 J.D. [Brody,W.&O.]
*PRACTICE AREAS: Real Estate; Debtor and Creditor; Contracts; Employment Law; Entertainment Law.
O'Connell, Philip R. .... '28 '56 C.433 B.A. L.178 LL.B. 40 Southport Woods Dr.
Pavlis, Alfred U., (AV) .... '58 '83 C.659 B.A. L.893 J.D. [Daly&P.]
*PRACTICE AREAS: Civil Litigation; Criminal Litigation.
Payne, S. Giles, (BV) .... '41 '66 C.976 B.A. L.659 LL.B. [Brody,W.&O.]
*PRACTICE AREAS: Estate Planning; Probate; Corporate Law; Real Estate; Entertainment Law.

Pepe & Hazard LLP, (AV)
30 Jelliff Lane, 06490-1436 ⊙
Telephone: 203-319-4000 FAX: 203-259-0251
URL: http://www.pepehazard.com
Members of Firm: Suzanne E. Baldasare; Mark I. Fishman; James C. Graham; Joseph W. Martini (Not admitted in CT); Harold James Pickerstein; Reed D. Rubinstein. Associates: James J. Flaherty, Jr.; Stephan B. Grozinger; Kristin B. Mayhew. Counsel: Jennifer L. Cox.
Commercial, Construction, Corporations, Taxation, Finance and Real Estate, Commercial and Asset Based Finance, Environmental Health/Safety, Fidelity and Surety, Securities, Labor/Employment and Education, Municipal, Administrative, Health Care, Intellectual Property, Patent, International Trade, Estate Planning, Probate, White Collar Crime, and Bankruptcy. Trials in all Courts.
Hartford, Connecticut Office: Goodwin Square, 06103-4302. Telephone: 860-522-5175. Fax: 860-522-2796.
Boston, Massachusetts Office: 150 Federal Street, 02110-1745. Telephone: 617-695-9090. Fax: 617-695-9255.

See Professional Biographies, SOUTHPORT, CONNECTICUT

Perles, Henry A., (BV) .... '42 '67 C.31 B.A. L.262 LL.B. [Kleban&S.]
*PRACTICE AREAS: Commercial Real Estate Law; Family Litigation; Residential Real Estate Law.
Pickerstein, Harold James, (AV) .... '46 '70 C.659 A.B. L.94 J.D. [Pepe&H.]
*PRACTICE AREAS: Civil Litigation; Criminal Litigation.

Pullman & Comley, L.L.C., (AV)
(Formerly Pullman, Comley, Bradley & Reeves)
200 Pequot Avenue, P.O. Box 510, 06490-0510 ⊙
Telephone: 203-254-5000 Telecopier: 203-254-5070
URL: http://www.pullcom.com
John S. Pullman (1871-1943); Arthur M. Comley (1883-1969); J. Kenneth Bradley (1903-1969); William Reeves (1906-1967). Members of Firm: Raymond E. Baldwin, Jr.; Deborah S. Breck; James B. Stewart. Associates: Katherine E. Caulfield; Richard S. DiPreta; Tracy Wheeler Lennon; Jennifer T. McGrath.
General Practice including Administrative, Antitrust, Banking, Bankruptcy and Creditors Rights, Bonds, Business and Commercial, Corporate, Education, Employee Benefits, Environmental, Hospital and Health Care, Labor and Employment, Municipal Finance, Real Estate, Securities, Tax, Trusts and Estates, and Zoning. Energy and Utilities, Litigation in all Courts.
Bridgeport, Connecticut Office: 850 Main Street. Telephone: 203-330-2000. Telecopier: 203-576-8888.
Hartford, Connecticut Office: 90 State House Square. Telephone: 860-424-4300. Telecopier: 860-424-4370.
New Haven, Connecticut Office: One Century Tower, 265 Church Street. Telephone: 203-773-3006. Telecopier: 203-776-7075.
Simsbury, Connecticut Office: 720 Hopmeadow Street. Telephone: 860-651-9348. Fax: 860-651-1431.
Stamford, Connecticut Office: 350 Bedford Street. Telephone: 203-324-5000. Telecopier: 203-363-8659.

See Professional Biographies, SOUTHPORT, CONNECTICUT

Rice, James E., (BV) .... '43 '69 C.262 B.S. L.477 J.D. [Brody,W.&O.]
*PRACTICE AREAS: Administrative Law; Public Utilities; Telecommunications Law; Commercial and Banking Law.
Rooney, Bethel Ann .... '41 '76 C.454 B.A. L.588 J.D. 411 Pequot Ave.
Rosen, Allan J., (BV) .... '36 '61 C.659 B.A. L.184 LL.B. [Kleban&S.]
*PRACTICE AREAS: Banking Law; Regulatory Law; Financing Law; Commercial Law; Real Estate Law.
Rubinstein, Reed D., (BV) .... '60 '85 C&L.477 A.B., J.D. [Pepe&H.] (⊙Hartford)
*PRACTICE AREAS: Environmental Liability; Real Estate Finance; Land Use and Zoning.
Saft, Stephen J., (BV) .... '44 '70 C.690 B.S. L.1009 J.D. [Kleban&S.]
*PRACTICE AREAS: Taxation Law; Estate Planning Law; Corporation Law.
Samor, Alexander W., (BV) .... '39 '64 C.1030 A.B. L.184 LL.B. [Kleban&S.]
*PRACTICE AREAS: Corporation Law; Securities Law.
Sanetti, Stephen L., (AV) '49 '75 C.885 B.A. L.902 J.D.
Vice President, General Counsel, Sturm, Ruger & Company, Inc.
Schneider, Paul Douglas .... '49 '92 C.569 B.A. L.262 J.D. P.O. Box 451
Schwartz, Alexander H. .... '57 '83 C.188 A.B. L.184 J.D. 3695 Post Road
Seeley, W. Parker, Jr., (AV) .... '37 '64 C.976 B.A. L.893 LL.B. [Seeley&B.]
Seeley & Berglass, (AV) .... 3695 Post Road (⊙New Haven)

Shaughnessey, Sheryl A., (BV) '54 '81 C.276 B.A. L.1029 J.D.
P.O. Box 1038, 06490
Telephone: 203-254-7544 Fax: 203-259-8755
Email: sheryl178@aol.com
***PRACTICE AREAS: Matrimonial Law; Criminal Law; Real Estate Law; Juvenile Law; Personal Injury.**

Shea, Gerald C. .... '59 '85 C.228 B.A. L.184 J.D. [Shea&S.] ⊙

Shea & Shea
181 Old Post Road, P.O. Box 577, 06490 ⊙
Telephone: 203-259-7522 Fax: 203-259-0864
URL: http://www.shea.com
Gerald C. Shea; Robert N. Shea (1932-1995).
International and Domestic Taxation, Corporate, Trusts and Estates, Civil and Criminal Tax Litigation, Personal Injury Law, Family Law, Probate, Private and Public Foundations.
New York, New York Office: 300 Park Avenue, Seventeenth Floor. Telephone: 212-572-6269. Fax: 212-935-1377.

See Professional Biographies, SOUTHPORT, CONNECTICUT

Silvestro, Brian T., (BV) .... '49 '74 C.918 B.A. L.818 J.D. [Kleban&S.]
*PRACTICE AREAS: Residential Real Estate Law; Zoning Law; Relocation Real Estate; Environmental Law; Estate Planning Law.
Stewart, James B., (AV) ..... '43 '68 C.918 B.A. L.880 J.D. [Pullman&C.] (⊙Bridgeport)
*PRACTICE AREAS: Estates and Trusts; Real Estate.
Strauss, Debra M. .... '62 '86 C.188 B.A. L.976 J.D. 990 Flintlock Rd.
Teicher, Robert L., (AV) .... '51 '77 C.976 B.A. L.880 J.D. [Brody,W.&O.]
*PRACTICE AREAS: Taxation; Business Law; Trusts and Estates.
Thorburn, James M., (AV) .... '46 '76 C.732 B.A. L.276 J.D. 135 Rennell Dr.
Tisdale, Thomas L., (AV) .... '56 '81 C.1030 B.S. L.724 J.D. [Tisdale&L.] ⊙

Tisdale & Lennon, LLC, (AV)
10 Spruce Street, 06490 ⊙
Telephone: 203-254-8474 Fax: 203-254-1641 URL: http://www.lawyers.com/tisdalelennon
Email: tl@tisdale-lennon.com URL: http://www.tisdale-lennon.com
Partners: Thomas L. Tisdale; Patrick F. Lennon. Associates: Charles E. Murphy; Kevin J. Lennon (Not admitted in CT).
Admiralty, Maritime, Insurance, Commercial, Products Liability, Bankruptcy Litigation and Personal Injury Litigation in all Courts.
New York, N.Y. Office: 36 West 44th Street, Suite 1111, 10036. Telephone: 212-354-0025.

See Professional Biographies, SOUTHPORT, CONNECTICUT

Tyma, Theodore R., (BV) .... '60 '85 C.1030 B.A. L.818 J.D. [Kleban&S.]
*PRACTICE AREAS: Civil Litigation.
Van Der Aue, Kathleen M., (BV) .... '41 '81 C.184 B.A. L.1029 J.D. 762 Mill Hill Rd.
Walsh, Thomas J., Jr., (BV) .... '61 '86 C&L.184 B.A., J.D. [Brody,W.&O.]
*PRACTICE AREAS: Commercial Transactions; Business Law; Real Estate Law; Municipal Law.
Weinstein, Judy K. .... '55 '80 C.914 B.A. L.184 J.D. [Neubert,P.&M.] ⊙
*PRACTICE AREAS: Health Law; Commercial Finance; Commercial Real Estate; Banking Law; Work-outs.
Wilkinson, Peter, (AV) .... '30 '55 C.976 B.A. L.309 LL.B. [Brody,W.&O.]
*PRACTICE AREAS: Probate Law; Trusts; Estate Planning.
Williams, Arthur C., (AV) .... '21 '48 C&L.976 B.A., LL.B. 2507 Post Rd.‡
Zacharias, Muriel E., (BV) .... '17 '41 C.821 A.B. L.976 LL.B. 2507 Post Rd.

SOUTH WINDSOR, 17,198, *Hartford Co.*

Bath, Candace V., (BV) ...... '51 '86 C.1103 B.S. L.184 J.D. Atty., Gerber Scientific, Inc.
Berman, Jon D., (BV) .... '51 '79 C.569 B.F.A. L.94 J.D. 819 Clark St.
Bonelli, Margaret .... '49 '89 C.725 B.A. L.184 J.D. Pro Se Legal Services, LLC
Carino, Francis J. .... '50 '75 C&L.184 B.A., J.D. P.O. Box 503‡
Cummings, Harold R., (BV) .... '45 '70 C.855 B.A. L.276 J.D. [Cummings&L.]
Cummings & Lanza, L.L.C., (BV) .... 1610 Ellington Rd.
Donnelly, Thomas J., Jr. .... '33 '64 C.1030 B.S.S. L.184 LL.B. 1400 Main St.
Fisher, Marianne Lassman .... '53 '86 C.93 B.A. L.1048 J.D. 194 Woodland Dr.
Gerber, David J. .... '61 '89 C.178 B.A. L.893 J.D. Atty., Gerber Scientific, Inc.
Gerlt, Wayne C., (BV) .... '48 '75 C.184 B.A. L.117 J.D. 435 Buckland Rd.
Kozik, Michael T. .... '50 '77 C.321 A.B. L.276 J.D. 395 Buckland Rd.
Kuehn, Edward R., (BV) .... '16 '48 C&L.184 B.A., J.D. 1610 Ellington Rd.‡
Lagassé, Jacques J. .... '49 '85 C&L.855 B.S., J.D. 29 Rockledge Dr.
Lanza, Michael J., (BV) .... '55 '83 C.184 B.S. L.1048 J.D. [Cummings&L.]
MacKinnon, James D. .... '37 '81 C.431 B.S. L.184 J.D. 360 Beelzebub Rd. (Pat.)
Molleur, R. Jay, (BV) .... '57 '83 C.31 B.A. L.184 J.D. 117 Wood Pond Rd.
Olson, Emily .... '47 '79 C.339 B.A. L.184 J.D. 117 Fairview Dr.
Paquin, Judith E., (BV) .... '59 '88 C.184 B.A. L.1048 J.D. P.O. Box 156
Percy, James D. .... '46 '74 C.860 B.A. L.184 J.D. 11 Kent Ln.
Purnhagen, Vincent John, (BV) .... '63 '88 C.184 B.A. L.1048 J.D. 1610 Ellington Rd.
Rennie, Kevin F., (BV) .... '58 '83 C.264 A.B. L.184 J.D. State Rep.
Russo, Frank W., (BV) .... '55 '81 C.976 B.A. L.276 J.D. 819 Clark St.
Sarnoski, Stephen R. .... '52 '85 C.1156 B.S. L.184 J.D. 31 Beldon Rd.★
Sessions, O. Thomas '43 '73
C.585 B.S.M.E. L.174 J.D. Sr. Pat. Coun., Gerber Scientific, Inc. (Pat.)
Treacy, Richard F., Jr. '45 '71 C.976 A.B. L.184 J.D.
Sr. V.P. & Gen. Coun., Gerber Scientific, Inc.
Wolf, Michael E., (BV) .... '46 '85 C.446 B.A. L.184 J.D. P.O. Box 1098
Woodcock, John J., III, (BV) .... '46 '74 C.708 B.A. L.818 J.D. 395 Buckland Rd.

STAFFORD SPRINGS, 4,100, *Tolland Co.*

Agranoff, Michael H., (CV) .... '42 '88 C.1033 B.A. L.184 J.D. 5 Burbank Rd.
Fiore, Thomas J., (BV) .... '49 '76 C.1030 B.A. L.1048 J.D. 14 West Stafford Road
Julian, John E., (CV) .... '43 '88 C.184 B.A. L.1048 J.D. 63 Main St.
Muska, Edward M., (CV) .... '49 '74 C.188 B.A. L.184 J.D. [Paradiso&M.]
*PRACTICE AREAS: Real Estate; Zoning; Municipal; Workers Compensation; Corporation.
Paradiso, F. Joseph, (BV) .... '35 '60 C.321 B.S. L.276 J.D. [Paradiso&M.]
*PRACTICE AREAS: Criminal; Estate; Real Estate; Family; Personal Injury.

Paradiso & Muska, (BV)
2 East Main Street, P.O. Box 22, 06076
Telephone: 860-684-4221 Fax: 860-684-4181
Members of Firm: F. Joseph Paradiso; Edward M. Muska.
General Civil and Criminal Practice before State and Federal Courts. Real Estate, Probate, Zoning, Corporation, Family, Workers Compensation, Personal Injury and Municipal Law. Trials in all Courts.
Representative Clients: Stafford Savings Bank; St. Edward's Church; Elm Water Co.; Borough of Stafford Springs; Goodhall's Garage, Inc.; Farmers Home Administration; Aqua Treatment & Service Co.; Workers Federal Credit Union; Glenville Development Corp.
See Professional Biographies, STAFFORD SPRINGS, CONNECTICUT

Prucker, Brian W., (BV) .... '50 '85 C.999 B.A. L.184 J.D. 510 Buckley Hwy.

STAFFORDVILLE, —, *Tolland Co.*

Lee, Susan N. .... '50 '75 C.30 B.A. L.446 J.D. P.O. Box 214-A

STAMFORD, 108,056, *Fairfield Co.*

Abate, Charles P. .... '70 '95 C.692 B.S. L.1048 J.D. [Abate&A.]
*PRACTICE AREAS: Commercial; Real Estate; Litigation; Personal Injury; Criminal Law.
Abate, Ernest N., (AV) .... '43 '69 C.884 B.S. L.602 J.D. [Abate&A.] (⊙Hartford)
*PRACTICE AREAS: Business; Trusts and Estates; Wills; Real Estate; Zoning.

Abate & Abate LLC, (AV)
607 Bedford Street, 06901
Telephone: 203-348-7770 Fax: 203-324-0057
URL: http://www.lawyers.com/abate&abate
Ernest N. Abate; Charles P. Abate.
Real Estate, Wills and Probate, Business Law, Estate Planning, Zoning, Divorce, Criminal Law and Civil Litigation, Personal Injury.
See Professional Biographies, STAMFORD, CONNECTICUT

Abbott, Preston H. ..... '47 '75 C&L.309 B.A., J.D. Coun., Coml. Fin., GE Capital Corp.
Ackerly, John A., (BV) .... '41 '68 C.708 B.A. L.128 J.D. 1318 Bedford St.
Adams, Elizabeth S. '53 '87 C.604 A.B. L.188 J.D.
Atty., Purdue Frederick Co./Purdue Pharma L.P.
*RESPONSIBILITIES: Corporate Law; Contracts; General Practice.
Adelstein, Robin D. '62 '88 C.165 A.B. L.569 J.D.
(adm. in NY; not adm. in CT)
V.P. & Asst. Gen. Coun., United Distillers & Vintners Ltd.
Adrian, Marcy J. '48 '77 C.994 B.A. L.245 J.D.
(adm. in GA; not adm. in CT) Crane Company
Albert, Martin J., (AV) '45 '70
C.659 B.S. L.94 J.D. [Cohen&W.] (⊙Bridgeport, Westport)
*PRACTICE AREAS: Taxation; Estate Planning; Probate.
Albert, Ward & Johnson, P.C.
(See Greenwich)
Albin, David I., (BV) .... '59 '84 C.855 B.A. L.976 J.D. [Finn D.&H.]
*PRACTICE AREAS: Corporate Law; Mergers and Acquisitions Law; Securities Law; Corporate Finance; Venture Capital Financing Law.
Albrecht, Richard L., (AV) '38 '62
C.105 B.S. L.188 J.D. [Cohen&W.] (⊙Bridgeport, Westport)
*PRACTICE AREAS: Litigation.
Alderucci, Dean '67 '95 C.94 B.S. L.184 J.D.
Chf. Coun., Intell. Prop., Walker Digital Corp.
*RESPONSIBILITIES: Intellectual Property.
Aleali, Roxana .... '73 '00 [Ⓐ Cummings&L.]
Alexander, Jack R. '26 '51 C.145 M.B.A. L.472 LL.B.
(adm. in FL; not adm. in CT) General Tel. & Electronics Corp.
Allen, Laura Morrison .... '66 '96 C.588 B.S. L.1040 J.D. [Ⓐ Cacace,T.&S.]
*PRACTICE AREAS: Zoning, Planning and Land Use; Telecommunications Law; Litigation.
Allison, Karen L. .... '67 '94 C.112 B.A. L.276 J.D. [Ⓐ Cummings&L.]
*PRACTICE AREAS: Litigation; Health Law; Hospital Law; Employment Law; Professional Licensing.
Alpert, Jane K. .... '— '80 C.67 B.A. L.588 J.D. Coun., GE Capital Real Estate
Alter, Lauren C. .... '65 '90 C.178 B.A. L.569 J.D. Swiss Bank Corporation
Altieri, Peter L., (AV) '55 '81 C.276 A.B. L.262 J.D.
[Epstein B.&G.] (⊙New York, NY)
Alvarez, Francis P. .... '63 '91 C.188 B.S. L.262 J.D. [Jackson L.S.&K.]
Amato, John '59 '85 C.478 B.A. L.930 J.D.
(adm. in MA; not adm. in CT) State Tax Coun., GE Capital Corp.
Ambrose, Stephen F., Jr. '54 '80 C.659 B.S. L.262 J.D.
(adm. in NY; not adm. in CT) V.P. & Assoc. Coun., GE Capital Corp.
Amendola & Amendola
(See Fairfield)
Ames, Morgan P., (AV) .... '19 '48 C&L.976 A.B., J.D. 1977 Shippan Ave.‡
Anastasia, Marsha L. '67 '92 C.860 B.S. L.184 J.D.
Sr. Corp. Coun., Pitney Bowes Inc.
*RESPONSIBILITIES: Commercial Law; Corporate Law; Real Estate.
Anderson, Jonathan S.R., (BV) '57 '83
C.183 B.A. L.1252 J.D. Title Coun., Ct. Aattys. Title Ins. Co.
Anderson, Lois B., (BV) .... '43 '75 C.823 B.A. L.831 J.D. 810 Bedford St.
Anderson, Scott W. '67 '95 C.692 B.A. L.838 J.D.
(adm. in XX; not adm. in CT) 677 Washington Blvd.
Andrade, Eduardo N. T. '69 '99 C.855 L.276 J.D.
(adm. in NY; not adm. in CT) [Ⓐ Paul,H.J.&W.]
*PRACTICE AREAS: Corporate Law.
Andrews, James F '56 '85 C.327 B.A. L.472 J.D.
(adm. in AL; not adm. in CT) Tax Coun., GE Capital Corp.
Andrews-Di Preta, Cynthia .... '71 '97 C.611 B.A. L.1252 J.D. [Ⓐ Ryan,R.J.&D.]
*PRACTICE AREAS: Civil Litigation.
Andriunas, Gregory G. .... '58 '94 C.184 B.A. L.1029 J.D. 1200 Summer Street
Angiolillo, Glenn J., (AV) .... '53 '79 C.659 B.S. L.276 J.D. [Cummings&L.]
*PRACTICE AREAS: Corporate Law; Mergers and Acquisitions; Banking and Finance.
Anner, John Lloyd, III
(See Greenwich)
Anthony, Lloyd W. .... '13 '42 C.608 L.569 LL.B. 301 Westwood Rd.‡
Antonetti, Matthew S. .... '71 '97 C.93 B.A. L.569 J.D. [Ⓐ Paul,H.J.&W.]
Apfelbaum, Marc J. '55 '84 C.659 B.A. L.276 J.D.
Sr. V.P., Gen. Coun. & Secy., Time Warner Cable
Apfeldorf, Morton '49 '76
C.102 B.A. L.1009 J.D. Sr. V.P. & Sr. Coun., CB Richard Ellis, Inc.
Arnowitz, Seth J., Law Offices of, (BV) '65 '89 C.569 B.A. L.1019 J.D.
733 Summer Street, Suite 202, 06901
Telephone: 203-348-7722 Fax: 203-978-1951 URL: http://www.ctattorney.com
Email: sja@ctattorney.com URL: http://www.lawyers.com/arnowitz
Associate: Juliet M. Nolta.
Residential Real Estate, Real Estate Litigation, Real Estate Foreclosure, Civil Litigation, Family Law.
See Professional Biographies, STAMFORD, CONNECTICUT

Arons, Howard, (BV) .... '06 '29 C&L.976 Ph.B., LL.B. 52 West View Ln.‡

Arpaia, Kimberly M. .... '58 '87 C.882 B.A. L.184 J.D. [Ⓐ Blair&P.]
*PRACTICE AREAS: Estate Planning; Estate Settlements; Trust Administration.
Arteaga, Mabél '69 '95 C.705 B.A. L.978 J.D.
(adm. in NJ; not adm. in CT) Corp. Coun., Pitney Bowes Inc.
*RESPONSIBILITIES: International Corporate.
Ashton, Harris J. '32 '60 C.976 B.A. L.178 LL.B.
(adm. in NY; not adm. in CT) Chmn. of the Bd., Pres. & CEO, General Host Corp.
Ashton, John F. .... '29 '54 C.309 A.B. L.976 LL.B. Stuyvesant Capital Mgmt. Corp.
Aulenti, Joseph J. .... '46 '78 C.128 B.A. L.262 J.D. 237 Pepper Ridge Rd.
Austin, Elizabeth J., (BV) '57 '83 C&L.546 B.A., J.D.
[Pullman&C.] (⊙Bridgeport, Hartford, New Haven)
*PRACTICE AREAS: Insolvency Law; Bankruptcy Litigation; Commercial Litigation.
Avery, G. Randall, (BV) .... '53 '78 C.228 B.A. L.184 J.D. [Avery&C.]
Avery & Crone, (BV) .... 25 Third St.
Ayres, Steven E., (BV) .... '45 '78 C.197 A.B. L.188 J.D. [Mead,B.&B.]
*PRACTICE AREAS: Trusts and Estates Law; Estate Settlement Law; Trust Administration Law; Probate Law; Tax Planning Law.
Babson-Smith, Stacey B. '61 '87 C.608 B.S. L.1398 J.D.
(adm. in NY; not adm. in CT) [Ⓒ Day,B.&H.]
*PRACTICE AREAS: Employment.
Badoyannis, Mary, (BV) .... '60 '85 C.855 B.A. L.896 J.D. 706 Bedford St.
Bailey, Robert G. '43 '73 C.431 B.A. L.823 J.D.
(adm. in NJ; not adm. in CT) 695 E. Main St.

Bainton McCarthy & Siegel, LLC
Three Stamford Landing 46 Southfield Avenue, 06902-7236 ⊙
Telephone: 203-323-8080 Facsimile: 203-325-9716
Email: info@baintonlaw.com URL: http://www.baintonlaw.com
John G. McCarthy.
Commercial Litigation, Intellectual Property, Product Liability, Trial Practice, Bankruptcy.
New York, N.Y. Office: 26 Broadway. Telephone: 212-480-3500. Facsimile: 212-480-9557.
Central Islip, New York Office: 320 Carleton Avenue. Telephone: 631-234-4900. Facsimile: 631-234-2886.
See Professional Biographies, STAMFORD, CONNECTICUT

Baird, Joan J. .... '33 '88 C.449 B.S. L.1029 J.D. 30 Oak St.
Baker, Frank Lewis, III, (AV) .... '— '73 C.976 B.A. L.893 J.D. [Robinson&C.]
*PRACTICE AREAS: Real Estate; Finance; Taxation.
Baldwin, James L., Jr., (AVⓉ) '61 '86 C.902 B.A. L.802 J.D.
(adm. in TX; not adm. in CT) Vice President, Legal Affairs, Motts, Inc.
Banahan, Thomas A. .... '55 '80 C&L.724 B.S., J.D. [Steefel,L.&W.]
*PRACTICE AREAS: Real Estate; Banking.
Banks-Urso, Kelly M. '65 '92 C.150 B.B.A. L.1187 J.D.
(adm. in NY; not adm. in CT) Tax Assoc., Price Waterhouse
Bannerman, Martha G. '43 '70 C.188 A.B. L.569 J.D.
Exec. V.P., Gen. Coun. & Secy., NAC Reinsurance Corp.
Barbaresi, George P. '54 '92 C.913 B.S. L.101 J.D.
(adm. in NY; not adm. in CT) [Ⓐ Pillsbury W.]
*PRACTICE AREAS: Mergers and Acquisitions; Securities; Corporate Law.
Barber, Staci B. '63 '89 C.860 B.A. L.262 J.D.
(adm. in NY; not adm. in CT)
Coun., Litigation & Legal Policy, Gen. Elec. Capital Corp.
Barker, M. Ridgway .... '55 '80 C.976 B.A. L.94 J.D. [Kelley D.&W.]
*PRACTICE AREAS: Joint Ventures; Mergers, Acquisitions and Divestitures; Securities; Public Offerings.
Barnett & Associates
(See Greenwich)

Baron, Steven J., (BV) '56 '84 C.184 B.A. L.1202 J.D.
600 Summer Street, 06901
Telephone: 203-353-0052 Fax: 203-357-7208
Email: SJBaron23@aol.com
***PRACTICE AREAS: Real Estate; Criminal Law; Personal Injury; Family Law.**
Real Estate, Residential Closings, Mortgage Closings, Commercial Real Estate. Family Law. Personal Injury and Criminal Law.
See Professional Biographies, STAMFORD, CONNECTICUT

Baronowski, Robert Jon .... '73 '98 C.478 B.A. L.184 J.D. Mgr., Ernst & Young LLP‡
Barr, Albert J., (BV) .... '49 '74 C.884 B.S. L.776 J.D. [Barr&L.]
*PRACTICE AREAS: Franchising Law (50%); Real Estate Law (20%); Family Law (10%); Environmental Law (10%).

Barr & LaCava, (BV)
22 Fifth Street, 06905
Telephone: 203-356-1505 Fax: 203-357-8397 URL: http://www.infolaw.com
Email: B&L@infolaw.com URL: http://www.lawyers.com/barr&lacava
Members of Firm: Albert J. Barr; John J. LaCava; John J. Morgan. Associates: Douglas R. Penn.
General Practice, Franchising and Franchise Law, Litigation in all State and Federal Courts, Real Estate, Probate, Corporate, Estate Planning, Family, Immigration, Petroleum Marketing Practices, Environmental Law, Workers Compensation, Appellate Practice, Personal Injury and Automobile Accidents.
See Professional Biographies, STAMFORD, CONNECTICUT

Barreca, Christopher A. .... '28 '54 C&L.94 J.D. [Ⓒ Paul,H.J.&W.]
*PRACTICE AREAS: Labor and Employment Law; Alternative Dispute Resolution; Bargaining Unit Certification Issues; Collective Bargaining; NLRB.
Bartlett, John F. .... '— '67 C&L.902 B.A., J.D. [Emmet,M.&M.]
Barto, Morris L. .... '48 '78 C.846 B.A. L.326 J.D. V.P., General Reins. Corp.
Barton, Nancy E., (AVⓉ) '50 '77 C.860 B.A. L.94 J.D.
(adm. in NY; not adm. in CT) Sr. V.P., Gen. Coun. & Secy., GE Capital Corp.
Basile, Richard J. '63 '95 C.867 B.S.M.E. L.146 J.D.
(adm. in NY; not adm. in CT; Pat.) [Ⓐ St. Onge S.J.&R.]
*PRACTICE AREAS: Intellectual Property; Patent Litigation; Trademark Litigation.
Bates, Elizabeth Lewis, (BV) .... '53 '78 C.788 A.B. L.588 J.D. [Roberts,R.&B.]
*PRACTICE AREAS: Real Estate; Zoning, Planning and Land Use; Trusts and Estates; Probate.
Battersby, Gregory J., (AV) '47 '73 C.776 A.B. L.262 J.D.
[Grimes&B.] (See Pat. Sect.)
Beal, Susan '70 '00 C.1139 B.S. L.1178 J.D.
(adm. in NY; not adm. in CT) [Ⓐ Goldberg&Assoc.] ⊙
*PRACTICE AREAS: Litigation.
Becker, Michael R. .... '62 '87 C.264 B.A. L.569 J.D. 2701 Summer St.
Becker-Lewke, Laura V. '55 '81 C.914 B.A. L.012 LL.B.
(adm. in NY; not adm. in CT) Secy., Coun. & Mgr., Admin., Navios Corp.
Beer, Robert Alexander, (AV) .... '36 '64 C&L.879 B.A., J.D. [Cummings&L.]
*PRACTICE AREAS: Estate Settlement Law; Trust Administration Law; Fiduciary Accounting Law; Taxation Law; Individual Tax Planning Law.
Beers, Christopher L. '64 '91 C.36 B.S. L.1040 J.D.
(adm. in NJ; not adm. in CT) 201 High Ridge Rd.
Begg, Tricia S. .... '69 '93 C&L.276 A.B., J.D. [Ⓐ Day,B.&H.]
*PRACTICE AREAS: Commercial Real Estate; Finance; Commercial Conveyancing.
Beggs, John F. '71 '96 C.1019 B.A. L.262 J.D.
(adm. in NY; not adm. in CT) [Ⓐ Kelley D.&W.]
*PRACTICE AREAS: Securities; Broker-Dealer.
Begun, Jason D. .... '70 '95 C.156 B.A. L.245 J.D. 1177 Summer Street

Belcamino, Beverly A. '— '81 C.1030 B.A. L.128 J.D.
Sr. Coun., GE Capital Card Servs.
Belkin, Steven C. .... '71 '96 C.367 L.306 Coun., Pitney Bowes Inc.
*RESPONSIBILITIES: Corporate.
Bellach, Andreana R. .... '74 '99 C.1372 B.A. L.880 J.D. [A Shipman&G.]
*PRACTICE AREAS: Litigation; Employment Litigation; Commercial Litigation.
Bellamy, William M., Jr. '31 '60 C&L.188 A.B., J.D.
(adm. in NY; not adm. in CT) 23 Stone Fence Lane‡
Bellavia, Melissa L. ....'74 '00 C.105 B.A. L.128 J.D. [A Day,B.&H.]
*PRACTICE AREAS: Commercial Litigation.
Belleau, Kathryn G. '54 '90 C.012 B.A. L.1009 J.D.
(adm. in NY; not adm. in CT) [A St. Onge S.J.&R.]
*PRACTICE AREAS: International Trademarks; International Copyright Law; International Intellectual Property.
Bello, Christopher R., (BV) '62 '87 C.216 B.A. L.1029 J.D.
2nd V.P. & Asst. Gen. Coun., Gen. Reinsurance Corp.
*RESPONSIBILITIES: Immigration; Insurance Regulation; Litigation; General Corporate 40 Act.
Bello, Robert S., (AV) .... '37 '61 C.1030 B.S.S. L.724 LL.B. [Bello,L.&C.] ⊙
*PRACTICE AREAS: Criminal Litigation; Real Estate; Family Law.

Bello, Lapine & Cassone, L.L.P., (AV)
600 Summer Street, 06901 ⊙
Telephone: 203-348-4244 Fax: 203-357-7208
Email: blclaw@lawyers.com URL: http://www.lawyers.com/bl&cllp
Robert S. Bello; Lawrence M. Lapine; Thomas M. Cassone;—Patrick D. McCabe (Not admitted in CT).
Personal Injury, Medical Malpractice, Product Liability, Auto Accidents and Injuries, Professional Negligence, Legal Malpractice, Real Estate, Criminal.
Ridgefield, Connecticut Office: 369 North Street. 06877. Telephone: 203 438-3974.
See Professional Biographies, STAMFORD, CONNECTICUT

Belson, Ellen Siev ......'46 '94 C.1036 B.A. L.1040 J.D. [A L.J.Levine] (⊙Purchase, NY)
*PRACTICE AREAS: Elder Law; Real Property; Trusts and Estates; Probate Law; Medicaid.
Benanti, Joseph P. .... '51 '82 C.454 A.B. L.94 J.D. 350 Bedford St.
Benedict, Peter B., (BV) .... '51 '76 C.829 B.A. L.1022 J.D. [Benedict&D.]
Benedict & Depuy, (BV) .... 84 West Park Place
Benjamin, Daniel A., (BV) .... '53 '78 C.575 B.A. L.790 J.D. [Benjamin&G.]
Benjamin, Scott P. '58 '85 C.1044 B.A. L.1398 J.D.
(adm. in NY; not adm. in CT) [A Spitzer S.&B.]
*PRACTICE AREAS: Civil Practice; Criminal Defense; Litigation.
Benjamin & Gold, P.C., (BV) ....350 Bedford Street
Bennett, J. Goodwin '51 '79 C.575 B.A. L.273 J.D.
(adm. in NY; not adm. in CT)
Vice President & Assistant General Counsel, GTE Service Corporation
Bennett, Jackson G. '51 '79 C.575 B.A. L.273 J.D.
(adm. in NY; not adm. in CT) GTE Serv. Corp.

Bentley, Mosher, Babson & Lambert, P.C.
(See Greenwich)

Benyus, Zolton A., Jr., (BV) .... '42 '69 C.69 B.B.A. L.623 J.D. 706 Bedford St.
Berg, Ira S. '69 '94 C.910 B.A. L.473 J.D.
(adm. in FL; not adm. in CT) World Wrestling Fed. Ent., Inc.
Berger, Garry A. '68 '95 C.1036 B.A. L.178 J.D.
(adm. in NY; not adm. in CT) Assoc. Gen. Coun., The Thomson Corp.
*RESPONSIBILITIES: Intellectual Property; Licensing; Commercial Law; Mergers and Acquisitions.
Bergman, Erik A. .... '64 '95 C.705 B.A. L.976 J.D. [A Finn D.&H.]
*PRACTICE AREAS: Corporate Law; Mergers and Acquisitions; Venture Capital; Corporate Finance; Securities.
Beri, Sandip K. '60 '95 C.999 B.A. L.966 J.D.
(adm. in IL; not adm. in CT) Coun., GE Capital Card Services
Berkman, Jerome, (AV) .... '41 '65 C&L.188 B.A., LL.B. [Day,B.&H.]
*PRACTICE AREAS: Real Estate Development; Commercial Leasing; Real Estate Finance.
Berkowitz, Eric S. '69 '95 C.103 B.A. L.178 J.D.
Litig. Coun., GE Capital Card Services
Berkowitz, Russell J., (BV) ....'58 '85 C&L.221 B.S., J.D. [Berkowitz,M.&M.]
*PRACTICE AREAS: Personal Injury; Medical Malpractice; Wrongful Deaths.

Berkowitz, Malowitz & Mullin, (BV)
Century Plaza South Tower, 100 Prospect Street, 06901-1207 ⊙
Telephone: 203-324-7909 Fax: 203-324-5067
URL: http://www.lawyers.com/bm&m
Members of Firm: Russell J. Berkowitz; Wesley M. Malowitz; Caryn L. Mullin.
Personal Injury Litigation, Medical Malpractice, Products Liability Law, Workers' Compensation, and Complex Civil Litigation.
See Professional Biographies, STAMFORD, CONNECTICUT

Berman, Edward M., (AV(T)) '34 '60 C&L.823 A.B., LL.B.
(adm. in NY; not adm. in CT) [C Rosenblum&T.] (⊙New York, NY)
Bernard, Christopher D., (AV) '54 '79
C.472 B.B.A. L.260 J.D. [Koskoff,K.&B.] (⊙Bridgeport)
*PRACTICE AREAS: Medical Malpractice; Personal Injury.
Berns, Philip E. .... '57 '94 C.188 B.S. L.1040 J.D. [P.E.Berns]
Berns, Philip E., L.L.C. ....1372 Summer St.
Bernstein, Andrew H. ....'65 '92 Four Stamford Plaza
Bernstein, Harold F., (BV) ....'61 '88 C&L.978 B.A., J.D. [Zone&B.]
Bernstein, Raymond M. ....'51 '76 C.188 B.S. L.575 J.D. [C Shipman&G.]
*PRACTICE AREAS: Intellectual Property; Trademarks; Copyrights; Entertainment Law; Employment Law.
Bernstein, Samuel J., (BV) ....'32 '56 C.103 B.A. L.976 LL.B. [Zone&B.]
Berson, Nancy S. '61 '87 C.976 B.A. L.309 J.D.
(adm. in NY; not adm. in CT) 1600 Summer St.
Bertrand, Raymond William '69 '95 C.999 B.A. L.982 J.D.
(adm. in NY; not adm. in CT) [A Paul,H.J.&W.]
*PRACTICE AREAS: Employment; Litigation.
Berzin, Steven M. '50 '77 C&L.309 A.B., J.D.
(adm. in NY; not adm. in CT) V.P., General Electric Credit Corp.
Bicks, James H. .... '62 '89 C.688 B.A. L.569 J.D. [Wiggin&D.]
Bills, Alexander ....'14 '59 C&L.569 B.S., J.D. 18 Gray Farms Rd.
Biondo, James F. ....'69 '95 C&L.1252 B.A., J.D. [A Rosenblum&T.] ⊙
Birch, Peter H. .... '56 '81 C.611 B.A. L.1029 J.D. 23 W. Haviland Ln.
Birch, Robert M. '17 '48 C.980 B.A. L.930 LL.B.
(adm. in OH; not adm. in CT) Div. Coun., General Electric Co.
Birch, Timothy A., (BV) .... '58 '83 C.529 A.B. L.94 J.D. [C Finn D.&H.]
*PRACTICE AREAS: Mergers and Acquisitions; Corporate Finance; Corporate Law.
Birenbaum, Jonathan .... '53 '79 C.165 A.B. L.982 J.D. [Paul,H.J.&W.]
*PRACTICE AREAS: Project Finance; Energy; Capital Markets Financing; Domestic and International Energy and Industrial Projects.
Biro, Steven G. M. '43 '74 C.178 B.A. L.262 J.D.
291 Vine Road, 06905-2106
Telephone: 203-329-9664 Fax: 203-329-1640
Email: SBIRO@optonline.NET URL: http://www.lawyers.com/stevenbiro
Personal Injuries, Divorce and Family, Accidents, Real Estate Transactions, Wills and Estates, Business Affairs, International and Domestic, Landlord-Tenant, Worker's Compensation, Collection.
(This Listing Continued)

Biro, Steven G. M. (Continued)
New York Office: 61 Broadway, 18th Floor, 10006, Telephone: 212-797-9100.
See Professional Biographies, STAMFORD, CONNECTICUT

Bishop, Stephen L., (BV) ....'49 '78 C.184 B.A. L.221 J.D. [Mead,B.&B.]
*PRACTICE AREAS: Real Estate Law; Commercial Law; Estate Planning; Administrative Law.
Bistor, Tad J. .... '67 '94 C.1349 B.A. L.1252 J.D. 1172 Bedford Street (⊙Newburgh, NY)
Black, Harris '60 '88 C.569 B.A. L.1009 J.D.
(adm. in NY; not adm. in CT) Assoc. Gen. Coun., ACNielsen Corporation
*RESPONSIBILITIES: Compensation and Benefits; General Corporate.
Blackwell, Barbara W. '59 '85 C.449 B.A. L.61 J.D.
Sr. Coun., GE Capital IT Solutions
Blair, Nancy E., (AV) ....'53 '81 C.881 B.A. L.94 J.D. [Blair&P.]
*PRACTICE AREAS: Estate Planning; Tax Planning; Estate Settlements; Trust Administration.
Blair, William H. '38 '63 C&L.174 B.A., LL.B.
(adm. in CO; not adm. in CT) Gen. Coun., IBM Retirement Funds

Blair & Potts, (AV)
Two Stamford Plaza, P.O. Box 1214, 06904
Telephone: 203-327-2333 Fax: 203-327-1731
Email: administrator@blairandpotts.com URL: http://www.lawyers.com/blair&potts
Nancy E. Blair; Arthur G. Potts, Jr. Associates: Kimberly M. Arpaia; Joan M. O'Brien; Robert A. Devellis; Catherine Vance Perusse; Moira A. Spollen; Michael L. Wolf; Anthony G. Dimaria.
Estate and Tax Planning and Estate Settlement and Trust Administration.
See Professional Biographies, STAMFORD, CONNECTICUT

Bliss, James R. .... '69 '95 C.569 B.A. L.262 J.D. [A Paul,H.J.&W.]
Blomberg, Jeffrey A. .... '71 '96 C.165 B.A. L.262 J.D. [A Finn D.&H.]
*PRACTICE AREAS: Mergers and Acquisitions; Venture Capital; Corporate Finance Law; Corporate Securities.

Bloomenthal, Melvin Lee '44 '69 C.882 B.A. L.1294 J.D.
600 Summer Street, 5th Floor, 06901
Telephone: 203-348-9595 Fax: 203-357-7208
Email: mlshot@aol.com
***PRACTICE AREAS: Workers Compensation; Products Liability; Medical Malpractice; Uninsured and Underinsured Motorists; Real Estate.**
General Practice, Domestic Relations, Personal Injury.
See Professional Biographies, STAMFORD, CONNECTICUT

Bloomfield, Elizabeth Anne ....'71 '00 C.881 A.B. L.569 [A Wiggin&D.]
Blume, Nancy B. '67 '92 C&L.309 A.B., J.D.
(adm. in NJ; not adm. in CT) Counsel, Xerox Corporation
Blume, Richard L. '42 '67 C.430 B.A. L.208 J.D.
(adm. in CO; not adm. in CT) 1600 Summer St.
Blumenthal, Richard, (AV) .... '46 '76 C.309 B.A. L.976 J.D. 184 Atlantic St.
Bockner, Gordon Judd '40 '67 C.367 B.A. L.976 LL.B.
(adm. in NY; not adm. in CT) Pres., Bus. Develop. Assocs.

Boeggeman, George, Hodges & Corde, P.C.
(See White Plains)

Bogan, David W. .... '— '86 C&L.1029 B.S., J.D. [Robinson&C.]
*PRACTICE AREAS: Administrative Law; Telecommunications; Energy.
Bollinger, Howard M., (AV) '22 '52 C.453 B.S. L.273 LL.B.
(adm. in NY; not adm. in CT; Pat.) 460 Summer St.
Bologna, Jenifer Magyar ....'67 '94 C.299 B.A. L.94 J.D. [A Paul,H.J.&W.]
*PRACTICE AREAS: Employment Law; Labor Law.
Bomzer, Lara Joy Schneider '69 '01 C.823 B.S. L.1398 J.D.
(adm. in MA; not adm. in CT) 123 Hoyt St.
Bonazzoli, M. Juliet ....'67 '99 [A Cummings&L.]
Bonner, Henry M., Jr. ....'64 '92 C.917 B.A. L.184 J.D. Asst. V.P., GE Equity
Boodman, Barry J., (P.A.), (BV) .....'41 '68 C.4 B.A. L.1009 LL.B. 70 Pepper Ridge Rd.
Bove, Nicholas J., Jr. ....'52 '81 C.1030 A.B. L.1029 J.D. Asst. State's Atty.
Bovino, Matthew A. ....'62 '87 C.262 B.A. L.569 J.D. [Cummings&L.]
*PRACTICE AREAS: Estate Planning Law; Estate Administration.
Bowman, Jonathan S., (AV) '42 '66
C.347 A.B. L.184 J.D. [Cohen&W.] (⊙Bridgeport, Westport)
*PRACTICE AREAS: Real Estate; Condominium; Property Tax Appeals; Bankruptcy; Title Insurance.

Bowman, Andrew B.
(See Westport)

Boynton, Sally J., (BV(T)) .... '51 '84 C.999 B.A. L.978 J.D. [C D.M.Wallman]
*PRACTICE AREAS: Matrimonial Law; Estate Planning; Estate Administration; Real Estate.
Bozek, Adam S. .... '67 '93 C.94 B.S. L.569 J.D. [A Paul,H.J.&W.]
*PRACTICE AREAS: Employment Law.
Bradley, David A. ....'72 '00 [A Cummings&L.]
Brady, Kevin R. .... '71 '00 C.184 B.A. L.1252 J.D. [A Diserio M.O.&C.]
*PRACTICE AREAS: Commercial Litigation; Complex Litigation.
Brandner, Geoffrey S., (CV) ....'48 '75 C.1029 B.A. L.184 J.D. [Brandner&P.]
*PRACTICE AREAS: Bankruptcy; Landlord and Tenant Law; Commercial Litigation; Real Estate; Probate.

Brandner & Ponzini, (BV)
24 Hoyt Street, 06905
Telephone: 203-327-6913; 203-327-5609 Fax: 203-327-6702
Email: BPLwyers@aol.com URL: http://www.lawyers.com/brandner&ponzini
Geoffrey S. Brandner; John Lino Ponzini.
General Civil and Criminal Litigation. Driving While Intoxicated, Personal Injury, Product Liability, Automobile Accidents, Domestic Relations, Commercial, Corporate, Real Estate and Estate Planning.
See Professional Biographies, STAMFORD, CONNECTICUT

Brandt, Jeffrey L., (BV) '54 '81 C.390 B.S. L.64 J.D.
(adm. in MD; not adm. in CT; Pat.) Coun., Priceline.com Inc.
Brandt, Kathleen L. .... '49 '96 C.1103 B.S.N. L.1040 J.D. [A Silver,G.&T.]
*PRACTICE AREAS: Medical Malpractice.
Brantner, Andrea J. '60 '90 C.164 B.A. L.93 J.D.
(adm. in NY; not adm. in CT) V.P. & Coun., GE Capital Aviation Servs. Inc.
Braun, Ann Lisa ....'67 '94 C.976 B.A. L.893 J.D. [A Day,B.&H.]
Breck, Deborah S., (BV) '53 '83
C.1102 B.A. L.184 J.D. [Pullman&C.] (⊙Bridgeport, Southport)
*PRACTICE AREAS: Estates and Trusts; Elder Law; Trust and Probate Litigation.
Breidbord, Paul L., (BV) ....'32 '58 C&L.184 B.S., LL.B. 123 Prospect St.
Brennan, Catherine M. .... '68 '94 C.321 A.B. L.1040 J.D. [A Shipman&G.]
*PRACTICE AREAS: Estate Planning; Trust Administration; Estate Settlements.
Brennan, E. Gaynor, Jr., (BV) ....'30 '56 C.276 B.S. L.262 LL.B. [Brennan,D.&B.]
Brennan, Elizabeth L. ....'— '87 C.855 B.A. L.184 J.D. [Robinson&C.]
*PRACTICE AREAS: Real Estate; Finance; Construction Law; Commercial Leasing.
Brennan, Dichter & Brennan, (BV) ....105 Bedford St.
Brey, Lewis ....'68 '95 C.1365 B.A. L.1040 J.D. [Spitzer S.&B.]
*PRACTICE AREAS: Labor and Employment Litigation; Commercial Contracts Litigation; Employment Arbitration.
Brinckerhoff, Richard L., (AV) .... '19 '49 C.951 B.A. L.178 LL.B. [C Curtis,B.&B.]
Brodrick, Richard G., (AV) .... '32 '59 C.103 A.B. L.309 LL.B. [Kelley D.&W.]
*PRACTICE AREAS: Securities; Closely Held Business Law; Business Acquisitions; Business Divestitures.

Brody, Frederic S. .... '51 '77 C.415 B.A. L.1048 J.D. 43 Edward Pl.
Brody, Robert G. ....'57 '82 C.385 B.A. L.880 J.D. [Brody&Assoc.]
Brody and Associates, LLC ....1177 Summer Street, Third Floor

Brody, Wilkinson and Ober, P.C.
(See Southport)

Bromberg, Cathy L. .... '53 '83 C.69 B.A. L.145 J.D. [[A] Shipman&G.]
*PRACTICE AREAS: Corporate Law; Commercial Finance; Securities Law.
Bromfield, Alicia B. .... '74 '99 C.367 B.A. L.1252 J.D. [[A] Diserio M.O.&C.]
*PRACTICE AREAS: Litigation; Commercial Litigation.
Bromley, Ellen E., (BV) .... '53 '81 C.228 B.A. L.276 J.D. 329 Vine Rd.
Bromley, J. Robert, (BV) .... '36 '62 C&L.976 B.A., LL.B. [[C] Mead,B.&B.]
*PRACTICE AREAS: Estate Settlement Law.
Bronsdon, James F., Jr. '56 '87 C.478 A.B. L.818 J.D.
V.P. - Legal, Sage Life Assurance of America, Inc.
Brotmann & Freedman ....6 Landmark Sq., 4th Floor (⊙White Plains, NY)
Brower, Elizabeth Adolff ....'61 '90 C.999 B.S. L.724 J.D. [[C] Paul,H.J.&W.]
*PRACTICE AREAS: Securities Law; Corporate Finance; Mergers and Acquisitions; Venture Capital; Emerging Growth Companies.
Brown, Celia Reznick '54 '80 C.1365 B.A. L.575 J.D.
(adm. in NY; not adm. in CT)
Sr. VP & Manager, Human Resources, NAC Reinsurance Corporation

Brown, Christopher G. '67 '92 C.659 B.A. L.724 J.D.
Suite 200 999 Summer Street, 06905-5513
Telephone: 203-964-9794 Fax: 203-964-9795 URL: http://www.cgbrown.com
Email: cgbrown@cgbrown.com URL: http://www.lawyers.com/cbrownlaw
Civil Litigation in all Courts, Business Law, Estate Planning, Real Estate and General Practice.
See Professional Biographies, STAMFORD, CONNECTICUT

Brown, Emmett E., III, (AV) ....'47 '78 C.659 B.S. L.188 J.D. [Tyler C.&A.]
*PRACTICE AREAS: Corporate Law; Intellectual Property; Emerging Growth Companies; Licensing Law; Franchise Law.
Brown, Stephen B. .... '39 '65 C.178 B.A. L.569 LL.B. Retired
Brown, Paindiris & Scott, LLP, (AV)
6 Landmark Square (⊙East Hampton, Glastonbury, Hartford, Hebron)
Browne, Colm Patrick ....'68 '94 C.602 B.A. L.823 J.D. [[A] F.J.Browne]
Browne, Edmond R., Jr. '47 '78 C.589 B.S. L.128 J.D.
(adm. in DC; not adm. in CT) Gen. Coun., Ct. Attys. Title Ins. Co.
Browne, Francis J., (BV) .... '59 '84 C.602 B.A. L.94 J.D. [F.J.Browne] (⊙Hartford)
Browne, Francis J., Esq., P.C., (BV) .... 112 Prospect Street
Brownrout, Harvey M. '35 '61
C.453 B.S. L.309 J.D. Dir., Software Lic., Xerox Corporation (Pat.)
Bruckmann, Joseph G. .... '56 '81 C.1030 B.S. L.184 J.D. Pub. Def.
Bryant, Marc R. '66 '93 C.165 B.A. L.245 J.D.
(adm. in MD; not adm. in CT) V.P. & Assoc. Gen. Coun., GE Asset Management
Buck, Michael P. ....'70 '96 C.676 B.A. L.1009 J.D. [[A] Kelley D.&W.]
*PRACTICE AREAS: Securities Law; Corporate Law.
Buckingham, Rob Roy, Jr. ....'67 '00 C.228 B.A. L.306 J.D. [[A] Day,B.&H.]
*PRACTICE AREAS: Real Estate.
Bucklan, Deborah Lynn ....'67 '93 C.865 B.A. L.1048 J.D. 11 Lewis Road
Budd, Martin L., (AV) ....'40 '69 C.197 A.B. L.309 LL.B. [Day,B.&H.]
*PRACTICE AREAS: Private Equity Funds; Mergers and Acquisitions; Strategic Joint Ventures; International Transactions; Securities Law.
Bujdud, Christian William ....'62 '92 C.1041 B.S. L.1252 J.D. 1200 Summer St.
Burdett, Christopher C., (AV) .... '43 '69 C.222 B.A. L.705 J.D. [C.C.Burdett]

Burdett, Christopher C., P.C., Law Offices of, (AV)
777 Summer Street, 06901
Telephone: 203-327-6767 Fax: 203-353-3392
Email: ccbesq@aol.com URL: http://www.lawyers.com/christopherburdett
Christopher C. Burdett.
Civil Litigation, Personal Injury, Automobile Accidents, Malpractice, Family, Divorce and Matrimonial Litigation.
See Professional Biographies, STAMFORD, CONNECTICUT

Burger, Barbara '60 '86 C.201 B.S. L.724 J.D.
(adm. in NY; not adm. in CT) V.P. & Gen. Coun., AIG Intl. Asset Mgmt. Inc.
Burke, David J., (BV) ....'— '88 C.321 B.A. L.1040 J.D. [[C] Robinson&C.]
*PRACTICE AREAS: Labor and Employment; Litigation; Health Care.
Burke, Nancy S. .... '38 '90 C.530 B.A. L.1029 J.D. Connecticut Legal Servs., Inc.
Burns, Mary Ellen, (AV) .... '52 '78 C.562 B.A. L.724 J.D. 7 Cogswell Lane
Burton, David K. '— '96 C.354 B.A. L.276 J.D.
Tax Coun., General Electric Capital Corporation
Bush, Samuel D., (CV) ....'59 '84 C.184 B.A. L.1029 J.D. 217 Bedford St.
Busó, Eduardo L. '— '78 C.112 B.A. L.1065 J.D.
(adm. in PR; not adm. in CT) Coun., GE Capital
Butler, Jennifer '69 '97 C.165 B.A. L.569 J.D.
(adm. in NY; not adm. in CT) 1055 Washington Blvd.

Byelas, Leslie
(See Westport)

Byrne, Elizabeth A. ....'75 '00 C.188 B.S. L.184 J.D. [[A] Paul,H.J.&W.]
*PRACTICE AREAS: Commercial Litigation.
Byrne, Michael P. ....'60 '87 C&L.93 B.S., J.D. [Day,B.&H.]
*PRACTICE AREAS: Real Estate Finance; Commercial Leasing; Real Estate Development; Real Estate Workouts and Restructuring.
Cacace, Michael J., (AV) ....'52 '78 C.262 B.A. L.564 J.D. [Cacace,T.&S.]
*PRACTICE AREAS: Zoning, Planning and Land Use; Administrative Law; Real Property; Litigation; Commercial Law.

Cacace, Tusch & Santagata, (AV) [BB]
777 Summer Street, P.O. Box 15859, 06901-0859
Telephone: 203-327-2000 Telecopier: 203-353-3392
Email: lawcts@lawcts.com
Members of Firm: Michael J. Cacace; Mark P. Santagata; Paul T. Tusch; Richard S. Fisher; Ronald E. Kowalski II. Of Counsel: Kenneth A. DellaRocco; Sherwood R. Spelke; Jane W. Freeman; Eric D. Grayson. Associates: Edward F. Nemchek; Alice Ann Fitzpatrick; Patrick L. Poeschl; Laura Morrison Allen; David J. Coviello; Joseph Todd Puhekker; Barbara S. Koteen (Not admitted in CT).
General Civil and Criminal Trial Practice in State and Federal Courts, Administrative Law, Elder Law, Probate, Civil Appeals, Business Law, Creditor and Collections, Commercial Law, Telecommunications Law, Entertainment and the Arts, Contracts, Government, Construction Law, Land Use Litigation, Commercial Litigation, Personal Injury, Domestic Relations, Real Estate, Corporation, Estate Planning, Commercial Leasing, Planning and Zoning, Land Use, Environmental, Eminent Domain and Real Estate Tax Appeals.
See Professional Biographies, STAMFORD, CONNECTICUT

Callagy, John M., (AV⊤) '44 '69
C.276 A.B. L.569 J.D. [Kelley D.&W.] (⊙New York, NY)
*PRACTICE AREAS: Business Torts; Complex Litigation; Contract Law.
Callahan, Jane B. .... '69 '00 C.524 B.A. L.1252 J.D. [[A] Ryan,R.J.&D.]
Callahan, Robert J. .... '30 '55 C.93 B.S. L.262 J.D. Chf. Supm. Ct. Jus.

Calvey, Brian J. '49 '74 C.602 A.B. L.893 J.D.
(adm. in NY; not adm. in CT) [Kelley D.&W.]
*PRACTICE AREAS: Corporate Law; Mergers, Acquisitions and Divestitures; Securities.
Campbell, Charles K., Jr., (AV) ....'49 '76 C.103 A.B. L.880 J.D. [Pullman&C.]
*PRACTICE AREAS: Environmental Law; Land Use Planning; Real Estate Law.
Campbell, Marvin N. '60 '87 C.103 B.A. L.1066 J.D.
(adm. in CA; not adm. in CT) Coun., GE Capital IT Solutions
Canaday, Mary Alice S. ....'65 '94 C.207 B.A. L.1040 J.D. [[A] Martin,L.&C.]
*PRACTICE AREAS: Commercial; Employment; Civil Litigation.
Canavan, Patricia M. ....'65 '91 C.390 B.A. L.1040 J.D. [[C] Day,B.&H.]
*PRACTICE AREAS: Wrongful Termination; Sexual Harassment; Employment Discrimination; Breach of Contract; Federal Civil Practice.
Canelos, Nicholas S. '59 '85 C.659 B.S. L.982 J.D.
(adm. in NY; not adm. in CT) V.P. & Asst. Gen. Coun., Gen. Reinsurance Corp.
*RESPONSIBILITIES: Reinsurance Litigation and Arbitration; General Insurance and Reinsurance Law; Corporate Law.
Cannavino, Deborah D. .... '65 '90 C.597 B.A. L.1065 J.D. [[C] Tyler C.&A.]
*PRACTICE AREAS: Employment Law; Civil Litigation.
Cannavino, John W., (AV) .... '51 '77 C.1044 B.A. L.823 J.D. [Cummings&L.]
*PRACTICE AREAS: Trial Practice; Civil Litigation; Commercial Law.
Cannella, Renée Mayerson .... '65 '91 C.1044 B.A. L.184 J.D. 150 Gary Rd.

Canner, Glen A., (BV) '53 '79 C.860 B.A. L.184 J.D.
112 Prospect Street, 06901
Telephone: 203-961-1080 Fax: 203-964-9509
URL: http://www.lawyers.com/canner
Trials and Appeals in State and Federal Courts. Employment Law, Personal Injury, Divorce, Real Estate and Probate.
See Professional Biographies, STAMFORD, CONNECTICUT

Cantore, J. Michael, Jr., (BV) '43 '71 C.415 B.A. L.818 J.D.
1172 Bedford Street, 06905
Telephone: 203-327-5040 Fax: 203-348-9220
URL: http://www.lawyers.com/cantorelaw
***PRACTICE AREAS: Medical Malpractice; Personal Injury; Auto Accident; Product Liability; Civil Litigation.**
Medical Malpractice, Personal Injury, Auto Accident, Product Liability, Civil and Commercial Litigation, Divorce, Family, Child Custody, Real Estate, Wills and Trust, Criminal Defense, DWI, Bankruptcy.
See Professional Biographies, STAMFORD, CONNECTICUT

Capalbo, Joseph J., II, (BV) ....'59 '85 C.184 B.A. L.1029 J.D. 1100 Summer St.
Capetta, John T., (BV) .... '55 '80 C.676 B.S. L.184 J.D. [Kelley D.&W.]
*PRACTICE AREAS: Corporate Law.
Carberry, John F., (BV) ....'57 '84 C.262 B.A. L.564 J.D. [Cummings&L.]
*PRACTICE AREAS: Bankruptcy Law; Creditors' Rights; Debtor and Creditor; Commercial Litigation.
Carey, Joseph, (BV) ....'— '75 C.1044 B.S. L.982 J.D. [[A] Robinson&C.]
Carlon, James P. .... '74 '99 C.1030 B.A. L.564 J.D. [[A] Diserio M.O.&C.]
*PRACTICE AREAS: Corporate Law.
Carpenter, Patricia A., (BV) ....'52 '81 C.282 B.A. L.188 J.D. [Day,B.&H.]
*PRACTICE AREAS: Trust and Estate Litigation; Commercial Litigation.
Carroll, Francis W. '34 '67 C.1041 B.B.A. L.262 LL.B.
(adm. in NY; not adm. in CT) I.R.S.
Carroll, Gretchen A. ....'70 '00 C.105 B.A. L.823 J.D. [[A] Kelley D.&W.]
*PRACTICE AREAS: Securities.
Carson, Kenneth A. '59 '85 C.1044 B.A. L.446 J.D.
(adm. in MD; not adm. in CT) Asst. Gen. Coun., The Thomson Corp.
Carswell, Bruce '30 '55 C.164 A.B. L.188 LL.B.
(adm. in NY; not adm. in CT) 1 Stamford Forum
Casino, Andrew Patrick Rivero '66 '96 C&L.662 B.A., LL.L.
(adm. in NY; not adm. in CT) 200 First Stamford Place
Caso, William J. '44 '69 C.884 B.S. L.93 J.D.
(adm. in MA; not adm. in CT) V.P., Taxes & Insurance, Lone Star Industries, Inc.
Casper, Stewart M., (AV) ....'53 '78 C.454 B.A. L.1019 J.D. [Casper&d.L.]
*PRACTICE AREAS: Personal Injury; Medical Malpractice; Product Liability; Workers' Compensation.

Casper & de Toledo LLC, (AV) [BB]
1111 Summer Street, 06905
Telephone: 203-325-8600 Fax: 203-323-5970 URL: http://www.lawyers.com/casperdetoledo
Email: info@casperdetoledo.com URL: http://www.casperdetoledo.com
Stewart M. Casper; Victoria de Toledo;—Anastasios T. Savvaides; Rhonna W. Rogol.
Civil Trial and Appellate Practice in all State and Federal Courts. Personal Injury, Medical Malpractice, Product Liability, Workers' Compensation, Employment Discrimination, Employee Rights and Benefits, Civil Rights, Contracts and Family Law.
See Professional Biographies, STAMFORD, CONNECTICUT

Cassone, John A. .... '61 '91 C.472 B.B.A. L.1029 J.D. [[A] Avery&C.]
Cassone, Thomas M., (BV) .... '56 '81 C.401 B.A. L.1048 J.D. [Bello,L.&C.] ⊙
*PRACTICE AREAS: Civil Litigation; Products Liability; Personal Injury; Medical Malpractice; Negligence Defense.
Castiglioni, Richard E., (AV) ....'52 '77 C&L.184 B.A., J.D. [Diserio M.O.&C.]
*PRACTICE AREAS: Commercial Litigation; Personal Injury Litigation; Labor Litigation.
Catalano, Michael A., (CV) .... '36 '62 C&L.454 B.A., LL.B. 733 Summer St.
Caulfield, Christine ....'69 '96 C.689 B.A. L.184 J.D. [[A] Emmett&G.] (⊙Stamford)
Cavaliero, Brooke A. ....'64 '89 C.184 B.A. L.1048 J.D. 84 W. Park Place

Cavallo, Victor J. '51 '91 C.273 B.A. L.1029 J.D.
750 Summer Street, 06901
Telephone: 203-602-0260 Fax: 203-602-0259
Email: victorjcavallo@lawyers.com URL: http://www.lawyers.com/victorcavallo
Practice limited to Family Law for Husbands and Fathers. Divorce, Child Support, Child Custody, Alimony and Domestic Violence.
See Professional Biographies, STAMFORD, CONNECTICUT

Centrella, Scott S., (BV) ....'58 '83 C.1030 B.A. L.184 J.D. [Diserio M.O.&C.]
*PRACTICE AREAS: Employment Law; Employment Litigation; Commercial Litigation; Family Law; Workers Compensation.
Cerrito, Christopher M. .... '71 '96 C&L.93 B.S., J.D. [[A] Cummings&L.]
*PRACTICE AREAS: Corporate Law; Mergers and Acquisitions.
Certilman, Steven A., (BV) .... '56 '82 C.183 B.A. L.1019 J.D. [S.A.Certilman] ⊙

Certilman, Steven A., P.C., (BV)
350 Bedford Street, 06901 ⊙
Telephone: 203-977-7800 Fax: 203-425-8600 URL: http://www.lawyers.com/certilman
Email: sac@certilman.com URL: http://www.certilman.com
Steven A. Certilman.
Corporation and Commercial Law, Alternative Dispute Resolution, Commercial Litigation, Computer Law, Trademark, Copyright and Licensing Law, Real Estate and Condominium Law.
Approved Attorney for: Countrywide Funding Corp. (CT and NY): Household Mortgage Corp.; BancBoston Mortgage Corp.; G.E. Capital Mortgage Services, Inc.
New York, New York Office: 640 Fifth Avenue, 4th Floor. Telephone: 212-956-3425.
See Professional Biographies, STAMFORD, CONNECTICUT

Chach, Kristin L. .... '72 '98 C.1103 B.A. L.575 J.D. [[A] Finn D.&H.]
*PRACTICE AREAS: Corporate Law; Mergers and Acquisitions; Securities; Venture Capital.

Champ, Norman B., III '63 '90 C.674 A.B. L.309 J.D.
(adm. in NY; not adm. in CT)
Managing Director & General Counsel, Chilton Investment Company , Inc.
Chang, Deborah S. ....'60 '86 C.378 B.A. L.221 J.D. [Cummings&L.]
*PRACTICE AREAS: Product Liability Litigation; Medical Malpractice Law.
Chapdelaine, Rosemarie ....'55 '90 C.1211 B.S. L.1029 J.D. 80 4th St.
Chargar, Richard S. ....'50 '76 C.659 B.S. L.823 J.D. [Kelley D.&W.]
*PRACTICE AREAS: Employee Benefits; Taxation.
Chayet, Julie Min ....'69 '99 C.311 B.A. L.262 J.D. [Ⓐ Wiggin&D.]
Chen, David ....'70 '00 C.184 B.S. L.564 J.D. [Ⓐ St. Onge S.J.&R.]
*PRACTICE AREAS: Patent Prosecution; Patent Litigation; Trademark Prosecution; Trademark Litigation; Copyright Prosecution.
Chequer, Nan Budde ....'38 '86 C.881 A.B. L.976 J.D. [Ⓒ Tyler C.&A.]
*PRACTICE AREAS: Real Estate; Trusts and Estates; Corporate.
Chinitz, Ross M. ....'67 '92 C.446 B.A. L.1019 J.D. 700 Canal St.
Chioffi, Mark P. ....'66 '91 C&L.184 B.S., J.D. [Martin,L.&C.]
*PRACTICE AREAS: Estate Planning; Tax Planning; Estate Settlement; Trust Administration.
Choate, John I. '46 '92 C.623 B.A. L.976 J.D.
(adm. in NY; not adm. in CT) 22 Powell Pl.
Choi, David Y. ....'73 '99 C.309 B.A. L.188 J.D. [Ⓐ Day,B.&H.]
*PRACTICE AREAS: Taxation; Trusts and Estates.
Christian, Jamene L. ....'65 '93 C.331 B.A. L.107 J.D. ESQ Construction, Inc.
Christiano, Lawrence A., (BV) ...... '41 '67 C.1029 B.A. L.1009 LL.B. [Macrides,Z.&C.]
Christie, Joanne F. '59 '87 C.602 B.A. L.228 J.D.
(adm. in NY; not adm. in CT) Coun., Xerox Corporation
Christman, David A. '59 '94 C&L.569 B.A., J.D.
(adm. in NY; not adm. in CT) Asst. Gen. Coun., Time Warner Cable
Christrup, G. Kenneth ....'24 '52 C&L.734 B.S., LL.B. Xerox Corp.
Cienava, Edmund J. ....'65 '94 C.818 B.S. L.1009 J.D. [Phelan&M.]
Ciocca, Henry G. '46 '71 C.116 B.A. L.602 J.D.
Pres., CEO Markborough Development
Ciottone, Jonathon ....'74 '99 C.454 B.A. L.1252 J.D. [Ⓐ Ryan,R.J.&D.]
*PRACTICE AREAS: Insurance Defense.
Ciuffo, John M. ....'63 '90 C.184 B.S. L.607 J.D. 112 Prospect St.
Clark, Robert B. ....'63 '88 C.197 B.A. L.184 J.D. Coun., GE Capital Card Servs.
Clarke, Martin A. ....'64 '94 C.401 B.A. L.262 J.D. [Ⓐ Cummings&L.]
Clarke, Peter J. ....'60 '89 C.433 B.A. L.1040 J.D. Price Waterhouse
Clasen, Joseph L., (AV) '— '81 C.93 A.B. L.893 J.D.
[Robinson&C.] (⊙New York, NY)
*PRACTICE AREAS: Litigation; Creditors' Rights; Bankruptcy.
Clauss, Thomas F., Jr., (AV) ....'53 '80 C.976 B.A. L.705 J.D. [Pillsbury W.]
*PRACTICE AREAS: Corporate Litigation; Arbitration; Corporate Governance; Life Sciences and Technology.
Clayton, Christina E. '47 '73 C.681 B.A. L.178 J.D.
(adm. in NY; not adm. in CT) V.P. & Gen. Coun., Xerox Corp.
*RESPONSIBILITIES: Antitrust; Litigation.

Clear, Michael Gene, Law Offices of, (AV) '44 '69 C.708 B.A. L.184 J.D. BR
184 Atlantic Street, P.O. Box 3292, 06905
Telephone: 203-973-0240 Facsimile: 203-973-0244
Email: MCLEAR9948@aol.com URL: http://www.lawyers.com/michaelclear
***PRACTICE AREAS: Automobile Accidents and Injuries; Personal Injury; Wills; Elder Law; Insurance Coverage.**
General Civil Trial Practice in State and Federal Courts. Personal Injury, Negligence, Environmental Law and Hazardous Waste Litigation, Insurance Coverage Litigation, Complex Litigation, Commercial Litigation, Alternative Dispute Resolution, Mediation, Municipal Law, Environmental Insurance Defense, Insurance Coverage, Probate Litigation, Wills, Elder Law, Incapacity Planning, Probate Administration.
See Professional Biographies, STAMFORD, CONNECTICUT

Cleary, Ward Frank, (BV) ....'43 '70 C&L.262 B.A., J.D. [Curtis,B.&B.]
*PRACTICE AREAS: Federal Taxation; International Taxation; Closely Held Corporations; Estate Planning; Commercial Real Estate Acquisitions.
Cleveland, Joan B. '32 '57 C.914 A.B. L.93 LL.B.
(adm. in MA; not adm. in CT) 9 W. Broad St.
Clifton, J. Christopher ....'71 '00 C.1044 B.S. L.880 J.D. [Ⓐ Pillsbury W.]
*PRACTICE AREAS: Corporate Law; Mergers and Acquisitions; Private Equity; Securities.
Coffin, John R. '49 '76 C.378 B.A. L.502 J.D.
(adm. in MO; not adm. in CT) Gen. Coun., Student Loan Corp., The
Cohen, Arlana S. '57 '82 C.1044 B.A. L.978 J.D.
(adm. in NY; not adm. in CT) [St. Onge S.J.&R.]
*PRACTICE AREAS: Litigation; Trademark; Unfair Competition; Copyrights.
Cohen, David M., (AV) ....'48 '73 C.309 A.B. L.976 J.D. [Wofsey,R.K.&K.]
*PRACTICE AREAS: Litigation; Employment Law; Civil Rights; Immigration and Naturalization.
Cohen, Mitchell H. ....'61 '86 C.823 B.S. L.1044 J.D. Ernst & Young

Cohen, Gary I.
(See Greenwich)

Cohen and Wolf, P.C., (AV)
112 Prospect Street, 06904 ⊙
Telephone: 203-964-9907 Facsimile: 203-576-8504
Email: cw@cohenandwolf.com URL: http://www.cohenandwolf.com
Richard L. Albrecht; Jonathan S. Bowman; Irving J. Kern; Martin J. Albert; Stewart I. Edelstein; Richard G. Kent; Richard Slavin; Richard J. Di Marco; David B. Zabel; Jocelyn B. Hurwitz. Of Counsel: Stuart A. Epstein; Jack E. McGregor.
General Practice. Business Transactions, Commercial Litigation, Employment and Labor, Family and Matrimonial, Land Use, Municipal, Personal Injury, Physicians Practice, Real Estate, Securities, Tax, Trusts and Estates. Litigation in all Courts.
Bridgeport, Connecticut Office: 1115 Broad Street. Telephone: 203-368-0211. Facsimile: 203-394-9901.
Danbury, Connecticut Office: 158 Deer Hill Avenue. Telephone: 203-792-2771. Facsimile: 203-791-8149.
Westport, Connecticut Office: 190 Main Street. Telephone: 203-222-1034.
See Professional Biographies, STAMFORD, CONNECTICUT

Cohn Birnbaum & Shea P.C., (AV)
350 Bedford Street, Suite 301 (⊙Hartford, Westport, CT; New York, NY)
Colbert, Richard P., (BV) ....'65 '90 C.1103 B.S. L.1194 J.D. [Ⓐ Day,B.&H.]
*PRACTICE AREAS: Complex Litigation; Real Estate Litigation.
Coleman, John Philip ....'64 '95 C.1030 B.A. L.1040 J.D. 1200 Summer St.
Collier, A. E. '21 '52 C&L.802 B.B.A., LL.B.
(adm. in TX; not adm. in CT) 32 Revonah Cir.‡
Collier, William J., Jr., (AV) ......'33 '60 C.321 B.A. L.262 LL.B. [Collier,H.N.N.&B.] ⊙
Collier, Halpern, Newberg, Nolletti & Bock, LLP, (AV)
970 Summer Street (⊙New York, White Plains, NY)
Collins, William T., (AVⓉ) '42 '67 C.321 A.B. L.893 J.D.
(adm. in NY; not adm. in CT) EQ Corp.

Collins, Hannafin, Garamella, Jaber & Tuozzolo, Professional Corporation
(See Danbury)

Comerford, Carolyn A. ....'59 '85 C.262 B.A. L.1029 J.D. Asst. Pub. Def.
Comerford, Richard F., Jr., (AV) ....'45 '69 C.1030 B.S. L.262 J.D. Supr. Ct. J.

Conlon, Jacquelyn A. ....'60 '93 C.273 B.A. L.1252 J.D. [Ⓐ Cummings&L.]
*PRACTICE AREAS: Professional Liability Law; General Litigation.
Connors, John T. '48 '79 C.870 B.S. L.724 J.D.
Chf. Oper. Offr./Chf. Legal Offr., Fortis Capital Holdings Inc.
Conroy, Douglas C., (AVⓉ) ....'42 '69 C.309 A.B. L.659 LL.B. [Paul,H.J.&W.]
*PRACTICE AREAS: Securities Litigation; Antitrust Litigation; Commercial Litigation; Class Actions; RICO.
Conroy, Edward A., Jr. .... '21 '59 C.994 B.S. L.273 LL.B. 1937 West Main St. (Pat.)
Conroy, Edward C. '68 '95 C.116 B.S. L.1187 J.D.
(adm. in MA; not adm. in CT) Ernst & Young LLP
Considine, Michael G., (AV) ....'58 '85 C.93 B.A. L.276 J.D. [Day,B.&H.]
*PRACTICE AREAS: Government Investigations; Commercial Litigation.
Cook, Richard F., Jr. '52 '80 C.951 B.A. L.880 J.D.
(adm. in NY; not adm. in CT) General Electric Credit Corp.
Cookney, Leonard E., (BV) ....'35 '61 C&L.262 B.S., LL.B. 300 Bedford St.
Cooper, George W. '27 '51 C&L.178 A.B., J.D.
(adm. in NY; not adm. in CT) [Grimes&B.]
Cooper & McCann, LLP, (AV) .... 700 Canal Street (⊙Elmsford, New York, NY)
Coplit, James G. '68 '94 C.188 B.S. L.94 J.D.
(adm. in NY; not adm. in CT; See Pat. Sect.) [Grimes&B.]
Cordone, James A. ....'72 '97 C.890 B.A. L.184 J.D. [Ⓐ Kelley D.&W.]
*PRACTICE AREAS: Real Estate.
Corn, Amy C. .....'53 '80 C.860 B.A. L.128 J.D. V.P. & Corp. Secy., Pitney Bowes Inc.
*RESPONSIBILITIES: Corporate Governance; Corporate; Securities.
Cornacchio, Elizabeth, (AVⓉ) '51 '82
C.354 B.Mus. Ed. L.724 J.D. [Heidell,P.M.&B.] ⊙
*PRACTICE AREAS: Medical Malpractice; Complex Litigation; Trial Practice; Professional Liability.
Corwin, Elizabeth ....'67 '99 C.674 L.1040 [Ⓐ Day,B.&H.]
Costa, John F. ....'60 '85 C.321 B.A. L.1009 J.D. [Heidell,P.M.&B.] ⊙
*PRACTICE AREAS: Trial Practice; Appellate Practice; Medical Malpractice; Products Liability; Professional Liability.
Costello, Mark '57 '82 C.459 B.S.E.E. L.930 J.D.
(adm. in OH; not adm. in CT) Gen Patent Coun., Zerox Corp.
*RESPONSIBILITIES: Intellectual Property.
Cottrell, Jane R. '47 '82 C.878 B.A. L.178 J.D.
(adm. in NY; not adm. in CT) Vice President & General Counsel, CBS Cable
Coughlin, Daniel F. '50 '92 C.860 B.A. L.46 J.D.
(adm. in IL; not adm. in CT; Pat.) [Cummings&L.]
*PRACTICE AREAS: Patents.
Coupe, Jeanne Dugan .... '64 '93 C.184 B.S. L.724 J.D. United Sys. Integrators Corp.
Courtney, Marian E. ....'70 '97 C.569 B.A. L.1019 J.D. [Ⓐ Heidell,P.M.&B.] ⊙
*PRACTICE AREAS: Medical Malpractice.

Cousins, Johnson & Desrosiers, P.C.
(See Stratford)

Coviello, David J. ....'72 '00 C.184 B.S. L.1194 J.D. [Ⓐ Cacace,T.&S.]
*PRACTICE AREAS: Zoning, Planning and Land Use; Litigation.
Covill, Thomas A. ....'46 '71 C.676 A.B. L.818 J.D. Chicago Title Ins. Co.
*RESPONSIBILITIES: Real Estate Law; Title Insurance Law.
Coyne, Jennifer M. ....'75 '01 [Ⓐ Cummings&L.]
Craddock-Lee, Vera M., (BV) ....'43 '87 C.054 B.A. L.569 J.D. [Ⓒ Cummings&L.]
*PRACTICE AREAS: Estate Planning; Estate Administration.
Craig, Christopher H. ....'61 '90 C.299 B.A. L.94 J.D. [Paul,H.J.&W.]
*PRACTICE AREAS: Banking; Financial Institutions; Asset-Based Financial Transactions; Letters of Credit; Restructurings.

Cramer & Ahern
(See Westport)

Creutzmann, Harry F. ....'43 '74 C.98 B.S. L.724 J.D. V.P., General Reins. Corp.
Crichton, Roni M. '56 '82 C.813 B.A. L.1065 J.D.
(adm. in CA; not adm. in CT) Assoc. Gen. Coun., Xerox Corp.
*RESPONSIBILITIES: Software Licensing; Distribution; Antitrust Law; Employment Law.
Crispino, Paul J. '65 '91 C.1040 B.B.A. L.569 J.D.
(adm. in NY; not adm. in CT) Tax Coun., GE Asset Management
Critelli, Michael J. '48 '74 C.966 B.A. L.309 J.D.
(adm. in IL; not adm. in CT)
V.P., Secy., Gen. Coun. & Chf. Pers. Offr., Pitney Bowes Inc.
Crone, Thor L., (BV) ....'52 '78 C.105 B.A. L.184 J.D. [Avery&C.]

Cuddy & Feder & Worby LLP
733 Summer Street, 06901 ⊙
Telephone: 203-348-4780
URL: http://www.cfwlaw.com
Of Counsel: Andrew A. Glickson.
General Practice. Corporate, Real Estate, Zoning, Environmental, Historic Preservation, Housing and Urban Development, Condominium, Municipal, Trusts, Estates, Probate, Estate Planning and Taxation, Elder, Commercial Litigation, Industrial Development Bond Financing and Secured Lending Law.
White Plains, New York Office: 90 Maple Avenue. Telephone: 914-761-1300. Telecopier: 914-761-5372.
New York, N.Y. Office: 500 Fifth Avenue, Suite 2900. Telephone: 212-944-2841. Telecopier: 212-944-2843.
Hudson Valley Office: Westage Business Center, 300 South Lake Drive, Fishkill, NY, 12524. Telephone: 845-896-2229. Telecopier: 845-896-3672.
Norwalk, Connecticut Office: One Marshall Street. Telephone: 203-853-8001. Telecopier: 203-831-8250.
See Professional Biographies, STAMFORD, CONNECTICUT

Cummings & Lockwood, (AV)
Four Stamford Plaza, P.O. Box 120, 06904-0120 ⊙
Telephone: (203) 327-1700 Telecopier: (203) 351-4535
Email: info@cl-law.com URL: http://www.cl-law.com
Members of Firm: Glenn J. Angiolillo; Foster Bam (Resident, Greenwich, Connecticut Office); Robert Alexander Beer; Donald L. Borod (Resident, Hartford, Connecticut Office); Paul L. Bourdeau (Resident, Hartford, Connecticut Office); Matthew A. Bovino; Lisa M. Boyle (Resident, Hartford, Connecticut Office); William H. Bright, Jr. (Resident, Hartford, Connecticut Office); John W. Cannavino; John F. Carberry; Deborah S. Chang; Daniel F. Coughlin (Not admitted in CT); Frank J. Coyle (Resident, Greenwich, Connecticut Office); Daniel L. Daniels; B. Cort Delany (Resident, Greenwich, Connecticut Office); Michael N. Delgass; Robert P. Dolian; Alison K. Douglas (Resident, Naples, Florida Office); Philip M. Drake (Resident, Greenwich, Connecticut Office); Lawrence A. Farese (Resident, Naples, Florida Office); Geoffrey F. Fay; Charles J. Filardi, Jr.; Timothy S. Fisher (Resident, Hartford, Connecticut Office); Jamie Johnson Fitzgerald (Resident, New Haven, Connecticut Office); John A. Flaherty; Thomas J. Freed; John R. French (Resident, Greenwich, Connecticut Office); Steven I. Frenkel; Keith Bradoc Gallant (Resident, New Haven, Connecticut Office); Charles R. Gehrke (Resident, Bonita Springs, Florida Office); Mark D. Giarratana (Resident, Hartford, Connecticut Office); Jessie A. Gilbert (Resident, Greenwich, Connecticut Office); Robert T. Gilhuly (Resident, Greenwich, Connecticut Office); Robert F. Grele (Resident, Greenwich, Connecticut Office); William O'C. Harnisch (Not admitted in CT); Michael J. Hinton; William N. Horowitz (Resident, Bonita Springs, Florida Office) (Board Certified Taxation Lawyer, Florida Bar Board of Legal Specialization and Education); Paul G. Hughes; Howard M. Hujsa (Resident, Naples, Florida Office); Robert B. Katz (Resident, Hartford, Connecticut Office); Wendi J. Kemp (Resident, Hartford, Connecticut Office); David W. Kesner (Resident, New Haven, Connecticut Office); Vincent M. Kiernan; Thad D. Kirkpatrick (Resident, Naples, Florida Office); Paul E. Knag; Jason Hunter Korn (Resident, Naples, Florida Office); Barry Kramer; Kenneth D. Krier (Resident, Naples, Florida Office); Gina S. Linstone (Resident, West Hartford, Connecticut Office); James I. Lotstein (Resident,

(This Listing Continued)

Cummings & Lockwood (Continued)

Hartford, Connecticut Office); William R. Lynch (Resident, Greenwich, Connecticut Office); John R. Mallin (Resident, Hartford, Connecticut Office); Stephen Marcovich; Nancy P. Marx; Richard P. McGrath; Jonathan B. Mills (Resident, Greenwich, Connecticut Office); John R. Musicaro, Jr.; Basam E. Nabulsi; William H. Narwold; Ralph A. Nichols; Gregory B. Nokes; Kevin D. O'Leary (Resident, Hartford, Connecticut Office); Douglas H. Olin (Resident, Greenwich, Connecticut Office); Margaret A. O'Neal; Willard J. Overlock; R. Thomas Payne (Not admitted in CT); Kelley G. Price (Resident, Naples, Florida Office); Charles D. Ray (Resident, Hartford, Connecticut Office); Robert W. Reeves; David A. Reif (Resident, New Haven, Connecticut Office); Cathy S. Reiman (Resident, Naples, Florida Office); Richard R. Rendeiro (Resident, Hartford, Connecticut Office); Edward F. Rodenbach (Resident, Greenwich, Connecticut Office); Timothy G. Ronan; Joel H. Schechter (Resident, Naples, Florida Office); Richard A. Siegal; Thomas P. Skidd, Jr.; Mark G. Sklarz (Resident, New Haven, Connecticut Office); Richard M. Solazzo; John F. Spindler; Ira B. Stechel (Not admitted in CT); Charles M. Tatelbaum (See Biography at Naples, Florida); Conrad Teitell (Not admitted in CT); Howard S. Tuthill; Howard S. Tuthill III; Richard Voigt (Resident, Hartford, Connecticut Office); Jane Kimball Warren (Resident at Hartford, Connecticut Office); William C. Weitzel, Jr. (Not admitted in CT); Eric Watt Wiechmann (Resident, Hartford, Connecticut Office); Gayle Brian Wilhelm; Holly J. Winger (Resident, Hartford, Connecticut Office); Scott D. Wofsy; Marc L. Zaken. Resident Counsel: Vera M. Craddock-Lee; Sanford J. Davis (Not admitted in CT); John D. Freeman; Harris S. Jaffe (Not admitted in CT); Evelyn M. Sommer (Not admitted in CT). Resident Associates: Roxana Aleali; Karen L. Allison; M. Juliet Bonazzoli; David A. Bradley; Christopher M. Cerrito; Martin A. Clarke; Jacquelyn A. Conlon; Jennifer M. Coyne; Tracy C. Daugherty; Margaret A. DeLuca; Ryan Charles Fisher; Daniel G. Johnson; Michael J. Kearney, Jr.; Andrew D. Kupinse; David T. Leibell; James J. Lillie (Not admitted in CT); Cassandra B. McDonald; Richard Newman; Carrie Webb Olson; Bart F. Peters; Yusef Poole; Carolyn Reers (Not admitted in CT); Elisa Shevlin Rizzo (Not admitted in CT); Claire E. Ryan; Joshua J. Sarner; Evan S. Seideman; Rachel B. Sherman; Robert J. Sickinger; David J. Silvia; Heather V. Taylor; Courtenay L. Tischer; Karen Wagshul; Mary Ellen C. Whiteman; Alison Jacobs Wice. Staff Attorney: Mady McSweeney.

General Practice. National and Regional Litigation Counsel, Corporate Law, Patent and Intellectual Property, Trusts and Estates, Labor and Employment, Mergers and Acquisitions, Partnerships and Joint Ventures, Commercial Lending, Corporate Finance, Creditors' Rights, Bankruptcy and Workouts, Securities Regulation and Litigation, Tax, Insurance, Banking and Financial Services, Leasing, Commercial and Residential Real Estate, Construction, Environmental, Toxic Torts, Health Law, Products Liability Litigation, Probate Litigation, Family Law, International Business.

Greenwich, Connecticut Office: Two Greenwich Plaza, P.O. Box 2505, 06836. Telephone: (203) 869-1200. Telecopier: (203) 869-3120.

Hartford, Connecticut Office: CityPlace I, 185 Asylum Street, 36th Floor, 06103-3495. Telephone: (860) 275-6700. Telecopier: (860) 724-3397.

New Haven, Connecticut Office: 700 State Street, P.O. Box 1960. 06509-1960. Telephone: (203) 782-3000. Telecopier: (203) 777-3347.

West Hartford, Connecticut Office: Town Center, 29 South Main Street, Suite 208, 06107. Telephone: (860) 275-6700. Telecopier: (860) 313-0293.

Bonita Springs, Florida Office: 24311 Walden Center, Suite 201, 34134. Telephone: (941) 947-8811. Telecopier: (941) 947-8025.

Naples, Florida Office: 3001 Tamiami Trail North, P.O. Box 413032, 34101-3032. Telephone: (941) 262-8311. Telecopier: (941) 263-0703.

See Professional Biographies, STAMFORD, CONNECTICUT

Cummiskey, Paul J. '58 '85 C.103 A.B. L.209 J.D.
(adm. in NY; not adm. in CT) V.P. & Coun., GE Capital Aviation Servs., Inc.

Cunningham, Richard H. G. ....'44 '70 C.453 B.S. L.228 J.D. 12 Keniworth Dr., E.

Curley, Stephen J., (BV) ....'67 '91 C.95 A.B. L.93 J.D. [Ⓐ Pillsbury W.]
*PRACTICE AREAS: Commercial Litigation.

Curry, Mary G. .... '61 '98 C.66 B.A. L.112 J.D. [Ⓐ Silver,G.&T.]
*PRACTICE AREAS: Medical Malpractice; Negligence; Commercial Litigation; Employment Law.

Curtin, Paul Sean '69 '94 C.93 B.A. L.982 J.D.
Sr. Coun., Purdue Frederick Co./Purdue Pharma L.P.
*RESPONSIBILITIES: Health Care; FDA Regulatory Law; Corporate Law; General Practice.

Curtis, Brinckerhoff & Barrett, P.C., (AV) BB
666 Summer Street, 06901-1416
Telephone: 203-324-6777 Telecopier: 203-324-9621
T. Ward Cleary (1916-1988); John Wayne Fox; Ward Frank Cleary; James D'Alton Murphy; Randolph T. Lovallo; Michael P. Murray; Susan L. Stratton. Of Counsel: Richard L. Brinckerhoff; John D. Hertz; Jane F. Donovan; Frederick M. Tobin; Patricia M. Gaug;—John J. Louizos; Joseph P. Sargent.
General Practice, Real Estate, Commercial Real Estate Acquisitions, Municipal Law, Zoning, Planning and Land Use, Banking, Administrative Law, Litigation, Civil Litigation, Commercial Litigation, Tax Appeals, Eminent Domain, Federal Taxation, International Taxation, State Taxation, Estate Planning, Trust and Estate, Probate, Elder Law, Family Law, Domestic Relations, Closely Held Corporations, Business Law, Corporate Law, Commercial Law, Commercial Leasing, Employment Law, Commercial Arbitration, Construction Law, Landlord and Tenant Law, Personal Injury and Negligence, Product Liability, Bankruptcy, Civil Trial and Appellate Practice in all State and Federal Courts.
Counsel for: Town of Darien; The F. A. Bartlett Tree Expert Co.; Miller Automobile Corp.; Bolliger, Inc.; People's Bank, Bridgeport; William Pitt Foundation; Manulife Wood Logan, Inc.
See Professional Biographies, STAMFORD, CONNECTICUT

Curtis, Mallet-Prevost, Colt & Mosle LLP, (AV)
Financial Centre, 695 East Main Street, 06901 ⊙
Telephone: 203-359-6200 Telecopier: 203-328-2617
Email: info@cm-p.com URL: http://www.cm-p.com
Resident Partner: Victor L. Zimmermann, Jr. Counsel: Peter E. Fleming, III; Remy A. Rodas; Michael K. Stanton, Jr. Associates: Jerrold A. Siskin (Not admitted in CT); D. Christine Woodhouse (Not admitted in CT).
General Practice, including the Laws of Latin American Countries.
New York, N.Y. Office: 101 Park Avenue. Telephone: 212-696-6000. Telecopier: 212-697-1559.
Washington, D.C. Office: Suite 1205L, 1801 K Street, N.W. Telephone: 202-452-7373. Telecopier: 202-452-7333.
Newark, New Jersey Office: One Gateway Center, Suite 403. Telephone: 973-622-0605. Telecopier: 973-622-5646.
Houston, Texas Office: 2 Houston Center, 909 Fannin Street, Suite 3725. Telephone: 713-759-9555. Telecopier: 713-759-0712.
Mexico City, D.F., Mexico Office: Curtis, Mallet-Prevost, Colt & Mosle, Ruben Dario 281, Pisos 8 & 9, Col. Bosque de Chapultepec, 11530 Mexico, D.F. Telephone: 52-55-5282-0444. Telecopier: 52-55-5282-0637.
Paris, France Office: 15 rue d'Astorg, 75008. Telephone: +33-1 42-66-39-10. Telecopier: +33-1 42-66-39-62.
London, England Office: One Cornhill, EC3V 3ND. Telephone: 0207-743-6310. Telecopier: 0207-743-6311.
Frankfurt am Main 1, Germany Office: Staufenstrasse 42. Telephone: +49-69-971-4420. Telecopier: +49-69-17 33 99.
Muscat, Sultanate of Oman Office: Jewel Beach-134. Telephone: 968-564-495. Telecopier: 968-564-497.
Milan, Italy Office: Curtis, Mallet-Prevost & Gilioli, Piazzale Principessa Clotilde 8, 20121. Telephone: +(39) 02 29 00 29 32. Telefax: +(39) 02 65 75 969.
Revisers of the Argentina, Bolivia, Brazil, Chile, Colombia, Costa Rica, Dominican Republic, Ecuador, El Salvador, Guatemala, Honduras, Mexico, Nicaragua, Peru, Uruguay and Venezuela Law Digests for this Directory.
See Professional Biographies, STAMFORD, CONNECTICUT

Daiuto, Ralph A. '38 '69 C.895 B.S. L.262 J.D.
(adm. in NY; not adm. in CT) V.P., Tax, Thomson U.S. Inc.

Dalfonso, Lisa M. ....'69 '96 C&L.107 B.A., J.D. Six High Ridge Park

Dallmeyer, Ford R. '47 '74 C.197 A.B. L.145 J.D.
(adm. in IL; not adm. in CT) Chf. Reg. Coun., ACNielsen Corporation
*RESPONSIBILITIES: International Law; Acquisitions/Joint Ventures.

D'Andrea, Frank H., Jr. ....'31 '55 C.976 B.A. L.309 LL.B. Supr. Ct. J.

Daniele, Barbara E. '51 '77
C&L.724 B.S., J.D. V.P. & Sr. Litig. Coun., GE Capital Corp.

Daniels, Daniel L., (AV) ....'62 '88 C.197 A.B. L.309 J.D. [Cummings&L.]
*PRACTICE AREAS: Estate Planning; Tax Planning; Estate Administration; Trust Administration; Probate Litigation.

Danile, Jeffrey John ....'75 '00 C.569 B.A. L.724 J.D. [Ⓐ Wiggin&D.]

Dattner, John W. '48 '78 C.994 B.A. L.724 J.D.
Vice President, General Reinsurance Corporation

Daugherty, Tracy C. ....'64 '89 C.280 B.B.A. L.94 J.D. [Ⓐ Cummings&L.]
*PRACTICE AREAS: Estate Planning and Administration.

Davey, Peter F. ....'42 '68 C.433 B.S. L.724 J.D. [Ⓐ Jones H.C.&B.] (⊙New York, NY)

Davidson, Robert E. '24 '52 C&L.986 B.A., LL.B.
(adm. in MO; not adm. in CT) 695 E. Main St.‡

D'Avino, Richard '— '80 C&L.659 B.S., J.D.
(adm. in PA; not adm. in CT) Sr. V.P., Taxes, GE Capital Corp.

Davis, F. Eugene, IV, (AV) ....'33 '58 C.453 S.B. L.309 LL.B. [F.E.Davis IV] (Pat.)

Davis, Leslie J. '50 '77 C.354 B.A. L.823 J.D.
V.P. & Asst. Gen. Coun., Gen. Reinsurance Corp.
*RESPONSIBILITIES: Litigation; Reinsurance; Insurance.

Davis, Polly DeVeau ....'63 '91 C.745 B.A. L.1194 J.D. [Ⓐ Pillsbury W.]
*PRACTICE AREAS: Commercial Real Estate; Property Law; Corporate Law.

Davis, Ricky B. W. ....'57 '88 C.259 B.S. L.569 J.D. Coun., GE Capital Card Servs.

Davis, Sanford J. '57 '85 C.659 L.904 J.D.
(adm. in NY; not adm. in CT) [Ⓒ Cummings&L.]
*PRACTICE AREAS: Corporate Law; Corporate Taxation; Mergers and Acquisitions; Partnership Taxation; International Taxation.

Davis, Tina A. '50 '76 C.910 B.A. L.597 J.D.
(adm. in IL; not adm. in CT) 290 Harbor Dr.

Davis, F. Eugene, IV, (AV) ....53 Harvest Hill Ln. (Pat.)

Davison, Endicott P. ....'23 '51 C.976 B.A. L.893 LL.B. 695 E. Main St.

Davoren, William M. ....'— '92 C.1030 B.S. L.982 J.D. [Ⓐ Wofsey,R.K.&K.]
*PRACTICE AREAS: Personal Injury; Medical Malpractice; Products Liability.

Dawkins, Jamal M. ....'71 '99 C.511 B.A. L.262 J.D. [Ⓐ Day,B.&H.]

Dawson, Laura E. B. ....'63 '89 C.112 B.A. L.976 J.D. Coun., GE Capital Card Servs.

Day, Berry & Howard LLP, (AV) BB
One Canterbury Green, 06901 ⊙
Telephone: 203-977-7300 Telecopier: 203-977-7301
Email: postmaster@dbh.com URL: http://www.dbh.com
Members of Firm in Stamford: Jerome Berkman; Martin L. Budd; Michael P. Byrne; Patricia A. Carpenter; Michael G. Considine; Kenneth W. Gage; Andrew P. Gaillard; Thomas D. Goldberg; Gregory A. Hayes; Robert J. Miller; Kenneth W. Ritt; Sabino Rodriguez III; Bonnie J. Roe (Not admitted in CT); Daniel L. Schwartz; James F. Stapleton; David A. Swerdloff; Stanley A. Twardy, Jr. Associates of Firm in Stamford: Tricia S. Begg; Melissa L. Bellavia; Ann Lisa Braun; Rob Roy Buckingham, Jr.; David Y. Choi; Richard P. Colbert; Elizabeth Corwin; Jamal M. Dawkins; Sarah Moore Fass; Kelly E. P. Flatt; Deborah S. Gordon; Joli Lyn Gross; Lorey Rives Leddy; Natasha M. Lipcan; Margaret A. McComish; Catherine Dugan O'Connor; Thomas J. O'Neill; Allen J. Roberts, III; Mark B. Robinson (Not admitted in CT); Jennifer L. Sachs (Not admitted in CT); Fritz Strohmeyer; Ray A. Wynter. Of Counsel in Stamford: Emil H. Frankel. Counsel in Stamford: Stacey B. Babson-Smith (Not admitted in CT); Patricia M. Canavan; Terence J. Gallagher III (Not admitted in CT); Derek Gilman; Benedicta S. McGrath; Roland A. Paul; Jonathan B. Tropp; Kathleen D. Warner; Paulette Wunsch.
Antitrust, Banking, Bank Lending, Bankruptcy, Bankruptcy Counseling, Benefits and Executive Compensation, Business Succession Planning, Business Transactions and Counseling, Closely Held Businesses, Credit Tenant Lease Financing, Commercial Litigation, Commercial Leasing, Construction, Direct Liability and Casualty Insurance, Disability, Emerging Companies, Energy, Environmental and Land Use, Equipment Finance and Leasing, Employment Law and Litigation, Environmental Law and Litigation, Executive Planning, Family Law, Finance and Investments, First Party Insurance, Franchise and Distributorship Litigation, Government Investigations, Health Care, Insurance Regulation and Proceedings, Insurance Litigation, International Tax, International Transactions, Life Insurance and Annuities, Low Income Housing Tax Credits, Medical and Professional Malpractice, Mergers and Acquisitions, Multi-Property Transactions, Municipal Finance, Negligence Defense, Planning for Entrepreneurs, Private Equity Funds, Product Liability, Real Estate Development, Real Estate Equity Investors, Real Estate Finance, Real Estate Workouts and Restructuring, Regulatory Insurance Proceedings and Litigation, Reinsurance, Securities Law, Securities Litigation, Strategic Joint Ventures, Structured Finance, Tax, Tax Litigation Group, Tax Exempt and Charity Giving, Tax Exempt Organizations, Technology and Intellectual Property Business and Litigation, Torts Litigation, Telecommunications, Trusts and Estates Administration, Trusts and Estates Litigation, Water Companies.
Greenwich, Connecticut Office: One East Putnam Avenue. Telephone: 203-862-7800. Telecopier: 203-862-7801.
Hartford, Connecticut Office: CityPlace I. Telephone: 860-275-0100. Telecopier: 860-275-0343.
Boston, Massachusetts Office: 260 Franklin Street. Telephone: 617-345-4600. Telecopier: 617-439-4453.
See Professional Biographies, STAMFORD, CONNECTICUT

Deans, Stuart R., (BV) ....'— '82 C.951 B.A. L.705 J.D. [Robinson&C.]
*PRACTICE AREAS: Environmental Law; Zoning, Planning and Land Use.

DeDona, Robert C. ....'68 '00 C&L.1040 B.B.A., J.D. [Ⓐ Sandak F.H.&G.]
*PRACTICE AREAS: Land Use; Zoning Law; Real Estate.

De Fina, Vincent R. '48 '74
C.994 B.A. L.1009 J.D. V.P./Mktg. & Coun., Chicago Title Ins. Co.

Dehmel, Paul R. .... '69 '98 C.951 B.A. L.724 J.D. [Ⓐ Paul,H.J.&W.]
*PRACTICE AREAS: Commercial Litigation.

Del Col, John V. '61 '90 C.197 A.B. L.309 J.D.
(adm. in NY; not adm. in CT)
Vice President, General Counsel & Secretary, Trenwick Group, Inc.

Delgass, Michael N. '69 '95 C.347 B.S.B.A. L.145 J.D.
[Cummings&L.] (⊙New Haven)
*PRACTICE AREAS: Trusts and Estates.

D'Elia, Susan F. ....'63 '89 C.829 B.S. L.306 J.D. 61 W. Hill Circle

DellaRocco, Kenneth A., (BV) .... '52 '83 C.1211 B.A. L.1029 J.D. [Ⓒ Cacace,T.&S.]
*PRACTICE AREAS: Business Law; Real Estate; Commercial Real Estate; Leases and Leasing; Corporate Law.

Dell'Isola, Mark A. '58 '85 C.588 B.S. L.818 J.D.
(adm. in MA; not adm. in CT) Arthur Andersen LLP

DelMonico, W. Bruce .....'69 '97 C.103 B.A. L.893 J.D. [Ⓐ Wiggin&D.] (⊙New Haven)

Deluca, Charles A., (AV) .... '50 '77 C.184 B.A. L.1009 J.D. [Ryan,R.J.&D.]
*PRACTICE AREAS: Complex and Multi-District Litigation; Professional Liability; Commercial Liability; Federal Practice.

DeLuca, Margaret A. ....'69 '96 C.674 A.B. L.276 J.D. [Ⓐ Cummings&L.]
*PRACTICE AREAS: Trusts and Estates.

DeLuca, Patricia A., (BV) '58 '84 C.30 B.S. L.1194 J.D.
Coun., GE Capital Real Estate

De Orchis, Walker & Corsa, LLP
24 Hoyt Street (⊙Miami, FL; Boston, MA; Union, NJ; New York, NY)

DePanfilis & Vallerie, LLC
(See Norwalk)

Depuy, Warner K., (BV) ....'51 '76 C.976 B.A. L.1017 J.D. [Benedict&D.]

DeStefanis, Jody L. ....'70 '99 C.184 B.S.E. L.1252 J.D. [Ⓐ Wiggin&D.] (Pat.)

de Toledo, Victoria, (AV) ....'56 '81 C.659 B.A. L.569 J.D. [Casper&d.L.]
*PRACTICE AREAS: Employment Law; Labor Law.

Devellis, Robert A. ....'69 '95 C.262 B.A. L.1252 J.D. [Ⓐ Blair&P.]
*PRACTICE AREAS: Estate Planning; Estate Settlements; Trust Administration.

DeVos, Joseph E. ....'33 '60 C.184 B.A. L.276 J.D. 117 Hubbard Ave.‡

Diamond, Mark .... '56 '86 C.102 B.S. L.1009 J.D. 24 W. Trail

DiBerardini-Albrecht, Danielle .... '70 '97 C.297 B.A. L.1252 J.D. [A Ryan,R.J.&D.]
*PRACTICE AREAS: Civil Litigation; Real Estate.
Dickson, Judge A. '40 '66 C&L.494 B.A., LL.B.
(adm. in MN; not adm. in CT) IBM Credit Corp.
Didamo, Valerie T. '61 '91 C.1040 B.S. L.107 J.D.
(adm. in NY; not adm. in CT) Pat. Coun., Cytec Industries Inc.
Diesa, Arthur L. .... '26 '50 C&L.564 B.A., J.D. 24 Smoke Hill Dr.
Di Giacomo, Anthony M. '62 '92 C.1139 B.S. L.178 J.D.
(adm. in NY; not adm. in CT) Region Coun., GE Capital Comm. Fin.
Di Marco, Richard J., (BV) '55 '84
C.1044 B.A. L.107 J.D. [Cohen&W.] (⊙Bridgeport, Westport)
*PRACTICE AREAS: Taxation; Estate Planning; Corporate.
Dimaria, Anthony G. .... '73 '98 C.1030 B.A. L.564 J.D. [A Blair&P.]
*PRACTICE AREAS: Estate Planning; Estate Settlements; Trust Administration.
DiNatale, Mario, (AV) .... '54 '80 C.178 B.A. L.569 J.D. [Silver,G.&T.]
*PRACTICE AREAS: Personal Injury; Medical Malpractice; Products Liability; Commercial Litigation; Criminal Defense.
Dinerstein, Robert C., (AVⓉ) '42 '66 C.309 B.A. L.477 J.D.
(adm. in NY; not adm. in CT)
Mng. Dir. & Gen. Coun., Warburg Dillon Read LLC, CT (⊙New York, NY)
Diserio, Eugene A., (AV) ....'27 '53 C&L.262 B.A., LL.B. [C Diserio M.O.&C.]

Diserio Martin O'Connor & Castiglioni LLP, (AV)
One Atlantic Street, 06901-2402
Telephone: 203-358-0800 Telecopier: 203-348-2321
Email: dmoc@dmoc.com
Members of Firm: Brian T. O'Connor; Richard E. Castiglioni; William A. Durkin III; Scott S. Centrella; Robert E. Murray, Jr.; Scott M. Harrington; Kevin T. Katske; Jonathan P. Whitcomb; David L. Dufort. Associates: Jason A. Marsh; Laura R. Shattuck; Merrie Fedor Hawley; James P. Carlon; Kevin R. Brady; Alicia B. Bromfield. Of Counsel: Eugene A. Diserio; Garry H. Morton; John V. A. Murray.
General Practice. Litigation and Trials in all Courts. Corporate, Commercial Finance, Securities, Taxation, Banking, Foreclosure and Workout, Real Estate Law, Personal Injury and Negligence, Employment Law, Wrongful Termination, Workers Compensation, Insurance Coverage and Defense, Family, Creditors Rights and Bankruptcy, Trusts, Probate, Estate and Tax Planning.
See Professional Biographies, STAMFORD, CONNECTICUT

Dix, Diane Stehle '62 '93 C.1161 B.A. L.150
(adm. in OH; not adm. in CT) Coun., GE Capital Equity Capital Group
Dixon, Brett W., (AV) .... '55 '82 C.951 B.A. L.188 J.D. [Finn D.&H.]
*PRACTICE AREAS: Taxation Law; Corporate Law.
Dize, Russell D. .... '71 '00 C.1369 B.B.A. L.1002 J.D. [A Grimes&B.]
*PRACTICE AREAS: Litigation; Intellectual Property.
Dluz, Peter M. .... '23 '52 C.976 A.B. L.477 LL.B. State's Atty.
Dolian, Robert P., (AV) ....'48 '75 C.228 B.A. L.309 J.D. [Cummings&L.]
*PRACTICE AREAS: Commercial Litigation; Construction Litigation; Probate Litigation.
Dolinsky, Nancy E. .... '56 '84 C.156 B.A. L.818 J.D. Asst. States Atty.
Dollarhide, Mary C. .... '57 '88 C.605 A.B. L.800 J.D. [Paul,H.J.&W.]
*PRACTICE AREAS: Sexual Harassment; Disability Discrimination; Employment Law; Reductions in Force; Employee Drug Testing.
Dominsky, John '39 '70 C.563 B.B.A. L.724 J.D.
(adm. in NY; not adm. in CT) Crane Co.
Donaher, Matthew M. .... '64 '93 C.602 B.B.A. L.930 J.D. [A Paul,H.J.&W.]
*PRACTICE AREAS: Secured Lending; Securitization; Corporate.
Donahue, Riker J. .... '68 '97 C.241 B.S.S.P. L.1040 J.D. [A Tooher&W.]
Donlon, Thomas J. ....'— '78 C.869 B.S. L.477 J.D. [A Robinson&C.]
Donnelly, Andrew P. '63 '89 C.973 B.A. L.150 J.D.
(adm. in OH; not adm. in CT) Coun., Taxes, GE Capital Corp.
Donovan, Jane F., (AV) ....'29 '67 C.103 A.B. L.262 J.D. [C Curtis,B.&B.]
Doonan, Lynn B. ....'69 '95 C.93 B.A. L.309 J.D. 707 Summer Street
Doppelt, Earl H. '53 '77 C.696 B.A. L.188 J.D.
(adm. in NY; not adm. in CT) Exec. V.P. & Gen. Coun., ACNielsen Corporation
*RESPONSIBILITIES: General Corporate.

Dougherty, Dougherty & Vecchiolla
(See Greenwich)

Dowd, Katherine ....'— '92 C.788 B.A. L.945 J.D. [A Robinson&C.]
Downey, Charles J., III, (BV) ....'64 '90 C.659 B.S. L.569 J.D. [Finn D.&H.]
*PRACTICE AREAS: Corporate Law; Mergers and Acquisitions Law; Securities Law; Venture Capital Financing Law.
Downs, Michael D...........'71 '00 C.264 B.A. L.309 J.D. Coun., Walker Digital Corp.
*RESPONSIBILITIES: Patent Prosecution.
Drake, Gregory S. '56 '81 C.684 B.A. L.1068 J.D.
(adm. in CA; not adm. in CT) Sr. Coun., Time Warner Cable
Dreimann, Ingrid A. '63 '90 C&L.352 B.A., J.D.
(adm. in NY; not adm. in CT) [ACNielsen]
*RESPONSIBILITIES: Corporate Law.
Dreyer, Peter Mason ....'71 '96 C.401 B.S. L.112 J.D. [A Silver,G.&T.]
Dreyfus, Ruth, (BV) ....'30 '55 C.477 B.A. L.309 J.D. 1200 Summer St.
Drummond, Elaine G. '52 '76 C.262 B.A. L.276 J.D.
Senior Counsel, Xerox Corporation
Dubin, Thomas I. H. '62 '88 C.31 B.A. L.569 J.D.
(adm. in NY; not adm. in CT) Vice President, General Counsel & Secretary, ChiRex Inc.
Duemmler, Frank L. '53 '77 C.165 B.A. L.902 J.D.
(adm. in NY; not adm. in CT) Merrill Lynch Realty, Inc.
Dufort, David L. .... '65 '91 C.1021 B.B.A. L.982 J.D. [Diserio M.O.&C.]
*PRACTICE AREAS: Trusts and Estates; Probate; Commercial Law; Corporate Law.
DuPont, Augustus I. '51 '78 C.813 A.B. L.145 J.D.
(adm. in MA; not adm. in CT) V.P., Gen. Coun. & Secy., Crane Co.

Dupont and Radlauer, L.L.P.
(See New London)

Durkin, Mark C., (BV) ....'59 '84 C.446 B.A. L.1040 J.D. [Durkin&P.] ⊙
*PRACTICE AREAS: Civil Litigation; Appellate Litigation; Personal Injury; Negligence; Commercial Law.
Durkin, William A., III, (BV) .... '54 '80 C.732 B.A. L.823 J.D. [Diserio M.O.&C.]
*PRACTICE AREAS: Corporate Law; Commercial Finance; Commercial Real Estate.

Durkin & Polera, P.C., (BV)
970 Summer Street, First Floor, 06905 ⊙
Telephone: 203-327-0044 Fax: 203-327-0088
URL: http://www.lawyers.com/durkin&polera
Mark C. Durkin; John C. Polera.
General Civil, Business, Litigation and Estates Practice. Business Transactions, Trusts and Estate Planning/Administration, Tax Planning and Compliance, Real Estate and Civil Litigation at the Trial and Appellate Levels in all Courts in the Personal Injury, Negligence, Contract, Commercial, Real Estate and Employment areas of the law, NASD and NYSE Arbitrations.
Tarrytown, New York Office: 14 North Broadway, 10591. Telephone: 914-631-1176.
See Professional Biographies, STAMFORD, CONNECTICUT

Dussault, Marilyn Black, (BV) .... '43 '80 C&L.184 B.A., J.D. 2777 Summer Street

Duval, Lee A. '75 '01 C.228 B.S.E. L.893 J.D.
(adm. in CA; not adm. in CT) [A Shipman&G.]
*PRACTICE AREAS: Litigation.
DuVernay, Valerie R. '67 '95 C&L.1040 B.B.A., J.D.
Coun., Corp. Consumer Rel., General Electric Capital Corporation
Dweck, Sari L. '62 '87 C.66 B.A. L.569 J.D.
(adm. in NY; not adm. in CT) Assoc. Gen. Coun., The Thomson Corp.
Dwelle, Cynthia L. ....'61 '89 C.529 B.A. L.1029 J.D. Stamford Computer Grp. Inc.
Eckweiler, Karl T. ....'61 '87 C.1145 B.A. L.1029 J.D. Senior Counsel, Xerox Corporation
Edelberg, Paul B., (AV) .... '50 '76 C.918 B.A. L.184 J.D. [Rucci,B.C.&E.]
*PRACTICE AREAS: Banks and Banking; Corporate Law; Business Law; Mergers, Acquisitions and Divestitures; Finance.
Edelstein, Stewart I., (AV) '48 '73
C.604 B.A. L.188 J.D. [Cohen&W.] (⊙Bridgeport, Westport)
*PRACTICE AREAS: Commercial Litigation; High Technology.
Edwards, Eugene T., Jr. .... '62 '92 C.188 B.S. L.1048 J.D. 91 Rachelle Ave.
Edwards, Frances E. '47 '79 C.788 B.A. L.564 J.D.
(adm. in NY; not adm. in CT) Asst. Secy. & Asst. Coun., Crane Co.

Effron, Wayne D., P.C.
(See Greenwich)

Egnatchik, Michael R. '47 '77 C.262 B.A. L.309 J.D.
(adm. in NY; not adm. in CT) Assoc. Gen. Coun., Int'l., Xerox Corp.
Ehlers, Dawn L. .....'61 '87 C.93 B.A. L.724 J.D. Asst. Gen. Coun., The Thomson Corp.
Ehring, Howard A., (BV) .... '53 '86 C.107 Ed.D. L.1029 J.D. Assoc. Pub. Def.
Einhorn, Diane M. '45 '73 C.659 B.A. L.564 J.D.
Assoc. Group Coun., Sara Lee Intimates, Sara Lee Corp.
Eisenberg, Seth F. '69 '96 C.867 B.A. L.982 J.D.
(adm. in NY; not adm. in CT) [A Jackson L.S.&K.]
Elbaum, Steven L. ....'— '92 C.918 B.A. L.94 J.D. [Robinson&C.]
*PRACTICE AREAS: Real Estate; Finance; Commercial Leasing.
Eldridge, Joan M. '53 '84 C.184 B.A. L.564 J.D.
(adm. in NY; not adm. in CT) Merrill Lynch Realty, Inc.
Elgee, Michael W. '42 '82 C.1030 B.A. L.1029 J.D.
V.P., Gen. Coun. & Secy., Gen. Reinsurance Corp.
*RESPONSIBILITIES: Life and Health Reinsurance; Regulatory Law; Corporate Law.
Elias, Michael E. '54 '85 C.184 B.S. L.1029 J.D.
V.P. & Dep. Gen. Coun., ACNielsen Corporation
Elkow, Pamela K. ....'— '89 C.165 B.A. L.273 J.D. [C Robinson&C.]
*PRACTICE AREAS: Environmental Law.
Ellenthal, Judith, (BV) ....'41 '84 C.102 B.A. L.1029 J.D. [Rapaport&E.]
Emerling, Sandra G. '57 '84 C.473 B.S. L.989 J.D.
(adm. in OH; not adm. in CT) State Tax Coun., GE Capital Corp.

Emmet, Marvin & Martin, LLP, (AV)
1351 Washington Boulevard, 06902 ⊙
Telephone: 203-425-1400 Fax: 203-425-1410
Email: postmaster@emmetmarvin.com URL: http://www.emmetmarvin.com
Members of the Firm: John F. Bartlett; Benjamin H. Green.
General Practice, including Banking and Finance, Real Estate, Corporate, Securities, Tax, Employee Benefits, Trusts, Estates, Commercial Litigation, Employment Law, Creditors Rights and Bankruptcy Law.
New York, New York Office: 120 Broadway. Telephone: 212-238-3000. Fax: 212-238-3100.
Morristown, New Jersey Office: 177 Madison Avenue. Telephone: 973-538-5600. Fax: 973-538-6448.
See Professional Biographies, STAMFORD, CONNECTICUT

Emmett, Kathryn, (AV) ....'44 '70 C.681 B.A. L.976 J.D. [Emmett&G.] ⊙
*PRACTICE AREAS: Litigation; Employee Rights and Benefits; Professional Negligence; Product Liability; Personal Injury.

Emmett & Glander, (AV)
45 Franklin Street, 06901 ⊙
Telephone: 203-324-7744 Facsimile: 203-969-1319 URL: http://www.emmettandglander.com
Email: offices@emmettandglander.com URL: http://www.lawyers.com/emmett&glander
Members of Firm: Kathryn Emmett; Jane W. Glander. Associate: Christine Caulfield.
Litigation, Employee Rights and Benefits, Personal Injury, Professional Negligence, Products Liability, Discrimination, Civil Rights, Workers Compensation, Small Business and Corporate, Banking, Family, Real Estate, Probate and Estate Planning, Education, Arbitration and Mediation.
Newtown, Connecticut Office: 17 Pond Brook Road, P.O. Box 724, 06470. Telephone: 203-270-9272. Facsimile: 203-426-1270.
See Professional Biographies, STAMFORD, CONNECTICUT

Engel, John H. '26 '52 C.860 A.B. L.724 LL.B.
(adm. in NY; not adm. in CT) Asst. V.P., Citizens Utilities Co.
Engelman, Steve T. '66 '92 C&L.1019 B.A., J.D.
Coun. & Global Compl. Off., GE Card Servs.
Engle, Arthur K. ....'— '94 C.309 A.B. L.262 J.D. [A Robinson&C.]
Ennis, Thomas A., Jr., (AV) '20 '49 C.976 B.A. L.178 LL.B.
(adm. in NY; not adm. in CT) V.P., Combustion Engg., Inc.
Epstein, Stuart A., (BV) '38 '62 C.945 B.A. L.976 LL.B.
[C Cohen&W.] (⊙Bridgeport)
*PRACTICE AREAS: Real Estate; Private Syndications of Real Estate Transactions.

Epstein Becker & Green, P.C., (AV)
Suite 1800, One Landmark Square, 06901-2601 ⊙
Telephone: 203-348-3737 Facsimile: 203-324-9291
Email: mail@ebglaw.com URL: http://www.ebglaw.com
Members of the Firm: Peter L. Altieri; David S. Poppick; Peter M. Stein; Michael R. Zeller. Senior Attorney: Mary A. Gambardella. Associates: Jonathan M. Plissner; Bradford J. Sullivan; Elizabeth Stebbins Torkelsen; Steven J. Younes.
General Practice. Corporation, Securities and Commercial Law. Health Care and Hospital Law. Management Labor Relations and Employee Benefits Law. Equal Employment Opportunity and Affirmative Action Law and Practice. Taxation, Insurance, Government Procurement, Municipal Finance, Real Estate, Political Activities, Legislation and Election Law. Arbitration, Administrative Proceedings, State and Federal Civil and Appellate Practice.
New York, N.Y. Office: 250 Park Avenue. Telephone: 212-351-4500.
Washington, D.C. Office: 1227 25th Street, N.W., Suite 700. Telephone: 202-861-0900.
San Francisco, California Office: Epstein Becker & Green, Two Embarcadero Center, Suite 1650. Telephone: 415-398-3500.
Los Angeles, California Office: Epstein Becker & Green, Suite 500, 1875 Century Park, East. Telephone: 310-556-8861.
Dallas, Texas Office: Park Central VII, 12750 Merit Drive, Suite 1320. Telephone: 972-628-2450.
Newark, New Jersey Office: Two Gateway Center, 12th Floor. Telephone: 973-642-1900.
Boston, Massachusetts Office: 75 State Street. Telephone: 617-342-4000.
Chicago, Illinois Office: 150 North Michigan Avenue, Suite 420. Telephone: 312-499-1400.
Atlanta, Georgia Office: Suite 1400, The Lenox Building, 3399 Peachtree Road, N.E. Telephone: 404-812-5680.
See Professional Biographies, STAMFORD, CONNECTICUT

Erdos, David C., (BV) .... '44 '75 C.178 M.B.A. L.724 J.D. 29 5th St.
Erdos, Pamela Ann, (BV) ....'58 '83 C.881 A.B. L.902 J.D. 29 5th St.
Esposito, Joseph A. '68 '95 C.262 B.A. L.569 J.D.
(adm. in NY; not adm. in CT) V.P. & Coun., GE Capital Aviation Servs., Inc.
Esposito, Shauna L. '63 '91 C.178 B.A. L.262 J.D.
(adm. in NY; not adm. in CT) Deloitte & Touche, LLP

Esses, Craig '61 '89 C.339 B.S. L.146 J.D.
(adm. in IL; not adm. in CT) Sr. Mgr., Taxes, GE Capital Corp.
Evans, John J., (CV) .... '56 '82 C.197 A.B. L.1194 J.D. 30 Oak St.
Eveleigh, Dennis G., (AV) .... '47 '72 C.967 A.B. L.184 J.D. State Ct. J.
Fallon, Yvette Pietruska .... '64 '93 C.1029 B.A. L.1252 J.D. 400 Main St.
Fanwick, Ernest .... '26 '52 C.645 B.S.E.E. L.178 J.D. 1403 Newfield Avenue (Pat.)
Farina, Guy J. .... '30 '55 C.184 B.A. L.94 LL.B. 98 Echo Hill Dr.
Farnsworth, John A. .... '72 '98 C.1036 B.A. L.818 J.D. [[A] Wofsey,R.K.&K.]
*PRACTICE AREAS: Commercial Litigation; Criminal Defense.
Farrington, James F., Jr. .... '52 '84 C.602 B.Ch.E. L.1252 J.D. [Wiggin&D.]
*PRACTICE AREAS: International Corporate; Pharmaceutical Strategic Alliances; Technology Transfer.
Fass, Sarah Moore .... '71 '96 C.882 B.A. L.472 J.D. [[A] Day,B.&H.]
*PRACTICE AREAS: Labor and Employment.
Fay, Geoffrey F. .... '52 '82 C&L.93 B.A., J.D. [Cummings&L.]
*PRACTICE AREAS: Commercial Real Estate; Construction Law.
Federici, James J. '50 '79 C.884 B.S. L.1049 J.D.
(adm. in CA; not adm. in CT) 40 Denise Dr.‡
Feeny, Christina Calise .... '71 '96 C.1044 B.A. L.262 J.D. [[A] Jackson L.S.&K.]
Fein, David B. .... '60 '87 C.197 A.B. L.569 J.D. [Wiggin&D.]
*PRACTICE AREAS: White Collar Defense; Internal and External Investigations; Corporate Compliance; Appellate; First Amendment.
Ferdinand, Edmund J., III .... '67 '94 C.867 B.A. L.861 J.D. [[A] Grimes&B.]
*PRACTICE AREAS: Intellectual Property Litigation; Internet Law.
Ferrante, Rosemarie .... '72 '96 C.188 B.S. L.1009 J.D. [[A] Fitzmaurice&F.]
Ferrer, Esteban A., III, (AV) .... '50 '76 C.216 B.A. L.178 J.D. [Paul,H.J.&W.]
*PRACTICE AREAS: Emerging Growth Capital; Corporate Governance; Securities Law and Compliance; Mergers and Acquisitions; Corporate Finance.
Ficarra, Troy .... '70 '95 C.569 B.A. L.978 J.D. [[A] Kelley D.&W.]
*PRACTICE AREAS: Employee Benefits.
Fickey, Charles J. '24 '63 C.923 B.S. L.273 LL.B.
(adm. in NY; not adm. in CT; Pat.) Sr. Pat. Coun., Amer. Cyanamid Co.
Filardi, Charles J., Jr. '56 '91 C.390 A.B. L.1029 J.D.
[Cummings&L.] (⊙New Haven)
*PRACTICE AREAS: Bankruptcy; Debtor and Creditor; Commercial Litigation; Creditors Rights.
Finn, Stephen A., (AV) .... '53 '79 C.910 A.B. L.893 J.D. [Wofsey,R.K.&K.]
*PRACTICE AREAS: Civil Litigation; Personal Injury; Commercial Law.

Finn Dixon & Herling LLP, (AV)
One Landmark Square, Suite 1400, 06901-2689
Telephone: 203-325-5000 Telecopier: 203-348-5777
Harold B. Finn III; Brett W. Dixon; Michael J. Herling; David I. Albin; Charles J. Downey III; James R. Hawkins, II; Donna Nelson Heller; Ernest M. Lorimer; Patrick J. McHugh; Edmund M. Remondino; Edward A. Weiss. Associates: Erik A. Bergman; Jeffrey A. Blomberg; Kristin L. Chach; Nancy L. Lomazzo; Laura J. Lutjen; Susan Powell; Marcia C. Sugrue; Grant S. Thompson (New York City Office); Sheryl A. Young. Senior Attorney: Cheryl Gabes Rice; Joyce H. Young. Of Counsel: Wilford R. Young (Not admitted in CT); Timothy A. Birch.
Corporate Law, Mergers and Acquisitions, Securities Law, Venture Capital Financing, Corporate Finance and Restructuring, Commercial Litigation, Banking and Lending Law, Bankruptcy and Workouts, Employee Benefits and the Federal and State Taxation of Businesses and Business Transactions.
See Professional Biographies, STAMFORD, CONNECTICUT

Finn III, Harold B., (AV) .... '38 '67 C.976 B.A. L.178 LL.B. [Finn D.&H.]
*PRACTICE AREAS: Securities Law; Banking Law; Corporate Law.
Fischer, A. Robert, (AV) .... '57 '84 C.843 B.B.A. L.846 J.D. [Jackson L.S.&K.]
Fisher, Amy H. '55 '81 C.918 B.A. L.178 J.D.
Managing Dir. & Sr. Coun., General Electric Capital Corporation
Fisher, Richard S., (AV) .... '37 '65 C.645 B.S. L.188 J.D. [Cacace,T.&S.]
*PRACTICE AREAS: Trusts and Estates; Elder Law; Taxation; Business Law.
Fisher, Ryan Charles .... '— '99 C.945 B.A. L.94 J.D. [[A] Cummings&L.]
Fitzmaurice, William T., (AV) .... '59 '84 C.1019 B.A. L.569 J.D. [Fitzmaurice&F.]
Fitzmaurice & Freeman, (AV) .... 1281 East Main Street
Fitzpatrick, Alice Ann, (BV) .... '55 '80 C.788 A.B. L.184 J.D. [[A] Cacace,T.&S.]
*PRACTICE AREAS: Probate; Trusts and Estates; Estate Administration; Estate Planning.
Flaherty, John A. .... '62 '91 C.93 A.B. L.145 J.D. [Cummings&L.]
*PRACTICE AREAS: Corporate Law; Securities.
Flaherty, Michael J. .... '47 '75 C.352 B.B.A. L.284 J.D. 1177 Summer St.
Flaherty, Walter T., Jr., (BV) .... '42 '67 C.884 B.S. L.184 J.D. 1318 Bedford St.
Flanagan, Eugene L., III '50 '76 C.433 B.E.E. L.724 J.D.
(adm. in NY; not adm. in CT; Pat.) [St. Onge S.J.&R.]
*PRACTICE AREAS: Intellectual Property.
Flatt, Kelly E. P. .... '74 '99 C&L.477 B.S.E., J.D. [[A] Day,B.&H.]
*PRACTICE AREAS: Intellectual Property; Business Law.
Fleming, Peter E., III .... '57 '86 C.882 B.A. L.276 J.D. [[C] Curtis,M.C.&M.]
*PRACTICE AREAS: Civil Litigation; Criminal Litigation; Securities Arbitration; Litigation.
Flood, James P. '54 '81 C.1019 B.B.A. L.262 J.D.
(adm. in NY; not adm. in CT) 25 Chapin Lane
Flynn, Allison T. '69 '98 C.497 B.A. L.1187 J.D.
(adm. in MD; not adm. in CT) Regis. Off., Union Bk. of Switzerland/Warburg
Flynn, Vincent J. .... '59 '87 C.823 B.A. L.1356 J.D. 777 Summer St.
Fogarty, John E. '47 '76 C.178 B.A. L.569 J.D.
(adm. in NY; not adm. in CT) V.P. & Asst. Gen. Coun., Time Warner Cable
Fogarty, Robert E. '44 '69 C&L.347 B.A., J.D.
Sr. Assoc. Coun. & Asst. Secy., Champion Intl. Corp.‡

Fogarty Cohen Selby & Nemiroff LLC
(See Greenwich)

Ford, Stefan P. '52 '86 L.188 J.D.
(adm. in NY; not adm. in CT)
Managing Dir. & Coun., GE Capital Servs. Structured Fin. Group, Inc.
Forrest, Michael '— '96 C.999 B.A. L.273 J.D.
(adm. in NY; not adm. in CT) [[A] Pillsbury W.]
*PRACTICE AREAS: Real Estate.
Forstadt, Matthew J., (AV) .... '46 '70 C&L.575 A.B., J.D. [Wofsey,R.K.&K.]
*PRACTICE AREAS: Commercial Litigation; Financial Law; Real Estate Litigation; Business Litigation; Construction Law.
Forster, Frederick T. .... '72 '00 C.724 B.S. L.262 J.D. [[A] Shipman&G.]
*PRACTICE AREAS: Corporate Law; Corporate Finance; Securities; Real Estate.
Foster, William C. '40 '66 C.712 B.A. L.262 LL.B.
Sr. Assoc. Coun., Champion International Corp.
Fowler, Joseph M. '47 '73 C.401 B.A. L.273 J.D.
(adm. in DC; not adm. in CT; Pat.) Pres., Amer. Actuator Corp.
Fox, Gerald M., III, (BV) .... '66 '92 C.676 B.A. L.365 J.D. [Fox&F.]
*PRACTICE AREAS: Litigation; Civil Practice; Family Law; Domestic Relations.
Fox, Gerald M., Jr., (AV) .... '44 '70 C.745 A.B. L.184 J.D. [Fox&F.]
*PRACTICE AREAS: Real Estate; Family Law; Estate Planning; Probate Law; Domestic Relations.
Fox, John Wayne, (AV) .... '47 '71 C.1030 B.A. L.276 J.D. [Curtis,B.&B.]
*PRACTICE AREAS: Litigation; Commercial Law; Family Law; Municipal Law; Tax Appeals.
Fox, Lawrence .... '48 '74 C.855 B.A. L.309 J.D. One Champion Plaza‡

Fox & Fox, L.L.P., (AV) [BR]
607 Bedford Street, 06901
Telephone: 203-348-7773 Fax: 203-324-0057
URL: http://www.lawyers.com/foxlaw
Gerald M. Fox, Jr.; Gerald M. Fox, III.
Real Estate, Probate, Estate Planning, Family Law, Criminal and Civil Litigation, Wills, Elder Law.
See Professional Biographies, STAMFORD, CONNECTICUT

Fragomen, Del Rey, Bernsen & Loewy, P.C., (AV)
One Atlantic Street, 06901 ⊙
Telephone: 203-352-1871 Facsimile: 203-352-1874
URL: http://www.fragomen.com
Noreen Quirk; Karin C. Lestelle (Not admitted in CT);—Peter D. Roberts (Not admitted in CT).
U.S. and Foreign Immigration and Nationality Law.
New York, New York Office: 515 Madison Avenue. Telephone: 212-688-8555. Facsimile: 212-758-7215; 212-319-5236.
Buffalo, New York Office: 50 Fountain Plaza, Suite 1320. Telephone: 716-856-5444. Facsimile: 716-856-5151.
Washington, D.C. Office: 1212 New York Avenue, N.W., Suite 850. Telephone: 202-223-5515. Facsimile: 202-371-2898.
Coral Gables, Florida Office: 241 Sevilla Avenue, Suite 802. Telephone: 305-774-5800. Facsimile: 305-774-6666.
Chicago, Illinois Office: 150 North Wacker Drive, Suite 1120. Telephone: 312-263-6101. Facsimile: 312-346-1970.
San Francisco, California Office: 100 Pine Street, Suite 1575. Telephone: 415-986-1446. Facsimile: 415-986-7964.
Los Angeles, California Office: 12121 Wilshire Boulevard, Suite 1001. Telephone: 310-820-3322. Facsimile: 310-820-2702.
Santa Clara, California Office: 2804 Mission College Boulevard, 2nd Floor. Telephone: 408-919-0600. Facsimile: 408-919-0615.
Irvine, California Office: 18401 Von Karman Avenue, Suite 255. Telephone: 949-261-0209. Facsimile: 949-261-2821.
Sacramento, California Office: 2399 Gateway Oaks Drive, Suite 200. Telephone: 916-564-6900. Facsimile: 916-564-5015.
Oakland, California Office: 1999 Harrison Street, Suite 1400. Telephone: 510-444-4208. Facsimile: 510-444-4873.
San Diego, California Office: 11512 El Camino Real, Suite 300. Telephone: 858-847-9060. Facsimile: 858-847-9119.
Iselin, New Jersey Office: Fragomen, Del Rey, Bernsen & Loewy, 99 Wood Avenue South. Telephone: 732-906-1230. Facsimile: 732-906-9190.
Troy, Michigan Office: Fragomen, Del Rey, Bernsen and Loewy, P.L.L.C., 2301 West Big Beaver Road, Suite 225. Telephone: 248-649-5404. Facsimile: 248-649-5121.
Atlanta, Georgia Office: 1175 Peachtree Street, N.E., 100 Colony Square, Suite 700. Telephone: 404-249-9300. Facsimile: 404-249-9291.
Dallas, Texas Office: 5000 Quorum Drive, Suite 215. Telephone: 972-233-6646. Facsimile: 972-233-3134.
Phoenix, Arizona Office: 3101 North Central Avenue, Suite 1470. Telephone: 602-631-9200. Facsimile: 602-631-9300.
Vienna, Virginia Office: 1595 Spring Hill Road, Suite 320. Telephone: 703-748-2380. Facsimile: 703-748-2387.
Brussels, Belgium Office: Vossendreef 6-B.I-Dreve Des Renards, 1180 Brussels, Belgium. Telephone: 011-322-374-7-37. Facsimile: 011-322-374-90-45.
See Professional Biographies, STAMFORD, CONNECTICUT

Franco, R. Kelley .... '— '95 C.276 B.A. L.184 J.D. [[A] Robinson&C.]

Franco & Associates
(See New Canaan)

Frankel, Emil H., (AV) .... '40 '65 C.918 B.A. L.309 LL.B. [[C] Day,B.&H.]
*PRACTICE AREAS: Transportation Law; Governmental Affairs; Environmental Law.
Franklin, Patricia M. '67 '92 C.860 B.A. L.178 J.D.
(adm. in NY; not adm. in CT) Dir. Lgl. & Ext. Afrs., Warburg Dillon Read LLC, CT
Fraulo, Anthony N., (BV) .... '42 '67 C.93 B.S. L.184 J.D. 1234 Summer St., 4th Fl.
Freccia, Vincent J., III, (BV) .... '55 '80 C.676 B.S. L.1029 J.D. 1200 Summer St.
Frederick, Robin G., (AV) .... '63 '88 C.188 B.A. L.569 J.D. [Shipman&G.]
*PRACTICE AREAS: Employment Law; Civil Litigation.
Frederick, Steven M., (AV) .... '64 '89 C.860 B.S. L.569 J.D. [Wofsey,R.K.&K.]
*PRACTICE AREAS: Civil Litigation; Commercial Law; Employment Law; Civil Rights Law.
Freed, Thomas J., (BV) .... '63 '88 C.1044 B.S. L.107 J.D. [Cummings&L.]
*PRACTICE AREAS: Corporate Law; Mergers and Acquisitions; Venture Capital; Securities Law.
Freedman, Joel E. .... '33 '59 C.976 B.A. L.309 LL.B. 29 Knapp‡
Freedman, Susan .... '52 '75 C&L.446 B.A., J.D. [Brotmann&F.] ⊙
Freeman, Jane W., (BV) .... '50 '76 C.289 B.A. L.184 J.D. [[C] Cacace,T.&S.]
*PRACTICE AREAS: Land Use; Litigation; Real Estate.
Freeman, John D., (BV) .... '64 '90 C.970 B.A. L.178 J.D. [[C] Cummings&L.]
*PRACTICE AREAS: Environmental Law; Land Use Planning Law; Commercial Real Estate Law.
French, Philip M., (CV) '44 '72 C.867 B.S. L.273 J.D.
1010 Washington Boulevard (Pat.)
Frenkel, Steven I., (BV) .... '64 '90 C.978 B.A. L.178 J.D. [Cummings&L.]
*PRACTICE AREAS: Litigation; Creditors' Rights; Bankruptcy Law.
Frenkel, William G. '64 '88 C.1138 B.A. L.564 J.D.
(adm. in NY; not adm. in CT) Metromedia International Telecommunications, Inc.
Friedland, Edward A. '56 '82 C.951 B.A. L.276 J.D.
V.P. & Dep. Gen. Coun., The Thomson Corp.
Friedman, Laura A. '53 '77 C&L.659 B.A., J.D.
(adm. in PA; not adm. in CT)
Assoc. Gen. Coun., Fin. Servs. Div., General Electric Credit Corp.
Friedman, Thomas P. '72 '99 C.860 B.A. L.1068 J.D.
(adm. in CA; not adm. in CT) [[A] Paul,H.J.&W.]
*PRACTICE AREAS: Litigation.
Frommer, Henry '43 '77 C.659 B.S. L.1009 J.D.
(adm. in NY; not adm. in CT) V.P., Fin., Executive Commercial Funding, Inc.
Frost, Matthew C. '67 '97 C.165 B.A. L.945 J.D.
(adm. in NY; not adm. in CT) [[A] Pillsbury W.]
Furman, Jesse M. '72 '99 C.309 A.B. L.976 J.D.
(adm. in NY; not adm. in CT) [[A] Wiggin&D.]
Furman, Susan S. '45 '86 C.783 B.A. L.564 J.D.
(adm. in NY; not adm. in CT) 695 E. Main St.
Gaffney, John B. .... '68 '96 C.676 B.S. L.262 J.D. [[A] Ryan,R.J.&D.]
*PRACTICE AREAS: Business Law.
Gage, Kenneth W. .... '66 '92 C&L.999 B.A., J.D. [Day,B.&H.]
*PRACTICE AREAS: Employment Law; Employment Litigation; Government Investigations.
Gaillard, Andrew P. .... '60 '85 C.197 A.B. L.659 J.D. [Day,B.&H.]
*PRACTICE AREAS: Commercial Litigation; Government Investigations.
Gaillard, William D. .... '31 '56 C.674 A.B. L.309 LL.B. [[C] Roberts,R.&B.]
*PRACTICE AREAS: Corporate Law; Commercial Law.
Gaines, Leonard P. '27 '53 C.976 B.A. L.309 LL.B.
(adm. in NY; not adm. in CT) 77 Lolly Ln.‡
Gall, Douglas Juster .... '59 '89 C.103 B.A. L.893 J.D. 184 Atlantic St.
Gallagher, Terence J., III '66 '94 C.659 B.A. L.800 J.D.
(adm. in NY; not adm. in CT) [[C] Day,B.&H.]
Galluzzi, David .... '74 '99 C.103 B.A. L.309 J.D. [[A] Paul,H.J.&W.]
*PRACTICE AREAS: Corporate Law.
Gambardella, Mary A., (BV) .... '58 '83 C.19 B.A. L.1252 J.D. [[A] Epstein B.&G.]
*PRACTICE AREAS: Employment Law; Commercial Litigation; Contracts; Sports; Entertainment.

Gamberdell, Joseph V., Jr. ....'54 '95 C.1029 B.S.E.E. L.1252 J.D. [Ⓐ Ohlandt,G.R.&P.]
*PRACTICE AREAS: Patents, Trademarks and Copyrights.

Gang, Arthur '48 '76 C.569 B.A. L.1009 J.D.
(adm. in NY; not adm. in CT) 2nd V.P. & Claims Litig., Gen. Reins. Corp.

Ganis, Stephen L., Law Offices of '51 '81 C.823 B.S. L.1009 J.D.
1234 Summer Street, 06905-5532
Telephone: 203-977-2465; Fax: 203-348-0196
Email: sganis@lawyers.com URL: http://www.lawyers.com/ganislaw
General Civil Practice, Business Law, Business Acquisitions and Sales, Contracts, Partnership, Family Business, Job Termination, Individuals with Disabilities, Wills and Probate, Estate Planning, Corporate Law, Intellectual Property, Labor and Employment and Trusts and Estates. Elder Law, Investments.
Representative Clients: Frymaster L.L.C.; Garland Commercial Industries; Seabury Securities; Enodis Corp.; The Delfield Co.
See Professional Biographies, STAMFORD, CONNECTICUT

Garofolo, Alfred J., (BV) '51 '81
C.855 B.A. L.184 J.D. Claims Coun., Ct. Attys. Title Ins. Co.

Gartmond, Joy A. '58 '91 C&L.705 B.S., J.D.
(adm. in NJ; not adm. in CT) Tax Consultant, GE Capital Corp.

Gass, Ronald S., (AV) '51 '80 C.228 B.A. L.446 J.D.
Assoc. Gen. Coun., 2nd V.P. & Asst. Secy., NAC Reinsurance Corp.

Gaug, Patricia M. .... '59 '85 C.1044 B.A. L.94 J.D. [Ⓒ Curtis,B.&B.]
*PRACTICE AREAS: Civil Litigation; General Practice.

Gazin, Glenn A. ....'54 '90 C.331 B.A. L.978 J.D. 75 Burwood Avenue

Gegelys, Chris '65 '91 C.264 B.A. L.659 J.D.
(adm. in NY; not adm. in CT) Div. Coun. & Asst. Secy., Cadbury Beverages, Inc.

Gelb, F. Gina ....'49 '85 C.978 B.A. L.184 J.D. IBM Credit Corp.

Genuario & Conover
(See Norwalk)

Gerardi, Joseph Lucian ....'53 '80 C.94 A.B. L.1029 J.D. 1074 Hope St.

Gershberg, Benjamin E., (CV) '59 '85 C.1036 B.A. L.184 J.D.
237 Strawberry Hill Ave.

Gibaldi, Laurel '61 '89 C.276 B.A. L.823 J.D.
(adm. in NY; not adm. in CT) [Ⓐ Kelley D.&W.]
*PRACTICE AREAS: Real Estate.

Gilbride, Tusa, Last & Spellane, LLC
(See Greenwich)

Gilland, Dana M. '61 '90 C.882 B.A. L.1048 J.D.
VP & Senior Counsel, Intellectual Property, United Distillers & Vinters, NA

Gillespie, James F. E. '25 '51 C.276 B.S. L.659 J.D.
(adm. in PA; not adm. in CT) 73 Harbor Dr.‡

Gilliam, Charles Phillips '50 '82 C.575 B.S. L.213 J.D.
(adm. in MI; not adm. in CT)
Vice President, Secretary & General Counsel, ContentGaurd, Inc.

Gilman, Derek ....'61 '92 C.870 B.S. L.184 J.D. [Ⓒ Day,B.&H.]
*PRACTICE AREAS: Business Law; Tax Law.

Gilson, Roger P., Jr. ....'52 '79 C&L.823 B.A., J.D. [Jackson L.S.&K.]

Ginsberg, Larry F., (CV) ....'51 '77 C.1350 B.A. L.107 J.D. 706 Bedford St.

Ginsky, Marvin H. ....'30 '55 C&L.569 A.B., LL.B. 1 Champion Plza.

Glander, Jane W., (BV) ....'54 '89 C.1030 B.A. L.724 J.D. [Emmett&G.] ⊙
*PRACTICE AREAS: Civil Litigation; Personal Injury; Workers Compensation; Corporate Law; Small Business Law.

Glennon, Philip N. '49 '80 C.1266 B.A. L.823 J.D.
(adm. in NY; not adm. in CT) Investment Advsr., Hynes, Himmelreich, Glennon & Co.

Glickson, Andrew A., (BV) '49 '75 C.309 A.B. L.94 J.D.
[Ⓒ Cuddy&F.&W.] (⊙Norwalk)
*PRACTICE AREAS: Condominiums and Property Owners Associations; Real Estate Transactions.

Glucksman, L. Morris, (BV) ....'47 '74 C.184 B.S. L.1009 J.D. 900 Bedford St.

Gochberg, Lawrence, (AV) ....'26 '51 C&L.273 LL.B. 101 Broad St.

Godlin, Harold N., (AV) ....'26 '53 C.103 A.B. L.309 LL.B. [Godlin&G.]

Godlin, Theodore, (BV) ....'29 '54 C.103 A.B. L.309 J.D. [Godlin&G.]

Godlin & Godlin, (AV) ....832 Bedford St.

Goggins, Glenn J. '60 '86 C.1044 B.S. L.575 J.D.
(adm. in NY; not adm. in CT) Coun., GE Capital Corp.

Gold, Andrew R. '65 '90 C.659 B.S. L.178 J.D.
(adm. in NJ; not adm. in CT) Labor & Employee Relations Counsel, Pitney Bowes Inc.

Gold, Frederick S., (AV) ....'52 '79 C.860 A.B. L.178 J.D. [Shipman&G.]
*PRACTICE AREAS: Business Litigation; Commercial Litigation; Business Torts; Real Estate Litigation.

Gold, Leo, (AV) ....'27 '60 C.569 B.A. L.564 LL.B. [Mackler&G.]

Gold, Peter A. '50 '76 C.860 B.A. L.569 J.D.
(adm. in NY; not adm. in CT) Princ. & Benefit Consultant, Buck Consultants, Inc.

Gold, Ronald M., (BV) ....'53 '79 C.174 B.S. L.823 J.D. [Benjamin&G.]

Gold, Steven M., (AV) ....'53 '79 C.319 B.A. L.188 J.D. [Shipman&G.]
*PRACTICE AREAS: Corporate Law; Commercial Finance; Computer Law.

Goldberg, Bruce A., (CV) ....'57 '83 C.705 B.A. L.1029 J.D. 733 Summer St.

Goldberg, Craig A. ....'64 '89 C.659 B.A. L.276 J.D. Sr. Coun., Time Warner Cable

Goldberg, Kenneth D., (AVⓉ) '49 '75 C.994 B.A. L.1009 J.D.
(adm. in NY; not adm. in CT) [Goldberg&Assoc.] ⊙
*PRACTICE AREAS: Litigation in all Courts; Commercial Law; Corporate Law; Insurance Law; Tort Law.

Goldberg, Marshall, (BV) ....'45 '76 C.103 A.B. L.184 J.D. [Wofsey,R.K.&K.]
*PRACTICE AREAS: Commercial Law; Creditors Rights; Creditor Bankruptcy; Real Estate.

Goldberg, Sara A. '70 '96 C.674 A.B. L.569 J.D.
(adm. in NY; not adm. in CT) [Ⓐ Wiggin&D.]

Goldberg, Thomas D., (AV) ....'54 '80 C.103 A.B. L.178 J.D. [Day,B.&H.]
*PRACTICE AREAS: Bankruptcy; Commercial Litigation; Securities Litigation; Bankruptcy Counseling.

Goldberg & Associates, (AVⓉ)
30 Oak Street, Suite 102, 06905 ⊙
Telephone: 212-968-2300 Fax: 212-968-2400
Email: kgoldberg@g-alaw.com URL: http://www.g-alaw.com
Kenneth D. Goldberg (Not admitted in CT). Associates: Russell B. Scarcella (Not admitted in CT); Robert Tambini; Andreas E. Theodosiou (Not admitted in CT); Susan Beal (Not admitted in CT). Of Counsel: Jack Gross (Not admitted in CT).
Corporate, Commercial and Insurance Law. Trial and Appellate practice in State Federal Courts; Mediation and Arbitration.
New York, N.Y. Office: 39 Broadway, 10006. Telephone: 212-968-2300. Fax: 212-968-2400.
Hoboken, New Jersey Office: 20 Hudson Place, 07030. Telephone: 201-420-1771. Fax: 201-420-7778.
See Professional Biographies, STAMFORD, CONNECTICUT

Goldstein, Bruce H. '66 '93 C.454 B.B.A. L.1019 J.D.
(adm. in NY; not adm. in CT) Tax Coun., GE Capital Corporate Tax

Goldstein, Daniel J. '61 '86 C.659 B.A. L.309 J.D.
(adm. in NY; not adm. in CT) Assoc. Gen. Coun., Pitney Bowes Inc.
*RESPONSIBILITIES: Litigation; Regulatory Law; Corporate Compliance.

Goldstein, Jennifer Cohen ....'59 '86 C.976 B.A. L.145 J.D. 184 Atlantic St.

Goldstein, Henry L.
(See New Canaan)

Golub, David S., (AV) ....'49 '73 C&L.976 B.A., J.D. [Silver,G.&T.]
*PRACTICE AREAS: Civil Litigation; Criminal Litigation; Civil Appeals; Criminal Appeals; Employment Litigation.

Good, David H. '58 '84 C.976 B.A. L.893 J.D.
(adm. in NY; not adm. in CT) 292 Long Ridge Rd.

Goodman, Joshua D. .... '63 '91 C.821 B.A. L.659 J.D. [Ⓐ Paul,H.J.&W.]
*PRACTICE AREAS: Employment Law; Labor Law.

Goodstein, Shari M. ....'59 '88 C.1036 B.A. L.569 J.D. [Shipman&G.]
*PRACTICE AREAS: Employment Law; Business Litigation; Commercial Litigation.

Goodwin, Lucia Lanzaro ....'50 '94 C.1030 B.A. L.724 J.D. P.O. Box 2246

Gordon, David P. ....'55 '81 C.976 B.S. L.276 J.D. [Gordon&J.] (Pat.)

Gordon, Deborah S. ....'65 '93 C.951 B.A. L.569 J.D. [Ⓐ Day,B.&H.]
*PRACTICE AREAS: Estate Planning; Estate Administration; Fiduciary Law; Trust Law.

Gordon & Jacobson, P.C. ....65 Woods End Road

Gorman, Sarah E. .....'48 '73 C&L.188 A.B., J.D. Assoc. Gen. Coun., GE Capital Corp.

Gottlieb, Scott E. ....'— '96 C.860 B.A. L.184 J.D. [Ⓐ Kelley D.&W.]
*PRACTICE AREAS: Corporate Law; Taxation; E-Commerce.

Gottlin, Sandra G. ....'60 '90 C.999 B.A. L.1178 J.D. 750 Summer St.

Gould, Barbara J. '59 '84 C.165 B.A. L.724 J.D.
(adm. in NY; not adm. in CT) Sr. V.P. & Dept. Coun., GE Equity

Graber, Howard R., (BV) .... '64 '90 C.415 B.S. L.1029 J.D. 196 North St.

Graber, Sarah J. '50 '75 C.807 B.A. L.378 J.D.
(adm. in KS; not adm. in CT) Sr. Legal Coun., Global Consumer Finance

Graham, Robert D. '48 '73 C.205 B.A. L.94 J.D.
Sr. V.P. & Asst. Gen. Coun., Gen. Reinsurance Corp.
*RESPONSIBILITIES: Insurance and Reinsurance; Corporation Law; Securities Law; General Business Contracts; Real Estate Law.

Grant, Julia F. ....'52 '77 C.770 B.A. L.276 J.D. 1177 High Ridge Rd

Graubard, Myra L., (BV) '43 '68 C&L.569 A.B., J.D.
1200 Summer Street, Suite 107, 06905
Telephone: 203-327-6720 Fax: 203-358-9904
Email: mgraubardesq@aol.com URL: http://www.lawyers.com/graubard
Commercial Law, Commercial Collections, Retail Collections, Enforcement of Judgements, Post Judgment Collections, Civil Litigation, General Civil Practice, Family Law, Divorce, Probate, Wills, Real Estate.
See Professional Biographies, STAMFORD, CONNECTICUT

Graubard, Naomi B. ....'71 '96 C.910 B.A. L.94 J.D. [Ⓐ Wiggin&D.]

Graves, Sarah E. ....'67 '92 C.01 B.A L.06 LL.B. [Ⓐ Paul,H.J.&W.]
*PRACTICE AREAS: Employment and Labor Law.

Gray, Samuel O. '46 '75 C.674 B.A. L.309 J.D.
(adm. in NY; not adm. in CT)
Managing Dir. & Gen. Coun., GE Capital Markets Services, Inc.

Grayson, Eric D., (BV) '57 '83 C.732 B.A. L.861 J.D.
[Ⓒ Cacace,T.&S.] (⊙Greenwich)

Grayson, Heath H. '62 '91 C.197 B.A. L.94 J.D.
(adm. in NY; not adm. in CT) V.P. & Legal Coun., MemberWorks Incorporated
*RESPONSIBILITIES: Corporate Law; Contracts; Securities; Mergers and Acquisitions; Intellectual Property.

Greco, Kevin M., (BV) ....'57 '89 C.829 B.S. L.1029 J.D. [Sandak F.H.&G.]
*PRACTICE AREAS: Personal Injury; Medical Malpractice; Civil Litigation; Labor Law.

Greeley, Paul D., (AV) '57 '82 C.183 B.A. L.285 J.D.
[Ohlandt,G.R.&P.] (See Pat. Sect.)

Green, Alan M. '53 '84 C.67 B.A. L.1292 J.D.
(adm. in NY; not adm. in CT) V.P. & Sr. Coun., GE Capital Markets Services

Green, Benjamin H., (AV) ....'— '78 C.1036 B.A. L.188 J.D. [Emmet,M.&M.]

Green, Robert W. '41 '71 C.347 A.B. L.145 J.D.
30 Oak Street, Suite 102, 06905-5313 ⊙
Telephone: 203-356-1399 Fax: 203-357-0908 http://www.bobgreenlaw.com
URL: http://www.lawyers.com/bobgreen
***PRACTICE AREAS: Probate (30%); Trusts and Estates (30%); Zoning, Planning and Land Use (15%); Administrative Law (15%); Appellate Practice (10%).**
Real Estate, Probate and Estate, Elder Law, Zoning, Planning and Land Use, Administrative Law, Financial Law and Legislative Practice.
Washington, D.C. Office: Eighth Floor, 1090 Vermont Avenue, N.W. Telephone: 202-682-9000. Fax: 203-682-0168.
See Professional Biographies, STAMFORD, CONNECTICUT

Green and Gross, P.C.
(See Bridgeport)

Greenberg, Kenneth S. '57 '82 C.188 A.B. L.94 J.D.
(adm. in NY; not adm. in CT) EQ Corp.

Greenberger, Richard E. ....'52 '81 C.569 B.S. L.1009 J.D. 26 Brodwood Dr.

Greene, Theodore J. ....'34 '60 C.994 B.S. L.893 LL.B. [Ⓒ Rosenblum&T.] ⊙

Gregory, Mark S. ....'61 '86 C.103 A.B. L.94 J.D. [Kelley D.&W.]
*PRACTICE AREAS: Commercial Litigation; Securities Litigation; Intellectual Property Litigation; Antitrust Class Actions.

Grenier, Christian A. ....'68 '97 C.262 B.A. L.724 J.D. [Ⓐ Jackson L.S.&K.]
*PRACTICE AREAS: Labor and Employment.

Grimes, Charles W., (AV) ....'51 '75 C.645 B.S. L.208 J.D. [Grimes&B.] (See Pat. Sect.)

Grimes & Battersby L.L.P., (AV)
3 Landmark Square, Suite 405, P.O. Box 1311, 06904-1311
Telephone: 203-324-2828 Telecopy: 203-348-2720
URL: http://www.gandb.com
Charles W. Grimes; Gregory J. Battersby; George W. Cooper (Not admitted in CT); Leora Herrmann; Melissa T. Rosse; James G. Coplit (Not admitted in CT);—Edmund J. Ferdinand, III; Gene J. Riccoboni (Not admitted in CT); Russell D. Dize. Of Counsel: Edward L. Justin (Not admitted in CT).
Patents, Trademarks, Copyrights, Unfair Competition, Trade Secrets, Multimedia, Licensing, Franchising, Litigation and Antitrust.
See Professional Biographies, STAMFORD, CONNECTICUT

Grinnell, Charles W., Law Offices of '37 '66 C.93 A.B. L.178 J.D.
41 Bank Street, 06901
Telephone: 203-363-7106 Fax: 203-363-7108
Email: grinlaw@aol.com URL: http://www.lawyers.com/grinnelllaw
***PRACTICE AREAS: General Corporate; Tax and Finance Law; Mergers and Acquisitions; Commercial Leasing; Executive Compensation.**
General Business, Corporate and Tax Law, Mergers and Acquisitions, Business Succession Planning, Commercial Leasing, Licensing, Executive Compensation and Benefits, Estate Planning, Probate and Administration of Estates.
See Professional Biographies, STAMFORD, CONNECTICUT

Grinshpun, Raisa '67 '92 C&L.569 B.S., J.D.
(adm. in NY; not adm. in CT) KPMG‡

Grobe, Bruce J. '50 '77 C.674 A.B. L.178 J.D.
(adm. in NY; not adm. in CT) Sr. V.P. & Gen. Coun., META Group, Inc.

Gross, Jack '56 '86 C.978 B.A. L.1019 J.D.
(adm. in NJ; not adm. in CT) [Ⓒ Goldberg&Assoc.] ⊙

Gross, Joli Lyn .... '69 '94 [🄰 Day,B.&H.]
*PRACTICE AREAS: Real Estate.
Gross, Stephen H., (AVⓉ) .... '40 '63 C.880 A.B. L.178 LL.B. Robinson & Cole
Grundei, Michael .... '64 '90 C.659 B.A. L.228 J.D. [Wiggin&D.]
*PRACTICE AREAS: Corporate Finance; Securities; Venture Capital; Public Offerings; Mergers and Acquisitions.
Grunow, John E. D. '19 '48 C.178 B.S. L.309 J.D.
(adm. in NY; not adm. in CT) 190 Davenport Dr.‡
Grushkin, Steven D., (BV) .... '47 '72 C.184 B.A. L.818 J.D. [Wofsey,R.K.&K.]
*PRACTICE AREAS: Real Estate; Business Law; Commercial Law; Finance.
Guaglianone, Victor F. '55 '80 C.112 A.B. L.145 J.D.
(adm. in CA; not adm. in CT) V.P. & Assoc. Gen. Coun., GE Capital Corp.
Guay, Joseph A. '68 '94 C.184 B.S. L.128 J.D.
(adm. in MD; not adm. in CT) [🄰 Paul,H.J.&W.]
Guider, Deborah L. '56 '84 C.518 A.B. L.273 J.D.
(adm. in NY; not adm. in CT)
V.P. & Corp. Coun., The Purdue Frederick Co./Purdue Pharma L.P.
*RESPONSIBILITIES: Licensing; Corporate Law; Securities Law; Banking Law; International Law.
Gustafson, Donald R., (AV) .... '53 '79 C.128 B.A. L.365 J.D. [Shipman&G.]
*PRACTICE AREAS: Real Estate Development; Commercial Leasing; Commercial Financing; Loan Workouts; Land Use.
Haave, Christian Rollow .... '71 '99 C.66 B.A. L.276 J.D. [🄰 Wofsey,R.K.&K.]
*PRACTICE AREAS: Landlord and Tenant Law; Family Law; Employment Law; Criminal Defense.
Hagan, Henry J. '31 '64 C.728 B.A. L.831 J.D.
(adm. in DC; not adm. in CT) Crane Co.
Hagan, John J. ....'22 '49 C.262 B.S. L.276 J.D. 1937 West Main St.‡
Hagner, Joseph C. '21 '48 C.423 A.B. L.446 LL.B.
(adm. in MD; not adm. in CT) 695 E. Main St.‡
Haine, Matthew D. .... '64 '91 C.882 B.A. L.910 J.D. 810 Bedford St.
Hall, Walter R., II '48 '73 C.659 B.A. L.893 J.D.
(adm. in PA; not adm. in CT) Citizens Utilities Co.
Hamlin, John W. .... '54 '89 C.970 B.A. L.184 J.D. [🄲 Paul,H.J.&W.]
*PRACTICE AREAS: Labor and Employment Law; Discrimination; Wrongful Termination; Executive Employment Contracts; Severance Agreements.
Hansson, Kurt W., (BV) .... '57 '86 C.860 B.A. L.904 J.D. [Paul,H.J.&W.]
*PRACTICE AREAS: Commercial Litigation; Tax Litigation; Intellectual Property Litigation; Employment Litigation; Alternative Dispute Resolution.
Haranzo, Mark E., (AVⓉ) .... '59 '86 C.1111 B.A. L.362 J.D. [Wiggin&D.]
*PRACTICE AREAS: Trusts Law; Estates Law; Estate Planning Law; Estate Litigation; Taxation of Trusts and Estates.
Harmer, Gregory E., (BV) ....'— '81 C.1030 B.A. L.365 J.D. [Robinson&C.]
*PRACTICE AREAS: Corporate; Finance; Bankruptcy; Banking Law; Corporate Law.

Harness, John R., (BV) '56 '88 C.93 B.S. L.1029 J.D.
1200 Summer Street, 06908
Telephone: 203-356-9975 Fax: 203-967-3028
***PRACTICE AREAS: Real Estate; Litigation; Family Law.**
Real Estate, Litigation, Family Law.
See Professional Biographies, STAMFORD, CONNECTICUT

Harnisch, William O'C., (AVⓉ) '40 '66 C.602 B.B.A. L.276 LL.B.
(adm. in DC; not adm. in CT) [Cummings&L.]
*PRACTICE AREAS: Taxation Law; Corporate Law; International Law.
Harrigan, Patricia Driscoll '61 '91 C.184 B.G.S. L.1029 J.D.
Sr. V.P. ,Asst. Gen. Coun. & Asst. Secy., Life Reassurance Corp. of America
*RESPONSIBILITIES: Corporate Law; Insurance Law; Securities Law.
Harrington, James J. '61 '92 C.754 B.S. L.1040 J.D.
(adm. in NJ; not adm. in CT) 1937 W. Main St.
Harrington, Scott M., (BV) .... '62 '87 C.165 B.A. L.184 J.D. [Diserio M.O.&C.]
*PRACTICE AREAS: Commercial Litigation; Construction Litigation; Bankruptcy.
Harris, Arthur Claborn '53 '84 C.39 B.S. L.502 J.D.
(adm. in MO; not adm. in CT) General Reins. Corp.
Harris, Michael S. '49 '75 C.569 B.A. L.724 J.D.
Sr. V.P., Gen. Coun. & Secy., The Thomson Corp.
Hart, Gordon L. ....'28 '57 C.862 B.S. L.623 LL.B. 77 Rocky Rapids Rd. (Pat.)‡
Harter, John L. '51 '82 C.918 B.A. L.982 J.D.
(adm. in NY; not adm. in CT) 66 Glenbrook Rd.‡
Hartje, John, (AVⓉ) '48 '77 C.967 B.A. L.107 J.D.
(adm. in NY; not adm. in CT) Senior Counsel - Litigation, International Paper Company
Hartwell, Olga '63 '92 C.976 B.A. L.813 J.D.
(adm. in NY; not adm. in CT) Sr. Tax Coun., GE Capital Corp.
Hatzis, Peter ....'61 '88 C.184 B.S. L.823 J.D. Sr. Mgr., Deloitte & Touche, LLP
Hauck, Cathy A. '55 '84 C.1031 B.S. L.724 J.D.
Assoc. Gen. Coun. & 2nd V.P., NAC Reinsurance Corp.
Hauhuth, Jennifer A. .... '61 '94 C.1029 B.A. L.1252 J.D. [🄰 Martin,L.&C.]
*PRACTICE AREAS: Real Estate; Corporate Law; Commercial Finance; Zoning.
Hawkins, Barry C., (AV) ....'43 '68 C.95 A.B. L.893 LL.B. [Shipman&G.]
*PRACTICE AREAS: Real Estate; Land Use Regulation; Community Association Law; Environmental Law; Business Litigation.
Hawkins, James R., II, (AV) .... '41 '67 C.999 A.B. L.823 LL.B. [Finn D.&H.]
*PRACTICE AREAS: Commercial Litigation; Securities; Antitrust; Alternative Dispute Resolution.
Hawkins, John D., Jr. .... '56 '81 C.401 B.A. L.575 J.D. [Paul,H.J.&W.]
*PRACTICE AREAS: Project Finance; Equipment Leasing; Asset-Based Finance.
Hawley, Merrie Fedor .... '65 '99 C.1030 B.A. L.1252 J.D. [🄰 Diserio M.O.&C.]
*PRACTICE AREAS: Litigation.
Hayes, Gregory A., (AV) .... '62 '88 C.976 B.S. L.893 J.D. [Day,B.&H.]
*PRACTICE AREAS: Estate Planning; Trust Administration; Estate Administration; Trust Litigation; Estate Litigation.
Hayman, Heather M. '55 '81 C.518 B.A. L.823 J.D.
(adm. in NY; not adm. in CT) Welbilt Corp.

Heagney, Lennon & Slane LLP
(See Greenwich)

Healy, Grace M., (AV) '48 '84 C.178 B.A. L.262 J.D.
(adm. in NY; not adm. in CT) Sr. Assoc. Coun., Champion International Corp.

Healy & Baillie, LLP
(See Norwalk)

Hedin, Randi-Jean G. ....'61 '88 C.66 B.A. L.1009 J.D. [Kelley D.&W.]
*PRACTICE AREAS: Securities Law; Corporate Law.

Heidell, Pittoni, Murphy & Bach, LLP, (AVⓉ) BR
30 Oak Street, 06905 ⊙
Telephone: 203-327-1800
Email: hpmb@hpmb.com
Luke M. Pittoni; Elizabeth Cornacchio; John F. Costa; Daniel S. Ratner;—Marian E. Courtney; Janice Kirsten Lunde; Carol L. Morris-Fox; Geraldine Koeneke Russell.
Trial and Appellate Practice in all Courts; Medical and Non-Medical Professional Liability; Health Care Law including Managed Care, Physician Licensing and Credentialing; Products Liability; Directors and Officers and Employment Practice Litigation; Toxic Tort and Environmental Litigation.
New York, New York Office: 99 Park Avenue. Telephone: 212-286-8585. Telecopier: 212-490-8966.
See Professional Biographies, STAMFORD, CONNECTICUT

Held, Gerald N. ..... '41 '70 C&L.823 B.A., J.D. Sr. Coun., Latin America, Xerox Corp.
*RESPONSIBILITIES: General Corporate; International.
Heller, Donna Nelson, (BV) .... '54 '81 C.104 A.B. L.659 J.D. [Finn D.&H.]
*PRACTICE AREAS: Commercial Litigation; Business Torts; Employment Law; Creditors' Rights Law; Bankruptcy Law.
Henderson, Mark H., (BV) ....'54 '85 C.855 B.S. L.1040 J.D. [Wofsey,R.K.&K.]
*PRACTICE AREAS: Litigation; Family Law; Criminal Law; Landlord and Tenant Law.
Hendrie, Donald A., Jr., (BV) ....'54 '81 C.652 B.A. L.1017 J.D. [🄰 Tooher&W.]
Hendrix, Eric V. '60 '86 C&L.446 B.S., J.D.
(adm. in MD; not adm. in CT) General Electric Capital Corp.
Hennessey, William J., Jr., (AV) .....'55 '81 C.1030 B.A. L.1040 J.D. [Sandak F.H.&G.]
*PRACTICE AREAS: Real Estate Law; Zoning Law; Land Use Law; Property Tax Appeals; Municipal Law.
Henock, Arlen F. ....'56 '88 C.999 B.B.A. L.1040 J.D. 44 Talmadge Ln.
Henry, Thomas Eugene, Jr. .... '59 '87 C.884 B.S. L.1040 J.D. 400 Atlantic St.‡
Herbert, Stephen R. .... '49 '75 C.1044 B.S. L.982 J.D. [Locke&H.] ⊙
Herde, Michael E. '63 '90 C.259 B.A. L.276 J.D.
(adm. in DC; not adm. in CT) Dir. & Sr. Coun., Warburg Dillon Read LLC
Herlihy, William F. '35 '62 C.446 B.A. L.477 J.D.
Assoc. Gen. Coun., The Purdue Frederick Co./Purdue Pharma L.P.
*RESPONSIBILITIES: FDA Law; Regulatory Law; Products Liability Litigation; General Law.
Herling, Michael J., (AV) .... '57 '82 C.165 A.B. L.813 J.D. [Finn D.&H.]
*PRACTICE AREAS: Corporate Law; Mergers and Acquisitions Law; Corporate Finance; Securities; Venture Capital Financing Law.

Herner, Donald A., Law Offices of, (AV) '43 '69 C.188 B.A. L.309 LL.B.
One Landmark Square, 4th Floor, 06901
Telephone: 203-351-1020 Fax: 203-351-1029
Email: herner@erols.com URL: http://www.lawyers.com/herner
***PRACTICE AREAS: General Corporate Law; Securities; Financing (Banking, Loans); International Law.**
Corporation, Finance and Securities, Venture Capital and International, Business Law, Mergers and Acquisitions.
See Professional Biographies, STAMFORD, CONNECTICUT

Herrera, Jorge Carlos '60 '93 L.262
(adm. in NY; not adm. in CT) 1633 Washington Blvd.
Herrmann, Leora ....'53 '79 C.112 A.B. L.976 J.D. [Grimes&B.]
*PRACTICE AREAS: Trademarks; Copyright; Intellectual Property Licensing; Intellectual Property Litigation.
Hertz, John D., (AV) .... '29 '55 C.264 B.A. L.262 J.D. [🄲 Curtis,B.&B.]
*PRACTICE AREAS: Real Estate; Administrative Law; Municipal Law; Commercial Law.
Hewitt, Peter E., (BV) ... '43 '72 C.385 A.B. L.94 J.D. General Counsel, The Ashforth Co.
Hickey, Robert O. .... '64 '97 C.184 B.A. L.1252 J.D. [🄰 Ryan,R.J.&D.]
*PRACTICE AREAS: Civil Litigation.
Hickey, Thomas J., (BV) .... '62 '88 C.262 B.A. L.128 J.D. [🄰 Sherman&R.]
Hickey, William F., Jr. ....'29 '55 C.433 A.B. L.262 J.D. Supr. J.
Higgins, Eric M., (BV) .... '63 '91 C.216 B.A. L.184 J.D. [Wofsey,R.K.&K.]
*PRACTICE AREAS: Civil Litigation; Commercial Litigation; Real Estate Litigation; Business Litigation; Landlord and Tenant Law.
Hinton, Michael J., (BV) ....'51 '76 C.276 A.B. L.188 J.D. [Cummings&L.]
*PRACTICE AREAS: Environmental Law; Commercial Real Estate Law; Construction Law; Franchise Law; Partnership Law.
Hirsh, Karen L. ....'65 '91 C.188 B.A. L.569 J.D. Asst. V.P., Thomson Corp., Tax Dept.
Hochman, Russell C. '64 '92 C.188 B.A. L.982 J.D.
Dep. Gen. Coun.-Intl. Legal & Govt. Affs., Pitney Bowes, Inc.
*RESPONSIBILITIES: International Law; International Government Relations; Commercial Law; Mergers and Acquisitions.
Hoddinott, Alfred H., Jr. '38 '64 C.276 A.B. L.569 LL.B.
Sr. Coun., Litig., Xerox Corporation (⊙Ridgefield)
Hodges, Kelly Warrick ....'73 '98 C.93 B.A. L.276 J.D. [🄰 Paul,H.J.&W.]
*PRACTICE AREAS: Corporate.
Hoffkins, Kevin L. ....'62 '88 C.696 B.A. L.1029 J.D. 700 Canal Street, 3rd Floor

Hoffman, Burt M., (BV) '42 '70 C.575 A.B. L.776 J.D.
1234 Summer Street, Suite 400, 06905
Telephone: 203-977-2490 Fax: 203-357-7669
Email: bhoffman@stamford-lawyer.com URL: http://www.lawyers.com/ctlawyer
***PRACTICE AREAS: Civil Practice; Real Estate; Corporate Law; Sports Law; Zoning and Land Use Law.**
Civil Practice emphasizing Commercial and Residential Real Estate, Corporate Law, Sports Law, and including Zoning Subdivisions Land Use and Debtor Creditor Rights, Real Estate Finance, Mortgage Financing and Refinancing.
See Professional Biographies, STAMFORD, CONNECTICUT

Hoffman, Kevin T.
(See Greenwich)

Hogan, Francis W., III .... '60 '87 C&L.94 B.A., J.D. 4 Landmark Sq.
Hogan, Frank W. '60 '87 C&L.94 B.A., J.D.
V.P., Gen. Coun. & Secy., Siligan Holdings, Inc.
Hogan, Leah Pavetti .... '64 '92 C.66 B.A. L.818 J.D. [🄰 M.E.Wynn]
*PRACTICE AREAS: Family Law; Matrimonial Law.
Hogan, Richard A. '61 '89 C&L.184 B.A., J.D.
Regulatory & Legis. Coun., Ct. Attys. Title Ins. Co.

Hoin, Stacey Weinsheimer '— '87 C.741 B.A. L.276 J.D.
1600 Summer Street, 06905-5125
Telephone: 818-346-2072 Fax: 818-346-1935
Email: staceyhoin@email.msn.com
(Not admitted in CT).
Employment Law.
See Professional Biographies, STAMFORD, CONNECTICUT

Holland Kaufmann & Bartels, LLC
(See Greenwich)

Holley, William A., III '61 '86 C.309 A.B. L.93 J.D.
General Electric Capital Corporation
Holmes, Andrew S. .... '55 '82 C.674 A.B. L.893 J.D. [🄲 Paul,H.J.&W.]
*PRACTICE AREAS: Asset Based Finance including; Equipment Leasing; Project Finance; Securitization of Transportation and Industrial Equipment; Co-Generation Power.
Hooper, Arthur W., Jr., (AV) ....'44 '70 C.264 A.B. L.188 J.D. [🄲 Pillsbury W.]
*PRACTICE AREAS: Commercial Real Estate, Leasing, Banking and Lending.
Hopkins, Zoe P. '50 '78 C.691 B.A. L.846 J.D.
V.P. & Asst. Gen. Coun., Gen. Reinsurance Corp.
*RESPONSIBILITIES: Employment Law; Employee Benefits; Executive Compensation; ERISA.

Hopper & Hopper
(See Greenwich)

Hryb, Deborah '51 '77 C.945 B.A. L.893 J.D.
(adm. in DC; not adm. in CT) [🄰 Paul,H.J.&W.]
*PRACTICE AREAS: Employment Law.
Hubbard, D. Seeley, (BV) ....'45 '71 C.855 B.A. L.184 J.D. [Neville S.H.&M.] ⊙
*PRACTICE AREAS: Commercial Real Estate; Computers and Software; Commercial Law; Business Law; Environmental Law.

Hubbard, Robert R. '37 '65 C.608 B.E.E. L.273 LL.B.
(adm. in DC; not adm. in CT; See Pat. Sect.) [Ⓒ Ohlandt,G.R.&P.]
Hudock, Bruce P., (BV) . . . . . '52 '77 C.30 B.A. L.128 J.D. Asst. State's Atty.
Huet, David R. '61 '86 C.645 B.S. L.61 J.D.
(adm. in CA; not adm. in CT) Gen. Coun., Capital Funding, Inc.
Huey, Mary Carroll '57 '84 C.976 B.A. L.659 J.D.
V.P. & Dep. Gen. Coun., Time Warner Cable
Hufford, Wendy Lynn '61 '86 C.165 B.A. L.976 J.D.
(adm. in PA; not adm. in CT) Sr. Lit. Coun., GE Capital Card Servs.
Hufziger, Paul T. '59 '85 C.477 B.B.A. L.912 J.D.
(adm. in MI; not adm. in CT) Tax Coun./Dir. of Taxes, GE Capital Card Servs.
Hughes, Paul G., (AV) . . . . . '47 '73 C.884 B.A. L.188 J.D. [Cummings&L.]
*PRACTICE AREAS: Corporate Law; Securities Law; Banking Regulatory.
Hume, Duncan B., (BV) . . . . . '45 '71 C.165 A.B. L.982 J.D. [Hume&Assoc.]
Hume & Associates, (BV) . . . . . One Landmark Square
Humphrey, Steven R., (AV) '— '66 C.918 B.A. L.880 J.D.
[Robinson&C.] (ⓞHartford)
*PRACTICE AREAS: Energy; Litigation; Telecommunications.
Hunt, Beverly J. . . . . . '45 '88 C.415 B.S. L.184 J.D. [Ⓐ Ryan,R.J.&D.]
*PRACTICE AREAS: Medical Malpractice.
Hunt, James G. '61 '86 C.589 B.S. L.352 J.D.
(adm. in IL; not adm. in CT) State Tax Coun., GE Capital Corp.
Hunter, Kathryn L. . . . . . '59 '87 C.1036 B.A. L.705 J.D. [Ⓐ Kelley D.&W.]
*PRACTICE AREAS: Real Estate.
Hurlbut, Terrill C. . . . . . '42 '67 C&L.352 B.B.A., J.D. One Champion Plz.
Hurley, Sarah M. . . . . . '72 '00 C.771 B.A. L.1040 J.D. [Ⓐ Robinson&C.]
Hurwitz, Jocelyn B. . . . '67 '92 C&L.188 B.S., J.D. [Cohen&W.] (ⓞBridgeport, Westport)
*PRACTICE AREAS: Family Law; Commercial Litigation; Divorce Mediation.
Hyde, Jeffrey L. '54 '80 C.645 B.S.B.A. L.1017 J.D.
(adm. in PA; not adm. in CT) Sr. Tax Coun., GE Capital Corp.
Hynes, Christopher J., (BV) . . . . . '53 '82 C.262 B.A. L.724 J.D. 106 Stamford Ave.
Hynes, Thomas W. '47 '76 C.262 B.A. L.724 J.D.
(adm. in NY; not adm. in CT) Pres., Hynes, Himmelreich, Glennon & Co.
Iacovo, Louis J., (AV) . . . . . '12 '38 C.262 B.A. L.178 LL.B. Ret. Prob. J.
Ibietatorremendía, José '68 '94 C&L.659 B.S., J.D.
(adm. in NJ; not adm. in CT) Mng. Dir. & Coun., GE Capital Structured Finance Group
Innis-Thompson, Janice '66 '91 C&L.260 B.S., J.D.
(adm. in FL; not adm. in CT) Coun., Lit., International Paper Co.
*RESPONSIBILITIES: Litigation.
Ippolito, Mario J., (AV) . . . . . '58 '84 C.276 B.S.B.A. L.178 J.D. [Paul,H.J.&W.]
*PRACTICE AREAS: Lending and Secured Transactions; Structured Finance; Asset-Based and Equipment Finance; Workouts; Bankruptcy.

Ivey, Barnum & O'Mara, LLC
(See Greenwich)

Izzillo, Joseph A. . . . . . '24 '51 C.262 L.724 J.D. [Ⓒ Roberts,R.&B.]
*PRACTICE AREAS: Guardianship and Conservatorship; Trusts and Estates.

Jachimczyk, Michael C. '52 '90 C.385 A.B. L.1029 J.D.
706 Bedford Street, P.O. Box 2442, 06906-0442
Telephone: 203-353-1769 Fax: 203-348-8092
Email: mcjesq@excite.com URL: http://www.lawyers.com/mcjesq
***PRACTICE AREAS: Real Estate; Zoning, Planning and Land Use; Criminal Defense; Probate. Real Estate, Zoning and Land Use Planning, Criminal Defense.**
See Professional Biographies, STAMFORD, CONNECTICUT

Jackson Lewis Schnitzler & Krupman, (AV)
177 Broad Street, 8th Floor, P.O. Box 251, 06904-0251 ⓞ
Telephone: 203-961-0404 Facsimile: 203-324-4704
Email: stamford@jacksonlewis.com URL: http://www.jacksonlewis.com
Francis P. Alvarez; A. Robert Fischer; Roger P. Gilson, Jr.; Conrad Shawn Kee; Michael J. Soltis. Associates: Seth F. Eisenberg (Not admitted in CT); Christina Calise Feeny; Joshua E. Greenberg (1970-1998); Christian A. Grenier; Edward V. Jeffrey; David P. Powilatis; Michelle H. Riordan (Not admitted in CT); Jeffrey M. Vona.
Labor Relations, Employment Discrimination, Wrongful Discharge and Other Employment-Related Litigation, Employee Benefits and Pension Law, Wage and Hour, OSHA, Immigration Law, Public Sector and State Labor Relations Law, On Behalf of Management.
Other offices located in: Atlanta, Georgia; Boston, Massachusetts; Chicago, Illinois; Dallas, Texas; Greenville, South Carolina; Hartford, Connecticut; Long Island, New York; Los Angeles, California; Miami, Florida; Minneapolis, Minnesota; Morristown, New Jersey; New York, New York; Orlando, Florida; Pittsburgh, Pennsylvania; Sacramento, California; San Francisco, California; Seattle, Washington; Washington, D.C.; White Plains, New York.
See Professional Biographies, STAMFORD, CONNECTICUT

Jacobs Partners LLC
(See Norwalk)

Jacobson, David S. '67 '95 C.477 B.A. L.273 J.D.
(adm. in NJ; not adm. in CT) [Gordon&J.]
Jacoby, Douglas M. '62 '98 C&L.910 B.S.B.A., J.D.
(adm. in NY; not adm. in CT) Assoc. Dir., Warburg Dillon Read LLC, CT
Jacques, Mary-Elizabeth . . . . . '— '53 C.881 A.B. L.309 J.D. [Ⓒ Roberts,R.&B.]
*PRACTICE AREAS: Probate; Trusts and Estates.
Jaffe, Harris S., (AVⓣ) '42 '67 C&L.145 B.A., J.D.
(adm. in IL; not adm. in CT) [Ⓒ Cummings&L.]
*PRACTICE AREAS: Finance (25%); Corporate Law (25%); Securities (25%); Mergers and Acquisitions (25%).
Janson, Charles E., (BV) . . . . . '— '81 C.951 B.A. L.184 J.D. [Ⓒ Robinson&C.]
*PRACTICE AREAS: Real Estate; Zoning, Planning and Land Use; Environmental Law; Museum Law; Affordable Housing.
Jarvis, Ora-Anne E. '66 '93 C.299 A.B. L.982 J.D.
Asst. Gen. Coun., The Purdue Frederick Co./Purdue Pharma L.P.
*RESPONSIBILITIES: Contracts; Employment; Licensing; Litigation; Technology.
Jauvin, Chantal C. '66 '93 C&L.018 B.S., LL.B.
(adm. in ON; not adm. in CT) Conair Corp.
Jeffrey, Edward V. . . . . . '— '96 C.1505 B.A. [Ⓐ Jackson L.S.&K.]
Jenks, Rodney P., Jr., (BVⓣ) '50 '76 C.112 A.B. L.1065 J.D.
(adm. in CA; not adm. in CT) Asst. Gen. Coun., Hexcel Corp.
*RESPONSIBILITIES: Corporate.
Jensen, Frode, (AV) . . . . . '50 '77 C.951 B.A. L.178 J.D. [Pillsbury W.]
*PRACTICE AREAS: Mergers, Acquisitions and Divestitures; Corporate Finance; Securities; Venture Capital; Corporate Governance.
Jepsen, George C., (BV) . . . . . '54 '82 C.197 B.A. L.309 J.D. [Ⓒ Shipman&G.]
*PRACTICE AREAS: General Practice; Tax Law; Estate Planning.

Jessen, Jon E. '63 '91 C.588 B.S. L.1252 J.D.
800 Summer Street, Suite 305, 06901
Telephone: 203-348-3262 Fax: 203-348-3264
Email: jonjessenlaw@aol.com URL: http://www.lawyers.com/usimmigrationlaw
***PRACTICE AREAS: Immigration and Naturalization.**
Immigration and Naturalization, Civil Litigation, Civil Rights, Personal Injury, Automobile Accidents, Wrongful Death, Criminal, DUI, Felonies, Homicides, Misdemeanors, Juvenile Crimes, Traffic Violations, Drug Crimes.
See Professional Biographies, STAMFORD, CONNECTICUT

Johnson, Daniel G. . . . . . '72 '97 C.276 A.B. L.893 J.D. [Ⓐ Cummings&L.]
Johnson, J. Paul, (AV) . . . . . '40 '66 C.976 B.A. L.309 J.D. [Ryan,R.J.&D.]
*PRACTICE AREAS: Family Law; Real Estate Law; Estate Planning; Estate Administration; Probate Litigation.
Johnson, John S. . . . . . '30 '55 C&L.976 B.A., LL.B. 300 First Stamford Pl.
Jones Hirsch Connors & Bull P.C.
6 Landmark Sq. (ⓞL.A., CA; East Brunswick, NJ; Mineola, New York, NY)
Josel, John D., (BV) . . . . . '60 '86 C.855 B.A. L.564 J.D. [Silver,G.&T.]
*PRACTICE AREAS: Medical Malpractice; Negligence; Criminal Law.
Junkin, Scott A., (AV) . . . . . '46 '73 C.976 B.A. L.659 J.D. [S.A.Junkin]
*PRACTICE AREAS: Business Law; Contracts; Corporate Law; Finance; Mergers, Acquisitions and Divestitures.

Junkin, Scott A., P.C., (AV)
One Stamford Landing, 62 Southfield Avenue, Suite 206, 06902-7229
Telephone: 203-356-9005 Fax: 203-967-3923
Email: SAJPC@aol.com URL: http://www.lawyers.com/scottjunkin
Scott A. Junkin.
Corporate, Business, Contracts.
See Professional Biographies, STAMFORD, CONNECTICUT

Justin, Edward L. '12 '34 C&L.569 B.S., J.D.
(adm. in NY; not adm. in CT) [Ⓒ Grimes&B.]
Kahn, Evans . . . . . '10 '49 C.976 B.A. L.273 LL.B. 225 Pinewood Rd.‡
Kalashian, James M. . . . . '58 '83 C.676 B.S. L.1194 J.D. Sr. Tax Coun., GE Capital Corp.
Kaliko, Joseph J. . . . . . '46 '75 C.555 B.A. L.117 J.D. 73 Rogers Rd. (Pat.)
Kamisar, Jonathan R. '62 '88
C.597 B.A. L.228 J.D. Sr. Coun., United Distillers & Vintner Ltd.
Kane, Edward M. . . . . . '61 '87 C.145 A.B. L.262 J.D. [Shipman&G.]
*PRACTICE AREAS: Corporate Law; Taxation; Securities Law.
Kane, John H. . . . . . '— '92 C.1030 B.S. L.262 J.D. [Ⓐ Robinson&C.]
Kane, Patricia, (BV) . . . . . '42 '76 C.783 B.S. L.1009 J.D. [Kane]
Kane Legal Group, LLC, (BV) . . . . . 230 High Ridge Rd.
Kapiloff, Arnold Y., (AVⓣ) '35 '61 C.575 B.S. L.276 J.D.
[Schwartzman G.W.K.&T.] ⓞ
Kaplan, Howard C., (AV) . . . . . '35 '60 C.477 A.B. L.976 LL.B. [Wofsey,R.K.&K.]
*PRACTICE AREAS: Construction Law; Business Law; Real Estate; Civil Litigation.
Kaplan, Seth L. . . . . . '69 '95 C.860 B.S. L.575 J.D. Sr. Corp. Coun., Hexcel Corp.
*RESPONSIBILITIES: Securities; Corporate Finance; Transactions; Corporate.
Kaplow, Mark D. '47 '74 C.569 B.A. L.94 J.D.
(adm. in NY; not adm. in CT) Business Gen. Coun., GE Capital Real Estate
Karakis, Bella '65 '94 C.659 B.A. L.1357 J.D.
(adm. in NJ; not adm. in CT) 1241 E. Main St.
Karazin, Edward R., Jr. . . . . . '40 '64 C.93 A.B. L.262 J.D. Supr. Ct. J.
Karp, Douglas M., (BV) . . . . . '55 '80 C.976 B.A. L.309 J.D. 70 New England Drive
Katske, Kevin T., (BV) . . . . . '60 '87 C.1365 B.A. L.1029 J.D. [Diserio M.O.&C.]
*PRACTICE AREAS: Commercial Finance; Corporate Law; Real Estate.
Katz, Joy A. . . . . . '64 '89 C.188 B.S. L.569 J.D. 48 Janes Lane
Katz, Mark F., (BV) . . . . . '45 '72 C.178 B.A. L.184 J.D. 196 North St.
Kauff, Russell G. . . . . . '69 '97 C.855 B.A. L.184 J.D. [Ⓐ Wiggin&D.]
Kaufman, Edward L. '59 '85 C.893 B.A. L.813 J.D.
Vice President & General Counsel, Titan Sports, Inc.
Kaufman, Mark S. '50 '74 C&L.188 B.A., J.D.
(adm. in MA; not adm. in CT) 200 Ingelside Dr.‡
Kaufman, Monty D. '53 '83 C&L.569 B.A., J.D.
(adm. in NY; not adm. in CT) V.P., Professional Mkts., Pitney Bowes Inc.

Kaye and Hennessey, LLC
(See Greenwich)

Kearney, Michael J., Jr. . . . . . '68 '96 C.884 B.S. L.128 J.D. [Ⓐ Cummings&L.]
Kee, Conrad Shawn . . . . . '62 '87 C&L.910 B.A., J.D. [Jackson L.S.&K.]
Keenan, Laura Marie '64 '91 C.188 B.S. L.1019 J.D.
(adm. in NY; not adm. in CT) Dir. Lgl. & Extrn. Aff., Warburg Dillon & Read LLC, CT
Keidel, James C. . . . . . '62 '88 C.1019 L.1009 J.D. 30 Oak St.
Keidel, James C. . . . . . '62 '88 C.1019 B.A. L.1009 J.D. [Lustig&B.] (ⓞNew York, NY)
*PRACTICE AREAS: Insurance Agents and Brokers Errors and Omissions; Litigation.
Kekac, Nancy A., (BV) . . . . . '53 '79 C.1030 B.A. L.128 J.D. Supr. Asst. Pub. Def.
Kelleher, William James, III . . . . . '70 '96 C.1030 B.A. L.724 J.D. [Ⓐ Wiggin&D.]
Kelley, Kenneth T., (BV) '39 '81
C.1033 B.S. L.1048 J.D. [Brown,P.&S.] (ⓞGlastonbury, Hartford)

Kelley Drye & Warren LLP, (AV)
Two Stamford Plaza, 281 Tresser Boulevard, 06901-3229 ⓞ
Telephone: 203-324-1400 Fax: (203) 327-2669; (203) 964-3188
Email: info@kelleydrye.com URL: http://www.kelleydrye.com
Connecticut Partners: M. Ridgway Barker; Richard G. Brodrick; John M. Callagy; Brian J. Calvey (Not admitted in CT); John T. Capetta; Richard S. Chargar; Mark S. Gregory; Randi-Jean G. Hedin; Paul F. McCurdy. Special Counsel: Michael J. Palmieri. Connecticut Associates: John F. Beggs (Not admitted in CT); Michael P. Buck; Gretchen A. Carroll; James A. Cordone; Troy Ficarra; Laurel Gibaldi (Not admitted in CT); Scott E. Gottlieb; Kathryn L. Hunter; Thomas M. Kelly; Delphine W. Knight-Brown; Nichelle Maynard-Elliott; James M. Moriarty; James E. Nealon; Christopher M. Parent; Christine E. Quier-Sheth (Not admitted in CT); Carol Weiss Sherman (Not admitted in CT); Christopher J. Twomey.
Litigation, Commercial Litigation, Emerging Growth Companies, Employee Benefits, Executive Compensation, Environmental Law, Financial Institutions, Health Care, Immigration, Insurance, Intellectual Property, Technology Litigation, International Law, Labor and Employment Law, Mergers and Acquisitions, Private Clients, Products Liability, Project Finance, Infrastructure, Real Estate Law, Restructuring, Creditors Rights, Securities, Securities Industry, Securities Litigation, Telecommunications, Trade Regulation, Antitrust, White Collar Crime, Corporate Investigations, Year 2000, Y2K.
New York, N.Y. Office: 101 Park Avenue. Telephone: 212-808-7800. Fax: (212) 808-7897.
Los Angeles, California Office: 777 South Figueroa Street, Suite 2700. Telephone: 213-689-1300. Fax: (213) 688-8150.
Washington, D.C. Office: 1200 19th Street, N.W., Suite 500. Telephone: 202-955-9600. Fax: (202) 955-9792.
Parsippany, New Jersey Office: 5 Sylvan Way. Telephone: 973-539-0099. Fax: (973) 539-3167.
Chicago, Illinois Office: 303 West Madison Street, Suite 1400. Telephone: 312-346-6350. Fax: (312) 346-8982.
Vienna, Virginia Office: 8000 Towers Crescent Drive, Suite 1200. Telephone: 703-918-2300. Fax: 703-918-2450.
Brussels, Belgium Office: 106 Avenue Louise, 1050. Telephone: (011) (32-2) 646-1110. Fax: (011) (32-2) 640-0589.
Hong Kong Office: Suite 1602, Fairmont House, 8 Cotton Tree Drive. Telephone: (011) (852) 2869-0821. Fax: (011) (852) 2869-0049.
Affiliated Offices:
Jakarta, Indonesia: Soebagjo, Jatim, Djarot, Plaza DM, 17th Floor, Jalan Jend. Sudirman Kav. 25, Jakarta 12920, Indonesia. Telephone: (011) (62-21) 5229765. Fax: (011) (62-21) 5229752.
Tokyo, Japan: Yumoto & Ota, Kioi Royal Heights, 3-29, Kioi-Cho, Chiyoda-Ku, Tokyo 102, Japan. Telephone: (011) (81-3) 3234-2441. Fax: (011) (81-3) 3262-2729.
Manila, Philippines: Oporto Reyes Suarez & Associates, 2111 BSA Suites, 103 C. Palanca Street, Legaspi Village, Makati City, Metro Manila. Telephone: (011) (63-2) 888-6951; 888-6953. Fax: (011) (63-2) 888-6945. E-Mail: oporto@pacific.net.ph.
Bangkok, Thailand: Dej-Udom & Associates, Charn Issara Tower, 9th Floor, 942/142-3 Rama IV Road, Bangkok 10500 Thailand. Telephone: (011) (66-2) 233-0055. Fax: (011) (66-2) 236-6681. E-Mail: dejudom@loxinfo.co.th.

(This Listing Continued)

Kelley Drye & Warren LLP (Continued)

Mumbai (Bombay) India: Wakhariya & Wakhariya, 41 Bajaj Bhawan, 226 Nariman Point, Mumbai 400021. Telephone: (91-22) 281-0336; 91-22-285-9820. Fax: (91-22) 281-0337. E-Mail: shabbirw@counsellor.com.

See Professional Biographies, STAMFORD, CONNECTICUT

Kellogg, Alfred C. '46 '72 C.705 B.A. L.188 J.D.
(adm. in NY; not adm. in CT) Dir., Warburg Dillon Read LLC, CT
Kelly, James B. '27 '54 C.1027 B.S. L.724 LL.B.
(adm. in NY; not adm. in CT) Combustion Engg., Inc.
Kelly, Janine M. . . . . '69 '94 C.321 B.A. L.1194 J.D. [🄰 Ryan,R.J.&D.]
*PRACTICE AREAS: Litigation.
Kelly, Karin Dai . . . .'71 '99 C.859 B.S. L.128 J.D. [🄰 Ohlandt,G.R.&P.]
*PRACTICE AREAS: Patent Law.
Kelly, Thomas M. . . . .'71 '97 C.823 B.A. L.776 J.D. [🄰 Kelley D.&W.]
*PRACTICE AREAS: Securities.
Kempson, Kenneth E. '51 '81 C.453 B.S. L.893 J.D.
(adm. in DC; not adm. in CT) Sr. Tax Coun. & Dir. Tax Exams, GE Capital Corp. Tax
Kent, Richard G., (AV) '51 '75
C.705 B.A. L.93 J.D. [Cohen&W.] (⊙Bridgeport, Westport)
*PRACTICE AREAS: Family; Civil; Criminal Litigation.
Kern, Irving J., (AV) . . . . '46 '71 C.184 B.S. L.893 J.D. [Cohen&W.] (⊙Bridgeport)
*PRACTICE AREAS: Real Estate; Commercial; Corporate; Estate Planning; Health Care.
Kesselman, Barry J. '41 '66 C.645 B.S.I.E. L.273 J.D.
Sr. Pat. Coun., Lic. & Litig., Xerox Corporation (Pat.)
Khan, Huma . . . .'70 '97 C&L.184 B.A., J.D. [🄰 Spitzer S.&B.]
*PRACTICE AREAS: Labor and Employment; Litigation; Civil Rights.
Khanna, Joe . . . .'70 '95 C.1044 B.A. L.107 J.D. Corp. Coun., Pitney Bowes Inc.
*RESPONSIBILITIES: Corporate Law.
Kidambi, Vaman B. '70 '97 L.273 LL.M.
(adm. in NY; not adm. in CT) [Kidambi&Assoc.]
*PRACTICE AREAS: Business Immigration; Corporate Law; Immigration and Naturalization; Employment Immigration; Employment Visas.

Kidambi & Associates, P.C.
800 Summer Street, Suite 209, 06901
Telephone: 203-961-1886 Fax: 203-961-1872 URL: http://www.lawyers.com/kidambi
Email: info@kidambi.com URL: http://www.kidambi.com
Vaman B. Kidambi (Not admitted in CT).
Corporate Law, Immigration and Naturalization.

See Professional Biographies, STAMFORD, CONNECTICUT

Kiefer, Donald R.
(See Greenwich)

Kiernan, Vincent M. . . . .'56 '82 C&L.569 B.A., J.D. [Cummings&L.]
*PRACTICE AREAS: Corporate Law; Securities Law; Mergers and Acquisitions; Emerging Technologies.
Kilkeary, Martin J. '47 '73 C&L.724 B.A., J.D.
(adm. in NY; not adm. in CT) Sr. Coun., Cushman & Wakefield, Inc.
King, Ronald, (AV) . . . .'26 '50 C&L.945 B.A., J.D. 79 Mather Rd.
Kipperman, Edward O. '51 '76 C.184 B.A. L.192 J.D.
(adm. in NJ; not adm. in CT) Citizens Utilities Co.
Kirban, Elise '61 '91 C.597 B.A. L.276 J.D.
(adm. in DC; not adm. in CT) Coun., Antitrust & Corp. Compl., International Paper Co.
*RESPONSIBILITIES: Antitrust; Trade Regulation; Federal Regulatory Compliance.
Kirby, Margaret Ann, (BV) . . . .'59 '84 C.321 B.A. L.818 J.D. 80 4th St.
Kissel, Neal H. '66 '94 C.473 B.Ph. L.813 J.D.
(adm. in CA; not adm. in CT) Marakon Assoc.
Klein, Gary S., (BV) . . . .'67 '91 C.893 B.A. L.472 J.D. [Sandak F.H.&G.]
*PRACTICE AREAS: Environmental Litigation; Commercial Litigation.
Klein, Matthew . . . . '55 '82 C.178 A.B. L.262 J.D. 350 Bedford St.
Kline, Harry H. '20 '51 C.102 B.A. L.30 LL.B.
(adm. in DC; not adm. in CT; Pat.) Amer. Cyanamid Co.
Kloster, Burton J., Jr. '31 '58 C&L.188 B.A., LL.B.
(adm. in NY; not adm. in CT) General Counsel, Global Opportunity Advisors, LLC‡
Knag, Paul E., (AV) . . . .'48 '71 C.994 B.A. L.309 J.D. [Cummings&L.]
*PRACTICE AREAS: Litigation; Bankruptcy Law; Health Law.
Knickerbocker, Jeffrey M. . . . .'66 '97 C.184 B.A. L.1048 J.D. [🄰 Sandak F.H.&G.]
Knight-Brown, Delphine W. . . . . '64 '90 C.674 A.B. L.724 J.D. [🄰 Kelley D.&W.]
*PRACTICE AREAS: Litigation.
Knopf, Gerald S. . . . . '58 '83 C.659 B.S. L.823 J.D. 350 Bedford St.
Koffsky, Bruce Donald, (BV) . . . .'60 '85 C.1044 B.A. L.978 J.D. 1200 Summer St.
Koga, Bond K. '56 '86 C.112 B.A. L.178 J.D.
(adm. in NY; not adm. in CT) Mng. Dir. & Sr. Coun., GE Capital Corporation
Koo, Steven J. . . . .'— '98 C.659 B.S. L.1009 J.D. [🄰 Robinson&C.]
Korsh, Kevin L. . . . . '60 '86 C.31 B.A. L.831 J.D. Coun., GE Capital Real Estate

Koskoff, Koskoff & Bieder, P.C., (AV)
1172 Bedford Street, 06905 ⊙
Telephone: 203-325-3686
Email: kkb@koskoff.com URL: http://www.koskoff.com
Christopher D. Bernard.
Litigation in all State and Federal Courts. Medical Malpractice, Equal Opportunity, Negligence, Products Liability, Civil Rights, Criminal Law and Class Actions.
Bridgeport, Connecticut Office: 350 Fairfield Avenue. Telephone: 203-336-4421.
Danbury, Connecticut Office: 1 Moss Avenue. Telephone: 203-792-7100.

See Professional Biographies, STAMFORD, CONNECTICUT

Kosowsky, Bernice Reisner, (CV) . . . .'40 '83 C.994 B.A. L.978 J.D. 1234 Summer St.
Koteen, Barbara S. '70 '96 C.454 B.A. L.1040 J.D.
(adm. in NY; not adm. in CT) [🄰 Cacace,T.&S.]
*PRACTICE AREAS: Probate; Estate Planning; Conservatorship; Elder Law.
Kouzoujian, Lisa B. . . . . '60 '89 C.165 B.A. L.1048 J.D. 810 Bedford St.
Kowalski, Ronald E., II . . . . '66 '91 C.1030 B.A. L.818 J.D. [Cacace,T.&S.]
*PRACTICE AREAS: Litigation; Appellate Practice; Tax Certiorari; Tax Valuation; Tax Appeals.
Kraemer, Brenna . . . . '61 '95 C.754 B.S. L.1252 J.D. [🄰 E.L.Reinken]
Krakower, Ira J. '40 '66 C.569 B.Ch.E. L.339 LL.B.
(adm. in NY; not adm. in CT; Pat.) Sr. V.P., Gen. Coun. & Secy., Hexcel Corp.
*RESPONSIBILITIES: Chief Legal Officer.
Kramer, Barry, (AV) . . . . '39 '66 C.688 B.Ch.E. L.569 J.D. [Cummings&L.] (Pat.)
*PRACTICE AREAS: Biotechnology; Intellectual Property; Patent; Trademark; Copyright.
Krantz, Richard A., (BV) . . . .'— '75 C.367 B.A. L.309 J.D. [Robinson&C.]
*PRACTICE AREAS: Corporate Law; Securities.
Krasnogor, Julie B. . . . .'— '95 C.1036 B.A. L.184 J.D. [Krasnogor&K.] ⊙
Krasnogor, Norine F. . . . .'— '86 C.188 B.F.A. L.564 J.D. [Krasnogor&K.]
Krasnogor & Krasnogor . . . . .706 Bedford St. (⊙New York, NY)
Krehbiel, Constance M. . . . .'44 '85 C.184 B.A. L.1029 J.D. 116 Woodmere Rd.
Krenicky, Michael W. . . . .'70 '00 C.1030 B.S. L.1218 J.D. 986 Bedford St.
Kretzman, Clare Attura . . . .'53 '80 C&L.724 B.S., J.D. [🄰 Shipman&G.]
*PRACTICE AREAS: Corporate Law; Business Law; Mergers and Acquisitions; Securities.

Kriegel, Samuel '34 '69 C.563 B.Ch.E. L.776 J.D.
(adm. in NJ; not adm. in CT)
Assoc. Gen. Coun., The Purdue Frederick Co./Purdue Pharma L.P.
*RESPONSIBILITIES: Patents and Trademarks; Licensing; Contracts; General Law.
Krinsky, Mary M. . . . . '46 '77 C.350 B.S. L.508 J.D. [St. Onge S.J.&R.] ⊙
*PRACTICE AREAS: Patent Law; Biotechnology.
Krup, Oleh A. '48 '74 C.262 B.S. L.724 J.D.
(adm. in NY; not adm. in CT) General Tax Counsel, Pitney Bowes Inc.
Kukowski, Thomas H. '63 '88 C.94 B.S. L.884 J.D. [Cooper&M.] ⊙
Kupinse, Andrew D. . . . .'70 '98 C.165 B.A. L.262 J.D. [🄰 Cummings&L.]
*PRACTICE AREAS: Corporate Law; Commercial Transactions; Real Estate.
Kwartin, Saul, (AV) . . . .'27 '52 C.197 A.B. L.188 LL.B. [🄲 Wofsey,R.K.&K.]
*PRACTICE AREAS: Real Estate; Zoning, Planning and Land Use; Litigation.
Kweskin, Edward M., (BV) . . . . '46 '71 C.659 A.B. L.273 J.D. [Wofsey,R.K.&K.]
*PRACTICE AREAS: Divorce; Real Estate; Family Law; Wills; Estate Planning.
LaCava, John J., (BV) . . . . '52 '80 C.860 B.A. L.184 J.D. [Barr&L.]
*PRACTICE AREAS: Civil Litigation Law; Personal Injury Law; Immigration Law.
Lachowicz, Mary Ellen . . . . '63 '88 C.860 B.A. L.982 J.D. Attorney, Xerox Corporation
Ladd, Daniel W., III '56 '88 C.550 B.S. L.178 J.D.
(adm. in NY; not adm. in CT) 677 Washington Blvd.
Ladestro, Gregory, (CV) . . . . '64 '90 C.588 B.S. L.1048 J.D. 1100 Summer St., 2nd Fl.
Lagano, Christopher . . . .'66 '92 C.1139 B.S./M.A. L.831 J.D. [🄰 Trow&S.]
*PRACTICE AREAS: Commercial Law; Collections; Landlord and Tenant Law; Civil Litigation; Personal Injury.
Lahiri, Yasho '68 '93 C.1365 B.A. L.262 J.D.
(adm. in NY; not adm. in CT) Gen. Coun., Quantitative Financial Strategies, Inc.
Laline, Daniel G., Jr. '49 '84 C.884 B.S. L.1029 J.D.
Princ., Towers, Perrin, Forster & Crosby, Inc.‡

Lane, Robert M.
(See Greenwich)

Laney, Robert C.E., (BV) . . . .'62 '88 C&L.945 B.A., J.D. [Ryan,R.J.&D.]
*PRACTICE AREAS: Civil Litigation.
Lang, Gregory F. . . . . '65 '93 C.951 B.A., L.184 J.D. [🄰 Paul,H.J.&W.]

Lange, Paul A., Law Offices of
(see Stratford)

Langham, James W. '60 '85 C.597 B.A. L.477 J.D.
(adm. in NY; not adm. in CT) V.P., Gen. Coun. & Secy., Lone Star Industries, Inc.
Lapin, Steven B. '45 '71 C&L.659 B.A., J.D.
(adm. in NY; not adm. in CT) Pres. & Chf. Oper. Offr., Geneve Corp.
Lapine, Lawrence M., (AV) . . . . '44 '69 C.103 B.A. L.184 J.D. [Bello,L.&C.] ⊙
*PRACTICE AREAS: Civil Litigation; Medical Malpractice; Dental Malpractice; Legal Malpractice; Personal Injury.
LaPorta, Jeanne M. '65 '95 C.1349 B.S. L.262 J.D.
(adm. in NY; not adm. in CT) V.P. & Assoc. Gen. Coun., GE Asset Management
Larobina, Michael D. . . . . '61 '88 C.1040 B.A. L.1029 J.D. [🄰 Tooher&W.]
Larson, Roy B. '53 '83 C.903 B.A. L.893 J.D.
(adm. in NY; not adm. in CT) Senior Counsel, Xerox Corporation
Laslo, Ruth G. '60 '85 C.367 B.A. L.1040 J.D.
(adm. in NY; not adm. in CT) Dir., Warburg Dillon Read LLC, CT

Lasnick, David P., (BV) '59 '86 C.184 B.A. L.823 J.D.
30 Oak Street, 06905
Telephone: 203-967-9111 Fax: 203-356-1383
***PRACTICE AREAS: Real Estate Law; Planning and Zoning Law.**
Civil and Commercial Litigation, and Probate and Estates.

Lathouris, Peter V., (CV) . . . .'56 '82 C&L.184 B.A., J.D. 1100 Summer St.
Laurentino, Vincent . . . .'64 '94 C.855 B.S. L.1325 J.D. 900 Long Ridge Road
Leader, Leonard, (AV) . . . . '50 '74 C.563 B.A. L.262 J.D. [Wiggin&D.]
*PRACTICE AREAS: Trusts and Estates.
Leddy, Lorey Rives . . . .'64 '90 C.319 B.A. L.188 J.D. [🄰 Day,B.&H.]
*PRACTICE AREAS: Commercial Litigation; Patent and Trademark Litigation; Year 2000 Issues.
Lee, Charles T., (AV) . . . . '50 '77 C.309 B.A. L.178 J.D. [Paul,H.J.&W.]
*PRACTICE AREAS: Trade Regulation; Insurance Coverage; Telecommunications; Environmental Law.
Lee, George M. '55 '84 C.563 B.S. L.705 J.D.
(adm. in NY; not adm. in CT) Merrill Lynch Realty, Inc.
Lee, Samuel K. '62 '89 C.112 B.A. L.564 J.D.
(adm. in NY; not adm. in CT) Coun., Xerox Corporation
Lee, Wendy H. '70 '97 C.188 B.S. L.184 J.D.
[🄰 Windels M.L.&M.] (⊙New York, NY)
Leibell, David T. . . . .'61 '90 C.855 B.A. L.262 J.D. [🄰 Cummings&L.]
*PRACTICE AREAS: Corporate Law.
Leibell, John J. '25 '50 C.276 B.S. L.178 LL.B.
(adm. in NY; not adm. in CT) Assoc. Gen. Coun., GE Capital Corp.
Leifer, Steven J. . . . . '38 '64 C.563 L.178 J.D. Sr. Coun., Insurance Alliances Grp., Inc.
Leitão, Kevin D. . . . .'64 '91 C.103 A.B. L.976 J.D. Coun., GE Capital Card Services
Lerner, Edward N., (BV) . . . .'47 '75 C.994 B.A. L.128 J.D. 112 Prospect St.
Lestelle, Karin C. '58 '83 C.569 B.A. L.273 J.D.
(adm. in NY; not adm. in CT) [Fragomen,D.B.&L.]

Lev & Berlin, P.C.
(See Norwalk)

Levene, Douglas B., (AV) '51 '82 C.453 S.B. L.477 J.D.
(adm. in NY; not adm. in CT) V.P., Gen. Coun. & Secy., Philip Morris Capital Corp.

Leventhal, Michael J.
(See Westport)

Levine, Eric T. . . . . '69 '95 C.103 B.A. L.184 J.D. [🄰 Paul,H.J.&W.]
Levine, Jonathan M., (BV) . . . . '64 '90 C.309 B.A. L.976 J.D. [Silver,G.&T.]
*PRACTICE AREAS: Medical Malpractice; Negligence; Commercial Litigation; Employment Law.
Levine, Linnea J. . . . .'47 '91 C.1044 B.A. L.564 J.D. [L.J.Levine] ⊙
*PRACTICE AREAS: Elder Care; Health Care; Medicare and Medicaid; Family Law; Estate and Probate Law.

Levine, Linnea J., P.C., Law Offices of
970 Summer Street, 06905 ⊙
Telephone: 203-348-8631 Fax: 203-359-0202
Email: linnealaw@aol.com URL: http://www.lawyers.com/linneajlevinelaw
Linnea J. Levine;—Ellen Siev Belson.
Elder Law, Health Law, Family Law, Estate and Probate Law, Social Security Disability, Medicare, Medicaid, Conservator Proceedings.
Purchase, New York Office: 3000 Westchester Avenue, 10577. Telephone: 914-251-1750; 800-828-1277. Fax: 914-251-1746.

See Professional Biographies, STAMFORD, CONNECTICUT

Levinson, Joseph . . . .'26 '53 C.339 B.S. L.273 LL.B. 460 Summer St. (Pat.)
Levister, Robert L. . . . .'18 '49 C.369 A.B. L.94 LL.B. Supr. Ct. J.
Levy, Lauren D. '69 '96 C.918 B.A. L.880 J.D.
(adm. in MA; not adm. in CT) 1055 Washington Blvd.
Lewis, Alan M. '46 '71 C.67 A.B. L.309 J.D.
Exec. V.P., Gen. Coun. & Secy., GE Asset Management

Leyden, Raymond William '46 '73 C.976 B.A. L.309 J.D.
(adm. in NY; not adm. in CT)
Mng. Dir. & Sr. Coun., GE Capital Servs. Structured Fin. Grp., Inc.
Leydon, Brenden P. . . . . '68 '95 C.860 B.A. L.705 J.D. [Ⓐ Tooher&W.]
Leydon, John F., Jr., (BV) . . . . '64 '91 C.309 A.B. L.262 J.D. [Ryan,R.J.&D.]
*PRACTICE AREAS: Business Law; Land Use; Real Estate; Trusts and Estates.
Lieb, Peter M. '56 '83 C.976 B.A. L.477 J.D.
(adm. in NY; not adm. in CT)
Assoc. Gen. Coun., Lit., Labor & Employment, International Paper Co.
*RESPONSIBILITIES: Litigation; Intellectual Property Law; Labor and Employment Law; Environmental Law; Health and Safety Law.
Ligelis, Gregory J. . . . . '— '76 C.1019 B.A. L.659 J.D. [Robinson&C.]
*PRACTICE AREAS: Admiralty and Maritime Law; Litigation; Arbitration; Insurance.
Lillie, James J. '65 '01 C.1133 B.S. L.724 J.D.
(adm. in NY; not adm. in CT; Pat.) [Ⓐ Cummings&L.] (⊙Stamford)
*PRACTICE AREAS: Intellectual Property.
Lindroos, Colleen Danehy, (BV) '53 '82 C.633 B.A. L.184 J.D.
Mgr., Legal Publications, Ct. Attys. Title Ins. Co.
Linnehan, Ann M. '71 '00 C.93 B.A. L.904 J.D.
(adm. in NY; not adm. in CT) One Elmcroft Rd.
Lipcan, Natasha M. . . . . '70 '95 C.881 A.B. L.184 J.D. [Ⓐ Day,B.&H.]
*PRACTICE AREAS: Employment Law; Employment Litigation; Labor and Employment.

Lipson, Jack S.
(See Westport)

Lipton, Amy N. '54 '79 C.1036 B.A. L.94 J.D.
(adm. in IL; not adm. in CT) CUC Intl. Inc.
Livolsi, Frank W., Jr., (BV) . . . . '38 '68 C.1338 B.A. L.262 J.D. [Plotkin&L.]
Llorca, Manuel R., (AVⓉ) . . . . '49 '75 C.176 A.B. L.262 J.D. [Skoufalos,L.&Z.] ⊙
Lloyd, James H., III, (AV) . . . . '43 '73 C.674 A.B. L.184 J.D. [Updike,K.&S.] (⊙Hartford)
Locke, Charles T., (P.C.), (AVⓉ) . . . . '49 '74 C.882 B.A. L.744 J.D. [Locke&H.] ⊙
Locke & Herbert, (AVⓉ) . . . . 1100 Summer Street (⊙New York, NY)
Lodato, Joseph M. . . . . '64 '89 C&L.276 B.S.B.A., J.D. [Pullman&C.]
*PRACTICE AREAS: Corporate Law; Partnership Law; Commercial Law; Nonprofit and Charitable Organizations; Securities Law.

Loforese, John T., LLC, Law Offices of
(See Greenwich)

Logan, W. Andrew P., III . . . . '66 '95 C.945 A.B. L.724 J.D. [Ⓐ Paul,H.J.&W.]
Lomazzo, Nancy L. . . . . '65 '94 C.197 A.B. L.145 J.D. [Ⓐ Finn D.&H.]
*PRACTICE AREAS: Real Estate; Corporate Finance; Mergers and Acquisitions.
London, Fredric S., (AVⓉ) '47 '74 C.976 B.A. L.705 J.D.
(adm. in XX; not adm. in CT) Sr. V.P., Secy. & Gen. Coun., OMI Corp.
London, Sheri Faith '55 '93 C.705 B.A. L.978 J.D.
(adm. in NY; not adm. in CT) Xerox Corporation
Lord, Michael H. '67 '93 C.1365 B.A. L.823 J.D.
(adm. in NY; not adm. in CT) 350 Bedford St.
Lorent, Marguerite . . . . '59 '85 43 Seaview Ave., #6
Lorenzo, Anthony R., (AV) . . . . '26 '61 C&L.569 B.S., J.D. [Ⓒ Wofsey,R.K.&K.]
*PRACTICE AREAS: Taxation; Corporate Law; Trusts and Estates.
Lorimer, Ernest M., (BV) . . . . '52 '79 C.674 A.B. L.976 J.D. [Finn D.&H.]
*PRACTICE AREAS: Public and Corporate Finance; Securities; Mergers and Acquisitions.
Louizos, John J. . . . . '72 '97 C.550 B.A. L.902 J.D. [Ⓐ Curtis,B.&B.]
*PRACTICE AREAS: Commercial Law; Civil Litigation; Real Estate.
Lovallo, Randolph T., (BV) . . . . '56 '81 C.367 B.A. L.1202 J.D. [Curtis,B.&B.]
*PRACTICE AREAS: Civil Litigation; Commercial Litigation; Landlord and Tenant Law; Corporate Law; Municipal Law.
Love, J. Michael '51 '77 C.477 B.A. L.215 J.D.
(adm. in NH; not adm. in CT) V.P., Citizens Utilities Co.
Lubash, Sharon June '61 '87 C.674 A.B. L.178 J.D.
(adm. in NY; not adm. in CT) P.O. Box 2147‡
Lucas, Scott R., (AV) . . . . '60 '85 C.688 B.S. L.982 J.D. [Martin,L.&C.]
*PRACTICE AREAS: Commercial; Employment; Civil Litigation.
Lucca, Marie J. '64 '88 C.309 A.B. L.94 J.D.
(adm. in MA; not adm. in CT) Editor in Chf., Intl. Mktg. Strategies

Lucey, Gordon M., (AV) '32 '58 C.301 B.A. L.309 J.D.
1177 Summer Street, 06905 ⊙
Telephone: 203-325-4448 Telefax: 203-359-2994
Of Counsel: Katherine M. Sortor; Barbara H. McWhirter.
General Practice. Corporate, International, Maritime, Environmental, Litigation, Federal Agencies and Real Estate.
New York, N.Y. Office: 122 East 42nd Street, Suite 1611, 10168-1699. Telephone: 212-557-9577. Telefax: 212-557-9580.

See Professional Biographies, STAMFORD, CONNECTICUT

Lunde, Janice Kirsten . . . . '53 '93 C.1044 B.S.N. L.564 J.D. [Ⓐ Heidell,P.M.&B.] ⊙
*PRACTICE AREAS: Professional Liability; Medical Malpractice; Litigation.
Luoma, Valerie A., (BV) . . . . '56 '81 C.918 B.A. L.184 J.D. Asst. Town Atty.

Lustig & Brown, LLP
1150 Summer Street, 06905 ⊙
Telephone: 203-977-7840 Fax: 203-977-8649
Email: firm@lustigbrown.com URL: http://www.lustigbrown.com
Member of Firm: James C. Keidel;—Christopher B. Weldon; Darren P. Renner.
General Insurance and Insurance Litigation, Casualty and Property Insurance, Professional Liability including Insurance Agents and Brokers Errors and Omissions, Insurance Coverage Analysis and Litigation including First and Third Party, Excess Coverage, Insurance Bad Faith, Insurance Products, Insurance Contracts, Civil Litigation, Trials and Appeals.
Buffalo, New York Office: Centerpointe Corporate Park, 400 Essjay Road, Suite 200, 14221-8228. Telephone: 716-626-2600. Fax: 716-626-2601.
New York, New York Office: 641 Lexington Avenue, 28th Floor, 10022. Telephone: 212-832-3235. Fax: 212-832-3155.
Newark, New Jersey Office: One Gateway Center, Suite 2600, 07102. Telephone: 973-645-9459. Fax: 973-645-0570.

See Professional Biographies, STAMFORD, CONNECTICUT

Lutjen, Laura J. . . . . '68 '96 C.999 B.B.A. L.976 J.D. [Ⓐ Finn D.&H.]
*PRACTICE AREAS: Taxation.
Lynam, William T. '34 '60 C.216 A.B. L.659 LL.B.
(adm. in DE; not adm. in CT) 3 High Ridge Park
Lyons, David A. . . . . '49 '75 C.999 B.A. L.365 J.D. 252 Brookdale Rd.‡
Lyons, Kirk M. H., (AVⓉ) '54 '81 C.1308 B.S. L.1202 J.D.
[Lyons,S.P.&F.] (⊙Boston, MA; New York, NY)
Lyons, Skoufalos, Proios & Flood, (AVⓉ)
999 Summer St., Ste. 200 (⊙Boston, MA; Englewood Cliffs, NJ; New York, NY)
Lytton, William B., (AVⓉ) '48 '73 C.276 A.B. L.30 J.D.
(adm. in DC; not adm. in CT) Sr. V.P. & Gen. Coun., International Paper Co.
Mackler, Isadore M., (AV) . . . . '18 '50 C.178 B.S. L.309 LL.B. [Mackler&G.]
Mackler and Gold, P.C., (AV) . . . . 460 Summer St.
MacMillan, Gary A., (AV) . . . . '47 '72 C.188 A.B. L.309 J.D. [Ⓒ Martin,L.&C.]
*PRACTICE AREAS: Commercial; Employment; Civil Litigation.
Macrides, Zezima & Christiano, (BV) . . . . 1516 Bedford St.

Madden, Michael J. . . . . '70 '95 C.676 B.A. L.724 J.D. [Ⓐ Paul,H.J.&W.]
*PRACTICE AREAS: Corporate.
Maddox, Matthew Morgen . . . . '64 '91 C.1030 B.S. L.818 J.D. 29 5th St.
Magida, Stephen A., (AVⓉ) . . . . '43 '68 C.659 B.S. L.178 LL.B. 105 Harbor Dr.
Magovern, John J. '49 '75 C.262 B.A. L.800 J.D.
(adm. in NY; not adm. in CT) Lgl. Coun., Warburg Dillon Read LLC, CT

Maher and Williams
(See Fairfield)

Maker, Joseph A. . . . . '66 '91 C.184 B.A. L.1029 J.D. 30 Oak St.
Malloy, Howard P. . . . . '23 '50 C.309 B.S. L.976 LL.B. 68 Eagle Dr.
Maloney, John P. '39 '68 C&L.724 B.B.A., J.D.
(adm. in NY; not adm. in CT) [Ⓐ Neville S.H.&M.] ⊙
*PRACTICE AREAS: Taxation; Trusts and Estates.
Malowitz, Wesley M. . . . . '64 '91 C.610 B.A. L.30 J.D. [Berkowitz,M.&M.] ⊙
*PRACTICE AREAS: Personal Injury; Medical Malpractice; Workers Compensation; Products Liability.

Mancuso, Rubin & Fufidio
(See White Plains, New York)

Mandel, Rolland A. . . . . '64 '89 C.569 B.A. L.978 J.D. 112 Prospect St., 3rd Fl.
Manfreda, Robert L., Jr. '— '94
C.602 B.A. L.184 J.D. Global Tax Dir., GE Capital Real Estate
Mannis, Bob D. '49 '75 C.705 A.B. L.276 J.D.
(adm. in NY; not adm. in CT) Assoc. Gen. Coun., Pitney Bowes Inc.
*RESPONSIBILITIES: Corporate Law; International; Commercial Law; Mergers and Acquisitions.
Mantel, Joan Licht '52 '76 C.66 B.A. L.569 J.D.
(adm. in NY; not adm. in CT) GE Capital Servs. Structured Fin. Grp., Inc.
Marcovich, Stephen, (BV) . . . . '53 '83 C.705 A.B. L.1029 J.D. [Cummings&L.]
*PRACTICE AREAS: Corporate; Securities; Venture Capital.
Margolis, Emanuel, (AV) . . . . '26 '57 C.575 A.B. L.976 LL.B. [Ⓒ Wofsey,R.K.&K.]
*PRACTICE AREAS: Civil Litigation; Discrimination; Criminal Law.
Marks, Wirt Peebles, III '29 '57 C&L.893 B.A., LL.B.
(adm. in VA; not adm. in CT) Combustion Engg., Inc.
Marrs, Peter B. '57 '86 C.867 B.S. L.976 J.D.
(adm. in CA; not adm. in CT) Sr. Tax Coun., GE Capital Corp.
Marsh, Jason A. . . . . '74 '99 C.860 B.A. L.184 J.D. [Ⓐ Diserio M.O.&C.]
*PRACTICE AREAS: Corporate Law; Commercial Leasing; Commercial Finance; Taxation; Trusts and Estates.
Marshall, Douglas H. '56 '81 C.97 B.A. L.608 J.D.
(adm. in OH; not adm. in CT) Senior Counsel, Xerox Corporation
Marshall, Peter W. '45 '73 C.659 B.S.E. L.1065 J.D.
(adm. in CA; not adm. in CT) Sr. Coun., Litig., Xerox Corporation
Martin, Christopher G., (AV) . . . . '61 '88 C.1211 B.S. L.1040 J.D. [Martin,L.&C.] ⊙
*PRACTICE AREAS: Business Law; Mergers and Acquisitions; Internet Law; Venture Capital; Taxation.
Martin, Jan Worthington '65 '91 C.454 B.B.A. L.276 J.D.
(adm. in NY; not adm. in CT) Tax Coun., GE Capital Corp.
Martin, Richard W., (AV) . . . . '22 '50 C.610 B.A. L.184 J.D. 1 Atlantic St.

Martin, Lucas & Chioffi, LLP, (AV)
1177 Summer Street, 06905 ⊙
Telephone: 203-324-4200 Fax: 203-324-8649 URL: http://www.mlc-law.com
Email: admin@mlc-law.com URL: http://www.lawyers.com/martinlucas&chioffi
Partners: Christopher G. Martin; Scott R. Lucas; Mark P. Chioffi. Of Counsel: Gary A. MacMillan; Robert M. Stephan. Associates: Mary Alice S. Canaday; Jennifer A. Hauhuth; George M. Melo; Amy L. Meyerson.
Business Law, Corporate Finance, Mergers and Acquisitions, Internet Law, Venture Capital, Commercial and Employment Litigation; Securities, Employment, Commercial Litigation, Real Estate, Commercial Leasing, Estate and Tax Planning, Estate Settlement and Trust Administration.
New York, N.Y. Office: 90 Park Avenue, Suite 1700, 10016. Telephone: 212-569-3300. Facsimile: 212-569-3700.

See Professional Biographies, STAMFORD, CONNECTICUT

Marx, Nancy P. . . . . '52 '84 C&L.846 B.F.A., J.D. [Cummings&L.]
*PRACTICE AREAS: Trusts and Estates Law and Tax Planning; Closely-Held Business Planning.

Marzik, Robert K., P.C., Law Offices of
(See Stratford)

Masanotti, Peter Louis, (BV) '55 '80
C.184 B.A. L.831 J.D. Intl. Telecomm. Data Systems, Inc.
Matt, Diane L. . . . . '69 '98 C.659 B.A. L.94 J.D. [Ⓐ Paul,H.J.&W.]
Matthews, Charles E., Jr., (AV) '46 '72 C.262 B.A. L.178 J.D.
(adm. in NY; not adm. in CT) Gen. Coun., EQ Corp.
Matthews, Marsha . . . . '— '84 C.1019 B.A. L.1040 J.D. 111 Prospect St.
Matz, Gary R. '54 '81 C.747 B.A. L.1035 J.D.
(adm. in MN; not adm. in CT) V.P. & Asst. Gen. Coun., Time Warner Cable
Maxon, Jodi M. . . . . '67 '92 C.401 B.A. L.823 J.D. 34 Highline Trail South
Maynard-Elliott, Nichelle . . . . '68 '95 C.103 B.A. L.178 J.D. [Ⓐ Kelley D.&W.]
*PRACTICE AREAS: Venture Capital; Emerging Growth Companies; Mergers and Acquisitions; Corporate Law.
Mazzella, Jennifer R. . . . . '70 '95 C.1030 B.A. L.724 J.D. [Ⓐ Ryan,R.J.&D.]
*PRACTICE AREAS: Civil Litigation.
McAllister, Terrence J. '55 '84 C.1044 B.A. L.1040 J.D.
(adm. in NY; not adm. in CT; See Pat. Sect.) [Ohlandt,G.R.&P.]
McAnaney, Brian T. '46 '72 C.893 B.A. L.178 J.D.
(adm. in NY; not adm. in CT) V.P. & Assoc. Gen. Coun., GE Capital Corp.
McAnerney, Robert M., (AV) . . . . '24 '54 C.951 B.A. L.893 J.D. [Ⓒ Wiggin&D.]
*PRACTICE AREAS: Estate Planning; Trusts and Estates; Family Law; Real Estate.
McArthur, Karen E. . . . . '68 '96 C.1044 B.A. L.564 J.D. [Ⓐ Paul,H.J.&W.]
McCabe, Daniel M., (BV) . . . . '49 '74 C.1029 B.A. L.723 J.D. 1200 Summer St.
McCabe, Patrick D. '71 '00 C.846 B.A. L.569 J.D
(adm. in NY; not adm. in CT) [Ⓐ Bello,L.&C.]
*PRACTICE AREAS: Litigation.
McCaffrey, Timothy T. '39 '65 C.309 B.A. L.178 LL.B.
Sr. V.P., Gen Coun. & Secy., General Reinsurance Corp.
*RESPONSIBILITIES: Corporate Law; Insurance Law.
McCaghey, Charles M., (AV) . . . . '40 '65 C.433 B.A. L.188 LL.B. [Ⓒ Ryan,R.J.&D.]
*PRACTICE AREAS: Commercial and Product Liability Litigation; Trials and Appeals.
McCarthy, John G. . . . . '66 '91 C&L.262 B.A., J.D. [Bainton M.&S.] ⊙
*PRACTICE AREAS: Litigation; Intellectual Property; Product Liability; Bankruptcy.
McCarty, Richard G. '54 '80 C.674 A.B. L.564 J.D.
(adm. in NY; not adm. in CT) V.P. & Asst. Gen. Coun., Gen. Reinsurance Corp.
*RESPONSIBILITIES: Insurance; Corporate; Reinsurance; International; Mergers and Acquisitions.
McCausland, Patricia N. '57 '92 C.054 B.S. L.1040 J.D.
Sr. Coun., Time Warner Cable
McClure, Kelly J. . . . . '66 '91 C.37 B.A. L.1029 J.D. [Pillsbury W.]
McComish, Margaret A. . . . . '69 '98 C.659 L.306 [Ⓐ Day,B.&H.]
*PRACTICE AREAS: Estate and Gift Taxation; Estate Administration; Estate Planning; Trust Administration; Trust Planning.
McCormick, Jeffrey V., (AV) '44 '70 C.103 A.B. L.823 J.D.
Branch Mgr & Title Cnsl, Ct. Attys. Title Ins. Co.
McCullough, Paul L., (BV) . . . . '45 '76 C.1033 B.A. L.1202 J.D. 460 Summer St.

McCurdy, Paul F., (BV) ....'60 '85 C.390 A.B. L.982 J.D. [Kelley D.&W.]
*PRACTICE AREAS: Corporate Law; Arbitration; Securities; Broker-Dealer Arbitration.
McDermott, Douglas C. '65 '90
C.299 A.B. L.262 J.D. Sr. Assoc., SBC/Warburg Dillon Read
McDonald, Andrew J., (BV) ....'66 '91 C.188 A.B. L.306 J.D. [Pullman&C.]
*PRACTICE AREAS: Commercial Litigation; Municipal Law; Property Valuation.
McDonald, Cassandra B. ....'63 '91 C.197 A.B. L.188 J.D. [Ⓐ Cummings&L.]
*PRACTICE AREAS: Commercial Litigation.
McEnroe, Mark T. '62 '90 C.813 A.B. L.262 J.D.
Sr. Vice President & General Counsel, Priceline WebHouse Club, Inc.
McGeady, Richard H. '56 '90 C.93 B.S. L.1029 J.D.
Tax Dir., GE Capital Servs. Structures Fin. Grp., Inc.
McGeeney, John S., (AV) ....'34 '60 C.31 A.B. L.309 LL.B. [Paul,H.J.&W.]
*PRACTICE AREAS: Commercial Litigation; Employment Law.
McGlynn, James J. .... '61 '90 C.1044 B.A. L.1048 J.D. Conn. Legal Servs., Inc.

McGovern & Associates
(See Greenwich)

McGrath, Benedicta S. ....'53 '91 C.605 B.A. L.184 J.D. [Ⓒ Day,B.&H.]
*PRACTICE AREAS: ERISA; Executive Compensation; Non-Qualified Benefits; Pension and Profit Sharing Plans; Employment Tax.
McGrath, Richard P., (AV) ....'29 '54 C.276 A.B. L.309 LL.B. [Cummings&L.]
*PRACTICE AREAS: Corporate Law; Securities Law; Mergers and Acquisitions.
McGregor, Jack E. ....'34 '63 C.976 B.S. L.665 LL.B. [Ⓒ Cohen&W.] (⊙Bridgeport)
*PRACTICE AREAS: Corporate; Finance; Real Estate Development.
McGuire, Mark M. '57 '83 C.273 B.A. L.893 J.D.
(adm. in PA; not adm. in CT) Assoc. Gen. Coun., International Paper Co.
*RESPONSIBILITIES: Mergers and Acquisitions; International Law; Antitrust and Competition Law; Compliance.
McHugh, Patrick J. .... '65 '90 C.262 B.A. L.188 J.D. [Finn D.&H.]
*PRACTICE AREAS: Commercial Litigation.
McKinney, Ivy Thomas '56 '81 C.674 B.A. L.976 J.D.
Assoc. Gen. Coun., Human Resources & Lit., Xerox Corporation
*RESPONSIBILITIES: Litigation; Employment Law.
McLaughlin, Stephanie A. ....'72 '00 C.30 B.A. L.209 J.D. [Ⓐ Sandak F.H.&G.]
McLean, Alan H., (AVⓉ) .... '38 '67 C.674 B.A. L.178 LL.B. [Neville S.H.&M.] ⊙
*PRACTICE AREAS: Commercial Litigation; Litigation; Environmental Law; Employment Law.
McMahon, David P., (BV) ....'39 '82 C.999 B.A. L.1040 J.D. 1318 Bedford St.
McMullin, Thomas R. '35 '63 C.893 B.A. L.659 LL.B.
(adm. in NY; not adm. in CT) 800 Long Ridge Road
McNamara, Francis J., Jr., (AV) '27 '52
C&L.276 A.B., J.D. Pres., Charles E. Culpeper Found.
McNamara, Stephen P., (AV) '58 '86
C.453 B.S.Ch.E. L.184 J.D. [St. Onge S.J.&R.] (Pat.)
*PRACTICE AREAS: Patent Law; Trademark Law; Copyright Law; Antitrust Law; Unfair Competition Law.
McPadden, Marybeth C. ....'69 '96 C.321 B.A. L.184 J.D. [Ⓐ Shipman&G.]
*PRACTICE AREAS: Litigation.
McSweeney, Mady ....'— '93 [Ⓢ Cummings&L.]
McWhirter, Barbara H. ....'52 '84 C.280 B.S.A. L.184 J.D. [Ⓒ G.M.Lucey]
*PRACTICE AREAS: Environmental Law.

Mead, Bromley & Bishop, (BV)
Mead Building, 41 Bank Street, 06901-3066
Telephone: 203-325-4477 Telefax: 203-323-3834
URL: http://www.lawyers.com/mb&b
Members of Firm: Benjamin H. Mead (1883-1971); Stephen L. Bishop; Donald B. Powers, Jr.; Steven E. Ayres. Of Counsel: J. Robert Bromley.
General Practice. Probate, Estate Planning, Real Estate, Negligence, Family, Commercial Law and Workers Compensation. Trials in all Courts.
See Professional Biographies, STAMFORD, CONNECTICUT

Meager, A. Pier '52 '78 C.311 B.A. L.178 J.D.
(adm. in NY; not adm. in CT) Bank of America
Meehan, Nancy A. ....'63 '99 C.1252 B.A. L.1243 J.D. [Ⓐ Ryan,R.J.&D.]
*PRACTICE AREAS: Civil Litigation.

Meehan, Meehan & Gavin
(See Bridgeport)

Melick, Patricia Kavee ....'62 '88 C.401 B.A. L.145 J.D. [Wiggin&D.]
*PRACTICE AREAS: Mergers, Acquisitions and Divestitures; Biotechnology Licensing; Commercial Transactions; Contracts; Corporate Law.
Mellis, Joel P. '34 '60 C.569 B.S. L.309 LL.B.
(adm. in NY; not adm. in CT) 1 Stamford Forum
Mellis, Jon Andrew '70 '95 C.367 B.A. L.880 J.D.
(adm. in MD; not adm. in CT) 280 Barncroft Rd.★
Melmed, Julian K., (BV) ....'39 '64 C.184 B.S. L.569 LL.B. [Melmed&T.]
Melmed & Trombly, (BV) .... 100 Prospect Street
Melo, George M. ....'73 '00 C.1374 B.S. L.1040 J.D. [Ⓐ Martin,L.&C.]
*PRACTICE AREAS: Corporate Law; Commercial Law.
Melzer, Franklin, (BV) '34 '61 C.184 B.A. L.564 J.D.
State Coun., Old Republic Natl. Title Ins. Co. (⊙New Canaan)
Meno, Richard A., (BV) ....'52 '78 C.250 B.A. L.215 J.D. 25 Third St.
Meo, R. Michael, Jr. ....'71 '95 C.855 B.A. L.659 J.D. [Ⓐ Shipman&G.]
*PRACTICE AREAS: Commercial Litigation.
Merken, Gary J. '63 '91 C.860 B.A. L.818 J.D.
(adm. in MA; not adm. in CT) Ernst & Young
Meyer, Charles H. ....'52 '77 C.494 B.S.B. L.309 J.D. 263 Tresser Blvd., 7th Fl.
Meyer, Frederick R. '55 '84 C.1349 B.A. L.569 J.D.
(adm. in NY; not adm. in CT) Grp. Coun., Chrysler Capital Corp.
Meyer, Mary D. '15 '71 C.66 A.B. L.823 J.D.
(adm. in NY; not adm. in CT) 340 Woodbine Rd.‡
Meyerson, Amy L. ....'67 '94 C.228 A.B. L.184 J.D. [Ⓐ Martin,L.&C.]
*PRACTICE AREAS: Internet Law; Computer Law; Corporate Law; Commercial Law; Telecommunications Law.
Michaelson, John O. '49 '83 C.1109 B.A. L.770 J.D.
(adm. in NY; not adm. in CT) 49 Bud Ln.
Miller, Robert J. ....'45 '71 C.31 B.A. L.893 J.D. [Day,B.&H.]
*PRACTICE AREAS: Trusts and Estate Administration; Planning for Entrepreneurs; Tax-Exempt Organizations; Estate Planning; Executive Planning.
Miller, Vernon C., Jr. '46 '73 C.885 B.A. L.188 J.D.
Business Development & General Counsel, Optimum Logistics
Miller, Victoria L. ..... '67 '95 C.207 B.A. L.790 J.D. Assoc. Coun., Time Warner Cable

Miller, Hilary B.
(See Greenwich)

Millian, Pamela R. .... '66 '91 C.1349 B.A. L.823 J.D. City Health Sys.
Mintz, Douglas C., (BV) ....'52 '78 C.477 B.G.S. L.1048 J.D. 123 Hoyt St.
Mitchell, Mark O. ....'57 '88 C.712 B.A. L.1040 J.D. P.O. Box 10354
Mitchell, Robert B., (AV) ... '53 '79 C.611 B.A. L.861 J.D. [Pullman&C.] (⊙Bridgeport)
*PRACTICE AREAS: General Civil Litigation; Trial Practice; Labor Law; Employment Law; Civil Rights Law.

Mitri, Michael F. ....'61 '87 C.602 B.S. L.262 J.D. [Phelan&M.]
Mittelstadt, David J. '59 '83 C.050 B.A. L.145 J.D.
(adm. in MA; not adm. in CT) Vice President Tax Counsel, Thomson Corporation
Mitten, L. Russell '51 '77 C.798 B.A. L.910 J.D.
(adm. in TX; not adm. in CT) V.P. , Gen. Coun. & Secy., Citizens Utilities Co.
*RESPONSIBILITIES: Public Utility Law; Telecommunications; Mergers and Acquisitions; Corporate Law; Business Law.
Modugno, Dominick, (BV) '59 '85 C.276 B.A. L.184 J.D.
General Counsel, United Systems Integrators Corporation
Moeller, Sheila AnnMarie '56 '84 C.426 B.A. L.990 J.D.
(adm. in WI; not adm. in CT) [Ⓒ Pillsbury W.]
*PRACTICE AREAS: Products Liability; Insurance; Commercial Litigation; Toxic Torts.
Moll, Steven A. ... '60 '86 C.264 B.A. L.1019 J.D. Asst. Gen. Coun., The Thomson Corp.
Mond, Richard H. '59 '85 C.390 A.B. L.978 J.D.
(adm. in NY; not adm. in CT) 90 Woodridge Dr. S.‡
Mooney, John F. ....'26 '51 C.262 L.724 LL.B. 2435 Bedford St.‡
Moore, Peggy Braden ....'44 '68 C.169 B.A. L.208 J.D. P.O. Box 3454
Moran, Brian E., (AV) ....'— '78 C.893 B.A. L.692 J.D. [Robinson&C.]
*PRACTICE AREAS: Litigation; Antitrust and Trade Regulation; Intellectual Property; Technology and Science.

More Phillips & Duncan, P.C.
(See Greenwich)

Morgan, John J. .... '67 '92 C.1044 B.A. L.884 J.D. [Barr&L.]
*PRACTICE AREAS: Litigation; Insurance; Franchise Law; Personal Injury; Products Liability.
Moriarty, James M. ....'69 '99 C.1266 B.A. L.1040 J.D. [Ⓐ Kelley D.&W.]
*PRACTICE AREAS: Litigation; Securities Arbitration.
Morris, D. Robert, (AV) ...... '50 '75 C&L.188 B.A., J.D. [Pullman&C.] (⊙Bridgeport)
*PRACTICE AREAS: Taxation Law; Corporate Law; Employee Benefits Law; Estate Planning; Computer Law.
Morris, Robert E. '22 '52 C.823 B.S. L.309 LL.B.
(adm. in NY; not adm. in CT) 208 Crystal Lake Rd.
Morris-Fox, Carol L. .... '64 '90 C.518 B.A. L.823 J.D. [Ⓐ Heidell,P.M.&B.] ⊙
*PRACTICE AREAS: Medical Malpractice; Products Liability.
Morrow, John C. '50 '78 C.472 B.G.S. L.809 J.D.
Chief Clk., Stamford/Norwalk Jud. Dist.
Morton, Garry H., (BV) .... '52 '77 C.197 A.B. L.178 J.D. [Ⓒ Diserio M.O.&C.]
*PRACTICE AREAS: Estate Planning; Estate Administration; Trust Administration; Fiduciary Taxation.
Moss, Sara E., (AVⓉ) '46 '75 C.454 B.A. L.569 J.D.
(adm. in NY; not adm. in CT) V.P. & Gen. Coun., Pitney Bowes, Inc.
Mothner, Jonathan S. '63 '90 C.319 B.A. L.569 J.D.
(adm. in NY; not adm. in CT) Litig. Coun., GE Capital Global Consumer Finance
Mottolese, A. William ....'35 '59 C.321 A.B. L.276 J.D. Supr. Ct. J.
Muhlbaum, Joel D., Law Offices of '63 '89
C.1044 B.A. L.978 J.D. 733 Summer Street, Suite 202
Mulderrig, Ann O. '51 '79 C.881 A.B. L.262 J.D.
(adm. in NY; not adm. in CT) 260 Long Ridge Rd.
Mullin, Caryn L. .... '61 '92 C.1102 B.S.R.N. L.1029 J.D. [Berkowitz,M.&M.]
*PRACTICE AREAS: Medical Malpractice; Personal Injury; Products Liability; Workers Compensation.
Mundinger, Paul C., II '59 '85 C.299 B.S. L.1049 J.D.
(adm. in NY; not adm. in CT) Coun., GE Capital Real Estate
Muñiz, Peter J. '64 '89 C.178 B.A. L.107 J.D.
(adm. in OH; not adm. in CT) V.P. & Dept. Coun., GE Capital, Equity Capital Group
Munro, Colin D., II .... '47 '73 C.210 B.A. L.215 J.D. 60 Long Ridge Rd. 4th Fl.
Munrow, Alfred E., III, (BV) .... '31 '61 C.1029 B.A. L.564 LL.B. P.O. Box 4162
Muraki, Hiroko ....'— '00 C.823 B.A. L.1040 J.D. [Ⓐ Robinson&C.]
Murchison, Allison Bloom ....'68 '95 C.1030 B.A. L.1252 J.D. 750 Summer St.
Murphy, Ambrose J. G. '63 '88 L.051 B.A.
(adm. in NY; not adm. in CT) 260 Long Ridge Rd.
Murphy, Barry J. '51 '77 C.309 A.B. L.1066 J.D.
(adm. in CA; not adm. in CT) Crane Co.
Murphy, James D'Alton, (BV) ....'52 '78 C.706 B.A. L.262 J.D. [Curtis,B.&B.]
*PRACTICE AREAS: Zoning, Planning and Land Use; Commercial Real Estate; Commercial Litigation; Construction Law.
Murphy, Richard E. '54 '83 C.299 B.A. L.262 J.D.
(adm. in NY; not adm. in CT) V.P. & Asst. Gen. Coun., Gen. Reinsurance Corp.
*RESPONSIBILITIES: Corporate Finance; Derivatives.
Murphy, Terrence J., Jr. .... '29 '56 C.276 B.S. L.724 LL.B. 115 Hoyt St.‡

Murphy and Karpie, LLC
(See Bridgeport)

Murray, Deirdre A. .... '71 '97 C.945 B.A. L.880 J.D. [Ⓐ Ryan,R.J.&D.]
*PRACTICE AREAS: Civil Litigation.
Murray, John V. A., (BV) '52 '77
C.103 A.B. L.184 J.D. [Ⓒ Diserio M.O.&C.] (⊙Greenwich)
*PRACTICE AREAS: Estate Planning; Estate Administration; Real Estate Law; Commercial Transactions.
Murray, Leanne E. .... '68 '94 C.228 B.A. L.1040 J.D. 156 Overlook Dr.
Murray, Michael P. ....'65 '91 C.884 B.A. L.262 J.D. [Curtis,B.&B.]
*PRACTICE AREAS: General Practice; Real Estate; Trust and Estate; Civil Litigation; Business Law.
Murray, Robert E., Jr., (BV) .... '58 '84 C.454 B.A. L.184 J.D. [Diserio M.O.&C.]
*PRACTICE AREAS: Commercial Real Estate; Residential Real Estate; Banking Law.
Murray, Robert W. '16 '49 C.273 B.A. L.276 J.D.
(adm. in DC; not adm. in CT) 144 Highline Trail‡
Murray, William J. ....'22 '46 C.882 B.S. L.597 J.D. 706 Bedford St.‡
Musicaro, John R., Jr., (AV) ....'49 '74 C.696 B.A. L.178 J.D. [Cummings&L.]
*PRACTICE AREAS: Estate and Trust Administration; Estate and Tax Planning; Probate Litigation.
Musilli, Mario P. ....'60 '86 C.184 B.A. L.345 J.D. P.O. Box 1273
Nabulsi, Basam E. .... '59 '86 C.816 B.E. L.262 J.D. [Cummings&L.] (Pat.)
*PRACTICE AREAS: Intellectual Property; Patent Licensing; Biotechnology; Emerging Technologies.
Nadler, Michael A. ....'58 '88 C.569 B.S. L.1040 J.D. Tax Mgr., Ernst & Young
Nadler-Sachs, Karen S. '66 '92 C.1365 B.A. L.280 J.D.
(adm. in NY; not adm. in CT) 27 Maple Tree Ave., Unit E
Nakian, Paul S., (BV) ....'37 '62 C.184 B.A. L.966 LL.B. 810 Bedford St.
Naples, Clement J. ....'— '00 C.1102 B.S. L.1252 J.D. [Ⓐ Wiggin&D.]
Napoli, Michelle M. ....'71 '97 C.1030 B.S. L.306 J.D. [Ⓐ Piazza&P.]
*PRACTICE AREAS: Criminal Litigation; Civil Litigation; Appellate Practice.
Narcisse, Robbie E. B. '58 '82 C.813 B.A. L.1066 J.D.
(adm. in CA; not adm. in CT) Dpty. Gen. Coun.-Corp. & Asst. Secy., Pitney Bowes Inc.
*RESPONSIBILITIES: Business; General Corporate; Commercial.
Narwold, William H., (AV) '52 '79 C.164 B.A. L.184 J.D.
[Cummings&L.] (⊙Hartford)
*PRACTICE AREAS: Appellate; Products and Professional Liability; Environmental Litigation.
Nealon, James E. ....'64 '91 C.1030 B.A. L.94 J.D. [Ⓐ Kelley D.&W.]
*PRACTICE AREAS: Commercial Litigation; Securities Litigation; Employment Litigation; Bankruptcy.

Neigher, Alan
(See Westport)

Nemchek, Edward F. ....'57 '91 C.706 B.A. L.262 J.D. [Ⓐ Cacace,T.&S.]
*PRACTICE AREAS: Real Estate; Criminal Defense.
Nepola, S. Richard ....'49 '79 C.94 B.S.B.A. L.767 J.D. P.O. Box 15189‡

Neuman, Andrea B. '67 '92 C.188 B.S. L.94 J.D.
(adm. in MA; not adm. in CT)
Sr. Asst. Gen. Coun., Purdue Frederick Co./Purdue Pharma L.P.
*RESPONSIBILITIES: Employment Law; Benefits Law; Contracts; Immigration Law.
Neville, Richard M. '42 '66 C&L.178 A.B., J.D.
(adm. in NY; not adm. in CT) [Neville S.H.&M.] ⊙
*PRACTICE AREAS: Securities; Corporate Finance; Corporate Law; Commercial Law; Business Law.

Neville Shaver Hubbard & McLean, (AVⓉ) BR
One Landmark Square, 06901 ⊙
Telephone: 203-363-5300 Telecopier: 203-363-5323
Email: firm@nevillaw.com URL: http://www.lawyers.com/nevillaw
Richard M. Neville (Not admitted in CT); Alan H. McLean; D. Seeley Hubbard;—Alan M. Shaver; John P. Maloney (Not admitted in CT).
General Practice, Corporate, Securities, Financing, Commercial and General Litigation, Government Contracts and Taxation.
New York, N.Y. Office: 477 Madison Avenue, 21st Floor. Telephone: 212-989-5300; Telecopier: 212-989-5323.
See Professional Biographies, STAMFORD, CONNECTICUT

Nevins, Kent S., (AV) .... '60 '85 C&L.1040 B.B.A., J.D. [Pillsbury W.]
*PRACTICE AREAS: Real Estate; Leasing; Business Law; Banking Law.
Newfield, James S. .... '67 '94 C.188 B.A. L.477 J.D. [Rosenblum&T.] ⊙
Newman, Jeffrey H. '56 '81 C.659 B.A. L.273 J.D.
Senior Vice President, W & M Properties of CT, Inc.
Newman, Richard .... '71 '00 [Ⓐ Cummings&L.]
Nichols, Ralph A., (AV) .... '19 '47 C.299 A.B. L.976 LL.B. [Cummings&L.]
*PRACTICE AREAS: Trust and Estate Administration, Estate Planning.
Nickel, Sandra E. '61 '90 C.83 B.Sc. L.352 J.D.
(adm. in NY; not adm. in CT)
Chf. Reg. Coun., Emerging Markets, ACNielsen Corporation
*RESPONSIBILITIES: Corporate Practice.
Nietzel, Catherine S. .... '64 '92 C.276 B.S.F.S. L.262 J.D. [Ryan,R.J.&D.]
*PRACTICE AREAS: Civil Litigation; Professional Liability; Products Liability; Appellate Practice.
Nigro, Martin L. .... '29 '54 C.1030 B.A. L.976 LL.B. Supr. Ct. J.
Noethiger, Robert A. '65 '92 C.1350 B.A. L.607 J.D.
(adm. in PA; not adm. in CT) Sr. Coun., CBS Cable
Noga, Joseph L. '68 '96 C.31 A.B. L.178 J.D.
(adm. in NY; not adm. in CT) General Electric Capital Corporation
Nokes, Gregory B., (AV) .... '51 '80 C.882 B.S. L.184 J.D. [Cummings&L.] (⊙Hartford)
*PRACTICE AREAS: Labor Law; Employment Law; Civil Litigation.
Nolan, Thomas M. '58 '95 C.1046 B.S. L.564 J.D.
General Counsel, International Masters Publishers Inc.
Nolin, Peter M., (BV) .... '56 '81 C.321 B.A. L.184 J.D. [Sandak F.H.&G.]
*PRACTICE AREAS: Civil Litigation; Commercial Litigation; Insurance Coverage; Environmental Law.
Nolta, Juliet M. .... '70 '99 C.477 B.A. L.1040 J.D. [Ⓐ S.J.Arnowitz]
Noonan, James J. .... '72 '97 C.1200 B.A. L.1252 J.D. [Ⓐ Rosenblum&T.]
Noone, Peter T. '62 '90 C.433 B.S. L.602 J.D.
(adm. in NY; not adm. in CT) Hungarian Telephone & Cable Corp.
Norris, Jonathan .... '66 '93 695 East Main Street
North, Cecil J., III '58 '88 C.882 B.A. L.982 J.D.
(adm. in NY; not adm. in CT) Counsel, Xerox Corporation
Northrop, Margaret D. .... '48 '75 C.103 A.B. L.424 J.D. 155 Mill Brook Road
Norton, Hunter .... '67 '93 C.184 B.S. L.831 J.D. 400 Atlantic St.‡
Nur-Vaccaro, Firouzeh '72 '97 C&L.880 B.A., J.D.
(adm. in TX; not adm. in CT) [Ⓐ Paul,H.J.&W.]
*PRACTICE AREAS: Litigation.

Nusbaum & Parrino, P.C.
(See Westport)

Oberdick, Todd M. ....'71 '97 C.401 B.S.M.E. L.365 J.D. [Ⓐ St. Onge S.J.&R.] (Pat.)
*PRACTICE AREAS: Intellectual Property; Litigation; Patent Prosecution; Mechanical Patents; Electrical Patents.
Oberhand, Sandra J. .... '51 '78 C.1349 B.A. L.1067 J.D. 37 Don Bob Rd.‡
O'Brien, Joan M. .... '42 '95 C.601 B.A. L.1040 J.D. [Ⓐ Blair&P.]
*PRACTICE AREAS: Estate Planning; Estate Settlements; Trust Administration.
O'Connor, Brian T., (BV) .... '42 '68 C.676 B.A. L.184 LL.B. [Diserio M.O.&C.]
*PRACTICE AREAS: Corporate Law; Taxation; Securities Regulation.
O'Connor, Catherine Dugan .... '68 '95 C.184 B.S. L.724 J.D. [Ⓐ Day,B.&H.]
*PRACTICE AREAS: Commercial Litigation; Intellectual Property; Federal Civil Practice.
O'Connor, Norman K. '57 '82
C.597 B.A. L.1194 J.D. [Ⓒ O'Connor,R.G.&S.] (⊙White Plains, NY)
O'Connor, Steven M., (AVⓉ) '58 '86 C.597 B.A. L.1040 J.D.
[O'Connor,R.G.&S.] (⊙Brookfield, CT; White Plains, NY)
O'Connor, Redd, Gollihue & Sklarin, LLP, LLP, (AVⓉ)
750 Summer St. (⊙Brookfield, CT; Hackensack, NJ; New York, White Plains, NY)
O'Donnell, Arianne .... '68 '97 C.1266 B.A. L.1252 J.D. 1234 Summer St.
O'Dwyer, Alison C. .... '— '99 C.562 B.S.N. L.1040 J.D. [Ⓐ Rosenblum&T.]
O'Farrell, William E. '67 '93
C&L.190 B.S.B.A., J.D. Asst. V.P., Berkshire Hathaway Grp.
Ogden, John V. '42 '69
C.309 B.A. L.477 J.D. V.P. & Assoc. Gen. Coun., GE Capital Corp.
O'Hanrahan, Ellenore '58 '81 C.058 B.C.L. L.976 LL.M.
(adm. in NY; not adm. in CT) V.P. & Dep. Gen. Coun., ACNielsen Corporation
*RESPONSIBILITIES: Corporate Transactions; Securities; Secretarial and Board; Corporate Miscellaneous.
O'Hearne, David B. '36 '65 C.321 A.B. L.309 LL.B.
(adm. in NY; not adm. in CT) V.P., Pitney-Bowes, Inc.
Ohlandt, John F. '23 '56 C.433 B.E.E. L.724 LL.B.
(adm. in NY; not adm. in CT; See Pat. Sect.) [Ⓒ Ohlandt,G.R.&P.]

Ohlandt, Greeley, Ruggiero & Perle, (AV)
Suite 903 One Landmark Square, 06901
Telephone: 203-327-4500 Facsimile: 203-327-6401
Email: 102001.3251@compuserve.com
Paul D. Greeley; Charles N. J. Ruggiero; Terrence J. McAllister (Not admitted in CT). Associates: John Yankovich (Not admitted in CT); Joseph V. Gamberdell, Jr.; Karin Dai Kelly. Senior Counsel: John F. Ohlandt (Not admitted in CT); E. Gabriel Perle. Of Counsel: George W. Rauchfuss, Jr. (Not admitted in CT); Robert R. Hubbard (Not admitted in CT).
Practice Limited to Intellectual Property Law and Related Matters.
See Professional Biographies, STAMFORD, CONNECTICUT

Olson, Carrie Webb .... '69 '01 C.380 B.A. L.1218 J.D. [Ⓐ Cummings&L.]
*PRACTICE AREAS: Intellectual Property; Trademarks.
O'Neal, Margaret A. .... '61 '90 C.264 B.A. L.262 J.D. [Cummings&L.]
*PRACTICE AREAS: Real Estate Law; Estate Planning; Administration.
O'Neill, Thomas J. .... '66 '91 C.1200 A.B. L.818 J.D. [Ⓐ Day,B.&H.]
*PRACTICE AREAS: Commercial Litigation; Medical Malpractice.
Onorato, Maria A. '64 '90 C.449 B.S. L.724 J.D.
Coun., Treas. Oper., GE Capital Corp.
Opalenik, Stanley J. '51 '76 C.829 B.A. L.127 J.D.
Dir. & Sr. Atty., Employee Rel. & Benefits, Lone Star Industries, Inc.

Ordway, David J., (CV) .... '52 '81 C.428 B.A. L.472 J.D. 441 Summer St., 2nd Fl.
Ormond, Wendy E. '43 '76 C.477 A.B. L.813 J.D.
(adm. in CA; not adm. in CT)
Mng. Dir. & Gen. Coun., GE Capital Servs. Structured Fin. Grp., Inc.
Orr, Donald E. '— '70 C.935 B.A. L.665 J.D.
(adm. in PA; not adm. in CT) Gen. Coun., Walsh Construction Co.
Orticelli, David J. .... '62 '90 C.1030 B.S. L.1029 J.D. Tax Atty., IBM Credit Corp.
Ortner, Melvin L. '46 '74 C.102 B.A. L.1009 J.D.
V.P. & Chf. Coun., Sara Lee Intimates, Sara Lee Corp. (⊙Winston-Salem, NC)
Osborne, Zachary R. .... '72 '98 C.1375 B.A. L.188 J.D. [Ⓐ Paul,H.J.&W.]
*PRACTICE AREAS: Employment Law; Reductions in Force Programs; Employee Benefit Litigation; Employment Discrimination Litigation.
O'Shaughnessy, Brian C. '60 '86 C.93 B.A. L.564 J.D.
(adm. in NY; not adm. in CT) Howard Systems Intl.
O'Sullivan, Anne M. '66 '94 C.1030 B.A. L.128 J.D.
(adm. in NY; not adm. in CT) Sr. Coun., Philip Morris Capital Corp.
Oswald, Alexandra '64 '90 C.276 B.S.F.S. L.597 J.D.
1177 Summer Street Second Floor
Overlock, Willard J., (AV) .... '22 '49 C.976 B.A. L.188 LL.B. [Cummings&L.]
*PRACTICE AREAS: Trusts and Estates.
Padilla, James E. '53 '78 C.597 B.A. L.228 J.D.
(adm. in IL; not adm. in CT) 1900 Summer St.
Palmer, Alison L. .... '64 '99 C.1211 B.S. L.1252 J.D. Atty., The Thomson Corp.
*RESPONSIBILITIES: Corporate Law; Commercial Real Estate.
Palmieri, Michael J. .... '66 '91 C.659 B.A. L.228 J.D. [Ⓒ Kelley D.&W.]
*PRACTICE AREAS: Securities; Corporate Law.
Panagrossi, Michael P. '67 '93 C.321 B.A. L.94 J.D.
Atty., Purdue Frederick Co./Purdue Pharma L.P.
Pankowski, Joseph M., Jr. .... '64 '90 C.259 B.S. L.893 J.D. [Ⓒ Wofsey,R.K.&K.]
*PRACTICE AREAS: Estate Planning; Estate Settlement; Trust Administration; Guardianship and Conservatorship; Charitable Giving.
Paolillo, Michael P. '65 '90 C&L.276 B.S., J.D.
(adm. in NJ; not adm. in CT) V.P. & Coun., GE Capital Markets Services, Inc.
Parent, Christopher M. .... '71 '00 C&L.602 B.A., J.D. [Ⓐ Kelley D.&W.]
*PRACTICE AREAS: Corporate; Securities; Litigation; International.
Parmelee, G. Kendall, (AV) ..... '22 '51 C.453 B.S.E.E. L.569 J.D. 460 Summer St. (Pat.)
Pastore, Michael M. '60 '85 C.31 B.A. L.178 J.D.
V.P. & Assoc. Gen. Coun., GE Asset Management
Paterson, Gordon R., (AV) .... '24 '50 C.164 A.B. L.262 LL.B. [Paterson&R.]
Paterson & Roberts, (AV) .... 733 Summer Street
Paul, Christina Chen .... '— '98 C.165 A.B. L.184 J.D. [Ⓐ Robinson&C.]
Paul, Matthew R. .... '72 '98 C.855 B.A. L.306 J.D. [Ⓐ Paul,H.J.&W.]
Paul, Richard S. .... '— '69 C.508 B.A. L.569 LL.B. Retired‡
Paul, Roland A. .... '37 '62 C.976 A.B. L.309 LL.B. [Ⓒ Day,B.&H.]
*PRACTICE AREAS: Business Law.

Paul, Hastings, Janofsky & Walker LLP, (AV) BR
A Limited Liability Partnership including Professional Corporations
1055 Washington Boulevard, 06901-2217 ⊙
Telephone: 203-961-7400 Fax: 203-359-3031
URL: http://www.paulhastings.com
Members of Firm: Jonathan Birenbaum; Douglas C. Conroy; Christopher H. Craig; Mary C. Dollarhide; Esteban A. Ferrer, III; Kurt W. Hansson; John D. Hawkins, Jr.; Mario J. Ippolito; Charles T. Lee; John S. McGeeney; Leslie A. Plaskon; David E. Rabin; Patrick W. Shea; David E. Snediker; John N. Turitzin (Not admitted in CT); Carla R. Walworth. Senior Counsel: Christopher A. Barreca. Of Counsel: Elizabeth Adolff Brower; John W. Hamlin; Andrew S. Holmes; Bonnie Pierson-Murphy; Arthur D. Rheingold (Not admitted in CT). Associates: Eduardo N. T. Andrade (Not admitted in CT); Matthew S. Antonetti; Raymond William Bertrand (Not admitted in CT); James R. Bliss; Jenifer Magyar Bologna; Adam S. Bozek; Elizabeth A. Byrne; Paul R. Dehmel; Matthew M. Donaher; Thomas P. Friedman (Not admitted in CT); David Galluzzi; Joshua D. Goodman; Sarah E. Graves; Joseph A. Guay (Not admitted in CT); Kelly Warrick Hodges; Deborah Hryb (Not admitted in CT); Gregory F. Lang; Eric T. Levine; W. Andrew P. Logan, III; Michael J. Madden; Diane L. Matt; Karen E. McArthur; Firouzeh Nur-Vaccaro (Not admitted in CT); Zachary R. Osborne; Matthew R. Paul; Mario A. Pena; Suzanne Marie Pepe-Robbins; Peter M. Schultz; Yolanda Seals-Coffield; Brit K. Seifert; H. William Smith III; John P. Staikos; Neil B. Stekloff; Jessica L. Sylvester; Dina A. Tolia-Gupta (Not admitted in CT); Joshua W. van Hulst.
Aircraft Finance Practice, Asia-Pacific, Banking and Financial Services, Computer Law, Creditor's Rights and Bankruptcy, Customs, International Trade and Export Control, Emerging Growth and Technology, Energy, Federal Legislative, Healthcare, Energy, Project Finance, International Trade, Internet and Electronic Commerce, Investment Management, Japan Practice for United States-Based Clients, Latin America, Lease and Asset-Based Finance, Mergers and Acquisitions, Structured Finance and Asset Securitization, Telecommunications and Media, Timber, Paper and Packaging, Trade Regulation and Proprietary Rights, Year 2000, Employee Benefits, Executive Practice, Immigration, Railroad Labor and Employment Law, Accountant's Liability, Alternative Dispute Resolution (ADR), Antidumping, Countervailing Duty and Related Trade Proceedings, Antitrust Litigation and Government Enforcement, Appellate, Entertainment, Environmental, Government Contracts, Insurance Coverage, Intellectual Property, Technology Licensing and Litigation, Trade Secret, Patent Litigation, Securities and Corporate Finance Litigation, White Collar Corporate Criminal Defense, Affordable Housing, Land Use, Real Estate Acquisition and Disposition, Resort, Restaurant and Recreation, Retail Leasing, International Tax and Tax Litigation.
Atlanta, Georgia Office: 24th Floor, 600 Peachtree Street, N.E. Telephone: 404-815-2400.
Los Angeles, California Office: 555 South Flower Street. Telephone: 213-683-6000.
New York, New York Offices: 399 Park Avenue. Telephone: 212-318-6000 and 75 East 55th Street. Telephone: 212-318-6000.
Orange County, California Office: 695 Town Center Drive, Costa Mesa. Telephone: 714-668-6200.
San Francisco, California Office: 345 California Street. Telephone: 415-835-1600.
Washington, D.C. Office: 1299 Pennsylvania Avenue, N.W. Telephone: 202-508-9500.
Tokyo, Japan Office: 27F Ark Mori Building, 12-32, Minato-Ku, Akasaka 1-Chome, P.O. Box 577 . Telephone: (03) 3556-4711.
London, England Office: Tower 42, 25 Old Broad Street. Telephone: +44 (0) 20 7562-4000.
See Professional Biographies, STAMFORD, CONNECTICUT

Payne, David M. .... '19 '48 C.976 A.B. L.178 LL.B. 695 E. Main St.
Payne, R. Thomas, (AVⓉ) '45 '81 C.870 B.S. L.201 J.D.
(adm. in OH; not adm. in CT; Pat.) [Cummings&L.]
*PRACTICE AREAS: Patents; Intellectual Property.

Pearl Professional Corporation
(See Westport)

Peeters, Robert S. .... '33 '67 C.37 B.S. L.724 J.D. 810 Bedford St.
Peikes, Lawrence .... '63 '87 C.446 B.A. L.273 J.D. [Wiggin&D.]
*PRACTICE AREAS: Labor and Employment Law; Alternative Dispute Resolution; Employee Benefits; Trade Secrets.
Peloso, John F. X., Jr., (BV) .... '— '89 C.951 B.A. L.262 J.D. [Ⓒ Robinson&C.]
*PRACTICE AREAS: Environmental Law; Taxation; Litigation.
Peluso, Frank N., (BV) .... '30 '57 C.93 B.S. L.262 J.D. [F.N.Peluso] ⊙
Peluso, Frank N., P.C., Law Offices of, (BV) .... 1799 Summer St. (⊙Pelham, NY)
Pena, Mario .... '71 '00 C.188 B.A. L.569 J.D. 1055 Washington Blvd
Pena, Mario A. .... '— '00 C.188 B.A. L.569 J.D [Ⓐ Paul,H.J.&W.]
*PRACTICE AREAS: Corporate; Securities.
Penn, Douglas R. .... '66 '95 C&L.208 B.A., J.D. [Ⓐ Barr&L.]
*PRACTICE AREAS: Immigration and Naturalization.
Pepe-Robbins, Suzanne Marie .... '66 '91 C.800 B.S. L.569 J.D. [Ⓐ Paul,H.J.&W.]
*PRACTICE AREAS: Tax.
Perkowski, Thomas J. .... '58 '86 C.158 B.S.E.E. L.1170 J.D. [T.J.Perkowski] (Pat.)

Perkowski, Thomas J., Esq., P.C.
Soundview Plaza, 1266 East Main Street, 06902
Telephone: 203-357-1950 Fax: 203-357-1959
Email: info@tjpatlaw.com URL: http://www.tjpatlaw.com
Thomas J. Perkowski; Jay P. Sbrollini (Not admitted in CT).
Patent, Intellectual Property, Trademarks, Copyrights, Trade Secrets.
See Professional Biographies, STAMFORD, CONNECTICUT

Perlah, Philip M. '45 '70 C.102 B.S. L.262 J.D.
Asst. Coun., Sara Lee Intimate Apparel
Perle, E. Gabriel, (AVⓉ) . . . . '22 '50 C.994 A.B. L.976 LL.B. [Ⓒ Ohlandt,G.R.&P.]
*PRACTICE AREAS: Publishing Law; Entertainment; Intellectual Property.
Perrone, William A., (BV) . . . . '52 '79 C.102 B.A. L.1048 J.D. [Wiggin&D.]
*PRACTICE AREAS: Corporate; Emerging Growth Companies; Information Technology; Mergers and Acquisitions; Securities.
Perrotta, Arnold Joseph . . . .'65 '98 C.1040 B.B.A. L.1252 J.D. State Dept. of Labor
Perry, Alice L. . . . . '31 '56 C&L.597 B.S.L., LL.B. Asst. Corp. Coun.
Perusse, Catherine Vance . . . .'58 '89 C.309 A.B. L.262 J.D. [Ⓐ Blair&P.]
*PRACTICE AREAS: Estate Planning; Estate Settlements; Trust Administration.
Peters, Bart F. . . . .'58 '93 C.999 B.A. L.184 J.D. [Ⓐ Cummings&L.]
*PRACTICE AREAS: Corporate; Commercial Finance.
Peters, Kristan L. . . . . '60 '87 C.188 B.S. L.846 J.D. [Pillsbury W.]
*PRACTICE AREAS: Employment Law; Commercial Litigation; Torts; Criminal Law.
Petre, David C. '39 '64 C&L.602 B.S., LL.B.
(adm. in NY; not adm. in CT; Pat.) Dir., Pat. Lic., Xerox Corporation
Petrie, James G. '57 '90 C.165 B.A. L.705 J.D.
(adm. in NY; not adm. in CT)
Dir., Legl. & Extern. Affrs., Warburg Dillon Read LLC, CT
Pettit, Aubrey L., Jr. '42 '70 C&L.846 B.A., LL.B.
(adm. in NY; not adm. in CT) Merrill Lynch Realty, Inc.
Phelan, William J., (AV) . . . .'51 '76 C.321 B.A. L.564 J.D. [Phelan&M.]
Phelan & Mitri, (AV) . . . . One Atlantic Street
Piazza, Anthony A., (AV) . . . .'42 '72 C.776 A.B. L.262 J.D. [Piazza&P.]
*PRACTICE AREAS: Family Law; Personal Injury; Wrongful Death.

Piazza & Pickel, (AV)
112 Prospect Street, P.O. Box 15390, 06901
Telephone: 203-348-2465 Fax: 203-964-9509
Email: Anthony.Piazza@piazza-pickel.com URL: http://www.lawyers.com/piazza&pickel
Anthony A. Piazza; Alan Scott Pickel. Associates: Tara C.F. Ryan; Michelle M. Napoli.
Trials and Appeals in State and Federal Courts, Negligence, Medical Malpractice, Divorce and Personal Injury Law, Wrongful Death, Legal Malpractice, Child Custody, Automobile Accidents, Product Liability, Adoption, Family Law.
See Professional Biographies, STAMFORD, CONNECTICUT

Pickel, Alan Scott . . . . '65 '90 C&L.823 B.S., J.D. [Piazza&P.]
*PRACTICE AREAS: Family Law; Personal Injury Litigation; Commercial Litigation; Real Estate.
Pierson-Murphy, Bonnie . . . .'67 '92 C.165 B.A. L.94 J.D. [Ⓒ Paul,H.J.&W.]
*PRACTICE AREAS: Employment Law; Employment Discrimination; Sexual Harassment; Wrongful Termination; Class Action Litigation Defense.
Pieterse, Sara T. . . . .'63 '88 C&L.801 B.A., J.D. 65 Northwood Lane

Pillsbury Winthrop LLP, (AV)
Financial Centre, 695 East Main Street, P.O. Box 6760, 06904-6760 ⊙
Telephone: 203-348-2300 Fax: 203-965-8226
URL: http://www.pillsburywinthrop.com
Members of Firm: Thomas F. Clauss, Jr.; Frode Jensen; Kelly J. McClure; Kent S. Nevins; Kristan L. Peters; Robert J. Rawn; G. William Sisley. Counsel: Arthur W. Hooper, Jr.; Sheila AnnMarie Moeller (Not admitted in CT). Associates: George P. Barbaresi (Not admitted in CT); J. Christopher Clifton; Stephen J. Curley; Polly DeVeau Davis; Michael Forrest (Not admitted in CT); Matthew C. Frost (Not admitted in CT); Donald J. Riccitelli; Vaya Sinha (Not admitted in CT); Henry K. Snyder; Cozata Solloway; Vicki E. Volper; Lori Iannotti Zyskowski.
General Practice with an emphasis on Administrative, Admiralty and Maritime, Alternative Dispute Resolution, Antitrust and Trade Regulation, Appellate Practice, Art, Aviation and Aerospace, Bankruptcy, Banking, Biotechnology, Business, Civil, Class Actions, Commerce & Technology, Commercial, Communications and Media, Complex and Multi-District Litigation, Construction, Contracts, Corporate, Creditor's Rights, E-Commerce, Emerging Companies, Employee Benefits, Energy, Environmental, Equipment Finance and Leasing, Executive Compensation, Finance, Guardianship and Conservatorship, Health Care and Hospital, International, International Trade, Internet, Labor and Employment, Leases and Leasing, Licensing, Life Sciences, Litigation, Medicare and Medicaid, Mergers, Acquisitions and Divestitures, Natural Resources, Nonprofit and Charitable Organizations, Partnership, Patents, Planning and Land Use, Political, Probate, Products Liability, Project Finance, Real Estate, Regulatory, RICO, Securities, Taxation, Torts, Toxic Torts, Trademark, Trust and Estates, Utility, White Collar Crime, Wills and Zoning Law.
San Francisco, California Office: 50 Fremont Street, 94105-2228. Telephone: 415-983-1000. Fax: 415-983-1200.
New York, New York Office: One Battery Park Plaza, 10004-1490. Telephone: 212-858-1000. Fax: 212-858-1500.
Los Angeles, California Office: 725 South Figueroa Street, Suite 2800, 90017-5406. Telephone: 213-488-7100. Fax: 213-629-1033.
Other Los Angeles, California Office: Century City, 10100 Santa Monica Boulevard, Suite 2300.
Orange County, California Office: 650 Town Center Drive, Seventh Floor, Costa Mesa, California 92626-7122. Telephone: 714-436-6800. Fax: 714-436-2800.
McLean, Virginia Office: 1600 Tysons Boulevard, 22102. Telephone: 703-905-2000. Fax: 703-905-2500.
Palm Beach, Florida Office: 125 Worth Avenue, 33480. Telephone: 561-655-7297. Fax: 561-833-6726.
Sacramento, California Office: 400 Capitol Mall, Suite 1700, 95814-4419. Telephone: 916-329-4700. Fax: 916-441-3583.
San Diego, California Office: 101 West Broadway, Suite 1800, 92101-8219. Telephone: 619-234-5000. Fax: 619-236-1995.
Other San Diego, California Office: 11975 El Camino Real, Suite 200, 92130-5000. Telephone: 619-234-5000. Fax: 858-509-4010.
Silicon Valley, California Office: 2550 Hanover Street, Palo Alto, California 94304-1115. Telephone: 650-233-4500. Fax: 650-233-4545.
Washington, D.C. Office: 1133 Connecticut Avenue, N.W., 20036. Telephone: 202-775-9800. Fax: 202-833-8491.
London, England Office: 54 Lombard Street, EC3V 9DH. Telephone: +44-171-648-9200. Fax: +44-171-283-1656.
Sydney, Australia Office: Level 10, 7 Macquarie Place, NSW2000. Telephone: +612-8214-2200. Fax: 612-8214-2211.
Tokyo, Japan Office: Fuerte Kojimachi Building, 5th Floor, 1-7-25 Kojimachi, Chiyoda-ku, 102-0083. Telephone: +011-81-3-5226-7260. Fax: +011-81-3-5226-7261.
Other Tokyo, Japan Office: 6 Gaikokuho Jimu Bengoshi Jimusho, Fifth Floor, Samon Eleven Building, 3-1, Samon-cho, Shinjuku-ku, 160. Telephone: +813-3354-3531. Fax: +813-3354-3534.
Hong Kong, China Office: 2504-6 Asia Pacific Finance Tower, Citibank Plaza, 3 Garden Road, Central Hong Kong. Telephone: +852-2530-3400. Fax: +852-2530-3355.
Singapore Office: 6 Battery Road #38-01B, 049909. Telephone: +65-227-4700. Fax: +65-227-4711.
See Professional Biographies, STAMFORD, CONNECTICUT

Pinard, Jeanette L. '56 '87 C.674 B.A. L.273 J.D.
(adm. in NY; not adm. in CT) V.P. & Coun., GE Capital Corp.
Pittoni, Luke M., (AVⓉ) . . . . '45 '72 C.321 B.A. L.262 J.D. [Heidell,P.M.&B.] ⊙
*PRACTICE AREAS: Trial Practice; Medical Malpractice; Products Liability; Professional Liability; Insurance Defense.
Plaskon, Leslie A. . . . . '63 '88 C.298 B.A. L.893 J.D. [Paul,H.J.&W.]
*PRACTICE AREAS: Creditors Rights; Bankruptcy; Commercial Lending; Foreclosure; Insolvency.
Plissner, Jonathan M. . . . . '64 '89 C.1349 B.A. L.1068 J.D. [Ⓐ Epstein B.&G.]
*PRACTICE AREAS: Commercial Litigation; Labor and Employment; First Amendment Law; Defamation; Privacy Law.

Plotkin, Ellery E., (BV) . . . . '52 '78 C.184 B.S. L.1019 J.D. [Plotkin&L.]
Plotkin & Livolsi, LLP, (BV) . . . . 1035 Washington Boulevard
Plotnick, Paul D., (BV) . . . . '33 '62 C.659 A.B. L.564 LL.B. [Plotnick&P.]
Plotnick, Scot Ethan . . . .'67 '92 C.273 B.A. L.564 J.D. [Ⓐ Brody&Assoc.]
Plotnick & Plotnick, (BV) . . . . .671 Bedford St.
Plouffe, Joan Freydberg . . . .'64 '89 C.273 B.A. L.823 J.D. 80 4th St.
Pocsik, Darren B. '66 '92 C.228 A.B. L.802 J.D.
(adm. in NY; not adm. in CT) Assoc. Gen. Coun., Thomson Corporation, The
Poeschl, Patrick L. . . . .'66 '95 C.723 B.A. L.994 J.D. [Ⓐ Cacace,T.&S.]
*PRACTICE AREAS: Estate Planning; Estate Administration; Elder Law; Estate Litigation; Conservatorship.
Poland, Susan L. '55 '82 C.771 B.A. L.050 B.A.
(adm. in NY; not adm. in CT) Reg. Coun., Coml. Fin., GE Capital Corp.
Polera, John C., (BV) . . . .'60 '86 C.861 B.S.M. L.472 J.D. [Durkin&P.] ⊙
*PRACTICE AREAS: Tax Planning; Trusts and Estates and Probate; Real Estate; Business Planning.
Pollack, Elliott B., (AV) '43 '65
C&L.178 A.B., LL.B. [Pullman&C.] (⊙Bridgeport, Hartford)
*PRACTICE AREAS: Health Care; Tax Appeal and Condemnation Law; Commercial Litigation.
Polsky, Tina Scott '68 '95 C.659 B.A. L.178 J.D.
(adm. in NY; not adm. in CT) Dir., Mediation Servs., Pitney Bowes Inc.
Ponzini, John Lino, (BV) . . . . '53 '81 C.1041 B.A. L.978 J.D. [Brandner&P.]
*PRACTICE AREAS: Civil Litigation; Criminal Law; Matrimonial Law; Personal Injury; Real Estate.
Poole, Yusef . . . .'73 '99 C.976 B.A. L.306 J.D. [Ⓐ Cummings&L.]
Poppick, David S., (BV) . . . .'54 '81 C.597 B.S.J. L.1048 J.D. [Epstein B.&G.]
*PRACTICE AREAS: Employment Law and Litigation.

Potash, Robert B.
(See Greenwich)

Potts, Arthur G., Jr., (AV) . . . .'49 '74 C.951 B.A. L.893 J.D. [Blair&P.]
*PRACTICE AREAS: Estate Litigation; Tax Planning; Estate Settlements; Trust Administration; Executive Compensation Taxation.
Povodator, Kenneth B., (BV) . . . .'48 '77 C.823 B.S. L.184 J.D. Asst. Corp. Coun.
Powell, Susan . . . .'— '97 C.569 B.S. L.178 J.D. [Ⓐ Finn D.&H.]
*PRACTICE AREAS: Executive Compensation; ERISA; Employee Benefits.
Powers, Donald B., Jr., (BV) . . . .'52 '79 C.860 B.A. L.818 J.D. [Mead,B.&B.]
*PRACTICE AREAS: Litigation; Real Estate Law; Estate Settlement Law; Family Law; Business Law.
Powers, Ruth L. '50 '77 C.937 B.A. L.273 J.D.
(adm. in NY; not adm. in CT) Citibank, N.A.
Powilatis, David P. . . . .'72 '98 C.276 A.B. L.93 J.D. [Ⓐ Jackson L.S.&K.]
*PRACTICE AREAS: Employment Law; Labor Law.
Procter, Arthur W., Jr. '29 '56 C.951 A.B. L.976 LL.B.
(adm. in NY; not adm. in CT) IBM Credit Corp.
Provetto, JoAnn . . . . '64 '95 C.562 B.A. L.818 J.D. [Ⓐ Rosenblum&T.]
Pruner, Mark, (BV) '55 '80 C.197 B.A. L.802 J.D.
(adm. in TX; not adm. in CT) President, Web Counsel, LLC
Puhekker, Joseph Todd . . . . '72 '98 C.1030 B.A. L.564 J.D. [Ⓐ Cacace,T.&S.]
*PRACTICE AREAS: Litigation; Zoning Law; Labor and Employment.
Pulitzer, Douglas S. '64 '92 C.569 B.A. L.978 J.D.
(adm. in NY; not adm. in CT) [Pulitzer] ⊙
Pulitzer Law Firm . . . . .34 Cascade Road, #1 (⊙Locust Valley, NY)

Pullman & Comley, L.L.C., (AV)
(Formerly Pullman, Comley, Bradley & Reeves)
350 Bedford Street, 06901-1743 ⊙
Telephone: 203-324-5000 Telecopier: 203-363-8659
URL: http://www.pullcom.com
John S. Pullman (1871-1943); Arthur M. Comley (1883-1969); J. Kenneth Bradley (1903-1969); William Reeves (1906-1967). Members of Firm: Elizabeth J. Austin; Deborah S. Breck; Charles K. Campbell, Jr.; Joseph M. Lodato; Andrew J. McDonald; Robert B. Mitchell; D. Robert Morris; Elliott B. Pollack; Margaret M. Sheahan; James T. Shearin.
General Practice including Administrative, Antitrust, Banking, Bankruptcy and Creditors Rights, Bonds, Business and Commercial, Corporate, Education, Employee Benefits, Environmental, Hospital and Health Care, Labor and Employment, Municipal Finance, Real Estate, Securities, Tax, Trusts and Estates, and Zoning. Energy and Utilities, Litigation in all Courts.
Bridgeport, Connecticut Office: 850 Main Street. Telephone: 203-330-2000. Telecopier: 203-576-8888.
Hartford, Connecticut Office: 90 State House Square. Telephone: 860-424-4300. Telecopier: 860-424-4370.
New Haven, Connecticut Office: One Century Tower, 265 Church Street. Telephone: 203-773-3006. Telecopier: 203-776-7075.
Simsbury, Connecticut Office: 720 Hopmeadow Street. Telephone: 860-651-9348. Fax: 860-651-1431.
Southport, Connecticut Office: 200 Pequot Avenue, P.O. Box 510. Telephone: 203-254-5000. Telecopier: 203-254-5070.
See Professional Biographies, STAMFORD, CONNECTICUT

Puzzuoli, R. Dante, (BV) . . . .'57 '83 C.178 B.A. L.184 J.D. 1100 Summer St.

Quatrella & Rizio, LLC
(See Fairfield)

Quier-Sheth, Christine E. '— '99 C.13 B.S. L.569 J.D.
(adm. in NY; not adm. in CT) [Ⓐ Kelley D.&W.]
*PRACTICE AREAS: Employee Benefits; Executive Compensation.
Quinn, Anne M. '55 '81 C.1031 B.A. L.724 J.D.
V.P. & Asst. Gen. Counsel; Gen. Reinsurance Corp.
*RESPONSIBILITIES: Corporate; Secretarial and Investor Relations.
Quinn, Carol A. '60 '86 C.229 B.S. L.1068 J.D.
(adm. in CA; not adm. in CT) Tax. Coun., GE Capital Corp.
Quinn, MJ . . . .'52 '92 C.1085 B.A. L.564 J.D. 22 Glenbrook Rd.
Quirk, Ashlin Carter . . . .'70 '95 C&L.276 B.A., J.D. Coun., Pitney Bowes Inc.
*RESPONSIBILITIES: Corporate.
Quirk, Noreen, (AV) . . . .'53 '79 C.569 B.A. L.705 J.D. [Fragomen,D.B.&L.]
Rabar, Maria E. '51 '78 C.696 B.A. L.273 J.D.
(adm. in NY; not adm. in CT) [Ⓒ Rosenblum&T.]
Rabin, David E. . . . . '62 '87 C.999 B.A. L.309 J.D. [Paul,H.J.&W.]
*PRACTICE AREAS: Commercial Real Estate; Real Estate Securitization; Real Estate Outsourcing; Asset Management; Mortgage Financing.
Rafsky, Gary D. . . . .'53 '79 C.611 B.A. L.1019 J.D. 1450 Washington Blvd.
Rakowitz, Leonard . . . . '58 '83 C.184 B.A. L.1029 J.D. 42 Fawn Dr.
Ramist, Roselyn B. . . . . '39 '67 C.823 B.A. L.659 J.D. Prob. Ct.
Ramos, Marilyn J., (BV) . . . . '45 '89 C.184 B.A. L.1040 J.D. [Ⓐ Silver,G.&T.]
*PRACTICE AREAS: Personal Injury Litigation.
Rapaport, James L., (BV) . . . .'47 '74 C.319 B.A. L.1019 J.D. 733 Summer St.
Rapaport, Jonathan I. . . . .'49 '75 C.197 B.A. L.107 J.D. 750 Summer St.
Rapaport, Ross S., (BV) . . . . '42 '67 C.319 B.A. L.188 LL.B. [Rapaport&E.]
Rapaport & Ellenthal, P.C., (BV) . . . . 750 Summer Street
Raspé, Adele M. R. '63 '88 C.788 A.B. L.880 J.D.
(adm. in NJ; not adm. in CT) Gen. Coun., Element Re Capital Products Inc.
Rathman, Marcy S. . . . . '65 '90 C.860 B.A. L.978 J.D. 1435 Bedford St.
Ratner, Daniel S. . . . . '64 '89 C.216 B.A. L.262 J.D. [Heidell,P.M.&B.] ⊙
*PRACTICE AREAS: Civil and Criminal Appellate Practice; Products Liability; Professional Liability; Medical Malpractice.
Ratner, Stuart B., (BV) . . . .'56 '81 C.184 B.S. L.823 J.D. [S.B.Ratner]
*PRACTICE AREAS: Tax Controversies (50%, 200); Criminal Taxation; Estate Planning (30%, 100); Corporate Law (20%, 90).

Ratner, Stuart B., P.C., (BV)
111 Prospect Street, 06901-1208
Telephone: 203-323-4900 Fax: 203-323-4141
Email: sbratner@hotmail.com URL: http://www.lawyers.com/stuartratner
Stuart B. Ratner.
Federal and State Tax Law, Estate Planning and General Corporate.
See Professional Biographies, STAMFORD, CONNECTICUT

Rauch, Susan H. '43 '83 C.915 A.B. L.569 J.D.
(adm. in NY; not adm. in CT) Amer. Cyanamid Co.
Rauchfuss, George W., Jr. '38 '68 C.645 B.S.Ch.E. L.904 J.D.
(adm. in DC; not adm. in CT; See Pat. Sect.) [Ⓒ Ohlandt,G.R.&P.]
Rawn, Robert J. .... '65 '91 C.674 A.B. L.569 J.D. [Pillsbury W.]
Reens, Louis H., (BV) .... '33 '64 C.216 B.S. L.184 LL.B. [St. Onge S.J.&R.] (Pat.)
*PRACTICE AREAS: Patent Law; Trademark Law; Copyright Law; Antitrust Law; Unfair Competition Law.
Reers, Carolyn '66 '92 C.93 B.A. L.276 J.D.
(adm. in MD; not adm. in CT) [Ⓐ Cummings&L.]
*PRACTICE AREAS: Trust Law; Wills; Taxation.
Reeves, Robert W., (AV) .... '51 '76 C.976 B.A. L.178 J.D. [Cummings&L.]
*PRACTICE AREAS: Corporate Law; Banking Law; Bankruptcy Law.

Regan, John P., (BV) '61 '89 C.1021 B.A. L.1029 J.D.
1200 Summer Street, Suite 103, 06905
Telephone: 203-324-4661 Fax: 203-359-4397
Email: jpreganesq@aol.com URL: http://www.lawyers.com/jprlaw
***PRACTICE AREAS: Commercial Law; Collections; Corporate Law; Business Law; Real Estate. General Civil and Criminal Trial Practice, Commercial Litigation, Landlord Tenant, Family, Personal Injury, Real Estate, Estates, Probate Law, Wills and Medical Malpractice.**
Reference: Gateway Bank.
See Professional Biographies, STAMFORD, CONNECTICUT

Reinken, Eric L., (BV) .... '56 '81 C.156 B.A. L.910 J.D. 1200 Summer Street Suite 101B
Remondino, Edmund M. .... '61 '87 C.1044 B.A. L.569 J.D. [Finn D.&H.]
*PRACTICE AREAS: Banking Law; Corporate Law; Mergers and Acquisitions; Securities Law.
Renck, Gary M. '58 '84 C&L.724 B.S., J.D.
(adm. in NY; not adm. in CT) Hewlett-Packard Co.
Renner, Darren P. .... '66 '95 C.1349 B.A. L.1170 J.D. [Ⓐ Lustig&B.]
*PRACTICE AREAS: Insurance Agents and Brokers Errors and Omissions; Insurance Litigation.
Reuben, Meredith B. '50 '76 C.860 B.A. L.94 LL.B.
(adm. in NY; not adm. in CT) 89 Sagamore Rd.‡
Rheingold, Arthur D. '42 '67 C.867 B.A. L.569 LL.B.
(adm. in NY; not adm. in CT) [Ⓒ Paul,H.J.&W.]
*PRACTICE AREAS: Environmental Law.
Riccitelli, Donald J. .... '64 '99 C.976 B.A. L.94 J.D. [Ⓐ Pillsbury W.]
Riccoboni, Gene J. '63 '01 C.1041 B.B.A. L.1040 J.D.
(adm. in MA; not adm. in CT) [Ⓐ Grimes&B.]
*PRACTICE AREAS: Domain Names; Computer Contracts; Internet Law.
Rice, Cheryl Gabes .... '61 '86 C.676 B.A. L.1019 J.D. [Ⓐ Finn D.&H.]
*PRACTICE AREAS: Asset Based Finance; Commercial Finance; Secured Finance; Unsecured Finance; Loan Workouts.
Richards, H. Ames, Jr. .... '19 '47 C&L.976 B.A., LL.B. 41 Long Close Rd.‡
Richichi, Joseph, (BV) .... '46 '73 C&L.184 B.A., J.D. [Sherman&R.]
Riehl, Edward J., (AVⓉ) '45 '77 C.93 B.A. L.276 J.D.
(adm. in PA; not adm. in CT) Chf. Reg. Coun., ACNielsen Corporation
Rights, Nancy S. '57 '88 C.92 B.S. L.790 J.D.
(adm. in NY; not adm. in CT)
Sr. Asst. Gen. Coun. & Asst. Secy., Philip Morris Mgmt. Corp.
Rinaldi, Charles J. ...... '67 '91 C.262 B.A. L.724 J.D. Dir. & Coun., UBS Warburg LLC
Riordan, Michelle H. '74 '00 C.93 B.A. L.800 J.D.
(adm. in MA; not adm. in CT) [Ⓐ Jackson L.S.&K.]
*PRACTICE AREAS: Labor and Employment; Benefits Law; Litigation.
Ritt, Kenneth W. .... '52 '77 C.103 A.B. L.309 J.D. [Day,B.&H.]
*PRACTICE AREAS: Commercial Litigation; Franchise and Distributorship Litigation; Antitrust.
Rizzo, Elisa Shevlin '70 '99 C.321 B.A. L.262 J.D.
(adm. in NY; not adm. in CT) [Ⓐ Cummings&L.]
*PRACTICE AREAS: Trusts and Estates; Tax Law.
Roberts, Adam D. '60 '87 C.882 B.A. L.262 J.D.
2nd V.P.& Asst. Gen. Coun., Gen. Reinsurance Corp.
*RESPONSIBILITIES: Insurance and Reinsurance; Litigation and Arbitration; Contracts.
Roberts, Allen J., III .... '67 '95 C.1030 B.S. L.1252 J.D. [Ⓐ Day,B.&H.]
*PRACTICE AREAS: Real Estate Acquisitions; Real Estate Contracts; Real Estate Finance; Real Estate Leasing; Real Estate Sales.
Roberts, Elinor Paterson, (BV) .... '55 '81 C.264 B.A. L.724 J.D. [Paterson&R.]
Roberts, John W., (AV) .... '32 '58 C.976 B.A. L.659 LL.B. [Roberts,R.&B.]
*PRACTICE AREAS: Trusts and Estates; Probate; Real Estate; Civil Litigation; Matrimonial.
Roberts, Peter D. '60 '91 C.103 B.A. L.588 J.D.
(adm. in MA; not adm. in CT) [Ⓐ Fragomen,D.B.&L.]

Roberts, Rose & Bates, P.C., (AV)
1055 Washington Boulevard Eighth Floor, P.O. Box 15630, 06901
Telephone: 203-324-6755 Telecopier: 203-348-5802
URL: http://www.lawyers.com/robertsrosebates
John W. Roberts; Richard L. Rose; Elizabeth Lewis Bates. Counsel: William D. Gaillard; Mary-Elizabeth Jacques; Joseph A. Izzillo; Amy L. Starobin.
General Practice, Litigation, Real Estate, Leasing, Banking, Matrimonial, Probate, Estate Planning and Trusts, International Business, Employment Law.
See Professional Biographies, STAMFORD, CONNECTICUT

Robinson, Mark B. '55 '96 C.893 B.A. L.276 J.D.
(adm. in NY; not adm. in CT) [Ⓐ Day,B.&H.]
*PRACTICE AREAS: Corporate; Securities; Secured Lending.
Robinson, Richard Allan, (BV) .... '57 '84 C.184 B.A. L.923 J.D. Asst. Corp. Coun.

Robinson & Cole LLP, (AV)
Financial Centre, 695 East Main Street, P.O. Box 10305, 06904-2305 ⊙
Telephone: 203-462-7500 Fax: 203-462-7599
Email: stam.rc.com URL: http://www.rc.com
Partners: Frank Lewis Baker, III; David W. Bogan; Elizabeth L. Brennan (Resident); Joseph L. Clasen; Stuart R. Deans; Steven L. Elbaum; Gregory E. Harmer; Steven R. Humphrey; Richard A. Krantz; Gregory J. Ligelis; Brian E. Moran. Counsel: David J. Burke; Pamela K. Elkow; Charles E. Janson; John F. X. Peloso, Jr. (Resident). Associates: Joseph Carey; Thomas J. Donlon; Katherine Dowd; Arthur K. Engle; R. Kelley Franco; Sarah M. Hurley; John H. Kane; Steven J. Koo; Hiroko Muraki; Christina Chen Paul; James M. Ruel; Regina M. Sweeney.
General Practice including Admiralty, Antitrust and Trade Regulation, Appellate, Banking and Institutional Finance, Bankruptcy and Creditors' Rights, Business Litigation, Business Workouts, Construction, Corporate and Closely Held Business, Criminal Litigation, E-Commerce and Intellectual Property, Employee Benefits and ERISA Litigation, Employment Litigation and Counseling, Environmental, Estate Planning and Probate, Government Relations, Healthcare, Immigration, Insurance, International, Labor Relations and Collective Bargaining, Land Use and Zoning, Personal Injury, Product Liability, Professional Liability, Public Finance, Real Estate Finance, Development and Leasing, Securities, Tax-Exempt Organizations, Tax Planning and Representation, Utilities and Telecommunications.
Other Offices: Hartford CT, Greenwich, CT, New London, CT, Boston, MA, New York, NY, and Manchester, NH.
See Professional Biographies, STAMFORD, CONNECTICUT

Rod, Einar M. '51 '77 C&L.262 B.S., J.D.
V.P., Gen. Coun. & Corp. Sec., Axel Johnson, Inc.
*RESPONSIBILITIES: Mergers and Acquisitions; Corporate; Commercial.
Rod, Helene Schlackman '60 '86 C.228 A.B. L.309 J.D.
(adm. in NY; not adm. in CT) 201 High Ridge Rd.
Rodas, Jane Frederick .... '56 '81 C.197 A.B. L.228 J.D. P.O. Box 10305
Rodas, Remy A., (BV) .... '56 '82 C.276 B.S.F.S. L.128 J.D. [Ⓒ Curtis,M.C.&M.]
*PRACTICE AREAS: Corporate Law; Commercial Law; Transportation; Joint Ventures; Mergers and Acquisitions.
Rodriguez, Sabino, III, (AV) .... '53 '79 C&L.309 A.B., J.D. [Day,B.&H.]
*PRACTICE AREAS: Strategic Joint Ventures; Tax; Benefits and Executive Compensation; Mergers and Acquisitions; Emerging Companies.
Rodwin, Roger M., (AVⓉ) .... '37 '61 C.674 A.B. L.178 LL.B. 60 Constance Lane
Roe, Bonnie J. '53 '83 C.788 A.B. L.569 J.D.
(adm. in NY; not adm. in CT) [Day,B.&H.]
*PRACTICE AREAS: Mergers and Acquisitions; Private Equity Funds; Benefit and Executive Compensation; Securities Law.
Rogers, Ilene S. .... '— '83 C.331 B.A. L.1040 J.D. 28 Haviland Rd.
Rogol, Rhonna W. .... '55 '79 C.1036 B.A. L.569 J.D. [Ⓐ Casper&d.L.]
*PRACTICE AREAS: Employment Law; Labor Law.
Ronan, Timothy G., (BV) .... '53 '84 C.321 B.A. L.564 J.D. [Cummings&L.]
*PRACTICE AREAS: Commercial Litigation; Alternative Dispute Resolution; Construction Law; Probate Litigation.
Rondepierre, Edmond F., (AV) '30 '59 C.1027 B.S. L.831 LL.B.
Sr. V.P., Gen. Coun. & Secy., General Reinsurance Corp.
Rose, Richard L., (AV) .... '36 '64 C.188 A.B. L.902 J.D. [Roberts,R.&B.]
*PRACTICE AREAS: Banking Law; Corporate Law; Securities; International Business Law.
Rose, Sharon H. .... '62 '93 C.1349 B.A. L.1398 J.D. [Ⓐ J.D.Muhlbaum]
Rosenberg, Burton S. .... '49 '75 C.401 B.A. L.569 J.D. City Corp. Coun.
Rosenberg, Judith, (BV) .... '43 '80 C.1044 B.S. L.1040 J.D. [Wofsey,R.K.&K.]
*PRACTICE AREAS: Employment Law; Workers Compensation; Accidents; Personal Injury; Discrimination.
Rosenberg, Meira .... '55 '80 C.347 B.A. L.978 J.D. 52 Boulder Brook Drive
Rosenblum, James B., (AVⓉ) '47 '73 C.976 B.A. L.188 J.D.
[Rosenblum&T.] & [Ⓒ Finkelstein B.W.M.&R.] ⊙
Rosenblum & Tannenbaum LLC, (AVⓉ)
One Landmark Square (⊙New York, White Plains, NY)
Rosenfeld, Brian D., (BV) .... '56 '82 C.611 B.A. L.564 J.D. 196 North St.

Rosenstein & Barnes
(See Fairfield)

Rosenzweig, Harlan J. '47 '72 C.994 B.A. L.184 J.D.
Westinghouse Bdcstg. & Cable Co.
Ross, Edmund T. '30 '56 C&L.976 B.A., LL.B.
(adm. in NY; not adm. in CT) IBM Credit Corp.
Rosse, Melissa T. .... '59 '86 C.188 A.B. L.262 J.D. [Grimes&B.]
Rossmoore, William .... '18 '48 C.309 A.B. L.178 LL.B. 448 Long Ridge Rd.‡
Rostain, Tanina, (BV) .... '60 '88 C.821 B.A. L.976 J.D. 184 Atlantic St.
Rothberg, Harvey J., (BV) ...... '40 '65 C.107 B.S.B.A. L.273 J.S.D. 126 Woodside Green
Rothenberg, Susan, (BV) .... '43 '82 C.882 B.A. L.1040 J.D. 25 3rd St.
Rothman, Saul A., (BV) .... '45 '72 C.103 A.B. L.273 J.D. 600 Summer St.
Royster, Constance L., (AVⓉ) .... '49 '78 C.976 B.A. L.705 J.D. [Ⓒ Cooper&M.] ⊙

Rubenstein, Green & Bass, LLC
(See Westport)

Rubin, David W. .... '66 '91 C.1044 B.A. L.1009 J.D. 750 Summer Street

Rubino, James M., (BV) '56 '82 C.1030 B.S. L.1029 J.D.
1100 Summer Street, 06905
Telephone: 203-327-4212 Fax: 203-973-0441
URL: http://www.lawyers.com/rubinolaw
Probate and Estate Planning and Administration, Corporations, Business and Real Estate Law. Federal and State Taxation. Landlord Tenant Law.
See Professional Biographies, STAMFORD, CONNECTICUT

Rubino, Michael A., Jr. .... '59 '91 C.999 — L.1029 J.D. 1100 Summer St.
Rucci, Joseph J., Jr., (AV) '41 '66 C.1030 A.B. L.884 J.D.
[Rucci,B.C.&E.] (⊙Darien)
*PRACTICE AREAS: Banking; Business Law; Commercial Law; Real Estate; Zoning, Planning and Land Use.

Rucci, Burnham, Carta & Edelberg, LLP, (AV)
6 Landmark Square, Suite 470, 06901 ⊙
Telephone: 203-359-5637
URL: http://www.rbce.com
Members of Firm: Joseph J. Rucci, Jr.; Paul B. Edelberg.
Commercial and Residential Real Estate, Trusts and Estates, Estate Planning, Civil Trial Practice including Fiduciary Disputes, Employment, Commercial, Construction and Personal Injury Litigation, Corporate, Commercial, Information Technology, Banking, Workouts and Bankruptcy, Business Law, Environmental Law, Pre-Nuptial Agreements, State, Local and Federal Taxation, Zoning, Pensions, ERISA Matters and Charitable Organizations.
Darien, Connecticut Office: 800 Post Road, P.O. Box 1107. Telephone: 203-655-7695.
New Canaan, Connecticut Office: 71 Elm Street, P.O. Box 1680. Telephone: 203-966-6500.
See Professional Biographies, STAMFORD, CONNECTICUT

Rudder-Taylor, Marva M. .... '55 '85 C.1030 B.Sc. L.1029 J.D. C
Rudnick, Rhoda L. .... '46 '89 C.563 B.A. L.1029 J.D. 202-1 Soundview Ave
Rudolph, Jeffrey P. '46 '72 C.604 A.B. L.930 J.D.
(adm. in OH; not adm. in CT) Coopers & Lybrand
Ruel, James M. .... '— '99 C.93 B.S. L.306 J.D. [Ⓐ Robinson&C.]
Ruggiero, Charles N. J. '49 '76
C.563 B.M.E. L.365 J.D. [Ohlandt,G.R.&P.] (See Pat. Sect.)
Ruskin, William A., (AVⓉ) '52 '78 C&L.188 B.A., J.D.
(adm. in NY; not adm. in CT) [Shipman&G.]
*PRACTICE AREAS: Environmental Law; Toxic Torts; Alternative Dispute Resolution; Environmental Litigation; Mediation.
Russell, David P. '65 '93 C.1145 B.S. L.184 J.D.
Coun. & Asst. Sec., Treas. Oper., GE Capital Corp.
Russell, Geraldine Koeneke ..... '63 '91 C.1019 B.A. L.724 J.D. [Ⓐ Heidell,P.M.&B.] ⊙
*PRACTICE AREAS: Trial Practice; Appellate Practice; Medical Malpractice; Products Liability; Insurance Defense.

Russell, Philip, P.C.
(See Greenwich)

Ryan, Claire E. .... '70 '99 C.385 B.A. L.904 J.D. [Ⓐ Cummings&L.]
Ryan, Daniel E., III, (AV) .... '55 '81 C.93 A.B. L.262 J.D. [Ryan,R.J.&D.]
*PRACTICE AREAS: Civil Litigation; Medical and Hospital Liability; Appeals.
Ryan, Daniel E., Jr., (AV) .... '28 '53 C.262 A.B. L.569 J.D. [Ⓒ Ryan,R.J.&D.]
*PRACTICE AREAS: Estate Administration; Probate Litigation.
Ryan, Michael D. '59 '86 C.1044 B.S. L.262 J.D.
(adm. in NY; not adm. in CT) Senior Counsel, Xerox Corporation
Ryan, Michael T., (BV) .... '57 '82 C&L.93 A.B., J.D. [Ryan,R.J.&D.]
*PRACTICE AREAS: Civil Litigation; Federal Practice; Professional Liability.

Ryan, Tara C.F. . . . . '67 '95 C.207 B.A. L.1252 J.D. [Ⓐ Piazza&P.]
*PRACTICE AREAS: Family Law; Personal Injury Litigation.
Ryan, W. Patrick, (AV) . . . . '30 '57 C&L.262 B.S., J.D. [Ⓒ Ryan,R.J.&D.]
*PRACTICE AREAS: Civil Litigation; Professional Liability; Hospital Law; Commercial Litigation.

Ryan, Ryan, Johnson & Deluca, LLP, (AV) BR
80 Fourth Street, P.O. Box 3057, 06905
Telephone: 203-357-9200 FAX: 203-357-7915
Email: info@rrjd-law.com
Members of Firm: J. Paul Johnson; Charles A. Deluca; Daniel E. Ryan, III; Michael T. Ryan; Kevin M. Tepas; Robert C.E. Laney; John F. Leydon, Jr.; Catherine S. Nietzel. Of Counsel: Daniel E. Ryan, Jr.; W. Patrick Ryan; Charles M. McCaghey. Associates: Beverly J. Hunt; Janine M. Kelly; Robert O. Hickey; Danielle DiBerardini-Albrecht; Jennifer R. Mazzella; Cynthia Andrews-Di Preta; Nancy A. Meehan; John B. Gaffney; Anthony D. Sutton; Deirdre A. Murray; Joseph C. Valdes; Jonathon Ciottone; Jane B. Callahan.
General and Trial Practice in all State and Federal Courts. Business and Corporate, Employment, Environmental and Hazardous Waste Law, Estate Planning, Family, Health and Hospital Law, Insurance, Litigation, Medical and Legal Malpractice, Negligence, Probate, Products Liability, Railroad, Real Estate, Wills, Zoning.
See Professional Biographies, STAMFORD, CONNECTICUT

Sachs, Jennifer L. '66 '94 C.976 L.813
(adm. in IL; not adm. in CT) [Ⓐ Day,B.&H.]
*PRACTICE AREAS: Labor and Employment; White Collar Crime; Commercial Litigation.
Sachs, Nancy Fairchild . . . . '55 '81 C.103 B.A. L.569 J.D. 100 Propect St., 2nd Fl.

St. John, Park & Scott
(See Greenwich)

St. Onge, Ronald J., (AV) . . . . . '30 '60 C.475 B.S. L.477 J.D. [Ⓒ St. Onge S.J.&R.] (Pat.)
*PRACTICE AREAS: Patent Law; Trademark Law; Copyright Law; Antitrust Law; Unfair Competition.

St. Onge Steward Johnston & Reens, LLC, (AV)
986 Bedford Street, 06905 ⊙
Telephone: 203-324-6155 Telecopier: 203-327-1096
Email: info@ssjr.com URL: http://www.ssjr.com
Louis H. Reens; Gene S. Winter; Stephen P. McNamara; Wesley W. Whitmyer, Jr.; Mary M. Krinsky; Arlana S. Cohen (Not admitted in CT); Eugene L. Flanagan III (Not admitted in CT);—Todd M. Oberdick; Kathryn G. Belleau (Not admitted in CT); Richard J. Basile (Not admitted in CT); David Chen. Of Counsel: Ronald J. St. Onge.
Patent, Trademark, Copyright, Computer, Antitrust, Unfair Competition Law and Litigation.
New Haven, Connecticut Office: 88 Prospect Street. Telephone: 203-562-4043.
See Professional Biographies, STAMFORD, CONNECTICUT

Sanchez, Daniel E. . . . . '63 '91 C.1033 B.A. L.94 J.D. 1100 Summer St.
Sandak, Jay H., (AV) . . . . '46 '71 C.164 A.B. L.823 J.D. [Sandak F.H.&G.]
*PRACTICE AREAS: Civil Litigation; Municipal Taxation; Mediation; Arbitration; Commercial Litigation.

Sandak Friedman Hennessey & Greco, LLP, (AV) BR
970 Summer Street, 06905
Telephone: 203-425-4200 Facsimile: 203-325-8608
URL: http://www.lawyers.com/sfh&g
Members of Firm: Kevin M. Greco; William J. Hennessey, Jr.; Gary S. Klein; Peter M. Nolin; Jay H. Sandak; Mary E. Sommer. Associates: Robert C. DeDona; Jeffrey M. Knickerbocker; Stephanie A. McLaughlin.
Trials and Appeals in all Connecticut and Federal Courts and Administrative Agencies. Personal Injury, Medical Malpractice, Commercial, Environmental Litigation, Real Estate, Zoning and Land Use, Property Tax Appeals.
See Professional Biographies, STAMFORD, CONNECTICUT

Sank, Mark A., (BV) . . . . '59 '84 C.999 B.S. L.1194 J.D. [Trow&S.]
*PRACTICE AREAS: Collections; Estate Planning; Probate; Landlord and Tenant Law; Real Estate.
Santagata, Mark P., (BV) . . . . '58 '84 C.184 B.A. L.1048 J.D. [Cacace,T.&S.]
*PRACTICE AREAS: Litigation; Personal Injury; Torts; Labor and Employment; Real Estate.
Santagata, Michael W., (BV) . . . . '64 '89 C.93 B.A. L.818 J.D. 22 5th St.
Santoro, Salvatore A., (AVⓉ) '47 '83 C&L.262 B.A., J.D.
(adm. in NY; not adm. in CT) GE Capital Servs. Structured Fin. Group, Inc.
Saperstein, Robert M. . . . . '52 '77 C.1350 B.A. L.1019 J.D. 34 Pony Trail Rd.
Sargent, Joseph P. . . . . '66 '94 C.1030 B.A. L.896 J.D. [Ⓐ Curtis,B.&B.]
*PRACTICE AREAS: Commercial Litigation.
Sarner, Joshua J. . . . . '71 '00 [Ⓐ Cummings&L.]

Sarner, Richard A., Law Offices of, (BV) '55 '82 C.197 B.A. L.1019 J.D.
184 Atlantic Street, 06901 ⊙
Telephone: 203-967-8899 Fax: 203-967-8886
Email: rsarner@aol.com
Estate Planning, Tax Planning, Trust Administration, Business Planning, Real Estate, Wealth Preservation, Family Wealth Transfer, Retirement Planning.
New York, New York Office: 465 Park Avenue, Suite 10C. Telephone: 800-392-8550.
See Professional Biographies, STAMFORD, CONNECTICUT

Sarnoff, Merton, (AVⓉ) '28 '57 C.867 A.B. L.178 LL.B.
(adm. in NY; not adm. in CT) 1 Shrewberry Hill Ave.‡
Sasser, Duffy A., II . . . . '45 '75 C&L.560 B.B.A., J.D. 21 Iron Gate Road
Satz, Cathy S., (BV) '63 '87 C.1349 B.S. L.94 J.D.
VP, Secretary & Corporate Counsel, Gartner Group Inc.
Savvaides, Anastasios T. . . . . '67 '92 C.308 B.A. L.818 J.D. [Ⓐ Casper&d.L.]
*PRACTICE AREAS: Personal Injury Litigation.
Sbrollini, Jay P. '65 '92 C.187 B.S. L.818 J.D.
(adm. in MA; not adm. in CT) [T.J.Perkowski]
*PRACTICE AREAS: Electrical Patent Prosecution; Computer and Software Patents; Patent Licensing.
Scarcella, Russell B. '69 '95 C.260 B.S. L.1009 J.D.
(adm. in NJ; not adm. in CT) [Ⓐ Goldberg&Assoc.] ⊙
*PRACTICE AREAS: Insurance Coverage; Litigation; Environmental Litigation.
Schaffer, Toby M. . . . . '53 '98 C.66 B.A. L.1009 J.D. [Ⓐ Shapiro&S.]

Schaffer, Stephen N.
(See Norwalk)

Schalick, Walton O., Jr. '31 '55 C.197 A.B. L.309 LL.B.
(adm. in NJ; not adm. in CT)
Assoc. Gen. Coun., Dist. Sales Fin. Div., General Electric Credit Corp.
Schatz & Schatz, Ribicoff & Kotkin . . . . 1 Landmark Square (⊙Hartford)

Scheffler, William L., & Associates
(See Westport)

Schelz, Stephen J., (BV) . . . . '58 '85 C.173 B.S. L.61 J.D. 1234 Summer St.
Scher, Lee T. . . . . '41 '66 C.178 A.B. L.184 LL.B. One Champion Plz.‡
Scherban, Jack S., (BV) . . . . '45 '70 C.823 B.A. L.94 J.D. 184 Atlantic St.
Schiaroli, Francis P., (AV) . . . . '11 '36 C&L.976 B.A., LL.B. 10 Stamford Forum
Schmidt, John T. '46 '76 C.884 B.A. L.276 J.D.
Director of Regulatory Postal Affairs, Pitney Bowes Inc.
Schmults, Edward C. '31 '59 C.976 B.S. L.309 J.D.
(adm. in NY; not adm. in CT) 1 Stamford Pl.
Schnaper, Kenneth '41 '62
C.331 B.A. L.569 LL.B. Assoc. Gen. Coun. & Asst. Secy., Crane Co.

Schoonmaker, George & Colin, P.C.
(See Greenwich)

Schott, Newton B., Jr., (AVⓉ) '42 '67 C.674 A.B. L.178 J.D.
(adm. in NY; not adm. in CT)
Ex. V.P., Chief Admn. Offr, Gen. Coun., Pimco Funds Distributors LLC
Schultz, Claire '60 '88 C.705 B.S. L.1292 J.D.
(adm. in NJ; not adm. in CT) Pat. Coun., Cytec Industries Inc.
Schultz, Peter M. . . . . '68 '94 C.118 B.A. L.1292 J.D. [Ⓐ Paul,H.J.&W.]
*PRACTICE AREAS: Employment Law.
Schwartz, Daniel L., (AV) . . . . '63 '89 C.674 B.A. L.1066 J.D. [Day,B.&H.]
*PRACTICE AREAS: Employment Law; Employment Litigation; Securities Litigation.
Schwartz, Ronald M., (BV) . . . . '33 '56 C&L.228 A.B., J.D. 1017 Washington Blvd.

Schwartzman Garelik Walker Kapiloff & Troy, P.C., (AVⓉ)
777 Summer Street, 06901 ⊙
Telephone: 203-325-1118 Fax: 203-353-3392
Arnold Y. Kapiloff.
General Civil Practice. Construction, Real Estate, Taxation, Estates, Trusts and Probate, Commercial and Tax Litigation.
New York, N.Y. Office: 335 Lexington Avenue. Telephone: 212-557-2900. Fax: 212-983-4193; 599-5067.
Hollywood, Florida Office: 2021 Tyler Street 33022. Telephone: 954-921-5500. Fax: 954-925-7013.
See Professional Biographies, STAMFORD, CONNECTICUT

Schwind, George S. '29 '57 C.602 B.S.M.E. L.276 J.D.
(adm. in IN; not adm. in CT; Pat.) Crane Co.
Sciglimpaglia, Robert, Jr. . . . . '66 '92 C.184 B.A. L.1040 J.D. 30 Oak St.
Scopac, Mari-Jo F. . . . . '48 '77 C.705 B.A. L.575 J.D. Corp. Coun., Lex Serv., Inc.
Seals-Coffield, Yolanda . . . . '71 '96 C.329 B.A. L.94 J.D. [Ⓐ Paul,H.J.&W.]
*PRACTICE AREAS: Employment Law.
Sedgwick, John A. '50 '80 C.860 B.A. L.37 J.D.
(adm. in AZ; not adm. in CT) V.P. & Intl. Div. Coun., Cadbury Beverages Inc.
Seeger, Stephan E. . . . . '66 '98 C.028 B.A. L.107 J.D. 27 5th Ave.
Segall, Maurice K., (BV) . . . . '62 '88 C.205 B.A. L.982 J.D. 733 Summer St.
Seideman, Evan S. . . . . '67 '96 C.276 B.S. L.978 J.D. [Ⓐ Cummings&L.]
Seifert, Brit K. . . . . '68 '95 C.62 B.A. L.1003 J.D. [Ⓐ Paul,H.J.&W.]
*PRACTICE AREAS: Employment Law; Litigation.

Selsberg, William, (AV) '37 '62 C&L.184 B.S., LL.B.
970 Summer Street, 06905-5518
Telephone: 203-353-1700 Fax: 203-352-1792 URL: http://www.earthlink.net/~wsels
Email: csels@earthlink.net
General Practice including Real Estate, Commercial and Residential, Corporate Law, Common Interest Community Law, Zoning and Subdivision Law, Environmental Law, Commercial and Residential Leases.
See Professional Biographies, STAMFORD, CONNECTICUT

Shafter, Robert L. '31 '58 C&L.276 B.S., J.D.
(adm. in DC; not adm. in CT) Sr. Coun., Xerox Corporation

Shanley, Thomas M., Law Office of
(See Greenwich)

Shapero, Paul D., Law Offices of, (AV) '20 '51
C.103 A.B. L.178 LL.B. 1100 Summer Street
Shapiro, Bernard L., (BVⓉ) . . . . '49 '76 C.102 B.A. L.724 J.D. [Shapiro&S.]
Shapiro, James A. '70 '95 C.976 B.A. L.880 J.D.
1 Elmcroft Road, Mail Stop MSC 6411
Shapiro & Siegel, P.C., (BVⓉ) . . . . 162 Bedford Street (⊙Great Neck, NY)
Sharp, Jacqueline . . . . '44 '97 C.1040 B.A. L.472 J.D. 1200 Summer Street Suite 103
Shattuck, Laura R. . . . . '69 '99 C.425 B.A. L.1252 J.D. [Ⓐ Diserio M.O.&C.]
*PRACTICE AREAS: Litigation.
Shaver, Alan M. . . . . '38 '64 C.197 A.B. L.976 LL.B. [Ⓐ Neville S.H.&M.] ⊙
*PRACTICE AREAS: Corporate Law; Business Law; Partnership Law; Limited Liability Company Law.
Shea, Patrick W. . . . . '57 '81 C.754 B.A. L.976 J.D. [Paul,H.J.&W.]
*PRACTICE AREAS: Employment Law; Employee Benefits; Employment Discrimination; Age Discrimination; Wrongful Termination.
Sheahan, Margaret M., (AV) '54 '80
C.262 B.A. L.569 J.D. [Pullman&C.] (⊙Bridgeport)
*PRACTICE AREAS: Labor Law; Employment Law; Civil Litigation.
Shearin, James T., (AV) '61 '86
C&L.184 B.A., J.D. [Pullman&C.] (⊙Bridgeport, Hartford)
*PRACTICE AREAS: Litigation; Intellectual Property; Admiralty; Securities.
Sheiman, Judith Ann . . . . '57 '81 C.184 B.A. L.94 J.D. 2437 Bedford St., D5‡
Sherer, Donald B., (BV) . . . . '47 '74 C.184 B.A. L.1009 J.D. 111 Prospect St.
Sherman, Alex K. '75 '00 C.787 B.A. L.904 J.D.
(adm. in MD; not adm. in CT) [Ⓐ Wofsey,R.K.&K.]
*PRACTICE AREAS: Litigation.
Sherman, Carol Weiss '63 '89 C.893 B.A. L.659 J.D.
(adm. in NY; not adm. in CT) [Ⓐ Kelley D.&W.]
*PRACTICE AREAS: Corporate Law; Securities.
Sherman, Michael, (AV) . . . . '46 '71 C&L.184 A.B., J.D. [Sherman&R.]
Sherman, Michael S., (AV) . . . . . '28 '51 C.477 A.B. L.569 LL.B. Comm., Workers' Comp.
Sherman, Rachel B. . . . . '73 '99 C.659 B.A. L.260 J.D. [Ⓐ Cummings&L.]
Sherman, William M., (BV) . . . . '37 '62 C.197 B.A. L.178 LL.B. 1100 Summer St.
Sherman & Richichi, (AV) . . . . 27 Fifth St.
Sherwood, Everett P., (BV) . . . . '26 '57 C.188 B.A. L.564 LL.B. [Sherwood&S.]
Sherwood, Michelle A. '57 '96 C.776 B.S. L.665 J.D.
(adm. in NY; not adm. in CT; Pat.) Pat. Coun., Cytec Industries Inc.
Sherwood and Sherwood, (BV) . . . . 30 Oak St.
Shiel, Samuel M. '68 '94 L.585 J.D.
Asst. V.P. & Natl. Underwriting Coun., Stewart Title Guaranty Co.- National Title Service
Shields, Day R., (BV) . . . . '47 '73 C&L.976 B.A., J.D. [Ⓒ Wofsey,R.K.&K.]
*PRACTICE AREAS: Estate Planning; Probate; Trust Law; Taxation.
Shiffman, Howard G., (BV) . . . . '41 '67 C.107 B.A. L.1009 LL.B. 30 Oak St.

Shipman & Goodwin LLP, (AV) BR
One Landmark Square, 06901 ⊙
Telephone: 203-324-8100 Telecopier: 203-324-8199
Email: www@goodwin.com URL: http://shipman-goodwin.com
Partners: Robin G. Frederick; Frederick S. Gold; Steven M. Gold; Shari M. Goodstein; Donald R. Gustafson; Barry C. Hawkins; Edward M. Kane; William A. Ruskin (Not admitted in CT); Michael L. Widland; Robert M. Wonneberger. Counsel: Raymond M. Bernstein. Of Counsel: George C. Jepsen. Associates: Andreana R. Bellach; Catherine M. Brennan; Cathy L. Bromberg; Lee A. Duval (Not admitted in CT); Frederick T. Forster; Clare Attura Kretzman; Marybeth C. McPadden; R. Michael Meo, Jr.; Steven Weinberger; Carolyn J. Zambelli; Andrew M. Zeitlin.
General Practice. Banking, Corporation, Tax, Antitrust, Trade Regulation, Finance and Securities, Venture Capital, Labor and Employment, Health Care, Environmental, Professional Liability, Pension and Profit Sharing, Estate Planning, Probate, Trust Administration and Financial Management, Municipal Law. Trials in all Courts.
Greenwich, Connecticut Office: 43 Arch Street. Telephone: 203-869-6222.
Hartford, Connecticut Office: One American Row. Telephone: 203-251-5000.
Lakeville, Connecticut Office: 12 Porter Street. Telephone: 203-435-2539.
See Professional Biographies, STAMFORD, CONNECTICUT

Sickinger, Robert J. ....'68 '94 C.855 A.B. L.184 J.D. [Ⓐ Cummings&L.]
*PRACTICE AREAS: Insurance Defense.
Siebert, Lawrence A. ....'56 '81 C.184 B.A. L.930 J.D. Pres., Siebert Capital Corp.
Siegal, Richard A., (AV) ....'47 '72 C&L.659 B.S., J.D. [Cummings&L.]
*PRACTICE AREAS: Federal and State Income Taxation; ERISA.
Siegel, John J., (BVⓉ) '40 '67 C.94 B.A. L.1009 J.D.
(adm. in NY; not adm. in CT) [Shapiro&S.] ⊙
Silberstein, Scott '64 '92 C.659 B.S. L.1068 J.D.
(adm. in NY; not adm. in CT) V.P. & Assoc. Gen. Coun., GE Asset Management
Silbert, Richard W. '59 '87 C&L.178 B.A., J.D.
V.P. & Assoc. Gen. Coun., The Purdue Frederick Co./Purdue Pharma L.P.
*RESPONSIBILITIES: Litigation; Contracts; General Law.
Silver, Bobbi L., Law Offices of, (BV) '43 '86 C.1029 B.S. L.184 J.D.
112 Prospect Street
Silver, Richard A., (AV) ....'36 '60 C.659 B.A. L.893 LL.B. [Silver,G.&T.]
*PRACTICE AREAS: Medical Malpractice; Personal Injury; Negligence; Business Litigation; Family Law.

Silver, Golub & Teitell LLP, (AV) BR
184 Atlantic Street, P.O. Box 389, 06904
Telephone: 203-325-4491 Fax: 203-325-3769
URL: http://www.sgtlaw.com
Members of Firm: Richard A. Silver; David S. Golub; Ernest F. Teitell; Patricia M. Haugh (1942-1988); John D. Josel; Mario DiNatale; Jonathan M. Levine;—Marilyn J. Ramos; Mary G. Curry; Kathleen L. Brandt; Paul A. Slager; Angelo A. Ziotas; Peter Mason Dreyer.
Trial Practice in all State and Federal Courts. Medical Malpractice, Negligence, Commercial Litigation, Family and Criminal Law.
See Professional Biographies, STAMFORD, CONNECTICUT

Silverman, Monroe, (AV) ....'31 '55 C.867 B.S. L.976 LL.B. [Wofsey,R.K.&K.]
*PRACTICE AREAS: Personal Injury; Contracts; Civil Litigation; Real Estate.
Silvestro, Tracie J. ....'72 '00 C.823 B.A. L.1040 J.D. 22 Fifth St.
Silvia, David J. ....'67 '00 [Ⓐ Cummings&L.] (Pat.)
Simon, James F., (BV) ....'31 '61 C.659 B.S. L.569 J.D. 196 North St.
Simon, Lisa T. '62 '86 C.1044 B.A. L.1009 J.D.
(adm. in NY; not adm. in CT) Asst. Vice Pres., NAC Reinsurance Corp.
Simon, Morton S. '35 '68 C.178 B.S. L.569 J.D.
(adm. in NY; not adm. in CT; Pat.) 1 Blachley Rd.
Simpson, Matthew J. '61 '87 C.659 B.A. L.262 J.D.
V.P. & Assoc. Gen. Coun., GE Asset Management & Gen. Coun., GE Fin. Assurance-Investment Servs. Group
Sincoff, Gregg M. '57 '82 C.94 B.S.B.A. L.1206 J.D.
(adm. in FL; not adm. in CT) Tax Coun., GE Capital Corp.
Sinha, Vaya '72 '01 C.1416 B.A. L.893 LL.M.
(adm. in NY; not adm. in CT) [Ⓐ Pillsbury W.]
Sirico, John A. .....'55 '80 C&L.93 B.S., J.D. Reg. Coun., Coml. Fin., GE Capital Corp.
Siskin, Jerrold A. '50 '76 C.1036 B.A. L.1009 J.D.
(adm. in NY; not adm. in CT) [Ⓐ Curtis,M.C.&M.]
*PRACTICE AREAS: Immigration and Nationality Law.
Sisley, G. William ....'44 '70 C.674 A.B. L.569 J.D. [Pillsbury W.]
*PRACTICE AREAS: Mergers, Acquisitions and Divestitures; Corporate Law; Business Law; Securities.

Sisson, Frank E., III, Law Offices of, (AV) '52 '76 C.165 B.A. L.309 J.D.
6 Landmark Square, 06901 ⊙
Telephone: 203-965-5965
Email: fsisson@compuserve.com URL: http://www.lawyers.com/frankesisson
Business Transactions, Corporate, Commercial, Probate, Estate Planning, Elder Law, Tax Law, Real Estate.
Westport, Connecticut Office: 180 Post Road East, 06881. Telephone: 203-965-5965. Telefax: 203-222-4869.
See Professional Biographies, STAMFORD, CONNECTICUT

Skidd, Thomas P., Jr., (AV) ....'36 '61 C.276 A.B. L.976 LL.B. [Cummings&L.]
*PRACTICE AREAS: Real Estate Law; Land Use Law; Zoning and Planning Law.
Skoufalos, Llorca & Ziccardi, LLP, (AVⓉ) ....2187 Atlantic Street (⊙New York, NY)
Skovgaard, Robert A., (BV) ....'52 '77 C.31 B.A. L.184 J.D. 1234 Summer St.
Slager, Paul A. ....'— '93 C&L.477 B.A., J.D. [Ⓐ Silver,G.&T.]
*PRACTICE AREAS: Civil Litigation; Medical Malpractice; Negligence; Products Liability.
Slater, William A. '43 '68 C.102 B.A. L.262 J.D.
(adm. in NY; not adm. in CT) V.P., Gen. Coun. & Secy., Donnelley Mktg., Inc.
Slavin, Richard, (BV) '47 '77 C.930 B.A. L.8 J.D.
[Cohen&W.] (⊙Bridgeport, Westport)
*PRACTICE AREAS: Securities Regulation; Banking Regulation; Securities, Banking and Corporate Litigation; Arbitrations.

Slavitt, Connery & Vardamis
(See Norwalk)

Slifkin, Irving ....'22 '48 C&L.477 A.B., J.D. 332 Mill Rd.‡
Smith, Alfred J., Jr. ....'43 '78 C.424 B.S.B.A. L.818 J.D. 706 Bedford St.
Smith, Barry Paul '43 '68 C.158 B.S.E.E. L.1009 J.D.
(adm. in NY; not adm. in CT; Pat.) Gen. Pat. Coun., Xerox Corporation
Smith, Brigid M. '52 '78 C.93 B.A. L.607 J.D.
Dir., Corp. Communications, Citizens Utilities Co.
Smith, Donald L. '47 '89 C.165 A.B. L.145 J.D.
(adm. in NY; not adm. in CT) Sr. V.P., & Gen. Coun., Odyssey Reinsurance Corp.
Smith, Edward A. ....'38 '63 C.188 B.A. L.893 LL.B. P.O. Box 3036‡
Smith, H. William, III ....'63 '92 C.696 B.A. L.930 J.D. [Ⓐ Paul,H.J.&W.]
*PRACTICE AREAS: Corporate; Corporate Finance.
Smith, Kevin M. '66 '93 C.976 B.A. L.30 J.D.
(adm. in NY; not adm. in CT) Assoc. Coun., Time Warner Cable
Smith, Kristen M. '73 '98 C.1031 B.S. L.982 J.D.
Atty., The Purdue Frederick Co./Purdue Pharma L.P.
*RESPONSIBILITIES: Corporate Law; Contracts; Litigation; Employment Law; General Law.
Smith, Philip E. '29 '57 C&L.262 A.B., LL.B.
(adm. in NY; not adm. in CT) 800 Long Ridge Rd.

Smith, Ranscht, Connors, Nordell & Mutino, P.C.
(See White Plains, New York)

Smithers, Barbara L. '52 '78 C.597 B.A. L.145 J.D.
(adm. in NY; not adm. in CT) V.P. & Corp. Secy., International Paper Co.
*RESPONSIBILITIES: Corporate Governance; Securities Law; Financing; Executive Compensation.
Smyth, John E., (BV) ....'34 '61 C.1030 B.A. L.262 LL.B. 1017 Washington Blvd.
Snediker, David E., (AV) ....'47 '76 C.602 B.S. L.724 J.D. [Paul,H.J.&W.]
*PRACTICE AREAS: Commercial Real Estate; Pension Fund Investments; Real Estate Investment; Real Estate Finance; Mortgage Finance.
Snover, Brian G. '62 '88 C.264 B.A. L.868 J.D.
(adm. in NY; not adm. in CT) V.P. & Gen. Coun., Berkshire Hathway Group
Snyder, Henry K. ....'67 '96 C.659 B.A. L.184 J.D. [Ⓐ Pillsbury W.]
*PRACTICE AREAS: Litigation; Life Sciences and Technology.
Solazzo, Richard M. ....'58 '84 C.188 B.S. L.276 J.D. [Cummings&L.]
*PRACTICE AREAS: Labor and Employment Litigation.

Solberg, Carl T., (AVⓉ) '46 '74 C.309 B.A. L.569 J.D.
(adm. in NY; not adm. in CT) V.P., Corp. & Legal Affs., Pitney Bowes Inc.
*RESPONSIBILITIES: Corporate Law.
Soli, Thomas R. ....'61 '92 C.1300 B.S. L.615 J.D. Assoc. Coun., Conair Corp.
Solloway, Cozata ....'72 '97 C&L.1040 B.A., J.D. [Ⓐ Pillsbury W.]
*PRACTICE AREAS: Real Estate; Corporate Law; Capital Markets.
Solomon, Stanley A., (AVⓉ) '44 '70 C&L.260 B.S.B.A., J.D.
(adm. in NY; not adm. in CT) Ernst & Young
Soltis, Michael J. ....'53 '79 C.184 B.A. L.564 J.D. [Jackson L.S.&K.]
Sommer, Evelyn M. '25 '56 C.331 B.A. L.1009 LL.B.
(adm. in NY; not adm. in CT; Pat.) [Ⓒ Cummings&L.] (⊙Stamford)
*PRACTICE AREAS: Patents; Trademarks; Unfair Competition; Copyrights; Licensing.
Sommer, Mary E., (BV) ....'49 '76 C.562 B.A. L.602 J.D. [Sandak F.H.&G.]
*PRACTICE AREAS: Civil Litigation; Commercial Litigation; Personal Injury.
Sortor, Katherine M. ....'34 '61 C.788 A.B. L.893 LL.B. [Ⓒ G.M.Lucey]
*PRACTICE AREAS: Corporate Law.
Sostman, Ellen L., (AV) '46 '75
C.108 B.A. L.184 J.D. Title Coun., Ct. Attys. Title Ins. Co.
Sparaco, Christine A. ......'69 '96 C.689 B.A. L.184 J.D. 45 Franklin Street (⊙Stamford)
Spelke, Sherwood R., (BV) ....'41 '67 C.178 A.B. L.94 LL.B. [Ⓒ Cacace,T.&S.]
*PRACTICE AREAS: Real Estate Law; Probate; Municipal Law.
Speranza, William J. ....'49 '76 C.602 B.S. L.262 J.D. [Wiggin&D.] (Pat.)
*PRACTICE AREAS: Patent Law; Intellectual Property; Litigation.
Spindler, John F., (AV) ....'29 '53 C&L.477 A.B., J.D. [Cummings&L.]
*PRACTICE AREAS: Fiduciary Law; Corporate Litigation; Legal Ethics.
Spitzer, Vlad G. ....'56 '88 C.569 B.A. L.1398 J.D. [Spitzer S.&B.]
*PRACTICE AREAS: Labor and Employment; Commercial Litigation.

Spitzer Sundheim & Brey LLC
Century Building, 350 Bedford Street, 4th Floor, 06901 ⊙
Telephone: 203-316-8422 Fax: 203-357-7856
URL: http://www.lawyers.com/ss&bllc
Vlad G. Spitzer; Steven R. Sundheim; Lewis Brey;—Huma Khan; Scott P. Benjamin (Not admitted in CT); Tara E. Smith (Resident, White Plains, New York Office).
Labor and Employment, Insurance Defense.
White Plains, New York Office: 123 Main Street, Suite 1700, 10601. Telephone: 914-949-5322. Fax: 914-946-5422.
See Professional Biographies, STAMFORD, CONNECTICUT

Spollen, Moira A. ....'74 '00 C.1030 B.A. L.262 J.D. [Ⓐ Blair&P.]
*PRACTICE AREAS: Estate Planning; Estate Settlements; Trust Administration.
Sprole, Jonathan K. '55 '82
C.813 B.A. L.893 J.D. Managing Dir. & Gen. Coun., GE Equity
Staikos, John P. ....'70 '98 C.1044 B.A. L.868 J.D. [Ⓐ Paul,H.J.&W.]
*PRACTICE AREAS: Corporate Law; Project Finance.
Stanton, Michael K., Jr., (BV) ....'61 '87 C.321 B.A. L.262 J.D. [Ⓒ Curtis,M.C.&M.]
*PRACTICE AREAS: Civil Litigation; Commercial Litigation; Construction Litigation; Probate Litigation; Torts.
Stapleton, James F., (AV) ....'32 '57 C.1030 B.S.S L.93 LL.B. [Day,B.&H.]
*PRACTICE AREAS: Commercial Litigation.

Starks, Samuel J. '51 '77 C.475 B.A. L.424 J.D.
1100 Summer Street, 06905
Telephone: 203-348-0441 Fax: 203-973-0441
Email: capjustice@aol.com URL: http://www.lawyers.com/samueljstarks
***PRACTICE AREAS: Health Law; Elder Law; Trusts and Estates.**
Elder Law, Health Law, Estate Administration and Probate.
See Professional Biographies, STAMFORD, CONNECTICUT

Starobin, Amy L. ....'60 '86 C.319 B.A. L.208 J.D. [Ⓒ Roberts,R.&B.]
*PRACTICE AREAS: Civil Litigation; Employment Law; Matrimonial.
Stechel, Ira B., (AVⓉ) '47 '73 C.563 B.A. L.188 J.D.
(adm. in NY; not adm. in CT) [Cummings&L.]

Steefel, Levitt & Weiss, A Professional Corporation
Six Landmark Square, Fourth Floor, 06901-2792 ⊙
Telephone: 203-359-5662 Fax: 203-359-5805
Email: slw@steefel.com URL: http://www.steefel.com
Richard J. Tannenbaum; Thomas A. Banahan.
General Civil and Trial Practice. Antitrust, Banking, Business, Corporate Financing, Reorganization, Corporation, Estate Planning and Probate Law, Public Utility, Real Estate, Taxation.
San Francisco, California Office: 30th Floor, One Embarcadero Center. Telephone: 415-788-0900. Fax: 415-788-2019.
See Professional Biographies, STAMFORD, CONNECTICUT

Stein, Peter M., (BV) ....'50 '76 C.105 B.A. L.273 J.D. [Epstein B.&G.]
*PRACTICE AREAS: Labor and Employment Law.
Stein, Richard H., (AV) ....'50 '75 C&L.150 B.A., J.D. [R.H.Stein]
*PRACTICE AREAS: Taxation; Estate Planning; Corporate; Business Law.

Stein, Richard H., LLC, (AV)
2777 Summer Street, 06905 ⊙
Telephone: 203-352-8300 Fax: 203-352-8303
URL: http://www.rhstein.com
Richard H. Stein.
Estate Planning, Taxation, Business Law, Corporate Law.
See Professional Biographies, STAMFORD, CONNECTICUT

Steinberg, Jeffrey G. '52 '77 C.188 B.S. L.262 J.D.
(adm. in NY; not adm. in CT) [Steinberg&C.] ⊙
Steinberg & Cavaliere, LLP ....6 Landmark Sq. (⊙New York, White Plains, NY)
Steiner, LaDonna L. '56 '86 C.608 B.S. L.208 J.D.
Sr. Asst. Gen. Coun., Purdue Frederick Co./Purdue Pharma L.P.
*RESPONSIBILITIES: Healthcare; FDA Regulatory; General Contracts.
Steinmayer, Janet L. '55 '81 C.104 A.B. L.145 J.D.
Corporate VP, General Counsel, & Secretary, Volume Service America, Inc.
Stekloff, Neil B. ....'72 '98 C.273 B.A. L.184 J.D. [Ⓐ Paul,H.J.&W.]
*PRACTICE AREAS: Employment Law.
Stephan, Robert M. ....'42 '67 C.399 B.A. L.966 J.D. [Ⓒ Martin,L.&C.] (⊙Stamford)
*PRACTICE AREAS: Corporate Law; Acquisitions; Securities Regulation; Licensing; Joint Ventures.
Stephan, Robert M. ......'42 '67 C.399 B.A. L.966 J.D. 1177 Summer Street (⊙Stamford)
Steward, Merrill F. ....'17 '50 C.976 B.E. L.184 J.D. 986 Bedford St. (Pat.)
Stitzer, H. Todd ....'52 '79 C.309 A.B. L.178 J.D. P.O. Box 3800
Stone, Mark P., (BV) ....'49 '77 C.569 B.E. L.724 J.D. 1100 High Ridge Rd. (Pat.)
Stone, Michael K., (AVⓉ) '54 '79 C&L.976 B.A., J.D.
(adm. in TX; not adm. in CT) Tax Coun., GE Capital Corp.
Stone, Robert N. '63 '89 C.659 B.A. L.262 J.D.
(adm. in NY; not adm. in CT) Coun., GE Capital Card Servs.
Strada, William E., Jr., (BV) ....'35 '62 C.1030 B.B.A. L.262 LL.B. 104 Atlantic St.
Strassburger, Philip C. '59 '88 C.860 B.S. L.184 J.D.
V.P., Intell. Prop. Coun., The Purdue Frederick Co./Purdue Pharma L.P. (Pat.)
*RESPONSIBILITIES: Patents; Trademarks; Copyrights; Trade Secrets; Litigation.
Stratton, Susan L., (BV) ....'44 '79 C&L.184 B.A., J.D. [Curtis,B.&B.]
*PRACTICE AREAS: Trusts and Estates; Probate; Elder Law; Real Estate.
Strohmeyer, Fritz ....'71 '98 C.1349 B.A. L.597 J.D. [Ⓐ Day,B.&H.]
*PRACTICE AREAS: Business Law.

Strone, Michael J. '53 '79 C.164 B.A. L.262 J.D.
V.P., Assoc. Gen. Coun. & Asst. Secy., GE Asset Management
Stuart, Harold E., (BV) ... '13 '39 C.569 B.S. L.178 J.D. 35 Skyview Dr.
Sugrue, Marcia C. ... '73 '98 C.367 B.A. L.273 J.D. [A Finn D.&H.]
*PRACTICE AREAS: Corporate Law; Securities; Mergers and Acquisitions; Venture Capital.
Sullivan, Bradford J. ... '69 '01 C.454 B.A. L.1252 J.D. [A Epstein B.&G.]
*PRACTICE AREAS: Labor and Employment; Litigation.
Sullivan-Walsh, Morgan T. '60 '87 C.569 B.S. L.262 J.D.
(adm. in NY; not adm. in CT) [ACNielsen]
*RESPONSIBILITIES: Internet Law; Technology Law; Privacy Law.
Summons, Sarah F., (CV) ... '42 '84 C&L.1040 B.S., J.D. 108 4th St.
Sundheim, Steven R. ... '58 '85 C.569 B.A. L.1398 J.D. [Spitzer S.&B.]
*PRACTICE AREAS: Insurance Defense; Torts Litigation; Commercial Contracts; Insurance Coverage; Labor and Employment Law.
Sutton, Anthony D. ... '71 '98 C.569 B.A. L.1252 J.D. [A Ryan,R.J.&D.]
*PRACTICE AREAS: Civil Litigation.
Sweeney, Regina M. ... '— '94 C.058 LL.B. L.276 LL.M. [A Robinson&C.]
Swerdloff, David A., (AV) ... '48 '79 C.103 A.B. L.184 J.D. [Day,B.&H.]
*PRACTICE AREAS: Emerging Companies; Technology and Intellectual Property - Business; Strategic Joint Ventures; Mergers and Acquisitions; Closely Held Businesses.
Sylvester, Jessica L. ... '71 '99 C.184 B.A. L.306 J.D. [A Paul,H.J.&W.]
*PRACTICE AREAS: Corporate Law.
Syrnyk, Irene M. '57 '81 C.597 B.A. L.276 J.D.
(adm. in DC; not adm. in CT) Gen. Coun., Service America Corp.
Tambini, Robert '69 '95 C.1040 B.A. L.564 J.D.
[A Goldberg&Assoc.] (⊙Hoboken, NJ)
*PRACTICE AREAS: Personal Injury; Litigation; Commercial Litigation; Insurance Subrogation; Toxic Torts.
Tannenbaum, Richard J. ... '54 '80 C.831 B.A. L.1009 J.D. [Steefel,L.&W.]
*PRACTICE AREAS: Commercial Bankruptcy; Equipment Finance; Real Estate Finance; Loan Workouts.
Tannenbaum, Samuel, (AVⓉ) ... '22 '49 C.563 B.S.S. L.569 LL.B. [Rosenblum&T.]
Taub, Melissa M. '63 '90 C.1350 B.A. L.982 J.D.
Gen. Coun., Sr. V.P. & Secy., Priceline.com Inc.
Tauber, Joseph N. ... '35 '60 C.178 A.B. L.976 LL.B. 99 Prospect St.
Taylor, Heather V. ... '70 '96 C.823 B.S. L.893 J.D. [A Cummings&L.]
*PRACTICE AREAS: Litigation.
Teig, Morris ... '13 '40 C.102 L.724 LL.B. 400 Main St.
Teitell, Conrad, (AVⓉ) '32 '58 C.477 A.B. L.178 LL.B.
(adm. in NY; not adm. in CT) [Cummings&L.]
*PRACTICE AREAS: Charitable Giving; Tax Exempt Organizations; Estate Planning.
Teitell, Ernest F., (AV) ... '52 '77 C.81 B.A. L.425 J.D. [Silver,G.&T.]
*PRACTICE AREAS: Medical Malpractice; Negligence; Criminal Law; Products Liability.
Tellalian & Tellalian
(See Bridgeport)
Tepas, Kevin M., (BV) ... '47 '72 C.321 B.S. L.184 J.D. [Ryan,R.J.&D.]
*PRACTICE AREAS: Professional Malpractice; Products Liability; Personal Injury; Litigation.
Tepper, Jacqueline G. ... '64 '90 C.659 B.A. L.569 J.D. 96 Old Mill Lane
Theodosiou, Andreas E. '68 '95 C.331 B.A. L.1325 J.D.
(adm. in NJ; not adm. in CT) [A Goldberg&Assoc.] ⊙
Thomas, George W. M. '63 '88
C.732 B.S.B.A. L.823 J.D. Gen. Coun., MemberWorks, Inc.
*RESPONSIBILITIES: Overall Supervision of Legal, Government Affairs and Public Affairs.
Thomas, John D., (BV) '51 '76 C.477 B.S. L.184 J.D.
Title Coun., Ct. Attys. Title Ins. Co.
Thomas, Milton C., II, (BV) ... '46 '75 C&L.184 B.A., J.D. 111 Prospect Street, 4th Floor
Thompson, Frank J., (AV) ... '32 '60 C.426 B.S.E.E. L.276 J.D. 111 Prospect St. (Pat.)
Thompson, Grant S. ... '70 '99 C.575 B.A. L.178 J.D. [A Finn D.&H.]
*PRACTICE AREAS: Corporate Law.
Tibbetts Keating & Butler, LLC
(See Darien)
Tierney, Kevin ... '38 '63 C.951 B.A. L.262 J.D. Supr. Ct. J.
Tierney, Zullo, Flaherty & Murphy, P.C.
(See Norwalk)
Timbers, John W. '42 '69 C.197 B.A. L.309 LL.B.
P.O. Box 3085, 06905
Telephone: 203-322-9553 Facsimile: 203-322-4505
***PRACTICE AREAS: Civil Litigation; Criminal Litigation.**
Civil Litigation, Criminal Litigation.
See Professional Biographies, STAMFORD, CONNECTICUT
Tirola & Herring ...
Tischer, Courtenay L. ... '73 '98 C.93 B.S. L.184 J.D. [A Cummings&L.]
*PRACTICE AREAS: Litigation; Zoning Law; Real Estate; Trusts and Estates.
Tisdale & Lennon, LLC
(See Southport)
Tobin, Frederick M., (AV) ... '36 '64 C.855 B.A. L.184 J.D. [C Curtis,B.&B.]
*PRACTICE AREAS: Corporate Law; Commercial Real Estate; Leases and Leasing; Real Estate; Business Law.
Tobin, Richard J., (AV) ... '34 '63 C&L.93 B.S., LL.B. Supr. Ct. J.
Tolia-Gupta, Dina A. '73 '96 C&L.999 B.A., J.D.
(adm. in NY; not adm. in CT) [A Paul,H.J.&W.]
*PRACTICE AREAS: Real Estate; Real Estate Finance.
Tomasetti, Robert J. '61 '87 C.746 B.B.A. L.436 J.D.
(adm. in MN; not adm. in CT) Tax Coun., GE Capital Corp.
Tooher, Joseph J., Jr., (BV) ... '30 '55 C&L.184 B.A., LL.B. [Tooher&W.]
Tooher & Wocl, L.L.C., (BV) ... 1100 Summer Street, 2nd Floor (⊙Fairfield)
Toomey, Priscilla R. '46 '72 C.331 B.A. L.893 J.D.
(adm. in NY; not adm. in CT) Merrill Lynch Realty, Inc.
Torkelsen, Elizabeth Stebbins ... '65 '92 C.67 B.A. L.92 J.D. [A Epstein B.&G.]
*PRACTICE AREAS: Labor and Employment Law; Litigation.
Torsone, Johnna G. '50 '76 C.881 A.B. L.982 J.D.
(adm. in NY; not adm. in CT) Pitney Bowes Inc.
Treanor, Janie L. ... '73 '98 C.846 B.A. L.802 J.D. [A Wiggin&D.]
Trent, Beth L. '57 '87 C.604 B.A. L.893 J.D.
(adm. in NY; not adm. in CT) 260 Long Ridge Rd.
Trombly, Angela M. ... '68 '93 C.787 B.A. L.1048 J.D. [Melmed&T.]
Tropp, Jonathan B. ... '67 '91 C&L.309 A.B., J.D. [C Day,B.&H.]
*PRACTICE AREAS: Commercial Litigation; Intellectual Property Litigation; Insurance Litigation; Alternative Dispute Resolution; Class Action Defense.
Trow, Griffith H., (BV) ... '51 '77 C.696 B.A. L.823 J.D. [Trow&S.] ⊙
*PRACTICE AREAS: Negligence; Personal Injury; Commercial Law; Real Estate; Civil Litigation.
Trow & Sank, P.C., (BV)
30 Oak Street, 06905 ⊙
Telephone: 203-357-1190 Fax: 203-356-1383
Email: trow.sank.pc@snet.net URL: http://www.lawyers.com/trow&sank
Griffith H. Trow; Mark A. Sank;—Christopher Lagano.
Trials in all Courts, Personal Injury, Collections, Negligence, Commercial Litigation, Landlord Tenant, Real Estate, Probate, Estate Planning, Tax, Commercial and Corporate Law, Workers Compensation.

(This Listing Continued)

Trow & Sank, P.C. (Continued)
References: First Fidelity Bank; Stamford Hospital, Inc.; Webster Bank; Mont Management; Toronto Dominion Bank.
White Plains, New York Office: 50 Main Street, Suite 1000. Telephone: 914-682-2611. Fax: 914-682-7784.
See Professional Biographies, STAMFORD, CONNECTICUT
Truebner, Peter L., (BV) '41 '67 C.976 B.A. L.477 J.D.
111 Prospect Street, Suite 206, 06901
Telephone: 203-323-4540 FAX: 203-323-4920
URL: http://www.lawyers.com/petertruebner
General Practice. Civil and Criminal Litigation, DUI, Juvenile, Personal Injury, Slip and Fall, Divorce and Family Law. Trials in all State and Federal Courts.
See Professional Biographies, STAMFORD, CONNECTICUT
Turitzin, John N. '55 '82 C.231 B.A. L.569 J.D.
(adm. in NY; not adm. in CT) [Paul,H.J.&W.] (⊙New York, NY)
*PRACTICE AREAS: Corporate.
Tusch, Paul T., (BV) ... '60 '85 C.1030 A.B. L.1029 J.D. [Cacace,T.&S.]
*PRACTICE AREAS: Real Property; Telecommunications Law; Zoning, Planning and Land Use; Family Law; Litigation.
Tuthill, Howard S., (AV) ... '18 '41 C&L.893 B.S., J.D. [Cummings&L.] (⊙Naples, FL)
*PRACTICE AREAS: Estate Settlement Law; Trust Administration Law; Executive Tax Planning Law; Post-Mortem Tax Planning Law.
Tuthill, Howard S., III, (AV) ... '47 '72 C.732 B.A. L.893 J.D. [Cummings&L.]
*PRACTICE AREAS: Estate Planning; Probate Law; Taxation; Trust and Estate Administration.
Twardy, Stanley A., Jr., (AV) ... '51 '76 C.855 B.S. L.893 J.D. [Day,B.&H.]
*PRACTICE AREAS: Government Investigation; Commercial Litigation.
Tweedy, Richard B., (AV) ... '19 '48 C&L.976 B.A., LL.B. 695 E. Main St.
Twomey, Christopher J. ... '72 '98 C.93 B.A. L.184 J.D. [A Kelley D.&W.]
*PRACTICE AREAS: Corporate; Litigation.
Tyler Cooper & Alcorn, LLP, (AV) BB
One Landmark Square, 06901-2501 ⊙
Telephone: 203-348-5555 Telecopier: 203-348-3875
URL: http://www.tylercooper.com
Members of Firm: Emmett E. Brown III (Resident); Christopher L. Ulrich (Resident). Counsel: Nan Budde Chequer (Resident); Deborah D. Cannavino.
Administrative Law, Alternative Dispute Resolution, Antitrust and Trade Regulation, Banking, Bankruptcy and Reorganization, Business Crimes, Business Organizations and Securities Law, Computer Law, Domestic Relations, Environmental Law, Financial Services, Franchising, Health Care, Immigration, Insurance Defense and Insurance Coverage Defense, Intellectual Property, Labor and Employment, Legislative Lawyering, Litigation, Media Law, Medical Malpractice Defense, Pension and Employee Benefits, Public Utilities, Real Estate, Taxation, Trusts and Estates and Workers' Compensation.
Hartford, Connecticut Office: CityPlace. Telephone: 860-725-6200. Telecopier: 860-278-3802.
New Haven, Connecticut Office: 205 Church Street. Telephone: 203-784-8200. Telecopier: 203-789-2133.
Greenwich, Connecticut Office: 675 Steamboat Road. Telephone: 203-869-2000. Telecopier: 203-869-2001.
Madison, Connecticut Office: 23 Woodland Road. Telephone: 203-318-3600. Telecopier: 203-318-3609.
See Professional Biographies, STAMFORD, CONNECTICUT
Tyree, Jane L. ... '62 '92 C.93 B.A. L.1040 J.D. [Rapaport&E.]
Udell, Howard R. '41 '66 C.331 B.A. L.569 LL.B.
Exec. V.P. & Gen. Coun., The Purdue Frederick Co./Purdue Pharma, L.P. (⊙New York, NY)
*RESPONSIBILITIES: Corporate Law; Labor and Employment Law; Litigation; International Law; Patents and Trademarks.
Ulrich, Christopher L., (BV) ... '53 '79 C.276 A.B. L.93 J.D. [Tyler C.&A.]
Unger, Michael E. '64 '91 C.222 B.A. L.724 J.D.
[De Orchis,W.&C.] (⊙New York, NY)
Ungerland, Thomas J., (AVⓉ) '39 '65 C.1030 B.S. L.276 J.D.
Assoc. Gen. Coun.& Asst. Secy., Crane Company
Updike, Kelly & Spellacy, P.C., (AV) ... 6 Landmark Sq., 4th Fl. (⊙Hartford, New Haven)
Valdes, Joseph C. ... '63 '93 C.184 B.A. L.1252 J.D. [A Ryan,R.J.&D.]
Van Benschoten, Birney M. '12 '35 C&L.477 A.B., J.D.
(adm. in MI; not adm. in CT) 59 Courtland Ave.‡
van Hulst, Joshua W. ... '66 '92 C.321 A.B. L.902 J.D. [A Paul,H.J.&W.]
*PRACTICE AREAS: Commercial Litigation.
Van Riet, Frank M. ... '33 '62 C.708 B.A. L.904 LL.B. Amer. Cyanamid Co. (Pat.)
Vasta, Donald J. ... '— '95 C.690 B.S. L.1040 J.D. Tax Coun., Exam., GE Capital Corp.
Volper, Vicki E. ... '55 '82 C.1044 B.A. L.94 J.D. [A Pillsbury W.]
Volpintesta, Louis, Jr., (BV) ... '53 '79 C.838 B.A. L.734 J.D. 1200 Summer St.
Vona, Jeffrey M. ... '67 '98 C.645 B.S.C.E. L.884 J.D. [A Jackson L.S.&K.]
*PRACTICE AREAS: Employment Law; Labor Law.
von Schilling, Julia, (CV) '51 '78 C.319 B.A. L.823 J.D.
832 Bedford Street, 06901
Telephone: 203-356-0011 Fax: 203-363-0199
Email: attyjvs@aol.com URL: http://www.lawyers.com/family_law
Family Law, Divorce, Child Custody, Domestic Relations, Alimony, Child Support, Commercial Litigation, Estate Planning, Wills and Trusts.
See Professional Biographies, STAMFORD, CONNECTICUT
Wachsstock, Suzanne E. ... '69 '94 C&L.309 A.B., J.D. [A Wiggin&D.]
Wagner, Martin S. '36 '61 C.994 B.A. L.178 LL.B.
Assoc. Gen. Coun., Corp. Fin. & Ventures, Xerox Corp.
*RESPONSIBILITIES: General Corporation Law; Corporate; Securities; Finance; Executive Compensation.
Wagshul, Karen ... '66 '95 C.813 B.A. L.809 J.D. [A Cummings&L.]
Wake, See, Dimes & Bryniczka
(See Westport)
Wallace, Robert A. '27 '62 L.904 LL.B.
(adm. in DC; not adm. in CT) 800 Long Ridge Rd.
Wallman, David M., (BV) '45 '70 C.659 A.B. L.184 J.D.
750 Summer Street, 06901-1020
Telephone: 203-348-7709 Fax: 203-357-1445
Email: wallmanlaw1@aol.com URL: http://www.lawyers.com/wallmanlaw
Of Counsel: Sally J. Boynton.
Business Litigation, Shareholder Lawsuits, Partnership Dissolution, Bankruptcy Litigation, Loan Workouts, Trials and Appeals in all State and Federal Courts.
Affiliate Office: Studio Legale Penta Ed Associati, via G. Puccini, 2, 1-20121, Milan, Italy. Telephone: +39-02-72020070.
See Professional Biographies, STAMFORD, CONNECTICUT
Wallman, Nathaniel B. '57 '80 C.659 B.A. L.94 J.D.
Coun. & Actuarial Specialist, Cologne Life Reins. Co.
Walser, Joni L. '59 '87 C&L.575 B.A., J.D.
(adm. in MA; not adm. in CT) Sr. Tax Coun., GE Capital
Walsh, David J., (BVⓉ) '49 '74 C.177 B.A. L.966 J.D.
(adm. in WI; not adm. in CT)
Exec. V.P., Corp. Coun. & Secy., Swiss RE Life & Health Amer. Inc.

Walsh, Ronald E. ....'40 '67 C.563 B.B.A. L.724 LL.B. V.P., Citizens Utilities Co.
Walworth, Carla R., (BV) ....'57 '85 C.976 B.S. L.184 J.D. [Paul,H.J.&W.]
*PRACTICE AREAS: Employment Law; Employee Benefits; Employment Discrimination; Age Discrimination; Wrongful Termination.
Ward, William W., (CV) ....'55 '81 C.1030 B.A. L.128 J.D. 1234 Summer St.
Warman, Ray, (AVⓉ) '48 '74 C.976 B.A. L.659 J.D.
(adm. in NY; not adm. in CT)
Sr. V.P. & Assoc. Gen. Coun., GE Capital Aviation Services, Inc.
Warner, Kathleen D. ....'64 '93 C.228 A.B. L.1009 J.D. [Ⓒ Day,B.&H.]
*PRACTICE AREAS: Litigation.

Warren, Elliot R.
(See Westport)

Wasserman, Philip M. '52 '79 C.569 B.A. L.564 J.D.
(adm. in NY; not adm. in CT) Tax Coun., General Signal Corp.
Watson, Gary W. '58 '87 C.494 B.A. L.1035 J.D.
(adm. in MN; not adm. in CT) Sr. Tax Coun., GE Capital Corp.
Watts, Roger H. ....'32 '69 C.350 B.S. L.184 J.D. Counsel, Rayonier Inc.‡
Webber, Don L. '57 '88 C.870 B.S. L.665 J.D.
(adm. in PA; not adm. in CT) Senior Patent Counsel, Xerox Corporation
Weinbaum, George ....'45 '72 C.102 B.A. L.564 J.D. [Ⓒ Rosenblum&T.]
Weinberger, Steven ....'64 '94 C.918 B.A. L.1398 J.D. [Ⓐ Shipman&G.]
*PRACTICE AREAS: Real Estate.
Weiner, Daniel P., (BV) ....'52 '77 C.860 B.A. L.1019 J.D. 24 Hoyt Street
Weiner, Elissa A. '68 '94 C.569 B.A. L.978 J.D.
(adm. in NY; not adm. in CT) [Ⓐ Cohn B.&S.]
Weinstein, Seymour N., (BV) ....'35 '63 C.976 B.A. L.184 LL.B. 671 Bedford St.

Weinstein, Weiner, Ignal, Napolitano & Shapiro, P.C.
(See Bridgeport)

Weisbard, James M. ....'66 '90 C.31 B.A. L.228 J.D. [Ⓐ Schatz&S.R.&K.]
Weiss, Edward A., (AV) ....'56 '82 C.821 B.A. L.813 J.D. [Finn D.&H.]
*PRACTICE AREAS: Banking Law; Lending Law; Corporate Law.
Weiss, Eric M. '55 '85 C.569 B.S. L.228 J.D.
(adm. in NY; not adm. in CT) Chief Operating Officer, iSolve Incorporated
Weiss, Tobias '18 '41 C.563 B.S.S. L.178 LL.B.
(adm. in NY; not adm. in CT) 130 Revonah Ave.‡
Weiss, William O. ....'56 '81 C.918 B.A. L.1119 J.D. Sr. Oper. Coun., Hexcel Corp.
*RESPONSIBILITIES: General Corporate Law.
Weitzel, William C., Jr. '35 '61 C&L.309 A.B., LL.B.
(adm. in DC; not adm. in CT) [Cummings&L.]
*PRACTICE AREAS: Litigation.

Welby, Brady & Greenblatt, LLP
(See White Plains, New York)

Weldon, Christopher B. ....'64 '90 C.128 B.A. L.180 J.D. [Ⓐ Lustig&B.]
*PRACTICE AREAS: Insurance Agents and Brokers Errors and Omissions; Civil Litigation and Trials.
Wells, Douglas J. ....'49 '77 C.882 B.A. L.1202 J.D. 111 Prospect Street
Wendell, Peg '— '96 C.209 B.A. L.365 J.D.
(adm. in IL; not adm. in CT) [ACNielsen]
*RESPONSIBILITIES: Contracts; Corporate.
Werner, Stacy Lynn ....'70 '96 C.1349 B.A. L.1202 J.D. [Ⓐ Benjamin&G.]
Wexton, Jane L. '43 '84 C.563 B.A. L.1019 J.D.
(adm. in NY; not adm. in CT)
Mng. Dir., Global Compliance, GE Capital Global Consumer Finance, Ltd.
Whitcomb, Jonathan P. ....'64 '90 C.319 B.A. L.1202 J.D. [Diserio M.O.&C.]
*PRACTICE AREAS: Commercial Litigation; Insurance Coverage; Insurance Defense; Intellectual Property; Personal Injury.
White, Barbara Glass '52 '79 C.66 B.A. L.178 J.D.
(adm. in NY; not adm. in CT) 2nd V.P. & Asst. Gen. Coun., Gen. Reinsurance Corp.
*RESPONSIBILITIES: Internet; E-Commerce and Technology; Intellectual Property; Reinsurance; Litigation.
White, Rebecca E. '65 '88 C.999 L.978 J.D.
(adm. in NJ; not adm. in CT) UBS AG
Whiteman, Mary Ellen C. ....'51 '84 C.690 B.S.N. L.831 J.D. [Ⓐ Cummings&L.]
Whitmyer, Wesley W., Jr. ....'63 '88 C.611 B.A. L.608 J.D. [St. Onge S.J.&R.] (Pat.)
*PRACTICE AREAS: Patent Law; Computer Law; Litigation.
Whittle, Jack J. '63 '89 C.174 B.A. L.823 J.D.
V.P. & Asst. Gen. Coun.; Gen. Reinsurance Corp.
*RESPONSIBILITIES: Insurance Regulatory.
Wice, Alison Jacobs ....'70 '97 C.659 B.A. L.1365 J.D. [Ⓐ Cummings&L.]
*PRACTICE AREAS: Labor; Employment.
Wicker, Cynthia '52 '77 C.808 B.A. L.1068 J.D.
(adm. in CA; not adm. in CT) 55 Ethan Allen Ln.
Widland, Michael L., (AV) ....'40 '65 C.28 B.A. L.94 LL.B. [Shipman&G.]
*PRACTICE AREAS: Business Reorganizations; Corporate Law and Commercial Financing; Public Transportation; Public Contract Law.

Wiggin & Dana LLP, (AV) ⓑⓥ
400 Atlantic Street, P.O. Box 110325, 06901-3234 ⊙
Telephone: 203-363-7600 Telefax: 203-363-7676
URL: http://www.wiggin.com
Members of Firm: James F. Farrington, Jr. (Resident); Leonard Leader (Resident); David B. Fein (Resident); William A. Perrone (Resident); Michael Grundei (Resident); Patricia Kavee Melick (Resident); William J. Speranza (Resident); Mark E. Haranzo; Lawrence Peikes; James H. Bicks (Resident). Resident Senior Counsel: Robert M. McAnerney (Resident). Associates: Elizabeth Anne Bloomfield (Resident); Julie Min Chayet (Resident); Jeffrey John Danile (Resident); W. Bruce DelMonico (Resident); Jody L. DeStefanis (Resident); Jesse M. Furman (Not admitted in CT); Sara A. Goldberg (Not admitted in CT); Naomi B. Graubard; Russell G. Kauff (Resident); William James Kelleher, III (Resident); Clement J. Naples; Janie L. Treanor (Resident); Suzanne E. Wachsstock (Resident).
Antitrust and Trade Regulation, Appellate, Automotive Industry Law, Banking and Financial Services, Bankruptcy Law, Biotechnology Law, Civil Litigation, Closely Held Business, Cogeneration, Construction Law, Employee Benefits and ERISA Law, Environmental Law, Estate Planning and Settlement Law, Franchise Law, Governmental Affairs, Health Care, Hospital Law, Institutional Finance, Insurance Coverage Litigation, Intellectual Property, Internal Corporate Investigations and White Collar Criminal Defense Law, International Transactions, Labor Law, Litigation, Long Term Care Facilities and Financing, Mental Health Law, Mergers and Acquisitions, National and Regional Litigation Counsel, Partnerships and Joint Ventures, Patent Prosecution and Litigation, Professional Malpractice Litigation, Public Finance, Public Utilities, Real Estate Leasing, Development and Finance, Secured Transactions, Securities Regulation, State and Federal Tax Law, Tax Exempt Organizations, Technology Licensing, Telecommunications, Trademarks and Copyright, Trust and Estates Administration, Venture Capital and Zoning.
New Haven, Connecticut Office: One Century Tower, P.O. Box 1832. Telephone: 203-498-4400. Telefax: 203-782-2889.
Hartford, Connecticut Office: One CityPlace. Telephone: 860-297-3700. Telefax: 860-525-9380.
Berwyn, Pennsylvania Office: 1055 Westlake Drive. Telephone: 610-727-4153. Telefax: 610-727-4085.
Cherry Hill, New Jersey Office: 402 Park Boulevard North, 08802. Telephone: 856-662-3331. Telefax: 856-662-1783.
See Professional Biographies, STAMFORD, CONNECTICUT

Wiggins, Rosalind Z. '59 '84 C.976 B.A. L.813 J.D.
Assistant General Counsel, Pitney Bowes Inc.

Wiles, Edward J., Jr. '48 '75 C.567 B.A. L.1065 J.D.
(adm. in CA; not adm. in CT) V.P. & Chief Compl. Off., GE Investment Servs., Inc.
Wilhelm, Gayle Brian, (AV) ....'36 '64 C&L.309 A.B., LL.B. [Cummings&L.]
*PRACTICE AREAS: Estate Settlement; Trust Administration; Probate Litigation; Estate Planning; Tax Planning.
Williams, Margaret A. '— '93 C.696 B.A. L.477 J.D.
(adm. in NY; not adm. in CT) Trademark & Copyright Coun., Xerox Corporation

Willinger, Willinger & Bucci, P.C.
(See Bridgeport)

Wilmer, Antje '66 '91 C.228 B.A. L.276 J.D.
Region Coun., GE Capital Commercial Finance, Inc.
Wilson, W. Weldon '61 '86 C.16 B.A. L.880 J.D.
(adm. in TX; not adm. in CT)
Exec. V.P. & Gen. Coun., Life Reassurance Corp. of Amer.
Windels Marx Lane & Mittendorf, LLP
Six Landmark Square (⊙Bonita Springs, FL; New Brunswick, Princeton, NJ; New York, NY)
Winter, Gene S., (AV) ....'50 '75 C.112 B.S. L.188 J.D. [St. Onge S.J.&R.] (Pat.)
*PRACTICE AREAS: Patent Law; Trademark Law; Copyright Law; Antitrust Law; Unfair Competition Law.
Witlin, Eric H. ....'67 '92 C.1029 B.A. L.823 J.D. 1177 High Ridge Rd.
Witmer, Melinda C. '61 '88 C.37 B.S. L.659 J.D.
(adm. in CA; not adm. in CT)
Asst. Gen. Coun., Programming/Corp., Time Warner Cable (⊙New York, NY)
Wiznitzer, Jane T. '51 '78 C.1036 A.B. L.178 J.D.
(adm. in NY; not adm. in CT)
Vice President, Legal Affairs & Secretary, Trenwick Group, Inc.
Wocl, Nicholas E., (BV) ....'59 '84 C.676 B.A. L.1029 J.D. [Tooher&W.] ⊙

Wofsey, Rosen, Kweskin & Kuriansky, LLP, (AV) ⓑⓥ
600 Summer Street, 06901
Telephone: 203-327-2300 Fax: 203-967-9273
URL: http://www.wrkk.com
Members of Firm: Abraham Wofsey (1915-1944); Michael Wofsey (1927-1951); David M. Rosen (1926-1967); Julius B. Kuriansky (1952-1992); Sydney C. Kweskin (1946-1998); Monroe Silverman; Howard C. Kaplan; Edward M. Kweskin; David M. Cohen; Marshall Goldberg; Stephen A. Finn; Judith Rosenberg; Mark H. Henderson; Steven D. Grushkin; Matthew J. Forstadt; Steven M. Frederick; Eric M. Higgins. Of Counsel: Saul Kwartin; Emanuel Margolis; Anthony R. Lorenzo. Counsel: Joseph M. Pankowski, Jr.; Day R. Shields. Associates: William M. Davoren; John A. Farnsworth; Daniel M. Young; Christian Rollow Haave; Alex K. Sherman (Not admitted in CT).
General Practice in all Courts. Civil and Criminal Litigation, Real Estate, Corporation, Family, Bankruptcy, Taxation, Estate Planning and Probate Law.
Representative Clients: Banque Paribas; Benenson Realty; Cellular Information Systems, Inc.; The Chase Manhattan Bank; First County Bank; Hartford Provision Co.; Louis Dreyfus Corp.; Norwalk Federation of Teachers; People's Bank; Ridgeway Shopping Center.
See Professional Biographies, STAMFORD, CONNECTICUT

Wofsy, Scott D. ....'67 '92 C.273 B.S.M.E. L.564 J.D. [Cummings&L.] (Pat.)
*PRACTICE AREAS: Patent Prosecution; Patent Litigation; Intellectual Property.
Wolf, Michael L. ....'— '00 C.867 B.A. L.312 J.D. [Ⓐ Blair&P.]
*PRACTICE AREAS: Estate Planning; Estate Settlements; Trust Administration.
Wolfman, June D. ....'61 '94 C.178 B.A. L.978 J.D. [Ⓐ Schatz&S.R.&K.]
Wonneberger, Robert M., (BV) ....'59 '84 C.184 B.A. L.659 J.D. [Shipman&G.]
*PRACTICE AREAS: Commercial Law; Commercial and Mortgage Lending; Loan Workouts and Debt Restructures; Real Estate.
Woodhouse, D. Christine '63 '91 C.813 B.A. L.893 J.D.
(adm. in NY; not adm. in CT) [Ⓐ Curtis,M.C.&M.]
*PRACTICE AREAS: International Finance.
Woods-King, Cathleen A. '63 '90 C.94 B.A. L.309 J.D.
(adm. in NY; not adm. in CT) Sr. Tax Coun., Pitney Bowes, Inc.
Wunsch, Paulette ....'61 '87 C.145 B.A. L.978 J.D. [Ⓒ Day,B.&H.]
*PRACTICE AREAS: Government Investigations; Federal Criminal Law; Criminal Taxation; Health Care Fraud.

Wynn, Mary Ellen, (AV) '46 '73 C&L.608 B.A., J.D.
1150 Summer Street, 06905-5530
Telephone: 203-356-1355 Fax: 203-356-9412
Email: mew1150@aol.com URL: http://www.lawyers.com/maryellenwynn
Associate: Leah Pavetti Hogan.
Domestic Relations, Matrimonial Law, Family Law, Divorce, Child Custody.
See Professional Biographies, STAMFORD, CONNECTICUT

Wynter, Ray A. ....'74 '01 C.309 M.A. L.262 J.D. [Ⓐ Day,B.&H.]
Xylas, George M. ....'58 '85 C.823 B.S. L.564 J.D. [Xylas&Assoc.]
*PRACTICE AREAS: Commercial Leasing; Real Estate; Mortgages; Loan Restructuring; Admiralty and Maritime Law.

Xylas & Associates, LLP
Clearwater House, 2187 Atlantic Street, 9th Floor, 06902 ⊙
Telephone: 203-348-5433 203-961-1183
Email: xylaslaw@mindspring.com URL: http://www.lawyers.com/xylaslaw
George M. Xylas.
Real Estate, Business Law, Corporate Law, Loans, Mortgages, Admiralty and Maritime Law.
New York Office: 11 East 44th Street, Suite 901, 10017. Telephone: 212-490-9352. Fax: 212-490-0502. E Mail: mail@xylaslaw.com.
See Professional Biographies, STAMFORD, CONNECTICUT

Yankovich, John '57 '96 C.667 M.S.E.E. L.1040 J.D.
(adm. in NY; not adm. in CT; See Pat. Sect.) [Ⓐ Ohlandt,G.R.&P.]
Yeomans, Ronald R. ....'62 '90 C.184 B.A. L.615 J.D. 69 Webb Ave.
Yonkman, Fredrick A. '30 '58 C.323 B.A. L.145 J.D.
(adm. in NY; not adm. in CT) 925 Rock Rimmon Rd.
Younes, Steven J. ....'66 '91 C.509 B.A. L.1029 J.D. [Ⓐ Epstein B.&G.]
*PRACTICE AREAS: Labor and Employment Law; Litigation.
Young, Carol K. ....'53 '80 C&L.421 B.A., J.D. [Schatz&S.R.&K.]
Young, Daniel M. ....'70 '95 C.188 B.S. L.569 J.D. [Ⓐ Wofsey,R.K.&K.]
*PRACTICE AREAS: Civil Litigation; Employment Law.
Young, Gaydell '53 '79 C.914 B.A. L.569 J.D.
(adm. in NY; not adm. in CT) Merrill Lynch Realty, Inc.
Young, Joyce H. ....'55 '84 C.174 B.S.B.A. L.262 J.D. [Ⓐ Finn D.&H.]
*PRACTICE AREAS: Commercial Litigation.
Young, Sheryl A. ....'67 '94 C.165 B.A. L.569 J.D. [Ⓐ Finn D.&H.]
*PRACTICE AREAS: Corporate Law; Mergers and Acquisitions; Securities.
Young, Wilford R. '10 '41 C.336 B.S. L.262 J.D.
(adm. in NY; not adm. in CT) [Ⓒ Finn D.&H.]
Yudain, Ted, (BV) ....'46 '73 C.354 B.A. L.724 J.D. 109 White Birch Lane
Yules, Robert B., (BV) ....'52 '78 C.611 B.A. L.851 J.D. [Yules&Y.] ⊙
*PRACTICE AREAS: Drugs and Medical Devices; Insurance Law; Products Liability; Professional Malpractice; Transportation.

Yules & Yules, LLC, (BV)
P.O. Box 522, 06904-0522 ⊙
Telephone: 203-327-9200
Email: yuleslaw@yuleslaw.com
Robert B. Yules.

(This Listing Continued)

Yules & Yules, LLC (Continued)

Trial Practice, Automobile, Mobile Carrier, Bad Faith, Corporate Business Torts, Drug and Medical Device Litigation, Fraud, Insurance, Products Liability, Professional Malpractice, Transportation, Workers' Compensation Law, Securities Arbitration and Financial Institutions Litigation.
Representative Clients: Aetna Casualty and Surety Co.; Allstate Insurance Co.; Nationwide Insurance Co.; Transamerica Insurance Group; Zurich-American Insurance Cos.
Hartford, Connecticut Office: P.O. Box 230278, 06123-0278. Telephone: 860-724-5815.
New Haven, Connecticut Office: 195 Church Street, Seventeenth Floor. 06510. Telephone: 203-789-1000. Fax: 203-789-6320.
New York, N.Y. Office: Grand Central Station, P.O. Box 4419. 10163-4419. Telephone: 203-327-9200.
See Professional Biographies, STAMFORD, CONNECTICUT

Zabel, David B., (AV) '57 '82 C.103 A.B. L.893 J.D. [Cohen&W.] (⊙Bridgeport, Westport)
*PRACTICE AREAS: Employment; Civil Litigation; Bankruptcy.
Zaken, Marc L., (BV) '58 '83 C.188 B.S. L.569 J.D. [Cummings&L.]
*PRACTICE AREAS: Labor Law; Employment Law.
Zambelli, Carolyn J. '74 '99 C.93 B.A. L.184 J.D. [Ⓐ Shipman&G.]
*PRACTICE AREAS: Real Estate; Corporate Law.
Zanfini, Maria L. '61 '88 C.183 B.A. L.1009 J.D. (adm. in NY; not adm. in CT) V.P. & Legal Coun., Memberworks, Inc.
*RESPONSIBILITIES: Litigation; Compliance; Regulatory Matters; Privacy.
Zeitlin, Andrew M. '68 '94 C.1036 B.A. L.659 J.D. [Ⓐ Shipman&G.]
*PRACTICE AREAS: Commercial Litigation.
Zeller, Michael R. '46 '75 C.994 B.S. L.724 J.D. [Epstein B.&G.] (⊙New York, NY)
*PRACTICE AREAS: Labor and Employment Law.
Zellmer, Jill A. G. '63 '89 C.66 B.A. L.978 J.D. Region Coun., GE Capital Comm. Fin.
Zezima, Donald F., (BV) '27 '53 C&L.94 B.S., LL.B. [Macrides,Z.&C.]
Zibelli, Ronald '34 '62 C.688 B.Mgt.Eng. L.276 J.D. (adm. in NY; not adm. in CT; Pat.) 800 Long Ridge Rd.
Ziehl, Catherine C., (BV) '57 '86 C.518 B.A. L.184 J.D. 184 Atlantic St.
Zimmer, Janet R. '49 '75 C.228 A.B. L.276 J.D. (adm. in DC; not adm. in CT) Exec. Dir., Warburg Dillon Read LLC NYC
Zimmerman, Jeffrey M. '59 '85 C.197 A.B. L.178 J.D. (adm. in NY; not adm. in CT) Asst. Gen. Coun., Timer Warner Cable
Zimmermann, Victor L., Jr., (AV) '52 '78 C.321 B.A. L.262 J.D. [Curtis,M.C.&M.]
*PRACTICE AREAS: Emerging Company Financings; Securities Litigation; Investment Partnerships; Financial Services Regulation.
Ziotas, Angelo A., (BV) '64 '91 C.183 B.A. L.184 J.D. [Ⓐ Silver,G.&T.]
*PRACTICE AREAS: Medical Malpractice; Product Liability; Negligence.
Zitter, Hillary Esbit, (BV) '48 '73 C.477 B.A. L.1009 J.D. 41 East Lane
Zlatkin, Lawrence J. '61 '86 C.012 B.A. L.145 J.D. (adm. in IL; not adm. in CT) Sr. Tax Coun., GE Capital Corp.
Zone & Bernstein, (BV) 123 Prospect Street
Zopfi, Gerard D. '56 '81 C.93 B.S. L.1292 J.D. (adm. in NJ; not adm. in CT) Hynes, Himmelreich, Glennon & Co.
Zuckert, Owen M. '32 '56 C.95 A.B. L.178 J.D. 67 W. Haviland Lane (⊙New York, NY)
Zyskowski, Lori Iannotti '71 '96 C.309 A.B. L.178 J.D. [Ⓐ Pillsbury W.]

STONINGTON, 1,100, *New London Co.*

Banister, Patience O. '45 '75 C.681 B.A. L.1019 J.D. 93 Flanders Rd.‡
Clegg, Alicia J. '55 '82 C.822 A.B. L.692 J.D. (adm. in WV; not adm. in CT) 48 Cove Side Lane‡
Delmhorst, Michele H. Jones, (BV) '49 '84 C.706 B.A. L.262 J.D. 173 Elm St.
Hinchey, Joseph M. '25 '80 C.867 B.S.E.E. L.93 J.D. (adm. in MA; not adm. in CT) 194 Wamphassuc Rd.‡
Huebner, Gary W. '67 '95 C.184 B.A. L.1048 J.D. 117 Water St. #7
Palmer, Richard C., Jr. '64 '91 C.999 B.A. L.1048 J.D. 224 Cove Rd.
Viering, Peter B. '51 '77 C.699 B.A. L.362 J.D. 158-B Water St.
Weeks, Louis S., Jr., (AVⓉ) '18 '47 C.674 A.B. L.178 LL.B. (adm. in NY; not adm. in CT) 12 Grand St.

STONY CREEK, —, *New Haven Co.*

Stamler, Joseph H. '11 '37 C.188 A.B. L.705 LL.B. (adm. in NJ; not adm. in CT) 14 Long Point Rd.‡

STORRS, 10,691, *Tolland Co.*

Bacon, Stephen M., (BV) '50 '75 C.103 A.B. L.184 J.D. 569 Middle Tpke.
Fox, Karla H. '46 '71 C&L.228 B.A., J.D. Univ. of Conn.
Hauslaib, Mark C., (BV) '46 '81 C.184 B.A. L.1048 J.D. 11 Russett Lane
Hill, George E. '36 '63 C.1030 B.S.S. L.184 LL.B. Univ. of Conn.
Mason, Deborah M. '59 '89 C.705 B.A. L.776 J.D. 1733 Storrs Rd.
Masterton, Reynold Peter '58 '83 C.550 B.A. L.184 J.D. 1 Ridge Rd.★
O'Conor, Suzanne M. '— '99 C.321 B.A. L.184 J.D. 2390 Alumni Drive, U-206
Reynolds, Richard R. '29 '54 C.309 A.B. L.477 J.D. (adm. in IL; not adm. in CT) Univ. of Conn.
Ritchings, Jon M. '44 '83 C.165 A.B. L.1048 J.D. 16 Fern Rd.
Schrager, Samuel L., (BV) '49 '74 C.156 B.A. L.472 J.D. 1733 Storrs Rd.
Shapiro, Paul M., (BV) '49 '74 C&L.930 B.A., J.D. Asst. Atty. Gen.
Taylor, Michael M. '44 '84 C.184 B.S. L.362 J.D. 12 Stone Mill Rd.

STRATFORD, 50,541, *Fairfield Co.*

Ahlberg, Kurt M., (BV) '52 '78 C.1030 B.A. L.184 J.D.
2885 Main Street, 06614
Telephone: 203-377-1311 Fax: 203-378-6756
***PRACTICE AREAS: Aged and Aging; Trusts and Estates; Probate; Real Estate; Wills.**
Real Estate, Probate, Trusts and Estates, Wills, Personal Injury, Zoning, Planning and Land Use.
See Professional Biographies, STRATFORD, CONNECTICUT

Ambrogio, Charles S., (BV) '48 '82 C.4 B.A. L.1029 J.D. [Ambrogio P.&Assoc.]
Ambrogio Pletter & Associates, (BV) 2019 Main Street
Aspinwall, James H., (BV) '30 '55 C.1030 B.A. L.184 J.D. 3200 Main St.
Barry, James E., Jr. '47 '73 C.321 A.B. L.184 J.D. V.P., Jim Barry Oldsmobile-Cadillac
Bashar, John P., (BV) '49 '73 C.1030 B.S. L.215 J.D. 2051 Main St.
Battaglia, Thomas V., Jr., (CV) '59 '84 C.1030 B.S. L.1040 J.D. 3267 Main St.
Beck, Dana K. '65 '92 C.1044 B.A. L.1252 J.D. [Beck&B.]
*PRACTICE AREAS: Business Law.
Beck, Kenneth A. '65 '91 C.1044 B.A. L.1029 J.D. [Beck&B.] ⊙
*PRACTICE AREAS: Civil Litigation; Intellectual Properties Law; Business Law.

Beck and Beck, LLC
83 Booth Street, 06614 ⊙
Telephone: 203-375-2222 Fax: 203-378-5263
URL: http://www.ctbecklaw.com
Members of Firm: Dana K. Beck; Kenneth A. Beck.
General Civil Litigation
New York, New York Office: 67 Will Street, Suite 2211, 10005-3198.
See Professional Biographies, STRATFORD, CONNECTICUT

Berlin, Patricia, (BV) '49 '85 C.994 B.A. L.1029 J.D. 3288 Main St.
Biafore, Joseph L., Jr. '27 '59 C.1029 B.S. L.1009 LL.B. 1825 Barnum Ave.
Biagiarelli, Lisa Anne P. '64 '89 C.1030 B.A. L.184 J.D. Town Collector of Rev.
Bigley, John F., (BV) '30 '56 C.1030 B.S. L.93 J.D. [Bigley&R.]
Bigley & Rosati, (BV) 3241 Main St.
Bishop, Timothy A., (BV) '61 '89 C&L.184 B.A., J.D. [Bishop&J.]
Bishop & Jackson, LLC, (BV) 80 Ferry Blvd., Ste. 103
Blake, Kevin M., (CV) '60 '85 C.676 B.A. L.61 J.D. [Shepro&B.]
Blando, Frank P., (BV) '42 '85 C.1156 B.S. L.1029 J.D. 972 E. Broadway
Bortolot, Richard V., Jr '46 '92 C.184 B.A. L.1029 J.D. [Bortolot&L.]
Bortolot & LaBrecque 3005 Main St.
Bougie, Roger M. '33 '62 C.550 B.A. L.93 LL.B. 6900 Main Street‡
Bowles, William R. '40 '69 C&L.734 B.S., J.D. Assoc. Gen. Coun., Sikorsky Aircraft
Brady, Edward P., III, (BV) '64 '89 C.184 B.S. L.818 J.D. [Coyne,v.B.&F.]
*PRACTICE AREAS: Litigation.
Broder, Matthew J. '67 '92 C.184 B.A. L.306 J.D. 2563 Main Street
Brown, Ridgely W., (BV) '46 '77 C&L.446 B.A., J.D. [Shepro&B.]
Chaplowe, M. Lewis, (BV) '34 '59 C.67 A.B. L.178 J.D. 120 Lantern Rd.
Connolly, James M., (BV) '51 '82 C&L.1029 B.A., J.D. [Rodie&C.]
Corcoran, Patrick J. '60 '90 C.93 B.A. L.724 J.D. Sr. Atty., Sikorsky Aircraft Corporation (Legal Department)
Coughlin, Thomas B., (BV) '11 '39 C.197 B.A. L.976 J.D. [Coughlin&C.]
Coughlin, Thomas C., (BV) '52 '77 C.855 B.A. L.818 J.D. [Coughlin&C.]
Coughlin & Coughlin, (BV) 1980 Main St.
Cousins, Donald C., (AV) '30 '55 C.855 B.A. L.309 J.D. [Cousins,J.&D.]
*PRACTICE AREAS: Workers' Compensation Law; Personal Injury Law; Trials Law.

Cousins, Johnson & Desrosiers, P.C., (AV)
2563 Main Street, 06615
Telephone: 203-386-1433 Fax: 203-386-9714
URL: http://www.lawyers.com/cousins&johnson
Donald C. Cousins; Norma S. Johnson; Albert E. Desrosiers; Patricia A. Morrissey;—Lawrence F. Morizio.
Language: Spanish
Workers' Compensation, Personal Injury, Trials, Real Estate, Probate.
See Professional Biographies, STRATFORD, CONNECTICUT

Coyne, James E., (AV) '49 '74 C.860 B.A. L.818 J.D. [Coyne,v.B.&F.]
*PRACTICE AREAS: Products Liability Litigation; Professional Liability Litigation; Municipal Liability; Commercial Law; Professional Injury Claims.
Coyne, Kevin S. '64 '92 C.184 B.A. L.1029 J.D. [Coyne,v.B.&F.]
*PRACTICE AREAS: Civil Litigation; Real Estate.

Coyne, von Kuhn, Brady & Fries, L.L.C., (AV)
999 Oronoque Lane, 06614
Telephone: 203-378-7100 Fax: 203-378-7711
Email: coynevkbf@snet.net URL: http://www.lawyers.com/coynevkbf
James E. Coyne; Philip F. von Kuhn; Edward P. Brady III; Colleen D. Fries; Kevin S. Coyne; Robert Philip Murphy.
Civil Litigation Practice including Personal Injury, Products Liability, Municipal Liability, Real Estate.
See Professional Biographies, STRATFORD, CONNECTICUT

Crossland, Roger L. '48 '77 C.178 A.B. L.262 J.D. [Shepro&B.]
Desrosiers, Albert E., (BV) '54 '84 C.184 B.A. L.1048 J.D. [Cousins,J.&D.]
*PRACTICE AREAS: Workers' Compensation Law; Personal Injury Law; Trial Law.
DiCicco, Margaret C. '61 '89 C.102 B.A. L.1029 J.D. 1825 Barnum Ave.
Dicicco, Mary '61 '89 C.102 B.A. L.1029 J.D. (adm. in NY; not adm. in CT) 1825 Barnum Avenue

Diserio Martin O'Connor & Castiglioni LLP
(See Stamford)

Drum, Joseph F. '50 '80 C.999 B.A. L.1029 J.D. Lawyers Title Ins. Corp.
Florek, John A., (BV) '51 '77 C.1029 B.A. L.184 J.D. [Florek&O.]
Florek & O'Neill, (BV) 2885 Main St.
Flynn, Richard J. '39 '85 C.869 B.S. L.1029 J.D. Dir., Sikorsky Aircraft
Framularo, Nicholas G., (BV) '51 '76 C.276 B.S. L.209 J.D. 3380 Main St.
Fries, Colleen D. '56 '93 C.1030 B.S. L.184 J.D. [Coyne,v.B.&F.]
*PRACTICE AREAS: Civil Litigation; Municipal Law.
Ganim, Davis W., (BV) '34 '62 C.1029 B.A. L.902 LL.B. 2192 Main St.
Ganim, Raymond W., (BV) '23 '47 L.477 LL.B. 2192 Main St.
Gardiner, Clinton L. '56 '86 C.976 B.A. L.1292 J.D. (adm. in PA; not adm. in CT) Dep. Gen. Coun., Sikorsky Aircraft Corp.
Gerety, Thomas C. '22 '59 C.1029 A.B. L.976 LL.B. 302 Bar Harbour Rd.‡
Giarniero, Richard P. '48 '95 C.1211 B.A. L.1252 J.D. 346 Prospect Dr.
Guerrera, Anthony M., (BV) '38 '63 C.321 B.S. L.184 LL.B. 1940 Main St.
Gust, James B. '52 '79 C.453 S.B. L.94 J.D. Merrill Anderson Co., Inc.
Hanley, J. Russell, (BV) '23 '62 C&L.184 B.S., J.D. 155 Peace Acre Lane

Harlow, Adams & Friedman, P.C.
(See Milford)

Harvey, Peter C., (BV) '58 '83 C.103 B.A. L.94 J.D. 1656 Main St.
Hillgen, Jennifer M.F. '73 '98 C.1030 B.A. L.1252 J.D. V.P. & Gen. Coun., Nat. Distrib. Syst., Inc.
Hnath, David M. '54 '84 C.107 B.S. L.1252 J.D. Convenant Tax Serv.
Hopko, Kathleen M. '60 '86 C.1030 B.S. L.184 J.D. V.P. & Gen. Coun., Sikorsky Aircraft Corporation
Ionescu, Istrate, II '50 '88 C.563 M.S.E.E. L.1029 J.D. P.O. Box 697
Jackson, Bruce D., (BV) '62 '89 C.282 B.A. L.1048 J.D. [Bishop&J.]
Jaekle, Robert G., (BV) '51 '76 C&L.184 B.A., J.D. State Auditor
Johnson, Norma S., (BV) '47 '83 C.207 B.A. L.1029 J.D. [Cousins,J.&D.]
*PRACTICE AREAS: Workers' Compensation Law; Personal Injury Law.
Jutila, Edwin J. '55 '85 C&L.184 B.A., J.D. Sr. Atty., Sikorsky Aircraft Corporation (Legal Department)
Kaiser, LLC, (BV) 972 East Broadway
Kaiser, John B., (BV) '64 '91 C.569 B.A. L.30 J.D. [Kaiser]
Kelly, John W., (BV) '35 '83 C.262 B.S. L.1029 J.D. 175 Peace Acre Lane
Knott, Barry C., (BV) '47 '74 C.276 B.S.B.A. L.724 J.D. [Knott&K.]
*PRACTICE AREAS: Real Estate; Zoning Law; Personal Injury.

Knott & Knott, (BV)
1656 Main Street, 06615
Telephone: 203-375-1433 Fax: 203-378-7192
URL: http://www.lawyers.com/knott&knott
Barry C. Knott. Associate: Kathleen M. Krygier.
General Practice. Civil and Criminal Litigation. Real Estate Development, Zoning, Summary Process, Probate, Personal Injury, Workers Compensation, Domestic Relations, Commercial Litigation, Title Opinions. Trials.
See Professional Biographies, STRATFORD, CONNECTICUT

Kochiss, Deborah A., (BV) '49 '83 C.1102 B.S. L.1029 J.D. 3000 Main St.
Krygier, Kathleen M. '71 '96 C.93 B.A. L.128 J.D. [Ⓐ Knott&K.]
*PRACTICE AREAS: Personal Injury; Domestic Relations; Civil Litigation; Workers Compensation.

Kryzanski, Daniel H. . . . . '68 '93 C.94 B.S. L.1202 J.D. 959 Main Street
LaBrecque, Koreen R. . . . . '52 '92 C.1211 B.S. L.1029 J.D. 2288 Main St.

Lange, Paul A., Law Offices of, (AV) '61 '86 C.415 B.A. L.1029 J.D.
2296 Main Street, Suite 2000, 06615-5938 ⊙
Telephone: 203-375-7724 FAX: 203-375-9397
Email: pal@lopal.com URL: http://www.lopal.com
Litigation and Transactions involving Aviation and Commercial Matters, Administrative Law, Insurance Defense and Coverage, Personal Injury, Products Liability, FAA Enforcement Defense and D.O.T. Regulatory Matters, General Civil Trial and Appellate Practice.
New York, N.Y. Office: 885 Third Avenue, Suite 2900. Telephone: 212-385-1215. FAX: 212-608-1215.
See Professional Biographies, STRATFORD, CONNECTICUT

Lennig, Edward N., III '45 '72
C.659 B.S.Econ. L.665 J.D. Sr. Atty., Sikorsky Aircraft Corp.
Little, Margaret A., (AV) . . . . '54 '85 C&L.976 B.A., J.D. 2268 Main St.
Little, Roger Skok . . . . '48 '74 C&L.976 B.A., J.D. 2149 Elm St.
Loew, Ralph S., (BV) . . . . '47 '71 C.645 B.S. L.184 J.D. [Milwe&L.]
Marzik, Robert K., (AV) . . . . '36 '61 C.321 B.A. L.276 LL.B. [R.K.Marzik] ⊙
*PRACTICE AREAS: Admiralty Law; Civil Litigation; Probate Law.

Marzik, Robert K., P.C., Law Offices of, (AV) [BR]
1512 Main Street, 06615-7097 ⊙
Mailing Address: New York, NY 10168-1700
Telephone: 203-375-4803 Telecopier: 203-386-0136
Email: marzikr@aol.com
Robert K. Marzik.
General Practice, Civil Litigation, Admiralty, Maritime, Aviation, Probate and Real Estate Law.
New York, New York Office: 380 Lexington Avenue, Suite 1700, 10168-1700. Telephone: 212-683-2805. Fax: 203-386-0136.
See Professional Biographies, STRATFORD, CONNECTICUT

McCarthy, James B., (BV) . . . . '49 '79 C.569 B.A. L.818 J.D. [Coughlin&C.]
McDonough, Sandra M., (BV) . . . . '39 '82 C.999 B.A. L.1029 J.D. 3333 Main St.
Mehta, Samir '72 '98 C.1200 B.A. L.184 J.D.
Atty., Sikorsky Aircraft Corporation (Legal Department)

Miller, Kent M. '63 '90 C.611 B.A. L.1029 J.D.
250 Rockwell Avenue, 06615
Telephone: 203-380-2161 Fax: 203-386-0432
Email: lexkantiae@aol.com URL: http://www.lawyers.com/kentmillerlaw
***PRACTICE AREAS: Landlord and Tenant Law; Mortgages; Collections.**
Landlord and Tenant Law, Mortgages, Collections.
See Professional Biographies, STRATFORD, CONNECTICUT

Mills, Winfield . . . . '44 '76 C.1159 B.S. L.1048 J.D. 919 Wilcoxson Ave.
Milwe, Jeffrey M., (BV) . . . . '40 '65 C.659 B.A. L.569 J.D. [Milwe&L.]
Milwe and Loew, (BV) . . . . 3638 Main St.
Minton, Richard E., (BV) . . . . '47 '75 C.478 B.A. L.276 J.D. 5725 Main St.

Miron, James R. '65 '94 C.829 B.A. L.1048 J.D.
125 Ferry Boulevard, 06615
Telephone: 203-377-4554
Arbitration.
See Professional Biographies, STRATFORD, CONNECTICUT

Monahan, Eugene J. . . . . '48 '73 C.754 B.S. L.1017 J.D. Sr. Atty., Sikorsky Aircraft
Montlick, Roslyn Z. P., (Mrs.) . . . . '23 '46 C.725 L.184 LL.B. 184/B Apache Ln.‡
Morizio, Lawrence F. . . . . '71 '98 C.705 B.A. L.1252 J.D. [[A] Cousins,J.&D.]
*PRACTICE AREAS: Workers Compensation; Labor and Employment; Personal Injury.
Morrissey, Caroline Nolting '59 '85
C.1030 B.A. L.1040 J.D. Sr. Atty., Sikorsky Aircraft Corporation
Morrissey, Patricia A., (BV) . . . . '63 '90 C.1156 B.S. L.1029 J.D. [Cousins,J.&D.]
*PRACTICE AREAS: Real Estate; Probate; Personal Injury; Premises Liability.
Murphy, Robert Philip . . . . '70 '97 C&L.184 B.A., J.D. [Coyne,v.B.&F.]
*PRACTICE AREAS: Products Liability Litigation; Professional Liability Litigation; Commercial Law; Municipal Liability.
O'Neill, Martin J., (BV) . . . . '53 '79 C.676 B.A. L.425 J.D. [Florek&O.]
O'Rourke, James G. . . . . '37 '80 C.1030 B.S.M.E. L.1252 J.D. 3406 Main St.
O'Rourke, James L. . . . . '58 '88 C&L.1029 B.S., J.D. 1825 Barnum Ave. (⊙Stratford)
O'Rourke, James L. . . . . '58 '88 C&L.1029 B.S., J.D. 1825 Barnum Ave. (⊙Stratford)

Piazza & Pickel
(See Stamford)

Pletter, Timothy M. . . . . '70 '95 C.1036 B.A. L.884 J.D. [[A] Ambrogio P.&Assoc.]
Radke, Terrance J. '44 '82 C.612 B.S. L.150 J.D.
(adm. in MN; not adm. in CT; Pat.) Coun.-Intell. Prop., Sikorsky Aircraft Corporation
Rice, Milton, (AV) . . . . '11 '45 C&L.976 B.A., LL.B. 644A Onondaga Ln.‡
Rodie, Wilfred J., Jr., (BV) . . . . '61 '86 C&L.276 A.B., J.D. [Rodie&C.]

Rodie & Connolly, P.C., (BV)
3380 Main Street, 06614
Telephone: 203-377-1010 Fax: 203-375-0203
Email: cons3380@aol.com URL: http://www.lawyers.com/rodie&connolly
Wilfred J. Rodie, Jr.; James M. Connolly.
Personal Injury, Death Claims, Auto Accidents and Medical Malpractice.
See Professional Biographies, STRATFORD, CONNECTICUT

Rosati, Robert T., (BV) . . . . '63 '88 C.1030 B.S. L.1252 J.D. [Bigley&R.]
Rosati, Thomas J., (BV) . . . . '36 '61 C.1030 B.S.S. L.262 LL.B. [Bigley&R.]
Rust, John B. . . . . '38 '85 C.378 B.A. L.1029 J.D. 2268 Main St.

Sandak Friedman Hennessey & Greco, LLP
(See Stamford)

Saylor, John F., (BV) . . . . '45 '90 C.1073 B.A. L.1029 J.D. 2885 Main St.
Sbriglio, Karen E. . . . . '61 '87 C.1029 B.A. L.184 J.D. 7003 Main St.
Schrandt, Curtis Leon . . . . '57 '97 C.878 B.S. L.1252 J.D. 803 Stratford Ave.
Shapiro, Michael L. . . . . '50 '76 C.1044 B.A. L.184 J.D. 1127 Essex Pl.
Shepro, Daniel, (BV) . . . . '42 '67 C.978 B.A. L.94 LL.B. [Shepro&B.]
Shepro & Brown, LLC, (BV) . . . . 2051 Main Street
Shull, J. Roger, (BV) . . . . '29 '55 C&L.228 A.B., LL.B. 355 Mt. Pleasant Ave.
Siciliano, Joseph A., (BV) . . . . '35 '62 C.1029 B.A. L.94 LL.B. 3333 Main St.
Simpson, Samuel S. . . . . '48 '77 C.184 B.A. L.724 J.D. Merrill Anderson Co., Inc.
Starkey, Patricia A., (BV) . . . . '63 '88 C.1102 B.A. L.1029 J.D. 108 Lighthouse Ave.
Stoddard, Elinor J. . . . . '63 '92 C.103 B.A. L.896 J.D. 17 Kathleen Dr.
Sussman, Everett G. . . . . '65 '90 C.855 B.A. L.1017 J.D. 1485 James Farm Rd.
Timpanelli, Chris A., (BV) . . . . '60 '85 C.945 B.A. L.940 J.D. 140 Peace Acre Ln.
Valentine, Mark C., Law Offices of, (BV) . . . . '48 '74 C.156 B.A. L.184 J.D. 2885 Main St.
von Kuhn, Philip F., (BV) . . . . '59 '85 C.1030 B.A. L.184 J.D. [Coyne,v.B.&F.]
Wnek, Robert E. . . . . '48 '77 C.884 B.S. L.1338 J.D. 3095 Main St.
Zanella, Vincent M., Jr., (BV) . . . . '27 '50 C.1029 A.B. L.184 LL.B. (J.P.)

SUFFIELD, 9,294, *Hartford Co.*

Alfano, Charles T., (AV) . . . . '20 '48 C.184 B.A. L.477 J.D. [[C] Alfano&F.]
*PRACTICE AREAS: Probate; Estate Administration; Planning; Real Estate Law; Corporate Law.
Alfano, Charles T., Jr., (BV) . . . . '59 '84 C.860 B.A. L.421 J.D. [Alfano&F.]
*PRACTICE AREAS: Real Estate; Personal Injury; Criminal Law; Domestic Law; Probate.

Alfano & Flynn, LLC, (BV)
53 Mountain Road, 06078
Telephone: 860-668-0221 Fax: 860-668-5413
Email: afsuffield@aol.com
Members of Firm: Joseph W. Flynn; Charles T. Alfano, Jr. Of Counsel: Charles T. Alfano.
General Practice. Trials, Negligence, Workers Compensation, Real Estate, Probate, Municipal and Corporation Law, Personal Injury and Domestic Law.
Representative Client: First Federal Bank.
See Professional Biographies, SUFFIELD, CONNECTICUT

Callahan, Lawrence '70 '97 C.183 B.A. L.378 J.D.
(adm. in MA; not adm. in CT) 185 N. Main St.
Daley, Timothy A., (BV) . . . . '55 '80 C.1145 B.S. L.1048 J.D. 157 Mountain Rd.
DiGennaro, Robert C. . . . . '47 '76 C.999 B.S. L.1048 J.D. 535 Halladay Ave.
Doran, James A. '52 '85 C.362 B.A. L.896 J.D.
(adm. in NC; not adm. in CT) 1290 East St., N.
Flynn, Joseph W., (BV) . . . . '55 '81 C.184 B.A. L.734 J.D. [Alfano&F.]
*PRACTICE AREAS: Real Estate Law; Personal Injury; Probate; Estate Administration; Planning.
Jentzen, Judith L., (BV) . . . . '— '82 C.399 B.A. L.94 J.D. 203 Suffield Village
Liquori, John J. . . . . '61 '86 C.184 B.A. L.1048 J.D. 93 Spring Lane
Mcananey, Joseph E. . . . . '57 '86 C.321 A.B. L.93 J.D. Suffield Vlg.
Spellman, Victoria . . . . '51 '78 C.518 B.A. L.306 J.D. 66 N. Main St.
Vassallo, Richard A. . . . . '63 '89 C.184 B.S. L.1048 J.D. [Williams&V.]
Williams, Robert J., Jr., (CV) . . . . '63 '89 C.999 B.S. L.1048 J.D. [Williams&V.]
Williams & Vassallo, (CV) . . . . 123 Mountain Rd.
Wyzik, John M., (BV) . . . . '49 '75 C.28 B.A. L.1048 J.D. 178 Mountain Rd.

TARIFFVILLE, 1,337, *Hartford Co.*

Blackford, John D. . . . . '34 '72 C.855 B.A. L.184 J.D. 42 Hayes Rd.

TERRYVILLE, 5,231, *Litchfield Co.*

Boylan, Christopher W. . . . . '57 '88 C.184 B.A. L.1029 J.D. 4 Steven St.

THOMASTON, 6,276, *Litchfield Co.*

Byers, Robert A. . . . . '64 '90 C.659 B.A. L.1292 J.D. 212 S. Main St.
Gilland, Richard D., (BV) . . . . '32 '57 C&L.184 B.A., LL.B. [Gilland,S.&M.]
Gilland, Richard D., Jr., (BV) . . . . '63 '89 C.882 B.S. L.1048 J.D. 97 Main St.
Gilland, Seabourne and Malley, (BV) . . . . 30 Main St.
Lyga, Peter H. . . . . '57 '84 C&L.184 B.A., J.D. 52 Main St.
Malley, Mark D., (BV) . . . . '59 '83 C&L.184 B.A., J.D. [Gilland,S.&M.]
Seabourne, George P., (BV) . . . . '49 '75 C.184 B.A. L.192 J.D. [Gilland,S.&M.]
Westby, Kie, (BV) . . . . '51 '79 C.918 B.A. L.192 J.D. 50 Union St.

THOMPSON, 8,141, *Windham Co.*

McNally, Timothy W., (BV) . . . . '43 '76 C.855 B.A. L.818 J.D. Corp. Coun., BCS Co., Inc.

TOLLAND, 8,141, *Tolland Co.*

Gill, Charles C., (BV) . . . . '55 '91 C.1030 B.S. L.1048 J.D. 6 Stone Pond Dr.
Goodwin, W. Bradford, (CV) . . . . '53 '88 C.999 B.A. L.1048 J.D. [Goodwin&P.]
Goodwin and Paul, (BV) . . . . 62 Hartford Tpke.
King, Robert D. . . . . '12 '58 C.352 B.A. L.976 LL.B. 55 Dimock Rd.‡
Palmer, Peter C., (BV) . . . . '48 '83 C.184 B.A. L.1048 J.D. 412 Hunter Rd.
Paul, JoAnn P., (BV) . . . . '56 '83 C.573 B.S. L.1048 J.D. [Goodwin&P.]

TORRINGTON, 33,687, *Litchfield Co.*

Blondin, Audrey B., (CV) . . . . '53 '80 C.1102 B.S. L.831 J.D. 21 Prospect St., Ste. A
Brower, Charles F., (AV) . . . . '38 '64 C.197 A.B. L.178 LL.B. [Brower&O.]
*PRACTICE AREAS: Civil Litigation; Copyright Infringement; Elder Law; Personal Injury.

Brower & Organschi, (AV)
445 Prospect Street, 06790
Telephone: 860-482-4979 Fax: 860-482-4701 URL: http://www.browerorganschi.com
Email: info@browerorganschi.com URL: http://www.lawyers.com/browerorganschi
Charles F. Brower; Marcus G. Organschi.
See Professional Biographies, TORRINGTON, CONNECTICUT

Conti, William A. . . . . '48 '73 C&L.93 A.B., J.D. [Febbroriello,C.&L.]
Cramer, Milton L. . . . . '28 '55 C.823 B.S. L.94 LL.B. P.O. Box 455
Donahue, Maureen E. . . . . '59 '88 C.1103 B.A. L.184 J.D. 30 Mason St.
Ebersol, Charles R., (AV) . . . . '16 '41 C.311 B.A. L.976 LL.B. [Ebersol&M.]
*PRACTICE AREAS: Estate Planning Law; Probate Law; Banking Law.
Ebersol, Charles R., Jr., (BV) . . . . '52 '77 C.311 B.A. L.880 J.D. [Ebersol&M.]
*PRACTICE AREAS: Real Estate Law; Planning and Zoning Law; Estate Planning Law.

Ebersol & McCormick, LLC, (AV)
24 Mason Street, P.O. Box 598, 06790
Telephone: 860-482-8557 FAX: 860-482-8089
Email: attys.ebersol@snet.net
Members of Firm: Charles R. Ebersol; Charles R. Ebersol, Jr.; Brian McCormick. Associate: Michael Keilty.
General Practice. Estate Planning, Corporation, Real Estate and Banking Law. Trials in all Courts.
Representative Clients: Eagle Federal Savings Bank; Town of Warren; Torrington Honda; WZBG.
See Professional Biographies, TORRINGTON, CONNECTICUT

Febbroriello, John P., (BV) . . . . '42 '67 C&L.184 A.B., J.D. [Febbroriello,C.&L.]
Febbroriello, Conti & Levy, (BV) . . . . 355 Prospect St.
Frauenhofer, David J., (AV) . . . . '41 '67 C.829 B.S. L.184 J.D. [Wall,W.&F.]
Gallicchio, Joseph J., (AV) . . . . '33 '62 C.1145 B.S. L.184 LL.B. [Gallicchio,M.&G.]
Gallicchio, Merati & Griffin, (AV) . . . . 157 Migeon Ave.
Garrity & Jordan, (BV) . . . . 387 Litchfield Street
Gawrych, John A., (BV) . . . . '45 '71 C&L.184 B.A., J.D. [Wall&G.]
Gregg, Jamie Vincent, (BV) '53 '79 C.478 A.B. L.818 J.D.
Pres. & CEO, Colonial Bronze
Griffin, Paul R., (BV) . . . . '51 '78 C.321 B.A. L.229 J.D. [Gallicchio,M.&G.]
Groppo, Ann Marie, (BV) . . . . '51 '89 C.184 B.G.S. L.1029 J.D. 8 Church St.
Gross, Steven R. . . . . '55 '82 C.273 B.A. L.1048 J.D. 179 Doman Dr.

Herbst, Peter C., Law Offices of, (BV) '48 '73 C.903 B.A. L.1294 J.D.
365 Prospect Street, 06790
Telephone: 860-489-9495 Fax: 860-489-5977
Email: pcherbst@imagine.com URL: http://www.lawyers.com/lawofficesofpetercherbst
Land Use Law, Land Development Law, Zoning Law, Wetlands Law, Real Estate Transactions.
References: Shawmut Bank; Northwest Bank for Savings; Winsted Savings Bank.
See Professional Biographies, TORRINGTON, CONNECTICUT

Hudson, John E. . . . . '64 '92 C.823 B.A. L.1194 J.D. P.O. Box 2026
Huntoon, David A., (CV) . . . . '62 '96 C.951 B.A. L.188 J.D. [D.A.Huntoon]
Huntoon, David A., LLC, Law Offices of, (CV) . . . . 30 Mason St.
Jenkins, Bridget G., (BV) . . . . '59 '84 C.1030 B.A. L.184 J.D. [Garrity&J.]
Jones, Gregory S., (BV) . . . . '64 '89 L.1194 J.D. 179 Water St.

Jordan, Susan F., (BV) ....'56 '91 C.6 B.A. L.306 J.D. [Garrity&J.]

Keefe, Joseph F., (AV) '42 '67 C.1030 B.A. L.184 J.D.
179 Water Street, 06790
Telephone: 860-482-7651 Fax: 860-482-7845
Email: email@skmwlaw.com URL: http://www.snetyp.com/skmw
***PRACTICE AREAS: Civil Litigation; Criminal Litigation.**
Civil Litigation, Criminal Litigation, Personal Injury, Commercial Litigation and Probate Litigation.
See Professional Biographies, TORRINGTON, CONNECTICUT

Keilty, Michael, (CV) ....'67 '92 C.184 B.A. L.1029 J.D. [Ⓐ Ebersol&M.]
*PRACTICE AREAS: Civil Litigation; Real Estate Law; Planning and Zoning; Environmental.
Kiel, Lawrence J., (BV) ....'57 '83 C&L.184 B.A., J.D. [Murphy,L.&K.] ⊙
Laudati, John L., (BV) ....'55 '81 C&L.184 B.A., J.D. [Murphy,L.&K.] ⊙
Lawrence, Peter L., (BV) ....'54 '80 C.156 B.A. L.1292 J.D. [Sivaslian&L.]
Leard, David C., (BV) ....'58 '84 C.105 B.A. L.184 J.D. [Manasse,S.&L.]
Lefebre, James B. ....'15 '52 C.976 B.S. L.262 LL.B. 47 Forest St.‡
Lefevre, Matthew J., (AV) ....'62 '87 C.1234 B.A. L.184 J.D. [M.J.Lefevre] ⊙
Lefevre, Regina Wexler, (CV) ....'62 '87 C.855 B.A. L.184 J.D. [Ⓒ M.J.Lefevre] ⊙
Lefevre, Matthew J., Esq., P.C., The Law Offices of, (AV)
94 Church Street (⊙Hartford)
Levy, Steven H., (BV) ....'56 '84 C.1044 B.A. L.1162 J.D. [Febbroriello,C.&L.]
Logan, John Reid, (BV) ....'56 '82 C.184 B.A. L.1048 J.D. [Sullivan,R.S.&L.]
Magistrali, Michael F., (BV) ....'53 '80 C&L.93 B.A., J.D. 30 Mason St.
Manasse, Edward W. ....'43 '71 C&L.184 B.A., J.D. 249 Winsted Rd.‡
Manasse, Slaiby & Leard, (BV) .... 249 Winsted Rd. (⊙Kent)
Marconi, Eugene A., (BV) ....'54 '79 C&L.184 B.A., J.D. 750 Pothier Rd.
McCormick, Brian, (BV) ....'51 '78 C.276 B.S. L.930 J.D. [Ebersol&M.]
*PRACTICE AREAS: Personal Injury Law; Family Law; Civil Litigation.
Merati, Michael A., (BV) .... '44 '73 C&L.184 B.A., LL.B. [Gallicchio,M.&G.]
Moraghan, David A., (BV) ....'58 '83 C.321 A.B. L.1048 J.D. 179 Water St.
Morrison, Christopher J. ....'58 '93 C.184 B.A. L.1048 J.D. O & G Industries, Inc.
Murphy, Neil F., Jr., (BV) ....'45 '70 C.93 A.B. L.184 J.D. [Murphy,L.&K.] ⊙
Murphy, Laudati & Kiel, P.C., (BV) ....249 Winsted Road (⊙Farmington)
Muschell, Victor M., (BV)....................'40 '66 C.390 B.A. L.94 LL.B. [Muschell&S.]
Muschell & Simoncelli, L.L.P., (BV) .... 104 Church Street
Nicholas, Jeffrey C., (CV) ....'60 '87 C&L.184 B.A., J.D. 373 Prospect St.
Oneglia, Gregory S. ....'47 '73 C.867 B.A. L.184 J.D. O & G Industries, Inc.
Oneglia, Roderic M. ......'51 '76 C.478 A.B. L.184 J.D. Burlington Construction Co., Inc.
Organschi, Marcus G., (BV) ....'52 '89 C.1033 B.A. L.188 J.D. [Brower&O.]
*PRACTICE AREAS: Civil Litigation; Family Law; Environmental Law; Real Estate; Personal Injury.
Peck, Lawrence M., Jr. ....'61 '88 C.1103 B.A. L.184 J.D. 179 Water St.
Perlotto, Joel D., (BV) ....'68 '95 C.1030 B.A. L.190 J.D. [Ⓐ Sullivan,R.S.&L.]
Reis, V. Peter, Jr., (BV) ....'47 '73 C.676 B.A. L.818 J.D. [Sullivan,R.S.&L.]
Roraback, Andrew W., (BV) ....'60 '87 C.976 B.A. L.893 J.D. [Roraback&R.]
*PRACTICE AREAS: Civil Litigation; Commercial Litigation; Municipal Law; Banking Law; Administrative Law.
Roraback, Charles E., (BV) ....'58 '85 C.976 B.A. L.184 J.D. [Roraback&R.]
*PRACTICE AREAS: Corporate Law; Commercial Finance Law; Municipal Law; Real Estate Law; Zoning Law.
Roraback, Charles W., (AV) .... '33 '58 C&L.976 B.A., LL.B. [Roraback&R.]
*PRACTICE AREAS: Estate Planning; Probate Law; Banking Law; Municipal Law; Real Estate Law.
Roraback, Margaret P., (BV) ....'61 '87 C.976 B.A. L.1194 J.D. [Roraback&R.]
*PRACTICE AREAS: Elder Law; Estate Planning; Probate Law; Real Estate Law.

Roraback & Roraback, (AV)
24 Mason Street, P.O. Box 925, 06790
Telephone: 860-489-6880 Fax: 860-489-5301
Members of Firm: Charles W. Roraback; Charles E. Roraback; Margaret P. Roraback; Andrew W. Roraback.
General Practice, Real Estate and Zoning, Corporate and Commercial Law, Civil and Commercial Litigation, Administrative Law, Banking Law, Municipal Law, Estate Planning and Probate Law.
Reference: Torrington Savings Bank.
See Professional Biographies, TORRINGTON, CONNECTICUT

Rosa, Alan A. ....'— '80 C.184 B.A. L.1029 J.D. 85 Lindbergh St.
Rozbicki, Zbigniew S. ....'42 '66 C.972 B.S. L.560 J.D. P.O. Box 419
Sanchy, Jerome J., (BV) ....'52 '77 C.178 B.A. L.184 J.D. [Sullivan,R.S.&L.]
Santore, Dennis A. ....'44 '99 C.745 B.S. L.306 J.D. 62 Cook St.
Simoncelli, George B., Jr., (BV) ....'56 '81 C.184 B.A. L.1202 J.D. 104 Church St.
Sivaslian, Peter K., (BV) .... '32 '57 C.855 B.A. L.145 J.D. [Sivaslian&L.]
Sivaslian & Lawrence, (BV) ....249 Winsted Rd.
Slaiby, Samuel E., (BV) ....'46 '76 C.1107 B.A. L.1194 J.D. [Manasse,S.&L.]
Smith, Jess H. ....'32 '57 C.164 A.B. L.94 LL.B. 179 Water St.‡
Sullivan, Robert J., (AV) ....'24 '51 C.829 L.93 LL.B. [Ⓒ Sullivan,R.S.&L.]
Sullivan, Reis, Sanchy & Logan, LLC, (BV) .... 9 Mason Street
Summers, Paul W., (BV) ....'64 '90 C.184 B.A. L.1048 J.D. 179 Water St., 2nd Fl.
Ugalde, Gregory F., (BV) '60 '85
C.1107 A.B. L.128 J.D. V.P. & Gen. Coun., T & M Bldg. Co., Inc.
Wall, Christopher G., (BV) ....'65 '94 C.276 B.S.B.A. L.184 J.D. [Ⓐ Wall,W.&F.]
Wall, R. Anthony, Jr., (BV) ....'45 '74 C.276 A.B. L.30 J.D. [Wall&G.]
Wall, Thomas F., (AV) ....'07 '30 C&L.309 A.B., LL.B. [Ⓒ Wall,W.&F.]
Wall, Thomas F., Jr., (BV) ....'38 '64 C.608 A.B. L.276 J.D. [Wall,W.&F.]
Wall and Gawrych, (BV) .... 8 Church St.
Wall, Wall & Frauenhofer, (AV) .... 117 Main St.
Zeller, James A. ....'68 '95 C.602 B.A. L.424 J.D. 616 Main St.

TRUMBULL, 32,989, *Fairfield Co.*

Abbamonte, David M., (BV) ....'46 '71 C&L.94 B.A., J.D. 14 Placid St.
Baldwin, Raymond G., Jr., (BV) ... '48 '84 C.1156 B.S. L.1029 J.D. 888 White Plains Rd.
Beckwith, Raymond W., (AV) ..... '27 '53 C.976 B.A. L.309 LL.B. 935 White Plains Rd.
Berta, Robert J., (BV) ....'39 '64 C.321 B.A. L.893 LL.B. [Ⓐ Owens,S.&N.]
*PRACTICE AREAS: Business Law; Tax and Estate Planning.
Biondi, David R. ....'41 '65 C.749 B.S. L.1009 LL.B. 940 White Plains

Bloom, Allison J., The Law Offices Of '68 '95 C.1030 B.A. L.1252 J.D.
35 Corporate Drive Suite 1155, 06611
Telephone: 203-452-8000 Fax: 203-452-7594
Email: emsatty@aol.com
***PRACTICE AREAS: Emergency Medical Services Law; Business Law; Wills; Trusts and Estates; Taxation.**
Contracts, Corporate Law, Emergency Medical Services Law, Taxation, Wills, Trusts and Estates, Business Law.
See Professional Biographies, TRUMBULL, CONNECTICUT

Braunstein & Todisco, LLC
(See Fairfield)

Brennan, Daniel E., Jr., (BV) ....'42 '81 C.1044 B.S. L.1029 J.D. 4 Daniels Farm Rd.
Brennan, Daniel Edward, (BV) ....'51 '80 C.1030 B.A. L.1029 J.D. [Brennan,M.&B.]
Brennan, Robert J., Jr., (BV) ....'43 '70 C.1030 B.A. L.1017 J.D. [Brennan,M.&B.] ⊙
Brennan, McNamara & Baldwin, P.C., (BV) .... 8 Daniels Farm Rd. (⊙Fairfield)
Brown, Christine Donahue ....'69 '96 C.93 B.A. L.1252 J.D. 888 White Plains Rd.
Burns, Kevin L., (BV) ....'52 '77 C.94 B.A. L.128 J.D. [Owens,S.&N.]
*PRACTICE AREAS: Probate; Estate Planning; Business Law; Bankruptcy; Commercial Litigation.
Caruso, Daniel F., (BV) ....'57 '83 C.184 B.A. L.1194 J.D. [Ⓐ Owens,S.&N.] ⊙
*PRACTICE AREAS: Trusts and Estates; Real Estate; Small Business Law; General Practice.
Cohen, Charles, (AVⓉ) '12 '35
(adm. in NY; not adm. in CT) 16 Colonial Dr.
Cooney, Robert J., (AV) ....'34 '60 C.1030 B.S.S. L.276 LL.B. [Williams,C.&S.]
*PRACTICE AREAS: Litigation; Defense; Environmental.
Cretella, Andrew D., (BV) ....'36 '61 C.321 B.A. L.724 LL.B. 965 White Plains Rd.
Crozier, John H. ....'35 '74 C.597 B.S.Ch.E. L.7 J.D. 1934 Huntington Tpke.
Curley, John T. ....'25 '55 C.1030 B.S. L.724 LL.B. 12 Carmel Rdg.‡
Derbyshire, George W., (CV) ....'63 '90 C.1211 B.S. L.1029 J.D. 2 Corporate Dr.
Fallon, John F., (AV) ....'50 '76 C.1030 B.A. L.262 J.D. [Ⓒ Owens,S.&N.] ⊙
*PRACTICE AREAS: Litigation; Zoning Law; Administrative Law.
Fatse, J. Brian, (BV) ....'58 '88 C.264 B.A. L.1048 J.D. [Ⓒ Owens,S.&N.] ⊙
*PRACTICE AREAS: Corporate Law; Bankruptcy; Real Estate.
Fatse, Susan E. ....'60 '93 C.184 B.S. L.1252 J.D. [Ⓐ Owens,S.&N.]
*PRACTICE AREAS: Litigation; Commercial Litigation; Family Law; Zoning Law; Land Use.
Furey, Robert H. '61 '96 C.800 B.S. L.276 J.D.
(adm. in CA; not adm. in CT) 53 Heritage Dr.
Gildea, William F., (BV) ....'55 '80 C.184 B.A. L.1029 J.D. 965 White Plains Rd.
Goldman, Ellen W. ....'61 '86 C.188 B.S. L.659 J.D. 11 Skytop Dr.
Goldstein, Stanley M., (BV) ....'46 '73 C&L.184 B.A., LL.B. [Palmesi K.G.&P.]
Gordon, Irwin J., (CV) ....'29 '65 C.569 B.A. L.1009 LL.B. 4154 Madison Ave.
Greenberg, Daniel ....'50 '94 C.1044 B.E. L.1252 J.D. [D.Greenberg]
Greenberg, Daniel, LLC, Law Offices of ....35 Corporate Dr.
Habansky, Ronald J., (BV) ....'32 '60 C.184 B.A. L.276 J.D. 799 Silver Lane
Hagani, James A. '63 '89 C.178 B.A. L.309 J.D.
(adm. in NY; not adm. in CT) 29 Red Barn Rd.
Hamaty, Gail J. '58 '85 C.665 B.A. L.1187 J.D.
(adm. in PA; not adm. in CT) 41 Bailey St.

Harlow, Adams & Friedman, P.C.
(See Milford)

Herman, H. Paul ....'37 '61 C&L.276 B.A., J.D. 144 Plymouth Ave.
Hoffmann, Abraham M., (BV) ....'52 '78 C.94 B.S. L.421 J.D. 4154 Madison Ave.
Huben, Kevin M. ....'58 '84 C.1044 B.A. L.1029 J.D. P.O. Box 49
Hunt, John J. ....'10 '40 C&L.262 B.S., LL.B. 44 Clover Hill Rd.‡
Hyde, John E. ....'61 '87 C.165 B.A. L.861 J.D. Rampart Fin. Grp.
Jankovic, Martha A. ....'59 '85 C.184 B.A. L.1029 J.D. 58 Regina St.
Jankovsky, Michael C. ....'69 '96 C.732 B.A. L.861 J.D. [Ⓐ Owens,S.&N.]
*PRACTICE AREAS: Civil Litigation; Criminal Litigation; Workers' Compensation.
Kascak, Richard G., Jr., (BV) ....'51 '83 C.184 B.A. L.1029 J.D. [Mihaly&K.]
*PRACTICE AREAS: Insurance; Negligence; Workers Compensation; Real Estate; Probate.
Kaufman, Richard N., (BV) ....'38 '62 C&L.94 A.B., LL.B. [Palmesi K.G.&P.]
Kearns, Burtsell J. ....'29 '58 C&L.262 B.S., J.D. 5 Maymont Lane (Pat.)
Kennedy, Timothy P. ....'69 '98 C.999 B.A. L.1252 J.D. [Ⓐ Mihaly&K.] ⊙
*PRACTICE AREAS: Insurance; Workers Compensation; Personal Injury; Negligence; Probate.
Lancia, Maurizio D. ....'63 '91 C.1041 B.A. L.1029 J.D. 2 Corporate Dr.

Laske, Arthur C., III, (BV) '62 '88 C.93 B.A. L.184 J.D.
8 Daniels Farm Road, 06611
Telephone: 203-452-9987 Fax: 203-452-7680
Email: laskelaw@aol.com URL: http://www.lawyers.com/aclaskelaw
Personal Injury, Contract Disputes, Criminal, Civil Trial Practice, Municipal Liability, Product Liability, Arbitration and Uninsured/Underinsured Motorists.
See Professional Biographies, TRUMBULL, CONNECTICUT

Lawler, George Joseph, Law Offices of, (BV) '47 '83
C.262 B.S. L.1029 J.D. 965 White Planis Rd., Ste 101
Linsey, Carolyn R., (AV) ....'53 '77 C&L.280 B.A., J.D. [Owens,S.&N.]
*PRACTICE AREAS: Civil Litigation; Employment Law; Education Law.

Lonergan, Dana P., (BV) '55 '83 C.454 B.S. L.1029 J.D.
4154 Madison Avenue, 06611
Telephone: 203-371-7023 Fax: 203-371-4452
Email: dloner1066@aol.com URL: http://www.lawyers.com/personalinjuryct
***PRACTICE AREAS: Personal Injury Law.**
Personal Injury.
See Professional Biographies, TRUMBULL, CONNECTICUT

Lopez, Lisa M. ....'52 '76 C.823 A.B. L.276 J.D. 51 Robinwood Road
Luedecker, Warren A., (BV) ....'23 '54 C.184 L.734 LL.B. 32 Glenarden Rd.
Lynch, Jeanine Maietta ....'64 '89 C.1349 B.A. L.273 J.D. 30 Pambar Rd.
Maguire, Jean Z. ....'57 '82 C&L.184 B.A., J.D. [Ⓐ Mihaly&K.]
*PRACTICE AREAS: Commercial Real Estate; Residential Real Estate; Estate Planning; Probate; Wills.

Malinowski, Johanna S., (BV) '40 '83 C.1211 B.S. L.1029 J.D.
8 Daniels Farm Road, 06611
Telephone: 203-268-8600 FAX: 203-261-4660
URL: http://www.lawyers.com/malinowskilaw
***PRACTICE AREAS: Real Property Law; Landlord and Tenant Law; Elder Law; Probate.**
Real Estate, Probate, Elder Law, Real Property, Estate Planning, Business.
See Professional Biographies, TRUMBULL, CONNECTICUT

Maria, Susan, (BV) ....'55 '83 C.540 B.A. L.724 J.D. Fidelity National Title Ins. Corp.
Marino, Anthony J. '59 '87
C.1236 B.A. L.362 J.D. Corp. Coun., Pitney Bowes Office System
Maxham, Kathleen N., (BV) ....'55 '83 C.702 B.A. L.1029 J.D. [Ⓒ Owens,S.&N.]
*PRACTICE AREAS: Real Estate (residential, commercial, zoning); Estate Planning; Probate.
Mcauley, Timothy J. ....'57 '92 C.415 B.A. L.1029 J.D. 78 Horse Tavern Rd.
Mihaly, Serge G., (BV) ....'33 '56 C&L.569 B.A., LL.B. [Mihaly&K.]
*PRACTICE AREAS: Insurance; Workers Compensation; Negligence; Probate; Trials and Appeals.

Mihaly & Kascak, (BV)
925 White Plains Road, 06611 ⊙
Telephone: 203-452-9077 Fax: 203-452-9087
URL: http://www.snetyp.com/mihaly-kascak
Members of Firm: Serge G. Mihaly; Richard G. Kascak, Jr. Associates: Jean Z. Maguire; Timothy P. Kennedy.
General Civil and Criminal Practice before State and Federal Courts. Negligence, Insurance, Workers Compensation, Real Estate, Probate, Zoning, Criminal Defense, Appellate, Domestic Relations Law and Divorce. Trials and Appeals.
Bethel, Connecticut Office: 93 Greenwood Avenue, 06801. Telephone: 203-748-9098.
See Professional Biographies, TRUMBULL, CONNECTICUT

Moore, Dion W., (AV) ....'39 '67 C.207 A.B. L.608 J.D. [Williams,C.&S.]
*PRACTICE AREAS: Litigation.
Nicola, Robert J., (BV) ....'42 '67 C.264 B.A. L.184 J.D. [Owens,S.&N.]
*PRACTICE AREAS: Matrimonial Law; Commercial Litigation; Workers Compensation; Personal Injury.
Nigro, Suzannah Kim ....'69 '94 C.299 B.A. L.184 J.D. [Williams,C.&S.]
*PRACTICE AREAS: Litigation; Appellate Practice.
Nucera, Joseph P., (BV) ....'31 '55 C.1030 B.A. L.276 LL.B. 965 White Plains Rd.

Owens, Schine & Nicola, P.C., (AV)
799 Silver Lane, P.O. Box 753, 06611-0753 ⊙
Telephone: 203-375-0600 FAX: 203-375-5003

(This Listing Continued)

Owens, Schine & Nicola, P.C. (Continued)

Howard T. Owens (1897-1986); Edward Schine (1928-1983); Robert M. Owens (1935-1997); Robert J. Nicola; Kevin L. Burns; Carolyn R. Linsey;—Robert J. Berta; Daniel F. Caruso; Michael C. Jankovsky; Susan E. Fatse. Of Counsel: J. Brian Fatse; John F. Fallon; Kathleen N. Maxham.
General Trial Practice in all Courts. Real Estate, Land Use and Planning, Environmental, Corporate, Probate, Personal Injury, Criminal, Family, Workers Compensation, Education Law, Labor Law, Foreclosures, Bankruptcy. Administrative Agency Proceedings and Appeals, Real Estate, Commercial Litigation, Construction Law, Arbitration.
Fairfield, Connecticut Office: 53 Sherman Street, 06430. Telephone: 203-259-6612. Fax: 203-256-8796.

See Professional Biographies, TRUMBULL, CONNECTICUT

Palmesi, Ralph L., (BV) .... '41 '66 C.184 B.A. L.276 J.D. [Palmesi K.G.&P.]
Palmesi Kaufman Goldstein & Petrucelli, PC, (BV) ....888 White Plains Rd.
Petrucelli, Robert R., (BV) .... '31 '59 C.1030 B.S. L.276 LL.B. [Palmesi K.G.&P.]
Riordan, Angela S. .... '61 '86 C.401 B.A. L.1029 J.D. 20 Kitcher Ct.
Rosenberg, Hiram ....'48 '91 C.569 B.A. L.1029 J.D. P.O. Box 110084
Sable, John D. '46 '85 C.58 B.A. L.1029 J.D.
General Counsel, Prudential Connecticut Realty
Sconziano, Matthew M. .... '73 '98 C.676 B.A. L.1252 J.D. 965 White Plains Rd.
Sheehy, Edward Maum, (AV) .... '40 '67 C.976 B.A. L.184 LL.B. [Williams,C.&S.]
*PRACTICE AREAS: Litigation.
Sheiman, Richard M., (BV) ....'42 '66 C&L.966 B.S., J.D. 883 White Plains Rd.
Spodnick, Jonathan E., (BV) .... '63 '89 C.184 B.S. L.1029 J.D. 965 White Plains Road
Stauder, Lloyd P. .... '35 '63 C.602 B.S. L.276 J.D. 470 Daniels Farm Rd. (Pat.)
Stern, Bruce E., (BV) .... '42 '67 C.659 B.S. L.569 J.D. 2400 Reservoir Avenue
Varese, William J., (BV) .... '47 '76 C.1102 B.S. L.192 J.D. 965 White Plains Rd.
Walkley, Nancy L., (BV) '56 '80 C.659 B.A. L.1048 J.D.
Branch Coun., Federal National Title Insurance Co. of New York

Watson, Lauri Giles '62 '89 C.349 B.S. L.705 J.D.
5415 Main Street, 06611
Telephone: 203-452-8030 Fax: 203-445-1900
Email: lawatson@aol.com URL: http://www.lawyers.com/lgwatson
***PRACTICE AREAS: Family Law; Labor and Employment; Civil Rights; Education Law; Entertainment Law.**
Family Law, Divorce, Child Custody, Employment Discrimination.

See Professional Biographies, TRUMBULL, CONNECTICUT

Williams, Ronald D., (AV) .... '27 '54 C&L.893 B.A., LL.B. [Williams,C.&S.]
*PRACTICE AREAS: Litigation; Defense.
Williams, Ronald D., Jr., (BV) ....'55 '82 C.184 B.A. L.1029 J.D. [Williams,C.&S.]
*PRACTICE AREAS: Litigation.

Williams, Cooney & Sheehy, (AV) BB
799 Silver Lane, 06611-0753
Telephone: 203-331-0888 Telecopier: 203-380-2327
Email: wilcooshee@aol.com URL: http://www.lawyers.com/wcs
Members of Firm: Ronald D. Williams; Robert J. Cooney; Edward Maum Sheehy; Dion W. Moore; Ronald D. Williams, Jr.; Francis A. Smith, Jr. (1951-1989); Suzannah Kim Nigro.
General Civil Practice with emphasis on Civil Litigation including Commercial Litigation, Insurance Defense, Personal Injury, Malpractice and Products Liability, Civil Rights, Zoning and Employment Litigation in State and Federal Courts. Trials and Appeals, OSHA, Environmental, Banking and Municipal.
Representative Clients: Connecticut Medical Insurance Co.; The Stop & Shop Companies, Inc.; Fleet Bank; Podiatry Insurance Company of America; Town of Easton, Conn.

See Professional Biographies, TRUMBULL, CONNECTICUT

Wolf, George, (BV) ...... '29 '57 C.184 B.A. L.94 LL.B. 4154 Madison Ave. (©Seymour)
Wright, Charlene M. ....'66 '95 C.216 B.A. L.1252 J.D. 799 Silver Lane

Yaffie, Burton S., (BV) '40 '65 C.659 B.S. L.184 J.D.
925 White Plains Road, 06611
Telephone: 203-261-0551 Fax: 203-459-0392
Email: bylawct@aol.com URL: http://www.lawyers.com/yaffielaw
General Practice. Real Estate, Zoning, Corporation, Probate, Administrative, Commercial, Negligence, Family and Estate Planning Law. Trials in all Courts.

See Professional Biographies, TRUMBULL, CONNECTICUT

UNCASVILLE, 1,750, *New London Co.*

Heller, Harry B., (BV) ....'49 '75 C&L.184 B.A., J.D. [Heller,H.&M.]
Heller, Heller & McCoy, (BV) ....736 Norwich-New London Tpke.
McCoy, William E., (BV) .... '50 '75 C.823 B.A. L.184 J.D. [Heller,H.&M.]
McMahon, Robert F. ....'41 '75 C&L.708 B.A., J.D. 106 Park Ave.
Meisner, Kevin W. ....'65 '90 C.273 B.A. L.930 J.D. 67 Sandy Desert Rd.
Wickwire, William B. ....'46 '78 C.976 B.A. L.174 J.D. Juv. Pros.

UNIONVILLE, 2,246, *Hartford Co.*

Colton, William Arthur, Jr .... '38 '65 C.197 B.A. L.1009 J.D. 5 Serra Dr.
Fentner, John Benz, Jr., (BV) ....'45 '81 C.829 B.A. L.184 J.D. 12 Washington Circle
Gillespie, Robert G., (BV) ....'20 '49 C&L.184 B.A., LL.B. [© Scully,N.M.&R.]
*PRACTICE AREAS: Real Estate; Wills; Probate.
Hanrahan, John K., (AV) ....'16 '46 C.976 B.A. L.659 LL.B. [© Scully,N.M.&R.]
*PRACTICE AREAS: Real Estate; Probate.
Martin, Kathleen B., (BV) ....'44 '82 C.184 B.S. L.1048 J.D. [Scully,N.M.&R.]
*PRACTICE AREAS: Family Law; Mediation; Trusts and Estates; Probate; Real Estate.
Nicksa, Walter C., Jr., (BV) .... '44 '69 C.976 B.A. L.184 J.D. [Scully,N.M.&R.]
*PRACTICE AREAS: Real Estate; Trusts and Estates; Probate; Corporate Law.
Reeve, Robert J., (BV) .... '58 '83 C.1145 B.S. L.1048 J.D. [Scully,N.M.&R.]
*PRACTICE AREAS: General Practice; Land Use; Real Estate; Personal Injury; Business Law.
Sanford, Robert Preston ....'59 '95 C.882 B.S. L.184 J.D. 25 W. Avon Rd.
Scully, Edward F., (AV) ....'40 '69 C.1030 B.S. L.184 J.D. [Scully,N.M.&R.]
*PRACTICE AREAS: Personal Injury; Litigation; Real Estate; General Practice; Business Law.
Scully, Patrick E. ....'67 '95 C.1030 B.A. L.1048 J.D. [Scully,N.M.&R.]
*PRACTICE AREAS: Personal Injury; Litigation; Real Estate; Criminal Law; Probate.

Scully, Nicksa, Martin & Reeve, LLP, (AV)
79 Main Street, P.O. Box 278, 06085-0278
Telephone: 860-673-7141 Telecopier: 860-675-8955
Email: scully.nicksa@snet.net
Members of Firm: Edward F. Scully; Walter C. Nicksa, Jr.; Kathleen B. Martin; Robert J. Reeve; Patrick E. Scully. Of Counsel: Robert G. Gillespie; John K. Hanrahan.
General Practice. Business Law, Negligence, Personal Injury, Real Estate, Commercial Law, Zoning, Planning and Land Use, Trusts and Estates, Probate, Estate Planning, Family Law and Mediation.

See Professional Biographies, UNIONVILLE, CONNECTICUT

Skripol, Paul G., (BV) .... '46 '76 C.1027 B.S. L.818 J.D. 1615 Farmington Ave.
Stuart, Mary Zimick .... '35 '77 C.521 B.A. L.1048 J.D. 11 Hemlock Notch Street
Weidemier, Larry E. .... '41 '97 C.299 B.A. L.1048 J.D. 25 New Britain Ave.

VERNON, * 27,974, *Tolland Co.*

Anderson, Donna L. .... '51 '81 C.878 B.S. L.1048 J.D. 77 Wildwood Rd.‡
Bars, Michael A., (BV) ....'55 '80 C.454 B.A. L.776 J.D. [Kahan,K.&C.]
*PRACTICE AREAS: Business Law; Real Property; Secured Finance; Employment Law.
Bartlett, Richard S., (BV) ....'50 '81 C.390 A.B. L.184 J.D. [McGann,B.&B.]
Boyan, Susan, (BV) ....'48 '83 C.999 B.S. L.184 J.D. [DuBeau,R.&B.]
Breslau, William E., (BV) ....'45 '72 C.823 B.A. L.184 J.D. [Kahan,K.&C.]
*PRACTICE AREAS: Real Estate; Real Estate Development; Business Law.
Brown, William C., (BV) .... '47 '74 C.128 B.A. L.184 J.D. [McGann,B.&B.]
Burke, Martin B., (BV) .... '40 '66 C.165 A.B. L.982 J.D. 130 Union Street
Butter, John A. ....'46 '79 C.1030 B.S. L.184 J.D. 203 Tracy Dr.
Capossela, Joseph P., (BV) .... '44 '69 C.676 B.S. L.184 J.D. [Kahan,K.&C.]
*PRACTICE AREAS: Land Use; Commercial Real Estate; Business Law; Administrative Law; Farm and Ranch Law.
Cardin, Patricia .... '70 '96 C.1200 B.A. L.306 J.D. 76 S. Frontage Rd.
Caron, Suzanne E., (BV) ....'56 '88 C.67 B.A. L.184 J.D. [Kahan,K.&C.]
*PRACTICE AREAS: Personal Injury Law; Family Law; Juvenile Law; Attorney Discipline.
Casey, John M. ....'29 '54 C.321 B.S. L.184 J.D. 21 Court St.‡
Chase, Kathleen F. ....'47 '85 C.725 B.A. L.1048 J.D. Chf. Clk., Supr. Ct.
Claunch, Helen F. .... '60 '88 C.918 B.A. L.966 J.D. P.O. Box 772
Cornish, Irene L., (BV) ....'41 '87 C&L.184 B.A., J.D. 76 S. Frontage Rd.‡
Courtney, Joseph D., (BV) ....'53 '78 C.860 B.A. L.184 J.D. [Flaherty,M.&C.]
*PRACTICE AREAS: Criminal Law; Personal Injury; Workers Compensation; Civil Practice; Real Estate.
Dakin, William J., (BV) ....'54 '79 C.184 B.A. L.472 J.D. [Kahan,K.&C.]
*PRACTICE AREAS: Estate Planning; Wills; Trusts and Estates; Probate; Taxation.
Davis, David C. ....'58 '87 C.1102 B.S. L.1048 J.D. [McGann,B.&B.]
Dietz, Mark W. ....'67 '93 C.1030 B.A. L.1048 J.D. [A Kahan,K.&C.]
*PRACTICE AREAS: Litigation; Real Estate; Family.
DuBeau, Robert C., (BV) ....'34 '62 C.309 A.B. L.184 LL.B. [DuBeau,R.&B.]
DuBeau, Ryan & Boyan, P.C., (BV) ....38 Park St.
Enright, Robert J., (BV) ....'50 '82 C.103 B.A. L.184 J.D. [McGann,B.&B.]
Finke, Amy L., (BV) .... '62 '90 C.659 B.S. L.174 J.D. 45 Hartford Turnpike

Flaherty, Meisler & Courtney, LLC, (BV)
62 Hyde Avenue, 06066-4503
Telephone: 860-872-7200 Fax: 860-875-6594
Email: FMACATTY@aol.com
Members of Firm: Leo B. Flaherty Jr. (1923-1998); Arthur P. Meisler (1945-2001); Joseph D. Courtney. Associate: Elizabeth C. Foran.
General Practice, Criminal, Real Estate, Estate Planning, Probate, Administrative, Workers Compensation, Municipal and Zoning, Family and Personal Injury Law. Civil and Criminal Trial Practice.
Reference: Savings Bank of Rockville.

See Professional Biographies, VERNON, CONNECTICUT

Foran, Elizabeth C. ....'55 '90 C.462 B.A. L.1048 J.D. [A Flaherty,M.&C.]
*PRACTICE AREAS: Criminal Law; Personal Injury; Civil Practice; Real Estate.
Ford, Steven M., (BV) ....'51 '78 C.30 B.S. L.1048 J.D. [Ford,O.M.&H.]
*PRACTICE AREAS: Commercial Law; Corporation Law; Personal Injury; Litigation; Criminal Law.

Ford, Oberg, Manion & Houck, P.C., (BV)
220 Hartford Turnpike, 06066
Telephone: 860-646-3141 Fax: 860-649-3532
Steven M. Ford; Mary C. Oberg; Douglas Kevin Manion; Cynthia D. Houck.
General Practice. Real Estate, Negligence, Divorce, Probate, Criminal, Commercial, Corporation and Zoning Law. Trials in all Courts.
Representative Clients: First Federal Savings & Loan Association of East Hartford, Conn.; Bolles Motors, Inc.; Countrywide Funding Corp.
Approved Attorneys For: Connecticut Attorney's Title Insurance Co.; Fidelity National Title Insurance Co.

See Professional Biographies, VERNON, CONNECTICUT

Giedraitis, Vincent J. ....'25 '58 C.012 B.A. L.184 LL.B. 76 Washington St.‡
Giulietti, John L. ....'42 '72 C.184 B.A. L.190 J.D. 20 beverly Rd.
Gorecki, John R. '23 '53 C&L.209 B.S., J.D.
(adm. in IL; not adm. in CT) 126 Evergreen Rd.‡
Hall, William E., (BV) ....'36 '64 C.1019 B.A. L.184 J.D. 130 Union St.
Hammer, Harry ....'26 '55 C.184 B.A. L.178 LL.B. Supr. Ct. J.
Hohenthal, Gary W. ....'58 '89 C.881 B.A. L.184 J.D. 45 Hartford Turnpike
Houck, Cynthia D., (BV) ....'50 '77 C.610 B.A. L.1194 J.D. [Ford,O.M.&H.]
*PRACTICE AREAS: Family Law; Real Estate Transactions.
Johnson, J. Thomas ....'42 '67 C.745 A.B. L.184 J.D. 281 Hartford Tpke.
Johnston, Timothy James, (BV) .... '49 '76 C&L.184 B.S., J.D. 7 Keynote Dr.

Kahan, Kerensky & Capossela, L.L.P., (BV)
45 Hartford Turnpike, P.O. Box K, 06066
Telephone: 860-646-1974 Fax: 860-647-8302
Email: attorneys@kkc-law.com URL: http://www.kkc-law.com
Members of Firm: Solomon Kerensky; Joseph P. Capossela; William E. Breslau; Michael A. Bars; William J. Dakin; Michael J. Kopsick; Suzanne E. Caron; Jeffrey M. Winnick. Associates: Mark W. Dietz; Dorian L. Reiser; Laurel D. Mangan; Stephen F. Sutton.
Business Law, Corporate Law, Elder Law, Estate Planning, Wills, Trusts and Estates, Family Law, Litigation, Personal Injury, Probate and Fiduciary Administration, Zoning, Planning and Land Use, Residential Real Estate, Commercial Real Estate, Taxation and Taxpayer Representation.

See Professional Biographies, VERNON, CONNECTICUT

Kerensky, Solomon, (BV) ....'37 '63 C.28 B.A. L.184 J.D. [Kahan,K.&C.]
*PRACTICE AREAS: Real Estate Development; Zoning Law; Business Law; Corporate Law.
Kopsick, Michael J., (BV) ....'63 '88 C.550 B.A. L.1048 J.D. [Kahan,K.&C.]
*PRACTICE AREAS: Commercial Litigation; Employment Law; Legal Malpractice.
Levine, Jerome D., (BV) ....'46 '72 C&L.184 B.A., J.D. 280 Talcottville Rd.
Mangan, Laurel D., (CV) ....'54 '85 C.184 B.A. L.306 J.D. [A Kahan,K.&C.]
*PRACTICE AREAS: Probate; Estate Planning for the Elderly; Estate Planning.
Manion, Douglas Kevin, (BV) ....'57 '83 C.902 B.A. L.900 J.D. [Ford,O.M.&H.]
*PRACTICE AREAS: Personal Injury Law; Real Estate Law; Divorce; Litigation; Criminal Law.
Marder, I. David, (BV) ....'45 '71 C.349 B.S. L.184 J.D. [Marder&K.]
Marder & Kallet, (BV) ....76 S. Frontage Rd.
McCoy, Frank J. .... '22 '57 C.976 B.A. L.184 LL.B. 310 Hartford Turnpike
McGann, Robert D., (BV) ....'43 '68 C.222 B.A. L.184 LL.B. [McGann,B.&B.]
McGann, Bartlett & Brown, (BV) ....Ste. 401, 281 Hartford Tpke.
Mierzwa, Mary Ann ....'59 '87 C.1111 B.A. L.990 J.D. P.O. Box 20484
Oberg, Mary C., (BV) ....'56 '81 C&L.184 B.A., J.D. [Ford,O.M.&H.]
*PRACTICE AREAS: Divorce Law; Probate Law.
O'Donnell, B. Patrick, Jr. ....'43 '68 C.108 B.A. L.347 J.D. 107 Range Hill Dr.
Purnell, Oliver James, III .... '49 '82 C.478 A.B. L.1048 J.D. 6 Forestview Dr.
Rady, Thomas F., III, (BV) ....'31 '58 C&L.184 B.A., LL.B. Prob. J.
Reik, Jonathan F., (BV) ....'52 '80 C.855 B.A. L.184 J.D. [McGann,B.&B.]
Reiser, Dorian L. ....'71 '96 C.676 B.A. L.1048 J.D. [A Kahan,K.&C.]
*PRACTICE AREAS: Land Use; Residential Real Estate; Commercial Real Estate; Secured Finance; Business Law.
Rivers, David H., (BV) ....'50 '75 C.184 B.A. L.306 J.D. 140 Union St.
Ryan, Atherton B., (BV) ....'34 '59 C&L.184 B.A., LL.B. [DuBeau,R.&B.]
Schwartz, Jeffrey G., (BV) .... '60 '85 C.659 B.A. L.245 J.D. 45 Hartford Tpk.
Stober, John M. '49 '84 C&L.184 B.A., J.D.
Executive Director, Vernon Area Community Health Center, Inc.
Stone, David T. ....'62 '88 C.184 B.A. L.306 J.D. 140 Union St.
Sutton, Stephen F. ....'66 '97 C.999 B.S. L.1048 J.D. [A Kahan,K.&C.]
*PRACTICE AREAS: Taxation; Corporate Law; Business Law; Estate Planning; Wills.
Winnick, Jeffrey M., (BV) ....'46 '73 C.95 B.A. L.93 J.D. [Kahan,K.&C.]
*PRACTICE AREAS: Estate Planning; Estate Administration; Business Planning; Pension Plans.

WALLINGFORD, 37,274, *New Haven Co.*

Abrams, James Wilson .... '56 '88 C.855 B.A. L.184 J.D. [Parsons&A.]
Balser, John J. '41 '76 C.570 B.S.Ch.E. L.776 J.D.
(adm. in NJ; not adm. in CT; Pat.) V.P. & Coun., Bristol-Myers Squibb Co.
Barry, Steven M., (CV) .... '64 '90 C.321 A.B. L.262 J.D. [Ⓐ Delaney,Z.D.D.&N.]
*PRACTICE AREAS: Litigation; Insurance Defense; Personal Injury Law; Products Liability; Employment Litigation.
Billings, John V. P., (BV) .... '38 '66 C&L.30 B.A., LL.B. [Billings&B.]
Billings and Billings, (BV) .... 155 N. Main St.
Borak, Jeffrey R., (BV) .... '53 '78 C.184 B.S. L.1194 J.D. 324 Main St.
Brennan, Stephen P., (BV) .... '61 '86 C.676 B.A. L.1194 J.D. 1062 Barnes Rd.
Carrozzella, Christopher .... '58 '87 C.602 B.B.A. L.184 J.D. 180 N. Main St.
Carruthers, Patricia B. .... '44 '90 C.1102 B.S. L.306 J.D. 37 Saw Mill Dr.
Conway, John F. .... '63 '89 C.401 B.S. L.262 J.D. [Loughlin F.]
*PRACTICE AREAS: Commercial Litigation; Municipal Law; Election Law; Insurance Defense.
Cronin, Jeremiah A. .... '19 '49 C&L.93 A.B., LL.B. 10 Research Pkwy.
David R. Seaver, Esq. .... 8 Amie Lane
Delaney, Joseph M., (AV) .... '24 '52 C.128 A.B. L.309 LL.B. [Delaney,Z.D.D.&N.]
*PRACTICE AREAS: Plaintiffs Trial Practice; Personal Injury Law; Negligence Tort Law; Litigation; Trial Practice.

Delaney, Zemetis, Donahue, Durham & Noonan, P.C., (AV)
111 South Main Street, P.O. Box 747, 06492 ⊙
Telephone: 203-269-1441 Fax: 203-284-9428
Email: dzddn@worldnet.att.net
Joseph M. Delaney; Terence A. Zemetis; Timothy W. Donahue; Michael G. Durham; Patrick M. Noonan (Resident Guilford); Edward W. Mayer, Jr.;—Steven M. Barry; Barbara M. Dunham; Andrew P. Dwyer, II; Tracey M. Lane.
Practice Primarily Limited to Professional Malpractice, Products Liability, Insurance Defense, Personal Injury, Employment and Commercial Litigation in all Courts.
Guilford, Connecticut Office: 741 Boston Post Road, 06437. Telephone: 203-458-9168. Fax: 203-458-4424.
See Professional Biographies, WALLINGFORD, CONNECTICUT

Del Sole & Del Sole, L.L.P., (AV)
46 South Whittlesey Avenue, 06492 ⊙
Telephone: 203-284-8000 Fax: 203-284-9800
Email: delsole@delsoledelsole.com URL: http://www.lawyers.com/delsoledelsole
Member of Firm: Denise Del Sole-Kennedy.
Trials and Appeals in all Courts. General, Tort and Malpractice, Litigation, Probate, Workers Compensation, Corporate, Real Estate Law and Insurance Law.
New Haven, Connecticut Office: 27 Elm Street, 06510. Telephone: 203-785-8500. Fax: 203-777-4485.
See Professional Biographies, WALLINGFORD, CONNECTICUT

Del Sole-Kennedy, Denise, (BV) .... '57 '90 C.1252 B.A. L.1029 J.D. [Del Sole&D.]
*PRACTICE AREAS: Litigation; Real Estate Law.
DePardo, Gerald L. '60 '94 C.588 B.S.E.E. L.184 J.D.
Vice President and Duputy General Counsel, CIDRA Corporation (Pat.)
Dickinson, William W., Jr., (BV) .... '46 '76 C.216 B.A. L.273 J.D. Mayor
Donahue, Timothy W., (AV) .... '52 '78 C.918 B.A. L.93 J.D. [Delaney,Z.D.D.&N.]
*PRACTICE AREAS: Plaintiffs Trial Practice; Health Care Law; Drug Law; General Negligence Law; Trials and Appeals.
Douglas, Marilyn P., (BV) .... '55 '80 C.184 B.A. L.1048 J.D. 1062 Barnes Rd.
DuBoff, Samuel J. '42 '72 C.563 M.Ch.E. L.1009 J.D.
(adm. in NY; not adm. in CT; Pat.) Assoc. Coun., Pat., Bristol-Myers Squibb Co.
Dunham, Barbara M. .... '54 '95 C.184 B.S. L.588 J.D. [Ⓐ Delaney,Z.D.D.&N.]
*PRACTICE AREAS: Civil Litigation; Medical Malpractice; Personal Injury.
Dwyer, Andrew P., II .... '65 '90 C.676 B.A. L.1029 J.D. [Ⓐ Delaney,Z.D.D.&N.]
Falsey, Marie T. .... '58 '85 C.976 B.A. L.1048 J.D. 333 Christian St.
Farrell, Gerald E., Jr. .... '68 '93 C.321 A.B. L.884 J.D. [Ⓐ Farrell,L.&G.]
*PRACTICE AREAS: Probate; Real Estate; Land Use.
Farrell, Gerald E., Sr., (AV) .... '42 '66 C&L.93 A.B., LL.B. [Farrell,L.&G.]
*PRACTICE AREAS: Probate; Criminal; Real Estate; Personal Injury; Corporate Law.
Farrell, Lynne S. .... '38 '01 C.19 B.A. L.1252 J.D. [Ⓐ Farrell,L.&G.]
*PRACTICE AREAS: Education Law; Family Law.

Farrell, Leslie & Grochowski, (AV)
375 Center Street, P.O. Box 369, 06492
Telephone: 203-269-7756 Fax: 203-269-1927
Email: info@wallingfordlawyers.com URL: http://www.lawyers.com/flglaw
Member of Firm: Gerald E. Farrell, Sr.;—Gerald E. Farrell, Jr.; Ann Farrell Leslie; Christine Farrell Grochowski; Lynne S. Farrell.
General Civil and Criminal Practice before State and Federal Courts. Personal Injury, Probate, Family, Real Estate, Land Use, Immigration, Employment, Criminal Defense, Social Security, Bankruptcy, Corporate, Commercial and General Litigation. Trials and Appeals.
Reference: Liberty Bank (Wallingford Office).
See Professional Biographies, WALLINGFORD, CONNECTICUT

Fay & Lunt, (AV) .... 46 South Whittlesey Avenue
Fishbein, Norman F., (BV) '41 '66 C.674 A.B. L.178 J.D.
100 South Main Street, P.O. Box 363, 06492
Telephone: 203-265-2895 Fax: 203-294-1396
***PRACTICE AREAS: Probate; Real Estate; Negligence; Domestic Relations.**
General Civil Practice before State Courts. Probate, Estate Planning, Real Estate, Zoning, Land Use, Negligence, Corporation, Domestic Relations and Bankruptcy Law. Trials.
References: First Union Bank; Fleet Bank.

FitzGerald, Edward B., (BV) .... '34 '59 C.188 A.B. L.184 LL.B. [Loughlin F.]
*PRACTICE AREAS: Civil Litigation; Insurance Defense; Personal Injury; Product Liability.
Gaffey, William J., (CV) .... '51 '77 C.228 B.A. L.884 J.D. 5 N. Main St.
Galligan, Matthew G., (BV) .... '23 '51 C.262 B.S. L.276 J.D. 300 Long Hill Rd.
Gamm, John R., Law Offices of, (BV) .... '45 '69 C.659 B.A. L.184 J.D. P.O. Box 20
Gee, Richard, (BV) .... '46 '72 C.81 B.A. L.273 J.D. 339 Main St. (Yalesville)
Gouin, Leon J., (BV) .... '27 '62 C&L.184 B.S., LL.B. 7 S. Elm St.
Greenberg, Nancy I. '57 '85 C&L.976 B.A., J.D.
(adm. in NY; not adm. in CT) Gaylord Hosp.
Grillo, Michael '60 '91 C.205 B.S.E.E. L.184 J.D.
Vice President, General Counsel & Secretary, CIDRA Corporation (Pat.)
Grochowski, Christine Farrell .... '68 '94 C.321 B.A. L.93 J.D. [Ⓐ Farrell,L.&G.]
*PRACTICE AREAS: Employment Law; Family Law; Immigration; Personal Injury; Litigation.
Gross, Leon O., (BV) .... '35 '60 C.918 B.A. L.184 J.D. 145 N. Main St.
Hannan, Gregg M. .... '69 '94 C.1107 B.A. L.1252 J.D. [Hannan]
Hannan, Richard C., Jr., (BV) .... '41 '66 C.976 B.A. L.184 J.D. [Hannan]
Hannan Law Firm, The, LLC, (BV) .... 850 N. Main St. Ext.
Henrici, Craig B., (BV) .... '53 '81 C.478 B.A. L.1029 J.D. [Loughlin F.]
*PRACTICE AREAS: Real Estate; Plaintiffs Personal Injury; Probate; Municipal Law; Landlord and Tenant Law.
Kamp, Michael P., (BV) .... '58 '84 C.93 B.A. L.245 J.D. [Loughlin F.]
*PRACTICE AREAS: Insurance Defense; Civil Litigation; Municipal Law.
Killen, James A., (BV) .... '60 '85 C.321 B.A. L.93 J.D. 11 Wisk Key Wind Rd.
Kusak, Walter R., (BV) .... '47 '73 C.273 B.A. L.184 J.D. 15 Liandina Rd.
Lane, Tracey M. .... '71 '97 C.569 B.A. L.306 J.D. [Ⓐ Delaney,Z.D.D.&N.]
*PRACTICE AREAS: Civil Litigation; Appellate Practice; Criminal Appeals.
Leslie, Ann Farrell .... '68 '94 C.321 A.B. L.93 J.D. [Ⓐ Farrell,L.&G.]
*PRACTICE AREAS: Family Law; Probate; Personal Injury; Real Estate; Social Security.
Lettick, Loren, (BV) .... '43 '71 C.831 B.S. L.184 J.D. 1062 Barnes Rd.
Lewis, Woodward F., Jr. .... '39 '74 C.976 A.B. L.184 J.D. [F.W.Lewis,Jr.]
Lewis, F. Woodward, Jr., P.C. .... 439 Main St. (Yalesville)
Longley, Christopher F., (CV) .... '59 '89 C.1102 B.S. L.1029 J.D. 1062 Barnes Rd.
Lord, Diane M. .... '56 '85 C.1102 B.A. L.1029 J.D. P.O. Box 865
Loughlin, E. James .... '64 '93 C.858 B.A. L.1194 J.D. [Loughlin F.]
*PRACTICE AREAS: Litigation; Real Estate; Zoning Law; Landlord and Tenant Law; Estates.
Loughlin, Edward P., (BV) .... '36 '62 C.976 B.A. L.184 LL.B. [Loughlin F.] ⊙
*PRACTICE AREAS: Real Estate; Probate; Corporate Law.

Loughlin FitzGerald, (BV)
150 South Main Street, 06492 ⊙
Telephone: 203-265-2035 Fax: 203-269-3487
Members of Firm: Edward P. Loughlin; Edward B. FitzGerald; Michael P. Kamp; Craig B. Henrici; Joan C. Molloy; Kate L. Rizzo; Charles P. Reed; E. James Loughlin; John F. Conway; W. Glen Pierson.
General Practice. Litigation, Real Estate, Insurance Defense, Corporation, Labor, Probate, Condominium, Municipal and Zoning, Family, Commercial, Products Liability, Negligence, Estate Planning, Contract and Criminal Law. Trials in all Courts.
Hamden, Connecticut Office: 1960 Whitney Avenue, 06517. Telephone: 203-288-2847.
See Professional Biographies, WALLINGFORD, CONNECTICUT

Lunt, Donald C., (AV) .... '30 '53 C.976 B.A. L.477 J.D. [Fay&L.]
Makujina, Shah R. '66 '96 C.446 B.A. L.575 J.D.
(adm. in NC; not adm. in CT) Asst. Coun., Patents, Bristol-Myers Squibb Co.
Mantzaris, Adam, (BV) .... '30 '61 C&L.184 B.A., LL.B. Corp. Coun.
Manuelidis, Emmanuel E. .... '67 '93 C.881 B.A. L.851 J.D. P.O. Box 310
Marriott, John F., Sr. .... '38 '84 C.725 B.S. L.1048 J.D. 33 Grieb Rd.
Mayer, Edward W., Jr., (BV) ..... '64 '89 C.589 B.S. L.1029 J.D. [Delaney,Z.D.D.&N.]
*PRACTICE AREAS: Litigation; Medical Malpractice; Insurance Defense Law; Employment Litigation.
Mazzarella, Joseph R. .... '63 '89 C.319 B.S. L.861 J.D. Conn. Telephone
McCann, James F., (BV) .... '48 '89 C.1102 B.S. L.1029 J.D. 300 Church St.
McManus, Vincent T., Jr., (BV) .... '41 '73 C.1252 B.A. L.818 J.D. [V.T.McManus,Jr.]
McManus, Vincent T., Jr., Professional Corporation, (BV) .... 116 S. Main St.
McNeil, Scott A. '56 '92 C&L.276 B.S., J.D.
(adm. in MA; not adm. in CT; Pat.) Assoc. Coun., Patents, Bristol-Myers Squibb
Mezzanotte, John F., (BV) .... '47 '73 C.1030 B.A. L.602 J.D. 256 N. Main St.
Miserendino, Anthony J. '27 '75 C.1149 B.S. L.818 J.D.
(adm. in MA; not adm. in CT) 35 Mulligan Drive
Mitchell, Lawrence W. .... '64 '90 C.150 B.A. L.608 J.D. KSI Inc.
Molloy, Joan C., (BV) .... '49 '83 C&L.184 B.A., J.D. [Loughlin F.]
*PRACTICE AREAS: Real Estate; Land Use and Development; Environmental Law; Family.
Morse, David M. '42 '79 C.696 B.S. L.823 J.D.
(adm. in NY; not adm. in CT; Pat.) Coun., Pat., Bristol-Myers Squibb Co.
Olevson, Ken '46 '83 C.768 B.S. L.770 J.D.
(adm. in CA; not adm. in CT) V.P., Quantum
Parsons, Kevin D., (BV) .... '62 '89 [Parsons&A.]
Parsons & Abrams, LLC, (BV) .... 45 Fair St.
Perez, Plinio .... '57 '83 C.352 B.B.A. L.823 J.D. Amphenol Corp.
Pierson, W. Glen .... '69 '96 C.674 A.B. L.276 J.D. [Loughlin F.]
Raccio, Lynn M., (BV) .... '64 '89 C.1030 B.A. L.1048 J.D. 1062 Barnes Rd., Ste. 110
Reed, Charles P., (BV) .... '64 '90 C.597 B.A. L.602 J.D. [Loughlin F.]
*PRACTICE AREAS: Personal Injury Litigation; Commercial Litigation; Insurance Defense.
Rizzo, Kate L. .... '60 '88 C.184 B.A L.1029 J.D. [Loughlin F.]
*PRACTICE AREAS: Domestic; Family Law; Real Estate.
Rockwell, Charles D. '58 '83 C.1156 B.A. L.930 J.D.
Van Court Prop. Mgmt. Servs., LTD
Rolla, Louis A .... '48 '77 C.724 B.A. L.602 J.D. P.O. Box 4191
Ryan, Richard P. .... '38 '93 C.383 L.184 J.D. Coun., Pat., Bristol-Myers Squibb Co.
Schuck, William '28 '52 C&L.472 A.B., LL.B.
(adm. in FL; not adm. in CT) 10 Research Pkwy.
Seaver, David R. .... '58 '94 C.463 B.S. L.184 J.D. [David R.S.]
Secol, Kenneth F., (BV) '46 '71
C.94 B.S. L.273 J.D. 850 N. Main Street Extension, Ste. 2A
Sheftel, Stephen M. .... '68 '93 C.1033 B.S. L.472 J.D. Connecticut Telephone
Shields, James F., (BV) .... '60 '85 C.21 B.A. L.1029 J.D. 35 Thorpe Ave.
Silverstein, Leila Ellen .... '67 '93 C.174 B.A. L.978 J.D. 1062 Barnes Rd.
Volpe, Mark F. .... '63 '89 C.184 B.A. L.306 J.D. 1062 Barnes Rd.
Wetmore, Robert G., Law Offices of, (BV) '52 '83
C.184 B.A. L.306 J.D. 339 Main Street-Yalesville
Woods, Dani Linn '61 '86 C.105 B.A. L.818 J.D.
(adm. in MA; not adm. in CT)
State Claims Counsel, Nationwide Mutual Insurance Company
Wright, Philip A., Jr. .... '54 '83 C.1102 B.S. L.823 J.D. Prob. J.
Zemetis, Terence A., (AV) .... '52 '77 C.184 B.A. L.982 J.D. [Delaney,Z.D.D.&N.]
*PRACTICE AREAS: Arbitration Law; Construction Law; Negligence Law; Insurance Law; Personal Injury Law.

WAREHOUSE POINT, 1,936, *Hartford Co.*

Butenkoff, George G., (CV) .... '32 '73 C.570 B.S. L.184 J.D. 169 Wells Rd.

WARREN, 1,027, *Litchfield Co.*

Abrahams, Richard K. .... '25 '48 C.309 A.B. L.178 LL.B. 111 Town Hill Rd.‡

WASHINGTON, 3,657, *Litchfield Co.*

DeRosa, David V. .... '73 '99 C.93 B.A. L.1252 J.D. P.O. Box 332
Greene, Marc Ford .... '49 '82 C.145 B.A. L.424 J.D. 16 Orchard Ln.
Hardee, Covington '19 '47 C.1365 A.B. L.309 LL.B.
(adm. in MA; not adm. in CT) 9 Mallory Brook Rd.‡
Lynch, David O. '23 '53 C.24 A.B. L.188 LL.B.
(adm. in NY; not adm. in CT) 28 Jupiter Meadow Rd.‡
Manning, Ecton R. .... '37 '63 C.880 B.E. L.893 LL.B. 49 Painter Ridge Rd.
Schaffner, Rosanne K. .... '37 '84 C.184 B.A. L.1040 J.D. 12 Painter Ridge Rd.

WASHINGTON DEPOT, —, *Litchfield Co.*

Blume, Elbaum, Collins & Kelly, P.C., (AV)
5 Green Hill Road, 2nd Floor (⊙West Hartford)
Cornell, Paul Lincoln, Jr., (BV) '30 '58
C.976 B.A. L.184 LL.B. Rte. 47, Washington Mews

Cramer & Anderson LLP, (AV)
Van Sinderen Building, 2 Green Hill Road, P.O. Box 321, 06794 ⊙
Telephone: 860-868-0527 Fax: 860-868-9342
Email: wfairbairn@cramer-anderson.com URL: http://www.cramer-anderson.com
Reginald William H. Fairbairn.
General Practice. Probate, Estate Planning, Municipal, Family and Real Estate. Trials. Planning and Zoning, Corporate, Banking, Securities.
Danbury, Connecticut Office: 68 North Street. Telephone: 203-790-7747. Email: danbury@crameranderson

(This Listing Continued)

Cramer & Anderson LLP (Continued)

Litchfield, Connecticut Office: 46 West Street. P.O. Box 278. Telephone: 860-567-8718. Email: litchfield@cramer-anderson.com
Kent, Connecticut Office: Kent Green, P.O. Box 333. Telephone: 860-927-3568. Email: gnelson@cramer-anderson.com
New Milford, Connecticut Office: 51 Main Street. Telephone: 860-355-2631. Email: newmilford@crameranderson.com
See Professional Biographies, WASHINGTON DEPOT, CONNECTICUT

Fairbairn, Reginald William H. .... '49 '75 C.504 B.A. L.862 J.D. [Cramer&A.]
*PRACTICE AREAS: Estate Planning; Probate Administration; Planning and Zoning; Elder Law; Real Estate.
Kelly, James G. .... '62 '88 C.184 B.A. L.724 J.D. 18 Titus Rd.
Peckerman, Edward R., Jr., (AV) '05 '29 C.674 A.B. L.178 LL.B.
(adm. in NY; not adm. in CT) 162 Sabbaday Lane‡

WATERBURY, 108,961, *New Haven Co.*

Agati, Salvatore C., (BV) .... '57 '82 C.1030 B.A. L.831 J.D. [Rinaldi,Z.B.A.&L.]
Alexander, Joan K. .... '62 '87 C.976 B.S. L.184 J.D. Asst. State's Atty.
Ambrozaitis, John J., (BV) .... '51 '76 C.309 A.B. L.790 J.D. [FitzMaurice&A.]
Andrew, Christine I. .... '42 '84 C.478 A.B. L.188 J.D. [[A] Carmody&T.]
*PRACTICE AREAS: Corporate Law; Commercial Law; Elder Law.
Antonacci, Raymond J., (BV) .... '48 '74 C&L.184 B.A., J.D. 301 Highland Ave.
Asman, Andrea Doyle .... '71 '97 C.518 B.A. L.306 J.D. 500 Chase Pkwy., 4th Fl.
Atkins, Richard F., (BV) .... '40 '70 C.184 B.S. L.1202 J.D. [Maloney,S.&A.]
Avitabile, Louis S., (BV) .... '43 '68 C&L.184 B.A., LL.B. 182 Grand St.
Berger, Mitchell M., (BV) .... '53 '80 C.321 A.B. L.184 J.D. 80 Phoenix Ave.
Bergin, Anthony P. .... '53 '79 C.602 B.A. L.128 J.D. 144 Buckingham St.
Blazi, John A., Law Offices of .... '53 '86 C.1156 B.S. L.1029 J.D. 1138 W. Main St.
Bozzuto, David J., (BV) .... '48 '81 C.319 B.A. L.1048 J.D. [Secor,C.&M.]
*PRACTICE AREAS: Civil Litigation; Criminal Law; Personal Injury; Workers Compensation; Divorce.
Brannelly, Catherine Caroline, (BV) '55 '81 C.1030 B.A. L.1029 J.D.
Asst. State's Atty.‡
Brayton, Thomas L., (AV) .... '32 '61 C.676 B.S. L.184 LL.B. [[A] Carmody&T.]
Breakstone, Douglas M. .... '52 '88 C.184 B.S. L.978 J.D. 69 Linden St.
Breg, Noël Ruggiero, (BV) .... '54 '81 C.788 A.B. L.1206 J.D. [Breg&B.]
Breg, William F., (BV) .... '52 '81 C.867 B.A. L.276 J.D. [Breg&B.]
Breg and Breg, (BV) .... 49 Leavenworth St.
Brenia, Bruce W., (BV) .... '48 '74 C.94 B.S. L.818 J.D. 192 Grand St.
Brennan, James P. .... '53 '85 C.1263 A.B. L.184 J.D. [Brennan&I.]
Brennan & Isaac, (BV) .... 37 Leavenworth St.
Broder, Gary L., (BV) .... '50 '75 C&L.184 B.A., J.D. 89 Roseland Ave.
Broderick, Michael, III, (BV) ..... '50 '80 C.433 B.A. L.823 J.D. [[A] Moynahan,R.M.&M.]
Brown, Louise Allen, (BV) .... '58 '83 C.562 B.A. L.823 J.D. Asst. Corp. Coun.
Brunnock, Thomas P., (BV) .... '48 '74 C.676 B.S. L.128 J.D. [Brunnock&C.]
Brunnock & Cicchetti, LLC, (BV) .... 58 Gaffney Pl.
Bruno, Richard, (BV) .... '40 '68 C.36 B.A. L.37 J.D. [Rinaldi,Z.B.A.&L.]
Buckley, Dennis M., (BV) .... '46 '72 C.524 B.S. L.93 J.D. 1062 Meriden Rd.
Budny, Joseph F., (AV) .... '41 '67 C.1062 B.A. L.276 J.D. [Carmody&T.]
*PRACTICE AREAS: Health Care; Corporate Law; Commercial Law.
Calabrese, John P. .... '65 '92 C.1033 B.S.B.A. L.823 J.D. [[A] Kernan&H.]
*PRACTICE AREAS: Civil Litigation; General Practice; Real Estate.
Calkins, Thomas W., (BV) .... '53 '81 C.537 B.A. L.1040 J.D. 35 Field St.
Capuano, Mark D., (BV) .... '51 '77 C.184 B.S. L.472 J.D. 49 Leavenworth St.
Carmody, Timothy R., (AV) .... '38 '63 C.1030 B.A. L.184 LL.B. [Carmody&T.]
*PRACTICE AREAS: Commercial Real Estate; Construction; Public Utilities.

Carmody & Torrance LLP, (AV) BB
50 Leavenworth Street, P.O. Box 1110, 06721-1110 ⊙
Telephone: 203-573-1200 Facsimile: 203-575-2600
Email: contactus@carmodylaw.com URL: http://www.carmodylaw.com
Partners: Timothy R. Carmody; Joseph F. Budny; Anthony M. Fitzgerald (Resident, New Haven Office); Norman K. Jellinghaus; Kenneth J. Pocius; Burton Z. Alter (Resident, New Haven Office); Charles F. Corcoran, III (Resident, New Haven Office); James K. Robertson, Jr.; Thomas R. Candrick, Jr. (Resident, New Haven Office); Trudie Ross Hamilton; Augustus R. Southworth III; David L. Sfara (Also at Southbury Office); John D. Yarbrough, Jr.; Maureen Danehy Cox; Mark J. Malaspina; Susan Seidler Chambers (Resident, New Haven Office); D. Charles Stohler; Ann Harris Rubin (Resident, New Haven Office); Marianne Barbino Dubuque; Thomas J. Sansone (Resident, New Haven Office); Joseph A. Wellington; Joseph L. Kinsella; Ann Hedges Zucker (Resident, New Haven Office); Kathleen Lenehan Nastri; Christopher Rooney (Resident, New Haven Office); Joseph E. Dornfried; M. Anne Peters; Michael J. Reardon (Also at Southbury Office); Brian T. Henebry; Arthur G. Schaier; Giovanna Tiberii Weller; John L. Cordani; Howard K. Levine (Resident, New Haven Office); John R. Horvack, Jr.; Kristin Connors; Richard L. Street. Of Counsel: G. Bradford Palmer; Walter F. Torrance, Jr.; Thomas L. Brayton; Jean B. Mauro. Counsel: J. Allen Kerr, Jr. Associates: Rona C. Lynch; Christine I. Andrew; Jennifer E. Sills; Mariella LaRosa; William M. O'Donnell, III; Leslie Gold McPadden; Domenico Zaino, Jr.; Michael L. Ferguson; Matthew R. Peterson; Susan LoFaso Henebry; David S. Hardy (Resident, New Haven Office); Isabella S. Murray; Pamela Levin Costa; Russell A. Green; William G. Lewis (Resident, New Haven Office); David T. Payne (Not admitted in CT); Anne D. Peterson (Resident, New Haven Office); Alexander G. Snyder; Douglas W. Royce (Not admitted in CT); Lucy M. Romeo (Resident, New Haven Office).
General Practice including Administrative, Alternative Dispute Resolution, Antitrust and Trade Regulation, Arbitration, Banking, Bankruptcy, Bond Finance, Closely Held Business, Commercial Real Estate, Commercial Litigation, Complex Litigation, Construction, Contracts, Corporate, Creditors' Rights, Employment Benefits, Employer Defense, Energy, Environmental, ERISA, Estate Planning, Family Business Successions, Finance, Freedom of Information, Government (State and Municipal Contracts), Health Care, Insurance, Intellectual Property, Patents and Trademarks, Labor and Employment, Land Use, Management Counseling, Medical Malpractice Defense, Municipal, Nonprofit Organizations, Pension, Privatization, Probate, Products Liability, Professional Liability Defense, Profit Sharing, Public-Private Finance, Public Utility, Securities, Tax, Toxic Torts, Zoning Law. General Civil, Criminal and Appellate Practice in all Courts.
Representative Clients: Algonquin Gas Transmission Co.; Anthem Blue Cross & Blue Shield of Connecticut, Inc.; Fleet Boston Financial Co.; MacDermid, Inc.; Northeast Utilities; Timex Corp.; Verizon Wireless; Waterbury Hospital.
Trial Counsel for: Aetna Life and Casualty; St. Paul Fire & Marine Insurance.
New Haven, Connecticut Office: 195 Church Street, P.O. Box 1950, 06509-1950. Telephone: 203-777-5501. Facsimile: 203-784-3199.
Southbury, Connecticut Office: 900 Main Street South. P.O. Box 410, 06488-0410. Telephone: 203-264-7882. Facsimile: 203-264-7847.
See Professional Biographies, WATERBURY, CONNECTICUT

Carrington, Mark, (BV) .... '52 '78 C.829 B.A. L.184 J.D. [Palumbo,P.&C.]
Casagrande, Anthony A. .... '53 '79 C.306 B.A. L.796 J.D. 144 Buckingham Street
Casagrande, Pamela J. .... '64 '92 C.911 B.S. L.1040 J.D. [[A] A.A.Casagrande]
Cassidy, John H., Jr., (AV) .... '24 '51 C.276 A.B. L.178 LL.B. [Secor,C.&M.]
*PRACTICE AREAS: Civil Litigation; Probate; Corporate Law; Real Estate.
Caulfield, James P., (BV) .... '35 '64 C.184 B.A. L.128 LL.B. 35 Field St.
Cavanaugh, Katie .... '66 '96 C.184 B.S. L.1252 J.D. P.O. Box 11106
Cetta, John Michael .... '70 '98 C.184 B.G.S. L.776 J.D. 300 Grand St.
Chase, Robert L., (BV) .... '42 '66 C.550 B.A. L.724 J.D. [Feeley,N.C.M.&P.]
Cicchetti, Carl R., (BV) .... '47 '74 C.676 A.B. L.188 J.D. [Brunnock&C.]
Cicchetti, Michael H., (BV) .... '46 '72 C.829 B.A. L.184 J.D. [Cicchetti&T.]
*PRACTICE AREAS: Real Estate; Planning and Zoning; Corporate/Business Law; Personal Injury; Municipal Law.

Cicchetti & Tansley, (BV)
500 Chase Parkway, 06708
Telephone: 203-574-4700 Fax: 203-574-2902
Email: cicchetti-tansley-law.com URL: http://www.lawyers.com/cicchetti-tansley
Members of Firm: Michael H. Cicchetti; Michael G. Tansley. Associate: Patrick J. McGrath; Mary Barile Pierce.
General Civil and Criminal Practice before State and Federal Courts; Trial and Appeals, Real Estate, Residential and Commercial, Real Estate Development, Planning and Zoning, Corporate/Business Law, Municipal Law, Commercial Litigation, Personal Injury, Domestic Relations, Workers Compensation Law, Criminal Law, Probate.
See Professional Biographies, WATERBURY, CONNECTICUT

Cohn, Barbara L. .... '48 '74 C.184 B.A. L.178 J.D. [Cohn&C.]
Cohn & Cohn, P.C. .... 534 Frost Rd.
Connors, Kristin .... '66 '93 C.884 B.A. L.184 J.D. [Carmody&T.]
*PRACTICE AREAS: Civil Litigation; Medical Malpractice Defense.
Cordani, John L. .... '63 '93 C.839 B.S. L.1252 J.D. [Carmody&T.] (Pat.)
*PRACTICE AREAS: Patents; Trademarks; Copyrights; Intellectual Property; Chemical Intellectual Property.
Costa, Pamela Levin .... '58 '00 C.94 B.S. L.1252 J.D. [[A] Carmody&T.]
*PRACTICE AREAS: Civil Litigation; Medical Malpractice Defense.

Coté, Andrew C., P.C.
(See Sharon)

Coviello, Leonard P., Jr., (BV) .... '45 '72 C&L.184 B.A., J.D. 299 Fairfield Ave.
Cox, Maureen Danehy, (BV) .... '54 '80 C.321 B.A. L.184 J.D. [Carmody&T.]
*PRACTICE AREAS: Civil Litigation; Public Utilities; Insurance; Freedom of Information; Insurance Defense.
Crean, Robert J., (BV) .... '40 '65 C.1030 B.S. L.306 LL.B. [Hertzmark&C.]
Crozier, Ralph C. .... '52 '77 C&L.472 B.A., J.D. 90 Riverport Rd.
Crutcher, William C., (AV) .... '29 '58 C.277 B.M.E. L.421 J.D. [Gager&P.] (Pat.)
*PRACTICE AREAS: Patent; Trademarks; Copyrights; Intellectual Property.
Daly, Kevin J., Jr., (BV) .... '61 '87 C&L.184 B.A., J.D. [Upson&D.]
Daly, M. J., III, (BV) .... '24 '57 C.453 B.S.M.E. L.184 LL.B. 50 Holmes Ave.
Danen, Richard A., (BV) .... '45 '70 C.1155 B.S.B.A. L.818 J.D. [Matzkin,K.&D.]
Diamond, Bruce W., (BV) ..... '58 '85 C.732 B.A. L.184 J.D. 625 Wolcott Street, Suite 21
Diebolt, Karen, (BV) .... '56 '82 C&L.37 B.A., J.D. 49 Leavenworth St.

Dodd, Lessack, Ranando & Dalton, L.L.C.
(See Cheshire)

Doherty, Margaret M. .... '60 '99 C.147 B.A. L.809 J.D. [[A] Tinley,N.R.&D.]
*PRACTICE AREAS: Personal Injury; Commercial Litigation.
Donnarumma, Francis M. .... '53 '78 C.1030 B.A. L.128 J.D. 100 Grand St.
Dornfried, Joseph E., (BV) .... '62 '87 C.1030 B.A. L.575 J.D. [Carmody&T.]
*PRACTICE AREAS: Corporate Law; Commercial Law; Energy; International Law; Project Finance.
Dost, Mark W., (AV) .... '55 '81 C.454 B.A. L.93 J.D. [Tinley,N.R.&D.]
*PRACTICE AREAS: Estate Planning; Probate; Taxation; Elder Law.
Doyle, Donald H., Jr. .... '54 '80 C.1057 B.A. L.1029 J.D. Wrkrs. Comp. J.
Drubner, Norman S., (AV) .... '39 '63 C.94 B.S. L.178 LL.B. [Drubner,H.O.&M.]
*PRACTICE AREAS: Finance; Real Estate Law; Commercial Transfers; Corporate Law; Zoning Law.

Drubner, Hartley, O'Connor & Mengacci, (AV) BB
500 Chase Parkway, 06708
Telephone: 203-753-9291 FAX: 203-753-6373
Email: drubner@dhom.com
Members of Firm: Norman S. Drubner; James E. Hartley, Jr.; Gary B. O'Connor; Joseph A. Mengacci; Gary D. Jones. Associates: Linda T. Wihbey.
Securities Litigation, Commercial and Business Litigation, Class Actions, Commercial Financing, Corporate Law, Mergers and Acquisitions, Commercial Law, Bonding Transactions, Administrative Law, Health Care Law, Real Estate, Condemnation, Tax Appeals, Zoning, Eminent Domain. General Civil Trial Practice in State and Federal Courts. Personal Injury, Product Liability, Medical Malpractice, Appellate Practice, Family Law.
See Professional Biographies, WATERBURY, CONNECTICUT

Dubuque, Marianne Barbino, (BV) .... '58 '83 C&L.184 B.A., J.D. [Carmody&T.]
*PRACTICE AREAS: Municipal Law; Zoning and Land Use; Real Estate; Public Utilities.
Duffy, Edward J., Jr., (BV) .... '50 '75 C.262 B.A. L.184 J.D. [Duffy&F.]
Duffy & Fasano, (BV) .... 37 Central Ave.

Engelman & Engelman
(See Southbury)

Errichetti, Christopher, (CV) '56 '85 C.178 B.S. L.184 J.D.
Gen. Coun., Errichetti Assocs.
Eschuk, Cara F., (BV) .... '51 '86 L.184 J.D. Asst. States Atty.
Fasano, Michael A., (BV) .... '49 '76 C.1211 B.A. L.669 J.D. [Duffy&F.]
Fasano, Michael Anthony, Jr. .... '74 '00 C.94 B.A. L.1526 J.D. 37 Central Ave.
Federer, Wendy R. .... '55 '92 C.273 B.A. L.1029 J.D. [Kernan&H.] ⊙
*PRACTICE AREAS: Trust Law; Estate Planning; Estate Administration; Probate.
Feeley, Francis B., (AV) .... '19 '43 C.321 A.B. L.184 J.D. 37 Leavenworth St.
Feeley, Nichols, Chase, McDermott & Pellett P.C., (BV) .... 37 Leavenworth Street
Ferguson, Michael L. .... '63 '98 C.829 B.S. L.184 J.D. [[A] Carmody&T.]
*PRACTICE AREAS: Corporate law; Litigation.
Finn, Patrick W., (BV) .... '63 '89 C.855 B.A. L.1048 J.D. [Secor,C.&M.]
*PRACTICE AREAS: Civil Litigation; Foreclosures; Commercial Litigation.
FitzMaurice, Sean G., (BV) .... '52 '76 C.184 B.S. L.585 J.D. [FitzMaurice&A.]
FitzMaurice & Ambrozaitis, (BV) .... 59 Central Ave.
Fraser, Antonio Flores, (BV) .... '46 '84 C.1030 B.A. L.208 J.D. 144 Buckingham St.
Frizzell, Thomas R., (BV) .... '47 '73 C.184 B.S.B.A. L.896 J.D. 41 Holmes Ave.

Gager & Peterson, LLP, (AV)
One Exchange Place, P.O. Box 2480, 06722-2480 ⊙
Telephone: 203-597-5100 Telecopier: 203-757-7888
William W. Gager (1892-1967); Carl A. Peterson; Curtis V. Titus; William C. Crutcher; Thomas J. McHale; Frank J. Scinto.
General Practice. Corporate Law, Mergers, Acquisitions and Divestitures, Business Law, Banks and Banking, Securities, Administrative Law, Litigation in all Courts, Insurance, Trusts and Estates, Probate, Health Care, Real Estate, Commercial Real Estate, Taxation, Zoning, Planning and Land Use, Patents, Trademarks, Copyrights, Intellectual Property, Consumer Law, Computers and Software, Information Technology, Electronic Commerce, Family Law, Environmental Law, Labor and Employment, Debtor and Creditor, Personal Injury.
Counsel for: BankBoston, NA.; First Union National Bank; The Eastern Co.; Risdon Corp.; Anamet, Inc.; The Platt Brothers & Co.; Caradon, Inc.
Bethel, Connecticut Office: 2 Stony Hill Road. Telephone: 203-207-5400. Telecopier: 203-207-5407.
Litchfield, Connecticut Office: 782 Bantam Road. Telephone: 860-567-0828. Telecopier: 860-567-5844.
Sharon, Connecticut Office: 25 West Main Street, P.O. Box 158. Telephone: 860-364-5531. Telecopier: 860-364-5805.
Southbury, Connecticut Office: 325 Main Street South. Telephone: 203-262-6600. Telecopier: 203-262-6780.
See Professional Biographies, WATERBURY, CONNECTICUT

Geghan, Carey R., (BV) .... '38 '64 C.262 B.S.S. L.128 J.D. [Mahaney&G.]
Geremia, Joseph A., Jr., (BV) .... '56 '83 C.1156 B.S. L.1029 J.D. 61 Holmes Ave.
Giardina, Giovanna Trocchi .... '69 '97 C.184 B.A. L.1252 J.D. [[A] Kernan&H.]
*PRACTICE AREAS: Civil Litigation.
Giordano, Phillip A. .... '63 '91 C.184 B.A. L.1187 J.D. 1169 W. Main St.

Goddard, Charles J., (BV) .... '48 '82 C.93 B.A. L.128 J.D. [Ⓐ Moynahan,R.M.&M.]
Goettel, Gerard L. '28 '55 C.228 B.A. L.178 LL.B.
(adm. in NY; not adm. in CT) Sr. U.S. Dist. J.
Goldberg, Jack R. .... '52 '92 C.588 L.184 J.D. 95 Westridge Dr.
Grady, Francis J., (BV) .... '44 '69 C.184 B.A. L.818 J.D. [Grady&R.]
Grady & Riley, (BV) .... 86 Buckingham St.
Gray, Donald A., Jr. '— '59 C.976 B.A. L.564 LL.B.
Pres. & Gen. Coun., Western Conn. Indus. Council, Inc.
Green, Russell A. .... '67 '94 C&L.184 B.A., J.D. [Ⓐ Carmody&T.]
*PRACTICE AREAS: Civil Litigation.
Griffin, David W., (BV) .... '56 '83 C.354 B.A. L.326 J.D. [Ⓐ Griffin&G.]
*PRACTICE AREAS: Commercial Law; Restructuring and Bankruptcy Law; Real Estate and Land Use Law; Corporate Law; Family Law.
Griffin, Stephen R., (BV) .... '53 '78 C.31 B.A. L.184 J.D. [Griffin&G.]
*PRACTICE AREAS: Real Estate; Banking Law; Collections; Foreclosures.
Griffin, Walter R., (AV) .... '21 '49 C.951 B.A. L.893 LL.B. [Griffin&G.]
*PRACTICE AREAS: Trust Law; Estate Planning; Banking Law; Real Estate; Corporate Law.

Griffin & Griffin, P.C., (AV)
Webster Plaza, Corner Bank and Grand Streets, P.O. Box 2184, 06702
Telephone: 203-755-1106 Fax: 203-596-7983
URL: http://wwwgriffinlawfirm.com
Walter R. Griffin; Stephen R. Griffin;—Linda N. Marini Mayo; David W. Griffin.
General Practice. Real Estate, Estate Planning, Probate and Commercial Law, Banks and Banking.
Representative Clients: Webster Bank; Web-Worx, LLC.; Dtec, Inc.; Webster Financial Corp.; Automotive Internet Management, Inc.
Approved Attorneys For: Connecticut Attorneys Title Insurance Co.

Hallum, Marcus V. .... '49 '75 C.575 B.A. L.861 J.D. 678 Chase Pkwy.
Hamilton, Trudie Ross, (AV) .... '44 '80 C.999 M.A. L.184 J.D. [Carmody&T.]
*PRACTICE AREAS: Civil Litigation; Medical Malpractice Defense; Products Liability Defense; Health Care; Professional Liability Defense.
Hanahan, Robert P., (BV) .... '47 '74 C.1102 B.A. L.184 J.D. 80 Phoenix Ave.
Harrigan, Dennis F. .... '30 '55 C&L.262 B.S., J.D. Supr. Ct. J.
Hartley, James E., Jr., (AV) .... '50 '75 C.94 B.S. L.178 J.D. [Drubner,H.O.&M.]
*PRACTICE AREAS: Commercial Litigation; Class Actions; Securities Litigation.
Hartley, Scott A. .... '53 '80 C.550 B.A. L.184 J.D. Trial Ct. Admr., State Jud. Branch
Healey, Frank T., Jr., (AV) .... '28 '51 C.321 A.B. L.93 LL.B. [Healey&P.] ‡
Healey & Phelan, (AV) .... 66 Linden St.
Healy, Jennifer R. .... '71 '96 C.787 B.A. L.945 J.D. 50 Leavenworth St.
Henebry, Brian T., (BV) .... '62 '90 C.659 B.S. L.893 J.D. [Carmody&T.]
*PRACTICE AREAS: Civil Litigation; Public Utility Regulation.
Henebry, Susan LoFaso .... '64 '92 C.823 B.S. L.262 J.D. [Ⓐ Carmody&T.]
*PRACTICE AREAS: Public Finance; Bond Finance.
Henry, Charles W., (AV) .... '49 '75 C.393 B.A. L.818 J.D. [Kernan&H.] ⊙
*PRACTICE AREAS: Trust Law; Estate Planning; Estate Administration; Probate.
Henry, Donald W., (AV) .... '17 '46 C&L.976 A.B., LL.B. [Ⓒ Kernan&H.]
Hershfield, Leonie .... '58 '88 C.855 B.A. L.184 J.D. Asst. V.P., Bank of Boston Conn.
Hertzmark, Alan H., (BV) .... '39 '64 C.184 B.A. L.893 LL.B. [Hertzmark&C.]
Hertzmark & Crean, P.C., (BV) .... 76 Center St.
Hickey, William F., III, (BV) .... '49 '74 C.93 B.A. L.818 J.D. 49 Leavenworth St.
Hodgson, Beverly J. .... '48 '76 C.103 A.B. L.976 J.D. Supr. Ct. J.
Holzberg, Robert L. .... '52 '78 C.103 A.B. L.184 J.D. Supr. J.
Horvack, John R., Jr. .... '67 '92 C.985 B.S. L.1252 J.D. [Carmody&T.]
*PRACTICE AREAS: Commercial Litigation; Intellectual Property Litigation; Personal Injury Litigation.
Isaac, Leonard M., (BV) .... '58 '86 C.1044 B.A. L.1066 J.D. [Brennan&I.]
Jellinghaus, Norman K., (AV) .... '39 '69 C.976 B.A. L.276 J.D. [Carmody&T.]
*PRACTICE AREAS: Corporate Law; Taxation; Project Finance.
Jones, Gary D. .... '55 '80 C.1036 B.A. L.569 J.D. [Drubner,H.O.&M.]
*PRACTICE AREAS: Commercial Financing; Corporate Law; Bond Finance; Mergers and Acquisitions; Administrative Law.
Kernan, James E., (AV) .... '47 '71 C.93 A.B. L.273 J.D. [Kernan&H.]
*PRACTICE AREAS: Civil Litigation.

Kernan & Henry, (AV)
207 Bank Street, 06702 ⊙
Mailing Address: P.O. Box 2156, Waterbury, Connecticut 06722
Telephone: 203-756-8961 FAX: 203-754-2353
Email: kernanandhenry@email.msn.com
Members of Firm: James E. Kernan; Charles W. Henry; David J. Scully; John K. McDonald; Wendy R. Federer. Associates: Giovanna Trocchi Giardina; Michael A. Giardina (Resident, Southbury Office); John P. Calabrese; Jonathan Kocienda. Of Counsel: Donald W. Henry.
Civil Trial Litigation, Estate Planning and Probate.
Representative Clients: ITT Hartford; Liberty Mutual Insurance Co.; LMI Insurance Co.; Hermitage Insurance Co.
Southbury Office: 9 Heritage Road. Telephone: 203-264-5606. Fax: 203-264-4409.
See Professional Biographies, WATERBURY, CONNECTICUT

Kerr, J. Allen, Jr. .... '44 '69 C.210 B.A. L.306 J.D. [Ⓒ Carmody&T.]
*PRACTICE AREAS: Municipal Law; Land Use; Commercial Real Estate.
Kinloch, William R., (BV) .... '48 '85 C.184 B.A. L.1048 J.D. P.O. Box 742
Kinsella, Joseph L., (BV) .... '59 '84 C.319 B.A. L.823 J.D. [Carmody&T.]
*PRACTICE AREAS: Banking; Bankruptcy; Commercial Law.
Kocienda, Jonathan .... '72 '97 C.321 B.a. L.184 J.D. [Ⓐ Kernan&H.]
*PRACTICE AREAS: Litigation; General Practice.
Kolesnik, Robert S. .... '41 '66 C.1030 B.S.S. L.276 J.D. [Kolesnik N.&R.]
Kolesnik Norris & Rado .... 80 Central Ave.
Kostecki, Mark, (BV) .... '50 '76 C.103 A.B. L.930 J.D. 63 Central Ave.
Krug, Frederick W., (AV) .... '42 '70 C&L.178 B.A., LL.B. [Matzkin,K.&D.]
LaRosa, Mariella .... '62 '94 C.938 B.A. L.306 J.D. [Ⓐ Carmody&T.]
*PRACTICE AREAS: Health Care.
Lawlor, James J., (AV) .... '42 '67 C.1030 A.B. L.93 LL.B. 193 Grand St.
Leder, Mark R. .... '48 '85 C.976 B.A. L.184 J.D. 141 E. Main St.
Lombard, Frank P., (BV) .... '47 '73 C.184 B.A. L.818 J.D. [St. John,S.L.&S.]
Lubus, Robert C., Jr., (BV) .... '63 '88 C.401 B.S. L.884 J.D. 86 Buckingham St.
Lugauskas, Lisa Jean, (BV) .... '61 '84 C.184 B.A. L.101 J.D. [Rinaldi,Z.B.A.&L.]
Lynch, Rona C., (BV) .... '57 '83 C.184 B.S. L.1048 J.D. [Ⓐ Carmody&T.]
*PRACTICE AREAS: Civil Litigation.
Mahaney, Daniel J., (BV) .... '54 '80 C.1030 B.A. L.285 J.D. [Mahaney&G.]
Mahaney, John D., (AV) .... '29 '57 C.1030 B.S.S. L.184 LL.B. [Ⓒ Mahaney&G.] ‡
Mahaney & Geghan, (BV) .... One Exchange Pl.
Malaspina, Mark J. .... '57 '82 C.1030 B.A. L.976 J.D. [Carmody&T.]
*PRACTICE AREAS: State Government; Municipal Government; Corporate; Commercial; Commercial Real Estate.
Maloney, Patrick E., (BV) .... '43 '71 C.433 B.S. L.1294 LL.B. [Maloney,S.&A.]
Maloney, St. John & Atkins, LLC, (BV) .... 21 State Street
Manning, John G. .... '44 '71 C.103 A.B. L.178 J.D. 33 Church St.
Maragos, Angelo .... '64 '89 C.184 B.S. L.902 J.D. 86 Buckingham St.
Marano, Richard M., (BV) .... '60 '85 C.1030 B.A. L.776 J.D. 61 Field Street
Marcuse, Peter, (BV) .... '28 '52 C.309 B.A. L.976 LL.B. 140 Greenwood Ave.‡
Mariani, Terence D., (BV) .... '33 '75 C.103 A.B. L.184 LL.B. Coun. to Gov.
Marryatt-Romaniello, Glorie .... '70 '96 C.999 B.A. L.1252 J.D. 61 Holmes Ave.
Martin, Edwin A. .... '34 '63 C.188 B.S. L.184 LL.B. Tr. Dept., Colonial Bk. & Tr. Co.
Martocchio, Louis .... '66 '91 C.1102 B.S. L.1029 J.D. 141 E. Main Street
Mascolo, Frederic E., (BV) .... '29 '54 C.776 B.S. L.276 J.D. [Moynahan,R.M.&M.]
Matasavage, Mark, (BV) .... '51 '82 C.454 B.B.A. L.1048 J.D. [Matasavage&M.]
Matasavage, Paul, (BV) .... '58 '84 C.321 A.B. L.818 J.D. [Matasavage&M.]
Matasavage, Vincent P. .... '12 '42 C.823 B.S. L.309 LL.B. 48 Stoddard Rd.‡
Matasavage & Matasavage, (BV) .... 38 Central Ave.
Matzkin, Krug & Danen, P.C., (AV) .... 76 Center St.
Mauro, Jean B. .... '36 '73 C.976 B.E. L.446 J.D. [Ⓒ Carmody&T.] (Pat.)‡
*PRACTICE AREAS: Corporate Law; Intellectual Property.
Mayo, Linda N. Marini, (BV) .... '66 '91 C.184 B.A. L.1048 J.D. [Ⓐ Griffin&G.]
*PRACTICE AREAS: Real Estate; Landlord and Tenant Law; Foreclosures.
McCarthy, John R. .... '47 '71 C.976 B.A. L.477 J.D. Conn. Legal Servs.
McCormack, James K., (BV) .... '32 '68 C&L.184 B.S., J.D. [McCormack,J.K.&M.D.M.]
McCormack, Matthew D. .... '60 '96 C.829 B.S. L.201 J.D. [McCormack,J.K.&M.D.M.]
McCormack, James K., and Matthew D. McCormack, (BV) .... 90 Pierpont Rd.

McCormick, Paulding & Huber, LLP
(See Hartford)

McDermott, Thomas F., Jr., (BV) .... '44 '69 C.93 A.B. L.184 J.D. [Feeley,N.C.M.&P.]
McDonald, John K., (BV) .... '60 '87 C.319 B.A. L.930 J.D. [Kernan&H.]
*PRACTICE AREAS: Civil Litigation.
McDonough, Thomas K., (BV) .... '54 '79 C.829 B.A. L.831 J.D. 144 Buckingham St.
McGill, Donald W., (BV) .... '46 '72 C.436 B.A. L.724 J.D. [McGill&M.]
McGill & McGill, (BV) .... 56 Gaffney Pl.
McGrath, Patrick J. .... '72 '98 C.676 B.A. L.818 J.D. [Ⓐ Cicchetti&T.]
*PRACTICE AREAS: Land Use; Municipal Law; Personal Injury; Civil Litigation.
McHale, Thomas J., (AV) .... '41 '67 C.745 B.A. L.128 J.D. [Gager&P.] (⊙Bethel)
*PRACTICE AREAS: Banking Law; Computer Law; Labor and Employment Law.
McPadden, Leslie Gold .... '69 '96 C.94 B.S. L.982 J.D. [Ⓐ Carmody&T.]
*PRACTICE AREAS: Insurance Defense; Health Law.
McPartland, Donald, (AV) .... '38 '62 C&L.976 B.A., LL.B. [Secor,C.&M.]
*PRACTICE AREAS: Civil Litigation; Medical Malpractice; Corporate Law; Real Estate.
McPartland, Donald C. .... '69 '97 C.241 B.A. L.1187 J.D. [Ⓐ Secor,C.&M.]
*PRACTICE AREAS: Personal Injury; Insurance Defense; Criminal Law; Land Use.
McTaggart, Gail E., (BV) .... '44 '81 C.267 B.A. L.184 J.D. [Secor,C.&M.]
*PRACTICE AREAS: Commercial Law; Real Estate; Municipal Law; Land Use; Banking.
Melchionne, Eugene S., (CV) .... '55 '82 C.184 B.A. L.221 J.D. 27 First Ave.
Mellon, Robert E., (BV) .... '25 '52 C.740 B.A. L.945 B.C.L. 49 Leavenworth St.
Mengacci, Joseph A., (AV) .... '50 '76 C.397 B.S. L.425 J.D. [Drubner,H.O.&M.]
*PRACTICE AREAS: Civil Litigation; Appellate Practice; Administrative Law.
Mezzy, Randi Faith .... '52 '78 C.659 B.A. L.178 J.D. Conn. Legal Servs.
Minnella, Martin J. .... '47 '74 C.831 B.B.A. L.1202 J.D. [Moynahan,R.M.&M.]
Mirkhani, Mary S. .... '60 '85 C.1030 B.A. P.O. Box 2244

Monagan, Philip H., (CV) '59 '85 C.184 B.S. L.472 J.D.
61 Holmes Avenue, P.O. Box 1817, 06722
Telephone: 203-754-7893 Fax: 203-754-3806
Email: monaganlaw@aol.com URL: http://www.lawyers.com/phmonagan
***PRACTICE AREAS: Personal Injury; Real Estate Settlements; Probate Administration; Elder Law; Commercial Litigation.**
Personal Injury, Commercial Litigation, Family Law, Collection Law, Real Estate, Probate, Elder Law.
See Professional Biographies, WATERBURY, CONNECTICUT

Montwell, Joseph F., (BV) .... '47 '72 C.276 A.B. L.184 J.D. 63 Central Ave.
Mosley, Maurice B., (BV) .... '46 '75 C.789 B.S. L.184 J.D. [Mosley&S.]
Mosley & Sinclair, (BV) .... 32 Linden St.
Mowad, George G., Jr. .... '68 '94 C.1145 B.S. L.1252 J.D. [Ⓐ St. John,S.L.&S.]
Moynahan, Timothy C., (BV) .... '40 '64 C.676 A.B. L.128 LL.B. [Moynahan,R.M.&M.]
Moynahan, Ruskin, Mascolo & Minnella, (BV) .... 141 E. Main St.
Murray, Isabella S. .... '73 '99 C.321 B.A. L.184 J.D. [Ⓐ Carmody&T.]
*PRACTICE AREAS: Civil Litigation; Medical Malpractice Defense; Public Utilities.
Narkis, Robert J., (AV) '34 '61
C.550 B.A. L.976 LL.B. Chm. & CEO, Center Financial Corporation
Nastri, Kathleen Lenehan, (AV) .... '61 '86 C&L.184 B.S., J.D. [Carmody&T.]
*PRACTICE AREAS: Civil Litigation; Personal Injury.
Nastri, Robert, Jr., (AV) .... '55 '85 C.918 B.A. L.184 J.D. [Tinley,N.R.&D.]
*PRACTICE AREAS: Personal Injury; Employment Litigation; Probate Litigation.
Nichols, Robert J. .... '44 '69 C&L.184 B.S., J.D. 3 Second Ave.
Norris, Maureen E. .... '60 '85 C.818 B.A. L.1252 J.D. [Kolesnik N.&R.]
O'Brien, Thomas M., (BV) .... '50 '76 C.745 B.A. L.1003 J.D. Chf. Juv. Pros.
O'Connor, Gary B., (AV) .... '55 '80 C&L.93 B.A., J.D. [Drubner,H.O.&M.]
*PRACTICE AREAS: Commercial and Business Litigation; Administrative Law; Class Actions; Health Care Law.
O'Donnell, William M., III .... '69 '95 C.976 B.A. L.184 J.D. [Ⓐ Carmody&T.]
*PRACTICE AREAS: Civil Litigation.
Oldakowski, Stephen J. .... '65 '91 C.999 B.S. L.1194 J.D. 58 Holmes Ave.
Oman, Charles E., III, (BV) .... '51 '86 C.184 B.S. L.1029 J.D. 100 Grand St.
Oneglia, Catherine S. .... '47 '78 C.706 B.A. L.184 J.D. 37 Leavenworth St.
Palmer, G. Bradford, (AV) .... '24 '52 C.674 A.B. L.976 LL.B. [Ⓒ Carmody&T.]
Palmeri, John J., (BV) .... '57 '84 C.102 B.S. L.1009 J.D. [Ⓒ Secor,C.&M.]
*PRACTICE AREAS: Estate Planning; Estate Administration; Commercial Transactions; Business Planning.
Palumbo, John R., (BV) .... '57 '83 C.184 B.A. L.436 J.D. [Palumbo,P.&C.]
Palumbo, Pasquale .... '22 '49 C.860 B.S. L.276 J.D. [Palumbo,P.&C.]
Palumbo, Palumbo & Carrington, P.C., (BV) .... 193 Grand St.
Parisot, Thomas G., (BV) .... '56 '81 C.754 B.S. L.1048 J.D. [Secor,C.&M.]
*PRACTICE AREAS: Civil Litigation; Workers Compensation.
Paul, Bette Lynn, (BV) .... '57 '85 C.588 B.A. L.1202 J.D. 137 Tower Rd.
Payne, David T. '71 '96 C.16 B.S. L.902 J.D.
(adm. in AL; not adm. in CT) [Ⓐ Carmody&T.]
*PRACTICE AREAS: Corporate Law; Commercial Law; Bankruptcy.
Pellett, Lawrence R., (BV) .... '56 '83 C.401 B.S. L.990 J.D. [Feeley,N.C.M.&P.]
Peters, M. Anne, (BV) .... '52 '83 C.914 B.A. L.93 J.D. [Carmody&T.]
*PRACTICE AREAS: Environmental Law; Underground Storage Tanks.
Peterson, Carl A., (AV) .... '35 '60 C.976 B.A. L.569 LL.B. [Gager&P.]
*PRACTICE AREAS: Real Estate Law; Corporate Law; Banking Law; Commercial Lending.
Peterson, Matthew R. .... '71 '98 C.855 B.A. L.184 J.D. [Ⓐ Carmody&T.]
*PRACTICE AREAS: Civil Litigation; Intellectual Property Licensing.
Petrokaitis, Gina M. .... '67 '94 C.184 B.S. L.1252 J.D. 678 Chase Pkwy.
Phelan, John F., (AV) .... '29 '54 C.321 A.B. L.976 J.D. [Healey&P.]

Pianka, Andrew J. '63 '96 C.999 B.A. L.1252 J.D.
86 Buckingham Street, 06710
Telephone: 203-575-1131 Fax: 203-754-1675
Email: ajpianka@snet.net URL: http://www.attorneypianka.com
***PRACTICE AREAS: Commercial Collections; Bank Collections; Foreclosures; Commercial Litigation; Contracts.**
Personal Injury, Commercial Litigation, Real Estate, Collections, Debtor Creditor, Foreclosure, Landlord/Tenant, Contracts.
See Professional Biographies, WATERBURY, CONNECTICUT

Pierce, Mary Barile ... '66 '91 C.105 B.A. L.128 J.D. [[A] Cicchetti&T.]
*PRACTICE AREAS: General Civil Litigation; Products Liability; Corporate Law.
Pliakas, Stephen E. ... '59 '96 C.676 B.A. L.306 J.D. [[A] Tinley,N.R.&D.]
Pocius, Kenneth J., (AV) ... '42 '70 C&L.184 B.A., J.D. [Carmody&T.]
*PRACTICE AREAS: Banking; Commercial Real Estate; Zoning; Land Use; Municipal Law.
Porzio, Audrey J., (CV) ... '59 '91 C.999 B.A. L.1029 J.D. [[A] Moynahan,R.M.&M.]
Porzio, Julie M., (BV) ... '63 '90 C.93 B.A. L.1014 J.D. [[A] Moynahan,R.M.&M.]
Rado, Danielle S. ... '68 '93 C.999 B.A. L.1048 J.D. [Kolesnik N.&R.]
Reardon, Michael J., (BV) '56 '84 C.183 B.A. L.1029 J.D. [Carmody&T.] (⊙Southbury)
*PRACTICE AREAS: Estate Planning; Business Succession; Trust Administration; Taxation; Probate.
Reilly, Allison Louise ... '62 '92 C.262 B.A. L.1029 J.D. 1138 W. Main St.
Renehan, Richard P., (BV) ... '60 '85 C.321 B.A. L.184 J.D. [Tinley,N.R.&D.]
*PRACTICE AREAS: Personal Injury; Workers Compensation.
Riley, Thomas V., (BV) ... '50 '76 C.884 B.S. L.831 J.D. [Grady&R.]
Rinaldi, Donald J., (BV) ... '38 '63 C.1030 A.B. L.184 J.D. [Rinaldi,Z.B.A.&L.]
Rinaldi, Zipoli, Bruno, Agati and Lugauskas, P.C., (BV) ... 80 Phoenix Ave.
Robertson, James K., Jr., (AV) ... '47 '74 C.976 B.A. L.184 J.D. [Carmody&T.]
*PRACTICE AREAS: Civil Litigation; Arbitration; Mediation.
Roosa, Gary S., (BV) ... '53 '86 C.184 B.a. L.1029 J.D. 1 Exchange Pl., 6th Fl.
Rosa, Nicholas W., (BV) ... '30 '56 C.262 B.S. L.276 J.D. 35 Field St.
Rosenbaum, Alvin, (BV) ... '30 '59 C.184 B.S. L.94 LL.B. 21 Church St.
Royce, Douglas W. '— '00 C.823 B.S. L.262 J.D. (adm. in NY; not adm. in CT) [[A] Carmody&T.]
*PRACTICE AREAS: Corporate Law; Commercial Law.
Rush, Mary Ann, (BV) ... '58 '85 C.93 B.A. L.818 J.D. 86 Buckingham St.
Ruskin, Stephen A., (BV) ... '29 '70 C.659 B.S. L.184 J.D. [Moynahan,R.M.&M.]
Russo, Vincent M. ... '61 '93 C.846 BBA L.8 J.D. 301 Highland Ave.
Ryan, Mary Jane, (BV) ... '45 '78 C.731 B.A. L.184 J.D. [Summa&R.]
*PRACTICE AREAS: Labor and Employment Law.
Ryan, William A. ... '65 '92 C.951 B.A. L.1019 J.D. [[A] Summa&R.]
*PRACTICE AREAS: Labor and Employment Law.
Sabelli, Veronica ... '56 '86 C.475 B.S. L.1187 J.D. Dep. Asst. Pub. Def.
St. John, Gregory G., (BV) ... '49 '75 C.93 B.A. L.1202 J.D. [Maloney,S.&A.]
St. John, William J., Jr., (AV) ... '41 '71 C.1102 B.A. L.818 J.D. [St. John,S.L.&S.]
St. John, Scappini, Lombard & Stevens, (AV) ... 13 1st Avenue
Santarsiero, Christopher G. ... '62 '92 C.262 B.A. L.1252 J.D. [[A] Moynahan,R.M.&M.]
Santucci, John P., (BV) ... '49 '74 C&L.273 B.S.F.S., J.D. [J.P.Santucci]
*PRACTICE AREAS: Real Estate; Torts; Civil Practice; Family Law; Criminal Law.

Santucci, John P., P.C., (BV)
35 Field Street, P.O. Box 2331, 06722-2331
Telephone: 203-574-5059; 574-5008 Facsimile: 203-574-3225
Email: John.P.Santucci.pc@snet.net
John P. Santucci.
General Practice including Alternative Dispute Resolution, Civil Trial Practice including Family Practice, Divorce, Juvenile Neglect, Juvenile Delinquency, Landlord-Tenant, Foreclosure, Real Estate Management Issues, Arbitration, Commercial Real Estate, Insurance, Torts and General Criminal Practice.
See Professional Biographies, WATERBURY, CONNECTICUT

Scappini, Richard J., (BV) ... '46 '71 C&L.184 B.A., J.D. [St. John,S.L.&S.]
Schaier, Arthur G. ... '65 '93 C.107 B.S.E.E. L.569 J.D. [Carmody&T.]
*PRACTICE AREAS: Patents; Trademarks; Copyrights; Intellectual Property.
Schellhardt, Donald Joseph ... '49 '75 C.918 B.A. L.273 J.D. 45 Bracewood Rd.
Scinto, Frank J., (BV) ... '53 '83 C.276 B.S. L.93 J.D. [Gager&P.] (⊙Bethel)
*PRACTICE AREAS: Business Law; Intellectual Property; Commercial Litigation; Employment Law.
Scully, David J., (BV) ... '59 '85 C.184 B.A. L.30 J.D. [Kernan&H.]
*PRACTICE AREAS: Civil Litigation.
Secor, W. Fielding, (BV) ... '42 '67 C.976 B.A. L.188 LL.B. [Secor,C.&M.]
*PRACTICE AREAS: Commercial Law; Banking Law; Real Estate.
Secor, William J., Jr., (AV) ... '14 '39 C&L.976 A.B., LL.B. [[C] Secor,C.&M.]

Secor, Cassidy & McPartland, P.C., (AV)
Successors to Bronson, Lewis, Upson & Secor; Lewis, Hart, Upson & Secor; Upson, Secor, Greene & Cassidy and Upson, Secor, Cassidy & McPartland, P.C.
41 Church Street, P.O. Box 2818, 06723-2818 ⊙
Telephone: 203-757-9261 Fax: 203-756-5762
Email: scm@ctlawyers.com URL: http://www.ctlawyers.com
Nath'l R. Bronson (1860-1949); Lawrence L. Lewis (1881-1965); Charles E. Hart (1884-1972); J. Warren Upson (1903-1992); John H. Cassidy, Jr.; Donald McPartland; W. Fielding Secor; James R. Healey (Resident, Southbury Office); Gail E. McTaggart; Thomas G. Parisot; Patrick W. Finn; David J. Bozzuto;—Donald C. McPartland. Special Tax Counsel: John J. Palmeri. Counsel: William J. Secor, Jr.
General Practice. Estate Planning, Probate, Corporation, Negligence, Real Estate, Land Use, Banking, Municipal, Commercial and Taxation Law. Criminal and Civil Trials in all Courts.
Attorneys for: The Mattatuck Museum; American Republican, Inc.; Hubbard-Hall, Inc.; The Siemon Co.; Engineered Sinterings and Plastics, Inc.; Boutin Industries; County Line Buick-Nissan, Inc.
Southbury, Connecticut Office: 900 Main Street South. Telephone: 203-264-8223. Fax: 203-264-6730.
See Professional Biographies, WATERBURY, CONNECTICUT

Sfara, David L., (AV) ... '52 '77 C.674 A.B. L.893 J.D. [Carmody&T.] (⊙Southbury)
*PRACTICE AREAS: Estate Planning; Business Succession; Taxation; Trust Administration; Probate.
Sheldon, Michael R. ... '49 '75 C.674 A.B. L.976 J.D. Supr. Ct. J.
Shortall, Joseph M. ... '39 '65 C.397 B.S. L.128 LL.B. Supr. Ct. J.
Sills, Jennifer E. ... '65 '93 C.951 B.A. L.184 J.D. [[A] Carmody&T.]
*PRACTICE AREAS: Environmental; OSHA; Commercial Real Estate; Municipal Law; Land Use.
Simmons, Donald C., (BV) ... '26 '67 C.597 B.S. L.184 LL.B. 440 Meadow St.
Sinclair, Roxanne Ellis, (BV) ... '49 '79 [Mosley&S.]
Smith, Marcia B. ... '31 '56 C.659 A.B. L.309 J.D. Asst. State's Atty.
Smolskis, Joseph V. ... '18 '53 C&L.276 B.S.S., J.D. 47 Holmes Ave.‡
Snyder, Alexander G. ... '69 '99 C.999 B.S. L.1252 J.D. [[A] Carmody&T.]
*PRACTICE AREAS: Civil Litigation; Intellectual Property; Utilities.
Southworth, Augustus R., III, (AV) ... '44 '73 C.197 B.A. L.94 J.D. [Carmody&T.]
*PRACTICE AREAS: Civil Litigation; Health Care; Professional Liability Defense; Medical Malpractice Defense; Products Liability Defense.

Spat, Meryl A., (CV) '63 '90 C.293 B.A. L.306 J.D.
182 Grand Street, 06722-2476
Telephone: 203-754-0732 Fax: 203-754-2404
Email: maspat1@yahoo.com URL: http://www.lawyers.com/maspat
***PRACTICE AREAS: Social Security; Workers Compensation; Family Law; Bankruptcy; Consumer Law.**
Social Security, Workers Compensation, Family Law, Bankruptcy, Consumer Protection.
See Professional Biographies, WATERBURY, CONNECTICUT

Stevens, William L., (BV) ... '55 '81 C.184 B.A. L.1048 J.D. [St. John,S.L.&S.]
Stohler, D. Charles, (AV) ... '56 '81 C.529 A.B. L.228 J.D. [Carmody&T.]
*PRACTICE AREAS: Labor and Employment; Employee Benefits; ERISA.
Street, Richard L. ... '68 '93 C.299 A.B. L.228 J.D. [Carmody&T.]
*PRACTICE AREAS: Civil Litigation; Public Utility; Land Use; Administrative Law; Municipal Law.
Sullivan, Christine A., (BV) ... '62 '88 C.321 B.A. L.184 J.D. [Duffy&F.]
Sullivan, John B., (BV) ... '29 '60 C.612 B.A. L.184 LL.B. [Sullivan&S.]
Sullivan & Sullivan, (BV) ... 36 Park Pl.

Summa, Joseph B., (AV) ... '49 '78 C.918 B.A. L.184 J.D. [Summa&R.]
*PRACTICE AREAS: Labor and Employment Law.

Summa & Ryan, P.C., (AV)
19-21 Holmes Avenue, 06710
Telephone: 203-755-0390 Fax: 203-756-8746
URL: http://www.lawyers.com/summa&ryanpc
Joseph B. Summa; Mary Jane Ryan;—William A. Ryan.
Management, Labor and Employment Law, Labor Relation, Equal Employment Opportunity.
See Professional Biographies, WATERBURY, CONNECTICUT

Tansley, Michael G., (BV) ... '57 '83 C.184 B.A. L.1292 J.D. [Cicchetti&T.]
*PRACTICE AREAS: Personal Injury; Commercial Litigation; Municipal Law; Workers Compensation; Criminal Law.
Tillona, Mary Anne B. '58 '87 C.184 B.S. L.1048 J.D. General Counsel, MacDermid Incorporated
Tinley, Jeffrey J., (AV) ... '55 '80 C.1044 B.A. L.724 J.D. [Tinley,N.R.&D.]
*PRACTICE AREAS: Commercial Litigation.

Tinley, Nastri, Renehan & Dost, LLP, (AV)
60 North Main Street, 2nd Floor, 06702
Telephone: 203-596-9030 Fax: 203-596-9036 URL: http://www.tnrdlaw.com
Email: thrdlaw@cs.com URL: http://www.lawyers.com/tnrd-attys
Jeffrey J. Tinley; Robert Nastri, Jr.; Richard P. Renehan; Mark W. Dost. Associates: Marilyn N. Toland; Stephen E. Pliakas; Margaret M. Doherty.
Trial Practice in State and Federal Courts. Commercial Litigation, Bankruptcy, Employment Law, Personal Injury, Workers Compensation, Collections, Elder Law, Estate Planning, Probate.
Representative Clients: Gar-San Corp.; General Electric Capital Commercial Automotive Finance, Inc.; Mobil Oil Corp.; Teikyo Post University; The May Department Stores Company; Watertown Construction Company, Inc.
See Professional Biographies, WATERBURY, CONNECTICUT

Titus, Curtis V., (AV) ... '33 '57 C.951 A.B. L.309 LL.B. [Gager&P.]
*PRACTICE AREAS: Corporate Law; Land Use Law; Health Care Law.
Tobin, William L., (BV) ... '22 '49 C.976 B.S. L.184 J.D. 77 Bank St.
Toland, Marilyn N. ... '55 '92 C.254 B.A. L.976 J.D. [[A] Tinley,N.R.&D.]
*PRACTICE AREAS: Elder Law; Medicaid Planning; Estate Administration.
Torrance, Walter F., Jr., (AV) ... '27 '51 C&L.976 B.S., LL.B. [[C] Carmody&T.]
Upson, Thomas F., (BV) ... '41 '69 C.901 B.A. L.184 LL.B. [Upson&D.]
Upson & Daly, (BV) ... 52 Holmes Ave.
Vallillo, Paul R., (BV) ... '65 '90 C.1030 B.A. L.1048 J.D. 1169 W. Main St.
Veller, Haley E. ... '65 '95 C.882 B.S. L.1252 J.D. [[A] Mahaney&G.]
Vencel, Marilyn A., (BV) ... '59 '84 C.788 B.A. L.184 J.D. 80 Phoenix Ave.
Vertefeuille, Christine S. ... '50 '75 C.855 B.A. L.184 J.D. Supr. Ct. J.
Villano, John A. ... '27 '58 C.976 B.E. L.184 LL.B. 135 W. Main St.
Vitale, Donald N. ... '23 '51 C.184 L.1009 LL.B. 49 Leavenworth St.
Wabiszczewicz, John M., (BV) ... '49 '76 C.165 B.A. L.184 J.D. 150 Prospect St.
Ward, Bradford J., (BV) ... '45 '70 C.156 A.B. L.184 J.D. Chief Asst. State's Atty.
Weiant, Bruce E. ... '59 '89 C.1211 B.S. L.1029 J.D. Asst. Pub. Def.
Weisman, H. John, (AV) ... '17 '46 C.976 A.B. L.659 LL.B. 76 Center St.‡
Weisman, Joseph H. ... '39 '66 C&L.184 B.A., LL.B. 25 Central Ave
Weller, Giovanna Tiberii, (BV) ... '65 '91 C&L.184 B.A., J.D. [Carmody&T.]
*PRACTICE AREAS: Civil Litigation; Employer Defense; Labor and Employment; Appellate Practice.
Wellington, Joseph A., (BV) ... '47 '78 C.871 B.S. L.818 J.D. [Carmody&T.]
*PRACTICE AREAS: Environmental; OSHA.
Werblin, Mary E. ... '49 '87 C.273 B.A. L.776 J.D. 585 Park Road
Wihbey, Linda T., (BV) ... '64 '89 C.687 B.A. L.818 J.D. [[A] Drubner,H.O.&M.]
*PRACTICE AREAS: Health Care Law; Family Law; Litigation; Insurance Defense.
Wrenn, Mark Mariner ... '55 '82 C.184 B.A. L.862 J.D. 35 Field St.
Yarbrough, John D., Jr., (AV) ... '50 '79 C.821 B.A. L.893 J.D. [Carmody&T.]
*PRACTICE AREAS: Public Finance; Bond Finance; Zoning and Land Use; Commercial Real Estate; Municipal Law.
Zailckas, F. Patrick ... '18 '44 C.321 A.B. L.128 LL.B. [Zailckas&Z.] ‡
Zailckas, Patrick ... '53 '80 C.321 A.B. L.276 J.D. [Zailckas&Z.]
Zailckas & Zailckas ... 51 Holmes Ave.
Zaino, Domenico, Jr. ... '71 '96 C.855 B.A. L.184 J.D. [[A] Carmody&T.]
*PRACTICE AREAS: Labor and Employment.
Zappone, Debra J. ... '54 '87 C.999 B.S. L.1048 J.D. 56 Gaffney Pl.
Zipoli, Richard P., (BV) ... '33 '59 C.676 B.A. L.262 LL.B. [Rinaldi,Z.B.A.&L.]

WATERFORD, 17,843, *New London Co.*

Alexander, Valerie, (CV) ... '42 '85 C.550 B.A. L.1048 J.D. 4 Percy Ave.
Avalos, Helen Elaine ... '62 '92 31 Colonial Dr.
Benoit, Gregory A. ... '51 '76 C.882 B.A. L.930 J.D. 143 Boston Post Rd.
Clark, Lawrence F. ... '49 '84 C.871 B.S. L.976 J.D. Treas. & Gen. Coun., Sonalysts, Inc.
Cory, Gerald A. ... '62 '97 C.183 B.S. L.1252 J.D. 42 Myrock Ave.
Fox, William C., (AV) ... '16 '41 C.976 B.A. L.306 LL.B. 161 Oswegatchie Rd.‡
Hauser, J. Vincent, (BV) ... '41 '67 C.884 A.B. L.262 LL.B. Asst. State's Atty.
Hendel, Myron H. ... '28 '53 C.976 B.A. L.309 LL.B. Hendel Petro. Co.
Kessler, Joel M. ... '55 '79 C.705 B.A. L.724 J.D. P.O. Box 1178
Kidder, Linda J., (BV) ... '60 '85 C.882 B.A. L.1048 J.D. 567 Vauxhall St. Extension
McGarry, John A., (BV) ... '30 '55 C.276 B.S. L.184 LL.B. [J.A.McGarry&Assoc.]
McGarry, John A., & Associates, P.C., (BV) ... P.O. Box 279
O'Brien, Donald, (CV) ... '14 '40 C.976 A.B. L.276 J.D. E. Conn. Cable Tele., Inc.
O'Brien, Edmund W., (AV) ... '15 '40 C.976 B.A. L.309 LL.B. E. Conn. Cable Tele., Inc.
Primus, Charles '46 '83 C.103 A.B. L.602 J.D. (adm. in IN; not adm. in CT) 58 Twin Lakes Dr.‡
Scillieri, Peter, (BV) ... '51 '76 C.264 B.A. L.669 J.D. Pub. Def.
Simones, Thomas C. ... '— '98 C.183 B.A. L.184 J.D. 728-A Broad Street Extension
Tytla, Lawrence J., (BV) ... '52 '80 C.1030 B.A. L.575 J.D. 220 Niantic River Rd.

WATERTOWN, 19,489, *Litchfield Co.*

Barrante, William T. ... '46 '72 C.855 B.A. L.184 J.D. 107 Scott Ave.
Butterly, Sean C., (BV) ... '51 '79 C.390 A.B. L.184 J.D. P.O. Box 714
D'Amico, Michael A., (BV) ... '62 '86 C.184 B.A. L.1252 J.D. [D'Amico,G.&P.]
*PRACTICE AREAS: Personal Injury; Medical Negligence; Products Liability; Workers Compensation.

D'Amico, Griffin & Pettinicchi, L.L.C., (BV)
465 Straits Turnpike, P.O. Box 670, 06798
Telephone: 860-945-6600 Fax: 860-945-6668
URL: http://www.dgplaw.com
Michael A. D'Amico; Mark F. Griffin; Thomas P. Pettinicchi.
Personal Injury, Medical Malpractice, Products liability, Family Law & Divorce Mediation.
See Professional Biographies, WATERTOWN, CONNECTICUT

Del Buono, John A. ... '28 '50 L.612 LL.B. 680 Main St.
De Leon, Patrick ... '11 '41 L.184 LL.B. 240 Skilton Rd.‡
Diorio, Edmond Michael, (BV) ... '51 '80 C.1211 B.S. L.1029 J.D. 51 Echo Lake Rd.
Griffin, Mark F., (BV) ... '58 '85 C.676 B.S. L.982 J.D. [D'Amico,G.&P.]
*PRACTICE AREAS: Personal Injury; Workers Compensation.
O'Connor, Leonard A. ... '26 '73 C.454 B.A. L.184 J.D. 141 Hamilton Ave.
Palladino, Eric J. ... '61 '86 C.901 B.A. L.1048 J.D. 459 Woodbury Rd.

Pettinicchi, Thomas P., (BV) '61 '86 C.676 B.A. L.1048 J.D. [D'Amico,G.&P.]
*PRACTICE AREAS: Matrimonial Law; Divorce Mediation; Personal Injury.
Pilicy, Franklin G., (BV) '47 '70 365 Main St.
Ricciardi, Edward T. '46 '81 C.1044 B.S. L.1029 J.D. Clk., Supr. Ct.
Scott, Robert A. '54 '94 [Slavin,S.&S.]
Sirica, Micheal R. '49 '86 C.30 B.A. L.1252 J.D. 51 Depot St.
Slavin, Sherman R., (BV) '22 '49 C&L.309 A.B., LL.B. [Slavin,S.&S.]
Slavin, Stauffacher & Scott, LLC, (BV) 680 Main Street
Stauffacher, Charles D., (BV) '43 '69 C.918 A.B. L.597 J.D. [Slavin,S.&S.]
Titley, John H. '41 '66 C.688 B.S. L.659 LL.B. 151 Hamilton Ave.

WEATOGUE, 2,396, *Hartford Co.*

Gordon, David S. '49 '76 C.184 B.A. L.1202 J.D. 25 Bob White Way
Greenblatt, Arthur N., (BV) '47 '73 C.28 B.A. L.184 J.D. Mng. Dir., Vesta Corp.‡
Johnson, Patricia B. '52 '78 C.477 B.A. L.188 J.D. 11 Westborough Dr.
Lissitzyn, Christine Beck, (BV) '48 '76
C.112 B.A. L.1066 J.D. Comsec Narragansett Security, Inc.
Merriam, Susan S. '57 '83 C.597 B.A. L.930 J.D. 80 Latimer Ln.
Rice, Charles M., Jr., (BV) '51 '76 C.276 B.A. L.184 J.D. P.O. Box 335
Rice, Hugh M. '60 '86 C.276 B.A. L.184 J.D. 23 Hopmeadow St.
Russo, Elizabeth DuBois, (CV) '55 '85 C.502 B.G.S. L.910 J.D. P.O. Box 332
Webber, Robert K., (BV) '48 '73 C.860 B.A. L.94 J.D. 237 Hopmeadow St.

WESTBROOK, 5,216, *Middlesex Co.*

Battistoli, Geraldine, (BV) '45 '76 C.97 B.S.Ed. L.184 J.D. 1509 Boston Post Rd.
Bushy, Willard F. '51 '77 C.95 A.B. L.818 J.D. 419 Pond Meadow Rd.
Frasure, Bonita C., (BV) '44 '79 C.665 B.A. L.184 J.D. [B.C.Frasure]
Frasure, Bonita C., P.C., (BV) P.O. Box 646
Hansen, Stefanie Alexis '67 '95 C.882 B.S. L.184 J.D. 50 Fishing Brook Rd.

Hoyt, Jonathan
(See Clinton)

Lee, Leighton, III '45 '74 C.401 B.S.M.E. L.190 J.D. Pres., The Lee Co.
Miano, Frederick J. '56 '81 C.1030 B.S. L.910 J.D. 1248 Post Rd.
Neidlinger, Olin E. '11 '37 C.103 Ph.B. L.94 LL.B. Ret. Prob. J.
Reisner, Samuel L. '17 '39 L.588 LL.B.
(adm. in MA; not adm. in CT) 16 Young Rd.‡
Rydholm, Daniel C. '58 '83 C.477 A.B. L.215 J.D.
(adm. in MI; not adm. in CT) 546 Stevenstown Rd.‡

WEST GRANBY, —, *Hartford Co.*

Locke, Arthur B., (AV) '36 '64 C.319 B.A. L.309 LL.B. 281 Simsbury Rd.‡

WEST HARTFORD, 61,301, *Hartford Co.*

Aaron, Barbara D. '57 '84 C.30 B.A. L.1009 J.D. [Berman,B.A.&D.]
*PRACTICE AREAS: Family Law; Alternative Dispute Resolution; Mediation.
Abery-Wetstone, Holly, (BV) '54 '80 C.725 B.A. L.1048 J.D. [Wetstone&D.]
Alfano, Alyce Lynn, (BV) '62 '87 C.659 B.A. L.112 J.D. [▣ H.M.Klebanoff]
Ancona, Benjamin, Jr. '64 '95 C.999 B.A. L.1187 J.D. 32 Jansen Ct.
Ankerman, Darcy W. '47 '84 C&L.607 B.A., J.D. 37 Montclair Drive
Apter, Morris, (AV) '08 '38 C.273 L.306 LL.B. 29 S. Main St.‡
Arciero, Christopher G., (CV) '59 '90 C.708 B.A. L.1048 J.D. [Sack,S.&K.]
Arnold, Jeffrey H. '67 '93 C&L.128 B.A., J.D. 433 S. Main St.
Arnold, Steven E., (BV) '50 '77
C.820 B.A. L.1048 J.D. 29 South Main Street (⊙Glastonbury)
Atlas, Neil E., (BV) '44 '71 C.823 B.S. L.184 J.D. [Atlas&H.]
*PRACTICE AREAS: Commercial Law; Business Law; Real Estate.

Atlas & Hudon, LLP, (AV)
95 South Main Street, P.O. Box 270670, 06127-0670
Telephone: 860-521-7800 Telecopier: 860-521-4783
URL: http://www.atlashudon.com
Neil E. Atlas; Paul A. Hudon; William C. Doran.
General Practice. Commercial, Banking, Corporate, Real Estate, Trust, Probate, Estate and Business Planning Law, Arbitration, Litigation.
See Professional Biographies, WEST HARTFORD, CONNECTICUT

Auburn, Travers T. '46 '72 C.951 B.A. L.184 [Reid&R.] (⊙Hartford, Lakeville)
*PRACTICE AREAS: Probate; Real Estate; Trusts and Estates.
Bailey, Elizabeth Dee, (BV) '44 '83 C.93 B.A. L.184 J.D. Asst. Corp. Coun.
Bannon, Edward C. '21 '50 C.976 B.A. L.309 LL.B. 61 Tunxis Rd.‡
Batchelor, Suzanne M., (BV) '61 '87 C.881 B.A. L.184 J.D. 29 Fawn Brk.
Baum, Edwin L., (BV) '32 '59 C&L.184 B.S., LL.B. P.O. Box 270027
Beauchemin, Joseph A. '26 '51 L.94 LL.B. 53 Burr St.‡
Beers, Sarah Russell '55 '84 C.860 B.S. L.976 J.D. 50 Lexington Rd.
Beizer, David B., (AV) '38 '64 C.309 A.B. L.178 LL.B. [Beizer&W.]
*PRACTICE AREAS: Civil Litigation; Personal Injury and Torts; Workers Compensation; Employment Law; Wrongful Termination.

Beizer & Weintraub, (AV)
345 North Main Street, 06117
Telephone: 860-236-5491 Fax: 860-236-5494
Email: beizerweintraub@mindspring.com URL: http://www.lawyers.com/beizerweintraub
Members of Firm: David B. Beizer; Jay B. Weintraub.
General Civil and Criminal Practice before State and Federal Courts. Personal Injury, Professional Malpractice, Workers Compensation, Employer/Employee Relations, Probate, Estate Planning, Real Estate, Business Entities, Commercial Loans, Domestic Relations, Foreclosures/Collections, Trials and Appeals.
References: Union Trust Co.; Connecticut Bank & Trust Co.; Burritt Interfinancial Bank Corp.
See Professional Biographies, WEST HARTFORD, CONNECTICUT

Bennett, Ealy A. '42 '75 C.326 B.F.A. L.325 J.D.
(adm. in TX; not adm. in CT) 104 Oakwood Ave., Apt. B3‡
Berliner, Lawrence W. '51 '83 C.472 B.B.A. L.1252 J.D. [▣ H.M.Klebanoff]
Berman, John A., (AV) '32 '57 C.937 A.B. L.184 J.D. [Berman,B.A.&D.]
*PRACTICE AREAS: Family Law; Probate Law; General Practice; Mediation.

Berman, Bourns, Aaron & Dembo, LLC, (AV)
970 Farmington Avenue, 06107
Telephone: 860-232-4471 Fax: 860-523-4605
John A. Berman; Courtney B. Bourns; Barbara D. Aaron; Steven R. Dembo. Associate: Jo-Ellen Zereski. Of Counsel: John K. Currie.
Family Law, Personal Injury, Litigation, Probate, Estate Planning, Real Estate, Corporate and General Practice.
See Professional Biographies, WEST HARTFORD, CONNECTICUT

Berry, William C., (BV) '47 '80 C.165 B.A. L.184 J.D. [Sack,S.&K.]
Birmingham, Alan, (AV) '43 '69
C.860 B.A. L.276 J.D. [Reid&R.] (⊙Hartford, Woodbury)
*PRACTICE AREAS: Probate; Real Estate; Trusts and Estates.
Blume, Daniel, (AV) '31 '59 C.184 A.B. L.276 J.D. [Blume,E.C.&K.]
Blume, Elbaum, Collins & Kelly, P.C., (AV)
433 South Main Street Suite 111 (⊙Washington Depot)
Bocchini, Suzanne S., (AV) '47 '73 C.128 B.A. L.734 J.D. [Reid&R.] (⊙Hartford)
*PRACTICE AREAS: Probate; Trusts and Estates.
Bourns, Courtney B., (AV) '36 '64 C.860 B.S. L.228 LL.B. [Berman,B.A.&D.]
*PRACTICE AREAS: Family Law; Mediation.
Brewer, James S. '— '87 C.1033 B.A. L.1029 J.D. 818 Farmington Ave.
Brick, Lawrence S., (BV) '45 '76 C.434 B.A. L.161 J.D. 433 S. Main St.
Brodigan, George D., (AV) '28 '57 C.918 B.A. L.893 J.D. 50 Timberwood Rd.‡
Brodsky, Mark W., (BV) '51 '77 C.860 B.A. L.184 J.D. Sr. Asst. States Atty.
Bronfman, Andrew I., (CV) '53 '79 C.276 B.A. L.564 J.D. 26 Borough Dr.
Buchwald, Deborah-Beth '56 '85 C.855 B.A. L.184 J.D. 15 Old Field Rd.
Campbell, Hugh S. '10 '37 C.855 B.A. L.306 LL.B. 275 Steele Rd.‡
Cantor, Shari J., (BV) '54 '81 C.882 B.S. L.184 J.D. 121 Federal St.
Carabillo, Elizabeth Heller '36 '79 C.705 B.A. L.184 J.D. 1405 Trout Brook Dr.‡
Carter, Suzanne M. '45 '81 C.725 B.A. L.1048 J.D. 240 Ridgewood Rd.
Clark, Newton A., Jr. '42 '84 C.67 B.S. L.184 J.D. 270 Bloomfield Ave.‡
Clementino, Valentino D., (AV) '11 '35 C&L.94 B.A., LL.B. 433 S. Main St.
Coccomo, Cynthia J. '62 '88 C.262 B.A. L.1029 J.D. CNA Ins. Cos.
Coleman, Elaine B., (BV) '50 '84 C.918 B.A. L.976 J.D. 73 Ringgold St.
Collins, Thomas W., (AV) '23 '55 C.918 B.A. L.184 LL.B. [Blume,E.C.&K.]
Conard, Frederick U., Jr., (AV) '18 '43 C.918 B.A. L.976 J.D. Trial Ref.‡
Connors, Susan A. '66 '91 C&L.184 B.S., J.D. [Krevolin,R.&C.L.] ⊙
*PRACTICE AREAS: Insurance; Personal Injury; Family Law; Divorce; Workers Compensation.
Courtney, Cynthia K., (BV) '53 '81 C.216 B.A. L.128 J.D. 49 Lexington Rd.
Croog, Martha E., (BV) '56 '82 C.477 B.A. L.1019 J.D. [M.Croog]
*PRACTICE AREAS: Creditors Rights; Foreclosures; Bankruptcy; Corporate Law; Securities Law.

Croog, Martha, LLC, Law Office of, (BV)
740 North Main Street, Suite N, 06117
Telephone: 860-236-9661 Fax: 860-233-9927
Email: martha.croog@mcroogllc.com URL: http://www.lawyers.com/crooglaw
Martha E. Croog.
Creditor's Foreclosure, Bankruptcy and Eviction, Securities Compliance, related Corporate and Banking Law.
See Professional Biographies, WEST HARTFORD, CONNECTICUT

Cummings, Jean Kelly '60 '85 C.321 B.A. L.128 J.D. 56 Brunswick Ave.

Cummings & Lockwood, (AV)
Town Center, 29 South Main Street Suite 205, 06107 ⊙
Telephone: (860) 275-6700 Telecopier: (860) 313-0293
Email: info@cl-law.com URL: http://www.cl-law.com
Partners: Gina S. Linstone; Paul L. Bourdeau (Resident, Hartford, Connecticut Office). Senior Attorney: Robert B. Fawber. Resident Associate: Kelley M. Galica Peck.
General Practice. National and Regional Litigation Counsel, Corporate Law, Patent and Intellectual Property, Trusts and Estates, Labor and Employment, Mergers and Acquisitions, Partnerships and Joint Ventures, Commercial Lending, Corporate Finance, Creditors' Rights, Bankruptcy and Workouts, Securities Regulation and Litigation, Tax, Insurance, Banking and Financial Services, Leasing, Commercial and Residential Real Estate, Construction, Environmental, Toxic Torts, Health Law, Products Liability Litigation, Probate Litigation, Family Law, International Business.
Stamford, Connecticut Office: Four Stamford Plaza, P.O. Box 120, 06904-0120. Telephone: (203) 327-1700. Telecopier: (203) 351-4535.
Greenwich, Connecticut Office: Two Greenwich Plaza, P.O. Box 2505, 06836. Telephone: (203) 869-1200. Telecopier: (203) 869-3120.
Hartford, Connecticut Office: CityPlace I, 185 Asylum Street, 36th Floor, 06103-3495. Telephone: (860) 275-6700. Telecopier: (860) 724-3397.
New Haven, Connecticut Office: 700 State Street, P.O. Box 1960. 06509-1960. Telephone: (203) 782-3000. Telecopier: (203) 777-3347.
Bonita Springs, Florida Office: 24311 Walden Center, Suite 201, 34134. Telephone: (941) 947-8811. Telecopier: (941) 947-8025.
Naples, Florida Office: 3001 Tamiami Trail North, P.O. Box 413032, 34101-3032. Telephone: (941) 262-8311. Telecopier: (941) 263-0703.
See Professional Biographies, WEST HARTFORD, CONNECTICUT

Currie, John K., (BV) '50 '77 C.477 B.G.S. L.107 J.D. [▣ Berman,B.A.&D.]
*PRACTICE AREAS: Litigation; Real Estate Law; General Practice.
Curry, Elizabeth A. '55 '84 C.1307 B.A. L.184 J.D. 10 Arnoldale Rd.
Cushner, Stephen S. '21 '52 C.900 B.B.A. L.1017 LL.B.
(adm. in DC; not adm. in CT) 93 Overbrook Rd.‡
D'Ambrosio, Doris B., (BV) '50 '84 C.829 B.A. L.1048 J.D. [Wetstone&D.]
Davidoff, Leon S. '62 '87 C.156 B.A. L.930 J.D. 3 Stoneham Dr.
Davis, Clifford '25 '52 C.145 B.S. L.309 LL.B.
(adm. in TX; not adm. in CT) Prof. of Law, Univ. of Conn.
Deans, John B. '43 '70 C.309 A.B. L.976 LL.B.
(adm. in NY; not adm. in CT) 89 Waterside Ln.‡
Delehanty, Garrett J., Jr., (AV) '52 '76 C.918 B.A. L.178 J.D. [Kroll,M.&E.]
*PRACTICE AREAS: Hotel Acquisitions, Sales; Finance, Management and Franchising; Real Estate Finance; Real Estate Acquisitions and Sales; Loan Workouts and Restructurings.

DeMarco, Robert A., (BV) '50 '84 C.1252 B.A. L.1029 J.D.
29 South Main Street, Suite 207, 06107-2103
Telephone: 860-561-2628 Telecopier: 860-521-6150
Civil Practice before State and Federal Courts with emphasis on Commercial Litigation, Creditor's Rights, Bankruptcy, Foreclosures and Commercial Collection Matters, Real Estate Transactions and Litigation, Personal Injury and Insurance Claims, Civil Trials and Appeals.
Representative Clients: The Travelers Bank FSB; Travelers Home Mortgage Services; Commercial Credit Corporation.
References: Webster Bank; Fleet Bank.

Dembo, Steven R. '65 '90 C.1349 B.S. L.1048 J.D. [Berman,B.A.&D.]
*PRACTICE AREAS: Litigation; Personal Injury; Family Law; Criminal Law; General Practice.
Dimock, Stanley W. '22 '51 C.659 B.S. L.184 LL.B. 21 Braintree Dr.‡
Donahue, Jeffrey O., (BV) '39 '70 C.659 A.B. L.184 J.D. 777 Farmington Ave.
Donnelly, Celia Moffie '58 '83
C.976 B.A. L.184 J.D. Pres. & CEO, Conn. Health Facilities
Dooley, Thomas H. '34 '64 C.158 B.B.A. L.306 LL.B. 109 Irene Dr.
Doran, William C., (AV) '45 '72 C.197 A.B. L.976 J.D. [Atlas&H.]
*PRACTICE AREAS: Estate Planning; Business Planning; Trusts and Estates; Probate.
Dorman, Nicole D. '53 '88 C.725 B.A. L.184 J.D. [Sack,S.&K.]
Dow, Linda A. '49 '74 C.242 B.A. L.818 J.D. Chief Coun., Prob. Ct.
Dowling, Pamela Jane '— '85 C.276 B.A. L.184 J.D. 77 Pilgrim Rd.
Downey, Robert F. '14 '39 C.321 B.A. L.306 LL.B. 97 S. Main St.‡
Dragat, John D., (AV) '27 '53 C.976 B.A. L.188 LL.B. [J.D.Dragat]
Dragat, John D., P.C., (AV) 345 N. Main St.
Driscoll, John H. '58 '87 C.184 B.A. L.1017 J.D. U.S. Trust Co. of CT
Droney, Patricia M. '48 '73 C.184 B.A. L.306 J.D. 75 Rockledge Dr.
Dunn, J. Morton, (BV) '26 '55 C.309 A.B. L.184 LL.B. 169 Oakwood Ave.
Dwyer, Lorna M. '47 '72 C.518 B.A. L.188 J.D. 62 Arnoldale Rd.
Eagan, Owen P., (BV) '60 '86 C.918 B.A. L.276 J.D. [Eagan&D.]
Eagan & Donohue, (BV) 24 Arapahoe Road
Eaton, Gordon & Sawyer 26 Mohegan Drive (⊙Tampa, FL)
Elbaum, Jerome D., (AV) '39 '64 C&L.188 A.B., J.D. [Blume,E.C.&K.]
Elkin, Sydney W., (BV) '46 '72 C.264 B.A. L.184 J.D. [S.W.Elkin]
Elkin, Sydney W., LLC, (BV) 1007 Farmington Avenue, Suite 4
Engel, Annie H. '70 '98 C.216 B.A. L.665 J.D. 304 Steele Rd.
Engel, Joan G. '54 '81 C.674 A.B. L.184 J.D. 43 Avondale Road

Evans, Douglas M., (BV) . . . .'63 '89 C.183 B.A. L.818 J.D. [Kroll,M.&E.]
*PRACTICE AREAS: Commercial Litigation; Real Estate Litigation; Contracts; Bankruptcy; Creditors' Rights.

Fawber, Robert B., (AV) . . . .'49 '75 C.855 B.A. L.276 J.D. [Ⓐ Cummings&L.]
*PRACTICE AREAS: Real Estate Law; Estate Planning Law; Probate Practice; Business Law.

Federman, David S. . . . .'43 '69 C.588 B.S. L.184 J.D. 1 Orchard Ln.‡
Felber, John H. . . . .'17 '80 C.999 M.D. L.184 J.D. 29 N. Main St.
Feldman, Samuel B., (BV) . . . .'54 '79 C.823 B.A. L.472 J.D. 433 S. Main St.
Ferguson, Dennis R. . . . .'44 '88 C.28 B.S. L.184 J.D. 31 Foxcroft Rd.
Ferraro, Mark J., (BV) . . . .'60 '86 C.827 B.A. L.362 J.D. [Lewis,L.&F.] ⊙
Fierer, Gayle . . . .'48 '81 C.569 B.A. L.184 J.D. 125 Cliffmore Rd.

Fink & Highmark, (BV)
8 Crossroads Plaza, P.O. Box 370038, 06137
Telephone: 860-236-6858 Fax: 860-236-6850
URL: http://www.lawyers.com/finkandhighmark
Members of Firm: Everett F. Fink (1923-1993); Louis A. Highmark, Jr.
Civil Trial and Appellate Practice in State and Federal Courts. Insurance, Subrogation, Fidelity and Surety, Products Liability, Environmental, Personal Injury, Business, Commercial, Probate, Estate Planning, Corporation, Real Estate, Construction and Workers Compensation.
Representative Clients: Royal Insurance Cos.; The Connecticut Light and Power Co.; BankAmerica Mortgage; Fidelity and Deposit Company of Maryland; North American Specialty Insurance Co.; Northeast Utilities; Colonial Spring Co.; Bevels Inc.; West Hartford Chamber of Commerce.
Reference: Fleet Bank.
See Professional Biographies, WEST HARTFORD, CONNECTICUT

Fiske, Carol E. . . . .'60 '88 C.197 A.B. L.262 J.D. 201 Fern St.
Fitzgerald, Mona A. . . . .'54 '88 C.1102 B.S. L.1048 J.D. 29 S. Main St.
Fitzgerald, Patrice M., (BV) . . . .'55 '83 C.860 B.A. L.904 J.D. 1 Mountainside Road
Flynn, Benedict D., Jr. . . . .'19 '51 C.976 B.S. L.184 LL.B. 54 Walbridge Rd.‡
Fox, Ronald A. . . . .'67 '93 C.472 B.A. L.1338 J.D. [Blume,E.C.&K.]
Franklin, Scott B., (BV) . . . .'56 '82 C.860 B.A. L.184 J.D. 68 S. Main St.
Friedeberg, William J. . . . .'40 '65 C.477 B.B.A. L.184 J.D. 76 Craigmoor Rd.
Friedman, Marsha Harris '65 '91 C.66 B.A. L.184 J.D.
(adm. in NJ; not adm. in CT) 49 W. Ridge Dr.‡
Frost, Albert W. . . . .'11 '40 C.95 B.S. L.93 LL.B. 25 Owings Rd.‡
Fundiller-Zweig, Doreen Lee, (BV) '52 '80 C.1350 B.S. L.184 J.D.
Exec. Dir, Jewish Federation of Greater Hartford, Inc.
Gaffey, Thomas E., (BV) . . . .'52 '80 C&L.184 B.A., J.D. Off. of Prob. Ct. Admn.
Garrison, Richard H., (AV) . . . .'46 '75 C.188 B.S. L.184 J.D. 57 Garfield Rd.
Gassner, Mark D. . . . .'35 '61 C&L.976 B.A., LL.B. J & S Develop. & Mgmt. Corp.
Gershman, Donald S., (AV) '56 '81 C.860 B.A. L.93 J.D.
Exec. V.P. & Gen. Coun., Konover Investments Corp.

Gersten, Ceil Saretta '59 '88 C.938 B.S. L.1048 J.D.
10 North Main Street, Suite 204, 06107
Telephone: 860-231-7455 Fax: 860-231-7461
URL: http://www.lawyers.com/ceilgersten
Family, Divorce, Custody, Child Support, Criminal, DUI, DWI, Misdemeanors, Personal Injury, Automobile Accidents, Slip and Fall, Dog Bites.
See Professional Biographies, WEST HARTFORD, CONNECTICUT

Gersten, Peter S. . . . .'62 '88 C.93 B.A. L.273 J.D. [Ⓐ S.P.Gersten]
Gersten, Sandra Pessin, (BV) . . . . . .'36 '60 C.881 B.A. L.184 LL.B. 75 North Main Street
Giddon, A. Arthur . . . .'09 '35 C.860 B.S. L.309 LL.B. 5 Beech Tree Ln.‡
Gipstein, M. Ted . . . .'54 '82 C.183 B.A. L.990 J.D. 49 S. Main St.
Gleeson, Marcia J., (BV) . . . .'51 '80 C&L.184 B.A., J.D. [Sack,S.&K.]
Goodman, Richard, (AV) . . . .'39 '64 C.604 B.A. L.309 LL.B. [Goodman,R.&M.]
*PRACTICE AREAS: Business Law; Real Estate; Estate Planning; Divorce.

Goodman, Rosenthal & McKenna, P.C., (AV)
68 South Main Street, 06106
Telephone: 860-231-2800 Fax: 860-523-9235
Email: grm@connix.com
Edward F. Rosenthal; Richard Goodman; John F. McKenna; Rebecca B. Lamont; Lee B. Ross.
Corporation, Real Estate, Pension, Employment, Antitrust, Litigation, Estate Planning.
See Professional Biographies, WEST HARTFORD, CONNECTICUT

Gordon, Howard A., P.A. . . . .'45 '69 C&L.184 B.A., J.D. [Eaton,G.&S.] (⊙Tampa, FL)
Gordon, Suzanne M., (CV) . . . .'32 '83 C.813 B.A. L.184 J.D. 9 Staples Place
Graham, John R., Jr., (BV) . . . .'49 '74 C.276 B.S.F.S. L.306 J.D. P.O. Box 270514
Grassick, Harry R. . . . .'21 '52 C.947 L.184 9 Walker Lane
Greenberg, Arnold C. . . . .'33 '58 C&L.309 A.B., LL.B. 61 S. Main St.‡
Greenspon, Maurice E. . . . .'06 '31 C&L.976 B.A., LL.B 19 Whitehill Dr.‡
Griner, Jerome M. . . . .'31 '59 C.976 A.B. L.94 LL.B. 47 N. Main St.
Guenter, Raymond A. '32 '58 C.823 B.A. L.309 LL.B.
(adm. in NY; not adm. in CT) 52 Wood Pond Rd.‡
Hagarty, Thomas J., (AV) . . . .'14 '39 C.855 B.A. L.306 LL.B. 115 Beacon Hill Dr.‡
Hamilton, Anne M., (BV) . . . .'39 '73 C.681 A.B. L.184 J.D. 105 Walden St.
Harding, Nicholas J., (AV) . . . .'47 '78 C.999 B.A. L.1218 J.D. [Kosloff&H.]
*PRACTICE AREAS: Environmental Law; Civil Litigation; Tax Litigation.

Havens, Catherine M. . . . .'47 '85 C.725 B.A. L.184 J.D. Univ. of Conn.
Hayes, Ivan E. . . . .'21 '49 C.178 B.S. L.188 J.D. 2247 Albany Ave.‡
Hershinson, Pamela R., (BV) . . . .'50 '75 C.569 B.A. L.128 J.D. 65 LaSalle Rd.
Hickey, James G. . . . .'29 '56 C&L.276 B.S.S., J.D. 135 Beacon Hill Dr.‡
Highmark, Louis A., Jr., (BV) . . . .'46 '74 C.197 A.B. L.477 J.D. [Fink&H.]
Hill, Robert L. '31 '55 C.920 L.608 J.D.
Dir., National Law Firm Mediation Network, Inc.
Hoffer, F. S., Jr. . . . .'08 '41 C.674 B.A. L.306 LL.B. 38 Foxridge Rd.‡
Hoffman, Hank D. . . . .'62 '87 C.867 B.A. L.569 J.D. 29 S. Main St.
Hoffman, Martin W., (AV) . . . .'33 '62 C.1033 B.S. L.306 J.D. 29 S. Main St.
Hoffman, Peter B. . . . .'42 '68 C.188 B.S. L.273 J.D. 16 Pilgram Rd.
Howley, Edward J. . . . .'57 '83 C.951 B.A. L.94 J.D. 920 Farmington Ave.
Hudon, Paul A., (AV) . . . .'45 '70 C.696 A.B. L.184 J.D. [Atlas&H.]
*PRACTICE AREAS: Trusts and Estates; Probate; Estate Planning; Business Planning.

Hurvitz, Henry B., (BV) '48 '74 C.966 B.A. L.184 J.D.
924 Farmington Avenue, 3rd Floor, 06107
Telephone: 860-232-8300 Fax: 860-232-2672
Email: hhurvitz@aol.com URL: http://www.lawyers.com/hhurvitz
***PRACTICE AREAS: Personal Injury; Real Estate; Family Law.**
Real Estate, Family Law, Personal Injury, Wills, Probate.
See Professional Biographies, WEST HARTFORD, CONNECTICUT

Ivimey, John R. . . . .'63 '91 C.165 B.A. L.184 J.D. [Reid&R.] (⊙Hartford)
*PRACTICE AREAS: Probate; Trusts and Estates.

Jackson, Jay W., (AV) . . . .'30 '58 C&L.902 B.A., LL.B. [Jackson,O.&P.] (⊙Hartford)
Jackson, O'Keefe and Phelan, (AV) . . . . .62 La Salle Road (⊙Bethlehem, Hartford)
Johnson, Eric W. . . . .'52 '77 C.546 B.A. L.188 J.D. [Ⓑ Kroll,M.&E.]
Karsten, Scott M., (BV) . . . .'51 '82 C.918 B.A. L.184 J.D. [Sack,S.&K.]
Katz, Kenneth B., (BV) . . . . . .'42 '85 C.1033 B.A. L.1048 J.D. 81 S Main Street, Suite 1A
Kaufman, Linda S., (BV) . . . .'63 '89 C.659 B.A. L.184 J.D. 41 N. Main St.
Kazarian, David J. . . . .'26 '50 C.696 A.B. L.184 LL.B. 79 Ridgewood Rd.‡

Kearns, John F. III, (AV) . . . .'57 '82 C.262 B.A. L.823 J.D. [Kearns&K.]
*PRACTICE AREAS: Elder Law; Probate; Estate Planning; Estate Planning for Parents of Handicapped Children; Estate Planning for the Disabled.

Kearns & Kearns, P.C., (AV)
1121 New Britain Avenue, 06110
Telephone: 860-233-1281 Fax: 860-523-5774
Email: attorney@ctelderlaw.com URL: http://www.ctelderlaw.com
John F. Kearns, Jr. (1930-1985); John F. III Kearns;—Lisa M. Vozzella Courser.
Elder Law, Estate Planning Administration and Probate.
See Professional Biographies, WEST HARTFORD, CONNECTICUT

Keily, Paul A., (BV) '55 '86 C.1145 B.S. L.1252 J.D.
12 North Main Street, 06107
Telephone: 860-561-9866 Fax: 860-561-9870
Email: pkeily@keilylaw.com URL: http://www.lawyers.com/keilylaw
Civil Litigation. Commercial Real Estate, Residential Real Estate, Landlord and Tenant Law, Bankruptcy, Probate and Family Law, Divorce, Child Custody, Child Support, Adoptions.
See Professional Biographies, WEST HARTFORD, CONNECTICUT

Klebanoff, Howard M., (AV) . . . .'37 '62 C.976 B.A. L.184 J.D. [H.M.Klebanoff]
Klebanoff, Howard M., P.C., (AV) . . . . 433 South Main Street
Klemonski, Edward S., (BV) . . . .'40 '65 C.262 A.B. L.184 J.D. 433 S. Main St.
Kone, Helen R., (CV) . . . .'27 '83 C.788 B.A. L.184 J.D. [H.R.Kone]
Kone, Helen R., P.C., Law Offices of, (CV) . . . . 10 N. Main St.
Kor, Robert J., (BV) . . . .'51 '77 C.184 B.A. L.1048 J.D. 81 S. Main St.
Kosloff, Alan M., (BV) . . . .'46 '71 C.184 B.A. L.273 J.D. [Kosloff&H.]
*PRACTICE AREAS: Environmental Law.

Kosloff & Harding, (AV)
28 North Main Street, 06107
Telephone: 860-521-7004 Fax: 860-521-3352
Email: amkandnjh@aol.com URL: http://www.lawyers.com/kosloff&harding
Alan M. Kosloff; Nicholas J. Harding. Associate: Mary McQueeney.
Environmental Law.
See Professional Biographies, WEST HARTFORD, CONNECTICUT

Krevolin, Andrew W., (AV) . . . .'55 '80 C.183 B.A. L.184 J.D. [Krevolin,R.&C.L.] ⊙
*PRACTICE AREAS: Personal Injury; Medical Malpractice; Products Liability; Insurance Coverage.

Krevolin, Roth & Connors LLC, (AV)
433 South Main Street, Suite 303, 06110 ⊙
Telephone: 860-561-7282 Fax: 860-561-7283
Members of Firm: Andrew W. Krevolin; Stuart M. Roth; Susan A. Connors. Of Counsel: Walter B. Schatz.
General Civil Litigation, Personal Injury, Medical Malpractice, Products Liability, Workers Compensation, Commercial Litigation, Matrimonial and Insurance.
Middletown, Connecticut Office: 100 Main Street, Suite 201, 06457. Telephone: 860-343-7260.
See Professional Biographies, WEST HARTFORD, CONNECTICUT

Kroll, Shelley A., (BV) . . . .'57 '84 C.105 B.A. L.823 J.D. [Kroll,M.&E.]
*PRACTICE AREAS: Commercial Leasing; Real Estate Acquisitions; Real Estate Sales; Commercial Finance; Loan Workouts.

Kroll, McNamara & Evans, LLP, (AV)
29 South Main Street, 06107
Telephone: 860-561-7070 Facsimile: 860-561-7075
URL: http://www.kmelaw.com
Shelley A. Kroll; Edward J. McNamara, III; Douglas M. Evans; Garrett J. Delehanty, Jr.;—Steven J. Meis; Richard M. Levy. Of Counsel: Eric W. Johnson.
General Practice, Commercial Real Estate, Commercial Litigation, Real Estate Development, Property Management, Real Estate Leasing, Real Estate Acquisitions and Dispositions, Real Estate Construction and Asset Management, Hotels, Real Estate Finance, Zoning, Planning and Land Use, Civil Litigation, Trial Practice, Appeals, Foreclosures, Creditors Rights, Bankruptcy, Contracts, Commercial Collections, Real Estate Litigation, Lender Liability, Landlord and Tenant Law, Trusts and Estates, Probate.
See Professional Biographies, WEST HARTFORD, CONNECTICUT

Kurmay, F. Paul . . . .'44 '69 C.893 B.A. L.276 J.D. Prob. J.
Lahm, Cynthia L., (BV) . . . .'56 '81 C.273 B.A. L.306 J.D. 24 Pilgrim Rd.
Lamont, Rebecca B., (BV) . . . .'45 '87 C.882 A.B. L.1048 J.D. [Goodman,R.&M.]
*PRACTICE AREAS: Personal Injury; Divorce; Bankruptcy; Real Estate; Housing.

Langenbach, John J. . . . .'38 '63 C.976 B.A. L.659 LL.B. Supr. Ct. J.
LaPlante, Joseph A. '23 '56 C.309 B.A. L.94 LL.B.
(adm. in MA; not adm. in CT) Prof. of Law, Univ. of Conn.
Laverty, Joanne Heslin . . . .'52 '92 C.184 B.A. L.1048 J.D. 777 Farmington Avenue
Lawlor, Richard P., (BV) . . . .'46 '75 C.829 B.A. L.306 J.D. 777 Farmington Ave.
Leedham, Edmond Francis, III . . . .'60 '95 C.694 B.A. L.1252 J.D. 41 Crossroads Plz.
Levine, Howard I. . . . .'46 '71 C.184 B.A. L.306 J.D. 29 S. Main St.
Levy, Mark W. . . . .'26 '51 C.855 A.B. L.94 LL.B. 290 N. Quaker Lane
Levy, Richard M. . . . .'65 '91 C&L.184 B.A., J.D. [Ⓐ Kroll,M.&E.]
*PRACTICE AREAS: Commercial Litigation; Real Estate Litigation; Foreclosure; Estate Planning; Probate.

Lewis, Scott Foster, (BV) . . . .'54 '81 C.855 B.A. L.818 J.D. [Lewis,L.&F.]

Lewis, Lewis & Ferraro, L.L.C., (BV)
28 North Main Street, 06107 ⊙
Telephone: 860-521-1500 Telecopier: 860-521-4500 URL: http://www.lewislewisferraro.com
Email: attorneys@lewislewisferraro.com URL: http://www.lawyers.com/lewislewisferraro
Members of Firm: Scott Foster Lewis; Mark J. Ferraro.
Family Law, Divorce, Personal Injury, Automobile Accidents, Real Estate, Medical Malpractice, Bankruptcy, Wills, Probate, Estate Planning, Trusts and Estates.
Bristol, Connecticut Office: 5 Maple Street. Telephone: 860-585-1500. Telecopier: Available Upon Request.
See Professional Biographies, WEST HARTFORD, CONNECTICUT

Linstone, Gina S., (AV) . . . .'64 '90 C.597 B.A. L.800 J.D. [Cummings&L.]
*PRACTICE AREAS: Estate Law; Tax Planning Law; Estate Settlement Law; Trust Administration Law.

Lissitzyn, Oliver J. '12 '36 C&L.178 A.B., LL.B.
(adm. in NY; not adm. in CT) 29 Highland St.‡
Locke, Aurelle S. '40 '65 C.906 B.A. L.309 J.D.
(adm. in MA; not adm. in CT) Univ. of Hartford
Lublin, Gerald R., (BV) . . . .'45 '70 C&L.930 B.A., J.D. 10 N. Main St.
Luby, Joan F. . . . .'19 '63 C.715 B.A. L.184 LL.B. 10 Northridge Dr.‡
Luca, George F. . . . .'49 '88 C.184 B.A. L.1029 J.D. 106 S. St.
Lukens, Ralph D. . . . .'29 '58 C.918 B.A. L.184 LL.B. Admin Prob. Ct. J.
Lynch, Daniel E., (BV) . . . .'33 '58 C.676 B.S. L.184 LL.B. 16 Arapahoe Rd.
Lynch, Karen Renzulli, (BV) . . . .'46 '81 C.706 B.A. L.1048 J.D. [Lynch]
Lynch, William J., (BV) . . . .'27 '63 C.1030 B.S.Bio. L.184 LL.B. 16 Arapahoe Rd.
Lynch Law Offices, (BV) . . . . .45 S. Main St.
Macrohon, M. P. . . . .'34 '73 C&L.262 B.S.S.S., LL.B. 59 Linbrook Rd.
Mahoney, Lynn Marie . . . .'74 '99 C.93 B.A. L.306 J.D. 10 North Main St.
Malinowski, S. John, (AV) . . . .'32 '61 C&L.184 B.S., J.D. [S.J.Malinowski]
Malinowski, S. John, P.C., (AV) . . . . 10 N. Main St.
Maltbie, Theodore M. . . . .'19 '45 C.951 B.A. L.976 LL.B. 22 Stratford Rd.‡
Mancuso, Ronald L. . . . .'46 '72 C.665 B.A. L.569 J.D. D&S Capital Group, LLC
McClure, Edith F., (BV) . . . .'38 '80 C.788 M.A. L.184 J.D. [Roisman&M.]
McHugh, Thomas D., IV, (BV) . . . .'51 '77 C.184 B.A. L.1048 J.D. 101 Hyde Rd.

McKenna, John F., (BV) . . . '38 '70 C.321 L.184 J.D. [Goodman,R.&M.]
*PRACTICE AREAS: Personal Injury; Insurance Defense; Criminal; Employment; Labor Relations.
Mclaughlin, Patricia L. . . . '44 '87 C.454 B.A. L.306 J.D. 29 S. Main St.

McLucas, Nancy '50 '87 C.309 A.B. L.184 J.D.
29 South Main Street, 06107
Telephone: 860-561-5621 Fax: 860-561-4204
URL: http://www.lawyers.com/mclucas
***PRACTICE AREAS: Probate; Wills; Trusts and Estates.**
Estate, Probate, Wills and Trusts.
See Professional Biographies, WEST HARTFORD, CONNECTICUT

McNamara, Edward J., III, (BV) . . . '61 '89 C.705 B.A. L.178 J.D. [Kroll,M.&E.]
*PRACTICE AREAS: Real Estate Finance; Real Estate Acquisitions; Commercial Leasing; Construction; Loan Workouts.
McQueeney, Mary . . . '67 '98 C.829 B.A. L.306 J.D. [Ⓐ Kosloff&H.]
*PRACTICE AREAS: Environmental Law; Civil Litigation.
Mead, Linda J. . . . '47 '74 C&L.107 B.A., J.D. 90 Sunny Reach Dr.
Meis, Steven J., (BV) . . . '61 '86 C.575 B.A. L.893 J.D. [Ⓐ Kroll,M.&E.]
*PRACTICE AREAS: Real Estate Acquisitions; Real Estate Sales; Commercial Leasing; Commercial Finance; Loan Workouts.
Melley, Maura L. . . . '51 '79 C.725 B.A. L.1048 J.D. 16 Old Oak Road
Meyer, Nancy L. . . . '65 '92 C.823 B.S. L.184 J.D. P.O. Box 370129
Miller, Grant H., Jr., (BV) . . . '53 '78 C.331 B.A. L.184 J.D. Mng. Trial Atty., CNA
Monahan, Jane B. . . . '45 '70 C.930 L.884 J.D. 18 N. Main St.
Morin, Kevin F. . . . '62 '89 C.164 B.A. L.896 J.D. [Blume,E.C.&K.]
Morris, John O. . . . '18 '49 C.976 B.A. L.893 LL.B. 40 Wood Pond Rd.‡
Morrissey, Ellen C., (CV) . . . '46 '82 C.550 B.A. L.1187 J.D. 65 La Salle Rd.
Moskowitz, Emily J. . . . '45 '88 C.994 B.A. L.306 J.D. 81 S. Main St.
Mullen, Frederick J., Jr., (AV) . . . '51 '77 C.976 B.A. L.893 J.D. [Reid&R.] (⊙Hartford)
*PRACTICE AREAS: Probate; Trusts and Estates.
Murray, George F., (BV) . . . '22 '56 C.823 B.A. L.184 LL.B. 737 Farmington Ave.

Nerenberg, Eliot J., Law Offices of, (AV) '49 '73 C.563 B.S. L.569 J.D.
10 North Main Street, Suite 214, 06107
Telephone: 860-232-4881 Fax: 860-233-5478
Email: enerenberg@rcn.com
***PRACTICE AREAS: Matrimonial Law (90%, 40); Real Estate (10%, 50).**
Associate: Robert D. Zaslow.
Family Law, Divorce, Child Custody, Divorce Mediation.
See Professional Biographies, WEST HARTFORD, CONNECTICUT

Newton, Germain D. . . . '31 '61 C.855 B.A. L.893 LL.B. 42 Castlewood Rd.‡
Nisimblat, Stephen . . . '71 '96 C.184 B.A. L.306 J.D. 23 Lilley Rd.
O'Connell, Flaherty & Attmore, L.L.C., (AV)
993 Farmington Avenue (⊙Danbury, Hartford, Moosup, Old Saybrook, CT; Springfield, MA)
O'Keefe, Andrew J., (AV) . . . '31 '56 C.321 B.S. L.184 J.D. [Jackson,O.&P.] ⊙
O'Keefe, Matthew J., (BV) . . . '57 '82 C.321 B.A. L.818 J.D. [Jackson,O.&P.] ⊙
Omilian, Susan M. '49 '79
C.477 B.A. L.545 J.D. Conn. Women's Educ. & Legal Fund, Inc.
Onacewicz, Walter J. . . . '66 '92 C.184 B.A. L.306 J.D. 29 S. Main St.
O'Neill, Dana Jones . . . '48 '75 C.560 B.A. L.174 J.D. 52 Westbrook Rd.
Parker, Nettie . . . '61 '91 C.1099 B.A. L.425 J.D. 14 Cumberland
Pascucci, Erminia . . . '47 '85 C&L.184 B.A., J.D. 71 Brightwood Lane
Pavano, Thomas A., (BV) . . . '63 '88 C.676 B.A. L.1029 J.D. 433 S. Main St.
Peck, Kelley M. Galica . . . '70 '97 C.258 B.S. L.1048 J.D. [Ⓐ Cummings&L.]
*PRACTICE AREAS: Trusts, Estates and Probate.
Phelon, Jeffrey V., (BV) . . . '60 '86 C.918 B.A. L.306 J.D. 29 S. Main St.
Pierce, Noble K., (AV) . . . '26 '52 C.976 B.A. L.184 LL.B. 109 Ridgewood Rd.‡
Preier, Katalin S. . . . '55 '91 C.276 B.S. L.184 J.D. 68 Harvest Lane

Reid and Riege, P.C., (AV)
65 La Salle Road, 06107 ⊙
Telephone: 860-232-6565 FAX: 860-232-6066
URL: http://www.reidriege.com
Travers T. Auburn; Suzanne S. Bocchini; Frederick J. Mullen, Jr.; Alan Birmingham; John R. Ivimey.
Alternative Dispute Resolution. Antitrust & Trade Regulation. Bankruptcy. Business Law. Commercial Law. Commercial Real Estate/Finance. Corporate Law. Employee Benefits/Pension Plans. Employee Benefits/Taft-Hartley Plans. Environmental Law. Health Care. Labor and Employment. Litigation. Mergers and Acquisitions. Nonprofit and Charitable Organizations. Occupational Safety & Health. Probate. Real Estate. Securities. Taxation. Trade and Professional Associations. Trusts & Estates. Zoning, Planning and Land Use.
Hartford, Connecticut Office: One State Street. Telephone: 860-278-1150. FAX: 860-240-1002.
Lakeville, Connecticut Office: 322 Main Street. Telephone: 860-435-9894. FAX: 860-240-1002.
Woodbury, Connecticut Office: 47 Sherman Hill Road. Telephone: 203-267-6680. FAX: 860-240-1002.
See Professional Biographies, WEST HARTFORD, CONNECTICUT

Reiter, Howard S. '36 '61 C.186 B.Mech.E. L.569 LL.B.
Corp. Pat. Coun., Garrison Liitg. Mgmt. Grp., Ltd (Pat.)
Richman, David M. . . . '54 '83 C.696 B.A. L.184 J.D. 40 Westcliff Dr.
RisCassi, Louis, (BV) . . . '29 '60 C.524 B.S. L.276 J.D. 16 Brace Rd.
RisCassi, Richard N., (BV) . . . '48 '75 C&L.276 B.A., J.D. 1010 Farmington Avenue
Roisman, Gerald A., (AV) . . . '37 '62 C.31 B.A. L.184 J.D. [Roisman&M.]
Roisman & McClure, P.C., (AV) . . . 433 S. Main Street
Rosenberg, Alan P., P.C., (BV) . . . '57 '82 C.867 B.S. L.184 J.D. 920 Farmington Ave.
Rosenberg, Elliott, (BV) . . . '34 '59 C.184 B.S. L.94 LL.B. 779 Farmington Ave.
Rosenblatt, Leon M., (BV) . . . '48 '84 C.550 B.A. L.184 J.D. 10 N Main St.
Rosenblit, Mark S., (CV) . . . '54 '79 C.228 B.A. L.128 J.D. 14 Coolidge Rd.
Rosenfield, Roslyne E. . . . '26 '71 C&L.184 B.S., J.D. 50 Lincoln Ave.‡
Rosenthal, Edward F., (AV) . . . '45 '70 C.103 B.A. L.184 J.D. [Goodman,R.&M.]
*PRACTICE AREAS: Business Law; Employment; Real Estate; ERISA; Business Estate Planning.
Rosenthal, Jan Carol . . . '54 '82 C.012 B.S. L.564 J.D. 65 LaSalle Rd.
Ross, Lee B. . . . '64 '96 C.867 B.A. L.306 J.D. [Goodman,R.&M.]
*PRACTICE AREAS: Personal Injury; Business Law; Real Estate; Elder; Regulatory.
Roth, Stuart M., (BV) . . . '45 '71 C&L.184 B.S., J.D. [Krevolin,R.&C.L.] ⊙
*PRACTICE AREAS: Products Liability; Medical Malpractice; Personal Injury; Family Law; Divorce.
Roy, Michael L. . . . '54 '79 C.855 B.A. L.188 J.D. 56 Lemay St.‡
Sack, Gerald S., (AV) . . . '53 '77 C.976 B.A. L.184 J.D. [Sack,S.&K.]

Sack, Spector & Karsten, LLP, (AV)
836 Farmington Avenue, 06119
Telephone: 860-233-8251 FAX: 860-232-8736
Members of Firm: Gerald S. Sack; Elliot B. Spector; Scott M. Karsten; Marcia J. Gleeson; William C. Berry; Nicole D. Dorman; Christopher G. Arciero. Associate: Marc Vidone.
Personal Injury, Insurance Defense, Law Enforcement Liability, Municipal Liability. General Civil Trial and Appellate Practice, Commercial Litigation, Risk Management Consulting.
See Professional Biographies, WEST HARTFORD, CONNECTICUT

Salafia, Brett J. . . . '66 '98 C.855 B.A. L.861 J.D. 54 Dover Rd.
Sandberg, John A. . . . '41 '67 C.105 A.B. L.94 J.D. 103 Walbridge Rd.
Sbarge, Arnold, (AV) . . . '31 '61 C.309 A.B. L.184 LL.B. 28 N. Main St.
Schatz, Nathan A., (BV) . . . '58 '86 C.1365 B.A. L.659 J.D. [Weinstein&W.]

Schatz, Robert F., (BV) '51 '77 C.188 B.A. L.818 J.D.
1007 Farmington Avenue, 06107
Telephone: 860-231-1050 Fax: 860-231-1052
Email: schatzlaw@aol.com
Corporate Law, Commercial Finance, Commercial Mortgages, Mortgage Finance, Mortgage Workouts, Asset Based Finance, Credit Enhancement, Debt and Equity Finance, Secured Finance, Structured Finance, Unsecured Finance, Employee Stock Ownership Plans (ESOP), Employee Stock Ownership Trusts, ERISA, Nonqualified Benefits, Fiduciary Law, Employee Benefits, Mergers, Acquisitions and Divestitures, Business Acquisitions, Business Divestitures, Leveraged Acquisitions, Leveraged Buyouts, Venture Capital.
See Professional Biographies, WEST HARTFORD, CONNECTICUT

Schatz, Walter B., (BV) . . . '22 '49 C&L.188 A.B., LL.B. [Ⓖ Krevolin,R.&C.L.] ⊙
*PRACTICE AREAS: Litigation.
Schatzki, Ralph D. . . . '59 '85 C.604 B.A. L.1119 J.D. 9 Walbridge Rd.‡
Schor, Robert M. . . . '31 '65 C.659 B.S.E. L.184 J.D. 993 Farmington Ave.
Schulman, Jed N., (BV) . . . '54 '80 C.184 B.A. L.1019 J.D. 433 S. Main St.
Seidman, Richard H., (BV) . . . '38 '64 C&L.976 B.A., LL.B. Ten Crossroads Plz.
Serafini, Cynthia A. St. Onge . . . '57 '91 C.788 B.A. L.306 J.D. 105 Raymond Rd.
Sexton, Terence P. . . . '66 '93 C.829 B.A. L.306 J.D. 924 Farmington Ave.
Shelton, Adam J. . . . '63 '89 C.1033 B.A. L.94 J.D. [Shelton&S.]
Shelton, Philip A., (BV) . . . '33 '79 C.178 A.B. L.184 J.D. [Shelton&S.]
Shelton & Shelton, (BV) . . . 29 N. Main St.
Sherfinski, John M. . . . '45 '74 C.966 B.A. L.1068 J.D. 27 Avalon Rd. (Pat.)

Sherman, Ralph D. '— '91 C.1103 B.A. L.184 J.D.
1001 Farmington Avenue, Suite 300, 06107
Telephone: 860-561-0695 Fax: 860-561-0896
Email: atty@ralphdsherman.com URL: http://www.ralphdsherman.com
Criminal and Civil Litigation. Civil Rights, Second Amendment Law, Firearms, Pistol Permits, Pardons, Landlord Tenant, Collections and Real Estate.
See Professional Biographies, WEST HARTFORD, CONNECTICUT

Shooshan, Charles H., III, (CV) . . . '55 '80 C.453 S.B. L.94 J.D. 846 Farmington Ave.
Sigal, Nathan A. . . . '26 '50 C.94 B.S. L.184 LL.B. 740 N. Main St.
Sinatro, Stephen J., (BV) '64 '89 C.184 B.A. L.1048 J.D.
[O'Connell,F.&A.] (⊙Hartford)
Singer, William . . . '27 '59 C.855 B.S. L.569 M.A. 31 Brown Leigh Rd.
Smith, Brian D. . . . '66 '92 C.156 B.A. L.1029 J.D. 98 Montclair Dr.
Smith, Richard P. . . . '14 '40 C.918 B.A. L.184 LL.B. 53 Hillsboro Dr.‡
Soifer, Aviam . . . '48 '74 C&L.976 B.A., J.D. Prof. of Law, Univ. of Conn.
Spahn, Elizabeth K. '49 '76
C.976 B.A. L.831 J.D. Prof. of Law, New England School of Law
Spector, Elliot B., (BV) . . . '47 '81 C.184 B.A. L.1033 J.D. [Sack,S.&K.]
Spiegel, David J., (BV) . . . '37 '69 C.563 A.B. L.976 LL.B. 62 King Philip Dr.

Stanger, Bruce H., (BV) '51 '77 C.1033 B.S.E.E. L.1048 J.D.
29 South Main Street, 06107
Telephone: 1-888-782-6437; 860-561-0650 Fax: 860-561-0646 URL: http://www.lawyers.com/bstangerlaw
Email: bstanger@stangerlaw.com URL: http://www.stangerlaw.com
***PRACTICE AREAS: Legal Malpractice; Medical Malpractice; Construction Law; Business Law; Civil Litigation.**
Legal Malpractice, Medical Malpractice, Construction, Business, Civil Litigation, Commercial Litigation, Personal Injury, Corporate Law, Automobile Accidents.
See Professional Biographies, WEST HARTFORD, CONNECTICUT

Steier, Mark S., (BV) . . . '47 '73 C.569 B.A. L.184 J.D. 65 LaSalle Rd.

Stein, Jeffrey W. '50 '75 C.1349 B.A. L.723 J.D.
28 North Main Street, Suite G-01, 06107
Telephone: 860-561-5671 Fax: 860-561-5681
Email: jeffrey.stein@usa.net
Estate Planning, Estate Administration, Wills, Trusts, Estate Litigation, Trust Litigation, Individual Taxation, Pensions.
See Professional Biographies, WEST HARTFORD, CONNECTICUT

Stevenson, Franklin W. '07 '35
C.275 B.A. L.383 LL.B. The Student Assoc., Univ. of Hartford
Storm, Robert W. . . . '51 '89 C&L.945 A.B., J.D. P.O. Box 271645
Sullivan, Paul W. . . . '— '93 433 S. Main St.
Svonkin, Mark J., (AV) . . . '39 '68 C.264 A.B. L.184 J.D. [M.J.Svonkin]
*PRACTICE AREAS: Commercial Real Estate; Zoning; Commercial Leasing Law; Condominium Law.

Svonkin, Mark J., P.C., The Law Offices of, (AV)
18 North Main Street, 06107
Telephone: 860-521-2811 Fax: 860-521-6448
Email: svonk@aol.com URL: http://www.lawyers.com/svonkin&godgelaw
Mark J. Svonkin.
Commercial Real Estate, Condominium Law, Financing, Zoning, Commercial Leasing, Corporate and LLC Law.
See Professional Biographies, WEST HARTFORD, CONNECTICUT

Swanson-Bowers, Rebecca L. . . . '53 '83 C.518 B.A. L.184 J.D. 5 Old Oak Rd.
Swerdloff, Ileen P., (BV) . . . '45 '79 C.107 B.A. L.1048 J.D. [Swerdloff&S.]
Swerdloff, Mark H., (BV) . . . '45 '75 C.107 B.A. L.184 J.D. [Swerdloff&S.]
Swerdloff & Swerdloff, (BV) . . . 61 S. Main St.
Tamoney, Thomas H., (AV) . . . '20 '50 C.855 B.S. L.306 LL.B. 580 Mountain Rd.‡
Teitenberg, Robert A., (BV) . . . '30 '68 C.1033 B.A. L.184 LL.B. [Teitenberg&W.]
Teitenberg & Wallace, (BV) . . . 902 S. Quaker Lane
Thibodeau, Richard E., (AV) . . . '47 '78 C.870 B.S. L.184 J.D. 91 S. Main St.
Thier, Clifford S. . . . '51 '75 C.1350 B.A. L.1338 J.D. [Thier]
*PRACTICE AREAS: Commercial Law; Business Law; Corporate Law; Real Estate Law; Wills.

Thier Law Offices, LLC
1007 Farmington Avenue, 06107
Telephone: 860-236-2600 Facsimile: 860-231-1052
Email: cliffthier@thierlaw.com
Clifford S. Thier.
Commercial Law, Business Law, Corporate Law and Real Estate Law.
See Professional Biographies, WEST HARTFORD, CONNECTICUT

Van Der Werff, Jan Peter, (CV) . . . '59 '87 P.O. Box 270697
Vidone, Marc . . . '69 '99 C.884 B.A. L.1187 J.D. [Ⓐ Sack,S.&K.]
*PRACTICE AREAS: Personal Injury.
Vozzella Courser, Lisa M. . . . '— '93 C.1030 B.A. L.1048 J.D. [Ⓐ Kearns&K.]
*PRACTICE AREAS: Elder Law; Probate; Estate Planning; Estate Planning for Parents of Handicapped Children; Estate Planning for the Disabled.
Wallace, Richard A., (BV) . . . '43 '67 C&L.184 B.A., LL.B. [Teitenberg&W.]
Walsh, Robert E., (BV) . . . '33 '62 C.95 A.B. L.184 J.D. 81 S. Main St.‡
Ward, Frederick F., II, (BV) . . . '52 '78 C.128 B.A. L.896 J.D. 433 S. Main St.
Waterman, Martin B., (CV) . . . '43 '71 C.569 B.A. L.184 J.D. 22 Forest Hills Dr.
Webb, Thomas R. . . . '46 '86 C.722 B.A. L.976 J.D. 197 Walden St.
Webber, Cori-Lynn S., (BV) . . . '63 '88 C.28 B.A. L.818 J.D. 29 S. Main St.
Wechsler, Alfred F., (AV) . . . '11 '35 C.569 L.94 LL.B. 10 N. Main St.
Wein, Alan, (BV) . . . '61 '87 C.183 B.A. L.93 J.D. 32 Park Rd.

Weinstein, Richard P., (AV) ....'46 '70 C.901 B.A. L.184 J.D. [Weinstein&W.]
*PRACTICE AREAS: Civil Litigation; Bank Litigation; Lender Liability Law; Debtor Rights Law.

Weinstein & Wisser, P.C., (AV) [BB]
29 South Main Street, 06107-2103
Telephone: 860-561-2628 Telecopier: 860-521-6150
Email: weinstein&wisser@dtg.net
Richard P. Weinstein; Kerry Marc Wisser; Nathan A. Schatz.
Litigation Practice including Commercial Specializing in Debtors Rights, Corporation, Personal Injury, Professional Malpractice, Real Estate and Bad Faith Law. Trials and Appeals in State and Federal Courts.
See Professional Biographies, WEST HARTFORD, CONNECTICUT

Weintraub, Jay B., (BV) ....'46 '71 C.882 B.A. L.276 J.D. [Beizer&W.]
*PRACTICE AREAS: Real Estate; Business Law; Commercial Law; Bankruptcy; Debtor and Creditor.
Weller, Harry D., (BV) ....'54 '79 C.823 B.A. L.184 J.D. Sr. Asst. State's Atty.
Werner, Howard M., (BV) ....'25 '52 C.855 B.S. L.184 LL.B. 924 Farmington Ave.
Wetstone & D'Ambrosio, (BV) ....784 Farmington Ave.
White, Richard S. ....'52 '77 C.930 B.A. L.94 J.D. 127 Park Rd.
Wiellette, Julia M. ....'64 '92 C.67 B.A. L.306 J.D. 33 Federal St.
Willard, John B. ....'16 '43 C.971 B.S. L.273 LL.B. 111 Hunter Dr. (Pat.)
Wisser, Kerry Marc, (AV) ....'60 '85 C.183 B.A. L.1029 J.D. [Weinstein&W.]
*PRACTICE AREAS: Civil Litigation; Personal Injury Litigation; Medical Malpractice; Commercial Litigation; Banking Litigation.
Zaccardi, Elizabeth Black ....'59 '89 C.588 B.A. L.818 J.D. 29 S. Main St.
Zaslow, Robert D. ....'68 '94 C.184 B.A. L.607 J.D. [[A] E.J.Nerenberg]
*PRACTICE AREAS: Family Law (80%); Juvenile Law (10%); Real Estate (10%).
Zereski, Jo-Ellen ....'71 '98 C.454 B.A. L.306 J.D. [[A] Berman,B.A.&D.]
*PRACTICE AREAS: Estate Planning; Probate; Real Estate; Corporate Law.

WEST HAVEN, 54,021, *New Haven Co.*

Abrams, Keith R. ....'61 '85 C.339 B.S. L.145 J.D. Sr. Coun., Bayer Corp.
Alderman, Stephen B., (BV) ....'47 '73 C.873 B.A. L.30 J.D. 201 Center St.
Altschuler, Donald L., (BV) ....'53 '80 C.597 B.S.S. L.184 J.D. [Altschuler&A.]
Altschuler, Richard P., (BV) ....'49 '74 C.860 B.A. L.306 J.D. [Altschuler&A.]
Altschuler & Altschuler, (BV) ....509 Campbell Ave.
Babbitz, David R. ....'68 '93 C.882 B.A. L.1252 J.D. 377 Main St.
Barrett, Peter C., (BV) ....'56 '81 C.184 B.S. L.884 J.D. [Mirto,K.&B.]
Benham, Christine ....'69 '01 L.1252 J.D. [[A] Umeugo&Assoc.]
*PRACTICE AREAS: Medical Malpractice; Personal Injury; Environmental Law.
Berry, Paul R. '54 '81 C.201 B.S. L.1035 J.D.
V.P., Asst. Gen. Coun. & Asst. Secy., Bayer Corp.
Bowerman, Richard H., (AV) ....'17 '46 C&L.976 B.A., LL.B. 612 Thorn Hill Lane‡
Brennan, James Thomas, (BV) ....'36 '63 C.976 B.A. L.309 LL.B. 14 Ashburton Pl.
Brewer, Alice A. ....'47 '91 C.347 A.B. L.1340 J.D. Pat. Coun., Bayer Corp. (Pat.)
Burns, Michael D. ....'57 '83 C.1156 B.S. L.982 J.D. 112 Bellevue Ave.
Carilli, Joseph F. ....'36 '79 C.869 B.S. L.183 J.D. V.P., Admn., Univ. of New Haven
Carmody, David C., (BV) ....'41 '76 C.976 B.A. L.818 J.D. 754 Savin Ave.
Carroll, Holly A. ....'48 '76 C.722 B.A. L.976 J.D. Yale Univ.
Chiu, Jerrie L. ....'67 '97 C.347 B.S. L.184 J.D. Pat. Coun., Bayer Corp. (Pat.)
Ciresi, Helen S. ....'42 '89 C.19 B.A. L.1029 J.D. [Ciresi&M.]
Ciresi & Mass, (BV) ....295 Main St.
Conway, Brian P. '62 '87 C.645 B.A. L.1017 J.D.
Sr. Coun., Bayer Corp. (⊙Pitts., PA)
DaBreo-Evans, Maria A. ....'71 '99 C.811 B.A. L.564 J.D. [[A] Umeugo&Assoc.]
*PRACTICE AREAS: Family Law; Employment Law; Debt Collection; Personal Injury; Real Estate Closings.
Damicis, Daniel, (BV) ....'26 '54 C.184 B.A. L.94 J.D. 251 Center St.
DeGennaro, Mark J., (BV) ....'56 '81 C.103 B.A. L.1029 J.D. [Donahue,V.&D.]
DiBenedetto, Alphonse S. ....'21 '50 C&L.262 B.S., LL.B. 367 Elm St.
Donahue, Dennis J., Jr., (BV) ....'35 '60 C&L.184 B.A., J.D. [Donahue,V.&D.] ⊙
Donahue, Votto & DeGennaro, P.C., (AV) ....415 Main St. (⊙Clinton)
Dorfman, Howard L. '49 '76 C.978 B.A. L.1009 J.D.
(adm. in NY; not adm. in CT) Sr. Coun., Bayer Corp.
Dorsi, Eugene J., (BV) ....'26 '53 C.184 B.S. L.262 LL.B. 251 Center St.
Falcone, Vincent R., (BV) ....'43 '71 C.309 A.B. L.188 J.D. [Falcone&L.]
Falcone & Lyons, P.C., (BV) ....336 Main Street
Feinberg, Michael L. ...'40 '66 C&L.184 B.A., LL.B. Corp. Coun., Premier Industries Inc.
Fischer, Brian T., (BV) ....'53 '79 C.692 B.S.B.A. L.1338 J.D. 259 Elm St.
Fischer, Herbert D., (AV) ....'19 '49 C&L.228 B.A., J.D. [Fischer&F.]
Fischer, James E., (BV) ....'55 '80 C.1145 B.S. L.1338 J.D. [Fischer&F.]
Fischer & Fischer, (AV) ....568 Washington Ave. (⊙Corpus Christi, TX)
Ginsberg, Kenneth S., (BV) ....'58 '83 C.276 B.S. L.930 J.D. 377 Main St
Gray, William F. '40 '81 C.679 B.S. L.818 J.D.
(adm. in MA; not adm. in CT; Pat.) Pat. Coun., Bayer Corp.
Greenman, Jeffrey M. '47 '75 C.816 B.E. L.262 J.D.
(adm. in NY; not adm. in CT; Pat.) V.P.-Patents & Lic., Bayer Corp.
Heffernan, E. Michael, (AV) ....'42 '67 C.165 A.B. L.184 J.D. [Heffernan&H.]
Heffernan, Gerald A., (BV) ....'49 '74 C.165 A.B. L.818 J.D. [Heffernan&H.]
Heffernan & Heffernan, (AV) ....295 Main St.
Ketaineck, Stephen R., (BV) ....'48 '73 C.95 A.B. L.184 J.D. [Mirto,K.&B.]
Lacobelle, Jerome A., (BV) ....'31 '59 C.676 B.A. L.276 J.D. [J.A.Lacobelle]
Lacobelle, Jerome A., Jr., (BV) ....'63 '89 C.676 B.A. L.1029 J.D. [J.A.Lacobelle]
Lacobelle, Jerome A., LLC, Law Offices of, (BV) ....537 Washington Ave.
Liberti, Vincent A., Jr. ....'66 '92 C.867 B.S. L.1048 J.D. 59 Elm Street
Lopez, Eric R. ....'66 '98 C.415 B.S. L.107 J.D. 205 Center St.
Lyons, Daniel A., Jr., (BV) ....'47 '76 C.184 A.B. L.1202 J.D. [Falcone&L.]
Malec, Thomas O., (BV) .....'42 '68 C.1252 B.S. L.1009 J.D. 140 Captain Thomas Blvd.
Mason, James M. '10 '39 C.128 B.S. L.537 LL.B.
(adm. in DC; not adm. in CT; Pat.) 460 Savin Ave.
Mass, Kathleen S., (BV) ....'59 '88 C.787 B.A. L.1029 J.D. [Ciresi&M.]
Mirto, Robert C., (BV) ....'38 '63 C.976 B.A. L.184 J.D. [Mirto,K.&B.]
Mirto, Ketaineck & Barrett, P.C., (BV) ....140 Captain Thomas Blvd.
Mitler, Laura S. ....'46 '88 C.1102 B.S. L.1048 J.D. 98 Elm St.
Peska, David J., (BV) ....'44 '73 C.1029 B.S. L.1294 J.D. 36 Windsock Rd.
Pizzola, Angelo ....'62 '90 C.184 B.A. L.1029 J.D. [[A] J.A.Lacobelle]
Rossi, Giancarlo, (BV) ....'49 '76 C.1030 B.A. L.352 J.D. 198 2nd Ave.
Salzo, Anthony, Jr. ....'50 '85 C.1156 B.A. L.1252 J.D. 645 Main St.
Scully, Thomas ....'29 '63 C&L.184 B.S., LL.B. 6 Cowpen Rd.‡
Shimei, Barbara A. .....'50 '81 C.475 B.S. L.1170 J.D. Sr. Pat. Coun., Bayer Corp. (Pat.)
Simonton, Pamela A. '49 '82 C.1278 B.S. L.1206 J.D.
(adm. in FL; not adm. in CT; Pat.) Bayer Corp.
Small, Stephen I., (CV) ....'55 '81 C.184 B.A. L.1252 J.D. 203 Campbell Ave.
Spitzbard, Kenneth S. ....'60 '85 C.1145 B.S. L.30 J.D. 375 Morgan Ln.
Stutman, Roni ....'— '95 C.645 B.A. L.1252 J.D. 367 Elm St.
Thomas, Kenneth L. ....'51 '86 C.1030 B.S. L.1029 J.D. 111 Ocean Ave.

Umeugo, Ikechukwu, (CV) ....'60 '89 C.1156 B.S. L.900 J.D. [Umeugo&Assoc.]
*PRACTICE AREAS: Collections; International Law; Medical Malpractice Law; Personal Injury Law; Workers Compensation.

Umeugo & Associates, P.C., (CV)
840 Orange Avenue 2nd Floor, P.O. Box 26373, 06516
Telephone: 203-931-2680 Fax: 203-931-2682
Email: umeugo@justice.com
Ikechukwu Umeugo;—Maria A. DaBreo-Evans; Christine Benham.
General Practice, Debt Collections, International Law, Personal Injury, Subrogation, Insurance Law and Civil Litigation, Automobile Accidents, Workers Compensation, Medical Malpractice, Commercial Collections, Employment Law, Immigration Law, Incorporation, Wills and Trusts, Landlord and Tenant Law, Business Law, Real Estate Closings and Trademarks and Copyrights.
See Professional Biographies, WEST HAVEN, CONNECTICUT

Votto, Louis Smith, (AV) ....'35 '61 C.262 B.S. L.184 J.D. [Donahue,V.&D.] ⊙
Weston, Vivian L. ....'51 '80 C.353 B.A. L.352 J.D. 11 Woody Crest

WESTON, 8,284, *Fairfield Co.*

Aron, Brad M. ....'63 '89 C.860 B.A. L.823 J.D. 211 Weston Rd. (⊙Westport)
Auchincloss, John W. ....'58 '84 C.976 B.A. L.893 J.D. 90 Kettle Creek Rd.
Blau, Barbara J. '56 '83 C.118 B.A. L.309 J.D.
(adm. in CA; not adm. in CT) 2 Rogues Ridge Rd.‡
Brufsky, Allen D., (AV) ....'39 '64 C.816 B.M.E. L.276 J.D. [A.D.Brufsky] ⊙
Brufsky, Allen D., P.A., (AV) ....124 Old Easton Tpke. (⊙Bokeelia, FL)
Cullen, Kevin J. '48 '73 C.724 B.S. L.569 J.D.
(adm. in NY; not adm. in CT) Sr. V.P., Boston Capital Servs., Inc.
Damin, Amy K. ....'55 '87 C.994 B.A. L.1040 J.D. 67 Godfrey Rd. W.
Finkelstein, Charles D. ....'51 '77 C.659 B.A. L.1202 J.D. 110 Lyons Plain Rd.

Guidera, George C., Law Offices of, (BV) '42 '67 C.165 B.A. L.276 J.D.
177 Weston Road, 06883-2113
Telephone: 203-227-5748 Fax: 203-227-0852
Email: westonlawfirm@aol.com URL: http://www.lawyers.com/guidera
***PRACTICE AREAS: Civil Practice; Criminal Law; Real Estate; Zoning, Planning and Land Use; Trusts and Estates.**
Associate: Suzanne K. Guidera.
Civil Practice, Criminal Law, Real Estate, Zoning, Planning and Land Use, Probate, Trusts and Estates, Corporate Law, Family Law, Personal Injury, Commercial Law, Mortgages and Wills.
References: First Fidelity Bank, Georgetown Office; Westport Bank & Trust Co., Weston Branch.
See Professional Biographies, WESTON, CONNECTICUT

Guidera, Suzanne K. ....'72 '99 C.36 B.S. L.1252 J.D. [[A] G.C.Guidera]
*PRACTICE AREAS: Real Estate; Probate; Trusts and Estates; Family Law; Zoning, Planning and Land Use.
Hart, Thomas G. ....'23 '51 C&L.228 B.A., J.D. 4 Wells Hill Rd.‡
Hover, Philip Brent ....'57 '82 C.216 B.S. L.564 J.D. 80 Beaverbrook Rd.
Israely, Martina Nicholls ....'48 '79 C.112 B.A. L.705 J.D. 20 Gray's Farm Rd.‡
Jaffe, Sharon E. ....'60 '85 C.846 B.A. L.1065 J.D. [[C] Levin&G.] ⊙
Joblin, Warren P., (BV) ....'38 '65 C.945 A.B. L.276 LL.B. 81 Old Easton Tpke.
Judge, George A. '41 '75 C.1041 B.A. L.29 J.D.
(adm. in VA; not adm. in CT) IBM
Levin & Glasser, P.C. ...............................P.O. Box 1098 (⊙New York, NY)
O'Shaughnessy, Maureen F. '50 '85 C.1140 B.A. L.1009 J.D.
(adm. in NY; not adm. in CT) 1 Hills End‡
Robbins, David L. '47 '72 C.610 A.B. L.178 J.D.
(adm. in OH; not adm. in CT) 13 Maple St.
Scheinman, Stanley B. '33 '61 C.188 A.B. L.178 J.D.
(adm. in NY; not adm. in CT) Mng. Dir., TTC Intl. Limited
Stires, Sally ....'50 '84 C.112 B.A. L.426 J.D. 9 Great Hill Rd.
Strauss, Ellen L. F., (CV) ....'— '83 C.1103 B.A. L.1218 J.D. 88 Ladder Hill Rd., N.
Thompson, Teresa D. ....'53 '96 C.45 B.A. L.978 J.D. 69 Georgetown Rd.
Wirtenberg, Alfred I. ....'46 '79 C.178 B.S. L.184 J.D. 15 Wilson Rd. (Pat.)
Workman, Mary B. '46 '83 C.922 B.S. L.923 J.D.
Coun., Intell. Prop. & Tech. Dept., Pitney Bowes, Inc.‡

WESTPORT, 25,290, *Fairfield Co.*

Ahern, Anthony E., (BV) ....'49 '79 C.1102 B.A. L.184 J.D. [Cramer&A.]
*PRACTICE AREAS: Civil Practice; Real Estate; Negligence; Probate; Estate Planning.
Albani, Suzanne B., (AV) ....'43 '78 C.788 B.A. L.724 J.D. [[C] Levett R.]
*PRACTICE AREAS: Health Law; Hospital Law; Commercial Real Estate Law; Corporate Law.
Albert, Martin J., (AV) '45 '70
C.659 B.S. L.94 J.D. [Cohen&W.] (⊙Bridgeport, Stamford)
*PRACTICE AREAS: Taxation; Estate Planning; Probate.

Albert, Ward & Johnson, P.C.
(See Greenwich)

Albrecht, Richard L., (AV) '38 '62
C.105 B.S. L.188 J.D. [Cohen&W.] (⊙Bridgeport, Stamford)
*PRACTICE AREAS: Litigation.
Aldrich, John H. ....'64 '90 C.165 B.A. L.569 J.D. [Aldrich&A.] ‡
Aldrich, Nancy, (BV) ....'59 '86 C.518 B.A. L.818 J.D. [Aldrich&A.]
Aldrich & Aldrich, (BV) ....830 Post Road East
Allison, Diane M. ....'53 '90 C.1030 B.S. L.1029 J.D. [Gunn,G.&A.]
Amschler, James R. ....'43 '68 C.966 B.S. L.813 LL.B. Diversified Legal Servs.
Andrew, Walter M., Jr., (BV) ....'32 '62 C.823 A.B. L.477 J.D. [[C] Wake,S.D.&B.]
*PRACTICE AREAS: Family Law; Trust Law; Estate Litigation; Wills; Probate.
Antonucci, Francis J., (AV) ....'47 '74 C.93 B.S. L.851 J.D. [Schine,J.&A.] ⊙
*PRACTICE AREAS: Taxation Law; Estate Planning Law; Corporate Law; Probate Law; Employee Benefits Law.
Aron, Brad M. ....'63 '89 C.860 B.A. L.823 J.D. 180 Post Road East (⊙Weston)
Avirom, Jonathan E., (AV) ....'38 '63 C.893 B.A. L.1009 LL.B. [Avirom&Assoc.] ⊙

Avirom & Associates, LLP, (AV)
38 Post Road West, 06880 ⊙
Telephone: 203-222-9355
Email: info@avirom.com
Jonathan E. Avirom.
Immigration and Nationality Law, Criminal and Matrimonial Law.
New York, N.Y. Office: 42 Broadway, Suite 1220. Telephone: 212-747-8787. Fax: 212-747-0857.
See Professional Biographies, WESTPORT, CONNECTICUT

Balbirer, Arthur E., (AV) ....'40 '66 C.867 B.S. L.569 J.D. [[C] Berkowitz,T.&T.]
*PRACTICE AREAS: Domestic Relations Law.
Baldwin, Thayer, (BV) ....'40 '65 C.976 B.A. L.276 LL.B. [Yost&Assoc.]
Barberi, Robert O. ....'45 '72 C.31 B.A. L.178 J.D. [Levett R.]
*PRACTICE AREAS: Corporate Law; Commercial Law; Mergers and Acquisitions.
Barndollar, Livia D., (BV) ....'56 '81 C.855 B.A. L.884 J.D. [[C] Weisman&L.]
*PRACTICE AREAS: Family Law; Appellate Practice.
Barrie, William J. ....'48 '74 C.1030 A.B. L.861 J.D. Pres., Mantrose-Haeuser Co.
Barton, James M., (AV) ....'42 '67 C.976 B.A. L.893 LL.B. CEO, Hematech, LLC
Bass, David I. ....'63 '95 C.569 B.F.A. L.1040 J.D. [Rubenstein,G.&B.]
*PRACTICE AREAS: Commercial Leasing; Land Use; Zoning; Real Estate.
Bass, Stacy Waldman ....'66 '93 C.66 B/A/ L.569 J.D. MHW Inc.

Battaglino, Nicholas A. . . . . '44 '70 C&L.184 B.A., J.D. 1 Pioneer Rd.
Begos, Patrick W., (AV⊤) . . . . '63 '88 C.367 B.A. L.178 J.D. [Begos&H.]
Begos & Horgan, LLP, (AV⊤) . . . . 25 Ford Rd. (⊙Bronxville, NY)
Beharry, Daniel P., (BV) '52 '77 C.976 B.A. L.800 J.D.
Dir. Envir. Affs., Caradon Inc. (Legal Department)
Belanger, Nora A. . . . . '53 '01 C.1102 B.S. L.1040 J.D. [Rutkin&O.]
*PRACTICE AREAS: Family Law; Litigation.
Belkin Burden Wenig & Goldman, LLP . . . . 125 Main St., 4th Fl. (⊙New York, NY)
Berg, Paul M., (BV) . . . . '50 '77 C.72 B.A. L.184 J.D. [Berkowitz,T.&T.]
*PRACTICE AREAS: Taxation Law; Intellectual Property; Antitrust Law.
Berger, Dina R. . . . . '47 '79 C.66 A.B. L.362 J.D. 6 Bayberry Common
Berger & Paul, LLP . . . . 125 Main Street (⊙New York, NY)
Berkowitz, Richard, (AV) . . . . . . '41 '66 C.197 A.B. L.184 J.D. [Berkowitz,T.&T.]
*PRACTICE AREAS: Executive Compensation and Contracts; Business Law; Real Estate Law; Sports Law; Corporate Law.
Berkowitz, Malowitz & Mullin, (BV) . . . . 8 St. John Place (⊙Stamford)

Berkowitz, Trager & Trager, LLC, (AV) BB
253 Post Road West, P.O. Box 808, 06881
Telephone: 203-226-1001 Fax: 203-226-3801
Email: btt@bertralaw.com URL: http://www.lawyers.com/berkowitztrager&tragerlic
Richard Berkowitz; Paul M. Berg; Samuel Febbraio, Jr.; Jay L. Goldstein; David A. Greenberg; Howard D. Komisar; Richard J. Preminger; Robert H. Rubin; Doris B. Shiller. Of Counsel: Arthur E. Balbirer.
General Business Practice. Executive Compensation and Contracts, Sports Law, Corporations, Commercial and Residential Real Estate, Banking Law, Estate Planning, Probate, Commercial and Business Law. Tax and Tax Planning Law, Creditors Rights and Bankruptcy Law.
See Professional Biographies, WESTPORT, CONNECTICUT

Bernhard, G. Kenneth, (BV) '44 '69 C.976 B.A. L.569 J.D.
[Cohen&W.] (⊙Bridgeport)
*PRACTICE AREAS: Civil Litigation; Municipal; Domestic; Criminal; Zoning Appeals.
Bernstein, Carole . . . . '63 '89 C.477 B.A. L.178 J.D. 41 Maple Ave., N.

Bershtein, Lippman, Bachman & McKeon, P.C.
(See New Haven)

Blackman, Lenard D., (CV) . . . . '36 '62 C.103 A.B. L.569 LL.B. [L.D.Blackman]
Blackman, Lenard D., P.C., (CV) . . . . 25 Sylvan Rd., S., Ste. M
Blazzard, Norse N., (BV) . . . . '37 '63 C.813 A.B. L.1065 J.D. [Blazzard,G.&H.] ⊙
*PRACTICE AREAS: Life Insurance Products; Securities Law; Corporations; Insurance Taxation; Employee Benefits.

Blazzard, Grodd & Hasenauer, P.C., (AV) BB
943 Post Road East, P.O. Box 5108, 06881 ⊙
Telephone: 203-226-7866 Telecopier: 203-454-4855
Email: BGHCT@mindspring.com
Norse N. Blazzard; Leslie E. Grodd; Judith A. Hasenauer; William E. Hasenauer; Raymond A. O'Hara, III; Lynn Korman Stone; Tina L. Lewert (Not admitted in CT); Ellen Mechlin-Levitt (Not admitted in CT).
Administrative, Corporation, Estate Planning, Insurance, Probate, Real Estate, Taxation and Securities Law.
Lauderdale-By-the-Sea Office: Suite 207, W. Tradewinds Avenue, 33308. Telephone: 954-771-6667. Facsimile: 954-771-7689. E-Mail: BGHFL@AOL.COM
See Professional Biographies, WESTPORT, CONNECTICUT

Bloom, Ira W., (BV) . . . . '53 '78 C.156 B.A. L.184 J.D. [Wake,S.D.&B.]
*PRACTICE AREAS: Municipal Law; Zoning, Planning and Land Use; Commercial Real Estate; Residential Real Estate; Civil Litigation.

Bochinski, Pamela D., (BV) '41 '77 C.105 B.A. L.184 J.D.
25 Ford Road, 06880
Telephone: 203-227-4484 Fax: 203-222-4833
Email: pamela.d.bochinski@snet.net
Trusts and Estates, Probate, Wills, Taxation.
See Professional Biographies, WESTPORT, CONNECTICUT

Bowman, Andrew B., (AV) '45 '70 C&L.184 B.S., J.D. BB
1804 Post Road East, 06880
Telephone: 203-259-0599 Fax: 203-255-2570
Email: andrew.bowman@snet.net URL: http://www.lawyers.com/bowmanlaw
General Civil and Criminal Litigation before all Federal and State Courts. Trials and Appeals. Criminal Defense, Tax Litigation, Employment Law, Construction Litigation, Civil Rights, Environmental Law, Personal Injury, Commercial Litigation and Negligence Law.
Reference: Peoples Bank.
See Professional Biographies, WESTPORT, CONNECTICUT

Bowman, Jonathan S., (AV) '42 '66
C.347 A.B. L.184 J.D. [Cohen&W.] (⊙Bridgeport, Stamford)
*PRACTICE AREAS: Real Estate; Condominium; Property Tax Appeals; Bankruptcy; Title Insurance.
Boyd, John W. . . . . '16 '42 C.299 B.S. L.178 LL.B. [Boyd&M.]
Boyd & Martin, P.C., (BV) . . . . 10 Bay Street
Boynton, Victoria L. . . . . . '— '82 C.454 B.A. L.61 J.D. 1200 Post Road East, Suite 110
Bradford, George J., (CV) . . . . '32 '82 C.178 A.B. L.569 J.D. [Bradford,T.&T.]
Bradford, Tudruj and Tomasky, (CV) . . . . 246 Post Rd. E., Suite 12
Brenneman, Frederica S. '26 '53 C.681 A.B. L.309 LL.B.
320 Bayberry Lane Extension‡

Brody, Wilkinson and Ober, P.C.
(See Southport)

Brophy, Joseph M., (BV) . . . . '41 '66 C.264 A.B. L.262 LL.B. 8 Myrtle Ave.
Brown, Carole D. . . . . '45 '74 C.172 B.A. L.705 J.D. [C.D.Brown]

Brown, Lawrence I., (AV) '31 '56 C.569 B.A. L.477 J.D.
611 Riverside Avenue, P.O. Box 2117, 06880
Telephone: 203-222-9099 Fax: 203-222-9008
Email: larrybrown@snet.net
Admiralty, Maritime and International Law.
See Professional Biographies, WESTPORT, CONNECTICUT

Brown, Linda S. . . . . '— '94 C.823 B.A. L.978 J.D. [Kove&K.]
*PRACTICE AREAS: Estate Planning; Estate Administration.
Brown, Michael K., Law Office of, (AV) '44 '69
C.860 A.B. L.569 J.D. 25 Ford Road 2nd Floor
Brown, Carole D., L.L.C., Law Office of . . . . Six Wilton Road
Bryniczka, Jacob P., (AV) . . . . '45 '71 C.918 B.A. L.184 J.D. [Wake,S.D.&B.]
*PRACTICE AREAS: Business Law; Taxation; Marketing Law; Promotion Law; Estate Planning.

Byelas, Leslie, (AV) '36 '61 C&L.94 B.S.B.A., LL.B.
1804 Post Road East, 06880
Telephone: 203-259-0599 Fax: 203-255-2570
General Civil Trial and Appellate Practice in all State and Federal Courts. Matrimonial, Real Estate.
See Professional Biographies, WESTPORT, CONNECTICUT

Campbell, Mark S. . . . . '69 '99 C.459 B.B.A. L.1040 J.D. Vice Pres., Knox & Co.
Capasse, Edward J., (AV) . . . . '30 '55 C.1030 B.S. L.93 J.D. [Nevas,N.C.&G.]
Capuano, Earl F., (AV) . . . . '31 '59 C.184 B.A. L.178 J.D. Ret. Prob. J.

Cardinali, Debra R. . . . . '57 '85 C.1083 B.S. L.893 J.D. [Levett R.]
*PRACTICE AREAS: Mergers and Acquisitions; Health Care Law; Corporate Law; Commercial Finance.
Carmichael, Martin '27 '53 C.575 B.S. L.976 LL.B.
(adm. in NY; not adm. in CT) 66 Weston Rd.‡
Carron, Mark S., (BV) . . . . '47 '86 C.667 B.S. L.1029 J.D. [Carron&F.]
Carron & Fink, (BV) . . . . 1698-A Post Road East
Carter, C. Michael, (AV) '43 '74 C.112 B.S. L.273 J.D.
[Tirola&H.] (⊙Oceanport, NJ)
*PRACTICE AREAS: Taxation; Corporate Law.

Casper & de Toledo LLC
(See Stamford)

Cavanaugh, Robert L., Jr. . . . . '67 '93 C.588 B.S. L.818 J.D. [Goldstein&P.] ⊙
Cederbaum, Eugene E., (BV) . . . . . . '42 '68 C.569 B.S. L.178 J.D. [Wake,S.D.&B.]
*PRACTICE AREAS: Business Law; Commercial Real Estate; Residential Real Estate; Commercial Litigation; Personal Injury Litigation.
Chang, Mary . . . . '70 '95 C.1349 B.A. L.724 J.D. [Levett R.]
*PRACTICE AREAS: Tax Law; Estate Planning; Corporate Law.
Chansky, Edward B., (AV) . . . . '60 '87 C.976 B.A. L.309 J.D. [Levett R.]
*PRACTICE AREAS: Copyright and Trademark; Internet Law; Advertising and Promotion; Antitrust and Unfair Competition.

Clear, Michael Gene, Law Offices of
(See Stamford)

Cobb & Eisenberg LLC
(See Westport)

Cohen, Amy S. . . . . '65 '97 C.882 B.A. L.262 J.D. [Sacks,M.P.&L.] ⊙
Cohen, Eric I '58 '84 C.1036 B.A. L.1398 J.D.
(adm. in NY; not adm. in CT) Sr. V.P., Secy. & Gen. Coun., Terex Corp.
*RESPONSIBILITIES: General Commercial; Contracts; Corporate Securities; Corporate Finance; Litigation Management.

Cohen and Wolf, P.C., (AV)
190 Main Street, 06880 ⊙
Telephone: 203-222-1034
Email: cw@cohenandwolf.com URL: http://www.cohenandwolf.com
Richard L. Albrecht; Jonathan S. Bowman; Martin J. Albert; Stewart I. Edelstein; G. Kenneth Bernhard; Greta E. Solomon; Richard G. Kent; Richard Slavin; Richard J. Di Marco; David B. Zabel; David M. Levine; Jocelyn B. Hurwitz; Patricia C. Sullivan.
General Practice. Business Transactions, Commercial Litigation, Employment and Labor, Family and Matrimonial, Land Use, Municipal, Personal Injury, Physicians Practice, Real Estate, Securities, Tax, Trusts and Estates. Litigation in all Courts.
Bridgeport, Connecticut Office: 1115 Broad Street. Telephone: 203-368-0211. Facsimile: 203-394-9901.
Danbury, Connecticut Office: 158 Deer Hill Avenue. Telephone: 203-792-2771. Facsimile: 203-791-8149.
Stamford, Connecticut Office: 112 Prospect Street. Telephone: 203-964-9907. Facsimile: 203-576-8504.
See Professional Biographies, WESTPORT, CONNECTICUT

Cohn Birnbaum & Shea P.C., (AV)
830 Post Road East, 2nd Floor, 06880 ⊙
Telephone: 203-341-9595 Fax: 203-341-9696
Richard J. Shea, Jr.; Matthew Feigenbaum; Robert H. Feigenbaum.
Banking, Bankruptcy, Business, Commercial, Communications, Condominium, Construction, Contracting, Corporation, Creditors Rights, Employment, Environmental, Finance, Health Care Administrative, Joint Ventures, Land Use, Media, Municipal, Professional Liability Defense, Real Estate, Securities, Shopping Center, Taxation, Technology, Litigation in all State and Federal Courts.
New York, New York Office: 67 Wall Street, Suite 2411. Telephone: 212-949-9555. Fax: 212-949-7997.
Hartford, Connecticut Office: 100 Pearl Street. Telephone: 860-493-2200. Fax: 860-727-0361.
See Professional Biographies, WESTPORT, CONNECTICUT

Colosimo, Louis A. '59 '84 C&L.262 B.A., J.D.
(adm. in NY; not adm. in CT) 27 Pequot Trail‡

Constantikes, George D. '26 '53 C.951 A.B. L.976 LL.B.
830 Post Road East, 06880
Telephone: 203-226-7716 Fax: 203-226-6445
General Civil Practice. Trusts, Wills, Estate Planning, Probate, Personal Injury, Family Law, Business Transactions, Real Estate and Zoning Law. Civil Litigation.
Approved Attorney for: Lawyers Title Insurance Corp.; First American Title Insurance Corp.

Copersino, Albert J. '33 '70 C.563 B.B.A. L.564 J.D.
(adm. in NY; not adm. in CT) 21 Side Hill Rd.
Corrigan, Bruce J., Jr., (CV) . . . . '48 '82 C.321 A.B. L.262 J.D. 1853 Post Rd., E.
Cott, Douglas M., (CV) . . . . '46 '72 C.823 A.B. L.262 J.D. [Spirer&C.]

Cousins, Johnson & Desrosiers, P.C.
(See Stratford)

Cowherd, Stephen M. . . . . '59 '91 C.1350 B.A. L.724 J.D. [Levett R.]
*PRACTICE AREAS: Health Care Law; Hospital Law; Civil Litigation.
Craft, Peter L., (CV) '57 '82 C.183 B.A. L.1048 J.D.
Sr. V.P., Gen. Coun. & Secy., D.W. Van Dyke & Co. of Conn., Inc.
*RESPONSIBILITIES: Taxation; Commercial Law; Corporate Law; Reinsurance; Joint Ventures.
Cramer, Allan P., (AV) . . . . '37 '64 C.659 B.A. L.184 J.D. [Cramer&A.]
*PRACTICE AREAS: Civil Practice; Real Estate; Negligence; Probate; Estate Planning.

Cramer & Ahern, (AV)
38 Post Road West, 06880
Telephone: 203-222-7000 Telecopier: 203-222-7788
Email: cramerandahern@lifeinvest.net URL: http://www.lawyers.com/calaw
Allan P. Cramer; Anthony E. Ahern. Of Counsel: Robert N. Grosby.
General Civil Practice. Real Estate, Negligence, Probate, Estate Planning, Business Law, Corporate Law, Art Law. Trials.
Reference: Fleet Bank, N.A.
See Professional Biographies, WESTPORT, CONNECTICUT

Cunnane, Kristine M. . . . . '75 '00 C.94 B.A. L.184 J.D. [Levett R.]
*PRACTICE AREAS: Corporate Law; Securities; Health Care Law; Mergers and Acquisitions.
Cusa, Thomas C. . . . . '69 '99 C.282 B.A. L.1252 J.D. [Tirola&H.]
*PRACTICE AREAS: Real Estate; Taxation.
Dale, E. Randolph '15 '43 C.843 B.A. L.846 J.D.
(adm. in TX; not adm. in CT) 70 Sylvan Rd., N.
Danaher, R. Cornelius, Jr., (AV) '47 '73
C&L.276 B.A., J.D. [Danaher,T.L.&N.] (⊙Hartford)
Danaher, Tedford, Lagnese & Neal, P.C., (AV) . . . . . . 3 Sylvan Rd. (⊙Hartford)
DaSilva, Eric S. . . . . '62 '87 C.1030 B.A. L.904 J.D. [DaSilva]
*PRACTICE AREAS: Litigation; Personal Injury; Real Estate; Negligence.

DaSilva Law Firm, The, LLC
830 Post Road E., 06880
Telephone: 203-226-0009 203-226-6445
Email: ericdasilva@lawyer.com URL: http://www.lawyers.com/ericdasilva
Eric S. DaSilva.
Real Estate, Litigation, Negligence, Personal Injury.
See Professional Biographies, WESTPORT, CONNECTICUT

Davidoff, Jerry, (BV) . . . . '26 '51 C.575 B.A. L.976 J.D. [Pober,R.&P.]

Day, Amy L. Y., (BV) .... '52 '77 C.788 A.B. L.184 J.D. [Wake,S.D.&B.]
*PRACTICE AREAS: Trust Law; Probate; Estate Planning; Real Estate.

DePanfilis & Vallerie, LLC
(See Norwalk)

Dephtereos, David L., (AV) '54 '80 C&L.188 B.A., J.D.
191 Post Road West, 06880
Telephone: 203-221-2852 Fax: 203-221-2853
Email: dephtereos@aol.com
General Corporate and Commercial Practice, Air Cargo, Maritime Law, Surface Transportation, International Trade and Transactions.

See Professional Biographies, WESTPORT, CONNECTICUT

Derrin, Stacie E. ....'67 '90 C.30 B.A. L.1029 J.D. 877 Post Rd. E., Ste. 2

Dietrich, Edward H., (AV) '44 '72 C.976 B.A. L.569 J.D.
125 Main Street, 06880 ⊙
Telephone: 203-222-7600 Fax: 203-222-1830
Email: ehdlaw@webquill.com URL: http://www.lawyers.com/dietrichlaw
Estate Tax Planning, Estate and Gift Taxation, Wills and Trusts, Probate and Administration.
Reference: The Bank of Darien at Westport.
New York, N.Y. Office: 780 Third Avenue, 12th Floor, 10017. Telephone: 212-599-5075.

See Professional Biographies, WESTPORT, CONNECTICUT

Dietz, John W. ....'68 '93 C.732 B.A. L.982 J.D. [Halloran&S.]
*PRACTICE AREAS: Products Liability; Transportation Litigation; Trucking Law; Indian Law.

Di Marco, Richard J., (BV) '55 '84
C.1044 B.A. L.107 J.D. [Cohen&W.] (⊙Bridgeport, Stamford)
*PRACTICE AREAS: Taxation; Estate Planning; Corporate.

Dimes, Edwin K., (AV) ....'23 '50 C.918 B.A. L.976 LL.B. [Wake,S.D.&B.]
*PRACTICE AREAS: Real Estate; Family Law; Estate Planning; Probate.

Diserio Martin O'Connor & Castiglioni LLP
(See Stamford)

Diviney, Richard J., (AV) .... '41 '67 C.1082 A.B. L.724 LL.B. [Sherwood&G.]
*PRACTICE AREAS: Estate and Trust Administration; Banking Law; Real Estate; Civil Litigation; Aviation.

Dobson, Richard E. '46 '72 C.112 A.B. L.1066 J.D.
(adm. in CA; not adm. in CT) V.P. & Gen. Coun., The Fund Amer. Cos., Inc.

Dzurik, John G., (AV) .... '50 '75 C&L.276 B.S.F.S., J.D. [Goldstein&P.] ⊙

Edelstein, Stewart I., (AV) '48 '73
C.604 B.A. L.188 J.D. [Cohen&W.] (⊙Bridgeport, Stamford)
*PRACTICE AREAS: Commercial Litigation; High Technology.

Ellis, Cynthia E. .... '54 '81 C.1103 B.S. L.1048 J.D. V.P., Ceruzzi Properties, Inc.

Elson, Edwin J., (BV) ....'28 '57 C.1029 B.S. L.184 J.D. 1555 Post Rd., E.

Fabbro, Richard M. '55 '82 C.976 A.B. L.276 J.D.
(adm. in NY; not adm. in CT) Tax Dir., AIG Fin. Products

Febbraio, Samuel, Jr., (BV) ....'58 '84 C.1030 B.S. L.1029 J.D. [Berkowitz,T.&T.]
*PRACTICE AREAS: Corporate Law; Securities; Taxation.

Feigenbaum, Matthew ....'43 '80 C.102 B.A. L.262 J.D. [Cohn B.&S.]

Feigenbaum, Robert H. ....'69 '96 C.1044 B.A. L.1049 J.D. [Cohn B.&S.]

Felder, Robert H. .... '48 '75 C.102 B.A. L.823 J.D. Commonfund Grp.

Ferguson, Russell S. .... '71 '99 C.676 B.A. L.184 J.D. [Ⓐ Wake,S.D.&B.]
*PRACTICE AREAS: Business Law; Marketing Law; Litigation.

Filan, Patrick J. ....'56 '82 C.228 A.B. L.608 J.D. [Pacifico&F.] ⊙
*PRACTICE AREAS: Personal Injury Law; Medical Malpractice; Product Liability; Civil Litigation; Health Care Fraud and Abuse.

Fink, Andrew F. ....'41 '69 C&L.477 B.A., J.D. [Carron&F.]

Fischel, Valerie S., (CV) ....'42 '89 C.569 B.A. L.1029 J.D. P.O. Box 5082

Fleischmann, Charles W., (AV) ....'45 '77 C.674 B.A. L.184 J.D. [Sherwood&G.]
*PRACTICE AREAS: Civil Litigation.

Flocken, Ann E. .... '58 '84 C.951 B.A. L.893 J.D. [Ⓐ Pearl]
*PRACTICE AREAS: Corporate Law.

Flynn, Walter A., Jr., (BV) ....'43 '68 C.93 B.S. L.276 J.D. [Goldstein&P.] ⊙

Fogarty Cohen Selby & Nemiroff LLC
(See Greenwich)

Fogerty, Stephen P., (BV) ....'61 '86 C.128 B.A. L.262 J.D. [Halloran&S.]
*PRACTICE AREAS: Civil Litigation; Municipal Liability; Employment Law.

Foodman, Bruce A. ....'64 '89 C.674 B.A. L.1019 J.D. 46 Riverside Dr.

Fowler-Cruz, Ann L. ....'64 '94 C.788 B.A. L.1252 J.D. [Hersh,F.] ⊙

Fredericks, Charles, Jr. ....'26 '49 C.674 A.B. L.309 LL.B. [Tirola&H.]
*PRACTICE AREAS: Commercial Law; Probate; Advertising Law; Corporate Real Estate; Trademarks.

Fredston, Dale Carol .... '52 '79 C.914 B.A. L.178 J.D. 18 Maple Avenue North

Freeburg, Dorothy M. ....'— '85 C.1133 B.S. L.262 J.D. [Ⓐ Kove&K.]
*PRACTICE AREAS: Estate Planning; Estate Administration.

Freedman, Theodore L., (BV) ....'47 '72 C.184 B.A. L.273 J.D. 225 Main St.

Friedman, Richard B. '57 '83 C.188 B.A. L.145 J.D.
(adm. in NY; not adm. in CT) Pres. & CEO, Legal Review Intl., U.C.

Funnell, James D., Jr., (AV) ....'60 '88 C.612 B.S. L.616 J.D. [Hermenze&M.]
*PRACTICE AREAS: Estate Planning; Estate Settlements; Probate; Trust Administration; Elder Law.

Gaboriault, Andrew L., (AVⓉ) .... '23 '55 C.128 B.Ch.E. L.569 J.D. 235 Post Road West

Gaboriault, Peter W., (BV) '56 '82
C.273 B.B.A. L.1040 J.D. [Gaboriault&P.] (⊙Brewster, NY)
*PRACTICE AREAS: Commercial Real Estate Acquisitions; Residential Real Estate Acquisitions; Land Use and Zoning; Commercial Real Estate Financing; Residential Real Estate Financing.

Gaboriault & Pearsall, P.C., (BV)
235 Post Road West, 06880
Telephone: 203-454-0773 Fax: 203-454-1284
Email: info@gaboriault-pearsall.com URL: http://www.lawyers.com/gaboriault&pearsall
Peter W. Gaboriault; Steven W. Pearsall.
Commercial Real Estate Finance, Asset Based Finance, Leasing, Loan Workouts, Loan Restructuring, Real Estate, Corporate Law, Corporate Collections.

See Professional Biographies, WESTPORT, CONNECTICUT

Garlick, Edward E., (AV) .... '24 '52 C&L.184 B.S., LL.B. [Sherwood&G.] ‡
*PRACTICE AREAS: Estate Planning; Wills; Probate; Real Estate.

Garskof, Deborah M. ....'69 '94 C.184 B.A. L.818 J.D. [Ⓐ Ury&M.]
*PRACTICE AREAS: Commercial Law; Banking Litigation; Civil Litigation; Employment Law; Construction Law.

Gasway, Susan Lake ....'65 '92 C.352 B.B.A. L.1035 J.D. 54 High Point Rd.

Gerard, Jamie Kay, (BV) ....'57 '80 C.1044 B.A. L.30 J.D. [Nevas,N.C.&G.]

Gershowitz, Jeffrey A. '64 '89 C.930 B.A. L.309 J.D.
(adm. in NY; not adm. in CT) Dep. Gen. Coun. & Asst. Secy., Terex Corp.
*RESPONSIBILITIES: Corporate Law; Commercial; Securities; Mergers and Acquisitions.

Gibbons, Richard S., (BV) .... '47 '72 C.874 B.A. L.1017 J.D. [Ⓒ Wake,S.D.&B.]
*PRACTICE AREAS: Zoning Law; Real Estate; Corporate Law.

Gilmore, Douglas, (BV) '51 '77 C.1030 B.A. L.884 J.D.
11 Harding Lane, 06880
Telephone: 203-226-6277 Fax: 203-222-0779
URL: http://www.douggatsnet.net
Criminal and Civil Litigation in the State and Federal Courts. Appellate Practice. Entertainment, Sports, Radio, TV, Communications, Trademarks, Copyrights, Unfair Competition, Corporate, Trade Regulation and Legislative Practice.

See Professional Biographies, WESTPORT, CONNECTICUT

Giordano, Thomas F. ....'64 '95 C.178 B.A. L.262 J.D. [Ⓐ Sacks,M.P.&L.] ⊙

Glazer, Steven .... '46 '73 C.178 B.A. L.401 J.D. [Ⓒ Rubenstein,G.&B.]
*PRACTICE AREAS: Commercial Real Estate; Zoning Law; Leasing; Corporate Law.

Godfrey, David L. .... '50 '90 C.299 A.B. L.1029 J.D. [Gunn,G.&A.]

Goelz, Virginia G. ....'57 '86 C.188 B.A. L.724 J.D. 3 Old Orchard Rd.

Goldberg, Martin A., (BV) ....'54 '80 C.156 B.A. L.184 J.D. [Ⓒ Nevas,N.C.&G.]

Goldberg, Richard M. .... '57 '86 C&L.184 B.S., J.D. Tax Coun., Salomon Inc.

Goldstein, Jay L. ....'56 '86 C.588 B.S. L.1202 J.D. [Berkowitz,T.&T.]
*PRACTICE AREAS: Taxation; Estate Planning; Trusts and Estates; ERISA; Pension and Profit Sharing Plans.

Goldstein and Peck, P.C., (AV) ....190 Main Street (⊙Bridgeport)

Goodbaum, Samuel ....'47 '81 C.1040 B.B.A. L.184 J.D. [Yost&Assoc.]

Gorman, Harold V. '43 '68 C.918 B.A. L.184 LL.B.
Sr. V.P. & Gen. Coun., Allied Domecq Spirits & Wine USA, Inc.
*RESPONSIBILITIES: Antitrust Law; Trademarks Law; Beverage Alcohol Law; International Practice.

Grace, Kenneth R., (BV) .... '54 '80 C.1200 B.A. L.734 J.D. 830 Post Rd. E.

Graham, Christopher M. ....'64 '92 C.401 B.S. L.184 J.D. [Ⓐ Levett R.]
*PRACTICE AREAS: Corporate Law; Mergers and Acquisitions; Securities Law; Emerging Growth Companies; Internet Law.

Grant, Robert E., (BV) '48 '77 C.276 B.A. L.30 J.D.
8 Myrtle Avenue, 06881
Telephone: 203-227-6769
URL: http://www.lawyers.com/robertgrant
***PRACTICE AREAS: General Practice; Real Estate; Probate; Estate Planning; Zoning Law.**
Real Estate, Probate, Corporate, Zoning, Estate Planning and Negligence.
Representative Clients: Prudential Relocation; Kowalsky Brothers, Inc.; Roseville Estates, Inc.; Westport Country Estates, Inc.
Reference: Fleet Bank.

See Professional Biographies, WESTPORT, CONNECTICUT

Green, Daniel, (BV) .... '50 '75 C.855 B.A. L.982 J.D. [Rubenstein,G.&B.]
*PRACTICE AREAS: Commercial Litigation; Tax Appeals; Real Estate; Personal Injury.

Green and Gross, P.C.
(See Bridgeport)

Greenberg, David A., (BV) ....'58 '83 C&L.273 B.A., J.D. [Berkowitz,T.&T.]
*PRACTICE AREAS: Commercial Law; Creditors Rights and Bankruptcy Law; Real Estate Law; Corporate Compliance; Banking Law.

Greene, Herbert B. .... '34 '59 C.309 A.B. L.178 LL.B. 1771 Post Rd. E.

Greene, Leslie M. .... '60 '87 C.951 B.A. L.145 J.D. 4 Vineyard Lane

Grodd, Leslie E., (AV) ....'46 '69 C.882 B.A. L.724 J.D. [Blazzard,G.&H.]
*PRACTICE AREAS: Income and Estate Taxation and Planning; Individuals; Corporations; Real Estate.

Grosby, Robert N., (BV) .... '27 '50 C.309 A.B. L.188 J.D. [Ⓒ Cramer&A.]

Grossman, Madeleine F., (AV) ....'39 '76 C.188 B.A. L.976 J.D. [Levett R.]
*PRACTICE AREAS: Civil Litigation.

Grundei, Jacqueline A. .... '64 '90 C.477 B.A. L.276 J.D. 4 Salem Rd.

Gunn, Colin, (AV) .... '21 '52 C.197 B.A. L.184 J.D. [Gunn,G.&A.]

Gunn, Godfrey & Allison, (AV) ....35 Church Lane

Haldeman, Harold W. ....'44 '74 C.951 B.A. L.184 J.D. [Ⓐ Nusbaum&P.]
*PRACTICE AREAS: Family Law; Military Law.

Halloran & Sage LLP, (AV)
315 Post Road West, 06880-4739 ⊙
Telephone: 203-227-2855 Fax: 203-227-6992
URL: http://www.halloran-sage.com
Resident Members: Stephen P. Fogerty; Thomas P. O'Dea, Jr.; Dan E. LaBelle; John W. Dietz.
Resident Counsel: Lisa M. Kowtko; Alan S. Rubenstein. Resident Associates: Thomas P. Lambert; Robert A. Rhodes; Brett Szczesny.
Administrative Law, Administrative Hearings and Appeals, Alternative Dispute Resolution, Appellate Practice, Aviation Products Liability, Bad Faith Litigation, Banking Law, Bankruptcy, Breach of Contract, Business Disputes, Business Law, Business Litigation, Business Planning, Casualty Insurance Litigation, Civil Appeals, Civil Litigation, Civil Rights Litigation, Class Action, Commercial Litigation, Complex Civil Litigation, Construction and Design Law, Construction Litigation, Corporate Contracts, Corporate Law, Criminal Litigation, Drug and Medical Device Litigation, Employment Law, Energy and Health Law, Environmental Law, Excess Insurance, Family Business Succession, Fidelity and Surety Law, Finance, Education Law, Employment Law, Environmental, Environmental Insurance Coverage, ERISA, ERISA Litigation, Estate Administration, Estate and Gift Taxation, Estates Law, Excess Insurance, General Corporate Law, General Liability, Government Contracts, Government Finance, Government Relations, Health and Life Insurance Litigation, Insurance Bad Faith Litigation, Insurance Coverage, Institutional Liability Law, Insurance Litigation, Insurance Regulation, Intellectual Property Litigation, International Law, Judicial Review, Labor and Employment, Land Use Planning Law, Lead Paint Litigation, Legislative Practice, Liquor Liability, Lobbying, Marine Insurance Defense, Medical Malpractice, Mergers and Acquisitions and Divestitures, Municipal Law, Municipal Liability, Probate Law, Products Liability Litigation, Professional Liability Litigation, Professional Regulation, Premises Liability, Property Insurance, Psychological Injury Claims, Public Utilities Law, Public Utility Regulation, Real Estate Transactions, Reinsurance Law, Risk Management Consulting, Secured Lending, Securities Law, Subrogation, Taxation Law, Telecommunications Law, Torts, Trade Association, Trucking Transportation Litigation, Trust Law, Unfair Trade, Uninsured and Underinsured Motorists, University Law, Workers Compensation Law, Zoning, Planning and Land Use.
Hartford, Connecticut Office: One Goodwin Square, 225 Asylum Street, 06103. Telephone: 860-522-6103. Fax: 860-548-0006.
Middletown, Connecticut Office: 300 Plaza Middlesex, 06457. Telephone: 860-346-8641. Fax: 860-344-1641.
Washington, D.C. Office: 1627 I Street, N.W., Suite 610, 20006. Telephone: 202-496-9270. Fax: 202-496-9279.

See Professional Biographies, WESTPORT, CONNECTICUT

Hammer, Tracey C. ....'65 '98 C.184 B.A. L.188 J.D. [Ⓐ Levett R.]
*PRACTICE AREAS: Mergers, Acquisitions and Divestitures; Securities; Corporate Law.

Hankin, Barbara L. ....'42 '86 C.66 A.B. L.1029 J.D. 191 Post Rd. West

Haroun, Julie Goldstick '62 '90 C.477 B.A. L.564 J.D.
(adm. in NY; not adm. in CT) 8 Broadview Rd.

Harrington, Christopher M. .... '61 '95 C.1373 B.A. L.1048 J.D. [Goldstein&P.] ⊙

Harrington, Joan C. ....'57 '84 C.813 B.A. L.659 J.D. 54 Wilton Rd.

Hart, Judith A. .... '55 '84 C.860 B.A. L.588 J.D. 7 E. Meadow Rd.

Hasenauer, Judith A., (AV) .... '46 '74 C.696 A.B. L.284 J.D. [Blazzard,G.&H.] ⊙
*PRACTICE AREAS: Life Insurance Products; Securities Law; Corporations; Insurance Taxation.

Hasenauer, William E., (BV) .... '49 '76 C.1122 B.A. L.365 J.D. [Blazzard,G.&H.]
*PRACTICE AREAS: Life Insurance Products; Securities Law; Corporations; Insurance Taxation; Employee Benefits.

Haskell, Grant P., (BV) ....'53 '81 C.31 B.A. L.228 J.D. 191 Post Rd., W.

Heagney, Lennon & Slane LLP
(See Greenwich)

Heimer, Dorit Schutzengel, (BV) ....'53 '79 C.914 B.A. L.309 J.D. [Levett R.]
*PRACTICE AREAS: Civil Litigation; Employment Law; Medical Malpractice.

Hermenze, David R., (AV) ....'60 '86 C.72 B.A. L.188 J.D. [Hermenze&M.]
*PRACTICE AREAS: Trusts and Estates; Wills; Probate; Taxation.

Hermenze & Marcantonio, (AV) BB
19 Ludlow Road, Suite 101, 06880
Telephone: 203-226-6552 Fax: 203-226-6035
David R. Hermenze; Edward Marcantonio; James D. Funnell, Jr.
Trusts and Estates, Wills, Probate, Taxation.

See Professional Biographies, WESTPORT, CONNECTICUT

Herring, Buddy O. H. .... '46 '71 C&L.896 B.A., J.D. [Tirola&H.]
*PRACTICE AREAS: Family Law; Real Property; Estate Planning; Sports Law; Entertainment Law.
Hersh, Fowler-Cruz, L.L.P. .... 25 Ford Rd. (⊙White Plains, NY)
Heyman, Ronnie F. .... '48 '73 C.309 B.A. L.976 J.D. Heyman Properties
Hodes, Joel C. '65 '92 C.659 B.A. L.309 J.D.
(adm. in NY; not adm. in CT) 100 Nyala Farm Road
Hogan, Kathleen A., (BVⓉ) '52 '77 C.1146 B.A. L.838 J.D.
[▣ Rutkin&O.] (⊙Denver, CO; Greenwich, CT)
*PRACTICE AREAS: Family Law; Litigation; Appeals.
Houliston-Otto, Deborah B. '54 '88 C&L.1161 B.A., J.D.
(adm. in OH; not adm. in CT) 285 Riverside Ave.
Hsieh, Charles Chia-Lin '69 '95 C.112 B.S., A.B. L.309 J.D.
(adm. in NY; not adm. in CT) V.P. & Coun., AIG Financial Prod. Corp.
Hurwitz, Jocelyn B. ... '67 '92 C&L.188 B.S., J.D. [Cohen&W.] (⊙Bridgeport, Stamford)
*PRACTICE AREAS: Family Law; Commercial Litigation; Divorce Mediation.
Ingber, Craig .... '59 '87 C.994 B.A. L.1009 J.D. [Belkin B.W.&G.] ⊙
Isaacs, Michael L. '47 '73 C.994 B.A. L.188 J.D.
(adm. in NY; not adm. in CT) 18 Bobwhite Dr.‡

Ivey, Barnum & O'Mara, LLC
(See Greenwich)

Jacobson, Paul F. .... '35 '61 C.197 A.B. L.976 J.D. 96 Myrtle Ave.
Jacobson, Susannah .... '68 '93 C.308 B.A. L.365 J.D. [▣ Tirola&H.]
Johnson, Charles M. '34 '60 C&L.976 B.A., LL.B.
(adm. in NY; not adm. in CT) 4 Berkeley Hill‡
Johnson, Charles Snowdon, (BV) .... '46 '78 C.188 B.A. L.61 J.D. [▣ Ottomano&J.]
*PRACTICE AREAS: Conveyancing; Easements; Real Estate Title Examination; Residential Real Estate; Estate Planning.
Johnson, Cheryl L. .... '61 '87 C.390 B.A. L.107 J.D. [Levett R.]
*PRACTICE AREAS: Tax Law; Corporate Law; Securities; Emerging Growth Companies.
Jones, Howard W. .... '27 '61 C.935 B.A. L.1003 J.D. 10 Bay St.
Jordon, Jane B. Lund '57 '85 C.938 B.A. L.818 J.D.
(adm. in MA; not adm. in CT) 31 Easton Rd.
Julianelle, Robert L., (AV) .... '40 '64 C.1030 B.S. L.276 J.D. [Schine,J.&A.] ⊙
*PRACTICE AREAS: Litigation; Estate Planning; Wills, Trusts and Probate Law; Business Law; Real Estate.
Kanaga, Lawrence W., (AV) '40 '65
C.951 A.B. L.309 LL.B. 830 Post Rd. East (⊙Orange)
Kaplan, Amanda J. .... '69 '94 C.165 B.A. L.184 J.D. 6 Carolyn Pl.‡
Katz, Bruce D., (BV) .... '59 '87 C.273 B.B.A. L.94 J.D. [B.D.Katz]
Katz, Bruce D., P.C., (BV) .... 53 Saugatuck Avenue
Keenan, Thomas M., (BV) .... '36 '64 C.276 B.S.S. L.893 J.D. 830 Post Rd., E.
Kelly, Gail .... '53 '82 C.94 B.A. L.724 J.D. 12 Canterbury Close
Kent, Lisa Kasden, (BV) .... '50 '86 C.659 B.A. L.1029 J.D. [▣ Rubenstein,G.&B.]
*PRACTICE AREAS: Real Estate; Leasing; Zoning; Banking.
Kent, Richard G., (AV) '51 '75
C.705 B.A. L.93 J.D. [Cohen&W.] (⊙Bridgeport, Stamford)
*PRACTICE AREAS: Family; Civil; Criminal Litigation.
Klein, Arthur O., (BV) .... '27 '59 C.569 B.C.E. L.1009 J.D. [Klein&V.]
Klein & Vibber, P.C., (BV) .... 7 Half Mile Common
Knapp, Beverly Stauffer, (BV) .... '59 '84 C.1211 B.S. L.184 J.D. [Shrader&K.]
*PRACTICE AREAS: Securities Litigation; Civil Litigation; Appellate Practice.
Knapp, Doris, (BV) .... '42 '84 C.102 B.A. L.1040 J.D. 830 Post Rd. E.
Koizim, John D. '52 '82 C.1168 B.A. L.800 J.D.
(adm. in FL; not adm. in CT) Castle Assocs.
Komisar, Howard D., (BV) .... '55 '80 C.659 B.S.Econ. L.472 J.D. [Berkowitz,T.&T.]
*PRACTICE AREAS: Commercial Real Estate Finance, Leasing and Development; Corporate Law.
Korn, Gary J. '63 '89 C.659 B.A. L.188 J.D.
(adm. in NY; not adm. in CT) 75 Cavalry Rd.
Kosakow, James M., (AV) .... '— '85 C.183 B.A. L.978 J.D. [Kove&K.] ⊙
*PRACTICE AREAS: Estate Planning; Probate; Estate Taxation.
Kovack, Mark J., (BV) .... '59 '85 C.732 B.A. L.982 J.D. [Wake,S.D.&B.]
*PRACTICE AREAS: Commercial Litigation (50%); Employment Law (15%); Real Estate Litigation (15%); Product Liability (15%); Personal Injury (5%).
Kove, Myron '— '61
(adm. in NY; not adm. in CT) [Kove&K.]
*PRACTICE AREAS: Estate Planning; Tax Planning; Business Planning; Real Estate.

Kove & Kosakow, LLC, (AV)
265 Post Road West, 06880 ⊙
Telephone: 203-454-0100 Fax: 203-454-3636
Email: jmk@kovkos.com URL: http://www.kovkos.com
Members of Firm: Myron Kove (Not admitted in CT; Resident, New York, New York Office); James M. Kosakow (. Associates: Dorothy M. Freeburg; Linda S. Brown.
Estate Planning, Probate, Estate Tax, Estate Administration.
New York, New York Office: 685 Third Avenue, 30th Floor. Telephone: 212-297-0255.
See Professional Biographies, WESTPORT, CONNECTICUT

Kowtko, Lisa M. .... '58 '87 C.1103 B.S. L.1029 J.D. [▣ Halloran&S.]
*PRACTICE AREAS: Medical Malpractice; Health Care; Liability.
Kozak, David M. '48 '81 C.393 B.A. L.424 J.D.
Coun., John W. Henry & Company, Inc.
Kramer, Sidney B. .... '15 '40 C.569 B.S. L.1009 J.D. 20 Bluewater Hill
Krenz, Donald A. '36 '59 C.107 B.S. L.178 LL.B.
(adm. in NY; not adm. in CT) 19 Beachside Common‡
Kritzer, Harry A. '54 '81 C.1365 B.B.A. L.978 J.D.
(adm. in NY; not adm. in CT) 16 Cross Hwy.
Kupinse, William J., Jr., (AV) .... '39 '64 C.197 A.B. L.188 LL.B. [Goldstein&P.] ⊙
Kurata, Stacy G. .... '63 '92 C.216 B.A. L.1252 J.D. Fairport Asset Mgmt. Corp.
Kurzman, Marc J., (BV) .... '58 '84 C.188 B.S. L.178 J.D. [Levett R.]
*PRACTICE AREAS: Civil Litigation; Commercial Real Estate Law; Health Law; Hospital Law.
LaBella, Anthony J. .... '64 '01 C.881 B.A. L.1252 J.D. [▣ Ury&M.]
*PRACTICE AREAS: Civil Litigation; Construction Law; Commercial Law; Personal Injury; Professional Malpractice.
LaBelle, Dan E., (BV) .... '55 '81 C.165 A.B. L.982 J.D. [Halloran&S.]
*PRACTICE AREAS: Civil Litigation; Environmental Law; Criminal Litigation.
Laccavole, Dennis M., (BV) .... '53 '78 C.1030 B.S. L.724 J.D. [Goldstein&P.] ⊙
Lake, Kimberly J. '60 '90 C.914 B.A. L.276 J.D.
(adm. in NY; not adm. in CT) 57 Kings Hwy., N.‡
Lalley, Edward P. '18 '54 C.707 B.S. L.862 LL.B.
(adm. in OK; not adm. in CT) 6 Onion Hill Rd.‡
Lambert, Thomas P. .... '67 '92 C.659 B.A. L.94 J.D. [▣ Halloran&S.] (⊙Hartford)
*PRACTICE AREAS: Insurance Defense Law; Civil Trial Law; Professional Liability.
Laplaca, Robert .... '67 '94 C.178 B.A. L.1009 J.D. [▣ Levett R.]
*PRACTICE AREAS: Commercial Litigation; Bankruptcy; Health Care Law; Advertising Law.

Laux, Michael A., (BV) '41 '67 C.31 B.A. L.262 LL.B.
Eight Myrtle Avenue, 06880
Telephone: 203-226-3392 Fax: 203-222-8023
Email: lauxlaw@aol.com URL: http://www.lawyers.com/michaelalaux

(This Listing Continued)

Laux, Michael A. (Continued)

General Practice before State and Federal Courts. Estate Planning, Probate, Residential Real Estate, Commercial Real Estate, Estate Planning, Personal Injury.
See Professional Biographies, WESTPORT, CONNECTICUT

Leepson, Peter L., (BV) .... '41 '66 C.1036 B.A. L.262 J.D. [P.L.Leepson]
Leepson, Peter L., P.C., (BV) .... 25 Ford Road

Leifer, Roger J., Law Offices of, (BV) '50 '74 C.176 B.A. L.309 J.D.
3 Sylvan Road South, P.O. Box 5180, 06881
Telephone: 203-227-8463 Fax: 203-226-3366
Real Estate, Planning, Zoning and Corporate.
See Professional Biographies, WESTPORT, CONNECTICUT

Leonard, Richard C. .... '29 '82 C.1030 B.A. L.1029 J.D. 3 Orchard Lane
Lerman, Lewis S., (BV) .... '55 '84 C.699 B.A. L.831 J.D. 8 Wright St.

Leventhal, Michael J., (BV) '56 '87 C.1293 B.A. L.1040 J.D.
155 Post Road East, Suite 6, 06881
Telephone: 203-227-9751 Fax: 203-227-9753
Email: levlaw@snet.net URL: http://www.lawyers.com/leventhallaw
***PRACTICE AREAS: Civil Litigation; Personal Injury; Construction; Workers Compensation; Family Law.**
Civil Litigation, Personal Injury, Family Law, Construction, Workers Compensation, Real Estate, Landlord Tenant; Collections.
See Professional Biographies, WESTPORT, CONNECTICUT

Levett, David R., (AV) .... '38 '62 C&L.976 B.A., LL.B. [Levett R.]
*PRACTICE AREAS: Corporate Law; Civil Litigation; Health Law; Hospital Law.

Levett Rockwood P.C., (AV)
33 Riverside Avenue, P.O. Box 5116, 06881
Telephone: 203-222-0885 Telecopier: 203-226-8025
URL: http://www.levettrockwood.com
Robert O. Barberi; Debra R. Cardinali; Edward B. Chansky; Stephen M. Cowherd; Madeleine F. Grossman; Dorit Schutzengel Heimer; Cheryl L. Johnson; Marc J. Kurzman; David R. Levett; Judy A. Rabkin; Sharon M. Schweitzer; Steven M. Siegelaub; Peter H. Struzzi; Barbara A. Young. Of Counsel: Suzanne B. Albani;—Mary Chang; Kristine M. Cunnane; Christopher M. Graham; Tracey C. Hammer; Robert Laplaca; John T. Shaban; Patricia D. Weitzman.
Corporate, Health Care and Hospitals, Litigation, Taxation, Employment, Information Technology, Intellectual Property, Mergers and Acquisitions, Securities, Capital Formation and Financing, Advertising, Promotion, Creditors' Rights, Estate Planning, Commercial Real Estate.
Representative Clients: Arch Chemicals, Inc.; Cannondale Corp.; Caradon, Inc.; DataViz, Inc.; Dooney & Bourke, Inc.; GAF Corporation; Heyman Properties; Hospital of Saint Raphael; Olin Corporation; St. Vincent's Medical Center.
See Professional Biographies, WESTPORT, CONNECTICUT

Levin, Glenn I. '58 '86 C.103 A.B. L.930 J.D.
(adm. in NY; not adm. in CT) 13 Godfrey Lane
Levine, Arnold ...... '34 '60 C.563 B.A. L.569 LL.B. Exec. V.P., Westport Bk. & Tr. Co.
Levine, David M., (BV) ...... '61 '86 C.1036 A.B. L.94 J.D. [Cohen&W.] (⊙Bridgeport)
*PRACTICE AREAS: Corporate; Commercial; Health Care; Real Estate.
Levine, Stuart M. .... '38 '64 C.674 A.B. L.659 LL.B. [Sacks,M.P.&L.]
Levy, Lisa M. .... '71 '97 C.401 B.A. L.1252 J.D. [▣ Wake,S.D.&B.]
*PRACTICE AREAS: Estate Planning; Probate; Real Estate.
Lewert, Tina L. '74 '00 C.1086 B.S. L.1206 J.D.
(adm. in FL; not adm. in CT) [Blazzard,G.&H.]
*PRACTICE AREAS: Life Insurance; Securities.
Lewis, Susan S., (BV) .... '47 '86 C.94 A.B. L.1029 J.D. [S.S.Lewis]
Lewis, Susan S., P.C., Law Offices of, (BV) .... 6 Wilton Road
Lindskog, David R., (AVⓉ) '36 '66 C.976 B.A. L.893 LL.B.
(adm. in NY; not adm. in CT)
Sr. Vice President, General Counsel, & Secretary, Leach Holdings Corporation
Link, Alan P., Law Offices of .... '62 '87 C.1030 B.S. L.1029 J.D. 830 Post Rd. E.

Lipson, Jack S., (BV) '48 '75 C.1029 B.A. L.472 J.D.
830 Post Road East, 06880
Telephone: 203-222-8775 Fax: 203-222-3872
Email: jlipson@mindspring.com URL: http://www.lawyers.com/lipsonlaw
Real Estate, Mortgage Finance, Estate Planning.
See Professional Biographies, WESTPORT, CONNECTICUT

LoMonte, Douglas E. .... '66 '91 C.855 B.A. L.306 J.D. [Wake,S.D.&B.]
*PRACTICE AREAS: Business Law; Taxation; Employment Law; Retirement Benefit Plans.
Long, Thomas R. .... '30 '56 C.882 B.A. L.976 J.D. 6 Palmieri Rd.
Lubell, Ellen B., (AV) .... '47 '72 C.569 B.A. L.184 J.D. [Weisman&L.]
*PRACTICE AREAS: Family; Appellate Practice.

Lynch, Trembicki, Martelon and Boynton, (BV)
225 Main Street, Suite 103, 06880 ⊙
Telephone: 203-227-6808 Fax: 203-226-6215
URL: http://www.lawyers.com/llmtblaw
Members of Firm: Alexander J. Trembicki.
General Practice. Probate, Real Estate, Zoning, Negligence, Workers' Compensation and Labor Relations, Domestic Relations and Municipal Law. Trials in all Courts.
Milford, Connecticut Office: 63 Cherry Street. P.O. Box 453. Telephone: 203-878-4669. Fax: 203-876-0644.
See Professional Biographies, WESTPORT, CONNECTICUT

Major, W. Glenn, (BV) .... '59 '83 C.321 B.A. L.190 J.D. [Sherwood&G.]
*PRACTICE AREAS: Residential and Commercial Real Estate; Zoning; Estate and Estate Planning; Probate.
Malowitz, Wesley M. .... '64 '91 C.610 B.A. L.30 J.D. [Berkowitz,M.&M.] ⊙
Manheim, Gene S., (BV) .... '51 '76 C.659 B.S. L.823 J.D. 175 Post Rd. W.
Mansolillo, A. Scott '62 '87 C.676 B.A. L.93 J.D.
V.P., Gen. Coun. & Secy., Xtra Corp.
Marcantonio, Edward, (BV) .... '65 '91 C.178 B.A. L.262 J.D. [Hermenze&M.]
*PRACTICE AREAS: Trusts and Estates; Wills; Probate; Taxation.
Martin, Heike S., (BV) .... '40 '88 C.1030 B.A. L.1029 J.D. [Boyd&M.]
Mason, James B. .... '40 '69 C&L.502 A.B., J.D. P.O. Box 5224
Matuszeski, John .... '37 '66 C.205 B.Ch.E. L.893 J.D. 212 Wilton Rd.‡
McBride, Ellen W. '40 '80 C.643 B.A. L.978 J.D.
(adm. in NY; not adm. in CT) 260 Hillspoint Rd.
McBride, Maureen, (AVⓉ) '53 '78 C.475 B.A. L.213 J.D.
(adm. in MI; not adm. in CT)
V.P. & Asst. Gen. Coun., Allied Domecq Spirits & Wine USA, Inc.
*RESPONSIBILITIES: Beverage Alcohol Law; Employment Law; Corporate Law; Commercial Law; Commercial Litigation.
McGeady, Bernard X., (AVⓉ) '25 '57 C.433 B.C.E. L.724 LL.B.
(adm. in NY; not adm. in CT; Pat.) 23 Compo Pkwy.
McGlynn, Louise A. .... '53 '92 C.184 B.G.S. L.1040 J.D. 5 Darbrook Road

McGovern & Associates
(See Greenwich)

McHugh, Lyn M. '54 '79 C.860 B.A. L.597 J.D.
(adm. in IL; not adm. in CT) 64 Bayberry Lane

McKeever, Stuart A., (AV) '36 '62 C&L.262 B.S., LL.B.
155 Post Road, East, 06880
Telephone: 203-227-4756 Fax: 203-454-2031

(This Listing Continued)

McKeever, Stuart A. (Continued)
Civil Trial Practice in State and Federal Courts. Probate, Estate, Tax and Real Estate Law.
Reference: Fleet Bank.

McKeon, Joseph F., Jr., (BV) .... '40 '65 C.1030 B.S.S. L.184 J.D. [J.F.McKeon,Jr.]
McKeon, Joseph F., Jr., P.C., (BV) .... 1200 Post Rd. E.
McNutt, Jan S. .... '53 '84 C.105 A.B. L.1029 J.D. 7 Half Mile Common
Meacham, Nancy K. '51 '74 C.597 B.S. L.986 J.D.
(adm. in KS; not adm. in CT) P.O. Box 214
Mechlin-Levitt, Ellen '60 '86 C.188 B.S. L.107 J.D.
(adm. in NY; not adm. in CT) [Blazzard,G.&H.]
*PRACTICE AREAS: Taxation; Insurance.
Melnick, Mark '58 '83 C.102 B.A. L.976 J.D.
(adm. in NY; not adm. in CT) V.P., Gen. Coun. & Secy., NCT Group, Inc.
Miller, Douglas A., Jr., (BV) .... '47 '77 C.475 B.A. L.184 J.D. [[A] Sargent&S.]
Millman, Arthur, (BV) .... '42 '70 C.102 B.A. L.823 LL.B. 234 Main St.
Moch, Susan A., (BV) .... '52 '77 C.518 A.B. L.472 J.D. [[C] Nusbaum&P.]
*PRACTICE AREAS: Family Law; Civil and Criminal Litigation.
Moks, Robert L. .... '45 '73 C&L.724 B.B.A., J.D. 191 Post Rd., W.
Moskow, Neal L., (BV) .... '64 '89 C.1044 B.A. L.94 J.D. [Ury&M.]
*PRACTICE AREAS: Construction Law; Construction Litigation; Commercial, Bank and Civil Litigation; Personal Injury; Employment Law.
Munro, J. B., Jr. .... '30 '83 C.103 B.S. L.1029 J.D. [Munro&M.]
Munro, Marilyn Fish .... '31 '83 C.788 A.B. L.1029 J.D. [Munro&M.]
Munro & Munro .... 45 Washington Ave.
Murphy, Alandra C. '64 '90 C.84 B.S. L.276 J.D.
(adm. in VA; not adm. in CT) Asst. Gen. Coun., IMS Health Inc.
*RESPONSIBILITIES: General Corporate; Securities; Technology Licensing.
Murray, Marianne F. .... '58 '84 C.1030 B.A. L.1040 J.D. [Rosner M.&T.] ⊙
Nadel, Irwin H. '20 '54 C&L.569 B.S., LL.B.
(adm. in NY; not adm. in CT) 1771 Post Rd. E., Box 338‡
Nayor, Michael A. .... '43 '69 C.188 B.S. L.569 J.D. 6 Robin Hill Road

Neigher, Alan, (AV) '41 '65 C.164 A.B. L.93 J.D. [BB]
1804 Post Road East, 06880
Telephone: 203-259-0599 Fax: 203-255-2570
Email: aneigher@snet.net URL: http://www.lawyers.com/neigherlaw
Of Counsel: Judith M. Trutt.
General Civil Practice before State and Federal Courts. Antitrust, Trade Regulation, Libel and Slander, Sports, Entertainment, Communications and Copyright Law.
See Professional Biographies, WESTPORT, CONNECTICUT

Nevas, Andrew B. '61 '90 C.867 B.A. L.276 J.D.
120 Post Road West, Suite 301, P.O. Box 2115, 06880
Telephone: 203-454-3843 Fax: 203-226-6077
Email: abn@iconn.net
(Also Of Counsel to Laurence Sarezky).
***PRACTICE AREAS: Litigation; Appellate Practice.**
General Practice.
See Professional Biographies, WESTPORT, CONNECTICUT

Nevas, Leo, (AV) .... '12 '36 C.477 B.A. L.188 LL.B. [Nevas,N.C.&G.]
Nevas, Stephen E., (CV) .... '38 '79 C.184 B.A. L.588 J.D. [[C] Nevas,N.C.&G.]
Nevas, Nevas, Capasse & Gerard, (AV) .... 246 Post Road East
Neville, Gregory J. '58 '86 C.951 B.A. L.446 J.D.
(adm. in NY; not adm. in CT) V.P. & Coun., AIG Fin. Products Corp.
Nusbaum, Edward, (AV) .... '48 '73 C.184 B.A. L.705 J.D. [Nusbaum&P.]
*PRACTICE AREAS: Family Law.

Nusbaum & Parrino, P.C., (AV) [BB]
212 Post Road West, 06880
Telephone: 203-226-8181 Fax: 203-454-9937
URL: http://www.lawyers.com/nusbaum&parrino
Edward Nusbaum; Thomas P. Parrino;—Harold W. Haldeman. Of Counsel: Susan A. Moch.
Trials in all Courts. Family, Negligence, Medical Malpractice, Criminal, Real Estate, Business and Commercial Law.
See Professional Biographies, WESTPORT, CONNECTICUT

O'Connell, Peter B., (BV) .... '44 '70 C.276 B.A. L.262 LL.B. [[C] Goldstein&P.] ⊙
O'Dea, Thomas P., Jr. .... '66 '91 C.676 B.S. L.180 J.D. [Halloran&S.]
*PRACTICE AREAS: Civil Litigation; Torts; Civil Rights; Government Tort Liability; Labor and Employment Law.

O'Donnell, McDonald and Cregeen, L.L.C.
(See Fairfield)

O'Grady, Kevin M., (BV) .... '46 '86 C.415 B.A. L.94 J.D. P.O. Box 383
O'Hara, Raymond A., III .... '55 '81 C.184 B.A. L.564 J.D. [Blazzard,G.&H.]
*PRACTICE AREAS: Life Insurance Products; Securities Law; Corporations; Insurance Taxation.
Oldham, Sarah S., (BV) .... '51 '88 C.918 B.S. L.184 J.D. [Rutkin&O.] ⊙
*PRACTICE AREAS: Family Law; Litigation.
Opinsky, Heidi E. .... '59 '85 C.732 B.S. L.1019 LL.B. [[C] Rutkin&O.]
*PRACTICE AREAS: Matrimonial Law; Divorce; Family Law; Alimony; Custody.
O'Sullivan, Christine B. .... '50 '75 C.478 A.B. L.776 J.D. 13 Hermit Ln.
Ottomano, Peter J., (BV) .... '54 '80 C.264 B.A. L.818 J.D. [Ottomano&J.]
*PRACTICE AREAS: Civil Litigation; Plaintiffs Personal Injury; Workers Compensation; Residential Real Estate.

Ottomano & Johnson, LLC, (BV)
111 Saugatuck Avenue, 06880
Telephone: 203-222-9900 Fax: 203-222-8504
Email: p.ottomano@snet.net
Peter J. Ottomano. Of Counsel: Charles Snowdon Johnson.
Litigation in all State and Federal Courts. Personal Injury, Worker's Compensation, Real Estate, Alternative Dispute Resolution.
See Professional Biographies, WESTPORT, CONNECTICUT

Pacifico, Paul J., (AV) '42 '66 C&L.262 B.S., J.D.
25 Ford Road (⊙Westport, CT; White Plains, NY)
Pacifico, Paul J., (AV) .... '42 '66 C&L.262 B.S., J.D. [Pacifico&F.] ⊙

Pacifico & Filan, L.L.P., (AV) [BB]
25 Ford Road, Suite 2, 06880 ⊙
Telephone: 203-221-8066 Fax: 203-222-4833
Paul J. Pacifico; Patrick J. Filan.
Trials and Appeals. Civil Litigation. Personal Injury, Medical Malpractice and Products Liability Law. General Civil Practice. Professional Licensure and Disciplinary Proceedings. Administrative Law, Medicare Fraud and Abuse.
White Plains, NY Office: 81 Main Street-Suite 118, 10601. Telephone: 914-949-7226. Facsimile: 914-949-7059.
See Professional Biographies, WESTPORT, CONNECTICUT

Paige, Candace D., (BV) ..... '56 '82 C.1030 B.A. L.1048 J.D. 1 Turkey Hill Road, South
Parker, John C., (BV) .... '39 '65 C.732 A.B. L.188 LL.B. 16 Loren Lane
Parrino, Thomas P., (BV) .... '61 '87 C.184 B.A. L.1029 J.D. [Nusbaum&P.]
*PRACTICE AREAS: Family Law; Personal Injury Litigation; Civil Litigation; Real Estate.
Pasquini, Gina A., (BV) .... '58 '85 C.67 B.S. L.184 J.D. [Pober,R.&P.]

Pate, Richard L. .... '68 '94 C.1029 B.A. L.1252 J.D. 155 Post Road East, Suite 11
Paul, Harold W .... '48 '76 C.1004 B.A. L.1009 J.D. [Berger&P.] ⊙
Pearl, Stewart W. .... '51 '77 C.165 A.B. L.309 J.D. [Pearl]
*PRACTICE AREAS: Aviation; Corporate and Commercial; Tax; Commercial Real Estate.

Pearl Professional Corporation
735 Post Road East, 06880
Telephone: 203-222-9000 Facsimile: 203-222-9100
Email: Thefirm@PearlPC.com URL: http://www.lawyers.com/pearlprofessionalcorp
Stewart W. Pearl. Associate Attorney: Ann E. Flocken.
Business, Corporate and Commercial, Aviation, Tax, Commercial Real Estate.
Representative Clients: Service America Corporation; BTR, Inc.; Shoreline Aviation, Inc.; Flight Services Group, Inc.; Columbia Air Services, Inc.; Grill and Partners, L.L.P.
See Professional Biographies, WESTPORT, CONNECTICUT

Pearsall, Steven W. .... '62 '88 C.602 B.B.A. L.262 J.D. [Gaboriault&P.]
*PRACTICE AREAS: Commercial Real Estate Financing; Commercial Real Estate Acquisitions and Sales; Leasing; Asset Based Lending; Equipment Finance and Leasing.
Peshkin, Joy Kony, (BV) .... '35 '80 C.881 A.B. L.1040 J.D. 46 Riverside Ave.

Piazza & Pickel
(See Stamford)

Plakins, Ava M. .... '54 '88 C.659 B.A. L.262 J.D. 3 Possum Run
Pober, Richard J., (BV) .... '53 '78 C.273 B.A. L.1202 J.D. [Pober,R.&P.]
Pober, Ross & Pasquini, (BV) .... 19 Ludlow Rd.
Polan, Lisa G. '58 '82 C.914 A.B. L.93 J.D.
Dep. Gen. Coun. & Asst. Secy., Terex Corp.
*RESPONSIBILITIES: Corporate Law; Commercial; Employment; Mergers and Acquisitions; Commercial Litigation.
Poling, Douglas L. '60 '86 C.860 B.A. L.976 J.D.
(adm. in NY; not adm. in CT) Gen. Coun., AIG Fin. Products
Powell, Robert T. '64 '89
C.378 B.S. L.880 J.D. V.P. & Coun., AIG Financial Prod. Corp.
Preminger, Richard J., (BV) .... '57 '81 C.1044 B.A. L.61 J.D. [Berkowitz,T.&T.]
*PRACTICE AREAS: Taxation; Estate Planning; Trusts and Estates; Corporate Law.
Quinlan, Robert F., Jr., (BV) .... '52 '83 C.524 B.S. L.1029 J.D. 180 Post Road East
Rabkin, Judy A., (BV) .... '44 '77 C.103 A.B. L.184 J.D. [Levett R.]
*PRACTICE AREAS: Commercial Real Estate Law; Creditors Rights Law; Bankruptcy Law.
Randel, James A., (BV) .... '49 '74 C&L.178 B.A., J.D. 175 Post Rd. W.
Raphael, Richard H., (BV) .... '54 '79 C.659 B.A. L.276 J.D. 19 Ludow Rd.
Rawitt, Peggy D. '57 '81 C.1044 B.A. L.564 J.D.
(adm. in NY; not adm. in CT)
Senior Vice President & General Counsel, Tower Realty Trust Inc.
Rhodes, Robert A. .... '67 '92 C.645 B.A. L.1048 J.D. [[A] Halloran&S.]
*PRACTICE AREAS: Municipal Law; Governmental Liability.
Richter, Robert E. '36 '60 C&L.569 B.S., LL.B.
(adm. in NY; not adm. in CT) 3 Ledgemoor Ln.
Ringel, Jed '51 '80 C.994 B.A. L.569 J.D.
(adm. in NY; not adm. in CT) 21 School Rd.‡
Rizza, Kimberly L. .... '67 '93 C.184 B.S. L.1048 J.D. 235 Post Road West

Roberts, Rose & Bates, P.C.
(See Stamford)

Rogers, Betty Ann .... '54 '91 C.1030 B.A. L.1029 J.D. [[A] Ury&M.]
*PRACTICE AREAS: Personal Injury; Medical Malpractice; Civil Litigation.
Rosenberg, Marvin B. '40 '65 C.1044 B.S. L.659 J.D.
(adm. in NY; not adm. in CT; Pat.) Terex Corp.
Rosenfeld, Marc S. .... '46 '70 C&L.472 B.B.A., J.D. 877 E. State St.
Rosenfeld, Roger C., (BV) .... '44 '69 C.472 B.A. L.818 J.D. P.O. Box 430
Rosner, Jonathan L., (AVⓉ) '32 '59 C.918 B.A. L.569 J.D.
(adm. in NY; not adm. in CT) [Rosner M.&T.] ⊙
Rosner Murray & Tucker LLP, (AVⓉ) .... 191 Post Rd. W. (⊙New York, NY)
Ross, David Eric, (BV) .... '54 '85 C&L.1029 B.E.S., J.D. [Pober,R.&P.]
Ross, Lois K., (CV) .... '34 '82 C.331 B.A. L.1029 J.D. [Ross&R.]
Ross, Raymond F., (BV) .... '30 '54 C&L.569 B.S., J.D. [Ross&R.]
Ross & Ross, P.C., (BV) .... 16 Taylor Pl.
Rubenstein, Alan S. .... '57 '91 C.696 B.A. L.1009 J.D. [[C] Halloran&S.]
*PRACTICE AREAS: Family Law; Matrimonial Law; Children; Mediation and Collaboration Law.
Rubenstein, Mark A., (BV) .... '46 '71 C&L.94 B.A., J.D. [Rubenstein,G.&B.]
*PRACTICE AREAS: Real Estate Law; Banking Law; Corporate Law; Estate Planning.

Rubenstein, Green & Bass, LLC, (BV)
315 Post Road West, P.O. Box 5143, 06881-5143
Telephone: 203-222-0022 Telecopier: 203-227-0766
Email: rubengreen@rubengreen.com URL: http://www.lawyers.com/rubensteingreen
Members of Firm: Mark A. Rubenstein; Daniel Green; David I. Bass;—Lisa Kasden Kent. Of Counsel: Steven Glazer.
General Civil Practice before State and Federal Courts, Real Estate, Corporation, Commercial and Banking, Personal Injury, Medical Malpractice, Estate Planning and Probate, Planning and Zoning Trials and Appeals, Banking Litigation.
References: Westport Bank & Trust Co.; Commonwealth Land Title Insurance Co.; Expressway Lubrication Centers; People's Bank.
See Professional Biographies, WESTPORT, CONNECTICUT

Rubin, Robert H., (AV) .... '32 '59 C.976 B.A. L.659 J.D. [Berkowitz,T.&T.]
*PRACTICE AREAS: Land Use Law; Commercial Law; Real Estate Law; Litigation.

Ruden, Morton R., (AV) '37 '62 C.867 B.A. L.569 LL.B.
19 Ludlow Road, 06880
Telephone: 203-454-0909 Telecopier: 203-341-0793
Email: attmr@aol.com
Real Estate, Banking, Corporate Law.
References: First Union National Bank; Peoples Bank.
See Professional Biographies, WESTPORT, CONNECTICUT

Ruffa, Gregory J. '62 '89 C.674 A.B. L.228 J.D.
(adm. in NY; not adm. in CT) V.P. & Coun., AIG Financial Prod. Corp.
Rutkin, Arnold H., (AV) .... '39 '65 C.659 B.S. L.94 LL.B. [Rutkin&O.] ⊙
*PRACTICE AREAS: Family Law; Litigation.

Rutkin and Oldham, L.L.C., (AV) [BB]
5 Imperial Avenue, P.O. Box 295, 06881 ⊙
Telephone: 203-227-7301 Fax: 203-222-9295
Email: law@rutkinoldham.com URL: http://www.lawyers.com/rutkinoldham
Arnold H. Rutkin; Sarah S. Oldham. Of Counsel: Kathleen A. Hogan; Heidi E. Opinsky; Nora A. Belanger.
Family, Trials and Appeals.
Greenwich Office: 125 Mason Street, 06830. Telephone: 203-869-7277.
See Professional Biographies, WESTPORT, CONNECTICUT

Sacks, Montgomery, Pastore & Levine, P.C.
1071 Post Road East, Suite 3 ⊙
Telephone: 203-291-6844
Stuart M. Levine (Resident); Stephen A. Stallings;—Thomas F. Giordano; Amy S. Cohen.
Construction, Government Contract and Surety Law, Commercial Litigation.
New York, N.Y. Office: Sacks Montgomery, P.C., 800 Third Avenue. Telephone: 212-355-4660.
See Professional Biographies, WESTPORT, CONNECTICUT

Salese, Anthony '56 '86 C.1349 B.A. L.569 J.D.
(adm. in NY; not adm. in CT) Coun., Philbro Energy Production, Inc.

Sandak Friedman Hennessey & Greco, LLP
(See Stamford)

Sands, R. Jeffrey, (BV) ....'55 '80 C.855 B.A. L.184 J.D. 1221 Post Road E.
Sarezky, Laurence, (BV) ... '49 '75 C.367 B.A. L.273 J.D. 120 Post Road West, Suite 301
Sargent, Hale C., (BV) ....'53 '79 C.37 B.A. L.184 J.D. [Sargent&S.]
Sargent, Murray, Jr. '13 '39 C.976 B.A. L.309 LL.B.
830 Post Rd. E. (⊙New York, NY)
Sargent, Thomas C. ....'43 '71 C.976 B.A. L.184 J.D. [Sargent&S.]
Sargent & Sargent, (BV) .... 830 Post Road East
Saverin, Kenneth A. ....'54 '79 C.154 B.A. L.262 J.D. Pres. & CEO, EMAC
Saxl, Richard H., (BV) ....'48 '76 C.659 B.A. L.1292 J.D. 5 Imperial Avenue
Scaccia, Tiziana M. ....'64 '90 C.1030 B.S. L.184 J.D. [Goldstein&P.] ⊙
Schadt, Barbara S., (BV) ....'38 '83 C.597 B.A. L.1252 J.D. 17 Owenoke Park

Scheffler, William L., & Associates, (AVⓣ) '48 '76 C.105 B.A. L.823 J.D. BB
P.O. Box 2773, 06880-0773
Telephone: 203-226-6600; 1-800-429-4480 Telecopier: 203-227-1873
Email: scheff@optonline.net URL: http://www.lawyers.com/williamscheffler&assoc
***PRACTICE AREAS: Corporate and Business Transactions involving non-publicly traded entities; Real Estate Development; Restaurant, Club and Hotel Licensing; Leasing and Zoning Law; Administrative.**
Corporate, Business Transactions, Real Estate Development, Zoning, Licensing, Administrative, Not For Profit Corporations.
See Professional Biographies, WESTPORT, CONNECTICUT

Schindler, Greg S. '59 '85 C.659 B.S. L.309 J.D.
(adm. in NY; not adm. in CT) Coun., Philbro Energy Production, Inc.

Schine, Julianelle & Antonucci, P.C., (AV)
Suite 100, 830 Post Road East, 06880 ⊙
Telephone: 203-226-6861 Fax: 203-226-6866
Email: sjalaw2@snet.net
Robert L. Julianelle; Francis J. Antonucci.
General Civil and Trial Practice in State and Federal Courts. Corporate, Commercial and Business Law, Probate, Personal Injury, Administrative, Estate Planning, Commercial and Residential Real Estate, Higher Education Law.
Representative Clients: Sacred Heart University, Incorporated; Unimin Corporation; Mariano Brothers, Inc.; Star Distributors, Inc.; General Electric Employees Federal Credit Union; Prime Bank; Slocum & Sons Inc.; Ocean Air Transportation, Inc.; South Central Regional Water Authority; Sonitrol Security Systems of Bridgeport.
Approved Counsel For: Connecticut Attorney's Title Insurance Co.; People's Bank; The New Haven Savings Bank; Bank of Boston; Westport Bank & Trust Co.; Norwalk Savings Society; Hudson United Bank; Connecticut Housing Finance Authority; Prime Bank; The Milford Bank; Fleet Bank, N.A.; Old Republic National Title Insurance Co.; First Union Home Equity Bank, N.A.
Reference: Fleet Bank, N.A.
Orange, Connecticut Office: 35 Old Tavern Road, P.O. Box 905. Telephone: 203-795-3563. Fax: 203-799-9655.
See Professional Biographies, WESTPORT, CONNECTICUT

Schlossberg, Joel ....'38 '64 C.184 B.A. L.94 LL.B. 6 E. Main St.
Schneider, Robert G. .... '30 '90 C.976 B.A. L.1029 J.D. 7 Whittney St., Exit 1
Scholl, Robert P., (BV) ....'31 '62 C.1029 B.S. L.976 J.D. J.P.

Schoonmaker, George & Colin, P.C.
(See Greenwich)

Schrage, Robert Alan '45 '72 C.112 A.B. L.1068 J.D.
(adm. in CA; not adm. in CT) [Stern&S.]
Schwarz, Ralph .... '49 '77 C.31 A.B. L.94 J.D. 965 Post Road, East
Schweitzer, Sharon M., (BV) ....'52 '77 C&L.659 B.A., J.D. [Levett R.]
*PRACTICE AREAS: Tax Law; Estate Planning Law.
See, Edgar T., (AV) ....'16 '41 C.918 B.A. L.976 LL.B. [Wake,S.D.&B.]
*PRACTICE AREAS: Estate Planning; Trust Law; Probate; Real Estate.
Seeley, Elizabeth C., (BV) '38 '63
C.659 B.S. L.893 LL.B. [Tirola&H.] (⊙New York, NY)
*PRACTICE AREAS: Corporate Law; Business Law; Banking Law; Commercial Real Estate.

Segore-Freshman, Nancy, (BV) '55 '81 C.696 B.A. L.982 J.D.
120 Post Road West, 06880
Telephone: 203-222-8686 Fax: 203-222-8857
Email: nesflaw@aol.com URL: http://www.lawyers.com/nancyfreshman
***PRACTICE AREAS: Family Law; Mediation; Real Estate.**
Family Law, Divorce Mediation, Collaborative Law, Estate Planning, Estate Administration.
See Professional Biographies, WESTPORT, CONNECTICUT

Senie, Alan H., (AV) .... '22 '48 C.893 B.A. L.976 LL.B. [Senie,S.&L.]
Senie, Stock & LaChance, P.C., (AV) .... 125 Main St.
Shaban, John T. .... '64 '94 C.174 B.A. L.1040 J.D. [A Levett R.]
*PRACTICE AREAS: Commercial Litigation; Employment Law; Sports Law.
Shaffer, Richard Allyn, (BV) ....'32 '58 C.966 B.A. L.477 LL.B. 965 Post Rd., E.
Shames, Jerry, (AV) ....'39 '64 C.994 B.A. L.569 LL.B. 16 Taylor Pl.

Sheiman, Ronald L., (AV) '48 '73 C.477 B.A. L.184 J.D. BB
1804 Post Road East, 06880
Telephone: 203-259-0599 Telecopier: 203-255-2570
URL: http://www.lawyers.com/ronaldsheiman
Federal Income, Estate and Gift Taxation. Partnership and Corporate Law. Probate and Estate Planning. International Business Law.
See Professional Biographies, WESTPORT, CONNECTICUT

Sherriff, Andrew R., (BV) ....'46 '71 C.262 B.S. L.94 J.D. [Sherriff&S.]
Sherriff, Andrew R., Jr. ....'72 '98 C.262 B.A. L.1009 J.D. [Sherriff&S.] (⊙Hartford)
Sherriff, Angela S., (BV) .... '48 '78 C.454 B.A. L.1202 J.D. [Sherriff&S.]
Sherriff & Sherriff, (BV) .... 225 Main Street

Sherwood & Garlick, P.C., (AV)
65 Jesup Road, P.O. Box 390, 06881-0390
Telephone: 203-227-9585 Fax: 203-227-7777
URL: http://www.lawyers.com/sherwoodgarlick
Harry R. Sherwood (1873-1966); Thaddeus G. Cowell, Jr. (1912-1991); Stanley P. Atwood (1937-2000); Richard J. Diviney; W. Glenn Major; Charles W. Fleischmann; Edward E. Garlick (Retired).
General Practice in all Courts. Real Property, Estate Planning, Probate, Municipal and Zoning Law, Aviation Law, Civil Litigation, and Appeals.
General Counsel for: The Westport Bank & Trust Co.
See Professional Biographies, WESTPORT, CONNECTICUT

Shiller, Doris B., (BV) ....'33 '79 C.66 B.A. L.976 J.D. [Berkowitz,T.&T.]
*PRACTICE AREAS: Banking Law; Real Estate Law; Corporate and Related Business Law.
Shirley, William A. '59 '87 C.813 A.B. L.178 J.D.
(adm. in NY; not adm. in CT) V.P. & Coun., AIG Financial Prod. Corp.
Shrader, L. Douglas, (AV) ....'35 '64 C&L.976 B.A., LL.B. [Shrader&K.]
*PRACTICE AREAS: Civil Litigation; Appellate Practice; Personal Injury; Medical Malpractice; Securities and Investment Fraud.

Shrader and Knapp, A Professional Corporation, (AV)
25 Ford Road, 06880
Telephone: 203-227-6628 Fax: 203-227-6922
Email: shrader.knapp@erols.com URL: http://www.lawyers.com/shraderknapplaw

(This Listing Continued)

Shrader and Knapp, A Professional Corporation (Continued)
L. Douglas Shrader; Beverly Stauffer Knapp.
Civil Trial and Appellate Practice in all State and Federal Courts. Medical Malpractice, Personal Injury, Securities and Investment Frauds, Fine Arts Claims, Commercial and Real Property Litigation.
See Professional Biographies, WESTPORT, CONNECTICUT

Siegel, Claudine F. ....'35 '59 C.66 B.A. L.569 J.D. Legal Aid Soc.
Siegelaub, Steven M., (BV) ....'56 '83 C.918 B.A. L.178 J.D. [Levett R.]
*PRACTICE AREAS: Commercial Real Estate Law.
Sisson, Frank E. ....'52 '77 C.165 B.A. L.309 J.D. 180 Post Rd., E.

Sisson, Frank E., III, Law Offices of, (AV) '52 '76 C.165 B.A. L.309 J.D.
180 Post Road East, Suite 202, 06881 ⊙
Telephone: 203-222-4844 Telefax: 203-222-4869
Email: fesisson3d@cs.com URL: http://www.lawyers.com/sisson
Estate Planning, Probate, Corporate, Commercial, Elder Law, Tax Law, Real Estate.
Stamford, Connecticut Office: 6 Landmark Square, 06901. Telephone: 203-965-5965.
See Professional Biographies, WESTPORT, CONNECTICUT

Skramstad, Robert C. '67 '94 C&L.477 B.A., J.D.
(adm. in MI; not adm. in CT)
Asst. Gen. Coun., Allied Domecq Spirits & Wine USA, Inc.
*RESPONSIBILITIES: Alcoholic Beverages; Employment Law; Litigation; Corporate Law; Commercial Litigation.
Slavin, Richard, (BV) '47 '77 C.930 B.A. L.8 J.D.
[Cohen&W.] (⊙Bridgeport, Stamford)
*PRACTICE AREAS: Securities Regulation; Banking Regulation; Securities, Banking and Corporate Litigation; Arbitrations.
Slez, Anthony F., Jr. ....'46 '79 C.1029 B.E.S. L.1048 J.D. [A Carron&F.]
Slez, Margaret J., (CV) ....'47 '88 C.876 B.A. L.1029 J.D. [A Carron&F.]
Sobel, Stacey Gladstone ....'60 '86 C.390 A.B. L.94 J.D. 19 Clover Lane
Solomon, Greta E., (AV) ......'51 '76 C.788 A.B. L.184 J.D. [Cohen&W.] (⊙Bridgeport)
*PRACTICE AREAS: Taxation; Estate Planning; Trusts and Estates; Elder Law; Retirement Planning.
Southwick, Michael J. '63 '89 C.276 A.B. L.93 J.D.
(adm. in NJ; not adm. in CT) V.P. & Coun., AIG Financial Prod. Corp.
Spiekermann, Gloria W. .... '— '79 C.555 B.A. L.705 J.D. 12 Great Marsh Rd.
Spirer, Alan R. ....'46 '72 C.367 B.A. L.273 J.D. [Spirer&C.]

Spirer & Cott, (CV)
830 Post Road East, P.O. Box 5201, 06880
Telephone: 203-454-1999 Fax:203- 454-9749
Email: arspirer@yahoo.com URL: http://www.lawyers.com/spirer
Members of Firm: Alan R. Spirer; Douglas M. Cott.
General Civil Practice before State and Federal Courts. Commercial Law, Appellate Practice, Litigation, Construction Law, Contracts, Zoning, Planning and Land Use, Environmental Law. Personal Injury, Family Law, Real Estate, Corporate Law, Business Law.
See Professional Biographies, WESTPORT, CONNECTICUT

Sporn, Judith B., (BV) '51 '80 C.1044 B.A. L.426 J.D.
125 Main Street, 06880-3303
Telephone: 203-226-6171 Fax: 203-227-5959
Email: jsporn@snet.net
Practice Limited to Immigration, Naturalization and Consular Law.
See Professional Biographies, WESTPORT, CONNECTICUT

Stallings, Stephen A. ....'58 '90 C.383 B.A. L.724 J.D. [Sacks,M.P.&L.] ⊙
Stammer, William '41 '64 C&L.569 B.A., LL.B.
Assoc. Gen. Coun., Playtex Products, Inc.
Steinberger, Rita A., (BV) ....'42 '81 C.94 B.A. L.1029 J.D 180 Post Rd. E.
Stern, Mark, (CV) ....'54 '79 C.260 B.A. L.426 J.D. [Stern&S.]
Stern & Schrage, (CV) .... 25 Ford Road, 2nd Floor
Stevens, John H. .... '30 '66 C.1030 B.S. L.1340 J.D. 26 Waterside Ter.
Stewart, Jeanne Fennell ....'47 '80 C.731 B.A. L.262 J.D. 7 Pan Handle Lane
Stock, Jack, (BV) ....'21 '48 C&L.976 B.A., LL.B. [Senie,S.&L.]
Stone, Lynn Korman ....'59 '85 C.30 B.A. L.1029 J.D. [Blazzard,G.&H.]
*PRACTICE AREAS: Life Insurance Products; Securities Law.
Struzzi, Peter H. ....'60 '86 C.951 B.A. L.659 J.D. [Levett R.]
*PRACTICE AREAS: Corporate Law; Securities.
Sullivan, Patricia C., (BV) ...... '59 '89 C&L.262 B.A., J.D. [Cohen&W.] (⊙Bridgeport)
Sullivan, Robert J., (BV) ....'52 '83 C.1211 B.S. L.284 J.D. [R.Sullivan]
*PRACTICE AREAS: Business Law; Litigation; Criminal Law.

Sullivan, Robert, Law Offices of, (BV)
190 Main Street, 06880
Telephone: 203-227-1404 V/TDD Facsimile: 203-226-6403 From San Francisco Bay Area: 510-820-0307
Robert J. Sullivan.
Business Transactions, Litigation, Criminal Law.
Danville, California Office: 375 Diablo Road, Suite 200. Telephone: 510-820-4141. Facsimile: 510-831-0155.
See Professional Biographies, WESTPORT, CONNECTICUT

Sussman, Robert C. .... '35 '60 C&L.309 A.B., LL.B. 64 Woodside Ave.
Sussmane, Kenneth S., (AVⓣ) .... '56 '81 C.472 A.B. L.276 J.D. [Sussmane&Z.]
Sussmane & Zapfel, P.C., (AVⓣ) ....735 Post Road, East
Swaim, Phillip B., (AV) .... '37 '62 C.197 B.A. L.178 LL.B. 46 Riverside Ave.
Swarts, William B., III .... '41 '65 C.103 A.B. L.659 LL.B. 27 Wright St.
Szczesny, Brett ....'72 '97 C.264 B.A. L.128 J.D. [A Halloran&S.]
*PRACTICE AREAS: Labor and Employment.
Tate, Stephen, (AV) .... '22 '50 C.197 A.B. L.309 LL.B. [C Nevas,N.C.&G.]
Tedford, Frederick B., (BV) '47 '72
C.184 B.A. L.818 J.D. [Danaher,T.L.&N.] (⊙Hartford)
Teixeira, Lisa '61 '87 C.4 B.A. L.724 J.D.
(adm. in NY; not adm. in CT) 22 Flower Farm Cir.

Thiemann, Nicholas W., (BV) '39 '64 C.184 A.B. L.893 LL.B.
830 Post Road East, P.O. Box 5169, 06881
Telephone: 203-227-2112 Fax: 203-227-2552
Email: nickthiemann@aol.com
***PRACTICE AREAS: Real Estate; Corporation; Probate and Estate Planning; General Civil Trial Practice.**
General Civil Practice. Real Estate, Corporation, Probate and Estate Planning.
Reference: People's Bank.

Thoren, Peter L. '56 '83 C.575 B.A. L.276 J.D.
(adm. in NY; not adm. in CT) V.P. & Gen. Coun., Philbro Energy Production, Inc.
Tirola, Vincent S., (AV) ....'37 '62 C.473 A.B. L.569 LL.B. [Tirola&H.]
*PRACTICE AREAS: Business Law; Executive Compensation; Real Property; Banking Law; Family Law.

Tirola & Herring, (AV)
1555 Post Road East, P.O. Box 631, 06881
Telephone: 203-255-5144 Fax: 203-255-5177
Email: tirolalaw@aol.com URL: http://www.lawyers.com/tirolalaw
Members of Firm: Vincent S. Tirola; Charles Fredericks, Jr.; Elizabeth C. Seeley; Buddy O. H. Herring;—Thomas C. Cusa. Of Counsel: Susannah Jacobson; C. Michael Carter; Michael E. Twomey; Gary Hoppe; Alan T. Gallanty; Gus Dimopoulos; John Logan O'Donnell; Diane K. Fernbach; Anthony Del Vecchio.

(This Listing Continued)

Tirola & Herring (Continued)

General Practice, Banking and Financial, Corporate, Executive Compensation, Real Estate, Land Use and Environmental Law, Family, Estate Planning and Probate and Litigation in all Courts.
Reference: U.S. Trust Co.
Affiliated Office: Twomey, Hoppe and Gallanty, LLP, 757 Third Avenue, New York, New York. 10017. Telephone: 212-688-0400. Fax: 212-688-1929.

See Professional Biographies, WESTPORT, CONNECTICUT

Toma, Michael Steven .... '70 '95 C.188 B.A. L.306 J.D. [Ⓐ Wake,S.D.&B.]
*PRACTICE AREAS: Municipal Law; Land Use Law; Real Estate; Civil Litigation.
Tomasky, Maria T., (CV) .... '48 '82 C&L.1029 B.S., J.D. [Bradford,T.&T.]
Tomeny, Lynne J. .... '45 '78 C.228 B.A. L.1009 J.D. Dep. Gen. Coun., Terex Corp.
*RESPONSIBILITIES: Product Liability; Environmental Law; Litigation; Management.
Trembicki, Alexander J., (BV) ....'55 '80 C&L.184 B.A., J.D. [Lynch,T.M.&B.]
*PRACTICE AREAS: Civil Litigation; Personal Injury; Commercial Litigation; Employment Law; Family Law.
Trutt, Judith M., (BV) ....'46 '81 C.66 B.A. L.1029 J.D. [Ⓒ A.Neigher]
Tucker, Joseph P. '58 '90 C.102 B.S. L.262 J.D.
(adm. in NY; not adm. in CT) [Rosner M.&T.] (ⓄNew York, NY)
Tudruj, Roman .... '49 '82 C&L.1029 B.A., J.D. [Bradford,T.&T.]
Ury, Frederic S., (AV) ....'52 '77 C.1155 B.S. L.818 J.D. [Ury&M.]
*PRACTICE AREAS: Trials and Appeals in all Courts; Banking and Commercial Law; Personal Injury Law; Medical Malpractice; Real Estate.

Ury & Moskow, (AV)
A Limited Liability Company
518 Riverside Avenue, P.O. Box 231, 06881
Telephone: 203-226-8088 Fax: 203-226-8437 URL: http://www.urymoskow.com
Email: law@UryMoskow.com URL: http://www.lawyers.com/ury&moskow
Members of Firm: Frederic S. Ury; Neal L. Moskow. Associates: Deborah M. Garskof; Betty Ann Rogers; Patricia Whiting Welch; Anthony J. LaBella. Special Counsel: Julia Cremin Wyman.
General Civil and Criminal Practice before State and Federal Courts. Real Estate, Corporation, Commercial and Banking Litigation, Personal Injury, Medical Malpractice, Construction Law and Litigation, Employment Law, Toxic Tort, Pharmaceutical and Devise Litigation, Trials and Appeals.

See Professional Biographies, WESTPORT, CONNECTICUT

Wake, See, Dimes & Bryniczka, (AV)
27 Imperial Avenue, P.O. Box 777, 06881
Telephone: 203-227-9545 Telecopier: 203-226-1641
Email: wsdb@wsdb.com URL: http://www.wsdb.com
Members of Firm: Hereward Wake (1905-1977); Edgar T. See; Edwin K. Dimes; Jacob P. Bryniczka; Amy L. Y. Day; Ira W. Bloom; Mark J. Kovack; Douglas E. LoMonte. Associates: Michael Steven Toma; Lisa M. Levy; Russell S. Ferguson. Special Counsel: Eugene E. Cederbaum. Of Counsel: Richard S. Gibbons; Walter M. Andrew, Jr.
Business and Corporate Law, Real Estate, Trusts and Probate, Estate Planning, Municipal, Zoning and Land Use Law, Litigation in all Federal and State Courts. Federal, State and Foreign Taxation, Pension and Profit Sharing, and Family Law.
General Counsel for: L.H. Gault & Son, Inc.; M.B.I., Inc.; The Danbury Mint; Beta Shim, Co.; Easton Press; Coverbind Corp.; D.L. Ryan Cos., Ltd.;
Approved Attorneys for: Lawyers Title Insurance Corporation of Richmond, Va.; Chicago Title Insurance Co.; Old Republic National Title Insurance Co.

See Professional Biographies, WESTPORT, CONNECTICUT

Walker, Robert G., (BV) .... '50 '80 C.855 B.A. L.588 J.D. 830 Post Rd. East

Warren, Elliot R., (BV) '50 '75 C.696 B.A. L.273 J.D.
1555 Post Road East, 06880 ⊙
Telephone: 203-254-9570 Fax: 203-255-5177
Email: ewarrenlaw@aol.com URL: http://www.lawyers.com/elliotrwarren
General Civil and Criminal Litigation before all State and Federal Courts. Trials and Appeals. Criminal Defense, Commercial and Tax Litigation, Personal Injury, Employment and Negligence Law.
Reference: Peoples Bank.

See Professional Biographies, WESTPORT, CONNECTICUT

Weisman, Lawrence P., (AV) ....'39 '63 C.1036 B.A. L.178 J.D. [Weisman&L.]
*PRACTICE AREAS: General Civil Practice; Zoning and Land Use Regulation; Family.

Weisman & Lubell, (AV)
5 Sylvan Road South, P.O. Box 3184, 06880
Telephone: 203-226-8307 Telecopier: 203-221-7279
Members of Firm: Lawrence P. Weisman; Ellen B. Lubell. Of Counsel: Livia D. Barndollar.
General Civil Practice. Litigation, Family, Appeals, Real Estate, Zoning and Land Use Regulation.

See Professional Biographies, WESTPORT, CONNECTICUT

Weitzman, Patricia D. .... '53 '94 C&L.184 B.S., J.D. [Ⓐ Levett R.]
*PRACTICE AREAS: Health Care; Hospital Law; Corporate Law; Employment Law.
Welch, Patricia Whiting .... '69 '99 C.1211 B.S. L.1252 J.D. [Ⓐ Ury&M.]
*PRACTICE AREAS: Personal Injury; Medical Malpractice; Products Liability; Wrongful Death.
Wessan, Sharon ....'60 '86 C.659 B.A. L.569 J.D. 253 Greens Farms Rd.
Wexler, Lisa K. ....'60 '85 C.367 B.A. L.569 J.D. 21 Poplar Plain Rd.
Wilkins, Jeffrey B., (BV) ....'53 '78 C.884 B.A. L.184 J.D. 1200 Post Rd. E.
Williams, Adrienne S. W. ....'62 '88 C.659 B.A. L.273 J.D. 4 Dover Road
Willick, Nelson H. .... '51 '77 C.367 B.A. L.1019 J.D. 8 Dorchester Dr.

Willinger, Willinger & Bucci, P.C.
(See Bridgeport)

Winkler, Linda J. ....'57 '85 C.184 B.A. L.1029 J.D. 17 N. Pasture‡
Wooters, J. Michael '44 '75 C.588 B.A. L.213 J.D.
Vice President & Counsel, Allied Domeq Spirits and Wine Limited
Wyman, Julia Cremin ....'64 '97 C.829 B.S. L.1048 J.D. [Ⓒ Ury&M.]
*PRACTICE AREAS: Drug and Medical Device Litigation; Medical Malpractice; Personal Injury.
Yestrumskas, Paul '51 '78 C.659 B.A. L.831 J.D.
Vice President, General Counsel & Secretary, Playtex Corporation
Yost, Byron Paul, (BV) ....'53 '78 C.1030 B.S. L.724 J.D. [Yost&Assoc.]
Yost & Associates, P.C., (BV) ....25 Ford Rd.
Young, Barbara A. ....'54 '80 C.118 B.A. L.893 J.D. [Levett R.]
*PRACTICE AREAS: Corporate Law; Business Law; Securities Law; Mergers and Acquisitions; Commercial Finance Law.
Young, Michael D. '47 '73 C.188 B.S. L.178 J.D.
(adm. in NY; not adm. in CT) V.P. & Gen. Coun., Phibro Div. of Salomon Bros. Inc.
Young, Michael David '— '73 C.188 B.S. L.178 J.D.
V.P. & Gen. Coun., Philbro Energy Production, Inc.
Zabel, David B., (AV) '57 '82
C.103 A.B. L.893 J.D. [Cohen&W.] (ⓄBridgeport, Stamford)
*PRACTICE AREAS: Employment; Civil Litigation; Bankruptcy.
Zapfel, Elaine B., (BVⓉ) ....'56 '82 C.1044 B.A. L.107 J.D. [Sussmane&Z.]
Zawacki, Edward W. .... '47 '73 C.602 B.Sc. L.724 J.D. 578 Post Road East, Suite 663
Zur, Grace L. ....'62 '92 C.95 B.A. L.1040 J.D. 37 Franklin St.

WEST REDDING, —, *Fairfield Co.*

Lancaster, Mary Dale ....'56 '90 C.322 B.A. L.262 J.D. 15 Mine Hill Rd.
Miller, Tina '47 '72 C.788 A.B. L.569 J.D.
(adm. in NY; not adm. in CT) 81 70 Acre Rd.‡
Russell, A. David ....'24 '52 C&L.976 B.A., LL.B. 9 Little River Lane‡

WEST SIMSBURY, —, *Hartford Co.*

Bauer, Patricia S. '46 '70 C&L.477 A.B., J.D.
(adm. in MI; not adm. in CT) 38 Rocklyn Dr.
Blackmon, Leon C. ....'27 '85 C.67 A.B. L.1048 J.D. 84 Drumlin Rd.
Falkowski, Anthony J. '46 '74 C.754 B.S. L.776 J.D.
(adm. in NJ; not adm. in CT) 104 N. Saddle Ridge Rd.‡
Gutman, Jewel A., (BV) ....'29 '79 C.788 A.B. L.184 J.D. 8 Daniel Lane‡
Heitman, Jane Hilary '52 '77 C.103 A.B. L.245 J.D.
(adm. in GA; not adm. in CT) 32 Old Stone Crossing‡
Herrlich, William M., Jr. ....'58 '87 C.178 A.B. L.990 J.D. P.O. Box 336
Kelly, Kenneth J. ....'32 '60 C.1024 B.A. L.184 LL.B. 12 Arrowhead Dr.‡
Lowman, Sharon P. '47 '76 C.881 B.A. L.178 J.D.
(adm. in CA; not adm. in CT) 18 Watson Dr.‡
Miller, Richard A., Jr. ....'57 '83 C.645 B.A. L.362 J.D. 239 W Mountain Rd
Penza, Jill ....'55 '84 C.390 A.B. L.776 J.D. 43 Canton Rd.
Tidd, Jonathan G. ....'45 '73 C&L.339 B.S., J.D. 9 Beaver Brook Rd.
Wall, Edward M. ....'16 '50 C&L.309 A.B., LL.B. 39 Quorn Hunt Rd.‡

WEST SUFFIELD, 8,634, *Hartford Co.*

Marmelstein, David D. ....'46 '88 C.1145 B.S. L.1029 J.D. 46 S. Stone St.

WETHERSFIELD, 26,013, *Hartford Co.*

Aaron, Arthur G., (BV) ....'42 '70 C.37 B.A. L.94 J.D. 1177 Silas Deane Hwy.
Acevedo, J. Martin ....'69 '92 C.999 B.A. L.306 J.D. [Ⓐ Mayo,G.&Z.]
*PRACTICE AREAS: Real Estate Litigation; Employment Defense Litigation; Public Housing Litigation.
Bagger, Jocelyn P., (BV) ....'43 '83 C.518 B.A. L.184 J.D. 261 Wolcott Hill Rd.
Baker, Alan Robert, (AV) ....'45 '74 C.311 B.A. L.184 J.D. [Baker O.&B.]
*PRACTICE AREAS: Litigation; Bankruptcy.

Baker O'Sullivan & Bliss PC, (AV)
Putnam Park, Suite 100 100 Great Meadow Road, 06109-2371
Telephone: 860-258-1993 Telecopier: 860-258-1991
Email: info@boblawyers.com
Alan Robert Baker; William J. O'Sullivan; Raymond C. Bliss;—Gale S. Dwyer; Denise R. Polivy.
Litigation, Bankruptcy and Creditors' Rights.
Representative Clients: The Aetna Casualty & Surety Company; Crown, Cork & Seal Company, Inc.; Eastman Kodak Company; Fidelity Investments; Heublein, Inc.; Nissan Motor Acceptance Corporation; Shawmut Bank Connecticut, N.A.; Sun Refining and Marketing Company; Tolland Bank.

See Professional Biographies, WETHERSFIELD, CONNECTICUT

Baldwin, Frederick D. ....'49 '76 C.831 B.A. L.184 J.D. 365 Silas Deane Highway
Barry, M. Peter, (BV) ....'33 '58 C.321 B.S. L.276 J.D. [Barry,H.&L.]
Barry, Michael P., (BV) ....'57 '82 C.1030 B.S. L.1202 J.D. [Barry,H.&L.]
Barry, Harvey & Later, P.C., (AV) .... 1177 Silas Deane Highway
Bascetta, Joseph R., (BV) ....'59 '86 C.676 B.A. L.1202 J.D. 1233 Silas Deane Hwy.
Biloon, Harold L., (BV) ......'25 '54 C.309 A.B. L.228 LL.B. 1177 Silas Deane Highway
Bliss, Raymond C., (BV) ....'54 '84 C.951 B.A. L.128 J.D. [Baker O.&B.]
*PRACTICE AREAS: Commercial Law; Bankruptcy; Creditors Rights.
Bobruff, Paul A. ....'62 '87 C.156 B.A. L.276 J.D. Dept. of Labor
Bumster, William J., (BV) ....'32 '58 C&L.184 B.S., LL.B. 786 Silas Deane Hwy.
Chorches, Martin, (AV) ....'35 '61 C.184 B.S. L.94 J.D. [Chorches&N.]
*PRACTICE AREAS: Bankruptcy; Asset Protection; Commercial Law; Real Estate; Foreclosure.

Chorches & Novak, P.C., (AV)
1260 Silas Deane Highway, 06109-4331
Telephone: 860-257-1980 Telecopier: 860-257-1988
Martin Chorches; Anthony S. Novak;—Teresa A. Fontaine.
Bankruptcy, Asset Protection, Commercial Transactions and Corporate. Civil Litigation in all State and Federal Courts. Representation before Internal Revenue Service.

See Professional Biographies, WETHERSFIELD, CONNECTICUT

Clark, Sean P., (BV) ....'65 '90 C.1021 B.S. L.1017 J.D. [Mayo,G.&Z.]
*PRACTICE AREAS: Civil Litigation; Commercial Litigation; Personal Injury; Real Estate; Bankruptcy.
Cramer, Richard S., (BV) ....'43 '69 C.012 B.A. L.93 J.D. 449 Silas Deane Hwy.
Crowe, William R., (BV) ....'59 '85 C.197 A.B. L.262 J.D. [Mayo,G.&Z.]
*PRACTICE AREAS: Commercial Real Estate; Business Law.
Cruz, Milagros S. ....'65 '92 C.518 B.A. L.184 J.D. [Ⓒ B.J.Ruhe]
*PRACTICE AREAS: General Practice; Civil Practice; Probate Litigation.
DeLuca, Crescenzo, (BV) ....'55 '80 C.184 B.A. L.273 J.D. 81 Wolcott Hill Rd.
DeManche, Gregory F., (BV) ....'52 '83 C.1019 B.A. L.345 J.D. [Mayo,G.&Z.]
*PRACTICE AREAS: Real Estate; Mortgage Lending; Consumer Lending; Regulatory Compliance; Business Law.
Dillman, Noreen A. ....'61 '91 C.1102 B.A. L.1252 J.D. [Ⓐ Mayo,G.&Z.]
*PRACTICE AREAS: Estate Planning and Administration; Elder Law; Taxation.
Dodd, Christopher J. ....'44 '73 C.676 B.A. L.421 J.D. (M.C)
Doerschler, G. Eric ....'28 '52 C&L.188 A.B., LL.B. 19 Reed Dr.
Donohue, James J. ....'16 '47 C.855 B.A. L.184 LL.B. 157 Nott St.‡
Dorros, Kenneth M. '59 '85 C.401 B.S. L.262 J.D.
Sr. V.P., Gen. Coun. & Secy., Shared Technologies Cellular, Inc.
Doyle, Edward R. ....'25 '50 C&L.976 A.B., LL.B. Supr. Ct. J.‡
Doyle, Paul R., (BV) ....'63 '90 C.164 B.A. L.184 J.D. 38 Thornbush Rd.
Dudley, Susan A. ....'68 '93 C.321 B.A. L.93 J.D. 251 Windmill Hill
Dwyer, Gale S. ....'70 '96 C.939 B.A. L.285 J.D. [Ⓐ Baker O.&B.]
*PRACTICE AREAS: Products Liability; Commercial Litigation; Bankruptcy.
Eisenman, Anne F.F. ....'62 '88 C.184 B.A. L.1029 J.D. Dept. of Labor, Bd. of Review
Fontaine, Teresa A. ....'66 '97 C.184 B.S. L.1252 J.D. [Ⓐ Chorches&N.]
*PRACTICE AREAS: Bankruptcy.
Gagne, J. William, Jr., (BV) ....'44 '71 C.820 B.A. L.818 J.D. [J.W.Gagne Jr.&Assoc.]
Gagne, J. William, Jr. & Associates, P.C., (BV) .... 1260 Silas Deane Highway
Gilligan, Robert G., (AV) ....'42 '72 C.1033 B.A. L.184 J.D. [Mayo,G.&Z.]
*PRACTICE AREAS: Real Estate; Commercial Law; Secured Finance; Banking; Estate Planning and Settlement.
Gundersen, Charles A. ....'32 '90 C.184 B.A. L.1048 J.D. 1260 Silas Deane Hwy.
Harvey, John F., Jr., (AV) ....'42 '68 C.745 B.A. L.128 J.D. [Barry,H.&L.]
Hennessey, Sheila M., (AV) ....'37 '61 C.19 B.A. L.93 J.D. 431 Wolcott Hill Rd.
Holmes, Brian R. '47 '79 C.012 B.A. L.770 J.D.
(adm. in CA; not adm. in CT) Dir., Reg. Affs., Conn. Construction Industries Assn.
Hoopes, David S., (BV) ....'57 '84 C.454 B.A. L.184 J.D. [Mayo,G.&Z.]
*PRACTICE AREAS: Commercial Litigation; Land Use; Real Estate.
Johnson, Lee N., Law Offices of, (BV) '56 '81
C.184 B.A. L.1048 J.D. 350 Silas Deane Highway
Joseloff, Gerald A., (BV) ....'45 '74 C.696 B.S. L.1009 J.D. [Joseloff&J.]
Joseloff & Joseloff, (BV) ....449 Silas Deane Hwy.
Kristofak, Stephen G., Jr., (BV) '39 '69 C.1030 B.S.S. L.128 J.D.
850 Silas Deane Hwy.
Krochmalny, Michael W. .... '49 '79 C.790 B.A. L.190 J.D. State Dept. of Motor Vehicles
Lazarek, Lisa S. ....'63 '94 C.783 B.A. L.184 J.D. Asst. Coun.
Lipes, Russell M., Jr. ....'21 '55 C.679 B.S. L.184 LL.B. 74 Boulder Rd. (Pat.)
Malesta, Michael ....'61 '86 C.454 B.B.A. L.472 J.D. Associate Counsel, Hartford
Malliet, Jerome T., (AV) ....'17 '48 C.262 B.S. L.184 LL.B. 43 Maxwell Dr.‡
Mayo, Walter H., (AV) ....'36 '61 C.674 A.B. L.309 LL.B. [Ⓒ Mayo,G.&Z.]

Mayo, Gilligan & Zito, LLP, (AV)
Putnam Park, 100 Great Meadow Road, 06109-2396
Telephone: 860-721-7725 Fax: 860-529-0493
URL: http://www.mayogilligan.com
Members of Firm: Edward A. Zito; Robert G. Gilligan; John J. Murphy; David S. Hoopes; William R. Crowe; James M. Scaramozza; Gregory F. DeManche; Glenn Powell; Sean P. Clark. Associates: Dean F. Radke; Noreen A. Dillman; J. Martin Acevedo. Of Counsel: Walter H. Mayo.
Trials in all Courts, Real Estate, Banking and Commercial Finance, Creditors' Rights and Bankruptcy, Employment, Business Law, Zoning, Environmental, Estate Planning, Elder Law, Probate and Personal Injury Law.
See Professional Biographies, WETHERSFIELD, CONNECTICUT

McCarthy, Patrice Ann, (BV) '57 '81 C.518 B.A. L.184 J.D. Gen. Coun., Conn. Assn. of Bds. of Educ.
McMahon, Nancy Owens . . . '66 '91 C.1102 B.S L.1029 J.D. [Rothenberg,R.&R.]
McQueeney, William A., (BV) . . . '27 '54 C&L.184 B.A., LL.B. Asst. Atty. Gen.
Mikol, Irene DiPietro '54 '84 C.829 B.A. L.1048 J.D. Claims Supervisor, Comm. on Victim Servs.
Moller, Charles E., Jr., (BV) . . . '28 '58 C.855 A.B. L.184 LL.B. 185 Broad St.
Murphy, John J., (BV) . . . '55 '81 C.299 A.B. L.262 J.D. [Mayo,G.&Z.]
*PRACTICE AREAS: Commercial Finance; Banking; Corporate Law; Business Law.
Myrun, Maurice . . . '12 '34 C.563 B.A. L.178 LL.B. 415 Silas Deane Hwy.
Napierata, Walter J., (BV) . . . '26 '59 C.623 B.S. L.184 LL.B. 123 Olney Rd.
Nichols, Peter . . . '16 '46 C&L.724 LL.B. 704 Ridge Rd.
Norsigian, Gregory C. . . . '62 '91 C.855 B.A. L.306 J.D. 334 Fox Hill Rd.
Novak, Anthony S., (BV) . . . '52 '82 C.184 B.A. L.1048 J.D. [Chorches&N.]
*PRACTICE AREAS: Bankruptcy Law; Commercial Law; Workouts; Representation before Internal Revenue Service.
O'Connell, Edward Y. . . . '30 '54 C&L.184 B.A., LL.B. Appl. Ct. J.
Odell, Frederick W., (BV) . . . '44 '69 C.829 B.A. L.184 J.D. 41 Oldham Rd.
O'Sullivan, William J., (BV) . . . '59 '90 C&L.184 B.A., J.D. [Baker O.&B.]
*PRACTICE AREAS: Business Litigation; Commercial Litigation; Creditors Rights.
Owen, Brent M. . . . '— '88 L.306 J.D. 42 Wells Farm Dr.
Pearlman, Susan T., (AV) . . . '46 '74 C.881 A.B. L.184 J.D. Asst. Atty. Gen.
Pelgrift, Robert Y. . . . '21 '49 C.309 A.B. L.184 LL.B. 24 Wolcott Hill Rd.‡
Petrelli, Frederick E., Jr. . . . '44 '75 C.434 B.A. L.184 J.D. 790 Wells Rd.
Pitt, Robert Francis, Jr. . . . '53 '79 C&L.602 B.A., J.D. Stewart Title Co.
Polivy, Denise R. . . . '53 '97 C.918 B.A. L.184 J.D. [Ⓐ Baker O.&B.]
*PRACTICE AREAS: Bankruptcy; Creditors Rights.
Powell, Glenn, (BV) . . . '53 '78 C.1019 B.A. L.188 J.D. [Mayo,G.&Z.]
*PRACTICE AREAS: Labor and Employment; Arbitration; Mediation; Alternative Dispute Resolution; Employment Litigation.
Pudlin, Bennett . . . '47 '78 C.197 B.A. L.976 J.D. Dept. of Labor - Exec. Dir.
Radke, Dean F., (BV) . . . '50 '75 C.688 B.S. L.184 J.D. [Ⓐ Mayo,G.&Z.]
*PRACTICE AREAS: Commercial Real Estate; Commercial Transactions; Loan Workouts; Foreclosures; Banking Law.
Ridolfo, James P., Jr. . . . '43 '77 C&L.184 B.A., J.D. Revenue Agent, I.R.S.
Roberts, Geraldine A. . . . '50 '82 C.725 B.A. L.1048 J.D. 64 Old Post Rd.
Rogers Parsons, A. Elaine . . . '63 '88 C.1048 B.A. L.184 J.D. Dept. of Labor
Rothenberg, Allan M. . . . '66 '90 C.184 B.S. L.1048 J.D. [Rothenberg,R.&R.]
Rothenberg, Seymour A., (BV) . . . '28 '53 C.184 B.A. L.94 LL.B. [Rothenberg,R.&R.]
Rothenberg, Rothenberg & Rothenberg, P.C., (BV) . . . 239 Silas Deane Hwy.

Ruhe, Barbara J., (BV) '48 '76 C&L.879 B.A., J.D.
415 Silas Deane Highway, Suite 304, 06109
Telephone: 860-513-5650 Fax: 860-513-5654
Email: rusoetal@courant.infi.net
***PRACTICE AREAS: Adoption; Matrimonial; Juvenile; Custody.**
Associate: Jonathan W. A. Ruhe. Of Counsel: Milagros S. Cruz.
Adoption, Matrimonial, Juvenile and Custody Law.
See Professional Biographies, WETHERSFIELD, CONNECTICUT

Ruhe, Jonathan W. A., (BV) . . . '62 '87 C&L.879 B.S., J.D. [Ⓐ B.J.Ruhe]
*PRACTICE AREAS: Real Estate; Juvenile; Matrimonial; Custody.

Sabatini and Associates, LLC
(See Newington)

Scaramozza, James M., (BV) . . . '59 '87 C.1030 B.A. L.1194 J.D. [Mayo,G.&Z.]
*PRACTICE AREAS: Commercial and Real Estate Finance; Affordable Housing; Nonprofit and Charitable Organizations; Corporate; Business Law.
Shaw, Keith S., (CV) . . . '56 '82 C.102 B.S. L.1048 J.D. 1160 Silas Dean Highway
Sikorsky, Igor I., Jr., (BV) . . . '29 '56 C&L.976 B.A., LL.B. 6 Chamberlain Rd.
Silver, Alan B., (BV) . . . '47 '73 C.184 B.A. L.818 J.D. [A.B.Silver]

Silver, Alan B., LLC, Law Offices of, (BV)
274 Silas Dean Highway, 06109
Telephone: 860-257-9327 Fax: 860-257-9324
Email: attyalansilver@cyberzone.net
Alan B. Silver.
Bankruptcy, Business Law, Commercial Law, Real Estate, Personal Injury.
See Professional Biographies, WETHERSFIELD, CONNECTICUT

Snider, William A. . . . '67 '95 C.823 B.A. L.1048 J.D. 280 Main St.
Spoll, Lisbeth R. . . . '57 '86 C.103 B.A. L.184 J.D. 1701 Asylum Ave.
Staines, Brian B. . . . '59 '89 C.1102 B.S. L.1029 J.D. [Ⓐ L.N.Johnson]
Streeto, James B. . . . '62 '87 C.855 B.A. L.184 J.D. 217 Highcrest Rd.

Strong, Patricia M. '50 '77 C.183 A.B. L.184 J.D.
415 Silas Deane Highway, Suite 220, 06109-1735
Telephone: 860-571-7440 Fax: 860-571-7436
Email: pstronglaw@aol.com URL: http://www.lawyers.com/pstronglaw
Employment and Labor Law, Civil Litigation in all State and Federal Courts, Administrative Law, Workers Compensation, Collections, Social Security Law.
See Professional Biographies, WETHERSFIELD, CONNECTICUT

Swafford, Roberta A. '44 '84 C.31 B.A. L.184 J.D. Sr. Admin. Hearings Atty., Dept. of Motor Vehicles
Sweeney, James M. . . . '21 '59 C.1033 B.S. L.184 LL.B. 82 Ridge Crest Circle‡
Sztaba, Stephen P., (CV) . . . '54 '79 C&L.184 B.A., J.D. 775 Ridge Rd.
Terk, Glenn T., (BV) . . . '49 '76 C.158 B.M.E. L.184 J.D. 81 Wolcott Hill Road
Theaker, Stephen B., (BV) . . . '52 '82 C.184 B.S. L.1048 J.D. 280 Main St.
Varano, Gina M., (BV) . . . '61 '88 C.183 B.A. L.184 J.D. 1260 Silas Deane Highway
Volk, John Pierce . . . '46 '83 C.976 B.A. L.93 J.D. Dept. of Labor
Yacavone, John P., Jr., (BV) . . . '46 '78 C&L.184 B.A., J.D. Asst. Atty. Gen.
Zanta, Jaye Bailey . . . '61 '87 C.690 B.A. L.306 J.D. Gen. Coun., State Bd. of Labor Rel.
Zito, Edward A., (AV) . . . '30 '59 C.855 B.A. L.184 LL.B. [Mayo,G.&Z.]
*PRACTICE AREAS: General Practice; Probate; Elder Law; Real Estate.

WILLIMANTIC, 14,652, *Windham Co.*

Bacharach, Pamela S. . . . '63 '89 C.904 B.A. L.818 J.D. 720 Main St.
Bates, Lawrence W., Jr. . . . '43 '77 C.1036 B.A. L.184 J.D. 14 Mansfield Ave.
Bergert, Shirley J., (BV) . . . '50 '75 C.446 B.G.S. L.1162 J.D. CT Legal Services, Inc.
Blanchard, Christopher, (CV) . . . '65 '90 C.67 B.A. L.184 J.D. 433 Valley St.

Boland, St. Onge & Brouillard
(See Putnam)

Brody, Paul I. . . . '48 '74 C&L.184 B.A., J.D. Excelsior Gaming, LLC
Chappell, Oliver S. . . . '— '64 C.103 A.B. L.145 J.D. 452 Jackson St.
Connors, Kevin C., (BV) . . . '54 '79 C&L.184 B.A., J.D. [Treiber,G.&C.]
*PRACTICE AREAS: Personal Injury Law; Civil Litigation; Criminal Law; Administrative Law; Probate.
Crockett, Douglas M., (BV) '39 '64 C.188 A.B. L.184 LL.B. Chf. Coun., Conn. Legal Servs.
Dale, Edward M. . . . '47 '75 C.550 B.A. L.1162 J.D. Dir., Conn. Legal Servs., Inc.
Dannehy, Joseph P. F. . . . '17 '43 C.93 A.B. L.188 LL.B. Ret. Assoc. Supm. Ct. Jus.
DeAngelis, Mark J., (BV) . . . '56 '81 C.184 B.S. L.818 J.D. 125 Mountain St.
Deschamps, Deborah A., (CV) . . . '57 '87 C.999 B.A. L.1029 J.D. 720 Main St.
Favreau, Pamala Jean, (CV) . . . '56 '89 C.999 B.S. L.1048 J.D. 756 Main St.
Gaucher, Harry S., Jr., (AV) . . . '25 '52 C&L.184 B.A., LL.B. 18 Selden St.‡
Gaucher and Peters, (BV) . . . 45 Church St.
Guarnaccia, Giacomo J., Jr., (BV) . . . '48 '74 C.1062 B.A. L.945 J.D. [Treiber,G.&C.]
*PRACTICE AREAS: Real Estate; Business Law; Corporate Law; Probate and Wills; Elder Law.
Heller, Paul A. . . . '38 '67 C.659 B.S.Ec. L.94 J.D. 366 Pleasant St.
Kelley, Richard A. . . . '32 '60 C&L.184 B.A., LL.B. Pub. Def.‡
Lamont, Daniel K., (BV) . . . '36 '65 C.602 B.S. L.424 J.D. 126 Storrs Rd.
Lane & Rosen, P.C., (AV) . . . 433 Valley Street
Lombardo, Michael J. . . . '27 '74 C&L.184 B.S., J.D. 6 Storrs Rd.‡
Magliocco, Michael C., (BV) . . . '51 '77 C.184 B.S. L.851 J.D. 14 Mansfield Ave.
Mandour, Laila A. . . . '56 '87 C.1156 B.S. L.1202 J.D. 720 Main St.
Mark, James R. . . . '53 '87 C.321 B.A. L.184 J.D. 452 Jackson St.
Mossberg, Sheldon A., (BV) . . . '47 '85 C.689 B.A. L.184 J.D. 90 S. Park St.
O'Brien, Dennis J., (BV) . . . '43 '72 C&L.184 B.A., J.D. [Ⓐ H.B.Schiller]

Paradiso & Muska
(See Stafford Springs)

Paun, Jerome W. . . . '50 '80 C.1044 B.S. L.107 J.D. 280 Jackson St.
Peters, Conrad A., (BV) . . . '46 '76 C.184 B.A. L.221 J.D. [Gaucher&P.]
Popple, Charles J. . . . '47 '72 C&L.184 B.A., J.D. 727 Main St.
Potter, Russell F., Jr. . . . '36 '61 C&L.184 B.A., LL.B. Supr. Ct. J.
Prue, Patrick M. . . . '51 '80 C.184 B.A. L.1048 J.D. [P.M.Prue&Assoc.]
Prue, Patrick M., & Associates, P.C., Law Offices of . . . 720 Main St.
Rosen, Jerome A., (AV) . . . '36 '61 C.976 B.A. L.309 J.D. [Lane&R.]
Sauer, Diane M., (BV) . . . '55 '80 C.339 B.S. L.352 J.D. 90 South Park
Schiller, Howard B., (BV) . . . '49 '75 C.918 B.A. L.184 J.D. 55 Church Street
Segarra, Miguel A. . . . '56 '94 L.306 J.D. 713 Main St.
Shepard, Omar H., Jr., (AV) . . . '32 '57 C&L.184 B.S., LL.B. 45 Church St.
Sinder, Joan B., (CV) . . . '49 '74 C.938 B.A. L.823 J.D. 756 Main St.
Stein, Judith Ann, (BV) '— '75 C.951 B.A. L.128 J.D. Exec. Dir., Ctr. for Medicare Advocacy, Inc.
Thoresen, Jean H. . . . '44 '89 C.518 B.A. L.1048 J.D. 243 Church St.
Treiber, David C., (BV) . . . '45 '70 C.745 B.A. L.184 J.D. [Treiber,G.&C.]
*PRACTICE AREAS: Real Estate; Probate and Wills; Elder Law; Civil Litigation; Personal Injury.

Treiber, Guarnaccia & Connors, (BV)
25 Church Street, P.O. Box 44, 06226
Telephone: 860-423-6308 Fax: 860-423-6344
Email: TGCLAW@NECA.COM
Members of Firm: David C. Treiber; Giacomo J. Guarnaccia, Jr.; Kevin C. Connors.
General Practice. Real Estate, Probate, Estate Planning, Commercial, Corporation, Personal Injury, Construction, Domestic Relations and Municipal Law. Civil and Criminal Trials in all Courts. Practice before Administrative Agencies.
See Professional Biographies, WILLIMANTIC, CONNECTICUT

WILTON, 15,351, *Fairfield Co.*

Adams, Edward M., Jr. '50 '76 C.262 B.S. L.1338 J.D. (adm. in NY; not adm. in CT) 23 Old Wagon Rd.‡
Adams, Thomas T., (AV) . . . '29 '57 C.107 A.B. L.188 J.D. [Gregory&A.] ⊙
*PRACTICE AREAS: Trusts and Estates; Probate; Real Estate; Zoning.
Aronoff, Carol R. '42 '67 C.914 A.B. L.659 LL.B. Secy. & Asst. Gen. Coun., Louis Dreyfus Holding Co. Inc. & V.P., Louis Dreyfus Corp.
Augenbraun, Sara Spielman . . . '53 '77 C.881 B.A. L.884 J.D. 3 Weathervane Lane‡
Barcan, Reina '51 '77 C.165 B.A. L.276 J.D. Asst. Gen. Coun., Louis Dreyfus Holding Co., Inc.
Bayer, Douglas I. . . . '68 '94 C.401 B.S. L.1009 J.D. [Ⓐ J.D.Paul&Assoc.]
Beebe, Marcus P., III '37 '67 C.165 B.A. L.477 LL.B. (adm. in NY; not adm. in CT) 41 Nod Hill Rd.‡
Bennett, Kirk A., (BV) . . . '53 '79 C.823 B.A. L.273 J.D. [Sinchak&B.]
*PRACTICE AREAS: Domestic Relations; Litigation; Trial Practice; Criminal and Civil.
Berg, Maxine R. . . . '64 '90 C.696 B.A. L.978 J.D. 20 Irmgard Lane
Birck, Karen A., (BV) . . . '53 '80 C.788 A.B. L.184 J.D. 239 Thunder Lake Rd.
Blakeslee, Katherine T., (BV) . . . '49 '88 C.914 B.A. L.1029 J.D. [Flynn&B.]
*PRACTICE AREAS: Family Law; Real Estate; Probate; Estates.
Blankmeyer, Kurt V. . . . '37 '73 C.309 A.B. L.976 J.D. 144 Signal Hill Road
Briody, Thomas A., (AV) . . . '29 '60 C.884 B.E.E. L.273 J.D. 225 Thayer Pond Rd. (Pat.)
Brotherton, Ronald P. '33 '58 C.659 B.S. L.309 J.D. (adm. in NY; not adm. in CT) 5 Saddle Ridge Rd
Buchanan, William H., Jr., (AVⓉ) '37 '64 C.674 A.B. L.309 LL.B. (adm. in NY; not adm. in CT) 187 Danbury Rd.
Busch, Jeffrey S., (BVⓉ) . . . '63 '88 C.156 B.A. L.1194 J.D. 31 Deforest Rd.
Cannella, Philip '33 '71 C.1138 B.B.A. L.724 J.D. (adm. in NY; not adm. in CT) 41 Ledgewood Dr.
Cardillo, Judith L. '63 '89 C.1040 B.A. L.569 J.D. (adm. in CA; not adm. in CT) Law Audit Servs.
Chulick, Andrew . . . '20 '57 C.1019 B.S. L.569 LL.B. 14 Bossy Ln.
Connelly, Andrew J. '37 '65 C.602 B.A. L.178 LL.B. (adm. in NY; not adm. in CT) V.P. & Gen. Coun., Louis Dreyfus Holding Co., Inc.
Cousins, W. James, Jr., (AV) . . . '53 '79 C.72 B.A. L.262 J.D. [McGowan&C.] ⊙
Crane, Anne E. . . . '56 '88 C.1349 B.A. L.569 J.D. [Gregory&A.]
*PRACTICE AREAS: Estate Planning; Trusts and Estates; Probate.
Creavin, Susan M. '58 '90 (adm. in NY; not adm. in CT) 49 Granite Dr.
Curtis, William R. . . . '14 '47 C.855 B.S. L.976 LL.B. 32 Old Farm Rd.‡
Delmar, Christine M. . . . '53 '82 C.914 B.A. L.276 J.D. 85 Rivergate Dr.
Dembitzer, Herbert M. . . . '34 '92 C.569 B.A. L.262 J.D. 94 Rivergate Dr.
DeSantis, Robert J. . . . '55 '82 C.659 B.S.E. L.93 J.D. 222 Dudley Rd.
Edwards, Elizabeth A. . . . '49 '86 C.1029 B.S. L.1040 J.D. 436 Danbury Rd.
Flynn, Charles P., (AV) . . . '39 '64 C.264 A.B. L.276 J.D. [Flynn&B.]
*PRACTICE AREAS: General Practice; Estate Planning; Real Estate; Business Law.

Flynn & Blakeslee, P.C., (AV)
80 Old Ridgefield Road, Wilton Center, P.O. Box 265, 06897
Telephone: 203-762-2451 Fax: 203-762-5537
Email: KTBESQ@aol.com
Charles P. Flynn; Katherine T. Blakeslee.
General Practice, Real Estate, Probate, Estate and Tax Planning, Business Organization, Planning and Zoning, Family, Common Ownership Communities, and Litigation.

Frees, Barbara S. '46 '76 C&L.262 B.A., J.D.
(adm. in NY; not adm. in CT) 5 River Rd.‡
Frisch, Patricia L. ....'55 '84 C.95 B.A. L.976 J.D. [Frisch&F.]
Frisch, Roger ....'33 '61 C.976 B.A. L.477 J.D. [Frisch&F.]
Frisch & Frisch .... 166 Ridgefield Road
Fuller, Robert A. ....'40 '64 C.197 B.A. L.659 LL.B. 75 E. Meadow Rd.
Gerlin, Robert A., (BV) .... '32 '61 C.732 B.A. L.178 LL.B. 190‡
Gill, Daren K. '66 '91 C&L.184 B.A., J.D.
(adm. in MA; not adm. in CT) 183 Westport Rd.‡
Goldman, Susan Lacy, (BV) ....'57 '85 C.174 B.A. L.1048 J.D. [Gregory&A.]
*PRACTICE AREAS: Real Estate; Zoning; Planning; Land Use.
Gordon, Stephanie Hack ....'64 '92 C.1044 B.S. L.1009 J.D. 65 Charter Oak Dr.
Grealy, Cornelius J. '58 '85 C.262 A.B. L.976 J.D.
Asst. Gen. Coun., Louis Dreyfus Holding Co., Inc.
Gregory, Julian A., (AV) .... '12 '39 C.674 A.B. L.477 J.D. [Gregory&A.] ⊙
*PRACTICE AREAS: Trusts and Estates.

Gregory and Adams, P.C., (AV)
190 Old Ridgefield Road, 06897 ⊙
Telephone: 203-762-9000 Telefacsimile: 203-834-1628
Thomas T. Adams; Anne E. Crane; Susan Lacy Goldman; J. Casey Healy; Michael P. Kaelin; Maryann D. Lally; Derrel M. Mason; Matthew C. Mason; Ralph E. Slater; Julie S. Schechter. Senior Counsel: Julian A. Gregory.
General Practice. Zoning, Planning and Land Use. Litigation. Commercial, Corporate/Transactional Law. Consumer Regulatory Matters. E-Commerce. General Counsel Services. Trusts and Estates. Taxation.
New York, N.Y. Office: 156 West 56th Street, 10019. Telephone: 212-757-0434. Telefacsimile: 212-977-9583.
See Professional Biographies, WILTON, CONNECTICUT

Harrison, Michael, III '57 '86 C.705 B.A. L.309 J.D.
(adm. in NJ; not adm. in CT)
V.P. & Gen. Coun., Danone Groupe-N. American Affiliates
Healy, J. Casey, (BV) .... '56 '83 C.812 B.S. L.245 J.D. [Gregory&A.]
*PRACTICE AREAS: Real Estate; Zoning; Planning; Land Use.
Higgins, Julianne McKenna '59 '86 C.433 B.S.B.A. L.262 J.D.
(adm. in NJ; not adm. in CT) 27 Briardale Pl.
Hojnacki, Cynthia L. ....'64 '90 C&L.724 J.D. 58 Range Rd.
Holt, Carl T. ....'46 '82 C.851 B.A. L.1048 J.D. P.O. Box 7278
Hughes, Raymond H. '45 '73 C&L.178 A.B., J.D.
(adm. in NY; not adm. in CT) Pres., Hyde Park Products, Inc.
Ipe, J. Bruce ....'38 '63 C.935 B.A. L.188 LL.B. 31 Rivergate Dr.‡
Johnson, Daniel R. '38 '63 C&L.477 B.A., LL.B.
(adm. in OH; not adm. in CT) 82 Kellogg Dr.‡
Jones, Valerie Brasswell ....'49 '95 C.1023 B.S. L.1252 J.D. 25 River Rd.
Joyce, Virginia M. '54 '81 C.881 A.B. L.724 J.D.
(adm. in NY; not adm. in CT) 201 Dudley Rd.
Kaelin, Michael P., (AV) ....'59 '85 C&L.228 B.A., J.D. [Gregory&A.] ⊙
*PRACTICE AREAS: Litigation; Employment Law.
Kemp, Gail M., (BV) ....'53 '79 C.1374 B.A. L.1049 J.D. 23 Hubbard Rd.
Klein, Gerald E. '48 '76 C.102 B.A. L.569 J.D.
Secretary & General Counsel, Mercator Software, Inc.

Kulawitz, Harvey J., LLC
(See Ridgefield)

Lally, Maryann D. ....'60 '95 C.390 B.A. L.1040 J.D. [Gregory&A.]
*PRACTICE AREAS: Corporate; Zoning; Planning; Land Use; Real Estate.
Lamb, Frederic D. ....'31 '57 C.894 B.A. L.477 J.D. 30 Keelers Ridge Rd.
Lane, George, (BV) ....'24 '52 C&L.276 B.S., J.D. 120 Old Ridgefield Rd.
Lovejoy and Rimer, P.C., (AV) .... 44 Old Ridgefield Road, Second Floor (⊙Norwalk)
Marquardt, Donald E. '22 '48 C.966 L.309 LL.B.
(adm. in MA; not adm. in CT) 24 Seir Hill Rd.‡
Mason, Derrel M. ....'60 '86 C&L.276 B.S.B.A., J.D. [Gregory&A.] ⊙
*PRACTICE AREAS: Corporate Law; Lending.
Mason, Matthew C., (BV) ....'56 '82 C.105 B.A. L.564 J.D. [Gregory&A.] ⊙
*PRACTICE AREAS: Litigation; Commercial Litigation; Employment Litigation; Securities Litigation.
McCartney, Terri J. ....'59 '86 John Frieda Prof. Hair Care, Inc.
McGowan, Frank A., Jr., (AV) ....'51 '79 C.884 B.A. L.262 J.D. [McGowan&C.] ⊙
McGowan & Cousins, P.C., (AV) ....15 Cannon Road (⊙White Plains, NY)
Melton, Ruby H. '50 '84 C.320 B.A. L.262 J.D.
Asst. Gen. Coun., Louis Dreyfus Holding Co., Inc.
Minor, James V. ....'47 '75 C.976 B.A. L.184 J.D. 27 Pelhan Lane‡
Murray, Harlan W. '33 '59 C.69 B.A. L.569 LL.B.
(adm. in NY; not adm. in CT) 25 Deacons Ln.‡
Neff, Deborah Jean '56 '85 C.914 B.A. L.178 J.D.
V.P. & Assoc. Coun., Louis Dreyfus Holding Co., Inc.
Nulty, Frank J. '29 '57 C&L.262 B.A., LL.B.
(adm. in NY; not adm. in CT) 240 Linden Tree Rd.‡
Olexo, George R., (CV) ....'25 '59 C.1029 B.A. L.273 J.D. (J.P.)
Paul, John D., (BV) .... '45 '71 C.659 B.S. L.262 J.D. [J.D.Paul&Assoc.]
Paul, John D., & Associates, P.C., (BV) .... 436 Danbury Rd.
Perry, Gregory M., (BV) ....'43 '68 C.674 A.B. L.188 J.D. [Perry&M.]
*PRACTICE AREAS: General Practice; Probate; Trusts; Estates; Real Estate.

Perry and McKendry, (BV)
44 Old Ridgefield Road, P.O. Box 517, 06897
Telephone: 203-762-3301 Fax: 203-762-3631
Members of Firm: Albert L. Perry (1907-1992); George F. McKendry (1917-1997); Gregory M. Perry.
General Practice. Probate, Trusts, Estate Planning and Real Estate.
Reference: The Wilton Bank, Wilton, Connecticut.
See Professional Biographies, WILTON, CONNECTICUT

Reuman, Alice C. '47 '74 C.910 B.A. L.966 J.D.
(adm. in IL; not adm. in CT) 15 Richdale St.‡
Roe, David '38 '64 C.659 B.S. L.569 LL.B.
(adm. in NY; not adm. in CT) 11 Bryants Brook Rd.‡
Salvin, Arthur H., (BV) ....'29 '54 C.184 B.S. L.94 LL.B. [Salvin&S.]
Salvin & Salvin, (BV) .... 259 Danbury Rd.
Sayegh, Miriam H. .... '61 '89 C&L.1040 B.B.A., J.D. P.O. Box 0217
Schaffer, John P. '45 '72 C.705 B.A. L.1009 J.D.
(adm. in NY; not adm. in CT) Lamorte Burns & Co., Inc.
Schechter, Julie S. ....'58 '85 C.103 A.B. L.846 J.D. [Gregory&A.] ⊙
*PRACTICE AREAS: Consumer Regulatory; Corporate; E-Commerce.

Scheuer, Thomas '28 '53 C.30 B.A. L.178 LL.B.
Coun., Louis Dreyfus Holding Co., Inc.
Seblatnigg, Renée F. '— '94
C.861 B.A. L.1040 J.D. Appeals Attorney, Law Audit Services, Inc.
Sinchak, Thomas M., (BV) ....'54 '79 C.93 B.S. L.823 J.D. [Sinchak&B.]
*PRACTICE AREAS: Residential Real Estate; Commercial Real Estate; Probate; Trusts and Estates; Corporate Law.

Sinchak & Bennett, (BV)
120 Old Ridgefield Road, P.O. Box 460, 06897
Telephone: 203-762-0741 Fax: 203-762-3827
Thomas M. Sinchak; Kirk A. Bennett.
General Practice. Real Estate, Corporate, Probate, Family and Personal Injury and Criminal Law.
Reference: Union Trust Co.
See Professional Biographies, WILTON, CONNECTICUT

Singewald, Robert A., (BV) ....'43 '67 C.602 B.A. L.273 J.D. [Singewald&V.]
*PRACTICE AREAS: Real Estate; Zoning Law; Administrative Law; Corporate and Commercial Law; Estate Planning.

Singewald and Valkenburgh, (BV)
87 Old Ridgefield Road, P.O. Box 796, 06897
Telephone: 203-762-0042 Telecopier: 203-762-2095 v
Email: assist@svlaw.com URL: http://www.lawyers.com/sandvlaw
Robert A. Singewald; Roger R. Valkenburgh.
General Practice. Real Estate and Zoning Law, Probate, Estate Planning, Federal and State Tax, Corporate and Commercial Matters. Litigation.
Reference: The Wilton Bank.
See Professional Biographies, WILTON, CONNECTICUT

Slater, Ralph E., (BV) ....'48 '73 C.674 A.B. L.659 J.D. [Gregory&A.]
*PRACTICE AREAS: Estate Planning; Trusts and Estates; Probate; Taxation.
Slutsky, Michael A., (BV(T)) ....'42 '73 C.665 B.A. L.94 J.D. 48 Old Highway
Stansbury, Karen A. .... '62 '88 C.880 B.A. L.1252 J.D. 75 E. Meadow Rd.
Tate, Robert T., Jr. '19 '49 C.674 A.B. L.309 J.D.
(adm. in NY; not adm. in CT) 63 Wolfpit Rd.‡
Valkenburgh, Roger R., (BV) ....'47 '76 C.696 A.B. L.188 J.D. [Singewald&V.]
*PRACTICE AREAS: Probate Matters; Real Estate; Estate Planning.
Verron, Kathleen M. '48 '79 C.94 B.A. L.569 J.D.
(adm. in NY; not adm. in CT) 70 Hulda Hill Rd.‡
Wackerman, Karen P. ....'57 '86 C.788 A.B. L.1009 J.D. 37 Mayapple Rd.‡
Waugh, Raymond G., Jr. '59 '89 C.1369 B.S.
(adm. in NY; not adm. in CT) 23 Appletree Lane
Wolff, Thomas G., (BV) .... '54 '85 C.976 B.A. L.184 J.D. [McGowan&C.] ⊙
Ziskind, Charles G. ....'60 '91 C.659 B.S.B.A. L.724 J.D. 119 Indian Hill Rd.
Zucker, Judith B., (BV) ....'29 '81 C.788 B.A. L.569 J.D. 436 Danbury Rd.

WINDHAM, 21,062, *Windham Co.*

Haggerty, Robert J. .... '27 '63 C&L.184 B.S., J.D. 43 Indian Hollow Rd.‡
Spector, John A., (BV) .... '30 '56 C.823 A.B. L.94 LL.B. 107 Babcock Hill Rd.
Stearns, Douglas T., (CV) ....'60 '95 C.184 B.S. L.306 J.D. 75 Murphy Hill Rd.

WINDSOR, 25,204, *Hartford Co.*

Anderson, Larry B. '48 '75 C.1042 B.A. L.426 J.D.
(adm. in CA; not adm. in CT) Regional Mgr., U.S. Postal Servc.
Bell, Robert S., Jr. '43 '78 C.188 B.Ch.E. L.184 J.D.
Vice President, General Counsel & Secretary, CE Nuclear Power LLC
Brophy, Thomas F. ....'27 '77 C.1044 B.A. L.1048 J.D. 25 Bradford Dr.‡
Brown, Stephen C., (BV) ....'59 '87 C.696 B.A. L.1218 J.D. [Johnson,D.&B.]
*PRACTICE AREAS: Probate; Estate Planning; Medicaid; Elder Law.
Burt, Richard M. '44 '70 C.282 B.A. L.1017 J.D.
(adm. in NY; not adm. in CT)
V.P., Gen. Coun. & Secy., Combustion Engg., Inc. (⊙Norwalk)
Buttler, Donna L. ....'56 '94 C.696 B.A. L.184 J.D. 15 Settlement Hill
Claussen, John H. '48 '74 C.688 B.S. L.982 J.D.
(adm. in NY; not adm. in CT) Sr. V.P. & Gen. Coun., TRC Cos., Inc.
Corbly, Mark T. '51 '86 C.550 B.A. L.1294 J.D.
(adm. in ME; not adm. in CT) U.S. Postal Serv.
Crawford, Anna V. .... '57 '86 C.788 A.B. L.184 J.D. U.S. Postal Serv.
Cullen, Jeffrey P. ....'51 '80 C.478 B.A. L.306 J.D. Sagemark Consulting
Deneen, Donald J., (BV) ....'34 '62 C.829 B.S. L.184 J.D. [O'Malley,D.L.M.&O.]
Deneen, Kevin M., (BV) ....'60 '87 C.321 B.A. L.184 J.D. [O'Malley,D.L.M.&O.]
Deneen, Michael P., (BV) ....'59 '84 C.93 B.A. L.184 J.D. [O'Malley,D.L.M.&O.]
Dowe, Everett B., III, (BV) ....'53 '85 C.184 B.A. L.1228 J.D. [Johnson,D.&B.]
*PRACTICE AREAS: Real Estate; Zoning; Corporations.
Dudek, Charles J. '50 '89 C.262 B.S. L.1048 J.D.
(adm. in PA; not adm. in CT) U.S. Postal Serv.
Ferraina, Dominic J., (BV) .... '32 '57 C.321 A.B. L.184 LL.B. 65 Maple Ave.
Fournier, Arthur E., Jr. ....'35 '66 2000 Day Hill Rd. (Pat.)
Freeman, Andrew L., (AV) ....'48 '76 C.966 B.A. L.128 J.D. U.S. Postal Serv.
Gallaudet, Anne M. '53 '91 C.205 B.A. L.966 J.D.
(adm. in WI; not adm. in CT) U.S. Postal Serv.‡
Grace, James P., (BV) ....'48 '78 C.184 B.A. L.1048 J.D. 110 Day Hill Rd.
Haverstock, John S. .... '62 '87 C&L.893 B.A., J.D. 340 Broad St.
Hennessey, David J. ... '55 '80 C.158 B.S. L.982 J.D. V.P., Assoc. Gen. Coun., Advo Inc.
Hoffberg, Robert J. ....'57 '83 C.178 B.S. L.184 J.D. AIW-Alton, Inc.
Jermn, Janis C. .... '65 '93 C.679 B.A. L.184 J.D. [O'Malley,D.L.M.&O.]
Johnson, Warren P., (AV) ....'39 '65 C.855 B.A. L.184 J.D. [Johnson,D.&B.]
*PRACTICE AREAS: Probate; Estate Planning.

Johnson, Dowe & Brown, LLC, (AV)
22 Elm Street, 06095
Telephone: 860-688-6060 Fax: 860-688-8787
Email: steveb@portone.com
Warren P. Johnson; Everett B. Dowe, III; Stephen C. Brown.
Probate, Estate Planning, Real Estate, Zoning, Corporations and Elder Law.
See Professional Biographies, WINDSOR, CONNECTICUT

Kolovson, Mark J., (BV) ....'53 '78 C.860 B.A. L.818 J.D. V.P., Blue Bell Mattress Co.
Lavine, Nancy B. ....'47 '75 C.914 B.A. L.893 J.D. U.S. Postal Serv.
Leary, William C., (BV) ....'38 '65 C.676 A.B. L.184 J.D. [O'Malley,D.L.M.&O.] ⊙
Lerman, Kenneth B. ....'61 '87 C.156 B.A. L.245 J.D. [K.B.Lerman]

Lerman, Kenneth B., P.C.
651 Day Hill Road, 06095-0040
Telephone: 860-285-0700 Telecopier: 860-285-0139
Kenneth B. Lerman.
Corporate, Securities, Real Estate, Mergers/Acquisitions, Business, Venture Capital Financing and Commercial Law.
See Professional Biographies, WINDSOR, CONNECTICUT

Liggett, Thomas E. '49 '76 C.381 B.A. L.7 J.D.
(adm. in OH; not adm. in CT) 2000 Day Hill Rd.

Machado, Arthur, & Associates, (BV) '60 '90 C.473 B.A. L.306 J.D. 242 Bloomfield Ave.
McCarthy, Denise '69 '95 C.380 B.A. L.1048 J.D. Atty., Konica Bus. Technologies Inc.
*RESPONSIBILITIES: Contracts; Commercial Litigation.
McCormack, Dennis A., (BV) .... '51 '76 C.321 B.A. L.184 J.D. [Wall&M.]
Mendizabal, Lorenzo, (BV) ..... '59 '90 C.308 B.A. L.93 J.D. Assoc. Coun., The Hartford
Messina, Andrew G., Jr., (BV) ...... '40 '65 C&L.184 B.A., LL.B. [O'Malley,D.L.M.&O.]
Morelli, Carmen, (BV) .... '22 '55 C&L.94 B.S., LL.B. 66 Maple Ave.
Morelli, Richard A., (BV) .... '45 '71 C.184 B.S. L.150 J.D. 66 Maple Ave.
Noble, Michael T. '49 '74 C&L.184 B.A., J.D. Assistant Chief Counsel-Labor Law, ABB Business Servs. Inc.
Oliva, Pamela A. '60 '89 C.184 B.S. L.818 J.D. Envir. Coun., TRC Environ. Consultants, Inc.
O'Malley, Thomas J., (BV) .... '26 '54 C.976 B.A. L.276 J.D. [O'Malley,D.L.M.&O.]
O'Malley, Deneen, Leary, Messina & Oswecki, (BV) ...20 Maple Ave. (⊙Windsor Locks)
Oswecki, Vincent W., Jr., (BV) .... '43 '68 C.855 B.A. L.276 J.D. [O'Malley,D.L.M.&O.]
Parker, Rebecca A. '72 '98 C.938 B.A. L.1048 J.D. (adm. in MA; not adm. in CT) OH Cas. Grp. Ins. Co.
Petitjean, Barbara A. .... '55 '88 C.518 B.A. L.184 J.D. 500 Day Hill Rd.
Platt, Robert A., (BV) .... '36 '63 C&L.184 B.A., J.D. 186 High St.
Probst, Valdemar B. ..... '62 '93 C.705 B.S. L.1009 J.D. Counsel, CE Nuclear Power LLC
Reardon, Jacqueline M. .... '65 '90 C.1200 B.A. L.818 J.D. P.O. Box 778
Sanders, Annette .... '60 '85 C.31 B.A. L.184 J.D. 19 Fox Meadow Lane
Sevarino, Angelo Paul, (AV) .... '50 '80 C.184 B.A. L.1048 J.D. Mag.
Stigler, David M. '43 '69 C.604 A.B. L.145 J.D. (adm. in NY; not adm. in CT) Sr. V.P., Legal, Gen. Coun. & Corp. Secy., Advo Inc.
Stone, Meredith Barg, (AV) '59 '85 C.882 B.A. L.724 J.D. V.P., Gen. Coun. & Secy., Konica Bus. Technologies, Inc.
*RESPONSIBILITIES: Legal; Compliance; Risk Management; Safety and Environmental Functions; Contracts.
Susen, John W. '48 '73 C.708 B.A. L.818 J.D. (adm. in MA; not adm. in CT) Chf. Coun.-Employ. & Labor Law, ABB Business Servs. Inc.
Tepley, Adelbert T. '32 '64 C.363 B.S. L.1003 J.D. Dir. of Transp., ABB Asea Brown Boveri
Thrall, Joseph B., II .... '64 '91 C.976 B.A. L.436 J.D. 65 Thrall Rd.
Venishnick, Joseph K. .... '45 '83 2000 Day Hill Rd.
Walker, Raymond A., Jr. .... '49 '89 C.999 B.A. L.1048 J.D. Fire Marshall
Wall, John A., (BV) .... '47 '75 C.93 B.A. L.184 J.D. [Wall&M.]
Wall & McCormack, P.C., (BV) .... 860 Prospect Hill Rd.
Windham, Eileen '65 '91 C.1175 B.S. L.838 J.D. (adm. in FL; not adm. in CT) 2000 Day Hill Road

WINDSOR LOCKS, 12,190, *Hartford Co.*

Bacon & Wilson, P.C.
334 Ella Grasso Turnpike, 06096 ⊙
Telephone: 860-623-6482 Fax: 860-654-1948
Email: bacon-wilson@bacon-wilson.com
—Jay A. Gabriel.
General Civil and Business Practice. Trials in all courts. Trust and Estate Planning, Elder Law, Product Liability, Personal Injury, Employment Law, Employers' Rights, Medical Negligence, Mergers and Acquisitions, Banking, Real Estate, Franchise Law, Bankruptcy and Commercial Reorganization, Health Care Law, Probate, Family Law, Immigration Law, OSHA Compliance, Criminal Law, Domestic Relations.
Springfield, Massachusetts Office: 33 State Street, 01103. Telephone: 413-781-0560. Fax: 413-739-7740.
Westfield, Massachusetts Office: 9 Chapel Street, 01085. Telephone: 413-562-9607. Fax: 413-562-7589.
Northampton, Massachusetts Office: 351 Pleasant Street, 01060. Telephone: 413-584-3280. Fax: 413-586-5959.
See Professional Biographies, WINDSOR LOCKS, CONNECTICUT

Banis, Lynn .... '55 '82 C.788 B.A. L.1048 J.D. Asst. Coun., Hamilton Standard
Blackburn, Stuart G., (BV) .... '55 '81 C&L.884 B.A., J.D. [S.G.Blackburn]
Blackburn, Stuart G., Law Offices of, (BV) .... 516 Spring St.
Bromson, Christopher W., (BV) .... '60 '85 C.94 B.S. L.1048 J.D. [Bromson&R.]
Bromson and Reiner, (BV) .... 546 Halfway House Road
Byrne, Margaret M., (BV) .... '65 '90 C.184 B.A. L.1048 J.D. [Ⓐ Bromson&R.]
Currier, Keith J. .... '71 '96 C.829 B.A. L.1252 J.D. [Ⓐ S.G.Blackburn]
Endrelunas, Richard M., (BV) ..... '42 '69 C.745 B.A. L.184 J.D. 546 Halfway House Rd.
Fahey, Thomas W., Jr., (BV) .... '47 '73 C.103 A.B. L.276 J.D. [Fahey,L.&Assoc.]
Fahey, Landolina & Associates, LLC, (BV) .... 487 Spring Street, Suite Two
Filip, Edwin P. .... '36 '76 C.1033 B.S.E.E. L.1048 J.D. 4 Olive St.‡
Gabriel, Jay A., (BV) '60 '86 C.93 B.A. L.861 J.D. [Ⓐ Bacon&W.] (⊙Springfield, MA)
*PRACTICE AREAS: Probate Law; Tax Law; Wills; Estate Planning; Elder Law.
Griffin, Brian T., (BV) .... '55 '80 C.021 B.A. L.425 J.D. 18 Suffield St.
Kelly, Robert H. '42 '78 C.864 B.E.M.E. L.472 J.D. (adm. in FL; not adm. in CT; Pat.) Asst. Coun., Hamilton Standard
Kervick, J. Christopher, (BV) .... '62 '87 C.262 B.A. L.128 J.D. [Post&K.]
Landolina, Carl, (BV) .... '58 '86 C.156 B.A. L.184 J.D. [Fahey,L.&Assoc.]
Leary, William C., (BV) .... '38 '65 C.676 A.B. L.184 J.D. [O'Malley,D.L.M.&O.] ⊙
Leis, Donald G., Jr., (BV) .... '45 '72 C.602 B.A. L.184 J.D. [Bromson&R.]
Linardos, George S. .... '24 '56 C.855 B.A. L.184 J.D. 546 Halfway House Rd.
Love, Joseph D. '40 '66 C&L.421 B.M.E., J.D. (adm. in KY; not adm. in CT) V.P., Contracts & Coun., Hamilton Standard
McManus, Dennis M. .... '69 '95 C.184 B.A. L.1048 J.D. [Ⓐ Bromson&R.]
O'Malley, Deneen, Leary, Messina & Oswecki, (BV) .... 487 Spring St. (⊙Windsor)
Post, Philip A., (BV) .... '31 '59 C.855 B.S. L.184 J.D. [Post&K.]
Post & Kervick, (BV) .... 3 Concorde Way
Reiner, Irving, (BV) .... '26 '59 C.855 B.A. L.184 LL.B. 546 Halfway House Rd.‡
Rosenthal, William E. '53 '79 C.665 B.A. L.365 J.D. (adm. in NY; not adm. in CT) Dep. Coun., Hamilton Standard
Sanderson, Harry N., Jr., (BV) .... '49 '75 C.184 B.A. L.1202 J.D. [Ⓐ Bromson&R.]
Stephenson, Gregory R. '64 '96 C.477 B.S.M.E. L.94 J.D. (adm. in CA; not adm. in CT; Pat.) Asst. Intellectual Property Coun., Hamilton Sundstrand Corp.
Storms, Dale Ann Feinblatt, (BV) .... '55 '81 C.529 B.A. L.1029 J.D. [Ⓐ Storms&S.]
Storms, Ronald F., (BV) .... '31 '60 C.855 B.A. L.184 J.D. [Storms&S.]
Storms, Scott A., (BV) .... '55 '80 C.1033 B.A. L.1029 J.D. [Storms&S.]
Storms & Storms, (BV) .... 18 Suffield St.
Ward, Anthony C. .... '09 '41 C.855 L.569 LL.B. Pres., Windsor Locks Svgs. & Loan
Wenc, David J., (BV) .... '51 '76 C.321 B.A. L.1048 J.D. [Wenc] ⊙

Wenc Law Offices, (BV)
44 Main Street, 06096-1435 ⊙
Telephone: 860-623-1195 Fax: 860-292-6705
Email: davidjwenc@dellnet.com
David J. Wenc.

(This Listing Continued)

Wenc Law Offices (Continued)
General Civil and Criminal Practice before State and Federal Courts. Business Law, Criminal Defense, Employment Law, Family Law, Personal Injury, Probate and Real Estate.
Springfield, Massachusetts Office: 175 State Street, Suite 500. Telephone: 413-746-1804.

WINSTED, 8,954, *Litchfield Co.*

Brooks, Donna J., (BV) .... '51 '77 C.293 B.A. L.184 J.D. [Dixon&B.]
Cusick, David M., (BV) .... '45 '69 C.299 B.A. L.893 LL.B. [Howd,L.&F.]
Dixon, Judith A., (BV) .... '48 '78 C.103 A.B. L.184 J.D. [Dixon&B.]
Dixon, Susan E., (CV) .... '51 '81 C&L.184 B.A., J.D. [Goring&D.]
Dixon & Brooks, P.C., (BV) .... 45 Center St.
Dougherty, Marlene A. .... '57 '97 C.1044 B.A. L.306 J.D. [Lavieri&D.] ‡
*PRACTICE AREAS: General Practice; Family Law; Litigation.
Fetzer, Timothy, (BV) .... '52 '91 C.829 B.A. L.1029 J.D. 65 Elm St.
Finch, Frank H., Jr., (AV) .... '33 '59 C&L.309 A.A., LL.B. [Howd,L.&F.]
Glynn, Jas. L., (BV) .... '08 '39 C.976 B.A. L.569 LL.B. 25 Center St.
Goring, Albert E. .... '25 '58 C.454 B.S. L.184 LL.B. [Goring&D.] ‡
Goring & Dixon, (CV) .... 40 Park Pl.
Herman, Stanley, (BV) .... '27 '53 C.823 A.B. L.309 LL.B. Pub. Def.
Howd, Lavieri & Finch, LLP, (AV) .... 682 Main Street
Jones, Mark K., (BV) .... '50 '75 C.918 B.A. L.184 J.D. 25 Center St.
Lavieri, Richard R., (BV) .... '52 '81 C.436 B.A. L.861 J.D. [Lavieri&D.]

Lavieri & Dougherty, LLC, (BV)
51 Elm Street, P.O. Box 983, 06098-0983
Telephone: 860-379-4343 Fax: 860-379-9279
Email: rlavieri@snet.net URL: http://www.lawyers.com/lavieri&doughertyllc
Richard R. Lavieri; Marlene A. Dougherty (Retired).
Civil and Criminal Litigation, Zoning and Land Use, Real Estate, Domestic Litigation, Business, Corporate Law, Estate Planning, Estate Administration.
See Professional Biographies, WINSTED, CONNECTICUT

Marino, Ellen C., (BV) .... '65 '90 C.1048 B.A. L.1040 J.D. 596 Main St.
Nader, Ralph .... '34 '58 C.674 A.B. L.309 LL.B. 53 Hillside Ave.‡
O'Connell, Douglas K., (BV) .... '58 '83 C.184 B.A. L.1048 J.D. [Howd,L.&F.]
Power, Patrick E. .... '45 '71 C.31 B.A. L.569 J.D. [Howd,L.&F.]
Renzullo, Patsy M. .... '46 '76 C&L.184 B.A., J.D. 72 Elm St.

Riiska, William O., (AV) '52 '77 C.732 B.A. L.982 J.D.
23 Union Street, 06098
Telephone: 860-379-7898 Fax: 860-379-3220
Email: woriiska@snet.net
Real Estate, Civil Litigation, Zoning and Land Use, Environmental Law, General Practice.
See Professional Biographies, WINSTED, CONNECTICUT

Rosenstein, Ronald S. .... '47 '75 C.705 B.A. L.184 J.D. 75 Park Pl.
Schmidt, Bruce C., (BV) .... '40 '71 C.611 B.A. L.472 J.D. [Howd,L.&F.]

WOLCOTT, 13,008, *New Haven Co.*

Iannone, Mark, (BV) .... '57 '85 C.999 B.S. L.1029 J.D. 250 Wolcott Rd.
Porzio, Salvatore D., (CV) .... '60 '86 C.1030 B.A. L.1040 J.D. Asst. Corp. Coun.
Procopio, Joseph .... '55 '79 C.1211 B.A. L.831 J.D. 33 Wolcott Rd.
Tynan, William F., (BV) .... '50 '75 C.573 B.A. L.184 J.D. 250 Wolcott Rd.

WOODBRIDGE, 7,761, *New Haven Co.*

Adams, Robert M., III '44 '69 C.282 A.B. L.273 J.D. (adm. in AR; not adm. in CT) 25 Punkin Patch‡
Asprelli, Ernest J., Jr. .... '63 '93 C.971 B.S.M.E. L.818 J.D. 32 Crestview Dr.
Axelrod, Eugene N. .... '46 '77 C&L.1019 B.A., J.D. [Employment]
Bakke, William Wight .... '42 '84 C.231 A.B. L.184 J.D. 55 Rimmon Rd.
Behnke, David W. .... '34 '85 C.184 B.A. L.950 J.D. 20 Dogwood Circle
Carter, Robert F., (AV) .... '— '74 C.309 A.B. L.976 J.D. [Carter&C.]
*PRACTICE AREAS: Workers Compensation Law; Occupational Disease Law; Personal Injury.

Carter & Civitello, (AV)
One Bradley Road, Suite 301, 06525
Telephone: 203-389-7000 Fax: 203-389-7004
Email: cartercivitello@bigplanet.com URL: http://www.lawyers.com/carter&civitellolaw
Members of Firm: Robert F. Carter; Donna Civitello.
Workers Compensation, Social Security, Disability Law, Personal Injury.
See Professional Biographies, WOODBRIDGE, CONNECTICUT

Civitello, Donna, (AV) .... '— '86 C.976 B.A. L.184 J.D. [Carter&C.]
*PRACTICE AREAS: Workers Compensation Law; Disabilities; Personal Injury; Social Security.
Crane, Hyla Flaks .... '61 '87 C.855 B.A. L.902 J.D. 34 Mulberry Rd.
D'Angelo, Joanne Milazzo .... '57 '82 C.788 A.B. L.306 J.D. P.O. Box 3688
Employment Law Group, The .... 8 Lunar Drive
Estes, Ellen G. .... '38 '64 C.569 B.A. L.976 LL.B. 41 Spoke Dr.‡
Gordon, Victor M., (AV) .... '11 '38 C.367 A.B. L.94 J.D. 21 Bradley Rd.‡
Gross, Melanie .... '46 '77 C.999 B.A. L.184 J.D. 52 Old Quarry Road
Harrison, Mark I., (AV) .... '60 '91 C.105 B.S.B.A. L.306 J.D. [M.I.Harrison]
Harrison, Mark I., P.C., (AV) .... 7 Research Dr.
Horowitz, Lisa S. .... '55 '83 C.103 B.A. L.178 J.D. 199 Rimmon Rd.
Hoyt, Joanna M. '50 '76 C.174 B.S. L.1188 J.D. (adm. in CO; not adm. in CT) 2 High St.‡
Hunter, Scott R., (CV) .... '58 '88 C.136 B.S. L.1252 J.D. 52 Indian Trl.
Jordan, Richard A., Jr. .... '62 '90 C.1030 B.S. L.306 J.D. 32 Old Barnabas Rd.
Lerner, Peter M., (BV) .... '52 '77 C.901 B.A. L.802 J.D. 270 Amity Rd.
Lesser, David M., (AV) .... '42 '67 C.31 B.A. L.976 LL.B. 1 Bradley Rd.
Longa, William C., (AV) .... '48 '79 C.178 B.A. L.184 J.D. [Longa&Assoc.]
Longa & Associates, LLC, (AV) .... 264 Amity Road, Suite 103
Maretz, Henry B., (BV) .... '33 '63 C.197 A.B. L.569 LL.B. 264 Amity Road
Perkins, Stacey Jackson, (BV) .... '56 '81 C.659 B.S. L.569 J.D. 11 Cleft Rock Ln.
Perlman, Lissa .... '55 '80 C.976 B.A. L.184 J.D. Old Racewick Rd.
Priest, Donald M., Jr. .... '59 '85 C.1312 B.A. L.831 J.D. Bud Priest Realtors
Resnik, John J., (AV) .... '35 '60 C&L.976 B.A., J.D. [Resnik&R.] ⊙
Resnik Conn, Emily, (BV) .... '63 '88 C.385 A.B. L.245 J.D. [Resnik&R.] ⊙
Resnik and Resnik, P.C., (AV) .... 270 Amity Rd. (⊙New Haven)
Saxe, Karen A. .... '50 '78 C.914 B.A. L.184 J.D. 1 Perkins Rd.
Skolnick, David W. .... '35 '62 C.976 A.B. L.178 J.D. Supr. Ct. J.
Stewart, John A. .... '42 '67 C.299 A.B. L.902 LL.B. 1 Bradley Rd., Ste 202
Stone, Ronald A. .... '44 '80 C.1030 A.B. L.184 J.D. 214 Amity Rd.
Teplitzky, Joshua A., (BV) .... '60 '86 C.1365 B.A. L.245 J.D. 40 Country Club Dr.
Wakeman, Marjorie Olencki, (BV) .... '53 '82 C.1211 B.S. L.1029 J.D. 1150 Johnson Rd.
Zolot, Norman, (AV) .... '20 '47 C&L.976 B.S., J.D. 264 Amity Rd.

WOODBURY, 6,942, *Litchfield Co.*

Birmingham, Alan, (AV) '43 '69 C.860 B.A. L.276 J.D. [Reid&R.] (⊙Hartford, West Hartford)
*PRACTICE AREAS: Probate Law; Real Estate; Trusts and Estates.

Clark, Peter M. '57 '83 C.299 A.B. L.904 J.D.
40 Main Street, 06798 ⊙
Telephone: 203-263-2131 Fax: 203-263-3858
Email: pmclaw@imagine.com URL: http://www.lawyers.com/pmclark
***PRACTICE AREAS: Real Estate; Estate Planning; Wills; Probate; Land Use.**
Real Estate, Estate Planning, Estate Administration, Commercial, Land Use, Municipal and Zoning.
See Professional Biographies, WOODBURY, CONNECTICUT

Clark, Peter M. .... '57 '83 C.299 A.B. L.904 J.D. [Sturges&M.] (⊙Woodbury)
Corsico, Deborah A. '62 '89 C.264 B.A. L.94 J.D.
(adm. in NJ; not adm. in CT) 36 Old Fair Ground Rd.
Einhorn, Joel J. '36 '62 C.197 A.B. L.309 J.D.
(adm. in NY; not adm. in CT) P.O. Box 432
Giuliano, Rosemary E., (AV) .... '53 '79 C.788 B.A. L.184 J.D. [Giuliano&R.]
Giuliano & Richardson, LLC, (AV) .... 39 Sherman Hill Rd.
Harley, Colin K. .... '53 '80 C.378 B.A. L.569 J.D. [Harley&D.] (⊙New York, NY)
Harley & Deickler ....P.O. Box 264
Hoey, William M., (BV) .... '56 '82 C.184 B.S. L.1170 J.D. P.O. Box 509
Hollon, Margaret C., (BV) .... '48 '86 C.184 L.306 J.D. 108 Main St. S.
Kaelin, Thomas A., (BV) .... '61 '89 C.228 A.B. L.910 J.D. P.O. Box 323
Marsching, Ronald '27 '54 C.674 B.A. L.309 J.D.
(adm. in NY; not adm. in CT) 41 E. Hill Rd.‡
Mathes, Carleton K., (AV) ....'13 '38 C.178 A.B. L.309 J.D. 244 Main St., S.‡
Mulligan, Lawrence R. ....'50 '76 C.884 A.B. L.262 J.D. 39 Sherman Hill Rd.

Reid and Riege, P.C., (AV)
47 Sherman Hill Road, 06798 ⊙
Telephone: 203-267-6680 FAX: 860-240-1002
URL: http://www.reidriege.com
Alan Birmingham.
Alternative Dispute Resolution. Antitrust & Trade Regulation. Bankruptcy. Business Law. Commercial Law. Commercial Real Estate/Finance. Corporate Law. Employee Benefits/Pension Plans. Employee Benefits/Taft-Hartley Plans. Environmental Law. Health Care. Labor and Employment. Litigation. Mergers and Acquisitions. Nonprofit and Charitable Organizations. Occupational Safety & Health. Probate. Real Estate. Securities. Taxation. Trade and Professional Associations. Trusts & Estates. Zoning, Planning and Land Use.
Hartford, Connecticut Office: One State Street. Telephone: 860-278-1150. FAX: 860-240-1002.
West Hartford, Connecticut Office: 65 LaSalle Road. Telephone: 860-232-6565. FAX: 860-232-6066.
Lakeville, Connecticut Office: 322 Main Street. Telephone: 860-435-9894. FAX: 860-240-1002.
See Professional Biographies, WOODBURY, CONNECTICUT

Richardson, Randolph E., II, (BV) .... '61 '86 C.293 A.B. L.184 J.D. [Giuliano&R.]
Ryan, James T., (BV) ....'39 '64 C.184 B.A. L.188 J.D. 175 Main St., S.
Stevens, Burton L. ....'49 '90 L.1029 J.D. P.O. Box 371
Sturges & Mathes, (BV) ....40 Main St., N. (⊙Southbury)
Williams, Walter J., Jr. ....'28 '53 C&L.724 B.S., LL.B. 223 Bacon Pond Rd.

WOODSTOCK, 5,117, *Windham Co.*

Monty, William J., (BV) .... '50 '79 C&L.184 B.S., J.D. 930 Rte. 169

DELAWARE

CAPITAL: DOVER

Delaware State Bar Association
1201 Orange St., Suite 1100
Wilmington, Delaware 19801-3233
Telephone: 302-658-5279
Fax: 302-658-5212

Index of Towns and Cities Listed by County

*Indicates County Seat

Kent County

Camden-Wyoming
* Dover
Harrington
Hartly
Magnolia
Milford
Smyrna
Wyoming

New Castle County

Bear
Claymont
Greenville
Hockessin
Middletown
Montchanin
Newark
New Castle
Newport
Odessa
Rockland
Smyrna
* Wilmington
Yorklyn

Sussex County

Bethany Beach
Dagsboro
Dewey Beach
Fenwick Island
* Georgetown
Laurel
Lewes
Milford
Millsboro
Milton
Ocean View
Rehoboth Beach
Seaford
Selbyville
South Bethany

BEAR, —, *New Castle Co.*

Bear Law Firm, The, P.A., (BV) .... 30 Little Mill Ln.
Brignola, Erin K. .... '63 '89 C.524 B.S. L.1338 J.D. 1701 Pulaski Hwy.
Christensen, Earl ....'19 '53 C.508 B.A. L.273 LL.B. 3014 Wrangle Hill Rd.‡
Harrison, Kimberly Ann ....'71 '97 C.205 B.A. L.1338 J.D. 1701 Pulaski Hwy.
Hitchings, Timothy L., (BV) ....'54 '90 C.1281 B.A. L.1338 J.D. 1218 Pulaski Hwy.
MacGray, Douglas R., (BV) ....'59 '88 C.999 B.A. L.818 J.D. [Bear]
Martone, Thomas F. .... '63 '90 C.205 B.A. L.1338 J.D. 103 Honora Dr.

BETHANY BEACH, 326, *Sussex Co.*

Bell, Charles W. '25 '59 C&L.30 J.D.
(adm. in MD; not adm. in DE) P.O. Box 734‡
Bodnar, Joseph J., (BV) ....'57 '84 C.705 B.A. L.564 J.D. [Walsh M.&M.] ⊙
Browder, Mary Elizabeth M. ....'62 '87 C.362 B.B.A. L.273 J.D. [Walsh M.&M.] ⊙
Mammarella, William C. ....'28 '58 C.205 A.B. L.273 LL.B. P.O. Box 1552
McLaughlin, Brian J. ....'60 '86 C.205 B.A. L.201 J.D. [Walsh M.&M.] ⊙
Mersky, Rachel B., (CV) ....'57 '81 C.205 B.A. L.285 J.D. [Walsh M.&M.] ⊙
Monaco, Francis A., Jr., (BV) ....'56 '81 C.205 B.A. L.884 J.D. [Walsh M.&M.] ⊙
Monzack, Melvyn I., (BV) ....'40 '66 C.690 B.S. L.273 LL.B. [Walsh M.&M.] ⊙

Mooney, Eric G., P.A.
(See Georgetown)

Murray, James P. '28 '51 C.976 B.S. L.276 LL.B.
(adm. in DC; not adm. in DE) P.O. Box 1050‡
Raskauskas, Joseph C., (CV) ....'53 '81 C.128 B.A. L.1338 J.D. P.O. Box 1509

Schab & Barnett, P.A.
(See Georgetown)

Scott, Kennedy William ....'70 '95 C&L.884 B.A., J.D. 400 Freeport Ct.
Steen, Tempe Brownell, (BV) ....'43 '83 C.228 A.B. L.1338 J.D. [Tunnell&R.]
Tunnell & Raysor, (BV) .... Ocean Hwy. (⊙Georgetown, Rehoboth Beach, Seaford)
Walcek, Stanley J. '28 '63 C&L.128 A.B., LL.B.
(adm. in MD; not adm. in DE) P.O. Box 557‡
Walsh, David I., (BV) ....'43 '70 C.276 B.S. L.64 J.D. [Walsh M.&M.] ⊙
Walsh Monzack and Monaco, P.A., (BV) ....Rt. 1 & Jefferson Bridge Rd. (⊙Wilmington)

CAMDEN-WYOMING, —, *Kent Co.*

Dean, Sandra W., (CV) ....'44 '90 C.204 B.S. L.1338 J.D. 12322 Willow Grove Rd.

CLAYMONT, —, *New Castle Co.*

Horsky, Eugene G. '26 '53 C.688 B.S. L.273 LL.B.
(adm. in DC; not adm. in DE; Pat.) 505 Maple Lane‡
Rokosz, Leon F. '17 '43 C.105 B.A. L.659 LL.B.
(adm. in PA; not adm. in DE) 718 N. Walnutree Lane‡

DAGSBORO, 344, *Sussex Co.*

Tuttle, Baldwin B. .... '43 '67 C.367 B.A. L.659 J.D. 282 Point Farm
Williams, Robert A. '26 '55 C&L.64 LL.B.
(adm. in MD; not adm. in DE) 330 Quail Lane‡

DEWEY BEACH, 176, *Sussex Co.*

Mooney, Eric G., P.A.
(See Georgetown)

DOVER, * 27,630, *Kent Co.*

Andrade, John C., (BV) ..... '51 '79 C.184 B.S.Ch.E. L.1338 J.D. [Parkowski&G.] (Pat.)
*PRACTICE AREAS: Patent Law; Product Liability Law; Environmental Law.
Arrington, Michael W. ....'57 '97 C.728 B.S. L.1338 J.D. [🄰 Parkowski&G.]
*PRACTICE AREAS: Domestic Relations; Environmental Law; Litigation; Transactional; Eminent Domain.

Bailey & Wetzel, P.A.
(See Wilmington)

Barros, A. Richard, (AV) ....'38 '65 C.205 B.A. L.1017 J.D. [Barros,M.S.M.&T.]
*PRACTICE AREAS: Personal Injury Law; Medical Malpractice; Workplace Injuries.

Barros, McNamara, Scanlon, Malkiewicz & Taylor, Professional Association, (AV)
State & Loockerman Streets, P.O. Box 1298, 19903-1298 ⊙
Telephone: 302-734-8400 Telefax: 302-734-4349; 302-734-8969
Email: bmsmt@dol.net
A. Richard Barros; Edward R. McNamara; Patrick Scanlon; Michael J. Malkiewicz; Robert J. Taylor; James J. Lazzeri; Bradley S. Eaby;—Elizabeth Y. Olsen.
Personal Injury, Medical Malpractice, Work Place Injury, Civil and Criminal Trial Practice. Family, Bankruptcy, Probate, Estate Planning and Corporate Law. Commercial Law. Litigation, Administrative, Zoning, Collections.
Representative Clients: Delaware State Music Teachers Assn.; Sears Roebuck & Co.
Lewes, Delaware Office: 1143 Savannah Road, 19958. Telephone: 302-644-8510.
See Professional Biographies, DOVER, DELAWARE

Barrows, Thomas I., (BV) ....'49 '75 L.896 J.D. [Hudson,J.J.&F.]
*PRACTICE AREAS: Civil Litigation; Automobile Personal Injury; Landlord-Tenant Law; Premises Liability.

Bayard Firm, The, (AV)
306 South State Street, 19901 ⊙
Telephone: 302-678-8787
URL: http://www.bayardfirm.com
Curtis P. Bounds.
Tax, Estate Planning, Corporation, Real Estate, Securities and Bankruptcy Law. Litigation, Administrative Law.
Wilmington, Delaware Office: 222 Delaware Avenue, Suite 900, P.O. Box 25130. Telephone: 302-655-5000. Telecopier: 302-658-6395.
See Professional Biographies, DOVER, DELAWARE

Becker, Doreen H., (CV) ....'59 '87 C.205 B.A. L.1338 J.D. [Holfeld&B.] ⊙
Best, Michael J.t. '74 '01 C.204 B.A. L.94 J.D.
(adm. in MA; not adm. in DE) 502 S. State St.
Blades, Lester H., Jr., (CV) ....'58 '85 C.205 B.S. L.1338 J.D. [Blades&R.]
Blades & Reisinger, P.A., (CV) .... 19 S. State St.
Boswell, Paul H., (AV) '38 '66 C.205 B.A. L.902 LL.B.
[Schmittinger&R.] (⊙Rehoboth Beach, Wilmington)
*PRACTICE AREAS: Corporate Law; Estate Planning; Estate Settlements; Taxation.
Bounds, Curtis P. ....'61 '90 C.893 B.A. L.1105 J.D. [Bayard] ⊙
*PRACTICE AREAS: Family Law; Employment Law; General Litigation.
Brainard, Mark Thomas '58 '97 C.952 B.A. L.1338 J.D.
(adm. in MD; not adm. in DE) Delaware Tech. & Community Coll.
Brown, Herman Cubbage, Jr., (CV) ....'49 '75 C.575 B.A. L.1338 J.D. [Brown,S.&C.]
Brown, Shiels & Chasanov, (BV)
108 East Water Street P.O. Drawer F (⊙Georgetown, Rehoboth Beach)
Carey, Crystal L., (BV) .....'62 '88 C.205 B.S. L.446 J.D. [Schmittinger&R.] (⊙Odessa)
*PRACTICE AREAS: Domestic Relations Law; Real Property Law.
Carey, Deborah L., (CV) .... '65 '90 C.585 B.A. L.1338 J.D. 1537 S. Governors Ave.
Catts, Douglas B., (BV) ....'47 '75 C&L.273 B.A., J.D. [Schmittinger&R.]
*PRACTICE AREAS: Personal Injury Law; Litigation; Labor Law.
Chambers, Scott E., (BV) '62 '88 C.205 B.S. L.1338 J.D.
[Schmittinger&R.] (⊙Odessa)
*PRACTICE AREAS: Criminal Law; Personal Injury Law; Real Estate; Veterans Law.
Clark, Jeffrey J., (CV) ....'68 '96 C.870 B.S. L.1338 J.D. [Schmittinger&R.]
*PRACTICE AREAS: Criminal Law; Personal Injury Law; Commercial Litigation.
Collins, April D. ....'68 '97 C.36 B.S. L.1338 J.D. Off. of Atty. Gen.

Connolly Bove Lodge & Hutz LLP
(See Wilmington)

Curley, Edward, (BV) .... '62 '87 C.705 B.A. L.1338 J.D. 502 S. State St.
Dalton, Gary F., (BV) ....'50 '76 C.205 B.A. L.245 J.D. 412 East Loockerman Street
de Bernard, Carolyn, (CV) ....'62 '86 C.1369 B.S. L.64 J.D. 300 S. State St.
Denman, William A., (BV) ....'52 '77 C.205 B.S. L.128 J.D. [Schmittinger&R.]
*PRACTICE AREAS: Litigation; Corporate Law; Commercial Law; Public Utility Law.
Dillard, Richard T. ....'56 '82 C.873 B.A. L.1338 J.D. State Sen. Atty.
Dodge, Gary R., (BV) ....'55 '80 C.264 B.A. L.1338 J.D. [G.R.Dodge]
Dodge, Gary R., P.A., (BV) .... 34 The Green
Dunkle, Mark F., (BV) ....'60 '85 C.893 B.A. L.245 J.D. [Parkowski&G.]
*PRACTICE AREAS: Commercial Real Estate Finance; Commercial Real Estate Development; Hotel and Resort Law; Hotel and Resort Development; Commercial Litigation.
Dunne, William J. .... '54 '95 C.205 B.S. L.942 J.D. Community Legal Aid Soc., Inc.
Eaby, Bradley S., (BV) ....'61 '89 C.656 B.A. L.1338 J.D. [Barros,M.S.M.&T.]
*PRACTICE AREAS: Bankruptcy Law; Business Law; Collections; Commercial Law; Civil Litigation.
Eisenberg, Jonathan ....'50 '74 C.367 B.A. L.446 J.D. 116 West Water St.
Eliassen, Craig T., (BV) ....'58 '84 C.1130 B.A. L.896 J.D. [Schmittinger&R.]
*PRACTICE AREAS: Domestic Relations Law; Workers Compensation Law; Litigation.
Elliott, Wayne N., (AV) '42 '67 C.309 A.B. L.893 LL.B.
[Prickett,J.&E.] (⊙Wilmington)
*PRACTICE AREAS: General Litigation; Personal Injury Litigation.
Ellis, John I., (BV) ....'48 '76 C.1083 B.S. L.945 J.D. Delaware Farm Credit, A.C.A.
Ennis, Bruce C., (BV) ..... '41 '69 C.924 B.A. L.1017 J.D. [Schmittinger&R.] (⊙Odessa)
*PRACTICE AREAS: Real Estate.
Farley, Emily A. ....'71 '00 C.1371 B.A. L.1338 J.D. 108 E. Water St.
Farren, Francis ....'63 '97 C.205 B.S.C.J. L.1338 J.D. Dep. Atty. Gen.
Fisher, Harry M., III, (BV) ....'52 '77 C.205 B.A. L.362 J.D. [Hudson,J.J.&F.]
*PRACTICE AREAS: Real Estate Law; School Law; Wills; Estates.
Fletcher, William D., Jr. '49 '75
C.205 B.A. L.902 J.D. [Schmittinger&R.] (⊙Wilmington)
*PRACTICE AREAS: Personal Injury Law; Employment Law.
Gardner, George F., III, (AV) ....'38 '63 C.216 B.A. L.273 LL.B. [🄶 Parkowski&G.]
*PRACTICE AREAS: Land Use Planning; Commercial Litigation; Commercial Real Estate.
Garey, John R., (CV) ....'61 '87 C.446 B.A. L.1338 J.D. Dep. Atty. Gen.
Gioia, Jennifer L. ....'71 '98 C.205 B.S. L.1338 J.D. [MacAnanny&G.]
*PRACTICE AREAS: Family Law; Workers Compensation; Personal Injury; Real Estate.
Glen, Robert A. ....'57 '87 C.951 B.A. L.659 J.D. 555 East Loockerman Street, #210
Grady, John S., (BV) ....'44 '69 C.728 A.B. L.276 J.D. [Grady&H.]
*PRACTICE AREAS: Personal Injury Law; Real Estate Law; Employment Law.

Grady & Hampton, P.A., (BV)
6 North Bradford Street, 19901
Telephone: 302-678-1265 Fax: 302-678-3544
John S. Grady; Stephen A. Hampton.
General Practice. Medical Malpractice, Negligence, Personal Injury, Social Security Disability, Family, Real Estate Law, Employment Law.
See Professional Biographies, DOVER, DELAWARE

Gregory, Donald E., (CV) ....'55 '80 C.205 B.A. L.884 J.D. 1537 S. Governors Ave.
Guerke, I. Barry, (BV) ....'48 '74 C.205 B.A. L.1017 J.D. [Parkowski&G.]
*PRACTICE AREAS: Personal Injury Law.
Hampton, Stephen A., (CV) .... '56 '87 C.645 B.A. L.1017 J.D. [Grady&H.]
*PRACTICE AREAS: Medical Dental Malpractice; Personal Injury Law; Social Security Disability Law.
Harpster, Robert A. ....'64 '96 C.205 B.A. L.1338 J.D. Off. of Pub. Def.
Hartnett, Anne E. ....'66 '93 C.205 B.A. L.1338 J.D. [🄰 Parkowski&G.]
*PRACTICE AREAS: Governmental Law; Collections; Wills.
Hartnett, Maurice A., III ....'27 '55 C.205 B.S. L.273 J.D. Chan. J.
Hickey, Catherine T., (BV) ....'49 '78 C.205 B.A. L.30 J.D. [Schmittinger&R.]
*PRACTICE AREAS: Employment Law; Administrative Law; Education Law; Litigation.
Hitchens, Glenn E., (BV) .... '42 '67 C.216 B.A. L.1017 J.D. [Morris,J.H.&W.]
*PRACTICE AREAS: General Practice.
Holfeld & Becker, (CV) ....5 East Reed Street, Suite 310 (⊙Wilmington)
Homer, Jeremy W., (BV) ....'47 '75 C.861 B.A. L.982 J.D. [Parkowski&G.]
*PRACTICE AREAS: Employment Law; Environmental Law; Administrative Law.
Horsey, Andrew T. '43 '74 C.869 B.S. L.472 J.D.
(adm. in FL; not adm. in DE) Mas. in Fam. Ct.
Horsey, Henry R. ....'24 '53 C&L.309 A.B., LL.B. Supm. Ct. Jus.
Hudson, William S., (BV) ....'34 '62 C.216 A.B. L.1017 J.D. [Hudson,J.J.&F.]
*PRACTICE AREAS: Family Law; Real Estate Law; Corporations Law; Foreign Investments in U.S. Real Estate.

Hudson, Bruce L., Law Office of
(See Wilmington)

Hudson, Jones, Jaywork & Fisher, (BV)
225 South State Street, 19901 ⊙
Telephone: 302-734-7401 Facsimile: 302-734-5532
URL: http://www.delawarelaw.com
Partners of Firm: William S. Hudson; R. Brandon Jones; John Terence Jaywork; Harry M. Fisher, III; Ronald D. Smith; Thomas I. Barrows; Daniel P. Myers, II (Resident, Rehoboth Beach Office); David J. Weidman (Resident, Georgetown Office).
General Civil and Criminal Practice. Real Estate, Corporation, Probate, Municipal, Zoning, Personal Injury, Family Law, Public Utilities Regulation.
Rehoboth Beach, Delaware Office: 309 Rehoboth Avenue, 19971. Telephone: 302-227-9441.
Georgetown, Delaware Office: 100 North Bedford Street, 19947. Telephone: 302-856-2256.
See Professional Biographies, DOVER, DELAWARE

Hurley, Joseph A., P.A.
(See Wilmington)

Jackson, Thomas C., (BV) ....'44 '70 C&L.575 A.B., J.D. 438 S. State St.
Jaworski, William F., Jr., (CV) ....'65 '92 C.299 B.A. L.607 J.D. [W.F.Jaworski]
Jaworski, William F., LLC, (CV) ....1679 South Dupont Highway, Suite 9
Jaywork, John Terence, (BV) ....'47 '75 C.1130 B.A. L.64 J.D. [Hudson,J.J.&F.]
*PRACTICE AREAS: Municipal Law; Zoning Law; Real Estate; Public Utility Law.
Jester, Clay T., (BV) ....'50 '80 C.454 B.A. L.1338 J.D. [Parkowski&G.]
*PRACTICE AREAS: Family Law; Personal Injury Law; Estate Planning.
Johnson, Karen L. ....'54 '84 C.683 A.B. L.128 J.D. Dir. of Pub. Safety‡
Jones, R. Brandon, (BV) ....'44 '70 C.205 B.A. L.893 J.D. [Hudson,J.J.&F.]
*PRACTICE AREAS: Estates Law; Real Estate Law; Commercial Law; Corporate Law; Personal Injury.
Karlsen, Steven R. ....'44 '72 C.205 B.A. L.831 J.D. 89 Kings Highway
Kelsey, Roger D. ....'40 '65 C.205 B.A. L.902 J.D. [Brown,S.&C.]
Kemmer, Kyle ......'70 '97 C.645 B.A. L.1338 J.D. [🄰 Schmittinger&R.] (⊙Wilmington)
*PRACTICE AREAS: Workers Compensation; Personal Injury.
Kiesel, Eleanor M. ....'53 '00 C.999 B.S. L.831 J.D. Community Legal Aid Soc., Inc.
Kinsley, Donald R. .....'54 '91 C.705 B.S. L.64 J.D. Legal Servs. Corp. of Delaware, Inc.

Knepper & Stratton
(See Wilmington)

Kollias, Basil C. ....'62 '99 C.874 B.S. L.1338 J.D. [[A] Parkowski&G.]
*PRACTICE AREAS: Environmental Law; Real Estate Law; Patent Law; Administrative Law; Contracts.

Laffey, Kathryn J., Law Office of
(See Wilmington)

Langdon, Jeanne L. '54 '81 C.367 B.A. L.446 J.D.
(adm. in MD; not adm. in DE) 89 Kings Highway‡

Lazzeri, James J., (BV) ....'51 '77 C.821 B.A. L.884 J.D. [Barros,M.S.M.&T.]
*PRACTICE AREAS: Workers' Compensation Law; Personal Injury Law.

Ligouri, Morris & Redding, (BV) .... 46 The Green
Liguori, James E., (BV) ....'50 '75 C.923 B.S. L.424 J.D. [Ligouri,M.&R.]
Little, Stefanie J. '67 '94 C.205 B.S.B.A. L.1338 J.D.
(adm. in PA; not adm. in DE) Citicorp Ins. Group
Longobardi, Cynthia J. '58 '94 C.525 B.A. L.1338 J.D.
(adm. in MD; not adm. in DE) 225 South State St.

MacAnanny, Glynis A., (BV) .... '57 '85 C.446 B.A. L.64 J.D. [MacAnanny&G.]
*PRACTICE AREAS: Family Law; Child Custody; Child Support; Marital Property Law; Divorce.

MacAnanny & Gioia, LLP, (BV)
1126 South State Street, 19901
Telephone: 302-730-3500 Fax: 302-730-0505
Email: glynis@erols.com URL: http://www.lawyers.com/macanannylaw
Glynis A. MacAnanny; Jennifer L. Gioia.
Family Law including Child Custody, Child Support, Divorce, Adoptions. Real Estate (Residential and Commercial), Landlord and Tenant, Creditors Rights, Collection, Personal Injury, Automobile Accidents, Business Law, Business Start-Ups, Contracts, Trusts and Estates, Wills and Probate. Worker's Compensation.
See Professional Biographies, DOVER, DELAWARE

MacArtor, June D. ....'30 '74 C.838 B.A. L.884 J.D. Dept. of Nat. Resources

Malik, John S.
(See Wilmington)

Malkiewicz, Michael J., (BV) ....'48 '81 C.204 B.A. L.602 J.D. [Barros,M.S.M.&T.]
*PRACTICE AREAS: Criminal Defense Law; Medical Malpractice; Personal Injury Law; Land Use Law; Administrative Law.

Malmberg, Constantine F., III, (CV) ....'58 '86 C.205 B.A. L.1338 502 S. State St.
Maybee, Joseph Whitmore, (BV) ....'37 '74 C.205 B.A. L.276 J.D. 10 S. Bradford St.
McCrystal, Michael J. .....'63 '88 C.645 B.A. L.1338 J.D. Community Legal Aid Soc., Inc.
McNamara, Edward R., (BV) ....'47 '71 C.205 A.B. L.884 J.D. [Barros,M.S.M.&T.] ⊙
*PRACTICE AREAS: Personal Injury Law; Estate Planning Law.

McNinch, Paul Longfellow ....'55 '97 C.916 B.S. L.1243 J.D. 108 E. Water St.
Miller, Barbara L. ....'28 '77 C.105 A.B. L.1338 J.D. 108 E. Water St.‡
Miller, Beth Buzzell ....'64 '93 C.550 B.S. L.61 J.D. [[A] Schmittinger&R.]
*PRACTICE AREAS: Corporate Law; Estate Planning; Estate Settlements; Probate Litigation; Trust Litigation.

Minott, Darrell J. ....'57 '82 C.1044 B.A. L.569 J.D. Delaware Develop. Off.
Morris, Gregory A., (CV) ....'65 '91 C.658 B.S. L.1338 J.D. [Ligouri,M.&R.]

Morris, James, Hitchens & Williams, LLP, (AV) [BB]
Suite 202, 32 West Loockerman Street, 19904-7356 ⊙
Telephone: 302-678-8815 Telecopier: 302-678-9063
URL: http://www.morrisjames.com
Resident Partner: Glenn E. Hitchens.
Litigation, Corporate Law, Commercial Law, Business Law, Administrative Law, Alternative Dispute Resolution, Bankruptcy, Commercial Real Estate, Computers and Software, Education Law, Environmental Law, Family Law, Health Care, Insurance, Insurance Defense, Intellectual Property, Labor and Employment, Medical Malpractice, Partnership Law, Personal Injury, Probate, Products Liability, Real Estate, Taxation, Torts, Trusts and Estates and Wills.
Wilmington, Delaware Offices: 222 Delaware Avenue, P.O. Box 2306, 19899-2306. Telephone: 302-888-6800. Telecopier: 302-571-1750 and 1010 North Bancroft Parkway, Suite 11, P.O. Box 2328, 19899-2328. Telephone: 302-655-2599. Fax: 302-655-8831.
Newark, Delaware Office: 16 Polly Drummond Hill Road, 19711-5703. Telephone: 302-368-4200. Fax: 302-368-6259.
See Professional Biographies, DOVER, DELAWARE

O'Brien, John E., (CV) ....'53 '79 C.205 B.A. L.1338 J.D. 942 Walker Sq.
Olsen, Elizabeth Y., (CV) ....'63 '93 C.787 B.A. L.1138 J.D. [[A] Barros,M.S.M.&T.]
*PRACTICE AREAS: Domestic Relations; Criminal Law; Domestic Violence.

O'Neill, Robert Joseph, Jr., (BV) ...'59 '85 C.205 B.S. L.884 J.D. Chf. Pros., Dept. of Jus.
Paradee, John W., (BV) ....'63 '89 C.893 B.A. L.692 J.D. [Prickett,J.&E.]
*PRACTICE AREAS: Commercial Litigation; Real Estate Law.

Parkowski, F. Michael, (AV) ....'45 '73 C.884 B.E. L.831 J.D. [Parkowski&G.]
*PRACTICE AREAS: Environmental Law; Administrative Law; Real Estate Development Law; Public Works Contract Law.

Parkowski & Guerke, Professional Association, (AV)
116 West Water Street, P.O. Box 598, 19903
Telephone: 302-678-3262 Telecopier: 302-678-9415
Email: png@dol.net URL: http://www.pnglaw.com
F. Michael Parkowski; I. Barry Guerke; Clay T. Jester; Jeremy W. Homer; John C. Andrade; Mark F. Dunkle;—Anne E. Hartnett; Michael W. Arrington; Basil C. Kollias. Of Counsel: George F. Gardner, III.
General Civil and Trial Practice in all Courts. Environmental, Administrative, Public Contract, Utility, Employment, Education, Real Estate, Personal Injury, Estate Planning, Commercial Law, Criminal and Family Law.
Representative Clients: Delaware Solid Waste Authority; Cabe Associates (Consulting Engineers).
Approved Attorneys for: Ticor Title Insurance Co.
Reference: First National Bank of Wyoming.
See Professional Biographies, DOVER, DELAWARE

Pepper Sr., William W., (BV) ....'59 '85 C.160 B.A. L.896 J.D. [Schmittinger&R.]
*PRACTICE AREAS: Municipal Law; Employment Law; Litigation; Personal Injury; Appellate Practice.

Pierce, Barry W. C. ....'49 '84 C.575 B.A. L.1218 J.D. 8 Baltray Rd.

Prickett, Jones & Elliott, P.A., (AV)
11 North State Street, 19901 ⊙
Telephone: 302-674-3841 Telecopier: 302-674-5864
Email: attorneys@prickett.com URL: http://www.prickett.com
Wayne N. Elliott; Gary F. Traynor (Resident); John W. Paradee (Resident);—D. Benjamin Snyder.
General Civil and Criminal Practice including: Commercial Law, Corporation Law, Estate Planning, Government Affairs, Insurance Defense, Personal Injury, Real Estate.
Wilmington, Delaware Office: 1310 King Street. Telephone: 302-888-6500.
Kennett Square, Pennsylvania Office: 217 West State Street. Telephone: 610-444-1573.
See Professional Biographies, DOVER, DELAWARE

Primos, Noel E., (BV) ....'64 '90 C.880 B.A. L.976 J.D. [Schmittinger&R.]
*PRACTICE AREAS: Civil Litigation; Employment Law.

Pryor, David T., (BV) ....'48 '82 C.205 B.S. L.1338 J.D. 225 South State Street
Redding, Laura A., (CV) ....'68 '94 C.884 B.S.B.A. L.174 J.D. [Ligouri,M.&R.]
Reisinger, Timothy A., (CV) ....'56 '82 C.820 B.A. L.1017 J.D. [Blades&R.]
Robb, James A. ....'47 '79 C.999 B.B.A. L.1338 J.D. Chief Dep. Ins. Commissioner
Rodriguez, Nicholas H., (AV) '34 '61 C.645 B.S. L.902 J.D.
[Schmittinger&R.] (⊙Rehoboth Beach, Wilmington)
*PRACTICE AREAS: Personal Injury Law.

Scanlon, Patrick, (BV) ....'43 '75 C.229 B.A. L.1292 J.D. [Barros,M.S.M.&T.]
*PRACTICE AREAS: Bankruptcy Collections; Retail Collections.

Schmid, Lloyd A., Jr. ....'56 '88 C.1335 B.S. L.312 J.D. 530 South State Street, Suite 108
Schmittinger, Harold, (AV) '28 '54 C.205 B.S. L.904 LL.B.
[Schmittinger&R.] (⊙Rehoboth Beach, Wilmington)
*PRACTICE AREAS: Personal Injury Law.

Schmittinger, John J., (AV) '41 '66 C.205 B.A. L.831 J.D.
[Schmittinger&R.] (⊙Rehoboth Beach, Wilmington)
*PRACTICE AREAS: Workers Compensation Law; Personal Injury.

Schmittinger, Walt F., (CV) ....'70 '95 C.216 B.A. L.1338 J.D. [Schmittinger&R.]
*PRACTICE AREAS: Personal Injury Law; Litigation; Workers Compensation Law.

Schmittinger & Rodriguez, P.A., (AV) [BB]
414 South State Street, 19901 ⊙
Telephone: 302-674-0140 FAX: 302-674-1830
Email: attorneys@schmittrod.com URL: http://www.schmittrod.com
Harold Schmittinger; Nicholas H. Rodriguez; Paul H. Boswell; John J. Schmittinger; Bruce C. Ennis; Douglas B. Catts; William D. Fletcher, Jr.; William A. Denman; Catherine T. Hickey; Craig T. Eliassen; William W. Pepper Sr.; Crystal L. Carey; Scott E. Chambers; Frederick A. Townsend III; Noel E. Primos; David A. Boswell (Resident, Rehoboth Beach, Delaware Office); Walt F. Schmittinger; R. Scott Kappes (Resident, Wilmington, Delaware Office); Jeffrey J. Clark; Beth Buzzell Miller; Kyle Kemmer (Resident, Wilmington, Delaware Office).
General Civil Practice. Personal Injury, Workers Compensation, Federal Practice, Corporation, Estate Planning, Real Estate and Commercial Law, Litigation, Criminal and Domestic Law.
Representative Clients: Chesapeake Utilities Corp.; City of Dover.
Wilmington, Delaware Office: 1300 North Market Street, Suite 205. Telephone: 302-652-3676. Fax: 302-652-8788.
Rehoboth Beach, Delaware Office: 4602 Highway One. Telephone: 302-227-1400. Fax: 302-645-1843.
Odessa, Delaware Office: Odessa Professional Park, P.O. Box 626. Telephone: 302-378-1697. Fax: 302-378-1659.
See Professional Biographies, DOVER, DELAWARE

Schranck, Frederick H., (BV) ....'53 '78 C.205 B.A. L.30 J.D. Dep. Atty. Gen.
Schreiber, Vicki Holmes ....'63 '00 C.205 B.S. L.1338 J.D. 208 S. Governors Ave.
Schwartz, Steven, (BV) ....'42 '74 C.831 B.A. L.1292 J.D. [S.Schwartz]
Schwartz, Steven, P.A., (BV) ....1140 S. State St.
Sherlock, Mary E., (BV) ....'58 '83 C.1031 B.A. L.1338 J.D. [Brown,S.&C.]
Shiels, Roy S., (BV) ....'39 '64 C.645 B.A. L.477 J.D. [Brown,S.&C.]
Sigler, John Charles, (CV) '45 '87
C.953 B.S. L.1338 J.D. Gen. Coun., Psychotherapeutic Servs. Inc.
Slomich, Joshua '72 '99 C.454 L.818 J.D.
(adm. in MA; not adm. in DE) Asst. Staff Judge Advocat

Smith, Ronald D., (BV) ....'51 '79 C.205 B.A. L.1338 J.D. [Hudson,J.J.&F.]
*PRACTICE AREAS: Bankruptcy Law; Domestic Relations Law.

Snyder, D. Benjamin ....'74 '01 C.1369 B.B.A. L.1017 J.D. [[A] Prickett,J.&E.]
*PRACTICE AREAS: Commercial Litigation; Commercial and Residential Real Estate Transactions; General Business; Corporate Practice; Administrative Law.

Soll, Melvin E. ....'34 '59 C&L.659 B.S., LL.B. 64 Liberto Lane
Stark, Alice W., (CV) ....'42 '95 C.952 B.S. L.1338 J.D. 735 Holly Dr.
Steele, Myron T. ....'45 '70 C&L.893 B.A., J.D. Justice, Supreme Court of DE
Stone, F. L. Peter, (BV) '35 '60 C.197 A.B. L.309 LL.B.
Dep. Atty. Gen., State Ins. Dept.

Street, Gerald I. H., (BV) ....'47 '73 C.205 B.A. L.904 J.D. [Twilley&S.]
*PRACTICE AREAS: Family Law; Real Estate; Personal Injury; Business Law.

Sunshine, Paul D., (CV) ....'66 '94 C.205 B.A.A.S. L.1338 J.D. [G.R.Dodge]
Swierzbinski, Paul S. ....'49 '75 C.205 B.A. L.796 J.D. Off. of Pub. Def.
Taylor, Robert J., (BV) ....'57 '83 C.181 B.A. L.1338 J.D. [Barros,M.S.M.&T.]
*PRACTICE AREAS: Criminal Defense Law; Personal Injury Law; Domestic Relations Law.

Terry, Harry K. F., (BV) ....'44 '74 C.205 B.A. L.421 J.D. [H.K.F.Terry] ⊙
Terry, Harry K. F., Professional Association, (BV) ....48 The Green (⊙Harrington)
Thompson, Robert R. '44 '74
C.197 A.B. L.472 J.D. State Dept. of Nat. Res. & Envir. Control

Townsend, Frederick A., III ....'62 '90 C.205 B.A. L.1338 J.D. [[A] Schmittinger&R.]
*PRACTICE AREAS: Insurance Regulation; Real Estate.

Trader, Merrill C. ....'32 '58 C.928 B.A. L.902 LL.B. Com. Pleas J.
Traynor, Gary F., (BV) ....'56 '82 C.197 A.B. L.1338 J.D. [Prickett,J.&E.]
*PRACTICE AREAS: Corporate Litigation; Commercial Litigation; Federal Litigation; Complex Criminal Defense.

Twilley, Joshua M., (BV) ....'28 '53 C&L.309 B.A., J.D. [Twilley&S.]
*PRACTICE AREAS: Estate Planning; Probate; Business Law; Real Estate.

Twilley & Street, P.A., (BV)
426 South State Street, P.O. Box 1366, 19903-1366
Telephone: 302-735-8400 1-800-253-8488 Fax: 302-735-8417
Joshua M. Twilley; Gerald I. H. Street.
General Civil and Trial Practice. Business Law, Real Estate, Probate, Trusts and Estates and Banking Law. Collections, Personal Injury, Zoning, Municipal, Family Law and Litigation, Elder Law.

Vari, Louann Jackson, (CV) ....'62 '91 C.205 B.A. L.1338 J.D. Dep. Atty. Gen.
Vaughn, James T., Jr., (BV) ....'49 '76 C.228 B.A. L.276 J.D. 414 S. State St.
Vaughn, William H., (AV) ....'35 '64 C.205 B.A. L.893 J.D. 11 Highview Ave.‡
Wagner, William C., II .... '43 '72 C.205 B.E.E. L.1017 J.D. Dir., Div. of Fish & Wildlife
Weeks-Tappan, Denise Lynn '62 '88
C.205 B.S. L.1338 J.D. Community Legal Aid Soc., Inc.
Welch, Charles W., III, (BV) ....'59 '85 C.205 B.S. L.884 J.D. [Brown,S.&C.]

Welch & Associates
(See Wilmington)

Whitehurst, Charles E., Jr. ....'52 '78 C.1047 B.A. L.273 J.D. 502 S. State St.
Williams, Donna Lee Harpster, (BV) ....'60 '84 C.945 B.A. L.1338 J.D. State Ins. Comm.
Williams, John, (BV) ....'48 '75 C.280 B.S. L.245 J.D. Dep. Atty. Gen.
Wilson, Lynn D. ....'41 '82 C.205 B.A. L.1338 J.D. Dep. Atty. Gen.
Wilson, P. Scott, (CV) ....'68 '94 C.205 B.A. L.216 J.D. 313 S. State St.
Witham, William L., Jr., (BV) ....'47 '75 C.205 B.A. L.446 J.D. 38 The Green
Wright, Janet A. '— '89 C&L.1338 B.A., J.D.
Comm. Coun., State Pub. Integrity Comm.

Young, Jeffrey A., (CV) ....'68 '95 C.821 B.A. L.884 J.D. [Young&Y.]
*PRACTICE AREAS: Insurance Defense; Criminal Law; Personal Injury.

Young, Kenneth J., (BV) ....'56 '81 C.94 B.A. L.1338 J.D. 502 South State Street
Young, Robert B., (AV) ....'43 '69 C.207 A.B. L.608 J.D. [Young&Y.]
*PRACTICE AREAS: Insurance Defense.

Young Conaway Stargatt & Taylor, LLP
(See Wilmington)

Young & Young, (AV) [BB]
300 South State Street, P.O. Box 1191, 19903
Telephone: 302-674-8822 Fax: 302-674-8251
Email: younglaw@intercom.net URL: http://www.lawyers.com/young-young
Members of Firm: Robert B. Young; Jeffrey A. Young.
Insurance Defense, Civil and Criminal Practice, Personal Injury.
See Professional Biographies, DOVER, DELAWARE

FENWICK ISLAND, 186, *Sussex Co.*

Buchanan & Bolte
(See Ocean City, Maryland)

Mooney, Eric G., P.A.
(See Georgetown)

Stumpf, Vickers & Sandy, P.A.
(See Georgetown)

Tomasetti, Raymond E., Jr., (BV) '54 '80 C.205 B.S. L.1338 J.D.
1209 Coastal Highway, 19944 ⊙
Telephone: 302-539-3041 Fax: 302-537-9986
Email: tomasetti@aol.com
***PRACTICE AREAS: General Civil Law; Trial Practice; Real Estate Law; Estate Planning Law; Personal Injury Law.**
General Civil and Trial Practice. Real Estate, Estate Planning, and Personal Injury.
Newport, Delaware Office: 16 West Market Street, P.O. Box 3058, 19804. Telephone: 302-995-2840. Fax: 302-995-9160.

See Professional Biographies, FENWICK ISLAND, DELAWARE

GEORGETOWN, * 3,732, *Sussex Co.*

Adkins, James W. ... '52 '78 C.205 B.A. L.1338 J.D. 114 E. Market St.
Andresen, Lisa M. ... '60 '96 C.205 B.A. L.644 J.D. 15 S. Race St.
Ayvazian, Kim E. ... '53 '87 C.976 B.A. L.145 J.D. Jud. Law Clk. to Supr. Ct.

Bailey & Wetzel, P.A.
(See Wilmington)

Baker, David W., P.A., (BV) ... '50 '75 C.205 B.A. L.945 J.D. 109 S. Race St.
Balliet, Heidi A. '69 '98 C.64 B.A. L.1002 J.D.
(adm. in MD; not adm. in DE) 30 E. Pine St.
Balliet, Heidi A. ... '69 '98 C&L.1002 B.A., J.D. [[A] Tunnell&R.]
*PRACTICE AREAS: Real Estate.
Barnett, Norman C., (BV) ... '42 '69 C.446 B.S. L.329 J.D. [Schab&B.] ⊙
*PRACTICE AREAS: Collections; Personal Injury; Real Estate; Mediation; Commercial Insurance Claims.
Barnett, Thomas David Hunter, (CV) ... '40 '76 C.1090 B.S. L.692 J.D. Asst. Pub. Def.
Bayard, Eugene H., (AV) ... '46 '74 C.674 B.A. L.893 J.D. [Wilson,H.&B.]
*PRACTICE AREAS: General Practice; Litigation.
Beauregard, Rosemary Betts, (BV) ... '58 '83 C.1369 B.A. L.1338 J.D. [Betts&B.]
Berl, Richard E. W., Jr., (BV) ... '54 '79 C.205 B.A. L.1338 J.D. [Smith O.P.&B.]
*PRACTICE AREAS: Personal Injury Law; Family Law; Business Law; Real Estate.
Betts, A. Dean, (BV) ... '26 '52 C&L.446 B.A., LL.B. [Betts&B.]
Betts, A. Dean, Jr., (CV) ... '65 '90 C.886 B.S. L.446 J.D. 15 S. Race St.
Betts & Beauregard, P.A., (BV) ... 15 S. Race St.
Brown, Shiels & Chasanov, (BV) ... 10 East Pine Street (⊙Dover, Rehoboth Beach)
Bruce & Mooney, P.C., (CV) ... 104 E. Pine St.
Bunting, Clayton E., (BV) ... '50 '76 C.692 B.S. L.64 J.D. [Wilson,H.&B.]
*PRACTICE AREAS: Personal Injury Law; Workers Compensation Law; Insurance; Premises Liability; Litigation.
Burke, Merritt, III, (CV) ... '43 '72 C.205 B.S. L.838 J.D. 1 South Race Street
Callaway, E. Stephen ... '48 '74 C&L.790 B.A., J.D. 101 S. Bedford St.
Campbell, Dean A. ... '60 '97 C.205 B.A. L.1338 J.D. [[A] Moore&R.] ⊙
*PRACTICE AREAS: Litigation; Real Estate Litigation; Landlord and Tenant Law; Collections; Construction Litigation.
Chandler, William B., III ... '51 '76 C.205 B.A. L.790 J.D. Chanc.
Chasanov, William M., (BV) ... '42 '67 C.659 B.S. L.276 J.D. [Brown,S.&C.]
Chorman, James R. ... '63 '89 C.100 B.A. L.607 J.D. 10 East Pine Street
Clark, Kenneth S., Jr. ... '54 '82 C.821 B.A. L.1065 J.D. Assoc. J., Ct. of Com. Pleas
Cooper, Margaret R. ... '61 '97 C.172 B.S. L.1338 J.D. [[A] Hudson,J.J.&F.]
Cordrey, John H., (BV) ... '55 '80 C.100 B.A. L.1338 J.D. [Cordrey&C.]
Cordrey & Clark, P.A., (BV) ... 16 S. Front St.
Cosgrove, Martin J. ... '71 '98 C.205 B.A. L.1360 J.D. Dep. Atty. Gen.
Csizmadia, Valerie S. ... '67 '00 C.999 B.S. L.446 J.D. Dep. Atty. Gen.
Davis, Alan G. ... '71 '00 C.893 B.A. L.1338 J.D. 207 E. Market St.
Davis, Henry Clay, III, (BV) ... '37 '73 C.205 B.A. L.1017 J.D. [H.C.Davis,III]
Davis, Henry Clay, III, P.A., (BV) ... 207 E. Market St.
DeBonte, Kim ... '68 '97 C.728 B.S. L.1338 J.D. [[A] Stumpf,V.&S.]
*PRACTICE AREAS: Family Law; Criminal Law.
Dignon, Neil Francis, (CV) ... '62 '96 C.1044 B.S. L.1252 J.D. 10 E. Pine St.
Dolan, Brian F., (CV) ... '58 '93 C.205 B.A. L.1017 J.D. [Stumpf,V.&S.]
*PRACTICE AREAS: General Civil and Trial Practice; Workman's Compensation; Personal Injury.
Dunlap, Jackson R., Jr., (BV) ... '31 '61 C&L.831 B.S., J.D. [Brown,S.&C.]
Ellis, Stephen P., (BV) ... '45 '72 C.1115 B.S. L.128 J.D. [Sergovic,E.&S.]
*PRACTICE AREAS: Taxation Law; Probate Law; Estate Planning.
Enterline, Paul G. ... '61 '92 C.205 B.S. L.64 J.D. 18 Chestnut St.
Fuqua, James A., Jr., (BV) ... '48 '73 C.205 B.A. L.446 J.D. [Fuqua&Y.]
Fuqua & Yori, P.A., (BV) ... The Circle
Gay, Thomas E. ... '65 '92 C.205 B.A. L.1338 J.D. [Stumpf,V.&S.]
*PRACTICE AREAS: Family Law.
Gelof, Adam David '67 '95 C.184 B.A. L.1338 J.D.
(adm. in MD; not adm. in DE) 114 E. Market St.
Gelof, Kelly Dunn, (CV) ... '69 '94 C.823 B.S. L.1338 J.D. [[A] Tunnell&R.]
*PRACTICE AREAS: Personal Injury; Medical Malpractice; Criminal Law; General Civil Litigation.
Gibbons, Kristin S. ... '68 '94 C.205 B.A. L.692 J.D. 205 S. Bedford St.
Gibbs, Robert G., (BV) ... '52 '85 C.222 B.A. L.64 J.D. [Wilson,H.&B.]
*PRACTICE AREAS: Banks and Banking; Business Law; Commercial Law; Civil Litigation; Real Estate.

Gill, Edward C., Law Office of, (BV) '57 '83 C&L.861 B.A., J.D.
16 North Bedford Street, 19947
Telephone: 302-854-5400 Fax: 302-854-5409
Email: egill@dmv.com
***PRACTICE AREAS: Criminal Law; Driving While Intoxicated; Drug Crimes; Automobile Accidents and Injuries; Workers Compensation.**
Associates: Theresa McQuaid Hayes; Lorraine K. Phillips.
General Practice.

See Professional Biographies, GEORGETOWN, DELAWARE

Graves, T. Henley ... '48 '73 C.205 B.A. L.446 J.D. Supr. Ct. J.
Gray, Gerry ... '63 '89 C.745 B.A. L.945 J.D. 13 E. Laurel St.

Green, Joseph B.
(See Wilmington)

Griffin, James D., (AV) ... '39 '69 C.45 B.S. L.560 J.D. [Griffin&H.]
*PRACTICE AREAS: General Civil and Trial Practice; Business Law; Real Estate Law; Wills, Trusts and Estates; Personal Injury.

Griffin & Hackett, P.A., (AV)
116 West Market Street, P.O. Box 612, 19947
Telephone: 302-856-9066 Fax: 302-856-9016
Email: gandh@ce.net URL: http://www.gandh.baweb.com
James D. Griffin; David R. Hackett;—Vincent G. Robertson. Of Counsel: Anne L. Naczi.
General Civil and Trial Practice. Corporate, Business, Banking, Real Estate, Probate, Family, Estate Planning, Personal Injury, Health Care, Zoning and Education Law.
Approved Attorneys for: Chicago Title Insurance Co.; Lawyers Title Insurance Corp.; TICOR Title Insurance Company of California.
Reference: Mellon Bank Delaware, The Circle, Georgetown, Delaware.

See Professional Biographies, GEORGETOWN, DELAWARE

Hackett, David R., (BV) ... '44 '69 C.244 B.A. L.902 J.D. [Griffin&H.]
*PRACTICE AREAS: Business Law; Real Estate Law; Health Care and Hospital Law; Commercial Loans; Corporate Law.
Halbrook, Robert L., (AV) ... '29 '57 C&L.477 B.A., J.D. [Wilson,H.&B.] ‡
Haller, Karl, (BV) ... '42 '68 C.893 A.B. L.276 J.D. Pub. Def.
Hayes, Theresa McQuaid ... '67 '93 C.692 B.A. L.1338 J.D. [[A] E.C.Gill]
*PRACTICE AREAS: Criminal Law; Family Law; Divorce; Child Custody; Child Support.
Holland, Randy J. ... '47 '72 C.821 B.A. L.659 J.D. Supr. Ct. J.
Howard, Alicia B., (BV) ... '56 '82 C&L.575 B.A., J.D. Comr., Supr. Ct.
Howard, Eric C., (BV) ... '56 '81 C.205 B.A. L.228 J.D. [Wilson,H.&B.]
*PRACTICE AREAS: Civil Litigation; Business Law; Construction Law.
Hudson, Howard W., Jr., (BV) ... '43 '70 C.205 B.A. L.446 J.D. Asst. Pub. Def.

Hudson, Bruce L., Law Office of
(See Wilmington)

Hudson, Jones, Jaywork & Fisher, (BV)
100 North Bedford St. (⊙Dover, Rehoboth Beach)

Hurley, Joseph A., P.A.
(See Wilmington)

Jacobs & Crumplar, P.A.
(See Wilmington)

Karsnitz, Craig A., (BV) ... '52 '78 C.205 B.A. L.884 J.D. [Young C.S.&T.]
*PRACTICE AREAS: Personal Injury; Workers' Compensation.
Lee, William Swain ... '35 '61 C.228 A.B. L.659 LL.B. Pres. J., Supr. Ct.
Longo, Vivian Medinilla, (CV) ... '66 '93 C.205 B.A. L.1338 J.D. [[A] Young C.S.&T.]
*PRACTICE AREAS: Personal Injury; Workers' Compensation; Criminal Defense; Medical Malpractice.
Lull, Margaret Ione ... '57 '86 C.942 B.S.W. L.375 J.D. Community Legal Aid Soc., Inc.

Malik, John S.
(See Wilmington)

Maull, Harry Edward, Jr., (BV) ... '39 '66 C.205 B.A. L.1017 J.D. [Maull&M.]
Maull & Maull, P.A., (BV) ... 406 S. Bedford St.
Millman, Kenneth M. ... '48 '73 C.316 A.B. L.896 J.D. Fam. Ct. J.
Mooney, Eric G., (CV) ... '68 '96 C.205 B.S. L.1252 J.D. [E.G.Mooney]
*PRACTICE AREAS: Criminal Defense; Driving While Intoxicated; Personal Injury.

Mooney, Eric G., P.A., (CV)
11 South Race Street, 19947
Telephone: 302-856-3070 Fax: 302-856-2177
Email: ericgmooney@aol.com URL: http://www.lawyers.com/ericgmooney
Eric G. Mooney.
Criminal Defense, Driving Under the Influence, Personal Injury.

See Professional Biographies, GEORGETOWN, DELAWARE

Moore, J. Everett, Jr., (BV) ... '50 '76 C.205 B.A. L.945 J.D. [Moore&R.] ⊙
*PRACTICE AREAS: Real Estate; Business Law.

Moore & Rutt, P.A., (BV)
122 West Market Street, P.O. Box 554, 19947 ⊙
Telephone: 302-856-9568 Fax: 302-855-9803 URL: http://www.mooreandrutt.com
Email: drutt@mooreandrutt.com URL: http://www.lawyers.com/moore&rutt
J. Everett Moore, Jr.; David N. Rutt;—Dean A. Campbell; Patrick E. Vanderslice.
General, Civil and Trial Practice. Real Estate, Planning and Zoning, Personal Injury, Automobile Accidents, Commercial Law, Wills and Probate, Construction Law, Family Law, Child Support, Child Custody, Divorce, Adoption, Trusts and Estates, Estate Planning, Landlord/Tenant Litigation.
Milford, Delaware Office: 109 North Walnut Street, 19963-1447. Telephone: 302-424-2240.

See Professional Biographies, GEORGETOWN, DELAWARE

Naczi, Anne L., (BV) ... '57 '82 C.276 B.A. L.884 J.D. [[C] Griffin&H.]
*PRACTICE AREAS: Negligence; Insurance; Workers Compensation; Products Liability; Medical Malpractice.
O'Donnell, Lynn R., (CV) ... '57 '92 C.205 B.A. L.884 J.D. [Smith O.P.&B.]
*PRACTICE AREAS: Estate Planning; Estate Administration; Elder Law; Guardianship; Real Estate.
Olson, Mark D., (AV) ... '45 '76 C.1044 B.A. L.659 J.D. [Wilson,H.&B.] (⊙Wilmington)
*PRACTICE AREAS: Taxation; Like Kind Exchanges; Estate Planning; Estate Administration; Family Business Planning.
Parker, Stephanie Kay ... '68 '94 P.O. Box 548
Phillips, Lorraine K. ... '56 '82 C.477 B.A. L.851 J.D. [[A] E.C.Gill]
*PRACTICE AREAS: Family Law; Divorce; Child Custody; Child Support; Labor and Employment.
Phillips, Ronald D., Jr. ... '68 '94 C&L.1338 B.A., J.D. [[A] Hudson,J.J.&F.]
Procino, Michele L., (CV) ... '69 '95 C.645 B.A. L.1338 J.D. [Smith O.P.&B.]
*PRACTICE AREAS: Taxation; Estate Planning; Estate Administration; Liquor Licensing; Guardianship.
Purnell, Harold W. T., II, (BV) ... '55 '80 C.282 B.A. L.1338 J.D. [Tunnell&R.]
*PRACTICE AREAS: Trusts and Estates; Real Estate; Tax; Business Organization.
Robertson, Vincent G., (CV) ... '69 '94 C.205 B.A. L.421 J.D. [[A] Griffin&H.]
*PRACTICE AREAS: Commercial Law; Real Estate Law; Education Law; Estate Planning; Landlord/Tenant Law.
Robinson, Battle Rankin, (Ms.) ... '38 '63 C.228 B.A. L.976 LL.B. Assoc. J., Family Ct.
Rogers, Bruce A., (CV) ... '61 '86 C.205 B.A.A.S. L.776 J.D. [Bruce&M.]
Rutt, David N., (BV) ... '52 '78 C.901 B.A. L.665 J.D. [Moore&R.] ⊙
*PRACTICE AREAS: Residential Real Estate; Commercial Real Estate; Real Estate Litigation; Construction Law; Estate Litigation.
Sandy, John P. M., (BV) ... '51 '77 C.205 B.A. L.64 J.D. [Stumpf,V.&S.]
*PRACTICE AREAS: Criminal Law; Personal Injury; Civil and Criminal Litigation.
Schab, William, (BV) ... '49 '75 C.728 B.A. L.446 J.D. [Schab&B.] ⊙
*PRACTICE AREAS: Real Estate; Collections; Probate and Estates.

Schab & Barnett, P.A., (BV)
9 Chestnut Street, P.O. Box 755, 19947 ⊙
Mailing Address: P.O. Box 755, Georgetown, Delaware 19947
Telephone: 302-856-9024 Fax: 302-856-6360
William Schab; Norman C. Barnett.
Commercial Collections, Commercial Law, Probate and Estates, Real Estate, Mortgage Foreclosures, Personal Injury, Commercial Insurance Claims and Defense, Products Liability, Admiralty, Maritime.
Lewes, Delaware Office: 1322 Kings Highway. Telephone: 302-645-6626.

See Professional Biographies, GEORGETOWN, DELAWARE

Schrader, Dennis L., (BV) ... '47 '72 C&L.923 B.A., J.D. [Wilson,H.&B.]
*PRACTICE AREAS: Municipal Law; Construction Law; Civil Litigation; Family Law.
Schrider, Mary Robin ... '74 '99 C.903 B.A. L.945 J.D. [[A] Tunnell&R.]
*PRACTICE AREAS: Civil Litigation; Debtor and Creditor; Homeowners Association Law.
Sergovic, John A., Jr., (BV) ... '48 '73 C.884 B.S. L.446 J.D. [Sergovic,E.&S.]
*PRACTICE AREAS: Real Property Law; Corporate Law.

Sergovic, Ellis & Shirey, P.A., (BV)
9 North Front Street, P.O. Box 875, 19947-0875
Telephone: 302-855-9500 FAX: 302-855-9509
Email: serg.ellis@dol.net
John A. Sergovic, Jr.; Stephen P. Ellis; Brian D. Shirey.
General Civil Practice. Real Property, Business, Probate, Taxation, Estate Planning and Corporate Law.

See Professional Biographies, GEORGETOWN, DELAWARE

Shirey, Brian D., (BV) ... '63 '90 C.204 B.S. L.1338 J.D. [Sergovic,E.&S.]
*PRACTICE AREAS: Commercial Law; General Business Law; Health Law.

Smith, George B., (BV) ....'48 '82 C.205 B.S. L.1338 J.D. [Smith O.P.&B.]
*PRACTICE AREAS: Elder Law; Guardianship; Real Estate; Estate Planning; Estate Administration.

Smith O'Donnell Procino & Berl, LLP, (BV)
406 South Bedford Street, P.O. Box 588, 19947
Telephone: 302-855-0551 Fax: 302-855-0553
George B. Smith; Lynn R. O'Donnell; Michele L. Procino; Richard E. W. Berl, Jr.
Corporate, Business Law, Probate and Estate Planning, Administrative, Tax, Real Estate, Elder Law, Personal Injury, Domestic Relations, Civil Litigation.
See Professional Biographies, GEORGETOWN, DELAWARE

Southmayd, Andrew K. ....'61 '91 C.205 B.A. L.1338 J.D. Comr., Fam. Ct.
Steele, Lawrence B., III, (BV) ....'43 '71 C.205 B.A.A.S. L.446 J.D. [L.B.Steele,III]
Steele, Lawrence B., III, Professional Association, (BV) .... 120 S. Bedford St.
Steiner, Paula Ryan ....'68 '93 C.659 B.A. L.276 J.D. State Dept. of Jus.
Stokes, Richard F. ....'46 '70 C.165 B.A. L.228 J.D. Com. Pleas J.
Stumpf, Thomas J., (BV) .... '48 '74 C.25 B.A. L.838 J.D. [Stumpf,V.&S.]
*PRACTICE AREAS: Personal Injury; Probate Law; Estate Planning Law; Litigation.

Stumpf, Vickers & Sandy, P.A., (BV)
8 West Market Street, 19947
Telephone: 302-856-3561 FAX: 302-856-0956
Thomas J. Stumpf; Vincent H. Vickers, II; John P. M. Sandy; Thomas E. Gay; Brian F. Dolan;—Kim DeBonte.
General Civil and Trial Practice. Personal Injury, Criminal Law, Workers' Compensation and Family Law.
See Professional Biographies, GEORGETOWN, DELAWARE

Tsantes, Stephanie Ann ....'66 '94 C.518 B.A. L.1338 J.D. Dept. of Jus.
Tunnell, Christine E., (CV) ...'56 '79 C.205 B.A. L.228 J.D. 114 East Market Street, #201
Tunnell, Robert W., (AV) .... '14 '41 C.532 A.B. L.228 LL.B. Pine & Race Sts.

Tunnell & Raysor, P.A., (BV)
30 E. Pine Street, P.O. Box 151, 19947 ⊙
Telephone: 302-856-7313; 1-800-533-2897 Fax: 302-856-7329; 856-3186
Email: info@tunnellraysor.com
John E. Messick (1959-1994); Harold E. Dukes, Jr. (Resident, Rehoboth Beach Office); James F. Waehler; Harold W. T. Purnell, II; Tempe Brownell Steen (Resident, Bethany Beach Office);—Kelly Dunn Gelof; Mary Robin Schrider; Heidi A. Balliet.
General Civil and Trial Practice. Labor and Employment Law, Corporate, Banking, Business, Commercial, Real Estate, Probate, Family, Tax and Estate Planning, Municipal, Negligence, Personal Injury and Criminal Law.
Bethany Beach, Delaware Office: Ocean Highway, P.O. Box 156. Telephone: 302-539-8222. Fax: 302-539-1089.
Rehoboth Beach, Delaware Office: Plaza Five, 323 East Rehoboth Avenue. Telephone: 302-227-1314. Fax: 302-227-5829.
Seaford, Delaware Office: 809 Norman Eskridge Highway. Telephone: 302-628-0123. Fax: 302-628-0125.
See Professional Biographies, GEORGETOWN, DELAWARE

Tyler, James B., III, (BV) '47 '74 C.855 B.A. L.893 J.D.
211 East Market Street, P.O. Box 555, 19947
Telephone: 302-856-6397; 1-800-758-0077 Fax: 302-856-6398
Email: jbtyler3@compuserve.com URL: http://www.lawyers.com/tylerlaw
***PRACTICE AREAS: General Civil Trial; Appellate Litigation; Business Law; Estate Planning Law; Bankruptcy.**
General, Civil, Trial and Appellate Litigation. Business and Estate Planning. Debtor-Creditor and Commercial Transactions, Collection and Real Estate Matters.
See Professional Biographies, GEORGETOWN, DELAWARE

Vanderslice, Patrick E. ....'67 '99 C.205 B.S. L.1338 J.D. [A Moore&R.]
*PRACTICE AREAS: Family Law; Civil Litigation; Wills; Contracts.
Vickers, Vincent H., II, (BV) .... '52 '83 C.205 B.S.B.A. L.945 J.D. [Stumpf,V.&S.]
*PRACTICE AREAS: Criminal Law; Personal Injury; Civil and Criminal Litigation.
Waehler, James F., (BV) .... '45 '70 C.885 B.A. L.276 J.D. [Tunnell&R.] (⊙Seaford)
*PRACTICE AREAS: Civil Litigation; Real Estate Law; Banking Law; Corporate Law; Commercial Law.

Walsh Monzack and Monaco, P.A.
(See Wilmington)

Weidman, David J. ....'67 '97 C.893 B.A. L.838 J.D. [Hudson,J.J.&F.]

Welch & Associates
(See Wilmington)

West, June Ellen .... '52 '77 C.903 B.A. L.1338 J.D. R.D. 1, Box 274
Willard, Timothy G. ....'61 '89 C.273 B.A. L.1338 J.D. 5 The Circle
Wilson, Sonja Truitt ....'67 '93 C.205 B.A.A.S. L.1338 J.D. Comr., Family Ct.

Wilson, Halbrook & Bayard, Professional Association, (AV) BB
107 West Market Street, P.O. Box 690, 19947
Telephone: 302-856-0015 Telecopier: 302-856-7116
Email: whbadmin@whblaw.com
Houston Wilson (1910-1980); Eugene H. Bayard; Clayton E. Bunting; Dennis L. Schrader; Robert G. Gibbs; Eric C. Howard; Mark D. Olson. Retired: Robert L. Halbrook.
General Practice. Personal Injury, Workers Compensation, Real Estate, Banks and Banking, Commercial Law, Civil Litigation, Municipal Law, Administrative Law, Construction Law, Estate Planning, Estate Administration and Taxation.
Representative Clients: Delaware National Bank; Townsend's Inc.; Allen Family Foods, Inc.; Burris Foods, Inc.; J.G. Townsend, Jr. & Co.; Sussex County; Nanticoke Homes, Inc.; First State Packaging, Inc.
Approved Attorneys for: Ticor Title Insurance Co.; First American Title Insurance Co.
References: Delaware National Bank; Wilmington Trust Co.
See Professional Biographies, GEORGETOWN, DELAWARE

Withers, Melanie C. ....'64 '90 C.893 L.245 J.D. Dept. of Jus.
Witsil, Robert V., Jr., (BV) ....'51 '81 C.95 B.A. L.1338 J.D. 120 S. Bedford St.
Yori, James August, (BV) ....'40 '79 C.524 B.S. L.64 J.D. [Fuqua&Y.]

Young Conaway Stargatt & Taylor, LLP, (AV) BB
110 West Pine Street, 19947 ⊙
Telephone: 302-856-3571 Telecopy: 302-856-9338
Email: ycst@ycst.com URL: http://www.ycst.com
Members of Firm: H. James Conaway, Jr. (1922-1990); Craig A. Karsnitz (Resident). Associate: Vivian Medinilla Longo (Resident).
General Practice.
Wilmington, Delaware Office: Eleventh Floor, Wilmington Trust Center, 1100 North Market Street, P.O. Box 391. Telephone: 302-571-6600. Telecopy: 302-571-1253.
See Professional Biographies, GEORGETOWN, DELAWARE

GREENVILLE, —, *New Castle Co.*

Bryan, Henry W. ....'12 '41 C.197 B.A. L.477 LL.B. P.O. Box 3735‡
Edell, Miriam Fost '46 '87 C.21 B.A. L.1338 J.D.
(adm. in NJ; not adm. in DE) P.O. Box 4280
Garthwaite, Patricia A. ....'59 '91 C.522 B.A. L.1338 J.D. 3828 Kennett Pike, Ste. 204
Langley, Van E. ....'36 '65 C.228 A.B. L.813 J.D. P.O. Box 3864
Lowicki, E. Scott ....'56 '87 C.260 B.A. L.356 J.D. 4000 Springfield Ln.
Malang, Robert J. ....'12 '38 C&L.262 A.B., LL.B. Ret. Civil Ct. J.
Measley, Harold F., Jr., (BV) ....'45 '71 C.205 B.A. L.880 J.D. [H.F.Measley,Jr.]
*PRACTICE AREAS: Taxation Law; Estate Planning Law; Estates Law.

Measley, Harold F., Jr., P.A., (BV)
Greenville Place, 124B Senatorial Drive, 19807
Telephone: 302-655-6362 Fax: 302-655-6363

(This Listing Continued)

Measley, Harold F., Jr., P.A. (Continued)
Harold F. Measley, Jr.
Taxation and Estate Planning Law.

Paolin, Gerald J. '23 '51 C.705 B.A. L.1292 LL.B.
(adm. in NJ; not adm. in DE) 11 Gale Ln.‡

HARRINGTON, 2,311, *Kent Co.*

Terry, Harry K. F., (BV) .... '44 '74 C.205 B.A. L.421 J.D. [H.K.F.Terry] ⊙
Terry, Harry K. F., Professional Association, (BV) ....Clark & Hanley Sts. (⊙Dover)

HARTLY, 107, *Kent Co.*

Stallings, Martin F. '46 '84 C&L.999 B.S., J.D.
(adm. in DC; not adm. in DE) Rte. 2, Box 105-B‡

HOCKESSIN, —, *New Castle Co.*

Adams, Charles C. '21 '49 C&L.902 A.B., J.D.
(adm. in AZ; not adm. in DE) 726 Loveville Rd.‡
Alexander, W. Stanley .... '29 '64 C.205 B.S. L.446 LL.B. 653 Woodview Dr. (Pat.)
Bryde, Gary A., (BV) ....'50 '76 C&L.838 B.S., J.D. [G.A.Bryde]
*PRACTICE AREAS: Commercial Real Estate; Residential Real Estate; Business Law; Personal Injury; Real Estate Development.

Bryde, Gary A., P.A., (BV)
Stone Mill Office Park, 724 Yorklyn Road, Suite 100, 19707
Telephone: 302-239-3700 Fax: 302-239-4015
Email: brydex4@aol.com URL: http://www.garybryde.homepage.com
Gary A. Bryde. Of Counsel: Charles Gruver, III.
Commercial and Residential Real Estate, Real Estate Development and Financing, Zoning and Subdivision, Transactional Law, Probate, Estate Planning, Corporate Law, Personal Injury and Business Law.
See Professional Biographies, HOCKESSIN, DELAWARE

Burt, Warren B., (AV) .... '34 '60 C.546 B.S. L.893 J.D. 886 Sharpless Rd.
Cardona, Virginia S. ....'55 '85 C.260 B.A. L.836 J.D. 146 Dantes Dr.
Duffy, William ....'16 '48 C.205 A.B. L.659 LL.B. Ret. Supm. Ct. Jus.
Froehlich, Mark H. ....'56 '81 C.216 B.A. L.1017 J.D. [Froehlich&Assoc.]
Froehlich & Associates, P.A. .... 724 Yorklyn Road, Suite 135
Gardiner, Scott G. '64 '91 C.1102 B.A. L.945 J.D.
(adm. in NC; not adm. in DE) 101 Cheltenham Rd.★
Gruver, Charles, III, (BV) .... '52 '77 C.107 B.S.B.A. L.1017 J.D. [© G.A.Bryde]
*PRACTICE AREAS: Personal Injury; Probate Law; Commercial Law; Collection Law; Estate Planning.
Hartnett, Jennifer Anne ....'68 '94 C.893 B.A. L.178 J.D. [Hartnett&H.]
*PRACTICE AREAS: Family Law; Criminal Law.
Hartnett, Lawrence F., (CV) ....'30 '59 C.205 B.A. L.1017 [Hartnett&H.]

Hartnett & Hartnett, (CV)
7301 Lancaster Pike, 19707
Telephone: 302-239-4220
URL: http://www.lawyers.com/hartnett&hartnett
Jennifer Anne Hartnett; Lawrence F. Hartnett.
Family Law, Criminal Law.
See Professional Biographies, HOCKESSIN, DELAWARE

Hyman, Jerry A., (CV) .... '49 '79 C.705 A.B. L.966 J.D. 724 Yorklyn Rd.
Locke, Christopher Ronald '62 '88 C.205 B.S.B.A. L.128 J.D.
(adm. in PA; not adm. in DE) 724 Yorklyn Rd.
Poole, Carroll F. .... '21 '51 C.821 B.A. L.893 LL.B. 647 Woodview Dr.‡
Rafferty, Timothy M., (P.A.), (CV) ... '47 '75 C.734 B.S. L.1338 J.D. 7189 Lancaster Pike
Rosini, Robert J. '47 '78 C.128 B.A. L.1338 J.D.
(adm. in PA; not adm. in DE) 35 Sage Way‡

Sobocinski, Edward Z., (BV) '39 '66 C.205 B.A. L.276 J.D.
3 Ashtree Lane, 19707
Telephone: 302-235-5773 Fax: 302-235-5708
General Civil Litigation, Real Estate, Wills and Estates, Personal Injury.

Weaver, June Heistand '51 '77 C.105 B.A. L.352 J.D.
(adm. in IA; not adm. in DE) 27 Kings Grant Rd.‡

Wendelburg, Allan, Law Office of, (BV) '54 '79 C.205 B.A. L.1338 J.D.
722 Yorklyn Road, Suite 300, 19707
Telephone: 302-235-0900 Fax: 302-235-2710
Email: awendelburg@wendelburglaw.com URL: http://www.lawyers.com/wendelburg
Civil Litigation, Criminal Litigation, Personal Injury, Professional Malpractice, Insurance Defense, Construction Law, Insurance, Probate, Estate Planning, Business Law, Commercial Law.
See Professional Biographies, HOCKESSIN, DELAWARE

Wright, Caleb M. ....'08 '33 C.205 B.A. L.976 LL.B. Sr. U.S. Dist. J.

LAUREL, 3,226, *Sussex Co.*

Lyon, Michael V. ....'44 '77 L.362 J.D. 212 W. 8th St.

LEWES, 2,295, *Sussex Co.*

Barnett, Norman C., (BV) ....'42 '69 C.446 B.S. L.329 J.D. [Schab&B.] ⊙
*PRACTICE AREAS: Collections; Personal Injury; Real Estate; Mediation; Commercial Insurance Claims.

Barros, McNamara, Scanlon, Malkiewicz & Taylor, Professional Association, (AV)
1143 Savannah Road, 19958 ⊙
Telephone: 302-644-8510
Edward R. McNamara.
Personal Injury, Medical Malpractice, Work Place Injury, Civil and Criminal Trial Practice. Family, Bankruptcy, Probate, Estate Planning and Corporate Law. Commercial Law. Litigation, Administrative, Zoning, Collections.
Representative Clients: Delaware State Music Teachers Assn.; Sears Roebuck & Co.
Dover, Delaware Office: State & Loockerman Streets, P.O. Box 1298, 19903-1298. Telephone: 302-734-8400. Telefax: 302-734-4349.
See Professional Biographies, LEWES, DELAWARE

Dyer, Preston L., (CV) .... '53 '80 C.205 B.S. L.1017 J.D. [© W.E.Wright]
Fifer, Larry W., (BV) ....'45 '73 C.901 B.A. L.902 J.D. 750 Kings Hwy.
Green, Joseph B., (BV) ..... '47 '72 C.216 B.A. L.229 J.D. 467 Hwy. One (⊙Wilmington)
Hitchens, J. Robert ....'46 '79 C.444 B.S. L.896 J.D. 27B Nassau Park‡
Kerkam, William B., Jr. '11 '35 C.674 B.S. L.273 LL.B.
(adm. in DC; not adm. in DE) 18 Shipcarpenter Sq.‡
McNamara, Edward R., (BV) .... '47 '71 C.205 A.B. L.884 J.D. [Barros,M.S.M.&T.] ⊙
*PRACTICE AREAS: Personal Injury Law; Estate Planning Law.

Mooney, Eric G., P.A.
(See Georgetown)

Reardon, Dennis A. ....'35 '65 C.205 B.A. L.128 LL.B. 108 Second Street, Suite 8
Schab, William, (BV) .... '49 '75 C.728 B.A. L.446 J.D. [Schab&B.] ⊙
*PRACTICE AREAS: Real Estate; Collections; Probate and Estates; Products Liability.

Schab & Barnett, P.A., (BV)
1322 Kings Highway, 19958 ⊙
Telephone: 302-645-6626

(This Listing Continued)

Schab & Barnett, P.A. (Continued)

William Schab; Norman C. Barnett.
Commercial Collections, Commercial Law, Probate and Estates, Real Estate, Mortgage Foreclosures, Personal Injury, Workers Compensation, Commercial Insurance Claims and Defense, Admiralty, Maritime, Beach Law.
Georgetown, Delaware Office: 9 Chestnut Street, P.O. Box 755. Telephone: 302-856-9024. Fax: 302-856-6360.

See Professional Biographies, LEWES, DELAWARE

Wright, William E., (BV) .... '42 '68 C.205 B.A. L.575 J.D. [W.E.Wright]
Wright, William E., P.A., (BV) ....1632 Savannah Road Suite 4
Zrake, Virginia A., (AVⓉ) '54 '85 C.1044 B.A. L.446 J.D.
(adm. in MD; not adm. in DE) 136 Henlopen Shores Circle

MAGNOLIA, 211, *Kent Co.*

Melvin, Gary S. ....'50 '79 C.204 B.A. L.1338 J.D. P.O. Box 99★

MIDDLETOWN, 3,834, *New Castle Co.*

Connolly, Beverley Burge .... '38 '64 C.903 B.A. L.831 LL.B. 139 E. Main St.
Delacy, Kathleen ....'57 '00 L.1338 J.D. 10 W. Green St.
Frumkin, Paul A., (AVⓉ) '52 '78 C.477 B.A. L.215 J.D.
(adm. in MI; not adm. in DE) 30 Manassas Drive
Hallsted, Robert H., Jr. .... '46 '73 C.205 B.A. L.705 J.D. 511 Saint Michael Drive
Murphy, Brian P., (CV) ....'39 '64 C.276 A.B. L.659 LL.B. 55 W. Main St.

MILFORD, 6,040, *Kent & Sussex Cos.*

Campbell, Dean A. ....'60 '97 C.205 B.A. L.1338 J.D. [🄰 Moore&R.] ⊙
Feindt, Walter G., (BV) .... '51 '83 C.205 B.A. L.1338 J.D. 4 Lakelawn Dr.
Moore, J. Everett, Jr., (BV) ....'50 '76 C.205 B.A. L.945 J.D. [Moore&R.] ⊙
Moore & Rutt, P.A., (BV) .... 109 N. Walnut St. (⊙Georgetown)
Prisco, Ronald J. ....'53 '79 C.205 B.A. L.1338 J.D. P.O. Box 625
Rutt, David N., (BV) ....'52 '78 C.901 B.A. L.665 J.D. [Moore&R.] ⊙
Snyder, John O., (BV) ....'16 '53 C&L.893 B.A., LL.B. 417 N. Walnut St.

MILLSBORO, 1,643, *Sussex Co.*

Reid, Samuel L., (CVⓉ) '20 '77 C.152 B.S. L.790 J.D.
(adm. in SC; not adm. in DE) 1321 Pot-Nets W.‡
Sweet, Rodney Don, (CV) ....'48 '74 C&L.823 B.S., J.D. P.O. Box 1555
Wilgus, William B., (CV) ....'53 '78 C.269 B.A. L.790 J.D. 221 E. Dupont Hwy.

MILTON, 1,417, *Sussex Co.*

Karsnitz, Kathi Ann, (BV) .... '53 '82 C.205 B.A.A.S. L.1338 J.D. 10 Heronwood

MONTCHANIN, —, *New Castle Co.*

Miller, Richard E. .... '64 '92 C.976 B.A. L.880 J.D. 3 Gunpowder Ln.‡

NEWARK, 25,098, *New Castle Co.*

Aaronson, Jennifer-Kate M. ....'70 '95 C.1053 B.A. L.1338 J.D. [Potter,C.&L.] ⊙
Amick, Steven H. .... '47 '72 C.903 B.A. L.1017 J.D. [🄲 Cooch&T.]
Baker, William R., Jr. ....'68 '98 C.205 B.A. L.1360 J.D. [🄰 Kimmel,C.R.&P.] ⊙
*PRACTICE AREAS: Civil Trial Practice; Insurance; Negligence; Workers Compensation; Construction Accidents.
Bartkowski, Matthew M., (BV) .... '67 '93 C.205 B.S. L.1338 J.D. [Kimmel,C.R.&P.] ⊙
*PRACTICE AREAS: General and Civil Trial Practice; Insurance; Negligence; Workers Compensation; Construction Accidents.
Bednash, Michael D., (BV) .... '64 '91 C.205 B.S. L.1338 J.D. [Kimmel,C.R.&P.] ⊙
*PRACTICE AREAS: General and Civil Trial Practice; Insurance; Negligence; Workers Compensation; Construction Accidents.
Bloxom, John M., IV, (CV) ......'56 '83 C.893 B.A. L.902 J.D. [Montgomery,M.W.&R.]
*PRACTICE AREAS: Real Estate-Commercial Law; Real Estate (Property) Law; Real Estate Development and Syndications Law; Commercial Lending; Mortgage Law.
Boarman, Charles H. '51 '78 C.197 B.A. L.64 J.D.
(adm. in MD; not adm. in DE) Maryland Bk., N.A.
Brennan, Mary Anna '60 '93
C.205 B.A. L.1338 J.D. Asst. V.P. & Coun., MBNA Amer. Bk., N.A.
Brown, James W. .... '48 '73 C.205 B.A. L.902 J.D. W.L. Gore & Assoc., Inc.
Burtch, Jeoffrey L., (BV) .....'50 '78 C.473 B.A. L.851 J.D. [Cooch&T.] (⊙Wilmington)
Cabell, Benjamin, IV '40 '65
C.276 A.B. L.893 J.D. V.P. & Gen. Coun., Maryland Bk., N.A.
Campbell, John S. '50 '80
C.999 B.S. L.1338 J.D. Pat. Coun., W.L. Gore & Assoc., Inc. (Pat.)
Carmine, Kenneth F. ....'48 '74 C.205 B.A. L.1017 J.D. [Potter,C.&L.] ⊙
Carter, Edward B., Jr., (AV) ......'46 '77 C.228 B.A. L.1338 J.D. [Kimmel,C.R.&P.] ⊙
*PRACTICE AREAS: General and Civil Trial Practice; Insurance; Negligence; Workers Compensation; Construction Accidents.
Civiletti, Andrew S. '61 '89 C.362 B.S. L.64 J.D.
(adm. in MD; not adm. in DE) Asst. V.P. & Coun., MBNA Amer. Bk., N.A.
Cole, Dezzie R. '59 '88 C&L.836 B.A., J.D.
(adm. in PA; not adm. in DE) Asst. V.P. & Coun., MBNA Amer. Bk., N.A.
Conner, Mark H., (BV) ....'64 '90 C.216 B.A. L.1338 J.D. [🄰 Morgan S.&L.]
*PRACTICE AREAS: Civil Litigation; Criminal Law; Workers Compensation; Family Law.
Cooch, Edward W., Jr., (AV) '20 '48
C.205 B.A. L.893 LL.B. [🄲 Cooch&T.] (⊙Wilmington)

Cooch and Taylor, (AV)
51 East Main Street, Suite B, P.O. Box 672, 19715-0672 ⊙
Telephone: 302-368-7200 Telecopier: 302-368-7491
URL: http://www/coochandtaylor.com
Members of Firm: Donald C. Taylor; H. Alfred Tarrant, Jr.; Robert W. Crowe; Bonnie H. Sheer; W. Jeffrey Whittle; Michael A. Friedberg; Jeoffrey L. Burtch; C. Scott Reese; Andrew P. Taylor (Also at Wilmington Office); Thomas D. Shellenberger;—Paula C. Witherow; Mary Ann P. Bazzano (Resident, Kennett Square, PA Office); Gregory J. Weinig; Adam Singer. Special Counsel: Steven H. Amick. Of Counsel: Edward W. Cooch, Jr.
General Practice, Banking, Litigation. Corporation, Real Estate, Environmental, Land Use and Development, Trial Practice in all Federal and Delaware Courts, Family, Personal Injury, Probate, Estate Planning, Taxation, Commercial, Bankruptcy and Changery Court Practice.
Representative Clients: Artisans' Bank; Trustees of the New Castle Common; CBI Industires, Inc. Approved Attorneys for: Ticor Title Insurance Co.; Lawyers Title Insurance Co.; Transnation Title Insurance Co.
References: PNC Bank, Delaware; Wilmington Trust Co.; First Union; Artisan's Bank.
Wilmington Office: Suite 1000, 824 Market Street Mall, P.O. Box 1680. Telephone: 302-652-3641. Telecopier: 302-652-5379.
Kennett Square, Pennsylvania Office: 502 West Cypress Street, P.O. Box 909. Telephone: 610-444-3700. Telecopier: 610-444-5446.

See Professional Biographies, NEWARK, DELAWARE

Coons, Christopher A. .... '63 '92 C.31 B.A. L.976 J.D. Atty., W.L. Gore & Assoc., Inc.
Crowe, John E. '26 '60 C.867 B.S. L.823 LL.B.
(adm. in NY; not adm. in DE; Pat.) 23 Dewalt Road
Crowe, Robert W., (BV) ... '39 '65 C.95 A.B. L.1017 LL.B. [Cooch&T.] (⊙Wilmington)
*PRACTICE AREAS: Estate Planning; Estate Settlements.
Daley, Robert E., (BV) .... '37 '63 C.602 B.A. L.893 J.D. [Daley,E.&v.] ⊙
Daley, Erisman & van Ogtrop, (AV) .... 206 E. Delaware Ave. (⊙Wilmington)
Danberg, Barbara Snapp '65 '92 C.205 B.A.A.S. L.1338 J.D.
[🄰 Trzuskowski,K.K.&P.]
*PRACTICE AREAS: Taxation; Estate Planning; Estate Administration; Commercial Litigation.
Drewry, Eric B. '48 '76 C.674 A.B. L.228 J.D.
(adm. in GA; not adm. in DE) 216 Planet Rd.‡
Dykes, James D. .... '52 '80 C.205 B.A.A.S. L.1017 J.D. 551 Paper Mill Rd.
Edwards, Duncan L. '54 '84 C&L.1049 B.A., J.D.
(adm. in CA; not adm. in DE) 551 Paper Mill Rd.
Erisman, James A., (AV) ....'40 '66 C.205 B.S. L.1017 J.D. [Daley,E.&v.] ⊙
Fanelli, Joseph M. '47 '96 C.276 B.S.L. L.1338 J.D.
(adm. in PA; not adm. in DE) Fin. Mgr., DuPont Co.
Ferry, Daniel B., (BV) ....'25 '64 C.205 B.S. L.831 LL.B. 299 E. Main St.‡
Ferry, Thomas B., (BV) .... '51 '81 C.205 B.S. L.1187 J.D. 299 E. Main St.
Flood, Susan E. .... '62 '87 C.205 B.A. L.1338 J.D. UAW Legal Servs. Plan
Forcina, Anthony N., Jr., (CV) '63 '89
C.884 B.A. L.1338 J.D. 131 Continental Drive, Suite 108
Ford, Eileen M., (CV) .... '63 '90 C.1093 B.S. L.1338 J.D. 9 Gilbert Ct.
Frank, John C. S., (CV) .... '43 '69 C.282 B.A. L.982 J.D. 125 E. Delaware Ave.
Friedberg, Michael A., (AV) .... '47 '72 C&L.893 B.A., J.D. [Cooch&T.] (⊙Wilmington)
Funk, Vance A., III, (BV) ...... '42 '68 C.205 B.S. L.902 J.D. [🄰 Trzuskowski,K.K.&P.]
Gallagher, Patricia A., (BV) '57 '89
C.645 B.S. L.831 J.D. V.P. & Coun., MBNA Amer. Bk., N.A.
Garvin, James W., Jr., (BV) ....'37 '70 C.205 B.S. L.831 J.D. 224 E. Del. Ave.
Genco, Victor M., Jr. '61 '91 C.871 B.S. L.1218 J.D.
(adm. in WI; not adm. in DE) W. L. Gore & Associates, Inc.
Giacco, Richard J., (BV) '52 '80
C.893 B.A. L.1338 J.D. V.P. & Gen. Coun., Axess Corporation
Guzzetta, Kathleen S. '64 '91 C&L.276 B.A., J.D.
(adm. in PA; not adm. in DE) Asst. V.P. & Coun., MBNA Amer. Bk., N.A.
Hall, Patricia E. .... '46 '81 C.228 A.B. L.1338 J.D. 500 Stanton Christiana Rd.
Hassan, Syed Jamshed Nasim ...... '47 '82 C&L.999 B.A., M.A. 102 Harmony Crest Dr.‡
Healy, Kevin G., (BV) .... '58 '86 C.205 B.A. L.1338 J.D. [Morris,J.H.&W.]
*PRACTICE AREAS: Civil Litigation; Construction Law; Personal Injury Litigation.
Hodesblatt, Alan .... '60 '84 C.696 B.A. L.665 J.D. 113 Fox Dr.
Hoffman, Sherry V. .... '46 '81 C.339 B.S. L.1338 J.D. 111 Dallas Ave.
Hubbard, Bruce E., (BV) .... '46 '77 C.300 B.A. L.851 J.D. 224 E. Delaware Ave.
James, Barbara M., (BV) '50 '76 C.945 A.B. L.276 J.D.
200 Continental Drive, Suite 212
Johns, David J. '58 '83 C.205 B.A. L.831 J.D.
(adm. in PA; not adm. in DE; Pat.) 551 Paper Mill Rd.
Jones, Francis J., Jr., (BV) ....'57 '83 C&L.128 B.A., J.D. [Morris,J.H.&W.]
*PRACTICE AREAS: Insurance Defense; Personal Injury; Litigation; Products Liability.
Kaeding, Konrad H. '59 '85 C.339 B.S. L.608 J.D.
(adm. in IL; not adm. in DE; Pat.) V.P. Legal Affrs. & Gen. Coun., Rodel, Inc.
Kennedy, James A. '58 '83 C.184 B.S. L.665 J.D.
(adm. in PA; not adm. in DE) Dir., Taxes & Tax Coun., W.L. Gore & Assoc., Inc.
Killheffer, Sharon C. '61 '86
C.174 B.S. L.276 J.D. 1st V.P. & Coun., MBNA Amer. Bk., N.A.
Kimmel, Morton Richard, (AV) .... '40 '65 C.831 A.B. L.273 J.D. [Kimmel,C.R.&P.] ⊙
*PRACTICE AREAS: General and Civil Trial Practice; Insurance; Negligence; Workers Compensation; Construction Accidents.

Kimmel, Carter, Roman & Peltz, P.A., (AV)
1400 Peoples Plaza, Suite 100, 19702 ⊙
Telephone: 302-838-5970
Morton Richard Kimmel; Edward B. Carter, Jr.; Thomas J. Roman; William R. Peltz; Michael D. Bednash; Matthew M. Bartkowski.
William R. Baker, Jr.
General Civil and Trial Practice in all Courts. Insurance, Negligence, Construction Accidents, Workers Compensation. Federal Practice.
References: Wilmington Trust Co.; PNC Bank.
Wilmington, Delaware Office: 913 Market Street, 12th Floor, P.O. Box 272, 19899-0272. Telephone: 302-571-0800. Fax: 302-571-8155.

See Professional Biographies, NEWARK, DELAWARE

Knepper & Stratton
(See Wilmington)

Kwarv, Melinda J. .... '58 '86 C.966 B.A. L.228 J.D. Univ. of Del.
Labovsky, Maxine S. '55 '88 C.94 A.B. L.564 J.D.
(adm. in NJ; not adm. in DE) MBNA Amer. Bk., N.A.
Lambiro, Chantel L. '71 '98 C.1292 B.A. L.1338 J.D.
(adm. in NJ; not adm. in DE) 500 Stanton- Christina Dr.
Latzko, David Michael '56 '82 C.205 B.A. L.273 J.D.
(adm. in VA; not adm. in DE) Attorney, W.L. Gore & Assoc., Inc.
Leonard, James R., (BV) ....'53 '78 C.205 B.A.A.S. L.831 J.D. [Potter,C.&L.] ⊙
Leoni, Robert J., (CV) '64 '90
C.205 B.A. L.1338 J.D. [Morgan S.&L.] (⊙Hunt Valley, MD)
*PRACTICE AREAS: Civil Trial Litigation.
McCann, Richard S., (CV) .... '38 '64 C&L.276 A.B., J.D. 94 E. Main St.
Messick, Sandra E. ..... '53 '78 C.205 B.A. L.1338 J.D. 200 Continental Drive, Suite 212
Meyer, Dena '54 '85 C.103 Sc.B. L.1338 J.D.
(adm. in PA; not adm. in DE) 551 Paper Mill Rd.
Milkovics, Krista A. ....'71 '98 C.205 B.A. L.1338 J.D. 72 Welsh Tract Rd.

Montgomery, McCracken, Walker & Rhoads, LLP, (CV)
Christiana Executive Campus, 131 Continental Drive, Suite 304, 19713 ⊙
Telephone: 302-894-7000 Fax: 302-733-7937
URL: http://www.mmwr.com
Partner: John M. Bloxom, IV. Associate: John H. Newcomer, Jr.
Litigation (including complex, class action and multi-district litigation, professional malpractice defense for all learned professions and healthcare institutions; products liability; toxic tort defense, insurance defense, First Amendment and media law); Intellectual Property; Information Technology; E-Commerce and Web-Based Businesses; Environmental Law; Antitrust; Government Investigations & White Collar Crime; Employment Law (including NLRB, Title VII, age discrimination, ADA, public employee labor relations, and workers' compensation); Government Relations; Business and Personal Counseling (including mergers and acquisitions; corporate, securities, corporate criminal investigations and computer law); Bankruptcy/Reorganization; Health Care; Nonprofit Corporations Law; Employee Benefits; Executive Compensation and Immigration; Taxation; Trusts and Estates; Real Estate; Sports Law.
Cherry Hill, New Jersey Office: LibertyView, Suite 600, 457 Haddonfield Road. Telephone: 856-488-7700. Facsimile: 856-488-7720.
Philadelphia, Pennsylvania Office: 123 South Broad Street. Telephone: 215-772-1500. Fax: 215-772-7620.

See Professional Biographies, NEWARK, DELAWARE

Morgan, Robert C., (AVⓉ) '55 '81 C.446 B.A. L.64 J.D.
(adm. in MD; not adm. in DE) [Morgan S.&L.] (⊙Hunt Valley, MD)
*PRACTICE AREAS: Civil Litigation; Insurance Defense; Health Care Law; Employment Discrimination; Officers and Directors Liability.

Morgan Shelsby & Leoni, A Professional Association, (AV)
131 Continental Drive, Suite 206, 19713
Telephone: 302-454-7430 Fax: 302-454-7437
Robert C. Morgan (Not admitted in DE); Gilbert F. Shelsby, Jr.; Robert J. Leoni;—Douglass Lee Mowrey; Mark H. Conner.
Civil and Criminal Trial Practice in all State and Federal Courts. Personal Injury, Medical Malpractice, Products Liability, Workers Compensation, Insurance and Health Care, Corporate and Commercial Litigation.
Affiliated Office: Morgan Shelsby Carlo Downs & Everton, P.A., 4 North Park Drive, 21031, Hunt Valley, Maryland. Telephone: 410-584-2800. Fax: 410-584-2020.
See Professional Biographies, NEWARK, DELAWARE

Morris, James, Hitchens & Williams, LLP, (AV) BR
16 Polly Drummond Hill Road, 19711-5703 ⊙
Telephone: 302-368-4200 Telecopier: 302-368-6259
URL: http://www.morrisjames.com
Resident Partners: Kevin G. Healy; Francis J. Jones, Jr.
Litigation, Corporate Law, Commercial Law, Business Law. Administrative Law, Alternative Dispute Resolution, Bankruptcy, Commercial Real Estate, Computers and Software, Education Law, Environmental Law, Family Law, Health Care, Insurance, Insurance Defense, Intellectual Property, Labor and Employment, Medical Malpractice, Partnership Law, Personal Injury, Probate, Products Liability, Real Estate, Taxation, Torts, Trusts and Estates and Wills.
Wilmington, Delaware Offices: 222 Delaware Avenue, P.O. Box 2306, 19899-2306. Telephone: 302-888-6800. Telecopier: 302-571-1750 and 1010 North Bancroft Parkway, Suite 11, P.O. Box 2328, 19899-2328. Telephone: 302-655-2599. Fax: 302-655-8831.
Dover, Delaware Office: Suite 202, 32 West Loockerman Street, 19904-7356. Telephone: 302-678-8815. Telecopier: 302-678-9063.
See Professional Biographies, NEWARK, DELAWARE

Mowrey, Douglass Lee, (BV) ....'59 '85 C.205 B.A. L.1017 J.D. [Ⓐ Morgan S.&L.]
*PRACTICE AREAS: Personal Injury Defense; Medical Malpractice Defense.
Murray, Brian T., (CV) .... '57 '83 C.205 B.A. L.1048 J.D. [B.T.Murray]
*PRACTICE AREAS: Real Estate; Leases and Leasing; Commercial Law; Residential Real Estate.

Murray, Brian T., P.A., (CV)
903 South College Avenue, 19713
Telephone: 302-731-1776 Fax: 302-731-1730
Brian T. Murray.
Commercial and Residential Real Estate, Landlord and Tenant Law, Leases and Leasing, Real Estate Development and Financing, Land Use and Zoning.
See Professional Biographies, NEWARK, DELAWARE

Newcomer, John H., Jr., (BV) '59 '84 C.216 B.A. L.896 J.D. [Ⓐ Montgomery,M.W.&R.]
*PRACTICE AREAS: Chancery Practice; Litigation; Mechanics Lien Law; Residential Real Estate.
Nowak, Stephen L. .... '62 '87 C.205 B.S. L.1338 J.D. P.O. Box 15006

Otlowski, Raymond J., (BV) '40 '74 C.205 B.A. L.1002 J.D.
224 East Delaware Avenue, 19711
Telephone: 302-368-8595 Fax: 302-368-8597
Personal Injury, Workers Compensation, Real Estate, Wills and Estates.
See Professional Biographies, NEWARK, DELAWARE

Peltz, William R., (BV) ....'62 '88 C.205 B.A. L.1338 J.D. [Kimmel,C.R.&P.] ⊙
*PRACTICE AREAS: General and Civil Trial Practice; Insurance; Negligence; Workers Compensation; Construction Accidents.
Phillips, Neal A. .... '47 '76 C.205 B.A. L.884 J.D. Univ. of Del.
Potter, Stephen B., (BV) .... '38 '64 C.205 B.A. L.128 LL.B. [Potter,C.&L.] ⊙
Potter, Carmine & Leonard, P.A., (BV)
1400 Peoples Plaza, Suite 101 (Glasgow/Bear) (⊙Wilmington)
Powell, Jacqueline Loughman '64 '91 C.903 B.A. L.902 J.D.
Sr. Pers. Bkg. Offr. & Coun., MBNA Amer. Bk., N.A.
Ravalese, Theresa Fennell .... '63 '90 11 Oak Knoll Circle
Reese, C. Scott, (BV) ....'55 '81 C.165 B.A. L.1338 J.D. [Cooch&T.] (⊙Wilmington)
*PRACTICE AREAS: Commercial Litigation; Products Liability; Tax Law.
Roman, Thomas J., (BV) ....'42 '77 C.205 B.A. L.1338 J.D. [Kimmel,C.R.&P.] ⊙
*PRACTICE AREAS: General and Civil Trial Practice; Insurance; Negligence; Workers Compensation; Construction Accidents.
Scheflen, John W., (AVⓉ) '46 '74 C.216 B.S. L.64 J.D.
(adm. in MD; not adm. in DE)
Sr. Exec. V.P., Gen. Coun. & Secy., MBNA Corp. & MBNA Amer. Bk., N.A.
Schoenfeld, Suzanne B. '62 '88 C.289 B.A. L.94 J.D.
(adm. in MA; not adm. in DE) 1 Sheldrake Rd.‡
Schreppler, John J., II, (BV) .... '56 '81 C.674 A.B. L.880 J.D. 664 Churchmans Rd.
Sheer, Bonnie H., (BV) ....'43 '68 C.105 B.A. L.273 J.D. [Cooch&T.] (⊙Wilmington)
*PRACTICE AREAS: Real Estate.
Shellenberger, Thomas D., (BV) '59 '85
C.205 B.A. L.1048 J.D. [Cooch&T.] (⊙Wilmington)
*PRACTICE AREAS: Family Law; Foreclosures.
Shelsby, Gilbert F., Jr., (AV) '59 '85
C&L.446 B.A., J.D. [Morgan S.&L.] (⊙Hunt Valley, MD)
*PRACTICE AREAS: Civil Litigation; Medical Malpractice; Insurance Defense.
Singer, Adam .... '60 '86 C.367 B.E.S. L.94 J.D. [Ⓐ Cooch&T.] (⊙Wilmington)
*PRACTICE AREAS: Commercial Credit; Bankruptcy Chapter 11; Bankruptcy Chapter 7.
Smith, Gary L., (BV) ....'52 '84 C.205 B.A. L.734 J.D. 1400 Peoples Plaza Suite 110
Squadron, Richard J. '57 '84 C.103 B.S. L.659 J.D.
Gen. Mgr., Delmarva Capital Investments, Inc.
Stanton, John P. '60 '89 C&L.276 B.S.F.S., J.D.
(adm. in MD; not adm. in DE) Asst. V.P. & Coun., MBNA Amer. Bk., N.A.
Sullivan, Larry D., (CV) ....'61 '91 C.205 B.S. L.1338 J.D. [L.D.Sullivan]
Sullivan, Larry D., P.A., (CV) ....111 Barksdale Professional Center
Tarrant, H. Alfred, Jr., (AV) '35 '61
C.902 A.B. L.446 LL.B. [Cooch&T.] (⊙Wilmington)
*PRACTICE AREAS: Domestic Relations.
Taylor, Andrew P., (BV) ....'58 '82 C.205 B.S. L.1017 J.D. [Cooch&T.]
*PRACTICE AREAS: Real Estate; Real Estate Brokerage Law.
Taylor, Donald C., (AV) ....'30 '54 C.216 A.B. L.1017 J.D. [Cooch&T.] (⊙Wilmington)
Testa, Cathy J., (BV) .... '62 '88 C.569 B.F.A. L.1338 J.D. W.L. Gore & Assoc., Inc.
Tilmon, Paula M. .... '44 '87 C.205 B.A. L.1338 J.D. Univ. of Del.
Trudel, Glen P., (BV) '62 '88
C.676 B.A. L.276 J.D. V.P. & Coun., MBNA Amer. Bk., N.A.

Trzuskowski, Kipp, Kelleher & Pearce, P.A., (AV)
273 East Main Street, 19711 ⊙
Telephone: 302-368-2561 Telefax: 302-368-9729
Associates: Vance A. Funk, III (Resident); Barbara Snapp Danberg.
General Practice. Civil Litigation, Personal Injury, Medical Malpractice, Commercial and Corporate, Real Estate, Estate Planning, Probate, Family, Matrimonial, Pension (ERISA).
Wilmington, Delaware Office: 1020 N. Bancroft Parkway, P.O. Box 429, 198999-0429. Telephone: 302-571-1782. Telefax: 302-571-1638.
See Professional Biographies, NEWARK, DELAWARE

van Ogtrop, Piet H., (BV) ....'39 '64 C.363 B.S. L.1017 LL.B. [Daley,E.&v.] ⊙
Ward, Michael P. '62 '90 C.205 B.S.B.A. L.1338 J.D.
(adm. in MD; not adm. in DE) 1413 Christina Mill Dr.‡
Watson, H. Camilla '50 '81 C.185 B.A. L.500 J.D.
(adm. in MS; not adm. in DE) Univ. of Del.
Weinig, Gregory J. ....'71 '96 C.198 B.A. L.902 J.D. [Ⓐ Cooch&T.] (⊙Wilmington)
Wheatcraft, Allan M. '65 '94 C.893 B.S.ChE. L.1170 J.D.
(adm. in PA; not adm. in DE; Pat.) Intell. Prop. Atty., W.L. Gore & Assoc., Inc.
White, Carol Ann Lewis '64 '89 C.205 B.S. L.1338 J.D.
(adm. in PA; not adm. in DE) W.L. Gore & Assoc., Inc.
Whittle, W. Jeffrey, (BV) ....'47 '72 C.658 B.A. L.383 J.D. [Cooch&T.] ⊙
Witherow, Paula C., (BV) ....'57 '90 C.645 B.S. L.1338 J.D. [Ⓐ Cooch&T.] ⊙
*PRACTICE AREAS: Personal Injury; Litigation.
Wolfe, Christopher B. '55 '84 C.205 B.A. L.1338 J.D.
Legal Studies Coord., Univ. of Del.

NEW CASTLE, 4,837, *New Castle Co.*

Allen, Deborah E. ....'68 '93 C.205 B.A.A.S. L.276 J.D. 910 West Basin Road
Camerota, Frank P. '39 '80 C.223 B.S.M.E. L.809 J.D.
(adm. in CA; not adm. in DE) 27 Skyline Dr.
Episcopo, Eric Leonard, (BV) ....'54 '83 C.205 B.S. L.1338 J.D. Co. Law Dept.
Eyster, Franklin S., II, (AV) '41 '67 C.951 B.A. L.659 LL.B.
Sr. V.P., Secy. & Gen. Coun., Atlantic Aviation Corp.
Frank & Rosen
2 Read's Way, Ste. 220 (⊙Voorhees, NJ; Bethlehem, Blue Bell, Bristol, North East, Phila., Southampton, PA)
Hilberg, Frank C. '— '46
(adm. in DC; not adm. in DE) 32 W. 5th St.‡
Levy, Roger M. '42 '72 C.1016 B.S.B.A. L.146 J.D.
Dir., V.P. & Treas., Miller's Furniture Industries, Inc.
Linarducci, Gary C., (BV) ....'50 '76 C.1046 B.S. L.1338 J.D. 92 Read's Way
McCarnan, John R. '46 '83 C.999 B.S. L.1338 J.D.
(adm. in PA; not adm. in DE) P.O. Box 71
Saltzman, Gordon '52 '92 C.205 B.A. L.1338 J.D.
(adm. in PA; not adm. in DE) 1 Penns Way
Snyder, Marc H. .... '61 '97 C.645 B.S. L.1338 J.D. [Ⓐ Frank&R.] (⊙Phila., PA)
Stansky, Joan M. '56 '90 C.884 B.A. L.1338 J.D.
(adm. in PA; not adm. in DE) 3 2nd St.‡
Thomas, John F., Jr. ....'68 '94 C.659 B.A. L.1338 J.D. [Ⓐ Frank&R.] (⊙Phila., PA)
Tracey, John E. .... '65 '90 C.205 B.A.A.S. L.446 J.D. Asst. Co. Atty.
Willard, Robert W., (BV) '51 '76
C.205 B.A. L.1017 J.D. Corp. Coun., Prison Health Servs., Inc.
Zlock, Tracy N. .... '71 '97 C.160 B.S. L.276 J.D. 187A Old Churchmans Rd.‡

NEWPORT, 1,240, *New Castle Co.*

Finkelman, Eric R. '57 '83 C.674 A.B. L.880 J.D.
(adm. in NY; not adm. in DE)
V.P., Legal & Regulatory Affs., Ciba Specialty Chemicals Corp.

Tomasetti, Raymond E., Jr., (BV) '54 '80 C.205 B.S. L.1338 J.D.
16 West Market Street, P.O. Box 3058, 19804 ⊙
Telephone: 302-995-2840 Fax: 302-995-9160
General Civil and Trial Practice. Real Estate, Estate Planning, Family Law and Personal Injury.
Fenwick Island, Delaware Office: 1209 Coastal Highway, 19944. Telephone: 302-539-3041.
See Professional Biographies, FENWICK ISLAND, DELAWARE

OCEAN VIEW, 606, *Sussex Co.*

Mooney, Eric G., P.A.
(See Georgetown)

Parsons, D. Stephen, (CV) ....'52 '80 C.682 B.S. L.1338 J.D. [D.S.Parsons]
Parsons, D. Stephen, P.A., (CV) .... Rte 26 & W. Ave.

ODESSA, 303, *New Castle Co.*

Aulgur, Robert T., Jr., (BV) .... '51 '77 C.63 B.A. L.823 J.D. [Whittington&A.]
Carey, Crystal L., (BV) ..... '62 '88 C.205 B.S. L.446 J.D. [Schmittinger&R.] (⊙Dover)
*PRACTICE AREAS: Domestic Relations Law; Real Property Law.
Chambers, Scott E., (BV) '62 '88 C.205 B.S. L.1338 J.D.
[Schmittinger&R.] (⊙Dover)
Ennis, Bruce C., (BV) ......'41 '69 C.924 B.A. L.1017 J.D. [Schmittinger&R.] (⊙Dover)
Hearn, Clifford B., Jr., (BV) .... '37 '62 C.205 B.A. L.893 LL.B. [C.B.Hearn,Jr.] ⊙
Hearn, Clifford B., Jr., P.A., (BV) ....Ste. 240 (⊙Wilmington)
Modica, Michael W., (BV) '57 '82 C.928 B.A. L.245 J.D.
[C.B.Hearn,Jr.] (⊙Wilmington)

Schmittinger & Rodriguez, P.A., (AV)
Odessa Professional Park, P.O. Box 626, 19730-0626 ⊙
Telephone: 302-378-1697 FAX: 302-378-1659
Email: attorneys@schmittrod.com URL: http://www.schmittrod.com
Bruce C. Ennis; Scott E. Chambers; Crystal L. Carey.
General Civil Practice. Personal Injury, Workers Compensation, Federal Practice, Corporation, Estate Planning, Real Estate and Commercial Law. Litigation.
Dover, Delaware Office: 414 South State Street. Telephone: 302-674-0140. Fax: 302-674-1830.
Wilmington, Delaware Office: 1300 North Market Street, Suite 205. Telephone: 302-652-3676. Fax: 302-652-8788.
Rehoboth Beach, Delaware Office: 4602 Highway One. Telephone: 302-227-1400. Fax: 302-645-1843.
See Professional Biographies, ODESSA, DELAWARE

Whittington, Thomas D., Jr., (BV) ..... '43 '71 C.205 B.S. L.665 J.D. [Whittington&A.] ⊙
Whittington & Aulgur, (BV) ....Ste. 110, 313 N. DuPont Hwy. (⊙Yorklyn)

REHOBOTH BEACH, 1,234, *Sussex Co.*

Beauregard, André M. ....'59 '86 C.676 B.S. L.1338 J.D. [Brown,S.&C.]
Becker, James Pahl ....'71 '98 C.797 B.A. L.846 J.D. [Ⓐ G.W.Williams]
Bierman, Daniel J. B. '27 '61 C.273 L.537 LL.B.
(adm. in MD; not adm. in DE) 20 Arnell Dr.‡
Boswell, David A., (CV) ....'— '93 C.945 B.A. L.659 J.D. [Schmittinger&R.]
*PRACTICE AREAS: Personal Injury; Labor and Employment Litigation; Criminal Law.
Boswell, Paul H., (AV) '38 '66
C.205 B.A. L.902 LL.B. [Schmittinger&R.] (⊙Dover, Wilmington)
Brady, John F. ....'59 '91 C.692 B.A. L.1338 J.D. [Brown,S.&C.]
Brown, Shiels & Chasanov, (BV)
401 Rehoboth Avenue P.O. Drawer B (⊙Dover, Georgetown)
Bucklin, Julie Griffith ....'70 '96 C.273 B.A. L.128 J.D. 3 Low Dow Circle Worth
Dukes, Harold E., Jr., (CV) .... '48 '74 C.269 B.A. L.790 J.D. [Tunnell&R.]

Griffin & Hackett, P.A.
(See Georgetown)

Hochholzer, Franklin D. '37 '69 C.966 B.S. L.945 J.D.
(adm. in VA; not adm. in DE) 24 Henlopen Ave.‡
Hudson, Jones, Jaywork & Fisher, (BV) ....309 Rehoboth Avenue (⊙Dover, Georgetown)
Hyde, John F., (CV) ....'30 '55 C.746 B.A. L.831 LL.B. 4129 Highway One
Kleinstuber, Dorian Rowe, (BV) ....'62 '88 C.205 B.A. L.1017 J.D. [G.W.Williams]

Marshall, Douglas D., (BV) ....'46 '76 C.446 B.S. L.64 J.D. [⊡ Hudson,J.J.&F.]
Mooney, Eric G., P.A.
(See Georgetown)

Myers, Daniel P., II, (CV) ....'62 '88 C.655 B.A. L.1017 J.D. [Hudson,J.J.&F.]
O'Leary, Barbara-Cherrix, (CV) ......'39 '68 C.103 A.B. L.273 LL.B. 413 Rehoboth Ave.
Ortolani, Frank R. '23 '51 C.645 B.S. L.273 LL.B.
(adm. in DC; not adm. in DE) 304 Sandalwood Dr.‡
Rago, Richard F. ....'46 '71 C&L.884 A.B., J.D. 145 Henlopen Ave. (⊙Wilmington)
Rodriguez, Nicholas H., (AV) '34 '61
C.645 B.S. L.902 J.D. [Schmittinger&R.] (⊙Dover, Wilmington)
Schmittinger, Harold, (AV) '28 '54
C.205 B.S. L.904 LL.B. [Schmittinger&R.] (⊙Dover, Wilmington)
Schmittinger, John J., (AV) '41 '66
C.205 B.A. L.831 J.D. [Schmittinger&R.] (⊙Dover, Wilmington)

Schmittinger & Rodriguez, P.A., (AV)
4602 Highway One, 19971 ⊙
Telephone: 302-227-1400 FAX: 302-645-1843
Email: attorneys@schmittrod.com URL: http://www.schmittrod.com
Harold Schmittinger; Nicholas H. Rodriguez; Paul H. Boswell; John J. Schmittinger; David A. Boswell (Resident).
General Civil Practice. Personal Injury, Workers Compensation, Federal Practice. Corporation, Estate Planning, Real Estate and Commercial Law. Litigation.
Dover, Delaware Office: 414 South State Street. Telephone: 302-674-0140. Fax: 302-674-1830.
Wilmington, Delaware Office: 1300 North Market Street, Suite 205. Telephone: 302-652-3676. Fax: 302-652-8788.
Odessa, Delaware Office: Odessa Professional Park, P.O. Box 626. Telephone: 302-378-1697. Fax: 302-378-1659.
See Professional Biographies, REHOBOTH BEACH, DELAWARE

Stumpf, Vickers & Sandy, P.A.
(See Georgetown)

Tunnell & Raysor, (BV)
323 E. Rehoboth Ave. Drawer G (⊙Bethany Beach, Georgetown, Seaford)

Tyler, James B., III
(See Georgetown)

Williams, Gregory W., (BV) ....'53 '78 C.999 B.A. L.896 J.D. [G.W.Williams]
Williams, Gregory W. Law Office of, (BV) .... 402 Rehoboth Ave.

ROCKLAND, —, *New Castle Co.*

Borin, Marsha Zutz, (BV) ....'44 '85 C.347 B.S. L.1338 J.D. P.O. Box 335
Johnson, J. R. L., Jr. ....'06 '32 C.945 M.A. L.309 LL.B. P.O. Box 400‡

SEAFORD, 5,689, *Sussex Co.*

McGroerty, Michael F., (CV) ....'48 '75 C.728 B.S. L.1338 J.D. [M.F.McGroerty]
McGroerty, Michael F., P.A., (CV)..110 Pine St.

Mooney, Eric G., P.A.
(See Georgetown)

Strott, George G., Jr., (BVⓉ) ....'48 '75 C.446 B.A. L.84 J.D. [G.G.Strott,Jr.] ⊙
Strott, George G., Jr., P.A., (BVⓉ) ....511 Bridgeville Rd. (⊙Salisbury, MD)

Stumpf, Vickers & Sandy, P.A.
(See Georgetown)

Tunnell & Raysor, (BV)
809 Norman Eskridge Hwy. (⊙Bethany Beach, Georgetown, Rehoboth Beach)
Waehler, James F., (BV) ....'45 '70 C.885 B.A. L.276 J.D. [Tunnell&R.] (⊙Georgetown)

SELBYVILLE, 1,335, *Sussex Co.*

Franz, Jack M. '13 '42 C.273 B.A. L.276 J.D.
(adm. in DC; not adm. in DE) Rt. 1‡

SMYRNA, 5,231, *Kent & New Castle Cos.*

Wright, George R. ....'29 '56 C.903 B.A. L.273 J.D. 147 S. Main St.‡

SOUTH BETHANY, 148, *Sussex Co.*

Kingsley, Thomas R. '26 '56 C&L.276 B.F.S., J.D.
(adm. in DC; not adm. in DE) 413 Victoria Rd.‡
O'Brien, Thomas J. '28 '59 C&L.276 B.S., J.D.
(adm. in VA; not adm. in DE) 301 W. 8th St.

WILMINGTON, * 71,529, *New Castle Co.*

Aaron, Kenneth E., (AVⓉ) '48 '73 C&L.659 B.S., J.D.
(adm. in PA; not adm. in DE) [Weir] (⊙Phila., PA)
Aaronson, Jennifer-Kate M. ....'70 '95 C.1053 B.A. L.1338 J.D. [Potter,C.&L.] ⊙
Abbott, Derek C., (CV) ....'65 '95 C.870 B.S. L.575 J.D. [🄰 Morris,N.A.&T.]
Abbott, Richard L., (BV) ....'64 '89 C.205 B.A. L.1017 J.D. [🄰 Bayard]
*PRACTICE AREAS: Commercial Litigation; Real Estate Law.
Abelson, Jeremy J. ....'56 '81 C.893 B.A. L.1338 J.D. Asst. V.P., PNC Bk., Del.
Aber, Gary W., (BV) ....'46 '72 C.205 B.S. L.273 J.D. [Heiman,A.G.&B.]
*PRACTICE AREAS: Litigation; Employment Law; Personal Injury Law; Medical Malpractice; Insurance Defense Law.
Ableman, S. Bernard, (BV) ....'22 '70 C.205 B.A. L.831 J.D. [⊡ Biggs&B.]
*PRACTICE AREAS: Corporate Law; Commercial Litigation.
Abramczyk, Jon E., (AV) ....'60 '85 C.659 B.S.B.A. L.861 J.D. [Morris,N.A.&T.]
Abramo, John G., (BV) ....'28 '67 C.686 B.S. L.659 LL.B. 307 Concord Ave. (Pat.)
Abrams, Kevin G., (BV) ....'56 '85 C.659 A.B. L.893 J.D. [Richards,L.&F.]
*PRACTICE AREAS: Mergers and Acquisitions; Corporate Law; Corporate Litigation; Securities Litigation.
Abrams, Richard D., (CV) ....'65 '91 C.273 B.A. L.1338 J.D. [Heckler&F.]
*PRACTICE AREAS: Personal Injury; Insurance Defense; Products Liability; Subrogation; Construction Law.
Ackermann-Swistara, Christina '65 '91 C.035 B.A. L.019 LL.B.
(adm. in ON; not adm. in DE) Asst. Gen. Coun., DuPont Pharmaceuticals Co.
Adamopoulos, Christos T. ....'74 '00 C.367 B.A. L.276 J.D. [🄰 Connolly B.L.&H.]
*PRACTICE AREAS: Business Law; Commercial Law; Bankruptcy.
Adams, James R. '51 '01 C.874 B.A. L.1338 J.D.
(adm. in WV; not adm. in DE) [🄰 Richards,L.&F.]
Aerenson, Andrew J. ....'62 '91 C.208 B.S.B.A. L.1017 J.D. 2213 Concord Pike

Agostini, Levitsky, Isaacs & Kulesza, (BV)
824 Market Street, Suite 810, P.O. Box 2323, 19899-2323
Telephone: 302-654-7444 Telecopier: 302-656-8920
Carl A. Agostini (1946-1994); Neal J. Levitsky; Michael J. Isaacs; Joseph D. Kulesza, Jr.;—L. Jason Cornell.
Commercial, Corporate and Civil Litigation. Bankruptcy, Personal Injury Law, Real Estate, Domestic Relations and Criminal Law, Collection.
See Professional Biographies, WILMINGTON, DELAWARE

Ahern, Andrew G., III, (BV) ....'49 '81 C.205 B.A. L.1338 J.D. [🄰 J.W.Benson]
*PRACTICE AREAS: Personal Injury; Criminal Defense; Business Law; General Litigation.
Akin, Roger A., (BV) ....'45 '77 C.823 B.A. L.446 J.D. [Sawyer,A.&H.]
*PRACTICE AREAS: Insurance Defense; Defense Litigation; Municipal Law; Automobile Insurance Defense; General Liability Defense.
Alazraki, Eliot, (BV) ....'49 '76 C.976 B.A. L.1338 J.D. [Weik,N.&D.] ‡
Alderson, Gary W. ....'57 '00 C.952 B.S. L.1338 J.D. State Dept. of Jus.
Aldrich, Debra C., (CV) ....'54 '89 C.656 B.A. L.1338 J.D. 1202 Kirkwood Hwy.
Alexander, Frederick H., (AV) ....'63 '89 C.446 B.A. L.276 J.D. [Morris,N.A.&T.]
Alford, Haile L. '49 '76 C.1160 B.A. L.1292 J.D.
Coun., Aqualon Company (Legal Department)
Allen, James B. '57 '83 C.732 B.S. L.1194 J.D.
(adm. in NY; not adm. in DE) Corp. Coun., E.I. du Pont de Nemours & Co.
*RESPONSIBILITIES: Environmental.
Allen, Joseph D., III '45 '73 C.659 B.A. L.705 J.D.
(adm. in NJ; not adm. in DE) Sr. V.P., Amer. Life Ins. Co.
Allen, Michael D. ....'70 '96 C.821 B.A. L.902 J.D. [🄰 Richards,L.&F.]
*PRACTICE AREAS: Corporate Law.
Allen, Richard D., (AV) ....'45 '74 C.902 B.A. L.276 J.D. [Morris,N.A.&T.]
Allen, Richard H. ....'32 '59 C.95 A.B. L.145 J.D. [⊡ Snyder&Assoc.]
*PRACTICE AREAS: Corporate Law; Probate and Estate Planning.
Allen-Berry, Lydia '56 '86 C.309 B.A. L.276 J.D.
(adm. in PA; not adm. in DE) Asst. Gen. Coun., AIG Life Cos.
Allingham, Thomas J., II, (BV) .....'53 '78 C.951 B.A. L.1338 J.D. [Skadden,A.S.M.&F.]
Allinson, Elihu E., III ....'62 '96 C.390 A.B. L.1338 J.D. [🄰 Potter A.&C.]
Allmond, Bayard W., III, (BV) ....'56 '86 C.205 B.A. L.1338 J.D. [Allmond&E.]
Allmond, Charles M., III, (BV) ....'31 '64 C.205 B.S. L.831 J.D. [Allmond&E.] ‡
Allmond & Eastburn, (BV) .... 1400 Market Street
Altizer, Delano E. '35 '62 C.181 B.S. L.923 LL.B.
(adm. in WV; not adm. in DE) E.I. du Pont de Nemours and Company
Altman, Paul M., (AV) ....'59 '83 C.401 B.S. L.884 J.D. [Richards,L.&F.]
*PRACTICE AREAS: Partnerships and Limited Liability Companies.
Ament, Albert John, Jr. '45 '90 C.205 B.A. L.831 J.D.
(adm. in DC; not adm. in DE) [🄰 Ament L.&C.]
Ament, Susan D., (BV) ....'52 '83 C.205 B.A. L.1338 J.D. [Morris,J.H.&W.]
*PRACTICE AREAS: Personal Injury Litigation; Insurance Law; Civil Litigation.
Ament Lynch & Carr, (BV) .... 6 Stone Hill Rd.
Amernick, Burton A., (AVⓉ) '40 '66 C.446 B.S.Ch.E. L.64 J.D.
(adm. in MD; not adm. in DE; See Pat. Sect.) [Connolly B.L.&H.]
*PRACTICE AREAS: Biotechnology Patents; Chemical Patents; Medical Patents; Metallurgical Patents; Pharmaceutical Patents.
Amorison, Allison L. ....'66 '93 C.401 B.S. L.608 J.D. [⊡ Skadden,A.S.M.&F.]
Amsterdam, Michael ....'46 '72 C.273 B.B.A. L.30 J.D. 4703 Center Ter.
Anderson, Alissa Balotti ....'— '97 C.183 B.A. L.1338 J.D. [🄰 Reed S.]
*PRACTICE AREAS: Corporate Law.
Anderson, David A. ....'46 '70 C.855 B.A. L.893 J.D. 2101 Gilpin Ave.‡
Anderson, John P. '31 '57 C&L.659 B.A., J.D.
(adm. in PA; not adm. in DE) Columbia Gas Sys. Serv. Corp.‡
Anderson, Lydia Constance Frank '46 '87 C.254 B.A. L.1338 J.D.
(adm. in PA; not adm. in DE) Law Clk. to Supr. Ct.
Anderson, Mary Jo '47 '72 C&L.383 B.A., J.D.
(adm. in KY; not adm. in DE) Corp. Coun., E.I. du Pont de Nemours and Company
Andrews, Richard G. ....'55 '83 C.311 B.A. L.1066 J.D. Asst. U.S. Atty.
Angelos, Peter G., (AVⓉ) '29 '61 C&L.1002 LL.B.
(adm. in MD; not adm. in DE) [P.G.Angelos] ⊙

Angelos, Peter G., A Prof. Corp., Law Offices of, (AVⓉ)
1300 North Market Street, Suite 212, 19801 ⊙
Telephone: 302-658-3301 Toll Free: 800-283-8193 Fax: 302-658-3319
Peter G. Angelos (Not admitted in DE);—Kathleen D. Hadley (Resident); Barbara J. Gadbois (Resident); Richard T. Wilson (Resident).
Asbestos Litigation, Tobacco Litigation, Fen-Phen Litigation, Products Liability, Medical Malpractice, Negligence, Workers Compensation, Commercial and Business Law, Real Estate, Criminal Law, Tax, Estates, Probate and Health Care.
Baltimore, Maryland Office: 100 North Charles Street, 22nd Floor, 21201. Telephone: 410-649-2000. Toll Free: 800-252-6622. Fax: 410-659-1780, 1781, 1782; 410-649-2111, 2112.
See Professional Biographies, WILMINGTON, DELAWARE

Anker, Daniel J., (BV) '55 '88 C.205 B.A.A.S. L.1338 J.D.
1100 Lovering Avenue, Suite 20, 19806
Telephone: 302-655-6263 Fax: 302-655-7138
Email: djankerlaw@aol.com URL: http://www.lawyers.com/djankerlaw
***PRACTICE AREAS: Bankruptcy; Personal Injury; Real Estate; General Commercial Transactional Law and Litigation; Administrative Law.**
Creditors Rights, Collections, Business Law, Business Startups, Business Planning, Bankruptcy, Foreclosures, Condominium Law, Landlord and Tenant Law, Administrative Law.
See Professional Biographies, WILMINGTON, DELAWARE

Annos, William, (BV) ....'47 '73 C.205 B.A. L.64 J.D. [W.Annos]
Annos, William, Esquire, P.A., (BV) .... 1208 King Street
Antoff, Carol J. ....'52 '97 C.339 B.S. L.1338 J.D. [🄰 Reger&R.]
Antonacci, Ross E. ....'74 '00 C.94 B.S. L.884 J.D. [🄰 Morris,J.H.&W.]
*PRACTICE AREAS: Business Transactions.
Aponik, Kimberly Ann '72 '97 C.646 B.A. L.884 J.D.
(adm. in PA; not adm. in DE) 844 King St.
Apostolico, James V., (CV) ....'64 '90 C.205 B.A. L.831 J.D. Dep. Atty. Gen.

Arcaro, Anthony R. '51 '89 C.205 B.A. L.1338 J.D.
31B Trolley Square, 19806
Telephone: 302-426-9665 Fax: 302-655-2087
Email: araraco@pop.net
***PRACTICE AREAS: Personal Injury Law; Worker's Compensation Law; Civil Litigation; Criminal Defense; Civil Rights Section 1983.**

Arrington, Roger W., (BV) '48 '73 C.674 A.B. L.208 J.D.
VP. & Assoc. Gen. Coun., E.I. du Pont de Nemours and Company
*RESPONSIBILITIES: Corporation; Securities; Commercial; Business; Patent.
Arsht, Roxana C. ....'15 '41 C.289 B.A. L.659 LL.B. Ret. Fam. Ct. J.
Ashby, Kelly C. ....'75 '01 C.1452 B.A. L.945 J.D. [🄰 Richards,L.&F.]
Ashby, Lawrence C., (AV) ....'45 '70 C.951 B.A. L.880 J.D. [Ashby&G.]

Ashby & Geddes, (AV) BB
222 Delaware Avenue, 17th Floor, P.O. Box 1150, 19899
Telephone: 302-654-1888 Fax: 302-654-2067
Members of Firm: Lawrence C. Ashby; James McC. Geddes; Stephen E. Jenkins; Randall E. Robbins; Steven J. Balick; Regina A. Iorii; William P. Bowden; Richard D. Heins; Philip Trainer, Jr.; Steven T. Margolin; Christopher S. Sontchi. Associates: Richard I. G. Jones, Jr.; Rafael X. Zahralddin-Aravena (Not admitted in DE); Ricardo Palacio; Carolyn S. Hake; Joseph Clement Handlon; Tiffany L. Geyer; Gregory Alan Taylor.
General Practice and Civil Litigation, including Corporate, Commercial, Bankruptcy, and Intellectual Property Law.
See Professional Biographies, WILMINGTON, DELAWARE

Astin, Daniel K. .... '64 '89 C.705 B.A. L.1292 J.D. [🄰 Bayard]
*PRACTICE AREAS: Bankruptcy Law; Creditors Rights; Commercial Litigation.
Aukamp, William M. '37 '63
C.390 A.B. L.188 LL.B. [🄲 Harvey,P.C.G.&R.] (⊙Phila., PA)
*PRACTICE AREAS: Banking Law; Corporate.
Austin, Jeffrey M., (BV) .... '57 '83 C.205 B.S.B.A. L.93 J.D. [Elzufon A.R.T.&M.]
*PRACTICE AREAS: Professional Liability Defense; Worker's Compensation Defense; Toxic Tort Defense.
Austin, Ross Edwin '40 '66 C&L.608 B.S., J.D.
(adm. in OH; not adm. in DE) Corp. Coun., E.I. du Pont de Nemours and Company
*RESPONSIBILITIES: Environmental.
Autman, W. Lee, Jr., (BV) .... '46 '72 C.205 B.A. L.904 J.D. [Autman&B.]
Autman & Bredt, P.A., (BV) .... 910 Gilpin Avenue (⊙Phila., PA)
Ayres, Caroline Patricia, (CV) '57 '85
C.890 B.A. L.893 J.D. 503 W. Ninth St. (⊙Dillwyn, VA)
Ayres, Monica M. .... '72 '00 C.659 B.A. L.945 J.D. [🄰 Richards,L.&F.]
Bab, Karen M. .... '68 '94 C.205 B.S.Ed. L.1017 J.D. Coun., Conectiv
*RESPONSIBILITIES: Contracts (90%); Bankruptcy (10%).
Babiarz, Francis S., (BV) .... '48 '73 C.205 B.A. L.477 J.D. 919 Market St., Suite 1400
Babiarz, John E., Jr. .... '41 '66 C.205 B.A. L.309 J.D. Supr. Ct. J.
Bacon, Richard G., (AV) .... '42 '68 C.884 B.S.Ec. L.228 LL.B. [Richards,L.&F.]
*PRACTICE AREAS: Trust Law; Probate Law; Taxation (Local, State) Law.
Bader, John Merwin, (AV) .... '19 '48 C.884 A.B. L.659 LL.B. [🄲 Tomar,O.K.J.&G.]
Bailey, James F., (BV) .... '50 '75 C&L.896 B.A., J.D. [Bailey&W.]
*PRACTICE AREAS: Insurance Defense; Environmental Law; Toxic Tort; Insurance Coverage; Asbestos.
Bailey, Mary Page .... '64 '94 C.205 B.S.B.A. L.1338 J.D. Dep. Atty. Gen.
Bailey, William D., Jr., (AV) .... '35 '60 C&L.602 A.B., J.D. [Bayard]
*PRACTICE AREAS: Litigation; Public Utility Law; Administrative Hearings and Appeals; Eminent Domain; Condemnation Law.

Bailey & Wetzel, P.A., (BV)
716 Tatnall Street, P.O. Box 2034, 19899-2034
Telephone: 302-658-5686 Telefax: 302-594-0612 URL: http://www.baileywetzel.com
Email: JBAILEY102@AOL.COM URL: http://www.lawyers.com/baileywetzel
James F. Bailey; Benjamin C. Wetzel, III;—Christopher J. Sipe; Natalie M. Ippolito. Of Counsel: Alan T. Boyd.
General Insurance Defense, Insurance Coverage, Corporate Law, Workers' Compensation, Professional Liability, Medical Malpractice, Social Security Disability, Product Liability, Personal Injury, Subrogation, Asbestos, Environmental and Toxic Substance Defense, Computer and Bankruptcy Law.
See Professional Biographies, WILMINGTON, DELAWARE

Baker, Darrell J., (CV) .... '58 '83 C.205 B.A. L.201 J.D. [Heiman,A.G.&B.]
*PRACTICE AREAS: Personal Injury; Real Estate Law; Zoning Law; Governmental Relations and Lobbying.
Baker, H. Garrett, (CV) .... '65 '90 C.1359 B.S. L.801 J.D. [🄰 Elzufon A.R.T.&M.]
*PRACTICE AREAS: Worker's Compensation; Insurance Defense; Litigation.
Baker, Kendra S. .... '68 '93 C.882 B.A. L.188 J.D. Sr. Coun., Astrazeneca Pharm., LP
*RESPONSIBILITIES: Corporate; Pharmaceuticals; Commercial.
Baker, William R., Jr. .... '68 '98 C.205 B.A. L.1360 J.D. [🄰 Kimmel,C.R.&P.] ⊙
*PRACTICE AREAS: Civil Trial Practice; Insurance; Negligence; Workers Compensation; Construction Accidents.
Balaguer, John D., (BV) .... '58 '85 C.205 B.A. L.1338 J.D. [White&W.]
Baldwin, David J., (BV) .... '51 '79 C.454 B.A. L.276 J.D. [Potter A.&C.]
Baldwin, Glen S. '47 '75 C.152 B.A. L.790 J.D.
(adm. in SC; not adm. in DE) Corp. Coun., E.I. du Pont de Nemours and Company
*RESPONSIBILITIES: Commercial Law; Antitrust; Products Liability; Corporate Law.
Balick, Adam, (BV) .... '63 '88 C.205 B.A. L.1017 J.D. [Balick&B.]
*PRACTICE AREAS: White Collar Criminal Defense; Health Care; Commercial Litigation.
Balick, Helen S. .... '35 '67 L.1017 J.D. Ret. Chf. U.S. Bkrptcy. J.
Balick, Jacob, (BV) .... '20 '47 C.223 B.S. L.831 LL.B. 1211 King St.
Balick, Samantha E., (BV) .... '— '96 C.205 B.A. L.1017 J.D. [🄰 Morris,J.H.&W.]
*PRACTICE AREAS: Residential Real Estate; Commercial Real Estate; Finance.
Balick, Sidney, (AV) .... '32 '56 C.205 B.A. L.1017 LL.B. [Balick&B.]
*PRACTICE AREAS: Personal Injury; Medical Malpractice; Workers Compensation; Criminal Law; Employment Law.
Balick, Steven J., (AV) .... '56 '82 C.205 B.A. L.94 J.D. [Ashby&G.]

Balick & Balick, (AV)
Suite 710 Mellon Bank Center, 919 Market Street, 19801
Telephone: 302-658-4265 Fax: 302-658-1682 Email: sbalick@balick.com
Email: abalick@balick.com
Sidney Balick; Adam Balick.
General Trial Practice with emphasis on Personal Injury, Workers' Compensation, Employment Law, Criminal Law, Commercial Litigation, Trials and Appeals.
See Professional Biographies, WILMINGTON, DELAWARE

Ballard, Stephani J. .... '— '96 C.205 B.A. L.1338 J.D. 1202 Kirkwood Hwy.
Balotti, R. Franklin, (AV) .... '42 '67 C.299 B.A. L.188 LL.B. [Richards,L.&F.]
Banks, Gloria J. '— '87 C&L.329 B.A., J.D.
(adm. in PA; not adm. in DE) 4601 Concord Pike
Barber, Jennifer .... '67 '95 C.1292 B.A. L.1338 J.D. [🄰 Wolf,B.S.&S-C.]
*PRACTICE AREAS: Business Litigation.
Barksdale, H. Gregory '64 '89 C.893 B.A. L.94 J.D.
(adm. in MD; not adm. in DE) Coun., Conectiv
*RESPONSIBILITIES: Federal Securities Law; Corporations; Mergers and Acquisitions.
Barnett, Anne Love .... '60 '91 C.555 B.A. L.262 J.D. [🄲 Connolly B.L.&H.]
Barnett, Larry D. '40 '76 C.112 B.A. L.260 J.D.
(adm. in FL; not adm. in DE) 4601 Concord Pike
Barnett, Robert P. .... '21 '48 C&L.228 B.A., J.D. [🄲 Potter A.&C.]
Barrera, Joseph '62 '99 C.999 B.A. L.560 J.D.
(adm. in NM; not adm. in DE; See Pat. Sect.) [🄰 Connolly B.L.&H.] ⊙
*PRACTICE AREAS: Intellectual Property.
Barron, Catherine A. .... '75 '00 C.997 B.A. L.884 J.D. [🄰 Morris,J.H.&W.]
*PRACTICE AREAS: Business Transactions.
Barron, Norman A. .... '42 '71 C.299 B.A. L.245 J.D. Supr. Ct. J.
Barry, Michael J. '70 '93 C.119 B.F.A. L.665 J.D.
(adm. in PA; not adm. in DE) [🄰 Grant&E.]
Bartels, Diane J. .... '58 '83 C.874 B.A. L.1017 J.D. 1807 N. Market St.
Bartels, Jeffrey K. .... '58 '83 C.205 B.A. L.1017 J.D. 401 S. Maryland Ave.
Bartholomaus, Carl G. '45 '71 C.197 A.B. L.188 J.D.
(adm. in NY; not adm. in DE) Corp. Coun., E.I. du Pont de Nemours and Company
*RESPONSIBILITIES: Mergers and Acquisitions; Joint Ventures; Antitrust; Commercial Law.
Bartkowski, Matthew M., (BV) .... '67 '93 C.205 B.S. L.1338 J.D. [Kimmel,C.R.&P.] ⊙
*PRACTICE AREAS: General and Civil Trial Practice; Insurance; Negligence; Workers Compensation; Construction Accidents.
Bartley, Brian J., (BV) .... '55 '80 C.205 B.A. L.1338 J.D. 1214 King St.
Bartoshesky, Philip B., (BV) .... '55 '82 C.602 B.S. L.1338 J.D. [Biggs&B.]
Batman, David R. '60 '91 C.205 B.S. L.1338 J.D.
Asst. V.P. & Coun., AIG Life Ins. Co.
Battaglia, Sandra Kaufmann, (BV) .... '51 '77 C.881 A.B. L.884 J.D. [🄲 Cozen O.]
*PRACTICE AREAS: Health Care; Nonprofit Organizations Law.

Battaglia, Victor F., (AV) .... '33 '58 C.205 B.S. L.276 J.D. [Biggs&B.]
*PRACTICE AREAS: General Litigation; Civil and Criminal; Legal and Medical Malpractice and Discipline; Hospital Litigation; Estate Planning and Probate.
Battaglia, Victor F., Jr., (BV) .... '58 '85 C.205 B.A. L.1338 J.D. [Biggs&B.]
Battista, Elio, Jr. .... '67 '99 C&L.1338 B.A., J.D. [🄰 Bayard]
*PRACTICE AREAS: Bankruptcy; Creditors Rights; Commercial Litigation.
Baum, Christopher F. .... '60 '86 C&L.262 B.A., J.D. Asst. Co. Atty.
Baumann, Julian H., Jr., (AV) .... '43 '68 C.160 B.S. L.709 J.D. [Richards,L.&F.]
*PRACTICE AREAS: Taxation Law.
Baumberger, David L., (BV) .... '55 '85 C.656 B.A. L.1338 J.D. [Chrissinger&B.]
Bayard, James A., Jr. .... '44 '77 C.393 B.A. L.744 J.D. Off. of Pub. Def.
Bayard, Richard H., (BV) .... '49 '79 C.575 B.A. L.1338 J.D. [🄲 Bayard]

Bayard Firm, The, (AV)
222 Delaware Avenue Suite 900, P.O. Box 25130, 19899 ⊙
Telephone: 302-655-5000 Telecopier: 302-658-6395
Email: bayardfirm.com URL: http://www.bayardfirm.com
Alexis I. duPont Bayard (1918-1985); Converse Murdoch (1919-1985); J. Caleb Boggs (1909-1993). Partners: William D. Bailey, Jr.; Vernon R. Proctor; Neil B. Glassman; Beverly J. Wik; Edmond D. Johnson; Charlene D. Davis; Curtis P. Bounds; Marla Hirshman Norton; Michael L. Vild; Kurt M. Heyman; Jeffrey M. Schlerf; Douglas M. Hershman. Associates: Richard L. Abbott; Daniel K. Astin; Felice Glennon Kerr; Francis J. Schanne; Ashley B. Stitzer; Steven M. Yoder; Patricia L. Enerio; Christopher P. Simon; Elio Battista, Jr.; James Tobia; Christopher A. Ward; Eric M. Sutty; George J. Danneman (Not admitted in DE); Anthony M. Saccullo. Of Counsel: Richard H. Bayard.
General Practice which includes Administrative, Regulatory, Legislative and Government Law, Bankruptcy and Creditor's Rights, Civil Rights Litigation, Commercial and Residential Real Estate, Commercial Transactions and Litigation, Corporate Litigation, Delaware Corporation, Partnership, Limited Liability Company and Business Trust Law, Employee Benefits Planning, Employment Law and Litigation, Environmental Law, Estate Planning and Administration, Family Law, Health Care Law, Holding Companies, Intellectual Property Protection, Mergers and Acquisitions, Personal Injury, Products Liability, Taxation, Toxic Tort Litigation, Utility Regulation, White Collar Crime, Zoning, Condemnation and Land Use Planning.
Dover, Delaware Office: 306 South State Street. Telephone: 302-678-8787.
See Professional Biographies, WILMINGTON, DELAWARE

Beach, Sean M. '70 '00 C.705 B.A. L.1019 J.D.
(adm. in NJ; not adm. in DE) [🄰 Young C.S.&T.]
*PRACTICE AREAS: Bankruptcy Litigation; Bankruptcy Chapter 11.
Beacom, Edward A., IV '49 '80 C.659 M.B.A.
(adm. in PA; not adm. in DE) du Pont Co.
Beam, Cynthia G. .... '— '87 C.205 B.A. L.1338 J.D. [🄰 Reger&R.]
Beardell, Lori Y. '62 '93 C.754 B.S. L.831 J.D.
(adm. in PA; not adm. in DE; Pat.) Sr. Coun., E.I. du Pont de Nemours and Company
*RESPONSIBILITIES: Intellectual Property; Licensing.
Beaver, Mark A. .... '75 '00 C.105 B.A. L.884 J.D. [🄰 Richards,L.&F.]
Bebko, Jennifer C. .... '72 '97 C.188 B.A. L.884 J.D. [🄰 Richards,L.&F.]
*PRACTICE AREAS: Labor and Employment Law; Civil Practice; Litigation.
Bechet, Leon Joseph '63 '92 C.329 B.A. L.309 J.D.
(adm. in NY; not adm. in DE) [E.I. d.d.]
*RESPONSIBILITIES: Trademark; Copyright; Unfair Competition.
Beck, Richard M., (BV) '38 '66 C.688 B.M.E. L.273 J.D.
(adm. in DC; not adm. in DE; See Pat. Sect.) [Connolly B.L.&H.]
Beck, Richard M., (BV) '64 '90 C.93 B.A. L.602 J.D.
[Klehr,H.H.B.&E.] (⊙Phila., PA)
*PRACTICE AREAS: Commercial Litigation; Bankruptcy Litigation.
Beck, Richard P., (AV) .... '43 '69 C.856 B.A. L.893 LL.B. [Morris,J.H.&W.]
*PRACTICE AREAS: Real Property; Commercial Transactions; Administration Law.
Beck, Thomas A., (BV) .... '56 '81 C.216 B.A. L.188 J.D. [Richards,L.&F.]
*PRACTICE AREAS: Litigation; Corporate Law; Chancery Practice.
Becker, Doreen H., (CV) .... '59 '87 C.205 B.A. L.1338 J.D. [Holfeld&B.] ⊙
Becker, Raymond L., (BV) .... '23 '51 C.645 B.A. L.831 LL.B. [Becker&B.]
Becker, Richard D., (BV) .... '58 '83 C.1036 B.A. L.904 J.D. [Becker&B.]
Becker & Becker, P.A., (BV) .... P.O. Box 8080
Bednash, Michael D., (BV) .... '64 '91 C.205 B.S. L.1338 J.D. [Kimmel,C.R.&P.] ⊙
*PRACTICE AREAS: General and Civil Trial Practice; Insurance; Negligence; Workers Compensation; Construction Accidents.
Behl, Catherine M. .... '61 '95 C.945 B.A. L.1338 J.D. 1310 King St.
Behringer, Alan W., (BV) .... '45 '70 C.205 B.A. L.1017 J.D. [Welch&Assoc.]
*PRACTICE AREAS: Commercial Collection Litigation; Banking Litigation; Bankruptcy Litigation; Mortgage Foreclosure-Residential; Real Estate And Title Insurance.
Belgam, Neal C., (BV) .... '63 '89 C.21 B.A. L.1017 J.D. [Blank R.C.&M.]
*PRACTICE AREAS: Litigation; Commercial Law; Corporate Law; Intellectual Property Litigation; Insurance Litigation.
Belohoubek, Klaus '59 '85 C&L.705 B.S., J.D.
(adm. in PA; not adm. in DE) V.P., Gen. Coun. & Secy., Rollins Truck Leasing Corp.
*RESPONSIBILITIES: Chief Legal Officer.
Belopolsky, Inna Y. '73 '96 C.018 B.S. L.1338 J.D.
(adm. in PA; not adm. in DE) Coun., E.I. du Pont de Nemours and Company
*RESPONSIBILITIES: Patents; Commercial Law.
Bender, Gretchen Ann, (CV) .... '60 '86 C.597 B.A. L.765 J.D. [Morris,J.H.&W.]
*PRACTICE AREAS: Civil Litigation.
Benjamin, Steven C. '64 '92 C.659 B.A./B.S.E. L.831 J.D.
(adm. in PA; not adm. in DE; Pat.) Sr. Coun., E.I. du Pont de Nemours and Company
*RESPONSIBILITIES: Intellectual Property.
Bennett, Calvin (Pete), Jr., (AV🅃) '48 '72 C&L.846 B.A., J.D.
(adm. in TX; not adm. in DE) Corp. Coun., E.I. du Pont de Nemours and Company
*RESPONSIBILITIES: Construction Law; Corporate Law; Contracts.
Bennett, Daniel P., (BV) .... '63 '90 C.896 B.S. L.945 J.D. [🄰 Heckler&F.]
*PRACTICE AREAS: Insurance Defense Law; Products Liability Law; Insurance Coverage Law.
Benseler, Stacey E. '71 '99 C.282 B.A. L.1338 J.D.
(adm. in PA; not adm. in DE) P.O. Box 7547
Benson, Joseph W., (BV) .... '42 '68 C.644 B.A. L.128 LL.B. [J.W.Benson]
*PRACTICE AREAS: Criminal Law; Personal Injury; Domestic Law.

Benson, Joseph W., P.A., (BV)
1701 North Market Street, P.O. Box 248, 19802
Telephone: 302-656-8811 Fax: 302-656-4230
Joseph W. Benson;—Andrew G. Ahern, III; Carl W. Heckert.
Criminal, Personal Injury, Family and Commercial Law.
See Professional Biographies, WILMINGTON, DELAWARE

Benton, Arlene M. '72 '97 C.205 B.A. L.1338 J.D.
(adm. in MD; not adm. in DE) [🄰 Morris,J.H.&W.]
Berg, Ted Martin .... '64 '90 C.205 B.A. L.94 J.D. First USA Bk., N.A.
Berger, Benjamin J. .... '58 '84 C.94 B.A. L.208 J.D. [Blank R.C.&M.]
*PRACTICE AREAS: Real Estate Law; Commercial Law.
Berger, Carolyn .... '48 '76 C.696 B.A. L.94 J.D. Supm. Ct. Jus.
Berkowitz, Alene, (BV) .... '38 '78 C.914 B.A. L.1338 J.D. [Berkowitz,S.C.&C.]
Berkowitz, Gerald Z., (BV) .... '32 '59 C.205 B.A. L.276 LL.B. [Berkowitz,S.C.&C.]
Berkowitz, Schagrin, Coonin & Cooper, (BV) .... 1218 Market St.
Bernstein, David K. '66 '94 C.705 B.A. L.1338 J.D.
(adm. in PA; not adm. in DE) Sr. Assoc., R.L.S. Associates, Inc.
Bernstein, Joseph M., (BV) '45 '70
C.205 B.A. L.1017 J.D. 300 Delaware Avenue, Suite 1130

Bernstein, Martina ....'54 '91 C&L.831 B.A., J.D. [Ⓐ Skadden,A.S.M.&F.]
*PRACTICE AREAS: Litigation.

Beste, Robert K., Jr., (BV) ....'50 '75 C&L.273 B.B.A., J.D. [Biggs&B.]
*PRACTICE AREAS: General Civil Litigation; Estate Planning and Probate.

Bettinger, Wilmer C., (BV) ....'40 '72 C.446 B.A. L.1119 J.D. [Ⓐ Pepper H.]
*PRACTICE AREAS: Banking Law; Creditors Rights.

Bevis, Antonia S. ....'56 '95 C.205 B.S. L.644 J.D. [Ferrara,H.&B.]

Bhaya, Shakuntla L., (CV) ....'60 '85 C.205 B.A. L.588 J.D. [Doroshow,P.K.S.&B.]

Biener, Steven L. ....'61 '87 C.188 B.S. L.569 J.D. [Cozen O.] (⊙Phila., PA)
*PRACTICE AREAS: Corporate; Commercial; Environmental; Real Estate.

Bifferato, Ian Connor, (BV) ....'67 '94 C.205 B.A. L.1338 J.D. [Bifferato,B.&G.]
*PRACTICE AREAS: Commercial Bankruptcy; Commercial Litigation; Insurance Litigation.

Bifferato, Karen C., (BV) ....'70 '94 C.576 B.A. L.945 J.D. [Connolly B.L.&H.]

Bifferato, Vincent A. ....'37 '63 C&L.884 B.A., LL.B. [Ⓒ Bifferato,B.&G.]

Bifferato, Vincent A., Jr., (BV) ....'61 '87 C.1365 B.A. L.884 J.D. [Bifferato,B.&G.]
*PRACTICE AREAS: Personal Injury; Insurance Defense Law; Worker's Compensation Law.

Bifferato, Bifferato & Gentilotti, (BV)
Buckner Building, 1308 Delaware Avenue, P.O. Box 2165, 19899-2165
Telephone: 302-429-1900 Telecopier: 302-429-8600
URL: http://www.bbglaw.com
Members of Firm: Vincent A. Bifferato, Jr.; Ian Connor Bifferato; Jeffrey M. Gentilotti. Associate: Megan N. Harper (Not admitted in DE); George T. Lees, III. Of Counsel: Vincent A. Bifferato.
Commercial Bankruptcy, Personal Injury, Insurance Litigation, Commercial Transactions, Products Liability, Workers Compensation.

See Professional Biographies, WILMINGTON, DELAWARE

Biggs, John, III, (BV) ....'27 '56 C.674 A.B. L.309 LL.B. [Ⓒ Biggs&B.]

Biggs and Battaglia, (AV)
1800 Mellon Bank Center, P.O. Box 1489, 19899-1489
Telephone: 302-655-9677
Email: B-B@DOL.NET
Members of Firm: Victor F. Battaglia; Robert D. Goldberg; Robert K. Beste, Jr.; Philip B. Bartoshesky; Victor F. Battaglia, Jr. Of Counsel: John Biggs, III; Gerard P. Kavanaugh, Sr.; S. Bernard Ableman.
General Practice. Trials. Negligence, Criminal, Insurance, Corporation, Tax, Probate, Real Estate, Products Liability and Family Law. Environmental Law.

See Professional Biographies, WILMINGTON, DELAWARE

Bigler, C. Stephen, (BV) ....'59 '84 C.902 B.S. L.893 J.D. [Richards,L.&F.]
*PRACTICE AREAS: Corporate Law; Corporate Transactions; Mergers and Acquisitions.

Bilynsky, Oleh V. ....'60 '95 C.659 B.S. L.831 J.D. [Ⓐ Connolly B.L.&H.]

Biondi, Mary Catherine ....'67 '92 C&L.659 B.A., J.D. Coun., First USA

Biondi, O. Francis, (AV) ....'33 '58 C.397 B.A. L.659 LL.B. [Ⓒ Morris,N.A.&T.]

Bischoff, Nicholas ....'66 '94 C.688 B.S. L.1338 J.D. 504 West Ninth Street

Bivins, Janet Y. '60 '86 C.864 B.S. L.659 J.D.
(adm. in PA; not adm. in DE) Corp. Counsel, E.I. du Pont de Nemours & Company

Bixby, Matilda B., (BVⓉ) '37 '81 C.518 B.A. L.1338 J.D.
(adm. in PA; not adm. in DE) 2 Bendford Ct.‡

Black, Lewis S., Jr., (AV) ....'38 '64 C.674 B.A. L.976 LL.B. [Morris,N.A.&T.]

Blancato, Lydia Cox ......'54 '79 C.881 A.B. L.659 J.D. Pres., Beishung Enterprises, Inc.

Blank Rome Comisky & McCauley LLP, (AV)
Chase Manhattan Centre, 1201 Market Street, Suite 800, 19801 ⊙
Telephone: 302-425-6400 FAX: 302-425-6464
Email: webmaster@blankrome.com URL: http://www.blankrome.com
Neal C. Belgam; Benjamin J. Berger; Michael D. DeBaecke; Bonnie Glantz Fatell; Richard K. Herrmann; Alan J. Hoffman; Mary B. Matterer; Mark J. Packel; Julian P. Rackow (Not admitted in DE); Cathy L. Reese; Lawrence R. Wiseman. Of Counsel: J. Caleb Boggs III; Julianne E. Hammond. Associates: A. Kimberly Rockwell Brosseit; William J. Burnett (Not admitted in DE); Steven L. Caponi; Dale R. Dubé; Andrea J. Faraone; Deborah Cirilla Sellis; Elizabeth A. Wilburn.
Administrative Law, Administrative Adjudications; Administrative Agency Practice, Administrative Hearings and Appeals, Administrative Litigation, Federal Administrative Law, Professional Licensing, Professional Licensing Regulation, Public Law, Admiralty and Maritime Law, Marine Law, Maritime Contracts, Maritime Finance, Maritime Law, Maritime Liens, Ship Sales and Mortgages, Aged and Aging, Age Discrimination, Elder Care, Elder Law, Agency and Distributorships, Distribution Agreements, International Distribution, Alcoholic Beverages, Liquor Licensing, Alternative Dispute Resolution, Arbitration, International Arbitration, International Dispute Resolution, Mediation, Antitrust and Trade Regulation, Antitrust, Business Combinations, Competition, Covenants Not To Compete, Deceptive Trade Practices, Noncompetition and Non-Solicitation Agreements, Price-Fixing, Restrictive Covenants, Trade Regulation, Unfair Trade, Appellate Practice, Civil Appeals, Art Law, Artists Rights, Museum Law, Asset Protection, International Asset Protection, Aviation and Aerospace, Aircraft Finance and Leasing, Aircraft Sales, Airline Labor Law, Aviation Law, Aviation Defense, Aviation Insurance, Aviation Litigation, Aviation Products Liability, Aviation Regulation, Bankruptcy, Bankruptcy Arbitration, Bankruptcy Chapter 7, Bankruptcy Chapter 11, Bankruptcy Chapter 12, Bankruptcy Chapter 13, Bankruptcy Collections, Bankruptcy Litigation, Bankruptcy Mediation, Bankruptcy Reorganization, Bankruptcy Taxation, Bankruptcy Trustees Rights, Commercial Bankruptcy, Commercial Foreclosure, Commercial Insolvency, Commercial Recovery, Commercial Workouts, Foreclosures, Fraudulent Conveyance, Insolvency, International Bankruptcy, International Insolvency, Liquidations, Out of Court Debt Restructuring, Pre-Bankruptcy Workouts, Receiverships, Repossessions, Workouts, Workouts Taxation, Banks and Banking, ATM Networks, Bank Collections, Bank Directors and Officers Liability, Bank Foreclosures, Bank Mergers and Acquisitions, Banking Antitrust, Banking Law, Banking Litigation, Commercial Banking, Commercial Credit, Commercial Loans, Consumer Banking, Credit Card Law, Credit Finance, Credit Law, Electronic Banking, Fair Lending, Financial Law, Interest and Usury, International Banking Law, International Loans, Lender Law, Lender Liability, Lender Regulation, Lenders Rights, Letters of Credit, Loan Restructuring, Loan Workouts, Loans, Savings and Loan Law, Secured Lending, Truth in Lending, Biotechnology, Biomedical Technology, Biotechnology Licensing, Business Law, Business Arbitration, Business Associations Law, Business Crimes, Business Development, Business Dissolutions, Business Estate Planning, Business Formation, Business Fraud, Business Litigation, Business Mediation, Business Organization, Business Planning, Business Regulation, Business Reorganization, Business Sales, Business Succession Planning, Business Successions, Business Syndication, Business Taxation, Business Torts, Business Transactions, Business Transfers, Business Trusts, Business Valuation, Buying and Selling of Businesses, Capital Formation, Closely Held Business Estate Planning, Closely Held Business Law, Closely Held Business Taxation, Complex Business Litigation, Emerging Business Law, Emerging Growth Companies, Entrepreneurial Business Law, Family Business Law, Family Business Mediation, Family Business Successions, International Business Law, International Joint Ventures, Joint Ventures, Limited Liability Company Law, Privatization, Professional Practices, Small Business Law, Sole Proprietorships, Strategic Alliances, Chancery and Equity, Chancery Practice, Children, Child Custody, Child Support, Civil Practice, Federal Civil Practice, Sex Discrimination, Commercial Collections, Post Judgment Collections, Commercial Law, Commercial Litigation, Complex Commercial Litigation, Secured Transactions, Uniform Commercial Code, Commercial Real Estate, Commercial Real Estate Acquisitions, Commercial Real Estate Development, Commercial Real Estate Finance, Commercial Real Estate Foreclosure, Commercial Real Estate Sales, Commercial Real Estate Syndication, Commercial Real Estate Workouts, Industrial Real Estate Law, Shopping Center Acquisitions, Shopping Center Development, Shopping Center Law, Complex and Multi-District Litigation, Computers and Software, Computer Contracts, Computer Law, Computer Security, Computer Software Law, Computer Technology, Electronic Commerce, Information Technology, Information Technology Contracts, Information Technology Licensing, International Computer Law, Internet Law, Software Copyright, Software Licensing, Software Protection, Year 2000 Computer Conversion, Constitutional Law, First Amendment Law, Construction Law, Construction Finance, Construction Litigation, Construction Workouts, Environmental Construction Law, International Construction Law, Public Construction Law, Consumer Law, Consumer Arbitration, Consumer Class Actions, Consumer Credit, Consumer Credit Compliance, Consumer Finance, Consumer Fraud, Consumer Litigation, Consumer Protection, Consumer Rights, Fair Credit Reporting Act, Contracts, Breach of Contract, Commercial Contracts, Contract Fraud, Contract Litigation, International Commercial Contracts, International Contracts, Copyrights, Copyright Infringement, Copyright Litigation, Copyright Prosecution, Copyright Protection, Copyright Registration, International Copyright Law, Corporate Law, Closely Held Corporations, Corporate Banking

(This Listing Continued)

Blank Rome Comisky & McCauley LLP (Continued)

Law, Corporate Commercial Law, Corporate Contracts, Corporate Control Contests, Corporate Criminal Law, Corporate Dissolutions, Corporate Ethics, Corporate Fiduciary Law, Corporate Finance, Corporate Formation, Corporate Governance, Corporate Income Tax, Corporate Insurance, Corporate Insurance Defense, Corporate Investigations, Corporate Litigation, Corporate Organization, Corporate Partnerships, Corporate Planning, Corporate Real Estate, Corporate Reorganization, Corporate Successions, Corporate Tax Controversies, Corporate Tax Planning, Corporate Taxation, Corporate Trusts, Corporate Workouts, Family Corporations, Foreign Sales Corporations, Hostile Takeovers, Incorporation, International Corporate Finance, International Corporate Law, International Corporate Taxation, Nonprofit Corporations, Offshore Corporations, Professional Corporations; Proxy Contests, Public Corporations, S Corporations, Securitization, Small Business Corporations, Takeovers, Tender Offers, Transfer Pricing, Criminal Law, Debtor and Creditor, Creditor Bankruptcy, Creditors Rights, Creditors Rights in Bankruptcy, Debtor and Creditor Bankruptcy, Debtor and Creditor Collections, Debtor and Creditor Remedies, Debtor and Creditor Reorganization, Debtor and Creditor Rights, Debtor and Creditor Workouts, Debtor Bankruptcy, International Creditors Rights, Secured Creditors Rights, Unsecured Creditors Rights, Disabilities, Americans with Disabilities Act, Academic Employment, College and University Law, Administrative Lobbying, Executive Lobbying, Legislative Lobbying, Lobbying, Eminent Domain, Employee Benefits, COBRA, Deferred Compensation, Employee Benefit Taxation, Employee Benefit Trusts, Employee Compensation, Employee Stock Ownership Plans, ERISA, Executive Compensation, Executive Compensation Taxation, Flexible Benefit Plans, Multi-Employer Benefits, Multi-Employer Pensions, Non-Qualified Benefits, Pension and Profit Sharing Plans, Pension Plans, Pension Taxation, Profit Sharing, Public Pension Plans, Qualified Retirement Plans, Retirement Benefit Plans, Taft-Hartley Plans, Unemployment Compensation, Music Copyright, Environmental Law, Environmental Compliance, Environmental Liability, Environmental Litigation, Environmental Mediation, International Environmental Law, Equipment Finance and Leasing, Equipment Finance, Equipment Leasing, Vehicle Leasing, Family Law, Divorce, Matrimonial Law, Finance, Asset Based Finance, Financial Institution Reorganization, Financial Institutions Law, Financial Institutions Taxation, Financial Restructuring, International Commercial Finance, International Finance, Franchises and Franchising, Franchise Law, Franchise Licensing, Franchise Litigation, Franchise Taxation, International Franchising, General Practice, Federal Practice, Government, County Government Law, Federal Government Law, Government Affairs, Government Agency Practice, Government Relations, Legislative Practice, Local Government Law, Public Policy, Qui Tam Litigation, State Government Law, State Legislative Practice, Township Law, Government Contracts, Government Construction Contracts, Government Contract Arbitration, Government Contract Fraud, Government Procurement, International Government Contracts, Local Government Contracts, Public Bidding, Public Contract Law, Public Works Contracts, Guardianship and Conservatorship, Health Care, Alternative Health Care Delivery System, Certificates of Need, Health Care Administration, Health Care Contracts, Health Care Corporate Law, Health Care Facility Licensing, Health Care Facility Regulation, Health Care Finance, Health Care Fraud, Health Care Legislation, Health Care Licensing, Health Care Mergers and Acquisitions, Health Care Regulation, Health Care Reimbursement, Health Care Taxation, Health Insurance, Health Insurance Coverage, Health Insurance Defense, Health Insurance Trusts, Health Law, Health Maintenance Organizations, Integrated Health Care Delivery Systems, Long Term Care, Managed Care, Managed Care Contracts, Medical Antitrust, Mental Health Law, Nursing Home Regulation, Pharmacy Law, Physicians Contracts, Hospital Law, Hospital Administration, Medical Staff Contracts, Medical Staff Credentialing, Housing Law, Affordable Housing, Apartment Projects, Housing Finance, Insurance, Commercial Insurance, Insurance Company Taxation, Insurance Litigation, Insurance Defense, Intellectual Property, Artistic Property, Chemical Intellectual Property, Electrical Intellectual Property, Intellectual Property Infringement, Intellectual Property Licensing, Intellectual Property Litigation, International Intellectual Property, International Licensing, Mechanical Intellectual Property, Medical Intellectual Property, Pharmaceutical Intellectual Property, Piracy, Proprietary Rights, Taxation of Intellectual Property, International Law, International Trade, Antidumping, Countervailing Duties, Customs Law, Export Regulation, Import and Export Law, International Trade Regulation, Latin America Trade, Russia Trade, Investments, Financial Services Law, Financial Services Regulation, Foreign Investment, Foreign Investment in the United States, International Investment, Investment Banking Law, Investment Company Law, Investment Partnerships, Investment Regulation, Labor and Employment, Affirmative Action, Collective Bargaining, Employee Drug Testing, Employer Liability, Employment at Will, Employment Contracts, Employment Discrimination, Employment Litigation, Employment Mediation, Executive Employment Law, Executive Severance Contracts, Fair Labor Standards, Family and Medical Leave Act, Federal Employment Law, Harassment, International Employment Contracts, International Labor Law, Labor Arbitration, Management Labor Law, National Labor Relations Act, Personnel Policies, Public Sector Collective Bargaining, Public Sector Labor Relations, Sexual Harassment, Unfair Labor Practices, Union Contract Negotiations, Union Elections, Union Organization, Wage and Hour Law, WARN Act, Workplace Violence, Wrongful Termination Defense, Leases and Leasing, Commercial Leasing, International Leasing, Landlord and Tenant Law, Lease Finance, Leasing, Leveraged Leasing, Office Leasing, Retail Leasing, Shopping Center Leasing, Legal Ethics and Professional Responsibility, Legal Ethics, Litigation, Civil Litigation, Complex Litigation, Defense Litigation, Federal Civil Litigation, Federal Litigation, International Litigation, Long-Arm Litigation, Trial Practice, U.S. Supreme Court Litigation, Newspaper Contracts, Publishing Contracts, Medical Malpractice, Medicare and Medicaid, Medicaid Planning, Medicare and Medicaid Reimbursement, Medicare Fraud and Abuse, Mergers, Acquisitions and Divestitures, Business Acquisitions, Business Divestitures, International Mergers and Acquisitions, Leveraged Acquisitions, Leveraged Buyouts, Merger Reorganization, Mergers and Acquisitions, Mergers and Acquisitions Finance, Mortgages, Commercial Mortgages, Mortgage Banking Law, Mortgage Bankruptcy, Mortgage Finance, Mortgage Foreclosure, Mortgage Insurance, Mortgage Lien Foreclosure, Mortgage Refinancing, Mortgage Securitization, Mortgage Tax, Mortgage Workouts, Secondary Mortgage Market, Municipal Bonds, Municipal Bonds Taxation, Municipal Contracts, Municipal Corporation Law, Municipal Derivative Products, Municipal Finance, Municipal Labor Law, Municipal Leasing, Municipal Pension Law, Municipal Redevelopment, Municipal Securities, Municipal Taxation, Tax Increment Finance, Natural Resources, Nonprofit and Charitable Organizations, Charitable Limited Partnerships, Charitable Organizations Law, Charitable Trusts and Foundations, Nonprofit Organizations Law, Nonprofit Tax Law, Private Foundations, Tax Exempt Organizations, Occupational Safety and Health, OSHA, Partnership Law, Family Limited Partnerships, Family Partnerships, Limited Liability Partnerships, Limited Partnerships, Partnership Dissolution, Partnership Formation, Partnership Organization, Partnership Syndication, Partnership Taxation, Patents, Biochemical Patents, Biotechnology Patent Prosecution, Biotechnology Patents, Chemical Patent Prosecution, Chemical Patents, Computer and Software Patents, Design Patents, Electrical Patent Prosecution, Electrical Patents, Electronic Patents, International Patents, Mechanical Patent Prosecution, Mechanical Patents, Medical Patents, Metallurgical Patents, Molecular Biology Patents, Patent Applications, Patent Infringement, Patent Interference Practice, Patent Licensing, Patent Litigation, Patent Prosecution, Patent Protection, Pharmaceutical Patents, Personal Injury, Premises Security, Probate, Ancillary Probate, International Probate, Probate Administration, Probate Litigation, Probate Taxation, Products Liability, Drug and Medical Device Defense, Firearms Products Liability, Professional Liability, Public Finance, Bond Finance, Economic Development, Housing and Urban Development, Industrial Development, International Economic Development, International Project Finance, Project Finance, Public Authority Finance, Public Finance Taxation, Public-Private Development, Tax Exempt Bonds, Tax Exempt Finance, Railway Labor Law, Real Estate, Condominium Association Law, Condominium Conversions, Condominium Development, Condominium Law, Conveyancing, Cooperative Association Law, Cooperative Conversions, Cooperative Housing Law, Easements, International Real Estate, Land Acquisitions, Land Sales, Land Trusts, Planned Unit Development Law, Real Estate Acquisitions, Real Estate Arbitration, Real Estate Banking Law, Real Estate Bankruptcy, Real Estate Brokers Licensing, Real Estate Contracts, Real Estate Development, Real Estate Finance, Real Estate Foreclosure, Real Estate Investment, Real Estate Investment Taxation, Real Estate Investment Trusts, Real Estate Joint Ventures, Real Estate Leasing, Real Estate Litigation, Real Estate Mediation, Real Estate Partnerships, Real Estate Restructuring, Real Estate Sales, Real Estate Secured Lending, Real Estate Securities, Real Estate Settlements, Real Estate Syndication, Real Estate Tax Appeals, Real Estate Tax Assessment, Real Estate Taxation, Real Estate Title, Real Estate Transfers, Real Estate Valuation, Real Estate Workouts, Real Property, Real Property Acquisitions, Real Property Development, Real Property Finance, Residential Real Estate, Residential Real Estate Development, Waterfront Development, Regulatory Law, Drug and Medical Device Regulation, Federal Regulatory Law, Regulated Industries, Regulatory Agency Practice, Regulatory Investigations, Religious Nonprofit Corporation Law, RICO, Securities, Bank Securities, Broker-Dealer Arbitration, Broker-Dealer Regulation, Initial Public Offerings, Private Placement, Private Placement Syndication, Public Offerings, SEC Enforcement, Securities Arbitration, Securities Litigation, Securities Offerings, Securities Registration, Securities Regulation, Shareholder Agreements, Shareholder Disputes, Tax Exempt Securities, Sports Contracts, Sports Licensing, Taxation, Employment Tax, Estate and Gift Taxation, Federal Income Tax, Federal Tax Controversies, Federal Taxation, Fiduciary Income Tax, Income Tax, Individual Taxation, International Tax Controversies, International Taxation, Like Kind Exchanges, Local Taxation, Low Income Housing Tax Credits, Property Tax Abatement, Property Tax Appeals, Sales and Use Tax, State Taxation, Tax Appeals, Tax Audits, Tax Collection, Tax Deferred Exchanges, Tax Planning, Tax Shelters, Trusts and Estates Taxation, Electronics, High Technology Contracts, Semi

(This Listing Continued)

Blank Rome Comisky & McCauley LLP (Continued)

conductor Technology, Technology Contracts, Technology Licensing, Technology Protection, Technology Transfers, Torts, Trade Association Law, Toxic Torts, Trade Secrets, Theft of Trade Secrets, Trademarks, International Trademarks, Trade Dress, Trade Names, Trademark Arbitration, Trademark Infringement, Trademark Licensing, Trademark Litigation, Trademark Prosecution, Trademark Protection, Trademark Registration, Transportation, Common Carrier Law, Mass Transit Law, Public Transportation Law, Transit Labor, Trusts and Estates, Decedents Estates, Estate Administration, Estate Litigation, Estate Planning, Family Trusts, Family Wealth Transfer, Fiduciary Law, Fiduciary Liability, Fiduciary Litigation, Financial Planning, International Estate Planning, International Trusts, Living Trusts, Offshore Trusts, Personal Planning, Retirement Planning, Trust Administration, Trust Law, Trust Litigation, Trust Planning, Wealth Preservation, Unfair Competition, Utility Law, Utility Acquisitions, Utility Contracts, Utility Taxation, White Collar Crime, Embezzlement, White Collar Criminal Defense, White Collar Fraud, Wills, Contested Wills, Inheritance, Living Wills, Successions, Zoning, Planning and Land Use, Building and Public Safety Codes, Cemetery Law, Environmental Land Use, Fire Districts, Improvement Districts, Land Conservation, Land Development, Land Entitlement, Land Use, Land Use Litigation, Land Use Permitting, Land Use Regulation, Rezoning, Special Districts, Subdivisions, Water Districts, Zoning Law, Zoning Variances, Retail Industry Development.

Media, Pennsylvania Office: Rose Tree Corporate Center, 1400 N. Providence Road, Building 1, Suite 301, 19063. Telephone: 610-891-7800. FAX: 610-891-7804.

Cherry Hill, New Jersey Office: Woodland Falls Corporate Park, 210 Lake Drive East, Suite 200, 08002-1164. Telephone: 856-779-3600. FAX: 856-779-7647.

Boca Raton, Florida Office: 1200 North Federal Highway, Suite 417, 33432. Telephone: 561-417-8100. FAX: 561-417-8101.

Allentown, Pennsylvania Office: 1620 Pond Road, Suite 200, 18104-2255. Telephone: 610-706-4300. FAX: 610-706-4343.

Philadelphia, Pennsylvania Office: One Logan Square, 19103-6998. Telephone: 215-569-5500. FAX: 215-569-5555.

Washington, D.C. Office: The Farragut Building, 900 17th Street, N.W., Suite 1000, 20006. Telephone: 202-530-7400. FAX: 202-463-6915.

Trenton, New Jersey Office: 200 West State Street, 08608. Telephone: 609-278-2320. FAX: 609-278-2323.

Baltimore, Maryland Office: 250 West Pratt Street, Suite 1100, 21201. Telephone: 410-659-1400. FAX: 410-659-1414.

New York, New York Office: The Chrysler Building, 405 Lexington Avenue, 10174. Telephone: 212-885-5000. FAX: 212-885-5001.

Cincinnati, Ohio Office: PNC Center, 201 East Fifth Street, Suite 1700, 45202. Telephone: 513-362-8700. Fax: 513-362-8787.

See Professional Biographies, WILMINGTON, DELAWARE

Blom, Deborah A. .... '58 '84 C.567 B.A. L.276 J.D. 207 Medford Rd.
Blumenfeld, Jack B., (AV) .... '52 '79 C.1044 B.A. L.976 J.D. [Morris,N.A.&T.]
Board, Charles L. .... '21 '50 C.885 B.S. L.1017 LL.B. 404 Stafford Rd.‡
Bodnar, Joseph J., (BV) .... '57 '84 C.705 B.A. L.564 J.D. [Walsh M.&M.] ⊙
*PRACTICE AREAS: Bankruptcy; Corporate; Commercial; Civil Litigation.
Boggs, J. Caleb, III '62 '87 C.692 B.A. L.180 J.D.
[Ⓒ Blank R.C.&M.] (⊙Wash., DC; Phila., PA)
*PRACTICE AREAS: Government Relations; Legislative Practice.
Bonanto, Paul J. '44 '69 C.884 A.B. L.188 J.D.
(adm. in PA; not adm. in DE) Corporate Counsel, E.I. du Pont de Nemours & Company
*RESPONSIBILITIES: Mergers and Acquisitions.
Bonczek, Robert R. '45 '70 C&L.575 B.S., J.D.
(adm. in FL; not adm. in DE; Pat.) du Pont Co.
Bonkowski, Michael F., (BV) .... '56 '83 C.178 A.B. L.831 J.D. [Ⓒ Saul E.]
*PRACTICE AREAS: Commercial Litigation; Limited Partnerships; Corporate Law.
Booker, Donald W., (BV) .... '21 '49 C.165 A.B. L.893 J.D. 118A Senatorial Dr.
Booth, Rebecca L. .... '75 '01 C.378 B.A. L.910 J.D. [Ⓐ Richards,L.&F.]
Booth-Barbarin, Ann V. '60 '84 C.659 B.A. L.262 J.D.
(adm. in PA; not adm. in DE) Sr. Coun. & Asst. Secy., Astrazeneca Pharm. LP
*RESPONSIBILITIES: Corporate; Commercial; Healthcare.
Boswell, Paul H., (AV) '38 '66 C.205 B.A. L.902 LL.B.
[Schmittinger&R.] (⊙Dover, Rehoboth Beach)
*PRACTICE AREAS: Corporate Law; Estate Planning; Estate Settlements; Taxation.
Bouchard, Andre G., (BV) .... '61 '86 C.93 A.B. L.309 J.D. [Bouchard M.&F.]
*PRACTICE AREAS: Corporate Litigation; Business Litigation; Intellectual Property Litigation.

Bouchard Margules & Friedlander, P.A., (BV)
222 Delaware Avenue, Suite 1102, 19801
Telephone: 302-573-3500 Telecopier: 302-573-3501
Andre G. Bouchard; David J. Margules; Joel Friedlander;—Joanne Pileggi Pinckney; Karen L. Pascale.
Corporate and Commercial Litigation.
See Professional Biographies, WILMINGTON, DELAWARE

Boudart, Mary C., (BV) .... '51 '76 C.205 B.A. L.831 J.D. 1202 Kirkwood Highway
Boudreaux, Gerald J. '53 '92 C.1036 Ph.D. L.1338 J.D.
(adm. in PA; not adm. in DE; Pat.)
Asst. Gen. Coun., The du Pont Merck Pharmaceutical Co.
Bounds, Curtis P. .... '61 '90 C.893 B.A. L.1105 J.D. [Bayard] ⊙
*PRACTICE AREAS: Family Law; Employment Law; General Litigation.
Bourke, Mary W. ... '59 '85 C.674 B.S.E. L.665 J.D. [Connolly B.L.&H.] (See Pat. Sect.)
Bove, Beverly L., (BV) .... '52 '80 C.205 B.A. L.1338 J.D. 1 Commerce Ctr.
Bove, Jeffrey B., (BV) .... '52 '79 C.205 B.A. L.1202 J.D. [Connolly B.L.&H.]
Bowden, Vivian G. '61 '89 C.1350 B.A. L.1338 J.D.
(adm. in PA; not adm. in DE) 1411 Foulk Rd.
Bowden, William P., (BV) .... '57 '89 C.205 B.S. L.1009 J.D. [Ashby&G.]
Bowen, Alanson G., Jr. '40 '71 C.688 B.S. L.273 J.D.
(adm. in VA; not adm. in DE; Pat.) Corp. Coun., E.I. du Pont de Nemours and Company
Bowler, Mary E. '56 '81 C.188 B.S. L.94 J.D.
(adm. in MA; not adm. in DE)
Corporate Counsel & Assistant Secretary, E.I. du Pont de Nemours & Company
*RESPONSIBILITIES: Corporate Law; Securities; Employment Law.
Bowman, John R., (BV) '38 '63 C.205 B.A. L.1017 LL.B.
Senior Counsel, E.I. du Pont de Nemours & Company
*RESPONSIBILITIES: Litigation Product Liability.
Bowser, William W., (BV) .... '57 '83 C.205 B.A. L.884 J.D. [Young C.S.&T.]
*PRACTICE AREAS: Collective Bargaining; Employee Drug Testing; Employment Disability Discrimination; Employment Discrimination; Employment Litigation.
Boyd, Alan T., (BV) .... '46 '73 C.105 B.S. L.823 J.D. [Ⓒ Bailey&W.]
*PRACTICE AREAS: Personal Injury.
Boyd, Don A. '26 '51 C&L.546 B.S., J.D.
(adm. in NE; not adm. in DE) 2008 Kynwyd Rd.‡
Boyd, Steven D. '57 '82 C.679 B.S.Ch.E. L.546 J.D.
(adm. in NE; not adm. in DE; Pat.) Coun., Hercules Incorporated
Boyer, Matthew F. .... '57 '87 C.309 B.A. L.893 J.D. [Ⓐ Connolly B.L.&H.]
*PRACTICE AREAS: Employment Law; Business Litigation; Professional Ethics.
Boyle, Leo J. .... '52 '79 C.205 B.S. L.1338 J.D. 5197 West Woodmill Drive, Suite 26
Bracegirdle, Thad J. .... '72 '98 C&L.659 B.A., J.D. [Ⓐ Richards,L.&F.]
Bradley, E. Scott .... '57 '87 C.205 B.S. L.1338 J.D. Assoc. J., Supr. Ct.
Bradley, Paul A., (BV) .... '55 '81 C.745 B.A. L.365 J.D. [McCarter&E.]
*PRACTICE AREAS: Litigation; Products Liability; Commercial; Life, Health and Disability Insurance; ERISA.
Bradley, William C. .... '37 '66 C.602 B.S.Ch.E. L.564 LL.B. Com. Pleas J.
Brady, Jennifer Gimler, (BV) .... '64 '90 C.945 B.A. L.1017 J.D. [Potter A.&C.]

Brady, John P. .... '26 '59 C.397 B.S. L.884 LL.B. 213 Welwyn Rd.‡
Brady, Keith R., (BV) .... '54 '82 C.937 B.A. L.128 J.D. Chf. Dep. Atty. Gen.
Brady, Kevin F., (AV) .... '51 '83 C.205 B.A. L.1338 J.D. [Ⓒ Skadden,A.S.M.&F.]
Brady, M. Jane, (BV) '51 '77 C.205 B.A. L.884 J.D.
Carvel State Office Building, 820 North French Street
Brady, Robert S., (BV) .... '64 '90 C.886 B.S. L.1017 J.D. [Young C.S.&T.]
*PRACTICE AREAS: Debtor and Creditor Reorganization; Debtor and Creditor Workouts; Debtor and Creditor Bankruptcy.
Brady, William P., (CV) .... '66 '95 C.999 B.S. L.1338 J.D. [Ⓐ Losco&M.]
Brancati, George A., (CV) .... '47 '72 C.205 B.A. L.923 J.D. 1324 King St.
Brand, David E., (BV) .... '43 '73 C.970 B.A. L.880 J.D. [Prickett,J.&E.]
*PRACTICE AREAS: Commercial Litigation; Alternate Dispute Resolution; Insurance Coverage Litigation; Intellectual Property Litigation; Professional Liability Litigation.
Brandt, Charles, (BV) .... '42 '71 C.205 B.A. L.1009 J.D. [Brandt&D.]
Brandt and Dalton, P.A., (BV) .... 919 Market St. Ste. 900
Brantley, Evelyn Hassinger '63 '91
C.228 B.A. L.16 J.D. E.I. dupont de Nemours & Company
*RESPONSIBILITIES: Employment; Personal Injury Law; Litigation.
Bredt, Alan M. '50 '75 C.472 B.B.A. L.831 J.D.
(adm. in PA; not adm. in DE) [Autman&B.] ⊙
Brehm, Karen S., (BV) .... '55 '84 C.884 B.A. L.1338 J.D. [Maron&M.]
*PRACTICE AREAS: Toxic Tort; Environmental Litigation; Product Liability; Personal Injury.
Bria, Robert S., (BV) .... '58 '88 C.1338 B.A. L.659 J.D. 1009 Closter Rd.
Brickley, Samuel D., II, (BV) ...... '67 '93 C.188 A.B. L.763 J.D. [Ⓐ Connolly B.L.&H.]
Bridge, Gary Alan '71 '01 C.502 B.S. L.1218 J.D.
(adm. in MA; not adm. in DE) [Ⓐ Connolly B.L.&H.]
*PRACTICE AREAS: Intellectual Property.
Bridgman, Victor H., III '38 '67 C.30 B.A. L.446 LL.B.
(adm. in MD; not adm. in DE) P.O. Box 4118‡
Brierley, Jennifer L. .... '70 '01 C.444 B.A. L.1338 J.D. [Ⓐ Morris,J.H.&W.]
*PRACTICE AREAS: Employment Rights; Civil Rights; Education Law; Domestic Relations.
Brightman, Kathleen Carlisle '61 '91 C.205 B.A. L.1338 J.D.
(adm. in PA; not adm. in DE)
Asst. Dean, External & Graduate Prog., Widener Univ. Sch. of Law
Brill, Leroy A. .... '14 '37 C&L.273 B.A., J.D. Pub. Serv. Comm.‡
Britton, Ann H. '49 '76 C.228 B.A. L.276 J.D.
(adm. in VA; not adm. in DE) Widener Univ.
Brockstedt, Chase T. .... '73 '99 C.953 B.A. L.1338 J.D. [Murphy S.&L.]
*PRACTICE AREAS: Commercial Litigation; Insurance Defense; Insurance Coverage; Civil Litigation.
Brodoway, Barbara A., (BV) .... '59 '85 C.205 B.A. L.884 J.D. [Nolte&B.]
*PRACTICE AREAS: Personal Injury; Real Estate; Insurance Defense; Asbestos; Toxic Torts.
Bromson, Debra L. '57 '82 C.188 A.B. L.276 J.D.
(adm. in NY; not adm. in DE) Sr. Coun., Astrazeneca Pharm. LP
*RESPONSIBILITIES: Information Technology; E-Commerce; Commercial; Pharmaceutical/Healthcare; Copyright.
Brosseit, A. Kimberly Rockwell ...... '68 '96 C.104 B.A. L.259 J.D. [Ⓐ Blank R.C.&M.]
*PRACTICE AREAS: Zoning, Planning and Land Use; Real Estate; Corporate Law; Environmental Law.
Broujos, Frank Nicholas, Jr. '61 '87 C.216 B.A. L.1338 J.D.
Asst. V.P. & Assoc. Legal Coun., PNC Bk., Del.
Browder, Mary Elizabeth M. .... '62 '87 C.362 B.B.A. L.273 J.D. [Walsh M.&M.] ⊙
*PRACTICE AREAS: Taxation Law; Federal, State and International Taxation; Estate Planning; Probate Law; Corporate Law.
Browder, Monte R. '58 '91 C.65 A.B. L.893 J.D.
(adm. in NJ; not adm. in DE; Pat.) Asst. Gen. Coun., DuPont Pharmaceuticals Co.
Brown, Calissa W. '62 '87 C.659 B.A. L.1149 J.D.
(adm. in PA; not adm. in DE) Corp. Counsel, E.I. du Pont de Nemours & Company
*RESPONSIBILITIES: Securities Law; Financing.
Brown, David B., (AV) .... '46 '73 C.575 A.B. L.893 J.D. [Potter A.&C.]
Brown, Don C. '51 '77 C.674 A.B. L.273 J.D.
Corp. Coun., E.I. du Pont de Nemours and Company
*RESPONSIBILITIES: Commercial Contracts; Intellectual Property; Healthcare.
Brown, Elizabeth A. .... '71 '96 C.1 B.A. L.494 J.D. [Ⓐ Morris,J.H.&W.]
Brown, Grover C., (AV) .... '35 '61 C.575 A.B. L.273 LL.B. [Ⓒ Gordon,F.&M.]
*PRACTICE AREAS: Corporate Fiduciary Law.
Brown, Paul D. .... '71 '00 C.659 B.A. L.665 J.D. [Ⓐ Richards,L.&F.]
Brown, Ronald A., Jr. .... '65 '90 C.105 B.S.B.A. L.1338 J.D. [Prickett,J.&E.]
*PRACTICE AREAS: Corporate Law; Chancery Court Litigation.
Brown, Spencer D. .... '69 '98 C.674 B.A. L.659 J.D. Coun., Astrazeneca Pharm. LP
*RESPONSIBILITIES: Corporate.
Brown, Stuart M., (BVⓉ) '63 '88 C.94 B.S. L.831 J.D.
(adm. in PA; not adm. in DE) [Buchanan I.] (⊙Phila., PA)
*PRACTICE AREAS: Bankruptcy; Creditors' Rights; Condominium Associations' Rights and Litigation.

Bryde, Gary A., P.A.
(See Hockessin)

Buchanan Ingersoll, Professional Corporation, (BVⓉ)
1201 North Market Street, Suite 1501, 19801 ⊙
Telephone: 302-428-5500 Fax: 302-428-3996
Shareholder: Stuart M. Brown (Not admitted in DE; Also at Philadelphia, Pennsylvania Office).
Associates: Frank B. Harrington (Not admitted in DE; Also at Princeton, New Jersey Office); Jami B. Nimeroff (Not admitted in DE; Also at Philadelphia, Pennsylvania Office).
Antitrust and Trade Regulation, Broadcasting and Cable TV, Commercial Transactions, Computer Law, Construction Industry Law, Corporate Law and Finance, Creditors' Rights and Bankruptcy, Energy, Environmental Law, ERISA and Employee Benefits, Family Law, Financial Institutions, Franchising, Government Relations, Healthcare, Insurance Regulation, Intellectual Property, International Transactions, Labor and Employment, Litigation, Mergers and Acquisitions, Municipal Law, Natural Resources Law, Public Finance, Real Estate, Security Alarm, Tax and Estate Planning, Technology Law, Trade Secret Litigation, Transportation Law, Trust and Estate Administration, Venture Capital.
Pittsburgh, Pennsylvania Office: One Oxford Centre, 301 Grant Street, 20th Floor. Telephone: 412-562-8800. Telecopier: 412-562-1041. URL: http://www.bipc.com.
Philadelphia, Pennsylvania Office: Eleven Penn Center, 14th Floor, 1835 Market Street. Telephone: 215-665-8700.
Bryn Mawr, Pennsylvania Office: 937 East Haverford Road, Suite 201. Telephone: 610-581-7004.
Harrisburg, Pennsylvania Office: One South Market Square, 213 Market Street, 3rd Floor. Telephone: 717-237-4800.
Tampa, Florida Office: SunTrust Financial Centre, 401 East Jackson Street, Suite 2500. Telephone: 813-222-8180.
Aventura, Florida Office: One Turnberry Place, 19495 Biscayne Boulevard, Suite 606. Telephone: 305-933-5600.
Miami, Florida Office: Bank of America Tower, 100 S.E. Second Street, Suite 2100. Telephone: 305-347-4080.
Princeton, New Jersey Office: 700 Alexander Park, Suite 300. Telephone: 609-987-6800.
Buffalo, New York Office: 268 Main Street, Suite 201. Telephone: 716-853-2330.
Washington, D.C. Office: 1776 K Street, N.W., Suite 800. Telephone: 202-452-7900.
Other Washington, D.C. Office: Silverstein and Mullens, 1776 K Street, N.W., Suite 800. Telephone: 202-452-7900.
New York, New York Office: 140 Broadway, 35th Floor. Telephone: 646-458-2340.
McLean, Virginia Office: 8280 Greensboro Drive, Suite 601. Telephone: 703-749-6060.
San Diego, California Office: First National Bank Center, 401 West A Street, Suite 1900. Telephone: 619-578-5000.
London, England Office: Tower 42, The International Financial Centre, Old Broad Street, EC2N 1HQ. Telephone: 44-207-920-3700.

(This Listing Continued)

Buchanan Ingersoll, Professional Corporation (Continued)
Dublin, Ireland Office: Level 1, 4 Custom House Plaza, IFSC, Dublin 1. Telephone: 011-353-1611-7266. Fax: 3531-836-9305.
See Professional Biographies, WILMINGTON, DELAWARE

Buckworth, Mark D. .... '56 '82 C.205 B.S. L.1338 J.D. Family Ct.
Bulman, Christine S. '66 '93 C.1369 B.S. L.602 J.D.
(adm. in MI; not adm. in DE) [A Grant&E.]
Bunitsky, Mark W., (BV) .... '55 '81 C.205 B.A. L.884 J.D. Dep. Atty. Gen.
Bunville, Kathryn L. .... '66 '94 C.205 B.A. L.665 J.D. Dept. of Jus.
Burgess, Richard H. .... '37 '63 C.576 B.S. L.161 J.D. Coun., du Pont Co. (Pat.)
Burkett, Lex J. '51 '82 C.999 B.A. L.1338 J.D.
(adm. in PA; not adm. in DE) 102 Somerset‡
Burleigh, Tracy A. .... '67 '97 C.205 B.A. L.1338 J.D. [A Marshall,D.W.C.&G.]
*PRACTICE AREAS: General Liability Defense.
Burnett, James F., (BV) .... '41 '69 C.649 B.A. L.276 J.D. [Potter A.&C.]
Burnett, William J. '69 '95 C.184 B.A. L.831 J.D.
(adm. in PA; not adm. in DE) [A Blank R.C.&M.]
*PRACTICE AREAS: Bankruptcy; Bankruptcy Chapter 11; Bankruptcy Reorganization; Bankruptcy Chapter 7; Bankruptcy Litigation.
Burt, David H., (BV) '58 '86 C.821 B.A. L.945 J.D.
Senior Counsel, E.I. du Pont de Nemours & Company
*RESPONSIBILITIES: Trial Practice; Commercial Litigation; Employment Litigation.
Burtch, Jeffrey L., (BV) .... '50 '78 C.473 B.A. L.851 J.D. [Cooch&T.] (⊙Newark)
*PRACTICE AREAS: Bankruptcy; Commercial Law; Banking Law.
Burton, Alan G. '45 '69 C&L.260 B.S., J.D.
Senior Counsel, E.I. dupont de Nemours & Company
*RESPONSIBILITIES: Labor and Employment.
Busenkell, Michael .... '68 '95 C.884 B.S. L.831 J.D. [A Morris,N.A.&T.]
Bussard, Donald A., (AV) .... '51 '76 C.951 B.A. L.831 J.D. [Richards,L.&F.]
Butcher, Rebecca L. .... '74 '99 C.893 B.A. L.880 J.D. [A Klett R.L.&S.]
*PRACTICE AREAS: Litigation.
Butler, A. Hays '50 '76 C.478 B.A. L.93 J.D.
(adm. in VT; not adm. in DE) 2106 Millers Rd.
Butzi, Fred F. '28 '59 C&L.966 B.S., J.D.
(adm. in WI; not adm. in DE; Pat.) 1102 Dardel Rd.‡
Caggiano, Nicholas J., Jr. .... '57 '88 C&L.884 B.ChE, J.D. [Morris,J.H.&W.]
Cain, Esta L. '43 '84 C.649 B.S.B.A. L.665 J.D.
(adm. in PA; not adm. in DE) Sr. V.P. & Gen. Coun., AIG Marketing, Inc.
Calder, Cynthia A. .... '65 '91 C.205 B.A. L.884 J.D. [A Grant&E.]
Calder, Peter D. .... '71 '00 C.339 B.A. L.659 J.D. [A Richards,L.&F.]
Caloway, Mary F., (BV) .... '60 '92 C.205 B.A.A.S. L.1338 J.D. [Klett R.L.&S.]
*PRACTICE AREAS: Banking Law; Commercial Law; Bankruptcy Law.
Campanelli, Lawrence E. '49 '78 C.999 B.A. L.1338 J.D.
(adm. in PA; not adm. in DE) 1333 Maple St.‡
Campbell, Mary Kate '68 '97 C.205 B.A. L.831 J.D.
(adm. in PA; not adm. in DE) [E.I. d.d.]
Campbell, Peter, (BV) .... '61 '87 C&L.128 B.A., J.D. [A Stewart&Assoc.]
*PRACTICE AREAS: Corporate Law; Litigation.
Canfield, Douglas B., (CV) '56 '81
C.205 B.A. L.1068 J.D. 100 West 10th Street, Suite 203
Cantor, Donna M. '65 '90 C.207 B.A. L.245 J.D.
(adm. in GA; not adm. in DE) Staff Atty., Community Legal Aid Soc., Inc.
Capodanno, Joseph F., Jr. '43 '74 C.397 B.S. L.500 J.D.
(adm. in MS; not adm. in DE) Off. of the Mayor
Capone, Jerome M., (BV) .... '51 '78 C.30 B.A. L.1338 J.D. 4 E. 8th St.
Caponi, Steven L. .... '68 '86 C.831 B.A. L.1338 J.D. [A Blank R.C.&M.]
*PRACTICE AREAS: Corporate Governance; Corporate Litigation; Complex Litigation; Intellectual Property.
Carey, Robert G., (BV) .... '34 '67 C.1062 B.A. L.831 J.D. 2304 Riddle Avenue, Suite 206
Carey, Wayne J., (AV) .... '48 '82 C.865 B.S. L.1338 J.D. [Prickett,J.&E.]
*PRACTICE AREAS: Corporate Law; Partnership; Limited Liability Companies; Delaware Investment Holding Companies; Business Trust Law.
Carickhoff, David W., Jr .... '72 '98 C.311 B.A. L.831 J.D. [A Pachulski,S.Z.Y.&J.]
*PRACTICE AREAS: Bankruptcy Chapter 11; Corporate Restructuring; Corporate Reorganization; Bankruptcy Litigation.
Carlino, Jodi-Ann .... '58 '90 C.205 B.S. L.1338 J.D. 1705 Sycamore Street
Carlson, Caryl L. '58 '90 C.97 B.S. L.851 J.D.
(adm. in OH; not adm. in DE) Jud. Law Clk. to U.S. Dist. J.
Carlton, Christopher F. .... '72 '98 C.280 B.B.A. L.884 J.D. [A Morris,N.A.&T.]
Carmichael, Linda M. .... '58 '97 C&L.1338 B.S., J.D. [A White&W.]
Carmine, Kenneth F. .... '48 '74 C.205 B.A. L.1017 J.D. [Potter,C.&L.] ⊙
Carpenter, David W., (AV Ⓣ) '58 '83 C.249 B.S. L.117 J.D.
(adm. in OH; not adm. in DE) Coun., First USA
Carpenter, Edmund N., II, (AV) .... '21 '49 C.674 B.A. L.309 LL.B. 600 Center Mill Rd.‡
Carpenter, William C., Jr. .... '51 '76 C.205 B.S. L.1338 J.D. Supr. Ct. J.
Carr, Michael D., (BV) .... '49 '78 C.1038 B.A. L.1338 J.D. [Ament L.&C.]
Carter, Edward B., Jr., (AV) ...... '46 '77 C.228 B.A. L.1338 J.D. [Kimmel,C.R.&P.] ⊙
*PRACTICE AREAS: General and Civil Trial Practice; Insurance; Negligence; Workers Compensation; Construction Accidents.
Casarino, Marc Stephen .... '72 '97 C.205 B.S. L.1338 J.D. [A White&W.]
Casarino, Stephen P., (AV) .... '41 '66 C.205 B.A. L.128 LL.B. [Casarino,C.&S.]
*PRACTICE AREAS: Civil Litigation; Personal Injury; Products Liability; Insurance Defense.

Casarino, Christman & Shalk, (AV)
800 King Street, Suite 200, P.O. Box 1276, 19801
Telephone: 302-594-4500 Telecopier: 302-594-4509
URL: http://www.casarino.com
Members of Firm: Stephen P. Casarino; Colin M. Shalk; Beth H. Christman; Donald M. Ransom;—Kenneth M. Doss; Diane M. Willette; Stacey L. Cummings; Thomas P. Leff.
Civil Litigation, including Personal Injury, Products Liability and Workers Compensation in all State and Federal Courts in the State of Delaware.
See Professional Biographies, WILMINGTON, DELAWARE

Casey, Timothy A., (BV) .... '52 '79 C.205 B.A. L.1017 J.D. [Marshall,D.W.C.&G.]
*PRACTICE AREAS: Workers Compensation.
Casner, Carol A. .... '40 '89 C.999 B.A. L.1338 J.D. Coun., Applied Card Systems
Castle, Ben T., (AV) .... '38 '64 C.659 A.B. L.276 J.D. [Young C.S.&T.]
*PRACTICE AREAS: Medical Negligence; Surgeons Liability; Obstetric Malpractice; Catastrophic Injury; Wrongful Death.
Cattie, William J., III, (AV) .... '46 '74 C.884 B.A. L.309 J.D. [Cattie&F.]
*PRACTICE AREAS: Insurance Defense Law; Asbestos and Toxic Tort Litigation; Professional Malpractice; Civil Practice; Trial Practice.

Cattie and Fruehauf, (AV)
1201 Orange Street, Suite 502, P.O. Box 588, 19899-0588
Telephone: 302-778-1200 Fax: 302-778-1400
Members of Firm: William J. Cattie, III; Barbara A. Fruehauf.
General Civil and Trial Practice. Insurance Defense, Insurance Coverage, Asbestos and Toxic Tort Litigation, Professional Malpractice.
See Professional Biographies, WILMINGTON, DELAWARE

Caulfield, Eileen F. .... '52 '79 C.728 B.A. L.862 J.D. 14 Brendle Ln.
Cavanagh, James B. '20 '50 C.976 B.A. L.831 LL.B.
(adm. in DC; not adm. in DE) 4031 Kennett Pike‡
Chaikin, Ellen R. .... '56 '82 C.1365 B.A. L.245 J.D. Dep. Atty. Gen.
Chamberlain, Gerard A. '55 '81 C&L.659 B.A., J.D.
(adm. in PA; not adm. in DE) V.P. & Coun., Wilmington Trust Company
Chapman, William Leonard '61 '87 C.103 B.A. L.276 J.D.
(adm. in PA; not adm. in DE) Mun. Ct. J.
Chappell, Harriet Lang ... '58 '84 C.205 B.A. L.1338 J.D. Bassett, Brosius & Dawson, Inc.
Charlton, Janet Z., (CV) .... '64 '89 C.569 B.S. L.831 J.D. [Young C.S.&T.]
*PRACTICE AREAS: Foreclosures; Workouts; Commercial Litigation; Construction Law; Landlord and Tenant Law.
Cheek, Teresa A., (BV) .... '— '88 C.205 B.A. L.1338 J.D. [Young C.S.&T.]
*PRACTICE AREAS: Affirmative Action; Employee Discipline; Employment Discrimination; Employment Termination; Immigration Discrimination.
Chehi, Mark S., (BV) .... '56 '90 C.311 B.A. L.145 J.D. [Skadden,A.S.M.&F.]
Cheney, Huddie L., III '53 '78 C.1365 B.A. L.245 J.D.
(adm. in GA; not adm. in DE) Sr. V.P., American Guaranty & Trust Co.
Cheney, Scott Brian .... '63 '94 C.380 B.S. L.1325 J.D. [A Roeberg,M.&Assoc.]
Chichi, C. Drue '68 '93 C.644 B.S. L.205 J.D.
Carvel State Office Bldg., 820 N. French St., 6th Fl.

Chimicles & Tikellis LLP, (BV)
One Rodney Square, 19801 ⊙
Telephone: 302-656-2500 Telecopier: 302-656-9053
Email: chimicles@aol.com URL: http://www.chimicles.com
Resident Partners: Pamela S. Tikellis; Robert J. Kriner, Jr.
Securities, Antitrust, Consumer, Environmental and Commercial Litigation, Mergers and Acquisitions, Class and Derivative Actions.
Haverford, Pennsylvania Office: One Haverford Centre, 361 West Lancaster Avenue, 19041-0100. Telephone: 610-642-8500. Telecopier: 610-649-3633.
See Professional Biographies, WILMINGTON, DELAWARE

Chipman, William E., Jr. .... '— '99 [A Greenberg T.]
Chismire, Lisa E. '58 '86 C.378 B.A. L.846 J.D.
(adm. in TX; not adm. in DE) Senior Counsel, E.I. dupont de Nemours & Co.
*RESPONSIBILITIES: Commercial Law; Antitrust; Mergers and Acquisitions.
Chopko, David A. '51 '76 C.1338 B.A. L.229 J.D.
(adm. in PA; not adm. in DE) du Pont Co.
Chrissinger, Nancy E., (BV) .... '60 '85 C.886 B.S.B.A. L.884 J.D. [Chrissinger&B.]
Chrissinger & Baumberger, (BV) .... 3 Mill Road, Suite 303
Christenbury, Lynne M. '59 '87 C.522 B.S. L.831 J.D.
(adm. in PA; not adm. in DE; Pat.) Senior Counsel, E.I. dupont de Nemours & Co.
*RESPONSIBILITIES: Intellectual Property; Patents.
Christman, Beth H., (BV) .... '55 '81 C.132 B.A. L.273 J.D. [Casarino,C.&S.]
*PRACTICE AREAS: Insurance Defense; Workers' Compensation; Civil Litigation.
Christman, Mark H. '55 '81 C.264 B.A. L.273 J.D.
(adm. in DC; not adm. in DE) Senior Counsel, E.I. depont de Nemours & Company
*RESPONSIBILITIES: Commercial Law.
Ciccarone, John A. .... '66 '94 C.205 B.S. L.1338 J.D. [A Potter A.&C.]
Ciconte, Edward T., (AV) .... '48 '73 C.728 B.S. L.884 J.D. [Ciconte,R.&W.]
*PRACTICE AREAS: Personal Injury; Collections; Medical Malpractice; Workers Compensation.

Ciconte, Roseman & Wasserman, (AV)
1300 King Street, 19801
Telephone: 302-658-7101 Fax: 302-658-4982
URL: http://www.lawyers.com/crw
Edward T. Ciconte; Kenneth M. Roseman; Jeffrey P. Wasserman.
Litigation, Commercial, Collection, Personal Injury, Domestic Relations, Wills and Estates, Bankruptcy and Workers Compensation Law, Medical Malpractice, Products Liability.
See Professional Biographies, WILMINGTON, DELAWARE

Clare, Laura S. .... '69 '94 C.262 B.A. L.884 J.D. [A Skadden,A.S.M.&F.]
*PRACTICE AREAS: Litigation.
Clark, Anthony W., (AV) .... '51 '79 C.1044 B.A. L.831 J.D. [Skadden,A.S.M.&F.]
Clark, David J. '52 '83 C.205 B.A. L.1338 J.D.
V.P., Secy. & Coun., Chase Manhattan Bk. Del.
Clark, Delia A. .... '61 '88 C.608 B.A. L.1338 J.D. [A Mattleman,W.&M.]
*PRACTICE AREAS: Civil Litigation; Personal Injury; Medical Malpractice; Premises Liability; Products Liability.
Clark, John A., III, (BV) .... '46 '72 C.262 B.A. L.273 J.D. [Connolly B.L.&H.]
Clark, Peter F., (CV) .... '54 '81 C.198 A.B. L.880 J.D. Gen. Coun., Conectiv
*RESPONSIBILITIES: Public Utility Regulation (40%); Labor and Employment (30%); Administrative Litigation (10%); General Corporate (10%).
Clark, Thomas L. .... '29 '59 C.896 B.A. L.309 LL.B. Barley Mill Plaza
Clarke, Michael L. '56 '81 C.967 B.A. L.893 J.D.
(adm. in PA; not adm. in DE) Senior Counsel, E.I. dupont de Nemours & Company
*RESPONSIBILITIES: Litigation.
Cleary, M. Blake .... '66 '97 C.893 B.A. L.1338 J.D. [A Young C.S.&T.]
*PRACTICE AREAS: Debtor and Creditor Reorganization; Debtor and Creditor Bankruptcy; Debtor and Creditor Workouts.
Cleghorn, Megan E. '69 '99 C&L.227 B.S., J.D.
(adm. in PA; not adm. in DE) [A Skadden,A.S.M.&F.]
*PRACTICE AREAS: Corporate Reorganization; Creditors Rights.
Clevenger, Redmond L., Jr. '68 '01 C.309 ALB L.276 J.D.
(adm. in MA; not adm. in DE) [A Connolly B.L.&H.]
*PRACTICE AREAS: Corporate Litigation.

Cline, David P., & Associates, (BV) '60 '87 C.732 B.A. L.1338 J.D.
1300 North Market Street, Suite 700, 19801
Telephone: 302-529-7848 Fax: 302-654-0884
Personal Injury, Civil Litigation, Products Liability, Workers Compensation, Medical Malpractice, Bankruptcy.
See Professional Biographies, WILMINGTON, DELAWARE

Cloutier, Philip D. .... '49 '83 C.454 B.S.M.E. L.1338 J.D. du Pont Co.
Cobb, Raymond W. .... '57 '82 C.205 B.A. L.884 J.D. [R.W.Cobb] ⊙
*PRACTICE AREAS: Insurance Defense; Litigation; Products Liability; Toxic Torts; Asbestos Litigation.
Cobb, Richard S. .... '64 '93 C.509 B.A. L.884 J.D. [A Klett R.L.&S.]
*PRACTICE AREAS: Commercial Litigation; Bankruptcy Litigation; Employment Litigation; Personal Injury Litigation.

Cobb, Raymond W., LLC
Three Mill Road Suite 206, 19806 ⊙
Telephone: 302-777-4100 Fax: 302-777-4111
Email: rwcobb@earthlink.net URL: http://www.lawyers.com/cobblaw
Raymond W. Cobb.
Products Liability, Admiralty and Maritime Law, Workers Compensation, Insurance Defense, Personal Injury Litigation, Medical Malpractice, Automobile Accidents.
Haddon Heights, New Jersey Office: 126 White Horse Pike. Telephone: 856-310-1100. Fax: 856-310-1212.
See Professional Biographies, WILMINGTON, DELAWARE

Cochran, Bryan M. .... '65 '93 C.205 B.S. L.1338 J.D. 3540 Old Capital Trl.
Cochran, C. Malcolm, IV, (BV) .... '59 '85 C.205 B.A. L.128 J.D. [Richards,L.&F.]
*PRACTICE AREAS: Complex Business Litigation; Governmental Relations; Administrative Law.

Coffey, Diane Marie, (BV) .... '59 '90 C.1376 B.S. L.1338 J.D. Dep. Atty. Gen.
Cohen, Amy S. ...... '59 '87 C.881 A.B. L.216 J.D. Chf. Coun., Fin. Servs., Hercules Inc.
Cohen, Elaina R. '70 '96 C.205 B.A. L.228 J.D.
(adm. in PA; not adm. in DE) Coun., Astrazeneca Pharm. LP
*RESPONSIBILITIES: Corporate; Commercial; Healthcare; Pharmaceuticals.
Cohen, Howard A. '74 '99 C.259 B.S. L.228 J.D.
(adm. in FL; not adm. in DE) [🄰 Skadden,A.S.M.&F.]
*PRACTICE AREAS: Corporate Restructuring; Corporate Bankruptcy.
Cohn, Donald A. '47 '72 C.645 B.A. L.569 J.D.
(adm. in PA; not adm. in DE) Corporate Counsel, E.I. dupont de Nemours & Company
*RESPONSIBILITIES: Computers and Software; Electronic Commerce; Internet Law; Procurement Law.
Collins, Cynthia S., (BV) '53 '79 C.205 B.A.A.S. L.1017 J.D.
BlueCross BlueShield of DE
Collins, James P., Sr., (BV) .... '18 '50 C.884 A.B. L.309 LL.B. P.O. Box 2030
Collins, Mark D., (BV) .... '65 '91 C.705 B.A. L.904 J.D. [Richards,L.&F.]
*PRACTICE AREAS: Bankruptcy Law; Creditors' Rights.
Collins, P. Clarkson, Jr., (AV) .... '50 '76 C.893 B.A. L.1017 J.D. [Morris,J.H.&W.]
*PRACTICE AREAS: Business; Fiduciary; Litigation; Corporate Law; Professional Liability.
Collins, Thomas P., (AV) '52 '78 C.692 B.A. L.1338 J.D.
V.P., Secy. & Gen. Coun., Wilmington Trust Comp.
Componovo, W. Christopher, (CV) '68 '94
C.602 B.A. L.1338 J.D. 125 Kimg St., Ste 1200
Conallen, Michael J., Jr. ....'70 '98 C&L.831 B.A., J.D. [🄰 Stewart&Assoc.]
Conaty, F. Peter, Jr., (BV) ....'67 '92 C.205 B.S.A.C. L.831 J.D. [Prickett,J.&E.]
*PRACTICE AREAS: Estate Planning; Probate; Taxation.
Conaty, Thomas P., IV, (CV) ......'67 '94 C.903 B.A. L.128 J.D. [Crossland,C.&Assoc.]
Conaway, Bernard G. ....'58 '90 C.1326 B.A. L.1338 J.D. [Maron&M.]
*PRACTICE AREAS: Toxic Tort; Alternative Dispute Resolution (60%); Products Liability; Personal Injury (20%); Commercial Law (20%).
Concha, Marcelo '45 '72 C.1222 M.P.A. L.999 J.D.
(adm. in PA; not adm. in DE) 2120 St. Francis St.
Conly, John James .... '44 '76 C.216 A.B. L.1017 J.D. 301 S. DuPont Rd.
Connell, Lawrence J. .... '— '79 C.1338 A.B. L.896 J.D. 4601 Concord Pike
Connolly, Anne E. ....'65 '91 C.197 A.B. L.228 J.D. [🄰 Skadden,A.S.M.&F.]
Connolly, Arthur G., (AV) '05 '32
C.453 B.S. L.309 LL.B. [Connolly B.L.&H.] (See Pat. Sect.)‡
Connolly, Arthur G., III, (BV) ...... '60 '88 C.951 B.A. L.276 J.D. [Connolly B.L.&H.]
Connolly, Arthur G., Jr., (AV) ....'37 '62 C&L.276 B.S., J.D. [Connolly B.L.&H.]
Connolly, Colm F. .... '64 '93 C.602 B.A. L.228 J.D. [Morris,N.A.&T.]

Connolly Bove Lodge & Hutz LLP, (AV) 🄱🄱
1220 Market Street, P.O. Box 2207, 19899-2207 ⊙
Telephone: 302-658-9141 Telecopier: 302-658-5614
Email: cblhlaw@cblhlaw.com URL: http://www.cblhlaw.com
Arthur G. Connolly (Retired); James M. Mulligan, Jr.; Arthur G. Connolly, Jr.; Rudolf E. Hutz; Harold Pezzner; Richard M. Beck (Not admitted in DE); Paul E. Crawford; Stanley C. Macel, III; Henry E. Gallagher, Jr.; George Pazuniak; N. Richard Powers; Richard David Levin; John A. Clark, III; Jeffrey B. Bove; James J. Woods, Jr.; Collins J. Seitz, Jr.; Edward F. Eaton; Charles J. Durante; Michael K. Newell; Patricia Smink Rogowski; Mary W. Bourke; Robert G. McMorrow, Jr. (Not admitted in DE); R. Eric Hutz; Arthur G. Connolly, III; William E. McShane (Not admitted in DE); James D. Heisman; Jeffrey C. Wisler; Ashley I. Pezzner; Karen C. Bifferato; Burton A. Amernick (Not admitted in DE); George R. Pettit (Not admitted in DE); Morris Liss (Not admitted in DE); Stanley B. Green (Not admitted in DE). Of Counsel: John D. Fairchild (Not admitted in DE); William E. Lambert (Not admitted in DE); M. Edward Danberg; Anne Love Barnett. Associates: Matthew F. Boyer; Gerard M. O'Rourke; Francis DiGiovanni; Samuel D. Brickley II; Thomas A. Stevens; Oleh V. Bilynsky; James M. Olsen; Eric J. Evain; Michelle McMahon; Daniel C. Mulveny; Christine M. Hansen; Judith M. Jones; Patrick H. Higgins (Not admitted in DE); Christos T. Adamopoulos; Gary Alan Bridge (Not admitted in DE); Adele Williams Gernsross (Not admitted in DE); Helena C. Rychlicki; Max B. Walton; Redmond L. Clevenger, Jr. (Not admitted in DE); Thomas F. Poche (Not admitted in DE; Resident, Washington, DC Office); Joseph Barrera (Not admitted in DE; Resident, Washington, DC Office); Elliott E. Mendelson; Michael L. Lovitz (Not admitted in DE); Daniel J. Harbison; Larry J. Hume (Not admitted in DE; Resident, Washington, DC Office); Patrick J. Wells (Not admitted in DE; Resident, Washington, D.C. Office); Michael L. Donner, Sr. (Not admitted in DE; Resident, Washington, D.C. Office).
General Practice, Corporations, Partnerships and Other Business Organizations, Intellectual Property, Antitrust, Commercial Transactions, Real Estate, Bankruptcy, Wills, Estates and Trusts, Taxation, Personal Injury, Family, Environmental and Construction Law, Labor and Employee Relations, Product Liability and Criminal Defense.
Washington, D.C. Office: Suite 800, 1990 M Street NW. Telephone: 202-331-7111. Facsimile: 202-293-6229.
See Professional Biographies, WILMINGTON, DELAWARE

Connors, Carolyn Gates '63 '97
C.105 B.A. L.1338 J.D. E.I. Dupont de Nemours & Co., Inc.
Connors, Kevin J., (BV) ....'55 '82 C.893 B.A. L.884 J.D. [Marshall,D.W.C.&G.]
*PRACTICE AREAS: Products Liability; General Liability Defense.
Cooch, Edward W., Jr., (AV) '20 '48 C.205 B.A. L.893 LL.B.
[🄲 Cooch&T.] (⊙Newark)
*PRACTICE AREAS: General Practice; Business Law; Estate Planning; Estate Settlements.
Cooch, Richard R. ....'48 '73 C.951 B.A. L.575 J.D. Supr. J.

Cooch and Taylor, (AV)
Suite 1000, 824 Market Street Mall, P.O. Box 1680, 19899-1680 ⊙
Telephone: 302-652-3641 Telecopier: 302-652-5379
URL: http://www.coochandtaylor.com
Members of Firm: Donald C. Taylor; H. Alfred Tarrant, Jr.; Robert W. Crowe; Bonnie H. Sheer; W. Jeffrey Whittle; Michael A. Friedberg; Jeoffrey L. Burtch; C. Scott Reese; Andrew P. Taylor (Also at Newark Office); Thomas D. Shellenberger;—Paula C. Witherow; Mary Ann P. Bazzano (Resident, Kennett Square, PA Office); Gregory J. Weinig; Adam Singer; Robert W. Pedigo. Special Counsel: Steven H. Amick (Resident, Newark Office). Of Counsel: Edward W. Cooch, Jr.
General Practice, Banking, Litigation. Corporation, Real Estate, Environmental, Land Use and Development, Construction and Asbestos Defense, Trial Practice in all Federal and Delaware Courts, Family, Personal Injury, Probate, Estate Planning, Taxation, Commercial, Bankruptcy and Chancery Court Practice.
Representative Clients: Artisans' Savings Bank; Trustees of the New Castle Common; Delaware Association of Realtors; CBI Industries; Ryder Truck Rental, Inc.
Approved Attorneys for: Ticor Title Insurance Co.; Lawyers Title Insurance Corp.
References: PNC Bank, Delaware; Wilmington Trust Co.
Newark Office: 51 E. Main Street, Suite B, P.O. Box 672. Telephone: 302-368-7200. Telecopier: 302-368-7491.
Kennett Square, Pennsylvania Office: 502 West Cypress Street, P.O. Box 909. Telephone: 610-444-3700. Telecopier: 610-444-5446.
See Professional Biographies, WILMINGTON, DELAWARE

Coombs, Douglas M. '22 '52 C.674 B.S. L.309 LL.B.
(adm. in DC; not adm. in DE) V.P. & Asst. Secy., Simmonds Precision Products, Inc.
Coonin, Robert Burton, (BV) ....'49 '75 C.205 B.A. L.365 J.D. [Berkowitz,S.C.&C.]
Cooper, Alan N., (BV) ....'52 '85 C.105 B.A. L.1338 J.D. [Berkowitz,S.C.&C.]
Cooper, Ellen Marie, (BV) .... '57 '90 C.205 B.A. L.831 J.D. [🄰 Morris,J.H.&W.]
*PRACTICE AREAS: Employment Law; Education Law; Health Law.
Copper, Mary E. .... '50 '77 C.914 A.B. L.94 J.D. [Potter A.&C.]
Corle, James T. '27 '55 C.679 B.S. L.1119 J.D.
(adm. in IN; not adm. in DE) 800 Sycamore Lane‡
Corliss, Cynthia L. '57 '82 C.104 A.B. L.188 J.D.
(adm. in PA; not adm. in DE) V.P. & Coun., Wilmington Trust Company

Cornell, L. Jason ....'— '99 C.259 B.A. L.1338 J.D. [🄰 Agostini,L.I.&K.]
*PRACTICE AREAS: Trial Practice; Commercial Litigation; Bankruptcy; Personal Injury.
Corrigan, Michael S. ....'70 '97 C.205 B.S. L.1338 J.D. 800 West St., 3rd Fl.
Corrodi, James A. '38 '63 C.918 B.A. L.477 LL.B.
(adm. in OH; not adm. in DE) [🄰 Skadden,A.S.M.&F.]
Corroon, Hugh, (BV) .... '29 '56 C.674 A.B. L.309 LL.B. [🄲 Potter A.&C.]
Costello, Kelly A., (CV) ..... '65 '95 C.205 B.S.B.A. L.1338 J.D. [🄰 Elzufon A.R.T.&M.]
*PRACTICE AREAS: Professional Liability Defense; Insurance Defense.
Cotreau, William J. '62 '95 C.951 B.A. L.30 J.D.
(adm. in VA; not adm. in DE) Sr. Coun., E.I. du Pont de Nemours & Co.
*RESPONSIBILITIES: Intellectual Property Licensing; Patent Preparation and Prosecution.
Cottrell, Frederick L., III, (BV) .... '63 '88 C.205 B.A. L.1017 J.D. [Richards,L.&F.]
*PRACTICE AREAS: Litigation; Intellectual Property.
Coulson, George T. ....'15 '46 C.722 B.A. L.893 LL.B. 3 Kings Ridge Rd.‡
Counihan, Victoria Watson, (CV) .... '71 '96 C.728 B.A. L.884 J.D. [🄰 Greenberg T.]
Courtney, Dawn R., (BVⓉ) '61 '87 C.397 B.A. L.831 J.D.
[Marks,O.O.&C.] (⊙Westmont, NJ; Norristown, Phila., PA)
Cousins, Scott D., (BV) ....'61 '92 C.1214 B.A. L.1338 J.D. [Greenberg T.]
Coyle, John J., 4th ....'72 '97 C.276 B.S.B.A. L.1338 J.D. [🄰 Kassab A.&O.] ⊙
Cozamanis, Steve C. '38 '76 C&L.1338 B.A., J.D.
(adm. in NJ; not adm. in DE)
Corp. Counsel & Assistant Secretary, E.I. depont de Nemours & Company

Cozen O'Connor, A Professional Corporation
Chase Manhattan Centre, 1201 North Market Street Suite 1400, 19801 ⊙
Telephone: 302-295-2000 888-207-2440 Fax: 302-295-2013
Email: postmaster@cozen.com URL: http://www.cozen.com
Firm Members in Wilmington: Mark E. Felger; Daniel V. Folt; Steven L. Biener. Firm Associates in Wilmington: Gary W. Lipkin; Jennifer L. Scoliard (Not admitted in DE). Firm Of Counsel in Wilmington: Sandra Kaufmann Battaglia.
Acquisitions and Divestitures, Admiralty and Maritime Law, Agents and Brokers Errors and Omissions, Alternative Dispute Resolution, Antitrust and Unfair Competition, Appellate Litigation, Appellate Practice, Arbitration and Alternative Dispute Resolution, Arson and Insurance Fraud, Asset Protection, Aviation Insurance, Aviation Law, Aviation Litigation, Aviation Products Liability, Bad Faith Litigation, Bankruptcy, Bankruptcy, Insolvency and Restructuring, Banks and Banking, Business Law, Casualty Insurance Defense, Civil Practice, Commercial Law, Commercial Litigation, Commercial Real Estate, Complex and Multi-District Litigation, Construction Claims, Construction Law, Construction Law and Litigation, Copyrights, Corporate and Partnership Law, Corporate Law, Corporate Planning, Creditors Rights, Crisis Management, Debtor and Creditor, Directors and Officers Errors and Omissions, E-Commerce and Internet Law, Electric Utility Regulation, Emerging Business and Venture Capital, Emerging Growth Companies, Employee Benefits, Employee Benefits and Executive Compensation, Employment Defense, Employment Practices, Energy, Energy Regulation, Environmental Insurance, Environmental Insurance Claims, Environmental Law, Estate Planning, Family Law, Finance, Financial Services, First and Third Party Insurance Defense, Gas Utility Regulation, Health Law, Healthcare, Healthcare Finance, Healthcare Litigation, Healthcare Regulation, Healthcare Reimbursement, Information Technology, Insurance, Insurance Bad Faith Defense, Insurance Corporate and Regulatory, Insurance Coverage, Insurance Coverage Defense, Insurance Defense, Insurance Mergers and Acquisitions, Insurance Regulation, Intellectual Property, Intellectual Property Litigation, Intentional Torts, International Estate Planning, International Tax and Estate Planning, International Trusts, Labor and Employment, Latin America Practice Group, Litigation, Management Labor Law, Marine and Maritime Law, Medical Devices Defenses, Medical Malpractice Defense, Mergers, Partnership Law, Patent Privacy Law, Planning and Land Use, Privacy Law and Regulation, Private Wealth Services, Products Liability, Professional Liability, Project Finance, Property Insurance, Property Subrogation, Public Finance, Public Utility Regulation, Punitive Damages, Punitive Damages Reinsurance, Real Estate, Real Estate Litigation, Reinsurance, RICO, Securities, Securities Litigation, Tax Litigation, Taxation, Torts, Toxic and Other Mass Torts, Toxic Torts, Trademarks, Trusts and Estates, Utility Law, Wealth Preservation, White Collar Crime, Zoning.
Representative Clients: Available upon request.
Philadelphia, Pennsylvania Office: 1900 Market Street, 19103. Telephones: 215-665-2000; 800-523-2900. Fax: 215-665-2013.
West Conshohocken, Pennsylvania Office: 200 Four Falls Corporate Center, Suite 400, P.O. Box 800, 19428. Telephone: 610-941-5400; 800-379-0695. Fax: 610-941-0711.
Charlotte, North Carolina Office: One First Union Center, 301 South College Street, Suite 2100, 28202. Telephones: 704-376-3400; 800-762-3575. Fax: 704-334-3351.
Dallas, Texas Office: BankOne Center, 1717 Main Street, Suite 2300, 75201. Telephones: 214-462-3000; 800-448-1207. Fax: 214-462-3299.
New York, N.Y. Office: 45 Broadway Atrium, 16th Floor, 10006. Telephones: 212-509-9400; 800-437-7040. Fax: 212-509-9492.
San Diego, California Office: Suite 1610, 501 West Broadway, 92101. Telephones: 619-234-1700; 800-782-3366. Fax: 619-234-7831.
Los Angeles, California Office: 777 South Figueroa Street, Suite 2850, 90017. Telephones: 213-892-7900; 800-563-1027. Fax: 213-892-7999.
Seattle, Washington Office: Suite 5200, Washington Mutual Tower, 1201 Third Avenue, 98101. Telephones: 206-340-1000; 800-423-1950. Fax: 206-621-8783.
Newark, New Jersey Office: One Newark Center, Suite 1900, 07102. Telephone: 973-286-1200; 888-200-9521. Fax: 973-242-2121.
Atlanta, Georgia Office: Suite 2200, SunTrust Plaza, 303 Peachtree Street, N.E., 30308. Telephones: 404-572-2000; 800-890-1393. Fax: 404-572-2199.
London, England Office: Tower 42, Level 23, 25 Old Broad Street, London EC2N 1HQ. Telephone: 011-44-20-7864-2000. Fax: 011-44-20-7864-2013.
Las Vegas, Nevada Office (Affiliated with the Law Offices of J. Goldberg, C. Stuart, III & D. Grossman): #1, 1000 East Sahara Avenue, 89104-3231. Telephone: 800-782-3366.
San Francisco, California Office: 425 California Street, Suite 1800, 94104-2203. Telephone: 415-617-6100; 800-818-0165. Fax: 415-617-6101.
Chicago, Illinois Office: 222 South Riverside, Suite 1500, 60606. Telephone: 312-382-3100; 877-992-6036. Fax: 312-382-8910.
Washington, D.C. Office: 1667 K Street, NW, 20006. Telephone: 202-912-4800; 800-540-1355. Fax: 202-912-4830.
Cherry Hill, New Jersey Office: LibertyView, Suite 300, 457 Haddonfield Road, P.O. Box 5459, 08002-2220. Telephone: 856-910-5000; 800-989-0499. Fax: 856-910-5075.
See Professional Biographies, WILMINGTON, DELAWARE

Crawford, Paul E., (BV) '40 '66
C&L.884 B.M.E., J.D. [Connolly B.L.&H.] (See Pat. Sect.)
Criscimagna, Matthew S. .... '75 '01 C.444 B.A. L.502 J.D. [🄰 Richards,L.&F.]
Crompton, Charles S., Jr., (AV) ...... '36 '62 C.205 B.A. L.893 LL.B. [🄲 Potter A.&C.]
Cronin, Laurence V., (BV) .... '59 '86 C.156 B.A. L.945 J.D. [Smith,K.&F.]
*PRACTICE AREAS: Litigation; Employment Law.
Cross, Caroline Lee .... '68 '96 C.205 B.A. L.945 J.D. 820 N. French St.
Cross, Richard H., Jr. ....'65 '97 C.1349 B.A. L.945 J.D. [🄰 Young C.S.&T.]
*PRACTICE AREAS: Commercial Litigation.

Crosse, Kester I. H., (BV) '45 '75 C.205 B.S. L.893 J.D.
1214 King Street Suite 300, 19801
Telephone: 302-658-3488 Fax: 302-652-3034
Email: kesterih@aol.com URL: http://www.lawyers.com/kihcrosselaw
Civil Litigation, Personal Injury, Automobile Accidents and Injuries, Medical Malpractice, Family Law, Divorce, Child Custody, Child Support, Adoption Law, Business Law, Collections, Real Estate, Wills, Probate, Trusts and Estates, Employment Law, Discrimination.
See Professional Biographies, WILMINGTON, DELAWARE

Crossland, Daniel T. ....'67 '92 C.696 B.A. L.884 J.D. [Crossland,C.&Assoc.]
Crossland, Lisa K. W. ....'66 '92 C.645 B.A. L.884 J.D. [🄲 Crossland,C.&Assoc.]

Crossland, Conaty & Associates, L.L.C., (CV)
1201 N. Orange Street, Suite 601, One Commerce Center, 19801
Telephone: 302-655-3000 Fax: 302-777-1218
Members of Firm: Daniel T. Crossland; Thomas P. Conaty, IV. Counsel: Lisa K. W. Crossland. Associate: David E. Matlusky.

(This Listing Continued)

Crossland, Conaty & Associates, L.L.C. (Continued)

General Civil Practice. Trusts and Estates, including Estate Planning, Estate Administration and Probate, Trust Planning and Wealth Preservation; Wills; Business Law and Commercial Law, including Business Start-Ups and Business Transfers; Construction Law; Contracts; Residential Real Estate and Commercial Real Estate; Civil Litigation, including Commercial Litigation, Contract Litigation, Personal Injury and Automobile Accidents and Injuries; Collections; Creditor Rights in Bankruptcy; Chancery Practice.

See Professional Biographies, WILMINGTON, DELAWARE

Crowe, Robert W., (BV) ....'39 '65 C.95 A.B. L.1017 LL.B. [Cooch&T.] (⊙Newark)
*PRACTICE AREAS: Estate Planning; Estate Settlements.
Crowell, Barbara D. ....'43 '80 C.518 A.B. L.659 J.D. Family Ct. J.
Crowther, Curtis J., (CV) ....'68 '94 C.999 B.A. L.1338 J.D. [Ⓐ White&W.]
Crumplar, Thomas C., (BV) ....'50 '75 C.477 A.B. L.893 J.D. [Jacobs&C.]
*PRACTICE AREAS: Asbestos Litigation; Products Liability Law; Toxic Substance Law; Negligence Law.
Culley, David G., (BV) ....'57 '82 C.205 B.A.A.S. L.273 J.D. [Tybout,R.&P.]
*PRACTICE AREAS: Negligence; Insurance; Workers Compensation; Products Liability; Medical Malpractice.
Culley, Mary M., (BV) ....'46 '85 C.741 B.A. L.1338 J.D. [Morris,J.H.&W.]
*PRACTICE AREAS: Estate and Gift Taxation; Estate Planning; Probate; Elder Law; Guardianship.
Culver, Donna L. ....'66 '91 C.205 B.A. L.94 J.D. [Morris,N.A.&T.]
Cummings, Courtney H., Jr. ....'26 '56 C.205 B.S. L.446 J.D. 1200 Pecksniff Road
Cummings, Stacey L., (BV) ....'68 '93 C.867 B.A. L.1338 J.D. [Ⓐ Casarino,C.&S.]
*PRACTICE AREAS: Insurance Defense; Workers' Compensation; Personal Injury; Insurance Coverage; Civil Litigation.
Currier, Teresa K. D., (BV) ....'60 '85 C.401 B.A. L.1017 J.D. [Klett R.L.&S.]
*PRACTICE AREAS: Bankruptcy and Reorganization; Creditors' Rights; Commercial Transactions; Banking.
Curtin, Christopher J., (BV) ....'51 '77 C.893 B.A. L.564 J.D. [Erisman&C.]
Curtin, Geo. M. '18 '46 C.205 B.A. L.893 LL.B.
(adm. in VA; not adm. in DE) 611 Amberley Rd.‡
Cutler, Julie Klein '56 '90 C.64 B.A. L.446 J.D.
(adm. in MD; not adm. in DE) Labor Law Enforce. Offr.
Czajkowski (Shy-kow-ski), Stanley T., (BV) '29 '57
C.205 B.S. L.273 LL.B. [Weik,N.&D.] ‡
*PRACTICE AREAS: Personal Injury; Wills; Estates; Real Estate; Corporations.
Czeschin, Brock E. ....'75 '00 C.134 B.A. L.884 J.D. [Ⓐ Richards,L.&F.]
Dafter, Edwin H., Jr. '22 '52 C.401 B.S. L.276 J.D.
(adm. in DC; not adm. in DE) 6 Little Leaf Ct.‡
Daley, Robert E., (BV) ....'37 '63 C.602 B.A. L.893 J.D. [Daley,E.&v.] ⊙
Daley, Erisman & van Ogtrop, (AV) .... 1224 King Street (⊙Newark)
Dalle Pazze, James P., (AV) ....'53 '78 C.693 B.A. L.1338 J.D. [Herdeg,D.&D.P.]
*PRACTICE AREAS: Estate Planning; Estate and Gift Taxation; Business Succession Planning; Federal and State Taxation Law.
Dalton, Bartholomew J., (BV) ....'52 '77 C.728 B.A. L.862 J.D. [Brandt&D.]
Daluz, Tobey M., (BVⓉ) '— '90 C.659 B.A. L.276 J.D.
(adm. in PA; not adm. in DE) [Reed S.]
*PRACTICE AREAS: Bankruptcy.
Damon, Doneene Keemer ....'67 '92 C.728 B.S. L.931 J.D. [Richards,L.&F.]
*PRACTICE AREAS: Business Law; Commercial Leasing; Asset-Based Lending; Business Trusts; Uniform Commercial Code.
Danberg, Barbara Snapp ...'65 '92 C.205 B.A.A.S. L.1338 J.D. [Trzuskowski,K.K.&P.]
*PRACTICE AREAS: Taxation; Estate Planning; Estate Administration; Commercial Litigation.
Danberg, Carl Christian, (CV) ....'64 '92 C.205 B.A.A.S. L.1338 J.D. Dep. Atty. Gen.
Danberg, M. Edward, (BV) ....'57 '82 C.205 B.A. L.128 J.D. [Ⓒ Connolly B.L.&H.]
D'Angelo, Alfred J., Jr., (AV) '48 '74
C.674 A.B. L.884 J.D. [Klett R.L.&S.] (⊙Phila., PA)
*PRACTICE AREAS: Labor and Employment Law.
D'Angelo, James P., (CV) ....'30 '55 C.205 B.S. L.276 J.D. 1807 Market St.
Daniello, John P. ....'68 '98 C.205 B.A. L.1338 J.D. [Ⓐ Maron&M.]
*PRACTICE AREAS: Personal Injury; Commercial Litigation.
Daniels, Steven J. ....'67 '96 C.994 B.A. L.178 J.D. [Ⓐ Skadden,A.S.M.&F.]
Danneman, George J. '— '01 C.273 B.A. L.1017 J.D.
(adm. in PA; not adm. in DE) [Ⓐ Bayard]
*PRACTICE AREAS: Corporate Transactions; Real Estate Law.
Dattani, Sheela P. ....'69 '97 C.205 B.S. L.884 J.D. [Ⓐ Stradley R.S.&Y.]
Davidson, S. Thomas '54 '95 C.205 B.A. L.1338 J.D.
(adm. in MD; not adm. in DE) V.P. & Coun., Wilmington Trust Company
Davies, Laura J. '55 '80 C.741 B.A. L.602 J.D.
(adm. in PA; not adm. in DE) Asst. Gen. Coun., Litig., Astrazeneca Pharm. LP
*RESPONSIBILITIES: Litigation; Products Liability.
Davis, Charlene D., (BV) ....'46 '84 C.611 B.A. L.1338 J.D. [Bayard]
*PRACTICE AREAS: Bankruptcy Law; Creditors Rights; Commercial Litigation; Business Crimes Law.
Davis, Eric M. ....'62 '92 C.893 B.A. L.245 J.D. [Ⓐ Skadden,A.S.M.&F.]
*PRACTICE AREAS: Bankruptcy; General Litigation.
Davis, James F., (BV) '47 '73 C.178 B.A. L.884 J.D.
Chf. Coun., Aqualon & Resins Div., Hercules Inc.
Davis, Michelle L. ....'67 '94 C&L.831 B.B.A., J.D. [Ⓐ Skadden,A.S.M.&F.]
Day, Grenville R. ....'69 '98 C.645 B.S. L.1338 J.D. [Ⓐ Skadden,A.S.M.&F.]
*PRACTICE AREAS: Corporate Reorganization.
Day, Melanie George ....'72 '97 C.659 B.A. L.276 J.D. [Ⓐ Richards,L.&F.]
Dayton, Carrie I. ....'70 '97 C.658 B.S. L.1338 J.D. [Ⓐ Seitz,V.&G.]
*PRACTICE AREAS: Civil Litigation.
Dearlove, Catherine G. ....'69 '94 C.276 B.S.F.S. L.813 J.D. [Richards,L.&F.]
DeBaecke, Michael D., (BV) ....'68 '93 C.728 B.S. L.945 J.D. [Blank R.C.&M.]
*PRACTICE AREAS: Bankruptcy; Chancery and Equity; Corporate Law; Commercial Litigation; Contracts.
De Carli, Silvio J. '49 '83 C.688 B.S. L.705 J.D.
(adm. in NJ; not adm. in DE) Corporate Counsel, E.I. dupont de Nemours & Company
*RESPONSIBILITIES: Litigation.
DeFranceschi, Daniel J., (BV) ....'62 '89 C.645 B.S. L.1338 J.D. [Richards,L.&F.]
*PRACTICE AREAS: Bankruptcy.
Dehney, Robert J. ....'65 '90 C.216 B.A. L.1040 J.D. [Morris,N.A.&T.]
Deitch, Gerald E. '47 '82 C.659 B.A. L.831 J.D.
(adm. in PA; not adm. in DE; Pat.) Corp. Coun., E.I. du Pont de Nemours and Company
*RESPONSIBILITIES: Patents.
Della Porta, Armand J., Jr., (AV) '55 '80
C.276 B.A. L.884 LL.B. [Kelley,J.M.&S.] (⊙Phila., PA)
*PRACTICE AREAS: Products Liability Law; Civil Litigation; Insurance Law; Reinsurance Law.
Del Pesco, Susan C. ....'46 '75 C.112 B.S. L.1338 J.D. Assoc. Supr. Ct. J.
Del Rossi, Stephen '44 '74 C.223 B.S. L.831 J.D.
(adm. in PA; not adm. in DE) [Ⓐ Gordon,F.&M.]
*PRACTICE AREAS: Estate Administration; Tax Law.
Demmy, John D., (BV) ....'61 '86 C.21 B.S. L.884 J.D. [Stevens&L.]
*PRACTICE AREAS: Bankruptcy; Commercial Litigation.
Dempsey, Bernard S. ....'29 '56 C.674 A.B. L.659 LL.B. 117 Delview Dr.‡

Demsey, Christine K., (BV) '49 '82 C.223 B.S. L.1338 J.D.
1328 King Street, 19801-3234
Telephone: 302-428-3190
Email: cdemsey@gte.com URL: http://www.lawyers.com/dss
***PRACTICE AREAS: Family Law; Probate; Wills.**
Family Law, Probate, Wills, Estate Administration, Guardianships and Conservatorships.

See Professional Biographies, WILMINGTON, DELAWARE

Denney, John X., Jr., (BV) ....'45 '74 C.321 A.B. L.893 J.D. [Ⓐ Tomar,O.K.J.&G.]
Denny, William R., (BV) ....'61 '88 C.674 A.B. L.893 J.D. [Potter A.&C.]
Dent, Arthur L., (BV) ....'56 '86 C.237 B.S. L.1338 J.D. [Potter A.&C.]
DePhillips, Kathleen Marshall '70 '00 C.128 B.A. L.273 J.D.
(adm. in PA; not adm. in DE) [Ⓐ Pachulski,S.Z.Y.&J.]
*PRACTICE AREAS: Bankruptcy.
Desgroseilliers, Mark L. '71 '99 C.367 B.A. L.446 J.D.
(adm. in MD; not adm. in DE) [Ⓐ Skadden,A.S.M.&F.]
*PRACTICE AREAS: Bankruptcy; Financial Restructuring.
Deshmukh, Sudhir G. '44 '89 C.999 B.T.Ch.E. L.1292 J.D.
(adm. in PA; not adm. in DE; Pat.) Sr. Coun., E.I. du Pont de Nemours and Company
*RESPONSIBILITIES: Intellectual Property Law; Patents, Licensing, Contracts; Infringement, Opinions, Secrecy, Agreements.
Detweiler, Donald J., (BV) ....'63 '92 C.884 B.A. L.1338 J.D. [Ⓒ Saul E.]
*PRACTICE AREAS: Bankruptcy Reorganization; Commercial Litigation; Personal Injury; Product Liability.
Devine, Donn ....'29 '75 C.205 B.S. L.1338 J.D. 2004 Kentmere Parkway
Deyerle, Kristie A. ....'64 '97 C.945 B.S. L.659 J.D. Law Clk., Dist. Ct.
DiCamillo, Raymond J. ....'68 '93 C.659 B.A. L.276 J.D. [Richards,L.&F.]
*PRACTICE AREAS: Business Law; Business Litigation; Corporate Law; Corporate Control Contests; Corporate Litigation.
Dickey, John F. '46 '75 C.277 B.S.Ch.E. L.326 J.D.
(adm. in TX; not adm. in DE) Corp. Coun., E.I. du Pont de Nemours and Company
*RESPONSIBILITIES: General Practice.
DiGiovanni, Francis '65 '93
C.105 B.S.M.E. L.665 J.D. [Ⓐ Connolly B.L.&H.] (See Pat. Sect.)
Di Gregorio, Michael A. '46 '79 C&L.831 B.A., J.D.
(adm. in PA; not adm. in DE) V.P. & Sr. Coun., Wilmington Trust Company
DiLiberto, Richard A., Jr., (BV) ....'61 '86 C.646 B.S.Ed. L.1338 J.D. [Young C.S.&T.]
*PRACTICE AREAS: Personal Injury; Automobile Liability; Trial Practice; Medical Negligence; Medicare Fraud and Abuse.
Dillione, Michelle T. '58 '84 C.103 B.A. L.36 J.D.
(adm. in AZ; not adm. in DE) Sr. Coun., Astrazeneca Pharm. LP
*RESPONSIBILITIES: Commercial; Regulatory/FDA.

Dilworth Paxson PLLC, (AVⓉ)
First Federal Plaza Suite 500, 19801 ⊙
Telephone: 302-571-9800 Fax: 302-571-8875
Email: lawyers@dilworthlaw.com URL: http://www.dilworthlaw.com
Member of the Firm: Robert Forrest Stewart, Jr.
General Practice in all Courts, Corporate, Litigation, Bankruptcy and Insolvency, Criminal and Regulatory Investigations, E-Commerce, Employment and Management Labor Relations, Entertainment, Environmental, Healthcare, Insurance Regulation, Intellectual Property, International, Public Finance, Real Estate Securities, Tax, Trust and Estates.
Cherry Hill, New Jersey Office: Liberty View Suite 700, 457 Haddonfield Road, 08002. Telephone: 856-663-8877. Fax: 856-663-8855.
Harrisburg, Pennsylvania Office: 305 N. Front Street, Suite 403, 17101-1236. Telephone: 717-236-4812. Fax: 717-236-7811.
Newtown Square, Pennsylvania Office: 11 Campus Boulevard, Suite 150, 19073. Telephone: 610-325-3200. Fax: 610-325-3293.
Philadelphia, Pennsylvania Office: 3200 Mellon Bank Center, 1735 Market Street, 19103-7595. Telephone: 215-575-7000. Fax: 215-575-7200.
Turnersville, New Jersey Office: P.O. Box 762, University Executive Campus Suite 201, 151 Fries Mill Road, 08012. Telephone: 856-227-6100. Fax: 856-227-7373.
Washington, D.C. Office: 1200 Nineteenth Street, N.W., 20036. Telephone: 202-452-0900. Fax: 202-452-0930.

See Professional Biographies, WILMINGTON, DELAWARE

Dinnage, James D. '50 '74 C.050 B.A. L.999
(adm. in Englan; not adm. in DE) Corp. Coun., E.I. du Pont de Nemours and Company
*RESPONSIBILITIES: Business Law.
DiPersio, Denise T. '55 '81 C.104 A.B. L.472 J.D.
(adm. in PA; not adm. in DE) [Ⓒ Grant&E.]
DiPrinzio, Eugene A., (AV) ....'56 '81 C.884 B.S. L.1338 J.D. [Young C.S.&T.]
*PRACTICE AREAS: Commercial Real Estate; Banks and Banking; Business Law; Leases and Leasing.
Director, Steven R., (BV) ....'52 '77 C.174 B.A. L.990 J.D. [Morris,J.H.&W.]
*PRACTICE AREAS: Business and Transactional Law; Taxation; Trusts, Estates and Estate Planning.
DiStefano, Nancy B. '48 '92 C.1040 B.A. L.1338 J.D.
(adm. in PA; not adm. in DE) 107 North Rd. Lindamere‡
Ditty, Bradley Nelson '70 '98 C&L.665 B.S., J.D.
(adm. in PA; not adm. in DE; Pat.) Pat. Atty., The Whitaker Corp.
Dixon, Gerald E., (BV) ....'49 '76 C.205 B.A. L.831 J.D. 1204 King St.
Dobson, Kevin S. '55 '98 C.512 B.S. L.326 J.D.
(adm. in TX; not adm. in DE; Pat.) Sr. Coun., E.I. du Pont de Nemours and Company
*RESPONSIBILITIES: Intellectual Property.
Doelze, Kurt J., (CV) ....'52 '77 C.205 B.A. L.1338 J.D. [K.J.Doelze]
Doelze, Kurt J., P.A., (CV) ....5143 W. Woodmill Dr.
Doerler, William L. ....'61 '97 C.205 B.A. L.1338 J.D. [Ⓐ Trzuskowski,K.K.&P.]
*PRACTICE AREAS: Appellate Practice; Civil Litigation; Insurance.
Dolan, Sean A., (BV) ....'58 '87 C.205 B.A. L.1338 J.D. [Ⓐ Marshall,D.W.C.&G.]
*PRACTICE AREAS: General Liability Defense.
Donald, Williamson P. '43 '69 C.674 A.B. L.477 J.D.
(adm. in NY; not adm. in DE) Corp. Coun., du Pont Co.
Donaldson, Richard M. '65 '91 C.105 B.A. L.1017 J.D.
(adm. in PA; not adm. in DE) [Ⓐ Grant&E.]
Donnelly, Rex A., IV '66 '96 C.886 B.S.M.E. L.1138 J.D.
[Ⓐ Ratner&P.] (See Pat. Sect.)
*PRACTICE AREAS: Intellectual Property.
Donner, Michael L., Sr. '61 '97 C.871 B.S. L.1356 J.D.
(adm. in VA; not adm. in DE) [Ⓐ Connolly B.L.&H.] ⊙
*PRACTICE AREAS: Intellectual Property.
Donnley-Evans, Deneen L. '64 '92 C.659 B.S. L.262 J.D.
General Counsel, ING USA Holding Corporation
Donoghue, Moira K. ....'51 '76 C.893 B.A. L.945 J.D. 800 King St.
Donovan, Keith E., (BV) ....'66 '91 C.205 B.S. L.1338 J.D. [Swartz,C.&D.]
*PRACTICE AREAS: Insurance Defense Litigation.
Doroshow, Eric M., (BV) ....'49 '74 C.21 A.B. L.365 J.D. [Doroshow,P.K.S.&B.]
Doroshow, Pasquale, Krawitz, Siegel & Bhaya, (BV) ....1202 Kirkwood Highway
Doss, Kenneth M., (BV) ....'65 '90 C.893 B.A. L.692 J.D. [Ⓐ Casarino,C.&S.]
*PRACTICE AREAS: Insurance Defense; Civil Litigation; Workers' Compensation; Insurance Coverage.
Dougherty, Paul J., III ....'70 '99 C.423 B.A. L.884 J.D. [Ⓐ McCarter&E.]
*PRACTICE AREAS: Bankruptcy; Creditors Rights.
Dougherty, Shawn, (BV) ....'61 '88 C.205 B.S.A.S. L.1338 J.D. [Weik,N.&D.]
*PRACTICE AREAS: Family Law.
Doughten, Nancy M. N., (CV) ....'32 '81 C.205 B.A. L.1338 J.D. 824 Market St.

Doughty, Stephen P. '62 '87 C.205 B.A. L.809 J.D.
[Lyons,D.&V.] (⊙Mount Laurel, NJ; Phila., PA)
*PRACTICE AREAS: Creditors Rights Law; Consumer Collections; Commercial Law; Foreclosure Law; Creditor Bankruptcy Law.
Doyle, Marjorie W., (AVⓉ) '48 '74 C.518 A.B. L.326 J.D.
(adm. in TX; not adm. in DE) Assoc. Gen. Coun. & Chf. Preventive Law Coun., E.I. du Pont de Nemours and Company
*RESPONSIBILITIES: Commercial Law; Patents; Litigation; Corporate Law.
Dozier, Bruce E. '48 '73 C&L.692 B.A., J.D.
(adm. in VA; not adm. in DE) V.P. & Gen. Coun., Amer. Life Ins. Co.
Drane, W. Harding, Jr., (BV) . . . . '49 '78 C.659 B.A. L.161 J.D. [Potter A.&C.]
Dreisbach, Daniel A. . . . . '56 '88 C.401 B.S.C.E. L.831 J.D. [Richards,L.&F.]
*PRACTICE AREAS: Litigation; Corporate Law; Corporate Transactions; Corporate Litigation; Business Law.
Drexler, David A., (AV) . . . . '30 '59 C.197 B.A. L.976 LL.B. [Ⓒ Morris,N.A.&T.]
Drexler, Lawrence S., (BV) . . . . '57 '84 C.264 B.A. L.1019 J.D. P.O. Box 26182
Drnec, James E. . . . . '59 '98 C.800 B.A. L.831 J.D. [Ⓐ Morris,J.H.&W.]
Drowos, Stuart B. . . . . '50 '76 C.205 B.A. L.64 J.D. Dep. Atty. Gen.
Dryden, Stephen F., (BV) . . . . '56 '82 C.205 B.A. L.1338 J.D. [Robinson&G.]

Duane, Morris & Heckscher LLP, (AV) BB
1100 North Market Street, Suite 1200, 19801 ⊙
Telephone: 302-657-4900 Fax: 302-657-4901
URL: http://www.duanemorris.com
Resident Partners: Michael R. Lastowski; Thomas P. McGonigle; Frank E. Noyes, II; John L. Reed; Richard W. Riley; Carl Schnee (Partner in Charge). Resident Associates: Timothy R. Dudderar; William K. Harrington; Ralph N. Sianni; John W. Weiss. Of Counsel: Judith Nichols Renzulli.
Alternative Dispute Resolution, Bankruptcy, Commercial Law, Corporate Law, Energy, Environmental Law, Estate and Asset Planning, Franchise Law, Health Care Law, Immigration Law, Intellectual Property, International Law, Labor and Employment, Litigation, Product Liability, Real Estate, Regulatory Compliance, Reorganization and Finance, Securities, Taxation and Telecommunications and Information Technologies.
Philadelphia, Pennsylvania Office: Suite 4200, One Liberty Place. Telephone: 215-979-1000. Fax: 215-979-1020.
New York, New York Office: 380 Lexington Avenue. Telephone: 212-692-1000. Fax: 212-692-1020.
London, England Office: 4 Chiswell Street, 5th Floor, EC1Y 4UP. Telephone: +44 20 7786 2100. Fax: +44 20 7786 2101.
Chicago, Illinois Office: 227 West Monroe Street, Suite 3400. Telephone: 312-499-6700. Fax: 312-499-6701.
Washington, D.C. Office: 1667 K Street, N.W., Suite 700. Telephone: 202-776-7800. Fax: 202-776-7801.
San Francisco, California Office: 100 Spear Street, Suite 1500. Telephone: 415-371-2200. Fax: 415-371-2201.
Boston, Massachusetts Office: 470 Atlantic Avenue, Suite 500. Telephone: 617-289-9200. Fax: 617-289-9201.
Atlanta, Georgia Office: 945 East Paces Ferry Road, Suite 2440. Telephone: 404-495-4900. Fax: 404-495-4901.
Miami, Florida Office: 200 South Biscayne Boulevard, Suite 3410. Telephone: 305-960-2200. Fax: 305-960-2201.
Harrisburg, Pennsylvania Office: 305 North Front Street, 5th Floor, P.O. Box 1003. Telephone: 717-237-5500. Fax: 717-232-4015.
Malvern, Pennsylvania Office: 200 Chesterfield Parkway, Suite 100. Telephone: 610-251-6900. Fax: 610-251-6901.
Cherry Hill, New Jersey Office: 51 Haddonfield Road, Suite 340. Telephone: 856-488-7300. Fax: 856-488-7021.
Newark, New Jersey Office: One Riverfront Plaza, 2nd Floor. Telephone: 973-424-2000. Fax: 973-424-2001.
Palm Beach, Florida Office: 249 Royal Palm Way, Suite 403. Telephone: 561-366-5400. Fax: 561-366-5401.
Allentown, Pennsylvania Office: 968 Postal Road, Suite 200, P.O. Box 90400. Telephone: 610-266-3650. Fax: 610-266-3651.
Houston, Texas Office: One Greenway Plaza, Suite 500. Telephone: 713-552-9900. Fax: 713-552-0109.
Bangor, Maine Office: 88 Hammond Street, Suite 500. Telephone: 207-262-5400. Fax: 207-262-5401.
Princeton, New Jersey Office: 100 College Road West, Suite 100. Telephone: 609-919-4400. Fax: 609-919-4401.
Westchester County, New York Office: 555 Pleasantville Road, Suite 200 North Building, Briarcliff Manor, New York. Telephone: 914-749-3700. Fax: 914-749-3701.
See Professional Biographies, WILMINGTON, DELAWARE

Dubé, Dale R. . . . . '50 '90 C.749 B.S. L.1338 J.D. [Ⓐ Blank R.C.&M.]
*PRACTICE AREAS: Intellectual Property Litigation; Employment Law; Employment Litigation; Commercial Litigation; Corporate Litigation.
Dubecq, Cheryl A. '68 '99 C.205 B.A. L.1338 J.D.
(adm. in PA; not adm. in DE) Licensing Coun., Tyco Electonics Corp.
Dudderar, Timothy R. . . . . '— '00 C.205 B.A. L.884 J.D. [Ⓐ Duane,M.&H.]
*PRACTICE AREAS: Complex Commercial Litigation; Corporate Litigation; Securities Litigation; Partnership Law.
Duffy, Roseanne Raimondo '59 '89 C.645 B.S. L.1338 J.D.
(adm. in PA; not adm. in DE; Pat.) Senior Counsel, E.I. dupont de Nemours & Company
*RESPONSIBILITIES: Intellectual Property; Litigation.
Dugan, J. Robert '65 '90 C.945 B.A. L.884 J.D.
(adm. in PA; not adm. in DE) Sr. Coun., PFPC, Inc.
Duggan, Michael F., (CV) . . . . '59 '94 C.205 B.S.M.E. L.1338 J.D. [Ⓐ Phillips,G.&S.]
Duhig, Peter J. . . . . '72 '01 C.280 B.A. L.128 J.D. [Ⓐ Pachulski,S.Z.Y.&J.]
*PRACTICE AREAS: Bankruptcy.
Dulin, Carol J. . . . . '53 '87 C.790 B.A. L.1338 J.D. Coun., Co. Council
Dunlavey, Colin Patrick . . . . '62 '95 C.128 B.A. L.1338 J.D. 2717 Bodine Dr.
du Pont, Pierre S., (AV) . . . . '35 '64 C.674 LL.B. L.309 J.D. [Richards,L.&F.]
Du Pont, William B., Jr., (BV) . . . . '46 '82 C.81 B.S. L.665 J.D. [Herdeg,D.&D.P.]
*PRACTICE AREAS: Estate Planning; Federal Estate and Gift Taxation; Trusts and Estates Taxation; Private Foundations; Estate Administration.
Durante, Charles J., (BV) . . . . '51 '77 C.311 B.A. L.884 J.D. [Connolly B.L.&H.]
Durkin, Daniel A., (BV) . . . . '42 '68 C.727 B.S. L.659 LL.B. 521 West St.
Durrier, Van C., II . . . . '70 '93 C.667 B.A. L.446 J.D. [Ⓐ Skadden,A.S.M.&F.]
*PRACTICE AREAS: Bankruptcy Litigation; Creditor's Rights; Real Estate.
Dvorak, Julie S. . . . . '69 '96 C.914 B.S. L.942 J.D. 704 N. King St.
Dwares, Rachel A. . . . . '60 '85 C.188 A.B. L.94 J.D. [Ⓒ Morris,N.A.&T.]
Eagle, David S. . . . . '60 '90 C.31 B.A. L.178 J.D. [Klehr,H.H.B.&E.]
*PRACTICE AREAS: Commercial Litigation; Corporate Litigation.
Eastburn, Thomas J., (BV) . . . . '47 '77 C.838 B.S. L.64 J.D. [Allmond&E.]
Easton, Richard L., (BV) '50 '76
C.914 B.A. L.276 J.D. [Skadden,A.S.M.&F.] (⊙New York, NY)
Eaton, Edward F., (BV) . . . . '48 '76 C.188 A.B. L.831 J.D. [Connolly B.L.&H.]
Eckman, Richard P., (BV) . . . . '51 '77 C.299 A.B. L.128 J.D. [Pepper H.]
*PRACTICE AREAS: Mergers and Acquisitions; Banking Law; Corporate Law; Real Estate.
Edinger, John Sinclear, Jr., (CV) . . . . . '59 '85 C.928 B.A. L.1338 J.D. Lead Atty., Fam. Ct.
Edwards, David '40 '74 C.912 B.S.Chem. L.64 J.D.
(adm. in PA; not adm. in DE; Pat.) Sr. Coun., Hercules Incorporated
Edwards, Mark A. '67 '94 C.385 B.A. L.1019 J.D.
(adm. in NJ; not adm. in DE; Pat.) Sr. Coun., E.I. du Pont de Nemours and Company
Eggen, Jean M '49 '83 C.183 A.B. L.823 J.D.
(adm. in NY; not adm. in DE) 4601 Concord Pike
Eisenhofer, Jay W. . . . . '56 '86 C.665 B.A. L.884 J.D. [Grant&E.]
Elgart, Adam R. . . . . '65 '94 C.705 B.A. L.1338 J.D. [Ⓐ Mattleman,W.&M.]
*PRACTICE AREAS: Civil Litigation; Immigration Law; Family Law.

Elliott, Richard G., Jr., (BV) . . . . '40 '66 C.902 B.S. L.575 LL.B. [Richards,L.&F.]
*PRACTICE AREAS: Labor and Employment; Media Law.
Elliott, Wayne N., (AV) . . . . . . '42 '67 C.309 A.B. L.893 LL.B. [Prickett,J.&E.] (⊙Dover)
*PRACTICE AREAS: General Litigation in State and Federal Courts.
Ellis, Richard W. . . . . '65 '98 C.576 B.S. L.1292 J.D. [Ⓐ Morris,N.A.&T.]
Ellis, Thomas H. '52 '84 C.216 L.1338 J.D.
Carvel State Office Building, 6th Floor, 820 North French Street
Elzufon, John A., (BV) . . . . '46 '74 C.701 B.S.Ch.E. L.276 J.D. [Elzufon A.R.T.&M.]
*PRACTICE AREAS: Professional Liability Defense; Products Liability Defense; Personal Injury.

Elzufon Austin Reardon Tarlov & Mondell, P.A., (BV)
300 Delaware Avenue Suite 1700, P.O. Box 1630, 19899-1630
Telephone: 302-428-3181 Fax: 302-428-3180
URL: http://www.elzufon.com
John A. Elzufon; Jeffrey M. Austin; Mark L. Reardon; Edward A. Tarlov; Scott R. Mondell; William D. Sullivan; William F. Taylor, Jr.;—H. Garrett Baker; Colleen D. Shields; Scott A. Simpson; Ann Poulios (Not admitted in DE); Kelly A. Costello; Katharine L. Mayer; Christian G. McGarry.
General Civil and Trial Practice in all State and Federal Courts, Professional Liability Defense, Real Estate, Banking Law, Bankruptcy, Business Law, Corporate Law, Asbestos Defense, Products Liability, Workers Compensation Defense, Estate Planning and Construction Law.
See Professional Biographies, WILMINGTON, DELAWARE

Enerio, Patricia L. . . . . '73 '98 C.1350 B.A. L.1338 J.D. [Ⓐ Bayard]
*PRACTICE AREAS: Corporate Governance Litigation; Partnership and Limited Liability Company Litigation; Commercial Litigation and Class and Derivative Actions.
Engelmann, Glenn M. '56 '80 C.1349 B.A. L.145 J.D.
(adm. in DC; not adm. in DE)
V.P., Gen. Coun. & Secy., Astrazeneca Pharmaceuticals LP
*RESPONSIBILITIES: Corporate Law; Antitrust.
Enna, Bradley James . . . . '50 '96 C.697 B.A. L.659 J.D. [Ⓐ Skadden,A.S.M.&F.]
*PRACTICE AREAS: Litigation.
Eppes, Sharon M., (CV) . . . . '64 '92 C.205 L.1338 [Ⓐ Becker&B.]
Epstein, Marsha J., (BV) . . . . '51 '83 C.705 B.A. L.1292 J.D. Dep. Atty. Gen.
Erenshteyn, Alisa . . . . '77 '01 C.205 B.A. L.831 J.D. [Ⓐ Morris,J.H.&W.]
*PRACTICE AREAS: Business Transactions.
Erhart, William W., (BV) . . . . '51 '82 C.205 B.A. L.705 J.D. [W.W.Erhart]
*PRACTICE AREAS: Personal Injury; Commercial; Construction; Railroad Law; Creditors Rights.

Erhart, William W., P.A., (BV)
300 Delaware Avenue Suite 1130, P.O. Box 234, 19899-0234
Telephone: 302-651-0113 Telecopier: 302-651-0331
URL: http://www.erhartlaw.com
William W. Erhart.
Personal Injury, General Civil Litigation, Construction, Commercial, Creditor's Rights, Bankruptcy.
See Professional Biographies, WILMINGTON, DELAWARE

Erisman, David H., (BV) . . . . '47 '74 C&L.575 B.A., J.D. [Erisman&C.]
Erisman, James A., (AV) . . . . '40 '66 C.205 B.S. L.1017 J.D. [Daley,E.&v.] ⊙
Erisman & Curtin, (BV) . . . . 629 Mt. Lebanon Rd.
Erlenbach, Elisa J. . . . . '74 '99 C.966 B.A. L.188 J.D. [Ⓐ Richards,L.&F.]
Eskin, Marla Rosoff, (CV) . . . . '66 '91 C&L.831 B.A., J.D. [Jacobs&C.]
*PRACTICE AREAS: Negligence Law; Products Liability Law; Toxic Substance Law; Business Law; Bankruptcy.
Estrin, Barry '45 '71 C.188 B.S. L.276 J.D.
(adm. in VA; not adm. in DE; Pat.)
Corporate Counsel, E.I. dupont de Nemours & Company
*RESPONSIBILITIES: Intellectual Property; Litigation; Patent Litigation.
Evain, Eric J. . . . . '60 '98 C.592 B.S. L.644 J.D. [Ⓐ Connolly B.L.&H.] (See Pat. Sect.)
Evans, Craig H. '43 '84 C.705 B.S. L.1292 J.D.
(adm. in NJ; not adm. in DE; Pat.) Corp. Coun., E.I. du Pont de Nemours and Company
*RESPONSIBILITIES: Intellectual Property; Patent Law; Licensing Law; Business Law.
Evans, Donald Elihu, (BV) . . . . '47 '82 C.94 B.A. L.1338 J.D. [Evans&Assoc.]
*PRACTICE AREAS: Insurance Defense Law; Personal Injury Law; Worker's Compensation Law; New Business; Medical Malpractice Law.
Evans, Elwyn, Jr., (BV) . . . . '27 '54 C.976 A.B. L.309 LL.B. 1210 King St.
Evans, George E., (CV) . . . . '47 '73 C.204 B.A. L.1292 J.D. 913 N. Market Street
Evans, Jane W., (CV) . . . . '— '82 C.205 B.S. L.1338 J.D. P.O. Box 778

Evans & Associates, (BV)
2 Mill Road, P.O. Box 550, 19899-0550
Telephone: 302-655-8807; 302-655-5025 Telefax: 302-655-5441
Email: donaldelihuevans@evanslawonline.com URL: http://www.lawyer.com/evans&associates
Member of Firm: Donald Elihu Evans.
General Civil Trial Practice in all Courts. Personal Injury, Negligence, Products Liability, Medical Malpractice, Automobile Accidents, Insurance Defense, Workers Compensation, Business Start-Ups, Commercial. Wills and Probate, Estate Planning, Trusts and Estates, Real Estate, Family Law, Child Custody, Child Support, Divorce, Bankruptcy.
Affiliated With: Hwang & Associates, P.C., 1325 Spruce Street, Philadelphia, Pennsylvania, 19107. Telephone: 215-790-5100 x100. Fax: 215-790-8300. Email: HWANG@HWANGLAWFIRM.COM
See Professional Biographies, WILMINGTON, DELAWARE

Eveland, Elwood T., Jr., (BV) . . . . '55 '81 C.705 B.A. L.1338 J.D. [Haase&E.]
*PRACTICE AREAS: Personal Injury; Workers Compensation; Contracts; Construction Litigation.
Everett, Carl B., (AVⓉ) . . . . '47 '74 C.453 B.S. L.326 J.D. [Saul E.] (⊙Phila., PA)
*PRACTICE AREAS: Environmental.
Facciolo, Philip J., Jr., (BV) . . . . '50 '79 C&L.1338 B.A., J.D. [Figliola&F.]
Facciolo, Richard J. . . . . '59 '96 C.208 B.S.E.E. L.446 J.D. [Ⓐ Richards,L.&F.]
*PRACTICE AREAS: Business Law; Asset Based Finance; Business Organization.
Fair, Tamera '— '90 C.119 B.S. L.273 J.D.
(adm. in PA; not adm. in DE) Sr. Coun., E.I. du Pont de Nemours and Company
*RESPONSIBILITIES: Patents.
Fairchild, John D., (AV) '32 '63 C.30 B.A. L.215 J.D.
(adm. in MI; not adm. in DE; See Pat. Sect.) [Ⓒ Connolly B.L.&H.]
Faix, Philip A., Jr. '37 '64 C.976 B.A. L.276 LL.B.
(adm. in DC; not adm. in DE) 115 E. 14th St.
Falasca, Angelo . . . . '37 '71 C.499 B.S. L.1292 J.D. Chief Dep. Pub. Def.
Falgowski, Edmond, (CV) '52 '81 C.205 B.A. L.1338 J.D.
1201 Market Street, Suite 1100
Fallon, Brett D., (BV) . . . . '61 '86 C&L.228 B.A., J.D. [Morris,J.H.&W.]
*PRACTICE AREAS: Bankruptcy; Corporate Litigation; Commercial Litigation.
Fallon, Sherry Ruggiero, (BV) . . . . '61 '86 C.659 B.A. L.1338 J.D. [Tybout,R.&P.]
*PRACTICE AREAS: Negligence; Insurance; Workers Compensation; Products Liability; Medical Malpractice.
Faraone, Andrea J. . . . . '72 '99 C.205 B.A. L.645 J.D. [Ⓐ Blank R.C.&M.]
*PRACTICE AREAS: Civil Litigation.
Faraone, John A., (CV) . . . . '34 '62 C.205 B.S. L.446 LL.B. 1213 King St.
Farnan, Joseph J., Jr. . . . . '45 '70 C.1113 A.B. L.851 J.D. Chf. J., U.S. Dist. Ct.
Farnan, Joseph James, III . . . . '72 '00 C.644 B.A. L.1338 J.D. [Ⓐ Phillips,G.&S.]
*PRACTICE AREAS: Personal Injury; Commercial Litigation; Real Estate.
Farr, Burke, Gambacorta & Wright, A Professional Corporation
5301 Limestone Rd., Ste. 123 (⊙Bellmawr, NJ; Phila., PA)
Farwell, Richard . . . . '45 '79 C.205 B.A. L.1338 J.D. 5 Garrett Rd.
Fasic, G. Kevin . . . . '65 '96 C.401 B.A. L.1338 J.D. [Ⓐ Tighe,C.&L.]
*PRACTICE AREAS: Labor & Employment; Construction Law; Employee Benefits; Disabilities.

Fatell, Bonnie Glantz, (AVⓉ) .... '51 '81 C.645 B.S. L.831 J.D. [Blank R.C.&M.]
*PRACTICE AREAS: Bankruptcy Reorganization; Bankruptcy Litigation; Out of Court Debt Restructuring; Secured Creditors Rights; Unsecured Creditors Rights.
Favata, R. David, (BV) .... '50 '88 C.666 B.S. L.1338 J.D. Asst. City Solr.
Feeny, Charles E. '25 '55 C.659 A.B. L.180 LL.B.
(adm. in DC; not adm. in DE; Pat.) Coun., du Pont Co.
Feibus, Phyllis Elaine '50 '75 C.94 B.A. L.615 J.D.
(adm. in OK; not adm. in DE) Blue Cross Blue Shield of DE
Feldman, Eric N. .... '71 '98 C.575 B.A. L.276 J.D. [Ⓐ Richards,L.&F.]
*PRACTICE AREAS: Business Law; Commercial Law; Business Organization; Limited Liability Company Law; Partnership Law.
Felger, Mark E. .... '63 '89 C.1213 B.S. L.94 J.D. [Cozen O.]
*PRACTICE AREAS: Bankruptcy Chapter 11; Insolvency; Workouts; Bankruptcy Litigation; Business Reorganization.
Feliceangeli, Peter S. .... '47 '72 C.170 B.A. L.884 J.D. Atty., Dept. of Jus.
Feltham, S. Neil '53 '98 C.529 B.S. L.1338 J.D.
(adm. in PA; not adm. in DE) Sr. Pat. Coun., E.I. du Pont de Nemours & Co.
*RESPONSIBILITIES: Intellectual Property.
Fenton, Laurence W. .... '34 '59 C&L.893 B.A., LL.B. 212 Hackney Cir.
Fenton, Wendell, (AV) .... '39 '66 C.976 B.A. L.309 LL.B. [Richards,L.&F.]
Ferguson, Blair Q. '— '91 C.276 Ph.D. L.1338 J.D.
(adm. in PA; not adm. in DE) Asst. Gen. Coun., The du Pont Merck Pharmaceutical Co.
Fernandes, Carl J. .... '35 '64 C.705 B.A. L.1065 J.D. [Ⓒ Stewart&Assoc.]
*PRACTICE AREAS: Corporate Law; Mergers and Acquisitions; Finance; Import and Export Law.
Ferrara, Louis B., (BV) .... '47 '72 C.205 B.A. L.1017 J.D. [Ferrara,H.&B.]
Ferrara, Haley & Bevis, (BV) .... 824 Market St. Mall, Ste. 800
Ferri, Dennis D., (BV) .... '46 '72 C.397 A.B. L.884 J.D. [Morris,J.H.&W.]
*PRACTICE AREAS: Personal Injury; Medical Malpractice Defense; Insurance Law; Products Liability; Professional Liability.
Ferry, David J., Jr., (BV) .... '53 '82 C.728 B.A. L.1338 J.D. [Ferry&J.]
*PRACTICE AREAS: Litigation; Negligence; Commercial; Trusts and Estates; Probate Litigation.

Ferry & Joseph, P.A., (AV)
824 Market Street, Suite 904, P.O. Box 1351, 19899
Telephone: 302-575-1555 Fax: 302-575-1714
Email: info@ferryjoseph.com URL: http://www.ferryjoseph.com
David J. Ferry, Jr.; Michael B. Joseph; Theodore J. Tacconelli; John D. Mattey; Rick S. Miller; Jason C. Powell; Edward F. Kafader.
General Practice. Litigation, Bankruptcy, Probate, Probate and Guardianship Litigation, Elder Law, Negligence, Business, Commercial and Collection Law.
Reference: First Union Bank.
See Professional Biographies, WILMINGTON, DELAWARE

Feuerhake, Herbert G., (BVⓉ) '56 '82 C.205 B.A. L.659 J.D.
521 West Street, 19801-2196
Telephone: 302-658-6101 Fax: 302-658-6105
Email: herblaw@verizonmail.com URL: http://www.lawyers.com/feuerhakelaw
Employment Law, Wrongful Termination, Discrimination, Harassment, Americans with Disabilities Act, Unemployment Compensation, Civil Litigation.
See Professional Biographies, WILMINGTON, DELAWARE

Fields, Gregory .... '49 '76 C.608 B.S.B.A. L.117 J.D. 3120 Kennett Pike‡
Figliola, Anthony A., Jr., (CV) .... '48 '78 C.223 B.S. L.1338 J.D. [Figliola&F.]
Figliola & Facciolo, (BV) .... 1813 Marsh Road
Figueras, I. Jaime '38 '85 C.999 D.V.M. L.831 J.D.
(adm. in PA; not adm. in DE) City Dep. Dir. of Pers.
Fillip, Joseph A., Jr., (BV) .... '58 '84 C.659 B.A. L.813 J.D. Siegfried Grp., LLP
Fineman, Steven J. .... '74 '01 C.874 B.A. L.861 J.D. [Ⓐ Richards,L.&F.]
Finestrauss, Philip M., (CV) .... '52 '90 C.205 B.A. L.1338 J.D. [P.M.Finestrauss]
Finestrauss, Philip M., P.A., (CV) .... 1300 N. Market Street, Suite 700
Finger, David L., (CV) .... '58 '88 C.659 B.A. L.893 J.D. [D.L.Finger]
Finger, Louis J., (AV) .... '20 '47 C.311 B.A. L.976 LL.B. 1 Rodney Sq.‡

Finger, David L., P.A., (CV)
One Commerce Center, 1201 Orange Street, Suite 725, 19801-1155
Telephone: 302-884-6766 Fax: 302-984-1294 URL: http://www.DavidFinger.com
Email: DLF@davidfinger.com URL: http://www.lawyers.com/fingerlaw
David L. Finger.
Commercial Litigation, Bankruptcy Litigation, Corporate Litigation, Intellectual Property Litigation, Media/First Amendment Law, Civil Litigation.
See Professional Biographies, WILMINGTON, DELAWARE

Finkelstein, Jesse A., (AV) .... '55 '80 C.696 B.A. L.93 J.D. [Richards,L.&F.]
Fioravanti, Paul A., Jr. .... '61 '97 C.205 B.A. L.446 J.D. [Ⓐ Prickett,J.&E.]
*PRACTICE AREAS: Corporate Litigation; Corporate Law.
Fischer, Matthew E. .... '66 '92 C.1369 B.A. L.896 J.D. [Ⓐ Potter A.&C.]

Fish & Richardson P.C., (AVⓉ)
919 North Market Street Suite 1000, P.O. Box 1114, 19801 ⊙
Telephone: 302-652-5070 Fax: 302-652-0607
Email: info@fr.com URL: http://www.fr.com
Frederick P. Fish (1855-1930); W. K. Richardson (1859-1951).
Thomas L. Halkowski (Not admitted in DE); William J. Marsden, Jr.; Frank P. Porcelli. Associates: J. Andrew Huffman; John T. Meli, Jr.; Keith A. Walter, Jr. (Not admitted in DE).
Intellectual Property, Complex Litigation, Technology Law: Patents, Trademarks, Copyrights, Trade Secrets, Intellectual Property Litigation, Business Litigation, Technology Regulations, Antitrust Law, Corporate and Securities, White Collar Crime.
Boston, Massachusetts Office: 225 Franklin Street. Telephone: 617-542-5070. Fax: 617-542-8906.
Washington, D.C. Office: 601 13th Street, N.W. Telephone: 202-783-5070. Fax: 202-783-2331.
Redwood City, California Office: 500 Aguello Street, Suite 500. Telephone: 650-322-5070. Fax: 650-854-0875.
Minneapolis, Minnesota Office: Fish & Richardson P.C., P.A., 60 South Sixth Street, 3300 Dain Rauscher Plaza. Telephone: 612-335-5070. Fax: 612-288-9696.
San Diego, California Office: 4350 La Jolla Village Drive, Suite 500. Telephone: 858-678-5070. Fax: 858-678-5099.
New York, New York Office: 45 Rockefeller Plaza, Suite 2800. Telephone: 212-765-5070. Fax: 212-258-2291.
Dallas, Texas Office: 5000 Bank One Center, 1717 Main Street. Telephone: 214-747-5070. Fax: 214-747-2091
See Professional Biographies, WILMINGTON, DELAWARE

Fitzgerald, Frank R. '27 '55 C.999 B.M.S. L.724 LL.B.
(adm. in NY; not adm. in DE) Simmonds Precision Products, Inc.
Fitzgerald, Raymond N. .... '37 '69 C.871 B.S. L.184 LL.B. 10 Tall Trees Ln.
Fitzgerald, Yvette C. .... '74 '00 C.1372 B.A. L.945 J.D. [Ⓐ Morris,N.A.&T.]
Fleming, Jeffrey E. '63 '88 C.610 B.S. L.884 J.D.
(adm. in PA; not adm. in DE) Sr. Coun., Astrazeneca Pharm. LP
*RESPONSIBILITIES: Commercial; Labor and Employment; Food and Drug.
Fletcher, William D., Jr. .... '49 '75 C.205 B.A. L.902 J.D. [Schmittinger&R.] (⊙Dover)
*PRACTICE AREAS: Personal Injury Law; Employment Law.
Fleury, Keith H. '56 '83 C.223 B.S. L.1338 J.D.
(adm. in PA; not adm. in DE) Montell USA Inc.
Flickinger, Joseph F., III, (BV) .... '48 '79 C.205 B.S. L.1338 J.D. P.O. Box 88
Flinn, C. Barr '61 '93 C.674 A.B. L.228 J.D.
(adm. in NY; not adm. in DE) [Young C.S.&T.]
*PRACTICE AREAS: Corporate Governance Litigation; Commercial Litigation; Antitrust; Privacy Law.

Flowers, Chipman Loyd, Jr. .... '74 '00 C.659 B.A. L.276 J.D. One Rodney Square
Floyd, Israel J., (BV) '46 '73 C.411 B.A. L.884 J.D.
Exec. V.P., Secy. & Gen. Coun., Hercules Inc.
Floyd, Linda Axamethy '53 '85 C.690 B.A. L.831 J.D.
(adm. in PA; not adm. in DE; Pat.) Corp. Coun., E.I. du Pont de Nemours and Company
*RESPONSIBILITIES: Intellectual Property; Licensing.
Flubacher, Todd A. .... '69 '99 C.223 B.S. L.446 J.D. [Ⓐ Morris,N.A.&T.]
Flynn, Anthony G., (BV) .... '52 '77 C.205 B.A. L.128 J.D. [Young C.S.&T.]
Flynn, James J. '25 '60 C.745 B.S. L.276 J.D.
(adm. in DC; not adm. in DE; Pat.) du Pont Co.

Foley, Thomas A., (BV) '60 '90 C.473 B.S. L.215 J.D.
1326 King Street, 19801
Telephone: 302-658-3077 Fax: 302-656-1993
Email: taf@taf-law.com URL: http://www.lawyers.com/foleylaw
***PRACTICE AREAS: Criminal Law (100%).**
Criminal Trial and Appellate Practice in all State and Federal Courts.
See Professional Biographies, WILMINGTON, DELAWARE

Folsom, James .... '43 '69 C&L.744 B.A., J.D. 1215 N. King St.
Folt, Daniel V. .... '57 '92 C.1306 B.S. L.464 J.D. [Cozen O.]
*PRACTICE AREAS: Corporate Litigation; Commercial Litigation; Complex Litigation.
Fontaine, Jennifer Williams '64 '91 C.645 B.A. L.273 J.D.
(adm. in NJ; not adm. in DE) Prof. of Law, Widener Univ.
Forrester, Zoe A. .... '67 '01 C.1349 B.A. L.188 J.D. [Ⓐ Richards,L.&F.]
Forsten, Richard A., (BV) .... '63 '88 C&L.893 B.S., J.D. [Klett R.L.&S.]
*PRACTICE AREAS: Land Use and Land Use Litigation; Construction Law and Mechanics' Liens; Commercial and Real Estate Transactions; Environmental Law and Permitting.
Fortunato, Kim Fremont '56 '89 C.228 B.A. L.1338 J.D.
(adm. in PA; not adm. in DE) 500 Field Ln.‡
Foster, Anne C., (BV) .... '61 '86 C&L.945 B.A., J.D. [Richards,L.&F.]
*PRACTICE AREAS: Litigation; Corporate Law.
Foster, Michael F., (BV) .... '47 '77 C.732 A.B. L.365 J.D. 1418 Lovering Ave.
Foster, Richard T. '41 '74 C.62 B.S. L.273 J.D.
(adm. in VA; not adm. in DE; Pat.) 2318 Shipley Rd.‡
Foulk, Gerald C., (BV) .... '34 '66 C.893 B.A. L.245 LL.B. [Miller&F.]
Fountain, Darryl K., (CV) .... '55 '84 C.205 B.A. L.893 J.D. 1225 N. King St., K#700
Fournaris, Emmanuel G., (BV) .... '58 '84 C.205 B.S. L.1338 J.D. [Gordon,F.&M.]
*PRACTICE AREAS: Commercial Law; Business Law; Business Formation; Mergers and Acquisitions; Taxation.
Fournier, David M., (BV) .... '64 '90 C.645 B.A. L.884 J.D. [Pepper H.]
*PRACTICE AREAS: Business Reorganization; Bankruptcy.
Fox, Stephanie A. .... '66 '91 C.205 B.A. L.1017 J.D. [Ⓐ Klehr,H.H.B.&E.]
*PRACTICE AREAS: Creditors Rights; Bankruptcy; Commercial Litigation.

Fox, Rothschild, O'Brien & Frankel, LLP
Mellon Bank Center, 919 North Market Street, Suite 1400, 14th Floor, 19801-3046 ⊙
Telephone: 302-655-7460 Cable Address: FROF Fax: 302-655-7004
Email: attorneys@frof.com URL: http://www.frof.com
Partner: Francis G. X. Pileggi. Associate: Sheldon K. Rennie.
Admiralty, Alternative Dispute Resolution, Antitrust, Banking, Bankruptcy, Civil Litigation, Commercial Litigation, Computer Law, Condominium Law, Construction, Corporate and Commercial, Condemnation Law, Corporate, Criminal Defense, Environmental, Estate Planning, Family Business, Family Law, Financial Services, Franchise, Governmental Affairs, Health Law, Insurance, Intellectual Property, Labor and Employment, General Litigation, Legal Malpractice Defense, Marine Finance, Municipal Finance, Nonprofit Institutions, Pension, Personal Injury, Probate, Products Liability, Professional Liability Defense, Profit Sharing and Employee Benefits, Public Utility, Real Estate, Securities, Sports Law, Taxation, Wills and Trusts, Zoning and Land Use.
Philadelphia, Pennsylvania Office: 2000 Market Street, Tenth Floor, 19103-3291. Telephone: 215-299-2000. Cable Address: FROF. Fax: 215-299-2150.
Atlantic City, New Jersey Office: CitiCenter Building, Suite 500, 1300 Atlantic Avenue, 08401. Telephone: 609-348-4515. Fax: 609-348-6834.
Doylestown, Pennsylvania Office: 102 North Main Street, P.O. Box 1589, 18901-0700. Telephone: 215-345-7500. Fax: 215-345-7507.
Exton, Pennsylvania Office: Eagleview Corporate Center, 760 Constitution Drive, Suite 104, P.O. Box 673, 19341-0673. Telephone: 610-458-7500. Fax: 610-458-7337.
Lansdale, Pennsylvania Office: 1250 South Broad Street, Suite 1000, P.O. Box 431, 19446. Telephone: 215-699-6000. Fax: 215-699-0231.
Trenton (Lawrenceville), New Jersey Office: Princeton Pike Corporate Center, 997 Lenox Drive, Building 3, 08648-2311. Telephone: 609-896-3600. Fax: 609-896-1469.
Voorhees, New Jersey Office: Laurelwood, Suite 103, 1103 Laurel Oak Road, 08043. Telephone: 856-782-6000. Fax: 856-346-9866.
See Professional Biographies, WILMINGTON, DELAWARE

Frabizzio, Anthony M., (BV) .... '55 '81 C.205 B.A. L.1017 J.D. [Heckler&F.]
*PRACTICE AREAS: Insurance Defense Law; Worker's Compensation Litigation; General Civil and Trial Practice.
Frabizzio, Samuel J. .... '45 '71 C.205 B.S. L.884 J.D. 1200 Pennsylvania Ave.
Fraczkowski, Alfred R. .... '26 '53 C.205 A.B. L.659 LL.B. Assoc. Com. Pleas J.
Frakt, Arthur N. '39 '65 C&L.705 B.S., LL.B.
(adm. in NJ; not adm. in DE) 4601 Concord Pike‡
Franta, Richard E., (BV) .... '45 '70 C.967 B.A. L.880 J.D. 1301 N. Harrison St.
Frazier, Shannon S. .... '75 '01 C.260 B.S. L.861 J.D. [Ⓐ Richards,L.&F.]
Freebery, James Joseph, IV .... '71 '96 C.205 B.S. L.602 J.D. [Ⓐ McCarter&E.]
*PRACTICE AREAS: Litigation; Corporate Law; Commercial Law; Bankruptcy; Environmental Law.
Freebery, Michael P., (BV) .... '57 '88 C.205 B.S. L.1338 J.D. [Freebery&H.]
Freebery & Houghton, (BV) .... 1232 King St., Ste. 300
Freibott, Frederick S., (BV) .... '63 '89 C.282 B.A. L.1338 J.D. [Woloshin,T.L.N.&F.]
Fresco, Brigitte V. .... '69 '96 C.645 B.A. L.273 J.D. [Ⓐ Richards,L.&F.]
Frey, Timothy A., (BV) .... '53 '78 C.197 B.A. L.659 J.D. [Saul E.]
*PRACTICE AREAS: Public Finance.
Fricke, Hilmar L. '35 '66 C.966 B.S.Ch.E. L.446 LL.B.
(adm. in DC; not adm. in DE; Pat.) [Ⓒ Potter A.&C.]
*PRACTICE AREAS: Patents; Contracts.
Friedberg, Michael A., (AV) .... '47 '72 C&L.893 B.A., J.D. [Cooch&T.] (⊙Newark)
*PRACTICE AREAS: Tax Law; Estate Planning; Business Law; Corporate Law.
Friedlander, Joel, (BV) .... '66 '93 C&L.659 B.S., J.D. [Bouchard M.&F.]
*PRACTICE AREAS: Corporate Litigation; Business Litigation.
Friedman, Jeffrey S. .... '67 '92 C.1044 B.A. L.1338 J.D. 10 Morgan Lane
Fruehauf, Barbara A., (CV) .... '51 '90 C.205 B.A. L.884 J.D. [Cattie&F.]
*PRACTICE AREAS: Insurance Defense Law; Civil Practice; Trial Practice; Subrogation Law.
Fullerton, Stuart L. '60 '88 C.112 B.S. L.276 J.D.
(adm. in NY; not adm. in DE) Sr. Litig. Coun., Astrazeneca Pharm. LP
*RESPONSIBILITIES: Litigation; Compliance (100%).
Furlow, Clark W., (BV) .... '45 '78 C.94 B.A. L.245 J.D. [Ⓒ Smith,K.&F.]
*PRACTICE AREAS: Litigation; Corporate Law.
Furr, Robert B., Jr. '57 '86 C.277 B.Ch.E. L.705 J.D.
(adm. in PA; not adm. in DE; Pat.) Corp. Coun., E.I. du Pont de Nemours & Co.
*RESPONSIBILITIES: Intellectual Property; Patents; Technology Licensing.
Fuzail, Kalim S. '69 '00 L.365 J.D.
(adm. in IL; not adm. in DE) 974 Centre Rd.
Gabay, Joseph A., (BV) .... '57 '83 C.728 B.A. L.1338 J.D. [J.A.Gabay]
Gabay, Joseph A., P.C., Law Office of, (BV) .... 901 Market Street, 4th Floor

Gadbois, Barbara J. .... '53 '88 C.205 B.A. L.1338 J.D. [Ⓐ P.G.Angelos]
*PRACTICE AREAS: Products Liability; Toxic Torts; Personal Injury Litigation.
Gagne, David C., (BV) .... '67 '92 C.205 B.S. L.1338 J.D. [Ⓐ Woloshin,T.L.N.&F.]
Galardi, Gregg M. .... '57 '91 C&L.659 B.A., J.D. [Skadden,A.S.M.&F.]
Gallagher, Henry E., Jr., (AV) .... '49 '75 C&L.884 A.B., J.D. [Connolly B.L.&H.]
Gallagher, John T. .... '24 '52 C.205 B.A. L.477 J.D. 901 Stuart Rd.‡
Galperin, Richard, (AV) .... '49 '75 C.205 B.A. L.884 J.D. [Morris,J.H.&W.]
*PRACTICE AREAS: Medical Malpractice Defense; Products Liability; Insurance.
Gamble, D. Geoffrey B. '45 '74 C.311 A.B. L.128 J.D.
Chf. Coun., Int'l. Trade, E.I. du Pont de Nemours and Company
*RESPONSIBILITIES: International Law; Trade Law.

Gangi, John F., (BV) '47 '79 C.378 B.S. L.1338 J.D.
712 West Street, 19801
Telephone: 302-656-4090 FAX: 302-656-4233
Email: jgangi1062@aol.com URL: http://www.lawyers.com/gangilaw
***PRACTICE AREAS: Civil Trial; Personal Injury Law; Family Law.**
General Civil and Trial Practice. Personal Injury, Auto Accidents and Family Law.
See Professional Biographies, WILMINGTON, DELAWARE

Garber, Aaron A. .... '68 '97 C.174 B.A. L.831 J.D. [Ⓐ Pepper H.]
*PRACTICE AREAS: Bankruptcy.
Gardner, Gary M. '51 '76 C.884 B.S. L.1338 J.D.
(adm. in PA; not adm. in DE) Sr. V.P., PFPC, Inc.
Garfield, Alan Evan '57 '83 C.1036 B.A. L.112 J.D.
(adm. in CA; not adm. in DE) P.O. Box 7474 Concord Pike
Garrett, David J., (AV) .... '36 '66 C.197 A.B. L.477 J.D. 350 Delaware Trust Bldg.
Garrett, William L., Jr., (BV) .... '51 '80 C.205 B.A. L.902 J.D. 18-B Trolley Sq.
Gattuso, Dominick T. .... '70 '97 C.1028 B.A. L.1338 J.D. [Ⓐ Richards,L.&F.]
*PRACTICE AREAS: Corporate Litigation; Commercial Litigation.
Gattuso, Kimberly L. .... '73 '98 C.205 B.A. L.1338 J.D. [Ⓐ Saul E.]
*PRACTICE AREAS: Litigation.
Gauthier, Frances, (CV) .... '66 '94 C.569 B.A. L.659 J.D. [Ⓐ Klett R.L.&S.]
*PRACTICE AREAS: Corporate Law; Intellectual Property Law.
Gauthier, Lindsey A. '65 '92 C.569 B.A. L.659 J.D.
(adm. in PA; not adm. in DE) Sr. Coun., E.I. du Pont de Nemours and Company
*RESPONSIBILITIES: Commercial Law; Antitrust.
Gaza, Anne Shea '72 '97 C.509 B.A. L.665 J.D.
(adm. in PA; not adm. in DE) [Ⓐ Richards,L.&F.]
*PRACTICE AREAS: Corporate Litigation; Commercial Litigation; Intellectual Property Litigation; Workmen's Compensation.
Gebelein, Richard S. .... '46 '71 C.665 B.S. L.884 J.D. Assoc. Supr. Ct. J.
Geddes, James McC., (BV) .... '49 '76 C.575 B.A. L.945 J.D. [Ashby&G.]
Gee, William S., (AV) .... '51 '77 C.976 B.A. L.902 J.D. [Saul E.]
*PRACTICE AREAS: Real Estate; Commercial Transactions; Public Finance.
Geiger, Kathleen W. .... '52 '90 C.966 L.1338 J.D. [Potter A.&C.] (Pat.)
*PRACTICE AREAS: Patents; Intellectual Property.
Gellert, Ronald S. '71 '97 C.705 B.A. L.1292
(adm. in PA; not adm. in DE) [Ⓐ Potter A.&C.]
*PRACTICE AREAS: Bankruptcy (100%).
Gentile, Mark J., (AV) .... '56 '82 C.1044 B.S. L.94 J.D. [Richards,L.&F.]
*PRACTICE AREAS: Corporate Law; Securities.
Gentilotti, Jeffrey M., (CV) .... '68 '95 C.401 B.S. L.1338 J.D. [Bifferato,B.&G.]
*PRACTICE AREAS: Insurance Defense; Personal Injury; Workers Compensation; Products Liability.
Geoghegan, Joseph H., (AV) .... '28 '56 C.976 A.B. L.178 LL.B. [© Potter A.&C.]
Gerard, Thomas J., (CV) .... '58 '91 C.415 B.A. L.1338 J.D. [Ⓐ Marshall,D.W.C.&G.]
*PRACTICE AREAS: General Liability Defense.
Gernsross, Adele Williams '56 '00 C.341 B.S. L.1338 J.D.
(adm. in NJ; not adm. in DE) [Ⓐ Connolly B.L.&H.]
*PRACTICE AREAS: Taxation; Estate Planning; Estate Administration; Trusts and Estates; Probate.
Geyer, Tiffany L. .... '75 '00 C.216 B.A. L.1338 J.D. [Ⓐ Ashby&G.]
Gibbs, Danielle B. .... '— '98 C.446 B.A. L.64 J.D. [Ⓐ Young C.S.&T.]
*PRACTICE AREAS: Corporate Litigation; Chancery Practice.
Glancy, Brian P., (BV) .... '61 '86 C.205 B.S.B.A. L.1338 J.D. [Hughes,S.&G.]
Glassman, Neil B., (AV) .... '52 '82 C.855 B.A. L.930 J.D. [Bayard]
*PRACTICE AREAS: Commercial Law; Insolvency and Bankruptcy Law; Law of Corporations; Partnerships; Business Trusts.
Glebe, David Curtis .... '52 '86 C&L.659 B.A., J.D. Chf. Disciplinary Coun., Supm. Ct.
Goddess, Jeffrey S., (AV) .... '45 '71 C.103 B.A. L.145 J.D. [Rosenthal,M.G.&G.]
*PRACTICE AREAS: Commercial Litigation; Corporate Litigation; Personal Injury; Civil Litigation.
Godowsky, Rory Colton, (CV) .... '50 '78 C.205 B.S. L.1338 J.D. [Green,G.&G.]
Goeller, Michael C. '54 '79 C.205 B.A.A.S. L.1017 J.D.
(adm. in PA; not adm. in DE) Gen. Coun. & Secy., Hatzel & Buehler, Inc.
Goldberg, Robert D., (BV) .... '46 '74 C.205 B.A. L.93 J.D. [Biggs&B.]
Goldberg, Steven D., (BV) .... '46 '71 C.205 B.A. L.273 J.D. [Saul E.]
*PRACTICE AREAS: Real Property Law; Corporate Law; Alternate Entities; Commercial Transactions.
Golde, Howard R. '50 '77 C.831 B.B.A. L.1338 J.D.
(adm. in PA; not adm. in DE) 2 E. 7th St.

Goldfein & Hosmer, A Professional Corporation, (BV)
PNC Bank Center, Suite 1110, 222 Delaware Avenue, P.O. Box 2206, 19899-2206 ⊙
Telephone: 302-656-3301 FAX: 302-656-0643
Email: gkaplan@goldfeinlawde.com URL: http://www.goldfeinlaw.com
Gary H. Kaplan; Richard K. Goll; Julie M. Sebring.
Civil Trial Practice, Casualty, Products Liability, Medical Malpractice, Insurance, Toxic Torts, Health Care, Subrogation, Hospital Liability, Insurance Coverage, General Corporate and Commercial Real Estate, Estate and Tax Planning.
Philadelphia, Pennsylvania Office: 1600 Market Street, 33rd Floor, 19103-7288. Telephone: 215-979-8200. Fax: 215-979-8201.
Princeton, New Jersey Office: Princeton Metro Center, Suite 115, 5 Vaughn Drive, 08540-6313. Telephone: 609-520-0400. Fax: 609-520-1450.
New York, New York Office: 5 Hanover Square, 21st Floor, 10004. Telephone: 212-791-0340. Fax: 212-791-0347.
Baltimore, Maryland Office: 217 East Redwood Street, 21st Floor, 21202. Telephone: 410-576-0200. Fax: 410-576-0887.
See Professional Biographies, WILMINGTON, DELAWARE

Goldlust, Perry F., (BV) .... '42 '66 C.1138 B.B.A. L.1009 J.D. [Heiman,A.G.&B.]
*PRACTICE AREAS: Labor (Union) Law; Commercial Law; Personal Injury; Workman's Compensation.
Goldman, Michael D., (AV) .... '42 '68 C.645 B.A. L.884 J.D. [Potter A.&C.]
Goldman, Robert S., (BV) .... '53 '79 C.184 B.S. L.472 J.D. [Phillips,G.&S.] ⊙
*PRACTICE AREAS: Insurance Defense Law; Toxic Tort; Environmental; Personal Injury Litigation; Bankruptcy Litigation.
Goldstein, Carl .... '38 '64 C&L.659 A.B., LL.B. Assoc. Supr. Ct. J.
Goldstein, Kevin W. .... '58 '91 C.688 B.S. L.1338 J.D. [Ratner&P.] (See Pat. Sect.)
*PRACTICE AREAS: Intellectual Property; Intellectual Property Litigation.

Goldstein, Lee C., (BV) '50 '76 C.205 B.A. L.796 J.D.
615 West 18th Street, P.O. Box 1957, 19899
Telephone: 302-654-2632 Fax: 302-654-2940
***PRACTICE AREAS: Personal Injury Law; Litigation; Domestic Relations Law.**
Civil Litigation, Wills & Probate and Real Estate.

Goldstein, Louis .... '18 '41 C.205 B.A. L.659 LL.B. 4 E. 13th St.
Golian, Andrew G. '38 '68 C.688 B.Ch.E. L.128 J.D.
(adm. in DC; not adm. in DE; Pat.) Corp. Coun., E.I. du Pont de Nemours and Company
Golian, Paul D. .... '73 '98 C.423 B.S. L.1194 J.D. [Ⓐ Potter A.&C.] (Pat.)
*PRACTICE AREAS: Intellectual Property; Patents.
Goll, Richard K., (BV) .... '40 '65 C.205 B.A. L.64 LL.B. [Goldfein&H.]
*PRACTICE AREAS: Personal Injury Defense; Estate Planning; Estate Administration; Commercial Litigation.

Gollatz, Griffin & Ewing, P.C.
1901 Superfine Lane Suite 2, 19802 ⊙
Telephone: 302-428-3761 Fax: 302-428-3766
Email: gge@ggelaw.com URL: http://www.ggelaw.com
J. Michael Johnson;—Nancy E. Whinnery.
General Civil Litigation in State and Federal Courts. Business, Technology, Intellectual Property, Transportation, Non Profit Organizations, Estate Planning and Administration, Real Estate, Employment, Environmental and Equine Law.
Philadelphia, Pennsylvania Office: 16th Floor, Two Penn Center Plaza. Telephone: 215-563-9400. Fax: 215-665-9988.
West Chester, Pennsylvania Office: 213 West Miner Street, P.O. Box 796. Telephone: 610-692-9116. Fax: 610-692-9177.
See Professional Biographies, WILMINGTON, DELAWARE

Gomez, Brian A. ... '65 '93 C.1119 B.A. L.1338 J.D. [Ⓐ Huntley&Assoc.] (See Pat. Sect.)
*PRACTICE AREAS: Intellectual Property; Patent; Trademark; Copyright.
Gondek, Francis C. .... '— '84 C.205 B.A.Ed. L.1338 J.D. [Ⓐ Wilbraham,L.&B.]
Gonser, William A., Jr. '47 '81 C.575 B.S.B.A. L.42 J.D.
Corp. Coun., E.I. du Pont de Nemours and Company
*RESPONSIBILITIES: Antitrust; Commercial Law.
Goodier, Rosemary .... '67 '97 C.878 B.S. L.1358 J.D. [Ⓐ Skadden,A.S.M.&F.]
Goodman, Donna L. '— '91 C.390 B.A. L.1017 J.D.
(adm. in PA; not adm. in DE) Attorney, LSE, E.I. dupont de Nemours & Company
*RESPONSIBILITIES: Appellate Practice.
Goodman, Lisa B. .... '63 '94 C.658 B.A. L.1338 J.D. [Ⓐ Young C.S.&T.]
*PRACTICE AREAS: Zoning, Planning and Land Use; Commercial Real Estate; Leases and Leasing.
Goodman, Todd L. .... '64 '92 C.205 B.A. L.1017 J.D. [© Potter A.&C.]
Goodrick, Michael J., (BV) .... '49 '74 C.276 A.B. L.420 J.D. 1118 West St.
Gordon, Peter S., (AV) .... '52 '77 C.276 A.B. L.262 J.D. [Gordon,F.&M.]
*PRACTICE AREAS: Taxation; Estate Planning; Probate; Commercial Law; Fiduciary Litigation.
Gordon, Susan M. .... '56 '97 C.205 B.S.N. L.1338 J.D. [Ⓐ Stevens&L.]
*PRACTICE AREAS: Health Law; Health Care Regulation.
Gordon, William C. .... '23 '51 C&L.477 A.B., J.D. HIMONT USA Inc.
Gordon, William E., Jr. '48 '76 C.641 B.S. L.796 J.D.
(adm. in TX; not adm. in DE) Corporate Counsel, E.I. dupont de Nemours & Company
*RESPONSIBILITIES: Litigation.

Gordon, Fournaris & Mammarella, P.A., (AV)
1220 North Market Street Suite 700, P.O. Box 1355, 19899-1355
Telephone: 302-652-2900 Fax: 302-652-1142
Peter S. Gordon; Thomas Mammarella; Emmanuel G. Fournaris. Special Counsel: Grover C. Brown;—Robert A. Penza; Bryan E. Keenan; Peter M. Sweeney; Stephen Del Rossi (Not admitted in DE).
Estate Planning, Estate and Trust Administration and Taxation, Guardianships, Limited Partnerships, Limited Liability Companies, Corporations, Tax and Business Planning, Succession Planning, Charitable Foundations, Litigation, Real Estate, Zoning, Land Development, Alternative Dispute Resolution.
See Professional Biographies, WILMINGTON, DELAWARE

Gorman, Francis X. .... '67 '98 C&L.893 B.A., J.D. [Ⓐ Klett R.L.&S.]
*PRACTICE AREAS: Commercial Transactions; Land Use Regulation; Litigation.
Gott, Michele C., (CV) .... '58 '88 C.205 B.A. L.1338 J.D. [Smith,K.&F.]
*PRACTICE AREAS: Corporate Litigation; Commercial Litigation.
Gouge, Donald L., Jr., (BV) .... '58 '84 C.205 B.A. L.61 J.D. [Heiman,A.G.&B.]
*PRACTICE AREAS: Personal Injury Law; Litigation; Insurance Defense Law; Real Estate Litigation.
Gould, David J. '43 '69 C.645 B.S. L.1292 J.D.
(adm. in DC; not adm. in DE)
Corporate Trademark Counsel, E.I. dupont de Nemours & Company
*RESPONSIBILITIES: Trademarks; International Intellectual Property.
Graham, Mary B., (BV) .... '52 '83 C.813 B.S. L.976 J.D. [Morris,N.A.&T.]
Grandell, Erik C. .... '58 '86 C.1338 B.S. L.884 J.D. [Ⓐ Heckler&F.]
*PRACTICE AREAS: Worker's Compensation.
Grant, M. Duncan, (AV) .... '50 '75 C.674 A.B. L.659 J.D. [Pepper H.] (⊙Phila., PA)
*PRACTICE AREAS: Corporate Litigation; Commercial Litigation.
Grant, Stuart M., (BV) .... '60 '86 C.1036 B.A. L.569 J.D. [Grant&E.]

Grant & Eisenhofer, P.A., (BV)
1220 North Market Street, Suite 500, 19801
Telephone: 302-622-7000 Fax: 302-622-7100
URL: http://www.gelaw.com
Jay W. Eisenhofer; Stuart M. Grant; Megan D. McIntyre. Of Counsel: Kurt N. Schacht (Not admitted in DE). Special Counsel: Denise T. DiPersio (Not admitted in DE); Geoffrey C. Jarvis; Abbott A. Leban; Diane T. Zilka (Not admitted in DE);—Michael J. Barry (Not admitted in DE); Christine S. Bulman (Not admitted in DE); Cynthia A. Calder; Richard M. Donaldson (Not admitted in DE); John C. Kairis; Sidney S. Liebesman; Stephan Matanovic (Not admitted in DE); Michelle N. Peterson (Not admitted in DE); C. Curtis Staropoli.
Litigation Boutique: Securities, Corporate, Bankruptcy, Insurance Coverage and Complex Commercial Litigation.
See Professional Biographies, WILMINGTON, DELAWARE

Gray, John Fisher '63 '87 C.347 B.A. L.309 J.D.
(adm. in PA; not adm. in DE) [Houghton,H.&G.]
Grayson, Eric L., (BV) .... '54 '79 C.205 B.S. L.1338 J.D. [Robinson&G.]
Grear, Craig D. .... '64 '90 C&L.276 B.S., J.D. [Young C.S.&T.]
*PRACTICE AREAS: Taxation; Business Law; Estate Planning; Partnership Law; Corporate Law.
Green, Derek S. '70 '99 C.893 B.A. L.831 J.D.
(adm. in PA; not adm. in DE) Asst. Dep. Atty. Gen.
Green, Harold N., (BV) .... '21 '43 C.216 L.1017 [Green,G.&G.]
Green, Jacqueline L. Jenkin '66 '93 C.205 B.A. L.1338 J.D.
(adm. in NJ; not adm. in DE) [Ⓐ Morris&M.]
*PRACTICE AREAS: Corporate Litigation; Securities Litigation.
Green, James S., (AV) .... '47 '72 C.674 A.B. L.864 J.D. [Seitz,V.&G.]
*PRACTICE AREAS: Construction Litigation; Commercial Litigation; Tort Litigation; Alternative Dispute Resolution.

Green, Joseph B., (BV) '47 '72 C.216 B.A. L.229 J.D.
Towne Center, 4 East 8th Street Suite 200, 19801 ⊙
Telephone: 302-654-4557 Fax: 302-655-5358
Email: joegreen@wserv.com URL: http://www.lawyers.com/joegreen
***PRACTICE AREAS: Personal Injury; Bankruptcy; Real Estate.**
Personal Injury, Bankruptcy and Real Estate.
Lewes, Delaware Office: 467 Highway One, 19958. Telephone: 302-644-1732.
See Professional Biographies, WILMINGTON, DELAWARE

Green, Scott A., (BV) ....'56 '80 C.205 B.A. L.904 J.D. 222 Dela. Ave.
Green, Stanley B., (AVⓉ) '41 '67 C.563 B.E.E. L.273 LL.B.
(adm. in DC; not adm. in DE; See Pat. Sect.) [Connolly B.L.&H.]
*PRACTICE AREAS: Patent Litigation; Patent Infringement; Electrical Patents; Electronic Patents; Computer and Software Patents.
Green, Green & Godowsky, (BV) ....4 E. 8th St.
Greenberg, Matthew M. ....'69 '97 C.855 B.A. L.30 J.D. [Ⓐ Skadden,A.S.M.&F.]
*PRACTICE AREAS: Corporate.
Greenberg Traurig, LLP, (BV)
1201 North Orange Street (⊙Phoenix, AZ; Santa Monica, CA; Denver, CO; Wash., DC; Boca Raton, Ft Laud., Miami, Orlando, Tallahassee, West Palm Beach, FL; Atlanta, GA; Chgo., IL; Boston, MA; New York, NY; Phila., PA; Tysons Corner, VA)
Greenstein, Garry G. ....'29 '55 C.205 B.A. L.659 LL.B. 64 Bancroft Estate Rd.‡
Gregory, Mark C. ....'65 '95 C.165 B.A. L.942 J.D. [Ⓐ Huntley&Assoc.]
*PRACTICE AREAS: Intellectual Property; Patent, Trademark and Copyright Law; Entertainment Law; Internet Law.
Gregory, Theodore C. '26 '68 C.645 B.S. L.8 J.D.
(adm. in OH; not adm. in DE; See Pat. Sect.) [Ⓒ Huntley&Assoc.]
*PRACTICE AREAS: Patent Law; Patent Applications; Litigation; Agreements.
Gregory, Theopalis K., (CV) '52 '78 C.205 B.A. L.260 J.D.
Carvel State Office Building, 820 North French Street
Grey, Joseph, (BV) ....'58 '86 C&L.893 B.A., J.D. [Stevens&L.]
*PRACTICE AREAS: Bankruptcy Chapter 11; Bankruptcy Litigation.
Grey, Teresa A. ....'61 '91 C.229 B.A. L.1338 J.D. 2646 W. Robino Dr.
Griffin, Randall V. ....'55 '79 C.136 B.S. L.276 J.D. Sr. Coun., Conectiv
*RESPONSIBILITIES: Regulatory (60%); Contract (25%).
Griffiths, John E. '53 '79 C.188 B.S. L.1338 J.D.
(adm. in PA; not adm. in DE; Pat.) Corp. Coun., E.I. du Pont de Nemours and Company
*RESPONSIBILITIES: Intellectual Property; Contracts; Intellectual Property Licensing.
Griffiths, John E. '25 '52 C.688 B.Mgt.E. L.188 D.J.
(adm. in NY; not adm. in DE) 2705 Marklyn Dr.‡
Griffiths, Norman D., (BV) '52 '83 C.30 B.S. L.128 J.D.
(adm. in DC; not adm. in DE) Corp. Coun., E.I. du Pont de Nemours and Company
*RESPONSIBILITIES: Commercial Transactions; Antitrust; Products Liability.
Grillo, Carolee M., (BV) ....'44 '83 C.645 B.A. L.1338 J.D. Comr., Fam. Ct.
Grimm, Eugene L. '25 '50
C&L.494 B.S.L., LL.B. Prof. of Law, Widener Univ. Sch. of Law
Grimm, John S. ....'65 '93 C.93 B.A. L.1338 130 Hitching Post Drive
Grimm, Thomas C., (BV) ....'54 '80 C.602 B.B.A. L.884 J.D. [Morris,N.A.&T.]
Grohsgal, Bruce ....'52 '81 C.1036 B.A. L.178 J.D. [Pachulski,S.Z.Y.&J.]
*PRACTICE AREAS: Bankruptcy; Real Property.
Gross, Kevin, (BV) ....'52 '78 C.205 B.A. L.30 J.D. [Rosenthal,M.G.&G.]
*PRACTICE AREAS: Bankruptcy; Corporate Litigation; Securities Litigation; Commercial Litigation; Business Litigation.
Grossbauer, John F., (BV) ....'61 '86 C.645 B.A. L.228 J.D. [Potter A.&C.]
*PRACTICE AREAS: Delaware Corporation Law/Transactions; Corporate; Acquisitions; Divestitures.
Grossman, Jerome K., (AV) ....'53 '77 C&L.276 A.B., J.D. [Young C.S.&T.]
*PRACTICE AREAS: Taxation; Estate Planning; Buying and Selling of Businesses; Mergers, Acquisitions and Divestitures; Business Law.
Gruccio, Philip A. '29 '52 C&L.276 A.B., J.D.
(adm. in NJ; not adm. in DE) 4601 Concord Pike
Gundersen, Mark J. ....'54 '79 C.188 A.B. L.94 J.D. [Klett R.L.&S.]
*PRACTICE AREAS: Mergers and Acquisitions; Licensing; Corporate Law.
Gunter, D. Shane ....'74 '00 C.999 B.S. L.1017 J.D. [Ⓐ Richards,L.&F.]
Gwynne, Kurt F. ....'— '92 C.1175 B.A. L.659 J.D. [Reed S.]
*PRACTICE AREAS: Bankruptcy.
Haase, Frederick T., Jr., (BV) ....'51 '76 C&L.884 B.A., J.D. [Haase&E.]
*PRACTICE AREAS: Personal Injury; Workers' Compensation; Medical Malpractice; Dental Malpractice; Divorce.

Haase & Eveland, (BV)
824 Market Street Mall, Suite 830, P.O. Box 393, 19899-0393
Telephone: 302-421-5900 Fax: 302-421-5909
Email: govbiggs@aol.com URL: http://www.lawyers.com/haaselegal
Frederick T. Haase, Jr.; Elwood T. Eveland, Jr.
Personal Injury and Workers' Compensation Litigation. Family Law, Wills, Estates, Real Estate Settlements, Medical and Dental Malpractice Law.
See Professional Biographies, WILMINGTON, DELAWARE

Habbart, Ellisa Opstbaum, (AV) ......'59 '86 C.831 B.B.A. L.884 J.D. [Stradley R.S.&Y.]
Hadley, Kathleen D. ....'48 '87 C.645 B.A. L.1338 J.D. [Ⓐ P.G.Angelos]
*PRACTICE AREAS: Products Liability; Toxic Torts; Personal Injury Litigation.
Hagedorn, Mark A. '71 '98 C.679 B.S.Ch.E. L.347 J.D.
(adm. in IL; not adm. in DE; Pat.) Coun., Hercules Incorporated
Hageman, Peggy K. ....'60 '86 C.112 B.A. L.884 J.D. Dep. Atty. Gen.
Haines, Kara R., (BV) ....'62 '89 C.659 B.A. L.831 J.D. Dep. Atty. Gen.
Hake, Carolyn S. ....'74 '99 C.205 B.A.A.S. L.1338 J.D. [Ⓐ Ashby&G.]
Halberstadt, Bertram S., (BV) ....'39 '65 C.994 B.A. L.178 J.D. [B.S.Halberstadt]
Halberstadt, Bertram S., P.A., (BV) ....Suite 301 1200 Pennsylvania Avenue
Haley, David J. ....'43 '73 C.714 B.B.A. L.744 J.D. 800 West St.
Haley, DeSales ....'61 '91 C.205 B.A. L.1338 J.D. Mas., Fam. Ct.
Haley, James J., Jr. ....'62 '91 C.309 A.B. L.644 J.D. [Ferrara,H.&B.]
Halkowski, Thomas L. '62 '89 C.436 B.S. L.966 J.D.
(adm. in WI; not adm. in DE) [Fish&R.]
*PRACTICE AREAS: Intellectual Property; Patent Litigation.
Hall, Eugene M. ....'46 '73 C.205 B.S. L.884 J.D. Delaware Dept. of Justice
Hall, James P., (CV) ....'66 '94 C.205 B.A. L.1338 J.D. [Phillips,G.&S.]
*PRACTICE AREAS: Toxic Tort Litigation; Insurance Defense; Personal Injury Litigation; Bankruptcy Litigation; Business Litigation.
Hamberger, Catherine M. ....'70 '98 C.174 B.A. L.1017 J.D. [Ⓐ Potter A.&C.]
*PRACTICE AREAS: Business Law; Mergers and Acquisitions; Joint Ventures; Financial Law; Commercial Law.
Hamby, Jane Obee '59 '89 C.821 B.S. L.128 J.D.
(adm. in VA; not adm. in DE; Pat.) Sr. Coun., E.I. du Pont de Nemours and Company
*RESPONSIBILITIES: Patent Prosecution; Patent Litigation; Intellectual Property Licensing.
Hamby, William H. '57 '84 C.477 B.S.E. L.215 J.D.
(adm. in MI; not adm. in DE; Pat.) Corp. Coun., E.I. du Pont de Nemours and Company
*RESPONSIBILITIES: Intellectual Property.
Hamermesh, Lawrence A., (AV) ......'52 '76 C.311 B.A. L.976 J.D. 4601 Concord Pike.
Hamilton, David Ley, (AV) ....'48 '75 C.311 B.A. L.245 J.D. [Morris,N.A.&T.]
Hammond, Julianne E., (BV) ....'49 '75 C.205 B.A. L.1017 J.D. [Ⓒ Blank R.C.&M.]
*PRACTICE AREAS: Bankruptcy; Real Estate; Commercial Real Estate; State, County and Municipal Government Law; Government.
Hanavan, Taylor W. ....'26 '51 C.262 A.B. L.309 LL.B. One Commerce Center
Handley, Earl L. '32 '60 C.174 B.A. L.273 J.D.
(adm. in DC; not adm. in DE; Pat.) du Pont Co.
Handlon, Joseph Clement ....'74 '99 C.658 B.S. L.1338 J.D. [Ⓐ Ashby&G.]
Hanley, James J., (CV) ....'41 '80 C.999 B.A. L.128 J.D. Dep. Atty. Gen.
Hannigan, Patricia C., (BV) ....'49 '82 C.454 B.A. L.1292 J.D. U.S. Atty. Off.
Hannum, Richard P. S., (BV) ....'44 '74 C.659 B.S. L.1017 J.D. [Phillips,G.&S.]
*PRACTICE AREAS: Civil Litigation; Personal Injury Litigation; Bankruptcy Litigation.

Hanrahan, Michael, (AV) ....'52 '78 C&L.178 B.A., J.D. [Prickett,J.&E.]
*PRACTICE AREAS: Corporate and Partnership Litigation; Corporate and Partnership Law.
Hansen, Christine M., (BV) '64 '92
C.674 A.B. L.659 J.D. [Ⓐ Connolly B.L.&H.] (See Pat. Sect.)
Hanson, Jeanne M. ....'46 '91 C.33 B.A. L.1338 J.D. [J.M.Hanson]
*PRACTICE AREAS: Family Law; Bankruptcy.
Hanson, Shannon Thee ....'64 '91 C.352 B.A. L.893 J.D. 1201 N. Market St.
Hanson, Thomas E., Jr. ....'71 '96 C.665 B.A. L.93 J.D. [Ⓐ Morris,J.H.&W.]
*PRACTICE AREAS: Corporate Litigation; Commercial Litigation.

Hanson, Jeanne M., Attorney At Law, LLC
521 West Street, 19801
Telephone: 302-777-7989 Fax: 302-571-8354 URL: http://www.hanson-law.com
Email: jeanne@hanson-law.com URL: http://www.lawyers.com/hanson-law
Jeanne M. Hanson.
Family Law, Bankruptcy Chapter 7.
See Professional Biographies, WILMINGTON, DELAWARE

Hanssen, John J. '59 '88 C.1490 B.S. L.999
Sr. Coun., E.I. du Pont de Nemours and Company
*RESPONSIBILITIES: Corporate; Commercial.
Harbison, Daniel J. ....'71 '00 C.679 b.S. L.1338 J.D. [Ⓐ Connolly B.L.&H.]
*PRACTICE AREAS: Patent Litigation; Trademark; Copyright; Trade Secret; Antiboycott Compliance.
Harker, James F., (BV) ....'46 '74 C.659 B.A. L.1017 J.D. [Herlihy,H.&K.]
*PRACTICE AREAS: Real Estate; Commercial Law; Civil Litigation.
Harper, Megan N. '69 '98 C.94 B.S. L.1338 J.D.
(adm. in PA; not adm. in DE) [Ⓐ Bifferato,B.&G.]
*PRACTICE AREAS: Bankruptcy; Insurance Defense; Personal Injury.
Harrington, Frank B. '66 '92 C.696 B.A. L.823 J.D.
(adm. in PA; not adm. in DE) [Ⓐ Buchanan I.] (⊙Princeton, NJ)
*PRACTICE AREAS: Litigation.
Harrington, William K. ....'68 '96 C.659 B.S. L.884 J.D. [Ⓐ Duane,M.&H.]
*PRACTICE AREAS: Reorganization; Finance Law.
Harris, David A. ....'71 '97 C.444 B.S. L.575 J.D. [Ⓐ Morris,N.A.&T.]
Harris, Donna L. ....'71 '98 C.776 B.A. L.1338 J.D. [Ⓐ Morris,N.A.&T.]
Harris, John G. '— '97 C.776 B.A. L.1338 J.D.
(adm. in NJ; not adm. in DE) [Ⓐ Reed S.]
*PRACTICE AREAS: Litigation.
Harrison, Walter J., Jr. '23 '53 C.178 A.B. L.564 LL.B.
(adm. in NY; not adm. in DE) 712 Hoper Lane, Sherwood Pk.‡
Harron, Edwin J. ....'68 '95 C.831 B.A. L.1338 J.D. [Ⓐ Young C.S.&T.]
*PRACTICE AREAS: Bankruptcy; General Litigation.
Harron, Susan Graham, (CV) ....'69 '95 C.651 B.A. L.1338 J.D. [Ⓐ White&W.]
Hartman, Brian J., (CV) ....'51 '76 C.205 B.A. L.884 J.D. Disabilities Law Prog.
Hartnett, Deborah I. '50 '84 C.446 B.S. L.831 J.D.
(adm. in PA; not adm. in DE) ICI Americas Inc.

Harvey, Pennington, Cabot, Griffith & Renneisen, Ltd.
1509 Gilpin Avenue, 19806 ⊙
Telephone: 302-428-0719 Fax: 302-777-4682
URL: http://www.harvpenn.com
—Jeffrey K. Martin (Resident). Of Counsel: William M. Aukamp.
General Civil Practice in all Courts. Admiralty, Civil and Criminal Antitrust, Environmental, Negligence, Corporation, Labor, Probate, Real Estate and Insurance Law. Trial and Appellate Practice. Financial Institutions, Transactions, Insolvency and Creditors' Rights.
Philadelphia, Pennsylvania Office: 11 Penn Center, 29th Floor, 1835 Market Street. Telephone: 215-563-4470. Fax: 215-568-1044.
Bryn Mawr, Pennsylvania Office: 26 South Bryn Mawr Avenue, Suite 200. Telephone: 610-527-9200. Fax: 610-527-5402.
Cherry Hill, New Jersey Office: Harvey, Pennington, Cabot, Griffith & Renneisen, P.C. Cherry Tree Corporate Center, Suite 360, 535 Route 38 East. Telephone: 856-317-9122. Fax: 856-317-2215.
New York, N.Y. Office: Park Avenue Atrium, 237 Park Avenue, Twenty-First Floor. Telephone: 212-682-4900. Fax: 212-697-8486.
See Professional Biographies, WILMINGTON, DELAWARE

Hatch, Denison H., Jr., (BV) ....'49 '80 C.188 A.B. L.597 J.D. [Morris,N.A.&T.]
Haubert, William J. ....'66 '91 C.884 B.S. L.188 J.D. [Richards,L.&F.]
*PRACTICE AREAS: Corporate Law; Corporate Transactions.
Hauge, Rhonda A. ....'56 '82 C.446 B.A. L.228 J.D. Coun., Dept. of Jus.
Haverly, Martin ....'67 '93 C.945 B.A. L.1017 J.D. 2 E. 7th St.
Hayes, Joyce Koria ....'45 '71 C.205 B.A. L.705 J.D. Columbia Gas Sys. Serv. Corp.
Hayes, Maureen A '58 '89 C.882 B.A. L.818 J.D.
(adm. in PA; not adm. in DE) 100 Haverford Rd.

Hayes, J. Stoddard, Jr.
(See Gollatz, Griffin & Ewing, P.C., West Chester, Pennsylvania)

Hayman, Selma ....'31 '86 C.33 B.S. L.1338 J.D. 1326 King St.
Hazeltine, William A., (CV) ....'58 '94 C.820 B.Mus. L.608 J.D. [Ⓐ Potter A.&C.]
Heaney, Julia, (BV) ....'66 '92 C.367 B.S. L.178 J.D. [Morris,N.A.&T.]
Hearn, Clifford B., Jr., (BV) ....'37 '62 C.205 B.A. L.893 LL.B. [C.B.Hearn,Jr.] ⊙
*PRACTICE AREAS: General Civil and Trial Practice; Personal Injury; Legislative and Regulatory Practice; Criminal; Family.

Hearn, Clifford B., Jr., P.A., (BV)
606 Market Street Mall, P.O. Box 1205, 19899 ⊙
Telephone: 302-575-0220 Fax: 302-575-0236
Clifford B. Hearn, Jr.
General Civil and Trial Practice. Business, Family, Labor, Personal Injury, Real Estate, Criminal, Wills, Estates and Administrative Law. Commercial and Collection Law. Legislative and Regulatory Practice. Workers Compensation.
Odessa, Delaware Office: Odessa Professional Park, Suite 240. Telephone: 302-378-4827. FAX: 302-378-4946.
See Professional Biographies, WILMINGTON, DELAWARE

Heath, Paul N. ....'68 '98 C.205 B.S. L.1338 J.D. [Ⓐ Richards,L.&F.]
*PRACTICE AREAS: Bankruptcy.
Heckert, Carl W. ....'64 '91 C.205 B.S.B.A. L.1338 J.D. [Ⓐ J.W.Benson]
*PRACTICE AREAS: Civil Litigation; Real Estate; Family Law; Estate Law; Business Law.
Heckler, George B., Jr., (AV) ....'47 '74 C.62 B.A. L.1017 J.D. [Heckler&F.]
*PRACTICE AREAS: Insurance Defense Law; Worker's Compensation Litigation; Asbestos and Toxic Tort Litigation; General Civil and Trial Practice.

Heckler & Frabizzio, (AV) BB
Mellon Bank Center, Suite 1300 919 North Market Street, P.O. Box 128, 19899-0128
Telephone: 302-573-4800 Fax: 302-573-4806
Members of Firm: George B. Heckler, Jr.; Anthony M. Frabizzio; Robert H. Richter; Maria Paris Newill; Richard D. Abrams; William D. Rimmer. Associates: Erik C. Grandell; Daniel P. Bennett; John W. Morgan; Timothy H. Rohs.
General Civil and Trial Practice. Insurance, Worker's Compensation, Negligence and Subrogation Law.
See Professional Biographies, WILMINGTON, DELAWARE

Hedrick, Vincent J. X., II, (CV) ....'64 '89 C.205 B.A. L.902 J.D. [Jacobs&C.]
Heffron, A. Richard '47 '79 C.831 B.S. L.1338 J.D.
(adm. in PA; not adm. in DE) Dir., Dept. of Real Estate & Housing

Hehn, Curtis A. '69 '97 C.112 B.A. L.1292 J.D.
(adm. in PA; not adm. in DE) [Ⓐ Pachulski,S.Z.Y.&J.]
*PRACTICE AREAS: Bankruptcy.
Heiman, Henry A., (BV) .... '42 '68 C.188 B.A. L.976 J.D. [Heiman,A.G.&B.]
*PRACTICE AREAS: Commercial Law; Bankruptcy Law; Commercial Real Estate; Chancery Practice.

Heiman, Aber, Goldlust & Baker, (BV)
First Federal Plaza, 702 King Street, P.O. Box 1675, 19899
Telephone: 302-658-1800 Fax: 302-658-1473
Members: Henry A. Heiman; Gary W. Aber; Perry F. Goldlust; Darrell J. Baker; Donald L. Gouge, Jr.; Susan Carol Over; Susan E. Kaufman.
General Civil and Trial Practice, Corporate, Negligence, Personal Injury, Medical Malpractice, Insurance (Defense) Law, Bankruptcy, Commercial Law, Employment Law, Construction Law, Commercial Real Estate, Labor and Zoning Law.
See Professional Biographies, WILMINGTON, DELAWARE

Heins, Richard D. ....'64 '89 C.724 B.S. L.659 J.D. [Ashby&G.]
Heinz, Peter D. '52 '76 C.264 A.B. L.145 J.D.
(adm. in IL; not adm. in DE) Chf. Coun., BethDearborn Div., Hercules Incorporated
Heiser, David E. '48 '83 C.178 B.S.Ch.E. L.966 J.D.
(adm. in WI; not adm. in DE; Pat.) Corp. Coun., E.I. du Pont de Nemours and Company
*RESPONSIBILITIES: Intellectual Property; Contracts.
Heisman, James D. .... '61 '89 C.354 B.A. L.884 J.D. [Connolly B.L.&H.]
Heister, Marcia E. '56 '81 C.322 B.A. L.229 J.D.
(adm. in PA; not adm. in DE) General Counsel, Concord EFS. Inc.
Helme, George W., IV ....'50 '75 C.311 B.A. L.188 J.D. 1100 N. Market St.
Henderer, Thomas D., (BV) '38 '69
C.821 B.S. L.659 LL.B. V.P. & Coun., Wilmington Trust Company
Hendrickson, John S. '54 '81 C.970 B.A. L.923 J.D.
(adm. in WV; not adm. in DE; Pat.)
Corp. Coun., E.I. du Pont de Nemours and Company
*RESPONSIBILITIES: Patent Filing and Prosecution; Advising; Agreements: Licensing, Joint Development.
Henrich, Christian J. .... '68 '99 C.197 B.A. L.659 J.D. [Ⓐ Morris,N.A.&T.]
Herak, Charles D. .... '34 '63 C.935 B.B.A. L.722 LL.B. Coun., Provident Mut.
Herdeg, John A., (AV) .... '37 '63 C.674 B.A. L.659 LL.B. [Herdeg,D.&D.P.]
*PRACTICE AREAS: Estate Planning; Estate and Gift Taxation; Trust Planning; Trust Administration; Estate Administration.

Herdeg, Du Pont & Dalle Pazze, LLP, (AV)
1201 Orange Street, Suite 500, 19801
Telephone: 302-655-6500
Email: hdd@dellaw.com URL: http://www.lawyers.com/dellaw
Partners: John A. Herdeg; William B. Du Pont, Jr.; James P. Dalle Pazze.
Estate and Tax Planning, Business Succession Planning, Trusts and Estates, Fiduciary Counseling, Wills and Probate, Estate Administration and Private Foundations.
See Professional Biographies, WILMINGTON, DELAWARE

Hering, George C., III, (AV) .....'30 '59 C.216 A.B. L.1017 LL.B. [Ⓒ Morris,J.H.&W.]
*PRACTICE AREAS: Health Care; Public Utilities; Government Lobbying.
Hering, Louis G., (BV) .... '60 '87 C.188 B.A. L.1068 J.D. [Morris,N.A.&T.]
Herlihy, Jerome O. ....'41 '66 C.197 A.B. L.659 LL.B. Assoc. Supr. Ct. J.
Herlihy, Mary Ann Hoff ....'49 '80 C.970 B.A. L.1338 J.D. Mas., Fam. Ct.
Herlihy, Thomas, III, (BV) ....'36 '60 C.197 A.B. L.893 LL.B. [Herlihy,H.&K.]
*PRACTICE AREAS: Wills and Estates; Elder Law; Civil Litigation; Commercial Law.

Herlihy, Harker & Kavanaugh, (BV)
Suite 400, 1300 North Market Street, P.O. Box 1597, 19899-1597
Telephone: 302-654-3111 FAX: 302-652-0226
Email: herharkav@aol.com
Members of Firm: Thomas Herlihy, III; James F. Harker; Gerard P. Kavanaugh, Jr.
General, Civil and Trial Practice, Business and Commercial Law and Transactions, Estate Planning and Administration, Elder Law, Corporate, Personal Injury, Real Estate, Family and Domestic Relations, Delaware Counsel in Federal and State Corporate and Admiralty Litigation.
Approved Attorneys For: Commonwealth Land Title Insurance; Transnation Title Insurance Co.

Herndon, Henry N., Jr., (AV) ....'30 '58 C.500 A.B. L.178 LL.B. [Morris,J.H.&W.]
*PRACTICE AREAS: Litigation; Corporate Law; Alternative Dispute Resolution.
Herndon, Randolph K., (BV) ....'53 '81 C&L.228 B.A., J.D. [Ⓒ Skadden,A.S.M.&F.]
Herring, Kelly A. ....'69 '97 C.1031 B.A. L.188 J.D. [Ⓐ Richards,L.&F.]
*PRACTICE AREAS: Corporate Law; Securities.
Herrmann, Richard K., (AV) .... '47 '71 C&L.823 B.S., J.D. [Blank R.C.&M.]
*PRACTICE AREAS: Internet Law; Technology Contracts; Trade Secrets; Technology Law; Commercial Litigation.
Herrmann, Stephen E., (AV) .... '44 '69 C.674 A.B. L.893 LL.B. [Richards,L.&F.]
Herron, Bruce C., (BV) ....'59 '85 C.893 B.A. L.1017 J.D. [Sawyer,A.&H.]
*PRACTICE AREAS: Insurance Defense; Civil Rights Defense; Defense Litigation; Municipal Law; Trial Practice.
Hershman, Douglas M., (BV) ....'61 '87 C.205 B.A. L.823 J.D. [Bayard]
*PRACTICE AREAS: Real Estate; Zoning, Planning and Land Use; Leases and Leasing; Business Law; Mortgages.
Hess, Peter E., The Law Office of '59 '85
C.893 B.A. L.861 J.D. 3 Mill Road, Suite 303 (⊙Maywood, NJ)
Heyden, Michael C., (CV) '55 '81 C.205 B.S. L.1338 J.D.
(adm. in PA; not adm. in DE) [Heyden,K.&O.]
Heyden, Kania & O'Neill, (CV) ....1201 North King Street
Heyman, Kurt M., (BV) ....'66 '92 C.477 A.B. L.145 J.D. [Bayard]
*PRACTICE AREAS: Corporate Governance Litigation; Partnership and Limited Liability Company Litigation; Securities Litigation; Commercial Litigation; Class and Derivative Actions.
Higgins, James K. '45 '73 C.321 B.A. L.309 J.D.
(adm. in NY; not adm. in DE) Corp. Coun., E.I. du Pont de Nemours and Company
*RESPONSIBILITIES: Antitrust; Commercial Law; International Law.
Higgins, Patrick H. '59 '93 C.446 B.S. L.1338 J.D.
(adm. in PA; not adm. in DE) [Ⓐ Connolly B.L.&H.]
*PRACTICE AREAS: Intellectual Property.
Higgs, W. Victor .... '30 '64 C.050 B.A. L.831 LL.B. 1007 Market St. (Pat.)‡
Highfield, Susan J. '50 '92 C.205 B.A. L.1338 J.D.
(adm. in PA; not adm. in DE) Asst. Coun., WSFS Fin. Corp.
Hilberg, Frank C., Jr. '35 '61 C.893 B.A. L.273 LL.B.
(adm. in VA; not adm. in DE) du Pont Co.‡
Hill, Robert Karl, (BV) ....'63 '89 C.205 B.A. L.1017 J.D. [Seitz,V.&G.]
*PRACTICE AREAS: Litigation; Bankruptcy.
Hiller, Adam '71 '97 C.154 B.A. L.446 J.D.
(adm. in MD; not adm. in DE) [Ⓐ Pepper H.]
*PRACTICE AREAS: Bankruptcy.
Hillis, Edmund M., (BV) ....'49 '80 C.397 B.A. L.1338 J.D. Off. of Pub. Def.
Hillis, Howard F. ....'44 '73 C.397 B.S. L.602 J.D. 1205 North King Street
Hoes, Donald A. ....'32 '60 C.150 B.S. L.273 LL.B. Mng. Coun., du Pont Co. (Pat.)
Hoffman, Abraham ....'08 '32 C.205 B.A. 1215 Shipley Rd.‡
Hoffman, Alan J., (AVⓉ) '48 '73
C.831 B.B.A. L.884 J.D. [Blank R.C.&M.] (⊙Phila., PA)
*PRACTICE AREAS: Trial Practice; Federal Litigation; Civil Litigation; Environmental Litigation; Litigation.
Hoffner, Tara J. ....'71 '96 C.529 B.A. L.1017 J.D. [Ⓐ Richards,L.&F.]
*PRACTICE AREAS: Business Law; Commercial Leasing; Asset-Based Lending; Business Trusts.

Hogan, Daniel K., Law Offices of, (BV) '64 '90 C.896 B.A. L.1338 J.D.
1701 Shallcross Avenue, Suite C, 19806
Telephone: 302-656-7540 Facsimile: 302-656-7604
Email: dkhogan@worldnet.att.net URL: http://www.lawyers.com/dkhogan
Commercial Litigation, Creditor Bankruptcy, Real Estate, General Civil and Trial Practice, Personal Injury, Medical Malpractice, Products Liability and Corporate Law.
See Professional Biographies, WILMINGTON, DELAWARE

Holfeld, Stephen J., (CV) .... '57 '85 C.205 B.A.A.F. L.1338 J.D. [Holfeld&B.]
Holfeld & Becker, (CV) ....1217 King Street (⊙Dover)
Holladay, Louis P. '43 '90 C.381 B. Arch L.1338 J.D.
(adm. in PA; not adm. in DE) Asst. Dep., Off. of the Prothonotary
Hollister, Michael T. '73 '01 C.205 B.A. L.1338 J.D.
(adm. in PA; not adm. in DE) [Ⓐ Tighe,C.&L.]

Hollstein Keating Cattell Johnson & Goldstein, P.C.
One Commerce Center, Suite 730, 12th and Orange Streets, 19801 ⊙
Telephone: 302-884-6700 Fax: 302-573-2507
Email: lmp@hkcjg.com
Lynne M. Parker.
Commercial and Casualty Litigation, Maritime Law, Products Liability.
Philadelphia, Pennsylvania Office: 1608 Walnut Street, Suite 1602, 19103. Telephone: 215-893-9488. Fax: 215-893-9480. Email: JFJ@HKCJG.com.
Marlton, New Jersey Office: Willow Ridge Executive Office Park, 750 Route 73 South, Suite 301, 08053. Telephone: 856-810-8860. Fax: 856-810-8861.
See Professional Biographies, WILMINGTON, DELAWARE

Holly, Lacy E., III .... '65 '91 C.999 B.S. L.945 J.D. [Houghton,H.&G.]
Holly, Timothy M. .... '74 '01 C.275 B.A. [Ⓐ Potter A.&C.]
*PRACTICE AREAS: Labor and Employment.
Holmes, Vera M. .... '— '89 C.656 B.S. L.1338 J.D. Coun., Hercules Inc.
Holt, Scott A. ....'62 '95 C.831 B.A. L.1338 J.D. [Ⓐ Young C.S.&T.]
*PRACTICE AREAS: Employment Law; Labor Law; Wage and Hour Law.
Holzman, James L., (AV) .... '49 '73 C.362 B.A. L.260 J.D. [Prickett,J.&E.]
*PRACTICE AREAS: Corporate Law and Litigation; Federal Litigation.
Hood, Michael J., (CV) .... '56 '82 C.436 B.A. L.1338 J.D. [Tigani&H.]
*PRACTICE AREAS: Civil Litigation; Criminal Law; Personal Injury.
Horn, Joanne L. '39 '81 C.205 B.S. L.1338 J.D.
Sr. Intell. Prop. Coun., Montell N. Amer. Inc. (Pat.)
Horn, Margaret A. '62 '88 L.884 J.D.
(adm. in PA; not adm. in DE; Pat.) du Pont Co.
Hornbeck, Sean K. ....'69 '97 C.867 B.A. L.982 J.D. One Rodney Square
Horowitz, Alan B. '67 '93 C.1349 B.A. L.904 J.D.
(adm. in NJ; not adm. in DE) Sr. Coun., Astrazeneca Pharm. LP
*RESPONSIBILITIES: Environmental Compliance and Litigation; Occupational Safety and Health Compliance.
Horwitz, Richard L., (BV) .... '57 '83 C.31 B.A. L.228 J.D. [Potter A.&C.]
Houghton, Mark, (BV) .... '54 '88 C.205 B.S. L.1049 J.D. [Freebery&H.]
Houghton, Michael, (BV) ....'56 '82 C&L.893 B.A., J.D. [Morris,N.A.&T.]
Houghton, Vivian A., (BV) .... '43 '80 C.205 B.A. L.1338 J.D. [Houghton,H.&G.]
Houghton, Holly & Gray, LLP, (BV) ....800 West St., 2nd Fl.
Houseal, Timothy Jay, (BV) ....'64 '90 C.999 B.A. L.1017 J.D. [Young C.S.&T.]
*PRACTICE AREAS: Environmental Law; Environmental Litigation; Insurance Coverage; Complex Litigation; Admiralty and Maritime Law.
Howard, Janine N. .... '70 '95 C.831 B.A. L.1338 J.D. [Ⓐ K.J.Laffey]
*PRACTICE AREAS: Family Law; Domestic Violence.
Howard, Neal J., (AV) '47 '74 C.659 B.A. L.309 J.D.
(adm. in NY; not adm. in DE) V.P. & Chf. Admin. Offr., Glenmede Trust Co.
Hubbard, Richard W., (CV) .... '52 '86 C&L.966 B.A., J.D. Dep. Atty. Gen.
Huber, Robert V. ....'17 '47 C.31 A.B. L.831 LL.B. 500 Bellevue Rd.‡

Hudson, Bruce L., Law Office of, (BV) '45 '78 C.205 B.S. L.1338 J.D.
300 Delaware Avenue, Suite 1130, 19801
Telephone: 302-656-9850 Fax: 302-656-9836
Email: delaw@aol.com URL: http://www.lawyers.com/delaw
***PRACTICE AREAS: Personal Injury; Negligence; Professional Liability; Products Liability; Premises Liability.**
Personal Injury Litigation, Medical/Dental Malpractice, Products Liability.
See Professional Biographies, WILMINGTON, DELAWARE

Huffman, J. Andrew ....'70 '95 C.1034 B.S.E.E. L.902 J.D. [Ⓐ Fish&R.]
Huggett, James E. .... '72 '00 C.646 B.A. L.831 J.D. [Ⓐ Klehr,H.H.B.&E.]
*PRACTICE AREAS: Bankruptcy; Creditors Rights; Insolvency; Reorganization.
Huggett, Laura H. '63 '88 C&L.1204 B.A., J.D.
(adm. in TN; not adm. in DE) [E.I. d.d.]
*RESPONSIBILITIES: Labor and Employment; Litigation.
Hughes, Thomas G., (BV) .... '32 '59 C&L.966 B.S., LL.B. [Ⓒ Hughes,S.&G.]
Hughes, Sisk & Glancy, P.A., (BV) ....522 Greenhill Ave.
Hume, Larry J. '56 '00 C.36 B.S.E.E. L.1209 J.D.
(adm. in VA; not adm. in DE; See Pat. Sect.) [Ⓐ Connolly B.L.&H.]
*PRACTICE AREAS: Patent; Trademark; Litigation Support; Copyright; Trade Secret.
Hunt, E. Leigh ....'38 '66 C&L.790 B.S.Ch.E., J.D. 1809 Wyckwood Ct. (Pat.)
Hunt, Thomas R., Jr., (AV) .... '48 '72 C.401 B.A. L.658 J.D. [Morris,N.A.&T.]
Hunt, Thomas R., Sr., (AV) .... '19 '47 C.401 A.B. L.309 LL.B. 2404 Grant Ave.‡
Hunter, Jeffrey W. .... '67 '95 C.645 B.S. L.1017 J.D. 1220 North Market St.
Huntley, Donald W. .... '42 '67 C&L.339 B.S., J.D. [Huntley&Assoc.] (See Pat. Sect.)
*PRACTICE AREAS: Intellectual Property Law; Patent, Trademark and Copyright Law.

Huntley & Associates
1105 North Market Street, P.O. Box 948, 19899-0948
Telephone: 302-426-0610 Facsimile: 302-426-0612
URL: http://www.monopolize.com
Donald W. Huntley. Associates: Mark C. Gregory; Brian A. Gomez. Of Counsel: Theodore C. Gregory (Not admitted in DE).
Intellectual Property; Patent, Trademark and Copyright Law.
See Professional Biographies, WILMINGTON, DELAWARE

Hurd, S. Mark .... '67 '94 C&L.276 B.S.F.S., J.D. [Morris,N.A.&T.]
Hurford, Mark T. .... '69 '94 C.347 B.A. L.942 J.D. [Ⓐ Swartz,C.&D.]
*PRACTICE AREAS: Personal Injury Defense; Worker's Compensation Defense.
Hurley, Joseph A., (AV) .... '43 '70 C.205 B.S. L.1017 J.D. [J.A.Hurley]
*PRACTICE AREAS: Criminal Law.
Hurley, Joseph P., Jr., (AV) .... '50 '77 Dep. Atty. Gen.

Hurley, Joseph A., P.A., (AV) BR
1215 King Street, 19801
Telephone: 302-658-8980 Fax: 302-658-8987
Joseph A. Hurley.
Criminal Trial Practice Only.
See Professional Biographies, WILMINGTON, DELAWARE

Huston, Joseph H., Jr., (AVⓉ) '49 '75
C.645 B.A. L.884 J.D. [Stevens&L.] (⊙Wayne, PA)
*PRACTICE AREAS: Bankruptcy; CHII; Commercial Workouts; International Bankruptcy.
Hutchinson, Shauneen Cruise, (BV) .... '42 '82 C.945 A.B. L.659 J.D. 132 Ponds Ln.
Hutz, R. Eric, (CV) .... '62 '88 C.401 B.A. L.273 J.D. [Connolly B.L.&H.]

Hutz, Rudolf E., (AV) '38 '64 C.674 A.B. L.276 J.D. [Connolly B.L.&H.] (See Pat. Sect.)
Iler, Arthur W. .... '61 '86 C.347 B.S. L.383 J.D. Columbia Gas Sys. Serv. Corp.
Inden, Arthur, (AV) '41 '65 C.205 A.B. L.1017 LL.B. 1225 North King Street, 6th Floor
Ingersoll, Josy W., (BV) .... '42 '80 C.705 B.A. L.831 J.D. [Young C.S.&T.]
*PRACTICE AREAS: Corporate Law; Corporate Litigation; Business Law; Patent Litigation; Trademark Litigation.
Inskip, Gregory A., (BV) .... '52 '77 C.976 B.A. L.309 J.D. [Potter A.&C.]
Iobst, Frederick William, (AV) .... '45 '72 C.228 B.A. L.884 J.D. [Young C.S.&T.]
*PRACTICE AREAS: Personal Injury; Litigation; Insurance; Products Liability; Construction Law.
Iorii, Regina A., (BV) .... '61 '87 C.205 B.S. L.1338 J.D. [Ashby&G.]

Ippoliti, Michael R., (CV) '61 '87 C.831 B.A. L.1338 J.D.
824 Market Street, Suite 412, P.O. Box 2284, 19899-2284
Telephone: 302-428-1400 Fax: 302-655-6827
URL: http://www.lawyers.com/ippolitilaw
***PRACTICE AREAS: Litigation; Workers Compensation; Employment Law.**
Litigation, Workers Compensation, Employment Law, Personal Injury.
See Professional Biographies, WILMINGTON, DELAWARE

Ippolito, Natalie M. .... '— '99 C&L.1338 B.A., J.D. [Ⓐ Bailey&W.]
Isaacs, Michael J., (BV) .... '60 '86 C.1369 B.S. L.1049 J.D. [Agostini,L.I.&K.]
*PRACTICE AREAS: Personal Injury; Real Estate.
Ishak, April Caso, (BV) .... '63 '89 C.705 B.A. L.1292 J.D. [Ⓒ Prickett,J.&E.]
*PRACTICE AREAS: Corporate Law; Litigation.
Isken, Donald Nelson, (BV) .... '53 '78 C.105 B.A. L.472 J.D. [Morris,N.A.&T.]
Ittel, Kathleen P. '— '96 C.473 B.S. L.1338 J.D. (adm. in PA; not adm. in DE) [Ⓐ Richards,L.&F.]
*PRACTICE AREAS: Real Estate.
Jackson, Roy V. '18 '48 C.05 B.A. L.012 B.C.L. (adm. in QU; not adm. in DE; Pat.) 15 Paladin Dr.
Jacobs, Jack B. .... '42 '68 C.145 A.B. L.309 LL.B. V. Chanc., Ct. of Chan.
Jacobs, Robert, (BV) .... '41 '68 C.563 B.S.Ch.E. L.831 J.D. [Jacobs&C.] (See Pat. Sect.)
*PRACTICE AREAS: Product Liability; Asbestos Litigation; Medical Malpractice; Business Litigation; Patent Law.

Jacobs & Crumplar, P.A., (BV)
2 East 7th Street, P.O. Box 1271, 19899
Telephone: 1-800-355-1818; 302-656-5445 FAX: 302-656-5875
Email: jcinbox@jacobsandcrumplar.com URL: http://www.jacobsandcrumplar.com
Robert Jacobs; Thomas C. Crumplar; Marla Rosoff Eskin; Elizabeth B. Lewis; Vincent J. X. Hedrick, II.
Personal Injury, Automobile Accidents, Medical Malpractice, Social Security Disability, Products Liability and Toxic Substance, Worker Compensation, Business Litigation, Bankruptcy, Patent and Copyright Law.
See Professional Biographies, WILMINGTON, DELAWARE

James, John E., (BV) .... '50 '79 C.198 A.B. L.575 J.D. [Potter A.&C.]
James-Roberts, Brenda .... '57 '86 C.4 B.S. L.1019 J.D. Asst. City Solr.
Jameson, Bruce E., (CV) .... '64 '91 C&L.665 B.A., J.D. [Prickett,J.&E.]
*PRACTICE AREAS: Corporate Law; Corporate and Commercial Litigation.
Jamison, Peter O., III, (CV) .... '58 '86 C.205 B.A. L.276 J.D. Dep. Atty. Gen.
Jarnholm, Arne R. '51 '81 C.339 B.S. L.365 J.D. (adm. in IL; not adm. in DE; Pat.) Sr. Coun., E.I. du Pont de Nemours and Company
*RESPONSIBILITIES: Patents.
Jarvis, Geoffrey C. .... '58 '85 C.188 B.A. L.309 J.D. [Ⓒ Grant&E.]
Jefferson, Andrew McK., (CV) .... '63 '93 C.205 B.A. L.1338 J.D. P.O. Box 7540
Jenkins, Cathy A., (CV) .... '64 '90 C.831 B.A. L.276 J.D. Dep. Atty. Gen.
Jenkins, David A., (BV) .... '53 '78 C.659 B.A. L.145 J.D. [Smith,K.&F.]
*PRACTICE AREAS: Litigation; Corporate Law.
Jenkins, Patricia Harris '45 '85 C.645 B.S. L.1338 J.D. (adm. in PA; not adm. in DE) Assoc. Prof., Temple Univ.
Jenkins, Stephen E., (BV) .... '54 '82 C&L.276 A.B., J.D. [Ashby&G.]
Jennings, Kathleen M., (AV) .... '53 '78 C.205 B.A. L.884 J.D. [Oberly&J.]
*PRACTICE AREAS: Criminal Law; Personal Injury; General Civil Litigation; Business.
Jensen, Scott J., (CV) .... '69 '95 C.846 B.A. L.1338 J.D. 222 Delaware Ave. Ste. 1200
Johnson, Ann Marie, (BV) .... '58 '84 C.104 B.A. L.184 J.D. Dep. Atty. Gen.
Johnson, Daniel P., (BV) .... '58 '87 C.205 B.S. L.1338 J.D. [Young C.S.&T.]
*PRACTICE AREAS: Real Estate Law; Zoning Law; Landlord Tenant; General Business.
Johnson, Edmond D., (BV) .... '41 '83 C.309 B.A. L.260 J.D. [Bayard]
*PRACTICE AREAS: Complex Commercial and Corporate Litigation; Class Action; Derivatives; Patent Matters.
Johnson, Guy V. '48 '81 C.472 B.S.C.E. L.1338 J.D. (adm. in PA; not adm. in DE) Corp. Coun., E.I. du Pont de Nemours and Company
*RESPONSIBILITIES: Environmental.
Johnson, J. Michael .... '52 '77 C.216 B.A. L.884 J.D. [Gollatz,G.&E.] (⊙Phila., PA)
Johnston, Andrew M., (BV) .... '57 '82 C.385 A.B. L.597 J.D. [Morris,N.A.&T.]
Johnston, John F., (AV) .... '46 '77 C.597 B.A. L.659 J.D. [Morris,N.A.&T.]
Johnston, Mary Miller, (BV) .... '57 '84 C.967 B.M. L.902 J.D. 3301 Coachman Rd.‡
Johnston, Patrick J. '55 '80 C.728 A.B. L.145 J.D. (adm. in PA; not adm. in DE) 4601 Concord Pike
Johnston, William D., (BV) .... '57 '82 C.165 A.B. L.902 J.D. [Young C.S.&T.]
*PRACTICE AREAS: Business Litigation; Chancery Practice; Mergers and Acquisitions; Limited Partnerships.
Jones, Christopher C. .... '67 '95 C.575 B.S. L.1338 J.D. [Ⓐ Young C.S.&T.]
*PRACTICE AREAS: Taxation; State Taxation; Local Taxation; Business Law; Corporate Law.
Jones, Judith M. .... '68 '96 C.1369 B.A. L.1338 J.D. [Ⓐ Connolly B.L.&H.]
Jones, Kenneth A. '56 '81 C.645 B.A. L.228 J.D. (adm. in PA; not adm. in DE) Corp. Coun., E.I. du Pont de Nemours and Company
*RESPONSIBILITIES: Commercial Transactions; Antitrust; Computer Law.
Jones, Laura Davis, (AV) ..... '61 '86 C.205 B.S.B.A. L.1017 J.D. [Pachulski,S.Z.Y.&J.]
*PRACTICE AREAS: Bankruptcy Chapter 11; Bankruptcy Litigation; Commercial Workouts; International Insolvency; Out of Court Debt Restructuring.
Jones, Richard I. G., (AV) '38 '64 C.976 B.A. L.659 LL.B. [Prickett,J.&E.] (⊙Kennett Square, PA)
*PRACTICE AREAS: Medical Malpractice Litigation; Personal Injury Litigation; Equine Law.
Jones, Richard I. G., Jr., (BV) .... '64 '94 C.205 B.S. L.338 J.D. [Ⓐ Ashby&G.]
Jordan, Kent A., (BV) '57 '84 C.101 B.A. L.276 J.D. Vice President & General Counsel, CSC - The United States Corporation
Joseph, Michael B., (AV) .... '50 '76 C.705 A.B. L.1338 J.D. [Ferry&J.]
*PRACTICE AREAS: Bankruptcy Law; Commercial Law.
Joseph, Pamela Davis .... '63 '90 C.893 B.A. L.1338 J.D. 800 King St.
Joung, J. Kenneth '69 '94 C.197 A.B. L.597 J.D. (adm. in IL; not adm. in DE; Pat.) Coun., E.I. du Pont de Nemours and Company
*RESPONSIBILITIES: Intellectual Property.
Juers, John W. '64 '91 C.645 B.S. L.107 J.D. (adm. in NY; not adm. in DE) Asst. V.P. & Coun., Wilmington Trust Co.
Julian, J. R., (AV) .... '43 '71 C.30 B.A. L.128 J.D. [J.R.Julian]
*PRACTICE AREAS: Civil Litigation; Negligence; Insurance; Workers Compensation; Products Liability.
Julian, Jessica L. .... '72 '98 C.205 B.A. L.1338 J.D. [Ⓐ Marshall,D.W.C.&G.]
*PRACTICE AREAS: Workers Compensation.

Julian, J. R., P.A., (AV)
Suite 1001, 824 Market Street Mall, P.O. Box 2171, 19899-2171
Telephone: 302-658-6700 Fax: 302-658-6708
J. R. Julian; Samantha P. Zazzo (Not admitted in DE); Jill Spevack DiSciullo (Not admitted in DE).
General Civil Practice. Personal Injury, Negligence and Tort Law. Insurance Litigation. Workers Compensation Defense, Products Liability, Toxic Substances Litigation, Real Estate, Asbestos Defense.
See Professional Biographies, WILMINGTON, DELAWARE

Kafader, Edward F., (BV) .... '49 '76 C.205 B.S. L.884 J.D. [Ⓐ Ferry&J.]
*PRACTICE AREAS: Insurance Defense; Wills; Estate Planning; Personal Injury; Government Affairs.
Kairis, John C., (CV) .... '62 '87 C.602 B.A. L.608 J.D. [Ⓐ Grant&E.]
Kaiser, Cynthia Deans, (BV) .... '59 '87 C.228 B.S.E. L.205 J.D. [Richards,L.&F.]
*PRACTICE AREAS: Asset Based Lending; Business Trusts; Securities Regulation Law (Blue Sky Law); Business Law; Commercial Law.
Kaminski, Cassandra Faline .... '58 '82 C.205 B.S. L.1017 J.D. [Young C.S.&T.]
*PRACTICE AREAS: Workers Compensation.
Kanaga, Lynn Thomas, (BV) .... '53 '82 2301 Penn. Ave.
Kane, John F. '45 '71 C.945 B.A. L.273 J.D. (adm. in VA; not adm. in DE) Corp. Coun., E.I. du Pont de Nemours and Company
Kane, Karen A. .... '55 '81 C.216 B.A. L.1338 J.D. 704 Abbey Rd.
Kania, Paul J., (CV) .... '49 '81 C.834 B.A. L.1338 J.D. [Heyden,K.&O.]
Kapalka, Robert J. '54 '86 C.884 B.S.M.E. L.1338 J.D. (adm. in PA; not adm. in DE; Pat.) Patent Atty., Tyco Electronics Corp.
Kaplan, Gary H., (BV) .... '54 '79 C.21 B.A. L.831 J.D. [Goldfein&H.]
Kaplit, Michael '39 '84 C.453 B.S. L.1338 J.D. (adm. in PA; not adm. in DE) du Pont Co.
Kappes, R. Scott, (CV) .... '66 '95 C.445 B.S. L.1338 J.D. [Schmittinger&R.]
*PRACTICE AREAS: Workers Compensation; Personal Injury; Employment Law.
Kapsalis, Sotiere S., (CV) .... '33 '60 C.645 B.A. L.1017 LL.B. 1216 King St.
Kasprzak, Brian L. .... '68 '99 C.1391 B.A. L.1339 J.D. [Ⓐ Marks,O.O.&C.]
Kassab Archbold & O'Brien, L.L.P. ...... 1326 King Street (⊙Wildwood, NJ; Media, PA)
Katz, Elliott A. '45 '71 C.696 B.S. L.276 J.D. (adm. in VA; not adm. in DE) Corp. Coun., E.I. du Pont de Nemours and Company
Katzenstein, Robert J., (AV) .... '51 '76 C.976 B.A. L.659 J.D. [Smith,K.&F.]
*PRACTICE AREAS: Litigation.
Kaufman, Susan E. .... '69 '95 C.205 B.S. L.884 J.D. [Heiman,A.G.&B.]
*PRACTICE AREAS: General Civil Practice; Bankruptcy; Contracts; Personal Injury; Real Estate.
Kavanaugh, Gerard P., Jr., (BV) ...... '43 '75 C.025 A.B. L.1017 J.D. [Herlihy,H.&K.]
*PRACTICE AREAS: Divorce Law; Family Law; Municipal Law.
Kavanaugh, Gerard P., Sr. .... '16 '41 C.025 A.B. L.276 J.D. [Ⓒ Biggs&B.]
Kavanaugh, Timothy S. '49 '80 C.945 B.A. L.1338 LL.B. (adm. in PA; not adm. in DE) Chf. Coun., Pulp & Paper Div., Hercules Chem. Specialties Co.
Keehan, Michael B. .... '35 '67 C.560 B.S. L.273 LL.B. [Ⓒ Potter A.&C.] (Pat.)
Keenan, Bryan E., (BV) .... '54 '79 C&L.823 B.S., J.D. [Ⓐ Gordon,F.&M.]
*PRACTICE AREAS: Taxation; Business Organization; Business Transactions; Charitable Trusts and Foundations.
Keener, Carmella Piscopo, (CV) .... '63 '88 C.390 B.A. L.705 J.D. [Rosenthal,M.G.&G.]
*PRACTICE AREAS: Insurance Coverage; Corporate Litigation; Securities Litigation; Business Litigation; Civil Litigation.
Keil, Charles K. .... '33 '61 C&L.659 B.S., J.D. Ret. Fam. Ct. J.
Keil, Ralph F., (CV) .... '30 '55 C.205 B.A. L.1017 J.D. 31 B Trolley Sq.
Keiter, John W. '47 '76 C.945 B.A. L.94 J.D. (adm. in MA; not adm. in DE) Corp. Coun., E.I. du Pont de Nemours and Company
*RESPONSIBILITIES: Commercial Law; Antitrust; Mergers and Acquisitions.
Kelleher, Daniel F., (BV) .... '35 '62 C.743 A.B. L.276 LL.B. [Trzuskowski,K.K.&P.]
*PRACTICE AREAS: Family Law; Litigation.
Kelleher, James F., (CV) .... '27 '53 C.397 B.A. L.128 LL.B. Dep. Atty. Gen.
Kelleher, Jennifer A. L. '— '97 C.205 B.A. L.1338 J.D. (adm. in MD; not adm. in DE) [Ⓐ Reed S.]
*PRACTICE AREAS: Litigation.
Kelley, Bernard J., (AV) .... '63 '89 C.821 B.A. L.659 J.D. [Richards,L.&F.]
*PRACTICE AREAS: Partnership Law; Limited Liability Company Law; Business Trust Law; Banking Law.
Kelley, Kathleen A. .... '72 '00 C.893 B.A. L.902 J.D. [Ⓐ Richards,L.&F.]

Kelley, Jasons, McGuire & Spinelli, L.L.P., (AV)
800 Delaware Avenue, P.O. Box 194, 19899 ⊙
Telephone: 302-652-8560 Fax: 302-652-8405
Email: adellaporta@kjms.com URL: http://www.KJMS.com
Armand J. Della Porta, Jr.
Civil Litigation, Personal Injury, Medical Malpractice Law, Collection Law, Products Liability Law, Environmental Law, Insurance Law, Reinsurance Law, Criminal Law, Commercial Law, Probate and Trust Law.
Philadelphia, Pennsylvania Office: Centre Square West, Suite 1500, 1500 Market Street, 19102. Telephone: 215-854-0658. Fax: 215-854-8434.
Marlton, New Jersey Office: One Greentree Centre, Suite 201, 08053. Telephone: 856-988-5543. Fax: 856-988-9165.
See Professional Biographies, WILMINGTON, DELAWARE

Kelly, Deanna H., (BV) '57 '84 C.67 B.A. L.1017 J.D. Sr. Coun., Montell N. Amer. Inc.
Kelly, Joseph C. '41 '67 C&L.884 B.S.Ec., J.D. Asst. Gen. Coun., Astrazeneca Pharm. LP
*RESPONSIBILITIES: Litigation; Environmental.
Kelly, Kathryn A. .... '66 '91 C.205 B.A. L.276 J.D. 800 King St.
Kelly, Michael P., (BV) .... '56 '84 C.178 B.A. L.1017 J.D. [McCarter&E.]
*PRACTICE AREAS: Environmental Law; Complex Civil Litigation; Personal Injury; Bankruptcy; Criminal Defense.
Kelly, Patricia L. '— '96 C.223 B.S. L.831 J.D. (adm. in PA; not adm. in DE) Sr. Coun., E.I. du Pont de Nemours and Company
*RESPONSIBILITIES: Patents; Intellectual Property.
Kelsey, Michael D., (BV) '53 '83 C.205 B.A. L.1338 J.D. Chf. Compl. Offr., PNC Bk., Del.‡
Kemmer, Kyle .... '70 '97 C.645 B.A. L.1338 J.D. [Ⓐ Schmittinger&R.] (⊙Dover)
*PRACTICE AREAS: Workers Compensation; Personal Injury.
Kennedy, Charles J., (CV) .... '48 '76 C.602 B.A. L.425 J.D. 902 Philadelphia Pike
Kenney, Frederic H. ...... '44 '78 C.205 B.A. L.1338 J.D. Chf. Mas. & Comr., Family Ct.
Kenny, Richard J., Jr. '58 '86 C&L.884 B. S., J.D. (adm. in PA; not adm. in DE) Asst. Gen. Coun., Astrazeneca Pharm. LP (⊙Wayne, PA)
*RESPONSIBILITIES: General/Corporate; Health/Medical; Contracts.

Kent & McBride, P.C.
Buckner, 1308 Delaware Avenue, P.O. Box 2165 ⊙
Telephone: 302-777-5477 Fax: 302-429-8600
George T. Lees, III.
General Civil Practice in State and Federal Courts of Pennsylvania, Delaware and New Jersey. Arson and Insurance Fraud, Property, Admiralty and Maritime Law, Insurance Law, Casualty, Products Liability, Medical Malpractice, Toxic Tort Litigation, Subrogation, Motor Vehicle Law, Commercial Premises.
Cherry Hill, New Jersey Office: 1040 Kings Highway North, Suite 403, 08034. Telephone: 856-667-3113. Fax: 856-667-4003.

(This Listing Continued)

Kent & McBride, P.C. (Continued)

Philadelphia, Pennsylvania Office: Two Logan Square, Suite 600, 18th and Arch Streets. Telephone: 215-568-1800. Fax: 215-568-1830.

See Professional Biographies, WILMINGTON, DELAWARE

Kenton, Glenn C., (BV) .... '43 '69 C.821 A.B. L.276 J.D. [Richards,L.&F.]
*PRACTICE AREAS: Administrative Law; Insurance; Communications Law; Government Relations; Derivative Products.

Kerber, Andrew G. .... '59 '84 C.861 B.A. L.575 J.D. [Ⓒ Stradley R.S.&Y.]

Kerr, Felice Glennon, (BV) ....'64 '89 C.884 B.A. L.818 J.D. [Ⓐ Bayard] (⊙Wilmington)
*PRACTICE AREAS: Family Law; Personal Injury; Real Estate; Family Mediation; Juvenile Law.

Kerr, Felice Glennon, (BV) '64 '89 C.884 B.A. L.818 J.D. 1225 King Street (⊙Wilmington)

Kessler, Frederick S., (CV) '42 '76 C.205 B.S. L.1338 J.D. V.P. & Gen. Coun., Associates Intl., Inc.

Keuler, Richard A., Jr. '— '99 C.674 A.B. L.276 J.D. (adm. in NJ; not adm. in DE) [Ⓐ Reed S.]
*PRACTICE AREAS: Bankruptcy.

Keyes, T. Richard, III ....'57 '88 C.205 B.S. L.1338 J.D. PFPC, Inc.

Kilcrease, Dawn B. ....'66 '94 C.1111 B.A. L.831 J.D. [Stewart&Assoc.] ⊙
*PRACTICE AREAS: Corporate Law; Commercial Law.

Killheffer, Theodore F. '38 '63 C.205 B.A. L.659 J.D. (adm. in PA; not adm. in DE) Assoc. Gen. Coun. & Chf. Coun., Antitrust, E.I. du Pont de Nemours & Co.
*RESPONSIBILITIES: Antitrust; Internet Law; International Trade.

Killian, Rosemary K., (BV) ....'42 '82 C.645 B.A. L.1338 J.D. Dep. Atty. Gen.

Kimmel, Edw. R. .... '21 '48 C.674 A.B. L.309 LL.B. 15 Wood Rd.‡

Kimmel, Morton Richard, (AV) ....'40 '65 C.831 A.B. L.273 J.D. [Kimmel,C.R.&P.] ⊙
*PRACTICE AREAS: General and Civil Trial Practice; Insurance; Negligence; Workers Compensation; Construction Accidents.

Kimmel, Carter, Roman & Peltz, P.A., (AV) BR
12th Floor, 913 Market Street, P.O. Box 272, 19899-0272 ⊙
Telephone: 302-571-0800 Fax: 302-571-8155
Morton Richard Kimmel; Edward B. Carter, Jr.; Thomas J. Roman; William R. Peltz; Michael D. Bednash; Matthew M. Bartkowski;—William R. Baker, Jr.
General Civil and Trial Practice in all Courts. Insurance, Negligence, Construction Accidents, Workers Compensation. Federal Practice.
References: Wilmington Trust Co.; PNC Bank.
Newark, Delaware Office: 1400 Peoples Plaza, Suite 100, 19702. Telephone: 302-838-5970.

See Professional Biographies, WILMINGTON, DELAWARE

King, Karen K. '— '89 C.575 B.A. L.329 J.D. (adm. in PA; not adm. in DE) Corp. Coun., E.I. du Pont de Nemours and Company
*RESPONSIBILITIES: Patents.

Kingery, Clark C. ....'52 '78 C.367 B.A. L.464 J.D. [C.C.Kingery]

Kingery, Clark C., P.A. ....914 North Walnut Street

Kinnard, Michael B. '57 '85 C&L.838 B.A., J.D. (adm. in TN; not adm. in DE) 2200 Concord Pike

Kinney, Judith M. .... '58 '97 C.705 B.A. L.831 J.D. Off. of U.S. Atty.

Kipp, James F., (AV) ....'37 '63 C.728 B.S. L.884 LL.B. [Trzuskowski,K.K.&P.]
*PRACTICE AREAS: Personal Injury; Tort Litigation.

Kirk, Richard D., (AV) .... '53 '78 C.276 A.B. L.893 J.D. [Morris,J.H.&W.]
*PRACTICE AREAS: General Litigation; Environmental Law; Alcoholic Beverages; Licensing and Regulation.

Kirk, William E., III, (BV) '50 '75 C.728 B.A. L.893 J.D. V.P., Gen. Coun. & Corp. Secy., Blue Cross Blue Shield of Del., Inc.

Kirk, William E., Jr. ....'21 '49 C.516 B.S. L.276 J.D. 302 Brockton Rd.‡

Kirkpatrick, Andrew B., Jr., (AV) '29 '54 C.198 B.S. L.309 LL.B. [Ⓒ Morris,N.A.&T.]

Kirsh, Peter S. .... '67 '93 C.823 B.S. L.1338 J.D. 1607 W. 9th St.

Kita, Gerald K. '41 '67 C.339 B.S. L.904 J.D. (adm. in DC; not adm. in DE; Pat.) 14 Steeplechase Rd.

Kittila, Theodore Allan '73 '00 C.205 B.A. L.494 J.D. 10th and King St., Daniel L. Hermann Courthouse

Kittredge, Amelia C. '49 '75 C.178 B.A. L.276 J.D. (adm. in NY; not adm. in DE) [E.I. d.d.]
*RESPONSIBILITIES: Toxic Torts; Product Liability Litigation.

Klayman, Barry M., (AVⓉ) .... '52 '77 C.178 B.A. L.309 J.D. [Wolf,B.S.&S-C.]
*PRACTICE AREAS: Commercial Litigation; Environmental Litigation; Toxic Torts Law.

Klehr, Harrison, Harvey, Branzburg & Ellers LLP, (BV)
Mellon Bank Center, 919 Market Street, Suite 1000, 19801 ⊙
Telephone: 302-426-1189 Fax: 302-426-9193
Email: mail@klehr.com URL: http://www.klehr.com
Members of Firm: Joanne B. Wills; David S. Eagle; Richard M. Beck; Steven K. Kortanek (Resident).
Associates: Stephanie A. Fox; James E. Huggett; Denise Seastone Kraft.
Banking, Corporate, Tax, Construction, Securities, Commercial, Probate, Employment, Estate Planning, Real Estate, Bankruptcy and Creditors Rights Law. Intellectual Property, General Civil Trial Practice in all Courts. Commercial Profit Sharing and Employee Benefit Law.
Philadelphia, Pennsylvania Office: 260 South Broad Street, Suite 400. Telephone: 215-568-6060. Fax: 215-568-6603.
Cherry Hill, New Jersey Office: LibertyView - Suite 510, 457 Haddonfield Road. Telephone: 856-486-7900. Fax: 856-486-4875.

See Professional Biographies, WILMINGTON, DELAWARE

Klein, Daniel L., (AV) ....'46 '72 C.659 B.S.Ec. L.665 J.D. [Richards,L.&F.]
*PRACTICE AREAS: Real Estate Law; Real Estate Finance; Privatization; Land Use.

Klett Rooney Lieber & Schorling, A Professional Corporation, (AV)
The Brandywine Building, 1000 West Street, Suite 1410, 19801 ⊙
Telephone: 302-552-4200 FAX: 302-552-4295
URL: http://www.klettrooney.com
Shareholders: Mary F. Caloway; Teresa K. D. Currier; Alfred J. D'Angelo, Jr.; Richard A. Forsten; Mark J. Gundersen; Adam G. Landis; William E. Manning; Bonnie L. Metz; Daniel B. Rath.
Associates: Rebecca L. Butcher; Richard S. Cobb; Frances Gauthier; Francis X. Gorman; Kathleen P. Makowski; Eric L. Schnabel; Katherine Randolph Witherspoon.
General Practice: Business Immigration; Creditor's Rights and Bankruptcy; Employee Benefits - ERISA; Environmental Law; Estate Planning and Administration; Finance; Government Affairs; Health Care; Labor and Employment; Litigation; Occupational Safety and Health; Mine Safety and Health; Public Finance; Railway Labor Act ; Real Estate; Securities Law; Taxation; Technology Law.
Pittsburgh, Pennsylvania Office: 40th Floor, One Oxford Centre, 15219-6498. Telephone: 412-392-2000. Fax: 412-392-2128, 2129.
Harrisburg, Pennsylvania Office: 240 North Third Street, Suite 600, 17101-1503. Telephone: 717-231-7700. Fax: 717-231-7712.
Philadelphia, Pennsylvania Office: 12th Floor, Two Logan Square, 19103-2756. Telephone: 215-567-7500. Fax: 215-567-2737.
Newark, New Jersey Office: 550 Broad Street, Suite 810, 07102-4517. Telephone: 973-273-9800. Fax: 973-273-9430.
Trenton, New Jersey Office: Mountain View Office Park, Suite 301, 810 Bear Tavern Road, 08628. Telephone: 609-883-6990. Fax: 609-883-7730.
Washington, D.C. Office: 600 Pennsylvania Avenue, S.E., 20003. Telephone: 202-544-4094. Fax: 202-544-9497.

See Professional Biographies, WILMINGTON, DELAWARE

Klusman, John J., Jr. ....'63 '89 C.884 B.S. L.1338 J.D. [Tybout,R.&P.]
*PRACTICE AREAS: Workers Compensation; Civil Practice.

Knauer, Lori Kettering '61 '89 C.105 B.A. L.659 J.D. (adm. in PA; not adm. in DE) Sr. Coun., E.I. du Pont de Nemours and Company
*RESPONSIBILITIES: Employee Benefits; ERISA.

Knepper, E. Martin, Jr., (BV) ....'55 '81 C.205 B.A.A.S. L.1017 J.D. [Knepper&S.]
*PRACTICE AREAS: Personal Injury Law; Criminal Law; Workers Compensation; Driving While Intoxicated; Traffic Violations.

Knepper & Stratton, (BV)
1225 King Street, Suite 1000, P.O. Box 1795, 19899
Telephone: 302-658-1717; 302-652-7717 Fax: 302-658-0631
Email: mknepper@lawyers.com URL: http://www.lawyers.com/knepper
Members of Firm: E. Martin Knepper, Jr.; Barbara H. Stratton.
General Civil and Trial Practice in all State and Federal Courts, Personal Injury, Automobile Accidents and Injuries, Workers Compensation, Criminal Law, Sexual Harassment, Employment Law, Employment Discrimination, Driving While Intoxicated, Traffic Violations, Wrongful Termination, Americans with Disabilities Act.

See Professional Biographies, WILMINGTON, DELAWARE

Knight, Gretchen S., (BV) .... '65 '90 C.205 B.A. L.884 J.D. [Morris,J.H.&W.]
*PRACTICE AREAS: Family Law; Education Law.

Knight, John H. ....'66 '94 C&L.446 B.S., J.D. [Ⓐ Richards,L.&F.]
*PRACTICE AREAS: Bankruptcy; Commercial Litigation.

Knothe, Charles S., (BV) '44 '81 C.971 B.S.M.E. L.1338 J.D. [C.S.Knothe] (See Pat. Sect.)
*PRACTICE AREAS: Real Estate Law; Collections; Commercial Law; Wills Law; Estates Law.

Knothe, Charles S., P.A., (BV)
#14 The Commons, 3516 Silverside Road, 19810-4932
Telephone: 302-478-8800 Fax: 302-478-8988
Email: cknothe@compuserve.com
Charles S. Knothe.
Real Estate, Collections, Commercial Law, Wills and Estates, Patent, Trademark and Copyright Law.

See Professional Biographies, WILMINGTON, DELAWARE

Kocks, Patrick J. '61 '86 C&L.477 B.A., J.D. (adm. in PA; not adm. in DE) Asst. Gen. Coun., DuPont Pharmaceuticals Co.

Kominkiewicz, Laura J. ....'72 '97 C.705 B.A. L.1338 J.D. [Ⓐ Brandt&D.]

Komissaroff, Julius ....'27 '53 C.415 L.1009 LL.B. First Federal Plz.‡

Kondrad, Karen H. '60 '92 C.999 B.S. L.1338 J.D. (adm. in PA; not adm. in DE; Pat.) Asst. Gen. Coun., The du Pont Merck Pharmaceutical Co.

Kopec, Julie Lynn '73 '00 C.205 B.A. L.1338 J.D. (adm. in NJ; not adm. in DE) [Ⓐ Tighe,C.&L.]
*PRACTICE AREAS: Insurance Defense; Contracts; Personal Injury; Construction Law; Workers Compensation.

Kortanek, Steven K., (CV) .... '66 '92 C.597 B.A. L.665 J.D. [Klehr,H.H.B.&E.]
*PRACTICE AREAS: Bankruptcy Law; Creditors' Rights.

Kosmowski, Edward J. .... '66 '99 C.645 B.S. L.705 J.D. [Ⓐ Young C.S.&T.]
*PRACTICE AREAS: Bankruptcy.

Kovach, Thomas H. ....'69 '97 C.205 B.A. L.1292 J.D. [Ⓐ Richards,L.&F.]
*PRACTICE AREAS: Litigation; Environmental Law; Administrative Law.

Kraft, Danya L. '68 '98 C.223 B.S. L.1338 J.D. (adm. in PA; not adm. in DE) Coun., E.I. du Pont de Nemours and Company

Kraft, Denise Seastone, (BVⓉ) ......'63 '89 C.924 B.S. L.128 J.D. [Ⓐ Klehr,H.H.B.&E.]
*PRACTICE AREAS: Commercial; Corporate; Securities; Bankruptcy Litigation.

Krahmer, Johannes R., (AV) .... '32 '59 C.197 A.B. L.309 J.D. [Morris,N.A.&T.]

Kramer, Seth Hamilton .... '74 '99 C&L.893 B.A., J.D. [Ⓐ Richards,L.&F.]
*PRACTICE AREAS: Alternative Entities.

Krapf, Daniel H., (BV) .... '48 '76 C.205 B.A. L.1017 J.D. [Saul E.]
*PRACTICE AREAS: Real Estate; Commercial Transactions; Leasing; Construction; Finance Law.

Krapf, Robert J., (AV) ....'51 '83 C.276 B.S.F.S. L.1338 J.D. [Richards,L.&F.]
*PRACTICE AREAS: Real Estate Law; Zoning Law; Commercial Leasing.

Krawitz, Arthur M., (BV) .... '59 '84 C.645 B.A. L.1338 J.D. [Doroshow,P.K.S.&B.]

Krepto, Laurie A. '67 '95 C&L.831 B.A., J.D. (adm. in PA; not adm. in DE) [Ⓐ Greenberg T.]

Kreshtool, Jacob ....'18 '58 C.205 B.A. L.472 LL.B. 8 Lori Lane‡

Krikelis, Basil S. '66 '95 C.679 B.S. L.365 J.D. (adm. in IL; not adm. in DE; Pat.) Pat. & Gen. Coun., DCV, Inc.

Krikelis, Costas S. ...... '37 '77 C.688 B.S.E.E. L.1338 J.D. [Ratner&P.] (See Pat. Sect.)
*PRACTICE AREAS: Intellectual Property Law.

Kriner, Robert J., Jr., (BV) ....'61 '88 C.205 B.S. L.1338 J.D. [Chimicles&T.]
*PRACTICE AREAS: Securities; Antitrust; Mergers and Acquisitions; Class and Derivative Actions.

Kristol, Daniel M., (AV) ....'36 '61 C&L.659 B.A., LL.B. [Richards,L.&F.]
*PRACTICE AREAS: Real Estate Law; Commercial Law.

Kron, James M. .... '53 '00 C.401 B.S.M.E. L.1338 J.D. [Ⓐ Potter A.&C.] (Pat.)
*PRACTICE AREAS: Intellectual Property; Commercial Litigation.

Krueger, Andreas G. '59 '89 C&L.999 (adm. in German; not adm. in DE) Sr. Coun., E.I. du Pont de Nemours and Company
*RESPONSIBILITIES: Antitrust; Corporate Law; Contracts.

Krukiel, Charles E. '46 '74 C.880 B.S. L.796 J.D. (adm. in TX; not adm. in DE; Pat.) Sr. Coun., E.I. du Pont de Nemours & Co.
*RESPONSIBILITIES: Intellectual Property; Technology Transfer and Licensing.

Kuehl, Robert S., (CV) ....'57 '85 C.93 B.S. L.174 J.D. Dep. Atty. Gen.

Kulesza, Joseph D., Jr., (CV) ....'61 '87 C.728 B.A. L.1338 J.D. [Agostini,L.I.&K.]
*PRACTICE AREAS: Domestic Law; Personal Injury; Criminal and Civil Litigation; Wills and Estates.

Kuller, Mark D., (AV) '59 '84 C.665 B.S.Ch.E. L.884 J.D. (adm. in PA; not adm. in DE; Pat.) [E.I. d.d.]
*RESPONSIBILITIES: Intellectual Property.

Kunz, Carl N., III, (BV) .... '67 '93 C.550 B.A. L.1338 J.D. [Ⓐ Morris,J.H.&W.]
*PRACTICE AREAS: Bankruptcy; Creditor's Rights; Insurance Defense; Civil Litigation; Commercial Litigation.

Kunz, Carolee Burton, (CV) .... '65 '91 C.205 B.A. L.93 J.D. 100 W. 10th St.

Kurey, Gregory S. ....'61 '87 C.216 B.A. L.1017 J.D. General Counsel, Avecia Inc.

Kutner, Dorothy G. '— '47 C.331 A.B. L.178 LL.B. (adm. in NY; not adm. in DE) Tr. Coun., Bank of Del.

Kwiatkowski, Joseph M., (AV) .... '30 '56 C.205 B.A. L.831 LL.B. 519 Falkirk Rd.

LaComb, Nathan J. .... '76 '01 C.732 B.A. L.659 J.D. [Ⓐ Potter A.&C.]
*PRACTICE AREAS: Commercial Real Estate; Business Transactions; Land Use; Zoning Law.

Ladig, Peter B. ....'71 '96 C.976 B.A. L.245 J.D. [Ⓐ Richards,L.&F.]
*PRACTICE AREAS: Corporate Litigation; Corporate Law.

Ladner, Gregory W. ....'64 '95 C.602 B.A. L.884 J.D. [Ⓐ Richards,L.&F.]
*PRACTICE AREAS: Partnership Law; Limited Liability Company Law; Commercial Law.

Lafferty, Gayle P. '65 '91 C.205 B.A. L.1017 J.D. Carvel State Office Bldg., 820 N. French Street

Lafferty, William M., (BV) ....'63 '89 C.205 B.S. L.1017 J.D. [Morris,N.A.&T.]

Laffey, Kathryn J., Law Office of, (BV) '56 '83 C.889 B.S.W. L.602 J.D.
1500 Shallcross Avenue, Suite 2-B, 19806-1432
Telephone: 302-651-7999 Fax: 302-651-7960
Email: KLaffeyatLK@aol.com
***PRACTICE AREAS: Family Law; Civil Litigation; Divorce and Family Mediation.**
Associate: Janine N. Howard.
Family Law, Civil Litigation, Divorce and Family Mediation.

See Professional Biographies, WILMINGTON, DELAWARE

Lahiff, Jeanne '60 '88 C.93 B.A. L.659 J.D.
(adm. in NJ; not adm. in DE) Dep. Atty. Gen.
Lamb, Christopher J., (BV) ....'62 '88 C.397 B.A. L.831 J.D. [Pepper H.]
*PRACTICE AREAS: Commercial Law; Real Estate; Bankruptcy.
Lamb, Stephen P. ....'49 '75 C.659 B.A. L.276 J.D. V.Chanc., Ct. of Chanc.
Lambert, William E. '41 '69 C.918 B.A. L.309 LL.B.
(adm. in DC; not adm. in DE; See Pat. Sect.) [[C] Connolly B.L.&H.]
LaMotte, William O., III, (AV) ....'43 '69 C.976 B.A. L.659 LL.B. [Morris,N.A.&T.]
Lancaster, Louise Bruce '46 '72 C.320 B.A. L.421 J.D.
(adm. in KY; not adm. in DE) Corp. Coun., E.I. du Pont de Nemours and Company
*RESPONSIBILITIES: Federal Securities; Corporation Law; Secretary of the Company.
Lanctot, Catherine J. '57 '81 C.103 B.A. L.276 J.D.
(adm. in DC; not adm. in DE) Prof. of Law, Villanova Univ.
Landis, Adam G., (BV) ....'63 '92 C.95 A.B. L.588 J.D. [Klett R.L.&S.]
*PRACTICE AREAS: Bankruptcy; Commercial Litigation.
Landon, Roger D., (BV) ....'61 '86 C.893 B.S. L.1338 J.D. [Murphy S.&L.]
*PRACTICE AREAS: Insurance Defense; Subrogation; Products Liability; Torts.
Langworthy, John A., (BVⓉ) '47 '72 C.378 B.A. L.846 J.D.
(adm. in TX; not adm. in DE) Sr. Coun., E.I du Pont de Nemours & Co.
*RESPONSIBILITIES: Intellectual Property.
Lank, Aubrey B., (AV) ....'25 '51 C.205 B.A. L.276 J.D. [Theisen,L.M.&G.]
Lank, David S., (BV) ....'49 '80 C.893 B.A. L.1338 J.D. 1118 West Street
Larsen, Scott K. '58 '99 C.770 B.S. L.831 J.D.
(adm. in PA; not adm. in DE) DuPont Pharmaceuticals Co.
Lassen, J. Kai ...... '42 '71 C.976 B.A. L.659 J.D. Vice Chmn. & CEO, Krapfcandoit Co.
Laster, J. Travis ....'69 '95 C.674 A.B. L.893 J.D. [[A] Richards,L.&F.]
*PRACTICE AREAS: Corporate Litigation; Corporate Law; General Litigation.
Lastowski, Michael R., (AVⓉ) ....'53 '80 C.103 B.A. L.659 J.D. [Duane,M.&H.]
*PRACTICE AREAS: Bankruptcy Law; Commercial Litigation.
Latchum, James L. ....'18 '42 C.674 A.B. L.893 LL.B. Sr. U.S. Dist. J.
Lattomus, Tara L. ....'70 '96 C.916 B.s. L.884 J.D. [[A] Saul E.]
*PRACTICE AREAS: Bankruptcy; Creditor Rights.
Lawson, Kimberly E. Connolly ....'70 '00 C.1296 B.A. L.1338 J.D [[A] Werb&S.]
*PRACTICE AREAS: Bankruptcy; Corporate Reorganization; Business Law; Corporate Law; Civil Litigation.
Layton, Jonathan ....'67 '97 C.945 B.A. L.1338 J.D. Dept. of Jus.
Lazarus, Lewis H., (BV) ....'56 '82 C.821 B.A. L.813 J.D. [Morris,J.H.&W.]
*PRACTICE AREAS: Litigation; Business Law; Corporate Law.
Leamy, Jane M. '70 '95 C.893 B.A. L.569 J.D.
(adm. in NJ; not adm. in DE) One Rodney Sq., 6th Fl.
Leary, John J., Jr. '45 '87 C&L.1338 B.S., J.D.
(adm. in PA; not adm. in DE) [[C] Stewart&Assoc.]
*PRACTICE AREAS: Corporate Taxation; Corporate Law.
Leathem, Patrick M. '73 '00 C.800 B.A. L.273 J.D.
(adm. in NY; not adm. in DE) [[A] Richards,L.&F.]
Leban, Abbott A. ....'33 '59 C.178 A.B. L.976 J.D. [[C] Grant&E.]
Ledyard, Lewis C., III, (CV) ....'64 '90 C.861 B.A. L.884 J.D. [Morris,J.H.&W.]
*PRACTICE AREAS: Business Trusts; Asset Secured Financing; Leveraged Leasing; Limited Liability Companies.
Ledyard, Michael M., (AV) ....'48 '82 C.312 B.A. L.1338 J.D. [Morris,J.H.&W.]
*PRACTICE AREAS: Business Trusts; Limited Liability Companies; Limited Partnerships; Joint Ventures; Structured Finance.
Lee, Mona A. ....'66 '94 C.659 B.A. L.831 J.D. [[A] Morris,N.A.&T.]
Lees, George T., III '71 '97 C.754 B.S. L.1338 J.D.
[[A] Bifferato,B.&G.] (⊙Wilmington, DE; Phila., PA)
*PRACTICE AREAS: Toxic Torts; Premises Liability; Products Liability; Automobile Insurance Defense; Employment Law.
Lees, George T., III '71 '97 C.754 B.S. L.1338 J.D.
[[A] Kent&M.] (⊙Wilmington, DE; Phila., PA)
*PRACTICE AREAS: Toxic Torts; Premises Liability; Products Liability; Automobile Insurance Defense; Employment Law.
Lefebvre, Kathleen M. ....'71 '00 C.884 B.A. L.904 J.D. [[A] Richards,L.&F.]
Leff, Thomas P. ....'50 '95 C.124 B.A. L.446 J.D. [[A] Casarino,C.&S.]
*PRACTICE AREAS: Insurance Defense; Personal Injury; Civil Litigation.

Lefton, Robert C., (BV) '38 '64 C.976 A.B. L.309 LL.B.
Suite 1011, 913 Market Street, P.O. Box 506, 19899-0506
Telephone: 302-656-0703
Email: lefton@compuserve.com
***PRACTICE AREAS: Taxation Law; Business Law; Corporate Law; Real Estate Law; Estate Planning Law.**
Taxation, Business, Corporate, Real Estate, Estate Planning and Probate Law.
See Professional Biographies, WILMINGTON, DELAWARE

Leichliter, Van H., Jr. '44 '69 C.976 B.A. L.477 J.D.
(adm. in OH; not adm. in DE) Corp. Coun., E.I. du Pont de Nemours and Company
Lein, Diane Smits ....'56 '82 C.741 B.A. L.276 J.D. Dep. Atty. Gen.
Leiper, Janice '61 '84
(adm. in Scotla; not adm. in DE) [E.I. d.d.]
*RESPONSIBILITIES: International Mergers and Acquisitions.
Leiser, Christie Day ....'60 '87 C&L.862 B.S., J.D. Sr. Coun., Conectiv
*RESPONSIBILITIES: Advertising, Antitrust and Consumer Law (45%); Regulatory (25%); Contracts (20%); Corporate/Securities (10%).
Leonard, James R., (BV) ....'53 '78 C.205 B.A.A.S. L.831 J.D. [Potter,C.&L.] ⊙
Lerman, Bart E. '60 '85 C.846 B.S.Ch.E. L.326 J.D.
(adm. in TX; not adm. in DE; Pat.) Corp. Coun., E.I. du Pont de Nemours and Company
*RESPONSIBILITIES: Intellectual Property; Licensing; Mergers and Acquisitions.
Lessner, Jonathan I. ....'61 '92 C.188 B.A. L.472 J.D. [Morris,N.A.&T.]
Lessner, Martin S., (BV) ....'63 '92 C.659 B.S.E. L.884 J.D. [Young C.S.&T.]
*PRACTICE AREAS: Corporate Litigation; Commercial Litigation; Civil Appeals; Business Law; Chancery Practice.
Letang, Peter N., (BV) ....'48 '74 C.105 B.A. L.69 J.D. 2612 W. 17th St.
Letcher, Ann Joyce ....'59 '84 C.884 B.S. L.1338 J.D. Tr. Coun., Comwlth. Tr. Co.
Levin, Richard David, (BV) ....'45 '70 C.205 B.A. L.276 J.D. [Connolly B.L.&H.]
Levine, Norman E., (BV) ....'43 '68 C&L.659 A.B., LL.B. [Levine&T.]
*PRACTICE AREAS: Family Law; Civil Litigation.
Levine, Richard A., (BV) ....'47 '72 C.94 A.B. L.659 J.D. [Young C.S.&T.]
*PRACTICE AREAS: Commercial Law; Commercial Real Estate; Banks and Banking; Leases and Leasing; Partnership Law.

Levine & Thompson, (BV)
1205 King Street, 19801
Telephone: 302-658-3070 Fax: 302-658-3031
Members of Firm: Norman E. Levine; John J. Thompson.
Family, Civil Litigation, Real Estate, General Business, Personal Injury, Collections Law, Criminal Law.
See Professional Biographies, WILMINGTON, DELAWARE

Levinson, Laurence I., (BV) '53 '79 C.205 B.A. L.1338 J.D.
1326 King Street, 19801
Telephone: 302-656-3393 Fax: 302-656-1993
Email: planlaw@aol.com URL: http://www.lawyers.com/planlaw
***PRACTICE AREAS: Estate Planning; Charitable Planning; Asset Protection Planning; Family Wealth Transfers.**
Estate Planning.
See Professional Biographies, WILMINGTON, DELAWARE

Levinson, Marilyn W. ....'49 '74 C&L.910 A.B., J.D. 8 Barley Mill Dr.
Levitsky, Neal J., (BV) '56 '81
C.205 B.A. L.472 J.D. [Agostini,L.I.&K.] (⊙Bellmawr, NJ)
*PRACTICE AREAS: Civil Trial; Commercial Litigation; Bankruptcy; Personal Injury.

Lew, Jeffrey C. '47 '81 C.186 B.S. L.831 J.D.
Silverside Professional Park, 1403 Silverside Road, 19810
Telephone: 302-475-7919 Fax: 302-475-7915
Email: lawoffice@jlew.com
***PRACTICE AREAS: Patents; Patent Applications; Patent Prosecution; Patent Licensing; Trademarks.**
Intellectual Property Law including: Patent, Trademark, Copyright and Related Matters.
See Professional Biographies, WILMINGTON, DELAWARE

Lewis, Elizabeth B., (CV) ....'56 '89 C.205 B.A. L.1338 J.D. [Jacobs&C.]
*PRACTICE AREAS: Products Liability; Negligence Law; Toxic Substance Law; Business Law.
Lewis, Gilbert R. '31 '56 C.645 B.S. L.659 LL.B.
(adm. in PA; not adm. in DE) 5823 Tupelo Turn‡
Lewis, Jacqueline A. '— '96 C.659 B.S. L.1040 J.D.
(adm. in CT; not adm. in DE) [[A] Potter A.&C.]
*PRACTICE AREAS: Corporate Law; Commercial Law; Banking.
Lewis, Lawrence W., (BV) ....'60 '88 C.445 B.S. L.1338 J.D. Dep. Atty. Gen.
Leyden, James G., Jr. ....'60 '88 C&L.884 B.S.A., J.D. [Richards,L.&F.]
*PRACTICE AREAS: Limited Liability Company Law; Limited Partnership Law; General Partnership Law; Business Law; Commercial Law.
Lhulier, Christopher J. ...... '70 '98 C.205 B.A.I.R. L.884 J.D. [[A] Pachulski,S.Z.Y.&J.]
*PRACTICE AREAS: Chapter 11 Bankruptcy; Corporate Restructuring and Reorganization.
Liebesman, Sidney S. ....'64 '95 C.205 B.A.A.S. L.884 J.D. [[A] Grant&E.]
Lilly, Edward M. ....'65 '97 C.210 B.A. L.188 J.D. [Walsh M.&M.]
*PRACTICE AREAS: Business Law; Corporate Law; Commercial Litigation; Real Property.
Lindh, Alfred J., (BV) .... '36 '62 C.205 B.A. L.276 J.D. 110 S. French St., Ste. 301A
Lindley, Daniel F., (AV) '50 '75 C.951 B.A. L.893 J.D.
Sr. V.P. & Trust Coun., U.S. Trust Co. of Delaware
Lipkin, Gary W. ....'71 '99 C.645 B.S. L.1338 J.D. [[A] Cozen O.]
*PRACTICE AREAS: Complex Commercial Litigation.
Lipton, Robert S., (AV) '42 '72 C.477 B.S.E. L.831 J.D.
(adm. in PA; not adm. in DE; Pat.) [Lipton,W.&H.] ⊙
Lipton, Weinberger & Husick, (AV) ...... 1020 N. Bancroft Parkway (Pat.) (⊙Media, PA)
Lisa, James P., Jr. '58 '86 C.205 B.S. L.930 J.D.
(adm. in OH; not adm. in DE) State Econ. Develop. Off.
Lisicky, Joseph G. ....'61 '88 C.645 B.S. L.831 J.D. [Morris,J.H.&W.]
*PRACTICE AREAS: Real Estate Law; Secured Lending Law.
Liss, Morris, (AVⓉ) '40 '70 C.563 B.E.E. L.128 J.D.
(adm. in DC; not adm. in DE; See Pat. Sect.) [Connolly B.L.&H.]
*PRACTICE AREAS: Computer and Software Patents; Electrical Patents; Electronic Patents; Mechanical Patents; Patent Licensing.
List, Susan A. ....'73 '98 C.208 B.S. L.884 J.D. [[A] Tybout,R.&P.]
*PRACTICE AREAS: Negligence; Insurance; Workers' Compensation; Products Liability; Civil Litigation.
Littman, James A. ..... '50 '75 C.228 B.A. L.245 J.D. Mgr., Blue Cross Blue Shield of DE
LoBue, Robert P., (CV) ....'51 '80 C.205 B.S. L.365 J.D. 803 Shipley St.
LoCastro, Jean D. '63 '88 C&L.884 J.D.
(adm. in PA; not adm. in DE) Dep. Atty. Gen.
Lockwood, Paul J. ....'68 '95 C.188 B.S. L.659 J.D. [[A] Skadden,A.S.M.&F.]
Lodge, Thomas S., (AV) ....'17 '53 C&L.893 A.B., LL.B. 1220 Market Street
Loftin, Monica Leigh, (CV) ....'65 '95 C.893 B.S. L.1338 J.D. [[A] Potter A.&C.]
*PRACTICE AREAS: Bankruptcy; Creditors Rights.
Logan, Donald L. ....'49 '87 C.459 B.S. L.1338 J.D. [Tighe,C.&L.] (⊙Towson, MD)
*PRACTICE AREAS: Construction Law; Contracts; Leases and Leasing.
Loizides, Christopher D. ....'66 '91 C.976 B.A. L.659 J.D. [[A] Richards,L.&F.]
*PRACTICE AREAS: Bankruptcy; Creditors Rights; Litigation.
Longobardi, Joseph J. ....'30 '57 C.903 B.A. L.831 LL.B Sr. U.S. Dist. J.

Longobardi, Joseph J., III, Law Office of, (BV) '57 '83 C.524 B.A. L.1338 J.D.
The Plaza, Suite 115, 1303 Delaware Avenue, 19806
Telephone: 302-575-1502 Telecopier: 302-575-1506
Email: longobardi@delnet.com URL: http://www.lawyers.com/longobardilaw
***PRACTICE AREAS: Personal Injury; Criminal Defense; Domestic Relations.**
Personal Injury including Automobile Accident, Medical Malpractice, Products Liability, Criminal Defense. Family Law including Child Support, Child Custody, Divorce, Adoptions.
See Professional Biographies, WILMINGTON, DELAWARE

Losco, Daniel R., (BV) ....'57 '84 C.645 B.S. L.1338 J.D. [Losco&M.]
Losco & Marconi, P.A., (BV) .... 1116 West Street
Louden, Karen Jacobs, (BV) ....'65 '90 C.659 B.A. L.309 J.D. [Morris,N.A.&T.]
Lovitz, Michael L. '64 '89 C.659 B.A. L.831 J.D.
(adm. in PA; not adm. in DE; See Pat. Sect.) [[A] Connolly B.L.&H.]
*PRACTICE AREAS: Trademarks; Unfair Competition; Copyrights.
Lowicki, Stanley C., (CV) ....'33 '59 C.205 B.A. L.276 J.D. 830 West St.
Lowy, Rachel Sarah ....'73 '98 C.280 B.A. L.1338 J.D. [[A] Pachulski,S.Z.Y.&J.]
Lucas, Hinton J., Jr. '48 '80 C.302 B.S. L.201 J.D.
(adm. in OH; not adm. in DE)
Assoc. Gen. Coun., E.I. du Pont de Nemours and Company
*RESPONSIBILITIES: Labor Law; Employment; Employee Benefits.
Lucas, Kathleen C. ....'50 '80 C.205 B.A. L.1338 J.D. Mag.
Luce, Edmund B. '67 '92 C.103 B.A. L.659 J.D.
(adm. in PA; not adm. in DE) Widener Law School
Luce, Thomas F., (CV) ....'22 '72 C&L.659 B.A., J.D. 1980 Saperfine Lane‡
Lugg, Sean P. '71 '96 C.205 B.A. L.884 J.D.
Carvel State Office Building, 820 North French Street
Luke, Maureen D. ....'— '92 C.999 B.A. L.884 J.D. [[A] Young C.S.&T.]
*PRACTICE AREAS: Bankruptcy.
Lukoff, Paul M., (AV) ....'44 '70 C.205 A.B. L.846 LL.B. [Prickett,J.&E.]
*PRACTICE AREAS: Premises Liability Litigation; Commercial Litigation; Product Liability Litigation; Medical Malpractice Litigation; Occupational Disease Litigation.
Lundblad, Douglas Wade, (BV) '50 '78 C.205 B.A. L.280 J.D.
Sr. Coun., PNC Bk., Del.
Lunger, William H. .... '69 '95 C.216 B.A. L.1338 J.D. [[A] Prickett,J.&E.]
*PRACTICE AREAS: Estate Planning; Estate Administration; Trust Administration; Family Business Planning; Tax.
Luria, Edward M., (AV) ....'41 '68 C&L.659 A.B., J.D. [[C] Moore&B.] ⊙
*PRACTICE AREAS: Tax Law; Estate Planning; Probate; Employee Benefits; Asset Protection.
Lynch, F. Edmund, (AV) ....'40 '65 C.524 B.S. L.692 J.D. [Woloshin,T.L.N.&F.]
Lynch, William F., II, (AV) ....'20 '49 C.918 A.B. L.659 LL.B. [[C] Morris,J.H.&W.]
*PRACTICE AREAS: Real Estate Law; Zoning and Planning Law; Wills Law; Probate Law.

Lynn, James T., III '47 '74 C.207 B.A. L.831 J.D.
(adm. in PA; not adm. in DE) E.I. du Pont de Nemours and Company
*RESPONSIBILITIES: Litigation; Public Policy; Government Relations.
Lyons, David J., (CV) .... '57 '85 C.273 B.A. L.1338 J.D. [Lyons]
*PRACTICE AREAS: Personal Injury; Workers Compensation; Social Security Disability.
Lyons, Edmund Daniel, (AV) .... '47 '74 C.31 B.A. L.276 J.D. [Lyons]
*PRACTICE AREAS: Personal Injury; Criminal Defense.
Lyons, Patricia M. .... '60 '91 C.728 B.S. L.1338 J.D. [Ⓐ W.E.Ward]

Lyons, Doughty & Veldhuis, P.C.
1148 Pulaski Highway (Bear), P.O. Box 313, 19701 ⊙
Telephone: 302-428-1670 URL: http://www/ldvlaw.com
Email: ldvlaw@ldvlaw.com URL: http://www.lawyers.com/ldvlaw
Stephen P. Doughty.
Creditors Rights, Consumer Collections, Creditor Bankruptcy, Mortgage Foreclosure, Commercial Mortgages, Mortgage Banking Law, Mortgage Bankruptcy, Mortgage Insurance, Mortgage Lien Foreclosure, Mortgage Workouts, Secondary Mortgage Market, Creditors Rights in Bankruptcy, Debtor and Creditor Collections, Debtor and Creditor Remedies, Debtor and Creditor Rights, Debtor and Creditor Workouts, Fair Debt Collection Practices Act, Secured Creditors Rights, Unsecured Creditors Rights, Foreclosures, Fraudulent Conveyance, Repossessions, Workouts, Bank Collections, Bank Foreclosures, Commercial Loans, Loan Workouts, Commercial Collections, Garnishments, Post Judgement Collections, Professional Collections, Retail Collections, Secured Collections, Unsecured Collections, Bankruptcy Chapter 7, Bankruptcy Chapter 11, Bankruptcy Chapter 13, Commercial Bankruptcy.
Mount Laurel, New Jersey Office: 1288 Route 73, Suite 310, P.O. Box 1269, 08054. Telephone: 856-802-1488. Fax: 856-802-2801.
Philadelphia, Pennsylvania Office: Telephone: 215-747-7735.
Pittsburgh, Pennsylvania Office: 7228 Baptist Road, #175, Bethel Park, 15102. Telephone: 412-765-2221.
See Professional Biographies, WILMINGTON, DELAWARE

Lyons Law Firm, The, (AV) BB
1526 Gilpin Avenue, P.O. Box 579, 19806
Telephone: 302-777-5698 Fax: 302-777-5051
Email: elyons@lyonslaw.com URL: http://www.lawyers.com/lyonslaw
Edmund Daniel Lyons; David J. Lyons.
Personal Injury including Wrongful Death, Catastrophic Injury, Automobile Accidents and Injuries, Medical Malpractice, Workers Compensation, Social Security Disability, Nursing Home Abuse and Neglect, Social Security Disability, Criminal Defense including Felonies, Misdemeanors, Juvenile Criminal Law, Traffic Offenses and Driving While Intoxicated.
See Professional Biographies, WILMINGTON, DELAWARE

Macauley, Thomas G. .... '66 '95 C.893 B.A. L.861 J.D. [Zuckerman S.]
*PRACTICE AREAS: Business Reorganization; Creditors Rights; Complex Civil Litigation; Corporate Governance.
Macchiaroli, Jean A. '49 '83 C.183 A.B. L.823 J.D.
(adm. in NY; not adm. in DE) Asst. Prof. of Law, Del. Law School
MacDonald, Barbara, (BV) .... '58 '84 C.205 B.A. L.276 J.D. [⊡ Morris,J.H.&W.]
*PRACTICE AREAS: Litigation; Appellate Practice; Utilities.
Macel, Stanley C., III, (BV) .... '38 '72 C.205 B.A. L.831 J.D. [Connolly B.L.&H.]
MacFarlane, Earl W. '60 '87 C&L.309 A.B., J.D.
(adm. in MD; not adm. in DE) Corp. Coun., E.I. du Pont de Nemours and Company
*RESPONSIBILITIES: Business Law; Commercial Transactions; Products Liability.
Mack, Carolyn D. .... '61 '85 C.446 B.A. L.537 J.D. 2024 Armour Drive
Maddock, Charles S., (AV) '11 '35 C.174 B.A. L.309 J.D.
Ste. 1000, 824 Market St. Mall‡
Magee, Thomas H. '43 '74 C.696 B.S.M.E. L.823 J.D.
(adm. in NJ; not adm. in DE; Pat.) Corp. Coun., E.I. du Pont de Nemours and Company
*RESPONSIBILITIES: Intellectual Property Law; Technology Transfers; Technology Licensing Law.
Magid, Laurie '60 '86 C.659 B.S. L.178 J.D.
(adm. in NY; not adm. in DE) Assoc. Prof., Widener Univ. School of Law
Mahoney, Daniel B. '45 '73 C.708 B.A. L.893 J.D.
(adm. in NY; not adm. in DE) du Pont Co.
Maimone, Michael J., (CV) .... '62 '90 C.527 B.A. L.893 J.D. [Morris,J.H.&W.]
*PRACTICE AREAS: Corporate Law; Corporate and Commercial Litigation.
Makowski, Kathleen P. .... '64 '96 C.205 B.A. L.1338 J.D. [Ⓐ Klett R.L.&S.]
*PRACTICE AREAS: Bankruptcy; Creditors' Rights.
Malatesta, Carl A. '57 '97 C.205 B.S.B.A. L.1338 J.D.
(adm. in PA; not adm. in DE) CFO., Color Proof Div., E. I. DuPont
Malatesta, David C., Jr. .... '70 '97 C.205 B.A. L.1338 J.D. [Ⓐ Tomar,O.K.J.&G.]
Malfitano, Joseph A. .... '75 '00 C.107 B.S. L.831 J.D. [Ⓐ Young C.S.&T.]
*PRACTICE AREAS: Bankruptcy Chapter 11; Bankruptcy Litigation.

Malik, John S., (AV) '58 '84 C.728 B.A. L.1338 J.D.
100 East 14th Street, 19801-3122
Telephone: 302-427-2247 Fax: 302-427-2414
URL: http://www.lawyers.com/johnmaliklaw
***PRACTICE AREAS: Criminal.**
Criminal Trial and Appellate Practice in all State and Federal Courts.
See Professional Biographies, WILMINGTON, DELAWARE

Malinowski, Andrea V. '60 '87 C.645 B.S. L.831 J.D.
(adm. in PA; not adm. in DE) Corp. Coun., E.I. du Pont de Nemours and Company
*RESPONSIBILITIES: Environmental; Patent.
Maloney, Kevin P., (BV) .... '58 '85 C.354 B.A. L.1194 J.D. Dep. Atty. Gen.
MaloneyHuss, Mary M., (BV) .... '60 '91 C.696 B.S. L.1035 J.D. [Wolf,B.S.&S-C.]
*PRACTICE AREAS: Bankruptcy; Business Litigation; Environmental Litigation; Environmental Counseling.
Mammarella, Thomas, (BV) .... '53 '78 C.205 B.A. L.228 J.D. [Gordon,F.&M.]
*PRACTICE AREAS: Real Estate; Zoning; Land Development.
Mancini, Lorenza .... '70 '00 C.952 B.S.N. L.1338 J.D. [Ⓐ Marshall,D.W.C.&G.]
*PRACTICE AREAS: Defense Litigation.
Mancini, Thomas R. '71 '99 C.823 B.A. L.1218 J.D.
(adm. in NJ; not adm. in DE) [Ⓐ Potter A.&C.]
*PRACTICE AREAS: Patents; Trademarks; Patent Applications; Patent Prosecution.
Mangan, Kevin J., (BV) .... '64 '89 C.754 B.S. L.884 J.D. [Walsh M.&M.]
*PRACTICE AREAS: Products Liability; Corporate Litigation; Civil Litigation; Bankruptcy.
Manning, Julia W. '56 '82 C.228 B.A. L.597 J.D.
(adm. in IL; not adm. in DE) Sr. Coun., Astrazeneca Pharm. LP
*RESPONSIBILITIES: Pharmaceutical; Commercial.
Manning, William E., (AV) .... '48 '76 C.205 B.A. L.421 J.D. [Klett R.L.&S.]
*PRACTICE AREAS: Land Use Regulation and Litigation; Commercial Law; Constitution Law; Legislative Representation and Drafting.
Mantzavinos, Megan Trocki .... '71 '99 C.205 B.A. L.1338 J.D. [Ⓐ Marks,O.O.&C.]
Marconi, Thomas C., (BV) .... '59 '89 C.205 B.S. L.1338 J.D. [Losco&M.]
Margolin, Christy J. .... '66 '94 C.893 B.A. L.1338 J.D. Coun., Hercules Incorporated
Margolin, Steven T. .... '67 '92 C.205 B.S. L.1017 J.D. [Ashby&G.]
Margules, David J., (BV) .... '56 '83 C.178 B.A. L.569 J.D. [Bouchard M.&F.]
*PRACTICE AREAS: Corporate Litigation; Bankruptcy Litigation.
Mariani, Erin '59 '88 C.264 B.A. L.884 J.D.
Sr. Coun., E.I. du Pont de Nemours and Company
*RESPONSIBILITIES: Litigation.

Marin, Bayard, (BV) '41 '67 C.205 A.B. L.823 LL.B.
521 West Street, 19801-2196
Telephone: 302-658-4200 Fax: 302-658-9075
Email: bmarin6655@aol.com URL: http://www.lawyers.com/bmarin
***PRACTICE AREAS: Civil Trial Practice; Personal Injury Law; Medical Malpractice; Products Liability Law; Insurance Law.**
Civil Trial Practice, Personal Injury, Medical Malpractice, Products Liability, Insurance Law, Workers Compensation, Administrative Law and Historic Preservation Law.
See Professional Biographies, WILMINGTON, DELAWARE

Marini, Gary J. '53 '78 C.665 M.B.A. L.229 J.D.
(adm. in PA; not adm. in DE)
Asst. Gen. Coun., Corp. & Comml. Law, Astrazeneca Pharm. LP
*RESPONSIBILITIES: Corporate Law/Commercial; Pharmaceutical/Healthcare; Antitrust; Mergers and Acquisitions.
Marks, O'Neill, O'Brien & Courtney, P.C., (BVⓉ)
2004 Foulk Road, Suite 7 (⊙Westmont, NJ; Norristown, Phila., Pitts., PA)
Maron, Elizabeth Daniello, (CV) '62 '88 C.205 B.A. L.1338 J.D.
Carvel State Office Building, 820 North French Street
Maron, James J., (BV) .... '57 '86 C.1044 B.A. L.1338 J.D. [Maron&M.]
*PRACTICE AREAS: Toxic Tort; Environmental Litigation; Product Liability; Complex Litigation; Commercial Litigation.

Maron & Marvel, P.A., (BV)
1300 North Broom Street, P.O. Box 288, 19899
Telephone: 302-425-5177 Telecopier: 302-425-0180
Email: info@mm-w.com URL: http://www.mm-w.com
James J. Maron; Wayne A. Marvel; Karen S. Brehm; Thomas C. Martin; Bernard G. Conaway; Philip L. Rothbart (Not admitted in DE);—John P. Daniello.
Civil Trial in all State and Federal Courts, Environmental, Toxic Tort, Neighborhood Exposure, Complex Litigation, Products Liability, Commercial Litigation, Medical Malpractice, Construction Law, Internet Law, Employment Law, Local, Multi-State and Federal Tax Planning, Antitrust, Corporations and Special Purpose Entities, Delaware Investment Holding Companies, Mediation Services. This litigation, tax and corporate boutique is dedicated to the delivery of efficient legal services through the leveraging of technology and alternative fee structures.
See Professional Biographies, WILMINGTON, DELAWARE

Marsden, William J., Jr., (BV) .... '55 '83 C.311 B.A. L.575 J.D. [Fish&R.]
*PRACTICE AREAS: Intellectual Property; Litigation.

Marshall, Dennehey, Warner, Coleman and Goggin, (BV)
1220 N. Market Street, Suite 202, 19801 ⊙
Telephone: 302-552-4300 Fax: 302-651-7905
URL: http://www.marshalldennehey.com
Resident Members: Timothy A. Casey; Kevin J. Connors. Resident Associates: Tracy A. Burleigh; Sean A. Dolan; Thomas J. Gerard; Jessica L. Julian; Lorenza Mancini; Christine P. O'Connor; Elizabeth A. Saurman; Scott L. Silar.
Defense Litigation Practice before all State and Federal Courts and Administrative Agencies. Appellate Advocacy, Arson, Fraud Litigation, Automotive Products Liability, Bad Faith, Disability, Employment Law, Commercial Litigation, Environmental and Toxic Torts, General Liability, Health Care Liability, Insurance Coverage, Insurance Law, Intellectual Property, Liquor Liability, Municipal Liability and Civil Rights, Construction Litigation, Medical Device and Pharmaceutical, Medical Malpractice, Products Liability, Professional Malpractice, Property Damage, Railroad Litigation, Retail Liability, Special Investigations Litigation, Amusement Park, Sports and Entertainment, Transportation Litigation, Workers' Compensation, Technology.
Bethlehem, Pennsylvania Office: 651 East Market Street. Telephone: 484-895-2300. Fax: 484-895-0208.
Doylestown, Pennsylvania Office: 10 North Main Street. Telephone: 267-880-2020. Fax: 215-348-5439.
Erie, Pennsylvania Office: 1001 State Street, 14th Floor. Telephone: 814-461-7800. Fax: 814-461-7818.
Harrisburg, Pennsylvania Office: 4200 Crums Mill Road. Telephone: 717-651-3500. Fax: 717-651-9630.
Newtown Square, Pennsylvania Office: 18 Campus Boulevard, Suite 250. Telephone: 610-355-7420. Fax: 610-355-7444.
Norristown, Pennsylvania Office: One Montgomery Plaza, Suite 1002. Telephone: 610-270-8500. Fax: 610-270-7444.
Philadelphia, Pennsylvania Office: 1845 Walnut Street. Telephone: 215-575-2600. Fax: 215-575-0856; 575-0857.
Pittsburgh, Pennsylvania Office: 600 Grant Street, USX Tower, Suite 2900. Telephone: 412-803-1140. Fax: 412-803-1188.
Scranton, Pennsylvania Office: 507 Linden Street, Suite 800. Telephone: 570-342-1999. Fax: 570-342-4999.
Williamsport, Pennsylvania Office: 33 W. Third Street, Suite 200. Telephone: 570-326-9091. Fax: 570-326-5507.
Roseland, New Jersey Office: 425 Eagle Rock Avenue, Suite 302. Telephone: 973-618-4100. Fax: 973-618-0685.
Cherry Hill, New Jersey Office: Woodland Falls Corporate Park, 200 Lake Drive East, Suite 300. Telephone: 856-414-6000. Fax: 856-414-6077.
Weirton, West Virginia Office: 3173 Main Street. Telephone: 304-748-7400. Fax: 304-748-0620.
Steubenville, Ohio Office: Sinclair Building, 10th Floor, 100 North 4th Avenue. Telephone: 740-282-6705. Fax: 740-282-8667.
Tampa, Florida Office: 100 North Tampa Street, Suite 3550. Telephone: 813-472-7800. Fax: 813-472-7811.
Orlando, Florida Office: 201 East Pine Street, Suite 675. Telephone: 407-246-0668. Fax: 407-839-3008.
See Professional Biographies, WILMINGTON, DELAWARE

Marston, Donald E., (BV) .... '51 '81 C.205 B.A. L.1338 J.D. [Sullivan&M.]
Martin, Colleen J. '56 '86 C.112 B.A. L.1068 J.D.
(adm. in PA; not adm. in DE) Assoc. Gen. Coun., Du Pont Pharmaceuticals Co.
Martin, Jeffrey K., (BV) '56 '81
C.390 A.B. L.1292 J.D. [J.K.Martin] & [Harvey,P.C.G.&R.]
*PRACTICE AREAS: Employment Law; Personal Injury; General Liability.
Martin, Joshua W., III, (AV) '44 '74
C.124 B.S. L.1292 J.D. Pres. & CEO, Bell Atlantic - Delaware (Pat.)
Martin, Linda D. .... '62 '00 C.1136 B.S. L.1148 J.D. [Ⓐ Morris,J.H.&W.]
*PRACTICE AREAS: Corporate Litigation.
Martin, Stacy J. '61 '93 C.223 B.S. L.1338 J.D.
(adm. in PA; not adm. in DE) J.P. Morgan
Martin, Susan E. '49 '80 C&L.69 B.A., J.D.
(adm. in TX; not adm. in DE) Asst. Gen. Coun., AIG Life Cos.
Martin, Thomas C. .... '52 '80 C.860 B.S. L.665 J.D. [Maron&M.]
*PRACTICE AREAS: Taxation; Multi-State Corporate Tax Planning; State and Local Taxation; Tax Planning; Federal Tax Planning.
Martin, William J., III, (BV) '53 '78
C.205 B.A. L.1292 J.D. [Prickett,J.&E.] (⊙Kennett Square, PA)
*PRACTICE AREAS: Taxation; Health Law; Employee Benefits; Estates and Trusts; Commercial.

Martin, Jeffrey K., P.A., (BV)
1509 Gilpin Avenue, 19806
Telephone: 302-777-4680 Facsimile: 302-777-4682
Email: jkmartin@nela.org URL: http://www.lawyers.com/jeffreykmartin
Jeffrey K. Martin.
Employment Law, Wrongful Termination, Discrimination, Harassment and Americans with Disabilities Act, Severance, Unemployment Compensation, Personal Injury, General Civil Litigation.
See Professional Biographies, WILMINGTON, DELAWARE

Martinelli, Adria B. '67 '98 C.945 B.A. L.1209 J.D.
(adm. in VA; not adm. in DE) [Ⓐ Young C.S.&T.]
*PRACTICE AREAS: Labor and Employment; Litigation.

Martino, Marie L. '60 '84 C.674 A.B. L.309 J.D.
(adm. in PA; not adm. in DE) Asst. Gen. Coun., Astrazeneca Pharm. LP
*RESPONSIBILITIES: Employment/Labor Law; Benefits; Commercial Law; Corporate Law.
Marvel, Wayne A., (BV) .... '55 '81 C.205 B.S. L.884 J.D. [Maron&M.]
*PRACTICE AREAS: Toxic Tort; Medical Malpractice; Products Liability; Personal Injury; Commercial Law.
Masom, Jeffrey Scott '68 '93 C.237 B.S. L.1338 J.D.
(adm. in PA; not adm. in DE) Atty., Smith Barney Inc.
Matanovic, Stephan '73 '99 C.893 B.A. L.831 J.D.
(adm. in PA; not adm. in DE) [Ⓐ Grant&E.]
Matlusky, David E. .... '70 '00 C.205 B.S. L.1338 J.D. [Ⓐ Crossland,C.&Assoc.]
Matterer, Mary B., (CV) ....'47 '88 C.205 B.A. L.1338 J.D. [Blank R.C.&M.]
*PRACTICE AREAS: Intellectual Property Litigation; Insurance Coverage Defense; Complex Litigation; Products Liability Defense.
Mattey, John D. .... '54 '92 C.205 B.S.B.A. L.1338 J.D. [Ferry&J.]
*PRACTICE AREAS: Litigation; Bankruptcy; Collections.
Matthews, Scott L. .... '73 '00 C.205 B.A. L.893 J.D. [Ⓐ Richards,L.&F.]

Mattleman, Weinroth & Miller, A Professional Corporation
200 Continental Drive Suite 211, 19713 ⊙
Telephone: 302-731-8349 Fax: 302-731-8753
URL: http://www.mwm-law.com
—Delia A. Clark (Resident); Melanie J. Thompson; Adam R. Elgart; John G. Mulford; Felicia M. Seaton; Holly M. Whitney.
Civil and Criminal Trial Practice in all courts. Commercial Litigation, Creditor Rights Litigation, Collections, Foreclosures, Repossessions, Workouts, Real Estate, Mortgages, Commercial Leasing, Personal Injury, Medical Malpractice, Consumer Law, Premises Liability, Products Liability, Professional Liability, Family Law, Business Law, Corporate Law, Environmental Law, Superfund Litigation, Sports Law, Entertainment Law, Immigration Law, Wills, Trusts and Estates.
Cherry Hill, New Jersey Office: 401 Route 70 East, 08034. Telephone: 856-429-5507. Fax: 856-429-9036.
Clifton, New Jersey Office: 1135 Broad Street, Suite 207, 07013. Telephone: 973-365-6140. Fax: 973-365-6143.
Philadelphia, Pennsylvania Office: 100 S. Broad Street, Suite 2226, 19110. Telephone: 215-923-2225. Fax: 215-567-4151.
See Professional Biographies, WILMINGTON, DELAWARE

Matuszewski, Mary Ann, (CV) '58 '84 C.205 B.S.B.A. L.1017 J.D.
1205 Chadwick Road
Maurer, Eugene J., Jr., (AV) ....'48 '75 C&L.831 B.A., J.D. [E.J.Maurer,Jr.]

Maurer, Eugene J., Jr., P.A., (AV) BR
1201-A King Street, 19801
Telephone: 302-652-7900 Fax: 302-652-2173
URL: http://www.lawyers.com/ejmaurerjr
Eugene J. Maurer, Jr.
Criminal Trial and Appellate Practice.
See Professional Biographies, WILMINGTON, DELAWARE

Maxwell, Edward B., 2nd, (AV) ......'37 '64 C.95 A.B. L.1017 J.D. [Ⓒ Young C.S.&T.]
*PRACTICE AREAS: Corporate Law; Litigation; Business Law; Chancery and Equity.
Maxwell, James Jeffrey .... '59 '90 C.205 B.S. L.1338 J.D. Dep. Atty. Gen.
May, James R. '62 '89 C&L.378 B.S.M.E., J.D.
(adm. in KS; not adm. in DE) 4601 Concord Pike
Maycen, Christina M. .... '75 '00 C.1369 B.S. L.1338 J.D [Ⓐ Morris,J.H.&W.]
*PRACTICE AREAS: Corporate Litigation; Commercial Litigation; Bankruptcy.
Mayer, Katharine L. ....'73 '98 C.205 B.A. L.1338 J.D. [Ⓐ Elzufon A.R.T.&M.]
*PRACTICE AREAS: Bankruptcy; Real Estate; Corporate Law.
Mayer, Nancy S. '48 '80 C.339 B.S. L.209 J.D.
(adm. in IL; not adm. in DE) [E.I. d.d.]
*RESPONSIBILITIES: Intellectual Property.
Mayes, Gregory T. '68 '95 C.823 B.S. L.831 J.D.
(adm. in PA; not adm. in DE) Coun., Astrazeneca Pharm. LP
*RESPONSIBILITIES: Labor and Employment; Commercial; Regulatory Compliance; Corporate.
Mayo, Jennifer L., (CV) .... '67 '95 C.692 B.A. L.1338 J.D. 2055 Limestone Rd.
Mazie, Eric A., (AV) .... '57 '84 C.223 B.S. L.945 J.D. [Richards,L.&F.]
*PRACTICE AREAS: Banks and Banking; Business Law; Commercial Law; Contracts; Corporate Law.
Mazza, Julie S. '57 '85 C.397 B.A. L.831 J.D.
(adm. in PA; not adm. in DE) Sr. Coun., E.I. du Pont de Nemours & Co.
*RESPONSIBILITIES: Drug & Medical Device Defense; Product Liability; Toxic Torts; Negligence Defense; Class Actions.
McAviney, Donald '50 '78 C.874 B.A. L.796 J.D.
(adm. in TX; not adm. in DE) Corp. Coun., E.I. du Pont de Nemours & Co.
McBride, David C., (AV) ....'48 '75 C.276 B.S.F.S. L.245 J.D. [Young C.S.&T.]
*PRACTICE AREAS: Litigation; Business Law; Corporate Law; Health Care; Mergers Acquisitions and Divestitures.
McCaffrey, Joseph F. '31 '91 C.1338 B.S. L.64 LL.B.
(adm. in PA; not adm. in DE) 2604 Forge Dr.‡
McCann, Douglas Edward .... '67 '99 C.871 B.S. L.262 J.D. 844 King St.

McCarter & English, LLP, (BV)
Mellon Bank Center, 919 Market Street, 19899 ⊙
Telephone: 302-654-8010 Telecopier: 302-654-0795
URL: http://www.mccarter.com
Resident Partners: Paul A. Bradley; Michael P. Kelly. Special Counsel: A. Richard Winchester. Associates: James Joseph Freebery, IV; Paul J. Dougherty, III; Thomas D. Walsh.
Administrative Law, Alternative Dispute Resolution, Antitrust and Trade Regulation, Appellate Practice, Aviation and Aerospace, Bankruptcy, Banks and Banking, Business Law, Civil Practice, Class Actions, Commercial Law, Commercial Real Estate, Communications and Media, Complex and Multi-District Litigation, Computers and Software, Contracts, Copyrights, Corporate Law, Debtor and Creditor, Education Law, Eminent Domain, Employee Benefits, Environmental Law, Equipment Finance and Leasing, Finance, General Practice, Health Care, Insurance, Insurance Coverage, Intellectual Property, International Law, Investments, Labor and Employment, Leases and Leasing, Litigation, Mergers, Acquisitions and Divestitures, Natural Resources, Nonprofit and Charitable Organizations, Patents, Probate, Products Liability, Professional Liability, Public Finance, Real Estate, Taxation, Torts, Toxic Torts, Trade Secrets, Trademarks, Transportation, Trusts and Estates, Unfair Competition, White Collar Crime, Wills, Zoning, Planning and Land Use.
Newark, New Jersey Office: Four Gateway Center, 100 Mulberry Street. P.O. Box 652. Telephone: 973-622-4444. Telecopier: 973-624-7070.
Cherry Hill, New Jersey Office: 1820 Chapel Avenue West, Suite 380. Telephone: 609-662-8444. Telecopier: 609-662-6203.
New York, New York Office: 300 Park Avenue, 18th Floor. Telephone: 212-466-9018. Telecopier: 212-432-6568.
Philadelphia, Pennsylvania Office: One Commerce Square, 2005 Market Street, Suite 3600. Telephone: 215-557-7700. Telecopier: 215-557-6544.
Baltimore, Maryland Office: 201 North Charles Street. Telephone: 410-385-1088.
Hartford, Connecticut Office: One Financial Plaza, 755 Main Street. Telephone: 860-493-3900.
See Professional Biographies, WILMINGTON, DELAWARE

McCauley, Michael B. ....'51 '79 C.1027 B.S. L.472 J.D. [Palmer B.&H.] ⊙
*PRACTICE AREAS: Admiralty Law; Insurance Law; Aviation Law; Litigation.
McCollom, Daniel P., (BV) .... '58 '83 C.264 B.A. L.665 J.D. [Morris,J.H.&W.]
*PRACTICE AREAS: Business Law; Taxation; Trusts and Estates.
McConnell, J. H. Tyler .... '14 '38 C.885 A.B. L.893 LL.B. 805 Snuff Mill Rd.‡
McCullough, Bruce W., (BV) ....'58 '83 C&L.659 B.A., J.D. [McCullough&M.]
McCullough & McKenty, P.A., (BV) ....824 Market Street, Suite 412

McCurdy, William A., Jr. '46 '71
C&L.659 B.S., J.D. Corp. Coun., E.I. de Pont de Nemours & Co.
McDaniel, John S. '55 '86 C.575 A.B. L.1017 J.D.
Carvel State Office Building, 820 North French Street
McDermott, Christine M. '47 '72
C.205 B.A. L.1017 J.D. Assoc. Prof. of Law, Widener Univ.
McDermott-Lundin, Shirley A. ....'64 '89 C.205 B.S. L.1338 J.D. [Ⓐ Roeberg,M.&Assoc.]
McDevitt, John F., Jr. '48 '74 C.728 A.B. L.1202 J.D.
(adm. in PA; not adm. in DE) Managing Attorney, CIGNA Companies
McDevitt, Sean P. .... '61 '90 C.205 B.S. L.831 J.D. [Pepper H.] (⊙Berwyn, PA)
*PRACTICE AREAS: Litigation; Labor Law.
McDonough, Kathleen Furey, (BV) .... '57 '85 C.728 A.B. L.831 J.D. [Potter A.&C.]
McDonough, Mary ....'53 '78 C.205 B.A. L.569 J.D. Community Legal Aid Soc., Inc.
Mc Donough, Thomas V., (BV) '58 '85
C.205 B.A. L.1338 J.D. Community Legal Aid Soc., Inc.
McDowell, Althea E. .... '63 '90 C.1305 B.A. L.884 J.D. Disabilities Law Program
McDowell, Charles S., (AV) .... '45 '75 C.674 A.B. L.893 J.D. [Potter A.&C.]
McEvilly, Walter P. .... '13 '40 C.205 B.A. L.659 LL.B. 1521 Barley Mill Rd.‡
McEvilly, Walter P., Jr., (BV) .... '45 '70 C.976 B.A. L.659 J.D. [Stevens&L.]
*PRACTICE AREAS: Health Care Law; Trusts and Estates.
McFadden, Bernard J., (BV) .... '46 '84 C.205 B.A. L.1338 J.D. 4 E. 8th St.
McGarry, Christian G. ....'74 '00 C.205 B.A. L.1338 J.D. [Ⓐ Elzufon A.R.T.&M.]
*PRACTICE AREAS: Workers Compensation.
McGee, Patricia '61 '92 C.401 B.S. L.1170 J.D.
(adm. in PA; not adm. in DE) Sr. Cuon., E.I. du Pont de Nemours & Co.
*RESPONSIBILITIES: Environmental Law; M & A.
McGeever, Elizabeth M., (AV) .... '56 '81 C.184 B.A. L.884 J.D. [Prickett,J.&E.]
*PRACTICE AREAS: Corporate Litigation; Commercial Litigation.
McGinnis, Doretta Massardo '63 '91 C.309 M.A. L.659 J.D.
(adm. in PA; not adm. in DE) Widener Univ. School of Law
McGonigle, Patricia P. .... '67 '92 C.1369 B.S. L.216 J.D. [Seitz,V.&G.]
*PRACTICE AREAS: Civil Litigation; Commercial Law; Construction Litigation; Bankruptcy; Business Torts.
McGonigle, Thomas P. .... '— '93 C.237 B.A. L.1017 J.D. [Duane,M.&H.]
*PRACTICE AREAS: Commercial Litigation; Administrative Law; Government Relations; Regulatory Law.
McGrory, Leanne C. .... '73 '00 C.205 B.A. L.276 J.D. [Ⓐ Stewart&Assoc.]
*PRACTICE AREAS: Corporate Law.
McHahon, Michelle ....'74 '00 C.999 B.B.A. L.276 J.D. 1220 Market St.
McIntyre, Megan D. ....'69 '94 C.645 B.S. L.1017 J.D. [Grant&E.]
McKelvie, Roderick R. .... '46 '73 C.309 B.A. L.659 J.D. U.S. Dist. J.
McKenty, Daniel L., (BV) .... '60 '88 C.970 B.A. L.1338 J.D. [McCullough&M.]
McKenzie, Allyson A. '74 '01 C.874 B.A. L.644 J.D.
(adm. in PA; not adm. in DE) [Ⓐ Prickett,J.&E.]
*PRACTICE AREAS: Corporate; Commercial Litigation; Corporate Litigation; Bankruptcy.
McLaughlin, Brian J. .... '60 '86 C.205 B.A. L.201 J.D. [Walsh M.&M.] ⊙
*PRACTICE AREAS: Business Law; Commercial Transactions; Environmental; Civil Litigation; Bankruptcy.
McLaughlin, Gordon L., (BV) ....'58 '83 C.205 B.A. L.838 J.D. 1203 Orange St.
McLaughlin, John D., Jr. '53 '85 C.893 B.A. L.1338 J.D.
(adm. in PA; not adm. in DE) [Ⓒ Young C.S.&T.]
*PRACTICE AREAS: Bankruptcy - Chapter 11 (100%, 2500).
McLaughlin, Lisa Cresci ....'65 '92 C.205 B.A. L.1338 J.D. [Phillips,G.&S.]
*PRACTICE AREAS: Personal Injury; Toxic Tort; Insurance Defense; Bankruptcy Litigation; Collections.
McMahon, Michelle .... '74 '00 C.932 B.B.A. L.276 J.D. [Ⓐ Connolly B.L.&H.]
McMahon, Richard L., (BV) .... '32 '56 C.918 B.A. L.659 LL.B. [Ⓒ Potter A.&C.]
McManamon, Mary Brigid '55 '80 C.976 B.A. L.188 J.D.
(adm. in OH; not adm. in DE) Assoc. Prof., Widener Univ. Sch. of Law
McMillan, James G., III .... '55 '00 C.311 B.A. L.659 J.D. [Ⓐ Morris,N.A.&T.]
McMorrow, Robert G., Jr. '58 '83 C.152 B.A. L.276 J.D.
(adm. in PA; not adm. in DE; See Pat. Sect.) [Connolly B.L.&H.]
McNally, Edward M., (AV) .... '47 '72 C.93 B.A. L.178 J.D. [Morris,J.H.&W.]
*PRACTICE AREAS: Litigation; Corporate Law; Alternative Dispute Resolution.
McNeice, Carolyn M., (CV) .... '46 '88 C.205 B.S. L.1338 J.D. 1225 N. King St.
McNeill, Omar Y. .... '67 '92 C.103 A.B. L.228 J.D. 1100 North King Street
McNew, R. Bruce, (BV) '53 '79
C.893 B.A. L.945 J.D. [Taylor&M.] (⊙Kennett Square, PA)
*PRACTICE AREAS: Corporate; Securities; Commercial; Antitrust; Consumer.
McRae, Arnetta '46 '78 C.512 B.S. L.930 J.D.
(adm. in OH; not adm. in DE) du Pont Co.
McReynolds, Sherry C., (BV) ... '46 '87 C.1205 B.S.N. L.1338 J.D. [Ⓒ Morris,J.H.&W.]
*PRACTICE AREAS: Medical Malpractice Defense; Personal Injury.
McShane, James A. ....'66 '96 C.205 B.A. L.831 J.D. [Ⓐ Morris&M.]
*PRACTICE AREAS: Corporate Litigation; Securities Litigation.
McShane, William E. '63 '89 C.205 B.S.Ch.E. L.1338 J.D.
(adm. in PA; not adm. in DE; See Pat. Sect.) [Connolly B.L.&H.]
Meadows, Robyn L. '58 '83 C.475 B.A. L.421 J.D.
(adm. in FL; not adm. in DE) 4601 Concord Pike
Medwick, George M. '47 '72 C.645 B.S.E.E. L.665 J.D.
(adm. in PA; not adm. in DE; Pat.) Corp. Coun., E.I. du Pont de Nemours & Co.
*RESPONSIBILITIES: Intellectual Property.
Meitner, Pamela, (AV) '50 '77 C.223 B.S. L.1338 J.D.
Corp. Coun., E.I. du Pont de Nemours & Co. (Pat.)
*RESPONSIBILITIES: Environmental.
Meixsell, Raymond K., Jr. '15 '51 C.951 A.B. L.1003 J.D.
(adm. in OH; not adm. in DE) 1912 Marsh Rd.‡
Mekler, Arlen, The Law Offices of '32 '72
C.112 B.S. L.831 J.D. 580 First Federal Plaza, 710 King St.
Meli, John T., Jr., (BV) ....'56 '93 C&L.1338 B.S.E.E., J.D. [Ⓐ Fish&R.]
*PRACTICE AREAS: Commercial Property; Intellectual Property; Litigation; Corporate Law; Computers and Software.
Melnik, Selinda A., (BVⓉ) .... '51 '85 C.831 B.A. L.564 J.D. [Smith,K.&F.]
*PRACTICE AREAS: Bankruptcy; Reorganization; Corporate Restructuring; Creditors Rights; International Insolvency.
Mendelson, Elliott E. ....'63 '00 C.893 B.S. L.276 J.D. [Ⓐ Connolly B.L.&H.]
*PRACTICE AREAS: Intellectual Property.
Menton, Dennis J., (CV) ....'55 '87 C.205 B.S. L.1338 J.D. [Tybout,R.&P.]
*PRACTICE AREAS: Worker's Compensation Defense; Personal Injury Defense.
Merchant, Michael J. .... '74 '99 C.645 B.S. L.884 J.D. [Ⓐ Richards,L.&F.]
*PRACTICE AREAS: Bankruptcy; Creditors Rights.
Mersky, Rachel B., (CV) .... '57 '81 C.205 B.A. L.285 J.D. [Walsh M.&M.] ⊙
*PRACTICE AREAS: Business Litigation; Commercial Bankruptcy; Commercial Litigation; Employment Law.
Messmore, Scott L. '47 '72 C.923 B.S. L.893 J.D.
(adm. in WV; not adm. in DE) [Ⓐ Tighe,C.&L.]
*PRACTICE AREAS: Corporate Law; Real Estate; General Practice.
Mester, Peter C. '60 '86 C.893 B.A. L.880 J.D.
(adm. in NY; not adm. in DE) Corp. Coun., E.I. du Pont de Nemours and Company
*RESPONSIBILITIES: Securities; Corporate Law; Banking Law.

Mette, Jacqueline Paradee '65 '91 C.881 B.A. L.884 J.D.
Legal Methods Prof., Widener Univ. School of Law
Mette, Luke W. .... '63 '88 C.311 B.A. L.273 J.D. Sr. Coun., AstraZeneca Pharm. LP
*RESPONSIBILITIES: Litigation; Environmental.
Metz, Bonnie L., (BV) .... '64 '91 C.1113 B.A. L.884 J.D. [Klett R.L.&S.]
*PRACTICE AREAS: Administrative Law; Public Utility Regulation; Healthcare Law; Immigration Law.

Meyer, Ellen Shaffer, (BV) '39 '81 C.103 A.B. L.1338 J.D.
521 West Street, 19801-2139
Telephone: 302-429-0344 Fax: 302-429-8806
Email: esmlaw@mindspring.com URL: http://www.lawyers.com/rsmlaw
Domestic Relations, Adoption Law.
See Professional Biographies, WILMINGTON, DELAWARE

Meyer, Geoffrey E. '49 '74 C.475 B.A. L.276 J.D.
Vice President & General Counsel, FiberVisions LLC
Mieczkowski, Francis E., Jr., (BV) '52 '79 C.205 B.A. L.564 J.D.
Sr. Coun., Blue Cross Blue Shield of Del., Inc.
Miller, Clinton F. .... '13 '41 C.401 B.S. L.659 LL.B. 800 Greenwood Rd.‡
Miller, Frank J., (BV) .... '20 '48 C&L.178 A.B., LL.B. [Miller&F.]
Miller, Kathleen M., (BV) .... '65 '90 C.884 B.S. L.1338 J.D. [Smith,K.&F.]
*PRACTICE AREAS: Bankruptcy Litigation; Personal Injury; Products Liability; General Litigation.
Miller, Laurence L. '44 '69 C&L.608 B.A., J.D.
(adm. in OH; not adm. in DE) du Pont Co.
Miller, Rick S. .... '65 '95 C.216 B.A. L.1338 J.D. [Ferry&J.]
*PRACTICE AREAS: Litigation; Veterans Law; Commercial Law; Bankruptcy; Probate.
Miller, Scott '56 '98 C.999 B.A. L.1338 J.D.
(adm. in NJ; not adm. in DE) Atty., AIG Marketing, Inc.
Miller, Stephen M., (BV) .... '60 '87 C.205 B.S. L.273 J.D. [Morris,J.H.&W.]
*PRACTICE AREAS: Commercial Law; Bankruptcy; Partnership Law; Limited Liability Company Law; Franchise Law.
Miller & Foulk, (BV) .... P.O. Box 70
Millikin, Margaret S. '62 '89 C&L.862 B.S.P.E., J.D.
(adm. in OK; not adm. in DE; Pat.) 1313 North Market Street
Minella, Louis A. '56 '80 C.188 B.S. L.884 J.D.
(adm. in PA; not adm. in DE) Group V.P. & Gen. Coun., Rollins Envir. Servs.
Minuti, Mark, (BV) .... '63 '88 C.205 B.S. L.1338 J.D. [Saul E.]
*PRACTICE AREAS: Bankruptcy.
Minutola, Lisa A. '70 '95 C.205 B.A. L.1209 J.D.
Daniel L. Herrmann Courthouse, 1020 North King Street, Ground Floor
Mitnick, Audy L. '65 '90 C.205 B.S.B.A. L.1338 J.D.
(adm. in PA; not adm. in DE) 4601 Concord Pike
Mobley, Stacey J. '45 '72 C&L.329 B.S.Ph., J.D.
(adm. in PA; not adm. in DE)
Sr. V.P., Chf. Admin. Off. & Gen. Coun., E.I. du Pont de Nemours and Company
Mock, Walter E. '17 '54 C.205 A.B. L.472 LL.B.
(adm. in FL; not adm. in DE) 703 S. Clayton St.‡
Modica, Michael W., (BV) .... '57 '82 C.928 B.A. L.245 J.D. 715 King St. (⊙Odessa)
Monaco, Francis A., Jr., (BV) .... '56 '81 C.205 B.A. L.884 J.D. [Walsh M.&M.] ⊙
*PRACTICE AREAS: Commercial Bankruptcy; Commercial Law.
Monahan, Jane T., (BV) .... '56 '85 C.893 B.A. L.665 J.D. 1100 North Market Street
Moncure, Henry, III, (BV) '60 '84 C.893 B.A. L.1338 J.D.
Senior Vice President & Counsel, MBNA America Bank, N.A.
Mondell, Scott R., (BV) .... '60 '85 C.205 B.S. L.1338 J.D. [Elzufon A.R.T.&M.]
*PRACTICE AREAS: Worker's Compensation Defense; Bankruptcy Litigation.
Mondros, Herbert W., (BV) .... '60 '89 C.1046 B.S. L.861 J.D. [[A] Morris&M.]
Mongan, William F. '58 '84 C.205 B.Ch.E. L.884 J.D.
Sr. Coun., Astrazeneca Pharm. LP
*RESPONSIBILITIES: Corporate Law; Commercial Law; Healthcare.
Monhait, Norman M., (AV) .... '48 '75 C.401 B.A. L.309 J.D. [Rosenthal,M.G.&G.]
*PRACTICE AREAS: Corporate Litigation; Securities Litigation; Business Litigation; Civil Litigation; Corporate Law.
Monroe, Bruce M. .... '40 '96 C.894 A.B. L.1338 J.D. [Ratner&P.] (See Pat. Sect.)
*PRACTICE AREAS: Intellectual Property; Chemical Intellectual Property.
Montgomery, Harrison K. '54 '87 C.831 B.B.A. L.1338 J.D.
(adm. in NJ; not adm. in DE) du Pont Co.
Monzack, Melvyn I., (BV) .... '40 '66 C.690 B.S. L.273 LL.B. [Walsh M.&M.] ⊙
*PRACTICE AREAS: Commercial Transactions; Business Reorganization; Real Estate; Civil Litigation.
Moore, David E. .... '69 '00 C.893 B.S. L.831 J.D. [[A] Potter A.&C.]
*PRACTICE AREAS: Litigation.
Moore, Paulette Sullivan .... '51 '77 C.938 B.A. L.705 J.D. 15 West Ct.
Moore, William X., Jr., (BV) .... '60 '87 C.884 B.S. L.1338 J.D. [Roeberg,M.&Assoc.]

Moore & Bruce, LLP, (AV)
2 East 7th Street, Suite 302, 19801 ⊙
Telephone: 302-655-0582 Fax: 302-655-9321
Of Counsel: Edward M. Luria.
Taxation, Corporate and Commercial Law, International Trade and Customs Law, Trusts and Estates, Civil and Criminal Tax Litigation.
Washington, D.C. Office: 1072 Thomas Jefferson Street, N.W. Telephone: 202-965-5300. Facsimile: 202-965-7745.
London, England Office: 43 Upper Grosvenor Street. Telephone: 011-44-207-493-4840. Fax: 011-44-207-493-4299.
See Professional Biographies, WILMINGTON, DELAWARE

Morabito, Christine M. .... '74 '99 C.264 B.A. L.884 J.D. [[A] Richards,L.&F.]
Moran, Joseph M. '29 '59 C.423 Ph.B. L.446 LL.B.
(adm. in MD; not adm. in DE) Rodney Sq. N.
Morgan, John W. .... '59 '92 C.205 B.A. Econ. L.1338 J.D. [[A] Heckler&F.]
*PRACTICE AREAS: Worker's Compensation; Labor and Employment.
Morgan, Pauline K., (AVⓉ) .... '56 '87 C.229 B.A. L.659 J.D. [Young C.S.&T.]
*PRACTICE AREAS: Bankruptcy; Debtor and Creditor.

Morgan Shelsby & Leoni, A Professional Association
(See Newark)

Morris, Geo. W. '16 '50 C.608 B.S. L.1003 J.D.
(adm. in OH; not adm. in DE) du Pont Co.
Morris, Irving, (AV) .... '25 '51 C.205 B.A. L.976 LL.B. [Morris&M.]
*PRACTICE AREAS: Corporate Litigation; Securities Litigation.
Morris, Karen L., (AV) .... '58 '84 C.976 B.A. L.228 J.D. [Morris&M.]
*PRACTICE AREAS: Corporate Litigation; Securities Litigation.
Morris, Patrick F. .... '55 '84 C.870 B.S. L.228 J.D. [Morris&M.]
*PRACTICE AREAS: Corporate Litigation; Securities Litigation.

Morris, James, Hitchens & Williams, LLP, (AV) BR
222 Delaware Avenue, P.O. Box 2306, 19899-2306 ⊙
Telephone: 302-888-6800 Telecopier: 302-571-1750
URL: http://www.morrisjames.com
Members of Firm: Henry N. Herndon, Jr.; Richard P. Beck; Glenn E. Hitchens (Resident, Dover, Delaware Office); Edward M. McNally; Norris P. Wright; James W. Semple; David H. Williams; P. Clarkson Collins, Jr.; Richard Galperin; Steven R. Director; Richard D. Kirk; Lewis H. Lazarus; Michael M. Ledyard; Francis J. Jones, Jr. (Resident, Newark, Delaware Office); Daniel P. McCollom; Robert L. Symonds, Jr.; Stephen M. Miller; Mary M. Culley; Laura Sunstein Murphy; Kevin G. Healy (Resident, Newark, Delaware Office); Nicholas J. Caggiano, Jr.; Michael J. Maimone; Lewis C.

(This Listing Continued)

Morris, James, Hitchens & Williams, LLP (Continued)
Ledyard, III; Gretchen Ann Bender; Norman M. Powell; Matthew J. O'Toole; Dennis R. Spivack; Joseph G. Lisicky; Dennis D. Ferri; Brett D. Fallon; Susan D. Ament (Resident, Bancroft Parkway Office); Gretchen S. Knight; Michael A. Weidinger. Associates: Ellen Marie Cooper; Carl N. Kunz, III; Thomas E. Hanson, Jr.; James E. Drnec; Samantha E. Balick; Elizabeth A. Brown; Arlene M. Benton (Not admitted in DE); Ross E. Antonacci; Catherine A. Barron; Paul H. Ostien, III; Christina M. Maycen; Linda D. Martin; Jennifer L. Brierley; Alisa Erenshteyn. Of Counsel: William F. Lynch, II; George C. Hering, III; Barbara MacDonald; Sherry C. McReynolds.
Litigation, Corporate Law, Commercial Law, Business Law. Administrative Law, Alternative Dispute Resolution, Bankruptcy, Commercial Real Estate, Computers and Software, Education Law, Environmental Law, Family Law, Health Care, Insurance, Insurance Defense, Intellectual Property, Labor and Employment, Medical Malpractice, Partnership Law, Personal Injury, Probate, Products Liability, Real Estate, Taxation, Torts, Trusts and Estates and Wills.
Other Wilmington, Delaware Office: 1010 North Bancroft Parkway, Suite 11, P.O. Box 2328, 19899-2328. Telephone: 302-655-2599. Fax: 302-655-8831.
Dover, Delaware Office: Suite 202, 32 West Loockerman Street, 19904-7356. Telephone: 302-678-8815. Telecopier: 302-678-9063.
Newark, Delaware Office: 16 Polly Drummond Hill Road, 19711-5703. Telephone: 302-368-4200. Fax: 302-368-6259.
See Professional Biographies, WILMINGTON, DELAWARE

Morris and Morris, (AV) BR
Suite 1600, 1105 North Market Street, P.O. Box 2166, 19899-2166
Telephone: 302-426-0400 Facsimile: 302-426-0406
Email: firm@morrisandmorrislaw.com
Irving Morris; Karen L. Morris; Patrick F. Morris; Seth D. Rigrodsky. Associates: Jacqueline L. Jenkin Green (Not admitted in DE); James A. McShane; Herbert W. Mondros.
Complex Representational Litigation, including Corporate, Securities and Consumer Law Litigation.
See Professional Biographies, WILMINGTON, DELAWARE

Morris, Nichols, Arsht & Tunnell, (AV) BR
1201 North Market Street, P.O. Box 1347, 19899-1347
Telephone: 302-658-9200 Telecopier: 302-658-3989
URL: http://www.mnat.com
Members of Firm: Johannes R. Krahmer; Lewis S. Black, Jr.; William O. LaMotte, III; Douglas E. Whitney; William H. Sudell, Jr.; Martin P. Tully; Thomas R. Hunt, Jr.; A. Gilchrist Sparks, III; Richard D. Allen; David Ley Hamilton; John F. Johnston; Walter C. Tuthill; Donald F. Parsons, Jr.; Jack B. Blumenfeld; Donald Nelson Isken; Donald E. Reid; Denison H. Hatch, Jr.; Thomas C. Grimm; Kenneth J. Nachbar; Andrew M. Johnston; Mary B. Graham; Michael Houghton; Thomas R. Pulsifer; Jon E. Abramczyk; Alan J. Stone; Louis G. Hering; Frederick H. Alexander; R. Judson Scaggs, Jr.; William M. Lafferty; Karen Jacobs Louden; Donna L. Culver; Julia Heaney; Jonathan I. Lessner; Robert J. Dehney; Colm F. Connolly; Jeffrey R. Wolters; Maryellen Noreika; David J. Teklits; S. Mark Hurd. Special Counsel: Rachel A. Dwares. Associates: Rodger D. Smith; Eric D. Schwartz; Mona A. Lee; Stanford L. Stevenson, III; Derek C. Abbott; Jessica Zeldin; David A. Harris; Patricia O'Neill Vella; Gregory W. Werkheiser; Wendy L. Walter; Christopher F. Carlton; Garfield B. Simms (Not admitted in DE); Michael Busenkell; Richard W. Ellis; John D. Pirnot; Megan E. Ward; Melissa Stone Myers; Jason W. Staib; Donna L. Harris; Todd A. Flubacher; Christian J. Henrich; Yvette C. Fitzgerald; James G. McMillan, III; Matt Neiderman; Scott Salerni; Patricia R. Uhlenbrock; Michael G. Wilson. Of Counsel: Andrew B. Kirkpatrick, Jr.; Richard L. Sutton; David A. Drexler; O. Francis Biondi; Walter L. Pepperman, II. Deceased Partners: Hugh M. Morris (1878-1966); Alexander L. Nichols (1906-1985); James M. Tunnell, Jr. (1910-1986); S. Samuel Arsht (1910-1999).
General Practice. Patent Litigation.
Representative Clients: Artesian Water Company, Inc.; AstraZeneca Inc.; The Coca-Cola Company; Delaware River and Bay Authority; The Dow Chemical Company; Ford Motor Company; Georgia-Pacific Corporation; J.P. Morgan Chase & Co. Incorporated; McDonald's Corporation; Merck & Co., Inc.
See Professional Biographies, WILMINGTON, DELAWARE

Morrissey, Bruce W. '42 '81 C.688 B.S. L.273 J.D.
(adm. in DC; not adm. in DE; Pat.) Corp. Coun., E.I. du Pont de Nemours and Company
*RESPONSIBILITIES: Intellectual Property Licensing; Commercial Law; Mergers and Acquisitions; Strategic Alliances.
Morse, Richard H., (BV) .... '48 '75 C.188 A.B. L.309 J.D. [Young C.S.&T.]
*PRACTICE AREAS: Civil Litigation; Contract Litigation; Tort Liability; Wrongful Death; Intellectual Property Litigation.
Mortenson, C. Walter, (BV) .... '15 '45 C.339 B.A. L.831 LL.B. 1601 Milltown Rd. (Pat.)
Morton, Edmon L. .... '74 '99 C.205 B.A. L.896 J.D. [[A] Young C.S.&T.]
*PRACTICE AREAS: Bankruptcy; Corporate.
Morton, Mark A., (BV) .... '63 '89 C.216 B.A. L.276 J.D. [Potter A.&C.]
Morton, Michael P., (BV) .... '55 '86 C.658 B.A. L.1338 J.D. [M.P.Morton]

Morton, Michael P., P.A., (BV)
1203 North Orange Street, 19801
Telephone: 302-426-1313 Fax: 302-426-1300 Mobile Text Email: 3024206333@page.nextel.com
Email: MPMPA@aol.com URL: http://www.lawyers.com/mpmpa
Michael P. Morton.
Business Dispute Resolution, Commercial Litigation, Complex Commercial Litigation, Corporate Law, L.L.C.'s, Partnerships, Business Organizations, Commercial Real Estate Acquisitions, Commercial Contracts, Bankruptcy, Secured Creditors Rights, Unsecured Creditors Rights, Environmental Insurance, Insurance Coverage, Commercial Leasing Evictions; Landlord and Tenant Law, Civil Litigation, Federal Civil Litigation, Mobile Home Law.
Affiliated Pennsylvania Offices:
Crawford, Wilson & Ryan L.L.C.: 220 West Gay Street, West Chester, Pennsylvania, 19380-2934. Telephone: 610-431-4500. FAX: 610-430-8718.
See Professional Biographies, WILMINGTON, DELAWARE

Mosholder, William '24 '52 C.861 B.B.A. L.608 LL.B.
(adm. in OH; not adm. in DE) 2203 W. 11th St.‡
Motter, Thomas J. .... '55 '81 C.205 B.A. L.884 J.D. 1205 North King Street
Moulton, H. Geoffrey, Jr. '58 '86 C.31 B.A. L.178 J.D.
(adm. in PA; not adm. in DE) 4601 Concord Pike
Moyer, Jeffrey L. .... '68 '94 C.205 B.S. L.831 J.D. [Richards,L.&F.]
Mulford, John G., (BV) .... '41 '67 C.896 B.A. L.575 J.D. [[A] Mattleman,W.&M.]
*PRACTICE AREAS: Civil Litigation; Personal Injury; Business Law; Environmental Law.
Mullen, Regina M., (AV) '48 '73 C.93 B.A. L.893 J.D.
Executive Vice President, Counsel, MBNA America Bank
Mullen, Thomas A. .... '67 '93 C.264 B.A. L.659 J.D. [Prickett,J.&E.]
*PRACTICE AREAS: Corporate Law and Litigation; Partnership; Limited Liability Company; Business Trust Law.
Mulligan, James M., Jr., (AV) .... '32 '58 C.728 B.S. L.659 J.D. [Connolly B.L.&H.]
Mulveny, Daniel C. .... '69 '98 C.205 B.Ch.E L.1017 J.D. [[A] Connolly B.L.&H.]
*PRACTICE AREAS: Patent Prosecution; Patent Litigation.
Munshi, Parth S. .... '69 '96 C.445 B.S. L.659 J.D. [[A] Skadden,A.S.M.&F.]
*PRACTICE AREAS: Corporate.
Murphy, Francis J., (BV) .... '52 '77 C.205 B.A. L.1017 J.D. [Murphy S.&L.]
*PRACTICE AREAS: Insurance Coverage; Bankruptcy Law.
Murphy, Laura Sunstein, (BV) .... '47 '90 C.659 B.A. L.884 J.D. [Morris,J.H.&W.]
*PRACTICE AREAS: Health Care Law.
Murphy, Patricia .... '74 '99 C.1338 B.S. L.884 J.D. [[A] Swartz,C.&D.]
*PRACTICE AREAS: Insurance Defense; Personal Injury; Subrogation.

Murphy Spadaro & Landon, (BV)
824 Market Street, Suite 700, P.O. Box 8989, 19899
Telephone: 302-654-4600 Telecopier: 302-654-4775
Email: msl@msllaw.com
Francis J. Murphy; John S. Spadaro; Roger D. Landon; Jonathan L. Parshall; Chase T. Brockstedt.

(This Listing Continued)

Murphy Spadaro & Landon (Continued)

Admiralty Law, Banking Law, Commercial Law, Bankruptcy and Creditor Rights, Civil Litigation, Commercial Litigation, Corporate Litigation, Employment Law. Environmental Law, Insurance Coverage, Insurance Defense, International Law, Labor Law, Products Liability, Public Utility Regulation and Tort Litigation.

See Professional Biographies, WILMINGTON, DELAWARE

Murray, Tanya M. .... '69 '96 C.1349 B.A. L.1019 J.D. [Ⓐ Stewart&Assoc.]
*PRACTICE AREAS: Corporate Law.
Myers, Melissa Stone ....'73 '98 C.1044 B.S. L.94 J.D. [Ⓐ Morris,N.A.&T.]
Nachbar, Kenneth J., (AV) .... '56 '81 C.311 B.A. L.569 J.D. [Morris,N.A.&T.]
Nardo, Francis X., (BV) .... '61 '88 C.645 B.A. L.1338 J.D. [Tybout,R.&P.]
*PRACTICE AREAS: Negligence; Insurance; Civil Litigation; Workers Compensation; Products Liability.
Nash, Paulette .... '46 '90 C.205 B.A. L.884 J.D. Off. of U.S. Atty.
Natalie, James A., Jr., (BV) .... '46 '71 C.918 B.A. L.893 J.D. [Woloshin,T.L.N.&F.]
Nathanson, Sheila G. '49 '85 C.381 B.S. L.446 J.D.
(adm. in MD; not adm. in DE) Coun., PNC Bk., Del.
Naylor, Joseph S. ....'73 '99 C.205 B.A. L.1338 J.D. [Ⓐ Pepper H.]
*PRACTICE AREAS: Commercial Litigation.
Neff, Wheeler K., (BV) ....'48 '74 C.105 B.A. L.831 J.D. Beneficial Corp.
Neiderman, Matt .... '71 '01 L.446 J.D. [Ⓐ Morris,N.A.&T.]
Neipris, Jonathan P. '49 '74 C.659 B.A. L.273 J.D.
Sr. Coun., Blue Cross Blue Shield of Del., Inc.
Ness, Anton P. '47 '72 C.237 B.A.B.S. L.1017 J.D.
(adm. in PA; not adm. in DE; Pat.) Pat. Atty., The Whitaker Corp.
Nestor, Michael R. ....'69 '95 C.446 B.A. L.1338 J.D. [Ⓐ Young C.S.&T.]
*PRACTICE AREAS: Bankruptcy; Debtor and Creditors Rights.
Neuberger, Thomas Stephen, (BV) ....'47 '74 C.728 B.A. L.276 J.D. [T.S.Neuberger]
Neuberger, Thomas S., P.A., (BV) ....2 East 7th Street
Newell, Michael K., (AV) ....'52 '82 C.205 B.A. L.1338 J.D. [Connolly B.L.&H.]
*PRACTICE AREAS: Family Law; Separation Agreements; Divorce; Marital Property Distribution; Alimony.
Newill, Maria Paris, (CV) ....'65 '91 C.205 B.S.A.S. L.616 J.D. [Heckler&F.]
*PRACTICE AREAS: Worker's Compensation Litigation; General Civil and Trial Practice.
Newnam, Benjamin T. ....'70 '96 C.884 B.A. L.1019 J.D. MBNA America Bk., N.A.
Nichols, Nathaniel C. '48 '74 C.329 B.A. L.178 J.D.
(adm. in PA; not adm. in DE) Assoc. Prof. of Law, Widener Univ. Sch. of Law
Nicholson, Joseph M., (BV) ....'45 '72 C.645 B.A. L.831 J.D. [Young C.S.&T.]
*PRACTICE AREAS: Business Law; Taxation; Trusts and Estates; Wills.
Niedzielski, Marc P. '51 '85 C.205 B.S. L.1338 J.D.
Carvel State Office Building, 820 North French Street
Niezgoda, Erica L. ....'74 '99 C.861 B.A. L.276 J.D. [Ⓐ Potter A.&C.]
*PRACTICE AREAS: Litigation.
Nimeroff, Jami B. '68 '93 C&L.94 B.A., J.D.
(adm. in NJ; not adm. in DE) [Ⓐ Buchanan I.] (⊙Phila., PA)
*PRACTICE AREAS: Bankruptcy; Creditors Rights; Commercial Litigation.
Ninan, Emilie R. ....'71 '95 C.831 B.A. L.276 J.D. [Ⓐ Potter A.&C.]
Nitsche, Gary S., (BV) .... '60 '87 C.205 B.A. L.1187 J.D. [Weik,N.&D.]
*PRACTICE AREAS: Personal Injury; Workers Compensation; Wrongful Death; Premises Liability.
Nivala, John F. '46 '73 C.323 B.A. L.477 J.D.
(adm. in MI; not adm. in DE) 4601 Concord Pike‡
Noah, Belinda ....'54 '83 C.1111 B.A. L.259 J.D. 2704 Blvd. Rd.
Noel, Jennifer R. .... '69 '00 C&L.1338 B.S., J.D. [Ⓐ Young C.S.&T.]
*PRACTICE AREAS: Taxation; Business Law; Intellectual Property Licensing; Employee Benefits; Tax Exempt Organizations.
Nolen, Samuel A., (AV) ....'54 '79 C.880 B.A. L.902 J.D. [Richards,L.&F.]
*PRACTICE AREAS: Corporate Law; Litigation; Mergers and Acquisitions; Chancery Practice.
Nolte, R. Stokes, (BV) ....'58 '84 C.205 B.S. L.61 J.D. [Nolte&B.]
*PRACTICE AREAS: Workers Compensation; Employment Law; Bankruptcy; Insurance Defense.

Nolte & Brodoway, P.A., (BV)
Three Mill Road Suite 304, 19806 ⊙
Telephone: 302-777-1700 Telecopier: 302-777-1705
Email: NOLBRO@AOL.COM
R. Stokes Nolte; Barbara A. Brodoway.
Employment Law, Insurance Defense, Workers Compensation, Commercial Litigation, Bankruptcy, Real Estate, Wills and Probate, Trusts and Estates, Asbestos, Toxic Torts.

See Professional Biographies, WILMINGTON, DELAWARE

Noreika, Maryellen ....'66 '93 C.401 B.S. L.665 J.D. [Morris,N.A.&T.]
Norman, Stephen C., (BV) ....'61 '85 C.651 B.A. L.1019 J.D. [Potter A.&C.]
Noronha, Preeya M. '76 '01 C.276 B.S.F.S. L.178 J.D.
Hon. Sue L. Robinson, U.S.C.D.J.
Norton, Marla Hirshman ....'62 '87 C.205 B.A. L.273 J.D. [Bayard]
*PRACTICE AREAS: Business Law; Commercial Law; Corporate Law; Trademark Law; Transactional Law.
Noyes, Frank E., II .... '58 '86 C.205 B.A. L.93 J.D. [Duane,M.&H.]
*PRACTICE AREAS: Product Liability; Civil Rights Liability; Tobacco Litigation; Insurance Coverage; Public Entity Liability.
Oberly, Charles M., III, (BV) ....'46 '71 C.645 B.A. L.893 J.D. [Oberly&J.]
*PRACTICE AREAS: Commercial; Corporate; Civil Litigation; Government Relations; Corporate Investigations.

Oberly & Jennings, P.A., (AV)
800 Delaware Avenue, P.O. Box 2054, 19899-2054
Telephone: 302-576-2000 Fax: 302-576-2004
Charles M. Oberly, III; Kathleen M. Jennings;—Karen Sullivan.
General Civil Litigation, Criminal Defense, Personal Injury, Commercial, Corporate, Business, Government Relations.

See Professional Biographies, WILMINGTON, DELAWARE

O'Brien, Robert P. O'Flynn '57 '90
C.205 B.A. L.1338 J.D. 1313 North Market Street (Pat.)
O'Connor, Christine P. ....'71 '99 C.658 B.S. L.1338 J.D. [Ⓐ Marshall,D.W.C.&G.]
*PRACTICE AREAS: Workers Compensation Defense.
O'Connor, David W., (BV) ....'61 '88 C.105 B.A. L.1017 J.D. Montell N. Amer. Inc.
O'Donnell, Bernard J., (BV) ....'52 '77 C.205 B.A. L.982 J.D. Asst. Pub. Def.
O'Donnell, Frank, (BV) ....'21 '50 C&L.831 B.S., LL.B. 1207 King St.
Oglesby, Nicholas E., Jr. '21 '52 C.688 B.Ch.E. L.273 LL.B.
(adm. in DC; not adm. in DE) 16 Perth Dr.‡
O'Hara, Robert C. ....'22 '48 C&L.659 B.A., LL.D. 902 Market St. 13th Fl.
O'Hare, Robert A., Jr. '64 '94 C.262 B.A. L.724 J.D.
(adm. in NY; not adm. in DE) Law Clk, U.S. Court of Appeals
Olsen, James M. '67 '98
C.659 B.S.M.E. L.273 J.D. [Ⓐ Connolly B.L.&H.] (See Pat. Sect.)
Olsen, John L., (BV) '58 '84
C.273 B.A. L.659 J.D. V.P. & Coun., Wilmington Trust Company
Olson, Mark D., (AV) ......'45 '76 C.1044 B.A. L.659 J.D. [M.D.Olson] (⊙Georgetown)

Olson, Mark D., & Company, L.L.C., (AV)
Suite 301, Little Falls Centre Two, 2751 Centerville Road, 19808
Telephone: 302-995-7080 Telecopier: 302-995-7075
Email: mark@markolsonlaw.com URL: http://www.markolsonlaw.com

(This Listing Continued)

Olson, Mark D., & Company, L.L.C. (Continued)

Mark D. Olson.
Like Kind Exchanges, Taxation, Estate Planning, Estate Administration, Family Business Planning, Business Succession Planning.

See Professional Biographies, WILMINGTON, DELAWARE

O'Neill, Andrew T. ....'59 '92 C.205 B.A.B.S. L.1338 J.D. [Ⓐ Potter A.&C.]
O'Neill, James E., III ....'60 '85 C.276 B.S. L.884 J.D. [Ⓐ Pachulski,S.Z.Y.&J.]
*PRACTICE AREAS: Corporate Law; Bankruptcy Law; Corporate Reorganizations; Commercial and Residential Foreclosures; Real Estate.
O'Neill, Kevin P., (CV) ....'56 '81 C.918 B.S. L.1292 J.D. [Heyden,K.&O.]
Orescan, Stephen D. '61 '99 C&L.1338 B.S., J.D.
(adm. in PA; not adm. in DE) [Ⓐ J.Williams]
Ormond, David L., Jr. '57 '89 C.575 B.A. L.280 J.D.
(adm. in GA; not adm. in DE) Dept. of Jus.
O'Rourke, Gerard M. '67 '94
C.367 B.S. L.884 J.D. [Ⓐ Connolly B.L.&H.] (See Pat. Sect.)
Ostien, Paul H., III ....'71 '99 C.216 B.S. L.1194 J.D. [Ⓐ Morris,J.H.&W.]
*PRACTICE AREAS: Business Transactions; Taxation; Trusts and Estates.
Ostroski, Janell Schoenbeck ....'68 '93 C.205 B.A. L.1338 J.D. [Ⓐ Schoenbeck&S.]
*PRACTICE AREAS: Family Law; Probate; Bankruptcy; Collections.
O'Toole, Matthew J. .... '63 '94 C.262 B.A. L.945 J.D. [Morris,J.H.&W.]
*PRACTICE AREAS: Corporate Law; Business Law; Intellectual Property.
Over, Susan Carol, (CV) ....'58 '86 C.205 B.A. L.1017 J.D. [Heiman,A.G.&B.]
*PRACTICE AREAS: Personal Injury; Medical Malpractice; Family Law.
Owen, James W., (BV) ....'54 '80 C.205 B.A. L.1017 J.D. [J.W.Owen]
Owen, James W., P.A., (BV) ....3411 Silverside Rd.
Ozolins, Ruth D. '51 '84
(adm. in ON; not adm. in DE) [E.I. d.d.]
*RESPONSIBILITIES: Commercial Law.

Pachulski, Stang, Ziehl, Young & Jones, Professional Corporation, (AV)
919 North Market Street, 16th Floor, P.O. Box 8705, 19899-8705 ⊙
Telephone: 302-652-4100 Telecopier: 302-652-4400
URL: http://www.pszyj.com
David W. Carickhoff, Jr; Kathleen Marshall DePhillips (Not admitted in DE); Peter J. Duhig; Bruce Grohsgal; Curtis A. Hehn (Not admitted in DE); Laura Davis Jones; Christopher J. Lhulier; Rachel Sarah Lowy; James E. O'Neill, III; Michael R. Seidl; Rosalie Spelman (Not admitted in DE).
Bankruptcy, Corporate Reorganization, Debtor-Creditor Matters, Insurance Insolvency, Civil Litigation, Business, Commercial Law, General Real Estate, and Corporate and Entertainment Transactions.
Los Angeles, California Office: 10100 Santa Monica Boulevard, 11th Floor. Telephone: 310-277-6910. Facsimile: 310-201-0760.
San Francisco, California Office: Three Embarcadero Center, Suite 1020. Telephone: 415-263-7000. Facsimile: 415-263-7010.
New York, New York Office: 461 Fifth Avenue, 25th Floor. Telephone: 212-624-9430. Facsimile: 212-624-9435.

See Professional Biographies, WILMINGTON, DELAWARE

Pacitti, Domenic E., (BVⓉ) .... '62 '87 C.1047 B.A. L.692 J.D. [Saul E.]
*PRACTICE AREAS: Bankruptcy; Commercial Litigation.
Packel, Mark J., (AVⓉ) ....'58 '83 C.216 A.B. L.831 J.D. [Blank R.C.&M.]
*PRACTICE AREAS: Bankruptcy Reorganization.
Page, John N., Jr. '38 '83 C.165 B.A. L.1234 J.D.
(adm. in GA; not adm. in DE) Wilmington Tr. Co.
Paikin, Susan F. ....'48 '78 C.477 B.A. L.1338 J.D. Mas., Fam. Ct.
Pala, Nina A. ....'56 '84 C.30 B.A. L.128 J.D. 125 Augustine Cut-Off
Palacio, Ricardo .... '71 '98 C.205 B.A. L.884 J.D. [Ⓐ Ashby&G.]
Pallace, Christine '68 '93
C.896 B.A. L.692 J.D. Claim Atty., State Farm Insurance Company

Palmer Biezup & Henderson LLP
1223 Foulk Road, 19803 ⊙
Telephone: 302-594-0895; 302-478-7443 FAX: 302-478-7625
Email: pbh1@pbh.com
Member of Firm: Michael B. McCauley.
Admiralty and Maritime, International, Insurance and Reinsurance, Commercial, Bankruptcy, Yachts and Recreational Craft, Aviation, Personal Injury, Product Liability, Professional Liability and Transportation Casualty Defense. General Civil, Trial and Appellate Practice in all Courts.
Philadelphia, Pennsylvania Office: 956 Public Ledger Building, 620 Chestnut Street, Independence Mall West, 19106-3409. Telephone: 215-625-9900. FAX: 215-625-0185.
New York, New York Office: 140 Broadway, 46th Floor, PMB 46030, 10005. Telephone: 212-406-1855. FAX: 212-858-7651.
Camden, New Jersey Office: 200 North 5th Street, 08102-1204. Telephone: 856-428-7717. FAX: 856-338-1008.

See Professional Biographies, WILMINGTON, DELAWARE

Palmeri, Barbara McDonald '58 '94 C.1169 B.A. L.1338 J.D.
Asst. V.P. & Compliance Coun., Wilmington Trust Comp.
Pankowski, Edward C., Jr., (BV) ....'46 '72 C.205 B.A. L.1017 J.D. 1211 N. King St.
Parker, Lynne M. .... '64 '89 C.223 B.S. L.884 J.D. [Hollstein K.C.J.&G.]
*PRACTICE AREAS: Commercial and Casualty Litigation; Products Liability; Maritime Law.
Parkins, John A., Jr., (AV) .... '46 '72 C.205 B.A. L.902 J.D. [Richards,L.&F.]
*PRACTICE AREAS: Litigation.
Parrish, Karl J. ....'27 '67 C.473 A.B. L.831 J.D. Ret. Family Ct. J.
Parshall, Jonathan L. ....'56 '92 C.205 B.A. L.1338 J.D. [Murphy S.&L.]
*PRACTICE AREAS: Insurance Coverage; Insurance Defense; Corporate Litigation; Civil Litigation.
Parson, Darryl A. '65 '99 C.309 B.A. L.178 J.D.
(adm. in NY; not adm. in DE) [Ⓐ Skadden,A.S.M.&F.]
*PRACTICE AREAS: Litigation.
Parsons, Donald F., Jr., (BV) ....'48 '77 C.401 B.S.E.E. L.276 J.D. [Morris,N.A.&T.]
Partnoy, Ronald A. '33 '62 C.976 B.A. L.309 LL.B.
(adm. in MA; not adm. in DE) Barley Mill Plaza
Pascale, Karen L., (BV) ....'60 '90 C.205 B.S. L.884 J.D. [Ⓐ Bouchard M.&F.]
*PRACTICE AREAS: Business Litigation; Corporate Litigation; Intellectual Property.
Paschetto, John J. ....'59 '98 C.705 B.A. L.309 J.D. [Ⓐ Young C.S.&T.]
*PRACTICE AREAS: Corporate Law; Alternative Entity Law; Chancery Court Litigation.
Pasquale, Robert, (BV) ....'49 '76 C.1046 B.S. L.1338 J.D. [Doroshow,P.K.S.&B.]
Passante, Lisa M. '59 '83 C.658 B.S. L.884 J.D.
(adm. in PA; not adm. in DE) Corp. Coun., E.I. du Pont de Nemours & Co.
Patel, Sonal C. '72 '99 C.205 B.A. L.1338 J.D.
(adm. in PA; not adm. in DE) 4601 Concord Pike
Patton, James L., Jr., (AV) ....'56 '83 C.198 B.A. L.1017 J.D. [Young C.S.&T.]
*PRACTICE AREAS: Bankruptcy; Commercial Workouts; Business Law.
Payson, Robert K., (AV) ....'39 '64 C&L.228 A.B., LL.B. [Potter A.&C.]
Pazuniak, George ....'52 '76 C.831 A.B. L.228 J.D. [Connolly B.L.&H.]
Pearce, Robert K., (BV) ....'49 '74 C.205 B.S. L.884 J.D. [Trzuskowski,K.K.&P.]
*PRACTICE AREAS: Tort Litigation; Insurance Law; Workers Compensation Law.
Pease, Donald E. ...'20 '47 C&L.276 B.S., J.D. Prof.of Law Emeritus, Widener Univ Sch.
Pease, Eleanor Thompson '23 '47 C.881 A.B. L.976 J.D.
(adm. in DC; not adm. in DE) 804 Princeton Rd.‡
Peck, Kevin T. '58 '83 C.205 B.A. L.884 J.D.
Assoc. Coun. & Asst. Secy., Household Retail Services USA
Pedigo, Robert W. ....'— '01 C.243 B.A. L.216 J.D. [Ⓐ Cooch&T.]

Peeling, Mary Alice '54 '91 C.322 A.B. L.1338 J.D.
(adm. in PA; not adm. in DE) Law. Libr., Widener Univ. Sch. of Law
Peet, J. Carlisle, III '52 '78 C.205 B.A. L.823 J.D.
(adm. in PA; not adm. in DE) Asst. Gen. Coun., Rollins Truck Leasing Corp.
Pelaia, Maria Theresa .... '68 '95 C.128 B.A. L.276 J.D. Off. of Atty. Gen.
Pell, Richard W., (AV) ....'41 '66 C.210 B.A. L.273 LL.B. [Tybout,R.&P.]
*PRACTICE AREAS: Negligence; Insurance; Products Liability; Medical Malpractice.
Peltz, William R., (BV) .... '62 '88 C.205 B.A. L.1338 J.D. [Kimmel,C.R.&P.] ⊙
*PRACTICE AREAS: General and Civil Trial Practice; Insurance; Negligence; Workers Compensation; Construction Accidents.
Pelzer, Robert E., (BV) '53 '80 C&L.02 B.Com., LL.B.
(adm. in AB; not adm. in DE) Sr. V.P. & Gen. Coun., DuPont Pharmaceuticals Co.
Penza, Robert A. .... '63 '89 C.223 B.S. L.884 J.D. [Ⓐ Gordon,F.&M.]
*PRACTICE AREAS: Commercial Litigation; Civil Litigation; Real Estate; Sports Contracts.

Pepper Hamilton LLP, (AV) BB
1201 Market Street, Suite 1600, P.O. Box 1709, 19899-1709 ⊙
Telephone: 302-777-6500 Telecopy: 302-656-8865
Email: phinfo@pepperlaw.com URL: http://www.pepperlaw.com
Partners: Richard P. Eckman; David M. Fournier; M. Duncan Grant; Christopher J. Lamb; Sean P. McDevitt; David B. Stratton; Benjamin Strauss. Associates: Wilmer C. Bettinger; Aaron A. Garber; Adam Hiller (Not admitted in DE); Joseph S. Naylor; Andrea Beth Unterberger.
General Practice.
Philadelphia, Pennsylvania Office: 3000 Two Logan Square, Eighteenth and Arch Streets, 19103-2799. Telephone: 215-981-4000. Fax: 215-981-4750.
Washington, D.C. Office: Hamilton Square, 600 Fourteenth Street, N.W. 20005-2004. Telephone: 202-220-1200. Fax: 202-220-1665.
Detroit, Michigan Office: 100 Renaissance Center, 36th Floor, 48243-1157. Telephone: 313-259-7110. Fax: 313-259-7926.
New York, New York Office: 1180 Avenue of the Americas, 14th Floor, 10036-8401. Telephone: 212-899-5090. Fax: 212-899-5091.
Pittsburgh, Pennsylvania Office: 500 Grant Street, 50th Floor, 15219-2502. Telephone: 412-454-5000. Fax: 412-281-0717.
Berwyn, Pennsylvania Office: 1235 Westlakes Drive, Suite 400, 19312-2401. Telephone: 610-640-7800. Fax: 610-640-7835.
Cherry Hill, New Jersey Office: LibertyView Building, Suite 420, 457 Haddonfield Road, 08002-2220. Telephone: 856-910-7200. Fax: 856-665-7743.
Harrisburg, Pennsylvania Office: 200 One Keystone Plaza, North Front and Market Streets, P.O. Box 1181, 17108-1181. Telephone: 717-255-1155. Fax: 717-238-0575.
Princeton, New Jersey Office: 300 Alexander Park, 08543-5276. Telephone: 609-452-0808. Fax: 609-452-1147.
Tysons Corner, Virginia Office: 8280 Greensboro Drive, Suite 800, 22102-3807. Telephone: 703-748-3900. Fax: 703-356-0005.
See Professional Biographies, WILMINGTON, DELAWARE

Pepukayi, Bernard '72 '99 C.155 B.A. L.352 J.D.
Deputy Attorney General for the State of Delaware
Pernick, Norman L., (AV) .... '59 '85 C.1036 B.A. L.537 J.D. [Saul E.]
*PRACTICE AREAS: Bankruptcy Law.
Perri, Jacqueline '53 '95 C.645 B.A. L.831 J.D.
(adm. in PA; not adm. in DE) Sr. Coun., AIG Life Ins. Cos. (US)

Perry, James T., (BV) '44 '69 C.645 A.B. L.884 J.D.
First Federal Plaza Suite 560, P.O. Box 1568, 19899
Telephone: 302-655-4482 Fax: 302-655-4043
Email: perrylaw@dol.net URL: http://www.perrylaw@dol.net
Associate: Michael L. Sensor.
Personal Injury, Workers Compensation, Products Liability, Insurance Coverage and Insurance Defense, Collections.

Person, Richard V. '64 '98 C.635 B.S. L.802 J.D.
(adm. in TX; not adm. in DE) Intell. Prop. Coun., Astrazeneca Pharm.LP
*RESPONSIBILITIES: Patents.
Peters, Allison Lynn '70 '96 C.178 B.A. L.644 J.D.
Carvel State Office Building, 6th Floor, 820 North French Street
Peterson, Michelle N. '72 '00 C.831 B.S. L.1338 J.D.
(adm. in NJ; not adm. in DE) [Ⓐ Grant&E.]
Pettit, George R., (BVⓉ) '45 '75 C.431 B.S.E.E. L.1009 J.D.
(adm. in IN; not adm. in DE; See Pat. Sect.) [Connolly B.L.&H.]
*PRACTICE AREAS: Electrical Intellectual Property; Intellectual Property Infringement; Intellectual Property Licensing; Computer and Software Patents; Electronic Patents.
Pezzner, Ashley I. ...... '59 '90 C.790 B.S. L.64 J.D. [Connolly B.L.&H.] (See Pat. Sect.)
Pezzner, Harold, (BV) '36 '62 C.645 B.S. L.273 J.D.
[Connolly B.L.&H.] (See Pat. Sect.)
Phillips, Blaine T., (AV) ....'30 '55 C&L.893 B.A., LL.B. [Ⓒ Potter A.&C.]
Phillips, John C., Jr., (AV) ....'48 '74 C.880 B.A. L.1017 J.D. [Phillips,G.&S.]
*PRACTICE AREAS: Bankruptcy Litigation; Business Litigation; Toxic Torts; Environmental; Insurance Coverage.
Phillips, Robert F., (CV) .... '58 '86 C&L.896 B.A., J.D. Dep. Atty. Gen.

Phillips, Goldman & Spence, P.A., (AV)
1200 North Broom Street, 19806 ⊙
Telephone: 302-655-4200 Telecopier: 302-655-4210
Email: pgs@pgslaw.com
John C. Phillips, Jr.; Robert S. Goldman; Stephen W. Spence; Richard P. S. Hannum; Lisa Cresci McLaughlin; James P. Hall;—Rosalind D. Williams; Michael F. Duggan; Joseph James Farnan, III.
Commercial, Corporate, Toxic Tort, Environmental, Superfund , Bankruptcy and Personal Injury Litigation, Insurance Coverage and Defense, Commercial Bankruptcy, Commercial Real Estate, Business Practice and Criminal Defense.
West Chester Office: 103 South High Street, 19382. Telephone: 610-701-9706. Telecopier: 610-701-9707.
See Professional Biographies, WILMINGTON, DELAWARE

Pietrafitta, Chris J. .... '60 '90 C.397 B.S. L.884 J.D. [Ⓐ Richards,L.&F.]
*PRACTICE AREAS: Corporate Trust; Asset Based Finance; Business Organization.
Pileggi, Francis G. X. .... '— '87 C.728 B.A. L.1338 J.D. [Fox,R.O.&F.]
*PRACTICE AREAS: Litigation; Commercial Transactions.
Pinckney, Joanne Pileggi ....'58 '94 C.999 B.S. L.1338 J.D. [Ⓐ Bouchard M.&F.]
*PRACTICE AREAS: Corporate Litigation; Business Litigation; Bankruptcy Litigation.
Pincus, Kathryn Ann ....'66 '91 C.205 B.A. L.276 J.D. Coun., Conectiv
*RESPONSIBILITIES: Litigation; Labor and Employment.
Pincus, Robert B., (AV) ....'55 '80 C.945 B.B.A. L.30 J.D. [Skadden,A.S.M.&F.]
Pirnot, John D. ....'60 '98 C.453 B.S. L.1338 J.D. [Ⓐ Morris,N.A.&T.]
Pittenger, Michael A. .... '68 '93 C.473 B.A. L.902 J.D. [Ⓐ Potter A.&C.]
Pizor, Andrew G. .... '70 '96 C.276 B.A. L.262 J.D. Legal Servs. Corp. of Del. Inc.
Plaza, Bernadette M. .... '63 '92 C.205 B.A. L.1338 J.D. 2205 Kentmere Pkwy.
Poche, Thomas F. '63 '95 C.659 B.A. L.94 J.D.
(adm. in IL; not adm. in DE) [Ⓐ Connolly B.L.&H.] ⊙
*PRACTICE AREAS: Patent Litigation.
Poehner, Maria J., (CV) ....'68 '93 C.831 B.B.A. L.1338 J.D. [Chrissinger&B.]
Poff, Adam W. ....'75 '00 C.205 B.A. L.884 J.D. [Ⓐ Young C.S.&T.]
Polesky, Joelle E. ....'70 '98 C.276 B.S.F.S. L.659 J.D. [Ⓐ Smith,K.&F.]
*PRACTICE AREAS: Corporate Litigation; Commercial Litigation.
Polite, Kenneth A., Jr. ....'76 '00 C.309 A.B. L.276 J.D. [Ⓐ Skadden,A.S.M.&F.]
*PRACTICE AREAS: Litigation.
Polk, John J., (BV) '50 '76
C.602 B.A. L.1338 J.D. Off. of Wkrs. Comp., DE Dept. of Labor

Polleck, Laurie Schenker '60 '88 C.205 B.A. L.1338 J.D.
(adm. in PA; not adm. in DE) Intrust Tech. Inc.
Pompian, Shawn Marc '73 '00 C.367 B.A. L.893 J.D.
(adm. in VA; not adm. in DE) 820 N. French St.
Pond, Nigel '60 '83 C.051 B.A. L.999
(adm. in Englan; not adm. in DE) Sr. Coun., E.I. du Pont de Nemours and Company
*RESPONSIBILITIES: Commercial Law.
Poole, Richard E., (AV) .... '40 '66 C.821 B.A. L.145 J.D. [Ⓒ Potter A.&C.]
Popp, Maura Crough '61 '86 C.93 B.A. L.884 J.D.
(adm. in PA; not adm. in DE) Asst. Gen. Coun., AIG Marketing, Inc.
Popper, Richard J. A., (AV) .... '52 '77 C.860 B.S. L.273 J.D. [Young C.S.&T.]
*PRACTICE AREAS: Trusts and Estates; Estate Planning; Estate Administration; Employee Benefits; Taxation.
Poppiti, Ciro C., (BV) .... '35 '61 C.205 A.B. L.659 J.D. 702 King St.
Poppiti, Michael A., (AV) .... '20 '48 C.205 B.A. L.659 J.D. 702 King St.
Poppiti, Vincent J. ....'45 '70 C.262 A.B. L.893 J.D. Chf. J., Family Ct.
Porcelli, Frank P., (AVⓉ) '47 '71 C.93 A.B. L.309 J.D.
[Fish&R.] (Pat.) (⊙Boston, MA)
*PRACTICE AREAS: Intellectual Property; Litigation; Appellate.
Poston, David S. '38 '65 C.388 B.A. L.347 LL.B.
(adm. in IN; not adm. in DE) Corp. Coun., E.I. du Pont de Nemours & Co.
Pott, Jeffrey A. '64 '90 C.937 B.A. L.884 J.D.
(adm. in PA; not adm. in DE) [Astrazeneca P.L.]
*RESPONSIBILITIES: Litigation; Antitrust; Products Liability.
Potter, Stephen B., (BV) .... '38 '64 C.205 B.A. L.128 LL.B. [Potter,C.&L.] ⊙

Potter Anderson & Corroon LLP, (AV)
Hercules Plaza, 1313 N. Market Street, P.O. Box 951, 19899-0951
Telephone: 302-984-6000 Fax: 302-658-1192
URL: http://www.potteranderson.com
Members of Firm: Robert K. Payson; Leonard S. Togman; Michael D. Goldman; James F. Burnett; Daniel F. Wolcott, Jr.; Charles S. McDowell; David B. Brown; Somers S. Price, Jr.; Donald J. Wolfe, Jr.; Gregory A. Inskip; David J. Baldwin; John E. James; W. Harding Drane, Jr.; Mary E. Copper; Richard L. Horwitz; Michael B. Tumas; Kathleen Furey McDonough; Laurie Selber Silverstein; Peter J. Walsh, Jr.; Stephen C. Norman; Arthur L. Dent; Harold I. Salmons, III; William R. Denny; Philip A. Rovner; Jennifer Gimler Brady; Scott E. Waxman; Mark A. Morton; John F. Grossbauer; Kathleen W. Geiger; Wendy K. Voss; Kevin R. Shannon. Counsel: Robert P. Barnett; Michael B. Keehan, Vice President-Law; Hilmar L. Fricke (Not admitted in DE); Todd L. Goodman. Of Counsel: John P. Sinclair; Blaine T. Phillips; Hugh Corroon; Joseph H. Geoghegan; Richard L. McMahon; Charles S. Crompton, Jr.; Richard E. Poole. Associates: Michael A. Pittenger; J. Breck Smith; Matthew E. Fischer; William A. Hazeltine; Emilie R. Ninan; Monica Leigh Loftin; Janine M. Salomone; Andrew T. O'Neill; John A. Ciccarone; John J. Quinn, III; Catherine M. Hamberger; Jacqueline A. Lewis (Not admitted in DE); Brian C. Ralston; Elihu E. Allinson, III; Paul D. Golian; Ronald S. Gellert (Not admitted in DE); James M. Kron; John M. Seaman; Thomas R. Mancini (Not admitted in DE); Rebecca L. Scalio; Erica L. Niezgoda; Nancy Waterman; David E. Moore; Michael W. Whittaker; Richard L. Renck; Timothy M. Holly; Nathan J. LaComb; Elizabeth D. Power; Michael J. Scali.
General Practice. Corporation Law.
Counsel for: ConRail; Conectiv, Inc.; Hercules Inc.; Corporation Trust Co.; General Motors Corp.; Chrysler Corp.; Citicorp.; Mazda Motor of America, Inc.; E.I. duPont de Nemours & Company, Inc.
See Professional Biographies, WILMINGTON, DELAWARE

Potter, Carmine & Leonard, P.A., (BV) ....840 North Union Street (⊙Newark)
Poulios, Ann '66 '92 C.1350 B.A. L.1338 J.D.
(adm. in PA; not adm. in DE) [Ⓐ Elzufon A.R.T.&M.]
*PRACTICE AREAS: Worker's Compensation; Subrogation.
Powell, Jason C. .... '72 '98 C.397 B.A. L.1338 J.D. [Ferry&J.]
*PRACTICE AREAS: Trusts and Estates; Mental Disability Law; Elder Law; Bankruptcy.
Powell, Norman M., (BV) ....'63 '90 C.276 B.S.B.A. L.884 J.D. [Morris,J.H.&W.]
*PRACTICE AREAS: Real and Personal Property; Business Law; Business Trusts; Limited Liability Companies; Structured Finance.
Power, Elizabeth D. .... '76 '01 C.205 B.A. L.575 J.D. [Ⓐ Potter A.&C.]
*PRACTICE AREAS: Bankruptcy.
Powers, N. Richard, (BV) ....'44 '72 C.728 B.S. L.884 J.D. [Connolly B.L.&H.]
Powlus, JoAnn Y. '61 '91 C.282 B.A. L.117 J.D.
(adm. in OH; not adm. in DE) Coun., First USA
Prestia, Joanne M. Scanlon '51 '89 C.116 B.A. L.309 J.D.
(adm. in DC; not adm. in DE) Coun., Conectiv
*RESPONSIBILITIES: Telecommunications (50%); Environmental Law (25%); Contracts (25%).
Prestia, Paul F., (AVⓉ) '37 '67 C.401 B.S.Ch.E. L.276 J.D.
[Ratner&P.] (See Pat. Sect.) (⊙Valley Forge, PA)
*PRACTICE AREAS: Intellectual Property; Litigation; Dispute Resolution; Patents.
Preston, Thomas P., (AV) .... '— '75 C.976 B.A. L.893 J.D. [Reed S.]
*PRACTICE AREAS: Litigation.
Price, Christopher '57 '82 C.881 A.B. L.945 J.D.
(adm. in VA; not adm. in DE) Pres., Brandywine Ins. Agcy., Inc.
Price, Somers S., Jr., (AV) .... '50 '75 C.198 B.A. L.188 J.D. [Potter A.&C.]
Prickett, William, (AV) ....'25 '55 C.674 B.A. L.309 LL.B. [Ⓒ Prickett,J.&E.]
*PRACTICE AREAS: Corporate Law; Chancery Litigation; Federal Litigation; Patent Litigation (Local Counsel).

Prickett, Jones & Elliott, P.A., (AV)
1310 King Street, P.O. Box 1328, 19899-1328 ⊙
Telephone: 302-888-6500 Telecopier: 302-658-8111; 658-7257
Email: attorneys@prickett.com URL: http://www.prickett.com
William S. Prickett (1862-1926); William Prickett (1894-1964); Richard I. G. Jones; Wayne N. Elliott; Mason E. Turner, Jr.; James L. Holzman; John H. Small; Michael Hanrahan; David E. Brand; Wayne J. Carey; Paul M. Lukoff; Elizabeth M. McGeever; William J. Martin, III; Gary F. Traynor (Resident at Dover Office); John W. Paradee (Resident at Dover Office); Ronald A. Brown, Jr.; Bruce E. Jameson; Thomas A. Mullen; F. Peter Conaty, Jr. Of Counsel: William Prickett; April Caso Ishak;—William H. Lunger; Paul A. Fioravanti, Jr.; Allyson A. McKenzie (Not admitted in DE); D. Benjamin Snyder (Resident, Dover, Delaware Office).
General Practice including: Trial and Appellate Litigation, Corporation, Partnership, Commercial, Banking, Business, Health Care Law, Personal Injury, Real Estate, Bankruptcy and Reorganization, Environmental, Probate, Trust and Estate Planning, Tax, Delaware Patent Litigation, Construction Law, Criminal Law, Medical Malpractice, Insurance Defense, Product Liability, Premises Liability, Occupational Disease Litigation, Labor and Employment, Government Affairs.
Representative Clients: Computer Associates International; Conectiv Power Delivery (Delmarva Power & Light); PHICO Insurance Company.
Dover, Delaware Office: 11 North State Street. Telephone: 302-674-3841.
Kennett Square, Pennsylvania Office: 217 West State Street. Telephone: 610-444-1573.
See Professional Biographies, WILMINGTON, DELAWARE

Pritzkur, Lewis Henry ....'47 '76 C.102 B.A. L.1338 J.D. 712 West St.
Procopio, Patricia C '61 '94 C.728 B.S. L.1338 J.D.
(adm. in PA; not adm. in DE) Atty., AIG Mktg. Inc.
Proctor, Margaret S. .... '54 '80 C.778 A.B. L.309 J.D. Dep. Atty. Gen.
Proctor, Vernon R., (BV) ....'54 '79 C&L.309 A.B., J.D. [Bayard]
*PRACTICE AREAS: Corporate and Commercial Litigation; Corporate Law; Partnership Law.
Pulsifer, Thomas R., (AV) .... '58 '85 C.478 B.A. L.569 J.D. [Morris,N.A.&T.]
Purpura, Mark V. .... '73 '99 C.800 B.S. L.575 J.D. [Ⓐ Richards,L.&F.]
*PRACTICE AREAS: Banks and Banking; Business Law.
Putnick, Mary E. .... '66 '00 C.104 A.B L.569 J.D 100 W. 10th Street
Quell Friedman, Tiffany .... '67 '92 C.903 B.A. L.1338 J.D. [Ⓐ Roeberg,M.&Assoc.]
Quinn, John J., III .... '55 '97 C.401 B.S,Ch.E. L.659 J.D. [Ⓐ Potter A.&C.]
Quinn, Michelle P. ....'73 '00 C.367 B.A. L.893 J.D. [Ⓐ Richards,L.&F.]

Quirk, Marion M. '72 '98 C.597 B.A. L.823 J.D.
(adm. in PA; not adm. in DE) [A Skadden,A.S.M.&F.]
*PRACTICE AREAS: Corporate Reorganization.
Rackow, Julian P., (AV①) '41 '66 C.188 A.B. L.309 J.D.
(adm. in PA; not adm. in DE) [Blank R.C.&M.] (⊙Phila., PA)
*PRACTICE AREAS: Retail Development; Commercial Real Estate Development; Commercial Real Estate Finance; Shopping Center Development; Public-Private Development.
Radulski, Raymond M. .... '49 '77 C.276 B.S. L.1202 J.D. 1225 N. King St. #301
Rago, Richard F. '46 '71 C&L.884 A.B., J.D.
1401 Pennsylvania Avenue, Suite 101 (⊙Rehoboth Beach)
Rahaim, Andrew D., (BV) .... '54 '80 C.205 B.A. L.1338 J.D. [Rahaim&S.]
Rahaim & Saints, (BV) ....2055 Limestone Rd.
Raju, Srinivas M. .... '68 '94 C.347 B.S. L.276 J.D. [Richards,L.&F.]
*PRACTICE AREAS: Business Law.
Ralston, Brian C. ....'73 '98 C.884 B.A. L.1017 J.D. [A Potter A.&C.]
Ralston, Robert W., (AV) ....'47 '72 C.874 B.A. L.1017 J.D. 10 East 13th Street
Ramunno, L. Vincent ....'39 '65 C.205 B.A. L.276 J.D. [Ramunno&R.]
Ramunno, Lawrence A. ....'51 '77 C.205 B.A. L.1338 J.D. [Ramunno&R.]

Ramunno, Leo John, (CV) '55 '80 C.205 B.A. L.1338 J.D.
1205 North King Street, 19801
Telephone: 302-654-0660 Fax: 302-425-5044
Personal Injury, Family Law, Criminal Law, Civil Litigation, Corporate and Business Law, Real Estate, Probate and Estate Planning, Collections, Bankruptcy.

Ramunno, Lorraine Mary '64 '94 C.205 B.A. L.1338 J.D.
(adm. in PA; not adm. in DE) 29 Shellburne Dr.‡
Ramunno & Ramunno, P.A. ....903 N. French St.
Ranalli, Kathleen M. '57 '89 C.831 B.A. L.889 J.D.
(adm. in PA; not adm. in DE) Sr. Litig. Coun., Astrazeneca Pharm. LP
*RESPONSIBILITIES: Employee Benefits.
Ransom, Donald M., (CV) ....'61 '87 C.205 B.A. L.884 J.D. [Casarino,C.&S.]
*PRACTICE AREAS: Civil Litigation; Personal Injury; Products Liability; Insurance Coverage; Arson and Insurance Fraud.
Rath, Daniel B. ....'63 '91 C.347 B.S. L.831 J.D. [Klett R.L.&S.]
*PRACTICE AREAS: Construction Litigation; Commercial Litigation.

Ratner & Prestia, A Professional Corporation, (AV①)
Suite 209, Webster Building, 3411 Silverside Road, P.O. Box 7228, 19803 ⊙
Telephone: 302-479-9470 Fax: 302-479-9480
Email: mail@ratnerprestia.com URL: http://www.ratnerprestia.com
Kevin W. Goldstein; Costas S. Krikelis (Resident Managing Partner); Bruce M. Monroe;—Rex A. Donnelly, IV. Consulting Attorney: Paul F. Prestia.
Domestic and International Intellectual Property Law including Patent, Trademark, Copyright, Unfair Competition, Trade Secret Matters and Related Litigation, Licensing and Antitrust, Biotechnology, Software and Computer Law, Internet Law, Protection and Entertainment Law.
Valley Forge, Pennsylvania Office: Suite 301, One Westlakes (Berwyn), P.O. Box 980. Telephone: 610-407-0700. Facsimile: 610-407-0701.
Allentown, Pennsylvania Office: Suite 265, Commerce Plaza II, 5100 Tilghman Street. Telephone: 610-530-8100. Fax: 610-530-8200.
See Professional Biographies, WILMINGTON, DELAWARE

Rau, James Thomas, Jr. ....'67 '95 C.105 B.S. L.1338 J.D. MBNA America Bk., N.A.
Ray, Laura K. '46 '81 C.104 A.B. L.976 J.D.
(adm. in CT; not adm. in DE) Prof. of Law, Widener Univ. Sch. of Law
Rea, Richard H. '31 '60 C.674 A.B. L.309 J.D.
(adm. in PA; not adm. in DE) Barley Mill Plaza
Reardon, Allison E., (BV) ....'59 '86 C.205 B.A. L.1338 J.D. Dep. Atty. Gen.
Reardon, Mark L., (BV) ....'60 '86 C.93 B.S. L.1338 J.D. [Elzufon A.R.T.&M.]
*PRACTICE AREAS: Civil Litigation; Construction Law; Torts and Insurance Law; Asbestos Litigation.
Redfearn, B. Wilson, (AV) ....'36 '62 C.473 B.A. L.597 J.D. [Tybout,R.&P.]
*PRACTICE AREAS: Negligence; Insurance; Worker's Compensation; Products Liability; Medical Malpractice.
Reed, John L., (BV) ....'64 '91 C.884 B.A. L.1338 J.D. [Duane,M.&H.]
*PRACTICE AREAS: Litigation; Corporate; Securities; Partnership Law; Complex Commercial Litigation.
Reed, Thomas J. '40 '69 C.436 A.B. L.602 J.D.
(adm. in IN; not adm. in DE) Prof. of Law, Widener Univ. School of Law

Reed Smith LLP, (AV)
1201 Market Street, Suite 1500, 19801 ⊙
Mailing Address: P.O. Box 2009, 15230-2009
Telephone: 302-778-7500 FAX: 302-778-7575
Email: reedsmith@reedsmith.com URL: http://www.reedsmith.com
Members of Firm: Tobey M. Daluz (Not admitted in DE); Kurt F. Gwynne; Thomas P. Preston; David S. Swayze; J. Richard Tucker (Not admitted in DE). Associates: Alissa Balotti Anderson; John G. Harris (Not admitted in DE); Jennifer A. L. Kelleher (Not admitted in DE); Richard A. Keuler Jr. (Not admitted in DE); Christine P. Schiltz; Michael W. Teichman; Jan A. T. Van Amerongen, Jr.
Antitrust and Trade Regulation, Asbestos, Bank Regulatory, Bankruptcy, China/Asia, Communications, Construction, Consumer Financial Services, Corporate and Securities, E-Commerce, Eminent Domain/Condemnation, Employee Benefits, Employment Discrimination Litigation, Employment Law, Energy and Natural Resources, Environmental, Equipment Leasing, Family Business, Financial Services, Financial Services Insurance, Financial Services Litigation, First Amendment, Food, Drug & Device, Franchise, Government Contracts & Export Compliance, Government Relations, Health Care, Higher Education, Immigration, Information Technology, Insurance, Insurance Coverage, Intellectual Property, International, Land Use, Litigation, Media and Entertainment, Mergers and Acquisitions, Non-Profit Organizations, Product Liability, Professional Liability, Project Finance, Public Finance, Real Estate, Restrictive Covenants/Trade Secrets, Satellite Transactions, Tax, Technology, Telecommunications, Tissue Engineering and Biomedical Applications, Trusts & Estates, Venture, White Collar Crime, Year 2000.
Pittsburgh, Pennsylvania Office: 435 Sixth Avenue, 15219-1886. Telephone: 412-288-3131. FAX: 412-288-3063.
Washington, D.C. Office: Suite 1100 - East Tower, 1301 K Street, N.W., 20005-3317. Telephone: 202-414-9200. FAX: 202-414-9299.
Philadelphia, Pennsylvania Office: 2500 One Liberty Place, 19103-7301. Telephone: 215-851-8100. FAX: 215-851-1420.
Harrisburg, Pennsylvania Office: 213 Market Street, 17101-2132. Telephone: 717-234-5988. FAX: 717-236-3777.
Princeton, New Jersey Office: 136 Main Street, Suite 250, 08540-5799. Telephone: 609-987-0050. FAX: 609-951-0824.
New York, N.Y. Office: 375 Park Avenue, 17th Floor, 10152. Telephone: 212-521-5400. FAX: 212-521-5450.
Newark, New Jersey Office: The Legal Center, One Riverfront Plaza, First Floor, 07102-5400. Telephone: 973-621-3200. FAX: 973-621-3199.
Falls Church, Virginia Office: Suite 1400, 3110 Fairview Park Drive, 22042. Telephone: 703-641-4200. FAX: 703-641-4340.
Leesburg, Virginia Office: 44084 Riverside Parkway, Suite 300, 20176. Telephone: 703-729-8500. Metro: 703-478-1992. FAX: 703-478-8003.
McLean, Virginia Office: Suite 1100, 8251 Greensboro Drive, 22102-3844. Telephone: 703-734-4600. FAX: 703-734-4699.
Richmond, Virginia Office: Riverfront Plaza, West Tower, 901 East Byrd Street, Suite 1700, 23219-4069. Telephone: 804-344-3400. FAX: 804-344-3410.
London, England Office: Reed Smith Warner Cranston, Pickfords Wharf, Clink Street, SE1 9DG. Telephone: +44-20-7403-2900. FAX: +44-20-7403-4221.
Coventry, England Office: Reed Smith Warner Cranston, Park House, Station Square, CV1 2FL. Telephone: +44 24 7629 3000. FAX: +44 24 7629 3030. DX: 11203 Coventry 1.
See Professional Biographies, WILMINGTON, DELAWARE

Rees, Marcia ....'41 '80 C.112 B.A. L.831 J.D. Dep. Atty. Gen.
Rees, Martha L. '52 '84 C.679 B.S. L.276 J.D.
(adm. in DC; not adm. in DE)
Assoc. Gen. Coun., E.I. du Pont de Nemours and Company
Reese, C. Scott, (BV) ....'55 '81 C.165 B.A. L.1338 J.D. [Cooch&T.] (⊙Newark)
*PRACTICE AREAS: Construction; Asbestos Defense; Products Liability; Commercial Litigation.
Reese, Cathy L., (BV) ....'60 '89 C.178 B.S. L.273 J.D. [Blank R.C.&M.]
*PRACTICE AREAS: Corporate Litigation; Securities Litigation; Commercial Litigation; Technology Litigation.
Reese, Judith R. ....'52 '89 C.114 B.A. L.982 J.D. 3317 Coachman Road
Reese, Leanne J. ....'70 '98 C&L.659 B.A., J.D. [A Richards,L.&F.]
Regan, Paul L. ....'57 '82 C.884 B.S. L.831 J.D. 4601 Concord Pike
Reger & Rizzo
1225 North King St., Ste. 900 (⊙Cherry Hill, NJ; King Of Prussia, Phila., PA)
Reichert, Robert J. '24 '53 C&L.477 B.S., LL.B.
(adm. in NY; not adm. in DE; Pat.) Pres., Robrei, Inc. Consultants
Reid, Donald E., (AV) ....'53 '79 C.659 B.A. L.884 J.D. [Morris,N.A.&T.]
Reidenberg, Seth J. ....'70 '97 C.645 B.S. L.1338 J.D. [A White&W.]
Reilly, Bernard J. '43 '77 C.870 B.S. L.893 J.D.
(adm. in VA; not adm. in DE) Corp. Coun., E.I. du Pont de Nemours and Company
*RESPONSIBILITIES: Environment; Mergers and Acquisitions.
Reilly, Michael K. ....'72 '98 C.884 B.A. L.188 J.D. [A Richards,L.&F.]
Reiver, Joanna, (AV) ....'46 '76 C.923 A.B. L.128 J.D. [Schlusser&R.]
*PRACTICE AREAS: Estate Planning; Probate Law.
Renck, Richard L. ....'70 '00 C.673 B.S. L.790 J.D. [A Potter A.&C.]
*PRACTICE AREAS: Corporate.
Rennie, Sheldon K. ....'71 '98 C.415 M.S./B.A. L.884 J.D. [A Fox,R.O.&F.]
*PRACTICE AREAS: Commercial Litigation; Creditors Rights in Bankruptcy; Corporate Litigation; Corporate Law.
Renzulli, Judith Nichols, (BV) ....'43 '80 C.400 B.A. L.659 J.D. [C Duane,M.&H.]
*PRACTICE AREAS: Commercial Litigation; Insurance Coverage Litigation; Real Estate Tax Assessment Litigation; Corporate Litigation.

Resnick, Abraham & Schwartzman, L.L.C.
100 East 14th Street, 19801 ⊙
Telephone: 302-655-1943
URL: http://www.ra-atty.com
—Andrew J. Witherell.
Commercial and Collection Law. Admiralty, Personal Injury, Immigration, Naturalization, Bankruptcy Law.
Baltimore, Maryland Office: One East Franklin Street, 21202. Telephone: 410-539-6087.
Fairfax, Virginia Office: 12600 Fair Lakes Circle, Suite 220. Telephone: 703-818-0223.
Washington, D.C. Office: 1730 K Street, N.W., Suite 304. Telephone: 202-452-1411.
Syosset, New York Office: 485 Underhill Boulevard, Suite 302. Telephone: 516-364-5300.
Glen Mills, Pennsylvania Office: 30 Regency Plaza. Telephone: 610-358-9600.
Burlington, New Jersey Office: 505 High Street, P.O. Box 1427. Telephone: 609-386-1911.
Roswell, Georgia Office: 1265 Minihinette Drive, Suite 150, P.O. Box 1870. Telephone: 770-840-8482.
Los Angeles, California Office: 2049 Century Park East, Suite 460. Telephone: 310-557-2599.
Deerfield Beach, Florida Office: 1701 West Hillsboro Boulevard, Suite 303. Telephone: 954-480-6220.
Charlotte, North Carolina Office: 1721 Norland Road. Telephone: 704-535-8440.
Cary, North Carolina Office: 140 Preston Executive Drive. Telephone: 919-781-1880.
See Professional Biographies, BALTIMORE, MARYLAND

Revit, Howard R. '43 '69 C.446 B.A. L.329 J.D.
(adm. in VA; not adm. in DE) du Pont Co.
Rhoades, Joseph J., (BV) ....'54 '81 C.205 B.A.A.S. L.1338 J.D. 1225 King St., Ste. 1200
Rhodes, Harry H., III, (BV) '44 '73 C&L.36 B.S., J.D.
Carvel State Office Building, 820 North French Street
Rice, Vernon R., (AV) '39 '67 C.877 B.S. L.273 J.D.
(adm. in VA; not adm. in DE; Pat.)
V.P. & Assoc. Gen. Coun., E.I. du Pont de Nemours and Company
*RESPONSIBILITIES: Intellectual Property; Environmental Law.
Richards, Ashby T., Jr. '45 '72 C.893 B.S. L.188 J.D.
(adm. in NY; not adm. in DE) Sr. Tax Coun., du Pont Co.
Richards, Charles F., Jr., (AV) ....'37 '63 C.674 A.B. L.976 LL.B. [Richards,L.&F.]
*PRACTICE AREAS: Business Law; Business Litigation; Corporate Law; Corporate Control Contests; Corporate Litigation.
Richards, Deirdre M. '62 '89 C.320 B.A. L.831 J.D.
(adm. in PA; not adm. in DE) [A Richards,L.&F.]
*PRACTICE AREAS: Bankruptcy; Creditors Rights; Litigation.
Richards, Helen M., (BV) ....'41 '89 C.788 B.A. L.1338 J.D. 1 Rodney Sq.
Richards, Robert H., III, (BV) ....'38 '62 C.674 A.B. L.309 LL.B. [Richards,L.&F.]

Richards, Layton & Finger, P.A., (AV) BR
One Rodney Square, P.O. Box 551, 19899
Telephone: 302-658-6541 Telecopier: 302-658-6548
Charles F. Richards, Jr.; Thomas P. Sweeney; Pierre S. du Pont; Robert H. Richards, III; R. Franklin Balotti; Richard G. Elliott, Jr.; Wendell Fenton; Allen M. Terrell, Jr.; Daniel M. Kristol; Glenn C. Kenton; Richard G. Bacon; Stephen E. Herrmann; Julian H. Baumann, Jr.; Daniel L. Klein; Donald A. Bussard; William J. Wade; Jesse A. Finkelstein; Samuel A. Nolen; Thomas A. Beck; Gregory P. Williams; John A. Parkins, Jr.; Paul M. Altman; Gregory V. Varallo; Mark J. Gentile; Robert J. Krapf; Kevin G. Abrams; Eric A. Mazie; Robert W. Whetzel; W. Donald Sparks, II; C. Stephen Bigler; C. Malcolm Cochran, IV; Anne C. Foster; Cynthia Deans Kaiser; Daniel A. Dreisbach; James G. Leyden, Jr.; Frederick L. Cottrell, III; Bernard J. Kelley; Robert J. Stearn, Jr.; William A. Yemc; Mark D. Collins; Lisa A. Schmidt; William J. Haubert; Doneene Keemer Damon; Daniel J. DeFranceschi; Raymond J. DiCamillo; Catherine G. Dearlove; Jeffrey L. Moyer; Srinivas M. Raju;—James R. Adams (Not admitted in DE); Michael D. Allen; Kelly C. Ashby; Monica M. Ayres; Mark A. Beaver; Jennifer C. Bebko; Rebecca L. Booth; Thad J. Bracegirdle; Paul D. Brown; Peter D. Calder; Matthew S. Criscimagna; Brock E. Czeschin; Melanie George Day; Elisa J. Erlenbach; Richard J. Facciolo; Eric N. Feldman; Steven J. Fineman; Zoe A. Forrester; Shannon S. Frazier; Brigitte V. Fresco; Dominick T. Gattuso; Anne Shea Gaza (Not admitted in DE); D. Shane Gunter; Paul N. Heath; Kelly A. Herring; Tara J. Hoffner; Kathleen P. Ittel (Not admitted in DE); Kathleen A. Kelley; John H. Knight; Thomas H. Kovach; Seth Hamilton Kramer; Peter B. Ladig; Gregory W. Ladner; J. Travis Laster; Patrick M. Leathem (Not admitted in DE); Kathleen M. Lefebvre; Christopher D. Loizides; Scott L. Matthews; Michael J. Merchant; Christine M. Morabito; Chris J. Pietrafitta; Mark V. Purpura; Michelle P. Quinn; Leanne J. Reese; Michael K. Reilly; Deirdre M. Richards (Not admitted in DE); Richard Philip Rollo (Not admitted in DE); Eric A. Schwartzman; Chad M. Shandler; Andrea K. Short; Russell C. Silberglied; Jason J. Solomon; Deborah E. Spivack; Lisa R. Stark; Michael R. Stein; Melissa K. Stubenberg.
General Civil Trial Litigation and Appellate Practice in all State and Federal Courts and Banking, Bankruptcy, Business, Corporations, Employee Benefits, Environment, Government Relations, Health Care, Intellectual Property, Labor and Employment, Partnership, Real Estate, Securities, Tax, and Trusts and Estates.
Revisers of the Delaware Law Digest for this Directory.
See Professional Biographies, WILMINGTON, DELAWARE

Richenderfer, Linda, (AV①) '59 '84 C&L.884 B.A., J.D.
(adm. in PA; not adm. in DE) [Saul E.] (⊙Phila., PA)
*PRACTICE AREAS: Environmental; White Collar Crime; Commercial Litigation.
Richter, Robert H., (BV) ....'53 '82 C.205 B.S. L.1338 J.D. [Heckler&F.]
*PRACTICE AREAS: Worker's Compensation Litigation; General Civil and Trial Practice.
Riegel, J. Kent '38 '64 C.24 B.A. L.823 LL.B.
(adm. in NY; not adm. in DE) Pres. & Gen. Coun., ICI Americas Inc.
Rigrodsky, Seth D., (CV) ....'63 '91 C.1036 B.A. L.276 J.D. [Morris&M.]
*PRACTICE AREAS: Corporate Litigation; Securities Litigation.
Riley, Richard W., (BV①) ....'62 '88 C.602 B.B.A. L.884 J.D. [Duane,M.&H.]
*PRACTICE AREAS: Bankruptcy Litigation; Civil Litigation; Commercial Litigation; Business Reorganization.

Rimmer, William D. .... '65 '91 C.222 B.A. L.1338 J.D. [Heckler&F.]
*PRACTICE AREAS: Worker's Compensation; Insurance Defense Litigation; General Litigation.
Ripple, Michael Leonard ....'71 '00 C.205 B.S. L.128 J.D. 820 N. French St.
Ripple, Raymond M. '46 '71 C.712 B.A. L.93 J.D.
(adm. in CT; not adm. in DE) Corp. Coun., E.I. du Pont de Nemours & Co.
*RESPONSIBILITIES: Appellate Practice; Civil Litigation.
Ripsom, David B., (AV) '49 '75 C.390 B.A. L.893 J.D.
Vice President & General Counsel, Nuclear Electric Ins. Ltd.
Rising, Wendy Anne ....'67 '92 C&L.823 B.A., J.D. Atty. General's Off.
Rittenhouse, David C. .... '31 '59 C&L.945 A.B., J.D. Sr. V.P., Del. Tr. Co.
Ritter, Judith L. '59 '79 C.107 B.A. L.276 J.D.
(adm. in NY; not adm. in DE) Assoc. Prof. of Law, Widener Univ. Sch. of Law
Riveros, Bettina Tweardy, (BV) ....'63 '88 C.372 B.S. L.884 J.D. Dep. Coun. to Gov.
Rizzo, Louis J., Jr. ....'67 '93 C.262 B.A. L.884 J.D. [Reger&R.]
Rizzo, Thomas M. '58 '96 C.188 B.S. L.823 J.D.
(adm. in MO; not adm. in DE) Sr. Coun., E.I. du Pont de Nemours and Company
*RESPONSIBILITIES: Biotechnology and Chemical Intellectual Property.
Robbins, Randall E., (BV) ....'56 '81 C&L.692 B.A., J.D. [Ashby&G.]
Roberts, Donald E., Jr. '64 '91 C.205 B.A. L.1338 J.D.
(adm. in PA; not adm. in DE) Atty., AIG Life Ins. Co.
Robinson, Eldon M. .... '17 '84 C.966 B.A. L.1338 J.D. 2513 Foulk Woods Rd.
Robinson, Stephen D. M., (BV) ....'48 '73 C&L.823 B.S., J.D. [Robinson&G.]
Robinson, Sue L. ....'52 '78 C.205 B.A. L.659 J.D. U.S. Dist. Ct.J.
Robinson & Grayson, P.A., (BV) .... 4001 Kennett Pike, Suite 300
Rocanelli, Andrea L., (BV) '64 '89
C.93 B.A. L.309 J.D. Dep. Coun., Off. of Discip. Coun.
Rodgers, Stephen J. '43 '90 C.397 B.A. L.1338 J.D.
(adm. in PA; not adm. in DE) 1701 Augustine Cut Off‡
Rodriguez, Nicholas H., (AV) '34 '61 C.645 B.S. L.902 J.D.
[Schmittinger&R.] (⊙Dover, Rehoboth Beach)
*PRACTICE AREAS: Personal Injury Law.
Roeberg, David, (AV) ....'37 '68 C.569 B.S. L.831 J.D. [Roeberg,M.&Assoc.]
Roeberg, Moore & Associates, P.A., (AV) ....910 Gilpin Avenue
Rogowski, Patricia Smink '62 '88
C.401 B.S.M.E. L.659 J.D. [Connolly B.L.&H.] (See Pat. Sect.)
Rohs, Timothy H. .... '67 '96 C.903 B.A. L.1338 J.D. [Ⓐ Heckler&F.]
*PRACTICE AREAS: Insurance Defense; Subrogation; Personal Injury.
Rollins, M. Metrinko ....'45 '69 C&L.276 B.S.F.S., J.D. 2200 Concord Pike
Rollo, Richard Philip '72 '99 C&L.260 B.S., J.D.
(adm. in FL; not adm. in DE) [Ⓐ Richards,L.&F.]
*PRACTICE AREAS: Corporate Litigation.
Roman, Thomas J., (BV) ....'42 '77 C.205 B.A. L.1338 J.D. [Kimmel,C.R.&P.] ⊙
*PRACTICE AREAS: General and Civil Trial Practice; Insurance; Negligence; Workers Compensation; Construction Accidents.
Rombach, Louis H. .... '26 '65 C.973 B.S. L.831 J.D. 201 N. Pembrey Dr.‡
Romero, Ramona E. '62 '88 C.66 B.A. L.309 J.D.
(adm. in PA; not adm. in DE) Corp. Coun., E.I. du Pont de Nemours and Company
*RESPONSIBILITIES: Commercial Litigation.
Roney, Donald E. '16 '40 C&L.585 B.S., LL.B.
(adm. in ND; not adm. in DE) 131 Cambridge Dr.‡
Ropp, James B. ....'54 '82 C.205 B.A. L.1017 J.D. Dept. of Jus.
Roseman, Kenneth M., (AV) ....'53 '78 C.831 B.A. L.1338 J.D. [Ciconte,R.&W.]
*PRACTICE AREAS: Personal Injury Law; Medical Malpractice.
Rosen, Robert '44 '76 C.659 D.M.D. L.1338 J.D.
(adm. in PA; not adm. in DE) 5505 Kirkwood Hwy.‡
Rosen, Steven Daniel ....'73 '99 C.205 B.A. L.1048 J.D. [Ⓐ Tybout,R.&P.]
*PRACTICE AREAS: Negligence; Insurance; Workers Compensation; Products Liability; Bankruptcy.
Rosenstein, I. David '52 '78 C&L.150 B.S.M.E., J.D.
(adm. in OH; not adm. in DE) Sr. Coun., Conectiv
*RESPONSIBILITIES: Contracts (40%); Regulatory (20%); Transactions (20%); Corporate Organization (20%).
Rosenthal, Edward B. ....'66 '92 C.264 B.A. L.884 J.D. [Ⓐ Rosenthal,M.G.&G.]
Rosenthal, Joseph A., (AV) ....'31 '56 C.976 B.A. L.309 J.D. [Rosenthal,M.G.&G.]
*PRACTICE AREAS: Corporate Litigation; Securities Litigation; Business Litigation; Corporate Law.

Rosenthal, Monhait, Gross & Goddess, P.A., (AV)
Suite 1401, Mellon Bank Center, P.O. Box 1070, 19899-1070
Telephone: 302-656-4433 Telecopier: 302-658-7567
Email: rmgg@rmgglaw.com
Joseph A. Rosenthal; Kevin Gross; Norman M. Monhait; Jeffrey S. Goddess; Carmella Piscopo Keener;—Edward B. Rosenthal.
Corporate, Securities and Commercial Litigation, Corporate Law, Bankruptcy, Personal Injury and General Civil Litigation.
Counsel for: Delaware Incorporating Co.
See Professional Biographies, WILMINGTON, DELAWARE

Ross, Angela Pinto ....'73 '99 C.223 B.S. L.1338 J.D. 1202 Kirkwood Hwy.
Rossi, Joanne '62 '98 C.1349 B.S. L.831 J.D.
(adm. in PA; not adm. in DE; Pat.) Coun., Hercules Incorporated
Roth, Jane R. ....'35 '65 C.788 B.A. L.309 LL.B. U.S. Cir. J
Roth, Wm. V., Jr. ....'21 '50 C.629 B.A. L.309 LL.B. U.S. Sen.
Rothbart, Philip L. '31 '86 C.623 B.A. L.1338 J.D.
(adm. in PA; not adm. in DE) [Maron&M.]
*PRACTICE AREAS: Toxic Tort; Medical Malpractice; Personal Injury.
Rothschild, Steven J., (AV) ....'44 '68 C.882 B.A. L.276 J.D. [Skadden,A.S.M.&F.]
Roulston, David C. '52 '81 C.197 B.A. L.564 J.D.
(adm. in NJ; not adm. in DE) V.P. & Coun., Wilmington Trust Company
Rovner, Philip A. ....'59 '88 C.659 B.A. L.262 J.D. [Potter A.&C.]

Rowland, Walter Speed, (AV) '39 '66 C.309 A.B. L.145 J.D.
2501 Willard Street, 19806
Telephone: 302-654-6526 Fax: 302-654-7823
Email: wrowland1@home.com
***PRACTICE AREAS: Corporate; Commercial; Arbitrations; Mediation; International.**
Corporate and Commercial Litigation, Arbitration & Mediation, Historic Preservation, International Law, Criminal Law.
See Professional Biographies, WILMINGTON, DELAWARE

Roy, Sharon C. '63 '96 C.205 B.A. L.1338 J.D.
(adm. in PA; not adm. in DE)
Asst. V.P. & Fiduciary Compliance Office, Wilmington Trust Company
Rubbert, William R. '34 '61 C&L.966 B.S., LL.B.
(adm. in WI; not adm. in DE) Barley Mill Plaza
Rubenstein, Harvey Bernard, (AV) '31 '56
C&L.831 A.B., J.D. 824 Market Street, Suite 901
Rubin, Gary A. '74 '99 C.367 B.A. L.145 J.D.
(adm. in MD; not adm. in DE) [Ⓐ Skadden,A.S.M.&F.]
*PRACTICE AREAS: Corporate Reorganization.
Ruckman, Norris E. '12 '45 C.453 S.M. L.273 J.D.
(adm. in DC; not adm. in DE) 314 Waycross Rd., Woodbrook‡

Ruiz Arthur, Giselle '65 '90
(adm. in Mexico; not adm. in DE) [E.I. d.d.]
*RESPONSIBILITIES: Trademarks; Internnet Law; Intellectual Property.
Rush-Milstead, Sheryl, (CV) ....'49 '83 C.610 B.A. L.1338 J.D. 702 N. King St.
Russo, Ronald R. ....'45 '82 C.728 B.S. L.1338 J.D. 4 Daylilly Ct.‡
Russo, Thomas M. '52 '77 C.688 B.S. L.884 J.D.
(adm. in PA; not adm. in DE) Corp. Coun., E.I. du Pont de Nemours and Company
*RESPONSIBILITIES: Corporate Law; Electronic Commerce; Litigation.
Ryan, Jeremy William '71 '97 C.901 B.A. L.665 J.D.
(adm. in PA; not adm. in DE) [Ⓐ Saul E.]
*PRACTICE AREAS: Commercial Litigation; Corporate Governance.
Rychlicki, Helena C. .... '60 '00 C.160 B.S. L.1338 J.D. [Ⓐ Connolly B.L.&H.]
*PRACTICE AREAS: Intellectual Property.
Saccullo, Anthony M. ....'76 '01 C.569 B.S. L.262 J.D. [Ⓐ Bayard]
*PRACTICE AREAS: Corporate Litigation; Bankruptcy.
Sager, Thomas L. '50 '76 C.575 B.A. L.896 J.D.
V.P. & Assoc. Gen. Coun., E.I. du Pont de Nemours and Company
*RESPONSIBILITIES: Litigation.
Saginaw, Robert B. '39 '65 C.563 B.A. L.569 LL.B.
(adm. in NY; not adm. in DE) Asst. Gen. Coun., AIG Life Cos.
Saints, Sheldon S. ....'57 '82 C.205 B.A. L.245 J.D. [Rahaim&S.]
Sale, Nell Graham, (BV) ....'46 '90 C.210 B.A. L.1338 J.D. [Schlusser&R.]
*PRACTICE AREAS: Estate Planning; Probate; Elder Law; Fiduciary Income Tax; Real Estate.
Salerni, Scott ....'74 '00 C.1372 B.A. L.1529 J.D. [Ⓐ Morris,N.A.&T.]
Salmons, Harold I., III ....'61 '86 C.282 B.A. L.1017 J.D. [Potter A.&C.]
Salomone, Janine M. .... '70 '96 C.645 B.S. L.1017 J.D. [Ⓐ Potter A.&C.]
*PRACTICE AREAS: Corporate Law.
Sampson, Tamara C. '59 '86
C.674 B.A. L.178 J.D. Corp. Coun., E.I. du Pont de Nemours & Co.
*RESPONSIBILITIES: Litigation.
Samuels, Gary A. ....'34 '61 C.473 A.B. L.608 LL.B. Sr. Coun., Hercules Incorporated
Sandler, Sheldon N., (AV) ....'41 '66 C.477 A.B. L.659 LL.B. [Young C.S.&T.]
*PRACTICE AREAS: Employment Discrimination; Employment Law; Management Labor Law; Title VII Discrimination; Union Elections.
Sandstrom, Theodore F., (BV) ....'31 '61 C.205 B.A. L.1017 LL.B. 1324 King St.
Sasso, Kelly J., (BV) ....'63 '89 C.923 B.S. L.930 J.D. 1200 Pennsylvania Ave.
Sattesahn, Keith R. ....'58 '85 C.372 B.S. L.831 J.D. [Ⓐ Stewart&Assoc.]
*PRACTICE AREAS: Information Technology; Intellectual Property.

Saul Ewing LLP, (AV)
A Delaware Limited Liability Partnership
222 Delaware Avenue, P.O. Box 1266, 19899-1266, For Courier Delivery: 222 Delaware Avenue, Suite 1200, 19801 ⊙
Telephone: 302-421-6800 Cable Address: "Bidsal" TWX: 83-4798. Telecopier: XEROX 7020 302-421-6813
Email: lawyers@saul.com URL: http://www.saul.com
Partners: Carl B. Everett; Timothy A. Frey; William S. Gee; Steven D. Goldberg; Daniel H. Krapf; Mark Minuti; Domenic E. Pacitti; Norman L. Pernick; Linda Richenderfer (Not admitted in DE); Pamela J. Scott; Wendie Cohen Stabler. Special Counsel: Michael F. Bonkowski; Donald J. Detweiler; Maria Aprile Sawczuk; J. Kate Stickles. Associates: Kimberly L. Gattuso; Tara L. Lattomus; Jeremy William Ryan (Not admitted in DE); Roger Lea Truemper.
Bankruptcy and Reorganization, Business, Construction, Criminal Defense and Government Enforcement, Education, Emerging Business, Employee Benefits, Environmental, Estates and Trusts, Financial Services, Golf, Government Relations and Regulatory Compliance, Health Law, Insurance, Intellectual Property, International, Labor and Employment, Litigation (Commercial and Civil), Products Liability, Public Finance, Real Estate, Securities, Tax, Technology, Telecommunications.
Philadelphia, Pennsylvania Office: Centre Square West, 1500 Market Street, 38th Floor, 19102-2186. Telephone: 215-972-7777. Cable Address: "Bidsal" TWX: 83-4798. Telecopier: XEROX 7020 215-972-7725.
New York, New York Office: Twenty-first Floor 237 Park Avenue, 10017. Telephone: 212-551-3502 TWX: 425170 Telecopier: 212-697-8486.
Chesterbrook, Pennsylvania Office: 1200 Liberty Ridge, Wayne, Pennsylvania 19087. Telephone: 610-251-5050. Cable Address: "BIDSAL". TWX: 83-4798. Telecopier: 610-651-5930.
Harrisburg, Pennsylvania Office: Penn National Insurance Tower, 2 North Second Street, 7th Floor, 17101. Telephone: 717-257-7500. Telecopier: 717-238-4622, 717-257-7516.
Princeton, New Jersey Office: 214 Carnegie Center, Suite 202, 08540. Telephone: 609-452-3100. Fax: 609-452-3122.
Baltimore, Maryland Office: 100 South Charles Street, Suite 1500, 21201-2773. Telephone: 410-332-8600. Fax: 410-332-8862.
See Professional Biographies, WILMINGTON, DELAWARE

Saunders, Barbara '60 '87 C.31 B.A. L.309 J.D.
(adm. in PA; not adm. in DE) Assoc. Gen. Coun., DuPont Pharmaceuticals Co.
Saunders, Robert S. ....'66 '91 C.197 A.B. L.893 J.D. [Skadden,A.S.M.&F.]
Saurman, Elizabeth A. ....'68 '93 C.611 B.A. L.1338 J.D. [Ⓐ Marshall,D.W.C.&G.]
*PRACTICE AREAS: Casualty Defense; Workers Compensation Defense.
Saville, Yvonne Takvorian, (BV) ....'70 '95 C.205 B.A. L.1338 J.D. [Ⓐ M.Weiss]
*PRACTICE AREAS: Civil Practice; Insurance; Negligence; Workers' Compensation; Personal Injury.
Sawczuk, Maria Aprile .... '67 '93 C.205 B.A. L.884 J.D. [Ⓒ Saul E.]
*PRACTICE AREAS: Bankruptcy; Corporate Law.
Sawyer, H. Murray, Jr., (AV) ....'46 '71 C.575 B.A. L.880 J.D. [Sawyer,A.&H.]
*PRACTICE AREAS: Estate Planning; Financial Planning; Living Trusts; Family Trusts; Family Wealth Transfer.

Sawyer, Akin & Herron, P.A., (AV)
1220 North Market Street Suite 608, P.O. Box 25047, 19899
Telephone: 302-655-5552 Telecopier: 302-655-3697
Email: sah@sahlaw.com URL: http://www.sahlaw.com
H. Murray Sawyer, Jr.; Roger A. Akin; Bruce C. Herron.
Trusts and Estates, Insurance Defense, Litigation.
See Professional Biographies, WILMINGTON, DELAWARE

Scaggs, R. Judson, Jr. ....'59 '89 C.902 B.A. L.945 J.D. [Morris,N.A.&T.]
Scali, Michael J. ....'76 '01 C.884 B.A. L.1017 J.D. [Ⓐ Potter A.&C.]
*PRACTICE AREAS: Corporate Opinion.
Scalio, Rebecca L. ....'67 '00 C.205 B.A. L.831 J.D. [Ⓐ Potter A.&C.]
*PRACTICE AREAS: Corporate Litigation; Commercial Litigation.
Scanlon, Rose Ann M. '63 '88 C.205 B.S. L.884 J.D.
(adm. in PA; not adm. in DE) Asst. Gen. Coun., Astrazeneca Pharm. LP
*RESPONSIBILITIES: Commercial; Healthcare; General/Corporate.
Scarlett, Dorothy K. '52 '92 C.787 B.S. L.831 J.D.
(adm. in PA; not adm. in DE) Wilmington Trust Co.
Scarpato, Peter A. '55 '81 C.705 B.A. L.1292 J.D.
(adm. in NJ; not adm. in DE) Sr. V.P. & Gen. Coun., Amer. Centennial Ins. Co.
Scerba, David R. ....'59 '86 C.659 Econ. L.1338 J.D. [Ramunno&R.]
Schacht, Kurt N., (BVⓉ) '54 '84 C&L.966 B.S., J.D.
(adm. in WI; not adm. in DE) [Ⓒ Grant&E.]
Schaeffer, Andrew L. '60 '87 C.401 B.S.Ch.E. L.1338 J.D.
(adm. in PA; not adm. in DE; Pat.) Corp. Coun., E.I. du Pont de Nemours & Co.
*RESPONSIBILITIES: Patent Litigation; Patent Prosecution; Patent Licensing.
Schaffer, Susan B. '48 '76 C.216 B.A. L.1292 J.D.
(adm. in PA; not adm. in DE) Sr. Coun., Litig., Astrazeneca Pharm. LP
*RESPONSIBILITIES: Litigation.
Schagrin, Martin A., (BV) ....'39 '69 C.861 B.A. L.446 LL.B. [Berkowitz,S.C.&C.]

Schanne, Francis J. .... '64 '89 C.184 B.S. L.884 J.D. [Ⓐ Bayard]
*PRACTICE AREAS: Estate Planning; Tax Planning; Commercial Law.
Schiltz, Christine P. .... '— '93 C.896 B.A. L.692 J.D. [Ⓐ Reed S.]
*PRACTICE AREAS: Government Relations.
Schiltz, Todd, (BV) .... '67 '94 C.210 B.A. L.597 J.D. [Ⓐ Wolf,B.S.&S-C.]
*PRACTICE AREAS: Litigation.
Schlecker, Carolyn R., (BV) .... '46 '78 C.205 B.S. L.1338 J.D. City Solr.
Schlerf, Jeffrey M. .... '59 '92 C.659 B.A. L.945 J.D. [Bayard]
*PRACTICE AREAS: Bankruptcy; Commercial Transactions; Creditors Rights; Business Law; Administrative Law.
Schlusser, Robert E., (AV) .... '42 '67 C.216 B.A. L.1017 J.D. [Schlusser&R.]
*PRACTICE AREAS: Taxation Law; Tax Controversies; Fiduciary Litigation.

Schlusser & Reiver, P.A., (AV) BR
1700 West 14th Street, 19806
Telephone: 302-655-8181 Fax: 302-655-8190
Robert E. Schlusser; Joanna Reiver; Nell Graham Sale.
Federal and State Income, Estate and Gift Taxation. Estate Planning. Probate, Tax and Fiduciary Litigation.
See Professional Biographies, WILMINGTON, DELAWARE

Schmidt, Lisa A. .... '66 '91 C.222 B.A. L.1017 J.D. [Richards,L.&F.]
Schmitt, Anita M. '— '86 C.1305 B.S. L.831 J.D.
(adm. in PA; not adm. in DE) Corp. Coun., E.I. du Pont de Nemours & Co.
*RESPONSIBILITIES: Litigation.
Schmittinger, Harold, (AV) '28 '54 C.205 B.S. L.904 LL.B.
[Schmittinger&R.] (⊙Dover, Rehoboth Beach)
*PRACTICE AREAS: Personal Injury Law.
Schmittinger, John J., (AV) '41 '66 C.205 B.A. L.831 J.D.
[Schmittinger&R.] (⊙Dover, Rehoboth Beach)
*PRACTICE AREAS: Workers Compensation Law; Personal Injury.

Schmittinger & Rodriguez, P.A., (AV)
1300 North Market Street, Suite 205, 19801 ⊙
Telephone: 302-652-3676 FAX: 302-652-8788
Email: attorneys@schmittrod.com URL: http://www.schmittrod.com
Harold Schmittinger; Nicholas H. Rodriguez; Paul H. Boswell; John J. Schmittinger; William D. Fletcher, Jr.; R. Scott Kappes (Resident); Kyle Kemmer (Resident).
General Civil Practice. Personal Injury, Workers Compensation, Federal Practice, Corporation, Estate Planning, Real Estate and Commercial Law. Litigation.
Dover, Delaware Office: 414 South State Street. Telephone: 302-674-0140. Fax: 302-674-1830.
Rehoboth Beach, Delaware Office: 4602 Highway One. Telephone: 302-227-1400. Fax: 302-645-1843.
Odessa, Delaware Office: Odessa Professional Park, P.O. Box 626. Telephone: 302-378-1697. Fax: 302-378-1659.
See Professional Biographies, WILMINGTON, DELAWARE

Schmucki, Ross F. '54 '80 C.674 A.B. L.665 J.D.
(adm. in PA; not adm. in DE) Corp. Coun., E.I. du Pont de Nemours & Co.
*RESPONSIBILITIES: Medical Products Litigation; Other Legal Advice.
Schnabel, Eric L. .... '68 '98 C.293 B.A. L.904 J.D. [Ⓐ Klett R.L.&S.]
*PRACTICE AREAS: Bankruptcy; Insolvency; Creditor's Rights; Debtors' Rights.
Schnee, Carl, (AV) .... '36 '62 C.529 B.A. L.884 J.D. [Duane,M.&H.]
*PRACTICE AREAS: Commercial Litigation; Health Care; Professional Liability; White Collar Criminal Defense; Corporate Investigations.
Schoell, Joseph C. .... '67 '92 C.205 B.A. L.976 J.D. 820 N. French St., 12th Fl.
Schoenbeck, Donna L. .... '— '87 C.831 B.A. L.1338 J.D. [Schoenbeck&S.]
*PRACTICE AREAS: Bankruptcy Chapters 7, 11, 13; Real Estate; Civil Litigation; Personal Injury; Probate.

Schoenbeck & Schoenbeck, P.A.
1211 Milltown Road, Suite A, 19808
Telephone: 302-999-9316 Fax: 302-999-8387 URL: http://www.schoenbeck.com
Email: schoenbeck@schoenbeck.com URL: http://www.lawyers.com/schoenbeck
Mark F. Schoenbeck (Deceased); Donna L. Schoenbeck;—Janell Schoenbeck Ostroski.
Civil Litigation, Personal Injury, Family Law, Probate and Estate Planning, Real Estate, Bankruptcy, Business Law, Corporate Law.
See Professional Biographies, WILMINGTON, DELAWARE

Schuenemeyer, Judith A. '39 '76
C.416 B.S. L.280 J.D. Exec. Dir., Community Legal Aid Soc., Inc.
Schuette, June B. '60 '94 C.188 B.S.E.E. L.818 J.D.
Pat. Atty., The Whitaker Corp. (Pat.)
Schwartz, Eric D. .... '62 '92 C.276 B.S.B.A. L.884 J.D. [Ⓐ Morris,N.A.&T.]
Schwartz, Murray M. .... '31 '56 C&L.659 B.S., LL.B. Sr. U.S. Dist. J.
Schwartz, Patricia Bartley '61 '90
C.884 B.A. L.724 J.D. 4425 North Market Street, 3rd Floor
Schwartz, Sol '26 '55 C.563 B.S. L.273 J.D.
(adm. in DC; not adm. in DE; Pat.) du Pont Co.
Schwartzman, Eric A. .... '72 '99 C.884 B.A. L.276 J.D. [Ⓐ Richards,L.&F.]
Schwind, Lisa M. .... '61 '90 C.205 B.S.N. L.1338 J.D. Off. of the Pub. Def.
Scialpi, Daniel W. .... '76 '01 C.884 B.A. L.1338 J.D. [Ⓐ R.R.Wier,Jr.]
Scoliard, Jennifer L. '71 '97 C.1338 B.A. L.469 J.D.
(adm. in GA; not adm. in DE) [Ⓐ Cozen O.]
*PRACTICE AREAS: Bankruptcy Chapter 11; Bankruptcy Reorganization; Commercial Bankruptcy; Debtor Bankruptcy; Creditor Bankruptcy.
Scott, Michelle Lee .... '71 '99 C.751 B.A. L.644 J.D. Pub. Def. Off.
Scott, Pamela J. .... '58 '84 C.205 B.S. L.1338 J.D. [Saul E.]
*PRACTICE AREAS: Commercial Real Estate; Real Estate; Zoning, Planning and Land Use; Administrative Law; Alcoholic Beverages.
Scovic, Stephen A. .... '70 '95 C.472 B.A. L.607 J.D. Dept. of Jus.
Seaman, John M. .... '69 '99 C.951 B.A. L.659 J.D. [Ⓐ Potter A.&C.]
*PRACTICE AREAS: Corporate Litigation.
Seaton, Felicia M. .... '69 '96 C.999 B.A. L.930 J.D. [Ⓐ Mattleman,W.&M.]
*PRACTICE AREAS: Family Law; Traffic Law; Estate Planning.
Sebree, Chyrrea Jackson '63 '97 C.1338 B.S. L.692 J.D.
(adm. in VA; not adm. in DE) Coun., E.I. du Pont de Nemours & Co.
*RESPONSIBILITIES: Intellectual Property; Patents.
Sebring, Julie M. .... '— '84 [Ⓐ Goldfein&H.]
*PRACTICE AREAS: Medical Malpractice; Litigation; Commercial; Insurance Defense.
Seidl, Michael R. .... '66 '96 C.1369 M.A. L.276 J.D. [Ⓐ Pachulski,S.Z.Y.&J.]
*PRACTICE AREAS: Business Litigation; Chapter 11 Bankruptcy.
Seitz, C. J. .... '14 '40 C.205 B.A. L.893 LL.B. Sr. U.S. Cir. J.
Seitz, Collins J., Jr., (BV) .... '57 '83 C.205 B.A. L.884 J.D. [Connolly B.L.&H.]
Seitz, George H., III, (BV) .... '45 '71 C.205 B.S. L.893 J.D. [Seitz,V.&G.]
*PRACTICE AREAS: Civil Litigation; Commercial Law; Construction Law; Environmental Insurance Litigation; Tort Litigation.

Seitz, Van Ogtrop & Green, P.A., (AV)
222 Delaware Avenue, Suite 1500, P.O. Box 68, 19899
Telephone: 302-888-0600 Fax: 302-888-0606
Email: svglaw.com URL: http://www.lawyers.com/svglaw
Bernard A. Van Ogtrop; George H. Seitz, III; James S. Green; Robert Karl Hill; Patricia P. McGonigle;—Carrie I. Dayton.
Bankruptcy, Construction, Corporate, Commercial, Insurance Coverage, Personal Injury, Transportation and Intellectual Property Litigation; General Civil Practice in all Courts.
See Professional Biographies, WILMINGTON, DELAWARE

Sellis, Deborah Cirilla .... '73 '98 C&L.884 B.A., J.D. [Ⓐ Blank R.C.&M.]
*PRACTICE AREAS: Bankruptcy; Bankruptcy Litigation; Financial Services Law; Civil Litigation; Commercial Litigation.
Semmelman, Andrew T. '52 '79 C.893 B.A. L.1338 J.D.
V.P. & Asst. Gen. Coun., J.P. Morgan Chase & Co.
Semple, James W., (AV) .... '43 '74 C.728 A.B. L.884 J.D. [Morris,J.H.&W.]
*PRACTICE AREAS: Commercial Litigation; Insurance; Alternative Dispute Resolution.
Sensor, Michael L. .... '70 '96 C.831 B.A. L.229 J.D. [Ⓐ J.T.Perry]
*PRACTICE AREAS: Personal Injury; Criminal Defense; Workers Compensation; Insurance Defense; Guardianships.
Seubert, Suzanne I. .... '55 '81 C.150 B.B.A. L.608 J.D. [S.I.Seubert]
*PRACTICE AREAS: Family Law; Divorce; Alimony; Child Support; Custody.

Seubert, Suzanne I., P.A.
1328 King Street, 19801-3234
Telephone: 302-661-0400 Fax: 302-428-3193
Email: s.seubert@worldnet.att.net URL: http://www.lawyers.com/suzanneiseubertpa
Suzanne I. Seubert.
Family Law, Divorce, Alimony, Child Support, Custody, Probate, Wills, Guardianships.
See Professional Biographies, WILMINGTON, DELAWARE

Shachtman, Douglas A., & Associates, (BV) '47 '74 C.260 B.S.B.A. L.659 J.D.
Suite 302, 1200 Pennsylvania Avenue, 19806
Telephone: 302-655-1800 Fax: 302-655-5244
Email: DoShack@aol.com URL: http://www.lawyers.com/shachtman
***PRACTICE AREAS: Civil Rights; Consumer Law; Professional Negligence; Commercial Law; Collections.**
Trial Practice in all Civil Courts. Civil Rights Law. Consumer Law and Construction Law, Commercial and Collection Law.
See Professional Biographies, WILMINGTON, DELAWARE

Shaffer, Brent C. .... '62 '87 C&L.896 B.A., J.D. [Young C.S.&T.]
*PRACTICE AREAS: Commercial Real Estate; Leases and Leasing; Affordable Housing; Commercial Mortgages; Real Estate Leasing.
Shalk, Colin M., (BV) .... '47 '78 C.205 B.A. L.1017 J.D. [Casarino,C.&S.]
*PRACTICE AREAS: Insurance Defense; Workers' Compensation; Civil Litigation.
Shamers, David S., (CV) .... '50 '82 C.205 B.S. L.1338 J.D. 15 Trolley Sq.
Shandler, Chad M. .... '72 '99 C&L.884 B.A., J.D. [Ⓐ Richards,L.&F.]
Shanley, Peter J., (BV) .... '45 '71 C.93 B.S. L.276 J.D. 222 Delaware Ave., Ste. 1200
Shannon, Brendan Linehan, (BV) ...... '64 '92 C.674 A.B. L.945 J.D. [Young C.S.&T.]
Shannon, Joseph Scott .... '64 '95 C.205 B.A.A.S. L.644 J.D. [Ⓐ Tighe,C.&L.]
*PRACTICE AREAS: Criminal Law; Insurance Defense; Litigation.
Shannon, Kevin R. .... '63 '92 C.884 B.S.A. L.1338 J.D. [Potter A.&C.]
Sharp, Melanie K., (BV) .... '60 '86 C.205 B.A. L.831 J.D. [Young C.S.&T.]
*PRACTICE AREAS: Litigation; Trial Practice; Personal Injury; Products Liability; Medical Malpractice.
Shaughnessy, Robert J. '57 '87 C.205 B.A. L.659 J.D.
Sr. Coun., Astrazeneca Pharm. LP
*RESPONSIBILITIES: Commercial; Healthcare; Regulatory Law.
Shaw, John W. .... '67 '95 C.645 B.S. L.665 J.D. [Ⓐ Young C.S.&T.]
*PRACTICE AREAS: Intellectual Property Litigation; Federal Civil Litigation; Information Technology; Electronic Commerce.
Shaw, Julia '54 '82 C.783 B.A. L.93 J.D.
(adm. in MA; not adm. in DE) Intl. Dept., du Pont Co.
Shay, Lucas K. '— '92 C.690 M.S. L.862 J.S.
(adm. in OK; not adm. in DE) Sr. Coun., E.I. du Pont de Nemours and Company
Sheehan, C. Ann '49 '90 C&L.216 B.A., J.D.
(adm. in DC; not adm. in DE)
Visiting Asst. Prof. & Dir., Academic, Widener Univ. Sch. of Law
Sheer, Bonnie H., (BV) .... '43 '68 C.105 B.A. L.273 J.D. [Cooch&T.] (⊙Newark)
*PRACTICE AREAS: Real Estate.
Shellenberger, Thomas D., (BV) '59 '85 C.205 B.A. L.1048 J.D.
[Cooch&T.] (⊙Newark)
*PRACTICE AREAS: Family Law; Foreclosures.
Shelton, David C. '63 '88 C.728 B.A. L.884 J.D.
(adm. in PA; not adm. in DE) Sr. Coun., E.I. du Pnot de Nemours & Co.
*RESPONSIBILITIES: Environmental Law.
Sheridan, John R. .... '44 '73 C.205 B.A. L.64 J.D. Asst. City Solr.
Shields, Colleen D. .... '67 '92 C.205 B.A. L.1338 J.D. [Ⓐ Elzufon A.R.T.&M.]
*PRACTICE AREAS: Civil Litigation; Professional Liability Defense; Commercial Litigation; Real Estate.
Shipley, James E. '42 '81 C.623 B.S.E.E. L.1338 J.D.
(adm. in PA; not adm. in DE; Pat.) Corp. Coun., E.I. du Pont de Nemours & Co.
Shoaf, Charles J. '30 '80 C.885 B.S. L.1338 J.D.
(adm. in PA; not adm. in DE; Pat.) du Pont Co.
Shomper, James D., Jr. '54 '80 C.502 B.A. L.665 J.D.
(adm. in PA; not adm. in DE)
Corp. Coun. & Mgr., Law Firm Partnering, E.I. du Pont de Nemours and Company
*RESPONSIBILITIES: Litigation.
Short, Andrea K. .... '73 '00 C.198 B.A. L.902 J.D. [Ⓐ Richards,L.&F.]
Sianni, Ralph N. .... '68 '96 C.659 B.A. L.94 J.D. [Ⓐ Duane,M.&H.]
*PRACTICE AREAS: Reorganization and Finance Law.
Siebold, Dennis J. ...... '49 '77 C.205 B.A. Fin. Legal Offr., New Castle Co. Dept. of Fin.
Siegel, Martin L. .... '— '84 C.105 B.A. L.1338 J.D. [Doroshow,P.K.S.&B.]
Siegell, Barbara C. '40 '81 C.994 B.S. L.1338 J.D.
Corp. Coun., E.I. du Pont de Nemours & Co. (Pat.)
*RESPONSIBILITIES: Intellectual Property; Patents; Contracts; Intellectual Property Licensing.
Silar, Scott L. ... '59 '92 C.820 B.A. L.1338 J.D. [Ⓐ Marshall,D.W.C.&G.] (⊙Phila., PA)
*PRACTICE AREAS: Products Liability.
Silberglied, Russell C. .... '70 '96 C.188 B.S. L.659 J.D. [Ⓐ Richards,L.&F.]
Silliman, Henry H., III '57 '82 C.178 B.A. L.245 J.D.
Corp. Coun., E.I. du Pont de Nemours and Company
*RESPONSIBILITIES: Real Estate.
Silverman, Michael I., (CV) .... '66 '91 C.823 B.S. L.1338 J.D. 1100 N. Grant Ave.
Silverstein, Bruce L., (BV) .... '61 '86 C.70 B.A. L.884 J.D. [Young C.S.&T.]
*PRACTICE AREAS: Corporate Law; Mergers, Acquisitions and Divestitures; Litigation; Appellate Practice; Chancery and Equity.
Silverstein, Laurie Selber, (BV) .... '59 '85 C.205 B.S. L.273 J.D. [Potter A.&C.]
Simms, Garfield B. '63 '98 C.204 B.S. L.588 J.D.
(adm. in MA; not adm. in DE) [Ⓐ Morris,N.A.&T.]
Simon, Christopher P. .... '70 '98 C.902 B.A. L.1338 J.D. [Ⓐ Bayard]
*PRACTICE AREAS: Commercial Litigation; Bankruptcy Law.
Simpson, Scott A. .... '67 '97 C.205 B.A. L.1338 J.D. [Ⓐ Elzufon A.R.T.&M.]
*PRACTICE AREAS: Workers Compensation Defense; Insurance Defense Litigation; General Liability Defense.
Sinclair, John P., (AV) .... '15 '40 C.821 A.B. L.659 LL.B. [Ⓒ Potter A.&C.]
Singer, Adam .... '60 '86 C.367 B.E.S. L.94 J.D. [Ⓐ Cooch&T.] (⊙Newark)
*PRACTICE AREAS: Creditors Rights; Bankruptcy Chapter 11; Bankruptcy Chapter 7.
Singewald, Christian J., (CV) .... '68 '94 C.692 B.A. L.365 J.D. [Ⓐ White&W.]
Sinnott, Jessica M. '64 '90 C.822 B.S. L.564 J.D.
(adm. in NY; not adm. in DE; Pat.) Corp. Coun., E.I. du Pont de Nemours & Co.
*RESPONSIBILITIES: Patents.
Sipe, Christopher J. .... '70 '95 C.205 B.A. L.942 J.D. [Ⓐ Bailey&W.]
*PRACTICE AREAS: Insurance Defense; Plaintiffs' Personal Injury; Insurance Subrogation; Collections.

Sisk, Mark D., (BV) .... '52 '79 C.311 B.A. L.884 J.D. [Hughes,S.&G.]
Siskin, Cheryl E. .... '— '95 [🄰 Skadden,A.S.M.&F.]

Skadden, Arps, Slate, Meagher & Flom LLP, (AV)
One Rodney Square, P.O. Box 636, 19899 ⊙
Telephone: 302-651-3000 Fax: 302-651-3001
URL: http://www.skadden.com
Partners: Steven J. Rothschild; Richard L. Easton; Edward P. Welch; Thomas J. Allingham, II; Anthony W. Clark; Robert B. Pincus; Karen L. Valihura; Gregg M. Galardi; Mark S. Chehi; Robert S. Saunders. Of Counsel: Rodman Ward, Jr. Counsel: Allison L. Amorison; Kevin F. Brady. Special Counsel: Randolph K. Herndon. Associates: Martina Bernstein; Laura S. Clare; Megan E. Cleghorn (Not admitted in DE); Howard A. Cohen (Not admitted in DE); Anne E. Connolly; James A. Corrodi (Not admitted in DE); Steven J. Daniels; Eric M. Davis; Michelle L. Davis; Grenville R. Day; Mark L. Desgrosseilliers (Not admitted in DE); Van C. Durrier, II; Bradley James Enna; Rosemary Goodier; Matthew M. Greenberg; Paul J. Lockwood; Parth S. Munshi; Darryl A. Parson (Not admitted in DE); Kenneth A. Polite, Jr.; Marion M. Quirk (Not admitted in DE); Gary A. Rubin (Not admitted in DE); Cheryl E. Siskin; Leonard P. Stark; James A. Stoltzfus; Julie Tostrup; Kara R. Yancey; Michael W. Yurkewicz (Not admitted in DE).
General Practice.
Firm/Affiliate Offices:
New York, New York: Four Times Square, 10036. Telephone: 212-735-3000. Fax: 212-735-2000.
Boston, Massachusetts: One Beacon Street, 02108. Telephone: 617-573-4800. Fax: 617-573-4822.
Washington, D.C.: 1440 New York Avenue, N.W., 20005. Telephone: 202-371-7000. Fax: 202-393-5760.
Los Angeles, California: 300 South Grand Avenue, 90071. Telephone: 213-687-5000. Fax: 213-687-5600.
Chicago, Illinois: Skadden, Arps, Slate, Meagher & Flom (Illinois), 333 West Wacker Drive, 60606. Telephone: 312-407-0700. Fax: 312-407-0411.
San Francisco, California: Four Embarcadero Center, 94111. Telephone: 415-984-6400. Fax: 415-984-2698.
Houston, Texas: 1600 Smith Street, Suite 4400, 77002. Telephone: 713-655-5100. Fax: 713-655-5200.
Newark, New Jersey: One Newark Center, 07102. Telephone: 973-639-6800. Fax: 973-639-6858.
Palo Alto, California: 525 University Avenue, Suite 1100, 94301. Telephone: 650-470-4500. Fax: 650-470-4570.
Reston, Virginia: 11911 Freedom Drive, Suite 550, 20190. Telephone: 703-796-2345. Fax: 703-796-2344.
Tokyo, Japan: ATT Main Tower 12F, 2-17-22, Akasaka, Minato-ku, 107-0052. Telephone: 011-813-3568-2600. Fax: 011-813-3568-2626.
London, England: One Canada Square, Canary Wharf, E14 5DS. Telephone: 011-44-20-7519-7000. Fax: 011-44-20-7519-7070.
Hong Kong, China: 30/F Tower Two, Lippo Centre, 89 Queensway, Central. Telephone: 011-852-2820-0700. Fax: 011-852-2820-0727.
Sydney, New South Wales 2000, Australia: Skadden, Arps, Slate, Meagher & Flom (International), Level 13, 131 Macquarie Street. Telephone: 011-61-2-9253-6000. Fax: 011-61-2-9253-6044.
Toronto, Ontario, Canada: Suite 1820, North Tower, P.O. Box 189, Royal Bank Plaza, M5J 2J4. Telephone: 416-777-4700. Fax: 416-777-4747.
Brussels, Belgium: 523 avenue Louise, Box 30, 1050. Telephone: 011-32-2-639-0300. Fax: 011-32-2-639-0339.
Frankfurt am Main, Germany: MesseTurm, 27th Floor, 60308. Telephone: 011-49-69-742200. Fax: 011-49-69-74220300.
Paris, France: 68, rue du Faubourg Saint-Honoré, 75008. Telephone: 011-331-55-27-11-00. Fax: 011-331-55-27-11-99.
Beijing, China: East Wing Office, Level 4, China World Trade Center, No. 1 Jian Guo Men Wai Avenue, 100004. Telephone: 011-86-10-6505-5511. Fax: 011-86-10-6505-5522.
Moscow, Russia: Degtyarniy Pereulok 4, Building 1, 103009. Telephone: 011-7-501-797-4600. Fax: 011-7-501-797-4601.
Singapore, Singapore: Skadden, Arps, Slate, Meagher & Flom (International), 9 Temasek Boulevard, Suite 29-01, Suntec Tower Two, 038989. Telephone: 011-65-434-2900. Fax: 011-65-434-2988.

See Professional Biographies, WILMINGTON, DELAWARE

Skiles, Nicholas E. .... '70 '98 C.347 B.A. L.1338 J.D. [🄰 Swartz,C.&D.]
*PRACTICE AREAS: Insurance Defense; Estate Planning; Plaintiffs Personal Injury; Contract Litigation.
Slanina, Charles, (BV) .... '54 '80 C.205 B.A. L.128 J.D. [Tybout,R.&P.]
*PRACTICE AREAS: Professional Responsibility; Personal Injury; Civil Litigation; Criminal Law.
Sleet, Gregory M. .... '51 '77 C.302 B.A. L.1292 J.D. Dist. J.
Slights, Ellen W., (BV) .... '64 '89 C.881 B.A. L.902 J.D. Asst. U.S. Atty.
Small, John H., (AV) .... '46 '73 C.276 B.A. L.893 J.D. [Prickett,J.&E.]
*PRACTICE AREAS: Corporate Law and Litigation; Business Entity Law.
Smalls, Alex J. .... '50 '78 C.512 B.A. L.1292 J.D. Chf. Com. Pleas J.
Smith, Craig B., (AV) .... '43 '75 C.118 B.A. L.823 J.D. [Smith,K.&F.]
*PRACTICE AREAS: Corporate Law; Securities; Corporate Litigation.
Smith, David C. '52 '84 C.050 B.A. L.184 J.D.
(adm. in CT; not adm. in DE) Int'l Coun., Amer. Life Ins. Co.
Smith, Gregory E. .... '75 '99 C.902 B.A. L.845 J.D. Dept. of Jus.
Smith, J. Breck .... '58 '90 C.197 B.A. L.1338 J.D. [🄰 Potter A.&C.]
*PRACTICE AREAS: Real Estate Acquisitions; Real Estate Development; Real Estate Finance; Commercial Leasing.
Smith, Kathleen Duffy .... '51 '93 C.205 B.A. L.1338 J.D. P.O. Box 547
Smith, Rodger D. .... '68 '94 C.659 B.S. L.569 J.D. [🄰 Morris,N.A.&T.]
Smith, Wilfred J., Jr., (CV) .... '29 '54 C.205 A.B. L.659 LL.B. 300 Delaware Avenue

Smith, Katzenstein & Furlow LLP, (AV) BR
The Corporate Plaza, 800 Delaware Avenue, P.O. Box 410, 19899
Telephone: 302-652-8400 Fax: 302-652-8405
Email: info@skfdelaware.com URL: http://www.SKFDelaware.com
Members of Firm: Craig B. Smith; Robert J. Katzenstein; David A. Jenkins; Laurence V. Cronin; Selinda A. Melnik; Michele C. Gott; Kathleen M. Miller. Associates: Joelle E. Polesky; Paranda B. Wiedemer. Of Counsel: Clark W. Furlow.
Corporate and Commercial Litigation, Corporation, Securities, Business, Limited Partnership, Limited Liability Companies, Insurance, Bankruptcy, and Employment Law.

See Professional Biographies, WILMINGTON, DELAWARE

Snyder, Bayard J., (BV) .... '51 '76 C.393 B.A. L.902 J.D. [Snyder&Assoc.]
*PRACTICE AREAS: Civil Litigation; Personal Injury; Corporate Law; Real Estate Law.
Snyder, Timothy J., (BV) .... '51 '81 C&L.1338 B.S., J.D. [Young C.S.&T.]
*PRACTICE AREAS: Employee Benefits; Nonprofit and Charitable Organizations; Probate; Taxation; Wills.

Snyder & Associates, P.A., (BV)
300 Delaware Avenue Suite 1014, 19899
Mailing Address: P.O. Box 90, Wilmington, Delaware 19899
Telephone: 302-657-8300 Telecopier: 302-657-8301
Email: snyder90@aol.com
Bayard J. Snyder. Of Counsel: Richard H. Allen.
Personal Injury, Bankruptcy, Products Liability, Medical Malpractice, Workers Compensation, Commercial Litigation, Real Estate, Wills & Probate, Trusts & Estates, Estate Planning, Admiralty.
Reference: Beneficial National Bank.

See Professional Biographies, WILMINGTON, DELAWARE

Snyderman, Charles, (BV) '48 '73 C.831 B.A. L.884 J.D.
5301 Limestone Road, Suite 214, 19808
Telephone: 302-239-1140 Fax: 302-239-2124
URL: http://www.lawyers.com/snyderman
Personal Injury, Birth Trauma, Obstetrical Negligence, Brain Injury, Misread Pap-Smears, Failure to Diagnose Cases, Medical Malpractice, Automobile Accidents. Business Litigation, Commercial Litigation, Business Formation, Business Planning, Incorporations, Limited Liability Corporations, Buying and Selling of Businesses, Registered Agent Services, Staffing Industry Law. Real Estate.

See Professional Biographies, WILMINGTON, DELAWARE

Solomon, Jason J. .... '74 '01 C.575 B.S.B.A. L.902 J.D. [🄰 Richards,L.&F.]
Sontchi, Christopher S., (CV) .... '66 '93 C.575 B.A. L.145 J.D. [Ashby&G.]

Spadaro, John S. .... '59 '86 C.524 B.A. L.262 J.D. [Murphy S.&L.]
*PRACTICE AREAS: Insurance Coverage; Commercial Litigation; Public Utility Regulation.
Sparks, A. Gilchrist, III, (AV) .... '44 '73 C.976 B.A. L.659 J.D. [Morris,N.A.&T.]
Sparks, W. Donald, II, (AV) .... '58 '83 C.197 B.A. L.976 J.D. [Richards,L.&F.]
*PRACTICE AREAS: Estate Planning and Estate Administration; Tax Exempt Organizations; Taxation.
Spelman, Rosalie '51 '81 C.339 B.A. L.276 J.D.
(adm. in NY; not adm. in DE) [🄲 Pachulski,S.Z.Y.&J.]
*PRACTICE AREAS: Bankruptcy.
Spence, Stephen W., (BV) .... '53 '81 C.205 B.S. L.1338 J.D. [Phillips,G.&S.]
*PRACTICE AREAS: Commercial Litigation; Bankruptcy; Commercial Real Estate; Small Business Practice.
Sperling, Robert B. '35 '62 C.597 B.A. L.813 LL.B.
(adm. in CA; not adm. in DE) Coun., du Pont Co.
Spevack DiSciullo, Jill '72 '99 C.886 B.A. L.1338 J.D.
(adm. in PA; not adm. in DE) [J.R.Julian]
*PRACTICE AREAS: Family Law.
Spivack, Deborah E. .... '65 '93 C.645 B.S. L.1338 J.D. [🄰 Richards,L.&F.]
Spivack, Dennis R., (BV) .... '47 '76 C.659 B.A. L.477 J.D. [Morris,J.H.&W.]
*PRACTICE AREAS: Real Estate Law; Commercial; Business Law.
Spoltore, Leslie .... '70 '97 C.874 B.A. L.1338 J.D. Family Ct. of the St. of Delaware
Springer-Messick, Joanne C. .... '66 '00 C.645 B.S. L.1338 J.D. [🄰 Young C.S.&T.]
*PRACTICE AREAS: Labor and Employment; Immigration Law.
Staats, David, (BV) .... '52 '82 C.918 B.A. L.309 J.D. [D.Staats]
*PRACTICE AREAS: Commercial Litigation; Franchise Law; Business Transactions; Internet Law; Appellate Practice.

Staats, David, P.A., Law Office of, (BV)
Suite 36, Professional Buildings, 1701 Augustine Cut-off, 19803
Telephone: 302-658-8188 Fax: 302-658-8168
Email: legal@staatslaw.com URL: http://www.staatslaw.com
David Staats; George Renos Tsakataras (Resident).
Commercial Litigation, Franchise Law, Business Transactions, Internet Law, Apellate Practice.

See Professional Biographies, WILMINGTON, DELAWARE

Stabler, Wendie Cohen, (BV) .... '58 '83 C.860 B.A. L.245 J.D. [Saul E.]
*PRACTICE AREAS: Commercial Law; Telecommunications; Zoning and Land Use; Real Estate Law; Administrative Law.
Staib, Jason W. .... '70 '98 C.205 B.A. L.1338 J.D. [🄰 Morris,N.A.&T.]
Stapleton, Walter K. .... '34 '59 C.674 A.B. L.309 LL.B. Ct. of App. J.
Stargatt, Bruce M., (AV) .... '30 '55 C.882 B.A. L.976 LL.B. [Young C.S.&T.]
*PRACTICE AREAS: Corporate Fiduciary Law; Corporate Governance; Civil Litigation.
Stark, Leonard P. .... '69 '97 C.205 B.A.B.S. L.976 J.D. [🄰 Skadden,A.S.M.&F.]
*PRACTICE AREAS: Litigation.
Stark, Lisa R. .... '73 '01 C.105 B.A. L.902 J.D. [🄰 Richards,L.&F.]
Staropoli, C. Curtis .... '65 '92 C.205 B.A.S. L.884 J.D. [🄰 Grant&E.]
Starr, Kristopher T. .... '72 '00 C.205 B.S.N. L.1338 J.D. 820 N. French St.
Stearn, Robert J., Jr., (BV) .... '62 '90 C.216 B.A. L.659 J.D. [Richards,L.&F.]
Stein, Michael R. .... '62 '89 C.216 B.A. L.1017 J.D. [🄰 Richards,L.&F.]
*PRACTICE AREAS: Estate Planning; Estate Administration; Taxation.
Steinberg, Thomas W. '54 '90 C.575 A.B. L.229 J.D.
(adm. in PA; not adm. in DE; Pat.) Sr. Coun., E.I. du Pont de Nemours & Co.
*RESPONSIBILITIES: Infringement/Counseling; Prosecution (Patent); Licensing Issues.
Stevens, Thomas A. .... '— '91 C.659 B.A. L.644 J.D. [🄰 Connolly B.L.&H.]

Stevens & Lee, A Professional Corporation, (AVⓉ)
300 Delaware Avenue Suite 800, 19801 ⊙
Telephone: 302-654-5180 Fax: 302-654-5181
Email: attys@stevenslee.com URL: http://www.stevenslee.com
Walter P. McEvilly Jr.; Joseph H. Huston, Jr.; Joseph Grey; John D. Demmy;—Susan M. Gordon; Thomas G. Whalen, Jr.
Antitrust, Securities, Tax-Exempt Finance, Tax, Employment Law, OSHA, ERISA, Mergers and Acquisitions, Litigation, Bankruptcy, Environmental Law, Banking, Insurance, Computer Law, Health Law, Complex Estate and Business Succession Planning, Government Affairs and Government Regulatory, Higher Education, Real Estate, International Law, Intellectual Property and e-Commerce Law.
Reading, Pennsylvania Office: 111 North Sixth Street, P.O. Box 679, 19603-0679. Telephone: 610-478-2000. Fax: 610-376-5610.
Wayne, Pennsylvania Office: One Glenhardie Corporate Center, 1275 Drummers Lane, P. O. Box 236, 19087-0236. Telephone: 610-964-1480. Fax: 610-687-1384.
Lancaster, Pennsylvania Office: 25 North Queen Street, Suite 602, P.O. Box 1594, 17608-1594. Telephone: 717-291-1031. Fax: 717-394-7726.
Allentown, Pennsylvania Office: 190 Brodhead Road, Suite 200, P.O. Box 20830, 18002-0830. Telephone: 610-691-7111. Fax: 610-691-7175.
Harrisburg, Pennsylvania Office: 208 North Third Street. Suite 310. P.O. Box 12090, 17108-2090. Telephone: 717-234-1250. Fax: 717-234-1939.
Off-Hill Harrisburg, Pennsylvania Office: 4750 Lindle Road, P.O. Box 11670, 17108-1670. Telephone: 717-561-5242. Fax: 717-561-5207.
Philadelphia, Pennsylvania Office: 1818 Market Street, 29th Floor, 19103. Telephone: 215-575-0100. Fax: 215-851-0214.
Scranton, Pennsylvania Office: Kane Building, Suite 2B, 116 North Washington Street, 18503. Telephone: 570-343-1827. Fax: 570-343-1892.
Wilkes-Barre, Pennsylvania Office: 120 South Franklin Street, 18701. Telephone: 570-823-6116. Fax: 570-823-1149.
Cherry Hill, New Jersey Office: 1415 Route 70 East, Suite 506, 08034. Telephone: 856-354-9200. Fax: 856-354-8111.

See Professional Biographies, WILMINGTON, DELAWARE

Stevenson, Robert B. '39 '73 C.352 Ph.D L.209 J.D.
(adm. in IL; not adm. in DE; Pat.) Corp. Coun., E.I. du Pont de Nemours & Co.
Stevenson, Stanford L., III, (BV) '68 '95 C.945 B.B.A. L.276 J.D.
[🄰 Morris,N.A.&T.]
Stewart, Gordon W., (BV) .... '53 '84 C.197 A.B. L.902 J.D. [Stewart&Assoc.] ⊙
*PRACTICE AREAS: Taxation; State and Local Taxation; Multi-State Corporate Tax Planning; Corporations; Property Tax Appeals.
Stewart, Robert Forrest, Jr., (AVⓉ) '43 '68
C.321 B.S. L.276 J.D. [Dilworth P.P.] (⊙Phila., PA)
*PRACTICE AREAS: Labor and Employment Law.

Stewart & Associates, A Professional Law Association, (BV)
Suite 1400 The Nemours Building, 1007 Orange Street, 19801 ⊙
Telephone: 302-652-5200 Telecopier: 302-652-7211
Email: info@delawarecorporatelaw.com URL: http://www.delawarecorporatelaw.com
Principal: Gordon W. Stewart. Director: Dawn B. Kilcrease. Counsel: Carl J. Fernandes. Associates: Peter Campbell; Keith R. Sattesahn; Tanya M. Murray; Michael J. Conallen, Jr.; Leanne C. McGrory; Elizabeth V. Thompson (Not admitted in DE). Of Counsel: S. Maynard Turk; John J. Leary, Jr. (Not admitted in DE).
State, Local and Federal Taxation, Corporations, Limited Liability Companies, Intellectual Property Law, Commercial Law, Mergers and Acquisitions, International Transactions, General Practice.
Las Vegas, Nevada Office: Hughes Center, Suite 460, 3993 Howard Hughes Parkway, 89109. Telephone: 702-836-3500. Fax: 702-836-0880. Email: info@nevadacorporatelaw.com

See Professional Biographies, WILMINGTON, DELAWARE

Steyermark, Paul R. .... '23 '68 C.014 Ph.D. L.273 J.D. Coun., du Pont Co. (Pat.)
Stickles, J. Kate, (BV) .... '62 '90 C.928 B.A. L.831 J.D. [🄲 Saul E.]
*PRACTICE AREAS: Bankruptcy Law; Commercial Law.
Stiftel, Albert J. .... '18 '41 C.205 A.B. L.893 LL.B. Ret. Supr. Ct. Pres. J.
Stilson, Ann E. Conaway, (BV) '54 '83 C.280 B.A. L.831 J.D.
Assoc. Prof. of Law, Widener Univ. School of Law

Stitzer, Ashley B. ... '69 '96 C.740 B.A. L.831 J.D. [Ⓐ Bayard]
*PRACTICE AREAS: Commercial Bankruptcy; Creditors Rights; Commercial Litigation.

Stoltzfus, James A. ... '67 '95 C.655 B.S. L.831 J.D. [Ⓐ Skadden,A.S.M.&F.]
*PRACTICE AREAS: Corporate.

Stone, Alan J., (BV) ... '61 '88 C&L.861 B.S.E., J.D. [Morris,N.A.&T.]

Stoner, Ronald L., (BV) ... '53 '92 C.953 B.S. L.942 J.D. 300Delaware Ave.

Stradley Ronon Stevens & Young, LLP, (AV)
919 North Market Street, Suite 600 (⊙Wash., DC; Cherry Hill, NJ; Malvern, Phila., PA)

Stratton, Barbara H., (BV) ... '56 '81 C.205 B.A. L.665 J.D. [Knepper&S.]
*PRACTICE AREAS: Personal Injury; Employment Law; Workers Compensation; Sexual Harassment; Automobile Accidents and Injuries.

Stratton, David B., (AV) ... '53 '78 C.282 A.B. L.665 J.D. [Pepper H.]
*PRACTICE AREAS: Bankruptcy Law; Creditors Rights; Commercial Banking.

Straub, Patrick W. ... '75 '00 C.821 B.A. L.1338 J.D. One Rodney Square

Strauss, Andrew L. '58 '88 C.674 B.A. L.569 J.D.
(adm. in NY; not adm. in DE) Assoc. Prof. of Law, Widener Univ. Sch. of Law

Strauss, Benjamin ... '55 '91 C.999 B.A. L.1338 J.D. [Pepper H.]
*PRACTICE AREAS: Corporate Law; Commercial Law; Securities.

Streett, Diane Clarke ... '50 '75 C&L.188 B.S., J.D. Asst. Pub. Def.

Strickland, Frederick D. '47 '94 L.831 J.D.
(adm. in PA; not adm. in DE; Pat.) Sr. Coun., E.I du Pont de Nemours & Co.
*RESPONSIBILITIES: Patent.

Stripling, Kathryn S. '63 '89 C.1350 B.A. L.273 J.D.
(adm. in CO; not adm. in DE) Sr. Coun., Astrazeneca Pharm. LP
*RESPONSIBILITIES: Health Law; Products Liability; General Commercial Law.

Strum, James C. ... '— '86 C.103 B.A. L.945 J.D. [Ⓒ Stradley R.S.&Y.]

Stubenberg, Melissa K. ... '70 '98 C.518 B.A. L.273 J.D. [Ⓐ Richards,L.&F.]

Stuhltrager, James Michael '67 '98 C.645 B.A. L.1338 J.D.
(adm. in PA; not adm. in DE) 4601 Concord Pike

Stull, John M. '34 '58 C.221 B.S.B.A. L.477 LL.B.
Suite 700, 1300 North Market Street, P.O. Box 1947, 19899-1947
Telephone: 302-654-0399 Fax: 302-654-0884
Email: jstullesq@AOL.COM
***PRACTICE AREAS: Employee Retirement Income Security Act (ERISA); Taxation (Federal and State); Estate Planning; Probate.**
ERISA, Taxation and Tax Litigation, Estate Planning, Probate, Pension and Profit Sharing and Corporate Law.
References: Wilmington Trust Co.; Christiana Bank.
See Professional Biographies, WILMINGTON, DELAWARE

Suddard, Oliver V., (AV) ... '26 '50 C&L.228 A.B., J.D. 8 E. 13th St.

Sudell, William H., Jr., (AV) ... '43 '71 C.103 B.S. L.659 J.D. [Morris,N.A.&T.]

Sullivan, Brian A., (BV) ... '55 '81 C.282 B.A. L.365 J.D. [Werb&S.]
*PRACTICE AREAS: Bankruptcy; Corporate Reorganization; Business Law; Corporate Law; Real Property.

Sullivan, John E., (BV) ... '50 '79 C.205 B.A. L.1338 J.D. [Sullivan&M.]

Sullivan, Karen ... '70 '98 C.205 B.A. L.276 J.D. [Ⓐ Oberly&J.]
*PRACTICE AREAS: Criminal Law; Personal Injury; Civil Litigation.

Sullivan, Lawrence M., (BV) '37 '65 C.1113 A.B. L.128 LL.B.
1010 Concord Ave., #201

Sullivan, William D., (BV) ... '62 '90 C.602 B.S. L.276 J.D. [Elzufon A.R.T.&M.]
*PRACTICE AREAS: Bankruptcy; Commercial Litigation.

Sullivan & Marston, P.A., (BV) ... 5301 Limestone Rd.

Summa, Leann Mattoscio ... '76 '00 C.655 B.A. L.1017 J.D. 900 King St.

Sundheim, Joanne K. '47 '76 C.298 B.A. L.831 J.D.
(adm. in PA; not adm. in DE) Sen. V.P. & Assoc. Gen. Coun., First USA

Supinski, Henry W. ... '49 '77 C.397 B.S. L.64 J.D. City Treas.

Surles, Robert H., (BV) ... '62 '90 L.229 J.D. Off. of Atty. Gen.

Sutton, Richard L., (AV) ... '35 '61 C.205 B.A. L.976 LL.B. [Ⓒ Morris,N.A.&T.]

Sutty, Eric M. ... '71 '00 C.945 B.B.A. L.1002 J.D. [Ⓐ Bayard]
*PRACTICE AREAS: Commercial Bankruptcy; Creditors Rights; Commercial Litigation.

Swain, Elizabeth Curtis '52 '81
C.205 B.S.B.A. L.1338 J.D. Sr. Coun., E.I. du Pont de Nemours & Co.
*RESPONSIBILITIES: Antitrust Law (30%); Government Contract Law (30%); Intellectual Property Law (20%); General Practice (18%); Copyright Law (2%).

Swartz, Campbell & Detweiler, (BV)
Mellon Bank Center, 919 Market Street, P.O. Box 330, 19899 ⊙
Telephone: 302-656-5935 Fax: 302-656-1434
Email: webmaster@scdlaw.com URL: http://www.scdlaw.com
Resident Partner: Keith E. Donovan. Resident Associates: Mark T. Hurford; Nicholas E. Skiles; Patricia Murphy.
General Civil and Trial Practice in State and Federal Courts including Insurance, Workers Compensation, Product Liability, Toxic Torts, Medical Malpractice, Legal Malpractice, Commercial and Bankruptcy Defense.
Philadelphia, Pennsylvania Office: 1601 Market Street, 34th Floor. Telephone: 215-564-5190. Telefax: 215-299-4301.
Media, Pennsylvania Office: 115 North Jackson Street. Telephone: 610-566-9222. Fax: 610-566-7351.
Harrisburg, Pennsylvania Office: 1631 North Front Street. Telephone: 717-233-3515. Fax: 717-233-3468.
Allentown, Pennsylvania Office: Suite 230. 5100 Tilghman Street. Telephone: 610-395-5903. Fax: 610-395-7097.
Mount Laurel, New Jersey Office: Bloom Court, Suite 101. 1300 Route 73. Telephone: 856-727-4777. Fax: 856-727-0464.
Scranton, Pennsylvania Office: Bank Towers, 6th Floor, 321 Spruce Street. Telephone: 570-343-0029. Fax: 570-343-1534.
West Chester, Pennsylvania Office: One South Church Street, Suite 400. Telephone: 610-692-9500. Fax: 610-692-4936.
Fort Myers, Florida Office: The Huntington Plaza, 2000 Main Street, Suite 805. Telephone: 941-790-7700. Fax: 941-332-5325.
Bedminster, New Jersey Office: Bedminster Center, 90 Washington Valley Road. Telephone: 908-719-8932. Fax: 908-719-6005.
See Professional Biographies, WILMINGTON, DELAWARE

Swayze, David S., (AV) ... '— '69 C.674 A.B. L.659 LL.B. [Reed S.]
*PRACTICE AREAS: Government Relations.

Sweeney, Peter M. ... '71 '97 C.602 B.A. L.884 J.D. [Ⓐ Gordon,F.&M.]
*PRACTICE AREAS: Commercial Litigation; Civil Litigation; Creditors Rights Litigation.

Sweeney, Thomas P., (AV) ... '36 '61 C.878 B.S. L.208 LL.B. [Richards,L.&F.]
*PRACTICE AREAS: Estate Planning; Taxation (Local, Personal Property, State, Federal or International) Law; Federal Income, Estate and Gift Taxation Law; Trust Law.

Symonds, Robert L., Jr., (AV) ... '53 '86 C.884 B.A. L.665 J.D. [Morris,J.H.&W.]
*PRACTICE AREAS: Business Law; Limited Liability Companies; Partnerships; Trusts; Joint Ventures.

Szanto, Ivan G. ... '34 '66 C.999 B.Ch.E. L.767 J.D. Hercules Plz. (Pat.)

Szymanski, Marilou A. ... '55 '80 C.524 B.A. L.831 J.D. 2211 Brookline Rd.

Tacconelli, Theodore J., (BV) ... '58 '88 C.205 B.S. L.1338 J.D. [Ferry&J.]
*PRACTICE AREAS: Commercial Law; Bankruptcy Law; Litigation; Creditors Rights.

Tarabicos, Larry J., (BV) ... '60 '86 C.205 B.A.A.S. L.245 J.D. [Young C.S.&T.]
*PRACTICE AREAS: Real Estate Development; Zoning Law; Real Estate Acquisitions; Real Estate Contracts; Leases and Leasing.

Tarlov, Edward A., (BV) ... '58 '85 C.354 B.S. L.221 J.D. [Elzufon A.R.T.&M.]
*PRACTICE AREAS: Real Estate Law; Commercial Law; Banking Law; Civil Litigation.

Tarrant, H. Alfred, Jr., (AV) '35 '61 C.902 A.B. L.446 LL.B.
[Cooch&T.] (⊙Newark)
*PRACTICE AREAS: Domestic Relations.

Taschner, Jeffrey M ... '62 '87 C&L.216 B.A., J.D. Dep. Atty. Gen.

Taylor, Andrew P. ... '58 '82 [Cooch&T.]
*PRACTICE AREAS: Real Estate; Real Estate Brokerage Law; Fair Housing; General Practice.

Taylor, Clarence W. ... '17 '42 C.205 A.B. L.976 LL.B. Ret. Supr. Ct. J.

Taylor, David M. ... '46 '82 C.205 B.A. L.1338 J.D. 1213 King St.

Taylor, Donald C., (AV) ... '30 '54 C.216 A.B. L.1017 J.D. [Cooch&T.] (⊙Newark)
*PRACTICE AREAS: Real Estate; Banking Law; Business Law.

Taylor, Gregory Alan ... '75 '00 C.205 B.A. L.1338 J.D. [Ⓐ Ashby&G.]

Taylor, Jonathan B., (BV) ... '50 '78 C.611 B.A. L.472 J.D. [Taylor&M.]
*PRACTICE AREAS: Real Estate Law; Zoning Law; Personal Injury Law; Business Law.

Taylor, Julia A. '57 '88 C.223 B.S. L.831 J.D.
(adm. in PA; not adm. in DE) Del. Div. of Rev.

Taylor, Vernon A. '46 '80 C.512 B.S. L.1338 J.D.
(adm. in PA; not adm. in DE) Del. Natl. Guard

Taylor, William F., (AV) ... '30 '54 C.216 A.B. L.1017 LL.B. [Ⓒ Young C.S.&T.]
*PRACTICE AREAS: Negligence; Civil Liability; Casualty Insurance; Insurance Arbitration; Drug and Medical Device Defense.

Taylor, William F., Jr., (BV) ... '64 '91 C.692 B.A. L.1017 J.D. [Elzufon A.R.T.&M.]
*PRACTICE AREAS: Bankruptcy; Reorganization; Commercial Litigation.

Taylor & McNew LLP, (BV)
Suite 210, 3711 Kennett Pike, 19807
Telephone: 302-655-9200 Fax: 302-655-9361
Email: mail@law-tm.com URL: http://www.taylormcnew.com
Jonathan B. Taylor; R. Bruce McNew.
General Practice. Commercial, Corporate and Securities Law, Real Estate (Commercial and Residential) and Zoning, Litigation, Personal Injury, Consumer Rights, Wills, Probate, Estate Planning, Class Actions, Complex Litigation, Environmental and Collection Law.
Agents for: Old Republic National Title Insurance Co.; Ticor Title Insurance Co.; Atlantic Title and Abstract Co.
Approved Attorneys for: Ataco, Inc.
See Professional Biographies, WILMINGTON, DELAWARE

Teichman, Michael W. ... '— '94 C.884 B.A. L.831 J.D. [Ⓐ Reed S.]
*PRACTICE AREAS: Financial Services Law.

Teklits, David J., (BV) ... '68 '93 C.659 B.S. L.276 J.D. [Morris,N.A.&T.]

Temin, Michael L., (AVⓉ) '33 '58
C.976 B.A. L.659 LL.B. [Wolf,B.S.&S-C.] (⊙Phila., PA)
*PRACTICE AREAS: Bankruptcy.

Tenenbaum, Harlan Scott ... '68 '94 C.860 B.A. L.1009 J.D. 1 Barley Mill Drive

Tenenbaum, Joel D., (BV) ... '40 '65 C.331 A.B. L.1009 LL.B. [Woloshin,T.L.N.&F.]

Tepe, John B., Jr., (BV) '47 '73 C.674 A.B. L.178 J.D.
(adm. in NY; not adm. in DE) Corp. Coun., E.I. du Pont de Nemours and Company
*RESPONSIBILITIES: Commercial; Antitrust and Trade Regulation; Joint Venture and Mergers and Acquisitions; Corporate; Finance.

Terrell, Allen M., Jr., (AV) ... '43 '69 C&L.309 B.A., LL.B. [Richards,L.&F.]
*PRACTICE AREAS: Litigation; Corporate Law.

Theisen, Vincent A., (AV) ... '14 '42 C.165 A.B. L.309 J.D. [Ⓒ Theisen,L.M.&G.] ‡

Theisen, Lank, Mulford & Goldberg, P.A., (AV) ... Ninth Floor, One Commerce Center

Thomas, Robert L., (BV) ... '46 '71 C.216 A.B. L.276 J.D. [Young C.S.&T.]
*PRACTICE AREAS: Closely Held Business Law; Commercial Real Estate Development; Condominium Development; Estate and Gift Taxation; Like Kind Exchanges.

Thompson, Catherine Hagerty, (BV) '55 '80
C.30 B.A. L.831 J.D. Corp. Coun., E.I. du Pont de Nemours & Co.
*RESPONSIBILITIES: Commercial Law; Employment Law; Litigation.

Thompson, Elizabeth V. '71 '98 C.970 B.A. L.1218 J.D.
(adm. in CO; not adm. in DE) [Ⓐ Stewart&Assoc.]

Thompson, John J., (BV) ... '51 '76 C.205 B.A. L.930 J.D. [Levine&T.]
*PRACTICE AREAS: General Business Law; Family Law; Civil Litigation; Personal Injury; Collections Law.

Thompson, Melanie J. ... '67 '97 C.550 B.A. L.1338 J.D. [Ⓐ Mattleman,W.&M.]
*PRACTICE AREAS: Family Law; Wills; Trusts and Estates.

Thornburg, Robin L., P.C., Law Offices of
(See West Conshohocken, Pennsylvania)

Tigani, Bruce W., (BV) ... '56 '81 C.205 B.S. L.884 J.D. [Tigani&H.]
*PRACTICE AREAS: Tax Planning; Estate Planning; Business Transactions; Real Estate; Closely Held Business Law.

Tigani, James V., Jr. ... '37 '62 C.397 B.A. L.276 J.D. 4604 Simon Rd.‡

Tigani, Janice Rowe, (BV) ... '55 '82 C.205 B.A. L.884 J.D. [Tigani&H.] ‡
*PRACTICE AREAS: Estate Planning; Estate Administration; Residential Real Estate; Business Organization; Administrative Law.

Tigani & Hood LLP, (BV)
1801 Mellon Bank Center, 919 Market Street, P.O. Box 1471, 19899
Telephone: 302-777-1000 Telecopier: 302-777-1098
URL: http://www.tiganihoodlaw.com
Bruce W. Tigani; Michael J. Hood; Janice Rowe Tigani.
Tax and Estate Planning, Business Transactions, Real Estate, Business Organization, Estate Administration, Civil Litigation, Criminal Trial Practice, Personal Injury, Administrative Law.
See Professional Biographies, WILMINGTON, DELAWARE

Tighe, Michael K., (BV) ... '47 '76 C.1021 B.A. L.128 J.D. [Tighe,C.&L.]
*PRACTICE AREAS: Commercial Law; Insurance Defense; Litigation; Personal Injury; Products Liability.

Tighe, Cottrell & Logan, P.A., (BV)
First Federal Plaza, Suite 500, P.O. Box 1031, 19801 ⊙
Telephone: 302-658-6400; 800-645-6401 Fax: 302-658-9836
Email: lawtcl@dol.net URL: http://www.lawtcl.com
Michael K. Tighe; Paul Cottrell (Resident, Philadelphia, Pennsylvania Office); Donald L. Logan; James S. Yoder;—G. Kevin Fasic; Joseph Scott Shannon; Scott L. Messmore (Not admitted in DE); Julie Lynn Kopec (Not admitted in DE); Michael T. Hollister (Not admitted in DE).
Civil Practice, Commercial Law, Construction Law, Insurance Defense, Debtor & Creditor.
Philadelphia, Pennsylvania Office: 2017 Spring Garden Street. Telephone: 215-564-0101.
Towson, Maryland Office: 110 West Road, Suite 245, 21204. Telephone: 410-539-7341.
Woodstown, New Jersey Office: 19 West Avenue, 08098. Telephone: 800-645-6401.
See Professional Biographies, WILMINGTON, DELAWARE

Tikellis, Pamela S., (BV) ... '52 '82 C.706 B.A. L.1338 J.D. [Chimicles&T.]
*PRACTICE AREAS: Securities Litigation; Partnership Litigation; Antitrust; Mergers and Acquisitions; Class Actions.

Tobia, James ... '73 '99 C.705 B.A. L.188 J.D. [Ⓐ Bayard]
*PRACTICE AREAS: Commercial Litigation; Corporate Litigation.

Togman, Leonard S., (AV) ... '39 '64 C.659 B.S.E. L.569 LL.B. [Potter A.&C.]

Toliver, Charles H., IV ... '51 '75 C.302 B.A. L.893 J.D. Supr. Ct. J.

Toll, Doris M. ... '— '64 C.518 B.A. L.325 LL.B. 11th Fl., Rodney Sq. N.

Tomar, O'Brien, Kaplan, Jacoby & Graziano
919 Market Street (⊙Atlantic City, Cherry Hill, Northfield, NJ; Media, PA)

Tostrup, Julie ... '— '97 C.477 B.A. L.884 J.D. [Ⓐ Skadden,A.S.M.&F.]
*PRACTICE AREAS: Litigation.

Toth, Kathleen '48 '93 C.608 B.A. L.117 J.D.
(adm. in OH; not adm. in DE) Coun., AIG Life Cos.

Trainer, Philip, Jr. ... '60 '89 C.945 B.A. L.1338 J.D. [Ashby&G.]

Trigg, Hastings S., Jr. '49 '75 C.105 B.S. L.262 J.D.
(adm. in NY; not adm. in DE) Corp. Coun., E.I. du Pont de Nemours & Co.
*RESPONSIBILITIES: Labor and Employment; OSHA.
Trostle, Keith A., (BV) .... '48 '75 C.49 B.A. L.607 J.D. Dep. Atty. Gen.
Trostle, Mary Pat, (BV) .... '51 '76 C.473 B.S. L.607 J.D. U.S. Mag. J.
Truemper, Roger Lea .... '60 '89 C.205 B.S. L.1338 J.D. [Ⓐ Saul E.]
*PRACTICE AREAS: Real Estate Law; Commercial and Business Law; Commercial Litigation.
Trzuskowski, Francis J., (BV) .... '37 '62 C.397 B.A. L.276 J.D. [Trzuskowski,K.K.&P.]
*PRACTICE AREAS: Pension Law; Commercial Law; General Litigation; Commercial Real Estate Law.

Trzuskowski, Kipp, Kelleher & Pearce, P.A., (AV)
1020 North Bancroft Parkway, P.O. Box 429, 19899-0429 ⊙
Telephone: 302-571-1782 Fax: 302-571-1638
Francis J. Trzuskowski; James F. Kipp; Daniel F. Kelleher; Robert K. Pearce; Vance A. Funk, III (Resident, Newark Office); Barbara Snapp Danberg; William L. Doerler.
General Practice. Civil Litigation, Personal Injury, Medical Malpractice, Commercial and Corporate, Real Estate, Estate Planning, Probate, Family, Matrimonial, Pension (ERISA).
Newark, Delaware Office: 273 East Main Street, 19711. Telephone: 302-368-2561. Telefax: 302-368-9729.
See Professional Biographies, WILMINGTON, DELAWARE

Tsakataras, George Renos .... '71 '97 C.205 B.S. L.884 J.D. [D.Staats]
*PRACTICE AREAS: Commercial Litigation; Franchise Law; Business Transactions; Music Law.
Tucker, J. Richard '— '69 C.205 B.A. L.796 J.D.
(adm. in TX; not adm. in DE) [Reed S.]
*PRACTICE AREAS: Corporate Law.
Tulloch, Rebecca W. '46 '93 C.125 A.B. L.1338 J.D.
Sr. Coun., E.I. du Pont de Nemours & Co. (Pat.)
*RESPONSIBILITIES: Intellectual Property.
Tully, Martin P., (AV) .... '44 '71 C.705 B.A. L.597 J.D. [Morris,N.A.&T.]
Tumas, Michael B., (BV) .... '59 '84 C.1044 B.A. L.659 J.D. [Potter A.&C.]
Turk, S. Maynard, (AV) ..... '25 '51 C.695 B.A. L.902 LL.B. [Ⓒ Stewart&Assoc.] (Pat.)
Turner, Mason E., Jr., (AV) .... '42 '67 C.299 A.B. L.893 LL.B. [Prickett,J.&E.]
*PRACTICE AREAS: Medical Malpractice; Products Liability; Insurance Defense Litigation.
Tussey, Susan P. .... '57 '94 C.205 B.A. L.1338 J.D. Atty., Dept. of Jus.
Tuthill, Walter C., (AV) .... '51 '77 C.207 B.A. L.597 J.D. [Morris,N.A.&T.]
Tybout, F. Alton, (AV) .... '29 '56 C.228 A.B. L.976 LL.B. [Ⓒ Tybout,R.&P.]
*PRACTICE AREAS: Negligence; Insurance; Products Liability; Medical Malpractice.

Tybout, Redfearn & Pell, (AV)
Suite 1100, 300 Delaware Avenue, P.O. Box 2092, 19899
Telephone: 302-658-6901 Fax: 302-658-4018
Email: trpmail@TRPLaw.com URL: http://www.trplaw.com
Partners: B. Wilson Redfearn; Richard W. Pell; David G. Culley; Sherry Ruggiero Fallon; Francis X. Nardo; John J. Klusman, Jr.; Danielle Kathleen Yearick; Charles Slanina; Dennis J. Menton. Associates: Susan A. List; Steven Daniel Rosen. Of Counsel: F. Alton Tybout.
General Practice. Litigation. Workers Compensation. Products Liability, Medical Malpractice, Insurance Coverage, and Construction.
Representative Clients: CIGNA Insurance Co.; Liberty Mutual Insurance Co.; Hartford Insurance Co.; Universal Underwriters; PHICO; State of Delaware; State Farm Insurance Co.; Insurance Guarantee Assn.; University of Delaware; First Delaware Insurance Co.
See Professional Biographies, WILMINGTON, DELAWARE

Uebler, E. Alan, (BV) .... '39 '74 C.205 Ph.D. L.446 J.D. 1601 Milltown Rd. (Pat.)
Uffelman, William H., Jr., (CV) ..... '35 '64 C.197 B.A. L.893 LL.B. 1303 Delaware Ave.
Uhlenbrock, Patricia R. .... '59 '00 C.665 B.A. L.1338 J.D. [Ⓐ Morris,N.A.&T.]
Undorf, Michael Andrew .... '75 '99 C.205 B.S. L.884 J.D. Dept. of Jus.
Unterberger, Andrea Beth .... '63 '98 C.103 B.A. L.1338 J.D. [Ⓐ Pepper H.]
*PRACTICE AREAS: Commercial Litigation; Corporate Litigation.
Unterberger, Robert M., (BVⓉ) '61 '89 C.860 B.A. L.93 J.D.
(adm. in PA; not adm. in DE) 101 Norris Rd.
Vahey, Maureen Patricia '70 '97 C.273 B.B.A. L.1338 J.D.
(adm. in PA; not adm. in DE) Coun., Hercules Incorporated
Valdes-Lora, Mario E. '64 '89 C.145 B.A. L.904 J.D.
(adm. in FL; not adm. in DE) Atty., AIG Life Cos.
Valihura, Karen L., (BV) .... '63 '88 C.901 B.A. L.659 J.D. [Skadden,A.S.M.&F.]
Valocchi, Beth Evans .... '54 '84 C.999 B.S. L.942 J.D. 1200 Pennsylvania Ave.
Van Amerongen, Jan A. T., Jr., (CV) .... '— '90 C.659 B.A. L.945 J.D. [Ⓐ Reed S.]
*PRACTICE AREAS: Litigation.
van Amerongen, Kathryn Castiglioni .... '66 '91 C.30 B.A. L.904 J.D. Dep. Atty. Gen.
Van Ogtrop, Bernard A., (AV) .... '44 '69 C.276 A.B. L.128 J.D. [Seitz,V.&G.]
*PRACTICE AREAS: Personal Injury; Litigation.
van Ogtrop, Piet H., (BV) .... '39 '64 C.363 B.S. L.1017 LL.B. [Daley,E.&v.] ⊙
Van Tassel, Emily Field '— '83 C.930 B.A. L.884 J.D.
(adm. in WI; not adm. in DE) Assoc. Prof. of Law, Widener Univ. Sch. of Law
Varallo, Gregory V., (BV) .... '59 '84 C.659 B.A. L.831 J.D. [Richards,L.&F.]
*PRACTICE AREAS: Corporate Control Litigation; Complex Business Litigation.
Veasey, E. Norman, (AV) .... '33 '58 C.197 A.B. L.659 LL.B. Chf. Supm. Ct. Jus.
Veatch, Ned P., (AVⓉ) '10 '34 C&L.145 Ph.B., J.D.
(adm. in IL; not adm. in DE) 2723 Shipley Rd.‡
Vella, Patricia O'Neill .... '70 '96 C.205 B.S.B.A. L.884 J.D. [Ⓐ Morris,N.A.&T.]
Vild, Michael L., (BV) .... '64 '91 C.608 B.Mus. L.602 J.D. [Bayard]
*PRACTICE AREAS: Bankruptcy Law; Corporate Litigation; Commercial Litigation; Equine Law.
Vinokur, Leon L. .... '71 '97 C.205 B.A. L.1017 J.D. [Ⓐ Young C.S.&T.]
*PRACTICE AREAS: Zoning, Planning and Land Use; Commercial Real Estate Law; Real Estate Leasing.
Voss, Wendy K. .... '52 '92 C.477 B.A. L.945 J.D. [Potter A.&C.]
Vye, H. Kemp .... '46 '78 C.205 B.A. L.1002 J.D. First Regiment Rd.
Wade, William J., (AV) .... '47 '76 C.205 B.A. L.659 J.D. [Richards,L.&F.]
Waite, Joel A., (BV) .... '65 '90 C.237 B.A. L.902 J.D. [Young C.S.&T.]
*PRACTICE AREAS: Bankruptcy; Commercial Law.
Wakefield, Robert W. .... '29 '54 C.674 A.B. L.893 LL.B. Fam. Ct. J.
Walker, P. Michael '58 '86 C.223 B.S.Ch.E. L.602 J.D.
(adm. in PA; not adm. in DE; Pat.)
Assoc. Gen. Coun.-Intell. Prop., E.I. du Pont de Nemours and Company
*RESPONSIBILITIES: Intellectual Property; Intellectual Property Licensing.
Walker, Wayne R. '59 '84 C.425 B.A. L.128 J.D.
(adm. in GA; not adm. in DE) du Pont Co.
Wallace, Paul R., (BV) .... '64 '90 C.446 B.A. L.128 J.D. Dep. Atty. Gen.
Walma, Kenneth D. '39 '70 C.477 B.A. L.273 J.D.
(adm. in VA; not adm. in DE) V.P. & Gen. Coun., AIG Life Cos.
Walsh, David I., (BV) .... '43 '70 C.276 B.S. L.64 J.D. [Walsh M.&M.] ⊙
*PRACTICE AREAS: Federal Taxation; International Taxation; Estate Planning; Corporate Law.
Walsh, Joseph T. .... '30 '54 C.397 B.A. L.276 J.D. Supm. Ct. J.
Walsh, Kevin E., (BV) '55 '81 C.205 B.A. L.1338 J.D.
V.P., Gen. Coun. & Secy., Montell N. Amer. Inc.
Walsh, Neilli Mullen, (CV) .... '62 '87 C.602 B.A. L.902 J.D. [Young C.S.&T.]
*PRACTICE AREAS: Medical Malpractice; Personal Injury; Premises Liability; Products Liability; Torts.
Walsh, Peter J. .... '34 '64 C.397 B.A. L.276 LL.B. U.S. Bkrptcy. J.
Walsh, Peter J., Jr., (BV) .... '60 '86 C.367 B.A. L.902 J.D. [Potter A.&C.]
Walsh, Thomas D. .... '— '98 C.205 B.A. L.1338 J.D. [Ⓐ McCarter&E.]
*PRACTICE AREAS: Commercial Bankruptcy; Complex Litigation; Criminal Defense.

Walsh Monzack and Monaco, P.A., (BV)
400 Commerce Center, Twelfth and Orange Streets, P.O. Box 2031, 19899 ⊙
Telephone: 302-656-8162 Fax: 302-656-2769
URL: http://www.lawyers.com/wmmlaw
David I. Walsh; Melvyn I. Monzack; Francis A. Monaco, Jr.; Rachel B. Mersky; Brian J. McLaughlin; Joseph J. Bodnar; Edward M. Lilly; Mary Elizabeth M. Browder; Kevin J. Mangan.
Taxation, Commercial Transactions, Business Reorganization, Commercial Bankruptcy, General Corporate, Real Estate. Civil Litigation in all Courts.
See Professional Biographies, WILMINGTON, DELAWARE

Walter, Keith A., Jr. '70 '99 C.338 B.S. L.831 J.D.
(adm. in NY; not adm. in DE) [Ⓐ Fish&R.]
*PRACTICE AREAS: Intellectual Property.
Walter, Wendy L. .... '71 '96 C.893 B.A. L.945 J.D. [Ⓐ Morris,N.A.&T.]
Walton, Max B. .... '72 '99 C.903 B.A. L.1338 J.D. [Ⓐ Connolly B.L.&H.]
*PRACTICE AREAS: Commercial Litigation; Construction Law; Real Estate.
Wang, Chen '68 '94 C.477 B.S.E. L.597 J.D.
(adm. in IL; not adm. in DE) Sr. Coun., E.I. du Pont de Nemours & Co.
*RESPONSIBILITIES: Patents; Intellectual Property.
Ward, Christopher A. .... '73 '99 C.509 B.A. L.1338 J.D. [Ⓐ Bayard]
*PRACTICE AREAS: Commercial Bankruptcy; Creditors Rights; Commercial Litigation.
Ward, John W. '54 '79 C.97 B.S. L.608 J.D.
(adm. in OH; not adm. in DE) Corp. Coun., E.I. du Pont de Nemours and Company
*RESPONSIBILITIES: Mergers and Acquisitions; Corporate Law; Securities; Banking Law.
Ward, Megan E. .... '73 '98 C.903 B.A. L.902 J.D. [Ⓐ Morris,N.A.&T.]
Ward, Rodman, Jr., (AV) ...... '34 '59 C.951 B.A. L.309 LL.B. [Ⓒ Skadden,A.S.M.&F.]
Ward, William E., (BV) .... '56 '81 C.1365 B.A. L.228 J.D. [W.E.Ward]
Ward, William E., P.A., (BV) .... 2751 Centerville Road Suite 212
Wasserbach, Robert B. '56 '92 C.205 B.S. L.1338 J.D.
(adm. in PA; not adm. in DE) 1100 N. Market St.
Wasserman, Jeffrey P., (BV) .... '55 '82 C.690 B.A. L.1338 J.D. [Ciconte,R.&W.]
*PRACTICE AREAS: Personal Injury Law; Commercial Law; Bankruptcy; Workmens' Compensation Law.
Waterland, Laura J. '59 '85 C&L.945 B.A., J.D.
Staff Atty., Disab. Law Prog./Community Legal Aid
Waterman, Nancy .... '69 '01 C.846 B.B.A. L.945 J.D. [Ⓐ Potter A.&C.]
*PRACTICE AREAS: Corporate.
Waters, Ophelia Michelle .... '62 '89 C.411 B.A L.902 J.D. Dept. of Jus.
Waxman, Scott E. .... '66 '91 C.367 B.A. L.276 J.D. [Potter A.&C.]
Weaver, John R., Jr., (BV) '53 '78
C.390 B.A. L.1292 J.D. [Ⓒ Farr,B.G.&W.] (⊙Bellmawr, NJ)
Weidinger, Michael A. .... '61 '94 C.473 A.B. L.273 J.D. [Morris,J.H.&W.]
*PRACTICE AREAS: Corporate Litigation; Commercial Litigation; Securities Disputes; Corporate Law.
Weigel, Charles A., Jr. '28 '57 C.446 B.S. L.831 J.D.
(adm. in DC; not adm. in DE; Pat.) du Pont Co.
Weik, Joseph W., (BV) .... '52 '79 C.205 B.A. L.1017 J.D. [Weik,N.&D.]
*PRACTICE AREAS: Personal Injury; Workers Compensation; Wrongful Death; Premises Liability.

Weik, Nitsche & Dougherty, (BV)
One Commerce Center, 3rd Floor, 12th and Orange Streets, P.O. Box 2324, 19899
Telephone: 302-655-4040 Fax: 302-654-4892 URL: http://www.weiknitsche.com
URL: http://www.lawyers.com/czajkowski
Joseph W. Weik; Gary S. Nitsche; Shawn Dougherty; Stanley T. Czajkowski (Shy-kow-ski) (Retired); Eliot Alazraki (Retired).
Personal Injury, Workers Compensation, Family Law, Insurance Law, Wrongful Death, Premises Liability, Motorcycle Accidents, Motor Vehicle Accidents and Injuries, Head Injury.
Reference: Wilmington Trust Co.
See Professional Biographies, WILMINGTON, DELAWARE

Weiler, Timothy Joseph, (BV) '58 '83 C.1044 B.A. L.1338 J.D.
727-B North Market Street, 19801
Telephone: 302-658-6900 Fax: 302-658-6909
Email: timweiler@aol.com URL: http://www.lawyers.com/weilerlaw
***PRACTICE AREAS: Bankruptcy; Civil Litigation; Personal Injury; Medical Malpractice; Corporate Law.**
Bankruptcy, Civil Litigation, Real Estate, Wills, Probate, Trusts and Estates, Estate Planning, Personal Injury, Automobile Accidents, Commercial Collections, Admiralty and Maritime, Business.
See Professional Biographies, WILMINGTON, DELAWARE

Weiner, Jeffrey M., (AV) .... '47 '72 C.823 B.A. L.93 J.D. [J.M.Weiner]
*PRACTICE AREAS: Civil Litigation; Commercial Litigation; Corporate Litigation; Personal Injury; Legal Malpractice Defense.
Weiner, Robert S., (BV) .... '50 '75 C.205 B.A. L.831 J.D. [Ⓐ Roeberg,M.&Assoc.]

Weiner, Jeffrey M., A Prof. Corp., The Law Offices of, (AV)
1332 King Street, 19801
Telephone: 302-652-0505 Telefax: 302-652-7824
Email: LegalW@aol.com
Jeffrey M. Weiner.
General Litigation (Commercial, Construction, Personal Injury, Legal Malpractice and Corporate) in the Delaware Superior, Chancery and Supreme Courts and the U.S. District Court for Delaware and General Civil Practice (Commercial, Corporate, Real Estate and Education).
Reference: Wilmington Trust Company.

Weinig, Gregory J. .... '71 '96 C.198 B.A. L.902 J.D. [Ⓐ Cooch&T.] (⊙Newark)
*PRACTICE AREAS: Estate Planning; Estate Settlements; Real Estate; Estate; Probate.
Weinstein, Sheldon A., (AV) .... '38 '64 C.205 B.A. L.1017 LL.B. [Young C.S.&T.]
Weir & Partners LLP, (AVⓉ) ..... 824 Market Street Mall (⊙Turnersville, NJ; Phila., PA)
Weiss, John W. .... '73 '01 C.608 B.A. L.1017 J.D. [Ⓐ Duane,M.&H.]
*PRACTICE AREAS: Reorganization and Finance.
Weiss, Michael, (BV) .... '49 '74 C.205 B.A. L.884 LL.B. [M.Weiss]
*PRACTICE AREAS: Civil Practice; Insurance; Negligence; Workers Compensation; Administrative Law.

Weiss, Michael, P.A., (BV)
1220 Market Street, Suite 604, P.O. Box 370, 19899
Telephone: 302-656-0400 Fax: 302-656-5011
Michael Weiss;—Yvonne Takvorian Saville.
General and Civil Trial Practice, Insurance, Negligence, Workers Compensation, Administrative Law, Federal Practice.
See Professional Biographies, WILMINGTON, DELAWARE

Welch, Charles E. .... '25 '51 C&L.608 B.S., J.D. du Pont Co.
Welch, Edward P., (AV) .... '50 '76 C.276 B.S. L.884 J.D. [Skadden,A.S.M.&F.]
Welch, Jeffrey S., (BV) .... '53 '79 C.205 B.S. L.1338 J.D. [Welch&Assoc.]
*PRACTICE AREAS: Commercial Litigation; Banking and Bankruptcy Litigation; Creditor's Rights; General Litigation; Corporate Litigation.
Welch, Jessica L. .... '66 '96 C.886 B.S. L.1338 J.D. 1202 Kirkwood Hwy.
Welch, John K., (CV) .... '53 '82 C.273 B.B.A. L.1338 J.D. Dep. of Jus.
Welch, Mary Madeline .... '41 '75 C.1031 B.S. L.262 J.D. 917 N. Madison St.
Welch, Michelle L. C., (BV) '53 '79 C.205 B.A. L.1338 J.D.
Chf. Coun., PNC Bk., Del.

Welch & Associates, (BV)
824 Market St., 8th Fl., Ste. 801, 19801
Telephone: 302-622-8900 Fax: 302-622-9046
Email: jwelch@welch-assoc.com
Jeffrey S. Welch; Alan W. Behringer.

(This Listing Continued)

Welch & Associates (Continued)

Commercial Litigation, Banking and Bankruptcy Litigation, Creditor's Rights, General Litigation, Corporate Litigation, Real Estate, Insurance Defense and Insurance Coverage.

See Professional Biographies, WILMINGTON, DELAWARE

Wells, Patrick J. '61 '99 C.436 B.S. L.30 J.D. (adm. in NY; not adm. in DE) [[A] Connolly B.L.&H.] ⊙
*PRACTICE AREAS: Intellectual Property; Patent Prosecution.

Wendelburg, Allan, Law Office of
(See Hockessin)

Wentz, Roy A., Jr. .... '20 '48 C.337 A.B. L.597 J.D. 101 Dexter Rd.‡
Werb, Duane D., (BV) .... '50 '79 C.999 B.A. L.1338 J.D. [Werb&S.]
*PRACTICE AREAS: Bankruptcy; Corporate Reorganization; Business Law; Corporate Law; Civil Litigation.

Werb & Sullivan, (BV)
Tenth Floor, 300 Delaware Avenue, P.O. Box 25046, 19899
Telephone: 302-652-1100 Telecopier: 302-652-1111
URL: http://www.lawyers.com/werb&sullivan
Duane D. Werb; Brian A. Sullivan. Associate: Kimberly E. Connolly Lawson.
Bankruptcy and Corporate Reorganization, Business and Corporate Law, Incorporation and Business Formation under Delaware Law, Civil and Criminal Litigation in all Courts, Business Planning, Estate Planning, and Real Property.
Representative Clients: Standard Distributing Co., Inc.; The Money Store/Delaware, Inc.; American Gypsum Floor Co., Inc.; Service America Corp.; Wesley Realty Co.

See Professional Biographies, WILMINGTON, DELAWARE

Werkheiser, Gregory W. ....'70 '96 C.645 B.S. L.1338 J.D. [[A] Morris,N.A.&T.]
Wernle, Paul A., Jr. .... '56 '86 C&L.705 B.A., J.D. 919 Market St.
West, Howard P., Jr. '26 '60 C.823 B.E.E. L.999 LL.B. (adm. in TN; not adm. in DE; Pat.) du Pont Co.
Wetzel, Benjamin C., III, (BV) ....'54 '79 C.923 B.A. L.884 J.D. [Bailey&W.]
*PRACTICE AREAS: General Insurance Defense; Product Liability; Personal Injury; Subrogation.
Whalen, Thomas G., Jr. ....'74 '01 C&L.831 B.A.P.S., J.D. [[A] Stevens&L.]
*PRACTICE AREAS: Bankruptcy Reorganization; Bankruptcy Litigation; Workouts; Foreclosures.
Whetzel, Robert W. ....'60 '84 C.205 B.Ch.E. L.884 J.D. [Richards,L.&F.] (Pat.)
*PRACTICE AREAS: Litigation; Environmental Law; Intellectual Property.
Whinnery, Nancy E. ....'56 '93 C.966 B.A. L.831 J.D. [[A] Gollatz,G.&E.] ⊙
*PRACTICE AREAS: Employment Law; Civil Litigation.
White, Michael J. '47 '75 C.338 B.A. L.446 J.D. (adm. in MD; not adm. in DE) 1 Alico Plaza

White and Williams LLP, (BV)
824 North Market Street, Suite 902, 19801-4938 ⊙
Telephone: 302-654-0424 Fax: 302-654-0245
URL: http://www.whitewms.com
Resident Partner: John D. Balaguer. Resident Counsel: David E. Wilks. Resident Associates: Linda M. Carmichael; Marc Stephen Casarino; Curtis J. Crowther; Susan Graham Harron; Seth J. Reidenberg; Christian J. Singewald.
General Practice, Civil Litigation (Business and Casualty), Computer Law, Corporate, Creditors' Rights, Director and Officers Liability, Environmental and Toxic Tort Litigation, Finance and Banking, Health Care and Medical Malpractice, Insurance Coverage and Reinsurance, Intellectual Property, Labor (Management), Products Liability, Professional Liability, Property and Subrogation Litigation, Real Estate, Securities, Taxation and Estates, Workers Compensation.
Paoli, Pennsylvania Office: 1500 Lancaster Avenue. Telephone: 610-251-0466. Fax: 610-296-4628.
Allentown, Pennsylvania Office: The Frederick Building, 3500 Winchester Road - 200. Telephone: 610-435-8414. Fax: 610-435-8420.
Westmont, New Jersey Office: 222 Haddon Avenue. Telephone: 856-858-5300. Fax: 856-858-0722.
Philadelphia, Pennsylvania Office: 18th Floor, 1650 Market Street. Telephone: 215-864-7000. Fax: 215-864-7523.
Pittsburgh, Pennsylvania Office: The Frick Building, 437 Grant Street, Suite 1001. Telephone: 412-566-3520. Fax: 412-566-3521.
New York, N.Y. Office: 11 East 44th Street, 9th Floor. Telephone: 888-458-1430.

See Professional Biographies, WILMINGTON, DELAWARE

Whitelaw, Jill Rouff '63 '88 C&L.659 B.A., J.D. (adm. in PA; not adm. in DE) Sr. Coun., PFPC, Inc.
Whitney, Douglas E., (AV) ....'39 '65 C.188 B.Ch.E. L.178 J.D. [Morris,N.A.&T.] (Pat.)
Whitney, Holly M. ....'58 '99 C.518 B.A. L.1338 J.D. [[A] Mattleman,W.&M.]
*PRACTICE AREAS: General Practice.
Whittaker, Michael W. .... '71 '00 C.150 B.S. L.776 J.D. [[A] Potter A.&C.]
Whittle, W. Jeffrey, (BV) ....'47 '72 C.658 B.A. L.383 J.D. [Cooch&T.] ⊙
*PRACTICE AREAS: Real Estate; Land Use Law; Estate Planning; Estate Settlements.
Wiedemer, Paranda B. ....'70 '01 C.999 B.S. L.1338 J.D. [[A] Smith,K.&F.]
*PRACTICE AREAS: Litigation; Bankruptcy.
Wier, Richard R., Jr., (AV) ....'41 '67 C.299 B.A. L.659 LL.B. [R.R.Wier,Jr.]
*PRACTICE AREAS: Employee/Employer Labor Law; Employment Law; Civil Litigation; Criminal Litigation; Personal Injury.
Wier, William J., Jr., (BV) ....'35 '60 C.165 B.A. L.976 LL.B. 55 Indian Field Rd.

Wier, Richard R., Jr., P.A., (AV) [BB]
1220 Market Street, Suite 600, 19801
Telephone: 302-888-3222 Fax: 302-888-3225 URL: http://www.wierlaw.com
Email: rwier@wierlaw.com URL: http://www.lawyers.com/richardrwier
Richard R. Wier, Jr.;—Daniel W. Scialpi.
Labor and Employment Law, Civil Rights, Sexual Harrassment, Discrimination, Civil and Criminal Litigation, DUI, Drug Abuse, Felonies, Homicides, Juvenile Misdemeanors, Parole and Probation, Sexual Assault, Traffic Violations, Personal Injury Law, Medical Malpractice, Auto Accidents, Sexual Abuse and Wrongful Death.

See Professional Biographies, WILMINGTON, DELAWARE

Wik, Beverly J., (AV) ....'52 '81 C.205 B.A. L.276 J.D. [Bayard]
*PRACTICE AREAS: Estate Planning; Trust Law; Local and Personal Property Taxation; Federal Income, Estate and Gift Taxation Law; Closely Held Businesses.

Wilbraham, Lawler & Buba, A Professional Corporation
Stoney Batter Office Building, 5301 Limestone Road, Suite 221, 19808-1251 ⊙
Telephone: 302-234-8217 Fax: 302-234-8218
Email: info@wlbdeflaw.com URL: http://www.wilbrahamlawlerandbuba.com
—Francis C. Gondek.
Appellate Practice, Civil Trial Practice, Commercial Litigation, Insurance Defense, Product Liability Law, Toxic Torts, Workers Compensation.
Philadelphia, Pennsylvania Office: 1818 Market Street, Suite 3100. Telephone: 215-564-4141. Fax: 215-564-4385.
Haddonfield, New Jersey Office: 24 Kings Highway West. Telephone: 856-795-4422. Fax: 856-795-4699.
Pittsburgh, Pennsylvania Office: First & Market Building, 100 First Avenue, Suite 325. Telephone: 412-255-0500. Fax: 412-255-0505.
New York, New York Office: 140 Broadway, 46th Floor. Telephone: 212-943-9245. Fax: 212-943-9246.

See Professional Biographies, WILMINGTON, DELAWARE

Wilburn, Elizabeth A. ....'70 '97 C.884 B.A. L.1338 J.D. [[A] Blank R.C.&M.]
*PRACTICE AREAS: Corporate Litigation; Commercial Litigation.
Wilcox, Scott George ..... '69 '00 C.205 B.A. L.1187 J.D. Dept. of Jus., Atty. Gen's. Off.
Wilks, David E., (BV) .... '64 '89 C.165 B.A. L.1017 J.D. [[C] White&W.]
Willard, John M., (BV) ....'46 '75 C.205 B.S. L.421 J.D. 104 E. 14th St.
Willette, Diane M., (CV) ....'63 '92 C.205 B.A. L.1338 J.D. [[A] Casarino,C.&S.]
*PRACTICE AREAS: Personal Injury; Products Liability; Insurance Defense; Workers Compensation.

Williams, David H., (AV) .... '50 '75 C.282 B.A. L.1017 J.D. [Morris,J.H.&W.]
*PRACTICE AREAS: Labor and Employment; Education Law; Litigation.
Williams, David Nicol, (AV) .... '35 '60 C.951 B.A. L.178 LL.B. [Williams]
*PRACTICE AREAS: Taxation; Trusts and Estates; Wills; Corporate Law.
Williams, Gregory P., (BV) .... '57 '82 C.205 B.A.A.S. L.945 J.D. [Richards,L.&F.]
*PRACTICE AREAS: Litigation; Corporate Law; Corporate Litigation; Partnership Litigation.

Williams, J. Calvin, Jr., (BV) '47 '78 C.1209 B.S. L.1202 J.D.
5307 Limestone Road, Suite 200, 19808
Telephone: 302-234-8656 Fax: 302-239-9154
General Civil Practice. Real Estate, Estate Planning, Business Law, Wills and Probate, Trusts and Estates.
Reference: Wilmington Savings Fund Society.

Williams, John, Jr., (BV) ....'49 '77 C.693 B.A. L.1338 J.D. [J.Williams]
Williams, Richmond L., (BV) .....'57 '82 C.951 B.A. L.1017 J.D. Sr. Coun., Hercules Inc.
Williams, Rosalind D. ....'66 '99 C.205 B.A. L.1338 J.D. [[A] Phillips,G.&S.]
*PRACTICE AREAS: Commercial Real Estate; Residential Real Estate; Small Business Law; Bankruptcy; Contracts.
Williams, John, P.A., (BV) ....1225 King Street, Suite 700

Williams Law Firm, The, P.A., (AV)
Suite 600, One Commerce Center, Twelfth and Orange Streets, P.O. Box 511, 19899-0511
Telephone: 302-575-0873 Toll Free: 800-759-2248 Telecopier: 302-575-1642
Email: dnwilliams@whw-de.com
David Nicol Williams.
Taxation, Commercial Law, Corporate Law, Real Estate, Estate Planning, Probate and General Civil Practice in Delaware, Florida and Federal Courts.

Williamson, James T. '51 '76 C&L.45 B.S., J.D. (adm. in AR; not adm. in DE) Corp. Coun., E.I. du Pont de Nemours & Co.
*RESPONSIBILITIES: OSHA; Environmental.
Willoughby, Barry M., (AV) ....'54 '79 C.205 B.A. L.1017 J.D. [Young C.S.&T.]
*PRACTICE AREAS: Management Labor Law; Employment Discrimination; Union Elections; Wrongful Termination Defense; Employer Rights.
Wills, Joanne B., (BV) ....'45 '85 C.188 B.A. L.1338 J.D. [Klehr,H.H.B.&E.]
*PRACTICE AREAS: Bankruptcy Law; Creditors' Rights Law; Commercial Litigation.
Wilson, A. Gary, (BV) ....'42 '72 C.766 B.A. L.665 J.D. 5307 Limestone Rd.
Wilson, Gregg E., (BV) ....'48 '73 C.205 B.A. L.1017 J.D. Dep. Atty. Gen.
Wilson, Michael G. ....'68 '01 C.1356 B.A. L.945 J.D. [[A] Morris,N.A.&T.]
Wilson, Richard T., (BV) ....'58 '89 C.655 B.A. L.446 J.D. [[A] P.G.Angelos]
*PRACTICE AREAS: Products Liability; Toxic Torts; Personal Injury Litigation; Criminal Law; Workers Compensation.
Wilton, James Henry '51 '76 C.339 B.A. L.424 J.D. Pres./CEO, Medical Network Management Services of Delaware, Inc.
Winchester, A. Richard ....'56 '82 C.645 B.A. L.659 J.D. [[C] McCarter&E.]
*PRACTICE AREAS: Litigation; Corporate Law; Commercial Law; Bankruptcy; Environmental Law.
Wingate, Gregory K. ....'60 '93 C.825 B.S. L.659 J.D. Rodney Sq. N.
Winslow, Don O. '27 '64 C.923 B.S.Chem.E. L.734 LL.B. (adm. in CA; not adm. in DE; Pat.) Barley Mill Plaza
Winslow, J. Dallas, Jr., (BV) ....'44 '73 C.216 B.A. L.229 J.D. 803 Shipley St.
Winslow, Julian D. ....'14 '41 C&L.575 B.S., LL.B. 102 Hermitage Rd.‡
Wiseman, Lawrence R., (AVⓉ) '52 '78 C&L.546 B.S., J.D. [Blank R.C.&M.] (⊙Phila., PA)
*PRACTICE AREAS: Securities; Business Law; Contracts; Corporate Law; Mergers, Acquisitions and Divestitures.
Wisler, Jeffrey C., (BV) .... '63 '89 C.205 B.S. L.1292 J.D. [Connolly B.L.&H.]
Witherell, Andrew J. ....'63 '93 [[A] Resnick,A.&S.]
*PRACTICE AREAS: Criminal Defense; Civil Debt Collection; General Practice; Personal Injury.
Witherell, Andrew J. ....'63 '93 C.205 B.A. L.1338 J.D. 100 E. 14th St.
Witherell, Victoria Roe ....'62 '94 C.205 B.A. L.1338 J.D. State Dept. of Jus.
Witherow, Paula C., (BV) ....'57 '90 C.645 B.S. L.1338 J.D. [[A] Cooch&T.] ⊙
*PRACTICE AREAS: Personal Injury; Litigation.
Witherspoon, Katherine Randolph .... '67 '95 C.228 A.B. L.569 J.D. [[A] Klett R.L.&S.]
*PRACTICE AREAS: Labor and Employment Law; Education Law.
Wittman, Paul S. '63 '89 C.999 B.S. L.276 J.D. (adm. in PA; not adm. in DE) Sr. Coun., E.I. du Pont de Nemours & Co.
*RESPONSIBILITIES: Computer Law; Procurement.
Woelfling, Frank Adam '47 '74 C.397 B.S. L.602 J.D. (adm. in PA; not adm. in DE) Asst. Secy. & Coun., The Whitaker Corp.
Wolcott, Daniel F., Jr., (BV) ....'46 '71 C.81 B.A. L.893 J.D. [Potter A.&C.]
Wolf, Natalie S., (BV) ....'68 '93 C.205 B.A. L.276 J.D. [[A] Young C.S.&T.]
*PRACTICE AREAS: Health Care Fraud; Qui Tam Actions; Workers' Compensation Defense; Automobile Accidents and Injuries; Medical Negligence.

Wolf, Block, Schorr and Solis-Cohen LLP, (AVⓉ)
One Rodney Square, 920 King Street, Suite 300, 19801 ⊙
Telephone: 302-777-5860 Fax: 302-777-5863
Email: wolfblock@wolfblock.com URL: http://www.wolfblock.com
Members of Firm: Barry M. Klayman (Resident); Mary M. MaloneyHuss; Michael L. Temin. Associate: Jennifer Barber; Todd Schiltz.
General Practice. Corporate, Real Estate, Taxation, Civil and Criminal Litigation, Estate Planning, Probate, Labor, Employment and Benefits, Antitrust, Securities, Banking, Municipal Finance, Patent, Trademark and Copyright, Bankruptcy, Family Law, Health Care, Intellectual Property and Information Technology, Communications, Financial Services, Government-Assisted and Affordable Housing, Utility Regulation, Surety, Fidelity and Liability, Mortgage Lending, Securitization and Environmental Law.
Philadelphia, Pennsylvania Office: 1650 Arch Street, 22nd Floor, 19103-2097. Telephone: 215-977-2000. Telecopier: 977-2334; 977-2346.
New York, New York Office: 250 Park Avenue, 10177. Telephone: 212-986-1116. Telecopier: 212-986-0604.
Camden, New Jersey Office: One Port Center, 2 Riverside Drive, Suite 502, 08103. Telephone: 856-225-1055. Fax: 856-225-9024.
Cherry Hill, New Jersey Office: 1940 Route 70 East, Suite 200, 08003. Telephone: 856-424-8200. Fax: 856-424-4446.
Harrisburg, Pennsylvania Office: 212 Locust Street, Suite 300, 17101. Telephone: 717-237-7160. Fax: 717-237-7161.
Newark, New Jersey Office: 744 Broad Street, Suite 1515, 07102. Telephone: 973-824-7723. Fax: 973-424-5740.
Norristown, Pennsylvania Office: 3 Penn Court, 325 Swede Street, P.O. Box 869, 19404. Telephone: 610-272-5555. Fax: 610-272-6976.

See Professional Biographies, WILMINGTON, DELAWARE

Wolfe, Donald J., Jr., (AV) ....'50 '76 C.205 B.A. L.813 J.D. [Potter A.&C.]
Wolfson, Herbert M. '23 '51 C.102 B.A. L.477 LL.B. 1213 Brook Dr., Normandy Manor (Pat.)
Woloshin, Melvyn A., (BV) .... '39 '65 C.205 B.A. L.1009 J.D. [Woloshin,T.L.N.&F.]
Woloshin, Tenenbaum, Lynch, Natalie & Freibott, P.A., (AV) .... 3200 Concord Pike
Wolters, Jeffrey R. .... '66 '94 C.205 B.A. L.893 J.D. [Morris,N.A.&T.]
Wood, Steven P., (BV) .... '59 '85 C.205 B.A. L.245 J.D. Dep. Atty. Gen.
Woods, James J., Jr., (BV) ....'56 '81 C.205 B.S. L.893 J.D. [Connolly B.L.&H.]
Woolfolk, Ann ....'57 '86 C.205 B.A.A.S. L.884 J.D. Dep. Atty. Gen.
Wren, Laurie O'Sullivan '60 '88 C.260 B.S. L.472 J.D. (adm. in MO; not adm. in DE) 1003 Berkeley Rd.‡

Wright, Christian Douglas ....'72 '96 C.205 H.B.A. L.228 J.D. [Ⓐ Young C.S.&T.]
*PRACTICE AREAS: Corporate Law; Business Law; Intellectual Property; Partnership Law; Chancery Practice.

Wright, Joelle Meredith ....'70 '96 C.831 B.A. L.1338 J.D. Off. of Atty. Gen.

Wright, Norris P., (AV) ....'45 '73 C.205 B.A. L.575 J.D. [Morris,J.H.&W.]
*PRACTICE AREAS: Taxation; Trusts and Estates; Business Law.

Yakob, Adrian F. '52 '76
C.216 B.A. L.884 J.D. Corp. Coun., E.I. du Pont de Nemours & Co.
*RESPONSIBILITIES: Commercial Law; Antitrust.

Yancey, Kara R. ....'73 '98 C.339 B.A. L.94 J.D. [Ⓐ Skadden,A.S.M.&F.]

Yearick, Danielle Kathleen ....'72 '97 C.433 B.A. L.884 J.D. [Tybout,R.&P.]
*PRACTICE AREAS: Workers Compensation; Insurance; Negligence; Civil Litigation; Bankruptcy.

Yemc, William A. ....'62 '90 C.602 B.B.A. L.884 J.D. [Richards,L.&F.]
*PRACTICE AREAS: Commercial Law; Secured Transactions; Business Trusts; Limited Liability Company Law; Partnership Law.

Yoder, James S., (BV) '61 '87 C.205 B.A. L.1338 J.D.
[Tighe,C.&L.] (ⓒWoodstown, NJ)
*PRACTICE AREAS: Bankruptcy; Medical Malpractice; Personal Injury; Products Liability; Professional Liability.

Yoder, Steven M. ....'67 '97 C.655 B.S. L.837 J.D. [Ⓐ Bayard]
*PRACTICE AREAS: Corporate Bankruptcy and Restructuring; Creditors' Rights; Commercial Litigation.

Young, Stuart B., (AV) ....'35 '62 C.951 B.A. L.893 LL.B. [Young C.S.&T.]
*PRACTICE AREAS: Litigation; Corporate Law; Construction Law; Products Liability; Intellectual Property.

Young Conaway Stargatt & Taylor, LLP, (AV) BR
Eleventh Floor, Wilmington Trust Center, 1100 North Market Street, P.O. Box 391, 19899-0391 ⊙
Telephone: 302-571-6600 Telecopy: 302-571-1253
Email: ycst@ycst.com URL: http://www.ycst.com
Members of Firm: H. Albert Young (1904-1982); H. James Conaway, Jr. (1922-1990); Bruce M. Stargatt; Stuart B. Young; Ben T. Castle; Sheldon A. Weinstein; Sheldon N. Sandler; Richard A. Levine; Richard A. Zappa; Frederick William Iobst; David C. McBride; Richard H. Morse; Joseph M. Nicholson; Barry M. Willoughby; Josy W. Ingersoll; Anthony G. Flynn; Jerome K. Grossman; Eugene A. DiPrinzio; James L. Patton, Jr.; Robert L. Thomas; William D. Johnston; Timothy J. Snyder; Bruce L. Silverstein; William W. Bowser; Larry J. Tarabicos; Richard A. DiLiberto, Jr.; Melanie K. Sharp; Cassandra Faline Kaminski; Richard J. A. Popper; Teresa A. Cheek; Neilli Mullen Walsh; Janet Z. Charlton; Robert S. Brady; Joel A. Waite; Brent C. Shaffer; Daniel P. Johnson; Craig D. Grear; Timothy Jay Houseal; Brendan Linehan Shannon; Martin S. Lessner; Pauline K. Morgan; C. Barr Flinn (Not admitted in DE). Special Counsel: John D. McLaughlin, Jr. (Not admitted in DE). Of Counsel: William F. Taylor; Edward B. Maxwell, 2nd. Associates: Sean M. Beach (Not admitted in DE); M. Blake Cleary; Richard H. Cross, Jr.; Danielle B. Gibbs; Lisa B. Goodman; Edwin J. Harron; Scott A. Holt; Christopher C. Jones; Edward J. Kosmowski; Maureen D. Luke; Joseph A. Malfitano; Adria B. Martinelli (Not admitted in DE); Edmon L. Morton; Michael R. Nestor; Jennifer R. Noel; John J. Paschetto; Adam W. Poff; John W. Shaw; Joanne C. Springer-Messick; Leon L. Vinokur; Natalie S. Wolf; Christian Douglas Wright; Sharon M. Zieg (Not admitted in DE). Georgetown, Delaware Office: Resident Partner: Craig A. Karsnitz. Resident Associate: Vivian Medinilla Longo (Resident).
General Practice.
Georgetown, Delaware Office: 110 West Pine Street. Telephone: 302-856-3571. Telecopy: 302-856-9338.

See Professional Biographies, WILMINGTON, DELAWARE

Yurkewicz, Michael W. '72 '98 C.696 B.A. L.94 J.D.
(adm. in MA; not adm. in DE) [Ⓐ Skadden,A.S.M.&F.]

Zaben, Lee B. '59 '85 C.443 B.S. L.64 J.D.
(adm. in MD; not adm. in DE) CEO, Kahunaville, Inc.

Zahralddin-Aravena, Rafael X. '67 '94 C.893 B.S. L.1338 J.D.
(adm. in PA; not adm. in DE) [Ⓐ Ashby&G.]

Zaleski, Matthew G., III ....'69 '96 C.21 A.B. L.446 J.D. 1201 N. Market St.

Zappa, Richard A., (AV) ....'48 '73 C.205 B.A. L.30 J.D. [Young C.S.&T.]

Zazzo, Samantha P. '70 '94 C.222 B.A. L.705 J.D.
(adm. in NJ; not adm. in DE) [J.R.Julian]
*PRACTICE AREAS: Defense Litigation; Environmental.

Zebe, Merril L. ....'55 '81 C.831 B.S. L.770 J.D. Community Legal Aid Soc., Inc.

Zeldin, Jessica ....'70 '96 C.597 B.A. L.910 J.D. [Ⓐ Morris,N.A.&T.]

Zepke, Brent E. '43 '74 C.1128 B.A. L.838 J.D.
(adm. in TN; not adm. in DE) Chf. Coun., Human Resources, Hercules Incorporated

Zieg, Sharon M. '72 '00 C.1128 B.S. L.896 J.D.
(adm. in NC; not adm. in DE) [Ⓐ Young C.S.&T.]
*PRACTICE AREAS: Bankruptcy.

Zilka, Diane T. '60 '86 C.1044 B.A. L.262 J.D.
(adm. in NY; not adm. in DE) [ⓒ Grant&E.]

Zuckerman, Richard M. '42 '66 C&L.910 A.B., J.D.
(adm. in MO; not adm. in DE) Sr. Atty., AIG Life Ins. Co.

Zuckerman Spaeder LLP
One Commerce Center, 1201 Orange Street, Suite 650, P.O. Box 1028, 19899 ⊙
Telephone: 302-427-0400 Fax: 302-427-8242
Email: counsel@zuckerman.com
Resident Member: Thomas G. Macauley.
Complex Civil Litigation, Business Restructuring and Reorganization.
Washington, D.C. Office: 1201 Connecticut Avenue, N.W., Suite 1200. Telephone: 202-778-1800. Fax: 202-822-8106.
Miami, Florida Office: 201 South Biscayne Boulevard, Suite 900. Telephones: 305-358-5000; Broward County: 305-523-0277. Fax: 305-579-9749.
Ft. Lauderdale, Florida Office: One East Broward Boulevard, Suite 700. Telephone: 954-356-0463. Fax: 954-356-0406.
Tampa, Florida Office: East Kennedy Boulevard, Suite 3140. Telephone: 813-221-1010. Fax: 813-223-7961.
Baltimore, Maryland Office: Suite 2440, 100 East Pratt Street. Telephone: 410-332-0444. Fax: 410-659-0436.
New York, N.Y. Office: 1114 Avenue of the Americas, 27th Floor, Grace Building. Telephone: 212-479-6500. Fax: 212-479-6512.

See Professional Biographies, WILMINGTON, DELAWARE

Zutz, Lawrence I., (BV) '46 '73
C.347 B.A. L.976 J.D. Gen. Coun., Harry David Zutz Ins., Inc.

WYOMING, 977, *Kent Co.*

DiMondi, William J. ....'55 '80 C.93 A.B. L.831 J.D. Wyoming Concrete Indus.

YORKLYN, 0, *New Castle Co.*

Doughty, Kristi J. ....'62 '87 C.508 B.S. L.1292 J.D. [Ⓐ Whittington&A.]
*PRACTICE AREAS: Bankruptcy; Foreclosures.

Whittington, Thomas D., Jr., (BV) ... '43 '71 C.205 B.S. L.665 J.D. [Whittington&A.] ⊙
*PRACTICE AREAS: Corporate Formation; Real Estate Development; Condominium Association Law; Residential Real Estate; Residential Real Estate Development.

Whittington & Aulgur, (BV)
2979 Barley Mill Road, 19736 ⊙
Telephone: 302-235-5800; 1-800-441-9459 Telecopier: 302-235-5900
Email: wa@delawarelawyer.com
Members of Firm: Thomas D. Whittington, Jr.; Robert T. Aulgur, Jr. (Resident, Odessa, Delaware Office). Associate: Kristi J. Doughty.
Real Estate, Foreclosure, Bankruptcy, Corporate, Environmental, Litigation, Zoning, Business Law, Condominium Association Law, Wills and Probate, Trust and Estates, Arbitration and Mediation.
Odessa, Delaware Office: Suite 110, Odessa Professional Park, 313 North DuPont Highway, 19730. Telephone: 302-378-1661. Fax: 302-378-1645.

See Professional Biographies, YORKLYN, DELAWARE

DISTRICT OF COLUMBIA

The District of Columbia Bar
6th Floor, 1250 H Street, N.W.
Washington, District of Columbia, 20005-5937
Telephone: 202-737-4700
Fax: 202-626-3471

Index of Towns and Cities Listed by County

*Indicates County Seat

WASHINGTON, 606,900

Aamoth, Robert J., (AV) ....'56 '82 C.477 A.B. L.309 J.D. [Kelley D.&W.]
*PRACTICE AREAS: Telecommunications Law; Appellate Practice.
Aaronson, David E. ....'40 '65 C.273 B.A. L.309 LL.B. Prof. of Law, Amer. Univ.
Aaronson, Donald W. '33 '75
C.339 B.A.B.S. L.209 J.D. [Ⓒ Powers,P.S.&V.] (⊙Chgo., IL)
Abbasi, A. Sonny ....'70 '96 C.273 B.A. L.904 J.D. [Ⓐ McKee N.]
*PRACTICE AREAS: Securitazation; Structured Finance.
Abbenante, Thomas, (AV) ....'50 '76 C.30 B.A. L.329 J.D. 1919 Pennsylvania Ave., N.W.
Abbey, Richard H. '38 '63 C.319 B.A. L.569 LL.B.
(adm. in NY; not adm. in DC) [Miller&C.]
*PRACTICE AREAS: Customs and International Trade.
Abbin, Byrle M. '31 '57 C.477 B.B.A. L.309 J.D.
(adm. in IL; not adm. in DC) 1666 K St. N.W.‡
Abbott, Frank L. ....'17 '56 C.133 B.A. L.273 J.D. 3805 Kanawha St., N.W.‡
Abed, Salah J. ....'56 '83 C.893 B.A. L.945 J.D. [Abed&S.]
Abed & Savage ....1101 17th St., N.W.
Abegg, Heidi K. .... '71 '96 C&L.879 B.A., J.D. [Ⓐ Webster,C.&B.]
*PRACTICE AREAS: Nonprofit Organizations Law; Charitable Organizations Law; Trade and Professional Associations; Constitutional Law; Election and Campaign Finance Law.
Abeles, Charles C., (AV) ....'29 '58 C.309 A.B. L.893 LL.B. 4531 Dexter St. N.W.‡
Abelow, Michael G. '74 '00 C.1369 B.A. L.902 J.D.
(adm. in MD; not adm. in DC) [Ⓐ Crowell&M.]
Abelson, Michael A., (AV) ....'49 '74 C.645 B.A. L.669 J.D. [Abelson] ⊙
*PRACTICE AREAS: Negligence; Products Liability; Medical Malpractice.

Abelson Law Firm, The, (AV) BB
1700 K Street, N.W. Suite 700, 20006 ⊙
Telephone: 202-331-0600 1-888-797-4242 Fax: 202-429-9088 URL: http://www.abelsonlaw.com
Email: maa@abelsonlaw.com URL: http://www.lawyers.com/abelsonlaw
Michael A. Abelson.
Plaintiffs Trial Practice. Negligence, Products Liability, Medical Malpractice, Wrongful Death, Insurance Bad Faith, Birth Trauma, Automobile Accidents.
Baltimore, Maryland Office: Harbor Place Tower, 111 South Calvert Street, Suite 2700, 21202. Telephone: 1-888-797-4242.
Boston, Massachusetts Office: 77 North Washington Street, 02114-1908. Telephone: 1-888-797-4242.
Pittsburgh, Pennsylvania Office: 510 Third Avenue, 15219. Telephone: 1-888-797-4242.
Philadelphia, Pennsylvania Office: 510 Walnut Street, 19106. Telephone: 1-888-797-4242.
See Professional Biographies, WASHINGTON, DISTRICT OF COLUMBIA

Aber, Robert E. '47 '73 C&L.276 B.S.B.A., J.D.
(adm. in VA; not adm. in DC)
V.P., Gen. Coun. & Secy., Nasdaq, Inc. & NASD Market Services, Inc.
Abernathy, Charles F. '69 '00 C&L.276 B.A., J.D.
(adm. in MD; not adm. in DC) [Ⓐ Miller&C.]
Ablard, Charles D., (AV) ....'30 '54 C&L.623 B.A., J.D. [Ⓒ Perkins,S.C.&C.]
*PRACTICE AREAS: Administrative Law; Government Contracts Law; Arbitration Law; Mediation Law.
Ablin, Karyn K. ....'66 '95 C.1288 B.S.B.A. L.893 J.D. [Ⓐ Wiley R.&F.]
Ablondi, Italo H., (AV) ....'29 '53 C.276 B.S. L.724 J.D. [Ablondi,F.S.&D.]
Ablondi, Foster, Sobin & Davidow, P.C., (AV)
1150 Eighteenth Street, N.W., Ninth Floor
Abod, Christopher P. ....'61 '87 C.446 B.S. L.904 J.D. MCI Communications Corp.
Abraham, Anil K. ....'69 '97 C.197 A.B. L.976 J.D. [Ⓐ Sidley A.B.&W.]
Abraham, Daniel '72 '00
(adm. in NY; not adm. in DC) [Ⓐ Swidler B.S.F.]
*PRACTICE AREAS: Telecommunications.
Abraham, E. Spencer '52 '79
C.475 B.A. L.309 J.D. Co-Chm., National Republican Comm.
Abraham, George D. ....'37 '61 L.500 J.D. 3045 N St., N.W.
Abraham, Philip, (BV) ......'46 '70 C.423 B.S. L.93 J.D. [Resnick,A.&S.] (⊙Balt., MD)
Abraham, Stephen H. ....'58 '84 C&L.902 B.A., J.D. [Greenstein D.&L.]
Abrahams, Daniel B., (BV) ....'55 '83 C.319 B.A. L.273 J.D. [Epstein B.&G.]
*PRACTICE AREAS: Government Contracts Law; Wage and Hour Law; Construction; Federal Employees Health Benefit Plan; Litigation.
Abrahams, Denise M., (BV) ....'64 '87 C&L.659 B.A., J.D. Asst. U.S. Atty.
Abrahams, Jessica C., (AV) ....'— '90 C.914 B.A. L.930 J.D. [Powell,G.F.&M.]
*PRACTICE AREAS: Government Contracts; International Government Contracts; Federal Litigation; Bid Protests.
Abrahamson, Jeffery Alan '58 '97 C.477 B.A. L.273 J.D.
(adm. in MD; not adm. in DC) Legis. Atty., U.S. Dept. of Treas.
Abram, Jonathan L. ....'56 '81 C.260 B.A. L.228 J.D. [Hogan&H.]
*PRACTICE AREAS: Complex Commercial Litigation; Constitutional Litigation; Technical Litigation; Oil and Gas Litigation; Contract Litigation.
Abramowitz, George R., (AV) ....'46 '70 C.165 A.B. L.276 J.D. [LeBoeuf,L.G.&M.]
*PRACTICE AREAS: Tax; Insurance.
Abrams, Andrew C. ....'66 '91 C.882 B.A. L.273 J.D. 750 17th St., N.W.
Abrams, Anessa ....'70 '95 C.112 B.A. L.273 J.D. [Schmeltzer,A.&S.]
*PRACTICE AREAS: Management Labor and Employment.
Abrams, David S., (AV) '37 '64
C.446 B.S. L.29 J.D. [Roylance,A.B.&G.] (See Pat. Sect.)
*PRACTICE AREAS: Litigation; Patent Law; Trademark Law.
Abrams, Jill M. ....'— '99 C.659 B.A. L.477 J.D. [Ⓐ Powell,G.F.&M.]
*PRACTICE AREAS: Health Law.
Abrams, Joseph M. ....'50 '80 C.1196 B.A. L.425 J.D. Bureau of Natl. Affs., Inc., The
*RESPONSIBILITIES: Contracts; Intellectual Property; Labor and Employment; Corporate Law.
Abrams, Robert G., (AV) ....'46 '72 C.165 A.B. L.273 J.D. [Howrey S.A.&W.]
*PRACTICE AREAS: Antitrust; Intellectual Property; Appellate Practice; Commercial Litigation.
Abrams, Ronald B. ......'46 '73 C&L.831 B.S., J.D. National Vets. Legal Servs. Program

Abrams, Adele L., P.C., Law Office of
(See Beltsville, Maryland)

Abramson, Jo Ann ....'52 '80 C.659 B.A. L.128 J.D. [Ⓑ Ross,D.&B.]
Abramson, Ronald D., (AV) ....'49 '75 C.569 B.A. L.276 J.D. [Silverstein&M.]
*PRACTICE AREAS: Business Planning; Taxation; Real Estate; Estate Planning.
Abramson, Ronald E., (AV) ....'41 '69 C.910 B.S. L.623 J.D. [Hurwitz&A.]
Abramson, Stanley H., (AV) ....'46 '73 C.223 B.S. L.1292 J.D. [Arent F.K.P.&K.]
*PRACTICE AREAS: Administrative Law; Biotechnology; Chemical Regulation; Environmental Law; Environmental Auditing.
Abramson, Steven M., (P.C.) ....'60 '86 C&L.273 B.B.A., J.D. [Silver,F.&T.]
*PRACTICE AREAS: Real Estate Leasing; Corporate Law.
Abravanel, Evelyn Ginsberg ....'51 '75 C&L.930 A.B., J.D. Amer. Univ.
Abrecht, Mary Ellen ....'45 '75 C.518 B.A. L.276 J.D. Assoc. Supr. Ct. J.
Abromson, Ellen Jane '51 '81 C.454 B.A. L.818 J.D.
(adm. in MA; not adm. in DC) [Cozen O.]
*PRACTICE AREAS: Contracts; Real Estate; Government Relations; Insurance; Corporate.
Abyad, Imad D. ....'63 '96 C.146 B.S.C.E. L.893 J.D. [Ⓐ Jenner&B.]
*PRACTICE AREAS: Antitrust; Complex Litigation; Telecommunications.
Acebal, Maria Laura ....'68 '95 C.228 A.B. L.976 J.D. 725 12th St., N.W.
Achenbach, Benjamin R., Jr. ....'33 '61 C.674 A.B. L.659 LL.B. [Ⓐ Steptoe&J.]
Acker, Lawrence G., (AV) ....'50 '74 C.823 B.A. L.276 J.D. [LeBoeuf,L.G.&M.]
*PRACTICE AREAS: Utilities.

Ackerley, Margaret L. '65 '92
C.309 A.B. L.976 J.D. Gen. Coun., World Wildlife Fund, Inc.
Ackerly, Dana T., II, (AV) ....'43 '70 C.951 B.A. L.309 J.D. [Covington&B.]
Ackerman, Debra L. ....'57 '85 C.689 B.A. L.904 J.D. 5335 Wisconsin Ave., N.W.
Ackerman, Howard B. ....'61 '86 C.881 B.A. L.30 J.D. 733 15th St., NW, Ste. 700
Ackerman, Jerome ....'21 '51 C.188 B.S. L.309 LL.B. 1201 Pennsylvania Ave. N.W.‡
Ackerman, Jonathan Z. ....'— '99 C.37 B.S.B.A. L.145 J.D. [Ⓐ McKee N.]
*PRACTICE AREAS: Taxation.
Ackerman, Kenneth D. ....'51 '76 C.103 B.A. L.276 J.D. [Ⓒ Olsson,F.&W.]
*PRACTICE AREAS: Agricultural Risk Management; Litigation.
Ackerman, Wendy E. ....'62 '90 C.66 B.A. L.145 J.D. [Ⓒ Shearman&S.]
Ackerman, William G. '68 '97 C&L.972 B.S., J.D.
(adm. in WY; not adm. in DC; Pat.) [Ⓐ Crowell&M.]
Ackerson, Nels, (AV) ....'44 '71 C.679 B.S. L.309 J.D. [Ackerson]
*PRACTICE AREAS: Litigation; Class Actions; International; Constitutional; Agricultural Law.

Ackerson Group, The, Chartered, (AV)
1666 K Street, N.W., Suite 1010, 20006
Telephone: 202-833-8833 202-833-8831 URL: http://www.ackersonlaw.com
Email: ackerson@ackersonlaw.com URL: http://www.lawyers.com/ackerson
Nels Ackerson;—Cecilia Fex; Kathleen Clubb Kauffman; Elaine A. Panagakos.
Litigation, Plaintiff Litigation, International, Legislative, Agricultural Law.
See Professional Biographies, WASHINGTON, DISTRICT OF COLUMBIA

Acquaah, Kwame ....'51 '82 L.831 LL.M. 2300 M St., N.W.
Adamo, Sonya A. ....'65 '90 C.94 B.A. L.30 J.D. D.C. Asst. Corp. Coun.
Adams, A. Hope ....'65 '92 C.999 B.M. L.1228 J.D. [Venable,A.B.H.&C.]
*PRACTICE AREAS: Corporate Transactions.
Adams, Arnold '22 '74 C.065 L.999
(adm. in NY; not adm. in DC) 3001 Veazey Terr., N.W.
Adams, Benjamin C. ....'71 '00 C.273 B.A. L.276 J.D. [Ⓐ Gibson,D.&C.]
Adams, Bruce A. ....'54 '83 C.821 B.A. L.94 J.D. [Arnold&P.]
*PRACTICE AREAS: Telecommunications Law.
Adams, Colleen L. ....'58 '94 L.575 J.D. 1801 L St. N.W.
Adams, Corliss V. ....'65 '93 C.999 B.S. L.1002 J.D. 1111 14th Street N.W.
Adams, David G., (AV) ....'53 '77 C.808 B.A. L.569 J.D. [Venable,A.B.H.&C.]
*PRACTICE AREAS: Food and Drug Law; Advertising Law.
Adams, Edwin M. '14 '39 C&L.339 A.B., LL.B.
(adm. in IL; not adm. in DC) 2540 Mass. Ave., N.W.‡
Adams, Eric S. '69 '99 C.164 B.A. L.477 J.D.
(adm. in NY; not adm. in DC) [Ⓐ Skadden,A.S.M.&F.]
Adams, Jasen Dean '71 '99 C.188 B.A. L.1209 J.D.
(adm. in VA; not adm. in DC) [Ⓐ Martin&A.]
*PRACTICE AREAS: Government Contracts; Internet Law; Asset Protection; Corporate Law; Civil Litigation.
Adams, Jennifer Collesano ....'72 '97 C.188 B.A. L.128 J.D. [Martin&A.]
*PRACTICE AREAS: Government Contracts; Complex Business Litigation; White Collar Criminal Defense; Intellectual Property Litigation; Software Licensing.
Adams, John J., (AV) ....'34 '59 C.207 B.A. L.893 LL.B. [Ⓒ Hunton&W.]
*PRACTICE AREAS: Corporate; Environmental Law.
Adams, Kenneth L. ....'46 '71 C.976 A.B. L.145 J.D. [Dickstein S.M.&O.]
*PRACTICE AREAS: Litigation; Toxic Torts; Governmental Affairs.
Adams, Kerry L., (AV) '50 '75 C.388 B.A. L.910 J.D.
Assoc. Gen. Coun., National Treasury Employees Union
Adams, Laurie B. ....'62 '87 C.188 B.S. L.659 J.D. 1800 M St., N.W.
Adams, Lee S., (AV) ....'49 '75 C.705 A.B. L.276 J.D. [Morrison&F.]
*PRACTICE AREAS: Financial Services.
Adams, Michael B., Jr. ....'— '95 C.951 B.A. L.273 J.D. [Ⓐ Blooston,M.D.D.&P.]
*PRACTICE AREAS: Telecommunications Law; FCC Regulation; PCS.
Adams, Robin C. '73 '00 C.259 B.S. L.945 J.D.
(adm. in CO; not adm. in DC) [Ⓐ Wiley R.&F.]
Adams, Vikki A. ....'— '86 C.45 B.A. L.284 J.D. [Duane,M.&H.]
*PRACTICE AREAS: International, Business and Trade; Intellectual Property; Immigration Law.
Adams and Reese LLP, (AV)
1455 Pennsylvania Avenue, N.W. Suite 200 (⊙Mobile, AL; Baton Rouge, New Orleans, LA; Jackson, MS; Hous., TX)

Adams, Whitney
(See McLean, Virginia)

Adamson, Alan W. '65 '93 C.205 B.A. L.446 J.D.
Associate General Counsel, CarrAmerica Realty Corporation
Adamson, Terrence B., (AV) '46 '73
C.1365 B.A. L.245 J.D. Exec. V.P., Natl. Geographic Soc.
Adcock, Eric William '71 '00
C.446 B.S. L.273 J.D. [Ⓐ Finnegan,H.F.G.&D.] (See Pat. Sect.)
*PRACTICE AREAS: Intellectual Property Litigation; Chemical Patents; Patent Litigation; Patent Prosecution; Pharmaceutical Patents.
Addis, David W. ....'53 '88 C.893 B.A. L.178 J.D. [Ⓒ Covington&B.]
Addison, Angela M. '64 '98 C.803 B.S.E.E. L.425 J.D.
(adm. in LA; not adm. in DC) [Ⓐ Van Ness F.]
*PRACTICE AREAS: Natural Gas Pipelines; Electric Energy; Public Utility Regulation.
Addison, Daniel R. ....'60 '89 C.154 B.A. L.128 J.D. [Patton B.]
Addlestone, David F. .....'41 '65 C.575 A.B. L.228 LL.B. National Vets. Legal Servs. Proj.
Adducci, Steven A., (BV) ....'65 '90 C&L.585 B.B.A., J.D. [Ⓐ Dorsey&W.]
*PRACTICE AREAS: Energy; Administrative Law.
Adduci, V. James, II, (AV) ....'50 '75 C.174 B.A. L.365 [Adduci,M.&S.]
*PRACTICE AREAS: International Trade Regulation; Imports and Exports; Customs; Litigation.

Adduci, Mastriani & Schaumberg, L.L.P., (AV) BB
1200 Seventeenth Street, N.W., Fifth Floor, 20036-3006
Telephone: 202-467-6300 Telefax: 202-466-2006
Email: ams@adduci.com URL: http://www.adduci.com
V. James Adduci, II; Louis S. Mastriani; Tom M. Schaumberg; Barbara A. Murphy; Harvey B. Fox; Gregory C. Anthes; Steven E. Adkins; Will E. Leonard; James Taylor, Jr.;—Michael L. Doane; Caridad Berdut (Not admitted in DC); Maureen F. Browne; Michael G. McManus (Not admitted in DC); David F. Nickel (Not admitted in DC); Sarah E. Hamblin (Not admitted in DC); Mark R. Leventhal. Of Counsel: Robert A. Westerlund; Raymond H. J. Powell, Jr. (Not admitted in DC); Philip L. Robins.
International Trade, Customs, Trade Regulation, Unfair Competition, Patent, Trademark and Copyright, and Government Contract Law.
A list of Representative Clients and References will be furnished upon request.
See Professional Biographies, WASHINGTON, DISTRICT OF COLUMBIA

Addy, Waltraut Susanne ....'44 '82 C.273 B.A. L.276 J.D. [Ⓒ Arnold&P.]
*PRACTICE AREAS: Complex Civil Litigation; Government Contracts.
Adelfio, Marco E., (AV) ....'56 '82 C.105 B.A. L.93 J.D. [Morrison&F.]
*PRACTICE AREAS: Investment Management; Corporate Finance; Financial Services.
Adelman, Martin J., (AV) '37 '63 C&L.477 A.B., J.D.
(adm. in MI; not adm. in DC) Prof. of Law, George Washington Univ.

Adelman, Roger M., The Law Offices of, (AV) '41 '67 C.197 A.B. L.659 LL.B.
1100 Connecticut Avenue, N.W., Suite 730, 20036
Telephone: 202-822-0600 Fax: 202-775-8702
Email: adelmarm@erols.com URL: http://www.lawyers.com/rogeradelmanlaw

(This Listing Continued)

Adelman, Roger M., The Law Offices of (Continued)
Civil Trials, Criminal Defense, White Collar Crimes, Business Fraud, Breach of Contract, Medical Malpractice, Wrongful Death, Personal Injury, Class Actions, Complex Litigation, Professional Malpractice, Arbitration, Mediation.
See Professional Biographies, WASHINGTON, DISTRICT OF COLUMBIA

Adelman-Pierson, Rachel '59 '86 C.604 B.A. L.477 J.D.
(adm. in MD; not adm. in DC) Off. of U.S. Atty.
Ades, Robert A., & Associates, P.C. '48 '73 C&L.472 B.A., J.D.
1140 Connecticut Ave NW (⊙Landover, MD; Springfield, VA)
Adewusi, Samuel Gbenga '60 '96 C.1280 B.A. L.999 J.D.
(adm. in MD; not adm. in DC) 601 Edgewood St. NE
Adkins, Alden S. '52 '81 C.367 B.A. L.30 J.D.
V.P. & Gen. Coun., National Assn. of Sec. Dealers, Inc.
Adkins, Larry Joseph '56 '81 C.604 B.A. L.124 J.D.
Dep. Gen. Coun., National Treasury Employees Union
Adkins, Steven E. .... '62 '91 C.278 B.A. L.692 J.D. [Adduci,M.&S.]
*PRACTICE AREAS: International Trade; Intellectual Property Litigation; Insurance Coverage Litigation; Complex Commercial Litigation; Reinsurance.
Adkinson, F. Keith .... '44 '69 C&L.893 B.A., J.D. P.O. Box 70495
Adler, Allan Robert ...... '53 '79 C.1044 B.A. L.273 J.D. V.P., Assn. of Amer. Publishers
Adler, Debra B. .... '60 '88 C.454 B.A. L.273 J.D. [Griggs&A.] ⊙
*PRACTICE AREAS: Corporate Law; Civil Litigation; Energy Regulation; Employment Law; Mediation.
Adler, Gary C. .... '57 '85 C.273 B.A. L.128 J.D. [O'Connor&H.]
Adler, Hans A. .... '21 '51 C.188 A.B. L.309 LL.B. Intl. Bk. for Reconstr. & Develop.
Adler, Howard, Jr., (AV) .... '25 '51 L.145 J.D. [Ⓒ Baker&M.]
*PRACTICE AREAS: Antitrust and Unfair Trade Practices Law; Litigation; Mergers and Acquisitions; Administrative Law.
Adler, Howard B., (AV) .... '51 '76 C.367 B.A. L.569 J.D. [Gibson,D.&C.]
*PRACTICE AREAS: Securities; Mergers, Acquisitions and Divestitures; Corporate Law; Banks and Banking; Finance.
Adler, Irving .... '13 '51 C.569 B.S. L.273 LL.B. 4101 Cathedral Ave., N.W.‡
Adler, Jessica .... '75 '00 C.966 B.A. L.608 J.D. [Ⓐ O'Connell&Assoc.]
*PRACTICE AREAS: Family Law; Taxation; Divorce Taxation; Estate and Gift Taxation; Estate Planning.
Adler, Lorraine J. .... '70 '95 C.188 B.S. L.880 J.D. LEXIS-NEXIS
Adler, M. Peter .... '— '83 C.610 B.S. L.1035 J.D. [Foley&L.]
*PRACTICE AREAS: E-health; HIPAA Compliance; E-Commerce; Information Security; Privacy.
Adler, Matthew D. .... '70 '96 C.477 A.B. L.188 J.D. [Ⓐ Clifford C.R.&W.]
*PRACTICE AREAS: Mergers and Acquisitions; Private Equity; Capital Markets.
Adler, Olivia P. .... '41 '67 C.681 A.B. L.309 LL.B. [Ⓐ Dechert]
*PRACTICE AREAS: Investment Management; Financial Services Law.
Adler, Reid G., (AV) .... '54 '82 C.446 B.S. L.273 J.D. [Morgan,L.&B.] (Pat.)
*PRACTICE AREAS: Intellectual Property; Technology Transfer.
Adler, Robert M., (AV) .... '43 '69 C.604 B.A. L.477 J.D. [O'Connor&H.]
Adler, Robert W. .... '55 '80 C.367 B.A. L.276 J.D. Natural Res. Def. Council
Adler, Spencer E. .... '65 '91 C.860 B.A. L.831 J.D. 1250 24th St., N.W.
Adlin, Michael B. .... '65 '91 C.228 A.B. L.94 J.D. [Manatt,P.&P.]
Adney, John T., (AV) .... '50 '75 C.357 B.A. L.976 J.D. [Davis&H.]
*PRACTICE AREAS: Taxation Law; Insurance Law; Legislation Law.
Adragna, John Michael, (AV) .... '53 '78 C.1044 B.A. L.273 J.D. [Miller,B.&O.]
*PRACTICE AREAS: Electric Power; Electric Utilities; Energy Regulation; Energy Contracts; Electric Cooperatives.
Adrian, Nadine D.Y. '73 '97 C.30 B.A. L.1117 J.D.
(adm. in CA; not adm. in DC) [Ⓐ Bonner K.T.&C.]
*PRACTICE AREAS: Civil Litigation.
Adrian, Stephen G. '63 '90
C.575 B.S. L.273 J.D. [Armstrong,W.H.M.&N.] (See Pat. Sect.)
Advocates at Law, Chartered, (AV) .... 5435 41st Pl., N.W.

Afridi, Angell & Pelletreau LLP
1025 Connecticut Avenue, N.W., Suite 904, 20036-5405 ⊙
Telephone: 202-518-8900 Fax: 202-518-8903
Email: rpelletreau@afridi.com URL: http://www.afridi-angell.com
Partner: Robert H. Pelletreau (Also Of Counsel to Baker Botts, L.L.P.). Of Counsel: A. John Radsan. The firm, including the New York, United Arab Emirates and Pakistan Offices, and Baker Botts L.L.P., independent law firms, have established a Strategic Alliance for purposes of enhancing their respective client service capabilities in the Middle East-North Africa-South Asia Region. Baker Botts has offices in Houston, Dallas and Austin, Texas, Washington, D.C., New York, London, Riyadh and Baku.
New York, N.Y. Office: 599 Lexington Avenue, Suite 2806, 10022-6030. Telephone: 212-697-0300. Fax: 212-697-0385. E-mail: nangell@afridi.com.
Abu Dhabi, United Arab Emirates Office: Al Ghaith Tower, Level 8, Suite 806, Hamdan Street. P.O. Box 3961. Telephone: +971-2-6275134. Fax: +971-2-6272905. E-mail: abudhabi@afridi-angell.com
Dubai, United Arab Emirates Office: Emirates Towers, 35th Floor, Sheikh Zayed Road, P.O. Box 9371. Telephone: +971-4-330-3900. Fax: +971-4-330-3800. E-mail: dubai@afridi-angell.com.
Jebel Ali, United Arab Emirates Office: Jebel Ali Free Trade Zone, P.O. Box 61276, Jebel Ali. Telephone: +971-4-8816010. Fax: +971-4-8816774.
Sharjah, United Arab Emirates Office: Al-Boorj Avenue, P.O. Box 5925. Telephone: +971-6-5544062. Fax: +971-6-5547336. E-mail: sharjah@afridi-angell.com.
Islamabad, Pakistan Office: Afridi Angell & Khan, 94 W. Jinnah Avenue, Blue Area, Islamabad 44000. Telephone: +92-51-2823-110. Fax: +92-51-2823-009. E-mail: islamabad@afridi-angell.com
Karachi, Pakistan Office: House D-3/1, Kehkashan, Clifton, Block 7. Telephone: +92-21-583 3585/583 3595. Fax: +92-21-5833-022/327. E-mail: karachi@afridi-angell.com.
See Professional Biographies, WASHINGTON, DISTRICT OF COLUMBIA

Agarwal, Pavan Kumar .... '— '96 C.446 B.S.E.E. L.273 J.D. [Ⓐ Foley&L.]
*PRACTICE AREAS: Electronics.
Agbe-Davies, Christopher Kole '— '97 C&L.329 B.B.A., J.D.
(adm. in GA; not adm. in DC) [Ⓐ King&S.]
*PRACTICE AREAS: Corporate.
Agee, Danielle C. .... '67 '92 C.339 B.A. L.477 J.D. [WorldCom]
Agenbroad, Aaron L. .... '69 '97 C.911 B.A. L.276 J.D. [Ⓐ Jones,D.R.&P.]
Aggarwal, Reggie K. '— '94 C.893 B.S. L.902 J.D.
(adm. in VA; not adm. in DC) 2300 N St. NW
Agin, Jonathan E. '71 '99 C.363 B.A. L.124 J.D.
[Ⓐ Bonner K.T.&C.] (⊙Rockville, MD)
*PRACTICE AREAS: Litigation.
Agin, Neely B. .... '72 '97 C.1365 B.A. L.930 J.D. [Ⓐ Fulbright&J.]
*PRACTICE AREAS: Antitrust; Litigation.
Agrawal, Swati .... '70 '96 C.477 A.B. L.976 J.D. 1001 Connecticut Ave., Suite 1035
Agresta, Steven J. .... '48 '77 C.575 A.B. L.309 J.D. [Swidler B.S.F.]
*PRACTICE AREAS: Regulatory Law; Utility Law.
Aguggia, Paul M. .... '63 '89 C.165 B.A. L.228 J.D. [Muldoon M.&F.]
*PRACTICE AREAS: Financial Institutions; Business Law; Mergers, Acquisitions and Divestitures; Securities.
Aguglia, Richard L., (AV) .... '45 '71 C.025 B.A. L.128 J.D. [Ⓒ Hunton&W.]
*PRACTICE AREAS: Real Estate; Property Tax Appeals; Land Use; Zoning Law; Historic Preservation.
Aguilar, Laura Ann '71 '98 C&L.37 B.A., J.D.
(adm. in AZ; not adm. in DC) 400 7th. St., S.W.
Agusti, Filiberto .... '53 '79 C.339 A.B. L.309 J.D. [Steptoe&J.]
Ahari, Leslie S. .... '63 '88 C.228 A.B. L.309 J.D. [Ross,D.&B.]

Ahern, Veronica M., (AV) .... '46 '73 C.702 B.A. L.276 J.D. [Nixon P.]
*PRACTICE AREAS: Communications and Media; Alternative Dispute Resolution (ADR); Antitrust; Nonprofit and Charitable Organizations.
Aherne, Elizabeth E. .... '73 '00 C.188 B.S. L.276 J.D. [Ⓐ Cadwalader,W.&T.]
*PRACTICE AREAS: Tax Law; Corporate Law.
Ahlers, Annette M. '59 '90 C.911 B.A. L.61 J.D.
(adm. in CA; not adm. in DC) Mgr., Ernst & Young, LLP
Ahlers, Clarke F., P.C.
(See Columbia, Maryland)
Ahmad, Aisha '— '97 C.446 BSEE L.989 J.D.
(adm. in MD; not adm. in DC; See Pat. Sect.) [Ⓐ Roylance,A.B.&G.]
*PRACTICE AREAS: Patent Prosecution.
Ahmad, Ali '65 '98 L.999 LL.B.
(adm. in NY; not adm. in DC) Lexis-Nexis
Ahmed, Syed I. '55 '86 C&L.999 B.A., J.D.
(adm. in NY; not adm. in DC) Sr. Coun., The World Bk.
Ahn, Cathy Haesang '74 '99 C&L.309 A.B., J.D.
(adm. in MA; not adm. in DC) [Ⓐ Wilmer,C.&P.]
Ahnen, Christi D. '60 '91 C.16 B.S./B.A. L.190 J.D.
Assoc. Gen. Coun., Group Hospitalization and Medical Services, Inc.
Ahnn, Michelle M. '73 '99 C.103 A.B. L.1068 J.D.
(adm. in CA; not adm. in DC) Georgetown Univ. Law Ctr.
Ahrens, Matthew G. .... '65 '93 C.691 B.A. L.273 J.D. [Wilkes A.]
*PRACTICE AREAS: Real Property Tax and Assessment Law.
Ailes, Stephen, (AV) .... '12 '36 C.674 A.B. L.923 J.D. 1330 Connecticut Ave., N.W.
Ain, Michael M., (AV) '— '75 C.107 B.A. L.273 J.D.
1155 15th Street, N.W., Suite 502, 20005 ⊙
Telephone: 202-828-9191 Fax: 202-371-9046 URL: http://www.lawyers.com/michaelainlaw
Email: info@ainlaw.com URL: http://www.ainlaw.com
(Also of Counsel, O'Reilly, Mark & Peelman, L.L.C.).
Medical Negligence, Automobile Accidents, Products Liability, Premises Liability, Police Brutality, Personal Injury.
Rockville, Maryland Office: 600 Jefferson Plaza, Suite 308.
See Professional Biographies, WASHINGTON, DISTRICT OF COLUMBIA
Ain, Sanford K., (AV) .... '47 '72 C.966 B.A. L.276 J.D. [Sherman,M.C.&A.]
*PRACTICE AREAS: Family Law; Commercial Transactions; Business Successions; Real Property.
Airasian, Lynn A. .... '69 '94 C.93 B.A. L.276 J.D. [Ⓐ Jones,D.R.&P.]
Aires, Randolf H. .... '35 '63 C.197 A.B. L.477 J.D. 1301 Pennsylvania Ave., N.W.
Aisenberg, Irwin M., (AV) '25 '58 C.119 B.S. L.276 J.D.
[Jacobson,H.] (See Pat. Sect.)
*PRACTICE AREAS: Intellectual Property Law; Biotechnology Patents; Chemical Patents.
Aistars, Sandra M. '68 '96 C.65 B.A. L.64 J.D.
(adm. in MD; not adm. in DC) [Ⓐ Weil,G.&M.]
Aitken, Andrew C. '61 '88 C.423 B.S. L.128 J.D.
[Venable,A.B.H.&C.] (See Pat. Sect.)
*PRACTICE AREAS: Patent Litigation; Patent Prosecution; Medical Patents; Mechanical Patents; Intellectual Property Litigation.
Aitken, Bruce, (BV) '47 '77
C.262 B.A. L.904 J.D. [Aitken I.B.&V.] (⊙Kyiv (Kiev),Ukraine)
*PRACTICE AREAS: Antitrust; Arbitration; Customs; International Trade Regulation and Policy; Congressional/Legislative.
Aitken, Richard L., (AV) '30 '56
C.188 B.E.E. L.273 J.D. [Venable,A.B.H.&C.] (See Pat. Sect.)
*PRACTICE AREAS: Intellectual Property; Patents; Trademarks; Computers and Software; Electronic Patents.

Aitken Irvin Berlin & Vroomán, LLP, (AV)
Suite 315 666 Eleventh Street, N.W., 20001 ⊙
Telephone: 202-331-8045; 202-331-3096 Telecopier: 202-331-8191; 202-573-8073 URL: http://www.aitkennirvinberlin&vrooman
Email: beaitken@aol.com URL: http://www.lawyers.com/aitkenirvinberlin&vrooman
Members of Firm: Evelyn F. Cohn (1948-1998); Bruce Aitken; Ben L. Irvin (Not admitted in DC); Alan D. Berlin (Not admitted in DC); Edward A. Vroomán (Not admitted in DC; Resident, White Plains, New York Office). Of Counsel: Kieran Sharpe (Not admitted in DC); Frederick R. Troncone; Brien E. Kehoe; Daniel Oliver (Not admitted in DC). Foreign Law Consultants/Associates: Elena Volochay (Not admitted in the United States); Jianping Zhang (Not admitted in United States).
Administrative and Commercial Practice before Federal Courts and Agencies and the U.S. Congress. International Trade Law and Policy, Customs, Export Control, Immigration, International Transactions and Project Finance, Government Affairs, Commercial Arbitration, Real Estate, Corporate Representation, Litigation, Arbitration, Maritime, Natural Resources and Energy Law.
White Plains, New York Office: 2 Gannett Drive, Suite 418. Telephone: 914-694-2226. Fax: 914-694-1647.
Kyiv, Ukraine Representative Office: c/o DDM, 25 Povitrof Avenue, 03049. Telephone: +380-67-449-4802. Fax: +380-44-245-4633.
Affiliated Offices: Beijing, Buenos Aires, Tokyo.
See Professional Biographies, WASHINGTON, DISTRICT OF COLUMBIA

Aiyetorro, Adjoa A. '46 '78 C.156 A.B. L.733 J.D.
(adm. in MO; not adm. in DC) ACLU National Prison Project
Aizawa, Motoko '59 '85 C.299 B.A. L.054 LL.M.
(adm. in NY; not adm. in DC) 1818 H Street Nw
Akaras, Andreas N. .... '70 '96 C.446 B.A. L.1002 J.D. [Sfikas,K.&A.] ⊙
Akard, Stephen J. '64 '89 C&L.347 B.A., J.D.
(adm. in IN; not adm. in DC) Indiana Univ. Sch. of Law
Akers, James E., (AV) '42 '67 C&L.178 A.B., LL.B.
Sr. V.P. & Assoc. Gen. Coun., Lit., Intell. Prop., Marriott Intl., Inc.

Akin, Gump, Strauss, Hauer & Feld, L.L.P., (AV) BR
A Registered Limited Liability Partnership including Professional Corporations
Robert S. Strauss Building 1333 New Hampshire Avenue, N.W., Suite 400, 20036 ⊙
Telephone: 202-887-4000 Fax: 202-887-4288
URL: http://www.akingump.com
Members of Firm: Donald C. Alexander; Keith R. Anderson; Richard N. Appel; James A. Barker, Jr.; Paul A. Belvin; Stephen S. Boochever; Sanjoy K. Bose; Janet C. Boyd; Rick L. Burdick (P.C.); David P. Callet (P.C.); J. David Carlin; Jay G. Cohen (Not admitted in DC); Joel M. Cohn (P.C.); Barry Conaty; Warren E. Connelly; Eileen M. Considine (Not admitted in DC); Colleen M. Coyle; Donald B. Craven; John J. D'Andrea (Not admitted in DC); Sean G. D'Arcy; Smith W. Davis (P.C.); Sylvia A. de Leon; David A. Donohoe (P.C.); Marilyn L. Doria; John M. Dowd; Keith A. Dunsmore (Resident); David H. Eisenstat; Joseph P. Esposito (P.C.); Allen V. Farber; Jeffrey T. Ganiban; Joseph V. Gatti; David Geanacopoulos; Richard M. Gittleman; Avrum M. Goldberg; Larry S. Gondelman; Philip D. Green; Spencer S. Griffith; Paul E. Gutermann; Scott M. Heimberg; Frank H. Henneburg; Paul B. Hewitt; William G. Hundley; Howard B. Jacobson; Joel Jankowsky (P.C.); Owen M. Johnson, Jr.; Ronald M. Johnson; Sheila D. Jones; Daniel Joseph; Stephen H. Kaplan (Not admitted in DC); Donald Michael Kaye; Sukhan Kim; Peter J. Kirsch; Merrill L. Kramer (P.C.); Lawrence L. Lamade; James C. Langdon, Jr.; Malcolm Lassman (P.C.); Vladimir Lechtman; Roy P. Lessy, Jr.; Lawrence D. Levien (P.C.); Donald R. Livingston; Jorge Lopez, Jr.; Terence J. Lynam; Alan S. Macdonald; Mark J. MacDougall; Michael J. Madigan (P.C.); Michael S. Mandel; Michael S. Marcus (P.C.); Robert W. McCann; R. Bruce McLean; Thomas P. McLish; Bruce S. Mendelsohn; Michael J. Mueller; Daniel L. Nash; Robin M. Nuschler; Neil S. Olderman; David B. Palmer; Jaemin Park (Not admitted in DC); Russell W. Parks, Jr.; J. Steven Patterson; Donald R. Pongrace; Michael Quigley; Dennis M. Race; Franz R. Rassman; Sarah M. Rockwell (Not admitted in DC); Perry M. Rosen; Steven R. Ross; Jerry E. Rothrock; Edward L. Rubinoff (P.C.); George R. Salem; Robert Salcido; Stanley J. Samorajczyk; Sanford M. Saunders, Jr.; Barney J. Skladany, Jr.; Valerie A. Slater; Roxane N. Sokolove; Jonathan S. Spaeth; Daniel L. Spiegel; C. Fairley Spillman; Robert S. Strauss; Larry E.

(This Listing Continued)

Akin, Gump, Strauss, Hauer & Feld, L.L.P. (Continued)

Tanenbaum; Henry A. Terhune; W. Randolph Teslik (P.C.); Thomas B. Trimble; James P. Tuite; Leslie M. Turner; Paul L. Uhrig; Charles L. Warren; S. Bruce Wilson; Samuel Wolff; Richard L. Wyatt, Jr. (P.C.); Clifford J. Zatz. Associates: Carrie Hill Allen; William F. Allen; Alison E. Barry (Not admitted in DC); Richard W. Black (Not admitted in DC); Robert T. Bradford; Maiysha R. Branch (Not admitted in DC); Katherine D. Brodie; Melanie R. Burkes (Not admitted in DC); Michael S. Caldwell (Not admitted in DC); David A. Catania; Risa B. Cherry; Alan Cohn; Michael L. Converse; Janis M. Crum; Jill F. Dash (Not admitted in DC); Erin Dozier; Angela M. Dusenbury (Not admitted in DC); Thomas F. Felton (Not admitted in DC); Michael Ferrans; Laura E. FitzRandolph; Charles William Frick (Not admitted in DC); Stephanie Agli Gallagher; Dirk R. Gardner; Fani Cyd Geroff; Jonathan L. Gold; Alison Leigh Gray; Michele S. Greif; Gregory J. Granitto; Nicole L. Hagenbuch; Keith A. Halpern (Not admitted in DC); Anne T. Hickey; Beth L. Hirschfelder; Elizabeth A. Holt (Not admitted in DC); Mary A. House (Not admitted in DC); James D. Humphrey, II (Not admitted in DC); Bernd Gunnar Janzen (Not admitted in DC); Janine L. Jones; Shelley E. Jones; Wendy E. Kamenshine; Glenn H. Kaminsky (Not admitted in DC); Kenneth P. Kaplan; Jeffrey M. King; Jo-Ellyn Sakowitz Klein; Robert H. Kluge, III (Not admitted in DC); Kerry E. Korody; Jonathan M. Krell; Xanthe M. Larsen; Thomas J. McCarthy; Scott D. McKinney; Erika Esterbrook Meadors; Byung Joon Min; Annamaria Locsin Nields (Not admitted in DC); Nathan J. Oleson; Michael J. Parini; J. David Park; David H. Quigley; Stacey A. Recht (Not admitted in DC); Aaron J. Reed; Daniel S. Reimer (Not admitted in DC); John M. Remy; Mark E. Ricardo; Reed L. Russell; Jeremy R. Schwer; Michael P. Seaman; Scott E. Seewald; Stacey Wruble Seewald; Rajat R. Shah; William Dixon Shay, III; John Sim; Dana E. Singiser; Nicole A. Smith; David G. Socie; Kimberly Stallings Suringa; Andrew T. Swers; Esther G. Tamburo; Joshua C. Toll; James R. Tucker, Jr.; Francesca Ugolini; Christopher J. VanArsdale; Aurore Y. Victor; Kristin J. Vollmers; Ernest Sylvain Voyard, Jr.; Robin Mahler Weisman. Counsel: Sam J. Alberts; Margaret D. Chisholm; Joel A. Christie; Timothy J. Choppin; Dmitri I. Dubograev; Shari L. Fleishman; Brian S. Gleicher; Karen Goldmeier Green; Stefan A. Hagerup; Jonathan H. Hambrick; Gary A. Heimberg; John R. Jacob; Polly B. Jessen (Not admitted in DC); Charles W. Johnson, IV; Robert G. Lian, Jr.; Elizabeth A. Matthews; Daniel F. McInnis; James J. Murphy; Michele Harrington Murphy; Evangeline C. Paschal; Laurent C. Pavageau; John E. Putnam; Bruce G. Rosen; Matthew A. Rossi; Wynn H. Segall; Todd M. Stenerson; Anthony W. Swisher; Mark D. Taylor; Karen Bland Toliver; Marilyn C. Vadon. Senior Counsel: Kenneth D. Alderfer; Richard P. Bonsignore; Marlene M. Colucci; Maryellen Connor; Joseph W. Cornelison; William J. Farah; Lars-Erik A. Hjelm; Michelle M. Hsu; Byron Keith Huffman, Jr.; Vernon E. Jordan, Jr.; Susan Heck Lent; Patrick F. J. Macrory; Paul E. Mirengoff; Tecla A. Murphy; Kenneth E. Natale; James C. Osborne, Jr.; W. Eric Pilsk; James P. Scanlan; Dawn E. Starr; Charles V. Stewart; James K. Stewart.

Antitrust, Banking and Financial Institutions, Bankruptcy, Capital Markets, Communications, Corporate and Securities, Employee Benefits, Energy, Entertainment, Environmental, Food and Drug, Government Contracts, Health Care, Insurance, Intellectual Property and Technology, International, Labor and Employment, Litigation, Mergers and Acquisitions, Privatization, Project Finance, Public Law and Policy, Real Estate and Taxation.

Dallas, Texas Office: 1700 Pacific Avenue, Suite 4100. Telephone: 214-969-2800. Fax: 214-969-4343.
Austin, Texas Office: Frost Bank Plaza, 816 Congress Avenue, Suite 1900. Telephone: 512-499-6200. Fax: 512-499-6290.
Houston, Texas Office: 1900 Pennzoil Place-South Tower, 711 Louisiana Street. Telephone: 713-220-5800. Fax: 713-236-0822.
San Antonio, Texas Office: 300 Convent Street, Suite 1500. Telephone: 210-281-7000. Fax: 210-224-2035.
New York, New York Office: 590 Madison Avenue. Telephone: 212-872-1000. Fax: 212-872-1002.
Philadelphia, Pennsylvania Office: One Commerce Square, 2005 Market Street, Suite 2200. Telephone: 215-965-1200. Fax: 215-965-1210.
Los Angeles, California Office: 2029 Century Park East, Suite 2400. Telephone: 310-229-1000. Fax: 310-229-1001.
Denver, Colorado Office: 1675 Broadway, Suite 2300. Telephone: 303-825-7000. Fax: 303-825-7005.
McLean, Virginia Office: 1676 International Drive. Telephone: 703-891-7500. Fax: 703-891-7501.
Brussels, Belgium Office: 65 Avenue Louise, P.B. #7. Telephone: (011) 32-2-535-2911. Fax: (011) 32-2-535-2900.
Moscow, Russia Office: Ducat Place II, 7 Gasheka Street, P.B. 20. Telephone: (011) 7-095 974-2411. Fax: (011) 7-095-974-2412.
London, England Office: One Angel Court. Telephone: (011) 44-20 7726-9600. Fax: (011) 44-20 7726-9610.
Affiliated Office:
Law Office of Abdulaziz H. Fahad, One Commerce Square, Jarir Plaza, 4th Floor, Olaya Street, P.O. Box 15870, Riyadh, Saudi Arabia, 11454. Telephone: (011) 966-1-464-8081. Telex: 406176 LAWS SJ. Telecopier: (011)-966-1-462- 4968.

See Professional Biographies, WASHINGTON, DISTRICT OF COLUMBIA

Akman, Jerome P., (AV) ....'44 '69 C.597 B.S.B.A. L.309 J.D. [Arent F.K.P.&K.]
*PRACTICE AREAS: Corporate Law; International Business (Trade and Finance); International Practice; Customs Law; Business Law.
Akman & Associates, P.C. ....1700 K St., N.W. (©Frederick, Lutherville, MD)
Akre, Charles T., (AV) ....'— '34 C.352 B.A. L.273 J.D. [▣ Miller&C.]
Aksman, Stanislaus, (AV) ....'50 '80 C.177 B.S. L.273 J.D. [Hunton&W.] (Pat.)
*PRACTICE AREAS: Intellectual Property Law.
Akyereko, Beth-Sherri ....'64 '95 C.674 B.A. L.273 J.D. [▣ Leventhal,S.&L.]
Alapati, Nanda K. ...... '59 '94 C.436 B.S.E.E. L.276 J.D. [▣ Pennie&E.] (See Pat. Sect.)
*PRACTICE AREAS: Intellectual Property; Patent.
Alberg, James L. ....'52 '78 C.867 B.A. L.94 J.D. [Shaw P.]
*PRACTICE AREAS: Information Technology; Corporate Law.
Alberse, Kristin R. '65 '90 C.886 B.A. L.1292 J.D.
Assoc. Gen. Coun., National Geographic Society
*RESPONSIBILITIES: Contracts; International Law; Intellectual Property; Commercial Law; Publishing Law.
Albert, Edie R. ....'67 '92 C.860 B.A. L.273 J.D. 1775 Eye St., N.W.
Albert, Jennifer A., (AV) ....'60 '85 C.679 B.S.E.E. L.790 J.D. [Hunton&W.] (Pat.)
*PRACTICE AREAS: Information Technology; Electronic Commerce; Intellectual Property; Patents; Trademarks.
Albert, Kenneth M., (BV) ....'— '83 C.1036 B.A. L.276 J.D. [▣ Brunenkant&H.]
*PRACTICE AREAS: Energy Law (100%).
Albert, Marc E., (AV) ....'48 '74 C&L.273 B.A., J.D. [Morrison&H.]
*PRACTICE AREAS: Bankruptcy; Tax; Real Estate.
Albert, Mary C. ....'51 '81 C.915 B.A. L.276 J.D. 3000 K St., NW, Ste. 300
Albert, Stacey Stern '69 '94
C.659 B.A. L.276 J.D. Pub. Policy Coun., Compaq Computer Corp.
Albert, Thomas L. ....'63 '88 C.1019 B.A. L.904 J.D. [Birch,H.B.&C.]
Alberta, Mark E., (AV) ....'50 '76 C.976 B.A. L.273 J.D. [Arent F.K.P.&K.]
*PRACTICE AREAS: Real Estate-Commercial Law.
Albertelli, Alyssa ....'65 '95 C.783 B.A. L.94 J.D. [▣ Ropes&G.]
Alberts, Sam J. ....'64 '92 C.569 B.A. L.273 J.D. [▣ Akin,G.S.H.&F.]
*PRACTICE AREAS: Financial Restructuring; Bankruptcy Chapter 11; Litigation.
Albertson, Fred W., (AV) ....'08 '34 C&L.477 A.B., J.D. [▣ Dow,L.&A.]
Albertson, Terry L., (AV) ....'46 '74 C.276 A.B. L.309 J.D. [Crowell&M.]
*PRACTICE AREAS: Contract Law; Government Contract Law; Public Contract Law; State and Federal Grants.
Albrecht, Michael R. ....'69 '96 C&L.734 B.S.B.A., J.D. [▣ Clifford C.R.&W.]
*PRACTICE AREAS: White Collar Crime; Regulatory Law; Litigation.
Albrecht, Ralph P. '65 '97
C.886 B.S.E.E. L.1356 J.D. [▣ Venable,A.B.H.&C.] (See Pat. Sect.)
*PRACTICE AREAS: Intellectual Property; Patents; Trademarks; Copyrights; Computers and Software.
Albrecht, Virginia S., (AV) .... '42 '81 C.966 B.S. L.880 J.D. [Hunton&W.]
*PRACTICE AREAS: Environmental Law; Administrative Law.
Albright, Ralph N., Jr., (AV) ....'42 '68 C.665 B.B.A. L.30 J.D. [Morgan,L.&B.]
Albritton, Erin '70 '97 C.019 B.A. L.861 J.D.
(adm. in LA; not adm. in DC) [▣ Jenner&B.]
*PRACTICE AREAS: Litigation.
Alcala, Marissa L. '76 '01 C.976 B.A. L.276 J.D.
(adm. in NY; not adm. in DC) [▣ Chadbourne&P.]
Alcorn, Linda E. ....'69 '94 C.188 B.S. L.94 J.D. [Sterne,K.G.&F.] (See Pat. Sect.)
*PRACTICE AREAS: Patent Litigation; Business Methods; Medical Devices; Consumer Products; Civil Appeals.
Alcorn, Wendell B., Jr., (AV) '39 '69 L.326 J.D.
1201 Pennsylvania Avenue, NW Suite 300 PMB 300, 20004 ©
Telephone: 202-661-4644 Fax: 202-661-4699 URL: http://www.lawyers.com/wendellalcorn
Email: walcorn@aol.com URL: http://www.alcornlawoffice.com
***PRACTICE AREAS: Agricultural Cooperatives; Antitrust and Trade Regulation; Business Law; Class Actions; Complex and Multi-District Litigation.**
Antitrust and Trade Regulation, Deceptive Trade Practices, Unfair Trade, Counterfeiting, Noncompetition and Non-Solicitation Agreements, Complex and Multi-District Litigation, Corporate Law, Business Litigation, Small Business Law, Trademark Protection, International Trademarks, Trade Secrets, Trade Association Law, Business Law.
Williamsburg, Virginia Office: 3107 Nathaniel's Green, 23185-7525. Telephone: 757-258-9563. Fax: 757-258-3448.

See Professional Biographies, WASHINGTON, DISTRICT OF COLUMBIA

Aldana-Pindell, Raquel E. .... '72 '97 C.36 B.A. L.309 J.D. Ctr. for Jus. & Intl. Law
Alden, Kristin D. ....'67 '92 C.367 B.A. L.30 J.D. [▣ Passman&K.]
*PRACTICE AREAS: Employment Law; Federal Civil Service; Equal Employment Opportunity Law; Labor Law.
Alderfer, Kenneth D. ....'57 '86 C.1124 B.S. L.893 J.D. [▣ Akin,G.S.H.&F.]
*PRACTICE AREAS: Taxation; Health Care.
Alderman, Elliott Carl ....'56 '83 C.705 B.A. L.30 J.D. [▣ Chavers]
*PRACTICE AREAS: Trademark; Copyright.
Aldock, Jessica Lauren '74 '99 C.311 B.A. L.893 J.D.
(adm. in MD; not adm. in DC) 333 Constitution Ave.
Aldock, John D., (AV) ....'42 '68 C.597 B.S. L.659 LL.B. [Shea&G.]
*PRACTICE AREAS: Complex Litigation; Class Actions; Products Liability; Toxic Torts; Legal Malpractice.
Aldrich, Katherine M. ....'64 '91 C.999 B.A. L.276 J.D. [▣ Boros&G.]
*PRACTICE AREAS: Airline Regulation; Aviation Law.
Aldrich, Robert F., (BV) ....'52 '79 C.976 B.A. L.893 J.D. [▣ Dickstein S.M.&O.]
*PRACTICE AREAS: Telecommunication Law.
Aldridge, Anna C. ....'67 '92 C.1350 B.A. L.823 J.D. Supr. Ct. Prob.
Alerding, Steven A. ....'66 '97 C.454 B.A. L.477 J.D. [▣ Fried,F.H.S.&J.]
*PRACTICE AREAS: Litigation; Government Contracts.
Alers, Jorge E. ....'59 '86 C.172 B.A. L.309 J.D. [Wilmer,C.&P.]
*PRACTICE AREAS: International Mergers and Acquisitions; Cross-Border Finance; Project Finance.
Alexander, Allison Leslie .... '69 '99 C.823 B.S. L.446 J.D. [▣ Piper M.R.&W.]
*PRACTICE AREAS: Corporate Finance; Securities; Venture Capital; Emerging Companies; Mergers, Acquisitions and Divestitures.
Alexander, Choi '68 '95 C.178 B.A. L.597 J.D.
Atty., Off. for Civil Rights, U.S. Dept. of Educ.
Alexander, Clifford J., (AV) ....'— '70 C.698 A.B. L.276 J.D. [Kirkpatrick&L.]
*PRACTICE AREAS: Investment Company Law; Investment Management; Broker-Dealer Regulation; Banking Law; Business Organizations.
Alexander, Clifford L., Jr., (AV) '33 '59
C.309 A.B. L.976 LL.B. Pres., Alexander & Assocs., Inc.
Alexander, Damien V. ....'73 '98 C.128 B.A. L.30 J.D. [▣ Smith C.]
*PRACTICE AREAS: Legal Malpractice; Litigation; Business Planning; Intellectual Property.
Alexander, David E. ....'54 '80 C.186 B.S. L.107 J.D. 2424 Pennsylvania Ave., N.W.
Alexander, Donald C., (AV) ....'21 '49 C.976 A.B. L.309 LL.B. [Akin,G.S.H.&F.]
*PRACTICE AREAS: Taxation.
Alexander, Eric L. ....'70 '96 C.385 B.A. L.228 J.D. [▣ Arnold&P.]
*PRACTICE AREAS: Litigation.
Alexander, James A. '59 '85
C.390 B.A. L.216 J.D. Sr. V.P. & Coun., Jonathan Woodner Co.
Alexander, Jay I. ....'63 '90 C&L.597 B.S., J.D. [Kirkland&E.]
*PRACTICE AREAS: Intellectual Property.
Alexander, Jay L. ....'61 '86 C.197 A.B. L.813 J.D. [Baker B.]
Alexander, Koteles, (AV) ....'55 '80 C.1086 B.A. L.325 J.D. [Alexander,B.H.&M.] ©
Alexander, Lee A., (AV) ....'51 '76 C.645 B.S. L.665 J.D. [Dickstein S.M.&O.]
*PRACTICE AREAS: Energy Law; Regulatory Law; Environment Law; Transportation Law.
Alexander, Philip M. ....'54 '85 C.276 B.S.F.S. L.128 J.D. 4912-43rd Place NW‡
Alexander, Richard M. ....'57 '82 C.1036 B.A. L.823 J.D. [Arnold&P.]
*PRACTICE AREAS: Financial Institutions.
Alexander, Robert W. ....'62 '92 C.1016 B.A. L.174 J.D. [▣ Bredhoff&K.]
Alexander, Sarira D. ....'62 '94 C.112 B.A. L.1065 J.D. [▣ Arent F.K.P.&K.]
*PRACTICE AREAS: Intellectual Property; Copyrights; Trademarks; Electronic Commerce; Licensing.
Alexander, Todd E. ....'69 '95 C.339 B.S. L.276 J.D. [▣ Chadbourne&P.]
Alexander, Bearden, Hairston & Marks, LLP, (AV)
2021 L Street, N.W., Suite 300 (©Silver Spring, MD)

Alexander & Cleaver, P.A.
(See Annapolis, Maryland)

Alexandri, Maya ....'75 '99 C.705 B.A. L.1494 J.D. [▣ Wilmer,C.&P.]
Alfano, Alphonse M. ....'47 '73 C.665 B.A. L.273 J.D. [Bassman,M.&A.]
Alfano, Anthony V., (AV) '56 '82
C.156 B.A. L.896 J.D. Sr. Litig. Coun., MCI WorldCom
Alford, James K. ....'49 '74 C.611 B.A. L.1202 J.D. [Vorys,S.S.&P.]
*PRACTICE AREAS: International Taxation; Corporate Taxation.
Alger, Jonathan R. '64 '89
C.821 B.A. L.309 J.D. Coun., American Assn. of Univ. Professors
Ali, Reema I. ....'58 '89 L.802 J.D. [Ali] (©Kuwait, Kuwait)
Ali, Zeba T. '74 '00 C.228 B.S. L.575 J.D.
(adm. in NC; not adm. in DC; See Pat. Sect.) [▣ Kenyon&K.]
*PRACTICE AREAS: Intellectual Property.
Ali & Partners .... 2121 K Street, N.W., Suite 800 (©Kuwait, Kuwait; Muscat, Oman)
Aliaskari, Mahsa .... '— '00 C.1356 B.A. L.30 J.D. 1100 Connecticut Avenue
Alison, John R. ....'56 '86 C.821 B.A. L.276 J.D. [Finnegan,H.F.G.&D.]
*PRACTICE AREAS: Patent Litigation; Trade Secrets.
Aljurf, Saladin A. '70 '98 C&L.352 B.A., J.D.
(adm. in VA; not adm. in DC) [▣ Kalbian H.]
Allan, Michael J. ....'72 '99 C.299 B.A. L.823 J.D. [▣ Arnold&P.]
*PRACTICE AREAS: Litigation.
Allan, Richmond F. ....'30 '57 C&L.508 B.A., J.D. [Duncan,W.G.&P.]
*PRACTICE AREAS: Public Land Law; Natural Resources; Public Utility Law.
Allard, Nicholas W., (AV) ....'— '80 C.674 A.B. L.976 J.D. [Latham&W.]
*PRACTICE AREAS: Communications and Media; Election, Campaign and Political Law; Government; Regulatory Law; Privacy Law.
Allbee, Michaela '72 '99 C.103 B.A. L.276 J.D.
(adm. in MA; not adm. in DC) [▣ Williams&C.]
*PRACTICE AREAS: Corporate Law.
Allen, Anita L. '53 '85 C.1275 B.A. L.309 J.D.
(adm. in NY; not adm. in DC) Prof.of Law, Georgetown Univ.
Allen, Brent H. ....'69 '95 C.659 B.A. L.880 J.D. [▣ Howrey S.A.&W.]
*PRACTICE AREAS: Commercial Litigation.
Allen, Carrie Hill ....'70 '95 C.472 B.A. L.588 J.D. [▣ Akin,G.S.H.&F.]
*PRACTICE AREAS: Energy Law.
Allen, Curtis Matthew '67 '93 C.612 B.A. L.862 J.D.
(adm. in OK; not adm. in DC) 716 Sicard St., S.E.★

Allen, David .... '48 '72 C.188 B.A. L.273 J.D. 1333 N. Hamps. Ave., N.W.
Allen, David W. '44 '70 C.309 B.A. L.178 J.D.
Gen. Coun., UMWA Health & Retirement Funds
Allen, Dennis L., (AV) .... '54 '80 C.57 B.A. L.602 J.D. [LeBoeuf,L.G.&M.]
*PRACTICE AREAS: Taxation; Insurance.
Allen, Donald R., (AV) .... '42 '68 C.188 A.B. L.1068 J.D. [Duncan&A.]
*PRACTICE AREAS: Electric Power; Energy Regulation; Utility Law.
Allen, Dwight L., Jr. .... '44 '72 C.608 B.A. L.309 J.D. Deloitte & Touche
Allen, Edwin H. .... '51 '79 C.112 A.B. L.813 J.D. 1101 17th St. NW, Ste. 803
Allen, Elizabeth A. .... '69 '96 C.309 B.A. L.276 J.D. [🄰 Nixon P.]
*PRACTICE AREAS: Litigation; Antitrust; Employment Law; Telecommunications.

Allen, Frank D., Jr., (BV) '37 '65 C.484 B.S. L.880 LL.B.
923 South Carolina Avenue, SE, P.O. Box 15539, 20003
Telephone: 202-544-0242 Fax: 202-547-1320
URL: http://www.lawyers.com/capitolhillallen
Retirement Planning, Trusts, Wills, Estate Planning and Estate Administration.
See Professional Biographies, WASHINGTON, DISTRICT OF COLUMBIA

Allen, George V., Jr., (AV) .... '35 '62 C.674 B.A. L.893 LL.B. 2300 N. St. NW
Allen, Jonathan E. '— '98 C.575 B.A. L.893 J.D.
(adm. in VA; not adm. in DC) [Manatt,P.&P.]
Allen, Kathryn B. '65 '95 C&L.846 B.A., J.D.
(adm. in CO; not adm. in DC) [🄰 McGuirewoods]
*PRACTICE AREAS: Energy; Utilities.
Allen, Kim M. .... '69 '00 C.732 B.A. L.145 J.D. [🄰 Hogan&H.]
Allen, Patrick H. '39 '64 C&L.378 B.A., J.D.
3248 Prospect Street, NW (⊙Mc Lean, VA)
Allen, Paul Shearman, & Associates, (BV) '38 '66 C&L.823 LL.B.
1329 18th Street, NW
Allen, Richard A., (AV) .... '45 '71 C.309 B.A. L.178 J.D. [Zuckert,S.&R.]
*PRACTICE AREAS: U.S. Supreme Court Litigation; Transportation Regulation; Motor Carrier Regulation; Civil Litigation; Railroad Labor Law.
Allen, Rosalind K. .... '57 '82 C.881 A.B. L.276 J.D. [🄲 Arnold&P.]
*PRACTICE AREAS: Telecommunications Law.
Allen, Susan Au .... '46 '84 L.1162 J.D. 1329 18th St. N.W.
Allen, Toni K., (AV) .... '40 '64 C.914 B.A. L.569 LL.B. [Piper M.R.&W.]
*PRACTICE AREAS: Public Utility Law; Environmental Law; Administrative Law.
Allen, W. David, (AV) '52 '81
C.282 B.A. L.734 J.D. 2121 K St. NW (⊙Crofton, Rockville, MD)
Allen, William F. .... '66 '96 C&L.893 B.S., J.D. [🄰 Akin,G.S.H.&F.]
*PRACTICE AREAS: Labor and Employment.
Allen, William H., (AV) .... '26 '58 C&L.813 B.A., LL.B. 1201 Penn. Ave., N.W.‡

Allen, Johnson, Alexander & Karp, P.A., (AV) BR
2120 L Street, N.W., Suite 701, 20037 ⊙
Telephone: 202-828-4141 Fax: 202-429-8798
Email: ajakdc@aol.com
D'Ana E. Johnson.
General Civil Trial Practice in all Courts. Insurance, Corporation, Insurance Defense, Products Liability, Civil Rights and Family Law.
Representative Clients: Scottsdale Insurance Co.; Nautilus Insurance Co.; Jefferson Insurance Co.; Liberty Mutual Insurance Co.; Avis Rent-A-Car; Otis Elevator Co.; Montgomery Elevator Co.; Admiral Insurance Co.; Local Government Insurance Trust; Penn National Insurance Co.
Baltimore, Maryland Office: Suite 1540, 100 East Pratt Street. Telephone: 410-727-5000.
See Professional Biographies, WASHINGTON, DISTRICT OF COLUMBIA

Allen, Robert G., P.C.
(See Manassas, Virginia)

Allenbaugh, Mark H '70 '00 C.800 B.A. L.30 J.D.
(adm. in MD; not adm. in DC) Staff Atty., U.S. Sentencing Comm.
Allera, Edward John .... '46 '74 C.923 B.S. L.276 J.D. [Buchanan I.]
*PRACTICE AREAS: Food, Drug and Cosmetic Law; Biomedical; Biotechnology.
Allis, Steven W. .... '67 '99 C.1111 B.S.M.E. L.273 J.D. [🄰 McDermott,W.&E.]
Allison, Bridget .... '73 '99 C.184 B.A. L.276 J.D. [🄰 Crowell&M.]
Allison, Ewen .... '63 '97 C.431 B.A. L.904 J.D. 3040 Idaho Ave., N.W.
Allison, Theodore S., (AV) .... '59 '84 C.907 B.A. L.800 J.D. [Karr&A.]
Allman-Dent, Alane R. .... '70 '99 C.329 B.A. L.128 J.D. 4312 19th Pl., N.E.
Almajan, Ariana .... '74 '99 C.976 B.A. L.145 J.D. [🄰 White&C.]
Almanza, Paul R. '66 '93 C.674 A.B. L.1066 J.D.
(adm. in CA; not adm. in DC) [🄰 McKenna&C.]
*PRACTICE AREAS: Litigation.
Almanzar, Quisaira Y. .... '69 '96 C.188 B.A. L.569 J.D. [🄰 Paul,H.J.&W.]
Almond, Calandra A. '74 '98 C&L.309 A.B., J.D.
(adm. in GA; not adm. in DC) [🄰 Ross,D.&B.]
*PRACTICE AREAS: Insurance.
Almstedt, Kermit W., (AV) .... '45 '70 C.798 B.S. L.986 J.D. [O'Melveny&M.]
*PRACTICE AREAS: Antitrust; Customs Law; International Trade.
Almy, Thomas B. .... '49 '78 C.103 B.A. L.276 J.D. [Dombroff&G.]
Alonge, Shauna E. .... '56 '79 C&L.861 B.A., J.D. [Crowell&M.]
*PRACTICE AREAS: Government Contract Law; Business Crimes Law; Health Care Law.
Alp, Paul .... '69 '95 C.893 B.S. L.273 J.D. [🄰 Crowell&M.]
Alper, Paul E. .... '48 '75 C.94 A.B. L.273 J.D. Asst. Corp. Coun.
Alper, Ty .... '74 '98 C.103 B.A. L.564 J.D. 111 F St. NW

Alper & Mann, P.C., (AV)
Suite 1107, 1730 K Street, N.W., 20006
Telephone: 202-298-9191 Fax: 202-298-9194
Email: Alpermann@INTR.NET URL: http://www.lawyers.com/alpermannweisbaum
Lawrence M. Mann.
General Practice before all Courts and Government Agencies. Railroad Safety Litigation, FELA Litigation, Personal Injury, Corporate, Utility, Labor, Transportation, Securities, Probate, Employment and Family Law. Trials.
See Professional Biographies, WASHINGTON, DISTRICT OF COLUMBIA

Alperin, Janice A. ...... '53 '78 C.645 B.A. L.273 J.D. Assoc. Gen. Coun., El Paso Corp.
Alpern, Erwin A. .... '29 '60 C.30 L.904 LL.B. 5040 Fulton St., N.W.‡
Alpern, Matthew '63 '90 C.1365 B.A. L.273 J.D.
(adm. in NJ; not adm. in DC) Staff Atty. to Pub. Def.
Alperstein, Brian Scott .... '68 '94 C.893 B.A. L.945 J.D. [Lasa,M.&V.]
Alpert, Brian L., (P.C.) .... '59 '87 C.197 A.B. L.276 J.D. [Silver,F.&T.]
*PRACTICE AREAS: Corporate Law; Probate Law; Estates and Trusts; Trademark Law.
Alpi, Donna Lady .... '65 '90 C.645 B.A. L.659 J.D. [Hogan&H.]
*PRACTICE AREAS: Corporate Taxation; Partnership Taxation; Real Estate Investment Taxation; Real Estate Taxation; Federal Income Tax.
Alpi, James V. .... '58 '88 C.1044 B.S. L.276 J.D. [Skadden,A.S.M.&F.]
Alprin, Brian D., (AV) .... '54 '79 C.976 B.A. L.273 J.D. [Duane,M.&H.]
*PRACTICE AREAS: Financial Institutions Law; Antitrust Law; Corporate Law.
Alprin, Geoffrey M. .... '39 '65 C.659 A.B. L.276 J.D. Supr. Ct. J.
Alprin, Michael Scott '70 '00 C.164 B.A. L.904 J.D.
(adm. in MD; not adm. in DC; See Pat. Sect.) [🄰 Armstrong,W.H.M.&N.]
*PRACTICE AREAS: Trademark; Patent Litigation; Research.

Alquist, Nancy V., (AV) '53 '78 C.659 B.A. L.831 J.D.
(adm. in PA; not adm. in DC) [Ballard S.A.&I.] (⊙Balt., MD)
*PRACTICE AREAS: Bankruptcy Law; Creditors Rights Law; Commercial Law; Debtor and Creditor; Litigation.

Alston & Bird LLP, (AV)
601 Pennsylvania Avenue, N.W., North Building, 10th Floor, 20004-2601 ⊙
Telephone: 202-756-3300 Telecopier: 202-756-3333 Cable Address: AMGRAM GA Telex: 54-2996 (AMG ATL) Easylink: 62985848
URL: http://www.alston.com
Members of Firm: Henry J. Birnkrant; Thomas M. Boyd; David E. Brown, Jr.; Robert T. Cole; Frank M. Conner III; Philip C. Cook; Thomas E. Crocker, Jr.; James E. Croker, Jr.; John L. Douglas (Not admitted in DC); Jonathan M. Fee (Not admitted in DC); Christopher D. Ford (Not admitted in DC); James S. Hutchinson; Frederick M. Joyce; Oscar N. Persons (Not admitted in DC); Thomas G. Schendt (Not admitted in DC); Margaret A. Sheehan; Jonathan H. Talcott; Charles W. Wheeler (Not admitted in DC). Senior Counsel: Brian E. Lebowitz; Edward M. Prince. Counsel: Robert A. Bauman; Mary Ann Capria; David R. Godofsky; Christine McLaughlin; Dwight C. Smith, III; Anne Wallace; Jonathan M. Winer. Associates: Pamela S. Ammermann; Gabrielle D. Bailey; Jennifer L. Butler; James J. Casey; Marianne Casserly; Lesley Ellen Hanchrow (Not admitted in DC); Mark O. Henry; Kathryn Cole Kling; Jay Krutulis (Not admitted in DC); Andrea Lane (Not admitted in DC); Emily W. Mao; William E. Morlan; Thomas P. Newman (Not admitted in DC); Ronald E. Quirk, Jr.; Michael P. Reed; Jason M. Waite (Not admitted in DC).
Administrative Law, Alternative Dispute Resolution, Antitrust and Trade Regulation, Appellate Practice, Bankruptcy, Banks and Banking, Biotechnology, Business Law, Class Actions, Commercial Real Estate, FCC Licensing, FCC Regulation, Wireless Communications, Complex and Multi-District Litigation, Computers and Software, Constitutional Law, Construction Law, Copyrights, Corporate Ethics, Corporate Governance, Corporate Law, Criminal Law, Debtor and Creditor, Electronic Commerce, Emerging Growth Companies, Employee Benefits, Entertainment Law, ERISA, ERISA Litigation, Energy, Environmental Law, Environmental Litigation, Finance, Immigration Law, International Finance, Franchises and Franchising, Health Care Corporate Law, Health Care Regulation, Insurance Defense, Intellectual Property, International Law, International Trade, Internet Law, Labor and Employment, Land Use, Legislative Practice, Life Sciences, Litigation, Medical Malpractice, Mergers, Acquisitions and Divestitures, Multimedia Law, Municipal Law, Nonprofit and Charitable Organizations, Occupational Safety and Health, Partnership Law, Patents, Privacy Law, Products Liability, Professional Liability, Public Finance, Public Policy, Real Estate Finance, Regulatory Law, RICO, Securities, Securities Litigation, Taxation, Tax Litigation, Technology and Science, Trademarks, Trusts and Estates, Utility Law, Venture Capital, White Collar Crime, Zoning.
Atlanta, Georgia Office: One Atlantic Center, 1201 West Peachtree Street 30309-3424. Telephone: 404-881-7000. Telecopier: 404-881-7777.
Charlotte, North Carolina Office: Bank of America Plaza, 101 South Tryon Street, Suite 4000, 28280-4000. Telephone: 704-444-1000. Fax: 704-444-1111.
Raleigh, North Carolina Office (Research Triangle Area): 3201 Beechleaf Court, Suite 600, 27604-1062. Telephone: 919-862-2200. Telecopier: 919-862-2260.
New York, New York Office: 90 Park Avenue, 10016-1387. Telephone: 212-210-9400. Fax: 212-210-9444.
(Liaison Office) Munich, Germany: Brienner Strasse 11/V, 80333 Munich. Telephone: (49) (89) 238-0-70. Telecopier: (49) (89) 238-0-7110.
See Professional Biographies, WASHINGTON, DISTRICT OF COLUMBIA

Alter, Michael J. .... '71 '97 C.867 B.A. L.273 J.D. [🄰 Fried,F.H.S.&J.]
*PRACTICE AREAS: Taxation.
Alter, Scott M. .... '62 '89 C.1365 B.S. L.273 J.D. [Hale&D.]
Alterman, Stephen A., (AV) .... '43 '68 C.103 A.B. L.94 J.D. [Meyers&A.]
Althen, William I., (AV) .... '46 '71 C&L.276 A.B., J.D. [Heenan,A.&R.]
Altherr, Robert F., Jr. '— '80 C.150 B.S.Ch.E. L.117 J.D.
[Banner&W.] (See Pat. Sect.)
*PRACTICE AREAS: Intellectual Property Litigation; Intellectual Property Law; Patents.
Altman, James B., (AV) .... '— '78 C.453 B.S. L.1066 J.D. [Miller&C.]
*PRACTICE AREAS: International Technology and Science; Intellectual Property; Federal Tax Controversies Litigation.
Altman, Jeffrey P. .... '49 '75 C.976 B.A. L.861 J.D. [McKenna&C.]
*PRACTICE AREAS: Trade Associations; Non-Profit Organizations; Technology; Insurance; Business.
Altman, Morris .... '20 '51 C.105 B.A. L.904 LL.B. 4100 Cathedral Ave., N.W.
Altman, Robert A., Law Offices of, (AV) '47 '71
C.966 B.A. L.273 J.D. 901-15th Street, N.W.
Altman, Victor A., (AV) .... '19 '42 C.145 B.A. L.309 LL.B. 1850 M St Nw # 400

Altmann and Vitt, (AV)
1616 H Street, N.W., 20006-4903
Telephone: 202-628-5093 Facsimile: 202-628-5932
Members of Firm: Andrew T. Altmann (1918-1988); A. Francis Vitt, Jr.
Estate Planning, Trust, Probate Small Business Law, Business Succession Planning and Corporation Law. Litigation.
See Professional Biographies, WASHINGTON, DISTRICT OF COLUMBIA

Altmiller, John C., (AV) '36 '71 C.884 B.E.E. L.188 J.D.
[Kenyon&K.] (See Pat. Sect.)
*PRACTICE AREAS: Intellectual Property.
Altongy, Alissa Jennifer .... '72 '97 C&L.692 B.A., J.D. [🄰 Kirkpatrick&L.]
*PRACTICE AREAS: Corporate Law; Securities; Mergers and Acquisitions.
Altschul, Michael F., (AV) '49 '75 C.165 B.A. L.569 J.D.
V.P. & Gen. Coun., Cellular Telecommunication Indus. Assn.
Altschuler, Aaron M. .... '74 '99 C.659 B.A. L.276 J.D. [🄰 Steptoe&J.]
Altschuler, Irwin P., (AV) .... '50 '75 C.273 B.A. L.446 J.D. [Manatt,P.&P.]
Alu, Sheryl Jones .... '53 '81 C.264 B.A. L.245 J.D. [🄲 Elias,M.T.&H.]
Aluise, Timothy J. .... '56 '80 C.276 B.A. L.602 J.D. [Hessel&A.]
Alvaré, Helen Michele '60 '84 C.884 B.S. L.188 J.D.
(adm. in PA; not adm. in DC) U.S. Catholic Conference
Alvarez, Karen D. '47 '85 C.569 B.A. L.276 J.D.
(adm. in PA; not adm. in DC) 1442 Foxhall Rd., N.W.
Alvord, Robert W., (AV) .... '33 '58 C.311 B.A. L.178 LL.B. [Alvord&A.]
*PRACTICE AREAS: Probate; Railroad Equipment Financing.

Alvord and Alvord, (AV)
1600 K Street Suite 200, 20006
Telephone: 202-393-2266 Fax: 202-393-2156
Email: alvordlaw@aol.com
Members of Firm: Elias C. Alvord (1860-1942); Ellsworth C. Alvord (1895-1964); Robert W. Alvord; Edward M. Luria.
Tax, Corporation, Probate Law, Railroad Equipment Financing.
See Professional Biographies, WASHINGTON, DISTRICT OF COLUMBIA

Amann, Amanda Ann .... '74 '99 C.197 B.A L.276 J.D 1440 New York Avenue N.W.
Amatruda, Matthew S. .... '70 '99 C.918 B.A. L.178 J.D. [🄰 Williams&C.]
*PRACTICE AREAS: Litigation.
Ambler, Diane E., (AV) .... '— '78 C.696 B.A. L.884 J.D. [Kirkpatrick&L.]
Ambrose, John P. '45 '71 C.745 B.A. L.1294 J.D.
(adm. in VT; not adm. in DC)
Dir., Legal & Govt. Affs., Amer. Assn. for Marriage & Family
Ambrose, Julie N. .... '71 '97 C.679 B.S. L.1218 J.D. [🄰 Clifford C.R.&W.] (Pat.)
*PRACTICE AREAS: Intellectual Property; Patent Litigation.
Ambrose, Kathleen A. .... '52 '84 C.446 B.A. L.904 J.D. 601 13th St. N.W.
Ambrose, Michael W., Jr. .... '65 '91 C.436 B.A. L.276 J.D. [🄰 Silverberg,G.&B.]
*PRACTICE AREAS: Air Transportation Law; Civil Rights Law; Litigation.
Ambrose, Myles J., (AV) .... '26 '52 C.433 B.B.A. L.564 J.D. [🄲 Arter&H.]
Ambrose, Patricia Riley, (AV) .... '51 '78 C.1031 B.A. L.276 J.D. [Hogan&H.]
*PRACTICE AREAS: Labor and Employment; Equal Employment Opportunity Law; Employment Contracts; Personnel Training; Personnel Policies.

Ambrose, W. Langhorne . . . . '70 '98 C.893 B.S. L.692 J.D. [[A] Ballard S.A.&I.]
*PRACTICE AREAS: Real Estate Finance; Health Care Finance.
Ambrosino, Michael T. '60 '86 C.1033 B.A. L.1019 J.D.
(adm. in NY; not adm. in DC) Asst. U.S. Atty.
Ambrozy, Rel S. . . . . '61 '95 C.896 B.S. L.128 J.D. [[A] Hunton&W.]
*PRACTICE AREAS: Litigation; Licensing; Electronic Commerce.
Amell, Laurie A. . . . . '63 '92 C.276 B.S. L.1209 J.D. [Stein,M.&M.]
*PRACTICE AREAS: Medical Malpractice; Personal Injury; Tort Litigation.
American Center For Law and Justice, The, (AV)
1000 Thomas Jefferson St., N.W. (⊙Mobile, AL; Scottsdale, AZ; New Milford, CT; New Hope, KY; Virginia Beach, VA; Strasbourg, France)

American Legal Center For Estate Planning, The, (AV)
1155 Connecticut Avenue N.W., Suite 400, 20036
Telephone: 202-429-6508 Fax: 202-467-4924
J. Nelson Happy.
Litigation, Corporate Law, Business Law, Mergers and Acquisitions.
See Professional Biographies, WASHINGTON, DISTRICT OF COLUMBIA

Amerine, David R., (AV) . . . . '53 '78 C.434 B.A. L.128 J.D. [Manatt,P.&P.]
Ames, Joanne . . . . '61 '87 C&L.276 B.S.B.A., J.D. 1225 Connecticut Ave NW
Ames, Matthew C. . . . . '59 '87 C.945 B.S. L.276 J.D. [Miller&V.]
*PRACTICE AREAS: Cable Franchising; Communications Law; Local Government Law; Information Technology; Contracts.
Ames, Pamela A. '45 '83 C&L.608 B.S.N., J.D.
(adm. in MO; not adm. in DC) Amer. Nurses Assn.
Ames, Robert G., (AV) '49 '73
C.831 B.B.A. L.273 J.D. [Venable,A.B.H.&C.] (⊙Balt., MD)
*PRACTICE AREAS: Labor Law (Management); Employment Discrimination; Wrongful Discharge; Employee Relations; Personnel Management Law.
Ames, Walter D., (AV) '25 '55
C.645 B.S. L.273 LL.B. 1400 K Street, N.W., 10th Floor (Pat.)
Amini, Bijan, (AV) . . . . '54 '82 C.112 A.B. L.477 J.D. [Storch A.&M.] (⊙New York, NY)
Amis, R. Thomas . . . . '56 '82 C.976 B.A. L.178 J.D. [Baker B.]
Amitay, Sharlene Petry . . . . '67 '95 C.659 B.S.E. L.276 J.D. KPMG Peat Marwick
Ammerman, Harris S., (AV) . . . . '45 '72 C.831 B.S. L.273 J.D. [Ammerman&G.]
*PRACTICE AREAS: Consumer Bankruptcy Law, Including: Chapters 7 and 13 Law; Commercial Bankruptcy; Foreclosure Law; Wage Garnishments; Creditors Rights.

Ammerman & Goldberg, (AV)
1115 Massachusetts Avenue, NW, 20005
Telephone: 202-638-0606 Fax: 202-638-3332
Email: hsaaba@aol.com
Harris S. Ammerman; Joseph M. Goldberg. Associate: Steven M. Assaraf.
Bankruptcy, Chapter 7, Chapter 13, Consumer Bankruptcy, Personal Bankruptcy, Consumer Rights, Foreclosure Law, Debtors Rights, Creditors Rights, Wage Garnishments, Car Repossessions.
See Professional Biographies, WASHINGTON, DISTRICT OF COLUMBIA

Ammermann, Pamela S. . . . . '69 '95 C.438 B.A. L.30 J.D. [[A] Alston&B.]
*PRACTICE AREAS: International Taxation; Federal Income Tax.
Ammons, Scott A. '69 '97 C.20 L.477 J.D.
(adm. in PA; not adm. in DC) 1025 Thomas Jefferson St. NW
Amodeo, John A. . . . . '52 '77 C&L.705 B.A., J.D. [[C] Skadden,A.S.M.&F.]
Amolsch, Regina B. . . . . '— '96 C.472 B.A. L.245 J.D. [[A] Piper M.R.&W.]
*PRACTICE AREAS: Franchise Law; Distribution.

Amolsch, Christopher B.
(See Alexandria)

Amorosi, Mark C. . . . . '68 '94 C.93 B.A. L.128 J.D. [[A] Kirkpatrick&L.]
*PRACTICE AREAS: Investment Management.
Amram & Hahn, P.C., (AV) .815 Connecticut Avenue, N.W., 6th Floor
Amron, Cory M., (AV) . . . '53 '77 C.696 B.A. L.309 J.D. [Vorys,S.S.&P.] (See Pat. Sect.)
*PRACTICE AREAS: Real Estate; Commercial Law; Trademark Law; Copyright Law; Licensing.
Amsellem, Jala Arlene . . . . '61 '86 C.569 L.1357 J.D. Harvard Law School
Amundson, Corey . . . . '— '98 C.347 B.A. L.1365 J.D. [[A] King&S.]
*PRACTICE AREAS: Government Investigations.
Amundson, Jan S. '46 '71 C.546 B.A. L.793 J.D.
V.P. & Gen. Coun., National Assn. of Manufacturers
Amuso, John Paul . . . . '72 '99 C.299 B.A. L.982 J.D. Legis. Coun.
An, Mildred H. '62 '93 C&L.309 A.B., J.D.
(adm. in NY; not adm. in DC) 1201 Penn. Ave., N.W.‡
Anand, Nalini P. . . . . '69 '96 C.188 B.A. L.813 J.D. [[A] Hogan&H.]
Anastasio, Julia '72 '99 C.264 B.A. L.30 J.D.
(adm. in PA; not adm. in DC) Dept. of Com., Off. of Gen. Coun.
Anawaty, William A., Jr. . . . . '45 '72 C.976 B.A. L.846 J.D. 1 St. Matthews Ct. NW

Andalman & Flynn, P.C.
(See Silver Spring, Maryland)

Anderberg, Karen L. . . . . '64 '92 C.165 B.A. L.94 J.D. [Dechert]
*PRACTICE AREAS: Investment Management; Financial Services Law.
Anders, Wolfram . . . . '59 '86 L.057 J.D. Princ. Invest. Offr., International Fin. Corp.
Andersen, Hans Ulfson . . . .'53 '87 L.999 J.D. [[C] Spirer&G.]
*PRACTICE AREAS: International Commercial Law.
Andersen, J. Carter . . . . '69 '98 C&L.260 B.S., J.D. [[A] Jones,D.R.&P.]

Anderson, Allan W., Jr., (AV) '46 '74 C.446 B.A. L.273 J.D.
4812 W Street, N.W., 20007
Telephone: 202-298-6910 Fax: 202-298-6914
Email: ALLANDER@EROLS.COM
Administrative Law, Energy Law, Electric Power, Hydroelectricity, Public Utilities, Oil and Gas, Pipeline Law.
See Professional Biographies, WASHINGTON, DISTRICT OF COLUMBIA

Anderson, Andrea . . . . '66 '97 C.893 B.A. L.273 J.D. [[A] Finnegan,H.F.G.&D.]
*PRACTICE AREAS: International Trademarks; Trademark Litigation; Trademark Prosecution; Trademark Infringement; Trademark Protection.
Anderson, Anthony A. . . . . '54 '79 C.367 B.A. L.893 J.D. [Thompson C.]
*PRACTICE AREAS: Mass Transit Federal Compliance; Americans with Disabilities Act; Administrative Law.
Anderson, Audrey J. . . . . '63 '90 C.597 B.S. L.477 J.D. [Hogan&H.]
*PRACTICE AREAS: Education Litigation; Appellate Litigation; Supreme Court Litigation; Litigation.
Anderson, Brian C. . . . . '59 '86 C.112 B.A. L.813 J.D. [O'Melveny&M.]
*PRACTICE AREAS: Litigation; Class Action Litigation.
Anderson, Byron E. '54 '84
C.665 B.A. L.1234 J.D. Sr. VP Govt. Affs., Amer. Gen. Corp.
Anderson, Carrie M. . . . . '72 '97 C.472 B.A. L.276 J.D. [[A] Clifford C.R.&W.]
*PRACTICE AREAS: Antitrust and Trade Regulation; Litigation.
Anderson, Chad C. '75 '00 C.576 B.S.E. L.692 J.D.
(adm. in VA; not adm. in DC; See Pat. Sect.) [[A] Venable,A.B.H.&C.]
*PRACTICE AREAS: Patent Prosecution; Intellectual Property Litigation.
Anderson, Darryl J. . . . . '44 '70 C&L.477 B.B.A., J.D. [O'Donnell,S.&A.]
Anderson, David L. '48 '73
C.445 B.S. L.446 J.D. 1919 Pennsylvania Ave., N.W., Suite 800
Anderson, David Sabin . . . . '64 '96 C.150 B.M. L.801 J.D. 600 14th St.

Anderson, Elizabeth B. '65 '91 C.228 B.A. L.904 J.D. 113 4th St., N.E.
Anderson, Elizabeth Hart '53 '80 C.518 A.B. L.262 J.D.
(adm. in VA; not adm. in DC) National Assn. of Sec. Dealers, Inc.
Anderson, Fiona Huang . . . . '71 '98 C.1375 B.A. L.309 J.D. [[A] Wilmer,C.&P.]
Anderson, Frank H. '44 '98 C.309 B.A. L.904 J.D.
(adm. in MD; not adm. in DC) Physician (Neurology)‡
Anderson, Frederick R., (AV) . . . . .'41 '69 C.575 B.A. L.309 LL.B. [Cadwalader,W.&T.]
*PRACTICE AREAS: Environmental Law; Natural Resources; Administrative Law; Government; Technology and Science.
Anderson, Gary D. . . . .'68 '97 C&L.602 B.B.A., J.D. [[A] Kirkland&E.]
*PRACTICE AREAS: Commercial Litigation; Trademarks.
Anderson, Heather H. . . . . '67 '95 C.976 B.A. L.893 J.D. [[A] Shea&G.]
Anderson, Howard T. . . . . '46 '71 C.197 A.B. L.309 J.D. [Stier,A.&M.]
*PRACTICE AREAS: Complex Litigation; Corporate Compliance; Civil RICO; Internal Corporate Investigations.
Anderson, James E., (AV) . . . . '42 '67 C.755 B.A. L.352 J.D. [Howe,A.&S.]
*PRACTICE AREAS: Antitrust Law; Trade Regulation Law; Association Law; Civil and Criminal Litigation.
Anderson, James E. . . . . '65 '92 C.878 B.A. L.101 J.D. [Wilmer,C.&P.]
*PRACTICE AREAS: Investment Management; Securities.
Anderson, Juan M. . . . . '67 '96 C.1280 B.A. L.180 J.D. [[A] Carr G.]
Anderson, Keith R. . . . . '57 '82 C.210 B.A. L.273 J.D. [Akin,G.S.H.&F.]
*PRACTICE AREAS: Health Care Law; Corporate Transactions; Corporate Law.
Anderson, Kenneth C. . . . .'36 '62 C.282 B.A. L.188 LL.B. [Anderson&G.]
Anderson, Kim Anglin '69 '96 C.945 B.A. L.273 J.D.
(adm. in VA; not adm. in DC) Lobbyist, National Education Assoc.‡
Anderson, L. Sue . . . . '— '81 C.747 B.A. L.1162 J.D. [[C] Emord&Assoc.]
Anderson, Lisa N. . . . . '— '99 C.674 A.B. L.276 J.D. 701 Pennsylvania Avenue, N.W.
Anderson, Lynne D. '— '94 C.831 B.S.E.E. L.1338 J.D.
(adm. in PA; not adm. in DC) [[A] Gardner,C.&D.]
*PRACTICE AREAS: Intellectual Property.
Anderson, M. Jean, (AV) . . . . '43 '75 C.597 B.A. L.276 J.D. [Weil,G.&M.]
*PRACTICE AREAS: International Trade Policy; Litigation; International Trade Negotiations; GATT; NAFTA.
Anderson, Merry C. . . . . '62 '88 C.309 A.B. L.813 J.D. [[C] Hogan&H.]
*PRACTICE AREAS: Banking Law; Mergers and Acquisitions; Corporate Law; Securities Law.
Anderson, Michael J. . . . . '58 '84 C.623 B.A. L.276 J.D. [Monteau,P.&C.]
*PRACTICE AREAS: Federal Indian Law; Contracts; Tribal Government; Gaming Law; Land Acquisitions.
Anderson, Nancy J. '67 '92 C.623 B.A. L.893 J.D.
(adm. in VA; not adm. in DC) Atty., Lawyers Comm. for Civil Rights Under Law
*RESPONSIBILITIES: Pro Bono Coordinator.
Anderson, Pamela J. . . . . '60 '90 C.173 B.S. L.208 J.D. [Van Ness F.]
*PRACTICE AREAS: Natural Gas Regulation; Taxation; Government Contracts.
Anderson, Phillip R. . . . . '68 '97 C.375 B.S. L.378 J.D. [[A] Shook,H.&B.]
Anderson, R. Jerome '49 '79 C.665 B.A. L.229 J.D.
(adm. in PA; not adm. in DC) Tech. Serv.(s) Grp., Chemonics Int'l, Inc.
Anderson, Reyn C. . . . .'70 '00 C.260 B.A. L.569 J.D. [[A] Cleary,G.S.&H.]
Anderson, Scott '67 '95 C.692 B.A. L.838 J.D.
(adm. in VA; not adm. in DC) The Nasdaq Stock Market, Inc.
Anderson, Stanton D., (AV) . . . .'40 '69 C.1239 B.A. L.950 J.D. [McDermott,W.&E.]
Anderson, Stephen S. (Todd), Jr. . . . . '69 '98 C.865 B.A. L.309 J.D. [[A] Patton B.]
Anderson, Thomas E. . . . .'62 '96 C.1213 B.S.E.E. L.776 J.D. [[C] Hunton&W.] (Pat.)
*PRACTICE AREAS: Patents; Trademarks; Copyrights; Electronic Commerce; Intellectual Property Licensing.
Anderson, Vicki Renee '63 '00 C.329 B.A. L.446 J.D.
(adm. in MD; not adm. in DC) 1200 Pennsylvania Ave.
Anderson, William A., II, (AV) . . . . '47 '74 C.575 A.B. L.309 J.D. [Winston&S.]
*PRACTICE AREAS: Environmental.
Anderson, William L. . . . .'53 '88 C.315 B.A. L.494 J.D. [Crowell&M.]
Anderson, Worth S. . . . .'70 '96 C.878 B.A. L.178 J.D. [[A] Skadden,A.S.M.&F.]

Anderson, Coe & King, L.L.P.
(See Baltimore, Maryland)

Anderson & Gingold . . . . 1201 Pennsylvania Avenue, N.W., Suite 821

Anderson Kill & Olick, L.L.P., (AV) BR
1275 K Street, N.W. Suite 1101, 20005 ⊙
Telephone: 202-218-0040 Fax: 202-962-3966
Email: akodc@andersonkill.com URL: http://www.andersonkill.com
Michele A. Gallagher; Daniel J. Healy (Not admitted in DC); Rhonda D. Orin.
General Practice including Litigation, Insurance, Environmental, Employment and Labor, Products Liability, Trademark, Unfair Competition and Intellectual Property.
New York, N.Y. Office: Anderson Kill & Olick, P.C., 1251 Avenue of the Americas. Telephone: 212-278-1000. Fax: 212-278-1733
Philadelphia, Pennsylvania Office: Anderson Kill & Olick, P.C., 1600 Market Street. Telephone: 215-568-4202. Fax: 215-568-4573.
Newark, New Jersey Office: Anderson Kill & Olick, P.C. One Gateway Center, Suite 901. Telephone: 973-642-5858. Fax: 973-621-6361.
Chicago, Illinois Office: Anderson Kill & Olick, 190 South La Salle Street, Suite 800. Telephone: 312-857-2500. Fax: 312-857-0122.
See Professional Biographies, WASHINGTON, DISTRICT OF COLUMBIA

Anderson & Quinn, LLC
(See Rockville, Maryland)

Andes, Phyllis E. . . . .'61 '93 C.1350 B.A. L.273 J.D. [[A] Fenwick&W.]
*PRACTICE AREAS: Corporate Trade; International Trade.
Andrade, Judith M. . . . . '73 '98 C.728 B.A. L.1360 J.D. [[A] Cameron M.]
*PRACTICE AREAS: Energy Utility Regulation; Gas Utility Regulation; Public Utility Rates.
Andreano, Richard J., Jr. . . . .'58 '83 C.1044 B.A. L.273 J.D. [Weiner B.S.K.]
*PRACTICE AREAS: Mortgage Banking; Financial Institutions; Consumer Credit; Regulatory Compliance; Mergers and Acquisitions.
Andreason, Cynthia T. . . . .'53 '84 C.174 B.Mus. L.878 J.D. [LeBoeuf,L.G.&M.]
*PRACTICE AREAS: Insurance; Litigation.
Andrew, Anne Slaughter, (AV) . . . .'55 '83 C.276 B.A. L.345 J.D. [Patton B.]
Andrew, John H. '36 '61 C.494 B.A. L.597 J.D.
(adm. in IL; not adm. in DC) J.C. Penney Co., Inc.
Andrew, Joseph J., (AV) '60 '85 C&L.976 B.A., J.D.
(adm. in IN; not adm. in DC) [Cadwalader,W.&T.] (⊙New York, NY)
*PRACTICE AREAS: Corporate; Government Affairs; Intellectual Property Law.
Andrews, Charles S. '39 '70 C.31 B.A. L.1294 J.D.
(adm. in ME; not adm. in DC) Mgr., Fed. Rels., AAA
Andrews, Elizabeth A. '60 '87 C&L.260 B.S., J.D.
(adm. in VA; not adm. in DC) V.P., Intl. Tax Plnng., Marriott Intl., Inc.
*RESPONSIBILITIES: Taxation-Domestic; Taxation-International.
Andrews, Kathleen I. . . . . '64 '89 C&L.1209 B.S., J.D. [Pascal&W.]
*PRACTICE AREAS: Labor; Lobbying; Bankruptcy; Alcoholic Beverage Control; Commercial Litigation.
Andrews, Kelli A. . . . .'70 '95 C.105 B.A. L.188 J.D. [[A] Verner,L.B.M.&H.]
*PRACTICE AREAS: White Collar Crime; Litigation; Criminal Law.
Andrews, Mark J., (AV) . . . . '— '70 C&L.309 A.B., J.D. [Strasburger&P.]
*PRACTICE AREAS: Cargo Claims; International Transportation Law; Logistics; Maritime Regulation; Motor Carrier Regulation.
Andrews, Mary E. '58 '92 C.923 B.A. L.902 J.D.
(adm. in MD; not adm. in DC) [[A] Hessel&A.]

Andrews, Michael A., (AV) . . . . '44 '71 C.846 B.A. L.802 J.D. [Vinson&E.]
*PRACTICE AREAS: Public Policy.
Andrews, Milton D. . . . . '37 '63 C.663 B.S. L.623 J.D. [Ⓒ Thompson C.]
*PRACTICE AREAS: International Trade; Business Law; Immigration Law.
Andrews, Paul J. '16 '42 C.31 A.B. L.1017 LL.B.
(adm. in PA; not adm. in DC) Asst. Gen. Coun., Dept. of Transp.
Andrews, Stephen D. . . . . '73 '00 C.309 A.B. L.145 J.D. [Ⓐ Williams&C.]
Andrews, William S. . . . . '49 '78 C.390 A.B. L.893 J.D. [Nixon P.] (⊙New York, NY)
*PRACTICE AREAS: Energy Finance; Project Finance.
Andrews, Wright H., Jr., (AV) . . . . '47 '74 C.1365 B.A. L.245 J.D. [Butera&A.]
*PRACTICE AREAS: Federal Legislation; Banking Law; Mortgages; Environmental Law; Nuclear Energy.

Andrews & Kurth L.L.P., (AV) BR
A Registered Limited Liability Partnership
Suite 300, 1701 Pennsylvania Avenue, N.W., 20006 ⊙
Telephone: 202-662-2700 Telecopier: 202-662-2739
Email: webmaster@akllp.com URL: http://www.akllp.com
Members of Firm: Michael J. Fremuth; Richard C. Green; Anthony J. Ivancovich; Thomas R. Kline; Shemin V. Proctor; Mark F. Sundback; Bruce A. Templeton; Kenneth L. Wiseman. Of Counsel: Scott A. Richie; Douglas V. Rigler; Thomas E. Starnes; Craig B. Young. Associates: Christopher Cobb (Not admitted in DC); Charles M. Crout; Marvin W. Ehrlich; Elaine L. Farris (Not admitted in DC); L. Eden Rood (Not admitted in DC); David S. Shaffer; Peter J. Thompson. Senior Attorney: Johanna S. Coulter (Not admitted in DC).
Administrative Law, Alternative Dispute Resolution, Antitrust and Trade Regulation, Appellate Practice, Banking Law, Bankruptcy, Business Law, Commercial Law, Construction Law, Contracts, Corporate Law, Debtor and Creditor, Education Law, Eminent Domain, Employee Benefits, Energy, Entertainment and Sports, Environmental Law, Finance, Government, Government Contracts, Health Care, Insurance, Intellectual Property International Law, International Trade, Investments, Labor and Employment, Leases and Leasing, Litigation, Mergers and Acquisitions, Natural Resources, Occupational Safety and Health, Patents, Products Liability, Professional Liability, Project Finance, Public Finance, Real Estate, Securities, Taxation, Technology and Science, Torts, Toxic Torts, Transportation, Trusts and Estates, Utility Law, White Collar Crime, Wills and Probates, Zoning, Planning and Land Use.
Houston, Texas Office: Suite 4200, 600 Travis, 77002. Telephone: 713-220-4200. Telecopier: 713-220-4285. E-Mail: webmaster@andrews-kurth.com.
Other Houston, Texas Office: 700 Louisiana, Suite 1900. Telephone: 713-225-7000. Fax: 713-225-7047.
Dallas, Texas Office: 1717 Main Street, Suite 3700. Telephone: 214-659-4400. Telecopier: 214-659-4401.
The Woodlands, Texas Office: Waterway Plaza Two, Suite 200, 10001 Woodloch Forest Drive, 77380. Telephone: 713-220-4801. Telecopier: 713-220-4815.
Austin, Texas Office: 9020 I Capital of Texas Highway, Suite 250, 78759. Telephone: 512-340-1360. Fax: 214-659-4401.
Other Austin, Texas Office: 111 Congress Avenue, Suite 1700. Telephone: 512-320-9200. Fax: 512-320-9292.
Los Angeles, California Office: Suite 1725, 601 South Figueroa Street. Telephone: 213-896-3100. Telecopier: 213-896-3137.
New York, N.Y. Office: 805 Third Avenue, 10022. Telephone: 212-850-2800. Telecopier: 212-850-2929.
London, England Office: Level 16 City Tower, 40 Basinghall Street, EC2V 5DE. Telephone: 011-20-7382-0550. Telecopier: 011-44-20-7614-0012.
See Professional Biographies, WASHINGTON, DISTRICT OF COLUMBIA

Andries, Edward M. . . . . '67 '96 C.477 B.B.A. L.273 J.D. [Ⓐ Pepper H.]
*PRACTICE AREAS: Commercial Litigation.
Andril, David T., (AV) . . . . '56 '80 C.276 B.S. L.893 J.D. [Vinson&E.]
*PRACTICE AREAS: Energy; Federal Energy Regulation; Contracts; Natural Gas Regulation; International Business Transactions.
Andrus, Katherine Boonin '60 '93 C.881 A.B. L.893 J.D.
Asst. Gen. Coun., Air Transport Assoc. of America
*RESPONSIBILITIES: Aviation; Administrative Law; Environmental Law.
Anenberg, Scott A., (P.C.), (AV) . . . . '53 '78 C.910 B.A. L.273 J.D. [Shaw P.]
*PRACTICE AREAS: Banking; International Transactions; Corporate Law.
Angeli, David H. . . . . '67 '97 C.94 B.S. L.276 J.D. [Ⓐ Williams&C.]
*PRACTICE AREAS: Criminal Litigation; Civil Litigation.
Angelis, Carl V. . . . . '48 '81 C.754 B.A. L.276 J.D. 1217 S. St., N.W.
Angelo, Amy M. . . . . '— '99 C.282 B.A. L.30 J.D. [Ⓐ King&S.]
*PRACTICE AREAS: Corporate.
Angelone, James J. . . . . '47 '74 C&L.705 B.A., J.D. Riggs Invest. Mgmt. Corp.
Anger, Scott P. '44 '71 C.966 B.S. L.436 J.D.
(adm. in WI; not adm. in DC) Coastal Corp.
Angert, Michael I. . . . . . '61 '99 C.645 B.S.E.E. L.64 J.D. [Ⓐ Kenyon&K.] (See Pat. Sect.)
*PRACTICE AREAS: Intellectual Property.
Angle, Connie M. . . . . '70 '00 C.1044 B.A. L.1187 J.D. Tax Mgr., Deloitte & Touche
Angle, Stephen, (AV) . . . . '49 '75 C.840 B.A. L.846 J.D. [Vinson&E.]
*PRACTICE AREAS: Electric Industry Restructuring; Public Utility Regulation; Hydroelectricity.
Angstreich, Scott H. . . . . '71 '99 C.674 A.B. L.309 J.D. [Ⓐ Kellogg,H.H.T.&E.]
*PRACTICE AREAS: Telecommunications.
Angulo, Carlos T. . . . . '64 '90 C.311 B.A. L.976 J.D. [Ⓐ Zuckerman S.]
*PRACTICE AREAS: Litigation; Legislative Practice.
Angus, Heather '70 '97
C.886 B.A. L.1364 J.D. Asst. Coun., American National Red Cross
*RESPONSIBILITIES: Labor and Employment; Contracts.
Angus, Kristen '71 '00 C.623 B.B.A. L.208 J.D.
(adm. in CO; not adm. in DC) [Ⓐ Coudert B.]
*PRACTICE AREAS: International Trade.
Anhang, George E. . . . . '63 '93 C.976 B.A. L.309 J.D. 1875 Connecticut Avenue, N.W.
Anikeeff, Anthony H. . . . . '52 '80 C.893 B.A. L.945 J.D. [Bracewell&P.]
*PRACTICE AREAS: Government Contracts; Commercial Litigation; International Trade.
Anillo, Alvaro I. . . . . '67 '92 C.228 B.A. L.880 J.D. [Ⓒ Groom]
Anker, Jerry D., (AV) . . . . '34 '58 C&L.309 A.B., J.D. Air Line Pilots Assn.
Anker, Philip D., (AV) . . . . '57 '83 C.659 B.A. L.273 J.D. [Wilmer,C.&P.]
*PRACTICE AREAS: Bankruptcy; Bankruptcy Litigation; Civil Practice.
Anklam, James E. . . . . '59 '87 C.893 B.A. L.188 J.D. [Ⓐ Jones,D.R.&P.]
Annand, Stephen Darley, (BV) '48 '72 C.923 B.S. L.902 J.D.
(adm. in VA; not adm. in DC) [Cohen,M.H.&T.]
*PRACTICE AREAS: Civil Litigation; Health Care Litigation.

Annis, Kenneth J., (AV) '43 '73 C.309 A.B. L.276 LL.B.
1100 Connecticut Avenue, N.W. Suite 800, 20036
Telephone: 202-785-2244 Fax: 202-785-2051
Email: kajannis@erols.com URL: http://www.lawyers.com/kennethannis
Civil, Administrative and Criminal Practice before all Courts, Agencies, Departments and Commissions with special emphasis on Plaintiff Trial Practice, Personal Injury, Automobile, Torts, Product Liability and Medical Negligence.
See Professional Biographies, WASHINGTON, DISTRICT OF COLUMBIA

Anolieh, Simon B. '65 '92 C.597 B.S.E.E. L.978 J.D.
(adm. in NY; not adm. in DC) 1100 New York Ave., N.W., 9th Fl., E. Twr.
Anolik, Stuart H. '59 '84 C.1138 B.B.A. L.1048 J.D.
(adm. in MD; not adm. in DC) 2000 M St Nw # 700
Anomnachi, Gordy N. . . . . '57 '92 L.999 LL.B. Asst. Corp. Coun.
Ansary, Cyrus A. . . . . '33 '59 C.30 B.S. L.178 LL.B. Pres., Investment Servs. Intl. Co.
Ansbacher, Richard I. . . . . '58 '84 C&L.260 B.S., J.D. [Fried,F.H.S.&J.]
*PRACTICE AREAS: Corporate Law.
Ansell, David L. . . . . '54 '79 C.659 B.S. L.831 J.D. [Fried,F.H.S.&J.]
Anstett, Michael J. . . . . '73 '00 C.670 B.A. L.228 J.D. [Ⓐ Fried,F.H.S.&J.]

Anthes, Gregory C. . . . . '61 '90 C.960 B.S. L.273 J.D. [Adduci,M.&S.]
*PRACTICE AREAS: Antidumping; Appellate Practice; International Trade Regulation; Customs.
Anthony, Beryl F., Jr., (AV) '38 '63 C&L.45 B.S.B.A., J.D.
(adm. in AR; not adm. in DC) [Ⓒ Winston&S.]
*PRACTICE AREAS: Legislative Law.
Anthony, David V., (AV) . . . . '29 '56 C.884 B.A. L.276 J.D. 1200 19th St. NW
Anthony, Demitrius M. '66 '00 C.577 B.A. L.329 J.D.
(adm. in NC; not adm. in DC) [Ⓐ Baker B.]
Anthony, Jason M. . . . . '70 '00 C.446 B.A. L.276 J.D. [Ⓐ Gibson,D.&C.]
Anthony, Kevin R. '59 '98 C.1278 B.P.S. L.472 J.D.
(adm. in FL; not adm. in DC) [Ⓐ Boies,S.&F.]
*PRACTICE AREAS: Complex Commercial Litigation; Antitrust Litigation; Intellectual Property Litigation; Employment Litigation.
Anthony, Stephen P. . . . . '61 '89 C.197 A.B. L.178 J.D. [Ⓒ Covington&B.]
Anthony, Willard S. "Kwame", II '71 '96 C&L.329 B.A., J.D.
[Ⓐ Firm of Larson-Jackson]
Antley, Bruce S. . . . . '67 '99 C.651 B.A. L.893 J.D. [Ⓐ Dow,L.&A.]
Antley, Corinne M. . . . . '55 '81 C.651 B.A. L.893 J.D. [Dow,L.&A.]
Antone, Thomas M., IV, (AV) . . . . '47 '75 C.576 B.A. L.273 J.D. [Mintz,L.C.F.G.&P.]
*PRACTICE AREAS: Health Law; Legislation.

Antonelli, Terry, Stout & Kraus, LLP
(See Arlington, Virginia)

Antonetti, Marc A. . . . . '66 '91 C.602 B.A. L.569 J.D. [Baker&H.]
*PRACTICE AREAS: Labor and Employment Law; Workers Compensation Law.
Antonides, Brett L. . . . . '54 '80 C.674 B.S.E. L.884 J.D. [Ⓒ McManus,S.A.&D.]
*PRACTICE AREAS: Business Planning; Commercial Litigation; Government Contracts; Intellectual Property Law; Technology Licensing.
Antonipillai, Justin S. . . . . '72 '98 C.188 B.A. L.904 J.D. [Ⓐ Arnold&P.]
*PRACTICE AREAS: Litigation; Products Liability; Corporate Law; Securities; Bankruptcy.
Antonucci, Thomas W. . . . . '72 '99 C.1265 B.B.A. L.245 J.D. [Ⓐ Wiley R.&F.]
Antton, D. Lee . . . . '59 '86 C.966 B.S. L.276 J.D. [O'Connor&H.] (Pat.)
*PRACTICE AREAS: Patents; Trademarks; Copyrights.
Anwah, Christopher . . . . '— '97 C.481 B.S. L.1364 J.D. [Ⓐ J.O.Iweanoge]
Anwyll, J. Bradford, (AV) . . . . '57 '82 C.367 B.A. L.228 J.D. [McKee N.]
*PRACTICE AREAS: Tax Litigation.
Anzaldi, Matthew A. . . . . '71 '96 C.228 A.B. L.880 J.D. [Ⓐ Shaw P.]
Anzaldúa-Montoya, Ricardo A. '53 '90
C.103 A.B. L.309 J.D. 2000 Pennsylvania Avenue, N.W.
Anzalone, Steven M., (BV) '57 '84
C.674 B.S.E. L.575 J.D. [Finnegan,H.F.G.&D.] (See Pat. Sect.)
*PRACTICE AREAS: Patent Infringement.
Aparisi, Jaime W. . . . . '67 '94 C.446 B.A. L.128 J.D. 3206 Grace St., N.W.
Apatoff, David B., (AV) . . . . '52 '77 C.771 B.A. L.145 J.D. [Arnold&P.]
*PRACTICE AREAS: Intellectual Property; Government Contracts; Administrative.
Appel, Richard N. . . . . '52 '76 C.575 B.A. L.128 J.D. [Akin,G.S.H.&F.]
*PRACTICE AREAS: Labor and Employment.
Appelbaum, Craig . . . . '70 '98 C.164 B.A. L.659 J.D. [Ⓐ Crowell&M.]
Apple, James G. '37 '62 C&L.893 B.A., J.D.
(adm. in VA; not adm. in DC) Pres. Intl. Jud. Academy
Applebaum, David . . . . '74 '01 C.659 B.A. L.880 J.D. [Ⓐ O'Melveny&M.]
Applebaum, Harvey M., (AV) . . . . '37 '62 C.976 B.A. L.309 LL.B. [Covington&B.]
Applebaum, Jill R. . . . . '67 '94 3811 39th St., N.W.
Applegarth, Paul V. . . . . '46 '74 C.976 B.A. L.309 J.D. The World Bk.
Apps, Antonia M. . . . . '69 '95 L.999 LL.B. [Kellogg,H.H.T.&E.]
*PRACTICE AREAS: Litigation; Telecommunications.
Aptaker, Edward, (AV) . . . . '22 '48 C&L.309 B.A., LL.B. [Ⓒ Schmeltzer,A.&S.]
*PRACTICE AREAS: Maritime Law; Administrative Law; Equipment Financing Law.
Aqua, Jocelyn A. . . . . '68 '95 C.645 B.A. L.273 J.D. [Ⓐ White&C.]
Aquino, John Thomas . . . . '49 '95 C&L.128 B.A., J.D. 1155 Conn. Ave., N.W.
Aquino, Monica A. . . . . '74 '99 C&L.472 B.A., J.D. [Ⓐ McKenna&C.]
*PRACTICE AREAS: Civil Litigation; Appellate Practice.
Aragon, Ray M. . . . . '59 '86 C.446 B.A. L.976 J.D. [McKenna&C.]
*PRACTICE AREAS: Business Litigation; Products Liability; Insurance Coverage.
Arata, John W., (AV) . . . . '40 '70 C.103 B.A. L.94 J.D. 3029 Dent Pl., N.W.
Araujo, Jaeleen Kookesh . . . . '73 '98 C.813 B.A. L.560 J.D. [Ⓐ Van Ness F.]
*PRACTICE AREAS: Federal Indian Law; Alaska Native Law; Legislative Practice.
Arbuckle, J. Gordon, (AV) . . . . '42 '68 C.446 B.A. L.273 LL.B. [Patton B.]
Arcadipane, Angelo V., (AV) . . . . '41 '69 C.693 B.S. L.276 J.D. [Dickstein S.M.&O.]
*PRACTICE AREAS: ERISA; Labor Law; Litigation.
Arcari, Michelle A. '73 '99
C.890 B.A. L.128 J.D. 900 Seventeenth Street, N.W., Suite 900
Arch, Rebekah R. '59 '96 C.331 B.S.N. L.128 J.D.
(adm. in VA; not adm. in DC) [Ⓐ Ashcraft&G.]
*PRACTICE AREAS: Pharmacy Law; Diet Drug Litigation.
Archibald, James K., (AV) '49 '75
C.367 B.A. L.446 J.D. [Venable,A.B.H.&C.] (⊙Balt., MD)
*PRACTICE AREAS: Civil Practice and Litigation; Products Liability Law; Professional Malpractice Law.
Archibald, Jeanne S., (AV) . . . . '51 '77 C.1350 B.A. L.276 J.D. [Hogan&H.]
*PRACTICE AREAS: International Trade Law; Financial Institution Regulation.
Archie, Jennifer C. . . . . '— '89 C.732 B.A. L.188 J.D. [Latham&W.]
*PRACTICE AREAS: Commercial Litigation; Internet Law; Health Care; Government Contract Fraud; Insurance Coverage.
Ard, Joel B. . . . . '73 '00 C.722 B.A. L.145 J.D. [Ⓐ Latham&W.]
*PRACTICE AREAS: Litigation.
Ardale, Erin K. '75 '01 C.611 B.A. L.188 J.D.
(adm. in NY; not adm. in DC) [Ⓐ Kirkpatrick&L.]
*PRACTICE AREAS: Securities Enforcement; Civil Litigation.
Ardia, David S. . . . . '66 '97 C.158 B.S. L.823 J.D. [Ⓐ Williams&C.]
*PRACTICE AREAS: Constitutional Law; Criminal Law; Environmental Law; Intellectual Property Litigation; Defamation.
Areen, Judith C. '44 '71 C.188 A.B. L.976 J.D.
(adm. in MA; not adm. in DC) Georgetown Univ. Law Center
Arend, Thomas E., Jr. . . . . '63 '94 C.385 B.A. L.904 J.D. [Ⓐ Shaw P.]
Arenson, Elizabeth '73 '00 C.228 A.B. L.30 J.D.
(adm. in CA; not adm. in DC) [Ⓐ Dickstein S.M.&O.]
*PRACTICE AREAS: Civil Litigation.
Arenson, Ethan . . . . '75 '00 C.30 B.A. L.273 J.D. [Ⓐ Holland&K.]
*PRACTICE AREAS: Commercial Litigation.
Arent, Albert E., (AV) . . . . '11 '35 C&L.188 B.A., LL.B. [Arent F.K.P.&K.] ‡

Arent Fox Kintner Plotkin & Kahn, PLLC, (AV) BR
1050 Connecticut Avenue, N.W., 20036-5339 ⊙
Telephone: 202-857-6000 Fax: 202-857-6395
URL: http://www.arentfox.com
Founding Members of Firm: Albert E. Arent (Retired); Henry J. Fox (1911-1990); Earl W. Kintner (1912-1992); Harry M. Plotkin (1913-1998); Edwin L. Kahn (Retired). Members of Firm: Stanley H. Abramson; Jerome P. Akman; Mark E. Alberta; William C. Basil; Richard L. Brand; Timothy F. Brown; Douglas R. Bush; Ronald L. Castle; William R. Charyk; Matthew J. Clark; Ronald H. Clark; Elizabeth H. Cohen; Earl M. Colson; John C. Culver; David T. Dekker; Kendra L. Dimond; D. Jeffrey Disbrow; Mary Joanne Dowd; Mark S. Dreux, Sr.; Alan S. Dubin; David L. Dubrow (Not admitted in DC); Michael M. Eaton; Harold J. Engel; Alan Gregg Fishel; Marc L. Fleischaker; Carol Connor

(This Listing Continued)

Arent Fox Kintner Plotkin & Kahn, PLLC (Continued)

Flowe; Stephen B. Forman; Jeremy B. Fox; Joseph M. Fries; Richard N. Gale; Sean W. Glynn; Douglas H. Goldhush; William W. Goodrich; Michael A. Gordon; Hervé Gouraige (Resident, New York, N.Y. Office); Jefferson M. Gray; Michael A. Grow; David C. Gryce; David C. Haas; James B. Halpern; Dennis J. Henderson (Not admitted in DC; Resident, New York, N.Y. Office); Lawrence F. Henneberger; Robert Charles Hill; Robert B. Hirsch; Robert H. Huey; James H. Hulme; Kenneth S. Jacob; Michael Evan Jaffe; Bryan W. Jardine (Resident, Bucharest, Romania Office); Quana C. Jew; Jeffrey E. Jordan; Stephen D. Kahn; Mark M. Katz; Bradley A. Kaufman (Resident, New York, N.Y. Office); Susan V. Kayser (Resident, New York, N.Y. Office); David L. Kelleher; Steven Kimelman (Resident, New York, N.Y. Office); Craig S. King; Sheldon H. Klein; Arlene Fine Klepper (Retired); Paul A. Koches; Richard J. Krainin (Resident, New York, N.Y. Office); George R. Kucik; Michael J. Kurman; Michael H. Leahy; Bernice K. Leber (Resident, New York, N.Y. Office); Gerard Leval; Lawrence A. Levit; Jerome T. Levy (Resident, New York, N.Y. Office); Anthony V. Lupo; John B. Madden, Jr. (Resident, New York, N.Y. Office); Stewart S. Manela; William E. Marames; Charles M. Marmelstein; Eugene A. Massey; Wayne H. Matelski; John C. McCoy; Donald C. McLean; William J. McSherry, Jr. (Resident, New York, N.Y. Office); Eugene J. Meigher; James P. Mercurio; John J. Meyer; Donald B. Mitchell, Jr.; Gerald L. Mitchell; Henry Morris, Jr.; Robert B. Murray; John N. Nassikas III; Richard A. Newman; George E. Oram, Jr.; David M. Osnos; Deanne M. Ottaviano; Lynn K. Pearle; Matthew S. Perlman; Jeffrey S. Peters; Elliott I. Portnoy; Howard B. Possick; Connie A. Raffa (Resident, New York, N.Y. Office); Deborah A. Randall; Marc Rauch (Resident, New York, N.Y. Office); Peter S. Reichertz; Alan E. Reider; Paul Jackson Rice; Stephanie A. Rigaux; Jeffrey B. Rosen (Not admitted in DC); Charles B. Ruttenberg; William A. Sarraille; Thomas Schattenfield; Joanne Schehl; Larri A. Short; Allen G. Siegel; Joel N. Simon; Howard V. Sinclair; Christopher Smith; Michael L. Stevens; Carter Strong; Kathy S. Taub; Gary C. Tepper; Carl A. Valenstein; Christopher Van Hollen, Jr.; David Vidal-Cordero; Kimberly A. Wachen; Barbara S. Wahl; Brian P. Waldman; Robert J. Waters; Richard J. Webber; Barbara G. Werther; Marsha C. Wertzberger; Arnold R. Westerman; M. Stephanie Wickouski; Breckinridge L. Willcox; Blair C. Woodside, III; David N. Wynn (Resident, New York, N.Y. Office); Harvey A. Yampolsky; Stephen C. Yohay; John J. Yurow; Gerald Zingone. Counsel: David J. Bardin; Dale L. Bumpers; Samuel K. Charnoff; Scott A. Cohn (Resident, New York, N.Y. Office); Abdullahi Massoud (Not admitted in United States); Carson P. Porter. Associates: Sarira D. Alexander; Melissa A. Bailey; Rhonda L. Barton (Not admitted in DC); Holly M. Bastian; Stephen M. Bellotti; Christina C. Benson; Richard Jason Berman; Alison J. Besunder (Not admitted in DC); Barb L. Bettenhausen; Darren T. Binder; Costina S. Bortes (Resident, Bucharest, Romania Office); Philip D. Brandt; Randall A. Brater; Lynn A. Bristol (Not admitted in DC); Diane Bui (Not admitted in DC); Karen F. Candreva (Resident, New York, N.Y. Office); Robert K. Carpenter; Cristina A. Carvalho (Not admitted in DC); Kathleen L. Carver-Cheney (Resident, New York, N.Y. Office); Thomas R. Castiello; Steven A. Cohen; Keli Colby; Sana D. Coleman; Daniel P. Conneen (Not admitted in DC; Resident, New York, N.Y. Office); Eve Corbin; Hans J. Crosby (Not admitted in DC); Michael S. Cryan (Resident, New York, N.Y. Office); James R. Davis, II; Mark R. Denicore; Peter James Dernbach (Not admitted in DC); Arthur S. Di Dio; Daniel J. Dowling; Kristine J. Dunne; D. Daniel Dzara, II (Not admitted in DC); Steven Robert Ebert (Resident, New York, N.Y. Office); Laurie Edberg; Felicia Efta (Resident, Bucharest, Romania Office); Craig M. Engle (Not admitted in DC); Caroline T. English; Lisa A. Estrada; Mugur Filipescu (Resident, Bucharest, Romania Office); Benjamin I. Fishman; Therese K. Francese; Hillary A. Frommer (Resident, New York, N.Y. Office); Joseph T. Gatewood; Christopher J. Giaimo Jr.; Barry R. Gogel (Resident, New York, N.Y. Office); Robin Freedman Gonzales; Christopher H. Grigorian; Louis John Grimmelbein, IV; Elizabeth Schickedanz Haile; E. L. Hambrick; Pamela Haughton-Denniston; Rustan J. Hill; Steven F. Hill; Sam Huang (Not admitted in DC); Suzy Chan Hung; Dana Isaroiu (Resident, Bucharest, Romania Office); Melanye K. Johnson; Eileen L. Kahaner; James A. Kaminski (Not admitted in DC); Gregory B. Kang; Katherine V. Kelley; Jonathan A. Kidney (Not admitted in DC); Jutta Klapisch; Susan Sonenshein Kleiman; Sunanda Kundra (Not admitted in DC); Alison L. Kutler; James F. Laboe (Not admitted in DC); Mark Bancroft Langdon; Brian C. Lansing; James M. Larkins, III; Rachel G. Lattimore; Ancuta Delia Leach (Resident, Bucharest, Romania Office); Patricia A. Leonard; Jo An Leonce; Melissa Callahan Lesmes; Brian Marc Lowinger (Not admitted in DC); Michael K. Lowman; Keith R. Marino; Ronan Joseph McHugh; Frederick D. McKalip (Not admitted in DC); Amy S. McNally; Michael T. McNamara; J. Marcus Meeks (Not admitted in DC); Anne L. Milem; Andra Musatescu (Resident, Bucharest, Romania Office); Jennifer L. Myron; James R. Newland, Jr. (Not admitted in DC); Nancy A. Noonan; Eugenia Ordynsky; Timothy D. Osterhaus; Murat Ozgu; Helene Pangalos (Resident, New York, N.Y. Office); Iulian Patrascanu (Resident, Bucharest, Romania Office); Matthew Scott Peeler (Resident, New York, N.Y. Office); Cosmin G. Predoiu (Resident, Bucharest, Romania Office); Joseph R. Price; Michael G. Rafferty; James R. Ravitz; Kerry E. Reichs (Not admitted in DC); Sheree D. Reinbach (Resident, New York, N.Y. Office); Michael J. Rhee (Resident, New York, N.Y. Office); Sandra A. Riley; Jeff Rosenblum (Not admitted in DC); Michael S. Rothman; Daniel C. Savitt (Resident, New York, N.Y. Office); Deborah M. Shelton; Allison Weber Shuren; Rebecca E. Silberbogen; Savalle C. Sims; D. Jacques Smith; Anna L. Spencer; Wanda R. Stansbury (Not admitted in DC); Michael A. Steinberg (Not admitted in DC); Evan S. Stolove; Courtney Ann Sullivan; Mark F. Tatelbaum; Flavia Stupcanu Teodosiu (Resident, Bucharest, Romania Office); Brian A. Tollefson (Not admitted in DC); Nicholas Tsoudis (Not admitted in DC); Ernest A. Tuckett III; Kevin F. Turner (Not admitted in DC); Fabricio Vayra (Not admitted in DC); Daniel Voicu (Resident, Bucharest, Romania Office); Natalie Stoney Walters; Robert E. Wanerman; Ivan J. Wasserman; Ronald L. Wisor, Jr.; Sarah M. Wolf; Jennifer S. Woodbury.

Advertising, Antitrust, Banking, Bankruptcy, Business Transactions, Construction, Electronic Commerce, Employment and Benefits, Energy, Environment, Food and Drug, Government Contracts, Health, Immigration, Intellectual Property, International, Legislation, Litigation, Municipal Finance, OHSA, Real Estate and Tax Law, Sports and Entertainment Law, Telecommunications, Telemedicine, White Collar Criminal. General Practice.

New York City Office: 1675 Broadway, 25th Floor. Telephone: 212-484-3900. Telecopier: 212-484-3990.

Bucharest Office: B-dul N. Titulescu, Nr.1 B1.A7, Sc. 1, Et. 6 Apt. 16, Sector 1, Bucharest, Romania. Telephone: 011-401-211-8797. Fax: 011-401-211-8771.

See Professional Biographies, WASHINGTON, DISTRICT OF COLUMBIA

Argrett, Loretta C., (AV) ...... '37 '76 C.329 B.S. L.309 J.D. 2900 Van Ness Street, N.W.
Arluk, Pamela S. .... '67 '92 C.473 B.A. L.945 J.D. 3000 K St., NW, Ste. 300
Arms, Abigail, (AV) ....'47 '84 C.30 B.A. L.1040 J.D. [Shearman&S.]
Armstrong, Anne C. '61 '97 C.880 B.S. L.128 J.D.
(adm. in MD; not adm. in DC) 3100 Connecticut Ave., N.W.★
Armstrong, James E., III, (AV) '29 '57
C.475 B.S.Ch.E. L.446 J.D. [Armstrong,W.H.M.&N.] (See Pat. Sect.)
Armstrong, James Elwood, IV '72 '97 C.367 B.S. L.30 J.D.
[Ⓐ Armstrong,W.H.M.&N.] (See Pat. Sect.) ⊙
*PRACTICE AREAS: Intellectual Property (100%).
Armstrong, Kara M. ....'66 '91 C.518 A.B. L.880 J.D. [Fisher,C.&S.] (See Pat. Sect.)
*PRACTICE AREAS: Patent; Trademark; Copyright; Unfair Competition and related Litigation.
Armstrong, Timothy K. .... '68 '93 C&L.846 B.A., J.D. [Ⓐ Howrey S.A.&W.]
*PRACTICE AREAS: Appellate Practice; Commercial Litigation.

Armstrong Teasdale LLP, (AV)

A Partnership including Professional Corporations
1747 Pennsylvania Avenue, N.W., Suite 300, 20006-4604 ⊙
Telephone: 202-293-0398 Facsimile: 202-393-0363 Twx: 910 761-2246 Cable: ATKV LAW
Email: armstrongteasdale@armstrongteasdale.com URL: http://www.armstrongteasdale.com
Members of Firm: Stephen A. Crystal.
Corporate Law, Real Estate, Project Finance, Venture Capital, Municipal Law, Government Affairs, Public Utility Law.
St. Louis, Missouri Office: One Metropolitan Square, Suite 2600, 63102. Telephone: 314-621-5070. Facsimile: 314-621-5065.
Kansas City, Missouri Office: 2345 Grand Boulevard, Suite 2000, 64108. Telephone: 816-221-3420. Facsimile: 816-221-0786.
Jefferson City, Missouri Office: 3405 W. Truman Blvd., Suite 210, 65109. Telephone: 573-636-8394.
Belleville, Illinois Office: 23 South First Street, 62220. Telephone: 618-397-4411.
Olathe, Kansas Office: 100 East Park, 66061. Telephone: 913-345-0706.
Shanghai, China Office: Suite 310, No. 12 Zhongshan Road (E1), Shanghai 200002 P.R.C. Telephone: 86-21-6326-7001. Facsimile: 86-21-6326-0626.
Sydney, Australia Office: C/Clayton Utz, Level 31, No. 1 O'Connell Street, Sidney, NSW 2000, Australia. Telephone: 61-29-262-6700. Facsimile: 61-29-262-3263.

See Professional Biographies, WASHINGTON, DISTRICT OF COLUMBIA

Armstrong, Westerman, Hattori, McLeland & Naughton, (AV)

1725 K Street, N.W., Suite 1000, 20006 ⊙
Telephone: 202-659-2930 Facsimile: 202-887-0357 (G.P.III); 202-331-7519 (G.P.III) Video: 202-728-6844
Email: information@armstrongpat.com URL: http://www.armstrongpat.com
James E. Armstrong, III; William F. Westerman; Ken-Ichi Hattori; William G. Kratz, Jr. (Resident, Pittsburgh, Pennsylvania); Mel R. Quintos; Donald W. Hanson; Stephen G. Adrian; Scott M. Daniels; William Lee Brooks. Associates: John P. Kong; James Elwood Armstrong, IV; Sadao Kinashi; Nicolas E. Seckel (Not admitted in DC); Thomas E. Brown (Not admitted in DC); Daniel A. Geselowitz; Michael Scott Alprin (Not admitted in DC); Joseph L. Felber; Kenneth Harry Salen (Not admitted in DC). Of Counsel: Le-Nhung McLeland; Ronald F. Naughton (Not admitted in DC); John F. Carney; Edward F. Welsh (Resident at Pittsburgh, Pennsylvania Office); Michael J. Caridi.
Languages: Japanese, French and Filipino.
Patent, Trademark, Copyright and Unfair Competition Law. Other Matters Involving Technology and Related Litigation in all Courts and Administrative Agencies including The U.S. International Trade Commission. United States and International Patent and Trademark Law.
Pittsburgh, Pennsylvania Office: 429 Fourth Avenue, Suite 707. Telephone: 412-281-2931. Facsimile: 412-281-1821.

See Professional Biographies, WASHINGTON, DISTRICT OF COLUMBIA

Arner, Erika Harmon .... '71 '99 C.945 B.S. L.902 J.D. [Ⓐ Finnegan,H.F.G.&D.]
*PRACTICE AREAS: Computer and Software Patents; Intellectual Property Portfolio Management; Patent Prosecution; Computer Architecture Patents.
Arner, Stephen M. .... '70 '95 C&L.945 B.A., J.D. [Ⓐ Beveridge&D.]
*PRACTICE AREAS: Litigation; Environmental Law.
Arness, John E., II, (BV) ....'57 '91 C.884 B.A. L.276 J.D. [Ⓐ Leibner&P.]
*PRACTICE AREAS: Civil Litigation; Real Estate; Collections; General Practice.
Arness, John P., (AV) .... '27 '52 C.309 A.B. L.276 J.D. [Ⓒ Hogan&H.]
*PRACTICE AREAS: Commercial Litigation; Construction Litigation; Excess Coverage; Extra Contractual Insurance Claims; Reinsurance.
Arnett, Angela Jones .... '41 '82 C.446 B.A. L.128 J.D. Amer. Council of Life Ins.
Arnholz, John C. ....'59 '86 C.95 B.A. L.276 J.D. [McKee N.]
*PRACTICE AREAS: Structured Finance.
Arnold, Deborah J. ....'63 '88 C.696 B.A. L.273 J.D. [Ⓒ Arter&H.]
Arnold, Eric A. .... '64 '92 C.103 Sc.B. L.880 J.D. [Sutherland A.&B.]
*PRACTICE AREAS: Broker-Dealer Regulation; Banking Law; Insurance Regulation; Corporate Law.
Arnold, Richard Alan, (AV) '46 '75 C.835 B.S. L.790 J.D.
(adm. in FL; not adm. in DC) [Kenny N.S.A.C.&S.] ⊙
*PRACTICE AREAS: Antitrust and Trade Regulation; Complex Commercial Litigation.
Arnold, Scott, (AV) ....'57 '82 C.1044 B.A. L.273 J.D. [Howrey S.A.&W.]
*PRACTICE AREAS: Government Contracts; Litigation.
Arnold, Wm. P. ....'09 '33 C.871 L.537 LL.B. 1601 Caton Pl., N.W.‡

Arnold & Porter, (AV) BR

Thurman Arnold Building, 555 Twelfth Street, N.W., 20004-1206 ⊙
Telephone: 202-942-5000 Cable Address: "Arfopo" Telecopy: 202-942-5999
URL: http://www.arnoldporter.com
Washington, D.C. Office: Partners: Bruce A. Adams; Richard M. Alexander; David B. Apatoff; Geoffrey F. Aronow; William J. Baer; Grant P. Bagley; Richard E. Baltz; Leonard H. Becker; Donald O. Beers; Kathleen A. Behan; Alexander E. Bennett; John T. Bentivoglio; Paul S. Berger; David B. Bergman; Michael L. Bernstein; Judith Bernstein-Gaeta; Blake A. Biles; Edward E. Bintz; Peter K. Bleakley; Brooksley Born; Jeffrey S. Bromme; Jeffrey A. Burt; Michael Caglioti; Susan Booth Cassidy; Howard Neil Cayne; Bruce M. Chadwick; Jerome I. Chapman; Martha L. Cochran; Robert B. Conley; William Edro Cook, Jr.; James L. Cooper; George E. Covucci; Michael D. Daneker; Patricia Ann Dean; Eli Whitney Debevoise, II; Jacqueline R. Denning; Steven S. Diamond; A. Patrick Doyle; Douglas A. Dworkin; David S. Eggert; Richard S. Ewing; Deborah L. Feinstein; Roger P. Fendrich; Richard M. Firestone; James F. Fitzpatrick; Samuel A. Flax; Sonia (Turcotte) Fois; Theodore D. Frank; Joel M. Freed; David F. Freeman, Jr.; Melvin C. Garbow; Murray R. Garnick; Robert A. Garrett; David P. Gersch; Jonathan Gleklen; Neil M. Goodman; Michael D. Goodwin; Patrick J. Grant; Julius M. Greisman; Peter T. Grossi, Jr.; Drew A. Harker; Cathy Hoffman; Philip W. Horton; Roberta Lazarus Horton; Joseph G. Howe, III; Richard L. Hubbard; Gary E. Humes; Darryl W. Jackson; Richard A. Johnson; Robert J. Jones; James P. Joseph; Sarah Elizabeth Kahn; Steven Kaplan; Andrew T. Karron; Hadrian R. Katz; David R. Kentoff; Abe Krash; Werner Kronstein; M. Sean Laane; Stuart J. Land; J. Stephen Lawrence, Jr.; Ronald D. Lee; Susan G. Lee; Kenneth A. Letzler; Arthur N. Levine; Daniel Martin Lewis; Jack L. Lipson; Robert S. Litt; Richard M. Lucas; Dennis G. Lyons; Helene B. Madonick; Robert E. Mannion; David R. Marsh; Jonathan S. Martel; John C. Massaro; Mark R. Merley; Michael B. Mierzewski; Thomas H. Milch; Bruce L. Montgomery; Susan T. Morita; S. Lee Narrow; Irvin B. Nathan; Anne J. O'Brien; Charles D. Ossola; Donna E. Patterson; Jennifer S. Perkins; Stephanie M. Phillipps; Stephen W. Porter; Claire E. Reade; Steven G. Reade; Thomas W. Richardson; Walter J. Rockler; William D. Rogers; Richard L. Rosen; Robert D. Rosenbaum; Stanford G. Ross; Julie B. Rottenberg; Eric A. Rubel; Blake D. Rubin; Michael J. Rufkahr; Stephen M. Sacks; James J. Sandman; Ronald A. Schechter; Lawrence A. Schneider; Scott B. Schreiber; Kenneth L. Schwartz; Matthew J. Seiden; Michael T. Shor; Norman M. Sinel; Edward H. Sisson; Jeffrey H. Smith; Michael N. Sohn; Michael J. Songer; Lester Sotsky; Mary Gabrielle Sprague; Mark H. Stumpf; Bryan J. Tomasek; Asim Varma; G. Duane Vieth; William W. Vodra; Douglas L. Wald; Daniel Waldman; Robert N. Weiner; Joseph D. West; Leslie Wharton; Robert H. Winter; Jay Kelly Wright; Walter F. Zenner. Of Counsel: Rosalind K. Allen; John P. Barker; J. Bradway Butler; Michael A. Lee; Robert Pitofsky; Victor L. Reid; Thomas E. Silfen; Melvin Spaeth; Jonathan L. Stern; James T. Walsh; Michele J. Woods; Robert Jones Worrall. Special Counsel: Waltraut Susanne Addy; Theodore S. Boone; Mary E. Cassidy; Peter J. Cinquegrani; March Coleman; Marcia Ann Cranberg; Lawrence E. Culleen; Beth S. DeSimone; Holly R. Fogler; Michael R. Geske; Howard L. Hyde; Jean E. Kalicki; David E. Korn; Rosemary Maxwell; Joan G. Ochs; Nancy L. Perkins; Randal M. Shaheen; Thomas D. Sydnor, II; Sharon L. Taylor. Associates: Eric L. Alexander; Michael J. Allan; Justin S. Antonipillai; Michael C. Augustini; Jonathan Batten; Jeanna M. Beck; Kristen E. Belz; Timothy C. Bickham; Laura Respess Biddle; Aruna K. Boppana; Monica Jahan Bose; Jennifer S. Brannan; Kathryn P. Caballero; Daniel A. Cantor; Arturo Caraballo; W. Jonathan Cardi; Erika R. Carmean; William J. Carmody; William P. Cejudo; Scott A. Chambers; Lisa ReVeal Chavarria; Eugene T. Chen; Yu Chen; Kwame A. Clement; June E. Cohan; Sharon Beth Cohn; Pelayo Coll; Robert S. Conway; Anika S. Cooper; Robert M. Cooper; D. Michael Cormaney; Kathleen M. Courtis; Anne W. Coventry; Harold Bryan Cunningham; John D. Daley; David G. Dargatis; Anne P. Davis; Jeffrey R. Denman; Ranjit S. Dhindsa; Mary M. Dixon; Clare H. Dooley; Rebecca L. Dubin; Cydonii V. Fairfax; Paul Scott Feira; Justine Anne Fitzgerald; Jeffrey K. Francer; Anthony J. Franze; John A. Freedman; Matthew L. Gannon; Cynthia A. Giordano; Eleazar A. Gonzalez; Jamie Z. Goodson; Ronna M. Govan; Ranjeev S. Guliani; Joel M. Gulick; Jeffrey L. Handwerker; Myles R. Hansen; Garrett M. Heenan; Scott D. Helsel; Thomas C. Indelicarto; Courtney E. Ingraffia; Brian D. Israel; Michael A. Johnson; Tracy L. Johnson; Stephen E. Jones; Simon Kann; Robert J. Katerberg; Matthew D. Keiser; Timothy J. Kelly; J. Benjamin King; Thomas L. Klein; Michael J. Klyce, Jr.; Christine E. Koh; Sarah B. Kotler; David W. Leary; Gordon Lederman; Wendy J. Levenson; Gregory H. Levine; Emma Kelton Lewis (Not admitted in DC); Virginia W. Liao; Jeffrey A. Liesemer; Franklin R. Liss; Kraig B. Long; Nick Malhotra; Lark T. Mallory; Christopher D. Man; Robert E. Mascola; Duane J. Mauney; Thaddeus R. McBride; Robert A. McCarter III; Amy L. McGinnis; Kathryn C. McGovern; Erica Taylor McKinley; Matthew Meisner; Kendall Millard; Randall K. Miller; Mark J. Montano; Amy Ralph Mudge; Wilson D. Mudge; Rebecca Nassab; Brad Newberg; Jeannie H. Nguyen; Son B. Nguyen; Leslie A. Nickel; Donna Norman; Ki O; Kathryn E. Olson (Not admitted in DC); David M. Orta; Anne M. Package; Emily Paquinelli; Amanda J. Paracuellos; Daniel S. Pariser; Douglas S. Pelley; Amy K. Phillips; Annalisa Pizzarello; Ian Plant; Kenneth L. Pollack; Stacy J. Pollock; Nicholas Porritt; Thorn L. Pozen; Elissa J. Preheim; Lisa A. Price; Michael D. Raibman; Kim Rappaport; Jeff Richman; Amy B. Rifkind; Richard R. Rodgers; Janice M. Rodriguez; James M. Rosenthal; Sidney A. Rosenzweig; Michael A. Rubin; Amy F. Ryan; Michael A. Sackey; Sheila B. Scheuerman; Peter J. Schildkraut; Karen K. Schwartz; P. Moni SenGupta; Jule L. Sigall; Fabio Roman Silva; S. Jnatel Simmons; Darren C. Skinner; Carey W. Smith; Sherrese M. Smith; Michael S. Solender; Sirak Solomon; Penny Somer-Greif; Michael L. Sozan; Marc A. Stanislawczyk; Tim Stelzig; Steve C. Suk; Eric Suter; Joy Taylor; Trent Taylor; Robert J. Wagman, Jr.; Anne McBride Walker; Andrea Macintosh Whiteway; Christy C. Wiegand; Erica Y. Williams; Christopher Winters; Elizabeth Wirick; Gillian C. Wood; Todd A. Wynkoop; Amy J. Yanoff; Michael D. Yeh; Kevin A. Zambrowicz; Elliott Zenick.

Antitrust/Competition and Trade Regulation, Bankruptcy, Consumer Products Safety, Corporate and Securities, Derivatives, Employee Benefits, Environmental, Financial Institutions, Food, Drug and Medical Devices, Government Contracts, Health Care, Intellectual Property and Technology, Inter

(This Listing Continued)

Arnold & Porter (Continued)

national Litigation and Arbitration, International Trade, Life Sciences, Litigation, National Security Law and Policy, Privacy, Product Liability, Project Finance, Public Policy and Legislative, Real Estate, Tax, Telecommunications.
Northern Virginia Office: 1600 Tysons Boulevard, Suite 900, McLean, Virginia, 22102-4865. Telephone: 212-715-1000. Fax: 212-715-1399.
Los Angeles, California Office: 44th Floor, 777 South Figueroa Street, 90017-2513. Telephone: 213-243-4000. Fax: 213-243-4199.
LA-Century City Office: Seventeenth Floor, 1900 Avenue of the Stars, Los Angeles, California, 90067-4403. Telephone: 310-552-2500. Fax: 310-552-1191.
Denver, Colorado Office: 370 Seventeenth Street, Suite 4500, 80202-1370. Telephone: 303-863-1000. Fax: 303-832-0428.
New York, New York Office: 399 Park Avenue, 10022-4690. Telephone: 212-715-1000. Fax: 212-715-1399.
The United Kingdom Office: Tower 42, 25 Old Broad Street, London, England, EC2N 1HQ. Telephone: 011-44-20-7786-6100. Fax: 011-44-20-7786-6299.
See Professional Biographies, WASHINGTON, DISTRICT OF COLUMBIA

Arnold, White & Durkee
(See Howrey, Simon, Arnold & White, LLP)

Arnopol, Scott D. .... '50 '77 C.30 B.A. L.64 J.D. 307 G St., N.W.
Arnsbarger, Linda A. .... '57 '85 C.385 B.A. L.228 J.D. [🄲 Morrison&F.]
*PRACTICE AREAS: Federal Taxation; State Taxation; Tax Controversies.
Arnwine, Barbara Ruth, (AV) '51 '77 C.773 B.A. L.228 J.D.
(adm. in NC; not adm. in DC) Exec. Dir., Lawyers Comm. for Civil Rights Under Law
*RESPONSIBILITIES: Civil Rights Law; Employment Discrimination Law; Housing Discrimination Law.
Aron, David E. ....'68 '94 C.477 B.A. L.823 J.D. [🄰 McDermott,W.&E.]
Aron, Nan .... '68 '74 C.604 B.A. L.930 J.D. Pres., Alliance for Justice
Aronie, Jonathan S. ....'68 '93 C.1036 B.A. L.228 J.D. [🄰 Fried,F.H.S.&J.]
*PRACTICE AREAS: Government Contracts; Litigation; Internal Investigations, Compliance and Monitoring; Qui Tam Defense.
Aronow, Geoffrey F. .... '55 '82 C&L.976 B.A., J.D. [Arnold&P.]
*PRACTICE AREAS: Litigation; Legislative Practice; Commodities; Securities.
Aronowitz, Daniel, (AV) .... '67 '91 C.608 B.A. L.880 J.D. [Ross,D.&B.]
Arons, Jessica Rachel '72 '00 C.103 B.A. L.945 J.D.
(adm. in VA; not adm. in DC) [🄰 James&H.]
*PRACTICE AREAS: Labor and Employment.
Aronson, Barton S. .... '67 '93 C.976 B.A. L.145 J.D. Asst. U.S. Atty.
Aronson, Bruce Jay ....'69 '94 C.597 B.A. L.273 J.D. Smithsonian Instit.
Aronson, Louis M. .... '65 '91 C.477 B.A. L.823 J.D. [Ruben&A.]
*PRACTICE AREAS: Corporate Finance; Securities; Transactional; Corporate Law; Real Estate.
Aronson, Mary Hudanish '— '98 C.289 B.A. L.30 J.D.
(adm. in MD; not adm. in DC) Aronson Wash. Research
Arp, D. Jarrett .... '66 '91 C.937 B.A. L.945 J.D. [🄰 Gibson,D.&C.]
*PRACTICE AREAS: Litigation; Antitrust and Trade Regulation.
Arpin, James B. .... '59 '89 C.659 B.A.S./B.S.E. L.94 J.D. [Baker B.] (See Pat. Sect.)
Arquit, Kevin J., (AV) '54 '78
C.732 B.A. L.188 J.D. [Clifford C.R.&W.] (⊙New York, NY)
Arrigo, Kimberley E. '58 '91 C.475 B.S. L.472 J.D.
(adm. in FL; not adm. in DC) U.S. Dept. of Agr.
Arrington, Leslie P. .... '67 '93 C.886 B.A. L.893 J.D. [Nixon P.]
*PRACTICE AREAS: Litigation; Labor and Employment.
Art, Andrew B. ....'69 '99 C.385 B.A. L.904 J.D. [🄰 Van Ness F.]
*PRACTICE AREAS: Energy; Electric Power; Administrative Law; Litigation; Adjudication.
Artabane, Joseph A., (AV) .... '49 '75 C&L.276 A.B., J.D. [Artabane&B.]
*PRACTICE AREAS: Civil Practice; Trial Practice; Corporate Litigation; Environmental Litigation; Employment Law.

Artabane & Belden, P.C., (AV)
818 18th Street, N.W., Suite 410, 20006
Telephone: 202-861-0070 Fax: 202-861-2939
Email: lawyers@artabane-belden.com URL: http://www.lawyers.com/artabane&belden
Joseph A. Artabane; W. Neil Belden; Robert F. Condon;—Luke C. Pingel (Not admitted in DC). Of Counsel: John A. McCahill.
Complex and Multi-Jurisdictional Commercial Litigation, Government Contracts, Employment Law, Wrongful Termination, Wrongful Discharge, Age Discrimination, Equal Employment Opportunity Law, Executive Compensation; Employment Compliance, Intellectual Property Litigation, Trade Secrets, Copyright, Patent Infringement, Trademarks, Securities Fraud, Grand Jury Practice, White Collar Crime, Qui Tam Litigation and Personal Injury.
See Professional Biographies, WASHINGTON, DISTRICT OF COLUMBIA

Arter & Hadden LLP, (AV)
1801 K Street, N.W., Suite 400K, 20006 ⊙
Telephone: 202-775-7100 Facsimile: 202-857-0172
URL: http://www.arterhadden.com
Members of Firm: Charles K. Arter (1875-1957); John A. Hadden (1886-1979).
William K. Dabaghi; Richard A. Dean; William L. Gehrig; Lawrence H. Gesner; Michael R. Goodstein; Philip M. Horowitz; James Grier Hoyt; Christopher H. Johnson; William K. Keane; Howard M. Liberman; John D. Maddox; Tom McDonald; David L. Miller; Jerry A. Moore III; Michael J. Pollack; Ted L. Ramirez (Not admitted in DC); Peter J. Riebling; Thomas K. Slattery; Francis R. Snodgrass. Of Counsel: Myles J. Ambrose; Deborah J. Arnold; Jerome A. Hochberg; Jodi Mintzer Krame; Jonathan W. Lipshie; Thomas H. Odom; Mark Van Bergh. Associates: Stephanie L. DeLong; Elizabeth A. Hammond; Donell A. Hicks; Darren E. Pogoda; Sarah P. Singleton; Amy Suski.
Appellate Litigation, Bankruptcy, Business Litigation, Commercial, Communications and Media, Construction, Corporate and Securities, Director and Officer Liability, Energy Deregulation, Employment, Environmental, Estates, Finance, Government Affairs, Health Care, Insurance Litigation, Intellectual Property, Customs, Trade and Technology, International, Professional and Product Liability, Real Estate, Tax Services and Workers' Compensation.
In Cleveland, Ohio: 1100 Huntington Building, 925 Euclid Avenue, 44115-1475. Telephone: 216-696-1100. Fax: 216-696-2645.
In Columbus, Ohio: Suite 2100, One Columbus, 10 West Broad Street, 43215-3422. Telephone: 614-221-3155. Fax: 614-221-0479.
In Dallas, Texas: 1717 Main Street, Suite 4100, 75201-4605. Telephone: 214-761-2100. Fax: 214-741-7139.
In Dayton, Ohio: Suite 2310, 40 North Main Street, 45423. Telephone: 973-223-4701. Fax: 937-223-0170.
In Los Angeles, California: 725 South Figueroa Street, Suite 3400, 90017. Telephone: 213-430-3000. Fax: 212-617-9255.
In Irvine, California: Five Park Plaza, Suite 1000, Jamboree Center, 92714. Telephone: 949-252-7500. Fax: 949-833-9604.
In San Francisco, California: Two Embarcadero Center, 5th Floor, 94111. Telephone: 415-617-2100. Fax: 415-912-3636.
In San Diego, California: 550 West C Street, 16th Floor, 92101. Telephone: 619-238-0001. Fax: 619-595-1313.
In Woodland Hills, California: 5959 Topanga Canyon Boulevard, Suite 244, 91367. Telephone: 818-712-0036. Fax: 818-346-6502.
Revisers of the Ohio Law Digest for this Directory
See Professional Biographies, WASHINGTON, DISTRICT OF COLUMBIA

Articola, Phillip John .....'— '94 C&L.446 M.S.E.E., J.D. [🄰 Foley&L.] (See Pat. Sect.)
*PRACTICE AREAS: Intellectual Property; Computer Law; Communications Law; Semiconductor Technology.

Artz, William E., A Professional Corporation
(See Arlington, Virginia)

Arumi, Ana Cristina .... '70 '96 C.575 A.B. L.228 J.D. [🄰 Hogan&H.]

Asbill, Henry W., (AV) .... '47 '76 C.674 B.A. L.276 J.D. [Asbill,J.M.&B.]
*PRACTICE AREAS: Appellate Practice; Civil Rights; Constitutional Law; Criminal Law; Drugs and Narcotics.

Asbill, Junkin, Moffitt & Boss, Chartered, (AV)
The Pacific House, 1615 New Hampshire Avenue, N.W., Second Floor, 20009
Telephone: 202-234-9000 Facsimile: 202-332-6480
Email: ajmchtd@erols.com URL: http://www.lawyers.com/asbill
Henry W. Asbill; Timothy deForest Junkin; William B. Moffitt (Not admitted in DC); Lenard B. Boss. Of Counsel: Oscar I. Dodek, Jr.; W. Louis Hennessy; William J. Mertens.
Criminal and Civil Trials and Appeals before all Courts.
See Professional Biographies, WASHINGTON, DISTRICT OF COLUMBIA

Asciolla, Gregory P. .... '65 '94 C.93 A.B. L.128 [Morgan,L.&B.]
Ash, Matthew G. .... '43 '73 C.477 B.A. L.276 J.D. [Cozen O.]
*PRACTICE AREAS: Banking Law; Corporate Law; Litigation.
Ash, Robert L. ....'51 '75 C&L.446 B.S., J.D. [Ober,K.G.&S.]

Ashcraft & Gerel, LLP, (AV)
A Limited Liability Partnership including Professional Corporations
Suite 400, 2000 L Street, N.W., 20036 ⊙
Telephone: 202-783-6400
URL: http://www.ashcraftandgerel.com
Members of Firm: Martin E. Gerel (P.C.) (Resident, Rockville, Maryland Office); James A. Mannino (P.C.) (Resident); Mark L. Schaffer (P.C.) (Resident); Wayne M. Mansulla (Resident); James F. Green (Resident); Allen J. Lowe (Resident); Michael H. Feldman (Resident); James M. Hanny (Resident); Michael V. Kowalski (Resident); H. Vincent McKnight, Jr. (Resident); Michelle A. Parfitt (Resident); George E. Swegman (Resident); Peter J. Vangsnes (Resident); Michael W. Heaviside (Resident); Christopher V. Tisi (Resident); Sidney Schupak (Resident); Martin Trpis (Resident);—Michael E. Gallant (Resident); Rebekah R. Arch (Not admitted in DC; Resident); Sotirios Basil Yanakakis; Jerry David Spitz (Resident); Keri A. Jones (Resident); Susan E. Fattig (Resident); Mohammad A. Syed (Not admitted in DC; Resident). Of Counsel: Altomease R. Kennedy (Resident).
Pharmaceutical Litigation, Negligence, Workers Compensation, Medical Malpractice, Social Security and Products Liability Law, AIDS Litigation, Asbestos Litigation, Breast Implant Litigation, Qui Tam.
Alexandria, Virginia Office: Suite 650, 4900 Seminary Road. Telephone: 703-931-5500.
Rockville, Maryland Office: Suite 1002, One Central Plaza, 11300 Rockville Pike. Telephone: 301-770-3737.
Baltimore, Maryland Office: Suite 1212, 10 East Baltimore Street. Telephone: 410-539-1122.
Landover, Maryland Office: Suite 301, 4301 Garden City Drive. Telephone: 301-459-8400.
Boston, Massachusetts Office: 440 Commercial Street, Suite 600. Telephone: 617-723-8544.
See Professional Biographies, WASHINGTON, DISTRICT OF COLUMBIA

Ashe, Mason P. '63 '91 C.299 B.A. L.107 J.D.
(adm. in NC; not adm. in DC) Strickland & Ashe Mgmt.
Asher, Robert H. .... '25 '51 C&L.174 J.D. 2000 M St., N.W.
Ashford, Deborah Taylor .... '50 '82 C.16 B.A. L.976 J.D. [Hogan&H.]
*PRACTICE AREAS: Corporate Law; Nonprofit and Charitable Organizations.
Ashford, Tamara W. '68 '95 C.228 B.A. L.880 J.D.
(adm. in NC; not adm. in DC) [🄰 Miller&C.]
*PRACTICE AREAS: Taxation; Tax Litigation; Tax Controversies; Federal Income Tax; International Taxation.
Ashley, Katherine D. ....'70 '96 C.228 B.A. L.477 J.D. [🄰 Skadden,A.S.M.&F.]
*PRACTICE AREAS: Corporate.
Ashton, Ann M. .... '54 '80 C.128 B.A. L.273 J.D. [🄲 Debevoise&P.] (⊙New York, NY)
*PRACTICE AREAS: Complex and Multi-District Litigation; Litigation; Securities Litigation; Class Action Defense.
Ashton, Robin C. .... '— '86 C.477 B.A. L.945 J.D. Asst. U.S. Atty.
Ashton, Sandra J. .... '44 '92 C.210 B.A. L.793 J.D. National Indian Gaming Comm.
Askenazy, Lisa J. .... '67 '95 C.1036 B.A. L.273 J.D. 1666 K St., N.W.‡
Askew, Delphine A. .... '58 '84 C&L.665 B.A., J.D. Gen. Coun., D.C. Bd. of Parole
Aslan, Shaoul ....'49 '76 C.994 B.A. L.276 J.D. [Patton B.]
Asmar, Charles M. .... '63 '91 C.882 B.S. L.128 J.D. [McManus,S.A.&D.]
*PRACTICE AREAS: Construction Law; Commercial Law; Civil Litigation.
Aspinall, Karen '74 '01 C&L.30 B.A., J.D.
(adm. in NY; not adm. in DC) [🄰 Dechert]
*PRACTICE AREAS: Investment Management; Financial Services Law.
Assaf, Eugene F. .... '62 '89 C.216 B.A. L.602 J.D. [Kirkland&E.]
*PRACTICE AREAS: Commercial Litigation; Trade Secrets; Antitrust; First Amendment.
Assaraf, Steven M. .... '65 '90 C.446 B.S. L.64 J.D. [🄰 Ammerman&G.]
*PRACTICE AREAS: Bankruptcy; Bankruptcy Chapter 7; Bankruptcy Chapter 13; Foreclosures; Consumer Credit.
Assatourians, Liza C. '71 '97 C.273 B.A. L.904 J.D.
Coun., Natl. Food Processors Assn.
Assey, James M., Jr. .... '68 '97 C.813 B.A. L.276 J.D. [🄰 Willkie F.&G.]
*PRACTICE AREAS: Communications; New Media.
Astin, Rainey L. ....'67 '95 C.575 B.A. L.280 J.D. [🄰 Shaw P.]
Astrove, David M., (AV) ......'57 '82 C.659 B.A. L.178 J.D. [🄲 Friedlander,M.S.K.&O.]
*PRACTICE AREAS: Commercial Finance; Commercial Real Estate; Commercial Leasing; Business Law.
Atallah, Amjad H. '65 '00 C.893 M.A. L.30 J.D.
(adm. in NY; not adm. in DC) [🄰 Kalbian H.]
*PRACTICE AREAS: Litigation; Probate; International Public Law; International Human Rights.
Atelsek, Paul '56 '92 C.446 B.S. L.280 J.D.
Office of Environmental Law, U.S. Coast Guard
Ates, John R. .... '68 '94 C.500 B.A. L.880 J.D. [🄰 Winston&S.]
Athari, Susan R. ....'67 '93 C.390 B.A. L.128 J.D. 1828 L St., N.W.
Athey, SueLyn Smith '— '86 C.446 B.A. L.1048 J.D.
(adm. in MD; not adm. in DC) [🄰 Reed S.]
*PRACTICE AREAS: Corporate; Finance.
Athy, Andrew, Jr., (BV) ....'48 '73 C.659 B.A. L.276 J.D. [O'Neill,A.&C.]
Atienza, Patricia J. '— '99 C.260 B.A. L.904 J.D.
(adm. in MD; not adm. in DC) [🄰 Jenkens&G.]
*PRACTICE AREAS: Health Law; Medicare Fraud and Abuse.
Atkin, Barbara A. '49 '75 C.821 B.A. L.893 J.D.
Dep. Gen. Coun., National Treasury Employees Union
Atkin, James B., (AV) .... '30 '59 C&L.893 B.A., LL.B. 1100 New York Ave., N.W.
Atkins, Alden L. .... '59 '85 C&L.893 B.A., J.D. [Vinson&E.]
*PRACTICE AREAS: Litigation; Complex and Multi-District Litigation; Antitrust and Trade Regulation; Trade Secrets; White Collar Crime.
Atkins, Pamela S. .... '57 '82 C.976 B.A. L.893 J.D. The Bureau of Natl. Affs., Inc.
Atkins, Paul S. '58 '84 C.968 A.B. L.880 J.D.
(adm. in FL; not adm. in DC) Price Waterhouse Coopers LLP
Atkins, Raymond A. ....'69 '99 C.119 B.A. L.271 J.D. [🄰 Covington&B.]
Atkins, Sean A. .... '69 '96 C&L.893 B.A., J.D. [🄰 Swidler B.S.F.]
*PRACTICE AREAS: Regulatory Law; Utility Law.
Atkins, Timothy B. .... '62 '00 C.1053 B.A. L.276 J.D. [🄰 Wilmer,C.&P.]
Atkinson, Kathryn Cameron ....'— '92 C.367 B.A. L.188 J.D. [🄲 Miller&C.]
*PRACTICE AREAS: Foreign Corrupt Practices Act; International Trade Regulation; Federal Litigation.
Atkinson, Michael K. .... '64 '91 C.823 B.A. L.188 J.D. [Winston&S.]
*PRACTICE AREAS: Trial Practice.
Atkinson, Theodore W. .... '70 '95 C.999 B.S. L.945 J.D. [🄰 Venable,A.B.H.&C.]
*PRACTICE AREAS: Intellectual Property Litigation.
Atlas, Harry I. .... '71 '97 C.999 B.T.L. L.446 J.D. [🄰 Venable,A.B.H.&C.] (⊙Balt., MD)
Atlas, Martin, (AV) ....'14 '45 C.569 A.B. L.273 LL.B. 1825 K St., N.W.

Atrokhov, Wendy .... '— '00 C.30 B.A. L.188 J.D. [Ⓐ Latham&W.]
*PRACTICE AREAS: Public Finance; Project Finance.
Attanasio, Donna M. .... '59 '88 C.788 A.B. L.309 J.D. [Dewey B.]
*PRACTICE AREAS: Energy Law.
Attaway, Fritz E., (AV) '46 '73 C.335 B.A. L.145 J.D.
Exec. V.P.- Govt. Rel. & Gen. Coun., Motion Picture Assn. of Amer., Inc.
Attaway, Scott K. .... '62 '98 C.1293 B.M. L.94 J.D. [Ⓐ Kellogg,H.H.T.&E.]
*PRACTICE AREAS: Telecommunications; Appellate Practice; Litigation.
Atticks, Ethan .... '74 '99 C.945 B.A. L.893 J.D. [Ⓐ Dow,L.&A.]
Attridge, Anne Asbill ....'55 '81 C.197 B.A. L.276 J.D. 1333 N. Hamps. Ave., N.W.‡
Attridge, Daniel F., (AV) .... '54 '78 C.659 B.A. L.273 J.D. [Kirkland&E.]
*PRACTICE AREAS: Litigation; Antitrust.
Attwell, Meredith M. .... '68 '95 C.902 B.A. L.326 J.D. 600 14th Street, N.W. Suite 75
Atwood, E. Barrett, IV '75 '00 C.259 B.S. L.276 J.D.
(adm. in FL; not adm. in DC) [Ⓐ Baker B.]
Atwood, James R., (AV) ....'44 '70 C.976 B.A. L.813 J.D. [Covington&B.]
Atwood, Mark W. .... '52 '79 C.423 A.B. L.800 J.D. [Sher&B.]
*PRACTICE AREAS: Transportation; Aviation; Administrative Law.
Atwood, Mary Pat ....'61 '89 C.893 B.A. L.276 J.D. 3000 K St., N.W.
Aubel, Leo J., (AV) '26 '56 C.546 B.S. L.564 J.D.
(adm. in NY; not adm. in DC) [Ⓒ Klayman&Assoc.]
Auberger, Marcia A., (BV) ....'63 '89 C.107 B.A. L.796 J.D. [Ⓐ Venable,A.B.H.&C.]
*PRACTICE AREAS: Trademark Prosecution; Trademarks; Trademark Litigation.
Auby, Scott N. ....'68 '93 C.399 B.Mus. L.309 J.D. [Ⓐ Debevoise&P.]
*PRACTICE AREAS: Class Actions; Litigation; Securities Litigation.
Auchincloss, Thomas M., Jr. .... '34 '68 C.276 B.A. L.128 J.D. [Rea,C.&A.]
*PRACTICE AREAS: Administrative Law; Interstate Commerce; Transportation; Freight Loss and Damage; Government Contracts.
Auchincloss-Lorr, Katharine A. '47 '74
C.771 B.A. L.705 LL.B. Amer. Immig. Law Found.
Audette, Rose Marie L. .... '59 '93 C&L.276 B.A., J.D. [Ⓐ Hogan&H.]
*PRACTICE AREAS: Litigation; Education Law.
Auerbach, Bethami ....'49 '74 C.668 B.A. L.813 J.D. [Ⓒ Bergeson&C.]
*PRACTICE AREAS: Clean Air Act; Resource Conservation and Recovery Act (RCRA); OSHA; Chemical Regulation; Environmental Compliance.
Auerbach, Dennis B. ....'61 '89 C.674 B.A. L.309 J.D. [Ⓒ Covington&B.]
Auerbach, Pamela J. .... '67 '94 C.178 B.A. L.145 J.D. [Kirkland&E.]
*PRACTICE AREAS: Litigation; Antitrust.
Auerbach, Randy P. .... '54 '79 C.696 B.A. L.64 J.D. Bur. of Natl. Affs., Inc.

Auerbach, Kenneth D.
(See Silver Spring, Maryland)

Augenblick, Mark, (P.C.), (AV) ....'46 '71 C.103 B.A. L.178 J.D. 2300 N. St. NW
Augustini, Michael C. .... '67 '95 C.95 B.A. L.1294 J.D. [Ⓐ Arnold&P.]
*PRACTICE AREAS: Litigation.
Augustino, Steven A., (BV) ....'66 '91 C.893 B.A. L.276 J.D. [Kelley D.&W.]
*PRACTICE AREAS: Telecommunications Law.
Aulick, Dean D., (P.C.) ....'45 '74 C.347 A.B. L.976 J.D. [Shaw P.]
*PRACTICE AREAS: Technology Outsourcing; Energy; Contracts.
Aurbach, Laurence Jay ....'37 '63 C.674 A.B. L.1066 J.D. 2811 McGill Terr., N.W.
Ausbrook, J. Keith '58 '86
C.674 A.B. L.893 J.D. Chief Coun. for Oversight & Investigations
Ausbrook, Perry C., (AV) .... '32 '61 C.659 B.S. L.309 LL.B. [Piper M.R.&W.]
*PRACTICE AREAS: International Franchising.
Ausrotas, Raymond P. .... '69 '98 C.103 A.B. L.273 J.D. [Ⓐ Jackson&C.]
*PRACTICE AREAS: Litigation; Insurance Coverage.
Austin, Bonnie J. ....'64 '89 C.197 A.B. L.602 J.D. [Ⓐ Skadden,A.S.M.&F.]
Austin, Jay '63 '98 C.475 B.A. L.893 J.D.
(adm. in OR; not adm. in DC) Sr. Atty., Environmental Law Institute
*RESPONSIBILITIES: International Environmental Law; Water Law.
Austin, John D., Jr., (AV) ....'46 '73 C.608 B.A. L.838 J.D. [Ⓒ Patton B.]
Austin, Page I., (AV) '42 '77 C.879 B.A. L.846 J.D.
(adm. in TX; not adm. in DC) 1455 Pennsylvania Ave., N.W.‡
Austin, Ronald R. '33 '57 C&L.724 B.A., J.D.
Exec. Dir. & Gen. Coun., Overseas Educ. Assn.
Austrian, Mark L., (AV) .... '45 '71 C&L.659 B.S., J.D. [Collier S.S.]
*PRACTICE AREAS: Federal Civil Litigation; Product Liability; Intellectual Property; Antitrust; Telecommunications.
Auyang, Heather Fai '72 '97 C.112 B.S. L.861 J.D. [Ⓐ Clifford C.R.&W.] (Pat.)
*PRACTICE AREAS: Patent Litigation.
Avakian, Michael E. '53 '79
C.732 B.A. L.1234 J.D. [Smetana&A.] (ⓞNorth Springfield, VA)
Avant, Yolanda Lanell '— '98 C.257 B.S. L.260 J.D.
(adm. in FL; not adm. in DC) 268 Luke Ave., S.W.★
Avendaño, Ana L. '62 '92 C.112 B.S.ChE L.276 J.D.
Asst. Gen. Coun., United Food & Comercial Workers International Union
Aveni, David J. .... '71 '99 C.276 B.S. L.228 J.D. [Ⓐ Wilmer,C.&P.]
Avery, Donald G. ....'43 '69 C.674 A.B. L.309 J.D. [Slover&L.]
Avery, Kevin J. '62 '88 C.309 A.B. L.813 J.D.
(adm. in NY; not adm. in DC) 430 South Capitol Se
Avery, Rosemary Boyd '45 '72 C.881 A.B. L.145 J.D. 5320 29th St., N.W.
Avil, Richard D., Jr., (AV) .... '48 '75 C.884 B.E.E. L.188 J.D. [Jones,D.R.&P.]
*PRACTICE AREAS: Energy; Energy Regulation; Energy Contracts; Utility Rates.
Avins, Jon '62 '01 C.771 B.A. L.276 J.D.
(adm. in NY; not adm. in DC) [Ⓐ Dewey B.]
*PRACTICE AREAS: International Trade; Litigation.
Avitabile, Gregg S. ....'— '89 C.855 B.A. L.273 J.D. [Ⓒ Verner,L.B.M.&H.]
*PRACTICE AREAS: Labor Law; Employment Law; Litigation; Commercial.
Avrakotos, Costas A. .... '— '87 C.665 B.S. L.128 J.D. [Kirkpatrick&L.]
*PRACTICE AREAS: Mortgage Banking Law; Consumer Law; Banking Regulation.
Awkard, Linda N. .... '48 '79 C.259 B.A.B.S. L.262 J.D. 1101 30th St. NW, Ste. 500
Axe, Judith W. ....'51 '80 C.518 B.A. L.569 J.D. 1990 M St Nw # 660
Axelrad, Maurice ....'34 '57 C.679 B.Ch.E. L.659 LL.B. 1800 M St., N.W.
Axelrod, Jonathan G., (AV) ....'46 '71 C.197 B.A. L.178 J.D. [Beins,A.&K.]
Axelson, Arthur B. ....'55 '80 C.264 B.A. L.884 J.D. [Morgan,L.&B.]
Axsmith, Christine ....'64 '00 C.223 B.S. L.128 J.D. 1920 N. St., N.W.
Ay-Lin Ong, Aryani '69 '99 C.1375 B.A. L.273 J.D.
(adm. in MD; not adm. in DC) 1140 Connecticut Ave. ,N.W.
Ayali, Noam '60 '89 L.999 LL.B.
(adm. in NY; not adm. in DC) [Chadbourne&P.]
Ayanian, John V. ....'68 '93 C.477 B.A. L.209 J.D. [Ⓐ Morgan,L.&B.]
Ayer, Donald B., (AV) ....'49 '75 C.813 B.A. L.309 J.D. [Jones,D.R.&P.]
*PRACTICE AREAS: Litigation; Appellate Practice; U.S. Supreme Court Litigation.
Ayer, Jeffrey D. ....'69 '96 C.691 B.A. L.37 J.D. [Ⓐ Wilmer,C.&P.]
Ayer, Victoria T. '72 '97 C.691 B.A. L.94 J.D.
(adm. in MA; not adm. in DC) Off. of Rep.
Ayers, Kimberly C. ....'— '98 C.276 B.A. L.861 J.D. [Ⓐ Smith C.]
*PRACTICE AREAS: Tax; Energy.
Ayers, Timothy '73 '98 C&L.276 B.A., J.D.
(adm. in MD; not adm. in DC) [Ⓐ Winston&S.]
*PRACTICE AREAS: Health Care.
Aylward, David K., (AV) .... '50 '76 C.197 B.A. L.273 J.D. 888 17th St., NW, 12th Fl.
Aylward, Jillian Kindlund '61 '88 C.454 B.A. L.818 J.D.
Assoc. Gen. Coun., Universal Services Administrative Group
Ayotte-Brennan, Christine ....'74 '96 C.93 B.A. L.128 J.D. [Ⓐ Sullivan&C.]
Ayres, Kenneth J. .... '53 '79 C.188 B.S. L.893 J.D. [Jones,D.R.&P.]
*PRACTICE AREAS: Mergers and Acquisitions; Securities; Corporate Finance.
Ayres, Margaret M., (AV) ....'43 '73 C.788 B.A. L.976 J.D. [Ⓒ Davis P.&W.]
Ayres, Richard E., (AV) .... '42 '72 C.674 A.B. L.976 LL.B. [Howrey S.A.&W.]
*PRACTICE AREAS: Environmental Law.
Azcuenaga, Mary L., (AV) ....'45 '73 C.813 A.B. L.145 J.D. [Heller E.W.&M.]
*PRACTICE AREAS: Antitrust; Advertising; Federal Trade Commission.
Azia, Stephen M., (BV) .... '— '89 C.165 B.A. L.306 J.D. [Duane,M.&H.]
*PRACTICE AREAS: Healthcare Law; Managed Care; Medicare and Medicaid Reimbursement and Coverage; Fraud and Abuse; Legislative and Regulatory Advocacy.
Azorsky, Tami Lyn .... '59 '84 C.645 B.A. L.273 J.D. [McKenna&C.]
*PRACTICE AREAS: Product Liability; Environmental Tort Litigation; Administrative Procedure Act Litigation; Environmental Claims; Commercial Litigation.
Baab, Craig H. '45 '77 C.238 B.A. L.904 J.D.
Staff Dir., Govt. Liason, Govt. Affs. Grp., Amer. Bar Assn.
Baach, Martin R., (AV) .... '48 '75 C.910 A.B. L.150 J.D. [Baach R.&L.P.]
*PRACTICE AREAS: Civil Litigation; Commercial Litigation; Insurance; Reinsurance; Product Liability.

Baach Robinson & Lewis PLLC, (AV)
One Thomas Circle, Suite 200, 20005-5803
Telephone: 202-833-8900 Telecopier: 202-466-5738
Email: baachrob@baachrobinson.com URL: http://www.baachrobinson.com
Senior Counsel: Robert L. Wald. Members of Firm: Martin R. Baach; Dwight P. Bostwick; Alan B. Croft; James P. Davenport; Mary E. Fechtig; Bruce R. Grace; Philip T. Inglima; Mark J. Leimkuhler; Eric L. Lewis; Stephen H. Marcus; Jeffrey D. Robinson; Joseph L. Ruby; James Sottile, IV; Duane K. Thompson; A. Katherine Toomey; Geovette E. Washington; Benjamin L. Zelenko. Associates: Randolph M. Collins; Charles A. Cowan; Thomas M. Glassic; H. Bradford Glassman; Helen F. Hiser; Sarah Leslie Knapp (Not admitted in DC); Melissa H. McNiven; Gina M. Saporito; Julie A. Schroeder; Elizabeth Torrant Sheldon; John L. Simpkins; Manuel S. Varela. Of Counsel: Russell M. Frank; Sally A. Regal; Sharon M. Schroer.
Litigation, International, Insurance, Employment, Banking, Government Relations, Antitrust, Trade, White Collar Crime.
London, England Office: At Lloyd's Building, 1 Lime Street, Room 735, EC3M 7DQ. Telephone: +011-44-207-327-4433. Facsimile: +011-44-207-327-4024.
See Professional Biographies, WASHINGTON, DISTRICT OF COLUMBIA

Babayi, Robert S. '59 '92
C.1222 B.S.E.E. L.472 J.D. [Ⓒ Venable,A.B.H.&C.] (See Pat. Sect.)
*PRACTICE AREAS: Intellectual Property; Patent Prosecution; Technology Licensing.
Babb, Margaret J. .... '53 '91 C.16 B.A. L.823 J.D. [Ⓐ Proskauer R.]
Babbin, Jed L., (AV) ....'50 '73 C.816 B.E. L.192 J.D. [O'Connor&H.]
*PRACTICE AREAS: Government Contracts; Complex Civil and Criminal Litigation.
Babbin, Sharon L. .... '54 '77 C.347 B.S. L.276 J.D. [O'Connor&H.]
*PRACTICE AREAS: Commercial Litigation; Corporate Transactions; Intellectual Property; Antitrust; Construction Law.
Babbitt, Bruce, (AV) '— '65 C.602 B.A. L.309 LL.B.
(adm. in AZ; not adm. in DC) [Ⓒ Latham&W.]
*PRACTICE AREAS: Natural Resources.
Babbitt, Harriet C. '47 '72 L.36 J.D.
(adm. in AZ; not adm. in DC) O.A.S.
Babby, Lon S., (AV) ....'51 '76 C.401 B.A. L.976 J.D. [Williams&C.]
*PRACTICE AREAS: Contracts; Employment Contracts; Entertainment Contracts; Executive Employment Law; Executive Severance Contracts.
Babby, Lorna '65 '95
(adm. in MT; not adm. in DC) Managing Atty., Native American Rights Fund
Babendreier, Gerard M. '— '98 C.178 B.A. L.309 J.D.
(adm. in MD; not adm. in DC) [Ⓐ Shaw P.]
Babiak, Nicholas J. '55 '80 C&L.262 B.A., J.D.
(adm. in NY; not adm. in DC) 614 5th Street N E
Babirak, Albert, Vangellow & Shaheen, P.C., (AV)
2121 K St., N.W. (ⓞAnnapolis, Bethesda, MD; Falls Church, Sterling, VA; London, England)
Babits, Joseph P. ....'63 '91 C.273 B.A. L.1209 J.D. 450 Fifth St., N.W.
Babitz, Alisa ....'68 '95 C.178 B.A. L.309 J.D. [Ⓐ Gibson,D.&C.]
*PRACTICE AREAS: Corporate.
Babson, Marshall B., (AV) ....'45 '75 C.659 A.B. L.178 J.D. [Jones,D.R.&P.]
*PRACTICE AREAS: Labor and Employment; Labor Relations; Labor Arbitration; Collective Bargaining.
Baca, B. Kurt '55 '91 C.560 B.S. L.276 J.D.
(adm. in VA; not adm. in DC) [Ⓐ Shearman&S.]
Bacaj, Faton A. ....'57 '91 C.722 B.A. L.128 J.D. [Winston&S.]
*PRACTICE AREAS: Business Law; Computers and Software; Corporate Law; Mergers, Acquisitions and Divestitures; Securities.
Bacelli, Frank ....'72 '99 C.107 B.A. L.128 J.D. [Ⓐ Hogan&H.]
Bach, Laura R. .... '75 '99 C.576 B.A. L.178 J.D. [Ⓐ Kirkland&E.]
*PRACTICE AREAS: Litigation.
Bach, Lucinda J., (AV) ....'— '81 C.597 B.S. L.94 J.D. [Ⓒ Piper M.R.&W.]
*PRACTICE AREAS: Civil and Commercial Litigation; Professional Liability Litigation; White Collar Criminal Litigation.
Bach, M. Stacey ....'75 '00 C.754 B.S. L.884 J.D. [Ⓐ Covington&B.]
Bach, William S. ....'35 '96 C.208 B.A. L.1162 J.D. 717 D St., N.W.
Bachenheimer, Cara C. ....'61 '87 C.855 B.A. L.276 J.D. [Ⓒ Epstein B.&G.]
*PRACTICE AREAS: Health; Government Relations.
Bachman, Allen R. ....'72 '99 C&L.945 B.A., J.D. [Ⓐ Clifford C.R.&W.]
*PRACTICE AREAS: Litigation; Antitrust.
Bachman, Christine D. .... '67 '92 C.367 B.A. L.273 J.D. [Ⓐ Proskauer R.]
Bachman, Gary D., (AV) ....'53 '78 C.105 B.A. L.904 J.D. [Van Ness F.]
*PRACTICE AREAS: Energy; Environment; Hydroelectricity; Electric Utilities; Public Lands.
Bachman, Kenneth L., Jr., (AV) ....'43 '68 C.610 A.B. L.309 J.D. [Cleary,G.S.&H.]
Bachman, William J. ....'61 '95 C.658 B.S. L.276 J.D. [Ⓐ Williams&C.]
Bachrach, Chelsea K. '69 '00 C.66 B.A. L.276 J.D.
(adm. in CA; not adm. in DC) [Ⓐ Davis&H.]
*PRACTICE AREAS: Taxation Law; Insurance Law.
Bachrach, Eve E., (AV) '51 '76 C.94 A.B. L.273 J.D.
Sr. V.P., Gen. Coun. & Secy., Consumer Healthcare Products Association
Bachrach, Max '68 '98 C.178 B.A. L.893 J.D.
(adm. in VA; not adm. in DC; See Pat. Sect.) [Ⓐ Pennie&E.]
*PRACTICE AREAS: Patent Prosecution; Patent Litigation; Pharmaceutical Patents.
Bacino, Birger Greg ....'59 '90 C.927 B.A. L.61 J.D. [B.G.Bacino] ⓞ
Bacino, Birger Greg, APC, The Law Offices of
1201 Pennsylvania Ave. Ste. 300 (ⓞSan Diego, CA; Hous., TX)
Backstrom, Kirsten ....'72 '97 C&L.273 B.A., J.D. [Ⓐ Epstein B.&G.]
*PRACTICE AREAS: Health Law.
Baco-Sanchez, Luis E. ....'67 '93 C.677 B.A. L.1087 J.D. [Ⓐ McDermott,W.&E.]
Bacon, Leonard L. '07 '32 C.976 B.A. L.309 LL.B.
(adm. in NY; not adm. in DC) 5011 Macomb St., N.W.‡

Bacon, Sylvia A. ....'31 '56 C.881 A.B. L.309 LL.B. Ret. Assoc. Supr. Ct. J.

Bacon, Thornton & Palmer, L.L.P.
(See Lanham, Maryland)

Badagliacca, Michael John '71 '97 C.188 B.S. L.990 J.D.
(adm. in NY; not adm. in DC; See Pat. Sect.) [🄰 Staas&H.]
*PRACTICE AREAS: Intellectual Property.
Badami, Heather Rheiner ....'70 '95 C.914 B.A. L.893 J.D. [🄰 Bryan C.]
*PRACTICE AREAS: Corporate; Securities; Finance.
Badami, Scott M. ....'63 '91 C.1369 B.A. L.502 J.D. [🄲 Bryan C.]
Bader, Hans '69 '95 C.893 B.A. L.309 J.D.
(adm. in CA; not adm. in DC) Sr. Coun., Center for Individual Rights
Bader, Michael H., (AV) .... '29 '54 C.273 L.537 LL.B. [🄲 Garvey,S.&B.]
*PRACTICE AREAS: Communications Law; Media Law; Telecommunications Law; Cable Law; Technology Law.
Badger, Leland J. ....'48 '73 C.197 A.B. L.309 J.D. [🄰 Howe&H.]
*PRACTICE AREAS: Not for Profit Corporations; Association Law; Health Care Law; Litigation; Antitrust Law.
Badiani, Purvi ....'74 '98 C.705 B.A. L.276 J.D. [🄰 Venable,A.B.H.&C.]
Badolato, Vincent J. ....'67 '93 C.103 B.A. L.1068 J.D. [🄰 Dechert]
*PRACTICE AREAS: Investment Management; Financial Services Law.
Badrich, Zlatana '73 '97 C.273 B.A. L.128 J.D.
(adm. in VA; not adm. in DC) 4614 Verplanck Pl., N.W.‡
Baek, Andrew C. .... '69 '95 C.569 B.A. L.1009 J.D. [🄰 Seward&K.]
*PRACTICE AREAS: Securities; Banking; Derivative Products.
Baek, Laura A. .... '70 '96 C.569 B.S. L.1019 J.D. [🄰 Silverstein&M.]
*PRACTICE AREAS: Tax Law; Estate Planning.
Baenen, Richard Anthony, (AV) '34 '59
C.723 A.B. L.477 J.D. 1735 New York Ave., N.W.
Baer, Teresa D. ....'— '86 C.659 B.A. L.813 J.D. [Latham&W.]
*PRACTICE AREAS: Communications and Media.
Baer, William E., Jr. ....'58 '83 C.945 B.A. L.188 J.D. [🄲 Morgan,L.&B.]
Baer, William J. ....'50 '75 C.399 B.A. L.813 J.D. [Arnold&P.]
*PRACTICE AREAS: Antitrust; Litigation.
Baez, Humberto Beau, III '65 '94 C.999 B.A.B.S. L.276 J.D.
(adm. in VA; not adm. in DC) Coun., Multistate Tax Comm.
Bagheri, Babak ....'73 '98 C.930 B.A. L.273 J.D. [🄰 Patton B.]
Bagileo, John R., (AV) ....'41 '66 C.276 B.S. L.93 LL.B. 1101 30th St. N.W.
Bagley, Andrew W. ....'63 '94 C.228 A.B. L.446 J.D. [🄰 Crowell&M.]
Bagley, Grant P. ....'41 '89 C&L.878 B.S., J.D. [Arnold&P.]
*PRACTICE AREAS: Health Care; Drug and Reimbursement; Health Policy and Practice.
Bagnall, Robert G. ....'56 '86 C.976 B.A. L.309 J.D. [🄲 Wilmer,C.&P.]
*PRACTICE AREAS: Securities Law.
Bagwell, Andrea Merritt ....'61 '92 C.302 B.A. L.276 J.D. [🄰 Harmon,W.&B.]
*PRACTICE AREAS: Lobbying; Corporate Law; Administrative Law.
Bahauddin, Anita M. '74 '99 C.477 B.A. L.904 J.D.
(adm. in VA; not adm. in DC) [🄰 Proskauer R.]
Bahena, Gary K., (AV) .... '59 '85 C.94 B.A. L.659 J.D. [Silverstein&M.]
*PRACTICE AREAS: Commercial Real Estate; Construction; Commercial Finance; Commercial Contracts; Real Estate Taxation.
Baheri, Leila M. '67 '94 C.228 B.A. L.30 J.D.
(adm. in PA; not adm. in DC) [🄰 Kelley D.&W.]
*PRACTICE AREAS: Telecommunications Law.
Bahin, Charlotte M, '56 '88 C.385 A.B. L.904 J.D.
(adm. in PA; not adm. in DC) Reg. Coun., America's Community Bnkers.

Bahr, Susan, PC, Law Offices of
(See Montgomery Village, Maryland)

Baik, Seung W. ....'— '00 C.188 B.A. L.597 J.D. [🄰 Latham&W.]
Bailen, Mark I. ....'69 '97 C.188 A.B. L.569 J.D. [🄰 Baker&H.]
*PRACTICE AREAS: Litigation; First Amendment; Libel Law.
Bailey, Anita Matyi .... '64 '94 C.823 B.S. L.64 J.D. 1201 New York Ave., N.W.
Bailey, Arthur L., (AV) ....'46 '72 C.823 B.A. L.30 J.D. [Steptoe&J.]
*PRACTICE AREAS: Insurance Taxation.
Bailey, Ashley N. ....'— '99 C&L.276 B.A., J.D. [🄰 Ropes&G.]
Bailey, Dori K. ....'— '00 C.1044 B.S. L.188 J.D. [🄰 Latham&W.]
*PRACTICE AREAS: Corporate.
Bailey, Edwin O., (AV) .... '40 '66 C.674 A.B. L.910 J.D. [Wiley R.&F.]
*PRACTICE AREAS: Litigation; Aviation.
Bailey, Gabrielle D. .... '73 '99 C.692 B.A. L.659 J.D. [🄰 Alston&B.]
*PRACTICE AREAS: Financial Services Law; Intellectual Property Licensing.
Bailey, Harold G., Jr. .... '59 '84 C.951 B.A. L.276 J.D. [Garvey,S.&B.]
*PRACTICE AREAS: Environmental Law; Legislative Process; Government Contracts; International Trade and Transactions.
Bailey, James C. .... '67 '93 C.754 B.A. L.1252 J.D. [🄰 Steptoe&J.]
Bailey, Julia K. ....'64 '96 C.802 B.A. L.45 J.D. [🄰 Williams M.]
*PRACTICE AREAS: International Business Transactions; International Trade; Customs Law; Export Regulation; International Anti-Corruption.
Bailey, Kathy D. ....'55 '85 C.326 B.S. L.30 J.D. [Bailey]
*PRACTICE AREAS: Environmental Law; Commercial Real Estate; Commercial Litigation.
Bailey, Kay '43 '67 C&L.846 LL.B.
(adm. in TX; not adm. in DC) 800 Independence Ave.‡
Bailey, Lyn Anne ....'69 '94 C.446 B.A. L.904 J.D. [🄰 Blank R.C.&M.]
*PRACTICE AREAS: Complex Commercial Litigation.
Bailey, Lynn Palmer '— '97 C.692 B.A. L.893 J.D.
(adm. in VA; not adm. in DC) 1730 Penn. Ave., N.W.‡
Bailey, Matthew T. .... '63 '89 C.688 B.S.E.E. L.128 J.D. [Hogan&H.] (Pat.)
*PRACTICE AREAS: Intellectual Property Law; Patent Law.
Bailey, Melissa A. ....'67 '95 C.597 B.A. L.378 J.D. [🄰 Arent F.K.P.&K.]
*PRACTICE AREAS: Occupational Safety and Health; Labor and Employment; Government Relations.
Bailey, Nora A., Law Office of, (AV) '41 '73
C.930 B.A. L.477 J.D. 1730 Rhode Island Ave. NW
Bailey, R. Gregory ....'61 '87 C&L.896 B.A., J.D. [Holland&K.]
*PRACTICE AREAS: ERISA and Employee Benefits; Executive Compensation; Federal Tax Legislation.
Bailey, R. Kevin .... '69 '99 C.228 B.A. L.597 J.D. [🄰 Wilmer,C.&P.]
Bailey, R. Russell, (AV) ....'51 '80 C.103 A.B. L.276 J.D. Air Line Pilots Assn.
Bailey, Robert A. '70 '98 C.112 B.A. L.273 J.D.
(adm. in WA; not adm. in DC) [🄰 Steptoe&J.]★
Bailey, Samuel, Jr. ....'49 '78 C&L.705 A.B., J.D. 1343 Pennsylvania Ave., S.E.
Bailey, Suzin C. '60 '93 C.101 B.S. L.273 J.D.
(adm. in MD; not adm. in DC; See Pat. Sect.) [🄰 Jacobson,H.]
*PRACTICE AREAS: Patent Prosecution; Litigation; Trademark; Copyright.
Bailey, William M. ....'63 '89 C&L.575 B.A., J.D. [🄰 Collier S.S.]
*PRACTICE AREAS: Litigation.

Bailey Law Group
1752 N Street, N.W., Suite 800, 20036
Telephone: 202-887-8040 Fax: 202-887-8044 URL: http://www.baileylawgroup.com
Email: kbailey@baileylawgroup.com
Kathy D. Bailey. Associates: Lisa M. Davenport; Dami Y. Odujinrin (Not admitted in DC); Alexa A. Cole.

(This Listing Continued)

Bailey Law Group (Continued)
Environmental Law, Clean Air Act, Environmental Litigation, Environmental Compliance, Environmental Permitting, Environmental Legislative Practice, Environmental Regulation, Risk Management, Commercial Real Estate, Leasing, Real Estate Joint Ventures, Commercial Real Estate Development, Federal Litigation.
See Professional Biographies, WASHINGTON, DISTRICT OF COLUMBIA

Baillif, Michael E. .... '66 '92 C.154 B.A. L.976 J.D. Sr. Mgr., Ernst & Young LLP‡
Bailor, Bernard S., (AV) ....'40 '77 C.717 B.S. L.276 J.D. [Caplin&D.]
*PRACTICE AREAS: Criminal Litigation.
Baim, Eric M. '72 '01 C.575 B.A. L.228 J.D.
(adm. in VA; not adm. in DC) [🄰 Shaw P.]
Bain, John W. .... '55 '98 C.679 B.S.E.E. L.345 J.D. [🄰 Sughrue M.] (See Pat. Sect.)
*PRACTICE AREAS: Intellectual Property.
Bain, Scott E. ....'— '97 C.494 B.E.E. L.1066 J.D. [🄰 Wiley R.&F.] (Pat.)
Baine, Kevin T., (AV) ....'49 '75 C.674 A.B. L.659 J.D. [Williams&C.]
Baird, Bruce A., (AV) ....'48 '76 C.188 B.A. L.569 J.D. [Covington&B.]
Baird, Elizabeth H. .... '— '96 C.103 A.B. L.276 J.D. [🄰 O'Melveny&M.]
Baird, Nancy D. .... '53 '89 C.280 B.S.Ed. L.276 J.D. 1440 New York Ave.
Baird, Orrin, (AV) '47 '77 C.918 B.A. L.1162 J.D.
Assoc. Gen. Coun., Service Employees Intl. Union
Baise, Gary H. ....'41 '68 C.927 B.S. L.345 J.D. [Baise&M.]
*PRACTICE AREAS: Environmental Law; Litigation.

Baise & Miller, P.C., (AV)
1020 19th Street NW, Suite 400, 20036
Telephone: 202-331-9100 Fax: 202-331-9060
Email: admin@dclaw.net URL: http://www.dclaw.net
Gary H. Baise; Eric P. Bock (Not admitted in DC); Anson M. Keller; Marshall Lee Miller; Mark L. Shaffer; Michael S. Levy;—Elizabeth S. Poliner; David G. Zanardi (Not admitted in DC); Stewart D. Fried; Michael C. Formica. Of Counsel: Guy Vander Jagt (Not admitted in DC); Alexander McMillan Bullock.
Environmental, Defamation, General Commercial and International Law.
See Professional Biographies, WASHINGTON, DISTRICT OF COLUMBIA

Baj, Alexandra E. P. ....'70 '00 C.385 B.A. L.145 J.D. [🄰 Steptoe&J.]
Bajefsky, Robert D., (AV) '43 '70
C.886 B.S.Ch.E. L.276 J.D. [Finnegan,H.F.G.&D.] (See Pat. Sect.)
*PRACTICE AREAS: Biotechnology Patents; Chemical Patents; Medical Patents; Patent Litigation; Pharmaceutical Patents.
Bajer, Edward R. '43 '80 C.476 B.S. L.1234 J.D.
Dir., Coalitions, Amer. Consulting Engineers Council
Bakari, Adisa P. .... '73 '98 C.204 B.A. L.966 J.D. [🄰 Dow,L.&A.]
Baker, Allyson '73 '01 C.178 B.A. L.569 J.D.
(adm. in NY; not adm. in DC) [🄰 Clifford C.R.&W.]
*PRACTICE AREAS: Litigation.
Baker, Brian W. .... '— '99 C.893 B.A. L.880 J.D. [🄰 Bracewell&P.]
*PRACTICE AREAS: Litigation; Government Contracts.
Baker, Daniele Allison '75 '01 C.853 B.A. L.276 J.D.
(adm. in VA; not adm. in DC) [🄰 Dechert]
*PRACTICE AREAS: Financial Services Law; Investment Management; Securities Litigation; Antitrust and Trade Regulation.
Baker, David H., (AV) ....'55 '79 C.299 B.A. L.273 J.D. [Thompson H.]
*PRACTICE AREAS: Transportation Law; Government Affairs; Regulatory Law; Product Safety Law.
Baker, Debra Ratterman '60 '85 C.475 B.A. L.309 J.D.
(adm. in CA; not adm. in DC) State Training Dir., ABA Ctr. on Children & the Law
Baker, Donald I., (AV) ....'34 '63 C.674 A.B. L.309 LL.B. [Baker&M.P.]
Baker, George D. ....'52 '78 C.299 B.A. L.128 J.D. [Williams&J.]
*PRACTICE AREAS: Energy and Environment Law; Agriculture Law; Trade Litigation.
Baker, Gregory L., (AV) ....'54 '79 C.893 B.A. L.846 J.D. [Howrey S.A.&W.]
*PRACTICE AREAS: Litigation; Antitrust Law; Intellectual Property.
Baker, Harold F., (AV) ....'21 '49 C.47 L.273 J.D. [Howrey S.A.&W.]
Baker, James A., IV .... '54 '82 C.188 B.S. L.846 J.D. [Baker B.]
Baker, James Addison, III, (AV) '30 '57 C.674 B.A. L.846 J.D.
(adm. in TX; not adm. in DC) Secy. [Baker B.] (⊙Hous., TX)
Baker, John M. .... '59 '85 C.138 B.A. L.309 J.D. [🄲 Stradley R.S.&Y.]
Baker, John S., Jr. ....'47 '72 C.1105 B.A. L.477 J.D. [M.E.Harrison]
Baker, June A. '46 '87 C.36 B.A. L.1066 J.D.
(adm. in CA; not adm. in DC) 1329 30th St., NW
Baker, M. Miller, (AV) ....'62 '84 C.420 L.861 J.D. [McDermott,W.&E.]
Baker, Marie C. '58 '01 C.446 B.A. L.30 J.D.
(adm. in NY; not adm. in DC) [🄰 Jorden B.]
*PRACTICE AREAS: Securities Law; Financial Services; Mutual Funds; Insurance Products; Corporate.
Baker, Marilyn L. .... '62 '89 C.429 B.A. L.30 J.D. [Mooney,G.B.&S.]
*PRACTICE AREAS: ERISA; Employee Benefits; Taft-Hartley Plans; Pension Plans; Health and Welfare Benefit Plans.
Baker, Mark E. ....'60 '85 C&L.893 B.A., J.D. [McGuiness N.&W.]
*PRACTICE AREAS: Employment Litigation; Equal Employment Opportunity Law; Labor Relations Law; Employment Law.
Baker, Mary M. ....'64 '90 C.160 B.A. L.276 J.D. [🄲 Kalbian H.]
*PRACTICE AREAS: Litigation.
Baker, Pamela Jean, (BV) '60 '85 C&L.420 B.S., J.D.
(adm. in LA; not adm. in DC) Vice President, American Arbitration Association
Baker, Raymond N., (AV) ....'24 '59 C.871 B.S. L.273 J.D. [Shanley&B.] (Pat.)
*PRACTICE AREAS: Patents; Trademarks; Copyrights; Patent Licensing; Patent Protection.
Baker, Reatha A. .... '— '96 C.880 B.A. L.734 J.D. [🄰 Kirkland&E.]
*PRACTICE AREAS: Corporate.
Baker, Robert C., Jr. ....'53 '79 C.282 A.B. L.537 J.D. 2031 Florida Ave., N.W.
Baker, Stewart A., (AV) ....'47 '77 C.103 A.B. L.1068 J.D. [Steptoe&J.]
*PRACTICE AREAS: Technology Law; International Law.
Baker, William B., (BV) ....'57 '83 C&L.893 B.A., J.D. [Wiley R.&F.]
*PRACTICE AREAS: Communications; Internet; Privacy; Postal.
Baker-Battist, Ruth S., Law Offices of, (AV) '33 '65 C.94 B.A. L.276 J.D.
1850 M Street, N.W. Suite 240 (⊙Chevy Chase, MD)

Baker Botts, L.L.P., (AV) BR
A Registered Limited Liability Partnership
The Warner, 1299 Pennsylvania Avenue, N.W., 20004-2400 ⊙
Telephone: 202-639-7700 Fax: 202-639-7832
Email: postmaster@bakerbotts.com URL: http://www.bakerbotts.com
Members of Firm: Jay L. Alexander; R. Thomas Amis; James B. Arpin; James A. Baker IV; James Addison Baker, III (Not admitted in DC); Michael J. Barta; J. Bradley Bennett; Ellen Fels Berkman; J. Patrick Berry; Stephen L. Braga; William M. Bumpers; Joe R. Caldwell, Jr.; John Joseph Cassidy; Christopher R. Cooper; Kelly Riley Donovan; James R. Doty; Thomas J. Eastment; Paul F. Enzinna; Michael A. Gold; Julia E. Guttman; James R. Heavner, Jr.; Steven R. Hunsicker; William H. Jeffress, Jr.; Debra J. Jezouit; Bruce F. Kiely; Jody Manier Kris; Niki Kuckes; Raymond G. Larroca; Steven L. Leifer; Mark K. Lewis; Randolph Quaile McManus; Herbert J. Miller, Jr.; Martin D. Minsker; R. Stan Mortenson; Harold D. Murry, Jr.; David N. Powers; Daniel J. Riley; James E. Rocap, III; Joanne C. Rutkowski; Mary C. Spearing; Jeffrey A. Stonerock; David A. Super; Randall J. Turk. Special Counsel: Diana L. Dietrich; Robert L. Troike; O. Kevin Vincent. Of Counsel: Evan R. Berlack; Jay M. Cantor; Thomas B. Carr; Theodore C. Jonas (Not admitted in DC); Robert H. Pelletreau (Also Member, Afridi, Angell & Pelletreau LLP); A. John Radsan. Associates: Demitrius M. Anthony (Not admitted in DC); E. Barrett Atwood, IV (Not admitted in DC); Brooksany Barrowes (Not admitted in DC); Jason Bennett (Not admitted in DC); Ryan Edward Bull (Not admitted in DC); James P. Calve

(This Listing Continued)

Baker Botts, L.L.P. (Continued)

(Not admitted in DC); Timothy J. Churna (Not admitted in DC); Glenn Frederick Elliott, Jr. (Not admitted in DC); Rebecca H. Ewing (Not admitted in DC); Jacqueline H. Fine; Joshua B. Frank; Gregory J. Golden; Renu K. Gupta (Not admitted in DC); Jacqueline Haberer (Not admitted in DC); Thomas E. Holmberg (Not admitted in DC); Jon B. Jordan; Richard C. King, Jr. (Not admitted in DC); Stephanie A. Martz; Melissa E. Maxwell; Kelli C. McTaggart; Mark A. Miller; Suhail Partawi (Not admitted in DC); Nikesh R. Patel; Clara M. Poffenberger; Mary Ann Poirier; Frank W. Rambo (Not admitted in DC); Almira P. Saenz (Not admitted in DC); Stephen M. Silver; Mark T. Stancil (Not admitted in DC); Tamar C. Stanley; Ramsey R. Taylor (Also at Riyadh, Saudi Arabia Office); Samuel J. Waldon; Wendy Barrett Warren; Matthew T. West; Stephanie L. Zucker (Not admitted in DC).
Antitrust, Construction, Securities, Mergers and Acquisitions, Energy, Environmental, Finance, White Collar Crime, Government Contracts, Intellectual Property, Patents, Trademarks, Copyrights, Trade Secrets, International Trade, Tax, Trial, Administrative Law, Alternative Dispute Resolution, Biotechnology, Business Law, Commercial Law, Computers and Software, Criminal Law, Fraud and Deceit, Government, Insurance, Regulatory Law, Technology and Science, Utility Law.
Houston, Texas Office: One Shell Plaza, 910 Louisiana. Telephone: 713-229-1234.
Austin, Texas Office: 1600 San Jacinto Center, 98 San Jacinto Boulevard. Telephone: 512-322-2500.
Dallas, Texas Office: 2001 Ross Avenue. Telephone: 214-953-6500.
New York, New York Office: 599 Lexington Avenue. Telephone: 212-705-5000.
London, England Office: 45 Ludgate Hill. Telephone: 0171-778-1400 (Local); 011-44-171-778-1400 (International).
Baku, Azerbaijan Office: 6-10 Vagif Mustafa-zadeh Street, Third Floor, Icheri Sheher, 370004. Telephone: 994-12-97-63-88 (Local); 011-994-12-97-63-88 (International). Fax: 994-12-97-63-91 (Local); 011-994-12-97-63-91 (International).
Associated Firm: Mohammed Bin Saud Al Rasheed, Attorneys and Legal Consultants, Le Cygne Commercial Center, No. 2, Olaya, Main Road, P.O. Box 62982, Riyadh 11595, Saudi Arabia. Telephone: (966-1) 464-3139. Facsimile: (966-1) 464-9264.

See Professional Biographies, WASHINGTON, DISTRICT OF COLUMBIA

Baker & Daniels, (AV)
805 15th Street, N.W., Suite 700, 20005 ⊙
Telephone: 202-312-7440 Fax: 202-312-7460
URL: http://www.bakerdaniels.com
Members of Firm: Albert R. Dawson; Joseph W. Kimmell, II (Not admitted in DC); Jana Lee Pruitt; Charles T. Richardson; Frank S. Swain; Mark W. Weller (Not admitted in DC); David R. Zook (Not admitted in DC). Counsel: Ted R. Mannen. Associates: Thomas A. Jensen; Kerri M. Willis (Not admitted in DC).
Antitrust, Bankruptcy, Business Planning, Commercial, Corporate Finance, Creditors Rights, Employee Benefits, Employment, Environment, Estate and Probate, Family, Financial, Food and Drug, Government Affairs, Health Care, Insurance, Intellectual Property, International, Legislative, Litigation, Medical Technology Regulation, Municipal, Nonprofit, Product Liability, Real Estate, Securities, Sports, Tax, Transportation, Utilities, Year 2000, Zoning and Land Use Law.
Indianapolis, Indiana Office: 300 North Meridian Street, Suite 2700, 46204. Telephone: 317-237-0300. Fax: 317-237-1000.
Fort Wayne, Indiana Office: 111 East Wayne Street, Suite 800, 46802. Telephone: 219-424-8000. Fax: 219-460-1700.
South Bend, Indiana Office: First Bank Building, 205 West Jefferson Boulevard, Suite 250, 46601. Telephone: 219-234-4149. Fax: 219-239-1900.
Elkhart, Indiana Office: 317 West Franklin Street, P.O. Box 507, 46515-0507. Telephone: 219-296-6000. Fax: 219-296-6001.
Indianapolis-96th Street, Indiana Office: Parkwood Six, 600 East 96th Street, Suite 600, 46240. Telephone: 317-569-9600. Fax: 317-569-4800.
Qingdao, China Office: Room A & C, 9th Floor, Qingdao Beer Building, May 4th Square, 35 Donghai Road, 266071. Telephone: +011-86-532-575-1051. Fax: +011-86-532-575-1055.

See Professional Biographies, WASHINGTON, DISTRICT OF COLUMBIA

Baker, Donelson, Bearman & Caldwell, (AV)
Lincoln Square, 6th Floor, 555 Eleventh Street, N.W., 20004 ⊙
Telephone: 202-508-3400 Telecopier: 202-508-3402
Email: info@bdbc.com URL: http://www.bakerdonelson.com
Managing Partner: James C. Duff. Partners: Lewis R. Donelson, III; Robert F. Worthington, Jr.; James W. McBride; Robert Engelbrecht Hauberg, Jr.; George Cranwell Montgomery; Joan M. McEntee; Anne M. Stolee; Charles Richard Johnston, Jr. Of Counsel: Albert B. Randall; Doreen M. Edelman; Raymond E. Mabus, Jr. Associate: Anne V. Winter (Not admitted in DC). Senior Foreign-Policy Advisor: Mark R. Parris.
General Practice, Civil Trial and Appellate Practice before all State and Federal Courts, Administrative Agencies and Commercial Arbitration Forums. Antitrust and Trade Regulation, Aviation, Banking and Finance, Bankruptcy, Business Compliance, Commercial Finance, Communications, Construction, Corporations, Employment and Labor, Entertainment, Environmental, Estate Planning and Administration, Family Law, Franchising, Healthcare, Immigration, Intellectual Property, International Law. Litigation including Commercial and Business, Personal Injury, Product Liability and Professional Malpractice, Mergers and Acquisitions, Municipal Finance, Municipal Law, Partnerships, Pensions and Employee Benefits, Real Estate Development, Securities, Federal, State and Local Taxation, Tax-Exempt Organizations, Transportation, Utilities, White Collar Crime, Zoning and Land Use Law.
Memphis, Tennessee Office: 20th Floor, First Tennessee Building, 165 Madison, 38103. Telephone: 901-526-2000. Telecopier: 901-577-2303.
Nashville, Tennessee Office: Commerce Center, Suite 1000, 211 Commerce Street, 37201. Telephone: 615-726-5600. Telecopier: 615-726-0464.
Chattanooga, Tennessee Office: 1800 Republic Centre, 633 Chestnut Street, 37450-1800. Telephone: 423-756-2010. Telecopier: 423-756-3447.
Knoxville, Tennessee Office: 2200 Riverview Tower, 900 South Gay Street, 37901. Telephone: 865-549-7000. Telecopier: 865-525-8569.
Johnson City, Tennessee Office: SunTrust Bank Building, 207 Mockingbird Lane, P.O. Box 3038, 37602. Telephone: 423-928-0181. Telecopier: 423-928-5694; 423-928-3654; Kingsport: 423-246-6191.
Huntsville, Tennessee Office: 3 Courthouse Square, 37756. Telephone: 423-663-2321. Telecopier: 423-663-2111.
Jackson, Mississippi Office: 4268 I-55 North, Meadowbrook Office Park, 39211. Telephone: 601-351-2400. Telecopier: 601-351-2424.
Atlanta, Georgia Office: 5 Concourse Parkway, Suite 900, 30328. Telephone: 770-396-2244. Telecopier: 770-399-9363.
Atlanta, Georgia Office: 3490 Piedmont Road, Suite 650, 30305. Telephone: 404-812-3100. Fax: 404-812-3101.

See Professional Biographies, WASHINGTON, DISTRICT OF COLUMBIA

Baker & Hostetler LLP, (AV)
Washington Square, Suite 1100, 1050 Connecticut Avenue, N.W., 20036-5304 ⊙
Telephone: 202-861-1500 Fax: 202-861-1783 To contact an attorney on the Internet use first initial and surname followed by @bakerlaw.com
URL: http://www.bakerlaw.com
Office Managing Partner: William H. Schweitzer (Managing Partner, Washington, D.C. Office). Partners: Marc A. Antonetti; Edward Jay Beckwith; Ralph G. Blasey, III; John J. Burke; Lee A. Casey; Bruce J. Casino; Frederick W. Chockley, III; William F. Conroy; William J. Conti; Barry J. Cutler; Mark A. Cymrot; Matthew J. Dolan; Lee T. Ellis, Jr.; Elliot J. Feldman; David J. Fischer; Peder A. Garske; Frederick H. Graefe; David Alistair Grant; Brian S. Harvey; Kenneth C. Howard, Jr.; Robert D. Lystad; David L. Marshall; Shelby F. Mitchell; Betty Southard Murphy; Roger A. Pies; David B. Rivkin; Bruce W. Sanford; Louis R. Sernoff; Lee H. Simowitz; David S. Wachen; Ronald F. Wick; Joanne W. Young; Henry G. Zapruder. Associates: Mark I. Bailen; Johnine P. Barnes; Darin R. Bartram; Bruce D. Brown; Marylou Brown (Not admitted in DC); David S. Chung; Arland DiGirolamo (Not admitted in DC); Robert M. Doherty (Not admitted in DC); Andrew J. Durkovic (Not admitted in DC); Adam Gropper (Not admitted in DC); Samuel L. Hendrix; Karen M. Kramer; Mandana Parsazad; Janis M. Penman; India J. Pinkney (Not admitted in DC); Elizabeth A. Scully (Not admitted in DC); Christopher T. Stephen. Of Counsel: E. Mark Braden; Jenifer M. Brown; Luis A. Galliani (Not admitted in United States); Kathleen M. Kerrigan; David M. Kirstein; Julia A. Oas; Madeleine B. Schaller; Guy Vander Jagt. Retired Partners: Richard H. Jones; Harlan Pomeroy.
General Practice.
In Cleveland, Ohio: 3200 National City Center, 1900 East Ninth Street. Telephone: 216-621-0200.
In Cincinnati, Ohio: 312 Walnut Street, Suite 2650. Telephone: 513-929-3400.
In Columbus, Ohio: Capitol Square, Suite 2100, 65 East State Street. Telephone: 614-228-1541.
In Costa Mesa, California: 600 Anton Boulevard, Suite 650. Telephone: 714-754-6600.
In Denver, Colorado: 303 East 17th Avenue, Suite 1100. Telephone: 303-861-0600.
In Houston, Texas: 1000 Louisiana, Suite 2000. Telephone: 713-751-1600.

(This Listing Continued)

Baker & Hostetler LLP (Continued)

In Los Angeles, California: 333 South Grand Avenue, Suite 1800. Telephone: 213-975-1600.
In Orlando, Florida: SunTrust Center, Suite 2300, 200 South Orange Avenue. Telephone: 407-649-4000.
In New York, N.Y.: 666 Fifth Avenue. Telephone: 646-496-1600.

See Professional Biographies, WASHINGTON, DISTRICT OF COLUMBIA

Baker, Lancianese, Campbell & Conaty, (AV)
1090 Vermont Avenue, N.W., Suite 800 (⊙Lexington, KY; Charleston, Huntington, WV)

Baker & McKenzie, (AV)
815 Connecticut Avenue, N.W., 20006-4078 ⊙
Telephone: (202) 452-7000 Int'l. Dialing: (1-202) 452-7000 Facsimile: (1-202) 452-7074
URL: http://www.bakernet.com
Members of Firm: Mary C. Bennett; David A. Clanton; Nicholas F. Coward; W. Warren Crowdus, III; Peter M. Daub; Edward E. Dyson; Thomas J. Egan, Jr.; Teresa A. Gleason; Daniel L. Goelzer; Jonathan W. Gottlieb; Mary B. Hevener; David J. Laing; Dennis I. Meyer; Kevin M. O'Brien; William D. Outman, II; Marc R. Paul; B. Thomas Peele III; Richard L. Slowinski; C. David Swenson; Leonard B. Terr; Eugene Theroux; A. Duane Webber; Lynda S. Zengerle; Michael J. Zimmer. National Partners: Marianna G. Dyson; Harry A. Franks, Jr.; Kenneth R. Hayduk; Rachael E. Schwartz; Stuart P. Seidel; Marc B. Tucker. Of Counsel: Howard Adler, Jr.; Anne G. Batter; Susan G. Braden; John W. Polk; John R. Reilly; Lee H. Spence. Resident Associates: Bill Batchelor (Not admitted in the United States); Robert H. Bethea; Margaret R. Blake; Gregory W. Bowman; Phoebe W. Brown; Brian F. Burke; John A. Cohen; David S. Cole; Thomas M. Cryan, Jr; Samir S. Desai; Roger M. Gibian; Dirk Gifford; Thomas Görgemanns (Not admitted in the United States); Kristi K. Hansen (Not admitted in DC); Mark R. Heilbrun; Joshua J. Izenberg (Not admitted in DC); Janet K. Kim; Juhong Kim (Not admitted in DC); Scott A. Knott; Matthew B. Landon; Micah A. Levy; Jeffrey P. Maydew (Not admitted in DC); Jean A. Milner (Not admitted in DC); Jennifer Barbee Molnar (Not admitted in DC); Michael E. Murphy; Allen Orr Jr.; Irene M. Recio (Not admitted in DC); Marni K. Rosenblatt; William Randolph (Randy) Rucker (Not admitted in DC); Jennifer Ancona Semko (Not admitted in DC); Neil K. Shapiro; Alison Stafford (Not admitted in the United States); Ronald David Trice; Adam C. Underwood (Not admitted in DC); Stephen H. Wagner; Thomas Edward Willis, II (Not admitted in DC).
Taxation. Customs, Tariff and International Trade Law. Corporate and Securities. Litigation. Practice before Governmental Departments, Commissions and Administrative Agencies. Patents and Trademark Law. Antitrust. Telecommunications. Banking.
Associated Offices of Baker & McKenzie in: Almaty, Amsterdam, Baku, Bangkok, Barcelona, Beijing, Berlin, Bogotá, Brasília, Brussels, Budapest, Buenos Aires, Cairo, Calgary, Caracas, Chicago, Dallas, Düsseldorf, Frankfurt, Geneva, Guadalajara, Hanoi, Ho Chi Minh City, Hong Kong, Houston, Juárez, Kuala Lumpur, Kyiv, London, Madrid, Manama, Manila, Melbourne, México City, Miami, Milan, Monterrey, Moscow, Münich, New York, Palo Alto, Paris, Porto Alegre, Prague, Rio de Janeiro, Riyadh, Rome, St. Petersburg, San Diego, San Francisco, Santiago, São Paulo, Singapore, Stockholm, Sydney, Taipei, Tijuana, Tokyo, Toronto, Valencia, Warsaw and Zürich.
Correspondent Law Firm: Hadiputranto, Hadinoto & Partners, Jakarta.

See Professional Biographies, WASHINGTON, DISTRICT OF COLUMBIA

Baker & Miller PLLC, (AV)
Suite 1000, 915 Fifteenth Street, N.W., 20005-2318
Telephone: 202-637-9499 Facsimile: 202-637-9394
URL: http://www.bakerandmiller.com
Donald I. Baker; W. Todd Miller; Deirdre L. Hay (Not admitted in DC);—Christine J. Sommer (Not admitted in DC). Special Counsel: Alice G. Glass.
Antitrust Counselling and Litigation, Government Investigations, Arbitration and Mediation, International Transactions and Disputes, Network Legal Problems, Electronic Banking Issues and Appeals.

See Professional Biographies, WASHINGTON, DISTRICT OF COLUMBIA

Baker-Shenk, Philip .... '57 '84 C.1124 B.S. L.128 J.D. [Dorsey&W.]
*PRACTICE AREAS: Native American Law; Federal Indian Law; Federal Civil Practice; Government Relations; Indian Gaming Law.
Bakich, Kathryn Louise .... '59 '85 C&L.502 B.A., J.D. 1350 Connecticut Ave. N.W.
Bakshian, Mary .... '— '42 C.273 L.537 LL.B. 4211 48th Pl., N.W.
Balaran, Alan '55 '92 C.273 B.A. L.1364 J.D.
1717 Pennsylvania Avenue, N.W., 12th Floor

Balch & Bingham LLP, (AV)
1275 Pennsylvania Avenue, N.W., 10th Floor, 20004 ⊙
Telephone: 202-347-6000 Facsimile: 202-347-6001
URL: http://www.balch.com
Counsel: Haley Barbour (Not admitted in DC); Lanny Griffith (Not admitted in DC); Edward M. Rogers, Jr. Resident Members of Firm: Frederick R. Eames (Not admitted in DC); Patrick J. McCormick, III; Barbara K. Olson (Not admitted in DC). Resident Associate: Kristi L. Remington (Not admitted in DC).
General Practice, Corporation, Public Utilities, Banking, Public Finance, Taxation, Securities, Antitrust, Litigation, Labor and Employment, Probate, Real Estate, Insurance, Intellectual Property, Environmental, Bankruptcy, Legislative Practice, Mergers and Acquisitions, Health Care, International Business Transactions, Criminal, Education, Construction, Products Liability, Coal and Natural Gas, and Personal Injury Law. Trials in all Courts. Alternative Dispute Resolution.
Counsel for: Alabama Power Co.; Blue Cross and Blue Shield of Alabama; The Boeing Co.; Brasfield & Gorrie, Inc.; Compass Bancshares, Inc.; Harbert Corp.; Kimberly-Clark Corp.; Southern Company Services, Inc.; Southern Research Institute; Vesta Insurance Group, Inc.
Birmingham, Alabama Offices: 1710 Sixth Avenue North, 35203. Telephone: 205-251-8100. Facsimile: 205-226-8798. 1901 Sixth Avenue North, 35203. Telephone: 205-251-8100. Facsimile: 205-226-8799.
Montgomery, Alabama Office: The Winter Building, 2 Dexter Avenue, 36104. Telephone: 334-834-6500. Facsimile: 334-269-3115.
Huntsville, Alabama Office: 655 Gallatin Street, 35801. Telephone: 205-551-0171. Facsimile: 205-512-0119.
Gulfport, Mississippi Office: 1310 Twenty-Fifth Avenue. P.O. Box 130. Telephone: 228-864-9900. Fax: 228-864-8221.
Jackson, Mississippi Office: 200 North Congress Street, Suite 310. Telephone: 601-961-9900. Fax: 601-961-4466.
Hattiesburg, Mississippi Office: 119 Hardy Street. P.O. Box 707. Telephone: 601-544-1215. Fax: 601-582-8732.
Bay St. Louis, Mississippi Office: 841 Highway 90. Telephone: 228-466-9905. Fax: 228-467-1079.

See Professional Biographies, WASHINGTON, DISTRICT OF COLUMBIA

Balderston, Scott D. '63 '89 C.884 B.S.E.E. L.659 J.D.
(adm. in PA; not adm. in DC; Pat.) [A Hunton&W.]
*PRACTICE AREAS: Intellectual Property.
Baldino, Frank S. ....'62 '87 C.529 B.A. L.776 J.D. [A Thompson H.]
*PRACTICE AREAS: Taxation; Corporate Law; Business Planning; Personal Planning; Successions.
Baldridge, J. Douglas ....'62 '87 C.259 B.A. L.273 J.D. [Howrey S.A.&W.]
*PRACTICE AREAS: Litigation.
Baldwin, James A. '68 '93 C.884 B.S. L.276 J.D.
(adm. in PA; not adm. in DC) [A Sutherland A.&B.]
*PRACTICE AREAS: Corporate Finance; Mergers and Acquisitions; Financial Institutions Law.
Baldwin, Jana V. T. ....'64 '91 C.47 B.A. L.893 J.D. [McDermott,W.&E.]
Baldwin, Kevin J. '39 '68 C.865 A.B. L.383 J.D.
Dept. Head - Lit. & Collections, Washington Gas Light Co.
Baldwin, Raymond C. '63 '96 C&L.466 B.A., J.D.
(adm. in MD; not adm. in DC) [A Seyfarth S.]
*PRACTICE AREAS: Labor and Employment.
Baldwin, Susan E. '74 '01 C.902 B.S. L.893 J.D.
(adm. in VA; not adm. in DC) [A Shaw P.]
Balis, Stanley W., (AV) .... '49 '75 C.94 B.S. L.276 J.D. [Miller,B.&O.]
*PRACTICE AREAS: Economic Regulatory Law; Energy Contracts; Gas Utilities.
Ball, Andrea '56 '91 C.112 B.A. L.29 J.D.
(adm. in CA; not adm. in DC) Nonprofit Advocacy Coun., Alliance for Justice

Ball, Angela Y. .... '74 '00 C.446 B.S. L.276 J.D. [[A] Kirkpatrick&L.]
*PRACTICE AREAS: Electronic Commerce; Corporate Law.

Ball, Hilary E. ....'64 '91 C.859 B.A. L.192 J.D. [Gardner,M.F.G.&K.]

Ball, John William, Jr. .... '64 '99 C.871 B.S. L.1243 J.D. [[A] Kilpatrick S.] (Pat.)
*PRACTICE AREAS: Intellectual Property.

Ball, Markham, (AV) .... '34 '61 C.31 B.A. L.309 LL.B. [Holland&K.]
*PRACTICE AREAS: International Arbitration; International Contracts.

Ball Janik LLP, (AV)
1455 F Street, N.W., Suite 225, 20005-1004 ⊙
Telephone: 202-638-3307 Telecopy: 202-783-6947
Email: info@balljanik.com URL: http://www.balljanik.com
Members of Firm: James A. Beall; Robert G. Hayes; Irene L. Ringwood. Of Counsel: Louis E. Gitomer (Not admitted in DC); Jay S. Johnson (Not admitted in DC); Karl Morell (Not admitted in DC).
Government Affairs, Legislative and Administrative Lobbying, Administrative Law, Federal Regulatory and Transportation Law.
Portland, Oregon Office: One Main Place, 101 S.W. Main Street, Suite 1100, 97204-3219. Telephone: 503-228-2525. Telecopy: 503-295-1058.
Bend, Oregon Office: 15 S.W. Colorado Avenue, Building 2, Suite K, 97702. Telephone: 541-617-1309. Telecopy: 541-617-8824.
See Professional Biographies, WASHINGTON, DISTRICT OF COLUMBIA

Ballantyne, Michèle S. ....'66 '97 C.034 B.A. L.276 J.D. 3050 K St., N.W.

Ballard, Frederic L., Jr., (AV) '41 '66
C&L.309 B.A., LL.B. [Ballard S.A.&I.] (⊙Phila., PA)
*PRACTICE AREAS: Finance; Health Care; Housing; Municipal Law; Taxation.

Ballard, Jeffrey S. ....'62 '90 C.813 B.A. L.273 J.D. [Ballard S.A.&I.]
*PRACTICE AREAS: Finance; Corporate Law; Securities.

Ballard Spahr Andrews & Ingersoll, LLP, (AV) [BR]
Suite 1000 South, 601 13th Street, N.W., 20005-3807 ⊙
Telephone: 202-661-2200 Fax: 202-661-2299
URL: http://www.ballardspahr.com
Nancy V. Alquist (Not admitted in DC); Frederic L. Ballard, Jr.; Jeffrey S. Ballard; Paul K. Casey; N. Beth Emery; Joseph A. Fanone; Mary Jo George (Not admitted in DC); W. Kimball Griffith; Charles S. Henck; Thomas L. Howard; F. Joseph Nealon; Constantinos G. Panagopoulos; Perry D. Robinson; Linda B. Schakel; Howard H. Shafferman; Daniel F. Stenger; Margo BeVier Stern; Allan R. Winn; Kelly Mitchell Wrenn. Of Counsel: Katherine L. Bishop; James P. Cooke; Eileen M. Greenbaum; Cynthia M. Hajost; B. Cheryl Terio; S. Elizabeth Weaver;—W. Langhorne Ambrose; Rhonda D. Bond-Collins; Marina K. Bowsher; Amy E. Campbell; Gwynne W. Guzzeau (Not admitted in DC); Steve N. Isser; Robert A. Kaplan; Kirsten E. Keating; Jeffrey W. Larroca; Paul J. Miller; Elizabeth G. Moulds (Not admitted in DC); Ann Marie H. Peters; Vicky Tsilas; Kurt E. Van Engen; John A. Washington, Jr.; Susan S. Yim.
General Practice.
Baltimore, Maryland Office: 300 East Lombard Street, 19th Floor. Telephone: 410-528-5600. Fax: 410-528-5650.
Camden, New Jersey Office: 800 Hudson Square, 5th Floor. Telephone: 856-541-5577. Fax: 856-541-8772.
Denver, Colorado Office: Seventeenth Street Plaza Building, Suite 2300, 1225 17th Street. Telephone: 303-292-2400. Fax: 303-296-3956.
Philadelphia, Pennsylvania Office: 1735 Market Street, 51st Floor. Telephone: 215-665-8500. Fax: 215-834-8999.
Salt Lake City, Utah Office: 201 South Main Street, Suite 600. Telephone: 801-531-3000. Fax: 801-531-3001.
Voorhees, New Jersey Office: Suite 500, Plaza 1000, Main Street. Telephone: 856-761-3400. Fax: 856-761-1020.
Revisers of the Pennsylvania Law Digest for this Directory.
See Professional Biographies, WASHINGTON, DISTRICT OF COLUMBIA

Ballen, Robert G. ....'56 '81 C.674 B.A. L.309 J.D. [Schwartz&B.]
*PRACTICE AREAS: Financial Services; Payments Law; International Banking; E-Commerce and Payments.

Ballenger, Laurie G. ....'67 '94 C.198 B.A. L.575 J.D. [[A] Shaw P.]

Baller, James, (AV) ....'47 '73 C.197 A.B. L.188 J.D. [B.Herbst] ⊙

Baller Herbst Law Group, The, (AV)
2014 P Street, N.W. Suite 200, 20036 ⊙
Telephone: 202-833-5300 Fax: 202-833-1180
Email: jimb@baller.com URL: http://www.baller.com
James Baller; Adrian E. Herbst (Not admitted in DC); Sean A. Stokes.
General Practice.
Minneapolis, Minnesota Office: 953 East Grain Exchange Building, 400 South Fourth Street. 55415-1413.
See Professional Biographies, WASHINGTON, DISTRICT OF COLUMBIA

Ballew, Steven E. .... '45 '78 C.228 A.B. L.800 J.D. [Hogan&H.]
*PRACTICE AREAS: Corporate and Public Finance; Securities Law; International Transactions; General Commercial.

Ballonoff, Paul A. '43 '92 C.112 B.A. L.1060 J.D.
(adm. in CA; not adm. in DC) [[A] Hunton&W.]
*PRACTICE AREAS: Energy; General.

Ballotta, Karen A. ....'68 '95 C.105 B.A. L.245 J.D. [[A] Covington&B.]
*PRACTICE AREAS: Litigation; Civil Litigation; Federal Litigation.

Ballou, Sandy M. '— '96 C.188 B.A. L.477 J.D.
(adm. in WI; not adm. in DC) [[A] Foley&L.]
*PRACTICE AREAS: Health Law.

Balto, David A. ....'52 '83 L.588 J.D. [White&C.]

Baltz, Richard E. ....'60 '85 C.216 B.A. L.276 J.D. [Arnold&P.]
*PRACTICE AREAS: Federal Securities Law; Corporate.

Baltzan, Elizabeth V. .... '70 '97 C.813 B.A. L.276 J.D. [[A] Hogan&H.]
*PRACTICE AREAS: International Trade.

Baluss, Jane E. ....'52 '85 C.575 B.A. L.228 J.D. [Buc&B.]

Baluss, Mary E., (AV) .... '48 '75 C.228 B.A. L.273 J.D. 1800 M St., NW

Bamberger, David H. ....'48 '81 C.855 B.A. L.273 J.D. [Piper M.R.&W.]
*PRACTICE AREAS: Litigation; Antitrust Law.

Bambino, Laurence M. '55 '83 C.178 B.A. L.823 J.D.
(adm. in NY; not adm. in DC) [Shearman&S.]

Bancroft, J. Gail, (AV) ....'49 '77 C.747 B.A. L.352 J.D. [Powell,G.F.&M.]
*PRACTICE AREAS: Corporate Law; Project Finance.

Band, Gary A. ....'65 '90 C.861 B.S.M. L.904 J.D. [Nixon P.]
*PRACTICE AREAS: Real Estate Syndication; Taxation.

Band, Ian P. ....'62 '87 C.446 B.A. L.904 J.D. [Hunton&W.]
*PRACTICE AREAS: Immigration.

Band, Jonathan .... '59 '85 C.309 A.B. L.976 J.D. [Morrison&F.]
*PRACTICE AREAS: Intellectual Property; Internet Regulation; Appellate Litigation.

Bandow, Doug ....'57 '79 C.259 B.S. L.813 J.D. Cato Institute

Baneman, Roger J., (AV) '51 '77 C.976 B.A. L.306 J.D.
(adm. in NY; not adm. in DC) [Shearman&S.]

Bang, Joyce .... '60 '86 C.597 B.A. L.276 J.D. 1722 I St., N.W.

Bangert, Beth A. '70 '01 C.72 B.A. L.128 J.D.
(adm. in MD; not adm. in DC) [[A] Slevin&H.]
*PRACTICE AREAS: ERISA; Employee Benefits.

Bangert, Philip A. .... '61 '91 C.1203 B.A. L.128 J.D. [Patton B.]

Bank, Richard K., (BV) .... '41 '66 C&L.188 B.S., J.D. [Thompson C.]
*PRACTICE AREAS: International Trade; Maritime Law; Legislative Law.

Bank, Rita M., (AV) .... '46 '78 C.331 B.A. L.128 J.D. [Feldesman,T.L.F.&B.]
*PRACTICE AREAS: Family Law; Business Law; Investments.

Banks, J. Taylor .... '49 '75 C.378 B.S. L.477 J.D. Natural Res. Def. Council

Banks, James T., (AV) ....'49 '76 C.378 B.S. L.477 J.D. [Hogan&H.]
*PRACTICE AREAS: Environmental; Regulation; Legislative; Litigation.

Banks, Jonathan B. ....'57 '83 C&L.477 B.A., J.D. Gen. Coun., BellSouth Corp.

Banks, Lisa J. .... '68 '95 C.855 B.A. L.208 J.D. [[A] Bernabei&K.]
*PRACTICE AREAS: Employment Discrimination; Civil Rights; Civil Liberties.

Banks, Quentin W. .... '22 '51 C&L.329 A.B., LL.B. 6411 16th St. N.W.

Banks, Sharon P. ....'42 '68 C.512 B.A. L.329 J.D. Howard Univ.

Banks, Terry M., (AV) ....'47 '73 C.477 B.S. L.128 J.D. Coun., EOP Group

Banks, Wyndell O. '64 '90 C.803 B.S. L.329 J.D.
(adm. in MI; not adm. in DC) [[C] Smith&Assoc.]

Banner, Brian E. ....'— '74 C.37 B.S.B.A. L.365 J.D. [Banner&W.] (See Pat. Sect.)
*PRACTICE AREAS: Intellectual Property Law; Trademarks; Copyrights; Intellectual Property Licensing.

Banner, Donald W., (AV) '— '53
C.679 B.S.E.E. L.215 J.D. [Banner&W.] (See Pat. Sect.)
*PRACTICE AREAS: Intellectual Property Law; Patents; Intellectual Property Litigation; Intellectual Property Licensing.

Banner, Pamela I., (AV) '— '87 C.679 B.S.E.E. L.273 J.D.
[Banner&W.] (See Pat. Sect.)
*PRACTICE AREAS: Intellectual Property Law; Patents; Intellectual Property Litigation; Appellate Practice; Electrical Intellectual Property.

Banner, Roy R. ....'15 '50 C.437 B.S. L.276 J.D. 3700 Massachusetts Ave., N.W.‡

Banner & Witcoff, Ltd., (AV) [BR]
Established In 1920 - Predecessor Parent
1001 G Street, N.W., 20001-4597 ⊙
Telephone: 202-508-9100 Facsimile: 202-508-9299
Email: cooperman@bannerwitcoff.com URL: http://www.bannerwitcoff.com
Robert F. Altherr, Jr.; Brian E. Banner; Donald W. Banner; Pamela I. Banner; Gary D. Fedorochko; William J. Fisher; Christopher R. Glembocki; Brian E. Hanlon; Patricia E. Hong; Dale H. Hoscheit; Thomas H. Jackson; Sarah A. Kagan; Robert S. Katz; Christopher L. McKee; Nina L. Medlock; Frederic M. Meeker; Helen Hill Minsker; Thomas L. Peterson; Joseph M. Potenza; Steven P. Schad; Joseph M. Skerpon; Susan A. Wolffe; Bradley C. Wright. Of Counsel: William W. Beckett; Edward F. McKie, Jr.; William F. Rauchholz; Douglas W. Robinson; Franklin D. Wolffe. Associates: Jordan N. Bodner; Steve S. Chang; Joseph P. Curtin; Michael David (Not admitted in DC); Catherine A. Ferguson; Holly M. Ford; Lisa M. Hemmendinger; Lin J. Hymel (Not admitted in DC); Richard C. Irving; Anthony W. Kandare (Not admitted in DC); David S. Lee (Not admitted in DC); Darrell Gilbert Mottley (Not admitted in DC); Ajay S. Pathak; Paul M. Rivard; Christopher B. Roth.
Intellectual Property including Procurement of Patents, Trademarks, Copyrights, Trade Secrets, Counseling & Opinions, Unfair Competition, Interferences, Licensing, Antitrust and International Trade Matters. Litigation including Trials and Appeals in Federal and State Courts and International Trade Commission.
Chicago, Illinois Office: Ten South Wacker Drive. Telephone: 312-715-1000. Facsimile: 312-715-1234.
Boston, Massachusetts Office: 28 State Street, 28th Floor. Telephone: 617-227-7111. Fax: 617-227-4399.
Portland, Oregon Office: 601 SW Second Avenue, Suite 1900. Telephone: 503-279-6330. Fax: 503-279-6328.
See Professional Biographies, WASHINGTON, DISTRICT OF COLUMBIA

Bannon, Brian A. ....'51 '81 C.102 B.A. L.273 J.D. [Dyer E.&J.]
*PRACTICE AREAS: Government Contracts; Intellectual Property; Proprietary Rights; Copyrights.

Banoun, Raymond, (AV) .... '45 '68 C.563 B.A. L.273 J.D. [Cadwalader,W.&T.]
*PRACTICE AREAS: White Collar Fraud; Civil Litigation; Criminal Law; SEC Enforcement.

Banov, Alan, and Associates, (AV) '— '71 C.575 A.B. L.273 J.D.
1400 K Street, N.W., Suite 1000, 20005-2403
Telephone: 202-842-9332 Fax: 202-842-9331 URL: http://www.banovlaw.com
Email: ab@banovlaw.com URL: http://www.lawyers.com/alanbanovlaw
***PRACTICE AREAS: Employment Law; Labor Law; Personal Injury; Litigation.**
Associate: Norberto Perez Salinas.
Labor and Employment, Employment Litigation, Wrongful Termination, Executive Compensation, Personnel Policies, Class Actions, Employment Contracts.
See Professional Biographies, WASHINGTON, DISTRICT OF COLUMBIA

Banowit, Donald R. '73 '98 C.477 B.S.E. L.276 J.D.
[[A] Sterne,K.G.&F.] (See Pat. Sect.)
*PRACTICE AREAS: Intellectual Property.

Banta, Carol J. .... '— '97 C.821 B.A. L.477 J.D. [[A] Wilmer,C.&P.]

Banta, Henry M., (AV) .... '37 '66 C&L.276 B.S., LL.B. [Lobel,N.&L.]
*PRACTICE AREAS: Anti-Trust; Federal Energy Law; Pipeline Law.

Banta, Teresa J. ....'53 '90 C.986 B.S. L.770 J.D. [Townsend&B.] (Pat.)

Bantham, Russel A. '— '67 C.299 B.A. L.145 J.D.
(adm. in NY; not adm. in DC) Pharmaceutical Research & Mnfct. of America

Banzhaf, John F., III '40 '65
C.453 B.S.E.E. L.178 LL.B. Prof. of Law, George Washington Univ.

Baptiste, Robert M., (AV) ....'41 '67 C.860 B.A. L.276 LL.B. [Baptiste&W.]
*PRACTICE AREAS: Labor Relations Law; Federal Civil Litigation; Administrative Law; Regulatory Law.

Baptiste & Wilder, P.C., (AV) [BR]
Suite 500, 1150 Connecticut Avenue, N.W., 20036
Telephone: 202-223-0723 Fax: 202-223-9677
URL: http://www.lawyers.com/baptiste&wilder
Robert M. Baptiste; Roland P. Wilder, Jr.; Patrick J. Szymanski; Christy Concannon; Susan Boyle; James F. Wallington; William R. Wilder.
Labor Relations, Federal Civil Litigation, Administrative, Regulatory, ERISA, Civil Rights Law, Aviation.
See Professional Biographies, WASHINGTON, DISTRICT OF COLUMBIA

Baquedano, Luis F. ....'64 '97 C.569 B.A. L.30 J.D. Natl. Gallery of Art

Bar, Richard B., (AV) .... '61 '86 C.787 B.A. L.273 J.D. [Galland,K.G.F.&S.] ⊙
*PRACTICE AREAS: Corporate; Real Estate; Business; Trade Association; Commercial Leasing.

Bar-Adon & Vogel, L.L.P., (BV) .... 1638 R Street, N.W.

Baraban, Cynthia ....'68 '99 C.210 B.A. L.347 J.D. [[A] Wilmer,C.&P.]

Barald, Patricia A., (AV) ....'48 '74 C.103 B.A. L.188 J.D. [Covington&B.]

Baran, Jan Witold, (AV) ....'48 '73 C.611 B.A. L.880 J.D. [Wiley R.&F.]
*PRACTICE AREAS: Election Law.

Baran, Kathryn K. ....'54 '00 C.103 A.B. L.276 J.D. [[A] Skadden,A.S.M.&F.]
*PRACTICE AREAS: Energy.

Baran, Tama Vail ....'66 '91 C.1376 B.A. L.1338 J.D. 2031 Florida Ave., N.W., 1st Fl.

Baranoff, Evan C. .... '71 '97 C.1349 B.A. L.107 J.D. 445 12th Street, SW

Baranowski, Joel M. ....'71 '97 C.659 B.A. L.276 J.D. [[A] Chadbourne&P.]

Barash, D. Scott '64 '88 C.976 B.A. L.145 J.D.
VP & General Counsel, Universal Service Administrative Company

Barash, Eyal Hanan '69 '97
C.347 B.S., B.A. L.597 J.D. [[A] Finnegan,H.F.G.&D.] (See Pat. Sect.)
*PRACTICE AREAS: Chemical Intellectual Property; Pharmaceutical Intellectual Property.

Barat, Dorothy A. ....'60 '86 C.276 A.B. L.188 J.D. 2300 N St., N.W.

Barba, Thomas M., (AV) .... '54 '79 C&L.831 B.A., J.D. [Steptoe&J.]
*PRACTICE AREAS: Litigation; Products Liability Law; Technology Law; Electronic Commerce.

Barbash, Barry P., (AV) ....'53 '78 C.95 A.B. L.188 J.D. [Shearman&S.]

Barber, Charles K., (BV) .... '54 '80 C&L.329 B.A., J.D. Dep. Gen. Coun., Howard Univ.

Barber, Jensen Egerton, II '45 '84 L.180 J.D.
The Jenifer Building, Suite 400, 400 Seventh Street, N.W., 20004-2206
Telephone: 202-737-8511 Fax: 202-628-0249
Email: jebarber@juno.com
***PRACTICE AREAS: Criminal Defense; Medical Malpractice; Personal Injury; Litigation.**
Federal Litigation Practice, Complex and Multi-District Civil and Criminal Litigation, Grand Jury Practice, Federal Criminal Law, Criminal Defense, Capital Criminal Defense, Criminal Conspiracy,

(This Listing Continued)

Barber, Jensen Egerton, II (Continued)

Money Laundering, RICO, White Collar Crime, Business Fraud, Mail Fraud, Wiretapping, Electronic Surveillance, Forgery, Theft, Drug Crimes, DWI, Homicide, Post-Conviction Remedies, Search and Seizure, Personal Injury, Auto Accidents, Wrongful Death, Medical Malpractice, Orthopedic Malpractice.

See Professional Biographies, WASHINGTON, DISTRICT OF COLUMBIA

Barber, Steven J. .... '63 '89 C.103 B.A. L.309 J.D. [Steptoe&J.]
*PRACTICE AREAS: Commercial Litigation; Insurance; E-Commerce; Intellectual Property.

Barber, Claudia, Law Offices of
(See Laurel, MD)

Barberic, Edward M. .... '49 '88 C.930 B.A. L.659 J.D. [Dyer E.&J.]
*PRACTICE AREAS: Tax Law; International Trade and Transactions; Mergers and Acquisitions.
Barbero, Carol L. .... '45 '78 C.25 B.A. L.276 J.D. [Hobbs,S.D.&W.]
Barbour, Haley, (AV) '47 '73 C&L.500 J.D.
(adm. in MS; not adm. in DC) [© Balch&B.] (⊙Birm., AL)
Barbulescu, Ruxandra ....'71 '99 C.94 B.A. L.188 J.D. [A Dickstein S.M.&O.]
*PRACTICE AREAS: Energy Project Finance; Energy Regulatory.
Barcella, E. Lawrence, Jr., (AV) .... '45 '71 C.197 A.B. L.880 J.D. [Paul,H.J.&W.]
*PRACTICE AREAS: White Collar Corporate Defense; Complex Litigation; White-Collar Criminal Investigation and Litigation; Bribery; Ethics Offenses.
Barclay, Erin Martha ...... '72 '99 C.1349 B.A. L.107 J.D. Network of East-West Women
Bard, Howard M. '63 '88 C&L.273 B.B.A., J.D.
(adm. in MD; not adm. in DC) [Feder,S.C.&B.]
*PRACTICE AREAS: Fiduciary Counseling; ERISA; Health Care.
Bard, Lawrence R. .... '65 '93 C.205 B.S. L.273 J.D. [Fried,F.H.S.&J.]
*PRACTICE AREAS: Corporate Law; Securities.
Bard, Nancy A., (AV) .... '56 '86 C.103 A.B. L.569 J.D. [© Harris,W.&G.]
*PRACTICE AREAS: Corporate.
Bardenwerper, Walter W. '51 '77 C&L.893 B.A., J.D.
V.P., Gen. Coun. & Secy., Watson Wyatt Worldwide
Bardin, David J., (AV) ....'33 '56 C.176 A.B. L.178 J.D. [© Arent F.K.P.&K.] ‡
Bardo, Thomas F. ....'63 '92 C&L.276 B.S.E.S., J.D. [A Carter,L.&M.]
Bardonille, Harold ....'36 '83 C.789 B.A. L.276 J.D. Recorder of Deeds
Bardsley, Catherine S. .... '— '74 C.914 B.A. L.94 J.D. [© Kirkpatrick&L.]
*PRACTICE AREAS: Investment Company Law; Investment Management; Mutual Funds; Financial Services Regulation; ERISA.
Barea, Adam L. '73 '00 C&L.178 B.A., J.D.
(adm. in NY; not adm. in DC) [A Drinker B.&R.]
Barefoot, Bartley L. .... '73 '99 C.228 A.B. L.575 [A Hogan&H.]
*PRACTICE AREAS: Health Law; Health Care Regulation.
Bares, Barbara H. ... '49 '79 C.881 A.B. L.188 J.D. Sr. Editor, Federal Publications, Inc.
Bares, Jacqueline C. .... '48 '90 C.436 B.A. L.597 J.D. [Jenner&B.]
*PRACTICE AREAS: Corporate Law.
Barfield, Issac R. ....'28 '68 C.824 B.A. L.329 LL.B. Prof., Howard Univ. Sch. of Law
Barg, Stanley M. ....'56 '81 C.103 B.A. L.309 J.D. 2300 N St., N.W.
Barger, Judith M. ....'68 '93 C.1208 B.S. L.276 J.D. [A Piliero,M.&P.]
*PRACTICE AREAS: Civil Litigation; Criminal Litigation; Native American Law; Labor and Employment; Government Contracts.
Barham, Jennifer M. '70 '99 C.446 B.A. L.904 J.D.
(adm. in MD; not adm. in DC) [Margolius,M.D.R.&T.]
Barkats, Pierre-Philippe, (AV) ....'54 '84 C&L.999 C.A.P.A., J.D. [Barkats&Assoc.]
Barkats & Associates, Chartered, Attorneys and Counselors At Law, (AV)
1250 Eye Street, N.W.
Barker, James A., Jr., (AV) .... '53 '85 C.103 B.A. L.893 J.D. [Akin,G.S.H.&F.]
*PRACTICE AREAS: Litigation; Libel Law; Health Care Law; Corporate Transactions; Trademarks.
Barker, James H., III ....'65 '90 C.902 B.A. L.893 J.D. [Latham&W.]
Barker, Jill M., (BV) ....'59 '83 C.259 B.S. L.904 J.D. [© Betts&H.]
*PRACTICE AREAS: Energy Regulation; Energy Contracts; Hydroelectricity; Administrative Law; Public Utility.
Barker, John P. .... '61 '87 C.197 A.B. L.477 J.D. [© Arnold&P.]
*PRACTICE AREAS: International Trade; Public Policy and Legislative; Intellectual Property; Technology Law; National Security Law and Policy.
Barker, Katherine Elizabeth '71 '97 C.823 B.S. L.818 J.D.
(adm. in MA; not adm. in DC) [A Kelley D.&W.]
Barker, Norman A. ....'47 '72 C&L.800 B.A., J.D. Assoc. Gen. Coun., Ernst & Young
Barker, Rosina B., (AV) .... '55 '90 C.309 A.B. L.276 J.D. [Ivins,P.&B.]
*PRACTICE AREAS: Employee Benefits; Employment Taxation; Executive Compensation; ERISA Litigation; ESOPs.
Barkin, Albert '11 '40 C.818 L.94 LL.B.
(adm. in MA; not adm. in DC) 4000 Cathedral Ave., N.W.‡
Barkin, Pamela L. '65 '91 C.228 A.B. L.477 J.D.
(adm. in MD; not adm. in DC) 2300 N St., N.W.‡
Barklind, Sharla Marie ....'72 '97 C.862 B.A. L.276 J.D. 1232 Longworth HOB‡
Barkow, Anthony S. ...'69 '96 C.477 A.B. L.309 J.D. Asst. U.S. Atty. at U.S. Atty. Office
Barkus, A. Neal, (AV) ....'47 '74 C.893 B.A. L.902 J.D. [Hunton&W.]
*PRACTICE AREAS: Labor; Employment; Business Immigration.
Barkus, Alexander N. ....'47 '74 C.893 B.A. L.902 J.D. 1900 K St., N.W.
Barletta, Thomas P., (AV) ....'51 '77 C.276 A.B. L.1066 J.D. [Steptoe&J.]
*PRACTICE AREAS: Government Contracts.
Barloon, Joseph L. ....'67 '96 C.309 A.B. L.276 J.D. [A Skadden,A.S.M.&F.]
Barlow, Andre '71 '97 C.923 B.A. L.273 J.D.
(adm. in VA; not adm. in DC) [A Powell,G.F.&M.]
*PRACTICE AREAS: Antitrust.
Barlow, Kathleen T., (BV) '62 '88 C.188 B.S. L.245 J.D.
General Counsel & Corporate Secretary, Bernstein Companies
Barlow, Kristi ....'66 '92 C.1111 B.A. L.999 J.D. 811 Vermont Avenue, N.W.
Barlow, Myron Paul ....'66 '95 C.367 B.A. L.472 J.D. [A Katten M.Z.]
*PRACTICE AREAS: Customs Law; International Trade; Export Regulation.
Barnako, Frank R. ....'12 '37 C.390 B.A. L.477 J.D. 1301 K St., N.W.
Barnard, Robert C., (AV) .... '13 '40 C&L.051 B.A., B.C.L. [© Cleary,G.S.&H.]
Barnard, William M., (AV) ....'39 '66 C.208 A.B. L.273 LL.B. [© Smithwick&B.]
*PRACTICE AREAS: Communication Law; Corporate Law.
Barner, Kevin M. '65 '97 C.205 B.E.E. L.64 J.D.
(adm. in MD; not adm. in DC; See Pat. Sect.) [A Sughrue M.]
*PRACTICE AREAS: Intellectual Property.
Barnes, Attison L., III ....'64 '89 C.893 B.A. L.692 J.D. [Gardner,C.&D.]
*PRACTICE AREAS: Commercial Law; Technology; Intellectual Property Litigation.
Barnes, Cheryl D. ....'70 '95 C.1298 B.A. L.446 J.D. [A Cadwalader,W.&T.]
Barnes, Clifford E., (AV) ....'50 '84 C.1040 B.B.A. L.893 J.D. [Epstein B.&G.]
*PRACTICE AREAS: Corporate Law; Health Law; Hospital Law; Managed Care Law; Mergers and Acquisitions.
Barnes, Donald M., (AV) ....'43 '70 C.645 B.S. L.273 J.D. [Seyfarth S.]
*PRACTICE AREAS: Antitrust Law; Complex Litigation; Agricultural Law; Trade Association Law.
Barnes, Johnine P. ....'70 '95 C&L.930 B.A., J.D. [A Baker&H.]
*PRACTICE AREAS: Labor Law; Employment Law; Sports Law.
Barnes, Julie A. .... '69 '99 C.352 B.A. L.904 J.D. [A King,P.&H.]
*PRACTICE AREAS: Health Law; Litigation.
Barnes, Mark ....'57 '81 C.36 B.S. L.1068 J.D. Asst. to Sen.
Barnes, Obren V. '61 '86 C&L.446 B.A., J.D.
(adm. in MD; not adm. in DC) 1828 18th St., N.W.
Barnes, Peter, (AV) .... '40 '66 C.976 A.B. L.309 LL.B. [© Swidler B.S.F.]
*PRACTICE AREAS: Real Estate; Civil Litigation; Complex Litigation.

Barnes, Richardson & Colburn, (AV)
Suite 1150, 1225 Eye Street, N.W., 20005 ⊙
Telephone: 202-457-0300 Facsimile: 202-331-8746
Email: barnes@brc-dc.com URL: http://www.barnesrichardson.com
Resident Members of Firm: Matthew T. McGrath; Robert A. Shapiro. Non-Resident Members of Firm: Rufus E. Jarman, Jr. (N.Y.); James S. O'Kelly (N.Y.); Robert E. Burke (Chicago); Donald J. Unger (Chicago); Sandra Liss Friedman (N.Y.); Brian F. Walsh (Chicago); Kazumune V. Kano (Chicago); Frederic D. Van Arnam, Jr. (N.Y.); Lawrence M. Friedman (Chicago); Alan Goggins (N.Y.). Resident Associates: Stephen W. Brophy; Michael J. Chessler; James B. Doran (Not admitted in DC). Special Counsel: Ansis M. Helmanis (Not admitted in DC). Counsel: Gunter von Conrad.
Customs and International Trade Law, Administrative Law. General Federal Litigation and Appellate Practice.
New York, New York Office: 475 Park Avenue South. Telephone: 212-725-0200.
Chicago, Illinois Office: 303 East Wacker Drive, Suite 1100. Telephone: 312-565-2000.

See Professional Biographies, WASHINGTON, DISTRICT OF COLUMBIA

Barnes & Thornburg, (AV) BB
750 17th Street, N.W. Suite 900, 20006 ⊙
Telephone: 202-289-1313 FAX: 202-289-1330
URL: http://www.btlaw.com
Partners: Randolph J. Stayin; Richard H. Streeter. Intellectual Property Department: Partners: Perry Palan; Joseph D. Lewis. Of Counsel: Mark M. Newman; Paul E. Fahrenkopf (Not admitted in DC); Karen A. McGee; Richard Paul Krinsky; Richard B. Lazarus.
Acquisitions and Divestitures, Ad Valorem Tax, Administrative Law, Affirmative Action, Agriculture Law, Americans with Disabilities Act, Antidumping, Antitrust, Antitrust and Trade Regulation, Appellate Practice, Attorney Grievances, Automotive Warranty Law, Aviation and Aerospace, Aviation Law, Banking Law, Banking Regulations, Bankruptcy, Bankruptcy Reorganization, Banks and Banking, Biochemical Patents, Biomedical Products Liability, Biomedical Technology, Biotechnology Patent Prosecution, Bond Law, Brain Injury, Breach of Warranty, Brown Fields Redevelopment, Business Immigration, Business Law, Business Litigation, Business Planning, Business Regulatory and Administrative, Business Start-ups, Business Succession Planning, Business Taxation, Business Torts, Business Transactions, Business Transfers, Buying and Selling of Businesses, Cable TV, Cargo Claims, Charitable Trusts and Foundations, Chemical Intellectual Property, Chemical Patent Prosecution, Chemical Patents, Chemical Products Liability, Civil Appeals, Civil Litigation, Civil Practice, Civil RICO, Class Action Defense, Clean Air Act, Clean Water Act, Closely Held Business Estate Planning, Closely Held Businesses, Closely Held Business Law, Closely Held Corporations, Collective Bargaining, Commercial Bankruptcy, Commercial Finance Law, Commercial Law, Commercial Leasing and Financing, Commercial Litigation, Commercial Conveyancing, Commercial Real Estate, Commercial Real Estate Acquisition, Commercial Real Estate Development, Commercial Real Estate Finance, Commercial Transactions, Commodities Fraud, Communications and Media, Complex Commercial Litigation, Complex Litigation, Computer and Software Patents, Computer Law, Computers and Software, Conflicts of Interest, Construction Labor Law, Construction Law, Consumer Credit, Contract Litigation, Cooperatives, Copyrights, Corporate Finance, Corporate Formation, Corporate Law, Corporate Taxation, Corporate Tax Planning, Countervailing Duties, Covenants Not To Compete, Creditors Rights, Creditors Rights in Bankruptcy, Criminal Defense, Criminal Law, Criminal Tax Audits, Customs Law, Dealer and Distributor Termination, Debt and Equity Finance, Decedents Estates, Defense Litigation, Design Patents, Disability Insurance Defense, Discrimination, Distribution, Drug and Medical Device Defense, Economic Development, Education Law, Elder Law, Election, Campaign and Political Law, Electric Power, Electric Utilities, Electrical Intellectual Property, Electrical Patents, Electro-mechanical Patents, Electronic Commerce, Electronic Patents, Eminent Domain, Employee Benefits, Employee Stock Ownership Plans, Employment Defense, Employment Discrimination, Employment Law, Employment Litigation, Energy, Energy Contracts, Energy Regulation, Environmental Administrative Law, Environmental Cleanup, Environmental Compliance, Environmental Criminal Defense, Environmental Law, Environmental Litigation, Environmental Permitting, Environmental Real Estate, Environmental Regulation, Environmental Risk Management, Equal Employment Opportunity Law, ERISA Litigation, Estate Administration, Estate and Gift Taxation, Estate Planning, Estate Planning and Taxation, Estate Planning and Administration, Estate Planning and Probate, Estate Planning for Parents of Handicapped Children, Estate Planning for Unmarried Individuals, Executive Compensation, Executive Severance Contracts, Export Regulation, Fair Employment Practices, Family and Medical Leave Act, Family Business Successions, Family Wealth Transfer, Federal and State Administrative Regulatory Practice, Federal and State Legislative Practice, Federal Civil Litigation, Federal Civil Practice, Federal Criminal Law, Federal Estate and Gift Taxation, Federal Litigation, Federal Tax Controversies, Federal Taxation, Fiduciary Income Tax, Finance, Financial Transactions, First Party Insurance, Foreign Investment in the United States, Freight Claims, Freight Loss and Damage, Gaming Law, Gaming Licensing, Gas Utilities, General Litigation, Government, Government Affairs, Government Agency Practice, Government Contracts, Government Investigations, Government Relations, Groundwater Contamination, Hazardous Materials and Substances, Hazardous Waste, Hazardous Waste Liability, Head Injury, Health Care, Health Care Corporate Law, Health Care Contracts, Health Care Fraud, Health Care Licensing, Health Care Litigation, Health Care Mergers and Acquisitions, Health Care Regulation, Health Care Reimbursement, Health Law, Heavy Equipment Products Liability, Immigration Law, Industrial Revenue Bond Law, Inheritance Tax, Initial Public Offerings, Insurance, Insurance Bad Faith, Insurance Coverage, Insurance Litigation, Insurance Regulation, Integrated Health Care Delivery Systems, Intellectual Property, Intellectual Property General Prosecution, Intellectual Property Infringement, Intellectual Property Licensing, Intellectual Property Litigation, Intellectual Property Procurement, Intellectual Property Protection, Intellectual Property Rights, International Business Law, International Intellectual Property, International Law, International Patents, International Trade, International Transportation Law, Internet Law, Internet Trademark Law, Joint Ventures, Labor and Employment, Labor Arbitration, Labor Law, Labor Relations, Land Use, Lease Law, Leasing, Legal Ethics and Professional Responsibility, Legal Malpractice Defense, Legislative Practice, Licensing, Life Insurance Defense, Limited Liability Company Law, Limited Partnerships, Liquor Licensing, Litigation, Loans, Lobbying, Local Government Law, Logistics, Long Term Care, Managed Care, Managed Care Contracts, Management Employment Law, Management Labor Law, Manufacturers Liability, Maritime Regulations, Mechanical Intellectual Property, Mechanical Patents, Media Law, Mediation, Medical Antitrust, Medical Intellectual Property, Medical Patents, Mental Health Law, Mergers, Acquisitions and Divestitures, Mergers and Acquisitions, Mineral Taxation, Molecular Biology Patents, Motor Carrier Law, Motor Carrier Regulation, Multi-Employer Pensions, Municipal Bonds, Municipal Bonds Taxation, Municipal Finance, Municipal Law, Municipal Leasing, Municipal Redevelopment, Municipal Securities, Municipal Taxation, National Labor Relations Act, Neurolaw, Nonprofit and Charitable Organizations, Nonprofit Organizations Law, North American Free Trade Agreement, Occupational Safety and Health, OSHA, Partnership Law, Partnership Taxation, Patent Infringement, Patent Interference Practice, Patent Litigation, Patent Prosecution, Patents, PCT Legal Export, Personal Injury, Personal Injury Defense, Pesticide Litigation, Pharmaceutical Intellectual Property, Pharmaceutical Patents, Physician Contracts, Physician Practices, Planning and Land Use, Power Line Contact Injury, Probate, Probate Litigation, Products Liability, Products Liability Defense, Professional Liability, Property Law, Property Tax, Property Tax Abatement, Property Tax Appeals, Psychological Injury, Public Finance, Public Sector Labor Relations, Public Utility Law, Railroad Law, Real Estate, Real Estate Acquisitions, Real Estate Contracts, Real Estate Development, Real Estate Finance, Real Estate Licensing, Real Estate Secured Lending, Real Estate Title Insurance, Real Property, Real Property Acquisitions, Real Property Finance, Reorganizations, Resource Conservation and Recovery Act (RCRA), Retirement Benefit Plans, School Law, Securities, Securities Litigation, Securitization, Semiconductor Technology, Sexual Harassment, Small Business Corporations, State Government Law, State Tax Controversies, State Taxation, Structured Finance, Succession Planning, Superfund, Tax Controversies, Tax Exempt Finance, Tax Exempt Organizations, Tax Increment Finance, Tax Law, Tax Litigation, Taxation, Technology and Science, Technology Law, Technology Licensing, Technology Transfers, Telecommunications Competition, Telecommunications Law, Theft of Trade Secrets, Title VII Discrimination, Title IX Discrimination, Tort Defense, Toxic Exposure, Toxic Tort Class Actions, Toxic Torts, Toxic Tort Defense, Trade Dress, Trade Secrets, Trademark Litigation, Trademarks, Trademark Prosecution, Trademark Protection, Trademark Registration, Transportation, Transportation Safety, Trial Practice, Trusts and Estates, Unfair Competition, Unfair Trade, Uniform Commercial Codes, Union Contract Negotiations, Union Elections, Utilities, Utility Law, Wage and Hour Law, WARN Act, Water Pollution, Water Quality, Water Utilities, Wetland Regulation, White Collar Crime, White Collar Criminal Defense, Wills, Workers Compensation, Workouts, World Trade Organization, Wrongful Death, Wrongful Termination, Wrongful Termination Defense, Zoning, Planning and Land Use.
Representative Intellectual Property Clients: CNF Transportation, Inc.; Food Processing Machinery and Supplies Association; Laidlaw, Inc.; National Candle Association; Water and Wastewater Equipment Manufacturers Association; Wheat Gluten Industry Council.

(This Listing Continued)

Barnes & Thornburg (Continued)

Indianapolis, Indiana Office: 11 South Meridian Street, 46204. Telephone: 317-236-1313. FAX: 317-231-7433.
Fort Wayne, Indiana Office: 600 One Summit Square, 46802. Telephone: 260-423-9440. FAX: 260-424-8316.
South Bend, Indiana Office: 600 1st Source Bank Center, 100 North Michigan, 46601-1632. Telephone: 574-233-1171. FAX: 574-237-1125.
Elkhart, Indiana Office: 121 West Franklin Street, Suite 200, 46516. Telephone: 574-293-0681. FAX: 574-296-2535.
Chicago, Illinois Office: 2600 Chase Plaza, 10 South LaSalle Street, 60603. Telephone: 312-357-1313. FAX: 312-759-5646.
See Professional Biographies, WASHINGTON, DISTRICT OF COLUMBIA

Barnett, Alexa Boonstra ....'70 '98 C.198 B.A. L.260 J.D. [A Keller&H.]
*PRACTICE AREAS: Food and Drug.
Barnett, D. Sean '63 '97 C.679 B.S.N.E. L.276 J.D.
(adm. in VA; not adm. in DC) [A Shaw P.] ‡
Barnett, Iris S. ....'58 '84 C.1044 B.A. L.309 J.D. 15 14th Street, SE
Barnett, James R. ....'47 '72 C&L.966 B.A., J.D. [Gordon&B.]
*PRACTICE AREAS: Government Contracts; Trial and Appellate Practice; Health Law; Employee Benefits Law; Insurance Law.
Barnett, Lisa M. '66 '96 C.569 B.A. L.564 J.D.
(adm. in CT; not adm. in DC) 471 H Street, N.W.
Barnett, Megan A. ....'— '98 C.893 B.A. L.976 J.D. [A Gibson,D.&C.]
*PRACTICE AREAS: Intellectual Property.
Barnett, Robert B., (AV) ....'46 '71 C.966 B.A. L.145 J.D. [Williams&C.]
*PRACTICE AREAS: Administrative Agency Practice; Commercial Law; Communications and Media; Contracts; Corporate Law.
Barnett, Robert Eugene, (AV) ....'35 '63 C&L.309 A.B., LL.B. [Barnett&S.]
*PRACTICE AREAS: Banking Law; Financial Institutions.
Barnett, Sarah E. ....'41 '84 C.102 B.S. L.276 J.D. V.P., Sugar Association, Inc., The
Barnett, Thomas O. ....'62 '89 C.976 B.A. L.309 J.D. [Covington&B.]

Barnett & Sivon, P.C., (AV)
2000 "M" Street, N.W., Suite 740, 20036-3113
Telephone: 202-463-6040 FAX: 202-785-5209
Robert Eugene Barnett; James C. Sivon.
Financial Institutions, General Regulatory and Legislative Law.
See Professional Biographies, WASHINGTON, DISTRICT OF COLUMBIA

Barnette, C. Kevin ....'59 '87 C&L.976 B.A., J.D. [Skadden,A.S.M.&F.]
Barnette, Curtis H., (AV) ....'35 '62 C.923 B.A. L.976 J.D. [C Skadden,A.S.M.&F.]
Barney, Daniel R. ....'51 '75 C.309 A.B. L.846 J.D. [Scopelitis,G.L.&H.]
*PRACTICE AREAS: Antitrust; Trade Regulation; Advertising and Marketing; Transportation; Transportation Safety.
Barney, James R. '68 '00 C.871 B.S. L.976 J.D.
(adm. in VA; not adm. in DC; See Pat. Sect.) [A Finnegan,H.F.G.&D.]
*PRACTICE AREAS: Patent Litigation; Chemical Intellectual Property; Pharmaceutical Intellectual Property.
Barnidge, Edward Coleman, III ....'71 '99 C.602 B.A. L.893 J.D. [A Williams&C.]
*PRACTICE AREAS: Litigation; Criminal Law.
Barnowski, Daniel D. ....'70 '95 C&L.477 B.A., J.D. [A Sonnenschein N.&R.]
*PRACTICE AREAS: General Litigation.
Baron, Alan I., (AV) ....'42 '66 C.674 B.A. L.309 LL.B. [Dorsey&W.]
*PRACTICE AREAS: White Collar Criminal Defense; Complex Civil Litigation.
Baron, David A. ....'70 '97 C.30 B.A. L.273 J.D. [A McDermott,W.&E.]
Baron, David S. ....'52 '77 C.367 B.A. L.188 J.D. Earthjustice Legal Defense Fund
Baron, Phyllis Joan, (AV) ....'46 '86 C.446 B.A. L.1162 J.D. 601 Indiana Ave. N.W.
Barondes, Anita, (AV) ....'50 '77 C.105 B.A. L.273 J.D. [Seyfarth S.]
*PRACTICE AREAS: Labor and Employment.
Barone, Elena C. ....'74 '99 C.228 B.A. L.273 J.D. [A Groom]
*PRACTICE AREAS: ERISA; Tax Law.
Barone, Michael '44 '70 C.309 A.B. L.976 LL.B.
Sr. Writer, U.S. News & World Report
Barr, Christopher J. ....'57 '83 C.976 B.A. L.273 J.D. [C Morgan,L.&B.]
Barr, Howard J., (AV) ....'61 '86 C.606 B.A. L.421 J.D. [Pepper&C.]
*PRACTICE AREAS: Cable TV; Cable Communications; Wireless Communications; Broadcast Radio.
Barr, Jeffrey N. '55 '80 C.976 B.A. L.309 J.D.
(adm. in MA; not adm. in DC) Adm. Off. of the U.S. Cts.
Barr, John Mills ....'62 '89 C.894 B.A. L.309 J.D. [C Morgan,L.&B.]
Barr, Karen L. '63 '88 C.659 B.A. L.477 J.D.
Gen. Coun., Investment Counsel Assoc. of America, Inc.
Barr, Kenneth S. ....'— '80 C.94 B.A. L.469 J.D. [C Reed S.]
*PRACTICE AREAS: Corporate; Finance.
Barr, Michael B., (AV) ....'48 '73 C.276 B.S. L.273 J.D. [Hunton&W.]
*PRACTICE AREAS: International; Investments; Energy; Finance.
Barr, Suzanne A. ....'66 '92 C&L.309 A.B., J.D. [Hogan&H.]
*PRACTICE AREAS: Emerging Growth Companies; Corporate Formation; Corporate Governance; Public Corporations; Initial Public Offerings.
Barracato, Louis J. ....'41 '66 L.128 J.D. Assoc. Prof., Catholic Univ. Law Sch.
Barratt-Brown, Elizabeth '59 '91 C.103 A.B. L.976 J.D.
(adm. in CT; not adm. in DC) Natural Res. Def. Council
Barre, Catherine Cloud '69 '98 C.659 B.A. L.893 J.D.
(adm. in VA; not adm. in DC) [A Covington&B.]
Barrera, Joseph ....'62 '99 C.999 B.A. L.560 J.D. [A Connolly B.L.&H.] (Pat.) ⊙
Barrera, Staci ....'69 '99 U.S. Dept. of Jus.
Barrett, David A. ....'— '88 C.1168 B.A. L.846 J.D. [C Latham&W.]
*PRACTICE AREAS: Insurance Coverage; Civil Litigation.
Barrett, David M., (AV) ....'37 '65 C.602 B.A. L.276 J.D. [Barrett&S.]
Barrett, James R. ....'62 '91 C.1168 B.A. L.276 J.D. [Latham&W.]
Barrett, Jane F., (AV) ....'52 '76 C.423 B.A. L.446 J.D. [Dyer E.&J.]
*PRACTICE AREAS: Litigation; White Collar Criminal Defense; Environmental Criminal Defense; Environmental Law; Environmental Compliance.
Barrett, Jesse M. '73 '99 C&L.602 B.A., J.D.
(adm. in MD; not adm. in DC) 17222 Eye Street, NW
Barrett, Judy Garcia ......'55 '90 C.508 B.S. L.560 J.D. 1300 I St., N.W., Suite 700 (Pat.)
Barrett, Melissa L. ....'54 '82 C.478 B.A. L.276 J.D. [C Goodwin P.]
*PRACTICE AREAS: International Commercial Law; Corporate and Finance Law.
Barrett, Shannon M. '72 '97 C.228 B.A. L.309 J.D.
(adm. in IL; not adm. in DC) [A O'Melveny&M.]
Barrett, St. John, (AV) ....'23 '49 C.668 B.A. L.1066 LL.B. 1850 M St., N.W.
Barrett, William A. ....'63 '92 C.563 B.B.A. L.188 J.D. [A Hughes H.&R.]
*PRACTICE AREAS: Litigation, Commercial; Legislative; Failed Bank Litigation.
Barrett, William H., (BV) ....'46 '78 C.550 B.A. L.273 J.D. [McDermott,W.&E.]
Barrett & Schuler, (AV) ....Suite 507 1000 Thomas Jefferson Street, N.W.
Barrie, John P., (AV) ....'47 '72 C.1494 A.B. L.1065 J.D. [Bryan C.]
*PRACTICE AREAS: Federal and State Taxation Controversy; Transactional Matters.
Barringer, Allen C. '43 '72 C.976 B.A. L.893 J.D.
Assoc. Gen. Coun., Potomac Electric Power Company
Barringer, Steven G. ....'55 '83 C.575 B.A. L.101 J.D. 201 Maryland Ave., N.E.
Barringer, William H., (AV) ....'48 '73 C.103 A.B. L.276 J.D. [Willkie F.&G.]

Barritt, Keith A. ....'61 '89 C&L.893 B.A., J.D. [Fish&R.]
*PRACTICE AREAS: Communications Law; Regulatory Affairs; Trademarks.
Barron, Fraser ....'37 '64 C.674 A.B. L.309 LL.B. National Endowment for the Arts
Barron, Jerome A. ....'— '59 C.860 B.A. L.976 J.D. 720 20th St., N.W.
Barron, John H. C., Jr., (AV) ....'46 '71 C.446 A.B. L.228 J.D. [Squire,S.&D.]
*PRACTICE AREAS: Real Estate; Finance; Foreign Investment.
Barron, Kathleen L. ....'70 '95 C.30 B.A. L.326 J.D. [A Skadden,A.S.M.&F.]
Barros, J. Darrel ....'60 '95 C&L.477 B.S., J.D. [A Piper M.R.&W.]
*PRACTICE AREAS: Venture Capital; Emerging Growth Companies.
Barros, Sonia Gupta '70 '97 C.1208 B.S. L.145 J.D.
(adm. in IL; not adm. in DC) [A Hogan&H.]
*PRACTICE AREAS: Corporate; Mergers and Acquisitions; Securities.
Barrow, Geoffrey A. ....'71 '97 C.399 B.S. L.273 J.D. [A Jenner&B.]
*PRACTICE AREAS: Terminations; Litigation; Bid Protests; Export Control.
Barrowes, Brooksany '75 '99 C.101 B.A. L.145 J.D.
(adm. in VA; not adm. in DC) [A Baker B.]
*PRACTICE AREAS: Energy.
Barry, Alison E. '63 '96 C.976 B.S. L.174 J.D.
(adm. in CO; not adm. in DC) [A Akin,G.S.H.&F.] (⊙Denver, CO)
Barry, Dennis M., (AV) ....'51 '76 C.611 B.A. L.893 J.D. [Vinson&E.]
*PRACTICE AREAS: Health Law; Medicare and Medicaid; Hospital Law.
Barry, F. Patrick '53 '79 C&L.629 B.S., J.D.
(adm. in AZ; not adm. in DC) P.O. Box 44378
Barry, Kenneth A. '48 '74 C&L.893 B.A., J.D.
(adm. in NY; not adm. in DC) [C Hunton&W.]
*PRACTICE AREAS: Energy Regulation; Energy Litigation; Energy Contracts; Electric Power; Natural Gas.
Barry, Kevin R., (AV) ....'— '81 C.1030 B.A. L.128 J.D. [Reed S.]
*PRACTICE AREAS: Health Care.
Barry, Kristin Pierce ....'73 '00 C.197 A.B. L.276 J.D. [A Collier S.S.]
*PRACTICE AREAS: Litigation.
Barry, Michael MacAdam '60 '96 C.910 B.S.C.E. L.734 J.D.
Pat. Coun., Samssung Electronics America, Inc. (Pat.)
*RESPONSIBILITIES: Intellectual Property Licensing; Intellectual Property Litigation; Telecommunications Law; Semiconductor Technology; Computer and Software Patents.
Barry, William P ....'69 '95 C.918 B.A. L.273 J.D. 504 7th St., S.E.
Barsh, Harry E., Jr., (AV) ....'30 '59 C.421 B.S. L.420 J.D. 700 13th St., N.W.
Barshefsky, Charlene, (AV) ....'50 '75 C.966 B.A. L.128 J.D. [Wilmer,C.&P.]
*PRACTICE AREAS: International Trade; International Business Law; Investments; Regulatory Law; Negotiable Instruments.
Barsky, David A. ....'59 '86 C&L.273 B.A., J.D. [Krooth&A.]
Barsness, George P. ....'55 '85 C&L.846 B.A., J.D. [Hogan&H.]
*PRACTICE AREAS: Corporate Law; Securities.
Barsukova-Spandau, Olesya Vladimirovna '— '00 C&L.280 B.B.A., J.D.
[A Hogan&H.]
Barta, Michael J., (AV) ....'63 '89 C.674 A.B. L.309 J.D. [Baker B.]
Bartelmay, Janet L. '54 '83 C.477 B.S. L.273 J.D.
Assoc. Gen. Coun. & Corp. Secy., Association of American Railroads
Barth, Roger V. ....'38 '63 C.674 A.B. L.107 LL.B. 1201L, 1801 K St., N.W.
Bartholomew, Michael J. '45 '74 C.156 B.A. L.669 J.D.
(adm. in MA; not adm. in DC) American Council of Life Insurance
Bartholomot, Henri D. '54 '83 C.446 B.S.C.E. L.309 J.D.
Sr. Atty., Edison Elec. Institute
Bartl, Timothy J. ....'68 '93 C.436 B.S. L.494 J.D. [A McGuiness N.&W.]
*PRACTICE AREAS: Labor Law; Employment Law; Legislation.
Bartlett, Charles J. ....'31 '61 C&L.276 B.S., J.D. 1401 New York Ave., N.W.
Bartlett, Christine A. ....'53 '80 C.763 B.S. L.982 J.D. [A Jones,D.R.&P.]
Bartlett, David C. ....'71 '99 C.902 B.A. L.180 J.D. 1615 L St.
Bartlett, Frederick B.H. ....'28 '59 C.102 B.A. L.30 LL.B. 1500 Massachusetts Ave.‡
Bartlett, John L., (AV) ....'42 '67 C.112 A.B. L.813 LL.B. [Wiley R.&F.]
*PRACTICE AREAS: Communications.
Bartlett, Kevin S. ....'60 '87 C.576 B.A. L.896 J.D. Tr. Offr., Crestar Bk., N.A.
Bartley, Margaret '59 '95
(adm. in MD; not adm. in DC) National Vets. Legal Servs. Program
Bartman, Thomas R. ....'53 '82 C.311 B.A. L.893 J.D. [A Shapiro,L.&S.]
*PRACTICE AREAS: Environmental Regulation; Litigation; Environmental Compliance Counseling; General Litigation.
Bartnoff, Judith ....'49 '75 C.681 A.B. L.178 J.D. Supr. Ct. J.
Bartoli-Cain, Michele ....'58 '84 C.576 B.A. L.896 J.D. [Claxton,S.&Q.]
*PRACTICE AREAS: Commercial Litigation; Personal Injury; Medical Malpractice; Dental Malpractice; Products Liability.
Barton, John L. '73 '99 C.846 B.A. L.893 J.D.
(adm. in CA; not adm. in DC) [A Shaw P.]
*PRACTICE AREAS: Technology.
Barton, Mary Catherine '55 '84 C.797 B.A. L.945 J.D.
(adm. in VA; not adm. in DC) Mgr., Graduate Progs., Sch. of Intl. Serv.
Barton, R. Joseph '69 '01 C&L.945 B.A., J.D.
(adm. in CA; not adm. in DC) [A Cohen,M.H.&T.]
*PRACTICE AREAS: Complex Civil Litigation; Class Action Litigation.
Barton, Rhonda L. '66 '99 C.329 B.S. L.446 J.D.
(adm. in MD; not adm. in DC) [A Arent F.K.P.&K.]
*PRACTICE AREAS: Patents.
Barton, William J. ....'24 '50 C.103 A.B. L.309 J.D. 818 Connecticut Ave., NW

Barton, Baker, McMahon & Tolle, L.L.P.
(See McLean, Virginia)

Bartone, David J., (AV) '58 '87 C.381 B.A. L.128 J.D. BB
Twelfth Floor, International Square, 1875 Eye Street, N.W., 20006
Telephone: 202-223-6200 Facsimile: 202-223-6220
Email: DJBARTONE@aol.com URL: http://www.lawyers.com/davidbartone
***PRACTICE AREAS: Electronic Banking; White Collar Criminal Defense; Commercial Law; General Litigation; Corporation Law.**
Complex Civil and Commercial Litigation, Securities Litigation, Electronic Banking, Mortgage and Finance, White Collar Criminal Defense, Business Fraud.
See Professional Biographies, WASHINGTON, DISTRICT OF COLUMBIA

Bartos, Jeffrey A. ....'65 '90 C.178 B.A. L.976 J.D. [Guerrieri,E.&C.]
Bartos, Mila F. '68 '93 C.966 B.A. L.30 J.D.
(adm. in MD; not adm. in DC) [A Finkelstein,T.&L.]
Bartram, Darin R. ....'68 '93 C.882 B.A. L.273 J.D. [A Baker&H.]
*PRACTICE AREAS: International Law; Environmental.
Bartsch, Adam H. '64 '99 C.454 B.A. L.273 J.D.
(adm. in NY; not adm. in DC) [A Huber L.&A.]
*PRACTICE AREAS: Energy Law; Public Utility Law.
Bartus, John J. ....'49 '75 C.433 B.S.E.E. L.724 J.D. [C Cameron M.]
*PRACTICE AREAS: Energy Law; Public Utilities Law; Administrative Law.
Bartz, Philip D. ....'56 '84 C.156 B.A. L.276 J.D. [Long A.&N.]
*PRACTICE AREAS: Antitrust; Litigation; Administrative Law.
Baruch, Douglas W. ....'62 '87 C.367 B.A. L.276 J.D. [Fried,F.H.S.&J.]
*PRACTICE AREAS: Civil and Criminal Fraud Litigation; Business Litigation; International Arbitration.
Baruch, Gregory ....'62 '88 C.976 B.A. L.477 J.D. [Berry&L.]

Baruch, Stephen D., (AV) ....'60 '85 C.893 B.S. L.94 J.D. [Leventhal,S.&L.]
*PRACTICE AREAS: Communications Law; International and Domestic Satellite Law.
Barusch, Ronald C. .... '53 '78 C&L.309 A.B., J.D. [Skadden,A.S.M.&F.] (⊙Reston, VA)
Barwind, Karie J. ....'72 '98 C.823 B.A./B.F.A. L.188 J.D. [Ⓐ White&C.]
Basch, Michelle J. ....'71 '96 C.1036 B.A. L.904 J.D. 555 Twelfth St., N.W.
Bascon, Hever M., Jr. '— '95 C.662 B.S.B.M. L.999 LL.B.
(adm. in NY; not adm. in DC) [Ⓐ Verner,L.B.M.&H.]
*PRACTICE AREAS: Mergers and Acquisitions; Corporate Law.
Basdekis, Thanos ....'71 '98 C.178 B.A. L.976 J.D. [Ⓐ Regan,H.&L.]
*PRACTICE AREAS: Personal Injury; Product Liability; Aviation Accidents; Medical Malpractice; Wrongful Death.
Bash, Jeremy B. '71 '98 C.276 A.B. L.309 J.D.
(adm. in VA; not adm. in DC) [Ⓐ O'Melveny&M.]
Basha, Leigh-Alexandra, (AV) ....'— '85 C.276 A.B. L.904 J.D. [Peterson&B.] ⊙
Basha, Steven L. '54 '79 C&L.472 B.B.A., J.D.
(adm. in FL; not adm. in DC) 1300 Pennsylvania Ave. N.W.
Basil, William C. ....'56 '81 C.867 B.S. L.245 J.D. [Arent F.K.P.&K.]
*PRACTICE AREAS: Bond Finance; Financial Institutions Law.
Basile, Edward M., (AV) ....'— '73 C.390 B.S. L.273 J.D. [King&S.]
*PRACTICE AREAS: Food and Drug Regulation.
Basile, James F. ....'64 '89 C&L.602 B.A., J.D. [Kirkland&E.]
*PRACTICE AREAS: Commercial Litigation; First Amendment; Libel and Defamation; Antitrust; Intellectual Property.
Basile, Michael D., (AV) ....'58 '83 C.390 B.A. L.904 J.D. [Dow,L.&A.]
Basile, Richard S. '63 '98 C.688 B.S.P.E. L.734 J.D.
(adm. in MO; not adm. in DC) [Ⓐ Proskauer R.]
Baskerville, Lisa C ....'69 '95 C.302 B.S. L.276 J.D. Asst. U.S. Atty.
Baskin, Maurice, (AV) ....'54 '78 C.309 B.A. L.260 J.D. [Venable,A.B.H.&C.]
*PRACTICE AREAS: Labor (Management) Law; Wrongful Discharge Law; Civil Rights Law; Litigation; Appellate Practice.
Bason, George Francis, Jr., (AV) '31 '56 C.198 A.B. L.309 J.D.
4910 Massachusetts Avenue, N.W., Suite 18 (⊙Chevy Chase, MD)
Bass, I. Scott, (AV) ....'51 '76 C.569 B.A. L.477 J.D. [Sidley A.B.&W.]
Bass, Kenneth C., III, (AV) '44 '70
C.228 A.B. L.976 LL.B. [Venable,A.B.H.&C.] (⊙Mc Lean, VA)
*PRACTICE AREAS: Appellate Practice; Intellectual Property Litigation; Constitutional Litigation; Civil Practice; Litigation.
Bass, Kenneth N., (AV) ....'58 '84 C.976 B.A. L.276 J.D. [Kirkland&E.]
*PRACTICE AREAS: Commercial Litigation-Corporate; Product Liability.
Bass, Susan Perkoff '57 '84 C.976 B.A. L.276 J.D.
Dir., Inter-American Prog., Environmental Law Institute
*RESPONSIBILITIES: Environmental Law; International Law.
Bass, Timothy C. ....'71 '96 C.228 B.S. L.276 J.D. [Ⓐ Greenberg T.]
Bass, Ursula C. ....'68 '97 C.66 B.A. L.904 J.D. [Ⓐ Wilmer,C.&P.]
Basseches, Robert T., (AV) ....'34 '59 C.31 B.A. L.976 LL.B. [Shea&G.]
*PRACTICE AREAS: Transportation Regulation; Administrative; Civil Litigation.
Bassman, Robert S. ....'47 '73 C.665 B.A. L.273 J.D. [Bassman,M.&A.]
Bassman, Mitchell & Alfano, Chartered ....1201 N.Y. Ave., N.W. Ste. 1275
Bastek, John A. '— '74 C.869 B.S. L.472 J.D.
(adm. in FL; not adm. in DC) [Ⓒ Preston G.E.&R.M.]
*PRACTICE AREAS: Military Law.
Bastiampillai, Harisha J. ....'67 '92 C.367 B.A. L.178 J.D. [Ⓐ Swidler B.S.F.]
*PRACTICE AREAS: Telecommunications Regulatory; Telecommunications Litigation; Telecommunications Appellate Litigation.
Bastian, Holly M. ....'64 '92 C.893 B.S. L.276 J.D. [Ⓐ Arent F.K.P.&K.]
*PRACTICE AREAS: Estate Planning; Estate and Gift Taxation; Wills; Trust Law; Corporate Law.
Bastianelli, Adrian L., III, (AV) .... '43 '71 C.679 B.C.E. L.421 J.D. [Bastianelli,B.&K.]
*PRACTICE AREAS: Construction Law; Government Contracts; Environmental Remediation; Alternative Dispute Resolution.

Bastianelli, Brown & Kelley, Chartered, (AV) [BR]
Two Lafayette Centre, 1133 21st Street, N.W., Suite 500, 20036
Telephone: 202-293-8815 Telecopier: 202-293-7994
Email: bbk@govconlaw.com URL: http://www.govconlaw.com
Adrian L. Bastianelli, III; J. Mitchell Brown; Philip R. Croessmann; James A. Kelley; Lawrence C. Melton; Charles M. Reifel; George W. Stiffler; Tina S. Tisinger; Donald A. Tobin; Ronald H. Uscher;—Nick R. Hoogstraten; Lori Ann Lange. Of Counsel: H. Clayton Cook, Jr.; Marcus W. Sisk, Jr.
Government Contracts and Construction Law, Environmental Remediation, Administrative and Legislative Practice, Admiralty and Maritime, Commercial, International and Corporate Law, Tax, Project Finance including U.S. and Foreign Flag Vessels and Aircraft and Litigation.
See Professional Biographies, WASHINGTON, DISTRICT OF COLUMBIA

Bastow, Thomas F. ....'42 '68 C.477 A.B. L.309 LL.B. Wash. Convention Ctr. Auth.
Bastress, Susan B. ....'52 '81 C.228 B.S. L.273 J.D. [Patton B.]
Basu, Ranu ....'43 '83 C.999 B.A. L.273 M.C.L. 419 7th St., N.W.
Batchelor, William C. ....'68 '95 C.893 B.S. L.945 J.D. 1990 18th St., N.W.
Bateman, Courtney R. ....'64 '89 C&L.585 B.S., J.D. [Ⓐ Dombroff&G.]
Bateman, Grace A. ....'43 '81 C.722 B.A. L.128 J.D. [Ⓒ Seyfarth S.]
*PRACTICE AREAS: Government Contract Law; Commercial Contract Law; Administrative Law.
Bateman, John W. ....'65 '90 C&L.893 B.A., J.D. [Kenyon&K.] (See Pat. Sect.)
*PRACTICE AREAS: Intellectual Property.
Bateman, Marguerite Cameron, (AV) '62 '87
C.228 A.B. L.896 J.D. Assoc. Coun., Investment Co. Inst.
*RESPONSIBILITIES: Securities; Governance.
Bates, Bradford L. '50 '75
C.378 B.A. L.629 J.D. Transp. Coun., Kimberly-Clark Corporation
Bates, Earle S. ....'32 '57 C.902 B.A. L.893 LL.B. 4441 MacArthur Blvd.‡
Bates, John D., (AV) ....'46 '76 C.918 B.A. L.446 J.D. [Miller&C.]
*PRACTICE AREAS: Federal Civil Litigation; Health Care Fraud; Government Contracts; False Claims Act; White Collar Crime.
Bates, Lawrence F. ....'54 '81 C.207 B.A. L.245 J.D. [Hughes H.&R.]
*PRACTICE AREAS: Banking; Bankruptcy.
Bates, Stephen ....'58 '88 C&L.309 A.B., J.D. Annenberg Washington Program
Bates, William B., (BV) '57 '82 C.802 B.B.A. L.502 J.D.
(adm. in MO; not adm. in DC) Hallmark Cards, Inc.
Batipps, Joyce Stanley ....'45 '97 C.329 B.S. L.1364 J.D. 1200 G St. N.W.
Batla, Raymond J., Jr. ....'47 '73 C&L.846 B.S.C.E., J.D. [Hogan&H.]
*PRACTICE AREAS: Corporate Finance; Project Finance; Mergers and Acquisitions; Technology.
Battaglia, John T. ....'69 '97 C&L.93 B.A., J.D. [Ⓐ Howrey S.A.&W.]
*PRACTICE AREAS: Commercial Litigation; Intellectual Property Litigation; Antitrust Litigation.
Batten, Jonathan ....'— '00 C.446 B.A. L.276 J.D. [Ⓐ Arnold&P.]
Batter, Anne G. ....'60 '85 C.446 B.A. L.309 J.D. [Ⓒ Baker&M.]
*PRACTICE AREAS: Tax Planning and Advice (Corporate and International).
Battino, Morris R. ....'54 '83 C.1213 B.S. L.1162 J.D. 1200 Perry Street, N.E.
Battista, Felicia C. ....'50 '93 C.273 B.B.A. L.128 J.D. [Malizia S.&F.]
*PRACTICE AREAS: Securities; Corporate; Banking.
Battles, Philip M., III, (AV) '44 '73 C.823 B.A. L.276 J.D. [Hunton&W.]
*PRACTICE AREAS: Project Finance; Leveraged Leasing; Real Estate; Finance; International.
Batts, Alicia J. ....'— '91 C.309 A.B. L.178 J.D. [Ⓒ Foley&L.]
*PRACTICE AREAS: Antitrust Litigation.
Baudhuin, Michael D. ....'39 '65 C&L.436 A.B., LL.B. Corp. V.P., AT&T

Bauer, Lee Anthony ....'44 '91 C.801 B.A. L.273 J.D. [Roller&B.]
*PRACTICE AREAS: Aviation Regulation; Aeronautical Regulation; Aviation Law; Federal Aviation Licenses; Customs Overflight Law.
Bauer, Richard P., (BV) ....'51 '84 C.870 B.S. L.128 J.D. [Katten M.Z.] (Pat.)
*PRACTICE AREAS: Intellectual Property; Intellectual Property Litigation; Internet Law; E-Commerce.
Bauer, Robert F., (AV) ....'52 '76 C.309 B.A. L.893 J.D. [Perkins C.]
*PRACTICE AREAS: Federal Election Law; Government Ethics; White Collar Criminal Law.
Bauer, Serge ....'62 '90 C.994 B.A. L.1048 J.D. [Bauer&Z.]
*PRACTICE AREAS: International Trade Law; Corporate Law; Immigration Law; Joint Ventures.
Bauer, Stephen R. ....'70 '96 C.674 A.B. L.309 J.D. [Ⓐ Fried,F.H.S.&J.]
*PRACTICE AREAS: Corporate Law; Securities; Private Equity.

Bauer & Zouaoui, LLP
2300 M Street N.W., Suite 800, 20037 ⊙
Telephone: 202-775-9344, 202-775-9344 Fax: 202-775-9341 http://www.bauerzouaoui.com
Email: bauerlaw@verizon.net URL: http://www.ilw.com/bauerlaw
Serge Bauer; Jamil Zouaoui.
Corporate Practice, International Business, Transactions, Joint Ventures, International Taxation Law, International Investment and Banking Law, Immigration Services, Business Immigration, Arbitration and Mediation.
Moscow, Russia Office: Novyi Arbat St., 2111. Telephone: 095-291-3941. Fax: 095-202-6063.
See Professional Biographies, WASHINGTON, DISTRICT OF COLUMBIA

Bauerly, Cynthia L. ....'71 '98 C.182 B.A. L.347 J.D. [Ⓐ Jones,D.R.&P.]
Baughan, Joan Sylvain ....'62 '91 [Keller&H.]
*PRACTICE AREAS: US and EU Food and Drug Law; Product Safety Law.
Baughman, Cynthia D. ....'68 '97 C.446 B.S. L.1017 J.D. [Ⓐ Dechert]
*PRACTICE AREAS: Financial Services Law; Investment Management.
Baughman, J. Steven ....'68 '94 C.674 B.S.E. L.309 J.D. [Ⓐ Ropes&G.]
Baulig, Laurie T. ....'58 '84 C&L.260 B.A., J.D. [Scopelitis,G.L.&H.]
Baum, Alissa ....'68 '93 C&L.846 B.A., J.D. One Massachusetts Avenue, N.W.
Baum, David J. ....'67 '96 C.276 B.S.F.S. L.904 J.D. [Ⓐ Ropes&G.]
*PRACTICE AREAS: Investment Management; Financial Services Law.
Baum, Deborah Brand ....'59 '83 C.945 B.A. L.893 J.D. [Shaw P.]
*PRACTICE AREAS: Litigation.
Baum, Lynne M. '— '00 C.966 B.A. L.276 J.D.
(adm. in NY; not adm. in DC) [Ⓐ Hogan&H.]

Baum, Hedlund, Aristei, Guilford & Schiavo, A Professional Corporation, (AV) [BR]
1250 24th Street, N.W., Suite 300, 20037 ⊙
Telephone: 202-466-0513; 800-827-0097 Fax: 202-466-0527
Email: info@baumhedlundlaw.com URL: http://www.baumhedlundlaw.com
Cara J. Luther.
Limited only to Plaintiff's Serious Personal Injury and Wrongful Death Accident Litigation nationwide and worldwide; including Aviation Accident Litigation, Airline Accidents, Bus Accidents, Tractor-Trailer Accidents, Train Accidents, Public Transportation Accidents, Mass Disaster Litigation, Complex Multi-District Litigation and Product Liability including Antidepressant Drug Litigation.
Los Angeles, California Office: Suite 950, 12100 Wilshire Boulevard. Telephones: 310-207-3233; 800-827-0087. Facsimile: 310-820-7444.
See Professional Biographies, WASHINGTON, DISTRICT OF COLUMBIA

Bauman, Barry H. ....'55 '81 C.16 B.S. L.192 J.D. Counsel, Lawyers for Civil Justice
Bauman, Gus ....'49 '75 C.156 A.B. L.910 J.D. [Ⓒ Beveridge&D.]
*PRACTICE AREAS: Land Use; Environmental Law; Inverse Condemnation; Trade Association Law.
Bauman, Jeffrey D., (AV) ....'37 '64 C&L.976 B.A., LL.B. 3125 Beech St., N.W.
Bauman, Robert A. ....'55 '84 C&L.945 B.B.A., J.D. [Ⓒ Alston&B.]
*PRACTICE AREAS: Employee Benefit Law; ERISA; Qualified Retirement Plans.
Baumann, David N. ....'59 '84 C.696 B.A. L.930 J.D. [Mintz,L.C.F.G.&P.]
*PRACTICE AREAS: Technology Contracts; Outsourcing; Intellectual Property; Telecommunications Law.
Baumann, Henry L., (AV) '44 '70 C.893 B.A. L.1017 J.D.
(adm. in PA; not adm. in DC) Exec. V.P., National Association of Broadcasters
Baumann, Linda A. ....'— '75 C.103 B.A. L.178 J.D. [Ⓒ Reed S.]
*PRACTICE AREAS: Health Care.
Baumann, Deseve & Landau ....16225 Massachusetts Avenue, N.W., Suite 450
Baumbusch, Peter L. ....'44 '72 C.197 A.B. L.309 J.D. [Gibson,D.&C.]
*PRACTICE AREAS: Corporate Taxation; Mergers and Acquisitions; Foreign Investment in the United States; Section 482 Intercompany Pricing; Executive Compensation.
Baumer, Catherine R., (AV) ....'46 '78 C.273 B.A. L.904 J.D. [Spriggs&H.]
*PRACTICE AREAS: Government Contracts; Banking Litigation; Litigation.
Baumgarten, Jon A., (AV) ....'42 '68 C.563 B.A. L.569 LL.B. [Proskauer R.]
Baumgarten, Ronald John, Jr. ....'70 '00 C.30 B.A. L.94 J.D. [Ⓐ Covington&B.]
Baur, Donald C. ....'54 '79 C.856 B.A. L.659 J.D. [Perkins C.]
*PRACTICE AREAS: Environmental Law; Litigation.
Baurley, Marion E., (BV) ....'— '79 C.472 B.A. L.30 J.D. [M.E.Baurley]
*PRACTICE AREAS: Family Law; Elder Law; School Law; Professional Licensing.

Baurley, Marion E., P.C., Law Offices of, (BV)
235 Massachusetts Avenue, N.E., 20002
Telephone: 202-544-9820 Fax: 202-544-9832
Email: baurley@erols.com URL: http://www.baurleylaw.com
Marion E. Baurley;—Kathy K.B. Dupuy-Bruno.
Adoption, Annulment, Child Custody, Child Visitation, Child Neglect, Child Support and Maintenance, Disability, Divorce, Domestic Relations, Father's Rights, Education, Elder Care, Employment, Estate and Probate, Legal Separation, Personal Injury, Professional Responsibility, Medical Malpractice, Small Business, Special Education.
See Professional Biographies, WASHINGTON, DISTRICT OF COLUMBIA

Bauser, Michael A. '43 '74 C.813 B.S.M.E. L.276 J.D.
Assoc. Gen. Coun., Nuclear Energy Institute, Inc.
*RESPONSIBILITIES: Nuclear Energy; Administrative Law; Corporate Law; Nonprofit and Charitable Organizations; Trade and Professional Organizations.
Bavender, Ann, (AV) ....'53 '85 C.928 B.A. L.273 J.D. [Ⓐ Fletcher,H.&H.] ⊙
*PRACTICE AREAS: Telecommunications Law; International Telecommunications Law; Internet Law; Satellite Communications; Mass Media Law.
Bavinger, William F., III, (AV) ....'— '68 C.976 B.E. L.477 J.D. [Bryan C.]
*PRACTICE AREAS: Corporate Law; Securities Regulation Law.
Baxley, Jean Male ....'63 '95 C.945 B.A. L.1209 J.D. [Ⓐ Steptoe&J.]
Baxt, Leonard J., (AV) ....'48 '73 C.665 B.A. L.477 J.D. [Dow,L.&A.]
Baxter, Allin P., (AV) ....'29 '57 C.893 B.A. L.273 LL.B. [Ⓒ Elias,M.T.&H.]
Baxter, Edward H. ....'48 '74 C&L.280 B.B.A., J.D. [Ⓐ Parry&R.]
Baxter, Graeme ....'47 '84 C.104 A.B. L.276 J.D. Pres., The Civil Tr.
Baxter, Michael St. Patrick, (AV) ....'— '81 L.028 LL.B. [Covington&B.]
Baxter, Thomas A., (P.C.) ....'46 '71 C.679 B.A. L.273 J.D. [Shaw P.]
*PRACTICE AREAS: Information Technology.
Bayer, Mark A., (AV) ....'47 '73 C.475 B.A. L.273 J.D. 1815 H St., N.W.
Bayer, Michael David ....'46 '78 C.94 B.A. L.823 J.D. 1200 K St., NW
Bayes, James R. W., (AV) ....'50 '76 C.228 B.A. L.893 J.D. [Wiley R.&F.]
*PRACTICE AREAS: Communications.
Bayles, Alan P. ....'47 '73 C.415 B.S. L.30 J.D. 1730 K St., N.W.
Bayles, Norman E., (AV) '31 '59 C&L.188 B.A., LL.B.
Suite 1000, 900 17th Street, N.W.
Baylis, Elena A. ....'72 '99 C.629 B.A. L.976 J.D. [Ⓐ Shea&G.]
Baylor, Bryneé Kyonne '74 '00 C.104 A.B. L.329 J.D.
(adm. in MD; not adm. in DC) [Ⓐ Dorsey&W.]
*PRACTICE AREAS: Corporate Law; Corporate Finance; Agricultural Cooperatives.

Baylor, Gregory S. '65 '90 C.197 A.B. L.228 J.D.
(adm. in TX; not adm. in DC) 815 Conn. Ave., N.W.‡
Bayly, John H., Jr. ....'44 '69 C.262 A.B. L.309 J.D. Supr. Ct. J.
Baynard, Ernest C., III ....'44 '71 C.855 B.A. L.276 J.D. 1825 I St.
Bayus, Richard M., II '68 '94 C.893 B.A. L.896 J.D.
(adm. in GA; not adm. in DC) Atty., Div. of Market Regulation, Sec. Exch. Comm.
Bayz, Panagiotis C. ....'62 '91 C.276 B.S.F.S. L.904 J.D. [🄲 Morrison&F.]
Bazan, S. Nicole '— '00 C.813 B.A. L.309 J.D.
(adm. in NY; not adm. in DC) [🄰 Hobbs,S.D.&W.]
Bazil, Paul J. ....'62 '88 C.197 A.B. L.94 J.D. [Pickard&D.]
Beach, Barbara N. ....'— '00 C.446 B.A. L.180 J.D. 407 Kentucky Avenue, S.E.
Beach, Danielle L. C. '55 '91 C.1163 B.A. L.64 J.D.
(adm. in MD; not adm. in DC) [Noto&O.]
*PRACTICE AREAS: Immigration Law.
Beach, Geoffrey K. ....'62 '92 C.604 B.A. L.128 J.D. [🄰 Jones,D.R.&P.]
Beadles, James C., (AV) ....'47 '72 C&L.273 B.A., J.D. [Willey&C.]
*PRACTICE AREAS: Probate Administration; Estates; Wills; Thrift Institutions Law.
Beahn, John M. ....'71 '99 C.93 B.A. L.128 J.D. [🄰 Skadden,A.S.M.&F.]
Beal, W. Ashby, Jr. ....'58 '86 C.976 B.A. L.276 J.D. [Singley&B.]
*PRACTICE AREAS: Antitrust; Trade Regulation; Telecommunications Law.
Beall, James A., (AV) ....'50 '76 C.628 B.A. L.629 J.D. [Ball J.] (⊙Port., OR)
*PRACTICE AREAS: Government Affairs; Legislative Lobbying; Administrative Lobbying Law.
Beals, Bart E. '— '00 L.329 J.D.
(adm. in IL; not adm. in DC) [🄰 Shaw P.]
Bean, Donald, Jr. ....'57 '82 C&L.145 B.A., J.D. [Fensterheim&B.]
Bean, J. Coleman, (AV) ....'28 '57 C.870 B.S. L.893 LL.B. [🄲 Webster,C.&B.]
*PRACTICE AREAS: Corporate Law.
Bean, Lori A. ....'69 '94 C.880 B.A. L.188 J.D. [🄰 Winston&S.]
Beard, Michael B. ....'63 '95 C.446 B.S. L.64 J.D. [🄰 Braude&M.]
*PRACTICE AREAS: Complex Litigation; Environmental Law; Construction Contracts; Government Contracts.
Beardsley, Kate C. ....'49 '75 C.788 B.A. L.245 J.D. [Buc&B.]
Beargie, Amy E. ....'64 '89 C.1118 B.A. L.421 J.D. 607 14th St., N.W.
Bearman, Michael James ....'73 '00 C.911 B.A. L.276 J.D. [🄰 McKenna&C.]
*PRACTICE AREAS: Litigation; Government Contracts; Life Sciences.
Bearse, Michael S., (AV) ......'45 '70 C&L.94 B.A., J.D. 905 16th. St. (⊙Providence, RI)
Beary, Roberta ....'54 '79 C.999 B.A. L.724 J.D. [🄰 Martell&Assoc.]
*PRACTICE AREAS: Real Estate Finance; Mortgage Finance; Housing and Urban Development; Secondary Mortgage Market; International Real Estate.
Beasley, Cecil A., Jr., (AV) ....'12 '40 C.674 A.B. L.976 LL.B. 1616 H St., N.W.‡
Beasley, Donna M. ....'62 '91 C.999 B.A. L.329 J.D. 419 7th St., N.W.
Beasley, Michele E. ....'64 '92 C.788 B.A. L.276 J.D. [🄲 Orrick,H.&S.]
Beasley, Vicky L. ....'— '99 C.893 B.A. L.178 J.D. [🄰 Latham&W.]
Beaston, Virgil Lee '63 '00 C.1095 B.S.E.E. L.1209 J.D.
(adm. in VA; not adm. in DC) [🄰 Sterne,K.G.&F.]
*PRACTICE AREAS: Patent Applications; Patent Prosecution; Patent Infringement; Patent Litigation.
Beato, Andrew Michael ....'69 '94 C.94 B.A. L.30 J.D. [Stein,M.&M.]
*PRACTICE AREAS: Antitrust; Trade Regulation.
Beattie, Lauralyn Elizabeth ....'72 '98 C.36 B.A. L.228 J.D. [🄰 Wilmer,C.&P.]
Beattie, Lisa C. '65 '97 C&L.813 B.A., J.D.
(adm. in NY; not adm. in DC) 725 12th St., N.W.
Beatty, George W., (AV) ....'32 '57 C.674 A.B. L.309 LL.B. 1200 18th St., N.W.
Beatty, Richard S., (AV) ....'34 '62 C.951 B.A. L.276 LL.B. [🄲 Shaw P.]
*PRACTICE AREAS: Corporate Law; Non-Profit Organizations; Trusts and Estates.
Beaty, John B. ....'53 '78 C.475 B.S. L.145 J.D. [Venable,A.B.H.&C.]
*PRACTICE AREAS: Financial Institutions; Business; Corporate.
Beauchamp, Edward E. '56 '87 C.1074 B.S. L.45 J.D.
(adm. in PA; not adm. in DC) Walter Reed Army Medical Center
Beaudin, Bruce D. ....'39 '64 C.1030 B.A. L.276 J.D. Sr. J., Supr. Ct.
Beaudreau, Tommy P. ....'72 '97 C.976 B.A. L.276 J.D. [🄰 Fried,F.H.S.&J.]
*PRACTICE AREAS: Litigation; Civil Fraud; White Collar Crime.
Beaumont, Meaghan McGrath ....'67 '93 C.178 B.A. L.276 J.D. [🄰 Chadbourne&P.]
Beauregard, Robert L. '45 '73 C.1122 B.B.A. L.93 J.D.
(adm. in MA; not adm. in DC)
Dir., Fed. Regulatory Affs., Southern California Gas Company
Beaver, Nathan A. ....'72 '97 C.37 B.A. L.276 J.D. [🄰 McDermott,W.&E.]
Beavers, Bonnie A., (AV) ....'58 '83 C.228 B.A. L.846 J.D. [Kleinfeld,K.&B.]
*PRACTICE AREAS: Food, Drug and Cosmetic Law; Food and Drug Regulation; Drug and Medical Device Regulation; Controlled Substances Law; Advertising Law.
Beazer, Craig T. '67 '93 C.1041 B.A. L.569 J.D.
(adm. in NY; not adm. in DC) [🄰 McKee N.]
*PRACTICE AREAS: Structured Finance; Lending; General Corporate; Public Finance.

Bebchick, Leonard N., (AV) '32 '58 C.188 A.B. L.976 LL.B.
1101 Connecticut Avenue, N.W., Suite 1000, 20036
Telephone: 202-822-6401 Fax: 202-822-6404
Email: beblaw@erols.com
Practice before all Federal Courts, Departments and Regulatory Agencies. Administrative Law, Civil Litigation and Appeals, Class Actions, Corporate Commercial Law.
See Professional Biographies, WASHINGTON, DISTRICT OF COLUMBIA

Bechky, Perry S. ....'68 '94 C.813 A.B. L.178 J.D. [🄰 Shearman&S.]
Becht, Tara S. ....'70 '96 C.354 B.S. L.128 J.D. 1730 Rhode Island Ave.
Bechtel, Gene A., (AV) ....'32 '58 C.467 B.S. L.273 J.D. [Bechtel&C.]
*PRACTICE AREAS: Communications Law; Telecommunications Law; Appellate Practice; Trademarks; Copyrights.
Bechtel, Philip E., (BV) ....'50 '75 C.264 A.B. L.276 J.D. [Williams&J.]
*PRACTICE AREAS: Financial Institutions; Banking.

Bechtel & Cole, Chartered, (AV)
Suite 250, 1901 L Street, N.W., 20036
Telephone: 202-833-4190 Telecopier: 202-833-3084
Email: info@coleslaw.com
Gene A. Bechtel.
Federal Administrative and Appellate Administrative Litigation Practice. Communications, Telecommunications and Intellectual Property.
See Professional Biographies, WASHINGTON, DISTRICT OF COLUMBIA

Beck, Candace N. '73 '99 C.10 B.A. L.30 J.D.
(adm. in TX; not adm. in DC) [🄰 Howrey S.A.&W.]
*PRACTICE AREAS: Commercial Litigation; Antitrust; White Collar Crime.
Beck, Douglas N. ....'59 '87 C.94 B.A. L.893 J.D. [LeBoeuf,L.G.&M.]
Beck, Edward A., III, (AV) ....'44 '74 C.198 A.B. L.692 J.D. [O'Connor&H.]
*PRACTICE AREAS: Legislation; Taxation Law; International Trade; Estate Planning; Probate.
Beck, George C. ....'— '93 C&L.276 B.S., J.D. [🄲 Foley&L.] (See Pat. Sect.)
*PRACTICE AREAS: Intellectual Property.
Beck, Jeanna M. ....'71 '98 C.473 B.A. L.209 J.D. [🄰 Arnold&P.]
*PRACTICE AREAS: Litigation.
Beck, John A., (AV) ....'— '51 C.862 B.A. L.273 J.D. [🄲 Reed S.]
*PRACTICE AREAS: Corporate; Finance.
Beck, Reagen ....'70 '97 C.367 B.A. L.904 J.D. [🄰 Orrick,H.&S.]
Beck, Stephen A. ....'73 '98 C&L.846 B.B.A., J.D. [🄰 Williams&C.]
*PRACTICE AREAS: Taxation.
Beck, Thomas M. ....'66 '92 C&L.893 B.A., J.D. [🄰 Jones,D.R.&P.]
Becker, Brandon, (AV) ....'54 '78 C.494 B.A. L.1049 J.D. [Wilmer,C.&P.]
*PRACTICE AREAS: Finance; Securities; Regulatory.
Becker, Daniel F. '55 '83 C.299 A.B. L.588 J.D.
(adm. in MA; not adm. in DC) Sierra Club of D.C.
Becker, Darby M.R. '68 '98 C.170 B.A. L.1209 J.D.
(adm. in VA; not adm. in DC) Gen. Coun., Gen. Aviation Manufacturers Assn.
Becker, David A. ....'— '96 C.976 B.A. L.145 J.D. [🄰 Latham&W.]
*PRACTICE AREAS: White Collar Criminal Defense; Congressional Investigations; Health Care Fraud; Insider Trading; Commercial Litigation.
Becker, Donna C. ....'62 '88 C.945 B.A. L.966 J.D. 1850 M St., N.W.
Becker, Evelyn ....'68 '94 C.800 A.B. L.145 J.D. [🄲 O'Melveny&M.]
Becker, Joanna Maxwell '22 '46 C.821 B.A. L.976 LL.B.
(adm. in NY; not adm. in DC) 5420 Connecticut Ave., N.W.‡
Becker, Julie C., (AV) '58 '84
C.108 B.S. L.273 J.D. Asst. Gen Coun., Alliance of Auto Mfrs.
Becker, Katherine L. '53 '80 C&L.276 A.B., J.D.
Asst. Dir., Govt. Rel., Amer. Psychiatric Assn.
Becker, Katherine M. Sutcliffe '76 '00 C.93 B.A. L.986 J.D.
(adm. in MO; not adm. in DC) [🄰 Morrison&H.]
Becker, Leonard H., (AV) ....'43 '69 C.309 B.A. L.976 LL.B. [Arnold&P.]
*PRACTICE AREAS: Litigation; Professional Responsibility.
Becker, Loftus E., Jr. ....'44 '70 C.309 A.B. L.659 LL.B. 1250 I St., N.W.
Becker, Merritt S. '61 '88 C.472 B.A. L.1162 J.D.
(adm. in PA; not adm. in DC) 1725 17th St., NW‡
Becker, Michael S. ....'62 '94 C.429 B.A. L.893 J.D. [Kirkland&E.]
*PRACTICE AREAS: Antitrust Law; Litigation.
Becker, Richard S., (AV) ....'42 '68 C.473 A.B. L.477 J.D. 1915 Eye Street, N.W.
Becker, Robert H., (AV) ....'30 '54 C.563 B.S. L.976 J.D. 1140 19th St., N.W.‡
Becker, Robert S. ....'48 '83 C.273 A.B. L.184 J.D. 3315 Morrison St., N.W.
Becker, Scott M. ....'63 '94 C.923 B.S.C.E. L.128 J.D. 3050 K St., N.W.
Becker, Stephan E., (BV) ....'57 '82 C.976 B.A. L.188 J.D. [Shaw P.]
*PRACTICE AREAS: International Trade.
Becker, Stephen A., (AV) ....'44 '75 C.46 B.S. L.273 J.D. [McDermott,W.&E.] (Pat.)
Becker, Steven R. ....'62 '87 C.390 A.B. L.273 J.D. [Vorys,S.S.&P.]
*PRACTICE AREAS: Professional Liability; Employment Law.
Becker, Sylvia M. ....'58 '87 C&L.276 B.S.F.S., J.D. [Kaye S.]
*PRACTICE AREAS: Foreign Investment; Commercial Litigation; Intellectual Property; Internet Law.
Becker, William W., (AV) ....'43 '68 C.197 A.B. L.309 LL.B. [W.W.Becker]
Becker, William W., Chartered, Law Offices of, (AV) .... 955-26th Street, N.W., Suite 801
Beckerman, Jason ....'— '99 C.184 B.A. L.426 J.D. [🄰 Kirkland&E.]
*PRACTICE AREAS: Litigation.
Beckers, J. Randall, (AV) '52 '80 C.10 B.S.E.E. L.192 J.D.
[Staas&H.] (See Pat. Sect.)
*PRACTICE AREAS: Intellectual Property Law; Patent, Trademark, Copyright and Unfair Competition.
Beckett, William W., (AV) '— '56 C.152 B.S. L.273 J.D.
[🄲 Banner&W.] (See Pat. Sect.)
*PRACTICE AREAS: Intellectual Property Law; Patents; Trademarks; Intellectual Property Licensing.
Beckett, William W., (AV) ...... '33 '58 C.446 B.A. L.276 LL.B. 1050 Conn. Ave., N.W.
Beckington, Jeffrey S., (AV) ....'48 '77 C.674 A.B. L.880 J.D. [Collier S.S.]
*PRACTICE AREAS: International Trade.
Beckler, Richard W., (AV) ....'40 '68 C.951 B.A. L.262 J.D. [Fulbright&J.]
*PRACTICE AREAS: Antitrust; Class Action Defense; Foreign Corrupt Practices Act; Complex Litigation; White Collar Crime.
Beckley, Catherine C. '63 '89 C.446 B.S. L.904 J.D.
Assoc. Gen. Coun., Cosmetic, Toiletry & Fragrance Assn.
Beckman, Barbara E. '50 '90 C.112 B.A. L.128 J.D.
(adm. in PA; not adm. in DC) Atty.
Beckman, John B. ....'71 '97 C.445 B.S. L.64 J.D. [🄰 Hogan&H.]
*PRACTICE AREAS: Corporate Finance; Securities; Mergers and Acquisitions.
Beckner, Clinton F. ....'65 '95 C.367 B.S. L.276 J.D. [🄰 Sidley A.B.&W.]
Beckner, Nancy M., (AV) ....'44 '79 C.446 B.A. L.312 J.D. [Carlsmith B.]
*PRACTICE AREAS: International Tax; International Estate Planning; Corporate and Partnership Tax; Tax Exempt Organizations.
Beckner, R. Bruce, (AV) ....'49 '78 C.674 A.B. L.893 J.D. [Fleischman&W.]
Beckwith, Edward Jay, (AV) ....'49 '75 C.645 B.S. L.276 J.D. [Baker&H.]
*PRACTICE AREAS: Tax Law; Closely Held Business Enterprises; Tax-Exempt and Charitable Organizations; Charitable and Personal Planning Law; Trusts and Estates Law.
Becton, Nicole J. '73 '98 C.893 B.A. L.228 J.D.
(adm. in NC; not adm. in DC) [🄰 Kaye S.]
*PRACTICE AREAS: Equal Rights Litigation and Compliance.
Beddard, Cameron W. '67 '01 C.910 B.S.E.E. L.276 J.D.
(adm. in MD; not adm. in DC; See Pat. Sect.) [🄰 Sughrue M.]
*PRACTICE AREAS: Patent Law.
Beddow, David T., (AV) ....'55 '79 C.165 A.B. L.893 J.D. [O'Melveny&M.]
*PRACTICE AREAS: Antitrust; Aviation; Transportation.
Bedell, Dennis P., (AV) ....'— '65 C.309 A.B. L.477 J.D. [Miller&C.]
*PRACTICE AREAS: Taxation; Corporate Taxation; Partnership Taxation; Federal Tax Controversies; Oil and Gas Taxation.
Bedell, Kevin B. ....'65 '89 C.309 B.A. L.893 J.D. [🄰 Dorsey&W.]
*PRACTICE AREAS: Litigation; Commercial Litigation.
Beder, Edward J., Jr., (AV) ....'48 '78 C.869 B.S. L.813 J.D. [Spriggs&H.]
*PRACTICE AREAS: Antitrust; International Arbitration; Complex Commercial Litigation; Insurance Coverage; Asbestos Defense.
Bednar, Richard J. ....'31 '54 C&L.190 LL.B. [🄲 Crowell&M.]
*PRACTICE AREAS: Government Contract Law; Public Contract Law; Contract Law; Court Martial.
Bednarz, Edward L., (BV) '42 '71 C.276 B.A. L.30 J.D.
Sr. V.P. & Assoc. Gen. Coun., Sr. Living Services, Marriott Intl., Inc.
*RESPONSIBILITIES: Real Estate Development; Health Care Law; Finance.
Beecher, Kathleen S. '68 '94 C.321 B.A. L.976 J.D.
(adm. in IL; not adm. in DC) 1722 Eye St., N.W.‡
Beeny, Sean T., (AV) ....'45 '79 C.118 B.A. L.276 J.D. [Miller,B.&O.]
*PRACTICE AREAS: Antitrust and Trade Regulation; Energy Contracts; Electric Power; Electric Utilities; Economic Regulatory Law.
Beer, Jennifer S. ....'67 '96 C.188 B.A. L.802 J.D. [🄰 Katten M.Z.]
*PRACTICE AREAS: Real Estate.
Beers, David Booth, (AV) ....'35 '61 C.855 B.A. L.1066 LL.B. [Shea&G.]
*PRACTICE AREAS: Litigation; Environmental; Products; Nonprofits.
Beers, Deborah M., (AV) ....'49 '76 C.66 A.B. L.178 J.D. [🄲 Silverstein&M.]
*PRACTICE AREAS: Tax Exempt Organizations; Estate Planning; Federal Taxation.
Beers, Donald O., (AV) ....'49 '75 C.197 A.B. L.178 J.D. [Arnold&P.]
*PRACTICE AREAS: Food and Drug Regulation.
Beesley, Susan L. '60 '88 C.198 B.A. L.228 J.D.
Asst. Gen. Coun., Nat. Assn. of Sec. Dealers, Inc.
Beggs, Kathleen L. ....'57 '83 C.914 B.A. L.309 J.D. [Williams&C.]
Begle, Howell E., Jr. ....'— '69 C.797 B.A. L.477 J.D. [🄲 Verner,L.B.M.&H.]
*PRACTICE AREAS: Corporate Law; Entertainment Law.

Begley, Ann Marie ... '64 '94 C&L.276 B.S.N., J.D. [Ⓐ Kirkpatrick&L.]
*PRACTICE AREAS: Food and Drug Law.
Begley, Dennis F., (AV) ... '43 '72 C.688 B.E.E. L.904 J.D. [Reddy,B.&M.] (Pat.)
*PRACTICE AREAS: Communications Law; Administrative Law.
Begun, Tammy ... '66 '91 C.446 B.A. L.128 J.D. 1350 Eye St., NW
Beh, James C., (AV) ... '58 '85 C&L.276 A.B., J.D. [Ⓒ Troutman S.]
*PRACTICE AREAS: Energy Law; Public Utility Law; Administrative Law; Regulatory Law.
Behan, Kathleen A., (AV) ... '63 '89 C.976 B.A. L.178 J.D. [Arnold&P.]
*PRACTICE AREAS: Civil Litigation; Criminal Litigation.
Behr, Douglas J., (AV) ... '47 '73 C.597 B.A. L.569 J.D. [Keller&H.]
*PRACTICE AREAS: Commercial Litigation; White-Collar Criminal Defense; General Business Disputes.
Behre, Kirby D., (AV) ... '60 '85 C.273 B.A. L.276 J.D. [Paul,H.J.&W.]
*PRACTICE AREAS: Corporate Criminal Defense; Corporate Compliance; Government Investigations; Government Contract Law.
Behrends, Samuel, IV, (BV) ... '51 '79 C.309 B.A. L.896 J.D. [LeBoeuf,L.G.&M.]
*PRACTICE AREAS: Utilities.
Behrens, Mark A. ... '65 '90 C.966 B.A. L.880 J.D. [Shook,H.&B.]
*PRACTICE AREAS: Torts; Insurance; Products Liability; Legislative Practice; Public Policy.
Behringer, John W., (AV) '38 '68
C.201 B.S.Chem. L.273 J.D. [Fitzpatrick,C.H.&S.] (See Pat. Sect.)
Beier, Bryan ... '69 '94 C.893 B.A. L.1209 J.D. [Ⓐ Covington&B.]
Beier, David W. '48 '74 C.165 B.A. L.982 J.D.
(adm. in NY; not adm. in DC) [Hogan&H.]
*PRACTICE AREAS: Health Law; Internet Law; Telecommunications Law; Trade; Legislative.
Beimers, Thomas W. ... '68 '99 C.429 B.A. L.494 J.D. [Ⓐ Covington&B.]
Beins, Hugh J., (AV) ... '32 '56 C&L.276 B.S., J.D. [Beins,A.&K.]
Beins, John J. ... '62 '89 C.205 B.A. L.276 J.D. [Beins,G.&G.]
Beins, Axelrod & Kraft, P.C., (AV) ... 1717 Massachusetts Avenue, N.W.
Beins, Goldberg & Gleiberman ... 5335 Wisconsin Avenue, N.W., Suite 910
Beisner, John H., (AV) ... '53 '78 C.378 B.A. L.477 J.D. [O'Melveny&M.]
*PRACTICE AREAS: Complex Civil Litigation; Class Actions; Communications Law.
Beizer, Nicholas M. '72 '99 C.390 B.A. L.128 J.D.
(adm. in VA; not adm. in DC) Assoc. Litig. Coun., WorldCom, Inc.
Beizer, Richard L., (AV) ... '42 '67 C.309 A.B. L.893 LL.B. [Crowell&M.]
*PRACTICE AREAS: Criminal Law; Criminal Trial Practice; Business Crimes Law; Litigation; Public Contract Law.
Beizer, Robert A., (AV) '39 '64 C.309 A.B. L.976 LL.B.
V.P., Law & Develope., & Secy., Gray Communications Systems, Inc.
*RESPONSIBILITIES: Communications Law.
Bela, Richard J ... '40 '66 C.843 B.A. L.846 LL.B. 2829 Connecticut Ave NW, Ste. 209
Belair, Robert R., (P.C.), (AV) ... '47 '73 C.373 B.A. L.178 J.D. [Mullenholz,B.&B.]
Belanger, Gregory P. '58 '89 C.1044 B.S. L.1188 J.D.
(adm. in NJ; not adm. in DC) J. Advoc. Gen. Off.
Belanger, Richard M., (AV) ... '47 '75 C.550 B.A. L.94 J.D. [Powell,G.F.&M.]
*PRACTICE AREAS: Customs; International Trade; Export Controls.
Belas, Richard S., (AV) ... '48 '74 C.855 A.B. L.893 J.D. [Davis&H.]
*PRACTICE AREAS: Taxation Law; Legislative Issues Law.
Belcher, Carl W., (AV) ... '23 '52 C.228 A.B. L.273 LL.B. 1100 H St., N.W.‡
Belcher, Scott F. '60 '91 C.684 B.A. L.893 J.D.
Mng. Dir., Envir. Affs. & Asst. Gen. Coun., Air Transport Association of America
*RESPONSIBILITIES: General Corporate; Environmental.
Belden, Roy S. ... '63 '91 C.67 B.A. L.273 J.D. [Ⓒ Chadbourne&P.]
Belden, W. Neil ... '64 '90 C.299 B.A. L.1194 J.D. [Artabane&B.]
*PRACTICE AREAS: Commercial Litigation; Employment Law; Intellectual Property.
Beldon, Jonathan A. ... '70 '95 C.659 B.A. L.846 J.D. [Ⓐ Shapiro,L.&S.]
*PRACTICE AREAS: Civil Litigation; Construction Law; Trial Practice.
Belendiuk, Arthur V., (AV) ... '55 '80 C.705 B.A. L.1019 J.D. [Smithwick&B.]
*PRACTICE AREAS: Administrative; Communications; Radio and TV; Cable; Common Carrier.
Belford, Kevin B. '48 '76 C.276 B.S. L.93 J.D.
Gen. Coun. & Corp. Secy., American Gas Assn.
Belilos, Elliot ... '61 '88 C.188 B.S. L.273 J.D. [Keller&H.]
*PRACTICE AREAS: Product Safety Law; Employment Law; Business Law; Commercial Law; Litigation.
Belinkie, Harris J. '48 '73 C.855 B.A. L.93 J.D.
Tax Coun., Blake Construction Co., Inc.
Belisle, Stephen E. '70 '00 C.158 B.S. L.273 J.D.
(adm. in VA; not adm. in DC) [Ⓐ Fitzpatrick,C.H.&S.]
Belkin, Leonard ... '25 '54 C.186 B.M.E. L.273 LL.B. 1828 L St., N.W.
Belkowitz, Harold G. ... '67 '94 C.1036 B.A. L.823 J.D. [Ⓐ Ober,K.G.&S.]
Bell, Bernard P., (AV) ... '59 '85 C.165 A.B. L.262 J.D. [Swidler B.S.F.]
*PRACTICE AREAS: Insurance Coverage; Insurance Litigation; Insurance Mediation; Environmental Litigation; Environmental Mediation.
Bell, Carol E. '59 '99 C.188 B.S. L.831 J.D.
(adm. in PA; not adm. in DC) [Ⓐ Eaton&M.] ⊙
*PRACTICE AREAS: Medical Malpractice; Products Liability.
Bell, Charles T. ... '18 '46 L.537 LL.B. 51 Louisiana Ave., N.W.
Bell, Christopher D. ... '67 '96 C&L.846 B.A., J.D. [Ⓐ Womble C.S.&R.]
*PRACTICE AREAS: Real Estate; Commercial Leasing.
Bell, Christopher L., (BV) ... '55 '85 C.475 B.A. L.477 J.D. [Sidley A.B.&W.]
Bell, David E. '75 '01 C.472 B.A. L.893 J.D.
(adm. in VA; not adm. in DC) [Ⓐ Crowell&M.]
Bell, Eleanor Lorraine ... '61 '93 C.696 B.A. L.107 J.D. 1775 Pennsylvania Ave., N.W.
Bell, Elizabeth Anne '71 '99 C.882 L.276 J.D.
(adm. in CA; not adm. in DC) [Ⓐ Troutman S.]
*PRACTICE AREAS: Indian Law; Environmental Law.
Bell, James F., (AV) ... '22 '49 C.674 A.B. L.309 J.D. 2103 R St., N.W.‡
Bell, Joseph C., (AV) ... '40 '68 C.174 B.A. L.976 J.D. [Hogan&H.]
*PRACTICE AREAS: Project Finance; Energy Regulation; Mergers and Acquisitions; International Law.
Bell, Kevin H. '46 '74 C.999 B.A. L.724 J.D.
Assoc. Gen. Coun., Securities Investor Protec. Corp.
Bell, Kevin M. '68 '99 C.472 B.A. L.1209 J.D.
(adm. in MD; not adm. in DC) [Ⓒ Piper M.R.&W.]
*PRACTICE AREAS: Intellectual Property Litigation; Technology Law.
Bell, L. Graeme, III, (AV) ... '44 '70 C.197 A.B. L.309 J.D. [Ⓒ Crowell&M.]
*PRACTICE AREAS: Public Contract Law; Business Crimes Law; Arbitration Law.
Bell, Michael A. ... '49 '81 C.446 B.S. L.128 J.D. [LeBoeuf,L.G.&M.]
*PRACTICE AREAS: Tax.
Bell, Michael D. ... '— '98 C.896 B.A. L.776 J.D. 701 Pennsylvania Avenue, N.W.
Bell, Michael J. ... '59 '89 C.602 B.S.M.E. L.276 J.D. [Howrey S.A.&W.] (See Pat. Sect.)
*PRACTICE AREAS: Intellectual Property.
Bell, Robert B., (BV) ... '53 '81 C.197 B.A. L.813 J.D. [Wilmer,C.&P.]
*PRACTICE AREAS: Antitrust; EU Competition; Litigation.
Bell, Robert L. ... '52 '78 C.638 B.S. L.329 J.D. 111 14th St., NW
Bell, Sheila Trice '49 '74 C.914 B.A. L.309 J.D.
(adm. in MA; not adm. in DC)
Exec. Dir. & CEO, National Association of College & Univ. Attys.
Bell, Stephen R., (AV) ... '42 '67 C.276 A.B. L.966 J.D. [Willkie F.&G.]

Bell, Boyd & Lloyd PLLC, (AV)
1615 L Street, N.W., Suite 1200, 20036 ⊙
Telephone: 202-466-6300 Fax: 202-463-0678
Email: dc@bellboyd.com URL: http://www.bellboyd.com
Resident Members: Edward A. Bloom; William H. Butterfield; A. Thomas Carroccio; Brian Cohen; Andrew N. Cook; Raymond C. Fay; Thomas R. Gibbon; Ronald E. Gilbertson; Peter M. Kilcullen; Christopher G. Mackaronis; Joel S. Rubinstein; Donald E. Santarelli; Robert J. Sciaroni; Walter A. I. Wilson; Charles A. Zielinski (Not admitted in DC). Of Counsel: Richard E. Hill; Edward J. Smith, Jr. Resident Associates: Laura C. Fentonmiller; Steven D. Hitchcock; Lawrence M. Prosen; Michael J. Schrier.
General Practice.
Chicago, Illinois Office: Bell Boyd & Lloyd LLC, Three First National Plaza, Suite 3300, 70 West Madison Street. Telephone: 312-372-1121. Fax: 312-372-2098.
See Professional Biographies, WASHINGTON, DISTRICT OF COLUMBIA

Bellamy, Everett '49 '80 C.958 B.S. L.1003 J.D.
(adm. in OH; not adm. in DC) [Ⓒ D.M.Temple]
Bellamy, Frederick R., (AV) ... '54 '79 C.893 B.A. L.188 J.D. [Sutherland A.&B.]
*PRACTICE AREAS: Insurance Products; Investment Company Law; Mutual Funds.
Bellamy, Galen D. '73 '00 C&L.260 B.A., J.D.
(adm. in CO; not adm. in DC) [Ⓐ Skadden,A.S.M.&F.]
*PRACTICE AREAS: Litigation.
Bellamy, Lorenzo M. ... '63 '96 C.893 B.A. L.128 J.D. [Bellamy]

Bellamy Law Firm, The, P.C.
1100 Conecticut Avenue, N.W., Suite 1000, 20036
Telephone: 202-785-5222 Fax: 202-785-5224
Email: bellamylaw@aol.com URL: http://www.lawyers.com/bellamylawfirm
Lorenzo M. Bellamy.
Legislative Practice, Labor and Employment, Wrongful Termination, Civil Litigation, Contracts, Corporate Law, Business Immigration, Small Business Law, Nonprofit Organizations Law, International Law, International Business Transactions.
See Professional Biographies, WASHINGTON, DISTRICT OF COLUMBIA

Bellan, Lori-Ann S. ... '70 '98 C.999 B.S. L.329 J.D. [Ⓐ Fulbright&J.]
*PRACTICE AREAS: Health Care Law; Health Care Fraud; Health Care Reimbursement.
Beller, Herbert N., (AV) ... '43 '67 C&L.597 B.S.B.A., J.D. [Sutherland A.&B.]
*PRACTICE AREAS: Federal Tax Planning; Tax Controversies; Exempt Organizations.
Beller, Margaret A. ... '32 '62 C&L.273 A.B., LL.B. 800 New Hampshire Ave., N.W.
Belles, Thomas A. ... '56 '81 C.273 B.A. L.228 J.D. [Swidler B.S.F.]
*PRACTICE AREAS: Antitrust; Business Combinations; Regulated Industries; Telecommunications Competition; Utility Acquisitions.
Bellinger, John B., III '60 '86 C.674 A.B. L.309 J.D.
U.S. Comm. on Roles & Capabil. U.S. Intellig. Commun.
Bellini, Christopher J., (BV) ... '61 '89 C.454 B.B.A. L.276 J.D. [Gibson,D.&C.]
*PRACTICE AREAS: Banking; Privacy Law.
Bello, Judith Hippler, (AV) ... '49 '75 C.575 B.A. L.976 J.D. 1722 Eye St., N.W.
Bellotti, Stephen M. ... '70 '95 C.93 B.A. L.30 J.D. [Ⓐ Arent F.K.P.&K.]
*PRACTICE AREAS: Commercial Real Estate; Finance; Business Planning.
Belman, Murray J., (AV) ... '35 '60 C.188 A.B. L.309 J.D. [Thompson C.]
*PRACTICE AREAS: International Trade; International Business; General Corporate.
Belmar, Warren, (AV) ... '42 '67 C.102 A.B. L.178 LL.B. [Fulbright&J.] ‡
*PRACTICE AREAS: Legislative Practice; Administrative Law; Energy; Litigation.
Belson, James A. ... '31 '56 C&L.276 A.B., J.D. Sr. Ct. App. J.
Belt, Bradley D. ... '58 '85 C.546 B.A. L.276 J.D. 1001 Pennsylvania Avenue, N.W.
Belt, David C. ... '70 '96 C.019 B.A. L.930 J.D. [Ⓐ Jenner&B.]
*PRACTICE AREAS: Litigation; Media and First Amendment Law; Appellate Practice.
Belt, Osborn S. ... '21 '51 C.25 A.B. L.273 LL.B. 20 Chevy Chase Cir.‡
Belter, Leonard W., (AV) ... '43 '68 C.712 B.A. L.178 LL.B. [Winston&S.]
*PRACTICE AREAS: Federal Energy Regulatory Law; Public Utility Law; Litigation.
Belvin, Paul A. ... '48 '73 C.896 B.A. L.945 J.D. [Akin,G.S.H.&F.]
*PRACTICE AREAS: Corporate Law; Securities.
Belz, John M. ... '48 '80 C.502 B.S.E.E. L.846 J.D. [Leydig,V.&M.] (See Pat. Sect.)
Belz, Kristen E. ... '72 '97 C.665 B.A. L.904 J.D. [Ⓐ Arnold&P.]
*PRACTICE AREAS: Employee Benefits; Tax Law.
Bemis, Douglas Knox, Jr., (AV) ... '— '63 C.976 B.A. L.309 J.D. [Ⓒ Verner,L.B.M.&H.]
*PRACTICE AREAS: Litigation; Energy.
Ben-Veniste, Richard, (AV) ... '43 '68 C.529 A.B. L.178 LL.B. [Weil,G.&M.]
*PRACTICE AREAS: Commercial Litigation; Securities Fraud; RICO; Tax Evasion; Antitrust.
Benach, Andres Cayetano '72 '99 C.93 B.A. L.273 J.D.
(adm. in NY; not adm. in DC) [Ⓐ Maggio&K.]
*PRACTICE AREAS: Immigration Law.
Bendall, Jennifer L. '64 '92 C.276 B.A. L.128 J.D.
(adm. in PA; not adm. in DC)
Sr. V.P., Gov. Affrs., Recording Industry Assoc. of America, Inc.
Bender, Brad P. '— '01 C.575 B.A. L.659 J.D.
(adm. in PA; not adm. in DC) [Ⓐ Reed S.]
Bender, Jonathan ... '62 '96 C.659 B.A. L.276 J.D. 1250 24th St. N.W.
Bender, Kathryn Christian '55 '85 C.471 B.A. L.818 J.D.
1735 New York Avenue, N.W.
Bender, Raymond G., Jr., (AV) ... '47 '73 C&L.276 B.S.F.S., J.D. [Dow,L.&A.]
Bender, Robyn R. ... '69 '97 C.228 B.A. L.276 J.D. [Ⓐ Dickstein S.M.&O.]
*PRACTICE AREAS: Litigation.
Bender, Susan K. ... '57 '86 C.478 B.A. L.309 J.D. Coun., The World Bk.
Bendernagel, James F., Jr., (BV) ... '51 '77 C.433 B.A. L.178 J.D. [Sidley A.B.&W.]
Benecke, Michelle Maria '61 '93
C.893 B.A. L.309 J.D. Servicemembers Legal Def. Network
Benedict, Scott N. ... '59 '85 C.103 A.B. L.309 J.D. [Ⓒ Cleary,G.S.&H.]
Benedict, Thane, IV '69 '99 C.183 B.A. L.188 J.D.
(adm. in NY; not adm. in DC) [Ⓐ Chadbourne&P.]
Benes, Keith J. '72 '00 C.546 B.A. L.276 J.D.
(adm. in MD; not adm. in DC) [Ⓐ Hogan&H.]
Benge, Malcolm L. ... '55 '83 C.918 B.A. L.659 J.D. [Zuckert,S.&R.]
*PRACTICE AREAS: Administrative Law; Aviation and Aerospace; Equipment Finance and Leasing; Transportation.
Benitez, Brigida ... '68 '93 C.260 B.S. L.93 J.D. [Wilmer,C.&P.]
*PRACTICE AREAS: Appellate Practice; Trial Practice; Internal Investigations; Alternative Dispute Resolution.
Benjamin, Tracy ... '66 '00 C.1177 B.S. L.273 J.D. [Ⓐ Dow,L.&A.]
Benjet, Brian H. '68 '93 C.1036 B.A. L.30 J.D.
Assoc. Coun., United Mine Workers of America Health and Retirement Funds
Benkin, Isaac D. ... '35 '60 C&L.309 A.B., LL.B. [Pillsbury W.]
*PRACTICE AREAS: Energy Law.
Benn, D. Randall ... '62 '87 C&L.228 B.A., J.D. [LeBoeuf,L.G.&M.]
*PRACTICE AREAS: Environmental; Hydropower; Legislative.
Benna, Robert H. ... '46 '82 C.563 B.M.E. L.273 J.D. [Ⓒ Wright&T.]
*PRACTICE AREAS: Alternative Dispute Resolution; Energy.
Benner, Brian J., (P.C.), (AV) '47 '75 C.625 B.A. L.912 J.D.
(adm. in MI; not adm. in DC) [Benner&B.] (⊙Farmington Hills, MI)
*PRACTICE AREAS: Personal Injury; Automobile; Aviation; Industrial Accidents; Medical Malpractice.
Benner, C. Jonathan, (AV) ... '48 '73 C.30 B.A. L.276 J.D. [Troutman S.]
*PRACTICE AREAS: Transportation; Administrative Law; Federal Regulation of Maritime Transportation; Litigation; Legislative and Governmental Affairs Representation.

Benner, Susan Carol .... '62 '88 C.446 B.A. L.128 J.D. [Seyfarth S.]
*PRACTICE AREAS: Labor and Employment Law.

Benner and Bilicki, (AV)
A Partnership including a Professional Corporation
1000 16th Street, NW, Suite 603, 20036 ⊙
Telephone: 202-546-6334 URL: http://www.bennerandbilicki.com
Email: bennerandbilicki@aol.com URL: http://www.lawyers.com/bennerandbilicki
Brian J. Benner (P.C.) (Not admitted in DC).
Personal Injury and Wrongful Death. Trial Practice in all State and Federal Courts. Automobile, Aviation, Industrial Accidents, Medical Malpractice, Premises Liability, Products Liability, Railroad, Workers Compensation.
Farmington Hills, Michigan Office: 28116 Orchard Lake Road, 48334. Telephone: 248-737-5544. Telefax: 248-737-5545.
Geneva, Switzerland Office: 17 Pictet-De-Rochemont, 1207. Telephone: +41 22 736-9603. Telefax: +41 22 736-9703.
See Professional Biographies, WASHINGTON, DISTRICT OF COLUMBIA

Bennet, Caressa Davison .... '61 '87 C.576 B.A. L.128 J.D. [Bennet&B.]
*PRACTICE AREAS: Communications Law.
Bennet, Michael R., (AV) .... '60 '86 C.659 B.A. L.228 J.D. [Bennet&B.]
*PRACTICE AREAS: Communications Law.

Bennet & Bennet, PLLC, (AV)
1000 Vermont Avenue, NW, 10th Floor, 20005
Telephone: 202-371-1500 Fax: 202-371-1558 URL: http://www.bennetlaw.com
Email: mail@benetlaw.com URL: http://www.lawyers.com/bennet&bennetlaw
Caressa Davison Bennet; Michael R. Bennet; Gregory W. Whiteaker; Marjorie Giller Spivak; Brent Weingardt. Senior Counsel: Howard S. Shapiro;—Donald L. Herman, Jr.; Kelvin L. Reaves; Rebecca L. Murphy.
Communications Law, Telecommunications Law, Wireless Communications, Cable Communications, Cable TV, Cellular Radio, Cellular Telephone, Satellite Communications, Broadcastings Law, FCC Licensing, FCC Regulation, Digital Communications, Telecommunications Regulation, Internet Law, E-Commerce Law, Emerging Business Law, Federal Administrative Law, Communications Common Carrier, Radio Common Carrier, Telephone Utility Regulation.
See Professional Biographies, WASHINGTON, DISTRICT OF COLUMBIA

Bennett, Alan R., (AV) .... '48 '73 C.184 B.A. L.178 J.D. [Bennett,T.&C.]
*PRACTICE AREAS: Food and Drug Regulation; Health Law; Product Safety.
Bennett, Alexander E., (AV) .... '40 '64 C&L.477 A.B., J.D. [Arnold&P.]
*PRACTICE AREAS: Litigation.
Bennett, Barbara, (BV) .... '52 '84 C&L.880 B.S., J.D. [Hogan&H.]
*PRACTICE AREAS: Health Care; Internet; Commercial Transactions; Corporate; Higher Education.
Bennett, Charles L. '56 '83 C.1111 B.A. L.767 J.D.
Dir., Corp. Fin., Natl. Assn. of Securities Dealers, Inc.
Bennett, Christopher L. '69 '96 C.886 B.S. L.893 J.D.
(adm. in NY; not adm. in DC) Vice President, Legal, MeriStar Hotels & Resorts
Bennett, Edward J. .... '64 '96 C.602 B.A. L.228 J.D. [[A] Williams&C.]
Bennett, J. Bradley .... '62 '89 C.732 B.A. L.276 J.D. [Baker B.]
Bennett, Jacqueline E. '— '91 C.681 A.B. L.276 J.D.
(adm. in MD; not adm. in DC) [[A] Reed S.]
*PRACTICE AREAS: Litigation.
Bennett, Jason '70 '00 C.846 B.A. L.276 J.D.
(adm. in NY; not adm. in DC) [[A] Baker B.]
Bennett, Jennifer B. .... '71 '99 C.692 B.A. L.276 J.D. [[A] Keller&H.]
*PRACTICE AREAS: Food and Drug; International Regulation; International Trade.
Bennett, Joel P., (AV) .... '46 '72 C.103 A.B. L.276 J.D. 1208 Eton Ct., N.W.
Bennett, Mary C., (AV) .... '54 '79 C.681 A.B. L.178 J.D. [Baker&M.]
*PRACTICE AREAS: Tax Planning and Advice (Corporate and International); Tax Controversies (Corporate and International).
Bennett, Michael S. '65 '91 C.918 B.A. L.178 J.D.
(adm. in NY; not adm. in DC) Coun., The World Bank
Bennett, Richard A., Jr. .... '51 '76 C.910 B.A. L.276 3524 K St., NW
Bennett, Richard D., (AV) ...... '47 '73 C.659 B.A. L.446 J.D. [Miles&S.] (⊙Balt., MD)
*PRACTICE AREAS: White Collar Criminal Defense Law; Federal Litigation; Internal Investigations.
Bennett, Robert S., (AV) .... '39 '64 C&L.276 B.A., LL.B. [Skadden,A.S.M.&F.]
Bennett, Stacey L. .... '70 '99 C.938 B.A. L.976 J.D. [[A] Kirkland&E.]
*PRACTICE AREAS: Litigation.
Bennett, Steven A. '60 '86
C&L.273 B.A., J.D. Sr. Coun., American Insurance Association
*RESPONSIBILITIES: Workers Compensation; Antitrust; Litigation.
Bennett, Susan Deborah '52 '80
C.976 B.A. L.178 J.D. Wash. College of Law, American Univ.

Bennett, Turner & Coleman, LLP, (AV)
1900 K Street N.W., Suite 750, 20006
Telephone: 202-833-4500 Fax: 202-833-2859
Email: info@btclaw.com URL: http://www.btclaw.com
Alan R. Bennett; Albert F. Cacozza, Jr.; Terry Coleman; Samuel D. Turner; Michael D. Petty; Jayne P. Bultena; Elizabeth Goss; Bruce S. Manheim, Jr. Associates: Kristi Elaine Schrode; Nathan Shawn Lee (Not admitted in DC); Praveen D. Fernandes; Kimberly E. McCutcheon (Not admitted in DC). Of Counsel: Kenneth P. Berkowitz (Not admitted in DC).
General Practice, Administrative Law, Civil Litigation and Legislative Practice at the Federal, State and International Levels with emphasis on Biomedical Research, Food, Drug and Cosmetic Regulation, Health Care, Medical Device Regulation, Medical Publishing and Communications Issues, and Medicare and Medicaid Law.
See Professional Biographies, WASHINGTON, DISTRICT OF COLUMBIA

Bennison, John Charles ....'39 '65 C.668 B.A. L.273 LL.B. 4861 Indian Lane, N.W.
Benoit, Philippe .... '59 '85 C.976 B.A. L.309 J.D. Intl. Bk. for Reconstr. & Develop.
Benoit, Roxanna '58 '86 C&L.02 B.A.
(adm. in AB; not adm. in DC) V.P. & Dep. Gen. Coun., American Corporate Counsel Association/Global Corporate Counsel Association
Benowitz, Howard A. .... '66 '94 C.228 B.A. L.910 J.D. [[A] Davis W.T.]
*PRACTICE AREAS: Energy Law; Administrative Law.
Bensfield, James A., (AV) .... '— '69 C.605 B.A. L.309 J.D. [Miller&C.]
Bensky, Eric A. .... '71 '97 C.477 B.A. L.145 J.D. [[A] Dickstein S.M.&O.]
*PRACTICE AREAS: Securities Litigation; Criminal Defense.
Bensley, Norman C. '— '69 C.674 A.B. L.178 J.D.
(adm. in NY; not adm. in DC) [[C] Foley&L.]
*PRACTICE AREAS: Taxation Law; Insurance Law; Corporate Law; Securities.
Benson, Carl Lynford '66 '99 C.477 B.S.E. L.276 J.D.
(adm. in MD; not adm. in DC; Pat.) [[A] Hunton&W.]
*PRACTICE AREAS: Intellectual Property; Patent Prosecution; Counseling.
Benson, Christina C. .... '67 '97 C&L.575 B.A., J.D. [[A] Arent F.K.P.&K.]
Benson, David K. '69 '01 C.36 B.S.
(adm. in MI; not adm. in DC; Pat.) [[A] Rader,F.&G.]
Benson, Glenn S. .... '68 '94 C.823 A.B. L.893 J.D. [[A] Fulbright&J.]
*PRACTICE AREAS: Natural Gas Pipelines; Energy Regulation; Oil and Gas Regulation; Public Utility Law; Energy Litigation.
Benson, Robert D., Jr. .... '59 '85 C.893 B.A. L.945 J.D. Pell Rudman Trust Co., N.A.
Benson, Steven P. .... '56 '81 C.454 B.A. L.273 J.D. [O'Brien,B.M.&S.]
*PRACTICE AREAS: Nonprofit and Charitable Organizations.
Benson, Stuart E., (AV) .... '— '72 C.112 A.B. L.1066 J.D. [Manelli,D.&S.]
*PRACTICE AREAS: Trademarks; International Trade.

Bent, Stephen A., (AV) .... '— '81 C.231 B.S. L.273 J.D. [Foley&L.] (See Pat. Sect.)
*PRACTICE AREAS: Biotechnology; Pharmaceutical; Intellectual Property.
Bentivoglio, John T. .... '63 '94 C.112 B.A. L.276 J.D. [Arnold&P.]
*PRACTICE AREAS: Privacy; Internet Healthcare; Food, Drug and Medical Devices; Public Policy and Legislative; Health Care and Pharmaceutical Fraud.
Bentley, David A. .... '53 '98 C.870 B.S. L.276 J.D. [[A] Dewey B.]
*PRACTICE AREAS: Litigation; Civil RICO; International Trade.
Benton, Janine Schollnick .... '— '95 C.1349 B.A. L.1209 J.D. [[A] Epstein B.&G.]
*PRACTICE AREAS: Commercial Litigation; Government Contracts Law; Technology Law.
Benton, Leslie Anne .... '63 '89 C.838 B.A. L.245 J.D. [[A] Hogan&H.]
*PRACTICE AREAS: Civil Litigation; Antitrust; Antitrust Class Actions; Federal Civil Practice; Complex Litigation.
Benton, Raymond S., (BV) .... '41 '66 C&L.352 B.A., J.D. 2875 Woodland Dr.
Bentz, Thomas H., Jr. .... '73 '98 C.477 B.A. L.424 J.D. [Vorys,S.S.&P.]
*PRACTICE AREAS: Litigation.
Bentzen, Michael P., (AV) '39 '65 C.210 B.A. L.273 J.D.
[Hughes&B.] (⊙Rockville, MD)
Benz, Steven F. .... '60 '90 C.367 B.A. L.813 J.D. [Kellogg,H.H.T.&E.]
*PRACTICE AREAS: Litigation; Antitrust.
Berardesco, Charles A., (AV) .... '58 '83 C.228 A.B. L.276 J.D. [[C] Piper M.R.&W.]
*PRACTICE AREAS: Securities Law; Corporate Law; Intellectual Property Law; Venture Capital; Technology.
Bercovici, Martin W., (AV) .... '42 '68 C.502 B.S. L.569 J.D. [Keller&H.]
*PRACTICE AREAS: Transportation Law; Telecommunications Law; Import and Export Law.
Berdo, Robert H., (AV) '30 '60
C.352 B.S. L.273 J.D. [Roylance,A.B.&G.] (See Pat. Sect.)
*PRACTICE AREAS: Patent Law; Pharmaceutical Patent Law; Chemical Patent Law.
Berdut, Caridad '59 '87 C.1222 B.A. L.904 J.D.
(adm. in FL; not adm. in DC) [[A] Adduci,M.&S.]
*PRACTICE AREAS: Customs; International Trade Regulation.
Berejka, Marc .... '63 '89 C.674 A.B. L.276 J.D. Sr. Atty., Microsoft Corp.
Berenson, Aimee Robin '61 '86 C.966 B.A. L.569 J.D.
Mng. Partner, Berenson Consulting Grp., LLC‡
Berenson, Bradford A. .... '65 '93 C.976 B.A. L.309 J.D. [Sidley A.B.&W.]
Berenson, D.S. .... '65 '90 C.174 B.A. L.228 J.D. [Johanson B.] (⊙Mc Lean, VA)
Berenson, Michael, (AV) .... '48 '74 C.367 B.A. L.276 J.D. [Morgan,L.&B.]
Berenson, William M. .... '47 '78 C.197 A.B. L.94 J.D. [[C] Lepon M.W.&H.]
Beresford, Douglas L. .... '56 '82 C.309 A.B. L.276 J.D. [Hogan&H.]
*PRACTICE AREAS: Energy; Public Utility Law; Electric Cooperatives Law; Administrative Law; Appellate Practice.
Beresford, Lori M. .... '63 '87 C.500 B.B.A. L.128 J.D. [Muldoon M.&F.]
*PRACTICE AREAS: Financial Institutions; Corporate Law; Mergers and Acquisitions; Banks and Banking; Securities.
Beresin, Marta Ilene .... '65 '91 C.645 B.A. L.273 J.D. 2219 38th St., N.W.
Berfield, Morton L., (AV) .... '33 '58 C.210 B.A. L.477 J.D. 2700 Calvert St., N.W.
Berg, Andrew .... '— '80 C.309 A.B. L.880 J.D. [King&S.]
*PRACTICE AREAS: Litigation and Trade.
Berg, David A., (AV) '54 '81 C.446 B.S. L.904 J.D.
Asst. Gen. Coun., Air Transport Association of America
*RESPONSIBILITIES: Aviation; Administrative Law; General Corporate.
Berg, Gracia M., (AV) .... '45 '80 C.55 B.A. L.602 J.D. [[C] Gibson,D.&C.]
*PRACTICE AREAS: International Trade.
Berg, Linda Breslau .... '48 '74 C.119 B.A. L.276 J.D. Natl. Organization For Women
Berg, Michael D., (AV) .... '— '74 C.823 B.A. L.276 J.D. [Verner,L.B.M.&H.]
*PRACTICE AREAS: Communications Law; International Law.
Bergan, Raymond W., (AV) .... '30 '54 C.321 B.S. L.276 LL.B. [[C] Williams&C.]
*PRACTICE AREAS: Administrative Litigation; Antitrust and Trade Regulation; Civil Practice; Criminal Law; Automotive Franchises and Dealerships.
Bergen, Robin M. .... '69 '95 C.893 B.S. L.569 J.D. [[A] Cleary,G.S.&H.]
Berger, Alexander B. .... '71 '97 C.893 B.A. L.846 J.D. [[A] Howrey S.A.&W.]
*PRACTICE AREAS: Commercial Litigation; Antitrust; Trademark Litigation.
Berger, Bruce J. .... '50 '76 C.184 B.A. L.309 J.D. [Spriggs&H.]
*PRACTICE AREAS: Toxic Torts; Litigation; Insurance Coverage; Environmental Law; Drug and Medical Device Defense.
Berger, Douglas L. '60 '89 C.234 B.A. L.910 J.D.
Dir., Public Affs., Advertising Mail Marketing Association
Berger, Eric .... '— '91 C.1036 B.A. L.107 J.D. [[A] Kirkpatrick&L.]
Berger, Glenn J. .... '53 '79 C.188 B.S. L.1194 J.D. [Skadden,A.S.M.&F.]
Berger, Henry R. .... '16 '39 C&L.537 J.D. 2801 New Mexico Ave., N.W.‡
Berger, Jeffrey L., (AV) '48 '74 C.1529 B.A. L.705 J.D.
[Berger] & [[C] Jackson&C.] (⊙Balt., Rockville, MD)
Berger, Jenifer .... '71 '99 C.264 B.A. L.1002 J.D. [[A] Bryan C.]
*PRACTICE AREAS: Commercial Litigation; Antitrust.
Berger, Marc S. .... '71 '99 C.645 B.S. L.472 J.D. [[A] Fenwick&W.]
*PRACTICE AREAS: Licensing and Online Commerce; Entertainment/New Media; Commercial Encryption Applications.
Berger, Mitchell R., (AV) .... '54 '80 C.659 A.B. L.309 J.D. [Patton B.]
Berger, Paul S., (AV) .... '32 '58 C.754 B.S. L.569 LL.B. [Arnold&P.]
*PRACTICE AREAS: International Finance; International Transactions; Tax; Government Relations.
Berger, Robert A. .... '66 '92 C.999 B.A. L.94 J.D. [Winston&S.]
Berger, Robert Glenn '54 '79 C.103 B.A. L.309 J.D.
V.P., Reg. & Legal Affs., WinStar Telecommunications, Inc.
Berger, Sanford David '38 '65 C.103 A.B. L.94 LL.B.
(adm. in MA; not adm. in DC) 2511 Q St., N.W.
Berger, Thomas C. .... '64 '93 C.475 B.S. L.273 J.D. [[A] Keller&H.]
*PRACTICE AREAS: Environmental Law; Occupational Safety and Health Law.

Berger Law Firm, The, P.C., (AV)
1120 20th Street, N.W., Suite 300 South Tower, 20036
Telephone: 202-861-1361 Fax: 202-861-1362
Email: bergerlaw@yahoo.com URL: http://www. bergerlaborlaw.com
Jeffrey L. Berger.
Management Labor Law, Employment Litigation, Wage and Hour, Discrimination and Harassment, OSHA, NLRA, FLSA, SCA, Affirmative Action, Employment Contracts, Trade Secrets and Personnel Policies for High Technology, Government Contract, Construction, Media, Professional, Executive, and Association Clients.
See Professional Biographies, WASHINGTON, DISTRICT OF COLUMBIA

Bergeson, Lynn L., (AV) .... '53 '80 C.475 B.A. L.128 J.D. [Bergeson&C.]
*PRACTICE AREAS: Federal Insecticide, Fungicide and Rodenticide Act (FIFRA); Toxic Substances Regulation; Clean Air Act; Resource Conservation and Recovery Act (RCRA); OSHA.

Bergeson & Campbell, P.C., (AV)
1203 19th Street, N.W., Suite 300, 20036-2401
Telephone: 202-962-8585 Fax: 202-962-8599
Email: bc@lawbc URL: http://www.lawyers.com/bergeson&campbelllaw
Partners: Lynn L. Bergeson; Lisa M. Campbell. Associates: Lisa Rothenberg Burchi. Of Counsel: Bethami Auerbach; Richard P. Bozof; Michael F. Cole; Cara S. Jablon; Eileen B. Salathé Gernhard.
General Civil Practice including Administrative Law, Civil Litigation, and Legislative Practice primarily including representation on Environmental, Chemical Regulation, and Occupational Health and Safety Law, Toxic Torts.
See Professional Biographies, WASHINGTON, DISTRICT OF COLUMBIA

Bergin, John T. .... '68 '93 C.128 B.A. L.30 J.D. [Ⓐ McManus,S.A.&D.]
*PRACTICE AREAS: Construction Law.
Bergin, Timothy W. .... '51 '78 C.276 B.S. L.659 J.D. [Squire,S.&D.]
*PRACTICE AREAS: Litigation; Antitrust.
Bergman, Alisa M. .... '72 '98 C.112 B.A. L.276 J.D. [Ⓐ Piper M.R.&W.]
*PRACTICE AREAS: Privacy Law; Electronic Commerce.
Bergman, David B. .... '63 '91 C.311 B.A. L.597 J.D. [Arnold&P.]
*PRACTICE AREAS: Civil Litigation; International Arbitration; White Collar Criminal Litigation.
Bergman, Edward J., (AV) '42 '74 C.659 B.A. L.178 J.D.
(adm. in NJ; not adm. in DC) [Bickerman D.R.] (⊙Princeton, NJ)
Bergman, Matthew Steven .... '66 '91 C.1036 B.A. L.273 J.D. [Dickstein S.M.&O.]
*PRACTICE AREAS: Banking; Real Estate; Corporate Law; Litigation.
Bergman, Max .... '16 '47 C.178 B.A. L.180 LL.B. 2905 Ellicott St., N.W.‡
Bergmanis, Imanta M. .... '68 '96 C.494 B.A. L.1035 J.D. [Ⓐ Sonnenschein N.&R.]
*PRACTICE AREAS: Corporate Law.
Bergmann, Michael R. .... '65 '93 C.309 B.A. L.893 J.D. [Ⓐ Skadden,A.S.M.&F.]
*PRACTICE AREAS: Employee Benefits.
Bergmark, Martha '48 '73 C.604 B.A. L.477 J.D.
(adm. in MS; not adm. in DC) Dir., Civil Div., Natl. Legal Aid & Defs. Assn.
Bergner, Alfred P., (AV) .... '42 '66 C.31 B.A. L.309 J.D. 1133 Connecticut Ave., N.W.
Bergner, Amy B. .... '— '83 C.788 B.A. L.904 J.D. [Ⓒ Reed S.]
*PRACTICE AREAS: Employee Benefits.
Bergner, Isidore '08 '35 C.178 M.A. L.1009 LL.B.
(adm. in NY; not adm. in DC) 3101 New Mexico Ave., N.W.‡

Bergner, Jane C., (AV) '43 '68 C.881 A.B. L.178 LL.B.
Suite 650, 1615 L Street, N.W., 20036
Telephone: 202-626-8215 Telecopier: 202-626-8233
Email: jbergnerlaw@abanet.org URL: http://www.lawyers.com/dctaxlaw
Federal and District of Columbia Tax Planning, Tax Controversies, Tax Litigation, Tax Collection. Tax Audits and Tax Appeals before Internal Revenue Service, Civil Litigation and Arbitration. Estate and Gift Taxation, Planning and Administration. Local Taxation.
See Professional Biographies, WASHINGTON, DISTRICT OF COLUMBIA

Bergquist, Robert A., (AV) .... '40 '64 C.585 B.A. L.309 LL.B. [Shearman&S.]
Bergsman, Marc A. .... '52 '77 C.473 B.A. L.1003 J.D. [Dickinson W.]
*PRACTICE AREAS: Trademark; Copyright; Unfair Competition.
Berk, Steven N. .... '59 '85 C.910 A.B. L.93 J.D. [Jenner&B.]
Berke, Elliot Stanton .... '71 '98 C.896 B.A. L.245 J.D. 1001 Pennsylvania Ave., N.W.
Berkeley, Alan J., (AV) .... '— '67 C.188 B.S. L.276 J.D. [Kirkpatrick&L.]
*PRACTICE AREAS: Securities; Corporate Law; Business Law.
Berkey, Judson O. .... '73 '98 C.893 B.A. L.309 J.D. Instit. of Intl. Fin.
Berkman, Ellen Fels, (AV) .... '64 '90 C.309 A.B. L.178 J.D. [Baker B.]
Berkow, Larry M. .... '33 '56 C.446 B.S. L.276 LL.B 1401 16th St., N.W.
Berkowitz, Edward C., (AV) .... '35 '60 C.188 B.A. L.309 LL.B. [Nixon P.]
*PRACTICE AREAS: Business Law; Real Estate; Litigation.
Berkowitz, Eric '65 '92 C.659 B.S.E.E. L.1292 J.D.
(adm. in PA; not adm. in DC) [Ⓐ Staas&H.]
*PRACTICE AREAS: Intellectual Property; Patents; Trademarks; Copyright Law.
Berkowitz, Ian M. '66 '92 C.966 B.S. L.1206 J.D.
(adm. in FL; not adm. in DC) 1714 N St., N.W.
Berkowitz, Jeffrey A. '63 '88
C.705 B.A. L.1325 J.D. [Finnegan,H.F.G.&D.] (See Pat. Sect.)
*PRACTICE AREAS: Patent Prosecution; Computer and Software Patents; Software Copyright.
Berkowitz, Kenneth P. '42 '67 C.331 B.A. L.1009 J.D.
(adm. in NY; not adm. in DC) [Ⓒ Bennett,T.&C.]
*PRACTICE AREAS: Food and Drug Law; Trade Regulation.
Berkowitz, Marvin C. '52 '95 C.277 B.I.E./B.E.E. L.1059 J.D.
(adm. in GA; not adm. in DC) [Ⓐ Nath&Assoc.]
Berkowitz, Philip J. .... '65 '89 C&L.178 A.B., J.D. [Ⓒ Womble C.S.&R.]
*PRACTICE AREAS: Commercial Litigation; Securities Litigation; Securities Arbitration; SEC Enforcement; Tax Litigation.
Berl, Joseph M., (AV) .... '42 '68 C.178 A.B. L.273 J.D. [Powell,G.F.&M.]
*PRACTICE AREAS: Corporate Law; Business Law; Securities Law.
Berlack, Evan R., (AV) .... '34 '63 C&L.309 A.B., LL.B. [Ⓒ Baker B.]
Berlin, Alan D., (AV) '39 '63 C.563 B.B.A. L.569 LL.B.
(adm. in NY; not adm. in DC) [Aitken I.B.&V.] (⊙White Plains, NY)
*PRACTICE AREAS: Natural Resources and Energy Law; Taxation; Corporate; Securities Law; International Commercial Transactions.
Berlin, Edward, (AV) .... '39 '61 C.563 B.B.A. L.178 LL.B. [Swidler B.S.F.]
*PRACTICE AREAS: Regulatory Law; Utility Law.
Berlin, Jeffrey S., (AV) .... '45 '69 C.604 B.A. L.309 J.D. [Sidley A.B.&W.]
Berlin, Kenneth, (AV) .... '47 '74 C.659 B.A. L.178 J.D. [Skadden,A.S.M.&F.]
Berlin, Kurt .... '26 '54 C.30 B.A. L.276 J.D. [Obergh&B.]
Berlin, Noah A. .... '73 '00 C.771 B.A. L.659 J.D. [Ⓐ Fried,F.H.S.&J.]
*PRACTICE AREAS: Securities.
Berlin, Seth D. .... '66 '91 C.103 B.A. L.309 J.D. [Levine S.&K.]
Berliner, Dana .... '67 '93 C&L.976 B.A., J.D. Institute for Jus.
Berliner, Henry A., Jr. .... '34 '65 C.477 B.A. L.273 J.D. [Ⓒ Berliner,C.&R.]
Berliner, Roger A., (AV) .... '51 '83 C.197 B.A. L.464 J.D. [Berliner,C.&J.] ⊙
*PRACTICE AREAS: Litigation; Administrative Law; North American Energy Law and Trade; Public Utility Law; Federal and State Legislation.

Berliner, Candon & Jimison, (AV) BR
1225 Nineteenth Street N.W., Suite 800, 20036 ⊙
Telephone: 202-955-6067 Telecopy: 202-822-0109
URL: http://www.bcjlaw.com
Members of Firm: Roger A. Berliner; John W. Jimison; Mary Eva Candon. Associates: Peter G. Hirst (Not admitted in DC); Megan Grant; Mark R. Gisler (Not admitted in DC). Of Counsel: Lucien Wulsin, Jr. (Not admitted in DC); Andy Schneider; Debra L. Roth (Not admitted in DC).
Administrative Law, Commercial Litigation, Appellate Advocacy, Intergovernmental Affairs, Legislative Practice, Health Policy, Maritime Law, International Trade, North American Energy Transactions, Oil and Gas Law, Public Utility Law, Pipeline Law, Telecommunications Law, Industrial Energy Use Law.
References: Canadian Embassy; City of Vernon, California; Pacific Gas Transmission Co.; Polyisocyanurate Insulation Manufacturers Assn.; Watson Cogeneration Co.
Berkeley, California Office: 2560 Ninth Street, Suite 316. Telephone: 510-549-6926. Telecopy: 510-649-9793.
Los Angeles, California Office: 1875 Century Park East, Suite 700. Telephone: 310-282-6848. Telecopy: 310-282-6841.
See Professional Biographies, WASHINGTON, DISTRICT OF COLUMBIA

Berliner, Corcoran & Rowe, L.L.P., (AV)
A Partnership including a Professional Corporation
1101 Seventeenth Street, N.W., Suite 1100, 20036-4798
Telephone: 202-293-5555 FAX: 202-293-9035
Email: bcr@bcr-dc.com URL: http://www.bcr-dc.com
Thomas G. Corcoran, Jr.; Wayne H. Rusch; Clemens Kochinke; Richard Landfield; Benjamin H. Flowe, Jr.; Bruce Zagaris; John A. Ordway, Jr.; James L. Marketos; Jay A. Rosenthal. Counsel: Thomas E. Wilson; Henry A. Berliner, Jr.; Neal E. Krucoff; Peter Heidenberger;—C. Ray Gold; Mary-Ellen Noone; Alexander Craig Vincent.
General Practice before all Courts and Government Agencies. International, Litigation, Corporate, e-Commerce Law, Internet Law, Emerging Business Law, Merger and Acquisitions, Computer, Real

(This Listing Continued)

Berliner, Corcoran & Rowe, L.L.P. (Continued)
Estate, Commercial Real Estate, Landlord and Tenant Law, Intellectual Property, Export Control, Criminal, Tax, Government Contracts, Entertainment, Family Law.
See Professional Biographies, WASHINGTON, DISTRICT OF COLUMBIA

Berlove, Michele Levy .... '68 '94 C.1044 B.A. L.1019 J.D. [Ⓐ Kirkpatrick&L.]
*PRACTICE AREAS: Insurance Coverage; Commercial Litigation.
Berman, Barbara A. .... '43 '85 C.102 B.A. L.284 J.D. The Bureau of Natl. Affs., Inc.
Berman, Barrie D. .... '60 '87 C.367 B.A. L.910 J.D. [Manatt,P.&P.]
Berman, Bruce M., (AV) .... '54 '80 C.951 B.A. L.976 J.D. [Wilmer,C.&P.]
*PRACTICE AREAS: Civil Practice; Educational Testing Law; Criminal Practice; Food, Drug and Cosmetic Regulation.
Berman, Daniel M., (AV) .... '57 '83 C&L.309 A.B., J.D. [Thelen R.&P.]
*PRACTICE AREAS: International Taxation; Tax Planning; International Law; Federal Legislative Practice; International Government Relations.
Berman, David S. .... '59 '93 C.910 B.A. L.128 J.D. [Ⓐ Wright&T.]
*PRACTICE AREAS: Energy.
Berman, Howard '54 '81 C.787 B.A. L.1194 J.D.
(adm. in NY; not adm. in DC) 510 11th St.
Berman, Jeffrey G. .... '57 '82 C.103 B.A. L.309 J.D. [Winston&S.]
*PRACTICE AREAS: Energy Law; Communications Law; Government Relations; Corporate Law.
Berman, Jonathan .... '68 '93 C.309 B.A. L.178 J.D. [Ⓐ Jones,D.R.&P.]
Berman, Kenneth J. .... '54 '80 C.216 B.A. L.145 J.D. [Debevoise&P.]
*PRACTICE AREAS: Investment Management Law; Securities Regulation Law.
Berman, Lawrence E. '44 '70
C.659 B.S. L.276 J.D. George Washington Univ. Health Plan, Inc.
Berman, Marshall F. .... '39 '67 C.893 B.A. L.273 J.D. [Ⓒ Ruben&A.]
*PRACTICE AREAS: Labor; Employment Relations.
Berman, Michael S., (AV) '39 '64 C&L.494 B.A., LL.B.
Pres., The Duberstein Grp., Inc.
Berman, Paul J., (AV) .... '51 '75 C&L.309 A.B., J.D. [Covington&B.] (See Pat. Sect.)
Berman, Richard Jason .... '69 '95 C.205 B.A. L.273 J.D. [Ⓐ Arent F.K.P.&K.] (Pat.)
*PRACTICE AREAS: Biochemical Patents; Biotechnology; Chemical; Pharmaceutical; Molecular Biology Patents.
Berman, William H. .... '24 '50 C&L.309 A.B., LL.B. 1776 K St., N.W.

Berman, Aisenberg & Platt, PLLC
(See Jacobson, Holman, PLLC)

Berman, Sobin & Gross, LLP
(See Gaithersburg, Maryland)

Bermingham, Maya J. .... '— '99 C.309 B.A. L.569 J.D. [Ⓐ Morgan,L.&B.]
Bernabei, Lynne, (AV) .... '50 '77 C.681 B.A. L.309 J.D. [Bernabei&K.]
*PRACTICE AREAS: Employment Discrimination Law; Whistleblower Law; Civil Rights; Civil Liberties.

Bernabei & Katz, PLLC, (AV)
1773 T Street, N.W., 20009-7139
Telephone: 202-745-1942 Telecopier: 202-745-2627 URL: http://www.bernabeiandkatz.com
Email: berkatzlaw@aol.com URL: http://www.lawyers.com/bernabei&katzlaw
Lynne Bernabei; Debra Susan Katz;—Lisa J. Banks; Ari M. Wilkenfeld; Alan R. Kabat; Gena E. Wiltsek (Not admitted in DC). Of Counsel: David J. Marshall.
Civil Rights Law, including sex, race, age and disability discrimination; Employment Law, Sexual Harassment Law; Whistleblower Litigation; General Civil Litigation.
See Professional Biographies, WASHINGTON, DISTRICT OF COLUMBIA

Bernanke, Jessica R. .... '67 '95 C.93 B.A. L.945 J.D. [Ⓐ Morgan,L.&B.]
Bernard, Eugene L., (AV) .... '28 '54 C.608 A.B. L.273 J.D. 2500 Virginia Ave. NW‡
Bernard, Joseph J., (BV) .... '44 '71 C.999 B.S. L.30 J.D. 601 Indiana Ave., NW
Bernard, Lawrence B., (AV) .... '48 '73 C.188 B.A. L.309 J.D. [Venable,A.B.H.&C.]
*PRACTICE AREAS: Litigation; Antitrust; Advertising Law.
Bernard, Lawrence J., Jr., (AV) '37 '64
C.575 B.S. L.273 LL.B. 5224 Chevy Chase Pkwy., N.W.
Bernard, Lloyd F. .... '62 '89 C.1350 B.A. L.569 J.D. [Ⓐ Sutherland A.&B.]
*PRACTICE AREAS: Investment Company Law; Mutual Funds; Insurance Products; Securities Regulation.
Bernardo, Ralph A. .... '59 '88 C.103 B.A. L.94 J.D. [Klein&C.]
Berner, Frederic G., Jr., (AV) .... '43 '73 C.478 B.A. L.273 J.D. [Sidley A.B.&W.]
Berner, Nicole G. .... '65 '97 C.112 B.A. L.1066 J.D. [Ⓐ Jenner&B.]
*PRACTICE AREAS: Civil Litigation; Civil Rights; E-Commerce Transactions.
Bernhard, Berl, (AV) .... '— '54 C.197 A.B. L.976 J.D. [Verner,L.B.M.&H.]
*PRACTICE AREAS: Corporate Law; Regulatory; Legislation; Transportation Law.
Bernhard, Darren B. .... '61 '86 C.264 B.A. L.30 J.D. [Howrey S.A.&W.]
*PRACTICE AREAS: Antitrust; Intellectual Property.
Bernius, Robert C., (AV) .... '46 '73 C.103 Sc.B.E.E. L.976 J.D. [Nixon P.]
*PRACTICE AREAS: Appellate Practice; Labor and Employment; Litigation; Media Law.
Bernsen, Sam .... '19 '50 C.563 L.1009 LL.B. [Ⓒ Fragomen,D.B.&L.]
Bernstein, Caryl S., (AV) .... '33 '68 C.188 B.A. L.276 J.D. [Bernstein]
*PRACTICE AREAS: Corporate; International; Mortgage Finance; Insurance; Arbitration.
Bernstein, Cyrus .... '11 '42 C.563 B.S. L.273 J.D. 4601 Reno Rd., N.W.
Bernstein, Daniel J., (AV) '44 '69
C.966 B.S. L.276 J.D. Asst. U.S. Atty. & Dep. Chf., Narcotics Sect.
Bernstein, David L. .... '29 '57 C.112 A.B. L.976 LL.B. P.O. Box 15216
Bernstein, Frank L., (AV) '59 '84 C.111 B.S. L.966 J.D.
[Sughrue M.] (See Pat. Sect.) ⊙
*PRACTICE AREAS: Intellectual Property Law; Litigation.
Bernstein, Gail C. .... '60 '88 C.999 B.A. L.309 J.D. [Wilmer,C.&P.]
Bernstein, George K., (AV) .... '33 '57 C&L.188 B.A., LL.B. [Bernstein] ⊙
*PRACTICE AREAS: Insurance Regulation; Insurance Rehabilitation and Liquidation; Insurance Mergers and Acquisitions; Reinsurance; International Insurance.
Bernstein, Glen S. .... '67 '92 C.880 B.S. L.659 J.D. [Ⓐ Skadden,A.S.M.&F.]
*PRACTICE AREAS: Energy.
Bernstein, Howard L., (P.C.), (AV) '43 '69
C.563 B.E.E. L.1009 J.D. [Sughrue M.] (See Pat. Sect.)
*PRACTICE AREAS: Intellectual Property Law; Litigation.
Bernstein, Jacob D. .... '— '00 C.769 B.A. L.276 J.D. [Ⓐ Latham&W.]
*PRACTICE AREAS: Corporate Law.
Bernstein, Joan Z. .... '26 '52 C.966 B.A. L.976 LL.D. [Ⓒ Bryan C.]
Bernstein, Joel H., (AV) .... '63 '88 C.165 B.A. L.1068 J.D. [Halprin,T.G.&M.]
*PRACTICE AREAS: Telecommunications Law; Legislative Law.
Bernstein, Jules, (AV) .... '35 '62 C.1036 B.A. L.145 J.D. [Bernstein&L.]
*PRACTICE AREAS: Labor Law.

Bernstein, Lawrence, (AV) '41 '73 C&L.912 A.B., J.D.
1818 N Street, N.W., Suite 700, 20036
Telephone: 202-296-1800; 202-331-7050 Fax: 202-331-9306
Email: LAWBERNS@erols.com URL: http://www.lawyers.com/lawrencebernsteinlaw
Practice before Federal and Local Courts and Administrative Agencies. Telecommunication Law, Transactional and Commercial Law, Intellectual Property. Emerging Technology Law, e-Commerce Law, Internet Law.
See Professional Biographies, WASHINGTON, DISTRICT OF COLUMBIA

Bernstein, Matthew C. .... '— '92 C.178 A.B. L.276 J.D. [Verner,L.B.M.&H.]
*PRACTICE AREAS: Legislative and Federal Affairs; Environmental.
Bernstein, Maya A. .... '63 '00 C.477 A.B. L.30 J.D. [Ⓐ Fried,F.H.S.&J.]
*PRACTICE AREAS: E-Commerce; Technology Transactions; Corporate Law.

Bernstein, Michael D. ... '60 '85 C&L.966 B.A., J.D. [A Hyman,P.&M.]
*PRACTICE AREAS: Food and Drug Regulation; Medical Device Regulation; Advertising Law; Trade Regulation.
Bernstein, Michael L., (AV) ... '64 '89 C.1036 B.A. L.597 J.D. [Arnold&P.]
*PRACTICE AREAS: Bankruptcy; Creditors' Rights.
Bernstein, Mitchell H., (AV) ... '49 '74 C.659 A.B. L.976 J.D. [Van Ness F.]
*PRACTICE AREAS: Environment; Clean Air Act; Hazardous Waste; Superfund.
Bernstein, Peter D. ... '— '95 C.273 B.A. L.7 J.D. [A Shook,H.&B.]
Bernstein, Richard D. ... '59 '88 C&L.178 B.A., J.D. [Sidley A.B.&W.]
Bernstein, Sandra ... '70 '96 C.454 B.A. L.30 J.D. Staff Atty., Univ. Legal Servs.
Bernstein, Tobie '60 '86 C.910 B.A. L.309 J.D.
(adm. in MD; not adm. in DC) Sr. Atty., Envirnomental Law Institute
Bernstein-Gaeta, Judith ... '50 '92 C.585 B.S. L.128 J.D. [Arnold&P.]
*PRACTICE AREAS: Commercial Litigation.

Bernstein Law Firm, The, PLLC, (AV)
1730 K Street, N.W., 20006 ⊙
Telephone: 202-452-8010 Telecopier: 202-296-2065
George K. Bernstein; Caryl S. Bernstein; Robert B. Shapiro.
New York, N.Y. Office: 30 Rockefeller Plaza. Telephone: 212-957-7634.
See Professional Biographies, WASHINGTON, DISTRICT OF COLUMBIA

Bernstein & Lipsett, (AV)
Suite 602, 1920 L Street, N.W., 20036
Telephone: 202-296-1798 Fax: 202-296-7220
URL: http://www.lawyers.com/bernstein&lipsett
Members of Firm: Jules Bernstein; Linda Lipsett.
Wage and Labor Standards, Labor Relations, ERISA, Legislative, Administrative, Civil Rights and Prepaid Legal Services.
See Professional Biographies, WASHINGTON, DISTRICT OF COLUMBIA

Bernthal, Eric L., (AV) ... '— '70 C.178 B.A. L.273 J.D. [Latham&W.]
Bernton, William P., (AV) ... '20 '48 C&L.309 A.B., LL.B. 321 N. Clark St., Suite 3400
Berrington, Craig A., (AV) '43 '69 C.30 B.A. L.597 J.D.
Sr. V.P. & Gen. Coun., American Insurance Association
Berrington, Lacy D. ... '72 '97 C.30 B.A. L.659 J.D. [A Clifford C.R.&W.]
*PRACTICE AREAS: Antitrust.
Berry, Cynthia E. ... '62 '87 C.893 B.A. L.880 J.D. Gen. Coun., Wexler Group
Berry, Danielle E. ... '73 '98 C.478 B.A. L.945 J.D. [A Wiley R.&F.]
Berry, George T. ... '53 '82 C.31 B.A. L.276 J.D. Georgetown Univ. Law Ctr.
Berry, J. Daniel, (AV) ... '51 '77 C.446 B.A. L.273 J.D. [Ropes&G.]
*PRACTICE AREAS: Environmental Law.
Berry, J. Patrick ... '49 '77 C&L.309 A.B., J.D. [Baker B.]
*PRACTICE AREAS: Environmental Law.
Berry, John V. ... '71 '97 C.477 B.A. L.215 J.D. 1320 "G" St., S.E.
Berry, Matthew B. '72 '98 C.197 A.B. L.976 J.D.
(adm. in VA; not adm. in DC) Institute for Jus.
Berry, Max N., Law Offices of, (AV) '35 '60 C&L.623 B.A., LL.B.
3213 O Street, N.W.
Berry, R. Stephen ... '47 '75 C.273 B.A. L.659 J.D. [Berry&L.]
Berry & Leftwich ... 2000 K Street, N.W., Suite 350
Berryman, Richard B., (AV) ... '32 '57 C.118 B.A. L.145 J.D. 655 15th St., N.W.
Berson, Eric C. ... '50 '76 C.696 B.A. L.813 J.D. Pres., Washington Realty Group, Inc.
Berson, Susan W. '61 '86 C.696 B.A. L.178 J.D.
(adm. in NY; not adm. in DC) [Mintz,L.C.F.G.&P.]
*PRACTICE AREAS: Health Law; Health Care Regulation; Health Care Mergers and Acquisitions; Health Care Contracts; Health Care Corporate Law.
Berthelsen, Richard A. '44 '69 C&L.966 B.S., J.D.
(adm. in WI; not adm. in DC) Gen. Coun., NFL Players Assn.
Bertin, Erik ... '71 '97 C.367 B.A. L.659 J.D. [A Dechert]
*PRACTICE AREAS: Intellectual Property.
Bertin, Erik ... '71 '97 C.367 B.A. L.659 J.D. [A Howrey S.A.&W.]
*PRACTICE AREAS: Commercial Litigation; Insurance Coverage; Trademark Litigation.
Bertin, Robert C. '68 '97 C.886 B.S.E.E. L.1209 J.D.
(adm. in VA; not adm. in DC; Pat.) [A Swidler B.S.F.]
*PRACTICE AREAS: Patent Prosecution; Intellectual Property Litigation; Intellectual Property Licensing.
Bertola, Marta ... '60 '93 C.446 B.S. L.128 J.D. 6925 4th St., N.W., 2nd Fl.
Bertoldo, Alejandro L. ... '70 '96 C.309 B.A. L.276 J.D. 1200 New Hampshire Ave. N.W.
Bertram, Catherine D. ... '64 '89 C.966 B.A. L.128 J.D. [C Whiteford,T.&P.]
*PRACTICE AREAS: Medical Malpractice; General Insurance Defense.
Bertram, Connie N., (BV) ... '65 '90 C.945 B.B.A. L.273 J.D. [Venable,A.B.H.&C.]
*PRACTICE AREAS: Labor and Employment.
Bertrand, Catherine E. ... '72 '97 L.508 J.D. Dept. of Commerce
Bertsch, Anne M. ... '— '98 C.205 B.S. L.276 J.D. [A Sonnenschein N.&R.]
*PRACTICE AREAS: Corporate Law.
Berube, Anne D. ... '68 '98 C.385 B.A. L.273 J.D. [A McKenna&C.]
*PRACTICE AREAS: Environmental.
Berwick, Philip C. '51 '78 C.659 B.A. L.851 J.D.
(adm. in OH; not adm. in DC) Georgetown Univ. Law Library
Berz, David R., (AV) ... '48 '73 C&L.273 B.A., J.D. [Weil,G.&M.]
*PRACTICE AREAS: Environmental Law and Litigation; Product Liability; Insurance Coverage Litigation.
Beske, Gavin A. '67 '96 C.674 A.B. L.178 J.D.
(adm. in CA; not adm. in DC) [A Gibson,D.&C.]
*PRACTICE AREAS: Corporate Law; Mergers, Acquisitions and Divestitures.
Besozzi, Paul C., (AV) ... '47 '72 C&L.276 B.S., J.D. [Patton B.]
Bess, Amy L. ... '60 '87 C.338 B.S. L.597 J.D. [Sonnenschein N.&R.]
*PRACTICE AREAS: Employment Litigation; Employment Counseling.
Bessette, Paul M. ... '— '00 C.94 B.S. L.352 J.D. [A Morgan,L.&B.]
Bessey, Melissa A. '58 '84 C.914 B.A. L.597 J.D.
(adm. in IL; not adm. in DC) 102 5th St., NE‡
Bessey, Terrance L. ... '57 '83 C.208 B.M. L.597 J.D. [Kirkland&E.]
*PRACTICE AREAS: Corporate; Securities.
Besson, Paul S. ... '53 '80 C.188 B.S. L.597 J.D. NBC, Inc.
Best, George C. '— '97 C&L.145 S.B., J.D.
(adm. in IL; not adm. in DC; See Pat. Sect.) [A Foley&L.]
*PRACTICE AREAS: Intellectual Property.
Best, Judah, (AV) ... '32 '59 C.188 A.B. L.178 LL.B. [Debevoise&P.]
*PRACTICE AREAS: Federal Criminal Law; Grand Jury Practice; Securities; Litigation; SEC Enforcement.
Best, Stephen A., (BV) ... '64 '89 C.902 B.A. L.846 J.D. [Coudert B.]
*PRACTICE AREAS: White Collar Criminal Defense; Complex Civil Litigation; Internal Investigations.
Bester, Margot F. ... '54 '79 C.1349 B.A. L.904 J.D. [C Perkins C.]
*PRACTICE AREAS: Telecommunications Law; Electronic Commerce; Wireless Communications; Electronic Surveillance; Information and Privacy.
Bestor, Geoffrey ... '55 '82 C.999 B.A. L.477 J.D. [C Dickstein S.M.&O.]
*PRACTICE AREAS: Energy; Y2K; Litigation.
Besunder, Alison J. '73 '99 C.107 B.A. L.1009 J.D.
(adm. in NY; not adm. in DC) [A Arent F.K.P.&K.]
*PRACTICE AREAS: Commercial Litigation; Professional Liability.
Betancourt, Ana-Mita '58 '81 C.276 A.B. L.813 J.D.
Deputy General Counsel, Darby Overseas Investments, Ltd.

Betaque, Andrew '69 '00 C.886 B.S. L.893 J.D.
(adm. in NY; not adm. in DC) [A Covington&B.]
*PRACTICE AREAS: Tax.
Bethea, Robert H. ... '66 '91 C&L.623 B.B.A., J.D. [A Baker&M.]
*PRACTICE AREAS: Trade Regulations and Customs Law.
Bethel, Pamela J., (BV) ... '49 '74 C.999 B.A. L.273 J.D. 2021 L St. N.W., Ste. 300
Bethune, Ed, (AV) ... '35 '63 C&L.45 B.S.B.A., J.D. [Bracewell&P.]
*PRACTICE AREAS: Government Relations; Government Strategies.
Betke, Todd W. ... '67 '94 C.165 B.A. L.146 J.D. [A Weil,G.&M.]
Betor, John G. '52 '77 C.610 B.S.Ed. L.851 J.D.
(adm. in OH; not adm. in DC) Fed. Deposit Ins. Corp.
Bettenhausen, Barb L. ... '56 '96 C.986 B.A. L.1209 J.D. [A Arent F.K.P.&K.]
*PRACTICE AREAS: Business Law; International Law; Commercial Real Estate.
Betts, Kirk Howard, (AV) ... '51 '80 C.273 B.A. L.904 J.D. [Betts&H.]
*PRACTICE AREAS: Energy Contracts; Wholesale Electric Contracts; Hydroelectricity; Energy Regulatory Law; Administrative Law.

Betts & Holt, (AV) BB
West Tower 10th Floor, 1333 H Street N.W., 20005-4707
Telephone: 202-530-3380 Fax: 202-530-3389
Kirk Howard Betts; James H. Holt. Of Counsel: Jill M. Barker; David E. Crawford.
Practice before federal and state energy regulatory agencies, commissions, and courts representing the interests of municipal, cooperative, university and industrial consumers of electricity and industrial consumers and producers of natural gas.
See Professional Biographies, WASHINGTON, DISTRICT OF COLUMBIA

Beuchert, George H., Jr., (AV) ... '24 '49 C&L.276 B.S., J.D. [Stohlman,B.E.&S.]
Beury, Robert N., Jr. '53 '80 C&L.309 A.B., J.D.
Vice President & General Counsel, Cogent Communications, Inc.
Bevan, Philip R. ... '54 '79 C.264 B.A. L.228 J.D. [Elias,M.T.&H.]
Beveridge, Albert J., III, (AV) ... '35 '63 C.674 A.B. L.309 J.D. [C Beveridge&D.]
*PRACTICE AREAS: Corporate; Estates and Trusts.

Beveridge & Diamond, P.C., (AV) BB
1350 I Street, N.W., Suite 700, 20005-3311 ⊙
Telephone: 202-789-6000 Telecopier: 202-789-6190
URL: http://www.beveridgediamond.com
Karl S. Bourdeau; Robert Brager; Dean H. Cannon; Richard S. Davis; Henry L. Diamond; David M. Friedland; Aaron H. Goldberg; John S. Guttmann, Jr.; Paul E. Hagen; John N. Hanson; Steven A. Herman (Not admitted in DC); Steven M. Jawetz; David S. Krakoff; Cynthia A. Lewis; Lorelie S. Masters; Donald J. Patterson, Jr.; Christopher F. Regan; Thomas Richichi; Harold L. Segall; James B. Slaughter; Gary J. Smith; Kathryn E. Szmuszkovicz; Mark A. Turco; Fred R. Wagner; Benjamin F. Wilson. Senior Counsel: Albert J. Beveridge, III; Jonathan Z. Cannon; Harold Himmelman. Of Counsel: Gus Bauman; Laura K. McAfee (Not admitted in DC); Michael R. Neilson;—Stephen M. Arner; Thomas A. Blaser (Not admitted in DC); Michele A. Boddy (Not admitted in DC); Christina E. Carey (Not admitted in DC); Scott R. Damelin; Brian L. Doster; Leah A. Dundon; James T. Esselman (Not admitted in DC); Alessio D. Evangelista; Richard J. Ferris, Jr.; Meredith L. Flax (Not admitted in DC); Matthew C. Holloran; Madeleine Boyer Kadas; Daniel M. Krainin; Kathleen Lennon (Not admitted in DC); Ruth Ann Lowery; Anthony L. Michaels; Bryan J. Moore (Not admitted in DC); James T. Parkinson (Not admitted in DC); Justin A. Savage; Ilana Z. Sultan; David W. Wagner (Not admitted in DC); David M. (Max) Williamson.
General Practice before Federal and State Courts, Departments and Agencies in the areas of Environmental Law, (including Clean Air Act, Clean Water Act, RCRA, solid waste, Superfund, toxic chemicals, pesticide regulation, wetlands and biotechnology), Litigation, Product Regulation, Land Use, International Environmental Law, Natural Resources, Corporate and Securities and Government Contracts.
New York, N.Y. Office: 15th Floor, 477 Madison Avenue, 10022-5802. Telephone: 212-702-5400. Telecopier: 212-702-5450.
San Francisco, California Office: Suite 1800, 456 Montgomery Street, 94104-1251. Telephone: 415-262-4000. Telecopier: 415-262-4040.
Saddle Brook, New Jersey Office: Beveridge & Diamond, Park 80 West, Plaza II Suite 200, 07663-5836. Telephone: 201-585-8162. Telecopier: 201-368-1944.
Baltimore, Maryland Office: Suite 2210, 201 North Charles Street, 21201-4150. Telephone: 410-230-3850. Telecopier: 410-230-3868.
See Professional Biographies, WASHINGTON, DISTRICT OF COLUMBIA

Beverly, Richard A. '53 '81
C.329 B.A. L.30 J.D. Gen. Coun., D.C. Off. of Employee Appeals
Bey, Dawn-Marie ... '— '99 C.264 B.A. L.1209 J.D. [A Kilpatrick S.] (Pat.)
*PRACTICE AREAS: Intellectual Property.
Beyda, C. Richard, (AV) ... '37 '62 C&L.273 B.Acct., LL.B. [Grossberg,Y.F.&B.]
Bhagat, Raj K. ... '46 '87 C&L.999 B.A., LL.B. [Bhagat&Assoc.]

Bhagat & Associates
1001 Connecticut Avenue N.W. Suite 1138, 20036
Telephone: 202-293-4044 Fax: 202-293-4046 URL: http://ww.visastous.com
Email: rkbhagat@bhagatandassociates.com URL: http://www.lawyers.com/rajbhagat
Raj K. Bhagat.
Immigration and Naturalization, Business Immigration, Family Immigration, Consular Law, Employment Visas, Permanent Visas, Citizenship, Political Asylum, Deportation, Refugee Law, Immigration Discrimination, Religious Visas, Personal Injury, Automobile Accidents and Injuries, Slip and Fall, Wrongful Death, Medical Malpractice, Bodily Injury.
See Professional Biographies, WASHINGTON, DISTRICT OF COLUMBIA

Bhat, Gouri ... '66 '97 C.846 B.A. L.966 J.D. [A Mehri,M.&R.]
*PRACTICE AREAS: Employment Discrimination; Civil Rights; False Claims Act; Consumer Fraud; Commercial Litigation.
Bhatia, Karan ... '68 '94 C.674 A.B. L.178 J.D. 2445 M Street, N.W.
Bhatt, Minaksi ... '63 '90 C.914 B.A. L.273 J.D. [C Rothwell,F.E.&M.] (See Pat. Sect.)
*PRACTICE AREAS: Intellectual Property Litigation.
Bhowmik, Rachana '70 '98 C.976 B.A. L.893 J.D.
Staff Atty., Ctr. to Prevent Handgun Violence
Biagini, Raymond B. ... '54 '79 C&L.602 B.A., J.D. [McKenna&C.]
*PRACTICE AREAS: Product Liability Litigation; Insurance Coverage Litigation.
Bianco, Michele J. ... '65 '93 C.289 B.A. L.1206 J.D. [A Patton B.]
Bianco, Ronni S. ... '66 '93 C&L.659 B.S., J.D. 655 15th St., N.W., Suite 1200
Bick, Thomas K. ... '48 '77 C.602 B.S. L.1162 J.D. [Kilpatrick S.]
*PRACTICE AREAS: Environmental; Insurance; Native American Law.
Bickart, David O., (AV) ... '44 '69 C.309 A.B. L.569 J.D. [Kaye S.]
*PRACTICE AREAS: Environmental Law; Trade Regulation; Administrative Law; Litigation.
Bickerman, John G. ... '56 '89 C.188 B.S. L.276 LL.B. [Bickerman D.R.]
Bickerman Dispute Resolution Group, PLLC, (AV) ... 1120 G Street, N.W., Suite 410
Bickham, Timothy C. ... '68 '94 C.947 B.Ch. L.502 J.D. [A Arnold&P.] (Pat.)
*PRACTICE AREAS: Intellectual Property; Technology Law.
Bicks, Mark S., (AV) '48 '77
C.588 B.S.M.E. L.128 J.D. [Roylance,A.B.&G.] (See Pat. Sect.)
*PRACTICE AREAS: Litigation; Patent Law; Trademark Law; Copyright Law; Mechanical Patent Law.
Bickwit, Leonard, Jr., (AV) ... '— '67 C.976 B.A. L.309 LL.B. [Miller&C.]
*PRACTICE AREAS: Energy; Environmental Law; Taxation; International Trade; Banks and Banking.
Biddle, Laura Respess ... '66 '96 C.945 B.B.A. L.128 J.D. [A Arnold&P.]
*PRACTICE AREAS: Financial Institutions.
Biddle, Nicole S. '72 '00 C.207 B.A. L.475 J.D.
(adm. in KY; not adm. in DC) [A Falk]
*PRACTICE AREAS: Securities; Commercial Contracts; Government Contracts; Corporate Law; Labor and Employment.

Biddle, Timothy M., (AV) ....'40 '71 C.276 A.B. L.128 J.D. [Crowell&M.]
*PRACTICE AREAS: Mine Safety and Health Law; Administrative Law; OSHA Law; Coal Law; Association Law.
Biden, R. Hunter '70 '96 C.276 B.A. L.976 J.D.
(adm. in CT; not adm. in DC) [Oldaker&B.]
*PRACTICE AREAS: Internet Law; International Trade; Information Technology; Intellectual Property.
Bidstrup, W. Richard ....'57 '82 C.453 S.B. L.309 J.D. [Ⓒ Cleary,G.S.&H.]
Bieber, Sander M., (AV) ....'50 '76 C.674 B.A. L.930 J.D. [Dechert]
*PRACTICE AREAS: Securities Law; Financial Services Law; Investment Management Law; Corporate Law.
Biebesheimer, Christina ....'58 '87 C.352 B.A. L.309 J.D. Atty., Inter-Amer. Develop. Bk.
Biedronski, Beth ....'70 '00 C.216 B.A. L.902 J.D. [Ⓐ Wilmer,C.&P.]
Biegel, Joseph D. ....'59 '85 C.367 B.A. L.273 J.D. 3900 Wisconsin Ave., N.W.
Bieging, David A. ....'49 '76 C.309 A.B. L.1035 J.D. [Dorsey&W.]
*PRACTICE AREAS: Legislation and Federal Regulatory Practice.
Biegon, Bradford E. ....'62 '96 C.276 B.S. L.893 J.D. [Ⓐ Kirkland&E.]
*PRACTICE AREAS: Intellectual Property; Litigation.
Bieke, James R., (AV) ....'45 '73 C.999 B.A. L.477 J.D. [Shea&G.]
*PRACTICE AREAS: Environmental Law; Natural Resources Law.
Biel, Michael, (P.C.) ....'46 '72 C.602 B.A. L.276 J.D. [Ⓒ O'Toole,R.N.&S.]
Bier, Stephen H. ....'63 '90 C.705 B.A. L.309 J.D. [Ⓐ Dechert]
*PRACTICE AREAS: Financial Services Law; Investment Management.
Bierbower, Mark B., (AV) ....'51 '80 C.597 B.A. L.276 J.D. [Hunton&W.]
*PRACTICE AREAS: Litigation.
Bierbower, William J. ....'53 '81 C.228 B.A. L.276 J.D. 888 17th St., N.W.
Bieri, Diane E. ....'70 '95 C.665 B.A. L.276 J.D. [Ⓐ Howrey S.A.&W.]
*PRACTICE AREAS: Antitrust; Commercial Litigation.
Bierlein, Lawrence W. ....'42 '68 C.367 B.A. L.659 J.D. [McCarthy,S.&H.]
*PRACTICE AREAS: Hazardous Materials and Substances; Transportation; Environmental Law.
Bierman, Chad A. '59 '01 C.959 B.A. L.30 J.D.
(adm. in NY; not adm. in DC) 1707 "H" St.
Bierman, James N., (AV) ....'— '70 C.910 A.B. L.309 J.D. [Foley&L.]
*PRACTICE AREAS: Federal Regulatory Law (75%); International Trade Law (25%).
Bierman, M. Elizabeth ....'55 '86 C.893 B.A. L.128 J.D. [Morgan,L.&B.]
Bierstein, Karin '54 '80 C.999 L.188 J.D.
(adm. in NY; not adm. in DC) Amer. Soc. of Anesthesiologists
Biersteker, Peter J. ....'55 '81 C&L.309 A.B., J.D. [Jones,D.R.&P.]
*PRACTICE AREAS: Litigation; Products Liability; Complex Commercial Litigation.
Bierut, Mary Beth ....'58 '87 C.924 B.A. L.276 J.D. Biotechnology Industry Organization
Bieter, Mark '67 '01 C.285 B.A. L.228 J.D.
(adm. in MD; not adm. in DC) [Ⓐ Wilmer,C.&P.]
Bigg, Dort S., III ....'56 '86 C.273 B.A. L.1209 J.D. Amer. Psychological Assn.
Biggins, John C. ....'52 '80 C&L.705 B.A., J.D. [Tendler&B.]

Bigham Englar Jones & Houston
818 Connecticut Avenue, N.W., Suite 1010, 20006 ⊙
Telephone: 202-293-3330 Telefax: 202-293-3515
Email: bejh.com
Daniel H. Murray.
General Practice. Admiralty, Insurance, Aviation, Banking, Bankruptcy, Personal Injury and Products Liability Law, Environmental and Reinsurance.
London, England Office: 107/112 Leadenhall Street, EC3A 4AH. Telephone: 207-891-2504. Telefax: 207-891-2401.
Newark, New Jersey Office: One Gateway Center, Suite 2600, 07102-5315. Telephone: 973-799-8545. Telefax: 973-799-8546.
See Professional Biographies, WASHINGTON, DISTRICT OF COLUMBIA

Bikoff, James L. ....'40 '67 C.150 B.A. L.178 LL.B. [Silverberg,G.&B.]
*PRACTICE AREAS: Intellectual Property Law; Internet Law; Technology Law; Customs and Trade Law.
Bilas, Kurt W. ....'59 '89 C.851 B.S.C.E. L.930 J.D. [Ⓐ Skadden,A.S.M.&F.]
Biles, Blake A., (AV) ....'46 '75 C&L.378 B.A., J.D. [Arnold&P.]
*PRACTICE AREAS: Environmental; Consumer Products; Administrative.
Bilich, Edward K.M., (AV) ....'64 '90 C.896 B.A. L.309 J.D. [Jones,D.R.&P.]
*PRACTICE AREAS: Litigation; Class Action Defense; Corporate Investigations.
Bill, Arthur H., (AV) ....'— '70 C.705 B.A. L.94 J.D. [Foley&L.]
*PRACTICE AREAS: Securities Law; Corporate Law.
Billauer, Barbara P., (AV) ....'51 '76 C.188 B.S. L.1019 J.D. 2011 Hillyer Pl. NW
Billett, Brian '66 '93 C&L.608 B.S.B.A., J.D.
(adm. in OH; not adm. in DC) PricewaterhouseCoopers LLP
Billingsley, Audrey ....'71 '99 C.145 B.A. L.276 J.D. [Ⓐ Levine S.&K.]
Bilsky, Eric A. ....'62 '91 C.976 B.A. L.309 J.D. 1121 12th St.
Bilzi, Carol J. ....'54 '86 C.1044 B.A. L.276 J.D. [Ⓒ Mayer,B.&P.]
Binder, Darren T. ....'68 '93 C.867 B.S. L.93 J.D. [Ⓐ Arent F.K.P.&K.]
*PRACTICE AREAS: Health Care Transactions; Health Care Regulation; Managed Care.
Binder, Elizabeth R. '60 '90 C.659 B.A. L.472 J.D.
(adm. in NY; not adm. in DC) [Ⓐ Kilpatrick S.]
*PRACTICE AREAS: Employee Benefits; Compensation; ERISA Litigation.
Binge, Brent E. ....'70 '99 C.678 B.A. L.276 J.D. [Ⓐ Cleary,G.S.&H.]

Bingham Dana LLP, (AV) BB
1120 20th Street, N.W., 20036 ⊙
Telephone: 202-778-6150 Telecopy: 202-778-6155
Email: info@bingham.com URL: http://www.bingham.com
Resident Partners: William H. Boger, III (Not admitted in DC); Roger D. Feldman; Yoshihide Ito (Not admitted in DC); Paul J. Lambert; J. Michael Pickett; Nancy M. Persechino; Paul S. Quinn; Barry P. Rosenthal; Peter D. Schellie; Roger L. Selfe; Neal E. Sullivan; Enid L. Veron; Erica H. Weiss. Of Counsel: Joseph P. Pelican; Wayne Pestone; Bonnie S. Temple; Mark C. Williams. Resident Associates: Matthew R. Bowsher (Not admitted in DC); Christian J. Clayton (Not admitted in DC); Margaret Kadel Eck; Gerard P. Finn; Jeffrey O. Himstreet; Thomas C. Klanderman (Not admitted in DC); Kara E. McCabe (Not admitted in DC).
Corporate and Securities Law, Banking and Financial Services, Financial Restructuring, Project/Structured Finance, Technology, Private Equity, Investment Management, Commercial and Criminal Litigation, Corporate Acquisitions, Real Estate, Entrepreneurial Services, Intellectual Property, Tax, Estate Planning, Securities Litigation, Business Regulation and White Collar Defense, Product Liability, Antitrust, Distribution and Franchising, Employment Law, Environmental Law, Sports, Media, Entertainment, International Transactions including International Trade, European, Japanese and Latin American Practices and Alternative Dispute Resolution.
Boston, Massachusetts Office: 150 Federal Street. Telephone: 617-951-8000. Telecopy: 617-951-8736.
New York, New York Office: 399 Park Avenue. Telephone: 212-318-7700. Fax: 212-752-5378.
Los Angeles, California Office: 444 South Flower Street, Suite 4500. Telephone: 213-817-3700. Fax: 213-817-3701.
Hartford, Connecticut Office: One State Street. Telephone: 860-240-2700. Fax: 860-240-2800.
London, England Office: 39 Victoria Street, SWIH 0EE. Telephone: 011-44-71-799-2646. Telecopy: 011-44-71-799-2654.
Singapore Office: Level 15 Prudential Tower, 30 Cecil Street, 049712. Telephone: 65 232-2768/2769. Fax: 65 232-2888.
See Professional Biographies, WASHINGTON, DISTRICT OF COLUMBIA

Bingler, Richard F. '54 '91 C.500 B.P.A. L.1187 J.D.
(adm. in VA; not adm. in DC) Bureau of National Affairs
Binkley, John C. '47 '83 C.424 B.A. L.209 J.D.
(adm. in IN; not adm. in DC) Resolution Tr. Corp.
Binstock, Daniel Brian ....'73 '00 C.446 B.A. L.904 J.D. [Ⓐ Finnegan,H.F.G.&D.]
*PRACTICE AREAS: Domain Name Infringement; Internet Trademark Law; Trademark Prosecution; Trademark Litigation.

Binstock, Torchinsky and Associates, P.C., Law Offices of
(See Chevy Chase, Maryland)

Bintz, Edward E. ....'58 '85 C.262 B.S. L.273 J.D. [Arnold&P.]
*PRACTICE AREAS: Benefits and Employment Law.
Birch, Elizabeth ....'56 '85 C.312 B.A. L.770 J.D. Human Rts. Campaign
Birch, Harold J., (AV) ....'20 '47 C.132 B.S. L.352 J.D. 1001 G St., N.W. (Pat.)
Birch, Ronald G., (AV) ....'41 '66 C.165 B.A. L.178 J.D. [Birch,H.B.&C.]
*PRACTICE AREAS: Litigation; Employment; Natural Resources.

Birch, Horton, Bittner & Cherot, P.C., (AV)
Suite 1200, 1155 Connecticut Avenue, N.W., 20036 ⊙
Telephone: 202-659-5800 Facsimile: 202-659-1027
Email: info@bhb.com URL: http://www.birchhorton.com
Thomas L. Albert; Ronald G. Birch; William P. Horn; Roy Stapleton Jones, Jr.; Harvey A. Levin; Elisabeth Hewitt Ross;—Douglas Scott Burdin; Allison M. Ellis.
General Practice
Anchorage, Alaska Office: 1127 West 7th Avenue. Telephone: 907-276-1550.
See Professional Biographies, WASHINGTON, DISTRICT OF COLUMBIA

Bird, John M. '73 '00 C&L.446 B.S.M.E., J.D.
(adm. in MD; not adm. in DC; See Pat. Sect.) [Ⓐ Sughrue M.]
*PRACTICE AREAS: Patents.
Birenbaum, David E., (AV) ....'37 '62 C.103 B.A. L.309 LL.B. [Fried,F.H.S.&J.]
Birenbaum, Joshua '74 '00 C.65 B.A. L.893 J.D.
(adm. in VA; not adm. in DC) [Ⓐ Howrey S.A.&W.]
Birenbaum, Joshua Daniel '74 '01 C.65 B.A. L.893 J.D.
(adm. in VA; not adm. in DC) 1297 Pennsylvania Ave., NW
Birg, Erika C. '— '95 C.575 B.A. L.245 J.D.
(adm. in GA; not adm. in DC) [Ⓐ Wiley R.&F.]
*PRACTICE AREAS: Litigation.
Birgisson, Gunnar ....'64 '96 C.112 B.A. L.228 J.D. [Ⓐ Cameron M.]
*PRACTICE AREAS: Energy Law; Administrative Law; Appellate Practice; International Law.
Birkel, Walter G., (AV) ....'47 '73 C.893 B.A. L.309 J.D. [Tighe P.A.T.]
*PRACTICE AREAS: Complex Civil Litigation; False Claims Act; Products Liability; Personal Injury Litigation; Government Contracts.
Birkenstock, Joseph M. ....'67 '92 C.524 B.A. L.273 J.D. Dem. Natl. Comm.
Birney, Arthur A., (AV) .....'27 '52 C&L.902 B.A., LL.B. 888 17th St., NW, Suite 1000‡
Birnkrant, Henry J., (AV) ....'55 '79 C.696 B.A. L.178 J.D. [Alston&B.]
*PRACTICE AREAS: Taxation Law; International Taxation; Federal Taxation.
Biros, Mark J., (AV) ....'48 '73 C.674 B.A. L.276 J.D. [Proskauer R.]
Bisceglie, Anthony P., (AV) ....'52 '78 C.174 B.A. L.1162 J.D. [Bisceglie&W.]
*PRACTICE AREAS: Corporate Counseling; Administrative Law; Commercial Litigation; Business Crimes; White Collar Criminal Defense.

Bisceglie & Walsh, (AV)
Suite 400, 1130 Seventeenth Street, N.W., 20036
Telephone: 202-778-1160 Facsimile: 202-659-9536
Email: bisc-walsh@worldnet.att.net URL: http://www.lawyers.com/bisceglie&walsh
Members of Firm: Anthony P. Bisceglie; William C. Walsh.
Civil, Criminal Trial, Appellate and Federal Agency Practice. Corporate Law, Government Relations, Media Law, International Human Rights.
See Professional Biographies, WASHINGTON, DISTRICT OF COLUMBIA

Bisgyer, Bert Neil, Law Offices of, (AV) '47 '73 C.910 A.B. L.273 J.D. BB
1025 Thomas Jefferson Street, N.W. Suite 525 East, 20007 ⊙
Telephone: 202-338-2172 Telecopier: 202-338-2447
Email: blsgyer@bisgyerlaw.com URL: http://www.lawyers.com/bisgyeremploymentlaw
***PRACTICE AREAS: Labor and Employment; Employment Discrimination.**
Of Counsel: Carl S. Silverman.
Labor and Employment Law for management including litigation.
See Professional Biographies, WASHINGTON, DISTRICT OF COLUMBIA

Bishop, Brant W. ....'— '96 C.101 B.A./M.A. L.309 J.D. [Ⓐ Kirkland&E.]
*PRACTICE AREAS: Litigation.
Bishop, Bruce C. ....'64 '96 C&L.893 B.A., J.D. [Ⓐ Steptoe&J.]
Bishop, Dennis W. '65 '95 C.165 B.A. L.990 J.D.
(adm. in NY; not adm. in DC) [Ⓐ Winston&S.]
*PRACTICE AREAS: Project Finance Law.
Bishop, James D. '57 '85 C.411 B.A. L.329 J.D.
Dir., Archdiocese Legal Network of Catholic Charities
Bishop, Katherine L., (AV) ....'52 '77 C.228 B.S.B.A. L.902 J.D. [Ⓒ Ballard S.A.&I.]
*PRACTICE AREAS: Health Care Finance; Commercial Real Estate; Business Finance; Secured Transactions; Commercial Real Estate Finance.
Bishop, Michael A. ....'74 '99 C.880 B.A. L.273 J.D. [Ⓐ Steptoe&J.]
Bishop, Miriam A. ....'56 '87 C.352 B.A. L.276 J.D. [Ⓐ Willkie F.&G.]
*PRACTICE AREAS: International Trade; Antitrust and Trade Regulation; Corporate; Federal Regulatory.
Bishop, Pascale J. '76 '01 C.502 B.A. L.477 J.D.
(adm. in IL; not adm. in DC) [Ⓐ McDermott,W.&E.]
Bishop, Robert W. '43 '76
C.871 B.S. L.184 J.D. V.P. & Gen. Coun., Nuclear Energy Institute
*RESPONSIBILITIES: Nuclear Energy; Administrative Law; Corporate Law; Nonprofit and Charitable Organizations; Trade and Professional Organizations.
Bisignano, Michael C. '— '97 C.659 B.A.B.S. L.309 J.D.
701 Pennsylvania Avenue, N.W.
Bisio, Peter R. ....'63 '92 C.1313 B.A. L.178 J.D. [Hogan&H.]
*PRACTICE AREAS: Litigation.
Bissegger, Michael R. ....'64 '92 C.101 B.A. L.188 J.D. [Ⓐ Epstein B.&G.]
*PRACTICE AREAS: Antitrust Law.
Bisset, Thomas E. ....'62 '86 C.884 B.S. L.94 J.D. [Ⓒ Sutherland A.&B.]
*PRACTICE AREAS: Insurance Products Regulation; Mutual Fund Regulation; Securities Regulation.
Bissonette, Matthew J. ....'68 '95 C.893 B.A. L.945 J.D. [Ⓐ Ritter E.&N.]
*PRACTICE AREAS: Public Finance Law.
Bitar, Neda E. ....'— '99 C.881 B.A. L.734 J.D. [Ⓐ Krupin O.]
*PRACTICE AREAS: Immigration Law; Litigation.
Bitol, Solange '— '93 C.740 B.A. L.1355 J.D.
(adm. in CA; not adm. in DC) Am. Civil Liberties Union
Bittman, Robert J., (BV) ....'62 '88 C.446 B.A. L.128 J.D. [Ⓒ White&C.]
*PRACTICE AREAS: Litigation; Criminal Law; Civil Litigation.
Bixler, John Mourer, (AV) ....'— '54 C.659 B.S. L.309 LL.B. [Ross,M.&F.]
*PRACTICE AREAS: Taxation; Tax Litigation; Trusts and Estates; Tax Exempt Organizations.
Bixler, Sidney R. ....'39 '68 C.31 B.A. L.309 J.D. 441 Fourth St. N.W.
Bjorge, Gerald H., (AV) '37 '66
C.597 B.S.Ch.E. L.273 LL.B. [Ⓒ Keil&W.] (See Pat. Sect.)
*PRACTICE AREAS: Patents; Trademark Law.
Bjorklund, Terrie M., Ms. ....'52 '84 C.1331 B.A. L.1162 J.D. [Ⓐ K.Nasseri]
*PRACTICE AREAS: Entertainment Law; Copyrights; Trademarks.
Bjornlund, Eric C. '58 '85 C.951 B.A. L.178 J.D.
(adm. in MA; not adm. in DC) Natl. Democratic Institute
Bjornson, Christopher R. '— '00 C.846 B.A. L.180 J.D.
701 Pennsylvania Avenue, N.W.
Blach, Andrzej M. ....'59 '93 [Cameron M.]
*PRACTICE AREAS: Energy Law; Corporate Law; International Law.
Blacher, Brian M. ....'69 '95 C&L.260 B.S., J.D. Ernst & Young

Black, Anthony M. ... '62 '91 C.352 B.A. L.893 J.D. [Ⓐ Tobin,O.&E.] ⊙
*PRACTICE AREAS: Telecommunications; Electronic Commerce.
Black, Colin L. ... '74 '99 C&L.861 B.A., J.D. [Ⓐ Gibson,D.&C.]
*PRACTICE AREAS: Appellate Practice; Constitutional Law.
Black, David M., (AV) ... '46 '73 C.477 A.B. L.30 J.D. 4000 Massachusetts Ave., N.W.
Black, Dennis M. ... '64 '90 C.839 B.S. L.145 J.D. [Williams&C.]
Black, Dorothy J. ... '44 '94 C.813 B.A. L.276 J.D. [Ⓐ Morgan,L.&B.]
Black, Edward J. '45 '72
C.529 B.A. L.30 J.D. Computer & Communications Industry Assn.
Black, H. Allen, III '57 '91 C.869 B.S. L.945 J.D.
(adm. in VA; not adm. in DC) [Ⓐ Winston&S.]
*PRACTICE AREAS: Maritime; Litigation; Admiralty Law; International Law.
Black, James J. ... '66 '98 C.801 B.A. L.893 J.D. [Ⓐ Clifford C.R.&W.]
*PRACTICE AREAS: Corporate; Securities; Mergers and Acquisitions; Cross-Border Finance.
Black, Jennifer Jewell ... '— '99 C.1375 B.A. L.893 J.D. [Ⓐ Fried,F.H.S.&J.]
*PRACTICE AREAS: Taxation.
Black, Joseph A. ... '44 '87 C.134 B.A. L.128 J.D. [Cullen]
*PRACTICE AREAS: International Trade Regulation; Customs Law; False Claims Act; Commercial Litigation; Motor Carrier Law.
Black, Laura L. ... '74 '00 C.105 B.A. L.309 J.D. [Ⓐ Cleary,G.S.&H.]
Black, Mark A. '73 '00 C.446 B.A. L.273 J.D.
(adm. in VA; not adm. in DC) [Ⓐ Steptoe&J.]
Black, Nathalie V. ... '35 '60 C.768 A.B. L.1066 LL.B. 3425 Porter St.‡
Black, Richard W. '71 '96 C&L.352 B.A., J.D.
(adm. in MN; not adm. in DC) [Ⓐ Akin,G.S.H.&F.]
*PRACTICE AREAS: Labor and Employment Litigation.
Black, Sam, (AV) ... '43 '73 C.976 B.A. L.276 J.D. [Squire,S.&D.]
*PRACTICE AREAS: Taxation; Corporate; Equipment Finance; International Acquisitions.
Black, Stephen F., (AV) ... '44 '69 C.309 A.B. L.477 J.D. [Wilmer,C.&P.]
*PRACTICE AREAS: Securities; Civil Practice.
Black, Thomas C. ... '48 '73 C.282 B.A. L.229 J.D. Asst. U.S. Atty.
Black, Wayne V. ... '37 '64 C.502 B.S. L.273 LL.B. [Keller&H.]
*PRACTICE AREAS: Telecommunications Law; Trade Regulation Law; Antitrust Law.
Blackburn, Thomas L., (AV) ... '48 '75 C.229 B.A. L.276 J.D. [Bruder,G.&M.]
*PRACTICE AREAS: Electric Utility.
Blackman, Scott H., (BV) ... '60 '89 C.999 B.S. L.188 J.D. [Ⓒ Lyon&L.] (Pat.)
*PRACTICE AREAS: Intellectual Property; Licensing; Litigation and Prosecution.
Blackman, Sean G. '71 '97 C.945 B.A. L.306 J.D.
(adm. in CT; not adm. in DC) [Ⓐ O'Melveny&M.]
Blackmer, Rebecca A. ... '56 '96 C.375 B.S. L.128 J.D. [Ⓐ Swidler B.S.F.]
*PRACTICE AREAS: Energy Law; Electric Power; Natural Gas; Utility Regulatory Law.
Blackmon, Leslie A. ... '58 '84 C.10 B.A. L.309 J.D. Asst. U.S. Atty.
Blacknell, Mark Eric '76 '00 C.1059 A.B. L.273 J.D.
(adm. in VA; not adm. in DC) [Ⓐ Pepper&C.]
Blacksher, Mary L. '73 '00 C.861 B.A. L.425 J.D.
(adm. in LA; not adm. in DC) U.S. Dept. of Justice
Blackstone, Liliah Rene ... '71 '00 C.1369 B.S. L.329 J.D. 301 G St., S.W.
Blackstone, Michael C., (AV) '42 '71
C.608 B.A. L.273 J.D. [King&N.] (⊙Arlington, VA)
*PRACTICE AREAS: Commercial Litigation; Corporate Litigation; Real Estate Litigation; Corporate Law; Labor and Employment.
Blackwell, Joel D., (AV) ... '06 '38 C&L.329 LL.B. 119 R St., N.W.
Blackwell, Robert J. ... '25 '54 C.823 B.S. L.309 LL.B. [Sher&B.]
*PRACTICE AREAS: Transportation; Government Relations.
Blad, Leiv H., Jr. ... '62 '90 C.112 B.A. L.94 J.D. [Clifford C.R.&W.]
*PRACTICE AREAS: Commercial Litigation; Intellectual Property Litigation; Antitrust.
Blagg, Christopher J. ... '66 '92 C.276 B.S.F.S. L.893 J.D. [Ⓐ Piper M.R.&W.]
*PRACTICE AREAS: Venture Capital; Emerging Growth Companies.
Blaha, Amber ... '72 '00 C&L.893 B.A., J.D. [Ⓐ Steptoe&J.]
Blaine, Jack H. ... '34 '61 C.201 B.S. L.966 LL.B. [Ⓒ Sutherland A.&B.]
*PRACTICE AREAS: Insurance Solvency; Insurance Mergers and Acquisitions; Insurance Products; Unfair Insurance Practices; Insurance Receiverships.
Blair, Bonnie S., (AV) ... '50 '76 C.918 B.A. L.309 J.D. [Thompson C.]
*PRACTICE AREAS: Energy; Complex Litigation; Utilities.
Blair, Charles T. ... '65 '90 C&L.893 B.A., J.D. [Ross,D.&B.]
Blair, David B. ... '— '90 C.276 A.B. L.188 J.D. [Miller&C.]
*PRACTICE AREAS: Federal Income Tax; Federal Tax Controversies; Tax Litigation; Tax Appeals; Taxation.
Blair, Lucrecia M. ... '73 '99 C.699 B.A. L.823 J.D. [Ⓐ Fragomen,D.B.&L.]
*PRACTICE AREAS: Immigration Law.
Blair, William McC., Jr. ... '16 '47 C.813 B.A. L.893 LL.B. 2510 Foxhall Rd., N.W.‡
Blake, David A. '69 '94 C&L.128 B.S., J.D.
(adm. in WA; not adm. in DC) [Ⓐ Seyfarth S.]
*PRACTICE AREAS: Construction; Government Contracts; Litigation.
Blake, Ernest L., Jr. (P.C.) ... '42 '73 C.871 B.S. L.228 J.D. [Shaw P.]
*PRACTICE AREAS: Energy; Administrative Law.
Blake, Jonathan D., (AV) ... '38 '65 C&L.976 B.A., LL.B. [Covington&B.]
Blake, Margaret R. ... '65 '93 C.886 B.A. L.128 J.D. [Ⓐ Baker&M.]
*PRACTICE AREAS: Securities and Financial Products; Regulatory Law; Mergers and Acquisitions; Corporate and Partnership Law.
Blake, Mona '34 '80 C.329 B.A. L.245 J.D.
Gen.Coun.,D.C.Lottery & Charitable Games Control Bd.
Blake, Weldon M. ... '40 '76 C&L.329 B.S., J.D. 1343 Pennsylvania Ave., S.E.
Blakely, Caroline E. ... '54 '80 C.893 B.A. L.276 J.D. V.P., National Coop. Bk.
Blakely, William D., (AV) ... '45 '77 C.966 B.A. L.215 J.D. [Piper M.R.&W.]
*PRACTICE AREAS: Aviation Litigation; Commercial Litigation; Construction; Government Contracts Litigation.
Blakeslee, Melise R. ... '61 '87 C.597 B.A. L.564 J.D. [McDermott,W.&E.]
Blakey, William A. ... '43 '69 C.389 B.A. L.329 J.D. [Dean B.&M.]
Blalack, K. Lee, II ... '64 '95 C&L.1015 B.A., J.D. [Ⓐ O'Melveny&M.]
*PRACTICE AREAS: Litigation.
Blalock, James A., III ... '58 '83 C.112 B.A. L.861 J.D. [Shaw P.]
*PRACTICE AREAS: Securitization; Structured Finance; Public Offerings; Securities Registration; Corporate Finance.
Blanc, Curtis D. ... '74 '99 C.910 B.S.B.A. L.273 J.D. [Ⓐ Shook,H.&B.]
Blanchard, Ellen '75 '00 C.611 B.A. L.904 J.D.
(adm. in VA; not adm. in DC) [Ⓐ Boies,S.&F.]
*PRACTICE AREAS: International Arbitration; Antitrust.
Blanchard, Hartman E., Jr. ... '69 '94 C.309 B.A. L.273 J.D. [Ⓐ McKee N.]
*PRACTICE AREAS: Tax Litigation; Taxation; Intellectual Property Litigation.
Blanchard, James J. ... '— '68 C.476 B.A. L.494 J.D. [Verner,L.B.M.&H.]
*PRACTICE AREAS: International Trade; Federal Affairs; Energy; Communications; Environmental.
Blanchard, Jerred G., Jr., (AV) '50 '76 C.976 B.A. L.880 J.D.
(adm. in TN; not adm. in DC) 1225 Connecticut Ave. N.W.
Blanchard, Lyle M. ... '58 '99 C.999 B.A. L.128 J.D. [Ⓐ Greenstein D.&L.]
*PRACTICE AREAS: Land Use; Estate Planning; Zoning Law; Historic Preservation; Municipal Law.
Blanchard, Tara Weinstock ... '70 '95 C.309 B.A. L.273 J.D. [Ⓐ Crowell&M.]
Blanchette, Katherine R. '70 '00 C.659 B.S. L.575 J.D.
(adm. in MD; not adm. in DC) [Ⓐ Long A.&N.]
*PRACTICE AREAS: Real Estate; Litigation.
Blanchette, Robert W. ... '32 '57 C.184 B.A. L.976 LL.B. 50 F St., N.W.
Bland, Gregory Brian ... '70 '95 C.1036 B.A. L.1398 J.D. 2000 L. Street N.W.
Blaner, Kathleen L. ... '53 '89 C.30 A.B. L.128 J.D. [Ⓒ Covington&B.]
Blanford, Thomas D. '— '97 C.273 B.A. L.245 J.D.
(adm. in MD; not adm. in DC) [Ⓐ King&S.]
*PRACTICE AREAS: Litigation; Trade Regulation.
Blank, Beverly L. ... '72 '97 C.893 B.A. L.477 J.D. [Ⓐ Hogan&H.]
*PRACTICE AREAS: Corporate Law; Securities; Private Equity.
Blank, Jennifer S. ... '62 '91 C.705 B.A. L.273 J.D. Business Software Alliance
Blank, Jonathan, (AV) ... '44 '71 C.319 B.A. L.309 J.D. [Preston G.E.&R.M.]
*PRACTICE AREAS: Aviation; Maritime.
Blank, Kathleen Alice '52 '98 C.973 B.A. L.446 J.D.
(adm. in MD; not adm. in DC) Program Spec., Natl. Council on Disability
Blank, Peter L. ... '54 '79 C.674 B.S.E. L.1338 J.D. Kiplinger Wash. Editors
Blank, Rhonda ... '50 '81 C.645 B.A. L.425 J.D. P.O. Box 1427

Blank Rome Comisky & McCauley LLP, (AV)
The Farragut Building, 900 17th Street, N.W., Suite 1000, 20006 ⊙
Telephone: 202-530-7400 FAX: 202-463-6915
Email: webmaster@blankrome.com URL: http://www.blankrome.com
Resident Members: Mark Blondman (Not admitted in DC); Herbert Cohen; Charles A. Cragin; Edward J. Farrell; Susan B. Flohr; Michael C. Greenbaum; Kathleen McDermott (Not admitted in DC); David A. Norcross; Victor M. Wigman; Charles R. Wolfe, Jr.; Joel Rothstein Wolfson. Senior, Special and Of Counsel: J. Caleb Boggs III; Donald R. Greene; George C. Myers, Jr. (Not admitted in DC); Lisa J. Savitt; Michael D. White. Resident Associates: Lyn Anne Bailey; David J. Edmondson (Not admitted in DC); Brooke Thomas Iley; Brian C. Jones; Denise Catherine Lane (Not admitted in DC); Rafael Perez-Pineiro (Not admitted in DC); Peter S. Weissman; Neil R. White (Not admitted in DC); John Yun (Not admitted in DC).
Administrative Law, Administrative Adjudications; Administrative Agency Practice, Administrative Hearings and Appeals, Administrative Litigation, Federal Administrative Law, Professional Licensing, Professional Licensing Regulation, Public Law, Admiralty and Maritime Law, Marine Law, Maritime Contracts, Maritime Finance, Maritime Law, Maritime Liens, Ship Sales and Mortgages, Aged and Aging, Age Discrimination, Elder Care, Elder Law, Agency and Distributorships, Distribution Agreements, International Distribution, Alcoholic Beverages, Liquor Licensing, Alternative Dispute Resolution, Arbitration, International Arbitration, International Dispute Resolution, Mediation, Antitrust and Trade Regulation, Antitrust, Business Combinations, Competition, Covenants Not To Compete, Deceptive Trade Practices, Noncompetition and Non-Solicitation Agreements, Price-Fixing, Restrictive Covenants, Trade Regulation, Unfair Trade, Appellate Practice, Civil Appeals, Art Law, Artists Rights, Museum Law, Asset Protection, International Asset Protection, Aviation and Aerospace, Aircraft Finance and Leasing, Aircraft Sales, Airline Labor Law, Aviation Law, Aviation Defense, Aviation Insurance, Aviation Litigation, Aviation Products Liability, Aviation Regulation, Bankruptcy, Bankruptcy Arbitration, Bankruptcy Chapter 7, Bankruptcy Chapter 11, Bankruptcy Chapter 12, Bankruptcy Chapter 13, Bankruptcy Collections, Bankruptcy Litigation, Bankruptcy Mediation, Bankruptcy Reorganization, Bankruptcy Taxation, Bankruptcy Trustees Rights, Commercial Bankruptcy, Commercial Foreclosure, Commercial Insolvency, Commercial Recovery, Commercial Workouts, Foreclosures, Fraudulent Conveyance, Insolvency, International Bankruptcy, International Insolvency, Liquidations, Out of Court Debt Restructuring, Pre-Bankruptcy Workouts, Receiverships, Repossessions, Workouts, Workouts Taxation, Banks and Banking, ATM Networks, Bank Collections, Bank Directors and Officers Liability, Bank Foreclosures, Bank Mergers and Acquisitions, Banking Antitrust, Banking Law, Banking Litigation, Commercial Banking, Commercial Credit, Commercial Loans, Consumer Banking, Credit Card Law, Credit Finance, Credit Law, Electronic Banking, Fair Lending, Financial Law, Interest and Usury, International Banking Law, International Loans, Lender Law, Lender Liability, Lender Regulation, Lenders Rights, Letters of Credit, Loan Restructuring, Loan Workouts, Loans, Savings and Loan Law, Secured Lending, Truth in Lending, Biotechnology, Biomedical Technology, Biotechnology Licensing, Business Law, Business Arbitration, Business Associations Law, Business Crimes, Business Development, Business Dissolutions, Business Estate Planning, Business Formation, Business Fraud, Business Litigation, Business Mediation, Business Organization, Business Planning, Business Regulation, Business Reorganization, Business Sales, Business Succession Planning, Business Successions, Business Syndication, Business Taxation, Business Torts, Business Transactions, Business Transfers, Business Trusts, Business Valuation, Buying and Selling of Businesses, Capital Formation, Closely Held Business Estate Planning, Closely Held Business Law, Closely Held Business Taxation, Complex Business Litigation, Emerging Business Law, Emerging Growth Companies, Entrepreneurial Business Law, Family Business Law, Family Business Mediation, Family Business Successions, International Business Law, International Joint Ventures, Joint Ventures, Limited Liability Company Law, Privatization, Professional Practices, Small Business Law, Sole Proprietorships, Strategic Alliances, Chancery and Equity, Chancery Practice, Children, Child Custody, Child Support, Civil Practice, Federal Civil Practice, Sex Discrimination, Commercial Collections, Post Judgment Collections, Commercial Law, Commercial Litigation, Complex Commercial Litigation, Secured Transactions, Uniform Commercial Code, Commercial Real Estate, Commercial Real Estate Acquisitions, Commercial Real Estate Development, Commercial Real Estate Finance, Commercial Real Estate Foreclosure, Commercial Real Estate Sales, Commercial Real Estate Syndication, Commercial Real Estate Workouts, Industrial Real Estate Law, Shopping Center Acquisitions, Shopping Center Development, Shopping Center Law, Complex and Multi-District Litigation, Computers and Software, Computer Contracts, Computer Law, Computer Security, Computer Software Law, Computer Technology, Electronic Commerce, Information Technology, Information Technology Contracts, Information Technology Licensing, International Computer Law, Internet Law, Software Copyright, Software Licensing, Software Protection, Year 2000 Computer Conversion, Constitutional Law, First Amendment Law, Construction Law, Construction Finance, Construction Litigation, Construction Workouts, Environmental Construction Law, International Construction Law, Public Construction Law, Consumer Law, Consumer Arbitration, Consumer Class Actions, Consumer Credit, Consumer Credit Compliance, Consumer Finance, Consumer Fraud, Consumer Litigation, Consumer Protection, Consumer Rights, Fair Credit Reporting Act, Contracts, Breach of Contract, Commercial Contracts, Contract Fraud, Contract Litigation, International Commercial Contracts, International Contracts, Copyrights, Copyright Infringement, Copyright Litigation, Copyright Prosecution, Copyright Protection, Copyright Registration, International Copyright Law, Corporate Law, Closely Held Corporations, Corporate Banking Law, Corporate Commercial Law, Corporate Contracts, Corporate Control Contests, Corporate Criminal Law, Corporate Dissolutions, Corporate Ethics, Corporate Fiduciary Law, Corporate Finance, Corporate Formation, Corporate Governance, Corporate Income Tax, Corporate Insurance, Corporate Insurance Defense, Corporate Investigations, Corporate Litigation, Corporate Organization, Corporate Partnerships, Corporate Planning, Corporate Real Estate, Corporate Reorganization, Corporate Successions, Corporate Tax Controversies, Corporate Tax Planning, Corporate Taxation, Corporate Trusts, Corporate Workouts, Family Corporations, Foreign Sales Corporations, Hostile Takeovers, Incorporation, International Corporate Finance, International Corporate Law, International Corporate Taxation, Nonprofit Corporations, Offshore Corporations, Professional Corporations; Proxy Contests, Public Corporations, S Corporations, Securitization, Small Business Corporations, Takeovers, Tender Offers, Transfer Pricing, Criminal Law, Debtor and Creditor, Creditor Bankruptcy, Creditors Rights, Creditors Rights in Bankruptcy, Debtor and Creditor Bankruptcy, Debtor and Creditor Collections, Debtor and Creditor Remedies, Debtor and Creditor Reorganization, Debtor and Creditor Rights, Debtor and Creditor Workouts, Debtor Bankruptcy, International Creditors Rights, Secured Creditors Rights, Unsecured Creditors Rights, Disabilities, Americans with Disabilities Act, Academic Employment, College and University Law, Administrative Lobbying, Executive Lobbying, Legislative Lobbying, Lobbying, Eminent Domain, Employee Benefits, COBRA, Deferred Compensation, Employee Benefit Taxation, Employee Benefit Trusts, Employee Compensation, Employee Stock Ownership Plans, ERISA, Executive Compensation, Executive Compensation Taxation, Flexible Benefit Plans, Multi-Employer Benefits, Multi-Employer Pensions, Non-Qualified Benefits, Pension and Profit Sharing Plans, Pension Plans, Pension Taxation, Profit Sharing, Public Pension Plans, Qualified Retirement Plans, Retirement Benefit Plans, Taft-Hartley Plans, Unemployment Compensation, Music Copyright, Environmental Law, Environmental Compliance, Environmental Liability, Environmental Litigation, Environmental Mediation, International Environmental Law, Equipment Finance and Leasing, Equipment Finance, Equipment Leasing, Vehicle Leasing, Family Law, Divorce, Matrimonial Law, Finance, Asset Based Finance, Financial Institution Reorganization, Financial Institutions Law, Financial Institutions Taxation, Financial Restructuring, International Commercial Finance, International Finance, Franchises and Franchising, Franchise Law, Franchise Licensing, Franchise Litigation, Franchise Taxation, International Franchising, General Practice, Federal Practice, Government, County Government Law, Federal Government Law, Government Affairs, Government Agency Practice, Government Relations, Legislative Practice, Local Government Law, Public Policy, Qui Tam Litigation, State Government Law, State Legislative Practice, Township Law, Government Contracts, Government Construction Contracts, Government Contract Arbitration, Government Contract Fraud, Government Procurement, International Government Contracts, Local Government Contracts, Public Bidding, Public Contract Law, Public Works

(This Listing Continued)

Blank Rome Comisky & McCauley LLP (Continued)

Contracts, Guardianship and Conservatorship, Health Care, Alternative Health Care Delivery System, Certificates of Need, Health Care Administration, Health Care Contracts, Health Care Corporate Law, Health Care Facility Licensing, Health Care Facility Regulation, Health Care Finance, Health Care Fraud, Health Care Legislation, Health Care Licensing, Health Care Mergers and Acquisitions, Health Care Regulation, Health Care Reimbursement, Health Care Taxation, Health Insurance, Health Insurance Coverage, Health Insurance Defense, Health Insurance Trusts, Health Law, Health Maintenance Organizations, Integrated Health Care Delivery Systems, Long Term Care, Managed Care, Managed Care Contracts, Medical Antitrust, Mental Health Law, Nursing Home Regulation, Pharmacy Law, Physicians Contracts, Hospital Law, Hospital Administration, Medical Staff Contracts, Medical Staff Credentialing, Housing Law, Affordable Housing, Apartment Projects, Housing Finance, Insurance, Commercial Insurance, Insurance Company Taxation, Insurance Litigation, Insurance Defense, Intellectual Property, Artistic Property, Chemical Intellectual Property, Electrical Intellectual Property, Intellectual Property Infringement, Intellectual Property Licensing, Intellectual Property Litigation, International Intellectual Property, International Licensing, Mechanical Intellectual Property, Medical Intellectual Property, Pharmaceutical Intellectual Property, Piracy, Proprietary Rights, Taxation of Intellectual Property, International Law, International Trade, Antidumping, Countervailing Duties, Customs Law, Export Regulation, Import and Export Law, International Trade Regulation, Latin America Trade, Russia Trade, Investments, Financial Services Law, Financial Services Regulation, Foreign Investment, Foreign Investment in the United States, International Investment, Investment Banking Law, Investment Company Law, Investment Partnerships, Investment Regulation, Labor and Employment, Affirmative Action, Collective Bargaining, Employee Drug Testing, Employer Liability, Employment at Will, Employment Contracts, Employment Discrimination, Employment Litigation, Employment Mediation, Executive Employment Law, Executive Severance Contracts, Fair Labor Standards, Family and Medical Leave Act, Federal Employment Law, Harassment, International Employment Contracts, International Labor Law, Labor Arbitration, Management Labor Law, National Labor Relations Act, Personnel Policies, Public Sector Collective Bargaining, Public Sector Labor Relations, Sexual Harassment, Unfair Labor Practices, Union Contract Negotiations, Union Elections, Union Organization, Wage and Hour Law, WARN Act, Workplace Violence, Wrongful Termination Defense, Leases and Leasing, Commercial Leasing, International Leasing, Landlord and Tenant Law, Lease Finance, Leasing, Leveraged Leasing, Office Leasing, Retail Leasing, Shopping Center Leasing, Legal Ethics and Professional Responsibility, Legal Ethics, Litigation, Civil Litigation, Complex Litigation, Defense Litigation, Federal Civil Litigation, Federal Litigation, International Litigation, Long-Arm Litigation, Trial Practice, U.S. Supreme Court Litigation, Newspaper Contracts, Publishing Contracts, Medical Malpractice, Medicare and Medicaid, Medicaid Planning, Medicare and Medicaid Reimbursement, Medicare Fraud and Abuse, Mergers, Acquisitions and Divestitures, Business Acquisitions, Business Divestitures, International Mergers and Acquisitions, Leveraged Acquisitions, Leveraged Buyouts, Merger Reorganization, Mergers and Acquisitions, Mergers and Acquisitions Finance, Mortgages, Commercial Mortgages, Mortgage Banking Law, Mortgage Bankruptcy, Mortgage Finance, Mortgage Foreclosure, Mortgage Insurance, Mortgage Lien Foreclosure, Mortgage Refinancing, Mortgage Securitization, Mortgage Tax, Mortgage Workouts, Secondary Mortgage Market, Municipal Bonds, Municipal Bonds Taxation, Municipal Contracts, Municipal Corporation Law, Municipal Derivative Products, Municipal Finance, Municipal Labor Law, Municipal Leasing, Municipal Pension Law, Municipal Redevelopment, Municipal Securities, Municipal Taxation, Tax Increment Finance, Natural Resources, Nonprofit and Charitable Organizations, Charitable Limited Partnerships, Charitable Organizations Law, Charitable Trusts and Foundations, Nonprofit Organizations Law, Nonprofit Tax Law, Private Foundations, Tax Exempt Organizations, Occupational Safety and Health, OSHA, Partnership Law, Family Limited Partnerships, Family Partnerships, Limited Liability Partnerships, Limited Partnerships, Partnership Dissolution, Partnership Formation, Partnership Organization, Partnership Syndication, Partnership Taxation, Patents, Biochemical Patents, Biotechnology Patent Prosecution, Biotechnology Patents, Chemical Patent Prosecution, Chemical Patents, Computer and Software Patents, Design Patents, Electrical Patent Prosecution, Electrical Patents, Electronic Patents, International Patents, Mechanical Patent Prosecution, Mechanical Patents, Medical Patents, Metallurgical Patents, Molecular Biology Patents, Patent Applications, Patent Infringement, Patent Interference Practice, Patent Licensing, Patent Litigation, Patent Prosecution, Patent Protection, Pharmaceutical Patents, Personal Injury, Premises Security, Probate, Ancillary Probate, International Probate, Probate Administration, Probate Litigation, Probate Taxation, Products Liability, Drug and Medical Device Defense, Firearms Products Liability, Professional Liability, Public Finance, Bond Finance, Economic Development, Housing and Urban Development, Industrial Development, International Economic Development, International Project Finance, Project Finance, Public Authority Finance, Public Finance Taxation, Public-Private Development, Tax Exempt Bonds, Tax Exempt Finance, Railway Labor Law, Real Estate, Condominium Association Law, Condominium Conversions, Condominium Development, Condominium Law, Conveyancing, Cooperative Association Law, Cooperative Conversions, Cooperative Housing Law, Easements, International Real Estate, Land Acquisitions, Land Sales, Land Trusts, Planned Unit Development Law, Real Estate Acquisitions, Real Estate Arbitration, Real Estate Banking Law, Real Estate Bankruptcy, Real Estate Brokers Licensing, Real Estate Contracts, Real Estate Development, Real Estate Finance, Real Estate Foreclosure, Real Estate Investment, Real Estate Investment Taxation, Real Estate Investment Trusts, Real Estate Joint Ventures, Real Estate Leasing, Real Estate Litigation, Real Estate Mediation, Real Estate Partnerships, Real Estate Restructuring, Real Estate Sales, Real Estate Secured Lending, Real Estate Securities, Real Estate Settlements, Real Estate Syndication, Real Estate Tax Appeals, Real Estate Tax Assessment, Real Estate Taxation, Real Estate Title, Real Estate Transfers, Real Estate Valuation, Real Estate Workouts, Real Property, Real Property Acquisitions, Real Property Development, Real Property Finance, Residential Real Estate, Residential Real Estate Development, Waterfront Development, Regulatory Law, Drug and Medical Device Regulation, Federal Regulatory Law, Regulated Industries, Regulatory Agency Practice, Regulatory Investigations, Religious Nonprofit Corporation Law, RICO, Securities, Bank Securities, Broker-Dealer Arbitration, Broker-Dealer Regulation, Initial Public Offerings, Private Placement, Private Placement Syndication, Public Offerings, SEC Enforcement, Securities Arbitration, Securities Litigation, Securities Offerings, Securities Registration, Securities Regulation, Shareholder Agreements, Shareholder Disputes, Tax Exempt Securities, Sports Contracts, Sports Licensing, Taxation, Employment Tax, Estate and Gift Taxation, Federal Income Tax, Federal Tax Controversies, Federal Taxation, Fiduciary Income Tax, Income Tax, Individual Taxation, International Tax Controversies, International Taxation, Like Kind Exchanges, Local Taxation, Low Income Housing Tax Credits, Property Tax Abatement, Property Tax Appeals, Sales and Use Tax, State Taxation, Tax Appeals, Tax Audits, Tax Collection, Tax Deferred Exchanges, Tax Planning, Tax Shelters, Trusts and Estates Taxation, Electronics, High Technology Contracts, Semiconductor Technology, Technology Contracts, Technology Licensing, Technology Protection, Technology Transfers, Torts, Trade Association Law, Toxic Torts, Trade Secrets, Theft of Trade Secrets, Trademarks, International Trademarks, Trade Dress, Trade Names, Trademark Arbitration, Trademark Infringement, Trademark Licensing, Trademark Litigation, Trademark Prosecution, Trademark Protection, Trademark Registration, Transportation, Common Carrier Law, Mass Transit Law, Public Transportation Law, Transit Labor, Trusts and Estates, Decedents Estates, Estate Administration, Estate Litigation, Estate Planning, Family Trusts, Family Wealth Transfer, Fiduciary Law, Fiduciary Liability, Fiduciary Litigation, Financial Planning, International Estate Planning, International Trusts, Living Trusts, Offshore Trusts, Personal Planning, Retirement Planning, Trust Administration, Trust Law, Trust Litigation, Trust Planning, Wealth Preservation, Unfair Competition, Utility Law, Utility Acquisitions, Utility Contracts, Utility Taxation, White Collar Crime, Embezzlement, White Collar Criminal Defense, White Collar Fraud, Wills, Contested Wills, Inheritance, Living Wills, Successions, Zoning, Planning and Land Use, Building and Public Safety Codes, Cemetery Law, Environmental Land Use, Fire Districts, Improvement Districts, Land Conservation, Land Development, Land Entitlement, Land Use, Land Use Litigation, Land Use Permitting, Land Use Regulation, Rezoning, Special Districts, Subdivisions, Water Districts, Zoning Law, Zoning Variances, Retail Industry Development.

Media, Pennsylvania Office: Rose Tree Corporate Center, 1400 N. Providence Road, Building 1, Suite 301, 19063. Telephone: 610-891-7800. FAX: 610-891-7804.

Philadelphia, Pennsylvania Office: One Logan Square, 19103-6998. Telephone: 215-569-5500. FAX: 215-569-5555.

Cherry Hill, New Jersey Office: Woodland Falls Corporate Park, 210 Lake Drive East, Suite 200, 08002-1164. Telephone: 856-779-3600. FAX: 856-779-7647.

Boca Raton, Florida Office: 1200 North Federal Highway, Suite 417, 33432. Telephone: 561-417-8100. FAX: 561-417-8101.

Allentown, Pennsylvania Office: 1620 Pond Road, Suite 200, 18104-2255. Telephone: 610-706-4300. FAX: 610-706-4343.

Wilmington, Delaware Office: Chase Manhattan Centre, 1201 Market Street, Suite 800, 19801. Telephone: 302-425-6400. FAX: 302-425-6464.

Trenton, New Jersey Office: 200 West State Street, 08608. Telephone: 609-278-2320. FAX: 609-278-2323.

Baltimore, Maryland Office: 250 West Pratt Street, Suite 1100, 21201. Telephone: 410-659-1400. FAX: 410-659-1414.

New York, New York Office: The Chrysler Building, 405 Lexington Avenue, 10174. Telephone: 212-885-5000. FAX: 212-885-5001.

(This Listing Continued)

Blank Rome Comisky & McCauley LLP (Continued)

Cincinnati, Ohio Office: PNC Center, 201 East Fifth Street, Suite 1700, 45202. Telephone: 513-362-8700. Fax: 513-362-8787.

See Professional Biographies, WASHINGTON, DISTRICT OF COLUMBIA

Blankenstein, Paul . . . . '46 '74 C.563 B.A. L.1009 J.D. [🄲 Gibson,D.&C.]
*PRACTICE AREAS: Litigation of Complex Commercial Cases.

Blankstein, Mitchell, (AV) '33 '58
C.273 B.A. L.309 LL.B. Gen. Coun., Parking Management, Inc.

Blanton, Alex . . . . '44 '73 C.869 B.S. L.128 J.D. [Dyer E.&J.]
*PRACTICE AREAS: Litigation; Maritime Law; Administrative Litigation; Shipbuilding and Repair; Appellate Practice.

Blase, Kurt E. . . . . '53 '79 C.160 B.A. L.276 J.D. [O'Connor&H.]
*PRACTICE AREAS: Environmental; Occupational Safety and Health.

Blaser, Thomas A. '74 '00 C.216 B.A. L.1194 J.D.
(adm. in MD; not adm. in DC) [🄰 Beveridge&D.]
*PRACTICE AREAS: Environmental Law.

Blasey, Ralph G., III . . . . '60 '87 C.228 B.A. L.575 J.D. [Baker&H.]
*PRACTICE AREAS: Litigation; Health Care.

Blasiak, James L., (AV) . . . . '51 '77 C&L.107 B.A., J.D. [McGuirewoods]
*PRACTICE AREAS: Energy Law; Utility Law.

Blask, Jerome K., (AV) . . . . '51 '80 C.216 B.A. L.276 J.D. [🄲 Kurtis&Assoc.]
*PRACTICE AREAS: Telecommunications Law.

Blassingame, Janet W. . . . . '52 '77 C.329 B.A. L.345 J.D. 1413 K Street, N.W.

Blaszak, James S., (AV) . . . . '46 '73 C.1105 B.A. L.846 J.D. [Levine,B.B.&B.]
*PRACTICE AREAS: Telecommunications Law; Administrative Law; Public Utility Law.

Blatch, Maralyn G. . . . . '42 '69 C&L.436 B.A., J.D. 7423 12th St., N.W.

Blatt, David S. . . . . '63 '90 C&L.976 B.A., J.D. [Williams&C.]
*PRACTICE AREAS: Banking Litigation; Commercial Litigation; Federal Civil Practice; Intellectual Property Litigation; Legal Professional Liability.

Blatt, Lisa Schiavo . . . . '65 '90 C&L.846 B.A., J.D. Sinclair Broadcast Group, Inc.

Blau, Russell M., (AV) . . . . '57 '82 C&L.309 A.B., J.D. [Swidler B.S.F.]
*PRACTICE AREAS: Telecommunications Competition; Telecommunications Regulation; Communications Finance.

Blauhut, Linda E. '65 '93
C.475 B.A. L.273 J.D. Asst. Gen. Coun., Paralyzed Vet. of Amer.

Blaya, Robbin K . . . . '68 '95 C.36 B.A. L.30 J.D. 625 Indiana Ave., N.W., 9th Fl.‡

Blaylock and Bleecker, Chartered, The Law Offices of
(See Bethesda, Maryland)

Blazek-White, Doris, (AV) . . . . '43 '69 C.289 B.A. L.276 J.D. [Covington&B.]

Blazer, John A., (AV) . . . . '48 '79 C&L.276 A.B., J.D. [🄲 Swartz&R.]

Blazina, Christine A. . . . . '69 '94 C.273 B.B.A. L.365 J.D. 1000 Navy Pentagon

Bleakley, Peter K., (AV) . . . . '36 '62 C&L.893 B.A., LL.B. [Arnold&P.]
*PRACTICE AREAS: Litigation; Products Liability; Antitrust and Trade Regulation.

Blecher, Melvin '22 '87 C.705 B.S. L.276 J.D.
4329 Van Ness Street, N.W., 2nd Floor (Pat.)

Blechman, William J., (AV) '57 '83
C.309 B.A. L.472 J.D. [Kenny N.S.A.C.&S.] (⊙Miami, FL)
*PRACTICE AREAS: Antitrust and Trade Regulation; Complex Commercial Litigation.

Bleeker, Ronald A., (AV) '49 '74
C&L.178 B.S., J.D. [Finnegan,H.F.G.&D.] (See Pat. Sect.)
*PRACTICE AREAS: Intellectual Property Litigation.

Bleicher, Samuel A., (AV) '42 '66 C.597 B.A. L.309 J.D.
[Miles&S.] (⊙Mc Lean, VA)
*PRACTICE AREAS: Environmental.

Bleichfeld, Howard S. . . . . '59 '91 C.188 B.S. L.1209 J.D. [🄲 Van Ness F.]
*PRACTICE AREAS: Environment; Clean Water Act; Wetlands Regulation; Clean Air Act.

Blevins, Don W. . . . . '63 '91 C&L.477 B.A., J.D. 3000 K St., N.W.

Blevins, J. Donald '28 '57 C&L.30 B.S., J.D.
(adm. in VA; not adm. in DC) 1819 H St., N.W., Ste. 500

Blier, William M. . . . . '58 '83 C.401 B.A. L.145 J.D. Asst. U.S. Atty.

Blinkova, Natalia V. '69 '99 C.976 B.A. L.276
(adm. in NY; not adm. in DC) [🄰 McDermott,W.&E.]

Bliss, Donald T., Jr., (AV) . . . . '41 '67 C.675 B.A. L.309 J.D. [O'Melveny&M.]
*PRACTICE AREAS: Aviation Law; Transportation Law; Healthcare Law; Appellate Litigation; Administrative Law.

Bliss, Richard W. . . . . '44 '68 C.205 B.A. L.273 LL.B. 1079 Papermill Ct., N.W.

Blitz, Gary P. . . . . '58 '84 C.477 B.B.A. L.569 J.D. [Piper M.R.&W.]
*PRACTICE AREAS: Financial Risks; Taxation; Insurance Law.

Blitz, James S., (AV) . . . . '57 '82 C.216 B.A. L.273 J.D. [Davis W.T.]
*PRACTICE AREAS: Cable Communications; Broadcast Television; Communications; Cable TV; Satellite Communications.

Bloch, Beate '28 '52 C.994 B.A. L.188 J.D.
(adm. in NY; not adm. in DC) 3001 Veazey Terr., N.W.‡

Bloch, David J. . . . . '— '93 C.178 B.A. L.659 J.D. [🄰 Reed S.]
*PRACTICE AREAS: Health Care.

Bloch, Richard I. . . . . '43 '69 C.197 A.B. L.477 J.D. 4335 Cathedral Ave., N.W.

Bloch, Robert E., (AV) . . . . '47 '73 C.264 B.A. L.273 J.D. [Mayer,B.&P.]

Bloch, Susan Low . . . . '44 '75 C.788 B.A. L.477 J.D. Prof., Georgetown Univ. Law Center

Block, Alan S., (BV) '66 '91 C.273 B.A. L.1209 J.D.
[🄲 Bonner K.T.&C.] (⊙Fairfax, VA)
*PRACTICE AREAS: Employment Litigation; Construction Litigation; Commercial Contracts; Commercial Litigation; Personal Injury.

Block, Brian A. '73 '98 C.659 B.A. L.1209 J.D.
(adm. in VA; not adm. in DC) [🄰 Firm of Larson-Jackson]

Block, Cheryl D. '55 '80 C.1019 B.A. L.107 J.D.
(adm. in NY; not adm. in DC) George Washington University

Block, Ellen G., (AV) . . . . '48 '75 C.1036 A.B. L.276 J.D. [Levine,B.B.&B.]
*PRACTICE AREAS: Telecommunications Law; Administrative Law; Litigation.

Block, Joseph G., (AV) . . . . '47 '72 C.477 B.A. L.309 J.D. [Venable,A.B.H.&C.]
*PRACTICE AREAS: Environmental Crimes; White Collar Crime; Internal Investigations; Environmental Auditing and Preventive Counseling; International Environmental Law.

Block, Lawrence P. . . . . '69 '95 C.183 B.A. L.273 J.D. [🄰 Morrison&H.]
*PRACTICE AREAS: Government Contracts; Bankruptcy Reorganization; Business Law; Commercial Litigation.

Block, Patricia L. '62 '99 C.651 B.A. L.180 J.D.
(adm. in MD; not adm. in DC) [🄰 Ropes&G.]
*PRACTICE AREAS: Business.

Block, Samuel B. . . . . '12 '37 L.537 LL.B. Asso. J., Supr. Ct.

Block, Stephen M. '36 '63 C.659 B.A. L.976 LL.B.
Staff Atty., ACLU of the National Capital Area

Block, Susan C. '50 '80 C.276 A.B. L.1068 J.D.
(adm. in CA; not adm. in DC) 620 Massachusetts Ave., N.E.‡

Blockinger, Jeffrey C. . . . . '— '97 C.679 B.A. L.472 J.D. [🄰 Morgan,L.&B.]

Blodgett, Timothy P. '66 '92 C.567 B.A. L.30 J.D.
(adm. in NY; not adm. in DC) [🄰 Krukowski&C.]
*PRACTICE AREAS: Labor and Employment Discrimination; Litigation.

Blonder, Seth J. '75 '01 C.1375 B.A. L.309 J.D.
(adm. in CA; not adm. in DC) [🄰 Wiley R.&F.]

Blondman, Mark '54 '80 C.659 B.S. L.378 J.D.
(adm. in MO; not adm. in DC) [Blank R.C.&M.] (⊙Phila., PA)
*PRACTICE AREAS: Age Discrimination; Sex Discrimination; Americans with Disabilities Act; Harassment; Sexual Harassment.
Blood, Laura .... '71 '97 C.896 B.A. L.846 J.D. [🄰 Wilmer,C.&P.]
Bloom, Adam S. .... '73 '00 C.477 B.A. L.273 J.D. [🄰 Buc&B.]
Bloom, Alan S. .... '65 '90 C.893 B.S. L.477 J.D. 1255 23rd St., NW
Bloom, Anne W. '62 '88 C.524 B.A. L.446 J.D.
(adm. in MD; not adm. in DC) Trial Lawyers for Public Justice, P.C.
Bloom, David I., (AV) .... '54 '78 C.103 A.B. L.976 J.D. [Mayer,B.&P.]
Bloom, Edward A., (AV) .... '58 '83 C&L.30 B.S., J.D. [Bell,B.&L.]
*PRACTICE AREAS: Real Estate; Corporate Law.
Bloom, Eric W. .... '62 '88 C&L.273 B.A., J.D. [Winston&S.]
*PRACTICE AREAS: Commercial Litigation; Criminal Litigation; Financial Institutions Litigation.
Bloom, Lauren M. .... '57 '86 C.976 B.A. L.128 J.D. Amer. Acad. of Actuaries
Bloom, Margaret L. '62 '91 C.273 B.A. L.128 J.D.
1250 Connecticut Avenue, N.W., Suite 700 (⊙Washington)
Bloom, Margaret L. '62 '91 C.273 B.A. L.128 J.D.
1250 Connecticut Avenue N.W., Suite 700 (⊙Washington)
Bloom, Peter M. ....'— '93 C.228 B.A. L.184 J.D. 701 Pennsylvania Avenue, N.W.
Bloom, Robert '22 '50 C.966 B.A. L.309 LL.B.
Gen. Coun., Fed. Retirement Thrift Invest. Bd.
Bloom, Sara Lynne '67 '92 C&L.378 B.A., J.D.
Asst. Gen. Coun., Washington Metropolitan Area Transit Authority
*RESPONSIBILITIES: Litigation.
Bloom, Sara Nelson .... '58 '83 C.112 B.A. L.1067 J.D. The NASDAQ Stock Market, Inc.
Bloomfield, Mark A. '49 '78
C.821 B.A. L.659 J.D. Pres., Amer. Coun. for Capital Formation
Bloomfield, Timothy J., (AV) .... '39 '67 C.918 B.A. L.893 LL.B. [Holland&K.]
*PRACTICE AREAS: Commercial Litigation; Construction Law; Antitrust and Trade Regulation.
Bloomquist, Christine E. ....'69 '95 C.299 B.A. L.910 J.D. [🄰 Morgan,L.&B.]
Bloomquist, Michael ....'69 '95 C.299 B.A. L.910 J.D. [🄰 Patton B.]

Blooston, Mordkofsky, Dickens, Duffy & Prendergast, (AV) [BB]
2120 L Street, N.W., Suite 300, 20037
Telephone: 202-659-0830 Fax: 202-828-5568
Email: jap@bloostonlaw.com URL: http://www.bloostonlaw.com
Members of Firm: Arthur Blooston (1914-1999); Harold Mordkofsky; Benjamin H. Dickens, Jr.; John A. Prendergast; Gerard J. Duffy; Richard D. Rubino. Of Counsel: Robert M. Jackson. Legislative Consultant: Perry W. Woofter (Not admitted in DC). Associates: David Cary Mitchell; Michael B. Adams, Jr.; Kathleen A. Kaercher (Not admitted in DC).
Practice is Limited to Telecommunications Law
See Professional Biographies, WASHINGTON, DISTRICT OF COLUMBIA

Blosser, Larry A., (AV) ....'46 '78 C.475 B.A. L.8 J.D. [🄲 Blumenfeld&C.]
*PRACTICE AREAS: Telecommunications.
Blouch, John W., (AV) .... '40 '69 C.976 B.A. L.273 J.D. [Jones&B.]
*PRACTICE AREAS: Securities Law; Corporate Law; Banking Law.
Blount, Gwendolyn A. '63 '89 C.228 B.A. L.245 J.D.
(adm. in GA; not adm. in DC) [Gray B.&Assoc.]
Blount, Sherri N. .... '55 '80 C.575 B.A. L.329 J.D. [Fitch,E.T.&F.]
*PRACTICE AREAS: Trademarks; Copyrights; Entertainment Law; New Media Law; Intellectual Property Licensing.
Blow, George, (AV) ....'28 '53 C.309 A.B. L.893 J.D. [Patton B.] ‡
Bloyd, Melissa M. ....'71 '96 C.884 B.S. L.273 J.D. Amer. Natl. Red Cross
Bloyer, Raymond K. '48 '78 C.488 B.A. L.362 J.D.
(adm. in FL; not adm. in DC) 35 Bryant St., N.E.‡
Blue, Elizabeth E. Appel ....'67 '94 C&L.976 B.A., J.D. [🄰 Jenner&B.]
Blue, Robert M. ....'67 '94 C.893 B.A. L.976 J.D. [🄰 Hogan&H.]
*PRACTICE AREAS: Civil Litigation; Insurance Litigation.

Bluestone Law International
(See Bethesda, Maryland)

Blum, Brian M. ....'63 '88 C.734 B.S.B.A. L.575 J.D. [Shaw P.]
*PRACTICE AREAS: Tax Law.
Blum, David E. .... '31 '58 C.165 B.A. L.309 J.D. 1401 16th St.
Blum, Dylana Leigh ....'73 '99 C.813 B.A. L.309 J.D. [🄰 Crowell&M.]
Blum, Jack A. ....'41 '67 C.65 B.A. L.178 J.D. [Lobel,N.&L.]
*PRACTICE AREAS: International Law and Taxation; Criminal Law; Money Laundering; Financial Fraud.
Blum, Jennifer L. ....'66 '95 C.856 B.A. L.128 J.D. [🄰 Drinker B.&R.]
Blum, Julie A. ....'60 '89 C.763 B.A. L.276 J.D. [🄲 Spriggs&H.]
*PRACTICE AREAS: Products Liability; Toxic Torts; Litigation; Drug and Medical Device Defense.
Blum, Royal I. ....'27 '55 C.273 L.30 LL.B. 601 Indiana Ave., N.W.‡
Blum, Steven '— '95 C.367 B.A. L.228 J.D.
(adm. in NJ; not adm. in DC) MCI Communications Corporation
Blum, William, Jr., (AV) '11 '42 C.659 B.S. L.276 J.D.
4201 Massachusetts Ave., N.W.‡
Blume, Jack P. .... '15 '37 C.563 B.S. L.569 LL.B. 4101 Cathedral Ave., N.W.‡
Blume, Robert C. ....'67 '93 C.103 B.A. L.276 J.D. [🄰 Gibson,D.&C.]
*PRACTICE AREAS: White Collar Crime; Litigation.
Blumenfeld, Jeffrey, (AV) ....'48 '73 C.103 A.B. L.659 J.D. [Blumenfeld&C.]
*PRACTICE AREAS: Antitrust; Telecommunications; Litigation.
Blumenfeld, Michael B. ....'59 '91 C.705 B.S. L.776 J.D. IRS Office of Chief Counsel
Blumenfeld, Norman L., (AV) '41 '66
C.188 B.A. L.976 LL.B. Suite 901, 1001 Connecticut Ave., N.W.
Blumenfeld, Sue D., (AV) ....'52 '77 C.1044 B.A. L.1292 J.D. [Willkie F.&G.]

Blumenfeld & Cohen, (AV) [BB]
1625 Massachusetts Avenue, N.W., Suite 300, 20036
Telephone: 202-955-6300 Facsimile: 202-955-6460
Email: info@technologylaw.com URL: http://www.technologylaw.com
Members of Firm: Jeffrey Blumenfeld; Gary M. Cohen; David M. Naseman (Not admitted in DC); Christy C. Kunin; Elise P.W. Kiely. Special Counsel: Larry A. Blosser; Michael D. McNeely. Associates: Jeremy D. Marcus (Not admitted in DC); Kristin L. Smith; Patrick J. O'Connor (Not admitted in DC).
Telecommunications, Communications Regulation, Antitrust, Economic and Business Regulation Legislation, Criminal Practice in State and Federal Courts, Trial and Appellate Litigation, Civil Litigation and Administrative Proceedings before State and Federal Agencies, Contract and Transactional Law.
See Professional Biographies, WASHINGTON, DISTRICT OF COLUMBIA

Blumenthal, Carol S., (AV) ....'51 '81 C.104 A.B. L.276 J.D. 1700 17th St., N.W.
Blumenthal, David A., (AV) '— '74
C.945 B.S. L.273 J.D. [Foley&L.] (See Pat. Sect.) (⊙L.A., CA)
*PRACTICE AREAS: Intellectual Property.
Blumenthal, Pamela Morris ....'— '95 C.188 B.S. L.477 J.D. [🄰 Hogan&H.]
*PRACTICE AREAS: Corporate and Securities; Commercial Practice.
Blumenthal, Susan G., (AV) .... '53 '80 C.477 B.A. L.930 J.D. [🄲 Steptoe&J.]
*PRACTICE AREAS: Estate Planning; Probate Administration; Trusts and Estates.
Blumenthal, William, (AV) .... '— '80 C.103 A.B. L.309 J.D. [King&S.]
*PRACTICE AREAS: Litigation and Trade.

Blumenthal, Paul S., P.A., Law Office of
(See Annapolis, Maryland)

Blunt, Jennifer M. ....'65 '91 C.821 L.180 J.D. [🄰 Kutak R.]
*PRACTICE AREAS: Complex Commercial Litigation; Securities; Antitrust; White Collar Crime.
Bly, William F. '64 '93 C.205 B.S./B.A. L.273 J.D.
(adm. in MD; not adm. in DC) [🄰 Cole,R.&B.] ⊙
*PRACTICE AREAS: Business Litigation; Communications Law; Entertainment Law; Regulatory Law; Public Policy.
Boalick, Scott R. .... '65 '99 C.659 B.S.E. L.276 J.D. [🄰 Fish&R.] (See Pat. Sect.)
Boardman, Deborah L. '74 '00 C.884 B.A. L.893 J.D.
(adm. in VA; not adm. in DC) [🄰 Hogan&H.]
Boardman, Ellen O. ....'57 '83 C&L.128 B.A., J.D. [O'Donoghue&O.]
Boardman, Michelle E. .... '— '99 C.103 B.A. L.145 J.D. [🄰 Wiley R.&F.]
Boardman, William J. '46 '72 C.454 B.S. L.588 J.D.
(adm. in MA; not adm. in DC) Pres., Concord Assocs., Inc.
Boasberg, James E. .... '63 '90 C&L.976 B.A., J.D. Asst. U.S. Atty.
Boatwright, Marc W. '65 '90 C.937 B.A. L.309 J.D.
(adm. in IL; not adm. in DC) Prison Fellowship Intl.
Bob, Rachel H. ....'74 '00 C.445 B.S. L.1002 J.D. [🄰 Jordan C.&S.]
*PRACTICE AREAS: Litigation; Insurance Defense.
Bobbish, Donna J. ....'57 '83 C.518 A.B. L.276 J.D. [🄲 Vinson&E.]
*PRACTICE AREAS: Energy Law; Energy Regulation.
Bobeck, Ann West '69 '98 C.918 B.A. L.273 J.D.
Staff Atty., National Association of Broadcasters
*RESPONSIBILITIES: Communications Law.
Bobeck, Joshua M. ....'67 '92 C.705 B.A. L.93 J.D. [🄰 Swidler B.S.F.]
*PRACTICE AREAS: Telecommunications.
Bocalandro, M. Laura ..... '55 '86 C.999 L.309 LL.M. Inter-American Development Bank
Bocchi, Linda Rosa '57 '80 C.1044 B.A.Econ. L.188 J.D.
V.P., Royalty Adm., Assoc. Gen. Coun., Recording Industry Assoc. of America, Inc.
Bock, Eric P. '57 '82 C.1074 B.S. L.809 J.D.
(adm. in CA; not adm. in DC) [Baise&M.]
*PRACTICE AREAS: Environmental Law; Natural Resources Law; Electric Utility Law; Public Policy.
Bockman, Jonathan ....'74 '00 C.188 B.S. L.174 J.D. [🄰 Morrison&F.] (Pat.)
*PRACTICE AREAS: Patents.
Bodansky, Robert L., (AV) .... '52 '78 C.823 A.B. L.273 J.D. [Nixon P.]
*PRACTICE AREAS: Business; Bankruptcy; Real Estate; Mergers and Acquisitions.
Boddie, Deborah D. '58 '88 C.446 B.S. L.329 J.D.
Admin. Law J., D.C. Dept. of Employ. Servs.
Boddy, Michele A. '63 '01 C.1042 B.S. L.1194 J.D.
(adm. in MA; not adm. in DC) [🄰 Beveridge&D.]
*PRACTICE AREAS: Environmental Law.
Bode, John W. '55 '83 C.623 B.A. L.1209 J.D.
(adm. in OK; not adm. in DC) [Olsson,F.&W.]
*PRACTICE AREAS: Agriculture Law; Food and Drug Law; Legislation.
Bode, William H., (AV) .... '42 '72 C.1070 B.S. L.273 J.D. [Bode&G.]
*PRACTICE AREAS: Environmental Law; Energy Law; Antitrust; Administrative Law; Intellectual Property.

Bode & Grenier, L.L.P., (AV)
1150 Connecticut Avenue, N.W., Ninth Floor, 20036
Telephone: 202-828-4100 Fax: 202-828-4130 Fax: 202-835-3219
Email: bodegrenier@bode.com URL: http://www.bode.com
Robert M. Beckman (1930-2000); William H. Bode; Peter C. Grenier; James M. Ludwig, III; Saul J. Singer; David H. Saffern. Associates: Clifton Merritt Mount; Marc Eric Pasekoff; Lori Jean Polacheck (Not admitted in DC); Darrin P. Sobin; Beth A. Bulgeron. Associate Counsel: William Conrad von Raab; John Umana. Of Counsel: Clark R. Silcox.
Antitrust, Commercial, Energy, Environmental, Intellectual Property, Internet/Technology, Complex Business Litigation, Insurance, Nationwide Civil Rights, Personal Injury, Wrongful Death, Real Estate, Construction.
See Professional Biographies, WASHINGTON, DISTRICT OF COLUMBIA

Bodendorf, Andrew F. '68 '98 C.228 B.S.E.E.
(adm. in VA; not adm. in DC; See Pat. Sect.) [🄰 Fish&R.]
*PRACTICE AREAS: Intellectual Property.
Bodenheimer, David Z. ....'55 '82 C&L.575 B.A., J.D. [Crowell&M.]
*PRACTICE AREAS: Government Contracts Law; Business Crimes Law; Litigation.
Bodensteiner, Dominic T. ....'60 '86 C.549 B.S. L.273 J.D. [Wiley R.&F.]
*PRACTICE AREAS: Business Law; Finance.
Bodner, John, Jr., (AV) ....'27 '53 C.188 L.597 J.D. [Howrey S.A.&W.]
*PRACTICE AREAS: Antitrust; Complex Litigation; Appellate Practice.
Bodner, Jordan N. ....'— '00 C.910 B.S.E.E. L.1209 J.D. [🄰 Banner&W.]
*PRACTICE AREAS: Intellectual Property Law; Electrical Intellectual Property; Patent Prosecution; Intellectual Property Litigation; Patents.
Bodoh, Devon M. ....'73 '98 C.477 B.B.A. L.215 J.D. [🄰 Dewey B.]
*PRACTICE AREAS: Federal Income Taxation; Corporate Taxation; Mergers and Acquisitions.
Bodor, Brian R. ....'70 '96 C.188 B.A. L.477 J.D. [🄰 Shaw P.]
Bodorff, Richard J., (AV) .... '49 '74 C.207 B.A. L.880 J.D. [Wiley R.&F.]
*PRACTICE AREAS: Communications.
Bodzin, Stephen A., (AV) ....'41 '67 C.347 B.S. L.477 J.D. 1156 15th St., N.W.
Boeckman, Ann M. ....'69 '98 C.612 B.S. L.128 J.D. [🄰 Hogan&H.]
*PRACTICE AREAS: Food Law; Administrative Law.
Boehler, Nicole B. '73 '99 C.339 A.B. L.273 J.D.
[🄰 Dillon,H.&L.] (⊙Stuttgart, Germany)
Boehlert, Garry R. '56 '81 C.893 B.A. L.945 J.D.
(adm. in VA; not adm. in DC) [Winston&S.]
*PRACTICE AREAS: Construction; Government Contracts; Litigation; Public-Private Development.
Boehling, D.E. ....'65 '91 C&L.893 B.A., J.D. [Levine,B.B.&B.]
*PRACTICE AREAS: Telecommunications Law; Administrative Law.
Boehm, Christine S. .... '69 '96 C.839 B.B.A. L.846 J.D. [🄰 Sullivan&W.]
*PRACTICE AREAS: Insurance Products; Mutual Funds.
Boehm, Steven B., (AV) ....'54 '78 C&L.705 B.A., J.D. [Sutherland A.&B.]
*PRACTICE AREAS: Securities Offerings; Investment Company Law; Investment Regulation; Venture Capital; SEC Enforcement.
Boese, John T., (AV) .... '47 '73 C.910 B.S. L.734 J.D. [Fried,F.H.S.&J.]
Bogan, Stephanie A. ....'74 '00 C.315 B.A. L.692 J.D. 1330 New Hampshire Ave., NW
Bogard, Lawrence J. ....'52 '77 C.881 A.B. L.276 J.D. [🄲 Neville,P.]
*PRACTICE AREAS: International Trade; Customs Law; Administrative Law.
Bogart, Amy L. ....'69 '99 C.65 B.A. L.94 J.D. [🄰 Greenberg T.]
Boger, William H., III '56 '83 C.608 B.A. L.851 J.D.
(adm. in OH; not adm. in DC) [Bingham D.]
*PRACTICE AREAS: Legislative Practice; Financial Institutions; Internet; Communications; Telecommunications Law.
Boggs, Bhavana S. ....'64 '91 C.390 B.A. L.1017 J.D. Sr. Coun., Marriott Intl, Inc.
*RESPONSIBILITIES: Labor and Employment Law.
Boggs, Carol Ann '62 '87 C.381 B.S. L.851 J.D.
(adm. in OH; not adm. in DC) LEXIS-NEXIS
Boggs, Douglas C. .... '67 '95 C.228 B.A. L.276 J.D. [🄲 Brobeck,P.&H.]
*PRACTICE AREAS: Corporate; Mergers and Acquisitions; Real Estate; Securities; Finance.
Boggs, George T., (AV) ....'47 '74 C.674 A.B. L.893 J.D. [Dickstein S.M.&O.]
*PRACTICE AREAS: International Business Law; International Law; Federal Taxation; International Taxation.

Boggs, J. Caleb, III '62 '87 C.692 B.A. L.180 J.D. [Ⓒ Blank R.C.&M.] (⊙Wilmington, DE; Phila., PA)
*PRACTICE AREAS: Government Relations; Legislative Practice.
Boggs, Thomas Hale, Jr., (AV) .... '40 '65 C&L.276 A.B., LL.B. [Patton B.]
Boggs, Virginia R. ....'70 '95 C.276 B.A. L.273 J.D. [Ⓐ Verner,L.B.M.&H.]
*PRACTICE AREAS: Legislative Practice; Federal Practice.
Bogorad, Cynthia Schneider, (AV) .... '53 '77 C.659 B.A. L.309 J.D. [Spiegel&M.]
*PRACTICE AREAS: Administrative Law; Antitrust; Energy; Litigation; Utility Law.
Bogorad, Saml. ....'06 '29 C&L.273 LL.B. 2501 Calvert St., N.W.‡
Bogorad, Stephen A., (AV) ....'59 '83 C.107 B.A. L.276 J.D. [Holland&K.]
*PRACTICE AREAS: Commercial Litigation; Bankruptcy Law.
Bohannon, Scott M. .... '69 '96 C.138 B.A. L.893 J.D. [Ⓐ Sidley A.B.&W.]
Bohlke, Gary L. .... '41 '67 C.911 B.A. L.30 J.D. [Duane,M.&H.]
*PRACTICE AREAS: International Law; Environmental Law; Corporate Law.
Bohman, John L. .... '51 '80 C.734 A.B. L.128 J.D. [O'Donoghue&O.]
Bohn, John W. .... '63 '93 C.976 B.A. L.893 J.D. [Ⓐ Dewey B.]
*PRACTICE AREAS: International Trade.
Bohr, Paul J. .... '66 '99 C.674 A.B. L.602 J.D. [Ⓐ Kirkland&E.]
*PRACTICE AREAS: Corporate Law; Mergers and Acquisitions; Private Equity; Venture Capital; Securities.

Boies, Schiller & Flexner LLP, (AV)
5301 Wisconsin Avenue, N.W., Suite 570, 20015 ⊙
Telephone: 202-237-2727 Facsimile: 202-237-6131
URL: http://www.bsfllp.com
Partners: David R. Boyd; Michael A. Brille; James P. Denvir, III; Donald L. Flexner; William A. Isaacson; Amy J. Mauser; Jonathan D. Schiller; W. Todd Thomas. Of Counsel: George T. Frampton, Jr.; Kimberly J. Tucker (Not admitted in DC). Resident Associates: Kevin R. Anthony (Not admitted in DC); Ellen Blanchard (Not admitted in DC); Kerri L. Boyer (Not admitted in DC); Dara Cacciamani (Not admitted in DC); Scott E. Gant; Seth A. Goldberg (Not admitted in DC); William C. Jackson (Not admitted in DC); Samuel C. Kaplan; Alfred P. Levitt; Carl John Nichols; Alison E. Peck (Not admitted in DC); Kenneth F. Rossman IV; Alanna Rutherford (Not admitted in DC); Jonathan Sherman; Hershel A. Wancjer (Not admitted in DC).
Litigation in all Federal and State Courts. Antitrust, Securities, Commercial and Banking Law, Bankruptcy, Criminal, Civil RICO, Appellate Practice, First Amendment and Civil Rights, Libel, Intellectual Property, Professional Liability, Employment, Environmental and Arbitration.
Armonk, New York Office: 80 Business Park Drive, Suite 110. Telephone: 914-273-9800. Facsimile: 914-273-9810.
Orlando, Florida Office: 390 North Orange Avenue, Suite 1890. Telephone: 407-425-7118. Facsimile: 407-425-7047.
Hollywood, Florida Office: 2435 Hollywood Boulevard. Telephone: 954-929-1190. Facsimile: 954-929-1185.
Hanover, New Hampshire Office: 26 South Main Street. Telephone: 603-643-9090. Facsimile: 603-643-9010.
Palm Beach Gardens, Florida Office: 11380 Prosperity Farms Road, Suite 110A. Telephone: 561-622-9700. Facsimile: 561-622-4400.
Albany, New York Office: 100 State Street, 12207. Telephone: 518-434-0600. Telecopier: 518-434-0665.
Oakland, California Office: 1970 Broadway, Suite 630, 94612. Telephone: 510-874-1000. Telecopier: 510-874-1460.
See Professional Biographies, WASHINGTON, DISTRICT OF COLUMBIA

Boinski, Patricia M. '51 '86 C.1047 B.A. L.273 J.D. (adm. in PA; not adm. in DC) Dir., Fed. Govt. Rel., ARCO
Boisture, Robert A. .... '52 '79 C.674 A.B. L.976 J.D. [Caplin&D.]
*PRACTICE AREAS: Tax Exempt Organizations Law.
Bokat, Stephen A., (AV) '46 '73 C.3 B.A. L.273 J.D. Sr. V.P. & Gen. Coun., U.S. Chamber of Comm.
Boland, Christopher T., (AV) ..... '15 '41 C.276 B.S. L.309 LL.B. [Ⓒ Gallagher,B.&M.]
*PRACTICE AREAS: Administrative Law; Energy; Utility Law.
Boland, Mark, (AV) ....'60 '85 C.321 B.A. L.128 J.D. [Sughrue M.] (See Pat. Sect.)
*PRACTICE AREAS: Intellectual Property Law; Litigation.
Boland, Michael J. '52 '87 C.128 B.C.E. L.273 J.D. (adm. in MD; not adm. in DC; Pat.) Asst. Gen. Coun., Potomac Electric Power Company
Boland, Sean F. X., (AV) ....'53 '78 C&L.276 A.B., J.D. [Howrey S.A.&W.]
*PRACTICE AREAS: Antitrust.
Boland, Thomas R., (AV) '36 '66 C.754 B.S. L.276 J.D. [Vorys,S.S.&P.] (See Pat. Sect.)
*PRACTICE AREAS: Intellectual Properties Law; Licensing Law; Trade Secret Law; Litigation.
Bolbach, Cynthia J. .... '47 '72 C.976 A.B. L.276 J.D. The Bureau of Natl. Affs., Inc.
Bolden, A. Scott ....'— '88 C.511 B.A. L.329 J.D. [Reed S.]
*PRACTICE AREAS: Litigation.
Bolek, Keith R. ....'72 '98 C.30 B.A. L.904 J.D. [Ⓐ O'Donoghue&O.]
*PRACTICE AREAS: Labor and Employment Law; ERISA.
Boles, James B. '69 '00 C.145 B.A. L.276 J.D. (adm. in MD; not adm. in DC) [Ⓐ Howrey S.A.&W.]
*PRACTICE AREAS: Commercial Litigation; Environmental Law.
Boley, Benjamin W., (AV) .... '34 '60 C.31 B.A. L.976 LL.B. [Shea&G.]
*PRACTICE AREAS: Employee Benefits; Corporate Law.
Bolger, Kathleen M. ....'61 '87 C.475 B.A. L.145 J.D. Gen. Coun., Forge Co.
Bolger, Robert J., Jr., (AV) '55 '82 C&L.893 B.A., J.D. [Venable,A.B.H.&C.] (⊙Balt., MD)
*PRACTICE AREAS: Business Law; Tax Law; Corporate Law; Technology Development; Emerging Businesses.
Bolkcom, Jerome V. .... '59 '89 C.589 B.A. L.352 J.D. [Jorden B.]
*PRACTICE AREAS: Life Insurance Class Actions; ERISA Litigation; Employee Benefits Counseling; Civil Rights Issues.
Bolling, Anne D. ....'57 '83 C.945 B.A. L.893 J.D. [Ⓐ Seyfarth S.]
*PRACTICE AREAS: Employee Benefits.
Bolling, Melinda M. .... '64 '98 C.277 B.S. L.128 J.D. [Ⓐ Gins&G.]
*PRACTICE AREAS: Bankruptcy Law; Insolvency Law; Commercial Litigation.
Bolling, Thomas Newton ....'60 '97 C.178 A.B. L.910 J.D. [Ⓐ Crowell&M.]
Bollini, Julia Alessandra ....'65 '94 C.112 B.A. L.30 J.D. Asst. Pub. Def.
Bollman, William H. .... '60 '93 C.205 B.E.E. L.273 J.D. [Manelli,D.&S.]
*PRACTICE AREAS: Patent Prosecution; Litigation; Design Patents; Trade Secrets; Trademarks.
Bolog, Erik D. .... '65 '91 C.1349 B.A. L.904 J.D. [Womble C.S.&R.]
*PRACTICE AREAS: Business Litigation; Professional Negligence; Civil Rights Litigation; Bankruptcy Litigation.
Bolton, Rhonda M. ....'— '96 C.326 B.S. L.945 J.D. [Ⓐ Steptoe&J.]
Bolton-Smith, Carlile, Jr. '37 '66 C.31 B.A. L.178 LL.B. V.P. & Secy., MCI WorldCom
Bolze, Ray S., (AV) ....'— '66 C.645 B.A. L.273 J.D. [Howrey S.A.&W.]
*PRACTICE AREAS: Antitrust; Complex Litigation; Energy.
Bomar, Anne E. '63 '91 C.188 B.A. L.945 J.D. (adm. in VA; not adm. in DC) Atty., Consolidated Nat. Gas Serv. Co.
Bonanno, Lisa ....'58 '83 C.276 B.S.F.S. L.976 J.D. [Hogan&H.]
*PRACTICE AREAS: Civil Litigation; Complex Litigation; Defense Litigation; Federal Civil Litigation; Federal Litigation.
Bonanno, Nona Jean '64 '90 C.128 B.A. L.329 J.D. [Ⓐ Martell,D.G.&G.] (⊙Rockville, MD)
Bonard, Glenn R., (AV) ....'43 '68 C.401 B.A. L.276 J.D. [Whiteford,T.&P.]
*PRACTICE AREAS: Business Law; Trusts and Estates; Taxation; Real Estate.

Bond, David M., (AV) ....'37 '66 C.446 B.S. L.273 LL.B. [Ⓒ Holland&K.]
*PRACTICE AREAS: Commercial Transactional Real Estate; Leasing; Condominium Law; Real Estate Sales.
Bond, Ferris R. ....'48 '74 C.208 B.A. L.796 J.D. [Bond,C.&N.]
Bond, Johanna E. ....'— '96 C.170 B.A. L.494 J.D. 600 New Jersey Ave., N.W.‡
Bond, Langhorne M., (AV) ....'37 '63 C&L.893 B.A., J.D. 1666 K St Nw # 1100
Bond, W. Michael, (AV) .... '56 '80 C.790 B.S. L.893 J.D. [Weil,G.&M.]
*PRACTICE AREAS: Real Estate; Securitization; Lending; Finance; Workouts and Restructurings.
Bond-Collins, Rhonda D. .... '60 '97 C.446 B.S. L.904 J.D. [Ⓐ Ballard S.A.&I.]
*PRACTICE AREAS: Public Finance; Real Estate.

Bond, Conte & Norman, P.L.L.C., (BV)
Suite 900, South Tower, 601 Pennsylvania Avenue, N.W., 20004
Telephone: 202-638-4100 Fax: 202-638-0062
URL: http://www.bondconte&norman
Ferris R. Bond; Joseph R. Conte; Jane Carol Norman.
Military Courts Martial, Military Administrative Law, Medical Malpractice Defense, Criminal Defense, Drug Crimes, Capital Crimes, Misdemeanors, Driving While Intoxicated, Business Fraud, White Collar Crime, Civil Practice, Small Business Law, Contracts, Wrongful Death, Personal Injury, Automobile Accidents and Injuries, Wrongful Termination, Employment Litigation, Terrorism Law, Federal Tort Claims.
See Professional Biographies, WASHINGTON, DISTRICT OF COLUMBIA

Bond, John
(See Fairfax, Virginia)

Bondareff, Joan M. ....'44 '75 C.273 B.A. L.904 J.D. [Ⓒ Dyer E.&J.]
*PRACTICE AREAS: Maritime Law; Environmental Law; Administrative Law.
Bonderman, Judith A. .... '44 '68 C.104 B.A. L.145 J.D. Catholic Univ. of Amer.
Bondi, Bradley J. ....'74 '99 C&L.260 B.S., J.D. [Ⓐ Williams&C.]
*PRACTICE AREAS: Litigation.
Bonds, Lorry B. ....'73 '98 C.302 B.A. L.329 J.D. [Ⓐ Cooper&Assoc.]
Bonello, John A. .... '66 '91 C.602 B.B.A. L.128 J.D. [Ⓐ McKenna&C.]
*PRACTICE AREAS: Commercial Litigation; Technology Law; Outsourcing; Software Licensing; Internet Law.
Boney, Kecia '65 '89 C.569 B.A. L.477 J.D. (adm. in PA; not adm. in DC) MCI Communications Corp.
Bonfiglio, Barbara Wixon .... '61 '88 C.446 B.S. L.64 J.D. [Williams&J.]
*PRACTICE AREAS: Government Contract Law; Administrative Law; Judicial Litigation; Construction Law; Federal and State Election Law.
Bonfiglio, Joel D., (BV) ....'58 '86 C.203 B.S. L.990 J.D. [Fleischman&W.]
Bonk, William A., III '64 '95 C.477 B.S.M.E. L.213 J.D. (adm. in MI; not adm. in DC; Pat.) [Ⓐ Dykema G.]
*PRACTICE AREAS: Intellectual Property.
Bonn, Denise ....'52 '77 C.1044 B.A. L.569 J.D. [Ⓒ Schmeltzer,A.&S.]
*PRACTICE AREAS: Health Care Law.
Bonner, Douglas G., (BV) .... '58 '83 C.105 B.A. L.128 J.D. [LeBoeuf,L.G.&M.]
*PRACTICE AREAS: Telecommunications; Litigation.
Bonner, Keith M., (AV) '54 '80 C.436 B.A. L.276 J.D. [Bonner K.T.&C.] (⊙Rockville, MD)
*PRACTICE AREAS: Medical Malpractice; Personal Injury; Product Liability; Construction; Toxic Torts.
Bonner, Leonard J., (BV) '38 '68 C.397 B.A. L.446 LL.B. 601 Pennsylvania Ave., N.W.
Bonner, Paul B. '70 '98 C.918 B.A. L.245 J.D. (adm. in VA; not adm. in DC) 2430 Wyoming Ave., N.W.
Bonner, Raymond A. ....'58 '87 C.446 B.A. L.569 J.D. [Sidley A.B.&W.]
Bonner, Robert C., (AV) ....'42 '66 C.446 B.A. L.276 J.D. [Gibson,D.&C.] (⊙L.A., CA)
*PRACTICE AREAS: White Collar Crime; Complex Business Litigation; Appellate Practice; Antitrust and Trade Regulation; Intellectual Property.
Bonner, Walter J., (AV) ....'— '55 C.128 A.B. L.276 LL.B. [Ⓒ Crowell&M.]
*PRACTICE AREAS: Complex Civil Litigation; Criminal Law; Trial Practice.

Bonner Kiernan Trebach & Crociata, (AV)
1250 Eye Street, N.W., 20005 ⊙
Telephone: 202-712-7000 FAX: 202-712-7100
URL: http://www.bktc.net
Members of Firm: John A. Kiernan (Resident, Boston, Massachusetts Office); Joseph S. Crociata; Barry D. Trebach; Keith M. Bonner; Michael D. Chefitz; Brian R. Ade (Certified Civil Trial Attorney, Supreme Court of New Jersey, Board on Trial Attorney Certification); Christopher E. Hassell; Stuart L. Peacock; Michael M. Hicks; Joseph J. Bottiglieri; Kenneth A. Schoen (At Parsippany, New Jersey and New York, New York Offices). Of Counsel: Andrew Butz; Alexander H. Gillespie; John P. Noyes; Ronald G. Guziak; Eric A. Spacek; Carolyn Israel Stein; Michael J. Smith; Tod W. Read; Hugh R. Curran; Alan S. Block. Associates: Alan G. White (Resident, Parsippany, NJ Office); Alan L. Korzen; Mary C. Commerton; Michele T. Oshman (Not admitted in DC); David C. Numrych; Sheri M. L. Collins; Anthony J. LaPorta; James Michael Dunphy, Jr. (Not admitted in DC); Stephen E. Hughes (Resident, Boston, MA Office); Felicity A. McGrath; William H. White Jr.; Kristin A. Sbarra (Resident, Boston, MA Office); Christopher L. Jefford; Ewan M. Clark; Musa L. Eubanks; Alison J. McGriff; Nadine D.Y. Adrian (Not admitted in DC); Jonathan E. Agin; Heather Shoaf Deane (Not admitted in DC); Jean-Marie Sylla, Jr.; Lucy C. Chiu; Shalini K. Kedia; Heather L. Parent (Not admitted in DC); Dana Denise M. Orquiza (Not admitted in DC).
General Civil Defense, Appellate and Trial Practice, Civil Mediation and Arbitrations, Product Liability, Malpractice, Property, Casualty, Insurance Law, Construction Litigation, Toxic and Environmental Litigation, Insurance Coverage Disputes, Railroad and Airline Litigation, Employment Law, Commercial Litigation and Counseling, Alternative Dispute Resolutions, Aviation, Computer Law, Technology Law, Consumer Fraud, White Collar Crime.
Rockville, Maryland Office: 51 Monroe Street. Telephone: 301-340-9155. Fax: 301-340-1310.
Fairfax, Virginia Office: 10511 Judicial Drive. Telephone: 703-691-0500. Fax: 703-591-5082.
Boston, Massachusetts Office: One Liberty Square. Telephone: 617-426-3900. Fax: 617-426-0380.
Parsippany, New Jersey Office: 140 Littleton Road, Suite 201. Telephone: 973-335-8480. Fax: 973-299-1337.
New York, New York Office: Empire State Building, Suite 3304. Telephone: 212-268-7535. Fax: 212-268-4965.
Providence, Rhode Island Office: 55 Pine Street. Telephone: 401-273-0100. Fax: 401-273-0101.
Hartford, Connecticut Office: 44 Capitol Avenue, Suite 402. Telephone: 860-249-9900. Fax: 860-246-3727.
See Professional Biographies, WASHINGTON, DISTRICT OF COLUMBIA

Bono, David A. .... '60 '87 C.228 B.A. L.309 J.D. [Harkins C.]
*PRACTICE AREAS: Litigation; Administrative Law; Regulated Industries.
Bono, Gaspare J., (AV) ....'50 '77 C.659 B.S. L.276 J.D. [Long A.&N.]
*PRACTICE AREAS: Antitrust; Complex Litigation; Commercial Litigation.
Bonomo, Philip A. .... '60 '97 C.446 B.S. L.276 J.D. [Ⓐ Leventhal,S.&L.]
*PRACTICE AREAS: Communications Law; Broadcasting Law; Satellite Communications.
Bonser, David W. ....'62 '87 C.228 B.S. L.846 J.D. [Hogan&H.]
*PRACTICE AREAS: Corporate Law; Securities Law.
Bonsignore, Richard P. .... '48 '75 C.323 A.B. L.421 J.D. [Ⓒ Akin,G.S.H.&F.]
*PRACTICE AREAS: Real Estate.
Boo, Shawn S., (Mr.) ...... '59 '84 C.923 B.A. L.659 J.D. Joint Oceanofraphic Insts., Inc.
Boochever, Stephen S., (AV) ....'56 '83 C.188 B.S. L.273 J.D. [Akin,G.S.H.&F.]
*PRACTICE AREAS: Health Care Law; Corporate Planning Law.
Boocker, Nancy E. '— '90 C.145 A.B. L.477 J.D. (adm. in IL; not adm. in DC) [Ⓐ Greenberg T.]
Boodman, Jeffrey R. ....'70 '99 C.910 A.B. L.276 J.D. [Ⓐ McKenna&C.]
Boog, Amanda L. .... '72 '99 C.859 B.S. L.208 J.D. U.S. Dept. of Justice, Tax Division
Bookey, Justin T. ....'66 '94 C.112 B.A. L.94 J.D. 2300 N St., N.W.
Bookhard, Bryan T. .... '— '98 C&L.329 B.A., J.D. 701 Pennsylvania Avenue, N.W.

Bookoff, Leslie I. '68 '93 C.446 B.S. L.659 J.D.
[A] Finnegan,H.F.G.&D.] (See Pat. Sect.)
*PRACTICE AREAS: Intellectual Property Portfolio Management; Intellectual Property Litigation; Mechanical Intellectual Property; Medical Intellectual Property; Patent Prosecution.
Bookshester, Steven A., (AV) .... '44 '76 C.174 B.A. L.30 J.D. 1771 N. St., N.W.
Booncharoen, Charlotte K. '72 '99 C.477 B.A. L.273 J.D.
(adm. in NY; not adm. in DC) [A] Lotstein B.]
*PRACTICE AREAS: Mortgage Banking.
Boone, Robert E., Jr. .... '40 '65 C&L.16 B.S., LL.B. [C] Wiley R.&F.]
Boone, Theodore S. .... '61 '88 C.339 B.A. L.178 J.D. [C] Arnold&P.]
*PRACTICE AREAS: Commercial Transactions.
Boorman, Ilene Baxt .... '60 '89 C.273 B.B.A. L.276 J.D. [Wilkes A.]
*PRACTICE AREAS: Real Property Tax Assessment Law; Condemnation; Construction Law.
Boot, Kevin Patrick '71 '01 C.352 B.A. L.273 J.D.
(adm. in NY; not adm. in DC) [A] Keller&H.]
*PRACTICE AREAS: Food and Drug Regulation; International Regulatory Law; Litigation.
Boote, Richard H. .... '48 '76 C.893 B.A. L.1162 J.D. 3125 38th St., N.W.
Booth, Christine W. .... '52 '89 C.477 A.B. L.930 J.D. KPMG Peat Marwick
Booth, Dawn R. '61 '91 C.674 B.A. L.893 J.D.
(adm. in NY; not adm. in DC) Sr. Coun., Marriott Intl., Inc.
*RESPONSIBILITIES: International; Contracts; Banking; Finance; Corporate.
Booth, Emily J. .... '74 '99 C.276 B.A. L.1017 J.D. [A] Kirkpatrick&L.]
*PRACTICE AREAS: Mortgage Banking.
Booth, James A. '46 '91 C.999 B.A. L.472 J.D.
(adm. in FL; not adm. in DC) USDA-Off. of Gen. Couns.,
Booth, Karyn A. .... '67 '93 C.354 B.S. L.823 J.D. [Thompson H.]
*PRACTICE AREAS: Transportation; Maritime Law; Administrative Law; Legislative.
Booth, Paul M. '59 '96 C.999 B.Sc. L.276 J.D.
[C] Heller E.W.&M.] (Pat.) (⊙Gaithersburg, MD)
Booth, Freret, Imlay & Tepper, P.C., (AV) ....5101 Wisconsin Ave., N.W. Ste 307
Boothby, Colleen L., (AV) .... '55 '80 C.668 A.B. L.1066 J.D. [Levine,B.B.&B.]
*PRACTICE AREAS: Telecommunications Law.
Boothby, Lee, (AV) .... '33 '57 C.243 L.912 J.D. [Boothby&Y.] ⊙
Boothby & Yingst, (AV) .... 4545 42nd St., N.W. (⊙Berrien Springs, MI)
Boothe, Jeffrey F. .... '55 '87 C.813 B.A. L.1209 J.D. [Holland&K.]
*PRACTICE AREAS: Health Care; Legislative Practice; Transportation; Federal Regulatory Law.
Booye, Sherri L. .... '51 '98 C&L.446 B.S., J.D. [A] Skadden,A.S.M.&F.]
Boozer, Travis P. '72 '98 C.228 B.A. L.280 J.D.
(adm. in FL; not adm. in DC) [A] Morgan,L.&B.]
Bopp, James, Jr., (AV) '48 '73 C.347 B.A. L.260 J.D.
(adm. in IN; not adm. in DC) [C] Webster,C.&B.] (⊙Terre Haute, IN)
*PRACTICE AREAS: Constitutional Law; Civil Litigation; Non-Profit Corporations Law; Election Law; Appeals.
Boppana, Aruna K. .... '— '01 C.188 B.A. L.880 J.D. [A] Arnold&P.]
Bor, M. Hossein ... '50 '88 C.30 Ph.D. L.273 M.C.L. [C] Entwistle&C.] (⊙New York, NY)
Bor, Victoria L., (AV) .... '52 '80 C.966 B.A. L.178 J.D. [Sherman,D.C.L.&Y.]
*PRACTICE AREAS: Labor and Employment Law; Union Labor Law.
Borababy, George M. .... '50 '79 C.188 B.A. L.309 J.D. [Patton B.]
Borak, Rachel D. '— '99 C.339 B.A. L.273 J.D.
(adm. in IL; not adm. in DC) [A] Foley&L.]
*PRACTICE AREAS: Financial Services; Bankruptcy.
Boraks, Robert A. W., (AV) ....'43 '68 C.659 B.S. L.273 J.D. [Garvey,S.&B.]
*PRACTICE AREAS: Criminal Law; Securities Law; Commodities Law; Malpractice; Negligence Law.
Borchert, John Witherspoon .... '74 '00 C.610 B.A. L.1365 J.D. [A] Crowell&M.]
Borden, George A. .... '61 '89 C.674 A.B. L.309 J.D. [Williams&C.]
*PRACTICE AREAS: Appellate Practice; Civil Practice; Class Action Defense; Commercial Litigation; Intellectual Property Litigation.
Borden, Neal D., (AV) '41 '66 C.309 A.B. L.446 LL.B.
(adm. in MD; not adm. in DC) [Venable,A.B.H.&C.] (⊙Balt., MD)
*PRACTICE AREAS: Franchise and Distribution Law; Corporate Law; Federal Taxation; State Taxation.
Borders, Brian T. .... '50 '80 C.870 B.S. L.1065 J.D. [C] Mayer,B.&P.]
*PRACTICE AREAS: Federal Regulation and Legislation; Securities Regulatory Policy and Controversies.
Boretsky, Askold ....'51 '91 C.119 B.A. L.128 J.D. 2814 University Ter., N.W.
Borgen, Lori Outzs '69 '96 C.309 B.A. L.178 J.D.
(adm. in NJ; not adm. in DC) Staff Atty., Lawyers Com. for Civil Rights Under Law
*RESPONSIBILITIES: Public Interest Law.
Borghesani, William H., Jr., (AV) .... '31 '57 C&L.93 J.D. [Keller&H.]
*PRACTICE AREAS: Transportation Law; Telecommunications Law; Environmental Law.
Borja, Mary E. .... '69 '93 C.367 B.A. L.472 J.D. [Wiley R.&F.]
*PRACTICE AREAS: Litigation; Insurance.
Borja, Paul D. .... '60 '90 C.602 B.B.A. L.273 J.D. [Kutak R.]
*PRACTICE AREAS: Corporate Law; Securities Law; Banking Law; Taxation Law.
Borke, Susan, (AV) '59 '86
C.659 B.S. L.831 J.D. Dep. Gen. Coun., Natl. Geographic Soc.
*RESPONSIBILITIES: Entertainment; Contracts; Intellectual Property; Rights Management.
Borman, Keith T. .... '48 '73 C.605 B.A. L.477 J.D. [Shook,H.&B.]
*PRACTICE AREAS: Products Liability.
Borman, Lance H., Jr. '70 '00 C.259 B.S. L.180 J.D.
(adm. in FL; not adm. in DC) 231 F St., N.E.
Born, Brooksley, (AV) .... '40 '66 C&L.813 A.B., J.D. [Arnold&P.]
*PRACTICE AREAS: Derivatives; Civil Litigation.
Bornstein, Katherine B. '75 '01 C.446 B.A. L.1365 J.D.
(adm. in MD; not adm. in DC) [A] Provost&U.]
*PRACTICE AREAS: Products Liability; Toxic Torts; Employment Discrimination.
Bornstein, Theodore H. .... '— '78 C.910 B.A. L.146 J.D. [Foley&L.]
*PRACTICE AREAS: Legislative Practice; Regulatory Law; Public Affairs.
Boros, Howard S., (AV) .... '29 '55 C.569 B.A. L.976 J.D. [C] Boros&G.]
Boros, Joan E. .... '36 '80 C.273 B.A. L.446 J.D. [Jorden B.]
*PRACTICE AREAS: Securities Law; Financial Services; Mutual Funds; Insurance Products; Corporate.

Boros & Garofalo, P.C., (AV)
Suite 550, 1201 Connecticut Avenue, N.W., 20036
Telephone: 202-822-9070 Cable Address: "Airlaw" Telecopier: 202-822-9075
Email: mail@bgairlaw.com
Gary B. Garofalo; Aaron A. Goerlich; Don H. Hainbach. Associates: Katherine M. Aldrich; John R. Copley; Victor H. Smith. Of Counsel: Howard S. Boros (Retired); R. Evan Smith (Not admitted in DC); Gregory S. Winton; Pierre E. Murphy.
Administrative Practice. Aviation, International, Transportation and Litigation. Corporation Law.
See Professional Biographies, WASHINGTON, DISTRICT OF COLUMBIA

Borovas, George .... '— '98 C.966 B.S. L.273 J.D. [A] Morgan,L.&B.]
Borowski, Irwin M., (AV) ....'35 '61 C.102 B.A. L.569 LL.B. 2415 20th St., N.W.
Borrasca, Adelia S., (BV) .... '48 '83 C.16 B.A. L.276 J.D. [C] Heller E.W.&M.]
*PRACTICE AREAS: Energy; Legislative.
Borrello, Ralph T. '58 '83 C.107 B.A. L.229 J.D.
(adm. in PA; not adm. in DC) V.P. & Tr. Offr., Security Tr. Co., N.A.
Bortz, Jason K. .... '69 '98 C.299 B.A. L.188 J.D. [A] Caplin&D.]
*PRACTICE AREAS: Employee Benefits Law; Tax.
Borzi, Phyllis C., (AV) .... '46 '78 C.999 B.A. L.128 J.D. [C] O'Donoghue&O.]
*PRACTICE AREAS: Employee Benefits (ERISA); Health Law.

Boscarino, Gina M. .... '74 '97 C.665 B.A. L.273 J.D. [A] Womble C.S.&R.]
*PRACTICE AREAS: Employee Benefits; Pensions; Executive Compensation; Health Care; Exempt Organizations.
Bosch, Michele C. '68 '93
C.893 B.A. L.945 J.D. [A] Finnegan,H.F.G.&D.] (See Pat. Sect.)
*PRACTICE AREAS: Pharmaceutical Patents; Chemical Patents; Biochemical Patents; Patent Interference Practice; Patent Prosecution.
Bosco, Joseph A., (AV) .... '38 '66 C&L.309 A.B., LL.B. 1150 Connecticut Ave.
Bosco, Mary Elizabeth .... '56 '83 C.976 B.A. L.273 J.D. [Patton B.]
Bose, Monica Jahan .... '64 '91 C.918 B.A. L.178 J.D. [A] Arnold&P.]
*PRACTICE AREAS: Environmental.
Bose, Sanjoy K. .... '64 '92 C.611 B.A. L.945 J.D. [Akin,G.S.H.&F.]
*PRACTICE AREAS: Corporate; Project Finance; Banking; Technology.

Bose Law Firm, PLLC
(See Arlington, Virginia)

Bose McKinney & Evans LLP, (AV)
700 North One Lafayette Centre, Suite N 700, 1120 20th Street, N.W., 20036 ⊙
Telephone: 202-973-1229 Fax: 202-973-1212
URL: http://www.boselaw.com
George Thomas Patton, Jr.
General Civil Practice in all Courts including Agricultural Law, Antitrust, Appellate Practice, Capital Strategies, Civil Rights, Commercial Law, Communications and Media, Constitutional Law, Corporate Law, Creditors Rights, Creditors Rights in Bankruptcy, Debtor Bankruptcy, Education Law, Employee Benefits, Entertainment and the Arts, Entrepreneurial Services, Environmental Law, Finance, Financial Institutions Law, Government Contracts, Government Relations, High Technology, Insurance, Intellectual Property, International Law, Labor and Employment, Legislative Practice, Litigation, Mergers and Acquisitions, Municipal Finance, Municipal Law, Planning and Land Use, Probate, Real Estate, Regulated Industries, Regulatory Agency Practice, Securities, Taxation, Trusts and Estates, Utility Law, Wills and Zoning.
Representative Clients: Duke Realty Corporation; Emmis Communications Corporation.; First Indiana Bank; Indianapolis Colts, Inc.; Hillenbrand Industries, Inc.; Indiana Bankers Assn.; Metropolitan Life Insurance Co.; Thomson Multimedia, Inc.; WOWemployers, Inc.; USX Corp.
Indianapolis, Indiana Offices: 2700 First Indiana Plaza, 135 North Pennsylvania Street, 46204. Telephone: 317-684-5000. Facsimile: 317-684-5173.
Indianapolis North Office: Suite 500, 600 East 96th Street, 46240. Telephone: 317-574-3700. Facsimile: 317-574-3716.
See Professional Biographies, WASHINGTON, DISTRICT OF COLUMBIA

Bosek, Ruth A., (AV) .... '49 '85 C.201 B.A. L.276 J.D. [Bosek]
*PRACTICE AREAS: Energy Law.

Bosek Law Firm, (AV)
1090 Vermont Avenue, N.W. Suite 800, 20005
Telephone: 202-326-5256 Fax: 202-289-7624
Email: rbosek@boseklaw.com
Ruth A. Bosek.
Administrative Law Practice before the Federal Energy Commission, Oil and Natural Gas Pipeline Law, Rate Structuring and Tariff Issues.
See Professional Biographies, WASHINGTON, DISTRICT OF COLUMBIA

Boskey, Bennett, (AV) '16 '40 C.951 A.B. L.309 LL.B.
1800 Massachusetts Avenue, N.W., Suite 600, 20036
Telephone: 202-737-6580 Fax: 202-737-6966
Email: BennettBos@aol.com
General Practice.
See Professional Biographies, WASHINGTON, DISTRICT OF COLUMBIA

Bosley & Hutzelman, P.C.
(See Alexandria, Virginia)

Boss, Brandon '73 '98 C.546 B.A. L.861 J.D.
(adm. in LA; not adm. in DC; See Pat. Sect.) [A] Smith,G.&R.]
*PRACTICE AREAS: Patent; Trademarks.
Boss, Lenard B., (AV) .... '60 '85 C.67 B.A. L.273 J.D. [Asbill,J.M.&B.]
*PRACTICE AREAS: Appellate Practice; Criminal Law; Drugs and Narcotics; Litigation; White Collar Crime.
Bosset, Eric C. .... '62 '87 C.118 B.A. L.976 J.D. [Covington&B.]
Bostick, George H., (AV) ....'44 '73 C.1365 B.A. L.893 J.D. [Sutherland A.&B.]
*PRACTICE AREAS: Employee Benefits; Executive Compensation; Taxation; ERISA.
Boston, Ellis A. ....'37 '74 C.446 B.A. L.64 J.D. D.C. Bd. of Educ.
Bostwick, Dwight P. .... '60 '89 C.813 B.A. L.267 J.D. [Baach R.&L.P.]
*PRACTICE AREAS: Litigation; White Collar Criminal.
Bostwick, Phillip D., (P.C.) ....'33 '62 C.813 A.B. L.309 J.D. 2300 N. St. NW
Boswell, Donna A., (BV) .... '50 '89 C.896 B.A. L.659 J.D. [Hogan&H.]
*PRACTICE AREAS: Health Law; Health Care Legislation; Medical Records Confidentiality; Health Care Reimbursement; Patients Rights.
Boswell, Mary Jane, (AV) ... '57 '86 C.880 B.E./E.E. L.209 J.D. [C] Morgan,L.&B.] (Pat.)
Both, Charles R., (AV) .... '43 '68 C.188 B.S. L.276 J.D. [Yablonski,B.&E.]
Bothell, Allison G. .... '72 '98 C.276 B.A. L.911 J.D. [A] Morrison&F.]
Botticelli, Catherine .... '63 '88 C&L.262 B.A., J.D. [Dechert]
*PRACTICE AREAS: Securities Litigation; Commercial Litigation.
Bottiglieri, Joseph J. '61 '87 C.754 B.S. L.128 J.D.
[Bonner K.T.&C.] (⊙Parsippany, NJ)
*PRACTICE AREAS: Products Liability; Medical Malpractice; Errors and Omissions.
Botvin, Victoria L. ....'69 '95 C.477 B.A. L.831 J.D. Assoc. Coun., U.S. House of Rep.
Bou, Edward C., (AV) .... '30 '58 C.659 B.S. L.30 LL.B. [E.C.Bou]
Bou, Lawrence K. .... '64 '92 C.855 B.A. L.904 J.D. 1700 K St., N.W.
Bou, Stephen A. .... '60 '85 C.207 B.A. L.128 J.D. 1700 K St., N.W.
Bouchard, Stephen A. .... '58 '82 C&L.846 B.B.A., J.D. [Fleischman&W.]
Boucher, Jamie L. .... '62 '96 C.604 B.A. L.276 J.D. [A] Skadden,A.S.M.&F.]
*PRACTICE AREAS: International.
Boucher, Michael .... '65 '94 C&L.276 A.B., J.D. [A] McKenna&C.]
*PRACTICE AREAS: Environmental Law; Environmental Litigation; Environmental Auditing; International Environmental Law; Joint Ventures.
Bou, Edward C., P.C., (AV) .... 1700 K St., NW
Boughner, Stephen T. '71 '98 C&L.8 B.S.E.E., J.D.
(adm. in OH; not adm. in DC; See Pat. Sect.) [A] Staas&H.]
*PRACTICE AREAS: Intellectual Property; Patents; Trademarks; Copyrights.
Bouknight, J. A., Jr., (AV) .... '44 '68 C.968 A.B. L.228 J.D. [Steptoe&J.]
*PRACTICE AREAS: Energy; Antitrust; Litigation.
Bouma, Herman B. .... '50 '79 C.114 B.A. L.846 J.D. [Caplin&D.]
*PRACTICE AREAS: International Taxation.
Bouquet, Christopher C. .... '61 '94 C.902 B.A. L.273 J.D. [A] McKenna&C.]
*PRACTICE AREAS: Government Contracts; Commercial Contracts.
Bourdeau, Karl S., (AV) .... '53 '78 C.529 B.S. L.309 J.D. [Beveridge&D.]
*PRACTICE AREAS: Environmental Law; Environmental Litigation; International Environmental Law.
Bourgault, Dennis P. .... '62 '88 C.684 B.A. L.93 J.D. Doolittle's Ltd.
Bourgeois, Julien M. '76 '01 C.055 L.1509 J.D.
(adm. in MD; not adm. in DC) [A] Dechert]
*PRACTICE AREAS: Investment Management; Financial Services Law.
Bourgeois, Ray M. '50 '75 C&L.500 B.A., J.D.
(adm. in MI; not adm. in DC) 1322 Patterson Avenue, S.E., Suite 1000
Bouton, Alexandre B. .... '63 '90 C&L.446 B.A., J.D. [A] Technology]

Boutrous, Theodore J., Jr. '60 '87 C.36 B.S. L.1049 J.D. [Gibson,D.&C.] (⊙L.A., CA)
*PRACTICE AREAS: Appellate Litigation; Media Law; Constitutional Law; Libel, Slander and Defamation; Legal Ethics and Professional Responsibility.
Bowcut, Brian Eugene '— '01 C.877 B.A. L.228 J.D. (adm. in MA; not adm. in DC) 555 12th St. NW
Bowden, Alan C. ...... '68 '98 C.886 B.S. L.209 J.D. [[A] Carr,M.&G.]
*PRACTICE AREAS: Business Law; Corporate Law; Civil Litigation.
Bowditch, Mark I. .... '63 '93 C&L.273 B.S., J.D. [[C] Rothwell,F.E.&M.] (See Pat. Sect.)
Bowe, James F., Jr., (AV) ...... '55 '82 C.951 B.A. L.597 J.D. [Dewey B.]
*PRACTICE AREAS: Energy; Project Finance.
Bowe, Richard W. ...... '49 '76 C.674 A.B. L.30 J.D. 5100 Wisconsin Ave., NW
Bowen, Vincent ...... '61 '86 C.93 B.A. L.273 J.D. [[A] White&C.]
Bower, David I. ...... '54 '79 C.205 B.A. L.659 J.D. [Weil,G.&M.]
Bower, Jean R. ...... '35 '70 C.881 A.B. L.276 J.D. 2500 Q St., N.W.
Bowers, Albert D. '41 '70 C.597 B.A. L.280 J.D. (adm. in NY; not adm. in DC) 1919 Pennsylvania Ave., N.W.
Bowers, Christopher P. ...... '72 '99 C.262 B.A. L.145 J.D. [[A] Wilmer,C.&P.]
Bowers, Josh F. ...... '53 '86 C.33 B.A. L.1162 J.D. [J.F.Bowers]
*PRACTICE AREAS: Employment Discrimination.
Bowers, Lynn A. ...... '56 '94 C.33 B.A. L.276 J.D. [[A] Slevin&H.]
*PRACTICE AREAS: Employee Benefits.

Bowers, Josh F., P.C.
1090 Vermont Avenue, N.W., Suite 500, 20005
Telephone: 202-408-8360
Email: jbdclaw@aol.com URL: http://www.lawyers.com/federal_employment_law
Josh F. Bowers.
An Employment practice limited to the representation of Federal Employees: Wrongful Termination, Harassment, Employment discrimination, Employee Rights, Wage and Hour Law, Whistleblower Defense, Family Medical Leave Act, Personal Injury, Automobile Accidents, Wrongful Death, Defective Products.
See Professional Biographies, WASHINGTON, DISTRICT OF COLUMBIA

Bowker, David W. '70 '99 C.1097 B.A. L.1066 J.D. (adm. in CA; not adm. in DC) Legal Advsr. Off.
Bowles, John Laing, Jr. '64 '91 C.880 B.A. L.128 J.D. Dir., Amer. Consulting Engineers Council
Bowles, Judson W. ...... '11 '34 C&L.276 J.D. 2934 Garfield St., N.W.‡
Bowling, G. Daniel, (BV) ...... '43 '71 C.269 B.A. L.309 LL.B. 3227 Klingle Rd., NW
Bowman, Gregory W. ...... '67 '94 C.923 B.A. L.597 J.D. [[A] Baker&M.]
*PRACTICE AREAS: Trade Regulations; Customs Law; NAFTA Trade; Administrative Law.
Bowman, Quinton V. '56 '85 C.870 B.S. L.893 J.D. (adm. in VA; not adm. in DC) V.P., Human Res. & Litig., Black Entertainment Television, Inc.★
*RESPONSIBILITIES: Employment Law; Litigation.
Bowman, Terri L. ...... '68 '93 C.475 B.A. L.273 J.D. [[A] Dechert]
*PRACTICE AREAS: Antitrust and Trade Regulation.
Bowman, William J., (AV) ...... '51 '76 C.309 A.B. L.276 J.D. [Hogan&H.]
*PRACTICE AREAS: Litigation.
Bowser, Renee Luvonia '49 '83 C.104 A.B. L.574 J.D. (adm. in PA; not adm. in DC) Asst. Gen. Coun., United Food & Comercial Workers International Union
Bowsher, David K. ...... '73 '00 C.103 A.B. L.228 J.D. [[A] Wilmer,C.&P.]
Bowsher, Marina K. ...... '71 '98 C.705 B.A. L.597 J.D. [[A] Ballard S.A.&I.]
*PRACTICE AREAS: Litigation.
Bowsher, Matthew R. '73 '98 C.477 A.B. L.597 J.D. (adm. in OH; not adm. in DC) [[A] Bingham D.]
*PRACTICE AREAS: Commercial Real Estate.

Bowytz, Savit & Szymkowicz, LLP
(See Bethesda, Maryland)

Boxerman, Samuel B. ...... '61 '87 C.339 B.A. L.309 J.D. [Sidley A.B.&W.]
Boyack, Andrea J. ...... '68 '97 C.101 B.A. L.893 J.D. [[A] Fried,F.H.S.&J.]
*PRACTICE AREAS: Finance.
Boyce, Bret T. ...... '— '95 C.976 B.A. L.597 J.D. 1800 M St. N.W.
Boyce, Gilbert W. ...... '— '88 C.329 B.B.A. L.128 J.D. [Kutak R.]
*PRACTICE AREAS: Litigation; Securities Law; Taxation Law.
Boyce, Katharine R. ...... '49 '80 C.938 B.A. L.128 J.D. [Patton B.]
Boyd, Alan M., (BV) ...... '59 '84 C.446 B.A. L.273 J.D. Asst. U.S. Atty.
Boyd, Alan S. '22 '47 C.260 L.893 LL.B. (adm. in VA; not adm. in DC) 1825 Eye St., N.W.
Boyd, Benjamin S. ...... '61 '87 C&L.45 B.S.B.A, J.D. [Piper M.R.&W.]
*PRACTICE AREAS: Business Litigation; Products Liability Law.
Boyd, David R., (AV) ...... '46 '73 C.880 B.A. L.893 J.D. [Boies,S.&F.]
*PRACTICE AREAS: Trial Litigation; Appellate Litigation; Corporate.
Boyd, Janet C., (BV) ...... '53 '85 C.846 B.J. L.273 J.D. [Akin,G.S.H.&F.]
*PRACTICE AREAS: Public Policy; Taxation.
Boyd, Roger N., (AV) ...... '29 '61 C.95 A.B. L.976 LL.B. [[C] Crowell&M.]
*PRACTICE AREAS: Government and Public Contract Law; Contract Law.
Boyd, Thomas M. ...... '46 '73 C.885 B.A. L.893 J.D. [Alston&B.]
*PRACTICE AREAS: Financial Services Law; Electronic Commerce; Legislative Advocacy.
Boyd, Walter Y., Jr., (AV) '56 '84 C.240 B.A. L.574 J.D. [Finnegan,H.F.G.&D.] (See Pat. Sect.)
*PRACTICE AREAS: Patent Prosecution; Patent Licensing.
Boyden, Bruce E. ...... '69 '98 C.45 B.A. L.976 J.D. [[A] Proskauer R.]
Boyer, J. Alton, (AV) ...... '26 '51 C&L.273 A.B., J.D. 1275 K St., N.W.
Boyer, Kerri L. '68 '93 C.893 B.A. L.420 J.D. (adm. in VA; not adm. in DC) [[A] Boies,S.&F.]
*PRACTICE AREAS: Litigation; International Arbitration.
Boyer, Spencer H. ...... '38 '67 C.329 B.S.E.E. L.273 LL.B. Howard Univ.
Boykin, Brenda J. ...... '59 '86 C.893 B.A. L.575 J.D. [[A] Cole,R.&B.]
*PRACTICE AREAS: Telecommunications; Environmental Law.
Boykin, Curtis A. ...... '62 '94 C.475 B.A. L.276 J.D. [[A] Leftwich&D.]
*PRACTICE AREAS: Commercial Litigation; Governmental Affairs; Government Contracts; Domestic Relations.
Boykin, Hamilton H., (AV) ...... '39 '64 C.855 B.A. L.276 J.D. 1620 L Street, N.W.
Boykins, James R. ...... '48 '89 1200 G St., N.W.
Boylan, Kim Marie Kozaczek ...... '59 '86 C.276 B.S. L.823 J.D. [Mayer,B.&P.]
Boylan, Virginia Walker ...... '41 '79 C.30 B.A. L.128 J.D. [Dorsey&W.]
*PRACTICE AREAS: Indians and Native Populations; Government Law; Casinos and Gambling; Legislative.
Boyle, Brian D. ...... '60 '86 C.276 A.B. L.309 J.D. [O'Melveny&M.]
*PRACTICE AREAS: Class Action Litigation; Health Care Litigation; Insurance Liability; Product Liability; Appellate Litigation.
Boyle, Cynthia W. ...... '63 '92 C.741 B.A. L.904 J.D. Coun., Watson Wyatt Worldwide
Boyle, Elizabeth Margaret '58 '83 C.499 B.A. L.500 J.D. 1155 Connecticut Ave., N.W., Ste. 500
Boyle, James J. '64 '99 C.1172 B.S. L.893 J.D. [[A] Finnegan,H.F.G.&D.] (See Pat. Sect.)
*PRACTICE AREAS: Patent Prosecution; Patent Protection; Electronics; Fiber Optics; Physics.
Boyle, James M., (AV) ...... '44 '69 C&L.276 B.S.B.A., J.D. [McDermott,W.&E.]
Boyle, Nicholas J. '72 '97 C.054 LL.B. L.309 LL.M. (adm. in NY; not adm. in DC) [[A] Williams&C.]
*PRACTICE AREAS: Practice Limited to Federal Litigation; Media and First Amendment; Antitrust.
Boyle, Peter M. ...... '66 '94 C.821 B.A. L.262 J.D. [Morgan,L.&B.]
Boyle, Susan ...... '65 '92 C.273 B.A. L.262 J.D. [Baptiste&W.]
*PRACTICE AREAS: Labor Relations Law; Civil Rights Law.
Boyle, Terrence J. ...... '41 '72 C&L.276 B.S.F.S., J.D. 1245 34th St., NW
Boyle, Timothy E. ...... '61 '86 C.207 B.A. L.228 J.D. [Howrey S.A.&W.]
*PRACTICE AREAS: Antitrust; Commercial and Intellectual Property Litigation; Products Liability Law.
Boyles, John H. ...... '21 '49 C.712 B.A. L.276 J.D. Prof. of Law, Georgetown Univ.
Boyles, Jonathan J. '73 '01 C.893 B.A. L.276 J.D. (adm. in NY; not adm. in DC) [[A] Groom]
*PRACTICE AREAS: Employee Benefits.
Bozof, Richard P. ...... '47 '77 C.197 B.A. L.1066 J.D. [[C] Bergeson&C.]
*PRACTICE AREAS: Federal Insecticide, Fungicide and Rodenticide Act (FIFRA); Toxic Substances Regulation; Food and Drug Regulation; Food, Drug and Cosmetic Law; Pesticide Regulation.

Bracewell & Patterson, L.L.P., (AV)
2000 K Street, N.W., Suite 500, 20006-1872 ⊙
Telephone: 202-828-5800 Fax: 202-223-1225
Joseph S. Bracewell (1892-1965); Harry W. Patterson (1922-1990). Founding Partners and Special Counsel: Searcy Bracewell; Fentress Bracewell. Partners: Michael L. Pate; Ed Bethune; Gene E. Godley; John R. Cope; James L. Chapman; Charles H. Shoneman; Marc Racicot (Not admitted in DC); George M. Foote; Stephen F. Hogwood; Nancy Morrison O'Connor; Anthony H. Anikeeff; Luis M. Nido; Randall S. Rich; Jeffrey D. Watkiss; Albert B. Krachman; Nancy A. Wodka; Nancy Jo Nelson; Scott H. Segal; Kevin A. Ewing. Counsel: Ronald N. Carroll; Richard D. Horn; Charles L. Ingebretson (Not admitted in DC). Associates: Brian W. Baker; Carlyn M. Carey (Not admitted in DC); Kimberly Curry (Not admitted in DC); Aryeh Fishman; Amauri Gaudensi Costa (Foreign Legal Consultant — Brazil); Kevin B. Hawkins (Not admitted in DC); Marc C. Hebert; Robert Housman (Not admitted in DC); Jason B. Hutt; Jacqueline R. Java; Shelby J. Kelley; Lori H. Schectel (Not admitted in DC); Andrea M. Settanni; Charlton C. Walker.
General Civil Practice, Trial and Appellate Practice in State and Federal Courts, Administrative Law, Antitrust, Bank Lending, Bankruptcy Reorganization and Creditors' Rights, Communications, Construction, Corporate and Securities, Early Stage Companies, Employee Benefits, Energy, Environmental, Financial Services, Health Care, Hospitality, Industrial Disaster, Insurance Bad Faith, Insurance Defense, Intellectual Property and Technology, International, Labor and Employment, Land Use and Zoning, Legislative and Governmental Relations, Lender Liability Litigation, Litigation and Alternative Dispute Resolution, Oil and Gas, Foundations and Not-for-Profit Organizations, Personal Injury, Power, Products Liability, Project Finance, Public Projects, Public Utilities, Real Estate, School Law, Taxation, Telecommunications, Trademark and Copyright, Trusts and Estates.
Houston, Texas Office: South Tower Pennzoil Place, 711 Louisiana Street, Suite 2900, 77002-2781. Telephone: 713-223-2900. Fax: 713-221-1212.
Austin, Texas Office: 111 Congress Avenue, Suite 2300, 78701-4052. Telephone: 512-472-7800. Fax: 512 472-9123.
Other Austin Office: Lakewood on the Park, 7600 B North Capital of Texas Highway, Suite 350, 78731. Telephone: 512-343-6116. Fax: 512-343-6002.
Corpus Christi, Texas Office: 2000 One Shoreline Plaza, South Tower, 800 North Shoreline Boulevard, 78401-3700. Telephone: 361-882-6644. Fax: 361-882-6659.
Dallas, Texas Office: Lincoln Plaza, 500 N. Akard Street, Suite 4000, 75201-3387. Telephone: 214-758-1000. Fax: 214-758-1010.
Fort Worth, Texas Office: 201 Main Street, Suite 1600, 76102. Telephone: 817-332-8143. Fax: 817-332-8409.
San Antonio, Texas Office: 800 One Alamo Center, 106 S. St. Mary's Street, 78205. Telephone: 210-226-1166. Fax: 210-226-1133.
Reston, Virginia Office: 12355 Sunrise Technology Park, Fifth Floor, 20191-3458. Telephone: 703-893-4670. Fax: 703-827-0545.
London, England Office: No. 1 Cornhill, EC3V 3ND. Telephone: 011-44-207-743-6250. Fax: 011-44-207-743-6251.
Almaty, Kazakhstan Office: 65 Kazybek bi str., Suite 410, 480091. Telephone: 73272-581-400. Fax: 73272-581-444.
Astana, Kazakhstan Office: Karaotkel Compound, Office C-7-2. Telephone: 011-7-3172-222-127.
See Professional Biographies, WASHINGTON, DISTRICT OF COLUMBIA

Bracey, Kali N. ...... '71 '97 C.811 B.A. L.976 J.D. Pub. Def. Serv.
Brack, William T. ...... '52 '82 C.173 B.A. L.862 J.D. [Brownstein H.&F.]
*PRACTICE AREAS: Taxation; Financial Institutions Law; Foreign Trade; Telecommunications; Health Care.
Brackshaw, Susan L., (AV) ...... '49 '82 C.454 B.A. L.904 J.D. [Webster,F.&B.]
*PRACTICE AREAS: Employment Law; Labor Law; Personal Injury; Litigation.
Bradbury, Steven Gill ...... '58 '88 C.813 B.A. L.477 J.D. [Kirkland&E.]
*PRACTICE AREAS: General Litigation; Antitrust; Telecommunications; Appellate Litigation; Constitutional Law.
Braden, E. Mark ...... '51 '76 C&L.902 B.A., J.D. [[C] Baker&H.]
*PRACTICE AREAS: Election Law; Legislative Law.
Braden, Susan G., (AV) ...... '48 '73 C&L.930 B.A., J.D. [[C] Baker&M.]
*PRACTICE AREAS: Administrative Law; Antitrust Law; Computers and Technology Law; Intellectual Property Law; Civil Litigation.
Bradfield, Michael, (AV) ...... '34 '61 C.867 B.A. L.178 J.D. [Jones,D.R.&P.]
*PRACTICE AREAS: Banks and Banking; International Banking Law.
Bradford, Lowell J., (AV) ...... '14 '35 C.276 Ph.B. L.273 LL.B. 1200 18th St., N.W.‡
Bradford, Martina L. ...... '52 '76 C.30 B.A. L.228 J.D. AT&T
Bradford, Robert T. ...... '65 '90 C.674 A.B. L.569 J.D. [[A] Akin,G.S.H.&F.]
*PRACTICE AREAS: Real Estate; Asset Backed Securities; Commercial Mortgage Backed Securities.
Bradford, Stacey A. ...... '67 '96 C.390 B.A. L.904 J.D. [[C] Calhoun] (⊙Washington)
Bradford, Stacey A. .... '67 '96 C.390 B.A. L.904 J.D. [[A] Sanders,S.&B.] (⊙Washington)
*PRACTICE AREAS: Employee Benefits; Trusts and Estates; Corporate.
Bradford, William H., Jr., (AV) ...... '37 '62 C&L.228 A.B., J.D. [[C] Sanders,S.&B.]
*PRACTICE AREAS: Taxation; Estate Planning; Probate; Business Law; Real Estate.
Bradham, John M. ...... '62 '89 C.198 B.A. L.188 J.D. [Nixon P.] (⊙New York, NY)
*PRACTICE AREAS: Civil Litigation; Corporate.
Bradley, Andrea Fish '60 '85 C.813 A.B. L.1068 J.D. V.P., Gen. Coun. & Corp. Secy., Carr Realty Corporation
Bradley, Eileen ...... '48 '80 C.856 A.B. L.273 J.D. Blue Cross Blue Shield Association
Bradley, James P. ...... '16 '41 C.722 A.B. L.799 LL.B. 7058 Eastern Ave.,N.W.
Bradley, Leigh A. ...... '56 '82 C&L.16 B.A., J.D. [Holland&K.]
*PRACTICE AREAS: Federal Government Contracts; Litigation; Privatization.
Bradley, William E. .... '69 '98 C.1369 B.S. L.1209 J.D. [[A] Fulbright&J.] (See Pat. Sect.)
*PRACTICE AREAS: Intellectual Property.

Bradley Arant Rose & White LLP, (AV)
801 Pennsylvania Avenue NW, Suite 230, 20004 ⊙
Telephone: 202-393-7150 Facsimile: 202-347-1684
Email: info@bradleyarant.com URL: http://www.bradleyarant.com
Members of Firm: Douglas E. Eckert (Not admitted in DC); Ben L. Erdreich; George Bryan Harris; Jeffrey D. Komarow; Jack W. Selden (Not admitted in DC); Luther J. Strange, III. Associate: David Stewart (Not admitted in DC).
Banking and Financial Services; Competitive Practices; Intellectual Property; Construction and Procurement; Corporate Law; Securities; Mergers and Acquisitions; Compliance; Environmental Law; Toxic Torts; Labor and Employment; ERISA; Litigation; Governmental Affairs; Health Care Law; Tax Exempt Facilities; Health Care Fraud; International Law; International Transactions; Public Finance; Real Estate Law; Finance; Land Use; Leasing; Workouts; Reorganization Restructuring and Insolvency; Tax Law; Trusts and Estates; White Collar Crime.
Birmingham, Alabama Office: 2001 Park Place, Suite 1400, 35203. Telephone: 205-521-8000. Facsimile: 205-521-8800.
Huntsville, Alabama Office: 200 Clinton Avenue West, Suite 900, 35801. Telephone: 256-517-5100. Facsimile: 256-517-5200.
Montgomery, Alabama Office: RSA Union Office Building, 100 North Union Street, Suite 650, 36104. Telephone: 334-261-4211. Facsimile: 334-261-4234. and 504 South Perry Street, 36102. Telephone: 334-834-6222. Facsimile: 334-834-7080.

(This Listing Continued)

Bradley Arant Rose & White LLP (Continued)

Jackson, Mississippi Office: 188 East Capitol Street, Suite 450, 39201. Telephone: 601-948-8000. Facsimile: 601-948-3000.
Revisers of the Alabama Law Digest for this Directory
See Professional Biographies, WASHINGTON, DISTRICT OF COLUMBIA

Bradner, Eileen P. . . . . . '59 '87 C.851 B.A. L.276 J.D. [Wiley R.&F.]
*PRACTICE AREAS: International Trade; Government Affairs.
Bradner, Robert H. . . . . . '62 '92 C.976 B.A. L.276 J.D. [Holland&K.]
*PRACTICE AREAS: Legislative; Health Law; Education Law; Employment Law; Environmental Law.
Bradshaw, Benjamin G. . . . . . '69 '97 C.976 B.A. L.800 J.D. [O'Melveny&M.]
Brady, Cathleen Russell '62 '88 C.160 B.A. L.790 J.D.
(adm. in SC; not adm. in DC) Asst. Dir., Govt. Rel., American Psychiatric Association
Brady, George M., III '59 '87 C.228 B.A. L.861 J.D.
(adm. in PA; not adm. in DC) Natl. Assn. of Ins. Comrs.
Brady, James W., Jr. . . . . . '57 '87 C.645 B.S. L.188 J.D. [Dickstein S.M.&O.]
*PRACTICE AREAS: Intellectual Property; Biotechnology Law; Litigation.
Brady, Joshua T. . . . . . '72 '99 C.276 A.B. L.976 J.D. [Wilmer,C.&P.]
Brady, Michael T. . . . . . '— '83 C.668 B.A. L.976 J.D. [Miller&C.]
*PRACTICE AREAS: Litigation; Patent Litigation; Complex Litigation; Intellectual Property Litigation.
Brady, Phillip D. '51 '76
C.602 B.A. L.426 J.D. V.P. & Gen. Coun., Amer. Auto. Mfrs. Assn.
Brady, Richard A., (AV) . . . . . '34 '60 C&L.976 B.S., LL.B. [Covington&B.]
Brady, Robert P., (AV) . . . . . '47 '72 C.696 B.A. L.273 J.D. [Hogan&H.]
*PRACTICE AREAS: Pharmaceutical; Biotechnology; Food Law.
Brafford, Anne . . . . . '70 '96 C.350 B.S. L.352 J.D. [Morgan,L.&B.]
Braga, Stephen L., (AV) . . . . . '55 '82 C.1030 B.A. L.276 J.D. [Baker B.]
Brager, Robert, (AV) . . . . . '54 '80 C&L.178 B.A., J.D. [Beveridge&D.] (⊙Balt., MD)
*PRACTICE AREAS: Litigation; Environmental Law; Media Law.
Bragin, Mitchell J., (AV) . . . . . '45 '70 C&L.831 B.S., J.D. [Kutak R.]
*PRACTICE AREAS: Taxation Law; Municipal Finance Law; Asset-Backed Securities Law.
Braker, Gregory S. . . . . . '62 '92 C.999 B.A. L.276 J.D. [Venable,A.B.H.&C.]
*PRACTICE AREAS: Environmental Law; Environmental Compliance; Internal Investigations; Criminal Defense.
Bralove, David H. . . . . . '53 '79 C.867 B.A. L.30 J.D. [Bralove]
Bralove Group, The . . . . . 5335 Wisconsin Avenue, Suite 440
Braman, Leonard . . . . . '25 '52 C.831 B.S. L.893 LL.B. Asso. J., Supr. Ct.
Bramble, Barbara J. . . . . . '47 '73 C.1209 B.A. L.273 J.D. National Wildlife Federation
Brame, J. Robert, III '42 '68 C.880 B.A. L.976 LL.B.
(adm. in VA; not adm. in DC) [Ogletree,D.N.S.&S.]
*PRACTICE AREAS: Labor; Employment; Litigation.
Brammer, James E. . . . . . '42 '70 C.942 B.A. L.276 J.D. [Jackson&C.]
*PRACTICE AREAS: Property Management; Asset Management; Loan Servicing; Real Estate; Compliance.
Brams, Robert S. . . . . . '59 '85 C.529 B.A. L.1029 J.D. [Patton B.]
Bran, Paul Bennett, (AV) . . . . . '58 '85 C.446 B.A. L.276 J.D. [Dickstein S.M.&O.]
*PRACTICE AREAS: Bankruptcy Law; Creditors Rights; Commercial Litigation.
Branch, Daniel H., (AV) '58 '83
C.1315 B.S.B.A. L.802 J.D. [Winstead S.&M.] (⊙Dallas, TX)
Branch, Maiysha R. '75 '00 C.597 B.S. L.273 J.D.
(adm. in PA; not adm. in DC) [Akin,G.S.H.&F.]
*PRACTICE AREAS: Litigation.
Branciforte, Jason M. . . . . . '65 '91 C.276 A.B. L.188 J.D. [Littler M.]
*PRACTICE AREAS: Labor and Employment; Litigation.
Brand, Joseph L., (AV) . . . . . '36 '63 C.477 A.B. L.273 J.D. [Patton B.]
Brand, Michael E., (AV) . . . . . '50 '75 C.696 A.B. L.128 J.D. [Loewinger&B.]
*PRACTICE AREAS: Real Estate Law; Landlord and Tenant Law; Complex Commercial Litigation.
Brand, Richard L., (AV) . . . . . '59 '84 C.276 B.S. L.659 J.D. [Arent F.K.P.&K.]
*PRACTICE AREAS: Real Estate; Electronic Commerce; Sports Law; Corporate Law; Business Law.
Brand, Stanley M., (AV) . . . . . '48 '75 C.264 B.A. L.276 J.D. [Brand&F.]
*PRACTICE AREAS: Criminal Law; Civil Litigation; Trade Associations; Trade Regulation; Administrative Law.
Brand, Wallace Edward, (AV) . . . . . '30 '58 C.112 B.S. L.309 J.D. 1730 K St., N.W.

Brand & Frulla, A Professional Corporation, (AV)
923 Fifteenth Street, N.W., 20005
Telephone: 202-662-9700 Facsimile: 202-737-7565
URL: http://www.lawyers.com/brand&frulla
Stanley M. Brand; David E. Frulla; Ross A. Nabatoff;—Andrew Dewald Herman; Jason S. Hadges; Corey A. Rubin; Deborah Y. Ho; Helen-Mary Bridget McGovern (Not admitted in DC). Of Counsel: Eugene Gressman; Margaret Colgate Love.
Criminal and Civil Litigation. Practice before Congress, Federal, State and Local Agencies. Appellate and Supreme Court Practice.
See Professional Biographies, WASHINGTON, DISTRICT OF COLUMBIA

Brandel, Abigail E. . . . . . '69 '94 C.105 B.A. L.446 J.D. [Buc&B.]
Brandenburg, Dan S., (AV) . . . . '49 '75 C.705 B.A. L.276 J.D. [Calhoun] (⊙Washington)
Brandenburg, Dan S., (AV) '49 '75
C.705 B.A. L.276 J.D. [Sanders,S.&B.] (⊙Washington)
*PRACTICE AREAS: Employee Benefits Law; Personal Service Organizations; Estate Planning.
Brandenburg, Stacey M. . . . . . '74 '01 C.577 B.A. L.569 J.D. [Steptoe&J.]
Brandolph, David B. . . . . . '56 '83 C.659 B.A. L.273 J.D. Bur. of Natl. Affs., Inc.
Brandon, Douglas I. '58 '87 C.893 B.A. L.880 J.D.
(adm. in NY; not adm. in DC)
V.P. & Chf. Coun., Federal Affs., AT&T Wireless Servs., Inc.
Brandon, Kevin P. . . . . . '67 '93 C.128 B.A. L.569 J.D. [Dow,L.&A.]
Brandriss, Ira Leo '52 '98 C.994 B.A. L.999 J.D.
(adm. in NY; not adm. in DC) 450 Fifth St. N.W.
Brands, Henk . . . . . '64 '91 C.999 LL.B. L.176 J.D. [Kellogg,H.H.T.&F.]
*PRACTICE AREAS: Telecommunications; Litigation.
Brandt, Philip D. . . . . . '65 '97 C.871 B.S. L.273 J.D. [Arent F.K.P.&K.]
*PRACTICE AREAS: Corporate Contracts; Corporate Real Estate; Corporate Organization; Land Sales.
Branfman, Eric J., (AV) . . . . . '47 '73 C.178 B.A. L.976 J.D. [Swidler B.S.F.]
*PRACTICE AREAS: Telecommunications Competition; Telecommunications Regulation; Telecommunications Law; Telecommunications Contracts; Complex Litigation.
Branitsky, Randy . . . . . '62 '92 C.188 B.S. L.1009 J.D. [Willkie F.&G.]
Brannan, Jennifer S. . . . . . '74 '00 C&L.378 B.S.J., J.D. [Arnold&P.]
*PRACTICE AREAS: Litigation.
Brannan, Patricia A., (AV) . . . . . '53 '80 C.436 B.A. L.309 J.D. [Hogan&H.]
*PRACTICE AREAS: Education Law; Civil Rights; Federal Civil Practice.
Brannigan, Vincent M. . . . . . '51 '76 C.446 B.A. L.276 J.D. Prof., Georgetown Univ.
Bransford, William L., (AV) . . . . . '47 '75 C.446 B.S. L.161 J.D. [Shaw,B.V.&R.]
*PRACTICE AREAS: Federal Employment Law; Employment Law; Litigation.
Bransilver, Edward, (AV) . . . . . '27 '60 C.659 B.S. L.477 LL.B. [Shearman&S.]
Branson, David J., (AV) '43 '73 C.128 A.B. L.276 J.D.
2100 M St., N.W. (⊙Washington)
Branson, David J., (AV) '43 '73
C.128 A.B. L.276 J.D. [Wallace K.M.&B.] (⊙Washington)
*PRACTICE AREAS: International Arbitration.
Branson, Robert E. '58 '83 C.893 B.A. L.309 J.D.
V.P., Chf. Legal Coun. & Dir., Post-Newsweek Stations, Inc.

Branton, Brian Edward '69 '97 C.575 B.A. L.30 J.D.
(adm. in VA; not adm. in DC) 1630 Longworth House Office Bldg.
Brashares, William C., (AV) . . . . . '39 '65 C.893 B.A. L.477 J.D. [Mintz,L.C.F.G.&P.]
*PRACTICE AREAS: Federal and State Litigation; Administrative Litigation; Securities Litigation; Commercial Arbitration; International Arbitration.
Brashear, Ann R. . . . . . '56 '85 C.273 B.S. L.276 J.D. [Squire,S.&D.]
*PRACTICE AREAS: Corporate; Public Finance.
Brasher, Lance T. . . . . . '60 '90 C.871 B.S. L.309 J.D. [Skadden,A.S.M.&F.]
Braswell, Jamila '— '98 C.309 A.B. L.893 J.D.
(adm. in VA; not adm. in DC) [Jenkens&G.]
*PRACTICE AREAS: Real Estate; Distribution.
Braswell, Marina Utgoff . . . . . '53 '82 C.228 B.A. L.1187 J.D. Asst. U.S. Atty.
Brater, Randall A. . . . . . '— '00 C.188 B.A. L.880 J.D. [Arent F.K.P.&K.]
Brathwaite, Van M. . . . . . '52 '90 C.999 B.A. L.329 J.D. Asst. Corp. Coun.
Bratton, William W., Jr. '51 '77 C&L.178 B.A., J.D.
(adm. in NY; not adm. in DC) Prof., George Washington Univ. Law Sch.
Braude, Herman M., (AV) . . . . . '39 '65 C.186 B.S. L.276 J.D. [Braude&M.]
*PRACTICE AREAS: Construction Law; Government Contracts; Administrative Law; Civil Trial Practice Law.
Braude, Lina A. '73 '96 L.999 J.D.
(adm. in Kazakh; not adm. in DC) [Coudert B.]
*PRACTICE AREAS: Corporate.

Braude & Margulies, P.C., (AV) ▣
The Brawner Building, 888 Seventeenth Street, N.W., Suite 500, 20006
Telephone: 202-293-2993 Fax: 202-331-7916
Email: Braudemarg@aol.com
Herman M. Braude; Samuel M. Morrison, Jr.; Gerson B. Kramer;—Michael B. Beard. Of Counsel: J. Richard Margulies.
Practice before all State, Federal Courts and Administrative Agencies, Government, Public and Private Construction Contracts, all facets of Government Contracts, Real Estate Development, Arbitration, Civil Litigation and Construction Insurance Law.
See Professional Biographies, WASHINGTON, DISTRICT OF COLUMBIA

Braue, Tim E. . . . . . '70 '97 C.1203 B.A. L.879 J.D. Spec. Asst. to the Asst. Atty. Gen.
Brauer, Lawrence M. '44 '70 C.30 B.S. L.273 J.D.
Tax Dept., MCI Communications Corp.
Brault, Albert E., (AV) . . . . . '06 '27 L.276 J.D. [Brault,G.S.&B.] (⊙Rockville, MD)‡

Brault, Graham, Scott & Brault, PLLC, (AV)
1140 Connecticut Avenue, N.W. Suite 250, 20036 ⊙
Telephone: 202-785-1200 Fax: 202-785-4301
Email: dcbgsb@aol.com URL: http://www.bgsb.com
Of Counsel: Laurence T. Scott; James Robert Miller (Not admitted in DC). Members of Firm: Denver H. Graham (1922-1987); Albert E. Brault (Retired); Albert D. Brault (Resident, Rockville, Maryland Office); Leo A. Roth, Jr.; James S. Wilson (Resident, Rockville, Maryland Office); Daniel L. Shea (Resident, Rockville, Maryland Office); M. Kathleen Parker (Resident, Rockville, Maryland Office); James M. Brault (Resident, Rockville, Maryland Office); David G. Mulquin (Not admitted in DC; Resident, Rockville, Maryland Office). Associates: Holly D. Shupert (Resident, Rockville, Maryland Office); Rhonda Ann Hurwitz (Resident, Rockville, Maryland Office); Joan F. Brault (Resident, Rockville, Maryland Office).
General, Civil, Trial and Appellate practice in all State and Federal Courts. Negligence, Insurance, Medical Malpractice, Personal Injury, Products Liability and Commercial Litigation.
Representative Clients: American Oil Co.; Crum & Forster Group; Fireman's Fund American Insurance Cos.; Kemper Group; Reliance Insurance Cos.; Safeco Group; Government Employees Insurance Co.; Medical Mutual Society of Maryland; Legal Mutual Liability Insurance Society of Maryland.
Brault, Graham, Scott & Brault, LLC:
Rockville, Maryland Office: 101 South Washington Street. Telephone: 301-424-1060. FAX: 301-424-7991.
Fairfax, Virginia Office: Suite 500, 11350 Random Hills Road, Fair Oaks Plaza, 22030-7429. Telephone: 202-785-1200.
See Professional Biographies, WASHINGTON, DISTRICT OF COLUMBIA

Brault Palmer Grove Zimmerman White & Steinhilber LLP
(See Fairfax, Virginia)

Braun, Daniel A. . . . . . '64 '92 C.674 A.B. L.976 J.D. [Comey B.&L.]
Braun, Eric M. . . . . . '58 '90 C.105 B.A. L.178 J.D. 725 12th St. NW
Braun, Howard J., (AV) . . . . . '37 '63 C.103 A.B. L.569 LL.B. [Rosenman&C.]
*PRACTICE AREAS: Telecommunications Law.
Braun, Joseph Lee . . . . . '48 '86 L.326 J.D. 2140 Pennsylvania Ave.
Braun, Theodore A. '27 '54 C&L.102 B.A., LL.B.
(adm. in NY; not adm. in DC) 1712 Taylor St., N.W.‡
Braunstein, Douglas E. . . . . . '67 '93 C.354 B.S. L.880 J.D. [Dow,L.&A.]
Braunstein, Richard L., (AV) . . . . . '33 '58 C.569 A.B. L.309 LL.B. [Dow,L.&A.]
Braunstein-Burgett, Karen L. . . . . . '66 '93 C.94 B.A. L.823 J.D. 1320 19th St., N.W.
Braverman, Burt A., (AV) . . . . . '46 '69 C.473 B.A. L.273 J.D. [Cole,R.&B.]
*PRACTICE AREAS: Commercial and Regulatory Litigation; Telecommunications; Antitrust; Unfair Trade; Competition.
Braverman, Joseph K. '64 '92 C.228 B.A. L.1066 J.D.
(adm. in CA; not adm. in DC) 1501 M St., N.W.‡
Bravin, Mark N. . . . . . '51 '79 C.112 B.A. L.309 J.D. [Morgan,L.&B.]
Bravo, Leonardo L. . . . . . '21 '70 L.999 J.D. 2121 Pennsylvania Avenue, N.W.‡
Braxton, Cathy A. . . . . . '66 '91 C.273 B.A. L.831 J.D. [Vorys,S.S.&P.]
*PRACTICE AREAS: Customs; International Trade.
Braxton, George P., II '65 '92 C.446 B.A. L.893 J.D.
(adm. in PA; not adm. in DC) Assoc. Dir., Georgetown Univ. Law Center
Bray, John M., (AV) . . . . . '— '62 C&L.734 B.A., LL.B. [King&S.]
*PRACTICE AREAS: Litigation and Trade.
Brazil, Harold E., (BV) . . . . . '48 '73 C&L.608 B.A., J.D. [Koonz,M.J.D.&L.]
Breads & Associates . . . . . 1700 K St., N.W. (⊙Rockville, Silver Spring, MD)
Breakman, Paul M. . . . . . '72 '98 C.112 B.A. L.861 J.D. [Rubin,W.D.H.&C.]
*PRACTICE AREAS: Communications Law; Media Law; Corporate Law.
Brecher, Mitchell F., (AV) . . . . . '48 '73 C.264 B.A. L.273 J.D. [Greenberg T.]
Brecher, Valerie . . . . . '69 '95 C.222 B.A. L.1194 J.D. U.S. E.P.A.
Bredhoff, Elliot, (AV) . . . . . '21 '49 C.563 B.S. L.976 LL.B. [Bredhoff&K.]
Bredhoff, Robert L., (AV) . . . . . '53 '80 C.674 B.A. L.276 J.D. [Stein,M.&M.]
*PRACTICE AREAS: Civil Litigation; Personal Injury; Criminal Law.

Bredhoff & Kaiser, P.L.L.C., (AV)
805 Fifteenth Street, N.W., Suite 1000, 20005
Telephone: 202-842-2600 Fax: 202-842-1888
URL: http://www.bredhoff.com
Members of Firm: George H. Cohen; Robert H. Chanin; Robert M. Weinberg; Jeffrey L. Gibbs; Julia Penny Clark; Jeffrey R. Freund; W. Gary Kohlman; Jeremiah A. Collins; Mady Gilson; Bruce R. Lerner; Andrew D. Roth; John M. West; Douglas L. Greenfield; Roger Pollak; Anne Ronnel Mayerson; Leon Dayan. Of Counsel: Laurence Gold; Patricia Polach; Constance Markakis; Laura Page Kennedy. Associates: Alice O'Brien; Devki K. Virk; Philip Hostak; Robert W. Alexander; Portia Yu-Jung Wu; Michael H. Sampson. Senior Counsel: Elliot Bredhoff.
General Appellate and Trial Practice, Civil and Criminal including practice before U.S. Supreme Court, Labor, Civil Rights, Constitutional Law, Bankruptcy, Occupational Safety and Health Law, Employee Benefit Law including Fiduciary and Tax Law, Antitrust, RICO, Attorney Discipline Law.
See Professional Biographies, WASHINGTON, DISTRICT OF COLUMBIA

Bredimus, Frank B., Jr., (BV) '62 '88 C.205 B.A. L.902 J.D.
(adm. in VA; not adm. in DC) [Bredimus&Assoc.] ⊙
*PRACTICE AREAS: Bankruptcy; Taxation; Estate Planning; Business Law.

Bredimus & Associates, P.C., (BV)
1718 "M" Street, Northwest, 20036-4505 ⊙
Telephone: 202-589-1885
Frank B. Bredimus, Jr. (Not admitted in DC).
General Business and Commercial Law, including Commercial Contracts, Taxation and Real Estate, Wills and Probate, Trusts and Estates and Estate Planning. General Civil and Criminal Trial Practice including Criminal Defense, Personal Injury and Bankruptcy.
Leesburg, Virginia Office: 11 West Market, 20176. Telephone: 703-777-9563. Fax: 703-771-3257.
Frederick, Maryland Office: 905 West 7th Street, Suite 321, 21701-8527. Telephone: 301-228-3695.
See Professional Biographies, WASHINGTON, DISTRICT OF COLUMBIA

Breed, Jerome A. ... '52 '78 C.178 B.A. L.309 J.D. [Powell,G.F.&M.]
*PRACTICE AREAS: Taxation Law.
Breed, Nathaniel P., Jr. (P.C.), (AV) ... '37 '67 C.1155 B.S.B.A. L.477 J.D. [🄲 Shaw P.]
*PRACTICE AREAS: Aviation; Administrative.
Breen, George B., (BV) ... '64 '89 C.183 B.A. L.128 J.D. [🄰 Epstein B.&G.]
*PRACTICE AREAS: Litigation; Professional Liability Defense; Health Law.
Breggin, Linda K., (BV) '62 '88
C.861 B.A. L.145 J.D. Sr. Atty, Environmental Law Institute
*RESPONSIBILITIES: Environmental.
Bregman, A. Randolph ... '46 '85 C.178 B.A. L.276 J.D. [Squire,S.&D.]
*PRACTICE AREAS: International Joint Ventures; International Business; Investment in Russia.
Bregman, Lynn, (AV) ... '49 '75 C.70 B.A. L.273 J.D. [Wilmer,C.&P.]
*PRACTICE AREAS: Insurance; Civil Practice; Litigation.
Bregman, Stanley I., Law Office of, (AV) '31 '58 C&L.273 B.A., LL.B.
2301 N. St., N.W.

Bregman, Berbert & Schwartz, L.L.C.
(See Bethesda, Maryland)

Breisach, Eric E., (AV) '57 '89 C.932 B.B.A. L.1187 J.D.
(adm. in MI; not adm. in DC) [Fleischman&W.]
Breitenbach, Douglas L. '44 '71
C.1150 B.A. L.150 J.D. Sr. Coun., Amer. Council of Life Ins.
Breithaupt, Harry J., Jr., (AV) ... '16 '41 C.695 A.B. L.273 J.D. 1026 16th St., N.W.‡
Brendel, John M. ... '71 '96 C.145 B.A. L.659 J.D. [🄰 Kelley D.&W.]
*PRACTICE AREAS: Telecommunications Law.

Breneman & Georges
(See Alexandria, Virginia)

Brennan, Janis H. ... '— '87 C.280 B.A. L.276 J.D. [Foley,H.&E.]
*PRACTICE AREAS: International Commercial Law; International Investment; Litigation; International Commercial Arbitration; Immigration.
Brennan, Jeffrey W. ... '59 '86 C.321 A.B. L.276 J.D. [Howrey S.A.&W.]
*PRACTICE AREAS: Antitrust; Trade Regulation; Civil Litigation.
Brennan, Jennifer A. '71 '99 C.118 B.A. L.30 J.D.
(adm. in MD; not adm. in DC) [🄰 Gilbert H.&R.]
*PRACTICE AREAS: Complex Dispute Resolution; Insurance Coverage.
Brennan, John J. '16 '41 C.423 L.446 LL.B.
(adm. in MD; not adm. in DC) 1120 20th St., NW‡
Brennan, John J., III, (AV) ... '51 '77 C&L.276 B.A., J.D. [Jackson&C.] ⊙
*PRACTICE AREAS: Property Rights Litigation; Business Litigation; Technology Law; Electronic Commerce; Property Management.
Brennan, John T., Jr., (AV) ... '49 '78 C.867 B.A. L.276 J.D. [Crowell&M.]
*PRACTICE AREAS: Health and Hospital Law; Fraud and Abuse; Administrative Law.
Brennan, Julie L. '— '01 C.245 B.A. L.273 J.D.
(adm. in VA; not adm. in DC) [🄰 Kirkland&E.]
*PRACTICE AREAS: Antitrust; Litigation.
Brennan, Kevin C. ... '72 '98 C.575 B.A. L.276 J.D. [🄰 Fleischman&W.]
Brennan, Shane J. '71 '96 C.273 B.A. L.30 J.D.
Director, Employment Law, MeriStar Hotels & Resorts

Brenneman, Diane M., (AV) '46 '80 C.770 B.A. L.276 J.D. BR
601 Pennsylvania Avenue, N.W., Ninth Floor, 20004
Telephone: 202-362-1161 Fax: 202-362-1171
Email: dmbrenneman46@aol.com URL: http://www.lawyers.com/dianembrennemanlaw
(Also Of Counsel, O'Reilly & Mark, L.L.C.).
***PRACTICE AREAS: Wills, Estates and Probate Law; Mediation; Arbitration; Family Law. Civil and Family Mediation and Arbitration, Divorce, Custody.**
See Professional Biographies, WASHINGTON, DISTRICT OF COLUMBIA

Brennen, Kimberly Dianna '66 '94 C.1086 B.A. L.259 J.D.
(adm. in FL; not adm. in DC) Lexis Publishing
Brenner, Barbara S., (AV) '42 '79 C.696 B.A. L.982 J.D.
(adm. in NY; not adm. in DC) [Couch W.] ⊙
*PRACTICE AREAS: Energy Law.
Brenner, Daniel L. ... '51 '76 C&L.813 A.B., J.D. National Cable Television Assn.
Brenner, Dean R. ... '60 '85 C.228 A.B. L.276 J.D. [Crispin&B.]
*PRACTICE AREAS: Communications Law; Commercial Litigation.
Brenner, Donald R. ... '24 '49 C&L.608 B.S., J.D. 5225 Wisconsin Ave., N.W.
Brenner, Janet M. ... '— '78 C.800 A.B. L.273 J.D. 3325 R St., N.W.‡
Brenner, Joel F., (AV) ... '47 '75 C.966 B.A. L.309 J.D. [Dilworth P.P.]
Brenner, Joseph K. ... '56 '82 C.188 A.B. L.276 J.D. [Wilmer,C.&P.]
*PRACTICE AREAS: Securities; Civil Practice; Criminal Practice.
Brenner, Randy Elizabeth ... '67 '98 C.788 A.B. L.339 J.D. [🄰 Foley&L.]
*PRACTICE AREAS: Intellectual Property; Litigation.
Brentani, Deborah C. ... '72 '98 C.659 B.A. L.188 J.D. [🄰 Wright&T.]
*PRACTICE AREAS: Energy.
Breskin, William Adam, (AV) '57 '87 C&L.276 B.A., J.D.
Chf. Washington Coun., BlueCross BlueShield Association
Bresler, Sidney M. ... '54 '79 C.611 B.A. L.607 J.D. Bresler & Reiner, Inc.
Breslow, Jeffrey Reid ... '68 '93 C.966 B.A. L.273 J.D. Smithsonian Institution
Bresnahan, Pamela A., (AV) ... '54 '80 C&L.446 B.A., J.D. [Vorys,S.S.&P.]
*PRACTICE AREAS: Professional Liability; Intellectual Property; Employment; Lawyer Discipline; Commercial Litigation.
Bresnick, William O. '49 '75 C.188 A.B. L.569 J.D.
(adm. in NY; not adm. in DC) Texaco Inc.
Bress, Joseph M. '44 '69 C.1349 B.A. L.107 J.D.
(adm. in NY; not adm. in DC) Spec. Asst. to Pres., AMTRAK
Bress, Richard P. ... '— '89 C.188 B.A. L.813 J.D. [Latham&W.]
*PRACTICE AREAS: Appellate Practice; Communications and Media; Constitutional Law; ERISA Litigation; U.S. Supreme Court Litigation.
Bressie, Kent D. ... '69 '94 C.813 A.B. L.145 J.D. [Harris,W.&G.]
*PRACTICE AREAS: Telecommunications Law; International Law.
Bretscher, Carl P. ... '62 '93 C.339 B.S. L.273 J.D. [🄰 Pennie&E.] (See Pat. Sect.)
*PRACTICE AREAS: Patent Law; Intellectual Property.
Bretschneider, Barry E., (AV) ... '47 '71 C.674 A.B. L.352 J.D. [Morrison&F.] (Pat.)
*PRACTICE AREAS: Intellectual Property; Patents; Trademarks; Litigation; Interference Practice.
Brett, Mary Ryder ... '59 '97 C.276 B.S. L.1356 J.D. P.O. Box 2309
Breuer, Lanny A., (AV) ... '58 '86 C&L.178 B.A., J.D. [Covington&B.]

Breuer, Nancy Robinson '58 '86
C.309 B.A. L.569 J.D. Assoc. Gen. Coun., National Gallery of Art
Brew, James W., (AV) ... '54 '80 C&L.276 A.B., J.D. [Brickfield B.R.&S.]
Brew, John B. ... '63 '88 C.105 B.A. L.216 J.D. [Collier S.S.]
*PRACTICE AREAS: Customs and International Trade Law.
Brewer, Katherine ... '55 '83 C.976 B.A. L.228 J.D. [Schmeltzer,A.&S.]
*PRACTICE AREAS: Labor and Employment Law; Litigation.
Brewer III, Hollis Bryan ... '67 '94 C.945 B.A. L.128 J.D. [🄰 Nixon P.]
*PRACTICE AREAS: Corporate; Emerging Growth Companies; Securities; Intellectual Property; Mergers and Acquisitions.
Brewster, Christopher R. ... '50 '75 C.197 A.B. L.893 J.D. [🄲 Kaye S.]
*PRACTICE AREAS: Legislation; Consumer Protection; Product Recall; Advertising Law; False Advertising.
Brewster, Jessica Y. ... '73 '98 C.813 B.A. L.329 J.D. [🄰 Swidler B.S.F.]
*PRACTICE AREAS: Litigation.
Brewster, Jody J. ... '55 '83 C&L.508 B.S., J.D. [🄲 Skadden,A.S.M.&F.]
Breyer, John F., Jr., (AV) '53 '79
C.659 B.S. L.861 J.D. [Breyer&Assoc.] & [🄲 Silver,F.&T.]
Breyer & Associates, P.C., (AV) ... 1100 New York Avenue
Breyfogle, Jon W. ... '60 '95 C.150 B.A. L.1209 J.D. [Groom]
*PRACTICE AREAS: Health Care; Employee Benefits; Pension and Profit Sharing; Legislative, Regulatory and Judicial Representations; ERISA.
Brick, Adam B. ... '64 '91 C&L.276 B.S.B.A., J.D. Georgetown Univ.
Brickel, Sandra L. ... '67 '99 C.645 B.S. L.128 J.D. [🄰 Coburn&S.]
*PRACTICE AREAS: Criminal Law; Civil Litigation.
Brickell, Beatrice A. ... '44 '73 C.446 B.A. L.904 J.D. [Sharretts,P.C.&B.]
*PRACTICE AREAS: Customs Law; International Trade; Imports and Exports; Antidumping; Countervailing Duties.
Brickfield, Cyril F., (AV) '19 '49
C.273 M.S. L.262 LL.B. Spec. Coun., Amer. Assoc. of Ret. Persons
Brickfield, Peter J. P. ... '43 '70 C.1044 B.S. L.564 J.D. [Brickfield B.R.&S.]
*PRACTICE AREAS: Energy; Steel.

Brickfield Burchette Ritts & Stone, P.C., (AV) BR
8th Floor, West Tower, 1025 Thomas Jefferson Street, N.W., 20007-5201 ⊙
Telephone: 202-342-0800 Fax: 202-342-0807
Email: bbrslaw.com URL: http://www.bbrslaw.com
James W. Brew; Peter J. P. Brickfield; William H. Burchette; Mark C. Davis (Not admitted in DC; Resident, Austin, Texas Office); Peter J. Mattheis; Michael N. McCarty; Frederick H. Ritts; Fernando Rodriguez (Resident, Austin, Texas Office); A. Hewitt Rose; Christine C. Ryan; Garrett A. Stone; Damon E. Xenopoulos. Of Counsel: Stephen J. Karina (Not admitted in DC); John H. Conway;—Malcolm A. Burke (Not admitted in DC); Eric M. Devito; Michael K. Lavanga; Shaun C. Mohler; Kathleen T. Mulville (Not admitted in DC); Nelson H. Nease (Resident, Austin, Texas Office); Stacey Walsh Thompson.
Austin, Texas Office: Suite 400, 1005 Congress Avenue. Telephone: 512-472-1081. Fax: 512-472-7473.
See Professional Biographies, WASHINGTON, DISTRICT OF COLUMBIA

Brickman, Rita L. ... '65 '94 C.659 B.S.B.A. L.94 J.D. [🄰 Venable,A.B.H.&C.]
*PRACTICE AREAS: Energy; Public Utility; Energy Project Development; Administrative Law.
Bride, James Rafferty '55 '88 C.611 B.S. L.1162 J.D.
(adm. in PA; not adm. in DC) 1700 K. St., NW.
Bridenbaugh, Thomas D. ... '65 '91 C.1375 B.A. L.29 J.D. [🄰 Leftwich&D.]
Bridgeland, John M. '60 '88 C.309 A.B. L.893 J.D.
Chf. Exec. Offr., Civic Solutions, Ltd.
Bridgeman, James D., (AV) ... '54 '81 C.1064 B.A. L.893 J.D. [McKee N.]
*PRACTICE AREAS: Taxation.
Bridgeman, Lester M., (AV) '— '52
C.823 A.B. L.178 LL.B. [Miller,H.S.O.&B.] (⊙Mobile, AL)
*PRACTICE AREAS: Litigation; Transportation Law; Antitrust Law; Aviation Law.
Bridges, Charles ... '48 '85 C.512 B.S. L.161 J.D. 441 Fourth Street, Suite 700
Bridgman, Linda B. ... '51 '76 C.575 B.A. L.896 J.D. 450 Fifth Street Nw
Brieger, George '66 '94 C.102 B.S. L.1398 J.D.
(adm. in NY; not adm. in DC) [🄰 Sughrue M.]
Brier, M. Claire S. ... '63 '88 C.602 B.A. L.276 J.D. Mng. Atty., Legal Aid Soc.
Brier, Wilma A. ... '50 '78 C.94 B.A. L.184 J.D. 601 Indiana Ave., N.W.
Brigati, Joseph J., (AV) ... '— '65 C.602 A.B. L.228 LL.B. [Kirkpatrick&L.]
*PRACTICE AREAS: Government Contracts; Shipbuilding and Repair; Construction Claims; Banking Litigation; Federal Litigation.
Briggerman, Steven L. ... '43 '68 C.145 B.A. L.273 J.D. [Seyfarth S.]
Briggs, Alan L., (AV) ... '42 '67 C.473 A.B. L.608 J.D. [Squire,S.&D.]
*PRACTICE AREAS: Complex Business Litigation; Corporate Litigation; Securities; Intellectual Property.
Briggs, David W., (AV) ... '46 '75 C.454 B.A. L.273 J.D. [Holland&K.]
*PRACTICE AREAS: Commercial Real Estate Acquisitions; Commercial Real Estate Sales; Commercial Real Estate Leasing; Land Use; Zoning Law.
Briggs, John DeQ., III, (AV) ... '43 '73 C.309 A.B. L.276 J.D. [Howrey S.A.&W.]
*PRACTICE AREAS: Antitrust; Intellectual Property Counseling and Litigation; Commercial and Civil Litigation; Products Liability Law; Appellate Practice.
Briggs, Rebecca S. '73 '01 C.665 B.A. L.276 J.D.
(adm. in NY; not adm. in DC) [🄰 Swidler B.S.F.]
*PRACTICE AREAS: Telecommunications Law.
Briggs, William H., Jr., (AV) ... '44 '69 C.198 A.B. L.228 J.D. [Ross,D.&B.]
Briggum, Sue M. ... '50 '80 C.665 B.A. L.309 J.D. Dir., Govt. Affs., Waste Mgmt.
Bright, Lauren W. ... '— '97 C.282 B.A. L.273 J.D. [🄰 Shaw P.]
Brightbill, Timothy C. ... '65 '94 C.597 B.S. L.276 J.D. [🄰 Wiley R.&F.]
Briglia, David M. ... '70 '97 C.705 B.A. L.446 J.D. [🄰 Lukas,N.G.&S.]
*PRACTICE AREAS: Corporate Law; Business Transactions; Civil Litigation; Securities.
Briglia, Shannon J., (AV) '62 '87 C.886 B.S. L.1209 J.D.
[Wickwire G.] (⊙Vienna, VA)
*PRACTICE AREAS: Construction, Bankruptcy, and Fidelity and Surety Law; Litigation.
Briley, John A., Jr. ... '34 '61 C.276 A.B. L.229 LL.B. 6205 30th, N.W.
Brill, Hillary '73 '00 C.309 B.A. L.276 J.D.
(adm. in MD; not adm. in DC) [🄰 Covington&B.]
*PRACTICE AREAS: Communications Law; Information Technology.
Brille, Michael A. ... '68 '94 C.1049 B.B.A. L.976 J.D. [Boies,S.&F.]
*PRACTICE AREAS: Antitrust; Commercial Litigation.
Brillhart, Ember A. '70 '95 C.1031 B.A. L.982 J.D.
(adm. in NY; not adm. in DC) Honda N. America
Brimsek, John R., (P.C.) ... '50 '78 C.429 B.A. L.30 J.D. [Mullenholz,B.&B.]
Brincefield, Barbara O. ... '52 '80 C.788 A.B. L.273 J.D. [🄰 Cahill G.&R.]

Brincefield Hartnett Maloof & Paleos, P.C.
(See Alexandria, Virginia)

Briney, Roger A. ... '49 '75 C.893 B.A. L.280 J.D. Gen. Atty., AT&T
*RESPONSIBILITIES: Government Contracts; Communications and Media; Commercial Law.
Brinig, F. Joseph, (AV) '46 '78
C.276 B.A. L.1209 J.D. 1818 N St., N.W. (⊙Arlington, VA)
Brinker, John T. '46 '72 C.605 B.A. L.945 J.D.
(adm. in CA; not adm. in DC) Assoc. Gen. Coun., Fannie Mae, Inc.
Brinkerhoff, Susan ... '53 '98 C.446 B.A. L.273 J.D. [🄰 Proskauer R.]
Brinkman, David W., (AV) '40 '65
C.688 B.Ch.E. L.273 J.D. 1100 New York Ave., N.W., 9th Fl. (Pat.)

Brinkman, Paul F. .... '66 '93 C.976 B.A. L.893 J.D. [Kirkland&E.]
*PRACTICE AREAS: International Trade; Customs; Commercial Litigation.
Brinkmann, Karen ....'— '89 C.103 A.B. L.569 J.D. [Latham&W.]
*PRACTICE AREAS: Communications Law.
Brinson, Clifton L. .... '72 '00 C.228 B.A. L.976 J.D. [▣ Wilmer,C.&P.]
Brinton, Mark A. '60 '89 C.878 B.A. L.101 J.D.
(adm. in VA; not adm. in DC) 1827 Jefferson Pl.
Briody, James J. ....'63 '90 C.276 B.A. L.893 J.D. [▣ Sutherland A.&B.]
*PRACTICE AREAS: Litigation; Construction Law; Contracts; Government Contracts; Commercial Law.
Briscuso, Raymond J., Jr. '59 '86 C.10 B.S. L.276 J.D.
(adm. in MD; not adm. in DC)
Dir., State Govt. Rel., Biotechnology Industry Organization
Briseno, Liliana O. '72 '97 C.276 B.S. L.813 J.D.
(adm. in MD; not adm. in DC) 1440 New York Ave., NW
Bristol, Lynn A. '58 '98 C.145 A.B. L.446 J.D.
(adm. in MD; not adm. in DC; Pat.) [▣ Arent F.K.P.&K.]
*PRACTICE AREAS: Intellectual Property; Patents.
Britner, Paul '58 '89 C.347 B.A. L.37 J.D.
(adm. in AZ; not adm. in DC) 1900 E Street, NW
Brittin, Alexander J., (AV) ....'56 '84 C.174 B.S. L.128 J.D. [Brittin]
Brittin, Michael D. .... '53 '79 C.902 B.A. L.945 J.D. U.S. Attys. Office
Brittin Law Group, P.L.L.C., (AV) .... 1900 K Street, Suite 100
Brittingham, Smith Rufus, IV ... '62 '87 C.604 B.A. L.608 J.D. [▣ Finnegan,H.F.G.&D.]
*PRACTICE AREAS: Intellectual Property Litigation; Patent Litigation.
Britton, Edward C. ....'55 '85 C.674 A.B. L.309 J.D. [Covington&B.]
Brizzolara, Margaret M. .... '66 '91 C.205 B.A. L.884 J.D. [▣ Baker,L.C.&C.]
Broadfield, Donald E., Jr. ....'— '96 C.383 B.G.S. L.930 J.D. [▣ Morgan,L.&B.]

Broadley, John H., (AV) '45 '71 C.453 B.S. L.1066 J.D.
1054 31st Street NW, Suite 200, 20007
Telephone: 202-333-6025 Fax: 202-333-5685
Email: jbroadley@alum.mit.edu URL: http://www.lawyers.com/broadley
***PRACTICE AREAS: Litigation; Transportation Law.**
Litigation, Transportation.
See Professional Biographies, WASHINGTON, DISTRICT OF COLUMBIA

Broadstone, James M., (AV) ....'45 '72 C&L.608 B.A., J.D. [Gallagher,B.&M.]
*PRACTICE AREAS: Alternative Energy; Energy; Gas Utilities; Public Utility Rates.
Broadstone, June ....'51 '77 C.608 B.A. L.117 J.D. [▣ Skadden,A.S.M.&F.]
Broadwater, Kenneth J., Jr. '62 '87 C.446 B.A. L.273 J.D.
(adm. in MD; not adm. in DC) 1801 K St., NW‡
Broadwater, Kevin M. .... '64 '89 C.1044 B.A. L.30 J.D. [▣ Seward&K.]
*PRACTICE AREAS: Investment Company Regulation; Investment Adviser Regulation.
Broadwater, Thomas D., Jr. '58 '86
C.790 B.A. L.93 J.D. Broadband Construction Servs., Inc.
Broas, Julia M. ....'60 '86 C.309 A.B. L.178 J.D. [▣ Jones,D.R.&P.]
Broas, Timothy M., (AV) ....'54 '79 C.93 B.A. L.945 J.D. [Winston&S.]
*PRACTICE AREAS: Criminal Litigation; Civil Litigation.

Brobeck, Phleger & Harrison LLP, (AV)
A Partnership including a Professional Corporation
1333 H Street, N.W. Suite 800, 20005 ⊙
Telephone: 202-220-6000 Facsimile: 202-220-5200
Email: info@brobeck.com URL: http://www.brobeck.com
Partners: Cono A. Carrano; Nora E. Garrote; John B. Missing; Stephen A. Riddick (Not admitted in DC); Anthony W. Shaw; Rodger L. Tate. Of Counsel: Laurence H. Posorske; Michael C. Todd; Douglas C. Boggs. Senior Associate: Kimberly B. Kiefer. Associates: Ada Fernandez; Akinyale S. Harrison; Cecil E. Key; Robert A. King; Daniel Lee; Mitchell D. Lee; Natalie K. Meyer; Dean S. Nordlinger (Not admitted in DC); Stephanie M. Pries; Craig L. Puckett (Not admitted in DC); Matthew M. Rosini; Armand J. Zottola.
General Practice, including Business and Technology, Business Litigation, Securities Litigation, Patent and Trademark Litigation; Technology Litigation, Environmental Litigation, Product Liability Litigation, Insurance Coverage Litigation on behalf of Policyholders, Intellectual Property (including Patent and Trademark Prosecution, Copyright, Trade Secrets and Licensing), Labor Law, Financial Services and Insolvency (including Bankruptcy and Loan Workout), Real Estate, and Tax, Executive Compensation, Employee Benefits and Estate Planning.
San Francisco, California Office: Spear Street Tower, One Market. Telephone: 415-442-0900. Facsimile: 415-442-0900.
Los Angeles, California Office: 550 South Hope Street. Telephone: 213-489-4060. Facsimile: 213-745-3345.
Palo Alto, California Office: Two Embarcadero Place, 2200 Geng Road. Telephone: 650-424-0160. Facsimile: 650-496-2885.
San Diego, California Office: 12390 El Camino Real. Telephone: 858-720-2500. Fax: 858-720-2555.
Irvine, California Office: 38 Technology Drive. Telephone: 949-790-6300. Facsimile: 949-790-6301.
Austin, Texas Office: 4801 Plaza on the Lake. Telephone: 512-330-4000. Facsimile: 512-330-4001.
Broomfield, Colorado Office: 370 Interlocken Boulevard, Suite 500. Telephone: 303-410-2000. Facsimile: 303-410-2199.
New York, N.Y. Office: 1633 Broadway, 47th Floor. Telephone: 212-581-1600. Facsimile: 212-586-7878.
Dallas, Texas Office: 300 Crescent Court, Suite 1400. Telephone: 972-715-2700. Fax: 972-715-2704.
Reston, Virginia Office: 2100 Reston Parkway, Suite 203. Telephone: 703-621-3000. Fax: 703-621-3001.
Associated International Offices:
London, England Office: Brobeck Hale and Dorr International, Hasilwood House, 60 Bishopsgate, London EC2N 4AJ. Telephone: + 44 171 638 6688. Facsimile: + 44 171 638 5888.
Oxford, England Office: Brobeck Hale and Dorr, Park Gate. 25 Milton Park. Abingdon. OX14 4RY. Telephone: +44 1235 82 30 00. Fax: +44 1235 82 30 30.
Munich, Germany Office: Brobeck Hale and Dorr, Maximilianstrasse 31. D-80539. Telephone: +49 89 24 213-0. Fax: +49 89 24 213-213.
See Professional Biographies, WASHINGTON, DISTRICT OF COLUMBIA

Brock, Noel P. ....'67 '96 C.181 B.S.B.A. L.923 J.D. [▣ Fried,F.H.S.&J.]
*PRACTICE AREAS: Federal Income Tax.
Brock, Thomas H., (AV) .... '53 '77 C.352 B.A. L.273 J.D. [▣ Proskauer R.]
Brockmeyer, Paul R. '66 '92 C.881 B.A. L.477 J.D.
(adm. in IL; not adm. in DC) [▣ Seyfarth S.]
*PRACTICE AREAS: Labor Litigation.
Broder-Feldman, Elena N. .... '72 '96 C.228 A.B. L.976 J.D. [▣ Jenner&B.]
*PRACTICE AREAS: Litigation.
Broderick, Katherine Shelton '51 '78
C.30 B.A. L.276 J.D. Dir., Univ. of Dist. of Columbia Law Sch.
Broderick-Sokol, Sam ....'67 '01 C.659 B.A. L.1494 J.D. [▣ Wilmer,C.&P.]
Brodie, Katherine D. .... '68 '97 C.95 A.B. L.273 J.D. [▣ Akin,G.S.H.&F.]
*PRACTICE AREAS: Public Policy.
Brodnax, Matilda A. '64 '91 C.1083 B.S. L.945 J.D.
(adm. in VA; not adm. in DC) Sr. Assoc. Coun., UMWA Health & Retirement Funds
Brodsky, Craig Stephen '70 '95 C.446 B.S. L.64 J.D.
[▣ Eccleston&W.] (⊙Fairfax, VA)
Brodsky, James A., (AV) .... '45 '73 C.188 B.S. L.276 J.D. [Weiner B.S.K.]
*PRACTICE AREAS: Mortgages; Real Estate Finance; Mortgage Banking; Mergers and Acquisitions; Asset Sales.
Brodsky, Reed Michael ....'69 '97 C.228 B.A. L.880 J.D. [▣ Wilmer,C.&P.]
Brody, David A., (AV) .....'16 '40 C.563 B.S.S. L.178 LL.B. 1140 Connecticut Ave., NW
Brody, David H., (AV) .... '63 '89 C.228 B.A. L.880 J.D. [Zuckerman S.]
*PRACTICE AREAS: Real Estate; Corporate; Business.

Brody, Melanie Hibbs .... '— '92 C.184 B.A. L.823 J.D. [Kirkpatrick&L.]
*PRACTICE AREAS: Privacy; Electronic Commerce; Mortgage Banking Law.
Brody, Peter M., (AV) ....'58 '85 C.674 A.B. L.309 J.D. [Ropes&G.]
Broeckel, Janet A. .... '— '90 C.911 B.A. L.904 J.D. [▣ Dechert]
*PRACTICE AREAS: SEC Enforcement; Securities Litigation; Securities Regulation; Broker-Dealer Regulation; Government Investigations.
Broeren, P. Robert, Jr. ....'69 '94 C.385 A.B. L.602 J.D. [▣ Covington&B.]
Brogan, Stephen J., (AV) ....'52 '77 C.93 A.B. L.602 J.D. [Jones,D.R.&P.]
*PRACTICE AREAS: Litigation; Complex Business Litigation; Corporate Investigations; Qui Tam Litigation.
Brogan, William J. '— '99
C.94 B.S.C.E. L.273 J.D. [▣ Finnegan,H.F.G.&D.] (See Pat. Sect.)
*PRACTICE AREAS: Computer and Software Patents; Intellectual Property Litigation; Software Protection; Patent Prosecution.
Bromberg, Daniel H., (AV) ....'68 '91 C.976 B.A. L.309 J.D. [Jones,D.R.&P.]
*PRACTICE AREAS: Litigation; Appellate Practice.
Bromberg, Neil S. .... '66 '92 C.1036 B.A. L.659 J.D. [Spriggs&H.]
*PRACTICE AREAS: Products Liability; Toxic Torts; Litigation; Drug and Medical Device Defense.
Bromberg, Richard S. ....'49 '75 C.597 B.S. L.424 J.D. 1815 H St Nw # 650
Bromberg, Todd Andrew ....'62 '92 C.604 B.A. L.978 J.D. [Littler M.]
*PRACTICE AREAS: Labor and Employment.
Bromberg, Rosenthal & Siegel, (AV) ... 1522 K. Steet, N.W., Suite 536 (⊙Rockville, MD)
Bromley, James F., (AV) .... '35 '60 C.299 B.A. L.309 LL.B. [▣ Thompson,O.M.N.&H.]
*PRACTICE AREAS: Life Insurance; Mediation and Arbitration; Trademark Law; Copyright Law; Transportation Law.
Bromme, Jeffrey S. ....'60 '86 C.999 B.S. L.846 J.D. [Arnold&P.]
Bromwich, Michael R. '53 '80 C&L.309 A.B., J.D.
[Fried,F.H.S.&J.] (⊙New York, NY)
*PRACTICE AREAS: Investigations, Monitoring and Oversight; White Collar Criminal Defense; Corporate Compliance.
Bronaugh, John W. '25 '56 C.674 A.B. L.893 LL.B.
(adm. in KY; not adm. in DC) 2475 Virginia Ave., N.W.‡
Brondfield, Ellen S. ....'— '92 C.930 B.A. L.477 J.D. 1330 Connecticut Ave., N.W.
Bronson, Rebecca B. '47 '80 C.861 B.A. L.846 J.D.
(adm. in TX; not adm. in DC) [Hogan&H.]
*PRACTICE AREAS: International Corporate and Financial Transactions; Project and Infrastructure Finance; Corporate Investments; Corporate Privatization Transactions.
Bronstein, Alvin J. '28 '52 C.563 B.B.A. L.564 LL.B.
(adm. in NY; not adm. in DC) Exec. Dir., The National Prison Proj.
Bronstein, Gary R. .... '53 '79 C.94 B.A. L.61 J.D. [Stradley R.S.&Y.]
Bronston, Robert L. .... '69 '96 C.659 B.S. L.477 J.D. [▣ Mayer,B.&P.]
*PRACTICE AREAS: Appellate and Trial Litigation; Antitrust.
Brooke, Edward W., (AV) '19 '48 C.329 B.S. L.94 LL.B.
1919 Pennsylvania Ave., N.W.
Brooke, Thomas Willcox .... '60 '91 C&L.945 B.A., J.D. [Holland&K.]
*PRACTICE AREAS: Intellectual Property Litigation; Intellectual Property Counseling; Trademark Prosecution; Copyright Prosecution; Technology Transfers.
Brookhart, Christopher J. ....'69 '99 C&L.101 B.A., J.D. [▣ Dow,L.&A.]
Brookhiser, Robert J., Jr. ....'49 '75 C.976 B.A. L.309 J.D. [Howrey S.A.&W.]
*PRACTICE AREAS: Antitrust; Complex Litigation.
Brookman, Justin J. ....'74 '00 C.893 B.A. L.569 J.D. [▣ Fried,F.H.S.&J.]
Brookner, Janine Marilyn ....'40 '99 C.703 B.A. L.273 J.D. 3645 St. Mary's Pl., N.W.
Brooks, B. Jeffrey '68 '93 C.1099 B.A. L.425 J.D.
(adm. in LA; not adm. in DC) [Adams&R.]
Brooks, B.G. '— '86 C.1365 B.B.A. L.945 J.D.
Asst. Gen. Coun., Nat. Assn. of Sec. Dealers, Inc.
Brooks, Brian P. .... '69 '94 C.309 A.B. L.145 J.D. [▣ O'Melveny&M.]
Brooks, Fredric M. ....'67 '93 C.976 B.A. L.178 J.D. [▣ Feinberg] ⊙
Brooks, Jessie Marie ....'— '89 C.1135 B.S. L.1009 J.D. [▣ Verner,L.B.M.&H.]
*PRACTICE AREAS: International Commerce; Litigation.
Brooks, Joseph, (AV) ....'— '82 C.651 B.A. L.893 J.D. [▣ Morgan,L.&B.]
Brooks, Marquita K. .... '63 '90 C.1369 B.S. L.329 J.D. [▣ D.A.Humphries]
Brooks, Mary Beth '70 '01 C.676 B.A. L.276 J.D.
(adm. in NY; not adm. in DC) [▣ Mayer,B.&P.]
*PRACTICE AREAS: Corporate Law.
Brooks, Robert J. ....'22 '53 C.754 B.S. L.178 J.D. 1815 H St., N.W.
Brooks, Samuel F. ....'62 '88 C.880 B.A. L.309 J.D. Deloitte & Touche LLP
Brooks, Sharon D. ....'— '00 C.339 B.A. L.276 J.D. [▣ Olsson,F.&W.]
*PRACTICE AREAS: Agricultural Law; Medical Device Law; Food and Drug Law.
Brooks, Teresa A., (AV) ....'46 '78 C.856 A.B. L.30 J.D. [Jones,D.R.&P.]
*PRACTICE AREAS: Health Care; Health Care Regulation; Health Care Legislation.
Brooks, Thomas A. ....'45 '70 C.170 B.A. L.420 J.D. [▣ Katten M.Z.]
*PRACTICE AREAS: Corporate; Financial Institutions.
Brooks, Virginia Navarrete ....'70 '94 C.145 A.B. L.597 J.D. [▣ Vinson&E.]
*PRACTICE AREAS: Litigation.
Brooks, William Lee '58 '87
C&L.893 B.S.E.E., J.D. [Armstrong,W.H.M.&N.] (See Pat. Sect.)

Brooks, Kimberly A.
(See Bethesda, Maryland)

Broom, R. Stuart ....'— '74 C.16 B.A. L.838 J.D. [Verner,L.B.M.&H.]
*PRACTICE AREAS: Municipal Solid Waste Resource Recovery Law; Environmental Law; Co-generation Law.
Brophy, Stephen W. ....'71 '98 C.754 B.S. L.276 J.D. [▣ Barnes,R.&C.]
*PRACTICE AREAS: International Trade; Customs.
Brose, Steven H., (AV) ....'48 '73 C.645 B.A. L.178 J.D. [Steptoe&J.]
*PRACTICE AREAS: Administrative Law; Energy Law; Oil and Gas Law; Public Utility Law; Pipeline Law.
Brosky, John C. '51 '76 C.665 B.S.E.E. L.229 J.D.
(adm. in PA; not adm. in DC; Pat.) [▣ R.E.Bushnell]
Brosnahan, Jennifer R. ....'73 '99 C&L.309 A.B., J.D. [▣ Kirkland&E.]
*PRACTICE AREAS: Litigation.
Brosnan, Thomas F., (AV) .... '21 '49 C.94 B.S. L.178 LL.B. [▣ LeBoeuf,L.G.&M.]
*PRACTICE AREAS: Federal Energy Law; Gas Utilities; Rates; Facility Siting; Taxation.
Brothers, Henry J., II, (AV) ....'57 '84 C.861 B.A. L.273 J.D. [Holland&K.]
*PRACTICE AREAS: Commercial Real Estate Development Law; Multifamily Housing; Finance Law; Housing Development; Community Development.
Brothers, Kenneth W. ....'62 '88 C.878 B.S. L.273 J.D. [Dickstein S.M.&O.]
*PRACTICE AREAS: Complex Litigation; Intellectual Property Litigation; Commercial Litigation; Antitrust; Appellate Practice.
Broughton, Brian K. '68 '96 C.446 B.A. L.665 J.D.
(adm. in NJ; not adm. in DC) 1235 W. Street, N.E.
Broun, Amanda Rachel '58 '83 C.66 B.A. L.569 J.D.
(adm. in NY; not adm. in DC) Public Edu. Network
Broussard, Vanessa H. '71 '99 C&L.420 B.S., J.D.
(adm. in LA; not adm. in DC) [▣ Keller&H.]
*PRACTICE AREAS: Intellectual Property; Electronic Commerce; Internet Law; Advertising Law.
Brovey, Jennifer P. ....'— '96 [▣ Skadden,A.S.M.&F.]

Browdy, Roger L., (AV) '45 '72 C.477 B.S.E. L.276 J.D.
[Browdy&N.] (See Pat. Sect.)
*PRACTICE AREAS: Pharmaceutical Intellectual Property; Medical Intellectual Property; Chemical Intellectual Property; International Intellectual Property; Intellectual Property Licensing.
Browdy and Neimark, (AV) ....Suite 300, 624 Ninth Street, N.W. (See Pat. Sect.)
Brower, Charles N., (AV) .... '35 '62 C&L.309 B.A., J.D. [[C] White&C.]
*PRACTICE AREAS: International Arbitration; International Dispute Resolution; International Investment.
Brower, Ronald P. .... '72 '96 C&L.273 B.A., J.D. [[A] Hogan&H.]
*PRACTICE AREAS: Aviation and Aerospace; Transportation Law; Administrative Law.
Brown, Adrienne A. ....'— '99 C.976 B.A. L.659 J.D. [[A] Morgan,L.&B.]
Brown, Alan C., (AV) .... '52 '77 C.602 B.A. L.273 J.D. [Duane,M.&H.]
*PRACTICE AREAS: Information and Privacy; Security; Healthcare; Government Contracts.
Brown, Alison J. '61 '86 C.280 B.A. L.30 J.D.
(adm. in MD; not adm. in DC) [[A] Maggio&K.]
*PRACTICE AREAS: Immigration and Nationality Law.
Brown, Alvin S. ....'32 '63 1925 Connecticut Ave.
Brown, Amy L. ....'69 '94 C.813 A.B. L.228 J.D. [[A] Squire,S.&D.]
Brown, Andrew M. ....'71 '97 C.276 B.S. L.893 J.D. [[A] Levine,B.B.&B.]
*PRACTICE AREAS: Telecommunications Law; Contracts; Information Technology; Outsourcing.
Brown, Anna L. ....'67 '92 C.446 B.A. L.188 J.D. [[B] Jones,D.R.&P.]
Brown, Arthur J., (AV) .... '— '74 C.563 B.S. L.569 J.D. [Kirkpatrick&L.]
*PRACTICE AREAS: Securities Regulation; Investment Company Law; Securities Registration; Investment Regulation; Hedge Funds.
Brown, B. Ervin, II, (AV) '44 '71 C&L.575 B.A., J.D.
(adm. in NC; not adm. in DC) [Moore&B.] ⊙
Brown, Barbara Berish, (AV) .... '46 '71 C.681 B.A. L.976 J.D. [Paul,H.J.&W.]
*PRACTICE AREAS: Employment Law; Sexual Harassment; Employment Discrimination; Class Actions; Wrongful Discharge.
Brown, Barbara E. ....'42 '80 C.831 B.S. L.128 J.D. [[A] Houston&H.]
Brown, Blair G., (AV) .... '57 '82 C.861 B.A. L.569 J.D. [Zuckerman S.]
*PRACTICE AREAS: Criminal and Civil Litigation.
Brown, Boyd J., II ....'62 '93 C.821 B.A. L.893 J.D. [[A] Morgan,L.&B.]
Brown, Brant K. .... '75 '00 C&L.880 B.A., J.D. [[A] Wilmer,C.&P.]
Brown, Bruce .... '48 '77 C.886 B.A. L.128 J.D. Edison Elec. Institute
Brown, Bruce D. ....'65 '96 C.813 A.B. L.309 J.D. [[A] Baker&M.]
*PRACTICE AREAS: Litigation; First Amendment.
Brown, Caroline M. .... '62 '93 C&L.309 A.B., J.D. [Covington&B.]
Brown, Catherine T. .... '— '99 C.802 B.B.A. L.904 J.D. [[A] Hogan&H.]
*PRACTICE AREAS: Corporate Law; Securities; Real Estate Securities.
Brown, Charles F. '14 '41 C&L.309 A.B., LL.B.
(adm. in MA; not adm. in DC) 3500 Macomb St., N.W.‡
Brown, Christopher '74 '01 C.494 B.A. L.273 J.D.
(adm. in VA; not adm. in DC) [[A] Emord&Assoc.]
*PRACTICE AREAS: Civil Litigation; Food and Drug Regulation; Administrative Law.
Brown, Daniel T. ....'67 '94 C.205 B.A. L.146 J.D. [[A] Clifford C.R.&W.]
*PRACTICE AREAS: Securities Litigation; Enforcement Defense; Regulatory Law.
Brown, David E., Jr. .... '61 '86 C.674 A.B. L.383 J.D. [Alston&B.]
*PRACTICE AREAS: Mergers and Acquisitions; Corporate Finance; Securities Regulation; Bank Mergers and Acquisitions; Electronic Banking.
Brown, David I. ....'73 '99 C.893 B.A. L.309 J.D. [[A] Latham&W.]
*PRACTICE AREAS: Mergers, Acquisitions and Divestitures; Corporate Law.
Brown, David N., (AV) ....'40 '67 C.188 A.B. L.145 J.D. [Covington&B.]
Brown, David W., (AV) ....'44 '74 C.911 B.A. L.94 J.D. [Knopf&B.]
*PRACTICE AREAS: Antitrust and Trade Regulation; Energy; Trade Associations; Litigation.
Brown, Donald A., (AV) ....'29 '52 C&L.273 B.A., LL.B. [Brown,G.&J.]
Brown, Donald C., Jr. ....'49 '89 C.802 B.F.A. L.184 J.D. [[C] Weiner B.S.K.]
*PRACTICE AREAS: Litigation.
Brown, Earl V., Jr., (AV) '47 '73 C.976 B.A. L.893 J.D.
Assoc. Gen. Coun., Intl. Brotherhood of Teamsters
Brown, Edsel M., Jr. ....'55 '92 C.610 B.A. L.851 1730 K St., N.W.
Brown, Eileen P. ....'— '93 C.884 B.A. L.128 J.D. [[A] Thompson C.]
*PRACTICE AREAS: Maritime Finance; Corporate Finance; Maritime Law.
Brown, Eilene .... '66 '92 C.1350 B.A. L.1009 J.D. 1133 N. Capitol St., N.E.
Brown, Eric D. ....'72 '99 C.976 B.A. L.309 J.D. [[A] Covington&B.]
Brown, Erica D. ....'— '94 C.575 B.A. L.228 J.D. 701 Pennsylvania Avenue, N.W.
Brown, Erin M. ....'73 '99 C.112 B.A. L.276 J.D. [[A] Clifford C.R.&W.]
*PRACTICE AREAS: Litigation.
Brown, Graeme .... '60 '98 C.184 B.S. L.1202 J.D. 1503 28th St. N.W.
Brown, J. Michael '46 '72 C&L.577 A.B., J.D.
(adm. in NY; not adm. in DC) V.P., AT&T
Brown, J. Mitchell, (AV) ....'30 '55 C.280 B.B.A. L.273 J.D. [Bastianelli,B.&K.]
*PRACTICE AREAS: Government Contracts; Litigation; Alternative Dispute Resolution.
Brown, James E. ....'38 '69 C.1286 B.S. L.329 J.D. [Murrell&B.]
*PRACTICE AREAS: Disabilities; Special Education.
Brown, Jamie E. ....'— '94 C.1111 B.A. L.276 J.D. [[A] Verner,L.B.M.&H.]
*PRACTICE AREAS: Legislative.
Brown, Janet A. .... '73 '98 C.724 B.A. L.273 J.D. [[A] Jackson&C.]
*PRACTICE AREAS: Real Property; Telecommunications Law.
Brown, Jason S. ....'71 '96 C.893 B.A. L.945 J.D. [[A] Dickstein S.M.&O.]
*PRACTICE AREAS: Insurance Litigation; Antitrust Litigation.
Brown, Jay S. .... '70 '95 C.770 B.S. L.823 J.D. [[A] Mayer,B.&P.]
Brown, Jay Ward .... '64 '92 C.494 B.A. L.569 J.D. [Levine S.&K.]
Brown, Jenifer M. ....'56 '86 C.893 B.A. L.966 J.D. [[C] Baker&H.]
*PRACTICE AREAS: Litigation; Trade Regulation Law.
Brown, John Patrick, Jr. ....'60 '88 C.93 B.A. L.276 J.D. [Greenstein D.&L.]
*PRACTICE AREAS: Real Estate Development; Zoning Law; Land Use; Historic Preservation; Municipal Law.
Brown, Joseph S. '74 '99 C.696 B.A. L.893 J.D.
(adm. in VA; not adm. in DC) [[A] Shaw P.]
Brown, Karen Kendrick .... '54 '80 C.94 B.A. L.273 J.D. [Lewis&M.]
*PRACTICE AREAS: Public Finance; Taxation Law.
Brown, Kathryn C. '52 '81 C.1266 B.A. L.823 J.D.
(adm. in NY; not adm. in DC) [Wilmer,C.&P.]
*PRACTICE AREAS: Communications Law; Telecommunications Law; Electronic Commerce; Public Utility Law; Consumer Protection Law.
Brown, Kent Masterson, (AV) '49 '74 C.138 B.A. L.902 J.D.
(adm. in KY; not adm. in DC) [[C] Webster,C.&B.] (⊙Lexington, KY)
*PRACTICE AREAS: Constitutional Law; Administrative Law; Civil Rights; Litigation; Health Care and Hospital Law.
Brown, Kimberly N. ....'68 '95 C.188 B.A. L.477 J.D. [[A] Caplin&D.]
*PRACTICE AREAS: Litigation.
Brown, Laurence W. '52 '82 C.145 B.A. L.1065 J.D.
(adm. in TX; not adm. in DC) Sr. Atty., Edison Elec. Institute
Brown, Leonard D., Jr. .... '67 '00 C.645 B.A. L.659 J.D. [[A] Williams&C.]
*PRACTICE AREAS: Corporate Law; Sports Law.
Brown, Lori J. .... '61 '88 C.999 B.S. L.1209 J.D. [Scribner,H.&T.]
Brown, Mark S., (AV) ....'— '85 C.477 A.B. L.734 J.D. [King&S.]
*PRACTICE AREAS: Food and Drug Regulation.
Brown, Mary L. '56 '83 C.454 B.A. L.823 J.D.
Dir., MCI Telecommunications Corp. (Regulatory Affairs)
Brown, Mary-Patrice, (AV) .... '56 '85 C&L.276 B.S.F.S., J.D. Asst. U.S. Atty.
Brown, Marylou '69 '98 C.860 B.A. L.893 J.D.
(adm. in MD; not adm. in DC) [[A] Baker&H.]
*PRACTICE AREAS: Trusts and Estates.
Brown, Melanie R. '— '00 C&L.36 B.S., J.D
(adm. in MD; not adm. in DC) 14th St. & Constitution, Rm. 3090
Brown, Michael A., (AV) ....'38 '62 C&L.744 B.B.A., LL.B. [Brown&F.]
*PRACTICE AREAS: Environmental Law; Product Safety Law.
Brown, Michael J. .... '51 '82 C.347 B.A. L.421 J.D. 1775 Pennsylvania Ave., N.W.
Brown, Michael T. ....'— '98 C.945 B.A. L.1209 J.D. [[A] Manatt,P.&P.]
Brown, Nata K. .... '65 '92 C.811 B.A. L.329 J.D. Off. of the City Admr.
Brown, Nathan A. ....'73 '99 C.446 B.A. L.309 J.D. [[A] Covington&B.]
*PRACTICE AREAS: Health Care; Biotechnology.
Brown, Omer F., II, (AV) ....'47 '72 C.705 A.B. L.188 J.D. [Harmon,W.&B.]
*PRACTICE AREAS: Environmental; Energy; Risk Management; Government Contracts; International.
Brown, Pamela J., (AV) '57 '82 C.1044 B.A. L.273 J.D.
Asst. Gen. Coun., Corp. for Pub. Broadcasting
Brown, Patricia Russell .... '67 '93 C.674 B.S.E. L.309 J.D. [[A] Dorsey&W.] (Pat.)
*PRACTICE AREAS: Intellectual Property; Trademark Prosecution; Trademark Licensing.
Brown, Paul H. .... '48 '74 C&L.878 B.S., J.D. [Wood,M.&B.]
*PRACTICE AREAS: Communications Law; Environmental Law.
Brown, Peter L. '60 '85 C.839 B.B.A. L.69 J.D.
(adm. in TX; not adm. in DC) MCI Communications Corporation
Brown, Phoebe W. .... '66 '97 C.103 A.B. L.588 J.D. [[A] Baker&M.]
*PRACTICE AREAS: Corporate and Partnership Law; Corporate Financings (Public and Private); Capital Markets.
Brown, Preston, (AV) ....'36 '62 C&L.309 B.A., LL.B. [Curtis,M.C.&M.]
*PRACTICE AREAS: Corporate Law; Regulatory Agency Practice; International Regulatory Law.
Brown, Rhonda R. ....'56 '98 C.446 B.A. L.999 J.D. 1730 K Street, N.W., Suite 304
Brown, Richard L., (AV) .... '44 '69 C.1365 B.A. L.569 J.D. [Brown N.&K.]
*PRACTICE AREAS: Telecommunications.
Brown, Sandra L. ....'68 '93 C.288 B.A. L.607 J.D. [[A] Troutman S.]
*PRACTICE AREAS: Transportation Regulation; Litigation; Government Relations; Transportation.
Brown, Scott A. '71 '97 C.105 B.A. L.273 J.D.
(adm. in MD; not adm. in DC) [[A] Muldoon M.&F.]
*PRACTICE AREAS: Corporate Law; Securities Regulation; Banking Law.
Brown, Sharie A. .... '— '82 C.659 B.A., M.A. L.276 J.D. [Foley&L.]
*PRACTICE AREAS: Environmental Litigation; General Commercial Litigation; Corporate.
Brown, Sommers T. .... '30 '57 C.602 B.S. L.276 J.D. 2321 Ashmead Pl., N.W.‡
Brown, Stephen D. '69 '95 C.367 B.A. L.659 J.D.
(adm. in CA; not adm. in DC) 2300 N St., N.W.‡
Brown, Stephen S., (AV) .... '50 '77 C.321 A.B. L.128 J.D. [Lipshultz&H.] ⊙
*PRACTICE AREAS: Civil Practice; Insurance; Automobile Insurance; Slip and Fall Defense; Personal Injury Insurance Defense.
Brown, Tamara Y. ....'66 '91 C.69 B.A. L.329 J.D. [[A] Shook,H.&B.]
Brown, Thomas E. '67 '98 C.107 B.S.E.E. L.1356 J.D.
(adm. in VA; not adm. in DC; See Pat. Sect.) [[A] Armstrong,W.H.M.&N.]
*PRACTICE AREAS: Patent Prosecution.
Brown, Timothy .... '56 '82 C&L.329 B.B.A., J.D. 107 P St. S.W.
Brown, Timothy F., (BV) ....'56 '82 C.988 B.A. L.309 J.D. [Arent F.K.P.&K.]
*PRACTICE AREAS: Commercial Litigation; Bankruptcy Litigation; Surety; Construction; Government Contracts Law.
Brown, Travis T., (AV) .... '08 '32 C&L.575 A.B., J.D. 4848 Dexter St., N.W.‡
Brown, Tyler S. .... '68 '95 C.152 B.S. L.280 J.D. [[A] Morrison&F.] (Pat.)
*PRACTICE AREAS: Intellectual Property; Technology Contracts; Litigation.
Brown, Tyrone, (AV) ....'42 '68 C.299 A.B. L.188 LL.B. [[C] Wiley R.&F.]
*PRACTICE AREAS: Communications Law.
Brown, Tyrone Anthony '73 '00 C.103 B.A. L.309 J.D.
(adm. in CA; not adm. in DC) [[A] Covington&B.]
*PRACTICE AREAS: Litigation.
Brown, Winthrop N., (AV) ....'48 '75 C.813 B.A. L.273 J.D. [Milbank,T.H.&M.]
*PRACTICE AREAS: Banking; Securities.
Brown, Zhonette .... '71 '98 C.1165 B.A. L.276 J.D. [[A] Kirkland&E.]
*PRACTICE AREAS: Litigation.

Brown & Freeston, (AV)
3201 New Mexico Avenue, N.W. Suite 242, 20016
Telephone: 202-237-6008 Fax: 202-237-5259
URL: http://www.brown-freeston.com
Michael A. Brown; Margaret A. Freeston.
Product Safety Law, Product Liability, Recalls, Administrative Law, Environmental Law, Expert Witnessing.
See Professional Biographies, WASHINGTON, DISTRICT OF COLUMBIA

Brown, Gildenhorn & Jacobs, (AV) .... 1250 Conn. Ave., N.W.

Brown Nietert & Kaufman, Chartered, (AV)
Suite 660, 1920 N Street, N.W., 20036
Telephone: 202-887-0600 Facsimile: 202-457-0126
Email: steve@bnkcomlaw.com URL: http://www.bnkcomlaw.com
Richard L. Brown; Robyn G. Nietert; Lorretta K. Tobin (Not admitted in DC); Rhonda L. Neil. Of Counsel: David J. Kaufman.
Practice before Federal and Local Courts, Government Departments and Commissions. Legislative and Committee Appearances. Public Utilities, State and Municipal Commissions and Agencies. Specializing in Telecommunications.
See Professional Biographies, WASHINGTON, DISTRICT OF COLUMBIA

Brown, Thomas P., III
(See Bethesda, Maryland)

Brown, Winick, Graves, Gross, Baskerville and Schoenebaum, P.L.C., (BV)
1133 21st Street, NW Suite M100 (⊙Des Moines, Pella, IA)
Browne, Judith A. ...... '66 '93 C.659 B.S. L.178 J.D. Sr. Attorney, Advancement Project
Browne, Maria T. .... '67 '92 C.575 B.A. L.273 J.D. [Cole,R.&B.]
*PRACTICE AREAS: Cable Television; Cable Programming; Telecommunications Competition; Telecommunications Regulation; Commercial Litigation.
Browne, Maureen F. ....'67 '92 C.321 B.A. L.273 J.D. [[A] Adduci,M.&S.]
*PRACTICE AREAS: Intellectual Property; Commercial; Trade Regulation.
Browne, Patrick J., Jr. ....'69 '96 C&L.861 B.S.M., J.D. [[A] White&C.]
Browne, Rachelle V. '52 '77
C.66 B.S. L.309 J.D. Asst. Gen. Coun., Smithsonian Institution
Browne, René E. ....'71 '98 C.228 A.B. L.276 J.D. [[A] Hogan&H.]
Brownell, Eileen L., (P.C.) .... '54 '82 C.893 B.S. L.309 J.D. [Shaw P.]
*PRACTICE AREAS: Tax; Corporate.
Brownell, F. William ....'52 '78 C&L.276 B.S., J.D. [Hunton&W.]
*PRACTICE AREAS: Environmental; Administrative Law; Appellate Practice; International Law.
Brownell, George R., (AV) '14 '39
C&L.188 A.B., LL.B. 1709 N St., N.W. (⊙New York, NY)
Brownell, Roy E., II .... '70 '99 C.475 B.A. L.30 J.D. [[A] Muldoon M.&F.]
Browner, Carol M. '55 '80 C&L.260 B.A., J.D.
(adm. in FL; not adm. in DC) 209 6th St., S.E.‡
Browning, Cheryl M. '49 '80
C.446 B.A. L.276 J.D. 1150 Connecticut Avenue, N.W., Suite 900

Browning, Dawn M '71 '97 C.205 B.A. L.904 J.D.
(adm. in TN; not adm. in DC) Asst. Gen. Coun., Legal Services Corp.
Browning, Edmund L., Jr., (AV) '16 '40
C.273 A.B. L.309 LL.B. 3315 Wisconsin Ave., N.W.‡
Browning, Linda K., (BV) '49 '82 C.1064 B.A. L.192 J.D.
(adm. in AL; not adm. in DC) [Miller,B.&O.]
*PRACTICE AREAS: Energy Law; Natural Gas Transactions; Energy Regulation.
Browning, Paul W. .... '68 '99 C.103 B.S. L.309 J.D. [Finnegan,H.F.G.&D.]
*PRACTICE AREAS: Chemical Intellectual Property; Chemical Patent Prosecution; Pharmaceutical Patents.
Browning, Susan J. '57 '82 C&L.1209 B.A., J.D.
(adm. in VA; not adm. in DC) Pension Benefit Guar. Corp.
Brownstein, Philip N., (AV) .... '17 '40 C.273 L.180 LL.B. 3000 K St., N.W.

Brownstein Hyatt & Farber, P.C., (AV)
1615 L Street, N.W. Suite 450, 20036
Telephone: 202-296-7353 Telecopier: 202-296-7009
URL: http://www.bhf-law.com
William T. Brack (Resident); Thomas H. Hudson (Resident). Of Counsel: Lee Cowen (Resident).
Administrative, Legislative, Regulatory.
Denver, Colorado Office: Twenty-Second Floor, 410 Seventeenth Street, 80202-4437. Telephone: 303-223-1100. Telecopier: 303-223-1111.
Glenwood Springs, Colorado Office: 715 Grand Avenue, Suite C, 81601. Mailing Address: P.O. Box 357, 81602-0357. Telephone: 970-945-5302. Telecopier: 970-384-2360.
See Professional Biographies, WASHINGTON, DISTRICT OF COLUMBIA

Brubaker, Raina E. .... '65 '96 C.170 B.A. L.930 J.D. [Skadden,A.S.M.&F.]
*PRACTICE AREAS: Litigation.
Bruce, Andrea M. .... '65 '93 C.367 B.A. L.1066 J.D. [Hogan&H.]
*PRACTICE AREAS: Food, Drug and Cosmetic Law; Food and Agriculture; Food Labeling and Inspection; Advertising and Labeling.
Bruce, Carol Elder, (AV) .... '49 '75 C&L.273 B.A., J.D. [Tighe P.A.T.]
*PRACTICE AREAS: White Collar Crime; Civil Litigation.
Bruce, Charles M., (AV) '45 '72
C.902 A.B. L.273 J.D. [Moore&B.] (London, England)
Bruce, E. Edward, (AV) .... '38 '67 C&L.976 B.A., LL.B. [Covington&B.]
Bruce, James T., III .... '47 '75 C.674 B.S.E. L.273 J.D. [Wiley R.&F.] (Pat.)
*PRACTICE AREAS: Government Affairs; Internet; Electronic Commerce; Energy.
Bruce, John F., (AV) .... '40 '66 C.273 B.A. L.893 LL.B. [Howrey S.A.&W.]
*PRACTICE AREAS: Antitrust; Complex Litigation; International Trade Law; Commercial Litigation.
Bruce, Patricia E. .... '55 '93 C.724 B.A. L.472 J.D. [Zuckert,S.&R.]

Bruce, Stephen R. '50 '79 C.575 B.A. L.276 J.D.
805 15th St. NW, Suite 210, 20005
Telephone: 202-371-8013 Fax: 202-371-0121
Email: stephen.bruce@prodigy.net
***PRACTICE AREAS: ERISA (100%).**
Pension Claims, Employee Benefit Claims. Represents Employees and Groups of Employees denied benefits. Consults with other attorneys on ERISA Law.

Bruch, Carl E. '67 '96 C.475 B.S. L.596 J.D.
(adm. in OR; not adm. in DC) Sr. Atty., Environmental Law Institute
Bruckmann, Barbara O. .... '45 '86 C.914 B.A. L.902 J.D. [Howrey S.A.&W.]
*PRACTICE AREAS: Antitrust.
Bruder, George F., (AV) .... '38 '64 C.197 A.B. L.145 J.D. [Bruder,G.&M.] ‡
*PRACTICE AREAS: Electric Utility; Hydroelectric Law; Appellate Practice.

Bruder, Gentile & Marcoux, L.L.P., (AV)
1100 New York Avenue, N.W., Suite 510 East, 20005-3934
Telephone: 202-783-1350 Telecopiers: 202-737-9117; 347-2644
Email: bgmstaff@brudergentile.com URL: http://www.brudergentile.com
George F. Bruder (Retired); Carmen L. Gentile; Albert R. Simonds, Jr. (Retired); J. Michel Marcoux; David E. Goroff; James H. McGrew; Thomas L. Blackburn;—Antonia A. Frost; David Martin Connelly; Gary D. Levenson. Of Counsel: Peter K. Matt.
General and Administrative Practice including Public Utility, Electric Power, Natural Gas, Cogeneration, Hydroelectric, Bulk Power Transmission, Energy and Antitrust. Appellate Practice.
See Professional Biographies, WASHINGTON, DISTRICT OF COLUMBIA

Brueckner, Leslie A. ...... '61 '89 C.112 A.B. L.309 J.D. Trial Lawyers for Pub. Jus. P.C.
Bruehs, Tracy L. .... '69 '99 C.1044 B.S. L.982 J.D. [Nixon P.]
*PRACTICE AREAS: Business Law.
Bruemmer, Russell J., (AV) .... '52 '78 C.427 B.A. L.477 J.D. [Wilmer,C.&P.]
*PRACTICE AREAS: Corporate Law; Finance; Banks and Banking.
Brugge, Parker E. .... '63 '88 C.893 B.S.Ch.E. L.945 J.D. [Patton B.]
Bruggeman, Linda S. .... '51 '79 C.473 A.B. L.276 J.D. [Crowell&M.]
*PRACTICE AREAS: Government Contract Law.
Brumskine, Charles Walker .... '51 '92 C.999 L.802 LL.M. 2300 M St. NW #800
Brun, Jean-Marc .... '59 '91 C.107 B.A. L.978 J.D. [Vorys,S.S.&P.]
*PRACTICE AREAS: Trademarks; Licensing; Unfair Competition.
Bruneau, Christopher T. .... '69 '95 C&L.276 B.A., J.D. [Wilmer,C.&P.]
Brunelli, Virginia A. '74 '00 L.228 LL.M.
(adm. in NY; not adm. in DC) [Troutman S.]
*PRACTICE AREAS: Project Finance; International Transactions.
Brunenkant, Jon L., (AV) .... '50 '75 C.597 B.A. L.273 J.D. [Brunenkant&H.]
*PRACTICE AREAS: Energy Law; Regulatory Law; Utility Law.

Brunenkant & Haskell, LLP, (AV)
805 15th Street, N.W., Suite 1101, 20005
Telephone: 202-408-0700 Fax: 202-408-5959
Email: brunenkant@bh-law.com URL: http://www.bh-law.com
Jon L. Brunenkant; Mark R. Haskell; James W. Moeller; Cheryl J. Walker. Senior Attorney: Kenneth M. Albert. Associates: Melissa L. Lauderdale; Christie L. Richart; Rebecca C. Moorehead.
Energy Law, Electricity and Natural Gas Regulation, Merger and Acquisition of Energy Companies, Natural Resource and Administrative Practice, Utility Law, Appellate Practice and Representation of Clients before the Federal and State Regulatory Commissions, Environmental Issues as related to Energy Law.
See Professional Biographies, WASHINGTON, DISTRICT OF COLUMBIA

Bruner, Becky M., (AV) .... '59 '85 C&L.846 B.A., J.D. [Vinson&E.]
*PRACTICE AREAS: Energy.
Bruner, Daniel, (AV) '52 '81 C.691 B.A. L.477 J.D.
Assoc. Dir., Lit. & Advocacy, Whitman-Walker Clinic Legal Servs. (Washington)
*RESPONSIBILITIES: Disability Discrimination; Employment Law; Health Insurance; Disability Insurance; Privacy Law.
Bruner, P. Daniel, (AV) '52 '81 C.691 B.A. L.477 J.D.
[Spiegel&M.] (Washington)
*PRACTICE AREAS: Energy; AIDS Litigation; Employment; Discrimination; Insurance.
Brunner, Jan M. '68 '99 C.856 B.A. L.893 J.D.
(adm. in MD; not adm. in DC) [Olsson,F.&W.]
*PRACTICE AREAS: Food and Drug Regulation.
Brunner, Thomas W., (AV) .... '45 '70 C.178 A.B. L.976 J.D. [Wiley R.&F.]
*PRACTICE AREAS: Insurance; Privacy Law; Health Care; Litigation.
Bruno, Jason M. .... '72 '00 C.953 B.A. L.575 J.D. [Dickstein S.M.&O.]
*PRACTICE AREAS: Complex Dispute Resolution.
Bruno, Philippe M. .... '55 '80 L.276 LL.M. [Dorsey&W.]
*PRACTICE AREAS: International Law.

Brunsvold, Brian G., (AV) '38 '67
C.350 B.S.Ch.E. L.273 J.D. [Finnegan,H.F.G.&D.] (See Pat. Sect.)
*PRACTICE AREAS: Antitrust and Trade Regulation; Chemical Intellectual Property; Intellectual Property Licensing; Intellectual Property Litigation; Pharmaceutical Intellectual Property.
Bruntel, Kenneth M., (AV) .... '49 '78 C.197 B.A. L.273 J.D. [Crowell&M.]
*PRACTICE AREAS: Public Contract Law; Wage and Hour Law; Business Crimes Law.
Brusca, Richard L. .... '56 '82 C.1044 B.A. L.904 J.D. [Skadden,A.S.M.&F.]
Bruse, J. Charles '46 '71
C.597 B.A. L.494 J.D. V.P. & Asst. Gen. Coun., Allstate Ins. Co.
Bruskin, Robert M. .... '46 '73 C.563 B.Ch.E. L.276 J.D. [Howrey S.A.&W.]
*PRACTICE AREAS: Intellectual Property; Antitrust Law; Complex Litigation.
Brustein, Michael L., (AV) .... '49 '74 C.569 B.A. L.184 J.D. [Brustein&M.]
*PRACTICE AREAS: Education; Civil Litigation.

Brustein & Manasevit, (AV)
3105 South Street, N.W., 20007
Telephone: 202-965-3652 Facsimile: 202-965-8913
Email: bruman@bruman.com URL: http://www.bruman.com
Members of Firm: Leigh M. Manasevit; Michael L. Brustein; Kristen Tosh Cowan. Associates: Christine M. Plagata-Neubauer (Not admitted in DC); Claire A. Milner (Not admitted in DC); Jonathan D. Tarnow; Melissa Clarry (Not admitted in DC).
See Professional Biographies, WASHINGTON, DISTRICT OF COLUMBIA

Bruton, James A., III, (AV) .... '49 '75 C.575 A.B. L.831 J.D. [Williams&C.]
Bruton, Jennifer J. .... '71 '97 C.575 B.A. L.896 J.D. [Venable,A.B.H.&C.]
*PRACTICE AREAS: Real Estate.
Bryan, Charles E. .... '46 '75 C.893 B.A. L.976 J.D. [Cadwalader,W.&T.]
*PRACTICE AREAS: Securitization; Corporate Finance; Securities Offerings.
Bryan, R. Timothy .... '57 '92 C.576 B.A. L.575 J.D. [Piper M.R.&W.]
*PRACTICE AREAS: Bankruptcy; Creditors Rights; Commercial Finance; Corporate Law; Mergers and Acquisitions.
Bryan, Richard W., (AV) .... '55 '80 C.945 B.A. L.273 J.D. [Jackson&C.]
*PRACTICE AREAS: Automobile Insurance Coverage; Casualty Insurance; Commercial Insurance; Excess Coverage; Insurance Bad Faith.

Bryan Cave LLP, (AV)
A Partnership including a Professional Corporation
700 Thirteenth Street, N.W., 20005-3960
Telephone: (202) 508-6000 Facsimile: (202) 508-6200 For attorney e-mails use: First initials of first and middle names, last name, firm name, e.g., rmsmith@bryancave.com
URL: http://www.bryancave.com
Partners: John P. Barrie; William F. Bavinger III; Richard A. Cohn; James M. Cole; John Michael Cooper; John C. Danforth (Not admitted in DC); Alan J. Dixon (Not admitted in DC); William C. Edgar; Robert M. Huber; Kenneth M. Kastner; Stanley J. Marcuss; LaDawn Naegle; Rodney F. Page; Therese D. Pritchard (Not admitted in DC); Daniel C. Schwartz; Eric F. Stoer; Kathleen E. Topelius; Robert F. Van Voorhees; John R. Wilner; Kevin J. Wolf. Of Counsel: Joan Z. Bernstein; Stephen S. Kaye; James J. Murphy; John J. O'Connor III; Jo Anne Peele; Robert P. Visser; Douglas E. Winter. Counsel: Scott M. Badami; Stuart M. Ginsberg; Scott R. Harrison; Dana B. Rosenfeld; Angela F. Williams; Jill M. Zucker. Resident Associates: Jenifer Berger; Vanessa Y. Chandler (Not admitted in DC); Daniel M. Fisher-Owens; Rebecca A. Ford; John Staley Heatly; Christopher C. S. Manning; Margaret G. Perl; Earl G. Pinto; Phillip A. Quatrini; Colleen M. Reddan; Heather Rheiner Badami; Sylvia A. Rhodes; Vasilios Salamandrakis; Sarah P. Swanz; Robert W. Tomilson; Tina R. Tyson; Whitney Wilson; Jami Wyatt.
General Civil Practice. Administrative, Antitrust, Aviation, Communications, Computer, Copyright, Corporate Finance, Corporation, Criminal Defense, Environmental, Financial Institutions, Government Contracts, Intellectual Property, International, International Trade and Customs, Legislative Patents, Life Sciences, Real Estate, Securities, Taxation, Technology, Trademark, Transportation, Trusts and Estates. General Civil Trial and Appellate Practice.
St. Louis, Missouri Office: One Metropolitan Square, 211 N. Broadway, 63102-2750. Telephone: (314) 259-2000. Facsimile: (314) 259-2020.
New York, N.Y. Office: 245 Park Avenue, 10167-0034. Telephone: (212) 692-1800. Facsimile: (212) 692-1900.
Kansas City, Missouri Office: 3500 One Kansas City Place, 1200 Main Street, 64105-2100. Telephone: (816) 374-3200. Facsimile: (816) 374-3300.
Jefferson City, Missouri Office: 221 Bolivar Street, 65102-1670. Telephone: (573) 556-6620. Facsimile: (573) 556-6630.
Overland Park, Kansas Office: 7500 College Boulevard, Suite 1100, 66210-4035. Telephone: (913) 338-7700. Facsimile: (913) 338-7777.
Phoenix, Arizona Office: Two North Central Avenue, Suite 2200, 85004-4406. Telephone: (602) 364-7000. Facsimile: (602) 364-7070.
Santa Monica, California Office: 120 Broadway, Suite 300, 90401-2305. Telephone: (310) 576-2100. Facsimile: (310) 576-2200.
Irvine, California Office: 2020 Main Street, Suite 600, 92614. Telephone: (949) 223-7000. Facsimile: (949) 223-7100.
Chicago, Illinois Office: Bryan Cave (Illinois), Chicago Title and Trust Building, 161 North Clark Street, Suite 2840, 60601. Telephone: 312-602-5000. Facsimile: 312-602-5050.
London, England Office: 33 Cannon Street, EC4M 5TE. Telephone: 44-20-7246-5800. Facsimile: 44-20-7246-5858.
Riyadh, 11465 Saudi Arabia Office: In Cooperation with Kadasah Law Firm, P.O. Box 20883. Telephone: 966-1-474-0888. Facsimile: 966-1-476-2881.
Kuwait City, Kuwait Office: Mashora Advocates & Legal Consultants, Sheraton Towers, Second Floor, P.O. Box 5902 Safat, 13060. Telephone: 965-240-4470. Facsimile: 965-242-4047.
Dubai, U.A.E. Office: Al-Mehairi Legal Consultants - Bryan Cave LLP, Dubai, Holiday Centre, Suite 1103, P.O. Box 13677, UAE. Telephone: 971-4-3314-123. Facsimile: 971-4-3318-287.
Abu Dhabi, U.A.E. Office: Al-Mehairi Legal Consultants - Bryan Cave LLP, Al Otaiba Tower, Suite 804, P.O. Box 47645. Telephone: 971-2-6340-322. Facsimile: 971-2-6340-522.
Hong Kong Office: Suite 2106, Tower One, Lippo Centre, 89 Queensway. Telephone: 852-2522-2821. Facsimile: 852-2522-3830.
Shanghai 200040, People's Republic of China Office: Suite 448, Shanghai Centre, 1376 Nan Jing West Road. Telephone: 8621-6279-8166. Facsimile: 8621-6279-8165.
See Professional Biographies, WASHINGTON, DISTRICT OF COLUMBIA

Bryant, Ann Lake, (BV) .... '49 '83 C.164 B.A. L.128 J.D. [Gordon&Br.]
*PRACTICE AREAS: Immigration Law; International adoptions; Citizenship; International Business Personnel Transfers.
Bryant, Arthur H. '54 '81
C.821 A.B. L.309 J.D. Exec. Dir., Trial Lawyers for Pub. Jus., P.C.
Bryant, Cathaleen Siunn '73 '99 C.1090 B.A. L.309 J.D.
(adm. in VA; not adm. in DC) 810 Vermont Ave. NW
Bryant, Dennis L. .... '46 '76 C.869 B.S. L.880 J.D. [Holland&K.]
*PRACTICE AREAS: Government Relations; Shipping Regulation; Admiralty; Regulatory; Legislative.
Bryant, Ellen Dunham .... '70 '98 C.25 B.A. L.228 J.D. [Hogan&H.]
*PRACTICE AREAS: Labor and Employment.
Bryant, James Sears, (AV) .... '53 '78 C.663 B.S. L.802 J.D. [Dow,L.&A.]
Bryant, Shawn D. .... '71 '98 C.164 B.A. L.228 J.D. [Spriggs&H.]
*PRACTICE AREAS: Litigation; Environmental Law; Toxic Torts.
Bryar, Marcel A. '65 '93 C&L.976 B.A., J.D.
(adm. in MA; not adm. in DC) Assoc. Gen. Coun., Fannie Mae
*RESPONSIBILITIES: E-Commerce; Technology; Intellectual Property; Telecommunications; Corporate Finance.
Brylawski, Henry H., (AV) .... '13 '40 L.537 LL.B. 316 Penn. Ave., S.E.
Bryson, John M., II .... '49 '77 C&L.893 B.S.N.E., J.D. [Holland&K.]
*PRACTICE AREAS: Litigation; Employment; Corporate Law.
Bryson, Molly R. .... '71 '99 C.128 B.A. L.180 J.D. [Nixon P.]
*PRACTICE AREAS: Real Estate Syndication; Taxation.
Bryson, Nancy S. .... '51 '75 C.94 B.A. L.276 J.D. [Crowell&M.]
Brzezinski, Mark F. '65 '97 C.197 B.A. L.893 J.D.
(adm. in VA; not adm. in DC) [McGuirewoods] ‡
*PRACTICE AREAS: International Transactions; International Law.

Brzezynski, Lora A. .... '68 '93 C.472 B.A. L.276 J.D. [[A] McKenna&C.]
*PRACTICE AREAS: Civil Litigation; Commercial Litigation; Products Liability.

Bubar, James S. '52 '78 C.1169 B.A. L.1065 J.D.
1667 K Street, NW, Suite 801, 20006
Telephone: 202-223-2060 Fax: 202-223-2061
Email: jbubar@aol.com URL: http://www.lawyers.com/jamesbubar
***PRACTICE AREAS: Communications (35%); Business Law (35%); Litigation (30%).**
Communications Law, FCC Law, Business Formations, Business Law, Securities Law, Securities Fraud, Business Transactions, Litigation, Commercial Litigation.
See Professional Biographies, WASHINGTON, DISTRICT OF COLUMBIA

Buc, Nancy L., (AV) .... '44 '69 C.103 A.B. L.893 LL.B. [Buc&B.]

Buc & Beardsley, (AV)
919 Eighteenth Street, N.W. Suite 600, 20006-5503
Telephone: 202-736-3600 Fax: 202-736-3608
Resident Partners: Kate C. Beardsley; Nancy L. Buc; Jane E. Baluss. Associates: Abigail E. Brandel; Julia C. Tierney; Adam S. Bloom; William LaFont Huie (Not admitted in DC).
Food, Drug, Medical Device, Biologics and Cosmetics Law. Advertising and Marketing Law. Consumer Products Safety Law.
See Professional Biographies, WASHINGTON, DISTRICT OF COLUMBIA

Bucca, Daniel .... '64 '00 C.645 Ph.D. L.30 J.D. [[A] McDermott,W.&E.] (Pat.)
Buch, Ronald L., Jr. .... '65 '93 C.999 B.B.A. L.213 J.D. [[A] McKee N.]
*PRACTICE AREAS: Tax Litigation.
Buchanan, James Randall .... '63 '89 C&L.893 B.A., J.D. [Sutherland A.&B.]
*PRACTICE AREAS: International Taxation; Federal Taxation; Tax Planning.
Buchanan, John G., III, (AV) .... '50 '79 C.674 A.B. L.309 J.D. [Covington&B.]
Buchanan, Thomas M., (AV) .... '53 '80 C.734 B.A. L.276 J.D. [Winston&S.]
*PRACTICE AREAS: White Collar Crime; Complex Litigation; Civil Litigation; Banking Litigation.

Buchanan Ingersoll, Professional Corporation, (AV)
1776 K Street, N.W., Suite 800, 20006-2365 ⊙
Telephone: 202-452-7900 Telecopier: 202-452-7989
URL: http://www.bipc.com
Shareholders: Edward John Allera; Steven M. Hilton; Andrew P. Loewinger; Robert G. Pinco; Donald E. Segal; Mark M. Yacura. Associates: Shannon Haaf; Todd H. Halpern; Paul J. Larsen (Not admitted in DC); Patrick A. Nickler (Not admitted in DC); Bradley K. Steinbrecher; Theodore M. Sullivan (Not admitted in DC).
Antitrust and Trade Regulation, Broadcasting and Cable TV, Commercial Transactions, Computer Law, Construction Industry Law, Corporate Law and Finance, Creditors' Rights and Bankruptcy, Energy, Environmental Law, ERISA and Employee Benefits, Family Law, Financial Institutions, Franchising, Government Relations, Healthcare, Insurance Regulation, Intellectual Property, International Transactions, Labor and Employment, Litigation, Mergers and Acquisitions, Municipal Law, Natural Resources Law, Public Finance, Real Estate, Security Alarm, Tax and Estate Planning, Technology Law, Trade Secret Litigation, Transportation Law, Trust and Estate Administration, Venture Capital.
Pittsburgh, Pennsylvania Office: One Oxford Centre, 301 Grant Street, 20th Floor. Telephone: 412-562-8800.
Philadelphia, Pennsylvania Office: Eleven Penn Center, 14th Floor, 1835 Market Street. Telephone: 215-665-8700.
Bryn Mawr, Pennsylvania Office: 937 East Haverford Road, Suite 201. Telephone: 610-581-7004.
Harrisburg, Pennsylvania Office: One South Market Square, 213 Market Street, 3rd Floor. Telephone: 717-237-4800.
Tampa, Florida Office: SunTrust Financial Centre, 401 East Jackson Street, Suite 2500. Telephone: 813-222-8180.
Aventura, Florida Office: One Turnberry Place, 19495 Biscayne Boulevard, Suite 606. Telephone: 305-933-5600.
Miami, Florida Office: Bank of America Tower, 100 S.E. Second Street, Suite 2100. Telephone: 305-347-4080.
Princeton, New Jersey Office: 700 Alexander Park, Suite 300. Telephone: 609-987-6800.
Buffalo, New York Office: 268 Main Street, Suite 201. Telephone: 716-853-2330.
New York, New York Office: 140 Broadway, 35th Floor. Telephone: 646-458-2340.
Other Washington, D.C. Office: Silverstein and Mullens, 1776 K Street, N.W., Suite 800. Telephone: 202-452-7900.
McLean, Virginia Office: 8280 Greensboro Drive, Suite 601. Telephone: 703-749-6060.
Wilmington, Delaware Office: 1201 North Market Street, Suite 1501. Telephone: 302-428-5500.
San Diego, California Office: First National Bank Center, 401 West A Street, Suite 1900. Telephone: 619-578-5000.
London, England Office: Tower 42, The International Financial Centre, Old Broad Street, EC2N 1HQ. Telephone: 44-207-920-3700.
Dublin, Ireland Office: Level 1, 4 Custom House Plaza, IFSC, Dublin 1. Telephone: 011-353-1611-7266. Fax: 3531-836-9305.
See Professional Biographies, WASHINGTON, DISTRICT OF COLUMBIA

Buchen, Philip W. .... '16 '41 C&L.477 A.B., J.D. 1775 Pennsylvania Ave.
Bucher, Jeffrey M. .... '— '58 C.605 A.B. L.813 J.D. [[C] Kozusko L.H.]
*PRACTICE AREAS: Financial Institution Regulation.
Bucher, Kathryn .... '58 '83 C.882 B.A. L.188 J.D. [Wiley R.&F.]
*PRACTICE AREAS: Health Care Regulation; Health Care Litigation; Insurance; Government Contracts; Privacy.
Buchet, Michael M. X. '47 '92 C.184 B.A. L.426 J.D.
(adm. in PA; not adm. in DC) Wkrs. Comp. Policy Coord., UBC Health & Safety Fund
Buchholz, Ross M. .... '48 '78 C.102 B.A. L.1202 J.D. 441 4th St. NW
Buchman, Barry I. .... '71 '97 C.347 B.A. L.904 J.D. [[A] Gilbert H.&R.]
*PRACTICE AREAS: Insurance Coverage; Personal Injury; Automobile Negligence; Premises Liability; Litigation.

Buchman & O'Brien, LLP
1331 Pennsylvania Avenue, N.W., Suite 1211, 20004 ⊙
Telephone: 202-638-6854 Telecopier: 202-638-2286
Email: dco@bev-alc-law.com URL: http://www.bev-alc-law.com
Resident Partner: Mark A. Koslowe.
General Civil Practice. Administrative, Corporate, Labor, Alcoholic Beverage Control and Business Law. Trade Regulation. Trademark, Copyright, Unfair Competition and Licensing, Food and Drug Law.
New York, New York Office: 10 East 40th Street, Suite 708. Telephone: 212-686-0440. Telecopier: 212-889-7622.
San Francisco, California Office: 505 Sansome Street, Suite 1500. Telephone: 415-398-0440. Telecopier: 415-394-9564.
Edison, New Jersey Office: 510 Thornall Street, Suite 200 (Metro Park). Telephone: 732-632-9463. Telecopier: 732-632-8760.
See Professional Biographies, WASHINGTON, DISTRICT OF COLUMBIA

Bucholtz, Harold R., (AV) .... '52 '76 C.705 B.A. L.893 J.D. [Holland&K.]
*PRACTICE AREAS: Tax Exempt Financing Law; Tax Exempt Organizations; Taxation (Local, State and Federal).
Bucholtz, Jeffrey S. .... '— '95 C.659 B.A. L.309 J.D. [[A] King&S.]
Buchovecky, John J., (BV) .... '60 '88 C.800 A.B. L.904 J.D. [Van Ness F.]
*PRACTICE AREAS: Electric Power; Energy.
Buck, Kara Brown '66 '94 C.112 B.A. L.1355 J.D.
(adm. in CA; not adm. in DC) Asst. Coun., Fed. Affs., State Farm Ins. Cos.
Buck, Karen A. .... '65 '91 C.415 B.A. L.128 J.D. Asst. Corp. Coun.
Buckelew, Brian J. .... '73 '99 C.37 B.A. L.1066 J.D. [[C] Williams&C.]
*PRACTICE AREAS: Litigation.
Buckhold, William C. .... '53 '85 C.823 B.A. L.107 J.D. 1000 16th St. NW
Buckle, Jane V. .... '33 '76 C.30 B.S. L.128 J.D. 1819 H St., N.W.
Buckles, Mary E. .... '— '81 C.914 B.A. L.30 J.D. [[C] Reed S.]
*PRACTICE AREAS: Intellectual Property; Copyrights; Patents; Trademarks; Trade Secrets.

Buckley, Carol Ann .... '60 '86 C.1031 B.S. L.188 J.D. 60 Massachusetts Ave., N.E.
Buckley, Christopher H., Jr., (AV) .... '40 '68 C.602 B.A. L.309 LL.B. [Gibson,D.&C.]
*PRACTICE AREAS: Litigation; Environmental Law; Toxic Torts; Class Actions; Construction Law.
Buckley, David W., (AV) .... '45 '74 C.602 B.A. L.273 J.D. [Statland&B.]
*PRACTICE AREAS: Commercial Litigation; Construction Law; Real Estate; Franchise Law.
Buckley, Jeremiah S., (AV) .... '44 '69 C.1030 B.A. L.893 J.D. [Goodwin P.]
*PRACTICE AREAS: Banking; Mortgage Finance; Consumer Finance; Regulatory; Real Estate.
Buckley, John J., Jr., (AV) .... '47 '72 C.276 A.B. L.145 J.D. [Williams&C.]
Buckley, Paul S. .... '59 '85 C.1019 B.A. L.446 J.D. Sr. Atty., Washington Gas Light Co.
Bucklin, Donald T., (AV) .... '38 '68 C.676 B.S. L.904 J.D. [Squire,S.&D.]
*PRACTICE AREAS: Civil Litigation; White Collar Criminal Litigation.
Buckman, Sally A., (AV) .... '57 '82 C.914 B.A. L.569 J.D. [Leventhal,S.&L.]
*PRACTICE AREAS: Communications Law; Media Law.
Buckman, Steven M., (AV) .... '53 '80 C.966 B.A. L.446 J.D. [Lotstein B.]
*PRACTICE AREAS: Real Estate; Real Estate Title; Real Estate Leasing; Foreclosures; Commercial Litigation.
Buckner, David M. .... '69 '95 C.705 B.A. L.309 J.D. 725 12th St., N.W.
Buczynski, Joseph J. '64 '94
C.1028 B.S.E.E. L.273 J.D. [Roylance,A.B.&G.] (See Pat. Sect.)
*PRACTICE AREAS: Intellectual Property Law; Electrical Patents; Mechanical Patents; Computer Law.
Budinetz, James A. .... '70 '95 C.276 B.S. L.30 J.D. [[A] Morgan,L.&B.]
Budoff, Robert S. '53 '80 C.299 B.A. L.276 J.D.
Asst. Gen. Coun., Distilled Spirits Council of the U.S.A.
Budoff, Sheila Kraft '55 '85 C.1044 B.A. L.904 J.D.
(adm. in MD; not adm. in DC) 1717 H St., N.W.

Budow and Noble, P.C.
(See Bethesda, Maryland)

Bue, Kara L. '64 '93 C.103 A.B. L.426 J.D.
(adm. in CA; not adm. in DC) [[A] Thacher P.&W.]
Buechner, Jack W., (AV) .... '40 '65 C.711 A.B. L.734 J.D. [Manatt,P.&P.]
Buehler, Lorien S. '74 '99 C.884 B.A. L.273 J.D.
D.C. Law Students in Court Prog., Inc.
Buek, Richard W., Jr. .... '45 '70 C.400 B.A. L.362 J.D. AlliedSignal Inc.
Buente, David T., Jr., (AV) .... '46 '75 C.401 B.S. L.659 J.D. [Sidley A.B.&W.]
Buerger, Christian A. .... '72 '96 C.674 A.B. L.309 J.D. [[A] Shaw P.]
Buffaloe, William T. '72 '00 C.976 B.A. L.178 J.D.
(adm. in VA; not adm. in DC) [[A] O'Melveny&M.]
Buffon, Charles E., (AV) .... '39 '65 C.197 A.B. L.309 LL.B. [Covington&B.]
Buffone, Samuel J., (AV) .... '46 '71 C.665 B.A. L.276 J.D. [Ropes&G.]
*PRACTICE AREAS: White Collar Crime Law; RICO; Complex Litigation.
Buford, Kevin A. .... '57 '86 C.869 B.S. L.846 J.D. [Holland&K.]
*PRACTICE AREAS: Technology Law; Commercial Law; Intellectual Property Law; Patents; Copyrights, Trademarks and Trade Secrets.
Bugaisky, Lawrence B. .... '51 '98 C.339 B.S. L.904 J.D. [[A] Sterne,K.G.&F.]
*PRACTICE AREAS: Intellectual Property.
Bui, Diane '75 '01 C.228 B.A. L.569 J.D.
(adm. in MD; not adm. in DC) [[A] Arent F.K.P.&K.]
*PRACTICE AREAS: International Transactions; International Trade.
Bui, Vu .... '73 '99 C.273 B.A. L.262 J.D. [[A] Morgan,L.&B.]
Buie, Alan M. .... '66 '92 C.846 B.A. L.309 J.D. [Jenner&B.]
Buik, Richard D., (AV) .... '52 '77 C.813 A.B. L.145 J.D. Pres., RDB Holdings, Inc.
Bukar, Nancy A. '63 '91 C.454 B.A. L.128 J.D.
State Gov't Coun., Consumer Healthcare Products Association
Buksbaum, Gregg S. .... '71 '97 C.477 B.A. L.1009 J.D. [[A] Weil,G.&M.]
*PRACTICE AREAS: Corporate Law; Private Equity.
Bulger, Michele L. .... '61 '91 C.264 B.A. L.273 J.D. [[A] Thompson,O.M.N.&H.]
*PRACTICE AREAS: General Practice; Personal Injury; Premise Liability; Products Liability; Insurance Coverage.
Bulgeron, Beth A. .... '71 '00 C.966 B.A. L.464 J.D. [[A] Bode&G.]
*PRACTICE AREAS: Complex Business Litigation; Appellate Practice; Construction Law.
Bulkley, Josephine A. '50 '79 C.477 B.A. L.1162 J.D.
Child Sexual Abuse Legal Specialist, Ctr. on Child. & the Law
Bull, Ryan Edward '72 '00 C.880 B.A. L.1341 J.D.
(adm. in TX; not adm. in DC) [[A] Baker B.]
Bulleit, Kristy A. Niehaus .... '57 '82 C.215 B.A. L.94 J.D. [Hunton&W.]
*PRACTICE AREAS: Environmental; Administrative Law.
Bulleit, Thomas N., Jr. .... '57 '87 C.976 A.B. L.477 J.D. [Hogan&H.]
*PRACTICE AREAS: Health Care Corporate Law; Health Care Mergers and Acquisitions; Medicare Fraud and Abuse; Medical Technology; Medicare and Medicaid Reimbursement.
Bullock, Alexander McMillan .... '60 '85 C.269 B.A. L.790 J.D. [[C] Baise&M.]
*PRACTICE AREAS: Environmental Law; Litigation.
Bullock, Alice Gresham '50 '75
C&L.329 B.A., J.D. Assoc. Dean, Howard Univ. Sch. of Law
Bullock, J. Jerome '— '75 C.864 B.S. L.329 J.D.
(adm. in IA; not adm. in DC) [Bullock&Assoc.]
Bullock, Robert S., (AV) .... '46 '72 C.390 B.A. L.659 J.D. [Glassman&B.]
*PRACTICE AREAS: Elder Law; Estate Planning; Administrative Law.
Bullock, Scott G. '66 '91 C.294 B.A. L.665 J.D.
(adm. in PA; not adm. in DC) Institute for Jus.
Bullock, Stephen C. .... '66 '94 C.154 B.A. L.178 J.D. [[A] Steptoe&J.]

Bullock & Associates, Inc.
5335 Wisconsin Ave, N.W., Suite 440, 20015-2034
Telephone: 202-966-5006 Fax: 202-686-3681 URL: http://www.bullockassociates.com
Email: JBullock@BullockAssociates.com URL: http://www.lawyers.com/bullockassociates
J. Jerome Bullock (Not admitted in DC).
Criminal Investigations, Business Fraud, Corporate Fraud, Fraud Investigations, Computer Fraud, Computer Forensics, Internal Investigations, Due Diligence and Anti-Corruption Investigations, Litigation Intelligence, Counterfeiting, Product Diversion, Internet Fraud, Telecommunications Fraud, Information Protection.
See Professional Biographies, WASHINGTON, DISTRICT OF COLUMBIA

Bulman, Dunie, Burke & Feld, Chartered
(See Bethesda, Maryland)

Bultena, Jayne P. .... '65 '91 C.793 B.S. L.309 J.D. [Bennett,T.&C.]
*PRACTICE AREAS: Food and Drug Regulation.
Bultena, Lance D. .... '63 '91 C.793 B.S. L.309 J.D. [[C] Hogan&H.]
*PRACTICE AREAS: Legislation; Federal Regulatory Law; Legal Reform; Internet Law; Communications.
Bumbalo, Linda K. '39 '82
(adm. in NY; not adm. in DC) 2103 1/2 S St Nw
Bumgardner, Eunice Lin '60 '86 C.1365 B.B.A. L.276 J.D.
V.P. & Gen. Coun., Bureau of National Affairs, Inc., The
*RESPONSIBILITIES: Employment Law; Contracts; Corporate Law; Intellectual Property.
Bumgarner, Carrie L. .... '59 '84 C.910 A.B. L.734 J.D. [Wright&T.]
*PRACTICE AREAS: Litigation; Energy.
Bumpers, Brooke .... '62 '92 C.881 A.B. L.276 J.D. [[C] Hogan&H.]
*PRACTICE AREAS: Medicare and Medicaid Reimbursement; Health Care Regulation; Health Law; Managed Care; Health Care Licensing.
Bumpers, Dale L., (AV) .... '25 '52 C.45 L.597 LL.B. [[C] Arent F.K.P.&K.]
*PRACTICE AREAS: Government Relations; Government Regulations.
Bumpers, Heidi Hughes .... '57 '82 C.112 B.A. L.1051 J.D. [[C] Jones,D.R.&P.]

Bumpers, William M., (AV) . . . '55 '84 C.315 B.A. L.893 J.D. [Baker B.]

Bundock, John P., Jr., (AV) '26 '51 C.860 B.S.E.E. L.273 LL.B. [Ⓒ Leydig,V.&M.] (See Pat. Sect.)

Bundren, William J. . . . '56 '83 C.838 B.A. L.902 J.D. [Cahn&S.] (See Pat. Sect.)
*PRACTICE AREAS: Intellectual Property Law.

Bundy, Thomas Robinson, III '73 '00 C.445 B.S. L.329 (adm. in MD; not adm. in DC) [Ⓐ Sutherland A.&B.]
*PRACTICE AREAS: Litigation; Intellectual Property Litigation.

Bungard, B. Chad '73 '99 C.999 B.S. L.1339 J.D. (adm. in VA; not adm. in DC) Coun., Committee on Gov. Reform

Bunker, John R. '— '98 C.259 B.S. L.724 J.D. (adm. in NY; not adm. in DC) [Ⓐ King&S.]
*PRACTICE AREAS: Business Litigation.

Bunkin, Dorann . . . '68 '96 C.112 B.A. L.976 J.D. [Ⓐ Wiley R.&F.]

Bunn, Robert, (AV) . . . '46 '72 C.512 A.B. L.309 J.D. 1200 19th St., N.W.

Buntrock, Ross A. . . . '70 '95 C.791 B.S. L.546 J.D. [Ⓐ Kelley D.&W.]
*PRACTICE AREAS: Telecommunications Law; Corporate Law.

Buonassissi, Henning & Lash, A Professional Corporation
(See Fairfax, Virginia)

Buono, Francis M. . . . '65 '92 C&L.276 B.A., J.D. [Willkie F.&G.]
*PRACTICE AREAS: Telecommunications Law; Internet Law; Intellectual Property Licensing.

Burack, James . . . '62 '91 C.197 A.B. L.174 J.D. 1120 Connecticut Ave., N.W.‡

Burack, Michael L., (AV) . . . '42 '71 C.918 B.A. L.813 J.D. [Ⓒ Wilmer,C.&P.]
*PRACTICE AREAS: Litigation; Civil Practice; Government Contracts; Computers and Software; Commercial Law.

Buratti, Jason R. '72 '00 C.893 B.A. L.1209 J.D. (adm. in VA; not adm. in DC) [Ⓐ Finnegan,H.F.G.&D.]
*PRACTICE AREAS: Genetics; Biotechnology Patents; Chemical Patents; Patent Litigation; Pharmaceutical Patents.

Burbach, Cristina . . . '74 '00 C.276 B.A. L.309 J.D. [Ⓐ Fried,F.H.S.&J.]

Burch, Dean, (AV) '27 '53 C&L.37 J.D. Dir., Intl. Telecommunications Satellite Organization

Burchette, William H., (AV) . . . '45 '71 C.296 B.A. L.896 J.D. [Brickfield B.R.&S.]

Burchfiel, Kenneth J., (AV) '51 '78 C.31 A.B. L.188 J.D. [Sughrue M.] (See Pat. Sect.)
*PRACTICE AREAS: Intellectual Property Law.

Burchfield, Bobby R., (AV) . . . '54 '80 C.896 B.A. L.273 J.D. [Covington&B.]

Burchi, Lisa Rothenberg . . . '68 '96 C.860 B.A. L.273 J.D. [Ⓐ Bergeson&C.]
*PRACTICE AREAS: Federal Insecticide, Fungicide and Rodenticide Act (FIFRA); Toxic Substances Regulation; Pesticide Regulation; Chemical Regulation; Environmental Compliance.

Burd, Daniel H. . . . '54 '83 C.813 A.B. L.145 J.D. [Malizia S.&F.]
*PRACTICE AREAS: Banking Law; Corporate Law.

Burdett, James R. '51 '84 C.871 B.S. L.1338 J.D. [Venable,A.B.H.&C.] (See Pat. Sect.)
*PRACTICE AREAS: Intellectual Property.

Burdick, Rick L., (P.C.), (AV) . . . '51 '76 C.770 B.S.C. L.945 J.D. [Akin,G.S.H.&F.]
*PRACTICE AREAS: Corporate and Securities Law; International Law.

Burdin, Douglas Scott . . . '60 '91 C.174 B.A. L.1065 J.D. [Ⓐ Birch,H.B.&C.]
*PRACTICE AREAS: Natural Resources; Wildlife Litigation; Employment; Communications.

Bureau, Lisa C. . . . '60 '86 C.164 A.B. L.276 J.D. [Dow,L.&A.]

Buren, Mindy . . . '55 '80 C.659 B.S. L.569 J.D. [Ⓒ Shaw P.]
*PRACTICE AREAS: Utility Regulation; Nuclear Waste Issues; Environmental Law.

Buresh, C. John . . . '45 '70 C.597 B.A. L.145 J.D. [Sidley A.B.&W.]

Burg, Michael S., (AV) '50 '76 C&L.208 B.A., J.D. [Burg S.E.H.&J.] (⊙Englewood, CO)

Burg Simpson Eldredge Hersh & Jardine, P.C., (AV) 227 Massachusetts Avenue, N.E., Suite 1 (⊙Englewood, Sterling, CO; Cody, WY)

Burgard, Nadia St. George . . . '60 '92 C.918 B.A. L.262 J.D. [O'Melveny&M.]
*PRACTICE AREAS: Loan Restructuring; Loan Workouts; Leveraged Acquisitions; Mergers and Acquisitions.

Burgdorf, Robert L., Jr. '48 '73 C&L.602 A.B., J.D. (adm. in IN; not adm. in DC) National Council on the Handicapped

Burgee, Kirk S. . . . '63 '88 C.790 B.A. L.276 J.D. [McDermott,W.&E.]

Burgee, Michael B. '46 '71 C.893 B.A. L.273 J.D. (adm. in VA; not adm. in DC) 801 Penn. Ave., N.W.‡

Burger, Arthur D., (AV) '48 '73 C.30 B.A. L.273 J.D. [Jackson&C.] (⊙Balt., Rockville, MD)
*PRACTICE AREAS: Insurance Coverage; Civil Litigation; Professional Responsibility.

Burger, Ethan S. '59 '89 C.309 A.B. L.276 J.D. [Ⓒ Ludwig&R.] & [Ⓒ Russin&V.] (⊙Washington)
*PRACTICE AREAS: Corporate Law; Commercial Law; Directors and Officers Liability; Professional Negligence; Domestic and International.

Burger, Ethan S. . . '59 '89 C.309 A.B. L.276 J.D. [Ⓒ Russian-Ukrainian] (⊙Washington)
*PRACTICE AREAS: Corporate Law; Commercial Law; Directors and Officers Liability; Professional Negligence; Domestic and International.

Burger, James M., (AV) . . . '46 '72 C&L.569 B.A., J.D. [Dow,L.&A.]

Burgess, Cathy L., Law Offices of, (BV) '58 '88 C.276 B.S.F.S. L.128 J.D.
1767 P Street, N.W. First Floor, 20036
Telephone: 202-265-5157 Fax: 202-265-5618
Email: cathy@clburgess.com URL: http://www.lawyers.com/cathyburgesslaw
Of Counsel: Michael O. Spivey.
Healthcare, Food and Drug, Corporate Compliance and Legislative Advocacy.
See Professional Biographies, WASHINGTON, DISTRICT OF COLUMBIA

Burgess, Frederick F., Jr. '36 '67 C.869 B.S. L.273 LL.B. 1875 Connecticut Ave., N.W.★

Burgess, Jack T., (AV) . . . '52 '80 C.30 B.A. L.128 J.D. [Burgess,K.&P.] ⊙

Burgess, William C. '— '00 C.128 B.A. L.273 J.D. (adm. in MD; not adm. in DC) [Ⓐ Epstein B.&G.]
*PRACTICE AREAS: Health.

Burgess, Kerrbach & Perigard, P.C., (AV) . . . 900 19th St., Ste. 200 (⊙Fairfax, VA)

Burgett, David W. . . . '55 '81 C.477 B.A. L.309 J.D. [Hogan&H.]
*PRACTICE AREAS: Government Contracts Law; Technology and Licensing Law; International Transactions.

Burgett, John M. . . . '67 '92 C.556 B.A. L.823 J.D. [Wiley R.&F.]
*PRACTICE AREAS: Communications Law.

Burgmeier, L. Dale, (AV) '35 '71 C.999 A.B. L.446 J.D. (adm. in MD; not adm. in DC) [Franch,J.B.&S.] ⊙
*PRACTICE AREAS: Commercial Litigation; Business Litigation; Family Law; Appellate Practice; Hospital Risk Management.

Burgoyne, Robert Anthony, (AV) . . . '56 '82 C.611 B.A. L.575 J.D. [Fulbright&J.]
*PRACTICE AREAS: Complex Business Litigation; Energy Contracts; International Arbitration; Federal Administrative Law; College and University Law.

Burgujian, Richard V. '49 '85 C.816 B.E. L.705 J.D. [Finnegan,H.F.G.&D.] (See Pat. Sect.)
*PRACTICE AREAS: Electronic Patents; Patent Infringement; Patent Prosecution.

Burk, Jeffrey Scot . . . '72 '00 C.846 B.A. L.276 J.D. [Ⓐ Steptoe&J.]

Burka, Alfred, (AV) . . . '28 '51 C&L.276 B.S., J.D. Ret. Supr. Ct. J.‡

Burka, Robert A., (AV) . . . '— '71 C.197 A.B. L.309 J.D. [Foley&L.]
*PRACTICE AREAS: Antitrust and Trade Regulation Law; Administrative Law; Litigation.

Burke, Ann Marie . . . '69 '98 C&L.893 B.A., J.D. [Ⓐ Shaw P.]

Burke, Beverly J. '51 '79 C.103 B.A. L.273 J.D. V.P. & Gen. Coun., Washington Gas Light Company

Burke, Brian E. . . . '59 '89 C.103 A.B. L.276 J.D. [Ⓒ Holland&K.]
*PRACTICE AREAS: Public Law; Environmental Law; Regulatory; Corporate Diversity; Municipal.

Burke, Brian F. . . . '72 '98 C.1369 B.A. L.276 J.D. [Ⓐ Baker&M.]
*PRACTICE AREAS: Antitrust Law.

Burke, Cheryl C., (AV) '47 '73 C.604 B.A. L.588 J.D. Gen. Coun., Washington Metropolitan Area Transit Authority.
*RESPONSIBILITIES: Management of Legal Department; Advise General Manager and Board.

Burke, Christopher . . . '75 '00 C.276 B.A. L.477 J.D. [Ⓐ Covington&B.]

Burke, D. Barlow '41 '67 C.309 A.B. L.659 LL.B. (adm. in PA; not adm. in DC) Prof. of Law, Amer. Univ.

Burke, Edmund W. . . . '48 '73 C&L.276 A.B., J.D. [Steptoe&J.]

Burke, Elizabeth Marie '— '00 C.128 B.S. L.180 J.D. (adm. in VA; not adm. in DC; See Pat. Sect.) [Ⓐ Finnegan,H.F.G.&D.]
*PRACTICE AREAS: Patent Prosecution.

Burke, F. William . . . '41 '68 C&L.902 B.A., J.D. V.P., Security Tr. Co., N.A.

Burke, Franklyn N. . . . '39 '76 C.446 B.A. L.329 J.D. 1050 17th St., N.W.

Burke, Frederic G. . . . '46 '81 C.973 B.S. L.1234 J.D. The Riggs Natl. Bk.

Burke, John . . . '61 '86 C.597 B.A. L.659 J.D. 1440 New York Ave., N.W.

Burke, John J. . . . '61 '86 C.597 B.A. L.659 J.D. [Baker&H.]
*PRACTICE AREAS: International Trade; Export Control; Product Safety.

Burke, John L., Jr., (AV) . . . '— '72 C.1030 B.A. L.276 J.D. [Foley,H.&E.]
*PRACTICE AREAS: Electronic Commerce; Corporate; Taxation; Trade Association; Law Firm Counselling.

Burke, Lisa Lavelle . . . '67 '92 C.741 B.A. L.602 J.D. [Ⓐ Patton B.]

Burke, Malcolm A. '73 '01 C&L.902 B.S., J.D. (adm. in VA; not adm. in DC) [Ⓐ Brickfield B.R.&S.]

Burke, R. Brian . . . '52 '77 C.602 A.B. L.352 J.D. [Rode&Q.] (⊙New York, NY)

Burke, Rebecca L. . . . '53 '82 C.103 B.A. L.276 J.D. [Ⓒ Powers,P.S.&V.]
*PRACTICE AREAS: Health Care Law.

Burke, Richard J. . . . '63 '90 C.309 A.B. L.276 J.D. [Ⓐ White&C.]

Burke, Susan L. . . . '62 '87 C.276 B.S.F.S. L.128 J.D. [Mintz,L.C.F.G.&P.]
*PRACTICE AREAS: Intellectual Property Litigation; Patent Litigation; Civil Litigation; Complex Litigation; Health Care Fraud.

Burke, Taylor L. . . . '73 '99 C.902 B.A. L.904 J.D. [Ⓐ Hogan&H.]

Burke, Thomas F. . . . '66 '91 C.103 A.B. L.273 J.D. [McKenna&C.]
*PRACTICE AREAS: Government Contracts; Construction Law.

Burke, William T. . . . '69 '95 C.674 B.A. L.893 J.D. [Ⓐ Williams&C.]
*PRACTICE AREAS: Litigation; White Collar Criminal Defense.

Burkes, Melanie R. '74 '01 C.228 A.B. L.893 J.D. (adm. in NY; not adm. in DC) [Ⓐ Akin,G.S.H.&F.]
*PRACTICE AREAS: Corporate Law.

Burkett, Paul A. . . . '65 '95 C.871 B.S. L.893 J.D. [Ⓐ Hogan&H.]
*PRACTICE AREAS: Tax; Corporate Law; Securities.

Burkman, John M. . . . '66 '92 C.665 B.A. L.276 J.D. [Ⓒ Holland&K.]
*PRACTICE AREAS: Federal Legislative; Federal Administrative Law.

Burley, Don O. . . . '49 '76 C.659 B.A. L.884 J.D. [Finnegan,H.F.G.&D.]
*PRACTICE AREAS: Intellectual Property Litigation; Intellectual Property Licensing.

Burley, Edward G. . . . '61 '91 C.602 B.A. L.893 J.D. Asst. U.S. Atty.

Burlingame, John A. '65 '91 C.886 B.A. L.692 J.D. [Squire,S.&D.] (⊙Tysons Corner, VA)

Burn, Brian '68 '01 C.387 B.S. L.1356 J.D. (adm. in VA; not adm. in DC; See Pat. Sect.) [Ⓐ Finnegan,H.F.G.&D.]
*PRACTICE AREAS: Chemical Intellectual Property; Pharmaceutical Intellectual Property; Chemical Patent Prosecution; Chemical Patents; Patent Litigation.

Burnes, John H., Jr. . . . '47 '72 C.855 B.A. L.184 J.D. [Van Ness F.]
*PRACTICE AREAS: Natural Gas; Energy; Administrative Law; Federal Energy Regulation.

Burnett, Marjorie A. . . . '— '96 C.659 B.S. L.262 J.D. [Ⓐ Miller&C.]
*PRACTICE AREAS: Taxation; Federal Tax Controversies; International Income Tax; Accounting Law; Tax Litigation.

Burney, David G. '38 '66 C.763 B.S. L.1065 J.D. (adm. in CA; not adm. in DC) U.S. Tuna Found.

Burnim, Ira A. '51 '78 C&L.309 A.B., J.D. Legal Dir., Buzelon, Judge David L., Center for Mental Health Law

Burnley, James H., IV, (AV) . . . '48 '73 C.976 B.A. L.309 J.D. [Winston&S.]
*PRACTICE AREAS: Administrative Law; Regulatory Law; Transportation Law; Government Relations.

Burns, Bethany M. . . . '69 '97 C.886 B.A. L.180 J.D. [Ⓐ Hunton&W.]

Burns, Brian R. . . . '59 '91 C.676 B.A. L.1209 J.D. 1225 Conn. Ave. NW, Ste. 800

Burns, Caleb P. . . . '74 '01 C.228 B.a. L.569 J.D. [Ⓐ Wiley R.&F.]

Burns, David D. . . . '60 '88 C.262 B.A. L.893 J.D. [Ⓒ Paul,H.J.&W.]

Burns, David Michael '74 '99 C.446 B.A. L.128 J.D. (adm. in MD; not adm. in DC) [Ⓐ Seyfarth S.]
*PRACTICE AREAS: Labor and Employment.

Burns, James M., (AV) . . . '61 '86 C.165 A.B. L.1068 J.D. [Vorys,S.S.&P.]
*PRACTICE AREAS: Antitrust; Commercial Litigation; Trademarks.

Burns, Robert Clifton . . . '53 '79 C&L.597 B.A., J.D. [Ablondi,F.S.&D.]

Burns, Robert L. '68 '95 C.674 B.S.A. & A.E. L.365 J.D. [Ⓐ Finnegan,H.F.G.&D.] (See Pat. Sect.)
*PRACTICE AREAS: Mechanical Intellectual Property; Aerospace Law; Technology Law.

Burns, Todd J. . . . '— '95 C.107 B.S.Ch.E. L.273 J.D. [Ⓒ Foley&L.] (See Pat. Sect.)
*PRACTICE AREAS: Intellectual Property; Chemical Patent; Pharmaceutical Patent Law.

Burns, Doane, Swecker & Mathis, L.L.P.
(See Alexandria, Virginia)

Burnside, Thomas B. '58 '87 C.611 B.A. L.128 J.D. (adm. in MD; not adm. in DC) [Ⓒ Mayer,B.&P.]

Buroker, Brian Mark . . . '69 '96 C.576 B.S.E.E. L.276 J.D. [Ⓐ Hunton&W.]

Burow, Richard-Scott, (BV) '49 '75 C.30 B.A. L.472 J.D. 1816 New Hampshire Ave. N.W.

Burr, Barbara A. . . . '62 '89 C.911 B.A. L.309 J.D. 1201 4th St., S.W.

Burr, J. Beckwith . . . '— '95 C.976 B.A. L.276 J.D. [Wilmer,C.&P.]
*PRACTICE AREAS: Electronic Commerce; Privacy Law; Security Clearances; Data Protection; Corporate Transactions.

Burr, Paula K. '62 '91 C.197 B.A. L.976 J.D. (adm. in NY; not adm. in DC) MCI Communications Corporation

Burroughs, Carol E. . . . '48 '87 C.273 B.A. L.128 J.D. Asst. Corp. Coun. & Claims Mgr.

Burrous, Beth A. . . . '— '93 C.188 B.S. L.276 J.D. [Foley&L.] (See Pat. Sect.)
*PRACTICE AREAS: Biotechnology; Strategic Business Planning; Patent Validity and Infringement Opinions.

Burrow, Christina Hosp . . . '63 '93 C.893 B.S. L.1209 J.D. [Ⓐ Dow,L.&A.]

Burrows, Damon, II . . . '70 '97 C.999 B.S. L.128 J.D. [Ⓐ Jenkens&G.]
*PRACTICE AREAS: Health Care Fraud; Health Care Litigation; White Collar Fraud.

Burstein, Ari '67 '92 C.994 B.A. L.273 J.D. (adm. in MD; not adm. in DC) Assoc. Coun., Investment Co. Institute
*RESPONSIBILITIES: Securities; Mutual Funds; Broker-Dealer Regulation.

Burstein, Diane B. '56 '83 C.918 B.A. L.276 J.D. Dep. Gen. Coun., National Cable Television Assn.

Burstein, Emanuel S. '54 '85 C.1036 B.A. L.93 J.D.
(adm. in NY; not adm. in DC) Publisher, Ins. Taxation & Regul. Publications, Inc.
Burstein, Joseph, (AV) ....'14 '40 L.537 LL.B. 700 New Hampshire NW‡
Burt, Dan, (AV) ....'42 '70 C.397 B.A. L.976 LL.B. [Burt,M.&M.]
*PRACTICE AREAS: Structured Finance; Litigation; Tax Audits.
Burt, Eric M. ....'69 '99 C.894 A.B. L.30 J.D. [🄰 Skadden,A.S.M.&F.]
*PRACTICE AREAS: Mergers and Acquisitions; Corporate Finance.
Burt, Franklin G., (AV) ....'48 '75 C.477 A.B. L.472 J.D. [Jorden B.] ⊙
*PRACTICE AREAS: Litigation; Class Action Defense; First Amendment and Environmental Law; Mergers and Acquisitions.
Burt, J. Keith ....'60 '85 C.446 B.S. L.273 J.D. [McKenna&C.]
*PRACTICE AREAS: Litigation; Government Contracts Law; International.
Burt, Jeffrey A., (AV) .... '44 '71 C.674 A.B. L.976 LL.B. [Arnold&P.]
*PRACTICE AREAS: International; Litigation.
Burt, Mary J. '— '89 C.931 B.A. L.208 J.D.
(adm. in CO; not adm. in DC) Dir., Govt. Rel., National Assn. of Mtge. Brokers

Burt, Maner & Miller, (AV)
975 East Tower, 1300 Eye Street, N.W., 20005
Telephone: 202-783-1500 Facsimile: 202-783-1523
Email: queries@bmmdc.com URL: http://www.lawyers.com/corporatetaxlaw
Members of Firm: Dan Burt; Henry B. Miller; Forbes Maner; Jonathan E. Jackel. Of Counsel: Alan L. Feld (Not admitted in DC). Associates: Susan Pecoraro Segar; David M. Oliver Jr. (Not admitted in DC).
Tax, both domestic and international, including international transactions, controversies, and litigation.
London, England Office: Suite 105/106 Hamilton House, 1 Temple Avenue, EC4Y OHA. Telephone: 020-7353-4722. Facsimile: 020-7353-4723.
See Professional Biographies, WASHINGTON, DISTRICT OF COLUMBIA

Burton, Alton K. ....'56 '90 C.446 B.S. L.273 J.D. [🄱 Quagliano&S.]
*PRACTICE AREAS: Small Business Law; Estate Planning; Estate Administration; Taxation; Intellectual Property.
Burton, Christopher John '76 '00 C.575 B.A. L.273 J.D.
(adm. in VA; not adm. in DC) 475 L'Enfant Plaza, S.W.
Burton, Daphne L. '67 '95 C&L.846 B.S.M.E., J.D.
(adm. in TX; not adm. in DC; Pat.) [🄰 Oppenheimer W.&D.]
*PRACTICE AREAS: Intellectual Property.
Burton, Debra F. ....'53 '92 C.546 B.A. L.276 J.D. 5234 42nd St.‡
Burton, Emma K. ....'72 '97 C.103 B.A. L.276 J.D. [🄰 Crowell&M.]
Burton, Harry W. ....'49 '75 C.674 A.B. L.276 J.D. [Morgan,L.&B.]
Burton, Joel S., (AV) ....'35 '61 C.319 B.A. L.276 LL.B. [🄱 O'Melveny&M.]
Burton, Michael L. ....'— '97 C.103 A.B. L.276 J.D. [🄰 Miller&C.]
*PRACTICE AREAS: International Trade; Foreign Asset Control; Foreign Corrupt Practices Act; Foreign Trade Sanctions; World Trade Organization.
Burton, Nancy E. ....'62 '96 C.518 B.A. L.276 J.D. [🄰 Fulbright&J.]
*PRACTICE AREAS: International Law.
Burton, Preston, (AV) ....'62 '89 C.228 A.B. L.893 J.D. [P.Cacheris] ⊙
*PRACTICE AREAS: White Collar Criminal Litigation.
Burton, William F., (AV) ....'62 '91 C.473 B.A. L.276 J.D. [Stein,M.&M.]
*PRACTICE AREAS: Civil Litigation; Business Litigation; Personal Injury Litigation.
Burwell, Clayton L., (AV) ....'10 '36 C.797 B.S. L.575 LL.B. [Burwell,P.&H.]
Burwell, L. Scott '69 '93 C.31 A.B. L.309 J.D.
[🄰 Finnegan,H.F.G.&D.] (See Pat. Sect.)
*PRACTICE AREAS: Intellectual Property Litigation; Pharmaceutical Intellectual Property; Biotechnology Patents; Patent Litigation.
Burwell, Peters & Houston, (AV) .... 1762 Church St., N.W.
Burzio, John M., (AV) ....'36 '60 C&L.623 B.B.A., LL.B. [Burzio&M.]
*PRACTICE AREAS: Federal Administrative Law; Postal Law; Aviation Regulatory Law.

Burzio & McLaughlin, (AV)
Canal Square Suite 540, 1054 Thirty-First Street, N.W., 20007
Telephone: 202-965-4555 Telecopier: 202-965-4432
Email: BMLaw@erols.com
Members of Firm: John M. Burzio; Thomas W. McLaughlin; Timothy L. Keegan. Of Counsel: Alvin H. Gandal.
Practice Before Postal Rate Commission, U.S Postal Service and Other Federal Administrative Agencies, Federal Appellate Litigation, Postal Law and Related Litigation, Lobbying, Business and Transactional Matters, Aviation Regulatory Law.
See Professional Biographies, WASHINGTON, DISTRICT OF COLUMBIA

Busby, David, (AV) ....'26 '50 C.976 A.B. L.623 LL.B. [Dorsey&W.]
Buscemi, Peter, (AV) ....'50 '77 C&L.178 B.A., J.D. [Morgan,L.&B.]
Buschner, Traci L. ....'69 '95 C.473 B.A. L.421 J.D. [🄰 Provost&U.]
*PRACTICE AREAS: General Civil and Trial Practice; False Claims Act Litigation; Employment and Labor Litigation; Civil Rights Litigation; Environmental Litigation.
Bush, Derek M. ....'67 '94 C.674 A.B. L.145 J.D. [🄰 Cleary,G.S.&H.]
Bush, Douglas R. .... '57 '86 C&L.101 B.S., J.D. [Arent F.K.P.&K.]
*PRACTICE AREAS: Trademarks; Copyrights.
Bush, Graeme W., (AV) ....'50 '76 C.918 B.A. L.446 J.D. [Zuckerman S.]
*PRACTICE AREAS: Civil; Securities; ERISA; Legal Malpractice; Criminal Litigation.
Bush, Guy K. '57 '82 C.1365 B.A. L.276 J.D.
(adm. in PA; not adm. in DC) 2828 Penn. Ave.‡
Bush, Ilsa K. '47 '73 C.309 B.A. L.36 J.D.
(adm. in AZ; not adm. in DC) 4353 Warren St., N.W.
Bush, Karen L. ....'58 '84 C.105 B.A. L.273 J.D. [Dickstein S.M.&O.]
*PRACTICE AREAS: General Litigation; Insurance Recovery; Insurance Litigation.
Bush, Michael J., (AV) ....'43 '68 C.813 A.B. L.309 LL.B. Director, Project REAP
Bush, Nathan Garrett '73 '00 C.893 B.A. L.309 J.D.
(adm. in VA; not adm. in DC) [🄰 O'Melveny&M.]
Bush, Zoe A. ....'54 '81 C.914 B.A. L.309 J.D. Supr. Ct. J.
Bushee, James M. ....'54 '82 C.846 B.B.A. L.128 J.D. [Sutherland A.&B.]
*PRACTICE AREAS: Energy; Environmental; Telecommunications Law.
Bushmiller, Ann E. ....'57 '82 C.67 B.A. L.145 J.D. [Sidley A.B.&W.]
Bushnell, Robert E. '— '74 C&L.446 B.S.E.E., J.D.
(adm. in MD; not adm. in DC; Pat.) [R.E.Bushnell]
Bushnell, R. E., & Law Firm ....1522 K Street, N.W., Suite 300 (Pat.)
Bushyeager, Amy L. ......'— '98 C.610 B.A. L.276 J.D. 701 Pennsylvania Avenue, N.W.
Busis, William L. ....'59 '91 C.976 B.A. L.309 J.D. Off. of U.S. Trade Rep.
Busman, Philip '75 '00 C.477 B.A. L.30 J.D.
(adm. in VA; not adm. in DC) [🄰 Dickstein S.M.&O.]
*PRACTICE AREAS: Insurance Litigation; Bankruptcy; Creditors Rights.
Bussey, Richard A., (AV) ....'50 '78 C.610 B.S.J. L.896 J.D. [Stein,M.&M.]
*PRACTICE AREAS: Personal Injury; Civil Litigation.
Busto, Felice ....'53 '80 C.105 B.A. L.128 J.D. Air Line Pilots Assn.
Butcher, Catherine Curran ....'69 '96 C.692 B.A. L.945 J.D. [🄰 Wilkinson B.K.]
*PRACTICE AREAS: Communications.
Butcher, Karen A. .... '66 '93 C&L.893 B.S., J.D. [Morgan,L.&B.]
Butcher, Peter F. ....'62 '93 C.831 B.A. L.276 J.D. [🄰 Clifford,L.&G.]
*PRACTICE AREAS: Civil Litigation; Employment; Medical Malpractice.
Butchman, Alan A. ....'38 '65 C.95 A.B. L.93 LL.B. 1000 Potomac St., N.W.
Butera, James J., (AV) ....'44 '73 C.728 B.A. L.276 J.D. [Butera&A.]
*PRACTICE AREAS: Government Relations; Financial Institutions Law; Regulation Law; Real Estate; Litigation.

Butera & Andrews, (AV)
1301 Pennsylvania Avenue, N.W., 20004-1701
Telephone: 202-347-6875 Fax: 202-347-6876 URL: http://www.butera-andrews.com
Email: info@butera-andrews.com URL: http://www.lawyers.com/butera-andrews
James J. Butera; Wright H. Andrews, Jr.; Stephen C. Leckar; Dennis M. Hart; Frank A. Tillotson (Not admitted in DC); Philip S. Corwin.
Banking, Other Legislative Matters, Federal Litigation.
See Professional Biographies, WASHINGTON, DISTRICT OF COLUMBIA

Butler, Alexandra V. ....'— '96 C.188 A.B. L.945 J.D. [🄰 Patton B.]
Butler, Benjamin T. ....'72 '98 C&L.228 A.B., J.D. [🄰 Crowell&M.]
Butler, Charles J. ....'68 '99 C.276 B.A. L.569 J.D. [🄰 Covington&B.]
Butler, Cynthia L. ....'60 '87 C.188 A.B. L.276 J.D. [Butler&S.]
Butler, David J., (AV) ....'50 '75 C.978 B.A. L.276 J.D. [Swidler B.S.F.]
*PRACTICE AREAS: Commercial Litigation; Mortgage Banking; Franchising; Employment Law.
Butler, Ellis M. ....'67 '93 C.893 B.A. L.309 J.D. [Hunton&W.]
*PRACTICE AREAS: Project Finance; Independent Power Development; Asset Finance; Leasing.
Butler, J. Bradway '41 '69 C.309 A.B. L.494 LL.B.
[🄱 Arnold&P.] (⊙Istanbul, Turkey)
*PRACTICE AREAS: Real Estate; International; Corporate; Securities.
Butler, Jennifer L. .... '73 '98 C.259 B.A. L.902 J.D. [🄰 Alston&B.]
*PRACTICE AREAS: Health Law; Corporate Law.
Butler, John W. ....'61 '91 C.170 B.A. L.273 J.D. [Sher&B.]
*PRACTICE AREAS: Transportation; Telecommunications; Litigation.
Butler, Mary Cathryn '59 '91 C.524 B.A. L.1209 J.D.
(adm. in VA; not adm. in DC) Asst. Editor, The Food & Drug Law Institute
Butler, Michelle L. ....'73 '98 C.813 A.B. L.276 J.D. [🄰 Hyman,P.&M.]
*PRACTICE AREAS: Food and Drug Regulation.
Butler, N. Sean '74 '01 C.277 B.S. L.180 J.D.
(adm. in MD; not adm. in DC) [🄰 Clifford C.R.&W.]
*PRACTICE AREAS: Litigation; Alternative Dispute Resolution.
Butler, Nathaniel E. ....'41 '66 C.164 B.A. L.145 J.D. [🄱 Kass&S.]
Butler, Patricia G. ....'58 '84 C.309 A.B. L.659 J.D. [Howrey S.A.&W.]
*PRACTICE AREAS: Commercial Litigation; Antitrust.
Butler, Paul V. ....'59 '90 C.1369 B.S. L.1209 J.D. [🄰 Dombroff&G.]
Butler, Robert J., (AV) ....'54 '79 C.475 B.A. L.309 J.D. [Wiley R.&F.]
*PRACTICE AREAS: Telecommunications; Internet; E-Commerce; Privacy Law.
Butler, Ronesha A. ....'73 '00 C.645 B.A. L.329 J.D. [🄰 Sutherland A.&B.]
*PRACTICE AREAS: Corporate Law.
Butler, Susan M. ....'66 '92 C.518 A.B. L.128 J.D. [Margolius,M.D.R.&T.]
*PRACTICE AREAS: Family Law.
Butler, William J., Jr., (AV) ....'33 '62 C&L.893 B.A., LL.B. [O'Brien,B.M.&S.]
*PRACTICE AREAS: Nonprofit Organizations Law.

Butler, Snow, O'Mara, Stevens & Cannada, PLLC
Suite 500, EOP Building, 819-7th Street N.W., 20001 ⊙
Telephone: 202-408-8668 Telecopier:202-408-8768
Email: first.last@butlersnow.com URL: http://www.butlersnow.com
Special Counsel: Mike Espy (Not admitted in DC).
General Civil Practice. Trials and Appeals before all State and Federal Courts. State and Federal Agency Practice, Administrative Law, Alternative Dispute Resolution, Antitrust and Trade Regulation, Appellate Litigation, Banking and Financial Services, Bankruptcy and Creditors' Rights, Business Planning and Operations, Civil Rights, Commercial Lending, Commercial Litigation, Construction, Criminal Defense, Director and Officer Liability, Drug and Medical Device Litigation, Economic Development Incentives, Employee Benefits, Environmental, Estate and Trust Administration, Estate and Wealth Transfer Tax Planning, Gaming Law and Regulation, Governmental Relations, Government Litigation, Healthcare, Insurance Defense, Insurance Law and Regulation, Intellectual Property, International Law, Labor and Employment Law (Management), Medical Professional Liability, Mergers and Acquisitions, Premises Liability, Products Liability, Professional Liability, Public Finance, Public Utilities, Real Estate, Securities, State and Municipal Bonds, Taxation, Technology and Intellectual Property, Toxic Torts, Transportation, and Workers' Compensation.
Jackson, Mississippi Office: 17th Floor, AmSouth Plaza, 210 East Capitol Street, 39201. Telephone: 601-948-5711. Telecopier: 601-985-4500.
Gulfport, Mississippi Office: Suite 204, Whitney National Bank Building, 1300 Twenty Fifth Avenue, P.O. Drawer 4248, 39502. Telephone: 601-864-1170. Telecopier: 601-868-1531.
Memphis, Tennessee Office: Suite 501, Forum I Building, 6750 Poplar Avenue, P.O. Box 171443, 38187-1443, 38187-1443. Telephone: 901-680-7200. Telecopier: 901-680-7201.
See Professional Biographies, WASHINGTON, DISTRICT OF COLUMBIA

Butler & Spears
1250 24th Street, N.W., Suite 300, 20037
Telephone: 202-467-2794
Email: butlercyn@aol.com
Members of Firm: Cynthia L. Butler; Byron P. Spears, Jr.
Employment Law, Employee Rights, Wrongful Termination, Harassment, Unfair Labor Practices, Employment Discrimination, Age Discrimination, Equal Employment Opportunity Law, Small Business Law, Complex Commercial Litigation, Breach of Contract, E-Commerce Law, High Technology and Internet Law, Employment Class Actions.
See Professional Biographies, WASHINGTON, DISTRICT OF COLUMBIA

Butler-Truesdale, Tonya M. ....'64 '95 C.893 B.A. L.329 J.D. 500 C St., N.W.
Butner, Blain B. ....'53 '80 C.198 A.B. L.228 J.D. [Dow,L.&A.]
Butrum, Roy W. ...... '25 '51 C.688 B.A.E. L.273 LL.B. 1400 K Street, N.W., 10th Floor
Butswinkas, Dane H., (AV) ....'61 '89 C.1369 B.S. L.893 J.D. [Williams&C.]
*PRACTICE AREAS: Commercial Litigation; Electronic Commerce Litigation; Employment Litigation; White Collar Litigation.
Butterfield, William H. ....'43 '67 C.93 B.S. L.276 J.D. [Bell,B.&L.]
*PRACTICE AREAS: Government Contracts; Federal Procurement; General Civil Litigation.
Butterfield, William P., (AV) ....'53 '78 C.97 B.S. L.851 J.D. [Finkelstein,T.&L.]
Butterworth, Barbara E. ....'66 '96 C.93 B.A. L.276 J.D. [🄰 Crowell&M.]
Button, Kristin K. ....'71 '97 C.475 B.A. L.477 J.D. 3000 K St., NW, Ste. 3000
Butz, Andrew ....'45 '76 C.674 A.B. L.276 J.D. [🄱 Bonner K.T.&C.] (⊙Fairfax, VA)
*PRACTICE AREAS: Insurance Coverage Law; Complex Litigation; Commercial Insurance; Excess and Reinsurance; Antitrust.
Buxton, C. Michael, (AV) ....'46 '71 C.691 B.A. L.383 J.D. [Vinson&E.]
*PRACTICE AREAS: White Collar Crime; Litigation; Antitrust and Trade Regulation.
Byam, John T. ....'56 '82 C.945 A.B., A.B. L.597 J.D. [Cleary,G.S.&H.]
Byers, Stephen M. ....'65 '92 C.896 B.A. L.893 J.D. [🄱 Crowell&M.]
*PRACTICE AREAS: Business Crimes; False Claims Act; Federal Criminal Law; Government Contract Fraud; Grand Jury Practice.
Bygrave, Daisy M. '74 '00 C.776 B.A. L.309 J.D.
(adm. in MD; not adm. in DC) [🄰 Shaw P.]
Byington, Lisa M. ....'65 '91 C.645 B.A. L.273 J.D. [🄱 Shaw P.]
Byrd, Adrienne P. ....'— '91 C.445 B.S. L.273 J.D. [🄰 Cole,R.&B.]
*PRACTICE AREAS: Corporate Transactions; New Media Law; Internet Law; Copyrights; Trademarks.
Byrd, James H., (AV) ....'54 '80 C.475 B.A. L.912 J.D. [Miller,B.&O.]
*PRACTICE AREAS: Energy Regulation; Hydroelectricity; Natural Gas Regulation; Energy; Contracts.
Byrd, Jerry S. ....'35 '65 C.254 B.A. L.329 LL.B. Mag., Supr. Ct. J.
Byrd, Kevin B., (AV) ....'51 '78 C.674 B.A. L.128 J.D. [🄱 Jones,D.R.&P.]
Byrd, Laura S. '52 '86 C.892 B.A. L.329 J.D.
(adm. in PA; not adm. in DC) Dept. of Consumer & Reg. Affairs
Byrd, Richard J., (AV) '37 '72 C&L.273 B.E.E., J.D.
[🄱 N.L.Blumenfeld] (⊙Fairfax, VA)
Byrd, William P. ....'73 '99 C.668 B.A. L.276 J.D. 1114 E St., S.E.
Byrne, Brian ....'70 '95 C.103 B.A. L.477 J.D. [🄰 Cleary,G.S.&H.]

Byrne, J. Peter .... '51 '81 C.597 B.A. L.893 J.D. Prof., Georgetown Law School
Byrne, John J., Jr. .... '53 '81 C.976 B.A. L.893 J.D. [Byrne G.&H.]
Byrne, Karen S., (BV) .... '51 '83 C.597 B.A. L.893 J.D. [Halberstein&B.]
Byrne, Patricia M. .... '71 '99 C&L.999 B.A., LL.B. [Ⓐ Wilmer,C.&P.]

Byrne Goldenberg & Hamilton, PLLC
1025 Connecticut Avenue NW, Suite 1012, 20036
Telephone: 202-857-9775 Fax: 202-857-9779
URL: http://www.lawyers.com/bghlaw
John J. Byrne, Jr.; Lloyd P Goldenberg; Thomas J. Hamilton.
General Practice.
See Professional Biographies, WASHINGTON, DISTRICT OF COLUMBIA

Byrnes, John T., Jr., (AV) .... '52 '77 C.276 B.S.B.A. L.659 J.D. [Dow,L.&A.]
Byrnes, Kristen A. .... '74 '99 C.273 B.S. L.94 J.D. [Ⓐ Hughes H.&R.]
*PRACTICE AREAS: Litigation.
Byrum, Lesa L. '62 '91 C.1369 B.S. L.1356 J.D.
(adm. in VA; not adm. in DC) [Ⓐ Keller&H.]
*PRACTICE AREAS: Occupational Safety and Health; Employment Law.
Caballero, Dilia M. .... '71 '95 C.309 B.A. L.276 J.D. [Ⓐ Dechert]
*PRACTICE AREAS: Financial Services Law; Investment Management.
Caballero, Kathryn P. .... '— '00 C.602 B.S. L.569 J.D. [Ⓐ Arnold&P.]
*PRACTICE AREAS: Environmental Law.
Cabassa, Ana María '— '01 C.276 B.S.B.A. L.569 J.D.
(adm. in NY; not adm. in DC) [Ⓐ Latham&W.]
*PRACTICE AREAS: Corporate Law; Taxation.
Cabezas-Gansler, Christine M. .... '73 '99 C.976 B.A. L.893 J.D. [Ⓐ Williams&C.]
*PRACTICE AREAS: Litigation.
Cabral, Neal J. .... '59 '88 C.867 B.A. L.945 J.D. [McGuirewoods]
*PRACTICE AREAS: Environmental Law.
Caccia, Ralph J., (AV) .... '61 '87 C.262 B.A. L.276 J.D. [Powell,G.F.&M.]
*PRACTICE AREAS: White Collar Criminal Defense; Health Care Fraud; Government Enforcement Litigation; Complex Civil Litigation.
Cacciamani, Dara '73 '00 C.646 B.A. L.574 J.D.
(adm. in NC; not adm. in DC) [Ⓐ Boies,S.&F.]
*PRACTICE AREAS: Copyright; Trademark; Antitrust; General Commercial Litigation.
Cacciatore, Giacomo .... '15 '43 C.588 L.818 LL.B. 700 New Hampshire Ave., N.W.‡
Cacheris, Plato, (AV) .... '29 '56 C&L.276 B.S., J.D. [P.Cacheris] ⊙
*PRACTICE AREAS: Criminal and Civil Litigation.

Cacheris, Plato, Law Offices of, (AV) BR
Suite 730, 1100 Connecticut Avenue, North West, 20036 ⊙
Telephone: 202-775-8700 Fax: 202-775-8702
Email: pcacheris@erols.com URL: http://www.lawyers.com/platocacheris
Plato Cacheris; Preston Burton; John F. Hundley. Associate: Erik A. Cox (Not admitted in DC). Of Counsel: Sydney J. Hoffmann.
Federal and State Criminal and Civil Trials and Appeals, International Criminal Law, including Extraditions.
Alexandria, Virginia Office: 120 North Alfred Street. Telephone: 703-549-8181.
See Professional Biographies, WASHINGTON, DISTRICT OF COLUMBIA

Cacozza, Albert F., Jr. .... '56 '82 C.103 A.B. L.145 J.D. [Bennett,T.&C.]
Cade, Denise R. .... '62 '90 C.436 B.A. L.276 J.D. [Shaw P.]

Cadeaux & Taglieri, P.C., (AV) BR
1100 Connecticut Avenue, N.W., Suite 800, 20036
Telephone: 202-785-3373
Email: jim@cadotag.com URL: http://www.lawyers.com/cadeaux&taglieri
Robert Cadeaux (1936-1994); James W. Taglieri; Joyce M. Notarius;—Nicholas S. Nunzio, Jr.; John G. Harnishfeger; Thomas M. Wochok. Of Counsel: Henry M. Lloyd.
Personal Injury, Negligence, Medical Malpractice, Products Liability, Wrongful Death, Automobile Accidents and Injuries, Workers Compensation, Police and Firemen's Retirement Law.
See Professional Biographies, WASHINGTON, DISTRICT OF COLUMBIA

Cader, M. Yasmin .... '67 '94 C.329 B.A. L.976 J.D. Pub. Def. Serv.

Cadwalader, Wickersham & Taft, (AV)
1201 F Street, N.W., Suite 1100, 20004 ⊙
Telephone: 202-862-2200 Fax: 202-862-2400
Email: cwtinfo@cwt.com URL: http://www.cadwalader.com
Members of Firm: Frederick R. Anderson; Joseph J. Andrew (Not admitted in DC; Also at New York, New York Office); Raymond Banoun; Charles E. Bryan; James P. Carroll; Diana R. de Brito; Mark C. Ellenberg; Mark P. Howe; Laurence S. Kirsch; Kenneth Klein; Edwin L. Lyon; Daniel J. Mulcahy; David F. Williams. Senior Counsel: Robert T. Lasky. Counsel: Peter M. Dodson. Special Counsel: Charles H. Camp; William T. Christian (Not admitted in DC); Robert A. Davis, Jr.; Geraldine E. Edens; Joyce J. Gorman. Senior Attorney: Jonathan R. Stone. Associates: Elizabeth E. Aherne; Cheryl D. Barnes; Stephen Chippendale; R. Campbell Connell; John Gutowski (Not admitted in DC); Gregg S. Jubin; Sophie A. Kozuch (Not admitted in DC); Susan A. McCarter (Not admitted in DC); D. David Parr, Jr.; Mary Randolph Sargent; Danielle K. Stinemetz (Not admitted in DC).
Capital Markets, Securitization, Corporate Law, Real Estate, Securities, Mergers, Acquisitions and Divestitures, Litigation, Finance, Project Finance, Bankruptcy, Banks and Banking, Taxation, Trusts and Estates, Health Care, Environmental Law, Nonprofit Charitable Organizations, Employee Benefits.
New York, N.Y. Office: 100 Maiden Lane, 10038. Telephone: 212-504-6000. Fax: 212-504-6666.
Charlotte, North Carolina Office: Suite 2400, 227 West Trade Street, 28202. Telephone: 704-348-5100. Fax: 704-348-5200.
London, England Office: Gracechurch House, First Floor, 55 Gracechurch Street, EC3V OEE. Telephone 0207-456-8500. Fax: 0207-456-8600.
See Professional Biographies, WASHINGTON, DISTRICT OF COLUMBIA

Caflisch, John Stephen .... '50 '75 C.309 A.B. L.276 J.D. Price Waterhouse
Cafritz, Diane Long .... '70 '95 C.860 B.A. L.893 J.D. [McDermott,W.&E.]
Cage, Kenneth L., (AV) .... '40 '71 C&L.502 B.S.M.E., J.D. [McDermott,W.&E.] (Pat.)
Caglioti, Michael .... '58 '91 C.1041 B.A. L.976 J.D. [Arnold&P.]
*PRACTICE AREAS: Financial Institutions; Litigation.
Cagna, Robert A. '59 '86 C&L.260 B.A., J.D.
(adm. in FL; not adm. in DC) A.A.R.P. Resch. Info. Ctr.
Cahill, John F., (BV) .... '52 '83 C.433 B.S. L.276 J.D. [Ⓒ Carter,L.&M.]
*PRACTICE AREAS: Technology; Environmental; Insurance; Litigation.
Cahill, Joseph M., (BV) '53 '78
C&L.128 B.A., J.D. Exec. Dir. Legal Affs., Riggs Bk. N.A.
Cahill, Robert A. .... '34 '62 C.966 B.S.E.E. L.273 J.D. 1300 I St., N.W., Suite 700 (Pat.)

Cahill Gordon & Reindel, (AV) BR
1990 K Street, N.W., 20006-1103 ⊙
Telephone: 202-862-8900 Facsimile: 202-862-8958
Resident Partner: Donald J. Mulvihill. Counsel: Corydon B. Dunham. Senior Attorney: Kirsten Emigholz (Not admitted in DC). Resident Associates: Barbara O. Brincefield; Kathy Silberthau Strom.
General Practice.
New York, N.Y. Office: 80 Pine Street. Telephone: 212-701-3000.
London, England Office: Augustine House, 6A Austin Friars, London, England EC2N 2HA. Telephone: +44-20 7920 9800. Facsimile: +44-20 7920 9825.
See Professional Biographies, WASHINGTON, DISTRICT OF COLUMBIA

Cahn, Mark D. .... '61 '87 C.860 B.A. L.976 J.D. [Wilmer,C.&P.]
*PRACTICE AREAS: Civil Practice; Securities; Antitrust; Criminal Law.
Cahn, Maurice U. .... '55 '82 C.401 B.A. L.128 J.D. [Cahn&S.] (See Pat. Sect.) ⊙
*PRACTICE AREAS: Intellectual Property Law.

Cahn & Samuels, LLP
2000 P Street, N.W., Suite 200, 20036 ⊙
Telephone: 202-331-8777 Fax: 202-331-3838
URL: http://www.pattmcopy.com
Maurice U. Cahn; Frederick N. Samuels; George A. Metzenthin; William J. Bundren.
Intellectual Property including procurement and protection of Patent, Trademark and Copyright, counseling and preparation of opinions, protection of trade secrets, litigation, International Patent Prosecution and Licensing, Patent Prosecution including Electrical, Mechanical, Medical, Biotechnology, Software, Business Methods, Electronic Commerce and Chemical.
Rockville, Maryland Office: P.O. Box 5565.
See Professional Biographies, WASHINGTON, DISTRICT OF COLUMBIA

Cail, Sylvester, Jr. .... '63 '94 C.1280 B.A. L.999 J.D. [Cail&Assoc.]
Cail & Associates, P.C. .... 1429 G Street, NW Suite 366
Cain, James M., (AV) .... '55 '80 C.602 A.B. L.276 J.D. [Sutherland A.&B.]
*PRACTICE AREAS: Corporate Law; Banks and Banking; Securities; Insurance; Commodities.
Cain, Michael A., (AV) .... '45 '70 C&L.128 B.A., J.D. [Hamilton&H.]
*PRACTICE AREAS: Land Use; Civil Litigation; Real Estate Tax; Municipal Law.
Cain, Simon L. .... '27 '57 C&L.329 B.A., LL.B. 4901 Klingle St., N.W.‡
Caine, Edward A. .... '43 '68 C.401 B.A. L.276 J.D. [Ⓒ Fletcher,H.&H.] ⊙
*PRACTICE AREAS: Telecommunications Law; Public Utility Law; Electricity and Natural Gas.
Caine, Wesley K., (AV) .... '42 '72 C.339 B.S. L.209 J.D. [Stewart&S.]
*PRACTICE AREAS: Customs Law; International Trade; International Trade Regulation; Import and Export Law; Antidumping.
Caira, Paula J. .... '62 '89 C.788 A.B. L.184 J.D. Intl. Brotherhood of Teamsters
Cairnie, Hilary Stephen .... '56 '89 C.679 B.S.M.S.E. L.128 J.D. [Dykema G.] (Pat.)
*PRACTICE AREAS: Government Contracts; Intellectual Property; Technology and Science.
Cairo, Deana L. .... '73 '99 C.446 B.S. L.273 J.D. [Ⓐ Howrey S.A.&W.]
*PRACTICE AREAS: Antitrust; Litigation.
Calabrese, Michael A. '57 '86 C.309 A.B. L.813 J.D.
(adm. in CA; not adm. in DC) Employee Benefits Coun., AFL-CIO
Calabrese, Michael R. .... '56 '82 C.276 B.S.F.S. L.893 J.D. [Coudert B.]
*PRACTICE AREAS: International Corporate; Commercial Regulation; Trade Regulation.
Calaby, Cecelia A. .... '60 '91 C.691 B.A. L.273 J.D. [Shaw P.]
Calaluca, Laura Hamilton .... '54 '87 C.428 B.A. L.893 J.D. [Ⓒ Dickstein S.M.&O.]
*PRACTICE AREAS: Commercial Litigation; Insurance Litigation; ERISA Litigation.
Calamari-Righi, Maryellen '— '80 C.724 B.S. L.262 J.D.
Assoc. Gen. Coun., Corp. Affrs., National Railroad Passenger Corp. (AMTRAK)
Calamaro, Raymond S., (AV) .... '44 '70 C.188 A.B. L.569 J.D. [Hogan&H.]
*PRACTICE AREAS: International Trade Law; Legislative and Regulatory Law.
Calcagno, Carla C. .... '57 '82 C&L.276 B.A., J.D. [Howrey S.A.&W.]
*PRACTICE AREAS: Trademarks; International Trademarks; Trademark Litigation; Trademark Prosecution; Trademark Protection.
Calderazzi, Kathrine L. .... '70 '97 C.1369 B.A. L.893 J.D. [Ⓐ Paul,H.J.&W.]
*PRACTICE AREAS: Telecommunications Law.
Calderwood, James A., (AV) .... '41 '70 C.446 B.S. L.273 J.D. [Zuckert,S.&R.]
*PRACTICE AREAS: Administrative Law; Antitrust and Trade Regulation; Energy; Government Contracts; Transportation.
Caldwell, Adam S. .... '66 '93 C.390 B.A. [Ⓐ Cole,R.&B.]
*PRACTICE AREAS: Commercial Litigation; Telecommunications Law; Cable Programming; Internet Law.
Caldwell, Joe R., Jr., (AV) .... '49 '74 C.823 A.B. L.705 J.D. [Baker B.]
Caldwell, John H., (AV) .... '36 '62 C.299 A.B. L.309 LL.B. [Caldwell]
Caldwell, Michael S. '70 '00 C.602 B.A. L.276 J.D.
(adm. in NY; not adm. in DC) [Ⓐ Akin,G.S.H.&F.]
*PRACTICE AREAS: Litigation.
Caldwell Associates, (AV) .... 888 17th St., N.W.
Calem, Andrea R. .... '57 '87 C.103 B.A. L.893 J.D. [Ⓐ Epstein B.&G.]
*PRACTICE AREAS: Labor and Employment Law.
Calemine, Guerino J. '74 '99
C&L.893 B.A., J.D. Atty., Communications Workers of America
Calender, John G., (AV) .... '51 '77 C.867 B.A. L.273 J.D. [Howrey S.A.&W.]
*PRACTICE AREAS: Antitrust; Commercial Litigation; Complex Litigation.
Calhoun, Bridget E. .... '71 '97 C.197 B.A. L.446 J.D. [Ⓐ Crowell&M.]
Calhoun, Carol V., (AV) .... '53 '80 C.367 B.A. L.276 J.D. [Calhoun]
Calhoun, George R., V .... '71 '97 C.880 B.A. L.446 J.D. [Ⓐ Steptoe&J.]
Calhoun, Martin C., (AV) .... '64 '89 C.976 B.A. L.276 J.D. [Spriggs&H.]
*PRACTICE AREAS: Products Liability; Toxic Torts; Litigation; Drug and Medical Device Defense; Insurance Coverage.
Calhoun Law Group, P.C., (AV) .... 900 Seventeenth Street, N.W.
Calkins, John J. .... '68 '93 C.367 B.A. L.30 J.D. [Sonnenschein N.&R.]
*PRACTICE AREAS: Litigation; Intellectual Property; Technology.
Calkins, Lynn Estes .... '68 '93 C.205 B.A. L.30 J.D. [Ⓐ Holland&K.]
*PRACTICE AREAS: Commercial Litigation; Real Estate Litigation.
Calkins, Stephen, (AV) .... '— '76 C.976 B.A. L.309 J.D. [Ⓒ Covington&B.]
Calkins, Troy M. .... '66 '91 C.475 B.A. L.477 J.D. [Gardner,C.&D.]
*PRACTICE AREAS: Securities; Mergers and Acquisitions; Corporate.
Callaghan, John L., (BV) '37 '64 C.674 A.B. L.188 LL.B.
(adm. in NY; not adm. in DC) 5126 Cathedral Ave., N.W.‡
Callahan, A. Renée .... '66 '95 C.309 B.A. L.30 J.D. [Ⓐ Willkie F.&G.]
*PRACTICE AREAS: Litigation.
Callahan, Celine T. '63 '91 C.128 B.Ch.E. L.273 J.D.
[Howrey S.A.&W.] (See Pat. Sect.)
*PRACTICE AREAS: Intellectual Property Law; Patent and Trademark Litigation; Counseling and Procurement.
Callahan, John J. .... '62 '94 C.93 B.A. L.128 J.D. [Ⓐ Hall,E.H.G.G.&N.]
*PRACTICE AREAS: Litigation.
Callahan, John T. .... '63 '90 C.128 B.Ch.E. L.64 J.D. [Sughrue M.] (See Pat. Sect.)
*PRACTICE AREAS: Intellectual Property Law.
Callahan, Mary Ellen .... '68 '98 C.665 B.Phil. L.145 J.D. [Ⓐ Hogan&H.]
*PRACTICE AREAS: Litigation; Antitrust; Consumer Protection.
Callaway, Claudia Treadwell .... '66 '92 C.104 A.B. L.276 J.D. [Ⓒ Paul,H.J.&W.]
*PRACTICE AREAS: Commercial Litigation; Complex Litigation; Class Action Defense; Consumer Finance; Employment Law.
Callaway, William H., Jr. .... '51 '76 C.228 B.A. L.893 J.D. [Zuckert,S.&R.]
*PRACTICE AREAS: International Aviation Law; Aircraft Finance and Leasing; Asset-Based Finance; International Commercial Finance.
Callery, T. Grant '46 '73 C.434 B.S. L.276 J.D.
Sr. V.P. & Gen. Coun., Nat. Assn. of Securities Dealers, Inc.
Callet, David P., (P.C.), (AV) .... '49 '73 C.645 B.A. L.273 J.D. [Akin,G.S.H.&F.]
*PRACTICE AREAS: Litigation.
Calligaro, Lee, (AV) .... '42 '67 C.478 B.A. L.705 J.D. [Ⓒ Epstein B.&G.]
*PRACTICE AREAS: Litigation; Health Law; Corporate Law.
Calsyn, Jeremy J. .... '73 '99 C.804 B.S. L.276 J.D. [Ⓐ Cleary,G.S.&H.]
Calvani, Terry, (AV) .... '47 '72 C.560 B.A. L.188 J.D. [Pillsbury W.] (⊙San Fran., CA)
*PRACTICE AREAS: Antitrust.
Calve, James P. '57 '85 C.870 B.S. L.188 J.D.
(adm. in MA; not adm. in DC) [Ⓐ Baker B.]

Calvert, Cynthia Thomas, L.L.C., Law Offices of
(See Ellicott City, Maryland)

Calvetti, Frederick F., (AV) '45 '78 C.474 B.S. L.64 J.D. [Smith,G.&R.] (See Pat. Sect.)
*PRACTICE AREAS: Intellectual Property.

Calvo, Gabriel .... '69 '99 C.228 A.B. L.276 J.D. [A Hunton&W.]
*PRACTICE AREAS: Environmental Law.

Camalier, Charles A., III, (AV) .... '51 '77 C.602 B.B.A. L.276 J.D. [Wilkes A.]
*PRACTICE AREAS: Real Property Tax and Assessment Law; Condemnation; Litigation.

Camarra, Christopher L. .... '72 '98 C.94 B.A. L.184 J.D. [A Holland&K.]
*PRACTICE AREAS: Real Property Law.

Cameron, Arthur E. '38 '66 C.30 B.A. L.904 J.D. (adm. in MD; not adm. in DC) 225 C St., N.E.‡

Cameron, Donald B., Jr., (AV) .... '49 '79 C.385 B.A. L.880 J.D. [Kaye S.]
*PRACTICE AREAS: International Trade.

Cameron, Duncan H., (AV) .... '34 '59 C.309 B.A. L.178 LL.B. [Cameron&H.] ⊙
*PRACTICE AREAS: International Business Transactions; International Banking Law.

Cameron, Kelly, (AV) .... '58 '83 C.860 B.A. L.276 J.D. [Powell,G.F.&M.]
*PRACTICE AREAS: Telecommunications; International Trade.

Cameron, Kelly A. .... '67 '95 C.101 B.A. L.902 J.D. [A Perkins C.]
*PRACTICE AREAS: Litigation; Telecommunications Law.

Cameron, Richard R. .... '— '95 C.188 A.B. L.273 J.D. [A Latham&W.]
*PRACTICE AREAS: Administrative Law; Communications and Media; Federal Legislative Practice; Telephone Utility Regulation.

Cameron, Robert H. .... '69 '98 C.228 B.A. L.273 J.D. [A Rothwell,F.E.&M.]

Cameron, Toryah S. .... '72 '98 C.309 A.B. L.329 J.D. [A Sullivan&C.]

Cameron & Hornbostel LLP, (AV)
Suite 700, 818 Connecticut Avenue, N.W., 20006 ⊙
Telephone: 202-293-4690 Cable Address: "Continent" Telecopier: 202-293-1877
Email: lawyersdc@cameron-hornbostel.com URL: http://www.Cameron-Hornbostel.com
Members of Firm: Duncan H. Cameron; Michele Sherman Davenport; Luiz Claudio Duarte (Not admitted in DC); Jim Tom Haynes; Dean Holbrook; Peter A. Hornbostel; Stephen L. Humphrey; William K. Ince; Dennis James, Jr.; Alexander W. Sierck; Thomas Silbiger; Frederick Simpich; Howard L. Vickery. Associates: Jayni L. Edelstein; Valerie Ellis; Ana V. Farach; Yong Lee (Not admitted in DC); Matthew J. Martin; Luiza Torresan Wilson (Not admitted in DC). Foreign Attorney: J. A. Antunes Maciel. Of Counsel: Bertrand J. Delanney (Resident, New York, N.Y. Office); Richard C. Katz.
International Law, Banking, Litigation, and General Practice.
New York, N.Y. Office: Suite 249, 866 United Nations Plaza. Telephone: 646-840-6666. Cable Address: "Continents, New York." Telecopier: 646-735-3759. Email: lawyersny@cameron-hornbostel.com.
See Professional Biographies, WASHINGTON, DISTRICT OF COLUMBIA

Cameron McKenna LLP, (AV) BB
2175 K Street, N.W. Fifth Floor, 20037-1850
Telephone: 202-466-0060 Fax: 202-466-0077
Email: info@cmcklaw.com URL: http://www.cmcklaw.com
Partners: Joel F. Zipp; George H. Williams, Jr.; Amy S. Koch; Andrzej M. Blach. Counsel: Reinier H. J. H. Lock; John J. Bartus; Robert C. Platt; Lena S. Zezulin. Senior Associates: Bridget Shahan; Nona S. Pucciariello (Not admitted in DC). Associates: Gunnar Birgisson; Matthew E. Ross; Judith M. Andrade.
Languages: English.
Practice focuses on Energy, Infrastructure, Environmental, Transportation, Public Utilities, Administrative, Litigation, International Trade, Transactions and Finance, and also represents clients before federal regulatory agencies and related federal appellate courts.
CMS offices and associated offices worldwide: Berlin, Brussels, London, Paris, Utrecht, Vienna, Zurich, Aberdeen, Amsterdam, Amhem, Beijing, Belgrade, Bratislava, Bristol, Bucharest, Budapest, Buenos Aires, Cape Town, Casablanca, Chemnitz, Dresden, Dusseldorf, Frankfort, Hamburg, Hilversum, Hong Kong, Johannesburg, Leipzig, Lyon, Madrid, Moscow, Munich, New York, Prague, Singapore, Stuttgart, Toronto, and Warsaw.
See Professional Biographies, WASHINGTON, DISTRICT OF COLUMBIA

Camet, Gregory W. .... '— '96 C.861 B.A. L.904 J.D. [A Morgan,L.&B.]

Camet, Lily A. .... '68 '96 C.276 A.B. L.904 J.D. [A Skadden,A.S.M.&F.]

Cammack, Ann B. .... '63 '90 C.682 A.B. L.902 J.D. [A Sutherland A.&B.]
*PRACTICE AREAS: Taxation.

Cammarata, Joseph, (AV) .... '58 '84 C.276 B.S. L.724 J.D. [A Chaikin&S.]
*PRACTICE AREAS: Litigation; Personal Injury; Medical Malpractice; Wrongful Death; Sexual Harassment.

Camp, Charles H., (AV) .... '57 '82 C.420 B.S. L.896 J.D. [C Cadwalader,W.&T.]
*PRACTICE AREAS: Litigation; International Dispute Resolution; Real Estate.

Camp, John C., (AV) .... '23 '48 C.88 L.420 J.D. [C Patton B.]

Campbell, Alan C., (AV) .... '40 '66 C.659 B.S. L.276 J.D. [Irwin,C.&T.]

Campbell, Amy E. .... '65 '94 C.378 B.A. L.1035 J.D. [A Ballard S.A.&I.]
*PRACTICE AREAS: Corporate Law; Public Securitization Finance; Securities.

Campbell, Angela J. '54 '81 C.1307 B.A. L.1068 J.D. Prof., Georgetown Univ. Law Sch.

Campbell, Ayoka A. .... '74 '00 C.329 B.A. L.802 J.D. 1400 Independence Ave., S.W.

Campbell, Benton J. '66 '91 C.976 B.A. L.145 J.D. (adm. in IL; not adm. in DC) 655 15th St., N.W., Suite 1200

Campbell, Bret A. .... '67 '95 C.319 B.A. L.1194 J.D. [A Clifford C.R.&W.]
*PRACTICE AREAS: Antitrust Litigation; Intellectual Property Litigation; Securities Litigation.

Campbell, Bruce D., Jr. .... '72 '98 C.665 B.A. L.273 J.D. [A Hogan&H.]

Campbell, C. Grace .... '69 '96 C.597 B.S. L.893 J.D. [A Skadden,A.S.M.&F.]
*PRACTICE AREAS: Corporate Law; Securities; Mergers and Acquisitions.

Campbell, Fred B., Jr .... '71 '97 C.569 B.A. L.546 J.D. [A Harris,W.&G.]
*PRACTICE AREAS: Telecommunications Law; Corporate Law.

Campbell, Gary J. .... '68 '99 C.93 B.S. L.1209 J.D. [A Hogan&H.]
*PRACTICE AREAS: Government Contracts.

Campbell, Glenn C., (AV) '— '85 C.896 B.A. L.575 J.D. (adm. in MD; not adm. in DC) [King&S.]
*PRACTICE AREAS: Corporate and Finance.

Campbell, Isaac R. '69 '99 C.1350 B.A. L.329 J.D. (adm. in MD; not adm. in DC) 1776 K St., N.W.

Campbell, Jack W., IV .... '69 '98 C.575 B.S. L.880 J.D. [A Jones,D.R.&P.]

Campbell, James S., (AV) .... '38 '66 C.976 B.A. L.813 LL.B. [C Wilmer,C.&P.]
*PRACTICE AREAS: Antitrust and Trade Regulation; Aviation; International Law.

Campbell, Jeffrey A. '65 '93 C.976 B.A. L.276 J.D. Assoc. Gen. Coun., Govt. Affs., Compaq Computer Corp.

Campbell, John W. .... '47 '72 C.602 B.B.A. L.276 J.D. [Epstein B.&G.]
*PRACTICE AREAS: Corporate Law; Mergers and Acquisitions Law; Health Law; Insurance Law.

Campbell, Julie A. '— '98 C.608 B.A. L.276 J.D. (adm. in VA; not adm. in DC) [A Manatt,P.&P.]

Campbell, Lisa M., (CV) .... '60 '85 C.36 B.S. L.813 J.D. [Bergeson&C.]
*PRACTICE AREAS: Federal Insecticide, Fungicide and Rodenticide Act (FIFRA); Toxic Substances Regulation; Resource Conservation and Recovery Act (RCRA); Pesticide Regulation; Chemical Regulation.

Campbell, Michael D. .... '— '67 C.390 B.A. L.276 J.D. [Miller&C.]

Campbell, Nancy Duff '43 '68 C.178 A.B. L.569 J.D. Co-Pres., National Women's Law Center

Campbell, Patricia L. .... '52 '96 C.836 B.S.M.E. L.273 J.D. [A Winston&S.]
*PRACTICE AREAS: Nuclear Energy (80%); Energy (20%).

Campbell, Patrick S. .... '71 '95 C.276 B.A. L.813 J.D. [A Paul,W.R.W.&G.]

Campbell, Rachel Danish .... '— '91 C.706 B.A. L.276 J.D. [Foley&L.]
*PRACTICE AREAS: Litigation.

Campbell, Thomas L. .... '53 '83 C.223 B.S.B.A. L.665 J.D. 530 8th St., S.E.

Campbell, Vivian L. '46 '81 C.280 A.B. L.276 J.D. Assoc Law Libr., Georgetown Univ. Law Ctr.

Camper, Anne B. .... '55 '81 C&L.893 B.A., J.D. [Powell,G.F.&M.]
*PRACTICE AREAS: Health Care; Corporate.

Campo, Laurent M. .... '70 '96 C.188 B.A. L.228 J.D. [A Dow,L.&A.]

Campoamor-Sanchez, Fernando .... '68 '94 C.276 B.S. L.228 J.D. [A Covington&B.]

Canaan, Karen '63 '97 C.846 B.A. L.1148 J.D. (adm. in CA; not adm. in DC; Pat.) [A Crowell&M.]

Canan, Russell F. .... '50 '76 C.823 B.A. L.1162 J.D. Supr. Ct. J.

Candon, Mary Eva, (AV) .... '50 '87 C.242 B.A. L.276 J.D. [Berliner,C.&J.]
*PRACTICE AREAS: Intergovernmental Affairs; Administrative Law.

Canetti, Craig W. .... '68 '96 C.976 B.A. L.276 J.D. [A Mayer,B.&P.]

Canfield, Edward F., (AV) '22 '49 C.728 B.A. L.659 J.D. 1815 H Street, N.W. Suite 1001 (⊙Phila., PA)

Canfield, William B., III, (AV) .... '46 '73 C.207 B.A. L.213 J.D. [Williams&J.]
*PRACTICE AREAS: Election, Campaign and Political Law; Legislative Practice; Congressional Investigations.

Cangelosi, Victor L. .... '61 '91 C.321 B.A. L.273 J.D. [Muldoon M.&F.]
*PRACTICE AREAS: Financial Institutions; Securities; Corporate Law.

Canis, Jonathan E., (AV) .... '54 '83 C.705 B.A. L.823 J.D. [Kelley D.&W.]
*PRACTICE AREAS: Communications; Corporate Law.

Cannata, Danielle L. '73 '00 C.165 B.A. L.30 J.D. (adm. in NY; not adm. in DC) [A O'Melveny&M.]

Cannon, Allen, III .... '52 '87 C.1083 B.A. L.276 J.D. [Perkins C.]
*PRACTICE AREAS: Government Contracts; Litigation.

Cannon, Daniel W. .... '20 '48 C&L.665 A.B., J.D. 611 Pennsylvania Ave., N.W.

Cannon, Dean H., (AV) .... '57 '81 C.16 B.S. L.276 J.D. [Beveridge&D.]
*PRACTICE AREAS: Environmental Law; Corporate Law.

Cannon, George D., Jr. .... '— '95 C.861 B.A. L.273 J.D. [A Latham&W.]
*PRACTICE AREAS: Energy.

Cannon, James R., Jr., (AV) .... '57 '82 C.893 B.A. L.30 J.D. [Williams M.]
*PRACTICE AREAS: Civil Litigation; Administrative; Trade Regulation; Antidumping; Customs Law.

Cannon, Jonathan Z., (AV) .... '45 '75 C.951 B.A. L.659 J.D. [C Beveridge&D.]
*PRACTICE AREAS: Environmental Law; Administrative Law.

Cannon, Kathleen Weaver, (AV) .... '55 '81 C.446 B.S. L.575 J.D. [C Collier S.S.]
*PRACTICE AREAS: International Trade.

Canter, Douglas M., (AV) .... '54 '79 C.105 B.A. L.64 J.D. [McCarthy,S.&H.]
*PRACTICE AREAS: Administrative Law; Public Utility Law; Energy Law.

Canter, MacKenzie, III, (AV) .... '49 '76 C.682 A.B. L.893 J.D. [Copilevitz&C.] ⊙
*PRACTICE AREAS: Tax Exempt Organizations; Civil Litigation; Real Estate; Trademark Law; Trade Regulation.

Canter, Mark A. '48 '75 C.94 A.B. L.818 J.D. Senior Counsel, American Council of Life Insurance

Canterman, Robert S. .... '58 '90 C.216 B.A. L.904 J.D. [C Crowell&M.]
*PRACTICE AREAS: Health Care Law; Antitrust Law.

Cantor, Alan I., (AV) .... '48 '75 C.186 B.E. L.64 J.D. [Foley&L.] (See Pat. Sect.)
*PRACTICE AREAS: Intellectual Property.

Cantor, Arthur I., (AV) .... '38 '63 C.178 A.B. L.309 LL.B. [Wiley R.&F.]
*PRACTICE AREAS: Franchise; Antitrust.

Cantor, Daniel A. .... '70 '96 C.67 B.A. L.904 J.D. [A Arnold&P.]
*PRACTICE AREAS: Environmental; Litigation.

Cantor, Herbert I., (AV) .... '35 '70 C.569 B.A. L.128 J.D. [Crowell&M.] (Pat.)
*PRACTICE AREAS: Patent Interferences; Litigation; Counseling.

Cantor, Jay M., (AV) .... '32 '60 C.659 B.S.E.E. L.273 J.D. [C Baker B.] (See Pat. Sect.)

Cantor, Richard Alan .... '49 '81 C.861 B.A. L.588 J.D. The Grizzle Co.

Cantrell, Melissa K. .... '69 '00 C.586 B.A.A.S. L.326 J.D. [A Vinson&E.]
*PRACTICE AREAS: Health Law; Medicare and Medicaid; False Claims Act; Antitrust and Trade Regulation; Technology and Science.

Cantu, Daniel A. .... '61 '99 C.112 B.A. L.145 J.D. [A Gibson,D.&C.]
*PRACTICE AREAS: Litigation.

Canzano, Peter L. .... '56 '82 C.477 A.B. L.893 J.D. [Sidley A.B.&W.]

Capizzi, Mary E. Devlin .... '66 '94 C.1105 B.A. L.245 J.D. [A Gardner,C.&D.]
*PRACTICE AREAS: Corporate; International.

Caplan, Bennett A. .... '56 '85 C.178 B.A. L.93 J.D. Joseph E. Seagram & Sons

Caplan, Corina R. .... '71 '96 C.1375 B.A. L.705 J.D. [A McKee N.]
*PRACTICE AREAS: Secured Fianace.

Caplan, Karen Anne '59 '88 C.477 B.A. L.912 J.D. Asst. Gen. Coun. Securities Inv., Securities Investor Protection Corporation

Caplan, Maia R. .... '62 '89 C&L.477 B.A., J.D. [A Kator,P.&W.]
*PRACTICE AREAS: Employment; Civil Rights; Litigation.

Caplan, Buckner & Kostecka, Chtd.
(See Bethesda, Maryland)

Caplin, Mortimer M., (AV) .... '16 '41 C&L.893 B.S., LL.B. [Caplin&D.]
*PRACTICE AREAS: Federal Tax Law; Tax Controversies; Tax Procedure; Corporate Law.

Caplin & Drysdale, Chartered, (AV) BB
One Thomas Circle, N.W., 20005 ⊙
Telephone: 202-862-5000 Cable Address: "Capdale" Telex: 904001 CAPL UR WSH Fax: 202-429-3301
URL: http://www.caplindrysdale.com
Mortimer M. Caplin; Douglas D. Drysdale; Bernard S. Bailor; Robert A. Boisture; Herman B. Bouma; Milton Cerny; Julie W. Davis; Michael Doran; Nathan D. Finch; Matthew W. Frank; Seth M. Green; Jessica L. Katz; Beth Shapiro Kaufman; Albert G. Lauber, Jr.; Patricia G. Lewis; Catherine E. Livingston; Peter Van N. Lockwood; Kent A. Mason; Scott D. Michel; Ralph A. Muoio; Cono R. Namorato; Marcus Sherman Owens (Not admitted in DC); Trevor Potter; Christopher S. Rizek; Daniel B. Rosenbaum; H. David Rosenbloom; James E. Salles; Walter B. Slocombe; Stafford Smiley; Trevor W. Swett III; Richard E. Timbie; Thomas A. Troyer; Douglas N. Varley; David N. Webster. Of Counsel: Ann C. McMillan; Rebecca I. Rosenberg (Not admitted in DC);—Jason K. Bortz; Kimberly N. Brown; Kristen M. Gurdin (Not admitted in DC); Diana R. Hartstein; Beth S. Heleman; H. Carter Hood; Kirk L. Jowers; William M. Klimon; Neal M. Kochman; Karin J. Lundell (Not admitted in DC); Lloyd H. Mayer.
Federal Tax Practice. Civil and Criminal Litigation, Corporations, Securities, International and Administrative Practice, Estate Planning.
New York, N.Y. Office: 399 Park Avenue, 36th Floor. Telephone: 212-319-7125. Fax: 212-644-6755.
See Professional Biographies, WASHINGTON, DISTRICT OF COLUMBIA

Capps, John E. '64 '96 C.880 B.A. L.846 J.D. (adm. in NY; not adm. in DC) [A Sullivan&C.]

Capps, Kelly J. .... '65 '93 C.846 B.B.A. L.30 J.D. [A Ravdin&W.]
*PRACTICE AREAS: Domestic Relations; Trusts and Estates.

Capretz, Colette M. .... '69 '95 C.846 B.S. L.602 J.D. [A Shaw P.]
*PRACTICE AREAS: Communications.

Capria, Mary Ann, (AV) .... '58 '84 C&L.790 B.S., J.D. [C Alston&B.] (Pat.)
*PRACTICE AREAS: Intellectual Property; Patents; Trademarks; Technology Licensing; Litigation.

Capron, Alexander M. '44 '70 C.821 B.A. L.976 LL.B. Prof. of Law, Georgetown Univ.

Capuano, David D. '67 '94 C.1369 B.A. L.128 J.D. (adm. in PA; not adm. in DC) [A O'Donoghue&O.] ⊙
*PRACTICE AREAS: Employee Benefits; Labor.

Capuano, Donald J., (AV) .... '34 '58 C.1044 B.S. L.276 LL.B. [O'Donoghue&O.]

Capuano, Vincent L. .....'64 '99 C.608 B.S. L.7 J.D. [A Sterne,K.G.&F.] (See Pat. Sect.)
*PRACTICE AREAS: Pharmaceutical Patent Procurement; Enforcement; FDA / ANDA.
Caputo, Andrew P ....'65 '90 C.103 A.B. L.976 J.D. Natural Resources Def. Coun.
Caputo, Kenneth J. '59 '85 C.1349 B.A. L.564 J.D.
(adm. in NY; not adm. in DC)
Assoc. Gen. Coun. & Sr. Trial Coun., Securities Investor Protec. Corp.
Caraballo, Arturo ....'71 '98 C&L.861 B.A., J.D. [A Arnold&P.]
*PRACTICE AREAS: Corporate; Securities; International; Capital Markets; Project Finance.
Carabillo, Joseph A., (AV) '46 '77
C.1174 B.A. L.776 J.D. V.P. & Chf. Legal Offr., ULLICO INC.
*RESPONSIBILITIES: Corporate; Securities; Group Life and Health Insurance; Managed Health Care; Financial Services.
Caramagno, Salvatore E., (AV) ....'32 '57 L.94 LL.B. 888 - 16th St., N.W.
Carb, Evan D., (AV) '60 '86
C.165 B.A. L.823 J.D. V.P. Legal Affairs, Wireless Holdings, Inc.
Carbaugh, William F. ....'64 '92 C&L.893 B.A., J.D. Sr. Coun., Marriott Intl., Inc.
*RESPONSIBILITIES: International Hotel Lodging Operations; Real Estate Development.
Carbone, Chad Anthony '71 '98 C.454 B.S. L.1194 J.D.
(adm. in MA; not adm. in DC) Atty., U.S. Envir. Protec. Agcy.
Cardaci, Christopher P. ....'69 '97 C.401 B.A., B.S. L.276 J.D. [A Hogan&H.]
*PRACTICE AREAS: Litigation; Insurance Coverage.
Cardaro, Thomas C., & Associates, (AV) '59 '85 C.446 B.S. L.128 J.D.
915 15th St., NW, 3rd Fl. (⊙Wash., DC; Balt., MD)
Cardaro, Thomas C., & Associates, (AV) '59 '85 C.446 B.S. L.128 J.D.
1155 Connecticut Avenue, N.W., Suite 300 (⊙Balt., MD)

Cardaro, Thomas C., & Associates
(See Baltimore)

Carder, Elizabeth B., (AV) ....'— '79 C.103 A.B. L.945 J.D. [Reed S.]
*PRACTICE AREAS: Health Care.
Cardi, W. Jonathan ....'69 '97 C.309 A.B. L.352 J.D. [A Arnold&P.]
*PRACTICE AREAS: Litigation; Intellectual Property.
Cardin, Sanford R., (BV) ....'57 '81 C.309 B.A. L.446 J.D. [C Heideman]
*PRACTICE AREAS: Corporate Law; Real Property; Professional Conduct; International Corporate Law.
Cardinale, Christopher T. '71 '99 C.676 B.A. L.30 J.D.
(adm. in NY; not adm. in DC) [A Weil,G.&M.]
*PRACTICE AREAS: International Trade; Corporate Law.
Cardman, Denise A. '51 '78 C.112 B.A. L.30 J.D.
(adm. in VA; not adm. in DC) Leg. Coord., Govt. Affs. Grp., Amer. Bar Assn.
Cardozo, Michael H., IV ....'10 '36 C.197 A.B. L.976 LL.B. 1001 Conn. Ave., N.W.‡
Cardozo, Michael H., V '40 '71
C.197 A.B. L.893 J.D. Manag. Dir., G. William Miller & Co., Inc.
Carey, Anthony M., (AV) '35 '63 C.674 A.B. L.309 LL.B.
(adm. in MD; not adm. in DC) [Venable,A.B.H.&C.] (⊙Balt., MD)
*PRACTICE AREAS: Environmental and Energy Law.
Carey, Carlyn M. '— '00 C.354 B.A. L.30 J.D.
(adm. in NY; not adm. in DC) [A Bracewell&P.]
*PRACTICE AREAS: Real Estate; Energy; Finance; Corporate Transactions.
Carey, Christina E. '72 '00 C.477 B.S. L.893 J.D.
(adm. in MI; not adm. in DC) [A Beveridge&D.]
*PRACTICE AREAS: Environmental Law; Litigation.
Carey, Jason A. '74 '99 C.951 B.A. L.893 J.D.
(adm. in VA; not adm. in DC) [A McDermott,W.&E.]
Carey, Kate ....'63 '91 C.770 B.A. L.180 J.D. V.P., Metropolitan Life Ins. Co.
Carey, Kathleen A., (AV) ....'52 '81 C.690 B.A. L.1162 J.D. [Jordan K.&J.]
Carey, Leslie '71 '96 C&L.339 B.A., J.D.
(adm. in IL; not adm. in DC) [A Kutak R.]
*PRACTICE AREAS: Public Finance; Corporate Finance.
Carey, Sarah C., (AV) ....'38 '66 C.309 B.A. L.276 LL.B. [Squire,S.&D.]
*PRACTICE AREAS: International Transactions; Privatization; Corporate Restructuring; International Investment Law.
Cari, Joseph A., Jr., (AV) '52 '78 C&L.602 B.A., J.D.
(adm. in IL; not adm. in DC) [Ungaretti&H.] ⊙
*PRACTICE AREAS: Business Law; Legislative Practice; Regulatory Law.
Carías-Troconis, Gabriela '68 '92 L.30 LL.M.
(adm. in NY; not adm. in DC) [A Thompson C.]
*PRACTICE AREAS: International Trade; Commercial Transactions; Tobacco Litigation.
Caridi, Michael J. '72 '97
C&L.128 B.A., J.D. [C Armstrong,W.H.M.&N.] (See Pat. Sect.)
*PRACTICE AREAS: Intellectual Property Litigation; International Trade; Commercial Litigation.
Carithers, Michael R., Jr. ....'66 '91 C.309 B.A. L.477 J.D. [A Collier S.S.]
*PRACTICE AREAS: Litigation; White Collar Defense.
Carl, David Lance '74 '99 C.860 B.A. L.273 J.D.
(adm. in MD; not adm. in DC) 1200 19th Street
Carlan, Janine A. ....'68 '98 C.576 B.S. L.1338 J.D. [A Shook,H.&B.] (Pat.)
Carleton, Gary A. '57 '83 C.347 A.B. L.107 J.D.
(adm. in NY; not adm. in DC) 1735 K St., N.W.
Carlin, J. David ....'62 '88 C.375 B.A. L.309 J.D. [Akin,G.S.H.&F.]
*PRACTICE AREAS: Public Policy.
Carlin, Joseph S. ....'65 '95 C.550 B.A. L.180 J.D. [A Gardner,C.&D.]
*PRACTICE AREAS: Securities; Mergers and Acquisitions; Corporate.
Carlin, Mark S., (AV) ....'53 '77 C.1044 B.A. L.976 J.D. [Sherman,M.C.&A.]
*PRACTICE AREAS: Civil Litigation; Family Law; Professional Malpractice.

Carlin, Bradshaw, Thomas & Yeatman L.L.P.
(See Bethesda, Maryland)

Carlineo, Daniel S. ....'— '98 C.1349 B.S.E.E. L.150 J.D. [A Morgan,L.&B.]
Carliner, David, (AV) ....'18 '40 C.30 L.537 LL.B. [Carliner,R.&M.]
*PRACTICE AREAS: Immigration Law.

Carliner, Remes and Mirbagheri-Smith, P.C., (AV) BB
Suite 903, 1700 K Street, N.W., 20006
Telephone: 202-223-0050 Fax: 202-223-0052 URL: http://www.carliner-remes.com
Email: info@carliner-remes.com URL: http://www.lawyers.com/carliner-remeslaw
David Carliner; Robert A. Remes; Ladan Mirbagheri-Smith.
Immigration and Nationality Law. Administrative Law. International Law.
See Professional Biographies, WASHINGTON, DISTRICT OF COLUMBIA

Carling, Duane D. '67 '95
(adm. in UT; not adm. in DC) PriceWaterhouseCoopers
Carlisle, Linda E., (AV) ....'48 '80 C.846 B.A. L.128 J.D. [White&C.]
*PRACTICE AREAS: Federal Income Tax; Federal Taxation; International Taxation.
Carlo, Juan C. ....'65 '90 C.454 B.A. L.30 J.D. Catholic Immigration Network, Inc.
Carlo, Meredith A. ....'— '97 C.1369 B.S. L.309 J.D. [A Morgan,L.&B.]
Carloni, Carla J. '61 '86 C.1030 B.A. L.945 J.D.
(adm. in VA; not adm. in DC) Assoc. Gen. Coun., Nat. Assn. of Sec. Dealers, Inc.

Carlsmith Ball LLP, (AV) BB
A Limited Liability Law Partnership
1201 Pennsylvania Avenue, N.W. Suite 300, 20004-2401 ⊙
Telephone: 202-628-2228 Fax: 202-628-2071
Email: execdirector@carlsmith.com URL: http://www.carlsmith.com

(This Listing Continued)

Carlsmith Ball LLP (Continued)

Resident Partner: Nancy M. Beckner.
Admiralty & Maritime, Administrative, Banking & Finance, Corporate, Environmental, Foreign Investment Interests, Hospitality, Hotel, Resort & Entertainment, Immigration, International, Labor & Employment, Litigation and Dispute Resolution, Public Utilities, Real Property and Land Use, Tax, Trusts, and Compensation Planning, Latin America Trade & Investment, Pacific Rim Trade & Investment, Energy Development & Regulations, Health Care, Medicare/Medicaid Fraud & Abuse, Telecommunications, Class Action Defense, E-Commerce, Internet Law, Intellectual Property Litigation, Construction Law, Appellate Practice, Estate Planning, Commercial Leasing, Product Liability, Professional Liability, Bank Regulatory Enforcement, Antitrust, Election and Campaign Finance, Government Contracts, Legislative Lobbying, Media Law, Franchise Law, Tax-Exempt Organizations, Foreign Sales Corporation, Project Finance.
Honolulu, Hawaii Office: Suite 2200, Pacific Tower, 1001 Bishop Street. P.O. Box 656, 96809-0656. Telephone: 808-523-2500. Fax: 808-523-0842.
Kapolei, Hawaii Office: Suite 318, Kapolei Building, 1001 Kamokila Boulevard, 96707. Telephone: 808-523-2500. Fax: 808-674-0850.
Wailuku, Maui Hawaii Office: Suite 400, One Main Plaza, 2200 Main Street, P.O. Box 1086, 96793-1086. Telephone: 808-242-4535. Fax: 808-244-4974.
Kailua-Kona, Hawaii Office: Suite 209, 75-1000 Henry Street, 96740. Telephone: 808-329-6464. Fax: 808-329-9450.
Hilo, Hawaii Office: 121 Waianuenue Avenue, P.O. Box 686, 96721-0686. Telephone: 808-935-6644. Fax: 808-935-7975.
Hagatna, Guam Office: Suite 401, Bank of Hawaii Building, 134 West Soledad Avenue, P.O. Box BF, 96932-5027. Telephone: 671-472-6813. Fax: 671-477-4375. Telex: 721-6445 CWCMI GM.
Saipan, Commonwealth of the Northern Mariana Islands Office: Carlsmith Building, Capitol Hill, P.O. Box 5241, 96950-5241. Telephone: 670-322-3455. Fax: 670-322-3368.
Los Angeles, California Office: 9th Floor, 444 South Flower Street, 90071-2901. Telephone: 213-955-1200. Fax: 213-623-0032.
Revisers of the Hawaii Law Digest for this Directory
See Professional Biographies, WASHINGTON, DISTRICT OF COLUMBIA

Carlson, Donald R. ....'61 '87 C.951 B.A. L.309 J.D. 725 12th St., N.W.
Carlson, Eileen Shannon .....'57 '83 C.846 B.A. L.276 J.D. 4937 Brandywine St., N.W.‡
Carlson, Jay L., (AV) ....'— '70 C.966 B.S. L.273 J.D. [Miller&C.]
*PRACTICE AREAS: Tax Litigation; International Tax Controversies; Federal Tax Controversies.
Carlson, Jim '52 '99 C.1070 B.S. L.494 J.D.
(adm. in MN; not adm. in DC) [A Piper M.R.&W.]
*PRACTICE AREAS: Business Law; Technology Law; Military Aviation; Computer Programming; Web Site Development.
Carlson, Lucy G. ....'68 '96 C.893 B.A. L.945 J.D. [A Willkie F.&G.]
Carlson, Marinn F. ....'72 '98 C.197 B.A. L.976 J.D. [A Powell,G.F.&M.]
*PRACTICE AREAS: Antitrust; International Corporate Law; International Trade.
Carlson, Mary Joyce '47 '73 C.498 B.A. L.228 J.D.
(adm. in GA; not adm. in DC) [C James&H.]
Carlson, Matthew W. ....'69 '94 C.446 B.S. L.128 J.D. [A Thompson,O.M.N.&H.]
*PRACTICE AREAS: Tort Defense; General Litigation; Workers' Compensation; Labor and Employment Law.
Carlton, Brandon Cash ....'75 '99 C.101 B.S. L.1142 J.D. 1225 Connecticut N.W.
Carlyle, Megan L. ....'70 '98 C.1365 B.A. L.228 J.D. [A Wilmer,C.&P.]
Carmean, Erika R. ....'69 '97 C&L.446 B.A., J.D. [A Arnold&P.]
*PRACTICE AREAS: Intellectual Property; Technology Law.
Carmean, Mark Wayne ....'71 '97 C.228 B.A. L.446 J.D. [A Piper M.R.&W.]
*PRACTICE AREAS: Telecommunications Litigation; Products Liability; Antitrust.
Carmel, Frank J., (AV) ....'54 '79 C.886 B.A. L.893 J.D. [Carmel&C.]
*PRACTICE AREAS: Real Estate Development; Regulatory Law; Internet Law; Information Technology; Corporate Law.

Carmel & Carmel, P.C., (AV)
4101 River Road NW, 20016-4617
Telephone: 202-237-1700 Fax: 202-237-1701 URL: http://www.carmeldc.com
Email: info@carmeldc.com URL: http://www.lawyers.com/carmel&carmel
Frank J. Carmel.
Real Estate Development, Acquisition and Finance including Resort, Hotel and Land Development, Golf Course Development, Condominiums and Timeshare Communities, Information Technology, Regulatory Law, Computers and Software, Copyrights, Trademarks, Internet Law, Domain Name Disputes, E-Commerce Issues, Entertainment and Sports Law, Immigration, Representation of clients before HUD and the FTC, Americans With Disabilities Act, Employment Law, Private Offerings, Venture Capital, Acquisitions, Divestitures and Strategic Alliances and General Counseling for Emerging Technology Companies.
See Professional Biographies, WASHINGTON, DISTRICT OF COLUMBIA

Carmen, Melinda L. ....'52 '78 C.1123 B.A. L.1218 J.D. [Carmen&M.]
Carmen & Muss, P.L.L.C. ....1901 Pennsylvania Ave., N.W.
Carmichael, James T. '62 '87 C.976 B.A. L.966 J.D.
(adm. in WI; not adm. in DC) [Lyon&L.]
*PRACTICE AREAS: Patents; Trademarks; Copyrights; Appellate Practice; Computer Law.
Carmody, Christine Waldmann ....'67 '95 C.914 B.A. L.276 J.D. [A Pepper H.]
*PRACTICE AREAS: Real Estate; Housing Finance; Affordable Housing.
Carmody, Stephanie Morris ....'69 '95 C.1356 B.S. L.276 J.D. [A Steptoe&J.]
Carmody, William J. ....'66 '94 C.893 B.A. L.128 J.D. [A Arnold&P.]
*PRACTICE AREAS: Real Estate; Corporate; Securities.
Carnahan, William A. ....'39 '64 C.116 B.S. L.107 LL.B. 2158 Fla. Ave., N.W.
Carneal, George U., (AV) ....'35 '61 C.674 A.B. L.893 LL.B. [Hogan&H.]
*PRACTICE AREAS: Aviation Law; Transportation Law; Trade Association Law; Foreign Governments.
Carneal, George U., III '59 '90 C.902 B.A. L.893 J.D.
(adm. in PA; not adm. in DC) Assoc. Gen. Coun., Group Health Assn. of Amer., Inc.
Carnegie, Les P. ....'73 '99 C&L.228 B.A., J.D. [A Covington&B.]
Carnell, William S. ....'— '97 C.1369 B.A. L.893 J.D. [A Latham&W.]
*PRACTICE AREAS: Communications and Media; Broadcasting Law; Communications Law; Telecommunications Competition; Wireless Communications.
Carney, Christopher James ....'73 '98 C.183 B.A. L.30 J.D. [A Swidler B.S.F.]
*PRACTICE AREAS: Litigation.
Carney, David E. ....'72 '99 C.821 B.A. L.945 J.D. [A Skadden,A.S.M.&F.]
Carney, Donald J. ....'63 '96 C.273 B.A. L.276 J.D. [A Perkins C.]
*PRACTICE AREAS: Government Contracts; Commercial Litigation.
Carney, Fred D., Jr. ....'55 '83 C.999 B.S. L.803 J.D. Neighborhood Legal Servs. Prog.
Carney, Jacqueline Ann ....'68 '94 C&L.893 B.A., J.D. 523 7th Street S.E.
Carney, John, (AV) ....'49 '76 C.424 B.A. L.425 J.D. [Carney&C.]
Carney, John F. ....'35 '62 C.588 B.S. L.273 J.D. [C Armstrong,W.H.M.&N.]
Carney, Peter J. ....'70 '96 C.164 B.A. L.904 J.D. [A White&C.]
Carney, Robert T., (AV) '47 '72 C.597 B.S. L.276 J.D.
801 Pennsylvania Ave., NW (Pat.)
Carney, Veta M. ....'49 '78 C.419 B.M.E. L.425 J.D. [Carney&C.]
Carney & Carney, (AV) ....601 Pennsylvania Ave., N.W.
Caro, Luisa ....'70 '97 C.659 B.S/B.A. L.276 J.D. [A Sidley A.B.&W.]
Carolla, Robert J. '56 '82 C.478 A.B. L.94 J.D.
(adm. in ME; not adm. in DC)
Dir. of Communications, Americans For Democratic Action
Carome, Patrick J., (BV) ....'57 '84 C.93 B.A. L.309 J.D. [Wilmer,C.&P.]
*PRACTICE AREAS: Communications and Media; Civil Practice.
Carp, Bertram W., (AV) ....'44 '69 C&L.813 B.A., J.D. [Williams&J.]
*PRACTICE AREAS: Communications Law; Federal Legislative Practice.
Carpenter, Charles H. ....'58 '91 C.506 B.S. L.128 J.D. [Pepper H.]
*PRACTICE AREAS: Civil Litigation; Government Contracts; Administrative Law.
Carpenter, Jeanne A. ....'53 '77 C.860 A.B. L.276 J.D. [McDermott,W.&E.]

Carpenter, JoAnn '48 '74 C.607 B.A. L.150 J.D.
V.P. & Dep. Gen. Coun., Fannie Mae
*RESPONSIBILITIES: E-Commerce and Technology.
Carpenter, Julia M. . . . . '61 '87 C.945 B.A. L.575 J.D. [Jenner&B.]
*PRACTICE AREAS: Litigation; Appellate Practice; Supreme Court Practice; Media and First Amendment; Technology Law.
Carpenter, Martin Dee . . . . '57 '81 C.959 B.A. L.966 J.D. Asst. U.S. Atty.
Carpenter, Robert K. . . . .'62 '89 C&L.446 B.S.Ch.E., J.D. [Ⓐ Arent F.K.P.&K.] (Pat.)
*PRACTICE AREAS: Patents; Trademarks; Copyrights; Unfair Competition.
Carpenter, Russell H., Jr., (AV) . . . . '41 '68 C.674 A.B. L.976 LL.B. [Covington&B.]
Carpenter, Sheila J., (AV) . . . . '50 '75 C.679 B.A. L.976 J.D. [Jorden B.]
*PRACTICE AREAS: Litigation; Arbitration; Insurance.
Carpenter-Holmes, Amy K. . . . . '72 '98 C.188 B.S. L.904 J.D. [Ⓐ Swidler B.S.F.]
*PRACTICE AREAS: General Litigation.
Carpentier, Deborah Ann . . . . '66 '92 C.446 B.A. L.273 J.D. [Ⓐ Dickstein S.M.&O.]
*PRACTICE AREAS: Energy Law.
Carr, Christopher K. . . . . '65 '96 C.103 B.A. L.178 J.D. [Ⓐ Vinson&E.]
Carr, Donald A., (AV) . . . . '48 '75 C.188 B.A. L.273 J.D. [Pillsbury W.]
*PRACTICE AREAS: Environmental Law; Natural Resources.
Carr, J. Robert . . . .'50 '75 C.511 B.A. L.178 J.D. Assoc. Of Trial Lawyers of Amer.
Carr, John F. '21 '49 C.951 B.A. L.309 LL.B.
(adm. in NY; not adm. in DC) 5070 Millwood Lane, N.W.‡
Carr, John L., Jr. . . . . '46 '78 C.10 B.S. L.280 J.D. [Shaw P.]
*PRACTICE AREAS: International Tax; Banking; Corporate.
Carr, Lawrence E., III, (AV) . . . . '51 '79 C&L.602 B.A., J.D. [Carr,M.&G.]
*PRACTICE AREAS: Civil Litigation; Personal Injury; Professional Liability; Products Liability; Insurance Defense.
Carr, Lawrence E., Jr., (AV) . . . . '23 '49 C&L.602 B.S., LL.B. [Carr G.]
*PRACTICE AREAS: Litigation; Environmental; Insurance Coverage.
Carr, Melanie K. '74 '00 C.446 B.A. L.145 J.D.
(adm. in MD; not adm. in DC) [Ⓐ Swidler B.S.F.]
*PRACTICE AREAS: Government Affairs; Antitrust and Trade Regulation; Real Estate Finance.
Carr, Thomas B., (AV) . . . .'43 '69 C.276 B.S. L.893 LL.B. [© Baker B.]

Carr Goodson, P.C., (AV) BR
1667 K Street, N.W., Suite 1100, 20006 ⊙
Telephone: 202-310-5500 Telecopier: 202-310-5555
Email: (attorney initials)@carrgoodson.com URL: http://www.carrgoodson.com
Lawrence E. Carr, Jr.; Robert W. Goodson; William J. Carter; Catherine A. Hanrahan; Paul J. Maloney; Thomas L. McCally; Kevin M. Murphy; Jan E. Simonsen; Mark M. Jones. Senior Counsel: Shadonna E. Hale. Of Counsel: Edward J. Krill;—Juan M. Anderson; David J. Finucane; Pamela S. Fox; Tina M. Maiolo; Valerie G. Preiss; Dennis J. Quinn; Angela W. Russell; William B. Schroeder; Michael J. Sepanik (Not admitted in DC); James P. Steele; Andrew J. Waghorn (Not admitted in DC).
Appellate, Business Transactions, Construction, Election, Employment and Labor, Environmental, Health Care, Insurance Coverage, Intellectual Property, Litigation (Commercial and Complex), Products Liability, Professional Liability, Tax, Technology, Toxic and Mass Tort, Trusts and Estates.
Vienna, Virginia Office: Tycon Towers, 8000 Towers Crescent Drive, Suite 1350, 22182. Telephone: 703-691-8818.
Baltimore, Maryland Office: 401 East Pratt Street, Suite 1622, The World Trade Center, 21202. Telephone: 410-752-1570.
Rockville, Maryland Office: 31 Wood Lane, 20850. Telephone: 301-424-7024.
See Professional Biographies, WASHINGTON, DISTRICT OF COLUMBIA

Carr, Morris & Graeff, P.C., (AV)
1120 G Street, N.W., Suite 930, 20005-3801 ⊙
Telephone: 202-789-1000 Facsimile: 202-628-3834
URL: http://www.cmgpc.com
Lawrence E. Carr III; Roy R. Morris; Stephen D. Graeff; Adam R. Wilk; Philip M. Schwartz;—Timothy R. Feely; Alan C. Bowden; Dana Suzanne Glynn; Brenda M. Hankins (Not admitted in DC). Of Counsel: Melville W. Feldman (1920-1998); Néstor Enrique Cruz.
General Business and Civil Litigation Practice. Corporate, Labor and Employment, Estate Planning, Malpractice, Products Liability and Negligence Law.
See Professional Biographies, WASHINGTON, DISTRICT OF COLUMBIA

Carrano, Cono A. . . . .'62 '94 C.1350 B.E.E.E. L.1019 J.D. [Brobeck,P.&H.] (Pat.)
*PRACTICE AREAS: Intellectual Property Law.
Carrier, Michael K. . . . . '66 '96 C&L.150 B.S., J.D. [Ⓐ Smith,G.&R.] (See Pat. Sect.)
*PRACTICE AREAS: Patent Prosecution; Patent Counseling.
Carrier, Michael Richard '64 '97 C.708 B.A. L.1356 J.D.
(adm. in VA; not adm. in DC) Amer. Community Bankers‡
Carrier, Rita M. . . . . '51 '84 C.706 B.A. L.128 J.D. [Ⓐ Sullivan&C.]
Carriere, Colin C. . . . . '52 '77 C.1031 B.S. L.190 J.D. 10 "G" St., N.E.
Carrigan, Daniel J., (AV) . . . . '49 '76 C&L.276 B.A., J.D. [Piper M.R.&W.]
*PRACTICE AREAS: Bankruptcy Law; Insolvency Law.
Carroccio, A. Thomas, (AV) . . . . '46 '71 C.524 B.S. L.128 J.D. [Bell,B.&L.]
*PRACTICE AREAS: Legislative, Communications Law.
Carroll, Amy E. . . . . '68 '96 C.112 B.A. L.904 J.D. [Ⓐ Drinker B.&R.]
Carroll, Catherine . . . .'— '96 C.951 B.A. L.893 J.D. 701 Pennsylvania Avenue, N.W.
Carroll, Christina M. . . . . '75 '01 C.309 A.B. L.276 J.D. [Ⓐ McKenna&C.]
Carroll, James P., (AV) '52 '77
C.276 B.A. L.128 J.D. [Cadwalader,W.&T.] (⊙Charlotte, NC)
*PRACTICE AREAS: Real Estate Finance; Real Estate Secured Lending; Real Estate Securities.
Carroll, Kevin M. . . . . '66 '96 C.999 B.S. L.446 J.D. [Ⓐ Wilmer,C.&P.]
Carroll, Margaret Ann . . . . '63 '91 C.1044 B.S. L.30 J.D. Asst. U.S. Atty.
Carroll, Mark J. . . . . '53 '84 C.184 B.S. L.262 J.D. Asst. U.S. Atty.
Carroll, Ramona R. '— '98 C.446 B.S. L.145 J.D.
(adm. in MD; not adm. in DC) [Ⓐ Latham&W.]
Carroll, Ronald N., (BV) . . . . '49 '76 C.446 B.A. L.64 J.D. [© Bracewell&P.]
*PRACTICE AREAS: Energy; Administrative; Regulatory; Antitrust; Litigation.
Carroll, William H. . . . . '38 '71 C.676 B.A. L.128 J.D. [© Dykema G.]
*PRACTICE AREAS: Government Contracts; Administrative Law.
Carson, Dylan M. . . . . '72 '97 [Ⓐ Howrey S.A.&W.]
*PRACTICE AREAS: Antitrust; Commercial Litigation.
Carstarphen, M.L. . . . . '54 '81 C.14 B.S. L.329 J.D. [Edwards&C.] ⊙
Carstens, John H., (AV) . . . .'57 '83 C&L.30 B.S., J.D. [Jordan C.&S.] (⊙Fairfax, VA)
*PRACTICE AREAS: Commercial Litigation; Tort Defense; Workers' Compensation; Professional Liability Defense.
Carter, Adam Augustine . . . . '65 '91 C&L.276 A.B., J.D. [Ⓐ Kelley D.&W.]
*PRACTICE AREAS: Litigation.
Carter, Barry E. . . . . '42 '70 C.813 A.B. L.976 J.D. Dept. of Commerce

Carter, Francis D., (AV) '46 '73 C.884 A.B. L.273 J.D.
Suite 717, The OFC Building, 1730 Rhode Island Avenue NW, 20036-3115
Telephone: 202-393-4330 Fax: 202-393-5657
Email: frank@fdcarter.com
General Civil and Criminal Practice, Litigation in all Courts, White Collar Criminal Defense, Business Fraud, Domestic Relations Law, Business Litigation, Employment Defense, Discrimination Defense.
See Professional Biographies, WASHINGTON, DISTRICT OF COLUMBIA

Carter, G. Scott . . . . '— '93 C.400 B.S. L.145 J.D. [Ⓐ Morgan,L.&B.]
Carter, Henry Wolfgang . . . . '63 '91 C.990 B.A. L.276 J.D. 607 14th St., N.W.
Carter, Lee C. . . . . '67 '93 C.207 B.A. L.145 J.D. [Ⓐ Shaw P.]
Carter, Richard D., (AV) . . . . '49 '80 C.1040 B.A. L.273 J.D. [Carter&C.] ⊙
*PRACTICE AREAS: Insurance Defense; Health Insurance; ERISA; Federal Litigation; Appeals.
Carter, Robert L., Jr., (AV) . . . .'65 '90 C.524 B.A.B.S. L.179 J.D. [McKenna&C.]
*PRACTICE AREAS: Insurance Coverage Litigation; Insurance Recovery.
Carter, Russell L. . . . . '14 '55 C.887 B.S. L.30 LL.B. 1409 Leegate Rd., N.W.‡
Carter, Tia M. '69 '96 C.178 B.A. L.659 J.D.
Assoc. Gen. Coun., Black Entertainment Television, Inc.
Carter, W. Burlette . . . . '61 '86 C.6 B.A. L.309 J.D. George Washington Univ. Law Ctr.
Carter, William J., (AV) . . . . '49 '74 C.886 B.S. L.945 J.D. [Carr G.]
*PRACTICE AREAS: Appellate; Litigation; Insurance Coverage.

Carter & Coleman, (AV)
700 E Street S.E., 20003 ⊙
Telephone: 202-682-7373 Fax: 202-682-7373
Email: info@cartercoleman.com URL: http://www.cartercoleman.com
Richard D. Carter; Douglas M. Coleman (Not admitted in DC); Juliane C. Miller; Gerald F. Ragland, Jr. Associates: Peggy E. Taylor (Not admitted in DC); Mikhael D. Charnoff (Not admitted in DC).
General Civil Practice, Professional Liability Insurance Defense, Insurance and Health Care Law, Medical Malpractice, Employment Law, Medical Benefits Coverage and Reimbursement, ERISA, Creditors Bankruptcy, Corporate and Commercial Law, Franchise Law, Business Law, Trial and Appellate Litigation in State and Federal Courts.
Representative Clients: CNA Insurance Company; Concord General Corporation; CIGNA; John P. Pearl & Associates, Ltd.; Journal Newspapers; Lloyd's of London; Principal Mutual Life Insurance Company; Penn-America Group, Inc.; Phyllis Wheatley YWCA, Inc.; Professional Indemnity Underwriters Corporation; Reliance Standard Life Insurance Co.
Alexandria, Virginia Office: 602 Cameron Street, 22314. Telephone: 703-739-4200. Fax: 703-739-4210.
See Professional Biographies, WASHINGTON, DISTRICT OF COLUMBIA

Carter, Ledyard & Milburn, (AV)
1401 Eye Street, NW, Suite 300, 20005 ⊙
Telephone: 202-898-1515 Fax: 202-898-1521
Email: info@clm.com URL: http://www.clm.com
Resident Members: Robert L. Hoegle; Timothy J. Fitzgibbon. Resident Of Counsel: John F. Cahill; Mary S. Diemer. Intellectual Property Counsel: L. Lawton Rogers, III; Mark Charles Comtois (Not admitted in DC); D. Joseph English (Not admitted in DC); Patrick Dennis McPherson (Not admitted in DC). Resident Associates: Thomas F. Bardo; Peter K. Killough; Bradley A. Farrell (Not admitted in DC).
General Practice.
New York, N.Y. Offices: 2 Wall Street, 10005. Telephone: 212-732-3200. Fax: 212-732-3232. Cable Address: "Ledyard" New York and Midtown Office: 570 Lexington Avenue, 10022. Telephone: 212-371-2720. Fax: 212-317-4234.
See Professional Biographies, WASHINGTON, DISTRICT OF COLUMBIA

Carton, Arthur B., (AV) . . . .'03 '33 C&L.724 A.B., J.D. 1225 19th St., N.W.

Cartwright, Wendy A., & Associates, P.C.
(See Bowie)

Carvalho, Cristina A. '63 '96 L.999 LL.B.
(adm. in NY; not adm. in DC) [Ⓐ Arent F.K.P.&K.]
*PRACTICE AREAS: Intellectual Property; Trademark Litigation; Trademark Protection; Trademark Licensing; International Trademark Protection.
Carver, Nancy C. '69 '97 C.1044 B.A. L.188 J.D.
(adm. in NY; not adm. in DC) Dept. of The Treasury, IRS
Carvin, Michael A., (AV) . . . .'56 '82 C.861 B.A. L.273 J.D. [Jones,D.R.&P.]
*PRACTICE AREAS: Litigation; Appellate Practice; U.S. Supreme Court Litigation.
Carwile, Stuart F. . . . . '42 '67 C&L.893 B.S., LL.B. [© Wiley R.&F.]
*PRACTICE AREAS: Corporate.
Cary, George D. . . . . '11 '37 C.659 B.S. L.276 J.D. 6323 Western Ave., N.W.‡
Cary, George S. . . . .'51 '76 C.112 A.B. L.1066 J.D. [Cleary,G.S.&H.]
Cary, Marticha L. . . . . '73 '99 C.597 B.A. L.309 J.D. Atty.
Cary, Robert M. . . . . '64 '90 C.197 A.B. L.893 J.D. [Williams&C.]
*PRACTICE AREAS: Commercial Litigation; Criminal Defense; Professional Liability Defense; Securities Litigation; Trial Practice.
Casale, Ralph L. . . . . '61 '88 C.145 B.A. L.188 J.D. Center for Individual Rights
Casalmir, June '— '99 C.228 B.A. L.910 J.D.
(adm. in GA; not adm. in DC) [Ⓐ Powell,G.F.&M.]
*PRACTICE AREAS: Antitrust.
Casano, William C., (AV) . . . .'53 '78 C.1030 B.A. L.665 J.D. [Greenstein D.&L.]
*PRACTICE AREAS: Civil Litigation; Employment Law; Administrative Law; Corporate Law; Trade Regulation.
Casden, Caryl L. '64 '90 C.518 B.A. L.904 J.D.
Asst. Coun., National Treasury Employees Union
Case, David T. . . . . '— '78 C&L.477 B.A., J.D. [Kirkpatrick&L.]
*PRACTICE AREAS: Civil Litigation; Environmental Coverage Litigation; Government Contracts; Construction Claims.
Case, Harlow R., (AV) . . . . '53 '79 C.823 B.A. L.273 J.D. [Ⓐ J.H.Olender&Assoc.]
*PRACTICE AREAS: Malpractice; Personal Injury.
Case, Stephen H., (AV) . . . . '42 '69 C&L.178 A.B., LL.B. [Davis P.&W.]
Casey, Bernard J., (AV) . . . . '— '67 C.676 A.B. L.128 J.D. [Reed S.]
*PRACTICE AREAS: Litigation.
Casey, Francis L., (AV) . . . . '54 '82 C&L.276 A.B., J.D. [Morgan,L.&B.]
Casey, Francis Lawton, Jr., (AV) '27 '53 C&L.276 B.S., LL.B.
2801 New Mexico Ave.‡
Casey, James J. . . . . '67 '95 C.602 B.A. L.329 J.D. [Ⓐ Alston&B.]
*PRACTICE AREAS: Electronic Commerce; Information and Technology Law.
Casey, James L., (AV) '50 '76 C.1350 B.A. L.724 J.D.
V.P. & Dep. Gen. Coun., Air Transport Association of America
Casey, Lee A. . . . . '57 '82 C.1154 B.A. L.477 J.D. [Baker&H.]
Casey, Martha Lincoln . . . . '55 '82 C.914 B.A. L.1294 J.D. [O'Neill,A.&C.]
Casey, Patricia A. . . . . '49 '82 C.477 B.A. L.228 J.D. Asst. Gen. Coun., INTELSAT
Casey, Paul K., (AV) . . . . . .'48 '77 C.708 B.A. L.893 J.D. [Ballard S.A.&I.] (⊙Balt., MD)
*PRACTICE AREAS: Housing and Community Development Law; Affordable Housing; Public Housing; Real Estate; Public Finance.
Casey, Robert J., (AV) . . . . '19 '49 C.823 B.A. L.128 J.D. [© Long]
Casey, Susan M. . . . . '— '85 C.103 B.A. L.976 J.D. [Kirkpatrick&L.]
*PRACTICE AREAS: Financial Services Regulation; Mutual Funds; Banking Regulation; Investment Management.
Casey, Tara Louise '72 '99 C.893 B.A. L.910 J.D.
(adm. in VA; not adm. in DC) 451 7th St. SW
Casey, Timothy D. '61 '88 C.549 B.S.E. L.770 J.D.
[Fried,F.H.S.&J.] (⊙New York, NY)
*PRACTICE AREAS: Intellectual Property; Technology Transactions; Litigation; Corporate Transactions.
Cash, Roderick W., Jr. '49 '75 C.918 B.A. L.30 J.D.
Pres., Roderick Cash Develop. Corp.
Cash, Steven Abram '62 '88 C.881 A.B. L.976 J.D.
(adm. in NY; not adm. in DC) Coun.
Cashdan, David R., (AV) . . . .'39 '67 C.604 B.A. L.477 J.D. [Cashdan,G.&K.]

Cashdan, Golden & Kane, PLLC, (AV)
1150 Connecticut Avenue, N.W., 9th Floor, 20036-4104
Telephone: 202-862-4330 Fax: 202-862-4331 URL: http://www.CGKLaw.com
URL: http://www.lawyers.com/cgklaw
Members of Firm: David R. Cashdan; Vicki G. Golden (1942-2001); Michael G. Kane. Associate: Meredith S. Francis.
Employment Law, Wrongful Termination, Employment Contracts, Executive Compensation, Employment Mediation, Fair Employment Practices, Discrimination, Harassment, College and Univer

(This Listing Continued)

Cashdan, Golden & Kane, PLLC (Continued)

sity Law, Whistleblower Litigation, Employee Rights, Executive Severance Contracts, Sexual Harassment, Disability Discrimination, Federal Employment Law, Handicapped Rights and Age Discrimination.

See Professional Biographies, WASHINGTON, DISTRICT OF COLUMBIA

Cashen, Henry C., II, (AV) ....'39 '64 C.103 A.B. L.477 J.D. [Dickstein S.M.&O.]
*PRACTICE AREAS: Administrative Law; Government Relations; Agency and Legislative Practice.
Casieri, Chris '68 '00 C.999 B.S. L.831 J.D.
(adm. in NJ; not adm. in DC) [🄰 Dorsey&W.]
*PRACTICE AREAS: Patent Prosecution; Patent Litigation.
Casino, Bruce J., (AV) ....'53 '88 C.446 B.S. L.276 J.D. [Baker&H.]
Casoni, Dava ....'69 '96 C.94 B.A.B.S. L.188 J.D. [🄰 Shaw P.]
*PRACTICE AREAS: Corporate Law; Securities; Entrepreneurial Law; Entertainment Law.
Cass, Kenneth R. '41 '68 C&L.215 A.B., J.D.
(adm. in MI; not adm. in DC) 60 Massachusetts Ave., N.W.
Cass, Richard W., (AV) ....'46 '71 C.674 A.B. L.976 J.D. [Wilmer,C.&P.]
*PRACTICE AREAS: Corporate Law; Securities Law; Finance; Mergers, Acquisitions & Divestitures; Sports Law.
Cassat, Peter C. ....'63 '89 C.67 B.A. L.966 J.D. [Dow,L.&A.]
Cassel, Eugene D. '47 '75 C.475 B.A. L.146 J.D.
(adm. in IL; not adm. in DC) Asst. Dir., Govt. Rel., American Psychiatric Association
Cassell, Paul R. ....'71 '96 C.945 B.A. L.893 J.D. [🄰 McKenna&C.]
*PRACTICE AREAS: Litigation.
Casserly, James L., (AV) ....'51 '76 C.860 A.B. L.178 J.D. [Mintz,L.C.F.G.&P.]
*PRACTICE AREAS: Communications Law; FCC Regulation; Telecommunications Competition.
Casserly, Marianne ....'— '00 [🄰 Alston&B.]
Cassidy, James M. ....'35 '63 C.276 B.S. L.128 LL.B. [Cassidy&Assoc.]
Cassidy, John Joseph, (AV) ....'30 '55 C&L.276 B.S., J.D. [Baker B.]
Cassidy, Kristan M. ....'67 '93 C.602 B.B.A. L.209 J.D. [🄰 Jackson&C.]
*PRACTICE AREAS: Insurance Coverage Litigation.
Cassidy, Lee W. ....'49 '85 C.604 B.A. L.128 J.D. [Cassidy&Assoc.]
Cassidy, Martha ....'58 '97 C.293 B.A. L.893 J.D. [🄰 Rothwell,F.E.&M.] (See Pat. Sect.)
Cassidy, Mary E. ....'55 '87 C.1044 B.A. L.273 J.D. [🄲 Arnold&P.]
*PRACTICE AREAS: Tax; Employee Benefits.
Cassidy, Robert C., Jr., (AV) ....'46 '73 C.367 B.A. L.659 J.D. [Wilmer,C.&P.]
*PRACTICE AREAS: International Aviation Law; Aviation Defense; Aerospace Law; International Trade; Legislative Practice.
Cassidy, Susan Booth ....'63 '89 C.459 B.S. L.904 J.D. [Arnold&P.]
*PRACTICE AREAS: Government Contracts; Litigation.
Cassidy, Thomas J., Jr. ....'53 '86 C.112 B.A. L.1065 J.D. Amer. Rivers
Cassidy & Associates ....1504 R Street NW
Casson, Joseph E., (AV) ....'43 '69 C.1030 B.A. L.276 J.D. [Proskauer R.]
Castaldi, Terra E. ....'72 '97 C.97 B.S. L.608 J.D. [🄰 Morgan,L.&B.]
Castanias, Gregory A. ....'65 '90 C.894 A.B. L.347 J.D. [Jones,D.R.&P.]
*PRACTICE AREAS: Litigation; Appellate Practice; Intellectual Property; International Arbitration.
Castanon, Richard G. '74 '99 C.813 A.B. L.309 J.D.
(adm. in CA; not adm. in DC) [🄰 Skadden,A.S.M.&F.]
*PRACTICE AREAS: Tax Law.
Casteel, Carroll K., Jr. '50 '79 C&L.502 B.S., J.D.
(adm. in MO; not adm. in DC)
Dir., State Reguls. & Govt. Affs., MCI Telecommunications Corp. (Regulatory Affairs)
Castellano, Kristina M. '71 '96 C.911 B.S. L.1218 J.D.
[🄰 Kenyon&K.] (See Pat. Sect.)
*PRACTICE AREAS: Intellectual Property.
Castellano, Michael L. '72 '99 C.367 B.A. L.309 J.D.
(adm. in NY; not adm. in DC) [🄰 Dewey B.]
*PRACTICE AREAS: International Trade; Litigation.
Castellitto, Paul V. ....'52 '83 C.1275 B.A. L.1068 J.D. 5505 Conn. Ave. N. W.
Castello, James E. ....'54 '87 C.976 B.A. L.1066 J.D. Assoc. Dep. Atty. Gen.
Castiello, Thomas R. ....'72 '97 C.951 B.A. L.276 J.D. [🄰 Arent F.K.P.&K.]
*PRACTICE AREAS: Business Law; Estate Planning.
Castiglia, Richard P., Jr. ....'66 '92 C.930 B.A. L.893 J.D. [🄰 McKenna&C.]
*PRACTICE AREAS: Government Contracts.
Castillo, Justin G. ....'— '94 C.976 B.A.M.A. L.276 J.D. [🄰 Levine,B.B.&B.]
*PRACTICE AREAS: Telecommunications Law; Corporate Contracts; International Law.
Castle, Gray C. ....'31 '55 C&L.902 B.A., J.D. 1850 K St., N.W.
Castle, Ronald L. ....'51 '82 C.1208 B.A. L.273 J.D. [Arent F.K.P.&K.]
*PRACTICE AREAS: Litigation; ERISA; Health; Hospital Law.
Castleton, Todd Bitner ....'69 '96 C.878 H.B.S. L.1356 J.D. [🄰 O'Donoghue&O.]
*PRACTICE AREAS: Employee Benefits; ERISA; Labor and Employment; Litigation.
Castner, Maria D. '— '00 C.30 B.A. L.472 J.D.
(adm. in MD; not adm. in DC) [🄰 Morgan,L.&B.]
Castro, Melissa R. ....'71 '98 C.546 B.A. L.276 J.D. [🄰 Swidler B.S.F.]
*PRACTICE AREAS: Antitrust; Consumer Protection; Litigation.
Castro, Tanja H., (AV) ....'59 '86 C.881 A.B. L.30 J.D. [Holland&K.]
*PRACTICE AREAS: Real Estate Tax Assessment; Eminent Domain; Condemnation; Guardianships and Conservatorships; Estate Planning.

Castro, Barros, Sobral, Vidigal, Gomes Advogados
801 Pennsylvania Avenue N.W. Market Square, Suite 747, 20004 ⊙
Telephone: (1 202) 638-7071 Facsimile: (1 202) 638-7072
Email: maildc@cbsvg.com.br
Associate: Guilherme Tepedino Hernandez (Not admitted in DC; Resident) (Not admitted in the United States).
Antitrust, Aviation, Finance and Capital Market, Civil, Entertainment, Corporate, Investment, Litigation, Environmental, Intellectual Property, International Trade, Labor, Maritime, Privatization, Tax, Infrastructure.
Other Offices in Brazil:
Rio de Janeiro: Praia de Botafogo, 228 - 15th Floor, 22359-900. Telephone: +(55 21) 2553-1855. Fax: +(55 21) 2552-1796. Email: mailrj@cbsvg.com.br.
São Paulo: Rua do Rocio, 291 - 11th Floor, 04552-000. Telephone: +(55 11) 3040-0908. Fax: +(55 11) 3040-0937/0938. Email: mailsp@cbsvg.com.br.
Porto Alegre: Avenida Carlos Gomes 11 6th Floor, 90480-903. Telephone: +(55 51) 328-7309. Fax: +(55 51) 328-3081. Email: mailpoa@cbsvg.com.br.
Brasília, D.F.: SQN Quadra 4, Bloco 404-A, 70714-900. Telephone: +(55 61) 326-0300. Fax: +(55 61) 328-6653. Email: maildf@cbsvg.com.br.
Offices Abroad:
Lisbon: Heron Castilho, Rua Braamcamp, 40-8° E, 1269-013, Lisbon, Portugal. Telephone: +351 21 387-5702. Fax: +351 21 387-5743.

See Professional Biographies, WASHINGTON, DISTRICT OF COLUMBIA

Casula, Denise M., (BV) '67 '94 C.352 B.A. L.128 J.D.
(adm. in IL; not adm. in DC) Veterans App. Bd., U.S. Dept. of Veterans Affs.
Catania, David A. ....'68 '94 C&L.276 B.S.F.S., J.D. [🄰 Akin,G.S.H.&F.]
*PRACTICE AREAS: Energy.

Cate, Charles I. '44 '70 C.276 A.B. L.128 J.D.
1730 K Street, N. W., Suite 304, 20006 ⊙
Telephone: 202-289-1006
Email: chascate@msn.com URL: http://www.lawyers.com/irsnemesis
***PRACTICE AREAS: Taxation; Tax Controversies; Probate; Wills; Exempt Organizations.**
Federal Tax Matters; Tax Controversies, Criminal Tax Litigation, Civil Tax Litigation, Income Tax Planning, Estate Tax Planning, Exempt Organizations.

(This Listing Continued)

Cate, Charles I. (Continued)

Arlington, Virginia Office: 2009 North 14th Street, Suite 306. 22201. Telephone: 703-522-2112. Fax: 703-522-5201.

See Professional Biographies, WASHINGTON, DISTRICT OF COLUMBIA

Cate, Fred H. ....'63 '87 C&L.813 A.B., J.D. [🄲 Hunton&W.] (Pat.)
*PRACTICE AREAS: Information and Privacy; Intellectual Property; Communications Law.
Cater, Gregorio B. ....'65 '93 C.623 B.A. L.976 J.D. [Wilmer,C.&P.]
*PRACTICE AREAS: Corporate Finance; Corporate Transactions; Electronic Commerce; International Aviation Law; Aviation Defense.
Cater, Rozan E. ....'53 '88 C.329 B.A. L.128 J.D. 601 Indiana Ave. N.W.
Cates, Clifton B., III ....'46 '75 C.976 B.A. L.309 J.D. [🄲 Ivins,P.&B.]
*PRACTICE AREAS: Taxation Law.
Catler, Susan L. ....'56 '82 C&L.309 B.A., J.D. [O'Donnell,S.&A.]
Catlin, Elizabeth J. ....'67 '94 C.309 A.B. L.228 J.D. 725 12th St., N.W.
Catliota, Thomas J., (AV) ....'53 '84 C.436 B.S. L.128 J.D. [Shaw P.]
*PRACTICE AREAS: Bankruptcy Law; Business Reorganization.
Catoe, Michael K. ....'63 '96 C.1280 B.B.A. L.329 J.D. [🄰 Covington&B.]
*PRACTICE AREAS: Computers and Software; Litigation.
Cattafesta, Maria L. ....'70 '96 C.575 B.A. L.128 J.D. [🄰 Swidler B.S.F.]
*PRACTICE AREAS: Telecommunications.
Cattalini, Gina '65 '96 C.681 B.A. L.276 J.D.
(adm. in CA; not adm. in DC) 2801 Quebec St., N.W.‡
Caudle, Larry W., Jr. '59 '94 C.1369 B.B.A. L.692 J.D.
(adm. in VA; not adm. in DC) [Jenkens&G.]
*PRACTICE AREAS: Construction Law; Insurance Defense; Surety Law; Commercial Litigation.
Caudle, Sheila R. '50 '87 C.549 B.A. L.128 J.D.
(adm. in CA; not adm. in DC) [🄰 Ross,D.&B.]
Cauman, Richard ....'49 '76 C.103 A.B. L.276 J.D. 1656 Monroe St., N.W.
Causey, C. Dawn '56 '84 C.357 B.A. L.273 J.D.
(adm. in VA; not adm. in DC) Gen. Coun., America's Community Bkrs.
Causey, William F., (AV) ....'49 '79 C.30 B.A. L.446 J.D. [Nixon P.]
*PRACTICE AREAS: Trial Practice; Appellate Practice.
Cavalier, Gina M. '71 '97 C.94 B.A. L.276 J.D.
(adm. in NY; not adm. in DC) [🄰 Shaw P.]
*PRACTICE AREAS: Health Care.
Cavaluzzi, Todd J. ....'74 '00 C.1349 B.A. L.276 J. D. [🄰 McDermott,W.&E.]
Cavanagh, Elizabeth A. ....'70 '96 C.197 A.B. L.976 J.D. [🄰 Jenner&B.]
*PRACTICE AREAS: Litigation.
Cavanagh, Rita A. ....'51 '87 C.1044 B.A. L.976 J.D. [McKee N.]
*PRACTICE AREAS: Tax Litigation.
Cavanaugh, Gordon, (AV) ....'28 '54 C.262 A.B. L.659 LL.B. [🄲 Reno&C.]
*PRACTICE AREAS: Legislation; Administrative Law; Public Housing.
Cavanaugh, J. Michael, (AV) ....'49 '74 C.608 B.A. L.813 J.D. [Holland&K.]
*PRACTICE AREAS: International Commercial Law; Mergers and Acquisitions; Transportation Law.
Cavanaugh, Karen Rothschild ....'64 '98 C.604 B.A. L.978 J.D. [🄰 Keller&H.]
*PRACTICE AREAS: Food and Drug.
Cavanaugh, Patrick O., (AV) ....'58 '83 C.1356 B.S. L.1209 J.D. [Dyer E.&J.]
*PRACTICE AREAS: Litigation; Product Liability; Environmental Law; Business Planning.
Cavanaugh, Theresa Zeterberg, (AV) ......'63 '89 C.890 B.A. L.128 J.D. [Cole,R.&B.]
*PRACTICE AREAS: Wireless Communications; Telecommunications Regulation; FCC Regulation; FCC Licensing.
Cave, Robert B., (AV) ....'48 '77 C&L.893 B.A., J.D. [Hogan&H.]
*PRACTICE AREAS: Litigation.
Cavelli, Grace ....'63 '95 C.1349 B.A. L.128 J.D. [🄰 Womble C.S.&R.]
*PRACTICE AREAS: Real Estate; Litigation; Corporate.
Cawley, Dennis P. '69 '00 C.754 B.S. L.1218 J.D.
(adm. in NJ; not adm. in DC) [🄰 Pepper H.]
*PRACTICE AREAS: Intellectual Property; Patents; Trademarks.
Cawley, Justin M. ....'— '99 C.692 B.A. L.276 J.D. [🄰 Verner,L.B.M.&H.]
*PRACTICE AREAS: International Law.
Cawley, Mark C. ....'72 '99 C&L.602 B.A., J.D. [🄰 Jones,D.R.&P.]
Cayne, Howard Neil ....'54 '80 C.696 B.A. L.910 J.D. [Arnold&P.]
*PRACTICE AREAS: Financial Institutions; Government Contracts; Litigation.
Cayne, Jonathan F. ....'62 '88 C.188 B.S. L.94 J.D. [🄲 Morrison&F.]
Cayton, Howard ....'12 '42 C.273 A.B. L.276 J.D. 2512 Q St. N.W.
Cecil, Erik J. '65 '97 C.174 L.446 J.D.
(adm. in MD; not adm. in DC) [🄰 Cole,R.&B.]
*PRACTICE AREAS: Telecommunications Law; Telecommunications Competition; Internet Law; Wireless Communications.
Cejudo, William P. ....'63 '89 C.802 B.B.A. L.846 J.D. [🄰 Arnold&P.]
*PRACTICE AREAS: Taxation.
Celestin, Jenny ....'70 '01 C.1353 B.A. L.1280 J.D. [🄰 Conlon,F.P.&P.]
*PRACTICE AREAS: Civil Rights; Class Actions.
Celestino, Carlos '55 '95 C.97 B.A. L.851 J.D.
(adm. in TX; not adm. in DC) [🄰 Keller&H.]
*PRACTICE AREAS: Food and Drug Regulation; Litigation.
Center, Judith A. ....'52 '83 C.472 A.B. L.273 J.D. [🄰 Skadden,A.S.M.&F.]
Ceplecha, Marcia Stuart ....'61 '94 C.381 B.A. L.945 J.D. [McDermott,W.&E.]
Cera, Alison B. ....'64 '99 C.188 B.S.I.L.R. L.276 J.D. [🄰 Hogan&H.]
*PRACTICE AREAS: Employee Benefits.
Ceresi, Diana Orantes '51 '79 C.1090 B.S. L.273 J.D.
Assoc. Gen. Coun., Service Employees Intl. Union
Cerf, Christopher D. ....'54 '86 C.31 B.A. L.178 J.D. 1776 K St., NW
Cerny, Milton, (AV) ....'33 '88 C.30 B.S. L.904 J.D. [Caplin&D.]
*PRACTICE AREAS: Tax Law; Non-Profit Organizations Law; International Law.
Certner, David M. '58 '83 C.659 B.A. L.273 J.D.
Sr. Coord., Econ. Issues, Amer. Assoc. of Ret. Persons
Cerutti, Stephen R., II '72 '99 C.645 B.S. L.629 J.D.
(adm. in OR; not adm. in DC) P.O. Box 14271
Ceruzzi, Leonard A. '38 '67 C.262 B.S. L.184 LL.B.
(adm. in CT; not adm. in DC) Mng. Atty., Rg. Affs., Continental Airlines, Inc.
Cervon, Kathryn L. ....'57 '90 C.170 B.A. L.273 J.D. [🅂 Chadbourne&P.]
Cesarano, Danielle R. ....'71 '99 C.692 B.A. L.30 J.D. [🄰 Reed S.]
*PRACTICE AREAS: Litigation.
Cestari, Kenneth C. ....'63 '94 C.105 B.A. L.692 J.D. [🄰 Hunton&W.]
*PRACTICE AREAS: Real Estate; Project Development; Project Finance; Corporate.
Chablais, Jean-Daniel '61 '91 L.999 LL.B.
(adm. in NY; not adm. in DC) Sr. Coun., International Fin. Corp.
Chabon, Robert S. '38 '76 C.273 B.S. L.446 J.D.
(adm. in PA; not adm. in DC) [🄲 J.H.Olender&Assoc.]
Chace, Stephen D. '57 '89 C.885 B.A. L.999 J.D.
(adm. in VA; not adm. in DC) [🄲 Goldstein&L.]
*PRACTICE AREAS: Trial Litigation; Appellate Litigation; Commercial Litigation; Banking Litigation; Casualty Defense Litigation.
Chachkin, Joseph ....'30 '59 C.705 L.1009 LL.B. 445 12th Street SW‡

Chadbourne & Parke LLP, (AV) BB
1200 New Hampshire Avenue, N.W., 20036 ⊙
Telephone: 202-974-5600 Facsimile: 202-974-5602

(This Listing Continued)

Chadbourne & Parke LLP (Continued)

Partners: Noam Ayali (Not admitted in DC); Carey G. Child; William S. D'Amico; Peter F. Fitzgerald; Andrew A. Giaccia; Cornelius J. Golden, Jr.; Kenneth W. Hansen (Not admitted in DC); Tracey W. Laws; Keith Martin; John B. O'Sullivan; William K. Perry; David M. Raim; David K. Schumacher; Robert F. Shapiro; Ellen H. Woodbury (Not admitted in DC). Resident Counsel: Roy S. Belden; J. Christopher Groobey; Lynn N. Hargis; Don J. Mros; Alejandro Silva. Resident Of Counsel: Edmund E. Harvey. Resident Associates: Marissa L. Alcala (Not admitted in DC); Todd E. Alexander; Joel M. Baranowski; Meaghan McGrath Beaumont; Thane Benedict IV (Not admitted in DC); Rohit Chaudhry (Not admitted in DC); Timothy E. Curley; Jennifer R. Devery; Timothy J. DiCintio; Benjamin T. Ford (Not admitted in DC); Philip J. Goodman; Kimberly J. Heimert (Not admitted in DC); Thomas G. Hohenthaner; Michelle A. Jones; Heléna M. Klumpp; Samuel R. Kwon (Not admitted in DC); Joy L. Langford; Ellen M. MacDonald; Kristin L. Meikle; W. Robertson Milbourne Jr. (Not admitted in DC); M. Katherine Montgomery; James W. Scarrow; William H. Schmidt, Jr.; John R. R. Tormey; Luis F. Torres; Steven E. Wagner. Staff Attorneys: Kathryn L. Cervon; Christopher T. Gallu, Jr.

Practice before all Federal and District of Columbia Trial and Appellate Courts, Federal Agencies and Departments.

New York, N.Y. Office: 30 Rockefeller Plaza, 10112. Telephone: 212-408-5100. Facsimile: 212-541-5369.

Los Angeles, California Office: Two California Plaza, 350 S. Grand Avenue, Suite 3300, 90071. Telephone: 213-892-1000. Facsimile: 213-622-9865.

Upper Montclair, New Jersey Office: 539 Valley Road, 07043. Telephone: 973-655-1550. Facsimile: 973-655-1558.

London, England Affiliate Office: Chadbourne & Parke, a multinational partnership of Registered Foreign Lawyers and Solicitors, Regis House, 45 King William Street, London EC4R 9AN. Telephone: 44-171-337-8000. Facsimile: 44-171-337-8001.

Moscow, Russia Office: 52/5 Kosmodamianskaya, 113054. Telephone: 7095-974-2424. Facsimile: 7095-974-2425. International satellite via US: Telephone: 212-408-1190. Facsimile: 212-408-1199.

Hong Kong, China Office: Suite 2203, Tower I, Lippo Centre, 89 Queensway. Hong Kong. Telephone: 852-2842-5400. Facsimile: 852-2521-7527.

See Professional Biographies, WASHINGTON, DISTRICT OF COLUMBIA

Chadwick, Bruce M. .... '46 '73 C.1154 B.A. L.477 J.D. [Arnold&P.]
*PRACTICE AREAS: Litigation; Products Liability.
Chadwick, G. A. "Jay", IV .... '— '96 C.945 B.A. L.893 J.D. [Ⓐ Shaw P.]
*PRACTICE AREAS: Commercial Real Estate Loans; Commercial Real Estate Leasing; Commercial Real Estate Development; Business.
Chafetz, Marc Edward .... '53 '80 C.604 B.A. L.893 J.D. 5105 Chevy Chase Pwy.
Chaikin, Donald J., (AV) '33 '64
C.446 B.A. L.904 LL.B. [Chaikin&S.] (⊙Bethesda, MD)
*PRACTICE AREAS: Auto Negligence; Premises Liability.
Chaikin, Lisa .... '68 '95 C.477 B.A. L.818 J.D. 1800 M St., N.W.
Chaikin, Lisa Ann .... '— '95 C.477 B.A. L.818 J.D. [Ⓐ Morgan,L.&B.]

Chaikin & Sherman, P.C., (AV) BB
The Law Building, 1232 Seventeenth Street, N.W., 20036 ⊙
Telephone: 202-659-8600 Fax: 202-659-8680
Email: Sherman@DC.law-net URL: http://www.lawyers.com/chaikin&sherman
Donald J. Chaikin; Ira Sherman;—Joseph Cammarata; Allan M. Siegel; Garrett V. Williams; Camellia Javadi Jacobs; Christine A Gray-Knight. Of Counsel: Silverio Coy.
Medical Malpractice, Wrongful Death, Automobile Negligence, Serious Personal Injury, Product Liability, Premises Liability, Class Action Lawsuits, Discrimination.
Bethesda, Maryland Office: 7315 Wisconsin Avenue, Suite 220-E. 20814.

See Professional Biographies, WASHINGTON, DISTRICT OF COLUMBIA

Chaires, Susan C. .... '48 '74 C.1365 B.A. L.280 J.D. 21 Dupont Cir. NW
Chajet, Henry .... '50 '76 C.930 B.A. L.229 J.D. [Patton B.]
Chalfie, Deborah M. .... '56 '83 C.608 B.A. L.273 J.D. Inst. for Public Representation
Chalk, Indra Sehdev '65 '93 C.813 B.A. L.893 J.D.
(adm. in TX; not adm. in DC) [Ⓐ Shaw P.]
*PRACTICE AREAS: Communications; Corporate; Business.
Chalker, Bruce Edward .... '48 '01 C.472 Ph.D. L.273 J.D. [Ⓐ Sterne,K.G.&F.]
*PRACTICE AREAS: Intellectual Property.
Chamberlain, Charles E. .... '17 '49 C&L.893 B.S., LL.B. [Ⓒ Webster,C.&B.]
*PRACTICE AREAS: Corporate Law.
Chambers, Andrea J. .... '59 '85 C.276 B.A. L.904 J.D. Sr. Coun., El Paso Corp.
Chambers, Jonathan Martin '60 '96 C.976 B.A. L.276 J.D.
(adm. in CT; not adm. in DC) 401 9th St. NW, Market Sq. N.
Chambers, Matthew A., (AV) .... '57 '82 C.228 A.B. L.477 J.D. [Ⓒ Wilmer,C.&P.]
*PRACTICE AREAS: Securities Regulation; Mutual Funds; Investment Partnerships; Investment Company Law; Derivative Products.
Chambers, Reid Peyton, (AV) .... '40 '68 C.051 B.A. L.309 LL.B. [Sonosky,C.S.E.&P.]
Chambers, Scott A. .... '52 '93 C.259 Ph.D. L.273 J.D. [Ⓐ Arnold&P.] (Pat.)
*PRACTICE AREAS: Intellectual Property.
Chambers, Tracey D. .... '66 '95 C.659 B.A. L.178 J.D. 325 7th St. NW, Suite 500

Chambers, Joy S.
(See Alexandria, Virginia)

Chamblee, Daryl A. (Sandy), (AV) .... '50 '77 C.276 B.S. L.128 J.D. [Steptoe&J.]
*PRACTICE AREAS: Biotechnology; Health Care; Toxic Torts; Corporate Counseling; Civil Litigation.
Chameides, Steven B., (AV) .... '— '71 C&L.477 B.S.E., J.D. [Foley&L.]
*PRACTICE AREAS: Corporate Law; Transactional Law; International Business Law; Maritime Law; Commercial Litigation.
Champagne, Margot J. .... '46 '72 C.766 B.A. L.1065 J.D. 818 18th St., N.W.
Champagne, Thomas M. '61 '92 C.690 B.S.E.E. L.273 J.D.
(adm. in VA; not adm. in DC) [IP S.]
Champion, Maxine C. '— '78
C.645 B.A. L.30 J.D. V.P., Govt. & Int'l Rel., Nestle USA, Inc.
Chan, May Y. .... '63 '00 C.178 B.S.E.E. L.818 J.D. [Ⓐ McDermott,W.&E.]
Chandler, Christian H. '72 '97 C.228 B.A. L.93 J.D.
(adm. in IL; not adm. in DC) [Ⓐ Thacher P.&W.]
*PRACTICE AREAS: ERISA; Employee Benefits.
Chandler, Elizabeth J. .... '65 '94 C.276 B.S.B.A. L.1209 J.D. [Ⓐ Howrey S.A.&W.]
*PRACTICE AREAS: Antitrust; Commercial Litigation.
Chandler, James P. .... '38 '78 C.112 A.B. L.1067 J.D. Prof. of Law, Geo. Wash. Univ.
Chandler, Robert E. '37 '00 C.1369 B.S. L.945 J.D.
(adm. in NY; not adm. in DC) [Ⓐ Sullivan&C.]
Chandler, Sterling W. '— '91 C.131 B.A. L.861 J.D.
(adm. in LA; not adm. in DC; See Pat. Sect.) [Ⓐ Lalos&K.]
*PRACTICE AREAS: Intellectual Property.
Chandler, Vanessa Y. '— '97 C.362 B.S. L.893 J.D.
(adm. in VA; not adm. in DC) [Ⓐ Bryan C.]
Chane, Jonathan C. '73 '97 C.260 B.A. L.362 J.D.
(adm. in FL; not adm. in DC) [Ⓐ Greenberg T.]
Chaney, John L. .... '74 '00 C&L.608 B.S., J.D. [Ⓐ Jones,D.R.&P.]
Chang, Deanna J. .... '70 '96 C.518 B.A. L.94 J.D. [Ⓐ Resolution]
*PRACTICE AREAS: Environmental Litigation; Civil Litigation; Toxic Torts.
Chang, Richard W. .... '72 '97 C.339 B.A. L.128 J.D. [Ⓐ Wasserman,M.&C.]
*PRACTICE AREAS: Immigration Law; Trademarks; Copyrights; Small Business Law.
Chang, Sam Hsien-Cheng .... '46 '81 L.999 LL.B. [Wasserman,M.&C.]
*PRACTICE AREAS: Immigration and Nationality Law.
Chang, Steve S. .... '— '99 C.608 B.S.E.E. L.831 J.D. [Ⓐ Banner&W.] (See Pat. Sect.)
*PRACTICE AREAS: Intellectual Property Law; Patents; Intellectual Property Litigation; Electrical Intellectual Property; Computer and Software Patents.

Chang, Ta-tung J. '51 '91 C.999 LL.B. L.1119 LL.M.
(adm. in NY; not adm. in DC) Coordination Council for N. Amer. Affs.
Chanin, Leah F. '29 '54 C.802 B.A. L.469 LL.B.
(adm. in GA; not adm. in DC) Dir. of Law Sch. Libr., Univ. of Dist. of Columbia
Chanin, Leonard N. .... '57 '84 C.30 B.A. L.910 J.D. [Ⓒ Morrison&F.]
*PRACTICE AREAS: Financial Services Law.
Chanin, Michael H. .... '43 '68 C.575 A.B. L.245 J.D. [Powell,G.F.&M.] (⊙Reston, VA)
*PRACTICE AREAS: Corporate; Corporate Finance; Government Contracts.
Chanin, Robert H. .... '34 '59 C.102 B.A. L.976 LL.B. [Bredhoff&K.]
Chanow, Linda Bray .... '70 '99 C.1134 B.A. L.904 J.D [Ⓐ Wilmer,C.&P.]
Chao, Fei-Fei .... '55 '97 C.999 B.S. L.446 J.D. [Ⓒ Venable,A.B.H.&C.] (See Pat. Sect.)
*PRACTICE AREAS: Patent Applications; Patent Prosecution; Patent Infringement; Technology Transfers; Technology Licensing.
Chapin, Douglas M., Jr. '64 '95 C.674 B.A. L.276 J.D.
(adm. in VA; not adm. in DC) [Ⓐ Skadden,A.S.M.&F.]
Chapin, Mary Carole .... '66 '93 C.1044 B.A. L.851 J.D. [McDermott,W.&E.]
Chapin, Peter A., (AV) .... '45 '71 C&L.8 B.A., J.D. [Sacks&C.]
*PRACTICE AREAS: Personal Injury Law; Family Law; Corporate Law.
Chaplin, Peggy Louie, (AV) '40 '73 C.367 B.S. L.446 J.D.
[Sandler,T.&R.] (⊙Balt., MD)
*PRACTICE AREAS: Customs Law; Administrative Agency Practice; International Commercial Law; Shipping and Transportation Law.
Chapman, Bryan A. .... '57 '82 C.197 B.A. L.966 J.D. 1117 Fern St., N.W.
Chapman, Dudley H., (AV) .... '34 '59 C&L.477 B.A., J.D. 1752 N St. N.W., Ste. 200
Chapman, Ernest F., (AV) '35 '72
C.754 B.S. L.831 J.D. [Ⓒ Finnegan,H.F.G.&D.] (See Pat. Sect.)
*PRACTICE AREAS: Patents; Chemical Patent Prosecution; Chemical Patents.
Chapman, Floyd B. .... '63 '93 C.277 B.E.E. L.472 J.D. [Wiley R.&F.] (Pat.)
*PRACTICE AREAS: Intellectual Property.
Chapman, James L., (AV) .... '45 '70 C.846 B.B.A. L.802 J.D. [Bracewell&P.]
*PRACTICE AREAS: Energy; Health Care; Environmental; Government; Public Policy.
Chapman, Jerome I., (AV) .... '39 '65 C.861 B.A. L.309 J.D. [Arnold&P.]
*PRACTICE AREAS: Antitrust; Civil Litigation.
Chapman, Linda S. '52 '77
C.679 B.A. L.1119 J.D. Admin. Law Judge, U.S. Dept. of Labor
Chapman, Paulette E., (AV) .... '54 '88 C.1356 B.A. L.273 J.D. [Koonz,M.J.D.&L.]
Chapman, Robert R., (AV) .... '42 '67 C&L.352 B.B.A., J.D. U.S. Attys. Off.
Chapman, Steven E. .... '62 '93 C.911 B.A. L.273 J.D. Prog. Mgr., Population Servs. Intl.
Chapman, Thomas B. '54 '82 C.415 B.F.A. L.30 J.D.
V.P. & Coun., Aircraft Owners & Pilots Assn.
Chappelle, Kasey '75 '01 C.16 B.A. L.180 J.D.
(adm. in NY; not adm. in DC) [Ⓐ Willkie F.&G.]
*PRACTICE AREAS: Telecommunications Law.
Chapper, Joy A. .... '46 '72 C.788 A.B. L.276 J.D. Chf. Dep. Clk., Ct. of App.
Chapple, Kevin L. .... '65 '95 C.886 B.S.E.E. L.329 J.D. [Ⓐ Dorsey&W.] (Pat.)
*PRACTICE AREAS: Intellectual Property; Intellectual Property Prosecution; Intellectual Property Litigation.
Charapp, Michael G., (AV) '49 '74
C.665 B.A. L.276 J.D. [Charapp,D.&W.] (⊙Vienna, VA)
*PRACTICE AREAS: Corporations and Commercial Transactions; Franchises; Real Estate; Commercial Law; Litigation.

Charapp, Deese & Weiss, LLP, (AV) BB
1901 Pennsylvania Avenue, N.W., Suite 1001, 20006 ⊙
Telephone: 202-463-9100 Fax: 202-463-2091
URL: http://www.cdw-law.com
Michael G. Charapp; C. Michael Deese; Brad D. Weiss;—Sarah Daly Jackowski; Michael C. Gartner; James B. St. John, III; Stephen F. Varholy (Not admitted in DC). Of Counsel: Edward H. Kim; Holmes C. Harrison (Not admitted in DC); Brenda Houck Harbison (Resident, Richmond, Virginia Office). Civil Litigation, Corporate Law and Government Contracts.
Vienna, Virginia Office: 8300 Boone Boulevard, Suite 500, 22182. Telephone 703-714-9576.
Bethesda, Maryland Office: 3 Bethesda Metro Center, Suite 700, 20814. Telephone: 301-657-6258.
Richmond, Virginia Office: 2201 West Broad Street, Suite 201, 23220. Telephone: 804-358-8003. Fax: 804-358-3889.

See Professional Biographies, WASHINGTON, DISTRICT OF COLUMBIA

Charen, Susan J. .... '65 '90 C&L.705 B.A., J.D. [Ⓐ Stier,A.&M.] ⊙
*PRACTICE AREAS: Complex Litigation; Internal Investigations; Corporate Compliance.
Charles, Robert H. '13 '38 C&L.976 A.B., LL.B.
(adm. in MO; not adm. in DC) 3259 R St., NW‡
Charlton, Suzan F. .... '66 '91 C.881 B.A. L.276 J.D. [Ⓒ Swidler B.S.F.]
Charnas, Douglas W., (AV) .... '53 '78 C.610 A.B. L.930 J.D. [McGuirewoods]
*PRACTICE AREAS: Business Acquisitions; Reorganizations; Divestitures; Charitable Giving; Tax Exempt Organizations.
Charnes, Adam H. '66 '93
C.674 A.B. L.309 J.D. Senior Litigation Counsel, MCI WorldCom
Charness, Michael R., (AV) .... '54 '79 C.659 B.A. L.276 J.D. [Vinson&E.]
*PRACTICE AREAS: Litigation.
Charnoff, Deborah B. .... '53 '78 C.104 B.A. L.228 J.D. 2300 N St., N.W.
Charnoff, Gerald, (P.C.), (AV) .... '30 '57 C.102 B.A. L.569 LL.B. [Ⓒ Shaw P.]
*PRACTICE AREAS: International Transactions; Litigation; Energy; Administrative.
Charnoff, Mikhael D. '73 '99 C.890 B.A. L.893 J.D.
(adm. in VA; not adm. in DC) [Ⓐ Carter&C.]
*PRACTICE AREAS: Civil Litigation; Insurance Defense.
Charnoff, Samuel K. .... '63 '89 C.178 B.A. L.276 J.D. [Ⓒ Arent F.K.P.&K.]
*PRACTICE AREAS: Labor and Employment Law; Civil Rights; Litigation.
Charnovitz, Steve .... '53 '99 C&L.976 B.A., J.D. [Ⓐ Wilmer,C.&P.]
Charrow, Robert P., (AV) .... '44 '70 C.1167 B.S. L.813 J.D. [Crowell&M.]
*PRACTICE AREAS: Science Law; Health and Hospital Law; Food, Drug and Cosmetic Law; Tort Law; Election Law.
Chartove, Alex, (AV) .... '54 '80 C.1036 B.A. L.228 J.D. [Morrison&F.] (Pat.)
*PRACTICE AREAS: Intellectual Property; Patent Prosecution.
Charyk, William R., (AV) .... '48 '73 C.367 B.A. L.273 J.D. [Arent F.K.P.&K.]
*PRACTICE AREAS: Pension and Profit Sharing Law; Taxpayer Representative Law; Professional Corporation Law; Partnership; Taxation of Individuals and Business Entities.
Charytan, Lynn R. .... '65 '91 C.178 B.A. L.309 J.D. [Wilmer,C.&P.]
*PRACTICE AREAS: Communications; Electronic Commerce.
Chasanov, Amy B. '66 '98 C.659 B.A.,B.S. L.477 J.D.
(adm. in MD; not adm. in DC) [Ⓐ Patton B.]
Chase, Adam Charles .... '74 '99 C.188 B.A. L.893 J.D. [Ⓐ Dow,L.&A.]
Chase, Catherine Babics '68 '96 C.705 B.A. L.273 J.D.
(adm. in MD; not adm. in DC) 750 First St., NE
Chase, Christopher F. .... '75 '00 C.878 B.S. L.904 J.D. 1826 Jefferson Pl., N.W.
Chase, Eugene A. .... '13 '50 C.329 A.B. L.1014 LL.B. 3413 13th St., N.W.
Chase, Judith L '43 '72 C&L.178 B.A., J.D.
(adm. in NY; not adm. in DC) 1719 19th Street, NW
Chase, Kerri J. .... '70 '99 C.446 B.S. L.477 J.D. [Ⓐ Cleary,G.S.&H.]
Chase, Linda J., (AV) .... '48 '83 C.1044 B.A. L.262 J.D. [Ⓒ Dickstein S.M.&O.]
*PRACTICE AREAS: Civil Litigation; Insurance Coverage.
Chase, Robert S., II .... '72 '97 C.878 B.S. L.273 J.D. [Ⓐ Sutherland A.&B.]
*PRACTICE AREAS: Federal Income Tax; Tax Litigation; Corporate Taxation; Federal Tax Controversies.
Chasen, Irving L., (AV) .... '23 '52 C.273 L.30 J.D. [Chasen&C.]

Chasen, Ronald L., (BV) ....'47 '72 C.354 B.A. L.276 J.D. [Chasen&C.]
Chasen & Chasen, (AV) ....5225 Wisconsin Avenue, N.W., Suite 500
Chasnow, Jeffrey B. '61 '88 C.309 A.B. L.145 J.D.
(adm. in WA; not adm. in DC) 1300 I St., N.W., Suite 700
Chasnow, Robert M. .... '48 '74 C.659 B.S. L.273 J.D. [Holland&K.]
*PRACTICE AREAS: Timeshare; Resort Community Development Law; Land Sales Law.
Chason, Anna P. '68 '96 C.228 B.A. L.953 J.D.
(adm. in VA; not adm. in DC)
Pub. Affairs Coun., Nat'l Assn. of Real Estate Investment Trusts, Inc.
Chason, Eric D. '70 '96 C.228 B.A. L.893 J.D.
(adm. in VA; not adm. in DC) [A Ivins,P.&B.]
*PRACTICE AREAS: Federal Estate and Gift Taxation; Federal Income Tax.
Chatain, Fabienne '66 '92 L.276 LL.M.
(adm. in NY; not adm. in DC) [A Elliot&M.]
Chatfield, Peter Wilson ....'61 '88 C.918 B.A. L.976 J.D. [Phillips&C.]
*PRACTICE AREAS: False Claims Act; Qui Tam Litigation.
Chatilovicz, Peter, (AV) .... '46 '74 C.72 B.A. L.472 J.D. [Seyfarth S.]
*PRACTICE AREAS: Labor Law; Employment Law.
Chatterjee, Aaron C. ....'— '98 C.999 B.S. L.1209 J.D. [A Foley&L.] (See Pat. Sect.)
*PRACTICE AREAS: Intellectual Property.
Chaturvedi, Anjali ....'68 '94 C.188 B.S. L.276 J.D. Asst. U.S. Atty.
Chaudhry, Rohit '67 '94 C.999 B.A. L.309 LL.M.
(adm. in NY; not adm. in DC) [A Chadbourne&P.]
Chavarria, Lisa ReVeal ....'64 '90 C.112 B.A. L.1066 J.D. [A Arnold&P.]
*PRACTICE AREAS: Financial Institutions; Corporate.
Chavers, Clayborne E., (AV) .... '47 '76 C&L.329 B.F.A., J.D. [Chavers]
*PRACTICE AREAS: Entertainment and Art Law; Civil Rights Law; Business Development.

Chavers Law Firm, The, P.C., (AV)
2600 Virginia Avenue, N.W., Suite 200, 20037
Telephone: 202-333-8575 Fax: 202-333-8226
URL: http://www.lawyers.com/chaverslaw
Clayborne E. Chavers;—Jean D. Meta (Not admitted in DC). Of Counsel: Elliott Carl Alderman. Corporate Diversity, Civil Rights Compliance, Women's Rights Issues, Employment Contracts, Discrimination, Sexual Harassment, Labor Law, Employment Law, Corporate Law, Commercial Transactions, Government Contracts, International Commercial Transactions, Arts and Entertainment Law, Internet Law, E-Commerce and Intellectual Property.
See Professional Biographies, WASHINGTON, DISTRICT OF COLUMBIA

Chaves, Lillian N. '74 '00 C&L.101 B.A., J.D.
(adm. in FL; not adm. in DC) U.S. Dept. of Labor
Chavez, Matthew .... '69 '94 C.556 B.A. L.178 J.D. [A Paul,W.R.W.&G.]
Chavis, Kami Nicole ....'74 '00 C.575 B.A. L.309 J.D. [A Fried,F.H.S.&J.]
*PRACTICE AREAS: Litigation.
Chawla, Tejpal Singh ....'73 '98 C.94 B.A. L.273 J.D. [A Crowell&M.]
Chay, Eugene F. .... '71 '98 C.659 B.A. L.904 J.D. [A Kirkland&E.]
*PRACTICE AREAS: Intellectual Property Litigation; Commercial Litigation.
Chazin, Rachel Lynn '74 '00 C.659 B.A. L.564 J.D.
(adm. in NJ; not adm. in DC) 4740 Connecticut Ave., N.W.
Cheatham, John H., III '38 '62 C&L.500 B.A., LL.B.
Exec. V.P., Gen. Coun. & Secy., Interstate Nat. Gas Assn. of Amer.
Cheek, Marney L. '72 '00 C.813 A.B. L.309 J.D.
(adm. in CA; not adm. in DC) [A Covington&B.]
Cheek, Warren M., Jr. ... '55 '83 C&L.260 B.S., J.D. [Wenderoth,L.&P.] (See Pat. Sect.)
*PRACTICE AREAS: Chemical Patents; Biotechnology and Pharmaceutical Patents.
Cheh, Mary M. ....'50 '75 C&L.705 B.A., J.D. Prof., The Natl. Law Ctr.
Chen, Anderson ....'66 '01 C.228 B.S.E.E. L.273 J.D. [A Wilmer,C.&P.]
Chen, Christine Suhming ....'— '00 C.197 B.A. L.659 J.D. [A Clifford C.R.&W.]
*PRACTICE AREAS: Corporate Banking Law; Corporate Finance.
Chen, Daniel S. '53 '90 L.999 LL.B.
(adm. in VA; not adm. in DC) [A White&C.]
Chen, Elizabeth '70 '01 C.477 A.B. L.178 J.D.
(adm. in NY; not adm. in DC) [A Clifford C.R.&W.]
*PRACTICE AREAS: Litigation.
Chen, Emily S. '— '01 C.197 B.A. L.93 J.D.
(adm. in NY; not adm. in DC) [A Piper M.R.&W.]
*PRACTICE AREAS: Corporate Law; Franchise Distribution.
Chen, Eugene T. .... '73 '99 C.178 B.A. L.813 J.D. [A Arnold&P.]
*PRACTICE AREAS: Food and Drug Regulation; Litigation.
Chen, James C. .... '65 '92 C.567 B.A. L.930 J.D. [G Hogan&H.]
*PRACTICE AREAS: Environmental; OSHA; Transportation Law; Government Regulatory.
Chen, Jennifer C. '67 '99 C.277 B.I.E. L.273 J.D.
(adm. in CA; not adm. in DC; Pat.) [A McDermott,W.&E.]
Chen, Jenny W. '73 '99 C.597 B.S.E.S. L.930 J.D.
(adm. in CA; not adm. in DC; See Pat. Sect.) [A Howrey S.A.&W.]
*PRACTICE AREAS: Intellectual Property; International Trade; Patent Law.
Chen, Jiwen '— '01
(adm. in China; not adm. in DC) [A Reed S.]
*PRACTICE AREAS: Intellectual Property; Patents; Copyrights; Trademarks; Trade Secrets.
Chen, Sophia Hue '— '97 C.999 B.A. L.276 J.D.
(adm. in GA; not adm. in DC) Assoc. Dir. of Admissions, Georgetown Law School
Chen, Sophy .... '71 '98 C&L.94 B.A., J.D. [A Pillsbury W.]
Chen, Yu ....'— '01 C.197 B.A. L.276 J.D. [A Arnold&P.]
Cheney, Elizabeth L. ....'66 '96 C.170 B.A. L.145 J.D. [A White&C.]
Cheng, David K. ....'73 '99 C.112 B.A. L.284 J.D. Dept. of Jus.
Cheng, J. Weili ...... '— '81 C.976 B.A. L.276 J.D. Asst. Gen. Coun., Marriott Intl., Inc.
*RESPONSIBILITIES: International Operations and Development.
Cheng, Lee ....'66 '96 C.477 B.S. L.823 J.D. [A Wenderoth,L.&P.] (See Pat. Sect.)
*PRACTICE AREAS: Biotechnology Patents; Pharmaceutical Patents; Chemical Patents; Patent Prosecution.
Chenoweth, Laura E. '72 '99 C.741 B.A. L.145 J.D.
(adm. in IL; not adm. in DC) [A Winston&S.]
*PRACTICE AREAS: Litigation (100%).
Chenoweth, Mark '72 '01 C.976 B.A. L.145 J.D.
(adm. in KS; not adm. in DC) [A Wilmer,C.&P.]
Cheplo, Thomas Z. ....'72 '99 C&L.446 B.A., J.D. [A Dyer E.&J.]
Cherecwich, Paul, Jr. ....'41 '71 C.688 B.E.E. L.818 J.D. [G Miller&C.]
*PRACTICE AREAS: Taxation.

Cherkasky, Clare
(See Falls Church, Virginia)

Chernack, Gregory Scott ....'71 '98 C.309 B.A. L.976 J.D. [A Wilmer,C.&P.]
Cherner, Abby Strongin ....'63 '89 C.188 B.A. L.276 J.D. 4145 Parkglen Ct., N.W.
Cherney, Colburn T. ....'48 '74 C&L.966 B.A., J.D. [Ropes&G.]
Chernick, Vanessa D. .....'— '87 C.788 B.A. L.276 J.D. Assoc. Gen. Coun., Fannie Mae
*RESPONSIBILITIES: Single-Family; Mortgage Finance; Affordable Housing.
Chernof, Kenneth L. ....'67 '91 C.309 A.B. L.276 J.D. [Heller E.W.&M.]
*PRACTICE AREAS: Litigation; Financial Institutions Law; Antitrust; Alternative Dispute Resolution.
Chernoff, Steven M. ....'69 '98 C.164 B.A. L.93 J.D. [A Lukas,N.G.&S.]
*PRACTICE AREAS: Telecommunications Law (100%).
Chernow, Stephen A. ....'61 '86 C.367 B.A. L.276 J.D. Asst. Gen. Coun., INTELSAT

Cherry, Risa B. .... '71 '96 C.188 B.A. L.659 J.D. [A Akin,G.S.H.&F.]
*PRACTICE AREAS: Labor and Employment.
Chesley, Carol B. .... '71 '96 C.165 B.A. L.659 J.D. [A Hogan&H.]
*PRACTICE AREAS: Real Estate.
Chesney, Charles W. ....'68 '98 C.645 B.S.E.E. L.893 J.D. [A Finnegan,H.F.G.&D.]
*PRACTICE AREAS: Software Protection; Electronic Intellectual Property; Electrical Patent Prosecution; Patent Litigation; Patent Protection.
Chesser, Wib .... '64 '93 C.659 B.A. L.446 J.D. [G Piper M.R.&W.] (Pat.)
*PRACTICE AREAS: Business Law; Technology Law; Intellectual Property; Patent Prosecution.
Chessick, Peter '70 '01 C.813 A.B. L.276 J.D.
(adm. in NY; not adm. in DC) [A Coudert B.]
*PRACTICE AREAS: Corporate; International; Project Finance.
Chessler, Michael J. .... '67 '95 C.273 B.A. L.365 J.D. [A Barnes,R.&C.]
*PRACTICE AREAS: Customs; International Trade.
Chester, George M., Jr., (AV) ....'47 '76 C.674 A.B. L.893 J.D. [Covington&B.]
Cheston, Sheila C. .... '58 '86 C.197 B.A. L.178 J.D. [Wilmer,C.&P.]
*PRACTICE AREAS: Congressional Investigations; Government Contracts; International Aviation Law; Aviation Defense; Aerospace Law.
Chettle, John H. ....'— '84 C.999 B.A. L.273 LL.M. [G Foley&L.]
*PRACTICE AREAS: International Trade Law; Immigration Law; Charitable Law.
Chetwynd, Frances J., (AV) .... '43 '75 C.446 B.A. L.273 J.D. [G Cole,R.&B.]
*PRACTICE AREAS: Commercial and Regulatory Litigation; Communications; Administrative Law; Cable Franchising; Intellectual Property.
Cheung, Katherine Y.K. ....'68 '94 C&L.309 A.B., J.D. [A McGuiness N.&W.]
*PRACTICE AREAS: Labor and Employment.
Chew, Benjamin G. ....'61 '88 C.674 B.Hist. L.893 J.D. [Patton B.]
Chhabra, Bhupinderpal S. .... '27 '93 L.999 LL.B. [A R.M.Price]
Chi, Patrick C. '69 '94 C.861 B.A. L.446 J.D.
(adm. in MD; not adm. in DC) 450 Fifth St., N.W.
Chiarello, Gustav ....'68 '99 C.128 B.A. L.1209 J.D. [A White&C.]
Chiarello, Katherine P. '72 '98 C.859 B.A. L.846 J.D.
(adm. in TX; not adm. in DC) [A Williams&C.]
Chicherio, Christine Marie '— '00 C.446 B.A. L.180 J.D.
(adm. in MD; not adm. in DC) 333 Constitution Ave.
Chierichella, John W., (AV) '47 '73
C.188 A.B. L.178 J.D. [Fried,F.H.S.&J.] (⊙L.A., CA)
*PRACTICE AREAS: Government Contracts; Litigation.
Child, Carey G. ....'65 '92 C.878 B.A., B.A. L.276 J.D. [Chadbourne&P.]
Childs, Stephanie '64 '90 C.893 B.A. L.659 J.D.
(adm. in PA; not adm. in DC) 2100 Pennsylvania Ave., N.W‡
Childs, William G. ....'71 '98 C.429 B.A. L.846 J.D. [A Williams&C.]
*PRACTICE AREAS: Business Crimes; Business Litigation; Civil Practice; Commercial Crimes; Commercial Litigation.
Chilton, John L. '74 '01 C.951 B.A. L.273 J.D.
(adm. in NY; not adm. in DC) [S Sullivan&W.]
*PRACTICE AREAS: Government Contracts.
Chin, Francis E. '71 '00 C.028 B.A. L.228 J.D.
(adm. in VA; not adm. in DC) [A Hale&D.]
Chin, Gordon C. F. '73 '99 C.472 B.B.A. L.30 J.D.
(adm. in WV; not adm. in DC) [A Krooth&A.]
*PRACTICE AREAS: Real Estate Finance; Mortgage Finance; Multi-Family Housing; Corporate Law.
Chin, Vina '70 '97 C.112 B.A. L.1066 J.D.
(adm. in CA; not adm. in DC) [A Howrey S.A.&W.]
*PRACTICE AREAS: Commercial Litigation; Insurance Coverage Litigation.
Chin, Yee Wah, (AV) '52 '78 C.453 S.B. L.178 J.D.
(adm. in NY; not adm. in DC) 701 Pennsylvania Avenue, N.W.
Chippendale, Stephen ....'— '01 [A Cadwalader,W.&T.]
Chisholm, Margaret D. ....'66 '94 C.788 A.B. L.276 J.D. [G Akin,G.S.H.&F.]
*PRACTICE AREAS: European Union Policy; International Trade.
Chiu, Grace R. ....'55 '96 C.103 A.B. L.30 J.D. [A Swidler B.S.F.]
*PRACTICE AREAS: Telecommunications.
Chiu, John C. '— '92 C.30 LL.M. L.861 J.D.
(adm. in PA; not adm. in DC) [G Miller&C.]
*PRACTICE AREAS: International Trade; Corporate Law.
Chiu, Lucy C. ....'71 '99 C.860 B.A. L.602 J.D. [A Bonner K.T.&C.] (⊙Fairfax, VA)
*PRACTICE AREAS: Civil Litigation; Trial Practice.
Chmara, Adam S. ....'66 '92 C.273 B.A. L.823 J.D. [Pepco,H.]
*RESPONSIBILITIES: Commercial Law; Corporate Law; International Law; Government Procurement.
Chmara, Theresa ....'63 '88 C.93 B.A. L.276 J.D. [Jenner&B.]
*PRACTICE AREAS: Media and First Amendment; Litigation; Civil Appeals; Advertising Law.
Chmielewski, Cynthia M. '71 '96
C.831 B.A. L.30 J.D. Staff Coun., NEA Office of Gen. Coun.
Cho, Albert S. ....'— '00 C.103 B.A. L.188 J.D. [A Shaw P.]
Cho, Albert Soo-Chang ....'71 '00 C.103 B.A. L.188 J.D. 2300 N Street, N.W.
Cho, Gregory D. '72 '00 C.966 B.A. L.352 J.D.
(adm. in NY; not adm. in DC) [A Clifford C.R.&W.]
*PRACTICE AREAS: Litigation.
Chockley, Frederick W., III, (AV) ....'54 '82 C.976 B.A. L.276 J.D. [Baker&H.]
*PRACTICE AREAS: Litigation.
Choharis, Peter C. .... '61 '93 C.309 B.A. L.976 J.D. [A Mayer,B.&P.]
Choi, Alicia M. '66 '99 C.608 B.S.E.E. L.08 J.D.
(adm. in OH; not adm. in DC; See Pat. Sect.) [A Staas&H.]
*PRACTICE AREAS: Patents.
Choi, Eun Ah '73 '00 C&L.276 B.F.S.F., J.D.
(adm. in VA; not adm. in DC) [A Hogan&H.]
Choi, Jennifer S. '— '93
C.659 B.S. L.273 J.D. Asst. Coun., Investment Company Institute
*RESPONSIBILITIES: International.
Choi, Richard T. .... '— '87 C.145 B.A. L.893 J.D. [Foley&L.]
*PRACTICE AREAS: Securities Law.
Choi, Sue J. ....'— '97 C&L.112 B.A., J.D. [A Latham&W.]
Choi, Zenas J. '72 '98 C.588 B.S. L.94 J.D.
(adm. in VA; not adm. in DC) [A Swidler B.S.F.]
*PRACTICE AREAS: Telecommunications.
Choiniere, Monique '68 '96 C.93 B.A. L.128 J.D.
(adm. in MD; not adm. in DC) The National Health Lawyers Assn.
Cholis, Thomas J. .... '46 '74 C.602 B.B.A. L.276 J.D. Sr. V.P., Crestar Bk., N.A.
Choné, Pierre .... '57 '96 C&L.446 B.S., J.D. [Choné&Assoc.]
*PRACTICE AREAS: Immigration Law; Business Law; Family Law; Estates and Trusts; Civil Litigation.

Choné & Associates, PLLC
206 Ninth Street, S.E., P.O. Box 15430, 20003
Telephone: 202-543-3066 Fax: 202-543-2836 URL: http://www.cabinetchone.com
Email: pchone@cabinetchone.com URL: http://www.lawyers.com/chonemauprivezlaw
Pierre Choné . Of Counsel: Bruno J. Mauprivez.
Small Business Corporate Counseling; Immigration (Business Immigration, Employment Visas, Family Immigration and Naturalization); Family Law (International Child Abductions, Prenuptial Agreements, Divorce); Estates and Trusts (International Wills); Civil Litigation.
See Professional Biographies, WASHINGTON, DISTRICT OF COLUMBIA

Chong, Sue Lin .... '48 '84 C.659 B.A. L.312 J.D. Georgetown Univ. Med. Ctr.

Chong, Suet M. .... '66 '91 C.446 B.S. L.273 J.D. [🄲 Lyon&L.] (Pat.)
*PRACTICE AREAS: Patent Prosecution; Litigation; Licensing.
Chopko, Mark E. .... '53 '77 C.754 B.S. L.188 J.D. Gen. Coun., U.S. Catholic Conference
Choppin, Timothy J. .... '63 '94 C.311 B.A. L.276 J.D. [🄲 Akin,G.S.H.&F.]
*PRACTICE AREAS: Real Estate.
Chopra, Marie ....'45 '95 C.051 B.A. L.276 J.D. [🄰 James&H.]
*PRACTICE AREAS: Labor Law; Employment Law; Civil Litigation.
Chopskie, Gregory A. '70 '99
C.276 B.S. L.1209 J.D. [🄰 Finnegan,H.F.G.&D.] (See Pat. Sect.)
*PRACTICE AREAS: Pharmaceutical Patents; Pharmaceutical Intellectual Property; Patent Litigation; Patent Prosecution.
Chorba, Timothy A. ....'46 '73 C.276 B.A. L.309 J.D. [Patton B.]
Chou, Jeremy C. .... '70 '97 C.69 B.A. L.30 J.D. [🄰 Wright,R.O.&T.]
*PRACTICE AREAS: Litigation; Employment.
Choukas-Bradley, James R., (AV) ....'50 '80 C.882 B.A. L.276 J.D. [Miller,B.&O.]
*PRACTICE AREAS: Energy Finance; Municipal Solid Waste; Energy Contracts; Natural Resources; Energy Regulation.
Chow, Christopher S. '64 '93 C.188 B.S. L.982 J.D.
(adm. in NJ; not adm. in DC; Pat.) [🄰 Dickstein S.M.&O.]
*PRACTICE AREAS: Intellectual Property.
Choy, Victoria ... '49 '87 C.926 B.A. L.178 J.D. Chf. Coun., Fin., International Fin. Corp.
Chriss, Margaret J. ....'69 '95 C.691 B.A. L.245 J.D. [🄰 Nixon P.]
*PRACTICE AREAS: Litigation.
Christakos, Nicholas T., (AV) ....'57 '82 C.309 A.B. L.276 J.D. [Sutherland A.&B.]
*PRACTICE AREAS: Civil Litigation; Insurance Litigation; Reinsurance; Employment Litigation; Banking Litigation.
Christen, Lee A., (BV) '51 '81
C.1290 B.A. L.1234 J.D. 601 Pennsylvania Ave., N.W., Ste. 900
Christensen, Wallace A., (AV) .... '50 '76 C.93 A.B. L.309 J.D. [Ross,D.&B.]
Christenson, Cass Walker, (CV) .... '69 '94 C.825 B.A. L.880 J.D. [🄰 McKenna&C.]
*PRACTICE AREAS: Insurance Litigation; Commercial Litigation.
Christian, Alphonso A., II, (AV) .... '45 '68 C.602 B.A. L.309 J.D. [Hogan&H.]
*PRACTICE AREAS: Corporate Law; Administrative Law.
Christian, Betty Jo, (AV) ....'36 '60 C&L.846 B.A., LL.B. [Steptoe&J.]
*PRACTICE AREAS: Transportation Law; Appellate Practice; Administrative Law; Railroad Law.
Christian, Christopher David ....'72 '99 C.1036 B.A. L.128 J.D. [🄰 Dechert]
*PRACTICE AREAS: Financial Services Law; Investment Management.
Christian, Claudette M. .... '54 '80 C.659 B.A. L.309 J.D. [Hogan&H.]
*PRACTICE AREAS: Project Finance; International Commercial Transactions.
Christian, Denise M. '62 '97 C.445 B.A. L.446 J.D.
Dep. Dir. & Coun., Annenberg/CPB
Christian, Ernest S., Jr., (AV) ....'37 '61 C&L.846 LL.B. 800 Connecticut Ave., NW
Christian, Gary C., (BV) .... '57 '84 C&L.329 B.A., J.D. 666 11th St. NW
Christian, James B., Jr., (AV) ....'47 '73 C.880 B.A. L.45 J.D. [Patton B.]
Christian, Jonathan F. ....'70 '00 C.886 B.A. L.904 J.D. [🄰 Jones,D.R.&P.]
Christian, Karen E. '73 '01 C.610 B.A. L.608 J.D.
(adm. in VA; not adm. in DC) [Vorys,S.S.&P.]
Christian, Kaye K. ....'53 '80 C&L.276 B.A., J.D. Supr. Ct. J.
Christian, Marguerite Tamberlaine '68 '94 C.888 B.A. L.329 J.D.
(adm. in VA; not adm. in DC) 2120 L.St., NW
Christian, William T. '43 '68 C.976 B.A. L.309 J.D.
(adm. in MA; not adm. in DC) [🄲 Cadwalader,W.&T.]
*PRACTICE AREAS: Environmental Law (70%); Energy (20%); Administrative Law (10%).
Christie, Jeffrey S. ....'54 '79 C.105 B.A. L.273 J.D. [Skadden,A.S.M.&F.]
Christie, Joel A. .... '67 '92 C.597 B.A. L.966 J.D. [🄲 Akin,G.S.H.&F.]
*PRACTICE AREAS: Antitrust and Trade Regulation; Public Policy.
Christie, John C., Jr., (AV) ....'36 '63 C.103 A.B. L.309 J.D. [Hale&D.]
*PRACTICE AREAS: Litigation.
Christmas, Patrick J., (AV) .... '45 '69 C.30 B.A. L.276 J.D. [P.J.Christmas&Assoc.]
Christmas, Patrick J., & Associates, P.C., (AV) ....750 Seventeenth Street, N.W.
Christner, Wallace E. '59 '85 C.228 B.A. L.945 J.D. [Venable,A.B.H.&C.]
Christopher, George L., (AV) ....'— '59 C&L.309 B.A., LL.B. [🄲 Kirkpatrick&L.]
*PRACTICE AREAS: Financial Institutions Law; Corporate Law.
Christy, David S., Jr. ....'62 '91 C.378 B.A. L.145 J.D. [🄲 Kaye S.]
*PRACTICE AREAS: Litigation; International Trade.
Chronis, Aristotelis A. '75 '00 C&L.893 B.A., J.D.
(adm. in VA; not adm. in DC) [🄰 Swidler B.S.F.]
*PRACTICE AREAS: Telecommunications.
Chryssikos, Telemac N. '44 '75 C.871 M.S.E. L.1049 J.D.
Dept. Head - Regulatory, Washington Gas Light Co.
Chu, Mable '51 '80 C.563 B.A. L.1162 J.D.
Asst. Gen. Coun., Washington Metropolitan Area Transit Authority
*RESPONSIBILITIES: Real Estate Transactions; Real Estate Development; Real Estate Sales; Real Estate Leasing; Eminent Domain.
Chuang, Janie A. ....'73 '99 C.976 B.A. L.309 J.D. [🄰 Cleary,G.S.&H.]
Chud, Adam Michael ....'72 '00 C.30 B.A. L.188 J.D. [🄰 Shea&G.]
Chuh, Patricia M. .... '64 '96 C.705 B.A. L.128 J.D. [🄰 Pepper&C.]
*PRACTICE AREAS: Broadcast Communications.
Chumnanvech, Alyssa ....'70 '96 C.105 B.A. L.273 J.D. [🄰 Perkins C.]
*PRACTICE AREAS: International Trade.
Chun, Jinny '58 '91 C.112 B.A. L.273 J.D.
(adm. in PA; not adm. in DC) Walter Reed Army Med. Ctr.
Chung, Betty Y. .... '72 '99 C.103 B.A. L.273 J.D. 409 Third St. S.W.
Chung, Cecil S. ....'62 '88 C.659 B.S. L.188 J.D. [🄰 Pillsbury W.]
Chung, David S. ....'— '99 C.1090 B.A. L.893 J.D. [🄰 Baker&H.]
Chung, Jennifer E. .... '68 '99 C.103 B.A. L.273 J.D. [🄰 Wiley R.&F.]
Chung, Kerwin ....'68 '94 C.312 B.B.A. L.309 J.D. Deloitte & Touche LLP
Chung Savidge, Jenny '68 '00 C.112 B.A. L.1178 J.D.
(adm. in NY; not adm. in DC) [🄰 Crowell&M.]

Church & Houff, P.A.
(See Baltimore, Maryland)

Churchill, David A. .... '52 '79 C.174 B.A. L.188 J.D. [Jenner&B.]
*PRACTICE AREAS: Government Contracts Litigation and Counseling; Arbitration; Bid Protests.
Churna, Timothy J. '73 '01 C.1349 B.S. L.945 J.D.
(adm. in VA; not adm. in DC) [🄰 Baker B.]
Chused, Richard H. '43 '68
C.103 A.B. L.145 J.D. Prof. of Law, Georgetown Univ. Law Center
Chuzi, George M., (AV) ....'44 '80 C.994 B.A. L.276 J.D. [Kalijarvi,C.&N.]
*PRACTICE AREAS: Labor and Employment; Civil Rights; Discrimination.
Chytla, Anna '64 '88 C.569 B.A. L.904 J.D.
(adm. in MD; not adm. in DC) The World Bank
Chyun, Mary Schneider ....'43 '75 C.696 B.S. L.128 J.D. [🄰 Grossberg,Y.F.&B.]
*PRACTICE AREAS: Estate Planning; Trust Planning.
Ciampa, Aileen Hurley '— '00 C.896 B.A. L.276 J.D.
(adm. in MD; not adm. in DC) [🄰 King&S.]
Cianci, Joy '62 '88 C&L.659 B.S., J.D.
(adm. in PA; not adm. in DC) Assoc. Gen. Coun., Fannie Mae
*RESPONSIBILITIES: Real Estate; Mortgage Banking; E-Commerce.

Ciatti, Michael J. .... '— '96 C&L.893 B.A., J.D. [🄰 King&S.]
*PRACTICE AREAS: Litigation; Trade Regulation.
Ciatto, Frank A. .... '66 '94 C&L.276 B.S.B.A., J.D. [🄰 Venable,A.B.H.&C.]
*PRACTICE AREAS: Corporate Law; Business Transactions.
Cibak, Craig M. .... '65 '96 C.779 B.S. L.273 J.D. [🄰 Schmeltzer,A.&S.]
*PRACTICE AREAS: Commercial Litigation.
Cibinic, John, Jr. '30 '61 C.665 A.B. L.273 J.D.
Assoc. Prof. of Law, George Wash. Univ.
Ciccarello, Sabrina '76 '01 C.446 B.S. L.902 J.D.
(adm. in VA; not adm. in DC) [🄰 Womble C.S.&R.]
*PRACTICE AREAS: Taxation; Banking Law; Finance; Property Law.
Cicchetti, Josephine, (AV) ....'55 '80 C.725 B.A. L.276 J.D. [Jorden B.] ⊙
*PRACTICE AREAS: Corporate; Securities; Insurance Regulatory; Insurance Products; Mergers and Acquisitions.
Cicconi, James W., (AV) .... '52 '77 C&L.846 B.A., J.D. 1120 20th St. NW
Ciccoretti, Eric '67 '99 C&L.477 A.B., J.D.
(adm. in MI; not adm. in DC) [🄰 Sutherland A.&B.]
*PRACTICE AREAS: Energy; Corporate Transactions.
Cicelski, Paul A. ....'69 '99 C.893 B.A. L.880 J.D. [🄰 Shaw P.]
*PRACTICE AREAS: Communications.
Cicero, Anita J. ....'65 '91 C.604 B.S. L.976 J.D. [Gardner,C.&D.]
*PRACTICE AREAS: International Treaty Law; Pharmaceutical Policy and Regulation.
Cicero, Michael J. ....'59 '91 C.602 B.A. L.145 J.D. [🄲 Covington&B.]
Cichowski, Carol A. ....'49 '78 C&L.659 B.A., J.D. Dept. of Education
Cicotte, George F. ....'67 '96 C.659 B.A. L.101 J.D. [🄰 Covington&B.]
*PRACTICE AREAS: Employee Benefits.
Cifuentes de Castro, Alvaro .... '— '75 C&L.677 B.B.A., J.D. [🄲 Verner,L.B.M.&H.]
*PRACTICE AREAS: Corporate Law; Commercial Law.
Cimbala, Michele A. .....'50 '91 C.645 B.S. L.273 J.D. [Sterne,K.G.&F.] (See Pat. Sect.)
*PRACTICE AREAS: Intellectual Property Law; Biotechnology Patents.
Cimbalo, Jeffrey L. '67 '99 C.276 B.S. L.893 J.D.
(adm. in NY; not adm. in DC) [🄰 Weil,G.&M.]
*PRACTICE AREAS: Litigation.
Ciminelli, Michael L. .... '55 '83 C.1213 B.S. L.107 J.D. Asst. Dist. Atty.
Cimino, Frank C., Jr. ..... '69 '96 C.223 B.S.M.E. L.64 J.D. [🄰 Clifford C.R.&W.] (Pat.)
*PRACTICE AREAS: Intellectual Property Law; Patent Litigation.
Cimko, John, Jr. ....'47 '72 C.30 B.A. L.309 J.D. [🄲 Greenberg T.]
Cinquegrani, Peter J. .... '59 '85 C.367 B.A. L.276 J.D. [🄲 Arnold&P.]
*PRACTICE AREAS: Tax.
Cipollone, Pat A. .... '66 '93 C.262 B.A. L.145 J.D. [Kirkland&E.]
Cipriani, Karen L. ....'69 '96 C.813 B.A. L.276 J.D. [🄰 Shaw P.]
Cirulnick, Arthur E., (AV) ....'54 '79 C.112 B.A. L.767 J.D. [Venable,A.B.H.&C.]
*PRACTICE AREAS: Corporate Law; Mergers and Acquisitions; Year 2000 Computer Conversion.
Cividanes, Emilio W., (AV) ....'56 '83 C.311 B.A. L.659 J.D. [Piper M.R.&W.]
*PRACTICE AREAS: E-Commerce; Privacy Law; Litigation; Legislative Practice.
Civiletti, Benjamin R., (P.C.), (AV) '35 '61
C.367 A.B. L.446 LL.B. [Venable,A.B.H.&C.] (⊙Balt., Towson, MD)
*PRACTICE AREAS: Litigation; Government Investigations and Special Investigations; Antitrust Law; Corporate Governance.
Claassen, Ann ....'— '89 C.170 B.A. L.560 J.D. [🄰 Latham&W.]
*PRACTICE AREAS: Chemical Regulation; Environmental Administrative Law; Environmental Health and Safety; Environmental Regulation; Toxic Substance Regulation.
Cladouhos, Harry W., (AV) '25 '54 C.276 B.S.F.S. L.309 LL.B.
[Oppenheimer W.&D.]
*PRACTICE AREAS: Government Relations.
Claffey, Theresa M. '— '99 C.95 A.B. L.228 J.D.
(adm. in MA; not adm. in DC) 701 Pennsylvania Avenue, N.W.
Clagett, A. C. Brooke ....'— '97 C.429 B.A. L.861 J.D. [🄰 Morgan,L.&B.]
Clagett, Brice M., (AV) ....'33 '58 C.674 A.B. L.309 J.D. [Covington&B.]
Clair, Adrienne E. ....'70 '96 C.302 B.A. L.273 J.D. [🄰 Morrison&H.]
*PRACTICE AREAS: Energy.
Clancy, Michael W., (AV) ....'57 '82 C.602 B.A. L.273 J.D. [Holland&K.]
*PRACTICE AREAS: Government Contracts; Government Investigations; FOIA Litigation; Commercial Litigation.
Clancy, Patrick J., (AV) ....'45 '72 C.446 B.A. L.276 J.D. [Krooth&A.]
Clancy, Sean Patrick ....'71 '96 C.401 B.A. L.1338 J.D. [🄰 Patton B.]
Clanton, David A., (AV) .... '44 '79 C.243 B.A. L.912 J.D. [Baker&M.]
*PRACTICE AREAS: Antitrust Law; Administrative Law; Franchise Law; Civil Litigation.

Clapp, R. Jack, & Assoc. Co., L.P.A.
Hall of States Building, 444 North Capital Street, N.W., Suite 828, 20001 ⊙
Telephone: 888-334-8500
Email: RJClappDC@aol.com URL: http://www.rjackclapp.com
—Douglas Desjardins.
Wrongful Death, Personal Injury, Medical Malpractice, Defective Products, Automobile Accidents and Aviation Law.
Cleveland, Ohio Office: One Cleveland Center, Suite 2420, 1375 East Ninth. Telephone: 216-861-1400. Fax: 216-861-1401.
Mentor, Ohio Office: 7784 Reynolds Road. Telephone: 216-946-1100. Fax: 216-946-1756.
See Professional Biographies, WASHINGTON, DISTRICT OF COLUMBIA

Clare, Thomas A. ....'70 '95 C&L.602 B.A., J.D. [Kirkland&E.]
*PRACTICE AREAS: Litigation.
Clark, Barkley, (AV) .... '39 '65 C.31 B.A. L.309 LL.B. [Shook,H.&B.]
*PRACTICE AREAS: Banking; Commercial Law; Uniform Commercial Code.
Clark, Barton B. ....'68 '95 C.309 B.A. L.145 J.D. [🄰 Latham&W.]
*PRACTICE AREAS: Securities Regulation; Corporate Law.
Clark, Cynthia H. .... '72 '98 C.329 B.A. L.976 J.D. [🄰 Wilmer,C.&P.]
Clark, Darrell W., (AV) ....'67 '93 C.183 B.A. L.910 J.D. [Morrison&H.]
*PRACTICE AREAS: Bankruptcy; Commercial Law; Real Estate; Banking and Finance.
Clark, David A. '64 '91 C.886 B.A. L.902 J.D.
(adm. in VA; not adm. in DC) [🄲 Steptoe&J.]
*PRACTICE AREAS: Litigation.
Clark, Denise M. ....'61 '87 C.436 B.A. L.574 J.D. [Feder,S.C.&B.]
Clark, Dennis D. .... '44 '71 C.611 B.A. L.477 J.D. [🄲 Peer&G.]
Clark, Donald E., Jr. ....'60 '96 C.228 B.S. L.896 J.D. [🄰 Wiley R.&F.]
Clark, Donald O. ....'— '63 C&L.790 A.B., J.D. [Reed S.]
*PRACTICE AREAS: International.
Clark, George R. ....'— '72 C.602 B.S. L.339 J.D. [Reed S.]
*PRACTICE AREAS: Litigation.
Clark, Gerard A. ....'62 '87 C.228 B.A. L.276 J.D. [🄲 Skadden,A.S.M.&F.]
Clark, Harry Lewis ....'63 '89 C.575 B.A. L.893 J.D. [🄲 Dewey B.]
Clark, Heather Doherty ....'72 '98 C.105 B.A. L.446 J.D. [🄰 Steptoe&J.]
Clark, Jeanette J. '48 '83 C.856 B.A. L.329 J.D.
Assoc. Gen. Coun., Washington Metropolitan Area Transit Authority
*RESPONSIBILITIES: Personal Injury; Employment and Discrimination; Labor, Transit.
Clark, Jesse '47 '74 C.512 B.A. L.477 J.D.
(adm. in SC; not adm. in DC) P.O. Box 50316‡
Clark, John F. '48 '74 C.976 B.A. L.878 J.D.
(adm. in UT; not adm. in DC) [🄰 Perkins C.]
*PRACTICE AREAS: Telecommunications Licensing; Environmental Regulation; Telecommunications Contracts; Digital Communications; Environmental Litigation.

Clark, Julia Penny, (AV) .... '48 '76 C&L.846 B.A., J.D. [Bredhoff&K.]
Clark, Kaija M. ....'— '99 C.602 B.S. L.273 J.D. [Ⓐ Hogan&H.]
*PRACTICE AREAS: Litigation.
Clark, Karen Renfree .... '— '89 C.770 B.A. L.273 J.D. [Ⓐ Hogan&H.]
*PRACTICE AREAS: Corporate.
Clark, Kathy M. ....'53 '86 C.575 B.A. L.790 J.D. 401 M St., S.W.
Clark, Kevin B. .... '54 '79 C&L.276 B.A., J.D. [Willkie F.&G.]
Clark, Kim M., (AV) .... '48 '74 C.165 A.B. L.982 J.D. [John&H.]
*PRACTICE AREAS: Energy Law.
Clark, Kimani .... '72 '97 C.453 B.S. L.813 J.D. [Ⓐ Finnegan,H.F.G.&D.]
*PRACTICE AREAS: Computer and Software Patents; Patent Prosecution; Patent Protection; Intellectual Property Rights; Intellectual Property Portfolio Management.
Clark, Lynn C. '45 '92 C.352 B.A. L.446 J.D.
(adm. in PA; not adm. in DC) Gen. Coun., Chamber of Com.
Clark, Mary Greer, (AV) .... '45 '82 C.813 A.B. L.976 J.D. [Williams&C.]
*PRACTICE AREAS: Administrative Litigation; Banking Litigation; Financial Institution Failures; Legal Ethics; Legal Malpractice Defense.
Clark, Matthew J., (AV) ....'58 '83 C.884 B.A. L.128 J.D. [Arent F.K.P.&K.]
*PRACTICE AREAS: International Trade Law; Import and Export Law.
Clark, Melvin E., Jr. '51 '76 C.645 B.A. L.597 J.D.
(adm. in PA; not adm. in DC) Pres. & CEO, Metroplex Corp.
Clark, Michael N. .... '67 '93 C.445 B.S. L.276 J.D. [Howrey S.A.&W.]
*PRACTICE AREAS: Commercial Litigation; Antitrust.
Clark, Nicholas W., (AV) '51 '77 C.1347 B.A. L.734 J.D.
Asst. Gen. Coun., United Food & Comercial Workers International Union
Clark, Paul T. .... '54 '80 C.112 A.B. L.1066 J.D. [Seward&K.]
*PRACTICE AREAS: Banking; Securities; Legislative and Regulatory Representation.
Clark, Rachel A. .... '— '00 C.914 B.A. L.309 J.D. [Ⓐ Gibson,D.&C.]
*PRACTICE AREAS: Litigation.
Clark, Richard R. ....'36 '67 C&L.329 B.A., LL.B. 7509 14th St., N.W.
Clark, Robert D. .... '— '81 C.446 B.A. L.329 J.D. [Ⓒ Reed S.]
*PRACTICE AREAS: Health Care.
Clark, Roger A., (AV) .... '32 '58 C&L.339 B.S., LL.B. 607 14th St., N.W.
Clark, Ronald H., (AV) ....'42 '77 C.112 A.B. L.117 J.D. [Arent F.K.P.&K.]
*PRACTICE AREAS: Health Care Fraud; Qui Tam Litigation; False Claims Act; Compliance Plans.
Clark, Sallye A. '67 '95 C.446 B.A. L.128 J.D.
(adm. in MD; not adm. in DC) 1730 Rhode Island Ave., N.W.
Clark, Shannon R. .... '68 '94 C.93 B.A. L.188 J.D. 607 14th St., N.W.
Clark, Sherman J. '63 '92 C.445 B.S. L.309 J.D.
(adm. in MD; not adm. in DC) 655 15th St., N.W., Suite 1200
Clark, W. Robinson H. .... '66 '96 C.945 B.S. L.30 J.D. [Ⓐ Dorsey&W.] (Pat.)
*PRACTICE AREAS: Chemical and Biotech Intellectual Property; Pharmaceutical Intellectual Property; Intellectual Property Licensing; Patent Law; Infringement Opinions.
Clark, Wendy A. .... '— '83 C.923 B.S. L.770 J.D. P.O. Box 1833
Clarke, David, Jr., (AV) ....'56 '81 C&L.309 A.B., J.D. [Piper M.R.&W.]
*PRACTICE AREAS: Securities Litigation; Business Litigation.
Clarke, David A. ....'43 '69 C.273 B.A. L.329 J.D. Chm., Council of D.C.
Clarke, Donald H., (AV) ....'49 '75 C.813 A.B. L.188 J.D. [GKRSE]
*PRACTICE AREAS: Energy; Natural Resources; International; Environmental.
Clarke, John O'B., Jr., (AV) ....'43 '68 C.524 B.S. L.276 J.D. [Highsaw,M.&C.]
*PRACTICE AREAS: Federal Court Trial and Appellate Practice; Supreme Court Practice; Railway Labor Act; Transportation; Bankruptcy.
Clarke, Julien E. ....'41 '94 C&L.999 B.A., J.D. Off. of Corp. Coun.
Clarke, Kathleen K. .... '43 '76 C.170 B.A. L.273 J.D. [Ⓒ Seward&K.]
*PRACTICE AREAS: Investment Companies; Securities; Corporations.
Clarke, Kay M. .... '66 '99 C.770 B.S. L.180 J.D. 601 Pennsylvania Avenue, N.W.
Clarke, Laurie A. .... '63 '91 C.788 A.B. L.813 J.D. [Ⓒ Hogan&H.]
*PRACTICE AREAS: Regulatory Law; Drug and Medical Device Regulation; Food and Drug Regulation; Food, Drug and Cosmetic Law.
Clarke, Peggy Ann .... '57 '91 C.273 B.A. L.276 J.D. [Ⓒ O'Melveny&M.]
*PRACTICE AREAS: International Trade.
Clarke, Thomas M. '63 '90 C.309 B.A. L.178 J.D.
(adm. in MA; not adm. in DC) 2445 M St., N.W.‡
Clarry, Melissa '71 '96 C.385 B.A. L.904 J.D.
(adm. in MD; not adm. in DC) [Ⓐ Brustein&M.]
*PRACTICE AREAS: Education Law; Federal Legislative Practice; Administrative Law.
Clasby, John .... '— '99 C.722 B.A. L.893 J.D. [Ⓐ Hogan&H.]
Class, Edgar, III ....'71 '96 C.30 B.A. L.904 J.D. [Ⓐ Shook,H.&B.]
Clause, C. Russell .... '69 '94 C.228 A.B. L.597 J.D. [Ⓐ Wilmer,C.&P.]
Claxton, Charles R. (Rick) ....'49 '78 C.502 B.J. L.94 J.D. [Claxton,S.&Q.]
*PRACTICE AREAS: Commercial Litigation; Medical Malpractice; Legal Malpractice; Employment Law.

Claxton, Sale & Quinn, P.C., (AV)
Fifth Floor, 910 Sixteenth Street, N.W., 20006
Telephone: 202-833-4170 Fax: 202-887-5137
URL: http://www.lawyers.com/claxtonsale&quinn
Stephen Sale; John D. Quinn; Charles R. (Rick) Claxton; Michele Bartoli-Cain.
Civil Litigation, Government Contracts, Energy, Telecommunication Law, Employment Law, Business Law; Business Litigation.
See Professional Biographies, WASHINGTON, DISTRICT OF COLUMBIA

Clay, Gordon M. ....'67 '96 C.886 B.S. L.276 J.D. [Ⓐ Steptoe&J.]
Clay, Khari M. '72 '98 C.821 B.A. L.309 J.D.
(adm. in NY; not adm. in DC) [Ⓐ Piper M.R.&W.]
*PRACTICE AREAS: Venture Capital; Commercial Litigation; Intellectual Property Litigation.
Clay, Sulee J. .... '— '98 C&L.309 A.B., J.D. [Ⓐ Piper M.R.&W.]
*PRACTICE AREAS: Corporate Finance; Securities; Venture Capital; Mergers and Acquisitions.
Clay, Tracy-Elizabeth .... '71 '97 C.813 B.A. L.309 J.D. [Ⓐ Hogan&H.]
*PRACTICE AREAS: Antitrust; Litigation; Health Care; Government Regulation.
Claybrook, Frederick W., Jr. ....'51 '76 C.937 B.A. L.228 J.D. [Crowell&M.]
*PRACTICE AREAS: Government Contract Law; Federal Practice; Contract Law; Railroad Law; Litigation.
Clayman, Robert S. ....'53 '78 C.860 B.A. L.245 J.D. [Guerrieri,E.&C.]
Clayton, Carol .... '58 '82 C.878 B.A. L.893 J.D. [Wilmer,C.&P.]
*PRACTICE AREAS: Environmental Law; Civil Practice; Complex Litigation.
Clayton, Carolyn Doozan .... '48 '90 C.477 B.A. L.1209 J.D. [Ⓒ Steptoe&J.]
*PRACTICE AREAS: Transportation Law; Administrative Law.
Clayton, Christian J. '73 '01 C.174 B.A. L.30 J.D.
(adm. in VA; not adm. in DC) [Ⓐ Bingham D.]
*PRACTICE AREAS: Business Corporate; Business Finance; Litigation.
Clayton, Kevin C. .... '70 '98 C&L.893 B.A., J.D. [Ⓐ Hogan&H.]
*PRACTICE AREAS: Corporate Law; Finance; Investments; Mergers, Acquisitions and Divestitures; Securities.
Clayton, Michael F. ....'54 '80 C.896 B.A. L.893 J.D. [Morgan,L.&B.]
Clayton, Mikeal M. ....'74 '99 C.623 B.A. L.846 J.D. [Ⓐ Vinson&E.]
*PRACTICE AREAS: Litigation.
Cleary, J. Michael, (AV) ......'43 '69 C.30 B.A. L.273 J.D. [Cleary&K.] (See Pat. Sect.)
*PRACTICE AREAS: Copyright Law; Trademark Law; Unfair Competition Law; Litigation.
Cleary, Jacqueline P. .... '63 '91 C.604 B.A. L.128 J.D. [Hogan&H.]

Cleary, Gottlieb, Steen & Hamilton, (AV) BB
2000 Pennsylvania Avenue, N.W. Suite 9000, 20006-1801 ⊙
Telephone: 202-974-1500 Facsimile: 202-974-1999
URL: http://www.cgsh.com
Of Counsel: Robert C. Barnard; Fred D. Turnage; J. Eugene Marans; Daniel B. Silver; Richard deC. Hinds. Washington, D.C. Partners: Donald L. Morgan; Kenneth L. Bachman, Jr.; Charles F. Lettow; Sara D. Schotland; John S. Magney; Mark Leddy; John C. Murphy, Jr.; George S. Cary; Janet L. Weller; Mitchell S. Dupler; Linda J. Soldo; Giovanni P. Prezioso; John T. Byam; Matthew D. Slater; Michael R. Lazerwitz; James R. Modrall† (Not admitted in DC); Michael A. Mazzuchi; Robert W. Cook. Special Counsel: W. Richard Bidstrup; Scott N. Benedict; Linda S. Matlack; Kevin A. Griffin. Senior Attorneys: Joyce E. McCarty; Karen A. Kerr; Scott R. Goodwin. Associates: Reyn C. Anderson; Robin M. Bergen; Brent E. Binge; Laura L. Black; Derek M. Bush; Brian Byrne; Jeremy J. Calsyn; Kerri J. Chase; Janie A. Chuang; Alexis L. Collins; L. Burton Davis; Jacob O. Davison; Tanya N. Dunne (Not admitted in DC); William S. Fultz; Michael Hershaft; Steven J. Kaiser; Elke M. Krauland; James D. Livingstone; Mutheu Maitha† (Not admitted in DC); Paul D. Marquardt; Patricia M. McDermott; John P. McGill, Jr.; Dipali B. Mehta; Pamela G. Meisel; Marc L. Mezey†; Mark W. Nelson; Andrew K. Niebler; Suzanne B. Perry; Stephen E. Pomper†; Mitchell L. Rabinowitz; Masha Smith†; Julie A. Southfield; Aliza Sperling† (Not admitted in DC); Patrick A. Tillou† (Not admitted in DC); Petia Vretenarova† (Not admitted in DC); Patricia J. Walsh; Wilbert H. Watts, Jr.
Antitrust, Banking and Financial Institutions, Business Litigation, Corporate, Derivatives and Commodities, Employee Benefits, Employment and Pensions, Energy, Environmental Law, Insurance Coverage, Intellectual Property, International Litigation and Arbitration, International Trade, Investment Funds, Joint Ventures, Litigation, Mergers and Acquisitions, Privatizations, Product Liability, Project Finance, Real Estate, Securities and Derivatives, Structured Finance, Taxation, Trusts and Estates, White Collar Defense, Workouts and Bankruptcy.
New York, New York Office: One Liberty Plaza, New York, N.Y. 10006. Telephone: 212-225-2000.
Paris, France Office: 41, Avenue de Friedland, 75008 Paris, France. Telephone: 33-1-40-74-68-00.
Brussels, Belgium Office: Rue de la Loi 57, 1040 Brussels, Belgium. Telephone: 32-2-287-2000.
London, England Office: City Place House, 55 Basinghall Street, London EC2V 5EH England. Telephone: 44-71-614-2200.
Hong Kong Office: 39th Floor, Bank of China Tower, One Garden Road, Hong Kong. Telephone: 852-2521-4122.
Tokyo, Japan Office: Cleary, Gottlieb, Steen & Hamilton Gaikokuho Jimu Bengoshi Jimusho, 20th Floor, Shin Kasumigaseki Building, 3-2, Kasumigaseki 3-Chome, Chiyoda-Ku, Tokyo 100-0013, Japan. Telephone: 81-3-3595-3911.
Frankfurt, Germany Office: Main Tower, Neue Mainzer Strasse 52, 60311 Frankfurt am Main, Germany. Telephone: 49-69-971-03-0.
Rome, Italy Office: Piazza de Spagna 15, 00187 Rome, Italy. Telephone: 39-06-69-52-22-1.
†Non-admitted attorneys working under the supervision of principals of the firm resident in the Washington, DC Office
See Professional Biographies, WASHINGTON, DISTRICT OF COLUMBIA

Cleary & Komen, LLP, (AV)
Suite 200, 600 Pennsylvania Avenue, S.E., 20003-4304
Telephone: 202-675-4700 Fax: 202-675-4716
Email: cleary-komen@cleary-komen.com
Members of Firm: J. Michael Cleary; Edwin Komen. Associates: Scott J. Major; Hae Park-Suk. Of Counsel: Bernard C. Dietz.
Copyright, Trademark and Unfair Competition Law, Foreign and Domestic. Practice before Federal Courts and Government Departments.
See Professional Biographies, WASHINGTON, DISTRICT OF COLUMBIA

Cleaver-Bascombe, Karen P. .... '65 '95 C.446 B.S. L.1364 J.D. P.O. Box 21550
Cleesattle, Jodi L. ....'68 '94 C&L.30 B.A., J.D. [Ⓐ Ross,D.&B.]
Clegg, Roger '55 '81 C.691 B.A. L.976 J.D.
V.P. & Gen. Coun., National Legal Center for the Public Interest
Cleghorn, Jeffery Melvin ....'62 '00 C.1039 B.A. L.273 J.D. P.O. Box 65301
Clememine, Guerino J. ....'74 '99 C&L.893 B.A., J.D. 501 3rd St., N.W.
Clement, Kelly A. ....'65 '93 C.823 B.A. L.659 J.D. [Howrey S.A.&W.]
*PRACTICE AREAS: Antitrust Law; Commercial Litigation; Intellectual Property Law.
Clement, Kwame A. ....'59 '94 C.999 B.Sc. L.273 J.D. [Ⓐ Arnold&P.]
*PRACTICE AREAS: Antitrust; Litigation.
Clemente, Ellen L. '64 '99 C.879 B.A. L.1356 J.D.
(adm. in MD; not adm. in DC) [Ⓐ Dombroff&G.]
Clements, Roxanne S. .... '59 '85 C.188 B.A. L.273 J.D. [Lachter&C.]
*PRACTICE AREAS: Antitrust Law; Commercial Litigation.
Clements, William L. '49 '76 C.188 B.S. L.818 J.D.
(adm. in MA; not adm. in DC) Sr. Mgr., Intl. Trade Reg., General Electric Co.
Clennon, Cary, (BV) .... '56 '82 C.276 A.B. L.33 J.D. P.O. Box 29302
Clerici, John M. .... '70 '95 C.128 B.A. L.575 J.D. [Ⓐ McKenna&C.]
*PRACTICE AREAS: Government Contracts; Insurance Coverage; Litigation.
Cleveland, David L. ....'49 '75 C.696 B.A. L.930 J.D. Off. of Corp. Coun.
Cleveland, Peter M. ....'65 '00 C.178 B.A. L.276 J.D. [Ⓐ Hunton&W.]
*PRACTICE AREAS: Project Development; Finance and Leasing.
Cleveland, Steven J. '67 '99 C.112 B.A. L.276 J.D.
(adm. in GA; not adm. in DC) [Ⓐ Skadden,A.S.M.&F.]
*PRACTICE AREAS: Corporate Law.
Click, Joseph O., (BV) ....'54 '86 C.763 A.B. L.1067 J.D. [Dyer E.&J.]
*PRACTICE AREAS: Litigation; Bankruptcy; Securities Fraud.
Clifford, Carol '52 '80 C.112 B.A. L.128 J.D.
Asst. Gen. Coun., United Food & Comercial Workers International Union
Clifford, John M., (AV) .... '47 '73 C.475 B.A. L.128 J.D. [Clifford,L.&G.]
*PRACTICE AREAS: Civil Litigation; Employment; Commercial; Personal Injury.
Clifford, Richard B., Jr. ....'65 '90 C.264 B.A. L.273 J.D. [Perkins C.]
*PRACTICE AREAS: Government Contracts; Litigation; International Law.

Clifford Chance Rogers & Wells LLP, (AV) BB
2001 K Street N.W., 20006-1001 ⊙
Telephone: 202-912-5000 Facsimile: 202-912-6000
URL: http://www.cliffordchance.com
Senior Partner: William P. Rogers (1913-2001). Partners: Kevin J. Arquit; Leiv H. Blad, Jr.; David D. DiBari; Jeremy A. Connick (Not admitted in United States); James C. Egan, Jr.; Anthony F. Essaye; David J. Evans; Kenneth A. Gallo; Ira D. Hammerman; Sara P. Hanks; John Paul Ketels; Steven A. Newborn; Michael A. O'Shea; Anthony J. Renzi, Jr.; Jon Randall Roellke; John E. Scribner; Ryan Trainer; Dale C. Turza; Laura A. Wilkinson. Counsel: Michael J. King; George Kleinfeld; Fred W. Reinke; Michael R. Silverman; John M. Sipple, Jr.; Kirsten A. Wolfe. Consultant: Virginia L. Snider. Associates: Matthew D. Adler; Michael R. Albrecht; Julie N. Ambrose; Carrie M. Anderson; Heather Fai Auyang; Allen R. Bachman; Allyson Baker (Not admitted in DC); Lacy D. Berrington; James J. Black; Daniel T. Brown; Erin M. Brown; N. Sean Butler (Not admitted in DC); Bret A. Campbell; Christine Suhming Chen; Elizabeth Chen (Not admitted in DC); Gregory D. Cho (Not admitted in DC); Frank C. Cimino, Jr.; Boyd Tristan Cloern; Charles M. Cole; Anthony M. Cooke; Sha-Shana N. L. Crichton; Patricia C. Crowley; Julia Symon de Kluiver; H.C. Eren; Benjamin M. Farber; Michael Fransella (Not admitted in DC); Paul R. Frontczak; Steven F. Gatti; Julie A. Goldman; Allyson Ann Gozycki (Not admitted in DC); Alissa S. Hecht (Not admitted in DC); Marc Jarsulic; Jennifer M. Jeannot; Gibbs A. Johnson; Thomas C. Koonce; Denise Landers (Not admitted in DC); Aimee D. Latimer (Not admitted in DC); Francesca D. Laursen; Julia Lee; Catherine McCarthy; Prakash H. Mehta; Katherine Wells Meighan; Ashley Anne Meise; Jennifer J. Mink; Hoda Atia Moustafa; Scott B. Murray; Joseph L. Musella; Gregory G. Nardini; Susan M. Petersen (Not admitted in DC); Timothy P. Peterson; Carlos E. Provencio; Jeneen Ramos (Not admitted in DC); Christopher D. Roberti; Kevin T. Roche (Not admitted in DC); Nicholas M. Roegner; Vincent Serpico (Not admitted in DC); Robyn Shields; Damon A. Terrill; Lee K. Van Voorhis; Mary F. Walters; Christopher Willott (Not admitted in DC); Glen M. Zwicker.
General Practice.
New York, N.Y. Office: Two Hundred Park Avenue, New York, N.Y. 10166-0153. Telephone: 212-878-8000. Facsimile: 212-878-8375.
Other Offices: Amsterdam, Bangkok, Barcelona, Beijing, Berlin, Brussels, Budapest, Dubai, Dusseldorf, Frankfurt, Hanoi, Ho Chi Minh City, Hong Kong, London, Madrid, Milan, Moscow, Munich, Padua, Paris, Prague, Rome, Sao Paulo, Shanghai, Singapore, Tokyo, Warsaw.
See Professional Biographies, WASHINGTON, DISTRICT OF COLUMBIA

Clifford, Lyons & Garde, (AV)
1620 L Street, N.W. Suite 625, 20036-5600
Telephone: 202-289-8990 Fax: 202-289-8992
URL: http://www.lawyers.com/clg-law
John M. Clifford; Mona Lyons; Billie Pirner Garde. Associate: Peter F. Butcher.
Civil Litigation, Labor and Employment (Employees and Employers, Public and Private), Wrongful Termination, Employment Discrimination, Civil Rights, Administrative Law-Nuclear and Energy Issues, Employment Investigations.
See Professional Biographies, WASHINGTON, DISTRICT OF COLUMBIA

Clifton, Jeffrey James '62 '97 C.10 B.S. L.945 J.D.
(adm. in AL; not adm. in DC) [Johnson&C.] (⊙Birm., AL)
*PRACTICE AREAS: Health Law; Administrative Law; Antitrust; Corporate Law; Business Law.
Clifton, Jill S. '45 '75 C.260 B.A. L.208 J.D.
(adm. in CO; not adm. in DC) Admin. Law J.
Clifton, Marcus Antoine '71 '98 C.887 B.S. L.1187 J.D.
(adm. in NY; not adm. in DC) [🄰 Smith C.]
*PRACTICE AREAS: Entertainment Law.
Climaco, John R., (AV) '41 '67 C.608 B.S. L.930 J.D.
(adm. in OH; not adm. in DC) [Climaco,L.P.W.&G.] ⊙
Climaco, Lefkowitz, Peca, Wilcox & Garofoli Co., L.P.A., (AV)
923 15th St., N.W. (⊙Cleve., Columbus, OH)
Cline, Andrew A. .... '67 '94 C.178 B.S. L.273 J.D. [🅂 Gibson,D.&C.]
*PRACTICE AREAS: Antitrust and Trade Regulation.
Cline, Andrew N. '72 '98 C.273 B.A. L.861 J.D.
(adm. in LA; not adm. in DC) [🄰 Weiner B.S.K.]
*PRACTICE AREAS: Mortgage Banking Law; Consumer Finance.
Clineburg, Stephen R. '41 '67 C.178 A.B. L.893 J.D.
(adm. in VA; not adm. in DC) V.P. & Reg. Gen. Coun., Boston Properties, Inc.
Clinton, William J. .... '53 '82 C&L.276 B.S., J.D. [White&C.]
Clissold, David B. .... '58 '96 C.112 B.S. L.446 J.D. [🄰 Hyman,P.&M.]
*PRACTICE AREAS: Food and Drug Regulation.
Cloern, Boyd Tristan .... '72 '98 C&L.383 B.A., J.D. [🄰 Clifford C.R.&W.]
*PRACTICE AREAS: Complex Litigation; Antitrust; Unfair Competition; Intellectual Property.
Close, David P., (AV) .... '15 '42 C.951 A.B. L.178 LL.B. [Dahlgren&C.]
*PRACTICE AREAS: General Practice; International Law; Corporate Law; Administrative Law.
Cloutier, Christopher T. '72 '00 C.477 B.A. L.273 J.D.
(adm. in NY; not adm. in DC) [🄰 Paul,H.J.&W.]
*PRACTICE AREAS: International Trade; E-Commerce; Commercial Litigation.
Clubb, Bruce E. .... '31 '59 C&L.494 B.B.A., LL.B. 815 Conn. Ave., N.W.
Clubok, Andrew B. .... '67 '94 C.309 A.B. L.477 J.D. [Kirkland&E.]
*PRACTICE AREAS: Litigation.
Clukey, Nathan Elliott .... '70 '97 C.886 B.A. L.128 J.D. [🄰 McKee N.]
*PRACTICE AREAS: Tax Controversies; Tax Litigation.
Clune, Kathryn L. .... '67 '94 C.732 B.A. L.982 J.D. [🄰 Dorsey&W.]
Coale, John P., (A Professional Corporation), (AV) '46 '72
C.446 B.A. L.64 J.D. [Coale C.L.M.]
*PRACTICE AREAS: Products Liability Law; Mass Disaster Litigation; Aviation Law.

Coale Cooley Lietz McInerny, A Professional Corporation, (AV) BB
818 Connecticut Avenue, N.W., Suite 857, 20006
Telephone: 202-887-4770 Facsimile: 202-887-4778
John P. Coale (A Professional Corporation); Diane E. Cooley; David K. Lietz; Julia Wernett McInerny;—Deborah St. Jean.
Aviation, Personal Injury, Wrongful Death, Product Liability, Mass Tort Litigation and General Litigation.
See Professional Biographies, WASHINGTON, DISTRICT OF COLUMBIA

Coan, Carl A. S., III, (AV) .... '56 '81 C.1356 B.A. L.276 J.D. [Coan&L.]
*PRACTICE AREAS: Housing and Urban Affairs; Real Estate; Litigation; Wills; Probate.
Coan, Carl A. S., Jr. .... '34 '58 C&L.276 A.B., LL.B. [Coan&L.]
*PRACTICE AREAS: Housing and Urban Affairs; Real Estate; Legislative Law; Fair Housing.

Coan & Lyons, (AV)
Suite 1000, 1100 Connecticut Avenue, N.W., 20036
Telephone: 202-728-1070 Facsimile: 202-293-2448
URL: http://www.lawyers.com/coan&lyons
Members of Firm: Carl A. S. Coan, Jr.; William S. Moorhead (1923-1987); Raymond K. James; Carl A. S. Coan, III. Associate: Sheila C. Salmon. Of Counsel: James A. Lyons, Jr.
General Practice. Federal, Administrative and Legislative Practice. Real Estate, Housing and Urban Affairs, Contracts, Banking Law, Litigation, Probate, Wills, Fair Housing.
See Professional Biographies, WASHINGTON, DISTRICT OF COLUMBIA

Coates, Melanie D. .... '70 '95 C.228 A.B. L.692 J.D. [🄰 Wilmer,C.&P.]

Coates, Davenport & Gurne, PLLC, (AV)
900 Nineteenth Street, N.W., 20006
Telephone: 202-778-0020 Fax: 202-778-0029
URL: http://www.lawyers.com/coates
David M. Davenport; Patricia D. Gurne;—Jennifer M. Porter. Counsel: Susan M. Gschwendtner; Stephen R. Yurek (Not admitted in DC). Special Counsel: Kathleen G. Gallagher; Sheila Trice Beil (Not admitted in DC).
Corporate Law, Business Law, Commercial Law, Small Business Law, Employment Law, Trade Association Law, Education Law, Merger and Acquisitions, Real Estate, Leasing, Commercial Transactions, Electronic Commerce.
See Professional Biographies, WASHINGTON, DISTRICT OF COLUMBIA

Coatzee, Theresa Adams .... '68 '96 C.165 A.B. L.1410 J.D. [🄰 Collier S.S.]
*PRACTICE AREAS: Antitrust; Litigation; Consumer Protection.
Cobb, Antoine P. .... '70 '96 C.1286 B.A. L.1209 J.D. [🄰 Troutman S.]
*PRACTICE AREAS: Government Affairs; Utility Regulation; Regulatory Law.
Cobb, Calvin H., III, (AV) .... '58 '85 C.674 A.B. L.276 J.D. [Craighill,M.F.C.&C.]
*PRACTICE AREAS: Estate Planning; Probate Law; Trusts.
Cobb, Calvin H., Jr., (AV) .... '24 '50 C.871 B.S. L.276 LL.B. [Steptoe&J.]
*PRACTICE AREAS: Corporate Planning, Transactions and Litigation; Securities.
Cobb, Christopher '73 '00 C.695 B.A. L.904 J.D.
(adm. in NY; not adm. in DC) [🄰 Andrews&K.]
*PRACTICE AREAS: Corporate; Securities.
Cobb, James F., Jr. '71 '99 C.101 B.A. L.276 J.D.
(adm. in UT; not adm. in DC) [🄰 Perkins C.]
*PRACTICE AREAS: Commercial Litigation; Telecommunications.
Cobb, Paul W. "Whit", Jr. .... '64 '91 C.228 A.B. L.976 J.D. [Jenner&B.]
Cobb, Susan A. .... '47 '79 C.550 B.A. L.201 J.D. [🄲 Powell,G.F.&M.]
*PRACTICE AREAS: Tax Exempt Organizations.
Cobb, Ty, (AV) .... '50 '79 C.309 A.B. L.276 J.D. [Hogan&H.] (⊙Denver, CO)
*PRACTICE AREAS: White Collar Criminal Defense; Congressional Investigations; Complex Litigation.
Cobb, Howard, Hayes & Windsor, (AV) .... 1511 K St., N.W., Ste. 440
Cobbs, Louise B., (AV) .... '47 '78 C.788 A.B. [Holland&K.]
*PRACTICE AREAS: Aviation Law; Aerospace Casualty Litigation; Products Liability; International Law.

Cobbs, Nicholas H., Law Offices of, (AV) '46 '75 C.31 A.B. L.659 J.D.
1776 K Street, N.W., Suite 300, 20006-2304
Telephone: 202-452-8222 Facsimile: 202-452-1659
Email: ncobbs@erols.com URL: http://www.cobbslaw.com
Administrative Law and Commercial Litigation, including Aviation, Admiralty, Insurance and Civil Appeals.
See Professional Biographies, WASHINGTON, DISTRICT OF COLUMBIA

Cober, Nicole M. .... '71 '96 C.1375 B.A. L.329 J.D. [🄰 Dickstein S.M.&O.]
*PRACTICE AREAS: Employment Litigation; Antitrust Litigation.
Coberly, Robert G. .... '54 '90 C.645 B.A. L.273 J.D. [🄰 Powell,G.F.&M.]
*PRACTICE AREAS: Tax; Affordable Housing.
Cobert, Ronald N., (AV) .... '35 '60 C.321 A.B. L.276 J.D. [Grove,J.&C.]
*PRACTICE AREAS: Business Law; Transportation; International Trade; Health Care.
Coburn, Barry, (AV) .... '56 '81 C.976 B.A. L.309 J.D. [Coburn&S.]
*PRACTICE AREAS: Criminal Litigation; Civil Litigation.
Coburn, David H., (AV) .... '51 '76 C.1036 B.A. L.276 J.D. [Steptoe&J.]
*PRACTICE AREAS: Administrative Law; Aviation Law; Transportation Law; Motor Carrier Law; Antitrust Law.
Coburn, Evelyn .... '45 '75 C.331 B.A. L.128 J.D. Supr. Ct. Comr.

Coburn, George M., (AV) '23 '49 C&L.309 A.B., LL.B.
1661 Crescent Place, N.W., Suite 208, 20009-4047
Telephone: 202-234-2054 Fax: 202-234-2054
Email: coburn.legalconsltg@erols.com
Government Contract Counseling and Litigation. Commercial Contract Arbitration, Neutral in Government Procurement Alternate Dispute Resolution (ADR).
See Professional Biographies, WASHINGTON, DISTRICT OF COLUMBIA

Coburn & Schertler, (AV)
1150 18th Street N.W., Suite 850, 20036
Telephone: 202-628-4199 Fax: 202-628-4177
Email: cobscher@aol.com
Barry Coburn; David Schertler; Russell D. Duncan. Associates: Sandra L. Brickel; Lisa A. F. Fishberg; Anne L. Saltzberg; Mark E. Schamel.
Criminal and Civil Litigation.
See Professional Biographies, WASHINGTON, DISTRICT OF COLUMBIA

Cocciardi, Thomas A. '57 '81
C&L.276 A.B., J.D. 1201 Pennsylvania Avenue, NW, Suite 300
Cochilla, Stephen J. '63 '89 C.705 B.A. L.477 J.D.
(adm. in NY; not adm. in DC) 1200 18th St., N.W.‡
Cochran, Andrew R. '56 '82
C.473 B.S. L.602 J.D. Room 7510, 14th St. & Constitution Avenue
Cochran, Johnnie L., Jr., (AV) '37 '63 C.112 B.S. L.426 LL.B.
(adm. in CA; not adm. in DC) [J.L.Cochran,Jr.] (⊙L.A., CA; New York, NY)
Cochran, Martha L., (AV) .... '48 '73 C&L.260 B.S., J.D. [Arnold&P.]
*PRACTICE AREAS: Corporate; Securities; SEC Enforcement Matters; Financial Institutions; Legislative.
Cochran, Johnnie L., Jr., A Prof. Corp., Law Offices of, (AV)
201 Massachusetts Ave., N.E. (⊙L.A., CA)
Cochrane, John E. .... '33 '61 C&L.477 A.B., J.D. 900 19th St., N.W., Ste. 400
Cochrane, Lisa L. '— '01 C.259 B.A. L.260 J.D.
(adm. in FL; not adm. in DC) [🄰 King&S.]
*PRACTICE AREAS: Litigation; Trade.
Cochrane, William M. '17 '41 C&L.575 A.B., LL.B.
(adm. in NC; not adm. in DC) 227 A St., N.E.
Cockrum, Carlynne S. .... '70 '98 C.976 B.A. L.276 J.D. [🄰 Steptoe&J.]
Codd, Bernard P. '61 '96 C.186 B.E. L.1002 J.D.
(adm. in MD; not adm. in DC; Pat.) [🄰 McDermott,W.&E.]
Coddington, Kipp A. .... '63 '92 C.679 B.S. L.276 J.D. [🄲 Covington&B.]
Codevilla, David A. .... '70 '96 C.1375 B.A. L.1209 J.D. [🄰 Kirkland&E.]
*PRACTICE AREAS: Environmental Transactions.
Codinha, J. William, (P.C.), (AV) '47 '72
C.611 B.A. L.94 J.D. [Nixon P.] (⊙Boston, MA)
*PRACTICE AREAS: White Collar Criminal Litigation; Civil Litigation; Environmental Litigation.
Cody, Daniel A. .... '— '99 C.821 B.A. L.945 J.D. [🄰 Reed S.]
*PRACTICE AREAS: Health Care.
Coe, Cheryl Miller .... '— '95 C.1365 B.A. L.276 J.D. [🄰 Latham&W.]
*PRACTICE AREAS: Taxation; Corporate Taxation; Partnership Taxation; Federal Taxation.
Coe, Michael I. '71 '97 C.138 B.S. L.945 J.D.
(adm. in VA; not adm. in DC; Pat.) [🄰 Crowell&M.]
Coerper, Milo G., (AV) .... '25 '54 C.871 B.S. L.477 J.D. 1627 I St., N.W.‡
Coffee, Gordon Alan, (AV) .... '58 '84 C.893 B.A. L.846 J.D. [Winston&S.]
*PRACTICE AREAS: Commercial Litigation; Health Care Litigation; Legal Malpractice; Criminal Defense.
Coffee, Roy C., III, (BV) '64 '92 C.846 B.J. L.990 J.D.
(adm. in CA; not adm. in DC) [O'Connor&H.]
Coffey, Carolyn .... '62 '98 C.446 B.S. L.180 J.D. [🄰 Dyer E.&J.]
Coffin, Linda .... '— '98 C.502 B.A. L.477 J.D. [🄰 Wilmer,C.&P.]
Coffin, Shannen W. .... '69 '94 C.425 B.B.A. L.276 J.D. [🄰 Steptoe&J.]
Coffman, Meredith C. .... '15 '48 C.428 A.B. L.537 LL.B. 406 5th St., N.W.
Cofrancesco, Juliana M. .... '58 '88 C.1044 B.A. L.276 J.D. [🄲 Howrey S.A.&W.]
*PRACTICE AREAS: International Trade Law; Import and Export Law.
Cogen, Edward S., (AV) .... '35 '60 C&L.188 B.A., J.D. [🄲 Whiteford,T.&P.]
*PRACTICE AREAS: Corporate Law; Business Law.
Coggins, Harman & Hewitt, (AV)
655 15th Street, N.W. (⊙Silver Spring, MD; Falls Church, VA)
Cohan, June E. .... '71 '97 C.893 B.A. L.276 J.D. [🄰 Arnold&P.] (Pat.)
*PRACTICE AREAS: Intellectual Property; Technology Law; Life Sciences.
Cohan, Marsha A. .... '55 '83 C.103 A.B. L.309 J.D. 2916 Fessenden St., N.W.
Cohan, Philip L., (AV) .... '39 '67 C.951 B.A. L.659 J.D. [Piper M.R.&W.]
*PRACTICE AREAS: Commercial Litigation; Patent Infringement Litigation; Product Liability; Defense Litigation.
Cohen, Adam .... '71 '96 C.893 B.A. L.309 J.D. [🄰 Sutherland A.&B.]
*PRACTICE AREAS: Employee Benefit Taxation; ERISA; Executive Compensation; Qualified Retirement Plans.
Cohen, Adam W. .... '66 '92 C.156 B.A. L.978 J.D. Asst. U.S. Atty., U.S. Dept. of Justice
Cohen, Allison G. .... '71 '99 C.311 B.A. L.893 J.D. 1201 Pennsylvania Ave., N.W.
Cohen, Arthur A., (AV) .... '54 '79 C.976 B.A. L.178 J.D. [🄲 Skadden,A.S.M.&F.]
Cohen, Barry E., (AV) .... '45 '71 C.339 B.S. L.597 J.D. [Crowell&M.]
*PRACTICE AREAS: International Business Law; Import and Export Law; Legal Ethics and Professional Responsibility.
Cohen, Benedict S. .. '59 '85 C.976 B.A. L.145 J.D. 2471 Rayburn House Office Building
Cohen, Brian .... '47 '72 C&L.446 B.A., J.D. [Bell,B.&L.]
*PRACTICE AREAS: Construction Law; Government Contracts Law.
Cohen, Charles I., (AV) .... '45 '71 C.861 B.A. L.665 J.D. [Morgan,L.&B.]
Cohen, Daniel .... '58 '89 C.354 B.A. L.1048 J.D. [🄰 Cuneo]
*PRACTICE AREAS: Litigation; Antitrust; Insurance; Alternative Dispute Resolution; Criminal Law.
Cohen, Daniel Eric, (BV) .... '61 '85 C.421 B.A. L.1340 J.D. [🄲 Swidler B.S.F.]
*PRACTICE AREAS: Insurance; Intellectual Property; Environmental; Construction.

Cohen, David A. '63 '88 C.912 B.A. L.1292 J.D.
(adm. in PA; not adm. in DC) [Cullen]
*PRACTICE AREAS: Class Actions; Property Litigation; Labor and Employment.
Cohen, David A. . . . . '— '95 C.1036 B.A. L.904 J.D. [🄰 King&S.]
*PRACTICE AREAS: Litigation; Trade Regulation.
Cohen, David B., (AV) . . . . '58 '83 C&L.846 B.A., J.D. [Vinson&E.]
*PRACTICE AREAS: Natural Resources Law; Business Law; Telecommunications Law; Project Financing Law.
Cohen, David E. . . . . '67 '92 C.966 B.B.A. L.436 J.D. [🄰 Sandler,T.&R.]
*PRACTICE AREAS: Customs Law; International Trade.
Cohen, David J. . . . . '53 '78 C&L.309 A.B., J.D. Asst. Dir. of Educ., AFL-CIO
Cohen, David S., (AV) . . . . '63 '90 C.188 B.A. L.976 J.D. 2555 M St.,NW
Cohen, David S., (AV) . . . . '49 '75 C&L.659 B.A., J.D. [Cohen M.]
*PRACTICE AREAS: Information Technology Contracts; Commercial Arbitration; Commercial Litigation; Information Technology Licensing; Government Contracts.
Cohen, David S. . . . . '68 '94 C.273 B.B.A. L.245 J.D. [🄰 Milbank,T.H.&M.]
*PRACTICE AREAS: Litigation.
Cohen, Debbi M. . . . . '60 '85 C.910 B.A. L.880 J.D. 601 Pennsylvania Ave., N.W.
Cohen, Edwin S., (AV) . . . . '14 '35 C.692 B.A. L.893 J.D. [🄲 Covington&B.]
Cohen, Elena N. . . . . '57 '85 C.681 B.A. L.569 J.D. Sr. Coun., Natl. Womens Law Ctr.
Cohen, Elizabeth H. . . . . '66 '92 C.289 B.A. L.569 J.D. [Arent F.K.P.&K.]
*PRACTICE AREAS: Trademark Law; Internet Law; Copyright Law; Litigation.
Cohen, Felice D. '38 '63 C&L.966 B.A., LL.B.
(adm. in WI; not adm. in DC) 1933-47th St., N.W.‡
Cohen, Gary B. . . . . '55 '81 C.1044 B.B.A. L.107 J.D. 1730 Kay St., N.W.
Cohen, Gary M., (AV) . . . . '43 '68 C.1044 B.A. L.107 J.D. [Blumenfeld&C.]
*PRACTICE AREAS: Criminal and Civil Antitrust Litigation and Counseling; Telecommunications Law; Civil Litigation.
Cohen, Gary N. . . . . '57 '82 C.477 A.B. L.107 J.D. Ernst & Young
Cohen, Gary O., (AV) . . . . '— '64 C.880 A.B. L.309 J.D. [Foley&L.]
*PRACTICE AREAS: Securities Law.
Cohen, George H., (AV) . . . . '34 '61 C&L.188 B.A., LL.B. [Bredhoff&K.]
Cohen, Giles T. . . . . '70 '98 C.188 B.A. L.659 J.D. [🄰 Wilmer,C.&P.]
Cohen, H. Rodgin, (AV) '44 '68 C&L.309 B.A., LL.B.
(adm. in NY; not adm. in DC) [Sullivan&C.] (⊙New York, NY)
Cohen, Harold D., (AV) . . . . '14 '37 C&L.188 A.B., LL.B. 1301 K St., N.W.
Cohen, Harvey B., (AV) . . . . '30 '59 C.472 A.B. L.276 J.D. [Cohen G.] ⊙
Cohen, Harvey J. . . . . '73 '98 C.1349 B.A. L.472 J.D. [Margolius,M.D.R.&T.]
*PRACTICE AREAS: Real Estate; Real Estate Title Insurance; Commercial Transactions.
Cohen, Herbert, (AV) '33 '69
C.477 B.S.C.E. L.904 J.D. [Blank R.C.&M.] (See Pat. Sect.)
*PRACTICE AREAS: Trademarks; International Trademarks; Patents; International Patents.
Cohen, Irving P., (AV) . . . . '41 '70 C.569 B.S. L.276 J.D. [Thompson H.]
*PRACTICE AREAS: Tax Law; Estate Planning; Business Law; Personal Planning; Successions.
Cohen, Irwin, (AV) . . . . '41 '70 C.477 B.B.A. L.64 J.D. [Fulbright&J.]
*PRACTICE AREAS: Health Care.
Cohen, Jay G., (BV) '59 '87 C.1044 B.A. L.273 J.D.
(adm. in NY; not adm. in DC) [Akin,G.S.H.&F.]
Cohen, Jeff M. . . . . '59 '84 C.1044 B.A. L.273 J.D. [Nixon P.]
*PRACTICE AREAS: Corporate Finance; Energy Finance; Project Finance; Mergers and Acquisitions.
Cohen, Jeffrey Scott . . . . '66 '95 C&L.273 B.S.E.E., J.D. [🄰 Wilkinson B.K.]
*PRACTICE AREAS: Internet Technology; Telecommunications; Administrative Litigation; Appellate Practice.
Cohen, Jill F. . . . . '67 '92 C.477 B.A. L.472 J.D. [Cohen&C.]
*PRACTICE AREAS: Personal Injury; Medical Malpractice; Product Liability.
Cohen, Jodi B. '— '96 C.813 B.A. L.893 J.D.
(adm. in MD; not adm. in DC) [🄰 Skadden,A.S.M.&F.]
Cohen, John A. . . . . '66 '93 C.30 B.A. L.64 J.D. [🄰 Baker&M.]
*PRACTICE AREAS: Public Contracts and Utilities; Regulatory Law; Administrative Law.
Cohen, Jonathan A., (AV) '51 '76
C.1036 B.A. L.276 J.D. Dir., Legal Dept., Air Line Pilots Assn.
Cohen, Jonathan M. . . . . '68 '97 C.145 B.A. L.1066 J.D. [🄰 Gilbert H.&R.]
*PRACTICE AREAS: Complex Dispute Resolution.
Cohen, Jonathan V., (AV) . . . . '56 '83 C.659 B.S. L.276 J.D. [Wilkinson B.K.]
*PRACTICE AREAS: Telecommunications Law; Administrative Law.
Cohen, Justin H. '75 '00 C.645 B.S. L.273 J.D.
(adm. in PA; not adm. in DC) [🄰 Jordan C.&S.]
*PRACTICE AREAS: Litigation.
Cohen, Kay Chopard '58 '83 C.784 B.A. L.352 J.D.
(adm. in IA; not adm. in DC) Dep. Exec. Dir., Natl. Crim. Jus. Assn.
Cohen, Laurence J., (AV) . . . . '32 '59 C.659 B.S. L.976 LL.B. [Sherman,D.C.L.&Y.]
*PRACTICE AREAS: Labor and Employment Law; Union Labor Law.
Cohen, Leslie R. . . . . '50 '75 C.1036 B.A. L.945 J.D. [Dickstein S.M.&O.]
*PRACTICE AREAS: Civil Litigation; Insurance.
Cohen, Lois J. . . . . '— '84 C.1059 B.S. L.245 J.D. 3271 C Sutton Pl., N.W.
Cohen, Louis R., (AV) . . . . '40 '67 C&L.309 A.B., LL.B. [Wilmer,C.&P.]
*PRACTICE AREAS: Appellate Practice; Federal Litigation; Corporate Law.
Cohen, Marc R. . . . . '59 '85 C&L.976 B.A., J.D. [Shaw P.]
*PRACTICE AREAS: Banks & Banking.
Cohen, Margaret L. . . . . '47 '84 C.102 B.A. L.1009 J.D. Bereau of Natl. Aff.
Cohen, Marjorie Fay . . . . '53 '78 C.860 B.A. L.128 J.D. The Bureau of Natl. Affs., Inc.
Cohen, Mary Louise . . . . '52 '77 C.575 A.B. L.309 J.D. [Phillips&C.]
*PRACTICE AREAS: False Claims; Qui Tam.
Cohen, Mia F. . . . . '72 '98 C.103 B.A. L.477 J.D. [🄰 Jones,D.R.&P.]
Cohen, Michael Paul Austern, (AV) '65 '90 C.886 B.A. L.902 J.D.
[Howrey S.A.&W.]
*PRACTICE AREAS: Antitrust Law; Appellate Practice; Commercial Law; Complex Litigation; Products Liability Law.
Cohen, Michelle Weisberg . . . . '67 '92 C.1036 B.A. L.245 J.D. [🄲 Paul,H.J.&W.]
*PRACTICE AREAS: Telecommunications Law.
Cohen, Nelson C., (AV) . . . . '47 '73 C.645 B.S. L.273 J.D. [Zuckerman S.]
*PRACTICE AREAS: Commercial Litigation; Bankruptcy and Creditor Rights.
Cohen, Richard S. '34 '60 C.674 A.B. L.976 LL.B.
(adm. in NJ; not adm. in DC) [Bickerman D.R.] (⊙New Brunswick, NJ)
Cohen, Robert H. '28 '63
C.563 B.A. L.564 LL.B. Gen. Coun., National Assn. of Social Wkrs.
Cohen, Sharon A. '60 '85 C.861 B.A. L.1049 J.D.
(adm. in IL; not adm. in DC) 2700 Virginia Ave., NW‡
Cohen, Sheldon S., (AV) . . . . '27 '52 C&L.273 A.B., J.D. [🄲 Morgan,L.&B.]
Cohen, Stanley B., (AV) . . . . '25 '50 C.102 A.B. L.309 LL.B. 7600 Marbury Rd.‡
Cohen, Stephen B. . . . . '47 '73 C.966 B.A. L.94 J.D. 1899 L St., N.W.
Cohen, Steven A. . . . . '70 '95 C.367 B.A. L.569 J.D. [🄰 Arent F.K.P.&K.]
*PRACTICE AREAS: E-Commerce; Interactive Marketing and Advertising; Internet Law; Corporate Law; Securities.
Cohen, Susan Jeanblanc . . . . '70 '95 C.205 B.S.B.A. L.472 J.D. [🄰 Seyfarth S.]
*PRACTICE AREAS: Labor and Employment Law.
Cohen, Tracey H. . . . . '73 '98 C&L.446 B.A., J.D. [🄰 Covington&B.]
Cohen, Victor L. . . . . '45 '71 C&L.446 B.S., J.D. [🄲 Howrey S.A.&W.]
*PRACTICE AREAS: Antitrust Law.

Cohen, Vincent H., (AV) . . . . '36 '60 C&L.823 A.B., LL.B. [Hogan&H.]
*PRACTICE AREAS: Litigation.
Cohen, Wayne R. . . . . '66 '91 C.477 B.B.A. L.472 J.D. [Cohen&C.]
*PRACTICE AREAS: Personal Injury; Medical Malpractice; Criminal Defense; Product Liability.

Cohen & Cohen, (BV)
1000 Connecticut Avenue, NW Suite 505, 20006
Telephone: 202-955-4529 Fax: 202-955-3142 http://www.lawyers.com/cohen&cohenlaw
URL: http://www.cohenandcohen.net
Members of Firm: Wayne R. Cohen; Jill F. Cohen; Thomas J. Simeone. Associate: Craig D Miller; Adam R. Leighton.
Personal Injury, Medical Malpractice, Automobile Accidents and Injuries, Product Liability and Criminal Defense Law.
See Professional Biographies, WASHINGTON, DISTRICT OF COLUMBIA

Cohen Gettings, P.C., (AV)
1225 19th St., N.W., 7th Fl. (⊙Silver Spring, MD; Alexandria, Arlington, VA)

Cohen, Jay L., P.C.
(See Chevy Chase, Maryland)

Cohen, Milstein, Hausfeld & Toll, P.L.L.C., (AV) 🄱🄱
West Tower, Suite 500, 1100 New York Avenue, N.W., 20005-3964 ⊙
Telephone: 202-408-4600 Facsimile: 202-408-4699
Email: lawinfo@cmht.com URL: http://www.CMHT.com
Members of Firm: Jerry S. Cohen (1925-1995); Herbert E. Milstein; Michael D. Hausfeld; Steven J. Toll; Ann C. Yahner; Lisa M. Mezzetti; Andrew N. Friedman; Richard S. Lewis; Daniel S. Sommers; Daniel A. Small; Gary E. Mason; Joseph M. Sellers; Sharon A. Snyder; Mark S. Willis; Stephen Darley Annand (Not admitted in DC); Marc I. Machiz; Paul T. Gallagher; Murray T. S. Lewis (Resident, Seattle, Washington); Linda P. Nussbaum (Not admitted in DC; Resident, New York, New York). Associates: Christine E. Webber; Alexander E. Barnett (Resident, New York, New York); Matthew James Ide (Resident, Seattle, Washington Office); Suzette M. Malveaux; Keelyn M. Friesen (Not admitted in DC; Resident, Seattle, Washington); Mary N. Strimel; Douglas J. McNamara (Not admitted in DC); Agnieszka M. Fryszman; Deborah J. Vagins; Charles E. Tompkins; Donna Solen; Tamara J. Driscoll (Resident, Seattle, Washington Office); Elizabeth Haines Cronise; Julie Goldsmith (Resident, Seattle, Washington Office); Lesli C. Esposito (Not admitted in DC); Jessica Glick Lyn; Victoria S. Nugent (Not admitted in DC); Brian A. Ratner; Megan E. Jones (Not admitted in DC); Robert J. Wozniak, Jr. (Not admitted in DC); Joshua S. Devore (Not admitted in DC); Justine J. Kaiser (Not admitted in DC); R. Joseph Barton (Not admitted in DC); James Pizzirusso (Not admitted in DC). Of Counsel: Margaret G. Farrell; Marlene F. Gibbons; Cheryl Hamer Mackell; Susan R. Schwaiger (Not admitted in DC; Resident, New York, New York).
General Civil Trial and Appellate Practice in State and Federal Courts. Antitrust and Unfair Trade Practices, Securities, Civil Rights and Employment Law, Consumer Product Liability, Franchising, Mass Torts, and Toxic Tort Litigation. Complex, Multi-District and Class Action Litigation.
Seattle, Washington Office: 999 Third Avenue, Suite 3600, 98104. Telephone: 206-521-0080. Facsimile: 206-521-0166.
New York, New York Office: 825 Third Avenue, 30th Floor, 10022. Telephone: 212-838-7797. Fax: 212-838-7745.
See Professional Biographies, WASHINGTON, DISTRICT OF COLUMBIA

Cohen Mohr LLP, (AV)
Suite 504, 1055 Thomas Jefferson Street, N.W., 20007 ⊙
Telephone: 202-342-2550 Facsimile: 202-342-6147
URL: http://www.cohenmohr.com
David S. Cohen; Daniel H. DuVal (Resident, McLean, VA Office); Russell J. Gaspar; Victor G. Klingelhofer (Resident, McLean, VA, Office); Andrew J. Mohr; William F. Savarino. Of Counsel: Brian J. Craig; Laurel Ann Hockey; John J. O'Brien. Associates: C. Kelly Kroll; Rowena E. Laxa.
Corporate and Business Practice. Government Contracts, Computer Law, Financing Transactions, Commercial Contracts, Acquisitions, Civil Litigation, Business Law, Employment Law, Construction Law.
McLean, Virginia Office: 1420 Beverly Road, Suite 330, 22101. Telephone: 703-761-1100. Telecopier: 703-761-0180.
See Professional Biographies, WASHINGTON, DISTRICT OF COLUMBIA

Cohick, Cameron . . . . '57 '85 C.502 B.J. L.893 J.D. [Long A.&N.]
*PRACTICE AREAS: Litigation.
Cohn, Alan . . . . '71 '97 C.178 B.A. L.276 J.D. [🄰 Akin,G.S.H.&F.]
Cohn, Herbert B. . . . . '12 '36 C.976 A.B. L.309 LL.B. 1800 M St., N.W.
Cohn, Jerald S. . . . . '59 '85 C.823 B.A. L.276 J.D. [Holland&K.]
*PRACTICE AREAS: Commercial Real Estate Acquisitions and Sales; Real Estate Finance; Loan Workouts; Foreclosure; Secured Creditor Bankruptcy Representation.
Cohn, Joel M., (P.C.) . . . . '49 '76 C.966 B.A. L.180 J.D. [Akin,G.S.H.&F.]
*PRACTICE AREAS: Labor and Employment.
Cohn, Lawrence N., (AV) . . . . '43 '69 C.118 A.B. L.188 J.D. [Cohn&M.]
*PRACTICE AREAS: Communications Law; Employment Law.
Cohn, Marcus, (AV) . . . . '13 '39 C&L.145 B.A., J.D. [🄲 Cohn&M.]
Cohn, Richard '61 '91 C.1044 B.A. L.273 J.D.
(adm. in MD; not adm. in DC) 607 14th St., N.W.‡
Cohn, Richard A. . . . . '— '74 C.276 B.S. L.910 J.D. [Bryan C.]
*PRACTICE AREAS: Real Estate and Real Estate Finance Law; Creditors Rights Law; Bankruptcy Law; Business Law.
Cohn, Robert E., (AV) . . . . '45 '69 C.823 B.A. L.276 J.D. [Shaw P.]
*PRACTICE AREAS: Aviation; Administrative; Transportation.
Cohn, Robin F. . . . . '59 '85 C.1036 B.A. L.276 J.D. [🄲 Swidler B.S.F.]
*PRACTICE AREAS: Telecommunications.
Cohn, Shanna Monique . . . . '74 '99 C.880 B.A. L.976 J.D. [🄰 McKee N.]
*PRACTICE AREAS: Corporate; Securities; Mergers and Acquisitions; Capital Markets.
Cohn, Sharon Beth . . . . '70 '97 C.893 B.A. L.309 J.D. [🄰 Arnold&P.]
*PRACTICE AREAS: International Trade; Litigation.
Cohn, Sherman L. . . . . '32 '57 C&L.276 B.S., J.D. [Bickerman D.R.]
Cohn-Connor, Jeanne T., (BV) '57 '85 C.659 B.A. L.145 J.D.
(adm. in NY; not adm. in DC) [🄲 Verrill&D.]

Cohn and Marks, (AV) 🄱🄱
1920 N Street, N.W., Suite 300, 20036-1622
Telephone: 202-293-3860 Fax: 202-293-4827
URL: http://www.cohnmarks.com
Members of Firm: Joel H. Levy; Robert B. Jacobi; Roy R. Russo; Ronald A. Siegel; Lawrence N. Cohn; Richard A. Helmick; Wayne Coy, Jr.; J. Brian De Boice; Jerold L. Jacobs. Associates: Susan Valerie Sachs; Kevin M. Goldberg; Joseph M. Di Scipio. Of Counsel: Marcus Cohn; Leonard H. Marks; Richard M. Schmidt, Jr.
Communications, Media, Trade Association Practice. Practice Before Federal Courts and Agencies.
See Professional Biographies, WASHINGTON, DISTRICT OF COLUMBIA

Colaianni, Joseph V., (AV) . . . . '35 '62 C.215 B.S.E.E. L.273 J.D. [Patton B.] (Pat.)
Colaianni, Joseph V., Jr. '69 '96 C.446 B.S.E.E. L.273 J.D.
[🄰 Fish&R.] (See Pat. Sect.)
*PRACTICE AREAS: Intellectual Property Litigation.
Colaizzi, Roger A. . . . . '58 '83 C.216 B.A. L.1338 J.D. [Venable,A.B.H.&C.]
*PRACTICE AREAS: Litigation; Technology; Intellectual Property; Electronic Commerce; Commercial Law.
Colangelo, Aaron Strider '— '00 C.645 B.A. L.309 J.D.
Staff Atty., Natural Resources Defense Council
Colapinto, David K., (AV) . . . . '58 '88 [Kohn,K.&C.]
*PRACTICE AREAS: Whistleblower Litigation; Civil Liberties; Privacy Law; Freedom of Information; Forensic Science.
Colarulli, Paul F. . . . . '50 '77 C.319 B.A. L.94 J.D. [Stier,A.&M.]
*PRACTICE AREAS: Complex Litigation; Corporate Compliance; Civil RICO; Employment Law; Internal Corporate Investigations.

Colatriano, Vincent J. ... '65 '90 C&L.273 B.A., J.D. [Cooper&K.]
*PRACTICE AREAS: Trial and Appellate Litigation; Administrative Law and Litigation; Litigation; Constitutional Law.

Colbert, Damon D. '76 '01 C.198 B.A. L.276 J.D.
(adm. in VA; not adm. in DC) [🄰 Shaw P.]

Colbert, Edward T., (AV) ... '47 '73 C&L.446 A.B., J.D. [Kenyon&K.] (See Pat. Sect.)
*PRACTICE AREAS: Intellectual Property Litigation; Trademark Counseling and Prosecution; Unfair Competition and Related Litigation.

Colbert, Lawr. L. ... '11 '35 C.273 B.S. L.276 J.D. 5139 33rd St., N.W. (Pat.)

Colby, Amie V. ... '72 '99 C.880 B.A. L.276 J.D. [🄰 Troutman S.]
*PRACTICE AREAS: Administrative Law; Energy; Environmental Law; Regulatory Law.

Colby, Keli ... '62 '91 C.822 B.A. L.904 J.D. [🄰 Arent F.K.P.&K.]
*PRACTICE AREAS: Real Estate Finance; Real Estate; Finance; Business Law.

Colclough, Jacqueline T. ... '65 '91 C.708 B.S.N. L.128 J.D. [🄰 Thompson C.]
*PRACTICE AREAS: General Corporate; Transportation; Commercial Finance.

Cole, Alexa A. ... '71 '00 C.012 B.A. L.1194 J.D. [🄰 Bailey]
*PRACTICE AREAS: Environmental Law; Commercial Litigation.

Cole, Carol L. '72 '00 C.446 B.S. L.904 J.D.
(adm. in VA; not adm. in DC; See Pat. Sect.) [🄰 Finnegan,H.F.G.&D.]
*PRACTICE AREAS: Biotechnology Patent Prosecution; Chemical Patent Prosecution; Patent Infringement; Patent Prosecution.

Cole, Charles G., (AV) ... '52 '76 C.976 B.A. L.309 J.D. [Steptoe&J.]
*PRACTICE AREAS: Pension and Profit Sharing Law; Administrative Law; Appellate Practice; Bankruptcy Law.

Cole, Charles M. ... '63 '94 C.401 B.S. L.30 J.D. [🄰 Clifford C.R.&W.]
*PRACTICE AREAS: Corporate.

Cole, Christopher A. ... '66 '94 C.976 B.S. L.94 J.D. [🄲 Paul,H.J.&W.]
*PRACTICE AREAS: Litigation; Environmental Law; False Advertising.

Cole, Daniel Randolph, Jr., (AV) ... '41 '67 C.902 A.B. L.273 J.D. [Krooth&A.]
*PRACTICE AREAS: Real Estate Development and Finance Law; Transactional Law.

Cole, David D. ... '58 '85 C&L.976 B.A., J.D. Prof. of Law, Georgetown Univ.

Cole, David S. ... '68 '95 C.696 B.A. L.273 J.D. [🄰 Baker&M.]
*PRACTICE AREAS: Mergers and Acquisitions; Corporate and Partnership Law; Securities and Financial Products; Aviation and Aerospace Technology; Entertainment, the Arts and Sports Law.

Cole, Eileen M. ... '72 '98 C&L.893 B.A., J.D. [🄰 White&C.]
*PRACTICE AREAS: Litigation.

Cole, Elliot H., (AV) ... '32 '60 C&L.94 B.S., J.D. [Patton B.]

Cole, James M., (AV) ... '— '79 C.1165 B.A. L.1065 J.D. [Bryan C.]
*PRACTICE AREAS: White Collar Criminal Defense; Corporate Investigations.

Cole, James V., II ... '67 '96 C.893 B.A. L.1209 J.D. [Counts,P.-D.&D.]

Cole, Janice L. '62 '91 C.910 B.A. L.64 J.D.
Asst. Gen. Coun., Washington Metro. Area Transit Auth.
*RESPONSIBILITIES: Litigation.

Cole, John P., Jr., (AV) ... '30 '56 C.10 B.S. L.273 LL.B. [Cole,R.&B.]
*PRACTICE AREAS: Communications; Cable Television; Cable Franchising; Appellate Litigation; Constitutional Law.

Cole, Keith N. ... '58 '88 C.228 B.S.E. L.893 J.D. [Swidler B.S.F.]
*PRACTICE AREAS: Governmental Law; Legislative Practice; Environmental Law.

Cole, Kenneth W. '47 '73 C.846 B.A. L.326 J.D.
(adm. in TX; not adm. in DC) V.P., AlliedSignal Inc.

Cole, Michael F. ... '— '66 C.880 B.A. L.569 LL.B. [🄲 Bergeson&C.]
*PRACTICE AREAS: Food and Drug Regulation; Food, Drug and Cosmetic Law; Chemical Regulation; Environmental Compliance; Environmental Regulation.

Cole, Montina M. ... '66 '92 C.900 B.A. L.893 J.D. 901 15th St., N.W.

Cole, Robert T., (AV) ... '32 '56 C.659 B.S. L.309 LL.B. [Alston&B.]
*PRACTICE AREAS: Transfer Pricing; International Taxation; International Tax Controversies; Corporate Taxation.

Cole, Tanisha M. ... '72 '98 C&L.910 B.A. [🄰 Passman&K.]
*PRACTICE AREAS: Employment Law; Federal Civil Service; Equal Employment Opportunity Law; Labor Law.

Cole Corette & Abrutyn, A Prof. Corp. ... 805 15th St., N.W.

Cole, Raywid & Braverman, L.L.P., (AV)
1919 Pennsylvania Avenue, N.W., 20006 ⊙
Telephone: 202-659-9750 Cable Address: "Crab" Telecopier: 202-452-0067
URL: http://www.crblaw.com
Partners: John P. Cole, Jr.; Alan Raywid (1930-1991); Burt A. Braverman; Robert L. James; John D. Seiver; Wesley R. Heppler; Paul Glist; David M. Silverman; James F. Ireland, III; Maurita K. Coley; Steven Jay Horvitz; Christopher W. Savage; Robert G. Scott, Jr.; Susan Whelan Westfall; Theresa Zeterberg Cavanaugh; Karlyn D. Stanley; John Davidson Thomas; John C. Dodge; Jeremy H. Stern (Also at El Segundo, California Office); Maria T. Browne; Donna C. Rattley; Edward L. Donohue; T. Scott Thompson; Madie D. Gustafson (Not admitted in DC). Associates: Adam S. Caldwell; William F. Bly (Not admitted in DC; Also at El Segundo, California Office); Christin S. McMeley (Not admitted in DC); Heidi Pearlman Salow; Erik J. Cecil (Not admitted in DC); Brenda J. Boykin; Robert Jystad (Not admitted in DC; Also at El Segundo, California Office); David N. Tobenkin; Rachael A. Galoob (Not admitted in DC); Laura G. Schloss; Brian M. Josef (Not admitted in DC); K. C. Halm (Not admitted in DC); Adrienne P. Byrd; Christopher W. Hembree; Felicia K. Watson; Genevieve D. Sapir; Gerie A. Miller; Jill M. Valenstein; Kristy J. Hall (Not admitted in DC); Danielle Frappier (Not admitted in DC); Steven J. Gerber; Cody Harrison (Not admitted in DC); Maria Celeste Moran (Not admitted in DC); Timothy Tobin (Not admitted in DC). Of Counsel: Frances J. Chetwynd; Ellen S. Deutsch; Ann E. Flowers; Frederick W. Giroux; Geoffrey C. Cook; Terence S. Cooke; Joel Pearlman (Not admitted in DC); James R. J. Scheltema (Not admitted in DC). Special Counsel: Suzanne E. Curtis (Not admitted in DC).
Telecommunications, Cable Television, Telephony, Wireless and Wireline Communications, Satellite Communications, Broadcast, Programming, Copyright, Trademark, Information and Privacy, Corporate and Commercial Law, Antitrust and Constitutional Law, Civil, Administrative and Commercial Practice in all Courts, State and Federal Agencies, State and Federal Legislatures.
El Segundo, California Office: 2381 Rosecrans Avenue, Suite 110. Telephone: 310-643-7999. Fax: 310-643-7997.

See Professional Biographies, WASHINGTON, DISTRICT OF COLUMBIA

Colella, Ugo ... '66 '97 C.813 B.A. L.861 J.D. [🄰 Patton B.]

Coleman, Brian A. ... '72 '97 C.105 B.A. L.273 J.D. [🄰 Drinker B.&R.]

Coleman, Brian R. '67 '98 C.112 B.S.E.E. L.1065 J.D.
(adm. in CA; not adm. in DC; Pat.) [Oppenheimer W.&D.]
*PRACTICE AREAS: Intellectual Property.

Coleman, Chritopher M. '71 '98 C.446 B.A. L.1202 J.D.
(adm. in MD; not adm. in DC) [🄰 Jordan C.&S.]

Coleman, Deborah R., (AV) ... '62 '89 C.893 B.A. L.945 J.D. [Leventhal,S.&L.]
*PRACTICE AREAS: Communications Law; Media Law.

Coleman, Donna Maria '60 '87 C.228 B.S. L.575 J.D.
(adm. in NC; not adm. in DC) Assoc. Gen. Coun., Fannie Mae
*RESPONSIBILITIES: Real Estate; Mortgage Banking Law; Finance.

Coleman, Dorothy Burke '49 '87 C.706 B.A. L.276 J.D.
(adm. in MD; not adm. in DC) 1666 K St., N.W.‡

Coleman, Douglas M., (AV) '60 '85 C.893 B.A. L.692 J.D.
(adm. in VA; not adm. in DC) [Carter&C.] ⊙
*PRACTICE AREAS: Professional Liability; Medical Malpractice; Insurance Law; Commercial Law; ERISA.

Coleman, Edward D. ... '34 '63 C&L.276 A.B., J.D. [Webster,C.&B.]
*PRACTICE AREAS: Taxation; Exempt Organizations.

Coleman, Francis T., (AV) ... '39 '65 C&L.276 A.B., J.D. [Williams M.]
*PRACTICE AREAS: Arbitration; Collective Bargaining; Discrimination; Employer Liability; Employment at Will.

Coleman, Jacqueline E. ... '70 '96 C.309 B.A. L.477 J.D. [🄰 Gibson,D.&C.]
*PRACTICE AREAS: General Litigation; Litigation; Securities Litigation; Antitrust.

Coleman, Lovida H., Jr., (AV) ... '49 '77 C.681 A.B. L.976 J.D. [Sutherland A.&B.]
*PRACTICE AREAS: Federal Practice; Business Litigation; Federal Criminal Law; Government Investigations; Discrimination.

Coleman, Lynn R., (AV) ... '39 '64 C.1 B.A. L.846 LL.B. [Skadden,A.S.M.&F.]

Coleman, March ... '42 '69 C.604 B.A. L.30 LL.B. [🄲 Arnold&P.]
*PRACTICE AREAS: Litigation; Antitrust.

Coleman, March Dolan '70 '97 C.276 A.B. L.665 J.D.
(adm. in VA; not adm. in DC) [🄰 Steptoe&J.]

Coleman, Paul D., (AV) ... '47 '73 C.575 B.S. L.276 J.D. [Hoppel,M.&C.]
*PRACTICE AREAS: Maritime Administrative Law; Shipping Regulations; Transportation; Energy Law.

Coleman, Sana D. ... '73 '98 C.228 A.B. L.276 J.D. [🄰 Arent F.K.P.&K.]
*PRACTICE AREAS: Telecommunications; Intellectual Property; Trademarks.

Coleman, Staci D. ... '70 '97 C.802 B.S. L.276 J.D. [🄰 Hobbs,S.D.&W.]

Coleman, Terry, (AV) ... '47 '73 C.494 B.A. L.309 J.D. [Bennett,T.&C.]
*PRACTICE AREAS: Health Law; Food and Drug Regulation.

Coleman, William T., Jr., (AV) ... '20 '47 C.659 A.B. L.309 LL.B. [🄲 O'Melveny&M.]
*PRACTICE AREAS: Constitutional Law; Appellate Practice; Trial Litigation; Corporate Law; Business Law.

Coleman, Wm. H., Jr. ... '17 '43 L.180 LL.B. 4445 13th St., N.E.

Coles, Terence A. '63 '96 C.1286 B.S. L.329 J.D.
(adm. in MD; not adm. in DC) Asst. Corp. Coun.

Coles, Todd R. ... '64 '91 C.339 B.A. L.904 J.D. [Troutman S.]
*PRACTICE AREAS: Energy; Project Finance; Project Development.

Coley, Maurita K., (AV) ... '56 '82 C.475 B.A. L.276 J.D. [Cole,R.&B.]
*PRACTICE AREAS: Media Law; Internet Law; Cable TV; Entertainment Law.

Colgate, Jessie M., (AV) '50 '77
C.681 A.B. L.276 J.D. Sr. V.P., New York Life Insurance Company

Coll, Carolina '70 '00 C.870 B.S. L.276 J.D.
(adm. in VA; not adm. in DC) [🄰 Thompson H.]
*PRACTICE AREAS: Customs Law; International Trade; Antitrust; FCC Regulation.

Coll, Pelayo ... '71 '97 C.446 B.A. L.904 J.D. [🄰 Arnold&P.]
*PRACTICE AREAS: Real Estate.

Coll, Robert W., (AV) ... '29 '58 C&L.273 B.A., LL.B. 2905 Davenport St., NW‡

Colleli, Ralph ... '52 '77 C.446 B.A. L.276 J.D. Sr. Atty., Amer. Petroleum Institute

Collery, Elizabeth D. ... '60 '87 C.976 B.A. L.309 J.D. 725 12th St. N.W.

Colley, Mark D., (AV) ... '55 '80 C.945 B.A. L.893 J.D. [Holland&K.]
*PRACTICE AREAS: Government Contracts Law; Litigation.

Colleye, Beth Hilliard ... '66 '97 C.178 B.A. L.145 J.D. [🄰 Fried,F.H.S.&J.]
*PRACTICE AREAS: Corporate Law; Securities.

Colleye, Elizabeth Hilliard '66 '97
C.178 B.A. L.145 J.D. 1001 Pennsylvania Ave., Nw, Suite 800

Collier, Anne E. ... '66 '92 C&L.477 B.A., J.D. [🄰 Miller&C.]
*PRACTICE AREAS: Taxation; Tax Accounting; Federal Tax Controversies; Tax Litigation; Tax Accounting of Technology.

Collier, Earl M., Jr. ... '47 '75 C.976 B.A. L.893 J.D. Vitas Healthcare Corp.

Collier, Frances ... '47 '74 C.112 B.A. L.180 J.D. 3833 Cathedral Ave., N.W.

Collier, H. Guy, (AV) ... '50 '76 C.893 B.A. L.692 J.D. [Shaw P.]
*PRACTICE AREAS: Health Law.

Collier, Tom, (AV) ... '51 '75 C.893 B.A. L.500 J.D. [Steptoe&J.]
*PRACTICE AREAS: Settlement Advocacy; Risk Analysis; Natural Resources; Indian Law; Technology Law.

Collier Shannon Scott, PLLC, (AV)
Suite 400, 3050 K Street, N.W., 20007 ⊙
Telephone: 202-342-8400 Facsimile: 202-342-8451
Email: lawyers@colliershannon.com URL: http://www.colliershannon.com
Members of Firm: Robert A. Collier (1917-1984); William W. Scott; David A. Hartquist; R. Timothy Columbus; Lauren R. Howard; Michael D. Sherman; Mark L. Austrian; John B. Williams; Paul C. Rosenthal; John L. Wittenborn; Jeffrey L. Leiter; Jeffrey S. Beckington; Judith L. Oldham; Laurence J. Lasoff; Patrick J. Coyne; William C. MacLeod; William J. Rodgers (Not admitted in DC); Michael J. Coursey; Robin H. Gilbert; William M. Guerry, Jr.; John B. Brew; Kerrie L. Hook; Russell S. Frye; Scott Sinder; John E. Villafranco; Thomas W. Mitchell; Thomas E. Gilbertsen; Richard H. Kjeldgaard; Michael H. Knight; David E. Johnston (Resident, Charlotte, North Carolina Office); Kathleen E. McDermott; Allan J. Weiner; Kathryn McMahon-Lohrer; Lewis Rose; John P. Feldman; Gregory M. Scott; Chet M. Thompson; D. Reed Freeman, Jr. Of Counsel: Thomas F. Shannon; Frank F. Murtha (Not admitted in DC); Michael R. Kershow; Kathleen Weaver Cannon; Mary Tuck Staley; David C. Smith, Jr.; R. Alan Luberda; Maureen Enright; Frank Koszorus, Jr.; Michael O. Hill; Mary C. Cronin (Not admitted in DC); Therese Marie Woods; Lynn Duffy Maloney. Associates: Stephanie Siegel; William M. Bailey; Michael R. McCarthy; Michael R. Carithers, Jr.; Katharine I. Matthews; David J. Ervin; Ann M. Plaza; Adam H. Gordon; Mark V. Wilson (Not admitted in DC); Mary Jean Fell; David R. Yohannan; Garrett B.M. Duarte; James M. Pacious (Not admitted in DC); Carl R. Katz; Christy Hallam DeSanctis; Adam B. Cramer; John N. Coulby, III; Joseph J. Green; Eric R. McClafferty; Theresa Adams Coatzee; John M. Herrmann; Grace W. Kim; Jeffrey A. Kauffman; Douglas S. Kantor (Not admitted in DC); Lisa Goldblatt; Lana L. Leiby; Thomas S. Cushing III (Not admitted in DC); Victoria L. Lippincott; Mercedes K. Kelley (Not admitted in DC); Nicholas A. Widnell; Alexander Zelikson; Christie L. Grymes; Christina Bechak Parascandola; Andrew M. Johnson (Resident, Charlotte, North Carolina Office); Elisa A. Nemiroff; Robert T.C. Vermylen; Sapna Delacourt; Kristin Pierce Barry; Halye Sugarman; Jennifer E. McCadney; John H.R. Lanou; Mark W. Rygiel (Not admitted in DC); Jason Edward Murphy (Resident, Charlotte, North Carolina Office); Gonzalo E. Mon.
Advertising and Marketing, Antitrust and Trade Regulation, Consumer Protection and Advertising, Energy, Environmental, Government Relations, Intellectual Property, International Trade, Labor and Employment, Litigation, Trade Associations, Taxation.
Reference: Riggs National Bank, Washington, D.C.
Charlotte, North Carolina Office: 277 West Trade Street, Suite 2020.

See Professional Biographies, WASHINGTON, DISTRICT OF COLUMBIA

Collins, Alexander R. '72 '00 C.103 B.A. L.93 J.D.
(adm. in MA; not adm. in DC) [🄰 Howrey S.A.&W.]
*PRACTICE AREAS: Antitrust.

Collins, Alexis L. ... '73 '99 C.604 B.A. L.145 J.D. [🄰 Cleary,G.S.&H.]

Collins, Angela F. ... '— '00 C.600 B.A. L.180 J.D. 701 Pennsylvania Avenue, N.W.

Collins, Bruce Dennis ... '51 '87 C.188 B.S. L.273 J.D. V.P. & Gen. Coun., C-SPAN

Collins, Charlotte '— '77 C.512 B.A. L.276 J.D.
(adm. in MD; not adm. in DC) [🄲 Powell,G.F.&M.]
*PRACTICE AREAS: Health Care.

Collins, Christopher H., (AV) ... '53 '79 C.93 A.B. L.128 J.D. [Holland&K.]
*PRACTICE AREAS: Land Use and Zoning Law; Real Estate; Municipal Law; Historic Preservation; Foreign Missions.

Collins, Christopher M., (BV) '60 '88 C.893 B.A. L.273 J.D.
(adm. in VA; not adm. in DC) [🄲 Stevens,D.M.&M.] (⊙Mc Lean, VA)
*PRACTICE AREAS: Intellectual Property.

Collins, Courtney Helen '71 '97 C.914 B.A. L.945 J.D.
(adm. in VA; not adm. in DC) Ernst & Young

Collins, Daniel F., (AV) '42 '68
C.1019 B.A. L.904 J.D. V.P. & Assoc. Gen. Coun., El Paso Corp.

Collins, Elizabeth C. ... '68 '96 C.165 B.A. L.30 J.D. [🄰 Squire,S.&D.]

Collins, J. Barclay, III ... '67 '94 C.103 A.B. L.178 J.D. [🄲 Wilmer,C.&P.]
*PRACTICE AREAS: Tax Law.

Collins, Jeremiah A., (AV) ... '49 '76 C.722 A.B. L.813 J.D. [Bredhoff&K.]

Collins, Jeremiah C., (AV) ... '29 '54 C&L.276 B.S., LL.B. [🄲 Williams&C.]

Collins, Jo Ann Petroziello ... '67 '92 C.645 B.S. L.607 J.D. Central Pension Fund, IUOE

Collins, John M. .... '63 '91 C.164 B.A. L.900 J.D. 1875 Connecticut Avenue, N.W.
Collins, John T., (AV) .... '46 '72 C.321 B.A. L.276 J.D. [Steptoe&J.]
*PRACTICE AREAS: Banking Law; Financial Institutions Law; Legislative Practice.
Collins, Kathleen W. .... '50 '75 C.645 B.A. L.831 J.D. [Morgan,L.&B.]
Collins, Kevin B. .... '65 '92 C.971 B.S. L.64 J.D. [Venable,A.B.H.&C.]
*PRACTICE AREAS: Intellectual Property Litigation; Commercial Litigation; Civil Litigation.
Collins, Leonard C., (AV) .... '21 '46 C.93 A.B. L.128 J.D. 471 H St., N.W.
Collins, Mark A. .... '64 '90 C.1163 B.A. L.800 J.D. [McDermott,W.&E.]
Collins, Martin J. '68 '98 C.128 B.A. L.64 J.D.
(adm. in MD; not adm. in DC) Atty., Pricewaterhouse Coopers LLP
Collins, Michael J. '69 '95 C&L.602 B.B.A., J.D.
(adm. in VA; not adm. in DC) [🄰 Gibson,D.&C.]
*PRACTICE AREAS: Employee Benefits; Taxation.
Collins, Ollie '— '30
(adm. in AR; not adm. in DC) 4201 Cathedral Ave., N.W.‡
Collins, Randolph M. .... '56 '91 C&L.273 B.A., J.D. [🄰 Baach R.&L.P.]
*PRACTICE AREAS: Commercial Litigation; Employment Law; Public Policy Legislation.
Collins, Scott P. .... '71 '97 C.696 B.A. L.823 J.D. [🄰 Piper M.R.&W.]
*PRACTICE AREAS: Real Estate; Commercial Leasing.
Collins, Sheri M. L. '66 '92
C.145 B.A. L.1365 J.D. [🄰 Bonner K.T.&C.] (⊙Rockville, MD)
*PRACTICE AREAS: Insurance Coverage Litigation; Professional Liability Defense; General Liability Defense.
Collins, Willis B., Jr. .... '16 '41 L.180 LL.B. 5444 Nebr. Ave., N.W.
Collyer, Rosemary M., (AV) .... '45 '77 C.856 B.A. L.208 J.D. [Crowell&M.]
Colman, Michelle L. .... '74 '99 C.228 B.A. L.602 J.D. [🄰 Fried,F.H.S.&J.]
*PRACTICE AREAS: Securities; Corporate Law.
Colman, Richard T., (AV) .... '35 '62 C.602 A.B. L.94 LL.B. [Howrey S.A.&W.]
*PRACTICE AREAS: Antitrust Law; Commercial Law; Litigation.

Colman, Susan E., (AV) '46 '81 C.477 B.S. L.1218 J.D.
International Square, PMB 400, 1825 I Street, N.W., Suite 400, 20006
Telephone: 202-775-4937 Fax: 301-469-7862
Email: colman@patriot.net
Information Technology and Computer Law including Software Licensing and Piracy Litigation (International and Domestic). Trademark Prosecution and Litigation, Copyrights and Intellectual Property Law.
See Professional Biographies, WASHINGTON, DISTRICT OF COLUMBIA

Colodny, Edwin I. .... '26 '51 C.696 A.B. L.309 LL.B. [🄲 Paul,H.J.&W.]
*PRACTICE AREAS: Business Law; Marketing; Advertising; Sales Promotion Law; Aviation Law.
Colon, Andres .... '70 '95 C.1507 B.A. L.107 J.D. [🄰 Dickstein S.M.&O.]
*PRACTICE AREAS: General Litigation.
Colson, David A., (BV) .... '43 '75 C.1073 B.A. L.1066 J.D. [LeBoeuf,L.G.&M.]
*PRACTICE AREAS: International Law; Environmental Law.
Colson, Earl M., (AV) .... '30 '57 C.823 B.S. L.309 LL.B. [Arent F.K.P.&K.]
*PRACTICE AREAS: Business Planning Law; Corporate Law; ESOPS; Estate Planning Law; Tax Law.
Colston, Fred .... '21 '54 C.414 A.B. L.30 LL.B. 4014 Georgia Ave., N.W.
Colston, Kristen M. .... '69 '97 C.518 A.B. L.569 J.D. [🄰 Shaw P.]
Colton, Barnum L., Jr., (AV) .... '30 '62 C.855 B.S. L.30 LL.B. 1000 16th St., N.W.
Colton, Carolyn '56 '81 C&L.101 B.S., J.D.
V.P. & Asst. Gen. Coun., Ramada Intl., Inc.
Colton, David S. .... '69 '96 C.446 B.S. L.64 J.D. 2300 N St. NW
Colton, Kendrew H., (AV) .... '55 '80 C.164 B.A. L.930 J.D. [Fitch,E.T.&F.] (Pat.)
*PRACTICE AREAS: Intellectual Property Law; Patents; Biotechnology; Chemicals; Trade Secrets.
Colucci, Marlene M. .... '62 '89 C.112 B.A. L.276 J.D. [🄲 Akin,G.S.H.&F.]
*PRACTICE AREAS: Public Policy.
Columbus, R. Timothy, (AV) .... '49 '74 C.309 A.B. L.893 J.D. [Collier S.S.]
Colwell, William J. .... '69 '99 C.597 B.A. L.228 J.D. [🄰 Wiley R.&F.]
Coman, Gabriela I. .... '68 '00 C.1138 B.S. L.1009 J.D. [🄰 Dickstein S.M.&O.]
*PRACTICE AREAS: Intellectual Property.
Combs, Ann Laine '56 '81 C.602 B.A. L.273 J.D.
V.P. & Chf. Coun., Retire. & Pens., Amer. Council of Life Ins.
*RESPONSIBILITIES: Retirement and Pensions; Long-Term Care.
Comer, Amy B. '71 '99 C.877 B.A. L.861 J.D.
(adm. in NY; not adm. in DC) [🄰 Thelen R.&P.]
*PRACTICE AREAS: Energy.
Comer, Edward H., (AV) '50 '74
C.145 B.A. L.659 J.D. V.P. & Gen. Coun., Edison Elec. Institute
Comess, Faye K. .... '60 '87 C.37 B.A. L.276 J.D. Law Clk., Supr. Ct. J.
Comey, Eugene J., (AV) .... '48 '77 C.728 A.B. L.145 J.D. [Comey B.&L.]
Comey Boyd & Luskin, (AV) .... 1025 Thomas Jefferson Street, N.W., Suite 420 East

Comiskey & Hunt
(See McLean, Virginia)

Comizio, V. Gerard, (BV) .... '55 '81 C.262 B.A. L.276 L.L.M [Thacher P.&W.]
*PRACTICE AREAS: Corporate and Financial Institutions; Securities.
Commerford, Cheryl B. '63 '88 C&L.378 B.G.S., J.D.
(adm. in KS; not adm. in DC) [Bassman,M.&A.]
Commins, Gregory J., Jr., (BV) ...... '65 '91 C.188 B.A. L.276 J.D. [Howrey S.A.&W.]
*PRACTICE AREAS: Antitrust; Commercial Law; Insurance Coverage.
Comstock, Earl W. '— '96 C.112 B.A. L.1209 J.D.
(adm. in AK; not adm. in DC) [Sher&B.]
*PRACTICE AREAS: Telecommunications; Government Relations; Legislative Practice; Marine Law; Environmental Law.
Comstock, Robert F., (AV) .... '36 '65 C&L.128 A.B., LL.B. [Comstock&R.]
Comstock & Reilly, L.L.P., (AV) .... 5225 Wisconsin Ave., N.W.
Comtois, Mark Charles '59 '96 C.871 B.S.M.E. L.1209 J.D.
(adm. in VA; not adm. in DC; Pat.) [🄲 Carter,L.&M.]
*PRACTICE AREAS: Intellectual Property; Litigation.
Conaboy, Richard P. '25 '51 C.754 B.A. L.128 LL.B.
(adm. in PA; not adm. in DC) Chmn., U.S. Sentencing Comm.
Conaghan, Thomas P. .... '70 '96 C&L.602 B.A., J.D. [🄰 Morgan,L.&B.]
Conaton, Erin Duffy .... '73 '00 C.276 B.A. L.180 J.D. [🄰 Dechert]
*PRACTICE AREAS: Investment Management; Financial Services Law.
Conaty, Barry .... '61 '89 C.976 B.A. L.273 J.D. [Akin,G.S.H.&F.] (⊙Denver, CO)
*PRACTICE AREAS: Environmental Law.
Conaway, Harry J. .... '52 '80 C.855 B.A. L.273 J.D. William M. Mercer, Inc.
Conboy, Brian .... '38 '63 C&L.262 B.S., LL.B. [🄲 Willkie F.&G.] ‡
Concannon, Christy .... '62 '87 C.264 B.A. L.128 J.D. [Baptiste&W.]
*PRACTICE AREAS: Labor Relations; ERISA; Employment Law.
Condit, Richard E. .... '58 '86 C.570 B.S. L.1162 J.D. Govt. Accountability Project
Condon, Robert F., (AV) '36 '61 C.724 B.A. L.276 J.D.
[Artabane&B.] (⊙Washington)
*PRACTICE AREAS: Commercial Litigation; Employment Law; Real Estate; Construction Law; Professional Ethics.
Condon, Robert F., (AV) '36 '61 C.724 B.A. L.276 J.D.
[🄲 Mitchell&D.] (⊙Washington)
*PRACTICE AREAS: Commercial Litigation; Employment Law; Real Estate; Construction Law; Professional Ethics.

Condon & Forsyth LLP, (AV)
1016 Sixteenth Street, N.W., 20036 ⊙
Telephone: 202-289-0500 Telecopier: 202-289-4524
Email: twhalen@condonlaw.com URL: http://www.condonlaw.com
Resident Partners: Thomas J. Whalen. Of Counsel: Evelyn D. Sahr. Senior Attorney: David G. Schryver. Resident Associates: John J. Delaney; Brenda A. Heffernan.
Civil and Commercial Litigation. Aviation, Business, Employment, International Trade, Products Liability, Administrative and Insurance Law.
New York, N.Y. Office: 685 Third Avenue, 14th Floor. Telephone: 212-921-5100. Telecopier: 212-370-4453; 212-370-4483; 212-370-4465.
Los Angeles, California Office: 1801 Avenue of the Stars, Suite 1450, 90067. Telephone: 310-557-2030. Telecopier: 310-557-1299.
See Professional Biographies, WASHINGTON, DISTRICT OF COLUMBIA

Condos, Barbara Moir .... '44 '77 C.999 B.A. L.273 J.D. [🄰 M.Heller&Assoc.]
*PRACTICE AREAS: Personal Injury; Divorce; Family Law.
Condray, Mattie Cohan '63 '88
C.66 B.A. L.276 J.D. Sr. Asst. Gen. Coun., Legal Services Corp.
Condrell, William K., (AV) .... '26 '51 C.976 B.S. L.309 LL.B. [🄲 Steptoe&J.]
*PRACTICE AREAS: Public School Law; Individuals with Disabilities Education Act; Americans with Disabilities Act.
Condron, Peter C. .... '62 '88 C.724 B.S. L.945 J.D. [🄲 Wallace K.M.&B.]
*PRACTICE AREAS: Litigation.
Conforti, David A. .... '64 '90 C.165 B.A. L.724 J.D. [🄰 Tobin,O.&E.]
*PRACTICE AREAS: Corporate; Business; Commercial Litigation.
Conkling, Carolyn W. .... '59 '89 C&L.276 B.S., J.D. [🄰 Willkie F.&G.]
Conlan, Robert J., Jr. .... '60 '88 C.446 B.S. L.273 J.D. [Sidley A.B.&W.]
Conley, James B. .... '51 '80 C.174 B.S. L.208 J.D. Ernst & Young
Conley, Lawrence E. '52 '82 C.602 B.Arch. L.823 J.D.
Sr. Consltn't, Warner Construction Consultants, Inc.
Conley, Robert B. .... '60 '93 C.197 B.A. L.893 J.D. [Arnold&P.]
*PRACTICE AREAS: Food and Drug Law; Products Liability.
Conlon, Michael J., (AV) .... '48 '74 C.602 A.B. L.276 J.D. [Conlon,F.P.&P.]
*PRACTICE AREAS: Corporate Law; Trade Association Law; Real Estate Law.

Conlon, Frantz, Phelan & Pires, LLP, (AV)
Suite 700, 1818 N Street, N.W., 20036
Telephone: 202-331-7050 Fax: 202-331-9306
Email: firm@CFPPLLAW.com URL: http://www.lawyers.com/conlonfrantzphelan&pires
Partners: David J. Frantz; Michael J. Conlon; Brian P. Phelan; Alexander J. Pires, Jr.; Mary Jean Fassett. Associates: Anurag Varma; Michelle A. Pilgrim; Ingrid Hutto (Not admitted in DC); James E. Fisher, II (Not admitted in DC); Malcolm C. Grace; Greg J. Kirschner (Not admitted in DC); Cassandra D. Mason (Not admitted in DC); Jenny Celestin.
General, Trial and Appellate Practice. Civil Rights, Complex Litigation, Agriculture, Real Estate, Trade Association, Government Contracts, Personal Injury, Medical Malpractice, Administrative, Antitrust, Wills and Estates and Family Law.
See Professional Biographies, WASHINGTON, DISTRICT OF COLUMBIA

Conn, Richard A., Jr., (AV) .... '— '82 C.197 B.A. L.262 J.D. [Latham&W.]
*PRACTICE AREAS: Bankruptcy; Debtor and Creditor; Insurance; Investment in Russia; Litigation.
Connall, Desmond D., Jr., (AV) ...... '54 '81 C.674 A.B. L.813 J.D. [Womble C.S.&R.]
*PRACTICE AREAS: Leasing; Workouts; Real Estate; Bankruptcy.
Connaughton, James L., (BV) .... '61 '89 C.976 B.A. L.597 J.D. [Sidley A.B.&W.]
Connaughton, Sean T. .... '61 '92 C.1027 B.S. L.1209 J.D. [🄲 Troutman S.]
*PRACTICE AREAS: Marine Transportation; Government Affairs; Environmental.
Connell, Margaret M. '65 '97 C.860 B.A. L.378 J.D.
(adm. in MA; not adm. in DC) [🄰 Sutherland A.&B.]
*PRACTICE AREAS: Corporate Law.
Connell, Paul W. .... '72 '98 C.1172 B.A. L.436 J.D. [🄰 Wilmer,C.&P.]
Connell, R. Campbell .... '67 '94 C.951 B.A. L.383 J.D. [🄰 Cadwalader,W.&T.]
*PRACTICE AREAS: Taxation; International Tax Planning; Financial Products Taxation.
Connell, Thomas F. .... '49 '79 C.674 A.B. L.659 J.D. [Wilmer,C.&P.]
*PRACTICE AREAS: Civil Practice; Trial Practice; Insurance.
Connella, Susan R. .... '— '93 C.420 B.A. L.425 J.D. [🄰 King&S.]
*PRACTICE AREAS: Environmental.
Connelly, Amy B. '70 '00 C.524 B.A. L.276 J.D.
(adm. in MD; not adm. in DC) [🄰 Krooth&A.]
*PRACTICE AREAS: Commercial Real Estate; Corporate Law.
Connelly, Christine E. .... '63 '88 C.446 B.S. L.276 J.D. [🄲 Wiley R.&F.]
*PRACTICE AREAS: Franchise Law.
Connelly, David Martin .... '70 '98 C.21 B.A. L.64 J.D. [🄰 Bruder,G.&M.]
*PRACTICE AREAS: Administrative Litigation.
Connelly, Jeanne K. '46 '77
C.831 A.B. L.705 J.D. V.P., Govt. Affs., Champion Intl. Corp.‡
Connelly, John J. .... '47 '75 C.433 B.A. L.724 J.D. 210 G St., NE
Connelly, Kevin P. .... '60 '85 C.446 B.A. L.237 J.D. [Seyfarth S.]
*PRACTICE AREAS: Government Contract Litigation and Counseling; Commercial Contract Litigation and Counseling.
Connelly, Mary T. '59 '86 C.994 B.A. L.276 J.D.
Staff Atty., Inernational Brotherhood of Teamsters
Connelly, Patricia E., (BV) .... '56 '82 C.1044 B.A. L.823 J.D. [🄰 Trout&R.]
*PRACTICE AREAS: Commercial Litigation; Civil Litigation; Civil Practice.
Connelly, Warren E., (AV) .... '46 '73 C.197 B.A. L.276 J.D. [Akin,G.S.H.&F.]
*PRACTICE AREAS: International Trade.
Conner, Frank M., III, (AV) .... '56 '81 C&L.893 B.A., J.D. [Alston&B.]
*PRACTICE AREAS: Financial Services Law; Financial Institution Regulation; Mergers, Acquisitions and Divestitures; Securities Regulation; Electronic Commerce.
Conner, J. Yost, Jr. .... '63 '97 C.886 B.Arch. L.893 J.D. [🄰 Patton B.]
Conner, John D., (AV) .... '11 '38 C.69 A.B. L.273 LL.B. [McKenna&C.]
Conner, John D., Jr. .... '48 '74 C&L.838 B.S., J.D. [McKenna&C.]
Conner, Patrick D. .... '72 '98 C&L.280 B.A., J.D. [🄰 Morgan,L.&B.]
Connerton, Robert J., (AV) .... '26 '52 C.754 B.A. L.273 J.D. [Connerton&P.]
Connerton, Tèrese M. .... '51 '80 C.608 B.A. L.117 J.D. [🄲 Schmeltzer,A.&S.]
*PRACTICE AREAS: Employee Benefits Law; Labor Law; Tax Exempt Entities.
Connerton & Payne, (AV) ....1401 New York Avenue, Suite 600
Connolly, Annemargaret .... '63 '88 C.823 A.B. L.273 J.D. [Weil,G.&M.]
Connolly, Charles F. .... '— '95 C.367 B.A. L.659 J.D. [🄰 O'Melveny&M.]
Connolly, Joseph G., Jr., (AV) .... '49 '74 C.433 B.A. L.276 J.D. [Hogan&H.]
*PRACTICE AREAS: Corporate Law; Securities.
Connolly, Michael J., (AV) '49 '73 C.686 B.A. L.500 J.D.
(adm. in MS; not adm. in DC) [Riley R.&C.] ⊙
*PRACTICE AREAS: Labor and Employment; Employment Benefits; Occupational Safety and Health; Gaming Law.
Connolly, Peter M., (AV) .... '51 '77 C.976 B.A. L.178 J.D. [Holland&K.]
*PRACTICE AREAS: Telecommunications Law.
Connolly, Thomas G. .... '61 '88 C.597 B.S. L.945 J.D. [Harris,W.&G.]
*PRACTICE AREAS: White Collar Criminal Defense; Civil Litigation.
Connolly Bove Lodge & Hutz LLP
Suite 800, 1990 M Street NW (Pat.) (⊙Wilmington, DE)

Connolly, John P.
(See Alexandria, Virginia)

Connor, G. Brent ....'62 '92 C.156 B.A. L.128 J.D. [Ⓐ Robins,K.M.&C.]
*PRACTICE AREAS: Governmental Affairs; Administrative Law; Military Base Closures; Military Base Conversions; Maritime.
Connor, J. Parker, (AV) .... '26 '54 C&L.276 B.S., J.D. [Ⓒ Mullin,R.E.&T.]
Connor, Maryellen .... '61 '90 C.401 B.A. L.276 J.D. [Ⓒ Akin,G.S.H.&F.]
*PRACTICE AREAS: Litigation.
Connor, Stephen C. '61 '90 C&L.228 B.A., J.D.
(adm. in NY; not adm. in DC) [Ⓒ Sullivan&C.]
Connor, Tracy E. '74 '00 C.188 B.A. L.659 J.D.
(adm. in PA; not adm. in DC) [Ⓐ Spiegel&M.]
*PRACTICE AREAS: Energy; Litigation.
Connors, John P., (BV) .... '47 '80 C.602 B.B.A. L.1209 J.D. 4418 Chesapeake N.W.
Connors, Paul J. ...... '43 '76 C.321 B.A. L.273 J.D. Armed Forces Institute of Pathology
Conover, David W. '60 '93 C.893 B.A. L.276 J.D.
(adm. in VA; not adm. in DC) 1250 H St., N.W.
Conrad, Andrew J. '63 '97 C.770 B.S. L.309 J.D.
(adm. in CA; not adm. in DC) [Ⓐ Dewey B.]
*PRACTICE AREAS: International Trade (100%).
Conrad, Robin S., (AV) '54 '80
C.518 A.B. L.180 J.D. V.P., National Chamber Litig. Ctr., Inc.
Conroy, John F., (AV) .... '42 '66 C.299 B.A. L.262 J.D. [Gordon&B.]
*PRACTICE AREAS: Criminal Law; Trial Practice.
Conroy, Kim '— '86 C&L.546 B.A., J.D.
(adm. in NE; not adm. in DC) Tax Dept., MCI Communications Corp.
Conroy, William F. ....'49 '75 C.262 B.A. L.128 J.D. [Baker&H.]
*PRACTICE AREAS: Tax and Personal Planning Law.
Considine, Eileen M., (BV) '55 '81 C.705 B.A. L.982 J.D.
(adm. in NY; not adm. in DC) [Akin,G.S.H.&F.]
*PRACTICE AREAS: Health Law.

Constangy, Brooks & Smith, LLC
(See Arlington, Virginia)

Constine, Jonathan A. .... '61 '86 C.309 A.B. L.893 J.D. [Hogan&H.]
*PRACTICE AREAS: Civil Litigation; Insurance Litigation; Commercial Insurance.
Conte, Christopher A. ....'60 '88 C.354 B.A. L.823 J.D. [Ⓐ Lipshultz&H.]
*PRACTICE AREAS: Insurance Coverage Defense; Insurance Agents and Brokers; Excess Insurance Carriers; Reinsurance Defense; Insurance Regulation.
Conte, Joseph R., (BV) .... '48 '82 C.923 B.S. L.1209 J.D. [Bond,C.&N.]
*PRACTICE AREAS: Criminal Law; Contracts Law; General Practice.
Content, Arthur L., (AV) '30 '54
C.299 A.B. L.145 J.D. 510 Wisconsin Ave., NW., Ste. 230
Conti, Pat S., (AV) .... '60 '86 C.569 B.A. L.1009 J.D. [Crowell&M.]
*PRACTICE AREAS: Broker-Dealer Regulation; SEC Enforcement; Investment Management; Self-Regulatory Agency Investigations.
Conti, William J., (AV) .... '53 '78 C&L.276 B.A., LL.B. [Baker&H.]
*PRACTICE AREAS: Corporate Law; Securities; Mergers and Acquisitions.
Contois, Thomas M. .... '64 '90 C&L.228 A.B., J.D. [Ⓐ Steptoe&J.]
Contract, Victor A. ....'68 '93 C.1365 B.A. L.94 J.D. [Ⓐ Skadden,A.S.M.&F.]
*PRACTICE AREAS: Energy.
Contratto, Dana C. ....'47 '73 C.801 B.S. L.910 J.D. [Crowell&M.]
Contreras, Amy Kathleen Tesar ....'70 '95 C.846 B.A. L.744 J.D. [Ⓐ McKee N.]
*PRACTICE AREAS: Taxation.
Contreras, Rudolph .... '62 '91 C.259 B.S. L.659 J.D. U.S. Atty. Off.
Converse, Michael L. .... '58 '92 C.276 B.A. L.273 J.D. [Ⓐ Akin,G.S.H.&F.]
*PRACTICE AREAS: Litigation.
Converse, Robert E., Jr., (AV) '45 '74
C.597 B.S.E.E. L.229 J.D. [Finnegan,H.F.G.&D.] (See Pat. Sect.)
*PRACTICE AREAS: Patent Prosecution; Patent Litigation.
Conway, Amy J. ....'— '93 C.882 B.A. L.180 J.D. [Ⓐ Morgan,L.&B.]
Conway, Caroline E. .... '71 '96 C.276 B.S. L.273 J.D. [Ⓐ Yodice]
Conway, Gregory K. ....'64 '90 C&L.276 B.S., J.D. [Ⓐ Willkie F.&G.]
*PRACTICE AREAS: Litigation.
Conway, John H. ....'48 '78 C.860 B.A. L.966 J.D. [Ⓒ Brickfield B.R.&S.]
*PRACTICE AREAS: Energy; Antitrust; Appellate Practice; Administrative Law; Litigation.
Conway, Melissa S. ....'72 '97 C.674 B.A. L.273 J.D. [Ⓐ Kelley D.&W.]
*PRACTICE AREAS: Telecommunications Law.
Conway, Richard J., (AV) ....'48 '73 C.93 B.S. L.276 J.D. [Dickstein S.M.&O.]
*PRACTICE AREAS: Government Contract Law.
Conway, Richard T., (AV) ....'26 '52 C.347 A.B. L.1119 LL.B. [Ⓒ Shea&G.]
Conway, Robert S. ....'67 '93 C.228 A.B. L.659 J.D. [Ⓐ Arnold&P.]
*PRACTICE AREAS: Corporate; International; Securities.
Conway, Shannon W. '68 '99 C.445 B.S. L.128 J.D.
(adm. in VA; not adm. in DC) [Ⓐ Patton B.]
Conyngham, William J., Jr. .... '56 '85 C.276 A.B. L.128 J.D. [Kellogg,H.H.T.&E.]
*PRACTICE AREAS: Telecommunications; Complex Litigation.
Cook, Andrew N., (BV) .... '59 '87 C.37 B.A. L.128 J.D. [Bell,B.&L.]
*PRACTICE AREAS: Government Contracts Law; Construction Law.
Cook, Bryson L., (P.C.), (AV) '48 '74 C.674 A.B. L.659 J.D.
(adm. in MD; not adm. in DC) [Venable,A.B.H.&C.] (⊙Balt., MD)
*PRACTICE AREAS: Corporate Law; Mergers and Acquisitions; Taxation Law; Estate Planning Law.
Cook, Christopher J. .... '69 '98 C.02 B.A. L.188 J.D. 2000 Penn. Ave., N.W.‡
Cook, David B. ....'46 '72 C.674 A.B. L.976 J.D. [Shea&G.]
*PRACTICE AREAS: Transportation Regulation; Administrative; Civil Litigation.
Cook, Elise A. '71 '96 C.280 B.B.A. L.469 J.D.
(adm. in NC; not adm. in DC) [Ⓐ Katten M.Z.]
*PRACTICE AREAS: Commercial Real Estate Finance; Commercial Real Estate Development; Commercial Real Estate Sales; Commercial Real Estate Acquisitions.
Cook, G. Mark ....'55 '81 L.999 LL.B. Assoc. Gen. Coun., El Paso Corp.
Cook, Geoffrey C. ....'63 '88 C&L.309 A.B., J.D. [Ⓒ Cole,R.&B.]
*PRACTICE AREAS: Commercial Litigation; Cable TV; Communications Law; Telecommunications Law.

Cook, H. Clayton, Jr., (AV) '35 '60 C.674 B.S.E. L.893 LL.B. BR
Two Lafayette Centre, 1133 21st Street, N.W., Suite 500, 20036
Telephone: 202-293-8815 Facsimile: 202-293-7994
Email: PlimsollDC@aol.com
(Also Of Counsel to Bastianelli, Brown & Kelley, Chartered).
Maritime Law, Maritime Finance, Shipbuilding and Repair, Project Finance, Administrative Law, Admiralty.
See Professional Biographies, WASHINGTON, DISTRICT OF COLUMBIA

Cook, Janine '70 '95 C.92 B.A. L.276 J.D.
(adm. in VA; not adm. in DC) [McDermott,W.&E.]
Cook, Jennifer E. .... '71 '99 C.103 B.S. L.904 J.D. [Ⓐ Sullivan&C.]
Cook, Kimberly L. .... '71 '97 C.1208 B.S., B.A. L.145 J.D. Atty. Advsr.
Cook, Michael H., (AV) ....'47 '73 C.831 B.A. L.884 J.D. [Jenkens&G.]
*PRACTICE AREAS: Health Care Law; Administrative Law.
Cook, Philip C., (AV) ....'46 '72 C.277 B.S. L.309 J.D. [Alston&B.] (⊙Atlanta, GA)
*PRACTICE AREAS: Federal Income Tax; Federal Tax Controversies; ERISA Litigation.

Cook, R. Christopher, (AV) '64 '89 C.1365 B.A. L.309 J.D.
(adm. in GA; not adm. in DC) [Jones,D.R.&P.]
*PRACTICE AREAS: Litigation; White Collar Crime; Corporate Investigations; Complex Business Litigation.
Cook, Robert N. .... '57 '90 C.367 B.A. L.1209 J.D. [Ⓒ Drinker B.&R.]
*PRACTICE AREAS: Antitrust; Trade Regulation; Administrative Law.
Cook, Robert W. ....'65 '92 C&L.309 A.B., J.D. [Cleary,G.S.&H.]
Cook, Roy C. .... '09 '49 C.790 A.B. L.276 J.D. 3370 Highwood Dr., S.E.‡
Cook, Stephen R. ....'71 '99 C.101 B.A. L.30 J.D. [Ⓐ Howrey S.A.&W.]
*PRACTICE AREAS: Commercial Litigation; Antitrust.
Cook, Susan M. ....'— '98 C.976 B.A. L.309 J.D. [Ⓐ Hogan&H.]
Cook, William Edro, Jr. .... '62 '90 C.228 A.B. L.309 J.D. [Arnold&P.]
*PRACTICE AREAS: Telecommunications.
Cook, William P. ....'52 '79 C.273 B.A. L.809 J.D. [Venable,A.B.H.&C.]
*PRACTICE AREAS: Legislative Practice; Public Policy; Corporate; Securities.
Cooke, Anthony M. ....'68 '95 C.276 B.A. L.861 J.D. [Ⓐ Clifford C.R.&W.]
Cooke, Edmund D., Jr., (AV) ....'42 '73 C.381 B.A. L.477 J.D. [Winston&S.]
*PRACTICE AREAS: Employment Relations; Labor Relations; Government Relations.
Cooke, Frederick D., Jr., (AV) ....'47 '73 C&L.329 B.S., J.D. [Rubin,W.D.H.&C.]
*PRACTICE AREAS: Communications; Legislative; Government Contracts.
Cooke, James P. .... '51 '81 C.999 B.S. L.802 J.D. [Ⓒ Ballard S.A.&I.]
*PRACTICE AREAS: Real Estate Law; Banking Law.
Cooke, James R. .... '42 '68 C.347 B.S. L.477 J.D. [Ⓒ Harris B.]
*PRACTICE AREAS: Telecommunications Law; Corporate Law; Legislation; Government Law.
Cooke, Terence S. ....'46 '76 C.1099 B.A. L.861 J.D. [Ⓒ Cole,R.&B.] ‡
*PRACTICE AREAS: Commercial Law; Zoning and Land Use; Insurance Law; Employment Law; Corporate Law.
Cooke, Thomas B., (BV) .... '49 '74 C.884 B.A. L.276 J.D. Dir., Georgetown Univ.
Cooksey, Paul H. .... '48 '82 C.301 B.A. L.1209 J.D. The Oliver Carr Co.
Cooleen, John J., (AV) ....'43 '68 C&L.276 B.A., J.D. [King&N.] (⊙Arlington, VA)
*PRACTICE AREAS: Commercial Litigation; Creditors Rights; Personal Injury; Landlord and Tenant Law.
Cooley, Diane E. ....'65 '91 C.94 B.A. L.276 J.D. [Coale C.L.M.]
*PRACTICE AREAS: Civil Litigation.
Coolidge, Bruce E., (AV) ....'47 '78 C.976 B.A. L.1066 J.D. [Wilmer,C.&P.]
*PRACTICE AREAS: Securities; Civil Practice; Criminal Practice.
Coolidge, David Gregory .... '65 '96 C.813 B.A. L.893 J.D. [Ⓐ Ivins,P.&B.]
*PRACTICE AREAS: Federal Tax; Employee Benefits; Corporate Taxation.
Coombs, Dianne C. ....'63 '95 C&L.273 B.A., J.D. [Ⓐ Paul,H.J.&W.]
*PRACTICE AREAS: Employment Law.
Coon, Jennifer E. '73 '01 C.118 L.823 J.D.
(adm. in NY; not adm. in DC) [Ⓐ Dechert]
*PRACTICE AREAS: Financial Services Law; Investment Management.

Coon, Curtis C., LLC, The Law Office of
(See Towson, Maryland)

Coonelly, Francis X. ....'60 '86 C.645 B.S. L.128 J.D. 1800 M St., N.W.
Cooney, John F. ....'49 '73 C.103 A.B. L.145 J.D. [Venable,A.B.H.&C.]
*PRACTICE AREAS: Regulatory, Environmental; Appellate; Constitutional.
Cooney, Paul E., (AV) .... '— '77 C.264 A.B. L.273 J.D. [Foley&L.]
*PRACTICE AREAS: Corporate Law; Health Law.
Cooney, Philip A. '59 '84 C.692 B.A. L.884 J.D.
Sr. Atty., American Petroleum Institute
Cooney, Thomas F., III, (AV) ....'— '78 C.197 A.B. L.477 J.D. [Kirkpatrick&L.]
*PRACTICE AREAS: Business Law; Corporate Law; Finance; Mergers, Acquisitions and Divestitures; Securities.
Cooney, Timothy J., (AV) .... '53 '79 C&L.276 A.B., J.D. [Wilkinson B.K.]
*PRACTICE AREAS: Communications Law; Administrative Law; Federal Regulatory Law.
Coony, Thomas E. ....'— '98 C.94 B.A. L.893 J.D. [Ⓐ Miller&C.]
Cooper, A. J., Jr. ....'44 '70 C.602 B.A. L.569 J.D. [Cooper&Assoc.]
Cooper, Aaron '73 '01 C.674 A.B. L.880 J.D.
(adm. in VA; not adm. in DC) [Ⓐ Covington&B.]
Cooper, Alan S., (AV) ....'42 '68 C&L.880 B.A., J.D. [Shaw P.]
Cooper, Andrew C. ....'64 '91 C.976 B.A. L.659 J.D. [Ⓒ Dickstein S.M.&O.]
*PRACTICE AREAS: Environmental.
Cooper, Anika S. .... '73 '97 C.302 B.A. L.976 J.D. [Ⓐ Arnold&P.]
*PRACTICE AREAS: Antitrust; Litigation.
Cooper, Charles J., (AV) .... '52 '77 C&L.16 B.S., J.D. [Cooper&K.]
*PRACTICE AREAS: Trial and Appellate Litigation.
Cooper, Christine M., (AV) ....'65 '90 C.174 B.S. L.273 J.D. [McGuiness N.&W.]
*PRACTICE AREAS: Civil Litigation; Employment Law; Agricultural Labor Law; Commercial Law; Administrative Law.
Cooper, Christopher R. .... '66 '94 C.976 B.A. L.813 J.D. [Baker B.]
Cooper, Clement T. ....'30 '60 C.410 A.B. L.329 J.D. P.O. Box 76135
Cooper, Deborah E. ....'72 '99 C.66 B.A. L.276 J.D. [Ⓐ Skadden,A.S.M.&F.]
*PRACTICE AREAS: Environmental Law; Litigation.
Cooper, Grover C., (AV) '30 '58 C.611 A.B. L.273 J.D.
2001 Pennsylvania Avenue, N.W.
Cooper, Howard A. ....'55 '80 C.575 B.S. L.893 J.D. [Thelen R.&P.]
*PRACTICE AREAS: Tax.
Cooper, Iver P., (AV) ......'53 '78 C.453 B.S. L.94 J.D. [Ⓒ Browdy&N.] (See Pat. Sect.)
*PRACTICE AREAS: Biotechnology and Biomedical Patents.
Cooper, Jacqueline Gerson ....'65 '93 C.145 B.A. L.911 J.D. [Sidley A.B.&W.]
Cooper, James Campbell .... '68 '00 C.790 B.A. L.1356 J.D. [Ⓐ Crowell&M.]
Cooper, James E., Jr. .... '25 '79 C.329 B.A. L.1209 J.D. 4461 S. Dakota Ave., N.E.
Cooper, James L. ....'64 '92 C.145 A.B. L.1119 J.D. [Arnold&P.]
*PRACTICE AREAS: Litigation; Antitrust.
Cooper, John Michael ....'— '73 C.821 B.A. L.309 J.D. [Bryan C.]
*PRACTICE AREAS: Administrative Law; Government Contracts Law; Antitrust Law; Litigation.
Cooper, Kathy L. .... '64 '94 C.446 B.S. L.128 J.D. [Ⓐ Swidler B.S.F.]
*PRACTICE AREAS: Telecommunication.
Cooper, Lawrence N. ....'61 '86 C.94 B.M. L.893 J.D. [Smith C.]
*PRACTICE AREAS: Tax Law; Corporate and Transactional Law; Finance Law; Business Law.
Cooper, Lindsey W. '— '00 C.30 B.A. L.904 J.D.
(adm. in TN; not adm. in DC) [Ⓐ Manatt,P.&P.]
Cooper, Mario M. ....'54 '87 C.478 B.A. L.276 J.D. [Cooper&Assoc.] ⊙
Cooper, Mary M. ....'12 '51 C.320 B.A. L.273 J.D. 5033 Kansas Ave., N.W.
Cooper, Michael J. '43 '69 C.911 B.A. L.878 J.D.
(adm. in UT; not adm. in DC) [Ⓒ Crowell&M.]
*PRACTICE AREAS: International Corporate Taxation.
Cooper, Mitchell J., (AV) '19 '49 C.659 B.A. L.976 LL.B.
1001 Connecticut Ave., N.W.
Cooper, Pamela C., (AV) ....'60 '86 C.893 B.A. L.128 J.D. [Davis W.T.]
*PRACTICE AREAS: Telecommunications; Broadcasting Transactions; FCC Regulation.
Cooper, Richard M., (AV) ....'42 '70 C.311 B.A. L.309 J.D. [Williams&C.]
*PRACTICE AREAS: Administrative Law; Constitutional Law; Criminal Law; Litigation; Drug and Medical Device Regulation.
Cooper, Robert Clayton '62 '87
C.329 B.B.A. L.273 J.D. [Jackson&C.] (⊙Balt., Rockville, MD)
*PRACTICE AREAS: Real Estate; Zoning, Planning and Land Use; Trusts and Estates; Corporate Law; Administrative Law.

Cooper, Robert M. .... '69 '94 C.178 B.A. L.245 J.D. [Ⓐ Arnold&P.]
*PRACTICE AREAS: Telecommunications; Litigation.
Cooper, Ronald S., (AV) .... '45 '69 C&L.280 A.B., J.D. [Steptoe&J.]
*PRACTICE AREAS: Employment Discrimination Law; Employment Law; Age Discrimination; Wage and Hour Law; Defense Litigation.
Cooper, Tasha L. ....'— '99 C.302 B.A. L.178 J.D. [Ⓐ Fried,F.H.S.&J.]
*PRACTICE AREAS: Corporate Law.
Cooper, Thomas J. ....'43 '75 C.273 A.B. L.861 J.D. [Venable,A.B.H.&C.]
*PRACTICE AREAS: Exports Control Law; International Trade Law; Election Law; Legislation Representation (Federal and District of Columbia).
Cooper, Vanessa J. .... '69 '97 C.329 B.A. L.180 J.D. [Ⓐ Finnegan,H.F.G.&D.]
*PRACTICE AREAS: Trademark Prosecution; International Intellectual Property.
Cooper, Ward R. .... '60 '85 C.976 B.A. L.309 J.D. Asst. Gen. Coun., Marriott Intl., Inc.
*RESPONSIBILITIES: Finance; Securities; Mergers and Acquisition.
Cooper and Associates, P.C. .... 1050 Seventeenth Street, N.W. (⊙New York, NY)

Cooper & Kirk, PLLC, (AV)
Suite 200, 1500 K Street, N.W., 20005
Telephone: 202-220-9600 Fax: 202-220-9601
Email: info@coopekirk.com URL: http://www.cooperkirk.com
Partners: Charles J. Cooper; Vincent J. Colatriano; Robert J. Cynkar; Michael W. Kirk; David H. Thompson. Associates: Hamish P. M. Hume; Victor J. Wolski (Not admitted in DC); Brian Stuart Koukoutchos (Not admitted in DC).
Administrative, Appellate, Constitutional, Employment, Litigation, Supreme Court, Trial.
See Professional Biographies, WASHINGTON, DISTRICT OF COLUMBIA

Cooperman, Leonard Jon ....'— '98 C.659 B.A. L.245 J.D. [Ⓐ Miller&C.]
*PRACTICE AREAS: Corporate Law; Business Law; International Trade; Investments; Intellectual Property.
Cooperstein, Theodore M., (BV) ....'63 '88 C.197 A.B. L.813 J.D. [T.M.Cooperstein]
*PRACTICE AREAS: Federal Litigation; Appellate Practice; Civil Rights Section 1983; Foreign Sovereign Immunities Act; International Litigation.

Cooperstein, Theodore M., P.C., (BV)
1815 Pennsylvania Avenue, N.W. Suite 501, 20006
Telephone: 202-331-7895 Fax: 202-331-9841 800-732-5118
Email: tmc@coopersteinlaw.com URL: http://www.coopersteinlaw.com
Theodore M. Cooperstein.
Commercial Litigation, Civil Litigation with International Emphasis, and Federal Constitutional and Civil Rights Litigation, in both Trial and Appeals Courts.
See Professional Biographies, WASHINGTON, DISTRICT OF COLUMBIA

Cooter, Dale A., (AV) .... '48 '75 C.1044 B.A. L.276 J.D. [Cooter,M.T.&W.]

Cooter, Mangold, Tompert & Wayson, L.L.P., (AV)
5301 Wisconsin Avenue, N.W., Suite 500, 20015
Telephone: 202-537-0700 Fax: 202-364-3664
Email: edwayson@waysonlaw.com URL: http://www.lawyers.com/cmt&w
Dale A. Cooter; Donna S. Mangold; James E. Tompert; Karen Simonek Karas; Elizabeth A. McFarland.
General Litigation, Commercial Transactions, Governmental Relations, Banking and Gaming Law.
Annapolis, Maryland Office: 191 Main Street. 21401. Telephone: 410-268-2020. Fax: 410-268-4576.
See Professional Biographies, WASHINGTON, DISTRICT OF COLUMBIA

Coots, John C. ....'67 '94 C.378 B.A. L.190 J.D. [Ⓢ Shook,H.&B.]
Copaken, Richard D., (AV) .... '41 '66 C&L.309 B.A., LL.B. [Covington&B.]
Cope, John R., (AV) ....'42 '66 C&L.846 B.B.A., LL.B. [Bracewell&P.]
*PRACTICE AREAS: Business Litigation; Intellectual Property Litigation; Litigation; Professional Liability; Securities Litigation.
Cope, Robert L., (AV) ....'47 '73 C.801 B.A. L.502 J.D. [Grove,J.&C.]
*PRACTICE AREAS: Transportation; Litigation; General Corporate.
Copenhaver, W. Andrew, (AV) '46 '72 C.228 A.B. L.575 J.D.
(adm. in NC; not adm. in DC) [Womble C.S.&R.] (⊙Winston-Salem, NC)
*PRACTICE AREAS: Antitrust Law; Unfair Trade Practices; Defamation; Intellectual Property Litigation.
Copilevitz, Errol, (AV) '43 '68 C&L.623 B.A., J.D.
(adm. in MO; not adm. in DC) [Copilevitz&C.] ⊙
*PRACTICE AREAS: Constitutional Law; Tax Exempt Organization Law; Civil Litigation; Charitable Giving Law; Non-Profit Tax Law.

Copilevitz & Canter, LLC, (AV)
1815 H Street NW Suite 501, 20006 ⊙
Telephone: 202-861-0740 Fax: 202-331-9841
Email: Copcandc@aol.com URL: http://www.exempttaxlaw.com
Errol Copilevitz (Not admitted in DC); MacKenzie Canter, III; Gregory B. Lam (Not admitted in DC); Mark J. Diskin;—Martin L. McCarthy (Not admitted in DC); William E. Raney (Not admitted in DC); Brian F. Ellis (Not admitted in DC).
Federal and State Tax-Exempt Organizations, Charitable Fund-raising, Registrations of Charities and Fund-raisers, Nonprofit, Not-For-Profit and Charity Organizations Practice, Nonprofit and Tax-Exempt Organization Counsel, Charitable Giving Law, Administrative Agency Practice, Constitutional and First Amendment Practice, Telemarketer and Telemarketing Law.
Kansas City, Missouri Office: 423 West 8th Street, Suite 400, 64105. Telephone: 816-472-9000. Fax: 816-472-5000.
See Professional Biographies, WASHINGTON, DISTRICT OF COLUMBIA

Copiz, Adrian B. '71 '99 C&L.446 B.A., J.D.
(adm. in MD; not adm. in DC) [Ⓐ McGuirewoods]
*PRACTICE AREAS: Telecommunications; Media.
Cople, William J., III .... '55 '81 C.902 B.A. L.724 J.D. [Spriggs&H.]
*PRACTICE AREAS: Products Liability; Toxic Torts; Litigation; Drug and Medical Device Defense.
Copley, John R. ....'63 '92 C.896 B.A. L.893 J.D. [Ⓐ Boros&G.]
*PRACTICE AREAS: Commercial Law; Transportation Law.
Copley, William E., III .... '74 '99 C.880 B.A. L.145 J.D. [Ⓐ Sonnenschein N.&R.]
*PRACTICE AREAS: Litigation.
Copus, David A., (AV) ....'42 '66 C.597 B.A. L.309 LL.B. [Ⓒ Jones,D.R.&P.]
Coran, Stephen E. ....'— '86 C.473 B.S. L.904 J.D. [Manatt,P.&P.]
Corazzini, Robert F., (AV) .... '36 '61 C.524 B.S. L.276 J.D. [Pepper&C.]
*PRACTICE AREAS: Communications and Media; Cable Communications; FCC Licensing; FCC Regulation.
Corber, Robert J., (AV) .... '26 '50 C.378 B.S. L.900 J.D. 1330 Conn. Ave., N.W.
Corbett, Bryan N. .... '72 '99 C.602 B.A. L.537 J.D. [Ⓐ Wilmer,C.&P.]
Corbett, Dennis P., (AV) ....'53 '79 C.309 A.B. L.275 J.D. [Leventhal,S.&L.]
*PRACTICE AREAS: Communications Law; Media Law.
Corbett, Gregory F. '74 '00 C.309 A.B. L.93 J.D.
(adm. in MA; not adm. in DC) [Ⓐ Kirkland&E.]
*PRACTICE AREAS: Litigation; Intellectual Property; Environmental; Appellate Practice.
Corbett, John J., Jr. .... '39 '68 C.128 Ph.B. L.276 J.D. [Spiegel&M.]
*PRACTICE AREAS: Transportation; Airport Law; Aviation and Aerospace; Legislative; Appellate Practice.
Corbin, Eve ....'73 '99 C.976 B.A. L.477 J.D. [Ⓐ Arent F.K.P.&K.]
*PRACTICE AREAS: Business; Commercial Leasing; Bond Finance; Tax Exempt Bond; Real Estate Contracts.
Corbitt, Aubria D. '66 '90 C.910 A.B. L.893 J.D.
(adm. in GA; not adm. in DC) 3930 Wisconsin Ave.
Corcoran, Brian H. ....'66 '92 C.197 A.B. L.893 J.D. [Ⓐ Katten M.Z.]
*PRACTICE AREAS: Litigation.
Corcoran, M. Evan ....'— '91 C.674 A.B. L.276 J.D. [Ⓐ Wiley R.&F.]
Corcoran, Peter J. '40 '77 C.128 A.B. L.262 J.D.
(adm. in NY; not adm. in DC) Edison Elec. Institute

Corcoran, Thomas G., Jr., (AV) ....'42 '69 C.103 A.B. L.309 LL.B. [Berliner,C.&R.]
*PRACTICE AREAS: Civil and Criminal Litigation; Appeals.
Cordell, Lisa Chandler .... '70 '96 C.347 B.A. L.209 J.D. [Ⓐ Fleischman&W.]
Cordell, Ruffin B., (AV) .... '63 '89 C.420 B.S.E.E. L.276 J.D. [Fish&R.] (See Pat. Sect.)
*PRACTICE AREAS: Litigation; Intellectual Property Law; International Trade Commission Proceedings.
Cordelli, B. Gerard .... '57 '83 C.273 B.B.A. L.1068 J.D. [Ⓐ Robins,K.M.&C.]
*PRACTICE AREAS: Commercial Insurance Litigation; Counseling and Litigation/Rehabilitation; Business and Commercial Litigation.
Corette, John E., III, (AV) ....'36 '61 C.508 B.S. L.893 J.D. [Piper M.R.&W.]
*PRACTICE AREAS: International Business Law; Domestic Business Law; Financial Law; Trade Law.
Corey, Ethan D. ....'63 '88 C.012 B.A. L.94 J.D. [Ⓐ Dechert]
*PRACTICE AREAS: Investment Management; Financial Services Law.
Corey, William S., (AV) ....'36 '62 C.216 A.B. L.273 J.D. [Ⓒ Sutherland A.&B.]
*PRACTICE AREAS: Federal Taxation; International Taxation; Tax Planning; Federal Tax Controversies.
Corey & Kime, P.C., (BV) ....1120 G. St. N.W., Ste. 200 (⊙Tucson, AZ)
Coriden, James A. '32 '72 C.999 S.T. L.128 J.D.
Prof. of Canon Law, Wash. Theological Union
Cork, Gregory M. .... '65 '93 C&L.893 B.A., J.D. [Ⓐ Zevnik H.]
*PRACTICE AREAS: Commercial Litigation; Insurance Coverage.
Cork, Jill Chessen ....'66 '92 C.597 B.S. L.659 J.D. [Ⓐ Hawkins,D.&W.]
*PRACTICE AREAS: Multifamily Housing Finance and Development; Low Income Housing.
Corley, Judith L. ....'52 '85 C.911 B.A. L.273 J.D. [Perkins C.]
*PRACTICE AREAS: Federal and State Election Law; Government Ethics; Non Profit Corporations; Congressional Investigations.
Cormaney, D. Michael .... '72 '97 C&L.352 B.A., J.D. [Ⓐ Arnold&P.]
*PRACTICE AREAS: Export Controls; International Trade; Ethics and Campaign Finance.
Cormier, Bruce M. '56 '82
C.818 B.A. L.188 J.D. Assoc. Gen. Coun., Ernst & Young LLP
Corn-Revere, Robert L., (AV) .... '54 '83 C.234 B.A. L.128 J.D. [Hogan&H.]
*PRACTICE AREAS: First Amendment Law; Internet Law; Communications Law.
Cornelison, Joseph W. ....'47 '77 C.870 B.S. L.276 J.D. [Ⓒ Akin,G.S.H.&F.]
*PRACTICE AREAS: International Business Law; Public Law; Public Policy; Environmental Law; Government Contracts.
Cornfield, Richard ....'47 '74 C.1029 B.S. L.128 J.D. The Bureau of Natl. Affs., Inc.
Cornish, Cornell D.M. Judge '29 '56
C.367 B.A. L.446 J.D. 1101 New Hampshire Ave., N.W. (Pat.)
Cornwell, David K.S. '58 '83 C&L.560 B.S.M.E., J.D.
[Sterne,K.G.&F.] (See Pat. Sect.)
*PRACTICE AREAS: Litigation; Intellectual Property Law.
Coroneos and Rubenstein, P.C., (AV) ....1818 N St., N.W., Ste. 701 (⊙Rockville, MD)
Corpuz, Marcelo N., III ....'— '95 C.276 B.A. L.273 J.D. [Ⓐ Latham&W.]
*PRACTICE AREAS: Health Care.
Corr, Christopher F., (BV) ....'61 '86 C.645 B.A. L.273 J.D. [White&C.]
*PRACTICE AREAS: International Trade Law; International Communications Law; International Business Law.
Correia, Edward, (AV) ....'— '76 C&L.623 B.A., J.D. [Ⓒ Latham&W.]
*PRACTICE AREAS: Government Relations; Antitrust; Consumer Protection; Civil Rights.
Correia, Linda M., (AV) ....'63 '91 C.94 B.A. L.904 J.D. [Webster,F.&B.]
*PRACTICE AREAS: Administrative Law; Labor and Employment; Commercial Litigation; Bankruptcy.
Cors, Dylan ....'— '97 C.453 S.B. L.228 J.D. [Ⓐ Verner,L.B.M.&H.]
Corsello, Kenneth R. ......'65 '92 C.1350 B.S. L.128 J.D. [Ⓐ Kenyon&K.] (See Pat. Sect.)
*PRACTICE AREAS: Intellectual Property.
Corsig, Julie Kaminski ....'66 '93 C.93 B.A. L.910 J.D. [Ⓒ Davis W.T.]
*PRACTICE AREAS: Telecommunications Law.
Corvo, Tara M. ....'— '94 C.188 B.A. L.228 J.D. 701 Pennsylvania Avenue, N.W.
Corwin, Carolyn F. ....'50 '77 C.604 A.B. L.976 J.D. [Covington&B.]
Corwin, Erik H. .... '63 '93 C&L.309 A.B., J.D. [Wilmer,C.&P.]
*PRACTICE AREAS: Taxation.
Corwin, Philip S. .... '50 '75 C.188 B.A. L.93 J.D. [Butera&A.]
*PRACTICE AREAS: Bankruptcy; Financial Services; Intellectual Property; Electronic Commerce.
Cory, Frederick W. ....'39 '70 C.923 A.B. L.838 J.D. 501 3rd St., NW‡
Cosby, Joseph G. ....'60 '89 C.145 A.B. L.477 J.D. [Ⓐ Tighe P.A.T.]
*PRACTICE AREAS: Complex Commercial Litigation; Criminal Litigation; Bankruptcy Litigation.
Cossack, Roger L., (AV) '41 '67 C.112 B.A. L.1068 J.D.
(adm. in CA; not adm. in DC) Legal Analyst, CNN
Cosson, David ....'41 '71 C.188 B.A. L.276 J.D. National Tel. Coop. Assn.
Costa, Christopher R. '58 '85
C.893 B.A. L.30 J.D. 1120 19th St.,N.W. (⊙Silver Spring, MD)
Costan, James M., (AV) .... '48 '74 C.893 B.A. L.902 J.D. [McGuirewoods]
*PRACTICE AREAS: Energy; Utility Law.
Costello, Ann S., (AV) .... '50 '79 C.228 B.A. L.273 J.D. V.P., Goldman, Sachs & Co.
Costello, Christopher J. .... '73 '98 C.93 B.A. L.128 J.D. [Ⓐ Kirkpatrick&L.]
*PRACTICE AREAS: Securities; Investment Management.
Costello, Frank J., (AV) ....'44 '70 C.197 A.B. L.276 J.D. [Zuckert,S.&R.]
*PRACTICE AREAS: Federal Administrative Law; Maritime Commercial Law; Aviation; Commercial Litigation.
Costello, Stacy E. ....'64 '90 C.1036 B.A. L.30 J.D. [Robins,K.M.&C.]
*PRACTICE AREAS: Business Transactions; Real Estate; Taxation; Wills; Trusts Planning.
Coston, William D., (AV) ....'50 '76 C.477 B.A. L.309 J.D. [Venable,A.B.H.&C.]
*PRACTICE AREAS: Litigation; Antitrust Law and Trade Regulation Law; Intellectual Property.
Cotten & Selfon, P.L.L.C., (BV) .... 1300 Pennsylvania Avenue, N.W.
Cotter, Francis P. ....'22 '55 C.569 B.S. L.128 LL.B. 1725 Desales St., N.W.
Cotter, Gregory A. ....'55 '80 C.597 B.A. L.228 J.D. 717 D Street, NW, 4th Fl.
Cottingham, Anne W. ....'51 '79 C.575 A.B. L.228 J.D. [Ⓐ Winston&S.]
*PRACTICE AREAS: Nuclear Energy; Energy Regulation; Nuclear Waste; Administrative Agency Practice.
Cottle, Jeffrey W. '64 '95 C.276 B.A. L.893 J.D.
(adm. in MD; not adm. in DC) 1875 Connecticut Avenue, N.W.
Cotton, Raymond D., (BV) ....'42 '68 C.1108 A.B. L.309 J.D. [Mintz,L.C.F.G.&P.]
*PRACTICE AREAS: Health Law; Public Health Law; Health Care Legislation; Biomedical Technology; College and University Law.

Couch White, LLP, (AV)
700 13th Street N.W., Suite 950, 20005 ⊙
Telephone: 202-434-4503 Fax: 202-434-4562
Email: CouchWhiteBrenn@Global2000.net URL: http://www.couchwhite.com
Members of Firm: Algird F. White, Jr. (Not admitted in DC); Barbara S. Brenner (Not admitted in DC); Robert M. Loughney (Not admitted in DC); Leonard H. Singer (Not admitted in DC); Doreen Unis Saia (Not admitted in DC).
Administrative and General Civil Practice before all Federal and State Courts and Administrative Agencies; Automotive Law; Construction; Surety; Energy Law; Environmental Law; Commercial; Real Estate; Probate and Bankruptcy Litigation; Appellate Practice; Labor; Health Care; Government Relations; Trusts; Estate Planning and Administration; Federal and New York Taxation; Internal Revenue Service Practice.
Albany, New York Office: 540 Broadway, P.O. Box 22222. Telephone: 518-426-4600. Telecopier: 518-426-0376.
See Professional Biographies, WASHINGTON, DISTRICT OF COLUMBIA

Coudert Brothers LLP, (AV)
1627 I Street, N.W., 20006 ⊙
Telephone: 202-775-5100 Telecopier: 202-775-1168 For attorney e-mails use: lastnamefirstinitial@coudert.com
URL: http://www.coudert.com

(This Listing Continued)

Coudert Brothers LLP (Continued)

Members of the Firm: Stephen A. Best; Michael R. Calabrese; William K. Coulter; Richard N. Dean; Kay Georgi; Tara Kalagher Giunta; John M. Gurley; Marian M. Hagler; Janet Hernandez (Not admitted in DC); Tedson J. Meyers; Robert F. Pietrowski, Jr.; Vera Ann Rechsteiner (Not admitted in DC); Roger D. Stark; Roger B. Wagner. Counsel: Matthew J. McConkey. Resident Associates: Kristen Angus (Not admitted in DC); Lina A. Braude (Not admitted in DC); Peter Chessick (Not admitted in DC); Markus Dausses (Not admitted in DC); Matthew R. Fowler (Not admitted in DC); Cathy J. Futrowsky; Elizabeth Holowinski; H. Rosemary Jeronimides; Alexander A. Kalinov (Not admitted in the United States); Kevin M. King; Mark P. Lunn; Julie N. Mack (Not admitted in DC); Kenneth E. Mack; Monica Restrepo (Not admitted in DC); Lynn Robitaille (Not admitted in DC); Yira Rodriguez-Creus (Not admitted in DC); Lisa Weiss Rosaya; Nancy J. Rosenfeld; Segei Vataev (Not admitted in United States); David M. Viscovich; Matthew J. Vitale.
General Practice.
Offices also at: New York; Los Angeles; Palo Alto; San Francisco; San Jose; Denver; Paris; London; Antwerp; Brussels; Ghent; Berlin; Frankfurt; Munich; Milan; Beijing; Hong Kong; Shanghai; Singapore; Sydney; Tokyo; Almaty; Moscow; St. Petersburg; Bangkok; Montreal.
Revisers of the France Law Digest for this Directory.

See Professional Biographies, WASHINGTON, DISTRICT OF COLUMBIA

Coughlan, James B. '63 '89 C.98 B.S.M.E. L.209 J.D.
(adm. in IL; not adm. in DC) 1800 M St., N.W.‡

Coughlin, Leo J. '35 '60 C.116 B.S. L.262 J.D.
Gen. Coun. & Dep. COO, Center for Strategic and International Studies

Coughlin, Paul J., Jr. .... '39 '64 C.276 A.B. L.178 LL.B. 3305 39th St., N.W.‡

Coughlin, R. Lawrence, (AV) ....'— '59 C.976 A.B. L.831 J.D. [Thompson C.]
*PRACTICE AREAS: Government Relations; Transportation; International Commerce.

Coughlin, Thomas A., (AV) '45 '70 C.1036 B.A. L.93 J.D.
1750 K Street, N.W., Suite 1200, 20006-2305
Telephone: 202-828-4968 Telecopier: 202-828-4966
Email: tac1@erols.com
Estate planning, and business practice in the District of Columbia, Virginia and Maryland. Specialized national practice in historic preservation, conservation easements, and non-profit organizations.

See Professional Biographies, WASHINGTON, DISTRICT OF COLUMBIA

Coukos, Pamela ....'68 '94 C.103 A.B. L.309 J.D. [Ⓐ Mehri,M.&R.]
*PRACTICE AREAS: Employment Discrimination; Civil Rights.

Coulby, John N., III .... '58 '96 C.903 B.S. L.1338 J.D. [Ⓐ Collier S.S.] (Pat.)
*PRACTICE AREAS: Intellectual Property; Litigation.

Coulter, Johanna S. '65 '91 C&L.893 B.A., J.D.
(adm. in TX; not adm. in DC) [Ⓐ Andrews&K.]
*PRACTICE AREAS: Environmental Law.

Coulter, William K., (AV) .... '46 '71 C.264 B.A. L.665 J.D. [Coudert B.]
*PRACTICE AREAS: Telecommunications; International; Commercial Transactions.

Counts, John P., (AV) ....'48 '73 C.205 B.A. L.273 J.D. [Counts,P.-D.&D.]

Counts, Potts-Dupre & Difede, Chartered, (AV)
Suite 444, 1125 Fifteenth Street, N.W., 20005
Telephone: 202-223-0888 Telecopier: 202-223-3868
John P. Counts; David H. Potts-Dupre; James R. Difede; James V. Cole II;—Jennifer Bush Hawkins; Shane N. Kramer; Kelly Huckno Gil; Katherine L. Jough; Melinda L. Emch (Not admitted in DC); Keith C. Ott (Not admitted in DC); Jeannine R. Shavitz (Not admitted in DC); William Gray Mitchell, Jr. (Not admitted in DC).
Pension and Labor Law. Real Estate, Tax and Commercial Transactions Law. Litigation.

See Professional Biographies, WASHINGTON, DISTRICT OF COLUMBIA

Coursen, Christopher D. .... '48 '75 C.902 B.A. L.273 J.D. Pres., Coursen Group, The

Coursey, Michael J., (AV) ....'54 '81 C.321 A.B. L.893 J.D. [Collier S.S.]
*PRACTICE AREAS: International Trade.

Courtis, Kathleen M. .... '65 '93 C.276 B.S.B.A. L.569 J.D. [Ⓐ Arnold&P.]
*PRACTICE AREAS: Trusts and Estates.

Courtland, Robert D., Chartered
(See, Bethesda, Maryland)

Courtney, Catherine A. '68 '01 C.446 B.A. L.180 J.D.
(adm. in MD; not adm. in DC) [Ⓐ Dechert]
*PRACTICE AREAS: Investment Management; Financial Services Law.

Courtney, Maryanne .... '63 '88 C.367 B.A. L.107 J.D. [Hogan&H.]
*PRACTICE AREAS: Commercial Law; International; Project Finance.

Courtot, George C. .... '43 '72 C.705 A.B. L.904 J.D. [Hughes&B.]

Covell, Colleen ....'64 '90 C.893 B.A. L.93 J.D. [Ⓒ Swidler B.S.F.]
*PRACTICE AREAS: Employment Discrimination; White Collar Criminal; Trial Attorney.

Coventry, Anne W. .... '73 '99 C.399 B.A. L.945 J.D. [Ⓐ Arnold&P.]
*PRACTICE AREAS: Tax Law; Estates.

Covert, John M. ....'63 '94 C.728 B.S. L.1209 J.D. [Sterne,K.G.&F.] (See Pat. Sect.)
*PRACTICE AREAS: Patent Law; Chemical Patent; Biotechnology.

Covey, Julia Fayngold .... '69 '97 C.309 A.B. L.976 J.D. 901 E Street, N.W.

Covey, Russell D. ....'65 '98 C.31 B.A. L.976 J.D. [Ⓐ Williams&C.]
*PRACTICE AREAS: General Civil; Criminal Litigation.

Coviello, Yvonne M. ....'67 '95 C.172 B.A. L.128 J.D. 1875 Connecticut Avenue, N.W.

Covington, Joseph P., (AV) ....'46 '74 C&L.893 B.A., J.D. [Jenner&B.]
*PRACTICE AREAS: Government Contracts; Litigation; Criminal Antitrust; White Collar Criminal Defense; Compliance Counseling.

Covington & Burling, (AV) BR
1201 Pennsylvania Avenue, N.W., 20004-2401 ⊙
Telephone: 202-662-6000 Fax: 202-662-6291
Email: postmaster@cov.com URL: http://www.cov.com
Partners: Dana T. Ackerly II; Mark H. Applebaum; James R. Atwood; Bruce A. Baird; Patricia A. Barald; Thomas O. Barnett; Michael St. Patrick Baxter; Bruce C. Bennett (Resident, New York, N.Y. Office); Paul J. Berman; Dr. Georg M. Berrisch (Resident, Brussels, Belgium Office); Jonathan D. Blake; Doris Blazek-White; Peter W. L. Bogaert (Resident, Brussels, Belgium Office); Eric C. Bosset; Richard A. Brady; Lanny A. Breuer; Edward C. Britton; Caroline M. Brown; David N. Brown; E. Edward Bruce; John G. Buchanan III; Charles E. Buffon; Bobby R. Burchfield; Kurt G. Calia (Resident, San Francisco, California Office); Russell H. Carpenter, Jr.; Warren G. Caywood, Jr. (Resident, New York, N.Y. Office); Leonard Chazen (Resident, New York, N.Y. Office); George M. Chester, Jr.; Brice M. Clagett; William R. Collins (Resident, New York, N.Y. Office); Richard D. Copaken; Carolyn F. Corwin; Evan R. Cox (Resident, San Francisco, California Office); Thomas L. Cubbage III; Michael E. Cutler; Roderick Allen De Arment; John B. Denniston; Mitchell F. Dolin; John C. Dugan; Julie M. Edmond; Clausen Ely, Jr.; Anna Engh; Nicholas W. Fels; Matthew E. Fishbein (Resident, New York, N.Y. Office); Peter L. Flanagan; Ellen J. Flannery; Andrew H. Friedman; Robert J. Gage; Marialuisa S. Gallozzi; Oscar M. Garibaldi; Theodore L. Garrett; Corinne A. Goldstein; Linda C. Goldstein (Resident, New York, N.Y. Office); Ellen P. Goodman; Saul B. Goodman; John P. Gourary (Resident, New York, N.Y. Office); William F. Greaney; Joanne B. Grossman; Eugene D. Gulland; John E. Hall; David W. Haller (Resident, New York, N.Y. Office); Newman T. Halvorson, Jr.; Robert P. Haney, Jr. (Resident, New York, N.Y. Office); David L. Harfst (Resident, Brussels, Belgium Office); J. Michael Hemmer; Anthony Herman; Timothy C. Hester; David H. Hickman; Harry G. Hives (Resident, New York, N.Y. Office); Michael B. Hopkins (Resident, New York, N.Y. Office); Michael S. Horne; Philip K. Howard (Resident, New York, N.Y. Office); John A. Hurvitz; Peter Barton Hutt; Jeffrey G. Huvelle; Michael X. Imbroscio; Stephen A. Infante (Resident, New York, N.Y. Office); William D. Iverson; O. Thomas Johnson, Jr.; Elizabeth T. Kessenides (Resident, New York, N.Y. Office); Mark F. Kightlinger (Resident, Brussels, Belgium Office); Richard F. Kingham (Resident, London, England Office); Bruce N. Kuhlik; Eugene I. Lambert; D. Michael Lefever; Bingham B. Leverich; Jack P. Levin (Resident, New York, N.Y. Office); Gregg H. Levy; Michael R. Levy; Charles E. Lister (Resident, London, England Office); S. William Livingston, Jr.; J. Jay Lobell (Resident, New York, N.Y. Office); Robert A. Long, Jr.; Mark H. Lynch; Daniel M. Mandil (Resident, New York, N.Y. Office); Aaron R. Marcu (Resident, New York, N.Y. Office); David Lawrence Meyer; Charles A. Miller; Allan B. Moore (Resident, London, England Office); Amy N. Moore; Peter J. Nickles; William M. Paul; C. William Phillips (Resident, New York,

(This Listing Continued)

Covington & Burling (Continued)

N.Y. Office); Mark E. Plotkin; Ethan M. Posner; Hilary Prescott (Resident, London, England Office); David H. Remes; Paul V. Rogers; Neil K. Roman; Steven J. Rosenbaum; John Peter Rupp; Robert N. Sayler; Laurie C. Self; Richard C. Shea; Laurence A. Silverman (Resident, New York, N.Y. Office); Christopher N. Sipes; William P. Skinner; Jay T. Smith; John Thomas Smith, II; Scott F. Smith (Resident, New York, N.Y. Office); James C. Snipes (Resident, San Francisco, California Office); Rebecca Snow; Stuart C. Stock; Philipp U. Tamussino (Resident, New York, N.Y. Office); Keith A. Teel; Phyllis D. Thompson; Lee J. Tiedrich; Henriette A. Tielemans (Not admitted in United States) (Resident, Brussels, Belgium Office); Allan J. Topol; Peter D. Trooboff; Seth A. Tucker; Kelly Vance (Resident, London, England Office); John Vanderstar; D. Jean Veta; John M. Vine; Ralph C. Voltmer, Jr.; Theodore Voorhees, Jr.; Gerard J. Waldron; J. D. Weinberg (Resident, New York, N.Y. Office); Harris Weinstein; Mark A. Weiss; Elizabeth Stotland Weiswasser (Not admitted in DC); Stephen A. Weiswasser; Albert L. Wells (Resident, New York, N.Y. Office); Reeves C. Westbrook; Robert Wick; Wesley S. Williams, Jr.; Thomas S. Williamson, Jr.; Bruce Sandness Wilson; Kurt A. Wimmer (Resident, London, England Office); Sonya D. Winner (Resident, San Francisco, California Office). Senior Counsel: Edwin S. Cohen; John L. Ellicott; Daniel M. Gribbon; David B. Isbell; James C. McKay; Alfred H. Moses; John H. Schafer; Stanley L. Temko; J. Randolph Wilson; Edwin M. Zimmerman. Of Counsel: David W. Addis; Stephen Calkins; Kipp A. Coddington; Patrick S. Davies; Edward H. Dixon; Ronald G. Dove, Jr.; Herbert Estreicher; Scott David Feldstein; Kathleen T. Gallagher-Duff; James A. Goold; David R. Grace; R. Laird Hart; Stuart Irvin; W. Andrew Jack; Anna D. Kraus; Benedict M. Lenhart; Richard A. Merrill; Alan A. Pemberton; Douglas E. Phillips; Andrea G. Reister; Jack Lee Schenendorf (Not admitted in DC); Elliott Schulder; Robert E. Shaw; Robert B. Stevens (Resident, London, England Office); Sarah E. Taylor; Edward S. West; Togo D. West, Jr. Special Counsel: Stephen P. Anthony; Dennis B. Auerbach; Kathleen L. Blaner; Michael J. Cicero; William H. Fitz; Thomas W. Krause; Michael Gary Michaelson; Julie Simon Miller; James S. Portnoy; Kevin Shortill; Elaine Wintroub Stone. Associates: Raymond A. Atkins; M. Stacey Bach; Karen A. Ballotta; Catherine Cloud Barre (Not admitted in DC); Ronald John Baumgarten, Jr.; Bryan Beier; Thomas W. Beimers; Andrew Betaque (Not admitted in DC); Hillary Brill (Not admitted in DC); P. Robert Broeren, Jr.; Eric D. Brown; Nathan A. Brown; Tyrone Anthony Brown (Not admitted in DC); Christopher Burke; Charles J. Butler; Fernando Campoamor-Sanchez; Les P. Carnegie; Michael K. Catoe; Marney L. Cheek (Not admitted in DC); George F. Cicotte; Tracey H. Cohen; Aaron Cooper (Not admitted in DC); Scott L. Cunningham (Not admitted in DC); Catherine Janine Dargan; James Robert Dean, Jr; John T. Delacourt; Christopher M. Denig; John V. Donnelly, III (Not admitted in DC); Kathleen J. Donnelly; Kenneth J. Drexler; Phillip E. Dube; Richard Dulik; Siobhan Elizabeth Dupuy; Erin M. Egan; Kimberly K. Egan; Christine E. Enemark; Juan Manuel Estrada; Michael J. Fanelli; Mark E. Feldman (Not admitted in DC); David Finkelson; Michael J. Francese; Richard L. Freuhauf; James M. Garland (Not admitted in DC); Laura B. Gasho; Jason P. Gluck; Adam W. Goldberg; Sara L. Gottovi; Eric Dodson Greenberg; Gideon Y. Grunfeld; Miriam J. Guggenheim; Michael Hadley; Stephen J. Hess; Elie Honig (Not admitted in DC); Marianna Horton; Camilla M. Jackson; Russell D. Jessee; Jennifer Anne Johnson; Julie L.B. Johnson; Emily Johnson Henn; Russell P. Kanjorski; Faith D. Kasparian; Georgia Kazakis; Timothy J. Keefer; Robert K. Kelner; Ann-Kelley Kemper; Laura M. Kim; Erika King; Karen Kizer (Not admitted in DC); Susan Koegel; Rukesh Korde; Douglas Kramer (Not admitted in DC); Karen Kramer; Joseph A. Kresse; Joan L. Kutcher; Michael Scott Labson; Monique J. La Fleur; Marie A. Lavalleye; Amy L. Levine; Jason A. Levine; Andrew D. Levy; Jason R. Litow; Catherine E. Long; John F. C. Luedke; Robert J. Lundman; C. Cecilia Macazana Barragan; Brooks Mackintosh; Simone Manigo-Truell (Not admitted in DC); Scott B. Markow (Not admitted in DC); Deborah J. Matties; James A. McLaughlin; C. Martin Meekins (Not admitted in DC); Nicole Jo Moss; Ralph M. Muoio; David G. Nason; Heather L. Nevin (Not admitted in DC); Robert S. Newman; Keith A. Noreika; David P. W. Orlin; Shaun M. Palmer (Not admitted in DC); Eric J. Pan; Elizabeth Pearsall; James B. Perrine; Jeannie M. Perron; Eric Phillips; Jennifer Plitsch; C. Edward Polk, Jr. (Not admitted in DC); Christopher J. Prokop; Benjamin J. Razi (Not admitted in DC); Roni R. Reed (Resident, San Francisco, California Office); Donald J. Ridings, Jr.; Edward Holden Rippey; Andrew Rittenberg; Jason F. Robinson (Not admitted in DC); Michael L. Rosenthal; Kristina Rosette; Simone Ross; Rochelle E. Rubin; Gary Rubman (Not admitted in DC); David P. Ruschke; James P. A. Ryan; Joel Samuels; John Scheib; Paul W. Schmidt; Andrew P. Schoeffler; Jennifer Schwartz (Not admitted in DC); Vijay Shanker; Fairlea Sheehy; Alexei M. Silverman; Grail Peyton Walsh Sipes; Richard W. Smith; Carl L. Spataro, Jr. (Not admitted in DC); Jalena G. Specht (Not admitted in DC); Jeremy D. Spector; Lisa J. Stevenson; Hisanari Tanaka (Not admitted in DC); Chad Y. Tang; Cametra Thompson; Henry P. Ting; Joseph E. Topmiller (Not admitted in DC); Emin Toro (Not admitted in DC); P. Andrew Torrez (Not admitted in DC); Terry L. Turnipseed; Nancy A. Udell; Debra R. Volland; Steven M. Warshawsky; George L. Washington, Jr.; Kashi Way (Not admitted in DC); Rachel Welch (Not admitted in DC); Christopher J. Wenk (Not admitted in DC); Grady Lee White; Jeffrey L. White; Gregory M. Williams; Jarrett Williams; Mary Newcomer Williams; Elizabeth I. Winston; Joshua D. Wolson (Not admitted in DC); Robert E. Wone; Rebecca Woods; D. Grayson Yeargin (Not admitted in DC); Anthony S. Yoo; Peter Zern.
General Practice, including, but not limited to: Antitrust and Competition, Appellate, Arbitration and Alternative Dispute Resolution, Banking and Financial Services, Bankruptcy and Insolvency, Business Law, Civil Rights, Communications and Media, Copyrights, Corporate, Criminal, Election and Campaign Finance, Emerging Companies, Employee Benefits, Employment, Energy, Environmental, Food, Drug and Cosmetics, Government Contracts, Health Services, Information Services, Insurance, Intellectual Property, International, Information Technology and Internet, Latin America, Legislative, Litigation, Mergers and Acquisitions, Petroleum, Products Liability, Professional Responsibility, Real Estate, Securities, Sports, Taxation, Toxic Torts, Trade Associations, Trade Regulation, Trademarks, Transportation, Trusts and Estates and Year 2000 Computer Conversion.
San Francisco, California Office: 601 California Street, Suite 1900, 94108. Telephone: 415-591-6000.
New York, N.Y. Office: 1330 Avenue of the Americas, 10019-5400. Telephone: 212-841-1000. Telecopier: 212-841-1010.
London, England Office: Leconfield House, Curzon Street, W1Y 8A5. Telephone: 011-44-71-495-5655. Fax: 011-44-71-495-3101.
Brussels, Belgium Office: 44 Avenue des Arts (Bte. 8), 1040. Telephone: 011-32-2-549-5230. Fax: 011-32-2-502-1598.

See Professional Biographies, WASHINGTON, DISTRICT OF COLUMBIA

Covucci, George E., (AV) .... '51 '76 C.563 B.A. L.276 J.D. [Arnold&P.]
*PRACTICE AREAS: Real Estate; Tax and Estates; Bankruptcy.

Cowan, Cameron L. .... '51 '82 C.823 B.A. L.893 J.D. [Orrick,H.&S.]
*PRACTICE AREAS: Corporate Finance Law; Structured Finance Law.

Cowan, Charilyn W. ....'50 '90 Gen. Coun., National Governors Assn.

Cowan, Charles A. .... '66 '91 C.69 B.A. L.309 J.D. [Ⓐ Baach R.&L.P.]
*PRACTICE AREAS: Litigation; Environmental.

Cowan, Joyce A., (BV) ....'61 '86 C.911 B.A. L.273 J.D. [Epstein B.&G.]
*PRACTICE AREAS: Governmental and Administrative Law; Health Law.

Cowan, Kristen Tosh .... '68 '93 C.228 B.A. L.904 J.D. [Brustein&M.]
*PRACTICE AREAS: Education; Administrative Litigation; Civil Litigation; Civil Rights.

Cowan, Lee W., (AV) .... '11 '40 C&L.799 LL.B. 1025 Vermont Ave., N.W.

Cowan, Mark D. ....'49 '77 C.494 B.A. L.180 J.D. [Patton B.]

Coward, Nicholas F., (AV) .... '52 '82 C.865 B.A. L.1209 J.D. [Baker&M.]
*PRACTICE AREAS: Trade Regulations and Customs Law; Regulatory Law; Information Technology/ Telecommunications; Administrative Law; Immigration Law.

Cowden, William R., (AV) .... '— '88 C.477 B.A. L.602 J.D. [Ⓒ Reed S.]
*PRACTICE AREAS: Health Care.

Cowen, Lee .... '64 '89 C.1036 B.A. L.245 J.D. [Ⓒ Brownstein H.&F.]
*PRACTICE AREAS: Legislative; Administrative.

Cowgill, Kenneth W., (AV) ....'50 '81 C.446 B.J. L.276 J.D. Asst. U.S. Atty.

Cowie, Michael G. ....'64 '92 C.319 B.A. L.276 J.D. [Howrey S.A.&W.]

Cox, David H., (AV) ....'53 '78 C.608 B.A. L.276 J.D. [Jackson&C.] ⊙
*PRACTICE AREAS: Business Law; Corporate Law; Real Estate Law; Title Insurance Law; Cooperative Housing Law.

Cox, Douglas R. .... '56 '82 C.674 A.B. L.309 J.D. [Gibson,D.&C.]
*PRACTICE AREAS: Litigation; Constitutional; Government; Regulatory Law.

Cox, Erik A. '75 '01 C.696 B.A. L.273 J.D.
(adm. in VA; not adm. in DC) [Ⓐ P.Cacheris] ⊙
*PRACTICE AREAS: Criminal Litigation; Civil Litigation.

Cox, Joseph P. ....'48 '77 C.112 B.A. L.1049 J.D. [Stein S.S.&O.] ⊙
*PRACTICE AREAS: Customs Law; International Trade Law; Export Law.

Cox, M. Elizabeth '51 '78 C.446 B.A. L.273 J.D.
Sr. Atty, American Petroleum Institute

Cox, Mary Carolyn, (AV) .... '49 '75 C.6 B.A. L.976 J.D. [Wilmer,C.&P.]
*PRACTICE AREAS: Employment Law; Ethics; Litigation.

Cox, Michael D. . . . .'48 '73 C.623 B.A. L.893 J.D. [🄲 Dickstein S.M.&O.]
*PRACTICE AREAS: Indian Law; Gaming Law; Government Law; Legislative Practice.
Cox, Robert H. . . . . '65 '91 C.228 A.B. L.893 J.D. [🄰 Howrey S.A.&W.]
*PRACTICE AREAS: Commercial Litigation; Antitrust.
Coxson, Harold P., Jr., (AV) . . . . '47 '72 C.264 B.A. L.904 J.D. [Ogletree,D.N.S.&S.]
*PRACTICE AREAS: Labor Legislation; Labor and Employment Law; Alternative Dispute Resolution; International Labor Law; Trade and Professional Associations.
Coy, Kevin L. . . . .'— '97 C&L.276 B.S., J.D. [🄰 Mullenholz,B.&B.]
Coy, Silverio . . . . '52 '86 C.1088 B.A. L.180 J.D. [🄲 Chaikin&S.]
*PRACTICE AREAS: International Law; Immigration Law.
Coy, Wayne, Jr., (AV) . . . . '38 '69 C.31 B.A. L.128 J.D. [Cohn&M.]
*PRACTICE AREAS: Communications Law; Intellectual Property Rights; Non-Profit Corporations.
Coye, Stephen E. . . . . '56 '90 C.311 A.B. L.276 J.D. Ctr. to Protect Wkrs. Rights
Coyle, Colleen M. . . . . '63 '90 C.276 B.A. L.128 J.D. [Akin,G.S.H.&F.]
*PRACTICE AREAS: Litigation.
Coyle, John P., (AV) . . . .'55 '80 C.860 B.A. L.276 J.D. [Duncan&A.]
*PRACTICE AREAS: Litigation; Energy Law; Bankruptcy; Labor and Employment Law.
Coyle, Kevin J. '50 '79 C.397 B.a. L.831 J.D.
(adm. in PA; not adm. in DC) Amer. Rivers
Coyle, Michael P. . . . .'68 '94 C.264 B.A. L.904 J.D. [🄰 Galland,K.G.F.&S.]
Coyne, Patrick J., (AV) . . . .'56 '82 C&L.893 B.S.C.E., J.D. [Collier S.S.] (Pat.)
*PRACTICE AREAS: Federal Civil Litigation; Patent, Trademark and Copyright; Antitrust.
Coyner, Kelley S. . . . . '60 '88 C.276 B.S.F.S. L.893 J.D. Dept. of Transp.

Cozen O'Connor, A Professional Corporation, (AV)
1667 K Street, NW, 20006 ⊙
Telephone: 202-912-4800; 800-540-1355 Fax: 202-912-4830
Email: postmaster@cozen.com URL: http://www.cozen.com
Firm Members in Washington, D.C.: Ellen Jane Abromson (Not admitted in DC); Edward B. Crosland, Jr.; Matthew G. Ash; Robert G. Rathbun (Not admitted in DC); Andrew B. Katz.
Acquisitions and Divestitures, Admiralty and Maritime Law, Agents and Brokers Errors and Omissions, Alternative Dispute Resolution, Antitrust and Unfair Competition, Appellate Litigation, Appellate Practice, Arbitration and Alternative Dispute Resolution, Arson and Insurance Fraud, Asset Protection, Aviation Insurance, Aviation Law, Aviation Litigation, Aviation Products Liability, Bad Faith Litigation, Bankruptcy, Bankruptcy, Insolvency and Restructuring, Banks and Banking, Business Law, Casualty Insurance Defense, Civil Practice, Commercial Law, Commercial Litigation, Commercial Real Estate, Complex and Multi-District Litigation, Construction Claims, Construction Law, Construction Law and Litigation, Copyrights, Corporate and Partnership Law, Corporate Law, Corporate Planning, Creditors Rights, Crisis Management, Debtor and Creditor, Directors and Officers Errors and Omissions, E-Commerce and Internet Law, Electric Utility Regulation, Emerging Business and Venture Capital, Emerging Growth Companies, Employee Benefits, Employee Benefits and Executive Compensation, Employment Defense, Employment Practices, Energy, Energy Regulation, Environmental Insurance, Environmental Insurance Claims, Environmental Law, Estate Planning, Family Law, Finance, Financial Services, First and Third Party Insurance Defense, Gas Utility Regulation, Health Law, Healthcare, Healthcare Finance, Healthcare Litigation, Healthcare Regulation, Healthcare Reimbursement, Information Technology, Insurance, Insurance Bad Faith Defense, Insurance Corporate and Regulatory, Insurance Coverage, Insurance Coverage Defense, Insurance Defense, Insurance Mergers and Acquisitions, Insurance Regulation, Intellectual Property, Intellectual Property Litigation, Intentional Torts, International Estate Planning, International Tax and Estate Planning, International Trusts, Labor and Employment, Latin America Practice Group, Litigation, Management Labor Law, Marine and Maritime Law, Medical Devices Defenses, Medical Malpractice Defense, Mergers, Partnership Law, Patent Privacy Law, Planning and Land Use, Privacy Law and Regulation, Private Wealth Services, Products Liability, Professional Liability, Project Finance, Property Insurance, Property Subrogation, Public Finance, Public Utility Regulation, Punitive Damages, Punitive Damages Reinsurance, Real Estate, Real Estate Litigation, Reinsurance, RICO, Securities, Securities Litigation, Tax Litigation, Taxation, Torts, Toxic and Other Mass Torts, Toxic Torts, Trademarks, Trusts and Estates, Utility Law, Wealth Preservation, White Collar Crime, Zoning.
Charlotte, North Carolina Office: One First Union Center, Suite 2100, 301 S. College Street, 28202. Telephones: 704-376-3400; 800-762-3575. Fax: 704-334-3351.
Dallas, Texas Office: 2300 BankOne Center, 1717 Main Street, 75201. Telephones: 214-462-3000; 800-448-1207. Fax: 214-462-3299.
New York, N.Y. Office: 45 Broadway Atrium, 16th Floor, 10006. Telephones: 212-509-9400; 800-437-7040. Fax: 212-509-9492.
West Conshohocken, Pennsylvania Office: 200 Four Falls Corporate Center, Suite 400, P.O. Box 800, 19428. Telephones: 610-941-5400; 800-379-0695. Fax: 610-941-0711.
San Diego, California Office: Suite 1610, 501 West Broadway, 92101. Telephones: 619-234-1700; 800-782-3366. Fax: 619-234-7831.
Los Angeles, California Office: 777 South Figueroa Street, Suite 2850, 90017. Telephones: 213-892-7900; 800-563-1027. Fax: 213-892-7999.
Seattle, Washington Office: Suite 5200, Washington Mutual Tower, 1201 Third Avenue, 98101. Telephones: 206-340-1000; 800-423-1950. Fax: 206-621-8783.
Newark, New Jersey Office: One Newark Center, Suite 1900, 07102. Telephone: 973-286-1200; 888-200-9521. Fax: 973-242-2121.
Atlanta, Georgia Office: Suite 2200, SunTrust Plaza, 303 Peachtree Street, N.E., 30308. Telephones: 404-572-2000; 800-890-1393. Fax: 404-572-2199.
London, England Office: Tower 42, Level 23, 25 Old Broad Street, London EC2N 1HQ. Telephone: 011-44-20-7864-2000. Fax: 011-44-20-7864-2013.
Wilmington, Delaware Office: Chase Manhattan Centre, 1201 North Market Street, Suite 1400, 19801. Telephone: 302-295-2000; 888-207-2440. Fax: 302-295-2013.
Las Vegas, Nevada Office (Affiliated with the Law Offices of J. Goldberg, C. Stuart, III & D. Grossman): #1, 1000 East Sahara Avenue, 89104-3231. Telephone: 800-782-3366.
San Francisco, California Office: 425 California Street, Suite 1800, 94104-2203. Telephone: 415-617-6100; 800-818-0165. Fax: 415-617-6101.
Chicago, Illinois Office: 222 South Riverside, Suite 1500, 60606. Telephone: 312-382-3100; 877-992-6036. Fax: 312-382-8910.
Philadelphia, Pennsylvania Office: 1900 Market Street, 19103. Telephones: 215-665-2000; 800-523-2900. Fax: 215-665-2013.
Cherry Hill, New Jersey Office: LibertyView, Suite 300, 457 Haddonfield Road, P.O. Box 5459, 08002-2220. Telephone: 856-910-5000; 800-989-0499. Fax: 856-910-5075.
See Professional Biographies, WASHINGTON, DISTRICT OF COLUMBIA

Crabtree, Michael A., (BV) '53 '78
C.339 B.A. L.424 J.D. Fund Coun., Central Pension Fund, IUOE
Craddock, Scott L. . . . . '72 '99 C.383 B.A. L.178 J.D. [🄰 Gibson,D.&C.]
Craft, Alice M. . . . .'47 '73 C.228 A.B. L.1119 J.D. Admin. Law J., U.S. Dept. of Labor
Craft, Carla Draluck . . . .'66 '91 C.659 B.A. L.245 J.D. [Venable,A.B.H.&C.]
*PRACTICE AREAS: Government Contracts.
Craft, Darrell Wayne '69 '00 C.695 B.A. L.1048 J.D.
(adm. in VA; not adm. in DC) Klimek, Kolodney &Casale, PC
Craft, Robert H., Jr., (AV) . . . . '39 '73 C.674 A.B. L.309 LL.B. [Sullivan&C.]
Craft, William C. . . . .'17 '40 C&L.546 A.B., LL.B. 3900 Watson Pl.‡
Cragin, Charles A., (AV) . . . .'43 '70 C.431 B.S. L.1294 J.D. [Blank R.C.&M.]
*PRACTICE AREAS: Government; Election, Campaign and Political Law; Health Care; Administrative Law; Regulatory Law.
Craig, Brian J. . . . .'64 '94 C.128 B.A. L.904 J.D. [🄲 Cohen M.]
*PRACTICE AREAS: Business Law; Corporate Law; Commercial Law; Government Contracts; Computers and Software.
Craig, Carolyn J. . . . . '57 '88 C.446 B.S. L.472 J.D. Trial Atty.
Craig, Gregory B., (AV) . . . . '45 '73 C.309 B.A. L.976 J.D. [Williams&C.]
*PRACTICE AREAS: Federal Administrative Law; Congressional Investigations; Criminal Law; Immigration Law; International Law.
Craig, Jeffrey L. . . . .'62 '90 C.651 B.S. L.831 J.D. [Feldesman,T.L.F.&B.]
*PRACTICE AREAS: Health Care Law; Criminal Law; Corporate Law.
Craig, Peter S., (AV) . . . . '28 '53 C.604 B.A. L.976 J.D. 3406 Macomb St., N.W.‡
Craig, Roger P. . . . . '40 '65 C.976 A.B. L.309 J.D. 3515 Idaho Ave., N.W.‡
Craig, Terence G. . . . .'46 '79 C.870 B.S. L.1066 J.D. [🄲 Feder,S.C.&B.]
*PRACTICE AREAS: ERISA; Litigation.

Craig, Vicki . . . . '57 '89 C.16 B.S. L.329 J.D. 1401 New York Ave., N.W.
Craighill, G. Bowdoin, Jr., (AV) . . . '14 '39 C.797 B.A. L.273 J.D. [Craighill,M.F.C.&C.]
*PRACTICE AREAS: Estate Planning; Probate Law; Trusts.

Craighill, Mayfield, Fenwick, Cromelin & Cobb, L.L.P., (AV)
Suite 215, 4910 Massachusetts Avenue, N.W., 20016-4300
Telephone: 202-364-4242 Facsimile: 202-966-1078
URL: http://www.lawyers.com/cmfcc
Members of Firm: G. Bowdoin Craighill, Jr.; Richard H. Mayfield; Francis E. Fenwick; Paul B. Cromelin, III; Calvin H. Cobb, III.
Estate Planning, Wills and Trusts, Probate, Living Wills, Wealth Preservation, Power of Attorney, Health Directives, Family Business Planning.
See Professional Biographies, WASHINGTON, DISTRICT OF COLUMBIA

Crain, Julie J. . . . . '69 '94 C.860 B.A. L.904 J.D. [🄰 Preston G.E.&R.M.]
*PRACTICE AREAS: Litigation; Telecommunications; Antitrust.
Crain, Michael David '72 '99 C.839 B.B.A. L.1363 J.D.
(adm. in TX; not adm. in DC) 412 First Street, SE
Cramer, Adam B. . . . . '70 '95 C.645 B.S. L.94 J.D. [🄰 Collier S.S.]
*PRACTICE AREAS: Environmental Law.
Cramer, Jill A. . . . .'74 '99 C.228 A.B. L.945 J.D. [🄰 Skadden,A.S.M.&F.]
*PRACTICE AREAS: International Trade.
Crampton, Scott P., (AV) . . . . . '13 '38 C.30 A.B. L.273 LL.B. 1815 H St., N.W., Ste. 1001
Cranberg, Marcia Ann, (AV) . . . . '55 '80 C.1036 B.A. L.352 J.D. [🄲 Arnold&P.]
*PRACTICE AREAS: Telecommunications.
Crandall, Deborah L. '67 '99 C.160 B.A. L.1002 J.D.
(adm. in VA; not adm. in DC) [🄰 Shaughnessy,V.&G.]
Crandall, Susan H. . . . . '60 '88 C.475 B.A. L.128 J.D. Asst. Gen. Coun., INTELSAT
Crane, Bernard F. . . . .'53 '84 C.273 B.A. L.128 J.D. 1742 N St., N.W. (⊙Washington)
Crane, Bernard F. . . . . '53 '84 C.273 B.A. L.128 J.D. [🄲 McFadden&S.] (⊙Washington)
Crane, Martin J. . . . .'63 '90 C.476 B.S. L.273 J.D. [Sherman,D.C.L.&Y.]
*PRACTICE AREAS: Labor and Employment Law; Union Labor Law.
Cravath, B. Jeffrey, (AV) '57 '88
C.30 B.S.B.A. L.128 J.D. V.P. & Dep. Gen. Coun., Fannie Mae
Cravath, Steven G. . . . . '59 '89 C.1369 B.A. L.128 J.D. [Morrison&F.]
*PRACTICE AREAS: Investment Management.
Craven, Donald B., (AV) . . . .'— '67 C.575 A.B. L.228 LL.B. [Akin,G.S.H.&F.]
*PRACTICE AREAS: Complex Litigation; Intellectual Property Litigation; Natural Resources; Appellate Practice; Administrative Law.
Craven, J. Jeffrey, (AV) . . . .'59 '88 C&L.276 A.B., J.D. [Patton B.]
Cravens, William S. D. '72 '98 C.674 A.B. L.902 J.D.
(adm. in MA; not adm. in DC) [🄰 Spriggs&H.]
*PRACTICE AREAS: Products Liability; Toxic Torts; Litigation; Drug and Medical Device Defense.
Craver, Brian W. . . . . '57 '83 C.674 A.B. L.893 J.D. [Person&C.]
Craver, Charles B. '44 '73 C&L.188 B.S., J.D.
(adm. in CA; not adm. in DC) Prof. of Law, George Washington Univ.
Crawford, David E. . . . .'55 '83 C.612 B.A. L.273 J.D. [🄲 Betts&H.]
*PRACTICE AREAS: Energy Contracts; Utilities.
Crawford, Henry E., (AV) . . . . '51 '81 C.994 B.A. L.273 J.D. 1150 Connecticut Ave. N.W.
Crawford, J. Craig '56 '81 C&L.362 B.A., J.D.
(adm. in FL; not adm. in DC) 1325 G St NW Ste 200
Crawford, Mark D. . . . . '64 '93 C.188 B.S. L.1356 J.D. [Friedlander,M.S.K.&O.]
*PRACTICE AREAS: Civil Litigation; Insurance Defense; Labor and Employment.
Crawford, Martha '65 '98 C.66 B.A. L.1209 J.D.
(adm. in VA; not adm. in DC) Law Clk., U.S. Claims Ct.
Crawford, Susan P. . . . . '63 '91 C&L.976 B.A., J.D. [Wilmer,C.&P.]
*PRACTICE AREAS: Electronic Commerce.
Creech, Amy Strain '67 '93 C&L.16 B.A., J.D.
(adm. in AL; not adm. in DC) Legis. Analyst, National Multi Housing Council
Creech, Catherine L., (AV) . . . .'— '87 C.853 B.A. L.309 J.D. [Miller&C.]
*PRACTICE AREAS: Employee Benefits; Executive Compensation Taxation; Taxation; Employment Tax; Federal Taxation.
Creeden, Wendy M. . . . .'70 '99 C.273 B.A. L.1209 J.D. [🄰 Swidler B.S.F.]
*PRACTICE AREAS: Telecommunications.
Cregan, James R. . . . .'49 '73 C.262 B.A. L.273 J.D. 1211 Connecticut Ave.
Cremen, Timothy P. '72 '00 C&L.475 B.S.M.E., J.D.
(adm. in MI; not adm. in DC) [🄰 Sughrue M.]
*PRACTICE AREAS: Intellectual Property.
Crenshaw, William C., (AV) '53 '77
C.860 B.A. L.893 J.D. [Powell,G.F.&M.] (⊙Reston, VA)
*PRACTICE AREAS: Commercial Litigation; Bankruptcy.
Creskoff, Stephen M., (AV) . . . . '39 '69 C.659 A.B. L.446 J.D. [Creskoff&D.]

Creskoff & Doram LLP, (AV)
1620 I Street, N.W., Suite 900, 20006 ⊙
Telephone: 202-463-1300 Fax: 703-709-9246
URL: http://www.internationalaw.com
Stephen M. Creskoff; Michael R. Doram. Of Counsel: Robert M. Green.
Customs, International Trade Law, Litigation, Trade Associations, Antidumping.
Pasadena, California Office: 1028 North Lake Avenue, Suite 202, 91104. Telephone: 626-296-9161
See Professional Biographies, WASHINGTON, DISTRICT OF COLUMBIA

Crespo, Richard . . . .'69 '94 C.188 B.S. L.273 J.D. Legal Aid Society of D.C.
Cresson, Catharine B. '58 '83 C.555 B.A. L.904 J.D.
(adm. in NJ; not adm. in DC) Coun., Tri-State Commercial Closing
Cresta-Savage, Patricia A. '51 '98
C.550 B.S. L.999 J.D. 1201 Pennsylvania Ave., NW, Ste. 300
Creston, Donald P. . . . .'65 '91 C.93 B.A. L.665 J.D. [Venable,A.B.H.&C.]
*PRACTICE AREAS: Securities Regulation; Corporate Finance.
Creswell, Clayton Michael '68 '94 C.1365 B.B.A. L.446 J.D.
(adm. in MD; not adm. in DC) Sr. Assoc. Coun., UMWA Health & Retirement Funds
Crew, Darren R. '— '93 C.223 B.S.E.E. L.1292 J.D.
(adm. in PA; not adm. in DC) [🄰 R.E.Bushnell]

Crews & Hancock, P.L.C.
(See Fairfax, Virginia)

Cribb, Troy . . . .'65 '95 C.597 B.S. L.276 J.D. [🄰 Steptoe&J.]
*PRACTICE AREAS: International Law.
Crichton, Sha-Shana N. L. . . . .'71 '99 C.999 B.A. L.329 J.D. [🄰 Clifford C.R.&W.]
*PRACTICE AREAS: Litigation.
Crickman, Kenneth C. '65 '98
C.296 B.S. L.1338 J.D. [🄰 Jackson&C.] (⊙Balt., Rockville, MD)
*PRACTICE AREAS: Cooperative Housing Law; Quiet Title; Real Estate Contracts; Real Estate Title Insurance; Real Property.
Crigler, John, (AV) . . . . '47 '81 C.918 B.A. L.276 J.D. [🄲 Garvey,S.&B.]
*PRACTICE AREAS: Communications Law; Television Law; First Amendment Law; Non-Profit Organizations; Radio Law.
Crimmins, Stephen J. . . . .'49 '74 C.262 B.A. L.178 J.D. [Holland&K.]
*PRACTICE AREAS: SEC Enforcement; Securities Litigation; Commercial Litigation.
Crisman, C. Benjamin, Jr., (AV) . . .'48 '75 C.823 B.A. L.190 J.D. [Skadden,A.S.M.&F.]
Crispin, William H., (AV) . . . .'46 '75 C.197 A.B. L.145 J.D. [Crispin&B.]
*PRACTICE AREAS: Commercial Litigation; Communications Law.

Crispin & Brenner, P.L.L.C., (AV)
1156 15th Street, N.W. Suite 1105, 20005
Telephone: 202-828-0152 Fax: 202-828-0158
Email: office@crispinandbrenner.com
William H. Crispin; Dean R. Brenner; Katherine Connor Linton; John L. Richardson.
Communications Law, with Special Emphasis on Wireless Communications, Common Carrier Law, Cellular, Radio and TV Licensing, and Commercial Litigation, with Special Emphasis on Communications Law, Copyright and Intellectual Property Law, Environmental Law, and Professional Liability and Insurance Law.
See Professional Biographies, WASHINGTON, DISTRICT OF COLUMBIA

Critchlow-Bentley, Carol .... '55 '80 C.112 B.A. L.276 J.D. 3000 K St., NW, Ste. 300
Crociata, Joseph S., (AV) '51 '82
C.1044 B.A. L.30 J.D. [Bonner K.T.&C.] (⊙Rockville, MD)
*PRACTICE AREAS: Aviation Litigation; Employers Liability; Insurance; Personal Injury; Railroad Liability.
Crocker, Saône Baron, (AV) '43 '83
C.999 B.A. L.276 J.D. 1200 G Street, N.W., Suite 600
Crocker, Thomas E., Jr., (AV) .... '49 '76 C.674 A.B. L.178 J.D. [Alston&B.]
*PRACTICE AREAS: Technology Law; Foreign Asset Control; Import and Export Law; Trade Regulation; Banking Regulation.
Crockett, Elizabeth S. .... '— '94 C.575 B.A. L.128 J.D. [A King&S.]
*PRACTICE AREAS: Food and Drug Regulation.
Croessmann, Jane Helen '55 '00 C.1322 B.A. L.986 J.D.
(adm. in MO; not adm. in DC) 1155 21st St., N.W.
Croessmann, Philip R., (BV) ...... '53 '81 C.629 B.Arch. L.823 J.D. [Bastianelli,B.&K.]
*PRACTICE AREAS: Construction Law; Architect and Engineer Malpractice; Environmental Law; Insurance Coverage.
Croft, Alan B. .... '45 '71 C.910 B.S.E.E. L.904 J.D. [Baach R.&L.P.]
*PRACTICE AREAS: Commercial Litigation; Criminal Litigation; Professional Malpractice; Banking Disputes; Construction Litigation.
Croker, James E., Jr. .... '57 '82 C.446 B.A. L.893 J.D. [Alston&B.]
*PRACTICE AREAS: Federal Taxation; International Taxation.
Cromartie, Martin L., Jr. '28 '56 C.228 A.B. L.575 LL.D.
(adm. in NC; not adm. in DC) 3700 N. Capitol St. N.W.
Cromelin, Paul B., III, (AV) .... '54 '79 C.902 B.A. L.692 J.D. [Craighill,M.F.C.&C.]
*PRACTICE AREAS: Estate Planning; Probate Law; Trusts.
Crompton, R. Michael '58 '94 C&L.112 B.A., B.A.
(adm. in CA; not adm. in DC) 700 Thirteenth St., N.W., Ste. 1200
Cronauer, Adrian, (BV) .... '38 '90 C.1313 B.A. L.659 J.D. 1200 19th St., N.W.
Cronheim, Craig T. '76 '01 C.692 B.A. L.309 J.D.
(adm. in VA; not adm. in DC) [A Hogan&H.]
Cronic, Jason P. .... '68 '93 C.861 B.A. L.145 J.D. [A Wiley R.&F.]
Cronin, Mary C. '57 '87 C.477 A.B. L.262 J.D.
(adm. in NY; not adm. in DC) [C Collier S.S.]
*PRACTICE AREAS: Commercial Litigation; Real Estate Transactions.
Cronise, Elizabeth Haines .... '71 '97 C.119 B.A. L.273 J.D. [A Cohen,M.H.&T.]
Croog, Elizabeth A. '40 '67
C.914 B.A. L.309 LL.B. Secy. & Gen. Coun., National Gallery of Art
Crook, Lowry A. .... '70 '99 C&L.846 B.A., J.D. [A Wilmer,C.&P.]
Crooke, Edward C. .... '— '99 C.311 B.A. L.893 J.D. [A Hogan&H.]
Crooms, Lisa A. '62 '91 C.329 B.A. L.477 J.D.
(adm. in CA; not adm. in DC) 2900 Van Ness St., N.W.
Crosby, Hans J. '— '98 C.886 B.S. L.884 J.D.
(adm. in PA; not adm. in DC; Pat.) [A Arent F.K.P.&K.]
*PRACTICE AREAS: Intellectual Property; Biotechnology; Patents.
Crosby, Lisa Ann .... '62 '95 C.413 B.A. L.276 J.D. [A Powell,G.F.&M.]
*PRACTICE AREAS: Customs; International Trade.
Crosland, David W., (AV) .... '36 '66 C.10 B.S. L.16 LL.B. [Crosland,S.F.&M.]
Crosland, Edward B. .... '12 '35 C.797 L.16 J.D. 1722 Eye St., N.W.
Crosland, Edward B., Jr., (AV) .... '44 '71 C&L.902 B.A., J.D. [Cozen O.]
Crosland, Strand, Freeman & Mayock, (AV) .... 2008 1/2 R St., N.W.
Cross, Gary E., (AV) .... '53 '79 C.945 B.A. L.276 J.D. [Dunaway&C.]
Cross, John J., III .... '56 '81 C.103 B.A. L.880 J.D. [Hawkins,D.&W.]
Cross, Meredith B., (AV) .... '57 '83 C.228 A.B. L.880 J.D. [Wilmer,C.&P.]
*PRACTICE AREAS: Corporate Law; Securities.

Cross, Murphy, Smuck & Houston, (AV) BB
1350 Connecticut Avenue, N.W., Suite 300, 20036
Telephone: 202-393-8668 Telecopier: 202-833-2351
Email: anwalt1350@aol.com URL: http://www.lawyers.com/cms&hlaw
Members of Firm: John W. Cross (1902-1971); James Russell Murphy (1905-1986); John C. Smuck; Stuart E. Houston.
Estate Planning, Tax Planning, Tax Law, Trust Law, Trust Administration, Wills, Probate and Probate Administration.
Reference: Sun Trust Bank, N.A.
See Professional Biographies, WASHINGTON, DISTRICT OF COLUMBIA

Crosswhite, Christopher L., (AV) .... '58 '83 C.691 B.A. L.846 J.D. [Duane,M.&H.]
*PRACTICE AREAS: Health Care Law; Medicare and Medicaid; Corporate Compliance Matters; Medicare Reimbursement Controversies and Appeals; Healthcare Fraud.
Crotteau, Craig A. .... '54 '87 C.285 B.S.C.E. L.273 J.D. V.P., IT Corp.
Crotty, Michael F. '47 '72 C.424 A.B. L.597 J.D.
Dep. Gen. Coun., Litig., American Bankers Association
Crouch, Christopher A. .... '— '99 C.840 B.A. L.569 LL.M. [A Shaw P.]
Crout, Charles M. .... '67 '95 C.880 B.A. L.273 J.D. [A Andrews&K.]
*PRACTICE AREAS: Litigation.
Crow, Sonia F. .... '42 '68 C.112 B.A. L.1066 J.D. 3600 Winfield Lane, N.W.‡
Crowder, Kimberly A. .... '69 '95 C&L.893 B.A., J.D. [A Shaw P.]
*PRACTICE AREAS: Tax; Real Estate.
Crowdus, W. Warren, III .... '58 '85 C.902 B.A. L.145 J.D. [Baker&M.]
*PRACTICE AREAS: Tax Planning and Advice (Corporate and International); Tax Controversies (Corporate and International).
Crowe, Alice M. '50 '80 C.259 B.A. L.128 J.D.
(adm. in FL; not adm. in DC) Amer. Petro. Institute
Crowe, Christine M. .... '67 '92 C.690 B.A. L.273 J.D. [A Paul,H.J.&W.]
*PRACTICE AREAS: Communications Law.
Crowe, Jaime M. .... '69 '94 C.1356 B.A. L.273 J.D. [A White&C.]
Crowe, Robert B., (P.C.), (AV) '47 '73
C.1030 B.A. L.818 J.D. [Perkins,S.C.&C.] (⊙Boston, MA)
*PRACTICE AREAS: Business Law; Corporate; Tax; Real Estate; Government Relations.
Crowe, Thomas K., (AV) .... '57 '84 C.569 B.A. L.273 J.D. [T.K.Crowe]

Crowe, Thomas K., P.C., Law Offices of, (AV)
2300 M Street, N.W. Suite 800, 20037
Telephone: 202-973-2890 Fax: 202-973-2891
Email: tkcrowe@bellatlantic.net URL: http://www.tkcrowe.com
Thomas K. Crowe.
Telecommunications Law, Commercial Transactions, Litigation and Legislative.
See Professional Biographies, WASHINGTON, DISTRICT OF COLUMBIA

Crowell, Dean W., (AV) .... '49 '75 C.1165 B.A. L.1065 J.D. [C Hogan&H.]
*PRACTICE AREAS: International Commercial Transactions.

Crowell, Eldon H., (AV) .... '24 '51 C.674 A.B. L.893 LL.B. [C Crowell&M.]
*PRACTICE AREAS: Public Contract Law; International Law.

Crowell & Moring LLP, (AV) BB
1001 Pennsylvania Avenue, N.W., 20004-2595 ⊙
Telephone: 202-624-2500 Fax: 202-628-5116
URL: http://www.crowell.com
Members of Firm: Brian C. Elmer; Patrick W. Lee; W. Stanfield Johnson; Peter B. Work; Donald D. Evenson; Ridgway M. Hall, Jr.; Harold J. Heltzer; John C. Lenahan; Richard L. Beizer; R. Bruce Keiner, Jr.; Steven P. Quarles; Robert P. Charrow; Jeffrey H. Howard; Thomas P. Humphrey; Michael M. Levy; John A. Macleod; Kent R. Morrison; Herbert I. Cantor; Barry E. Cohen; Marc F. Efron; James F. McKeown; Timothy M. Biddle; Gary R. Edwards; Herbert J. Martin; Joseph I. Goldstein; Richard McMillan, Jr.; Dana C. Contratto; George D. Ruttinger; Richard E. Schwartz; Howard M. Weinman; Karen Hastie Williams; Terry L. Albertson; Joseph D. Evans; Richard J. Morvillo; Nancy S. Bryson; JoAnn E. Macbeth; David W. O'Brien; Wm. Randolph Smith; Fred S. Souk; John I. Stewart, Jr.; Frederick W. Claybrook, Jr.; Robert T. Ebert; Thomas P. Gies; Arthur N. Lerner; Andrew H. Marks; James J. Regan; Jennifer N. Waters; Rosemary M. Collyer; David Florin; John T. Brennan, Jr.; Kenneth M. Bruntel; Robert C. Davis, Jr.; Warren J. DeVecchio; Clifford B. Hendler; Michael L. Martinez; Thomas C. Means; Shauna E. Alonge; Clifton S. Elgarten; Lorraine Berman Halloway; Susan M. Hoffman; Laurel Pyke Malson; Stuart H. Newberger; David B. Siegel; Robert M. Halperin; Raymond F. Monroe; Robert L. Willmore; Alan W.H. Gourley; Wilma A. Lewis; Mark D. Plevin; David Z. Bodenheimer; Robert L. Roth; R. Timothy McCrum; Kent A. Gardiner; Pat S. Conti; Ellen Moran Dwyer; Cathy Gebhard; Luther Zeigler; Paul William Kalish; J. Michael Klise; James R. Stuart, III; William D. Wallace; Scott L. Winkelman; William L. Anderson; Charles C. Hwang; Keith T. Sampson; Jeffrey D. Sanok; Kathryn Dean Kirmayer; David M. Schnorrenberg; Jeane A. Thomas; Alexandre de Gramont; Kathleen E. Karelis; Kris David Meade; Philip Katz. Senior Counsel: Eldon H. Crowell; Richard J. Bednar; Roger N. Boyd; L. Graeme Bell, III; Irving B. Yoskowitz; Joseph M. Oliver, Jr. Counsel: Walter J. Bonner; Edward M. Green; Michael J. Cooper (Not admitted in DC); Thomas A. Guidoboni; Lloyd M. Weinerman; Mark R. Eaton; Thomas R. Lundquist; Vincent J. Sunderdick (Not admitted in DC); Linda S. Bruggeman; Anne M. ("Nancy") Wheeler; Daryl A. Lander; Richard E. Mendales; Eileen M. Gleimer; Richard J. Mannix; Kathleen M. Stratton; Kathryn A. Underhill; Barbara H. Ryland; Steven P. Taub; Edward Jackson; John E. McCarthy, Jr.; Margit H. Nahra; Robert S. Canterman; Terence F. Flynn; Glenn D. Grant; Jonathan Hale Pittman; Ellen B. Steen; Stephen M. Byers; Peter W. Paulsen; Tracy A. Roman; Monica G. Parham; Jeffrey F. Robertson; Christopher H. Wood; Robert L. Grabarek, Jr. Associates: Jody Goodman; Bazil Facchina; Linn Kaiser Redway; Brian J. Weber; Richard R. Diefendorf; Christine C. D'Alessandro; Ariel R. David; Cheryl B. Grandy; Jerome A. Murphy; Elizabeth W. Newsom; Karen A. Rosenthal; Gloria Martinez Trattles; Warren A. Zitlau; Andrew W. Bagley; Christopher E. Kaczmarek; Paul Alp; Tara Weinstock Blanchard; Kevin P. Forjette; Kimberly J. Gold; Beth M. Kramer; Alicia J. Palmer; Barry M. Parsons; Felicia Goldberg Schweitzer; Kimberly A. Tolhurst-Lapp; William G. Ackerman (Not admitted in DC); Thomas Newton Bolling; Barbara E. Butterworth; Jeffrey E. Greene; Sarah J. Zimmerman; Craig Appelbaum; Emma K. Burton; Benjamin T. Butler; Bridget E. Calhoun; Karen Canaan (Not admitted in DC); Michael I. Coe (Not admitted in DC); Daniel R. Forman; L. Rachel Gervin; Edward B. Glennon; Christopher J. Huber; Daniel A. Sasse; Dylana Leigh Blum; Tejpal Singh Chawla; Miguel H. Del Toro; Adam C. Gajadharsingh; David L. Haga; Kay Lee Kim (Not admitted in DC); Donald J. Kochan (Not admitted in DC); Peter G. Korytnyk (Not admitted in DC); Sarah C. Lindsey; Joseph P. Mastrosimone; Kirsten L. Nathanson; Aryeh S. Portnoy; Bradford K. Watts (Not admitted in DC); Bridget Allison; John Witherspoon Borchert; Jenny Chung Savidge (Not admitted in DC); J. Chris Haile; Matthew C. Hans; Karen C. Hermann; Valerie Hinko; Burke W. Kappler; J. Catherine Kunz; Amy E. Laderberg (Not admitted in DC); Shari Ross Lahlou (Not admitted in DC); William M. Mann; Christina M. Mireles; Katherine Nesbitt; Monya A. Phillip; Miguel E. Rodriquez; Jennifer Kane Schwartz; Rebecca L. Springer; Michael G. Van Arsdall; Adam Daley Wilson; Michael G. Abelow (Not admitted in DC); James Campbell Cooper; Parul P. Desai; Patricia J. B. DeWitt; F. Ryan Keith; Bridget E. Littlefield (Not admitted in DC); Edward R. Murray; Amy B. Newman; Heidi Piranian (Not admitted in DC); David E. Bell (Not admitted in DC); Jennifer A. Gruda (Not admitted in DC); Jennifer E. Schlosser (Not admitted in DC).
General Practice.
Irvine, California Office: 2010 Main Street, Suite 1200. Telephone: 949-263-8400. Fax: 949-263-8414.
London, England Office: Crowell & Moring, 180 Fleet Street, EC4A 2HG. Telephone: 44-207-413-0011. Fax: 44-207-413-0333.
Brussels, Belgium Office: Crowell & Moring, 27, Avenue Des Arts, B-1040. Telephone: 32 2 231 1799. Fax: 32 2 230 6399.
See Professional Biographies, WASHINGTON, DISTRICT OF COLUMBIA

Crowley, Conor R. '69 '97 C.446 B.S. L.128 J.D.
(adm. in VA; not adm. in DC) 1055 Thomas Jefferson St. N.W.
Crowley, Daniel H., (AV) .... '37 '66 C.976 A.B. L.446 J.D. [Crowley,H.&F.]
*PRACTICE AREAS: Probate; Estate Planning; Trust Administration.
Crowley, James I. '57 '91 C.869 B.S. L.276 J.D.
(adm. in PA; not adm. in DC) Assoc. Coun., State & Local Legal Ctr.
Crowley, Juanita A. .... '53 '77 C.856 B.A. L.276 J.D. [Wilmer,C.&P.]
*PRACTICE AREAS: Civil Practice; Employment Law; Complex Litigation.
Crowley, M. Lisanne, (AV) .... '59 '85 C.914 B.A. L.597 J.D. [Troutman S.]
*PRACTICE AREAS: Energy Law; Federal Regulation.
Crowley, Margaret A. .... '51 '88 C.232 B.S.N. L.128 J.D. Georgetown Univ. Med. Ctr.
Crowley, Patricia C. .... '— '94 C.859 B.A. L.180 J.D. [A Clifford C.R.&W.]
*PRACTICE AREAS: Litigation; Antitrust.
Crowley, William J. .... '69 '97 C.951 B.A. L.1209 J.D. [A Piper M.R.&W.]
*PRACTICE AREAS: Government Contracts; Litigation; Alternative Dispute Resolution.

Crowley, Hoge & Fein, P.C., (AV)
1710 Rhode Island Avenue, NW, Seventh Floor, 20035-3125
Telephone: 202-483-2900 Fax: 202-483-1365
URL: http://www.chf-law.com
Daniel H. Crowley; Christopher G. Hoge; Leslie G. Fein.
General Civil and Criminal Law Practice including Counselling, Negotiations, Trial and Appellate Work in Family Law, Estate Planning, Probate, Fiduciary Matters, Negligence and Small Businesses.
See Professional Biographies, WASHINGTON, DISTRICT OF COLUMBIA

Crowne, James D. '49 '80 C.446 B.A. L.1234 J.D.
(adm. in GA; not adm. in DC) Mng. Editor, The Bureau of Natl. Affs., Inc.
Crownover, Blair '33 '59 C.674 A.B. L.477 J.D.
(adm. in MI; not adm. in DC) 1101 Vermont Ave., N.W.‡
Crowson, Celine Jimenez .... '65 '90 C.228 B.S.E.E. L.276 J.D. [Hogan&H.] (Pat.)
*PRACTICE AREAS: Intellectual Property.
Cruise, Warren M. '39 '73
C.512 A.B. L.329 J.D. Chf. Adm. Law J., Off. of Employee App.
Crum, Janis M. .... '68 '98 C.1060 B.A. L.112 J.D. [A Akin,G.S.H.&F.]
*PRACTICE AREAS: Election Law; Political Compliance; Federal Ethics Compliance; State Ethics Compliance; Local Ethics Compliance.
Crumlish, Joseph D., (AV) .... '22 '67 C.276 B.S.S. L.128 J.D. [C Dahlgren&C.]
*PRACTICE AREAS: General; Corporate; Administrative; Government Contracts; Wills and Estates.
Crump, Anne Goodwin .... '62 '87 C.198 B.A. L.893 J.D. [A Fletcher,H.&H.] ⊙
*PRACTICE AREAS: Communications Law; Mass Media Law; Communications Transactions; FCC Licensing; FCC Regulation.
Crump, Jason C. .... '72 '99 C.511 B.A. L.329 J.D. [Murray,P.&C.]
Crutchfield, Firmadge W. '64 '89 C.302 B.A. L.245 J.D.
(adm. in VA; not adm. in DC) 888 17th St Nw # 1000
Crutchfield, Sam S., Jr. '34 '63 C&L.273 B.A., LL.B.
Exec. Dir., Phi Delta Phi Intl. Legal Fraternity
Cruz, Agustin .... '33 '68 L.209 J.D. The World Bk.
Cruz, Anatolio B., III '58 '92 C.446 B.S. L.128 J.D.
V.P. & Dep. Gen. Coun., Black Entertainment Television, Inc.
*RESPONSIBILITIES: Corporate Transactions; Corporate Governance; Banking; Real Estate; External Affairs.
Cruz, Leslie Sperling .... '— '97 C&L.446 B.A., J.D. [A Morgan,L.&B.]

Cruz, Néstor Enrique .... '45 '72 C.844 B.A. L.188 J.D. [🄲 Carr,M.&G.]
*PRACTICE AREAS: Estate Planning; International Estate Planning; Labor and Employment; International Law; Immigration.
Cryan, Thomas M., Jr .... '72 '97 C.902 B.A. L.1209 J.D. [🄰 Baker&M.]
Crystal, Stephen A. '65 '92 C.197 A.B. L.904 J.D.
[Armstrong T.] (⊙Kansas City, MO)
*PRACTICE AREAS: Corporate; Gaming; Governmental Affairs; Municipal; Project Finance.
Cubbage, Thomas L., III .... '66 '92 C.802 B.A. L.846 J.D. [Covington&B.]
Cubert, Jack S. '31 '67 C.563 B.E.E. L.831 J.D.
(adm. in NJ; not adm. in DC; See Pat. Sect.) [🄰 Fitzpatrick,C.H.&S.]
Cubert, Jeremy A. .... '66 '95 C.705 B.A. L.1209 J.D. [🄰 Dickstein S.M.&O.]
*PRACTICE AREAS: Patent; Licensing; Technology Transfer; Antitrust.
Cubeta, David B., (AV) .... '— '78 C.165 B.A. L.982 J.D. [Miller&C.]
*PRACTICE AREAS: Taxation; Partnership Taxation; Mineral Taxation; Corporate Law; Business Law.
Cuca, Roberto E. .... '— '94 C.674 A.B. L.187 J.D. 1800 M St., NW
Cuccias, Matthew J. .... '66 '94 C.893 B.S. L.273 J.D. [🄰 Jacobson,H.]
*PRACTICE AREAS: Trademarks and Litigation.
Cuervo, Raul A., (BV) .... '54 '85 C&L.260 B.A., J.D. [Jorden B.] ⊙
*PRACTICE AREAS: Commercial Insurance Litigation; Insurance Regulation; Bankruptcy; Workouts.
Cuffe, Ronald F., (BV) '50 '86
C.273 B.A. L.904 J.D. Asst. Gen. Coun., Smithsonian Institution
Culbertson, Robert E. .... '— '82 C.976 B.A. L.309 J.D. [King&S.]
*PRACTICE AREAS: Tax.
Culleen, Lawrence E. .... '58 '83 C&L.273 B.A., J.D. [🄲 Arnold&P.]
*PRACTICE AREAS: Environmental; Administrative.
Culleiton, Joseph E. .... '71 '98 C&L.276 B.S.B.A., J.D. [🄰 Kirkland&E.]
*PRACTICE AREAS: Litigation.
Cullen, Elizabeth A. '63 '90 C.103 B.A. L.569 J.D.
(adm. in MA; not adm. in DC)
Asst Dir., Legal & Regulatory Affs., Amer. Psychological Assn.
Cullen, Lawrence '70 '00 C.645 L.128 J.D.
(adm. in PA; not adm. in DC; Pat.) [🄰 McDermott,W.&E.]
Cullen, Michael S. '55 '86 C.276 B.S. L.1194 J.D.
(adm. in PA; not adm. in DC) National Pub. Radio
Cullen, Paul D., Jr. .... '67 '99 C.945 B.A. L.276 J.D. [Cullen]
*PRACTICE AREAS: Transportation Law; False Claims Act; Class Action Litigation; Partnership Law; Government Affairs.
Cullen, Paul D., Sr., (AV) .... '40 '65 C&L.276 A.B., J.D. [Cullen]
*PRACTICE AREAS: Transportation; Class Actions; False Claims Act; International Trade Law; Whistleblower Litigation.
Cullen, Thomas F., Jr., (AV) .... '49 '74 C&L.309 A.B., J.D. [Jones,D.R.&P.]
*PRACTICE AREAS: Litigation; Complex Business Litigation; Antitrust.

Cullen and Dykman LLP, (AV)
1101 Fourteenth Street, N.W., Suite 550, 20005 ⊙
Telephone: 202-223-8890 Telecopier: 202-457-1405
Email: cullenanddykman.com URL: http://www.cullendykman.com
Member of Firm: Kenneth T. Maloney. Of Counsel: Robert G. Hardy.
General Practice.
Brooklyn, New York Office: 177 Montague Street. Telephone: 718-855-9000. Telecopier: 718-855-4282.
Garden City, New York Office: Garden City Center, 100 Quentin Roosevelt Boulevard. Telephone: 516-357-3700. Telecopier: 516-357-3792.
Newark, New Jersey Office: One Gateway Plaza, Suite 2600. Telephone: 973-353-8410. Telecopier: 973-353-8411.
See Professional Biographies, WASHINGTON, DISTRICT OF COLUMBIA

Cullen Law Firm, The, PLLC, (AV)
1101 30th Street N.W., Suite 300, 20007
Telephone: 202-944-8600 Fax: 202-944-8611 URL: http://www.cullenlaw.com
Email: pdc@cullenlaw.com URL: http://www.lawyers.com/cullenlaw
Paul D. Cullen, Sr.; Joseph A. Black; David A. Cohen (Not admitted in DC); Paul D. Cullen, Jr.; Joseph A. Hennessey; Joyce E. Mayers; Claire L. Shapiro; James J. Whittle;—Belinda Rodriguez Harrison (Not admitted in DC).
Class Actions, Transportation Litigation, Motor Carrier Law, Interstate Commerce, Trade Association Law, Legislative Practice, Administrative Agency Practice, International Trade Regulation, Asia Trade, Customs Law, Antidumping, False Claims Act, Whistleblower Litigation, Constitutional Law, Commercial Litigation. Civil Litigation and Appeals in all State and Federal Courts.
See Professional Biographies, WASHINGTON, DISTRICT OF COLUMBIA

Cullinan, Paul H. '12 '42 C.976 B.A. L.306 LL.B.
(adm. in CT; not adm. in DC) 2475 Va. Ave., N.W.‡
Cullins, Jeanna ...'54 '81 V.P. & Deputy Gen. Counsel, Independent Fiduciary Servs., Inc.
Culotta, Jennifer Hinkebein '62 '88 C&L.421 B.A., J.D.
(adm. in LA; not adm. in DC) [🄲 Hunton&W.]
*PRACTICE AREAS: Litigation.
Culpepper, Kerry '75 '00 C.277 B.E.E. L.273 J.D.
(adm. in VA; not adm. in DC; Pat.) [🄰 D.G.Posz]
Culvahouse, Arthur B., Jr., (AV) .... '48 '73 C.838 B.S. L.569 J.D. [O'Melveny&M.]
*PRACTICE AREAS: Litigation; Corporate Law.
Culver, John C., (AV) .... '32 '63 C.309 A.B. L.707 J.D. [Arent F.K.P.&K.]
*PRACTICE AREAS: International Law; Government Relations.
Culyba, Basil C., (BV) .... '49 '78 C.901 B.A. L.1292 J.D. [Howrey S.A.&W.]
*PRACTICE AREAS: Antitrust Law; Appellate Practice; Commercial Law; Complex Litigation; Government Regulation.
Cumins, Gail T., (AV) '39 '63 C.477 A.B. L.309 J.D.
(adm. in NY; not adm. in DC) [Sharretts,P.C.&B.] ⊙
*PRACTICE AREAS: Customs Law; International Trade; Imports and Exports; Antidumping; Countervailing Duties.
Cummings, Amy Claudine '71 '99
C.197 B.A L.893 J.D 1300 I Street, N.W., 12th Floor East
Cummings, Andrea T. '— '98 C&L.893 B.A., J.D.
(adm. in VA; not adm. in DC) [🄰 Hogan&H.]
Cummings, Frank, (P.C.), (AV) '29 '59 C.319 B.A. L.178 LL.B.
[🄲 LeBoeuf,L.G.&M.]
*PRACTICE AREAS: Employee Benefits; Employment; Labor; Litigation.
Cummings, H. Don, (AV) .... '15 '43 C.604 B.A. L.309 LL.B. 1700 K St., N.W.
Cummings, Jasper L., Jr., (AV) .... '46 '72 C.228 A.B. L.976 J.D. Chf. Couns. Off.
Cummings, Jill, (AV) .... '36 '70 C.881 A.B. L.273 J.D. 1666 Connecticut Ave., N.W.
Cummings, Jody Allen '75 '00 C.228 A.B. L.178 J.D.
(adm. in MD; not adm. in DC) [🄰 Steptoe&J.]
Cummings, Philip T. '45 '71 C.813 A.B. L.976 LL.B.
(adm. in WV; not adm. in DC) 1101 Pennsylvania Ave., N.W.‡
Cumpiano, Flavio .... '67 '94 C.276 B.A. L.677 J.D. [🄰 Hughes H.&R.]
*PRACTICE AREAS: Litigation; Government Affairs; International.
Cunard, Jeffrey P., (AV) .... '55 '81 C.112 B.A. L.976 J.D. [Debevoise&P.]
*PRACTICE AREAS: Computers and Software; Technology and Science; Telecommunications Law; Communications Law; Copyright Law.
Cuncannan, Jacqueline K. .... '67 '97 C.477 A.B. L.910 J.D. [🄰 Ross,D.&B.]
Cundra, Steven D. .... '49 '75 C.665 B.A. L.569 J.D. [O'Rourke&C.]
Cuneo, Jonathan W., (AV) .... '52 '77 C.178 B.A. L.188 J.D. [Cuneo]
*PRACTICE AREAS: Litigation; Government Relations.

Cuneo, Sandra W. '48 '83 C.771 A.B. L.276 J.D.
Exec. Dir., Robert F. Kennedy Memorial

Cuneo Law Group, The, P.C., (AV) BR
317 Massachusetts Avenue, N.E. Suite 300, 20002
Telephone: 202-789-3960 Fax: 202-789-1813
Email: contact@cuneolaw.com URL: http://www.cuneolaw.com
Jonathan W. Cuneo; James J. Schweitzer; David W. Stanley; Michael G. Lenett;—Daniel Cohen; Charles J. LaDuca (Not admitted in DC). Of Counsel: Jon Anders Tostrud (Not admitted in DC).
Civil Litigation in Federal and State Courts. General Commercial Practice. Administrative, Antitrust, Copyright, Franchise, Health Care, Civil Rights, White Collar Criminal and Securities Law. Government Relations.
See Professional Biographies, WASHINGTON, DISTRICT OF COLUMBIA

Cunliffe, Robert W. '27 '58
C.529 A.B. L.831 LL.B. Coun./Legal Research, Transp. Research Bd.
Cunniff, Martin F. .... '61 '90 C.425 B.B.A. L.260 J.D. [Howrey S.A.&W.]
Cunningham, Andrew Paul '63 '90 C.93 B.A. L.823 J.D.
(adm. in NY; not adm. in DC) 1155 21st Street N.W.
Cunningham, Camille M. .... '73 '01 C.165 B.A. L.273 J.D. [🄲 Schwartz,W.&M.]
*PRACTICE AREAS: Trademarks; Communications Law; Contracts.
Cunningham, Edward I. '33 '63 C.436 A.B. L.276 J.D.
(adm. in NY; not adm. in DC) Secy., Intl. Travel Corp.
Cunningham, Harold Bryan .... '— '90 C.352 B.A. L.893 J.D. [🄰 Arnold&P.]
Cunningham, Jean M. .... '71 '97 C.602 B.A. L.273 J.D. [🄰 Spriggs&H.]
*PRACTICE AREAS: Products Liability; Toxic Torts; Litigation; Insurance Coverage; Asbestos Defense.
Cunningham, Lynn E. .... '44 '73 C.188 B.A. L.178 J.D. Neighborhood Legal Servs. Prog.
Cunningham, Nelson W. ... '59 '84 C.976 B.A. L.813 J.D. 1775 Pennsylvania Ave., N.W.
Cunningham, Paul A., (AV) .... '46 '72 C.939 B.A. L.911 J.D. [Harkins C.]
Cunningham, Richard O., (AV) .... '42 '68 C&L.273 A.B., J.D. [Steptoe&J.]
*PRACTICE AREAS: International Trade Law.
Cunningham, Scott L. '72 '01 C&L.659 B.A., J.D.
(adm. in NY; not adm. in DC) [🄰 Covington&B.]
Cunningham, Susan O. .... '62 '87 C&L.352 B.B.A., J.D. [Nixon P.]
*PRACTICE AREAS: Real Estate; Affordable Housing; Small Business Representation; Commercial Transactions.
Cunningham, Thomas F. .... '58 '83 C.575 B.A. L.128 J.D. Pres., Lanman Companies
Cunningham-Bowers, Kelly '65 '91 C.473 B.A. L.945 J.D.
(adm. in NY; not adm. in DC)
Staff Atty., National Law Ctr. on Homelessness & Poverty
Cuomo, Paul C. .... '70 '95 C.884 B.A. L.30 J.D. [🄰 Howrey S.A.&W.]
*PRACTICE AREAS: Antitrust.
Curley, Robert P. '53 '89 C.273 B.A. L.831 J.D.
(adm. in PA; not adm. in DC) [O'Donoghue&O.] ⊙
*PRACTICE AREAS: Labor and Employment; ERISA.
Curley, Thomas .... '68 '00 C.228 B.A. L.276 J.D. [🄰 Levine S.&K.]
Curley, Timothy E. .... '70 '96 C.228 B.A. L.982 J.D. [🄰 Chadbourne&P.]
Curran, Alice T. Valder .... '67 '93 C.668 B.A. L.178 J.D. [🄰 Hogan&H.]
*PRACTICE AREAS: False Claims Act; Qui Tam Litigation; Government Investigations; Civil Fraud; Health Care Fraud.
Curran, Christopher M. .... '60 '86 C.893 B.A. L.659 J.D. [White&C.]
*PRACTICE AREAS: Corporate Litigation; International Litigation; Foreign Corrupt Practices Act.
Curran, Diane J., (BV) .... '— '81 C.976 B.S. L.446 J.D. [Harmon,C.S.&E.]
Curran, Patrick M., Jr. .... '— '98 C.95 A.B. L.276 J.D. [🄰 Morgan,L.&B.]
Currie, Andrew J. .... '69 '96 C.477 B.A. L.475 J.D. [🄰 Wilmer,C.&P.]
Currie, L. Rodger '68 '93 C&L.276 A.B., J.D.
Assist. Gen. Coun., Pharmaceutical Research & Mnfct. of America
Curry, Kathleen '58 '84 C.754 B.S. L.128 J.D.
(adm. in PA; not adm. in DC) National Assn. of Independent Colleges & Univs.
Curry, Kimberly '72 '01 C.446 B.A. L.273 J.D.
(adm. in MD; not adm. in DC) [🄰 Bracewell&P.]
*PRACTICE AREAS: Energy.
Curry, William E. '58 '97 C&L.446 B.S.E.E., J.D.
(adm. in MD; not adm. in DC; See Pat. Sect.) [🄰 Kenyon&K.]
*PRACTICE AREAS: Intellectual Property.
Curtin, David J., (AV) .... '47 '72 C&L.734 B.A., J.D. [McKee N.]
*PRACTICE AREAS: Litigation.
Curtin, Joseph P., (BV) '— '91
C.576 B.S.E.E. L.446 J.D. [🄰 Banner&W.] (See Pat. Sect.)
*PRACTICE AREAS: Intellectual Property Law; Patents; Electrical Intellectual Property; Computer and Software Patents; Electronic Patents.
Curtin, Michael F., (AV) .... '40 '66 C.1031 B.S. L.128 J.D. [Sherman,M.C.&A.]
*PRACTICE AREAS: Probate; Estate Planning; Trust and Estate Litigation.
Curtin, Peter J., (BV) .... '67 '91 C.150 B.A. L.276 J.D. [Venable,A.B.H.&C.]
*PRACTICE AREAS: Intellectual Property Litigation; General Litigation.
Curtin, William J., (AV) .... '31 '56 C&L.276 B.S., J.D. 1800 M St., N.W.
Curtin, William J., III .... '69 '96 C.228 A.B. L.893 J.D. [🄰 Hogan&H.]
*PRACTICE AREAS: International Business Transactions; Corporate and Securities Law.
Curtis, Kenneth W., (BV) .... '42 '73 C.107 B.S. L.273 J.D. [Finnegan,H.F.G.&D.]
*PRACTICE AREAS: Civil Litigation; Intellectual Property Litigation; Federal Litigation; Trial Practice.
Curtis, Lee P., (AV) .... '53 '78 C.645 B.A. L.665 J.D. [Perkins C.]
*PRACTICE AREAS: Government Contract Law; Commercial Law and Litigation.
Curtis, Rena I. .... '71 '99 C.446 B.A. L.180 J.D. [🄰 Dechert]
*PRACTICE AREAS: Commercial Litigation; SEC Enforcement; Antitrust.
Curtis, Suzanne E. '64 '92 C.951 B.A. L.770 J.D.
(adm. in CA; not adm. in DC) [🄲 Cole,R.&B.]
*PRACTICE AREAS: Communications Law; Cable TV; Telecommunications Law.
Curtis, Vincent J., Jr., (AV) .... '39 '65 C.749 B.S. L.276 J.D. [Fletcher,H.&H.] ⊙
*PRACTICE AREAS: Communications Law; FCC Licensing; FCC Regulation; Communications Transactions.
Curtis, Wendy Butler '73 '98 C.550 B.A. L.446 J.D.
(adm. in TX; not adm. in DC) [🄰 Fulbright&J.]
*PRACTICE AREAS: Litigation; Health Law.

Curtis, Mallet-Prevost, Colt & Mosle LLP, (AV) BR
Suite 1205L, 1801 K Street, N.W., 20006 ⊙
Telephone: 202-452-7373 Telecopier: 202-452-7333
Email: info@cm-p.com URL: http://www.cm-p.com
Resident Partners: Preston Brown; Samuel Rosenthal; Jeffrey I. Zuckerman.
General Corporate Practice including Securities, Investment Management, International Transactions and Finance, Antitrust and Trade Regulation, Regulation of International Transactions, Employment. Civil Trial and Appellate Practice, Criminal Defense. Consultants on Laws of Latin American Countries.
New York, N.Y. Office: 101 Park Avenue. Telephone: 212-696-6000. Telecopier: 212-697-1559.
Newark, New Jersey Office: One Gateway Center, Suite 403. Telephone: 973-622-0605. Telecopier: 973-622-5646.
Houston, Texas Office: 2 Houston, Center, 909 Fannin Street, Suite 3725. Telephone: 713-759-9555. Telecopier: 713-759-0712.
Stamford, Connecticut Office: Financial Centre, 695 East Main Street. Telephone: 203-359-6200. Telecopier: 203-328-2617.
Mexico City, D.F., Mexico Office: Curtis, Mallet-Prevost, Colt & Mosle, Ruben Dario 281, Pisos 8 & 9, Col. Bosque de Chapultepec, 11530 Mexico, D.F. Telephone: 52-55-5282-0444. Telecopier: 52-55-5282-0637.

(This Listing Continued)

Curtis, Mallet-Prevost, Colt & Mosle LLP (Continued)

Paris, France Office: 15 rue d'Astorg, 75008. Telephone: +33-1 42-66-39-10. Telecopier: +33-1 42-66-39-62 .
London, England Office: One Cornhill, EC3V 3ND. Telephone: 0207-743-6310. Telecopier: 0207-743-6311.
Frankfurt am Main 1, Germany Office: Staufenstrasse 42. Telephone: +49-69-971-4420. Telecopier: +49-69-17 33 99.
Muscat, Sultanate of Oman Office: Jewel Beach-134. Telephone: 968-564-495. Telecopier: 968-564-497.
Milan, Italy Office: Curtis, Mallet-Prevost & Gilioli, Piazzale Principessa Clotilde 8, 20121. Telephone: +(39) 02 29 00-29 32. Telefax: +(39) 02 65 75 969.
Revisers of the Argentina, Bolivia, Brazil, Chile, Colombia, Costa Rica, Dominican Republic, Ecuador, El Salvador, Guatemala, Honduras, Mexico, Nicaragua, Peru, Uruguay and Venezuela Law Digests for this Directory.
See Professional Biographies, WASHINGTON, DISTRICT OF COLUMBIA

Curtiss, Catherine, (AV) ....'50 '80 C.477 B.A. L.276 J.D. [Hughes H.&R.]
*PRACTICE AREAS: International Trade and Investment Law; Federal Litigation; Customs Law.
Curtiss, James R. .... '53 '79 C&L.546 B.A., J.D. [Winston&S.]
*PRACTICE AREAS: Energy Law; Electric Power; Nuclear Energy Law.
Curto, Michael A. ....'58 '83 C.276 A.B. L.128 J.D. [Patton B.]
Curzon, Elliott Rowles, (BV) .... '55 '83 C.763 B.A. L.464 J.D. [Ⓒ Dechert]
*PRACTICE AREAS: Securities Law; Regulatory Policy; Securities Regulation; Broker-Dealer Regulation.
Cushing, David J., (AV) '52 '77 C.602 B.S.E.E. L.446 J.D.
[Sughrue M.] (See Pat. Sect.)
*PRACTICE AREAS: Intellectual Property Law; Litigation.
Cushing, Michael .... '47 '75 C&L.309 A.B., J.D. 1900 E Street, NW
Cushing, Thomas S., III '67 '97 C.880 B.A. L.1209 J.D.
(adm. in VA; not adm. in DC) [Ⓐ Collier S.S.]
*PRACTICE AREAS: Litigation.
Custer, B. H. '43 '81 C.309 A.B. L.178 J.D.
(adm. in NY; not adm. in DC) 5032 Belt Rd., N.W.
Custer, B. Scott, Jr. .... '37 '65 C&L.309 A.B., LL.B. [Shaw P.]
*PRACTICE AREAS: Technology and Telecommunications Outsourcing; International Transactions; Project Finance; Privatization; Corporate Law.
Cutler, Barry J. ....'43 '68 C.188 A.B. L.178 J.D. [Baker&H.]
*PRACTICE AREAS: Litigation; Trade Regulation; Consumer Law.
Cutler, Christopher M. '72 '00 C.276 B.S. L.260 J.D.
(adm. in FL; not adm. in DC) 450 5th Street, NW
Cutler, Jay B. '30 '56 C.569 B.S. L.1009 LL.B.
Special Counsel & Director-Government Relations, American Psychiatric Association
Cutler, John A. '53 '78 C.893 B.A. L.280 J.D.
(adm. in GA; not adm. in DC) Amer. Assn. of Ret. Persons
Cutler, John M., Jr., (AV) ....'47 '76 C.797 B.A. L.276 J.D. [McCarthy,S.&H.]
*PRACTICE AREAS: Transportation Law; Energy Law.
Cutler, Lloyd N., (AV) ....'17 '40 C&L.976 B.A., LL.B. [Ⓒ Wilmer,C.&P.]
*PRACTICE AREAS: Alternative Dispute Resolution; Business Law; Constitutional Law; International Law; Regulatory Law.
Cutler, Michael E., (AV) ....'55 '82 C.881 A.B. L.813 J.D. [Covington&B.]
Cutler, Stephanie, (BV) ....'— '84 C.188 B.A. L.276 J.D. [Ⓒ Foley,H.&E.]
*PRACTICE AREAS: Business; Real Estate.
Cutler, Thomas P. ....'45 '80 C.976 B.A. L.273 J.D. P.O. Box 18423
Cutlip, Meikka A., (CV) ....'66 '92 C.352 B.A. L.273 J.D. [Ⓐ Heenan,A.&R.] ‡
*PRACTICE AREAS: Labor and Employment; Trade Association Law; Litigation.
Cutrone, Roseann M. ....'61 '86 C.105 B.A. L.309 J.D. [Ⓒ Skadden,A.S.M.&F.]
Cutter, David F. .... '67 '95 C.477 B.G.S. L.128 J.D. [Ⓐ Hogan&H.]
*PRACTICE AREAS: Litigation.
Cutts, Matthew D. '71 '97 C&L.893 B.A., J.D.
(adm. in MD; not adm. in DC) [Ⓐ Patton B.]
Cwalina, Christopher G. ....'71 '97 C.282 B.A. L.1002 J.D. [Ⓐ Spriggs&H.]
*PRACTICE AREAS: Products Liability; Toxic Torts; Litigation; Drug and Medical Device Defense.
Cymrot, Mark A., (AV) ....'47 '73 C.273 B.A. L.178 J.D. [Baker&H.]
*PRACTICE AREAS: International; Litigation; Fraud Law.
Cymrot, Steven L. '42 '68 C.103 A.B. L.309 LL.B.
(adm. in NY; not adm. in DC) 410 A St., S.E.
Cynamon, David J., (P.C.), (AV) ....'49 '73 C.103 A.B. L.309 J.D. [Shaw P.]
*PRACTICE AREAS: Litigation.
Cynkar, Robert J. ....'52 '77 C.674 A.B. L.569 J.D. [Cooper&K.]
*PRACTICE AREAS: Trial and Appellate Litigation; Regulatory Litigation; Constitutional Litigation.
Cys, Richard L., (AV) ....'44 '69 C.174 B.S. L.276 J.D. [Davis W.T.]
*PRACTICE AREAS: Communications and Media; Litigation; White Collar Criminal Defense.
Czaban, James Nicholas ....'66 '92 C.112 B.A. L.893 J.D. [Heller E.W.&M.]
*PRACTICE AREAS: Food, Drug and Cosmetics; Advertising; Litigation; Intellectual Property Litigation.
Czarra, Edgar F., Jr., (AV) .... '28 '54 C&L.976 B.S., LL.B. 1201 Penn. Ave., N.W.
Czelen, John C. .... '48 '74 C.119 B.A. L.665 J.D. 3411 30th St., N.W.
Dabaghi, William K. ...... '45 '72 C.1284 L.846 J.D. [Arter&H.] (⊙Geneva, Switzerland)
*PRACTICE AREAS: Financial Services; International Trade Policy; World Trade Organization Dispute Settlement; Government Relations.
Dabney, Jasmin A. ....'63 '96 C.645 B.A. L.904 J.D. [Ⓐ J.M.Riddick&Assoc.]
*PRACTICE AREAS: Employment Discrimination (30%); Family Law (30%); Personal Injury (25%); Corporate Law (10%); General Practice (5%).
Dabney, John Jay '70 '98 C&L.893 B.A., J.D.
(adm. in NY; not adm. in DC) [Ⓐ McDermott,W.&E.]
Dacek, Raymond F. .... '30 '56 C.659 B.S. L.309 LL.B. [Ⓒ Thelen R.&P.]
*PRACTICE AREAS: Tax.
Daddario, Emilio Q. .... '18 '42 C.918 B.A. L.184 LL.B. 3133 Conn. Ave., N.W.‡
Dadey, Kristin Marie .... '73 '99 C&L.823 B.A., J.D. 200 Constitution Ave. NW
Dadlani, Jack B. .... '63 '89 C&L.93 B.A., J.D. Aspen Systems Corp.
Daebeler, Paul F. '66 '91
C.401 B.S.E.E. L.1338 J.D. [Ⓒ Venable,A.B.H.&C.] (See Pat. Sect.)
*PRACTICE AREAS: Intellectual Property.
Dahlberg, Julia A. ....'60 '87 C.112 B.A. L.1065 J.D. [Gibson,D.&C.]
*PRACTICE AREAS: Litigation; Securities; Labor and Employment; Communications.

Dahlgren and Close, (AV) BB
1000 Connecticut Avenue, N.W., Suite 204, 20036
Telephone: 202-659-1440 Fax: 202-659-5755
Email: dahlgrenclose@cs.com URL: http://www.lawyers.com/dahlgrencloselaw
Members of Firm: John O. Dahlgren (1913-1989); David P. Close. Of Counsel: Joseph D. Crumlish. General, International, Corporate and Administrative Practice, Retirement Planning, Wills, Estates, Trusts, Probate, Family Wealth Transfer, Expert Witnessing for Wills, Estates and Probate.
See Professional Biographies, WASHINGTON, DISTRICT OF COLUMBIA

Dai, Miwako '71 '97 L.999 LL.B.
(adm. in NY; not adm. in DC) 1155 21st St., N.W.‡
Daigle, Lesley E. ....'70 '98 C.976 B.A. L.846 J.D. [Ⓐ Long A.&N.]
*PRACTICE AREAS: Commercial Real Estate; Secured Lending.
Dailard, Cynthia B. .... '68 '95 C.309 A.B. L.1375 J.D. Alan Guttmacher Inst.
Dailard, Scott D. .... '68 '94 C.309 B.A. L.1066 J.D. [Ⓐ Dow,L.&A.]
Daileader, Robert L., Jr. ....'54 '80 C.602 B.B.A. L.982 J.D. [Nixon P.]
*PRACTICE AREAS: Energy Finance; Project Finance.
Dailey, Jonathan Christian .... '69 '94 C.951 B.A. L.30 J.D. [Dailey&Assoc.]
Dailey, Margaret S. ... '54 '84 C.188 B.F.A. L.276 J.D. MCI Communications Corporation
Dailey, Rosemary E. ....'72 '97 C.473 B.A. L.128 J.D. [Ⓐ Venable,A.B.H.&C.]
*PRACTICE AREAS: Labor and Employment; Immigration.
Dailey, Virginia C. '— '00 C&L.259 B.S., J.D.
(adm. in FL; not adm. in DC) [Ⓐ Verner,L.B.M.&H.]
*PRACTICE AREAS: International Trade; International Dispute Resolution.
Dailey & Associates, Chtd. ....Suite 200 2900 M Street
Daines, Kendall W. ....'56 '87 C.951 B.A. L.477 J.D. [Ⓒ Groom]
*PRACTICE AREAS: Employee Benefits.
Dajani, F. Martin ....'66 '91 C.378 B.A. L.502 J.D. [Ⓒ Piper M.R.&W.]
*PRACTICE AREAS: Antitrust and Trade Regulation; Litigation.
Dakolias, Maria M. '65 '91 C.311 B.A. L.1209 J.D.
(adm. in VA; not adm. in DC) The World Bk.
Dale, Frank M., Jr. ....'67 '95 C.577 B.A. L.228 J.D. [Ⓐ Swidler B.S.F.]
*PRACTICE AREAS: Energy; Litigation.

Dale, G. Allen, (AV) '51 '78 C.34 B.A. L.276 J.D. BB
307 G Street, N.W., 20001
Telephone: 202-638-2900 Fax: 202-783-1654
Email: gallendale@aol.com URL: http://www.lawyers.com/gallendalelaw
***PRACTICE AREAS: Criminal Law (100%).**
Criminal Defense, Drug Crimes, Sex Crimes, Domestic Violence, Assault and Battery, Homicide, Criminal Appeals, White Collar Crimes, Business Fraud, Driving While Intoxicated, Traffic Violations, Police Misconduct, Federal Criminal Defense.
See Professional Biographies, WASHINGTON, DISTRICT OF COLUMBIA

Dale, Kathleen C. '72 '00 C.966 B.A. L.276 J.D.
(adm. in MD; not adm. in DC) [Ⓐ Dewey B.]
*PRACTICE AREAS: Tax Litigation and Controversy.
Dale, Mitchell W. ....'49 '76 C.228 B.A. L.276 J.D. [Ⓒ Miller&C.]
*PRACTICE AREAS: International Trade.
Dale, William P., (AV) ....'49 '74 C.788 A.B. L.276 J.D. [McChesney&D.] ⊙
d'Alelio, Ellen ....'38 '75 C.741 B.A. L.309 J.D. [Steptoe&J.]
*PRACTICE AREAS: Electronic Banking; Electronic Commerce; Banking; Banking Regulation; Corporate.
D'Alessandro, Christine C. ....'65 '91 C.823 B.A. L.569 J.D. [Ⓐ Crowell&M.]
D'Alessandro, David, (AV) '51 '77 C.321 B.A. L.818 J.D.
(adm. in MA; not adm. in DC) [Morrison&H.]
*PRACTICE AREAS: Public Utility Regulation; Energy.
Daley, Henry J. '— '97 C.971 B.S. L.588 J.D.
[Ⓐ Pillsbury W.] (See Pat. Sect.) (⊙Mc Lean, VA)
*PRACTICE AREAS: Intellectual Property; Patent Prosecution; Patent Litigation.
Daley, John D. .... '— '00 C.145 A.B. L.309 J.D. [Ⓐ Arnold&P.]
*PRACTICE AREAS: Litigation; International Law; Public Policy and Legislative.
Daley, Kathleen Alice '66 '93
C.188 B.S. L.276 J.D. [Ⓐ Finnegan,H.F.G.&D.] (See Pat. Sect.)
*PRACTICE AREAS: Intellectual Property Licensing; Intellectual Property Litigation; Mechanical Intellectual Property; Biomedical Technology.
Dallett, Estelina L. ....'64 '94 C&L.309 A.B., J.D. [Ⓐ Dickstein S.M.&O.]
*PRACTICE AREAS: Alternative Dispute Resolution; Mass Tort Settlements; Insurance.
Dalton, Carol Ann, Law Office '50 '86
C.563 B.A. L.564 J.D. 1150 Connecticut Ave., 9th Fl.
Daly, John A. '48 '83 C.259 B.A. L.1209 J.D.
Dir. Atty. Place., Stone Legal Resources Grp.
Daly, Joseph P. .... '57 '82 C.1350 B.A. L.273 J.D. [Muldoon M.&F.]
*PRACTICE AREAS: Financial Institutions Regulation; Holding Companies Regulation; Regulation; Savings and Loan Regulation; Thrift Institutions Regulation.
Daly, Kelly A. .... '64 '89 C&L.602 B.A., J.D. [Morrison&H.]
*PRACTICE AREAS: Energy; Public Utility Law; Telecommunications Law; Litigation.
Daly, Thomas R. .... '53 '80 C.712 B.A. L.1209 J.D. [Ⓒ Hewes,G.L.&D.] (⊙Fairfax, VA)
Damari, Tamir D. .... '— '95 C.1349 B.A. L.273 J.D. [Ⓐ S.H.Goldschmidt]
Damato, Joseph R., (AV) ....'56 '81 C.676 B.A. L.273 J.D. [Seyfarth S.]
*PRACTICE AREAS: Labor Law; Employment Law.
D'Ambrosio, Peter M., (AV) '50 '76 C&L.276 B.A., J.D.
(adm. in VA; not adm. in DC) [Winston&S.]
*PRACTICE AREAS: Construction Claims; Construction and Surety Law; Public Construction Law.
Damelin, Harold, (AV) ....'46 '72 C&L.93 B.S., J.D. [Powers,P.S.&V.]
*PRACTICE AREAS: Criminal Law; Health Care Fraud; Grand Jury Practice; Administrative Law.
Damelin, Rachel B. ....'72 '98 C.860 B.A. L.93 J.D. [Ⓐ Morgan,L.&B.]
Damelin, Scott R. ....'69 '95 C.860 B.A. L.93 J.D. [Ⓐ Beveridge&D.]
*PRACTICE AREAS: Civil Litigation; Criminal Litigation; Environmental Law.
Dameron, Del Stiltner ....'53 '77 C.1319 B.A. L.150 J.D. [McKenna&C.]
Damico, Nicholas P., (AV) ....'37 '63 C.728 B.S. L.659 LL.B. [Damico&Assoc.]
*PRACTICE AREAS: Employee Benefits; Estate Planning; Taxation.
D'Amico, Thomas J., (AV) '47 '74 C.910 B.S.E.E. L.273 J.D.
[Dickstein S.M.&O.] (Pat.)
*PRACTICE AREAS: Intellectual Property Law.
D'Amico, William S., (AV) .... '38 '67 C&L.93 B.S., J.D. [Chadbourne&P.]

Damico & Associates, (AV)
1101 - 17th Street, N.W. Suite 820, 20036-4704
Telephone: 202-872-1045 Fax: 202-872-1141
URL: http://www.lawyers.com/damico&associates
Nicholas P. Damico. Of Counsel: Edward M. Luria.
Employee Benefits, Pension and Profit Sharing Plans, Employee Stock Ownership Plans, Executive Compensation, Estate Planning.
See Professional Biographies, WASHINGTON, DISTRICT OF COLUMBIA

Dana, Jane T. .... '53 '79 C.575 B.A. L.178 J.D. 3105 36th St., N.W.
Dana, Jonathan M., (AV) .... '55 '84 C.966 B.A. L.1162 J.D. [Feldesman,T.L.F.&B.]
*PRACTICE AREAS: Family Law.
Danaher, Brian E. ....'61 '91 C&L.276 A.B., J.D. Sr. Coun., Marriott Intl., Inc.
*RESPONSIBILITIES: Health Care Law; Regulatory.
Danas, Andrew M., (AV) ....'55 '82 C.184 B.A. L.273 J.D. [Grove,J.&C.]
*PRACTICE AREAS: Maritime; Transportation; Antitrust; Litigation; International Law.
Dance, Simon E. ....'— '91 C.999 B.Sc. L.602 J.D. [Ⓒ Foley&L.]
*PRACTICE AREAS: Litigation; Intellectual Property Litigation; Environmental Law.
Dandeker, Rebecca L. ....'67 '94 C.999 B.S. L.276 J.D. [Ⓐ Kirkpatrick&L.]
*PRACTICE AREAS: Food and Drug Law; Pharmaceuticals; Dietary Supplements; Clinical Research.
D'Andrea, Elisa A. .... '64 '96 C.259 B.A. L.273 J.D. 1800 M St., NW
D'Andrea, John J. '65 '91 C.321 B.A. L.982 J.D.
(adm. in NY; not adm. in DC) [Akin,G.S.H.&F.]
*PRACTICE AREAS: Health and Hospital Law; Health Insurance Law.
Daneker, Michael D. .... '65 '92 C.976 B.A. L.880 J.D. [Arnold&P.]
*PRACTICE AREAS: Environmental; Litigation.
Danello, Daniel F., (AV) '57 '85 C.309 A.B. L.228 J.D.
Assoc. Gen. Coun., Fannie Mae
Danforth, John C., (AV) '— '64 C.674 A.B. L.976 LL.B.
(adm. in NY; not adm. in DC) [Bryan C.] (⊙St. Louis, MO)
*PRACTICE AREAS: Corporate Law; Health Care Law; International Law.
Dang, Thu A. '66 '95 C.893 B.S.E.E. L.273 J.D.
(adm. in VA; not adm. in DC) [Ⓐ Kenyon&K.]
*PRACTICE AREAS: Intellectual Property.
d'Angelo, George V. ....'54 '83 L.056 J.D. 1730 K St., N.W.
Daniel, Aubrey M., III, (AV) .... '41 '66 C.893 B.A. L.692 LL.B. [Williams&C.]

Daniel, John E. .... '43 '68 C&L.16 B.S., J.D. [Ⓒ Morgan,L.&B.]
Daniel, Paul G. .... '53 '78 C.982 B.A. L.188 J.D. MCI Communications Corp.
Daniel-Grobler, Anne M. .... '— '89 C.309 A.B. L.893 J.D. 2722 Poplar St., N.W.
Daniels, Brooke '76 '01 C.145 B.A. L.861 J.D.
(adm. in VA; not adm. in DC) [Ⓐ Shaw P.]
Daniels, David W.T. .... '67 '94 C.674 A.B. L.145 J.D. [Ⓐ Gibson,D.&C.]
*PRACTICE AREAS: Securities Litigation; Intellectual Property Litigation; Complex Commercial Litigation.
Daniels, Denise A. .... '56 '85 C&L.446 B.S., J.D. [Ⓒ Zuckert,S.&R.]
*PRACTICE AREAS: Aviation Law; Aviation Regulation; Airport Law; Aviation Accidents; Transportation Safety.
Daniels, Diana M., (AV) '49 '75 C.188 B.A. L.309 J.D.
V.P., Gen. Coun. & Secy., Washington Post Co., The
Daniels, Kara L. .... '73 '98 C.311 B.A. L.273 J.D. [Ⓐ Holland&K.]
*PRACTICE AREAS: Commercial Litigation; Trade Secrets Litigation; Media Law.
Daniels, Rhonda L. '55 '81 C.112 B.A. L.1065 J.D.
Corp. Coun., American Resort Develop. Assn.
Daniels, Scott M., (AV) '52 '77
C.118 B.A. L.188 J.D. [Armstrong,W.H.M.&N.] (See Pat. Sect.)
*PRACTICE AREAS: Intellectual Property Law.
Danish, Kyle W. .... '67 '96 C.311 B.A. L.831 J.D. [Ⓐ Van Ness F.]
*PRACTICE AREAS: Environment; International Environment.
Dankner, Donald K., (AV) .... '47 '73 C.966 B.A. L.273 J.D. [Winston&S.]
*PRACTICE AREAS: Energy Law; Litigation.
Dann, Thomas S., (AV) .... '52 '79 C.813 B.A. L.904 J.D. [Hewes,G.L.&D.]
Dannenbaum, Daniel G., (BV) '62 '90 C.309 A.B. L.273 J.D.
[Ⓐ Lewis] (☉Fairfax, VA)
*PRACTICE AREAS: Family Law; Civil Litigation.
Dannenberg, Elizabeth Kate Derting '72 '00 C.838 B.A. L.273 J.D.
(adm. in VA; not adm. in DC) 1401 H St., N.W.
Dannenmaier, Eric R. '59 '85
C.225 B.A. L.94 J.D. Dir., North-South Ctr. Envir. Law Prog.
Danner-Riccardi, Jennifer '69 '94 L.273
(adm. in MD; not adm. in DC) 1775 Pennsylvania Ave., N.W.
Dansky, Stacey .... '73 '98 C.880 B.A. L.846 J.D. [Ⓐ Williams&C.]
*PRACTICE AREAS: Litigation.
Dantzic, David S. .... '— '95 C.188 B.A. L.309 J.D. [Ⓐ Latham&W.]
*PRACTICE AREAS: Mergers and Acquisitions; General Corporate; Venture Capital Financings.
Danyliw, Bohdan .... '24 '54 C.128 A.B. L.276 LL.B. 1575 Eye St. N.W.‡
Danziger, Martin B. .... '31 '58 C&L.560 B.A., LL.B. [Ⓐ Danziger,M.&F.] ‡

Danziger, Mak and Fu, LLP
Suite 420, 5301 Wisconsin Avenue, N.W., 20015
Telephone: 202-686-9958 Fax: 202-686-9790
Email: immlaw@dmfllp.com URL: http://www.lawyers.com/danzigermak
Members of Firm: Pamela J. Mak; K. N. Minnie Fu. Associates: Denise Ann Thomasson (Not admitted in DC); Martin B. Danziger (Retired).
Immigration and Consular Matters.
See Professional Biographies, WASHINGTON, DISTRICT OF COLUMBIA

Darby, Joan M. .... '53 '79 C.914 B.A. L.273 J.D. [Ⓒ Dickstein S.M.&O.]
*PRACTICE AREAS: Energy.
Darby, Timothy J. '47 '88 C.1356 B.I.S. L.1209 J.D.
(adm. in VA; not adm. in DC) Acquisition Mgr., The Bureau of Natl. Affs., Inc.
D'Arcy, Sean G. .... '62 '92 C.1030 B.A. L.128 J.D. [Akin,G.S.H.&F.]
*PRACTICE AREAS: Public Policy.
Darden, Eric J., (AV) .... '63 '89 C.446 B.A. L.228 J.D. [McManus,S.A.&D.]
*PRACTICE AREAS: Construction Law; Civil Litigation; Administrative Law.
Dargan, Catherine Janine .... '70 '94 C.813 A.B. L.309 J.D. [Ⓐ Covington&B.]
Dargatis, David G. .... '64 '97 C.645 B.S. L.352 J.D. [Ⓐ Arnold&P.]
*PRACTICE AREAS: Corporate Law; Securities.
Darling, Erin Lewis '— '99 C.575 B.A. L.276 J.D
(adm. in NC; not adm. in DC) 701 Pennsylvania Avenue, N.W.
Darneille, Hopewell H., III, (AV) .... '— '74 C.976 A.B. L.276 J.D. [Verner,L.B.M.&H.]
*PRACTICE AREAS: Government Contracts Law; Litigation; Maritime Law.
Daroff, William C. .... '68 '99 C&L.930 B.A., J.D. 415 Second Street, N.E.
Daron, Threet T. .... '73 '00 C.174 B.S. L.602 J.D. 2300 "M" St., N.W.
Darr, Charles V. .... '65 '01 C.1027 B.S. L.273 J.D. Sr. Milit Coun.
Darr, Kurt J. .... '40 '64 C.182 B.A. L.494 J.D. Prof. of Hosp. Adm., George Wash. Univ.
Darrah, Dorothy A. .... '50 '78 C.681 A.B. L.94 J.D. 1440 New York Ave. N.W.
Darrow, James D., (AV) .... '49 '76 C.95 B.A. L.273 J.D. [Sutherland A.&B.]
*PRACTICE AREAS: Mergers and Acquisitions; Debt and Equity Finance; Securities; Commercial Contracts.
Daschbach, Richard J. .... '36 '65 C&L.276 B.A., J.D. Seafarers Intl. Union
Dasef, David .... '— '81 C.373 B.A. L.477 J.D. Coun., Watson Wyatt Worldwide
Dash, Jill F. '75 '00 C.188 B.A. L.228 J.D.
(adm. in MD; not adm. in DC) [Ⓐ Akin,G.S.H.&F.]
*PRACTICE AREAS: Labor.
Dash, Samuel .... '25 '50 C.831 S.B. L.309 J.D. Prof. of Law, Georgetown Univ.
Dashefsky, Michael '70 '97 C.696 B.A. L.276 J.D.
(adm. in NJ; not adm. in DC) [Ⓐ Morrison&F.]
*PRACTICE AREAS: Antitrust.
Dashoff, Brad M. '75 '00 C.477 B.A. L.659 J.D.
(adm. in MD; not adm. in DC) [Ⓐ Shaw P.]
*PRACTICE AREAS: Corporate Law; Securities.
Dattu, Firoz '71 '96 C.025 B.A. L.309 J.D.
(adm. in NY; not adm. in DC) Corp. Exec. Bd., The
Daub, Harold J., Jr. '41 '66 C.910 B.S.B.A. L.546 J.D.
(adm. in NE; not adm. in DC) Princ., Dir., Govt. Affs., Deloitte & Touche
Daub, Peter M. .... '56 '82 C.309 A.B. L.976 J.D. [Baker&M.]
*PRACTICE AREAS: Tax Planning and Advice (Corporate and International); Tax Controversies (Corporate and International).
Daubert, Gail L. '65 '99 C.597 B.S. L.30 J.D.
(adm. in IL; not adm. in DC) [Ⓐ Reed S.]
*PRACTICE AREAS: Health Care.
Daubert, Todd D. .... '67 '94 C.612 B.A.E. L.228 J.D. [Ⓐ Kelley D.&W.]
*PRACTICE AREAS: Telecommunications Law.
Dauphinais, Richard .... '53 '79 C&L.602 B.B.A., J.D. 1712 N St., N.W.
Dausses, Markus '— '01 C.869 B.S. L.276 J.D.
(adm. in NY; not adm. in DC) [Ⓐ Coudert B.]
*PRACTICE AREAS: Project Finance; Energy; Privatization.
Davé, Raj S. .... '58 '97 C.999 B.S. L.306 J.D. [Ⓐ Morrison&F.]
Davenport, David M., (AV) '44 '68 C.524 B.S. L.273 J.D.
[Coates,D.&G.] & [Ⓒ Coates&D.] (☉Richmond, VA)
*PRACTICE AREAS: Corporate Law; Mergers and Acquisitions; Business Law; Commercial Law; Civil Litigation.
Davenport, James P., (AV) .... '44 '71 C&L.228 A.B., J.D. [Baach R.&L.P.]
*PRACTICE AREAS: Scientific and Technical Litigation; Product Liability; Medical Malpractice; Legal Malpractice; Environmental Insurance Coverage.
Davenport, Lisa M. .... '63 '94 C.347 B.S. L.174 J.D. [Ⓐ Bailey]
*PRACTICE AREAS: Commercial Real Estate.
Davenport, Michele Sherman, (AV) .... '63 '89 C.276 B.S.F.S. L.178 J.D. [Cameron&H.]
*PRACTICE AREAS: International Trade Regulation; Litigation.
Daves, George L., (AV) .... '43 '67 C&L.280 B.B.A., J.D. [Nixon P.]
*PRACTICE AREAS: Real Estate; Real Estate Finance; Housing and Urban Affairs.
David, Ariel R. .... '64 '91 C.966 B.B.A. L.831 J.D. [Ⓐ Crowell&M.]
David, Joseph M., Jr. .... '43 '73 C.820 B.A. L.602 J.D. [Jones,D.R.&P.]
*PRACTICE AREAS: Litigation; Products Liability.
David, Michael '— '00 L.446 J.D.
(adm. in MD; not adm. in DC; See Pat. Sect.) [Ⓐ Banner&W.]
*PRACTICE AREAS: Patents; Patent Licensing; Pharmaceutical Intellectual Property; Medical Intellectual Property Law.
David, Richard G., (AV) .... '41 '67 C.659 B.S.E. L.309 LL.B. [Womble C.S.&R.]
*PRACTICE AREAS: Commercial Real Estate Transactions; Contracts; Leasing; Business Formation and Planning; Taxation.
Davidow, Charles E., (AV) .... '54 '80 C.31 B.A. L.309 J.D. [Wilmer,C.&P.]
*PRACTICE AREAS: Securities; Civil Practice.
Davidow, Joel, (AV) .... '38 '65 C.674 B.A. L.178 LL.B. [Miller&C.]
*PRACTICE AREAS: Antitrust Law; International Litigation; Intellectual Property Litigation; Trade Regulation Law.
Davidson, Daniel I., (AV) .... '36 '59 C&L.178 A.B., J.D. [Spiegel&M.]
*PRACTICE AREAS: Administrative Law; Antitrust; Energy; Hydroelectricity; Qui Tam.
Davidson, Daniel M. .... '50 '75 C.951 B.A. L.309 J.D. [Hogan&H.]
*PRACTICE AREAS: Taxation Law; Business Law.
Davidson, Diane Hofbauer .... '57 '83 C.228 B.A. L.880 J.D. The Walt Disney Co.
Davidson, Garber A., Jr. '39 '72 C.112 A.B. L.575 J.D.
(adm. in MD; not adm. in DC) Checchi & Co. Consulting, Inc.
Davidson, Howard A. '45 '70 C.94 B.A. L.93 J.D.
(adm. in MA; not adm. in DC)
Staff Dir., Nat. Legal Res. Ctr. for Child Advo. & Prot., Amer. Bar Assn.
Davidson, Jeffery S. .... '67 '98 C.1326 B.S. L.831 J.D. [Ⓐ Howrey S.A.&W.]
*PRACTICE AREAS: Antitrust and Trade Regulation; Commercial Litigation; Copyright Litigation.
Davidson, Jeffrey J. .... '50 '77 C&L.228 A.B., J.D. [Hale&D.]
*PRACTICE AREAS: Environmental Law.
Davidson, Jennifer A. .... '69 '94 C.477 B.A. L.893 J.D. [Ⓐ Kleinfeld,K.&B.]
*PRACTICE AREAS: Food, Drug and Cosmetics Law; Food and Drug Regulation; Drug and Medical Device Regulation; Advertising Law; Civil Litigation.
Davidson, Joel R. .... '59 '85 C.94 B.A. L.976 J.D. 414 6th St. N.E.
Davidson, Nestor M. '— '99 C.309 A.B. L.178 J.D.
(adm. in NY; not adm. in DC) [Ⓐ Latham&W.]
*PRACTICE AREAS: Affordable Housing; Commercial Real Estate; Civil Appeals.
Davidson, Seth A., (AV) .... '53 '78 C.893 B.A. L.178 J.D. [Fleischman&W.]
Davidson, Steven K. .... '60 '85 C.94 B.A. L.597 J.D. [Steptoe&J.]
*PRACTICE AREAS: Civil Litigation; Commercial Litigation; White Collar Crime; Bankruptcy Law; Insurance Coverage.

Davidson, Michael M.
(See Arlington, Virginia)

Davies, Amy G. .... '56 '84 C.604 B.A. L.966 J.D. [Ⓐ Thompson H.]
*PRACTICE AREAS: Employee Benefits Law; ERISA.
Davies, Charles R. '40 '68 C.229 B.S. L.276 J.D.
Sr. V. P. & Gen. Coun., GEICO Corp.
Davies, Christopher R.L. .... '70 '98 C.918 B.A. L.813 J.D. [Ⓐ Wilmer,C.&P.]
Davies, Patrick S. .... '61 '88 C.754 B.S. L.602 J.D. [Ⓒ Covington&B.]
Davies, Ross E. .... '62 '97 C.910 B.A. L.145 J.D. [Ⓐ Shea&G.]
Davila-Bloise, Edwin G., (BV) .... '57 '84 C&L.276 B.S.B.A., J.D. [Ober,K.G.&S.]
Davine, Amy C. .... '72 '97 C.990 B.A. L.602 J.D. [Ⓐ Patton B.]
Davis, Alison N. .... '66 '91 C.012 B.A. L.309 J.D. [Ⓐ Krupin O.]
*PRACTICE AREAS: Labor and Employment.
Davis, Angela Jordan .... '56 '82 C.329 B.A. L.309 J.D. Dir., Pub. Def. Serv.
Davis, Anne P. .... '67 '97 C.197 A.B. L.893 J.D. [Ⓐ Arnold&P.]
*PRACTICE AREAS: Litigation; Antitrust.
Davis, Bruce N., (AV) .... '57 '84 C.893 B.A. L.309 J.D. [White&C.]
*PRACTICE AREAS: Taxation; International Income Tax; International Taxation.
Davis, Christopher M., (AV) .... '54 '84 C.1350 B.A. L.128 J.D. [Davis&D.]
Davis, Clarence, Jr. '38 '75 C.873 B.S. L.64 J.D.
(adm. in NJ; not adm. in DC) Union Medical Ctr., Inc.
Davis, Drew M. '47 '73 C.695 B.A. L.273 J.D.
V.P., Fed. Affs., National Soft Drink Assn.
Davis, F. Nikki '— '99 C&L.1243 B.S., J.D.
(adm. in AR; not adm. in DC) [Ⓐ Morgan,L.&B.]
Davis, Garrett V. ...... '54 '84 C.923 B.S. L.64 J.D. [Roylance,A.B.&G.] (See Pat. Sect.)
*PRACTICE AREAS: Patent Law; Chemical Patent Law.
Davis, Geoffrey G. .... '58 '85 C.31 B.A. L.893 J.D. [Patton B.]
Davis, Glenn E. .... '49 '74 C.464 A.B. L.1066 J.D. [Kleinfeld,K.&B.] ☉
*PRACTICE AREAS: Food, Drug and Cosmetic Law; Drug and Medical Device Regulation; Advertising Law.
Davis, James F., (AV) '34 '64
C.339 B.S.Ch.E. L.276 J.D. [Howrey S.A.&W.] (See Pat. Sect.)
*PRACTICE AREAS: Intellectual Property; Patent Law; Patent, Trademark and Copyright Law.
Davis, James R., II .... '67 '98 C.1369 B.B.A. L.378 J.D. [Ⓐ Arent F.K.P.&K.]
*PRACTICE AREAS: Intellectual Property; Internet Law; Cyberspace Law; Trademark; Copyright.
Davis, Jeffrey G. .... '68 '94 C.1064 B.S. L.990 J.D. [McKee N.]
*PRACTICE AREAS: Taxation.
Davis, Jeffrey S. .... '66 '92 C.1349 B.S. L.145 J.D. Atty., NASD Regulation, Inc.
Davis, Jennifer B. .... '68 '94 C.228 B.A. L.245 J.D. [Ⓐ Hyman,P.&M.]
Davis, Jennifer Leigh '71 '97 C&L.16 B.S., J.D.
(adm. in AL; not adm. in DC) Atty., Southern Co.
Davis, John E. .... '— '91 C&L.893 B.A., J.D. [Ⓒ Miller&C.]
*PRACTICE AREAS: Foreign Corrupt Practices Act; Import and Export Law; International Trade Regulation; Foreign Trade Sanctions; Federal Litigation.
Davis, Joseph G. .... '65 '92 C.31 B.A. L.1066 J.D. [Ⓐ Willkie F.&G.]
*PRACTICE AREAS: Litigation.
Davis, Julie W., (AV) .... '40 '80 C.228 B.A. L.276 J.D. [Caplin&D.]
*PRACTICE AREAS: Federal Tax Controversies and Litigation; Health Care Taxation; Estate Planning.
Davis, Karl E. .... '30 '59 C.301 B.A. L.273 J.D. 1828 L Street, N.W., Suite 500‡
Davis, Kimberly M. .... '71 '97 C.893 B.A. L.472 J.D. [Ⓐ Kalbian H.]
*PRACTICE AREAS: State, Federal and International Taxation; Corporate Law; Business Law.
Davis, L. Burton .... '70 '96 C.575 B.A. L.976 J.D. [Ⓐ Cleary,G.S.&H.]
Davis, Lanny J., (AV) .... '45 '70 C&L.976 B.A., LL.B. [Patton B.]
Davis, Linda Kay .... '44 '73 C.112 B.A. L.309 J.D. Assoc. J., Supr. Ct.
Davis, Mark David, (AV) .... '56 '83 C&L.101 B.A., J.D. [Davis&L.]
*PRACTICE AREAS: International Trade; Commercial Arbitration; Business Immigration; Russian Legal Development.
Davis, Mark G. .... '62 '87 C.128 B.A. L.273 J.D. [McDermott,W.&E.]
Davis, Mary E., (AV) .... '53 '84 C.1350 B.A. L.128 J.D. [Davis&D.]
Davis, Melissa Hall '73 '01 C.188 B.A. L.893 J.D.
(adm. in VA; not adm. in DC) [Ⓐ Wilmer,C.&P.]
Davis, Michael R., (AV) '42 '70
C.1213 B.S.Chem. L.273 J.D. [Wenderoth,L.&P.] (See Pat. Sect.)
*PRACTICE AREAS: Chemicals; Pharmaceuticals; Metallurgy; Biochemicals.

Davis, Mindy G. .... '62 '87 C&L.665 B.A., J.D. [Howrey S.A.&W.]
*PRACTICE AREAS: Commercial Litigation; Insurance Coverage.
Davis, Patricia L. '59 '85 C.375 B.S. L.900 J.D.
(adm. in KS; not adm. in DC) 1901 Columbia Rd., N.W.
Davis, Peter J. .... '63 '94 C.188 A.B. L.128 J.D. [[C] Morrison&F.] (Pat.)
*PRACTICE AREAS: Intellectual Property.
Davis, Philip J. .... '48 '73 C.855 B.A. L.273 J.D. [Wiley R.&F.]
*PRACTICE AREAS: Government Contracts; Litigation.
Davis, Rhonda L. '52 '83 C.339 B.S.B.A. L.209 J.D.
(adm. in IL; not adm. in DC) William M. Mercer, Inc.
Davis, Richard L. .... '71 '97 C.1 B.B.A. L.273 J.D. [[A] Fleischman&W.]
Davis, Richard L. .... '72 '00 C.999 B.S L.446 J.D. [[A] Hogan&H.]
Davis, Richard S., (BV) .... '53 '80 C.823 A.B. L.128 J.D. [Beveridge&D.]
*PRACTICE AREAS: Environmental Law; Clean Water Act; Water Quality; Litigation.
Davis, Rikke K. '64 '91 C.289 B.A. L.64 J.D.
(adm. in MD; not adm. in DC) 1850 M St., N.W.
Davis, Robert A., Jr. .... '50 '92 C.831 B.Mus.Ed. L.813 J.D. [[C] Cadwalader,W.&T.]
*PRACTICE AREAS: Tax.
Davis, Robert C., Jr. .... '52 '78 C.623 B.B.A. L.616 J.D. [Crowell&M.]
*PRACTICE AREAS: Environmental Law; Hazardous Materials Law; Natural Resources Law; Toxic Substances Law; Toxic Torts.
Davis, Robert P., (AV) .... '49 '80 C.103 A.B. L.276 J.D. [Mayer,B.&P.]
Davis, Sarah E. .... '71 '97 C.197 A.B. L.472 J.D. [[A] Howrey S.A.&W.]
*PRACTICE AREAS: Commercial Litigation.
Davis, Sharon L. .... '67 '91 C.88 B.S. L.145 J.D. [[A] Williams&C.]
Davis, Shelley F. .... '52 '78 C.704 B.A. L.127 J.D. Farmworker Justice Fund, Inc.
Davis, Smith W., (P.C.), (AV) .... '48 '78 C&L.976 B.A., J.D. [Akin,G.S.H.&F.]
*PRACTICE AREAS: Public Policy.
Davis, Sylvia D. .... '66 '98 C.273 B.S. L.276 J.D. [[A] Katten M.Z.]
*PRACTICE AREAS: Intellectual Property.
Davis, Terry G., (AV) ..... '53 '81 C.14 B.A. L.192 J.D. [Davis&H.] (⊙Montgomery, AL)
Davis, Thomas A., (AV) .... '38 '63 C&L.260 B.A., LL.B. [Davis&H.]
*PRACTICE AREAS: Taxation Law; Legislation Law; Commodities Futures Law; Administrative Law.
Davis, Virginia A. .... '66 '91 C.10 B.A. L.309 J.D. [Katten M.Z.]
*PRACTICE AREAS: Commercial Real Estate.
Davis, Warren N. .... '47 '75 C&L.276 B.S., J.D. [Sutherland A.&B.]
*PRACTICE AREAS: Derivative Products; Corporate Finance; Equipment Leasing; Corporate Fiduciary Law; Securities Disclosure.
Davis, William A. .... '11 '44 C.887 A.B. L.329 LL.B. 5254 Chillum Pl., N.E.
Davis, William A. .... '63 '87 C.665 B.A. L.178 J.D. [Mintz,L.C.F.G.&P.]
*PRACTICE AREAS: Complex Business Litigation; Intellectual Property Litigation; Telecommunications Litigation; Securities Litigation.
Davis, William E., (AV) .... '43 '68 C.575 A.B. L.945 J.D. [Ross,M.&F.]
*PRACTICE AREAS: Estate Planning; Estate Administration; Real Estate; Small Business Corporations.
Davis, William Woodhouse '69 '00 C.902 B.A. L.896 J.D.
(adm. in VA; not adm. in DC) [[A] Hunton&W.]
*PRACTICE AREAS: International Project Finance; Domestic Project Finance; Leveraged Lease Financing.

Davis & Campbell L.L.C.
1828 L Street, N.W., Suite 660, 20036 ⊙
Telephone: 202-293-5690 Fax: 202-296-5706
URL: http://www.dcamplaw.com
Of Counsel: Carlos M. Recio.
Management Labor Law, Corporate Law, Trial Practice, Employee Benefits, Mergers and Acquisitions, Employer Rights, Local Government Rights, Employment Law, Commercial Law, Commercial Litigation, Complex Litigation, Intellectual Property, Securities Regulation, Antitrust, Immigration and Naturalization, Real Estate, Zoning Planning and Land Use, Tax Law, Estate Planning, Probate.
Peoria, Illinois Office: 401 Main Street, Suite 1600, 61602-1241. Telephone: 309-673-1681. Telecopier: 309-673-1690.
Chicago, Illinois Office: 135 South La Salle Street, Suite 1424, 60603. Telephone: 312-795-1681; 312-201-0999. Fax: 312-201-0749.
See Professional Biographies, WASHINGTON, DISTRICT OF COLUMBIA

Davis & Davis, (AV) .... 601 Indiana Avenue, N.W.

Davis & Harman LLP, (AV)
Suite 1200, 1455 Pennsylvania Avenue, N.W., 20004
Telephone: 202-347-2230 Fax: 202-393-3310
Members of Firm: Thomas A. Davis; William B. Harman, Jr.; John T. Adney; Joseph F. McKeever, III; Richard S. Belas; Barbara N. Seymon-Hirsch; Randolf Hurst Hardock; Craig R. Springfield; Kirk Van Brunt; Mark E. Griffin. Of Counsel: Thomas W. Ewing (Not admitted in DC); Thomas L. Stapleton. Associates: Bryan W. Keene; Daniela Stoia; John J. O'Neill, Jr. (Not admitted in DC); John J. Spina; Chelsea K. Bachrach (Not admitted in DC).
General Practice including Administrative, Agricultural, Commodities, Insurance and Tax Law. Legislative Practice.
See Professional Biographies, WASHINGTON, DISTRICT OF COLUMBIA

Davis & Hatcher, L.L.C., (AV)
1201 Pennsylvania Ave., Ste. 300 (⊙Montgomery, AL; Atlanta, GA)

Davis & Leiman, P.C., (AV)
5108 34th Street, N.W., 20008
Telephone: 202-296-4790 Fax: 202-296-4791
Email: dltrade@aol.com URL: http://www.lawyers.com/davis&leiman
Mark David Davis.
International Trade Law with special emphasis in the area of U.S. Import and Export Law, Anti-Dumping, Countervailing Duties Law, W.T.O. & GATT. International Commercial Arbitration.
See Professional Biographies, WASHINGTON, DISTRICT OF COLUMBIA

Davis Polk & Wardwell, (AV) [BB]
1300 I Street, N.W., 20005 ⊙
Telephone: 202-962-7000 Fax: 202-962-7111
URL: http://www.dpw.com
Members of Firm: Stephen H. Case; Scott W. Muller; Jordan Luke; Dana L. Trier. Resident Counsel: Margaret M. Ayres; Theodore A. Doremus, Jr.; Robert W. Weaver. Resident Associate: Margaret E.M. Paulsen (Not admitted in DC).
General Practice.
New York, N.Y. Office: 450 Lexington Avenue, 10017. Telephone: 212-450-4000. Fax: 212-450-3800.
Menlo Park, California Office: 1600 El Camino Real, Menlo Park, California, 94025. Telephone: 650-752-2111.
London, England Office: 99 Gresham Street, London, EC2V 7NG, England. Telephone: 44-171-418-1300. Fax: 44-171-418-1400.
Paris, France Office: 15, avenue Matignon, 75008 Paris, France. Telephone: 33-01-56-59-36-00. Fax: 33-01-56-59-36-90.
Frankfurt, Germany Office: MesseTurm, 60308 Frankfurt am Main, Germany. Telephone: 49-69-97-57-03-0. Fax: 49-69-74-77-44.
Tokyo, Japan Office: Akasaka Twin Tower East, 11th Floor, 17-22, Akasaka 2-Chome, Minato-ku, Tokyo 107-0052, Japan. Telephone: 81-3-5561-4421. Fax (main): 81-3-5561-4425.
Hong Kong, China Office: The Hong Kong Club Building, 3A Chater Road, Hong Kong. Telephone: 852-2533-3300. Fax: 852-2533-3388.
See Professional Biographies, WASHINGTON, DISTRICT OF COLUMBIA

Davis-Smith, Yvonne .... '— '00 C.329 B.S. L.1364 J.D. 2501 Northampton St.

Davis Wright Tremaine LLP, (AV)
1500 K Street, N.W. Suite 450, 20005 ⊙
Telephone: 202-508-6600 FAX: 202-508-6699
URL: http://www.dwt.com

(This Listing Continued)

Davis Wright Tremaine LLP (Continued)

Partners: James S. Blitz; Pamela C. Cooper; Richard L. Cys; Laura R. Handman; Keith M. Korenchuk (Not admitted in DC); Randall B. Lowe; Richard D. Marks; James B. Vasile; Daniel Waggoner. Resident Associates: Howard A. Benowitz; Constance M. Pendleton; Rebecca R. Reed; Holly Rachel Smith. Counsel: Julie Kaminski Corsig; Mary Lawless Plantamura; Daniel W. Pugh.
Administrative; Banking; Communications; Corporate; Customs Law; Domestic and International Trade Regulation Law; Employee Benefits; Environmental; Government Contracts Law; Government Investigations; Labor; Legislative Practice; Litigation; Maritime; Media Law; Nuclear Energy; Securities; Tax.
Anchorage, Alaska Office: Suite 800, 701 West 8th Avenue. 99501-3408. Telephone: 907-257-5300. FAX: 907-257-5399.
Bellevue, Washington Office: 1800 Bellevue Place, 10500 NE 8th Street. 98004. Telephone: 425-646-6100. FAX: 425-646-6199.
Honolulu, Hawaii Office: 1360 Pauahi Tower, 1001 Bishop Street, 96813. Telephone: 808-538-3360. FAX: 808-526-0101.
Los Angeles, California Office: 865 South Figueroa Street, Suite 2400, 90017-2566. Telephone: 213-633-6800. FAX: 213-633-6899.
New York, N.Y. Office: 1740 Broadway, 10019. Telephone: 212-489-8230. FAX: 212-489-8340.
Portland, Oregon Office: 2300 First Interstate Tower, 1300 SW Fifth Avenue. 97201. Telephone: 503-241-2300. FAX: 503-778-5299.
San Francisco, California Office: One Embarcadero Center, Suite 600, 94111. Telephone: 415-276-6500. FAX: 415-276-6599.
Seattle, Washington Office: 2600 Century Square, 1501 Fourth Avenue. 98101. Telephone: 206-622-3150. FAX: 206-628-7040.
Shanghai, China Office: Suite 450 E. Tower, Shanghai Centre, 1376 Nanjing Xi Lu, 200040. Telephone: 011-8621-6279-8560. FAX: 011-8621-6279-8547.
See Professional Biographies, WASHINGTON, DISTRICT OF COLUMBIA

Davish, Patrick T. '61 '87 C.659 B.A. L.309 J.D.
(adm. in PA; not adm. in DC) Asst. Coun., Merck & Co., Inc.
Davison, Calvin, (AV) .... '32 '59 C.473 A.B. L.309 LL.B. 1001 Penn. Ave., N.W.
Davison, Dennis A., (AV) .... '48 '74 C.273 B.A. L.1292 J.D. [Long A.&N.]
*PRACTICE AREAS: Real Estate Development; Business Law; Business Litigation.
Davison, Douglas J. .... '68 '93 C&L.645 B.S., J.D. [[C] Wilmer,C.&P.]
*PRACTICE AREAS: Securities Law.
Davison, Jacob O. .... '— '99 C&L.276 B.A., J.D. [[A] Cleary,G.S.&H.]
Dawe, Christopher M. '63 '95 C.118 B.A. L.893 J.D.
(adm. in ME; not adm. in DC) [[A] Vinson&E.]
Dawson, Albert R. .... '44 '79 C.560 B.A. L.564 J.D. [Baker&D.]
*PRACTICE AREAS: Insurance; Regulatory.
Dawson, Donald S., & Associates, (AV) '08 '38
C.502 B.S. L.273 J.D. 1133 Connecticut Ave., NW
Dawson, Rhett B. '43 '72 C.340 B.A. L.910 J.D.
(adm. in MO; not adm. in DC) 4207 Linnean Ave. N.W.
Dawson, Robert K. '46 '71 C.861 B.S. L.192 J.D.
(adm. in AL; not adm. in DC) Vice Chmn., Cassidy & Assocs., Inc.
Dawson, Teresa E. .... '62 '91 C.98 B.A. L.276 J.D. [[C] O'Melveny&M.]
*PRACTICE AREAS: Litigation; Regulatory Law.
Day, Charles Williamson, Jr. .... '65 '98 C.976 B.A. L.273 J.D. [[A] Gebhardt&Assoc.]
*PRACTICE AREAS: Employment Law; Employment Discrimination; Civil Rights; Federal Civil Practice; Civil Litigation.
Day, Christopher William '69 '00 C.576 B.S. L.180 J.D.
(adm. in MD; not adm. in DC; See Pat. Sect.) [[A] Finnegan,H.F.G.&D.]
*PRACTICE AREAS: Intellectual Property Infringement; Intellectual Property Litigation; International Intellectual Property; Mechanical Intellectual Property; Computer and Software Patents.
Day, James E. .... '60 '90 C.311 B.A. L.659 J.D. [[A] Kirkpatrick&L.]
*PRACTICE AREAS: Civil Litigation; SEC Enforcement; Securities Litigation; Employment Litigation; Securities Class Action.
Day, James M., (AV) '30 '59
C.664 B.A. L.30 LL.B. 1001 Connecticut Ave., NW, Ste. 819‡
Dayan, Jeannette '— '96 C.951 B.A. L.976 J.D.
(adm. in NY; not adm. in DC) [[A] Miller&C.]
*PRACTICE AREAS: Employee Benefits; Taxation.
Dayan, Leon .... '63 '91 C.813 A.B. L.1066 J.D. [Bredhoff&K.]
Dayanim, Behnam .... '67 '93 C.978 B.A. L.309 J.D. [[A] Paul,H.J.&W.]
*PRACTICE AREAS: Technology and Electronic Commerce Law and Policy; International Trade; Intellectual Property; False Advertising.
Dayle, Aldys A. .... '70 '96 C.276 B.S. L.904 J.D. [[A] Goodwin P.]
Days, Drew S., III '41 '66 C.299 A.B. L.976 LL.B.
(adm. in IL; not adm. in DC) [[C] Morrison&F.]
*PRACTICE AREAS: Civil Appeals; Criminal Appeals.
Dazé, Michel A., (AV) ..... '— '83 C.688 B.S. L.982 J.D. Assoc. Gen. Coun., Fannie Mae
*RESPONSIBILITIES: Tax.
Deacon, James W., II '73 '98 C.861 B.A. L.276 J.D.
(adm. in LA; not adm. in DC) [[A] Kelley D.&W.]
*PRACTICE AREAS: Telecommunications Law; Commercial Litigation.
Deal, David T. '44 '73 C.884 B.C.E. L.273 J.D.
Dir., Lgl Svc & Asst. Gen. Cnsl, American Petroleum Institute
Deal, Jill B. .... '41 '79 C.112 B.S. L.128 J.D. [Fish&R.]
*PRACTICE AREAS: Food and Drug Regulation; European Union Law; Drug and Medical Device Litigation.
Dean, Benjamin Masur .... '71 '98 C.197 A.B. L.893 J.D. [[A] Shaw P.]
Dean, Danell Palladine, (AV) '63 '88 C.659 B.A. L.1338 J.D.
[[A] Feldesman,T.L.F.&B.]
*PRACTICE AREAS: Family Law; Commercial Litigation; Construction Litigation.
Dean, David P. .... '55 '91 C.145 B.A. L.178 J.D. [James&H.]
Dean, Howard .... '61 '94 C.767 B.A. L.464 J.D. Coun., World Bank
Dean, James Robert, Jr .... '72 '99 C.228 A.B. L.309 J.D. [[A] Covington&B.]
Dean, Jennifer L. .... '71 '97 C.928 B.A. L.94 J.D. [[A] Drinker B.&R.]
Dean, John E. .... '50 '83 C&L.276 B.A., J.D. [Dean B.&M.]
Dean, John P. .... '49 '80 C.999 B.A. L.178 J.D. 1155 21st Street, N.W.
Dean, Karen Sullivan .... '72 '97 C.228 A.B. L.904 J.D. [[A] Ivins,P.&B.]
Dean, Patricia Ann .... '49 '81 C&L.276 B.S.B.A., J.D. [Arnold&P.]
*PRACTICE AREAS: Litigation.
Dean, Richard A., (AV) .... '48 '73 C.210 B.A. L.1119 J.D. [Arter&H.]
*PRACTICE AREAS: Litigation; Products Liability Law; Toxic Tort; Insurance Coverage.
Dean, Richard N. .... '55 '81 C.880 B.A. L.893 J.D. [Coudert B.]
*PRACTICE AREAS: Russian Law; Corporate; Foreign Corrupt Practices Act.
Dean, S. Bobo .... '32 '63 C&L.976 B.A., LL.B. [Hobbs,S.D.&W.]
Dean, Warren L., Jr. .... '47 '75 C&L.446 B.A., J.D. [Thompson C.]
*PRACTICE AREAS: Antitrust and Trade Regulation; Transportation; Aviation and Aerospace.
Dean Blakey & Moskowitz, (AV) .... 1101 Vermont Ave., N.W.
Deane, Heather Shoaf '72 '97 C.645 B.A. L.904 J.D.
(adm. in VA; not adm. in DC) [[A] Bonner K.T.&C.] (⊙Fairfax, VA)
Deane, John Russell, III, (AV) .... '43 '72 C.30 B.A. L.276 J.D. [Trainum,S.&D.]
*PRACTICE AREAS: Corporate Law; Administrative Law; Nonprofit and Charitable Organizations.
Deane, Sherry C. .... '47 '81 C.28 B.A. L.184 J.D. Children's Def. Fund

de Angeli, Michael M., P.C.
(See Rockville, Maryland)

DeAngelis, Ildiko P. '47 '80
C.705 B.A. L.30 J.D. Asst. Gen. Coun., Smithsonian Institution‡

Dearborn, Philip M., III .... '60 '87 C.199 B.A. L.945 J.D. [Piliero,M.&P.]
*PRACTICE AREAS: Government Contracts; Employment Law; Commercial Leasing; Native American Law; Civil Litigation.
De Arment, Roderick Allen, (AV) ....'48 '73 C.855 B.A. L.893 J.D. [Covington&B.]
De Armond Mucchetti, Suzanne ....'69 '00 C.788 B.A. L.30 J.D. [Ⓐ Weiner B.S.K.]
*PRACTICE AREAS: Mortgage Banking Law; Real Estate Finance; Regulatory Compliance.
de Arteaga, Jose A. '63 '98 C.959 B.S. L.966 J.D.
(adm. in WI; not adm. in DC) AFL-CIO
Deasy, Oonagh L. '67 '95 C.1369 B.B.A. L.861 J.D.
(adm. in VA; not adm. in DC) [Ⓐ Katten M.Z.]
*PRACTICE AREAS: Public Finance.
de Bernardo, Mark A., (AV) ....'53 '79 C.436 B.A. L.276 J.D. [Littler M.]
*PRACTICE AREAS: Drug and Alcohol Testing; Labor and Employment.
Deberry, Sharon Y. Christmas '63 '94 L.446 J.D.
(adm. in MD; not adm. in DC) 1700 K St., N.W.
Debevoise, Eli Whitney, II, (AV) ....'53 '77 C.976 B.A. L.309 J.D. [Arnold&P.]
*PRACTICE AREAS: International Law.

Debevoise & Plimpton, (AV) BB
555 13th Street N.W., 20004 ⊙
Telephone: 202-383-8000 Telecopier: 202-383-8118
URL: http://www.debevoise.com
Members of Firm: Judah Best; Ralph C. Ferrara; Jeffrey P. Cunard; Colby A. Smith; Kenneth J. Berman; Jonathan R. Tuttle. Counsel: Ann M. Ashton; Phillip D. Parker; Herbert Thomas. Retired Partner: Robert J. Geniesse. Associates: Scott N. Auby; Rachel H. Graham; Elizabeth N. Kaplan; Philip S. Khinda.
Class Actions, Commercial Law, Communications and Media, Corporate Law, Government, Intellectual Property, Litigation, Securities, White Collar Crime.
New York, N.Y. Office: 919 Third Avenue, 10022-3904. Telephone: 212-909-6000. Telex: (Domestic) 148377 DEBSTEVE NYK. Telecopier: (212) 909-6836.
Paris, France Office: 21 Avenue George V 75008. Telephone: (33-1) 40 73 12 12. Telecopier: (33-1) 47 20 50 82. Telex: 648141F DPPAR.
London, England Office: Old Broad Street, EC2N 1HQ. Telephone: (44-71) 786-9000. Telex: 884569 DPLON G. Telecopier: (44-71) 588-4180.
Hong Kong Office: 13/F Entertainment Building, 30 Queen's Road Central. Telephone: 852-2160-9800. Fax: 852-2810-9828.
Moscow, Russia Representative Office: Debevoise & Plimpton, LLC, Bolshoi Palashevsky Pereulok 13/2, 4th Floor, 103104. Telephone: 7 (095 or 503) 956-3858. Fax: 7 (095 or 503) 956-3868.
Frankfurt am Main, Germany Office: Börsencenter, Taubenstrasse 7-9, 60313. Telephone: +49-69-20 97 5000. Fax: +49-69-20 97 555.
See Professional Biographies, WASHINGTON, DISTRICT OF COLUMBIA

De Boeck, Pascale ....'61 '87 C.999 L.362 J.D. Intl. Monetary fund
DeBoer, James W., (BV) '46 '71 C.1090 B.A. L.945 J.D.
(adm. in VA; not adm. in DC) Sr. Legal Coun., First American Title Insurance Co.
De Boice, J. Brian, (AV) ....'51 '79 C.385 A.B. L.339 J.D. [Cohn&M.]
*PRACTICE AREAS: Communications Law; Broadcasting Law; Cable Television Litigation.
DeBok, Sandra Jean '71 '96 C.446 B.S. L.1209 J.D.
(adm. in VA; not adm. in DC) Lt. U.S. Coast Guard
Debolt, Paul A. ....'63 '89 C.363 B.A. L.608 J.D. [Venable,A.B.H.&C.]
*PRACTICE AREAS: Government Contracts; Complex Litigation.
de Brito, Diana R. .... '57 '84 C.976 B.A. L.276 J.D. [Cadwalader,W.&T.]
*PRACTICE AREAS: Corporate Law; Securities; Finance; Joint Ventures; Business Acquisitions.
DeBruin, David W., (AV) ....'55 '80 C.347 B.A. L.477 J.D. [Jenner&B.]
*PRACTICE AREAS: Civil, Criminal and Appellate Litigation.
DeBry, Kristine ....'67 '97 C.878 B.A. L.276 J.D. [Ⓐ Swidler B.S.F.]
*PRACTICE AREAS: Government Relations; Telecommunications.
DeBusk, F. Amanda ....'55 '81 C.692 B.A. L.309 J.D. [Miller&C.]
*PRACTICE AREAS: International Trade.
deButts, Thomas M. .... '59 '91 C.228 A.B. L.1209 J.D. [Ⓐ Pillsbury W.]
*PRACTICE AREAS: International Trade.
Decaire, William J. ....'73 '01 C.1458 B.A. L.982 J.D. Mngr. Govt. Rel., PWIA
DeCamp, Antoinette '72 '96 C.309 B.A. L.178 J.D.
(adm. in NY; not adm. in DC) [Ⓐ Gibson,D.&C.]
*PRACTICE AREAS: General Litigation; Securities Litigation.
DeCamp, Paul '71 '95 C.309 A.B. L.178 J.D.
(adm. in CA; not adm. in DC) [Ⓐ Gibson,D.&C.] (⊙L.A., CA)
*PRACTICE AREAS: Appellate Practice; Labor and Employment.
De Carbonnières, Tanguy '66 '98 C.999 L.30 J.D.
(adm. in NY; not adm. in DC) Assoc. Gen. Coun., Fannie Mae
*RESPONSIBILITIES: International Law; Intellectual Property Law.
DeCarlo, Michael J. ....'56 '89 C.10 B.A. L.192 J.D. [Ⓒ Dickstein S.M.&O.]
*PRACTICE AREAS: Health Care.
DeCarlo, Nicholas ....'69 '99 C.893 B.S. [Ⓐ Milbank,T.H.&M.]
De Carlo, Connor & Selvo, A Professional Corporation
101 Constitution Ave., N.W., Suite 322 (⊙L.A., CA)

DeCaro, Doran, Siciliano, Gallagher & DeBlasis, LLP
(See Lanham, Maryland)

Dechert, (AV) BB
1775 Eye Street, N.W., 20006-2401 ⊙
Telephone: 202.261.3300 Telefax: 202.261.3333
URL: http://www.dechert.com
Resident Partners: Karen L. Anderberg; Sander M. Bieber; Catherine Botticelli; Frank J. Eisenhart; Ruth S. Epstein; Susan C. Ervin; Paul H. Friedman; David J. Harris; Robert W. Helm; Jane A. Kanter; Bettina M. Lawton; Allan S. Mostoff; Jack W. Murphy; Jeffrey S. Puretz; Keith T. Robinson; Melvin A. Schwarz; Theodore Sonde; Paul Schott Stevens; Wallace L. Timmeny; Patrick W.D. Turley; David A. Vaughan; Donald Zarin. Resident Counsel: Elliott Rowles Curzon; Edward B. Horahan III; Reid B. Horwitz (Not admitted in DC); Elizabeth M. Knoblock; Paul J. Mason; Ralph Oman; Kimberly Dopkin Rasevic; Robert A. Robertson (Not admitted in DC); Alan Rosenblat; R. Michael Smith. Resident Associates: Olivia P. Adler; Karen Aspinall (Not admitted in DC); Vincent J. Badolato; Daniele Allison Baker (Not admitted in DC); Cynthia D. Baughman; Erik Bertin; Stephen H. Bier; Julien M. Bourgeois (Not admitted in DC); Terri L. Bowman; Janet A. Broeckel; Dilia M. Caballero; Christopher David Christian; Erin Duffy Conaton; Jennifer E. Coon (Not admitted in DC); Ethan D. Corey; Catherine A. Courtney (Not admitted in DC); Rena I. Curtis; James Gregory Dyer (Not admitted in DC); Bryan Isaac Eder (Not admitted in DC); Taylor Vinson Edwards (Not admitted in DC); Jennifer O. Epstein; Jeffrey A. Foor (Not admitted in DC); John K. Forst (Not admitted in DC); Brendan C. Fox; Wendy Fox; Eric B. Garvey (Not admitted in DC); R. William Hawkins (Not admitted in DC); Nandita Hogan (Not admitted in DC); Richard R. Holley, III (Not admitted in DC); Hugh Hollman (Not admitted in the United States); Jesse Kanach; Sanjay Lamba (Not admitted in DC); Robert S. Lamont, Jr.; Dennis J. Lawson; Carolyn S. Lee; Randy G. Legg; J. Christophe Leitz; Bennett A. MacDougall; Maureen Magner (Not admitted in DC); Andrea R. Mango (Not admitted in DC); Rebecca B. Martin; Brian Scott Masterson (Not admitted in DC); Lisa McCrea; Michael J. McDonough; Kathryn A. McElroy; Carolyn M. McPhillips (Not admitted in DC); Christian Natiello; Mariam A. Nawabi; Laura A. Novack; Michael D. Pappas; Reza Pishva (Not admitted in DC); Margaret Riley; Michelle C. Roberts; Roland St. Paul; John I. Sakhleh; Caroline Schaefer; Adam Matthew Schoeberlein (Not admitted in DC); Michael Lauren Sherman (Not admitted in DC); Christopher Smith (Not admitted in DC); Janene M. Smith; Robert J. Smith (Not admitted in DC); Cristina M. Sorgi (Not admitted in the United States); Victoria M. Szybillo (Not admitted in DC); Petros L. Tsirigotis; Clifford J. Turbitt; Erin Gibson Wagner; Richard Wei; Trayne S. Wheeler; Yueyao (George) Zhao. Of Counsel: Arthur W. Leibold Jr.
Antitrust, Banking, Bankruptcy and Reorganization, Business and Technology, Commercial Litigation, Complex Litigation, Copyrights, Corporate Finance, Competition, Construction, Customs and Excise, Criminal and Civil Fraud, Defamation, Domestic Taxation, Employee Benefits and Executive Compensation, Employment, Environmental, Estate Planning, EU Legislation, Financial Services, First Amendment, Government Affairs, Health Care, Immigration, Insurance, Intellectual Property, Internet and e-Commerce, Information Technology, Insurance, International Business, International

(This Listing Continued)

Dechert (Continued)
Taxation, International Trade, Investment Management, Labor, Latin America, Life Sciences, Mass Torts, Media, Mergers and Acquisitions, Patent Law and Litigation, Privacy, Private Equity, Products Liability, Property Planning, Real Estate and Mortgage Finance, Retail, Securities Litigation and Enforcement, Securitization, State and Local Taxation, Tax-Exempt Organizations, Trademarks, Venture Capital.
Philadelphia, Pennsylvania: 4000 Bell Atlantic Tower, 1717 Arch Street, 19103-2793. Telephone: 215.994.4000.
New York, New York: 30 Rockefeller Plaza, 10112. Telephone: 212.698.3500.
Harrisburg, Pennsylvania: Thirty North Third Street, 17101-1603. Telephone: 717.237.2000.
Princeton, New Jersey: Princeton Pike Corporate Center, P.O. Box 5218, 08543-5218. Telephone: 609.620.3200.
Boston, Massachusetts: Ten Post Office Square South, 12th Floor, 02109-4603. Telephone: 617.728.7100.
Hartford, Connecticut: 90 State House Square, 06103-3702. Telephone: 860.524.3999.
Newport Beach, California: 4675 MacArthur Court, Suite 1400, 92660-8842. Telephone: 949.442.6000.
London, England: 2 Serjeants' Inn, EC4Y 1LT. Telephone: +44 20 7583 5353.
Brussels, Belgium: 65 Avenue Louise 1050. Telephone: +32 2 535 5411.
Paris, France: 55, avenue Kléber, 75116. Telephone: +33 1 53 65 05 00.
Luxembourg: Brucher & Seimetz in association with Dechert, Avocats a la Cour, 10 rue de Vianden B.P. 709, L-2017. Telephone: +352 45 62 62.
See Professional Biographies, WASHINGTON, DISTRICT OF COLUMBIA

Deckelbaum, David A. ....'55 '82 C.228 B.A. L.276 J.D. Pres., Settlement Corp.

Deckelbaum Ogens & Raftery, Chartered
(See Bethesda, Maryland)

Decker, Audrey G. ....'67 '01 C.1349 B.A. L.893 J.D. Atty. Office of the General Counsel
Decker, John S. ....'69 '94 C.228 A.B. L.893 J.D. [Ⓐ Vinson&E.]
*PRACTICE AREAS: Energy; Administrative Law; Business Law.
DeConcini, Christina ....'62 '88 C.112 B.A. L.588 J.D. Dir., Amer. Bar Assn.
DeConcini, Dennis, (AV) ....'37 '64 C&L.37 B.A., LL.B. [DeConcini M.Y.&L.]
DeConcini McDonald Yetwin & Lacy, P.C., (AV)
233 Constitution Ave., N.E. (⊙Phoenix, Tucson, AZ)
DeCosta, Frank A., III '63 '96
C.188 B.S. L.276 J.D. [Ⓐ Finnegan,H.F.G.&D.] (See Pat. Sect.)
*PRACTICE AREAS: Intellectual Property; Computers and Software; Litigation; Patent Licensing; Patent Prosecution.
DeCosta, Janet K., (AV) ....'47 '79 C.454 B.A. L.209 J.D. [J.K.DeCosta]
*PRACTICE AREAS: Securities; Arbitration; Litigation; Employment Law.

DeCosta, Janet K., P.C., (AV)
601 Thirteenth Street, N.W. Suite 500 North, 20005
Telephone: 202-638-3344 Fax: 202-824-8126
Email: JanetKDC@aol.com URL: http://www.lawyers.com/decostalaw
Janet K. DeCosta.
Securities Litigation, Securities Fraud, NASD Arbitration and Mediation, Class Action, Complex and Multijurisdictional Litigation, Commercial Litigation, Employment Law, Civil Trial and Appellate Practice.
See Professional Biographies, WASHINGTON, DISTRICT OF COLUMBIA

Deeley, Elizabeth Lee ....'— '98 C.280 B.B.A. L.273 J.D. [Ⓐ Kirkland&E.]
*PRACTICE AREAS: Litigation.
Deem, Patricia A. ....'— '97 C.629 B.A. L.446 J.D. [Ⓐ Verner,L.B.M.&H.]
*PRACTICE AREAS: Environmental.
Dees, C. Stanley, (AV) ....'38 '63 C.674 A.B. L.893 LL.B. [McKenna&C.]
*PRACTICE AREAS: Government Contracts; Litigation.
Dees, Elizabeth A. ....'71 '96 C&L.93 B.A., J.D. 701 Penn. Ave., N.W., Ste. 900
Deese, C. Michael ....'51 '76 C.198 A.B. L.659 J.D. [Charapp,D.&W.]
*PRACTICE AREAS: Trade Association Law; Litigation; First Amendment.
Deese, Crystal S. ....'69 '96 C.956 B.A. L.30 J.D. [Ⓐ Whiteford,T.&P.]
*PRACTICE AREAS: Litigation; Medical Malpractice.
Deese, Pamela M., (AV) ....'58 '84 C.30 B.S. L.904 J.D. [Dorsey&W.]
*PRACTICE AREAS: Intellectual Property; Advertising Law; Litigation.
DeFeo, Morris F., Jr. ...'59 '85 C.659 B.A. L.94 J.D. [Ⓒ Morrison&F.] (⊙Mc Lean, VA)
*PRACTICE AREAS: Corporate Finance; Securities; Mergers and Acquisitions.
De Franco, Joseph ....'29 '55 C.262 B.S. L.309 LL.B. 1200 K Street Nw
Degenhart, Lara A. ....'67 '92 C.810 B.S.S.S. L.790 J.D. [Ⓐ Howrey S.A.&W.]
*PRACTICE AREAS: Commercial Litigation; Insurance Coverage.
DeGeorge, Steven W., (AV) ...,.................'57 '82 C.128 B.A. L.273 J.D. AT&T
*RESPONSIBILITIES: Government Contracts; Internet Security; Commercial Transactions.
DeGette, Diana L., (AV) '57 '82 C.170 B.A. L.569 J.D.
(adm. in CO; not adm. in DC) 1339 Longworth H.O.B.
Degnan, Frederick H., (AV) ....'— '74 C.321 B.A. L.276 J.D. [King&S.]
*PRACTICE AREAS: Food and Drug Regulation.
Degnan, Lauren A. .... '70 '95 C.188 B.S. L.880 J.D. [Ⓐ Fish&R.] (See Pat. Sect.)
DeGooyer, John G., (AV) .... '— '68 C.228 A.B. L.30 J.D. [Foley&L.]
*PRACTICE AREAS: Litigation; Government Contracts Law.
de Gracia, Evangeline '73 '99 C.145 B.A. L.904 J.D.
(adm. in CA; not adm. in DC) [Ⓐ Steptoe&J.]
DeGraffenreidt, James H., Jr. '53 '80 C.976 B.A. L.178 J.D.
Chair & Chf. E.O., Washington Gas Light Co.
de Gramont, Alexandre ....'63 '90 C.918 B.A. L.569 J.D. [Crowell&M.]
*PRACTICE AREAS: Litigation.
de Gramont, Jacqueline ....'— '98 C.30 B.A. L.276 J.D. [Ⓐ Miller&C.]
*PRACTICE AREAS: International Trade; International Law; International Trade Regulation; Foreign Corrupt Practices Act; Import and Export Law.
DeGrandis, William D. ....'55 '80 C.645 B.A. L.1068 J.D. [Paul,H.J.&W.]
*PRACTICE AREAS: Energy Regulatory and Transactions; Project Finance and Privatizations; Federal Energy Regulatory Commission Matters.
de Gravelles, Patrick P. .... '— '95 C.276 B.S.F.S. L.1068 J.D. [Ⓐ Miller&C.]
*PRACTICE AREAS: Business Litigation; Contract Litigation.
DeHaan, Robert A. ....'69 '94 C&L.339 A.B., J.D. [Ⓐ Zuckert,S.&R.]
DeHart, June Langston (Walton) ....'52 '81 C.484 B.A. L.496 J.D. [Manatt,P.&P.]
Deinoff, Pelle ....'42 '82 C&L.999 LL.B. 1730 K St., N.W.
De Jager, Charles F. ....'71 '00 C.103 A.B. L.262 J.D. [Ⓐ Miller&C.]
*PRACTICE AREAS: International Trade; Antidumping; Customs Law; World Trade Organization; Export Control.
DeJordy, Eugene A. '58 '92 C.446 B.S. L.128 J.D.
(adm. in RI; not adm. in DC) 3000 K St., N.W.‡
deKieffer, Donald E., (AV) ....'45 '71 C.174 B.A. L.276 J.D. [deKieffer&H.]
*PRACTICE AREAS: International Trade and Regulation; Export and Customs Law; Foreign Asset Control; Unfair Trade; Antidumping.

deKieffer & Horgan, (AV)
Suite 800, 729 Fifteenth Street, N.W., 20005
Telephone: 202-783-6900; 800-787-1600 Facsimile: 202-783-6909
Email: khorgan@dhlaw.com URL: http://www.dhlaw.com
Members of Firm: Donald E. deKieffer; J. Kevin Horgan. Of Counsel: John J. Kenkel; Marc E. Montalbine (Not admitted in DC; Resident, Saarbrücken, Germany); Kevin C. Kennedy (Not admitted in DC); Charles H. Nalls; Frank A. Orban, III. Foreign Attorneys: Alejandro N. Gomez-Strozzi (Not admitted in United States); Judith L. Holdsworth (Resident, Saarbrücken, Germany).
International Trade Law, Customs Law, Antidumping Law, Import and Export Regulation, International Commercial Transactions.
Saarbrucken, Germany Office: Beethovenstrasse 13, D-66111. Telephone: 011 49 681379 3220. Fax: 011 496 681390 7219.

(This Listing Continued)

deKieffer & Horgan (Continued)

Monterey, Nuevo León, Mexico Office: Rio Mississippi 51, San Pedro, Garza Garcia, 66220. Telephone: 011-52-8-378-1990. Fax: 011-52-8-378-1991.

See Professional Biographies, WASHINGTON, DISTRICT OF COLUMBIA

Dekker, David T. ... '56 '81 C.207 B.A. L.188 J.D. [Arent F.K.P.&K.]
*PRACTICE AREAS: Litigation; Insurance; Construction; RICO; ERISA.
de Kluiver, Julia Symon ... '68 '94 C.860 B.A. L.861 J.D. [Ⓐ Clifford C.R.&W.]
*PRACTICE AREAS: Antitrust; Intellectual Property; Complex Litigation.
Delacourt, John T. ... '71 '97 C.276 B.A. L.309 J.D. [Ⓐ Covington&B.]
Delacourt, Sapna ... '73 '00 C.477 B.A. L.276 J.D. [Ⓐ Collier S.S.]
*PRACTICE AREAS: Competition; Antitrust.
de la Cruz, Peter L., (AV) ... '47 '76 C.188 A.B. L.851 J.D. [Keller&H.]
*PRACTICE AREAS: Environmental Law; Trade Association Law; Antitrust and Trade Regulation.
DeLancey, Merle Miller, Jr. ... '66 '91 C.269 B.A. L.896 J.D. [Dickstein S.M.&O.]
*PRACTICE AREAS: Government Contract/Regulation; Litigation/Complex and Multi-District; ERISA/Employee Benefits; Leases and Leasing; Health Care.
Delancy, Benjamin I. '51 '78 C.197 A.B. L.280 J.D.
(adm. in CA; not adm. in DC) [Thelen R.&P.]
*PRACTICE AREAS: Employee Benefits; Executive Compensation.
Delaney, Duane B. ... '54 '89 C.329 B.A. L.276 J.D. Clk. of Supr. Ct.
Delaney, John J. ... '57 '84 C.602 B.A. L.128 J.D. [Ⓐ Condon&F.]
Delaney, Joshua C. ... '64 '96 C.276 B.A. L.64 J.D. [Ⓐ Wilmer,C.&P.]
Delaney, Kathleen Marie ... '59 '87 C&L.893 B.A., J.D. [Ropes&G.]
Delaney, Patrick R. ... '63 '00 C.446 B.S. L.128 J.D. [Ⓐ Smith,G.&R.] (See Pat. Sect.)
Delaney, Thomas J. ... '57 '87 C.276 B.A. L.30 J.D. [Shaw P.]
*PRACTICE AREAS: Banks & Banking.
Delany, William J., (AV) ... '31 '60 C&L.276 A.B., J.D. [Ⓒ Krooth&A.]
*PRACTICE AREAS: Real Estate Law; Real Estate Finance; Affordable Housing Law; Probate Law.
de la Peña, Nuria '— '88 C.904 LL.M. L.999 J.D.
(adm. in NY; not adm. in DC) 4401A Connecticut Avenue, P.M.B. 199
Delaporta, Gregg A. '55 '81 C.999 B.S. L.818 J.D.
(adm. in NY; not adm. in DC; Pat.) 1300 I St., N.W., Suite 700
DeLargy, Krista '69 '97 C.502 B.S. L.276 J.D.
(adm. in MD; not adm. in DC) [Ⓐ Morrison&F.]
*PRACTICE AREAS: Financial Services.
de Laurentiis, Jennifer ... '66 '92 C.20 B.A. L.904 J.D. [Ⓐ Harris E.&L.]
*PRACTICE AREAS: Customs Law; International Trade Regulation; Unfair Competition; Antitrust Law; Legislative Practice.
Delbert, Susan M. ... '51 '78 C.207 B.A. L.851 J.D. [Fontaine,S.K.&D.]
Del Bianco, Mark C. ... '56 '80 C.446 B.A. L.976 J.D. [Ⓒ Skadden,A.S.M.&F.]
Del Buono, Brian J. '61 '00 C.372 B.S. L.276 J.D.
(adm. in VA; not adm. in DC) [Ⓐ Sterne,K.G.&F.]
*PRACTICE AREAS: Intellectual Property Law; Civil Appeals; Biotechnology; Life Sciences; Medical Technology.
Del Duca, Maureen F. ... '60 '87 C.821 B.A. L.569 J.D. [Jenner&B.]
*PRACTICE AREAS: Appellate Practice; Regulatory Law; Telecommunications Law; New Media Law; Internet Law.
Delea, Molly A. '71 '00 C.692 B.S.B.A. L.1509 J.D.
(adm. in VA; not adm. in DC) [Ⓐ Venable,A.B.H.&C.]
*PRACTICE AREAS: Trusts and Estates.

Delehanty, Andrew J. J., (BV) '46 '83 C.569 B.S. L.276 J.D.
5315 Connecticut Avenue, N.W., 20015-1829
Telephone: 202-244-5551
Email: dfnsatty@erols.com URL: http://www.lawyers.com/delehantylaw
***PRACTICE AREAS: Criminal Law; Civil Law; Probate Law.**
Criminal Defense Practice including White Collar Crime, Drug Crimes, Major Felonies, Probate Litigation, Estate Planning & Administration.

See Professional Biographies, WASHINGTON, DISTRICT OF COLUMBIA

de Leon, Leon M. '58 '92 C.472 B.B.A. L.276 J.D.
(adm. in FL; not adm. in DC) Atty. & Analyst, National Assn. of Sec. Dealers, Inc.
de Leon, Sylvia A., (AV) ... '50 '76 C.985 B.A. L.846 J.D. [Akin,G.S.H.&F.]
*PRACTICE AREAS: Public Policy.
Delery, Stuart F. ... '68 '93 C.893 B.A. L.976 J.D. [Wilmer,C.&P.]
*PRACTICE AREAS: Litigation; Securities Law.
Delfin, Ricardo R. ... '74 '00 C.188 B.A. L.597 J.D. [Ⓐ Wilmer,C.&P.]
DelGiorno, Matthew ... '71 '96 C.886 B.S.E.E. L.893 J.D. [Ⓐ Finnegan,H.F.G.&D.]
*PRACTICE AREAS: Patent Litigation; Electrical Intellectual Property; Patent Infringement.
Delibert, Arthur C. ... '— '80 C.188 B.S.E.E. L.569 J.D. [Kirkpatrick&L.]
*PRACTICE AREAS: Investment Company Law; Investment Management; Mutual Funds; Business Trusts; Securities Regulation.
Deligiorgis, Maria '64 '90 C.352 B.M. L.904 J.D.
(adm. in VA; not adm. in DC)
Corporate Counsel, American Resort Development Association
Delinsky, Eric R. ... '69 '97 C.860 B.A. L.276 J.D. Asst. Fed. Pub. Def.
de Lisser, Margaret A. ... '61 '88 C&L.659 B.A., J.D. [Hogan&H.]
*PRACTICE AREAS: Executive Compensation; Equity Incentives; Employee Benefits.
Dell'Aglio, Brandon M. '74 '00 C.273 B.A. L.276 J.D.
(adm. in MD; not adm. in DC) [Ⓐ Schwartz&B.]
*PRACTICE AREAS: Banking; Financial Services.
DelliCarpini, Christopher J. ... '71 '97 C.602 B.A. L.178 J.D. [Ⓐ Howrey S.A.&W.]
*PRACTICE AREAS: Litigation; Antitrust.
Dellinger, Walter E., (AV) '41 '70 C.575 A.B. L.976 J.D.
(adm. in NC; not adm. in DC) [O'Melveny&M.]
Dellon, Leslie K. ... '54 '78 C.30 B.A. L.273 J.D. [Lepon M.W.&H.]
Delmore, John R. ... '69 '94 C.1369 B.B.A. L.790 J.D. [Ⓐ McDermott,W.&E.]
Delogu, Nancy N. ... '— '94 C.860 B.A. L.945 J.D. [Ⓐ Littler M.]
De Long, Allen R. ... '19 '47 C.902 A.B. L.273 LL.B. 6200 Oregon Ave., N.W.‡
DeLong, James V., (AV) ... '38 '64 C&L.309 B.A., LL.B. 1417 44th St., N.W.
DeLong, Stephanie L. ... '71 '00 C.112 B.A. L.273 [Ⓐ Arter&H.]
*PRACTICE AREAS: Real Estate; Real Estate Finance; Corporate.
DeLony, Rieyn ... '65 '94 C.914 B.A. L.64 J.D. Natl. Tr. for Historic Preservation
DeLorenzo, James T. ... '74 '99 C.228 A.B. L.569 J.D. [Ⓐ Swidler B.S.F.]
*PRACTICE AREAS: Government Affairs; Telecommunications; Internet Law.
DeLorme, Gilbert E., Jr., (AV) ... '45 '68 C.103 A.B. L.659 LL.B. [Greenstein D.&L.]
DeLorme, M. Carter ... '70 '95 C.659 B.A. L.276 J.D. [Ⓐ Winston&S.]
del Rio, Jorge A. ... '71 '97 C.425 B.A. L.1206 J.D. [Ⓐ Kutak R.]
*PRACTICE AREAS: Tax Law.
Del Rio, Olga L. ... '67 '95 L.472 J.D. [Ⓐ Holland&K.]
*PRACTICE AREAS: Corporate; International; Transactional.
Del Sesto, Ronald W., Jr. ... '68 '98 C.276 B.A. L.128 J.D. [Ⓐ Swidler B.S.F.]

Delston, Ross S., (AV) '51 '76 C&L.273 B.A., J.D. BB
3013 Beech Street, N.W., 20015-2203
Telephone: 202-362-2260 Fax: 202-362-2754
Email: rdelston@delston.com URL: http://www.delston.com
Financial Services Law, Banking Law, Banking Regulation, Electronic Banking, Bank Mergers and Acquisitions, Consumer Banking, International Banking Law, Bank Insolvency, Bank Failures, International Finance, Trade Finance.

See Professional Biographies, WASHINGTON, DISTRICT OF COLUMBIA

Deltergo, Michael J. ... '62 '97 C.454 B.A. L.818 J.D. [Ⓐ Skadden,A.S.M.&F.]
Del Toro, Miguel H. ... '72 '99 C.309 B.A. L.813 J.D. [Ⓐ Crowell&M.]
DeLuca, John P., (AV) ... '44 '69 C.433 B.E.E. L.274 J.D. [Dykema G.] (Pat.)
*PRACTICE AREAS: Electrical Patent; Mechanical Patent; Computer Science Patent; Trademarks; Copyrights.
DeLuca, Vincent M. '60 '87
C.178 B.S.E.E. L.1209 J.D. [Rothwell,F.E.&M.] (See Pat. Sect.)
*PRACTICE AREAS: Intellectual Property.
DeLucia, Robert J. '52 '77 C.205 B.A. L.276 J.D.
V.P. & Gen. Coun., Airline Industrial Relations Conference
DeMarcus, M. Rachel '53 '77 C&L.280 A.B., J.D.
(adm. in GA; not adm. in DC) 441 G. Street NW
Demarest, William F., Jr., (AV) ... '47 '73 C.754 B.S. L.94 J.D. [Shook,H.&B.]
*PRACTICE AREAS: Energy; Natural Gas Regulation and Litigation; Legislation; Environment.
De Martino, Ralph V., (AV) ... '54 '79 C.105 B.S.B.A. L.273 J.D. [De Martino F.R.&V.]
*PRACTICE AREAS: Securities Law; Corporate Financing Law; Broker Dealer Regulation.

De Martino Finkelstein Rosen & Virga, (AV) BB
Suite 400, 1818 N Street, N.W., 20036 ⊙
Telephone: 202-659-0494 Telecopier: 202-659-1290
Email: BUSLAW@dfrv.com URL: http://www.demartinolaw.com
Members of Firm: Ralph V. De Martino (Resident); Steven R. Finkelstein (Not admitted in DC; Resident, New York, N.Y. Office); Jeffrey S. Rosen (Resident); Gerard A. Virga (Not admitted in DC; Resident, New York, N.Y. Office);—Keith H. Peterson (Not admitted in DC; Resident, New York, N.Y. Office); F. Alec Orudjev (Not admitted in DC); Valerie J. Pelton (Not admitted in DC).
Securities and Commodities Law. Administrative Practice. Business, Corporate, Corporate Financing. Trial Practice. Estate Administration and Planning, Real Estate, Banking Law, and Elder Law.
New York, N.Y. Office: Suite 1700, 90 Broad Street. Telephone: 212-363-2500. Telecopier: 212-363-2723. Email: info@DFRV-NY.com

See Professional Biographies, WASHINGTON, DISTRICT OF COLUMBIA

DeMasi, Deborah A., (AV) ... '56 '80 C.776 B.A. L.262 J.D. [Thelen R.&P.]
*PRACTICE AREAS: Infrastructure Development; Project Finance.
Dembling, Paul G., (AV) ... '20 '52 C.705 A.B. L.273 J.D. [Schnader H.S.&L.] ‡
DeMeo, Regina A. ... '72 '98 C.276 B.S. L.273 J.D. [Ⓐ Liotta,D.&E.]
*PRACTICE AREAS: Family Law; Wills; Real Estate.
Demianczuk, Yolanda M. ... '71 '98 C.976 B.A. L.178 J.D. [Ⓐ Wilmer,C.&P.]
Deming, Stuart H., (AV) ... '51 '77 C&L.477 B.A., J.D. [Inman D.] ⊙
*PRACTICE AREAS: Foreign Corrupt Practices Act; Foreign Asset Control; Corporate Litigation.
DeMita, Michael A. '33 '63 C.569 B.S. L.724 LL.B.
(adm. in NY; not adm. in DC) V.P., Philip Morris Cos. Inc.
DeMond, Gorton M., Jr. '46 '73 C&L.813 A.B., J.D.
(adm. in CA; not adm. in DC) World Bank
Dempsey, John C. ... '42 '74 C.172 B.A. L.276 J.D. 1101 17th St., N.W.
Dempsey, Kevin M. ... '62 '87 C.910 A.B. L.309 J.D. [Dewey B.]
*PRACTICE AREAS: International Trade.
Dempsey, Melissa ... '69 '96 C.882 B.A. L.982 J.D. [Ⓐ King&S.]
*PRACTICE AREAS: Litigation; Trade Regulation.
Dempsey, William H., (AV) ... '30 '55 C.602 A.B. L.976 LL.B. [Ⓒ Shea&G.]
Dempster, William J., (AV) '52 '82
C.401 B.A. L.564 J.D. Asst. Gen. Coun., Marriott Intl., Inc.
*RESPONSIBILITIES: Civil Litigation; Labor and Employment Law.
DeMuth, Christopher C. ... '46 '73 C.309 A.B. L.145 J.D. 1150 Seventeenth St., N.W.

Denbo, James R. '41 '68 C.477 B.A. L.273 J.D.
1801 K Street, N.W., Suite 1205L, 20006
Telephone: 202-452-7373 Facsimile: 202-452-7333
Email: denbojim@aol.com
Management Labor Law. General Practice. Representing Employers in Labor and Employment Law.

See Professional Biographies, WASHINGTON, DISTRICT OF COLUMBIA

Denbo, Mark B. ... '70 '98 C.659 B.A. L.904 J.D. [Ⓐ Fleischman&W.]
de Neuville, Helene '71 '97 C.61 J.D. L.861 L.L.M.
(adm. in NY; not adm. in DC) [Ⓐ Duncan&A.]
*PRACTICE AREAS: International Mining Law; Energy Law; Admiralty Law.
Deng, Donald M. '73 '00 C.31 B.A. L.976 J.D.
(adm. in MD; not adm. in DC) [Ⓐ Patton B.]
Denger, Michael L., (AV) ... '45 '70 C.597 B.S. L.309 J.D. [Gibson,D.&C.]
*PRACTICE AREAS: Antitrust and Trade Regulation Law; False Advertising Law; Administrative Law; Litigation.
Denicore, Mark R. ... '62 '96 C.158 B.S.C.E. L.904 J.D. [Ⓐ Arent F.K.P.&K.]
*PRACTICE AREAS: Construction Counseling and Litigation.
Denig, Christopher M. ... '70 '96 C.821 B.A. L.178 J.D. [Ⓐ Covington&B.]
DeNigris, Stephen G. '52 '92 C.1086 L.1206 J.D.
(adm. in NY; not adm. in DC) [S.G.DeNigris]

De Nigris, Stephen G., Law Offices of
2117 L Street, N.W., Suite 283, 20037-1524
Telephone: 800-791-9908 Telecopier: 888-791-4441
Email: sgd853@aol.com URL: http://www.lawyers.com/denigrislaw
Stephen G. DeNigris (Not admitted in DC). Associate: Michael L. Michetti, Jr. (Not admitted in DC).
Labor law, Employment Law, Civil Litigation, Administrative Law.

See Professional Biographies, WASHINGTON, DISTRICT OF COLUMBIA

Denis, Paul T., (AV) ... '58 '85 C.884 B.A. L.477 J.D. [Swidler B.S.F.]
*PRACTICE AREAS: Antitrust and Trade Regulation.
Denison, George L. ... '53 '81 C.476 B.S. L.1187 J.D. [Ⓒ Hopkins R.C.H.&H.]
Denison, Mary Boney ... '56 '82 C.228 A.B. L.575 J.D. [Manelli,D.&S.]
*PRACTICE AREAS: Intellectual Property; Trademarks; Copyrights; Commercial Litigation.
Denman, Jeffrey R. ... '66 '92 C.446 B.A. L.1068 J.D. [Ⓐ Arnold&P.]
*PRACTICE AREAS: Intellectual Property; Technology Law.
Denney, George ... '21 '48 C.913 B.S. L.309 J.D. 2604 36th St., N.W.‡
Dennin, Joseph F., (AV) ... '43 '69 C&L.813 A.B., J.D. [McKenna&C.]
*PRACTICE AREAS: International Trade and Investment; Government Relations.
Denning, Jacqueline R. ... '48 '76 C.1365 B.S. L.945 J.D. [Arnold&P.]
*PRACTICE AREAS: Litigation.

Denning & Wohlstetter, (AV)
1700 K Street, N.W., Suite 301, 20006
Telephone: 202-833-8884 Fax: 202-833-8886
Members of Firm: William I Denning (1883-1977); Alan F. Wohlstetter; Stanley I. Goldman.
General Practice before Federal Courts, including U.S. Court of Federal Claims, Administrative Agencies. Motor Carrier, Maritime, Aviation, Government Contract and Trademark Law.

See Professional Biographies, WASHINGTON, DISTRICT OF COLUMBIA

Dennis, Jeanne M. ... '66 '93 C.821 B.A. L.1068 J.D. [Ⓐ Winston&S.]
Dennis, Patricia Diaz, (AV) '46 '73 C.112 A.B. L.426 J.D.
1701 Pennsylvania Ave. N.W.
Dennis, Sandra J.P. ... '56 '84 C.645 B.A. L.790 J.D. [Morgan,L.&B.]
Dennis, Warren L., (AV) ... '48 '72 C&L.659 B.A., J.D. [Proskauer R.]
Dennison, Sean '74 '00 C.1090 B.S. L.659 J.D.
(adm. in MD; not adm. in DC) [Ⓐ Shaw P.]
*PRACTICE AREAS: Real Estate.
Denniston, John B., (AV) ... '36 '63 C.188 B.E.P. L.309 J.D. [Covington&B.]

Dent, G. Richard '60 '85 C.893 B.A. L.846 J.D.
V.P. & Asst. Gen. Coun., College Construction Loan Ins. Assn.
Denvir, James P., III, (AV) . . . . '50 '75 C.976 B.A. L.260 J.D. [Boies,S.&F.]
*PRACTICE AREAS: Antitrust; Commercial Litigation.
De Paso, Thomas J. '56 '84 C.645 B.S. L.128 J.D.
Staff Coun., National Football League Players Assn.
De Prest, Geert, (BV) . . . . '54 '82 L.999 J.D. [Stewart&S.]
*PRACTICE AREAS: International Trade; International Trade Regulation; Antidumping; European Union Law; Import and Export Law.
DePuy, Jacques B., (AV) . . . . '43 '75 C.30 B.A. L.276 J.D. [Greenstein D.&L.]
Depuy, Michelle R. . . . . '68 '00 C.1056 B.A. L.273 J.D. [Ⓐ Thelen R.&P.]
*PRACTICE AREAS: Construction; Government Contracts; International.
Dequina, Carlos T. . . . . '— '99 C.705 B.A. L.276 J.D. [Dequina&Assoc.]
Dequina & Associates . . . . 1768 Church St. NW, Suite 200-B
Derasmo, William R. '69 '94 C.165 B.A. L.896 J.D.
(adm. in NJ; not adm. in DC) [Ⓐ Troutman S.]
*PRACTICE AREAS: Energy; Administrative Law; Regulatory Law; Utility Law.
Derbes, Elizabeth K. . . . . '70 '99 C.309 B.A. L.145 J.D. [Ⓐ Wilmer,C.&P.]
Derbis, Joseph R. . . . . '72 '98 C.903 B.A. L.602 J.D. [Ⓐ Jones,D.R.&P.]
Derby, Michael D. '54 '80 C&L.588 B.S., J.D.
House Coun., Marine Engrs. Beneficial Assn.
De Reyes, Jose '73 '97 C.999 L.178 LL.M.
(adm. in Mexico; not adm. in DC) [Ⓒ Miller&C.]
*PRACTICE AREAS: International Trade; Investments; Alternative Dispute Resolution.
de Ridder, Craig A. . . . . '54 '84 C&L.4 B.A., LL.B. [Shaw P.]
*PRACTICE AREAS: Technology Transactions; Technology Outsourcing; Telecommunications and Broadband; Technology; Partnership Law.
Dernbach, Peter James '70 '98 C.273 B.A. L.893 J.D.
(adm. in CA; not adm. in DC) [Ⓐ Arent F.K.P.&K.]
*PRACTICE AREAS: Intellectual Property; Trademarks; Copyrights.
De Roche, Chas. P. . . . . '16 '52 C&L.276 B.S., J.D. 3211 McKinley St., N.W.‡
DeRoche, Jo A. . . . . '49 '91 C.477 B.A. L.213 J.D. [Weiner B.S.K.]
*PRACTICE AREAS: Railway Labor Act; Collective Bargaining Agreement; Negotiation and Arbitration; Transportation; Regulatory Compliance.
de Rosa, Barth X. . . . . . '55 '82 C.273 B.A. L.280 J.D. [Stevens,D.M.&M.] (See Pat. Sect.)
*PRACTICE AREAS: Intellectual Property; Trademarks; Copyrights; Litigation; Mergers and Acquisitions.
Derrevere, Suzette W. . . . . '70 '98 C.788 B.A. L.188 J.D. [Ⓐ Perkins C.]
*PRACTICE AREAS: Government Contracts; Construction Litigation.
Derrick, Butler C., Jr. . . . . '36 '65 C.790 L.280 J.D. [Powell,G.F.&M.]
*PRACTICE AREAS: Administrative.
Derstine, Ann K. '— '00 C.1053 B.A. L.569 J.D.
(adm. in MD; not adm. in DC) [Ⓐ Morgan,L.&B.]
Derzko, Natalie M. . . . . '70 '95 C.025 B.Sc. L.035 LL.B. [Ⓐ Fitzpatrick,C.H.&S.]
Desai, Parul P. . . . . '74 '00 C.705 B.S. L.564 J.D. [Ⓐ Crowell&M.]
Desai, Samir S. . . . . '68 '95 C.311 B.A. L.982 J.D. [Ⓐ Baker&M.]
*PRACTICE AREAS: Project Finance; Asset Based Finance.
DeSanctis, Christy Hallam . . . . '70 '96 C.228 B.A. L.569 J.D. [Ⓐ Collier S.S.]
*PRACTICE AREAS: Litigation; Government Relations.
DeSanctis, Joseph J. '58 '83 C.229 B.A. L.930 J.D.
(adm. in OH; not adm. in DC) [Ⓒ Kirkland&E.]
*PRACTICE AREAS: Litigation.
De Sanctis, Lisa M. '71 '96 C&L.1375 B.A., J.D.
Assoc. Prof., Clinical Law, George Washington University
DeSanctis, Michael B. . . . . '69 '98 C.93 B.A. L.569 J.D. [Ⓐ Jenner&B.]
*PRACTICE AREAS: Litigation.
DeSantis, Karen McCartan . . . . '60 '86 C.674 A.B. L.602 J.D. [Kirkland&E.]
*PRACTICE AREAS: Commercial Litigation; Products Liability.
DeSantis, Victor J. . . . . '60 '86 C.976 B.A. L.309 J.D. [White&C.]
*PRACTICE AREAS: Infrastructure Development; Project Finance; International Investment.
Deschauer, John J., Jr. . . . . '50 '78 C.602 B.A. L.569 J.D. [Patton B.]
DeSeve, Karren A. . . . . '48 '96 C.999 B.A. L.831 J.D. [Baumann,D.&L.]
DeSilva, Eric W., (BV) . . . . '65 '89 C.446 B.S. L.477 J.D. [Wiley R.&F.]
*PRACTICE AREAS: Communications.
DeSimone, Beth S. . . . . '59 '84 C.937 B.A. L.945 J.D. [Ⓒ Arnold&P.]
*PRACTICE AREAS: Financial Institutions; Corporate.
Desio, Paula J. '50 '80 C.105 B.A. L.436 J.D.
Dep. Gen. Coun., U.S. Sentencing Comm.
Desjardins, Douglas '64 '93 C.198 B.A. L.930 J.D.
[Ⓐ R.J.Clapp&Assoc.] (⊙Cleve., OH)
*PRACTICE AREAS: Aviation Law; Products Liability; Personal Injury; Automobile Negligence; Complex Litigation.
Desmarais, Edward S., Jr. . . . . '64 '89 C&L.260 B.A., J.D. [Hogan&H.]
*PRACTICE AREAS: Federal Estate and Gift Taxation; Fiduciary Income Tax; Generation Skipping Tax; Trusts and Estates Taxation.
Desmond, Michael J. . . . . '68 '94 C.112 B.A. L.128 J.D. [Ⓐ McKee N.]
*PRACTICE AREAS: Tax Controversies; Tax Litigation.
Deso, Robert E., (AV) . . . . '43 '68 C.276 B.S.F.S. L.893 J.D. [Deso,T.&S.]
Deso, Thomas & Stein, P.C., (AV) . . . . 1828 L Street N.W.
DeSoto, Kurt E., (AV) . . . . '56 '84 C.276 A.B. L.178 J.D. [Ⓒ Wiley R.&F.]
*PRACTICE AREAS: Communications Law.
Determan, Sara-Ann, (AV) . . . . '38 '68 C.205 A.B. L.273 LL.B. [Hogan&H.]
*PRACTICE AREAS: Wills; Trusts and Estates; Estate and Gift Taxation; Non-profit and Charitable Organizations; Estate Planning.
Detwiler, Alice W. '— '95 C.974 A.B. L.309 J.D.
(adm. in CA; not adm. in DC) [Ⓐ Gibson,D.&C.]
*PRACTICE AREAS: Litigation; Securities; Appellate Practice.
Detzner, John A. . . . . '55 '80 C&L.309 A.B., J.D. [Ⓒ Neville,P.]
*PRACTICE AREAS: International Trade Regulation; International Transactions.
Deuser, Jon . . . . '65 '92 C.347 B.A. L.893 J.D. Chief of Staff & Coun.
Deutch, Philip J. . . . . '64 '92 C.31 B.A. L.813 J.D. 725 12th St., N.W.
Deutsch, Brad . . . . '65 '95 C.103 A.B. L.262 J.D. [Ⓐ Hogan&H.]
*PRACTICE AREAS: Communications Law; FCC Regulation; Television Law; Radio Law.
Deutsch, Ellen S. . . . . '43 '77 C.33 B.A. L.128 J.D. [Ⓒ Cole,R.&B.]
*PRACTICE AREAS: Telecommunications Regulation; Litigation; Legislative Practice.
Deutsch, Morris H., (AV) . . . . '53 '82 C.94 B.A. L.93 J.D. [Osborne&D.]
*PRACTICE AREAS: Immigration and Nationality; General Business Law.
Devall, James L. . . . . '41 '68 C.378 B.A. L.1066 J.D. [Ⓒ Zuckert,S.&R.]
*PRACTICE AREAS: Airline Regulation; Aviation Law; International Aviation Law.
DeVan, William A., (BV) '64 '93 C&L.945 A.B., J.D.
(adm. in VA; not adm. in DC) [Ⓒ Thelen R.&P.]
*PRACTICE AREAS: Construction; International Law; Commercial Law.
Devaney, Dennis M., (AV) '46 '76 C.446 B.A. L.276 J.D.
Comr., U.S. Intl. Trade Comm.
Devaney, John M. . . . . '57 '83 C.93 B.A. L.128 J.D. [Perkins C.]
*PRACTICE AREAS: Commercial Litigation; Telecommunications Law; Employment Litigation; Environmental Insurance Coverage.
DeVecchio, Warren J. . . . . '52 '78 C.228 B.A. L.128 J.D. [Crowell&M.]
*PRACTICE AREAS: Government (or Public) Contract Law.
Dever, Mark F. . . . . '68 '93 C.93 B.A. L.228 J.D. [Ⓐ Drinker B.&R.]

Devereaux, Kathleen M. '76 '01 C.477 B.A. L.597 J.D.
(adm. in MD; not adm. in DC) [Ⓐ Sutherland A.&B.]
*PRACTICE AREAS: Litigation; Corporate Law.
Devery, Jennifer R. . . . . '73 '98 C.645 B.A. L.446 J.D. [Ⓐ Chadbourne&P.]
Devine, M. Colette . . . . '65 '97 C.276 B.A. L.893 J.D. [Ⓐ Hogan&H.]
Devine, Thomas R. . . . . '— '79 C&L.813 A.B., J.D. [Foley&L.]
*PRACTICE AREAS: Airport Law (Regulatory, Environmental, Financing).
Devinsky, Paul, (AV) . . . . '48 '78 C.563 B.S.E.E. L.128 J.D. [McDermott,W.&E.] (Pat.)
Devito, Eric M. . . . . '71 '98 C.608 B.S.B.A. L.446 J.D. [Ⓐ Brickfield B.R.&S.]
*PRACTICE AREAS: Energy.
Devlin, Frank C., Jr. . . . . '40 '72 C&L.30 B.S., J.D. 555 12th St.
Devlin, Thomas C. . . . . '49 '75 C.262 B.A. L.724 J.D. 305 H St., N.W.
Devlin, Timothy M. . . . . '70 '97 C.645 B.S. L.477 J.D. [Ⓐ Kenyon&K.] (See Pat. Sect.)
*PRACTICE AREAS: Intellectual Property.
Devlin-Brown, Arlo '— '00 C.178 B.A. L.309 J.D.
(adm. in NY; not adm. in DC) [Ⓐ Wilmer,C.&P.]
Devore, Joshua S. '75 '00 C.691 B.A. L.276 J.D.
(adm. in VA; not adm. in DC) [Ⓐ Cohen,M.H.&T.]
*PRACTICE AREAS: Securities Litigation; Consumer Protection.
De Vore, Lawrence M. . . . . '28 '54 C&L.477 B.A., J.D. 4973 Hillbrook La. N.W.
De Vries, Rosalee J. . . . . '70 '96 C.893 B.A. L.30 J.D. 1225 Connecticut Ave., N.W.
DeWald, Ronald G., (AV) . . . . '45 '72 C.473 B.A. L.273 J.D. [Lipshultz&H.] ⊙
*PRACTICE AREAS: Automotive; Tire/Rim Mismatch; Elevator Liability; Product Defects; Products Liability.
DeWeese, Mary Jane . . . . '67 '93 C.604 B.A. L.145 J.D. [Ⓐ Piper M.R.&W.]
*PRACTICE AREAS: Real Estate.
Dewey, Elizabeth R. . . . . '67 '93 C.862 B.A. L.904 J.D. [Ⓒ Piper M.R.&W.]
*PRACTICE AREAS: Commercial Litigation; White Collar Crime.

Dewey Ballantine LLP, (AV) BB
1775 Pennsylvania Avenue, N.W., 20006-4605 ⊙
Telephone: 202-862-1000; Telecopier: 202-862-1093 Cable Address: "Dewbalaw"
URL: http://www.deweyballantine.com
Resident Partners: Donna M. Attanasio; James F. Bowe, Jr.; Kevin M. Dempsey; Joseph K. Dowley; Anna-Liza B. Harris; Thomas R. Howell; Andrew W. Kentz; Felix B. Laughlin; John R. Magnus; W. Clark McFadden II; Herbert V. Morais; Earle H. O'Donnell; Joseph M. Pari; John A. Ragosta; John J. Salmon; Martha J. Talley; Alan Wm. Wolff. Counsel: Harry Lewis Clark; Julia Dryden English; Laurel W. Glassman; Keith M. Schwartz; Michael H. Stein; Bradford L. Ward. Of Counsel: Zori G. Ferkin. Associates: Jon Avins (Not admitted in DC); David A. Bentley; Devon M. Bodoh; John W. Bohn; Michael L. Castellano (Not admitted in DC); Andrew J. Conrad (Not admitted in DC); Kathleen C. Dale (Not admitted in DC); Lisa E. Epifani; Jon G. Finkelstein (Not admitted in DC); Emily Sanford Fisher (Not admitted in DC); Nathaniel Friends, Jr. (Not admitted in DC); Bruce A. Grabow; Matthew P. Haskins; Hugh Edwin Hillard, Jr. (Not admitted in DC); Diara M. Holmes (Not admitted in DC; Century City, CA Office); Robert G. Lorndale Jr.; Andrea S. Miano; Alyson M. Petroni (Not admitted in DC); Douglas L. Poms; Rory F. Quirk; John D. Renneisen; Jennifer Danner Riccardi; William E. Rice; Roger L. St. Vincent; Charles C. Thompson (Not admitted in DC); James Wickett (Not admitted in DC); Andrew B. Young; Hui Yu.
General Practice.
Other offices: New York, New York; Los Angeles and Menlo Park, California; Houston, Texas, London, England; Hong Kong; Budapest, Hungary; Prague, Czech Republic; and Warsaw, Poland.
See Professional Biographies, WASHINGTON, DISTRICT OF COLUMBIA

Dewire, Mark A. . . . . '— '87 C.276 B.S. L.94 J.D. [Wilmer,C.&P.] (⊙Balt., MD)
*PRACTICE AREAS: Corporate Law; Securities Law.
DeWitt, Patricia J. B. . . . . '74 '00 C.112 B.A. L.309 J.D. [Ⓐ Crowell&M.]
Dewitty, Robert Michael '73 '00 C.302 B.A. L.64 J.D.
(adm. in MD; not adm. in DC) 1000 6th St., SW, Apt. 505
De Young, Kyle . . . . '72 '99 C&L.477 B.A., J.D. [Ⓐ Wilmer,C.&P.]
Deza, Paula . . . . '— '95 C.64 B.A. L.128 J.D. 701 Pennsylvania Avenue, N.W.
Dhima, Artan '64 '97 C.999 L.276 M.L.
(adm. in NY; not adm. in DC) 3306 Ross Pl., N.W.
Dhindsa, Ranjit S. . . . . '69 '95 C&L.446 B.S., J.D. [Ⓐ Arnold&P.]
*PRACTICE AREAS: Litigation.
Dial, Alan R. . . . . '65 '93 C.112 B.A. L.329 J.D. 1730 Pennsylvania Ave., N.W.
Diamond, Benjamin D. . . . . '52 '77 C.309 A.B. L.229 J.D. [Ⓐ Swidler B.S.F.]
*PRACTICE AREAS: Transactional; Real Estate; Finance.
Diamond, Bruce M., (AV) . . . . '47 '74 C.659 B.A. L.477 J.D. 3000 K St., N.W.
Diamond, Henry L., (AV) . . . . '32 '59 C.880 B.A. L.276 LL.B. [Beveridge&D.]
*PRACTICE AREAS: Environmental Law.
Diamond, Louis H., (AV) . . . . '32 '57 C&L.273 B.A., J.D. [Silverstein&M.]
*PRACTICE AREAS: Taxation; Employee Benefits; Employee Stock Ownership Plans (ESOPs); Business; Estate Planning.
Diamond, Marvin J., (AV) . . . . '41 '68 C.674 A.B. L.976 LL.B. [Ⓒ Hogan&H.]
*PRACTICE AREAS: Communications Law.
Diamond, Michael R. . . . . '45 '69 C.823 B.A. L.262 J.D. Georgetown Univ.
Diamond, Richard, (AV) . . . . '44 '74 C.674 A.B. L.976 LL.B. [Ⓒ Steptoe&J.]
Diamond, Robert A. . . . . '33 '76 C.951 B.A. L.128 J.D. 6251 29th St., N.W.
Diamond, Robert M. . . . . '49 '73 C.665 B.S. L.659 J.D. [Whitten&D.]
Diamond, Steven S. . . . . '56 '81 C&L.477 B.A., J.D. [Arnold&P.]
*PRACTICE AREAS: Government Contracts; Corporate Transactions; Commercial Arbitration; Intellectual Property.
Diaz, Amy Sobba '75 '00 C.413 B.A. L.276 J.D.
(adm. in MD; not adm. in DC) [Ⓐ Ropes&G.]
*PRACTICE AREAS: Corporate Law; Financial Services Law.
Diaz, Steven A., (AV) . . . . '48 '74 C.766 B.A. L.770 J.D. [Dykema G.]
*PRACTICE AREAS: Transportation; Infrastructure Development; Government Contracts.
Diaz-Asper, Jose A. . . . . '43 '69 C.276 B.S. L.260 J.D. ATC Equity & Mtge. Inc.
DiBari, David D. . . . . '64 '90 C.165 A.B. L.982 J.D. [Clifford C.R.&W.]
*PRACTICE AREAS: Litigation; Regulatory; White Collar Defense; International Arbitration; Foreign Corrupt Practices Act.
DiBattiste, Carol . . . . '51 '82 C.397 B.A. L.831 J.D. [Holland&K.]
*PRACTICE AREAS: Corporate Diversity; Counseling; Government Relations; Government Contracts; Criminal Litigation.

Dibble, John C., (AV) '46 '74 C.178 B.A. L.1119 J.D.
Suite 175, 3050 K Street NW, 20007
Telephone: 202-944-4524 Fax: 202-944-4525
Email: jdibble@wdn.com URL: http://www.lawyers.com/johndibble
International Trade Regulation, Export Regulation, Customs Law, Foreign Asset Control, Unfair Trade Practices, Foreign Corrupt, Practices Act, Export Compliance, Foreign Trade Sanctions.
See Professional Biographies, WASHINGTON, DISTRICT OF COLUMBIA

DiBiagio, Thomas M., (BV) . . . . '60 '85 C.216 B.A. L.692 J.D. [Dyer E.&J.]
*PRACTICE AREAS: White Collar Crime; Environmental Law; Commercial Litigation.
DiBianco, Gary . . . . '68 '97 C.976 B.A. L.276 J.D. [Ⓐ Skadden,A.S.M.&F.]
DiCarlo, Dana M. . . . . '55 '91 C.788 B.A. L.188 J.D. 2101 L St., N.W.
Dicello, Francis P., (AV) . . . . '— '66 C.602 A.B. L.262 LL.B. [Reed S.]
*PRACTICE AREAS: Bankruptcy.
DiCintio, Timothy J. . . . . '68 '93 C.976 B.A. L.309 J.D. [Ⓐ Chadbourne&P.]
Dick, Edison Warner, (AV) '37 '62
C.976 B.A. L.893 LL.B. 1620 L Street, N.W., Suite 825
Dick, James V. . . . . '47 '75 C.31 B.A. L.813 J.D. [Squire,S.&D.]
*PRACTICE AREAS: Antitrust; Litigation; Regulatory.
Dick, Jerome J., (AV) . . . . '16 '40 C&L.477 A.B., J.D. 1200 18th St., N.W.

Dick, Rebecca P. . . . .'47 '78 C.207 B.A. L.107 J.D. [Swidler B.S.F.]
*PRACTICE AREAS: Antitrust.

Dicke, Stephen P. . . . . '42 '67 C.674 A.B. L.659 J.D. [Scribner,H.&T.]

Dickens, Benjamin H., Jr., (AV) . . . '— '77 C.469 B.A. L.259 J.D. [Blooston,M.D.D.&P.]
*PRACTICE AREAS: Telecommunications Law; International Telecommunications.

Dickens, Dorrance D. . . . . '58 '96 C.1044 B.A. L.496 J.D. [Luxenberg,J.&D.]
*PRACTICE AREAS: Family Law; Domestic Relations; Gay and Lesbian Family Law; Divorce; Child Custody.

Dicker, Ross T. . . . . '43 '70 C.103 B.A. L.880 J.D. Asst. Bar Coun.

Dickerman, John M. . . . . '14 '40 C&L.339 A.B., J.D. 1201 L St., N.W.

Dickerson, Elizabeth B. . . . . '54 '96 C.914 A.B. L.30 J.D. 1875 Connecticut Avenue, N.W.

Dickey, Martha L. . . . .'43 '83 C.846 B.A. L.1234 J.D. 5932 Utah Ave., N.W.

Dickey-Tomlinson, Margaret L. . . . . '29 '63 C.788 A.B. L.564 J.D. 3314 P St., N.W.‡

Dickieson, David H., (AV) . . . . '55 '80 C.188 B.A. L.477 J.D. [Silverstein&M.]
*PRACTICE AREAS: Litigation; Tax Controversies; Bankruptcy.

Dickinson, Dwight . . . . '57 '82 C&L.659 B.A., J.D. 5416 Galena Pl., N.W.

Dickinson, Timothy L., (AV) . . . .'54 '80 C&L.477 A.B., J.D. [Dickinson L.]
*PRACTICE AREAS: Foreign Corrupt Practices Act; International Joint Ventures; Foreign Asset Control; Agency and Distributorships; International Arbitration.

Dickinson, William C. . . . . '25 '50 C&L.16 J.D. [Haas&N.]

Dickinson Landmeier LLP, (AV)
1900 K Street, N.W., Suite 1150, 20006
Telephone: 202-457-5970 Facsimile: 202-785-1226
Email: tdickinson@dllaw.com
Timothy L. Dickinson; Lisa M. Landmeier; William F. Pendergast;—Natalia H. Jordan (Not admitted in DC); Robin B. First.
International Law, Foreign Corrupt Practices Act, Foreign Asset Control, Export Regulation, Export Compliance, Antiboycott Compliance, Economic Sanctions, Foreign Claims, Foreign Sales and Investment, Foreign Sovereign Immunities Act, International Arbitration, International Distribution, International Joint Ventures, Public International Law, Corporate Law, White Collar Criminal Defense, Corporate Compliance.
See Professional Biographies, WASHINGTON, DISTRICT OF COLUMBIA

Dickinson, Mackaman, Tyler & Hagen, P.C.
Suite 506 1660 L Street, NW, 20036-5603 ⊙
Telephone: 202-463-1260 Fax: 202-463-6328
Of Counsel: Gene C. Lange; John W. Thomas; Christopher Wheeler.
General Civil Practice. Corporation, Securities, Real Estate, Probate, Trials and Appeals, Taxation, Antitrust, Banking, Administrative, Fidelity and Surety Law, Labor and Employment Law, Casualty Insurance and Workers Compensation, Public Utility, Environmental, Energy and Telecommunications, Intellectual Property.
Representative Clients: Board of Water Works Trustees, Des Moines, Iowa; Merchants Bonding Co. (Mutual); Norwest Bank, N.A.; Adventure Lands of America; American Insurance Association; Associated Builders and Contractors of Iowa; Budget Marketing, Inc.; Burlington Northern Railroad Co.; Central Iowa KFC.
Des Moines, Iowa Office: Suite 1600 Hub Tower, 699 Walnut Street. Telephone: 515-244-2600. Fax: 515-246-4550.
See Professional Biographies, WASHINGTON, DISTRICT OF COLUMBIA

Dickinson Wright PLLC, (AV)
Suite 800, 1901 L Street, N.W., 20036-3506 ⊙
Telephone: 202-457-0160 Facsimile: 202-659-1559
URL: http://www.dickinson-wright.com
Resident Members: Marc A. Bergsman; William E. Elwood; David R. Haarz; Samuel D. Littlepage; Stephen L. Sulzer. Resident Of Counsel: Laurinda L. Hicks; J. John Shimazaki. Resident Associate: Nicole M. Meyer (Not admitted in DC).
Alternative Dispute Resolution, Antitrust, Appellate Litigation, Banking and Financial Services, Bankruptcy, Business Criminal Defense and Internal Investigations, Commercial and Business Litigation, Construction Law, Corporate, Corporate Finance, Ebusiness, Education and School Law, Employee Benefits, Employment Litigation, Energy and Public Utilities, Environmental, Family and Matrimonial Law, Gaming Law, Immigration, Insurance Industry, Intellectual Property, International, Labor and Employment Relations, Mergers and Acquisitions, Municipal Law and Finance, Private Capital, Product Liability/Personal Injury Litigation, Railroads and Transportation, Real Estate, Regulatory and Administrative Law, Risk Management, Securities, Taxation, Telecommunications, Trade Regulation, Trusts and Estate Planning.
Detroit, Michigan Office: 500 Woodward Avenue, Suite 4000. Telephone: 313-223-3500. Facsimile: 313-223-3598.
Ann Arbor, Michigan Office: 101 North Main Street, Suite 535. Telephone: 734-623-7075. Fax: 734-623-7568.
Bloomfield Hills, Michigan Office: 38525 Woodward Avenue, Suite 2000. Telephone: 248-433-7200. Facsimile: 248-433-7274.
Grand Rapids, Michigan Office: 200 Ottawa Avenue, N.W., Suite 900. Telephone: 616-458-1300. Facsimile: 616-458-6753.
Lansing, Michigan Office: Suite 200, 215 South Washington Square. Telephone: 517-371-1730. Facsimile: 517-487-4700.
See Professional Biographies, WASHINGTON, DISTRICT OF COLUMBIA

Dickman, David G. . . . . '52 '86 C.869 B.S. L.734 J.D. [Venable,A.B.H.&C.]
*PRACTICE AREAS: Environmental Law; Environmental Criminal Defense; Maritime International Law; Administrative; Regulatory Law.

Dickman, Marjorie J. . . . . '71 '97 C.228 A.B. L.276 J.D. [Wiley R.&F.]

Dickson, R. Bruce, (AV) . . . .'47 '73 C&L.178 B.A., J.D. [Paul,H.J.&W.]
*PRACTICE AREAS: False Advertising Litigation; Lanham Act; Intellectual Property Litigation; Food and Drug Law; Federal Trade Commission.

Dickstein, Jason A. '67 '93 C.860 B.A. L.904 J.D.
(adm. in NY; not adm. in DC) 1707 H St., N.W.

Dickstein, Sidney, (AV) . . . . '25 '49 C.264 A.B. L.178 J.D. [Dickstein S.M.&O.] ⊙
*PRACTICE AREAS: Antitrust Law; Corporate Law; Mergers and Acquisitions Law; Securities Litigation.

Dickstein Shapiro Morin & Oshinsky LLP, (AV) BR
2101 L Street, N.W., 20037-1526 ⊙
Telephone: 202-785-9700 Fax: 202-887-0689
URL: http://www.legalinnovators.com
Members of Firm: Kenneth L. Adams; Lee A. Alexander; Angelo V. Arcadipane; Matthew Steven Bergman; George T. Boggs; James W. Brady, Jr.; Paul Bennett Bran; Kenneth W. Brothers; Karen L. Bush; Henry C. Cashen II; Leslie R. Cohen; Robin L. Cohen (Resident, New York, N.Y. Office); Richard J. Conway; Thomas J. D'Amico; Merle Miller DeLancey, Jr.; Ida Wurczinger Draim; Stephen A. Dvorkin (Resident, New York, N.Y. Office); Larry F. Eisenstat; David L. Elkind; David L. Engelhardt; Emanuel Faust, Jr.; Margaret Feinstein; Howard N. Feldman; Barry J. Fleishman; Lawrence D. Garr; Allan B. Goldstein; Howard Graff (Resident, New York, N.Y. Office); G. Michael Green; Donald A. Gregory; Jon David Grossman; Katherine J. Henry; Robert J. Higgins; Gary M. Hoffman; R. Bruce Holcomb; J. Andrew Jackson; Howard S. Jatlow; Jeffrey M. Johnson; Peter Hafner Jost; Peter J. Kadzik; Leslie A. Kaplan; George Kaufmann (1931-1990); Leon B. Kellner; Deborah P. Kelly; James D. Kelly; William D. Kingery, Jr.; Joel B. Kleinman; Joseph E. Kolick, Jr.; Mark H. Kolman; Ira L. Kotel (Resident, New York, N.Y. Office); John T. Kotelly; Albert H. Kramer; Stefan M. Krantz; Arthur J. Lafave III; Neil Lefkowitz; Richard J. Leveridge; Barry Wm. Levine; Daniel M. Litt; Frederick M. Lowther; Patrick Winston Lynch; Kenneth M. Lyons; Matthew G. Maloney; Elaine Metlin; Andrew P. Miller; G. Joseph Minetti (1907-1993); M. J. Mintz; Ira R. Mitzner; Peter W. Morgan; Kenneth R. Morrow; David M. Nadler; Michael E. Nannes; Bernard Nash; Eric Oliver; Jerold Oshinsky; Randy Paar (Resident, New York, N.Y. Office); Lewis J. Paper; David Patton Parker; Corrine Propas Parver; Woody N. Peterson; George R. Pitts; Ira H. Polon; Charles M. Pratt (Resident, New York, N.Y. Office); Adam Proujansky; Frank C. Razzano (Not admitted in DC); Todd M. Roberts (Resident, New York, N.Y. Office); Gabrielle S. Roth; Charles W. Saber; Francis J. Sailer; Howard Schiffman; Gary L. Schoenbrun (Resident, New York, N.Y. Office); Richard Schramm (1941-1991); L. Kevin Sheridan, Jr. (Resident, New York, N.Y. Office); Elizabeth A. Sherwin (Resident, New York, N.Y. Office); Justin D. Simon (1947-2001); Kenneth M. Simon; James vanR. Springer; Paul R. Taskier; Edward Tessler (Resident, New York, N.Y. Office); Mark J. Thronson; Stephanie Karen Wade; Beth L. Webb; Stephan G. Weil; Kent T. Withycombe; Rebecca Wright; L. Andrew Zausner. Senior Counsel: Sidney Dickstein; Seymour Glanzer; Sallie H. Helm;

(This Listing Continued)

Dickstein Shapiro Morin & Oshinsky LLP (Continued)

Charles H. Morin; David I. Shapiro; Joseph D. Tydings. Of Counsel: Robert F. Aldrich; Laura Hamilton Calaluca; Michael D. Cox; Joan M. Darby; Michael I. Gilman; Douglas N. Jacobson (Not admitted in DC); George E. Johnson; Robert Mangas; Amy Marmer Nice; Stanford E. Parris; Richard P. Perrin; Mark L. Perlis; Steven John Roman; Michael J. Rustum; Laura J. V. Szabo. Counsel: Geoffrey Bestor; John J. Carr (Resident, New York, N.Y. Office); Linda J. Chase; Andrew C. Cooper; Michael J. DeCarlo; Michael R. Engleman (Not admitted in DC); Robert C. Fallon; Joseph Francis Fields (Resident, New York, N.Y. Office); Joel A. Fischman; Allan C. Hubbard; Andrew S. Kersting; Mark Kotlarsky; Harold K. McCombs, Jr.; Edward G. Modell; James Richard O'Neill; John P. Pierce (Not admitted in DC); Charlotte Rothenberg Rosen; Lawrence P. Sandor; Edward Still; Laura A. Vikander; Carla Perantoni Walsh; Alexander D. Widell (Resident, New York, N.Y. Office); Nicholas J. Zoogman (Resident, New York, N.Y. Office). Associates: Peter J. Andrews (Resident, New York, N.Y. Office); Constance Elaine Arabatzis (Resident, New York, N.Y. Office); Elizabeth Arenson (Not admitted in DC); Ruxandra Barbulescu; Robyn R. Bender; Eric A. Bensky; Jason S. Brown; Jason M. Bruno; Philip Busman (Not admitted in DC); Deborah Ann Carpentier; Christopher S. Chow (Not admitted in DC); Nicole M. Cober; Andres Colon; Gabriela I. Coman; Jeremy A. Cubert; Eli Curi, Jr. (Resident, New York, N.Y. Office); Estelina L. Dallett; William C. Dennis (Resident, New York, N.Y. Office); Kirsten Lea Doolittle (Not admitted in DC); Jennifer M. Eck; Charles Ernest Edgar, IV; Carmela N. Edmunds; Steven R. Eichel (Resident, New York, N.Y. Office); Jason R. Eig; Jacob S. Farber; Maria Farinella; Laura Beth Feigin; Robert N. Felgar; Laurence E. Fisher; Ryan H. Flax (Not admitted in DC); Kenneth H. Frenchman (Resident, New York, N.Y. Office); Robert Friedman (Resident, New York, N.Y. Office); Valerie M. Furman; Keisha A. Gary; John A. Gibbons (Not admitted in DC); Andrew Gilman (Resident, New York, N.Y. Office); Jonathan M. Goodman (Resident, New York, N.Y. Office); David H. Greenberg; Edward S. Hammerman; Walker G. Harman, Jr. (Resident, New York, N.Y. Office); Teresa L. Harvey; Elizabeth B. Haywood; Bridget M. Healy (Resident, New York, N.Y. Office); Maria Colsey Heard; Jennifer Tara Geter Holubar; Samuel L. Jefferson, Jr.; Patrick J. Kealy (Not admitted in DC); Michael S. Kimberling; J. Brian King; Paul W. Kisslinger; Jorge Kotelanski; Malathi Krishnamachari (Resident, New York, N.Y. Office); Victoria A. Kummer (Resident, New York, N.Y. Office); Gregory D. Kwan (Not admitted in DC); Christopher Leonardo (Not admitted in DC); Selena J. Linde; Susan A. Littell; Darren E. Long (Not admitted in DC); Paul R. Lucey; Marilyn T. Lynch (Not admitted in DC); Joseph R. Magnas (Resident, New York, N.Y. Office); Shibani Malhotra; Carla M. Marcolin; Keith A. Markel (Resident, New York, N.Y. Office); James Robertson Martin; Andrew J. McFarland; Charles V. Mehler, III (Not admitted in DC); Charles L. Miller, Jr.; Frances J. Miller; Lisa M. R. Miller; Steven L. Miller (Not admitted in DC); Gianni Minutoli; Christopher A. Monsey (Not admitted in DC); Robert James Moss; Sabrina A. Nelson; Tara L. Newmyer; Jonathan C. Odell; Benjamin R. Ogletree (Not admitted in DC); Edwin Oh (Not admitted in DC; Resident, New York, N.Y. Office); Christopher C. O'Hara; C. Todd Piczak (Not admitted in DC); Eden M. Polatnick (Not admitted in DC); R. Edward Poole; William E. Powell III; Debra H. Rednik; Tina D. Reynolds; Jeffrey Rhodes; Cara Romanzo; Meredith J. Ross (Not admitted in DC); Carrie M. Safford; Andra E. Schnabolk (Not admitted in DC); David T. Schur (Not admitted in DC); Julie P. Seamon; Edward E. Sharkey; Michael T. Sharkey; Bernard F. Sheehan, Jr.; April Everette Shelton; Kristi Singleton; Patrick T. Skacel (Not admitted in DC); Michael J. Slattery; John Charles Snodgrass (Not admitted in DC); Paul Spackman (Not admitted in DC); Leslie H. Spiegel (Not admitted in DC); Salvatore P. Tamburo; Christopher Mark Tanner; Kate Tapley; Jeffrey H. Tignor; Kenneth B. Trotter; Jodi Trulove; Brian D. Unroe (Resident, New York, N.Y. Office); Gabriel B. Valle (Not admitted in DC); Adam Vann; Gary L. Veron; Peter A. Veytsman; Nicole M. Vorrasi (Not admitted in DC); Steven Walter; Katherine A. Walther; Andrew M. Weiner; Steven M. Weinstein; Michael J Wentworth (Not admitted in DC); Mialeeka C. Williams-Bibbs (Not admitted in DC); Bradley D. Wine; James M. Wines; John P. Winsbro (Resident, New York, N.Y. Office); Becki L. Young; Adam S. Ziffer (Resident, New York, N.Y. Office); Jean E. Zimmerman (Resident, New York, N.Y. Office).
General Practice, including: Antitrust, Bankruptcy and Creditors' Rights, Banking, Business Crimes/Regulatory Enforcement, Civil Litigation, Construction, Communications, Alternative Dispute Resolution, Corporate, Financial Institutions, Intellectual Property, Employee Benefits (ERISA), Energy, Environmental Law, Finance, Government Affairs, Government Contracts, Health Care, Immigration and Naturalization, Insurance, Intellectual Property, International Trade, Labor and Employment, Litigation, Mergers and Acquisitions, Natural Resources, Patents, Real Estate, Securities, Sports Law, Tax, Trademarks, Trusts and Estates, Utility Law, and White Collar Crime.
New York, New York Office: 1177 Avenue of the Americas, 10036-2714. Telephone: 212-835-1400. Fax: 212-997-9880.
Correspondent Office, St. Petersburg, Russia: Russian-American Law Firm, Lermontovsky Prospect 7/12, 190008. Local Telephone: 114-5660. International Telephone: 850-1430.
See Professional Biographies, WASHINGTON, DISTRICT OF COLUMBIA

DiCrescenzo, Mary V. '56 '89 C.449 B.A. L.275 J.D.
(adm. in CT; not adm. in DC) Sr. Staff Coun., National Association of Home Builders

Didden, George A., III '45 '73 C.93 B.A. L.128 J.D.
Chmn. of the Bd. CEO & Gen. Coun., The National Capital Bk. of Wash.

Di Dio, Arthur S. . . . .'65 '98 C.851 B.S. L.276 J.D. [Arent F.K.P.&K.]
*PRACTICE AREAS: Health Care Law; Health Care Regulation; Health Care Litigation.

Diebold, David K. . . . .'42 '67 C.107 B.A. L.188 J.D. 1775 Eye St., N.W.

Diefendorf, Richard R. . . . .'59 '89 C.696 B.S.M.E. L.1209 J.D. [Crowell&M.] (Pat.)

Diemer, Mary S. . . . .'63 '88 C.273 B.A. L.94 J.D. [Carter,L.&M.]
*PRACTICE AREAS: Telecommunications; Litigation.

Dienelt, John F., (AV) . . . . '43 '70 C.893 B.A. L.976 LL.B. [Hogan&H.]
*PRACTICE AREAS: Complex Commercial Litigation; Class Actions; Franchise and Distribution Litigation; Antitrust; Trade Regulation Litigation.

Dienes, C. Thomas '40 '64 C.424 B.S. L.597 J.D.
(adm. in IL; not adm. in DC) George Washington Univ. Natl. Law Ctr.

Diercks, Walter E., (AV) . . . . '45 '72 C.688 B.Ch.E. L.893 J.D. [Rubin,W.D.H.&C.]
*PRACTICE AREAS: Media; Civil Litigation; Trade Regulation; General Corporate.

Diesenhouse, Samantha '73 '99 C.860 B.A. L.1040 J.D.
(adm. in CT; not adm. in DC) Atty., Environmental Law Institute
*RESPONSIBILITIES: Environmental Law.

Diess, Louis W., III '67 '92 C.282 B.A. L.1338 J.D.
(adm. in MD; not adm. in DC) [McCarron&D.]
*PRACTICE AREAS: Perishable Agricultural Commodities Act (PACA).

Dieter, Richard C. '46 '92
C.602 B.S. L.276 J.D. Exec. Dir., Death Penalty Information Center

Dieterich, L. Elise . . . .'62 '88 C.1331 B.A. L.309 J.D. [Swidler B.S.F.]
*PRACTICE AREAS: Telecommunications.

Dietrich, Diana L. . . . .'58 '86 C.228 B.A. L.378 J.D. [Baker B.]

Dietrich, Julie S. . . . .'70 '95 C.321 B.A. L.028 J.D. 1700 K St., Ste. 200

Dietrich, Paul George '49 '89 C.1291 B.A. L.999 J.D.
(adm. in VA; not adm. in DC) 1201 Pennsylvania Ave., N.W.‡

Dietz, Bernard C. . . . . '42 '68 C.1030 B.S. L.128 J.D. [Cleary&K.]
*PRACTICE AREAS: Copyrights; Entertainment Law; Unfair Competition Law.

Dietze, Paul E. . . . . '53 '99 C.1178 B.S. L.446 J.D. [Pennie&E.] (See Pat. Sect.)
*PRACTICE AREAS: Intellectual Property; Patents.

Difede, James R. . . . .'59 '87 C.04 B.A. L.276 J.D. [Counts,P.-D.&D.]

diGenova, Joseph E., (AV) . . . .'45 '70 C.150 B.A. L.276 J.D. [diGenova&T.]

diGenova & Toensing, (AV) . . . . .901 15th Street NW, Suite 430

DiGiovanni, Joseph A., Jr. '51 '77
C.734 B.A. L.818 J.D. Sr. V.P., St. Govt. Affs., Amer. Ins. Assn.

DiGirolamo, Arland '72 '98 C.93 B.A. L.1292 J.D.
(adm. in NJ; not adm. in DC) [Baker&H.]
*PRACTICE AREAS: International Trade Law; International Law.

DiGiulian, Maria T. '66 '99 C.299 B.A. L.1209 J.D.
(adm. in VA; not adm. in DC) [Powell,G.F.&M.]
*PRACTICE AREAS: International Trade; Litigation; Health.

DiLallo, Kevin S. . . . . '59 '87 C.893 B.A. L.930 J.D. [Levine,B.B.&B.]
*PRACTICE AREAS: Telecommunications Law; Commercial Law; Technology Law.

Dilcher, Amy J. '73 '00 C.665 B.S. L.329 J.D.
(adm. in NY; not adm. in DC) [Proskauer R.]

Dildine, Diane K., (AV) . . . . '47 '72 C.207 B.A. L.831 J.D. 419 7th St., N.W.

Di Leva, Charles E. . . . . '54 '78 C.690 B.A. L.1194 J.D. 1545 18th St., N.W.
Dilley, Dean M., (BV) . . . .'55 '80 C.188 A.B. L.128 J.D. [Patton B.]

Dillingham & Murphy, LLP, (AV)
1155 Connecticut Ave., N.W., Suite 1120, 20036-3419 ⊙
Telephone: 202-835-9880 Cable Address: "Paladin" Fax: 202-835-9885
Email: DM@wirepaladin.com URL: http://www.wirepaladin.com
Albert A. Foster, Jr.; Laurie A. Erdman. Of Counsel: John J. Lynch (Not admitted in DC). Associate: Grace M. Lee (Not admitted in DC).
General Civil Trial Practice, Business Planning, Litigation, Commercial Law, Intellectual Property, Internet Law, Technology and Science, Employment Law, Products Liability, Environmental Law, Toxic Torts, Real Estate Law, Insurance Law, Labor and Employment, Contracts, Business Law, Corporate Law, Investments, Probate, Trust and Estate, Securities, Civil Rights, Construction Law, Personal Injury and Torts, International Law, Admiralty and Maritime, Creditors Rights, Bankruptcy, Landlord and Tenant Law.
San Francisco, California Office: 225 Bush Street, Sixth Floor, 94104-4207. Telephone: 415-397-2700. Fax: 415-397-3300.
See Professional Biographies, WASHINGTON, DISTRICT OF COLUMBIA

Dillon, Sheri . . . .'62 '99 C.502 B.A. L.276 J.D. [Ⓐ McKee N.]
*PRACTICE AREAS: Taxation; Tax Controversies; Tax Litigation.
Dillon, Thomas Joseph, Jr. '63 '91 C&L.280 B.A., J.D.
(adm. in GA; not adm. in DC) [Dillon,H.&L.] ⊙
Dillon, Veronica '49 '77 C.724 B.A. L.262 J.D.
(adm. in NY; not adm. in DC) Sr. V.P. & Gen. Coun., Kaplan Educational Centers, Inc.
Dillon, Hall & Lungershausen LLC
601 Pennsylvania Avenue NW North Building, Suite 540 (⊙Hong Kong, China; Stuttgart, Germany)
DiLorenzo, Jack T. . . . . '21 '48 C.116 L.107 LL.B. 3801 Conn. Ave., N.W.‡

Dilworth Paxson PLLC, (AV)
1200 Nineteenth Avenue, N.W., 20036 ⊙
Telephone: 202-452-0900 Fax: 202-452-0930
Email: lawyers@dilworthlaw.com URL: http://www.dilworthlaw.com
Joel F. Brenner; Michael J. Dixon; Rebecca A. Donnellan; George R. A. Doumar; Richard S. Kraut; Ralph Drury Martin; Jon S. Nicholas; Allen H. Orenberg; Irving M. Pollack; Max Riederer von Paar (Not admitted in DC; Resident, Arlington, Virginia Office); Laurence Storch; John A. Whitney.
General Practice in all Courts, Corporate, Litigation, Bankruptcy and Insolvency, Criminal and Regulatory Investigations, E-Commerce, Employment and Management Labor Relations, Entertainment, Environmental, Healthcare, Insurance Regulation, Intellectual Property, International, Public Finance, Real Estate Securities, Tax, Trust and Estates.
Cherry Hill, New Jersey Office: Liberty View Suite 700, 457 Haddonfield Road, 08002. Telephone: 856-663-8877. Fax: 856-663-8855.
Harrisburg, Pennsylvania Office: 305 N. Front Street, Suite 403, 17101-1236. Telephone: 717-236-4812. Fax: 717-236-7811.
Newtown Square, Pennsylvania Office: 11 Campus Boulevard, Suite 150, 19073. Telephone: 610-325-3200. Fax: 610-325-3293.
Philadelphia, Pennsylvania Office: 3200 Mellon Bank Center, 1735 Market Street, 19103-7595. Telephone: 215-575-7000. Fax: 215-575-7200.
Turnersville, New Jersey Office: P.O. Box 762, University Executive Campus Suite 201, 151 Fries Mill Road, 08012. Telephone: 856-227-6100. Fax: 856-227-7373.
Wilmington, Delaware Office: First Federal Plaza, Suite 500, 19801. Telephone: 302-571-9800. Fax: 302-571-8875.
See Professional Biographies, WASHINGTON, DISTRICT OF COLUMBIA

DiMartino, Horace R. . . . . '18 '54 C&L.273 LL.B. 4432 Brandywine St., N.W.‡
DiMichael, Nicholas J., (AV) . . . .'48 '78 C.436 B.A. L.276 J.D. [Thompson H.]
*PRACTICE AREAS: Transportation; Energy; Administrative Law; Litigation.
Dimock, Whiting G. . . . . '71 '96 C.951 B.A. L.174 J.D. [Ⓐ Dow,L.&A.]
Dimond, Kendra L., (BV) . . . . '47 '79 C.282 B.A. L.1017 J.D. [Arent F.K.P.&K.]
*PRACTICE AREAS: Health Law; Health Care Fraud; Health Care Litigation; Public Health Law; Health Care Regulation.
Dimopoulos, Arthur . . . . '58 '91 C.128 B.F.A. L.809 J.D. [© Preston G.E.&R.M.]
*PRACTICE AREAS: Transportation; Maritime Law.

Dimos, C. L.
(See Middleburg, Virginia)

Dinan, Donald R., (BV) . . . .'49 '75 C.659 B.S. L.276 J.D. [Hall,E.H.G.G.&N.]
*PRACTICE AREAS: International Trade; Litigation; Trademarks; Copyrights.
Dinan, James H., (AV) . . . . '58 '86 C.692 B.A. L.221 J.D. Asst. U.S. Atty.
Dinan, Kevin M., (AV) . . . .'— '85 C.882 B.A. L.245 J.D. [King&S.]
*PRACTICE AREAS: Litigation and Trade.
DiNardo, John A. '36 '60 C&L.602 A.B., J.D.
(adm. in OH; not adm. in DC)
Grp. V.P. & Gen. Coun., American Institute of Architects, The
Dinerstein, Paula N. . . . .'49 '80 C.446 B.S. L.273 J.D. [© Duncan,W.G.&P.]
Dinerstein, Robert D. '53 '78 C.188 A.B. L.976 J.D.
Prof., American Univ., Wash. College of Law
Dingilian, Timothy R. '55 '83
C.112 B.A. L.990 J.D. [Jackson&C.] (⊙Balt., Rockville, MD)
*PRACTICE AREAS: Insurance Coverage Litigation; Medical Malpractice.
Dingwall, Craig D. . . . .'56 '83 C.763 B.A. L.1049 J.D. Gen. Atty., Sprint Corp.
Dinneen-Long, Christian B. '— '95 C.966 B.B.A. L.146 J.D.
(adm. in IL; not adm. in DC) [Ⓐ Foley&L.]
*PRACTICE AREAS: Business Law.
Dinning, Brian R. . . . .'65 '90 C.294 B.A. L.1339 J.D. [Robins,K.M.&C.]
*PRACTICE AREAS: Mergers, Acquisitions and Consolidations; Business Law; Emerging Growth Companies; Tax and Employee Benefits.
Dinsmore, Courtney A. '66 '93 C.821 B.A. L.893 J.D.
(adm. in NY; not adm. in DC) [© Mayer,B.&P.]
DiNunzio, Nicholas Paul '63 '98 C.886 B.S. L.1356 J.D.
(adm. in VA; not adm. in DC) Dept. of Energy
DiPentima, Margaret E. . . . . '73 '99 C.674 A.B. L.893 J.D. [Ⓐ Hogan&H.]
DiPietro, Ralph J. . . . . '63 '90 C.94 B.A. L.273 J.D. 1325 18th St., N.W.
Director, Mark D., (AV) '58 '85 C&L.309 A.B., J.D.
Exec. V.P. & Gen. Coun., U.S. Off. Prod. Co.
Direnfeld, Barry B., (AV) . . . .'49 '76 C.365 B.A. L.180 J.D. [Swidler B.S.F.]
*PRACTICE AREAS: Legislative Lobbying; Governmental Affairs; Environmental Law.
DiResta, Anthony E., (AV) . . . .'53 '84 C.699 B.A. L.259 J.D. [© Fulbright&J.]
*PRACTICE AREAS: Antitrust; Business Litigation; Securities; Communications and Media Law.
DiSalvo, Samuel C. '59 '85 C&L.107 B.Acct., J.D.
(adm. in NY; not adm. in DC) Sr. Mgr., Price Waterhouse
Disbrow, D. Jeffrey . . . .'60 '85 C.477 B.A. L.273 J.D. [Arent F.K.P.&K.]
*PRACTICE AREAS: Tax Law.
Disch, Robert M. . . . .'55 '81 C.121 B.A. L.597 J.D. [© Kutak R.]
*PRACTICE AREAS: Litigation; Antitrust.
Discher, Gregory S. '60 '96 C.679 B.S. L.1356 J.D.
(adm. in VA; not adm. in DC; Pat.) [Ⓐ Hale&D.]
*PRACTICE AREAS: Intellectual Property Law.
Di Scipio, Joseph M. . . . .'67 '96 C.208 B.A. L.823 J.D. [Ⓐ Cohn&M.]
*PRACTICE AREAS: Communications Law; Telecommunications Law; Common Carrier; Mass Media Law.
DiSciullo, Jeffrey G., (AV) . . . . '54 '84 C.260 B.A. L.128 J.D. [Wright&T.]
*PRACTICE AREAS: Energy.

Disenhaus, Helen E., (BV) . . . .'48 '77 C.518 A.B. L.976 J.D. [Swidler B.S.F.]
*PRACTICE AREAS: Regulatory Law; Telecommunications Law.
Diskin, Mark J. . . . . '54 '80 C.477 B.A. L.273 J.D. [Copilevitz&C.] ⊙
*PRACTICE AREAS: Tax Exempt Organizations; Civil Litigation; Estate Planning and Probate; Real Estate.
Disselkamp, Linda B. '55 '81 C.188 B.A. L.30 J.D.
Legal Index Editor, Bur. of Natl. Affs.
di Stefano, James Michael '61 '86 C.160 B.S. L.64 J.D.
(adm. in MD; not adm. in DC) Sr. Tax Mgr., Deloitte & Touche
DiStefano, Robert P. '55 '84 C.1044 B.A. L.1206 J.D.
(adm. in FL; not adm. in DC) 1250 24th St., N.W., Ste. 350
Ditchek, Neil I. . . . .'64 '90 C.1349 B.A. L.273 J.D. 1101 17th St Nw # 1210
Ditkoff, James H. '46 '72 C.976 B.A. L.178 J.D.
(adm. in NY; not adm. in DC) Danaher Corp.
Divoll, Vicki J. . . . . '51 '78 C.518 B.A. L.893 J.D. 3839 Livingston St., N.W.‡
Dix, Katherine M. . . . .'70 '98 C.575 B.A. L.309 J.D. Legal Aid Society of D.C.
Dixon, Alan J. '— '49 C.339 B.S. L.910 LL.B.
(adm. in MO; not adm. in DC) [Bryan C.] (⊙Chgo., IL; St. Louis, MO)
*PRACTICE AREAS: Corporate Law; Government Contracts.
Dixon, Amy T. . . . .'72 '97 C.575 B.A. L.602 J.D. [Ⓐ Weil,G.&M.]
Dixon, Ben F. . . . . '18 '56 C.575 A.B. L.273 J.D. 3282 North St., N.W.‡
Dixon, Edward H. . . . .'64 '93 C.178 B.A. L.477 J.D. [© Covington&B.]
Dixon, Gary V., (AV) . . . . '50 '75 C.105 B.S.B.A. L.893 J.D. [Ross,D.&B.]
Dixon, Heather O. . . . .'74 '99 C.886 B.S. L.893 J.D. [Ⓐ Wiley R.&F.]
Dixon, Herbert B., Jr. . . . .'46 '73 C.329 B.S. L.276 J.D. Supr. Ct. J.
Dixon, Lee J., II . . . . '46 '73 C.381 B.B.A. L.930 J.D. Pres., Dixon Capital Associates, Inc.
Dixon, Mary M. . . . .'66 '98 C.882 B.A. L.880 J.D. [Ⓐ Arnold&P.]
Dixon, Michael J. . . . .'53 '93 C.945 B.A. L.273 J.D. [Dilworth P.P.]
Dixon, Monique L. '70 '96 C.331 B.A. L.446 J.D.
(adm. in MD; not adm. in DC) Staff Atty., Advancement Project
Dixon, Richard D., Jr . . . . '40 '65 C.228 A.B. L.575 J.D. 450 E. St., N.W.
Dixon, Ronald . . . .'49 '78 C.1032 B.A. L.1162 J.D. 2119 2nd St., N.W.
Djinis, Anthony W., (AV) . . . .'49 '75 C.688 B.S. L.724 J.D. [Pickard&D.]
Djordjevich, Alexander . . . . '66 '92 C.112 A.B. L.904 J.D. [Griffin,F.T.&M.]
*PRACTICE AREAS: Business Transactions (35%); Real Estate (20%); Litigation (20%); Wills (20%); Trust Law.

DKW Law Group, PC, (AV)
1620 L Street, N.W., Suite 1210, 20036 ⊙
Telephone: 202-955-5080 Telecopier: 202-955-6070
Email: dkwlaw@dkwlaw.com URL: http://www.dkwlaw.com
Jeffrey W. Letwin; Michael A. Weiss (Not admitted in DC); Leo A. Keevican, Jr. (Not admitted in DC); Clyde H. Slease, III. Of Counsel: John J. McGovern, Jr.
Pittsburgh, Pennsylvania Office: 58th Floor, USX Tower, 600 Grant Street. Telephone: 412-355-2600. Fax: 412-355-2609.
Southfield, Michigan Office: 4000 Town Center, Suite 1500. Telephone: 248-358-2090. Fax: 248-358-3599.
Cleveland, Ohio Office: 26th Floor, BP Tower, 200 Public Square. Telephone: 216-875-4800. Fax: 216-875-4809.
Harrisburg, Pennsylvania Office: 4th Floor, Locust Court, 212 Locust Street. Telephone: 717-232-9500. Fax: 717-232-3524.
See Professional Biographies, WASHINGTON, DISTRICT OF COLUMBIA

Doan, Kathryn M. . . . .'62 '91 C.188 B.A. L.128 J.D. Legal Aid Soc.
Doane, Michael L. . . . .'64 '90 C.381 B.A. L.911 J.D. [Ⓐ Adduci,M.&S.]
*PRACTICE AREAS: International Trade Regulation; Corporate and Business Transactions; Intellectual Property; Litigation.
Dobbins, Alexander W. . . . .'42 '71 C&L.329 B.A., J.D. 1206 Madison St., N.W.
Dobbins, M. David . . . .'70 '98 C.502 B.A. L.477 J.D. [Ⓐ Shea&G.]
Dobeck, Robert B. '54 '81 C.184 B.S. L.276 J.D.
Prelaw Advisor, Georgetown University
Dobek, Robert F. . . . .'48 '79 C.976 B.A. L.276 J.D. 2844 Wisconsin Ave., N.W.
Dobin, Phyllis J., (AV) . . . . '52 '76 C.910 B.A. L.446 J.D. [Dobin&S.] ⊙
*PRACTICE AREAS: Elder Law; Estate Planning; Estates; Trusts; Probate.

Dobin & Senatore, P.C., (AV)
1025 Connecticut Avenue, N.W., Suite 515, 20036 ⊙
Telephone: 202-659-3232 Facsimile: 202-296-1064 URL: http://www.dobinlaw.com
Email: info@dobinlaw.com URL: http://www.lawyers.com/dobinlaw
Members of Firm: Phyllis J. Dobin; E. Taylor Senatore (Not admitted in DC).
Elder Law, Estate Planning, Estates, Trusts, Probate Law, Estate and Gift Taxation, Wealth Preservation, Family Business Succession, Disability and Retirement Planning, Will Contests, Medicaid, Small Business Law, Corporate Law, Business Planning, Nonprofit Law, Real Estate.
Reference: Crestar Bank, N.A., 20th St. Branch, Washington, D. C.
Silver Spring, Maryland Office: 8701 Georgia Avenue. Suite 750. Telephone: 301-585-6677.
See Professional Biographies, WASHINGTON, DISTRICT OF COLUMBIA

Dobranski, Bernard '39 '64 C.602 B.B.A. L.893 J.D.
(adm. in VA; not adm. in DC) Dean & Prof. of Law, Catholic Univ.
Dobson, Lisa S. . . . .'73 '98 C.608 B.A. L.362 J.D. Office of Chief Coun.
Docter, Charles A., (AV) . . . .'31 '56 C.385 B.A. L.145 J.D. [Docter,D.&L.]
*PRACTICE AREAS: Reorganization Law; Bankruptcy Law; Insolvency Law.
Docter, Henry David Will '60 '96 C.118 B.A. L.569 J.D.
(adm. in MD; not adm. in DC) [Ⓐ Docter,D.&L.]
*PRACTICE AREAS: Elder Law; Probate; Consumer Law.
Docter, Marcia K. . . . . '33 '57 C&L.659 B.S., LL.B. [Docter,D.&L.]
*PRACTICE AREAS: Reorganization Law; Creditors Rights Law; Commercial Litigation.

Docter, Docter & Lynn, P.C., (AV)
666 Eleventh Street, N.W., Suite 1010, 20001-4542
Telephone: 202-628-6800 Telefax: 202-628-5445
Email: ddl@bankruptcy-docter.com URL: http://www.lawyers.com/docterdocter&lynn
Charles A. Docter; Marcia K. Docter; David E. Lynn;—Henry David Will Docter (Not admitted in DC).
Bankruptcy, Reorganization, Creditors Rights, Insolvency Matters, Commercial Law, Corporation Law.
See Professional Biographies, WASHINGTON, DISTRICT OF COLUMBIA

Dodd, Quin D. '67 '95 C.560 B.A. L.276 J.D.
(adm. in NM; not adm. in DC) 1501 M St., N.W.
Dodds, John H . . . .'53 '97 C.054 B.S. L.1187 J.D. 1742 N St., NW
Dodek, Oscar I., Jr. . . . . '31 '85 C.477 B.A. L.273 J.D. [© Asbill,J.M.&B.]
*PRACTICE AREAS: Medical Malpractice.
Dodge, Garen E., (AV) . . . . '57 '82 C.1171 B.A. L.945 J.D. [Littler M.]
*PRACTICE AREAS: Labor and Employment.
Dodge, John C., (BV) . . . . '60 '86 C.431 B.A. L.128 J.D. [Cole,R.&B.]
*PRACTICE AREAS: Telecommunications; Administrative Law; Rate Regulation.
Dodge, John D. . . . .'53 '96 C.1012 B.S. L.273 J.D. City Atty.
Dodson, G. Diane . . . .'47 '73 C.691 B.A. L.846 J.D. Dep. Dir., Women's Legal Def. Fund
Dodson, Mary Jane . . . .'54 '82 C.674 A.B. L.893 J.D. [© Shaw P.]
*PRACTICE AREAS: Corporate Finance.
Dodson, Peter M. . . . .'54 '80 C&L.893 B.A., J.D. [© Cadwalader,W.&T.]
*PRACTICE AREAS: Bankruptcy; Bankruptcy Reorganization; Insolvency.

Doherty, Cornelius H., Jr., (AV) '35 '59 C&L.276 B.S., LL.B. [Doherty,S.&P.] (⊙Vero Beach, FL; Fairfax, VA)
*PRACTICE AREAS: Probate; Corporate Law; Estate Planning.

Doherty, David '73 '01 C&L.602 B.A., J.D. (adm. in NY; not adm. in DC) [[A] Dow,L.&A.]

Doherty, Dennis O. '52 '91 C.1044 B.S. L.128 J.D. (adm. in NJ; not adm. in DC) [Smith,G.&R.] (⊙Atlanta, GA)

Doherty, Karen M. . . . . '61 '94 C.696 B.S.N. L.446 J.D. [[A] Regan,H.&L.]
*PRACTICE AREAS: Medical Malpractice; Wrongful Death; Products Liability.

Doherty, Robert M. '73 '99 C.945 B.A. L.1509 J.D. (adm. in VA; not adm. in DC) [[A] Baker&H.]
*PRACTICE AREAS: Litigation.

Doherty, Thomas J. '49 '74 C.436 B.A. L.128 J.D. Asst. Gen. Coun., Medlantic Healthcare Group

Doherty, W. Patrick '73 '00 C.276 B.S.F.S. L.273 J.D. (adm. in MD; not adm. in DC) [[A] Venable,A.B.H.&C.]
*PRACTICE AREAS: Government Contracts; Litigation.

Doherty-Minicozzi, Colleen . . . . '68 '94 C.674 A.B. L.813 J.D. [[C] Wilmer,C.&P.]
*PRACTICE AREAS: Securities Law.

Doherty, Sheridan & Persian, L.L.P., (AV)
1050 17th Street NW Suite 1250, 20036 ⊙
Email: ds.law@erols.com
Members of Firm: Cornelius H. Doherty, Jr.; Edwin A. Sheridan; Eric M. Persian.
General Civil and Trial Practice, Probate, Insurance, Corporation, Creditors Rights, Negligence.
Fairfax, Virginia Office: Suite 200, 8408 Arlington Boulevard, 22031. Telephone: 703-698-7700. Facsimile: 703-641-9645.
Bethesda, Maryland Office: 4701 Sangamore Road, Suite S-225, 20816.
Vero Beach, Florida Office: 1701 Highway AIA, Suite 220, 32963.
See Professional Biographies, WASHINGTON, DISTRICT OF COLUMBIA

Doherty Taylor, Tracy . . . .'63 '96 C.1375 B.A. L.273 J.D. [[A] Williams&J.]
*PRACTICE AREAS: Telecommunications Law; Technology Law.

Doig, Amy S. '74 '01 C.188 B.A. L.477 J.D. (adm. in OR; not adm. in DC) [[A] Kirkpatrick&L.]

Dola, Mark S. . . . .'58 '94 C.976 B.A. L.276 J.D. [[A] Orrick,H.&S.]

Dolan, Edward C., (AV) . . . . '53 '78 C.178 B.A. L.276 J.D. [Hogan&H.]
*PRACTICE AREAS: Bankruptcy; Commercial Law; Finance; Real Estate.

Dolan, Kathleen S. . . . .'72 '98 C.436 B.A. L.128 J.D. [[A] Venable,A.B.H.&C.]
*PRACTICE AREAS: Environmental; White Collar Crime.

Dolan, Louis E., Jr. . . . .'64 '92 C.276 B.A. L.1209 J.D. [[A] Nixon P.]
*PRACTICE AREAS: Corporate Litigation; Commercial Litigation; Real Estate.

Dolan, Matthew J. . . . .'60 '86 C.976 B.A. L.893 J.D. [Baker&H.]
*PRACTICE AREAS: Corporate; Tax; Health Care.

Dolan, Thomas J. . . . .'65 '91 C.262 B.A. L.602 J.D. Assoc. Gen. Coun., Fannie Mae
*RESPONSIBILITIES: Real Estate; Finance.

Doland, Marie N., (AV) . . . .'49 '77 C.788 B.A. L.273 J.D. [Shaw P.]
*PRACTICE AREAS: Outsourcing; Technology.

Dold, Elizabeth Thomas '69 '94 C.645 B.S. L.1017 J.D. (adm. in NJ; not adm. in DC) [[A] Groom]
*PRACTICE AREAS: Taxation Law; Employee Benefits; Pension and Profit Sharing; ERISA.

Dole, Robert J., (AV) '— '52 C&L.900 A.B., LL.B. (adm. in KS; not adm. in DC) [[C] Verner,L.B.M.&H.]

Dolgoff, Eliana Debra '68 '97 C.66 B.A. L.276 J.D. (adm. in NY; not adm. in DC) IRS, Chf. Couns. Off.

Dolin, Mitchell F., (AV) . . . .'56 '82 C.860 B.A. L.569 J.D. [Covington&B.]

Dolphin, Verginald L., (BV) . . . '22 '52 C.329 A.B. L.1014 LL.B. 4308 Georgia Ave., NW

Dols, Jonathan Reidy '68 '00 C.870 B.S. L.1209 J.D. (adm. in VA; not adm. in DC) 400 Seventh St. S.W.

Doman, Latif '70 '98 C.511 B.A. L.659 (adm. in PA; not adm. in DC) [[A] Howrey S.A.&W.]
*PRACTICE AREAS: Intellectual Property Litigation.

Dombek, Brooke Amy '75 '01 C.597 B.A. L.569 J.D. (adm. in NY; not adm. in DC) [[A] Shaw P.]
*PRACTICE AREAS: Technology Transactions; Technology Licensing; Intellectual Property; Commercial Transactions; Internet Law.

Dombo, Frederick T. '67 '93 C.222 B.A. L.1338 J.D. Leg. Coun., HALT-An Organization of Americans for Legal Reform

Dombo, Frederick T., III . . . .'67 '93 C.222 B.A. L.1338 J.D. [O'Connor&H.]
*PRACTICE AREAS: Lobbying; Administrative Law.

Dombroff, Mark A., (AV) . . . . '47 '71 C.30 B.A. L.904 J.D. [Dombroff&G.]

Dombroff & Gilmore, (AV) 1025 Thomas Jefferson St., N.W. (⊙Miami, FL; New York, NY)

Domenech, Mildred '73 '00 C.276 B.S.F.S. L.178 J.D. (adm. in MD; not adm. in DC) [[A] Shaw P.]
*PRACTICE AREAS: Communications Law; Technology Law.

Domenici, David '64 '92 C.893 B.A. L.813 J.D. (adm. in PA; not adm. in DC) Off. of City Admin.

Domer, Cindy Kendrick '66 '91 C.484 B.A. L.309 J.D. (adm. in MD; not adm. in DC) 1776 K St., N.W.‡

Domike, Julie Ronder . . . .'54 '86 C.518 A.B. L.276 J.D. [Wallace K.M.&B.]
*PRACTICE AREAS: Environmental.

Dominguez, Christopher E. . . . .'60 '97 C.556 B.B.A. L.128 J.D. [[A] Kirkpatrick&L.]
*PRACTICE AREAS: Securities Litigation; Civil Litigation; NASD Arbitration; Employment Litigation; Export Regulation.

Dominguez, John P., (AV) . . . .'52 '77 C.150 B.A. L.128 J.D. Asst. U.S. Atty.

Dominitz, Erica Jill . . . .'70 '97 C.1036 B.A. L.276 J.D. 1015 18th St., N.W.

Dominy, Mary Ann . . . . . . '69 '94 C.280 B.B.A. L.893 J.D. 1701 Pennsylvania Ave., N.W.

Dommers, Christa L. '68 '97 C.19 B.A. L.1252 J.D. (adm. in CT; not adm. in DC) [[A] Powell,G.F.&M.]
*PRACTICE AREAS: Real Estate; Environmental.

Don, David M. . . . .'71 '96 C&L.276 B.S.F.S., J.D. [[A] Willkie F.&G.]
*PRACTICE AREAS: Communications Law.

Don, Michael E. . . . . . .'43 '69 C.860 A.B. L.30 J.D. Pres., Securities Investor Protec. Corp.

Donahue, Joseph P. '54 '85 C.602 B.B.A. L.273 J.D. (adm. in VA; not adm. in DC) Mng. Tax Dir., Resch. & Planning, Marriott Intl., Inc.

Donahue, Maureen E. . . . .'67 '94 C.882 B.A. L.910 J.D. [[A] Gardner,C.&D.]
*PRACTICE AREAS: International Environmental Law.

Donahue, Michael P. . . . .'67 '96 C.800 B.A. L.128 J.D. [[A] Swidler B.S.F.]
*PRACTICE AREAS: Telecommunications.

Donahue, Nancy A. . . . .'56 '82 C.1030 B.A. L.30 J.D. [[A] Katz&R.]

Donahue, Pierre M. '62 '88 C.93 B.A. L.1068 J.D. Asst. Gen. Coun., Mariott International, Inc.
*RESPONSIBILITIES: Counseling; Commercial.

Donahue, Stephanie '55 '87 C.608 B.S. L.1209 J.D. (adm. in MD; not adm. in DC) [[A] Donahue] ⊙
*PRACTICE AREAS: Civil Litigation; Banking Law; Products Liability Defense.

Donahue Law Firm, The, (AV)
Suite 930 1120 G. Street, N.W., 20005 ⊙
Telephone: 202-371-1080 URL: http://www.thedonahuelawfirm.com
URL: http://www.lawyers.com/thedonahuelawfirm

(This Listing Continued)

Donahue Law Firm, The (Continued)
Associate: Stephanie Donahue (Not admitted in DC).
Wrongful Death, Products Liability, Medical Malpractice, Major Personal Injury, Banking Law, Bank Transactions, Family Law, Business Law and Litigation, Criminal, Probate and Estate Planning.
Annapolis, Maryland Office: 18 West Street. 21401. Telephone: 410-280-2023. Fax: 410-280-0905.
See Professional Biographies, WASHINGTON, DISTRICT OF COLUMBIA

Donaldson, Richard C. '59 '85 C.188 B.A. L.145 J.D. (adm. in VA; not adm. in DC) [Shaw P.]
*PRACTICE AREAS: Tax; REIT; Corporate Finance.

Donaldson, Timothy B. '70 '00 C.896 B.S. L.1209 J.D. (adm. in VA; not adm. in DC) [[A] Finnegan,H.F.G.&D.]
*PRACTICE AREAS: Biotechnology Patent Prosecution; Biotechnology Patents; Chemical Patent Prosecution; Molecular Biology Patents; Patent Interference Practice.

Donath, Glen . . . . '70 '98 C.976 B.A. L.145 J.D. [[A] Williams&C.]
*PRACTICE AREAS: Litigation.

Donath, Nicole B. . . . .'66 '92 C.951 B.A. L.309 J.D. [[A] Keller&H.]
*PRACTICE AREAS: Telecommunications.

Donavan, Mary Sue . . . . '44 '91 C.999 B.Mus. L.107 J.D. [[A] R.M.Price]

Donegan, Charles E. . . . . . .'33 '68 C.1016 B.S.C. L.329 J.D. 601 Pennsylvania Ave., N.W.

Donelly, Shannon A. . . . .'74 '00 C.478 B.A. L.904 J.D. 2829 Connecticut Ave.

Donelson, Lewis R., III, (AV) '17 '40 C.806 B.A. L.276 LL.B. [Baker,D.B.&C.] (⊙Chattanooga, Huntsville, Knoxville, Memphis, Nashville, TN)
*PRACTICE AREAS: Tax; Corporate Law; School Equal Protection.

Doner, Karen A. . . . .'71 '97 C.205 B.A. L.424 J.D. [[A] Williams M.]
*PRACTICE AREAS: Labor and Employment; Commercial Litigation.

Doniger, David D. '51 '77 C.976 B.A. L.1066 J.D. White House Off. on Environ. Policy

Donilon, Thomas E., (BV) '55 '86 C.128 B.A. L.893 J.D. Exec. V.P. & Corp. Secy., Fannie Mae, Inc.

Donley, Charles F., II . . . .'58 '88 C.188 A.B. L.339 J.D. [Squire,S.&D.]
*PRACTICE AREAS: International Aviation Law; Commercial Law; Contracts; Airline Regulation; Transportation Regulation.

Donley, Marshall O., III '73 '98 C.790 B.A. L.880 J.D. (adm. in GA; not adm. in DC) [[A] Sutherland A.&B.]
*PRACTICE AREAS: Litigation; Securities.

Donley-Hoopes, Maureen A. . . . . '54 '80 C.893 B.A. L.276 J.D. [Kirkland&E.]
*PRACTICE AREAS: Futures Law; Derivative Products; Financial Services.

Donlon, Donna M. . . . .'70 '97 C.893 B.A. L.945 J.D. [[A] Long A.&N.]
*PRACTICE AREAS: Litigation.

Donnellan, Rebecca A. . . . . '50 '75 C.453 S.B. L.309 J.D. [Dilworth P.P.]
*PRACTICE AREAS: Environmental; Corporate Litigation; Personal Injury Litigation; Securities Litigation; Litigation.

Donnelly, John V., III '75 '01 C&L.309 A.B., J.D. (adm. in MA; not adm. in DC) [[A] Covington&B.]

Donnelly, Kathleen J. . . . .'71 '97 C.309 A.B. L.145 J.D. [[A] Covington&B.]

Donnelly, Kenneth W. . . . . '68 '93 C.472 B.S. L.259 J.D. [[A] Howrey S.A.&W.]
*PRACTICE AREAS: Antitrust; Complex Commercial Litigation.

Donnelly, Shannon . . . .'74 '00 C.478 B.A. L.904 J.D. 5324 43rd Street, N.W.

Donnelly, William J., Jr., (AV) . . . . .'23 '50 C.1027 B.S. L.273 J.D. [[C] Martell,D.G.&G.]

Donnenfeld, Charles R., (AV) . . . .'35 '60 C.102 B.S. L.178 LL.B. [[C] Schwalb,D.&S.]

Donner, Irah H. . . . .'62 '91 C.124 B.S. L.930 J.D. [Hale&D.] (Pat.)
*PRACTICE AREAS: Intellectual Property.

Donner, Michael L., Sr. '61 '97 C.871 B.S. L.1356 J.D. (adm. in VA; not adm. in DC) [[A] Connolly B.L.&H.] ⊙

D'Onofrio, Steven J. '56 '81 C.102 B.S. L.1068 J.D. Exec. V.P. & Dir., Anti-Piracy, Recording Industry Assoc. of America, Inc.

Donoghue, John J. '71 '00 C&L.276 B.A., J.D. (adm. in MD; not adm. in DC) [[A] O'Melveny&M.]

Donoghue, Kristen A. . . . .'68 '96 C.276 B.A. L.477 J.D. [[A] Hogan&H.]

Donohoe, Charles R., (AV) '41 '70 C.608 B.S. L.273 J.D. Sr. V.P., Gen.Coun. & Pat. Coun., Samsung Electronics (Pat.)

Donohoe, David A., (P.C.), (AV) . . . .'37 '63 C&L.128 A.B., LL.B. [Akin,G.S.H.&F.]
*PRACTICE AREAS: Litigation; Antitrust; Securities.

Donohue, Daniel J., (AV) '52 '79 C.321 B.A. L.128 J.D. [Wickwire G.] (⊙Vienna, VA)
*PRACTICE AREAS: Government Contracts; Construction Law; Commercial Law.

Donohue, Edward L. . . . . '60 '86 C.1102 B.S.B.A. L.904 J.D. [Cole,R.&B.]
*PRACTICE AREAS: Zoning; Land Use; Historic Preservation; Transactional Real Estate.

Donohue, Mark J. . . . . '69 '95 C.423 B.B.A. L.64 J.D. Atty. Sec. Exch. Comm.

Donohue, Kaufmann, Shaw & Kligman, (AV) . . . . 503 D St., N.W.

Donovan, Daniel T. . . . .'71 '97 C.884 B.S. L.273 J.D. [[A] Kirkland&E.]
*PRACTICE AREAS: Litigation.

Donovan, Edward C. . . . .'— '94 C.1350 B.E. L.273 J.D. [Kirkland&E.]
*PRACTICE AREAS: Intellectual Property.

Donovan, Kelly Riley . . . . '66 '92 C.339 B.S. L.910 J.D. [Baker B.]

Donovan, Patrick J., (BV) . . . .'48 '76 C.1036 A.B. L.276 J.D. [[C] Swidler B.S.F.]
*PRACTICE AREAS: Telecommunications; Administrative Law.

Donovan, Paul M., (AV) . . . .'41 '68 C.1031 B.A. L.94 LL.B. [LaRoe,W.M.&D.]
*PRACTICE AREAS: Transportation Law; Environmental Law; Antitrust Law.

Donovan, Tiffany F. . . . .'69 '00 C.20 B.A. L.188 J.D. [[A] Jones,D.R.&P.]

Donovan, William J., Jr. '49 '78 C.321 B.A. L.128 J.D. V.P., Govt. Affs., National Assn. of Fed. Credit Unions

Donovan, William P., Jr. '66 '91 C.178 B.A. L.1068 J.D. Senior Litigation Counsel, MCI WorldCom, Inc.

Dooley, Clare H. . . . .'67 '97 C.691 B.A. L.426 J.D. [[A] Arnold&P.]
*PRACTICE AREAS: Products Liability.

Dooley, Helen I. . . . . '71 '95 C&L.228 B.A., J.D. [[A] Williams&C.]
*PRACTICE AREAS: Business Law; Corporate Law.

Doolittle, J. William, (AV) . . .'29 '54 C.210 A.B. L.309 LL.B. 4000 Cathedral Ave., N.W.

Doolittle, Kirsten Lea '74 '00 C.197 B.A. L.800 J.D. (adm. in VA; not adm. in DC) [[A] Dickstein S.M.&O.]
*PRACTICE AREAS: Litigation; Labor.

Dopp, Mark D., (AV) . . . .'57 '84 C.966 B.S. L.502 J.D. 555 13th St., N.W.

Dopsovic, David A. . . . . '51 '78 C.401 B.S. L.276 J.D. 2121 K St., NW

Doram, Michael R., (AV) . . . .'40 '67 C.813 A.B. L.276 J.D. [Creskoff&D.] ⊙
*PRACTICE AREAS: Customs Law; International Trade.

Doran, James B. '64 '00 C.999 L.276 J.D. (adm. in MD; not adm. in DC) [[A] Barnes,R.&C.]
*PRACTICE AREAS: Food and Drug; International Trade; Customs.

Doran, Kelley Patrick . . . . '67 '93 C.67 B.A. L.902 J.D. [[A] Preston G.E.&R.M.]
*PRACTICE AREAS: Government Contracts.

Doran, Michael . . . . '66 '93 C.918 B.A. L.976 J.D. [Caplin&D.]
*PRACTICE AREAS: Employee Benefits; Taxation.

Doran, William K. . . . .'63 '89 C.893 B.A. L.128 J.D. [Heenan,A.&R.]
*PRACTICE AREAS: Occupational Safety and Health; Employment Law; Litigation.

Doremus, Theodore A., Jr. . . . .'40 '69 C.902 B.A. L.362 J.D. [[C] Davis P.&W.]

Dorfman, Marc B., (AV) . . . . '— '76 C.976 A.B. L.309 J.D. [Foley&L.]
*PRACTICE AREAS: Litigation; Securities Law.

Dori, Yaron ... '70 '96 C.1036 B.A. L.93 J.D. [Ⓐ Hogan&H.]
*PRACTICE AREAS: Communications.
Doria, Marilyn L., (AV) ... '44 '74 C.1036 A.B. L.831 J.D. [Akin,G.S.H.&F.]
*PRACTICE AREAS: Energy.
Dorman, Carolyn K. ... '69 '99 C.67 B.A. L.1194 J.D. 1726 M Street, NW, Suite 703
Dormer, Robert A. ... '45 '72 C.197 A.B. L.893 J.D. [Hyman,P.&M.]
Dorn, Joseph W., (AV) ... '— '74 C.575 A.B. L.893 J.D. [King&S.]
*PRACTICE AREAS: Litigation and Trade.
Dorn, Susan E., (AV) ... '56 '85 C.945 B.A. L.1162 J.D. [Dorn&K.]

Dorn & Klamp, P.C., (AV)
1625 Massachusetts Avenue, N.W., Suite 450, 20036
Telephone: 202-986-3300 Fax: 202-986-0823
Email: DORNKLMP@EROLS.COM URL: http://www.DK-Law.com
Susan E. Dorn; Carolyn Klamp;—Michelle A. Hanson (Not admitted in DC).
Non-Profit Association Law.
See Professional Biographies, WASHINGTON, DISTRICT OF COLUMBIA

Dornbrand, Faith D., (AV) ... '52 '79 C.976 B.A. L.1066 J.D. [Sherman,M.C.&A.]
*PRACTICE AREAS: Family Law; Civil Litigation.
Dornburg, Erica M. '71 '96
(adm. in MA; not adm. in DC) Gen. Coun.
Dorotheo, Lakandula Duke '72 '97 C.1350 B.A. L.128 J.D.
(adm. in NJ; not adm. in DC) 1901 Pennsylvania Ave., N.W.
Dorr, Lisa C. '64 '93 C.367 B.A. L.309 J.D.
Staff Atty., Securities Investor Protection Corporation
Dorrian, Krista Bean ... '56 '82 C&L.893 B.A., J.D. NHP Inc.
Dorrier, Thomas B. '43 '75
C.277 B.M.E. L.692 J.D. Washington Metro. Area Transit Auth.
Dorris, Gregory C. ... '61 '86 C&L.280 B.A., J.D. [Pepper H.]
*PRACTICE AREAS: Customs Law; International Trade Regulation.
Dorrough, Stephen B. '67 '94 C.101 B.A. L.878 J.D.
(adm. in WA; not adm. in DC) Asst. Regional Coun., Marriott International, Inc.
Dorsen, David M., (AV) ... '35 '60 C&L.309 A.B., LL.B. [Ⓒ Wallace K.M.&B.]
*PRACTICE AREAS: Civil Litigation; Libel and Slander Law.
Dorsey, Daniel K. '58 '90 C.1048 B.S.E.E. L.1162 J.D.
[Ⓐ Jacobson,H.] (See Pat. Sect.)
*PRACTICE AREAS: Criminal Law; Intellectual Property Law.
Dorsey, Jay B. ... '51 '77 C&L.665 B.S., J.D. 146 Tennessee Ave., N.E.
Dorsey, Joy Johnson ... '60 '85 C.329 B.A. L.1019 J.D. [Potomac C.I.]
Dorsey, Mark J. ... '53 '84 C.1161 B.A. L.564 J.D. [Fried,F.H.S.&J.]

Dorsey & Whitney LLP, (AV)
1001 Pennsylvania Avenue, N.W., Suite 300 South, 20004 ⊙
Telephone: 202-824-8800 Facsimile: 202-824-8990
URL: http://www.dorseylaw.com
Members of Firm: Philip Baker-Shenk; Alan I. Baron; David A. Bieging; Virginia Walker Boylan; Philippe M. Bruno; Pamela M. Deese; Frederick S. Frei; Mark L. Hogge; Creighton R. Magid (Not admitted in DC); J. Gary McDavid; Aldo Noto; Richard E. Powers, Jr.; Delbert D. Smith; George Y. Sugiyama; Ralph A. Taylor, Jr.; Raymond Van Dyke (Not admitted in DC); Lance L. Vietzke; Kevin J. Wadzinski. Of Counsel: Daniel E. Fisher; Munford Page Hall, II; Martha K. Landesberg (Not admitted in DC); Stefan M. Lopatkiewicz. Associates: Steven A. Adducci; Bryneé Kyonne Baylor (Not admitted in DC); Kevin B. Bedell; Patricia Russell Brown; Chris Casieri (Not admitted in DC); Kevin L. Chapple; W. Robinson H. Clark; Kathryn L. Clune; Brian Gunn; Tania W. Hanna; John K. Harrop; Rosa S. Jeong (Not admitted in DC); Julia A. Jones (Not admitted in DC); Christopher A. Karns; Robin P. Levine; Victor Mroczka; Trystan Phifer O'Leary; Linda B. Popejoy; Rebecca Roby (Not admitted in DC); Ami P. Shah (Not admitted in DC); Bruce K. Trauben; Sean Wooden. Retired Member: David Busby; John B. Rehm.
International Trade, International Transactions, Intellectual Property, Energy, Environmental and Natural Resources, Federal Indian, Administrative and Legislative Law, Litigation, Project Finance, Agricultural, Cooperatives, Telecommunications.
Minneapolis, Minnesota Office: Suite 1500, 50 South Sixth Street, 55402-1498. Telephone: 612-340-2600.
Seattle, Washington Office: U.S. Bank Building Centre, 1420 Fifth Avenue, Suite 3400, 98101. Telephone: 206-903-8800.
New York, New York Office: 250 Park Avenue, 10177. Telephone: 212-415-9200.
Denver, Colorado Office: 370 Seventeenth Street, Republic Plaza Building, Suite 4700, 80202-5647. Telephone: 303-629-3400.
London, England Office: 21 Wilson Street, EC2M 2TD. Telephone: 011-44-207-588-0800.
Brussels, Belgium Office: 35 Square De Meeûs 1000. Telephone: 011-32-2-504-4611.
Hong Kong Office: Suite 3008, One Pacific Place, 88 Queensway. Hong Kong. Telephone: 011-852-252-65000. Fax: 011-852-252-43000.
Tokyo, Japan Office: Shiroyama JT Mori Building 16F, 4-3-1 Toranomon Minato-Ku, 105-6016. Telephone: 81 3 5403 4876. Fax: 81 3 5403 4877.
Shanghai, China Office: Suite 6211-12, Plaza 66, No. 1266 Nanjing Xi Lu, Shanghai, 200040. Telephone: 86-21-6288-2323. Fax: 86-21-6288-3222.
Toronto, Ontario Office: BCE Place, 161 Bay Street, Suite 4310. M5J 2S1. Telephone: 416-367-7370. Fax: 416-367-7371.
Vancouver, British Columbia Office: 666 Burrard Street, Suite 500, V6C 3P6. Telephone: 604-687-5151.
Anchorage, Alaska Office: 1031 West 4th Avenue, Suite 600, 99501. Telephone: 907-276-4557.
Des Moines, Iowa Office: 801 Grand, Suite 3900, 50309. Telephone: 515-283-1000.
Salt Lake City, Utah Office: Wells Fargo Plaza, 170 South Main Street, Suite 900, 84101. Telephone: 801-933-7360.
Orange County, California Office: Center Tower, 650 Town Center Drive, Suite 1850, P.O. Box 5066, Costa Mesa, 92626. Telephone: 714-662-7300.
Billings, Montana Office: 1200 First Interstate Center, 401 North 31st Street, P.O. Box 7188, 59103. Telephone: 406-252-3800.
Fargo, North Dakota Office: Dakota Center, 51 North Broadway, Suite 402, P.O. Box 1344, 58107-1344. Telephone: 701-235-6000.
Great Falls, Montana Office: 507 Davidson Building, 8 Third Street North, P.O. Box 1566, 59401. Telephone: 406-727-3632.
Rochester, Minnesota Office: 201 First Avenue, S.W., Suite 340, 55902. Telephone: 507-288-3156.
Missoula, Montana Office: 125 Bank Street, Suite 600, 59802. Telephone: 406-721-6025.
Paramus, New Jersey Office: East 80, Route 4, 07652. Telephone: 201-291-8904. Fax: 201-712-9444.
See Professional Biographies, WASHINGTON, DISTRICT OF COLUMBIA

Dort, David Bogart ... '68 '98 C.103 B.A. L.930 J.D. [Ⓐ Oppenheimer W.&D.]
*PRACTICE AREAS: Intellectual Property.
Doses, Michelle Debra ... '66 '95 C.1036 B.A. L.273 J.D. 811 Vermont Ave., N.W.
Doshi, Urvi M. ... '— '99 C.477 B.A. L.569 J.D. [Ⓐ Fried,F.H.S.&J.]
*PRACTICE AREAS: Taxation.
Doster, Brian L. ... '69 '95 C&L.228 A.B., J.D. [Ⓐ Beveridge&D.]
*PRACTICE AREAS: Environmental Law; Air Quality; Water Quality; Administrative Litigation.
Dottori, Mario F. ... '61 '87 C.207 B.A. L.1029 J.D. [Shaw P.]
Doty, James R., (AV) ... '40 '69 C.691 B.A. L.976 LL.B. [Baker B.]
Doub, William O., (AV) ... '31 '56 C.901 B.A. L.446 LL.B. 1800 M St., N.W.‡
Doud, Alden L. '35 '59 C.353 B.A. L.309 LL.B.
(adm. in IL; not adm. in DC) Intl. Bk. for Reconstr. & Develop.
Doud, Mary Teresa Anastasia ... '70 '97 C.311 B.A. L.659 J.D. [Ⓐ Dow,L.&A.]
Douds, H. James ... '30 '55 C&L.923 A.B., J.D. 1922 F St., N.W.
Dougherty, Thomas J., Jr., (AV) ... '53 '81 C.207 B.A. L.128 J.D. [Gardner,C.&D.]
*PRACTICE AREAS: Communications and Media; Telecommunications Contracts; Telecommunications Licensing; Utility Law; Telephone Utility Regulation.
Douglas, Bradley D ... '61 '88 C.947 B.A. L.502 J.D. Home Builders Instit.
Douglas, Frederick A., (AV) ... '47 '74 C.262 B.A. L.569 J.D. [Leftwich&D.]

Douglas, James D. '73 '98 C.260 B.A. L.982 J.D.
(adm. in NY; not adm. in DC) [Ⓐ Dow,L.&A.]
Douglas, James D. '49 '83 C.999 B.A. L.1209 J.D.
(adm. in VA; not adm. in DC) Dep. Gen. Coun., Smithsonian Institution
Douglas, John L., (AV) '50 '77 C.198 B.A. L.280 J.D.
(adm. in GA; not adm. in DC) [Alston&B.] (⊙Atlanta, GA)
*PRACTICE AREAS: Mergers and Acquisitions; Banks and Banking.
Douglas, John W., (AV) '21 '48 C.674 A.B. L.976 LL.B.
1201 Pennsylvania Ave., N.W.‡
Douglas, Kevin H. ... '— '98 C.893 B.A. L.880 J.D. [Ⓐ Latham&W.]
*PRACTICE AREAS: Mergers and Acquisitions; Corporate Law; Securities.
Douglas, Patricia W. S. ... '50 '81 C.1102 B.A. L.900 J.D. [Ⓢ Thompson H.]
*PRACTICE AREAS: Employee Benefits; ERISA.
Douglas, Rodney Scott ... '56 '85 C.225 A.B. L.904 J.D. 1752 S St. N.W., Apt 1
Douglass, David L. ... '59 '85 C.976 B.A. L.309 J.D. [Porter W.M.&A.]
Douglass, Joseph D. ... '52 '78 C.477 B.A. L.659 J.D. [Whiteford,T.&P.]
*PRACTICE AREAS: Community Association Law; Condominium Association Law; Cooperative Housing Law; Homeowners Association Law.
Doumar, George R. A. ... '61 '86 C.276 B.S.F.S. L.893 J.D. [Dilworth P.P.]
Dove, Ronald G., Jr. ... '64 '91 C.482 B.A. L.309 J.D. [Ⓒ Covington&B.]
Dover, Agnes Pek ... '53 '81 C.62 B.A. L.128 J.D. [Hogan&H.]
*PRACTICE AREAS: Government Contracts; Energy; Intellectual Property.

Dow, Lohnes & Albertson, PLLC, (AV) BR
1200 New Hampshire Avenue, N.W. Suite 800, 20036-6802 ⊙
Telephone: 202-776-2000 Facsimile: 202-776-2222
Email: info@dlalaw.com URL: http://www.dlalaw.com
Members of the Firm: Corinne M. Antley; Michael D. Basile; Leonard J. Baxt (Chairman, Board of Directors); Raymond G. Bender, Jr.; Richard L. Braunstein; Lisa C. Bureau; James M. Burger; Blain B. Butner; John T. Byrnes, Jr.; Peter C. Canfield (Resident, Atlanta, Georgia Office); Peter C. Cassat; Thomas M. Clyde (Resident, Atlanta, Georgia Office); James A. Demetry (Resident, Atlanta, Georgia Office); William S. Dudzinsky Jr.; Peter H. Feinberg; John R. Feore, Jr.; Patricia A. Francis; Linda A. Fritts; Jonathon C. Glass; Michael B. Goldstein; Todd D. Gray; Joyce Trimble Gwadz; Ralph W. Hardy, Jr.; J.G. Harrington; Jonathan D. Hart; Michael D. Hays; Michael A. Hepburn; Jonathan B. Hill; J. Michael Hines; R. Dale Hughes (Resident, Atlanta, Georgia Office); John C. Jost; Timothy J. Kelley; Kevin J. Kuzas; Paul R. Lang; John S. Logan; Bernard J. Long, Jr.; Stephanie M. Loughlin; Judith A. Mather; Elizabeth Anne McGeary; Richard P. McHugh; John W. McNamara (Resident, Atlanta, Georgia Office); Margaret L. Miller; David E. Mills; Edward J. O'Connell; Timothy J. O'Rourke; B. Dwight Perry (Chair, Management Committee); Thomas J. Peters IV (Resident, Atlanta, Georgia Office); Laura Hathaway Phillips; John H. Pomeroy; Mary K. Qualiana; J. Christopher Redding; Kevin F. Reed; Curtis A. Ritter; Kenneth D. Salomon; James R. Saxenian; Stuart A. Sheldon; Sean R. Smith (Resident, Atlanta, Georgia Office); Mitchell H. Stabbe; M. Anne Swanson; Thomas D. Twedt; John D. Ward; Leslie H. Wiesenfelder; David Daniel Wild; Richard A. Wilhelm (Resident, Atlanta, Georgia Office); David J. Wittenstein;—Bruce S. Antley; Chester H. Arter, III (Resident, Atlanta, Georgia Office); Ethan Atticks; Adisa P. Bakari; Tracy Benjamin; Matthew A. Block (Resident, Atlanta, Georgia Office); Steven E. Blumenthal (Resident, Atlanta, Georgia Office); Kevin P. Brandon; Douglas E. Braunstein; Christopher J. Brookhart; Denice Sayers Burch (Resident, Atlanta, Georgia Office); Christina Hosp Burrow; Laurent M. Campo; Adam Charles Chase; Jill C. Coan (Resident, Atlanta, Georgia Office); Peter D. Coffman (Resident, Atlanta, Georgia Office); Scott D. Dailard; Richard S. Denning (Resident, Atlanta, Georgia Office); Whiting G. Dimock; David Doherty (Not admitted in DC); Mary Teresa Anastasia Doud; James D. Douglas (Not admitted in DC); Marci J. Finkelstein; Jason E. Friedrich; Suzanne R. Garment (Not admitted in DC); Jeffrey J. Gee; Barbara A. Goffman; Lars Golumbic; Lisa A. Gomez (Not admitted in DC); Carolyn R. Greer (Not admitted in DC); Harold Hancock (Not admitted in DC); Michael R. Heath; Shannan E. Higgins; Michael C. Hochman; John B. Hoover; Lawrence T. Humphrey (Resident, Atlanta, Georgia Office); Aaron Kanter; Nam Eun Kim; Todd B. Klessman; Jason Paul Langley; Kevin P. Latek; John M. Lee (Resident, Atlanta, Georgia Office); Mark E. Liniado; Kara D. Little; Rebecca A. Littleton (Resident, Atlanta, Georgia Office); Tracy Anderson Locklin; Stephen E. Lopez; Gary S. Lutzker; Jason S. McCarter (Resident, Atlanta, Georgia Office); Rogelyn D. McLean (Not admitted in DC); Barbara K. Miller (Resident, Atlanta, Georgia Office); J. Kevin Mills; Francesca Muratori (Not admitted in DC); Carlos M. Nalda; Harry S. Pangas (Not admitted in DC); Scott S. Patrick; Barry Persh; Daniel D. Prichard (Not admitted in DC); Jason E. Rademacher; Theodore L. Radway; Maureen M. Richardson (Not admitted in DC); Christopher D. Romaine; Elisa P. Rosen; Michael D. Rothberg; David M. Rudin; Heather Berner Sachs; Brian M. Salb (Not admitted in DC); Elizabeth M. R. Salgado; Carolyn Schafer; Christopher A. Schwab (Resident, Atlanta, Georgia Office); Nina Shafran; Randall R. Smith (Resident, Atlanta, Georgia Office); Marcia Bull Stadeker (Resident, Atlanta, Georgia Office); Michael J. Stawasz (Not admitted in DC); Philip R. Strzalka (Not admitted in DC); Kathleen M. Tomcho (Resident, Atlanta, Georgia Office); Suzanne M. Underwald; E. Adam Webb (Resident, Atlanta, Georgia Office); Beth D. Wilkinson (Resident, Atlanta, Georgia Office); Brian J. Winterfeldt; Jill M. Wood (Resident, Atlanta, Georgia Office); Lawrence K. Workman, Jr.; Nicole Wynn. Senior Counsel: Christina S. Wadyka; To-Quyen Truong. Of Counsel: Fayette B. Dow (1881-1962); Gaylen D. Kemp (Resident, Atlanta, Georgia Office); Horace L. Lohnes (1897-1954); Fred W. Albertson. Consultant: James Sears Bryant.
General Civil and Administrative Practice including Antitrust, Aviation, Cable Television, Commercial TV and Radio Broadcasting, Communications, Compensation and Benefits, Corporate, Employee Relations/Benefits, Environmental, Estate Planning and Administration, Financial Institutions, Government Contracts, Government Relations, Health Care, Intellectual Property, Media and Information Technology, Labor, Legislation, Litigation, Mergers and Acquisitions, Non-Profit Institutions, Public Broadcasting and Telecommunications, Real Estate, Satellite Communications, Securities, Telecommunications and Telephones and Tax.
Atlanta, Georgia Office: One Ravinia Drive, Suite 1600. Telephone: 770-901-8800. Telecopier: 770-901-8874.
See Professional Biographies, WASHINGTON, DISTRICT OF COLUMBIA

Dowd, David F. ... '66 '92 C&L.276 A.B., J.D. [Mayer,B.&P.]
*PRACTICE AREAS: Government Contracts; Litigation.
Dowd, James M. ... '72 '97 C.745 B.A. L.94 J.D. [Ⓐ Hale&D.]
*PRACTICE AREAS: Litigation.
Dowd, John M., (AV) ... '41 '67 C.1244 A.B. L.245 J.D. [Akin,G.S.H.&F.]
*PRACTICE AREAS: Litigation; White Collar Criminal Defense.
Dowd, Kelvin J. ... '56 '81 C.1044 B.A. L.904 J.D. [Slover&L.]
Dowd, Mary Joanne, (AV) ... '54 '81 C.1044 B.A. L.107 J.D. [Arent F.K.P.&K.]
*PRACTICE AREAS: Bankruptcy Law; Debtor Creditor Law.
Dowd, Terry Bancroft ... '— '74 C.966 B.A. L.184 J.D. [Ⓒ Miller&C.]
*PRACTICE AREAS: Government Contracts; Government Procurement; Federal Litigation.
Dowd, Theodore J. ... '73 '01 C.676 B.A. L.180 J.D. 1155 21st Street N.W.
Dowdell, Thomas E., (BV) ... '59 '87 C.659 B.A. L.273 J.D. [Fulbright&J.]
*PRACTICE AREAS: Health Care.
Dowden, Lisa G., (AV) ... '61 '86 C.910 B.A. L.309 J.D. [Spiegel&M.]
*PRACTICE AREAS: Utility Law; Environmental Law; Energy.
Dowdey, Landon Gerald, (AV) ... '23 '48 C.659 B.S. L.276 LL.B. 2000 L St., N.W.

Dowell & Dowell, P.C.
(See Arlington, Virginia)

Dower, Jennifer C. ... '66 '92 C.518 B.A. L.273 J.D. 555 13th St Nw # 701E
Dowley, Joseph K., (AV) ... '46 '76 C&L.276 A.B., J.D. [Dewey B.]
*PRACTICE AREAS: Tax; Trade; Health.
Dowling, Daniel J. ... '53 '90 C.870 B.S. L.893 J.D. [Ⓐ Arent F.K.P.&K.]
Dowling, Timothy J. ... '57 '82 C.602 B.A. L.276 J.D. Community Rights Coun.
Downey, Arthur T., (AV) '37 '63
C.757 B.A. L.884 LL.B. V.P., Baker Hughes Incorporated
Downey, Jeffrey J. ... '63 '89 C.1044 B.A. L.1019 J.D. [Ⓒ Robins,K.M.&C.]
*PRACTICE AREAS: Personal Injury; Medical Malpractice.
Downey, Kevin M., (AV) ... '65 '90 C.172 B.A. L.1017 J.D. [Ⓒ Hogan&H.]
*PRACTICE AREAS: Energy; Utility Law.
Downey, Kevin M., (AV) ... '67 '91.C.197 A.B. L.309 J.D. [Williams&C.]
Downey, Richard Morgan ... '46 '72 C.1030 B.A. L.276 J.D. [Hoffheimer&D.]

Downie, Brian T. . . . . '55 '81 C.205 B.C.E. L.276 J.D. Dir., Western Develop. Corp.
Downs, Clark Evans . . . . '46 '73 C&L.94 A.B., J.D. [Jones,D.R.&P.]
*PRACTICE AREAS: Energy; Energy Regulation; Utility Law.
Downs, Mary E. . . . . '48 '74 C&L.93 B.A., J.D. Assoc. Gen. Coun., Fannie Mae
*RESPONSIBILITIES: New Products; Contracts; Corporate.
Downs, Thomas C. . . . . '61 '95 C.103 A.B. L.904 J.D. [[A] Patton B.]
Dowton, Tamara Y. '69 '97 C.893 B.A. L.1188 J.D.
(adm. in MD; not adm. in DC) [[A] Wasserman,M.&C.]
*PRACTICE AREAS: Immigration and Naturalization.
Doyal, Stephanie E. '72 '97 C.228 B.S. L.846 J.D.
(adm. in TX; not adm. in DC) 1100 Fifteenth Street, NW, Suite 700
Doyle, A. Patrick, (AV) . . . . '48 '76 C.1044 B.A. L.823 J.D. [Arnold&P.]
*PRACTICE AREAS: Financial Institutions; Corporate; Securities.
Doyle, Alison L., (AV) . . . . '55 '84 C.659 B.A. L.276 J.D. [McKenna&C.]
*PRACTICE AREAS: Government Contracts Law.
Doyle, Austin J., (AV) . . . . '41 '74 C.602 B.B.A. L.904 J.D. [Doyle]
Doyle, Bernard E. . . . . '55 '85 C.273 B.A. L.64 J.D. [[A] Shaw,B.V.&R.]
*PRACTICE AREAS: Federal Employment Law; Employment Law; Military Law; Litigation.
Doyle, Francis X., Jr. '33 '63 C.321 A.B. L.724 J.D.
(adm. in NY; not adm. in DC)
Assoc. Gen. Secy., National Conference of Catholic Bishops
Doyle, James A. '57 '83 C.446 B.S. L.1209 J.D.
(adm. in VA; not adm. in DC) Pres., National Paint & Coatings Association
Doyle, John F. . . . . '17 '46 C.698 A.B. L.276 J.D. Sr. Supr. Ct. J.
Doyle, Rani E. . . . . '67 '95 C.705 B.A. L.564 J.D. [[A] Morgan,L.&B.]
Doyle, Robert W., Jr., (AV) . . . . '47 '76 C&L.831 B.A., J.D. [Powell,G.F.&M.]
*PRACTICE AREAS: Antitrust; Mergers and Acquisitions; Litigation.
Doyle, Stephen P., (AV) . . . . '50 '77 C.309 A.B. L.846 J.D. [Wilmer,C.&P.]
*PRACTICE AREAS: International Law; Corporate Law; Aviation.
Doyle, Trent M. . . . . '66 '00 C.171 B.S. L.945 J.D. [[A] Keller&H.]
*PRACTICE AREAS: Environmental Law.
Doyle Law Firm, (AV) . . . . 3201 New Mexico Avenue, N.W.
Dozier, Erin . . . . '70 '99 C.1307 B.A. L.276 J.D. [[A] Akin,G.S.H.&F.]
*PRACTICE AREAS: Communications Law.
Drabkin, Murray, (AV) . . . . '— '53 C.299 A.B. L.309 LL.B. [Foley&L.] ‡
*PRACTICE AREAS: Bankruptcy; Bankruptcy Reorganization; State and Local Taxation.
Dragon, Edward A. . . . . '28 '56 C.676 A.B. L.276 J.D. [[C] Inman D.]
*PRACTICE AREAS: International.
Drahozal, Christopher R. . . . . '61 '88 C.910 B.A. L.352 J.D. 1722 Eye St., N.W.
Draim, Ida Wurczinger, (AV) . . . . '55 '82 C.705 B.A. L.309 J.D. [Dickstein S.M.&O.]
*PRACTICE AREAS: Securities.
Drake, Donna . . . . '65 '93 C.1042 B.S. L.1522 J.D. [[A] Howrey S.A.&W.]
*PRACTICE AREAS: Commercial Litigation; Insurance Coverage.
Drake, Jody Haller . . . . '55 '81 C.264 B.A. L.1048 J.D. [Sughrue M.]
*PRACTICE AREAS: Trademark Law; Copyright Law.
Drake, Stuart A. C. . . . . '54 '83 C&L.976 B.A., J.D. [Kirkland&E.]
*PRACTICE AREAS: Environmental and Regulatory Counseling; Government Litigation.
Drake, Susan D. . . . . '70 '97 C.30 B.S. L.128 J.D. [[A] Wiley R.&F.]
Dranitzke, Alan, (AV) . . . . '42 '68 C.918 B.A. L.976 LL.B. [Liotta,D.&E.]
*PRACTICE AREAS: Real Estate; General Practice.
Draper, Kenneth J. . . . . '60 '88 C.797 B.A. L.260 J.D. 1110 VT Ave.,NW, Ste. 405
Draper, Robert Linn . . . . '64 '90 C.951 B.A. L.802 J.D. [Winston&S.]
*PRACTICE AREAS: Corporate Law; Project Finance; Energy Project Development; Cogeneration; Electric Power.
Drasner, Fred, (AV) '43 '71 C.569 B.S. L.904 J.D.
Pres. & Co-Publisher, N.Y. Daily News & U.S. News & World Report
Drath, Constance M. . . . . '47 '83 C.174 B.A. L.809 J.D. [Drath&D.]
Drath & Dwyer . . . . 1056 Paper Mill Ct. N.W.
Draude, James T. . . . . '47 '73 C.276 B.A. L.309 J.D. [Driscoll&D.]
*PRACTICE AREAS: Civil Litigation; Land Use Regulation; Environmental Law.
Draughn, James Worth, Jr. . . . . '66 '91 C.575 B.A. L.309 J.D. [Kirkland&E.]
*PRACTICE AREAS: Commercial Litigation; Energy Litigation; Antitrust; Product Liability.
Drazin, Russell S. '74 '99 C.696 B.A. L.273 J.D.
(adm. in VA; not adm. in DC) 2031 Florida Avenue, NW
Drea, Tracy D. . . . . '69 '99 C.240 B.S. L.1065 J.D. Smithsonian Institute
Dreben, Ron N. . . . . '61 '88 C&L.309 A.B., J.D. [Morgan,L.&B.]
Drefke, Kristi D. . . . . '68 '92 C&L.546 B.S., J.D. [[A] Jones,D.R.&P.]
Drefke, Kyle W. '69 '94 C&L.352 B.B.A., J.D.
(adm. in IA; not adm. in DC) [[A] Orrick,H.&S.]
Dreher, Robert G. . . . . '51 '81 C.309 A.B. L.976 J.D. [[C] Troutman S.]
*PRACTICE AREAS: Environmental Law; Litigation.
Dreier, Alexander E. . . . . '66 '97 C.309 A.B. L.976 J.D. [[A] Hogan&H.]
*PRACTICE AREAS: Education Law; College and University Law; Public School Law; Special Education; Litigation.
Drennan, D. Jane, (AV) . . . . '44 '69 C.347 B.A. L.1119 J.D. [Drennan&Assoc.]

Drennan & Associates, (AV)
1216 Sixteenth Street, N.W., 20036
Telephone: 202-835-2600 Facsimile: 202-835-0452
Email: jdrennan@drennanassoc.com URL: http://www.lawyers.com/janedrennanlaw
D. Jane Drennan.
Energy, Transportation, Environmental Law and related Regulatory Matters.
See Professional Biographies, WASHINGTON, DISTRICT OF COLUMBIA

Dressing, Julie Stumpe . . . . '57 '82 C.679 B.A., B.S. L.188 J.D. 51 Louisiana Ave.
Dreux, Anthony . . . . '64 '96 C.329 B.S.E.E. L.273 J.D. [[A] Finnegan,H.F.G.&D.]
*PRACTICE AREAS: Patent Litigation; Computer Architecture Patents; Electrical Patent Prosecution; Computer and Software Patents.
Dreux, Mark S., Sr., (AV) . . . . '54 '82 C.276 B.A. L.128 J.D. [Arent F.K.P.&K.]
*PRACTICE AREAS: Occupational Safety and Health; Litigation; White Collar Crime.
Drew, Natasha L. '73 '98 C.112 B.A. L.61 J.D.
(adm. in CA; not adm. in DC) [[A] Keller&H.]
*PRACTICE AREAS: Litigation.
Drew, Shakun M. . . . . '46 '84 C.1313 M.A. L.1162 J.D. 5301 Wisconsin Ave., N.W.
Drewry, James S. W. . . . . '44 '69 C.682 B.A. L.893 LL.B. [Dyer E.&J.]
*PRACTICE AREAS: Legislative Practice; Lobbying; Technology and Science.
Drexler, Kenneth J. . . . . '62 '93 C.309 A.B. L.276 J.D. [[A] Covington&B.]
Driesen, George B., (AV) . . . . . . '33 '61 C.309 B.A. L.976 LL.B. [Zwerdling,P.L.K.T.&D.]
Driggers, William Gerald . . . . '55 '91 C.846 B.A. L.276 J.D. [Powell,G.F.&M.]
*PRACTICE AREAS: Real Estate; Tax Law.
Drimmer, Allison '69 '99 C.813 B.A. L.276 J.D.
(adm. in MD; not adm. in DC) [[A] Wilmer,C.&P.]
Drinan, Robert F. . . . . '20 '50 C.93 A.B. L.276 J.D. Prof., Georgetown Univ. Law Ctr.

Drinker Biddle & Reath LLP, (AV) [BB]
A Pennsylvania Limited Liability Partnership
1500 K Street, N.W., Suite 1100, 20005-1208 ⊙
Telephone: 202-842-8800 Fax: 202-842-8465. Cable Address: "Debemac"
URL: http://www.dbr.com
Resident Partners: Joe D. Edge; Michael L. Gassmann; John C. Hockenbury; Alan J. Joaquin; Joseph F. Johnston, Jr.; Douglas M. Mangel; Joaquin A. Marquez; Philip J. Mause; Michael J. McManus; M. Howard Morse; Mark L. Pelesh; Michael J. Remington; Richard M. Singer; Robert A. Skitol; Norm D. St. Landau. Counsel: Stephen G. Janoski; John R. Przypyszny. Of Counsel: Robert N. Cook;

(This Listing Continued)

Drinker Biddle & Reath LLP (Continued)
Henry W. Leeds; Kenneth E. Ryan. Resident Associates: Adam L. Barea (Not admitted in DC); Jennifer L. Blum; Amy E. Carroll; Brian A. Coleman; Jennifer L. Dean; Mark F. Dever; Alisa M. Everts; Janet Fries; Laura S. Gallagher; Dina M. Gold; Timothy R. Hughes (Not admitted in DC); Jeffrey J. Lopez; Elizabeth A. Marshall; Janet R. McFadden; Kathleen S. O'Neill (Not admitted in DC); Tina M. Pidgeon; Jennifer G. Smith (Not admitted in DC); Patricia N. Vercelli (Not admitted in DC); Mary Patricia Weyback.
Federal Administrative, Legislative and Litigation Practice including: Communications, common carrier, satellite, telephony, emerging technologies, broadcast and cable; Antitrust, including merger approval, treble damage litigation, and practice before the Federal Trade Commission; Insurance including directors' and officers' liability, fidelity bond, environmental and other forms of business insurance; Intellectual Property; Education Law; Legislative Advocacy and Commercial Litigation.
Philadelphia, Pennsylvania Office: One Logan Square, 18th & Cherry Streets. Telephone: 215-988-2700. Telefax: 215-988-2757. Cable Address: "Debemac."
Florham Park, New Jersey Office: Drinker Biddle & Shanley LLP, 500 Campus Drive, Telephone: 973-360-1100. Fax: 973-285-1625.
Princeton, New Jersey Office: Drinker Biddle & Shanley LLP, Suite 300, 105 College Road East. Telephone: 609-716-6500. Telefax: 609-799-7000.
Berwyn, Pennsylvania Office: Suite 300, 1000 Westlakes Drive. Telephone: 610-993-2200. Telefax: 610-993-8585.
See Professional Biographies, WASHINGTON, DISTRICT OF COLUMBIA

Driscoll, Benjamin D. '68 '00 C.659 B.S.E.E. L.1209 J.D.
(adm. in VA; not adm. in DC; See Pat. Sect.) [[A] Fish&R.]
*PRACTICE AREAS: Patent Prosecution; Patent Litigation.
Driscoll, Brian G., (AV) . . . . '48 '73 C.31 B.A. L.178 J.D. [Driscoll&D.]
*PRACTICE AREAS: Commercial Law; Construction Law; Computer Law.
Driscoll, Kevin J. '47 '75 C.93 B.A. L.818 J.D.
(adm. in NY; not adm. in DC) Sr. Legis. Coun., Amer. Bar Assn.
Driscoll, Richard W. . . . '59 '90 C.878 B.A. L.904 J.D. [[A] Eccleston&W.] (⊙Fairfax, VA)
*PRACTICE AREAS: Insurance Defense Law; Professional Malpractice Law; Legal Malpractice Law; Insurance Coverage.
Driscoll, Timothy S. . . . . '66 '92 C.1019 B.A. L.309 J.D. 725 12th St., N.W.
Driscoll, William J. . . . . '32 '57 C.433 B.B.A. L.273 LL.B. 122 5th St., SE

Driscoll & Draude, (AV)
Second Floor, 1230 Thirty-First Street, N.W., 20007
Telephone: 202-333-0330 Cable Address: "Driscoll" Telecopier: 202-298-6699
Members of Firm: Brian G. Driscoll; James T. Draude.
General Corporate, Government Contracts, Construction, Computer Law and Licensing, Environmental Law, Real Property Law and Land Use Regulation, Civil Litigation in Federal and State Courts.
See Professional Biographies, WASHINGTON, DISTRICT OF COLUMBIA

Driver, Kenneth B. . . . . '67 '95 C.1369 B.S. L.276 J.D. [[A] Jones,D.R.&P.]
Drogin, Jack P. '63 '90 C.659 B.A. L.309 J.D.
(adm. in NY; not adm. in DC) [[C] Morgan,L.&B.]
Drogula, Jennifer M. . . . . '64 '92 C.846 B.A. L.228 J.D. [Wilmer,C.&P.]
*PRACTICE AREAS: Latin America; Corporate.
Droller, Lester W. . . . . '51 '76 C.597 B.A. L.273 J.D. [Jones,D.R.&P.]
*PRACTICE AREAS: Taxation; Corporate Tax Planning; Mergers and Acquisitions.
Drozen, Melvin S., (AV) . . . . '49 '76 C.276 B.A. L.1009 J.D. [Keller&H.]
*PRACTICE AREAS: Food and Drug Law; Trade Regulation Law.
Dryer, Edwin Jason . . . . '— '40 C&L.976 B.A., LL.B. [Foley&L.] ‡
*PRACTICE AREAS: Energy (Oil and Gas and Electric Power); Antitrust Law.
Drysdale, Douglas D., (AV) . . . . '24 '52 C&L.893 B.A., LL.B. [Caplin&D.]
Duane, Jennifer A. . . . . '63 '89 C.645 B.A. L.273 J.D. Atty., Sprint Corp.

Duane, Morris & Heckscher LLP, (AV) [BB]
1667 K Street, N.W., Suite 700, 20006-1608 ⊙
Telephone: 202-776-7800 Fax: 202-776-7801
URL: http://www.duanemorris.com
Partners: Vikki A. Adams; Brian D. Alprin; Stephen M. Azia; Gary L. Bohlke; Alan C. Brown; Christopher L. Crosswhite; Valerie J. Eastwood (Not admitted in DC); Keith H. Ellis; John W. Griffin; Sheila Slocum Hollis (Partner-in-Charge, Washington, D.C.); Brad C. Johnson; Laurence S. Lese; Christopher W. Mahoney; William R. Mapes, Jr.; Andrew E. Mishkin; Mark F. Pretzat; Terry F. Quill; David H. Robbins; Denyse Sabagh; Stephen L. Teichler; Daniel P. Weitzel; Douglas Woloshin. Associate: Gregg K. Stepan. Special Counsel: Catherine Carl Wakelyn. Regulatory Counsel: Mary Ann Ralls.
Alternative Dispute Resolution, Bankruptcy, Commercial Law, Corporate Law, Energy, Environmental Law, Estates and Asset Planning, Franchise Law, Health Care Law, Immigration Law, Intellectual Property, International Law, Labor and Employment, Litigation, Product Liability, Real Estate, Regulatory Compliance, Reorganization and Finance, Securities Taxation and Telecommunications.
Philadelphia, Pennsylvania Office: Suite 4200, One Liberty Place. Telephone: 215-979-1000. Fax: 215-979-1020.
New York, New York Office: 380 Lexington Avenue. Telephone: 212-692-1000. Fax: 212-692-1020.
London, England Office: 4 Chiswell Street, 5th Floor, EC1Y 4UP. Telephone: +44 20 7786 2100. Fax: +44 20 7786 2101.
Chicago, Illinois Office: 227 West Monroe Street, Suite 3400. Telephone: 312-499-6700. Fax: 312-499-6701.
San Francisco, California Office: 100 Spear Street, Suite 1500. Telephone: 415-371-2200. Fax: 415-371-2201.
Boston, Massachusetts Office: 470 Atlantic Avenue, Suite 500. Telephone: 617-289-9200. Fax: 617-289-9201.
Atlanta, Georgia Office: 945 East Paces Ferry Road, Suite 2440. Telephone: 404-495-4900. Fax: 404-495-4901.
Miami, Florida Office: 200 South Biscayne Boulevard, Suite 3410. Telephone: 305-960-2200. Fax: 305-960-2201.
Wilmington, Delaware Office: 1100 North Market Street, Suite 1200. Telephone: 302-657-4900. Fax: 302-657-4901.
Harrisburg, Pennsylvania Office: 305 North Front Street, 5th Floor, P.O. Box 1003. Telephone: 717-237-5500. Fax: 717-232-4015.
Malvern, Pennsylvania Office: 200 Chesterfield Parkway, Suite 100. Telephone: 610-251-6900. Fax: 610-251-6901.
Cherry Hill, New Jersey Office: 51 Haddonfield Road, Suite 340. Telephone: 856-488-7300. Fax: 856-488-7021.
Newark, New Jersey Office: One Riverfront Plaza, 2nd Floor. Telephone: 973-424-2000. Fax: 973-424-2001.
Palm Beach, Florida Office: 249 Royal Palm Way, Suite 403. Telephone: 561-366-5400. Fax: 561-366-5401.
Allentown, Pennsylvania Office: 968 Postal Road, Suite 200, P.O. Box 90400. Telephone: 610-266-3650. Fax: 610-266-3651.
Houston, Texas Office: One Greenway Plaza, Suite 500. Telephone: 713-552-9900. Fax: 713-552-0109.
Bangor, Maine Office: 88 Hammond Street, Suite 500. Telephone: 207-262-5400. Fax: 207-262-5401.
Princeton, New Jersey Office: 100 College Road West, Suite 100. Telephone: 609-919-4400. Fax: 609-919-4401.
Westchester County, New York Office: 555 Pleasantville Road, Suite 200 North Building, Briarcliff Manor, New York. Telephone: 914-749-3700. Fax: 914-749-3701.
See Professional Biographies, WASHINGTON, DISTRICT OF COLUMBIA

Duarte, Garrett B.M. . . . . '68 '95 C.674 A.B. L.477 J.D. [[A] Collier S.S.]
*PRACTICE AREAS: Antitrust; Litigation.
Duarte, Maria Cristina '62 '95 C.472 A.B. L.276 J.D.
(adm. in FL; not adm. in DC) MCI
Dubé, Lawrence E., Jr., (AV) '48 '73 C.388 B.A. L.352 J.D.
(adm. in IA; not adm. in DC) [Dubé&G.] & [[C] Grove,J.&C.] ⊙
Dube, Phillip E. . . . . '72 '99 C.692 B.A. L.893 J.D. [[A] Covington&B.]
*PRACTICE AREAS: Insurance; Insurance Arbitration; Insurance Coverage; Litigation; Civil Litigation.

Dube, Steven L. '66 '98 C.321 B.A. L.569 J.D.
(adm. in MA; not adm. in DC) [A Holland&K.]
*PRACTICE AREAS: Real Estate Development and Finance; Zoning Law; Land Use.

Dubé & Goodgal, P.C., (AV)
Suite 400, 1730 M Street, N.W., 20036 ⊙
Telephone: 202-331-2183 Telecopier: 410-276-8807
Email: firm@dubelaw.com URL: http://www.lawyers.com/dubelaw.com
Lawrence E. Dubé, Jr. (Not admitted in DC); Paula A. Goodgal (Not admitted in DC).
Labor and Employment Law and Litigation (Employer and Employee), Equal Employment Opportunity, Wage and Hour Law, Wrongful Discharge and Employment Rights Litigation, Employee Benefits, Collective Bargaining, Civil and Administrative Litigation and Arbitration.
Baltimore, Maryland Office: The Can Company, Suite 407, 2400 Boston Street. Telephone: 410-276-8801. Telecopier: 410-276-8807.
See Professional Biographies, WASHINGTON, DISTRICT OF COLUMBIA

Dubeck, John B., (AV) ... '49 '76 C.188 B.S. L.276 J.D. [Keller&H.]
*PRACTICE AREAS: Food and Drug Law; Environmental Law; Trade Regulation Law.
Dubelier, Eric A., (AV) ... '— '81 C&L.861 B.A., J.D. [Reed S.]
*PRACTICE AREAS: White Collar Crime; Government Contracts; Export Compliance; Civil Litigation.
Dubert, Carl A. ... '66 '92 C.475 B.A. L.145 J.D. Price Waterhouse LLP
Dubin, Alan S., (AV) ... '51 '76 C.696 B.A. L.273 J.D. [Arent F.K.P.&K.]
*PRACTICE AREAS: Business Law; Corporate Financing Law; Real Estate-Commercial Law.
Dubin, Rebecca L. ... '73 '99 C&L.446 B.A., J.D. [A Arnold&P.]
*PRACTICE AREAS: Litigation.
Dubitsky, Alexander A. ... '65 '93 L.976 J.D. 555 13th St Nw
DuBoff, Scott M., (AV) ... '47 '73 C&L.966 B.A., J.D. [Wright&T.]
*PRACTICE AREAS: Environmental Regulation; Appellate Practice.
Dubograev, Dmitri I. ... '67 '94 L.902 J.D. [C Akin,G.S.H.&F.]
*PRACTICE AREAS: Corporate Law.
Dubois, Pascale Hélène ... '62 '88 L.999 LL.M. Sr. Coun., World Bank, The‡
DuBray, Katherine M. '73 '99 C.1322 B.A. L.276 J.D.
(adm. in MD; not adm. in DC) [S Fulbright&J.]
*PRACTICE AREAS: Intellectual Property.
Dubroff, Andrew J. ... '56 '82 C&L.659 B.S., J.D. 1225 Conn. Ave., N.W.
Dubrow, David L. '51 '87 C.103 B.A. L.569 J.D.
(adm. in NY; not adm. in DC) [Arent F.K.P.&K.]
*PRACTICE AREAS: Public Finance; Secured Lending; Structured Finance.
Dubrow, Eve L. '63 '88 C.860 B.A. L.266 J.D.
Mgr. Partner, Strag. Part., Geo. Wash. Uni.
Dubrow, Jon B., (AV) ... '66 '92 C.893 B.A. L.659 J.D. [McDermott,W.&E.]
Dubuc, Steven C. ... '68 '94 C.188 B.A. L.276 J.D. [A Wallace K.M.&B.]
*PRACTICE AREAS: Environmental Law; Litigation; Education; Environmental Regulation.
Duchelle, John W. ... '50 '90 C.1375 B.A. L.893 J.D. [Ross,D.&B.]
Duchesne, Matthew S. ... '64 '99 C.473 B.A. L.575 J.D. [A Jones,D.R.&P.]
Duchovny, Daniel F. ... '69 '98 C.446 B.S. L.276 J.D. [A Wilmer,C.&P.]
Duckers, Edward C. ... '57 '85 C.378 B.S. L.276 J.D. [Hogan&H.]
*PRACTICE AREAS: Antitrust Law; Litigation.
Duckett, Tracey Lenhardt '69 '94 C&L.893 B.A., J.D.
(adm. in VA; not adm. in DC) 1900 K St., N.W.‡
Duckworth, Frank A. '21 '48 C&L.260 B.S., J.D.
(adm. in FL; not adm. in DC) 700 New Hampshire Ave. N.W.‡
Duclaux, Duane K. '63 '98
C.425 B.B.A. L.1209 J.D. Coun., Dominion Resources Services, Inc.
Dudek, Jean K., (BV) '57 '85
C.788 A.B. L.569 J.D. [A Fitzpatrick,C.H.&S.] (See Pat. Sect.)
Dudley, Godfrey D. ... '44 '71 C.864 B.S. L.329 J.D. 1801 L Street NW‡
Dudley, Jane Saindon ... '49 '97 C.30 B.A. L.1209 J.D. [A Whiteford,T.&P.]
*PRACTICE AREAS: Business Law; Estate Planning; Community Association Law.
Dudley, John A. ... '32 '58 C.665 B.B.A. L.276 J.D. [Sullivan&W.]
*PRACTICE AREAS: Mutual Funds; Investment Regulation.
Dudzinsky, William S., Jr. ... '62 '88 C.276 B.S.F.S. L.659 J.D. [Dow,L.&A.]
Dueffert, Paul K. ... '63 '88 C.494 B.A. L.309 J.D. [Williams&C.]
*PRACTICE AREAS: Administrative Law; Civil Litigation; Copyright Litigation; First Amendment; Food and Drug Regulation.
Dufek, Robert A., (AV) ... '51 '76 C.966 B.A. L.276 J.D. [Morgan,L.&B.]
Duff, Daniel '44 '71 C.276 B.A. L.665 J.D.
Chf. Coun. & V.P., Govt. Affs., American Public Transit Assn.
Duff, James, P.C., (AV) ... '23 '49 C.645 B.A. L.273 J.D. Admin. Asst. Chief Jus.
Duff, James C. ... '53 '81 C.383 B.A. L.276 J.D. [Baker,D.B.&C.]
Duffey, Robert Michael, (AV) '54 '79 C.276 B.A. L.744 J.D.
(adm. in TX; not adm. in DC) Asst. Gen. Coun., Ernst & Young
Duffield, Cara Tseng '— '00 C.681 A.B. L.144 J.D.
(adm. in IL; not adm. in DC) [A Kirkland&E.]
*PRACTICE AREAS: Litigation.
Duffield, Steven J. '— '01 C.276 B.A. L.145 J.D.
(adm. in TX; not adm. in DC) [A Mayer,B.&P.]
*PRACTICE AREAS: Appellate Practice.
Duffy, Gerard J., (AV) ... '— '76 C.884 B.A. L.273 J.D. [Blooston,M.D.D.&P.]
*PRACTICE AREAS: Telecommunications Law; Cable TV; FCC Regulation; PCS.
Duffy, John J. ... '44 '70 C.103 A.B. L.188 J.D. [C Steptoe&J.]
*PRACTICE AREAS: Natural Resources; Government Contract; Federal and State Election Law; Native American Law.
Duffy, Michael F. '49 '76 C.128 B.A. L.273 J.D.
Dep. Gen. Coun., National Mining Association
Dufresne, Alexandra Felder '— '99 L.145 J.D.
(adm. in IL; not adm. in DC) [A Latham&W.]
*PRACTICE AREAS: Litigation.
Dugan, Christopher F. ... '48 '82 C.367 B.A. L.276 J.D. [Jones,D.R.&P.]
*PRACTICE AREAS: International Trade; International Arbitration; International Litigation.
Dugan, John C., (AV) ... '55 '81 C.477 B.A. L.309 J.D. [Covington&B.]
Dugan, John R. "Jay", (AV) '43 '68 C.321 A.B. L.273 J.D.
1912 Sunderland Pl., N.W. (⊙Rockville, MD)

Dugan, Jakubowski, Babij & Spector, LLC
(See Timonium, Maryland)

Dugan, John R. "Jay"
(See Rockville, Maryland)

Dugas, Julian R. ... '18 '50 C.789 B.S. L.329 LL.B. 2020 Trumbull Terr., NW
Duggan, Lisa M. ... '69 '96 C.893 B.A. L.659 J.D. [A Williams&C.]
*PRACTICE AREAS: Civil Litigation.
Duggin, Sarah H. '54 '80
C.788 A.B. L.659 J.D. Vice President & General Counsel, Amtrak
Duhig, Diane, (BV) ... '59 '87 C.734 A.B. L.128 J.D. [A Swick&S.]
Duke, Charles E. '37 '63 C.893 B.A. L.692 LL.B.
(adm. in VA; not adm. in DC) Coun., Ticor Title Ins. Co.
Duke, David M. '67 '92 C.420 B.A. L.356 J.D.
(adm. in PA; not adm. in DC) Congressional Quarterly
Duke, Douglas A. '67 '93
(adm. in MD; not adm. in DC) PETA

Duke, Hilary ... '63 '99 C.273 B.B.A. L.276 J.D. [A Sonnenschein N.&R.]
*PRACTICE AREAS: Employee Benefits; Executive Compensation.
Duke, Nicole Chapin ... '68 '94 C.976 B.A. L.276 J.D. [A Williams&C.]
Duke, Paul R., (AV) ... '29 '54 C.728 A.B. L.659 LL.B. 1201 Pennsylvania Ave., N.W.
Duke, Rebecca F., (BV) ... '64 '90 C.806 B.A. L.273 J.D. [C Holland&K.]
*PRACTICE AREAS: Telecommunications; Government; Municipal Law; Land Use.
Dukic, Aleksandar ... '70 '99 C.1214 B.A. L.273 J.D. [A Hogan&H.]
Dulany, Benjamin W., (AV) '19 '48
C.893 A.B. L.276 LL.B. [Jackson&C.] (⊙Vienna, VA)
*PRACTICE AREAS: Estate Planning Law; Probate Law; Trust Law.
Dulik, Richard ... '55 '86 C.930 B.S. L.976 J.D. [A Covington&B.]
Dumas, Nkeisha J. ... '74 '00 C.512 B.S.C.E. L.276 J.D. [A Jackson&C.]
*PRACTICE AREAS: Insurance Coverage; Business Litigation.
Dumler, Johnna Brooke ... '— '99 C.787 B.A. L.904 J.D. [A Steptoe&J.]
Dunaway, Elizabeth Johnson '70 '93 C.145 B.A. L.659 J.D.
(adm. in IL; not adm. in DC) [A Steptoe&J.]
Dunaway, Mac S., (AV) ... '42 '67 C.12 B.A. L.16 LL.B. [Dunaway&C.]
Dunaway, Sally Putnam '53 '80 C.893 B.A. L.831 J.D.
(adm. in PA; not adm. in DC) Amer. Bar Assn.

Dunaway & Cross, A Professional Corporation, (AV) BR
1700 K Street, N.W. Suite 800, 20006-3819
Telephone: 202-862-9700 Fax: 202-862-9710
Email: duncross@msn.com
Mac S. Dunaway; Gary E. Cross; Matthew F. Hall. Counsel: Raymond P. Shafer (Not admitted in DC).
Litigation in all Federal and State Courts. Administrative Law, Antitrust, Aviation Law, General Business and Commercial Law, Insurance and Insurance Defense, Product Safety, Products Liability, Real Estate Law, Trade Association and International Trade Law.
See Professional Biographies, WASHINGTON, DISTRICT OF COLUMBIA

Dunbar, Mary M. ... '63 '91 C.546 B.S. L.893 J.D. Atty., Nasdaq Regulation
Duncan, Alison MacDonald, (BV) ... '53 '84 C.999 B.Ed. L.273 J.D. [Porter W.M.&A.]
*PRACTICE AREAS: Health Care Fraud; White Collar Crime; Government Contracts.
Duncan, Debra J. ... '56 '86 C.945 B.A. L.273 J.D. [C Vinson&E.]
*PRACTICE AREAS: Federal Taxation; Tax Controversies; Tax Litigation; International Taxation.
Duncan, Deidre G. ... '71 '96 C.228 A.B. L.150 J.D. [A Hunton&W.]
*PRACTICE AREAS: Environmental Law; Land Use.
Duncan, Jack G. '41 '63 C.269 B.A. L.790 J.D.
(adm. in SC; not adm. in DC) Gen. Coun., Council of State Administrators
Duncan, Jack G. ... '38 '63 C.269 A.B. L.790 J.D. 1213 29th St., N.W.
Duncan, Lawrence, III ... '— '94 C.309 B.A. L.893 J.D. [A Verner,L.B.M.&H.]
*PRACTICE AREAS: Legislative; Federal Affairs; Communications.
Duncan, Mallory B. '49 '76 C.668 B.A. L.976 J.D.
Vice President & General Counsel, National Retail Federation
Duncan, Robert B. ... '56 '87 C.659 B.A. L.893 J.D. [Hogan&H.] (⊙Mc Lean, VA)
*PRACTICE AREAS: Commercial Litigation; Intellectual Property Litigation; Technology Litigation; Employment Litigation; Real Estate Litigation.
Duncan, Russell D., (AV) ... '56 '82 C&L.309 A.B., J.D. [Coburn&S.]
*PRACTICE AREAS: Litigation; Government Contracts; White Collar Crime; Insurance Fraud.
Duncan, Wallace L., (AV) ... '37 '61 C&L.30 A.B., J.D. [Duncan,W.G.&P.]
*PRACTICE AREAS: Administrative Law; Natural Resources; Public Utility Law.

Duncan & Allen, (AV)
1575 Eye Street, N.W., 20005-1105
Telephone: 202-289-8400 Facsimile: 202-289-8450
Members of Firm: C. Emerson Duncan, II (1919-2000); Donald R. Allen; Gregg D. Ottinger; John P. Williams; John P. Coyle. Associates: Jon R. Stickman (Not admitted in DC); Helene de Neuville (Not admitted in DC); Norma Jean Vidal.
Practice before Courts, Federal Agencies and Departments and the U.S. Congress. Electric Power, Energy Regulation, Hydroelectric Licensing, Natural Resources, Utility Law, Water Rights, Mineral Law, Petroleum Law. International Business, Finance, Labor, Regulatory Affairs at State and Federal Levels, Business Litigation.
See Professional Biographies, WASHINGTON, DISTRICT OF COLUMBIA

Duncan-Peters, Stephanie ... '53 '77 C.529 B.A. L.128 J.D. Assoc. Supr. Ct. J.

Duncan, Weinberg, Genzer & Pembroke, P.C., (AV)
Suite 800, 1615 M Street, N.W., 20036-3203 ⊙
Telephone: 202-467-6370 Fax: 202-467-6379
Email: dwgp@dwgp.com
Wallace L. Duncan; Edward Weinberg (1918-1995); James D. Pembroke; Richmond F. Allan; Robert Weinberg; Janice L. Lower; Jeffrey C. Genzer; Thomas L. Rudebusch; Michael R. Postar; Tatjana M. Shonkwiler; Eli D. Eilbott;—Lisa S. Gast; Sean M. Neal; Joseph C. Hall (Not admitted in DC). Of Counsel: Frederick L. Miller, Jr.; Barry F. McCarthy (Resident, San Jose, CA Office; also practicing individually, San Jose, CA); Thomas J. Lynch (Resident, Syracuse, NY Office; also practicing individually, Syracuse, NY); Terry E. Singer; James F. Flug; Paula N. Dinerstein; Kathleen L. Mazure.
Energy, Natural Resources, Public Utility, Antitrust, Public Lands, Indian Affairs, Water Rights, Municipal, Land Use, Legislative, General Administrative, Environmental, Patent and Trademark, Hazardous Materials, Transportation and Communications Law before Federal and State Courts and Agencies.
San Jose, California Office: 2105 Hamilton Avenue, Suite 140, 95125. Telephone: 408-558-0950. Fax: 408-558-0955.
Associated Law Firm: Syracuse, New York, Thomas J. Lynch, 2700 Bellevue Avenue, 13219. Telephone: 315-471-1318. Fax: 315-471-1409.
See Professional Biographies, WASHINGTON, DISTRICT OF COLUMBIA

Dundon, Leah A. ... '70 '97 C.30 B.A. L.880 J.D. [A Beveridge&D.]
*PRACTICE AREAS: White Collar Criminal Defense; Environmental Law.
Dunham, Corydon B., (AV) ... '27 '51 C.95 B.A. L.309 LL.B. [C Cahill G.&R.] ⊙
Dunham, Thomas M. '63 '95 C.1349 B.S. L.884 J.D.
[Howrey S.A.&W.] (See Pat. Sect.)
*PRACTICE AREAS: Intellectual Property Law.
Dunigan, Thomas E., (BV) ... '50 '76 C&L.276 B.A., J.D. [Sherman,M.C.&A.]
*PRACTICE AREAS: Real Property; Corporate Law; Estate Planning.
Dunkelberger, H. Edward, Jr., (AV) '30 '57
C&L.976 A.B., J.D. 1201 Pennsylvania Ave., N.W.
Dunkin, Denise M. ... '71 '97 C.1349 B.A. L.262 J.D. [Woodley,G.&M.]
*PRACTICE AREAS: Labor and Employment Law; Fair Labor Standards Law; Public Sector Labor Relations Law.
Dunlop, John E. ... '37 '68 C.475 B.A. L.215 J.D. National Educ. Assn.
Dunn, Alan M., (AV) ... '53 '80 C.1356 B.S. L.893 J.D. [Stewart&S.]
*PRACTICE AREAS: International Trade.
Dunn, Alvin ... '62 '89 C.846 B.A. L.309 J.D. [C Shaw P.]
*PRACTICE AREAS: Litigation; Antitrust.
Dunn, Brian J. '74 '00 C.885 B.A. L.127 J.D.
(adm. in MA; not adm. in DC) U.S. Securities and Exchange Commission
Dunn, Christopher A., (AV) ... '51 '75 C.103 A.B. L.276 J.D. [Willkie F.&G.]
Dunn, David E., III ... '49 '75 C&L.16 B.A., J.D. [Patton B.]
Dunn, H. Stewart, Jr., (AV) ... '29 '54 C.976 A.B. L.309 LL.B. [Ivins,P.&B.]
*PRACTICE AREAS: Federal Tax.
Dunn, Jeffrey A., (AV) '51 '76
C.378 B.A. L.276 J.D. [Venable,A.B.H.&C.] (⊙Balt., MD)
*PRACTICE AREAS: Intellectual Property; Commercial Litigation; Public Contract Law.
Dunn, Reagan B. ... '71 '98 C.36 B.A. L.911 J.D. 950 Pennsylvania Ave.
Dunn, Thomas F. ... '35 '65 C&L.276 B.A., LL.B. [Mitchell&D.]
*PRACTICE AREAS: Criminal; Drug Crimes; Lobbying; Personal Injury.

Dunnaville, Andrew M. '75 '00 C.31 B.A. L.893 J.D.
(adm. in MD; not adm. in DC) [Kelley D.&W.] (⊙New York, NY)
*PRACTICE AREAS: Telecommunications.
Dunne, Bruce W. ... '49 '75 C.951 B.A. L.273 J.D. [Jones&B.]
*PRACTICE AREAS: Securities Law; Corporate Law.
Dunne, Elizabeth M. '77 '01 C.698 B.A. L.1365 J.D.
(adm. in GA; not adm. in DC) [Holland&K.]
*PRACTICE AREAS: Litigation.
Dunne, Kristine J. ... '67 '00 C.999 B.A. L.893 J.D. [Arent F.K.P.&K.]
*PRACTICE AREAS: Employment Law; Civil Litigation; Education Law.
Dunne, Susan S. ... '67 '92 C.188 B.S. L.273 J.D. [Morgan,L.&B.]
Dunne, Tanya N. '68 '01 C.999 B.S. L.276 J.D.
(adm. in NY; not adm. in DC) [Cleary,G.S.&H.]
Dunnells, G. Richard, (AV) ... '37 '67 C.197 B.A. L.893 LL.B. [Holland&K.]
*PRACTICE AREAS: Housing Development and Financing; Commercial Real Estate Transactions; Housing and Urban Development; Federal Housing Law; Affordable Housing Finance.
Dunner, Donald R., (AV) '31 '58
C.679 B.S.Ch.E. L.276 J.D. [Finnegan,H.F.G.&D.] (See Pat. Sect.)
*PRACTICE AREAS: Intellectual Property Litigation; Intellectual Property Appeals.
Dunner, Lisa A. ... '61 '96 C.699 B.A. L.365 J.D. [McDermott,W.&E.]
Dunnings, Susan E. '57 '85 C.813 B.A. L.477 J.D.
Assoc. Gen. Coun., National Public Radio, Inc.
Dunphy, James Michael, Jr. '68 '95 C.884 B.A. L.1202 J.D.
(adm. in MA; not adm. in DC) [Bonner K.T.&C.]
*PRACTICE AREAS: Premises Liability; Dram Shop Liability; Insurance Defense.
Dunsmore, Keith A. ... '57 '82 C.951 B.A. L.880 J.D. [Akin,G.S.H.&F.]
*PRACTICE AREAS: Real Estate Finance (66%); Tax Law (34%).
Dunst, Isabel P., (AV) ... '47 '71 C.966 B.S. L.569 J.D. [Hogan&H.]
*PRACTICE AREAS: Medicare and Medicaid; Health Care; Regulatory Law; Government.
Dunstan, James E. ... '58 '83 C.154 B.A. L.276 J.D. [Garvey,S.&B.]
*PRACTICE AREAS: Television Law; Cable Law; Space Law; Computer Law; Copyrights.
Dupart, Louis H. '50 '85 C.895 B.A. L.904 J.D.
(adm. in VA; not adm. in DC) [Fleischman&W.]
Dupler, Mitchell S. ... '55 '79 C&L.309 A.B., J.D. [Cleary,G.S.&H.]
Dupree, David H. ... '59 '85 C&L.329 B.B.A., J.D. 6722 3rd St., N.W.
Dupree, Thomas H., Jr. ... '70 '98 C.951 B.A. L.145 J.D. [Gibson,D.&C.]
DuPuy, Carolyn M. ... '50 '83 C.518 B.A. L.276 J.D. [Weil,G.&M.]
Dupuy, R. René ... '56 '93 C.845 B.A. L.904 J.D. P.O. Box 5663
Dupuy, Siobhan Elizabeth ... '71 '97 C.420 B.A. L.276 J.D. [Covington&B.]
Dupuy-Bruno, Kathy K.B. ... '— '99 C.724 B.A. L.30 J.D. [M.E.Baurley]
*PRACTICE AREAS: Family Law; Medical Malpractice; Employment Discrimination; Special Education.
Durbin, David P., (AV) ... '48 '77 C&L.276 B.S.F.S., J.D. [Jordan C.&S.]
*PRACTICE AREAS: Professional Liability Defense; Appellate Practice; Defense Litigation; Insurance Defense; Insurance Coverage.
Durden, Daniel E. ... '60 '87 C.1161 B.A. L.904 J.D. 1747 Pennsylvania Ave., NW
Durkin, David L. ... '59 '88 C.363 A.B. L.128 J.D. [Olsson,F.&W.]
*PRACTICE AREAS: Food, Drug and Medical Device Law; Litigation.
Durkin, Tracy-Gene Graveline, (BV) '61 '89
C.1316 B.S. L.273 J.D. [Sterne,K.G.&F.] (See Pat. Sect.)
*PRACTICE AREAS: Intellectual Property Law; Mediation; Trademarks; Unfair Competition; Patents.
Durkovic, Andrew J. '60 '93 C.112 B.A. L.426 J.D.
(adm. in CA; not adm. in DC) [Baker&H.]
*PRACTICE AREAS: Real Estate Litigation; Business Litigation.
Durling, James P. ... '58 '84 C.311 B.A. L.569 J.D. [Willkie F.&G.]

Durney, Michael C., Law Offices of, (AV) '43 '69 C.112 A.B. L.1065 J.D. BR
1072 Thomas Jefferson Street, N.W., 20007
Telephone: 202-965-7744 Fax: 202-965-7745
Email: mcd@mdurney.com
Civil and Criminal Tax Controversy, Federal Fraud Practice in Federal Courts and Before Federal Departments and Agencies, Mediation and Arbitration, International Tax Controversies.
See Professional Biographies, WASHINGTON, DISTRICT OF COLUMBIA

Duross, Jeanne M. Moore ... '68 '96 C.668 B.A. L.273 J.D. [Shaw P.]
*PRACTICE AREAS: Environmental; Litigation; Antitrust.
DuRoss, William H., III ... '41 '68 C.976 B.A. L.273 J.D. [Shainis&P.]
*PRACTICE AREAS: Labor and Employment Law; Employment Discrimination; Employee Benefits.
Durrah, Fred D. ... '16 '49 C.329 B.S. L.705 LL.B. 1937 Vermont Ave., N.W.
Durst, Michael C. ... '— '81 C.951 B.A. L.1066 J.D. [King&S.]
*PRACTICE AREAS: Tax.
Durst, Ron L. '53 '87 C&L.923 B.S., J.D.
(adm. in VA; not adm. in DC) [Hanson&M.]
*PRACTICE AREAS: Federal Taxation; Corporate Taxation; Estate and Trusts; Exempt Organizations.
Duru, N. Jeremi ... '73 '99 C.103 B.A. L.309 J.D. [Wilmer,C.&P.]
Dusenbury, Angela M. '73 '99 C.454 B.A. L.846 J.D.
(adm. in NY; not adm. in DC) [Akin,G.S.H.&F.]
*PRACTICE AREAS: Environmental Law.
Dussman, Seymour H. '40 '65 C.912 A.B. L.145 J.D.
(adm. in MI; not adm. in DC) 2123 California St. N.W., #G-6‡
Dustin, Kimberley K. ... '68 '96 C.1369 B.A. L.945 J.D. William M. Mercer, Inc.
Duston, Robert L., (AV) ... '60 '84 C.1209 B.A. L.893 J.D. [Schmeltzer,A.&S.]
*PRACTICE AREAS: Management Labor Law; Employment Law; Employee Benefits Law; Civil Rights Law; School Law.
Dutton, Brian Keith ... '58 '00 C.223 B.S.E.E. L.273 J.D. [Rader,F.&G.]
Dutton, Frederick G. ... '23 '49 C.112 B.S. L.813 LL.B. [Dutton&D.]
Dutton, Nancy Hogan ... '38 '75 C.706 B.A. L.276 J.D. [Dutton&D.]
Dutton & Dutton, P.C. ... 5017 Tilden St., N.W.
DuVall, Amy L. ... '73 '99 C.910 B.S. L.107 J.D. [Piper M.R.&W.]
*PRACTICE AREAS: Solid Waste Regulation; Hazardous Waste Regulation; Legislative Practice; Regulatory Law; Appellate Practice.
Duvall, Donald Knox ... '25 '54 C.976 A.B. L.893 J.D. 1025 Connecticut Ave., N.W.
Duvall, Susan E., (AV) ... '53 '78 C.105 B.A. L.659 J.D. [Swidler B.S.F.]
*PRACTICE AREAS: Real Estate Finance; Structured Finance; Mortgage-Backed Securities; Housing.
Dwan, Ralph H., Jr., (AV) ... '32 '57 C&L.477 A.B., LL.B. 729 8th St., S.E.
Dwares, David R., (AV) ... '63 '88 C.880 B.A. L.659 J.D. [Ross,D.&B.]
Dweck, Jacob ... '51 '76 C.102 B.A. L.276 J.D. [Sutherland A.&B.]
*PRACTICE AREAS: Business Law; Business Regulation; Agency and Distributorships; Energy Regulation; Technology Law.
Dweck, Ralph S. ... '41 '65 C&L.30 B.A., J.D. 1730 M St., N.W.
Dworkin, Douglas A. ... '47 '77 C.604 B.A. L.976 J.D. [Arnold&P.]
*PRACTICE AREAS: Litigation; International; International Litigation; Arbitration; Public Policy and Legislative.
Dwyer, Amy S. ... '64 '91 C.321 B.A. L.93 J.D. [Stewart&S.]
*PRACTICE AREAS: International Trade; International Trade Regulation; Import and Export Law; Antidumping; North American Free Trade Agreement.
Dwyer, Daniel R., (BV) ... '55 '85 C.1044 B.A. L.276 J.D. [Kleinfeld,K.&B.]
*PRACTICE AREAS: Food, Drug and Cosmetic Law; Drug and Medical Device Regulation; Food Labeling and Inspection; Advertising Law; Corporate Investigations.
Dwyer, Ellen Moran ... '60 '86 C.732 B.A. L.188 J.D. [Crowell&M.]
Dwyer, Jeffry R., (AV) ... '46 '71 C&L.276 B.S.F.S., J.D. [Greenberg T.]
Dwyer, John J. ... '64 '90 C.676 B.A. L.276 J.D. [Piper M.R.&W.]
*PRACTICE AREAS: Litigation; Franchise.

Dwyer, Kevin C. ... '58 '85 C.602 B.A. L.228 J.D. [Jenner&B.]
*PRACTICE AREAS: Government Contract Law; Government Contract Cost Accounting; Health Care Contracting.
Dwyer, Lisa M. ... '71 '99 C.918 B.A. L.273 J.D. [Patton B.]
Dwyer, Maureen Ellen, (AV) ... '51 '79 C.788 B.A. L.128 J.D. [Shaw P.]
*PRACTICE AREAS: Real Estate; Zoning, Planning and Land Use; Municipal Law; Historic Preservation; Lobbying.
Dwyer, Roderick T. '44 '77 C.93 A.B. L.128 J.D.
Dep. Gen. Coun., National Mining Association
Dwyer, William F., II ... '35 '83 L.809 J.D. [Drath&D.]
Dyckman, Matthew '69 '94 C.893 B.A. L.228 J.D.
(adm. in MD; not adm. in DC) [Thacher P.&W.]
Dye, Alan L., (AV) ... '53 '78 C.1365 B.A. L.280 J.D. [Hogan&H.]
*PRACTICE AREAS: Corporate Law; Securities.
Dye, Alan P., (AV) ... '46 '71 C.228 B.A. L.260 J.D. [Webster,C.&B.]
*PRACTICE AREAS: Exempt Organizations; Taxation; Election Law; General Corporate; Association Law.
Dye, Stuart S., (AV) ... '39 '67 C.878 B.S. L.893 LL.B. [Holland&K.]
*PRACTICE AREAS: International Transactions; International Finance; Transportation Law; Energy Law.
Dyer, James Gregory '74 '01 C&L.101 B.S., J.D.
(adm. in CA; not adm. in DC) [Dechert]
*PRACTICE AREAS: Civil Litigation; Complex Litigation; Defense Litigation; Trial Practice; Bank Securities.
Dyer, Jocelyn Y. ... '68 '93 C.575 B.A. L.273 J.D. 1250 24th St., N.W.
Dyer, Joseph J. '54 '79 C&L.446 B.A., J.D.
(adm. in MD; not adm. in DC) [Seyfarth S.]
*PRACTICE AREAS: Government Contracts Law; International Law.
Dyer, Richard J. ... '74 '00 C.273 B.A. L.128 J.D. [O'Melveny&M.]
Dyer, Thomas M., (AV) ... '45 '73 C.276 B.A. L.273 J.D. [Dyer E.&J.]
*PRACTICE AREAS: Maritime Law; Transactions; Ship Finance.

Dyer Ellis & Joseph, A Professional Corporation, (AV)
Watergate - Eleventh Floor, 600 New Hampshire Avenue, N.W., 20037
Telephone: 202-944-3000 Telecopier: 202-944-3068 URL: http://www.dyerellis.com
Email: info@dejlaw.com URL: http://www.dejlaw.com
Thomas M. Dyer; James B. Ellis II; Michael Joseph; Brian A. Bannon; Edward M. Barberic; Jane F. Barrett; Alex Blanton; Patrick O. Cavanaugh; Joseph O. Click; Thomas M. DiBiagio; James S. W. Drewry; Brett M. Esber; Jeanne Marie Grasso; John E. Graykowski; John G. Henderson (Not admitted in DC); Paul M. Honigberg; John F. Kearney; Wayne A. Keup; Richard A. Kirby; Barbara D. Linney; Edward L. Lublin; William R. Martin; R. Anthony Salgado; Lawrence S. Sher; Duncan C. Smith III; Jonathan K. Waldron; Marcus R. Wyler; Pat Munroe Woodward, Jr. Of Counsel: Joan M. Bondareff; Geoffrey P. Gitner; Nathalia S. A. Hardy (Not admitted in DC); Debra M. Robbins; Linda K. Rosenthal; William L. Schachte, Jr.; Todd D. Snyder; Sidney A. Wallace;—Thomas Z. Cheplo; Carolyn Coffey; Katia I. Fano (Not admitted in DC); Alan M. Freeman; Christopher T. Furlow (Not admitted in DC); Natalia W. Geren; Peter R. Johnson (Not admitted in DC); Lara Bernstein Mathews; J. Christopher Naftzger; Shaila Lakhani Ohri; Kristine L. Sendek; Steven P. Steinberg; Luis Vernaza (Not admitted in DC); Susan L. Watson (Not admitted in DC); Shawn M. Wright.
Practice before Federal Courts and Agencies, Legislative Practice, Shipping, Government Contracts, Healthcare, Antitrust, International Transactions, General Corporate, Securities Regulation, Tax, Environmental, White Collar Crime, Litigation, Trademark and Copyright.
See Professional Biographies, WASHINGTON, DISTRICT OF COLUMBIA

Dykema, Peter Kryn ... '56 '85 C.118 B.A. L.477 J.D. 1400 L St., N.W.

Dykema Gossett PLLC, (AV) BR
Franklin Square, Suite 300 West, 1300 I Street, N.W., 20005-3353 ⊙
Telephone: 202-906-8600 Fax: 202-906-8669
Email: mstarrs@dykema.com URL: http://www.dykema.com
Resident Members: Hilary Stephen Cairnie; Steven A. Diaz; John P. DeLuca; Edward A. Groobert; Donald N. Huff; D. Biard MacGuineas; Howard E. O'Leary, Jr.; Lawrence R. Radanovic; Richard H. Tushin; Fred L. Woodworth; Stephen H. Zimmerman (Not admitted in DC). Of Counsel: William H. Carroll; Sanford B. Ring. Resident Associates: William A. Bonk, III (Not admitted in DC); Judy Parker Jenkins; Sandra Snapp.
General Practice. Antitrust and Trade Regulation, Commercial Litigation, Intellectual Property, Trademark Law, Trade Associations, Energy Law, Transportation Law, Government Contracts, Health Care Law, White Collar Crime, Regulatory Law and Legislative Practice.
Ann Arbor, Michigan Office: 315 East Eisenhower Parkway, Suite 100, 48108-3336. Telephone: 734-214-7660. Fax: 734-214-7696.
Bloomfield Hills, Michigan Office: 39577 Woodward Avenue, Suite 300, 48304-2820. Telephone: 248-203-0700. Fax: 248-203-0763.
Chicago, Illinois Office: 55 East Monroe Street, Suite 3050, 60603-5709. Telephone: 312-551-4900. Fax: 312-551-4919.
Detroit, Michigan Office: 400 Renaissance Center, 48243-1668. Telephone: 313-568-6800. Fax: 313-568-6545.
Grand Rapids, Michigan Office: Suite 700, 300 Ottawa Avenue, N.W., 49503-2306. Telephone: 616-776-7500. Fax: 616-776-7573.
Lansing, Michigan Office: 800 Michigan National Tower, 48933-1742. Telephone: 517-374-9100. Fax: 517-374-9191.
See Professional Biographies, WASHINGTON, DISTRICT OF COLUMBIA

Dykes, Teresa E. ... '66 '98 C.277 B.Ch.E. L.904 J.D. [Piper M.R.&W.] (Pat.)
*PRACTICE AREAS: Environmental.
Dymowski, Julianne Erin '67 '92
C.273 B.A. L.904 J.D. [Whiteford,T.&P.] (⊙Columbia, MD)
*PRACTICE AREAS: Community Association Law; Cooperative Association Law; Real Estate Collections; Contracts; Accreditation Law.
Dynes, Andrea F., (AV) ... '60 '89 C.347 B.A. L.904 J.D. [Gibson,D.&C.]
*PRACTICE AREAS: International Trade.
Dyson, Edward E., (AV) ... '39 '66 C&L.273 B.B.A., LL.B. [Baker&M.] (Pat.)
Dyson, Elizabeth D. '39 '64
C.681 A.B. L.378 LL.B. 3601 Connecticut Ave. N.W., Apt. 816
Dyson, Marianna G. ... '53 '80 C&L.421 B.A., J.D. [Baker&M.]
*PRACTICE AREAS: Litigation; Tax Controversies (Corporate and International); Tax Planning and Advice (Corporate and International); Employee Benefits.
Dyson, Michael Thomas ... '66 '96 C.1369 B.A. L.276 J.D. [Winston&S.]
*PRACTICE AREAS: Litigation.
Dzara, D. Daniel, II '74 '99 C.575 B.A. L.861 J.D.
(adm. in IL; not adm. in DC) [Arent F.K.P.&K.]
*PRACTICE AREAS: Patents; Trademarks; Copyrights.
Dziak, Douglas ... '70 '99 C.610 A.B. L.945 J.D. [Hunton&W.]
*PRACTICE AREAS: Antitrust; International Trade; Regulatory Litigation.
Dziedic-Leonard, Jennifer ... '72 '99 C.107 B.A. L.273 J.D. [Feldesman,T.L.F.&B.]
*PRACTICE AREAS: Health Care; Federal Grants; Corporate Litigation.
Dzubow, Jason A. ... '69 '97 C.831 B.A. L.276 J.D [Sherman,M.C.&A.]
*PRACTICE AREAS: Litigation.
D'Zurilla, David ... '59 '91 C.645 B.S. L.30 J.D. [Hunton&W.] (Pat.)
Dzwonczyk, Michael R. ... '62 '90 C.831 B.S. L.1017 J.D. [Morgan,L.&B.] (Pat.)
Eadie, Johanna '69 '00 C.1375 B.A. L.473 J.D.
(adm. in NY; not adm. in DC) [Orrick,H.&S.]
Eager, Robert C. ... '46 '81 C.880 B.A. L.276 J.D. [Gibson,D.&C.]
*PRACTICE AREAS: Gram-Leach-Bliley and Financial Institutions Law; Financial Institutions Law; Bank and Savings Association Regulation; Legislation; Transactional Matters for Banks and Thrift Law.
Eagle, Jacqueline H. ... '— '78 C.228 B.A. L.276 J.D. [Olsson,F.&W.]
*PRACTICE AREAS: Litigation.

Eames, Frederick R. '64 '94 C.25 B.A. L.273 J.D. (adm. in PA; not adm. in DC) [Balch&B.]
*PRACTICE AREAS: Legislative Practice; Energy; Environmental.
Earhart, Farleigh H. '66 '92 C&L.575 B.A., J.D. Asst. Gen. Coun., Smithsonian Institution
Earle, Richard Alan, (AV) .... '41 '68 C&L.477 B.B.A., J.D. [Patton B.]
Easley, Peter R. '63 '91 C.30 B.S. L.128 J.D. (adm. in MD; not adm. in DC) World Bank, The
Easley, Stephen J. '57 '84 C.893 B.S. L.280 J.D. Vice President & General Counsel, American Cellular Corporation
Easlick, David K., Jr., (BV) .... '47 '77 C.476 B.A. L.213 J.D. 2238 47th Street, N.W.
Eastin, Keith E. .... '40 '67 C.150 A.B. L.145 J.D. Deloitte& Touche, LLP
Eastman, James L. .... '70 '96 C.431 B.A. L.309 J.D. [🄰 Schiff H.&W.]
Eastman, Michael J. '68 '98 C.165 B.A. L.1209 J.D. (adm. in VA; not adm. in DC) [🄰 McGuiness N.&W.]
*PRACTICE AREAS: Labor Law; Employment Law; Legislative Practice.
Eastment, Thomas J. .... '50 '76 C.433 B.Ch.E. L.477 J.D. [Baker B.]
Easton, Amy L. .... '73 '99 C.477 B.A. L.608 J.D. [🄰 Squire,S.&D.]
Easton, Jack C. .... '73 '99 C.367 B.A. L.893 J.D. [🄰 Fried,F.H.S.&J.]
*PRACTICE AREAS: Corporate.
Easton, John O., (AV) .... '43 '77 C.69 B.A. L.1209 J.D. [Jordan C.&S.] (⊙Fairfax, VA)
*PRACTICE AREAS: Architects and Engineers Malpractice; Legal Malpractice; Medical Malpractice; Products Liability; Sexual Assault/Abuse.
Eastwood, Elizabeth Ann .... '66 '90 C.945 B.A. L.893 J.D. [🄲 Wiley R.&F.]
*PRACTICE AREAS: Insurance.
Eastwood, James A. .... '53 '87 C.604 B.A. L.276 J.D. [🄰 Dombroff&G.]
Eastwood, Valerie J., (BV) '55 '87 C.1222 B.F.A. L.472 J.D. (adm. in FL; not adm. in DC) [Duane,M.&H.]
*PRACTICE AREAS: Healthcare Law; Fraud and Abuse; Medicare and Medicaid Reimbursement; Compliance Reviews and Guidance.
Eaton, Alison H. .... '— '97 C.945 B.A. L.245 J.D. [🄰 Hogan&H.]
Eaton, Allen T., (AV) .... '35 '70 C.561 B.S. L.273 J.D. [Eaton&M.] ⊙
*PRACTICE AREAS: Professional Negligence (Medical, Dental, Legal); Directors and Officers Liability Claims; Products Liability.
Eaton, Geoffrey P. '71 '99 C.945 B.A. L.893 J.D. (adm. in NY; not adm. in DC) [🄰 Sullivan&C.]
Eaton, Holly R. .... '59 '91 C.197 A.B. L.588 J.D. Georgetown Law Ctr.
Eaton, Mark R., (AV) .... '50 '75 C.918 B.A. L.178 J.D. [🄲 Crowell&M.]
*PRACTICE AREAS: Corporate Law; Securities Law.
Eaton, Michael M., (AV) .... '46 '71 C.893 B.A. L.145 J.D. [Arent F.K.P.&K.]
*PRACTICE AREAS: Antitrust; Health and Hospital Law; Franchise Law; Litigation; Covenants Not To Compete.
Eaton, Robert E. L., Jr., (AV) .... '41 '68 C&L.446 B.S., LL.B. Asst. U.S. Atty.

Eaton & McClellan, (AV)
1111 14th Street, N.W., Suite 777, 20005 ⊙
Telephone: 202-789-0088 Fax: 202-789-1377
Email: apeem@earthlink.net
Members of Firm: Allen T. Eaton; Frank M. McClellan. Associates: La' Vern D. Wiley; Emmanuel O. Iheukwumere (Not admitted in DC); Carol E. Bell (Not admitted in DC).
Civil Litigation. Professional Liability, Medical Malpractice, Auto Torts, Aviation Law, Products Liability, Insurance, Wrongful Death, Commercial Employment and Labor Law, Toxic Torts Insurance Law, General Practice.
Philadelphia, Pennsylvania Office: 230 South Broad Street, Third Floor, 19102. Telephone: 215-875-0600. Fax: 215-875-0617.
See Professional Biographies, WASHINGTON, DISTRICT OF COLUMBIA

Ebb, Carmel P. '24 '45 C.66 A.B. L.178 LL.B. (adm. in NY; not adm. in DC) 4532 Broad Branch Rd., N.W.‡
Ebb, Lawrence F. .... '18 '47 C&L.309 A.B., LL.B. 4532 Broad Branch Rd., N.W.
Ebb, Nancy Elizabeth '50 '76 C.681 A.B. L.1066 J.D. (adm. in NH; not adm. in DC) Children's Defense Fund
Eberle, William S., (P.A.) '23 '50 C.813 B.A. L.309 J.D. (adm. in ID; not adm. in DC) [🄲 Kaye S.]
*PRACTICE AREAS: International Trade.
Ebersole, Joseph L. .... '30 '66 C.484 A.B. L.800 J.D. 2101 Conn. Ave., N.W.
Ebert, Allan '52 '88 C.102 B.A. L.1162 J.D. (adm. in PA; not adm. in DC) 2607 24th St., NW
Ebert, Eugene, (AV) '30 '55 C&L.273 B.A., J.D. 1025 Connecticut Avenue, N.W., Suite 515 (⊙Silver Spring, MD)
Ebert, Paul S. .... '71 '96 C.1044 B.S. L.273 J.D. [🄰 Winston&S.]
*PRACTICE AREAS: Government Contracts; Litigation.
Ebert, Robert T. .... '51 '76 C.216 B.A. L.1017 J.D. [Crowell&M.]
*PRACTICE AREAS: Government Contract Law.
Ebner, Lawrence S. .... '47 '73 C.197 B.A. L.309 J.D. [McKenna&C.]
*PRACTICE AREAS: Appellate Practice; Complex Civil Litigation; Toxic Torts; Product Liability.
Eburuche-Ekeanyanwu, Thecla .... '65 '91 C.215 B.A. L.1187 J.D. Kalorama Station
Eccles, Robert N., (AV) .... '47 '72 C&L.309 A.B., J.D. [O'Melveny&M.]
*PRACTICE AREAS: ERISA; ERISA Litigation; Employee Benefits; Employee Benefits Litigation.
Eccleston, Lynn E., (AV) .... '48 '88 C.597 B.A. L.912 J.D. [Morgan,L.&B.] (Pat.)

Eccleston and Wolf, A Professional Corporation, (AV)
1750 K Street, N.W., Suite 450, 20006-2300 ⊙
Telephone: 202-857-1696 Fax: 202-857-0762
Aaron L. Handleman; Ronald W. Fuchs; Jeffrey J. Hines;—Richard W. Driscoll; Craig Stephen Brodsky; Heather Shanan O'Connor (Not admitted in DC); Matthew William Lee; Juli Z. Simonyi; Theresa M. Hummel; George S. Mahaffey, Jr. (Not admitted in DC).
General Trial and Appellate Practice in all Courts with concentration in Insurance Defense Litigation including Legal Malpractice, Medical Malpractice, Claims against Architects, Engineers, Accountants, Realtors, School Boards and other Professionals and Products Liability, Pharmaceutical Manufacturer's Liability, Automobile Tort, Workers Compensation and General Aviation. Additional areas of concentration: Insurance Coverage, Corporate, Contract, Commercial Law, Labor and Employment Law.
Baltimore, Maryland Office: 729 E. Pratt Street - 7th Floor, Scarlett Place. Telephone: 410-752-7474. Fax: 410-752-0611.
Fairfax, Virginia Office: 10875 Main Street, Suite 201. Telephone: 703-218-5330.
See Professional Biographies, WASHINGTON, DISTRICT OF COLUMBIA

Echikson, Thomas G. .... '62 '88 C.197 A.B. L.597 J.D. [Sidley A.B.&W.]
Echols, F. Stanley .... '45 '78 C.260 B.S. L.276 J.D. [Winston&S.]
*PRACTICE AREAS: Energy Law; Environmental Law; Regulatory Law; Administrative Law.
Echols, Marsha A. .... '43 '68 C.329 B.A. L.276 J.D. Howard Univ.
Eck, F. Thomas, IV .... '64 '89 C&L.800 B.A., J.D. [Eck] ⊙
Eck, Jennifer M. .... '65 '95 C.645 B.S. L.575 J.D. [🄰 Dickstein S.M.&O.]
*PRACTICE AREAS: Mergers and Acquisitions; Corporate; Securities.
Eck, Margaret Kadel .... '65 '95 C.692 B.S. L.990 J.D. [🄰 Bingham D.]
*PRACTICE AREAS: Commercial Real Estate; Real Estate Finance.

Eck Law Firm, The
1101 30th Street, N.W., Suite 500, 20007 ⊙
Telephone: 202-625-4342 Fax:202-318-1136
Email: teck@ecklawfirm.com URL: http://www.ecklawfirm.com
F. Thomas Eck, IV.

(This Listing Continued)

Eck Law Firm, The (Continued)
Business Litigation, Emerging Business Law, Electronic Commerce Law, Internet Law, Complex Litigation, Small Business Law, Financial Planning, Commercial Transactions, Uniform Commercial Code.
San Francisco, California Office: 50 California Street, Suite 1500, 94111. Telephone: 415-399-9797. Fax: 415-276-2870.
See Professional Biographies, WASHINGTON, DISTRICT OF COLUMBIA

Ecker, N. Boyd '25 '54 C.976 B.A. L.174 LL.B. (adm. in CO; not adm. in DC) 1250 H St. N.W.‡
Eckert, Ann Marie .... '67 '93 C.118 B.A. L.326 J.D. 1825 T. St., N.W.
Eckert, Douglas E. '66 '93 C&L.893 B.A., J.D. (adm. in AL; not adm. in DC) [Bradley A.R.&W.] (⊙Birm., AL)
*PRACTICE AREAS: International; Litigation; Construction; Governmental Affairs.
Eckert, Paul R. .... '67 '97 C.861 B.A. L.945 J.D. [🄰 Wilmer,C.&P.]

Eckert Seamans Cherin & Mellott, LLC, (AV) [BR]
Suite 700, 1250 24th Street, N.W., 20037 ⊙
Telephone: 202-659-6600 Facsimile: 202-659-6699
Email: escm@escm.com URL: http://www.escm.com
Members of Firm: Edward J. Longosz, II; Edward R. Noonan; George J. Wallace; Michael A. Wiegard. Associate: Emily A. Nack.
General Practice including Alternative Dispute Resolution, Antitrust and Trade Regulations, Appellate, Bankruptcy, Construction, Corporate and Finance, Creditors' Rights, E-Commerce and Information Technology, Education, Employee Benefits/ERISA, Energy, Environmental, Estate Planning and Administration, Government Contracts, Government Relations, Health Care, Immigration, Insurance, Intellectual Property, including Patents, Trademarks, Trade Secrets, Licensing and Copyrights, Intellectual Property Litigation, International Business and Trade, Labor and Employment, Land Use, Litigation, Municipal Law and Municipal Finance, Product Liability, Public Utilities Law, Real Estate, Religious Organizations, Securities, Sports and Entertainment, Taxation, Toxic Tort Litigation, Transportation, Trusts and White Collar Criminal Defense Law.
Pittsburgh, Pennsylvania Office: 44th Floor, 600 Grant Street. Telephone: 412-566-6000. Facsimile: 412-566-6099.
Harrisburg, Pennsylvania Office: 213 Market Street, Eighth Floor. Telephone: 717-237-6000. Facsimile: 717-237-6019.
Philadelphia, Pennsylvania Office: 1515 Market Street, Ninth Floor. Telephone: 215-851-8400. Facsimile: 215-851-8383.
Boston, Massachusetts Office: One International Place, 18th Floor. Telephone: 617-342-6800. Facsimile: 617-342-6899.
Haddonfield, New Jersey Office: 36 Tanner Street, Second Floor. Telephone: 856-427-6240. Facsimile: 856-427-0611.
Morgantown, West Virginia Office: 2400 Cranberry Square. Telephone: 304-594-1000. Facsimile: 304-594-1181.
See Professional Biographies, WASHINGTON, DISTRICT OF COLUMBIA

Eckland, William S. .... '54 '79 C.446 B.A. L.273 J.D. [Sidley A.B.&W.]
Eckstein, Gabriel E. '67 '96 C.381 B.A. L.904 J.D. Coun., American Crop Protection Assoc.
*RESPONSIBILITIES: Environmental Law; Regulatory Law; Antitrust and Trade Regulation; General Corporate.
Edberg, Laurie .... '70 '96 C.66 B.A. L.1009 J.D. [🄰 Arent F.K.P.&K.]
*PRACTICE AREAS: Intellectual Property.
Eddie, Relinda '48 '86 C.999 B.A. L.1162 J.D. Staff Atty., Organization of American States, Inter-American Comm. Human Rights
Edelman, Daniel B., (AV) .... '44 '69 C&L.309 A.B., J.D. [Yablonski,B.&E.]
Edelman, Doreen M. .... '63 '87 C&L.273 B.A., J.D. [🄲 Baker,D.B.&C.]
*PRACTICE AREAS: International Trade; Customs; International Transactions; Corporate; Legislative.
Edelman, Henry D. '48 '74 C.165 B.A. L.188 J.D. (adm. in NY; not adm. in DC) Pres., Federal Agricultural Mortgage Corp.
Edelman, Mira Vayda .... '69 '97 C.367 B.A. L.30 J.D. [🄰 Hughes H.&R.]
*PRACTICE AREAS: Securities Law; Advertising Law; Litigation; Trademark; White Collar Crime.
Edelman, Richard S., (AV) .... '53 '79 C.188 B.S. L.94 J.D. [O'Donnell,S.&A.]
*PRACTICE AREAS: Labor Law; Administrative Law; Transportation Law; Employment Discrimination Law; Federal District Court and Appellate Litigation.
Edelschick, Douglas G. .... '72 '97 C&L.597 B.A., J.D. [🄰 McDermott,W.&E.]
Edelstein, Jan M., (Ms.) .... '49 '75 C.1108 B.A. L.776 J.D. Amer. Intl. Grp., Inc.
Edens, Geraldine E. .... '51 '91 C&L.472 B.S., J.D. [🄲 Cadwalader,W.&T.]
*PRACTICE AREAS: Environmental Law; Litigation.
Eder, Bryan Isaac '75 '01 C.475 B.A. L.145 J.D. (adm. in MD; not adm. in DC) [🄰 Dechert]
*PRACTICE AREAS: Investment Management; Financial Services Law.
Eder, Elliot D. .... '58 '87 C.309 A.B. L.94 J.D. [VanCleve&E.]
Ederington, L. Benjamin .... '70 '96 C.976 B.A. L.309 J.D. [🄰 Steptoe&J.]
Edgar, Charles Ernest, IV ..... '65 '94 C.885 B.S.C.E. L.893 J.D. [🄰 Dickstein S.M.&O.]
*PRACTICE AREAS: Government Contracts; Environmental; Construction.
Edgar, George L., (AV) .... '41 '70 C.197 A.B. L.273 J.D. [Morgan,L.&B.]
Edgar, Jonathan '74 '00 C.674 A.B. L.273 J.D. (adm. in VA; not adm. in DC) [🄰 Patton B.]
Edgar, Kevin R. '71 '99 C.93 B.A. L.201 J.D. Spec. Coun., New York Stock Exchange, Inc.
*RESPONSIBILITIES: Securities.
Edgar, William C. .... '62 '89 C.787 B.A. L.273 J.D. [Bryan C.]
*PRACTICE AREAS: Commercial Litigation; Products Liability.
Edge, Joe D., (AV) .... '48 '73 C.10 B.S. L.16 J.D. [Drinker B.&R.]
*PRACTICE AREAS: Telecommunications Law; Regulatory Law; Antitrust Law.
Edge, William Brian '70 '98 C.574 B.S. L.347 J.D. (adm. in NC; not adm. in DC) [🄰 Sterne,K.G.&F.]
*PRACTICE AREAS: Intellectual Property.
Edgeworth, Arthur B., Jr. ..... '29 '53 C.951 A.B. L.893 LL.B. 1500 K Street, N.W., #500
Edick, William D. .... '66 '94 C&L.30 B.S.B.A., J.D. [🄰 Pickard&D.]
Edidin and LaPlaca, P.C., (AV) .... 1819 H Street, N.W.
Edinger, Brook A. .... '68 '95 C&L.945 B.A., J.D. [🄰 Wiley R.&F.]
Edlavitch, Susan T. .... '48 '76 C.910 B.A. L.1119 J.D. [Venable,A.B.H.&C.]
*PRACTICE AREAS: Federal Taxation Law.
Edles, Gary J. '41 '66 C.994 B.A. L.569 J.D. (adm. in NY; not adm. in DC) Wash. Coll. of Law
Edlund, Taina E. M. .... '58 '85 C.976 B.A. L.276 J.D. [Womble C.S.&R.]
Edmond, John A., (AV) .... '56 '81 C.477 B.A. L.273 J.D. [Guerrieri,E.&C.]
*PRACTICE AREAS: Litigation.
Edmond, Julie M. .... '55 '83 C.976 B.A. L.309 J.D. [Covington&B.]
Edmondson, David J. '62 '92 C.367 B.A. L.477 J.D. (adm. in VA; not adm. in DC; See Pat. Sect.) [🄰 Blank R.C.&M.]
*PRACTICE AREAS: Intellectual Property; Electrical Intellectual Property; Electrical Patent Prosecution; Computer and Software Patent Protection; International Patents.
Edmondson, James W. '57 '88 C.870 B.S. L.276 J.D. [Finnegan,H.F.G.&D.] (See Pat. Sect.)
*PRACTICE AREAS: Intellectual Property Infringement; Intellectual Property Licensing; Intellectual Property Litigation; Mechanical Intellectual Property; Proprietary Rights.
Edmondson, Joseph D., Jr. .... '— '91 C&L.273 B.A., J.D. [Foley&L.]
*PRACTICE AREAS: General Commercial and Securities Litigation; Regulatory Law; Food and Drug Law.
Edmondson, Mary E. '68 '93 C.378 B.A. L.623 J.D. Sr. Coun., Marriott International, Inc.
*RESPONSIBILITIES: Healthcare Operations; Healthcare Regulatory.

Edmondson, Paul W. '55 '81 C.188 A.B. L.30 J.D.
V.P. & Gen. Coun., National Trust for Historic Preservation
Edmunds, Carmela N. ....'63 '92 C.302 B.A. L.228 J.D. [[A] Dickstein S.M.&O.]
*PRACTICE AREAS: Litigation.
Edmundson, Ellen Mandell, (AV) ......'52 '81 C.994 B.A. L.724 J.D. [[C] Smithwick&B.]
*PRACTICE AREAS: Telecommunications Law.
Edmundson, James K., (AV) ....'38 '63 C&L.923 B.A., J.D. [[C] Smithwick&B.]
*PRACTICE AREAS: Telecommunications Law.
Edsall, Michael T. ....'58 '86 C&L.477 B.G.S., J.D. [Kirkland&E.]
*PRACTICE AREAS: Corporate-Mergers and Acquisitions; Venture Capital; Corporate Finance.
Edson, Charles L., (AV) ....'34 '59 C&L.309 A.B., J.D. [Nixon P.]
*PRACTICE AREAS: Affordable Housing; Community Development.
Edwards, Amy L., (AV) ....'53 '78 C.788 A.B. L.273 J.D. [Holland&K.]
*PRACTICE AREAS: Environmental.
Edwards, Bridnetta D. ....'— '91 C.329 B.B.A. L.128 J.D. [[A] Reed S.]
*PRACTICE AREAS: Labor and Employment.
Edwards, Eric '67 '95 C.679 B.A. L.365 J.D.
(adm. in IL; not adm. in DC) Coun., U.S. House Bkg. Committee
Edwards, Gary R. ....'45 '71 C.679 B.S.E.E. L.276 J.D. [Crowell&M.] (Pat.)
*PRACTICE AREAS: Patents; Trademarks; Copyrights; Trade Secrets; Intellectual Property Licensing.
Edwards, Jack ....'28 '54 C&L.16 B.S., J.D. [Hand A.] (⊙Mobile, AL)
Edwards, Jean C. ....'57 '95 C.376 B.S. L.472 J.D. [[C] Sonnenschein N.&R.] (Pat.)
*PRACTICE AREAS: Intellectual Property.
Edwards, Karen M. '58 '88 C&L.329 B.A., J.D.
Dept. of Consumer & Regulatory Affairs
Edwards, Katherine B., (AV) ....'47 '81 C.682 B.A. L.846 J.D. [GKRSE]
*PRACTICE AREAS: Energy Law; Natural Gas Pipelines; Public Utilities Regulation; Administrative Law.
Edwards, Kerry Lynn ....'57 '86 C.1044 B.S. L.276 J.D. [Mayer,B.&P.]
Edwards, Krista L. ....'61 '88 C.589 B.A. L.597 J.D. [Sidley A.B.&W.]
Edwards, Monte R. ....'40 '72 C.446 B.S. L.273 J.D. 1100 H St.‡
Edwards, Robert H., Jr. ....'61 '91 C.309 A.B. L.813 J.D. [[A] Hunton&W.]
*PRACTICE AREAS: Project Finance; Energy Acquisitions; Divestitures.
Edwards, Taylor Vinson '67 '00 C.512 B.S. L.124 J.D.
(adm. in MD; not adm. in DC) [[A] Dechert]
*PRACTICE AREAS: Financial Services Law; Investment Management; Corporate Law.
Edwards, Tony M., (AV) '50 '75 C.401 B.A. L.472 J.D.
Sr. V.P. & Gen. Coun., Natl. Assn. of Real Estate Investment Trust Inc.
Edwards, William D. '15 '40 C&L.813 A.B., LL.B.
(adm. in CA; not adm. in DC) 2700 Virginia Ave., N.W.‡
Edwards & Carstarphen ....1332 E. Capitol St. (⊙Miami, FL)
Edwardson, Eric John ....'69 '95 C&L.893 B.A., J.D. [[A] Kirkpatrick&L.]
*PRACTICE AREAS: Mortgage Banking Law; Financial Institutions Law; Corporate Law; Securities Law; Business Law.
Efron, Marc F., (AV) ....'42 '70 C.197 A.B. L.309 J.D. [Crowell&M.]
*PRACTICE AREAS: Government/Public Contract Law; Litigation; Criminal Law.
Efros, Ellen A., (BV) ....'50 '78 C.930 B.A. L.1019 J.D. [Rader,F.&G.] (Pat.)
*PRACTICE AREAS: Antitrust Law; Federal Civil Litigation; Commercial Litigation; Intellectual Property Litigation.
Efrusy, Michael ....'70 '97 C.259 B.S. L.260 J.D. Gen. Coun., Amer. Secs. Inc.
Egan, Erin M. ....'69 '94 C.966 B.B.A. L.273 J.D. [[A] Covington&B.]
Egan, James C., Jr., (AV) ....'43 '71 C.1111 B.A. L.724 J.D. [Clifford C.R.&W.]
*PRACTICE AREAS: Antitrust; General Litigation.
Egan, Kimberly K. ....'71 '98 C.66 A.B. L.228 J.D. [[A] Covington&B.]
Egan, Leonard ....'41 '66 C&L.309 A.B., LL.B. [[C] Slater&Z.]
*PRACTICE AREAS: Antitrust Law; Litigation; Ship Financing.
Egan, Thomas J., (AV) ....'31 '56 C&L.276 B.S.S., J.D. [Stohlman,B.E.&S.]
Egan, Thomas J., Jr. ....'57 '83 C.893 B.A. L.902 J.D. [Baker&M.]
*PRACTICE AREAS: Mergers and Acquisitions; Securities; Investments; Corporate Law; Partnership Law.

Egan & Associates, PLLC
(See McLean, Virginia)

Ege, Stephen M. ....'43 '73 C&L.145 A.B., J.D. [Elias,M.T.&H.]
Egge, George V., Jr., (AV) ....'37 '62 C.10 B.S. L.276 J.D. [G.V.Egge,Jr.]
Egge, George V., Jr., P.C., (AV) ....Ste. 400, 1825 Eye St., N.W.
Egger, Matt E., (AV) ....'49 '78 C.893 B.S. L.245 J.D. 1775 Pennsylvania Ave., N.W.
Eggers, Susan E. ....'— '95 C.93 B.A. L.339 J.D. [[A] Nixon P.]
*PRACTICE AREAS: Affordable Housing; Real Estate.
Eggert, Benjamin C. ....'74 '00 C&L.893 B.A., J.D. [[A] Ross,D.&B.]
Eggert, David S. ....'60 '84 C.425 B.A. L.228 J.D. [Arnold&P.]
*PRACTICE AREAS: Litigation; Antitrust; Products Liability; Class Actions.
Eggert, Jesse '76 '01 C&L.188 A.B., J.D.
(adm. in VA; not adm. in DC) [[A] Shaw P.]
Eggleston, W. Neil, (AV) ....'53 '79 C.228 A.B. L.597 J.D. [Howrey S.A.&W.]
Ehinger, John A., Jr. '73 '99 C.10 B.A. L.880 J.D.
(adm. in VA; not adm. in DC) 450 5th St. N.W.
Ehlenberger, Mona E. ....'56 '83 C.696 B.A. L.659 J.D. [[C] Skadden,A.S.M.&F.]
Ehrenberg, Daniel S. '58 '93 C.231 B.A. L.976 J.D.
Deputy General Counsel, Neighborhood REinvestment
Ehrenberg, Jason H. ....'74 '00 C.188 B.S. L.477 J.D [[A] Steptoe&J.]
Ehrenhaft, Peter D. ....'33 '58 C&L.178 B.A., LL.B. [Miller&C.]
*PRACTICE AREAS: International Trade Law; Transnational Business Transactions; Licensing Law.
Ehrgood, Thomas A., Jr. '51 '78
C.31 B.A. L.273 J.D. Inter. Trade Coun., Compaq Computer Corp.
Ehrig, Lenore G. ....'24 '51 C.273 L.537 J.D. 3017 Cleveland Ave., N.W.
Ehrlich, Andrew L. ....'63 '88 C.420 B.S. L.425 J.D. 1919 Pennsylvania Ave. N.W.
Ehrlich, Mark B. ...'69 '95 C.477 B.S.E. L.309 J.D. Assoc. Legal Coun., WorldCom, Inc.
Ehrlich, Marvin W. ....'— '92 C.705 B.A. L.30 J.D. [[A] Andrews&K.]
*PRACTICE AREAS: Commercial Mortgage Finance; Secured Lending; Mortgage Loans; Workouts; Foreclosures.
Ehrlich, Stacy L. ....'68 '94 C.1365 B.A. L.309 J.D. [[A] Kleinfeld,K.&B.]
*PRACTICE AREAS: Food, Drug and Cosmetic Law; Food and Drug Regulation; Drug and Medical Device Regulation; Advertising Law; Federal Civil Litigation.
Ehrman, Christopher C. ....'66 '93 C.473 B.A. L.383 J.D. 2445 M St., N.W.
Eichberg, Ross E. ....'59 '85 C.228 B.A. L.893 J.D. [Patton B.]
Eichelburg, Robert J., (AV) '35 '63
C.262 B.S. L.273 J.D. [[C] Finnegan,H.F.G.&D.] (See Pat. Sect.)
*PRACTICE AREAS: Chemical Patent Prosecution; Coatings Technology; Inorganic Chemistry; Organic Chemistry; Polymers.
Eichenberg, Timothy K. ...'46 '74 C.231 B.A. L.910 J.D. Coun., Ctr. for Marine Conserv.
Eichenberger, John C. ....'62 '90 C.1044 B.A. L.276 J.D. [[C] Shaw P.]
Eichinger, Katja M. ....'66 '97 C.1032 B.A. L.862 J.D. U.S. Dept. of Justice, Tax Division
Eichner, Richard A. ....'53 '80 C.188 B.A. L.893 J.D. [Ritter E.&N.]
*PRACTICE AREAS: Public Finance Law; Federal Income Taxation; Housing.
Eide, Peter J. '52 '86 C.259 B.A. L.446 J.D.
(adm. in MD; not adm. in DC) Mgr., Labor Law Policy, U.S. Chamber of Com.
Eidson, Walter J., Jr. ....'54 '86 C.276 B.S. L.273 J.D. [[C] McKenna&C.]
*PRACTICE AREAS: Information Technology; Licensing; Corporate; Commercial; International.
Eig, Jason R. ....'72 '99 C&L.276 B.A.S., J.D. [[A] Dickstein S.M.&O.]
*PRACTICE AREAS: Corporate; Mergers and Acquisitions; Securities.

Eig, Michael J., and Associates, P.C.
(See Chevy Chase, Maryland)

Eilbott, Eli D. ....'61 '87 C.659 B.A. L.30 J.D. [[C] Duncan,W.G.&P.] (Pat.)
*PRACTICE AREAS: Intellectual Property; Patents; Trademarks; Energy; Public Utility Law.
Eilperin, Stephen F. ....'37 '63 C&L.178 B.A., LL.B. J., Supr. Ct. of D.C.
Einaudi, Carol P., (AV) '37 '85
C.783 B.S. L.273 J.D. [Finnegan,H.F.G.&D.] (See Pat. Sect.)
*PRACTICE AREAS: Patent Prosecution.
Eisen, Bruce Alan, (AV) ....'44 '70 C.823 A.B. L.904 J.D. [[C] Kaye S.]
*PRACTICE AREAS: Communication Law; Telecommunications Law; Internet Law.
Eisen, Charles Lee, (AV) ....'— '67 C.674 B.A. L.976 LL.B. [Kirkpatrick&L.]
*PRACTICE AREAS: Complex Litigation; Federal Civil Litigation; Trial Practice; Securities Fraud; Arbitration.
Eisen, Norman L. ....'60 '91 C.103 A.B. L.309 J.D. [Zuckerman S.]
*PRACTICE AREAS: Civil (General Civil) Practice; White Collar Criminal Defense.
Eisen, Richard C., (AV) ....'50 '80 C.597 B.A. L.128 J.D. [Eisen&R.]
Eisen & Rome, P.C., (AV) ....1 Thomas Circle, N.W.
Eisenberg, Elisa A. '65 '91 C&L.861 B.A., J.D.
[[A] Jackson&C.] (⊙Balt., Rockville, MD)
*PRACTICE AREAS: Insurance Coverage Litigation; Litigation.
Eisenberg, Henry C. ....'59 '85 C.918 B.A. L.309 J.D. [[C] Skadden,A.S.M.&F.]
Eisenberg, Maureen ....'64 '89 C.339 B.S. L.273 J.D. National Assn. of Sec. Dealers, Inc.
Eisenberg, Milton, (P.C.), (AV) ....'28 '50 C&L.188 B.A., J.D. [[C] Fried,F.H.S.&J.]
Eisenberg, Ruth E., (AV) ....'53 '80 C.910 A.B. L.734 J.D. [Harmon,C.S.&E.]
Eisenbud, Robert E. ......'— '72 C.903 B.A. L.273 J.D. Dir. of Legis. Affs., Waste Mgmt.
Eisenhart, Frank J., (AV) ....'45 '72 C.93 B.S. L.831 J.D. [Dechert]
*PRACTICE AREAS: Securities Litigation; Commercial Litigation; Product Liability Litigation.
Eisenhaure, Jessica L. ....'70 '98 C.311 B.A. L.276 J.D. [[A] Gardner,C.&D.]
*PRACTICE AREAS: Health Transactions; Health Reimbursement; Health Regulation; Health Fraud; Health Abuse.
Eisenmann, James M. ....'64 '91 C.923 B.A. L.180 J.D. [Passman&K.]
*PRACTICE AREAS: Employment Law; Federal Civil Service; Equal Employment Opportunity Law; Labor Law; Security Clearances.
Eisenstat, David H., (BV) ....'51 '76 C.659 B.A. L.823 J.D. [Akin,G.S.H.&F.]
*PRACTICE AREAS: Health Care.
Eisenstat, Larry F., (AV) ....'53 '85 C&L.145 B.A., J.D. [Dickstein S.M.&O.]
*PRACTICE AREAS: Energy; Utilities; Litigation; Antitrust; Eminent Domain.
Eisenstein, Jeffrey N., (AV) '48 '75 C.188 B.S. L.818 J.D.
(adm. in MA; not adm. in DC) [Perkins C.]
*PRACTICE AREAS: Government Contracts Law.
Eisenstein, Laurence J., (AV) ....'60 '85 C&L.309 B.A., J.D. [Swidler B.S.F.]
*PRACTICE AREAS: Insurance Coverage; Litigation.
Eisgrau, Adam M. ....'58 '85 C.197 B.A. L.309 J.D. Legis. Asst.
Eizenstat, Jay L. '70 '98 C.823 B.A. L.1365 J.D.
(adm. in GA; not adm. in DC) [[A] Patton B.]
Ekman, John C. '70 '97 C.604 B.A. L.966 J.D.
(adm. in WI; not adm. in DC) [[A] Goodwin P.]
Elam, Mark R. '53 '80 C&L.790 B.A., J.D.
(adm. in SC; not adm. in DC)
C.O.O. & Exec. V.P., Govt. Rel., Amer. Council of Life Ins.
Elardo, Donald J., (AV) '42 '69 C.62 B.A. L.1003 J.D.
Asst. Regulatory Coun., MCI Telecommunications Corp. (Regulatory Affairs)
Elbaor, David W., (AV) ......'46 '71 C.339 A.B. L.893 J.D. 1133 Connecticut Ave., N.W.
Elberfeld, Donald N. '26 '51 C.674 A.B. L.309 LL.B.
(adm. in NY; not adm. in DC) 1818 H St., N.W.‡
Elcano, Mary S. ....'49 '76 C.428 B.A. L.180 J.D. [Sidley A.B.&W.]
Elder, Albert L., III '51 '74 C.789 B.S. L.273 J.D.
(adm. in PA; not adm. in DC) Coun., America's Community Bkrs.
Elder, William L. ....'58 '97 C.871 B.S. L.276 J.D. [[A] Hogan&H.]
*PRACTICE AREAS: Administrative Agency Practice; Aviation Law; Aviation Regulation; Hazardous Materials Transportation.
El Dorrado, Felicia R. '59 '90 C.911 B.A. L.1066 J.D.
(adm. in CA; not adm. in DC) Howard Univ. Law Sch.
Eldred, John S., (AV) ....'45 '69 C.880 B.A. L.383 J.D. [Keller&H.]
*PRACTICE AREAS: Food and Drug Law; Trade Regulation Law; Litigation.
Eldred, Nina R. ....'54 '83 C.105 B.S. L.128 J.D. Asst. Gen. Coun., Marriott Intl., Inc.
*RESPONSIBILITIES: Commercial Real Estate; Transactional; Franchise.
Eleftheriou, Demetrios ....'70 '00 C.476 B.A. L.446 J.D. [[A] Willkie F.&G.]
Eley, Claud v. S. ....'57 '82 C.945 B.A. L.245 J.D. [Hogan&H.]
*PRACTICE AREAS: Commercial Law; Contracts; Corporate Law; International Corporate Law; International Law.
Elgarten, Clifton S. ....'50 '80 C.563 B.A. L.978 J.D. [Crowell&M.]
Elgin, Arthur C., Jr., (AV) '38 '66
C.674 B.S.E. L.273 J.D. [Jackson&C.] (⊙Balt., Rockville, MD)
*PRACTICE AREAS: Business Law; Corporate Law; Civil Litigation; Family Wealth Transfer; Estate Administration.
El Guindi-Rosenbaum, Magda ....'— '96 C.788 B.A. L.597 J.D. [[A] Morgan,L.&B.]
Elhassan, Khalid A. '73 '00 C.1209 B.A. L.893 J.D.
(adm. in VA; not adm. in DC) 1530 P St., N.W.
Elias, Jack I., (AV) ....'18 '50 C.1138 B.B.A. L.273 LL.B. [[C] Elias,M.T.&H.]
Elias, Marc E. ....'69 '93 C.299 A.B. L.228 J.D. [[A] Perkins C.]
*PRACTICE AREAS: White Collar Criminal Defense; Election and Campaign Finance; Election Law; Administrative Litigation.

Elias, Matz, Tiernan & Herrick L.L.P., (AV)
12th Floor The Walker Building, 734 15th Street, N.W., 20005
Telephone: 202-347-0300 Fax: 202-347-2172
URL: http://www.emth.com
Members of Firm: Timothy B. Matz; Stephen M. Ege; Raymond A. Tiernan; Gerard L. Hawkins; John P. Soukenik, Jr. (Not admitted in DC); Gerald F. Heupel, Jr.; Jeffrey A. Koeppel; Philip R. Bevan; Hugh T. Wilkinson; Kevin M. Houlihan; Kenneth B. Tabach;—Patricia J. Wohl; David Teeples; Eric M. Marion. Special Counsel: W. Michael Herrick. Of Counsel: Allin P. Baxter; Jack I. Elias; Sheryl Jones Alu.
Banking, Thrift Institution, Securities, Corporate, Taxation Law. Administrative Practice before Federal Agencies.
See Professional Biographies, WASHINGTON, DISTRICT OF COLUMBIA

Eliason, Randall D., (AV) ....'61 '85 C.585 B.A. L.309 J.D. Asst. U.S. Atty.
Elitzur, Ofer '73 '00 C.112 B.A. L.309 J.D.
(adm. in CA; not adm. in DC) [[A] Swidler B.S.F.]
*PRACTICE AREAS: Corporate; Securities.
Elkin, Molly Ann ....'68 '93 C.966 B.A. L.273 J.D. [Woodley,G.&M.]
*PRACTICE AREAS: Public Sector Labor Relations; Employment Discrimination; Fair Labor Standards Law.
Elkind, David L., (BV) ....'57 '84 C.273 B.A. L.276 J.D. [Dickstein S.M.&O.]
*PRACTICE AREAS: Insurance Litigation; Commercial Litigation.
Ell, Douglas W., (AV) ....'49 '79 C.453 B.A. L.184 J.D. [Groom]
*PRACTICE AREAS: Labor and Employment; Insurance Defense; Mergers and Acquisitions; Tax; Employee Benefits.
Ellard, George '48 '84 C.262 B.A. L.976 J.D.
Chief Counsel to US Senator Joseph Biden

Ellenberg, Mark C., (AV) ....'50 '75 C.188 B.S. L.276 J.D. [Cadwalader,W.&T.]
*PRACTICE AREAS: Insolvency; Complex Litigation.
Ellenbogen, David H. '76 '01 C.273 B.A. L.910 J.D.
(adm. in MO; not adm. in DC) Atty./Advisor, J. John F. Dean, U.S. Tax Court
Ellentuck, Albert B. ...... '32 '56 C.569 B.S. L.309 LL.B. [© King&N.] (©Arlington, VA)
*PRACTICE AREAS: Taxation; Tax Planning; Trusts and Estates.
Ellentuck, Robert P. '66 '91 C.183 B.A. L.904 J.D.
(adm. in PA; not adm. in DC) Gen. Coun., Aviation Facilities Co., Inc.
Eller, Jennifer E. '71 '00 L.276 J.D.
(adm. in MD; not adm. in DC) [A Groom]
*PRACTICE AREAS: Employee Benefits.
Ellerman, Whitney C. .... '61 '88 C&L.893 B.A., J.D. [Janis,S.&W.]
*PRACTICE AREAS: White Collar Criminal Defense.
Ellett, E. Tazewell, (AV) .... '52 '77 C.198 B.A. L.893 J.D. [Hogan&H.]
*PRACTICE AREAS: Aeronautical Regulation; Aerospace Law; Airline Regulation; Airport Law; Airport Privatization.
Ellickson, Dale R. '47 '76 C.494 B.A. L.51 J.D.
(adm. in GA; not adm. in DC) President & Counsel, Ellickson & Associates
Ellicott, John L., (AV) .... '29 '54 C.674 A.B. L.309 LL.B. [© Covington&B.]
Elliot, Thomas A., (AV) ....'49 '74 C.860 B.A. L.930 J.D. [Elliot&M.]
Elliot & Mayock, LLP, (AV) ....1629 K Street, Twelfth Floor (©San Fran., CA)
Elliott, E. Donald ....'48 '75 C&L.976 B.A., J.D. [Paul,H.J.&W.]
*PRACTICE AREAS: International Environmental Law; Clean Air Act; Toxic Torts; Resource Conservation and Recovery Act; National Environmental Policy Act.
Elliott, Glenn Frederick, Jr. '73 '01 C.659 B.S. L.276 J.D.
(adm. in VA; not adm. in DC) [A Baker B.]
Elliott, James D. ....'67 '96 C.105 B.A. L.1040 J.D. [A Hunton&W.]
*PRACTICE AREAS: Environmental; Litigation; Energy.
Elliott, Randolph Lee .... '57 '83 C.453 S.B. L.309 J.D. [Miller,B.&O.]
*PRACTICE AREAS: Energy Law; Antitrust; Judicial Review.
Elliott, Richard S. .... '55 '81 C.855 B.A. L.178 J.D. [© Paul,W.R.W.&G.]
*PRACTICE AREAS: International Trade; International Investment; International Finance; Intellectual Property.
Elliott, Robert J., (AV) .... '34 '61 C.999 A.B. L.276 J.D. [© Hogan&H.]
*PRACTICE AREAS: Real Estate; Business Law.
Elliott, Warren G., (AV) .... '27 '52 C.174 A.B. L.477 LL.B. [© Nossaman,G.K.&E.]
*PRACTICE AREAS: Government Relations.
Ellis, Allison M. .... '70 '96 C.260 B.A. L.424 J.D. [A Birch,H.B.&C.]
*PRACTICE AREAS: Litigation; Telecommunications; Corporate; Lobbying; Child Advocacy.
Ellis, Brian F. '69 '00 C.999 B.A. L.986 J.D.
(adm. in MO; not adm. in DC) [A Copilevitz&C.] ©
*PRACTICE AREAS: Nonprofit Organizations Law; Charitable Trusts and Foundations; Telemarketing Law; Administrative Agency Practice.
Ellis, Courtenay, (AV) .... '46 '73 C.051 B.A. L.273 LL.M. [Murphy E.W.]
*PRACTICE AREAS: International Business Law; Litigation; Administrative Law; Government Relations.
Ellis, James B., II, (AV) .... '44 '73 C.869 B.S. L.273 J.D. [Dyer E.&J.]
*PRACTICE AREAS: Maritime Law; Maritime Finance; Corporate Finance.
Ellis, Keith H. ....'50 '76 C.273 B.A. L.904 J.D. [Duane,M.&H.]
*PRACTICE AREAS: Financial Institutions; Administrative Law; Corporate Law.
Ellis, Lee T., Jr., (AV) ....'45 '70 C.838 B.A. L.276 J.D. [Baker&H.]
*PRACTICE AREAS: Litigation.
Ellis, Neil R. .... '55 '81 C.188 A.B. L.976 J.D. [Powell,G.F.&M.]
*PRACTICE AREAS: International Trade Regulation; Antitrust.
Ellis, Pamela K. ....'63 '88 C.914 B.A. L.880 J.D. [A Sutherland A.&B.]
*PRACTICE AREAS: Securities Regulation; Securities Registration; Securities Disclosure; Mutual Funds.
Ellis, Valerie ....'68 '01 C.30 M.P.A. L.861 J.D. [A Cameron&H.]
*PRACTICE AREAS: International Trade; International Business Law.
Ellis, Van W. .... '69 '94 C&L.228 A.B., J.D. [© Wilmer,C.&P.]
Ellis, William T. .... '— '75 C.339 B.S.E.E. L.128 J.D. [Foley&L.] (See Pat. Sect.)
*PRACTICE AREAS: Electronics; Patents; Computer Law; E-commerce; Contracts.
Ellison, Dawn A. '71 '98 C.645 B.A. L.575 J.D.
(adm. in NC; not adm. in DC) [A Howrey S.A.&W.]
*PRACTICE AREAS: Commercial Law; Insurance Coverage.
Ellison, Jennifer S. .... '71 '96 C.188 B.S. L.276 J.D. 409 3rd St., SW
Ellison, Mark C. '50 '78 C&L.472 B.A., J.D.
(adm. in GA; not adm. in DC) [© Maloney&K.] (©Burke, VA)
Ellrod, Frederick E., III ....'53 '86 C.128 B.A. L.309 J.D. [Miller&V.]
*PRACTICE AREAS: Cable Franchising; Local Government Law; Municipal Leasing; Municipal Utility Regulation; Telephone Utilities.
Ellsworth, Cheryl, (AV) .... '55 '81 C.239 B.A. L.107 J.D. [Harris E.&L.]
*PRACTICE AREAS: Customs Law; International Trade Regulation; Unfair Competition; Antitrust Law; Legislative Practice.
Elman, Stephan A. .... '48 '73 C.477 B.A. L.339 J.D. D.C. Supr Ct.
Elmer, Brian C., (AV) ....'36 '63 C.188 A.B. L.477 J.D. [Crowell&M.]
Elmi, Salman H. ....'— '00 C.477 B.A. L.245 J.D. [A Morgan,L.&B.]
Elmont, David L. '68 '98 C.101 B.A. L.178 J.D.
(adm. in MD; not adm. in DC) [A Milbank,T.H.&M.]
Elrod, Eugene R., (AV) .... '49 '74 C.197 A.B. L.245 J.D. [Sidley A.B.&W.]
Elsbernd, Brian .... '64 '97 C.339 B.A. L.734 J.D. [A Proskauer R.]
Elsberry, Knight ....'— '97 C.145 B.A. L.477 J.D. [A Wilmer,C.&P.]
Elsea, Erik H. ....'72 '98 C.210 B.A. L.880 J.D. [A Skadden,A.S.M.&F.]
*PRACTICE AREAS: Corporate Law (45%); Mergers and Acquisitions.
Elwell, William C. '72 '01 C.101 B.A. L.276 J.D.
(adm. in MD; not adm. in DC) [A Miller&C.]
*PRACTICE AREAS: Corporate Taxation; Technology and Science; International Taxation; Federal Tax Controversies; Exempt Organizations.
Elwood, William E. ....'43 '69 C.645 B.S. L.659 J.D. [Dickinson W.]
*PRACTICE AREAS: Taxation Law; Partnerships; Corporate Law; Communications Law.
Ely, Clausen, Jr., (AV) ....'45 '73 C.332 B.A. L.16 J.D. [Covington&B.]
Embrey, Diana L. ....'69 '96 C.446 B.A. L.309 J.D. [A Paul,H.J.&W.]
Emch, Melinda L. '71 '00 C&L.190 B.A., J.D.
(adm. in CO; not adm. in DC) [A Counts,P.-D.&D.]
Emden, Craig A. ....'55 '80 C.472 B.S. L.273 J.D. [Venable,A.B.H.&C.]
*PRACTICE AREAS: Taxation Law; Affordable Housing; Real Estate.
Emeka, Uzoamaka S. ....'75 '00 C.597 B.S. L.569 J.D. [A Patton B.]
Emerson, Eric C. ....'64 '91 C.352 B.A. L.893 J.D. [Steptoe&J.]
*PRACTICE AREAS: International Business Law; International Law.
Emery, N. Beth ....'52 '77 C.623 B.A. L.309 J.D. [Ballard S.A.&I.]
*PRACTICE AREAS: Energy Finance; Energy Project Development; Business Law; Finance.
Emge, Kirk J. '49 '74 C.367 B.A. L.446 J.D.
(adm. in MD; not adm. in DC) Dep. Gen. Coun., Potomac Electric Power Company
Emigholz, Kirsten '49 '83 C.823 B.A. L.705 J.D.
(adm. in NJ; not adm. in DC) [A Cahill G.&R.] ©
Emley, Sara E. ....'67 '93 C.477 B.A. L.228 J.D. [© Wilmer,C.&P.]
*PRACTICE AREAS: Securities Law; Investment Management; Broker-Dealer Regulation.
Emmer, Matthew D. .... '62 '88 C.1365 B.A. L.94 J.D. [Fleischman&W.]
Emmert, Steven M. '57 '82 C&L.608 B.A., J.D.
(adm. in OH; not adm. in DC) Reed Elsevier, Inc.
Emmott, Erin Weber ....'74 '99 C.692 B.A. L.588 J.D. [A Kelley D.&W.]
*PRACTICE AREAS: Telecommunications.

Emnett, William M. ....'71 '98 C.1142 B.A. L.276 J.D. [A Skadden,A.S.M.&F.]
Emord, Jonathan W., (AV) ....'61 '85 C.339 B.A. L.209 J.D. [Emord&Assoc.] ©
*PRACTICE AREAS: Constitutional Law; Food and Drug Law; False Advertising Law; General Civil Litigation; Libel Law.

Emord & Associates, P.C., (AV)
1050 Seventeenth Street, N.W. Suite 600, 20036 ©
Telephone: 202-466-6937 Fax: 202-466-6938 URL: http://www.emord.com
Email: emordal1@erols.com URL: http://www.lawyers.com/emordlaw
Jonathan W. Emord;—Claudia A. Lewis-Eng (Not admitted in DC); Andrea Gallimore Ferrenz; Christopher Brown (Not admitted in DC). Of Counsel: L. Sue Anderson.
Constitutional Law, Food and Drug Law, False Advertising Law, General Civil Litigation, First Amendment Law, Libel Law, Administrative Law, Communications Law, and Corporate Law.
Burke, Virginia Office: Burke Professional Center, 5282 Lyngate Court. Telephone: 202-466-6937.
See Professional Biographies, WASHINGTON, DISTRICT OF COLUMBIA

Employment Law Group, PLLC
1850 M Street NW, Suite 920, 20036-5832
Telephone: 202-331-3911 Fax: 202-261-2835
Email: inquiry@employmentlawgroup.net URL: http://www.lawyers.com/employmentlawgroup
R. Scott Oswald;—Kenneth H. Fails, II (Not admitted in DC). Of Counsel: David H. Martin.
Labor and Employment, Discrimination, Harassment, Wrongful Termination Defense, Personnel Policies, Executive Compensation, Wage and Hour Law, Retirement Benefit Plans, Americans with Disabilities Act, Breach of Contract, Employment Claims, Age Discrimination, Sexual Harassment.
See Professional Biographies, WASHINGTON, DISTRICT OF COLUMBIA

Ende, Asher H. .... '14 '38 C.102 B.A. L.1009 LL.B. 1615 M St., N.W.
Ende, Neil S., (AV) .... '56 '80 C.696 B.A. L.93 J.D. [Technology]
*PRACTICE AREAS: Communication Law; Civil Litigation.
Endick, Jeffrey S., (AV) .... '57 '82 C.1044 B.A. L.188 J.D. [Slevin&H.]
*PRACTICE AREAS: Employee Benefits.
Endres, Barbara Jean ....'66 '92 C.1350 B.A. L.945 J.D. [A Sidley A.B.&W.]
Endreson, Douglas B. L. ....'53 '78 C.164 B.A. L.966 J.D. [Sonosky,C.S.E.&P.]
Enemark, Christine E. ....'69 '97 C.659 B.A. L.178 J.D. [A Covington&B.]
Enferadi, Kimberly Knight ....'56 '96 C.273 B.A. L.1206 J.D. Vet. Appeals Brd.
Eng, Vincent A. '70 '95 C.1036 B.A. L.30 J.D.
(adm. in MD; not adm. in DC) 1140 Connecticut Ave., Suite 1200
Engel, Charles J. (Tim), III ....'55 '81 C.276 B.A. L.823 J.D. [Howrey S.A.&W.]
*PRACTICE AREAS: Antitrust; Complex Litigation; Energy.
Engel, David ....'44 '68 C.331 A.B. L.705 LL.B. 3731 Northampton St., N.W.
Engel, Diana R., (AV) .... '37 '84 C.66 A.B. L.276 J.D. [Liotta,D.&E.]
*PRACTICE AREAS: Family Law; Wills; Estates; Probate; Mediation.
Engel, Harold J. .... '43 '69 C.446 L.329 J.D. [Arent F.K.P.&K.]
*PRACTICE AREAS: OSHA; MSHA; Toxic Torts; Labor.
Engel, John, (P.C.), (AV) ....'43 '71 C.976 B.A. L.276 J.D. [Shaw P.]
*PRACTICE AREAS: Commercial Real Estate.
Engel, John M. .... '63 '92 C.128 B.A. L.276 J.D. [Foxkiser]
*PRACTICE AREAS: Biotechnology; Food and Drug Regulation; Intellectual Property.
Engel, Kirsten '61 '86 C.103 B.A. L.597 J.D.
(adm. in IL; not adm. in DC) Sierra Club of D.C.
Engel, Michael C. '69 '00 C.804 B.S. L.128 J.D.
(adm. in NY; not adm. in DC) [A Kelley D.&W.]
*PRACTICE AREAS: Telecommunications.
Engel, Tala, (AV) ....'33 '57 C&L.472 B.A., J.D. 2800 Quebec St., N.W.
Engelhardt, David L. ....'62 '89 C.105 B.A. L.276 J.D. [Dickstein S.M.&O.]
*PRACTICE AREAS: Complex Civil Litigation; Energy; Construction; Insurance Coverage; Administrative Law.
Engelstein, Larry, (AV) .... '54 '83 C.966 B.S. L.597 J.D. 815 16th St. N.W.
Engh, Anna ....'— '89 C.198 B.A. L.945 J.D. [Covington&B.]
Engle, Craig M. '60 '86 C.150 B.A. L.276 J.D.
(adm. in OH; not adm. in DC) [A Arent F.K.P.&K.]
*PRACTICE AREAS: Government Relations; Election Law; Public Affairs.
Engle, James W. ....'60 '86 C&L.1209 B.A., J.D. Sen. Coun.
Engledow, Wells .... '73 '00 C.1369 B.S. L.276 J.D. [A Orrick,H.&S.]
Engleman, Michael R., (BV) '61 '88 C&L.421 B.S., J.D.
(adm. in KY; not adm. in DC) [© Dickstein S.M.&O.]
*PRACTICE AREAS: Energy Law; Litigation.
Englert, Roy T., Jr., (AV) .... '58 '81 C.674 A.B. L.309 J.D. [Robbins,R.E.O.&U.]
English, A. Scott '71 '99 C.902 B.A. L.923 J.D.
(adm. in VA; not adm. in DC) [S Fulbright&J.]
*PRACTICE AREAS: Litigation; Administrative; Oil and Gas.
English, Anne M. '60 '88 C.611 B.A. L.477 J.D.
(adm. in CO; not adm. in DC) Assoc. Gen. Coun., Fannie Mae
*RESPONSIBILITIES: Employment Litigation; Employment Law Counseling; Commercial Litigation.
English, Caroline T. ....'70 '96 C.207 B.A. L.273 J.D. [A Arent F.K.P.&K.]
*PRACTICE AREAS: Civil Litigation; Criminal Litigation.
English, Charles M., Jr., (AV) .... '59 '84 C&L.893 B.S., J.D. [Thelen R.&P.]
*PRACTICE AREAS: Government Affairs.
English, D. Joseph '63 '98 C.871 B.S.M.E. L.128 J.D.
(adm. in VA; not adm. in DC; Pat.) [© Carter,L.&M.]
*PRACTICE AREAS: Intellectual Property; Litigation.
English, Donald E., Jr. ....'— '00 C.1070 B.S. L.273 J.D. [A Morgan,L.&B.]
English, Elaine Patton ....'49 '83 C.683 A.B. L.273 J.D. [Graybill&E.]
English, Julia Dryden ....'59 '89 C.893 B.A. L.276 J.D. [© Dewey B.]
*PRACTICE AREAS: Energy Regulation.
Englund, Lara A. .... '70 '96 C.945 B.A. L.145 J.D. [A Wilmer,C.&P.]
Engman, Patricia Hanahan '42 '69
C.163 A.B. L.260 J.D. Exec. Dir., The Business Roundtable
Ennis, Gail Susan .... '62 '98 C.575 B.S. L.1009 J.D. [A Wilmer,C.&P.]
Ennis, James G., (AV) ....'47 '77 C.197 A.B. L.276 J.D. [A Steptoe&J.]
Enright, Donald J. '71 '96 C.222 B.A. L.273 J.D.
(adm. in MD; not adm. in DC) [A Finkelstein,T.&L.]
Enright, Maureen ....'59 '88 C.262 B.A. L.893 J.D. [© Collier S.S.]
*PRACTICE AREAS: Trade Regulation.
Enslein, Peter T. ....'53 '79 C.124 B.A. L.1003 J.D. [Sutter&E.]
Enslen, Alan F. ....'— '97 C.10 B.S. L.16 J.D. [A King&S.]
*PRACTICE AREAS: International Transportation Law; International Business; Dispute Resolution.
Ensor, Richard F. '72 '98 C.1356 B.S. L.945 J.D.
(adm. in VA; not adm. in DC) [A Venable,A.B.H.&C.]
*PRACTICE AREAS: Government Contracts; Construction Law; Commercial Litigation.

Enterprise Business Law Group LLC
(See McLean, Virginia)

Entezari, Shirin O., & Associates ....'— '77 L.146 J.D. 1250 24th St., NW
Entwistle & Cappucci LLP
1735 New York Avenue, NW (©Tallahassee, FL; Chgo., IL; Princeton, NJ; New York, NY; Austin, TX)
Enzinna, James B. '61 '94 C.107 B.A. L.1209 J.D.
(adm. in VA; not adm. in DC) National Geographic T.V.
Enzinna, Paul F., (AV) ....'58 '89 C.262 B.A. L.893 J.D. [Baker B.]
Epifani, Lisa E. ....'71 '97 C.846 B.A. L.976 J.D. [A Dewey B.]
*PRACTICE AREAS: Energy Law.

Eppard, Julia K. .... '70 '98 C.1369 B.A. L.273 J.D. [Ⓐ Willkie F.&G.]
Epps Edwards, Marsha .... '51 '83 C.1204 B.S. L.329 J.D. 7306 Georgia Ave., N.W.
Epstein, Amy L. .... '58 '84 C&L.446 B.A., J.D. 1101 17th St., NW
Epstein, Anthony C., (AV) .... '52 '78 C&L.976 B.A., J.D. [Steptoe&J.]
*PRACTICE AREAS: Antitrust; Telecommunications; Litigation.
Epstein, Bart S. .... '— '99 C.1349 B.A. L.893 J.D. [Ⓐ Latham&W.]
*PRACTICE AREAS: Computer Law; Communications Law; Internet Law; Electronic Commerce; Business Law.
Epstein, Carol Paskin .... '57 '82 C.597 B.A. L.904 J.D. Asst. Corp. Coun.
Epstein, David, (AV) .... '— '60 C&L.309 A.B., J.D. [Feith&Z.] (⊙Jerusalem, Israel)
Epstein, Edwin N. .... '15 '46 C&L.569 B.S., LL.B. 1227 25th St., NW
Epstein, Elliot S. '26 '51 C&L.339 Ph.B., J.D.
(adm. in IL; not adm. in DC) 1403 28th St. NW
Epstein, Gary M., (AV) .... '— '71 C.401 B.S.E.E. L.309 J.D. [Latham&W.]
*PRACTICE AREAS: Administrative Law; Communications and Media; Corporate Law; Intellectual Property; Technology and Science.
Epstein, Jennifer O. .... '70 '97 C.352 B.B.A. L.178 J.D. [Ⓐ Dechert]
*PRACTICE AREAS: Investment Management; Financial Services Law; Securities Regulation.
Epstein, Jenny E. .... '66 '94 C.882 B.A. L.818 J.D. P.O. Box 53224
Epstein, Jerome L. .... '61 '86 C&L.659 B.S., J.D. [Jenner&B.]
*PRACTICE AREAS: Civil Litigation; Telecommunications Law.
Epstein, Jodi H. .... '66 '93 C.813 B.A. L.309 J.D. [Ivins,P.&B.]
*PRACTICE AREAS: Employee Benefits.
Epstein, Jonathan M. .... '63 '95 C.299 B.A. L.276 J.D. [Ⓐ Holland&K.]
*PRACTICE AREAS: Telecommunications Law; Space Law; International Law; Export Compliance.
Epstein, Nicole A. '73 '99 C.228 B.A. L.477 J.D.
(adm. in NC; not adm. in DC) [Ⓐ Skadden,A.S.M.&F.]
Epstein, Richard D. '50 '77 C.800 B.A. L.1066 J.D.
(adm. in CA; not adm. in DC) Assoc. Technology Coun., MCI WorldCom
Epstein, Ross A. '61 '87 C.674 A.B. L.94 J.D.
(adm. in CA; not adm. in DC) [Nath&Assoc.]
*PRACTICE AREAS: Corporate Law; Business Transactions; Intellectual Property; Business Formation; Real Estate.
Epstein, Ruth S., (AV) .... '52 '79 C.188 B.A. L.309 J.D. [Dechert]
*PRACTICE AREAS: Financial Services Law; Investment Management.
Epstein, Steven B., (AV) .... '43 '69 C.860 B.A. L.178 LL.B. [Epstein B.&G.]
*PRACTICE AREAS: Health Law; Strategic Alliances; Mergers and Acquisitions; Venture Capital Law.

Epstein Becker & Green, P.C., (AV)
1227 25th Street, N.W., Suite 700, 20037 ⊙
Telephone: 202-861-0900 Facsimile: 202-296-2882
Email: mail@ebglaw.com URL: http://www.ebglaw.com
Members of the Firm: Daniel B. Abrahams; Clifford E. Barnes; John W. Campbell; Joyce A. Cowan; Steven B. Epstein; Raymond Fioravanti; Stuart M. Gerson; Brian D. Gradle; Carolyn Doppelt Gray; Marcia S. Handler; Douglas A. Hastings; Jean Marie Jones; Ann Leopold Kaplan; Mark E. Lutes; David E. Manoogian; David A. Matyas; Frank C. Morris, Jr.; John M. Murdock; Robert D. Reif; Lynn Shapiro Snyder; David B. Tatge; Daly D. E. Temchine; Carrie Valiant; Kenneth B. Weckstein. Senior Counsel: William G. Kopit; Helen E. Quick. Of Counsel: Cathie A. Shattuck; Kathleen M. Williams. Special Counsel: Cara C. Bachenheimer; Lee Calligaro. Senior Associate: Brian W. Steinbach. Associates: Kirsten Backstrom; Janine Schollnick Benton; Michael R. Bissegger; George B. Breen; William C. Burgess (Not admitted in DC); Andrea R. Calem; Ryan M. Faden (Not admitted in DC); Robert B. Fox; Karen Russell Gally; Alicia M. Hawkins (Not admitted in DC); Tina Batra Hershey; Tammy Hopkins; Robert J. Hudock (Not admitted in DC); Teresa L. Jakubowski; JoAnna Jesperson; Shlomo D. Katz; Kimberly S. Keith (Not admitted in DC); Tiffany Natasha Kithcart (Not admitted in DC); Michael B. Lehrhoff; Michael D. Maloney; Mary R. Marta; Cori Fisher McRae (Not admitted in DC); John B. Moriarty, Jr.; Elizabeth Kondonijakos Murphy; Nicholas A. Nardi; Clayton J. Nix; Leslie V. Norwalk; Kenya Parrish-Dixon; Corey M. Perman; Kathleen A. Peterson; Michael S. Portnoy; Kathy Potter; John S. Rah (Not admitted in DC); Lena Robins; Leslie Burris Thorpe; Tanya B. Vanderbilt; Patricia M. Wagner; Jonathan D. Weinberg; Constance A. Wilkinson; Brian J. Wise (Not admitted in DC); Howard A. Wolf-Rodda.
Health Care and Hospital Law. Government Procurement, Management Labor Relations and Employee Benefits Law. Equal Employment Opportunity and Affirmative Action Law and Practice. Insurance, Political Activities, Legislation and Election Law. Arbitration, Administrative Proceedings, State and Federal Civil and Appellate Practice. General Practice. Corporation.
New York, N.Y. Office: 250 Park Avenue. Telephone: 212-351-4500.
San Francisco, California Office: Epstein Becker & Green, Two Embarcadero Center, Suite 1650. Telephone: 415-398-3500.
Los Angeles, California Office: Epstein Becker & Green, Suite 500, 1875 Century Park, East. Telephone: 310-556-8861.
Dallas, Texas Office: Park Central VII, 12750 Merit Drive, Suite 1320. Telephone: 972-628-2450.
Stamford, Connecticut Office: Suite 1800, One Landmark Square. Telephone: 203-348-3737.
Newark, New Jersey Office: Two Gateway Center, 12th Floor. Telephone: 973-642-1900.
Boston, Massachusetts Office: 75 State Street. Telephone: 617-342-4000.
Chicago, Illinois Office: 150 North Michigan Avenue, Suite 420. Telephone: 312-499-1400.
Atlanta, Georgia Office: Suite 1400, The Lenox Building, 3399 Peachtree Road, N.E. Telephone: 404-812-5680.
See Professional Biographies, WASHINGTON, DISTRICT OF COLUMBIA

Epstein, Edell, Shapiro, Finnan & Lytle, LLC
(See Rockville, Maryland)

Epstien, Jay A., (AV) .... '51 '76 C.124 B.S. L.188 J.D. [Piper M.R.&W.]
*PRACTICE AREAS: Real Estate.
Epting, John T. .... '50 '82 C.160 B.A. L.904 J.D. [Ⓒ Shaw P.]
*PRACTICE AREAS: Real Estate; Zoning, Planning and Land Use; Municipal Law; Historic Preservation; Building Codes.
Erb, Nicole .... '67 '99 C.685 B.A. L.178 J.D. [Ⓐ White&C.]
Erbe, Bonnie G. '54 '88 C.66 B.A. L.276 J.D.
(adm. in NY; not adm. in DC) UPI Radio Network
Erckert, Christopher P. B. .... '— '92 C.606 B.A. L.178 J.D. [Vinson&E.]
*PRACTICE AREAS: Project Finance; International Business Law; Energy; Capital Markets.
Erdman, Laurie A. .... '67 '94 C.112 B.S. L.464 J.D. [Dillingham&M.]
*PRACTICE AREAS: Labor and Employment; Civil Rights; Litigation.
Erdmann, Carl R. .... '66 '96 C.1369 B.B.A. L.705 J.D. [Ⓒ Skadden,A.S.M.&F.]
Erdreich, Ben L. .... '38 '63 C.976 B.A. L.16 J.D. [Bradley A.R.&W.] (⊙Birm., AL)
*PRACTICE AREAS: Government Affairs; Election Law; Campaign Law; Political Law.
Eren, H.C. .... '60 '98 C.446 B.A. L.30 J.D. [Ⓐ Clifford C.R.&W.]
*PRACTICE AREAS: Economic Sanctions; International Public Law; International Regulatory Law; International Trade; Project Finance.
Erickson, John F. .... '40 '66 C.378 B.A. L.900 J.D. 437 N.J. Ave., S.E.
Erickson, Sally A. '61 '91 C.855 B.A. L.1294 J.D.
Associate International Counsel, MCI WorldCom
Ericson, Christine F. .... '— '92 C.228 L.910 J.D. [Ⓐ Swidler B.S.F.]
*PRACTICE AREAS: Public Utilities; Energy; Environmental; Litigation.
Ericson, Connie M. '50 '99 C.297 B.A. L.326 J.D.
(adm. in TX; not adm. in DC) [Ⓐ Weil,G.&M.]
*PRACTICE AREAS: Environmental Law.
Eriksen, Richard E. .... '45 '75 C&L.705 A.B., J.D. Special Ct., RRRA
Erikson, George W., Jr. .... '72 '99 C.893 B.A. L.880 J.D. [Ⓐ McGuirewoods]
*PRACTICE AREAS: Mergers and Acquisitions; Emerging Growth Companies; Technology Law; Corporate Finance; Securities.
Erkelenz, William F. '45 '72 C.178 B.A. L.309 J.D.
Gen. Solr., National Railroad Passenger Corp. (AMTRAK)
Ermer, David M. .... '54 '79 C.184 B.A. L.276 J.D. [Gordon&B.]
*PRACTICE AREAS: Trial and Appellate Practice; Government Contract Law; Health Law; Employee Benefits Law; Insurance Law.

Ermer, Marilyn S. .... '55 '79 C.783 B.A. L.273 J.D. MCI Communications Corp.
Ernst, Barbara G. ..... '55 '80 C.928 B.A. L.446 J.D. [Rothwell,F.E.&M.] (See Pat. Sect.)
*PRACTICE AREAS: Intellectual Property.
Ernst, Christopher G. '66 '00 C.308 B.A. L.180 J.D.
(adm. in MD; not adm. in DC) [Ⓐ Wilkinson B.K.]
*PRACTICE AREAS: Telecommunications Law; Wireless Communications.
Ertel, Raymond D. .... '53 '81 C.569 B.A. L.61 J.D. The Bureau of Natl. Affs., Inc.
Erulkar, Benjamin .... '60 '92 C.309 A.B. L.659 J.D. [Ⓐ Vinson&E.]
*PRACTICE AREAS: Project Finance; International Business Transactions; Business Law.
Erville, Pierre '54 '90 C.860 B.A. L.588 J.D.
Dir.of Housing & Envir. Policy, Alliance To End Childhood Lead Poisoning
Ervin, Carlton C. '70 '97 C.228 B.A. L.309 J.D.
(adm. in NY; not adm. in DC) Corp. Coun., Marriott International, Inc.
*RESPONSIBILITIES: International Economic Development.
Ervin, David J. .... '67 '92 C.30 B.A. L.904 J.D. [Ⓐ Collier S.S.]
*PRACTICE AREAS: Intellectual Property; Litigation.
Ervin, Susan C. .... '51 '77 C.518 B.A. L.705 J.D. [Dechert]
*PRACTICE AREAS: Derivative Products; Financial Services Law; Securities Regulation; Investment Management.
Esber, Brett M. .... '58 '84 C.608 B.S. L.276 J.D. [Dyer E.&J.]
*PRACTICE AREAS: Maritime Law; Commercial Law; Corporate Law; Finance.
Esber, Eva Petko .... '59 '84 C.728 B.A. L.276 J.D. [Williams&C.]
*PRACTICE AREAS: Banking Litigation; Check Fraud; Fraud and Deceit; Hospital Liability Defense; Employment Discrimination.
Esch, Michael D., (BV) .... '54 '80 C&L.309 A.B., J.D. [Hale&D.]
*PRACTICE AREAS: International Trade Law.
Escobar, Elisabeth Roth .... '63 '90 C.976 B.A. L.178 J.D. Sr. Coun., Marriott Intl., Inc.
*RESPONSIBILITIES: Intellectual Property.
Escoto, Henry A. .... '65 '95 C.1141 B.A. L.1364 J.D. 600 F St. NW
Esfahani, Houtan Khalili '64 '95
C.178 B.S.E.E. L.1292 J.D. [Ⓐ Finnegan,H.F.G.&D.] (See Pat. Sect.)
*PRACTICE AREAS: Intellectual Property; Patents.
Eshelman, J. William .... '— '69 C.16 A.B. L.192 J.D. [Feith&Z.] (⊙Jerusalem, Israel)
Eskay, Robert L., Jr. '65 '98 C.945 B.A. L.37 J.D.
(adm. in AZ; not adm. in DC) [Ⓐ Morrison&H.]
*PRACTICE AREAS: Commercial Litigation; Appellate Practice; Bankruptcy Litigation; Fraudulent Conveyance; Energy Deregulation.
Eskelsen, Todd R. .... '59 '85 C.878 B.A. L.276 J.D. [Sonnenschein N.&R.]
*PRACTICE AREAS: Corporate Law; Real Estate; Cooperatives.
Eskildsen, Paul M. .... '54 '80 C&L.893 B.A., J.D. MCI Communications Corp.
Eskin, Andrew D. .... '— '85 C.813 B.A. L.1065 J.D. [Verner,L.B.M.&H.]
*PRACTICE AREAS: Federal Practice; Antitrust and Trade Regulation; Transportation; Financial Services; Tax Law.
Eskin, Otho E. .... '35 '60 C.95 A.B. L.273 LL.B. 1614 19th St., N.W.‡
Eskovitz, Sean .... '70 '97 C.659 B.A. L.569 J.D. 725 12th St., N.W.
Esmond, Robert W. ...... '53 '89 C.446 B.Sc. L.273 J.D. [Sterne,K.G.&F.] (See Pat. Sect.)
*PRACTICE AREAS: Intellectual Property Law.
Espaldon, Karen M. .... '64 '96 C&L.1356 B.S., J.D. [Ⓐ Jones,D.R.&P.]
Espey-Romero, Ruth .... '46 '79 C.443 B.S. L.180 J.D. [Ⓒ Greenberg T.]
Espinosa, William H. .... '45 '79 C.309 A.B. L.276 J.D. [Ⓐ Pillsbury W.]
Esposito, Denise .... '67 '92 C.705 B.A. L.477 J.D. [Wilmer,C.&P.]
*PRACTICE AREAS: Biotechnology; Complex Contract Disputes; Litigation; Products Liability; Product Safety.
Esposito, Frank M. '70 '98 C.94 B.A. L.1398 J.D.
(adm. in NY; not adm. in DC) [Ⓐ King,P.&H.]
*PRACTICE AREAS: Employment Law; Commercial Law; Contracts; Constitutional Law.
Esposito, Joseph P., (P.C.), (AV) ...... '53 '79 C.1044 B.A. L.569 J.D. [Akin,G.S.H.&F.]
*PRACTICE AREAS: Litigation.
Esposito, Lesli C. '— '98 C.93 B.A. L.930 J.D.
(adm. in MD; not adm. in DC) [Ⓐ Cohen,M.H.&T.]
*PRACTICE AREAS: Antitrust.
Esposito, Peter G., (AV) '54 '79 C.690 B.S. L.276 J.D.
V.P. & Regul. Coun., NGC Corp.
Esposito, Sante J. .... '47 '73 C.1030 B.A. L.184 J.D. [Metzger&M.]
Espy, Mike '53 '78 C.329 B.A. L.770 J.D.
(adm. in MS; not adm. in DC) [Ⓒ Butler,S.O.S.&C.] (⊙Jackson, MS)
*PRACTICE AREAS: International Law; Government Relations; Governmental Liability; Agribusiness; Business Planning.
Esquenet, Margaret A. .... '73 '99 C.112 B.A. L.904 J.D. [Ⓐ Finnegan,H.F.G.&D.]
*PRACTICE AREAS: Software Licensing; Intellectual Property Litigation; Trademark Prosecution.
Essaye, Anthony F., (AV) .... '34 '62 C.276 B.S.S. L.309 LL.B. [Clifford C.R.&W.]
Esselman, James T. '69 '00 C.30 B.A. L.893 J.D.
(adm. in VA; not adm. in DC) [Ⓐ Beveridge&D.]
*PRACTICE AREAS: Environmental Law.
Esser, Peter Joseph Christian '68 '97
C.1350 B.A. L.802 J.D. Gen. Coun., Rep. of German Indus. & Trade
Esslinger, J. Thomas, (AV) .... '43 '73 C.976 B.A. L.276 J.D. [Schmeltzer,A.&S.]
*PRACTICE AREAS: Litigation; Business Law; Business Transactions; Corporate Law; Maritime Law.
Estes, John N., III .... '57 '83 C.861 B.A. L.420 J.D. [Skadden,A.S.M.&F.]
Estes, Matthew W. S. .... '58 '84 C.228 B.A. L.893 J.D. [Ⓒ Skadden,A.S.M.&F.]
Estrada, Juan Manuel .... '75 '01 C.910 B.A. L.273 J.D. [Ⓐ Covington&B.]
Estrada, Lisa A. .... '66 '99 C.651 B.A. L.1209 J.D. [Ⓐ Arent F.K.P.&K.]
*PRACTICE AREAS: Health; White Collar Crime; Civil Litigation; Civil Fraud; Legislative Practice.
Estrada, Miguel A. '61 '87 C.178 A.B. L.309 J.D.
(adm. in NY; not adm. in DC) [Gibson,D.&C.]
*PRACTICE AREAS: Appellate Practice; White Collar Crime.
Estreicher, Herbert .... '54 '89 C.1036 B.A. L.569 J.D. [Ⓒ Covington&B.]
Etienne-Cummings, Shamita D. '69 '00 C.659 B.S.E.E. L.801 J.D.
[Ⓐ McDermott,W.&E.]
Etkind, Barbara E. .... '50 '75 C.1036 B.A. L.477 J.D. [Ross,D.&B.]
Ettinger, David J. .... '67 '93 C.1044 B.A. L.1040 J.D. [Ⓐ Keller&H.]
*PRACTICE AREAS: Food and Drug Law; Litigation; Trademarks.
Ettinger, Mitchell S., (AV) .... '58 '83 C.35 B.S. L.128 J.D. [Skadden,A.S.M.&F.]
Eubanks, Musa L. '— '99
C.1356 B.A. L.273 J.D. [Ⓐ Bonner K.T.&C.] (⊙Rockville, MD)
*PRACTICE AREAS: Insurance Defense; Civil Litigation.
Euben, Donna R. '62 '94 C.604 B.A. L.1009 J.D.
Assoc. Coun., American Assn. of Univ. Professors
Eure, Cary Ann '58 '90 C&L.893 B.A., J.D.
Asst. Coun., Washington Post-Newsweek Interactice
*RESPONSIBILITIES: Intellectual Property; Entertainment Law; Trademarks; Copyrights; Communications Law.
Eustice, Robert C. .... '63 '88 C&L.477 A.B., J.D. [Ⓐ Lewis]
*PRACTICE AREAS: Family Law; Commercial Litigation.
Evale, Colleen M. .... '72 '97 C.602 B.S. L.884 J.D. [Ⓐ Keller&H.]
*PRACTICE AREAS: Food and Drug Law.
Evangelista, Alessio D. .... '70 '96 C.1044 B.A. L.823 J.D. [Ⓐ Beveridge&D.]
*PRACTICE AREAS: White Collar Criminal Litigation; Civil Litigation.

Evans, Alexander M. '75 '00 C.45 B.A. L.1375 J.D.
(adm. in CA; not adm. in DC) [🄰 Vinson&E.]
*PRACTICE AREAS: Project Finance; Securities; General Corporate Law.
Evans, Billy L. '41 '64 C&L.280 A.B., LL.B.
(adm. in GA; not adm. in DC) 407 1st St., SE
Evans, Constance G. ... '50 '80 C&L.329 B.A., J.D. Reg. of Wills, Supr. Ct.
Evans, Cynthia H. ... '58 '84 C&L.665 B.S., J.D. 1111 19th St., NW
Evans, David C. ... '— '71 C.347 B.S. L.1119 J.D. [Reed S.]
*PRACTICE AREAS: Government Relations.
Evans, David H. ... '— '95 C&L.597 B.A., J.D. [🄰 Jones,D.R.&P.]
Evans, David J. ... '53 '78 C.94 B.S. L.1294 J.D. [Clifford C.R.&W.]
*PRACTICE AREAS: Project Finance; Utility Law; Energy Law.
Evans, Donald J., (AV) ... '51 '77 C.93 B.A. L.276 J.D. [🄲 Fletcher,H.&H.] ⊙
*PRACTICE AREAS: Mass Media Law; Broadcast; Wireless Cable; Common Carrier Law; Cellular Radio.
Evans, H. Malloy, III '73 '01 C.198 B.S. L.902 J.D.
(adm. in VA; not adm. in DC) [🄰 Hunton&W.]
Evans, Hugh C. ... '28 '52 C&L.383 LL.B. 108 5th St., N.E.‡
Evans, Jeremy Paul '72 '00 C.112 B.A. L.276 J.D.
(adm. in VA; not adm. in DC) 1875 Connecticut Avenue, N.W.
Evans, Joseph D., (AV) ... '46 '75 C.877 B.S. L.273 J.D. [Crowell&M.] (Pat.)
*PRACTICE AREAS: Patents; Trademarks; Copyrights; Trade Secrets; Litigation.
Evans, K. Stewart, Jr., (AV) '45 '72
C&L.893 B.A., J.D. [Pepper H.] (⊙Tysons Corner, VA)
*PRACTICE AREAS: Intellectual Property Litigation; Noncompetition and Non-Solicitation Agreements; Business Torts.
Evans, Karen E. ... '58 '90 C.232 B.S.N. L.575 J.D. [🄰 J.H.Olender&Assoc.]
*PRACTICE AREAS: Medical Malpractice; Personal Injury.
Evans, Kesha D. ... '73 '99 C.112 B.A. L.813 J.D. [🄰 Piper M.R.&W.]
Evans, Linda S. ... '61 '91 C.608 B.S. L.1209 J.D. 1300 I St., Suite 700 (Pat.)
Evans, Marianne '58 '86 C&L.616 B.S., J.D.
(adm. in OK; not adm. in DC) Ernst & Young
Evans, Mark L., (AV) ... '42 '68 C.299 A.B. L.188 [Kellogg,H.H.T.&E.]
*PRACTICE AREAS: Telecommunications; Supreme Court and Appellate Litigation.
Evans, Mary E. ... '58 '85 C&L.276 A.B., J.D. Asst. Gen. Coun., Disclosure Incorporated
Evans, Michael Brock ... '37 '64 C.674 B.A. L.477 L.L.B. Endangered Species Coalition
Evans, Michael R. '70 '95 C.260 B.S. L.472 J.D.
(adm. in FL; not adm. in DC) Coun., Marriott Intl.
Evans, Philip Tucker ... '60 '93 C.951 B.A. L.276 J.D. [Holland&K.]
*PRACTICE AREAS: Civil Litigation; Commercial Litigation; Bankruptcy; Creditor's Rights; E-Commerce.
Evans, Rachel Cohen ... '41 '80 C.477 A.B. L.128 J.D. [Jordan K.&J.]
Evans, Richard W. ... '66 '93 C.164 A.B. L.128 J.D. [Evans A.&C.] ⊙
Evans, Robert B. ... '46 '84 C.282 B.A. L.665 J.D. Atty., Washington Gas Light Co.
Evans, Robert D. '45 '69 C.976 B.A. L.477 J.D.
(adm. in IL; not adm. in DC)
Assoc. Exec. Dir., Govt. Affs. & Pub. Serv., Amer. Bar Assn.
Evans, Sheila T. ... '70 '95 C.880 B.A. L.472 J.D. [🄰 Shaw P.]
Evans, Terri L. '66 '94 C&L.273 B.B.A., J.D.
1200 New Hampshire Ave., N.W., Suite 800
Evans, Thomas B., Jr. '31 '56 C&L.893 B.A., LL.B.
(adm. in VA; not adm. in DC) 1010 Wisconsin Ave., N.W.
Evans, Thomas L. ... '52 '84 C.339 B.S. L.145 J.D. [Kirkland&E.]
*PRACTICE AREAS: Tax; Corporate.
Evans, William C., (AV) ... '— '66 C&L.575 B.S., LL.B. [Verner,L.B.M.&H.]
*PRACTICE AREAS: Aviation Law; Surface Transportation; Administrative.
Evans, William M. ... '59 '86 C.101 B.A. L.893 J.D. [Groom]
*PRACTICE AREAS: Employee Benefits; Labor and Employment; Pension and Profit Sharing; Tax Law; ERISA.
Evans Antonelli & Cox, LLC ... 601 Indiana Ave. NW Ste. 1001 (⊙Bethesda, MD)
Evens, Mark Fox ... '49 '75 C.575 A.B. L.893 J.D. [Thelen R.&P.]
*PRACTICE AREAS: Litigation.
Evenson, Donald D., (AV) ... '40 '66 C&L.494 B.S., J.D. [Crowell&M.] (Pat.)
*PRACTICE AREAS: Patents; Trademarks; Copyrights; Trade Secrets; Litigation.
Everett, J. Clayton, Jr. ... '— '99 C&L.893 B.A., J.D. [🄰 Morgan,L.&B.]
Everett, Ralph B., (AV) ... '51 '77 C.511 B.A. L.228 J.D. [Paul,H.J.&W.]
*PRACTICE AREAS: Federal Legislative Practice; Independent Regulatory Agencies; Administrative Policy Initiatives; Preparing Witnesses for Congressional Hearings; Federal Communications Commission.
Everley, Douglas R. '49 '74 C.378 L.900 J.D.
(adm. in KS; not adm. in DC) MCI Communications Corp.
Evers, Robert Allen, (AV) ... '45 '70 C.597 B.A. L.178 J.D. [R.A.Evers]
Evers, Robert Allen, Law Offices, Chartered, (AV) ... 1155 Connecticut Ave., N.W.
Everts, Alisa M. ... '66 '96 C.446 B.A. L.880 J.D. [🄰 Drinker B.&R.]
Ewart, Andrea M. ... '57 '00 C.999 B.A. L.472 J.D. [🄰 Holland&K.]
*PRACTICE AREAS: International Trade and Customs; Administrative; Regulatory; Legislative.
Ewing, Brenda S. ... '48 '87 C&L.446 B.S., J.D. V.P., Seabury & Smith
Ewing, Kenneth P. ... '64 '91 C.976 B.A. L.477 J.D. [Steptoe&J.]
*PRACTICE AREAS: Antitrust; International Law.
Ewing, Kevin A. ... '66 '92 C.975 B.A. L.276 J.D. [Bracewell&P.]
*PRACTICE AREAS: Environmental Law; Environmental Criminal Defense; Environmental Lender Liability; Hazardous Waste; Mergers and Acquisitions.
Ewing, Ky P., Jr., (AV) ... '35 '59 C.69 B.A. L.309 LL.B. [Vinson&E.]
*PRACTICE AREAS: Litigation; Antitrust and Trade Regulation.
Ewing, Rebecca H. '74 '00 C&L.309 A.B., J.D.
(adm. in PA; not adm. in DC) [🄰 Baker B.]
Ewing, Richard S., (AV) ... '38 '65 C.188 B.A. L.569 LL.B. [Arnold&P.]
*PRACTICE AREAS: Health Care; Government Contracts.
Ewing, Thomas W., (BV) '35 '68 C.357 B.S. L.365 J.D.
(adm. in IL; not adm. in DC) [🄲 Davis&H.]
*PRACTICE AREAS: Legislative Practice; Business Law; Agricultural Law; General Practice.
Ewing, Todd, (P.C.) ... '65 '92 C.350 B.S. L.221 J.D. [Tobin,O.&E.]
*PRACTICE AREAS: Real Estate; Transaction; Business; Corporate; Wills.
Exposito, Lorenzo F. ... '65 '94 C.184 B.A. L.128 J.D. [🄰 Powell,G.F.&M.]
*PRACTICE AREAS: Public Contract Law; Construction Contracts; Litigation.
Exposito, Patricia A. ... '66 '96 C.893 B.A. L.128 J.D. [🄰 Venable,A.B.H.&C.]
*PRACTICE AREAS: Labor; Litigation.
Eyman, Barbara D.A. ... '60 '90 C.478 B.A. L.309 J.D. [🄲 Powell,G.F.&M.]
*PRACTICE AREAS: Health Law.
Eyster, Rodney E. '28 '58 C.871 B.S. L.976 LL.B.
(adm. in NY; not adm. in DC) 5041 Sedgwick St., N.W.‡
Faber, Michael ... '59 '87 C.1044 B.A. L.145 J.D. 701 Pennsylvania Ave., N.W.
Faberman, Edward P. ... '46 '70 C.30 B.S. L.724 J.D. [Ungaretti&H.] ⊙
*PRACTICE AREAS: Administrative Agency Practice; Airline Regulation; Airport Regulation; Aviation Law; Environmental Law.
Fabrikant, Marvin, (AV) ... '45 '71 C.659 B.A. L.30 J.D. 5149 Tilden St NW
Fabrikant, Melinda '48 '85
C&L.705 B.A., J.D. 1025 Thomas Jefferson St., NW, East Lobby
Fabrizio, Steven B. '63 '89 C&L.276 B.S.B.A., J.D.
Sr. V.P., Dir. Civil Litig., Recording Industry Assoc. of America, Inc.

Facchina, Bazil ... '60 '87 C.94 B.S.B.A L.893 J.D. [🄰 Crowell&M.]
Facer, Eric F. ... '53 '80 C.101 B.A. L.276 J.D. [Facer&S.]
Facer & Stamoulas ... 1155 Connecticut Avenue, Suite 300
Faden, Ryan M. '— '00 C.112 B.A. L.776 J.D.
(adm. in NJ; not adm. in DC) [🄰 Epstein B.&G.]
*PRACTICE AREAS: Health.
Fagan, Joseph C. '25 '52 C&L.966 B.S., LL.B.
(adm. in WI; not adm. in DC) 3315 Wisconsin Ave., Suite 301‡
Fagan, Joseph H. ... '66 '93 C.918 B.A. L.273 J.D. [🄰 Heller E.W.&M.]
Fagg, Brad ... '62 '90 C.896 B.A. L.178 J.D. [Morgan,L.&B.]
Fagre, Danielle '72 '99 C.678 B.A. L.904 J.D.
(adm. in MD; not adm. in DC) [🄰 Venable,A.B.H.&C.]
*PRACTICE AREAS: Legislative Practice; Election Law; Privacy Law.
Fahey, A. Kevin, (BV) ... '39 '74 C.676 B.S. L.128 J.D. 601-A Indiana Ave., N.W.
Fahey, John J. ... '64 '99 C.390 B.A. L.537 J.D. [🄰 Sutherland A.&B.]
*PRACTICE AREAS: Securities.
Fahrenkopf, Frank J., Jr., (AV) ... '39 '65 C.549 B.A. L.1066 J.D. [Hogan&H.]
*PRACTICE AREAS: International Law; Legislative Law; Corporate Law.
Fahrenkopf, Leslie A. '68 '95 C.976 B.A. L.893 J.D.
(adm. in NY; not adm. in DC) [🄰 O'Melveny&M.]
Fahrenkopf, Paul E. '— '79 C.30 B.A. L.472 J.D.
(adm. in NJ; not adm. in DC; See Pat. Sect.) [🄲 Barnes&T.]
*PRACTICE AREAS: Trademark Protection; Trademark Registration; Trade Dress.
Faibish, Laura F. ... '59 '87 C&L.846 B.B.A., J.D. Sr. Coun., Marriott International, Inc.
Fails, Kenneth H., II '71 '96 C.273 B.A. L.1209 J.D.
(adm. in VA; not adm. in DC) [🄰 Employment]
*PRACTICE AREAS: Labor and Employment; Civil Rights; Corporate Law.
Fain, Deidre Susan '50 '91 C.1276 B.A. L.276 J.D.
(adm. in MD; not adm. in DC) Asst. Prof. of Justice, Amer. Univ.

Fairchild, Pamela B., Law Offices of
(See Alexandria, Virginia)

Fairey, Wm. Fletcher ... '65 '98 C.198 B.A. L.904 J.D. [🄰 Steptoe&J.]
Fairfax, Cydonii V. ... '72 '98 C.446 B.S. L.309 J.D. [🄰 Arnold&P.]
*PRACTICE AREAS: Corporate Law; Securities.
Fairley, Trina L. ... '71 '96 C.893 B.A. L.273 J.D. [🄰 King,P.&H.]
*PRACTICE AREAS: Management Labor and Employment Law; Commercial Litigation; Litigation.
Fajfar, Mark ... '66 '92 C.910 B.A. L.276 J.D. [🄲 Fried,F.H.S.&J.]
Falb, Robert E., (AV) ... '43 '68 C.103 B.A. L.309 LL.B. [Robins,K.M.&C.]
*PRACTICE AREAS: Taxation; Real Estate; Trusts; Estate Planning; Probate.
Fales, Lisa J. ... '62 '90 C.446 B.A. L.64 J.D. [Howrey S.A.&W.]
*PRACTICE AREAS: Antitrust; Trade Regulation.
Faley, R. Scott ... '47 '73 C&L.276 B.A., J.D. [S.R.Faley]
Faley, R. Scott, P.C. ... 5100 Wisconsin Ave., N.W.
Falk, Andrew E. ... '65 '93 C&L.276 A.B., J.D. [🄲 Fulbright&J.]
*PRACTICE AREAS: Aircraft Finance and Leasing.
Falk, Donald M. ... '57 '90 C.1375 B.A. L.1066 J.D. [Mayer,B.&P.]
Falk, Erin M. '60 '88 C.846 B.A. L.904 J.D.
(adm. in VA; not adm. in DC) [Mintz,L.C.F.G.&P.]
*PRACTICE AREAS: Intellectual Property; Intellectual Property Litigation; Intellectual Property Portfolio Management; Trademarks; Trademark Litigation.
Falk, James H., Jr., (AV) ... '60 '87 C.902 B.A. L.922 J.D. [Falk]
*PRACTICE AREAS: Business Transactions; Civil Trials; Labor and Employment; Commercial Contracts; Government Contracts.
Falk, James H., Sr., (AV) ... '38 '65 C&L.37 B.S.B.A., J.D. [Falk]
*PRACTICE AREAS: Civil Trials; Government Contract Law; Intellectual Property; Insurance; Labor and Employment.
Falk, John M. ... '64 '91 C&L.902 B.A., J.D. [Falk]
*PRACTICE AREAS: Civil Trials; Government Contracts; International Trade; High Technology; Law Enforcement.
Falk, Robert N. ... '63 '90 C.674 A.B. L.976 J.D. [🄲 Powell,G.F.&M.]
*PRACTICE AREAS: Health Care.

Falk Law Firm, The, PLLC, (AV) BR
A Professional Limited Liability Corporation
Suite 260 One Westin Center, 2445 M Street, N.W., 20037
Telephone: 202-833-8700 Telecopier: 202-872-1725
Email: falklaw@falklawfirm.com
James H. Falk, Sr.; James H. Falk, Jr.; John M. Falk;—Meredith N. Long (Not admitted in DC); Nicole S. Biddle (Not admitted in DC).
General Civil and Criminal Practice in all Federal, State and Local Courts in the District of Columbia, Virginia, Maryland, Pennsylvania and West Virginia.
See Professional Biographies, WASHINGTON, DISTRICT OF COLUMBIA

Fallas, Thomas M. ... '73 '00 C.705 B.A. L.276 J.D. [🄰 Fried,F.H.S.&J.]
*PRACTICE AREAS: Corporate Law.
Fallon, James M. ... '41 '72 C.276 A.B. L.128 J.D. 503 11th St., S.E.
Fallon, Jeffrey E. ... '71 '96 C.276 B.A. L.273 J.D. [🄰 Webster,F.&B.]
*PRACTICE AREAS: Litigation; Employment and Labor; Public Utilities; Personal Injury.
Fallon, Robert C., (BV) ... '56 '86 C&L.421 B.A., J.D. [🄲 Dickstein S.M.&O.]
*PRACTICE AREAS: Energy.
Fallow, Katherine A. ... '69 '96 C.112 B.A. L.309 J.D. [🄰 Jenner&B.]
*PRACTICE AREAS: Litigation; Appellate Practice.
Falon, Paul H. ... '51 '83 C&L.477 B.A., J.D. [Fried,F.H.S.&J.]
*PRACTICE AREAS: Insurance.
Falstrom, Jeanne K. '67 '00 C.150 B.A. L.893 J.D.
(adm. in VA; not adm. in DC) [🄰 Miller&C.]
*PRACTICE AREAS: Taxation; Employee Benefits.
Fam, Samia, (AV) ... '60 '85 C.813 B.A. L.569 J.D. Pub. Def. Serv.
Fama, James P. ... '53 '81 C.893 B.A. L.64 J.D. [🄲 LeBoeuf,L.G.&M.]
*PRACTICE AREAS: Energy Law; Regulatory Law; Mergers and Acquisitions; Corporate Law.
Fanelli, Michael J. ... '70 '96 C.1349 B.A. L.273 J.D. [🄰 Covington&B.]
Fang, William L., (AV) '51 '75
C.597 B.S.J. L.893 J.D. Dep. Gen. Coun., Edison Elec. Institute
Fannell, Jeffery B ... '62 '97 Assoc. Gen. Coun., AFL-CIO
Fanning, Michael R. ... '47 '75 C.188 B.S. L.276 J.D. CEO, Central Pension Fund
Fano, Katia I. '67 '00 C.446 B.S. L.30 J.D.
(adm. in MD; not adm. in DC) [🄰 Dyer E.&J.]
Fanone, Joseph A. ... '49 '74 C&L.276 A.B., J.D. [Ballard S.A.&I.]
Fant, Lester G., III, (AV) ... '41 '66 C.880 B.A. L.309 LL.B. 1722 Eye st.
Fanucci, Allan A., (AV) '53 '82
C.1028 B.S. L.724 J.D. [Winston&S.] (Pat.) (⊙New York, NY)
*PRACTICE AREAS: Intellectual Property; Patents.
Farabow, Ford F., Jr., (AV) '38 '63
C.160 B.S.Ch.E. L.273 J.D. [Finnegan,H.F.G.&D.] (See Pat. Sect.)
*PRACTICE AREAS: Chemical Intellectual Property; Intellectual Property Arbitration; Intellectual Property Infringement; Intellectual Property Litigation; Pharmaceutical Intellectual Property.
Farabow, Sara Beiro, (AV) ... '63 '90 C.886 B.S. L.945 J.D. [Seyfarth S.]
*PRACTICE AREAS: Contract Law; International Litigation.
Farach, Ana V. ... '69 '98 C.276 B.S./B.A. L.273 J.D. [🄰 Cameron&H.]
*PRACTICE AREAS: Corporate Law; International Business Transactions.

Farah, William J. '57 '89 C.696 B.M. L.30 J.D. [Ⓒ Akin,G.S.H.&F.]
*PRACTICE AREAS: Public Policy.
Farano, Gerald P. '66 '92 C.105 B.A. L.273 J.D. [Winston&S.]
Farber, Alan J. '43 '69 C&L.421 B.S.L., J.D.
Asst. Prof., Columbus Sch. of Law, Catholic Univ. of Amer.
Farber, Allen V., (AV) '50 '75 C.228 B.A. L.273 J.D. [Akin,G.S.H.&F.]
*PRACTICE AREAS: Litigation; First Amendment Law; Libel Law; Commercial Leasing Law.
Farber, Benjamin M. '74 '00 C.178 B.A. L.982 J.D. [Ⓐ Clifford C.R.&W.]
*PRACTICE AREAS: Corporate Law.
Farber, David J. '61 '88 C.569 B.A. L.276 J.D. [Patton B.]
Farber, Evan R. '72 '98 C.1349 B.A. L.273 J.D.
(adm. in NY; not adm. in DC) [Ⓐ Hogan&H.]
*PRACTICE AREAS: Corporate Law; Securities; Mergers and Acquisitions; Private Equity; Public Offerings.
Farber, Jacob S. '69 '94 C.477 B.A. L.273 J.D. [Ⓐ Dickstein S.M.&O.]
*PRACTICE AREAS: Communications.
Farber, Michael D. '69 '95 C.645 B.S. L.273 J.D. [Ⓐ Swidler B.S.F.]
*PRACTICE AREAS: Antitrust.
Farha, B.D. Eddie '52 '77 C.986 B.A. L.623 J.D. [Farha&S.]
Farha & Sanders, (AV) 1725 K St.
Faria, Teresa Maurea Pantoja da Costa '74 '97 L.276 J.D.
(adm. in NY; not adm. in DC) [Ⓐ Hogan&H.]
*PRACTICE AREAS: Business Law; Finance; Project Finance.
Faria, Wendell M. '55 '88 C.1138 B.B.A. L.1066 J.D. [Ⓒ Paul,H.J.&W.]
*PRACTICE AREAS: Investment Management Regulation; Securities Law.
Farina, Benga, (BV) '64 '89 C.216 B.A. L.537 J.D. [Ⓐ Skadden,A.S.M.&F.]
*PRACTICE AREAS: Energy Law.
Farina, Richard H. '47 '70 C&L.602 A.B., J.D.
Gen. Coun., Thrift Depositor Protec. Oversight Bd.
Farina, Steven M. '66 '92 C.228 A.B. L.477 J.D. [Williams&C.]
*PRACTICE AREAS: Class Action Defense; Complex and Multi-District Litigation; Libel and Slander; Defamation; Products Liability Defense.
Farinella, Maria '70 '95 C.788 B.A. L.904 J.D. [Ⓐ Dickstein S.M.&O.]
*PRACTICE AREAS: Energy.
Faris, Dawn E. '66 '96 C.347 B.A. L.178 J.D. [Ⓐ Fried,F.H.S.&J.]
*PRACTICE AREAS: Corporate.

Faris, James J. '38 '66 C&L.228 B.A., LL.B.
Suite 350 3201 New Mexico Avenue, N.W., 20016-2756
Telephone: 202-895-1372 Fax: 301-292-0720
URL: http://www.lawyers.com/jamesjfaris
Estate Planning and Administration, Probate, Wills, Trusts and Taxation Law.
See Professional Biographies, WASHINGTON, DISTRICT OF COLUMBIA

Farley, Brian P. '— '96 C.170 B.A. L.273 J.D.
(adm. in CO; not adm. in DC) 3050 K St.
Farley, Michael J. '65 '92 C&L.436 B.A., J.D. [Ⓐ Mayer,B.&P.]
Farley, Robert C., Jr. '— '96 C.838 B.A. L.831 J.D.
(adm. in PA; not adm. in DC) [Ⓐ Morgan,L.&B.]
Farley, William P. '63 '96 C.1349 B.S. L.107 J.D. 900 Seventeenth St. N.W.
Farmer, Donald A., Jr., (AV) '— '70 C&L.813 B.A., J.D. [Reed S.]
*PRACTICE AREAS: Antitrust; Litigation.
Farmer, F. Scott '— '82 C.576 B.A. L.575 J.D. [McKee N.]
*PRACTICE AREAS: Taxation; International Taxation; Tax Litigation.
Farmer, Jonathan L., (AV) '52 '77 C.103 A.B. L.477 J.D. [Griffin,F.T.&M.]
*PRACTICE AREAS: Zoning, Planning and Land Use; Municipal Law; Environmental Law.
Farmer, Thomas L., (AV) '23 '51 C&L.309 A.B., LL.B. 2121 K St. NW
Farmer, Tyler L. '73 '00 C&L.602 B.A., J.D.
(adm. in CA; not adm. in DC) [Ⓐ Jones,D.R.&P.]
Farnsworth, James R. '65 '91 C.604 B.A. L.569 J.D. [Ⓐ Vinson&E.]
*PRACTICE AREAS: Litigation.
Farnum, David M. '69 '00 C.145 A.B. L.976 J.D.
(adm. in CT; not adm. in DC) [Ⓐ Venable,A.B.H.&C.]
Farquhar, Douglas B., (AV) '54 '83 C.94 B.S. L.976 J.D. [Hyman,P.&M.]
Farquhar, Michele C., (AV) '57 '84 C.228 B.A. L.893 J.D. [Hogan&H.]
*PRACTICE AREAS: Communications.
Farquhar, Thomas W., (AV) '35 '67 C&L.273 A.B., LL.B. 600 F St. N.W.
Farr, Alec W. '66 '91 C&L.276 B.A., J.D. [Ⓒ Proskauer R.]
Farr, H. Bartow, III, (AV) '44 '74 C.674 A.B. L.36 J.D. [Farr&T.]
*PRACTICE AREAS: Appellate Practice.

Farr & Taranto, (AV)
Suite 800, 1220 19th Street, N.W., 20036-2435
Telephone: 202-775-0184 Telecopier: 202-223-8679
Members of Firm: H. Bartow Farr, III; Richard G. Taranto.
Supreme Court and Appellate Practice in all substantive areas, including Constitutional Law, Telecommunications Law.
See Professional Biographies, WASHINGTON, DISTRICT OF COLUMBIA

Farrah, Elias G., (AV) '51 '78 C.708 A.B. L.1048 J.D. [LeBoeuf,L.G.&M.]
*PRACTICE AREAS: Energy; Utilities.
Farrand, Judith A. '71 '97 C.802 B.A. L.1194 J.D. [Ⓐ Paul,H.J.&W.]
*PRACTICE AREAS: Environmental Law.
Farrell, Bradley A. '— '00 C.999 B.S. L.831 J.D.
(adm. in NJ; not adm. in DC) [Ⓐ Carter,L.&M.]
Farrell, Edward J., (AV) '45 '70 C.401 B.A. L.276 J.D. [Blank R.C.&M.]
*PRACTICE AREAS: International Trade; Antidumping; Countervailing Duties; Customs Law; Import and Export Law.
Farrell, J. Michael '41 '67 C&L.276 B.S.B.A., J.D. 1730 K. St. N.W.
Farrell, Joseph P. '13 '40 C.674 A.B. L.831 LL.B. 3001 Veazey Terr., N.W.‡
Farrell, Lawrence M. '34 '66 C.116 A.B. L.128 LL.B. [Ⓒ McKenna&C.]
*PRACTICE AREAS: Government Contracts Law; Litigation.
Farrell, Margaret G. '39 '65 C.188 B.A. L.145 J.D. [Ⓒ Cohen,M.H.&T.]
*PRACTICE AREAS: Health Law; Products Liability; Insurance; Employment Disability Law.
Farrell, Michael W. '38 '74 C.602 B.A. L.30 J.D. Assoc. J., Ct. of App.
Farren, J. Michael '52 '82 C.1030 B.A. L.184 J.D.
Exec. Asst., Republican Natl. Comm.
Farren, Mary Margaret '66 '95 C.401 B.S. L.184 [Ⓐ Skadden,A.S.M.&F.]
*PRACTICE AREAS: Electric Power.
Farres, Ozzie A. '69 '98 C.259 B.S. L.472 J.D.
(adm. in FL; not adm. in DC; Pat.) [Ⓐ Hunton&W.]
*PRACTICE AREAS: Intellectual Property Litigation.
Farrington, Daniel E. '73 '98 C.260 B.A. L.276 J.D. [Ⓐ O'Melveny&M.]
Farrington, Rebecca H. '71 '97 C.112 B.A. L.1066 J.D. [Ⓐ O'Melveny&M.]
Farrington, Sandra Jill '74 '99 C.276 B.A. L.893 J.D. [Ⓐ Gardner,C.&D.]
*PRACTICE AREAS: Environmental Law.
Farris, Elaine L. '71 '97 C.446 B.A. L.945 J.D.
(adm. in VA; not adm. in DC) [Ⓐ Andrews&K.]
Farthing, Penelope S., (AV) '— '70 C.679 B.A. L.1119 J.D. [Patton B.]
Farwell, Donald F. '24 '78 C.33 B.S. L.273 J.D. 3608 35th St. N.W.‡
Farzan, Leila '66 '94 C.696 B.A. L.893 J.D.
(adm. in VA; not adm. in DC) Ctr. for Science in the Pub. Interest

Fassett, Mary Jean '62 '87 C.105 B.A. L.276 J.D. [Conlon,F.P.&P.]
*PRACTICE AREAS: Litigation; Agricultural Law; Probate; Guardianship Law.
Fast, Kevin L. '60 '86 C.446 B.A. L.893 J.D. [Hunton&W.]
*PRACTICE AREAS: Environmental.
Fasulo, Albert J., II '62 '97 C.054 B.S. L.1002 J.D.
(adm. in MD; not adm. in DC; See Pat. Sect.) [Ⓐ Sterne,K.G.&F.]
*PRACTICE AREAS: Patent Law.
Fattig, Susan E. '55 '80 C.543 B.S. L.602 J.D. [Ⓐ Ashcraft&G.]
Fattman, Stephen P. '67 '92 C.659 B.A.B.S. 1275 Pennsylvania Ave Nw # 800
Faucette, Douglas P. '46 '72 C.454 B.A. L.818 J.D. [Muldoon M.&F.]
*PRACTICE AREAS: Government; Finance; Banks and Banking; Corporate Law; Securities.
Faughnan, James J. '58 '90 C.1040 B.B.A. L.273 J.D. [Quagliano&S.]
*PRACTICE AREAS: Commercial Litigation; Corporate.
Faulk, Page C. '— '97 C.802 B.A. L.1017 J.D.
(adm. in MD; not adm. in DC) [Ⓐ Ungaretti&H.]
Faulkner, York Moody '65 '92 C&L.101 B.S., J.D. [Ⓐ Finnegan,H.F.G.&D.]
*PRACTICE AREAS: Intellectual Property Infringement; Intellectual Property Litigation; Patent Litigation; Trade Secrets.
Faulkner, Shands & Stupar, (AV) 5225 Wisconsin Ave.
Faunce, Marisa Gallehr '70 '94 C.893 B.A. L.659 J.D. [Ⓐ Wiley R.&F.]
Faust, Emanuel, Jr., (BV) '58 '83 C.790 B.A. L.228 J.D. [Dickstein S.M.&O.]
*PRACTICE AREAS: Corporate Law; Securities Law; Corporate Finance, Mergers and Acquisitions.
Faust, John M. '67 '94 C.951 B.A. L.893 J.D. [Ⓐ Vinson&E.]
*PRACTICE AREAS: Litigation; Antitrust and Trade Regulation.
Faust, Marcus G., (AV) '53 '77 C.878 B.A. L.101 J.D. [M.G.Faust]
*PRACTICE AREAS: Legislative Law (Federal); Natural Resources Law; Energy Law; Water Law; Aviation Law.
Faust, Michelle M. '— '98 C.823 B.A. L.30 J.D.
(adm. in NY; not adm. in DC) [Ⓐ Ungaretti&H.]

Faust, Marcus G., P.C., (AV)
332 Constitution Avenue, N.E., 20002
Telephone: 202-547-5400 Facsimile: 202-543-5740
Email: MarcusFaust@msn.com
Marcus G. Faust.
Legislative Practice. Natural Resources, Environmental, Public Utility and Water Law. International Aviation Law.
Representative Clients: Sierra Pacific Resources; Public Service Company of New Mexico; Clark County, Nevada; Montana Department of Conservation and Natural Resources; Central Utah Water Conservancy District; Las Vegas Valley Water District; Las Vegas McCarran Airport; Colorado River Commission of Nevada; Contra Costa Water District.

Fausti, John J. '55 '81 C.178 B.A. L.1019 J.D. 4301 Connecticut Avenue, N.W.
Fauth, Laurence C. '64 '97 C.105 B.A. L.1209 J.D. [Ⓐ Lee&M.]
*PRACTICE AREAS: Commercial Litigation; Architects and Engineers Liability; Construction Law.
Favretto, Richard J., (AV) '41 '66 C.1041 B.A. L.128 LL.B. [Mayer,B.&P.]
Fawcett, Myrna, (BV) '48 '74 C.66 A.B. L.276 J.D. 1763 R St., N.W.
Fawcett, Wilford H. "Buzz", (BV) '53 '80
C.800 A.B. L.809 J.D. [Ⓒ Perkins C.] (⊙Boise, ID)
*PRACTICE AREAS: Government; Environmental Law; Natural Resources; Endangered Species; Water Rights.
Fay, Jeannine J. '55 '87 C.321 A.B. L.1292 J.D.
(adm. in NJ; not adm. in DC) Catholic Univ. of Amer. Law School
Fay, Raymond C., (AV) '47 '74 C.734 A.B. L.276 J.D. [Bell,B.&L.]
*PRACTICE AREAS: Labor and Employment Law; Age Discrimination.
Fay, Thomas Fortune, (AV) '40 '67 C.602 A.B. L.705 J.D. [T.F.Fay]
Fay, Thomas Fortune, P.C., (AV) 601 Pennsylvania Ave. NW
Fayad, Michael L., (AV) '45 '70 C&L.215 B.A., J.D. [McKenna&C.]
*PRACTICE AREAS: Corporate Criminal Law; Civil Fraud Defense; Criminal Trials; Corporate Investigations; Government Contracts.
Fazzone, Patrick B. '53 '82 C.184 B.A. L.228 J.D. [Tighe P.A.T.]
*PRACTICE AREAS: Commercial Law; Commercial Transactions; Corporate Law; Intellectual Property; International Trade.
Feagles, Prentiss E., (BV) '51 '76 C.188 B.A. L.228 J.D. [Hogan&H.]
*PRACTICE AREAS: Taxation Law; Real Estate Investment Trusts; Partnership Taxation; Corporate Taxation.
Featherstone, Donald J. '64 '99
C.390 B.S.E.E. L.1356 J.D. [Ⓐ Sterne,K.G.&F.] (See Pat. Sect.)
*PRACTICE AREAS: Intellectual Property Law.
Fechtig, Mary E. '65 '91 C&L.347 B.S., J.D. [Baach R.&L.P.]
*PRACTICE AREAS: Insurance Coverage Litigation; Litigation.

Fedders, John M., (AV) '41 '67 C.436 B.A. L.128 LL.B.
1742 N Street, N.W., 20036
Telephone: 202-659-2424 Facsimile: 202-785-2210 URL: http://www.fedderssecuritieslaw.com
Email: JFedders@erols.com URL: http://www.lawyers.com/johnfeddersslaw
***PRACTICE AREAS: Securities Law; Commodities Law; Business Crimes; Corporate Law; Business Litigation.**
Federal Court Practice and before the Securities and Exchange Commission and Commodity Futures Trading Commission. Corporate, Securities, Commodities and Finance Practice. Litigation, Arbitration and Reparations.
See Professional Biographies, WASHINGTON, DISTRICT OF COLUMBIA

Feder, Gerald M., (AV) '36 '66 C.67 B.A. L.178 LL.B. [Feder,S.C.&B.]
*PRACTICE AREAS: Employee Benefits.
Feder, Gregory S. '70 '97 C&L.893 B.A., J.D. [Ⓐ Mayer,B.&P.]
*PRACTICE AREAS: Financial Services Law; Regulatory Law; E-Commerce; Privacy Law.

Feder, Semo, Clark & Bard, P.C., (AV)
Suite 600, 1350 Connecticut Avenue, N.W., 20036-1712
Telephone: 202-955-8305 Facsimile: 202-955-8311; 202-466-5109
URL: http://www.lawyers.com/federsemoclarkbard
Gerald M. Feder; Joseph Semo; Denise M. Clark; Howard M. Bard (Not admitted in DC); Mark C. Nielsen (Not admitted in DC). Of Counsel: Terence G. Craig.
Employee Benefits, Labor Law, Health Care, Civil Litigation, Appellate Litigation, Administrative and Legislative Practice.
See Professional Biographies, WASHINGTON, DISTRICT OF COLUMBIA

Federico, Philip C., (AV) '57 '83 C.367 B.S. L.64 J.D. [Schochor,F.&S.] ⊙
*PRACTICE AREAS: Medical Malpractice; Product Liability Law; Civil Litigation.
Federman, Michael K. '— '96 C.188 B.S. L.273 J.D. [Ⓐ Swidler B.S.F.]
*PRACTICE AREAS: Real Estate; Structured Finance; Construction.
Fedigan, John T., (AV) '32 '67
C.1031 B.S.Chem. L.128 LL.B. [Ⓒ Wenderoth,L.&P.] (See Pat. Sect.)‡
*PRACTICE AREAS: Patents; Chemical Patents; Prosecution; Interference Practice.
Fedorochko, Gary D. '— '90 C.688 B.S. L.273 J.D. [Banner&W.] (See Pat. Sect.)
*PRACTICE AREAS: Intellectual Property Law; Patents; Intellectual Property Licensing; Electrical Intellectual Property; Computer and Software Patents.
Fee, Denise A. '55 '90 C.446 B.S. L.128 J.D. [Ⓒ Jorden B.]
*PRACTICE AREAS: Class Action Defense Litigation; General Civil Litigation.
Fee, John '68 '95 C.101 B.A. L.145 J.D. [Ⓐ Sidley A.B.&W.]
Fee, Jonathan M., (AV) '49 '74 C.659 B.S. L.245 J.D.
(adm. in GA; not adm. in DC) [Alston&B.]
*PRACTICE AREAS: Customs Law; International Trade Regulation.

Feely, Timothy R. .... '67 '97 C.890 B.S. L.128 J.D. [Ⓐ Carr,M.&G.]
*PRACTICE AREAS: Business Law; Commercial Law; Corporate Law; Labor and Employment; Litigation.
Feeney, Jean I. .... '48 '78 C.502 B.A. L.273 J.D. NASD Regul., Inc.
Feeney, Thomas J. .... '53 '78 C.453 S.B. L.659 J.D. Coun., Fed. Deposit Ins. Corp.
Feffer, Gerald A., (AV) .... '42 '68 C.401 B.A. L.893 J.D. [Williams&C.]
*PRACTICE AREAS: Criminal Defense; Criminal Law; Criminal Taxation.
Fehrenbach, John .... '52 '78 C.205 B.A. L.128 J.D. [Winston&S.]
*PRACTICE AREAS: Environmental Law; Regulatory Law; Energy Law; Government; Administrative Law.
Feidelman, Joel R., (P.C.), (AV) .... '34 '58 C.823 B.A. L.976 LL.B. [Ⓒ Fried,F.H.S.&J.]
Feig, Erik M. .... '71 '97 C.188 B.S. L.262 J.D. [Ⓐ Piper M.R.&W.]
*PRACTICE AREAS: Business Law; Technology Law; Information Technology; Venture Capital; Emerging Growth Companies.
Feigen, Georgina L.O. '66 '93 C.94 B.S. L.128 J.D.
(adm. in MD; not adm. in DC) [Ⓐ Wilkinson B.K.]
*PRACTICE AREAS: Communications; Telecommunications Law; International Telecommunications.
Feigen, Philip G. .... '65 '93 C.94 B.S. L.128 J.D. [Patton B.]
Feigin, Laura Beth .... '59 '90 C.103 A.B. L.813 J.D. [Ⓐ Dickstein S.M.&O.]
*PRACTICE AREAS: Criminal and Civil Litigation.
Fein, Bruce .... '76 '00 C&L.145 A.B., J.D. [Ⓐ Sullivan&C.]
Fein, Laura E. .... '69 '96 C.309 A.B. L.178 J.D. [Ⓐ Wilmer,C.&P.]
Fein, Leslie G., (AV) .... '46 '71 C.861 B.A. L.838 J.D. [Crowley,H.&F.]
*PRACTICE AREAS: Family Law; Personal Injury Law; Elder Law.
Feinberg, Adam P. .... '— '94 C&L.276 A.B., J.D. [Ⓐ Miller&C.]
*PRACTICE AREAS: Government Contract Fraud; White Collar Crime; Government Contracts; False Claims Act.
Feinberg, Elizabeth H. .... '71 '98 C.1044 B.A., B.S. L.30 J.D. [Ⓐ Gilbert H.&R.]
*PRACTICE AREAS: General Litigation; Insurance.
Feinberg, Joel D. .... '68 '94 C.446 B.A. L.276 J.D. [Ⓐ Sidley A.B.&W.]
Feinberg, Kenneth R., (AV) .... '45 '71 C.454 B.A. L.569 J.D. [Feinberg] ⊙
*PRACTICE AREAS: Arbitration and Mediation; Products Liability.
Feinberg, Peter H., (AV) .... '46 '73 C.569 B.A. L.273 J.D. [Dow,L.&A.]

Feinberg Group, The, LLP, (AV) BB
1120 20th Street, N.W. Suite 740 South, 20036-3437 ⊙
Telephone: 202-371-1110 Fax: 202-962-9290
Email: kfeinberg@thefeinberggroup.com URL: http://www.thefeinberggroup.com
Partners: Kenneth R. Feinberg; Deborah E. Greenspan; Michael K. Rozen (Resident, New York Office); Peter H. Woodin (Resident, New York Office). Associate: Fredric M. Brooks. Senior Counsel: Jacqueline E. Zins.
Mediation and Arbitration, Products Liability.
New York, N.Y. Office: 780 3rd Avenue, Suite 2202. Telephone: 212-527-9600. Fax: 212-527-9611. Email: kfeinberg@thefeinberggroup.com.
See Professional Biographies, WASHINGTON, DISTRICT OF COLUMBIA

Feiner, Wendy P. .... '73 '98 C.260 B.A. L.273 J.D. [Ⓐ Fried,F.H.S.&J.]
*PRACTICE AREAS: Litigation.
Feinstein, Andrew A. '50 '76 C.918 B.A. L.569 J.D.
(adm. in NY; not adm. in DC) Prof., Georgetown Univ.
Feinstein, Deborah L., (AV) .... '60 '87 C.112 B.A. L.309 J.D. [Arnold&P.]
*PRACTICE AREAS: Antitrust.
Feinstein, Margaret .... '58 '88 C.918 B.A. L.904 J.D. [Dickstein S.M.&O.]
*PRACTICE AREAS: Civil Litigation; Government Affairs.
Feinstein, Nathan B., (AV) .... '29 '55 C.645 B.A. L.976 LL.B. [Piper M.R.&W.]
*PRACTICE AREAS: Bankruptcy Law.
Feira, Paul Scott .... '67 '94 C.309 A.B. L.976 J.D. [Ⓐ Arnold&P.]
*PRACTICE AREAS: Telecommunications; Corporate.
Feiring, Marshall .... '51 '79 C.569 B.A. L.1009 J.D. [Ⓐ Sidley A.B.&W.]
Feirman, Steven B., (AV) .... '55 '81 C.165 A.B. L.910 J.D. [Piper M.R.&W.]
*PRACTICE AREAS: Antitrust; Franchising and Distribution; Litigation.
Feis, Gregory S. .... '56 '81 C.112 A.B. L.1068 J.D. [Shaw P.]
Feist, John W. .... '36 '62 C.378 B.A. L.813 J.D. 3050 K St.
Feisthamel, Karen L. .... '65 '90 C.103 Sc.B. L.276 J.D. [Ⓐ Kenyon&K.] (See Pat. Sect.)
*PRACTICE AREAS: Intellectual Property.
Feit, Rona F. .... '32 '75 C.104 B.A. L.178 J.D. 604 7th St., S.W.
Feitel, Robert A. .... '58 '82 C.1044 B.A. L.273 J.D. Asst. U.S. Atty
Feith, Douglas J., (AV) ..... '— '78 C.309 A.B. L.276 J.D. [Feith&Z.] (⊙Jerusalem, Israel)
Feith & Zell, P.C., (AV) .... 1300 19th Street, N.W. (⊙Jerusalem, Tel Aviv, Israel)
Felber, Joseph L. '61 '00
C.893 B.S. L.128 J.D. [Ⓐ Armstrong,W.H.M.&N.] (See Pat. Sect.)
*PRACTICE AREAS: Patent.
Feld, Alan L. '40 '63 C.178 A.B. L.309 LL.B.
(adm. in NY; not adm. in DC) [Ⓒ Burt,M.&M.]
*PRACTICE AREAS: International Tax; Structured Finance.
Feldblum, Chai Rachel '59 '86 C.66 B.A. L.309 J.D.
(adm. in MA; not adm. in DC) Georgetown Univ. Law Ctr.
Felde, Jon R. '53 '81 C.309 A.B. L.383 J.D.
Gen. Coun., National Conference of State Legis.
Felder, Thomas Wesley, II '— '97 C.999 B.A. L.329 J.D.
Asst. Gen. Coun., Black Entertainment Television, Inc.
*RESPONSIBILITIES: Litigation; Corporate and Transactional Law; Entertainment Law; Vendor Agreements.
Feldesman, James L., (AV) .... '39 '66 C.659 B.S. L.276 J.D. [Feldesman,T.L.F.&B.]
*PRACTICE AREAS: Administrative Law; Health Care Law; Federal Grant and Contract Matters; Federal Inspector General Problems.

Feldesman, Tucker, Leifer, Fidell & Bank LLP, (AV) BB
2001 L Street, N.W., 2nd Floor, 20036 ⊙
Telephone: 202-466-8960 Telefax: 202-293-8103
Email: info@feldesmantucker.com URL: http://www.feldesmantucker.com
Members of Firm: James L. Feldesman; Marna S. Tucker; Jacqueline C. Leifer; Eugene R. Fidell; Rita M. Bank; Mary S. Pence; Jonathan M. Dana; Edward T. Waters; Roger A. Schwartz; Michael B. Glomb; Tanya A. Harvey; Richard C. Shadyac, Jr.; Bruce F. Hoffmeister; Jeffrey L. Craig. Associates: Jennifer B. Pennington; Marcie H. Zakheim; Kathy S. Ghiladi; Daniel L. Gray; Jennifer Dziedic-Leonard; Michael D. Golde; Danell Palladine Dean; Holly A. Whittier; Jessica S. Walton; Steven H. Wishod; Alane A. Peragallo; Jordana J. Hughes (Not admitted in DC); Karen L. Hecker (Not admitted in DC).
Family Law, Matrimonial Law and Domestic Relations, Health Care Law, Business, Corporate, Complex Commercial Litigation, Special Education Law and Disability Rights, Trial and Appellate Practice before Federal and State Courts, Court Martial and Administrative Agencies, Estate Planning, Trusts, Wills, Probate.
Rockville, Maryland Office: One Church Street, Suite 800. Telephone: 301-279-6770.
Falls Church, Virginia Office: 5661 Columbia Pike, Suite 200. Telephone: 703-671-5800. Fax: 703-671-5805.
See Professional Biographies, WASHINGTON, DISTRICT OF COLUMBIA

Feldgarden, Robert, (AV) .... '40 '66 C.103 B.Sc. L.569 LL.B. [McDermott,W.&E.]
Feldhaus, John J., (AV) '— '80 C.688 B.S. L.1209 J.D.
(adm. in VA; not adm. in DC; See Pat. Sect.) [Foley&L.]
*PRACTICE AREAS: Electrical and Mechanical Intellectual Property Procurement; Litigation.
Feldhaus, Stephen M., (AV) .... '45 '73 C.602 A.B. L.813 J.D. [Fulbright&J.]
*PRACTICE AREAS: International Law; Taxation; Corporate Law.

Feldhausen, Daniela P. '66 '93 C.112 B.S. L.1066 J.D.
Assoc. Gen. Coun., Fannie Mae
*RESPONSIBILITIES: E-Commerce; Technology Law; Corporate.
Feldheim, Mark S. .... '47 '73 C.608 B.A. L.161 J.D. Gen. Coun., JMW Settlements
Feldman, Cary M., (AV) .... '49 '75 C.696 B.A. L.273 J.D. [Ⓒ Piper M.R.&W.]
*PRACTICE AREAS: White Collar Crime; Litigation; Commercial Litigation.
Feldman, Clarice R., (AV) '41 '65 C&L.966 B.S., LL.B.
1050 Thomas Jefferson St., N.W.
Feldman, Daniel '72 '98 C.659 B.A. L.846 J.D.
(adm. in TX; not adm. in DC) [Ⓐ Krupin O.]
*PRACTICE AREAS: Labor and Employment.
Feldman, Darryl Alan .... '69 '94 C.861 B.S.M. L.64 J.D. [Ⓐ Sherman,M.C.&A.]
*PRACTICE AREAS: Family Law.
Feldman, Elliot J., (AV) .... '47 '88 C.145 B.A. L.309 J.D. [Baker&H.]
*PRACTICE AREAS: International Trade; International Law; Intellectual Property Infringement.
Feldman, Gabriel '73 '00 C&L.228 B.A., J.D.
(adm. in NY; not adm. in DC) [Ⓐ Williams&C.]
Feldman, Howard J., (AV) .... '39 '64 C&L.966 B.B.A., LL.B. [Van Ness F.]
*PRACTICE AREAS: Taxation; Public Lands; Federal Legislative Practice.
Feldman, Howard N. .... '58 '83 C.1044 B.A. L.904 J.D. [Dickstein S.M.&O.]
*PRACTICE AREAS: Litigation: Securities, Commercial, Product Liability and Intellectual Property.
Feldman, Jodi L. .... '66 '97 C.31 B.A. L.276 J.D. [Whitman-Walker]
*RESPONSIBILITIES: Social Security.
Feldman, John P. .... '64 '90 C.647 A.B. L.188 J.D. [Collier S.S.]
*PRACTICE AREAS: Advertising and Promotion; Sweepstakes; Electronic Commerce; Trademark; Copyright.
Feldman, Mark B., (AV) '— '61 C.918 A.B. L.309 LL.B.
[Feith&Z.] (⊙Jerusalem, Israel)
Feldman, Mark E. '70 '00 C.966 B.A. L.178 J.D.
(adm. in NY; not adm. in DC) [Ⓐ Covington&B.]
Feldman, Michael H., (AV) .... '49 '75 C.30 B.A. L.273 J.D. [Ashcraft&G.]
*PRACTICE AREAS: Medical Malpractice; Personal Injury; Products Liability.
Feldman, Myer, (AV) .... '17 '39 C&L.659 B.S., LL.B. 1250 Connecticut Ave., N.W.
Feldman, Paul J., (AV) .... '56 '88 C.178 B.A. L.1068 J.D. [Fletcher,H.&H.] ⊙
*PRACTICE AREAS: Broadcast Television; Cable TV; Communications; Common Carrier; Digital Communications.
Feldman, Roger D., (AV) .... '43 '66 C.103 B.A. L.976 LL.B. [Bingham D.]
Feldman, Stacey Ann .... '74 '99 C.477 B.A. L.904 J.D. [Ⓐ McKenna&C.]
*PRACTICE AREAS: Litigation; White Collar Crime; Employment Law; Insurance Recovery.
Feldman, Stephen M., (AV) '48 '75
C.1036 B.A. L.128 J.D. 601 Pennsylvania Avenue, N.W.
Feldman, Stuart F. .... '37 '62 C&L.659 B.A., LL.B. 1305 30th St., N.W.
Feldman, Ted J. .... '66 '93 C.1349 B.A. L.1019 J.D. [Ⓐ Gilbert H.&R.]
*PRACTICE AREAS: Complex Dispute Resolution.

Feldman, Nancy Lee
(See Arlington, Virginia)

Feldmann, Linda Danielle .... '66 '93 C.367 B.A. L.273 J.D. [Ⓐ Leventhal,S.&L.]
*PRACTICE AREAS: Broadcast; Communications.
Feldstein, Scott David .... '59 '85 C.188 B.A. L.659 J.D. [Ⓒ Covington&B.]
Feldstein, Stuart F., (AV) .... '38 '64 C&L.477 B.B.A, J.D. [Fleischman&W.]
Feldstein-Soto, Luis A. .... '60 '96 C.311 B.A. L.813 J.D. [Ⓐ Wilmer,C.&P.]
Feldt, Judith M. '— '81 C.116 B.A. L.107 J.D.
(adm. in NY; not adm. in DC) [Ⓐ Vinson&E.]
*PRACTICE AREAS: Health Law; Medicare and Medicaid; Commercial Law; Bankruptcy Reorganization.
Felgar, Robert N. .... '70 '98 C.012 B.A. L.273 J.D. [Ⓐ Dickstein S.M.&O.]
*PRACTICE AREAS: Telecommunications Law; Broadcasting Law.
Felice, Andrew N., (AV) .... '60 '86 C.867 B.A. L.273 J.D. [Katz&S.] ⊙
*PRACTICE AREAS: Construction Law; Public Contract Law; Fidelity and Surety Law.
Felix, James Clarence '39 '67 C.602 B.A. L.151 J.D.
(adm. in OH; not adm. in DC) F.B.I.
Fell, Mary Jean .... '63 '95 C.321 B.A. L.128 J.D. [Ⓐ Collier S.S.]
*PRACTICE AREAS: Antitrust.
Feller, Mary Capuano .... '61 '86 C.790 B.S. L.128 J.D. [O'Donoghue&O.]
Feller, Peter Buck, (AV) .... '37 '65 C.659 A.B. L.904 J.D. [McKenna&C.]
Fellman, Douglas A. .... '62 '87 C.367 B.A. L.188 J.D. [Hogan&H.]
*PRACTICE AREAS: Complex Civil Litigation; White Collar Criminal Defense; Professional Liability; Attorney Malpractice.
Fellman, Steven John, (AV) .... '38 '62 C.951 A.B. L.569 LL.B. [Galland,K.G.F.&S.] ⊙
*PRACTICE AREAS: Antitrust; Trade Association Law; ADA; FDA.
Fellner, Baruch A., (AV) .... '44 '69 C.273 A.B. L.309 J.D. [Gibson,D.&C.]
*PRACTICE AREAS: Labor Relations Law; Employee Benefits Law; Occupational Safety and Health Law; Litigation.
Fels, Adam S. .... '— '00 C.178 A.B. L.145 J.D. [Ⓐ Latham&W.]
*PRACTICE AREAS: Litigation.
Fels, Nicholas W., (AV) .... '43 '68 C&L.309 B.A., LL.B. [Covington&B.]
Felsen, Daniel K. .... '66 '91 C&L.893 B.A., J.D. [McManus,S.A.&D.]
*PRACTICE AREAS: Construction Law; Fidelity and Surety.
Felton, Thomas F. '70 '00 C.893 B.A L.128 J.D.
(adm. in VA; not adm. in DC) [Ⓐ Akin,G.S.H.&F.]
*PRACTICE AREAS: Health Care.
Femia, Nicholas R. .... '58 '85 C.674 A.B. L.569 J.D. [O'Donoghue&O.]
*PRACTICE AREAS: Labor and Employment Law.
Fendrich, Roger P. .... '43 '80 C.472 A.B. L.976 J.D. [Arnold&P.]
*PRACTICE AREAS: Litigation.
Fenimore, David L. .... '47 '90 C.95 B.A. L.180 J.D. [Ⓒ Fried,F.H.S.&J.]
*PRACTICE AREAS: Securities Law Enforcement; Broker-Dealer Compliance; Corporate.
Fennell, Lee Anne .... '66 '90 C.69 B.B.A. L.276 J.D. 444 N. Capitol St., N.W.
Fennell, Stephen A., (AV) .... '52 '78 C.446 B.A. L.276 J.D. [Steptoe&J.]
*PRACTICE AREAS: Litigation, Construction and Insurance Law.
Fennell, William A., (AV) .... '48 '77 C.674 A.B. L.30 J.D. [Stewart&S.]
*PRACTICE AREAS: International Trade; International Trade Regulation; Import and Export Law; Antidumping; Export Regulation.
Fenske, Scott A. .... '65 '90 C.723 B.A. L.904 J.D. 1920 N St., N.W.
Fenster, Herbert L., (AV) '35 '61
C.659 A.B. L.893 LL.B. [McKenna&C.] (⊙Denver, CO)
Fensterheim, G. David .... '57 '81 C.976 B.A. L.893 J.D. [Fensterheim&B.]
Fensterheim & Bean, P.C. .... 1250 Connecticut Avenue, N.W., Suite 700
Fenton, Kathryn M., (AV) .... '53 '78 C.1030 B.A. L.276 J.D. [Jones,D.R.&P.]
*PRACTICE AREAS: Antitrust and Trade Regulation; Competition.
Fentonmiller, Laura C. .... '70 '94 C&L.477 B.S., J.D. [Ⓐ Bell,B.&L.]
*PRACTICE AREAS: Employment Law.
Fentress, Lisa D. '62 '88 C.862 B.S. L.904 J.D.
Asst. Gen. Coun., Washington Metropolitan Area Transit Authority
*RESPONSIBILITIES: Litigation.
Fenwick, Francis E., (AV) .... '45 '75 C&L.276 B.A., J.D. [Craighill,M.F.C.&C.]
*PRACTICE AREAS: Estate Planning; Probate Law; Trusts.

Fenwick & West LLP, (AV)
1920 N Street, N.W., Suite 650, 20036 ⊙
Telephone: 202-261-0400 Fax: 202-463-6520; 202-887-5143
URL: http://www.fenwick.com

(This Listing Continued)

Fenwick & West LLP (Continued)

Roger M. Golden; Garry S. Grossman; Brian S. Kelly (Not admitted in DC); C. Kevin Kelso (Not admitted in DC). Associates: Phyllis E. Andes; Marc S. Berger; Christopher M. Tobin (Not admitted in DC).

General Practice. Corporate, Securities, Mergers and Acquisitions, Executive Compensation and Employee Benefits, Intellectual Property, Including Patent, Trademark and Copyright, Licensing and Online Commerce, Computer and High Technology Law, Government Contracts and Procurement, Litigation and Alternative Dispute Resolution, Antitrust and Trade Regulation, Trade Secrets, Employment and Labor Law and Domestic and International Taxation.

Palo Alto, California Office: Two Palo Alto Square. Telephone: 650-494-0600. Fax: 650-494-1417.

San Francisco, California Office: 275 Battery Street, Suite 1500. Telephone: 415-875-2358. Fax: 415-281-1350.

Boise, Idaho Office: 877 West main Street, suite 706, 83702. Telephone: 208-331-0700. Fax: 208-331-7723.

See Professional Biographies, WASHINGTON, DISTRICT OF COLUMBIA

Feola, Phil T., (AV) ...'47 '79 C.602 B.A. L.128 J.D. [Shaw P.]
*PRACTICE AREAS: Real Estate; Zoning, Planning and Land Use; Municipal Law.
Feore, John R., Jr., (AV) ... '46 '75 C.93 A.B. L.276 J.D. [Dow,L.&A.]
Ferber, David ...'12 '36 C.659 B.S. L.982 LL.B. 1200 18th St., N.W.
Ferber, Judith R. '48 '76 C.145 B.A. L.1162 J.D.
George Washington Univ. Natl. Law Ctr.
Ferenchak, Brett P. ...'72 '97 C.228 A.B. L.692 J.D. [Ⓐ Swidler B.S.F.]
*PRACTICE AREAS: Telecommunications.
Ferger, Kathryn ...'53 '81 C.604 B.A. L.1119 J.D. 1337 Hamilton St., N.W.
Ferguson, Brian E. ...'66 '92 C.867 B.S.E.E. L.982 J.D. [McDermott,W.&E.] (Pat.)
Ferguson, Catherine A. '— '93 C.550 B.A. L.1338 J.D.
[Ⓐ Banner&W.] (See Pat. Sect.)
*PRACTICE AREAS: Intellectual Property.
Ferguson, Edward L., Jr. ... '60 '92 C.732 B.S. L.128 J.D. [Ⓐ Howrey S.A.&W.]
*PRACTICE AREAS: Environmental Law; Regulatory; Litigation; Legislative Practice.
Ferguson, Edward T., III '56 '82 C.178 B.A. L.309 J.D.
(adm. in NY; not adm. in DC) [Ⓒ T.F.Lenzner]
*PRACTICE AREAS: Investigations; Litigation; Transactions.
Ferguson, James ... '60 '99 C.640 B.S. L.329 J.D. [Ⓐ Swidler B.S.F.]
*PRACTICE AREAS: Telecommunications.
Ferguson, John R., (AV) ...'34 '63 C.608 B.A. L.930 J.D. [Swidler B.S.F.]
*PRACTICE AREAS: Litigation; Antitrust.
Ferguson, Lewis H., III, (AV) ... '44 '71 C.976 B.A. L.309 J.D. [Williams&C.]
*PRACTICE AREAS: Asset Sales; Biomedical Technology; Biotechnology Licensing; Business Dissolutions; Business Formation.
Ferguson, Sheila Lowery ...'55 '90 C.999 B.A. L.112 J.D. [Ⓐ Smith&Assoc.]
Ferkin, Zori G., (BV) ...'57 '81 C.165 A.B. L.276 J.D. [Ⓒ Dewey B.]
*PRACTICE AREAS: Energy.
Ferman, Irving '19 '48 C.569 B.S. L.309 LL.B.
Prof., Emeritus, Howard Univ. Law Sch.
Fernandes, Gregg Joseph '68 '99 C&L.446 B.A., J.D.
(adm. in MD; not adm. in DC) Washington Post, The
Fernandes, Praveen D. ...'72 '00 C.103 B.A. L.575 J.D. [Ⓐ Bennett,T.&C.]
*PRACTICE AREAS: Health Law; Legislative Practice; Biomedical Technology.
Fernandez, Ada ... '— '98 C.103 A.B. L.276 J.D. [Ⓐ Brobeck,P.&H.]
*PRACTICE AREAS: Securities Litigation.
Fernandez, Charles M. ... '56 '97 C.390 B.A. L.188 J.D. 555 12 St., N.W.
Fernandez, Jose Ignacio ... '45 '92 L.276 J.D. 1701 Pennsylvania Ave., N.W.
Fernandez, Lillian '54 '79 C.563 B.A. L.659 J.D.
(adm. in PA; not adm. in DC) Corporation for Public Broadcasting
Ferrans, Michael ... '71 '96 C.861 B.A. L.273 J.D. [Ⓐ Akin,G.S.H.&F.]
*PRACTICE AREAS: Labor and Employment.
Ferrara, Ralph C., (AV) ... '45 '70 C.276 B.S. L.150 J.D. [Debevoise&P.]
*PRACTICE AREAS: Corporate Financing Law; Mergers and Acquisitions; SEC Enforcement; Securities Litigation; Securities Regulation Law.
Ferrari, Paul L. ...'60 '98 C.477 B.A. L.273 J.D. [Ⓐ Hyman,P.&M.]
*PRACTICE AREAS: Food and Drug Regulation.
Ferrario, Matias ...'72 '00 C.477 B.S. L.124 J.D. 1299 Pennsylvania Ave.
Ferraro, Donald P. ...'57 '93 C.260 B.S. L.1202 J.D. [Ⓐ Winston&S.] (Pat.)
*PRACTICE AREAS: Energy; Nuclear; Administrative.
Ferrate, Alejandro ... '69 '95 C.695 B.A. L.1209 J.D. [Ⓐ Shaw P.]
Ferreira, Cristina M. L. ...'65 '94 C.999 B.C.H.L. L.146 J.D. [Ⓐ Skadden,A.S.M.&F.]
*PRACTICE AREAS: Energy; Project Finance.
Ferreira, Penelope S. '39 '85 C.999 B.A. L.229 J.D.
(adm. in PA; not adm. in DC) Assoc. Dir., Pub. Servs. Div., Amer. Bar Assn.
Ferrell, Elizabeth A., (AV) ... '57 '82 C&L.790 B.A., J.D. [Sonnenschein N.&R.]
*PRACTICE AREAS: Government Contract Law; Commercial Litigation.
Ferren, John M. ... '37 '62 C&L.309 A.B., LL.B. Assoc. J., Ct. of App.
Ferrenz, Andrea Gallimore ...'71 '98 C.890 B.S. L.273 J.D. [Ⓐ Emord&Assoc.]
*PRACTICE AREAS: Civil Litigation; Administrative Law; Food and Drug Regulation; Intellectual Property; Constitutional Law.
Ferrera, Tess J. ... '57 '90 C.273 B.A. L.276 J.D. [Kilpatrick S.]
*PRACTICE AREAS: ERISA.
Ferrigno, Thomas A., (AV) ...'49 '75 C&L.276 A.B., J.D. [Hughes H.&R.]
*PRACTICE AREAS: Securities Regulation and Enforcement; Litigation.
Ferrin, Richard P. ...'61 '97 C.597 B.A. L.30 J.D. [Ⓐ Hunton&W.]
*PRACTICE AREAS: International Trade Regulation (100%).
Ferris, Charles D., (AV) ... '33 '61 C&L.93 A.B., J.D. [Mintz,L.C.F.G.&P.]
*PRACTICE AREAS: Litigation; Telecommunications; Legislation.
Ferris, Gail A., (Mr.) '53 '79 C.976 B.A. L.150 J.D.
(adm. in CT; not adm. in DC)
Exec. Dir., Alumni/Develop. Records, George Washington University
Ferris, Richard J., Jr. ...'62 '96 C.156 B.A. L.228 J.D. [Ⓐ Beveridge&D.]
*PRACTICE AREAS: International Environmental Law; China Trade; Asia Trade; United Nations Law; International Finance.
Ferro, Albert L. '66 '98 C.871 B.S.A.E. L.446 J.D.
(adm. in MD; not adm. in DC) [Ⓐ Sterne,K.G.&F.]
*PRACTICE AREAS: Patent Litigation; Patent Prosecution.

Ferry, Daniel R., & Associates '41 '65 C.999 B.A. L.502 J.D.
600 14th Street, N.W. Suite 600, 20005-2004
Telephone: 202-659-0146 Fax: 202-659-0148
Email: ftasinc@aol.com URL: http://www.lawyers.com/danielrferrylaw
International Private Law, International Commercial Transactions, International Personal Injury Law, Corporate and Business Law.

See Professional Biographies, WASHINGTON, DISTRICT OF COLUMBIA

Ferster, Andrea C. ...'58 '84 C.771 B.A. L.273 J.D. 1100 17th St, N.W., 10th Fl.
Ferstl, Kurt D. '64 '99 C.945 B.A. L.1209 J.D.
(adm. in VA; not adm. in DC) [Ⓐ Reed S.]
*PRACTICE AREAS: Government Contracts; Export Compliance.
Fetter, Leslie D. ...'74 '99 C.237 B.A. L.665 J.D. [Ⓐ Wiley R.&F.]
Feuer, Semi ...'36 '62 C&L.273 B.A., LL.B. Asst. Corp. Coun.
Feuer, Stacy A. ...'65 '91 C.188 B.S. L.569 J.D. Fed. Trade Comm.
Feuerle, Peter '40 '78 C.378 Ph.D. L.976 J.D.
(adm. in NY; not adm. in DC) 1747 Pennsylvania Ave., N.W.
Feuerstein, Adam S. ...'71 '97 C.188 B.S. L.309 J.D. [Ⓐ Hogan&H.]
*PRACTICE AREAS: Tax; Corporate.
Feuerstein, Ronald A., (AV) ...'47 '73 C.94 B.A. L.30 J.D. [Kilpatrick S.]
*PRACTICE AREAS: Taxation; Estate Planning; Pension and Profit Sharing.
Fex, Cecilia ... '57 '92 C.446 B.A. L.309 J.D. [Ⓐ Ackerson]
*PRACTICE AREAS: Complex Litigation; Class Actions; Appellate Practice.
Fiala, Thomas C. ...'67 '98 C.688 B.S. L.306 J.D. [Ⓐ Sterne,K.G.&F.] (See Pat. Sect.)
*PRACTICE AREAS: Patent Law; Intellectual Property Law.
Fichthorn, Norman W. ... '58 '85 C.97 B.A. L.813 J.D. [Hunton&W.]
*PRACTICE AREAS: Environmental; Administrative.
Fick, Philip J. ... '— '98 C.734 B.S.B.A. L.276 J.D. [Ⓐ Reed S.] (⊙Washington)
*PRACTICE AREAS: Real Estate.
Fickett, Joel A. '57 '91 C.1155 B.S. L.94 J.D.
(adm. in MA; not adm. in DC) Atty., Nat. Assn. of Sec. Dealers, Inc.
Ficklin, Patrice Alexander '61 '91
C.276 A.B. L.309 J.D. Dir., Off. of Corp. Jus., Fannie Mae
Fidell, Eugene R., (AV) ...'45 '68 C.994 B.A. L.309 LL.B. [Feldesman,T.L.F.&B.]
*PRACTICE AREAS: Civil Litigation; Administrative Litigation; Military Litigation.
Fidelman, Morris, (AV) ... '23 '51 C.563 B.Ch.E. L.276 LL.B. 1233 20th St., N.W. (Pat.)
Fiedler, Marc, (AV) ... '55 '85 C&L.309 B.A., J.D. [Koonz,M.J.D.&L.]
Field, Andrea Bear, (AV) ... '49 '74 C.976 B.A. L.893 J.D. [Hunton&W.]
*PRACTICE AREAS: Environmental.
Field, Charles G., (BV) '40 '78 C.188 B.A. L.276 J.D.
Staff V.P. & Regulatory Coun., National Association of Home Builders
Field, Deborah M. ... '69 '96 C.823 B.A. L.273 J.D. [Ⓐ Wilmer,C.&P.]
Field, Ingrid L. Dietsch '72 '98
C.1049 B.A. L.1002 J.D. U.S. Equal Employment Opportunity Comm.
Field, John J. '67 '96 C.216 B.A. L.273 J.D.
(adm. in NY; not adm. in DC) 607 14th St., N.W.‡
Fielding, Fred F., (AV) ... '39 '65 C.282 A.B. L.893 J.D. [Wiley R.&F.]
*PRACTICE AREAS: Government Affairs; Business Law; Crisis Management; White Collar Litigation.
Fields, Beverly Ann '65 '94 C&L.329 B.S.M.E., J.D.
(adm. in MD; not adm. in DC) 1523 Longworth Bldg.
Fields, Debra F. ...'62 '87 C.1036 B.A. L.309 J.D. The Geo. Wash. Univ.
Fields, Rhonda C. '50 '73 C.569 B.A. L.276 J.D.
(adm. in MD; not adm. in DC) Asst. U.S. Atty.
Fields, Wendy L., (AV) ... '46 '76 C&L.273 B.A., J.D. [Katten M.Z.]
*PRACTICE AREAS: Commercial Real Estate Law.
Fierberg, Douglas E. ... '59 '88 C.477 B.A. L.904 J.D. [Sherman,M.C.&A.]
*PRACTICE AREAS: Commercial Litigation; Products Liability; Hazing; Campus; Personal Injury.
Fierst, David U., (AV) ... '50 '75 C.659 B.A. L.273 J.D. [Stein,M.&M.]
*PRACTICE AREAS: General Civil Litigation; Antitrust; Trade Regulation.
Fierst, Edith U., (AV) ... '25 '49 C.788 B.A. L.273 LL.B. 1225 19th St. N.W.
Fierst, Herbert A., (AV) ...'14 '39 C.309 A.B. L.976 LL.B. 1200 18th St., N.W.
Fife, Joan B. Tucker, (AV) ...'61 '86 C.597 B.A. L.880 J.D. [Winston&S.]
*PRACTICE AREAS: Employment Litigation; Employment Law; Title VII Discrimination; Sexual Harassment; Employment Disability Discrimination.
Fife, K. Scott ... '60 '86 C.301 B.A. L.245 J.D. 1220 19th St Nw # 700
Figel, Reid M., (AV) ...'56 '82 C.478 A.B. L.569 LL.B. [Kellogg,H.H.T.&E.]
*PRACTICE AREAS: Litigation; Securities.
Figg, E. Anthony, (AV) '46 '73
C.701 B.S. L.345 J.D. [Rothwell,F.E.&M.] (See Pat. Sect.)
*PRACTICE AREAS: Intellectual Property.
Figueiras, Dawn '66 '00 C.886 B.A.Ed. L.945 J.D.
(adm. in VA; not adm. in DC) [Ⓐ Gibson,D.&C.]
Figueroa, John J. '59 '99 C.350 B.S. L.262 J.D.
(adm. in NY; not adm. in DC) [Ⓐ Wenderoth,L.&P.]
*PRACTICE AREAS: Patent Prosecution; Chemical Patents.
Filipek, Jeffrey R. '70 '00
C.645 B.S.E.E. L.180 J.D. [Ⓐ Wenderoth,L.&P.] (See Pat. Sect.)
*PRACTICE AREAS: Patents.
Filipos, John M. '51 '83 C.645 B.S. L.1356 J.D.
Asst. V.P., Barnes, Morris, Pardoe & Foster, Inc.

Filler & Weller, P.C.
(See Alexandria, Virginia)

Fillinger, Tamera A. '59 '90 C.769 B.A. L.1068 J.D.
(adm. in NY; not adm. in DC) [Ⓒ Sonenthal&O.]
*PRACTICE AREAS: Nonprofit Organizations Law; Federal Grants; Government Contracts; Government Procurement; International Contracts.
Filou, Rosemary A. '63 '90 C.976 B.A. L.1066 J.D.
U.S. Securities and Exchange Comm.
Filpi, James D. ... '— '99 [Ⓐ Goodwin P.]
Filpi, Mark ... '— '94 C&L.893 B.S., J.D. [Ⓐ King&S.]
*PRACTICE AREAS: Taxation.
Fimea, Victoria E. '61 '88 C.35 B.S. L.904 J.D.
Sr. Coun., Litig., Amer. Coun. of Life Ins.
Fina, Marielena '— '90 C.477 B.A. L.588 J.D.
Staff Atty., Cambridge & Somerville Legal Servs. Inc.
Fina, Thomas D. ...'60 '89 C.309 A.B. L.893 J.D. [Howrey S.A.&W.]
*PRACTICE AREAS: Antitrust.
Finan, Thomas M. ...'70 '96 C.893 B.A. L.494 J.D. [Ⓐ Hunton&W.]
*PRACTICE AREAS: Telecommunications Litigation.
Finch, Arthur W. ... '38 '74 C.33 B.A. L.309 J.D. State Pub. Serv. Comm.
Finch, Brian E. ...'74 '99 C.188 B.S. L.273 J.D. [Ⓐ Long A.&N.]
*PRACTICE AREAS: Litigation; Government/Administrative.
Finch, David L. ...'68 '94 C.294 B.A. L.285 J.D. [Ⓐ Robins,K.M.&C.]
*PRACTICE AREAS: Taxation; Partnerships; Corporations.
Finch, Glenda S. '49 '84 C.577 B.A. L.128 J.D.
Dep. Gen. Coun., UMWA Health & Retirement Funds
Finch, Nathan D. ... '67 '92 C&L.893 B.A., J.D. [Caplin&D.]
*PRACTICE AREAS: Commercial Litigation; Civil Litigation; Criminal Litigation; Tax Litigation.
Finch, Ruth Mae, (CV) '52 '78 C.446 B.A. L.64 J.D.
(adm. in MD; not adm. in DC) [Ⓒ Stevens,D.M.&M.]
*PRACTICE AREAS: Intellectual Property; Litigation.
Finder, Jodi ...'73 '98 C.228 B.A L.273 J.D. [Ⓐ Kirkpatrick&L.]
Findlay, Jon C., Jr. '65 '00 C.1128 B.A. L.192 J.D.
(adm. in NC; not adm. in DC) [Ⓐ Muldoon M.&F.]
*PRACTICE AREAS: Securities Law; Corporate Law; Banking Law.
Fine, Alexander D. '72 '01 C.228 A.B. L.893 J.D.
(adm. in NY; not adm. in DC) [Ⓐ Sullivan&C.]
Fine, Jacqueline H. ... '65 '92 C.494 B.S. L.188 J.D. [Ⓐ Baker B.]
Fine, Lisa R. '70 '99 C.860 B.A. L.276 J.D.
(adm. in NY; not adm. in DC) [Ⓐ Weil,G.&M.]
Fine, Michael E. ... '54 '83 C.705 B.A. L.94 J.D. [Powell,G.F.&M.]
*PRACTICE AREAS: Legislative; International Trade; Government Ethics.
Fineberg, Todd C. ...'44 '68 C.188 A.B. L.94 J.D. [Ⓒ Rodriguez O.F.G.&W.]
*PRACTICE AREAS: International Trade; International Transactions; International Investment; Business; Trusts and Estates.

Fineman, Stanley J., (AV) .... '39 '64 C.477 B.A. L.178 LL.B. [Wilkes A.]
*PRACTICE AREAS: Real Property Tax and Assessment Law; Condemnation; Litigation.
Finerfrock, James S., (AV) .... '57 '83 C.874 B.A. L.276 J.D. 4510 Q Place N.W.
Finger, Shelley .... '74 '00 C.30 B.A. L.904 J.D. [Ⓐ Fried,F.H.S.&J.]
*PRACTICE AREAS: Corporate.
Fingerhut, Michael B. .... '46 '72 C&L.273 B.A., J.D. Gen. Atty., Sprint Corp.
Fink, Jeanne Martyn '61 '98 C.561 B.S. L.446 J.D.
(adm. in MD; not adm. in DC) Assoc. Gen. Coun., National Geographic Society
*RESPONSIBILITIES: Contracts; Intellectual Property; Entertainment Law.
Fink, Marc J., (AV) .... '47 '73 C.1044 B.A. L.273 J.D. [Sher&B.]
*PRACTICE AREAS: Transportation; Maritime Law; Antitrust; Government Relations.
Fink, Matthew P. .... '41 '66 C.103 B.A. L.309 LL.B. Pres., Investment Co. Inst.
Finkel, E. Jay .... '31 '66 C.821 B.A. L.273 J.D. [Porter W.M.&A.]
*PRACTICE AREAS: Bank and Thrift Regulation Law; International Finance and Trade Law.
Finkelson, David .... '71 '99 C&L.893 B.A., J.D. [Ⓐ Covington&B.]
Finkelstein, Anita J. .... '57 '82 C.967 B.A. L.976 J.D. [Venable,A.B.H.&C.]
*PRACTICE AREAS: Securities Regulation; Corporate; Corporate Finance.
Finkelstein, Ben, (AV) .... '57 '82 C.311 B.S. L.976 J.D. [Spiegel&M.]
*PRACTICE AREAS: Administrative Hearings and Appeals; Energy; Hydroelectricity; Federal Energy Regulation; Litigation.
Finkelstein, Burton H., (AV) .... '37 '62 C.563 B.B.A. L.659 LL.B. [Finkelstein,T.&L.]
Finkelstein, Jay Gary .... '53 '78 C.674 A.B. L.309 J.D. [Piper M.R.&W.]
*PRACTICE AREAS: Corporate Law; Corporate Partnerships; Workouts; Securities Regulation Law; Mergers and Acquisitions Law.
Finkelstein, Jay M., (AV) '37 '64
C.223 B.S.E.E. L.273 J.D. [Ⓒ Browdy&N.] (See Pat. Sect.)
*PRACTICE AREAS: Intellectual Property.

Finkelstein, Joel M., (AV) '39 '64 C.861 B.B.A. L.188 LL.B.
1742 N Street, N.W., 20036
Telephone: 202-659-3322 FAX: 202-785-2210
Email: attorneydc@aol.com URL: http://www.lawyers.com/joelfinkelstein
(Also of Counsel to Karp, Frosh, Lapidus & Wigodsky, P.A.).
General Negligence, Trials and Appeals. Medical Malpractice, Personal Injury, Automobile Accidents, Legal Malpractice, Professional Malpractice, Premises Liability, Wrongful Death, Products Liability Law.
See Professional Biographies, WASHINGTON, DISTRICT OF COLUMBIA

Finkelstein, Jon G. '72 '01 C.178 B.A. L.494 J.D.
(adm. in NY; not adm. in DC) [Ⓐ Dewey B.]
*PRACTICE AREAS: Tax.
Finkelstein, Marci J. .... '70 '00 C.475 B.A. L.477 J.D. [Ⓐ Dow,L.&A.]
Finkelstein, Nathan I.
(See Bethesda, Maryland)
Finkelstein, Thompson & Loughran, (AV)
1055 Thomas Jefferson Street, N.W. Suite 601
Finkle, Rachel L. '73 '00 C&L.93 B.A., J.D.
(adm. in MD; not adm. in DC) [Ⓐ Venable,A.B.H.&C.]
*PRACTICE AREAS: Legislative Practice; Regulatory.
Finlator, Martha D. .... '50 '76 C&L.896 B.A., J.D. Natl. Treasury Employees Union
Finley, Timothy T. .... '70 '95 C.37 B.A. L.597 J.D. [Ⓐ Howrey S.A.&W.]
Finn, Gerard P. .... '66 '94 C.105 B.A. L.273 J.D. [Ⓐ Bingham D.]
*PRACTICE AREAS: Environmental Law; Commercial Litigation; Bankruptcy.
Finn, John M. '— '60
(adm. in MA; not adm. in DC) Legis. Coun., Congressional Affairs
Finn, Kelley A., (P.A.) '58 '86 C.260 B.S. L.362 J.D.
(adm. in FL; not adm. in DC) [Richter,M.&F.] (⊙Miami Beach, FL)
Finn, Tamar E. .... '69 '94 C.105 B.A. L.276 J.D. [Ⓐ Swidler B.S.F.]
*PRACTICE AREAS: Telecommunications Regulation; Local Telecommunications Competition.
Finn, Timothy J. .... '50 '77 C&L.309 A.B., J.D. [Jones,D.R.&P.]
*PRACTICE AREAS: Litigation; Administrative Litigation.
Finnegan, David B. .... '33 '61 C&L.93 B.S., LL.B. [Ⓒ Mayer,B.&P.]

Finnegan, Henderson, Farabow, Garrett & Dunner, L.L.P., (AV) BR
1300 I Street, N.W., Suite 700, 20005 ⊙
Telephone: 202-408-4000 Facsimile: 202-408-4400
Email: info@finnegan.com URL: http://www.finnegan.com
Members of Firm: Marcus B. Finnegan (1927-1979); Douglas B. Henderson; Ford F. Farabow Jr.; Arthur S. Garrett; Donald R. Dunner; Brian G. Brunsvold; Jerry D. Voight (Resident Partner, Palo Alto, California Office); Laurence R. Hefter; Herbert H. Mintz; C. Larry O'Rourke (Resident Partner, Palo Alto, California Office); Albert J. Santorelli; Michael C. Elmer (Resident Partner, Palo Alto, California Office); Richard H. Smith; Stephen L. Peterson; John M. Romary; Bruce C. Zotter; D. Patrick O'Reilley; Allen M. Sokal; Robert D. Bajefsky; Richard Lee Stroup; David W. Hill; Thomas L. Irving; Charles E. Lipsey; Thomas W. Winland; Basil J. Lewris; Martin I. Fuchs; E. Robert Yoches; Barry W. Graham; Susan Haberman Griffen; Richard B. Racine; Thomas H. Jenkins III; Robert E. Converse Jr.; Clair X. Mullen Jr.; Christopher P. Foley; John C. Paul; Roger D. Taylor (Resident Partner, Atlanta, Georgia Office); Griffith B. Price Jr.; John F. Hornick; Robert D. Litowitz; David M. Kelly; Kenneth John Meyers; Carol P. Einaudi; Walter Y. Boyd Jr.; Steven M. Anzalone; Darrel C. Karl; Jean Burke Fordis (Resident Partner, Palo Alto, California Office); Barbara Clarke McCurdy; James K. Hammond; Richard V. Burgujian; John Michael Jakes; John C. Lowe; Thomas W. Banks (Resident Partner, Cambridge, Massachusetts Office); Christopher P. Isaac; Bryan C. Diner (Resident Partner, Brussels, Belgium Office); M. Paul Barker (Resident Partner, Palo Alto, California Office); Andrew Chanho Sonu; Mark Sommers; Kenneth M. Frankel; William H. Pratt; David S. Forman; Vincent P. Kovalick; Don O. Burley; Gerson S. Panitch; James W. Edmondson; Michael R. McGurk; Cheri M. Taylor; Joann M. Neth; Linda A. Wadler; Liam O'Grady (Not admitted in DC); Charles E. Van Horn; Jeffrey A. Berkowitz; Michael R. Kelly (Resident Partner, Tokyo, Japan Office); James B. Monroe; Doris Johnson Hines; David Avrum Manspeizer; Lori-Ann Johnson (Resident Associate, Atlanta, Georgia Office); Lisa Peller London; John R. Alison; Allen R. Jensen; Scott R. Mosko (Resident Partner, Palo Alto, California Office); Ronald A. Bleeker; John A. Rissman (Not admitted in DC; Resident Partner, Cambridge, Massachusetts Office); Gerald F. Ivey; James H. Johnson, Jr. (Resident Partner, Atlanta, Georgia Office); R. Bruce Bower (Resident Partner, Atlanta, Georgia Office); Julia Anne Matheson (Resident Partner, Palo Alto, California Office); Yitai Hu; Virginia L. Carron (Resident Partner, Atlanta, Georgia Office); Martin F. Majestic (Resident Partner, Palo Alto, California Office); Therese A. Hendricks (Resident Partner, Cambridge, Massachusetts Office); M. Lawrence Oliverio (Resident Partner, Cambridge, Massachusetts Office); Kenneth W. Curtis. Senior Counsel: Tipton D. Jennings IV; Kenneth E. Payne. Of Counsel: Smith Rufus Brittingham IV; Ernest F. Chapman; William B. Dyer, III (Resident Counsel, Atlanta, Georgia Office); Robert J. Eichelburg; C. Edward Good (Not admitted in DC); Wayne W. Herrington; George E. Hutchinson; Thomas L. Jarvis; Mary C. Kennedy; Arthur J. Levine; Laura P. Masurovsky; Robert F. McCauley, III (Resident Counsel, Palo Alto, California Office); William T. McClain; Leslie A. McDonell (Resident Counsel, Boston, Massachusetts Office); Steven H. Morrissett (Resident Counsel, Palo Alto, California Office); Robert F. Rotella; Russell L. Sandidge (Resident Counsel, Atlanta, Georgia Office); Robert F. Ziems. Associates: Jennifer R. Adams Draffen (Resident Associate, Palo Alto, California Office); Eric William Adcock; Andrea Anderson; Erika Harmon Arner; Adam Avrunin (Resident Associate, Atlanta, Georgia Office); Eyal Hanan Barash; James R. Barney (Not admitted in DC); Kenneth D. Bassinger (Resident Associate, Atlanta, Georgia Office); F. Leslie Bessenger III (Resident Associate, Atlanta, Georgia Office); Barry D. Biddle (Resident Associate, Atlanta, Georgia Office); Daniel Brian Binstock; Leslie I. Bookoff; Michele C. Bosch; James J. Boyle; William J. Brogan; Walter W. Brown (Resident Associate, Atlanta, Georgia Office); Paul W. Browning; Jason R. Buratti (Not admitted in DC); Elizabeth Marie Burke (Not admitted in DC); Brian Burn (Not admitted in DC); Robert L. Burns; L. Scott Burwell; Kelly A. Casey (Resident Associate, Atlanta, Georgia Office); Charles W. Chesney; Gregory A. Chopskie; Kimani Clark; Carol L. Cole (Not admitted in DC); Vanessa J. Cooper; Christopher L. Crumbley (Resident Associate, Atlanta, Georgia Office); Kathleen Alice Daley; Christopher William Day (Not admitted in DC); Frank A. DeCosta III; Matthew DelGiorno; Timothy B. Donaldson (Not admitted in DC); Anthony Dreux; José A. Duthil (Resident Associate, Atlanta, Georgia Office); Houtan Khalili Esfahani; Margaret A. Esquenet; York Moody Faulkner; Michael J. Flibbert; David Penn Frazier; Susan M. Freedman; Lawrence Francis

(This Listing Continued)

Finnegan, Henderson, Farabow, Garrett & Dunner, L.L.P. (Continued)
Galvin; Stephanie S. Conis Gauthier (Resident Associate, Atlanta, Georgia Office); Jonathan M. Gelchinsky; Jason E. Gorden (Resident Associate, Palo Alto, California Office); Paul C. Goulet; Troy Edwin Grabow; C. Gregory Gramenopoulos (Resident Associate, Brussels, Belgium Office); Anthony M. Gutowski; Anthony A. Hartmann; Kristen M. Healey; B. Brett Heavner; Christie Baty Heinze (Resident Associate, Atlanta, Georgia Office); Scott A. Herbst (Resident Associate, Palo Alto, California Office); Rebecca D. Hess (Not admitted in DC); Christina J. Hieber; Timothy M. Hsieh; John A. Hudalla (Resident Associate, Atlanta, Georgia Office); Lynn M. Jordan; D. Brian Kacedon (Not admitted in DC); Vamsi K. Kakarla (Not admitted in DC); Lara Chapman Kelley; Sang Hui Michael Kim (Resident Associate, Palo Alto, California Office); Paul Alan Larson (Not admitted in DC); Lionel M. Lavenue; Christine E. Lehman; Kenneth M. Lesch (Not admitted in DC); Howard Warren Levine; Louis J. Levy; Esther H. Lim; Kurt Albert Luther; Keith Douglas MacMillan; Elizabeth McGoogan Magnuson; Phil N. Makrogiannis (Resident Associate, Palo Alto, California Office); Robert W. Mann (Resident Associate, Palo Alto, California Office); Geoffrey Colbourne Mason; Matthew Jerald Mason; Robert A. Matthews, Jr.; Timothy James May (Not admitted in DC); Roland George McAndrews, Jr.; Kevin William McCabe; Michael J. McCabe II (Resident Associate, Atlanta, Georgia Office); Ellen Kathleen McDonnell; Rebecca McNeill; Courtney Beth Meeker; Arie M. Michelsohn (Not admitted in DC); Michael A. Morin; Carolyn E. Morris; Allen J. Moss (Not admitted in DC); Sean Christopher Myers-Payne (Not admitted in DC); William Nakhleh (Not admitted in DC); Charles D. Niebylski (Not admitted in DC); Elizabeth Ann Niemeyer (Not admitted in DC); Karna Jean Nisewaner (Resident Associate, Palo Alto, California Office); Michelle O'Brien (Not admitted in DC); Steven P. O'Connor; Kristen Rae Jakobsen Osenga; Steven L. Park (Resident Associate, Atlanta, Georgia Office); Robert A. Pollock; Scott J. Popma; Montia Givens Pressey; Erik R. Puknys (Resident Associate, Palo Alto, California Office); Eric P. Raciti; Richard L. Rainey (Resident Associate, Atlanta, Georgia Office); Aaron M. Raphael; Evan A. Raynes; Douglas A. Rettew; Monica Anne Riva; Rafael E. Rosado (Resident Associate, Cambridge, Massachusetts Office); Barbara R. Rudolph; Christopher S. Schultz (Resident Associate, Cambridge, Massachusetts Office); Steven J. Scott (Resident Associate, Brussels, Belgium Office); Julie M. Seaman (Not admitted in DC); Robert Frederic Shaffer; Parmanand "Anand" K. Sharma; Patricia Ann Shatynski; Michael T. Siekman; Ranjeev Singh; Leonard Smith, Jr.; Jemy Soegeng; Jay A. Stelacone; Daniel Kent Stier (Resident Associate, Atlanta, Georgia Office); Kara Farnandez Stoll; William L. Strauss; Pedro F. Suarez (Not admitted in DC); Sanya Sukduang; Jennifer S. Swan (Not admitted in DC); Mark D. Sweet; Jeanne M. Tanner; Linda Jean Thayer (Resident Associate, Palo Alto, California Office); Susanne C. Tinker (Not admitted in DC); Rachel H. Townsend; Anthony C. Tridico (Not admitted in DC; Resident Associate, Brussels, Belgium Office); Louis M. Troilo; Andrew Joseph Vance; Thalia V. Warnement; Douglas Scott Weinstein (Resident Associate, Atlanta, Georgia Office); Charlena L. Williams (Resident Associate, Atlanta, Georgia Office); James T. Wilson (Not admitted in DC); Bart W. Wise (Resident Associate, Palo Alto, California Office); Naoki Yoshida.
Patents, Trademarks, Copyrights, Trade Secrets, Chemical IP, Electrical IP, IP Infringement, IP Licensing, IP Litigation, IP Portfolio Management, IP Procurement, IP Rights, International IP, Mechanical IP, Pharmaceutical IP, Biotechnology IP, Information Technology Licensing.
Reference: Crestar Bank, N.A., Washington, D.C.
Atlanta, Georgia Office: 3200 SunTrust Plaza, 303 Peachtree Street, N.E., 30308. Telephone: 404-653-6400. Facsimile: 404-653-6444.
Cambridge, Massachusetts Office: 55 Cambridge Parkway, 02142. Telephone: 617-444-8508. Facsimile: 617-444-8608.
Palo Alto, California Office: 700 Hansen Way, 94304. Telephone: 650-849-6600. Facsimile: 650-849-6666.
Brussels, Belgium Office: Avenue Louise 326, Box 37, B-1050. Telephone: 011-322-646-0353. Facsimile: 011-322-646-2135.
Tokyo, Japan Office: Toranomon No. 45 Mori Building, Third Floor, 1-5, Toranomon 5-Chome Minato-Ku, 105-0001. Telephone: 011-813-3431-6943. Facsimile: 011-813-3431-6945.
See Professional Biographies, WASHINGTON, DISTRICT OF COLUMBIA

Finney, P. Dustin, Jr. .... '52 '85 C.884 B.A. L.273 J.D. 555 13th St., N.W.
Finucane, David J. .... '62 '94 C.801 B.S. L.831 J.D. [Ⓐ Carr G.]
Fioravanti, Raymond, (AV) .... '63 '88 C.800 B.S. L.823 J.D. [Epstein B.&G.]
*PRACTICE AREAS: Commercial Litigation; Construction Law; Government Contracts.
Fiordalisi, Amy Lynn '72 '99 C.423 B.A. L.64 J.D.
(adm. in MD; not adm. in DC) Commodity Futures Trading Comm.
Fiorini, John E., III, (AV) .... '46 '71 C.276 B.S. L.659 J.D. [Wiley R.&F.]
*PRACTICE AREAS: Communications Law.
Fireison, Scott E. .... '67 '96 C.446 B.S. L.273 J.D. [Ⓐ Pepper H.]
*PRACTICE AREAS: Real Estate; Finance; Affordable Housing.
Firestone, Richard M., (AV) .... '48 '73 C&L.477 B.A., J.D. [Arnold&P.]
*PRACTICE AREAS: Telecommunications; International; Legislative.
First, Robin B. .... '69 '96 C.178 B.A. L.228 J.D. [Ⓐ Dickinson L.]
*PRACTICE AREAS: International Law; Foreign Corrupt Practices Act; International Arbitration; White Collar Crime; Export Compliance.
First, Stanley A., (AV) .... '27 '57 C.472 B.B.A. L.273 LL.B. 1232 17th St. N.W.
Firvida, Cristina Begona .... '69 '95 C.976 B.A. L.188 J.D. Nat. Women's Law Ctr.
Fisch, Alan M. .... '66 '95 C.846 B.A. L.861 J.D. [Howrey S.A.&W.]
*PRACTICE AREAS: Litigation; Intellectual Property.
Fisch, Fredrick Lee '55 '87 C.174 B.A. L.972 J.D.
(adm. in WY; not adm. in DC) F.D.I.C.
Fisch, Richard .... '57 '85 C.188 B.S.I.L.R. L.276 J.D. [Malizia S.&F.]
*PRACTICE AREAS: Securities; Banking; Corporate; Tax; Employee Benefits.
Fischer, David J. .... '58 '83 C.475 B.A. L.273 J.D. [Baker&H.]
*PRACTICE AREAS: Tax.
Fischer, David Timothy .... '74 '99 C.473 B.A. L.276 J.D. [Ⓐ Porter W.M.&A.]
*PRACTICE AREAS: Complex Litigation; Commercial Litigation.
Fischer, Henry G. .... '11 '38 C.659 B.S. L.309 LL.B. 2161 Florida Ave., N.W.‡
Fischer, L. Richard .... '43 '71 C.767 A.B. L.1065 J.D. [Morrison&F.]
*PRACTICE AREAS: Financial Services and Administrative Law.
Fischer, Lynn M. .... '— '99 C.30 B.A. L.813 J.D. [Ⓐ Wilmer,C.&P.]
Fischer, Nancy A. .... '67 '93 C.280 B.B.A. L.823 J.D. [Ⓒ Shaw P.]
Fischer, Paul A., (AV) .... '50 '74 C&L.659 B.S., J.D. [Jorden B.]
*PRACTICE AREAS: SEC, NASD and NYSE Enforcement; Securities; Securities Litigation; Insurance Litigation.
Fischer, Wolfram .... '57 '84 C.999 L.339 J.D. Sr. Coun., International Fin. Corp.
Fischler, Keith S. .... '57 '83 C.188 B.S. L.276 J.D. [Ⓒ Thelen R.&P.]
*PRACTICE AREAS: Employment Law; Labor Law.
Fischman, Joel A. .... '62 '88 C.477 A.B. L.575 J.D. [Ⓒ Dickstein S.M.&O.]
*PRACTICE AREAS: Civil Litigation; Complex Commercial Litigation.
Fischman, Noam B. .... '— '99 C.705 B.A. L.273 J.D. 701 Pennsylvania Avenue, N.W.
Fise, Thomas F. '50 '78 C.276 B.A. L.446 J.D.
(adm. in MD; not adm. in DC) 3016 Q St., N.W.‡
Fish, Andrew C. .... '67 '95 C.976 B.A. L.813 J.D. [Ⓒ Foxkiser]
*PRACTICE AREAS: Biotechnology; Life Sciences; Regulatory Law; Government Affairs.
Fish, Paul W. .... '33 '65 C.128 B.E.E. L.273 LL.B. [Ⓒ Rader,F.&G.] (Pat.)

Fish & Richardson P.C., (AV)
601 13th Street N.W., 20005 ⊙
Telephone: 202-783-5070 Fax: 202-783-2331
Email: info@fr.com URL: http://www.fr.com
Frederick P. Fish (1855-1930); W. K. Richardson (1859-1951).
Keith A. Barritt; Ruffin B. Cordell; Jill B. Deal; Alexander J. Hadjis; John F. Hayden; Linda Liu Kordziel; Terry G. Mahn; Michael J. McKeon; Ralph A. Mittelberger. Of Counsel: James E. Mrose; Rene D. Tegtmeyer; Robert J. Ungar. Associates: Scott R. Boalick; Andrew F. Bodendorf (Not admitted in DC); Joseph V. Colaianni, Jr.; Lauren A. Degnan; Benjamin D. Driscoll (Not admitted in DC); Harold H. Fox; Richard G. Green; William D. Hare; Joseph Franklin Key; Andrew Kopsidas (Not admitted in DC); Phyllis Kristal (Not admitted in DC); Kevin J. McNeely; Heather Morin; Brian R. Nester (Not admitted in DC); Brian T. Racilla (Not admitted in DC); Robert V. Racunas (Not admitted in DC); W. Karl Renner (Not admitted in DC); Gary Savitt; Mark Edward Wadrzyk (Not admitted in DC); Gregory A. Walters; R. Whitney Winston.

(This Listing Continued)

Fish & Richardson P.C. (Continued)

Intellectual Property, Complex Litigation, Technology Law: Patents, Trademarks, Copyrights, Trade Secrets, Intellectual Property Litigation, Business Litigation, Technology Regulations, Antitrust Law, Corporate and Securities, White Collar Crime.
Boston, Massachusetts Office: 225 Franklin Street. Telephone: 617-542-5070. Fax: 617-542-8906.
Redwood City, California Office: 500 Aguello Street, Suite 500. Telephone: 650-322-5070. Fax: 650-854-0875.
Minneapolis, Minnesota Office: Fish & Richardson, P.C., P.A., 60 South Sixth Street, 3300 Dain Rauscher Plaza. Telephone: 612-335-5070. Fax: 612-288-9696.
San Diego, California Office: 4350 La Jolla Village Drive, Suite 500. Telephone: 858-678-5070. Fax: 858-678-5099.
New York, N.Y. Office: 45 Rockefeller Plaza, Suite 2800. Telephone: 212-765-5070. Fax: 212-258-2291.
Wilmington, Delaware Office: 919 North Market Street, Suite 1000, P.O. Box 1114. Telephone: 302-652-5070. Fax: 302-652-0607.
Dallas, Texas Office: 5000 Bank One Center, 1717 Main Street. Telephone: 214-747-5070. Fax: 214-747-2091

See Professional Biographies, WASHINGTON, DISTRICT OF COLUMBIA

Fishbein, Allen V. '47 '77
C.994 B.A. L.1162 J.D. Gen. Coun., Center for Community Change
Fishberg, David B. .... '75 '00 C.165 B.A. L.273 J.D. [A Fried,F.H.S.&J.]
*PRACTICE AREAS: Litigation.
Fishberg, Lisa A. F. .... '72 '98 C.1044 B.A. L.273 J.D. [A Coburn&S.]
*PRACTICE AREAS: Criminal Litigation; Civil Litigation.
Fishburne, Benjamin P., III, (AV) .... '43 '68 C.602 B.A. L.893 LL.B. [Winston&S.]
*PRACTICE AREAS: International Commercial Transactions; Corporate Finance; High Technology; International Dispute Resolution.
Fishel, Alan Gregg .... '59 '86 C.264 B.A. L.228 J.D. [Arent F.K.P.&K.]
*PRACTICE AREAS: Telecommunications; Litigation.
Fisher, Adrian S. .... '14 '38 C.674 A.B. L.309 LL.B. Georgetown Univ. Law Sch.
Fisher, Ben C., (AV) .... '23 '51 C.339 A.B. L.309 J.D. [C Shaw P.]
*PRACTICE AREAS: Communications.
Fisher, Brian T. .... '64 '94 C.999 B.S. L.1202 J.D. [A McKenna&C.]
*PRACTICE AREAS: Government Contracts; Commercial Law; Litigation.
Fisher, Daniel E. .... '47 '78 C.367 B.S.E. L.273 J.D. [C Dorsey&W.] (Pat.)
*PRACTICE AREAS: Intellectual Property Law; Patents; Intellectual Property Licensing; Electrical Intellectual Property; Computer and Software Patents.
Fisher, Daniel Philip .... '71 '98 C.1036 B.A. L.273 J.D. IRS
Fisher, David J. '59 '85 C.1044 B.A. L.276 J.D.
(adm. in NY; not adm. in DC) [Piper M.R.&W.] (⊙New York, NY)
*PRACTICE AREAS: Finance; Corporate; Securities.
Fisher, Emily Sanford '75 '00 C.273 B.A. L.276 J.D.
(adm. in MD; not adm. in DC) [A Dewey B.]
*PRACTICE AREAS: Energy; Administrative Law.
Fisher, George A. .... '36 '61 C.976 B.A. L.276 LL.B. [C Stein,M.&M.]
Fisher, Ilana R. .... '72 '98 C.112 B.A. L.188 J.D. [A Troutman S.]
*PRACTICE AREAS: Complex and Multi-District Litigation; Labor and Employment.
Fisher, James E., II '69 '99 C.329 B.B.A. L.446 J.D.
(adm. in MD; not adm. in DC) [A Conlon,F.P.&P.]
*PRACTICE AREAS: Civil Rights; Class Actions.
Fisher, Jane A. .... '57 '86 C.276 B.A. L.273 J.D. 4436 Sedgwick St NW
Fisher, Janet C. .... '73 '98 C.188 B.S. L.309 J.D. [A Williams&C.]
*PRACTICE AREAS: Litigation; Constitutional Law.
Fisher, Jocelyn .... '68 '93 C&L.446 B.A., J.D. Atty, AFL-CIO Housing Investment Tr.
Fisher, Joel Hilton, (AV) .... '18 '41 C&L.823 A.B., J.D. [Fisher,J.H.]
Fisher, Karen S. .... '62 '89 C&L.665 B.S., J.D. Assn. of Amer. Medical Colleges
Fisher, Laurence E. .... '51 '89 C.446 B.S. L.276 J.D. [A Dickstein S.M.&O.] (Pat.)
*PRACTICE AREAS: Intellectual Property.
Fisher, Louis K. '71 '98 C&L.976 B.A., J.D.
(adm. in CT; not adm. in DC) [A Jones,D.R.&P.]
Fisher, Marjorie P. '68 '97 C.918 B.A. L.1068 J.D.
(adm. in CA; not adm. in DC) [A Piper M.R.&W.]
*PRACTICE AREAS: Commercial Real Estate.
Fisher, Miriam L. .... '60 '85 C.423 B.A. L.446 J.D. [Hogan&H.]
*PRACTICE AREAS: Tax Controversies; Tax Litigation; Tax Fraud.
Fisher, Ralph E. '55 '80 C.138 B.A. L.64 J.D.
V.P., Frederick Div., Washington Gas Light Co.
Fisher, Robert C., (AV) ..... '59 '87 C.446 B.A. L.273 J.D. Asst. Gen. Coun., INTELSAT
Fisher, Robert M. .... '54 '91 C.228 A.B. L.309 J.D. [C Fried,F.H.S.&J.]
*PRACTICE AREAS: Securities Law; Banking; Antitrust.
Fisher, William B., (BV) '52 '86 C.24 B.A. L.1209 J.D.
[Wickwire G.] (⊙Vienna, VA)
*PRACTICE AREAS: Construction, Public Contract, Environmental, and Fidelity and Surety Law; Litigation.
Fisher, William J. ...... '— '86 C.46 B.S.Ch.E. L.776 J.D. [Banner&W.] (See Pat. Sect.)
*PRACTICE AREAS: Intellectual Property Law; Patents; Intellectual Property Licensing; Chemical Intellectual Property; Pharmaceutical Intellectual Property.

Fisher, Christen & Sabol, (AV)
Suite 1401, 1725 K Street, N.W., 20006
Telephone: 202-659-2000 Fax: 202-659-2015
Email: FCSabol@aol.com URL: http://www.lawyers.com/fisherchristen&sabol
Martin T. Fisher (1890-1964); Arnold B. Christen (1915-1980); Eugene Sabol (1928-1993); Virgil H. Marsh; Kara M. Armstrong.
Patent, Trademark, Copyright, Unfair Competition and related Litigation. Mechanical Patents, Chemical Patents, Biotechnology Patents.

See Professional Biographies, WASHINGTON, DISTRICT OF COLUMBIA

Fisher, Joel Hilton, P.C., (AV) .... 800 25th St., N.W. #604
Fisher Law Group, The, PLLC
(See Upper Marlboro, Maryland)

Fisher-Owens, Daniel M. .... '70 '00 C.197 A.B. L.276 J.D. [A Bryan C.]
Fishgold, Herbert, (AV) '41 '67 C.563 B.A. L.976 LL.B.
1730 Rhode Island Ave., N.W.
Fishman, Aryeh .... '69 '97 C.103 B.A. L.273 J.D. [A Bracewell&P.]
*PRACTICE AREAS: Energy Law; Electricity; Natural Gas Transportation; Administrative Law; Appellate Litigation.
Fishman, Benjamin I. .... '67 '92 C.976 B.A. L.800 J.D. [A Arent F.K.P.&K.]
*PRACTICE AREAS: Commercial Litigation; Antitrust; Construction Law; Patent; International Arbitration.
Fishman, Burton J., (AV) .... '42 '79 C.605 B.A. L.976 J.D. [Ogletree,D.N.S.&S.]
*PRACTICE AREAS: Labor Law; Employment Discrimination Law; ERISA.
Fishman, Carol H., (AV) .... '41 '78 C.914 B.A. L.273 J.D. [C Wilmer,C.&P.]
*PRACTICE AREAS: Insurance; Civil Practice.
Fishman, Craig .... '60 '88 C.188 B.A. L.893 J.D. [A Orrick,H.&S.]
Fishman, Edward .... '69 '96 C.228 B.A. L.273 J.D. [A Kirkpatrick&L.]
*PRACTICE AREAS: Transportation; Litigation; Health Care.
Fishman, Eric, (AV) .... '49 '77 C.145 A.B. L.178 J.D. [Holland&K.]
*PRACTICE AREAS: Telecommunications; Corporate.
Fishman, Ira .... '57 '82 C.976 B.A. L.309 J.D. [Patton B.]
Fishman, Jarred A. '— '98 C.1036 B.A. L.273 J.D.
(adm. in MD; not adm. in DC) 101 G St., SW
Fishman, Meryl S. .... '39 '85 C.1040 B.P.S. L.564 J.D. [A Howrey S.A.&W.]
Fishman, Vicki Bajefsky .... '71 '97 C.821 B.A. L.477 J.D. [A Ross,D.&B.]
Fishman, William L., (AV) .... '41 '66 C.103 B.A. L.309 J.D. [C Swidler B.S.F.]
*PRACTICE AREAS: Privacy Law; Communications Law.
Fisk, Robert C. .... '41 '71 C.976 B.A. L.273 LL.B. Neighborhood Legal Servs. Prog.
Fiske, David G., (AV) .... '44 '69 C.367 B.A. L.276 J.D. [Shaw P.]
*PRACTICE AREAS: Commercial Litigation; Federal Practice.
Fiske, David H. '40 '69 C.918 B.A. L.659 LL.B.
(adm. in PA; not adm. in DC) Edward Aycoth & Co., Inc.
Fitch, Elaine L. '66 '96 C.1375 B.S. L.1065 J.D.
(adm. in CA; not adm. in DC) [A Gebhardt&Assoc.]
Fitch, John H., Jr. '45 '72 C.893 B.A. L.500 J.D.
(adm. in MS; not adm. in DC) V.P., National Assn. of Wholesalers
Fitch, Rebecca April .... '48 '72 C.184 B.A. L.945 J.D. Georgetown Law Ctr.
Fitch, Susan Kathleen .... '62 '92 C&L.846 B.A., J.D. [A Kirkland&E.]
*PRACTICE AREAS: White Collar Crime; Government Contracts; Health Care.
Fitch, Warren Anthony, (AV) .... '44 '70 C.674 A.B. L.309 J.D. [Swidler B.S.F.]
*PRACTICE AREAS: Civil Litigation; Criminal Litigation; Professional Liability; Telecommunications Law.

Fitch, Even, Tabin & Flannery, (AV) BB
1801 K Street, N.W., Suite 401L, 20006-1201 ⊙
Telephone: 202-419-7000 Fax: 202-419-7007
Email: email@fitcheven.com URL: http://www.fitcheven.com
Edward W. Gray, Jr.; Sherri N. Blount; Kendrew H. Colton; Charles W. Peterson, Jr. (Not admitted in DC);—Christopher E. George; Ramon R. Hoch (Not admitted in DC; Also at Chicago, Illinois Office).
Intellectual Property and Technology-Related Law including United States and International Patents, Trademarks, Trade Secret, Copyrights and Unfair Competition, Antitrust and International Trade Commission Causes and Related Litigation.
Chicago, Illinois Office: 120 South La Salle, Suite 1600. 60603. Telephone: 312-577-7000. Fax: 312-577-7007.
San Diego, California Office: 4250 Executive Square, Suite 510. Telephone: 858-552-1311. Telecopier: 858-552-0095.

See Professional Biographies, WASHINGTON, DISTRICT OF COLUMBIA

Fithian, John F. .... '61 '87 C.945 B.A. L.893 J.D. [Patton B.]
Fitterman, Mark D. .... '42 '74 C.604 A.B. L.276 J.D. [Morgan,L.&B.]
Fitts, Jane Gale .... '— '78 C&L.262 B.A., J.D. Coun., Fed. Nat. Mortgage Assn.
Fitz, Marshall .... '68 '99 C&L.893 B.A., J.D. [A Hogan&H.]
*PRACTICE AREAS: Immigration Law.
Fitz, William H., (AV) .... '42 '68 C.902 B.A. L.273 J.D. [C Covington&B.]
Fitzgerald, Ari Q. .... '62 '91 C.309 A.B. L.976 J.D. [Hogan&H.]
*PRACTICE AREAS: Communications Law; Project Finance.
Fitzgerald, Brandon M. .... '— '97 C.659 B.A. L.893 J.D. [A Piper M.R.&W.]
*PRACTICE AREAS: Mergers and Acquisitions; Venture Capital; Securities.
Fitzgerald, Brian W. .... '54 '81 C.347 B.A. L.1162 J.D. [Swidler B.S.F.]
*PRACTICE AREAS: Government Affairs; Intellectual Property; Federal Election Law; Federal Practice.
Fitzgerald, David A. .... '— '95 C.170 B.A. L.128 J.D. [A Verner,L.B.M.&H.]
*PRACTICE AREAS: Energy.
Fitzgerald, Donald J. '45 '73
C.575 A.B. L.228 J.D. [Manatt,P.&P.] (⊙L.A., Palo Alto, CA)
*PRACTICE AREAS: Taxation.
Fitzgerald, Jayne T. .... '55 '80 C&L.276 B.A., J.D. [Washington C.]
Fitzgerald, Justine Anne .... '69 '98 C.659 B.S./B.A. L.276 J.D. [A Arnold&P.]
*PRACTICE AREAS: Real Estate.
Fitzgerald, Kevin C. .... '62 '91 C&L.273 B.A., J.D. [Troutman S.]
*PRACTICE AREAS: Energy; Legislative Corporate Reorganization; Regulatory Law.
Fitzgerald, Mark R. .... '57 '82 C.1030 B.A. L.128 J.D. [Gardner,C.&D.]
*PRACTICE AREAS: Health Care Law; Corporate Law.
Fitzgerald, Mary Clare .... '46 '94 C.945 B.A. L.1209 J.D. [C Troutman S.]
*PRACTICE AREAS: Electronic Commerce; Banking; Government Relations; Communications and Media.
Fitzgerald, Peter F. .... '56 '82 C.602 B.A. L.705 J.D. [Chadbourne&P.]
Fitzgerald, Richard V. .... '36 '65 C.903 B.A. L.446 LL.B. 5101 Wisconsin Ave.
Fitzgerald, Sarah B. '73 '99 C.473 B.S. L.424 J.D.
(adm. in IL; not adm. in DC) KPMG Washington Nat'l Tax
FitzGerald, Scott J. '67 '92 C.367 B.A. L.262 J.D.
(adm. in CT; not adm. in DC) [Fragomen,D.B.&L.]
Fitzgerald, T. Jeffrey .... '71 '97 C.174 B.A. L.602 J.D. [A Jones,D.R.&P.]
Fitzgerald, Thomas F. .... '53 '81 C.728 B.A. L.276 J.D.C. [Groom]
*PRACTICE AREAS: Employee Benefits Law; Health Care Law; ERISA; Civil Litigation.

Fitzgerald, Henry St. John
(See Arlington, Virginia)

Fitzgibbon, Timothy J., (AV) .... '55 '83 C&L.276 B.S.F.S., J.D. [Carter,L.&M.]
*PRACTICE AREAS: Litigation; Telecommunications; Federal Government Law.
Fitzhugh, Joshua D. .... '70 '98 C.164 B.A. L.276 J.D. [A Shaw P.]
Fitzner, Catherine Hubbard '59 '85 C&L.575 B.A., J.D.
(adm. in NC; not adm. in DC) American Insurance Association
Fitzpatrick, Amy R. .... '70 '96 C.103 B.A. L.945 J.D. [A Howrey S.A.&W.]
*PRACTICE AREAS: Commercial Litigation; Patent Litigation; Antitrust Litigation.
Fitzpatrick, Bridget M. '— '00 C.188 B.A. L.276 J.D.
(adm. in CA; not adm. in DC) [A Piper M.R.&W.]
*PRACTICE AREAS: Litigation; White Collar Crime.
Fitzpatrick, Donna R. .... '48 '80 C.30 B.A. L.273 J.D. 4393 Embassy Park Dr., NW
Fitzpatrick, James F., (AV) .... '33 '59 C.347 A.B. L.1119 J.D. [Arnold&P.]
*PRACTICE AREAS: Legislation; Public Policy; Administrative Law.
Fitzpatrick, James F. '45 '77
C.229 B.A. L.273 J.D. Mng. Editor, The Bur. of Natl. Affs., Inc.
Fitzpatrick, Robert B., (AV) .... '41 '68 C&L.273 B.A., LL.B. [Fitzpatrick&Assoc.]
*PRACTICE AREAS: Employment Law; International Employment Law; Labor Law.

Fitzpatrick & Associates, (AV)
Universal Building North, 1875 Connecticut Avenue, N.W. Suite 1140, 20009-5728
Telephone: 202-588-5300 Facsimile: 202-588-5023
Email: fitzlaw@erols.com URL: http://www.lawyers.com/fitzpatricklaw
Robert B. Fitzpatrick.
Labor, Employment and International Employment Law.

See Professional Biographies, WASHINGTON, DISTRICT OF COLUMBIA

Fitzpatrick, Cella, Harper & Scinto, (AV) BB
1900 K Street, N.W., 20006-1110 ⊙
Telephone: 202-530-1010 Facsimile: 202-530-1055 URL: http://www.fitzpatrickcella.com
Resident Partners: John W. Behringer; Lawrence A. Stahl; William M. Wannisky; Warren E. Olsen; Scott D. Malpede; Thomas J. O'Connell; Steven E. Warner; Mark A. Williamson; Anne M. Maher; Daniel S. Glueck; Brian L. Klock. Counsel: Robert C. Kline. Resident Associates: Christopher Philip Wrist; Gary M. Jacobs; Jack S. Cubert (Not admitted in DC); Jean K. Dudek; Natalie M. Derzko; Shawn W. Fraser; Edmund J. Haughey, III; Justin J. Oliver (Not admitted in DC); Stephen E. Belisle (Not admitted in DC); Simon D. Roberts (Not admitted in DC).
Intellectual Property Practice. Patent, Trademark, Copyright, Trade Secret, Unfair Competition, Computer, Licensing, Antitrust and International Trade Law. Trials and Appeals in Federal and State Courts and Administrative Agencies.
New York, N.Y. Office: 30 Rockefeller Plaza. Telephone: 212-218-2100. Facsimile: 212-218-2200.

(This Listing Continued)

Fitzpatrick, Cella, Harper & Scinto (Continued)
Orange County, California Office: 650 Town Center Drive, Suite 1600, Costa Mesa. Telephone: 714-540-8700. Facsimile: 714-540-9823.
See Professional Biographies, WASHINGTON, DISTRICT OF COLUMBIA

FitzRandolph, Laura E. . . . . '69 '98 C.112 B.A. L.273 J.D. [Ⓐ Akin,G.S.H.&F.]
*PRACTICE AREAS: Labor and Employment.
Fitzsimmons, Mark P., (AV) . . . . '55 '80 C.882 B.A. L.597 J.D. [Steptoe&J.]
*PRACTICE AREAS: Toxic Tort; Product Liability; Environmental; Civil Litigation.
Fitzsimmons, Paul A. . . . . '58 '85 C&L.477 A.B., J.D. [Wright,R.O.&T.]
*PRACTICE AREAS: Insurance Coverage Litigation; Insurance Defense Litigation; Commercial Litigation; Libel Litigation.
Flack, Brian L. . . . . '72 '99 C.645 B.S. L.1040 J.D. [Ⓐ Venable,A.B.H.&C.]
*PRACTICE AREAS: Environmental; Energy; White Collar Crime.
Flack, Howard I., (AV) . . . . '51 '77 C.705 A.B. L.564 J.D. [Hogan&H.]
*PRACTICE AREAS: Mergers, Acquisitions and Divestitures; Business Law; Corporate Law; Securities; Financial Institutions.
Flack, Jill D. '59 '87 C.188 B.S. L.128 J.D.
Assistant General Counsel, Potomac Electric Power Company
Flagg, Ronald S. . . . . '53 '78 C.145 A.B. L.309 J.D. [Sidley A.B.&W.]
Flaherty, Barbara M. . . . . '— '97 C.446 B.S. L.128 J.D. [Ⓐ Morgan,L.&B.]
Flaherty, Marion Heyna '— '91 C.112 B.A. L.1068 J.D.
(adm. in MD; not adm. in DC) Federal Publications, Inc.
*RESPONSIBILITIES: Government Contract Law (100%).
Flam, Anne Kurtz . . . . '69 '97 C.93 B.A. L.128 J.D. [Ⓐ Gardner,C.&D.]
*PRACTICE AREAS: Health Care; Administrative Law; Legislative Practice.
Flanagan, E. Michael, (AV) . . . . '49 '79 C.871 B.S. L.273 J.D. [Weil,G.&M.]
*PRACTICE AREAS: Health Law; Regulatory Law; Corporate Law.
Flanagan, Michael F. . . . . '64 '91 C.188 A.B. L.477 J.D. [Gibson,D.&C.]
*PRACTICE AREAS: Litigation; Securities.
Flanagan, Peter L. . . . . '65 '94 C.966 B.A. L.569 J.D. [Covington&B.]
Flanagan, Steven M. '60 '91 C.93 B.A. L.1202 J.D.
(adm. in MA; not adm. in DC) Ernst & Young LLP
Flanagan, T. Mark, Jr., (AV) . . . . '54 '81 C.602 B.A. L.893 J.D. [McKenna&C.]
*PRACTICE AREAS: White Collar Criminal Defense Law; General Civil Litigation.
Flanagan, William J. . . . . '52 '77 C&L.276 B.S.F.S., J.D. [Ⓒ Wilmer,C.&P.]
*PRACTICE AREAS: Employee Benefits.
Flanders, John M. '57 '00 C.103 B.A. L.306 J.D.
(adm. in CT; not adm. in DC) 2000 M St. N.W.
Flannery, Dennis M., (AV) . . . . '39 '64 C.262 A.B. L.659 LL.B. [Ⓒ Wilmer,C.&P.]
*PRACTICE AREAS: Civil Practice.
Flannery, Ellen J., (AV) . . . . '51 '78 C.518 A.B. L.94 J.D. [Covington&B.]
Flax, Meredith L. '69 '01 C&L.477 B.A., J.D.
(adm. in MI; not adm. in DC) [Ⓐ Beveridge&D.]
*PRACTICE AREAS: Environmental.
Flax, Ryan H. '73 '99 C.896 B.S. L.802 J.D.
(adm. in MD; not adm. in DC) [Ⓐ Dickstein S.M.&O.]
*PRACTICE AREAS: Intellectual Property Litigation and Prosecution.
Flax, Samuel A., (AV) . . . . '56 '81 C.277 B.I.E. L.902 J.D. [Arnold&P.]
*PRACTICE AREAS: Corporate; Securities; Bankruptcy; Real Estate.
Flax-Davidson, Cheryl '54 '80 C.1275 B.A. L.362 J.D.
(adm. in NY; not adm. in DC) 3738 Jenifer St., N.W.
Flaxman, Lisa J. . . . . '65 '94 C.103 B.A. L.276 J.D. 1200 New Hampshire Ave., N.W.
Fleck, Mary Ellen '66 '96 C.597 B.A. L.180 J.D.
1333 New Hampshire Avenue, N.W., Suite 400
Fleder, John R., (AV) . . . . '47 '73 C.364 B.A. L.569 J.D. [Hyman,P.&M.]
*PRACTICE AREAS: Litigation; Food, Drug and Cosmetic Law; White Collar Crime; Administrative Law.
Fleet, Leslie G. . . . . '43 '69 C.30 B.A. L.273 J.D. The Bureau of Natl. Affs., Inc.
Flegel, Laura M. '55 '84 C&L.966 B.A., J.D.
Dir. of Legal Servs., Whitman-Walker Clinic Legal Servs.
*RESPONSIBILITIES: Disability Discrimination; Immigration and Naturalization; Social Security; Medicare and Medicaid; Child Custody.

Fleig, Susan Findling, Law Office of '— '91 C.446 B.A. L.276 J.D.
1025 Connecticut Avenue NW, Suite 1012, 20036
Telephone: 202-857-9707 Fax: 301-656-8646 URL: http://www.estatehelp.com
Email: sffleig@erols.com URL: http://www.fleiglaw
***PRACTICE AREAS: Estate Planning; Estate and Gift Taxation; Generation Skipping Tax; Charitable Trusts and Foundations; Estate Administration.**
Trusts and Estates, Wills, Taxation, Charitable Giving, Probate, Wealth Preservation, Estate and Gift Taxation.
See Professional Biographies, WASHINGTON, DISTRICT OF COLUMBIA

Fleischaker, Marc L., (AV) . . . . '45 '71 C.659 B.S. L.273 J.D. [Arent F.K.P.&K.]
*PRACTICE AREAS: Toxic Torts; Environmental Law; Antitrust; Trade Association Law; Civil Rights.
Fleischer, James S., (P.C.), (AV) . . . . '51 '76 C.197 B.A. L.228 J.D. [Silver,F.&T.]
*PRACTICE AREAS: Securities Law; Mergers and Acquisitions; Banking Law; Corporate Law.

Fleischer, Walter H.
(See McLean)

Fleischman, Aaron I., (AV) . . . . '39 '65 C.855 B.A. L.309 LL.B. [Fleischman&W.]

Fleischman and Walsh, L.L.P., (AV)
1400 Sixteenth Street, N.W., 20036
Telephone: 202-939-7900 Facsimile: 202-745-0916
Email: fw@fw-law.com
Partners: Aaron I. Fleischman; Charles S. Walsh; Arthur H. Harding; Stuart F. Feldstein; Jeffry L. Hardin; Stephen A. Bouchard; R. Bruce Beckner; Christopher G. Wood; Seth A. Davidson; James F. Moriarty; Matthew D. Emmer; Louis H. Dupart (Not admitted in DC); Sharon O'Malley Monahan (Not admitted in DC); Lawrence R. Freedman; Eric E. Breisach (Not admitted in DC); Joel D. Bonfiglio. Associates: Jill Kleppe McClelland; Regina Famiglietti Pace; Craig A. Gilley; Susan A. Mort; Mark D. Pihlstrom; Brian C. Malady; Thomas E. Knight; Seth M. Warner; Mark B. Denbo; Cara E. Sheppard; Steven J. Hamrick; Kevin C. Brennan; Richard L. Davis; Shari L. Wilkozek (Not admitted in DC); Lisa Chandler Cordell; David J. Lavan (Not admitted in DC); Aimee E. Knapp; Peter B. Sanchez (Not admitted in DC).
General Practice before Federal and State Administrative Agencies and Courts. Communications, Utilities, Legislative, Litigation, Transportation, Corporate and Securities Practice.
See Professional Biographies, WASHINGTON, DISTRICT OF COLUMBIA

Fleishman, Barry J. . . . . '56 '81 C&L.569 B.A., J.D. [Dickstein S.M.&O.]
*PRACTICE AREAS: Insurance Litigation; Electric Power Products Liability.
Fleishman, Rishona '— '01 C.659 B.A. L.1365 J.D.
(adm. in NY; not adm. in DC) [Ⓐ King&S.]
Fleishman, Robert W., (AV) . . . . '45 '73 C.383 B.A. L.477 J.D. [Steptoe&J.]
*PRACTICE AREAS: Antitrust; Acquisitions, Divestitures, Mergers; Franchise Relations; International Business Law; Complex Litigation.
Fleishman, Shari L. . . . . '67 '93 C.228 A.B. L.309 J.D. [Ⓒ Akin,G.S.H.&F.]
*PRACTICE AREAS: Litigation; Patent Litigation; Technology.
Fleisig, Leonard L. . . . . '53 '91 C.999 B.A. L.569 J.D. [Ⓒ Troutman S.]
*PRACTICE AREAS: Transportation; Trade; Customs.
Fleming, Britt S. . . . . '72 '97 C.197 B.A. L.30 J.D. [Ⓐ Van Ness F.]
*PRACTICE AREAS: Energy; Environment.
Fleming, Carey W. . . . . '59 '98 C.999 B.S. L.574 J.D. [Ⓐ Winston&S.]
*PRACTICE AREAS: Nuclear Energy.
Fleming, Christopher T. . . . . '63 '88 C.951 B.A. L.276 J.D. 2122 Mass. Ave., N.W.
Fleming, Elizabeth Wallace, (AV) . . .'— '81 C&L.280 B.A., J.D. [Ⓒ Preston G.E.&R.M.]
*PRACTICE AREAS: Litigation; Health Care Fraud; Government Contracts.
Fleming, Erika M. '71 '96 C.188 B.S. L.1066 J.D.
(adm. in CA; not adm. in DC) [Ⓐ Winston&S.]
*PRACTICE AREAS: Real Estate; Real Estate Finance; Public Finance; Electricity and Energy Law.
Fleming, Joe W., II (P.C.) . . . . '37 '63 C.45 B.A. L.273 LL.B. 1606 20th St Nw # 3
Fleming, Linda P. '61 '86 C.477 B.B.A. L.273 J.D.
(adm. in MD; not adm. in DC) 4360 G. St., N.W.‡
Fleming, Michael W. . . . . '61 '94 C&L.893 B.A., J.D. [Ⓐ Swidler B.S.F.]
*PRACTICE AREAS: Telecommunications Regulation; Local Telecommunications Competition.
Fleming, Peter Carlton . . . . '— '98 C.659 B.A. L.309 J.D. [Ⓐ King&S.]
*PRACTICE AREAS: Antitrust.
Fleming, Philip A., (AV) . . . . '30 '57 C.188 A.B. L.477 J.D. 1001 Penn. Ave., N.W.
Fleming, Timothy B. . . . . '55 '80 C&L.846 B.A., J.D. [Ⓐ Gordon,S.W.&C.]
*PRACTICE AREAS: Civil Rights Litigation; Employment Discrimination.
Fleps, Christina W. . . . . '52 '78 C.668 B.A. L.1066 J.D. [O'Connor&H.]
Fletcher, David E. '71 '01 C.945 A.B. L.339 J.D.
(adm. in VA; not adm. in DC) [Ⓐ Piper M.R.&W.]
*PRACTICE AREAS: Government Contracts.
Fletcher, Eric L. '67 '98 C.1375 B.S. L.893 J.D.
(adm. in IL; not adm. in DC) [Ⓐ Kirkland&E.]
*PRACTICE AREAS: Corporate.
Fletcher, Francis E., Jr., (AV) . . . . '43 '68 C&L.945 A.B., J.D. [Gardner,C.&D.]
*PRACTICE AREAS: Communications and Technology; International Telecommunications Law; Telecommunications and Technology Contracts; Telecommunications Law; Telecommunications Licensing.
Fletcher, Lynne M. '62 '91 C.674 A.B. L.276 J.D.
(adm. in NJ; not adm. in DC) The du Pont Merck Pharmaceutical Co.
Fletcher, Robert P. . . . . '58 '83 C.674 A.B. L.228 J.D. [Nixon P.]
*PRACTICE AREAS: Litigation; Labor and Employment; Employment Litigation; Contracts; Contract Litigation.
Fletcher, Ronald R., (AV) . . . .'40 '69 C&L.221 B.S., J.D. 4125 Parkglen Ct., N.W.

Fletcher, Heald & Hildreth, P.L.C., (AV)
2000 L Street, NW, Suite 200, 20036 ☉
Telephone: 202-828-5700
Email: office@fhhlaw.com URL: http://www.fhhlaw.com
Members of Firm: James P. Riley; Leonard R. Raish; Vincent J. Curtis, Jr.; Frank R. Jazzo; Howard M. Weiss; Harry C. Martin; Paul J. Feldman; Kathleen Victory; Eugene M. Lawson, Jr. Special Counsel: Susan A. Marshall. Senior Associates: Ann Bavender; Anne Goodwin Crump; Liliana Estevez Ward. Associates: Alison J. Shapiro (Not admitted in DC); Raymond J. Quianzon (Not admitted in DC); Jennifer Dine Wagner. Of Counsel: Edward A. Caine; Mitchell Lazarus; Edward S. O'Neill; Donald J. Evans.
Practice before Federal and State Courts and Federal and State Administrative Agencies primarily in the fields of Domestic and International Communications Law, including radio and television broadcasting, satellites, telephone, commercial wireless communications, cable television, private land mobile, microwave, maritime, aeronautical radio, new technology and equipment authorizations. Practice also in the fields of Antitrust, Energy Law, Public Utility Law, Trademark, Copyright, Trade Associations, EEO, Privacy, Computer, Entertainment, Transactional and Emerging Technology Law, as well as Bankruptcy, Estate Planning, Business Law and Civil Litigation.
Arlington, Virginia Office: 1300 North 17th Street, 11th Floor. Telephone: 703-812-0400. Fax: 703-812-0486.
See Professional Biographies, WASHINGTON, DISTRICT OF COLUMBIA

Flexner, Donald L., (AV) . . . . '41 '67 C&L.569 B.A., LL.B. [Boies,S.&F.]
*PRACTICE AREAS: Antitrust; Litigation.
Flibbert, Michael J. '64 '94
C.276 B.S. L.273 J.D. [Ⓐ Finnegan,H.F.G.&D.] (See Pat. Sect.)
*PRACTICE AREAS: Chemical Intellectual Property; Chemical Patents; Patent Litigation; Pharmaceutical Patents.
Flick, Lauren Lynch, (BV) . . . . '65 '90 C.276 B.A. L.128 J.D. [Shaw P.]
*PRACTICE AREAS: Communications; Litigation; Intellectual Property.
Flick, Scott E., (AV) . . . . '52 '76 C.477 A.B. L.597 J.D. [Howrey S.A.&W.]
*PRACTICE AREAS: Antitrust Law; Complex Litigation.
Flick, Scott R. . . . . '63 '88 C.347 B.A. L.1068 J.D. [Shaw P.]
*PRACTICE AREAS: Communications.
Flicker, Scott M. . . . . '63 '88 C.112 B.A. L.1068 J.D. [Paul,H.J.&W.]
*PRACTICE AREAS: International Trade; Commercial Regulation; Competition Law; Antidumping; Trade Agreements and Disputes.
Flickinger, Charles M., (BV) '53 '83 C.893 B.A. L.309 J.D.
(adm. in IN; not adm. in DC) [Ⓒ Sutherland A.&B.]
*PRACTICE AREAS: Securities Regulation; Environmental Regulation; Mergers and Acquisitions; Corporate Law.
Flickinger, David '68 '96
C.597 B.Mus. L.813 J.D. Dep. Gen. Coun., World Wildlife Fund, Inc.
Flint, James F., (AV) . . . . '43 '73 C.602 B.A. L.276 J.D. [Ⓒ Grove,J.&C.]
*PRACTICE AREAS: Administrative Law; Litigation; Railroads; Transportation; Children Law.
Flint, Myles E. '33 '63 C.685 B.A. L.174 LL.B.
(adm. in NM; not adm. in DC) [Ⓒ Sidley A.B.&W.]
Floam, D. Andrew '65 '93 C.446 B.S.E.E. L.128 J.D.
(adm. in MD; not adm. in DC; Pat.) [Sonnenschein N.&R.]
*PRACTICE AREAS: Electrical Intellectual Property; Electrical Patents; Information Technology; Computers and Software.
Flocks, Karl W., (AV) '10 '33 C.367 B.E. L.273 J.D.
3110 Chain Bridge Rd., N.W. (Pat.)
Flohr, Susan B. . . . . '53 '79 C.1356 B.A. L.904 J.D. [Blank R.C.&M.] (See Pat. Sect.)
*PRACTICE AREAS: Trademark Law; Copyright Law; Computer Law; Unfair Competition Law; Licensing.
Flood, Edward F. . . . . '66 '97 C.588 B.S. L.818 J.D. 2430 E. St., N.W.
Flood, Emmet T. . . . . '56 '92 C.1105 B.A. L.976 J.D. [Williams&C.]
Flood, James G. '63 '90 C.188 B.S. L.276 J.D.
U.S. Attorney's Office for District of Columbia
Flood, James J., Jr., (AV) . . . . . . '31 '59 C.602 B.A. L.273 J.D. 1000 Thomas Jefferson St.‡
Flood, John J., (AV) '51 '77 C&L.276 B.A., J.D.
Assoc. Gen. Coun., Nat. Assn. of Securities Dealers, Inc.
Floom, John P. '74 '99 C.575 B.A. L.94 J.D.
(adm. in VA; not adm. in DC) [Ⓐ GKRSE]
*PRACTICE AREAS: Energy.
Florenzo, David B. . . . . '— '98 C.602 B.A. L.276 J.D. [Ⓐ Kirkland&E.]
*PRACTICE AREAS: Litigation; Antitrust and Trade Regulation.
Flores, Deanna J. '64 '91
C.763 B.A. L.273 J.D. Assoc. Coun., Investment Company Institute
*RESPONSIBILITIES: Mutual Funds; International Taxation; Derivative Products.
Florin, David, (AV) . . . . '52 '77 C.1044 B.A. L.273 J.D. [Crowell&M.]
*PRACTICE AREAS: Health Law; Litigation; Insurance; Antitrust Law; Association Law.
Florini, Karen L., (AV) '57 '84 C.604 B.A. L.309 J.D.
Sr. Atty., Environmental Def. Fund
Flournoy, Todd '69 '94 C&L.893 B.A., J.D.
Coun. & Dir., State Legis. Affs., Motion Picture Assn. of Amer., Inc.
Flowe, Benjamin H., Jr., (AV) . . . . '56 '81 C.228 A.B. L.575 J.D. [Berliner,C.&R.]
*PRACTICE AREAS: International; Corporate; Commercial Transactions; Maritime.
Flowe, Carol Connor, (AV) . . . . '50 '77 C.531 B.M.E. L.1119 J.D. [Arent F.K.P.&K.]
*PRACTICE AREAS: ERISA; Litigation; Employment Law; Employee Benefits Litigation; ERISA Litigation.

Flowers, Ann E. .... '56 '83 C.575 B.A. L.276 J.D. [Ⓒ Cole,R.&B.]
*PRACTICE AREAS: Transactional Matters; Acquisitions and Finance; Corporate Organization and Governance Issues.
Flowers, Holly J. .... '71 '00 C.800 B.A. L.904 J.D. 1429 G. St. N.W.
Floyd, Eldora Ellison '66 '99 C.311 B.S. L.276 J.D.
(adm. in MD; not adm. in DC; See Pat. Sect.) [Ⓐ Sterne,K.G.&F.]
*PRACTICE AREAS: Patent Law.
Fluet, Joseph E., III '67 '99 C.401 B.A. L.260 J.D.
(adm. in FL; not adm. in DC) Pension Benefit Guaranty Corp.
Flug, James F., (AV) .... '39 '63 C&L.309 A.B., LL.B. [Ⓒ Duncan,W.G.&P.]
*PRACTICE AREAS: Energy; Administrative Law; Federal Litigation; State Representation.
Flyer, Michael R., (AV) .... '37 '63 C&L.477 B.A., J.D. [Venable,A.B.H.&C.]
*PRACTICE AREAS: Business Law; Tax Law.
Flyger, John .... '61 '87 C.429 B.A. L.228 J.D. [Ⓒ Steptoe&J.]
*PRACTICE AREAS: Litigation; Insurance Coverage.
Flynn, Blair E. '74 '99 C.692 B.A. L.893 J.D.
(adm. in AL; not adm. in DC) [Ⓐ Sutherland A.&B.]
*PRACTICE AREAS: Securities; Mergers and Acquisitions; Corporate Law.
Flynn, Christopher .... '65 '92 C.273 B.A. L.128 J.D. [King,P.&H.]
*PRACTICE AREAS: Litigation; Health Care Law; Employment Law.
Flynn, Claudia J. '54 '82 C.103 B.A. L.569 J.D.
(adm. in NY; not adm. in DC) U.S. Dept. of Jus.
Flynn, Colin T. .... '— '93 C.262 B.A. L.128 J.D. [Ⓐ Morgan,L.&B.]
Flynn, Darcy Evans Robert .... '59 '96 C.932 B.B.A. L.477 J.D. U.S. Secs. Exch. Comm.
Flynn, Kathleen A. .... '50 '76 C.446 B.A. L.930 J.D. 5345 Broad Branch Rd., NW
Flynn, Kevin W. '69 '00 C.164 B.A. L.446 J.D.
(adm. in MD; not adm. in DC) [Ⓐ Van Ness F.]
*PRACTICE AREAS: Electric Power; Natural Gas.
Flynn, Kristen M. .... '68 '99 C.31 B.A. L.477 J.D. [Ⓐ Zuckerman S.]
*PRACTICE AREAS: Civil Litigation; Criminal Litigation.
Flynn, Martin J., (AV) .... '37 '62 C.347 A.B. L.1119 J.D. [Shea&G.]
*PRACTICE AREAS: Banking; Corporate; Commercial Litigation.
Flynn, Paul M. .... '60 '85 C.734 B.A. L.273 J.D. [Wright&T.]
*PRACTICE AREAS: Energy Regulation; Hydroelectricity Licensing.
Flynn, Ruth S., (AV) .... '44 '83 C.597 B.S. L.146 J.D. [McKenna&C.]
*PRACTICE AREAS: Estate Planning; Estate Administration; Charitable Giving.
Flynn, Tegan M. .... '63 '88 C.788 A.B. L.309 J.D. [Vinson&E.]
*PRACTICE AREAS: Litigation.
Flynn, Terence F., (AV) .... '60 '90 C.446 B.A. L.902 J.D. [Ⓒ Crowell&M.]
*PRACTICE AREAS: Labor and Employment; Civil Litigation; Employee Benefits; Communications and Media; Corporate Law.
Flynt, Richard A., (AV) .... '46 '73 C.893 B.A. L.500 J.D. [Roylance,A.B.&G.]
*PRACTICE AREAS: Trademark Law; Litigation; Copyright Law.
Fobe, Nicholas M. .... '61 '93 C.1038 B.M. L.262 J.D. [Verstegen&F.] ⊙
Fogarty, Marie .... '62 '88 C.1349 B.A. L.188 J.D. One Thomas Circle
Fogarty, Michael E. .... '62 '92 C.1133 B.S.E.E. L.724 J.D. [McDermott,W.&E.] (Pat.)
Fogel, J. Cathy, (AV) .... '— '77 C.966 B.S. L.128 J.D. [Verner,L.B.M.&H.]
*PRACTICE AREAS: Energy Law.
Fogelson, Richard J. .... '67 '93 C.165 B.A. L.823 J.D. [Ⓐ B.J.Klores&Assoc.]
*PRACTICE AREAS: Civil Trial Practice; Professional Negligence; Emergency Medicine.
Foggan, Laura A. .... '58 '83 C.659 B.A. L.273 J.D. [Wiley R.&F.]
*PRACTICE AREAS: Appellate; Insurance; Litigation.
Fogleman, Dannie B., (AV) .... '48 '75 C.575 B.A. L.790 J.D. [Ⓒ Ford&H.]
*PRACTICE AREAS: Litigation; Management Labor Law; Discrimination.
Fogleman, Krista M. .... '52 '78 C.914 B.A. L.276 J.D. 1825 I St., N.W.
Fogleman, Stephen C. '48 '82
C.885 B.A. L.1148 J.D. 1919 Pennsylvania Ave., N.W., Suite 800
Fogler, Holly R. .... '67 '93 C&L.846 B.B.A., J.D. [Ⓒ Arnold&P.]
*PRACTICE AREAS: Antitrust.
Fogt, Howard W., Jr., (AV) .... '— '67 C.674 A.B. L.893 J.D. [Foley&L.]
*PRACTICE AREAS: Antitrust Law; European Community Law; International Trade Law.
Fohrman, Elizabeth P. '62 '87 C.861 B.A. L.273 J.D.
Resch Atty., MCI Communications Corporation
Fois, Sonia (Turcotte) .... '58 '88 C.164 A.B. L.276 J.D. [Arnold&P.]
*PRACTICE AREAS: Public Policy; Legislative.
Folds, J. David .... '66 '93 C.797 B.A. L.575 J.D. [Ⓐ Womble C.S.&R.]
*PRACTICE AREAS: Commercial Litigation; Bankruptcy.
Foley, Cheryl M. '47 '78 C.518 B.A. L.117 J.D.
(adm. in TX; not adm. in DC) [Ⓒ Skadden,A.S.M.&F.]
Foley, Christopher P., (AV) '53 '83
C.871 B.S. L.276 J.D. [Finnegan,H.F.G.&D.] (See Pat. Sect.)
*PRACTICE AREAS: Trademark Registration; Trademark Litigation; Patent Litigation; Patent Prosecution.
Foley, Colin .... '71 '99 C.659 B.A. L.93 J.D. [Ⓐ Howrey S.A.&W.]
*PRACTICE AREAS: Trademarks; Copyrights; Commercial Litigation.
Foley, John F. .... '58 '93 C.94 B.A. L.276 J.D. [Ⓐ Keller&H.]
*PRACTICE AREAS: Food and Drug Law; Environmental Law.
Foley, John P. .... '62 '89 C.09 B.A. L.025 LL.B. [Ⓐ Shook,H.&B.]
Foley, John R., Jr., (AV) .... '17 '47 C.755 A.B. L.276 LL.B. [Foley&F.]
Foley, Thomas S., (AV) '29 '57 C&L.911 A.B., LL.B.
1333 New Hampshire Ave., N.W.

Foley & Foley, (AV)
624 Bowen Building, 815 15th Street, N.W., 20005
Telephone: 202-737-8055
John R. Foley (1890-1953); John R. Foley, Jr.
General and Administrative Practice. Energy, Trusts, Probate, Labor, Tax and Commercial Law.
See Professional Biographies, WASHINGTON, DISTRICT OF COLUMBIA

Foley, Hoag & Eliot LLP, (AV) BR
1747 Pennsylvania Avenue, N.W., 20006 ⊙
Telephone: 202-223-1200 Telecopier: 202-785-6687
URL: http://www.foleyhoag.com
Members of Firm: Janis H. Brennan; John L. Burke, Jr.; Gary S. Guzy; James T. Montgomery, Jr.; Paul S. Reichler. Counsel: Stephanie Cutler; Traci Duvall Humes; Alima Joned; Gare A. Smith. Associates: Lawrence H. Martin (Not admitted in DC); Mariana Prieto (Not admitted in DC).
General and Administrative Practice, International; International Arbitration; Government Affairs; Tax and Commercial Law, Real Estate, Corporate, Trust and Estate Planning.
Boston, Massachusetts Office: One Post Office Square. Telephone: 617-832-1000. Telecopier: 617-832-7000.
See Professional Biographies, WASHINGTON, DISTRICT OF COLUMBIA

Foley & Lardner, (AV) BR
Washington Harbour, Suite 500, 3000 K Street, N.W., 20007-5109 ⊙
Telephone: 202-672-5300 Facsimile: 202-672-5399
Email: webmaster@foleylaw.com URL: http://www.foleylardner.com
Partners: M. Peter Adler; Stephen A. Bent; James N. Bierman; Arthur H. Bill; David A. Blumenthal; Theodore H. Bornstein; Sharie A. Brown; Robert A. Burka; Beth A. Burrous; Rachel Danish Campbell; Alan I. Cantor; Steven B. Chameides; Richard T. Choi; Gary O. Cohen; Paul E. Cooney; John G. DeGooyer; Thomas R. Devine; Marc B. Dorfman; Murray Drabkin; Joseph D. Edmondson, Jr.; William T. Ellis; John J. Feldhaus (Not admitted in DC); Howard W. Fogt, Jr.; Jay W. Freedman; Thomas E. Hartman; Donald M. Itzkoff; Thomas L. James; Mary Cynthia Atchley Jester; Michael D. Kaminski; Lyle Kimms; Kenneth E. Krosin; Johnny A. Kumar; Jack L. Lahr; Steven C. Lambert; Thomas C. Lauerman; Glenn Law; Jerris Leonard; Melinda F. Levitt; Peter G. Mack; Stephen B. Maebius; Lisa S. Mankofsky; Lawrence G. McBride; Francis O. McDermott; Brian J. McNamara;

(This Listing Continued)

Foley & Lardner (Continued)
Robert J. Meyer; Cleta Deatherage Mitchell Mitchell; Paul R. Monsees; Philip A. Nacke; Richard C. Peet; George E. Quillin (Not admitted in DC); David T. Ralston, Jr.; Andrew E. Rawlins; Jamie Palter Rennert; Richard F. Riley, Jr.; David A. Sacks; Jacqueline Marie Saue; Bernhard D. Saxe; Charles F. Schill; Richard L. Schwaab; Larry L. Shatzer II; Michele M. Simkin; Samuel B. Sterrett, Jr.; Richard G. Stoll; Paul E. Sullivan (Not admitted in DC); Charles Michael Tobin; Sheldon L. Trubatch; Jay N. Varon; Robert P. vom Eigen; J. Mark Waxman (Not admitted in DC); Harold C. Wegner; Martin J. Weinstein; Kenneth B. Winer; Samuel J. Winer; Michael D. Wolk (Not admitted in DC); Jeff Zimmerman; Gary M. Zinkgraf. Retired Partners: Edwin Jason Dryer; Donald D. Jeffery; Arthur Schwartz. Of Counsel: John H. Chettle; Walter Freedman; Mary Gayle Holden; Peter C. Linzmeyer; Barbara Ann McDowell (Not admitted in DC); Peter E. Panarites. Special Counsel: Norman C. Bensley (Not admitted in DC); Karen M. Grane; Jayme A. Huleatt; Nina M. Osseiran (Not admitted in DC). Senior Counsel: Alicia J. Batts; George C. Beck; Todd J. Burns; Simon E. Dance; Allison C. George; Bryan B. House; Patrick J. Kearney; Mary Michelle Kile; Jeffrey G. Micklos (Not admitted in DC); Jeffrey S. Newman; Leo F. Orenstein; Patrick W. Reilly; Alan D. Rutenberg. Resident Associates: Pavan Kumar Agarwal; Phillip John Articola; Sandy M. Ballou (Not admitted in DC); George C. Best (Not admitted in DC); Rachel D. Borak (Not admitted in DC; 888 Sixteenth Street, N.W. Office); Randy Elizabeth Brenner; Aaron C. Chatterjee; Christian B. Dinneen-Long (Not admitted in DC); Robert M. Hansen (Not admitted in DC); Juliet Dawn Hiznay (Not admitted in DC); Parvin Huda (Not admitted in DC); Kristen Grim Hughes; Joo-Mee Kim (Not admitted in DC); Susan M. C. Kovarovics; Marvin C. Lunde, III; Thomas W. Mac Allister; Geoffrey M. McNutt (Not admitted in DC); Amy Wilsey Miller; Nalini K. Pande; Arden T. Phillips; John C. Pisa-Relli; Leon Radomsky; Irwin Perry Raij; Norman J. Rich (Not admitted in DC); Garth D. Richmond; Gregg H. Rosenblatt (Not admitted in DC); Heidi Elisabeth Rosenberg; Gary S. Rovner; David Seth Sanders; Ankur D. Shah; Morgan Wayne Shelton (Not admitted in DC); Howard N. Shipley; James M. Silbermann; Anthony H. Son; Todd N. Spalding (Not admitted in DC); Frederic T. Tenney (Not admitted in DC); Cynthia E. Tidler; C. Anthony Trambley; Heather M. Trew; Marc K. Weinstein (Not admitted in DC); Roderick B. Williams.
General Practice, International and Domestic Patent, Trademark and Copyright, Biotechnology and related Intellectual Property Law, Health Law, Litigation, including Intellectual Property Litigation, Insurance, Telecommunications, International Trade.
Other Washington, D.C. Office: 888 Sixteenth Street, N.W. Telephone: 202-835-8000. Fax: 202-835-8136.
Los Angeles, California Office: 2029 Century Park East, 35th Floor. Telephone: 310-277-2223. Fax: 310-557-8475.
Sacramento, California Office: 300 Capitol Mall, Suite 1125. Telephone: 916-443-8005. Fax: 916-443-2240.
San Diego, California Office: 402 West Broadway, 23rd Floor. Telephone: 619-234-6655. Fax: 619-234-3510.
San Diego/North County, California Office: 11250 El Camino Real, Suite 200. Telephone: 858-847-6700. Facsimile: 858-792-6773.
San Francisco, California Office: One Maritime Plaza, Sixth Floor. Telephone: 415-434-4484. Fax: 415-434-4507.
Denver, Colorado Office: 1999 Broadway, Suite 2560. Telephone: 303-297-0260. Fax: 303-297-0266.
Jacksonville, Florida Office: The Greenleaf Building, 200 Laura Street. P.O. Box 240. Telephone: 904-359-2000. Facsimile: 904-359-8700.
Orlando, Florida Office: Suite 1800, 111 North Orange Avenue, P.O. Box 2193. Telephone: 407-423-7656. Facsimile: 407-648-1743.
Tallahassee, Florida Office: 106 East College Avenue, Highpoint Center, Suite 900, P.O. Box 1819. Telephone: 850-222-6100. Facsimile: 850-561-6475.
Tampa, Florida Offices: Suite 2700, 100 N. Tampa Street, P.O. Box 3391. Telephones: 813-229-2300; Pinellas County: 813-442-3296. Facsimile: 813-221-4210.
West Palm Beach, Florida Office: 777 South Flagler Drive, Suite 901, West Tower. Telephone: 561-655-5050. Facsimile: 561-655-6925.
Chicago, Illinois Office: One IBM Plaza, 330 N. Wabash Avenue, Suite 3300. Telephone: 312-755-1900. Facsimile: 312-755-1925.
Other Chicago, Illinois Office: Three First National Plaza, 70 West Madison, Suite 4100. Telephone: 312-558-6600. Fax: 312-558-6676.
Annapolis, Maryland Office: Suite 102, 175 Admiral Cochrane Drive. Telephone: 410-266-8077. Facsimile: 410-266-8664.
Detroit, Michigan Office: 150 West Jefferson, Suite 1000. Telephone: 313-963-6200. Fax: 313-963-9308.
Madison, Wisconsin Office: Verex Plaza, 150 East Gilman Street, P.O. Box 1497. Telephone: 608-257-5035. Facsimile: 608-258-4258.
Milwaukee, Wisconsin Office: Firstar Center, 777 East Wisconsin Avenue. Telephone: 414-271-2400. Facsimile: 414-297-4900.
Brussels, Belgium Office: Avenue Louise, 283. Telephone: 32-2-646-2777. Facsimile: 32-2-646-7574.
See Professional Biographies, WASHINGTON, DISTRICT OF COLUMBIA

Follette, Lysle S., III .... '62 '95 C.999 B.A. L.325 J.D. 7603 Georgia Ave. N.W.
Folsom, Suzanne Rich .... '— '94 C.228 A.B. L.276 J.D. [Ⓒ O'Melveny&M.]
*PRACTICE AREAS: Strategic Alliances; Litigation; Trade Association Law.
Foltin, Richard '52 '77 C.569 B.A. L.309 J.D.
Legis. Dir. & Coun., American Jewish Comm.
Fones, Michael R. '59 '84 C.945 B.A. L.1209 J.D.
(adm. in VA; not adm. in DC) 4119 Brandywine St. N.W.‡
Fonseca, Michael D. .... '54 '82 C.563 B.A L.276 J.D. [O'Brien&L.]
*PRACTICE AREAS: Alcoholic Beverage Licensing; Liquor Licensing; Municipal Law.
Fonstein, Cliff H. '57 '84 C.112 B.A. L.1068 J.D.
[O'Melveny&M.] (⊙New York, NY)
*PRACTICE AREAS: Labor and Employment.
Fonsworth Coles, Janell P. .... '70 '96 C&L.329 B.A., J.D. 701 Penn. Ave., N.W., Ste. 900
Fontaine, Donald C., Jr. .... '57 '97 C.446 B.S. L.990 J.D. 1730 K St., N.W.
Fontaine, Monita W. .... '52 '78 C.890 B.A. L.744 J.D. [Fontaine,S.K.&D.]
Fontaine, Shimkin, King & Delbert, L.L.P. .... 4720 44th St., N.W.
Fontein, Douglas J. '22 '60 C.255 M.A. L.276 J.D.
(adm. in VA; not adm. in DC) Intl. Bk. for Reconstr. & Develop.
Fontham, John H. .... '— '96 C&L.893 B.A., J.D. [Ⓐ King&S.]
*PRACTICE AREAS: Commercial Litigation; Oil and Gas Law.
Foor, Jeffrey A. '73 '01 C.659 B.A. L.273 J.D.
(adm. in FL; not adm. in DC) [Ⓐ Dechert]
*PRACTICE AREAS: Investment Management; Financial Services Law.
Foote, George M., (AV) .... '49 '75 C.902 B.A. L.276 J.D. [Bracewell&P.]
*PRACTICE AREAS: International Transactions; Telecommunications; Nonprofit Organizations.
Foote, Joseph .... '32 '60 C.951 B.A. L.309 LL.B. 66 G St., S.W.
Foote, Susan Bartlett '46 '77 C.930 B.A. L.1066 J.D.
(adm. in CA; not adm. in DC) 1330 Connecticut Ave., N.W.‡
Forch, Jeanne Marie, (BV) .... '50 '82 C.886 B.A. L.128 J.D. 3050 K St., N.W.
Forchilli, Cheryl E. '74 '01 C.846 B.A. L.260 J.D.
(adm. in FL; not adm. in DC) [Ⓐ Jones,D.R.&P.]
Ford, Ann K., (AV) .... '54 '81 C.276 B.A. L.228 J.D. [Piper M.R.&W.]
*PRACTICE AREAS: Intellectual Property.
Ford, Benjamin T. '— '01 C.1335 B.A. L.309 J.D.
(adm. in NY; not adm. in DC) [Ⓐ Chadbourne&P.]
Ford, Christopher A. '67 '96 C.309 A.B. L.976 J.D.
Russell Senate Office Bldg., Rm. 100
Ford, Christopher D. '65 '93 C.893 B.S. L.245 J.D.
(adm. in GA; not adm. in DC) [Alston&B.]
*PRACTICE AREAS: Information Technology; Telecommunications Contracts; Outsourcing Transactions; Strategic Alliances; Joint Ventures.
Ford, David A. '59 '84 C&L.1243 B.A., J.D.
(adm. in AR; not adm. in DC) 935 Pennsylvania Ave., N.W.
Ford, Gary M., (AV) .... '50 '77 C.309 A.B. L.94 J.D. [Groom]
*PRACTICE AREAS: Employee Benefits Law; Insurance Litigation; Pension and Profit Sharing; Mergers and Acquisitions; Labor and Employment.

Ford, Holly M. .... '— '92 C.128 B.A. L.93 J.D. [Ⓐ Banner&W.]
*PRACTICE AREAS: Intellectual Property Law; Trademarks; Copyrights; Intellectual Property Licensing.
Ford, John C. '71 '97 C.813 B.A. L.477 J.D.
(adm. in MI; not adm. in DC) [Ⓐ Wilmer,C.&P.]
Ford, John M. .... '— '94 C.728 B.S. L.705 J.D. [Ⓐ Morgan,L.&B.]
Ford, Kathleen J., (AV) '55 '87 C.140 B.S. L.190 J.D.
(adm. in NE; not adm. in DC)
Assoc. Gen. Coun., Labor & Employ., Natl. Railroad Passenger Corp. (AMTRAK)
Ford, Laura A. .... '73 '98 C.367 B.A. L.228 J.D. [Ⓐ Swidler B.S.F.]
*PRACTICE AREAS: Environmental Law.
Ford, Marie R. '63 '89 C.892 B.A. L.1209 J.D.
(adm. in PA; not adm. in DC) 1919 Pennsylvania Ave.‡
Ford, Paul H. .... '30 '67 C.446 B.S. L.273 J.D. Wash. Gas Light Co.
Ford, Peter J. '56 '82 C.178 B.A. L.273 J.D.
Asst. Gen. Coun., United Food & Comercial Workers International Union
Ford, Rebecca A. .... '69 '01 C.502 B.A. L.1439 J.D. [Ⓐ Bryan C.]
Ford, William D. .... '27 '53 C&L.208 B.S., LL.B. 2550 M St. N.W.

Ford & Harrison LLP, (AV) BB
1300 19th Street, N.W., Suite 700, 20036 ⊙
Telephone: 202-719-2000 Fax: 202-719-2077
Email: firm@fordharrison.com URL: http://www.fordharrison.com
Members of Firm: Ronald C. Henson; Joshua M. Javits; Peter J. Petesch; David A. Rosenberg. Resident Senior Counsel: Dannie B. Fogleman. Resident Associates: Kevin M. Kraham; Darlene H. Smith (Not admitted in DC); Randy C. Sparks, Jr. (Not admitted in DC); Mark Wise (Not admitted in DC).
Labor and Employment Law representing Employers, including Employment Litigation, Discrimination, Harassment, Class Action Litigation, Affirmative Action, Wrongful Termination, Wage and Hour Law, ADA/FMLA, Airline Labor Law, Labor Union Organizing, Collective Bargaining, Arbitration, Layoffs and Plant Closings, Mergers and Acquisitions (Labor), Employment Contracts, Alternative Dispute Resolution, Business Immigration, Employee Benefits, Workplace Safety and Environmental Law.
Representative Clients: Coca-Cola Enterprises; Delta Air Lines, Inc.; Federal Express Corp.; Knight Publishing Co.; Landmark Communications, Inc.; LIN Television Corp.; Regional Airline Assn.; Rheem Manufacturing Co.; The Standard Register Co.
Atlanta, Georgia Office: 600 Peachtree at the Circle Building, 1275 Peachtree Street, N.E., 30309. Telephone: 404-888-3800. Fax: 404-888-3863.
Denver, Colorado Office: 1675 Broadway, Suite 2150, 80202. Telephone: 303-592-8860. Fax: 303-592-8861.
Los Angeles, California Office: 333 South Grand Avenue, Suite 3680, 90071. Telephone: 213-680-3410. Fax: 213-680-4161.
Memphis, Tennessee Office: 6750 Poplar Avenue, Suite 600, 38138. Telephone: 901-291-1500. Fax: 901-291-1501.
Miami, Florida Office: 516 Ingraham Building, 25 S.E. 2nd Avenue, 33131. Telephone: 305-379-3811. Fax: 305-358-5933.
Orlando, Florida Office: 300 South Orange Avenue, Suite 1300, 32801. Telephone: 407-418-2300. Fax: 407-418-2327.
Tampa, Florida Office: 101 E. Kennedy Boulevard, Suite 900, 33602. Telephone: 813-261-7800. Fax: 813-261-7899.
Jacksonville, Florida Office: 121 West Forsyth Street, Suite 1000, P.O. Box 41566, 32203. Telephone: 904-356-8073. Fax: 404-358-2319.
Birmingham, Alabama Office: 505 North 20th Street, Suite 1201, 35203. Telephone: 205-254-9480. Fax: 205-254-9848.
See Professional Biographies, WASHINGTON, DISTRICT OF COLUMBIA

Forde-Mazrui, Kim A. '68 '93 C&L.477 B.A., J.D.
(adm. in MI; not adm. in DC) 1722 Eye St.
Forest, Janet A. .... '51 '78 C.297 B.A. L.494 J.D. [Ⓒ Miller&C.]
*PRACTICE AREAS: Customs Law.
Forester, G. Yasué .... '68 '93 C.575 B.A. L.930 J.D. Jud. Law Clk, to Supr. Ct.

Forester, J. Gordon, Jr., (AV) '33 '62 C.575 B.S. L.273 LL.B.
1742 N Street, N.W., 20036
Telephone: 202-293-3353 Facsimile: 202-785-2210
Email: jgfcadence@earthlink.net
Civil and Criminal Litigation, General and Appellate Practice, Trusts and Estates.
See Professional Biographies, WASHINGTON, DISTRICT OF COLUMBIA

Forgotson, Elizabeth, P.C.
(See Rockville, Maryland)

Forjette, Kevin P. .... '69 '96 C.273 B.A. L.1194 J.D. [Ⓐ Crowell&M.]
Forkner, David A. .... '71 '97 C&L.208 B.A., J.D. [Ⓐ Williams&C.]
Forlini, Emidio J., Jr. '72 '97 C.477 B.A. L.896 J.D.
(adm. in MD; not adm. in DC) JM Zell Partners, Ltd.
Forman, Daniel R. .... '72 '98 C.881 B.A. L.978 J.D. [Ⓐ Crowell&M.]
Forman, David S., (BV) '42 '87
C.309 B.A. L.273 J.D. [Finnegan,H.F.G.&D.] (See Pat. Sect.)
*PRACTICE AREAS: Patent Law.
Forman, James, Jr. .... '67 '94 C.103 B.A. L.976 J.D. Pub. Def. Serv.
Forman, Johanna Mendelson '47 '89 C.994 B.A. L.30 J.D.
Amer. Univ. Sch. of Intl. Serv.
Forman, Stephen B., (AV) .... '40 '72 C.178 B.S. L.273 J.D. [Arent F.K.P.&K.]
*PRACTICE AREAS: Employment Law; Employment Discrimination; Wrongful Termination; Sexual Harassment; Wage and Hour Law.
Formica, Frank J. '43 '72 C.610 A.B. L.30 J.D.
(adm. in NY; not adm. in DC) V.P., Nat. Assn. of Securities Dealers, Inc.
Formica, Michael C. .... '71 '99 C.690 B.A. L.1194 J.D. [Ⓐ Baise&M.]
*PRACTICE AREAS: Environmental Law; International Law; Litigation; Legislative Practice.
Fornaci, Philip J. ....'58 '91 C.178 B.A. L.273 J.D. Natl. Assocaition for Pub. Interest Law
Fornaciari, John R., (AV) .... '46 '71 C.676 A.B. L.93 J.D. [Ross&H.]
Fornelli, Cynthia M. .... '60 '91 C.679 B.A. L.273 J.D. 1775 Eye St., N.W.
Forrer, Graydon J. .... '58 '86 C.228 B.A. L.910 J.D. [Ⓒ Foxkiser]
*PRACTICE AREAS: Food and Drug Regulation; Health Care.
Forrester, Nathan A. '66 '97 C.260 B.S. L.145 J.D.
(adm. in VA; not adm. in DC) 1722 Eye St., N.W.‡
Forseth, Mark B. '60 '91 C.1369 B.A. L.446 J.D.
(adm. in TX; not adm. in DC) Sr. Coun., Marriott Intl., Inc.
*RESPONSIBILITIES: Franchising and Distribution.
Forseth, Scott L. .... '62 '89 C.276 B.S.F.S. L.893 J.D. 1775 Pennsylvania Ave., N.W.
Forshay, Paul F., (AV) .... '59 '84 C.311 B.A. L.904 J.D. [Sutherland A.&B.]
*PRACTICE AREAS: Energy; Administrative Law; Regulatory Law; Utility Law; Transportation.
Forst, John K. '60 '91 C.273 B.B.A. L.117 J.D.
(adm. in FL; not adm. in DC) [Ⓐ Dechert]
*PRACTICE AREAS: Banking Regulation; Securities Regulation; Broker-Dealer Regulation; Federal Regulatory Law; Trust Administration.
Forsythe, L. B. '66 '92 C.112 B.A. L.262 J.D
(adm. in CA; not adm. in DC) The Natl. Political Action Comm.
Fort, Joanne Doddy, (AV) .... '50 '72 C.104 B.A. L.659 J.D. [Ⓒ Jordan K.&J.]
Forte, Patrick A. .... '42 '82 C.608 B.A. L.1162 J.D. 5034 Overlook Rd., N.W.
Fortenberry, Amy E. .... '70 '97 C.1059 B.A. L.93 J.D. [Ⓐ Kilpatrick S.]
*PRACTICE AREAS: Environmental Law; Food and Drug.
Fortenberry, Monique Y. .... '70 '97 C.597 B.A. L.276 J.D. [Ⓐ Jackson L.S.&K.]
*PRACTICE AREAS: Labor and Employment.
Fortine, Carol A., (AV) .... '58 '85 C.473 A.B. L.273 J.D. Asst. U.S. Atty.

Fortney, Anne Price .... '44 '69 C.890 B.A. L.276 J.D. [Lovells]
*PRACTICE AREAS: Consumer Financial Services; Privacy; Federal Regulatory Compliance.
Fortney, David S., (AV) .... '54 '80 C.645 B.A. L.229 J.D. [Ogletree,D.N.S.&S.]
*PRACTICE AREAS: Labor; Employment; Litigation.
Fortune, Terence J. .... '46 '75 C&L.276 B.A., J.D. [Paul,W.R.W.&G.]
*PRACTICE AREAS: International Trade; International Telecommunications; Government Procurement; Federal Administrative Law.
Fortuno, Victor M., (AV) '52 '77 C&L.178 B.A., J.D.
V.P., Legal Affs., Gen. Coun. & Corp. Secy., Legal Services Corp.
Forville, Janet Benson '73 '00
C.886 B.A. L.945 J.D. Smithsonian Institute, Contracting Office
Foscarinis, Maria '56 '82 C.66 A.B. L.178 J.D.
Exec. Dir., National Law Ctr. on Homelessness & Poverty
Fosnocht, David J. .... '62 '87 C.884 B.A. L.276 J.D. George Washington Univ.
Foster, Albert A., Jr. .... '57 '84 C.1350 B.S. L.107 J.D. [Dillingham&M.]
*PRACTICE AREAS: Employment Law; Toxic Torts; Civil Rights; Insurance Defense.
Foster, Alexandra .... '72 '99 C.309 B.A. L.846 J.D. [Ⓐ Zuckerman S.]
*PRACTICE AREAS: Litigation.
Foster, Bernard A., III .... '42 '68 C.797 A.B. L.273 LL.B. [Ross,M.&F.]
*PRACTICE AREAS: Energy Law; Administrative Law.
Foster, C. Allen, (AV) .... '41 '67 C.674 A.B. L.309 J.D. [Greenberg T.]
Foster, Catherine Crystal '65 '92 C.976 B.A. L.309 J.D.
Proj. Dir., National Assn. of Child Advocates
Foster, David M., (AV) .... '53 '81 C&L.893 B.A., J.D. [Fulbright&J.]
*PRACTICE AREAS: Antitrust and Trade Regulation; Litigation.
Foster, Dennis A. .... '49 '88 C.575 B.A. L.813 [Wolf,A.&C.] (⊙New York, NY)
*PRACTICE AREAS: International Business Law; International Arbitration; International Mediation; International Copyright Law; International Trademarks.
Foster, F. David, (AV) .... '46 '73 C&L.36 B.A., J.D. [Miller&C.]
*PRACTICE AREAS: International Trade Law; Unfair Competition Law.
Foster, Hope S., (AV) .... '48 '73 C.914 B.A. L.273 J.D. [Mintz,L.C.F.G.&P.]
*PRACTICE AREAS: Health Care Fraud; Health Care Legislation; Health Care Regulation; Health Care Reimbursement; Health Law.
Foster, Jody M. .... '58 '93 C.623 B.A. L.1066 J.D. [Ⓐ Hogan&H.]
*PRACTICE AREAS: Environmental Regulation; Clean Air Act; Clean Water Act; National Environmental Policy Act (NEPA); Endangered Species.
Foster, John D. ... '43 '70 C.350 B.S.Ch.E. L.276 J.D. [Ⓒ Leydig,V.&M.] (See Pat. Sect.)
Foster, Katharine V. .... '70 '98 C.165 B.A. L.30 J.D. [Ⓐ Galland,K.G.F.&S.]
*PRACTICE AREAS: Corporate Law; Association; Transportation.
Foster, Louise T. .... '— '24 C.357 A.B. L.273 LL.B. 1445 New York Ave. N.W.‡
Foster, Mark M. .... '63 '96 C.1333 B.S. L.285 J.D. [Ⓐ Nixon P.]
*PRACTICE AREAS: Business; Nonprofit and Charitable Organizations; Tax Law.
Foster, Mark W., (AV) .... '42 '71 C.976 B.A. L.309 J.D. [Zuckerman S.]
*PRACTICE AREAS: Complex Commercial Transactions; Civil Litigation; Business Organization; Legal Ethics and Lawyer Discipline; Partnership Law.
Foster, Robert A., (AV) .... '58 '83 C.597 B.A. L.339 J.D. [Ⓐ Shapiro,L.&S.]
*PRACTICE AREAS: Commercial Real Estate; Commercial Transactions.
Foster, Stephanie M. .... '— '94 C.918 B.A. L.1009 J.D. [Ⓐ Morgan,L.&B.]
Foster, Stephen M., (AV) .... '47 '78 C.31 B.A. L.276 J.D. 1924 47th St., N.W.
Foti, Nancy L. '73 '01 C.1142 B.A. L.101 J.D.
(adm. in MD; not adm. in DC) Jud. Clk., US Court of Appeals for Veterans Claims
Fotis, Stephen C., (BV) .... '55 '86 C.197 B.A. L.30 J.D. [Van Ness F.]
*PRACTICE AREAS: Environment; Clean Air Act; Natural Resources; Air Pollution; Air Quality.
Fountain, Edwin L. .... '64 '90 C.575 B.A. L.893 J.D. [Jones,D.R.&P.]
*PRACTICE AREAS: Litigation; Antitrust.
Fountain, Elizabeth L. .... '50 '85 C.16 B.A. L.923 J.D. [Tendler&B.]
Fountain, Sharon F. .... '62 '90 C.158 B.S. L.273 J.D. Bur. of National Affairs, Inc.
Fournier, James J. .... '70 '97 C.112 B.A. L.262 J.D. [Ⓐ Howrey S.A.&W.]
*PRACTICE AREAS: Insurance Coverage; Commercial Litigation.
Fournier, Paul A. .... '— '98 C.431 B.S.E.E. L.273 J.D. [Ⓐ Morgan,L.&B.] (Pat.)
Foushee, Trudi McCollum '56 '82 C.574 B.A. L.276 J.D.
[Green&F.] (⊙St. Louis, MO)
*PRACTICE AREAS: Corporate Law; Human Resources; Employment; Communications Law.
Fowler, Brian D. .... '74 '99 C.886 B.A. L.228 J.D. [Ⓐ Hogan&H.]
Fowler, Debra-Lynn Gargano '60 '86 C.705 L.893 J.D.
Asst. Gen. Coun., Nat. Assn. of Sec. Dealers, Inc.
Fowler, Donald W. .... '51 '75 C.188 B.A. L.976 J.D. [Spriggs&H.]
*PRACTICE AREAS: Environmental Law; Litigation; Toxic Torts; Products Liability; Civil Appeals.
Fowler, Gregory M. .... '54 '79 C.1074 B.A. L.990 J.D. Price Waterhouse
Fowler, J. Edward, (AV) '31 '60 C.674 A.B. L.976 LL.B.
(adm. in NY; not adm. in DC) 10 Kalorama Circle, N.W.‡
Fowler, Matthew R. '72 '01 C.547 B.A. L.477 J.D.
(adm. in NY; not adm. in DC) [Ⓐ Coudert B.]
*PRACTICE AREAS: Project Finance; Energy; International Finance.
Fowler, Tillie K. .... '42 '67 C&L.1365 A.B., J.D. [Holland&K.] (⊙Jacksnvl., FL)
*PRACTICE AREAS: Public Law; Federal Appropiations.
Fox, Allan M., (AV) .... '48 '72 C&L.831 B.A., J.D. [Foxkiser]
Fox, Allen H., (AV) .... '51 '76 C.910 A.B. L.273 J.D. [Hale&D.]
*PRACTICE AREAS: Real Estate Law.
Fox, Arthur L., II .... '43 '68 C&L.893 B.A., LL.B. [Ⓒ Lobel,N.&L.]
*PRACTICE AREAS: Litigation; Labor and Employment.
Fox, Brendan C. .... '69 '93 C.1044 B.A. L.273 J.D. [Ⓐ Dechert]
*PRACTICE AREAS: Financial Services Law; Investment Management.
Fox, David E., and Associates, (AV) .... '47 '73 C.1044 B.A. L.276 J.D. 1325 18th St.
Fox, David M. '64 '90 C.945 B.A. L.569 J.D.
(adm. in NY; not adm. in DC) [Hogan&H.]
*PRACTICE AREAS: Food and Drug Law.
Fox, Eric R., (AV) .... '39 '64 C.31 B.A. L.309 LL.B. [Ivins,P.&B.]
*PRACTICE AREAS: Corporate Taxation; International Taxation; Tax Litigation; Estate and Gift Taxation.
Fox, Hamilton P., III, (AV) .... '45 '71 C.893 B.A. L.976 LL.B. [Sutherland A.&B.]
*PRACTICE AREAS: Litigation; White Collar Criminal Defense; Civil Litigation.
Fox, Harold H. .... '67 '99 C.453 B.S. L.94 J.D. [Ⓐ Fish&R.] (See Pat. Sect.)
*PRACTICE AREAS: Patent Law.
Fox, Harvey B. .... '41 '66 L.64 J.D. [Adduci,M.&S.]
*PRACTICE AREAS: Customs and International Trade Law; Domestic and Foreign Administrative Law; International Business; Federal Practice Litigation.
Fox, Howard, (AV) '55 '80
C.976 B.A. L.569 J.D. Mng. Atty., Earthjustice Legal Defense Fund

Fox, Jacqueline '66 '91 C.771 B.A. L.276 J.D.
5746 MacArthur Boulevard, N.W., 20016-5303
Telephone: 202-966-5610 Fax: 202-966-5476 URL: http://www.lawyers.com/jacquelinefox
Email: jfox@jacquelinefox.com URL: http://www.jacquelinefox.com
***PRACTICE AREAS: Managed Care; Health Insurance Coverage; Health Maintenance Organizations; Patients Rights; Health Care Reimbursement.**
Managed Care - Patient Advocate - Elder Law.
See Professional Biographies, WASHINGTON, DISTRICT OF COLUMBIA

Fox, Jeremy B., (AV) .... '59 '84 C.454 B.B.A. L.273 J.D. [Arent F.K.P.&K.]
*PRACTICE AREAS: Commercial Real Estate; Transactional Law; Commercial Leasing; Secured Finance.
Fox, Judith .... '58 '86 C.309 B.A. L.893 J.D. [Ⓐ Dombroff&G.]
Fox, Julius I., (AV) .... '28 '57 C.422 B.S. L.30 J.D. [Grossberg,Y.F.&B.] ‡

Fox, Katherine L. '59 '91 C.918 B.A. L.273 J.D.
(adm. in VA; not adm. in DC) Prog. Offr.
Fox, Pamela S. .... '68 '94 C.112 B.A. L.273 J.D. [Ⓐ Carr G.]
Fox, Renee Isla, (AV) '36 '79 C.1036 A.B. L.128 J.D.
1725 K Street N.W. 12th Floor, Suite 1202, 20006
Telephone: 202-429-0444 Fax: 202-429-9340
Email: rif@reneefox.com URL: http://www.lawyers.com/reneeislafoxlaw
Estate Planning, Estate Administration and Litigation. Conservatorship and Guardianship Law, Elder Law, Wills and Trusts, Probate.
See Professional Biographies, WASHINGTON, DISTRICT OF COLUMBIA
Fox, Robert B. ....'— '95 C.884 B.A. L.273 J.D. [Ⓐ Epstein B.&G.]
*PRACTICE AREAS: Corporate Law; Health Law.
Fox, Russell H., (AV) ....'57 '81 C.696 B.A. L.228 J.D. [Mintz,L.C.F.G.&P.]
*PRACTICE AREAS: Telecommunications Law; Telecommunications Licensing; Telecommunications Regulation; Wireless Communications.
Fox, Samuel L., (AV) ....'41 '67 C.446 B.S. L.273 LL.B [Ⓒ Sterne,K.G.&F.]
*PRACTICE AREAS: Intellectual Property Law.
Fox, Steven J., (BV) .... '50 '74 C&L.446 B.A., J.D. [Pepper H.]
Fox, Thomas A. ....'66 '91 C.228 A.B. L.276 J.D. [Schwartz&B.]
*PRACTICE AREAS: Banking; Financial Services; E-Commerce and Payments.
Fox, Thomas C., (AV) .... '— '66 C.532 B.A. L.273 LL.B. [Reed S.]
*PRACTICE AREAS: Health Care.
Fox, Wendy ....'51 '77 C.951 B.A. L.178 J.D. [Ⓐ Dechert]
*PRACTICE AREAS: Investment Management; Financial Services Law; Securities; Corporate Law.
Foxkiser, (AV)
750 Seventeenth Street, N.W. Suite 1100, 20006
Telephone: 202-778-2300 Telecopier: 202-778-2330
Allan M. Fox; John Daniel Kiser; Michael B. Waitzkin; John M. Engel; Matthew D. Peterson; Diane E. Robertson, Ph.D. Associates: William E. Holtz; Anita D. Novitt (Not admitted in DC); Genine C. Swanzey. Of Counsel: Andrew C. Fish; David E. Meade; Graydon J. Forrer.
General Civil Practice, Administrative Law, Civil Litigation and Legislative Practice at the Federal, State and International Levels, with emphasis on Biomedical Research, Environmental Compliance, Food, Drug and Cosmetic Regulation, Health Care Reimbursement, Medical Publishing and Communications Issues.
See Professional Biographies, WASHINGTON, DISTRICT OF COLUMBIA
Fraas, Phillip L. .... '43 '69 C.698 A.B. L.502 J.D. [Ⓒ Tuttle,T.&H.]
Frable, Ralph E. ....'52 '81 C.273 B.S. L.1218 J.D. 5101 Wisconsin Ave. N.W.
Fracassi, Michael A., (P.C.), (AV) ....'57 '83 C&L.107 B.S., J.D. [Fracassi M.] ⊙
Fracassi • Mahdavi • LLP, (AV)
2001 L Street, N.W., Suite 610 (⊙New York, NY; Falls Church, VA)
Fraedrich, Laura .... '— '95 C.945 B.A. L.1209 J.D. [Ⓐ Kirkland&E.]
*PRACTICE AREAS: International Trade; Customs Law.
Fragomen, Del Rey, Bernsen & Loewy, P.C., (AV)
1212 New York Avenue, N.W., Suite 850, 20005 ⊙
Telephone: 202-223-5515 Facsimile: 202-371-2898
URL: http://www.fragomen.com
Scott J. FitzGerald (Not admitted in DC);—Lucrecia M. Blair; Randall K. Hulme; Stacy Shore (Not admitted in DC). Of Counsel: Sam Bernsen; Gary N. Merson (Not admitted in DC).
U.S. and Foreign Immigration and Nationality Law.
New York, New York Office: 515 Madison Avenue. Telephone: 212-688-8555. Facsimile: 212-758-7215; 212-319-5236.
Buffalo, New York Office: 50 Fountain Plaza, Suite 1320. Telephone: 716-856-5444. Facsimile: 716-856-5151.
Coral Gables, Florida Office: 241 Sevilla Avenue, Suite 802. Telephone: 305-774-5800. Facsimile: 305-774-6666.
Chicago, Illinois Office: 150 North Wacker Drive, Suite 1120. Telephone: 312-263-6101. Facsimile: 312-346-1970.
San Francisco, California Office: 100 Pine Street, Suite 1575. Telephone: 415-986-1446. Facsimile: 415-986-7964.
Los Angeles, California Office: 12121 Wilshire Boulevard, Suite 1001. Telephone: 310-820-3322. Facsimile: 310-820-2702.
Santa Clara, California Office: 2804 Mission College Boulevard, 2nd Floor. Telephone: 408-919-0600. Facsimile: 408-919-0615.
Irvine, California Office: 18401 Von Karman Avenue, Suite 255. Telephone: 949-261-0209. Facsimile: 949-261-2821.
Sacramento, California Office: 2399 Gateway Oaks Drive, Suite 200. Telephone: 916-564-6900. Facsimile: 916-564-5015.
Oakland, California Office: 1999 Harrison Street, Suite 1400. Telephone: 510-444-4208. Facsimile: 510-444-4873.
San Diego, California Office: 11512 El Camino Real, Suite 300. Telephone: 858-847-9060. Facsimile: 858-847-9119.
Stamford, Connecticut Office: One Atlantic Street. Telephone: 203-352-1871. Facsimile: 203-352-1874.
Iselin, New Jersey Office: Fragomen, Del Rey, Bernsen & Loewy, 99 Wood Avenue South. Telephone: 732-906-1230. Facsimile: 732-906-9190.
Troy, Michigan Office: Fragomen, Del Rey, Bernsen and Loewy, P.L.L.C., 2301 West Big Beaver Road, Suite 225. Telephone: 248-649-5404. Facsimile: 248-649-5121.
Atlanta, Georgia Office: 1175 Peachtree Street, N.E., 100 Colony Square, Suite 700. Telephone: 404-249-9300. Facsimile: 404-249-9291.
Dallas, Texas Office: 5000 Quorum Drive, Suite 215. Telephone: 972-233-6646. Facsimile: 972-233-3134.
Phoenix, Arizona Office: 3101 North Central Avenue, Suite 1470. Telephone: 602-631-9200. Facsimile: 602-631-9300.
Vienna, Virginia Office: 1595 Spring Hill Road, Suite 320. Telephone: 703-748-2380. Facsimile: 703-748-2387.
Brussels, Belgium Office: Vossendreef 6-B.I-Dreve Des Renards, 1180 Brussels, Belgium. Telephone: 011-322-374-7-37. Facsimile: 011-322-374-90-45.
See Professional Biographies, WASHINGTON, DISTRICT OF COLUMBIA
Fraidin, Matthew I. ....'65 '93 C.311 B.A. L.966 J.D. Legal Aid Soc. of D.C
Fraiser, Leigh ....'— '96 C.276 B.S. L.880 J.D. [Ⓐ Powell,G.F.&M.]
*PRACTICE AREAS: Customs Law; Export Regulation.
Frampton, George T., Jr., (AV) ....'44 '70 C.976 B.A. L.309 J.D. [Ⓒ Boies,S.&F.]
*PRACTICE AREAS: Litigation; Civil Litigation; Criminal Defense; Non-Profit Law; Environmental Law.
Franasiak, David E. ....'51 '78 C&L.107 B.A., J.D. [Williams&J.]
*PRACTICE AREAS: Federal Tax Policy; Tax Law; Environmental; Energy; Securities Law.
France, Jill ....'71 '99 C.311 B.A. L.273 J.D. [Ⓐ Latham&W.]
*PRACTICE AREAS: Corporate Finance; Corporate Governance; Private Placement; Public Offerings.
Francer, Jeffrey K. .... '— '01 C.103 A.B. L.893 J.D. [Ⓐ Arnold&P.]
*PRACTICE AREAS: Food, Drug and Medical Devices.
Francescani, Donna M. .... '68 '97 C.93 B.A. L.273 J.D. 1440 New York Avenue
Francesconi, Michael J. ....'65 '97 C.870 B.S. L.128 J.D. [Ⓐ Kelley D.&W.]
*PRACTICE AREAS: Telecommunications Law.
Francese, Michael J. ....'66 '92 C.228 A.B. L.273 J.D. [Ⓐ Covington&B.]
Francese, Therese K. .... '64 '92 C.276 B.S.F.S. L.273 J.D. [Ⓐ Arent F.K.P.&K.]
*PRACTICE AREAS: Trademark Prosecution; Trademark Protection; Trademark Litigation; Copyright Protection.
Franceski, Larry G., (AV) ....'55 '80 C.420 B.A. L.309 J.D. [Fulbright&J.]
*PRACTICE AREAS: International Law; Bankruptcy; Corporate Law.
Franch, Jarashow, Burgmeier & Smith, P.A., (AV)
Suite 514, 2600 Virginia Avenue, N.W., 20036 ⊙
Telephone: 202-337-3080 Fax: 202-337-1185
Email: fjhlaw@erols.com URL: http://www.FJBSlaw.com
Ronald H. Jarashow; Robert R. Smith; L. Dale Burgmeier (Not admitted in DC). Of Counsel: Frank T. Laznovsky; L. Harvey Poe, Jr.
(This Listing Continued)

Franch, Jarashow, Burgmeier & Smith, P.A. (Continued)
General Civil and Trial Practice in all State and Federal Courts. Family Law, Divorce, Custody, Negligence, Personal Injury, Equipment Leasing, Corporation, Business Law, Bankruptcy, Insurance Law. Insurance Defense, Employment Law.
Annapolis, Maryland Office: 111 Cathedral Street. P.O. Box 827. Telephone: 410-268-5600; 410-269-0463; 301-261-1332. Fax: 410-269-1446.
Baltimore, Maryland Office: Suite 900, 210 N. Charles Street. Telephone: 410-269-0463.
Affiliated With: Coston & Lichtman, New York, Los Angeles, San Francisco, South Florida and Boston.
See Professional Biographies, WASHINGTON, DISTRICT OF COLUMBIA
Francis, Frances E., (AV) .... '40 '65 C.216 B.A. L.976 LL.B. [Spiegel&M.]
*PRACTICE AREAS: Administrative Hearings and Appeals; Energy; Hydroelectricity; Energy Project Development; Utility Law.
Francis, Lauren L. ....'72 '98 C.659 B.A. L.477 J.D. [Ⓐ Shaw P.]
*PRACTICE AREAS: Corporate Law.
Francis, Meredith S. ....'73 '97 C&L.659 B.A., J.D. [Ⓐ Cashdan,G.&K.]
*PRACTICE AREAS: Labor and Employment.
Francis, Patricia A. .... '63 '89 C.497 B.A. L.893 J.D. [Dow,L.&A.]
Franck, Susan D. ....'73 '98 C.1215 A.A. L.494 J.D. [Ⓐ Wilmer,C.&P.]
Franco, Antonio R. .... '60 '87 C.861 B.A. L.276 J.D. [Piliero,M.&P.]
*PRACTICE AREAS: Government Contracts; Civil Litigation; Minority Business.
Franco, Patricia A. '61 '89
C.860 B.S. L.569 J.D. Philips Electronics North America Corp.
Franco, Sandra '74 '99 C.145 B.S. L.276 J.D.
(adm. in MD; not adm. in DC) [Ⓐ Swidler B.S.F.]
*PRACTICE AREAS: Environmental Law.
Franco, Vincenzo ....'70 '01 C&L.999 LL.B. [Ⓐ Van Ness F.]
*PRACTICE AREAS: International Trade; International Environment; Energy.
Franey, Leo C. .... '38 '64 C.276 B.A. L.893 LL.B. [Rea,C.&A.]
*PRACTICE AREAS: Administrative Law; Interstate Commerce; Transportation.
Frangie, Paul D. '72 '98 C.1044 B.A. L.188 J.D.
(adm. in NY; not adm. in DC) [Ⓐ Swidler B.S.F.]
*PRACTICE AREAS: Antitrust.
Frank, Arthur J. .... '46 '71 C.1155 B.S.B.A. L.339 J.D. [Breads&Assoc.]
Frank, Carl R. ....'59 '83 C.823 B.S. L.30 J.D. [Ⓒ Wiley R.&F.]
*PRACTICE AREAS: Communications Law.
Frank, Daniel E. ....'67 '94 C.911 B.A. L.145 J.D. [Ⓐ Sutherland A.&B.]
*PRACTICE AREAS: Energy Contracts; Energy Regulation; Electric Utilities; Electric Cooperatives Law; Public Utility Regulation.
Frank, Joshua B. .... '71 '98 C.188 A.B. L.477 J.D. [Ⓐ Baker B.]
Frank, Lauren D. '62 '87 C.860 B.A. L.30 J.D.
Major Gifts Offr., Natl. Assoc. of Pub. Interest Law‡
Frank, Mary J. ....'— '00 C.804 B.F.A. L.262 J.D. [Ⓐ Morgan,L.&B.]
Frank, Matthew W. ....'62 '87 C.821 B.A. L.477 J.D. [Caplin&D.]
*PRACTICE AREAS: Tax Litigation; General Tax.
Frank, Melanie A. '72 '98 C.260 B.A. L.128 J.D.
(adm. in MD; not adm. in DC) [Ⓐ Weil,G.&M.]
*PRACTICE AREAS: International Trade.
Frank, Michele Van Patten .... '66 '95 C.867 B.S.M.E. L.904 J.D. [Morgan,L.&B.] (Pat.)
Frank, Richard A., (AV) ....'36 '62 C&L.309 A.B., J.D. 1120 19th St., N.W.
Frank, Richard L., (AV) .... '51 '76 C&L.477 B.A., J.D. [Olsson,F.&W.]
*PRACTICE AREAS: Food and Drug Law; Advertising Law; Agriculture Law.
Frank, Robert J., (AV) '24 '60
C.188 B.E.E. L.1009 LL.B. [Venable,A.B.H.&C.] (See Pat. Sect.)
*PRACTICE AREAS: Patent Law; Trademark Law.
Frank, Russell M. .... '49 '78 C.228 A.B. L.128 J.D. [Ⓒ Baach R.&L.P.]
*PRACTICE AREAS: Civil Litigation; Commercial Litigation; Insurance Coverage Litigation.
Frank, Theodore D., (AV) ....'41 '66 C.688 B.S. L.846 LL.B. [Arnold&P.]
*PRACTICE AREAS: Telecommunications; Communications; Administrative Law.
Frank, Theodore H. ....'68 '94 C.1036 B.A. L.145 J.D. [Ⓐ O'Melveny&M.]
Frankel, Jonathan J. ....'69 '95 C.309 A.B. L.976 J.D. [Ⓒ Wilmer,C.&P.]
Frankel, Jonathan S. ....'70 '95 C.477 B.A. L.1356 J.D. [Ⓐ Swidler B.S.F.]
*PRACTICE AREAS: Telecommunications.
Frankel, Kenneth M., (AV) .... '48 '73 C.659 B.S.M.E. L.273 J.D. [Finnegan,H.F.G.&D.]
*PRACTICE AREAS: Antitrust and Trade Regulation; Intellectual Property Litigation.
Frankel, Roger, (AV) ....'46 '71 C.1036 B.A. L.273 J.D. [Swidler B.S.F.]
*PRACTICE AREAS: Bankruptcy Law; Financial Restructuring; Creditors Rights; Workouts.
Frankhauser, Mahlon M., (AV) .... '— '58 C.21 A.B. L.659 LL.B. [Kirkpatrick&L.]
Franklin, Darryl L. ....'74 '99 C.30 B.A. L.945 J.D. [Ⓐ Venable,A.B.H.&C.]
*PRACTICE AREAS: Commercial Litigation; Labor and Employment.
Franklin, Eric J. ....'64 '91 C.112 B.S. L.30 J.D. [Ⓒ Swidler B.S.F.] (Pat.)
Franklin, Gretchen ....'58 '88 C&L.112 B.A., J.D. Pub. Def. Serv.
Franklin, Jonathan S. .... '64 '90 C.309 A.B. L.976 J.D. [Hogan&H.]
*PRACTICE AREAS: Litigation; U.S. Supreme Court Litigation; Appellate Practice.
Franklin, William J., (BV) '45 '77
C.679 B.S.M.E. L.276 J.D. 1200 G Street, N.W. Suite 800
Franks, Harry A., Jr. ....'63 '88 C&L.893 B.A., J.D. [Baker&M.]
*PRACTICE AREAS: Tax; International Tax.
Fransella, Michael '76 '01 C.951 B.A. L.976 J.D.
(adm. in VA; not adm. in DC) [Ⓐ Clifford C.R.&W.]
*PRACTICE AREAS: Mergers and Acquisitions; Securities.
Frantz, David J., (AV) .... '48 '74 C&L.276 B.S.B.A., J.D. [Conlon,F.P.&P.]
*PRACTICE AREAS: Litigation; Trade Association Law; Commercial Law.
Frantz, John Peter '72 '97 C.93 B.A. L.309 J.D.
V.P. & Assoc. Gen. Coun., Strategic Broadband Int., Verizon Communications
Frantz, Steven P. .... '54 '79 C&L.893 B.S.N.E., J.D. [Morgan,L.&B.]
Franze, Anthony J. ....'70 '95 C.625 B.S. L.602 J.D. [Ⓐ Arnold&P.]
*PRACTICE AREAS: Litigation; White Collar Crime.
Franzel, Brent S. .... '61 '88 C.502 B.J. L.228 J.D. [Tighe P.A.T.]
*PRACTICE AREAS: International Business Transactions; International Government Relations; Legislation.
Frappier, Danielle '74 '00 C.477 B.A. L.904 J.D.
(adm. in MD; not adm. in DC) [Ⓐ Cole,R.&B.]
*PRACTICE AREAS: Domestic and International Telecommunications Law; Internet Law; Telecommunications Competition.
Fraser, Anne H. S., P.C., (AV) .... '54 '81 C.999 B.A. L.1162 J.D. 1501 M St., NW
Fraser, Shawn W. ....'68 '94 [Ⓐ Fitzpatrick,C.H.&S.]
Frazer, James A. ....'56 '87 C.103 B.A. L.145 J.D. [Ⓢ Skadden,A.S.M.&F.]
Frazer, Monica O. .... '75 '00 C.174 B.A. L.276 J.D. [Ⓐ Nixon P.]
*PRACTICE AREAS: Business Law.
Frazier, David Penn '66 '00
C.645 B.S. L.276 J.D. [Ⓐ Finnegan,H.F.G.&D.] (See Pat. Sect.)
*PRACTICE AREAS: Intellectual Property Portfolio Management; Pharmaceutical Intellectual Property; Biotechnology Patents; Patent Litigation; Pharmaceutical Patents.
Frazier, James Larry ....'48 '80 C.178 A.B. L.276 J.D. 918 Maryland Ave., N.E.
Frazier, Thomas A., Jr., (AV) ....'34 '59 C&L.893 B.A., LL.B. [Ⓒ Trainum,S.&D.]
*PRACTICE AREAS: Federal and State Taxation; Probate; Trusts and Estates.
Freas, Monica A. ....'72 '98 C.1175 B.S. L.911 J.D. [Ⓐ Spriggs&H.]
*PRACTICE AREAS: Banking Litigation; Government Contracts; Complex Commercial Litigation.

Frechtel, Eric A. '71 '96 C.165 B.A. L.64 J.D.
(adm. in MD; not adm. in DC) [Ⓐ Spriggs&H.]
*PRACTICE AREAS: Construction Law; Litigation.
Freda, Dominick V. . . . . '72 '00 C.705 B.A. L.659 J.D. [Ⓐ Jones,D.R.&P.]
Freda, Dominik . . . . . . '72 '00 C.705 B.A. L.659 J.D. 1800 Massachusetts Avenue, N.W.
Freda, Robert Joseph, (AV) '52 '77
C&L.276 B.S.B.A., J.D. [Ⓒ Garfinkle&Assoc.] (⊙Mc Lean, VA)
Frederick, David C. . . . . '61 '89 C.665 B.A. L.846 J.D. [Kellogg,H.H.T.&E.]
*PRACTICE AREAS: Litigation.
Fredman, I. Jay . . . . '— '83 C.870 B.S. L.276 J.D. [I.J.Fredman]
Fredman, I. Jay, P.C., Law Offices of . . . . 1750 K Street, N.W., Suite 325
Fredrickson, Bruce A., (AV) . . . . . . '51 '76 C.197 B.A. L.273 J.D. [Webster,F.&B.]
*PRACTICE AREAS: Employment Law; Labor Law; Personal Injury; Litigation.
Fredrickson, Jodi Kyung . . . . '72 '98 C.221 B.S. L.180 J.D. 555 13th St. N.W.

Fredrikson & Byron, P.A., (AV)
1825 I Street N.W. Suite 400, 20006 ⊙
Telephone: 202-828-6280 Fax: 202-429-2727
Email: smurphy@fredlaw.com URL: http://www.fredlaw.com
Of Counsel: John E. Mullen (Resident).
General Practice including: Advertising, Alternative Dispute Resolution, Aviation, Banking and Commercial, Business Litigation, Business Risk Management and Compliance, Business and Tax Planning, Business Technology, Commercial Litigation, Commercial Transactions, Communications and Entertainment, Condemnation, Corporate Acquisitions and Securities, Creditor Remedies and Bankruptcy, Directors and Officers Services, Emerging Business, Eminent Domain, Employee Benefits, Employment and Labor, Environmental, Estate Planning, Probate and Trusts, Executive and Professional Compensation, Family Business, Family Law, Finance, Franchise Law, Health Care and Hospitals, High Technology and Communications, Immigration, Insurance, Intellectual Property, International Law, Litigation, Local Government and Education, Medicare Fraud and Compliance, Mergers and Acquisitions, Non-Profit Organizations, Partnerships, Property Tax, Shareholder Rights, Software Licensing, Syndications and Tax Shelters, Professional Corporations, Real Estate, Regulatory Defense, Sports Law, Travel, White Collar.
Minneapolis, Minnesota Office: 1100 International Centre, 900 Second Avenue South, 55402-3397. Telephone: 612-347-7000. Telecopier: 612-347-7077.
London, England Office: 16 Bedford Street, Covent Garden, WC2 9HF. Telephone: 011-44-207-395-3030. Fax: 011-44-207-836-9966.
See Professional Biographies, WASHINGTON, DISTRICT OF COLUMBIA

Free, Douglas J. '— '00 C.276 B.A. L.128 J.D.
(adm. in MD; not adm. in DC) [Ⓐ Morgan,L.&B.]
Freed, Charles L., (AV) . . . . '49 '74 C.473 B.A. L.597 J.D. [Thompson H.]
*PRACTICE AREAS: Antitrust and Trade Regulation; Franchising; Competition; Health Care.
Freed, Joel M., (AV) . . . . '43 '70 C.401 B.A. L.276 J.D. [Arnold&P.] (Pat.)
*PRACTICE AREAS: Intellectual Property; Litigation; Patent Law; Patent, Trademark and Copyright Law; Trade Secrets.
Freedman, Anthony S. . . . . '45 '68 C.563 B.S. L.813 LL.B. [Hawkins,D.&W.]
*PRACTICE AREAS: Public Finance; Low-Income Housing Tax Credits; Multifamily Housing Finance and Development; Military Housing; Low Income Housing.
Freedman, Beth A. . . . . '66 '92 C.881 B.A. L.904 J.D. [Silver,F.&T.]
*PRACTICE AREAS: Financial Institutions; Regulatory & Securities Law.
Freedman, Dara L. '66 '92 C.691 B.A. L.245 J.D.
Natl. Assn. of Real Estate Investment Trust Inc.
Freedman, James J., (AV) . . . . '58 '84 C.385 B.A. L.608 J.D. [Silverstein&M.]
*PRACTICE AREAS: Real Estate; Banking Law.
Freedman, Jared O. . . . . '69 '99 C.309 A.B. L.976 J.D. [Ⓐ Jenner&B.]
*PRACTICE AREAS: Litigation.
Freedman, Jay W., (AV) . . . . '— '68 C.951 B.A. L.976 J.D. [Foley&L.]
*PRACTICE AREAS: Corporate Law; Securities Law; Probate; Estate Planning Law.
Freedman, John A. . . . . '69 '95 C.951 B.A. L.309 J.D. [Ⓐ Arnold&P.]
*PRACTICE AREAS: Litigation.
Freedman, Lawrence R. . . . . '56 '85 C.668 B.S. L.904 J.D. [Fleischman&W.]
Freedman, Mark F. '69 '95 C.165 B.A. L.188 J.D.
(adm. in NY; not adm. in DC) Asst. Gen. Coun., Legal Services Corporation
Freedman, Michael H. . . . . '67 '95 C.228 B.A. L.30 J.D. [Ⓐ Orrick,H.&S.]
Freedman, Robert L., (P.C.), (AV) . . . . . . '39 '64 C.446 A.B. L.477 J.D. [Silver,F.&T.]
*PRACTICE AREAS: Financial Institutions Law; Securities Law; Mergers and Acquisitions.
Freedman, Roberta, (P.C.), (AV) . . . . . . '58 '83 C.823 A.B. L.64 J.D. [Pederson&F.]
*PRACTICE AREAS: Immigration and Nationality Law; Consular Issues.
Freedman, Susan M. . . . . '62 '92 C.299 B.A. L.273 J.D. [Ⓐ Finnegan,H.F.G.&D.]
*PRACTICE AREAS: Trademark Infringement; Trademark Litigation; Trademark Prosecution; Trademark Protection; Trademark Registration.
Freedman, Walter, (AV) . . . . '— '37 C&L.910 A.B., J.D. [Freedman,L.K.&S.]
Freedman, William D., (AV) . . . . '49 '76 C.94 B.S. L.150 J.D. [Morrison&F.]
*PRACTICE AREAS: Communications Law; Litigation; Appellate Advocacy; Business Transactions.
Freedman, Levy, Kroll & Simonds, (AV)
1050 Connecticut Avenue, N.W. (⊙Lincolnshire, IL)
Freedson, Brett Heather . . . . '75 '00 C.145 B.A. L.273 J.D. [Ⓐ Kelley D.&W.]
*PRACTICE AREAS: Telecommunications.
Freeman, Alan M. . . . . '71 '96 C.178 B.A. L.273 J.D. [Ⓐ Dyer E.&J.]
*PRACTICE AREAS: Commercial Litigation; Alternative Dispute Resolution.
Freeman, Carol Garfiel, (AV) . . . . '37 '61 C.914 A.B. L.178 LL.B. U.S. Dist. Ct.
Freeman, D. Reed, Jr. . . . . '68 '93 C.692 B.A. L.893 J.D. [Collier S.S.]
*PRACTICE AREAS: Advertising; Electronic Commerce; Privacy and Publicity; Federal Trade Commission Investigations and Litigation; Unfair Trade Practices.
Freeman, David F., Jr. . . . . '59 '87 C&L.893 B.A., J.D. [Arnold&P.]
*PRACTICE AREAS: Financial Institutions; Securities.
Freeman, George Clemon, Jr., (AV) '29 '56
C.880 B.A. L.976 LL.B. [Ⓒ Hunton&W.] (⊙Richmond, VA)
Freeman, James J., (AV) . . . . '40 '66 C.321 A.B. L.309 LL.B. [Ⓒ Kelley D.&W.]
*PRACTICE AREAS: Telecommunications Law; Communications Law.
Freeman, Lauren E. . . . . '62 '90 C.95 A.B. L.945 J.D. [Hunton&W.]
*PRACTICE AREAS: Environmental; Administrative Law.
Freeman, Leo . . . . '09 '33 C&L.724 LL.B. 3715 Ingomar St., N.W.‡
Freeman, Martin H., (AV) . . . . '40 '65 C.401 B.S.M.E. L.273 J.D. [Freeman&J.] ⊙
Freeman, Neil M. . . . . '67 '93 C.228 B.A. L.276 J.D. 1440 New York Ave., N.W.
Freeman, Orville L. '18 '46 C&L.494 A.B., LL.B.
(adm. in MN; not adm. in DC) 655 15th St., N.W., Suite 800
Freeman, Paul C. '73 '99 C.732 B.A. L.1194 J.D.
(adm. in NY; not adm. in DC) 1875 Connecticut Avenue, N.W.
Freeman, Peter G. . . . . '74 '99 C.178 B.A. L.273 J.D. [Ⓐ Shaw P.]
*PRACTICE AREAS: Corporate Law; Securities.
Freeman, Stanley A., (AV) . . . . '56 '82 C.477 B.A. L.276 J.D. [Powers,P.S.&V.]
*PRACTICE AREAS: Education Law; Litigation; Administrative Law.
Freeman & Jenner, P.C., (AV) . . . . . . 1000 16th St., N.W. (⊙Aspen, CO; Rockville, MD)
Freeston, Margaret A. . . . . '44 '69 C.518 B.A. L.276 J.D. [Brown&F.]
*PRACTICE AREAS: Product Safety Law; Administrative Law.
Frei, Frederick S., (AV) . . . . '45 '74 C.188 B.S. L.276 J.D. [Dorsey&W.] (Pat.)
*PRACTICE AREAS: Patent; Intellectual Property; Antitrust; Litigation.
Freideman, Robert S. . . . . '49 '75 C.976 B.A. L.276 J.D. [Freideman,I.W.&L.]
*PRACTICE AREAS: Taxation Law; Estate Planning and Probate; Non-Profit Organizations Law.

Freideman, Irelan, Ward & Lamberton, P.C., (AV)
1000 Potomac Street, N.W., Suite 400, 20007-3551
Telephone: 202-625-1800 Fax: 202-625-1616
Email: r.freideman@fiwllaw.com URL: http://www.fiwllaw.com
Robert S. Freideman; William T. Irelan; Nicholas D. Ward; Benjamin P. Lamberton.
Charities, Non-Profit Associations Law, Employment Law, Education Law, Trusts and Estate Planning and Administration, Taxation, Corporate Law, International Business and Commercial Law. Civil Litigation including Commercial Trial Work, Fiduciary and Discrimination Litigation.
See Professional Biographies, WASHINGTON, DISTRICT OF COLUMBIA

Freilich, Harold I., (AV) . . . . '— '77 C.529 B.A. L.228 J.D. [Verner,L.B.M.&H.]
*PRACTICE AREAS: International Finance; Project Finance; Corporate Law; Security Law.
Freilicher, Miriam S., (AV) . . . . '41 '80 C.446 B.A. L.273 J.D. [Freilicher&H.]
*PRACTICE AREAS: Immigration and Nationality Law.

Freilicher & Hoffman, P.C., (AV)
Suite 200, 1925 K Street, N.W., 20006
Telephone: 202-331-9450 Telecopier: 202-466-8151
URL: http://www.lawyers.com/freilicher&hoffmanpc
Miriam S. Freilicher; Linda M. Hoffman.
Immigration and Nationality Law Specialist practicing before all agencies involved in Immigration for U.S. and International Corporations, Law Firms, Universities and Research Institutions, International Organizations and Individuals.
See Professional Biographies, WASHINGTON, DISTRICT OF COLUMBIA

Freire, Bettina Veronica '— '91 C.999 L.178 LL.M.
(adm. in NY; not adm. in DC) [Ⓒ Latham&W.]
*PRACTICE AREAS: Project Finance; Investment in Latin America; International Finance; International Mergers and Acquisitions; Energy Project Development.
Freire, Juan Carlos '72 '00 C.563 B.A. L.1158 J.D.
(adm. in FL; not adm. in DC) [Ⓐ Salgado&Assoc.]
*PRACTICE AREAS: Immigration; Visas; Political Asylum; Deportation.
Freitag, Edward G. '46 '73 C.674 A.B. L.178 J.D.
(adm. in NY; not adm. in DC) General Counsel, NeuStar, Inc.
Frekko, Matthew T. '72 '00 C.165 B.A. L.276 J.D.
(adm. in MD; not adm. in DC) [Ⓐ Keller&H.]
*PRACTICE AREAS: Food and Drug Regulation.
Fremuth, Michael J., (AV) . . . . '47 '76 C.674 A.B. L.813 J.D. [Andrews&K.]
*PRACTICE AREAS: Energy; Administrative Law; Antitrust.
Frenkel, Jacob S. '60 '85 C&L.861 B.A., J.D.
(adm. in LA; not adm. in DC) [Ⓒ Smith,G.&R.] (⊙Atlanta, GA)
*PRACTICE AREAS: Securities Litigation; SEC, NASD and State Enforcement; White Collar Crime; Internal Investigations; Securities Arbitration.
Freret, Julian P., (AV) . . . . '18 '42 C&L.861 B.S., LL.B. [Booth,F.I.&T.] ‡

Freshfields Bruckhaus Deringer LLP, (AV)
1300 I Street, NW, 12th Floor East, 20005-3314 ⊙
Telephone: 202-969-4500; 202-777-4500 Fax: 202-969-4555; 202-777-4555
Email: email@freshfields.com URL: http://www.freshfields.com
Partners: Ellen L. Hayes (Not admitted in the United States); Thomas P. Hechl (Not admitted in DC); Gregory Evers May; Claude B. Stansbury.
Competition and Trade; Corporate; Dispute Resolution; Employment, Pensions and Benefits; Finance; Intellectual Property; Real Estate; Tax.
Freshfields Bruckhaus Deringer offices in: Amsterdam, Bangkok, Barcelona, Beijing, Berlin, Bratislava, Brussels, Budapest, Cologne, Düsseldorf, Frankfurt, Hamburg, Hanoi, Ho Chi Minh City, Hong Kong, London, Madrid, Milan, Moscow, Munich, New York, Paris, Prague, Rome, ★Shanghai, Singapore, Tokyo, Vienna, Washington.
★associate office.
See Professional Biographies, WASHINGTON, DISTRICT OF COLUMBIA

Freuhauf, Richard L. . . . . '67 '97 C.276 B.S.F.S. L.893 J.D. [Ⓐ Covington&B.]
*PRACTICE AREAS: International Law; International Trade; Banks and Banking; Administrative Law.
Freund, Jeffrey R., (AV) . . . . '45 '70 C.597 B.A. L.1066 J.D. [Bredhoff&K.]
Freund, Leigh M. P. . . . . '67 '99 C.373 B.A. L.276 J.D. [Ⓐ Kirkpatrick&L.]
*PRACTICE AREAS: Civil Litigation; Securities Litigation; SEC Enforcement.
Frey, Andrew L., (AV) '38 '62
C.821 B.A. L.178 LL.B. [Mayer,B.&P.] (⊙New York, NY)
*PRACTICE AREAS: Civil Appeals; Criminal Appeals; Constitutional Law; Complex Civil Litigation; Products Liability.
Frey, Elizabeth Jesukiewicz . . . . '58 '87 C.446 B.S.N. L.64 J.D. [Ⓐ J.H.Olender&Assoc.]
*PRACTICE AREAS: Civil Trial Practice; Medical Malpractice; Personal Injury.
Fricano, John C., (AV) . . . . . . '30 '56 C.524 B.S. L.262 LL.B. 1440 New York Ave., N.W.
Frick, Charles William '74 '01 C.597 B.A. L.309 J.D.
(adm. in MD; not adm. in DC) [Ⓐ Akin,G.S.H.&F.]
*PRACTICE AREAS: Litigation.
Frick, G. William, (AV) '44 '69 C&L.378 B.A., J.D.
V.P., Gen Cnsl & Sec., American Petroleum Institute
Fried, Alfred S., (AV) . . . . '26 '50 C&L.273 LL.B. 1725 K St., NW
Fried, Bruce M., (AV) . . . . '49 '75 C&L.260 B.A., J.D. [Shaw P.]
*PRACTICE AREAS: Health Care.
Fried, Jeffrey S. . . . . '57 '86 C.102 B.S. L.30 J.D. [Fried]
Fried, Michael S. . . . . '70 '96 C.477 B.A. L.178 J.D. [Ⓐ Jones,D.R.&P.]
Fried, Neil . . . . '— '96 C.597 B.S.J. L.910 J.D. [Ⓐ Verner,L.B.M.&H.]
*PRACTICE AREAS: Telecommunications; Media.
Fried, Stewart D. . . . . '69 '95 C.367 B.A. L.472 J.D. [Ⓐ Baise&M.]
*PRACTICE AREAS: Civil Litigation; Commercial Litigation; Environmental Litigation; Personal Injury.
Fried & Company, P.C. . . . . 700 Thirteenth Street, N.W. Suite 325

Fried, Frank, Harris, Shriver & Jacobson, (AV) BR
A Partnership including Professional Corporations
Suite 800, 1001 Pennsylvania Avenue, N.W., 20004-2505 ⊙
Telephone: 202-639-7000 Telecopy: 202-639-7008
Email: info@ffhsj.com
Washington, D.C. Partners: Richard I. Ansbacher; David L. Ansell; Lawrence R. Bard; Douglas W. Baruch; David E. Birenbaum; John T. Boese; Michael R. Bromwich; Timothy D. Casey; John W. Chierichella; Mark J. Dorsey; Paul H. Falon; Deborah A. Garza; Jack B. Gordon; Karl A. Groskaufmanis; David B. Hardison; Lanae Holbrook; Dixie Lynn Johnson; Alan S. Kaden; Kevin M. Keyes; Jay R. Kraemer; Robert H. Ledig; Daniel E. Loeb; James J. McCullough; Deneen J. Melander; Matt T. Morley; Bernard A. Nigro, Jr.; Douglas E. Perry; Elliot E. Polebaum; Michael J. Rivera; Charles F. (Rick) Rule; Richard A. Sauber; James H. Schropp; Richard A. Steinwurtzel; Vasiliki B. Tsaganos; Andrew P. Varney; Thomas P. Vartanian; Michael L. Waldman. Of Counsel: Milton Eisenberg (P.C.); Joel R. Feidelman (P.C.); Martin D. Ginsburg (P.C.); Max M. Kampelman; Marcus A. Rowden; Sargent Shriver; Daniel M. Singer; Michael A. Vatis; Louis D. Victorino. Special Counsel: Mark Fajfar; David L. Fenimore; Robert M. Fisher; Karen T. Grisez; Jonathan M. Jacobs; Deborah Miller; Anne B. Perry; Catherine Evans Pollack; Paul M. Rothstein. Associates: Steven A. Alerding; Michael J. Alter; Michael J. Anstett; Jonathan S. Aronie; Stephen R. Bauer; Tommy P. Beaudreau; Noah A. Berlin; Maya A. Bernstein; Jennifer Jewell Black; Andrea J. Boyack; Noel P. Brock; Justin J. Brookman; Cristina Burbach; Kami Nicole Chavis; Beth Hilliard Colleye; Michelle L. Colman; Tasha L. Cooper; Urvi M. Doshi; Jack C. Easton; Thomas M. Fallas; Dawn E. Faris; Wendy P. Feiner; Shelley Finger; David B. Fishberg; Rex Y. Fujichaku (Not admitted in DC); David S. Gallagher (Not admitted in DC); Janet G. Gamer; Joshua J. Gessler (Not admitted in DC); Gejaa Temesgien Gobena; Michelle Berk Gold; Kevin J. Harnisch; Taylor Young Hong; John R. Ingrassia; David Wilson Jolly (Not admitted in DC); Jonathan S. Kanter; Rachel S. Katz; Walid A. Khuri; Melissa E. Lamb; JoEllen Lotvedt Legg; Ron Leviner (Not admitted in DC); Russell Light (Not admitted in DC); Charles W. Lockyer, Jr.; Bradford Lucas (Not admitted in DC); Natasha R. Luddington; Jeff L. Magenau; Jay D. Majors; Beth C. McClain (Not admitted in DC); Julia A. McDonough; David Myers (Not admitted in DC); John S. Nargiso; David A. Neuman; Abram J. Pafford; Julie J. Panigrahi (Not admitted in DC); George B. Parizek; Richard C. Park; Steven C. Parker; Paul H. Pashkoff; Stacy L. Paxson;

(This Listing Continued)

Fried, Frank, Harris, Shriver & Jacobson (Continued)

Ducchi T. Quan; Louis Ramos; Donyale Y. Hooper Reavis (Not admitted in DC); James E. Rhilinger; René L. Rocque; Eric P. Rubenfeld; Christopher M. Salter; Jonathan P. Scott; Matthew L. Skidmore; Andrew Dieter Skowronek; Thomas Peter Smith, Jr.; Jacqueline Stephens; Tricia Chwenchii Su; Sharan K. Suri; Larisa Avner Trainor; Michael Arthur Umayam (Not admitted in DC); C. Tucker Waldruff (Not admitted in DC); Karin E. Weiner; Pyong W. Yoon.
General Practice.
New York, New York Office: One New York Plaza. Telephone: 212-859-8000. Cable Address: "Steric New York." W.U. Intl. Telex: 662119. W.U. Domestic: 128173. Telecopier: 212-859-4000 (Dex 6200).
Los Angeles, California Office: 350 South Grand Avenue, 32nd Floor. Telephone: 213-473-2000.
London, England Office: 99 City Road, London EC1Y 1AX. Telephone: 011-44-171-972-9600. Fax: 011-44-171-972-9602.
Paris, France Office: 7, Rue Royale, 75008. Telephone: (011 331) 40-17-04-04. Fax: (011 331) 40-17-08-30.

See Professional Biographies, WASHINGTON, DISTRICT OF COLUMBIA

Friedel, Loren Andrea '66 '00 C.797 B.A. L.1360 J.D.
(adm. in MD; not adm. in DC) U.S. Coast Guard
Friedenthal, Jack H. '31 '59
C.813 A.B. L.309 J.D. Dean, George Washington Univ. Law Sch.
Friedland, David M. .... '57 '83 C&L.276 B.S.F.S., J.D. [Beveridge&D.]
*PRACTICE AREAS: Environmental Law; Clean Air Act; Litigation.
Friedlander, Charles .... '53 '78 C.280 B.A. L.893 J.D. [Squire,S.&D.]
*PRACTICE AREAS: Energy; Project Finance; Privatization; International Law; Corporate Law.
Friedlander, Lisa L. .... '69 '96 C.659 B.A. L.904 J.D. [🄰 Preston G.E.&R.M.]
*PRACTICE AREAS: Telecommunications Law; Litigation.
Friedlander, Stephen H., (AV) '37 '63 C.902 B.A. L.276 J.D.
[Friedlander,M.S.K.&O.]
*PRACTICE AREAS: Commercial Real Estate; Commercial Leasing; Business Associations Law.

Friedlander & Friedlander, P.C.
(See McLean, Virginia)

Friedlander, Misler, Sloan, Kletzkin & Ochsman, PLLC, (AV)
1101 Seventeenth Street, N.W., Suite 700, 20036-4704
Telephone: 202-872-0800 Cable Address: "FMSHLAW" Telex: 64273 Facsimile: 202-857-8343
URL: http://www.dclawfirm.com
Members of Firm: Stephen H. Friedlander; Leonard A. Sloan; Morris Kletzkin; Jeffrey W. Ochsman; Jerome Ostrov; Jana Kay Guggenheim; Alan Dean Sundburg; Mark D. Crawford. Associates: Philippa T. Gasnier; Todd S. Sapiro; Joan M. Luria (Not admitted in DC); Thomas Francis Murphy; Denise E. Jackson; Barbara J. Prasse (Not admitted in DC). Of Counsel: Robert E. Greenberg; David M. Astrove; Deborah G. Segal; Lois J. Vermillion.
Real Estate, Corporate, Creditors' Rights and Bankruptcy Law, Estate Planning. General Civil Practice, including Trial, Administrative and Appellate, Insurance Law, Tax, Probate and Worker's Compensation.

See Professional Biographies, WASHINGTON, DISTRICT OF COLUMBIA

Friedlob, Raymond L., (AV) '45 '69 C.174 B.A. L.208 J.D.
[Friedlob S.P.&T.] (⊙Phoenix, AZ; Denver, Englewood, CO)
Friedlob Sanderson Paulson & Tourtillott, LLC, (AV)
1776 I Street, N.W., Suite 900 (⊙Phoenix, AZ; Santa Cruz, CA; Denver, Englewood, CO)

Friedman, Alvin, (AV) '31 '57 C.188 B.A. L.976 LL.B.
700 New Hampshire Avenue, N.W., 20037
Telephone: 202-255-8383 Fax: 202-333-6328
Email: afwins@aol.com
Litigation and Counseling in Domestic and International Corporate and Commercial Transactions including Acquisitions, Dispositions and Financing of Aircraft.

See Professional Biographies, WASHINGTON, DISTRICT OF COLUMBIA

Friedman, Amy L. .... '73 '01 C.976 B.A. L.30 J.D. [🄰 Squire,S.&D.]
Friedman, Andrew H., (AV) ....'55 '80 C.855 B.A. L.309 J.D. [Covington&B.]
Friedman, Andrew M. ....'68 '93 C.188 B.A. L.273 J.D. [McDermott,W.&E.]
Friedman, Andrew M. ....'66 '94 C.103 A.B. L.494 J.D. [🄰 Patton B.]
Friedman, Andrew N., (AV) .... '58 '83 C.860 B.A. L.273 J.D. [Cohen,M.H.&T.]
*PRACTICE AREAS: Securities Litigation; Securities Fraud Class Actions; Civil Litigation.
Friedman, Barbara A. .... '53 '83 C.1044 B.A. L.273 J.D. [🄲 Morgan,L.&B.] (Pat.)
Friedman, Barry A., (AV) ....'51 '76 C.1044 B.A. L.94 J.D. [Thompson H.]
*PRACTICE AREAS: Communications Law; Commercial Law; Administrative Law; Corporate Law; Securities.
Friedman, Donald J., (AV) ....'45 '73 C.309 A.B. L.976 J.D. [Perkins C.]
*PRACTICE AREAS: Computer Law; Civil Litigation; Commercial Arbitration; Telecommunications Law.
Friedman, Edward A. '56 '87 C&L.999 H.L.E., LL.B.
(adm. in NY; not adm. in DC) [🄲 Ruben&A.]
*PRACTICE AREAS: Securities; Mergers and Acquisitions; International Transactions; Corporate; Business.
Friedman, Edward J., (AV) .... '51 '77 C.382 B.B.A. L.64 J.D. [Weinstock,F.&F.] ⊙
Friedman, Emily R. '75 '00 C.860 B.A. L.276 J.D.
(adm. in MD; not adm. in DC) [🄰 Seyfarth S.]
*PRACTICE AREAS: Litigation; Employment Law; Labor Law.
Friedman, Francine E. .... '73 '99 C.276 B.A. L.945 J.D. [🄰 Hunton&W.]
*PRACTICE AREAS: Commercial Litigation.
Friedman, Harvey G. ....'40 '65 C&L.472 B.A., J.D. 1701 Q Street NW
Friedman, Howard ....'42 '68 C.831 B.S. L.546 J.D. 2827 28th St., NW
Friedman, Ian C. '56 '85 C.309 A.B. L.976 J.D.
(adm. in NY; not adm. in DC) U.S. Tax Court
Friedman, Jeffrey '67 '97 C&L.446 B.A., J.D.
(adm. in MD; not adm. in DC) Tax Coun., Comm. on State Taxation
Friedman, Jonathan A. .... '64 '98 C.309 B.A. L.276 J.D. [🄰 Willkie F.&G.]
Friedman, Lee A. .... '64 '97 C.550 B.S. L.596 J.D. [🅂 Jones,D.R.&P.]
Friedman, Lyman G., (AV) ....'18 '43 C&L.900 A.B., LL.B. [🄲 Williams&C.]
Friedman, Margery Sinder, (AV) ......'50 '78 C.930 B.A. L.276 J.D. [🄲 Morgan,L.&B.]
Friedman, Neal J., (AV) .... '40 '85 C.645 B.A. L.30 J.D. 1776 K. St N.W.
Friedman, Paul H., (AV) ....'54 '79 C.145 A.B. L.94 J.D. [Dechert]
*PRACTICE AREAS: Antitrust and Trade Regulation; Complex Litigation; Complex Commercial Litigation.
Friedman, Paula G. '64 '89
C.446 B.A. L.904 J.D. Exec. Dir., Fed. Communications Bar Assn.
Friedman, Peter M. '72 '98 C.855 B.A. L.597 J.D.
(adm. in IL; not adm. in DC) [🄰 Weil,G.&M.]
*PRACTICE AREAS: Litigation; Public Policy.
Friedman, Philip S., (AV) .... '60 '87 C.112 B.A. L.813 J.D. [Friedman]
*PRACTICE AREAS: Civil Litigation; Election Law; Consumer Class Actions.
Friedman, Sanford A., (AV) ....'61 '86 C.446 B.A. L.30 J.D. 1050 17th Street
Friedman, Steven E. ....'71 '96 C.910 B.A. L.273 J.D. [🄰 Piper M.R.&W.]
*PRACTICE AREAS: Business Law; Technology Law; Corporate Finance.
Friedman, Steven G., (AV) ....'48 '75 C.659 B.S.E. L.276 J.D. [Grossberg,Y.F.&B.]
Friedman, Susan Meyers, (AV) .... '43 '82 C.102 B.A. L.276 J.D. [Kuder,S.&F.] ⊙
*PRACTICE AREAS: Domestic Relations Law.

Friedman Law Offices P.L.L.C., (AV) [BR]
1735 New York Avenue, N.W., Suite 500, 20006
Telephone: 202-661-3925 Fax: 202-331-1024
Email: friedman@consumerlawhelp.com URL: http://www.consumerlawhelp.com

(This Listing Continued)

Friedman Law Offices P.L.L.C. (Continued)

Member of the Firm: Philip S. Friedman.
Civil Litigation, Election Law and Consumer Class Actions.

See Professional Biographies, WASHINGTON, DISTRICT OF COLUMBIA

Friedmann, Peter A. .... '52 '78 C&L.911 B.A., J.D. [🄲 Lindsay,H.N.&W.]
Friedrich, Jason E. .... '— '99 C.273 L.128 [🄰 Dow,L.&A.]
Friel, Brian G. ....'68 '94 C.93 B.A. L.724 J.D. [🄰 Swidler B.S.F.]
*PRACTICE AREAS: Insurance; Insurance Litigation; Litigation.
Friends, Nathaniel .... '46 '71 C.424 B.S.B.A. L.966 J.D. Gen. Atty., AT&T
*RESPONSIBILITIES: Federal Procurement (Domestic and International); Commercial Transactions.
Friends, Nathaniel, Jr. '73 '00 C.893 B.A. L.966 J.D.
(adm. in NY; not adm. in DC) [🄰 Dewey B.]
*PRACTICE AREAS: Investment Management; Private Equity.
Fries, Janet ....'49 '95 C.788 B.A. L.273 J.D. [🄰 Drinker B.&R.]
Fries, Joseph M., (AV) ....'37 '61 C.188 A.B. L.309 LL.B. [Arent F.K.P.&K.]
*PRACTICE AREAS: Real Estate (Property) Law.
Fries, Kenneth E. '41 '67
C.813 A.B. L.1066 LL.B. Gen. Coun., U.S. Trade & Develop. Agcy.
Friess, Katherine Elizabeth .... '67 '93 C.494 B.A. L.208 J.D. 1801 K St. N.W.
Frings-Kolstad, Carole L. '46 '70 C.339 B.S. L.846 J.D.
Dir., Fed. Affs., American Dental Association
Frisby, Bradford V. '69 '94 C.446 B.A. L.273 J.D.
(adm. in MD; not adm. in DC) Assoc. Gen. Coun., National Mining Association
Frisby, R. Larson .... '62 '88 C.446 B.A. L.597 J.D. Legis. Coun., Amer. Bar Assn.
Frisch, Michael S. ....'50 '75 C.930 B.A. L.276 J.D. Asst. Bar Coun., D.C. Bar
Frischkorn, Marci Lynn '69 '94 C.923 B.A. L.1017 J.D.
(adm. in VA; not adm. in DC) [🄰 Miller&V.]
*PRACTICE AREAS: Cable Franchising; Cable TV; Communications Law; Telecommunications Competition; Telecommunications Regulation.
Frisk, Frank W., Jr., (AV) ....'39 '70 C&L.911 B.A., J.D. [F.W.Frisk,Jr.]

Frisk, Frank W., Jr., P.C., (AV) [BR]
Suite 125, Canal Square, 1054 Thirty-First Street, N.W., 20007
Telephone: 202-333-8433 Fax: 202-333-8431
Email: ffrisk@gslink.com
Frank W. Frisk, Jr.
Energy, Environmental, Natural Resources, Municipal, Administrative and Legislative Law. Hydroelectric Regulation and Licensing, Cogeneration and Electric Utility Rates. General Practice before all Courts and Government Agencies.

See Professional Biographies, WASHINGTON, DISTRICT OF COLUMBIA

Fritts, Jonathan C. ....'— '98 C.893 A.B. L.276 J.D. [🄰 Morgan,L.&B.]
Fritts, Linda A. .... '54 '79 C.239 B.A. L.893 J.D. [Dow,L.&A.]
Fritz, Jerald N., (AV) '51 '76 C.597 B.S. L.602 J.D.
Sr. V. P., Legal & Strategic Affairs, Allbritton Communications Company
Fritze, Elizabeth ....'75 '00 C.902 B.A. L.976 J.D. [🄰 Fulbright&J.]
Froelich, Edward L. ....'66 '94 C.999 B.A. L.893 J.D. [🄰 Steptoe&J.]
Froelich, F. Edwin ....'57 '89 C.623 B.S. L.276 J.D. 2300 N St., N.W.
Froemming, John G., (BV) ....'59 '85 C.197 A.B. L.597 J.D. [Howrey S.A.&W.]
*PRACTICE AREAS: Complex Litigation; Antitrust Law; Intellectual Property Litigation.
Frohlich, David ....'52 '89 C.1288 B.A. L.352 J.D. 450 5th St., NW
Fronabarger, Paige K. ....'70 '95 C.420 B.A. L.425 J.D. [🄰 Wilkinson B.K.]
*PRACTICE AREAS: Corporate; Commercial Transactions; Finance.
Frontczak, Paul R. ....'71 '96 C.529 B.A. L.982 J.D. [🄰 Clifford C.R.&W.]
*PRACTICE AREAS: Antitrust; Antitrust Litigation.
Frosh, Brian E., (AV) '46 '71 C.918 B.A. L.178 J.D.
1232 17th St. N.W. (⊙Bethesda, Rockville, MD)
Frost, Amanda '71 '98 C&L.309 B.A., J.D.
(adm. in MD; not adm. in DC) Staff Atty., Public Citizen Litig. Grp.
Frost, Antonia A. ....'68 '95 C&L.1356 B.A., J.D. [🄰 Bruder,G.&M.]
*PRACTICE AREAS: Electric Utilities; Administrative Law.
Frost, Don Joaquin, Jr. ....'61 '89 C.118 B.A. L.228 J.D. [🄲 Skadden,A.S.M.&F.]
Frost, Edmund B., (AV) ....'42 '67 C.197 A.B. L.477 J.D. [Leonard H.F.L.&L.]
*PRACTICE AREAS: Environmental Law; Litigation; Antitrust Law; Transportation Law; Real Estate.
Frost, James W. ....'67 '95 C.604 B.A. L.30 J.D. [🄰 Wilmer,C.&P.]
Frost, Laurie A., (BV) '57 '83 C.790 B.A. L.893 J.D.
1801 K Street Northwest, Suite 1200
Frouman, Barbara Ann '48 '77 C.994 B.A. L.1019 J.D.
(adm. in NY; not adm. in DC) Assoc. Gen. Coun., Fannie Mae
*RESPONSIBILITIES: Multi-Family Housing Finance; Credit Enhancement.
Frulla, David E. .... '62 '87 C.197 A.B. L.893 J.D. [Brand&F.]
*PRACTICE AREAS: Regulatory Litigation; Small Business Law; Natural Resources; Campaign Ethics; Criminal.
Frumin, Matthew .... '59 '88 C.477 B.A. L.273 J.D. [🄲 Steptoe&J.]
*PRACTICE AREAS: International Trade; International Arbitration; Litigation; Antitrust.
Frutkin, Jonathan B. '73 '98 C.30 B.A. L.893 J.D.
(adm. in OH; not adm. in DC) Gen. Coun., Doceus, Inc.
Fry, Howard M. ....'31 '57 C.976 A.B. L.309 LL.B. 1156 15th St., N.W.
Fry, Norman J. ....'50 '94 C.339 A.B. L.273 J.D. [🄰 Shaw P.]
Fry, William R. '32 '59 C.197 B.A. L.178 LL.B.
(adm. in NY; not adm. in DC) HALT- Americans for Legal Reform
Frye, Eric T. ....'66 '95 C.478 B.A. L.273 J.D. Corp. Coun., Marriott Intl., Inc.
Frye, Russell S., (BV) ....'53 '78 C.674 A.B. L.208 J.D. [Collier S.S.]
*PRACTICE AREAS: Environmental; Administrative.
Frysiak, John M. ....'32 '57 C.116 B.A. L.107 J.D. 445 12th Street SW‡
Fryszman, Agnieszka M. .... '— '97 C.103 B.A. L.276 J.D. [🄰 Cohen,M.H.&T.]
*PRACTICE AREAS: Antitrust.
Fu, K. N. Minnie .... '61 '98 C.999 B.A. L.904 J.D. [Danziger,M.&F.]
*PRACTICE AREAS: Business Immigration; Citizenship; Consular Law.
Fuchs, Beatrice G. ....'22 '45 L.1009 LL.B. 5315 Conn. Ave., NW‡
Fuchs, Diane J., (AV) ....'47 '74 C&L.705 B.A., J.D. [Womble C.S.&R.]
*PRACTICE AREAS: Taxation; Employee Benefits; Executive Compensation; Employment Law; Exempt Organizations.
Fuchs, Martin I., (AV) '52 '78
C.705 B.A. L.273 J.D. [Finnegan,H.F.G.&D.] (See Pat. Sect.)
*PRACTICE AREAS: Patent Infringement.
Fuchs, Meredith ....'66 '94 C.054 B.S. L.569 J.D. [🄰 Wiley R.&F.]
Fuchs, Ronald W., (AV) .... '44 '74 C.893 B.S. L.64 J.D. [Eccleston&W.]
*PRACTICE AREAS: Insurance Defense Law; Professional Malpractice Law; Accounting Malpractice Law; Legal Malpractice Law; Architectural Malpractice Law.
Fuentes, Dominique C. ....'— '98 [🄰 Shearman&S.]
Fuentes, José A. ....'— '81 C.825 B.S. L.1088 J.D. [🄲 Reed S.]
*PRACTICE AREAS: Government Relations.
Fuentes, Rudy '66 '90 C.813 B.A. L.1066 J.D.
(adm. in TX; not adm. in DC) [🄰 Shaw P.]
Fuerst, Mitchell S., (AV) '53 '78 C.30 B.S.B.A. L.472 J.D.
(adm. in FL; not adm. in DC) [Rodriguez O.F.G.&W.] (⊙Miami, FL)
*PRACTICE AREAS: Income Tax; Federal Income Tax; Excise Tax; Tax Litigation; Administrative Law.
Fues, Eric J. .... '62 '95 C.597 B.S. L.424 J.D. [🄰 Pennie&E.] (See Pat. Sect.)
*PRACTICE AREAS: Intellectual Property; Patent Litigation.

Fugate, Wilbur L., (AV) '13 '36
C.198 B.A. L.893 LL.B. 1050 Connecticut Ave. (⊙Alexandria, VA)
Fugere, Patricia Mullahy '59 '84 C&L.276 A.B., J.D.
Wash. Legal Clinic for the Homeless
Fugh, John L. ....'34 '60 C.276 B.S.F.S. L.273 J.D. 1627 Eye St., N.W.
Fuisz, John R. ....'67 '92 C.276 B.S. L.128 J.D. [McDermott,W.&E.] (Pat.)
Fujichaku, Rex Y. '69 '98 C.605 A.B. L.312 J.D.
(adm. in HI; not adm. in DC) [Ⓐ Fried,F.H.S.&J.]
*PRACTICE AREAS: Antitrust.
Fujimoto, Shirley S., (AV) ....'51 '77 C.597 B.A. L.1162 J.D. [McDermott,W.&E.]

Fulbright & Jaworski L.L.P., (AV)
801 Pennsylvania Avenue, N.W., 20004-2604 ⊙
Telephone: 202-662-0200 Fax: 202-662-4643
Email: info@fulbright.com URL: http://www.fulbright.com
Partners: R. C. Fulbright (1881-1940); Richard W. Beckler; Robert Anthony Burgoyne; Irwin Cohen; Thomas E. Dowdell; Stephen M. Feldhaus; David M. Foster; Larry G. Franceski; Jeffrey H. Goodman; John F. Harrington; Gregg W. Harris; Peter F. Healey, Jr.; Robert J. Koch (Not admitted in DC); L. Poe Leggette; Alan B. Levenson; Kerry B. Long; John E. Lynch; Michael J. Manning; Stephen M. McNabb; Marilyn Mooney; Dan M. Peterson; Steven B. Pfeiffer; Craig T. Redinger; Frederick Robinson; Lance L. Shea (Not admitted in DC); John M. Simpson; Joseph T. Small, Jr.; Julie A. Tassi; Michael D. Trager; Peter V.B. Unger; Mark E. Ungerman; Carl W. Vogt; Daniel L. Wellington; Charles R. Wenner; William A. Williams. Retired Partner: Warren Belmar. Senior Counsel: Anthony E. DiResta; Allen K. Halperin; James P. White. Counsel: Andrew E. Falk; Thomas S. Hahn; Arthur A. Impastato; Maha S. Jadallah (Not admitted in DC); Amy Kertgate (Not admitted in DC); John C. Letteri; Karen M. Moran; Janet S. Nolan; Brenda J. Oliver; Michael J. Strauss. Senior Associates: Glenn S. Benson; Nancy E. Burton; Yeages Cowan (Not admitted in the United States); Cynthia C. Henderson (Not admitted in DC); Lisa Zeiler Joiner; Sean J. Klein; Robert Jeffrey Layne; Seth H. Lundy; Laura S. Morton (Not admitted in DC); Nancy L. Pell; Mary Anne Schofield (Not admitted in DC). Associates: Neely B. Agin; Lori-Ann S. Bellan; William E. Bradley; Wendy Butler Curtis (Not admitted in DC); Elizabeth Fritze; Gabriele Haist Fuqua (Not admitted in the United States); Joseph E. Hartman; Jeremy Ambler Hushon; Erica D. Jones; Matthew H. Kirtland; Ben Konop (Not admitted in DC); Kerry Elizabeth Larsen; Joshua R. Martin; Kristin McGovern (Not admitted in DC); Letitia W. McKoy; Caroline Marie Mew; Michelle Ciszak Pardo; René Y. Quashie; Einar Stole (Not admitted in DC); Bret A. Sumner; Yan Wang (Not admitted in DC); Steven War (Not admitted in DC); Carol I. Wicks (Not admitted in DC). Staff Attorneys: Katherine M. DuBray (Not admitted in DC); A. Scott English (Not admitted in DC); Christopher M. Gerlach (Not admitted in DC); Dimitri Seletzky.
General Civil Practice. Trial and Appellate Practice before Federal and State Courts, Departments and Agencies. Administrative and Legislative, Antitrust and Trade Regulations, Banking, Corporate and Securities, Customs, Education and Intercollegiate Sports Law, Energy, Environmental, Health Care, Immigration and Export Law, International, Labor and Employment, Patent, Project Finance, Trademark and Copyright, Taxation, Transportation, White Collar Criminal Law.
Houston, Texas Office: 1301 McKinney, Suite 5100, 77010. Telephone: 713-651-5151. Fax: 713-651-5246.
Austin, Texas Office: 600 Congress Avenue, Suite 2400, 78701. Telephone: 512-474-5201. Fax: 512-536-4598.
San Antonio, Texas Office: 300 Convent Street, Suite 2200, 78205. Telephone: 210-224-5575. Fax: 210-270-7205.
Dallas, Texas Office: 2200 Ross Avenue, Suite 2800, 75201. Telephone: 214-855-8000. Fax: 214-855-8200.
New York, New York Office: 666 Fifth Avenue, 31st Floor. 10103. Telephone: 212-318-3000. Fax: 212-318-3400.
Los Angeles, California Office: 865 South Figueroa Street, 29th Floor, 90017. Telephone: 213-892-9200. Fax: 213-680-4518.
Minneapolis, Minnesota Office: 225 South Sixth Street, Suite 4850, 55402. Telephone: 612-321-2800. Fax: 612-321-9600.
London, England Office: 2 St. James's Place, SW1A 1NP Telephone: 011-4420-7629-1207. Fax: 011-4420-7493-8259.
Hong Kong Office: The Hong Kong Club Building, Nineteenth Floor, 3A Chater Road, Central. Telephone: 011-852-2523-3200. Fax: 011-852-2523-3255.
See Professional Biographies, WASHINGTON, DISTRICT OF COLUMBIA

Fuller, Charles F. ....'58 '85 C.999 B.S. L.1048 J.D. [McChesney&D.] (⊙Bowie, MD)
Fuller, David R. '57 '83 C.992 B.A. L.150 J.D.
(adm. in OH; not adm. in DC) [McDermott,W.&E.]
Fuller, James T., III, (AV) ....'46 '71 C.10 B.S. L.893 J.D. [Williams&C.]
*PRACTICE AREAS: Taxation; Business Law; Nonprofit and Charitable Organizations.
Fuller, Kathryn S. ......'46 '77 C.103 B.A. L.846 J.D. Pres. & CEO, World Wildlife Fund
Fuller, Vincent J., (AV) ....'31 '56 C.951 B.A. L.276 LL.B. [Ⓒ Williams&C.]
Fullerton, Lawrence R., (AV) ....'52 '78 C.674 A.B. L.893 J.D. [Powell,G.F.&M.]
*PRACTICE AREAS: Antitrust.

Fullerton & Wise
(See Fairfax)

Fullum, Karen Yvonne '— '92 C.271 B.A. L.276 J.D.
(adm. in PA; not adm. in DC)
V.P., Regulatory Affs., National Association of Broadcasters
*RESPONSIBILITIES: Communications Law and Policy; FCC Regulation; Executive Lobbying.
Fulton, Ellen K. ....'71 '00 C.802 B.S. L.145 J.D. [Ⓐ Wilmer,C.&P.]
Fulton, Harry J. '40 '71 C.4 B.A. L.904 J.D.
Chf., Pub. Def. Serv. of DC, Mental Hlth. Div.
Fulton, Laurie S. ....'49 '89 C.627 B.A. L.276 J.D. [Williams&C.]
Fulton, Shana LaVerne '76 '01 C.575 B.A. L.178 J.D.
(adm. in NC; not adm. in DC) [Ⓐ Williams&C.]
*PRACTICE AREAS: Litigation.
Fultz, William S. ....'71 '98 C.575 B.A. L.893 J.D. [Ⓐ Cleary,G.S.&H.]
Funger, W. Scott, (AV) ....'57 '83 C.228 B.A. L.273 J.D. [Funger&K.]
Funger & Kirsch, (AV) .... 5301 Wisconsin Ave., N.W.
Funk, Larry Edward ...'47 '72 C&L.446 B.A., J.D. Sr. Atty., Washington Gas Light Co.
Funk, Robert E., Jr. '44 '68 C&L.862 LL.B.
Assoc. Gen. Coun., United Food & Comercial Workers International Union
Funkhouser, Cameron '58 '84 C.276 B.S.B.A. L.1209 J.D.
(adm. in VA; not adm. in DC)
Asst. Dir., Market Surveillance, National Assn. of Sec. Dealers, Inc.
Funkhouser, Robert B., (AV) ....'59 '88 C.309 A.B. L.262 J.D. [Ⓒ Hughes H.&R.]
*PRACTICE AREAS: Banking Litigation; Insurance Coverage; Antitrust.
Furey, Joseph M. ....'55 '84 C.93 B.A. L.64 J.D. [Ⓒ Hughes H.&R.]
*PRACTICE AREAS: Securities Litigation; Securities Regulation Law; Insurance; Litigation; Corporate Law.
Furey, Roger P. ....'54 '83 C.1356 B.S.P.A. L.893 J.D. [Katten M.Z.]
*PRACTICE AREAS: Intellectual Property; Intellectual Property Litigation.

Furey, Doolan & Abell, L.L.P.
(See Chevy Chase, Maryland)

Furlow, Christopher T. '— '00 C&L.893 B.A., J.D.
(adm. in MD; not adm. in DC) [Ⓐ Dyer E.&J.]
Furlow, Walter S., Jr., (AV) ....'25 '51 C.674 A.B. L.309 LL.B. [Lambert&F.] ⊙
Furman, Ann Began ....'56 '87 C.112 B.S. L.276 J.D. [Jorden B.]
*PRACTICE AREAS: Securities Law; Mutual Funds; Insurance Products; Investment Management.
Furman, Pamela J. ....'66 '95 C.976 B.A. L.813 J.D. [Olsson,F.&W.]
*PRACTICE AREAS: Medical Device Law; Food, Drug and Cosmetics Law.
Furman, Valerie M. .... '— '95 C.1036 B.A. L.904 J.D. [Ⓐ Dickstein S.M.&O.]
*PRACTICE AREAS: Communications Law; Administrative Law; Corporate Law.
Fusfield, Eric A. '67 '96 C.178 B.A. L.30 J.D.
(adm. in VA; not adm. in DC) 1301 15th St., N.W.

Fuss, David ....'11 '36 C&L.309 A.B., J.D. 5412 31st St., N.W.‡
Fuss, David A. ....'58 '87 C.477 A.B. L.128 J.D. [Wilkes A.]
*PRACTICE AREAS: Real Property Tax Litigation; Federal and State Condemnation; Federal and State Tax Controversy; Administrative Law.
Futrell, J. William, (AV) '35 '60 C.861 B.A. L.178 LL.B.
(adm. in LA; not adm. in DC) Pres., CEO & Pub., Environmental Law Institute
*RESPONSIBILITIES: Federal/State Regulations on Environment (30%, 10); International Environmental Management (30%, 4); Corporate Governance (30%, 20).
Futrowsky, Cathy J. .... '62 '92 C.188 B.S. L.910 J.D. [Ⓐ Coudert B.]
*PRACTICE AREAS: Patent Law; Litigation.
Fuzesi, Stephen, Jr. ...'48 '75 C.674 A.B. L.659 J.D. V.P. & Chf. Coun., Newsweek, Inc.
Gaary-Holran, Pamela C. ....'65 '91 C.390 A.B. L.273 J.D. [Ⓐ Lukas,N.G.&S.]
*PRACTICE AREAS: Telecommunications Law; FCC Regulation; FCC Licensing.
Gaba, Carmody Ann '— '00 C.886 B.A. L.904 J.D.
(adm. in VA; not adm. in DC) [Ⓐ Verner,L.B.M.&H.]
*PRACTICE AREAS: Labor and Employment; Transportation.
Gaba, Michael M. ....'61 '87 C.265 B.A. L.273 J.D. [Holland&K.]
*PRACTICE AREAS: Government Relations; Health Care.
Gabaldon, Theresa A., (AV) '54 '78
C.37 B.S. L.309 J.D. Prof. of Law, George Washington Univ.
Gabardi, Jeffrey L. '51 '79 C&L.878 B.A., J.D.
(adm. in UT; not adm. in DC) Health Ins. Assn. of Amer.
Gabauer, Peter A., Jr. '45 '73 C&L.823 B.A., J.D.
Dep. Gen. Coun., National Mining Association
Gabig, A. John, (AV) ....'— '63 C.282 A.B. L.1017 LL.B. [Ⓒ Miller&C.]
Gabrielson, Ann E., (CV) ....'61 '95 C.55 B.A. L.494 J.D. 3200 Havana Pl.
Gacek, Christophe M. '61 '95
C.659 B.S. L.893 J.D. Fed. Communications Comm., Wireless Bur.
Gacek, Stanley A. '52 '79
Asst. Dir., Intl. & Foreign Affs. Dept., United Food & Comercial Workers International Union
Gadiano, Willem F. .... '67 '92 C.967 B.A. L.904 J.D. [McDermott,W.&E.] (Pat.)
Gaede, Brooke L. ....'71 '99 C.1222 B.S. L.472 J.D. [Ⓐ Steptoe&J.]
Gaffney, Donna Lynn, (BV) ... '62 '90 C.367 B.A. L.904 J.D. 4200 Wisconsin Ave. N.W.
Gaffney, Michael Dean ....'61 '87 C.112 B.A. L.818 J.D. [Ⓒ Rosenman&C.]
Gaffney, P. Terrence ....'58 '91 C.363 B.A. L.161 J.D. [Ⓒ Womble C.S.&R.]
Gaffney, Paul B. ....'64 '92 C.228 A.B. L.145 J.D. [Williams&C.]
Gage, Larry S., (AV) ....'47 '73 C.309 B.A. L.178 J.D. [Powell,G.F.&M.]
*PRACTICE AREAS: Health Care; Administrative Law; Government Relations.
Gage, Robert J., (AV) ....'51 '77 C.381 B.A. L.309 J.D. [Covington&B.]

Gagliardo, Thomas J.
(See Silver Spring, Maryland)

Gagnebin, Rachel '71 '99 C.299 B.A. L.1398 J.D.
(adm. in NY; not adm. in DC) [Ⓐ Paul,H.J.&W.]
*PRACTICE AREAS: Corporate.
Gagner, Jana P. '64 '88 C.900 B.A. L.378 J.D.
(adm. in KS; not adm. in DC) Off. Gen. Coun., Finance & Litigation
Gagner, Philip A. ....'50 '84 C.588 B.A. L.276 J.D. [Shaughnessy,V.&G.]
Gagnier, Paul O., Jr. ....'69 '94 C.696 B.A. L.659 J.D. [Ⓐ Swidler B.S.F.]
*PRACTICE AREAS: Telecommunications.
Gagnon, Richard J., Jr. ....'66 '93 C.477 A.B. L.880 J.D. [Ⓐ Shearman&S.]
Gaguine, Benito, (AV) ....'12 '34 C&L.178 A.B., LL.B. 2300 M St Nw # 900
Gaine, John G. .... '42 '68 C.602 A.B. L.309 LL.B. 1150 Connecticut Ave, N.W.
Gainer, Ronald L. ....'34 '60 C.475 B.A. L.477 J.D. [Gainer&R.]
Gainer, Terracne William, Jr. ....'72 '97 C.363 B.A. L.365 J.D. Corp. Coun. of D.C.
Gainer and Rient ....Suite 690 1875 Connecticut Ave., N.W.
Gaines, Donald H. ....'30 '66 C&L.329 B.A., LL.B. 329 Oglethorpe St., N.W.‡
Gaines, Rachele M. .... '69 '96 C.645 B.S. L.64 J.D. [Ⓒ A.S.Toppelberg&Assoc.]
Gainor, Edward E. ....'54 '90 C.423 B.A. L.273 J.D. [McKee N.]
*PRACTICE AREAS: Securitization; Securities; Corporate.
Gajadharsingh, Adam C. ....'73 '98 C.861 B.A. L.245 J.D. [Ⓐ Crowell&M.]
Galambos, L. Denise ....'62 '90 C.674 B.A. L.966 J.D. [Ⓒ Morgan,L.&B.]
Galarowicz, Dennis C., (BV) ....'47 '85 C.966 B.S. L.128 J.D. 601 Indiana Ave., N.W.
Galat, Judy D. ......'54 '82 C.1168 B.A. L.588 J.D. Amer. Federation of Govt. Employees
Galbraith, J. Alan, (AV) ....'41 '66 C.309 B.A. L.477 J.D. [Williams&C.]
*PRACTICE AREAS: Civil Practice; Commercial Litigation; ERISA Litigation; Federal Civil Practice; Legal Malpractice Defense.
Galbraith, Mark R. '60 '93 C.494 B.A. L.1209 J.D.
(adm. in VA; not adm. in DC) [Ⓐ Quinn,R.&G.]
Galbreath, Andrew .... '67 '00 C.676 B.A. L.1364 J.D. [Ⓐ Rosenau&R.]
Galbreath, Philip L. '62 '91 C.836 B.B.A. L.880 J.D.
(adm. in GA; not adm. in DC) KPMG Peat Marwick
Galbreath, Robert L. ....'65 '91 C.918 B.A. L.902 J.D. [Ⓐ Powell,G.F.&M.]
*PRACTICE AREAS: Communications Law.
Gale, Richard N. ....'56 '81 C.228 B.S. L.893 J.D. [Arent F.K.P.&K.]
*PRACTICE AREAS: Health Care; Mergers and Acquisitions; Business Acquisitions; Business Law; Taxpayer Representative Law.
Galeota, William R., (AV) ....'48 '77 C&L.309 A.B., J.D. 1800 Mass. Ave. NW
Galer, Russell G. ......'61 '87 C.976 B.A. L.569 J.D. Sr. Coun., Investment Co. Institute
*RESPONSIBILITIES: Pension.
Gallagher, Catherine S., (AV) ....'60 '86 C.976 B.A. L.276 J.D. [Vinson&E.]
*PRACTICE AREAS: Securities; Corporate Law; Structured Finance; Business Law; Mergers, Acquisitions and Divestitures.
Gallagher, Daniel M., Jr. ....'72 '99 C.276 B.A. L.180 J.D. [Ⓐ Wilmer,C.&P.]
Gallagher, David S. '72 '01 C.878 B.A. L.30 J.D.
(adm. in VA; not adm. in DC) [Ⓐ Fried,F.H.S.&J.]
*PRACTICE AREAS: Litigation; Government Contracts; False Claims Act.
Gallagher, Donna Ann ....'69 '96 C.1350 B.A. L.128 J.D. Staff Atty., Ayuda Inc.
Gallagher, Edward G. .... '45 '74 C.951 B.A. L.273 J.D. [Wickwire G.] (⊙Vienna, VA)
*PRACTICE AREAS: Fidelity and Surety and Construction Law.
Gallagher, George R. ....'15 '37 C.273 L.180 LL.B. Sr. J., D. C. Ct. of App.
Gallagher, Henry T. ....'39 '71 C.723 B.A. L.276 J.D. 214 Massachusetts Ave., N.E.
Gallagher, James L. ....'66 '95 C.128 B.A. L.276 J.D. [Ⓐ Pillsbury W.]
Gallagher, John J. ....'47 '72 C.754 B.S. L.188 J.D. [Paul,H.J.&W.]
Gallagher, Kathleen G., (AV) '48 '73
C.706 B.A. L.818 J.D. [Ⓒ Coates,D.&G.] (⊙Mc Lean, VA)
*PRACTICE AREAS: Business Organizations; Real Estate Finance and Acquisitions; Corporate Finance and Securities; General Corporate; Partnership Law.
Gallagher, Kevin P. ....'58 '85 C.602 B.A. L.276 J.D. MCI Communications Corp.
Gallagher, Laura S. ....'68 '94 C.93 B.A. L.904 J.D. [Ⓐ Drinker B.&R.]
Gallagher, Lynn Monk ....'56 '85 C.260 B.A. L.276 J.D. [Ⓒ Swidler B.S.F.]
*PRACTICE AREAS: Water Pollution; Pesticides; Environmental Compliance; Environmental Enforcement.
Gallagher, Michael G. ....'36 '64 C&L.273 A.B., J.D. George Washington Univ.
Gallagher, Michele A. ....'66 '96 C.128 B.A. L.276 J.D. [Anderson K.&O.]
*PRACTICE AREAS: General Litigation; Insurance Litigation.
Gallagher, Paul T. ....'61 '93 C.1209 B.A. L.945 J.D. [Cohen,M.H.&T.]
*PRACTICE AREAS: Antitrust Class Actions; Securities Class Actions.

Gallagher, Raymond E., Jr. '32 '61
C&L.262 A.B., LL.B. Assoc. Prof., Catholic Univ. Law School
Gallagher, Robert P., (AV) ....'45 '71 C&L.273 B.A., J.D. [Groom]
*PRACTICE AREAS: Health Care; Employee Benefits; Pension and Profit Sharing; ERISA.
Gallagher, Stephanie Agli .... '72 '97 C.276 B.A. L.309 J.D. [A Akin,G.S.H.&F.]
*PRACTICE AREAS: Litigation.
Gallagher, Virginia H. ....'43 '68 C.424 B.S. L.228 J.D. Pres., Conreg Inc.
Gallagher, Wade J., (AV) '40 '67
C.276 A.B. L.128 J.D. [Martell,D.G.&G.] (⊙Rockville, MD)

Gallagher, Boland and Meiburger, (AV)
1023 15th Street, N.W., Suite 900, 20005-2602
Telephone: 202-289-7200 Fax: 202-289-7698
URL: http://www.GBMDC.com
Members of Firm: Richard J. Connor (1901-1984); Walter E. Gallagher (1910-1996); James M. Broadstone; Frank X. Kelly; Peter C. Lesch; Steve Stojic. Senior Counsel: Christopher T. Boland; George J. Meiburger.
Federal Energy Regulation, Natural Gas, Natural Gas Pipelines, Electric Utility Regulation, Gas Utilities, Hydroelectricity Licensing, Alternative Energy, Independent Power.
See Professional Biographies, WASHINGTON, DISTRICT OF COLUMBIA

Gallagher-Duff, Kathleen T. ....'53 '85 C.1057 B.A. L.276 J.D. [C Covington&B.]

Galland, Kharasch, Greenberg, Fellman & Swirsky, P.C., (AV)
Canal Square, 1054 Thirty-First Street, N.W., 20007-4492 ⊙
Telephone: 202-342-5200 Telecopier: 202-342-5219
Email: gkglaw@gkglaw.com URL: http://www.gkglaw.com
George F. Galland (1910-1985); Edward D. Greenberg; David K. Monroe; David P. Street; Steven John Fellman; Keith G. Swirsky; Martin Jacobs; Richard B. Bar; William F. Krebs; Stuart M. Schabes (Not admitted in DC; Resident, Baltimore, Maryland Office);—Katharine V. Foster; Michael P. Coyle; Cynthia J. Hurwitz. Of Counsel: Robert N. Kharasch; Rex E. Reese (Not admitted in DC).
Advertising, Alternative Dispute Resolution, Antitrust, Aviation, Commercial, Corporate, Employment Law, Energy, Food and Drug, Gaming, Government Contracts, Information Technology, Intellectual Property, International Trade, Legislative Affairs, Litigation, Maritime, Real Estate, Securities, Surface Transportation, Taxation, Tax Controversy, representation before IRS and State Taxing Authorities, Telecommunications, Trade and Professional Associations, and Wildlife.
Baltimore, Maryland Office: 9199 Reisterstown Road, Suite 200B, 21117. Telephone: 443-394-6310. Fax: 443-394-6320.
See Professional Biographies, WASHINGTON, DISTRICT OF COLUMBIA

Gallant, Gary G., Jr. ....'67 '92 C&L.1292 B.A., J.D. [A Swidler B.S.F.]
*PRACTICE AREAS: Legislative Practice.
Gallant, Michael E. .... '67 '95 C.262 B.A. L.128 J.D. [A Ashcraft&G.]
*PRACTICE AREAS: Products Liability; Personal Injury; Pharmacy Law; Diet Drug Litigation.
Gallas, Philip S. ....'53 '78 C.910 A.B. L.904 J.D. [Sandler,T.&R.]
*PRACTICE AREAS: International Trade; Customs Law; Export Law.
Gallen, Kevin P. ....'46 '75 C.884 B.C.E. L.309 J.D. [Morgan,L.&B.]
Galler, Eric S. ....'64 '95 C.685 B.A. L.904 J.D. [A Wilmer,C.&P.] (⊙Balt., MD)
Galli, Thomas, (AV) .... '62 '88 C.659 B.S. L.813 J.D. [Winston&S.]
*PRACTICE AREAS: Commercial Real Estate.
Galligan, Arthur J., (AV) .... '26 '54 C.178 A.B. L.569 LL.B. 2101 L St., N.W.
Gallo, Joseph ....'34 '63 C.964 B.A. L.494 LL.B. [Gallo B.&R.]
Gallo, Kenneth A. ....'56 '83 C&L.280 B.A., J.D. [Clifford C.R.&W.]
*PRACTICE AREAS: Antitrust Law; Complex Litigation; Intellectual Property.
Gallo Brown and Ross, L.L.P., (AV) ....Suite 1014 1025 Connecticut Avenue, N.W.
Gallop, David H. '50 '78 C.25 B.A. L.1048 J.D.
(adm. in PA; not adm. in DC) The Bureau of Natl. Affs., Inc.
Gallozzi, Marialuisa S. ....'61 '87 C.309 A.B. L.569 J.D. [Covington&B.]
Gallu, Christopher T., Jr. ....'70 '97 C.645 B.A. L.273 J.D. [B Chadbourne&P.]
Gallup, David M. '65 '92 C.910 A.B. L.30 J.D.
(adm. in MD; not adm. in DC) Pres. & Gen. Coun., World Service Authority
Gally, Karen Russell ....'— '97 C.197 B.A. L.446 J.D. [A Epstein B.&G.]
*PRACTICE AREAS: Health Law; Government Investigations; Health Care Fraud and Abuse.
Galoob, Rachael A. '70 '97 C.93 B.A. L.615 J.D.
(adm. in FL; not adm. in DC) [A Cole,R.&B.]
*PRACTICE AREAS: Regulatory Law; International Communications Law; Corporate Law; Satellite Communications.
Galotto, John A. ....'67 '94 C.367 B.A. L.178 J.D. [A McKee N.]
*PRACTICE AREAS: Tax Litigation; White Collar Crime.
Galt, George ....'63 '93 C.174 B.A. L.29 J.D. Associated Press
Galvin, Lawrence Francis '55 '98
C.871 B.S. L.276 J.D. [A Finnegan,H.F.G.&D.] (See Pat. Sect.)
*PRACTICE AREAS: Mechanical Intellectual Property; Design Patents; Electrical Patent Prosecution; Mechanical Patents; Patent Prosecution.
Gamble, Bruce ....'53 '89 C.421 B.S. L.276 J.D. DC Retire. Bd.
Gamer, Janet G., (AV) ....'38 '65 C.788 B.A. L.569 LL.B. [A Fried,F.H.S.&J.]
Gammon, Elinor W., (AV) .... '— '69 C.914 B.A. L.893 LL.B. [Kirkpatrick&L.]
*PRACTICE AREAS: Investment Company Law; Investment Regulation; Mutual Funds; Securities Regulation.

Gammon & Grange, P.C.
(See McLean, Virginia)

Gamse, Alan N., (AV) ......'42 '67 C.453 B.S. L.446 J.D. [Semmes,B.&S.] (⊙Balt., MD)
*PRACTICE AREAS: Insurance Corporate and Regulatory Law; Insurance Coverage; Insurance Insolvency; Administrative Law.
Gamson, Miriam R. ....'59 '84 C.112 B.A. L.861 J.D. [C Hale&D.]
*PRACTICE AREAS: Real Estate.
Gan, Michael J., (BV) ....'65 '90 C.477 B.A. L.94 J.D. [Peer&G.]
Gandal, Alvin H. ....'32 '56 C&L.930 A.B., LL.B. [C Burzio&M.]
Gandal, Larry N., (AV) '39 '69
C&L.910 B.S.B.A., J.D. [Shulman,R.G.P.&E.] (⊙Rockville, MD)
Gandy, Kim A. '54 '78 C.418 B.S. L.425 J.D.
Exec. V.P., National Organization for Women
Gani, Paula '— '94 C.813 B.A. L.966 J.D.
(adm. in CA; not adm. in DC) 1800 M St., N.W.‡
Ganiban, Jeffrey T. ....'64 '89 C.860 B.A. L.273 J.D. [Akin,G.S.H.&F.]
*PRACTICE AREAS: Health Care Law.
Gannett, Sarah Sargent ....'69 '97 C&L.813 A.B., J.D. Pub. Def. Servs.
Gannon, Curtis E. ....'73 '98 C.309 A.B. L.145 J.D. [A Gibson,D.&C.]
*PRACTICE AREAS: Appellate Practice.
Gannon, Jonathan W. '73 '01 C.321 B.A. L.880 J.D.
(adm. in VA; not adm. in DC) [A Shaw P.]
*PRACTICE AREAS: Litigation.
Gannon, Kerri B. '74 '01 C.93 B.A. L.30 J.D.
(adm. in MA; not adm. in DC) [A Sonnenschein N.&R.]
Gannon, Matthew L. ....'— '98 C.602 B.A. L.352 J.D. [A Arnold&P.]
*PRACTICE AREAS: Legislative Practice; Litigation.
Gans, Jeffrey R. ....'66 '95 C.260 B.A. L.128 J.D. [A Thelen R.&P.]
*PRACTICE AREAS: Commercial Litigation; Construction Litigation; White Collar Criminal Defense.
Ganslaw, Lawrence S. ....'67 '98 C&L.446 B.S., J.D. [A Morgan,L.&B.]
Gansler, Douglas F. ....'62 '89 C.976 B.A. L.893 J.D. U.S. States Atty.
Gant, Scott E. ....'69 '95 C.918 B.A. L.309 J.D. [A Boies,S.&F.]
*PRACTICE AREAS: Commercial Litigation; Antitrust; Constitutional Law; Media Law.
Ganther, James S., (AV) ....'61 '88 C&L.602 B.A., J.D. [Ganther&F.] ⊙
Ganther & Fee, P.A., (AV) ....910 17th Street, N.W. (⊙Tampa, FL)
Gantt, John B. ....'39 '65 C.119 B.S. L.893 LL.B. [Mizrack&G.] ⊙
*PRACTICE AREAS: Civil Practice; International Trade; Public International Law; Commercial Law; Space and Telecommunications Law.
Gantt, W. Andrew H., III ....'— '94 C.112 B.A. L.893 J.D. [A Latham&W.]
*PRACTICE AREAS: Health Care; Corporate Law; Intellectual Property; Mergers, Acquisitions and Divestitures; Privacy Law.
Gantz, David A., (AV) ..... '42 '67 C.309 A.B. L.813 J.D. 1001 Pennsylvania Ave., N.W.
Gantz, Jule L '68 '97 C.309 A.B. L.893 J.D.
Lawyers' Comm. for Civil Rights Under Law
Ganzfried, Jerrold J., (BV) ....'48 '75 C.976 B.A. L.813 J.D. [Howrey S.A.&W.]
*PRACTICE AREAS: Supreme Court and Appellate Litigation; Complex Litigation; Antitrust; Intellectual Property.
Ganzglass, Martin R. .... '41 '64 C.563 B.A. L.309 LL.B. [O'Donnell,S.&A.]
Garb, Sarah H. ....'70 '96 C.966 B.A. L.494 J.D. [A Howrey S.A.&W.]
*PRACTICE AREAS: Antitrust; Litigation.
Garber, Everett M., III ....'53 '80 C.893 B.A. L.692 J.D. 1133 19th St., N.W., 10th Fl.
Garber, Margaret E. ....'52 '80 C&L.446 B.S., J.D. Sr. Coun., SBC Communications
Garber, William J., (AV) ....'28 '52 C.30 L.537 LL.B. 717 D St. N.W.
Garbow, Melvin C., (AV) ....'33 '60 C.679 B.S. L.273 J.D. [Arnold&P.]
*PRACTICE AREAS: Antitrust; Litigation; Government Contracts; Real Estate.
Garces, Rafael L. ....'58 '84 C.597 B.A. L.128 J.D. MCI Telecom. Corp.
Garcia, Brian N. '62 '88 C.776 B.A. L.179 J.D.
(adm. in MD; not adm. in DC) 888 17th St Nw # 1100
Garcia, Joe, Jr. ....'57 '86 C.586 B.S. L.846 J.D. [McKee N.]
*PRACTICE AREAS: Taxation.
Garcia, Kathleen Quimby .... '67 '94 C.197 B.A. L.893 J.D. [A Williams&C.] (Pat.)
Garcia, Loretta J. ....'55 '85 C.1165 B.A. L.276 J.D. [Irwin,C.&T.]
Garcia, Oliver ....'70 '95 C.178 A.B. L.846 J.D. [A Williams&C.]
Garcia-Bokor, Amybeth .... '68 '95 C.916 B.A. L.569 J.D. [A Proskauer R.]
Garde, Billie Pirner ....'53 '86 C.619 B.A. L.1162 J.D. [Clifford,L.&G.]
*PRACTICE AREAS: Civil Litigation; Toxic Torts; Employment; Work Environment Training and Consulting.
Garden, Kevin ....'64 '89 C.602 B.A. L.904 J.D. [Saltman&S.]
*PRACTICE AREAS: Government Contracts; Environmental Law; Natural Resources Law; Timber and Logging Law; Corporate Law.
Gardiner, James S. '28 '56
C&L.276 B.S.S., J.D. Commr. on Mental Health, Supr. Ct. of D.C.
Gardiner, Kent A. ....'58 '85 C.1044 B.A. L.276 J.D. [Crowell&M.]
*PRACTICE AREAS: Litigation; Antitrust Law; Criminal Law.
Gardner, Allen M. ....'— '96 C.101 B.A. L.178 J.D. [A Latham&W.]
Gardner, Barbara K., (AV) ....'39 '82 C.273 B.A. L.276 J.D. [Leventhal,S.&L.]
*PRACTICE AREAS: Communications Law; Media Law.
Gardner, Bruce E. ....'53 '81 C.112 B.A. L.823 J.D. [Gardner]
*PRACTICE AREAS: Taxation; Labor Law; Bankruptcy Law.
Gardner, Bryant E. ....'74 '01 C&L.861 B.A., J.D. [A Winston&S.]
*PRACTICE AREAS: Admiralty Law; Maritime Administrative Law; Maritime Regulation; Carriage of Goods by Sea; Marine Environmental Law.
Gardner, Catherine B. ....'69 '94 C&L.276 B.A., J.S. [A Sonnenschein N.&R.]
*PRACTICE AREAS: Corporate.
Gardner, Dirk R. ....'66 '98 C.101 B.A. L.910 J.D. [A Akin,G.S.H.&F.]
*PRACTICE AREAS: Corporate; Securities; Banking.
Gardner, Jamie S. ....'58 '83 C.860 B.A. L.276 J.D. [Patton B.]
Gardner, Joan Marie, (AV) '54 '80 C.45 B.A. L.902 J.D.
(adm. in VA; not adm. in DC) Dir., State Servs., Blue Cross & Blue Shield Assn.
Gardner, Jody M. ....'75 '01 C.1055 B.A. L.425 J.D. [A Jones,D.R.&P.]
Gardner, Michael R., (AV) ....'42 '77 C&L.276 B.A., J.D. [M.R.Gardner]
Gardner, R. Scott .... '48 '73 C.659 B.A. L.94 J.D. [Spencer,G.&H.]
Gardner, Richard D. '73 '01 C.309 B.A. L.893 J.D.
(adm. in MA; not adm. in DC) [A O'Melveny&M.]
Gardner, Stephen K., (BV) .... '49 '76 C.208 B.A. L.1065 J.D. [McKenna&C.]
*PRACTICE AREAS: Energy Law.
Gardner, Warner W., (AV) ....'09 '35 C.705 M.A. L.178 LL.B. [C Shea&G.]
Gardner, William C. .... '17 '51 C.329 A.B. L.309 LL.B. Sr. Assoc. J., Supr. Ct.
Gardner, William L., (AV) ....'42 '68 C.228 A.B. L.30 J.D. [Morgan,L.&B.]

Gardner, Carton & Douglas, (AV)
Suite 900, East Tower, 1301 K Street, N.W., 20005-3317 ⊙
Telephone: 202-408-7100 Facsimile: 202-289-1504
URL: http://www.gcd.com
Members of Firm: Francis E. Fletcher, Jr. (Resident); Arthur G. House; M. Scott Johnson (Resident); W. N. Harrell Smith IV; Patrick C. Rock; Rodney H. Glover; Ballard Jamieson, Jr.; James M. Jorling; Laura C. Mow; Thomas J. Dougherty, Jr.; Kathleen M. Nilles; T. J. Sullivan; Attison L. Barnes III; George N. Grammas; Philip G. Hampton, II (Not admitted in DC); Carin J. Sigel; Anita J. Cicero; Mark R. Fitzgerald; Troy M. Calkins. Associates: Lynne D. Anderson (Not admitted in DC); Mary E. Devlin Capizzi; Joseph S. Carlin; Maureen E. Donahue; Jessica L. Eisenhaure; Sandra Jill Farrington; Laurie A. Holmes; Anne Kurtz Flam; Demetrios Kouzoukas (Not admitted in DC); Holley Thames Lutz; Neela A. Paykel; Lee G. Petro; Jason Schlosberg (Not admitted in DC); Corey A. Stewart.
Administrative Law, Affirmative Action, Alternative Dispute Resolution, Antitrust and Trade Regulation, Appellate Practice, Bankruptcy, Banks and Banking, Broadcasting Law, Broadcasting Television, Broker-Dealer Arbitration, Broker-Dealer Regulation, Business Dispute Resolution, Business Law, Business Reorganization, Business Successions, Cable TV, Civil Litigation, Clean Water Act, Closely Held Business Law, Coastal Environmental Law, COBRA, Collective Bargaining, Commercial Banking, Commercial Law, Commodities, Communications and Media, Complex Litigation, Computer Law, Computers and Software, Constitutional Law, Consumer Law, Contested Trusts and Estate, Contracts, Cooperate Fiduciary Law, Copyright Protection, Copyrights, Corporate Commercial Law, Corporate Contracts, Corporate Governance, Corporate Law, Corporate Tax Planning, Criminal Antitrust, Criminal Law, Custom Law, Debtor and Creditor, Deferred Compensation, Drug and Medical Device, Educational Law, Employee Benefits Trusts, Employee Benefits, Employee Compensation, Employee Stock Ownership Plans, Employment Civil Rights, Employment Discrimination, Employment Litigation, Energy, Entertainment and the Arts, Environmental Auditing, Environmental Cleanup, Environmental Compliance, Environmental Cost Recovery, Environmental Insurance, Environmental Law, Environmental Litigation, Environmental Permitting, Equal Employment Opportunity Law, Equipment Finance and Leasing, ERISA Compliance, ERISA, Estate and Gift Taxation, Estate Planning, Executive Compensation, Executive Employment, Export Regulation, False Claims Act, Family Wealth Transfer, FCC Regulation, Federal Civil Litigation, Federal Energy Regulation, Federal Income Tax, Finance, Foreign Corrupt Practices Act, Foreign Investment, Government, Health Benefits, Health Care Finance, Health Care Mergers and Acquisitions, Health Care Regulation, Health Care Reimbursement, Health Care Taxation, Health Care, Health Insurance, Health Law Fraud, Health Law, Indians and Native Populations, Information Technology, Infringement Intellectual Property Litigation, Initial Public Offerings, Insurance Defense, Insurance, Integrated Health Care Delivery Systems, Intellectual Property Litigation, Intellectual Property, Intellectual Technology Contracts, International Corporate Finance, International Corporate Law, International Dispute Resolution, International Energy Law, International Environmental Law, International Law, International Mergers and Acquisitions, International Telecommunication Law, International Trade, Internet Law, Investment Management, Investment Partnerships, Investments, Labor and Employment, Labor Relations, Land Acquisitions, Land Sales, Leases and Leasing, Legal Ethic and Professional Responsibility, Literary Property, Litigation, Loans, Long Term Care, Managed Care, Management Labor Law, Mass Media Law, Media Antitrust, Medicare and Medicaid, Mental Health Law, Mergers and Acquisitions, Mergers, Acquisitions and Divestitures, Municipal Law, Music Law, Mutual Funds, National Environmental Law, New Media Law, Non-Qualified Benefits, Nonprofit and Charitable Organizations, Nonprofit Corporations, Partnership Law, Pension and Profit Sharing Plan, Personnel Policies, Physicians Contracts, Planning and Land Use, Private Placement, Probate, Products Liability, Professional Liability, Public Finance, Public Offerings,

(This Listing Continued)

Gardner, Carton & Douglas (Continued)

Qualified Retirement Plans, Qui Tam Litigation, Radio Common Carrier, Real Estate Acquisitions, Real Estate Brokerage Law, Real Estate Development, Real Estate Finance, Real Estate Leasing, Real Estate Sales, Real Estate Secured Lending, Real Estate Zoning, Real Estate, Regulatory Law, Religious Institutions, Resource Conservation and Recovery Act, Retirement Benefit Plans, Secured Lending, Securities Arbitration, Securities Fraud Arbitration, Securities Fraud Class Actions, Securities Litigation, Securities Offerings, Securities, Sports Law, State Taxation, Tax Controversies, Tax Exempt Finance, Tax Law, Tax Planning, Taxation, Technology and Science, Technology Licensing, Telecommunications Contracts, Telecommunications Law, Telecommunications Licensing, Telecommunications Regulation, Telephone Utility Regulation, Title VII Discrimination, Toxic Torts, Trademark Infringement, Trademarks, Tribal Taxation, Trust and Estates, Underground Storage Tanks, University Finance, Utility Acquisitions Utility Finance, Utility Law, Venture Capital, White Collar Criminal Defense Litigation, Wills, Wireless Communications, Wrongful Termination Defense, Zoning, Planning and Land Use.
Chicago, Illinois Office: Quaker Tower, Suite 3400, 321 North Clark Street, 60610-4795. Telephone: 312-644-3000.
See Professional Biographies, WASHINGTON, DISTRICT OF COLUMBIA

Gardner Law Firm, The, P.C.
601 Pennsylvania Avenue NW, Suite 900, 20004
Telephone: 202-271-0552; 301-249-8820 Fax: 301-249-6234
Email: beegard@aol.com
Bruce E. Gardner.
Taxation, IRS Controversies, Estate & Gift Taxation, Tax Appeals, Tax Audits, Tax Fraud, Tax Planning, Non-Profit Tax Law, Charitable Giving, Tax Exempt Organizations, Estates & Trusts, Wills, Probate, Power of Attorney, Wealth Preservation, Business Successions, Family Wealth Transfer, Financial Planning, Contracts, Negotiations and Review, Small Business Law, Criminal Tax Law.
See Professional Biographies, WASHINGTON, DISTRICT OF COLUMBIA

Gardner, Michael R., P.C., The Law Offices of, (AV)
1150 Connecticut Avenue, Suite 710

Gardner, Middlebrooks, Fleming, Gibbons & Kittrell, P.C.
1919 S Street NW, 20009 ⊙
Telephone: 202-667-8278
Samuel H. Heldman; Hilary E. Ball.
General Civil Trial Practice. Labor, Personal Injury, Toxic Torts, Admiralty, F.E.L.A., Insurance, Workers' Compensation, Longshore and Harbor Worker's Compensation Act, Employee Benefits.
Representative Clients: Alabama AFL-CIO; Southwest Alabama Labor Council, AFL-CIO; Greater Mobile Port Council, AFL-CIO; Mobile/Pensacola; Building Trades Council, AFL-CIO; Paper Allied-Industrial Chemical Energy Workers International Union, AFL CIO, CLC; International Organization of Masters, Mates & Pilots, AFL-CIO; International Brotherhood of Boilermakers, AFL-CIO; International Alliance of Theatrical Stage Employees & Moving Picture Machine Operators, AFL-CIO; UAW Local 1639.
Birmingham, Alabama Office: Suite 450, 2013 1st Avenue, North. Telephone: 205-250-7776.
Mobile, Alabama Office: 1119 Government Street. Telephone: 334-433-8100. Fax: 334-433-8181.
See Professional Biographies, WASHINGTON, DISTRICT OF COLUMBIA

Gardner, Ohlrich & Vlach, (AV) .... 1050 Seventeenth Street, N.W.
Garfinkle, Ann M., (AV) .... '42 '68 C.966 B.S. L.1009 J.D. [Garfinkle&Assoc.]
*PRACTICE AREAS: Art Law; Intellectual Property; Family Law; Wills; Trusts and Estates.
Garfinkle, Morris R., (AV) ....'48 '73 C.659 B.S.E. L.276 J.D. 1054 31st St. N.W.

Garfinkle & Associates, Law Offices of, (AV) BR
1150 Connecticut Avenue, N.W., Suite 505, 20036
Telephone: 202-457-0200 Facsimile: 202-857-0550
Email: agarfinkle@garfinklelaw-com URL: http://www.lawyers.com/washingtonartlaw
Ann M. Garfinkle. Of Counsel: Robert Joseph Freda; Allie Johnson Sheffield.
Art Law, Intellectual Property, Entertainment and the Arts, Wills, Trusts and Estates, Probate, Family Law, Real Estate, General Practice.
See Professional Biographies, WASHINGTON, DISTRICT OF COLUMBIA

Garibaldi, Oscar M., (AV) .... '46 '78 C&L.999 B.B., J.D. [Covington&B.]
Garland, James M. '73 '00 C.674 A.B. L.893 J.D.
(adm. in OH; not adm. in DC) [Ⓐ Covington&B.]
Garment, Leonard, (AV) .... '— '49 C.102 A.B. L.1009 LL.B. [Ⓒ Verner,L.B.M.&H.]
*PRACTICE AREAS: Litigation; Government Relations.
Garment, Suzanne R. '46 '00 C.681 B.A. L.276 J.D.
(adm. in MD; not adm. in DC) [Ⓐ Dow,L.&A.]
Garmisa, Gregg A. ....'59 '86 C.813 B.A. L.276 J.D. 700 13th St. NW
Garner, Gene M., II ....'58 '88 C&L.446 B.S.E.E., J.D. [Staas&H.] (See Pat. Sect.)
*PRACTICE AREAS: Intellectual Property Law; Patents; Trademarks; Copyright Law.
Garner, Mary M. ....'— '42 C&L.273 LL.B. 2510 Virginia Ave., N.W.‡
Garner, Stephanie Diane ....'47 '77 C.994 B.A. L.569 J.D. 1801 L St., N.W.
Garner, William W. ....'42 '70 C.659 B.S.E. L.966 J.D. 1155 Connecticut Ave., N.W.
Garnick, Murray R. .... '59 '86 C&L.280 B.A., J.D. [Arnold&P.]
*PRACTICE AREAS: Litigation; Products Liability.
Garofalo, Gary B., (AV) ....'40 '65 C.688 B.S.A.E. L.893 LL.B. [Boros&G.]
*PRACTICE AREAS: Federal Aviation Regulation; Airline Regulation.
Garofoli, Anthony J., (AV) ....'36 '61 C.363 L.1003 J.D. [Climaco,L.P.W.&G.] ⊙
Garr, Lawrence D., (AV) ....'45 '71 C.659 B.A. L.831 J.D. [Dickstein S.M.&O.]
*PRACTICE AREAS: Taxation (Local, State, Federal or International) Law; Federal Income Estate and Gift Taxation Law; Taxation of Individuals and Business Entities; IRS Collection Procedures; Litigation.
Garr, Sally D. .... '52 '80 C.1059 B.A. L.280 J.D. [Patton B.]
Garrett, Arthur S., (AV) '38 '64
C.688 B.S.Ch.E. L.273 LL.B. [Finnegan,H.F.G.&D.] (See Pat. Sect.)
*PRACTICE AREAS: International Patent Prosecution; International Licensing; Trademark Registration.
Garrett, Arthur S., III ....'65 '90 C.390 B.A. L.692 J.D. [Keller&H.]
*PRACTICE AREAS: Litigation; Insurance Recovery.
Garrett, Mark G. '71 '98 C.257 B.S. L.846 J.D.
(adm. in MD; not adm. in DC) [Ⓐ McDermott,W.&E.]
Garrett, Patrick E. '62 '96
C.1338 B.S.E.E. L.446 J.D. [Ⓐ Sterne,K.G.&F.] (See Pat. Sect.)
*PRACTICE AREAS: Intellectual Property Law.
Garrett, Ranji Martelli ....'71 '97 C.790 B.A. L.902 J.D. [Ⓐ Kirkpatrick&L.]
*PRACTICE AREAS: Insurance Coverage Litigation.
Garrett, Robert A., (AV) ....'48 '73 C&L.597 B.A., J.D. [Arnold&P.]
*PRACTICE AREAS: Telecommunications Law; Communications; Intellectual Property; Sports and Entertainment; Litigation.
Garrett, Theodore L., (AV) ....'43 '68 C.976 B.A. L.178 J.D. [Covington&B.]
Garrett, Thomas S. ....'68 '99 C.692 B.A. L.893 J.D. [Ⓐ Wiley R.&F.]
Garrett-Nelson, LaBrenda, (AV) .... '53 '79 C.1139 B.A. L.569 J.D. [Washington C.]
Garrigues, Shinobu K. ....'— '98 C.174 B.A. L.494 J.D. [Ⓐ Hogan&H.]
Garris, Troy W. ....'66 '98 C.326 B.A. L.30 J.D. [Ⓐ Weiner B.S.K.]
*PRACTICE AREAS: Transportation; Corporate Law; Mergers and Acquisitions; Railway Labor Law; Surface Transportation.
Garrison, Charles W., III ......'44 '78 C.62 B.A. L.851 J.D. Pres., Garrison & Sisson, Inc.
Garrity, Wm. P. .... '36 '61 C.436 L.276 J.D. 1545 18th St., N.W.
Garrote, Nora E. ....'58 '83 C.104 A.B. L.178 J.D. [Brobeck,P.&H.]
*PRACTICE AREAS: Intellectual Property; Technology Law; Computer Law; Telecommunications Law.
Garske, Peder A. .... '62 '88 C&L.893 B.A., J.D. [Baker&H.]
Gart, Ronald S., (AV) .....'54 '79 C&L.273 B.A., J.D. [Powell,G.F.&M.] (⊙Reston, VA)
*PRACTICE AREAS: Real Estate; Finance Law; Securitization; Real Estate Law; Condominium Law.
Gartman, Grant Alan '72 '99 C.990 B.A. L.904 J.D.
(adm. in NY; not adm. in DC) 450 5th Street

Gartner, Michael C. .... '71 '97 C.886 B.A. L.1035 J.D. [Ⓐ Charapp,D.&W.]
*PRACTICE AREAS: Civil Litigation; Employment Law; Corporate Law.
Garvey, Eric B. '73 '01 C.446 B.A. L.128 J.D.
(adm. in MD; not adm. in DC) [Ⓐ Dechert]
*PRACTICE AREAS: Investment Management; Financial Services Law.
Garvey, George E. '42 '72 C.339 B.A. L.966 J.D.
(adm. in WI; not adm. in DC) Prof. of Law, Catholic Univ.
Garvey, John C., (AV) ...... '53 '79 C.228 B.S.E. L.273 J.D. [Staas&H.] (See Pat. Sect.)
*PRACTICE AREAS: Intellectual Property Law; Patent, Trademark, Copyright and Unfair Competition.
Garvey, John L. ...'27 '48 C.973 A.B. L.128 LL.B. Prof. of Law, Catholic Univ. of Amer.

Garvey, Schubert & Barer, (AV) BR
Fifth Floor, 1000 Potomac Street, N.W., 20007 ⊙
Telephone: 202-965-7880 Telecopier: 202-965-1729
URL: http://www.GSBlaw.com
Members of Firm: Harold G. Bailey, Jr.; Robert A. W. Boraks; Richard D. Gluck; Eldon V. C. Greenberg; Paul S. Hoff; Matthew R. Schneider; Richard A. Wegman. Of Counsel: Michael H. Bader; John Crigler; James E. Dunstan; John Wells King; Benjamin J. Lambiotte; John M. Pelkey; William E. Perry; Henry A. Solomon; Melodie A. Virtue. Associates: Michael Ian Goulding; John C. Kalitka; Amy B. Levenson; Lisa M. Patera Sterling; Carolyn A. Prince.
Languages: English, French, German, Japanese, Korean, Italian, Mandarin Chinese, Marshallese and Spanish.
Administrative Process, Legislative Process, Government Relations, Bankruptcy and Creditors' Rights, Business, and Litigation. Admiralty, Antitrust, Commercial Transactions, Communications, Customs, E-Commerce and Emerging Technologies, Employee Benefit Plans, Environmental Law, Estate Planning and Probate, Ethics/Scientific Misconduct, Federal Election Law, Fisheries, Government Contracts, Health and Safety Regulation, Health Care, Housing, Immigration, Insurance Coverage and Defense, Intellectual Property and Information Regulation, International Trade and Business, Maritime, Mergers and Acquisitions, Natural Resources, Securities, Federal Taxation, State and Local Taxation, Technology and Transportation.
Representative Clients: Boston Transit Group; China Ocean Shipping (Group) Company; Embassy of Canada; International Federation of Freight Forwarders Association (FIATA); Japan Fisheries Assn.; National Fisheries Institute; Primavera Laboratories, Inc.; The Prudential Group; Totem Ocean Trailer Express, Inc.; USX Corporation.
Seattle, Washington Office: 1191 Second Avenue, 18th Floor, 98101. Telephone: 206-464-3939. Telecopier: 206-464-0125.
Portland, Oregon Office: Eleventh Floor, 121 S.W. Morrison Street, 97204. Telephone: 503-228-3939. Telecopier: 503-226-0259.
New York, N.Y. Office: Eighth Floor, 599 Broadway, 10012. Telephone: 212-431-8700. Telecopier: 212-334-1278.
See Professional Biographies, WASHINGTON, DISTRICT OF COLUMBIA

Garvie, Pamela Jeanne, (AV) ....'48 '77 C&L.629 B.A., J.D. [Preston G.E.&R.M.]
*PRACTICE AREAS: Transportation Law; Governmental Relations Law; Administrative Law.
Garvin, Peter F., III, (AV) .... '51 '78 C.93 B.S. L.128 J.D. [Jones,D.R.&P.]
*PRACTICE AREAS: Litigation; Contracts; Government Contracts; Construction Contracts.
Garwood, Suzanne Fay '71 '97 C.1145 B.S. L.607 J.D.
(adm. in VA; not adm. in DC) [Ⓐ Kirkpatrick&L.]
*PRACTICE AREAS: Mortgage Banking Law.
Gary, Keisha A. ....'70 '95 C.681 A.B. L.276 J.D. [Ⓐ Dickstein S.M.&O.]
*PRACTICE AREAS: Civil Litigation; Insurance Litigation.
Gary, Michelle Kravtin ....'55 '80 C&L.276 B.A., J.D. 4802 32nd St., N.W.
Garza, Deborah A., (AV) ....'56 '82 C.589 B.A. L.145 J.D. [Fried,F.H.S.&J.]
*PRACTICE AREAS: Antitrust; Litigation.
Garziglia, John F., (AV) ....'50 '79 C.734 B.A. L.910 J.D. [Pepper&C.]
*PRACTICE AREAS: Broadcast Radio; Broadcast Station Transfers; Broadcast Applications; FCC Regulation; FCC Licensing.
Gasaway, Robert R. .... '— '94 C.597 B.A. L.145 J.D. [Kirkland&E.]
*PRACTICE AREAS: Appellate Litigation; Environmental Litigation.
Gasho, Laura B. ....'66 '94 C.813 B.A. L.1066 J.D. [Ⓐ Covington&B.]
Gaskin, Lillian B. '46 '72 C.216 B.A. L.1017 J.D.
Sr. Legal Coun., Govt. Affs. Grp., Amer. Bar Assn.
Gasnier, Philippa T. ....'61 '88 C.446 B.A. L.276 J.D. [Ⓐ Friedlander,M.S.K.&O.]
*PRACTICE AREAS: Banking; Commercial Law; Business Associations Law; Creditors' Rights.
Gaspar, Russell J. ....'50 '75 C&L.276 B.S.F.S., J.D. [Cohen M.]
*PRACTICE AREAS: Civil Litigation and Appeals; Employment Litigation; Employment Law; Federal Administrative Litigation; Commercial Arbitration.
Gasper, Gary J., (AV) ....'58 '83 C.339 B.S. L.209 J.D. [Ⓒ Washington C.]
Gassmann, Michael L., (AV) ....'52 '78 C.893 B.A. L.309 J.D. [Drinker B.&R.]
*PRACTICE AREAS: Directors & Officers Liability and Insurance Law; Professional Liability Insurance Law.
Gassner, Allison S. '72 '98 C.896 B.A. L.861 J.D.
(adm. in PA; not adm. in DC) 401 9th St., NW
Gast, Lisa S. .... '70 '97 C.645 B.S. L.1292 J.D. [Ⓐ Duncan,W.G.&P.]
*PRACTICE AREAS: Energy.
Gasteyer, Philip ....'38 '73 C.145 B.A. L.128 J.D. 900 19th St., N.W., Ste. 400
Gaston, Paul G. .... '53 '79 1150 Connecticut Avenue, N.W., Ninth Floor

Gaston, Paul G., Law Offices of, (AV) '53 '79 C&L.976 B.A., J.D.
1120 Nineteenth Street, N.W., Suite 750, 20036
Telephone: 202-296-5856 Fax: 202-296-4154
Email: pgaston@attglobal.net
Complex Commercial Litigation emphasizing International Trade, Copyright, Trademark, Banking, Contracts and Antitrust.
See Professional Biographies, WASHINGTON, DISTRICT OF COLUMBIA

Gately, Mary E. ....'63 '88 C.93 B.A. L.309 J.D. [Piper M.R.&W.]
*PRACTICE AREAS: Commercial Litigation.
Gates, Jennifer L. '75 '01 C&L.352 B.A., J.D.
(adm. in VA; not adm. in DC) [Ⓐ Ross,D.&B.]
Gates, Kimberly A. .... '74 '00 C.893 B.A. L.309 J.D. [Ⓐ Steptoe&J.]
*PRACTICE AREAS: Litigation.
Gatewood, Christopher E. '72 '00 C.896 B.A. L.893 J.D.
(adm. in VA; not adm. in DC) [Ⓐ Venable,A.B.H.&C.]
*PRACTICE AREAS: Litigation; Intellectual Property; Antitrust Law; Trade Regulation Law.
Gatewood, Joseph T. ....'69 '90 C.446 B.A. L.30 J.D. [Ⓐ Arent F.K.P.&K.]
*PRACTICE AREAS: Health Care; Administrative Law; Litigation; Health Care Fraud.
Gatje, Michael A. ....'61 '86 C.880 B.S. L.945 J.D. [Wickwire G.] (⊙Vienna, VA)
*PRACTICE AREAS: Construction, Public Contract, and Fidelity and Surety Law; Litigation.
Gatti, Joseph V. .... '62 '87 C.367 B.A. L.273 J.D. [Akin,G.S.H.&F.]
*PRACTICE AREAS: Asset Securitization; Corporate Securities.
Gatti, Steven F. ....'68 '95 C.945 B.A. L.273 J.D. [Ⓐ Clifford C.R.&W.]
*PRACTICE AREAS: Securities Regulation and Enforcement; Technology Law; E-Commerce.
Gattuso, Christina M. .... '57 '84 C.1113 B.S. L.64 J.D. [Muldoon M.&F.]
*PRACTICE AREAS: Business Law; Financial Institution Regulations; Holding Companies; Nonprofit and Charitable Organizations; Thrift Institutions.
Gauch, Bonnie Lynn '65 '99
C.1155 B.S. L.1202 J.D. Secs. & Exch. Comm., Div. of Mkt. Regul.
Gauch, James E. ....'64 '89 C.608 B.A. L.145 J.D. [Jones,D.R.&P.]
*PRACTICE AREAS: Litigation.
Gaudet, Caroline .... '54 '94 L.999 LL.B. [Steptoe&J.]
*PRACTICE AREAS: Commercial Transactions; Commercial Real Estate.
Gaudreau, Russell A., Jr., (AV) ....'43 '68 C.454 B.A. L.818 LL.B. [Ropes&G.]
*PRACTICE AREAS: Employee Benefits.
Gauger, Jeffrey A. '70 '95
C.347 B.A. L.665 J.D. Atty., U.S. Merit Systems Protection Board

Gaukler, Paul A. ....'47 '75 C.585 B.S. L.309 J.D. [Shaw P.]
*PRACTICE AREAS: Energy; Administrative; Litigation.

Gaul, John F. ....'68 '94 C&L.276 B.S., J.D. [Ⓐ Hogan&H.]
*PRACTICE AREAS: Corporate; Securities.

Gauthier, Pamela L. ....'72 '97 C.884 B.A. L.273 J.D. [Ⓐ Keller&H.]
*PRACTICE AREAS: Food and Drug Law.

Gavil, Andrew I., (BV) ....'57 '81 C.994 B.A. L.597 J.D. [Ⓒ Powell,G.F.&M.]
*PRACTICE AREAS: Antitrust Law; Civil Litigation.

Gavin, Donald G., (AV) ...... '42 '69 C&L.659 B.S., J.D. [Wickwire G.] (⊙Vienna, VA)
*PRACTICE AREAS: Construction; Public Contract Law; Fidelity and Surety; Environmental; Federal Grants.

Gavin, James H. '61 '91 C.597 B.S. L.262 J.D.
(adm. in NJ; not adm. in DC) 1445 New York Ave., N.W.

Gavin, Stephen Diaz, (AV) ....'55 '84 C.918 B.A. L.128 J.D. [Patton B.]

Gaybrick, Robert J., (AV) .... '50 '78 C.475 B.S. L.128 J.D. [Morgan,L.&B.] (Pat.)

Gaye, Thomas J. ....'48 '76 C.276 A.B. L.724 J.D. Comr., Supr. Ct. of D.C.

Gayle, Alana Patrice .... '52 '86 C.411 B.A. L.273 J.D. Off. of the People's Coun.

Gaylor, Diane C. ....'62 '96 C.37 B.S.E.E. L.309 J.D. [Ⓐ Paul,W.R.W.&G.]

Gaynes, Martin Jay, (AV) ....'33 '60 C.477 A.B. L.569 LL.B. [Ⓒ Schmeltzer,A.&S.]
*PRACTICE AREAS: Health Care Law.

Gaynor, Kevin A., (AV) ....'48 '73 C.184 B.A. L.893 J.D. [Vinson&E.]
*PRACTICE AREAS: Alternative Dispute Resolution; Environmental Law; White Collar Crime; Litigation.

Gayton, Cynthia M. '61 '96 C.273 B.A. L.1209 J.D.
(adm. in VA; not adm. in DC) [Ⓐ Morgan,L.&B.]

Gaziano, Todd F. '63 '90 C.923 B.A. L.145 J.D.
(adm. in TX; not adm. in DC) The Heritage Found.

Gazzola, Robert A., (AV) ....'38 '84 C.262 B.A. L.273 J.D. [Quinn,R.&G.]
*PRACTICE AREAS: Estate Planning; Fiduciary Law; Probate Law; Elder Law; Business Law.

Gdanski, Jeffrey Isaac '72 '95 C.978 L.1040
(adm. in NY; not adm. in DC) [Ⓐ S.Z.Gdanski]

Gdanski, Sam Zalman '48 '72 C.415 B.A. L.1009 J.D.
1101 30th Street, N.W., Suite 500 (⊙Suffern, NY)

Gdanski, Scott Howard '71 '95 C.978 L.1040
(adm. in NY; not adm. in DC) [Ⓐ S.Z.Gdanski]

Gdula, James M. '48 '74 C.645 B.A. L.229 J.D.
(adm. in PA; not adm. in DC) Sr. V.P. & Gen. Coun., Western Develop. Corp.

Geale, Nicholas C. ....'74 '99 C.154 B.A. L.276 J.D. [Ⓐ Thelen R.&P.]
*PRACTICE AREAS: Labor and Employment; Litigation.

Geanacopoulos, David .... '55 '83 C.309 A.B. L.276 J.D. [Akin,G.S.H.&F.]
*PRACTICE AREAS: Public Policy.

Geary, William L., Jr. '56 '92 C.861 B.S.E.E. L.902 J.D.
Asst. Gen. Pat. Coun., Samsung Electronics (Pat.)
*RESPONSIBILITIES: Intellectual Property Licensing; Patents; Litigation.

Geating, Gary C. ....'73 '99 C.276 B.S. L.1375 J.D. [Ⓐ Steptoe&J.]

Gebhard, Cathy ....'52 '85 C.604 B.A. L.659 J.D. [Crowell&M.]
*PRACTICE AREAS: Biotechnology Licensing; Mergers and Acquisitions; Corporate Law.

Gebhardt, Joseph D., (AV) ....'46 '72 C.187 B.A. L.309 J.D. [Gebhardt&Assoc.]
*PRACTICE AREAS: Employment Law; Employment Discrimination; Civil Rights; Federal Civil Practice; Civil Litigation.

Gebhardt & Associates, LLP, (AV) BB
1101 17th Street N.W., Suite 607, 20036
Telephone: 202-496-0400 Fax: 202-496-0404
Email: cday@pressroom.com URL: http://www.lawyers.com/gebhardt
Joseph D. Gebhardt;—Charles Williamson Day, Jr.; Lori N. Nacht; Elaine L. Fitch (Not admitted in DC). Of Counsel: Susan C. Lee.
Employment Law in the District of Columbia and Maryland (Representing Institutions, Corporations, Managers, Employees including Federal and Private Employees and Unions), Discrimination Law, Civil Rights and Women's Rights. General Civil Litigation in all Courts. Matters before the Equal Employment Opportunity Commission, the Merit Systems Protection Board and Local Human Rights Agencies.
See Professional Biographies, WASHINGTON, DISTRICT OF COLUMBIA

Geckle, Robert A., Jr. ....'70 '96 C.478 B.A. L.93 J.D. [Ⓐ Hogan&H.]
*PRACTICE AREAS: Corporate Law; Securities Law.

Gedeon, Richard '70 '00 C.690 B.A. L.818 J.D.
(adm. in MA; not adm. in DC) Supr. Ct.

Gee, Jeffrey J. ....'— '99 C.823 B.A. L.276 J.D. [Ⓐ Dow,L.&A.]

Geer, John J., Jr. '44 '69 C&L.262 B.S., J.D.
(adm. in NY; not adm. in DC) Vice President of Claims, GEICO Corporation

Geffert, Garry G. '48 '77 C.831 B.A. L.33 J.D.
(adm. in FL; not adm. in DC) Migrant Legal Action Program

Gegenheimer, Gary A. '53 '81 C.462 B.A. L.1294 J.D.
(adm. in MA; not adm. in DC) Barents Group, LLC

Gehlmann, Gregory A. ....'— '88 C.201 B.A. L.608 J.D. [Manatt,P.&P.]

Gehman, Julian P. .... '55 '92 C.800 B.A. L.276 J.D. [Ⓒ Mayer,B.&P.]

Gehrig, William L. ....'53 '81 C&L.893 B.A., J.D. [Arter&H.]
*PRACTICE AREAS: Municipal Finance; Corporate Finance; Federal Taxation.

Gehring-Flores, Gaela K. .... '71 '96 C.339 B.A. L.276 J.D. [Ⓐ Paul,W.R.W.&G.]
*PRACTICE AREAS: Litigation.

Gehringer, Michael E. '50 '79 C.229 A.B. L.128 J.D.
(adm. in VA; not adm. in DC) International Monetary Fund‡

Geier, David N. .... '63 '89 C.910 B.S. L.260 J.D. [Ⓐ Schwalb,D.&S.]
*PRACTICE AREAS: Commercial Litigation.

Geier, Jon A., (BV) .... '55 '85 C.119 B.A. L.273 J.D. [Paul,H.J.&W.]
*PRACTICE AREAS: Labor and Employment Law; Title VII; Age Discrimination; Fair Labor Standards Act; Family Medical Leave Act.

Geiger, Susan B. .... '47 '83 C.696 B.A. L.276 J.D. [Preston G.E.&R.M.]

Geimer, William W., (AV) .... '37 '63 C.436 B.S. L.597 J.D. Jamestown Found.

Geise, Elizabeth Runyan ....'55 '81 C.477 B.A. L.309 J.D. [Shea&G.]
*PRACTICE AREAS: Toxic Torts; Environmental; Insurance Coverage.

Gelb, Joseph D., (AV) ....'23 '54 C.754 B.S. L.273 J.D. [Gelb&G.]
*PRACTICE AREAS: Personal Injury; Medical Malpractice; Trials.

Gelb, Roger K. ....'65 '92 C.790 B.A. L.1206 J.D. [Gelb&G.]
*PRACTICE AREAS: Personal Injury; Medical Malpractice; Automobile Accidents; Dental Malpractice; Wrongful Death.

Gelb & Gelb, P.C., (AV)
1120 Connecticut Avenue, N.W., Suite 421, 20036
Telephone: 202-331-7227 Fax: 202-452-1855
Email: lawyers@gelbandgelb.com URL: http://www.lawyers.com/gelbandgelb
Joseph D. Gelb; Roger K. Gelb.
Personal Injury, Medical Malpractice Law, Automobile Accidents, Truck Accidents, Motorcycle Accidents, Bus Accidents, Surgeons Liability.
See Professional Biographies, WASHINGTON, DISTRICT OF COLUMBIA

Gelband, Stephen L., (AV) .... '31 '55 C.976 A.B. L.309 J.D. [Hewes,G.L.&D.]

Gelbman, Tessa J. ....'74 '99 C.188 B.S. L.309 J.D. [Ⓐ Littler M.]
*PRACTICE AREAS: Labor and Employment.

Gelchinsky, Jonathan M. .... '73 '00 C.1036 B.A. L.904 J.D. [Ⓐ Finnegan,H.F.G.&D.]
*PRACTICE AREAS: Domain Name Infringement; Internet Trademark Law; Trademark Infringement; Trademark Prosecution; Trademark Protection.

Geldon, Anne W. ....'47 '75 C.188 B.A. L.309 J.D. [Ⓒ Sutherland A.&B.]
*PRACTICE AREAS: Estate Planning; Estate and Gift Taxation; Living Trusts; Estate Administration; Trust Administration.

Geldzahler, Janet Thiele .... '54 '80 C&L.893 B.A., J.D. [Ⓒ Sullivan&C.]

Gelenian, Milton C., (AV) ....'31 '58 C.1016 B.A. L.276 J.D. 1634 Eye St., N.W.

Gelfond, Frederic J. '65 '91 C.1044 B.S. L.94 J.D.
(adm. in NY; not adm. in DC) 555 12th Street, NW

Gell, Stephen N., (BV) .... '38 '63 C.197 A.B. L.659 LL.B. [S.N.Gell]

Gell, Stephen N., P.C., (BV)
1101 30th Street, N.W., Suite 500, 20007
Telephone: 202-625-8311 Fax: 703-522-5503
Email: sgell@his.com
Stephen N. Gell.
Land Use, Zoning, Boundary Disputes, Building Permits, Street and Alley Closings, Real Estate Tax Appeals, Alcoholic Beverage Commission Licenses, Property Issues.
See Professional Biographies, WASHINGTON, DISTRICT OF COLUMBIA

Geller, Kenneth S., (AV) .... '47 '72 C.563 B.A. L.309 J.D. [Mayer,B.&P.]

Gellhorn, Ernest .... '35 '62 C&L.494 B.A., LL.B. 2907 Normanstone Ln., N.W.

Gelman, Jeffrey H., (AV) ....'59 '84 C.156 B.A. L.273 J.D. [Greenstein D.&L.]

Geltman, Edward A., (AV) .... '46 '71 C.264 A.B. L.273 J.D. [Squire,S.&D.]
*PRACTICE AREAS: Antitrust and Trade Regulation; Advertising and Marketing Law; Complex Litigation; Grand Jury Practice; Medical Antitrust.

Geltner, Michael E. ....'41 '66 C.659 B.A. L.178 LL.B. 10 E St., SE

Genasci, Matthew '74 '01 C.1239 B.S. L.813 J.D.
(adm. in NY; not adm. in DC) [Ⓐ McKee N.]
*PRACTICE AREAS: Taxation.

Genderson, Bruce R., (AV) .... '52 '77 C.228 B.A. L.659 J.D. [Williams&C.]
*PRACTICE AREAS: Civil Litigation; Complex Litigation; Government Contracts; Intellectual Property; Patent Litigation.

Geneson, David F., (AV) .... '47 '74 C.688 B.S. L.472 J.D. [Hunton&W.]
*PRACTICE AREAS: Litigation.

Genetski, Christian S. ....'70 '95 C.88 B.A. L.880 J.D. [Ⓐ Kirkland&E.]
*PRACTICE AREAS: Cyber Law; Information Technology; Intellectual Property; Litigation.

Geniesse, Robert J., (AV) ....'29 '58 C.951 B.A. L.309 LL.B. [Debevoise&P.] ‡
*PRACTICE AREAS: Litigation; International Trade Law; Securities Regulation Law.

Géno, Sharon Wilson ....'67 '92 C.861 B.A. L.276 J.D. [Reno&C.]
*PRACTICE AREAS: Legislative Practice; Administrative Law; Affordable Housing; Real Estate Transactions; Corporate Law.

Genser, Erick J., (BV) .... '53 '79 C.30 B.S.B.A. L.94 J.D. [Woodley,G.&M.]
*PRACTICE AREAS: Collective Bargaining; Employment Discrimination Law; Public Sector Labor Relations Law; Railway Labor Act Law; Employee Benefit Plans Law.

Gentemann, Evelynn M. '61 '90
C.893 B.A. L.30 J.D. Sr. Atty., MCI Communications Corporation

Gentile, Beth-Ann F. ....'43 '69 C.771 B.A. L.94 J.D. 3519 Rodman St., N.W.

Gentile, Carmen L., (AV) ....'40 '68 C.309 A.B. L.659 LL.B. [Bruder,G.&M.]
*PRACTICE AREAS: Utility Law; Appellate Practice; Antitrust Law.

Gentin, Andrew N. ....'— '97 C.31 B.A. L.276 J.D. [Ⓐ Manatt,P.&P.]

Gentner, Marsha G. .... '54 '78 C.347 B.S. L.276 J.D. [Jacobson,H.]
*PRACTICE AREAS: Intellectual Property Law; Information Technology; Computer Law; Trade Regulation; Trademarks.

Genzer, Jeffrey C., (AV) .... '56 '83 C.311 B.A. L.904 J.D. [Duncan,W.G.&P.]
*PRACTICE AREAS: Energy; Legislative Law; Environmental Law.

Geolot, Alan C. ....'54 '79 C.103 A.B. L.893 J.D. [Sidley A.B.&W.]

George, Allison C. .... '— '93 C.976 B.A. L.228 J.D. [Ⓒ Foley&L.]
*PRACTICE AREAS: International Business Law (40%); White Collar Crime (40%); Commercial Litigation (20%).

George, Christopher E. .... '67 '93 C.893 B.A. L.245 J.D. [Ⓐ Fitch,E.T.&F.]
*PRACTICE AREAS: Trademark; Intellectual Property; Litigation; Corporate Law; Environmental Law.

George, J. Russell '63 '89 C.329 B.A. L.309 J.D.
(adm. in NY; not adm. in DC) U.S. House of Rep., Committee on Govt. Reform

George, Keith E. '55 '91 C&L.273 B.S.E.E., J.D.
(adm. in VA; not adm. in DC; Pat.) [McDermott,W.&E.]

George, Latrice A. ....'— '00 C.188 B.S. L.178 J.D. [Ⓐ Morgan,L.&B.]

George, Leo I., P.C., (AV) '36 '63
C.546 B.A. L.276 J.D. WinStar Telecommunications, Inc.

George, Louis J. .... '67 '92 C.461 B.S. L.276 J.D. Natl. Veterans Legal Servs. Prog.

George, Mary Jo, (BV) '60 '85 C.276 A.B. L.273 J.D.
(adm. in MD; not adm. in DC) [Ballard S.A.&I.]
*PRACTICE AREAS: Real Estate; Housing.

George, Ryan L. .... '73 '99 C.901 B.A. L.665 J.D. [Ⓐ Ritter E.&N.]
*PRACTICE AREAS: Public Finance; Federal Income Tax.

George, Susan M. '60 '88 C&L.560 B.A., J.D.
(adm. in NM; not adm. in DC) Biodiversity Coun., Defenders of Wildlife

George, Tracey E. ....'67 '94 C.802 B.A.B.S. L.813 J.D. 2555 M. St., N.W.

Georgi, Kay, (AV) .... '63 '90 C&L.188 B.A., J.D. [Coudert B.]
*PRACTICE AREAS: International Trade.

Georis, Fabrice ....'65 '95 C&L.893 B.A., J.D. 1775 Pennsylvania Ave.

Gerald, Tilman L. .... '46 '77 C&L.329 B.B.A., J.D. 2021 L St., N.W.

Geraldo, Manuel R., (AV) ....'50 '78 C.776 B.S. L.705 J.D. [Robinson&G.]

Gerber, Marc S. .... '67 '94 C.659 B.S. L.276 J.D. [Ⓐ Skadden,A.S.M.&F.]

Gerber, Melanie K. ....'47 '89 C.446 B.A. L.276 J.D. [Ⓒ Patton B.]

Gerber, Steven J. ....'69 '95 C.367 B.A. L.30 J.D. [Ⓐ Cole,R.&B.]
*PRACTICE AREAS: Telecommunications Law; Cable TV; CLEC Franchising; Pole Attachments.

Gerdes, Gregory C. .... '72 '98 C.475 B.A. L.477 J.D. [Ⓐ Gibson,D.&C.]
*PRACTICE AREAS: International Trade.

Gerdes, Ronald W. '47 '72
C.201 B.A. L.477 J.D. [Sandler,T.&R.] (⊙L.A., San Fran., CA)
*PRACTICE AREAS: Customs Law; International Trade Law.

Gerdine, Clint A. '70 '98 C.813 B.S. L.705 J.D.
(adm. in VA; not adm. in DC; See Pat. Sect.) [Ⓐ Kenyon&K.] ‡
*PRACTICE AREAS: Intellectual Property.

Gere, Elizabeth Sarah, (AV) ....'47 '73 C.207 B.A. L.273 J.D. [Ross,D.&B.]

Geren, Natalia W. ....'73 '99 C.326 B.B.A. L.796 J.D. [Ⓐ Dyer E.&J.]
*PRACTICE AREAS: International Trade and Transactions.

Gerg, Ann Marie ....'64 '90 C.25 B.A. L.188 J.D. 2300 N St., N.W.

Gergen, Michael J. ....'60 '93 C.33 B.A. L.569 J.D. [Ⓐ Latham&W.]
*PRACTICE AREAS: Regulated Industries; Utility Law; Energy; Antitrust and Trade Regulation; Administrative Law.

Gerhardt, Bonnie R. .... '70 '97 C.951 B.A. L.902 J.D. [Ⓐ Levine,B.B.&B.]
*PRACTICE AREAS: Telecommunications.

Gerkin, Daniel J. .... '75 '01 C.276 B.A. L.273 J.D. [Ⓐ Kirkland&E.]
*PRACTICE AREAS: Customs Law; International Trade.

Gerlach, Christopher M. '72 '98 C.174 B.S. L.208 J.D.
(adm. in MD; not adm. in DC) [Ⓢ Fulbright&J.]
*PRACTICE AREAS: Intellectual Property; Litigation.

Gerlach, Helmut E. ....'64 '97 C.445 B.A. L.446 J.D. [Ⓐ Shapiro,L.&S.]
*PRACTICE AREAS: Real Estate; Business Law; Commercial Transactions; Secured Lending; Commercial Loans.

Germain, Regina '61 '89 C.276 B.S.F.S. L.665 J.D.
(adm. in PA; not adm. in DC) United Nations High Comm. for Refergees

Germanis, Intra L. . . . . '67 '92 C.188 B.S. L.893 J.D. [B Paul,H.J.&W.]
*PRACTICE AREAS: Employment Law.
Gernhard, Eileen B. Salathé . . . . '65 '92 C.938 B.A. L.276 J.D. [B Bergeson&C.]
*PRACTICE AREAS: Federal Insecticide, Fungicide and Rodenticide Act (FIFRA); Resource Conservation and Recovery Act (RCRA); Superfund; Pesticide Regulation; Chemical Regulation.
Geroe, Michael R. . . . . '68 '94 C.276 B.S.F.S. L.178 J.D. [Williams M.]
*PRACTICE AREAS: International Business Law; Corporate Law; Export Regulation; Antitrust.
Geroff, Fani Cyd . . . . '74 '99 C.188 B.S. L.659 J.D. [A Akin,G.S.H.&F.]
*PRACTICE AREAS: Litigation.
Gerrish, Jeffrey D. . . . . '69 '94 C.1044 B.A. L.228 J.D. [A Skadden,A.S.M.&F.]
Gersch, David P., (AV) . . . . '56 '82 C.604 A.B. L.569 J.D. [Arnold&P.]
*PRACTICE AREAS: Litigation; Antitrust.
Gersh, Victor B. . . . . . '47 '73 C.475 B.A. L.273 J.D. 1150 Connecticut Ave., N.W., 9th Fl.
Gershengorn, Ian Heath . . . . '67 '94 C&L.309 A.B., J.D. [Jenner&B.]
*PRACTICE AREAS: Civil Litigation; Appellate Practice; Communications.
Gershoni, Tammy '59 '00 C.569 B.S. L.273 J.D.
(adm. in VA; not adm. in DC) [A Shaw P.]
*PRACTICE AREAS: Communications Law.
Gerson, Marc J. . . . . '68 '93 C.1365 B.B.A. L.273 J.D. [A Skadden,A.S.M.&F.]
*PRACTICE AREAS: Taxation.
Gerson, Stuart M., (AV) '44 '68
C.645 B.A. L.276 J.D. [Epstein B.&G.] (©New York, NY)
*PRACTICE AREAS: Civil Litigation; Criminal Law; Antitrust; Health Care; Securities Fraud.
Gerstein, John R., (AV) . . . . '51 '75 C&L.477 A.B., J.D. [Ross,D.&B.]
Gerstell, Glenn S. . . . . '51 '77 C.569 B.A. L.178 J.D. [Milbank,T.H.&M.]
Gertler, Nicholas B. . . . . '— '99 C.893 B.S. L.309 J.D. [A Latham&W.]
*PRACTICE AREAS: Environmental Law.
Gertz, Gary D. . . . . '49 '76 C.276 B.S. L.64 J.D. GEICO Corp.
Gervasio, Phyllis Jo '53 '78 C.262 B.S. L.1209 J.D.
(adm. in VA; not adm. in DC) 3200 Chestnut St., N.W.‡
Gervin, L. Rachel . . . . '69 '98 C.1494 B.A. L.329 J.D. [A Crowell&M.]
Gerwin, Edward F., Jr. . . . . '55 '80 C.884 B.A. L.276 J.D. [Winston&S.]
*PRACTICE AREAS: International Trade; Administrative Law; Government.
Gery, Yoav Karel . . . . '68 '94 C.228 A.B. L.273 J.D. Sr. Coun., Marriott International, Inc.
*RESPONSIBILITIES: Lodging Development.
Geselowitz, Daniel A. . . . . '55 '82 C.311 B.S. L.813 [A Armstrong,W.H.M.&N.]
*PRACTICE AREAS: Preparation and Prosecution of Patent Applications; Appeals before Board of Patent Appeals and Interferences; Petitions to Commissioner of Patents and Trademarks.
Geske, Alvin J., (AV) . . . . '42 '67 C.802 B.A. L.145 J.D. [B Holland&K.]
*PRACTICE AREAS: Federal Income; Estate Law; Excise Tax Law.
Geske, Michael R. . . . . '61 '90 C.999 B.A. L.1119 J.D. [B Arnold&P.]
*PRACTICE AREAS: Antitrust; Litigation.
Gesner, Lawrence H., (AV) . . . . '58 '83 C.273 B.B.A. L.276 J.D. [Arter&H.]
Gessler, Joshua J. '69 '00 C.30 B.A. L.1209 J.D.
(adm. in PA; not adm. in DC) [A Fried,F.H.S.&J.]
Gessner, William J. '50 '83 C.443 B.A. L.64 J.D.
(adm. in MD; not adm. in DC) [A A.F.Konopka]
*PRACTICE AREAS: Commercial Real Estate; Residential Real Estate; Landlord and Tenant Law; Probate; Lender Representation.
Getlan, Myles S. . . . . '— '95 C.390 B.A. L.665 J.D. [A Miller&C.]
*PRACTICE AREAS: International Trade.
Gewirtz, Joel D. . . . . '46 '71 C.569 A.B. L.309 J.D. National Educ. Assn.
Gewirz, Bernard S. . . . . '26 '53 C.871 B.S. L.276 J.D. 1730 K St., N.W.‡
Geyer, Laura Talley . . . . '68 '98 C.604 B.A. L.904 J.D. [A Jones,D.R.&P.]
Ghatt, Jeneba Jalloh . . . . '73 '98 C.446 B.A. L.128 J.D. [A Willkie F.&G.]
*PRACTICE AREAS: Telecommunications Law; Administrative Law; Federal Regulatory Law.
Gherardi, Thomas G., (AV) . . . . '42 '66 C.262 A.B. L.569 J.D. [T.G.Gherardi]

Gherardi, Thomas G., P.C., (AV)
1229 Nineteenth Street, N.W., 20036
Telephone: 202-223-1535 FAX: 202-429-4912
Email: tomg@counsellor.com URL: http://www.lawyers.com/thomasgherardi
Thomas G. Gherardi.
General Practice including Negotiation of Complex Transactions; Television, Music and Multi Media Acquisition, Production and Distribution; Communications Law; and Licensing of Copyrights, Trademarks and Intellectual Properties.
See Professional Biographies, WASHINGTON, DISTRICT OF COLUMBIA

Ghiladi, Kathy S. . . . . '67 '91 C.30 B.A. L.446 J.D. [A Feldesman,T.L.F.&B.]
*PRACTICE AREAS: Government Contracts; Federal Grants; Health Care Law; Litigation; Employment Law.
Ghosh, Paramita . . . . '67 '99 C.659 B.S.E.E. L.276 J.D. [A Wilmer,C.&P.] (Pat.)
Giaccia, Andrew A. . . . . '59 '84 C&L.276 A.B., J.D. [Chadbourne&P.]
Giaimo, Christopher J., Jr. . . . . '69 '95 C.728 B.S. L.724 J.D. [A Arent F.K.P.&K.]
*PRACTICE AREAS: Creditors Rights; Bankruptcy; Litigation.
Giammichele, Carla N. '63 '89 C.1044 B.A. L.904 J.D.
(adm. in PA; not adm. in DC) One Massachusetts Ave., N.W.
Giancarlo, Angela Elizabeth '63 '96 C.856 B.A. L.128 J.D.
(adm. in VA; not adm. in DC) [A Hogan&H.]
*PRACTICE AREAS: Telecommunications; Wireless; Common Carrier.
Giannetti, John A., Jr. '64 '95 C.105 B.S. L.446 J.D.
(adm. in MD; not adm. in DC) [A Jackson&C.]
*PRACTICE AREAS: Telecommunications Law; Real Property; Litigation.
Giannotto, Michael S., (AV) . . . . '53 '79 C.659 B.A. L.309 J.D. [Shea&G.]
*PRACTICE AREAS: Environmental Law; Environmental Litigation; Complex Insurance Litigation; Products Liability Litigation; Government Contracts Litigation.
Gibbens, Wayne '36 '67
C.845 B.A. L.846 LL.B. Pres., Mid-Continent Oil & Gas Association
Gibbon, Frederick B. . . . . '45 '72 C.976 B.A. L.893 J.D. [Thompson H.]
*PRACTICE AREAS: Employee Benefits Law.
Gibbon, Thomas R. . . . . '48 '74 C.105 B.A. L.1294 J.D. [Bell,B.&L.]
*PRACTICE AREAS: Communications Law.
Gibbons, Boyd H., III '37 '62 C&L.37 B.S., LL.B.
(adm. in AZ; not adm. in DC) National Geographic Magazine
Gibbons, David A., (AV) . . . . '— '91 C.893 B.A. L.245 J.D. [King&S.]
*PRACTICE AREAS: Corporate and Finance.
Gibbons, Jean M. . . . . '64 '95 C.788 B.A. L.1209 J.D. 3000 K St., NW, Ste. 300
Gibbons, John A. '73 '98 C.446 B.A. L.128 J.D.
(adm. in MD; not adm. in DC) [A Dickstein S.M.&O.]
*PRACTICE AREAS: Litigation.
Gibbons, Kathleen . . . . '49 '81 C.741 B.A. L.273 J.D. Federal Natl. Mtge. Assn.
Gibbons, Lance E. . . . . '— '00 C.473 B.S. L.607 J.D. [A Morgan,L.&B.]
Gibbons, Marlene F. . . . . '51 '81 C.1109 B.A. L.692 J.D. [B Cohen,M.H.&T.]
*PRACTICE AREAS: Civil Litigation; Health Care.
Gibbons, Richard F., Jr. '62 '87 C.321 A.B. L.945 J.D.
Asst. Comwlth. Atty. [A Lewis]
*PRACTICE AREAS: Family Law (95%); Commercial Litigation (5%).
Gibbons, Sam M. . . . . '20 '47 C&L.260 J.D. [Gibbons,M.G.&G.] (©Tampa, FL)
Gibbons, Melendi, Gibbons and Garcia, (AV)
1455 Pennsylvania Ave. (©Tallahassee, Tampa, FL)
Gibbs, Jeffrey L. . . . . '45 '73 C.102 B.A. L.597 J.D. [Bredhoff&K.]
Gibbs, Jeffrey N., (AV) . . . . '53 '78 C.674 B.A. L.569 J.D. [Hyman,P.&M.]
Gibbs, Kirstin E. . . . . '68 '97 C.1031 B.A. L.128 J.D. [A Sutherland A.&B.]
*PRACTICE AREAS: Energy and Commodities Division.
Gibbs, Lawrence B., (AV) . . . . '— '63 C.976 B.A. L.846 LL.B. [Miller&C.]
*PRACTICE AREAS: Taxation; Tax Litigation; Legislative Practice; Corporate Taxation; International Taxation.
Gibian, Barbara M. . . . . '— '94 C.300 B.A. L.276 J.D. [A Latham&W.]
Gibian, Craig J. '70 '97 C.674 A.B. L.309 J.D.
(adm. in NY; not adm. in DC) [A Shearman&S.]
Gibian, Roger M. . . . . '68 '96 C.881 B.A. L.930 J.D. [A Baker&M.]
*PRACTICE AREAS: Public Contracts and Utilities; Regulatory Law; Administrative Law.
Giblin, Jennifer A. . . . . '66 '92 C.976 B.A. L.659 J.D. [B Shaw P.]
Giblin, Mary E. '62 '88 C.103 B.A. L.30 J.D.
Asst. Gen. Coun., CareFirst Blue Cross Blue Shiels
Gibson, Douglas G. '65 '90 C.367 B.S. L.309 J.D. 6151 30th St. NW
Gibson, Frederick W., Jr. . . . . '55 '81 C&L.846 B.A., J.D. F.D.I.C.
Gibson, James . . . . '68 '97 C.976 B.A. L.893 J.D. [A Williams&C.]
*PRACTICE AREAS: Copyrights; Criminal Defense; Federal Civil Practice; Legal Ethics and Professional Responsibility.
Gibson, Kumiki . . . . '59 '88 C.309 A.B. L.588 J.D. [Williams&C.]
*PRACTICE AREAS: Civil Litigation; Criminal Defense; Employment Discrimination.
Gibson, Richard W. . . . . '65 '90 C.262 A.B. L.128 J.D. [Beins,A.&K.]
Gibson, Sharon Lynn . . . . '63 '92 C.839 B.S. L.245 J.D. [S Ross,D.&B.]
Gibson, Stephen L., (AV) '42 '67
C.352 A.B. L.309 LL.B. 1050 Connecticut Avenue, N.W.‡
Gibson, William F., II . . . . '68 '97 C.893 B.A. L.1019 J.D. [A McManus,S.A.&D.]
*PRACTICE AREAS: Construction Law; Litigation.

Gibson, Dunn & Crutcher LLP, (AV)
1050 Connecticut Avenue, N.W., 20036-5306 ©
Telephone: 202-955-8500 Telecopier: 202-467-0539
URL: http://www.gibsondunn.com
Partners: John F. Olson; Robert C. Bonner (Washington, D.C. and Los Angeles, California Offices); William J. Kilberg; Peter L. Baumbusch; Joseph H. Price; Cantwell Faulkner Muckenfuss III; Christopher H. Buckley Jr.; David R. Johnson; Donald Harrison; Wayne A. Schrader; Peter H. Turza; Michael L. Denger; F. Joseph Warin; Daniel J. Plaine; James R. Loftis, III; Howard B. Adler; Larry L. Simms; John H. Sturc; Joseph Kattan; Robert C. Eager; Stephen I. Glover (Also at Los Angeles, CA); Baruch A. Fellner; Arthur David Pasternak; Terence P. Ross; John C. Millian; Raymond B. Ludwiszewski; Amy G. Rudnick; Brian J. Lane (Not admitted in DC); Julia A. Dahlberg; Theodore J. Boutrous, Jr. (Los Angeles, California and Washington, D.C. Offices); Judith A. Lee; Ronald O. Mueller; Douglas R. Cox; Thomas G. Hungar; Michael F. Flanagan; Stephanie Tsacoumis; Miguel A. Estrada (Not admitted in DC); Christopher J. Bellini; Peter P. Murphy. Advisory Counsel: Stephen E. Tallent; Theodore B. Olson (Washington, D.C. and Los Angeles, California Offices); Peter J. Wallison; Aulana L. Peters (Not admitted in DC; Los Angeles, California and Washington, D.C. Offices). Of Counsels: Gracia M. Berg; Paul Blankenstein; Andrea F. Dynes; Amy L. Goodman; Linda Noonan; Malcolm R. Pfunder; Diana Gale Richard; Victoria P. Rostow; Richard A. Zimmer (Not admitted in DC). Special Counsel: Derry Dean Sparlin Jr. Associates: Elise C. Keegan; Daniel W. Nelson; Peter E. Seley; D. Jarrett Arp; Jonathan K. Tycko; Alice W. Detwiler (Not admitted in DC); David W.T. Daniels; Delwen A. Jones (Not admitted in DC); Todd D. Kantorczyk; Hassan A. Zavareei; Gavin A. Beske (Not admitted in DC); Antoinette DeCamp (Not admitted in DC); Hill B. Wellford, III; Paul DeCamp (Not admitted in DC); Michael J. Collins (Not admitted in DC); Alisa Babitz; Robert C. Blume; Deborah J. Katz; Jacqueline E. Coleman; David B. Salmons (Not admitted in DC); Lisa A. Murray; Andrew S. Tulumello; Christopher E. Humber; Corinne A. Lammers; James D. Slear; Montgomery N. Kosma; Thomas H. Dupree, Jr.; John Christopher Wood (Not admitted in DC); Megan A. Barnett; Michael J. Scanlon; Gillian McPhee; Scott E. Silverstein; Jason C. Schwartz; Albert Y. Kim; Mark E. Papadopoulos; Curtis E. Gannon; Rachel A. Clark; Scott L. Craddock; Jeffrey W. Gladstone; Gregory C. Gerdes; Harry M. Gruber; Colin L. Black; Joshua Lipton; Michael K. Murphy; Daniel A. Cantu; Lauren S. Goodman; Brian J. Rohal; Mark K. Moller (Not admitted in DC); Anne H. Lee; Kathleen M. Kedian; Nicolle Sciara (Not admitted in DC); Jeffrey A. Wadsworth; Jennifer G. Loy (Not admitted in DC); Lauren Elizabeth Schmidt (Not admitted in DC); Jason M. Anthony; Elizabeth A. Ising; Benjamin H. Rippeon; Kevin M. St. John (Not admitted in DC); Benjamin C. Adams; Tanya Axenson Macallair; Dawn Figueiras (Not admitted in DC); Cory J. Skolnick (Not admitted in DC). Staff Attorneys: Andrew A. Cline; Danielle K. Moskowitz; Sydney M. Smith.
General Civil Trial and Appellate Practice, State and Federal Courts. Antitrust Law. Specialized Criminal Defense. General Corporation, Securities, Administrative, Labor and Employment, Employee Benefits, Taxation, Estate Planning, Probate and Trust, International Business, Entertainment, Real Estate Development and Financing, Banking, Commercial, Insolvency, Bankruptcy and Reorganization, Natural Resources, Oil and Gas, Environmental, Energy, Municipal and Public Utility Law.
Los Angeles, California Office: 333 South Grand Avenue. Telephone: 213-229-7000. Telecopier: 213-229-7520; 213-229-7268.
See Professional Biographies, WASHINGTON, DISTRICT OF COLUMBIA

Gick, Thomas A. . . . . '56 '82 C.999 B.B.A. L.1044 J.D. [Sutherland A.&B.]
*PRACTICE AREAS: Federal Taxation; Federal Tax Controversies; Insurance.
Gideon, Kenneth W., (AV) . . . . '46 '71 C.309 A.B. L.976 J.D. [Skadden,A.S.M.&F.]
Gidley, J. Mark, (AV) . . . . '61 '87 C.378 B.S. L.178 J.D. [White&C.]
*PRACTICE AREAS: Antitrust; Mergers and Acquisitions; Commercial Litigation.
Gies, Thomas P., (AV) . . . . '50 '76 C.602 B.A. L.273 J.D. [Crowell&M.]
Giese, Robert B., (AV) . . . . '49 '77 C.30 B.A. L.767 J.D. 3811 Garfield St., N.W.
Giffin, Christina P. '67 '99 C.685 B.A. L.273 J.D.
(adm. in VA; not adm. in DC) [A Williams&C.]
Giffin, Gordon D., (AV) . . . . '49 '74 C.228 B.A. L.245 J.D. [Long A.&N.] ©
*PRACTICE AREAS: Administrative Law; Energy; Utilities; Communications and Media; Contracts.
Gifford, C. Nichole '74 '99 C.834 B.S. L.836 J.D.
(adm. in TN; not adm. in DC; See Pat. Sect.) [A Rothwell,F.E.&M.]
*PRACTICE AREAS: Intellectual Property.
Gifford, Dirk . . . . '68 '93 C.659 B.S. L.770 J.D. [A Baker&M.]
*PRACTICE AREAS: Commercial Litigation; Taxation.
Gigot, Thomas S., (AV) . . . . '58 '84 C.436 B.S. L.276 J.D. [Groom]
*PRACTICE AREAS: Employee Benefits; Labor and Employment; Pension and Profit Sharing; Insurance Defense; ERISA.
Giguere, Paul G. . . . . '31 '59 C.1107 A.B. L.276 J.D. [B Sandler,T.&R.]
*PRACTICE AREAS: Customs Law; International Trade Law.
Gihring, Susan . . . . '76 '01 C.494 B.A. L.145 J.D. [A Steptoe&J.]
*PRACTICE AREAS: International Law; International Trade.
Gil, Kelly Huckno . . . . '70 '97 C.1349 B.A. L.64 J.D. [A Counts,P.-D.&D.]
Gilbert, Jan S., (BV) . . . . '65 '90 C.012 B.A. L.94 J.D. [Jenkens&G.]
*PRACTICE AREAS: Franchising; Product Distribution.
Gilbert, John A., Jr. . . . . '57 '92 C.462 B.A. L.128 J.D. [Hyman,P.&M.]
Gilbert, Peter R. . . . . '— '65 C.31 A.B. L.309 LL.B. [Feith&Z.] (©Jerusalem, Israel)
Gilbert, Rebecca L. '69 '94 C.264 B.A. L.464 J.D.
(adm. in MD; not adm. in DC) 3018 Q. St. NW #2
Gilbert, Robin H. . . . . '52 '86 C.1356 B.S. L.276 J.D. [Collier S.S.]
*PRACTICE AREAS: Customs Law; International Trade.
Gilbert, Scott D., (AV) . . . . '53 '79 C.597 B.A. L.145 J.D. [Gilbert H.&R.]
*PRACTICE AREAS: Arbitration; Alternative Dispute Resolution; Mediation; Insurance; Products Liability.

Gilbert Heintz & Randolph LLP, (AV) BR
1350 I Street, NW Suite 200, 20005-3324
Telephone: 202-772-2200 Facsimile: 202-772-3333
URL: http://www.ghrdc.com
Members of Firm: Scott D. Gilbert; John E. Heintz; David B. Killalea; Rachel S. Kronowitz; Craig J. Litherland (Not admitted in DC; Resident, Austin Office); Richard D. Milone, Jr.; Bette M. Orr; Mark A. Packman; Jerome C. Randolph (Not admitted in DC); Richard D. Shore; Gary Thompson. Associates: Jennifer A. Brennan (Not admitted in DC); Barry I. Buchman; Jonathan M. Cohen;
(This Listing Continued)

Gilbert Heintz & Randolph LLP (Continued)

Elizabeth H. Feinberg; Ted J. Feldman; Erin Elizabeth Johnson (Not admitted in DC); Richard D. Martindale (Not admitted in DC); Glenn Schlactus (Not admitted in DC); Lara Hope Schwartz; Divonne Smoyer; Jason D. Wallach.
Insurance Coverage, Commercial Litigation, Alternative Dispute Resolution.
See Professional Biographies, WASHINGTON, DISTRICT OF COLUMBIA

Gilbertsen, Thomas E. ....'61 '89 C.608 B.A. L.188 J.D. [Collier S.S.]
*PRACTICE AREAS: Intellectual Property; Antitrust; Litigation; Commercial Law; Employment Law.
Gilbertson, Larry R. '47 '73
C.301 B.A. L.30 J.D. Gen. Coun., Global Vacation Group, Inc.
Gilbertson, Ronald E. .... '54 '79 C&L.446 B.A., J.D. [Bell,B.&L.]
*PRACTICE AREAS: Black Lung Disability Defense; Coal; Mining Law; Government Contracts; Construction Claims.
Gilbreath, Karen Griffith ....'65 '90 C.1034 B.S. L.276 J.D. Ernst & Young
Gilbride, Ann DeBaets ....'56 '90 C.1049 B.A. L.276 J.D. 1233 Kearney St., N.E.
Gilburt, Tony '70 '97 C.994 B.A. L.724 J.D.
(adm. in NY; not adm. in DC) 1200 New Hampshire Ave., N.W.
Gilchrist, Bruce W., (AV) .... '51 '81 C&L.178 B.A., J.D. [Hogan&H.]
*PRACTICE AREAS: Corporate Finance; Securities Offerings; Mergers and Acquisitions; Real Estate Investment Trusts; Bankruptcy Reorganization.
Gilchrist, Gregory M. ....'— '00 C.813 A.B. L.178 J.D. [Ⓐ Williams&C.]
Gildenhorn, Joseph B. ....'29 '54 C.446 B.S. L.976 LL.B. [Brown,G.&J.]
Gilder, Mark A. ....'48 '76 C.128 B.A. L.64 J.D. 500 Morse St. N.E.
Giles, John E. '25 '52 C&L.575 B.S., J.D.
(adm. in NC; not adm. in DC) The Wexler Grp.
Giles, Sharon Cummings ....'— '85 C.790 B.A. L.276 J.D. [Robins,K.M.&C.]
*PRACTICE AREAS: Commercial Litigation; Business Litigation; Employment Law; Civil Litigation; Antitrust.
Gilfoyle, Nathalie F. P., (AV) '49 '74 C.320 B.A. L.893 J.D.
Dep. Gen. Coun., American Psychological Association
Gilgore, Lance S. .... '57 '84 C.156 B.A. L.802 J.D. [L.S.Gilgore]
Gilgore, Lance S., Law Office of ....1050 17th Street, NW
Giliberti, Mary T. '66 '92 C.309 B.A. L.976 J.D.
Staff Atty., Bazelon Ctr. for Mental Health Law
Gill, Christine Meagher, (AV) ....'49 '76 C.1044 B.A. L.904 J.D. [McDermott,W.&E.]
Gill, Edward J., Jr. ....'47 '74 C.276 A.B. L.128 J.D. [Thompson C.]
*PRACTICE AREAS: Administrative Law; Construction Law; Legislative Law.
Gill, John J. ... '39 '64 C.524 B.S. L.276 J.D. Gen. Coun., American Bankers Association
Gill, Patrick D., (AV) ...... '44 '68 C.994 B.A. L.569 J.D. [Rode&Q.] (⊙New York, NY)
Gill, Robert C., II ....'60 '86 C.886 B.A. L.1209 J.D. [Slavit&G.]
Gill, T. Nicholas .... '54 '82 C.902 B.S. L.30 J.D. 1722 Wisconsin Ave., N.W.
Gill, Vernon S. .... '42 '67 C&L.329 B.A., LL.B. Gen. Coun., Wash. Met. Police Dept.
Gilleece, Mary Ann, (AV) ....'40 '72 C.184 B.A. L.818 J.D. [Manatt,P.&P.]
Gillen, Bradley K. '76 '00 C.301 B.A. L.893 J.D.
(adm. in VA; not adm. in DC) [Ⓐ Wiley R.&F.]
Gillen, Neal P., (AV) '37 '65 C.569 B.S. L.276 J.D.
Exec. V.P. & Gen. Coun., American Cotton Shippers Association
Gillespie, Alexander H. '59 '86
C.745 B.A. L.910 J.D. [Ⓒ Bonner K.T.&C.] (⊙New York, NY)
*PRACTICE AREAS: Federal Civil Practice; Insurance; Casualty Insurance; Insurance Coverage; Environmental Law.
Gillespie, Gardner F., (AV) .... '45 '73 C.951 B.A. L.893 J.D. [Hogan&H.]
*PRACTICE AREAS: Communications and Media; Cable TV; Cable Franchising; Telecommunications Law; Civil Litigation.
Gillespie, James P. ....'63 '90 C.294 B.S. L.602 J.D. [Kirkland&E.]
*PRACTICE AREAS: Commercial Litigation; Antitrust.
Gillespie, Samuel H., III '42 '73 C.478 B.A. L.880 J.D.
(adm. in NY; not adm. in DC) [Ⓒ Skadden,A.S.M.&F.]
Gilley, Craig A. .... '69 '95 C.103 A.B. L.276 J.D. [Ⓐ Fleischman&W.]
Gillice, Thomas A. .... '64 '94 C.529 B.A. L.128 J.D. Asst. Corp. Coun.
Gillick, John E., (AV) ....'45 '71 C.165 A.B. L.276 J.D. [Pillsbury W.]
*PRACTICE AREAS: Aviation Law; Regulatory Law; International Law.
Gilligan, Charles W. .... '60 '85 C.1036 B.A. L.128 J.D. [O'Donoghue&O.]
*PRACTICE AREAS: Labor and Employment.
Gilligan, Joseph E. ....'— '97 C.423 B.B.A. L.276 J.D. [Ⓐ Hogan&H.]
*PRACTICE AREAS: Corporate Law; Securities; Mergers and Acquisitions; Corporate Finance.
Gilliland, C. Michael ....'52 '80 C.16 B.S. L.192 J.D. [Hogan&H.]
*PRACTICE AREAS: Election Campaign and Political Law; Lobbying; Government Relations; Legislative Practice; Public Policy.
Gillon, Kara '72 '97 C.276 B.A. L.1194 J.D.
(adm. in MA; not adm. in DC) Defenders of Wildlife
Gillon, Peter M., (AV) ....'57 '83 C.228 A.B. L.276 J.D. [Greenberg T.]
Gilman, Cynthia L. ....'60 '85 C.1365 B.A. L.1049 J.D. [Weiner B.S.K.]
*PRACTICE AREAS: Mortgage Banking Law; Financial Institutions; Corporate Litigation.
Gilman, Denise L. '68 '94 C.595 B.A. L.178 J.D.
(adm. in TX; not adm. in DC) Wash. Lawyers' Comm. for Civil Rights
Gilman, John H. '43 '89 C.112 B.A. L.1065 J.D.
(adm. in CA; not adm. in DC) 1329 30th St., NW
Gilman, Michael I. ....'62 '91 C&L.893 B.A., J.D. [Ⓒ Dickstein S.M.&O.]
*PRACTICE AREAS: Tax.
Gilman, Neil K. ....'68 '95 C.31 B.A. L.477 J.D. [Ⓒ O'Melveny&M.]
*PRACTICE AREAS: Antitrust; Securities; Litigation.
Gilman, Nicholas, (AV) ....'38 '72 C.813 B.A. L.273 J.D. [Gilman&Assoc.]
*PRACTICE AREAS: Aviation Law; Aviation Accidents; Airplane Crash Litigation; Aviation Disasters; Aviation Torts.

Gilman & Associates, (AV)
600 Pennsylvania Avenue S.E., Suite 410, 20003 ⊙
Telephone: 202-547-9080 Fax: 202-547-8944
Email: ndgilman@aol.com URL: http://www.lawyers.com/gilmanairlaw
Members of Firm: Nicholas Gilman; John J. Carlino (1946-1987). Associate: John M. Green (Not admitted in DC). Of Counsel: William J. Olson.
Aviation Law, Airplane Crash Litigation, Aviation Accidents, Automobile, Maritime, Railroad and other Transportation Litigation. Medical Malpractice, Product Liability, Negligence, Insurance and International Law. Civil, Criminal and Administrative Trials and Appeals in all Courts, including Multi-national and Multi-District Tort Disasters, U.S. and Foreign Personal Injuries and Wrongful Deaths.
McLean, Virginia Office: Suite 1070, 8180 Greensboro Drive. Telephone: 703-356-5070. Fax: 703-356-5085.
See Professional Biographies, WASHINGTON, DISTRICT OF COLUMBIA

Gilmore, Craig Edward ....'68 '93 C.94 B.A. L.128 J.D. [Wilkinson B.K.]
*PRACTICE AREAS: Communications; Telecommunications Law; Administrative Law; Appellate Practice.
Gilmore, David M. .... '69 '97 C.1110 B.A. L.475 J.D. [Ⓢ Preston G.E.&R.M.]
*PRACTICE AREAS: Maritime Regulation; Shipping Regulation; Corporate Finance.
Gilmore, Jeffrey G., (AV) '57 '82 C.473 B.A. L.945 J.D.
[Wickwire G.] (⊙Vienna, VA)
*PRACTICE AREAS: Construction, Commercial, and Fidelity and Surety Law; Litigation.
Gilmore, Patricia K. .... '50 '79 C&L.770 B.A., J.D. [Dombroff&G.]

Gilpatric, Kenneth D. '50 '94 C.273 B.B.A. L.30 J.D.
(adm. in PA; not adm. in DC) 1615 Manchester Lane N.W.
Gilsdorf, Christine J. .... '61 '98 C.886 B.S. L.150 J.D. [Ⓐ Staas&H.] (See Pat. Sect.)
*PRACTICE AREAS: Intellectual Property Law; Patents; Trademarks; Copyrights.
Gilson, Anne E. '68 '94 C.674 A.B. L.477 J.D.
(adm. in IL; not adm. in DC) 1722 Eye St.
Gilson, Mady, (AV) .... '51 '76 C.103 B.A. L.1162 J.D. [Bredhoff&K.]
Gilson, Thomas A. ....'63 '93 C.309 A.B. L.597 J.D. [Ⓐ Skadden,A.S.M.&F.]
*PRACTICE AREAS: Litigation.
Gimbel, Holly A. ....'68 '95 C.260 B.A. L.494 J.D. [Ⓐ Skadden,A.S.M.&F.]
*PRACTICE AREAS: International Trade.
Gimble, Glenn S. '56 '84 C.94 B.A. L.1048 J.D.
Program Mgr. & Coun., America's Community Bkrs.
Gimer, Richard H., (AV) ....'40 '65 C.350 B.S. L.273 J.D. [Ⓒ Semmes,B.&S.]
*PRACTICE AREAS: Insurance Coverage; Trade Associations; Trade Regulation.

Gingell & Jenkins, P.C.
(See Silver Spring, Maryland)

Gingerich, Tara R. .... '73 '00 C.659 B.A. L.30 J.D. [Ⓐ Steptoe&J.]
Gingold, Dennis M. .... '49 '74 C.699 B.A. L.776 J.D. [Anderson&G.]
Gingrás, Rosario C. .... '— '94 C.112 B.A. L.999 J.D. [Eisen&R.]
Gins, Richard H., (AV) .... '42 '68 C.575 A.B. L.273 J.D. [Gins&G.] ⊙
*PRACTICE AREAS: Bankruptcy Law; Insolvency Law; General Commercial Law.

Gins & Greenfeld, P.C., (AV)
5028 Wisconsin Avenue, N.W., Suite 300, 20016 ⊙
Telephone: 202-537-7050 Fax: 202-364-5165
URL: http://www.ginsandgreenfeld.lawoffice.com
Richard H. Gins; Steven H. Greenfeld;—Melinda M. Bolling.
Bankruptcy, Reorganization and Commercial Law.
Gaithersburg, Maryland Office: Fourth Floor, 806 West Diamond Avenue, 20878 Telephone: 301-258-9777. Fax: 301-670-9026.
See Professional Biographies, WASHINGTON, DISTRICT OF COLUMBIA

Ginsberg, Benjamin L., (AV) ....'51 '83 C.659 B.A. L.276 J.D. [Patton B.]
Ginsberg, Ellen C. '58 '85
C.860 B.A. L.30 J.D. Dep. Gen. Coun., Nuclear Energy Institute
*RESPONSIBILITIES: Nuclear Energy; Administrative Law; Corporate Law; Nonprofit and Charitable Organizations; Trade and Professional Organizations.
Ginsberg, Peter R. ....'53 '81 C.659 B.A. L.178 J.D. [P.R.Ginsberg]
*PRACTICE AREAS: White Collar Criminal Defense; Securities; Commercial Litigation; Sports Law.
Ginsberg, Stuart M. ....'— '85 C.951 B.A. L.659 J.D. [Ⓒ Bryan C.]
*PRACTICE AREAS: Real Estate; Commercial Law; Business Law.

Ginsberg, Peter R., P.C.
Suite 600, 1201 Connecticut Avenue, N.W., 20036
Telephone: 202-293-1410 Fax: 202-293-1484
URL: http://www.lawyers.com/pginsberglaw
Peter R. Ginsberg.
White Collar Criminal Defense, Complex Commercial Litigation, Sports Law, Appellate Practice, Business Fraud.
See Professional Biographies, WASHINGTON, DISTRICT OF COLUMBIA

Ginsburg, David, (AV) .... '12 '35 C.923 B.A. L.309 LL.B. [Ⓒ Powell,G.F.&M.]
*PRACTICE AREAS: International Law; Corporate Law.
Ginsburg, Elizabeth A. .... '57 '83 C.112 B.A. L.1066 J.D. Sr. Atty., Air Line Pilots Assn.
Ginsburg, Gilbert J., (AV) ....'36 '57 C&L.145 B.A., J.D. 1227 25th St., NW
Ginsburg, Martin D., (P.C.), (AV) ....'32 '59 C.188 A.B. L.309 J.D. [Ⓒ Fried,F.H.S.&J.]
Giobbi, Herbert V. '47 '77 C.390 B.A. L.776 J.D.
(adm. in NJ; not adm. in DC) V.P., The Narragansett Grp., Inc.
Giordano, Cynthia A., (AV) .... '54 '79 C.966 B.A. L.273 J.D. [Ⓐ Arnold&P.]
*PRACTICE AREAS: Zoning; Land Use; Historic Preservation; Real Property; Tax Appeals.
Giovannoni, Catherine M. ....'56 '95 C&L.446 B.S., J.D. [Ⓐ Steptoe&J.]
Gira, Thomas R. '61 '86 C.896 B.A. L.446 J.D.
Assoc. Gen. Coun., The Nasdaq Stock Market, Inc.
Giral, Teresa M. ....'66 '91 C&L.276 B.A., J.D. 2000 K St Nw # 500
Girard, Cathryn Clark '44 '89 C.829 B.S. L.184 J.D.
(adm. in CT; not adm. in DC) 420 7th St., N.W.‡
Girard, Victoria W. ....'62 '88 C.222 B.A. L.276 J.D. [Ⓐ Hogan&H.]
*PRACTICE AREAS: Food and Drug Regulation; Food, Drug and Cosmetic Law.
Giroux, Danielle .... '74 '00 C.1369 B.A. L.1209 J.D. [Ⓐ Sutherland A.&B.]
*PRACTICE AREAS: Civil Litigation.
Giroux, Frederick W. .... '62 '87 C.676 B.A. L.128 J.D. [Ⓒ Cole,R.&B.]
*PRACTICE AREAS: Communications Law; Rate Regulation; Cable Franchising; Signal Carriage; Telecommunications Regulation.
Gische, David M., (AV) .... '49 '78 C.309 A.B. L.976 J.D. [Ross,D.&B.]
Gish, Carrie E. '60 '91 C.573 B.S. L.64 J.D.
(adm. in PA; not adm. in DC) Crestar Bk., N.A.
Gisler, Mark R. '— '88 C.628 B.A. L.30 J.D.
(adm. in MD; not adm. in DC) [Ⓐ Berliner,C.&J.]
Gist, Pamela L., (AV) .... '57 '80 C.836 B.F.A. L.45 J.D. [Lukas,N.G.&S.]
*PRACTICE AREAS: Wireless Communications; Cable TV; Trademark Registration.
Gitell, Seth A. '68 '94 C.309 B.A. L.569 J.D.
(adm. in MA; not adm. in DC) 1049 Natl. Press Bldg.
Gitelman, Sheldon J. ..... '29 '52 C&L.494 B.S.L., LL.B. 1000 Potomac St., N.W., 5th Fl.
Gitelman, Steven R. '61 '87 C.918 B.A. L.145 J.D.
(adm. in NY; not adm. in DC) Sr. Corp. Coun., US Off. Prod. Co.
*RESPONSIBILITIES: Corporate Law.
Gitenstein, Mark H., (AV) ....'46 '72 C.228 A.B. L.276 J.D. [Mayer,B.&P.]
Gitner, Geoffrey P., (AV) .... '44 '70 C.339 B.S. L.276 J.D. [Ⓒ Dyer E.&J.]
*PRACTICE AREAS: Business Litigation; Professional Malpractice; Securities Litigation; Real Estate Litigation; Arbitration.
Gitomer, Louis E. '51 '76 C&L.64 B.S., J.D.
(adm. in MD; not adm. in DC) [Ⓒ Ball J.]
*PRACTICE AREAS: Transportation Law.
Gittings, Thomas Morton, Jr., (AV) '27 '51 C&L.273 LL.B.
1620 Eye Street, N.W., Suite 716 (⊙Potomac, MD)
Gittleman, Richard M. .... '55 '83 [Akin,G.S.H.&F.]
*PRACTICE AREAS: Project Finance; Infrastructure Development; International Transactions.
Giunta, Claudia '67 '98 L.659 LL.M.
(adm. in NY; not adm. in DC) Coun., Intl. Monetary Fund
Giunta, Tara Kalagher, (AV) .... '59 '86 C.860 B.A. L.128 J.D. [Coudert B.]
*PRACTICE AREAS: Telecommunications; Satellites; Aerospace.
Giventer, Lorrie A. ....'69 '95 C.103 B.A. L.893 J.D. [Ⓐ Piper M.R.&W.]
*PRACTICE AREAS: Civil Litigation; Criminal Litigation.

GKRSE, (AV)
1500 K Street, N.W., Suite 330, 20005
Telephone: 202-408-5400 Telecopier: 202-408-5406
Email: gkrse@gkrse-law.com URL: http://www.gkrse-law.com
Members of Firm: Elisa J. Grammer; Peter C. Kissel; Alan I. Robbins; Nancy J. Skancke; Katherine B. Edwards; Donald H. Clarke. Associates: Elizabeth Teuwen (Not admitted in DC); John P. Floom (Not admitted in DC).

(This Listing Continued)

GKRSE (Continued)

Energy, Administrative, Litigation, Environmental Law. General Practice before Administrative Agencies, Government Departments and Federal Appellate Courts and Congress.

See Professional Biographies, WASHINGTON, DISTRICT OF COLUMBIA

Gladstone, Brandon M. '68 '93 C.893 B.S. L.347 J.D. [Ⓐ Lee&M.]
*PRACTICE AREAS: Personal Injury; Negligence; Civil Litigation; Insurance Law; Commercial Litigation.
Gladstone, James W. '60 '84 C&L.846 B.A., J.D. [Ⓐ Womble C.S.&R.]
*PRACTICE AREAS: Civil Litigation.
Gladstone, Jeffrey W. '73 '99 C.659 B.S. L.276 J.D. [Ⓐ Gibson,D.&C.]
*PRACTICE AREAS: Corporate Law; Securities.
Gladstone, Richard A. '42 '71 C.197 A.B. L.128 J.D. 1818 N St., NW
Glakas, Nicholas J. '44 '73 C.945 B.A. L.276 J.D. 10 G St.
Glancz, Ronald R., (AV) '43 '68 C&L.477 B.A., J.D. [Venable,A.B.H.&C.]
*PRACTICE AREAS: Banking Regulation; Thrift Institution Regulation; Bank Mergers and Acquisitions; Electronic Banking; Fair Lending.
Glanzer, Seymour, (AV) '26 '61 C.999 B.S. L.564 LL.B. [Ⓒ Dickstein S.M.&O.]
*PRACTICE AREAS: Litigation; White Collar Criminal Defense; Complex Civil Litigation; Grand Jury Practice; Federal Regulatory Law.
Glaser, Christopher A. '73 '98 C.446 B.A. L.1040 J.D. [Ⓐ Wright,R.O.&T.]
*PRACTICE AREAS: Civil Litigation.
Glaser, Mara '73 '98 C&L.190 B.S.B.A., J.D. [Ⓐ Swidler B.S.F.]
*PRACTICE AREAS: Corporate.
Glaser, Peter S., (AV) '53 '80 C.478 B.A. L.273 J.D. [Ⓒ Shook,H.&B.]
*PRACTICE AREAS: Energy Law; Utility Law; Environmental Law; Litigation.
Glasgow, James A., (AV) '45 '69 C&L.37 B.A., J.D. [Morgan,L.&B.]
Glasgow, Norman M., Jr., (AV) '52 '77 C&L.276 B.A., J.D. [Holland&K.]
*PRACTICE AREAS: Real Estate; Zoning, Planning and Land Use; Municipal Law; Historic Preservation.
Glasgow, Norman M., Sr., (AV) '22 '49 C.446 B.S. L.273 J.D. [Holland&K.]
*PRACTICE AREAS: Real Estate; Zoning, Planning and Land Use; Municipal Law; Government Relations; Legislative Affairs.
Glasgow, Peter R. '71 '98 C.446 B.A. L.1209 J.D. CACI
Glasheen, Megan '66 '91 C.690 B.A. L.309 J.D. [Reno&C.]
*PRACTICE AREAS: Affordable Housing; Real Estate Transactions; General Corporate; Nonprofit Organizations; Administrative Law.
Glasmann, Jay W., (AV) '24 '50 C&L.309 LL.B. [Ⓒ Ivins,P.&B.]
Glass, Alice G. '55 '92 C.819 B.S. L.846 J.D. [Ⓒ Baker&M.P.]
Glass, Jennifer G. '73 '98 C.188 B.S. L.273 J.D. [Ⓐ Shaw P.]
Glass, Jonathon C. '53 '91 C.118 B.A. L.276 J.D. [Dow,L.&A.]
Glassberg, Brian L. '74 '99 L.309 J.D. [Ⓐ Latham&W.]
*PRACTICE AREAS: Communications Law; Corporate Law; Technology Law.
Glasser, Caryn '66 '96 C&L.1019 B.A., J.D.
(adm. in NY; not adm. in DC) [Ⓐ Shearman&S.]
*PRACTICE AREAS: Litigation.
Glassic, Thomas M. '70 '97 C.945 A.B. L.273 J.D. [Ⓐ Baach R.&L.P.]
*PRACTICE AREAS: Insurance; Litigation.
Glassie, Jefferson C. '53 '85 C.893 B.A. L.273 J.D. [Shaw P.]
*PRACTICE AREAS: Association Law; International Law; Government Relations; Nonprofit Organizations.
Glassman, H. Bradford '67 '94 C.103 B.A. L.893 J.D. [Ⓐ Baach R.&L.P.]
*PRACTICE AREAS: Litigation.
Glassman, Jeffrey R. '70 '96 C.966 B.A. L.904 J.D. 2001 Pennsylvania Ave., N.W.
Glassman, Laurel W. '49 '74 C.788 A.B. L.705 J.D. [Ⓒ Dewey B.]
*PRACTICE AREAS: Energy.
Glassman, Mark L. '67 '98 C.378 B.A. L.904 J.D. [Ⓐ Jones,D.R.&P.]
Glassman, Stephen C., (AV) '42 '67 C.30 B.A. L.276 J.D. [Glassman&B.] ⊙
*PRACTICE AREAS: Military Law.

Glassman & Bullock, (AV)
1111 19th Street, N.W. Suite 1200, 20036-3603 ⊙
Telephone: 202-452-0000 Fax: 202-835-9846
Email: gblawdc@erols.com URL: http://www.lawyers.com/glassman&bullock
Members of Firm: Stephen C. Glassman; Robert S. Bullock.
Elder Law, Commercial Transactions and Litigation; Civil Trial Law. Military Law. Veterinary and Equine Law; Family Law (including Military Divorce and International Custody Law). Probate, Estate Planning and Administration; Legal and Medical Malpractice; Tax Controversies, Employment Law; General Counsel Services.
Vienna, Virginia Office: 1950 Old Gallows Road, Suite 700, Tysons Corner. Telephone: 703-902-9500. Fax: 703-902-9501. Email: gblaw@erols.com
Laytonsville, Maryland Office: 5515 Riggs Road. Telephone: 301-670-9200. Fax: 301-670-9246. Email: gblaw@erols.com

See Professional Biographies, WASHINGTON, DISTRICT OF COLUMBIA

Glaze, James E. '61 '93 C.330 B.A. L.1067 J.D.
(adm. in CA; not adm. in DC) [Ⓐ Sonosky,C.S.E.&P.]
*PRACTICE AREAS: Native American Law; Employment Law; Immigration Law.
Glazer, Reena N. '69 '95 C.66 B.A. L.228 J.D. [Ⓐ Shea&G.]
Gleason, Carolyn B. '56 '81 C.367 B.A. L.276 J.D. [McDermott,W.&E.]
Gleason, Edward M., Jr. '64 '89 C.262 B.A. L.1017 J.D. [Beins,A.&K.]
Gleason, Jean Wilbur, (AV) '43 '69 C.914 B.A. L.309 LL.B.
801 Pennsylvania Ave., N.W.
Gleason, Kathryn L. '56 '81 C.367 B.A. L.276 J.D. [Morgan,L.&B.]
Gleason, Teresa A. '63 '88 C.319 B.A. L.767 J.D. [Baker&M.]
*PRACTICE AREAS: Trade Regulations and Customs Law.

Gleason, Flynn, Emig & Fogleman, Chartered
(See Rockville, Maryland)

Gleiberman, Paul D. '58 '85 C&L.276 B.S.F.S., J.D. [Beins,G.&G.]
Gleicher, Brian S. '70 '95 C.260 B.S. L.276 J.D. [Ⓒ Akin,G.S.H.&F.]
*PRACTICE AREAS: Taxation.
Gleimer, Eileen M., (AV) '57 '82 C.30 B.S. L.245 J.D. [Ⓒ Crowell&M.]
Gleklen, Jonathan '66 '93 C.976 B.A. L.145 J.D. [Arnold&P.]
*PRACTICE AREAS: Antitrust; Intellectual Property.
Glembocki, Christopher R. '— '95
C.893 B.S.E.E. L.904 J.D. [Banner&W.] (See Pat. Sect.)
*PRACTICE AREAS: Intellectual Property Law; Patents; Electrical Intellectual Property; Computer and Software Patents; Electronic Patents.
Glendening, John W., Jr., (AV) '17 '41 C.165 B.A. L.188 J.D. [Ⓒ Schiff H.&W.]
Glennon, Edward B. '68 '97 C.893 B.A. L.945 J.D. [Ⓐ Crowell&M.]
Glennon, Robert E., Jr., (AV) '48 '74 C.339 B.S. L.260 J.D. [Williams&J.]
*PRACTICE AREAS: Federal Tax Policy; Tax Law; Financial Institutions and Banking.
Glew, William B., Jr. '56 '84 C.976 B.A. L.893 J.D. [Ⓒ Swidler B.S.F.]
*PRACTICE AREAS: Federal Legislative Practice; Electric Utility Regulation.
Glick, Helene L. '— '90 C.1365 B.A. L.273 J.D. 1800 M St., NW
Glick, Leslie Alan, (AV) '46 '71 C&L.188 B.S., J.D. [Porter W.M.&A.]
*PRACTICE AREAS: International Trade Law; Customs Law; Imports and Exports; Food, Drug and Cosmetic Law; NAFTA Anti Dumping.
Glick, Warren W. '27 '52 C.367 B.A. L.309 J.D. [Vorys,S.S.&P.]
*PRACTICE AREAS: International Law; Finance; Commercial Law.
Glickfield, Cheryl R. '56 '86 C.145 B.A. L.659 J.D. 2939 28th St., N.W.
Glickman, Susan '— '94 C.94 B.S. L.563 J.D.
(adm. in PA; not adm. in DC) Education Dir., ACLU of the National Capital Area

Glist, Paul, (AV) '53 '78 C.188 A.B. L.813 J.D. [Cole,R.&B.]
*PRACTICE AREAS: Cable Communications; Telecommunications Law; Rate Regulation; Compulsory Copyrights; Cable Franchising.
Glitzenstein, Eric R. '57 '81 C.367 B.A. L.276 J.D. 1601 Connecticut Ave. N.W.
Glock, Earl F. '52 '80 C.602 B.A. L.276 J.D. [O'Connell&G.]
*PRACTICE AREAS: Real Estate; Taxation; Corporate; International Law.
Glomb, Michael B. '44 '70 C&L.276 A.B., J.D. [Feldesman,T.L.F.&B.]
*PRACTICE AREAS: Health Care Law; Nonprofit Organizations; Business Law; Commercial Law.
Glosserman, Michael J. '45 '71 C.659 B.E. L.846 J.D. [Brown,G.&J.]
Glover, Gregory J. '59 '89 C&L.309 A.B., J.D. [Ropes&G.] (Pat.)
Glover, Mildred M. '— '94
C.273 B.C.S. L.276 J.D. Asst. Gen. Coun., Smithsonian Institution
Glover, Rodney H., (BV) '51 '78 C.446 B.A. L.692 J.D. [Gardner,C.&D.]
*PRACTICE AREAS: Intellectual Property Litigation; Employment Litigation; Privacy Law.
Glover, Stephen I. '55 '82 C.31 B.A. L.309 J.D. [Gibson,D.&C.] (⊙L.A., CA)
*PRACTICE AREAS: Corporate Law; Securities; Mergers, Acquisitions and Divestitures.
Glowinski, Robert W. '54 '82 C.705 B.A. L.64 J.D. Amer. Forest & Paper Assn.
Gluck, Amy Epstein '70 '95 C.860 B.A. L.537 J.D. [O'Rourke&C.]
Gluck, Jacquelyn N. '61 '91 C.473 B.A. L.30 J.D.
(adm. in NY; not adm. in DC) [Ⓐ L.D.Wasko]
*PRACTICE AREAS: Aviation Law; International Aviation Law; Aeronautical Regulation; Contracts; Litigation.
Gluck, Jason P. '71 '98 C.597 B.A. L.477 J.D. [Ⓐ Covington&B.]
*PRACTICE AREAS: Civil Litigation.
Gluck, Richard D., (AV) '50 '78 C.145 B.A. L.276 J.D. [Garvey,S.&B.]
*PRACTICE AREAS: Government Contracts Law; Transportation Law; Maritime Law; International Trade; E-Commerce.
Glueck, Daniel S. '66 '93 C&L.309 A.B., J.D. [Fitzpatrick,C.H.&S.] (See Pat. Sect.)
Glymph, Darrin Lewis '64 '94 C.951 B.A. L.861 J.D. [Ⓐ Hunton&W.]
*PRACTICE AREAS: Public Finance; Real Estate.
Glynn, Dana Suzanne '74 '99 C.893 B.A. L.861 J.D. [Ⓐ Carr,M.&G.]
*PRACTICE AREAS: Civil Litigation; Corporate Law; Business Law.
Glynn, Edward F., Jr., (AV) '47 '72 C.012 B.A. L.188 J.D. [Venable,A.B.H.&C.]
*PRACTICE AREAS: Antitrust, Consumer Protection and Trade Regulation.
Glynn, Sean W. '64 '90 C.228 B.A. L.446 J.D. [Arent F.K.P.&K.]
*PRACTICE AREAS: Public Finance and Real Estate.
Gnazzo, Patrick J. '46 '71 C.363 A.B. L.1003 J.D.
(adm. in OH; not adm. in DC) V.P., United Technologies Corp.
Gobena, Gejaa Temesgien '74 '99 C.893 B.A. L.178 J.D. [Ⓐ Fried,F.H.S.&J.]
*PRACTICE AREAS: Litigation.
Goch, David P. '66 '91 C.477 B.G.S. L.446 J.D. [Webster,C.&B.]
*PRACTICE AREAS: Trade and Professional Associations; Nonprofit and Charitable Organizations; Government Relations.
Goddard, Claude P., Jr. '52 '79 C.871 B.S. L.659 J.D. [Wickwire G.] (⊙Vienna, VA)
*PRACTICE AREAS: Government Contracts; Civil Litigation.
Goddard, Henry B., Jr. '47 '93 C.836 B.A. L.273 J.D. [Ⓐ Dombroff&G.]
Godfrey, E. Malia '72 '99 C&L.101 B.A., J.D. [Ⓐ Vinson&E.]
*PRACTICE AREAS: Public Finance Law.
Godfrey, Merrill C. '— '99 C.878 B.A. L.1375 J.D. [Ⓐ Shearman&S.]
*PRACTICE AREAS: Litigation.
Godles, Joseph A., (AV) '55 '80 C.188 B.S. L.659 J.D. [Goldberg,G.W.&W.]
*PRACTICE AREAS: Communications and Media.
Godlewski, Kenneth A. '63 '91 C.970 B.A. L.608 J.D. [Kilpatrick S.] (Pat.)
*PRACTICE AREAS: Patent Law; Intellectual Property Litigation; Litigation.
Godley, Gene E., (AV) '39 '63 C&L.802 B.A., J.D. [Bracewell&P.]
*PRACTICE AREAS: Business Law; International Trade; Energy; Government; International Law.
Godley, Patricia Fry, (AV) '48 '79 C.859 B.A. L.846 J.D. [Van Ness F.]
*PRACTICE AREAS: Energy; Government; Natural Resources.
Godofsky, David R. '58 '82 C.999 B.S. L.893 J.D. [Ⓒ Alston&B.]
*PRACTICE AREAS: Employee Benefits.
Godschalk, David K. '67 '94 C&L.575 B.A., J.D. [Ⓐ Vinson&E.]
*PRACTICE AREAS: Public Finance.
Godwin, Michael W. '56 '90
C&L.846 B.A., J.D. Sr. Legal Editor, American Lawyer Media
Goebes, Robert L. '46 '75 C&L.128 A.B., J.D. The Bureau of Natl. Affs., Inc.
Goeken, Richard W. '63 '91 C.436 B.A. L.945 J.D. [Saltman&S.]
*PRACTICE AREAS: Government Contracts; Timber and Logging; Litigation; Natural Resources Law.
Goekjian, Samuel V. '27 '58 C.823 B.A. L.309 J.D. [Kile G.L.&R.P.]
*PRACTICE AREAS: International Trade and Investment; Commercial Transactions.
Goel, Ankur J., (AV) '64 '90 C.339 B.S. L.309 J.D. [McDermott,W.&E.]
Goelzer, Angela C. '55 '80 C.676 B.A. L.309 J.D. [Ⓒ Morgan,L.&B.]
Goelzer, Daniel L., (AV) '47 '73 C&L.966 B.B.A., J.D. [Baker&M.]
*PRACTICE AREAS: Capital Markets; Regulatory Law; Asset Management; Corporate Financings (Public and Private).
Goerlich, Aaron A., (AV) '55 '80 C&L.861 B.A., J.D. [Boros&G.]
*PRACTICE AREAS: Aviation; Aeronautical Regulation.
Goetz, Janet L. '54 '82 C.188 B.S. L.569 J.D. [Skadden,A.S.M.&F.]
Goetzl, Katherine Anne '70 '97 C.31 B.A. L.276 J.D. [Ⓐ Littler M.]
Goewey, David W. '62 '87 C.893 B.A. L.945 J.D. [Venable,A.B.H.&C.]
*PRACTICE AREAS: Litigation.
Goff, Jacquelyn A. '45 '73 C.338 B.S. L.339 J.D. 441 G Street NW
Goffe, William G. '49 '78 C.659 B.S. L.273 J.D. 4100 Massachusetts Ave., NW
Goffman, Barbara A. '69 '99 C.477 B.A. L.228 J.D. [Ⓐ Dow,L.&A.]
Goffman, Joseph '54 '80 C&L.976 B.A., J.D.
(adm. in NY; not adm. in DC) Environmental Def. Fund
Goins, Cer Gladwyn '51 '76 C&L.930 B.A., J.D.
(adm. in PA; not adm. in DC) [Ⓒ Miller,C.P.&S.]
*PRACTICE AREAS: Securities; Banking Law; Litigation.
Gold, C. Ray '66 '93 C.575 B.A. L.276 J.D. [Ⓐ Berliner,C.&R.]
*PRACTICE AREAS: Export Controls; Trademarks.
Gold, Denise S. '66 '91 C.477 A.B. L.276 J.D. Associated Gen. Contractors of America
Gold, Dina M. '67 '94 C.188 B.S. L.273 J.D. [Ⓐ Drinker B.&R.]
Gold, Harold '10 '33 C.563 A.B. L.262 J.D. V.P., Hill & Knowlton, Inc.
Gold, Jack A. '61 '92 C.477 B.A. L.276 J.D. [Karp,F.L.W.&N.]
*PRACTICE AREAS: Appellate Practice.
Gold, Jonathan L. '67 '94 C.446 B.S. L.64 J.D. [Ⓐ Akin,G.S.H.&F.]
*PRACTICE AREAS: Bankruptcy.
Gold, Kimberly J. '70 '95 C.1036 B.A. L.904 J.D. [Ⓐ Crowell&M.]
Gold, Laurence, (AV) '36 '61 C.674 A.B. L.309 LL.B. [Ⓒ Bredhoff&K.]
Gold, Laurence E., (AV) '53 '80 C.31 B.A. L.188 J.D. Assoc. Gen. Coun., AFL-CIO
Gold, Leslie J. '54 '81 C.604 A.B. L.273 J.D. The Bur. of Natl. Affs., Inc.
Gold, Marc S. '64 '89 C.1044 B.A. L.273 J.D.
Asst. Gen. Coun., National Academy of Sciences
Gold, Martin B. '47 '76 C&L.30 B.A., J.D. [Schwabe,W.&W.]
*PRACTICE AREAS: Legislation.
Gold, Michael '73 '00 C.1036 B.A. L.659 J.D.
(adm. in NY; not adm. in DC) [Ⓐ Patton B.]
Gold, Michael A. '66 '94 C.659 B.S.E. L.145 J.D. [Baker B.]
Gold, Michelle Berk '71 '97 C.1036 B.A. L.276 J.D. [Ⓐ Fried,F.H.S.&J.]
*PRACTICE AREAS: Tax.

Gold, Peter F., (AV) ... '45 '72 C.188 A.B. L.569 J.D. [Gold]
Gold, Richard M., (AV) ... '64 '88 C.882 B.S. L.273 J.D. [Holland&K.]
*PRACTICE AREAS: Environmental Law; Federal Practice; Federal Litigation; Legislative Law; Administrative Law.
Gold, Stephanie J. ... '69 '98 C.103 A.B. L.477 J.D. [[A] Hogan&H.]
*PRACTICE AREAS: Education Law; College and University Law; School Law; Student Loans.
Gold, Stephen V. '59 '99 C.36 B.S. L.1209 J.D.
(adm. in VA; not adm. in DC) 3050 K St., NW, Suite 400

Gold Group, The, Chartered, (AV)
1319 F Street, N.W. Suite 1000, 20004
Telephone: 202-347-5542; 301-963-1148 Telefax: 202-628-1258; 301-963-1168
Peter F. Gold.
Antitrust, Trade Regulations, General Legislative and Merchant Banking Services.
See Professional Biographies, WASHINGTON, DISTRICT OF COLUMBIA

Gold Morrison & Laughlin PC, (AV)
1200 G Street, N.W., Suite 800, 20003 ⊙
Telephone: 703-836-7004
Email: info@goldmorrison.com URL: http://www.goldmorrison.com
Valerie P. Morrison.
Restructures, Insolvency, Bankruptcy, Creditors' Rights, Foreclosures, Banking Law, Federal Court Litigation.
Tysons Corner, Virginia Office: 1660 International Drive, Suite 450, Telephone: 703-836-7004. Facsimile: 703-548-9430.
Alexandria, Virginia Office: 1800 Diagonal Road, Suite 600. 22314-2808.
See Professional Biographies, WASHINGTON, DISTRICT OF COLUMBIA

Goldberg, Aaron H., (BV) ... '57 '85 C.976 B.S. L.813 J.D. [Beveridge&D.]
*PRACTICE AREAS: Environmental Law; Administrative Law; Hazardous Waste; Resource Conservation and Recovery Act (RCRA).
Goldberg, Adam W. ... '69 '95 C.860 B.A. L.309 J.D. [[A] Covington&B.]
Goldberg, Alfred M. ... '32 '61 C.188 B.S. L.1009 LL.B. 1920 N. St., N.W.‡
Goldberg, Avrum M., (AV) ... '43 '70 C.645 B.S. L.884 J.D. [Akin,G.S.H.&F.]
*PRACTICE AREAS: Labor and Employment.
Goldberg, Daniel S., (AV) ... '47 '72 C.696 A.B. L.309 J.D. [[C] Piper M.R.&W.]
*PRACTICE AREAS: Business Taxation; Business; Technology; Venture Capital; Emerging Growth Companies.
Goldberg, Eric M. '64 '92 C.273 B.A. L.910 J.D.
(adm. in PA; not adm. in DC) Asst. Gen. Coun., American Insurance Association
*RESPONSIBILITIES: Legislative/Regulatory; Property Insurance; Intellectual Property; Workers' Compensation; Occupational Safety and Health.
Goldberg, Fred B., (AV) ... '51 '76 C.446 B.A. L.365 J.D. [Spirer&G.]
*PRACTICE AREAS: Civil Litigation; Personal Injury; Products Liability; Medical Malpractice; Commercial Law.
Goldberg, Fred T., Jr., (AV) ... '47 '74 C&L.976 B.A., J.D. [Skadden,A.S.M.&F.]
Goldberg, Henry, (AV) ... '39 '65 C.94 A.B. L.178 LL.B. [Goldberg,G.W.&W.]
*PRACTICE AREAS: Communications and Media.
Goldberg, James M., (AV) ... '40 '68 C.823 B.S. L.273 J.D. 888 16th St., N.W.
Goldberg, Jeffrey A. ... '70 '98 C.401 B.S. L.569 J.D. [[A] Skadden,A.S.M.&F.]
Goldberg, Jennifer Anne ... '72 '99 C.681 A.B. L.309 J.D. 111 F Street, N.W.

Goldberg, Joel J. '53 '83 C.705 B.A. L.477 J.D.
1050 17th Street, N.W. Suite 1200, 20036
Telephone: 202-822-4668 Fax: 202-822-4676
Email: jgoldlaw@worldnet.att.net URL: http://www.lawyers.com/joelgoldberglaw
Commercial Real Estate, Real Estate Finance, Leasing, Landlord and Tenant Law, Commercial Transactions, Corporate Law, Commercial Law.
See Professional Biographies, WASHINGTON, DISTRICT OF COLUMBIA

Goldberg, Joseph M., (AV) ... '47 '80 C.264 A.B. L.276 J.D. [Ammerman&G.]
*PRACTICE AREAS: Bankruptcy Law; Bankruptcy Chapter 7; Bankruptcy Chapter 13; Foreclosures; Consumer Credit.
Goldberg, Joshua L. '— '99 C.910 B.S. L.273 J.D.
(adm. in VA; not adm. in DC; See Pat. Sect.) [[A] Nath&Assoc.]
Goldberg, Katie G. ... '71 '98 C.188 B.S. L.893 J.D. 1350 I St., N.W.
Goldberg, Kevin M. ... '71 '95 C.1369 B.A. L.273 J.D. [[A] Cohn&M.]
*PRACTICE AREAS: Communications Law; First Amendment Law.
Goldberg, M. Roy ... '62 '87 C.378 B.A. L.174 J.D. [[C] Schnader H.S.&L.]
*PRACTICE AREAS: Civil Litigation; Administrative Law; Antitrust Law; Media Law; Aviation Law.
Goldberg, Marion Kristal ... '47 '95 C.696 B.A. L.446 J.D. [[A] Winston&S.]
*PRACTICE AREAS: Business; Health Care; Life Sciences; Biotechnology; Mergers and Acquisitions.
Goldberg, Matthew Falk '72 '97 C.311 B.A. L.597 J.D.
(adm. in MD; not adm. in DC) [[A] Hunton&W.]
*PRACTICE AREAS: Environmental; Administrative.
Goldberg, Monica B. '67 '94 C.1375 B.A. L.309 J.D.
Ocean Law Proj. Earthjustice LDF
Goldberg, Neal M., (AV) '46 '72
C.156 A.B. L.178 J.D. Gen. Coun., National Cable Television Assn.
Goldberg, Neal N. '59 '00 C.107 B.A. L.893 J.D.
(adm. in VA; not adm. in DC) [[A] Hale&D.]
*PRACTICE AREAS: Intellectual Property Litigation; Patent Prosecution; Intellectual Property.
Goldberg, Reuben, (AV) ... '12 '34 L.537 LL.B. 110 15th St., N.W.
Goldberg, Sandra '61 '88 C.860 B.S. L.1097 J.D.
(adm. in CA; not adm. in DC) Sierra Club Legal Def. Fund
Goldberg, Seth, (AV) ... '53 '79 C.1044 B.A. L.813 J.D. [Steptoe&J.]
*PRACTICE AREAS: Environmental Law; Pesticide Regulation; Administrative Law; Litigation.
Goldberg, Seth A. '71 '99 C&L.831 B.A., J.D.
(adm. in FL; not adm. in DC) [[A] Boies,S.&F.]
*PRACTICE AREAS: Antitrust; Complex Litigation.
Goldberg, Seth D. '67 '94 C.446 B.S. L.1019 J.D.
(adm. in MD; not adm. in DC) [Beins,G.&G.]
Goldberg, Steve ... '46 '72 C.156 B.A. L.184 J.D. [Jorden B.]
*PRACTICE AREAS: Insurance Law; ERISA Litigation; Corporation Law; Securities Law.
Goldberg, Susan G. ... '55 '86 C.104 A.B. L.276 J.D. [Knopf&B.]
*PRACTICE AREAS: Non-profit Organizations; Corporate Law; Litigation.

Goldberg & Finnegan, LLC
(See Silver Spring, Maryland)

Goldberg, Godles, Wiener & Wright, (AV)
1229 Nineteenth Street, N.W., 20036
Telephone: 202-429-4900 Telecopier: 202-429-4912
Email: general@G2W2.com URL: http://www.2w2.com
Members of Firm: Henry Goldberg; Joseph A. Godles; Jonathan L. Wiener. Associates: Sheryl J. Lincoln; Michael A. McCoin (Not admitted in DC); Eric J. Schwalb (Not admitted in DC). Counsel: Henrietta Wright; Thomas G. Gherardi, P.C.
Communications and Media, Broadcasting Law, FCC Regulation, International Telecommunications Law, Mass Media Law, Satelite Communications, Telecommunications Contracts, Telecommunications Law, Telecommunications Licensing, Wireless Communications.
See Professional Biographies, WASHINGTON, DISTRICT OF COLUMBIA

Goldberger, Aaron N '74 '99 C.475 B.A. L.1119 J.D.
(adm. in MI; not adm. in DC) Atty. Adviser
Goldblatt, Craig T. ... '68 '94 C.276 B.A. L.145 J.D. [Wilmer,C.&P.]
*PRACTICE AREAS: Bankruptcy; Litigation.
Goldblatt, Jason L. ... '70 '96 C.228 A.B. L.273 J.D. [[A] Venable,A.B.H.&C.]
*PRACTICE AREAS: Business Law; Partnership Law.
Goldblatt, Lisa ... '69 '97 C.976 B.A. L.273 J.D. [[A] Collier S.S.]
*PRACTICE AREAS: Litigation; Securities; Banking.
Golde, Michael D. ... '70 '98 C.112 B.A. L.273 J.D. [[A] Feldesman,T.L.F.&B.]
*PRACTICE AREAS: Health Care; Corporate Law; Nonprofit Organizations Law.
Golden, Cornelius J., Jr., (AV) ... '48 '73 C&L.813 B.A., J.D. [Chadbourne&P.]
Golden, David A. ... '60 '84 C.1059 B.B.A. L.280 J.D. Ernst & Young
Golden, Deborah M. ... '72 '98 C.659 B.S. in B.A. L.477 J.D. 1400 20th St., N.W.
Golden, Gregory J. ... '69 '96 C.902 B.A. L.692 J.D. [[A] Baker B.]
Golden, King, Jr. ... '46 '75 C.112 A.B. L.893 J.D. 2860 28th Street N.W.
Golden, Michael D., (AV) ... '40 '65 C.188 B.A. L.569 J.D. [Golden&N.] ⊙
*PRACTICE AREAS: Corporate Law; Business Law; Mergers, Acquisitions and Divestitures; Securities Law; Education Law.
Golden, Michael Joseph ... '— '98 C.893 B.S. L.276 J.D. [[A] Latham&W.]
*PRACTICE AREAS: Litigation; Appellate Practice; Consumer Law; Intellectual Property; Computers and Software.
Golden, Roger M., (AV) ... '42 '67 C.674 A.B. L.477 J.D. [Fenwick&W.]
*PRACTICE AREAS: International Business; Trade; Customs Law; Export Control; Internet Law.
Golden, Ronald D. '49 '81 C.870 B.S. L.128 J.D.
(adm. in MD; not adm. in DC) [[A] Yodice]

Golden & Nelson, PLLC, (AV)
1420 K Street N.W. Suite 500, 20005 ⊙
Telephone: 202-842-0456 Fax: 703-751-4583
URL: http://www.lawyers.com/golden&nelsonlaw
Michael D. Golden; Hedy L. Nelson.
Corporate Law, Business Law, International Business Law, Securities, Taxation, Commercial Law, Contracts, Mergers, Acquisitions and Divestitures, Finance, Commercial Leasing.
Maryland, Millersville Office: 8285 Highglade Court, 21108. Telephone: 410-729-4285. Fax: 410-729-2246.
See Professional Biographies, WASHINGTON, DISTRICT OF COLUMBIA

Goldenberg, Lloyd P ... '47 '72 C.966 B.A. L.309 J.D. [Byrne G.&H.]
Goldfarb, Brooke Deratany ... '69 '96 C.893 B.A. L.309 J.D. [[A] Swidler B.S.F.]
*PRACTICE AREAS: Corporate; Mergers and Acquisitions.
Goldfarb, Ronald L., (AV) ... '33 '56 C&L.823 A.B., LL.B. 918 16th St., NW
Goldfield, Harold P. ... '51 '77 C.183 B.A. L.276 J.D. [Swidler B.S.F.]
*PRACTICE AREAS: International Practice; Trade Regulation Law; Government Affairs.
Goldfrank, Amy '72 '00 C.118 B.A. L.145 J.D.
(adm. in MD; not adm. in DC) [[A] Shaw P.]
*PRACTICE AREAS: Litigation.
Goldhush, Douglas H. ... '62 '91 C.1133 B.T. L.818 J.D. [Arent F.K.P.&K.] (Pat.)
*PRACTICE AREAS: Intellectual Property; Electronic Commerce; Patents; Trademarks; Copyrights.
Goldin, Elizabeth E. ... '69 '99 C.966 B.A. L.221 J.D. [[A] Wiley R.&F.]
Golding, Glenn W. D. ... '62 '91 C.165 B.A. L.904 J.D. [Singer&Assoc.]
Goldman, Charles D. ... '43 '67 C.477 B.A. L.1009 J.D. 1155 15th St., N.W.
Goldman, Eugene I., (AV) ... '51 '77 C.30 B.A. L.128 J.D. [McDermott,W.&E.]
Goldman, Gerald, (AV) ... '— '68 C&L.309 A.B., LL.B. [[C] McKee N.]
*PRACTICE AREAS: Tax Litigation; Litigation; Appellate Practice.
Goldman, Jennifer Monday '73 '00 C&L.846 B.A., J.D.
(adm. in TX; not adm. in DC) [[A] Vinson&E.]
*PRACTICE AREAS: Employee Benefits; ERISA.
Goldman, Joseph A. ... '67 '92 C.978 B.S. L.178 J.D. [Jones,D.R.&P.]
*PRACTICE AREAS: Taxation; International Tax; Federal Income Tax; Transfer Pricing.
Goldman, Joseph B., (AV) ... '17 '40 C.273 A.B. L.309 J.D. 5250 Linnean Ave., N.W.‡
Goldman, Judith R., (AV) ... '51 '82 C.30 B.S. L.273 J.D. [Greenstein D.&L.]
Goldman, Julie A. ... '66 '00 C.172 B.A. L.276 J.D. [[A] Clifford C.R.&W.]
*PRACTICE AREAS: Corporate.
Goldman, Leslie Ayn '63 '90 C.910 B.A. L.665 J.D.
(adm. in MD; not adm. in DC) The Bureau of Natl. Affs., Inc.‡
Goldman, Leslie J. ... '45 '70 C&L.477 B.A., J.D. [Skadden,A.S.M.&F.]
Goldman, Loretta M. ... '16 '40 C.331 B.A. L.569 LL.B. 5250 Linnean Ave., N.W.‡
Goldman, Marc A. ... '66 '94 C&L.309 A.B., J.D. [[A] Jenner&B.]
*PRACTICE AREAS: Civil Litigation; Appellate Practice; Telecommunications Law.
Goldman, Michael F., (AV) ... '46 '71 C.831 B.A. L.309 J.D. [Silverberg,G.&B.]
*PRACTICE AREAS: Air Transportation Law; Commercial Transportation Law; Airport Law; International Air Law; Export Controls.
Goldman, Neil D., (AV) ... '53 '78 C.659 B.A. L.273 J.D. [Young,G.&V.] ⊙
*PRACTICE AREAS: Civil Litigation; Business Law; Commercial Law; Employment Law; Real Estate Law.
Goldman, Rebecca A. ... '67 '96 C.860 B.S.E.E. L.1218 J.D. [[A] Long A.&N.] (Pat.)
*PRACTICE AREAS: Intellectual Property; Patents; Technology Licensing; Litigation.
Goldman, Roger S., (AV) ... '55 '80 C&L.893 B.A., J.D. [Latham&W.]
*PRACTICE AREAS: Government Contract Fraud; Health Care Fraud; Bid Protests; Foreign Military Sales.
Goldman, Stanley I., (AV) ... '39 '65 C&L.893 B.A., LL.B. [Denning&W.]
*PRACTICE AREAS: Transportation Law; Government Contracts; Maritime Law; Trademark Law.
Goldman, Stephen Mark ... '46 '71 C.228 A.B. L.477 J.D. [[C] McKenna&C.]
*PRACTICE AREAS: Insurance Coverage.
Goldman, Stephen P. ... '40 '65 C.145 B.A. L.976 LL.B. 2013 O St., N.W.
Goldman, Steven M., (AV) '60 '86
C.882 B.A. L.280 J.D. V.P. & Asst. Gen. Coun., Marriott Int'l., Inc.
*RESPONSIBILITIES: Franchising and Licensing.
Goldman, William L., (AV) ... '40 '65 C.188 B.A. L.309 LL.B. [McDermott,W.&E.]
Goldschmidt, Stanley H., (AV) '53 '78
C.978 B.A. L.276 J.D. 1025 Connecticut Avenue, Suite 220
Goldsmith, Barry R. ... '49 '75 C.659 B.S.E. L.276 J.D. N.A.S.D.
Goldsmith, Barry S. '62 '94 C.886 B.S.E.E. L.260 J.D.
[[A] Kenyon&K.] (See Pat. Sect.)
*PRACTICE AREAS: Intellectual Property.
Goldsmith, Kenneth '67 '94 C.446 B.A. L.64 J.D.
(adm. in MD; not adm. in DC) Amer. Bar Assn., Governmental Affs.
Goldsmith, Leizer Z., (BV) ... '62 '88 C.477 B.A. L.93 J.D. [Goldsmith]
Goldsmith, Rebecca L. ... '71 '97 C.1036 B.A. L.904 J.D. [[A] Venable,A.B.H.&C.]
*PRACTICE AREAS: Intellectual Property; Patent Litigation.
Goldsmith, Willis J., (AV) ... '47 '73 C.103 B.A. L.569 J.D. [Jones,D.R.&P.]
*PRACTICE AREAS: Labor and Employment; Employment Litigation; Management Labor Law; Employee Benefits Litigation.

Goldsmith Law Firm, The, (BV)
1900 L Street, N.W., Suite 614, 20036
Telephone: 202-775-0040 Fax: 202-775-0005
Email: lgoldsmith@goldsmithfirm.com
Leizer Z. Goldsmith. Associate: Julie Glass Martin.
Labor and Employment, Litigation, Discrimination, Sexual Harassment, Contracts, Torts, Unpaid Wages, Overtime, Federal Civil Service, Wrongful Termination, Torts, Civil Rights.
See Professional Biographies, WASHINGTON, DISTRICT OF COLUMBIA

Goldson, Amy Robertson ... '53 '76 C.788 B.A. L.128 J.D. 4015 28th Pl. Northwest
Goldstein, Allan B., (AV) ... '48 '74 C.273 B.A. L.982 J.D. [Dickstein S.M.&O.]
*PRACTICE AREAS: Banking Law; Real Estate (Property) Law; Taxation of Individuals Law; Business Entities Law.
Goldstein, Andrew P. ... '34 '59 C.25 L.94 LL.B. [McCarthy,S.&H.]
*PRACTICE AREAS: Transportation Law; Antitrust Law.

Goldstein, Anne T. '57 '83 C.674 A.B. L.309 J.D.
(adm. in MA; not adm. in DC) Intl. Human Rights Law Grp.
Goldstein, Bruce, (AV) .... '44 '69 C.575 A.B. L.273 J.D. [Zuckerman S.]
*PRACTICE AREAS: Bankruptcy.
Goldstein, Corinne A., (AV) .... '51 '76 C.914 B.A. L.477 J.D. [Covington&B.]
Goldstein, David S. .... '55 '81 C.1307 B.A. L.94 J.D. [Sutherland A.&B.]
*PRACTICE AREAS: Securities Regulation; Investment Company Law; Investment Management; Insurance Regulation; Retirement Benefit Plans.
Goldstein, Frank R., (AV) .... '43 '67 C.228 A.B. L.446 LL.B. [Sidley A.B.&W.]
Goldstein, Irving .... '38 '64 C.994 B.A. L.569 LL.B. Dir. Gen. & CEO, INTELSAT
Goldstein, Jeffrey M. .... '57 '83 C.105 B.A. L.94 J.D. [Goldstein&L.]
*PRACTICE AREAS: Franchise Law; Complex Litigation; Antitrust; Securities.
Goldstein, Jennifer A. .... '71 '96 C.893 B.A. L.945 J.D. [Ⓐ Patton B.]
Goldstein, Jorge A., (AV) '49 '83
C.688 B.S. L.273 J.D. [Sterne,K.G.&F.] (See Pat. Sect.)
*PRACTICE AREAS: Agrochemicals; Life Sciences; Technology Transfers; Biotechnology; Intellectual Property.
Goldstein, Joseph I., (AV) .... '42 '73 C.705 B.A. L.477 J.D. [Crowell&M.]
*PRACTICE AREAS: Broker-Dealer Arbitration; Broker-Dealer Regulation; Securities Arbitration; Securities Disclosure; Securities Fraud.
Goldstein, Kelly D. '— '98 C.696 B.A. L.273 J.D.
(adm. in CA; not adm. in DC) [Ⓐ Piper M.R.&W.]
*PRACTICE AREAS: Business; Technology; Venture Capital; Emerging Growth Companies.
Goldstein, Melissa M. .... '70 '96 C.893 B.A. L.976 J.D. [Ⓐ Skadden,A.S.M.&F.]
Goldstein, Melissa Michele '70 '95 C.893 B.A. L.976 J.D.
(adm. in NY; not adm. in DC) 2219 California St., N.W.
Goldstein, Melvin, (AV) .... '40 '66 C.659 B.A. L.309 J.D. [Goldstein&Assoc.]
*PRACTICE AREAS: Energy Law; Environmental Law; Litigation.
Goldstein, Melvin '34 '70 C.831 A.B. L.276 J.D.
(adm. in MD; not adm. in DC; See Pat. Sect.) [Ⓒ Keil&W.]
*PRACTICE AREAS: Patents.
Goldstein, Michael B. .... '43 '67 C.188 A.B. L.569 J.D. [Dow,L.&A.]
Goldstein, N. Linda, (AV) .... '53 '79 C.30 B.A. L.1218 J.D. [Ⓒ Goulston&S.]
*PRACTICE AREAS: Real Estate Law; Housing Law; Affordable Housing.
Goldstein, Nick '73 '01 C.319 B.A. L.1194 J.D.
(adm. in MA; not adm. in DC) [Ⓐ Van Ness F.]
*PRACTICE AREAS: Energy; Environment.
Goldstein, Richard S., (AV) .... '48 '74 C.1044 B.A. L.93 J.D. [Nixon P.]
*PRACTICE AREAS: Real Estate; Housing Law; Real Estate Securities.
Goldstein, Thomas C. .... '70 '95 C.575 A.B. L.904 J.D. 4607 Asbury Pl., N.W.

Goldstein & Associates, P.C., (AV)
1757 P Street, N.W., 20036
Telephone: 202-872-8740 Telecopier: 202-872-8744
Melvin Goldstein;—William L. Miller.
Energy, Environmental, Administrative and International Law. Civil Litigation.
See Professional Biographies, WASHINGTON, DISTRICT OF COLUMBIA

Goldstein Handler & Levine, P.C.
(See Bethesda, Maryland)

Goldstein & Loots, PC, (AV)
1700 K Street, N.W., Suite 801, 20006 ⊙
Telephone: 202-223-1983 Facsimile: 202-223-2002
Email: info@goldlootslaw.com URL: http://www.goldlootslaw.com
Members: James M. Loots; Jeffrey M. Goldstein. Of Counsel: Stephen D. Chace (Not admitted in DC). Associates: Matthew J. Kreutzer (Not admitted in DC); Brian A. Loffredo (Not admitted in DC); David G. Ross (Not admitted in DC).
Franchise Law, Franchise Litigation, Dealership Law, Franchise Arbitration, Franchise Termination, Hotel Franchise Law, Franchise Distribution and Licensing, Small Business Law, Commercial Leasing, Corporate Law, Emerging Business Law, Commercial Litigation, Employment Law, Employment Dispute Resolution, Executive Compensation, Employment Policy Review and Development, Wrongful Termination.
Union, New Jersey Office: 2042 Morris Avenue. Telephone: 908-688-7281. Fax: 908-688-7284.
See Professional Biographies, WASHINGTON, DISTRICT OF COLUMBIA

Goldstone, David J. .... '68 '95 C.453 B.S. L.309 J.D. [Ⓐ Skadden,A.S.M.&F.]
*PRACTICE AREAS: Computer and Software Patents; Litigation.
Goldwert, Joshua S. .... '73 '00 C.659 B.A. L.569 J.D. [Ⓐ Wilmer,C.&P.]
Goley, Sharon M. .... '62 '89 C.516 B.A. L.904 J.D. [Margolius,M.D.R.&T.]
*PRACTICE AREAS: Commercial Litigation; Residential and Commercial Landlord-Tenant Law; Employment Law.
Golightly, Kim O. .... '58 '85 C.101 B.S. L.276 J.D. Ernst & Young, LLP
Gollatz, Christine M. .... '— '00 C.823 B.A. L.659 J.D. [Ⓐ Shaw P.]
Gollhofer, Richard A. .... '55 '81 C.701 B.S. L.146 J.D. [Staas&H.] (See Pat. Sect.)
*PRACTICE AREAS: Intellectual Property Law; Patent, Trademark, Copyright and Unfair Competition.
Gollin, Michael A., (AV) '57 '85
C.674 A.B. L.94 J.D. [Venable,A.B.H.&C.] (See Pat. Sect.)
*PRACTICE AREAS: Intellectual Property; Patent Law; Biotechnology; Trademarks; Environmental Law.
Gollomp, Jeffrey A. .... '64 '90 C.945 B.A. L.245 J.D. Sr. Coun., Cinergy Servs.
Golob, Barry P. .... '61 '91 C.472 B.S. L.904 J.D. [Shook,H.&B.]
*PRACTICE AREAS: Patent, Trademark, Copyright and Trade Secret Litigation; Intellectual Property Counseling.
Golomb, Jonathan I. '55 '81 C.1349 B.A. L.477 J.D.
(adm. in NY; not adm. in DC) NASD Regulation, Inc.
Golub, Arnold P. '68 '93 C.30 B.S.B.A. L.1019 J.D.
(adm. in NY; not adm. in DC) Nasdaq
Golub, Jonathan M. .... '63 '99 C.1036 B.A. L.999 J.D. 1007 K Street, N.W.
Golub, Martin J. .... '47 '77 C.674 A.B. L.93 J.D. [Seyfarth S.]
*PRACTICE AREAS: Government Contracts Law; International Commercial Transactions; International Arbitration and Litigation.
Golub, Michael J. .... '60 '85 C.228 B.A. L.276 J.D. 1156 15th St., N.W.
Golubock, Carol R. '48 '73 C.681 B.A. L.813 J.D.
Assoc. Gen. Coun, Service Employees Intl. Union
Golumbic, Lars .... '67 '98 C.597 B.A. L.659 J.D. [Ⓐ Dow,L.&A.]
Gombar, Robert C. .... '48 '75 C.1040 B.B.A. L.262 J.D. [McDermott,W.&E.]
Gomez, Armando .... '70 '94 C.228 A.B. L.276 J.D. [Ⓐ Skadden,A.S.M.&F.]
*PRACTICE AREAS: Federal Taxation.
Gomez, Lisa A. '71 '96 C.477 B.A. L.94 J.D.
(adm. in IL; not adm. in DC) [Ⓐ Dow,L.&A.]
Gomez, Marisa A. .... '68 '94 C&L.477 B.A., J.D. [Ⓐ Sidley A.B.&W.]
Gomez-Pinzon, Enrique .... '— '83 [Ⓒ Wilmer,C.&P.]
*PRACTICE AREAS: Mergers and Acquisitions; International Arbitration; International Trade; Project Finance; Privatization.
Gomperts, John S. .... '56 '83 C.112 A.B. L.276 J.D. 3751 Jenifer St NW
Gondelman, Larry S., (AV) .... '52 '77 C.1036 B.A. L.276 J.D. [Akin,G.S.H.&F.]
*PRACTICE AREAS: Litigation.
Gonsalves, Gregory J. '60 '97 C.823 Ph.D. L.276 J.D.
(adm. in VA; not adm. in DC; See Pat. Sect.) [Ⓐ Pennie&E.]
*PRACTICE AREAS: Intellectual Property.
Gonson, Paul .... '— '54 C&L.107 LL.B. [Ⓒ Kirkpatrick&L.]
*PRACTICE AREAS: Securities Litigation; Securities Regulation; SEC Enforcement; Insider Trading; U.S. Supreme Court Litigation.

Gonsoulin, John P. '76 '01 C.846 B.A. L.309 J.D.
(adm. in TX; not adm. in DC) [Ⓐ Kirkland&E.]
*PRACTICE AREAS: Litigation; Appellate Practice.
Gonzales, Robin Freedman .... '64 '99 C.945 B.A. L.273 J.D. [Ⓐ Arent F.K.P.&K.]
*PRACTICE AREAS: Business; Commercial Real Estate; Corporate Law; Leases and Leasing; Nonprofit and Charitable Organizations.
Gonzalez, Cecilia H., (AV) .... '55 '80 C.012 B.A. L.276 J.D. [Howrey S.A.&W.]
*PRACTICE AREAS: International Trade; Intellectual Property; Litigation.
Gonzalez, Daniel '65 '91 C.1044 B.A. L.1019 J.D.
(adm. in XX; not adm. in DC) Next Link Communications
Gonzalez, Edward .... '53 '91 C.1165 B.A. L.276 J.D. [E.Gonzalez]
Gonzalez, Eleazar A. .... '— '99 C.1222 B.A. L.1119 J.D. [Ⓐ Arnold&P.]
*PRACTICE AREAS: Corporate Law; Securities; International Law.
Gonzalez, Henry P. '55 '86 C.262 B.A. L.1162 J.D.
(adm. in NY; not adm. in DC) [Rodriguez O,F.G.&W.] (⊙New York, NY)
*PRACTICE AREAS: International Transportation; Admiralty and Maritime Law; Export Regulation; International Commercial Transactions; Surety Bonds.
Gonzalez, Jennifer R. .... '69 '96 C.309 A.B. L.976 J.D. [Ⓐ Kirkpatrick&L.]
*PRACTICE AREAS: Investment Management; Mutual Funds; Blue Sky Law.
Gonzalez, Kate Jesberg '55 '97 C.339 B.S.W. L.276 J.D.
(adm. in MD; not adm. in DC) D.C. Dept. of Human Servs.
Gonzalez, Silvia Laura .... '59 '83 C.4 B.A. L.273 J.D. Asst. U. S. Atty.
Gonzalez, Edward, P.C. .... 1400 16th St., NW, Ste. 500
González-Magaz, José Ramón .... '70 '97 C.31 B.A. L.178 J.D. [Ⓐ Steptoe&J.]
Gonzalez-Scarano, Frances G. '51 '93 C.677 B.S. L.128 J.D.
2725 Connecticut Ave., N.W.
Gooch, R. Gordon, (AV) '34 '61 C.902 A.B. L.846 LL.B.
Suite 750, 1310 G Street, N.W.
Gooch, Raymond L., (AV) .... '38 '64 C.910 B.S. L.276 J.D. [Ross,M.&F.]
*PRACTICE AREAS: Real Estate Law (50%); Decedents Estates (25%); Estate Planning Law (25%).
Good, C. Edward '45 '71 C.575 A.B. L.893 J.D.
(adm. in VA; not adm. in DC) [Ⓒ Finnegan,H.F.G.&D.] ‡
Goode, Coralyn .... '56 '81 C.276 A.B. L.945 J.D. [Squire,S.&D.]
*PRACTICE AREAS: International Law; Project Finance; Construction Law; Public Contract Law.
Goode, Ryan W. '— '01 C.602 B.B.A. L.309 J.D.
(adm. in IL; not adm. in DC) [Ⓐ Kirkland&E.]
*PRACTICE AREAS: Litigation.
Goode, Scott W. '66 '94 C.1365 B.A. L.1206 J.D.
(adm. in IL; not adm. in DC) [Ⓐ Stevens,D.M.&M.]
*PRACTICE AREAS: Trademark; Trademark Litigation; Unfair Competition; Copyright.
Goode, Thomas E. '67 '91 C.423 B.A. L.276 J.D.
(adm. in MD; not adm. in DC) UTC, The Telecommunications Assn.
Goodell, Rebecca Ellen '65 '93 C.602 B.S. L.893 J.D.
Senior Manager, Management Consultant KDMG Peat Marwick‡
Goodgal, Paula A. '48 '74 C.289 B.A. L.597 J.D.
(adm. in IL; not adm. in DC) [Dubé&G.] ⊙
Goodheart, Rebecca P. .... '74 '00 C.276 B.S.F.S. L.893 J.D. [Ⓐ Wiley R.&F.]
Goodin, Mark A. ....'— '92 C.893 B.A. L.273 J.D. [Ⓐ Morgan,L.&B.]
Goodkind, Arthur B., (AV) .... '35 '60 C.918 B.A. L.309 LL.B. [Holland&K.]
*PRACTICE AREAS: Telecommunications Law.
Goodling, Monica Marie '73 '99 C.1053 B.A. L.1339 J.D.
(adm. in VA; not adm. in DC) 310 First St., SE
Goodman, Alfred N., (AV) '45 '70
C.696 B.S.M.E. L.276 J.D. [Roylance,A.B.&G.] (See Pat. Sect.)
*PRACTICE AREAS: Litigation; Patent Law; Trademark Law; Copyright Law; Mechanical Patent Law.
Goodman, Amy L., (AV) .... '51 '75 C&L.94 A.B., J.D. [Ⓒ Gibson,D.&C.]
*PRACTICE AREAS: Securities; Corporate Law.
Goodman, Andrea Pierce '66 '94 C.597 B.A. L.93 J.D.
(adm. in MA; not adm. in DC) U.N. Mission for Kosora
Goodman, Collette C., (AV) .... '44 '75 C.914 B.A. L.309 J.D. [Shea&G.]
*PRACTICE AREAS: Domestic Taxation; International Taxation.
Goodman, Craig G., (BV) .... '50 '75 C.446 B.A. L.472 J.D. 3254 O Street, N.W.
Goodman, Ellen P. .... '65 '92 C&L.309 A.B., J.D. [Covington&B.]
Goodman, Jack N., (AV) '51 '75 C.367 A.B. L.575 J.D.
Sr. V.P. & Gen. Coun., National Association of Broadcasters
*RESPONSIBILITIES: Communications Law; Appellate.
Goodman, Janine F. .... '66 '92 C.103 B.A. L.145 J.D. [Ⓐ Levine,B.B.&B.]
*PRACTICE AREAS: Telecommunications Law; Administrative Law; Commercial Law.
Goodman, Jeffrey H., (AV) .... '52 '79 C.31 B.A. L.477 J.D. [Fulbright&J.]
*PRACTICE AREAS: Project Finance; International Law; Real Estate; Corporate Law.
Goodman, Jeffrey M. '73 '98 C.183 B.A. L.30 J.D.
(adm. in NJ; not adm. in DC) [Ⓐ Swidler B.S.F.]
*PRACTICE AREAS: Antitrust and Trade Regulation.
Goodman, Jennifer F .... '70 '95 C.205 B.A.A.S. L.1048 J.D. 810 First Street N.E.
Goodman, Jody, (BV) .... '58 '85 C.976 B.A. L.472 J.D. [Ⓐ Crowell&M.]
Goodman, John M., (AV) '47 '74 C.674 A.B. L.309 J.D.
Asst. Gen. Coun., Fed. Reg. & Legis. Matters, Verizon Communications
Goodman, Lauren S. .... '75 '99 C.188 B.S. L.309 J.D. [Ⓐ Gibson,D.&C.]
Goodman, Leonard S. .... '33 '57 C.645 B.A. L.309 LL.B. 7119 16th St., N.W.
Goodman, Lois R. .... '45 '71 C.681 B.A. L.659 J.D. 5712 Nebraska Ave. N.W.
Goodman, Mary Beth ...... '73 '00 C.1369 B.A. L.146 J.D. 1300 Pennsylvania Ave., NW
Goodman, Neil M. .... '57 '84 C.103 A.B. L.178 J.D. [Arnold&P.]
*PRACTICE AREAS: Corporate; International.
Goodman, Philip J. .... '61 '92 C.871 B.S. L.659 J.D. [Ⓐ Chadbourne&P.]
Goodman, Randolph M., (AV) '48 '74
C.264 B.A. L.705 J.D. [Morrison&F.] (⊙Irvine, CA)
Goodman, S. Mark ... '59 '85 C.502 B.J. L.228 J.D. Exec. Dir., Student Press Law Center
Goodman, Saul B., (AV) .... '53 '80 C.976 B.A. L.893 J.D. [Covington&B.]
Goodman, Sharon McNeilly .... '63 '89 C.367 B.A. L.588 J.D. [Slevin&H.]
Goodman, Stephen J. .... '58 '85 C.309 B.A. L.976 J.D. [Ⓒ Jones,D.R.&P.]
Goodman, Stephen L., (AV) .... '56 '80 C.688 B.S. L.188 J.D. [Halprin,T.G.&M.]
*PRACTICE AREAS: Telecommunications Law; Antitrust Law.
Goodman, Timothy H. .... '70 '99 C.276 B.S. L.930 J.D. [Ⓐ Schmeltzer,A.&S.]
*PRACTICE AREAS: Litigation; Civil Litigation; Business Law; Franchise Law.
Goodrich, George H. .... '25 '53 C.951 B.A. L.893 LL.B. Sr. Supr. Ct. J.
Goodrich, Jennifer A. .... '69 '95 C&L.276 B.A., J.D. [Ⓐ Holland&K.] (⊙New York, NY)
*PRACTICE AREAS: Real Estate; Commercial Leasing.
Goodrich, Nathaniel H., (AV) .... '14 '36 C&L.188 A.B., LL.B. [Ⓒ Seyfarth S.]
Goodrich, Robert D. .... '56 '81 C.696 B.A. L.273 J.D. 3003 Van Ness St., N.W.
Goodrich, William W. .... '47 '75 C.228 A.B. L.273 J.D. [Arent F.K.P.&K.]
*PRACTICE AREAS: Government (Public) Contract Law; Intellectual Properties Law; Litigation.
Goodson, Jamie Z. .... '— '01 C.309 B.A. L.976 J.D. [Ⓐ Arnold&P.]
*PRACTICE AREAS: Real Estate.
Goodson, Robert W., (AV) .... '50 '76 C&L.602 A.B., J.D. [Carr G.] ⊙
*PRACTICE AREAS: Professional Liability; Health Care; Litigation.
Goodson, Vivian B. .... '14 '43 C.788 A.B. L.273 LL.B. 1300 19th St., N.W.
Goodstein, Michael D. .... '59 '84 C.103 B.A. L.188 J.D. [Resolution]
*PRACTICE AREAS: Environmental Litigation.

Goodstein, Michael R. .... '64 '89 C.1036 B.A. L.904 J.D. [Arter&H.]
*PRACTICE AREAS: Litigation.
Goodwin, Charles .... '08 '32 C.563 B.S. L.1009 LL.B. 3601 Connecticut Ave., N.W.‡
Goodwin, Lee M., (AV) .... '50 '75 C.197 A.B. L.477 J.D. [Thelen R.&P.]
*PRACTICE AREAS: Electric Power and Infrastructure Project Acquisition; Development and Finance; Electric Power Regulation.
Goodwin, Michael D., (AV) .... '60 '84 C.145 B.A. L.309 J.D. [Arnold&P.]
*PRACTICE AREAS: Real Estate.
Goodwin, Scott R. .... '57 '92 C.188 B.S. L.276 J.D. [Ⓐ Cleary,G.S.&H.]

Goodwin Procter LLP, (AV)
A Partnership including Professional Corporations
1717 Pennsylvania Avenue, N.W., 20006 ⊙
Telephone: 202-974-1000 Telecopier: 202-331-9330
URL: http://www.goodwinprocter.com
Members of Firm: Jeremiah S. Buckley; Joseph M. Kolar; Keith D. Shugarman; Thomas M. Hefferon; Jeffrey P. Naimon; Andrea Lee Negroni; John P. Kromer; Margo H.K. Tank; David L. Permut. Counsel: Melissa L. Barrett. Of Counsel: R. David Whitaker (Not admitted in DC). Associates: Jonathan D. Jerison; Patricia S. Mugavero; Peter N. Koufos (Not admitted in DC); Aldys A. Dayle; Anthony Tu-Sekine (Not admitted in DC); James D. Filpi; Jacob G. Thiessen (Not admitted in DC); Christopher M. Witeck; Vincent D. Schaper (Not admitted in DC); Michael P. Whalen (Not admitted in DC); John C. Ekman (Not admitted in DC); Nakita M. Pastor (Not admitted in DC); Ellen M. Quattrucci; Ray Christian Witter; Maureen C. Yap (Not admitted in DC).
Alternative Dispute Resolution, Antitrust and Trade Regulation, Banking, Bankruptcy, Corporate, Corporate Finance, Corporate Governance, Securities, Litigation and Mergers and Acquisitions, ERISA/Employee Benefits, Energy, Environmental and Environmental Litigation, Estate Planning, Consumer Financial Services, Financial Services, Housing, Finance and Economic Development, Insurance, Intellectual Property/Technology, Labor and Employment, Intellectual Property Litigation, Litigation, Private Equity/Emerging Companies, Patent and Trademarks, Real Estate Development, Real Estate Investment Management, Real Estate Securities and Capital Markets, Regulatory Compliance, Securities, Tax, Electronic Commerce, Legislative and Economic Development.
Boston, Massachusetts Office: Exchange Place, Telephone: 617-570-1000. Telecopier: 617-523-1231.
New York, N.Y. Offices: 599 Lexington Avenue. Telephone: 212-813-8800. Telecopier: 212-355-3333; 1285 Avenue of the Americas. Telephone: 212-956-1500. Telecopier: 212-956-3252.
Roseland, New Jersey Office: Seven Becker Farm Road. Telephone: 973-992-1990. Fax: 973-992-4643.
See Professional Biographies, WASHINGTON, DISTRICT OF COLUMBIA

Goodwyn, R. Tyler, IV .... '60 '94 C.885 B.S.E.E. L.945 J.D. [Morgan,L.&B.]
Goodwyn, Suzanne Spink .... '64 '94 C.861 B.A. L.564 J.D. [Ⓐ Pepper&C.]
*PRACTICE AREAS: Cable Communications; FCC Licensing; FCC Regulation; Communications and Media; Wireless Communications.
Goold, James A., (AV) .... '50 '76 C.918 B.A. L.145 J.D. [Ⓒ Covington&B.]
Gootman, Marek Drell '70 '00 C.659 B.S.E. L.276 J.D.
(adm. in MD; not adm. in DC) [Ⓐ Patton B.]
Goraya, Victor S. .... '38 '85 C&L.999 B.A., J.D. Asst. Corp. Coun.
Gordin, Richard H. .... '48 '74 C.679 B.S. L.597 J.D. [Tighe P.A.T.]
*PRACTICE AREAS: Complex Litigation; Criminal Law.
Gordon, Adam H. .... '66 '93 C.976 B.A. L.273 J.D. [Ⓐ Collier S.S.]
*PRACTICE AREAS: International Trade.
Gordon, Alvin .... '18 '42 C.999 L.878 LL.B. 1511 K St., N.W.
Gordon, Bernard, (AV) .... '23 '51 C.273 A.B. L.276 J.D. 1025 Thomas Jefferson St. N.W.
Gordon, Christopher H. .... '72 '98 C&L.893 B.A., J.D. [Ⓐ Squire,S.&D.]
Gordon, David Louis '68 '97 C.112 B.A. L.309 J.D.
(adm. in MA; not adm. in DC) 1200 Penn Ave.
Gordon, Denis F., (AV) .... '39 '68 C.390 A.B. L.659 J.D. [Gordon&B.]
*PRACTICE AREAS: Trial and Appellate Practice; Corporate Law; Labor Law; Employee Benefits.
Gordon, George I., (AV) .... '30 '54 C&L.178 A.B., J.D. [Ⓒ Swidler B.S.F.]
*PRACTICE AREAS: Structured Finance; Real Estate.
Gordon, Jack B., (AV) .... '55 '80 C.1044 B.A. L.273 J.D. [Fried,F.H.S.&J.]
Gordon, Jacqueline M. .... '56 '82 C.260 B.A. L.893 J.D. [Ⓐ Weil,G.&M.]
*PRACTICE AREAS: Real Estate; Real Estate Finance; Corporate Transactions; Secondary Financing; Health Care.
Gordon, Jeffrey B. '47 '74 C.446 B.S. L.64 J.D.
(adm. in TX; not adm. in DC) 3001 Veazey Ter., N.W.‡
Gordon, Julia R. ...... '63 '92 C&L.309 A.B., J.D. Sr. Coun., Ctr. for Law and Soc. Policy
Gordon, Keara M. .... '68 '94 C.1041 B.A. L.276 J.D. [Ⓐ Piper M.R.&W.]
*PRACTICE AREAS: Securities Litigation; Business Litigation.
Gordon, Leonard L. .... '63 '88 C&L.273 B.A., J.D. [Piper M.R.&W.]
*PRACTICE AREAS: Antitrust and Trade Regulation.
Gordon, Michael A., (AV) .... '52 '77 C.165 A.B. L.30 J.D. [Arent F.K.P.&K.]
*PRACTICE AREAS: Real Estate-Commercial Law.
Gordon, Michael E. .... '69 '97 C.309 A.B. L.477 J.D. [Ⓐ Wilmer,C.&P.]
Gordon, Rebecca H. '75 '01 C.945 B.A. L.273 J.D.
(adm. in VA; not adm. in DC) [Ⓐ Perkins C.]
*PRACTICE AREAS: Political Law.
Gordon, Richard K, Jr '56 '85 C.976 B.A. L.309 J.D.
(adm. in MA; not adm. in DC) 700 19th St., N.W.
Gordon, Steven D., (AV) .... '49 '75 C.821 B.A. L.309 J.D. [Holland&K.]
*PRACTICE AREAS: White Collar Criminal Litigation; Civil Litigation; Administrative Procedure Act Litigation.
Gordon, Stuart J., (AV) .... '30 '57 C&L.569 B.S., J.D. 1667 K St. N.W.
Gordon, Todd S. .... '— '99 C.1369 B.B.A. L.880 J.D. [Ⓐ Latham&W.]

Gordon & Barnett, (AV)
Suite 450, Two Lafayette Centre, 1133 21st Street, N.W., 20036
Telephone: 202-833-3400 Telecopier: 202-223-0120
Members of Firm: Denis F. Gordon; James R. Barnett; Frank Petramalo, Jr.; John F. Conroy; David M. Ermer; Brad W. Spencer; Scott R. Jamison. Associates: Mary M. Siffermann; Robert G. Iadicicco.
Trial and Appellate Practice in all Courts. Labor and Employee Benefits Law including Commercial Law, Government Contracts, Insurance Law, Health Law, Criminal Law.
See Professional Biographies, WASHINGTON, DISTRICT OF COLUMBIA

Gordon & Bryant, (BV)
Curtis House, 1742 S Street, N.W., 20009-6145
Telephone: 202-833-8011 Fax: 202-833-0352
Email: albryant@clark.net URL: http://www.lawyers.com/gordon&bryantlaw
Charles Gordon (1905-1999); Ann Lake Bryant.
Immigration and Nationality Law. Business Immigration.
See Professional Biographies, WASHINGTON, DISTRICT OF COLUMBIA

Gordon, Silberman, Wiggins & Childs, P.C.
1621 Connecticut Avenue, N.W., Suite 400, 20009 ⊙
Telephone: 202-238-0690 Facsimilie: 202-238-0968
URL: http://www.gswc.com
Resident Associates: David W. Sanford; Timothy B. Fleming; Lori B. Kisch (Not admitted in DC); S. Nicole Nardone (Not admitted in DC).
General Civil Trial and Appellate Practice in all State and Federal Courts. Class Action Litigation, Corporate/Business, Acquisitions and Mergers, Corporate Finance, Banking, Real Estate, Taxation, Securities, Administrative, Estate Planning, Labor, Employment Discrimination, Sex Harassment, ERISA, Wage and Hour, Employee Benefits, Disability, Discrimination, Special Education Law.
Birmingham, Alabama Office: 1400 South Trust Tower, 420 North 20th Street, 35203. Telephone: 205-328-0640. Facsimile: 205-254-1500.
See Professional Biographies, WASHINGTON, DISTRICT OF COLUMBIA

Gore, Gabriel E. '69 '94 C.804 B.A. L.145 J.D.
(adm. in MO; not adm. in DC) [Ⓐ Williams&C.]
*PRACTICE AREAS: White Collar Criminal Defense; Complex Commercial Litigation; Manufacturers Liability.
Gore, Russell H. .... '68 '93 C.269 B.A. L.276 J.D. [Ⓒ Seyfarth S.]
*PRACTICE AREAS: Labor and Employment.

Gorelick, Philip A.
(See McLean, Virginia)

Goren, Robert K., (AV) .... '49 '74 C.216 B.A. L.128 J.D. [Goren,W.&O.] ⊙
Goren, Wolff & Orenstein, L.L.C., (AV) .... 1730 K St., N.W. (⊙Rockville, MD)
Gorham, Robert L., (AV) .... '42 '74 C.473 B.A. L.273 J.D. [Holland&K.]
*PRACTICE AREAS: Commercial Transactional Real Estate; Commercial Real Estate Acquisitions and Sales; Finance; Leasing; Loan Workouts.
Gorinson, Stanley M., (AV) .... '45 '74 C.102 B.A. L.705 J.D. [Kilpatrick S.]
*PRACTICE AREAS: Antitrust; Litigation.
Gorman, Edward J., III '54 '82 C.93 B.A. L.128 J.D.
Exec. Dir., United Brotherhood of Carpenters Health & Safety Fund
Gorman, John J., (AV) .... '54 '79 C.103 B.A. L.880 J.D. [Luse L.G.P.&S.]
*PRACTICE AREAS: Banking and Financial Institutions; Mergers and Acquisitions; Corporate Law; Securities.
Gorman, Joyce J., (AV) .... '52 '77 C.788 A.B. L.446 J.D. [Ⓒ Cadwalader,W.&T.]
Gorman, Leo N., (AV) .... '38 '66 C.602 A.B. L.276 J.D. Asst. Corp. Coun.
Gorman, Nancy Yaeger, (BV) .... '60 '85 C.502 B.A. L.846 J.D. 1722 Eye St., N.W.
Gorman, Robert A. '37 '62 C&L.309 B.A., LL.B.
(adm. in NY; not adm. in DC) [Ⓒ Meyer&K.]
Gorman, Thomas O., (AV) .... '48 '73 C.363 A.B. L.161 J.D. [Porter W.M.&A.]
*PRACTICE AREAS: Complex Litigation; Antitrust; Securities; Commercial; International.
Gorman, Walter .... '37 '64 C.676 A.B. L.94 LL.B. 3660 Winfield Lane, NW

Gorman & Williams
(See Baltimore, Maryland)

Gormley, F. Joseph .... '68 '93 C.550 B.A. L.446 J.D. [Ⓐ Hogan&H.]
*PRACTICE AREAS: Antitrust.
Gormley, Joseph L. .... '14 '48 C.93 B.S. L.276 LL.B. 3817 Kanawha St., N.W.‡
Gormley, W. Paul .... '26 '58 C.768 A.B. L.273 J.D. 1629 16th St., N.W.‡
Gormly, Charles F. .... '67 '96 C.918 B.A. L.30 J.D. 1899 L St., N.W.
Goroff, David E. .... '52 '77 C.860 B.A. L.818 J.D. [Bruder,G.&M.]
*PRACTICE AREAS: Electric Utility; Cogeneration; Energy Contracts.
Gorrell, J. Warren, Jr., (AV) '54 '79
C.674 A.B. L.893 J.D. [Hogan&H.] (⊙New York, NY)
*PRACTICE AREAS: Corporate Finance; Securities Offerings; Mergers and Acquisitions; Real Estate Investment Trusts.
Gorski, Joseph M. '61 '96 C.475 B.S.M.E. L.1209 J.D.
(adm. in VA; not adm. in DC; See Pat. Sect.) [Ⓐ Wenderoth,L.&P.]
*PRACTICE AREAS: Mechanical Patent Prosecution; Electrical Patent Prosecution.
Gorsuch, Neil M. .... '67 '92 C.178 A.B. L.309 J.D. [Kellogg,H.H.T.&E.]
*PRACTICE AREAS: Litigation.
Gosain, Carol R. .... '61 '98 C.1356 B.A. L.1209 J.D. [Ⓐ Steptoe&J.]
Gosliner, Michael L. '53 '81 C.112 A.B. L.1065 J.D.
(adm. in CA; not adm. in DC) Gen. Coun., Marine Mammal Comm.
Goss, Elizabeth .... '56 '93 C.681 A.B. L.276 J.D. [Bennett,T.&C.]
Goss, Roland C., (AV) .... '53 '78 C.475 B.A. L.597 J.D. [Jorden B.]
*PRACTICE AREAS: Class Action Litigation; Insurance Coverage Litigation; Environmental Litigation.
Gosselink, Robert G. .... '64 '95 C.604 B.A. L.93 J.D. [Ⓐ White&C.]
Gossett, David M. .... '69 '97 C.685 B.A. L.145 J.D. [Ⓐ Mayer,B.&P.]
Gothard, Crystal .... '66 '97 C&L.208 B.A., J.D. [Ⓐ Patton B.]
Gottesdiener, Eli .... '61 '87 C.30 B.A. L.276 J.D. [Gottesdiener]
*PRACTICE AREAS: Class Actions; Complex Litigation; ERISA.

Gottesdiener Law Firm
3901 Yuma Street, N.W., 20016
Telephone: 202-243-1000 Fax: 202-537-1989
Email: egottesdiener@gottesdienerlaw.com URL: http://www.gottesdienerlaw.com
Eli Gottesdiener.
Civil and Criminal Litigation in Federal and State Court. Class Action, ERISA, White Collar, Criminal Defense, Consumer Fraud, Business Fraud, Professional Malpractice, Complex Civil.
See Professional Biographies, WASHINGTON, DISTRICT OF COLUMBIA

Gottesman, Evan R. '65 '93 C.976 B.A. L.178 J.D.
(adm. in NY; not adm. in DC) 1615 L. Street, N.W.
Gottesman, Milton M., (AV) .... '22 '48 C.178 A.B. L.976 LL.B. 1818 N St., N.W.‡
Gottfried, Barry H., (AV) .... '48 '77 C.918 B.A. L.309 J.D. [Shaw P.]
*PRACTICE AREAS: Litigation; Communications.
Gottlieb, Jonathan W. .... '59 '86 C.209 B.A. L.564 J.D. [Baker&M.]
*PRACTICE AREAS: Infrastructure Development; Project Finance.
Gottlieb, Robert Gene, (AV) .... '51 '76 C.645 B.A. L.273 J.D. [Venable,A.B.H.&C.]
*PRACTICE AREAS: Real Estate; Tax Law; Business Law.
Gottlieb, Sharon E., (BV) '42 '82 C.645 B.A. L.276 J.D.
900 New Hampshire Ave., N.W.
Gottovi, Sara L. .... '69 '97 C.860 B.A. L.945 J.D. [Ⓐ Covington&B.]
Gottscho, Christopher M. '63 '90 C.276 B.S. L.893 J.D.
(adm. in NJ; not adm. in DC) 3000 K St. NW
Gould, Dana L. .... '— '94 C.165 B.A. L.30 J.D. Assoc. Gen. Coun., Fannie Mae
*RESPONSIBILITIES: Financial Institutions.
Gould, James C., (AV) .... '54 '79 C.902 A.B. L.309 J.D. 801 Pennsylvania Ave NW #730
Gould, Jason H. .... '70 '96 C&L.276 B.A., J.D. [Ⓐ Jorden B.]
*PRACTICE AREAS: Litigation; General Practice; Insurance Law.
Gould, Kingdon, Jr. .... '24 '51 C&L.976 B.A., LL.B. 1725 DeSales, N.W.
Gould, William F. .... '65 '90 C.901 B.A. L.893 J.D. 1440 New York Ave., N.W.
Goulding, Michael Ian .... '64 '97 C.604 B.A. L.128 J.D. [Ⓐ Garvey,S.&B.]
*PRACTICE AREAS: Maritime; Environmental; Legislative Practice.
Goulet, Paul C. .... '72 '97 C&L.659 B.A., J.D. [Ⓐ Finnegan,H.F.G.&D.]
*PRACTICE AREAS: Patent Litigation; Patent Infringement; International Intellectual Property.

Goulston & Storrs, A Professional Corporation
Counsellors at Law
1717 Pennsylvania Avenue, 20006 ⊙
Telephone: 202-721-0011 Fax: 202-721-1111
Email: info@goulstonstorrs.com URL: http://www.goulstonstorrs.com
—Cynthia Langelier Paine (Not admitted in DC). Counsel: N. Linda Goldstein.
Affordable Housing, Commercial Law, Commercial Lending, Bankruptcy. Corporate, Business Formation, E-Commerce, Securities Law, Mergers and Acquisitions, Equity and Debt Financing, Closely-Held Businesses, Investment Funds, Intellectual Property, Emerging Technologies, Retail Businesses, Manufacturing Businesses, Employment Law, Non-Profit Organizations. Health Care, Assisted Living, Telemedicine, Hospitals/Health Centers, Professional Associations, Long Term Care, Corporate Compliance, Healthcare Practitioners, Managed Care, Home Health Providers. International, Joint Ventures, Tax Planning, Acquisitions/Financing, Latin American Group. Litigation, Land Use/Environmental, Intellectual Property, Employment Law, ADR, Construction, Regulatory Compliance, Tax Abatement, Insurance, Business and Commercial. Philanthropic Advisors. Real Estate/Environmental, Retail/Shopping Centers, Office, Real Estate Finance, Leasing, REIT/Securities, Development/Permitting, Environmental, Hospitality/Recreation, Affordable Housing, Multi-Family. Tax, Business Transactions, Real Estate Transactions, International Planning, Individual Tax Planning,

(This Listing Continued)

Goulston & Storrs, A Professional Corporation (Continued)

Wealth Transfer, Tax-Exempt Entities, Tax Incentive Programs, Executive Compensation, ERISA/ Employee Benefits. Trusts and Estates, Estate Planning, Fiduciary Administration, Charitable Planning.
Boston, Massachusetts Office: 400 Atlantic Avenue. Telephone: 617-482-1776. Fax: 617-574-4112.
See Professional Biographies, WASHINGTON, DISTRICT OF COLUMBIA

Gourley, Alan W.H. ... '55 '81 C.72 B.A. L.893 J.D. [Crowell&M.]
*PRACTICE AREAS: Public Contract Law; Litigation; Business Crimes Law; International Law.
Govan, Amelia G. ... '51 '81 C.329 B.A. L.362 J.D. Dept. of Employ. Servs.
Govan, Ronna M. ... '— '00 [Ⓐ Arnold&P.]
Gover, Kevin, (AV) ... '55 '81 C.674 A.B. L.560 J.D. [Steptoe&J.]
*PRACTICE AREAS: American Indian Law; Administrative Law.
Gowdey, Peter W., (AV) ... '43 '69 C.158 B.S. L.982 J.D. [Shook,H.&B.] (Pat.)
*PRACTICE AREAS: Intellectual Property Litigation; Intellectual Property Audits; International Law.
Gowen, Anne Elizabeth '70 '96 C.309 A.B. L.94 J.D.
(adm. in MA; not adm. in DC) P.O. Box 11380
Gowetski, Jennifer L. ... '— '99 C&L.276 B.S.F.S., J.D. [Ⓐ Latham&W.]
*PRACTICE AREAS: Corporate Law; Communications and Media.
Gozycki, Allyson Ann '74 '01 C.321 B.A. L.180 J.D.
(adm. in MD; not adm. in DC) [Ⓐ Clifford C.R.&W.]
*PRACTICE AREAS: Litigation.
Graae, Steffen W. ... '40 '73 C.976 B.A. L.276 J.D. Assoc. J., Supr. Ct.
Grabarek, Robert L., Jr. ... '59 '95 C.871 B.S. L.64 J.D. [Ⓒ Crowell&M.] (Pat.)
Graber, Elysa L. ... '67 '92 C.188 B.A. L.273 J.D. Asst. Corp. Coun.
Graber, Kathleen M. ... '69 '94 C&L.276 A.B., J.D. [Ⓐ Steptoe&J.]
Grable, Michael G. ... '70 '97 C.228 A.B. L.945 J.D. [Ⓐ Harris,W.&G.]
*PRACTICE AREAS: Telecommunications Law; Litigation.
Grabow, Bruce A. ... '63 '94 C.260 B.S. L.1338 J.D. [Ⓐ Dewey B.]
*PRACTICE AREAS: Energy.
Grabow, Troy Edwin ... '71 '01 C.867 B.S. L.273 J.D. [Ⓐ Finnegan,H.F.G.&D.]
*PRACTICE AREAS: Intellectual Property Litigation; Electro-Mechanical Patents; Patent Infringement; Patent Litigation; Patent Prosecution.
Grabow-Wallace, Gayle ... '— '99 C.1044 B.A. L.982 J.D. [Ⓐ Morgan,L.&B.]
Grace, Bruce R. ... '57 '89 C.145 B.A. L.178 J.D. [Baach R.&L.P.]
*PRACTICE AREAS: Civil Litigation; Commercial Litigation; Insurance Coverage Disputes; Reinsurance Coverage Disputes; Professional Malpractice.
Grace, David R., (AV) ... '56 '81 C.674 A.B. L.309 J.D. [Ⓒ Covington&B.]
Grace, Kevin M. '63 '93 C&L.425 B.B.A., J.D.
(adm. in LA; not adm. in DC) [Ⓐ Porter W.M.&A.]
*PRACTICE AREAS: Insurance Coverage Litigation.
Grace, Malcolm C. ... '72 '98 C&L.823 B.A., J.D. [Ⓐ Conlon,F.P.&P.]
*PRACTICE AREAS: Civil Rights; Class Actions.
Grace, Michael J. ... '54 '81 C.339 B.S. L.477 J.D. [Ⓒ Powell,G.F.&M.]
*PRACTICE AREAS: Taxation Law; Business Succession Planning.
Grace, Valerie S. ... '56 '81 C.681 A.B. L.309 J.D. William M. Mercer, Inc.
Gracyalny, Patricia A. '63 '94
C.119 B.A. L.128 J.D. Asst. Gen. Coun., D.C. Housing Auth.
Gradia, A. Kenneth '50 '76 C.216 B.A. L.276 J.D.
(adm. in MD; not adm. in DC) National Railway Labor Conference
Gradle, Brian D. ... '61 '87 C.951 B.A. L.276 J.D. [Epstein B.&G.]
*PRACTICE AREAS: Health Law.
Gradoville, Savery M. ... '47 '70 C.1295 B.A. L.276 LL.B. [Steptoe&J.]
*PRACTICE AREAS: Intellectual Property; Computer Law; Transactions; Licensing.
Grady, David F. ... '56 '82 C.951 B.A. L.893 J.D. 3801 Conn. Ave., N.W.
Grady, Gregory, (AV) ... '45 '73 C.893 B.A. L.861 J.D. [Wright&T.]
*PRACTICE AREAS: Energy Regulation.
Graefe, Frederick H., (AV) ... '44 '73 C.425 A.B. L.276 J.D. [Baker&H.]
*PRACTICE AREAS: Health Law; Legislative Law; Telecommunications; Tax; International Trade.
Graeff, Stephen D. ... '50 '75 C.30 B.A. L.273 J.D. [Carr,M.&G.]
*PRACTICE AREAS: Labor and Employment; Civil Litigation; Criminal Defense.
Graf, Marguerite L. '66 '95 C.914 B.A. L.665 J.D.
Asst. Coun., National Treasury Employees Union
Graf, Richard M. ... '57 '84 C.145 B.A. L.93 J.D. [Mintz,L.C.F.G.&P.]
*PRACTICE AREAS: Mergers & Acquisitions; Internet Law; Securities Offerings; Corporate Finance.
Graff, Edmund D. ... '64 '89 C.901 B.A. L.893 J.D. [Shaw P.]
Grafman, Stephen W., (AV) ... '— '65 C.575 A.B. L.893 LL.B. [Kirkpatrick&L.]
*PRACTICE AREAS: Commercial Litigation; Commercial Arbitration; Federal Criminal Law.
Graham, Barry W., (AV) '47 '77
C.893 B.S.E.E. L.280 J.D. [Finnegan,H.F.G.&D.] (See Pat. Sect.)
*PRACTICE AREAS: Electronic Intellectual Property; Intellectual Property Infringement; Intellectual Property Litigation; Computer and Software Patents; Technology Protection.
Graham, Cheryl K. '67 '92 C.1356 B.A. L.128 J.D.
(adm. in VA; not adm. in DC) [Margolius,M.D.R.&T.]
*PRACTICE AREAS: Domestic Relations; Mediation.
Graham, Donald K., (AV) ... '29 '55 C.383 B.S. L.893 J.D. [Spencer,G.&H.]
Graham, Felicia B. ... '52 '78 C.66 B.A. L.1194 J.D. [Orrick,H.&S.]
*PRACTICE AREAS: Structured Finance Law; Public Finance Law.
Graham, Grace '73 '00 C.88 B.A. L.93 J.D.
(adm. in AL; not adm. in DC) [Ⓐ Howrey S.A.&W.]
*PRACTICE AREAS: Commercial Litigation.
Graham, James J. ... '46 '71 C.93 B.A. L.846 J.D. [Jones,D.R.&P.]
*PRACTICE AREAS: Litigation; White Collar Crime; Corporate Investigations.
Graham, Jennifer F. ... '52 '80 C&L.999 B.A., LL.B. 601 13th St. N.W.
Graham, John S., III, (AV) ... '44 '74 C.902 B.A. L.976 J.D. [Ober,K.G.&S.] ⊙
Graham, Jonathan P., (AV) ... '60 '88 C.1168 B.A. L.846 J.D. [Williams&C.]
*PRACTICE AREAS: Civil Appeals; Commercial Litigation; Complex Litigation; Employment Discrimination; Environmental Criminal Defense.
Graham, Lori E. ... '72 '99 C.862 B.A. L.276 J.D. [Ⓐ Sonnenschein N.&R.]
*PRACTICE AREAS: Corporate Transactions.
Graham, Neil E. '55 '92 C.1356 B.A. L.1209 J.D.
(adm. in VA; not adm. in DC) [Stephens] ⊙
Graham, Rachel H. ... '66 '93 C.164 B.A. L.575 J.D. [Ⓐ Debevoise&P.]
*PRACTICE AREAS: Securities Regulation; Corporate Law.
Graham, Robert A. ... '68 '94 C.575 A.B. L.477 J.D. [Ⓐ Reno&C.]
*PRACTICE AREAS: Litigation; Administrative Agency Practice; Nonprofit Organizations Law; Affordable Housing.
Graham, Thomas R. ... '— '70 C.347 B.A. L.309 J.D. [King&S.]
*PRACTICE AREAS: Litigation and Trade.
Grambow, Martin E. '49 '74 C.188 B.S. L.734 J.D.
V.P. & Gen. Atty., SBC Communications Inc.
Grammas, George N. ... '64 '89 C.399 B.A. L.1035 J.D. [Gardner,C.&D.]
*PRACTICE AREAS: Corporate Law; Export Regulation; International Trade; Customs Law; Technology and Science.
Grammer, Elisa J., (AV) ... '52 '76 C.390 A.B. L.945 J.D. [GKRSE]
*PRACTICE AREAS: Administrative Law; Environmental Law; Oil and Gas; Natural Gas.
Granados, Luis L., III ... '53 '79 C.103 A.B. L.276 J.D. [McDermott,W.&E.]
Granados, Patricia D. ... '— '87 C.94 B.A. L.446 J.D. [Heller E.W.&M.] (Pat.)
*PRACTICE AREAS: Biotechnology and Pharmaceutical Patent Law.
Grandinetti, Paul, (AV) ... '52 '83 C.608 B.S. L.117 J.D. [Levy&G.] (Pat.)
Grandis, Edward S. ... '50 '77 C.280 B.A. L.692 J.D. 1735 20th St., N.W.

Grandison, W. George, (AV) ... '42 '72 C.870 B.S. L.976 J.D. [Steptoe&J.]
*PRACTICE AREAS: International Trade Law.
Grandon, Rodney A. ... '60 '85 C.350 B.A. L.221 J.D. [Patton B.]
Grandy, Cheryl B. ... '— '92 C.276 B.S. L.1209 J.D. [Ⓐ Crowell&M.]
Grandy, H. Clifton ... '53 '80 C.918 B.A. L.276 J.D. Sr. Court Mngr.
Grane, Karen M. ... '— '88 C.607 B.A. L.1209 J.D. [Ⓒ Foley&L.]
*PRACTICE AREAS: Civil Practice; Banking Law.
Grange, Lori ... '65 '94 C.800 B.A. L.112 J.D. Natl. Assn. for Public Interest Law

Granger, David I., (AV) '32 '59 C.674 A.B. L.309 LL.B.
1800 Massachusetts Avenue, N.W., Suite 600, 20036
Telephone: 202-785-1274 Fax: 202-785-1631
Email: grangerdi@aol.com
General Practice.
See Professional Biographies, WASHINGTON, DISTRICT OF COLUMBIA

Granison, Terri D. '73 '00 C.446 B.A. L.273 J.D.
(adm. in IL; not adm. in DC) 2120 "L" St., N.W.
Granitto, Gregory J. ... '59 '87 C.363 B.A. L.128 J.D. [Ⓐ Akin,G.S.H.&F.] ‡
*PRACTICE AREAS: Litigation.
Grannis, Mark A., (AV) ... '63 '89 C.276 A.B. L.477 J.D. [Harris,W.&G.]
*PRACTICE AREAS: Communications.
Grannon, Eric ... '72 '99 C.102 B.A. L.329 J.D. [Ⓐ White&C.]
*PRACTICE AREAS: Trial and Appellate Litigation; Antitrust Litigation; Foreign Corrupt Practices Act.
Grano, Elisabeth ... '70 '96 C.205 B.S.B.A. L.1365 J.D. [Ⓐ Sutherland A.&B.]
*PRACTICE AREAS: Securities.
Granoff, Nadine ... '55 '90 C&L.30 B.A., J.D. 2939 Van Ness St., N.W.
Grant, Andrea Jill ... '— '75 C&L.910 B.A., J.D. [Verner,L.B.M.&H.]
*PRACTICE AREAS: Legislative Law; Energy Law.
Grant, Christopher L. ... '50 '77 C.309 B.A. L.280 J.D. 2000 L St., NW
Grant, David Alistair, (AV) ... '54 '78 C.95 A.B. L.276 J.D. [Baker&H.]
*PRACTICE AREAS: Employment Law; Benefits Law.
Grant, Davida M. ... '71 '96 C.446 B.A. L.329 J.D. 1776 K St., N.W.
Grant, Glenn D. ... '64 '90 C.105 B.A. L.273 J.D. [Ⓒ Crowell&M.]
Grant, Jill Elise ... '55 '81 C.976 B.A. L.309 J.D. [Nordhaus,H.T.T.&B.]
*PRACTICE AREAS: Administrative Law; Environmental Law; Indian Law; Federal Litigation.
Grant, K. Denise ... '65 '91 C.853 B.A. L.383 J.D. 1800 M St., NW
Grant, Lauryn Guttenplan '55 '81
C.188 A.B. L.276 J.D. Asst. Gen. Coun., Smithsonian Institution
Grant, Lori K. ... '70 '95 C.1369 B.A. L.273 J.D. Special Serv. Staff
Grant, Megan ... '66 '95 C.1049 B.A. L.336 J.D. [Ⓐ Berliner,C.&J.]
Grant, Patrick J., (AV) ... '51 '77 C&L.276 A.B., J.D. [Arnold&P.]
*PRACTICE AREAS: Telecommunications; Cable Television; Litigation.
Grant, Paula DiMeo, (AV) ... '43 '85 C.93 B.S. L.999 J.D. [Ⓒ Ross&H.]
Grant-Wilkinson, Patti L. ... '63 '88 C&L.276 B.A., J.D. [Hunton&W.]
*PRACTICE AREAS: Municipal Finance; Real Estate.
Granwell, Alan W. ... '44 '68 C.478 A.B. L.94 J.D. [Ivins,P.&B.]
*PRACTICE AREAS: International Taxation; Federal Income Tax.
Grassi, Joseph J., III '63 '88 C&L.884 B.S.B.A., J.D.
(adm. in PA; not adm. in DC) Assoc. Gen. Coun., Fannie Mae
*RESPONSIBILITIES: Real Estate; Community Development; Mortgage Banking; Finance.
Grassi, Lia Silva '63 '96 C.886 B.A. L.705 J.D.
(adm. in NJ; not adm. in DC) [Ⓐ Morgan,L.&B.]
Grasso, Fred ... '66 '97 C.893 B.S.C.E. L.904 J.D. [Ⓐ Kenyon&K.] (See Pat. Sect.)
*PRACTICE AREAS: Intellectual Property.
Grasso, Jeanne Marie ... '61 '94 C.602 B.S. L.446 J.D. [Dyer E.&J.]
*PRACTICE AREAS: Environmental Law; Maritime Law; Environmental Compliance; Federal Regulatory Law.
Grau, Caren A. ... '71 '99 C.659 B.A. L.128 J.D. [Ⓐ Keller&H.]
*PRACTICE AREAS: Food and Drug.
Graves, Donet D., (AV) '46 '79 C.161 B.S. L.1003 J.D.
(adm. in OH; not adm. in DC) [Graves&H.] ⊙
Graves, Donet D., Jr. '70 '95 C.951 B.A. L.276 J.D.
(adm. in MD; not adm. in DC) [Ⓐ Graves&H.]
Graves, Thomas J. '51 '77 C.813 B.A. L.893 J.D.
V.P. & Gen. Cnsl, National Paint & Coatings Association
Graves & Horton, LLC, (AV) ... 1111 14th Street, N.W. Third Fl. (⊙Cleve., OH)
Gray, Alison Leigh ... '59 '84 C&L.575 B.A., J.D. [Ⓐ Akin,G.S.H.&F.]
*PRACTICE AREAS: Labor and Employment.
Gray, Bernard A., Sr., (CV) ... '41 '78 C.30 B.S.B.A. L.276 J.D. 2009 18th St., S.E.
Gray, C. Boyden, (AV) ... '43 '69 C.309 B.A. L.575 J.D. [Wilmer,C.&P.]
*PRACTICE AREAS: International Law; Environmental Law.
Gray, Carolyn Doppelt ... '— '79 C.502 B.J. L.345 J.D. [Epstein B.&G.]
*PRACTICE AREAS: Labor; Employment; Disability Law; Construction Law.
Gray, Dan L., Jr. ... '65 '90 C.576 B.A. L.575 J.D. 888 17th St Nw # 4
Gray, Daniel D. ... '65 '90 C.454 B.A. L.818 J.D. Assoc. Gen. Coun., Fannie Mae
*RESPONSIBILITIES: Real Estate; Servicing; Bankruptcy; Litigation; E-Commerce.
Gray, Daniel L. ... '70 '97 C.893 B.A. L.1356 J.D. [Ⓐ Feldesman,T.L.F.&B.]
*PRACTICE AREAS: Domestic Relations; Litigation.
Gray, Daniel M. '56 '81 C.880 B.A. L.910 J.D.
(adm. in MD; not adm. in DC) [Ⓒ Swick&S.]
Gray, Edward W., Jr., (AV) ... '46 '70 C.145 B.A. L.178 J.D. [Fitch,E.T.&F.]
*PRACTICE AREAS: Trademarks; Trademark Licensing; Litigation; Copyrights; Taxation.
Gray, Frank M., Jr. '38 '70 C.103 A.B. L.902 J.D.
(adm. in VA; not adm. in DC) 1903 S. St., N.W.‡
Gray, Heiskell R. ... '32 '59 C.575 A.B. L.276 J.D. 2809 Sunset Ln.
Gray, Jefferson M., (AV) ... '56 '84 C.976 B.A. L.309 J.D. [Arent F.K.P.&K.]
*PRACTICE AREAS: White Collar Criminal Defense Litigation.
Gray, John W., Jr. ... '30 '57 C.886 B.S. L.893 LL.B. Corp. V.P., AT&T
Gray, Peter L. ... '57 '85 C.446 B.S. L.276 J.D. [McKenna&C.]
Gray, Robert Reed, (AV) ... '21 '48 C.197 A.B. L.309 LL.B. [Ⓒ Pillsbury W.]
*PRACTICE AREAS: Aviation Law.
Gray, Sherry Mastrostefano ... '— '90 C.94 B.A. L.273 J.D. [Ⓒ Powers,P.S.&V.]
*PRACTICE AREAS: Education Law; Administrative Law.
Gray, T. Wayne, (AV) ... '44 '69 C.885 B.A. L.893 LL.B. [Holland&K.]
*PRACTICE AREAS: Project Finance; Construction; Government Contracts; International Law.
Gray, Terry ... '73 '01 C.893 B.A. L.813 J.D. [Ⓐ Wilmer,C.&P.]
Gray, Todd D., (AV) ... '54 '79 C.937 B.A. L.309 J.D. [Dow,L.&A.]
Gray Blount & Associates, LLP ... 1801 K St., NW
Gray-Knight, Christine A ... '61 '87 C.446 B.A. L.329 J.D. [Ⓐ Chaikin&S.]
*PRACTICE AREAS: Personal Injury.
Graybill, Nina ... '41 '87 C.30 B.A. L.273 J.D. [Graybill&E.]
Graybill & English, L.L.C. ... 1920 N Street, N.W. Suite 620
Grayer, Cara T. ... '75 '01 C.811 B.A. L.30 J.D. 445 12th St., S.W.
Graykowski, John E. ... '53 '89 C.1044 B.Sc. L.128 J.D. [Dyer E.&J.]
*PRACTICE AREAS: Maritime Finance; Maritime Law; Transportation; Legislative; Government.
Grayson, Dean, (AV) ... '64 '89 C.659 B.A. L.276 J.D. Corporate Counsel, Avaya Inc.
Grdina, Betty, (BV) ... '54 '81 C.930 B.A. L.1003 J.D. International Teamsters Union
Greaney, William F. ... '56 '81 C.446 B.A. L.309 J.D. [Covington&B.]

Greco, Gary J. '— '95 C.645 B.A. L.30 J.D.
(adm. in MD; not adm. in DC) [Ⓐ King&S.]
Greco, R. Douglas '50 '78 C.597 B.A. L.1065 J.D.
(adm. in CA; not adm. in DC) Overseas Private Invest. Corp, Overseas Educ. Assn.
Green, Allen B. . . . . '47 '75 C&L.893 B.A., J.D. [Howrey S.A.&W.]
*PRACTICE AREAS: International Arbitration and Litigation; International Law; Government Contracts.
Green, Anthony C. . . . . '74 '99 C.659 B.A. L.188 J.D. [Ⓐ McKee N.]
*PRACTICE AREAS: Securities.
Green, Carl J. . . . . '39 '65 C.309 A.B. L.976 J.D. Hitachi Ltd.
Green, Donald H., (AV) . . . . '29 '57 C.823 A.B. L.309 LL.B. [Pepper H.]
*PRACTICE AREAS: Litigation; Mediation; Arbitration.
Green, Donald L. . . . . '44 '77 C.928 B.A. L.446 J.D. 1350 Connecticut Ave., N.W.
Green, Douglas G., (AV) . . . . '47 '73 C.95 B.A. L.276 J.D. [Steptoe&J.]
*PRACTICE AREAS: Energy; Antitrust; Litigation.
Green, Douglas H., (AV) . . . . '56 '83 C.183 B.A. L.273 J.D. [Piper M.R.&W.]
*PRACTICE AREAS: Environmental.
Green, Edward M. . . . . '43 '68 C&L.94 A.B., LL.B. [Ⓒ Crowell&M.]
*PRACTICE AREAS: Mining or Mineral Law; Trade Association Law; Mine Safety and Health Law; Administrative Law; Natural Resources Law.
Green, Eric M. '72 '00 C&L.659 B.A., J.D.
(adm. in VA; not adm. in DC) [Ⓐ Shaw P.]
*PRACTICE AREAS: Securities; Corporate Law.
Green, G. Michael . . . . '58 '83 C&L.276 B.S.B.A., J.D. [Dickstein S.M.&O.]
*PRACTICE AREAS: Tax Law.
Green, George R. '48 '75 C.994 B.A. L.1009 J.D.
Vice President & Assistant General Counsel, Food Marketing Institute
Green, Griffith L. '68 '95 C.659 B.A. L.145 J.D. [Ⓐ Sidley A.B.&W.]
Green, Iris M. . . . . '54 '77 C.30 B.A. L.273 J.D. [Green&F.]
Green, James F. . . . . '48 '73 C.1263 B.A. L.818 J.D. [Ashcraft&G.]
*PRACTICE AREAS: Products Liability; Pharmaceutical & Medical Device Litigation.
Green, Jason . . . . '43 '69 C.473 B.S. L.1003 J.D. [Ⓒ Kalbian H.]
*PRACTICE AREAS: Bankruptcy; Probate; Bankruptcy Litigation; Probate Litigation.
Green, Jeffrey T., (AV) . . . . '60 '89 C.188 A.B. L.1067 J.D. [Sidley A.B.&W.]
Green, John M. '48 '99 C.800 M.S. L.273 J.D.
(adm. in MD; not adm. in DC) [Ⓐ Gilman&Assoc.]
*PRACTICE AREAS: Aviation Law; Aviation Accidents; Personal Injury; Family Law; Negligence.
Green, Joseph H., Jr. . . . . '53 '92 C.329 B.A. L.1162 J.D. 1730 K St., N.W.
Green, Joseph J. . . . . '71 '96 C.893 B.A. L.309 J.D. [Ⓐ Collier S.S.]
*PRACTICE AREAS: Environmental.
Green, Karen Goldmeier . . . . '65 '93 C.188 B.S. L.446 J.D. [Ⓒ Akin,G.S.H.&F.]
*PRACTICE AREAS: Legislative.
Green, Karin L. '64 '95 C.429 B.A. L.309 J.D.
(adm. in MD; not adm. in DC) [Ⓐ Sidley A.B.&W.]
Green, Lauson C. . . . . '66 '94 C.732 B.A. L.823 J.D. [Ⓐ McDermott,W.&E.]
Green, Lora M. '— '98 C.688 B.S. L.273 J.D.
(adm. in MD; not adm. in DC) [Ⓐ Morgan,L.&B.]
Green, Pamela K. . . . . '52 '77 C.813 B.A. L.273 J.D. 3738 Huntington St., N.W.
Green, Paul A., (AV) . . . . '57 '82 C.145 A.B. L.446 J.D. [Mooney,G.B.&S.]
*PRACTICE AREAS: ERISA; Employee Benefits; Health and Welfare Benefit Plans; Qualified Retirement Plans; Multiemployer Plans.
Green, Philip D., (AV) . . . . '50 '74 C.659 B.A. L.273 J.D. [Akin,G.S.H.&F.]
*PRACTICE AREAS: Health Care Law; Corporate Transactional; Corporate Planning.
Green, Reuben '— '00 C.1051 B.A. L.1365 J.D.
(adm. in GA; not adm. in DC) [Ⓐ King&S.]
Green, Richard A. . . . . '26 '54 C&L.309 A.B., LL.B. [Stohlman,B.E.&S.]
Green, Richard C., (AV) . . . . '44 '76 C.976 B.A. L.276 J.D. [Andrews&K.]
*PRACTICE AREAS: Energy Law.
Green, Richard G. . . . . '70 '99 C.188 B.A. L.273 J.D. [Ⓐ Fish&R.]
*PRACTICE AREAS: Intellectual Property.
Green, Robert L., Jr. . . . . '51 '76 C.659 B.S. L.446 J.D. [Howrey S.A.&W.]
*PRACTICE AREAS: Antitrust; Complex Litigation; Litigation.
Green, Robert M., (BV) . . . . '53 '81 C.282 A.B. L.1234 J.D. [Ⓒ Creskoff&D.]
Green, Robert S. . . . . '61 '95 C.1213 B.S. L.904 J.D. [Ⓐ Rader,F.&G.] (Pat.)
*PRACTICE AREAS: Patent Law.
Green, Robert W. . . . . '41 '71 C.347 A.B. L.145 J.D. [Ⓒ Tendler&B.] (⊙Stamford, CT)
Green, Sandra Helena . . . . '64 '89 C.1365 B.A. L.273 J.D. Ernst & Young
Green, Seth M. . . . . '67 '91 C.309 A.B. L.446 J.D. [Caplin&D.]
*PRACTICE AREAS: Federal Income Taxation; Corporate Tax; Partnership Tax.
Green, Sharilyn Maphis '— '95 C.245 B.A. L.145 J.D.
(adm. in VA; not adm. in DC) 3000 K St., N.W.‡
Green, Stanley J. . . . . '33 '62 C.679 B.S. L.178 J.D. [Hughes&B.]
Green, Theodore T., (AV) '48 '74
C.604 B.A. L.893 J.D. Laborers' Intl. Union of North Amer.
Green, Thomas C., (AV) . . . . '41 '65 C.197 B.A. L.976 LL.B. [Sidley A.B.&W.]
Green, William J. . . . . '38 '77 C.728 B.S. L.884 J.D. 4875 Loughboro Rd. N.W.
Green, William Shalom, (AV) . . . . '24 '52 C&L.976 B.A., LL.B. 1301 K St., N.W.

Green, Carol Lynn
(See Bethesda, Maryland)

Green and Foushee
1130 Seventeenth Street, N.W., Suite 210, 20036
Telephone: 202-785-1171 Fax: 202-785-8108
Email: irisеagain@aol.com URL: http://www.lawyers.com/greenandfoushee
Iris M. Green; Trudi McCollum Foushee.
Civil Trial Practice including Personal Injury (Medical Malpractice), Probate, Family, Appellate and Educational Law. Civil Rights and Constitutional Law including Women's Rights Issues and Sexual Harassment. Complex Commercial and Business Litigation. Telecommunications Law including Cable Regulatory Issues. Employment Law, Wrongful Termination, Race Discrimination.
See Professional Biographies, WASHINGTON, DISTRICT OF COLUMBIA

Greenan, Kathleen L. . . . . '69 '95 C.446 B.S. L.128 J.D. [Ⓐ Swidler B.S.F.]
Greenbaum, Eileen M. . . . . '51 '76 C.1036 B.A. L.107 J.D. [Ⓒ Ballard S.A.&I.]
*PRACTICE AREAS: Commercial Real Estate; Affordable Housing; Commercial Conveyancing; Commercial Real Estate Acquisitions; Commercial Real Estate Development.
Greenbaum, Michael C. '51 '76
C.971 B.S.E.E. L.1292 J.D. [Blank R.C.&M.] (See Pat. Sect.)
*PRACTICE AREAS: Software Protection; Year 2000 Computer Conversion; Copyright Infringement; Electrical Intellectual Property; Biomedical Technology.
Greenbaum, Robert B. . . . . '38 '64 C&L.910 LL.B. 1440 NY Ave., N.W.
Greenbaum, Samuel M., (AV) . . . . '16 '39 C&L.276 J.D. 2840 Brandywine St., N.W.‡
Greenberg, Bennett D. . . . . '56 '81 C.1044 B.A. L.276 J.D. [Seyfarth S.]
*PRACTICE AREAS: Construction Law; Government Contracts Law.
Greenberg, David H. . . . . '75 '00 C.823 B.A. L.30 J.D. [Ⓐ Dickstein S.M.&O.]
*PRACTICE AREAS: Complex Civil Litigation; Insurance Coverage.
Greenberg, Edward D., (AV) . . . . '42 '68 C.367 B.A. L.128 J.D. [Galland,K.G.F.&S.]
Greenberg, Eldon V. C., (AV) . . . . '44 '70 C&L.309 B.A., J.D. [Garvey,S.&B.]
*PRACTICE AREAS: Litigation; Administrative Law; Environmental Law; Natural Resources Law; Ethics/Scientific Misconduct.
Greenberg, Eric Dodson . . . . '64 '92 C.860 B.A. L.273 J.D. [Ⓐ Covington&B.]
*PRACTICE AREAS: Corporate Law; Mergers, Acquisitions and Divestitures.

Greenberg, Lauren A. . . . . '71 '99 C.197 A.B. L.128 J.D. [Ⓐ Thaler L.]
*PRACTICE AREAS: Litigation.
Greenberg, Robert E., (AV) '49 '72 C.1160 A.B. L.260 J.D.
[Ⓒ Friedlander,M.S.K.&O.]
*PRACTICE AREAS: Commercial Law; Real Estate; Litigation; Commercial Leasing; Creditors Rights Law.
Greenberg, Sally Joan . . . . '54 '87 C.33 B.A. L.128 J.D. Consumers Union
Greenberg, Susan R. . . . . '54 '78 C.1044 B.A. L.273 J.D. 5225 Wisconsin Ave., NW

Greenberg & Lieberman
(See Takoma Park, Maryland)

Greenberg Traurig, LLP, (AV)
800 Connecticut Avenue, N.W. (Pat.) (⊙Phoenix, AZ; Santa Monica, CA; Denver, CO; Wilmington, DE; Boca Raton, Ft Laud., Miami, Orlando, Tallahassee, West Palm Beach, FL; Atlanta, GA; Chgo., IL; Boston, MA; New York, NY; Phila., PA; Tysons Corner, VA)
Greenberger, Marcia D. . . . . . . '46 '70 C&L.659 A.B., J.D. National Women's Law Center
Greenblatt, Jonathan L., (AV) '55 '81
C.184 B.A. L.273 J.D. [Shearman&S.] (⊙New York, NY)

Greenblum & Bernstein, P.L.C.
(See Reston, Virginia)

Greenburg, Douglas N. . . . . '66 '93 C.103 A.B. L.145 J.D. [Ⓐ Winston&S.]
Greenburg, Jan Crawford '65 '97 C.16 B.A. L.145 J.D.
(adm. in NY; not adm. in DC) Journalist, Chicago Tribune
Greene, Adam H. '76 '00 C.367 B.A. L.273 J.D.
(adm. in MD; not adm. in DC) [Ⓐ Powers,P.S.&V.]
*PRACTICE AREAS: Medicare and Medicaid; Health Care; Administrative Law.
Greene, Ava D. . . . . '62 '88 C.575 B.A. L.329 J.D. 1301 K St., N.W.
Greene, Charles S., III '— '97 C.228 B.A. L.1066 J.D.
(adm. in CA; not adm. in DC) [Ⓐ Hogan&H.]
*PRACTICE AREAS: Litigation.
Greene, Donald R., (AV) '31 '66
C.472 B.S.E.E. L.273 LL.B. [Ⓒ Blank R.C.&M.] (See Pat. Sect.)
*PRACTICE AREAS: Electronic Patents; Intellectual Property Licensing; Semiconductor Technology; Technology Licensing; Electronics.
Greene, Gerrie S. . . . . '47 '73 C&L.930 B.A., J.D. National Assn. of Counties
Greene, Glenn S. . . . . '65 '95 C.186 B.S. L.846 J.D. [Ⓐ Spriggs&H.]
*PRACTICE AREAS: Government Contracts; Construction Law; Federal Claims; Litigation; Toxic Torts.
Greene, Henry F. . . . . '41 '67 C.309 A.B. L.178 LL.B. Supr. Ct. J.
Greene, James W. . . . . '40 '64 C.31 A.B. L.477 J.D. [Thompson,O.M.N.&H.]
*PRACTICE AREAS: Litigation; Insurance Coverage; Environmental Law; Arbitration.
Greene, Jeffrey E. . . . . '69 '96 C.94 B.A. L.446 J.D. [Ⓐ Crowell&M.]
Greene, Marcy . . . . '69 '95 C.378 B.A. L.30 J.D. Excel Communications, Inc.
Greene, Peter A., (AV) . . . . '37 '66 C.724 B.B.A. L.276 J.D. [Thompson H.]
*PRACTICE AREAS: Transportation Law; Government Affairs; Regulatory Agency Practice; Administrative and Regulatory Law.
Greene, Ronald J., (AV) . . . . '42 '68 C&L.309 A.B., LL.B. [Wilmer,C.&P.]
*PRACTICE AREAS: Antitrust and Trade Regulation; Banks and Banking; Consumer Credit.
Greene-Buckner, SueCarol . . . . '54 '85 C.610 B.S. L.276 J.D. ULLICO INC.
*RESPONSIBILITIES: Litigation; Life and Health Insurance; Mergers and Acquisitions.
Greenfeld, Steven H., (AV) . . . . '62 '89 C.861 B.S.M. L.1209 J.D. [Gins&G.] ⊙
*PRACTICE AREAS: Bankruptcy Law; Insolvency Law; General Commercial Litigation.
Greenfield, Andrew B. . . . . '67 '92 C.659 B.A. L.273 J.D. [Ⓐ Shaw P.]
*PRACTICE AREAS: Immigration and Nationality Law.
Greenfield, Deborah . . . . '54 '81 C.821 B.A. L.659 J.D. Assoc. Gen. Coun., AFL-CIO
Greenfield, Douglas L. . . . . '59 '86 C.813 B.A. L.831 J.D. [Bredhoff&K.]
Greenfield, James Peter . . . . '63 '90 C.892 B.A. L.276 J.D. 502 2nd St.,N.W.
Greenfield, Leon B. . . . . '64 '90 C.645 B.S. L.145 J.D. [Ⓒ Wilmer,C.&P.]
*PRACTICE AREAS: Antitrust; Corporate Investigations; Securities Law.
Greenfield, Marsha R. '48 '74 C.881 A.B. L.705 J.D.
(adm. in NY; not adm. in DC) [Ⓒ Leonard H.F.L.&L.]
*PRACTICE AREAS: Association Law; Corporate Law; Health Law; Energy Law.
Greenhouse, Robin L., (AV) . . . . '59 '84 C.446 B.S. L.831 J.D. [McDermott,W.&E.]
Greenlaw, Hollis M. '64 '90 C.95 A.B. L.178 J.D. 725 12th St., N.W.
Greenlee, Diane . . . . '56 '81 C.1036 B.A. L.276 J.D. [Ⓐ Powell,G.F.&M.]
*PRACTICE AREAS: Law Income Housing Tax Credit Transactions.
Greenlees, Lisa T. . . . '62 '92 C.860 B.A. L.276 J.D. Sr. Coun., Mariott International, Inc.
*RESPONSIBILITIES: Counseling; Contracts; General Corporate.
Greenman, Gilbert O. . . . . '67 '94 C.178 B.A. L.309 J.D. [Ⓐ Williams&C.]
*PRACTICE AREAS: Civil Fraud; Civil RICO; Federal Criminal Law; Grand Jury Practice; Professional Liability Defense.
Greenspan, Deborah E. . . . . '55 '81 C&L.477 B.S., J.D. [Feinberg] ⊙
*PRACTICE AREAS: Alternative Dispute Resolution; Products Liability.
Greenspan, John P. . . . . '40 '68 C.399 B.A. L.446 J.D. 445 12th Street SW‡
Greenspan, Michael A., (AV) . . . . '40 '65 C.188 B.A. L.178 LL.B. [Thompson C.]
*PRACTICE AREAS: Financial Institutions; Mergers and Acquisitions; Administrative.
Greenspoon, Benjamin . . . . '28 '55 C.502 Bk.A. L.276 J.D. 1500 K St., N.W.
Greenspun, Katerina '68 '95 C.93 B.A. L.1202 J.D.
(adm. in NY; not adm. in DC) [Ⓐ Katten M.Z.]
*PRACTICE AREAS: Real Estate.
Greenstein, Abraham J., (AV) . . . . '45 '68 C.569 B.A. L.273 J.D. [Greenstein D.&L.]
Greenstein, Louis D. . . . . '72 '98 C.823 B.S. L.1398 J.D [Ⓐ Skadden,A.S.M.&F.]
*PRACTICE AREAS: SEC Enforcement.
Greenstein, Marci E. '54 '83 C.604 B.A. L.1162 J.D.
(adm. in PA; not adm. in DC) 1111 19th St Nw # 1200
Greenstein, Seth D. . . . . '55 '85 C.446 B.A. L.1162 J.D. [McDermott,W.&E.]

Greenstein DeLorme & Luchs, P.C., (AV)
1620 L Street, N.W., Suite 900, 20036-5605
Telephone: 202-452-1400 Facsimile: 202-452-1410
William H. Harris, Jr.; Richard G. Wise; Abraham J. Greenstein; Gilbert E. DeLorme, Jr.; Vincent Mark J. Policy; Richard W. Luchs; Judith R. Goldman; Jacques B. DePuy; Jeffrey H. Gelman; Alan S. Weitz; William C. Casano; Stephen H. Abraham; Lewis F. Morse; John Patrick Brown, Jr.;—Lyle M. Blanchard; Donald F. Holmes, Jr.; Miriam Hellen Jones; Sarae T. Leuckel; Isabel P. Ruiz de Gamboa (Not admitted in DC); James D. Sadowski.
General and Business Practice including Civil Litigation, Real Estate, Banking and Savings and Loan, Creditors Rights, Financial Institutions, Development Law, Housing and Urban Development, Condominiums and Cooperatives, Local Government, Securities, Taxation, Trade Organizations, Zoning, Land Use, Real Property Assessment Appeals, Municipal Government and Public Finance Law.
See Professional Biographies, WASHINGTON, DISTRICT OF COLUMBIA

Greenwald, Eliot J., (AV) . . . . '51 '77 C.188 A.B. L.209 J.D. [Ⓒ Swidler B.S.F.]
*PRACTICE AREAS: Telecommunications Law; Wireless Communications; FCC Licensing; FCC Regulation; Cellular Telephone.
Greenwald, Gerald B., (AV) . . . . '29 '51 C&L.145 A.B., J.D. 1050 Conn. Ave., N.W.‡
Greenwald, John D. '45 '73 C.575 B.A. L.178 J.D.
(adm. in NY; not adm. in DC) [Wilmer,C.&P.]
*PRACTICE AREAS: International Trade.
Greenwood, Mark A., (AV) . . . . '51 '78 C&L.477 B.A., J.D. [Ropes&G.]
Greer, Carolyn R. '67 '00 C.273 B.B.A. L.276 J.D.
(adm. in MD; not adm. in DC) [Ⓐ Dow,L.&A.]

Greer, Cynthia D. ....'66 '90 C.131 B.A. L.30 J.D. [🄲 Shaw P.]
*PRACTICE AREAS: Intellectual Property; Internet and World Wide Web; Communications.
Greer, William H., Jr., (AV) ....'28 '54 C.976 A.B. L.309 LL.B. 910 16th St., N.W.
Greeves, Geoffrey J. '70 '97 C.1369 B.A. L.902 J.D.
(adm. in VA; not adm. in DC) [🄰 Greenberg T.]
Grefe, Ronald D. '39 '66
C.886 B.S.M.E. L.904 J.D. Gen. Coun., Patent Reproduction Co. (Pat.)
Gregg, Donna Coleman, (AV) .... '48 '75 C.477 B.A. L.228 J.D. [Wiley R.&F.]
*PRACTICE AREAS: Communications; Internet; Electronic Commerce.
Gregg, James C., (AV) .... '24 '50 L.273 LL.B. [Macleay,L.G.&L.]
*PRACTICE AREAS: Insurance Defense; Architectural and Engineering Law; Insurance Liability.
Gregg, John P., (AV) .... '57 '83 C.319 B.A. L.30 J.D. [Miller,B.&O.]
*PRACTICE AREAS: Energy Contracts; Energy Legislation; Energy Regulation; Public Utility Regulation.
Gregg, Timothy W. ....'70 '99 C.575 B.A. L.880 J.D. [🄰 Latham&W.]
*PRACTICE AREAS: Corporate Law; Securities.
Gregoire, Brent J. ....'66 '93 C.494 B.A. L.208 J.D. [🄰 McDermott,W.&E.]
Gregory, Donald A. .... '51 '79 C.893 B.S. L.945 J.D. [Dickstein S.M.&O.] (Pat.)
*PRACTICE AREAS: General Practice; Licensing Law; Patent, Trademark and Copyright Law.
Gregory, Keith A. '59 '90 C.94 B.S.B.A. L.1149 J.D.
U.S. Sec. and Exch. Comm., Div. of Invest. Mgmt.
Greif, Michele S. ....'69 '97 C.446 B.S. L.776 J.D. [🄰 Akin,G.S.H.&F.]
*PRACTICE AREAS: Products Liability; General Litigation.
Greif, William G. '26 '52 C.276 L.602 J.D.
1333 New Hampshire Ave., N.W., Suite 400
Greiner, Daniel James .... '69 '97 C.893 B.A. L.477 J.D. [🄰 Jenner&B.]
*PRACTICE AREAS: Agency Law; Constitutional Law; Employment Discrimination; Commercial Litigation; Government Contracts.
Greisman, Julius M., (AV) ....'14 '37 C.563 B.S. L.1009 LL.B. [Arnold&P.]
*PRACTICE AREAS: Tax.
Gremminger, Steven L. ....'50 '77 C.112 B.A. L.30 J.D. KPMG Peat Marwick
Grenier, Edward J., Jr., (AV) ...... '33 '59 C.433 B.A. L.309 LL.B. [Sutherland A.&B.]
*PRACTICE AREAS: Federal Energy Regulation; Energy Regulation; Energy Contracts; Federal Administrative Law.
Grenier, Peter C. ....'63 '88 C&L.602 B.A., J.D. [Bode&G.]
*PRACTICE AREAS: Business Litigation; Real Estate Construction Litigation; Personal Injury; Medical Malpractice; Wrongful Death.
Gressman, Eugene, (AV) .... '17 '48 C&L.477 A.B., J.D. [🄲 Brand&F.]
*PRACTICE AREAS: Constitutional Law; Federal Litigation; Professional Practice.
Greszes, Mario .... '57 '86 C.1365 B.A. L.273 J.D. [🄰 Hessel&A.]
*PRACTICE AREAS: HUD Administrative Proceedings; Real Estate Litigation; Bankruptcy; Multi-Family Housing.
Grewal, Gurbir Singh '73 '99 C.276 B.S.F.S. L.945 J.D.
(adm. in NJ; not adm. in DC) [🄰 Howrey S.A.&W.]
*PRACTICE AREAS: Commercial Litigation; Antitrust and Trade Regulation.
Gribbin, D.J., IV '63 '92 C&L.276 A.B., J.D.
(adm. in VA; not adm. in DC) Legal Repres., Natl. Fed. of Independent Bus.
Gribbon, Daniel M., (AV) .... '17 '42 C.930 A.B. L.309 LL.B. [🄲 Covington&B.]
Grieff, Edward D. ....'66 '93 C.216 B.S. L.831 J.D. [🄰 Hale&D.] (Pat.)
*PRACTICE AREAS: Intellectual Property.
Grier, Phillip M. '41 '69 C.269 B.A. L.790 J.D.
(adm. in SC; not adm. in DC)
Exec. Dir. & CEO, National Association of College & University Attorneys
Griff, Marvin T., (AV) ....'55 '81 C.1036 B.A. L.861 J.D. [🄲 Swidler B.S.F.]
*PRACTICE AREAS: Federal and State Regulated Energy and Pipeline Law; Utility Law.
Griffen, Michael C. ....'64 '93 C.1031 B.A. L.107 J.D. [Morgan,L.&B.]
Griffen, Susan Haberman, (AV) '56 '82
C.350 B.S. L.352 J.D. [Finnegan,H.F.G.&D.] (See Pat. Sect.)
*PRACTICE AREAS: Biotechnology Patents.
Griffin, Benjamin J., (AV) ....'52 '76 C&L.790 B.A., J.D. [Mintz,L.C.F.G.&P.]
*PRACTICE AREAS: Communications and Media; Satellite Communications; Cable Programming; Cable Communications.
Griffin, John W. ....'46 '73 C.855 B.A. L.276 J.D. [Duane,M.&H.]
*PRACTICE AREAS: Corporate and Securities Law; Litigation; Transactional Matters; Securities; Exchange Commission Enforcement Matters.
Griffin, Kevin A. ....'56 '80 C.685 B.A. L.309 J.D. [🄲 Cleary,G.S.&H.]
Griffin, Lisa B. ....'65 '90 C.188 B.S. L.309 J.D. 445 12th St.
Griffin, Mark E. ....'59 '85 C.299 B.A. L.823 J.D. [Davis&H.]
*PRACTICE AREAS: Taxation Law; Insurance Law.
Griffin, Mark G., (AV) ....'47 '73 C&L.276 A.B., J.D. [Griffin,F.T.&M.]
*PRACTICE AREAS: Real Estate; Estate Planning; Probate; Business Law; Corporate Law.
Griffin, Maura E. ....'67 '96 C.321 B.A. L.861 J.D. [🄰 Wilmer,C.&P.]
Griffin, Michael C. ....'69 '00 C.152 B.A. L.537 J.D. [🄰 Schmeltzer,A.&S.]
*PRACTICE AREAS: Labor and Employment.
Griffin, Paul G. ....'67 '97 C&L.276 A.B., J.D. [🄰 O'Melveny&M.]
Griffin, Richard F. '56 '81
C.976 B.A. L.588 J.D. Gen. Coun., Intl. Union of Oper. Engrs.
Griffin, Sean C. ....'68 '93 C.309 B.A. L.178 J.D. [🄰 Steptoe&J.]
*PRACTICE AREAS: Litigation; Government Contracts.
Griffin, Thomas C. '47 '75
C.604 B.A. L.838 J.D. Staff Atty., American Academy of Actuaries
Griffin, William L. ....'37 '74 C.871 B.S. L.30 J.D. 888 16th St., N.W.
Griffin, Yolanda C. ....'70 '96 C.205 B.A. L.309 J.D. [🄰 Zevnik H.]
*PRACTICE AREAS: Environmental; Insurance Coverage; Litigation.

Griffin, Farmer, Tarby & Murphy, LLP, (AV)
1912 Sunderland Place, N.W., 20036-1608 ⊙
Telephone: 202-429-9000 Telefax: 202-232-7365
Email: gglaw1912@aol.com URL: http://www.washlaw.com
Mark G. Griffin; Jonathan L. Farmer; Brian P. Murphy; Alexander Djordjevich. Associates: David K. McRae; James T. Heise (Not admitted in DC). Of Counsel: Dale L. Jernberg.
Commercial Transactions, Corporate Law, Commercial and Residential Real Estate, Land Use and Zoning, Federal and State Taxation, Estate Planning and Probate, Civil and Administrative Litigation before all Courts, Departments and Agencies, General Practice.
Fairfax, Virginia Office: 10476 Armstrong Street, 22030. Telephone: 703-591-4300. Fax: 703-591-4323.
See Professional Biographies, WASHINGTON, DISTRICT OF COLUMBIA

Griffis, Kirby T. .... '67 '95 C.1365 B.A. L.893 J.D. [🄰 Spriggs&H.]
*PRACTICE AREAS: Products Liability; Toxic Torts; Insurance Coverage; Drug and Medical Device Defense.
Griffis, Monika Krizek .... '62 '90 C.66 B.A. L.94 J.D. 2111 Bancroft Pl. NW
Griffith, Donald E. .... '64 '92 C.8 B.S. L.823 J.D. 607 14th St., N.W.
Griffith, Kelly Call '68 '98 C.1349 B.A. L.724 J.D.
(adm. in NY; not adm. in DC) [🄰 Reed S.]
*PRACTICE AREAS: Bankruptcy.
Griffith, Lanny '51 '76 C&L.500 B.A., J.D.
(adm. in MS; not adm. in DC) [🄲 Balch&B.] (⊙Birm., AL)
Griffith, Spencer S., (AV) .... '56 '82 C.103 A.B. L.569 J.D. [Akin,G.S.H.&F.]
*PRACTICE AREAS: International Trade.
Griffith, W. Kimball, (AV) ....'49 '74 C.198 B.A. L.575 J.D. [Ballard S.A.&I.]
*PRACTICE AREAS: Credit Enhancement; Structured Finance; Tax Exempt Bonds; Tax Exempt Finance.

Grigera Naon, Horacio A. '47 '86 L.999 J.D.
(adm. in NY; not adm. in DC) [🄲 White&C.]
*PRACTICE AREAS: International Commercial Arbitration; Project Finance; Oil and Gas Law; Corporate; International Sales.
Grigg, Kenneth A., Jr. ....'59 '84 C.178 B.A. L.896 J.D. [Patton B.]
Griggs, John Wyeth, (AV) ....'47 '73 C.165 B.A. L.178 J.D. [Griggs&A.] ⊙
*PRACTICE AREAS: Energy Regulation; Civil Litigation; Commercial Real Estate; Natural Resources.
Griggs, Linda L. ....'49 '74 C.788 B.A. L.150 J.D. [Morgan,L.&B.]

Griggs & Adler, (AV)
1225 Eye Street, N.W., Suite 500, 20005 ⊙
Telephone: 202-682-4766; 888-317-0853 Fax: 703-716-2865
Email: GRIGGSLAW@AOL.COM URL: http://www.lawyers.com/griggs&adlerlaw
John Wyeth Griggs; Debra B. Adler.
Energy Regulation, Administrative Agency Practice, Natural Resources, Commercial Leasing.
Reston, Virginia Office: Griggs & Adler, P.C., 1801 Robert Fulton Drive, Suite 400. Telephone: 703-758-6701.
See Professional Biographies, WASHINGTON, DISTRICT OF COLUMBIA

Grigorian, Christina J. .... '68 '96 C&L.273 B.A., J.D. [🄰 Sidley A.B.&W.]
Grigorian, Christopher H. ....'64 '89 C.273 B.B.A. L.904 J.D. [🄰 Arent F.K.P.&K.]
*PRACTICE AREAS: Antitrust; Trade Regulation; Complex Litigation; Business Litigation; Motor Vehicle Safety Law.
Grigsby, McGee ....'— '71 C.420 B.A. L.309 J.D. [Latham&W.]
*PRACTICE AREAS: International Tax Controversies; Tax Controversies; Tax Planning.
Grill, Andrea S. ....'64 '89 C.94 B.A. L.276 J.D. [Klimaski&G.]
*PRACTICE AREAS: Employment Law; Labor Relations; Police Misconduct; Civil Rights; Discrimination.
Grill, Jeffrey B. .... '71 '95 C.1044 B.A. L.659 J.D. [🄰 Shaw P.]
Grillon, Jacquelyn E. ....'— '85 C.454 B.S. L.128 J.D. [🄲 Hogan&H.]
*PRACTICE AREAS: Corporate Law; Commercial Law; Communications Law.
Grima, Angelo M. '57 '84 C.918 B.A. L.145 J.D.
Dep. Gen. Coun., Natl. Geographic Soc.
*RESPONSIBILITIES: Corporate Transactions; Commercial Law; Litigation; Intellectual Property.
Grimaldi, Alan M., (AV) '44 '72
C.563 B.Ch.E. L.128 J.D. [Howrey S.A.&W.] (See Pat. Sect.)
*PRACTICE AREAS: Antitrust; Commercial Law; Intellectual Property; Arbitration; Insurance Coverage.
Grimaldi, Anthony E., (AV) '30 '58
C.645 B.A. L.276 LL.D. [🄰 Martell,D.G.&G.] (⊙Fairfax, VA)
*PRACTICE AREAS: Civil Practice; General Liability; Malpractice; Products Liability; Employment Law.
Grimaldi, David F., (AV) ....'39 '64 C.1062 B.A. L.128 J.D. [Martell,D.G.&G.]
Grime, Richard W. ....'64 '91 C.999 L.051 3000 K St., N.W.
Grimmelbein, Louis John, IV ....'60 '90 C.197 A.B. L.602 J.D. [🄰 Arent F.K.P.&K.]
*PRACTICE AREAS: Commercial Transactions; Real Estate.
Grimson, Jeffrey S. ....'67 '92 C.339 B.A. L.904 J.D. [🄰 Grunfeld,D.L.&K.]
Grincewich, Katherine G., (AV) '56 '82
C.205 B.A. L.128 J.D. Asst. Gen. Coun., U.S. Catholic Conference
Grindal, H. Theodore '53 '80 C.55 B.A. L.494 J.D.
(adm. in MN; not adm. in DC) [Lockridge G.N.] ⊙
Grindle, John, Jr., (AV) ....'16 '47 C&L.309 A.B., LL.B. 1400 K St., N.W.
Griner, G. Christopher ....'44 '73 C.401 B.A. L.1292 J.D. [Kaye S.]
*PRACTICE AREAS: International Transactions; National Security Law; Technology Licensing; Export Regulation; Export Compliance.
Grinnell, Jason Eltinge '70 '95 C.197 B.A. L.629 J.D.
(adm. in WI; not adm. in DC) 1666 K Street, N.W.
Grinstead, Darrel J., (AV) .... '40 '69 C.228 B.A. L.477 J.D. [Hogan&H.]
*PRACTICE AREAS: Health Law; Medicare and Medicaid.
Grise, Jacqueline I. ....'70 '95 C.1145 B.S. L.1202 J.D. [🄰 Howrey S.A.&W.]
*PRACTICE AREAS: Antitrust; Mergers and Acquisitions; Commercial Litigation.
Grisez, Karen T. ....'55 '90 C.446 B.A. L.128 J.D. [🄲 Fried,F.H.S.&J.]
Grishkin, Jennifer E. ....'72 '98 C.896 B.A. L.976 J.D. [🄰 Wilmer,C.&P.]
Griswold, Donald M. '58 '83 C.145 A.B. L.94 J.D.
(adm. in MA; not adm. in DC) [McDermott,W.&E.]
Gritzmacher, Thomas A. ....'45 '73 C.885 B.A. L.276 J.D. 600 N. J. Ave., N.W.‡
Groark, Paul D. ....'62 '90 C.197 A.B. L.273 J.D. [🄰 Dombroff&G.]
Groben, Carol A. ....'57 '88 C.260 B.S. L.893 J.D. MCI Communications Corp.
Grochowski, Raymond B. ....'— '92 C.945 B.A. L.276 J.D. [🄰 Latham&W.]
*PRACTICE AREAS: Telecommunications Regulation; Corporate Finance; Corporate Governance; Venture Capital; Mergers and Acquisitions.
Grody, Miles H. ....'56 '86 C.309 B.A. L.976 J.D. [Rowan&G.]
Groen, Clifford J. ......'47 '73 C.197 A.B. L.309 J.D. Princ. Coun., International Fin. Corp.
Grogan, Stephanie J. ....'49 '78 C.890 B.A. L.575 J.D. 4900 Massachusetts Ave, N.W.
Grohl, Renie Yoshida '50 '76 C.681 A.B. L.1066 J.D.
Sr. V.P. & Dep. Gen. Coun., Fannie Mae Inc.
Grohowski, Robert C. '68 '94
C&L.893 B.A., J.D. Assoc. Coun., Investment Company Institute
*RESPONSIBILITIES: International.
Gromfine, Isadore J. ....'20 '44 C.107 B.A. L.273 LL.B. 1101 15th St. N.W.
Groner, Felicia M. ....'66 '91 C.477 B.A. L.273 J.D. 1850 M St Nw # 400
Gronlund, Mary ....'60 '87 C.893 B.A. L.945 J.D. 1001 G St., N.W.
Groobert, Edward A., (AV) .... '35 '60 C&L.178 A.B., LL.B. [Dykema G.]
*PRACTICE AREAS: Trade and Professional Associations; Equipment Leasing.
Groobey, J. Christopher .... '65 '91 C.1307 B.A. L.145 J.D. [🄲 Chadbourne&P.]
*PRACTICE AREAS: Project Finance; Capital Markets; Corporate Law.
Groom, Theodore R., (AV) ....'34 '60 C.105 A.B. L.309 LL.B. [Groom]
*PRACTICE AREAS: ERISA; Tax Law; Employee Benefits; Pension and Profit Sharing; Health Care.

Groom Law Group, Chartered, (AV)
Suite 1200 1701 Pennsylvania Avenue, N.W., 20006-5893
Telephone: 202-857-0620 Telecopier: 202-659-4503
Email: info@groom.com URL: http://www.groom.com
Theodore R. Groom; Louis T. Mazawey; Gary M. Ford; Robert P. Gallagher; Stephen M. Saxon; Douglas W. Ell; Charles W. Sherman, Jr.; Thomas F. Fitzgerald; Ian D. Lanoff; Lonie Hassel; Thomas S. Gigot; William M. Evans; Andrée M. St. Martin; Jon W. Breyfogle; David W. Powell; Roberta J. Ufford; Mark L. Lofgren; Edward A. Scallet; Richard K. Matta. Of Counsel: William F. Hanrahan; John P. McAllister; Michael A. Thrasher; Robert D. Valer; Alvaro I. Anillo; Kendall W. Daines;—Michael J. Prame; Elizabeth Thomas Dold (Not admitted in DC); Daniel Lee Hogans; Stephanie L. Napier; David N. Levine; Christy A. Tinnes (Not admitted in DC); Jennifer E. Eller (Not admitted in DC); Elena C. Barone; C. Duncan MacRae; Jason O. Keene (Not admitted in DC); Jonathan J. Boyles (Not admitted in DC).
Employee Benefits, Health, Litigation, Tax and Legislation.
See Professional Biographies, WASHINGTON, DISTRICT OF COLUMBIA

Groomes, Cynthia A., P.C.
(See Bethesda, Maryland)

Grooms, Odell ....'54 '83 C.999 B.A. L.362 J.D. 1614 S St., S.E.★
Groppe, Charles P. ....'— '97 C.276 B.A. L.273 J.D. [🄰 Morgan,L.&B.]
Gropper, Adam '73 '00 C.260 B.S. L.273 J.D.
(adm. in NY; not adm. in DC) [🄰 Baker&H.]
*PRACTICE AREAS: Tax Controversies; Tax Planning.
Grosberg, Joel ....'70 '97 C.477 B.A. L.188 J.D. [🄰 McDermott,W.&E.]
Groseclose, Steven J. ....'67 '94 C.691 B.A. L.446 J.D. [🄰 Piper M.R.&W.]
*PRACTICE AREAS: Environmental.

Groskaufmanis, Karl A. .... '61 '88 C.188 B.S. L.659 J.D. [Fried,F.H.S.&J.]
Gross, Clifford R. .... '63 '89 C.976 B.S.E.E. L.145 J.D. [Skadden,A.S.M.&F.]
Gross, David A. ....'— '79 C.659 B.A. L.178 J.D. Sr. Coun., AirTouch Comm.
Gross, Diane L. '69 '95 C.112 B.A. L.569 J.D.
(adm. in NY; not adm. in DC)
Pub. Policy Coord., Lawyers Comm. for Civil Rights Under Law
Gross, Gary Paul '58 '84 C.1044 B.A. L.564 J.D.
(adm. in NY; not adm. in DC) Natl. Assn. of Advocacy Systems
Gross, Harold J. .... '56 '81 C.1044 B.A. L.276 J.D. Sp. Asst. U.S. Atty.
Gross, Joel M. ....'52 '78 C.978 B.A. L.569 J.D. 555 12th Street, N.W.
Gross, Kenneth A., (AV) ....'51 '75 C.1029 B.A. L.245 J.D. [Skadden,A.S.M.&F.]
Gross, Leslie Marie '— '98 C.329 B.A. L.273 J.D.
(adm. in MD; not adm. in DC) Atty., Lawyers Comm. for Civil Rights Under Law
*RESPONSIBILITIES: Equal Educational Opportunities; Affirmative Action.
Gross, Nina G. .... '— '78 C.273 B.A. L.1209 J.D. Deloitte & Touche
Gross, Richard A., (AV) ....'49 '73 C.918 B.A. L.309 J.D. [Rosenman&C.]
Gross, Robert J. '69 '98 C.319 B.A. L.665 J.D.
(adm. in NY; not adm. in DC) [A] Sidley A.B.&W.]
Gross, Thomas P. .... '49 '79 C.124 B.S. L.930 J.D. [B] Ruddy&M.]
*PRACTICE AREAS: Energy; Environmental; Project Finance; International; Intellectual Property.
Grossberg, Gerald P., (AV) ....'40 '66 C.645 B.A. L.273 LL.B. [Grossberg,Y.F.&B.]
Grossberg, Israel .... '10 '36 C.424 L.64 LL.B. 4545 Conn. Ave., N.W.
Grossberg, James E. ....'56 '85 C&L.893 B.A., J.D. [Levine S.&K.]

Grossberg, Yochelson, Fox & Beyda, LLP, (AV)
2000 L Street, N.W., Suite 675, 20036-4907
Telephone: 202-296-9696 Telecopier: 202-296-7777
URL: http://www.GYFB.com
Members of Firm: Solomon Grossberg (1905-1994); Irving B. Yochelson (1906-1983); Isadore Brill (1905-1964); C. Richard Beyda; Lawrence A. Miller; Gerald P. Grossberg; Steven G. Friedman; Richard F. Levin; Linton W. Hengerer; Brett D. Orlove. Associates: Bruce C. Johnson (Not admitted in DC); Michael D. Ravitch; Mary Schneider Chyun; Sidney Jerome Rosenbaum IV. Retired: Julius I. Fox.
Commercial Real Estate, Real Estate Finance, Real Estate Tax, Corporate Taxation, Probate and Estate Planning, Health Care Law.
See Professional Biographies, WASHINGTON, DISTRICT OF COLUMBIA

Grossenbacher, Karla ....'67 '92 C.436 B.A. L.276 J.D. [Seyfarth S.]
*PRACTICE AREAS: Employment and Labor Law; Litigation.
Grosser, James M. ....'66 '93 C.197 A.B. L.659 J.D. [B] Shaw P.]
Grossi, Peter T., Jr. ....'47 '74 C.855 B.A. L.976 J.D. [Arnold&P.]
*PRACTICE AREAS: Litigation; Products Liability; Antitrust; Food and Drug.
Grossman, Alison E. ....'66 '94 C.309 A.B. L.893 J.D. 2555 M St. N.W.
Grossman, Donna Brown '51 '83
C.976 B.A. L.276 J.D. Amer. Coll. of Preventive Medicine
Grossman, Garry S. ....'50 '82 C.477 A.B. L.273 J.D. [Fenwick&W.]
*PRACTICE AREAS: Government Contracts; Technology Transfers; Computer Law; Privacy Law; Information Security.
Grossman, Joanna L. .... '68 '95 C.31 B.A. L.813 J.D. 725 12th St., N.W.
Grossman, Joanne B., (AV) ....'49 '75 C.681 A.B. L.1066 J.D. [Covington&B.]
Grossman, Jon David ....'55 '88 C.145 B.A. L.904 J.D. [Dickstein S.M.&O.] (Pat.)
*PRACTICE AREAS: Patent Law; Copyright Law; Computer Law.
Grossman, Jonathan M. ....'70 '00 C.477 B.A. L.309 J.D. [A] Hogan&H.]
Grossman, Marla '68 '93 C.976 B.A. L.309 J.D.
Dir., Fed. Affairs, Verner, Liipfert, Bernhard, McPherson & Hand, Chtd. (⊙Washington)
Grossman, Marla ....'— '93 C.976 B.A. L.309 J.D. [Verner,L.B.M.&H.] (⊙Washington)
*PRACTICE AREAS: Internet Ventures; Federal Affairs; Entertainment Law.
Grossman, Milton J. ....'36 '60 C.367 A.B. L.309 LL.B. [B] Miller,B.&O.]
*PRACTICE AREAS: Energy Law; Antitrust Law; Appellate Practice.
Grossman, Neil M. ....'49 '75 C.339 B.A. L.276 J.D. William M. Mercer, Inc.
Grossman, Scott M. '73 '99 C.260 B.S. L.273 J.D.
(adm. in FL; not adm. in DC) P.O. Box 14198

Grosso, Andrew, (AV) '53 '81 C.688 B.S. L.602 J.D. [BR]
2121 K Street, N.W., Suite 800, 20037
Telephone: 202-261-3593 Fax: 202-261-3595
Email: agrosso@acm.org
Civil and Criminal Litigation, including Health Care and Defense Procurement Fraud, and Qui Tam and Corporate Compliance Matters. Electronic Commerce, including Computer and Information Security, Internet Law, Digital Copyrights, Trademarks, Domain Name Registration, and Financial, Medical and Electronic Privacy.
See Professional Biographies, WASHINGTON, DISTRICT OF COLUMBIA

Grove, Jaskiewicz and Cobert, (AV) [BR]
Suite 400, 1730 M Street, N.W., 20036 ⊙
Telephone: 202-296-2900 Telecopier: 202-296-1370
Email: rcobert@gjcobert.com URL: http://www.gjcobert.com
Members of Firm: William J. Grove (1914-1988); Ronald N. Cobert; Edward J. Kiley; Robert L. Cope; Andrew M. Danas. Of Counsel: Leonard A. Jaskiewicz; James F. Flint; Lawrence E. Dubé, Jr.; James K. Jeanblanc; Edmund M. Jaskiewicz.
General Practice and Administrative Law, including Practice before United States Trial and Appellate Courts, Government Departments, Federal and State Agencies. Antitrust, Trade Regulation, Corporate, Copyright, Customs, Health Care, International Trade, Labor, Legislative, Litigation, Patent, Pension, Tax, Trademark, and Transportation Law.
Baltimore, Maryland Office: Suite 407, 2400 Boston Street, 21224. Telephone: 410-522-3200.
See Professional Biographies, WASHINGTON, DISTRICT OF COLUMBIA

Grover, Robin W. '53 '82 C.216 B.A. L.893 J.D.
1747 Pennsylvania Avenue N.W. Suite 1000, 20006-4693
Telephone: 202-302-1653
Email: RGrover716@aol.com URL: http://www.lawyers.com/robingrover
***PRACTICE AREAS: International Trade and Investment Law; Trade Associations Law; Administrative Law.**
All aspects of international trade including export licensing issues (BXA and ODTC); OFAC regulations and licensing; Customs import requirements (country of origin, classification, marking, FTA, tariff preference and policy issues); CFIUS, foreign investment reporting and sectoral limitations. The full range of issues involving trade association law, including those of organization, governance, membership, codes and standards. Practice before federal, state and local regulatory agencies.
See Professional Biographies, WASHINGTON, DISTRICT OF COLUMBIA

Groves, Carolyn W. ....'67 '92 C.754 B.A. L.180 J.D. [Wilkinson B.K.]
*PRACTICE AREAS: Communications; Telecommunications Law; Administrative Law.
Groves, Marilyn W. '38 '67 C.597 A.B. L.477 J.D.
(adm. in NY; not adm. in DC) 1700 Q St. N.W.
Groves, William A. '53 '82 C.381 B.S. L.7 J.D.
(adm. in OH; not adm. in DC)
Asst. Gen. Coun., Procurement, Ballistic Millile Defense Organization★
Grow, Michael A., (AV) .... '47 '75 C.1085 B.A. L.273 J.D. [Arent F.K.P.&K.]
*PRACTICE AREAS: Litigation; Trademark; Copyright; Unfair Competition.
Grubb, Ronald S., Jr. '66 '00 C.1034 B.S.E.E. L.836 J.D.
[A] Oppenheimer W.&D.] (Pat.)
*PRACTICE AREAS: Intellectual Property.
Grubber, Karen L. '65 '92 C.446 B.A. L.180 J.D.
Sr. Coun., Marriott International, Inc.
*RESPONSIBILITIES: Litigation.

Grubbs, Wendy J. ....'61 '87 C.1128 B.A. L.896 J.D. U.S. Senate
Grube, Brian K. ....'72 '97 C.610 B.B.A. L.145 J.D. [A] Jones,D.R.,&P.]
Gruber, Gregory A. ....'64 '89 C.911 B.A. L.36 J.D. Asst. U.S. Atty.★
Gruber, Harry M. ....'73 '99 C.477 B.B.A. L.273 J.D. [A] Gibson,D.&C.]
*PRACTICE AREAS: Litigation; Appellate Practice.
Gruda, Jennifer A. '76 '01 C.1036 B.A. L.276 J.D.
(adm. in VA; not adm. in DC) [A] Crowell&M.]
Gruhin, Mark I. ....'56 '81 C.705 B.A. L.904 J.D. [Schmeltzer,A.&S.]
*PRACTICE AREAS: Business Law; Transactions; High Technology; Biotechnology; Venture Capital.
Grummer, Mark E. .... '50 '76 C.597 B.A. L.145 J.D. [Kirkland&E.]
*PRACTICE AREAS: Environmental Litigation; Environmental Due Diligence; CERCLA.
Grundeman, Fredric Edward '38 '65 C&L.900 B.B.A., J.D.
(adm. in KS; not adm. in DC) Ernst & Young
Gruner, Heidi S. '68 '99 C.273 B.A. L.276 J.D.
(adm. in NY; not adm. in DC) 1875 Connecticut Avenue, N.W.
Grunfeld, Gideon Y. ....'65 '93 C.659 B.A. L.1065 J.D. [A] Covington&B.]

Grunfeld, Desiderio, Lebowitz, Silverman & Klestadt LLP, (AV)
A Partnership
Suite 975, 1500 K Street, N.W., 20005 ⊙
Telephone: 202-783-6881 Telecopy: 202-783-0405
URL: http://www.GDLSK.com
Partners: Harold M. Grunfeld (Resident Partner, New York, N.Y. Office); Frank J. Desiderio (Resident Partner, New York, N.Y. Office); Alan G. Lebowitz (Resident Partner, New York, N.Y. Office); Robert B. Silverman (Resident Partner, New York, N.Y. Office); Peter W. Klestadt (Resident Partner, New York, N.Y. Office); Steven P. Florsheim (Resident Partner, New York, N.Y. Office); Bruce M. Mitchell (Resident Partner, New York, N.Y. Office); Max F. Schutzman (Resident Partner, New York, N.Y. Office); Alan R. Klestadt (Resident Partner, New York, N.Y. Office); Barry E. Powell (Resident Partner, Los Angeles, California Office); Mary Elizabeth Wright (Resident Partner, Boston, Massachusetts Office); Richard M. Wortman (Resident Partner, Los Angeles, California Office); Andrew B. Schroth (Resident Partner, New York, N.Y. Office); David M. Murphy; Edward B. Ackerman (Resident Partner, New York, N.Y. Office). Associates: Jeffrey S. Grimson (Resident); Erik D. Smithweiss (Resident Associate, New York, N.Y. Office); David J. Evan (Resident Associate, New York, N.Y. Office); Mark E. Pardo (Not admitted in DC; Resident); Brett Ian Harris (Resident Associate, New York, N.Y. Office); Laurence M. Friedman (Resident Associate, New York, N.Y. Office); Michael T. Cone (Resident Associate, New York, N.Y. Office); Ellen A. DiLapi (Resident Associate, New York, N.Y. Office); Stephanie A. Goldfischer (Resident Associate, New York, N.Y. Office); Anthony A. Tonucci (Resident Associate, New York, N.Y. Office); Stacy L. Weinberg (Resident Associate, New York, N.Y. Office); Adam M. Dambrov (Not admitted in DC; Resident Associate, New York, N.Y. Office). Of Counsel: Harold I. Loring (Resident Of Counsel, New York, N.Y. Office). Principal: Barry Hipshman (Resident, New York, N.Y. Office).
Customs Law, International Trade Law, Trade Regulations and Administrative Law. Trials and Appeals.
New York, N.Y. Office: 245 Park Avenue, 33rd Floor. Telephone: 212-557-4000. Fax: 212-557-4415.
Boston, Massachusetts Office: Grunfeld, Desiderio, Lebowitz, Silverman, Klestadt & Wright, LLP, Old City Hall, 45 School Street, 2nd Floor. Telephone: 617-742-8550. Telecopy: 617-523-9429.
Los Angeles, California Office: 707 Wilshire Boulevard, Suite 4900. Telephone: 213-624-1970. Telecopy: 213-624-1678.
See Professional Biographies, WASHINGTON, DISTRICT OF COLUMBIA

Gruskin, Steven M. .....'66 '91 C.472 B.S.M.E. L.273 J.D. [Sughrue M.] (See Pat. Sect.)
*PRACTICE AREAS: Intellectual Property Law.
Gryce, David C., (AV) ....'55 '83 C.103 A.B. L.208 J.D. [Arent F.K.P.&K.]
*PRACTICE AREAS: Information Technology Contracts; Software Licensing; Trademarks; International Trademarks; Unfair Competition.
Grymes, Christie L. .... '72 '98 C.846 B.B.A. L.273 J.D. [A] Collier S.S.]
*PRACTICE AREAS: Advertising and Marketing; Consumer Protection; Promotion Law; Internet Law.
Grymes, Susan Page ....'69 '00 C.893 B.A. L.1209 J.D. [A] Olsson,F.&W.]
*PRACTICE AREAS: Legislation; Food and Drug Law; Litigation.
Grynberg, Michael ....'71 '00 C.118 B.A. L.893 J.D. [A] Hogan&H.]
Gschwendtner, Susan M., (AV) .... '— '83 C.338 B.A. L.309 J.D. [B] Coates,D.&G.]
*PRACTICE AREAS: Real Estate Law; Corporate Law; Business Law.
Guan, Yue '66 '99 C.999 B.A. L.904 LL.M.
(adm. in NY; not adm. in DC) [A] White&C.]
Guandolo, John, (AV) ....'19 '44 C.339 A.B. L.446 J.D. 1815 H St., N.W.
Guarino, Elizabeth Toni, (AV) ....'47 '77 C.1044 B.A. L.902 J.D. [Vorys,S.S.&P.]
*PRACTICE AREAS: Food and Drug; Advertising.
Guarisco, Annette J. ....'58 '84 C&L.1019 B.B.A., J.D. 1775 Pennsylvania Ave., N.W.
Guben, Jan K., (AV) '42 '67 C.863 B.A. L.1002 LL.B.
(adm. in MD; not adm. in DC) [Venable,A.B.H.&C.] (⊙Balt., MD)
*PRACTICE AREAS: Real Estate Law; Corporate Law; Partnership Law; Tax Law.
Gubinsky, Louis, (P.C.), (AV) '41 '67
C.446 B.S. L.276 LL.B. [Sughrue M.] (See Pat. Sect.)
*PRACTICE AREAS: Intellectual Property Law; Biotechnology.
Gude, Kalpak S. '66 '95
C.1213 B.S.E.E. L.347 J.D. V.P. & Assoc. Gen. Coun., Panamsat
Guerin, Charles A. ....'17 '48 C.014 B.A. L.128 J.D. 3040 Idaho Ave., N.W.‡
Guerra, Joseph R. ....'58 '85 C.893 B.A. L.276 J.D. [Sidley A.B.&W.]
Guerrera, Joanne M. ....'69 '94 C.93 B.A. L.273 J.D. [A] Weil,G.&M.]
Guerrera, Mark P. ....'69 '94 C.276 B.A. L.273 J.D. [A] Sidley A.B.&W.]
Guerrieri, Joseph, Jr., (AV) ....'47 '73 C.477 B.A. L.273 J.D. [Guerrieri,E.&C.]

Guerrieri, Edmond & Clayman, P.C., (AV)
1625 Massachusetts Avenue, N.W., Suite 700, 20036-2243
Telephone: 202-624-7400 Facsimile: 202-624-7420
Joseph Guerrieri, Jr.; John A. Edmond; Robert S. Clayman; Jeffrey A. Bartos;—Jonathan P. Rolfe (Not admitted in DC); Soye Kim; Eleanore A. Irwin.
Litigation, Labor, Tort, Bankruptcy and Employee Benefits Law.
See Professional Biographies, WASHINGTON, DISTRICT OF COLUMBIA

Guerrina, Britton B. '68 '99 C&L.145 B.A./M.A., J.D.
(adm. in IL; not adm. in DC) [A] Mayer,B.&P.]
Guerry, William M., Jr. ....'61 '87 C&L.893 B.A., J.D. [Collier S.S.]
*PRACTICE AREAS: Environmental Law.
Guervitz, Maurice A. ....'14 '40 C.273 L.180 LL.B. 1025 Vermont Ave., N.W.
Guggenheim, Achiezer '72 '96 C.978 B.A. L.178 J.D.
(adm. in NJ; not adm. in DC) [A] Sidley A.B.&W.]
Guggenheim, Jana Kay ....'58 '87 C.959 B.A. L.904 J.D. [Friedlander,M.S.K.&O.]
*PRACTICE AREAS: Commercial Real Estate; Banking; Commercial Law; Business Associations; Creditors' Rights.
Guggenheim, Miriam J. ....'70 '96 C.659 B.A. L.178 J.D. [A] Covington&B.]
Guggenheim, Seth M., (BV) .... '50 '77 C.94 B.A. L.30 J.D. Off. of the Corp. Coun.
Guida, Alfonso, Jr. '58 '87 C.30 B.A. L.809 J.D.
(adm. in PA; not adm. in DC) [A] Kalbian H.]
Guidoboni, Thomas A., (AV) ....'46 '72 C&L.893 B.A., J.D. [B] Crowell&M.]
*PRACTICE AREAS: Litigation; Appellate Practice; Criminal Law.
Guidry, Eric C. '69 '98 C.94 B.A. L.477 J.D.
(adm. in CO; not adm. in DC) 555 13th St., N.W.‡
Guiffre, Michael ....'69 '93 C.556 B.A. L.276 J.D. [A] Patton B.]
Guilfoyle, Joan S. '62 '92 C.188 B.A. L.273 J.D.
(adm. in VA; not adm. in DC) [Stradley R.S.&Y.]
Guilfoyle, Patrick S. .... '50 '79 C.385 A.B. L.276 J.D. 4715 17th St., NW
Guinivan, James M. ....'54 '88 C&L.893 B.A., J.D. [B] Harkins C.]
*PRACTICE AREAS: Regulated Industries; Administrative Law; Litigation.

Guinot, Luis, Jr. .... '35 '68 C.569 B.A. L.128 J.D. [Shapiro,S.&G.]
*PRACTICE AREAS: International Law; Commercial Law.
Guldi, Virginia Whitehill .... '63 '89 C.659 B.S.E. L.1338 J.D. [[A] Zuckerman S.]
*PRACTICE AREAS: Bankruptcy.
Guliani, Ranjeev S. .... '74 '00 C&L.893 B.A., J.D. [[A] Arnold&P.]
*PRACTICE AREAS: Mergers and Acquisitions.
Gulick, Joel M. .... '— '01 C.282 B.A. L.273 J.D. [[A] Arnold&P.]
*PRACTICE AREAS: Employee Benefits; Tax Law.
Gulick, Karen Lynn .... '66 '93 C.813 B.A. L.976 J.D. [Harris,W.&G.]
*PRACTICE AREAS: Telecommunications Law; Administrative Law; Appellate Practice.
Gulin, Frank C. .... '63 '91 C.165 A.B. L.30 J.D. [[A] Piliero,M.&P.]
*PRACTICE AREAS: Labor and Employment; Government Contracts; Civil Litigation.
Gulland, Eugene D., (AV) .... '47 '73 C.674 A.B. L.976 J.D. [Covington&B.]
Gulya, Brigitta Rianna ..... '65 '89 C.309 B.A. L.145 J.D. 1775 Pennsylvania Ave., N.W.
Gunion, John B. .... '12 '37 C&L.273 LL.B. 3408 Wisconsin Ave., N.W.
Gunn, Brian .... '73 '99 C.906 B.A. L.911 J.D. [[A] Dorsey&W.]
*PRACTICE AREAS: Indian Law; Litigation; Government Relations; Federal Administrative Law.
Gunnarson, R. Shawn '65 '95 C&L.101 B.A., J.D.
(adm. in UT; not adm. in DC) [[A] White&C.]
*PRACTICE AREAS: Government Investigations; Complex Litigation; Appellate Litigation.
Gunsalus, D. Brent '54 '85 C.1124 B.A. L.902 J.D.
[Hudson C.] (⊙Linthicum, MD; Charlottesville, VA)
Gunter, Sue D., (AV) .... '54 '79 C.1365 B.S. L.245 J.D. [Sherman,D.C.L.&Y.]
*PRACTICE AREAS: Labor and Employment Law; Union Labor Law.
Gunzburger, Ronald M., (BV) '63 '88 C.273 B.A. L.1194 J.D.
908 Pennsylvania Ave. S.E.
Gupta, Renu K. '67 '94 C.691 B.A. L.326 J.D.
(adm. in TX; not adm. in DC) [[A] Baker B.]
Gura, Alan .... '71 '95 C.188 B.A. L.276 J.D. 1730 K Street, N.W., Suite 304
Gurdak, Michael P. .... '62 '87 C&L.602 B.A., J.D. [Jones,D.R.&P.]
*PRACTICE AREAS: Litigation.
Gurdin, Kristen M. '74 '00 C.103 A.B. L.831 J.D.
(adm. in PA; not adm. in DC) [[A] Caplin&D.]
*PRACTICE AREAS: Taxation; Tax Exempt Organizations.
Gurley, John M. .... '55 '84 C&L.378 B.A., J.D. [Coudert B.]
*PRACTICE AREAS: International Trade; Customs Law.
Gurman, Louis, (AV) '47 '74 C.1044 B.A. L.273 J.D.
[Morrison&F.] (⊙Mc Lean, VA)
*PRACTICE AREAS: PCS and Wireless Communications; Appellate Advocacy; Litigation; Business Transactions.
Gurne, Patricia D., (AV) .... '41 '69 C.430 A.B. L.273 J.D. [Coates,D.&G.]
*PRACTICE AREAS: Association Law; Employment Law; Education Law; Corporate Law; Civil Litigation.
Gurney, Brent J. .... '59 '85 C.373 B.A. L.309 J.D. [[C] Wilmer,C.&P.]
*PRACTICE AREAS: Complex Litigation; White Collar Crime.
Gurny, Susan Lynn .... '53 '85 C.690 B.A. L.128 J.D. 1801 K St. NW
Gurss, Robert M., (AV) .... '57 '82 C&L.477 B.A., J.D. [[C] Shook,H.&B.]
*PRACTICE AREAS: Telecommunications Law.
Gurwitz, Adam W. '67 '93 C.228 B.A. L.93 J.D.
(adm. in MA; not adm. in DC) 1500 K St., N.W.‡
Gustafson, Albert Katsuaki '49 '81 C.813 B.A. L.911 J.D.
(adm. in NY; not adm. in DC) 1250 Eye St.,N.W.
Gustafson, Charles H. .... '37 '64 C.107 B.S. L.145 J.D. Prof., Georgetown Univ.
Gustafson, John H. .... '52 '81 C&L.276 B.A., J.D. D.C. Comm. on Human Rights
Gustafson, Katharine Herber '51 '79 C&L.285 B.A., J.D.
(adm. in WA; not adm. in DC) 2300 N. St., N.W.‡
Gustafson, Kristen L. .... '71 '98 C.674 A.B. L.569 J.D. Trial Atty./ Litigator
Gustafson, Madie D. '49 '81 C.597 B.S. L.208 J.D.
(adm. in CO; not adm. in DC) [Cole,R.&B.]
*PRACTICE AREAS: Cable TV Law; Communications Law; Cable Franchising.
Gustavson, Karen Ruth .... '66 '94 C.446 B.A. L.425 J.D. [[A] Weiner B.S.K.]
*PRACTICE AREAS: Mortgage Banking; Real Estate Finance; Financial Institutions Law; Regulatory Compliance.
Gustini, Raymond J. .... '43 '70 C&L.184 B.A., J.D. [Nixon P.]
*PRACTICE AREAS: Banking Law; Privacy Law.
Gutermann, Paul E., (BV) .... '56 '81 C.156 A.B. L.124 J.D. [Akin,G.S.H.&F.]
*PRACTICE AREAS: Environmental Law; Land Use; Project Finance.
Guthrie, Carolyn N. .... '55 '92 C.273 B.A. L.276 J.D. [[A] Skadden,A.S.M.&F.]
*PRACTICE AREAS: Antitrust.
Guthrie, W. Theodore, (BV) '52 '77 C.303 B.A. L.629 J.D.
(adm. in OR; not adm. in DC) 1849 Kalorama NE Apt. 2
Gutierrez, Franca Harris .... '68 '95 C&L.178 B.A., J.D. [[C] Wilmer,C.&P.]
Gutierrez, Jay M. .... '51 '79 C.276 B.A. L.1292 J.D. [Morgan,L.&B.]
Gutierrez, Patrick .... '72 '00 C.893 B.A. L.659 J.D. [[A] Wilmer,C.&P.]
Gutierrez, Thomas, (AV) .... '50 '79 C.446 B.S. L.128 J.D. [Lukas,N.G.&S.]
*PRACTICE AREAS: Administration Law; Communications and Media; Contracts.
Gutman, Howard W., (AV) .... '56 '82 C.178 B.A. L.309 J.D. [Williams&C.]
*PRACTICE AREAS: Commercial Litigation; Federal Civil Practice; Legal Malpractice; Litigation; Real Estate Litigation.
Gutmann, Peter, (AV) .... '49 '78 C.918 B.A. L.273 J.D. [Pepper&C.]
*PRACTICE AREAS: Telecommunications Law; Broadcast Station Transfers; Broadcast Applications; Telecommunications Contracts; Broadcast Television.
Gutowski, Anthony M. '67 '94
C.884 B.M.E. L.273 J.D. [[A] Finnegan,H.F.G.&D.] (See Pat. Sect.)
*PRACTICE AREAS: Mechanical Patents; Electro-Mechanical Patents; Medical Patents; Patent Protection; Patent Prosecution.
Gutowski, John '76 '01 C.340 B.A. L.893 J.D.
(adm. in VA; not adm. in DC) [[A] Cadwalader,W.&T.]
*PRACTICE AREAS: Corporate; Financial Restructuring.
Gutter, Samuel I., (AV) .... '52 '77 C.860 B.A. L.273 J.D. [Sidley A.B.&W.]
Gutterman, Alvin H. .... '45 '72 C.454 B.S. L.569 J.D. [Morgan,L.&B.]
Guttman, Julia E., (AV) .... '60 '85 C.309 B.A. L.976 J.D. [Baker B.]
Guttman, Reuben A. .... '59 '85 C.696 B.A. L.245 J.D. [Provost&U.]
*PRACTICE AREAS: General Civil and Trial Practice; False Claims Act Litigation; Antitrust Litigation; Securities Litigation; Commercial Litigation.
Guttman-McCabe, Catherine R. .... '68 '95 C.821 B.A. L.309 J.D. [[A] Hogan&H.]
*PRACTICE AREAS: Education Law; College and University Law; School Law; Employment Discrimination; Employment Law.
Guttmann, John S., Jr., (AV) '53 '78
C.659 B.A. L.188 J.D. [Beveridge&D.] (⊙New York, NY)
*PRACTICE AREAS: Complex Litigation; Product Liability; Toxic Tort Defense; Environmental Law.
Guy, Jonathan P. .... '61 '94 C.054 B.S. L.813 J.D. [[A] Swidler B.S.F.]
*PRACTICE AREAS: Litigation; Bankruptcy.
Guy-Jackson, Carol .... '65 '94 C.329 B.B.A. L.1280 J.D. [[A] Piper M.R.&W.]
*PRACTICE AREAS: Litigation; Real Estate.
Guymon, CarrieLyn D. .... '69 '99 C.976 B.A. L.276 J.D. [[A] O'Melveny&M.]
Guziak, Ronald G. .... '46 '71 [[C] Bonner K.T.&C.] (⊙Rockville, MD)
*PRACTICE AREAS: General Litigation; Medical Malpractice; Construction Litigation; Toxic Tort Litigation; Product Liability.
Guzman, Javier Manuel .... '66 '91 C.420 B.S. L.861 J.D. Dept. of Jus.

Guzman, Michael J. .... '64 '94 C.101 B.A. L.309 J.D. [Kellogg,H.H.T.&E.]
*PRACTICE AREAS: Litigation; Telecommunications.
Guzy, Gary S. .... '— '83 C&L.188 B.A., J.D. [Foley,H.&E.]
*PRACTICE AREAS: Environmental Law; Government; Strategic Alliances.
Guzzeau, Gwynne W. '66 '99 C.914 B.A. L.276 J.D.
(adm. in VA; not adm. in DC) [[A] Ballard S.A.&I.]
*PRACTICE AREAS: Real Estate Finance.
Gwadz, Joyce Trimble .... '49 '76 C.788 A.B. L.477 J.D. [Dow,L.&A.]
Haaf, Shannon .... '72 '98 C.446 B.A. L.64 J.D. [[A] Buchanan I.]
*PRACTICE AREAS: Franchise Law.
Haag, Susan White ....'55 '85 C.454 B.A. L.569 J.D. 1722 Eye St., N.W.
Haanes, Elizabeth J. .... '56 '01 C.477 B.S. L.174 J.D. [[A] Sterne,K.G.&F.]
*PRACTICE AREAS: Biotechnology Patents; Biotechnology Patent Prosecution; Patent Applications; Intellectual Property.

Haar, Paul S., Law Offices of, (BV) '53 '83 C.477 B.A. L.30 J.D.
1150 Connecticut Avenue, N.W., Ninth Floor, 20036
Telephone: 202-862-4328 Fax: 202-862-4397
Email: paulhaar@aol.com URL: http://www.lawyers.com/haarlaw
Immigration and Nationality Law, Immigration Litigation, Business Immigration, Employment Visa, International Corporate, Transnational Litigation, Arbitration.
See Professional Biographies, WASHINGTON, DISTRICT OF COLUMBIA

Haarz, David R. .... '50 '76 C.1154 B.A. L.477 J.D. [Dickinson W.]
*PRACTICE AREAS: International Trademarks; International Patents; Domestic Trademarks.
Haas, Alfred M. .... '71 '97 C.228 B.A. L.273 J.D. [[A] Piper M.R.&W.] (Pat.)
*PRACTICE AREAS: Patent Law; Intellectual Property.
Haas, Christa .... '71 '00 C.323 B.A. L.902 J.D. [[A] Littler M.]
*PRACTICE AREAS: Labor and Employment.
Haas, Darlene Marie '70 '00 C.97 B.A. L.851 J.D.
(adm. in MI; not adm. in DC) National Labor Relations Board
Haas, David C., (AV) .... '59 '84 C.945 B.B.A. L.644 J.D. [Arent F.K.P.&K.]
*PRACTICE AREAS: International Project Development; International Finance; Construction; Technology Joint Ventures; International Trade.

Haas & Anderson, P.C.
(See McLean, Virginia)

Haas & Najarian, (AV) .... 1200 19th Street, N.W., Suite 401 (⊙San Fran., CA)
Haber, Kenneth J. .... '45 '70 C&L.477 B.A., J.D. [K.J.Haber]
Haber, Kenneth J., Law Offices of, P.C. .... 1730 K St., NW
Haberer, Jacqueline '73 '00 C.696 B.A. L.309 J.D.
(adm. in NY; not adm. in DC) [[A] Baker B.]
Haberman, Michael H. '60 '86 C.1036 B.A. L.276 J.D.
1050 17th St. NW, Ste. 1100 (⊙Tel Aviv, Israel)
Habib, Amy M. .... '68 '96 C.93 B.A. L.107 J.D. [[A] McGuiness N.&W.]
*PRACTICE AREAS: Litigation; Labor Law; Employment Law.
Hackbarth, Margaret A. .... '66 '92 C.105 B.A. L.665 J.D. [[A] Holland&K.]
Hacker, Jonathan .... '68 '96 C.309 A.B. L.477 J.D. [[A] O'Melveny&M.]
Hacker, Robert C., (AV) .... '— '65 C&L.339 A.B., J.D. [Kirkpatrick&L.]
*PRACTICE AREAS: Financial Services Law; Investment Management; Investment Regulation; Mutual Funds; Broker-Dealer Regulation.
Hackett, Jacqueline Suzanne '74 '00 C.276 B.S. L.228 J.D.
(adm. in NY; not adm. in DC) [[A] Sullivan&C.]
Hackett, Susan J. '61 '86 C.475 B.A. L.477 J.D.
Sr. V.P., Gen. Coun. & Asst. Secy., Amer. Corp. Coun. Assn.
*RESPONSIBILITIES: Legal Affairs; Amicus Work; Legal Issues Affecting Corporate Counsel; Advocacy (Public Policy, Diversity and Pro Bono); ACCA Online.
Hackney, James V. .... '50 '75 C&L.659 B.A., J.D. 601 13th St., N.W.
Haddad, Mark E. .... '56 '87 C.813 A.B. L.976 J.D. [Sidley A.B.&W.]
Haddaway, Keith G. '58 '97
C.1203 B.S. L.273 J.D. [[A] Venable,A.B.H.&C.] (See Pat. Sect.)
*PRACTICE AREAS: Intellectual Property.
Hadden, Charles I. .... '50 '75 C.475 B.S. L.477 J.D. [Ross,D.&B.]
Haddon, Jonathan W. .... '58 '85 C.659 B.A. L.94 J.D. [[C] Orrick,H.&S.]
Haden, Mabel D., P.C. .... '14 '48 C.887 B.S. L.329 LL.B. 724 9th St., N.W.
Hadges, Jason S. .... '69 '95 C.228 B.A. L.30 J.D. [[A] Brand&F.]
*PRACTICE AREAS: Criminal Litigation; Civil Litigation; Employment Law; Administrative Law.
Hadjis, Alexander J. .... '67 '95 C.608 B.S.E.E. L.665 J.D. [Fish&R.] (See Pat. Sect.)
*PRACTICE AREAS: Intellectual Property Law.
Hadley, Amy L. '73 '98 C&L.945 B.A., J.D.
(adm. in VA; not adm. in DC) [[A] Lewis] (⊙Fairfax, VA)
*PRACTICE AREAS: Family Law.
Hadley, Joseph E., Jr., (AV) .... '43 '73 C.676 A.B. L.904 J.D. [Hadley&M.]
Hadley, Michael .... '74 '00 C.945 B.A. L.893 J.D. [[A] Covington&B.]
*PRACTICE AREAS: Litigation; Employee Benefits.
Hadley & McKenna, (AV) ....1815 H Street, N.W., Suite 500 (⊙Fairfax, VA)
Haemer, Robert '61 '99 C.911 B.S. L.276 J.D.
(adm. in VA; not adm. in DC) [[A] Shaw P.]
Hafeli, Susan M. .... '55 '87 C.477 B.A. L.846 J.D. [[A] Shaw P.]
*PRACTICE AREAS: Communications.
Hafemeister, Jason Todd .... '65 '99 C.112 B.A. L.276 J.D. 600 17th St., S.E.
Hafner, Elizabeth Cole, (AV) .... '60 '89 C.112 A.B. L.94 J.D. [Powell,G.F.&M.]
*PRACTICE AREAS: International Trade Law; Customs Law.
Haft, Robert J. .... '30 '55 C.563 B.A. L.178 J.D. Georgetown Univ. Law Ctr.
Haft, William S. .... '64 '99 C.118 B.A. L.309 J.D. [[A] Hogan&H.]
*PRACTICE AREAS: Education Law; School Law; Legislative Practice; Litigation.
Haga, David L. .... '73 '98 C&L.893 B.A., J.D. [[A] Crowell&M.]
Haga, Robert '— '96 C.178 B.S. L.1065 J.D.
(adm. in CA; not adm. in DC) Neca Inc.
Hagan, Christopher J. .... '61 '86 C.20 B.A. L.228 J.D. [Hogan&H.]
*PRACTICE AREAS: Corporate Law; Securities Law; Mergers and Acquisitions; Venture Capital Transactions.
Hage, Joseph K., III, (BV) '50 '79 C.299 B.A. L.982 J.D.
(adm. in NY; not adm. in DC) [[C] Lukas,N.G.&S.] (⊙Utica, NY)
*PRACTICE AREAS: Public Utility Law; Municipal Law; Business Law; Corporate Law; Partnership Law.
Hagedorn, William D. .... '73 '98 C.674 A.B. L.893 J.D. [[A] McDermott,W.&E.]
Hagel, Lawrence B. '47 '76
C.871 B.S. L.464 J.D. Dep. Gen. Coun., Paralyzed Vet. of Amer.
Hagen, Katherine .... '44 '82 C.604 B.A. L.575 J.D. V.P.; Fed. Govt. Affs., AT&T
Hagen, Paul E., (BV) .... '64 '90 C.676 B.A. L.904 J.D. [Beveridge&D.]
*PRACTICE AREAS: International Environmental Law; Environmental Law.
Hagenbuch, Nicole L. .... '74 '99 C.390 A.B. L.128 J.D. [[A] Akin,G.S.H.&F.]
*PRACTICE AREAS: Litigation; White Collar Crime.
Hager, Mark M. '55 '83
C.31 A.B. L.309 J.D. Washington College of Law, American Univ.
Hager, Robert A. .... '65 '91 C&L.276 B.S.F.S., J.D. [Patton B.]
Hagerty, James R. .... '57 '86 C.30 B.A. L.809 J.D. [Kalbian H.]
*PRACTICE AREAS: Federal, State and International Taxation; Corporate Law; Business Law; Exempt Organizations; Government Relations.
Hagerty, Thomas G., (AV) .... '50 '78 C.105 B.S. L.904 J.D. [Semmes,B.&S.]
*PRACTICE AREAS: Litigation; Insurance Defense Law; Workers Compensation Law.

Hagerup, Stefan A. ....'62 '91 C&L.966 B.A., J.D. [Ⓒ Akin,G.S.H.&F.]
*PRACTICE AREAS: Litigation; Labor and Employment Law.
Haggerty, Robert J., (AV) ....'43 '69 C&L.276 A.B., J.D. 1100 New York Ave. N.W.
Haggerty, Thomas J. '44 '70 C&L.276 B.S.F.S., J.D.
(adm. in MD; not adm. in DC) [Muldoon M.&F.]
*PRACTICE AREAS: Business Law; Banks and Banking; Corporate Law; Mergers, Acquisitions and Divestitures; Securities.
Hagle, George H. '36 '62 C.976 B.E. L.846 LL.B.
(adm. in TX; not adm. in DC) Chmn., Connoisseur Travel, Ltd.‡
Hagler, Marian M. ....'62 '90 C.112 A.B. L.276 J.D. [Coudert B.]
*PRACTICE AREAS: Corporate; Russia; Kazakhstan.
Hagner, John D., (AV) ....'45 '73 C.150 B.S.M.E. L.276 J.D. [Womble C.S.&R.]
*PRACTICE AREAS: Commercial Real Estate; Corporate; Business; Insurance Law.
Hague, Kurt '72 '99 C.689 B.A. L.128 J.D.
(adm. in MA; not adm. in DC) [Ⓐ Willkie F.&G.]
Hahm, Kevin ....'67 '96 C.821 B.A. L.861 J.D. [Ⓐ Skadden,A.S.M.&F.]
*PRACTICE AREAS: Antitrust.
Hahm, W. Douglas '68 '00 C.645 B.S.M.E. L.1356 J.D.
(adm. in VA; not adm. in DC; See Pat. Sect.) [Ⓐ Wenderoth,L.&P.]
*PRACTICE AREAS: Patent Prosecution; Mechanical Patents.
Hahn, Benjamin W. ....'53 '79 C&L.813 A.B., J.D. [Hahn K.&H.]
Hahn, Gilbert, Jr., (AV) ....'21 '48 C.674 A.B. L.976 LL.B. [Amram&H.]
Hahn, John S. ....'52 '77 C.228 A.B. L.976 J.D. [Mayer,B.&P.]
Hahn, Martin J. ....'63 '89 C.608 B.S. L.597 J.D. [Hogan&H.]
*PRACTICE AREAS: Food, Drug and Cosmetic Law; Food and Drug Regulation; Food and Agriculture; Food Labeling and Inspection; Food Processing.
Hahn, Robert A. ....'58 '85 C.103 A.B. L.178 J.D. [Ⓐ Olsson,F.&W.]
*PRACTICE AREAS: Banking Law; Food and Drug Regulation; Lobbying.
Hahn, Thomas S. .... '44 '77 C.645 B.S. L.1209 J.D. [Ⓒ Fulbright&J.] (See Pat. Sect.)
*PRACTICE AREAS: Intellectual Property; Patents; Trademarks; Copyrights.
Hahn-Burkett, Tracy '66 '96
C.860 B.A. L.893 J.D. Legis. Coun., People for the Amer. Way
Hahn Kyle & Hollrah, LLP .... 1667 K Street, N.W., Suite 480
Haifley, John F. .... '45 '71 C.446 B.A. L.325 J.D. 400 Seventh Street, SW, Romm 3318
Haile, Elizabeth Schickedanz ....'75 '99 C.347 B.S.P.A. L.276 J.D. [Ⓐ Arent F.K.P.&K.]
*PRACTICE AREAS: OSHA; Employment Law; ERISA.
Haile, J. Chris ....'79 '99 C.880 B.A. L.276 J.D. [Ⓐ Crowell&M.]
Hailes, Edward A., Jr. ....'54 '83 C&L.329 B.A., J.D. Coun., NAACP Wash. Bur.
Hailey, Gary D. ....'52 '78 C.691 B.A. L.309 J.D. [Venable,A.B.H.&C.]
*PRACTICE AREAS: Advertising; Trade Regulation; Direct Marketing.
Hails, Robert L., Jr. ....'68 '93 C.446 B.S. L.273 J.D. [Ⓐ Kenyon&K.] (See Pat. Sect.)
*PRACTICE AREAS: Intellectual Property.
Hainbach, Don H., (AV) ....'55 '80 C.103 A.B. L.477 J.D. [Boros&G.]
*PRACTICE AREAS: Transportation Regulation; International Aviation.
Haines, Jerry V., (AV) ....'44 '81 C.494 B.S. L.229 J.D. [Wiley R.&F.]
*PRACTICE AREAS: Communications.
Haines, Susan Q. ....'68 '96 C.722 B.A. L.273 J.D. [Ⓐ Jones,D.R.&P.]
Hainline, Forrest A., III, (AV) ....'46 '74 C.602 B.A. L.477 J.D. [F.A.Hainline,III]

Hainline, Forrest A., III, Law Office of, (AV)
Suite 440, 5335 Wisconsin Avenue, N.W., 20015
Telephone: 202-966-1962 Fax: 202-966-1891
Email: aikidoLaw@aol.com URL: http://www.lawyers.com/hainline
Forrest A. Hainline III.

See Professional Biographies, WASHINGTON, DISTRICT OF COLUMBIA

Hair, Penda D. .... '54 '80 C.838 B.S. L.309 J.D. Co-Dir., The Advancement Project
Haire, Dirk ....'67 '94 C.63 B.S. L.273 J.D. [Ⓒ Holland&K.]
*PRACTICE AREAS: Construction.
Hairston, Abbey Gail, (AV) ....'55 '82 C.221 B.A. L.352 J.D. [Seyfarth S.]
*PRACTICE AREAS: Litigation; Labor and Employment Law; Education Law.
Hairston, Joseph H. ....'22 '60 C.446 B.S. L.30 J.D. 1316 Floral St., N.W.‡
Hajek, Luther L. ....'70 '99 C.197 B.A. L.273 J.D. [Ⓐ Keller&H.]
*PRACTICE AREAS: Litigation; Unfair Trade; Food and Drug.
Hajjar, Anton G., (AV) ....'47 '75 C.262 B.A. L.861 J.D. [O'Donnell,S.&A.]
*PRACTICE AREAS: Labor and Employment Law.
Hajjar, David R. ....'62 '91 C&L.339 B.S., J.D. Prison Fellowship Intl.
Hajost, Cynthia M. ....'— '85 C.150 B.A. L.273 J.D. [Ⓒ Ballard S.A.&I.]
*PRACTICE AREAS: Real Estate Finance; Housing Law.
Hajost, Theresa W. ....'54 '85 C.1105 B.A. L.273 J.D. [Halloran&S.]
*PRACTICE AREAS: Litigation; Insurance; Reinsurance; Commercial Litigation.
Hakim, Shazmah '69 '99 C.773 B.A. L.273 J.D.
(adm. in NY; not adm. in DC) [Ⓐ Orrick,H.&S.]
Hakimi, Shahryar '64 '90 C&L.273 B.A., J.D.
(adm. in PA; not adm. in DC) 5018 Weaver Ter. N.W.‡
Hakura, Dima S. ....'67 '93 C.821 B.A. L.477 J.D. [Ⓐ Sidley A.B.&W.]
Halber, Eric P. ......'63 '90 C.390 B.S.M.E. L.1202 J.D. [Ⓐ Sughrue M.] (See Pat. Sect.)
*PRACTICE AREAS: Intellectual Property.
Halberstein, Richard ....'42 '67 C.401 B.A. L.477 J.D. [Halberstein&B.]
Halberstein & Byrne, (BV) .... 705 D St., S.E.
Haldane, Elise ....'51 '76 C.659 B.A. L.1209 J.D. 303 E St., N.E.
Hale, Christopher ....'73 '00 C.472 B.A. L.228 J.D. [Ⓐ Wiley R.&F.]
Hale, Marian F. ....'53 '89 C.1044 B.A. L.276 J.D. MCI Telecom. Corp.
Hale, Marilyn F. ....'31 '56 C.856 A.B. L.276 J.D. 4201 Cathedral Ave., N.W.
Hale, Mary L. ....'54 '85 C.276 B.S. L.273 J.D. [Ⓐ Jones,D.R.&P.]
Hale, Shadonna E., (BV) ....'56 '90 C.30 B.S.N. L.446 J.D. [Ⓒ Carr G.]
*PRACTICE AREAS: Professional Liability; Health Care.

Hale and Dorr LLP, (AV) BB
A Partnership including Professional Corporations
1455 Pennsylvania Avenue, N.W., 20004 ⊙
Telephone: 202-942-8400 Cable Address: "Hafis Wsh" Telecopier: 202-942-8484
URL: http://www.haledorr.com
Resident Members: John C. Christie, Jr.; Jeffrey J. Davidson; Irah H. Donner; Michael D. Esch; Allen H. Fox; Mark A. Heller; Louise Nicholson Howe; Gilbert B. Kaplan; Michael J. Levitin; Meghan H. Magruder; William G. McElwain; Kenneth R. Meade; James L. Quarles III; Kenneth H. Slade; Steven S. Snider; Jay P. Urwitz; Paul G. Wallach; Kathleen M. Weinstein; David A. Wilson; Henry N. Wixon. Scott M. Alter; Barry J. Hurewitz; Cynthia K. Nicholson; James G. Votaw; Deborah M. Wiggin. Counsel: Miriam R. Gamson; Paul W. Jameson; Cris R. Revaz; Wendy Anderson Terry. Resident Associates: Francis E. Chin (Not admitted in DC); Gregory S. Discher (Not admitted in DC); James M. Dowd; Neal N. Goldberg (Not admitted in DC); Edward D. Grieff; Michael Q. Hyde; Anthony H. Kahng (Not admitted in DC); Karen Lowy Tinsky (Not admitted in DC); Aimen Mir (Not admitted in DC); Brent M. Mitchell; Stephanie Philbin; Natalie L. Reed; Kerry Pyle Rubin; James P. Sheesley, II (Not admitted in DC); Nancy K. Stade; David A. Suski; Luke J. Yeh. Staff Attorney: Hy David Rubenstein.
General Practice. Corporate, Securities, Trusts, Real Estate, Taxation, Probate, Estate Planning, Pension, Bankruptcy, Reorganization and Creditors Rights, Antitrust and Trade Negotiation, Government Contracts and Legislative, International, State and Federal Trial and Appellate Practice including Complex Commercial Transactions, Antitrust, Securities Regulation, Unfair Competition and Trade Secrets, Product Liability, Environmental Claims, Other Civil and Criminal Litigation, Biotechnology, Family Business, Finance, Emerging Companies, Publicly Traded Companies, Telecommunication and Software, Venture Capital, Initial Public Offerings, Intellectual Property, Trademarks, Investment Management, Labor and Employment, Employee Benefits, ERISA and Real Estate Capital Management.

(This Listing Continued)

Hale and Dorr LLP (Continued)
Boston, Massachusetts Office: 60 State Street. Telephone: 617-526-6000. Cable Address: "Hafis." Telex: 94-0472. Telecopier: Domestic 617-526-5000; 617-742-9108.
Waltham, Massachusetts Office: Bay Colony Corporate Center, 1100 Winter Street, Suite 4650. Telephone: 781-966-2000. Telecopier: 781-966-2100.
Princeton, New Jersey Office: 650 College Road East. Telephone: 609-750-7600. Telecopier: 609-750-7700.
New York, N.Y. Office: 300 Park Avenue. Telephone: 212-937-7200. Fax: 212-937-7300.
Reston, Virginia Office: One Freedom Square, 11951 Freedom Drive, Suite 1400. Telephone: 703-654-7000. Fax: 703-654-7100.

See Professional Biographies, WASHINGTON, DISTRICT OF COLUMBIA

Haley, Kathleen M. ....'68 '97 C.855 B.A. L.893 J.D. [Ⓐ McDermott,W.&E.]
Hall, Charles S. ....'09 '53 C.465 A.B. L.912 J.D. 1300 I St., N.W. (Pat.)
Hall, Christopher R. ....'70 '98 C.69 B.A. L.846 J.D. [Ⓐ Hogan&H.]
*PRACTICE AREAS: Litigation.
Hall, Debra J. '57 '80 C.801 B.A. L.365 J.D.
Sr. V.P. & Gen. Coun., Reins. Assn. of America
Hall, Douglas W. ....'— '89 C.665 B.A. L.276 J.D. [Verner,L.B.M.&H.]
*PRACTICE AREAS: Labor and Employment Law; Litigation.
Hall, Francis L. '10 '35 L.537 LL.B.
(adm. in MS; not adm. in DC) 1719 Varnum St., N.W.‡
Hall, James E. ....'41 '67 C&L.838 B.A., LL.B [Dillon,H.&L.]
Hall, John E., (AV) ....'57 '85 C&L.309 A.B., J.D. [Covington&B.]
Hall, John R., (AV) ....'46 '75 C.228 B.A. L.30 J.D. [Muldoon M.&F.]
*PRACTICE AREAS: Financial Institutions; Thrift Insurance; Corporate Banking; Mergers, Acquisitions and Reorganizations; Federal Regulatory.
Hall, Joseph C. '73 '00 C.880 B.S. L.861 J.D.
(adm. in MD; not adm. in DC) [Ⓐ Duncan,W.G.&P.]
*PRACTICE AREAS: Energy Law; Telecommunications.
Hall, Joseph Solomon '73 '00 C.228 A.B. L.276 J.D.
(adm. in NY; not adm. in DC) [Ⓐ Kellogg,H.H.T.&E.]
*PRACTICE AREAS: Litigation.
Hall, Kristy J. '74 '00 C.624 B.A. L.1356 J.D.
(adm. in VA; not adm. in DC) [Ⓐ Cole,R.&B.]
*PRACTICE AREAS: Communications Law; Commercial Litigation; Antitrust.
Hall, Matthew F. ....'60 '87 C.917 B.A. L.276 J.D. [Dunaway&C.]
Hall, Melissa R.H. ....'71 '00 C.311 B.A. L.846 J.D. [Ⓐ Vinson&E.]
*PRACTICE AREAS: Project Finance; International Business Transactions; Business Law; Corporate Law.
Hall, Munford Page, II, (AV) ....'48 '80 C.228 B.A. L.904 J.D. [Ⓒ Dorsey&W.]
*PRACTICE AREAS: International Trade Law; Customs Law; Civil Litigation.
Hall, Ridgway M., Jr., (AV) ....'41 '66 C.976 B.A. L.309 LL.B. [Crowell&M.]
*PRACTICE AREAS: Environmental Law; Litigation.
Hall, Robert M. ....'50 '75 C.602 B.A. L.884 J.D. [Ⓒ Piper M.R.&W.]
*PRACTICE AREAS: Reinsurance; Insurance; Insolvency.
Hall, Robert S., Jr., (AV) '40 '64
C.976 B.S. L.893 LL.B. 900 Seventeenth Street, N.W. Suite 900
Hall, Robert T. '70 '00 C.311 B.A. L.846 J.D.
(adm. in MD; not adm. in DC) [Ⓐ Winston&S.]
*PRACTICE AREAS: Health Care Contracts; Health Care Regulation; Health Care Corporate Law; Health Care Facility Regulation; Physicians Contracts.
Hall, Robert T., III ....'45 '71 C.902 B.S. L.276 J.D. [Thelen R.&P.]
*PRACTICE AREAS: Infrastructure Development; Project Finance.
Hall, Rochelle S., (AV) ....'58 '84 C.93 A.B. L.309 J.D. [Ⓒ McGuirewoods]
*PRACTICE AREAS: Securities.
Hall, Stephen M. ....'65 '99 C.945 B.A. L.893 J.D. [Ⓐ Ross,D.&B.]
Hall, William N. ....'53 '78 C.105 B.A. L.276 J.D. [Winston&S.]
*PRACTICE AREAS: Environmental Law; Sports Law.

Hall, Estill, Hardwick, Gable, Golden & Nelson, A Professional Corporation, (AV)
Suite 700, North Building, 1120 20th Street, N.W., 20036-3406 ⊙
Telephone: 202-973-1200 Facsimile: 202-973-1212
Email: attorney_name@HallEstill.Com URL: http://www.HallEstill.Com
John B. Rudolph; Joseph R. Membrino, Jr.; Donald R. Dinan; John J. McDermott; James B. Wilcox, Jr.; Craig A. Koenigs; John J. Callahan; Sandeep Kathuria. Of Counsel: David L. Hill; Audrey P. Rasmussen.
General and Administrative Practice before all Courts and Administrative Agencies. Energy Regulatory and Natural Resources Law. Indian Law and Water Law. Government Relations.
Tulsa, Oklahoma Office: 320 South Boston Avenue, Suite 400, 74103. Telephone: 918-594-0400. Facsimile: 918-594-0505.
Oklahoma City, Oklahoma Office: Bank One Center, Suite 2900, 100 North Broadway, 73102-8827. Telephone: 405-553-2828. Facsimile: 405-553-2855.
Fayetteville, Arkansas Office: One East Center Street, Suite 315, 72701. Telephone: 501-973-5200. Facsimile: 501-973-0520.

See Professional Biographies, WASHINGTON, DISTRICT OF COLUMBIA

Hall & Evans, L.L.C., (AV)
Suite 610, 1341 G. Street, N.W., 20005 ⊙
Telephone: 202-638-4633 Fax: 202-408-5146
Email: hallevans@hallevans.com URL: http://www.hallevans.com
Member: F. Gregory McKenna.
General Civil and Trial Practice in all State and Federal Courts, including Administrative Law; Alternative Dispute Resolution; Complex and Multi-District Litigation; Environmental Law; Government Contracts; Litigation; Regulatory Law.
Denver, Colorado Office: Suite 1700, 1200 Seventeenth Street, 80202. Telephone: 303-628-3300. Fax: 303-628-3368.
Colorado Springs, Colorado Office: Suite 600, 102 South Tejon Street, 80903-2264. Telephone: 719-578-5600. Fax: 719-635-7458.

See Professional Biographies, WASHINGTON, DISTRICT OF COLUMBIA

Hall, Priddy, Myers & Vande Sande
(See Potomac, Maryland)

Halladay, Roberta L., (AV) ....'49 '75 C.717 A.B. L.602 J.D. [Morgan,L.&B.]
Hallagan, John B., (BV) ....'55 '85 C.550 B.S. L.30 J.D. [D.R.Thompson]
Hallberlin, Cynthia J. ....'57 '82 C.577 B.S. L.1162 J.D. [Ⓒ Sidley A.B.&W.]
Hallcom, Danielle D. ....'— '99 C&L.178 B.A., J.D. [Ⓐ Howrey S.A.&W.]
*PRACTICE AREAS: Commercial Litigation; Environmental; Insurance Coverage.
Halle, Peter E., (AV) ....'44 '73 C.569 B.A. L.472 J.D. [Morgan,L.&B.]
Haller, Susan C. ....'67 '92 C.945 B.A. L.273 J.D. [Mullenholz,B.&B.]
Halley, D. Gunnar ....'67 '95 C&L.276 B.S.F.S., J.D. [Ⓐ Willkie F.&G.]
*PRACTICE AREAS: Telecommunications.
Halliday, Stephen D. ....'48 '74 C.228 B.A. L.945 J.D. [Ⓒ Wiley R.&F.]
Hallmark, James B. ....'67 '93 C&L.846 B.A., J.D. [Ⓐ Piper M.R.&W.]
*PRACTICE AREAS: Business and Technology; Corporate and Securities; Venture Capital and Emerging Companies; Mergers and Acquisitions; Intellectual Property.
Hallmark, Sandra W. ....'— '84 C.1036 B.A. L.978 J.D. [King&S.]
*PRACTICE AREAS: Tax.
Halloran, Deirdre Dessingue '51 '75 C&L.128 B.A., J.D.
Assoc. Gen. Coun., U.S. Catholic Conference

Halloran & Sage LLP
1627 I Street, N.W., Suite 610, 20006 ⊙
Telephone: 202-496-9270 Fax: 202-496-9279
URL: http://www.halloran-sage.com
Members of Firm: James C. Stearns; Theresa W. Hajost. Of Counsel: Gina L. Schaecher.

(This Listing Continued)

Halloran & Sage LLP (Continued)

Administrative Law, Arbitration, Commercial Litigation, Construction Law, Employment Law, Government Contracts, Insurance, International Trade and Reinsurance Law.
Hartford, Connecticut Office: One Goodwin Square, 225 Asylum Street, 06103. Telephone: 860-522-6103. Fax: 860-548-0006.
Middletown, Connecticut Office: 300 Plaza Middlesex, 06457. Telephone: 860-346-8641. Fax: 860-344-1641.
Westport, Connecticut Office: 315 Post Road West, 06880-4739. Telephone: 203-227-2855. Fax: 203-227-6992.
See Professional Biographies, WASHINGTON, DISTRICT OF COLUMBIA

Halloway, Lorraine Berman, (AV) ....'47 '79 C.966 B.A. L.128 J.D. [Crowell&M.]
*PRACTICE AREAS: Aviation Law; Import and Export Law; Transportation Law.
Hallowell, Andrew P. ....'59 '86 C.347 B.A. L.30 J.D. [Piliero,M.&P.]
*PRACTICE AREAS: Corporate Law; Government Contracts; Trade Association Law; Native American Law; Civil Litigation.
Hallward-Driemeier, Douglas H. '— '95 C.210 B.A. L.309 J.D.
(adm. in MA; not adm. in DC) 1301 K St. N.W., Suite 800 E.
Halm, K. C. '67 '99 C.354 B.A. L.30 J.D.
(adm. in MD; not adm. in DC) [Ⓐ Cole,R.&B.]
*PRACTICE AREAS: Telecommunications Law; Telecommunications Competition; Administrative Law; Administrative Litigation.
Halperin, Allen K., (AV) ....'42 '68 C&L.893 B.S., LL.B. [Ⓒ Fulbright&J.]
*PRACTICE AREAS: Taxation; Aircraft Finance and Leasing; Equipment Finance and Leasing.
Halperin, Eliot J., (AV) ....'40 '65 C.319 B.A. L.309 J.D. [Manelli,D.&S.]
*PRACTICE AREAS: Transportation Law; Maritime Law; Legislation; Administrative Law.
Halperin, Jonathan E., (AV) ....'64 '91 C.273 B.A. L.128 J.D. [Regan,H.&L.] ⊙
*PRACTICE AREAS: Personal Injury; Aviation Accidents; Medical Malpractice; Wrongful Death; Legal Malpractice.
Halperin, Robert M., (AV) ....'54 '80 C.309 B.A. L.228 J.D. [Crowell&M.]
Halpern, Don J. ....'62 '88 C.659 B.A. L.1292 J.D. [Weiner B.S.K.]
*PRACTICE AREAS: Mortgage and Real Estate Finance; Mortgage Banking; Mergers and Acquisitions; Asset Sales; Corporate Law.
Halpern, James B., (AV) ....'36 '61 C&L.309 B.A., J.D. [Arent F.K.P.&K.]
*PRACTICE AREAS: Securities; Mergers, Acquisitions and Divestitures; Business Law; High Technology; Corporate Law.
Halpern, Jay L. ....'64 '89 C.1365 B.A. L.228 J.D. [Pillsbury W.] (⊙Mc Lean, VA)
*PRACTICE AREAS: Finance; Venture Capital; Mergers and Acquisitions; Corporate Structuring; Joint Ventures.
Halpern, Keith A. '70 '99 C.860 B.A. L.1365 J.D.
(adm. in MD; not adm. in DC) [Ⓐ Akin,G.S.H.&F.]
*PRACTICE AREAS: Labor and Employment.
Halpern, Naomi Joy Levan ....'63 '92 C.477 B.A. L.273 J.D. [Ⓐ Olsson,F.&W.]
*PRACTICE AREAS: Food, Drug and Cosmetic Law.
Halpern, Samuel W. '50 '75 C.103 B.A. L.273 J.D.
Exec. V.P. & Gen. Coun., Independent Fiduciary Servs., Inc.
Halpern, Todd H. ....'70 '96 C.966 B.A. L.262 J.D. [Ⓐ Buchanan I.]
*PRACTICE AREAS: Food, Drug and Cosmetics Law; Regulatory Law; Corporate Law; Biotechnology; Consumer Protection.
Halpert, James J. ....'63 '90 C.976 B.A. L.309 J.D. [Piper M.R.&W.]
*PRACTICE AREAS: Electronic Commerce; Privacy; Communications; Intellectual Property.
Halprin, Albert, (AV) ....'47 '75 C.907 B.A. L.309 J.D. [Halprin,T.G.&M.]
*PRACTICE AREAS: Communications Law; International Communications Law; Internet Litigation.
Halprin, Jack A. '69 '94 C.976 B.A. L.1068 J.D.
(adm. in CA; not adm. in DC) 1150 18th St. N.W. Lower Level
Halprin, Lawrence P. ....'52 '77 C.659 B.S. L.229 J.D. [Keller&H.]
*PRACTICE AREAS: Occupational Safety and Health Law; Environmental Law; Hazardous Materials and Substances; Commercial Transactions; Employment Law.

Halprin, Temple, Goodman & Maher, (AV)
950 North, 555 12th Street, N.W., 20004
Telephone: 202-371-9100 Fax: 202-371-1497
Email: htgm@htgm.com URL: http://www.htgm.com
Members of Firm: Albert Halprin; Riley K. Temple; Stephen L. Goodman; William F. Maher, Jr.; Joel H. Bernstein. Of Counsel: Janice I. Obuchowski.
Domestic and International Telecommunications Law, Communication Legislative Advocacy, Wireless, Cellular, Satellite, PCS, Administrative Legal Practice.
See Professional Biographies, WASHINGTON, DISTRICT OF COLUMBIA

Halsey, James D., Jr., (AV) ....'35 '64 C.446 B.S. L.904 J.D. [Staas&H.] (See Pat. Sect.)
*PRACTICE AREAS: Intellectual Property Law; Patent, Trademark, Copyright and Unfair Competition.
Halstead, Gloria J. ....'— '01 C.896 B.A. L.30 J.D. [Ⓐ Hunton&W.]
Halverson, James T., (AV) ....'40 '65 C&L.309 B.A., LL.B. [Steptoe&J.]
*PRACTICE AREAS: Antitrust; Complex Litigation.
Halvorson, Newman T., Jr., (AV) ......'36 '62 C.674 A.B. L.309 LL.B. [Covington&B.]
Ham, Yoon S. ....'61 '94 C.999 B.S.E.E. L.264 J.D. [Jacobson,H.] (See Pat. Sect.)
*PRACTICE AREAS: Intellectual Property Law; Electrical Patents; Mechanical Patents.
Hamberger, Robert S. '59 '84 C.188 B.A. L.178 J.D.
(adm. in NY; not adm. in DC) 1899 L St Nw, Suite 500‡
Hamble, Frederick J. ....'71 '97 C.188 B.S. L.262 J.D. [Ⓐ Morgan,L.&B.]
Hambley, Gwyneth E. ....'60 '93 C.945 B.A. L.1066 J.D. [Ⓐ McKee N.]
*PRACTICE AREAS: Corporate Law; Securities.
Hamblin, Sarah E. '69 '00 C.890 B.S. L.180 J.D.
(adm. in VA; not adm. in DC; See Pat. Sect.) [Ⓐ Adduci,M.&S.]
*PRACTICE AREAS: Intellectual Property Litigation.
Hambrick, E. L. ....'53 '98 C.659 B.S.B.A. L.273 J.D. [Ⓐ Arent F.K.P.&K.]
*PRACTICE AREAS: Health Law; Emergency Medical Services Law.
Hambrick, Jonathan H. ....'67 '94 C.976 B.A. L.945 J.D. [Ⓒ Akin,G.S.H.&F.]
*PRACTICE AREAS: Litigation.
Hambrick, Kathryn W. '66 '94 C.223 B.S L.945 J.D.
(adm. in VA; not adm. in DC) [Ⓐ Patton B.]
Hamburger, Paul M. ....'58 '83 C&L.477 B.A., J.D. [McDermott,W.&E.]
Hamburger, Philip A. '57 '82 C.674 B.A. L.976 J.D.
(adm. in PA; not adm. in DC) Prof. of Law, George Washington Univ.
Hamelburg, Mark E. ....'63 '88 C.659 B.S. L.477 J.D. William M. Mercer, Inc.
Hamill, David R. '59 '88 C.105 B.A. L.276 J.D.
(adm. in NY; not adm. in DC) [Ⓒ Miller&C.]
Hamilton, Anne M. ....'65 '92 C.93 B.A. L.273 J.D. 1050 Conn. Ave., N.W.
Hamilton, Eugene N. ....'33 '59 C&L.339 B.A., LL.B. Chf. Supr. Ct. J.
Hamilton, Francis M., III ....'72 '98 C.806 B.A. L.902 J.D. [Ⓐ Williams&C.]
Hamilton, Heather D. ....'— '97 C.473 B.A. L.879 J.D. [Ⓐ Piper M.R.&W.]
*PRACTICE AREAS: Electronic Commerce; Privacy Law; Health Care; State Legislative Practice; Public Policy.
Hamilton, James, (AV) ....'38 '63 C.198 A.B. L.976 LL.B. [Swidler B.S.F.]
*PRACTICE AREAS: Civil Litigation; White Collar Criminal Defense; Congressional Investigations; Government Investigations; Government Affairs.
Hamilton, Michele Claire '70 '98 C.893 B.A. L.1356 J.D.
(adm. in VA; not adm. in DC) Def. of Prop. Rights
Hamilton, Palmer C., (AV) '47 '74 C.16 B.A. L.228 J.D.
(adm. in AL; not adm. in DC) [Miller,H.S.O.&B.] (⊙Mobile, AL)
*PRACTICE AREAS: Bank Regulatory Law; Bankers Blanket Bond Claims; Directors and Officers Liability Litigation; Legislative Representation.

Hamilton, Shane T. ....'— '97 C&L.893 B.A., J.D. [Ⓐ Miller&C.]
*PRACTICE AREAS: Taxation; Federal Income Tax; Federal Tax Controversies; Tax Litigation; Tax Exempt Organizations.
Hamilton, Shelby G. ....'59 '98 C.232 B.A. L.273 J.D. [Ⓐ Firm of Larson-Jackson]
Hamilton, Stephen W. ....'52 '78 C.309 A.B. L.352 J.D. [Skadden,A.S.M.&F.]
Hamilton, Thomas J. ....'54 '79 C.976 B.A. L.893 J.D. [Byrne G.&H.]

Hamilton and Hamilton, LLP, (AV)
Suite 1100 1775 Pennsylvania Avenue, N.W., 20006
Telephone: 202-463-8282 Telecopier: 202-463-7282; 202-659-8285
Email: mailbox@hamiltonlaw.com URL: http://www.hamiltonlaw.com
South Trimble, III (1925-2000). Partners: Michael A. Cain; Richard E. Jordan; Patrick Kavanaugh; George T. Masson, Jr.; Stephen W. Nealon; James B. Sarsfield; E. Tillman Stirling; Philip J. Sweeney, III. Associate: Diane P. Pritchett. Special Counsel: Thomas D. Quinn, Jr.; Stephen A. Trimble. Of Counsel: Allen Jones, Jr.; Harry J. Jordan; Edward R. Kump.
Civil Litigation, Complex Multi-District Litigation, Business Law, Corporate Law, Education Law, Employment Law, Estate Planning, Trusts, Wills, Probate, Tax Exempt Organizations, Insurance Coverage Disputes, Municipal Law, Personal Injury, Professional Malpractice, Real Estate Law, Real Estate Tax, Taxation, Land Use and Zoning, Transportation.
Representative Clients: First American Bank, N.A.; Potomac Electric Power Co.; The Catholic University of America; Southern Railway Co.; Richmond, Fredericksburg & Potomac Railroad Co.; Consolidated Rail Corp.; The Medlantic Healthcare Group; Crawford & Co.
See Professional Biographies, WASHINGTON, DISTRICT OF COLUMBIA

Hamlin, Barney T. ....'43 '70 C.608 B.A. L.161 J.D. 2718 32nd St., S.E.

Hammack, Paul W., Jr.
(See Fairfax, Virginia)

Hammar, Patricia K. '64 '00 C.453 S.B. L.64 J.D
(adm. in XX; not adm. in DC) Nat'l Sec. Research, Inc.
Hamme, Joel M. ....'49 '73 C.216 B.A. L.659 J.D. [Powers,P.S.&V.]
*PRACTICE AREAS: Health Care Law; Litigation.
Hammer, Michael H. ....'54 '80 C.705 B.A. L.273 J.D. [Willkie F.&G.]
Hammer, Rachael ....'68 '99 C.999 B.A. L.178 J.D. [Ⓐ Jones,D.R.&P.]
Hammer, Stacey Beth ....'72 '99 C.1036 B.A. L.564 J.D. 2301 N St., N.W.
Hammerman, Edward S. ....'69 '94 C.1365 B.A. L.128 J.D. [Ⓐ Dickstein S.M.&O.]
*PRACTICE AREAS: Communications; Transactional; Intellectual Property.
Hammerman, Ira D. ....'60 '86 C.1365 B.A. L.276 J.D. [Clifford C.R.&W.]
*PRACTICE AREAS: Securities Regulation and Enforcement.
Hammerschmidt, Judith L. '54 '83 C.228 A.B. L.665 J.D.
Exec. V.P., International Chf. Coun., Herbalife International of America, Inc.
Hammett, Mary Ann, (AV) ....'45 '79 C.500 B.A. L.836 J.D. [Ⓒ Heggestad&W.]
*PRACTICE AREAS: Insurance Coverage; Civil Litigation; Contracts; Torts; Administrative.
Hammock, A. Statton, Jr. ....'67 '95 C.893 B.A. L.1294 J.D. [Ⓐ O'Brien,B.M.&S.]
*PRACTICE AREAS: Media Libel; Corporate Law; Nonprofit Organizations Law; Trademarks; Copyrights.
Hammond, Alan W. ....'60 '93 C.446 B.S.E.E. 1300 I St., N.W., Suite 700
Hammond, Benton R., (BV) ....'50 '75 C.966 B.A. L.178 J.D. [Hogan&H.]
*PRACTICE AREAS: Banking Law; Commercial Real Estate Law; Commercial Law.
Hammond, David C. .... '59 '88 C.20 B.A. L.477 J.D. [Powell,G.F.&M.] (⊙Reston, VA)
*PRACTICE AREAS: Government Contracts Law; Health Care Procurement Law; Legislative Law.
Hammond, Elizabeth A. ....'65 '96 C.846 B.B.A. L.273 J.D. [Ⓐ Arter&H.]
*PRACTICE AREAS: Corporate; Communications; Telecommunications Law.
Hammond, James K., (BV) '52 '78
C&L.893 B.S., J.D. [Finnegan,H.F.G.&D.] (See Pat. Sect.)
*PRACTICE AREAS: Patent Prosecution; Patent Litigation.
Hammond, Timothy '55 '82 C.327 B.S. L.87 J.D.
(adm. in AL; not adm. in DC) V.P., Crestar Bk.
Hampe, Carl W. ....'60 '92 C.813 B.A. L.276 J.D. [Ⓒ Paul,W.R.W.&G.]
*PRACTICE AREAS: Legislative; Immigration.
Hampel, Larry ....'51 '86 C.112 B.A. L.64 J.D. [Ⓐ F.L.Ikenson]
*PRACTICE AREAS: Customs and International Trade Law.
Hampton, Philip G., II, (AV) '54 '81 C.453 B.S.Chem.E. L.145 J.D.
(adm. in NY; not adm. in DC; Pat.) [Gardner,C.&D.]
*PRACTICE AREAS: Intellectual Property.
Hamrick, Cameron Street ....'58 '85 C&L.228 B.A., J.D. [Mayer,B.&P.]
Hamrick, Mary '57 '87 C.228 B.A. L.575 J.D.
(adm. in NC; not adm. in DC) New York Life Ins. Co.
Hamrick, Steven J. ....'65 '94 C.30 B.A. L.904 J.D. [Ⓐ Fleischman&W.]
Hamrock, Kurt J. ....'66 '92 C.802 B.A. L.846 J.D. [McKenna&C.]
*PRACTICE AREAS: Appellate Litigation.
Han, Cora Tung ....'70 '96 C.309 B.A. L.145 J.D. [Ⓐ Wilmer,C.&P.]
Han, Edward ....'58 '85 C.367 B.A. L.276 J.D. [Howrey S.A.&W.]
*PRACTICE AREAS: Antitrust; Intellectual Property; Insurance Coverage; Complex Litigation.
Han, Joanna ....'73 '98 C.976 B.A. L.273 J.D. [Ⓐ Holland&K.]
*PRACTICE AREAS: Labor and Employment; Corporate Diversity Counseling.
Hanback, Christopher B., (AV) ....'50 '75 C.228 A.B. L.597 J.D. [Holland&K.]
*PRACTICE AREAS: Real Estate; Fair Housing; Americans with Disabilities Act; Telecommunications; Senior Citizen Housing.
Hance, Kenneth G., Jr. ....'40 '66 C.475 B.A. L.597 J.D. [Nixon P.]
*PRACTICE AREAS: Real Estate; Real Estate Finance; Housing and Urban Development.
Hance, Kent R. '42 '68 C.845 B.B.A. L.846 LL.B.
(adm. in TX; not adm. in DC) [Hance S.W.G.&B.] (⊙Austin, TX)
Hance Scarborough Wright Ginsberg & Brusilow, L.L.P.
1150 Seventeenth Street N.W., Suite 500 (⊙Austin, Dallas, TX)
Hanchrow, Lesley Ellen '71 '99 C.228 A.B. L.276 J.D.
(adm. in NY; not adm. in DC) [Ⓐ Alston&B.]
*PRACTICE AREAS: Mergers and Acquisitions; Securities.
Hancock, Amy E. ....'59 '84 C.502 B.A. L.276 J.D. [McDermott,W.&E.]
Hancock, D. Michael ....'52 '81 C.612 B.S. L.45 J.D. 1300 Pennsylvania Ave. NW‡
Hancock, Harold '71 '00 C.1169 B.A L.966 J.D.
(adm. in VA; not adm. in DC) [Ⓐ Dow,L.&A.]
Hancock, Mark S. ....'74 '00 C&L.823 B.A., J.D. [Ⓐ Jones,D.R.&P.]
Hancock, Mary Ann ....'43 '83 C.612 B.S. L.128 J.D. 308 C St., N.E.
Hancock, Thomas F. ....'44 '77 C&L.339 B.A., J.D. [Ⓐ Sullivan&C.]
Hand, Elisabeth J. ....'26 '58 C.183 A.B. L.569 LL.B. 2700 Virginia Ave., N.W.
Hand, Emma F. '— '01 C.893 B.A. L.276 J.D.
(adm. in VA; not adm. in DC) [Ⓐ Verner,L.B.M.&H.]
*PRACTICE AREAS: Energy.
Hand, Gregg A. ....'62 '88 C.264 B.A. L.94 J.D. [Ⓐ White&C.]
Hand, Lloyd N., (AV) ....'— '57 C&L.846 B.A., J.D. [Verner,L.B.M.&H.]
*PRACTICE AREAS: Corporate; Legislative; Trade.

Hand, Patrick T., (AV) '58 '84 C.128 B.A. L.262 J.D.
3201 New Mexico Avenue, N.W., Suite 350, 20016
Telephone: 202-895-1332 Fax: 202-537-1200
Email: patrickthand@aol.com
***PRACTICE AREAS: Trusts and Estates; Mental Health Law.**
Wills, Estates, Trusts, Probate, Powers of Attorney, Contested Wills, Conservatorships, Guardianships, Estate and Gift Taxation, Estate Litigation, Retirement Planning, Family Business Succession Planning.
See Professional Biographies, WASHINGTON, DISTRICT OF COLUMBIA

Hand Arendall, L.L.C., (AV)
Suite 300 410 Frist Street, S.E. (⊙Birm., Foley, Mobile, AL)
Hand, Little, Pennington & Codrington ....2121 K Street, N.W., Suite 800 (⊙Newark, NJ)
Handleman, Aaron L., (AV) ....'46 '71 C.434 B.A. L.273 J.D. [Eccleston&W.]
*PRACTICE AREAS: Insurance Defense Law; Professional Malpractice Law; Legal Malpractice Law; Insurance Coverage; Complex Litigation.
Handler, Allyson B. ....'71 '96 C.659 B.A. L.276 J.D. [Ⓐ Sonnenschein N.&R.]
*PRACTICE AREAS: Litigation.
Handler, Marcia S. ....'64 '89 C.264 B.A. L.273 J.D. [Epstein B.&G.]
*PRACTICE AREAS: Health Law.
Handman, Christopher Todd .... '72 '98 C.30 B.A. L.976 J.D. [Ⓐ Hogan&H.]
*PRACTICE AREAS: Appellate Litigation; Litigation.
Handman, Laura R., (AV) '51 '77
C.976 B.A. L.94 J.D. [Davis W.T.] (⊙New York, NY)
*PRACTICE AREAS: Libel Law; Privacy Law; Media Law; Intellectual Property; Litigation.
Handrigan, Melissa R. '74 '99 C.823 B.A. L.273 J.D.
(adm. in MD; not adm. in DC) 1299 Pennsylvania Ave. N.W.
Handwerker, Jeffrey L. ....'70 '95 C.705 B.A. L.273 J.D. [Ⓐ Arnold&P.]
*PRACTICE AREAS: Government Contracts; Litigation.
Handzo, David A., (AV) .... '54 '80 C.674 B.A. L.477 J.D. [Jenner&B.]
*PRACTICE AREAS: Civil Law; Criminal Law; Bankruptcy Litigation; Advertising Law.
Hani, George A. ....'— '94 C.228 A.B. L.128 J.D. [Ⓒ Miller&C.]
*PRACTICE AREAS: Federal Tax Controversies; Corporate Taxation; International Taxation; Employment Tax.
Hanifin, Sean M., (AV) .... '57 '81 C.821 B.A. L.145 J.D. [Ross,D.&B.]
Hankin, Nancy L. ....'57 '83 C.577 B.A. L.910 J.D. [Ⓒ Sutherland A.&B.]
*PRACTICE AREAS: Trademarks; Copyrights; Unfair Competition.
Hankins, Brenda M. '74 '01 C.628 B.S. L.30 J.D.
(adm. in NY; not adm. in DC) [Ⓐ Carr,M.&G.]
*PRACTICE AREAS: Business Law; Corporate Law; Estate Planning.
Hankins, John A. .... '60 '85 C.859 B.S. L.1292 J.D. [McDermott,W.&E.] (Pat.)
Hankinson, Kymberly D. ....'66 '99 C.264 B.A. L.128 J.D. [Ⓐ Jones,D.R.&P.]
Hanks, Sara P. ....'57 '85 C.051 B.A. L.999 [Clifford C.R.&W.]
Hanley, Thomas L. ....'59 '85 C.893 B.A. L.945 J.D. [Piper M.R.&W.]
*PRACTICE AREAS: Finance; Corporate Law; Securities; Mergers and Acquisitions; Business Law.
Hanlon, Brian E. ....'— '95 C.971 B.S.M.E. L.128 J.D. [Banner&W.] (See Pat. Sect.)
*PRACTICE AREAS: Intellectual Property Law; Patents; Design Patents; Mechanical Intellectual Property; Medical Intellectual Property.
Hanlon, Patrick M. ....'46 '78 C.145 A.B. L.309 J.D. [Shea&G.]
*PRACTICE AREAS: Environmental; Toxic Torts; Legislative Practice; Civil Litigation; International.
Hanlon, R. Timothy, (P.C.), (AV) .... '37 '61 C.734 B.S. L.309 J.D. [Shaw P.]
*PRACTICE AREAS: Government Contracts; Outsourcing Contracts; Dispute Resolution.
Hanlon, William R. ....'53 '81 C.945 B.A. L.659 J.D. [Shea&G.]
*PRACTICE AREAS: Complex Litigation; Class Actions; Mass Torts; Professional Malpractice; Products Liability.
Hanna, James R. ....'66 '96 C.840 B.A. L.1066 J.D. [Ⓐ Latham&W.]
*PRACTICE AREAS: Telecommunications; Mergers and Acquisitions; Securities.
Hanna, Ray L., (AV) ......'34 '61 C&L.911 B.A., LL.B. 1000 Thomas Jefferson St., N.W.
Hanna, Tania W. ....'68 '95 C.276 B.S. L.30 J.D. [Ⓐ Dorsey&W.]
*PRACTICE AREAS: International Telecommunications Law; E-Commerce; Internet Licensing.
Hannes, Steven P., (AV) ....'45 '70 C.31 B.A. L.569 J.D. [McDermott,W.&E.]
Hannon, Brian W. ....'57 '87 C.884 B.S.M.E. L.128 J.D. [Sughrue M.] (See Pat. Sect.)
*PRACTICE AREAS: Intellectual Property Law; Litigation.
Hannon, J. Michael, (AV) .... '50 '81 C.674 A.B. L.904 J.D. [Thompson,O.M.N.&H.]
*PRACTICE AREAS: Premises Liability; Grand Jury Practice; ERISA; Professional Liability; White Collar Crime.
Hanny, James M., (AV) .... '42 '72 C.116 B.A. L.446 J.D. [Ashcraft&G.]
*PRACTICE AREAS: Personal Injury.
Hanrahan, Catherine A., (AV) ....'59 '85 C.1369 B.S. L.64 J.D. [Carr G.] ⊙
*PRACTICE AREAS: Health Care; Products Liability.
Hanrahan, Karen ....'69 '00 C.347 B.A. L.910 J.D. [Ⓐ White&C.]
Hanrahan, William F., (AV) ....'48 '73 C.112 B.A. L.1065 J.D. [Ⓒ Groom]
*PRACTICE AREAS: Employee Benefits Law; Civil Trial Practice; Pension and Profit Sharing; Appellate Practice; ERISA.
Hans, Matthew C. ....'74 '99 C.973 B.A. L.128 J.D. [Ⓐ Crowell&M.]
Hansell, Herbert J. '25 '49 C.453 B.S. L.976 LL.B.
(adm. in OH; not adm. in DC) [Ⓒ Jones,D.R.&P.]
Hansen, Camille ....'69 '95 C&L.1335 B.A., J.D. [Ⓐ Wilkinson B.K.]
*PRACTICE AREAS: Communications Law; Administrative Law.
Hansen, Christopher A., (AV) '34 '63
C.188 B.S. L.446 J.D. [Ⓒ Heggestad&W.] (⊙Towson, MD)
*PRACTICE AREAS: Civil Litigation; Insurance Law; Products Liability Law.
Hansen, Cynthia L. '70 '98 C&L.112 B.A., J.D.
(adm. in CA; not adm. in DC) [Ⓐ Winston&S.]
*PRACTICE AREAS: Corporate Law; International Law; Business Transactions.
Hansen, Keith E. ....'60 '89 C.976 B.A. L.813 J.D. The World Bk.
Hansen, Kenneth W. '51 '84 C.309 A.B. L.659 J.D.
(adm. in MA; not adm. in DC) [Chadbourne&P.]
Hansen, Kristi K. '74 '01 C.352 B.A. L.273 J.D.
(adm. in NY; not adm. in DC) [Ⓐ Baker&M.]
*PRACTICE AREAS: Trade Regulations and Customs Law; Intellectual Property Law.
Hansen, Mark C., (AV) .... '56 '83 C.197 A.B. L.309 J.D. [Kellogg,H.H.T.&E.]
*PRACTICE AREAS: Litigation.
Hansen, Myles R. .... '— '92 C.176 A.B. L.477 J.D. [Ⓐ Arnold&P.]
*PRACTICE AREAS: Antitrust and Trade Regulation.
Hansen, Orval, (AV) ....'26 '54 C.336 B.A. L.273 J.D. [Ⓒ Hopkins R.C.H.&H.]
*PRACTICE AREAS: Energy; Litigation.
Hansen, Robert M. '— '99 C.260 M.S. L.1209 J.D.
(adm. in VA; not adm. in DC) [Ⓐ Foley&L.]
*PRACTICE AREAS: Intellectual Property Law.
Hansen, Walter D., (AV) '27 '52
C&L.273 B.A., LL.B. 1762 Churst St., N.W. (⊙Manassas, VA)
Hanser, Russell P. .... '72 '97 C.31 B.A. L.309 J.D. [Ⓐ Wilmer,C.&P.]
Hanson, Donald W., (AV) '46 '74
C.350 B.S.Ch.E. L.273 J.D. [Armstrong,W.H.M.&N.] (See Pat. Sect.)
Hanson, John N., (AV) .... '45 '70 C&L.273 A.B., J.D. [Beveridge&D.]
*PRACTICE AREAS: Litigation; Environmental and Administrative Law.
Hanson, John T. '70 '96 C.966 B.A. L.276 J.D.
(adm. in MD; not adm. in DC) Ste. 400, 1125 15th St., N.W.
Hanson, Melinda M. .... '44 '84 C.112 B.A. L.378 J.D. Legal Editor, U.S. Law Week
Hanson, Michelle A. '— '98 C.488 B.A. L.585 J.D.
(adm. in MN; not adm. in DC) [Ⓐ Dorn&K.]
*PRACTICE AREAS: Nonprofit Organizations Law.

Hanson & Molloy, (AV)
1250 Eye Street, N.W., Suite 701, 20005-3922
Telephone: 202-842-1116 Facsimile: 202-842-1597
Email: hanson-molloy.com URL: http://www.lawyers.com/h&mlaw
Arthur B. Hanson (1916-1989); James Dennis Molloy; Arthur D. McKey; Michael B. McGovern. Of Counsel: Ron L. Durst (Not admitted in DC). Special Legal Consultant: Bala Nadarajah (Not admitted in the United States).

(This Listing Continued)

Hanson & Molloy (Continued)
General counsel to both profit and non-profit corporations. Internet litigation and governance, civil litigation with substantive concentration in insurance and reinsurance, labor and employment, anti-trust, media, First Amendment, tax, government, commercial contracts, real estate, trusts and estates.
See Professional Biographies, WASHINGTON, DISTRICT OF COLUMBIA

Hanten, Linda K. .... '49 '74 1700 17th St., N.W.
Hanzlik, Rayburn .... '38 '75 C.675 B.S. L.893 J.D. [Ⓒ Trainum,S.&D.]
*PRACTICE AREAS: Corporate Law; Business Law; Energy; Environmental Law.
Happy, J. Nelson, (AV) .... '43 '67 C.823 B.S. L.178 J.D. [American,E.P.]
*PRACTICE AREAS: Litigation; Corporate Law; Business Law; Mergers and Acquisitions.
Harb, Kimberly A. ....'66 '91 C.903 B.A. L.823 J.D. [Ⓐ Jones,D.R.&P.]
Harbeck, Stephen P. '46 '74
C.321 B.A. L.188 J.D. Gen. Coun., Securities Investor Protec. Corp.
Harbinger, Bonny ....'51 '97 C.999 B.A. L.276 J.D. [Ⓐ Phillips&C.]
*PRACTICE AREAS: False Claims Act; Qui Tam Litigation.
Harburg, Stephen J. ....'60 '85 C.976 B.A. L.659 J.D. [O'Melveny&M.]
*PRACTICE AREAS: Antitrust; Class Action Litigation; Insurance Coverage.
Harcar, Mary V. .... '— '76 C&L.776 B.A., J.D. 5101 Wisconsin Ave., NW
Hardesty, C. Howard, Jr. .... '22 '49 C.228 B.S. L.923 LL.B. 1701 Penn. Ave., N.W.
Hardie, Jeffrey B. ....'62 '94 C.886 B.A. L.861 J.D. [Ⓐ Hunton&W.]
Hardiman, Joseph R. '37 '62 C&L.446 A.B., LL.B.
(adm. in MD; not adm. in DC) Pres., National Assn. of Sec. Dealers, Inc.
Hardin, Jeffry L. ....'54 '79 C.966 B.A. L.178 J.D. [Fleischman&W.]
Hardin, Mark A. '45 '73 C.112 B.A. L.629 J.D.
(adm. in CA; not adm. in DC) Dir., Child Welf., ABA Ctr. on Children & the Law
Harding, Arthur H., (AV) .... '50 '75 C.906 B.A. L.911 J.D. [Fleischman&W.]
Harding, Barbara Mack ....'63 '88 C.16 B.A. L.276 J.D. [Kirkland&E.]
*PRACTICE AREAS: Civil Litigation; Criminal Litigation.
Harding, Bertrand M., Jr., (AV) '46 '75 C.228 B.A. L.273 J.D.
815 Connecticut Ave., NW
Harding, Robert B., (AV) ....'42 '67 C.210 A.B. L.893 J.D. [McDermott,W.&E.]
Hardison, David B. ....'59 '84 C.674 A.B. L.178 J.D. [Fried,F.H.S.&J.]
Hardman, Kenneth E., (AV) ....'44 '69 C.347 A.B. L.276 J.D. [Moir&H.]
*PRACTICE AREAS: Telecommunication Law; Communications Law; Antitrust Law; Administrative Law.
Hardock, Randolf Hurst, (AV) .... '56 '81 C.696 B.A. L.659 J.D. [Davis&H.]
*PRACTICE AREAS: Taxation Law; Pensions; Employee Benefits; Legislation; Employment Tax Law.
Hardwick, John C., Jr. ....'66 '92 C.228 A.B. L.93 J.D. [Kilpatrick S.]
*PRACTICE AREAS: Employment Law; Labor Law; Immigration Law.
Hardwick, Karen M. ....'63 '89 C.893 B.S.E. L.309 J.D. [Hogan&H.]
*PRACTICE AREAS: Commercial Litigation.
Hardy, G. Todd ....'49 '74 C.679 B.S. L.904 J.D. [Ⓒ Maloney&K.] (⊙Burke, VA)
Hardy, Kevin ....'74 '00 C.188 A.B. L.178 J.D. [Ⓐ Williams&C.]
Hardy, Nathalia S. A. '63 '91 C.1356 B.A. L.930 J.D.
(adm. in MI; not adm. in DC) [Ⓒ Dyer E.&J.]
*PRACTICE AREAS: Environmental; White Collar Crime; Litigation.
Hardy, Nathaniel J. ....'73 '98 C.896 B.A. L.180 J.D. 1730 Rhode Island Avenue, N.W.
Hardy, Ralph W., Jr., (AV) ....'41 '69 C.878 B.S. L.1066 J.D. [Dow,L.&A.]
Hardy, Robert G., (AV) .... '44 '69 C.288 B.A. L.575 J.D. [Ⓒ Cullen&D.]
*PRACTICE AREAS: Administrative Law; Energy Law.
Hardy, Timothy S., (AV) ....'47 '72 C.31 B.A. L.976 J.D. [Kirkland&E.]
*PRACTICE AREAS: Environmental Law; Toxic Substance Regulation, Litigation and Counseling; Commercial Litigation-Environmental, Product Liability; Product Liability-Product Defect.
Hardy, William J. ....'44 '70 C.93 B.S. L.276 J.D. [Karalekas&N.]
*PRACTICE AREAS: Federal Civil Litigation; Federal Criminal Law; White Collar Criminal Defense; Qui Tam Litigation; Corporate Investigations.
Hare, Jeffrey L. '72 '97 C&L.923 B.S., J.D.
(adm. in WV; not adm. in DC) [Ⓐ Thacher P.&W.]
*PRACTICE AREAS: Corporate; Banking; Securities; Limited Liability Company Law.
Hare, William D. .... '63 '95 C.160 B.S. L.326 J.D. [Ⓐ Fish&R.] (See Pat. Sect.)
*PRACTICE AREAS: Intellectual Property Law.
Harfst, David L. ....'50 '83 C.918 B.A. L.976 J.D. [Covington&B.]
Hargis, Lynn N. .... '43 '75 C.802 B.A. L.1066 J.D. [Ⓒ Chadbourne&P.]
Harig, Lisa A. ....'68 '93 C.645 B.A. L.228 J.D. [Ⓐ Hogan&H.]
*PRACTICE AREAS: Corporate Law; Securities Law; Aviation Law.
Harkavy, Anne ....'73 '99 C&L.309 A.B., J.D. [Ⓐ Wilmer,C.&P.]
Harker, Drew A. ....'56 '86 C.112 B.A. L.276 J.D. [Arnold&P.]
*PRACTICE AREAS: Government Contracts; Litigation; Legislative.
Harkins, Charles J., Jr., (AV) ....'43 '69 C.524 B.S. L.128 J.D. Asst. U.S. Atty.
Harkins, Joseph P. ....'54 '83 C.674 A.B. L.276 J.D. [Littler M.]
*PRACTICE AREAS: Labor and Employment; Litigation.
Harkins, Malcolm J., III ....'51 '76 C.722 A.B. L.734 J.D. [Proskauer R.]
Harkins, Patrick R. ....'55 '82 C.57 B.A. L.30 J.D. [Spriggs&H.]
*PRACTICE AREAS: Products Liability; Toxic Torts; Litigation; Asbestos Defense.
Harkins, Tanya E. '68 '99 C.1090 B.A. L.127 J.D.
(adm. in MD; not adm. in DC) [Ⓐ Nath&Assoc.]
*PRACTICE AREAS: Patent Prosecution; Trademark Prosecution; Copyright Prosecution.

Harkins Cunningham, (AV)
Suite 600, 801 Pennsylvania Avenue, N.W., 20004-2615 ⊙
Telephone: 202-973-7600 Facsimile: 202-973-7610
Email: dhirsh@harkinscunningham.com URL: http://www.harkinscunningham.com
Members of Firm: Paul A. Cunningham; David A. Bono; Richard B. Herzog; David A. Hirsh; A. Carl Kaseman, III; Gerald P. Norton; James G. Rafferty. Of Counsel: James M. Guinivan; Julie A. Waddell. Associates: Robert A. Wimbish.
Complex and Multi-District Litigation, Economic Regulation, Legislative Policy, Antitrust and Trade Regulation, Biotechnology, Corporate Governance, Corporate and Securities Transactions, Business Law, Energy, Administrative Law, Taxation, Transportation, Utility Law and Alternative Dispute Resolution.
Philadelphia, Pennsylvania Office: 2800 One Commerce Square, 2005 Market Street, 19103-7042. Telephone: 215-851-6700. Facsimile: 215-851-6710.
New York, New York Office: 10 Rockefeller Plaza, Suite 1250, 10020. Telephone: 212-218-1990. Facsimile: 212-218-1999.
See Professional Biographies, WASHINGTON, DISTRICT OF COLUMBIA

Harkless, James M. ....'31 '56 C&L.309 A.B., LL.B. 3029 M St., NW
Harkrader, Carleton A., (AV) ....'17 '53 C.885 B.A. L.976 LL.B. 1300 19th St., N.W.
Harles, Charles W. ....'46 '72 C&L.575 A.B., J.D. 1018 South Carolina Avenue, S.E.
Harley-Boyce, Atina S. ....'69 '94 C.886 B.S. L.976 J.D. [Ⓐ Shaw P.]
*PRACTICE AREAS: Litigation.
Harllee, John, Jr., (AV) .... '41 '68 C.309 B.A. L.276 J.D. 1812 Wyoming Ave., N.W.
Harlow, David Stuart ....'60 '86 C.945 B.A. L.893 J.D. [Ⓐ Hunton&W.]
Harmala, Robert C. ....'69 '95 C.112 A.B. L.800 J.D. [Ⓒ Venable,A.B.H.&C.]
*PRACTICE AREAS: Legislative Practice.
Harman, John H., (AV) '44 '70 C.576 B.S. L.904 J.D.
[Coggins,H.&H.] & [Ⓒ Nikaido,M.M.&O.] (Pat.) (⊙Silver Spring, MD)
Harman, Scott A. .... '50 '77 C.478 B.A. L.184 J.D. [Ⓒ Steptoe&J.]
*PRACTICE AREAS: Energy; Business Transactions.
Harman, Thomas E. '39 '65 C.885 B.A. L.30 LL.B.
(adm. in VA; not adm. in DC) Legal Coun., Amer. Home Products Corp.

Harman, Thomas S. ....'57 '82 C.228 A.B. L.893 J.D. [Morgan,L.&B.]
*PRACTICE AREAS: Mutual Funds; Securities Law; Banking.
Harman, William B., Jr., (AV) .... '30 '56 C&L.945 A.B., J.D. [Davis&H.]
*PRACTICE AREAS: Taxation Law; Insurance Law; Legislation Law.
Harmatz, Hugo R. ......'63 '94 C.705 B.S. 1429 G St., N.W., Ste. 550 (⊙New York, NY)
Harmon, Gail M., (AV) ....'43 '70 C.681 B.A. L.178 J.D. [Harmon,C.S.&E.]
Harmon, Herbert N., (AV) ....'44 '73 C.216 A.B. L.276 J.D. [Harmon,W.&B.]
*PRACTICE AREAS: Personal Injury; General Corporate Law; Business Law; Commercial Litigation; Civil Practice.
Harmon, Jewel M. '56 '94 C.860 B.A. L.93 J.D.
1350 Connecticut Ave., N.W., Suite 301
Harmon, John H., III ....'31 '61 C.105 A.B. L.329 LL.B. 729 8th St., S.E.
Harmon, Curran, Spielberg & Eisenberg, LLP, (AV) ...... 1726 M Street, N.W., Suite 600

Harmon, Wilmot & Brown, L.L.P., (AV)
Suite 810, 1010 Vermont Avenue, N.W., 20005
Telephone: 202-783-9100 Facsimile: 202-783-9103
Herbert N. Harmon; David W. Wilmot; Omer F. Brown, II. Associate: Andrea Merritt Bagwell.
Legislative Advocacy, Corporate, Commercial and Municipal Government and Litigation, Environmental, Energy, Government Contracts, Risk Management.
See Professional Biographies, WASHINGTON, DISTRICT OF COLUMBIA

Harned, Karen R. ....'67 '95 C.623 B.A. L.273 J.D. [[A] Olsson,F.&W.]
*PRACTICE AREAS: Legislation; Food and Drug Law; Agriculture Law.
Harness, Suzanne '45 '98 C.128 B.S. L.273 J.D.
(adm. in VA; not adm. in DC) [[A] Seyfarth S.]
*PRACTICE AREAS: Construction; Government Contracts.

Harness, Dickey & Pierce, P.L.C.
888 Sixteenth Street, N.W., 20006 ⊙
Telephone: 202-835-7480
Email: info@hdp.com URL: http://www.hdp.com
W. R. Duke Taylor.
Patent, Trademark, Copyright, Unfair Competition, Computer Law, Trade Secrets, Trade Regulation. Trial and Appellate Practice in State and Federal Courts.
Representative Clients: The Black and Decker Manufacturing Co.; Daimler-Chrysler Corp.; Emerson Electric Co.; General Motors Corp.; La-Z-Boy Chair Co.; Matsushita Electric; Monroe Auto Equipment Co.; Sun Microsystems; University of Michigan.
Troy, Michigan Office: 5445 Corporate Drive, Suite 400. Telephone: 248-641-1600. Telefacsimile: 248-641-0270.
St. Louis, Missouri Office: 7700 Bonhomme, Suite 400. Telephone: 314-726-7500. Fax: 314-726-7501.
See Professional Biographies, WASHINGTON, DISTRICT OF COLUMBIA

Harnett, Andrea L. ....'48 '74 C.597 B.A. L.178 J.D. Supr. Ct.
Harney, John R. ....'55 '89 C.112 B.A. L.966 J.D. [O'Donoghue&O.]
*PRACTICE AREAS: Employee Benefits.
Harnisch, Kevin J. ....'69 '95 C.602 B.B.A. L.988 J.D. [[A] Fried,F.H.S.&J.]
*PRACTICE AREAS: Securities Enforcement and Regulation; Securities Litigation; Corporate Internal Investigations.
Harnishfeger, John G. ....'67 '93 C.473 B.A. L.607 J.D. [[A] Cadeaux&T.]
*PRACTICE AREAS: Workers Compensation; Personal Injury; Products Liability.
Harold, Rosemary C., (BV) .... '58 '91 C.945 B.A. L.276 J.D. [Wiley R.&F.]
*PRACTICE AREAS: Communications; Internet; Electronic Commerce.
Harper, Blaney ....'60 '92 C.477 B.S. L.276 J.D. [Jones,D.R.&P.] (See Pat. Sect.)
*PRACTICE AREAS: Intellectual Property; Intellectual Property Litigation.
Harper, Emery W., (AV) '36 '62 C.31 B.A. L.976 LL.B.
(adm. in NY; not adm. in DC) [[C] Inman D.]
*PRACTICE AREAS: Ship Finance; International Maritime; Maritime Law.
Harper, Keith M. .... '66 '94 C.112 B.A. L.569 J.D. Native American Rights Fund
Harper, Laura S. ....'— '91 C.878 B.S. L.188 J.D. [[C] Kirkland&E.]
*PRACTICE AREAS: Corporate; Mergers and Acquisitions; Securities; Venture Capital; Private Equity.
Harpole, J. Marinda ....'46 '77 C.518 B.A. L.1162 J.D. Antioch Sch. of Law
Harr, Timothy A., (AV) ....'50 '76 C.674 B.A. L.893 J.D. Sr. Coun., Motorola, Inc.
Harrell, Dorothy J. '— '90 C.597 B.S. L.966 J.D.
(adm. in WI; not adm. in DC) National Educ. Assn.
Harrell, Richard S., (AV) '26 '56 C.682 B.A. L.893 LL.B.
1700 Pennsylvania Ave., N.W.
Harrigan, Cecil C., II ....'48 '85 C&L.329 B.A., J.D. [C.C.Harrigan II]
Harrigan, Cecil C., II, P.C. ....1638 R St., N.W., Ste 220
Harriman, Jansak & Wylie, (BV)
1155 Connecticut Ave., N.W., Ste. 300 (⊙Towson, MD)
Harrington, Clifford M., (AV) ....'47 '72 C.808 B.A. L.174 J.D. [Shaw P.]
*PRACTICE AREAS: Communications.
Harrington, David A. .... '65 '94 C&L.893 B.A., J.D. [[A] Ross,D.&B.]
Harrington, J.G., (AV) ....'60 '87 C.705 B.S. L.569 J.D. [Dow,L.&A.]
Harrington, John F., (AV) ....'44 '69 C.164 A.B. L.94 J.D. [Fulbright&J.]
*PRACTICE AREAS: Administrative Law; Energy; Natural Resources.
Harrington, Paul H. .... '43 '69 C.205 B.A. L.1017 J.D. Potomac Electric Power Company
Harrington, Phillip H. ....'40 '91 C.871 B.S. L.1209 J.D. [[C] Wiley R.&F.]
*PRACTICE AREAS: Government Contracts.
Harris, Anna-Liza B. ....'61 '89 C&L.276 B.S.F.S., J.D. [Dewey B.]
Harris, Archie L., Jr. ....'64 '90 C&L.945 B.A., J.D. 17 Hawthorne Ct. N.E.
Harris, Carole C., (AV) ....'47 '73 C.446 B.A. L.128 J.D. [McDermott,W.&E.]
Harris, Cathy A. '71 '98 C.103 A.B. L.273 J.D.
(adm. in NY; not adm. in DC) [[A] Kator,P.&W.]
*PRACTICE AREAS: Employment Law; Civil Rights; Civil Service.
Harris, David J. ....'56 '82 C.679 B.S., B.A. L.276 J.D. [Dechert]
*PRACTICE AREAS: Financial Services Law; Investment Management.
Harris, Don V., Jr., (AV) '21 '47 C.210 A.B. L.309 J.D.
1201 Pennsylvania Ave., N.W.‡
Harris, Elizabeth A. ....'72 '98 C&L.178 B.A., J.D. [[A] Shaw P.]
*PRACTICE AREAS: Taxation; Corporate Law.
Harris, George Bryan, (AV) '64 '89 C.16 B.A. L.893 J.D.
[Bradley A.R.&W.] (⊙Birm., Montgomery, AL)
*PRACTICE AREAS: Corporations; Business Litigation; Alternative Dispute Resolution.
Harris, George N., Jr. .... '— '90 C.839 B.A. L.61 J.D. [Kozusko L.H.]
*PRACTICE AREAS: Tax Controversies; Dispute Resolution; Tax Legislation; Tax Planning.
Harris, Gregg W., (AV) ....'59 '84 C.951 B.A. L.597 J.D. [Fulbright&J.]
*PRACTICE AREAS: Project Finance; Real Estate.
Harris, Herbert E., II, (AV) .... '26 '52 C.698 A.B. L.276 J.D. [Harris E.&L.]
*PRACTICE AREAS: Customs Law; International Trade Regulation; Unfair Competition; Antitrust Law; Legislative Practice.
Harris, James A. ....'57 '82 C.1032 B.A. L.911 J.D. [Zuckert,S.&R.]
*PRACTICE AREAS: Tax Exempt Organizations; Nonprofit Tax Law; Charitable Giving; Tax Controversies; Estate Planning.
Harris, James Warden '66 '94 C.367 B.A. L.1209 J.D.
(adm. in VA; not adm. in DC) V.P., Prop. Mgmt., National Multi Housing Council
Harris, Jeffrey ....'44 '69 C.569 B.S. L.823 J.D. [Rubin,W.D.H.&C.]
*PRACTICE AREAS: White Collar Crime; Criminal Antitrust; Civil Litigation; Construction; Banking.
Harris, Jessie M. ....'37 '71 C.228 A.B. L.276 J.D. 4401 W St., N.W.‡
Harris, Joe H. .... '27 '53 C&L.846 B.A., J.D. 3900 Wisconsin Ave., N.W.
Harris, Judith L. ....'— '73 C.477 B.A. L.976 J.D. [Reed S.]
*PRACTICE AREAS: Communications; Antitrust; Litigation.
Harris, Kelly J. ....'66 '92 C.602 B.A. L.569 J.D. Assoc. Gen. Coun., CareFirst BCBS

Harris, Larry D., (AV) .... '50 '75 C.201 B.S. L.273 J.D. [Piper M.R.&W.]
*PRACTICE AREAS: Government Contracts; Construction; Commercial Litigation.
Harris, Laurence E. '36 '74 C.178 B.A. L.276 J.D.
(adm. in PA; not adm. in DC) [Patton B.]
Harris, Matthew S. '67 '99 C.156 B.A. L.229 J.D.
Atty., Natl. Assoc. of Broadcast Employees & Technicians
Harris, Pamela A. ....'62 '92 C&L.976 B.A., J.D. [[C] O'Melveny&M.]
*PRACTICE AREAS: Appellate Practice.
Harris, Richard C., (AV) .... '23 '52 C.350 B.S. L.273 LL.B. 1400 K St.,NW (Pat.)
Harris, Robert O. ....'29 '56 C.178 A.B. L.976 LL.B. 1100 17th St. NW
Harris, Ronald B. .... '51 '83 C.329 B.A. L.128 J.D. Asst. Gen. Coun., Metro Police Dept.
Harris, Samuel J. ....'20 '52 C&L.329 LL.B. 7116 7th St., N.W.
Harris, Scott Blake, (AV) .... '51 '77 C.103 A.B. L.309 J.D. [Harris,W.&G.]
*PRACTICE AREAS: Communications; International; Intellectual Property; Commercial; Telecommunications.
Harris, Stuart H. ....'50 '75 C.860 B.A. L.273 J.D. [Howrey S.A.&W.]
*PRACTICE AREAS: Antitrust Law; Complex Litigation; Franchise Law.
Harris, Susan Banes ....'42 '79 C.273 B.A. L.904 J.D. Dir., United Jewish Appeal
Harris, William H., Jr., (AV) ....'42 '69 C.974 B.A. L.329 J.D. [Greenstein D.&L.]

Harris Beach LLP
Suite 300, 1776 K Street, N.W., 20006 ⊙
Telephone: 202-861-0001 Fax: 202-861-0011
URL: http://www.harrisbeach.com
Of Counsel: James R. Cooke.
General Practice.
Rochester, New York Office: Granite Building, 130 East Main Street. Telephone: 716-419-8800. Fax: 716-419-8801.
Pittsford, New York Office: 99 Garnsey Road. Telephone: 716-419-8800. Fax: 716-419-8801.
Plattsburgh, New York Office: One Cumberland Avenue. Telephone: 518-561-4400. Fax: 518-561-4848.
Ithaca, New York Office: 119 East Seneca Street. Telephone: 607-273-6444.
Albany, New York Office: 20 Corporate Woods Boulevard. Telephone: 518-427-9700. Fax: 518-427-0235.
Hamburg, New York Office: One Grimsby Drive. Telephone: 716-646-5050. Fax: 716-648-8201.
Syracuse, New York Office: Suite 400, One Park Place, 300 South State Street. Telephone: 315-423-7100. Fax: 315-422-9331.
New York, N.Y. Office: 500 Fifth Avenue, 5th Floor. Telephone: 212-687-0100. Fax: 212-687-0659.
Newark, New Jersey Office: 2 Gateway Center, 12th Floor. Telephone: 973-848-1244. Fax: 973-848-1594.
See Professional Biographies, WASHINGTON, DISTRICT OF COLUMBIA

Harris Ellsworth & Levin, (AV)
The Watergate, 2600 Virginia Avenue, N.W., Suite 1113, 20037
Telephone: 202-337-8338 Facsimile: 202-337-6685
Email: hel@idt.net URL: http://www.internationaltrade-law.com
Members of Firm: Herbert E. Harris II; Cheryl Ellsworth; Jeffrey S. Levin;—John Burt Totaro, Jr.; Jennifer de Laurentiis.
Customs, International Trade Regulation, Unfair Competition and Antitrust Law. Legislative Practice.
See Professional Biographies, WASHINGTON, DISTRICT OF COLUMBIA

Harris-Newton, Ghita '— '99 C.1369 B.A. L.276 J.D.
(adm. in VA; not adm. in DC) 701 Pennsylvania Avenue, N.W.

Harris, Wiltshire & Grannis LLP, (AV)
1200 Eighteenth Street, N.W. Suite 1200, 20036
Telephone: 202-730-1300 Fax: 202-730-1301
Email: info@harriswiltshire.com URL: http://www.harriswiltshire.com
Members of Firm: Scott Blake Harris; John T. Nakahata; William M. Wiltshire; Thomas G. Connolly; Mark A. Grannis; Kent D. Bressie; Jonathan B. Mirsky; Karen Lynn Gulick; Christopher J. Wright. Associates: Timothy J. Simeone; Kelly Sweeney McGinn; Michael G. Grable; Patrick O'Donnell; Fred B. Campbell, Jr. Of Counsel: Nancy A. Bard.
Communications, Intellectual Property, International, Corporate, Commercial Transactions, Litigation, Appellate.
See Professional Biographies, WASHINGTON, DISTRICT OF COLUMBIA

Harrison, Akinyale S. ....'72 '99 C.893 B.S. L.477 J.D. [[A] Brobeck,P.&H.]
*PRACTICE AREAS: Corporate Law; Venture Capital; Mergers and Acquisitions.
Harrison, Allison W. ....'73 '98 C.236 B.A. L.976 J.D. [[A] Kirkpatrick&L.]
*PRACTICE AREAS: Investment Management; Mutual Funds.
Harrison, Benjamin N. '61 '98 C.886 B.A. L.30 J.D.
(adm. in CO; not adm. in DC) Dep. COO, Enterpriseworks Worldwide
Harrison, Cody '70 '99 C.837 B.S. L.1364 J.D.
(adm. in MD; not adm. in DC) [[A] Cole,R.&B.]
*PRACTICE AREAS: Cable TV; Telecommunications Law; Pole Attachments; Litigation.
Harrison, Craig S. .... '48 '84 C.112 A.B. L.312 J.D. [[C] Hunton&W.]
*PRACTICE AREAS: Environmental.
Harrison, Debra A. ....'67 '92 C.608 B.S. L.273 J.D. [McDermott,W.&E.]
Harrison, Donald, (AV) .... '46 '72 C&L.309 B.A., J.D. [Gibson,D.&C.]
*PRACTICE AREAS: International Trade Law; Customs Law.
Harrison, Ellen K., (AV) ....'46 '73 C.477 B.A. L.309 J.D. [Shaw P.]
*PRACTICE AREAS: Tax Law; Estate Planning; Estate Administration; Tax Controversies.
Harrison, Holmes C., (AV) '41 '66 C.301 B.A. L.692 J.D.
(adm. in VA; not adm. in DC) [[C] Charapp,D.&W.]
*PRACTICE AREAS: Civil Litigation.
Harrison, Keith J. .... '58 '86 C.945 B.A. L.893 J.D. [King,P.&H.]
*PRACTICE AREAS: Complex Civil Litigation; Intellectual Property Litigation; Employment Law; Health Care Law; Government Contracts.
Harrison, Lisa M. ....'72 '98 C.951 B.A. L.309 J.D. [[A] Shea&G.]
Harrison, Marion Edwyn, (AV) '31 '54
C.893 B.A. L.273 LL.B. [M.E.Harrison] (⊙Falls Church, VA)
Harrison, Mark B., (BV) '53 '77
C.1044 B.A. L.1292 J.D. [Venable,A.B.H.&C.] (See Pat. Sect.)
*PRACTICE AREAS: Trademark Law; Copyright Law; Computer Law.
Harrison, Scott R. ....'58 '86 C.999 B.A. L.818 J.D. [[C] Bryan C.]

Harrison, Allen H., Jr.
(See Arlington, Virginia)

Harrison, Marion Edwyn, Law Offices, (AV) .... 1700 K Street, Suite 700
Harrop, John K. ....'49 '95 C.871 B.S.A.E. L.1356 J.D. [[A] Dorsey&W.] (Pat.)
*PRACTICE AREAS: Intellectual Property; Electronic Intellectual Property; Mechanical Intellectual Property; Computer and Software Patents; Design Patents.
Harroun, John A. '69 '99 C.160 B.S.E.E. L.446 J.D.
(adm. in MD; not adm. in DC; See Pat. Sect.) [[A] Sterne,K.G.&F.]
*PRACTICE AREAS: Intellectual Property.
Hart, Ann Marie .... '— '97 C.1369 B.S. L.276 J.D. [[A] King&S.]
*PRACTICE AREAS: Litigation; Trade Regulation.
Hart, Barry J. ....'48 '73 C.197 B.A. L.273 J.D. [Winston&S.]
*PRACTICE AREAS: International Taxation; Tax Exempt Organizations; Nonprofit Corporations; International Corporate Law; International Corporate Transactions.
Hart, Christopher J. ....'60 '86 C.309 B.A. L.893 J.D. [Katten M.Z.]
*PRACTICE AREAS: Real Estate; Finance.
Hart, Dennis M., (AV) ....'49 '74 C.339 B.A. L.326 J.D. [Butera&A.]
*PRACTICE AREAS: Appellate Practice; Criminal Trial; Civil Trial.

Hart, Henry A., (AV) ... '— '75 C.31 B.A. L.276 J.D. [Reed S.]
*PRACTICE AREAS: Government Relations; Trade Association Law; Banking Law; Business Law.
Hart, J. Steven ... '53 '79 C.623 B.B.A. L.276 J.D. [Williams&J.]
*PRACTICE AREAS: Transportation Law; Labor & Employee Benefits; Communications.
Hart, Jonathan D., (AV) ... '56 '85 C.478 B.A. L.813 J.D. [Dow,L.&A.]
Hart, Marvin E. ... '59 '85 C&L.383 B.A., J.D. D.C. Off. of Human Rights
Hart, R. Laird ... '53 '81 C.674 A.B. L.976 J.D. [Ⓒ Covington&B.]
Hart, Thomas A., Jr. ... '56 '81 C.103 B.A. L.276 J.D. [Shook,H.&B.]
*PRACTICE AREAS: Telecommunications; Entertainment; Legislative; Corporate.
Hart, Thomas J., (AV) ... '45 '71 C.604 A.B. L.273 J.D. [Slevin&H.]
*PRACTICE AREAS: Employee Benefits.
Harth, David, (AV) ... '— '79 C&L.966 B.A., J.D. [Heller E.W.&M.] (⊙Madison, WI)
*PRACTICE AREAS: Intellectual Property and Commercial Litigation.
Harthill, Susan ... '63 '94 C.999 B.A. L.150 J.D. [Ⓐ Steptoe&J.]
Harthoorn, Ruth ... '54 '80 C.1304 B.A. L.273 J.D. 419 7th St., N.W.
Hartland, Michelle L. '— '97 C.945 A.E. L.904 J.D.
(adm. in VA; not adm. in DC) [Ⓐ Nath&Assoc.]
*PRACTICE AREAS: Trademarks; Copyrights.
Hartley, Roger C. '43 '70 C.188 B.S. L.665 J.D.
Assoc. Prof., Catholic Univ. of America Law Sch.
Hartman, Barry M., (AV) ... '— '79 C.659 B.A. L.273 J.D. [Kirkpatrick&L.]
*PRACTICE AREAS: Environmental Litigation; Criminal Litigation; Appellate Litigation; Administrative Litigation.
Hartman, Gerald S. ... '44 '73 C.178 A.B. L.273 J.D. [Swidler B.S.F.]
*PRACTICE AREAS: Employment Law; Employment Litigation.
Hartman, Joseph E. ... '75 '99 C.893 B.A. L.145 J.D. [Ⓐ Fulbright&J.]
*PRACTICE AREAS: Litigation.
Hartman, Laurie A. ... '67 '94 C.94 B.A. L.945 J.D. [Ⓐ White&C.]
Hartman, Thomas E. ... '— '91 C.477 B.S.E. L.966 J.D. [Foley&L.]
*PRACTICE AREAS: Securities; Mergers & Acquisitions; General Corporate.
Hartmann, Anthony A. '66 '96
C.893 B.S. L.602 J.D. [Ⓐ Finnegan,H.F.G.&D.] (See Pat. Sect.)
*PRACTICE AREAS: Intellectual Property Litigation; Chemical Intellectual Property.
Hartmann, Charles J., Jr. '38 '66 C.910 A.B. L.502 J.D.
(adm. in MO; not adm. in DC) Georgetown Univ.
Hartnett, F. Douglas '61 '97 C.787 B.S. L.1364 J.D.
(adm. in MD; not adm. in DC) 1421 Van Buren St., N.W.
Hartnett, Mary E. '59 '85 C.293 B.A. L.276 J.D.
Exec. Dir. & Adjunct Prof., Georgetown Univ. Law Ctr.‡
Hartquist, David A., (AV) ... '41 '66 C.800 B.S. L.309 J.D. [Collier S.S.]
*PRACTICE AREAS: International Trade.
Hartsoe, Joseph R. ... '54 '80 C.198 B.S. L.893 J.D V.P. Fed. Reg. Aff., Enron Corp.
Hartstein, Diana R. ... '71 '98 C.446 B.S. L.178 J.D. [Ⓐ Caplin&D.]
*PRACTICE AREAS: Election, Campaign and Political Law; Exempt Organizations.
Hartwell, Ray V., III, (AV) '47 '75 C&L.902 B.A., J.D.
[Hunton&W.] (⊙Richmond, VA)
*PRACTICE AREAS: Antitrust; Intellectual Property.
Hartwig, Jahna M. '71 '00 C&L.273 B.A., J.D.
(adm. in CA; not adm. in DC) [Ⓐ Weil,G.&M.]
*PRACTICE AREAS: International Trade.
Hartwig, Lawrence E. '06 '36 C&L.477 B.A., J.D.
(adm. in NY; not adm. in DC) 3540 39th St., N.W.‡
Hartzenbusch, Catharine A. ... '64 '95 C.893 B.A. L.309 J.D. [Ⓐ Skadden,A.S.M.&F.]
Harvey, Amy Marie ... '67 '97 C.665 B.A. L.273 J.D. [Ⓐ Kirkland&E.]
*PRACTICE AREAS: Corporate Law.
Harvey, Brian S., (AV) ... '52 '79 C.437 B.A. L.930 J.D. [Baker&H.]
*PRACTICE AREAS: Employment and Labor Law; Litigation.
Harvey, Edmund E., (AV) ... '20 '48 C.602 A.B. L.262 LL.B. [Ⓒ Chadbourne&P.]
Harvey, Scott A. ... '66 '91 C&L.893 B.A., J.D. [Ⓐ Thompson H.]
*PRACTICE AREAS: Environmental; Administrative Law; Litigation.
Harvey, Sheila McC. ... '54 '79 C.104 A.B. L.477 J.D. [Shaw P.]
*PRACTICE AREAS: Environmental.
Harvey, Tanya A. ... '57 '83 C.566 B.S. L.107 J.D. [Feldesman,T.L.F.&B.]
*PRACTICE AREAS: Estate Planning; Special Education; Disability Rights.
Harvey, Teresa L. ... '65 '93 C.1096 B.S. L.802 J.D. [Ⓐ Dickstein S.M.&O.]
*PRACTICE AREAS: Civil Litigation; Insurance Coverage Litigation; Employment Law; Constitutional Law.
Harvie, Christopher J. ... '59 '89 C.103 A.B. L.112 J.D. [Mintz,L.C.F.G.&P.]
*PRACTICE AREAS: Communications; Legislation.
Harwell, Lori E. ... '62 '87 C.259 B.S. L.260 J.D. [Ⓒ Sutherland A.&B.]
*PRACTICE AREAS: Corporate Income Tax; Tax Planning; Tax Controversies.
Harwood, John H., II, (AV) ... '45 '73 C.309 A.B. L.178 J.D. [Wilmer,C.&P.]
*PRACTICE AREAS: Communications and Media; Electronic Commerce; International Law.
Hasan, Jannette E. ... '69 '96 C.999 B.A. L.615 J.D. 1875 Connecticut Avenue, N.W.
Haseley, John ... '63 '91 C.610 B.A. L.273 J.D. 336 Cannon HOB
Haselkorn, David L. ... '61 '88 C&L.145 A.B., J.D. 3211 44th St., N.W.
Haskell, Boris, (AV) ... '23 '50 C.309 A.B. L.273 LL.B. 655 15th St., N.W. (Pat.)
Haskell, Floyd K., (AV) ... '16 '46 C&L.309 A.B., LL.B. 133 North Carolina Ave., S.E.
Haskell, Mark R., (AV) ... '60 '85 C.431 B.A. L.309 J.D. [Brunenkant&H.]
*PRACTICE AREAS: Energy Law; Environmental Law; Natural Resources; Regulatory Law; Utility Law.
Haskin, Benjamin J. ... '— '91 C.674 A.B. L.145 J.D. [Kirkpatrick&L.]
*PRACTICE AREAS: Investment Management; Securities; Mutual Funds; Investment Company Law.
Haskins, Matthew P. ... '67 '96 C.473 B.S. L.309 J.D. [Ⓐ Dewey B.]
*PRACTICE AREAS: Taxation.
Hassel, Lonie, (AV) ... '55 '80 C.128 B.A. L.893 J.D. [Groom]
*PRACTICE AREAS: Mergers and Acquisitions; Pension and Profit Sharing; Insurance Litigation; Employee Benefits; ERISA.
Hassell, Christopher E., (AV) '54 '79 C.319 B.A. L.276 J.D.
[Bonner K.T.&C.] (⊙Rockville, MD; Fairfax, VA)
*PRACTICE AREAS: Insurance Defense; Employment Discrimination; Products Liability; Medical Malpractice Law.
Hasselman, Allen J. ... '34 '91 C.712 B.A. L.276 J.D. 1630 R St., N.W.
Hasselman, Scot T. ... '— '98 C.1169 B.A. L.29 J.D. [Ⓐ Reed S.]
*PRACTICE AREAS: Health Care.
Hassett, Joseph M., (AV) ... '43 '67 C.116 A.B. L.309 LL.B. [Hogan&H.]
*PRACTICE AREAS: Litigation; Securities Litigation.
Hassett, Kristie S. ... '61 '86 C.821 B.A. L.659 J.D. [Ⓐ Reboul,M.H.M.&K.]
*PRACTICE AREAS: Regulatory; Telecommunications and Energy; Tort Defense/Product Liability.
Hassler, William T. ... '54 '82 C.575 B.A. L.976 J.D. [Steptoe&J.]
*PRACTICE AREAS: Litigation; White Collar Criminal Matters; Environmental Law.
Hasson, Kevin J. ... '57 '85 C&L.602 A.B., J.D. 725 12th St.
Hastings, Douglas A., (AV) ... '49 '81 C.228 A.B. L.893 J.D. [Epstein B.&G.]
*PRACTICE AREAS: Managed Care; Integrated Delivery Systems; Health Law; Hospital Law.
Hastings, Karis A., (AV) ... '62 '88 C.477 B.A. L.228 J.D. [Ⓒ Hogan&H.]
*PRACTICE AREAS: Communications Law; Satellite Communications; Telecommunications Law; Telecommunications Licensing; Telecommunications Regulation.
Hasty, Robert E. ... '64 '90 C.228 B.S.E. L.893 J.D. [Shaw P.]
Hatcher, Julia A. ... '— '87 C.518 B.A. L.276 J.D. [Latham&W.]
*PRACTICE AREAS: Environmental Law; Administrative Law; Litigation; Occupational Safety and Health.
Hatcher, Michael R. ... '62 '87 C.197 A.B. L.276 J.D. [Holland&K.]
Hatchett, Michael E. '66 '93 C.894 A.B. L.178 J.D.
(adm. in NY; not adm. in DC) [Ⓐ Shearman&S.]
Hatfield, Rachel '74 '01 C.174 B.A. L.902 J.D.
(adm. in VA; not adm. in DC) [Ⓐ Jenkens&G.]
*PRACTICE AREAS: Health Law; White Collar Crime.
Hathaway, Carolyne R. ... '— '88 C.999 B.S. L.276 J.D. [Latham&W.]
Hatheway, Gordon W., Jr., (AV) ... '— '68 C.105 B.S. L.273 J.D. [Reed S.]
*PRACTICE AREAS: Litigation.
Hathway, John J., (AV) '55 '85
C.128 B.A. L.64 J.D. [Whiteford,T.&P.] (⊙Columbia, MD)
*PRACTICE AREAS: Insurance Litigation; Business Litigation.
Hatti, Vivek '71 '99 C.945 A.B. L.537 J.D.
(adm. in OH; not adm. in DC) [Ⓐ Spriggs&H.]
*PRACTICE AREAS: Litigation; Banking Litigation.
Hattori, Ken-Ichi, (BV) '44 '90
C.999 B.A. L.1209 J.D. [Armstrong,W.H.M.&N.] (See Pat. Sect.)
Hauberg, Robert Engelbrecht, Jr., (AV) '43 '71
C.500 B.A. L.976 J.D. [Baker,D.B.&C.] (⊙Jackson, MS)
*PRACTICE AREAS: Antitrust; White Collar Crime; Financial Institutions; Civil Litigation.
Hauch, Jeanne M., (AV) ... '63 '89 C.674 A.B. L.976 J.D. U.S. Atty. Off.
Hauck, Dolly Bowman ... '41 '91 C.860 B.A. L.30 J.D. 1437 Foxhall Rd., N.W.
Hauck, Sheldon J., Jr. '68 '95 C.597 B.S.J. L.128 J.D.
(adm. in MD; not adm. in DC) Acct. Exec., Hauck & Assoc., Inc.
Haughey, Edmund J., III '72 '98
C.659 B.S.E. L.945 J.D. [Ⓐ Fitzpatrick,C.H.&S.] (See Pat. Sect.)
Haughton-Denniston, Pamela ... '— '98 C.732 B.A. L.276 J.D. [Ⓐ Arent F.K.P.&K.]
*PRACTICE AREAS: Computer and Software; Electronic Commerce; Trademarks; Copyright.
Hauptman, Gregory B. ... '51 '76 C.910 A.B. L.273 J.D. [Venable,A.B.H.&C.]
*PRACTICE AREAS: Real Estate-Commercial Law; Finance Law.
Hausfeld, Michael D., (AV) ... '46 '69 C.102 A.B. L.273 J.D. [Cohen,M.H.&T.]
*PRACTICE AREAS: Environmental Class Actions; Antitrust; Consumer Rights; Discrimination.
Hausman, Dale E. ... '61 '89 C.188 B.A. L.276 J.D. [Wiley R.&F.]
*PRACTICE AREAS: Insurance; Litigation.
Hausman, Robert M., (AV) ... '31 '57 C.659 B.S. L.178 J.D. 3308 35th St., N.W.
Havens, Charles W., III (P.C.), (AV) '36 '61
C.264 A.B. L.893 LL.B. [Ⓒ LeBoeuf,L.G.&M.]
*PRACTICE AREAS: Insurance; Antitrust.
Havermann, Donald L. ... '54 '80 C&L.893 B.S., J.D. [Morgan,L.&B.]
Havlicek, Franklin J. '47 '74 C&L.178 B.A., J.D.
V.P., Indus. Rel. & Envir. Servs., The Washington Post Co.
Hawkes, Timothy D. ... '71 '98 C.101 B.A. L.178 J.D. 1722 Eye St., N.W.
Hawkins, Alicia M. '63 '91 C.1077 B.A. L.665 J.D.
(adm. in PA; not adm. in DC) [Ⓐ Epstein B.&G.]
*PRACTICE AREAS: Managed Care Law.
Hawkins, Gerard L. ... '53 '78 C.93 A.B. L.276 J.D. [Elias,M.T.&H.]
Hawkins, Jennifer Bush ... '66 '94 C.724 B.S. L.1019 J.D. [Ⓐ Counts,P.-D.&D.]
Hawkins, Kevin B. '66 '98 C.95 A.B. L.184 J.D.
(adm. in CT; not adm. in DC) [Ⓐ Bracewell&P.]
*PRACTICE AREAS: Energy; Finance.
Hawkins, R. William '74 '01 C.880 B.A. L.273 J.D.
(adm. in MD; not adm. in DC) [Ⓐ Dechert]
*PRACTICE AREAS: Financial Services Law; Investment Management.
Hawkins, Rebecca Bowles ... '10 '35 C.99 L.260 LL.B. 3600 Macomb St., N.W.‡
Hawkins, Robert W., (AV) ... '49 '76 C.31 B.A. L.893 J.D. [Hunton&W.]
*PRACTICE AREAS: Litigation; International Commercial Arbitration.
Hawkins, Stacy Holmes ... '— '98 C.893 B.A. L.276 J.D. [Ⓐ Littler M.]

Hawkins, Delafield & Wood
601 13th Street, N.W. Suite 800 South, 20005 ⊙
Telephone: 202-682-1480 Fax: 202-682-1497
Resident Members: John M. McNally; John J. Cross, III; Florence A. Wood; Anthony S. Freedman.
Associates: Jill Chessen Cork; Aviva M. Roth (Not admitted in DC).
General Practice. Law of State, Municipal and Public Financing, Federal Securities, Tax, Litigation, Domestic and International Corporate and Banking, Real Estate, Probate.
New York, N.Y. Office: 67 Wall Street. Telephone: 212-820-9300. Fax: 212-514-8425.
Hartford, Connecticut Office: City Place, 185 Asylum Street. Telephone: 860-275-6260. Fax: 860-527-5786.
Newark, New Jersey Office: One Gateway Center. Telephone: 973-642-8584. Fax: 973-642-6773.
Los Angeles, California Office: 633 West Fifth Street, Suite 3550. Telephone: 213-236-9050. Fax: 213-236-9060.
San Francisco, California Office: One Embarcadero, Suite 1040. Telephone: 415-486-4200. Fax: 415-397-1513.

See Professional Biographies, WASHINGTON, DISTRICT OF COLUMBIA

Hawley, Noelle Montano ... '— '97 C.228 B.A. L.1209 J.D. [Ⓐ Verner,L.B.M.&H.]
*PRACTICE AREAS: Legislative.
Haworth, Jennifer L. '— '98 C.939 B.A. L.1065 J.D.
(adm. in CA; not adm. in DC) [Ⓐ Powell,G.F.&M.]
*PRACTICE AREAS: International Law; International Trade; Customs Law.
Hawthorne, W. Aaron ... '71 '97 C.1356 B.S. L.623 J.D. Assoc., PricewaterhouseCoopers
Hay, Deirdre L. '65 '90 L.999 LL.B.
(adm. in NY; not adm. in DC) [Baker&M.P.]
Hayden, Brian A. '71 '99 C.216 B.A. L.446 J.D.
(adm. in MD; not adm. in DC) [Ⓐ Jaeger&T.]
Hayden, Christopher G. '57 '97 C.339 B.S. L.326 J.D.
(adm. in TX; not adm. in DC; See Pat. Sect.) [Ⓐ Pennie&E.]
*PRACTICE AREAS: Intellectual Property.
Hayden, John F. ... '66 '92 C.150 B.S. L.309 J.D. [Fish&R.] (See Pat. Sect.)
*PRACTICE AREAS: Intellectual Property; Patents.
Hayduk, Kenneth R. ... '60 '89 C.693 B.S.C. L.273 J.D. [Baker&M.]
*PRACTICE AREAS: Taxation.
Hayes, Benjamin S. ... '70 '99 C.882 B.A. L.608 J.D. [Ⓐ Kirkpatrick&L.]
*PRACTICE AREAS: Electronic Commerce; Privacy Law; Copyrights.
Hayes, David J., (AV) ... '— '78 C.602 A.B. L.813 J.D. [Latham&W.]
*PRACTICE AREAS: Environmental Law; Natural Resources; Indians and Native Populations; Energy.
Hayes, David P. ... '50 '88 C.347 B.A. L.1029 J.D. 7709 Alaska Ave Nw
Hayes, Donald R. ... '52 '78 C.886 B.S. L.893 J.D. Sr. Atty., Washington Gas Light Co.
Hayes, Gina Clark ... '67 '95 C.128 B.A. L.180 J.D. [Ⓐ Cooper&Assoc.]
Hayes, James A. '46 '71 C.808 L.861 J.D.
(adm. in LA; not adm. in DC) [Ⓒ Adams&R.]
Hayes, Jennifer M. ... '68 '94 C&L.329 B.S., J.D. [Ⓐ Sughrue M.] (See Pat. Sect.)
*PRACTICE AREAS: Patent Law.
Hayes, John C., Jr., (AV) ... '47 '73 C.951 B.A. L.273 J.D. [Nixon P.]
*PRACTICE AREAS: Litigation.
Hayes, Robert G. ... '46 '74 C.94 B.S. L.128 J.D. [Ball J.]
*PRACTICE AREAS: Government Relations Law; International Trade Law; Natural Resources.
Hayes, Robin Belton ... '59 '86 C.575 B.A. L.260 J.D. [Holland&K.]
*PRACTICE AREAS: Commercial Leasing; Zoning; Land Use; Commercial Leasing.
Haynes, Bryan M. ... '71 '93 C.886 B.A. L.1209 J.D. [Ⓐ Sutherland A.&B.]
*PRACTICE AREAS: Litigation.
Haynes, Burton J., (AV) ... '48 '79 C&L.446 B.A., J.D. 1156 15th St., N.W.

Haynes, Fred E. . . . . '44 '73 C.95 A.B. L.309 J.D. Asst. U.S. Atty.
Haynes, Jim Tom, (AV) . . . . '43 '68 C&L.846 B.A., LL.B. [Cameron&H.]
*PRACTICE AREAS: Immigration Law.
Haynes, Kimberley H. . . . . '71 '98 C.675 B.A. L.734 J.D. [Ⓐ Kirkpatrick&L.]
*PRACTICE AREAS: Investment Management; Securities; Mutual Funds; Hedge Funds.
Haynes, Kristie G. . . . . '72 '97 L.1202 J.D. [Ⓐ Slavit&G.]
*PRACTICE AREAS: Civil Litigation.
Haynes, Margaret Campbell '56 '81
C.198 B.A. L.575 J.D. Dir., Child Support Proj., Amer. Bar Assn.
Haynes, R. Michael . . . . '40 '69 C&L.705 B.A., J.D. [Semmes,B.&S.]
*PRACTICE AREAS: Venture Capital; Small Business Investment Companies; Government Regulation; White Collar Crime.

Haynes and Boone, LLP, (AV)
555 Eleventh Street, N.W. Suite 650, 20004 ⊙
Telephone: 202-654-4500 Telecopy: 202-654-4501
URL: http://www.haynesboone.com
Members of Firm: Ellen Gibson McGinnis; Kenneth B. Reisenfeld. Associate: Hale E. Sheppard (Not admitted in DC).
Languages: English, French, German, Hebrew, Italian, Korean, Spanish, Japanese, Vietnamese, Chinese (Mandarin, Cantonese, Shanghainese).
Antitrust, Appellate, Business Litigation, Business Reorganization and Bankruptcy, Commercial Litigation, Corporate/Securities, Employee Benefits/ERISA, Energy, Environmental, Finance, Government Contracts, Government Investigations, Health Care, Insurance Litigation, International, Labor and Employment, Mergers and Acquisitions, Real Estate, Securities Litigation, Tax, Technology/Intellectual Property, White Collar Criminal Defense.
Austin, Texas Office: 600 Congress Avenue, Suite 1600. Telephone: 512-867-8400. Telecopy: 512-867-8470.
Other Austin, Texas Office: 7501 North Capital of Texas Highway, Building A, Suite 130, 78731. Telephone: 512-692-8300. Fax: 512-692-8370.
Dallas, Texas Office: 901 Main Street, Suite 3100. Telephone: 214-651-5000. Telecopy: 214-651-5940. Telex: 73-0187.
Fort Worth, Texas Office: 201 Main Street, Suite 2200. Telephone: 817-347-6600. Telecopy: 817-347-6650.
Houston, Texas Office: 1000 Louisiana Street, Suite 4300. Telephone: 713-547-2000. Telecopy: 713-547-2600.
Richardson, Texas Office: 2505 North Plano Road, Suite 400. Telephone: 972-739-6900. Telecopy: 972-680-7551.
San Antonio, Texas Office: 112 East Pecan Street, Suite 1600. Telephone: 210-978-7000. Telecopy: 210-978-7450.
Mexico City, Mexico Office: Haynes and Boone, S.C., Blvd. Manuel Avila Camacho, No. 40, Despacho 1801 Lomas de Chapultepec. Telephone: (525) 540-5558. Telecopy: (525) 540-0630.
See Professional Biographies, WASHINGTON, DISTRICT OF COLUMBIA

Hays, Margaret T. '64 '89 C.893 B.S. L.1017 J.D.
(adm. in VA; not adm. in DC) Sr. Atty., MCI Communications Corporation
Hays, Michael D., (AV) . . . . '48 '77 C.674 B.A. L.276 J.D. [Dow,L.&A.]
Haywood, Elizabeth B. . . . . '69 '94 C&L.575 A.B., J.D. [Ⓐ Dickstein S.M.&O.]
*PRACTICE AREAS: Legislative Practice; Regulatory Law; Health Care.
Haywood, Margaret A. . . . . '12 '42 L.999 LL.B. Sr. Supr. Ct. J.
Hazard, John W., Jr. . . . . '53 '80 C.886 B.A. L.607 J.D. [Webster,C.&B.]
*PRACTICE AREAS: Trademark and Copyright Law; Publishing Law; Artist Rights; Entertainment Law.
Hazel, George J. . . . . '75 '99 C.511 B.A. L.276 J.D. [Ⓐ Weil,G.&M.]
*PRACTICE AREAS: Litigation.
Hazel, Kim Alison '59 '85 C.589 B.A. L.1292 J.D.
(adm. in PA; not adm. in DC) 600 5th Street, N.W.
Hazelton, David R. . . . . '— '83 C.912 A.B. L.477 J.D. [Latham&W.]
*PRACTICE AREAS: Government Contracts; Litigation; Administrative Law; Intellectual Property.
Hazen, Edwin R. '37 '70 C.401 B.A. L.228 J.D.
(adm. in PA; not adm. in DC) Assoc. Dean, Wash. Coll. of Law, Amer. Univ.
Hazlett, Katharine B. . . . . '72 '97 C.575 B.A. L.976 J.D. [Ⓐ O'Melveny&M.]
Heacock, Mark A., (BV) '53 '79 C.893 B.A. L.276 J.D.
V.P. & Asst. Reg. Coun., 1st Amer. Title Ins. Co.
Healey, Kristen M. . . . . '69 '99 C.103 B.A. L.904 J.D. [Ⓐ Finnegan,H.F.G.&D.]
*PRACTICE AREAS: Intellectual Property; Patents; Patent Litigation.
Healey, Peter F., Jr., (AV) . . . . '42 '67 C.103 A.B. L.276 J.D. [Fulbright&J.]
*PRACTICE AREAS: Labor and Employment; Litigation.
Healey, Thomas J., Jr. '63 '98 C.363 B.S./B.A. L.339 J.D.
(adm. in IL; not adm. in DC) [Ⓒ Troutman S.]
*PRACTICE AREAS: Railroad Regulatory; Labor and Employment; Litigation; Commercial Law; Contracts.
Healy, Amy D. . . . . '— '99 C.198 B.A. L.273 J.D. [Ⓐ Kilpatrick S.]
*PRACTICE AREAS: Employee Benefits.
Healy, Daniel J. '73 '99 C.1367 B.A. L.262 J.D.
(adm. in NY; not adm. in DC) [Anderson K.&O.] (⊙New York, NY)
Healy, Eugene P. . . . . '70 '99 C.276 B.A. L.145 J.D. 1299 Pennsylvania Ave. N.W.
Healy, Gene . . . . '70 '99 C.276 B.A. L.145 J.D. [Ⓐ Howrey S.A.&W.]
*PRACTICE AREAS: Commercial Litigation.
Healy, Jason M. . . . . '72 '99 C.165 B.A. L.128 J.D. [Ⓐ Reed S.]
*PRACTICE AREAS: Health Care.
Healy, Michael F. . . . . '51 '77 C.569 B.A. L.309 J.D. [Morgan,L.&B.]
Healy, Robert W., (AV) . . . . '33 '60 C.262 B.S. L.276 J.D. 1990 M Street, NW, Ste. 510
Healy, Terence Michael . . . . '65 '92 C.575 B.A. L.30 J.D. [Ⓐ Dombroff&G.]
Healy, Thomas Joseph, Jr. '63 '96 C.401 B.S. L.564 J.D.
(adm. in CT; not adm. in DC) Princ., Bessemer Trust Co., N.A.
Heard, Frank Lane, III, (AV) . . . . '50 '79 C&L.976 B.A., J.D. [Williams&C.]
*PRACTICE AREAS: Appellate Practice; Civil Practice; Class Actions; Complex and Multi-District Litigation; Litigation.
Heard, Maria Colsey . . . . '68 '94 C.397 B.A. L.273 J.D. [Ⓐ Dickstein S.M.&O.]
*PRACTICE AREAS: Public Sector Litigation; Civil Litigation; Alternative Dispute Resolution.
Hearne, Steven G. . . . . '70 '98 C.118 B.A. L.602 J.D. Securities & Exchange Commission
Heasley, David K. . . . . '53 '81 C.367 B.A. L.446 J.D. [Ⓐ Silverberg,G.&B.]
*PRACTICE AREAS: Trademarks; Civil Litigation.
Heath, Michael R. . . . . '75 '00 C.939 B.A. L.228 J.D. [Ⓐ Dow,L.&A.]
Heatly, John Staley . . . . '72 '01 C.69 B.A. L.861 J.D. [Ⓐ Bryan C.]
Heaton, J. Andrew '60 '87
C.98 B.A.,B.S. L.145 J.D. Asst. Gen. Coun., Ernst & Young LLP
Heaviside, Michael W., (AV) . . . . '53 '80 C.276 B.A. L.945 J.D. [Ashcraft&G.]
*PRACTICE AREAS: Pharmacy Law; Diet Drug Litigation.
Heavner, B. Brett . . . . '66 '93 C.722 B.A. L.228 J.D. [Ⓐ Finnegan,H.F.G.&D.]
*PRACTICE AREAS: Trademark Litigation; Trademark Prosecution; Copyright Infringement; International Trademarks; Trademark Infringement.
Heavner, James R., Jr. . . . . '59 '91 C.870 B.S. L.276 J.D. [Baker B.]
Heberlig, Brian M. . . . . '71 '96 C.197 A.B. L.276 J.D. [Ⓐ Steptoe&J.]
Hebert, Jay H., (AVⓉ) '61 '86 C.691 B.A. L.309 J.D.
(adm. in TX; not adm. in DC) [Vinson&E.]
*PRACTICE AREAS: Securities; Corporate Law; Telecommunications Law; Mergers, Acquisitions and Divestitures; Partnership Law.
Hebert, Lorane F. . . . . '64 '95 C.766 B.A. L.813 J.D. [Ⓐ Hogan&H.]
*PRACTICE AREAS: Litigation.
Hebert, Marc C. . . . . '69 '94 C.861 B.A. L.425 J.D. [Ⓐ Bracewell&P.]
*PRACTICE AREAS: Legislation (5%); International Law (80%); Environmental Law (10%); Election Law (5%).

Hechinger, Brian M. '60 '86 C.861 B.A. L.424 J.D.
(adm. in IL; not adm. in DC) ULLICO INC.
*RESPONSIBILITIES: Property and Casualty Insurance; ERISA; Financial Services; Litigation.
Hechl, Thomas P. '58 '87 C.057 J.D. L.1049 M.C.L.
(adm. in CA; not adm. in DC) [Freshfields B.D.]
Hecht, Alissa S. '70 '97 C.112 B.A. L.145 J.D.
(adm. in NY; not adm. in DC) [Ⓐ Clifford C.R.&W.]
*PRACTICE AREAS: Antitrust.
Hecht, James C. . . . . '66 '91 C.893 B.A. L.976 J.D. [Skadden,A.S.M.&F.]
Hecht, Philip H. . . . . '— '80 C.31 B.A. L.477 J.D. [Kirkpatrick&L.]
*PRACTICE AREAS: Insurance Coverage; Complex Litigation.
Hecker, James M. . . . . '51 '77 C&L.339 A.B., J.D. Trial Lawyers for Pub. Jus., P.C.
Hecker, Karen L. '65 '93 C.188 B.S. L.174 J.D.
(adm. in CO; not adm. in DC) [Ⓐ Feldesman,T.L.F.&B.]
*PRACTICE AREAS: Military Law; Litigation.
Heckman, Jerome H., (AV) . . . . '27 '53 C&L.276 B.S., LL.B. [Keller&H.]
*PRACTICE AREAS: Food and Drug Law; Antitrust Law; Trade Regulation Law.
Heckman, Michael D. . . . . '62 '92 C.604 B.A. L.273 J.D. Thompson Publishing Grp.
Hedge, Brook . . . . '48 '75 C.112 B.A. L.128 J.D. Supr. Ct. J.
Hedlund, James W. . . . . '65 '93 C.276 A.A. L.861 J.D. Atty., Sprint Corp.
Hedstrom, John E. . . . . '70 '98 C.902 B.A. L.436 J.D. [Ⓐ Porter W.M.&A.]
Heenan, Garrett M. . . . . '— '00 C.94 B.A. L.30 J.D. [Ⓐ Arnold&P.]
*PRACTICE AREAS: Litigation; Intellectual Property; Technology Law.
Heenan, Michael T., (AV) . . . . '42 '67 C.524 B.S. L.665 J.D. [Heenan,A.&R.]
*PRACTICE AREAS: Mine Safety and Health; Occupational Safety and Health; Regulatory Agency Practice; Government Inspections and Investigations.

Heenan, Althen & Roles, LLP, (AV)
1110 Vermont Avenue, N.W., Suite 400, 20005 ⊙
Telephone: 202-887-0800 Fax: 202-775-8518
Email: info@harlaw.com URL: http://www.harlaw.com
Members of Firm: Michael T. Heenan; William I. Althen; Forrest H. Roles (Resident, Charleston, West Virginia Office); Ronald E. Meisburg; John R. Woodrum; Anna Marie Dailey (Resident, Charleston, West Virginia Office); Mark A. Carter (Resident, Charleston, West Virginia Office); William K. Doran; Donna Colberg Kelly (Resident, Charleston, West Virginia Office); Mark E. Heath (Resident, Charleston, West Virginia Office); David J. Hardy (Resident, Charleston, West Virginia Office). Associates: Margaret S. Lopez; W. Gregory Mott; Allison S. Williams (Resident, Charleston, West Virginia Office); Meikka A. Cutlip. Counsel: Timothy B. McBride.
General Litigation and Administrative Practice before Federal Courts, Departments and Agencies. Corporate, Labor Relations and Employment, Mining, Trade Association, Pension and Employee Benefits (ERISA), Taxation, Real Estate, Safety and Environmental Law.
Charleston, West Virginia Office: BB&T Square, 300 Summers Street. Telephone: 304-342-8960. Fax: 304-342-5761.
See Professional Biographies, WASHINGTON, DISTRICT OF COLUMBIA

Heffernan, Barbara K., (AV) . . . . '53 '78 C.446 B.A. L.128 J.D. [Schiff H.&W.]
*PRACTICE AREAS: Energy; Energy Regulatory; Administrative Law.
Heffernan, Brenda A. . . . . '64 '90 C.690 B.A. L.1040 J.D. [Ⓐ Condon&F.]
Heffernan, David . . . . '63 '96 C.031 B.A. L.128 J.D. [Ⓐ Wilmer,C.&P.]
Heffernan, Edward D., (AV) '33 '61
C.339 A.B. L.209 J.D. One Massachusetts Ave., N.W.
Heffernan, Elizabeth Blossom, (AV) . . . . '52 '80 C.681 B.A. L.276 J.D. [Hogan&H.]
*PRACTICE AREAS: Education Law; Government Contracts Law.
Heffernan, James V., (AV) . . . . '26 '53 C&L.188 A.B., J.D. [Sutherland A.&B.]
*PRACTICE AREAS: Federal Income Tax; Federal Estate and Gift Tax; Federal Tax Controversies; Tax Planning; Tax Litigation.
Heffernan, Patricia Ann . . . . '65 '90 C.93 B.A. L.602 J.D. Asst. U.S. Atty.‡
Hefferon, Thomas M. . . . . '60 '86 C.855 B.A. L.145 J.D. [Goodwin P.]
*PRACTICE AREAS: Civil Litigation; Consumer Finance; Class Actions; Insurance.
Heffler, James M., (AV) . . . . '45 '71 C.264 A.B. L.276 J.D. 915 15th St., N.W.
Heffner, Douglas J. . . . . '57 '83 C.20 B.A. L.215 J.D. [Ⓒ Hunton&W.]
*PRACTICE AREAS: International Law.
Heffner, John D., (BV) . . . . '45 '72 C.893 B.A. L.245 J.D. [Rea,C.&A.]
*PRACTICE AREAS: Administrative Law; Interstate Commerce; Transportation; Railroads.
Heffron, Howard A., (AV) . . . . '27 '53 C.178 A.B. L.309 LL.B. 1850 K St. NW, Ste. 500
Heflin, H. Ray '67 '97 C.277 B.S. L.1218 J.D.
(adm. in VA; not adm. in DC; See Pat. Sect.) [Ⓐ Sughrue M.]
Hefter, Laurence R., (AV) '35 '64
C.688 B.M.E. L.273 J.D. [Finnegan,H.F.G.&D.] (See Pat. Sect.)
*PRACTICE AREAS: Trademarks; Trademark Litigation; Unfair Competition; Intellectual Property Litigation; Alternative Dispute Resolution.
Hefty, Andrew J. '70 '97 C.475 B.A. L.902 J.D.
(adm. in MD; not adm. in DC) [Ⓐ Steptoe&J.]
Heggestad, Robert E. . . . . '46 '72 C&L.352 B.B.A., J.D. [Heggestad&W.]
*PRACTICE AREAS: Personal Injury; Professional Liability; Insurance Coverage.

Heggestad & Weiss, P.C., (AV)
Suite 600, 1320 19th Street, N.W., 20036
Telephone: 202-289-8333 Fax: 202-289-8307
Email: heggestad@radix.net
Robert E. Heggestad; Alexander Wilson Whitaker. Of Counsel: Christopher A. Hansen; Mary Ann Hammett.
Federal and State Civil Trial and Appellate Practice including Administrative, Contracts, Corporate, Trade Regulation, Insurance, International, Construction, Insurance Coverage, Environmental, Medical Malpractice, Professional Malpractice, Corporation.
See Professional Biographies, WASHINGTON, DISTRICT OF COLUMBIA

Hegland, Paul G. . . . . '43 '71 C&L.494 B.A., J.D. [Ⓐ White&C.]
*PRACTICE AREAS: Customs; International Trade.
Hegyi, Bruce R. . . . . '54 '84 C.945 A.B. L.838 J.D. U.S. Atty's. Off for the Dist. of DC
Heideman, Richard D. . . . . '47 '72 C.477 B.A. L.273 J.D. [Heideman]
*PRACTICE AREAS: Criminal Defense; Civil Trial; Personal Injury; Wrongful Death; International Trade.

Heideman Law Group, The, P.C.
1714 N Street, N.W., 20036-2907
Telephone: 202-462-8990 Fax: 202-462-8995
Email: attorneys@heidemanlaw.com URL: http://www.Heidemanlaw.com
Richard D. Heideman; Noel J. Nudelman;—Tracy Reichman Kalik. Of Counsel: Sanford R. Cardin. Special Counsel: Avigdor Warsha.
Criminal Defense and Civil Trial Practice. Personal Injury, Wrongful Death, Corporate Law, Real Property, Civil Rights, Military, Sports, Health Care. Ethics, Government Relations, International Trade and International Corporate Transactions.
See Professional Biographies, WASHINGTON, DISTRICT OF COLUMBIA

Heidenberger, Peter, (AV) . . . . '22 '57 C.060 L.273 [Ⓒ Berliner,C.&R.]
Heiderscheit, John W., III . . . . '62 '87 C.813 A.B. L.1068 J.D. 1200 G. St. N.W.
Heifetz, Kimberly R. . . . . '— '98 C.788 B.A. L.904 J.D. [Ⓐ Miller&C.]
*PRACTICE AREAS: Government Contracts; Commercial Law; Government Procurement; Bid Protests.
Heifetz, Stephen R. . . . . '71 '96 C.813 A.B. L.276 J.D. [Ⓐ Wilmer,C.&P.]
Heilbrun, Mark R. . . . . '63 '91 C.245 B.A. L.846 J.D. [Ⓐ Baker&M.]
*PRACTICE AREAS: Litigation.
Heim, Joan L. . . . . '— '68 C.914 A.B. L.494 J.D. [Ⓒ Heller E.W.&M.]
*PRACTICE AREAS: Antitrust.
Heiman, Bruce J., (AV) . . . . '56 '80 C.1036 B.A. L.309 J.D. [Preston G.E.&R.M.]
*PRACTICE AREAS: Technology; Trade; Transportation; Federal Policy.

Heiman, Lee C. '58 '85 C.813 A.B. L.426 J.D.
(adm. in CA; not adm. in DC) [A] Nath&Assoc.]
*PRACTICE AREAS: Civil Litigation; Probate Litigation.
Heiman, Richard J., (AV) '31 '56 C.339 A.B. L.477 LL.B.
Suite 200, 1925 K Street, N.W.
Heimann, Christopher M. ....'61 '91 C.128 B.A. L.945 J.D. 1401 H. St. N.W.
Heimann-McGhee, Robin .... '64 '89 C.893 B.A. L.945 J.D. [A] Powell,G.F.&M.]
*PRACTICE AREAS: Real Estate Law; Commercial Lending; Tax Credits.
Heimberg, Gary A. ....'62 '92 C&L.273 B.A., J.D. [C] Akin,G.S.H.&F.]
*PRACTICE AREAS: Public Policy.
Heimberg, Scott M. .... '59 '85 C.264 B.A. L.273 J.D. [Akin,G.S.H.&F.]
*PRACTICE AREAS: Government Contracts; Construction Law.
Heimert, Kimberly J. '69 '94 C.30 B.A. L.309 J.D.
(adm. in NY; not adm. in DC) [A] Chadbourne&P.]
Hein, Werner J. ....'42 '86 L.178 LL.M. [Mayer,B.&P.]
Heinrichs, Jane G. .... '68 '94 C.1349 B.A. L.904 J.D. [A] Shearman&S.]
*PRACTICE AREAS: Investment Management.
Heins, Jeffrey J. ....'— '94 C.1031 B.A. L.823 J.D. [A] Piper M.R.&W.]
*PRACTICE AREAS: Business; Technology; Communications.
Heintz, James M. .... '65 '97 C.1350 B.E.E.E. L.724 J.D. [A] Piper M.R.&W.] (Pat.)
*PRACTICE AREAS: Patent; Trademark; Trade Secrets; Intellectual Property Licensing.
Heintz, John E., (AV) .... '48 '77 C.188 B.A. L.569 J.D. [Gilbert H.&R.]
*PRACTICE AREAS: Insurance Coverage; Commercial Litigation; Torts; Mediation and Arbitration.
Heinzerling, Lisa E. .... '61 '88 C.674 A.B. L.145 J.D. 600 New Jersey Ave., N.W.
Heise, James T. '71 '99 C&L.1002 B.S., J.D.
(adm. in MD; not adm. in DC) [A] Griffin,F.T.&M.]
*PRACTICE AREAS: Real Property; Business Law; Trusts and Estates.
Heiss, Marjorie A. '58 '85 C&L.477 B.A., J.D.
(adm. in IL; not adm. in DC) 1359 28th St. NW
Heitmann, John J. ....'67 '95 C.602 B.A. L.569 J.D. [A] Kelley D.&W.]
*PRACTICE AREAS: Telecommunications Law.
Hekman, Mary A., (BV) ....'57 '84 C.114 B.A. L.904 J.D. [C] Miller,B.&O.]
*PRACTICE AREAS: Cogeneration; Hydroelectricity; Energy Project Development; Electric Power; Electric Utilities.
Heland, Kenneth V. '46 '71 C.976 B.A. L.659 J.D.
(adm. in MD; not adm. in DC)
Assoc. Dir., Amer. Coll. of Obstetricians & Gynecologists
Heldman, Samuel H. .... '65 '90 C&L.309 B.A., J.D. [Gardner,M.F.G.&K.]

Helein Law Group, The, P.C.
(See McLean, Virginia)

Heleman, Beth S. .... '71 '96 C.705 B.A. L.659 J.D. [A] Caplin&D.]
*PRACTICE AREAS: Civil Litigation.
Helfrich, George F. '33 '70 C.861 B.S. L.420 J.D.
(adm. in LA; not adm. in DC; See Pat. Sect.) [C] Keil&W.]
*PRACTICE AREAS: Chemical Patents; Litigation; Licensing; Trade Secret and Trademark Law.
Helfrich, Lee Ellen .... '55 '80 C.611 B.A. L.904 J.D. [Lobel,N.&L.]
*PRACTICE AREAS: Federal Energy; Natural Resources; Public Lands; Oil and Gas; Complex Civil Litigation.
Helget, Kasha '52 '77 C.963 B.S. L.69 J.D.
(adm. in TX; not adm. in DC) 888 E. First Street, N.E.
Hellbeck, Eckhard R. ....'— '96 L.999 J.D. [A] White&C.]
Heller, Barry M., (AV) ....'53 '77 C.569 B.A. L.276 J.D. [Piper M.R.&W.]
*PRACTICE AREAS: Litigation; Franchising; Antitrust.
Heller, Caroline J. '73 '01 C.104 B.A. L.597 J.D.
(adm. in NY; not adm. in DC) [A] Steptoe&J.]
Heller, Harry, (AV) .... '09 '34 C&L.178 A.B., LL.B. Legal Aid Soc.‡
Heller, J. Roderick, III, (AV) '37 '64 C.674 A.B. L.309 LL.B.
Chmn. & CEO, NHP, Inc.
Heller, Jack I., (AV) .... '32 '62 C.145 B.A. L.178 LL.B. [Heller&R.]
*PRACTICE AREAS: Business Law; International Transactions.
Heller, Mark A. .... '47 '73 C&L.966 B.A., J.D. [Hale&D.]
*PRACTICE AREAS: Drug and Medical Device Regulation.
Heller, Martha E. .... '70 '98 C.188 B.A. L.893 J.D. [A] Wiley R.&F.]

Heller, Milton, & Associates, (AV) '29 '58 C&L.273 B.S., J.D.
927 15th Street, N.W., 20005
Telephone: 202-737-4300 Fax: 202-628-4608
Email: mheller@erols.com URL: http://www.lawyers.com/miltonhellerlaw
***PRACTICE AREAS: Product Liability; Medical Malpractice; Personal Injury; Civil Litigation.**
Associate: Barbara Moir Condos.
General Civil Trial Practice before all Courts of the District of Columbia and Maryland. Malpractice, Products Liability and Negligence Law, Family Law.
Reference: First Union National Bank.
See Professional Biographies, WASHINGTON, DISTRICT OF COLUMBIA

Heller Ehrman White & McAuliffe LLP, (AV)
A Partnership of Professional Corporations
1666 K Street, NW, Suite 300, 20006-1228 ⊙
Telephone: 202-912-2000 Facsimile: 202-912-2020
URL: http://www.hewm.com
Shareholders: Mary L. Azcuenaga††; Kenneth L. Chernof††; James Nicholas Czaban; Patricia D. Granados††; David Harth††; John P. Isacson, Jr.††; Bruce F. Mackler††; Monica P. Medina††; Kit A. Pierson††; Brent N. Rushforth††; Colin G. Sandercock; John S. Skilton; Michael A. Stosser††. Special Counsel: Paul M. Booth (Also at Gaithersburg, Maryland Office); Adelia S. Borrasca; Joan L. Heim; Paul B. Mohler (Not admitted in DC); David F. Smutny; Jane E. Stelck. Associates: Joseph H. Fagan; John A. Jurata, Jr. (Not admitted in DC); Hyun Sun Kim (Not admitted in DC); Natasha V. Leskovsek; Mireya A.R. Llaurado; Martina M. Stewart (Not admitted in DC); John P. Wunderli.
General Practice.
Gaithersburg, Maryland Office: 101 Orchard Ridge Drive. Telephone: 301-721-6100. Facsimile: 301-721-6299.
San Francisco, California Office: 333 Bush Street. Telephone: 415-772-6000. Facsimile: 415-772-6268. Cable Address: "Helpow". Telex: 340-895; 184-996.
Anchorage, Alaska Office: 550 West 7th Avenue, Suite 1900. Telephone: 907-277-1900. Facsimile: 907-277-1920.
Los Angeles, California Office: 601 S. Figueroa Street. Telephone: 213-689-0200. Facsimile: 213-614-1868.
Menlo Park, California Office: 275 Middlefield Road. Telephone: 650-324-7000. Facsimile: 650-324-0638.
San Diego, California Office: 4350 La Jolla Village Drive, Suite 700. Telephone: 858-450-8400. Facsimile: 858-450-8499.
Madison, Wisconsin Office: One East Main Street, Suite 201. Telephone: 608-663-7460. Facsimile: 608-663-7499.
New York, New York Office: 120 West 45th Street, 21st Floor. Telephone: 212-832-8300. Facsimile: 212-763-7600.
Portland, Oregon Office: 200 S.W. Market Street, Suite 1750. Telephone: 503-227-7400. Facsimile: 503-241-0950.
Seattle, Washington Office: 701 Fifth Avenue, Suite 6100. Telephone: 206-447-0900. Facsimile: 206-447-0849.
Hong Kong Office: 6308-09 The Center, 99 Queens Road Central, Hong Kong. Telephone: (011) 852-2526-6381. Facsimile: (011) 852-2810-6242.
Singapore Office: 50 Raffles Place, 17-04 Singapore Land Tower. Telephone: (011) 65 538-1756. Facsimile: (011) 65 538-1537.
Affiliated Carnelutti Office: Cabinet Carnelutti, 6, Avenue George V, Paris, France 75008. Telephone: (1) 4723-3181. Fax: (1) 4720-2509.

(This Listing Continued)

Heller Ehrman White & McAuliffe LLP (Continued)

Affiliated Carnelutti Office: Studio Legale associato con Carnelutti, Via Parigi, 11, Rome, Italy 00185. Telephone: (06)473-901. Fax: (06) 481-9833. Email: CARNELUTTIROME@FLASH.NET.it.
Affiliated Carnelutti Office: Studio Legale associato Carnelutti, Corso Matteotti, Via Principe Amedeo, 3, 20121 Milan, Italy. Telephone: (011) 3902-655851. Fax: (011) 3902-6558-5585. Email: CARNELUTTI@carnelutti.com
††Lawyer who is a stockholder and an employee of a professional corporation which is a member of the firm
See Professional Biographies, WASHINGTON, DISTRICT OF COLUMBIA

Heller & Rosenblatt, (AV)
1101 15th Street, Suite 205, 20005
Telephone: 202-466-4700 Telecopier: 202-223-4826 E-Mail: ffddprosenblatt@erols.com
Email: ffddjheller@erols.com
Members of Firm: Peter R. Rosenblatt; Jack I. Heller.
International and U.S. Government Practice. Domestic and International Corporation and Finance, Arbitration.

Hellewell, Robert John .... '67 '96 C&L.101 B.S., J.D. [A] Skadden,A.S.M.&F.]
*PRACTICE AREAS: Antitrust and Trade Regulation.
Hellman, Richard A. ....'40 '66 C.116 B.S. L.276 J.D. 2013 Que St., N.W.
Hellmich, Christopher '67 '93 C.436 B.S. L.190 J.D.
(adm. in NE; not adm. in DC) [A] Patton B.]
Helm, Jacquelyn V. .... '52 '77 C.879 B.A. L.273 J.D. 700 E St., SE
Helm, Robert W., (AV) .... '57 '84 C&L.813 A.B., J.D. [Dechert]
*PRACTICE AREAS: Investment Management; Securities Regulation; Financial Services Law.
Helm, Sallie H., (AV) .... '31 '75 C.419 B.S. L.276 J.D. [C] Dickstein S.M.&O.]
*PRACTICE AREAS: Commercial Litigation; Intellectual Property; Insurance Litigation; Antitrust and Trade Regulation; Unfair Competition.
Helmanis, Ansis M., (BV) '45 '73 C.94 B.A. L.669 J.D.
(adm. in NH; not adm. in DC) [C] Barnes,R.&C.]
*PRACTICE AREAS: Food and Drug Regulation.
Helmes, Jacquenette M. '— '00 C.823 B.S. L.276 J.D.
(adm. in MD; not adm. in DC) [A] Morgan,L.&B.]
Helmick, Richard A., (AV) ....'42 '71 C.973 A.B. L.150 J.D. [Cohn&M.]
*PRACTICE AREAS: Communications Law.
Helsel, Kathleen L. .... '55 '83 C.119 B.S. L.276 J.D. The World Bk.
Helsel, Scott D. .... '70 '95 C.237 B.A. L.945 J.D. [A] Arnold&P.]
*PRACTICE AREAS: Litigation; Legislative.
Heltzer, Harold J., (AV) ....'42 '67 C.563 B.A. L.569 LL.B. [Crowell&M.]
*PRACTICE AREAS: Taxation Law.
Helvey, Jeffrey T. '65 '97 C.645 B.S.E.E. L.846 J.D.
(adm. in TX; not adm. in DC) [A] Sterne,K.G.&F.]
*PRACTICE AREAS: Patent Law.
Hembree, Christopher W. ....'69 '97 C.30 B.A. L.128 J.D. [A] Cole,R.&B.]
*PRACTICE AREAS: Communications and Media; Zoning, Planning and Land Use; Property Law.
Hemby Jr., Joseph K. '58 '99 C.302 B.A. L.273 J.D.
(adm. in MD; not adm. in DC) [A] Nath&Assoc.]
*PRACTICE AREAS: Patent Prosecution.
Hemmendinger, Lisa M. '— '98 C.788 A.B. L.446 J.D.
[A] Banner&W.] (See Pat. Sect.)
*PRACTICE AREAS: Intellectual Property Law; Patents; Biotechnology; Pharmaceutical Intellectual Property.
Hemmendinger, Noel, (AV) .... '13 '37 C.674 A.B. L.309 LL.B. [C] Willkie F.&G.] ‡
Hemmer, J. Michael ....'49 '76 C.813 B.A. L.1066 J.D. [Covington&B.]
Hemmersbaugh, Paul A. ....'61 '92 C.747 B.A. L.494 J.D. [A] Sidley A.B.&W.]
Hemond, Kerry F. '58 '85 C.914 B.A. L.818 J.D.
(adm. in MA; not adm. in DC) Intl. Fin. Corp.
Hemphill, Cynthia B. .... '61 '95 C.976 B.A. L.329 J.D. [A] Trow&K.]
*PRACTICE AREAS: Immigration and Nationality Law.
Hemphill, Holly K. ....'45 '77 C.623 B.A. L.276 J.D. [McDermott,W.&E.]
Hemrich, Veronica E. '65 '90
C.454 B.A. L.276 J.D. The ABA CenterFor Children and The Law
Henault, John F., Jr. '70 '00 C.734 B.A. L.1209 J.D.
(adm. in VA; not adm. in DC) [A] Venable,A.B.H.&C.]
*PRACTICE AREAS: Commercial Litigation; White Collar Crime.
Henault, Roberta Kathryn '68 '99 C.1200 B.A. L.818 J.D.
(adm. in MA; not adm. in DC) [A] Lewis]
*PRACTICE AREAS: Family Law.
Henck, Charles S. ....'47 '75 C.1365 B.A. L.245 J.D. [Ballard S.A.&I.]
*PRACTICE AREAS: Taxation; Project Finance; Tax Exempt Finance.
Hendel, David P. .... '57 '83 C.1036 B.A. L.569 J.D. [Wickwire G.] (⊙Vienna, VA)
*PRACTICE AREAS: Government Contracts and Commercial Law; Litigation.
Henderson, Alma C. '65 '93
C.910 B.A. L.569 J.D. Staff Atty., People for the American Way
Henderson, Amy Catherine '62 '89 C.846 B.A. L.326 J.D.
(adm. in TX; not adm. in DC) 703 Hart Senate Ofc. Bldg.‡
Henderson, Cynthia C. '69 '95 C.893 B.A. L.276 J.D.
(adm. in MD; not adm. in DC) [A] Fulbright&J.]
*PRACTICE AREAS: Intellectual Property.
Henderson, Donna Jean, (BV) '56 '82 C.338 B.S. L.734 J.D.
Asst. Gen. Coun., Washington Metropolitan Area Transit Authority
*RESPONSIBILITIES: Personal Injury; Workers Compensation.
Henderson, Douglas B., (AV) '35 '62
C.645 B.S. L.273 J.D. [Finnegan,H.F.G.&D.] (See Pat. Sect.)
*PRACTICE AREAS: Intellectual Property Litigation; Patents; Technology Licensing; Trade Secrets; Trademarks.
Henderson, Frances J. .... '57 '85 L.999 LL.B. [Sonnenschein N.&R.]
*PRACTICE AREAS: International Trade.
Henderson, James L., III, (AV) '51 '76 C.575 B.A. L.280 J.D.
(adm. in GA; not adm. in DC) [Sutherland A.&B.] (⊙Atlanta, GA)
*PRACTICE AREAS: Finance; Government; Health Care; Non Profit and Charitable Organizations; Securities.
Henderson, James Matthew, Sr. .... '58 '87 C.953 B.A. L.734 J.D. [American L.&J.]
Henderson, John D. ....'57 '84 C.763 B.A. L.1066 J.D. 50 E. Street, SW
Henderson, John G. '62 '90 C.393 B.A. L.30 J.D.
(adm. in VA; not adm. in DC) [Dyer E.&J.]
*PRACTICE AREAS: Structured Finance; Aircraft Finance and Leasing; Project Finance; Financial Restructuring; Debtor and Creditor Workouts.
Henderson, Matthew T. ....'70 '99 C.674 B.S.E. L.145 J.D. Kirkland & Ellis
Henderson, Nick A. .... '65 '90 C.190 B.A. L.904 J.D. [A] Sidley A.B.&W.]
Henderson, Thomas H., Jr. .... '39 '66 C.10 B.S. L.16 J.D. Exec. Dir., A.T.L.A.
Henderson, Thomas J., (AV) '52 '77 C.970 B.A. L.665 J.D.
(adm. in PA; not adm. in DC)
Dep. Dir. Litig., Lawyers Comm. for Civil Rights Under Law
*RESPONSIBILITIES: Civil Rights/Constitutional Law; Education Law; Employment Law; Housing Law.
Henderson, Wade J. ....'48 '73 C.329 B.A. L.705 J.D. 2325 First St., N.W.

Henderson & Sturm LLP, (AV)
1301 Pennsylvania Avenue, N.W. Suite 1020, 20004-1707 ⊙
Telephone: 202-296-3854 Fax: 202-223-9606
URL: http://www.hsllp.com

(This Listing Continued)

Henderson & Sturm LLP (Continued)

Members of Firm: William H. Wright; Michael O. Sturm (Not admitted in DC).
Patent, Trademark, Copyright and Unfair Competition Law and Federal Trial Practice Exclusively, Intellectual Property.
Other Offices: Des Moines, Iowa; Davenport, Iowa; Omaha, Nebraska.

See Professional Biographies, WASHINGTON, DISTRICT OF COLUMBIA

Hendler, Clifford B., (AV) ....'53 '78 C.976 B.A. L.813 J.D. [Crowell&M.]
Hendricks, Beatice E. ....'— '73 C.512 B.S. L.329 J.D. Asst. Corp. Coun.
Hendrix, R. Brian ....'73 '99 C.838 B.A. L.880 J.D. [Ⓐ Patton B.]
Hendrix, Samuel L. ....'70 '95 C.228 B.A. L.893 J.D. [Ⓐ Baker&H.]
Hengerer, Edward W., (AV) ....'45 '73 C.165 B.A. L.273 J.D. [John&H.]
*PRACTICE AREAS: Energy Law.
Hengerer, Linton W. ....'54 '80 C.94 B.S.B.A. L.273 J.D. [Grossberg,Y.F.&B.]
Henke, Michael J., (AV) ....'40 '65 C&L.69 B.A., LL.B. [Vinson&E.]
*PRACTICE AREAS: Litigation; Antitrust and Trade Regulation; Administrative Law; Federal Energy Regulation; Alternative Dispute Resolution.
Henley, Robert P. '— '99 C.893 B.A. L.208 J.D.
(adm. in VA; not adm. in DC) [Ⓐ Morgan,L.&B.]
Henneberger, Lawrence F. ....'38 '62 C&L.425 B.B.A., LL.B. [Arent F.K.P.&K.]
*PRACTICE AREAS: Antitrust; Motor Vehicle Safety Law; Transportation Law; Trade Association Law.
Henneberry, Edward P., (AV) ....'45 '70 C&L.93 B.A., J.D. [Howrey S.A.&W.]
*PRACTICE AREAS: Antitrust; Commercial Litigation; Products Liability Law.
Henneberry, Lisa G. ....'67 '92 C.104 B.A. L.273 J.D. [Squire,S.&D.]
*PRACTICE AREAS: International Corporate Law; International Finance; Energy Law; Project Finance.
Henneburg, Frank H., (AV) ....'49 '75 C.276 A.B. L.145 J.D. [Akin,G.S.H.&F.]
*PRACTICE AREAS: Real Estate.
Hennessee, Karl Kiffin '74 '98 C&L.802 B.A., J.D.
(adm. in TX; not adm. in DC) [Ⓐ Vinson&E.]
*PRACTICE AREAS: Litigation; Antitrust and Trade Regulation; Mergers, Acquisitions and Divestitures; Aviation and Aerospace; International Business Transactions.
Hennessey, Joseph A. ....'65 '96 C.860 B.A. L.180 J.D. [Cullen]
*PRACTICE AREAS: International Arbitration; Commercial Law; Litigation; Privacy Law; Regulatory Law.
Hennessy, Ellen A. .... '49 '78 C.475 B.A. L.128 J.D. 601 Pennsylvania Ave. NW
Hennessy, W. Louis ....'55 '97 C.064 B.A. L.446 J.D. [Ⓒ Asbill,J.M.&B.]
*PRACTICE AREAS: Criminal Law; Law Enforcement; Personal Injury; Premises Liability; Civil Rights.
Henri, Anita L. '57 '87 C.30 B.A. L.329 J.D.
(adm. in CA; not adm. in DC) 1050 Conn. Ave., N.W.‡
Henrichsen, Neil L., (AV) '63 '89 C.331 B.A. L.30 J.D.
[Henrichsen S.] (⊙Jacksnvl., FL)
*PRACTICE AREAS: Construction and Surety Law; Commercial Torts; Employment Law; Civil Rights; Civil Litigation.

Henrichsen Siegel, P.L.L.C., (AV) BB
1850 M Street N.W., Suite 250, 20036 ⊙
Telephone: 202-293-7766 Facsimile: 202-293-7778
Email: administrator@hslawyers.com URL: http://www.hslawyers.com
Neil L. Henrichsen; Eric L. Siegel; Dawn C. Stewart; Aaron Nisenson; William J. Moore, III (Resident, Jacksonville, Florida Office). Associates: Helen H. Albee (Resident, Jacksonville, Florida Office); Colleen M. Leyrer; Joel M. Long. Of Counsel: Lorraine M. Magee; Joanna R. Onorato.
Construction and Surety Law, Government Contracts, Employment and Labor Law, Civil Rights, Creditors Rights, Commercial Torts, General Civil Litigation, Environmental Litigation, Products Liability, Class Action, Litigation.
Jacksonville, Florida Office: 200 East Forsyth Street, 32202. Telephone: 904-355-2233. Fax: 904-596-5705.

See Professional Biographies, WASHINGTON, DISTRICT OF COLUMBIA

Henricks, Tiffany A. ....'72 '98 C.112 B.A. L.904 J.D. [Ⓐ Malizia S.&F.]
*PRACTICE AREAS: Securities; Corporate; Banking.
Henry, Jeanett P. ....'60 '87 C.1141 B.A. L.276 J.D. [Ⓐ D.M.Temple]
Henry, John A., Jr. ....'72 '98 C.105 B.A. L.902 J.D. [Ⓐ Holland&K.]
*PRACTICE AREAS: Real Estate Transactions; Development and Finance; Leasing; Affordable Housing.
Henry, John C., Jr. ....'48 '75 C.976 A.B. L.309 J.D. [Squire,S.&D.]
*PRACTICE AREAS: Corporate; Financial Institutions; International Acquisitions; Joint Ventures.
Henry, Katherine J. ....'58 '90 C.613 B.A. L.145 J.D. [Dickstein S.M.&O.]
*PRACTICE AREAS: Civil Litigation; Insurance Coverage Litigation; Complex Commercial Litigation; White Collar Crime; Appellate Practice.
Henry, Mark J. ....'67 '92 C.645 B.S.C.E. L.1338 J.D. [Staas&H.] (See Pat. Sect.)
*PRACTICE AREAS: Intellectual Property Law; Patent, Trademark, Copyright and Unfair Competition.
Henry, Mark O. ....'73 '00 C.608 B.S.B.A. L.575 J.D. [Ⓐ Alston&B.]
*PRACTICE AREAS: Banking Law; Mergers and Acquisitions; Financial Institutions Law; Securities.
Henry, Reginald Keith '60 '88 C.329 B.A. L.93 J.D.
(adm. in PA; not adm. in DC) Educ. Prog. Specialist, D.C. Educ. Licensure Comm.‡
Henry, Ronald K. ....'51 '76 C&L.477 B.A., J.D. [Kaye S.]
*PRACTICE AREAS: Government Contracts; Litigation; Intellectual Property.
Henry, Roxann E., (AV) ....'53 '79 C.881 A.B. L.1292 J.D. [Howrey S.A.&W.]
*PRACTICE AREAS: Antitrust; Complex Litigation; White Collar Criminal Defense.
Henry, William A., (BV) ....'56 '84 C.309 A.B. L.178 J.D. [Howrey S.A.&W.]
*PRACTICE AREAS: Antitrust; Trade Regulation.
Hens, Tanja E. ....'69 '93 C.276 B.S. L.145 J.D. [Wiley R.&F.]
*PRACTICE AREAS: Franchise Law; Litigation.
Henschel, Evan S. '69 '01 C.659 B.A. L.273 J.D.
(adm. in NY; not adm. in DC) [Ⓐ Wiley R.&F.]
Henschel, Rouget F. ....'59 '00 C.563 B.S. L.276 J.D. [Ⓐ Lyon&L.] (Pat.)
*PRACTICE AREAS: Intellectual Property; Pro Bono.
Hensler, David J., (AV) ....'43 '67 C&L.734 A.B., J.D. [Hogan&H.]
*PRACTICE AREAS: Civil Litigation; Commercial Litigation; Complex Litigation; Corporate Litigation; Insurance Coverage Litigation.
Henson, Jacqueline A. ....'55 '83 C.659 B.A. L.904 J.D. [McKenna&C.]
*PRACTICE AREAS: Nonprofit Organization Law; Taxation Law; Corporation Law.
Henson, Ronald C. ....'42 '73 C.575 B.A. L.245 J.D. [Ford&H.]
*PRACTICE AREAS: Management Labor Law; Contracts; Collective Bargaining; Arbitration.
Henteleff, Thomas O., (AV) ....'43 '69 C.878 B.S. L.1066 J.D. [Kleinfeld,K.&B.]
*PRACTICE AREAS: Food, Drug and Cosmetic Law; Drug and Medical Device Regulation; Controlled Substances Law; Advertising Law; Food Labeling and Inspection.
Hentoff, Thomas G. ....'64 '92 C.918 B.A. L.178 J.D. [Williams&C.]
*PRACTICE AREAS: Copyrights; Complex Litigation; Intellectual Property; Media and First Amendment; Media Libel.
Hentrel, Michael L. ....'67 '92 C.477 B.A. L.329 J.D. [Ⓐ Shaw P.]
Hepburn, Michael A. ....'63 '88 C.928 B.A. L.273 J.D. [Dow,L.&A.]
Heppen, Bruce P. '53 '78 C.188 B.S. L.273 J.D.
Assoc. Gen. Coun., Washington Metropolitan Area Transit Authority
*RESPONSIBILITIES: Civil Rights; Personnel; First Amendment.
Heppler, Wesley R., (AV) ....'54 '79 C.475 B.A. L.945 J.D. [Cole,R.&B.]
*PRACTICE AREAS: Cable Television; Communications Common Carrier; Copyright; Cable Programming; Cable Franchise Renewals and Transfers.

Hepworth, Joanne Roney, (AV) '48 '80 C&L.128 B.A., J.D.
305 H Street, N.W., 20001
Telephone: 202-789-0037 Fax: 202-408-1606
Email: jrhepworth@erols.com URL: http://www.lawyers.com/jrhepworthlaw
***PRACTICE AREAS: Criminal Law; Civil Rights; Personal Injury; Family Law.**

(This Listing Continued)

Hepworth, Joanne Roney (Continued)

Civil Rights and Constitutional Tort Civil Litigation, Personal Injury, Premises Liability, Auto Negligence, Criminal Defense, Drug Crimes, White Collar Criminal Defense, Alternatives to Criminal Prosecution, Domestic Relations, Divorce, Separation, Custody Issues, Auto Accidents, Drunk Driving.

See Professional Biographies, WASHINGTON, DISTRICT OF COLUMBIA

Herbert, Douglas C., Law Office of, (AV) '53 '79 C.497 B.A. L.145 J.D.
1000 Connecticut Avenue, N.W., Suite 301, 20036
Telephone: 202-659-1400 Telecopier: 202-659-2435
Email: dougherbert@mindspring.com URL: http://www.lawyers.com/herbertlaw
Employment Law, Civil Litigation.

See Professional Biographies, WASHINGTON, DISTRICT OF COLUMBIA

Herbert, Eugene T. ....'34 '58 C.674 A.B. L.309 J.D. 1150 Connecticut Ave., N.W.
Herbert, Ian A. '61 '85 C.910 B.A. L.339 J.D.
(adm. in IL; not adm. in DC) [Ⓒ Sutherland A.&B.]
*PRACTICE AREAS: Employee Benefit Taxation; ERISA; Executive Compensation; Qualified Retirement Plans.
Herbert, Karen Jones .... '47 '89 C.302 B.A. L.276 J.D. D.C.Taucab Comm.
Herbert, William F. ....'56 '81 C.93 B.A. L.128 J.D. [Staas&H.] (See Pat. Sect.)
*PRACTICE AREAS: Intellectual Property Law; Patent, Trademark, Copyright and Unfair Competition.
Herbst, Adrian E., (AV) '39 '65 C.494 B.S. L.1035 J.D.
(adm. in MN; not adm. in DC) [B.Herbst] ⊙
*PRACTICE AREAS: Telecommunications Law; Cable Television; Municipal Law; Utilities; Planning & economic dev. activities (cities), incl. "Mall of America" in Bloomington, MN.
Herbst, Lisa D. ....'— '98 C.1102 B.S. L.180 J.D. [Ⓐ Morgan,L.&B.]
Herdrich, Madeline A. '59 '90 C.449 B.B.A. L.904 J.D.
(adm. in VA; not adm. in DC) Contract Spec., Corp. for Public Broadcasting

Herge, Sparks & Christopher, LLP
(See McLean, Virginia)

Herlach, Mark D., (AV) ....'50 '75 C.813 B.A. L.477 J.D. [Sutherland A.&B.]
*PRACTICE AREAS: International Law; International Trade; Litigation; Communications and Media.
Herman, Alan I. ....'36 '59 C.569 B.S. L.823 J.D. AARP
Herman, Andrew Dewald ....'68 '97 C.477 B.A. L.1067 J.D. [Ⓐ Brand&F.]
*PRACTICE AREAS: Criminal Litigation; Civil Litigation; Administrative Law.
Herman, Andrew M. ....'69 '95 C.575 B.S.B.A. L.178 J.D. [Ⓐ Wilmer,C.&P.]
Herman, Anthony, (AV) ....'50 '89 C.790 B.A. L.309 J.D. [Covington&B.]
Herman, Donald L., Jr. ....'71 '96 C.846 B.J. L.16 J.D. [Ⓐ Bennet&B.]
*PRACTICE AREAS: Communications Law.
Herman, Elizabeth A. ..... '49 '77 C.289 B.A. L.1162 J.D. Asst. Coun., Off. of Bar Coun.

Herman, Mario L. '58 '83 C.30 B.A. L.276 J.D.
5335 Wisconsin Avenue, N.W., Suite 440, 20015-2003
Telephone: 202-686-2886 Fax: 301-874-1585 URL: http://www.franchise-law.com
Email: mherman@franchise-law.com URL: http://www.lawyers.com/franchiselaw
Franchise Law, Franchise Litigation, Franchise Arbitration, Franchise Mediation, Franchise Termination.

See Professional Biographies, WASHINGTON, DISTRICT OF COLUMBIA

Herman, Melanie L. '65 '94 C.30 B.A. L.1209 J.D.
Exec. Dir., Nonprofit Risk Mgmt. Ctr.
Herman, Robert Neil '57 '88
C.540 B.S. L.276 J.D. Advocacy Atty., Paralyzed Vet. of Amer.
Herman, Steven A. '44 '70 C&L.705 B.A., J.D.
(adm. in AR; not adm. in DC) [Beveridge&D.]
*PRACTICE AREAS: Environmental; Public Land Law.
Hermann, Karen C. ....'72 '99 C.261 B.A. L.273 J.D. [Ⓐ Crowell&M.]
Hermann, Richard L. ....'46 '75 C.976 B.A. L.188 J.D. President, Federal Reports, Inc.
Hermiz, Aram D. '69 '97 C.436 B.S.M.E. L.365 J.D.
(adm. in IL; not adm. in DC) 1920 N. Street N.W., Suite 650
Hernandez, Alan N. ....'— '90 C.918 B.A. L.309 J.D. [Verner,L.B.M.&H.]
*PRACTICE AREAS: Corporate; Transactional; Securities; International Business.
Hernandez, Cynthia M. .... '66 '94 C.477 B.A. L.30 J.D. 1050 17th St., NW
Hernandez, David M. ....'65 '97 C.1070 B.S. L.597 J.D. [Ⓐ Pillsbury W.]
*PRACTICE AREAS: Regulatory; Litigation; Aviation; Corporate Law.
Hernandez, Guilherme Tepedino '— '98
(adm. in Brazil; not adm. in DC) [Ⓐ Castro,B.S.V.G.A.]
Hernandez, Hector I., Sr. '60 '86 C&L.276 A.B., J.D.
(adm. in PA; not adm. in DC) 1353 Ingraham St., N.W.‡
Hernandez, Janet '66 '92 C.1222 B.A. L.659 J.D.
(adm. in FL; not adm. in DC) [Coudert B.]
*PRACTICE AREAS: Telecommunications.
Hernandez, Sunshine '— '95 C.1111 B.S. L.537 J.D.
(adm. in NY; not adm. in DC) [Ⓐ Winston&S.]
*PRACTICE AREAS: Energy.
Hernandez-Chapman, Cynthia M. '66 '98 C.477 B.A. L.904 J.D.
480 National Press Bldg.
Herndon, Diane L. '46 '80 C.329 B.S. L.273 J.D.
Sr. Assoc. Gen. Coun., Corp. Affs., Natl. Railroad Passenger Corp.
Herold, Arthur L., (AV) ....'41 '66 C&L.861 B.A., LL.B. [Webster,C.&B.]
*PRACTICE AREAS: Association Law; Antitrust and Trade Regulation; General Corporate; Employment; Election Law.
Heron, Julian B., Jr., (AV) ....'39 '65 C&L.383 B.S., LL.B. [Ⓒ Tuttle,T.&H.]
Herren, Karen Hassell ....'71 '97 C.232 B.A. L.770 J.D. [Ⓐ Slover&L.]
Herrera, Anita M. '57 '92 C.945 B.B.A. L.831 J.D.
(adm. in PA; not adm. in DC) [Ⓒ McGuirewoods]
*PRACTICE AREAS: Energy; Utilities; Securities.
Herrera, Mitsuko R. '69 '00 C.112 B.A. L.276 J.D.
(adm. in CA; not adm. in DC) [Ⓐ Miller&V.]
*PRACTICE AREAS: Telecommunications Law; Cable TV; Local Government Law; Copyrights; Trademarks.
Herrick, W. Michael ....'43 '77 C.205 B.S. L.904 J.D. [Ⓒ Elias,M.T.&H.]
Herring, Charniele '69 '97 C.1356 B.A. L.128 J.D.
(adm. in VA; not adm. in DC) [Ⓐ Leftwich&D.]
*PRACTICE AREAS: Telecommunications; Civil Litigation; Criminal Defense.
Herrington, Matthew J. ....'67 '94 C.823 B.A. L.976 J.D. [Ⓐ Williams&C.]
*PRACTICE AREAS: Commercial Litigation; Constitutional Law; International Criminal Law; Congressional Investigations; Media Libel.
Herrington, Wayne W., (AV) '45 '71
C.500 B.A. L.178 J.D. [Ⓒ Finnegan,H.F.G.&D.] (See Pat. Sect.)
*PRACTICE AREAS: Intellectual Property Litigation; Patent Litigation; Patent Protection; International Intellectual Property.
Herrling, Christopher J. ....'54 '81 C.696 B.A. L.128 J.D. [Ⓒ Wilmer,C.&P.]
Herrmann, John M. ....'69 '97 C.813 A.B. L.893 J.D. [Ⓐ Collier S.S.]
*PRACTICE AREAS: International Trade; Customs.
Herrmann, William H., III '62 '87 C.610 A.B. L.930 J.D.
(adm. in OH; not adm. in DC)
Assoc. Gen. Coun., Labor & Employ., Natl. Railroad Passenger Corp. (AMTRAK)

Herron, David E., II '— '92 C.375 B.S. L.986 J.D.
(adm. in KS; not adm. in DC; See Pat. Sect.) [Ⓒ Stevens,D.M.&M.]
*PRACTICE AREAS: Patent Prosecution; Electro-Mechanical Patents; Patent Litigation.
Herron, Sharon R. '63 '98 C.208 B.A. L.446 J.D.
(adm. in MD; not adm. in DC) [Ⓐ J.M.Riddick&Assoc.]
*PRACTICE AREAS: Family Law; Personal Injury; Medical Malpractice; Disability Benefits; Managed Care Contracts.
Herrup, Andrew R. ....'66 '91 C.477 B.A. L.1068 J.D. 1201 New York Ave., N.W.
Herschthal, Raymond ....'53 '80 C.102 B.A. L.1095 J.D. [Klein&C.]
Hersh, Matthew ....'67 '99 C.178 B.A. L.276 J.D. [Ⓐ Jenner&B.]
*PRACTICE AREAS: Litigation.
Hershaft, Michael ....'73 '00 C.597 B.S. L.145 J.D. [Ⓐ Cleary,G.S.&H.]
Hershey, J. Alexander ....'72 '99 C.604 B.A. L.273 J.D. [Ⓐ Patton B.]
Hershey, Tina Batra ....'74 '99 C.884 B.A. L.273 J.D. [Ⓐ Epstein B.&G.]
*PRACTICE AREAS: Health Law.
Hertz, Michelle D. ....'67 '98 C.732 B.A. L.1356 J.D. [Ⓐ Holland&K.]
*PRACTICE AREAS: Government Contracts; Litigation.
Hertz, Mitchell F., (AV) ....'64 '90 C.30 B.A. L.178 J.D. [Kirkland&E.]
*PRACTICE AREAS: Corporate Law; Energy; Communications.

Hertz & McElwaine, P.A.
(See Greenbelt, Maryland)

Hertzberg, Elisabeth M. '71 '98 C.893 B.S. L.273 J.D.
(adm. in MD; not adm. in DC) [Ⓐ Shaw P.]
*PRACTICE AREAS: Technology Law; Corporate Law.
Herzog, Mark E. '62 '87 C.260 B.S. L.273 J.D.
Adjunct Law Prof., D.C. Law Students in Court
Herzog, Richard B., (AV) ....'39 '64 C.951 B.A. L.309 LL.B. [Harkins C.]
*PRACTICE AREAS: Regulated Industries; Administrative Law; Appellate Litigation; Antitrust Law; Advertising.
Herzstein, Robert E., (AV) ....'31 '55 C&L.309 A.B., LL.B. [Miller&C.]
*PRACTICE AREAS: International Trade and Investment; Administrative Law; Litigation; Antitrust.
Heslep, Katherine W. ....'49 '87 C.216 B.A. L.128 J.D. 419 7th St., N.W.
Heslep, Thomas T., (BV) ....'49 '80 C.216 B.A. L.128 J.D. 419 7th St., N.W.
Hess, Catherine L. '73 '00
C.1128 B.S.W. L.124 J.D. [Ⓐ Porter W.M.&A.] (⊙Columbus, OH)
*PRACTICE AREAS: Litigation; Government Investigations; Health Care Fraud.
Hess, Edward D. '47 '71 C.260 B.S. L.893 J.D.
(adm. in VA; not adm. in DC) 3628 Reservoir Rd., NW‡
Hess, Michael A. ....'52 '77 C.602 B.A. L.273 J.D. Chf. Coun., Republic Natl. Comm.
Hess, Rebecca D. '72 '99 C.478 B.A. L.494 J.D.
(adm. in MN; not adm. in DC) [Ⓐ Finnegan,H.F.G.&D.]
*PRACTICE AREAS: Patent Prosecution; Pharmaceutical Patents; Biotechnology Patents; Patent Litigation.
Hess, Stephen J. ....'71 '99 C.227 B.A. L.976 J.D. [Ⓐ Covington&B.]
Hess, Wayne G. '63 '95 C.188 B.S. L.724 J.D.
(adm. in NJ; not adm. in DC) [Ⓐ Shaw P.] (⊙Mc Lean, VA)
*PRACTICE AREAS: Corporate.
Hessel, Arthur R., (AV) ....'42 '67 C.309 A.B. L.976 LL.B. [Hessel&A.]

Hessel and Aluise, P.C., (AV)
1050 Seventeenth Street, N.W., Suite 900, 20036
Telephone: 202-466-5300 Telecopier: 202-466-5508
Email: firm@hapc.com URL: http://www.lawyers.com/hesselandaluise
Arthur R. Hessel; Timothy J. Aluise. Of Counsel: Morton W. Schomer;—Kristin M. Neun; Mary E. Andrews (Not admitted in DC); Mario Greszes; Eric M. Keifer (Not admitted in DC); Christopher W. Hornig.
Housing and Urban Development Law, Real Estate and Real Estate Finance including Residential, Commercial and Health Care Facilities. Partnership and Business Association Matters, Legislative Services, Construction Law, Administrative Enforcement and Fair Housing Matters, Dispute Resolution and Litigation.
See Professional Biographies, WASHINGTON, DISTRICT OF COLUMBIA

Hessler, Stephen O., (BV) ....'50 '75 C.529 A.B. L.273 J.D. [Hessler&Assoc.]
Hessler & Associates, Chartered, (BV) ....729 15th Street, N.W., Suite 200
Hester, Theodore M., (AV) ....'— '70 C.280 A.B. L.309 J.D. [King&S.]
*PRACTICE AREAS: Governmental Practice.
Hester, Timothy C., (AV) ....'55 '83 C.951 B.A. L.477 J.D. [Covington&B.]
Heupel, Gerald F., Jr. ....'56 '80 C.1338 B.A.B.S. L.94 J.D. [Elias,M.T.&H.]
Hevener, Mary B., (AV) ....'52 '78 C.914 B.A. L.893 J.D. [Baker&M.]
*PRACTICE AREAS: Executive Compensation; Stock Options; Nonqualified Deferred Compensation Plans; Workforce Wide Benefits; Fringe Benefits.
Hewes, C. Alexander, Jr. ....'42 '70 C.30 B.A. L.904 J.D. [Hewes,G.L.&D.]
Hewes, Gelband, Lambert & Dann, P.C., (AV) .....1000 Potomac Street, N.W., Suite 300
Hewitt, Jason I. ....'69 '97 C.499 B.A. L.846 J.D. [Ⓐ Morgan,L.&B.]
Hewitt, Paul B., (AV) ....'49 '74 C.597 B.A. L.966 J.D. [Akin,G.S.H.&F.]
*PRACTICE AREAS: Antitrust; Trade Regulation; Litigation.
Heyder, Markus B. ....'62 '94 C.478 B.A. L.178 J.D. [Ⓐ Lovells]
*PRACTICE AREAS: Consumer Financial Services; Privacy; Federal Regulation; Commercial Litigation; Reinsurance.
Heyer, Thomas N. ....'56 '81 C.867 B.A. L.188 J.D. [Howrey S.A.&W.]
*PRACTICE AREAS: Antitrust; Complex Litigation; Intellectual Property.
Heylman, Paul M., (AV) ....'52 '78 C.722 B.A. L.904 J.D. [Schmeltzer,A.&S.]
*PRACTICE AREAS: Management Labor and Employment Law; ERISA; Maritime Law.
Heyward, Peter E. ....'53 '80 C.918 B.A. L.178 J.D. [Venable,A.B.H.&C.]
*PRACTICE AREAS: Financial Institutions; Corporate.
Heywood, Christopher M. ....'73 '98 C&L.128 B.A., J.D. [Ⓐ Pillsbury W.]
*PRACTICE AREAS: Property Tax Litigation; Civil Litigation.
Heywood, John Quentin '60 '87 C.35 B.S. L.30 J.D.
(adm. in MD; not adm. in DC) American Univ., Wash. Coll. of Law
Hiatt, Jonathan P ....'— '75 Gen. Coun., AFL-CIO
Hibbert, Robert G., (AV) ....'50 '75 C.178 B.A. L.904 J.D. [McDermott,W.&E.]
Hibey, David M. ....'— '98 C&L.276 B.A., J.D. [Ⓐ Morgan,L.&B.]
Hibey, Richard A., (AV) ....'41 '65 C.1031 A.B. L.276 J.D. [Winston&S.]
*PRACTICE AREAS: Litigation.
Hickerson, David A. ....'61 '87 C.880 B.A. L.477 J.D. [Weil,G.&M.]
*PRACTICE AREAS: Tax Litigation; Contract Disputes; Business and Partnership Disputes; Patent, Copyright and Trademark Litigation; White Collar Criminal Litigation.
Hickey, Anne T. ....'71 '98 C.385 B.A. L.228 J.D. [Ⓐ Akin,G.S.H.&F.]
Hickey, David T. '— '98 C.885 B.A. L.128 J.D.
(adm. in VA; not adm. in DC) [Ⓐ Reed S.]
*PRACTICE AREAS: Government Contracts; Export Compliance.
Hickey, J. Patrick, (P.C.), (AV) ....'39 '63 C.120 B.A. L.309 LL.B. [Shaw P.]
*PRACTICE AREAS: Litigation; Internal Investigations; Employment Litigation; White-Collar Crime; Criminal Law.
Hickey, Michael B. '65 '93 C.446 B.S. L.64 J.D.
(adm. in MD; not adm. in DC) Leg. Dir. & Coun., Health Ins. Assn. of Amer.
Hickey, Robert J. ....'37 '62 C.676 A.B. L.309 LL.B. 733 15th St. N.W.
Hickey, Robert N. ....'41 '66 C.116 B.S. L.276 J.D. [Sullivan&W.]
*PRACTICE AREAS: Business Law; Securities.
Hickman, David H., (AV) ....'41 '68 C&L.309 B.A., LL.B. [Covington&B.]

Hickman, Stephen D. '58 '89 C.425 B.S.S. L.1209 J.D.
(adm. in PA; not adm. in DC) Corp. Secy., National Assn. of Sec. Dealers, Inc.
Hickox, Kenneth N., Jr. ....'60 '95 C.276 B.S.F.S. L.945 J.D. [Ⓐ Howrey S.A.&W.]
*PRACTICE AREAS: Commercial Litigation; Insurance Coverage; Employment Discrimination; Civil Rights.
Hicks, Donell A. ....'75 '00 C.188 B.A. L.273 J.D. [Ⓐ Arter&H.]
*PRACTICE AREAS: Communications; Telecommunications.
Hicks, Kirkland L. '71 '97 C.1378 B.S. L.228 J.D.
(adm. in MD; not adm. in DC) Coun., Watson Wyatt Worldwide
Hicks, Laurinda L. ....'44 '87 C.575 B.A. L.999 LL.B. [Ⓒ Dickinson W.]
*PRACTICE AREAS: Intellectual Property; International Law.
Hicks, Michael M., (AV) '56 '82
C.311 B.A. L.273 J.D. [Bonner K.T.&C.] (⊙Rockville, MD)
*PRACTICE AREAS: Bank Directors and Officers Liability; Lender Liability; Legal Malpractice Defense; Medical Malpractice Defense; Negligence Defense.
Hicks, Perry '69 '01 C.30 B.A. L.893 J.D.
(adm. in NY; not adm. in DC) [Ⓐ Milbank,T.H.&M.]
*PRACTICE AREAS: Project Finance; Capital Markets; Banking Law.
Hieber, Christina J. ....'72 '99 C.197 B.A. L.273 J.D. [Ⓐ Finnegan,H.F.G.&D.]
*PRACTICE AREAS: Trademarks; Internet Law; Unfair Competition.
Hiebert, Peter N. ....'49 '81 C.178 B.A. L.276 J.D. [Winston&S.]
*PRACTICE AREAS: International Trade Law; Administrative Law; Legislative Practice.
Higdon, Robert E., (AV) ......'39 '73 C.446 B.A. L.904 J.D. 5027 Eskridge Terr., N.W.‡
Higginbotham, Patricia G. '52 '79 C.45 B.A. L.245 J.D.
Asst. Gen. Coun., Air Transport Assoc. of Americ.
*RESPONSIBILITIES: General Corporate.
Higgins, Anthony S. ....'69 '95 C.475 B.S. L.64 J.D. [Ⓐ Shaw P.]
*PRACTICE AREAS: Financial Institutions; Investment Companies; Securities Regulation; Electronic Commerce; Year 2000 Computer Conversion.
Higgins, Brian W. ....'64 '96 C.950 B.A. L.273 J.D. [Ⓐ Wilkinson B.K.]
*PRACTICE AREAS: Communications; Telecommunications Law.
Higgins, Lawrence P. '47 '73 C.734 B.S. L.502 J.D.
(adm. in MO; not adm. in DC) [Higgins,M.&S.]
Higgins, Mary B. ....'17 '40 L.180 LL.B. 3900 Watson Pl., N.W.
Higgins, Michael H. '72 '00 C.821 B.A. L.30 J.D.
(adm. in MD; and limited adm. in DC) [Ⓐ Thompson H.]
*PRACTICE AREAS: Transportation.
Higgins, Paul M. ....'68 '96 C.550 B.A. L.128 J.D. [Ⓐ Sughrue M.]
*PRACTICE AREAS: Trademark.
Higgins, Robert J., (AV) ....'41 '69 C.1113 A.B. L.276 J.D. [Dickstein S.M.&O.]
*PRACTICE AREAS: Securities Litigation; General Commercial Litigation; ERISA; RICO; Labor Litigation.
Higgins, Shannan E. ....'74 '99 C.103 B.A. L.276 J.D. [Ⓐ Dow,L.&A.]
Higgins, McGovern & Smith, L.L.C. ....1620 L Street, N.W. Suite 1210
High, Lance W. ....'66 '93 C.197 B.A. L.945 J.D. [Ⓐ Kirkpatrick&L.]
*PRACTICE AREAS: Litigation; Environmental Law.

Highsaw, Mahoney & Clarke, P.C., (AV) BB
Suite 590, 1050 Seventeenth Street, N.W., 20036
Telephone: 202-296-8500 Fax: 202-296-7143
Email: hmcjobc@worldnet.att.net URL: http://www.lawyers.com/highsawmahoneyclarke
James L. Highsaw (1970-1992); John O'B. Clarke, Jr. Of Counsel: William G. Mahoney.
General Practice before all Federal Courts, Departments and Agencies. Interstate Commerce, Labor Law, Aviation Law, Employee Benefits, Pension Plans, ERISA, Employment Discrimination, Complex Litigation.
See Professional Biographies, WASHINGTON, DISTRICT OF COLUMBIA

Hight, Helen M. '70 '00 C.696 B.S. L.1356 J.D.
(adm. in VA; not adm. in DC) [Ⓐ Vinson&E.]
*PRACTICE AREAS: Energy Law.
Hightower, Wanda Morris '— '87 C&L.930 B.S., J.D.
(adm. in GA; not adm. in DC) 60 Massachusetts Ave. N.E.
Hilbert, John W., III '70 '97 C.608 B.S.B.A. L.902 J.D.
(adm. in OH; not adm. in DC) 900 2nd St., N.E.
Hildebrandt, David A., (AV) ....'43 '70 C.101 B.S. L.966 J.D. [White&C.]
*PRACTICE AREAS: International Compensation; International Benefits.
Hildebrandt, Stephen Austin ....'47 '75 C.309 A.B. L.228 J.D. [Ⓒ Leventhal,S.&L.]
Hildebrant, Jeffrey P. ....'53 '87 C.262 B.S. L.425 J.D. [Ⓒ Holland&K.]
Hildreth, Linda A. ....'57 '88 C.881 A.B. L.893 J.D. [Ⓐ Venable,A.B.H.&C.]
*PRACTICE AREAS: Real Estate; Commercial Transactions.
Hiler, Bruce A. ....'52 '77 C.602 B.A. L.477 J.D. [O'Melveny&M.]
*PRACTICE AREAS: Securities Law; Securities Regulation and Enforcement; Litigation.
Hill, A. Karen, (AV) '43 '76 C.352 B.A. L.326 J.D.
V.P., Regul. Affs., American Gas Association (Law Department)
Hill, Brian A. ....'— '96 C.804 B.A. L.276 J.D. [Ⓐ Miller&C.]
*PRACTICE AREAS: Litigation; Defense Contract Fraud; Health Care Fraud; Civil Practice; Appellate Practice.
Hill, David J. ....'48 '73 C.276 B.S.F.S. L.309 J.D. [Ⓒ Skadden,A.S.M.&F.]
*PRACTICE AREAS: Energy; Litigation; Antitrust.
Hill, David W., (AV) '46 '77
C.870 B.S. L.273 J.D. [Finnegan,H.F.G.&D.] (See Pat. Sect.)
*PRACTICE AREAS: Alternative Dispute Resolution; Intellectual Property; Patents; Trademarks; Unfair Competition.
Hill, Dean G. ....'35 '62 C.352 B.A. L.276 LL.B. 1330 New Hampshire Ave., N.W.
Hill, Domiento C.R. '72 '00 C&L.446 B.S., J.D.
(adm. in MD; not adm. in DC) [Ⓐ Murrell&B.]
*PRACTICE AREAS: Complex Litigation; Class Actions.
Hill, Eleanor J. ....'— '75 C&L.259 B.A., J.D. [King&S.]
*PRACTICE AREAS: Special Matters/Government Investigations.
Hill, George E. '19 '51 C&L.339 B.S., J.D.
(adm. in IL; not adm. in DC) 3001 Veazey Terr., N.W.‡
Hill, Jerry C. ....'43 '71 C.112 B.A. L.128 J.D. [McDermott,W.&E.]
Hill, Jonathan B. ....'44 '69 C.164 A.B. L.94 J.D. [Dow,L.&A.]
Hill, Linda G. ....'65 '93 C.705 B.S./B.A. L.893 J.D. [Ⓐ Schmeltzer,A.&S.]
*PRACTICE AREAS: Employment Law; Management Labor Law.
Hill, Michael O. ....'57 '85 C.951 B.A. L.976 J.D. [Ⓒ Collier S.S.]
*PRACTICE AREAS: Environmental Law and Litigation.
Hill, Myron G., Jr. ....'36 '62 C&L.276 B.S., J.D. 3900 Calvert, N. W.
Hill, Rachael ....'74 '01 C&L.145 B.A., J.D. [Ⓐ Wilmer,C.&P.]
Hill, Richard E. ....'28 '55 C.885 B.S. L.902 LL.B. [Ⓒ Bell,B.&L.]
Hill, Robert Charles, (AV) ....'52 '80 C.1160 B.A. L.276 J.D. [Arent F.K.P.&K.]
*PRACTICE AREAS: Immigration and Nationality Law; Business Immigration; Employment Authorizations; Employment Visas; Labor Certifications.
Hill, Robert J. ....'— '87 C&L.477 B.A., J.D. [Reed S.]
*PRACTICE AREAS: Health Care.
Hill, Rustan J. ....'61 '95 C.446 B.S.A.E. L.911 J.D. [Ⓐ Arent F.K.P.&K.] ‡
*PRACTICE AREAS: Intellectual Property; Patents; Trademarks; Copyrights.
Hill, Stephen S., (AV) ....'51 '77 C&L.309 A.B., J.D. [Sidley A.B.&W.]
Hill, Steven F. ....'68 '97 C.880 B.A. L.597 J.D. [Ⓐ Arent F.K.P.&K.]
*PRACTICE AREAS: Commercial Litigation; International Trade.
Hill, Thomas C., (P.C.), (AV) ....'50 '76 C.674 A.B. L.188 J.D. [Shaw P.]
*PRACTICE AREAS: Litigation.

Hillard, Hugh Edwin, Jr. '56 '00 C.245 B.A. L.276 J.D.
(adm. in MD; not adm. in DC) [Ⓐ Dewey B.]
*PRACTICE AREAS: Energy.
Hilleboe, Douglas L. ... '57 '83 C.691 B.A. L.145 J.D. [Ⓒ Steptoe&J.]
*PRACTICE AREAS: Antitrust; Litigation; International Trade.
Hilliard, David E., (AV) ... '50 '75 C.383 B.B.A. L.893 J.D. [Wiley R.&F.]
*PRACTICE AREAS: Communications.
Hilliard, Thomas P. ... '65 '96 C&L.128 B.M.E., J.D. [Ⓐ Pillsbury W.] (See Pat. Sect.)
*PRACTICE AREAS: Intellectual Property Law; Patent Law.
Hills, Carla Anderson, (AV) ... '34 '59 C.813 A.B. L.976 LL.B. [Hills&S.]
Hills, Megan E. ... '66 '92 C.276 B.A. L.813 J.D. 725 12th St., N.W.
Hills, Roderick M., (AV) ... '31 '57 C&L.813 B.A., LL.B. [Hills&S.]

Hills & Stern, (AV)
1200 Nineteenth Street, N.W., 20036
Telephone: 202-822-1600 Fax: 202-822-1622
Roderick M. Hills; Carla Anderson Hills; Samuel A. Stern. Of Counsel: Irina Paliashvili.
International Finance, International Trade, Corporate Finance.
Reference: First Chicago Corp.
See Professional Biographies, WASHINGTON, DISTRICT OF COLUMBIA

Hilton, Steven M. ... '58 '86 C.674 B.A. L.276 J.D. [Buchanan I.]
*PRACTICE AREAS: Government Relations.
Himelfarb, P.J. ... '65 '91 C&L.446 B.S, J.D. [Ⓐ Weil,G.&M.]
Himelstein, Julieanne ... '56 '86 C.241 B.A. L.1162 J.D. Asst. U.S. Atty.
Himmelberg, John M., (AV) ... '46 '75 C.321 A.B. L.128 J.D. [O'Connor&H.]
Himmelman, Harold, (AV) ... '42 '67 C.951 B.A. L.569 LL.B. [Ⓒ Beveridge&D.]
*PRACTICE AREAS: Alternative Dispute Resolution; Mediation; Arbitration; Environmental and Administrative Law; Litigation.
Himstreet, Jeffrey O. ... '67 '93 C&L.950 B.S., J.D. [Ⓐ Bingham D.]
*PRACTICE AREAS: Securities.
Hinckle, Michael Henry ... '65 '96 C.888 B.S. L.273 J.D. [Ⓐ Kirkpatrick&L.]
*PRACTICE AREAS: FDA Regulatory.
Hinderliter, Jay D. ... '60 '85 C.225 B.A. L.623 J.D. 1440 New York Ave., N.W.
Hindin, Barbara A., (BV) '49 '74 C.966 B.A. L.1068 J.D.
Asst. Gen. Coun., Reg. Affs., Edison Elec. Institute
Hindin, Jennifer D. ... '71 '97 C.276 B.S.F.S. L.569 J.D. [Ⓐ Wiley R.&F.]
Hinding, John E. ... '72 '97 C.602 B.A. L.228 J.D. [Ⓐ Sutherland A.&B.]
*PRACTICE AREAS: Tax; Federal Tax; Tax Controversies; International Tax.
Hindman, Richard A. ... '53 '90 C.352 B.A. L.128 J.D. [Ⓒ Skadden,A.S.M.&F.]
Hinds, Richard deC., (AV) ... '41 '67 C.860 B.A. L.178 LL.B. [Ⓒ Cleary,G.S.&H.]

Hines, Deborah K., (AV) '54 '78 C.659 B.A. L.273 J.D.
1700 K Street, N.W., 20036
Telephone: 202-824-8124 Facsimile: 202-628-7220
Email: dkhines@aol.com URL: http://www.lawyers.com/lawyerhines
***PRACTICE AREAS: Personal Injury; Medical Malpractice; Premises Liability; Products Liability; Wrongful Death.**
Automobile Accidents, Motorcycle Accidents, Slip and Fall, Premises Liability, Wrongful Death, Product Liability, Lead Paint Poisoning, Asbestos, Inadequate Security Liability, Criminal Defense, Domestic Abuse, Personal Injury, Medical Malpractice.
See Professional Biographies, WASHINGTON, DISTRICT OF COLUMBIA

Hines, Doris Johnson '64 '91
C.688 B.S.E.E. L.273 J.D. [Finnegan,H.F.G.&D.] (See Pat. Sect.)
*PRACTICE AREAS: Patent Litigation; Electrical Patent Prosecution.
Hines, Eugene E. ... '26 '52 C.208 B.S. L.383 LL.B. 5303 29th St., N.W.‡
Hines, J. Michael, (AV) ... '45 '71 L.309 J.D. [Dow,L.&A.]
Hines, Jeffrey J., (AV) ... '59 '85 C&L.446 B.A., J.D. [Eccleston&W.] (⊙Fairfax, VA)
*PRACTICE AREAS: Insurance Defense Law; Professional Malpractice Law; Securities Litigation; Legal Malpractice Law; Appellate Practice.
Hines, William J. '23 '48 C.800 L.424 LL.B.
(adm. in IL; not adm. in DC) 5232 Macomb St., N.W.‡
Hinger, Cathy A. ... '73 '01 C&L.446 B.A., J.D. [Ⓐ Piper M.R.&W.]
Hinko, Valerie ... '69 '99 C.976 B.A. L.273 J.D. [Ⓐ Crowell&M.]
Hinsch, Claudia '67 '95 C.119 B.A. L.276 J.D.
(adm. in MD; not adm. in DC) [Ⓐ Latham&W.]
*PRACTICE AREAS: Employee Benefits; ERISA.
Hinshaw, Scot A. ... '74 '99 C.446 B.A. L.276 J.D. [Ⓐ Hunton&W.]
*PRACTICE AREAS: Labor and Employment; Litigation.
Hinson, Dale B., (AV) ... '31 '59 C.623 B.B.A. L.846 LL.B. 1400 Sixteenth Street, N.W.
Hinton, Shirley A. ... '67 '95 C&L.339 B.A., J.D. [Ⓐ Kirkpatrick&L.]
*PRACTICE AREAS: Investment Company Law; Securities.
Hirasuna, Robert Y. ... '50 '78 C.103 B.A. L.128 J.D. [Leonard,S.&D.]
*PRACTICE AREAS: Energy; Public Utility Law.
Hird, David B. ... '50 '77 C.188 A.B. L.569 J.D. [Weil,G.&M.]
*PRACTICE AREAS: Litigation; Environmental Law; Insurance Law; Superfund; RCRA.

Hird, Frederick S., Jr., (AV) '35 '60 C&L.309 A.B., LL.B.
1850 M Street, N.W., Suite 280, 20036
Telephone: 202-778-0878 Fax: 202-778-0688
Federal Administrative and Regulatory Law; General Practice.
See Professional Biographies, WASHINGTON, DISTRICT OF COLUMBIA

Hirn, Richard J. ... '54 '79 C.311 B.A. L.904 J.D. 5335 Wisconsin Ave., NW, Ste. 440
Hirsch, Andrea E. ... '56 '84 C.813 A.B. L.770 J.D. [Ⓐ Kuder,S.&F.]
*PRACTICE AREAS: Domestic Relations; Trust and Estates.
Hirsch, Emil, (AV) ... '51 '76 C&L.446 B.S., J.D. [O'Connor&H.]
*PRACTICE AREAS: Business Litigation; Bankruptcy Law; Corporate Law.
Hirsch, Rebecca L. ... '68 '94 C.597 B.A. L.861 J.D. [Ⓐ Sutherland A.&B.]
*PRACTICE AREAS: Commercial Litigation; Business Litigation.
Hirsch, Robert B., (AV) ... '26 '50 C&L.273 LL.B. [Arent F.K.P.&K.]
*PRACTICE AREAS: Mergers and Acquisitions; Securities Litigation; Corporate Law; Commercial Real Estate.
Hirsch, Sam ... '62 '95 C.691 B.A. L.309 J.D. [Jenner&B.]
*PRACTICE AREAS: Litigation.
Hirsch, Sara Wynne '74 '99 C.893 B.S. L.945 J.D.
(adm. in VA; not adm. in DC) Securities and Exchange Commission
Hirschberg, D. Jeffrey ... '45 '71 C.966 B.S. L.436 J.D. 1225 Connecticut Ave. NW
Hirschfelder, Beth L. ... '73 '98 C.659 B.A. L.309 J.D. [Ⓐ Akin,G.S.H.&F.]
*PRACTICE AREAS: Litigation.
Hirschhorn, Eric L., (AV) ... '46 '68 C.145 B.A. L.178 J.D. [Winston&S.]
*PRACTICE AREAS: Export Regulation; Customs Law; Legal Ethics and Professional Responsibility; Federal Litigation; Foreign Asset Control.
Hirselj, Rebecca A. '74 '99 C.201 B.A L.910 J.D.
(adm. in MD; not adm. in DC) [Ⓐ Schmeltzer,A.&S.]
*PRACTICE AREAS: Commercial Litigation; Franchise Law.
Hirsh, David A. ... '59 '83 C.1036 B.A. L.276 J.D. [Harkins C.]
*PRACTICE AREAS: Transportation Law; Regulated Industries; Administrative Law; Commercial Contracts; Appellate Litigation.
Hirsh, Harold L. ... '17 '73 C.446 B.S. L.904 J.D. 2801 New Mexico Ave., N. W.‡
Hirsh, Merril Jay, (AV) ... '57 '82 C.604 B.A. L.309 J.D. [Ross,D.&B.]
Hirshberg, Robert L. ... '19 '76 C.604 A.B. L.273 J.D. 2122 Bancroft Pl., N.W.‡

Hirst, Peter G. '50 '81 C.668 B.A. L.809 J.D.
(adm. in CA; not adm. in DC) [Ⓐ Berliner,C.&J.]
*PRACTICE AREAS: Commercial Litigation; Oil and Gas Law; State Public Utility Proceedings; Natural Gas Pipeline Litigation.
Hise, James C. ... '26 '51 C.339 A.B. L.273 J.D. Chief Coun., Natl. Guard Bur.
Hiser, Helen F. ... '56 '89 C.970 B.A. L.904 J.D. [Ⓐ Baach R.&L.P.]
*PRACTICE AREAS: Insurance Law; Environmental Law.
Hiskey, Timothy Grant '60 '96 C.277 B.A. L.1280 J.D.
(adm. in VA; not adm. in DC) Staff Atty., Council of the Dist. of Columbia
Hissong, Drew, Ph.D. ... '67 '99 C.381 B.S. L.930 J.D. [Ⓐ Sughrue M.] (See Pat. Sect.)
*PRACTICE AREAS: Intellectual Property Law.
Hitchcock, Cornish F. ... '51 '75 C.145 B.A. L.276 J.D. 1100 17th St., NW, 10th Fl.
Hitchcock, Steven D. ... '67 '94 C.696 B.A. L.893 J.D. [Ⓐ Bell,B.&L.]
*PRACTICE AREAS: Communication Law; Civil Litigation.
Hiznay, Juliet Dawn '— '97 C.93 B.A. L.1356 J.D.
(adm. in VA; not adm. in DC) [Ⓐ Foley&L.]
*PRACTICE AREAS: Litigation; Commercial Law; Business Law; Misdemeanors; Theft.
Hjelm, Lars-Erik A. ... '63 '89 C.659 B.A. L.245 J.D. [Ⓒ Akin,G.S.H.&F.]
*PRACTICE AREAS: International Trade.
Hnath, Gary M., (AV) ... '58 '85 C.475 B.A. L.309 J.D. [Venable,A.B.H.&C.]
*PRACTICE AREAS: Intellectual Property and Complex Civil Litigation.
Ho, Deborah Y. ... '69 '96 C.813 B.A. L.500 J.D. [Ⓐ Brand&F.]
*PRACTICE AREAS: Civil Litigation; Regulatory Law; Legislative Practice; Election Law.
Ho, Raymond J. ... '69 '94 C.277 B.S.E.E. L.1059 J.D. [Ⓐ Sonnenschein N.&R.] (Pat.)
*PRACTICE AREAS: Patents; Trademarks; Copyrights; Trade Secrets.

Ho, Jane, The Law Offices of
(See North Potomac)

Hoag, Aaron D. '71 '96 C.367 B.A. L.309 J.D.
(adm. in MD; not adm. in DC) Trial Atty., US Dept. of Justice
Hoare, Michael J. ... '41 '68 C.94 B.A. L.904 J.D. [M.J.Hoare]
Hoare, Michael J., P.C. ... 530 F St. Terr. SE
Hobbes, Carol G. '54 '81 C.893 B.A. L.896 J.D.
(adm. in MD; not adm. in DC) Children's Foundation
Hobbes, Thomas B. ... '50 '79 C.902 B.A. L.420 J.D. 3000 Connecticut Avenue N.W.
Hobbet, Richard Duane ... '27 '51 C&L.352 B.A., J.D. 1440 New York Ave. N.W.
Hobbie, Charles A. ... '45 '77 C.197 B.A. L.273 J.D. Dep. Gen. Coun., AFGE, AFL-CIO
Hobbs, Caswell O., III, (AV) ... '41 '67 C.378 B.S. L.659 LL.B. [Morgan,L.&B.]
Hobbs, Charles A., (AV) ... '28 '57 C.976 B.A. L.273 J.D. [Hobbs,S.D.&W.]
Hobbs, Howard C.M. '49 '76 C&L.425 B.A., J.D.
(adm. in FL; not adm. in DC) [Ⓐ Seyfarth S.]
*PRACTICE AREAS: Labor and Employment.
Hobbs, J. Timothy, (AV) ... '41 '69 C.911 B.A. L.30 J.D. [Wiley R.&F.]
*PRACTICE AREAS: Trademarks; Copyrights; Unfair Competition.
Hobbs, Straus, Dean & Walker, LLP, (AV)
2120 L Street, N.W., Suite 700 (⊙Oklahoma City, OK; Port., OR)
Hobday, George F., Jr. ... '67 '94 C.197 A.B. L.276 J.D. [Ⓐ Hogan&H.]
Hobelman, Carl D., (P.C.) ... '31 '60 C.188 B.C.E. L.309 LL.B. [Ⓒ LeBoeuf,L.G.&M.]
*PRACTICE AREAS: Utilities; Trade and Professional Associations.
Hobson, Carol P. M. ... '66 '95 C.040 B.A. L.188 J.D. 1225 11th St., N.W.
Hobson, Everett K. ... '38 '74 C.922 B.S. L.329 J.D. 8220 Eastern Ave., N.W.
Hobson, James R., (AV) ... '37 '72 C.188 B.A. L.767 J.D. [Ⓒ Miller&V.]
*PRACTICE AREAS: Communications Law; Administrative Law; Public Utilities Law.
Hoch, Ramon R. '59 '91 C.378 B.S.Ch.E. L.1209 J.D.
(adm. in VA; not adm. in DC; Pat.) [Ⓐ Fitch,E.T.&F.] (⊙Chgo., IL)
*PRACTICE AREAS: Intellectual Property.
Hochberg, Jerome A., (AV) ... '33 '60 C.188 B.A. L.309 J.D. [Ⓒ Arter&H.]
Hochberg, Philip R., (AV) ... '— '66 C.823 B.S. L.273 LL.B. [Ⓒ Verner,L.B.M.&H.]
*PRACTICE AREAS: Sports Law; Entertainment Law; Communications Law.
Hochberg, Sheldon E., (AV) ... '43 '68 C.178 A.B. L.309 LL.B. [Steptoe&J.]
*PRACTICE AREAS: Administrative Law; International Law; Title Insurance Law.
Hochman, Michael C. ... '69 '96 C.659 B.A. L.93 J.D. [Ⓐ Dow,L.&A.]
Hockenberry, John F. '45 '74
C.674 A.B. L.976 J.D. Assoc. Gen. Coun., Washington Post, The
Hockenbury, John C. ... '51 '87 C.509 B.A. L.276 J.D. [Drinker B.&R.]
*PRACTICE AREAS: Directors and Officers Liability Insurance.
Hockey, Laurel Ann ... '64 '89 C.945 B.A. L.273 J.D. [Ⓒ Cohen M.] ⊙
*PRACTICE AREAS: Small Business Law; Business Law; Corporate Law; Government Contracts.

Hodes, Ulman, Pessin & Katz, P.A., (AV)
1025 Thomas Jefferson Street NW, 20007 ⊙
Telephone: 202-338-2172
Email: Hupk@Hupk.com URL: http://www.HUPK.com
Carl S. Silverman. Of Counsel: Bert Neil Bisgyer.
Estates and Trusts, Elder Law, Probate, Taxation, Corporate, Environmental, Health Law, Franchise Law, Litigation, Family Law, White Collar Criminal Defense, Intellectual Property, E-Commerce, Executive Compensation, Banking and Commercial Transactions, Real Estate, Construction and Land Use/Zoning, Associated Civil Trial and Appellate Practice Before all State and Federal Courts and Administrative Agencies. Labor and Employment, Bankruptcy and Creditors Rights.
Towson, Maryland Office: 901 Dulaney Valley Road, Suite 400, 21204. Telephone: 410-938-8800. FAX: 410-938-8806.
Columbia, Maryland Office: 10500 Little Patuxent Parkway, Suite 650. Telephone: 410-740-2000; D.C. Direct: 301-596-1717. FAX: 410-740-2005.
Havre de Grace, Maryland Office: 131 South Union Avenue, Second Floor, 21078. Telephone: 410-938-8800.
Bethesda, Maryland Office: 3 Bethesda Metro Center, 7th Floor, 20814. Telephone: 301-596-1717.
Bel Air, Maryland Office: 112 South Main Street, Suite 102, 21014-3818. Telephone: 410-893-2333.
Cambridge, Maryland Office: 317 Crusader Road, 21613. Telephone: 410-228-1040.
See Professional Biographies, WASHINGTON, DISTRICT OF COLUMBIA

Hodge, Michael V. ... '47 '92 C.705 Ed.M. L.276 J.D. D.C. Revenue Bond Program
Hodges, Ann C. '63 '95 C.893 B.A. L.1209 J.D.
(adm. in VA; not adm. in DC) 2300 N St., N.W.‡
Hodges, John A., (AV) ... '40 '68 C.309 A.B. L.178 LL.B. [Wiley R.&F.]
*PRACTICE AREAS: International Trade; Product Liability; Energy; Environmental.
Hodges, Kevin M. ... '65 '90 C.103 Sc.B. L.276 J.D. [Williams&C.]
*PRACTICE AREAS: Commercial Litigation; False Claims Act; Government Contracts; Litigation; Professional Liability.
Hodgson, Morgan D., (AV) ... '47 '73 C.681 A.B. L.813 J.D. [Steptoe&J.]
*PRACTICE AREAS: Labor and Employment Law; Employee Benefits; Civil Litigation; Whistleblower Litigation.
Hodson, Kenneth J. '13 '38 C&L.378 A.B., LL.B.
(adm. in WY; not adm. in DC) Mag. Gen.‡
Hodson, Robert E. ... '08 '47 C.273 A.B. L.904 LL.B. 1200 18th St., N.W.
Hoe, E. Sanderson, (AV) ... '47 '73 C.164 B.A. L.188 J.D. [McKenna&C.]
*PRACTICE AREAS: Governments Contracts; Telecommunications; Litigation.
Hoecker, James J. ... '— '78 C.592 B.A. L.966 J.D. [Swidler B.S.F.]
*PRACTICE AREAS: Energy; Administrative Law; Corporate.
Hoefling, Matthew J. '74 '00 C&L.602 B.A., J.D.
(adm. in NC; not adm. in DC) [Ⓐ Jones,D.R.&P.]
Hoegle, Robert L. ... '52 '77 C&L.276 A.B., J.D. [Carter,L.&M.]
*PRACTICE AREAS: Litigation; Telecommunications; Federal Agency Law.
Hoekstra, Kathlyn B. ... '52 '81 C.20 B.A. L.365 J.D. Address Unknown

Hoel, John E. '42 '74 C.502 B.S. L.276 J.D.
(adm. in VA; not adm. in DC; See Pat. Sect.) [Morgan&F.]
Hoenicke, Jeanne E. '58 '85 C.674 A.B. L.145 J.D.
V.P. & Dep. Gen. Coun., Amer. Council of Life Ins.
*RESPONSIBILITIES: Federal Taxes.
Hofer, Patrick F. .... '61 '86 C&L.893 B.A., J.D. [Hogan&H.]
*PRACTICE AREAS: Insurance; Insurance Coverage Litigation; Litigation.
Hoff, Martha W. '49 '78 C.966 B.A. L.276 J.D.
Asst. Dean & Dir. of Graduate Studies, Georgetown Univ. Law Ctr.
Hoff, Paul S., (AV) ....'42 '68 C.309 B.A. L.976 LL.B. [Garvey,S.&B.]
*PRACTICE AREAS: International Trade; Export Regulation; Administrative Law; Legislative Process.
Hoff, William J. '07 '32 C.976 B.A. L.178 LL.B.
(adm. in NY; not adm. in DC) 1529 29th St., N.W.‡
Hoff-Patrinos, Kathryn E., (AV) ....'52 '83 C.918 B.A. L.309 J.D. [Ⓐ Milbank,T.H.&M.]
Hoffheimer, Lawrence S., (AV) .... '37 '62 C.473 B.S. L.150 LL.B. [Hoffheimer&D.]
Hoffheimer & Downey, P.C., (AV) ....1250 24th St., N.W.
Hoffinger, Adam S., (AV) ....'56 '83 C.855 B.A. L.262 J.D. [Piper M.R.&W.]
*PRACTICE AREAS: White Collar Crime; Securities; Health Care; Complex Civil Litigation.
Hoffman, Cathy .... '59 '89 C.165 B.A. L.494 J.D. [Arnold&P.]
*PRACTICE AREAS: Antitrust; Litigation.
Hoffman, Christy ....'55 '90 C.569 B.A. L.563 J.D. [Ⓒ James&H.]
*PRACTICE AREAS: Labor Law.
Hoffman, E. Leslie, III '47 '72 C&L.923 A.B., J.D.
(adm. in WV; not adm. in DC) [Piper M.R.&W.]
*PRACTICE AREAS: Litigation; White Collar Crime; White Collar Defense.
Hoffman, Gary M., (AV) '46 '71 C.659 B.S.E.E. L.273 J.D.
[Dickstein S.M.&O.] (Pat.)
*PRACTICE AREAS: Intellectual Property Law; Computer Law; Litigation.
Hoffman, Greer '68 '94 C.831 B.A. L.273 J.D.
(adm. in PA; not adm. in DC) Sr. Atty. & Advsr.
Hoffman, Jason Foster ....'— '97 C.1036 B.A. L.659 J.D. [Ⓐ Howrey S.A.&W.]
*PRACTICE AREAS: Intellectual Property; Commercial Litigation.
Hoffman, Joel E., (AV) ....'37 '60 C.569 B.A. L.976 LL.B. [Ⓒ Sutherland A.&B.]
*PRACTICE AREAS: Food, Drug and Cosmetic Law; Drug and Medical Device Regulation; Food and Drug Regulation; Product Safety; Deceptive Trade Practices.
Hoffman, Julie K. ....'— '95 C.610 B.B.A. L.150 J.D. [Ⓐ Latham&W.]
*PRACTICE AREAS: Securities.
Hoffman, Kenneth R., (AV) '52 '77
C.443 B.S. L.446 J.D. [Venable,A.B.H.&C.] (⊙Balt., MD)
*PRACTICE AREAS: Taxation Law; Employee Benefits Law.
Hoffman, Laura L. .... '66 '94 C.94 B.S. L.273 J.D. [Ⓐ Kilpatrick S.]
*PRACTICE AREAS: Government Contracts; Litigation.
Hoffman, Leora K. .... '— '83 C.659 B.A. L.1019 J.D. 1714 N St., N.W.
Hoffman, Leslie R. .... '72 '97 C&L.260 B.A., J.D. [Ⓐ Steptoe&J.]
Hoffman, Linda M., (AV) .... '53 '85 C.597 B.A. L.1209 J.D. [Freilicher&H.]
*PRACTICE AREAS: Immigration and Nationality Law.
Hoffman, Matthew M. ....'69 '96 C.309 A.B. L.976 J.D. [Ⓐ Shea&G.]
Hoffman, Richard B. '45 '72 C.188 B.S. L.309 J.D.
Dir. & Sr. Coun., The Justice Manaagement Institute
Hoffman, Richard S., (AV) .... '19 '48 C.16 L.724 LL.B. 1800 M St., N.W.
Hoffman, Steven J. '53 '80
C.33 B.A. L.569 J.D. Sr. Legis. Coun., N.Y.S. Off. of Fed. Affairs
Hoffman, Steven K., (AV) ....'48 '84 C.228 B.A. L.976 J.D. [James&H.]
*PRACTICE AREAS: Litigation; Labor and Employment; Insurance; College and University Law.
Hoffman, Susan M., (AV) ....'54 '80 C.347 B.A. L.273 J.D. [Crowell&M.]
*PRACTICE AREAS: Adoption Law; Child Abuse and Neglect; Child Custody; Domestic Violence; Mediation.
Hoffman, Tara Laster '71 '99 C.886 B.S. L.128 J.D.
(adm. in VA; not adm. in DC; See Pat. Sect.) [Ⓐ Roylance,A.B.&G.]
*PRACTICE AREAS: Intellectual Property; Intellectual Property Litigation.
Hoffman, Whitney S. ....'66 '94 C.659 B.A. L.1017 J.D. [Ⓐ Madden&P.]

Hoffman, Wasson & Gitler, P.C.
(See Arlington, Virginia)

Hoffmann, Joseph L. '57 '85 C.309 B.A. L.911 J.D.
(adm. in PA; not adm. in DC) [Maines&L.]
Hoffmann, Sandra A. ....'57 '86 C.350 B.S. L.477 J.D. Res. for the Future
Hoffmann, Sydney J., (AV) .... '52 '86 C&L.276 B.A., J.D. [Ⓒ P.Cacheris] ⊙
*PRACTICE AREAS: Criminal Litigation.
Hoffmeister, Bruce F. ....'61 '86 C.339 B.S. L.910 J.D. [Feldesman,T.L.F.&B.]
*PRACTICE AREAS: Estate Planning; Probate; Individual and Corporate Tax; Tax-Exempt Organizations.
Hoffmeister, Thaddeus A. '70 '98 C.512 B.A. L.588 J.D.
(adm. in IN; not adm. in DC) Soldier's Legal Coun./Admin Law Atty.
Hoffpauir, Norma Briscoe ....'64 '94 C.446 B.S. L.329 J.D. [Ⓐ Trow&K.]
*PRACTICE AREAS: Immigration and Nationality Law.
Hofmann, Tina F. ....'60 '90 L.309 J.D. [Ⓐ Morrison&F.]
Hogan, E. Desmond .... '68 '96 C.25 B.A. L.329 J.D. [Ⓐ Hogan&H.]
*PRACTICE AREAS: Litigation; Civil Rights.
Hogan, Janice Marchiafava '66 '95 C.453 B.S. L.276 J.D.
[Ⓐ Hogan&H.] (⊙Phila., PA)
*PRACTICE AREAS: Biotechnology.
Hogan, Nandita '71 '96 C.264 B.A. L.831 J.D.
(adm. in PA; not adm. in DC) [Ⓐ Dechert]
*PRACTICE AREAS: Investment Management; Financial Services Law.

Hogan & Hartson L.L.P., (AV) BR
555 13th Street, N.W., 20004-1109 ⊙
Telephone: 202-637-5600 Telex: 89-2757 Cable Address: "Hogander Washington" Fax: 202-637-5910
URL: http://www.hhlaw.com
Members of Firm: Frank J. Hogan (1877-1944); Nelson T. Hartson (1887-1976); Jonathan L. Abram; Gil A. Abramson (Resident, Baltimore, Maryland Office); Donna Lady Alpi; Patricia Riley Ambrose; Audrey J. Anderson; Jeanne S. Archibald; Edwin P. Aro (Resident, Denver, Colorado Office); Deborah Taylor Ashford; Helen Clark Atkeson (Resident, Denver, Colorado Office); Matthew T. Bailey; Steven E. Ballew; James T. Banks; Suzanne A. Barr; George P. Barsness; Raymond J. Batla, Jr.; George Beall (Resident, Baltimore, Maryland Office); Richard K.A. Becker (Resident, McLean, Virginia Office); David W. Beier (Not admitted in DC); Joseph C. Bell; Barbara Bennett; Douglas L. Beresford; Lee E. Berner (Resident, McLean, Virginia Office); Laura Besvinick (Resident, Miami, Florida Office); Peter R. Bisio; Lisa Bonanno; David W. Bonser; John W. Borkowski (Also practicing in New Orleans, Louisiana); Donna A. Boswell; Christine Bougis (Resident, Paris, France Office); William J. Bowman; Marc H. Bozeman (Resident, Los Angeles, California Office); Robert P. Brady; Dr. Max Braeuer (Resident, Berlin, Germany Office); Patricia A. Brannan; Dr. Eckhard Bremer (Resident, Berlin, Germany Office); Rebecca B. Bronson (Not admitted in DC); Stanley J. Brown (Resident, McLean, Virginia Office); Andrea M. Bruce; Thomas N. Bulleit, Jr.; David W. Burgett; Carol W. Burton (Resident, Denver, Colorado Office); Raymond S. Calamaro; Alan F. Cariddi (Resident, Paris, France); George U. Carneal; Robert B. Cave; Michael L. Cheroutes (Not admitted in DC; Resident, Denver, Colorado Office); Alphonso A. Christian, II; Claudette M. Christian; Jacqueline P. Cleary; Nancy Andreas Clodfelter (Resident, Denver, Colorado Office); Ty Cobb; Vincent H. Cohen; Michael D. Colglazier (Resident, Baltimore, Maryland Office); Joseph G. Connolly, Jr.; Jonathan A. Constine; John W. Cook (Resident, Colorado Springs, Colorado Office); Robert L. Corn-Revere; Maryanne Courtney; Michele C. Coyle (Resident, Los Angeles, California Office); Colin W. Craik (Prague, Czech Republic and London, England Offices); Celine Jimenez Crowson; Daniel M. Davidson; W. Sidney Davis, Jr. (Resident at 100 Park Avenue, New York, New York Office);

(This Listing Continued)

Hogan & Hartson L.L.P. (Continued)

Margaret A. de Lisser; Edward S. Desmarais, Jr.; Sara-Ann Determan; John F. Dienelt; Edward C. Dolan; Agnes Pek Dover; Edward C. Duckers; Robert B. Duncan; David Dunn (Resident at 100 Park Avenue, New York, New York Office); Isabel P. Dunst; Alan L. Dye; Steven M. Edwards (Resident at 100 Park Avenue, New York, New York Office); Bijan-Emmanuel Eghbal (Resident, Paris France Office); Claud v. S. Eley; E. Tazewell Ellett; Kevin D. Evans (Resident, Denver, Colorado Office); Frank J. Fahrenkopf, Jr.; Michele C. Farquhar; Prentiss E. Feagles; Ira M Feinberg (Resident at 100 Park Avenue, New York, New York Office); Douglas A. Fellman; Miriam L. Fisher; Ari Q. Fitzgerald; Howard I. Flack; William P. Flanagan (Resident, McLean, Virginia Office); David M. Fox (Not admitted in DC); Jonathan S. Franklin; Amy Bowerman Freed (Resident, Baltimore, Maryland Office); Sean R. Gallagher (Resident, Denver, Colorado Office); Aleksander Galos (Resident, Warsaw, Poland Office); John M. Gardner (Resident, Denver, Colorado Office); Mark D. Gately (Resident, Baltimore, Maryland Office); James A. Gede, Jr. (Resident, Baltimore, Maryland Office); Jeffrey S. George (Resident, Colorado Springs, Colorado Office); Jay E. Gerber (Resident at 100 Park Avenue, New York, New York Office); James R. Ghiselli (Resident, Boulder, Colorado Office); Gerald E. Gilbert (Resident, McLean, Virginia Office); Bruce W. Gilchrist; Gardner F. Gillespie; C. Michael Gilliland; J. Warren Gorrell, Jr.; Kevin G. Gralley (Resident, Baltimore, Maryland Office); Darrel J. Grinstead; Christopher J. Hagan; Martin J. Hahn; William F. Haigney (Resident at 100 Park Avenue Office); Benton R. Hammond; Karen M. Hardwick; Michele Sasse Harrington (Resident, McLean, Virginia Office); Joseph M. Hassett; Catriona Hatton (Resident, Brussels, Belgium Office); Kenneth J. Hautman (Resident, McLean, Virginia Office); Elizabeth Blossom Heffernan; Dr. Jan Hegemann (Resident, Berlin, Germany Office); David J. Hensler; Patrick F. Hofer; Steven P. Hollman; Whitney A. Holmes (Resident, Denver, Colorado Office); Howard M. Holstein; Janet Pitterle Holt; Craig A. Hoover; Richard T. Horan, Jr. (Resident, McLean, Virginia Office); James A. Hourihan; William Mike House; Eve N. Howard; George F. Hritz (Resident at 100 Park Avenue, New York, New York Office); James A. Hutchinson; Stephen J. Immelt (Resident, Baltimore, Maryland Office); Maciej Jamka (Resident, Warsaw, Poland Office); Harry T. Jones, Jr.; Jonathan S. Kahan; Henry D. Kahn (Resident, Baltimore, Maryland Office); Robert H. Kapp; Mark A. Kass; Steven M. Kaufman; John C. Keeney, Jr.; Nevin J. Kelly; J. Hovey Kemp; Robert J. Kenney, Jr.; Michael L. Kidney; David A. Kikel; Carol Weld King; David P. King (Resident, Baltimore, Maryland Office); Sandra Folsom Kinsey; Duncan S. Klinedinst (Resident, McLean, Virginia Office); Edward L. Korwek; Joseph G. Krauss; William J. Kubida (Resident, Colorado Springs, Colorado Office); Dr. Wolfgang Kuhla (Resident, Berlin, Germany Office); S. Gregg Kunzi; Raymond A. Kurz; Gary Jay Kushner; Robert D. Kyle; Stuart M. Langbein; Kevin J. Lanigan; Philip C. Larson; C. Stephen Lawrence (Resident, Irvine, California Office); Mitchell J. Lazris; Dirk Leermakers (Resident, Brussels, Belgium Office); Robert F. Leibenluft; Lewis E. Leibowitz; Craig A. Lewis; Scott R. Lilienthal; John R. Lilyestrom; Kevin J. Lipson; Timothy A. Lloyd; Laura E. Loeb; Walter G. Lohr, Jr. (Resident, Baltimore, Maryland Office); Milan Lovíšek (Resident, Prague, Czech Republic Office); Jeffrey Alan Lowe; David L. Lubitz (Resident, Los Angeles, California and Tokyo, Japan Offices); Stuart Lubitz (Resident, Los Angeles, California Office); Daniel H. Maccoby (Resident, London, England Office); Paul D. Manca; Thene M. Martin (Resident, Baltimore, Maryland Office); Warren H. Maruyama; Mary Anne Mason; George W. Mayo, Jr.; Mark E. Mazo; Scott D. McClure; Mark S. McConnell; Janet L. McDavid; Thomas L. McGovern III; James G. McMillan; David Medine; Bruce C. Mee (Resident, Paris, France); Dr. Gernod Meinel (Resident, Berlin, Germany Office); George H. Mernick, III; Martin Michaelson; Georg Miggel (Resident, Berlin, Germany Office); Evan Miller; George W. Miller; H. Todd Miller; Barbara F. Mishkin; Austin S. Mittler; William L. Monts, III; Jean S. Moore; Dennis K. Moyer (Resident, McLean, Virginia Office); Jeffrey W. Munk; Kornelia Nagy-Koppany (Not admitted in United States); Helen A. Nastasia (Resident, McLean, Virginia Office); William L. Neff; J. Patrick Nevins; Karol Lyn Newman; David Newmann; William D. Nussbaum; Gerald E. Oberst, Jr. (Resident, Brussels, Belgium Office); Maureen O'Bryon; Bob Glen Odle; Linda L. Oliver; Nancy Doerr O'Neil; Christopher D. Ozeroff (Resident, Boulder, Colorado Office); Christine M. Pallares (Resident, Third Avenue New York, N.Y. Office); Jeffrey D. Pariser; Bruce E. Parmley; Richard J. Parrino (Resident, McLean, Virginia Office); Bert R. Peña; Robert B. Pender, Jr.; Patrick K. Perrin (Resident, Boulder, Colorado Office); M. Elizabeth Peters; Peter J. Pettibone (Resident at Moscow, Russia and Third Avenue, New York, N.Y. Offices); John E. Porter (Not admitted in DC); Philip D. Porter (Resident, McLean, Virginia Office); John M. Potter (Resident, Los Angeles, California Office); Sharis Arnold Pozen; E. Barrett Prettyman, Jr.; Michael A. Proett (Resident, London, England Office); Gerard J. Prud'homme; Patrick M. Raher; Prof. Dr. Peter Raue (Resident, Berlin, Germany Office); John A. Redmon (Resident at 100 Park Avenue, New York, New York Office); Jonathan T. Rees; Scott H. Reisch (Resident, Denver, Colorado Office); Terri Steinhaus Reiskin; Thomas E. Repke (Resident, Baltimore, Maryland Office); Marissa G. Repp; Jai H. Rho (Resident, Los Angeles, California Office); Leslie S. Ritts; John G. Roberts, Jr.; William R. Roberts (Resident, Boulder, Colorado Office); Steven N. Robinson; Richard S. Rodin; Paul G. Rogers; Peter A. Rohrbach; Peter J. Romeo; James J. Rosenhauer; Mace J. Rosenstein; Howard J. Rosenstock; Steven J. Routh; Fabrice Rué (Resident, Paris, France); James P. Ruggeri; George A. Salter (Resident at 100 Park Avenue, New York, New York Office); David J. Saylor; Todd D. Schafer; William C. Schmidt; Jeffrey G. Schneider (Resident, Third Avenue New York, N.Y. Office); Friedrich Tobias Schöne (Resident, Berlin, Germany Office); Dr. Carl-Stephan Schweer (Resident, Berlin, Germany Office); David J. Scott (Resident, Denver, Colorado Office); Lawrence R. Seidman (Resident, Baltimore, Maryland Office); Dr. Hans M. Seiler (Resident, Berlin, Germany Office); Jeffrey N. Shane; Jeffrey K. Shapiro; James E. Showen; David L. Sieradzki; Howard S. Silver; Michael J. Silver (Resident, Baltimore, Maryland Office); Richard S. Silverman; Paul C. Skelly; Edward C. Sledge (Resident, Baltimore, Maryland Office); David W. Smail; Maree F. Sneed; Lorraine Sostowski; Peter S. Spivack; Timothy Charles Stanceu; John S. Stanton; Stuart G. Stein; Steven B. Steinborn; Mark A. Sterling; John T. Stough, Jr.; Clifford D. Stromberg; Mary Anne Sullivan; Thomas J. Sweeney, III (Resident at 100 Park Avenue, New York, New York Office); Jan Tanzer (Resident, Prague, Czech Republic Office); Dennis H. Tracey, III (Resident at 100 Park Avenue, New York, New York Office); Lyndon M. Tretter (Resident at 100 Park Avenue, New York, New York Office); Helen R. Trilling; Andrew J. Trubin (Resident, Third Avenue New York, N.Y. Office); Shawna R. Tunnell; Albert W. Turnbull; Niki Frangos Tuttle (Resident, Denver, Colorado Office); Ralph S. Tyler (Resident, Baltimore, Maryland Office); Craig H. Ulman; Craig A. Umbaugh (Resident, Denver, Colorado Office); Christine A. Varney; Ann Morgan Vickery; Christian von Hammerstein (Resident, Berlin, Germany Office); Eric Von Salzen; Dr. Christoph Wagner (Resident, Berlin, Germany Office); Morris Waisbrot (Resident, 100 Park Avenue, New York, N.Y. Office); Robert J. Waldman; Donis G. Walker (Denver and Colorado Springs, Colorado Offices); Nicola S. Walker (Resident, London, England Office); Christopher J. Walsh (Resident, Denver, Colorado Office); Phyllis V. Wan (Resident, Denver, Colorado Office); Howard S. Weber (Resident at 100 Park Avenue, New York, New York Office); Richard L.A. Weiner; David F. Wertheimer (Resident at 100 Park Avenue, New York, New York Office); T. Clark Weymouth; Douglas P. Wheeler; Zdzislaw W. Wieckowski (Resident, Warsaw, Poland Office); Marcy J. Wilder; Michael Cunningham Williams; Edward C. Wilson, Jr.; Ronald J. Wiltsie, II; Joel S. Winnik; David A. Winter; Pamela G. Winthrop; Marcia A. Wiss; William H. Wright (Resident, Los Angeles, California Office); Erik B. Wulff; Michael K. Wyatt; Emily M. Yinger (Resident, McLean, Virginia Office); Joseph H. Young (Resident, Baltimore, Maryland Office). Counsel: Merry C. Anderson; Steven F. Barley (Resident, Baltimore, Maryland Office); Dale E. Bonner (Resident, Los Angeles, California Office); Pavel Bradac (Resident, Prague, Czech Republic Office); Lance D. Bultena; Brooke Bumpers; James C. Chen; Laurie A. Clarke; Donald B. Dillport (Resident at 100 Park Avenue, New York, New York Office); Kevin M. Downey; Cynthia A. Feigin (Resident at 100 Park Avenue, New York, New York Office); Kathryn L. Goetz (Resident at 100 Park Avenue, New York, N.Y. Office); Jacquelyn E. Grillon; James C. Hansen (Resident at 100 Park Avenue, New York, New York Office); Karis A. Hastings; Sten A. Jensen; Lynn G. Kamarck; Michele A. Kulerman; Gerald J.S. Laporte; Melvin E. Lefkowitz; Norma B. Levy (Resident at 100 Park Avenue, New York, New York Office); Timothy J. Lockhart (Resident, McLean, Virginia Office); Helen P. McClure; Gordon L. Miller (Not admitted in DC); Douglas R. M. Nazarian (Resident, Baltimore, Maryland Office); Stephen B. Parker (Resident, McLean, Virginia Office); Steven C. Petersen (Resident, Boulder, Colorado Office); Aurel Pinter (Resident, Budapest, Hungary Office); John Houston Pope (Resident at 100 Park Avenue, New York, New York Office); Robert N. Rabecs; Beth L. Roberts; Margaret E. Roggensack; Robert C. Satrom (Resident, Moscow, Russia Office); Ellen Siegler; Frank T. Spano (Resident at 100 Park Avenue, New York, New York Office); Robert L. Spencer; Jolanta Sterbenz; Lowell R. Stern; Christopher S. Stokes; J. Michael Thesz, Jr.; Stephen G. Vaskov; Paul W. Virtue; Mitchell E. Zamoff; Stephen J. Zempolich. European Counsel: Vuong Van Bac (Resident, Paris, France Office). Of Counsel: John P. Arness; Kathryn Webb Bradley (Resident, Denver, Colorado Office); Dean W. Crowell; Marvin J. Diamond; Robert J. Elliott; Andrew J. Kilcarr; Bogudar Kordasiewicz (Resident, Warsaw, Poland Office); Dennis J. Lehr; Lee Loevinger; Sherwin J. Markman; Seymour S. Mintz; William S. Reyner, Jr.; John J. Ross; David E. Skaggs; Jac K. Sperling (Resident, Denver, Colorado Office); Peter W. Tredick; Bruce S. Wolff; Clayton K. Yeutter. Resident Associates: Kim M. Allen; Nalini P. Anand; Ana Cristina Arumi; Rose Marie L. Audette; Frank Bacelli; Elizabeth V. Baltzan; Bartley L. Barefoot; Sonia Gupta Barros (Not admitted in DC); Olesya Vladimirovna Barsukova-Spandau; Lynne M. Baum (Not admitted in DC); John B. Beckman; Keith J. Benes (Not admitted in DC); Leslie Anne Benton; Beverly L. Blank; Robert M. Blue; Pamela Morris Blumenthal; Deborah L. Boardman (Not admitted in DC); Ann M. Boeckman; Ronald P. Brower; Catherine T. Brown; René E. Browne; Ellen Dunham Bryant; Taylor L. Burke; Paul A. Burkett; Mary Ellen Callahan; Bruce D. Campbell Jr.; Gary J. Campbell; Christopher P. Cardaci; Alison B. Cera;

(This Listing Continued)

Hogan & Hartson L.L.P. (Continued)

Carol B. Chesley; Eun Ah Choi (Not admitted in DC); Kaija M. Clark; Karen Renfree Clark; John Clasby; Tracy-Elizabeth Clay; Kevin C. Clayton; Helene F. Combe (Not admitted in the United States); Susan M. Cook; Craig T. Cronheim (Not admitted in DC); Edward C. Crooke; Andrea T. Cummings (Not admitted in DC); Alice T. Valder Curran; William J. Curtin, III; David F. Cutter; Richard L. Davis; Brad Deutsch; M. Colette Devine; Margaret E. DiPentima; Kristen A. Donoghue; Yaron Dori; Alexander E. Dreier; Aleksandar Dukic; Alison H. Eaton; William L. Elder; Evan R. Farber (Not admitted in DC); Teresa Maurea Pantoja da Costa Faria (Not admitted in DC); Adam S. Feuerstein; Marshall Fitz; Ute Foshag (Not admitted in the United States); Jody M. Foster; Brian D. Fowler; Shinobu K. Garrigues; John F. Gaul; Robert A. Geckle, Jr.; Angela Elizabeth Giancarlo (Not admitted in DC); Joseph E. Gilligan; Victoria W. Girard; Stephanie J. Gold; F. Joseph Gormley; Charles S. Greene, III (Not admitted in DC); Jonathan M. Grossman; Michael Grynberg; Catherine R. Guttman-McCabe; William S. Haft; Christopher R. Hall; Christopher Todd Handman; Lisa A. Harig; Lorane F. Hebert; George F. Hobday, Jr.; E. Desmond Hogan; Janice Marchiafava Hogan; Brian H. Hook; Alex Hortis (Not admitted in DC); Theresa M. Howald; Deborah James (Not admitted in DC); LaShawn M. Johnson (Not admitted in DC); Mary L. Johnson; Kathleen Marie Joyce; William P. Kahn; Jonathan S. Kallmer; H. Deen Kaplan; David P. Kassebaum; Elizabeth L. Katkin; R. Daniel Keating; Ellen Swennes Kennedy; Behnaz L. Kibria; Christopher L. Killion; Alethia N. King; Josh Klatzkin; Audrey E. Klein; Douglas A. Klein; Maya Renata Kobersy; Ajay Kuntamukkala; Anna J. Kurian; Keith D. Larson; Mark D. Learn; F. William LeBeau; Katherine R. Leibowitz; Adam K. Levin; Melissa B. Levine; Erik J. Lichter; Ronald G. London; Harriette H. Lopp; Robert Mahini; Robert G. Malkin; Timothy C. Maples; Lynda K. Marshall; David L. Martin; Michael F. Mason; Brian E. Mazurek; Susan Rotatori McAuliffe; John E. McCarrick; S. Tovan McDaniel; John J. McDonald; Shelly Lynn McGee; Scott A. McIntosh; Cynthia M. McKnight; Margaret E.K. Middleton; Kathy Marlo Miljanic; Emily A. Miller; Erica S. Mintzer; Anthony L. Miranda; Arthur C. Mok; R. Latane Montague, IV; Jeremy Todd Monthy; Audrey Elaine Moog; Thomas C. Morey; Natasha T. Muhammad; Theresa K. Nabors; James Namiki; David D. Nelson (Not admitted in DC); Jeffrey C. Nelson; William F. Nixon; Jeffrey S. O'Dwyer; Benjamin K. Olson (Not admitted in DC); Gregory F. Parisi; Alexander J. Park; Edward B. Parks, II; Aarti J. Patel; Mark Paulding; Scott D. Peterman; G. Laurence Plaisted; Martin A. Price; Stephen F. Propst; Jennifer A. Purvis; John M. Rafferty; Omyra M. Ramsingh; Siobhan C. Rausch; Marcos Rios (Not admitted in the United States); Margaret Rhinelander Rizzi; Mark J. Robertson; Dean A. Romhilt; Evan L. Rosenfeld; Corey W. Roush; Andrew M. Rowell; Martha L. Russo (Not admitted in DC); Amit Saluja; Sherri A. Braden Sampson; David R. San Martin; Atul Saran; Nathan H. Saunders; Catherine Schenker; Christopher A. Schindler; Jodi K. Scott; Kelleen McGinnis Scott; Sumeet Seam; Lori J. Searcy; Catherine S. Seery; Scott A. Shail; Tamar Shapiro (Not admitted in DC); Kevin G. Shaw; Brian L. Shiker; Charles E. Sieving; Kerri R. Sikorski; Elizabeth J. Silva; Melanie A. Simmons; Paula Primost Skalaban; James O. Smith; Melinda A. Sossamon; Gina M. Spade; Kimberly J. Stahlman; Deborah Kim Staudinger; Gabriel Stephen Sterling, III; Catherine E. Stetson; Joy E. Sturm; Marta I. Tanenhaus; Adam B. Tankel; Sharon L. Tasman; Farinaz S. Tehrani; C. Jeffrey Tibbels; Patrick D. Traylor; Robert Tyler; Natalie S. Tynan; Ann M. Ungvarsky; Michael J. Vernick; Katharine T. Vestal; Emily C. Vitan (Not admitted in DC); Naomi Abe Voegtli; Kevin L. Vold; Peggy Yu Ping Wang; Te Mika S. Warner (Not admitted in DC); Shaundra L. Watson; Steven P. Willmore (Not admitted in DC); Gordon C. Wilson; Kevin J. Wolff; Grace Sing-Fein Yeh; Jenny Wu Yeh; Lucinda T. Yeh (Not admitted in DC).

Antitrust and Trade Regulation, Appellate and Supreme Court Practice, Arbitration, Mediation and Alternative Dispute Resolution, Communications, Corporate and Securities, Education, Election Law, Energy and Natural Resources, Environmental, Estate Planning and Administration, Financial Institutions and Transactions, Food, Drug and Medical Devices, Franchise Law, Government Contracts, Health, Immigration, International Trade, Internet Law, Labor and Employment, Legislation, Litigation, Privatization, Private Equity, Project Finance, Public Finance, Real Estate, Sports Law, Sports Facilities Law, Tax, Technology Licensing and Intellectual Property (Copyright, Trademark and Patent Law), Transportation, and Venture Capital.

Berlin, Germany Office: Potsdamer Platz 1, 10785. Telephone: 49-30 726 115-0. Fax: 49-30 726 115-100.
Brussels, Belgium Office: Avenue des Arts 41, 1040. Telephone: (32.2) 505.09.11. Fax: (32.2) 505.09.96.
Budapest, Hungary Office: Nagy & Pintér, Hogan & Hartson Law Office, Budapest V., Szabadság tér 7-9, 1054. Telephone: (36-1) 302-9050. Fax: (36-1) 302-9060.
London, England Office: One Angel Court, EC2R 7HJ. Telephone: +(44) 207-367-0200. Fax: +(44) 207-367-0220.
Moscow, Russia Office: 14, Prechistenskiy Pereulok, 119034. Telephone: 7 (095) 797-9900. Fax: 7 (095) 797-9961.
Paris, France Office: Cariddi, Mee, Rué, Avocats Associés à la Cour de Paris, 12, rue de la Paix, 75002. Telephone: (33-1) 42.61.57.71. Fax: (33-1) 42.61.79.21.
Prague, Czech Republic Office: Hogan & Hartson, advokátní kanceláře, Tržiště 13, 118 00. Telephone: (420-2) 2211-7111. Fax: (420-2) 2211-7222.
Tokyo, Japan Office: Shinjuku Center Building, 46th Floor, 25-1 Nishi-Shinjuku 1-Chome, Shinjuku-ku, 163-0646. Telephone: 813-5908-4070. Fax: 813-5908-4071.
Warsaw, Poland Office: Kancelaria Prawna Hogan & Hartson M. Jamka, A. Galos i Wspólnicy Spólka Ko., Al. Jana Pawla II 25, 00-854. Telephone: (48-22) 653-4200. Fax: (48-22) 653-4250.
Baltimore, Maryland Office: 111 South Calvert Street. Telephone: 410-659-2700. Fax: 410-539-6981.
Boulder, Colorado Office: 1800 Broadway. Telephone: 720-406-5300. Fax: 720-406-5301.
Colorado Springs, Colorado Office: Two North Cascade Avenue. Telephone: 719-448-5900. Fax: 719-448-5922.
Denver, Colorado Office: 1200 Seventeenth Street. Telephone: 303-899-7300. Fax: 303-899-7333.
Irvine, California Office: 3 Park Plaza. Telephone: 949-250-4550. Fax: 949-833-0976.
Los Angeles, California Office: 500 S. Grand Avenue. Telephone: 213-337-6700. Fax: 213-337-6701.
McLean, Virginia Office: 8300 Greensboro Drive. Telephone: 703-610-6100. Fax: 703-610-6200.
Miami, Florida Office: 1111 Brickell Avenue. Telephone: 305-459-6500. Fax: 305-459-6550.
New York, New York Office: 885 Third Avenue. Telephone: 212-409-9800. Fax: 212-409-9801.
Other New York, New York Office: 875 Third Avenue. Telephone: 212-918-3000. Fax: 212-918-3100.
Philadelphia, Pennsylvania Office: 1515 Market Street. Telephone: 215-864-8087. Fax: 215-569-4963

See Professional Biographies, WASHINGTON, DISTRICT OF COLUMBIA

Hogans, Daniel Lee . . . . . '67 '93 C.1356 B.S. L.945 J.D. [[A] Groom]
*PRACTICE AREAS: Retirement Benefit Plans; Executive Compensation; Securities.
Hoge, Christopher G., (AV) . . . . . '48 '75 C.575 B.A. L.30 J.D. [Crowley,H.&F.]
*PRACTICE AREAS: Civil Law; Criminal Litigation; Professional Negligence.
Hogen, Philip N. '44 '70 C.56 B.S. L.793 J.D.
(adm. in SD; not adm. in DC) [[G] Holland&K.]
*PRACTICE AREAS: Indian Law; Gaming Law; Administrative Law.
Hogge, Mark L. . . . . . '53 '84 C&L.1209 B.A., J.D. [Dorsey&W.] (Pat.)
*PRACTICE AREAS: Unfair Competition Litigation; Patent Infringement; Antitrust; Trademark Infringement; Trade Dress.
Hoghooghi, Babak . . . . . '63 '95 C.769 B.S. L.276 J.D. [[A] Skadden,A.S.M.&F.]
Hogwood, Stephen F., (AV) . . . . . '52 '77 C.797 B.A. L.228 J.D. [Bracewell&P.]
*PRACTICE AREAS: Energy Project Development; Energy Finance; Energy Acquisitions; International Transactions; International Finance.
Hohengarten, William A. . . . . . '60 '95 C.685 B.A. L.976 J.D. [[A] Jenner&B.]
*PRACTICE AREAS: Litigation.
Hohenthaner, Thomas G. . . . . . '59 '90 C.793 B.A. L.893 J.D. [[A] Chadbourne&P.]
Hoing, Debra H. . . . . . '59 '85 C.867 B.A. L.94 J.D. Assn. of Trial Lawyers of Amer.
Holbein, James R. . . . . . '51 '79 C.112 B.A. L.45 J.D. [[G] Stewart&S.]
*PRACTICE AREAS: International Trade; Alternative Dispute Resolution; Customs Law; Regional Trade Agreements.
Holbrook, Lanae . . . . . '65 '93 C.463 B.S. L.472 J.D. [Fried,F.H.S.&J.]
*PRACTICE AREAS: Corporate; Securities.
Holcomb, R. Bruce, (AV) . . . . . '56 '81 C.354 B.A. L.273 J.D. [Dickstein S.M.&O.]
*PRACTICE AREAS: Litigation; Antitrust Law; Securities Law; Insurance Law.
Holdaway, Jeffrey A. . . . . . '58 '85 C.101 B.S. L.178 J.D. Marriott Drive (⊙Washington)
Holdaway, Jeffrey A. '58 '85 C.101 B.S. L.178 J.D.
V.P. & Ass. Gen. Coun., Marriott Intl., Inc. (⊙Washington)
*RESPONSIBILITIES: General Corporate; Hotel Development and Operations; Acquisitions.
Holden, James P., (AV) . . . . . '32 '60 C.174 B.S. L.276 [Steptoe&J.]
*PRACTICE AREAS: Tax Controversies.
Holden, Mary Gayle . . . . . '— '80 C.695 B.A. L.893 J.D. [[G] Foley&L.]
*PRACTICE AREAS: Corporate Law; Business Law; Trusts and Estates; Real Estate Law.
Holderman, Richard A., (AV) . . . . . '38 '68 C.692 B.A. L.893 LL.B. [Spencer,G.&H.]

Holdmann, Lee F., Chartered
(See Bethesda, Maryland)

Holiday, Edith E. . . . . . '52 '77 C&L.260 B.S., J.D. 3239 38th St., N.W.
Holik, Susan Z. . . . . . '55 '79 C.951 B.A. L.273 J.D. 3900 Wisconsin Ave. N.W.
Holinsky, Ronald A. '70 '97 C.923 B.S.B.A. L.64 J.D.
(adm. in MD; not adm. in DC) [[A] Kirkpatrick&L.]
*PRACTICE AREAS: Investment Management; Securities.
Holladay, Marcus B. . . . . . '66 '92 C.88 B.S. L.245 J.D. [[S] Ross,D.&B.]
Holland, Brendan . . . . . '73 '99 C.893 B.A. L.945 J.D. [[A] Shaw P.]
*PRACTICE AREAS: Communications.
Holland, H. Brian . . . . . '66 '00 C.860 B.A. L.904 J.D. [[A] Jones,D.R.&P.]
Holland, J. Kent, Jr., (AV) '53 '79
C.658 B.S. L.884 J.D. [[G] Wickwire G.] (⊙Vienna, VA)
*PRACTICE AREAS: Public Contract, Federal Grant, Environmental and Construction Law.
Holland, John G. . . . . . '— '95 C.101 B.A. L.178 J.D. [[A] Latham&W.]
Holland, Pamela . . . . . '62 '88 C.454 B.A. L.128 J.D. 3900 Wisconsin Ave., N.W.
Holland-Chatman, Jan A. . . . . . '64 '91 C.811 B.A. L.276 J.D. Off. of Corp. Coun.

Holland & Knight LLP, (AV) BR
2099 Pennsylvania Avenue, N.W., Suite 100, 20006 ⊙
Telephone: 202-955-3000 Fax: 202-955-5564
URL: http://www.hklaw.com

Washington, D.C. Members and Associates: R. Gregory Bailey; Markham Ball; Timothy J. Bloomfield; Stephen A. Bogorad; Jeffrey F. Boothe; Leigh A. Bradley; David W. Briggs; Thomas Willcox Brooke; Henry J. Brothers II; John M. Bryson, II; Harold R. Bucholtz; Kevin A. Buford; Tanja H. Castro; J. Michael Cavanaugh; Robert M. Chasnow; Michael W. Clancy; Louise B. Cobbs; Jerald S. Cohn; Mark D. Colley; Christopher H. Collins; Peter M. Connolly; Stephen J. Crimmins; Carol DiBattiste; G. Richard Dunnells; Stuart S. Dye; Amy L. Edwards; Philip Tucker Evans; Eric Fishman; Tillie K. Fowler; Michael M. Gaba; Norman M. Glasgow, Sr.; Norman M. Glasgow, Jr.; Richard M. Gold; Arthur B. Goodkind; Steven D. Gordon; Robert L. Gorham; T. Wayne Gray; Christopher B. Hanback; Michael R. Hatcher; Robin Belton Hayes; Eric B. Holmberg; Dennis M. Horn; Edward W. Hummers, Jr.; Margot Smiley Humphrey; Thomas J. Hutton; David S. Kahn; Samuel P. Kastner; Paul J. Kiernan; Paul F. Kilmer; Bernard Koteen; Deborah L. Kramm; Weldon H. Latham; Richard E. Lear; Lawrence R. Liebesman; George T. Magee; Kenneth L. Marcus; Carol L. B. Matthews; Donald H. Meiers; Peter T. Meszoly; David P. Metzger; Nelson F. Migdal; William J. Mutryn; Christopher A. Myers; Alan Y. Naftalin; Charles R. Naftalin; La Fonte Nesbitt; Stephen D. Niles; Ronald A. Oleynik; Timothy P. O'Shea (Not admitted in DC); Mark J. Palchick; Alan K. Palmer; Frank K. Peterson; Whayne S. Quin; Robert L. Rhodes, Jr.; Marvin Rosenberg; Steven S. Rosenthal; Michael J. Ruane; Alban Salaman; Tara A. Scanlon; Janis B. Schiff; Christopher "Kip" Schwartz; Stephen Brett Shapiro; Gerald E. Sikorski; Richard P. Sills; Theodore S. Silva, Jr.; David C. Silver; Andrew W. Stephenson; Scott Andrew Sterling; Jeffrey B. Stern; Janet R. Studley; John E. Theberge; Paul M. Thomas; Charles D. Tobin; Jeffery A. Tomasevich; Charles Welch Tiedemann; Alan P. Vollmann; Susan Lee Voss; Frederick P. Waite; Mel S. Weinberger; Stephen J. Weiss; George Y. Wheeler, III; Joseph B. Whitebread, Jr.; David L. Winstead; Lawrence J. Wolk; Robert T. Wray; Xiaohua Zhao. Senior Counsel: Robert H. Bradner; Dennis L. Bryant; Brian E. Burke; John M. Burkman; Rebecca F. Duke; Stephanie A. Lipinski Galland (Not admitted in DC); Alvin J. Geske; Dirk Haire; Jeffrey P. Hildebrant; Lloyd J. Jordan (Not admitted in DC); Keith D. Lind; Jim J. Marquez; Madonna A. McGwin; Douglas J. Patton; Sung Park Reynolds; Miguel Eugenio Rubio; Steven A. Sadel; Kevin J. Smith; Roderic L. Woodson;—Ethan Arenson; Lynn Estes Calkins; Christopher L. Camarra; Kara L. Daniels; Olga L. Del Rio; Steven L. Dube (Not admitted in DC); Elizabeth M. Dunne (Not admitted in DC); Jonathan M. Epstein; Andrea M. Ewart; Jennifer A. Goodrich (Also at New York, N.Y. Office); Margaret A. Hackbarth; Joanna Han; John A. Henry, Jr.; Michelle D. Hertz; Craig A. Holman; Dennis R. Hughes; Karlyn J. Hunter (Not admitted in DC); Kristen Schmeelcke Ittig; Lisa L. Jackson; Stephen J. Jeffries; John G. Kelly; Joseph L. Kitto; Eileen C. Lee; Michael L. Lefkowitz; Thomas D. Leland; Kelly Lodde (Not admitted in DC); Christopher G. Margand; Anthony R. Masiello; Selwa Masri (Not admitted in DC); Geraldine R.S. Mataka; David M. Matuszewski; Leslie S. McAdoo-Brobson; Marc E. Miller; David A. O'Connor; Rafe Petersen; Bryan R. Phillips (Not admitted in DC); Scott M. Pritchett; Christopher S. Reynolds (Not admitted in DC); Femi S. Richards (Not admitted in DC); Leo G. Rydzewski; Curtis L. Sano; Amee A. Shah; Christine Moseley Shiker (Not admitted in DC); C. Kristopher Simpson; Dorothy C. Slovak; Bernard L. Smith; C. Dennis Southard IV; Leslie S. Spitalney; Damien G. Stewart; Sarah E. Tippet; Douglas A. Tucker; Maria A. Whitehorn (Not admitted in DC); David C. Whitestone (Not admitted in DC); Kimberly Young. Of Counsel: Stuart Marshall Bloch; David M. Bond; Philip N. Hogen (Not admitted in DC); William B. Ingersoll; Marc Levy; Thomas F. Railsback; Richard S. Weinstein (Not admitted in DC).

General Practice including: Administrative and Rulemaking, Agriculture, Aircraft Finance and Leasing, Alternative Dispute Resolution, American Continental Group Strategic Affiliation, Antitrust, Trade Regulation and Competition, Appropriations, Asia Practice, Automotive and Automotive Finance, Aviation, Bankruptcy and Creditors' Rights and Workouts, Beverage Alcohol, Bond Financing, Brownfields, Cash Flow and Asset-Based Lending, Charitable Giving, Civil Rights, Computer Law, Construction and Design, Consumer Fraud, Contests and Sweepstakes, Corporate and Securities, Corporate Compliance, Corporate Finance, Corporate Relocation and Expansion, Corporate Trust, Customs and International Trade, Development of Regional Impact, Directors' and Officers' Liability, Diversity Counseling, Drug & Medical Devices, E-Commerce, Education, Elder Law, Elections-State, Eminent Domain and Condemnation, Energy, Entertainment, Environmental, Equipment Financing & Leasing, ERISA, Employee Benefits and Executive Compensation, Financial Institutions, Franchise, Gaming, Government (GSA) Real Estate Contracting, Government - Illinois State & Local, Government - State and Local, Government Contracts, Grants and Infrastructure, Growth Management, Concurrency and Land Use, GSA Holdovers and Condemnation Disputes, Health Care, Hospitality, Hotel, Timeshare and Resort Development, Housing, Immigration, Nationality and Consular Law, Indian Law, Individual and Private Business, Insurance, Intellectual Property, Intellectual Property - Copyright, Intellectual Property - Patent, Intellectual Property - Trademark, International, International Procurement, Internet Resource Team, Investment Funds and Asset Management, Israel Practice, Labor and Employment Relations, Legislation - Federal, Legislation - State, Litigation - Airline Accident, Litigation - Appellate, Litigation - Class Action, Litigation - Commercial, Litigation - Criminal Defense, Litigation - Environmental, Litigation - International, Litigation - Securities, Marital and Family Law, Maritime and Shipping, Media & Communications, Mergers and Acquisitions, Mexico Practice, Mining, Minority Initiative, Money Laundering, Mortgage Banking, Natural Gas, OSHA, Personal Injury and Wrongful Death, Power Plant and Transmission Line Siting, Privatization, Product Liability, Project Finance, Public Finance, Public Law, Public Utilities, Rapid Response Team, Real Estate Investment Trusts (REITs), Real Estate Environmental and Land Use, Retail Development, Retail Real Estate, Securitization of Financial Assets, Space Law, Sports - Amateur, Sports - Collegiate Administration and Compliance, Sports Practice, Syndication and Partnership, Taxation - Federal, Taxation - State and Local, Taxation - Tax-Exempt Organizations, Technology, Technology Transfers & Licensing, Telecommunications, Transportation, Trusts and Estates, U.S. Export Compliance, Venture Capital, Water/Wastewater Practice, White Collar Crime.

Annapolis, Maryland Office: State Circle Building, 47 State Circle, Suite 400, 21401. Telephone: 410-263-7800. Fax: 410-263-3768.
Atlanta, Georgia Office: One Atlantic Center, 1201 West Peachtree Street, N.E., Suite 2000, 30309. Telephone: 404-817-8500. Fax: 404-881-0470.
Bethesda, Maryland Office: 3 Bethesda Metro Center, Suite 800, 20814. Telephone: 301-654-7800. Fax: 301-656-3978.
Boston, Massachusetts Office: 10 St. James Avenue, 02116. Telephone: 617-523-2700. Fax: 617-523-6850.
Bradenton, Florida Office: 1001 3rd Avenue West, Suite 600, 34205. Telephone: 941- 748-7076. Fax: 941-747-9774.
Chicago, Illinois Office: 55 West Monroe Street, Suite 800, 60603. Telephone: 312-263-3600. Fax: 312-578-6666.
Fort Lauderdale, Florida Office: One East Broward Boulevard, Suite 1300, 33301. Telephone: 954-525-1000. Fax: 954-463-2030.
Helsinki, Finland Office: Holland & Knight Oy, Pohjoisesplanadi 33, FIN-00100. Telephone: 358-9-684-1520. Fax: 358-9-6841-5252.
Jacksonville, Florida Office: 50 North Laura Street, Suite 3900, 32202. Telephone: 904-353-2000. Fax: 904-358-1872.
Lakeland, Florida Office: 92 Lake Wire Drive, 33815. Telephone: 863-682-1161. Fax: 863-688-1186.
Los Angeles, California Office: 633 West Fifth Street, 21st Floor, 90071. Telephone: 213-896-2400. Fax: 213-896-2450.
Melbourne, Florida Office: 1499 South Harbor City Boulevard, Suite 201, 32901. Telephone: 321-951-1776. Fax: 321-951-1849.

(This Listing Continued)

Holland & Knight LLP (Continued)

Mexico City, Mexico Office: Paseo de los Tamarindos 400-B, Piso 2, Delegación Cuajimalpa, Bosques de las Lomas, 05120, Mexico, D.F. Telephone: 011-525-261-1866. Fax: 011-525-261-1867.
Miami, Florida Office: 701 Brickell Avenue, Suite 3000, 33131. Telephone: 305-374-8500. Fax: 305-789-7799.
New York, New York Office: 195 Broadway, 10007. Telephone: 212-513-3200. Fax: 212-385-9010.
Northern Virginia: 1600 Tyson Boulevard, Suite 700, McLean, Virginia, 22102. Telephone: 703-720-8600. Fax: 703-720-8610.
Orlando, Florida Office: 200 South Orange Avenue, Sun Trust Building, Suite 2600, 32801. Telephone: 407-425-8500. Fax: 407-244-5288.
Portland, Oregon Office: 2300 U.S. Bancorp Tower, 111 Southwest Fifth Avenue, 97204. Telephone: 503-243-2300. Fax: 503-241-8014.
Providence, Rhode Island Office: One Financial Plaza, Suite 1800, 02903. Telephone: 401-751-8500. Fax: 401-553-6850.
Rio de Janeiro, Brazil Office: Rua de Assembléia, 58-10th Floor, 20011-000. Telephone: 011-55-21-2509-5050. Fax: 011-55-21-2221-9035.
San Antonio, Texas Office: Weston Centre, 112 East Pecan Street, Suite 2700, 78205. Telephone: 210-229-3000. Fax: 210-229-1194.
San Francisco, California Office: 50 California Street, Suite 2800, 94111. Telephone: 415-743-6900. Fax: 415-743-6910.
São Paulo, Brazil Office: Rua Pedroso Alvarenga, 1,284 - 10th Floor, Suite 102, 04531-000. Telephone: 011-55-11-3079-2300. Fax: 011-55-11-3079-2004.
Seattle, Washington Office: 2600 Pike Tower, 520 Pike Street, 98101. Telephone: 206-340-1825. Telecopier: 206-623-4363.
St. Petersburg, Florida Office: 200 Central Avenue, Suite 1600, 33701. Telephone: 727-896-7171. Fax: 727-822-8048.
Tallahassee, Florida Office: 315 South Calhoun Street, Suite 600, 32301. Telephone: 850-224-7000. Fax: 850-224-8832.
Tampa, Florida Office: 400 North Ashley Drive, Suite 2300, 33602. Telephone: 813-227-8500. Fax: 813-229-0134.
Tokyo, Japan Office: Suite 613, New Otemachi Building, 2-2-1 Otemachi, Chiyoda-ku, 100-0004. Telephone: 011-81-3-3-242-1289. Fax: 011-81-3-3-242-1290.
West Palm Beach, Florida Office: 625 North Flagler Drive, Suite 700, 33401. Telephone: 561-833-2000. Fax: 561-650-8399.
Representative Offices:
Caracas, Venezuela Office: Tinoco, Travieso, Planchart & Núñez, Avenida Francisco De Miranda, Torre Country Club, Piso 1 y 2, Chacaito, 1050. Telephone: 011-582-12-952-9033 (Master). Fax: 011-582-12-953-1053/8365/7583. Email: ttpn@ttpn.com.ve.
Tel Aviv, Israel Office: 23 Derech Petach-Tikva, 18th Floor, 66184. Telephone: 011-972-3-566-7666. Fax: 011-972-3-566-7667.

See Professional Biographies, WASHINGTON, DISTRICT OF COLUMBIA

Hollander, Lauren T. '74 '01 C.860 B.A. L.245 J.D
(adm. in NY; not adm. in DC) [Ⓐ Paul,H.J.&W.]
*PRACTICE AREAS: Employment Law.

Hollander Law Firm, P.L.C.
(See Fairfax, Virginia)

Hollaway, William R. .... '64 '98 C.277 B.S. L.276 J.D. [Ⓐ Skadden,A.S.M.&F.]
*PRACTICE AREAS: Energy Law.
Holleran, Linda M. ....'73 '00 C.1372 B.A. L.276 J.D. [Ⓐ McDermott,W.&E.]
Holley, Richard R., III '75 '01 C.67 B.A. L.575 J.D.
(adm. in NC; not adm. in DC) [Ⓐ Dechert]
*PRACTICE AREAS: Investment Management; Financial Services Law.
Holliday, Richard E., Jr. .... '57 '85 C.763 B.A. L.329 J.D. 1604 6th St., N.W.
Hollingshead, Robert J. ....'— '99 C.446 B.S.E.E. L.180 J.D. [Ⓐ Morgan,L.&B.] (Pat.)
Hollingsworth, Joe G., (AV) .... '49 '75 C.210 B.A. L.276 J.D. [Spriggs&H.]
*PRACTICE AREAS: Products Liability; Toxic Torts; Litigation; Drug and Medical Devices; Insurance Coverage.
Hollis, Bobby J., II .... '74 '00 C.260 B.A. L.352 J.D. [Ⓐ Jenner&B.]
*PRACTICE AREAS: Corporate.
Hollis, Sheila Slocum, (AV) ....'48 '74 C.174 B.S. L.208 J.D. [Duane,M.&H.]
*PRACTICE AREAS: Energy Transactions; Energy Regulatory Law; International Law; Administrative Law.
Hollman, Lawrence D., (AV) ....'32 '56 C&L.309 A.B., LL.B. [Ober,K.G.&S.]
Hollman, Steven P., (AV) .... '58 '83 C.309 B.A. L.893 J.D. [Hogan&H.]
*PRACTICE AREAS: Civil Litigation; Commercial Litigation; Patent Litigation; Trademark Litigation; Trade Secret Litigation.
Holloran, Matthew C. ....'69 '95 C.423 B.A. L.945 J.D. [Ⓐ Beveridge&D.]
*PRACTICE AREAS: Litigation; White Collar Crime; Commercial Litigation.
Holloway, Claire ....'— '00 C.880 B.S. L.477 J.D. [Ⓐ Latham&W.]
Holloway, James P. .... '61 '86 C.94 B.A. L.1065 J.D. [Ⓒ Proskauer R.]
Holloway, Oscar M., II '71 '97 C.577 B.A. L.575 J.D.
(adm. in NC; not adm. in DC) U.S. Equal Employ. Opportunity Comm.
Hollrah, Russell A. ....'58 '84 C.446 B.S. L.862 J.D. [Hahn K.&H.]
Holman, Charles F., III '57 '81
C.477 B.G.S. L.912 J.D. Director, D.C. Office of Human Rights
Holman, Craig A., (AV) ....'68 '93 C.93 B.A. L.273 J.D. [Ⓐ Holland&K.]
*PRACTICE AREAS: Government Contracts; Litigation.
Holman, John Clarke, (AV) '38 '66 C.966 B.S. L.30 J.D.
[Jacobson,H.] (See Pat. Sect.)
*PRACTICE AREAS: Intellectual Property Law; Chemical Patents; Metallurgical Patents; Mechanical Patents; Trademarks.
Holman, Kristin A. .... '71 '99 C.518 A.B. L.800 J.D. 2262 Rayburn House Office

Holman & Stern, Chartered, PLLC
(See Jacobson, Holman, PLLC)

Holmberg, Eric B. .... '60 '89 C.645 B.S. L.1209 J.D. [Holland&K.]
Holmberg, Thomas E. '71 '00 C.37 B.A. L.276 J.D.
(adm. in MD; not adm. in DC) [Ⓐ Baker B.]
Holmer, Alan F., (AV) ....'49 '80 C.674 A.B. L.276 J.D. 1722 Eye St., N.W.
Holmes, Diara M. '70 '99 C.659 B.A. L.309 J.D.
(adm. in NY; not adm. in DC) [Ⓐ Dewey B.]
Holmes, Donald F., Jr. ....'66 '94 C.831 B.B.A. L.128 J.D. [Ⓐ Greenstein D.&L.]
Holmes, Doreen Randi '63 '88
C.659 B.A. L.178 J.D. Asst. Gen. Coun., Ernst & Young LLP
Holmes, Jacqueline M. .... '69 '95 C.111 B.S. L.426 J.D. [Ⓐ Jones,D.R.&P.]
Holmes, John E., (AV) '53 '78
C.688 B.S.E.E. L.273 J.D. [Roylance,A.B.&G.] (See Pat. Sect.)
*PRACTICE AREAS: Patent, Trademark and Copyright Law; Technology Licensing; Electrical and Computer Patent Law.
Holmes, Laurie A. .... '62 '93 C.706 B.A. L.276 J.D. [Ⓐ Gardner,C.&D.]
*PRACTICE AREAS: Litigation.
Holmes, Mark van Dyke ....'60 '84 C.309 B.A. L.145 J.D. [Ⓒ Miller&C.]
*PRACTICE AREAS: Federal Litigation; Tax Litigation; International Trade; Litigation.
Holmes, Melinda K. .... '70 '96 C.597 B.A. L.276 J.D. [Ⓐ O'Donnell,S.&A.]
Holmes, Miriam R. .... '40 '75 C&L.329 B.S., J.D. Off. of Corp. Coun.
Holmes, Norman L., (AV) .... '28 '58 C.966 B.S. L.178 LL.B. 1156 15th St., N.W.
Holmes, Priscilla, (AV) ......'— '55 C.821 A.B. L.309 LL.B. 4710 Woodway Ln., N.W.‡
Holmes, Rhonda C. ....'— '98 C.228 A.B. L.262 J.D. [Ⓐ Morgan,L.&B.]

Holmes, Schwartz & Gordon
(See Rockville, Maryland)

Holowinski, Elizabeth .... '71 '96 C.696 B.A. L.982 J.D. [Ⓐ Coudert B.]
*PRACTICE AREAS: Telecommunications Law; Agency Law; International Law.
Holstein, Howard M., (AV) ....'46 '73 C.690 B.S. L.276 J.D. [Hogan&H.]
*PRACTICE AREAS: Regulatory Law; Medical Device Regulation; Food and Drug Regulation; Food, Drug and Cosmetic Law.
Holt, Elizabeth A. '75 '01 C.269 B.A. L.228 J.D.
(adm. in GA; not adm. in DC) [Ⓐ Akin,G.S.H.&F.]
*PRACTICE AREAS: Labor and Employment.
Holt, James H., (AV) ....'53 '79 C.691 B.A. L.477 J.D. [Betts&H.]
*PRACTICE AREAS: Administrative Law; Natural Gas; Litigation.
Holt, Janet Pitterle .... '55 '81 C.276 B.S.B.A. L.893 J.D. [Hogan&H.]
*PRACTICE AREAS: Commercial Litigation; Insurance Law; Employment Litigation; Securities Litigation; Special Education.
Holt, Reginald L., (AV) ....'38 '73 C.512 B.S. L.329 J.D. 4308 Georgia Ave., N.W.
Holt, Thaddeus, (AV) '29 '56 C.797 B.A. L.309 LL.B.
1201 Pennsylvania Ave., N.W. (⊙Point Clear, AL)
Holt, Veronice A. .... '48 '73 C.477 B.A. L.273 J.D. 3003 Van Ness N.W.
Holtz, H. Edward '38 '67 C.446 B.A. L.30 J.D.
Asst. Gen. Coun., Potomac Electric Power Company
Holtz, William E. ....'72 '01 C.665 B.S. L.276 J.D. [Ⓐ Foxkiser]
*PRACTICE AREAS: Food and Drug Regulation; Health Law.

Holtz & Foret, LLC
(See Chevy Chase, Maryland)

Holtzinger, John E., Jr., (AV) .... '28 '56 C.645 B.S. L.273 J.D. 701 Pennsylvania Ave.
Holtzman, Jill '70 '96 C.945 B.A. L.209 J.D.
(adm. in VA; not adm. in DC) Assoc. Coun., Republican Nat.Comm.
Holubar, Jennifer Tara Geter ..... '69 '95 C.446 B.S. L.276 J.D. [Ⓐ Dickstein S.M.&O.]
*PRACTICE AREAS: Civil Litigation; Securities Litigation; Insurance Litigation.
Holway, James R. ....'29 '53 C.602 A.B. L.477 LL.B. 1015 20th St., N.W.
Holzworth, David, (AV) ....'51 '79 C.951 B.A. L.813 J.D. [Lepon M.W.&H.]
Hom, Frances M. '64 '89 C.94 B.A. L.273 J.D.
(adm. in MD; not adm. in DC) Staff Dir., D.C. Coun.
Homer, Gregory W., (AV) ....'54 '79 C.976 B.A. L.893 J.D. [Swidler B.S.F.]
*PRACTICE AREAS: Labor and Employment; Litigation.
Hone, John Llewellyn, (AV) ....'39 '68 C.431 B.A. L.276 J.D. [Lipshultz&H.] ⊙
*PRACTICE AREAS: Farm Equipment Liability; Environmental Defense; Toxic Torts; Products Liability, Lead Paint Poisoning; Premises Liability Defense.
Hong, Jennifer L. .... '69 '96 C.273 B.A. L.276 J.D. [Ⓐ Paul,H.J.&W.]
*PRACTICE AREAS: Energy; Administrative Law.
Hong, Ki P. ....'67 '93 C.188 B.A. L.309 J.D. [Ⓒ Skadden,A.S.M.&F.]
Hong, Patricia E. ....'— '93 C.886 B.S.M.E. L.180 J.D. [Banner&W.] (See Pat. Sect.)
*PRACTICE AREAS: Intellectual Property Law; Patents; Design Patents; Intellectual Property Litigation.
Hong, Taylor Young ....'69 '00 C.75 B.A. L.178 J.D. [Ⓐ Fried,F.H.S.&J.]
*PRACTICE AREAS: Corporate Law; Securities.
Honig, Daniel A. ....'32 '75 C.260 B.S. L.273 J.D. 4479 Connecticut Ave., N.W.
Honig, Elie '75 '00 C.705 B.A. L.309 J.D.
(adm. in PA; not adm. in DC) [Ⓐ Covington&B.]
Honigberg, Paul M. ....'55 '80 C.228 A.B. L.880 J.D. [Dyer E.&J.]
*PRACTICE AREAS: Litigation; Environmental Law; Toxic Torts; Products Liability; Government Contracts.
Honigman, Steven S. ....'48 '73 C.569 B.A. L.976 J.D. [Ⓒ Thelen R.&P.]
*PRACTICE AREAS: Commercial Litigation; Securities Litigation; Environmental Law; Nuclear Regulation; Government Contracts.
Honikel, Kevin Charles '68 '94 C.867 B.A. L.30 J.D.
(adm. in MD; not adm. in DC) 6021 Western Ave., N.W.‡
Honnold, Edward E. ....'49 '78 C.118 B.A. L.976 J.D. 527 Fern Place, N.W.
Hood, Constance Kleiner '59 '89 C.1051 B.A. L.990 J.D.
(adm. in CA; not adm. in DC) 3801 Connecticut, N.W.‡
Hood, H. Carter ....'69 '98 C&L.309 A.B., J.D. [Ⓐ Caplin&D.]
*PRACTICE AREAS: Tax.
Hoogstraten, Nick R. ....'61 '86 C.378 B.A. L.276 J.D. [Ⓐ Bastianelli,B.&K.]
*PRACTICE AREAS: Government Contracts; Construction.
Hook, Brian H. .... '68 '00 C.755 B.A. L.352 J.D. [Ⓐ Hogan&H.]
Hook, Kerrie L. .... '62 '87 C.1209 B.A. L.904 J.D. [Collier S.S.]
*PRACTICE AREAS: Litigation.
Hooper, June E. ....'72 '00 C.232 B.S.B.A. L.1002 J.D. 1500 "K" St., N.W.
Hoover, Craig A., (AV) ....'56 '84 C.684 B.A. L.228 J.D. [Hogan&H.]
*PRACTICE AREAS: Civil Litigation; Commercial Litigation; Health Care Litigation.
Hoover, Craig M. '68 '98 C.477 B.S. L.426 J.D.
(adm. in VA; not adm. in DC) Prog. Offr., Policy & Law, World Wildlife Fund
Hoover, John B. ....'60 '85 C.893 B.S. L.280 J.D. [Ⓐ Dow,L.&A.]
Hoover, Joseph S., Jr. ....'59 '86 C.893 B.A. L.273 J.D. [Ⓒ Miller T.W.&L.]
*PRACTICE AREAS: Commercial Law; Environmental Law; Litigation; Administrative Law.
Hoover, Kimberly Hill .... '58 '84 C.69 B.A. L.228 J.D. [Hoover]
*PRACTICE AREAS: Financial Institutions Law; Financial Infrastructures; Banking Law; International Finance; Information and Privacy.
Hoover, Lesa Noblitt '56 '84 C.446 B.A. L.1002 J.D.
(adm. in MD; not adm. in DC) Apt. & Off. Bldg. Assn. of Metro. Wash.

Hoover Partners
1101 Connecticut Avenue, N.W., Suite 1000, 20036
Telephone: 202-828-2428 Fax: 202-318-2657 URL: http://www.hooverpartners.com
Email: kim@hooverpartners.com URL: http://www.lawyers.com/hoover
Kimberly Hill Hoover.
Banks and Banking, International Financial Institutions, Federal Regulatory Privacy, Information Security.

See Professional Biographies, WASHINGTON, DISTRICT OF COLUMBIA

Hope, Anthony J. '40 '66 C.276 B.A. L.309 J.D.
(adm. in CA; not adm. in DC) 2801 New Mexico Ave., N.W.
Hope, Judith Richards, (AV) .... '40 '64 C.914 A.B. L.309 J.D. [Paul,H.J.&W.]
*PRACTICE AREAS: Corporate Law; Alternative Dispute Resolution; Biotechnology; Privatization Transactions.
Hopeman, M. Jennifer '70 '96 C.118 B.A. L.309 J.D.
(adm. in MN; not adm. in DC) [Ⓐ Shaw P.]
*PRACTICE AREAS: Litigation; Labor and Employment Law; Antitrust.
Hopfl, Karen M. ....'68 '98 C.881 B.A. L.174 J.D. Physicians for Soc. Responsibility
Hopkins, Albert R., Jr. .... '41 '69 C&L.329 B.S., J.D. 2041 M L King Jr. Ave., S.E.
Hopkins, Brenda L. ....'50 '83 C&L.574 B.S., J.D. 3724 12th St., N.E.
Hopkins, Charles I., Jr. '27 '58
C&L.339 B.S., J.D. Chmn., National Railway Labor Conference
Hopkins, George C. ....'59 '85 C.860 B.A. L.93 J.D. [Vinson&E.]
*PRACTICE AREAS: Administrative Law; Environmental Law.
Hopkins, Martha J. .... '— '99 C.923 B.S.E.E. L.128 J.D. [Ⓐ Morgan,L.&B.]
Hopkins, Michael A. ....'61 '93 C.1107 B.A. L.273 J.D. [McKenna&C.]
*PRACTICE AREAS: Government Contracts; Telecommunications.
Hopkins, Peter J. ....'57 '87 C.951 B.A. L.276 J.D. [Spiegel&M.]
*PRACTICE AREAS: Energy; Qui Tam Litigation; Telecommunications Law.

Hopkins, Tammy ....'— '97 C.934 B.S. L.945 J.D. [Ⓐ Epstein B.&G.]
*PRACTICE AREAS: Government Contracts.

Hopkins Roden Crockett Hansen & Hoopes, PLLC, (AV)
8 East Street, S.E., 20003 ⊙
Telephone: 202-546-0360 Fax: 202-546-6294
Resident Of Counsel: Orval Hansen; George L. Denison.
General Civil, Trial and Appellate Practice before all State and Federal Courts and Administrative Agencies, Administrative Law, Agricultural Law, Alcoholic Beverages, Banking Law, Bankruptcy, Business Law, Civil Rights, Contracts, Construction Law, Corporate Law, Criminal Law, Debtor and Creditor, Election, Campaign and Political Law, Eminent Domain, Employment Law, Family Law, Government, Insurance, Health Care, Hospital Law, Immigration Law Intellectual Property, Natural Resources, Negligence, Patents, Trademarks and Copyrights, Personal Injury (plaintiffs and defense), Real Estate, Social Security, Taxation, Trusts and Estates, Utility Law, Wills and Probate, Workers' Compensation Law, and Zoning, Planning and Land Use.
Idaho Falls, Idaho Office: 428 Park Avenue, P.O. Box 51219, 83405-1219. Telephone: 208-523-4445. Fax: 208-523-4474. Email: Iflaw@hrchh.com.
Boise, Idaho Office: 802 West Bannock, Suite 900, P.O. Box 2110, 83701-2110. Telephone: 208-336-7930. Fax: 208-336-9154. Email: BoiseLaw@hrchh.com.
See Professional Biographies, IDAHO FALLS, IDAHO

Hopp, R. Richard .... '64 '90 C.911 B.A. L.446 J.D. [O'Donoghue&O.]
Hopp, Rachel M. .... '52 '79 C.446 B.A. L.180 J.D. [Hopp&Assoc.]
*PRACTICE AREAS: Environmental Law; Environmental Compliance; Environmental Litigation; Conservation Law; Land Trusts.

Hopp & Associates, P.L.L.C., The Law Offices of
1250 24th Street, N.W. Suite 300, 20037
Telephone: 202-467-8339 Fax: 202-467-8340 URL: http://www.ecolaw.com
Email: hopp&associates@ecolaw.com URL: http://www.ecolaw.com
Rachel M. Hopp;—Eric Louis Napoli (Not admitted in DC).
Domestic and International Environmental, Natural Resources and Related Business Law, Including:: Air Pollution, Water Pollution (TMDL's, Criteria), Climate Change/Joint Implementation, Ozone Depletion, Endangered Species, Compliance Counseling, Enforcement, Contractor Debarment, Litigation, Sustainable Development Finance, Environmental Commodity Transactions and Permits (Effluent Trading, Acid Rain Allowances, International Greenhouse Gas Offsets), Conservation Easements, Renewable Energy, Environmental Due Diligence, Regulatory Flexibility.
See Professional Biographies, WASHINGTON, DISTRICT OF COLUMBIA

Hoppel, Robert G., Jr., (AV) '21 '55
C.754 B.S. L.276 J.D. 3600 Massachusetts Ave., N.W.‡

Hoppel, Mayer & Coleman, (AV) BB
1000 Connecticut Avenue, N.W., Suite 400, 20036
Telephone: 202-296-5460 Telecopier: 202-296-5463
Email: hmc@hmc-law.com URL: http://www.lawyers.com/hmc-law
Members of Firm: Neal Michael Mayer; Paul D. Coleman.
Maritime Administrative Law, Maritime Commercial Law, Transportation Regulations, Administrative Law, Transportation Arbitration.
See Professional Biographies, WASHINGTON, DISTRICT OF COLUMBIA

Hopson, Mark D., (AV) .... '58 '84 C.362 B.A. L.276 J.D. [Sidley A.B.&W.]
Hora, Sundeep .... '73 '00 C.1044 B.A. L.904 J.D. 555 12th St., NW
Horahan, Edward B., III, (AV) .... '51 '76 C.397 B.A. L.976 J.D. [Ⓒ Dechert]
*PRACTICE AREAS: Civil Litigation; Securities Law; Employee Benefits Law; Administrative Law; ERISA.
Horan, John G. .... '60 '86 C.705 B.A. L.276 J.D. [McDermott,W.&E.]
Horan, Mern '62 '89 C.165 B.A. L.904 J.D.
Asst. Dir., Gov. & Pub. Interest, Georgetown Univ. Law Ctr.
Horan, Michael P. '55 '89
C.649 B.A. L.273 J.D. Assoc. Gen. Coun., Paralyzed Vet. of Amer.
Hordell, Michael A., (AV) .... '48 '73 C.150 B.B.A. L.94 J.D. [Kilpatrick S.]
*PRACTICE AREAS: Government Contracts; Government; Business.
Horgan, J. Kevin, (AV) .... '52 '82 C.665 B.A. L.564 J.D. [deKieffer&H.]
*PRACTICE AREAS: International Trade and Regulation; Export and Customs Law; Unfair Trade Practices; Antidumping; Countervailing Duties.
Horin, William A. .... '54 '79 C.597 B.S. L.276 J.D. [Winston&S.]
*PRACTICE AREAS: Administrative Law; Administrative Agency Practice; Federal Administrative Law; Energy; Energy Regulation.
Horkitz, Peter D. '63 '92
C.918 B.A. L.273 J.D. 1200 New Hampshire Ave., N.W., Suite 800
Horlick, Gary N., (AV) .... '47 '74 C.197 A.B. L.976 J.D. [O'Melveny&M.]
*PRACTICE AREAS: International Trade Law.
Horn, Bernard P. .... '56 '81 C.367 B.A. L.276 J.D. Dir., Handgun Control, Inc.
Horn, Charles M. .... '51 '76 C.309 A.B. L.188 J.D. [Mayer,B.&P.]
*PRACTICE AREAS: Financial Services Law; Securities; Corporate Law.
Horn, Dennis M., (AV) .... '50 '76 C.696 B.A. L.659 J.D. [Holland&K.]
*PRACTICE AREAS: Commercial Real Estate Development; Finance Law; Commercial Leasing; Business and Financial Restructuring.
Horn, Mary '69 '95 C&L.221 B.A., J.D.
(adm. in VA; not adm. in DC) [Ⓐ Greenberg T.]
Horn, Maurita Elaine .... '68 '97 C.839 B.A. L.145 J.D. [Ⓐ Williams&C.]
*PRACTICE AREAS: Labor and Employment; Litigation.
Horn, Meredith Kersey '70 '93 C.260 B.S. L.228 J.D.
(adm. in TX; not adm. in DC) 2300 N St. NW
Horn, Richard D. .... '62 '89 C.576 B.A. L.904 J.D. [Ⓒ Bracewell&P.]
Horn, Robert J. '43 '67 C.563 B.A. L.262 J.D.
(adm. in NY; not adm. in DC) [Patton B.]
Horn, Stephen, (AV) '46 '74
C.705 B.S. L.776 J.D. [Ⓒ Schmeltzer,A.&S.] (⊙Randolph, MA)
*PRACTICE AREAS: Civil Litigation; Franchise Law.
Horn, William P. .... '50 '83 C&L.30 B.A., J.D. [Birch,H.B.&C.]
Hornblower, Marshall, (AV) .... '17 '44 C.674 A.B. L.976 LL.B. 2445 M St., N.W.‡
Hornbostel, Peter A., (AV) .... '36 '62 C.103 B.A. L.178 J.D. [Cameron&H.]
*PRACTICE AREAS: International Business Transactions; International Finance; Reinsurance.
Horne, Frederick J. .... '63 '88 C.309 A.B. L.477 J.D. [Ⓒ Steptoe&J.]
*PRACTICE AREAS: Antitrust; Complex Litigation.
Horne, Michael S., (AV) .... '38 '63 C.494 B.A. L.309 J.D. [Covington&B.]
Horne, Scott J. '55 '81 C.1365 B.A. L.365 J.D.
(adm. in IL; not adm. in DC) Institute of Scrap Recycling Inds.
Hornick, John F. .... '56 '84 C.831 B.A. L.128 J.D. [Finnegan,H.F.G.&D.]
*PRACTICE AREAS: Intellectual Property Litigation; Software Protection; Software Licensing; Copyright Litigation; Trade Secrets.
Hornig, Christopher W., (AV) .... '53 '79 C.309 B.A. L.813 J.D. [Ⓐ Hessel&A.]
*PRACTICE AREAS: Affordable Housing; Real Estate.
Horning, Mark F., (AV) .... '46 '75 C&L.976 B.A., J.D. [Steptoe&J.]
*PRACTICE AREAS: Antitrust; Insurance Regulatory Law; Class Actions; Constitutional and Appellate Litigation.
Hornstein, Michael D. .... '54 '81 C.1044 B.A. L.724 J.D. [Orrick,H.&S.]
*PRACTICE AREAS: Project Finance; Energy Regulation.
Hornstein, Roger A. '27 '54 C.674 A.B. L.976 LL.B.
(adm. in NY; not adm. in DC) The World Bk.
Hornyak, Joseph P. .... '64 '90 C&L.446 B.S., J.D. [Sonnenschein N.&R.]
*PRACTICE AREAS: Government Contracts Law; Commercial Litigation; Labor and Employment Litigation.

Horowitz, Alan I., (AV) .... '— '77 C.453 B.S. L.178 J.D. [Miller&C.]
*PRACTICE AREAS: Appellate Practice; Litigation; U.S. Supreme Court Litigation; Tax Appeals; Tax Litigation.
Horowitz, Eugene G., (AV) ..... '36 '61 C&L.273 A.B., J.D. [Ⓒ Margolius,M.D.R.&T.] ‡
*PRACTICE AREAS: Commercial Transactions; Federal Income, Estate and Gift Taxation; Estate Planning; Probate; Real Estate.
Horowitz, Howard B., (BV) .... '41 '68 C.446 B.S. L.273 J.D. Asst. Corp. Coun.
Horowitz, Karen G. '68 '95 C.674 B.S.E. L.262 J.D.
(adm. in NY; not adm. in DC; See Pat. Sect.) [Ⓐ Pennie&E.]
*PRACTICE AREAS: Patent Prosecution; Patent Opinions.
Horowitz, Michael J. .... '38 '64 C.563 A.B. L.976 LL.B. Hudson Institute
Horowitz, Pamela S., (AV) .... '46 '74 C.429 B.A. L.94 J.D. [Advocates]
Horowitz, Philip M., (AV) .... '46 '73 C.873 A.B. L.276 J.D. [Arter&H.]
Horowitz, Robert M. '50 '75 C.1036 B.A. L.276 J.D.
Assoc. Dir., Ctr. of Children & the Law, Amer. Bar. Assoc.
Horrigan, Daniel M. .... '65 '91 C.276 A.B. L.273 J.D. [Ⓐ Piper M.R.&W.]
*PRACTICE AREAS: Venture Capital.
Horsky, Charles A., (AV) .... '10 '35 C.911 A.B. L.309 LL.B. 1201 Penn. Ave., N.W.
Hortis, Alex '72 '01 C.429 B.A. L.569 J.D.
(adm. in MD; not adm. in DC) [Ⓐ Hogan&H.]
Horton, Earle C., (BV) '43 '68 C.254 B.A. L.161 J.D.
(adm. in OH; not adm. in DC) [Graves&H.] ⊙
Horton, Frank, (AV) ...... '19 '47 C.420 B.A. L.188 LL.B. M.C. [Ⓒ Venable,A.B.H.&C.]
*PRACTICE AREAS: Government Contracts.
Horton, Marianna .... '76 '01 C.1349 B.A. L.273 J.D. [Ⓐ Covington&B.]
Horton, Philip W. .... '55 '80 C.976 A.B. L.309 J.D. [Arnold&P.]
*PRACTICE AREAS: Litigation; Telecommunications.
Horton, Roberta Lazarus .... '61 '88 C&L.976 B.A., J.D. [Arnold&P.]
*PRACTICE AREAS: Intellectual Property; Litigation.
Horton, Thomas J. .... '55 '81 C.309 A.B. L.930 J.D. [Orrick,H.&S.]
Horton, Tonya D. '75 '00 C.329 B.A. L.575 J.D.
(adm. in MD; not adm. in DC) [Ⓐ Venable,A.B.H.&C.]
*PRACTICE AREAS: Trademark Prosecution; Intellectual Property Litigation.
Horton, William L., Jr. .... '69 '96 C.896 B.A. L.893 J.D. [Ⓐ Shaw P.]
Horvitz, Alissa A. .... '66 '90 C.188 B.S. L.273 J.D. [Ⓒ Morgan,L.&B.]
Horvitz, Steven Jay .... '59 '84 C.103 B.A. L.813 J.D. [Cole,R.&B.]
*PRACTICE AREAS: Cable Television Law, including Cable Franchising, Copyright and FCC Regulatory Matters; Home Satellite Industry Issues; Copyright and Communications Law Litigation.
Horwitz, Paul .... '69 '98 C.012 B.A. L.025 LL.B. [Ⓐ O'Melveny&M.]
Horwitz, Paul Stephen .... '69 '00 C.012 B.A. L.025 LL.B. 555 13th St., N.W.
Horwitz, Reid B. '57 '82 C&L.150 B.A., J.D.
(adm. in OH; not adm. in DC) [Ⓒ Dechert]
*PRACTICE AREAS: Antitrust; Competition.
Horwood, James N., (AV) .... '36 '61 C&L.659 B.S., LL.B. [Spiegel&M.]
*PRACTICE AREAS: Communications Law; Contracts; Electric Power; Energy Regulation; Media and First Amendment.
Hoscheit, Dale H., (AV) .... '— '56 C&L.339 B.S., J.D. [Banner&W.] (See Pat. Sect.)
*PRACTICE AREAS: Intellectual Property Law; Patents; Intellectual Property Licensing; Intellectual Property Litigation; Biotechnology.
Hosking, Wayne Frederick, Jr. .... '66 '95 C.264 B.A. L.208 J.D. Roy F. Weston, Inc.
Hoskins, Anne E. .... '62 '94 C.188 B.S. L.309 J.D. Coun., Regulatory, Verizon Wireless
Hostak, Philip .... '64 '99 C.846 B.A. L.188 J.D. [Ⓐ Bredhoff&K.]
Hostetler, Darrin .... '67 '98 C.36 B.S. L.813 J.D. [Ⓐ Wilmer,C.&P.]
Hostetler, James S., (AV) .... '34 '58 C.976 B.A. L.309 J.D. [Ⓒ Kirkland&E.]
*PRACTICE AREAS: Government Contracts; Association Law; Legislative; Administrative Law.
Hostetler, Zona F., (AV) .... '36 '60 C.945 A.B. L.309 LL.B. [O'Toole,R.N.&S.]
Hotchkiss, Ryan Block .... '74 '00 C.966 B.A. L.904 J.D. [Ⓐ Steptoe&J.]
Hotes, David W. .... '65 '95 C.401 B.S. L.446 J.D. [Ⓐ Zuckerman S.]
*PRACTICE AREAS: Business Law; Corporate Law; Real Estate; Taxation.
Hotine, Susan J., (AV) .... '48 '74 C.915 B.A. L.188 J.D. [Scribner,H.&T.]
Hotvedt, Richard C., (AV) .... '35 '62 C.436 B.S. L.309 LL.B. [Ⓒ Morgan,L.&B.]
Hou, William C. .... '55 '82 C.881 B.A. L.228 J.D. 900 Seventeen St.
Houck, Caryn Blythe '71 '99 C.788 A.B. L.893 J.D.
(adm. in VA; not adm. in DC) [Ⓐ Preston G.E.&R.M.]
*PRACTICE AREAS: Litigation; Maritime Law.
Houck, Larry K. '58 '96 C.1356 B.A. L.596 J.D.
(adm. in OR; not adm. in DC) [Ⓐ Hyman,P.&M.]
*PRACTICE AREAS: Pharmaceutical Law; Drug Law; Chemical Law.
Houck, Victoria E. .....'— '94 C.674 A.B. L.145 J.D. Assoc. Gen. Coun., MedStar Health
Hougen, Eric J. .... '71 '98 C.427 B.A. L.352 J.D. [Ⓐ Wilmer,C.&P.]
Hough, Clayton Lee .... '58 '90 C.112 B.A. L.276 J.D. [Patton B.]
Hough, Gina A. '58 '86 C.788 A.B. L.93 J.D.
(adm. in MA; not adm. in DC) V.P. Dep Gen. Coun., Fannie Mae Inc.
*RESPONSIBILITIES: Intellectual Property.
Hough, Jessica A. .... '— '97 C.846 B.B.A. L.145 J.D. [Ⓐ Skadden,A.S.M.&F.]
*PRACTICE AREAS: Tax Law.
Houlihan, David P., (AV) .... '37 '65 C.980 B.S. L.276 LL.B. [White&C.]
*PRACTICE AREAS: International Trade.
Houlihan, Katharine B. .... '— '95 C.610 A.B. L.276 J.D. [Ⓐ Morgan,L.&B.]
Houlihan, Kevin M. .... '61 '86 C.884 B.A. L.276 J.D. [Elias,M.T.&H.]

Houlon & Berman, LLC
(See New Carrollton)

Houlton, Sabrina .... '— '98 C.918 B.A. L.813 J.D. [Ⓐ Wilmer,C.&P.]
Hourcle, Laurent R. '46 '71 C.94 B.S. L.228 J.D.
(adm. in NC; not adm. in DC) George Washington Univ. Law Sch.
Hourihan, James A., (AV) .... '36 '61 C.390 A.B. L.477 J.D. [Hogan&H.]
*PRACTICE AREAS: Civil Litigation; Commercial Litigation; Environmental Law; Product Liability.
Hourihan, Paul T. .... '67 '95 C&L.893 B.A., J.D. [Ⓐ Williams&C.]
Houry, Diane Michelle '74 '00 C.1356 B.S. L.1209 J.D.
(adm. in VA; not adm. in DC) Gen. Coun. Off.
House, Arthur G., (AV) .... '47 '72 C.860 B.A. L.893 J.D. [Gardner,C.&D.]
House, Bryan B. .... '— '93 C.347 B.A. L.494 J.D. [Ⓒ Foley&L.]
*PRACTICE AREAS: Litigation; Securities Litigation; Securities Enforcement; White Collar Crime.
House, Deborah M. '51 '76 C.339 B.S. L.904 J.D.
V.P. & Dep. Gen. Coun., Fannie Mae
*RESPONSIBILITIES: Multifamily Transactions.
House, Joseph R. .... '— '96 C.321 B.A. L.128 J.D. [Ⓐ Morgan,L.&B.]
House, Mary A. '67 '00 C.1369 B.S. L.30 J.D.
(adm. in MD; not adm. in DC) [Ⓐ Akin,G.S.H.&F.]
*PRACTICE AREAS: Civil Litigation; Products Liability; Antitrust.
House, Michael P., (AV) .... '57 '82 C.802 B.F.A. L.846 J.D. [Kaye S.]
*PRACTICE AREAS: International Trade; Administrative Law.
House, William Mike .... '45 '71 C.10 B.A. L.16 J.D. [Hogan&H.]
*PRACTICE AREAS: Legislation and Government Regulation.
Houseman, Alan W. .... '43 '68 C.604 B.A. L.569 J.D. 1616 P. St., N.W.
Housley, Allan D., (AV) '29 '53 C&L.64 J.D.
(adm. in MD; not adm. in DC) [Ⓒ Stradley R.S.&Y.]

Housman, Robert '65 '91 C.732 B.A. L.904 J.D.
(adm. in PA; not adm. in DC) [Ⓐ Bracewell&P.]
Houston, Stuart E. ...... '49 '74 C&L.902 B.A., J.D. [Burwell,P.&H.] & [Cross,M.S.&H.]
Houston & Howard .... 2021 L Street, N.W. Suite 304
Howald, Theresa M. ....'— '98 C.112 B.S. L.276 J.D. [Ⓐ Hogan&H.]
*PRACTICE AREAS: Health Law; White Collar Crime; Litigation.
Howard, Eve N. .... '62 '88 C.197 A.B. L.228 J.D. [Hogan&H.]
*PRACTICE AREAS: Corporate Law; Securities Law.
Howard, Glen S., (AV) '50 '74 C.309 A.B. L.145 J.D.
Sr. V.P. & Gen. Coun., Fannie Mae Foundation
Howard, Jasper A. .... '62 '87 C.383 B.S. L.228 J.D. [McKee N.]
*PRACTICE AREAS: Taxation; Federal Taxation.
Howard, Jeffrey H., (AV) .... '44 '69 C.682 B.A. L.893 LL.B. [Crowell&M.]
*PRACTICE AREAS: Energy, Environmental and Industrial Disease; Toxic Torts; Antitrust; Litigation.
Howard, John M. .... '44 '80 C.860 B.A. L.128 J.D. 1532 Upshur St., N.W.
Howard, Johnny M. .... '52 '77 C&L.329 B.S., J.D. [Houston&H.]
Howard, Kenneth C., Jr., (AV) .... '47 '75 C&L.846 B.A., J.D. [Baker&H.]
*PRACTICE AREAS: Business Law; Communications Law.
Howard, Lauren R., (AV) ....'45 '75 C.66 B.A. L.276 J.D. [Collier S.S.]
*PRACTICE AREAS: International Trade.
Howard, Renee M. .... '74 '99 C&L.602 B.A., J.D. [Ⓐ Jones,D.R.&P.]
Howard, Robert P., Jr. .... '66 '96 C.665 B.A. L.893 J.D. [Ⓐ McGuirewoods]
*PRACTICE AREAS: Securities Litigation; Securities Regulation.
Howard, Theodore A. .... '56 '82 C.602 B.A. L.309 J.D. [Wiley R.&F.]
*PRACTICE AREAS: Insurance.
Howard, Thomas L., (AV) ....'46 '71 C.902 B.A. L.880 J.D. [Ballard S.A.&I.]
*PRACTICE AREAS: Tax Law.
Howard, Timothy K. .... '71 '97 C.378 B.A. L.477 J.D. [Ⓐ Steptoe&J.]
Howe, Jerald S., Jr. .... '56 '83 C.674 A.B. L.309 J.D. [Steptoe&J.]
*PRACTICE AREAS: Aerospace Law; Appellate Practice; Government Contract Law; Space Law.
Howe, Jonathan T., (AV) .... '40 '66 C.597 B.A. L.228 J.D. [Howe&H.] (⊙Chgo., IL)
*PRACTICE AREAS: Not For Profit Corporations; Travel, Tourism, Hotel and Meetings Liability; Arbitration; Alternative Dispute Resolution; Trial and Appellate.
Howe, Joseph G., III, (AV) .... '52 '78 C&L.893 B.A., J.D. [Arnold&P.]
*PRACTICE AREAS: International Taxation; International Joint Ventures; Real Estate Investment Taxation; Taxation Law; Real Estate Finance Law.
Howe, Louise Nicholson .... '61 '87 C.674 A.B. L.893 J.D. [Hale&D.]
*PRACTICE AREAS: Government; Regulatory Law.
Howe, Mark P. .... '55 '87 C.309 A.B. L.276 J.D. [Cadwalader,W.&T.]
*PRACTICE AREAS: Corporate Tax Planning; Corporate Taxation; Federal Income Tax; Federal Taxation; Income Tax.
Howe, Shippen ....'55 '82 C.94 B.A. L.930 J.D. [Ⓒ Van Ness F.]
*PRACTICE AREAS: Energy; Natural Gas.
Howe, William H., (AV) ....'44 '70 C.197 A.B. L.893 LL.B. [Howe,A.&S.]
*PRACTICE AREAS: Labor Law; Legislative Law; Employment Law; Association Law.

Howe, Anderson & Steyer, P.C., (AV)
815 Connecticut Avenue, N.W., Suite 620, 20006
Telephone: 202-296-5680 Facsimile: 202-331-8049
Email: info@haspc.com URL: http://www.haspc.com
William H. Howe; James E. Anderson; Richard Alan Steyer; Mary Lou Smith; Robert J. Weil.
Administrative, Association, Labor and Employment, Legislative, Civil and Criminal Litigation, Antitrust and Trade Regulation, Nonprofit Taxation, Trademark and Pension Law.
See Professional Biographies, WASHINGTON, DISTRICT OF COLUMBIA

Howe & Hutton, Ltd., (AV)
1054 Thirty-First Street, N.W., Suite 200, 20007 ⊙
Telephone: 202-466-7252 Fax: 202-466-5829
Email: hh@howehutton.com URL: http://www.howehutton.com
Jonathan T. Howe;—Leland J. Badger.
General Representation of Not for Profit Organizations, Associations and Related Entities, Antitrust, Corporate, Employment, Contract, Administrative, Tax, Travel, Transportation, Meetings, Expositions and Hospitality Industry, Intellectual Property Law, Arbitration, Alternative Dispute Resolution, Trial and Appellate Practice.
Chicago, Illinois Office: 20 North Wacker Drive, Suite 4200, 60606-9833. Telephone: 312-263-3001. Fax: 312-372-6685.
Ballwin (St. Louis), Missouri Office: 1421 Buckhurst Court, 63021. Telephone: 636-256-3351. Fax: 636-256-3727.
See Professional Biographies, WASHINGTON, DISTRICT OF COLUMBIA

Howell, Christopher S. .... '40 '68 C.216 B.A. L.128 J.D. 16 7th St., S. E.
Howell, Deneen C. .... '71 '97 C.976 B.A. L.813 J.D. [Ⓐ Williams&C.]
*PRACTICE AREAS: Business Formation; Business Transactions; Copyright Licensing; Copyright Registration; Entertainment Law.
Howell, Jeffrey J. '70 '99 C.367 B.S.M.E. L.64 J.D.
(adm. in MD; not adm. in DC; See Pat. Sect.) [Ⓐ Roylance,A.B.&G.]
*PRACTICE AREAS: Patent Law; Patent Litigation.
Howell, John A., (AV) .... '50 '75 C&L.228 A.B., J.D. [Squire,S.&D.]
*PRACTICE AREAS: Government Contracts Law; Construction Law; National Security and Defense Procurement Law; Commercial Contracts.
Howell, John E. .... '40 '66 C&L.477 B.A., J.D. [Ⓐ Sperduto]
*PRACTICE AREAS: Litigation; Veterans Benefits.
Howell, Kyra Fischbeck '— '97 C.706 B.A. L.262 J.D.
(adm. in NY; not adm. in DC) [Ⓐ Powell,G.F.&M.]
*PRACTICE AREAS: Government Relations; Internet Law; Election Law.
Howell, Rachel '75 '01 C.30 B.A. L.904 J.D.
(adm. in VA; not adm. in DC) [Ⓐ Morrison&F.]
*PRACTICE AREAS: Financial Services Law.
Howell, Roy C. .... '54 '79 C.382 B.A. L.329 J.D. The Consulate
Howell, Thomas R., (AV) .... '49 '77 C.309 A.B. L.94 J.D. [Dewey B.]
*PRACTICE AREAS: International Trade.

Howes & Kinnane, P.C.
(See Annapolis, Maryland)

Howie, Brian A. ....'71 '96 C.478 B.A. L.902 J.D. [Ⓐ Howrey S.A.&W.]
*PRACTICE AREAS: Antitrust; Commercial Litigation.
Howie, Tami J. '72 '97 C.445 B.S. L.446 J.D.
(adm. in MD; not adm. in DC) [Ⓐ Piper M.R.&W.]
*PRACTICE AREAS: Corporate; Venture Capital.
Howie, Teresa A. .... '58 '88 C.575 B.A. L.329 J.D. U.S. Atty's. Off.

Howie, Irene E.
(See Annapolis, Maryland)

Howley, Patrick J. .... '69 '94 C.93 B.A. L.128 J.D. [Spencer,G.&H.]
Howrey, Edward F., (AV) '03 '27 C.352 A.B. L.273 J.D.
1299 Pennsylvania Ave., N.W.

Howrey Simon Arnold & White, LLP, (AV)
1299 Pennsylvania Avenue, N.W., 20004-2402 ⊙
Telephone: 202-783-0800 Fax: 202-383-6610
URL: http://www.howrey.com
William Simon; David C. Murchison; Harold F. Baker. Counsel: Victor L. Cohen; Terrence C. Sheehy. Members of Firm: Robert G. Abrams; Scott Arnold; Richard E. Ayres; Gregory L. Baker; J. Douglas Baldridge; Michael J. Bell; Darren B. Bernhard; John Bodner, Jr.; Sean F. X. Boland; Ray S. Bolze; Timothy E. Boyle; Jeffrey W. Brennan; John DeQ. Briggs, III; Robert J. Brookhiser, Jr.; John F.

(This Listing Continued)

Howrey Simon Arnold & White, LLP (Continued)

Bruce; Barbara O. Bruckmann; Robert M. Bruskin; Patricia G. Butler; Carla C. Calcagno; John G. Calender; Celine T. Callahan; Michael N. Clark; Kelly A. Clement; Michael Paul Austern Cohen; Richard T. Colman; Gregory J. Commins, Jr.; Michael G. Cowie; Basil C. Culyba; Martin F. Cunniff; James F. Davis; Mindy G. Davis; Thomas M. Dunham; W. Neil Eggleston; Charles J. (Tim) Engel, III; Lisa J. Fales; Thomas D. Fina; Alan M. Fisch; Scott E. Flick; John G. Froemming; Jerrold J. Ganzfried; Cecilia H. Gonzalez; Allen B. Green; Robert L. Green, Jr.; Alan M. Grimaldi; Edward Han; Stuart H. Harris; Edward P. Henneberry; Roxann E. Henry; William A. Henry; Thomas N. Heyer; Thomas A. Isaacson; Marcia Press Kaplan; Roger A. Klein; James G. Kress; Joseph P. Lavelle; Ezra C. Levine; Mark I. Levy; Karen M. Lockwood; Charles A. Loughlin; Karen Louise Manos; Christopher J. MacAvoy; Elizabeth B. McCallum; Rosemary H. McEnery; Virginia R. Metallo; Helen Katherine Michael; Victor J. Miller; Peter E. Moll; P. Todd Mullins; Reed W. Neuman; John W. Nields, Jr.; William R. O'Brien; James W. Olson; Joseph A. Ostoyich; John C. Peirce; Keith E. Pugh, Jr.; Bert C. Reiser; William Bradford Reynolds; James F. Rill; Richard A. Ripley; Howard T. Rosenblatt; John J. Rosenthal; Robert F. Ruyak; Lisa J. Saks; Richard H. Saltsman; Ralph J. Savarese; Mark C. Schechter; Marc G. Schildkraut; Edward B. Schwartz; Frederick F. Shaheen; Harvey G. Sherzer; Laura S. Shores; Robert H. Shulman; Tracy A. Heinzman Smith; Koorosh Talieh; Peter L. Tracey; William L. Webber; Mark D. Wegener; David B. Weinberg; William K. West, Jr.; J. Paul Williamson; A. Duncan Whitaker; Alan M. Wiseman; Carmine R. Zarlenga; Margaret M. Zwisler. Of Counsel: Gregory F. Intoccia; Hillary L. Snyder; James R. Wagner; Mark L. Whitaker. Special Counsel: Juliana M. Cofrancesco; Gilbert S. Keteltas; Jeffrey M. Lenser; Rachel Lisa Strong. Associates: Brent H. Allen; Timothy K. Armstrong; John T. Battaglia; Candace N. Beck (Not admitted in DC); Alexander B. Berger; Erik Bertin; Diane E. Bieri; Joshua Birenbaum (Not admitted in DC); James B. Boles (Not admitted in DC); Deana L. Cairo; Dylan M. Carson; Elizabeth J. Chandler; Jenny W. Chen (Not admitted in DC); Vina Chin (Not admitted in DC); Alexander R. Collins (Not admitted in DC); Stephen R. Cook; Robert H. Cox; Paul C. Cuomo; Jeffery S. Davidson; Sarah E. Davis; Lara A. Degenhart; Christopher J. DelliCarpini; Latif Doman (Not admitted in DC); Kenneth W. Donnelly; Donna Drake; Dawn A. Ellison (Not admitted in DC); Edward L. Ferguson, Jr.; Timothy T. Finley; Meryl S. Fishman; Amy R. Fitzpatrick; Colin Foley; James J. Fournier; Sarah H. Garb; Grace Graham (Not admitted in DC); Gurbir Singh Grewal (Not admitted in DC); Jacqueline I. Grise; Danielle D. Hallcom; Gene Healy; Kenneth N. Hickox, Jr.; Jason Foster Hoffman; Brian A. Howie; Robert P. Jacobs; James K. Kaleigh; Pamela S. Kane; Melissa B. Kimmel; Donna D. King; Stacey H. King; Mark Andrew Klapow (Not admitted in DC); Erik T. Koons; Aaron M. Levine (Not admitted in DC); Margaret D. Macdonald; James A. Maysonett; Eric J. McCarthy; Jennifer K. McDannell; Laura C. Miller (Not admitted in DC); Polly A. Myers; Matthew J. Moore; Danielle R. Oddo; Douglas S. Onley; Hae-Chan Park (Not admitted in DC); Edward I. Richards; Jason C. Raofield; Brian Rosenthal (Not admitted in DC); Scott D. Russell; Christina Guerola Sarchio; Jon Schiffrin; Bradley J. Schlozman; Brian Sherwood Seal; Jason D. Smith; Timothy Martin Smith (Not admitted in DC); John F. Stanton; Coke Morgan Stewart; Terry L. Sullivan; Steven A. Susswein (Not admitted in DC); Alan B.T. Sutton (Not admitted in DC); Jennifer A. Tunick; Jennifer M. Vasta; Margaret M. Vierbuchen; Tara M. Vold; Jonathan Michael Weinrieb; Stephen Weissman; Evan Jeffrey Werbel; Ramsey J. Wilson; Matthew M. Wolf; John H. Zacharia; Jennifer A. Zenker. Staff Attorney: Philip M. Ingeneri (Not admitted in DC).
General and Trial Practice including Antitrust, Commercial Litigation, Corporate and Transactional, Environmental, Government Contracts, Insurance Coverage, Intellectual Property, International Trade, Products Liability, Securities Litigation, Supreme Court and Appellate and White Collar Criminal Defense.
Century City, California Office: 1925 Century Park East, Suite 2100, 90067-2512. Telephone: 310-712-1000. Fax: 310-712-1099.
Los Angeles, California Office: Suite 1400, 550 South Hope Street, 90071-2604. Telephone: 213-892-1800. Fax: 213-892-2300.
Menlo Park, California Office: 301 Ravenswood Avenue, 94025. Telephone: 650-463-8100. Fax: 650-463-8400.
Houston, Texas Office: 750 Bering Drive, 77057-2198. Telephone: 713-787-1400. Fax: 713-787-1440.
Minneapolis, Minnesota Office: 4850 U.S. Bank Place, 601 Second Avenue South, 55402-4320.
Irvine, California Office: 2020 Main Street, Suite 1000. Telephone: 949-721-6900.
Chicago, Illinois Office: 321 North Clark Street, Suite 800, 60610. Telephone: 312-595-1239. Fax: 312-595-2250.
London Office: City Point, One Ropemaker Street, EC2Y 9HS. Telephone: 011 44 207 6283303. Fax: 011 44 207 065 6650.
See Professional Biographies, WASHINGTON, DISTRICT OF COLUMBIA

Hoyle, Peggy A. .... '65 '90 C.575 A.B. L.228 J.D. 1875 Connecticut Avenue, N.W.
Hoyt, Helen F. .... '20 '51 C.280 A.B. L.245 LL.B. 224 M St., S.W.
Hoyt, James Grier ....'58 '84 C.280 B.A. [Arter&H.]
Hoyt, Robert F. .... '64 '90 C.188 B.S. L.659 J.D. [Wilmer,C.&P.]
*PRACTICE AREAS: Securities; Corporate; Litigation.
Hrabosky, Kimberly .... '75 '00 C.890 B.A. L.1209 J.D. [Ⓐ Wiley R.&F.]
Hrozenchik, Mark W. '62 '97
C.816 B.E.E.E. L.1252 J.D. [Ⓐ Roylance,A.B.&G.] (See Pat. Sect.)
*PRACTICE AREAS: Electronics; Intellectual Property.
Hruby, Timothy .... '68 '95 C.37 B.A. L.276 J.D. [Ⓐ Weil,G.&M.]
*PRACTICE AREAS: International Trade.
Hsieh, Timothy M. '61 '98
C.367 B.E.S. L.893 J.D. [Ⓐ Finnegan,H.F.G.&D.] (See Pat. Sect.)
*PRACTICE AREAS: Patent Litigation; Patent Prosecution; Fiber Optics; Semiconductor Technology.
Hsu, Amber Wong ....'69 '95 C.691 B.A. L.276 J.D. [Ⓒ Powell,G.F.&M.]
*PRACTICE AREAS: Tax Exempt Organizations; Tax Exempt Litigation.
Hsu, Christine P. ....'71 '96 C.309 A.B. L.276 J.D. [Ⓐ Weil,G.&M.]
Hsu, Jeffrey T. .... '60 '94 C.918 B.A. L.188 J.D. 1133 19th St., N.W.
Hsu, John K. '— '00 C.367 B.A. L.446 J.D.
(adm. in VA; not adm. in DC; Pat.) [Ⓐ Shook,H.&B.]
Hsu, Michelle M. .... '63 '92 C.66 B.A. L.276 J.D. [Ⓒ Akin,G.S.H.&F.]
Hu, Shoufen .... '73 '97 [Ⓐ Mayer,B.&P.]
*PRACTICE AREAS: Financial Services Law; Corporate Law; Mergers and Acquisitions.
Hu, Yitai ....'65 '94 C.378 B.A. L.446 J.D. [Finnegan,H.F.G.&D.] (See Pat. Sect.)
*PRACTICE AREAS: Intellectual Property Litigation; Intellectual Property Licensing; International Intellectual Property; International Licensing.
Huang, Benjamin '69 '95 C.846 B.S. L.228 J.D.
(adm. in TX; not adm. in DC; Pat.) [Ⓐ Levine,B.B.&B.]
*PRACTICE AREAS: Intellectual Property.
Huang, David C. ....'56 '83 C.1073 B.S. L.1065 J.D. 1775 Pennsylvania Ave., N.W.
Huang, Sam '64 '96 C.823 B.S. L.1292 J.D.
(adm. in NJ; not adm. in DC) [Ⓐ Arent F.K.P.&K.]
*PRACTICE AREAS: Intellectual Property; Patents; Trademarks; Copyrights.
Huang, Stuart T. F. .... '57 '89 C.367 B.E.S. L.904 J. D. [Steptoe&J.]
*PRACTICE AREAS: Intellectual Property.
Huang, William S. .... '60 '87 C.309 A.B. L.976 J.D. [Spiegel&M.]
*PRACTICE AREAS: Energy; Hydroelectricity; Administrative Law; Contracts.
Huard, Paul R. ....'44 '69 C.93 A.B. L.276 J.D. Sr. V.P., National Assn. of Manufacturers
Hubbard, Allan C. ....'43 '72 C.902 B.A. L.893 J.D. [Ⓒ Dickstein S.M.&O.]
*PRACTICE AREAS: Telecommunications.
Hubbard, Heidi K. .... '61 '86 C.101 B.A. L.813 J.D. [Williams&C.]
*PRACTICE AREAS: Complex Litigation; Litigation; Mass Torts; Products Liability.
Hubbard, Michael B. .... '54 '79 C&L.902 B.A., J.D. [Seyfarth S.]
*PRACTICE AREAS: Government Contract Law; Commercial Contract Law; Contract Litigation.
Hubbard, Nerman Dobynes '51 '82 C.829 B.S. L.128 J.D.
Sr. Coun., Marriott Intl., Inc.
*RESPONSIBILITIES: Compensation and Employee Benefits.
Hubbard, Patrick L. ....'62 '88 C.1105 B.A. L.128 J.D. [Ⓢ Jones,D.R.&P.]
Hubbard, Richard L., (AV) .... '43 '68 C.951 B.A. L.309 LL.B. [Arnold&P.]
*PRACTICE AREAS: Tax; Employee Benefits.
Huber, Christopher J. ....'72 '97 C.976 B.A. L.276 J.D. [Ⓐ Crowell&M.]
Huber, Elizabeth A. .... '48 '80 L.1137 J.D. [Hudson C.] (⊙Gardena, CA; Linthicum, MD)
Huber, Jennifer S. .... '68 '96 C.276 B.A. L.1355 J.D. [Ⓐ Wiley R.&F.]
Huber, John J., (BV) .... '— '75 C&L.966 B.A., J.D. [Latham&W.]

Huber, Peter W., (AV) . . . .'52 '85 C.453 B.S. L.309 J.D. [Kellogg,H.H.T.&E.]
*PRACTICE AREAS: Telecommunications.
Huber, Robert M. . . . .'54 '82 C.446 B.A. L.893 J.D. [Bryan C.]
*PRACTICE AREAS: Antitrust and Trade Regulation.

Huber Lawrence & Abell, (AV)
1001 G Street, N.W., Twelfth Floor, 20001 ⊙
Telephone: 202-737-3880
Members of Firm: Barbara S. Jost; Richard M. Lorenzo (Not admitted in DC); Jonathan D. Schneider (Not admitted in DC; Resident). Associates: Adam H. Bartsch (Not admitted in DC; Resident); John R. Matson, III (Resident. Counsel: Heidi Marie Werntz (Resident).
General Practice, Corporate, Securities, Litigation, Public Utility, Energy, Communications, Taxation, Corporate Finance and Environmental Law.
New York, N.Y. Office: 605 Third Avenue, 27th Floor. Telephone: 212-682-6200.
See Professional Biographies, WASHINGTON, DISTRICT OF COLUMBIA

Huberman, David A. . . . . '70 '96 C.228 A.B L.276 J.D. 1776 K St., N.W.
Huberman, Gisela . . . .'42 '81 C.273 B.A. L.904 J.D. 1090 Vermont Ave., NW
Huckert, John W. '25 '52 C.884 B.S.M.E. L.276 J.D.
7400 Benjamin Franklin Sta. (Pat.)‡
Huda, Parvin '70 '99 C&L.276 B.A., J.D.
(adm. in IL; not adm. in DC) [[A] Foley&L.]
*PRACTICE AREAS: Communications Law; Regulatory law; International Trade.

Huddles & Jones, P.C.
(See Columbia, Maryland)

Huddleson, Edwin E., III, (AV) '45 '70 C.813 B.S. L.144 J.D.
316 F Street, N.E., 20002
Telephone: 202-543-2233 Fax: 202-543-2257
Email: huddlesone@aol.com URL: http://www.lawyers.com/huddleson
***PRACTICE AREAS: Trial and Appellate Practice in State and Federal Courts; Administrative Law; Corporate and Business Law; Employment; Equipment Leasing.**
General Civil Practice.
See Professional Biographies, WASHINGTON, DISTRICT OF COLUMBIA

Hudes, Karen . . . . '48 '77 C.569 B.A. L.976 J.D. Sr. Coun., The World Bk.

Hudgins Law Firm
(See Alexandria)

Hudock, Robert J. '73 '00 C.732 L.188 J.D.
(adm. in NY; not adm. in DC) [[A] Epstein B.&G.]
*PRACTICE AREAS: Health; Litigation; Antitrust.
Hudson, Brian M. . . . .'71 '99 C.575 B.A. L.276 J.D. [[A] Venable,A.B.H.&C.]
*PRACTICE AREAS: Labor Law; Employment Litigation; Employee Benefits.

Hudson, Daryl J., III, (AV) '52 '79 C.623 B.A. L.276 J.D.
1042 31st Street, NW, 20007
Telephone: 202-342-1700 Fax: 202-342-7234
Email: dhudson@starpower.net URL: http://www.lawyers.com/djhudsonlaw
***PRACTICE AREAS: Transactions; Litigation; Securities.**
Associate: Thomas F. Stollman.
Litigation, S.E.C. Enforcement, Corporate and Partnership Law, International Litigation, Corporate Transactions, Investments.
See Professional Biographies, WASHINGTON, DISTRICT OF COLUMBIA

Hudson, Michael E., (AV) '43 '73 C.870 B.S. L.846 J.D.
(adm. in TX; not adm. in DC) 25 E St. NW
Hudson, Paul B. . . . .'72 '98 C.228 B.A. L.813 J.D. [[A] Swidler B.S.F.]
*PRACTICE AREAS: Telecommunications.
Hudson, Rodney E. . . . .'55 '85 C.629 B.S. L.800 J.D. 6900 Georgia Avenue★
Hudson, Rodney M. . . . . '71 '97 C.1228 B.A. L.823 111 F St., N.W.
Hudson, Thomas B., (AV) '43 '73 C.280 B.A. L.276 J.D.
[Hudson C.] (⊙Linthicum, MD)
Hudson, Thomas H., (BV) . . . .'46 '73 C&L.420 B.A., J.D. [Brownstein H.&F.]
*PRACTICE AREAS: State and Federal Legislative Practice; Administrative; Regulatory.
Hudson Cook, LLP, (AV)
1612 K Street, N.W., Suite 204 (⊙Gardena, CA; New Haven, CT; Linthicum, MD; Clifton Park, NY; Charlottesville, VA)
Huerta, John E. '43 '70 C.1097 B.A. L.1066 J.D.
(adm. in CA; not adm. in DC) Gen. Coun., Smithsonian Institution
Huey, Erik V. . . . .'67 '93 C.472 B.B.A. L.602 J.D. [[C] Venable,A.B.H.&C.]
*PRACTICE AREAS: Telecommunications; Government Relations; Legislative Practice; Regulatory.
Huey, Robert H., (AV) . . . .'43 '68 C.319 B.A. L.893 LL.B. [Arent F.K.P.&K.]
*PRACTICE AREAS: International Trade Law; Import and Export Law; International Law.
Huey-Burns, Paul . . . .'56 '82 C.367 B.A. L.659 J.D. [Morgan,L.&B.]
Huff, Donald N., (AV) . . . .'45 '73 C.24 B.S. L.276 J.D. [Dykema G.] (Pat.)
*PRACTICE AREAS: Trademarks; Copyrights; Unfair Competition; Patents.
Huff, Kevin B. . . . .'71 '97 C.878 B.S. L.178 J.D. [[A] Kellogg,H.H.T.&E.]
*PRACTICE AREAS: Litigation.
Huffman, Byron Keith, Jr. . . . .'41 '67 C&L.976 B.A., LL.B. [[C] Akin,G.S.H.&F.]
*PRACTICE AREAS: Corporate Law; Environmental Law.
Huffman, Thad S. . . . . '52 '84 C.208 B.A. L.923 J.D. [Jackson&K.P.]
*PRACTICE AREAS: Natural Resources; Administrative and Commercial Law.

Huffman, Byron L., P.C.
(See Columbia, Maryland)

Huffstetler, Michael R. . . . .'54 '83 C.790 B.S. L.477 J.D. [Ivins,P.&B.]
*PRACTICE AREAS: Employee Benefits; Employment Taxation; Executive Compensation; ERISA Litigation; ESOPs.
Huge, Harry, (AV) . . . . '37 '63 C.547 A.B. L.276 LL.B. [Powell,G.F.&M.]
*PRACTICE AREAS: Commercial Litigation; Civil and Criminal Litigation; Corporate and International Transactions.
Huggins, Matthew . . . .'64 '97 C.197 B.A. L.309 J.D. [[A] Wilmer,C.&P.]
Hughes, Cheryl Risley . . . .'69 '96 C.1044 B.A. L.608 J.D. [Sanders,S.&B.]
*PRACTICE AREAS: Employee Benefits.
Hughes, Dennis R. . . . .'69 '95 C.880 B.A. L.861 J.D. [[A] Holland&K.]
*PRACTICE AREAS: Real Estate; Zoning, Planning and Land Use; Municipal Law; Historic Preservation.
Hughes, Elizabeth, (BV) . . . .'63 '88 C.446 B.A. L.378 J.D. [Hughes&B.]
Hughes, Gary E., (BV) '47 '73 C.675 B.A. L.945 J.D.
(adm. in VA; not adm. in DC) Sr. V.P., Gen. Coun., Amer. Council of Life Ins.
*RESPONSIBILITIES: Corporate; Legislative.
Hughes, George J., (AV) . . . . '32 '60 C.128 B.A. L.276 J.D. [Hughes&B.]
Hughes, J. David, & Associates, PLLC '35 '64
C.846 B.B.A. L.30 J.D. [J.D.Hughes&Assoc.]
Hughes, J. Vance, (AV) . . . . '46 '71 C.198 A.B. L.280 J.D. [Kilpatrick S.]
*PRACTICE AREAS: Environmental; Natural Resources.
Hughes, Jennifer P. . . . . '68 '95 C.276 B.A. L.823 J.D. 1730 Rhode Island Ave., N.W.
Hughes, John C. C. . . . .'71 '99 C.990 B.A. L.477 J.D. [[A] Mayer,B.&P.]
*PRACTICE AREAS: Tax Controversies.
Hughes, John K. . . . .'53 '84 C.93 B.A. L.823 J.D. [Sidley A.B.&W.]
Hughes, Jordana J. '71 '00 C.446 B.A. L.273 J.D.
(adm. in VA; not adm. in DC) [[A] Feldesman,T.L.F.&B.] ⊙
*PRACTICE AREAS: Domestic Relations.
Hughes, Kent H. . . . .'41 '71 C.976 B.A. L.309 LL.B. 14th & Constitution Aves., N.W.

Hughes, Kristen Grim . . . . '— '98 C.112 B.A. L.276 J.D. [[A] Foley&L.]
*PRACTICE AREAS: Litigation.
Hughes, Mary Rose . . . .'50 '79 C.276 B.S. L.128 J.D. [Perkins C.]
*PRACTICE AREAS: Product Liability Litigation; General Civil Litigation.
Hughes, Nicole '73 '98 C.884 B.A. L.1301 J.D.
(adm. in MD; not adm. in DC) [[A] McNary,M.&S.]
*PRACTICE AREAS: Immigration Law; Litigation.
Hughes, Philippa Pham Bates '68 '97 C.893 B.A. L.692 J.D.
Coun., Investment Counsel Assoc. of America, Inc.
Hughes, Shantelle Denise . . . .'73 '98 C.302 B.A. L.273 J.D. [[A] Shaw P.]
*PRACTICE AREAS: Commercial Real Estate.
Hughes, Thomas M. . . . .'65 '96 C.1145 B.A. L.818 J.D. [[A] Hunton&W.]
Hughes, Timothy R. '72 '97 C.276 B.S.F.S. L.945 J.D.
(adm. in MD; not adm. in DC) [[A] Drinker B.&R.]
Hughes, William F. . . . .'64 '91 C&L.276 B.A., J.D. [[C] Wallace K.M.&B.]
*PRACTICE AREAS: Environmental Law; Litigation.
Hughes & Bentzen, PLLC, (AV) . . . . . . 1667 K. Street, NW (⊙Tampa, FL; Rockville, MD)

Hughes Hubbard & Reed LLP, (AV)
1775 I Street, N.W., 20006-2401 ⊙
Telephone: 202-721-4600 Telex: 89-2674 Telecopier: 202-721-4646
Email: info@hugheshubbard.com URL: http://www.hugheshubbard.com
Resident Partners: Lawrence F. Bates; Catherine Curtiss; Thomas A. Ferrigno; Dennis S. Klein; Robert P. Reznick; Kathleen M. Russo; William R. Stein; John M. Townsend. Special Counsel: Robert B. Funkhouser; Joseph M. Furey; Alan G. Kashdan. Resident Associates: William A. Barrett; Kristen A. Byrnes; Flavio Cumpiano; Mira Vayda Edelman; Robert M. Kennedy, Jr.; Roberta Koss; Mary Kathleen O'Connor; Kelsey Schaefer (Not admitted in DC).
General Practice.
New York, New York Office: One Battery Park Plaza, 10004. Telephone: 212-837-6000. Telex: 427120. Telecopier: 212-422-4726.
Los Angeles, California Office: 350 S. Grand Avenue, Suite 3600, 90071-3442. Telephone: 213-613-2800. Telecopier: 213-613-2950.
Miami, Florida Office: 201 South Biscayne Boulevard, Suite 2500, 33131-4332. Telephone: 305-358-1666. Fax: 305-371-8759. Telex: 518785.
Paris, France Office: 47, Avenue Georges Mandel, 75116. Telephone: 33 1 44 05 80 00. Telex: 645440. Telecopier: 33 1 45 53 15 04.
See Professional Biographies, WASHINGTON, DISTRICT OF COLUMBIA

Hughes, J. David, & Associates, PLLC
1815 Pennsylvania Avenue N.W. Suite 550, 20006
Telephone: 202-347-3100 Fax: 202-331-8893; 703-370-1760
Email: jdavehughes@home.com
J.D. Hughes & Associates, PLLC.
Arbitration, Mediation, Civil Litigation, Federal Energy Regulation, Immigration.
See Professional Biographies, WASHINGTON, DISTRICT OF COLUMBIA

Hugie, Steven E. . . . .'69 '97 C.101 B.A. L.976 J.D. [[A] Wilmer,C.&P.]
Huhn, Nan R. . . . . '45 '70 C.1044 B.A. L.30 J.D. Supr. Ct. J.
Huhta, Susan E. '66 '94 C.188 B.A. L.966 J.D.
WA Layers Comm. for Civil Rights & Urban Affairs
Huie, William LaFont '73 '98 C&L.846 B.A., J.D.
(adm. in TX; not adm. in DC) [[A] Buc&B.]
*PRACTICE AREAS: FDA Regulatory; Healthcare LTC Regulatory.
Huizinga, James Alan . . . .'57 '81 C.605 A.B. L.1065 J.D. [Sidley A.B.&W.]
Huleatt, Jayme A. . . . .'— '88 C.658 B.A. L.128 J.D. [[C] Foley&L.] (See Pat. Sect.)
*PRACTICE AREAS: Patents; Trademarks; Copyrights; Intellectual Property.
Hulina, Amy L. '64 '97 C.645 B.S. L.30 J.D.
(adm. in VA; not adm. in DC; See Pat. Sect.) [[A] Kenyon&K.]
*PRACTICE AREAS: Intellectual Property.
Hulkower, Mark J., (AV) . . . .'57 '85 C.188 B.S. L.276 J.D. [Steptoe&J.]
*PRACTICE AREAS: White Collar; Criminal Matters.
Hull, John Daniel, IV, (AV) . . . . '53 '80 C.228 B.A. L.150 J.D. [Hull M.] ⊙
*PRACTICE AREAS: Complex Business Litigation; Environmental Law; Natural Resources; Intellectual Property; Federal Legislative Practice.

Hull McGuire PC, (AV)
1155 Connecticut Avenue, N.W. Suite 300, 20036-4306 ⊙
Telephone: 202-429-6520 Fax: 202-429-0977
Email: info@hullmcguire.com URL: http://www.hullmcguire.com
John Daniel Hull, IV; Julie E. McGuire (Not admitted in DC).
Corporate Law, Taxation, International Law, Intellectual Property, Complex Business Litigation and Arbitrations, Employment Law, Environmental Law and Natural Resources, Federal Courts, Federal Legislative Practice.
Pittsburgh, Pennsylvania Office: 32nd Floor, USX Tower, 600 Grant Street, 15219-2702. Telephone: 412-261-2600. Fax: 412-261-2627.
See Professional Biographies, WASHINGTON, DISTRICT OF COLUMBIA

Hulme, James H., (AV) . . . .'53 '79 C.478 B.A. L.904 J.D. [Arent F.K.P.&K.]
*PRACTICE AREAS: Intellectual Property Infringement; Patent Infringement; Entertainment Litigation; Arbitration; Insurance Litigation.
Hulme, Randall K. . . . .'56 '90 C.30 B.A. L.128 J.D. [[A] Fragomen,D.B.&L.]
Humber, Christopher E. . . . .'69 '98 C.145 B.A. L.309 J.D. [[A] Gibson,D.&C.]
*PRACTICE AREAS: Labor and Employment; Litigation.
Hume, Hamish P. M. . . . .'68 '95 C.976 B.A. L.893 J.D. [[A] Cooper&K.]
*PRACTICE AREAS: Trial and Appellate Litigation; Constitutional Litigation; Tax Litigation.
Hume, John P., (AV) . . . . '42 '70 C.602 B.B.A. L.273 J.D. 607 14th St., N.W.
Hume, Patrick H., (AV) . . . .'11 '35 C&L.537 LL.B. 3830 Macomb St., N.W. (Pat.)‡
Hume, Robert T. . . . .'46 '72 C.976 B.A. L.30 J.D. 1620 I Street, N.W., Suite 900
Humes, Gary E., (AV) . . . . '50 '81 C.918 B.A. L.188 J.D. [Arnold&P.]
*PRACTICE AREAS: Real Estate.
Humes, Traci Duvall . . . .'— '90 C&L.276 B.A., J.D. [[C] Foley,H.&E.]
*PRACTICE AREAS: Securities; Corporate Law; International Trade.
Hummel, Jeffrey M. . . . . '67 '95 C.1369 B.S. L.893 J.D. [[A] Seyfarth S.]
*PRACTICE AREAS: Construction Law; Government Contracts.
Hummel, Theresa M. . . . .'73 '99 C.957 B.A. L.221 J.D. [[A] Eccleston&W.]
*PRACTICE AREAS: Insurance Defense.
Hummers, Edward W., Jr., (AV) . . . . '36 '64 C.401 B.S. L.273 J.D. [Holland&K.]
*PRACTICE AREAS: Telecommunications.
Humphrey, James D., II '66 '97 C.502 B.A. L.477 J.D.
(adm. in NY; not adm. in DC) [[A] Akin,G.S.H.&F.]
Humphrey, John J. . . . .'14 '69 C.1044 B.S. L.128 J.D. 1324 18th St., N. W.
Humphrey, Margot Smiley, (AV) . . . .'44 '69 C.914 B.A. L.309 J.D. [Holland&K.]
*PRACTICE AREAS: Telecommunication Law.
Humphrey, Stephen L. . . . . '49 '74 C.960 B.S. L.421 J.D. [Cameron&H.]
*PRACTICE AREAS: International Trade; International Project Finance; International Banking; Trademark Law; Technology Transfers.
Humphrey, Thomas P., (AV) . . . .'44 '69 C&L.976 B.A., LL.B. [Crowell&M.]
*PRACTICE AREAS: Government Contracts Law; Natural Resources Law; Litigation.
Humphries, Derrick A., (AV) . . . .'47 '73 C.477 B.A. L.912 J.D. [D.A.Humphries]
Humphries, Laura B. . . . .'59 '85 C.880 B.A. L.228 J.D. 2000 K St. N.W., Ste. 600
Humphries, Nathaniel A., (AV) '34 '65
C.790 B.S. L.273 J.D. [[C] Jacobson,H.] (See Pat. Sect.)
*PRACTICE AREAS: Intellectual Property; Mechanical Patents.
Humphries, Derrick A., P.C., (AV) . . . . Suite 910 1025 Vermont Avenue N.W.

Hundley, John F. ....'67 '93 C.893 B.A. L.276 J.D. [P.Cacheris] ⊙
*PRACTICE AREAS: Criminal and Civil Litigation.
Hundley, William G., (AV) ....'25 '51 L.262 LL.B. [Akin,G.S.H.&F.]
*PRACTICE AREAS: Litigation.
Hung, Suzy Chan ....'57 '94 C.112 B.A. L.276 J.D. [Ⓐ Arent F.K.P.&K.]
*PRACTICE AREAS: Immigration; International Trade.
Hungar, Thomas G. .... '62 '89 C.950 B.S. L.976 J.D. [Gibson,D.&C.]
*PRACTICE AREAS: Appellate Practice; Constitutional Law; Litigation.
Hunkler, Jennifer A. .... '73 '99 C.705 B.S. L.602 J.D. [Ⓐ Jones,D.R.&P.]
Hunnicutt, Charles A., (AV) .... '50 '75 C.30 B.S. L.280 J.D. [Robins,K.M.&C.]
*PRACTICE AREAS: Government Affairs; Transportation; Maritime; Aviation; International Trade.
Hunsader, Joseph E. '59 '85 C.436 B.A. L.1066 J.D.
(adm. in CA; not adm. in DC) [Ⓐ Vinson&E.]
*PRACTICE AREAS: Litigation.
Hunseder, Michael J. ....'69 '94 C.228 A.B. L.276 J.D. [Ⓐ Sidley A.B.&W.]
Hunsicker, Karen K. ....'62 '87 C.802 B.A. L.846 J.D. 3083 Ordway St., N.W.
Hunsicker, Steven R., (AV) ....'50 '76 C.352 B.B.A. L.1049 J.D. [Baker B.]
Hunt, David W. ....'52 '77 C&L.893 B.A., J.D. [White&C.]
*PRACTICE AREAS: Corporate Transactions; Project Finance; Public Utilities; Utility Acquisitions.
Hunt, Lisa A. ....'69 '96 C.893 B.A. L.30 J.D. [Ⓐ Patton B.]
Hunt, Paul D. ....'65 '93 C.339 B.A. L.273 J.D. Autonomy Legal Servs.
Hunt, Paul J. ....'— '92 C.105 B.A. L.893 J.D. [Latham&W.]
*PRACTICE AREAS: Project Finance; Energy Project Development; Infrastructure Development; Energy Contracts; Independent Power.
Hunt, Sean R. ....'67 '99 C.893 B.S. L.30 J.D. [Ⓐ Kirkpatrick&L.]
*PRACTICE AREAS: Corporate Law; Technology and Science; Securities.
Hunt, Vicki Jean, (BV) '52 '83
C.1356 B.A. L.1209 J.D. The George Washington Univ. Med. Ctr.
Hunter, Allan O. '16 '40 C.267 A.B. L.1066 LL.B.
(adm. in CA; not adm. in DC) Dir., Fed. Natl. Mtge. Assn.
Hunter, Daniel R. ....'35 '61 C.188 B.Ch.E. L.597 J.D. 1155 21st St., N.W.
Hunter, James H, IV '62 '89
C.966 B.S.ChE. L.178 J.D. V.P. & Asst. Gen. Coun., Marriott Intl., Inc.
*RESPONSIBILITIES: International Lodging Development; Real Estate.
Hunter, Jerry L., (BV) ....'42 '68 C.1378 B.S. L.329 J.D. [Roundtree,H.&P.]
Hunter, Justin R. '68 '00 C.497 B.A. L.836 J.D.
(adm. in TN; not adm. in DC) [Ⓐ Powers,P.S.&V.]
Hunter, Karlyn J. '74 '99 C.302 B.S. L.178 J.D.
(adm. in MD; not adm. in DC) [Ⓐ Holland&K.]
*PRACTICE AREAS: Litigation.
Huntington, Mary Ann K. ....'64 '90 C&L.276 A.B., J.D. [Morgan,L.&B.]

Hunton & Williams, (AV)
1900 K Street, N.W., 20006-1109 ⊙
Telephone: 202-955-1500 Telex: 350 362 H&W WASH UD FAX: 202-778-2201 (Rapicom); 202-778-2202 (Ricoh230)
URL: http://www.hunton.com
Senior Counsel: John J. Adams; George Clemon Freeman, Jr.; William A. Pusey. Members of Firm: Stanislaus Aksman; Jennifer A. Albert; Virginia S. Albrecht; Ian P. Band; A. Neal Barkus; Michael B. Barr; Philip M. Battles, III; Mark B. Bierbower; F. William Brownell; Kristy A. Niehaus Bulleit; Ellis M. Butler; Kevin L. Fast; Norman W. Fichthorn; Andrea Bear Field; Lauren E. Freeman; David F. Geneson; Patti L. Grant-Wilkinson; Ray V. Hartwell III; Robert W. Hawkins; Juan C. Iturregui (Director of Governmental Affairs); Thomas F. Kaufman; Darryl S. Lew; C. King Mallory, III; Jeffrey N. Martin; Richard Edward May; James Forrest Miller; Jack A. Molenkamp; Eric J. Murdock; Kimberly A. Newman; Henry V. Nickel; Bruce D. Peterson; Arnold H. Quint; John Jay Range; John M. Ratino; Scott L. Robertson; Pauline A. Schneider; Robert M. Schulman; Thomas J. Scott, Jr.; William Silverman; Laurence E. Skinner (Not admitted in DC); Turner T. Smith, Jr.; Michael L. Teague; Mark G. Weisshaar; William F. Young; Lee B. Zeugin. Counsel: Richard L. Aguglia; Thomas E. Anderson; Kenneth A. Barry (Not admitted in DC); Fred H. Cate; Jennifer Hinkebein Culotta (Not admitted in DC); Craig S. Harrison; Douglas J. Heffner; Lucinda Minton Langworthy; Maida Oringher Lerner; John J. Rhodes; John J. Rhodes, III; Linda L. Walsh; O. Julia Weller; Susan Frier Wiltsie. Associates: Rel S. Ambrozy; Scott D. Balderston (Not admitted in DC); Paul A. Ballonoff (Not admitted in DC); Carl Lynford Benson (Not admitted in DC); Bethany M. Burns; Brian Mark Buroker; Gabriel Calvo; Kenneth C. Cestari; Peter M. Cleveland; William Woodhouse Davis (Not admitted in DC); Deidre G. Duncan; Douglas Dziak; David D'Zurilla; Robert H. Edwards, Jr.; James D. Elliott; H. Malloy Evans, III (Not admitted in DC); Ozzie A. Farres (Not admitted in DC); Richard P. Ferrin; Thomas M. Finan; Francine E. Friedman; Darrin Lewis Glymph; Matthew Falk Goldberg (Not admitted in DC); Gloria J. Halstead; Jeffrey B. Hardie; David Stuart Harlow; Scot A. Hinshaw; Thomas M. Hughes; Makram Jaber; Herbert V. Kerner; Ryan T. Ketchum; Gregory L. Kinzelman; Raymond Krncevic; Lewis E. Lamb III; Bradley T. Lennie; R. Andrew Lien; Jonathan Link; Peter J. Loughlin (Not admitted in DC); Audrey C. Louison (Not admitted in DC); Tyler Maddry (Not admitted in DC); David T. McIndoe (Not admitted in DC); David H. Milligan (Not admitted in DC); Devin S. Morgan; Ted J. Murphy; Andrew H. Murray; Kerry H. Owens (Not admitted in DC); Beth H. Regas; Richard A. Rice, Jr.; Adam J. Rosser; Stephen T. Schreiner (Not admitted in DC); Elizabeth (Nena) C. Shaw; James R. Simoes (Not admitted in DC); Yisun Song; Linda C. Trees; Andrew J. Turner; Samson Vermont (Not admitted in DC); Stephen J. Wenderoth; Michelle R. Wildstein (Not admitted in DC); Blake H. Winburne; Allison D. Wood; Russell G. Wood, Jr.; Scott F. Yarnell (Not admitted in DC).
General Practice.
Miami, Florida Office: Barclays Financial Center, 1111 Brickell Avenue, Suite 2500, 33131. Telephone: 305-810-2500. Fax: 305-810-2460.
Atlanta, Georgia Office: Bank of America Plaza, 600 Peachtree Street, N.E., Suite 4100, 30308-2216. Telephone: 404-888-4000. Fax: 404-888-4190 and Georgia-Hill Office: Southside Legal Center, 250 Georgia Avenue, S.E., Suite 211, 30312. Telephone: 404-688-5512; 404-688-5513.
New York, New York Office: 200 Park Avenue, 43rd Floor, 10166-0136. Telephone: 212-309-1000. Cable Addresses: "Huntwand, New York" and "Dialboard." Telex: 424 549 HUNT UI. Fax: 212-309-1100.
Charlotte, North Carolina Office: Bank of America Plaza, 101 South Tryon Street, Suite 3500, 28280. Telephone: 704-3778-4700. Telecopier: 704-378-4890.
Raleigh, North Carolina Office: One Hannover Square, 421 Fayetteville Street Mall, Suite 1400, 27601. Telephone: 919-899-3000. Fax: 919-833-6352.
Knoxville, Tennessee Office: 2000 Riverview Tower, 900 South Gay Street, Suite 2000, 37902. Telephone: 865-549-7700. Fax: 865-549-7704.
McLean, Virginia Office: 1751 Pinnacle Drive, Suite 1700, Tysons Corner, 22102. Telephone: 703-714-7400. Fax: 703-714-7410.
Norfolk, Virginia Office: SunTrust Center, Suite 1000, 500 East Main Street, 23510-3889. Telephone: 757-640-5300. FAX: 757-625-7720.
Richmond, Virginia Office: Riverfront Plaza, East Tower, 951 East Byrd Street, 23219-4074. Telephone: 804-788-8200. Cable Address: "Huntwand". Telex: 804-684-4251. Fax: 804-788-8218. TWX: 710-956-0061 and Church Hill Office: 2300 East Marshall Street, 23223. Telephone: 804-775-2248.
Brussels, Belgium Office: Ave Louise 326, B6, 1050 Brussels, Belgium. Telephone: 32(0)-2-643-5800. Fax: 32(0)-2-643-5822.
Hong Kong, Office: 23/F CITIC Tower, 1 Tim Mei Avenue, Central, Hong Kong. Telephone: (852) 2841-9100. Fax: (852) 2841-9191.
Bangkok, Thailand Office: Hunton & Williams (Thailand) Limited, 34/F Abdulrahim Place, 990 Rama IV Road, Bangkok, Thailand, 1050. Telephone: 011 (662) 636-2366. Fax: 011 (662) 636-2377.
Warsaw, Poland Office: Warsaw Stock Exchange Building, Ksi ążęca 4, 00-498 Warsaw, Poland. Telephone: 011 (48-22) 690 61 00. Telecopier: 011 (48-22) 690 62 22.
London, England Office: Fleetway House, 25 Farringdon Street, London EC4A 4AB, England. Telephone: 44 (0)20 7246 5700. Fax: 44 (0)20 7246 5772.
See Professional Biographies, WASHINGTON, DISTRICT OF COLUMBIA

Huntoon, Stephen L. '56 '82 C&L.893 B.A., J.D.
Dir. & Reg. Coun., Dynegy Inc. (⊙Hous., TX)
Huntsman, Lawrence D., (AV) '34 '59
C.645 B.S. L.273 LL.B. 1101 17th St., N.W. (⊙Fairfax, VA)
Huppe, Michael J. '68 '95 C.893 B.A. L.309 J.D.
Anti-Piracy Counsel, Recording Industry Association of America
Huppert, Michael S. '58 '90 C.506 B.S. L.1209 J.D.
[Wenderoth,L.&P.] (See Pat. Sect.)
*PRACTICE AREAS: Patent Law; Mechanical Patents; Patent Prosecution.
Hurdle, Paul C., III ....'48 '74 C&L.893 B.A., J.D. [Ⓒ McKee N.]
*PRACTICE AREAS: Securitization; Capital Markets; Structured Finance; Commercial Real Estate.
Hurewitz, Barry J. ....'69 '94 C.228 A.B. L.276 J.D. [Hale&D.]
*PRACTICE AREAS: Government Contracts; Federal Administrative Law; Export Regulation.
Hurewitz, Lane Steven ....'62 '87 C.30 B.A. L.273 J.D. [Ⓒ Stewart&S.]
*PRACTICE AREAS: International Trade; C.I.T.; CAFC; Administrative Law; ITA.
Hurlbut, Stephen B., (AV) '55 '81 C.893 B.A. L.910 J.D.
[Wickwire G.] (⊙Vienna, VA)
*PRACTICE AREAS: Public Contract Law; Construction Law; Litigation.
Hurme, Sally Balch ....'46 '77 C.861 B.A. L.30 J.D. Amer. Assoc. of Ret. Persons
Hurson, Daniel J., (AV) ....'47 '72 C.276 A.B. L.309 J.D. [Ⓒ Williams&C.]
*PRACTICE AREAS: SEC Enforcement; White Collar Criminal Defense.
Hurst, Andrew L. ....'— '96 C.776 B.A. L.276 J.D. [Ⓐ Reed S.]
*PRACTICE AREAS: Litigation.
Hurst, Melissa B. '71 '96 C.884 B.A. L.273 J.D.
Sr. Coun., American National Red Cross
*RESPONSIBILITIES: Employment.
Hurst, Paul R. ....'70 '96 C.205 B.A. L.659 J.D. [Ⓐ Steptoe&J.]
Hurst, Veta P. '71 '98 C.1139 B.S. L.1187 J.D.
Atty., Equal Employment Opportunity Commission
Hurt, Patricia E. '65 '99 C.1356 B.S. L.128 J.D.
(adm. in VA; not adm. in DC) [Ⓐ Paul,H.J.&W.]
*PRACTICE AREAS: Energy; Federal Energy Regulatory Commission Matters.
Hurt, Valerie E. ....'— '99 C.691 B.A. L.893 J.D. 701 Pennsylvania Avenue, N.W.
Hurvitz, John A. ....'64 '91 C.311 B.A. L.976 J.D. [Covington&B.] (See Pat. Sect.)
Hurwich, Evelyn M. '54 '90 C.999 B.A. L.1066 J.D.
Dir. & Coun., Circumpolar Conservation Union
Hurwitz, Cynthia J. ....'72 '00 C.104 B.A. L.208 J.D. [Ⓐ Galland,K.G.F.&S.]
*PRACTICE AREAS: Transportation; Maritime Law; Customs.
Hurwitz, Ely, (AV) ....'42 '68 C.620 B.A. L.623 J.D. [Hurwitz&A.]
Hurwitz, Kenneth G., (AV) '52 '76
C.178 B.A. L.659 J.D. [Venable,A.B.H.&C.] (⊙Balt., MD)
*PRACTICE AREAS: Energy; Telecommunications.
Hurwitz & Abramson, (AV) ....1735 20th Street, N.W.
Husband, Phillip L., (BV) '62 '87 C.497 B.B.A. L.861 J.D.
Health & Hosp. Benefit Corp.
Hushon, Jeremy Ambler ....'71 '97 C.103 A.B. L.228 J.D. [Ⓐ Fulbright&J.]
*PRACTICE AREAS: International; Project Finance; Commercial Real Estate.
Husisian, Gregory ....'64 '92 C&L.188 B.A., J.D. [Ⓒ Weil,G.&M.]
Hussain, Tasneem ....'70 '95 C&L.910 B.A., J.D. [Ⓒ Rogers&M.]

Huston & Angus
(See Arlington, Virginia)

Hut, A. Stephen, Jr., (AV) .... '46 '74 C.659 B.A. L.309 J.D. [Wilmer,C.&P.]
*PRACTICE AREAS: Appellate Litigation; Civil Practice; Insurance.
Hutchings, Jeffrey D. ....'57 '83 C&L.228 A.B., J.D. [Shaw P.]
*PRACTICE AREAS: Technology; Corporate.
Hutchins, Jeremy Todd ..... '69 '96 C.685 B.A. L.276 J.D. 1001 Pennsylvania Ave., N.W.
Hutchins, John R. ...... '70 '96 C.477 B.S.E. L.309 J.D. [Ⓐ Kenyon&K.] (See Pat. Sect.)
*PRACTICE AREAS: Intellectual Property.
Hutchins, Kate '75 '01 C.477 B.A. L.976 J.D.
(adm. in NY; not adm. in DC) [Ⓐ Wilmer,C.&P.]
Hutchinson, George E., (AV) .....'23 '55 C&L.273 A.B., LL.B. [Ⓒ Finnegan,H.F.G.&D.]
*PRACTICE AREAS: Federal Civil Litigation; Appellate Practice.
Hutchinson, James A. .... '66 '93 C.659 B.A. L.276 J.D. [Hogan&H.]
*PRACTICE AREAS: Corporate Mergers and Acquisitions; Corporate Finance; Corporate Securities.
Hutchinson, James S., (AV) .... '52 '79 C.732 B.A. L.880 J.D. [Alston&B.]
*PRACTICE AREAS: Pension and Profit Sharing Plans; Employee Stock Ownership Plans; Executive Compensation.

Hutchinson, Barbara B.
(See New Carrollton, Maryland)

Huther, Christopher S. ....'66 '92 C.888 B.S. L.276 J.D. [Preston G.E.&R.M.]
*PRACTICE AREAS: Telecommunications; Litigation.
Hutson, Harrison D. ....'26 '51 C.1055 A.B. L.273 J.D. [Ⓒ Preston G.E.&R.M.]
*PRACTICE AREAS: Maritime and Shipping Regulation Law; Environmental Law; Corporate Finance Law.
Hutt, Jason B. .... '73 '99 C.165 B.A. L.1194 J.D. [Ⓐ Bracewell&P.]
*PRACTICE AREAS: Environmental Law; Environmental Litigation; Mergers and Acquisitions.
Hutt, Peter B., II, (BV) ....'— '90 C.976 B.A. L.813 J.D. [Miller&C.]
*PRACTICE AREAS: False Claims Act; Qui Tam Litigation; Government Contracts; Health Care Litigation; Federal Civil Litigation.
Hutt, Peter Barton, (AV) .... '34 '59 C.976 B.A. L.309 LL.B. [Covington&B.]
Hutter, Allen M., (AV) ....'35 '61 C&L.178 B.A., LL.B. 1115 Mass. Ave., N.W.
Huttler, Stephen B., (P.C.), (AV) ....'49 '75 C.823 B.A. L.276 J.D. [Shaw P.]
*PRACTICE AREAS: Commercial Real Estate.
Hutto, F. Chase, III '69 '97 C&L.477 B.B.A., J.D.
(adm. in MD; not adm. in DC) 1201 New York Ave., N.W.‡
Hutto, Ingrid '67 '99 C.968 B.A. L.276 J.D.
(adm. in NY; not adm. in DC) [Ⓐ Conlon,F.P.&P.]
*PRACTICE AREAS: Civil Rights; Class Actions.
Hutton, Thomas E.M. '— '00 C.183 B.A. L.276 J.D.
(adm. in MD; not adm. in DC) [Ⓐ Powell,G.F.&M.]
*PRACTICE AREAS: Tax Exempt Organizations.
Hutton, Thomas J., (AV) ....'56 '81 C.276 B.S.F.S. L.1066 J.D. [Holland&K.]
*PRACTICE AREAS: Communications.
Hutton, Thomas P. ....'63 '88 C.10 B.S. L.192 J.D. [Muldoon M.&F.]
*PRACTICE AREAS: Employee Benefits; Federal Taxation; ERISA.
Huvelle, Jeffrey G., (AV) ....'46 '73 C.309 B.A. L.178 J.D. [Covington&B.]
Hwa, James '69 '97 C.178 B.S.E.E. L.273 J.D.
(adm. in NY; not adm. in DC; See Pat. Sect.) [Ⓐ Morgan&F.]
*PRACTICE AREAS: Intellectual Property.
Hwang, Charles C. ....'62 '89 C.309 A.B. L.178 J.D. [Crowell&M.]
*PRACTICE AREAS: Taxation.
Hyatt, Thomas K., (AV) .... '57 '82 C.93 B.A. L.665 J.D. [Ober,K.G.&S.]
Hyde, Howard L. ....'57 '83 C.197 A.B. L.309 J.D. [Ⓒ Arnold&P.]
*PRACTICE AREAS: Financial Institutions; Corporate; Securities.
Hyde, Michael Q. .... '70 '96 C.770 B.S. L.273 J.D. [Ⓐ Hale&D.]
*PRACTICE AREAS: Litigation.
Hyde, Myra B. '52 '93 C.846 B.A. L.208 J.D.
(adm. in CO; not adm. in DC) Mgr., Envir. Affs., National Cattlemen's Association
Hyde, Terrill A., (AV) ....'47 '79 C.999 B.S. L.546 J.D. [Wilmer,C.&P.]
*PRACTICE AREAS: Taxation.
Hydeman, Lee M., (AV) ....'28 '51 C.951 B.A. L.309 LL.B. 2550 M. St., N.W.
Hydrick, Jeffrey S. ....'71 '96 C.472 B.B.A. L.309 J.D. [Ⓐ Wilmer,C.&P.]

Hyland, William H., Jr. '50 '93 C.831 B.A. L.1376 J.D.
(adm. in CA; not adm. in DC) Federal Tax Managment
Hylden, Thomas, (AV) .... '46 '76 C.691 B.A. L.273 J.D. [Powers,P.S.&V.]
*PRACTICE AREAS: Education Law; Mergers, Acquisitions and Divestitures; Administrative Law; Litigation.
Hylton, Michelle L. .... '69 '97 C.94 B.A. L.180 J.D. [A McKenna&C.]
*PRACTICE AREAS: Commercial Litigation; Civil Litigation.
Hylton, Patrick C. .... '47 '86 C&L.329 B.A., J.D. D.C. Council
Hyman, David .... '61 '89 C&L.145 B.A., J.D. [© Mayer,B.&P.]
Hyman, Elizabeth A. '66 '92 C.860 B.A. L.904 J.D.
1333 New Hampshire Avenue, N.W., Suite 400
Hyman, Lester S., (AV) .... '31 '55 C.103 A.B. L.178 LL.B. [© Swidler B.S.F.]
Hyman, Paul M., (AV) .... '40 '66 C.145 B.A. L.976 LL.B. [Hyman,P.&M.]

Hyman, Phelps & McNamara, P.C., (AV)
700 Thirteenth Street, N.W., Suite 1200, 20005 ⊙
Telephone: 202-737-5600 Fax: 202-737-9329
URL: http://www.hpm.com
Robert T. Angarola (1945-1996); James R. Phelps; Paul M. Hyman; Robert A. Dormer; Stephen H. McNamara; Roger C. Thies; Thomas Scarlett; Jeffrey N. Gibbs; Brian J. Donato (Resident, Irvine, California Office); Frank J. Sasinowski; Diane Barber McColl; A. Wes Siegner, Jr.; Alan M. Kirschenbaum; Douglas B. Farquhar; John A. Gilbert, Jr.; John R. Fleder;—Marc H. Shapiro (Resident, Durham, North Carolina Office); Jennifer B. Davis; Frances K. Wu; David B. Clissold; Cassandra A. Soltis; Josephine M. Torrente; Michelle L. Butler; Patricia Ann Ades Vanstory; Thomas R. Gibson (Resident, Irvine California Office); Paul L. Ferrari; Jeffrey N. Wasserstein; Brian J. Malkin; Anne Marie Murphy; Michael D. Bernstein; Dara Susan Katcher; Larry K. Houck (Not admitted in DC). Of Counsel: Mary Kate Whalen.
Practice before all Courts, Government Agencies and International Regulatory Authorities involving Foods, Drugs, Cosmetics, Medical Devices, Biologics, Pesticides, Controlled Substances and Consumer Products.
Irvine, California Office: Hyman, Phelps & McNamara. 2603 Main Street, Suite 760. Telephone: 949-553-7400. Fax: 949-553-7433.
Durham, North Carolina Office: Hyman, Phelps & McNamara., P.C. 4819 Emperor Boulevard, Suite 400. Telephone: 919-313-4750. Fax: 919-313-4751.
See Professional Biographies, WASHINGTON, DISTRICT OF COLUMBIA

Hymel, Lin J. '— '01 L.276 J.D.
(adm. in MD; not adm. in DC; See Pat. Sect.) [A Banner&W.]
*PRACTICE AREAS: Intellectual Property; Patents; Pharmaceutical Intellectual Property; Medical Intellectual Property; Intellectual Property Litigation.
Hymo, Lawrence A., (AV) '29 '57
C.823 A.B. L.276 LL.B. 1100 New York Ave., N.W. (Pat.)

Hynak & Associates, P.C.
(See Arlington, Virginia)

Hyndman, Kelly G. .... '60 '97 C.870 B.S. L.276 J.D. [A Sughrue M.] (See Pat. Sect.)
Hynds, Joseph A. ..... '64 '91 C.894 B.A. L.273 J.D. [Rothwell,F.E.&M.] (See Pat. Sect.)
*PRACTICE AREAS: Intellectual Property.
Hynes, John L. .... '67 '00 C.231 B.A. L.276 J.D. [A Sutherland A.&B.]
*PRACTICE AREAS: Federal Taxation.
Hynes, Terence M., (AV) .... '54 '79 C.705 A.B. L.228 J.D. [Sidley A.B.&W.]
Hyun, Montgomery K. .... '22 '61 C.821 A.B. L.276 LL.B. 3637 Van Ness St., N.W.‡
Iadicicco, Robert G. .... '63 '96 C.1044 B.A. L.1209 J.D. [A Gordon&B.]
*PRACTICE AREAS: Employee Benefits; Health Law; Government Contracts; Insurance.
Ianniello, Antonia B., (AV) .... '52 '80 C.188 B.A. L.276 J.D. [Steptoe&J.]
*PRACTICE AREAS: Insurance; Insurance Defense; Insurance Coverage; Malpractice Defense; RICO.
Iannucci, Joseph S., (AV) .... '31 '56 C.569 B.A. L.309 J.D. [Jones,D.R.&P.]
*PRACTICE AREAS: Taxation; Corporate Tax Planning; International Taxation; Transfer Pricing.

Ice Miller, (AV)
1090 Vermont Avenue, N.W. Suite 920, 20005 ⊙
Telephone: 202-824-8600 Fax: 202-824-8601
Email: info@icemiller.com URL: http://www.icemiller.com
Member of Firm: G. Daniel Miller (Not admitted in DC). Of Counsel: Henry Rose; Erica L. Summers. Associate: Jason E. Levine.
Administrative Law, Antitrust, Appellate Practice, Architectural Malpractice Law, Banking, Bankruptcy, Broadcasting and Communications, Cable TV, Cable TV Franchising, Civil and Criminal Litigation, Civil Rights, Coal Law, College and University Law, Commercial and Business Litigation, Complex Litigation, Computer Law, Contracting and Litigation, Construction Law, Corporate Law, Corporate Finance, Creditors Rights Law, Drug and Medical Device Litigation, Economic Development and Incentives, Education Law, Employee Benefits Law, Entrepreneurial Services, Environmental Law, Estate Development and Finance, Franchise Law, Gaming Law, Gift and Estate Tax, Governmental Affairs, Governmental Relations, Governmental Services and Lobbying, Government Law, Government (Public) Contract Law, Government Procurement, Guardianship, Health Care Law, Immigration Law, Insurance Law, Intellectual Property and Licensing, International Law, Labor and Employment Law (including Equal Employment Litigation, ERISA Practice and Occupational Safety and Health Matters), Liability Risk Management, Licensing, Management Labor Relations Law, Mergers and Acquisitions, Minerals and Mining, Municipal Finance (Bond) Law, Municipal Finance (Bond), Dispute Resolution and Litigation, Municipal Litigation, Municipal Solid Waste Resource Recovery, Municipal Utility Regulation, Occupational Hazards Law (Black Lung, Asbestosis, etc.), Patent, Trademark and Copyright, Plaintiff's Trial Practice, Probate Law, Product Liability Law, Public Agency, Public Authority Financing Law, Public Contract Law, Public Employment Relations, Public Entity Law, Public Finance, Public Health Law, Public Housing Law, Public Schools, Public Sector Collective Bargaining, Public Utility Law, Public Works, Professional Malpractice Law, Real Estate Law (including Sales, Development and Financing, Mortgage Banking, Secured Transactions, Sale/Leasebacks, Condominiums and Zoning), Regulation, Risk and Claims Management, Securities Regulation Law, Sports Law, Taxation (Federal, State and Local), Tax Exempt Organizations, Tort Law, Toxic Torts, Transportation Law, Utility Law, Venture Capital, Venture Finance Services, Workers' Compensation.
Counsel for: American United Life Insurance Co.; Chrysler Corp.; Ford Motor Company; General Electric Company; Indiana Bankers Assn.
Indianapolis, Indiana Office: One American Square, Box 82001. Telephone: 317-236-2100. Fax: 317-236-2219. Internet E-mail: info@icemiller.com. Web Site Address: http://www.icemiller.com.
Chicago, Illinois Office: 135 South LaSalle Street, Suite 4100. Telephone: 312-726-1567. Fax: 312-641-6263. Internet E-mail: info@icemiller.com. Web Site Address: http://www.icemiller.com.
Granger, Indiana Office: 51323 Pebble Beach Court. Telephone: 219-234-7955. Fax: 219-234-7965. Internet E-mail: info@icemiller.com. Web Site Address: http://www.icemiller.com.
Mission Hills, Kansas Office: 6430 Norwood. Telephone: 913-403-8788. Email: info@icemiller.com. Web Site Address: http://www.icemiller.com.
Revisers of the Indiana Law Digest for this Directory
See Professional Biographies, WASHINGTON, DISTRICT OF COLUMBIA

Ickes, Harold, (AV) '39 '73 C.813 B.A. L.178 J.D.
(adm. in NY; not adm. in DC) [Meyer,S.E.&K.] (⊙Mineola, NY)
*PRACTICE AREAS: Government Relations; Employment and Labor Law; Election Law; FEC Law.
Idzelis, Rima '— '01 C.475 B.A. L.1194 J.D.
(adm. in WI; not adm. in DC) [A Morgan,L.&B.]
Ifft, Richard A., (AV) .... '59 '85 C.945 B.A. L.276 J.D. [Wiley R.&F.]
*PRACTICE AREAS: Insurance.
Ifrah, A. Jeff .... '68 '93 C&L.978 B.A., J.D. [A Paul,H.J.&W.]
*PRACTICE AREAS: White Collar Criminal Litigation; Government Contracts; International Trade Litigation.
Iheukwumere, Emmanuel O. '62 '95 C.648 B.A. L.831 J.D.
(adm. in PA; not adm. in DC) [A Eaton&M.] ⊙
*PRACTICE AREAS: Medical Malpractice; Products Liability; Personal Injury.
Ihnen, Jeffrey L., (AV) '51 '80
C.898 B.A. L.273 J.D. [© Rothwell,F.E.&M.] (See Pat. Sect.)
*PRACTICE AREAS: Intellectual Property Law.

Ikenson, Frederick L., (AV) .... '40 '68 C.188 B.A. L.564 J.D. [F.L.Ikenson]
*PRACTICE AREAS: Customs and International Trade Law.

Ikenson, Frederick L., P.C., (AV)
1621 New Hampshire Avenue, N.W., 20009
Telephone: 202-483-8900 Facsimile: 202-483-9368
Email: Fikenson@ikenson.com URL: http://www.lawyers.com/ikensonlaw
Frederick L. Ikenson;—Larry Hampel.
Practice before Federal Courts, Government Agencies and Congressional Committees. International Trade and Customs Law.
See Professional Biographies, WASHINGTON, DISTRICT OF COLUMBIA

Iley, Brooke Thomas .... '69 '94 C.446 B.S. L.180 J.D. [A Blank R.C.&M.] (⊙Balt., MD)
*PRACTICE AREAS: Labor and Employment Law.
Illingworth, Jennifer J. '72 '98 C&L.188 B.S., J.D.
(adm. in NY; not adm. in DC) [A Porter W.M.&A.]
*PRACTICE AREAS: Litigation.
Imbroscio, Michael X. .... '68 '94 C.608 B.A. L.309 J.D. [Covington&B.]
Imlay, Christopher D., (AV) .... '53 '78 C.855 B.A. L.904 J.D. [Booth,F.I.&T.]
Impastato, Arthur A. .... '54 '87 C.273 B.A. L.128 J.D. [© Fulbright&J.]
*PRACTICE AREAS: International Trade; Securities.
Imperial, Eric H. .... '64 '89 C.228 A.B. L.1068 J.D. P.O. Box 15842
Imundo, Aimee L. '64 '92 C.66 B.A. L.276 J.D.
Assoc. Gen. Con., Antitrust, General Electric Co.
Imus, Neil W., (AV) .... '53 '85 C.198 B.S. L.276 J.D. [Vinson&E.]
*PRACTICE AREAS: Litigation; Antitrust and Trade Regulation.
Inbar, Jill Ilan Berger .... '69 '97 C.188 B.A. L.978 J.D. [A Shea&G.]
Inbar, Tomer J. .... '— '97 C.1349 B.A. L.569 J.D. [A Morgan,L.&B.]
Ince, William K., (AV) .... '36 '62 C.674 A.B. L.976 LL.B. [Cameron&H.]
*PRACTICE AREAS: International Trade Law; Customs Law.
Incorvaia Mroz, Denise '69 '95 C.444 B.A. L.128 J.D.
V.P. Anti-Piracy Coun., Recording Industry Assoc. of America, Inc.
Indelicarto, Thomas C. .... '— '97 C.651 B.S. L.665 J.D. [A Arnold&P.]
*PRACTICE AREAS: Litigation; Product Liability.
Infante, Marie Catherine '49 '86 C.446 B.S.N. L.128 J.D.
701 Pennsylvania Avenue, N.W.

Ing, Edwin T.C., (AV) '49 '75 C.154 B.A. L.273 J.D.
Suite 800, 2121 K Street, N.W., 20037
Telephone: 202-457-6630 Telecopier: 202-293-0027
Federal Taxation and Corporate Practice.
See Professional Biographies, WASHINGTON, DISTRICT OF COLUMBIA

Ingall, Seth M. .... '65 '92 C.30 B.A. L.904 J.D. Dir.- Staff Coun. Dept., GEICO Corp.
Ingalls, Dorothy M. '64 '90
C.546 B.S. L.378 J.D. Sr. Coun. & Corp. Secy., Marriott Intl. Corp.
*RESPONSIBILITIES: Real Estate and Development.
Ingber, Kathy Kresch .... '— '86 C.188 B.A. L.94 J.D. [© Kirkpatrick&L.]
*PRACTICE AREAS: Investment Management; Corporate; Securities.
Inge, John R., (AV) .... '46 '74 C.119 B.S. L.818 J.D. [Sughrue M.] (See Pat. Sect.)
*PRACTICE AREAS: Intellectual Property Law.
Ingebretson, Charles L. '55 '87 C.228 A.B. L.602 J.D.
(adm. in VA; not adm. in DC) [© Bracewell&P.]
*PRACTICE AREAS: Public Utility Regulation; Regulated Industries; Trade Regulation.
Ingeneri, Philip M. '73 '99 C.771 B.A. L.94 J.D.
(adm. in NY; not adm. in DC) [S Howrey S.A.&W.]
*PRACTICE AREAS: Antitrust; Intellectual Property; International Trade.
Inglima, Philip T., (AV) .... '62 '88 C&L.276 A.B., J.D. [Baach R.&L.P.]
*PRACTICE AREAS: White Collar Crime; Criminal Defense; Civil Litigation.
Ingoldsby, Thomas M. .... '— '70 C.103 B.A. L.228 J.D. [Verner,L.B.M.&H.]
*PRACTICE AREAS: Project Finance; Public Finance; International Finance.
Ingraffia, Courtney E. .... '67 '95 C.164 B.A. L.861 J.D. [A Arnold&P.]
*PRACTICE AREAS: Toxic Tort Litigation; Environmental Litigation; Pharmaceutical; Products Liability.
Ingram, John M. .... '57 '86 C.546 B.S. L.128 J.D. Assoc. Gen. Coun., Fannie Mae
Ingram, Kenneth J., (BV) .... '45 '70 C.31 B.A. L.910 J.D. [Whiteford,T.&P.]
*PRACTICE AREAS: Government Contracts; Community Association Law; Civil Practice.
Ingrassia, John R. .... '67 '96 C.1040 B.A. L.1019 J.D. [A Fried,F.H.S.&J.]
*PRACTICE AREAS: Antitrust.
Ingrisano, Joseph A. .... '55 '80 C.1044 B.A. L.904 J.D. [Kutak R.]
*PRACTICE AREAS: Securities Litigation and Arbitration; Insurance Defense; General Litigation.
Inkellis, Steven A. '48 '79 C.454 B.A. L.273 J.D.
V.P., Legal & Pub. Pol., MCI Telecommunications Corp. (Regulatory Affairs)
Inman, Harry A., (AV) ..... '— '52 C.309 A.B. L.893 LL.B. [Inman D.] (⊙Honolulu, HI)
*PRACTICE AREAS: International Business; Business Transactions; Government Relations.

Inman Deming LLP, (AV)
Hamilton Square, 600 Fourteenth Street, N.W., Suite 600, 20005-2004 ⊙
Telephone: 202-347-6800 Facsimile: 202-347-6013
Email: Inman.Deming@InmanDeming.com URL: http://www.InmanDeming.com
Harry A. Inman; Stuart H. Deming. Of Counsel: Robert Layton (Not admitted in DC); Edward A. Dragon; Joseph P. Smith III; Emery W. Harper (Not admitted in DC); Garry L. Walton (Not admitted in DC).
International Transactions, Investments, Trade and Procurement, Corporate, Securities, Legislative and Administrative Law, Civil, White Collar and International Litigation, International and Domestic Arbitration, Commercial Transactions, Probate and Estates, Admiralty, International Maritime and Maritime Finance Law, and Special Matters Relating to Foreign Corrupt Practices Issues, Economic Sanctions and Visas.
Kalamazoo, Michigan Office: 229 East Michigan Avenue, Suite 145, 49007-6411. Telephone: 616-382-8080. Facsimile: 616-382-8083. E-Mail: Inman.Deming@InmanDeming.com.
See Professional Biographies, WASHINGTON, DISTRICT OF COLUMBIA

Inokon, Charles M. .... '71 '99 C.446 B.S. L.188 J.D. [A Piper M.R.&W.]
*PRACTICE AREAS: Venture Capital; Emerging Technologies.
International Business Law Firm, P.C., The .... 1155 Conn. Ave., N.W.
Intoccia, Gregory F. .... '56 '85 C.1070 B.S. L.208 J.D. [© Howrey S.A.&W.]
*PRACTICE AREAS: Telecommunications.
IP Strategies, P.C. .... 806 7th Street, N.W., Suite 301
Ipeker, Baris H. .... '69 '94 C.893 B.S. L.1365 J.D. [A Venable,A.B.H.&C.]
*PRACTICE AREAS: Real Estate; Business Transactions; Telecommunications.
Irelan, William T. .... '40 '66 C.504 A.B. L.893 J.D. [Friedeman,I.W.&L.]
*PRACTICE AREAS: Corporate Law; Non-Profit Organizations Law; Litigation; Employer-Employee Relations Law.
Ireland, James F., III, (AV) .... '54 '80 C.732 B.A. L.945 J.D. [Cole,R.&B.]
*PRACTICE AREAS: Telecommunications Law and Regulation; Cable Communications; Franchising; Wireless Communications; Internet Law.
Ireland, Kathy Davidson '55 '80
C.400 B.S. L.945 J.D. Assoc. Coun., Investment Company Institute
*RESPONSIBILITIES: Securities.
Ireland, Oliver I. '48 '74 C.976 B.A. L.846 J.D.
(adm. in MA; not adm. in DC) [© Morrison&F.]
*PRACTICE AREAS: Financial Services Law.
Irish, Herbert A. '53 '78 C.893 B.A. L.902 J.D.
(adm. in VA; not adm. in DC) Coun., National Paint & Coatings Association

Irish, Robert W. '— '99 C.860 B.A. L.966 J.D.
(adm. in IL; not adm. in DC) [Ⓐ Kirkland&E.]
*PRACTICE AREAS: International Trade.
Irizarry-Díaz, Carmen, (AV) .... '56 '82 C&L.677 B.B.A., J.D. [Ⓒ Silverstein&M.]
*PRACTICE AREAS: Estate Planning.
Irons, R. Elizabeth '— '79
C.657 B.A. L.128 J.D. V.P. & Asst. Gen. Coun., Marriott Intl., Inc.
Irvin, Ben L., (AV) '35 '68 C.645 B.A. L.1002 LL.B.
(adm. in MD; not adm. in DC) [Aitken I.B.&V.]
*PRACTICE AREAS: Customs; International Trade; Food and Drug; Immigration Law.
Irvin, Kenneth W. ....'64 '93 C.158 B.S.E.E. L.823 J.D. [Morrison&F.]
Irvin, Stuart ....'61 '89 C.1365 B.A. L.273 J.D. [Ⓒ Covington&B.]
Irvin, Wm Robert .... '59 '83 C.877 B.S. L.629 J.D. Ctr. for Marine Conserv.
Irving, John S., Jr., (AV) .... '40 '65 C.103 A.B. L.276 J.D. [Kirkland&E.]
*PRACTICE AREAS: Civil Rights; Labor and Employment.
Irving, Margaret A. '49 '78 C.67 A.B. L.30 J.D.
(adm. in VA; not adm. in DC) 2234 47th St. N.W.
Irving, Richard C. .... '— '93 C.588 B.S. L.273 J.D. [Ⓐ Banner&W.] (See Pat. Sect.)
*PRACTICE AREAS: Intellectual Property Law; Patents; Computer and Software Patents; Electrical Patents; Patent Prosecution.
Irving, Thomas L., (AV) '51 '77
C.878 B.A.Chem. L.228 J.D. [Finnegan,H.F.G.&D.] (See Pat. Sect.)
*PRACTICE AREAS: Chemical Intellectual Property; Chemical Patent Prosecution; Chemical Patents; Patent Interference Practice.
Irwin, Andrew D. ....'71 '96 C.674 A.B. L.273 J.D. [Ⓐ Latham&W.]
*PRACTICE AREAS: Government Contracts; White Collar Crime; Health Care Fraud; Litigation; Government Ethics.
Irwin, David A., (AV) .... '40 '67 C.30 B.A. L.904 J.D. [Irwin,C.&T.]
Irwin, Eleanore A. ....'73 '98 C.999 B.A. L.329 J.D. [Ⓐ Guerrieri,E.&C.]
Irwin, Geoffrey S. .... '70 '96 C.276 B.A. L.846 J.D. [Ⓐ Kirkland&E.]
*PRACTICE AREAS: Litigation.
Irwin, Campbell & Tannenwald, P.C., (AV) ....1730 Rhode Island Ave., N.W.
Isa, John P. .... '71 '99 C.1356 B.A. L.30 J.D. [Ⓐ Paul,H.J.&W.]
*PRACTICE AREAS: Employee Benefits; ERISA; Employment Law.
Isaac, Christopher P., (BV) '59 '87
C.665 B.S. L.273 J.D. [Finnegan,H.F.G.&D.] (See Pat. Sect.)
*PRACTICE AREAS: Patent Prosecution.
Isaacs, Davida H. ....'71 '96 C.1036 B.A. L.569 J.D. [Ⓐ Venable,A.B.H.&C.]
*PRACTICE AREAS: Intellectual Property Litigation; Patent Litigation; Trademark Litigation; Trademark Prosecution.
Isaacson, Thomas A. ....'58 '84 C.197 A.B. L.659 J.D. [Howrey S.A.&W.]
*PRACTICE AREAS: Antitrust; Complex Litigation; Environmental Law.
Isaacson, William A., (AV) .... '60 '87 C.684 B.A. L.893 J.D. [Boies,S.&F.]
*PRACTICE AREAS: Commercial Litigation; Arbitration.
Isacson, John P., Jr. .... '— '88 C.446 B.A. L.273 J.D. [Heller E.W.&M.] (Pat.)
*PRACTICE AREAS: U.S. and Foreign Patent Law; Regulatory Law.
Isakoff, Peter D., (AV) ....'51 '79 C&L.178 B.A., J.D. [Weil,G.&M.]
*PRACTICE AREAS: Civil, Criminal and Tax Litigation; Government Contracts Fraud; Securities Fraud; Antitrust; Trade Secret Litigation.
Isbell, David B., (AV) .... '29 '56 C&L.976 B.A., J.D. [Ⓒ Covington&B.]
Isele, Michele A. '63 '88 C.867 B.A. L.128 J.D.
V.P., Develop., Citizens for a Sound Economy
Isenberg, Beth Ann .... '70 '98 C.865 B.S. L.982 J.D. 1722 Eye Street, NW
Isenberg, Clifford Scott '72 '97 C.910 A.B. L.893 J.D.
(adm. in VA; not adm. in DC) 4850 Connecticut Ave., N.W.
Isenberg, Craig ....'70 '97 C.31 B.A. L.861 J.D. [Ⓐ Mayer,B.&P.]
Isenberg, Jerry A. '50 '75 C.846 B.A. L.659 J.D.
(adm. in TX; not adm. in DC) [McGuirewoods]
*PRACTICE AREAS: Securities Litigation; Compliance and Enforcement.
Isenberg, Robin ....'47 '78 C.550 B.A. L.273 J.D. Millin Publicaions
Isenman, Michael K. ....'66 '93 C.309 A.B. L.477 J.D. [Shea&G.]
*PRACTICE AREAS: Securities; Litigation.
Ishida, Natsue '73 '99 C.103 B.A. L.273 J.D.
(adm. in NY; not adm. in DC) KPMG LLP
Isicson, Anita ....'49 '76 C.659 B.S. L.276 J.D. Auditor Master - D.C. Supr. Ct.
Ising, Elizabeth A. .... '70 '00 C.1369 B.S. L.575 J.D. [Ⓐ Gibson,D.&C.]
Isla, Ruby M. .... '72 '97 C.259 B.S. L.273 J.D. Atty-Advsr., Dept. of Energy
Isles, Adam Revere '69 '98 C.976 B.A. L.309 J.D.
(adm. in MA; not adm. in DC) U.S. Dept. of Jus.
Israel, Benjamin Lee ....'62 '87 C.823 B.A. L.273 J.D. [Troutman S.]
*PRACTICE AREAS: Electric, Natural Gas and Independent Power Development and Regulation; Federal and State Election Law; Energy; Real Estate; Finance.
Israel, Brian D. .... '67 '97 C.1275 B.A. L.569 J.D. [Ⓐ Arnold&P.]
*PRACTICE AREAS: Environmental; Litigation.
Israel, Deborah J. ....'64 '90 C&L.705 B.A., J.D. [Piper M.R.&W.]
*PRACTICE AREAS: Commercial Litigation; Business Litigation; Intellectual Property.
Israel, Sheryl R., (AV) ....'61 '87 C.861 B.A. L.94 J.D. [Ⓒ Shaw P.]
*PRACTICE AREAS: Transportation; Aviation; Administrative Law.
Isser, Steve N. ....'55 '00 C.659 B.A. L.846 J.D. [Ⓐ Ballard S.A.&I.]
*PRACTICE AREAS: Business Law; Mergers and Acquisitions; Utility Law; Antitrust.
Isserles, Marc E. '71 '01 C.771 B.A. L.309 J.D.
(adm. in MD; not adm. in DC) [Ⓐ Jenner&B.]
*PRACTICE AREAS: Litigation.
Iszard, Alexis S. C. '52 '78 C&L.30 B.S., J.D.
Sr. V.P. & Gen. Coun., Combined Properties, Incorporated
Itkin, David .... '62 '89 C&L.273 B.A., J.D. Legal Aid Soc.
Ito, Yoshihide '55 '91 C.999 M.P.P. L.309 LL.B.
(adm. in NY; not adm. in DC) [Bingham D.]
Ittig, Gerard W., (AV) ....'45 '75 C.107 B.A. L.838 J.D. 1901 18th St., N.W.
Ittig, Judith B., (AV) ....'46 '72 C&L.107 B.A., J.D. 1901 18th St., N.W.
Ittig, Kristen Schmeelcke ....'68 '97 C.30 B.A. L.880 J.D. [Ⓐ Holland&K.]
*PRACTICE AREAS: Litigation.
Iturregui, Juan C. ....'— '90 C.454 B.A. L.128 J.D. [Hunton&W.]
*PRACTICE AREAS: Government Affairs; Legislative Practice; Trade and Commerce Issues; Project Development.
Itzkoff, Donald M. .... '— '87 C.103 A.B. L.273 J.D. [Foley&L.]
*PRACTICE AREAS: Transportation; Legislative; Regulatory.
Itzkoff, Mark L. ....'55 '89 C.696 B.A. L.365 J.D. [Ⓒ Olsson,F.&W.]
*PRACTICE AREAS: Food and Drug Regulation; Administrative Law; Environmental Law.
Iuculano, Russel P. ....'52 '87 C.128 B.A. L.64 J.D. V.P., Metropolitan Life Ins. Co.
Ivancovich, Anthony J., (BV) ....'59 '84 C.1375 B.A. L.273 J.D. [Andrews&K.]
*PRACTICE AREAS: Natural Gas Pipelines; Natural Gas Regulation; Natural Gas Contracts; Public Utility Regulation; Administrative Hearings and Appeals.
Ivers, Melissa L. .... '71 '97 C.183 B.A. L.128 J.D. [Ⓐ Morrison&F.]
Iverson, William D., (AV) .... '42 '69 C.659 B.S. L.976 LL.B. [Covington&B.]
Ives, Stephen B., Jr., (AV) ....'24 '52 C.309 A.B. L.976 LL.B. 1300 19th St., N.W.
Ivey, Carole Jean ...... '48 '78 C.502 B.A. L.273 J.D. National Assn. of Sec. Dealers, Inc.
Ivey, Gerald F. ....'57 '82 C&L.893 B.A., J.D. [Finnegan,H.F.G.&D.]
*PRACTICE AREAS: Biotechnology Patents; Medical Intellectual Property; Mechanical Patents; Intellectual Property Litigation.
Ivey, Glenn F. .... '61 '87 C.674 A.B. L.309 J.D. [Preston G.E.&R.M.]
*PRACTICE AREAS: Legislative; Utilities Regulation; Criminal Litigation; Telecommunications Law.
Ivins, Benjamin F. P., II, (AV) '47 '77 C.210 B.A. L.276 J.D.
Sr. Assoc. Gen. Coun., National Association of Broadcasters
*RESPONSIBILITIES: Copyright; Trademark; Communications Law; Administrative Law.
Ivins, Steven D. .... '37 '62 C&L.659 B.S., LL.B. Kiplinger Wash. Editors

Ivins, Phillips & Barker, Chartered, (AV) BB
Suite 600, 1700 Pennsylvania Avenue, N.W., 20006
Telephone: 202-393-7600 Fax: 202-393-7601; 347-4256
Email: IPB@ipbtax.com URL: http://www.ipbtax.com
James S. Y. Ivins (1885-1960); Percy W. Phillips (1892-1969); Richard B. Barker (1906-1988); H. Stewart Dunn, Jr.; Carroll J. Savage; Eric R. Fox; William L. Sollee; Carol K. Nickel; Alan W. Granwell; Leslie Jay Schneider; Robert H. Wellen; Kevin P. O'Brien; Daniel B. Stone; Patrick J. Smith; Michael R. Huffstetler; Laurie E. Keenan; Jeffrey E. Moeller; Steven H. Witmer; Rosina B. Barker; Jodi H. Epstein;—Dean R. Morley, IV; David Gregory Coolidge; Eric D. Chason (Not admitted in DC); Robin M. Solomon; Lisa M. Robinson; Colleen L.S. Markham; Marlene Ellen Laro; David D. Sherwood (Not admitted in DC); Karen Sullivan Dean. Of Counsel: Jay W. Glasmann; Clifton B. Cates, III; Alan J. J. Swirski; Jeannie Leahy (Not admitted in DC).
Tax Law, Employee Benefits, Estate Planning and Related Litigation.
See Professional Biographies, WASHINGTON, DISTRICT OF COLUMBIA

Iweanoge, Charles C ..... '64 '99 C.999 L.1280 J.D. 1010 Vermont Avenue, NW, Ste. 600
Iweanoge, John O. '63 '93 C.999 B.S.C. L.1280 J.D.
1010 Vermont Avenue NW Suite 600
Izenberg, Joshua J. '73 '01 C.012 B.Sc. L.025 LL.B.
(adm. in MA; not adm. in DC) [Ⓐ Baker&M.]
*PRACTICE AREAS: Information Technology/Telecommunications; Corporate and Partnership Law.
Jabara, Abdeen M. ....'40 '66 C.477 A.B. L.912 J.D. ADC Resch. Inst.
Jaber, Makram ....'63 '96 C.999 B.E. L.1365 J.D. [Ⓐ Hunton&W.]
*PRACTICE AREAS: Environmental Law.
Jablon, Cara S. ....'43 '78 C.518 A.B. L.273 J.D. [Ⓒ Bergeson&C.]
*PRACTICE AREAS: Federal Insecticide, Fungicide and Rodenticide Act (FIFRA); Toxic Substances Regulation; Pesticide Regulation; Chemical Regulation; Environmental Compliance.
Jablon, Robert A., (AV) ....'39 '65 C.401 B.S. L.309 LL.B. [Spiegel&M.]
*PRACTICE AREAS: Antitrust; Energy; Municipal Utility Regulation; Complex Litigation; Regulatory Agency Practice.
Jacewicz, Benjamin R. .... '67 '93 C.228 A.B. L.893 J.D. [Ⓐ O'Melveny&M.]
Jack, W. Andrew .... '62 '86 C&L.276 B.A., J.D. [Ⓒ Covington&B.]
Jackel, Jonathan E. ....'65 '91 C.94 B.S. L.276 J.D. [Burt,M.&M.]
*PRACTICE AREAS: Tax Litigation; International Taxation; Taxation.
Jackins, Alexander X. .... '69 '00 C.446 B.A. L.128 J.D. 1133 19th St., NW
Jackman, Jennifer S. ....'73 '98 C.205 B.A. L.64 J.D. [Ⓐ Whiteford,T.&P.]
*PRACTICE AREAS: Insurance Defense Litigation; Litigation; Medical Malpractice Defense.
Jackman, Peter A. ......'71 '98 C.884 B.S. L.64 J.D. [Ⓐ Sterne,K.G.&F.] (See Pat. Sect.)
*PRACTICE AREAS: Intellectual Property Law.
Jackowski, Sarah Daly '68 '93
C.1369 B.S. L.276 J.D. [Ⓐ Charapp,D.&W.] (⊙Bethesda, MD)
*PRACTICE AREAS: Corporate Law; Commercial Transactions; Trade and Professional Associations Law.
Jackson, Amy Berman, (AV) ....'54 '79 C&L.309 A.B., J.D. [Trout&R.] ⊙
*PRACTICE AREAS: Complex Litigation; Criminal Investigations and Defense; Criminal Trials; Civil Trials; Appeals.
Jackson, Anne Marie ....'69 '94 C.1365 B.A. L.904 J.D. [Ⓐ Sherman,M.C.&A.]
*PRACTICE AREAS: Family Law.
Jackson, Camilla M. ....'72 '98 C&L.178 B.A., J.D. [Ⓐ Covington&B.]
Jackson, Chadwick A. '70 '99 C&L.823 B.S., J.D.
(adm. in NY; not adm. in DC) [Ⓐ Swidler B.S.F.]
*PRACTICE AREAS: Intellectual Property; Licensing; Litigation.
Jackson, Clinton A. .... '56 '84 C.511 B.A. L.276 J.D. 1828 18th St., N.W.
Jackson, Darryl W., (AV) ....'53 '77 C.411 B.A. L.329 J.D. [Arnold&P.]
*PRACTICE AREAS: Litigation; White Collar Criminal Defense.
Jackson, David W. ....'55 '88 C.645 B.A. L.276 J.D. Pres., Northridge Capital‡
*RESPONSIBILITIES: U.S. and U.K. Commercial Real Estate; Acquisitions, Financing and Development; Transactions; International Investment; Venture Capital and Private Equity.
Jackson, Denise E. ....'60 '94 C.30 B.S. L.446 J.D. [Ⓐ Friedlander,M.S.K.&O.]
*PRACTICE AREAS: Commercial Real Estate; Commercial Finance; Commercial Leasing.
Jackson, Edward ....'53 '88 C.803 B.S. L.446 J.D. [Ⓒ Crowell&M.]
Jackson, Eric S. ....'66 '93 C.813 A.B. L.966 J.D. [Robins,K.M.&C.]
*PRACTICE AREAS: Business Litigation; Intellectual Property Litigation; Employment Law; Civil Litigation.
Jackson, J. Andrew ....'59 '84 C.885 B.S.E.E. L.923 J.D. [Dickstein S.M.&O.]
*PRACTICE AREAS: Government Contract Law; Government Contract Litigation; Federal Litigation.
Jackson, James K. .... '40 '66 C.802 B.B.A. L.846 LL.B. [Ⓒ Verner,L.B.M.&H.]
*PRACTICE AREAS: Taxation; Business Entities Law; Tax Controversies.
Jackson, Jerome D. '56 '87 C.453 B.S. L.818 J.D.
1101 Pennsylvania Avenue, N.W., Suite 800 (Pat.) ⊙
Jackson, Jerry L. ....'52 '77 C.1365 B.A. L.280 J.D. [Ⓒ Skadden,A.S.M.&F.]
Jackson, John Henry, IV '72 '98 C.974 B.A. L.339 J.D.
(adm. in LA; not adm. in DC) Program Analyst, U.S. Dept. of Labor
Jackson, Judith ....'38 '90 C.446 B.S. L.904 J.D. 2745 29th St., N.W.‡
Jackson, Julie M. .... '69 '97 C.282 B.A. L.893 J.D. [Ⓐ Steptoe&J.]
Jackson, Kevin T. '57 '82 C&L.259 B.A., J.D.
(adm. in FL; not adm. in DC) Georgetown Univ. Sch. of Bus. Admn.
Jackson, Kristie '72 '00 C.362 B.A. L.1209 J.D.
(adm. in VA; not adm. in DC) [Ⓐ Preston G.E.&R.M.]
*PRACTICE AREAS: Litigation.
Jackson, Lee W. .... '50 '75 C.355 B.A. L.273 J.D. [O'Donnell,S.&A.]
*PRACTICE AREAS: Labor Law; Civil Rights Law.
Jackson, Lisa L. ....'66 '93 C.893 B.A. L.446 J.D. [Ⓐ Holland&K.]
*PRACTICE AREAS: Real Estate; Land Use; Environmental.
Jackson, Mark D., (AV) .... '59 '85 C.30 B.S. L.245 J.D. [Sutherland A.&B.]
*PRACTICE AREAS: Real Estate; Secured Transactions Law; Debtor Creditor Law; Corporate Law.
Jackson, Neal A., (AV) '43 '68 C.575 A.B. L.276 J.D.
Vice President for Legal Affairs, National Public Radio
Jackson, Rebecca L., (AV) ....'51 '78 C.502 B.S. L.276 J.D. [Shaw P.]
*PRACTICE AREAS: Health Care; Technology; Corporate.
Jackson, Richard F. .... '62 '87 C&L.276 B.S., J.D. [Ⓒ Morgan,L.&B.]
Jackson, Robert H. ....'51 '76 C.755 B.A. L.494 J.D. [Ⓒ Reed S.]
*PRACTICE AREAS: Communications.
Jackson, Robert M., (AV) ....'— '78 C.273 B.A. L.128 J.D. [Ⓒ Blooston,M.D.D.&P.]
*PRACTICE AREAS: Telecommunications Law; Cellular Communications; FCC Licensing; FCC Regulation.
Jackson, Suzanne H. ......'63 '90 C.914 B.A. L.309 J.D. Dir., Ayuda Clinica Legal Latina
Jackson, Thomas C. ....'59 '84 C.31 B.A. L.309 J.D. [Kelley D.&W.]
*PRACTICE AREAS: Environmental Law; Endangered Species; Litigation.
Jackson, Thomas H. .... '— '82 C.659 B.S.E.E. L.776 J.D. [Banner&W.] (See Pat. Sect.)
*PRACTICE AREAS: Intellectual Property Law; Patents; Electrical Intellectual Property; Intellectual Property Litigation; Computer and Software Patents.
Jackson, Vicki C. ....'51 '76 C&L.976 B.A., J.D. 600 Nj Ave Nw
Jackson, William C. '69 '98 C.309 B.A. L.178 J.D.
(adm. in MA; not adm. in DC) [Ⓐ Boies,S.&F.]
*PRACTICE AREAS: Litigation; International Arbitration.

Jackson & Campbell, P.C., (AV) BB
One Lafayette Centre, 300 South Tower, 1120-20th Street, N.W., 20036 ⊙
Telephone: 202-457-1600 Telecopier: 202-457-1678
Email: info@jackscamp.com URL: http://www.jackscamp.com
James E. Brammer; John J. Brennan, III; Richard W. Bryan; Arthur D. Burger; Robert Clayton Cooper; David H. Cox; Timothy R. Dingilian; Benjamin W. Dulany; Arthur C. Elgin, Jr.; Vernon W. Johnson, III; Robert N. Kelly; Richard S. Kuhl; Peter Lipresti; Warren C. Lutz; John J. Matteo; Nicholas S. McConnell; M. Elizabeth Medaglia; James R. Michal; Robert E. Rider, Jr.; James P. Schaller; Alan R. Swendiman; Donald L. Uttrich;—Raymond P. Ausrotas; Janet A. Brown; Kristan M. Cassidy; Kenneth C. Crickman; Nkeisha J. Dumas; Elisa A. Eisenberg; John A. Giannetti, Jr. (Not admitted in DC); Ngoc H. Lam; Daniel J. Lynn; Barbara M.R. Marvin; Erin N. McGonagle; Syeda B. Naqvi; Robert Notigan; Jason A. Pardo; Susan Phillips; Ann Marie Terzaken. Of Counsel: Jeffrey L. Berger; Roy L. Kaufmann; Michael Paige.
Antitrust and Trade Regulation, Corporate and Securities, Employment, Environmental, Estates and Trusts, Hospitals and Health Care, Insurance Coverage, Intellectual Property, International Telecommunications and International Trade, Litigation, Professional and Medical Malpractice Defense, Property and Asset Management, Tax, Title Insurance, Trade Associations and Charitable Foundations Law. General Practice.
Rockville, Maryland Office: Suite 225, 200 A Monroe Street. Telephone: 301-340-0450.
Baltimore, Maryland Office: 111 S. Calvert Street, Suite 2700. Telephone: 410-385-5343.
Vienna, Virginia Office: 8300 Boone Boulevard, Suite 500. Telephone: 703-522-1330.
See Professional Biographies, WASHINGTON, DISTRICT OF COLUMBIA

Jackson & Jessup, P.C.
(See Arlington, Virginia)

Jackson & Kelly PLLC, (AV) BB
2401 Pennsylvania Avenue, N.W., Suite 400, 20037 ⊙
Telephone: 202-973-0200 Fax: 202-973-0232
Email: info@jacksonkelly.com URL: http://www.jacksonkelly.com
Members of Firm: Thad S. Huffman; G. Lindsay Simmons; John K. McDonald. Of Counsel: Dennis J. Whittlesey.
Health, Safety and Environmental, Regulatory and Legislative, Litigation, Corporate, Public Utilities, Coal, Metal and Minerals Development, Construction, Oil and Gas, Natural Resources, Endangered Species and Marine Mammals, Taxation, Municipal Bond, Labor and Employment, Insurance, Estate Planning, Real Estate, Securities, Bankruptcy, Banking, Federal Lands and Royalties, Health Care, Workers Compensation, Federal Black Lung, Admiralty, Government Contracts Law; Intellectual Property.
Charleston, West Virginia Office: 1600 Laidley Tower, P.O. Box 553. Telephone: 304-340-1000. Fax: 304-340-1130.
Martinsburg, West Virginia Office: 217 West Burke Street, P.O. Box 1068. Telephone: 304-263-8800. Fax: 304-263-7110.
Morgantown, West Virginia Office: 6000 Hampton Center, P.O. Box 619. Telephone: 304-599-3000. Fax: 304-285-2040.
New Martinsville, West Virginia Office: 256 Russell Avenue, P.O. Box 68. Telephone: 304-455-1751. Fax: 304-455-6314.
Parkersburg, West Virginia Office: 412 Market Street, Suite 202, P.O. Box 1144. Telephone: 304-424-3490. Fax: 304-424-3499.
Fairmont, West Virginia Office: 1000 Technology Drive, Suite 1310. Telephone: 304-368-2000. Fax: 304-368-2020.
Lexington, Kentucky Office: 175 East Main Street, Suite 500, P.O. Box 2150. Telephone: 859-255-9500. Fax: 859-281-6478.
Denver, Colorado Office: Denver Place-Plaza Tower, 1099 Eighteenth Street, Suite 2150. Telephone: 303-390-0003. Fax: 303-390-0177.
Wheeling, West Virginia Office: 1144 Market Street. Telephone: 304-233-4000. Fax: 304-233-4077.
Revisors of the West Virginia Law Digest for this Directory
See Professional Biographies, WASHINGTON, DISTRICT OF COLUMBIA

Jackson Lewis Schnitzler & Krupman, (AV)
1156 Fifteenth Street, N.W. Suite 500, 20005 ⊙
Telephone: 202-347-5200 Facsimile: 202-223-8557
Email: washingtondc@jacksonlewis.com URL: http://www.jacksonlewis.com
Members of Firm: Michael N. Petkovich; Harold R. Weinrich. Associate: Monique Y. Fortenberry; Daria E. Neal (Not admitted in DC).
Labor Relations, Employment Discrimination, Wrongful Discharge and Other Employment-Related Litigation, Employee Benefits and Pension Law, Wage and Hour, OSHA, Immigration Law, Public Sector and State Labor Relations Law On Behalf of Management.
Other offices located in: Atlanta, Georgia; Boston, Massachusetts; Chicago, Illinois; Dallas, Texas; Greenville, South Carolina; Hartford, Connecticut; Long Island, New York; Los Angeles, California; Miami, Florida; Minneapolis, Minnesota; Morristown, New Jersey; New York, New York; Orlando, Florida; Pittsburgh, Pennsylvania; Sacramento, California; San Francisco, California; Seattle, Washington; Stamford, Connecticut; White Plains, New York.
See Professional Biographies, WASHINGTON, DISTRICT OF COLUMBIA

Jacob, Fred ....'25 '55 C.563 B.E.E. L.273 J.D. 2475 Virginia Ave., N.W. (Pat.)‡
Jacob, John R. .... '66 '93 C.165 A.B. L.904 J.D. [Ⓒ Akin,G.S.H.&F.]
*PRACTICE AREAS: Health Care.
Jacob, Kenneth S. .... '67 '92 C.276 B.S.F.S. L.893 J.D. [Arent F.K.P.&K.]
*PRACTICE AREAS: Commercial Real Estate; Business Law.
Jacob, Matthew M., (AV) '39 '70
C.102 B.S.Chem. L.904 J.D. [Wenderoth,L.&P.] (See Pat. Sect.)
*PRACTICE AREAS: Chemical Patent Prosecution; Patent Interference Practice; Patent Licensing.
Jacobi, Robert B., (AV) .... '30 '54 C.904 A.B. L.902 LL.B. [Cohn&M.]
*PRACTICE AREAS: Communications Law.
Jacobovitz, Jeffrey S., (AV) .... '55 '81 C.107 B.A. L.30 J.D. [Kutak R.]
*PRACTICE AREAS: Antitrust Law; Criminal Defense; Civil Litigation; Appellate Practice.
Jacobs, Benjamin R., (AV) .... '40 '66 C&L.30 B.S., J.D. [Brown,G.&J.]
Jacobs, Brenda A., (AV) .... '55 '80 C.188 B.S. L.273 J.D. [Powell,G.F.&M.]
*PRACTICE AREAS: Customs and International Trade Law.
Jacobs, Bruce D., (AV) .... '55 '80 C.1275 B.A. L.309 J.D. [Shaw P.]
*PRACTICE AREAS: Communications; Internet and World Wide Web.
Jacobs, Camellia Javadi .... '76 '00 C.861 B.A. L.904 J.D. [Ⓐ Chaikin&S.]
*PRACTICE AREAS: Wrongful Death; Medical Malpractice; Automobile Negligence; Personal Injury.
Jacobs, David H. .... '62 '89 C&L.446 B.A., J.D. [Ⓒ Miller,C.P.&S.] (⊙Detroit, MI)
*PRACTICE AREAS: Labor and Employment Law; Products Liability; Construction Litigation; Commercial Litigation.
Jacobs, Gary M. .....'51 '76 C&L.846 B.A., J.D. [Ⓐ Fitzpatrick,C.H.&S.] (See Pat. Sect.)
Jacobs, Harry W. .... '31 '68 C.276 B.S.F.S. L.273 J.D. Archdiocese of Washington
Jacobs, Harvey S., (AV) ....'58 '84 C.273 B.B.A. L.1009 J.D. [Jacobs&Assoc.] ⊙
*PRACTICE AREAS: Internet Law; Corporate Law; Real Estate Law; Intellectual Property.
Jacobs, J. David '61 '89 C&L.178 B.A., J.D.
(adm. in NY; not adm. in DC) Sr. Coun., American National Red Cross
*RESPONSIBILITIES: Business Transactions; Tax Law; Securities; Antitrust; Contracts.
Jacobs, Jerald A., (AV) .... '45 '71 C&L.276 A.B., J.D. [Shaw P.]
*PRACTICE AREAS: Association Law; Health Care Law; Antitrust Law.
Jacobs, Jerold L., (AV) .... '43 '69 C.31 B.A. L.309 J.D. [Cohn&M.]
*PRACTICE AREAS: Communications Law; Telecommunications Law; Cable Communications Law.
Jacobs, Jonathan M. ....'62 '88 C.228 A.B. L.659 J.D. [Ⓒ Fried,F.H.S.&J.]
*PRACTICE AREAS: Civil Litigation.
Jacobs, Kurt H. .... '60 '90 C&L.976 B.A., J.D. [Ⓐ Sidley A.B.&W.]
Jacobs, Lorenzo W., Jr. ....'29 '60 C.887 A.B. L.329 LL.B. 1414 Juniper St., N.W.
Jacobs, Martin, (AV) .... '40 '64 C.563 B.B.A. L.564 LL.B. [Galland,K.G.F.&S.] ⊙
*PRACTICE AREAS: Business and Corporate; Gaming; Real Estate.
Jacobs, Matthew L., (AV) ....'— '82 C.674 B.A. L.893 J.D. [Kirkpatrick&L.]
*PRACTICE AREAS: Environmental Insurance Coverage; Insurance; Products Liability; Complex Litigation; Year 2000 Computer Conversion.
Jacobs, Michael H. ....'62 '96 C.884 B.E.E. L.276 J.D. [Ⓐ Milbank,T.H.&M.]
*PRACTICE AREAS: Litigation; Patent Law.
Jacobs, Neil I., (AV) '57 '84 C.1044 B.A. L.1009 J.D.
(adm. in NY; not adm. in DC) [Ⓒ Jacobs&Assoc.]
*PRACTICE AREAS: Corporate; Securities; International; Transactional.
Jacobs, Robert D., (AV) .... '46 '71 C.454 B.A. L.30 J.D. [Swidler B.S.F.]
*PRACTICE AREAS: Antitrust and Trade Regulation.
Jacobs, Robert P. .... '63 '88 C.260 B.S. L.276 J.D. [Ⓐ Howrey S.A.&W.]
*PRACTICE AREAS: Insurance Coverage Litigation; Commercial Litigation.
Jacobs, Stephen I. '52 '88 C.30 B.S. L.128 J.D.
V.P., National Association of Broadcasters
Jacobs, W. Michael, (BV) .... '51 '83 C.112 B.A. L.273 J.D. 1232 17th St., N.W.

Jacobs & Associates, (AV)
2000 L Street N.W., Suite 200, 20036 ⊙
Telephone: 202-457-0100 Fax: 202-457-0186 URL: http://www.internet-law-firm.com
Email: lawyer@internet-law-firm.com
Harvey S. Jacobs. Of Counsel: Donna Maria Coles Johnson (Not admitted in DC); Neil I. Jacobs (Not admitted in DC).
Internet Law, Corporate Law, Intellectual Property, Securities Law.
Rockville, Maryland Office: 50 West Montgomery Avenue, Suite 330, 20850. Telephone: 301-251-5294.
See Professional Biographies, WASHINGTON, DISTRICT OF COLUMBIA

Jacobsen, Bernice H. ....'17 '61 C.962 B.Ed. L.273 LL.B. 560 North St., S.W.
Jacobsen, Jennifer '67 '95 C.976 B.A. L.893 J.D.
Dep. Dir., Dom. Policy, America Online, Inc.‡
Jacobsen, Raymond A., Jr., (AV) ......'49 '75 C.205 B.A. L.276 J.D. [McDermott,W.&E.]
Jacobsohn, David B., (AV) .... '— '68 C&L.188 B.A., J.D. [Ⓒ Verner,L.B.M.&H.]
*PRACTICE AREAS: Financial Institutions; Federal Legislative and Administrative Matters; Securities Law.
Jacobson, Clarence A. ....'40 '66 C.976 B.A. L.309 LL.B. 400 7th St., N.W.
Jacobson, David E. ....'49 '75 C.696 B.A. L.107 J.D. [Thelen R.&P.]
*PRACTICE AREAS: Tax.
Jacobson, Douglas N. '61 '90 C.846 B.A. L.904 J.D.
(adm. in MD; not adm. in DC) [Ⓒ Dickstein S.M.&O.]
*PRACTICE AREAS: International Trade; Aviation Law.
Jacobson, Erica R. .... '72 '00 C.446 B.A. L.180 J.D. [Ⓐ Wiley R.&F.]
Jacobson, Harvey B., Jr., (AV) '36 '62
C.976 B.Ch.E. L.309 LL.B. [Jacobson,H.] (See Pat. Sect.)
*PRACTICE AREAS: Intellectual Property Litigation; Chemical Patents; Mechanical Patents.
Jacobson, Howard B., (AV) .... '55 '79 C.477 A.B. L.309 J.D. [Akin,G.S.H.&F.]
*PRACTICE AREAS: Taxation.
Jacobson, Joanne G. ....'61 '88 C&L.05 B.Sc., LL.B. [Ⓒ Calhoun] (⊙Washington)
Jacobson, Joanne G. .... '61 '88 C&L.05 B.Sc., LL.B. [Ⓐ Sanders,S.&B.] (⊙Washington)
*PRACTICE AREAS: ERISA; Employee Benefits Law; Tax Law.
Jacobson, Kasen H. '63 '95 C.446 B.S.M.E. L.128 J.D.
(adm. in MD; not adm. in DC; Pat.) 400 7th St., N.W.

Jacobson, Holman, PLLC, (AV) BB
400 Seventh Street, N.W., 20004
Telephone: 202-638-6666 Cable Address: "Lawpat" Telefax: 202-393-5350; 202-393-5351; 202-393-5352
Email: IP@JHIP.COM URL: http://www.JHIP.COM
Members of Firm: Harvey B. Jacobson, Jr.; John Clarke Holman; Simor L. Moskowitz; Allen S. Melser; Michael R. Slobasky; Marsha G. Gentner; Jonathan L. Scherer; Irwin M. Aisenberg; George William Lewis; William E. Player; Yoon S. Ham; Philip L. O'Neill. Associates: Linda J. Shapiro; Leesa N. Weiss; Suzin C. Bailey (Not admitted in DC); Matthew J. Cuccias; Daniel K. Dorsey; Suzannah K. Sundby (Not admitted in DC). Of Counsel: Marvin R. Stern; Nathaniel A. Humphries.
Patent, Trademark, Unfair Competition, Copyright, Computer and Antitrust Law. International Patent and Trademark Practice. Practice before all Federal Courts, U.S. Patent and Trademark Office and other Administrative Agencies.
See Professional Biographies, WASHINGTON, DISTRICT OF COLUMBIA

Jacobus, John L. .... '63 '89 C&L.309 A.B., J.D. [Ⓒ Steptoe&J.]
*PRACTICE AREAS: Civil Litigation; Antitrust.
Jacoby, Conrad J. .... '68 '93 C.976 B.A. L.276 J.D. [Ⓒ Spriggs&H.]
*PRACTICE AREAS: Litigation; Information Technology.
Jacokes, Paul D. ....'53 '79 C.575 B.A. L.976 J.D. [Sutherland A.&B.]
*PRACTICE AREAS: Federal Taxation.
Jacqmotte, Benoit N. ....'— '99 C.012 B.A. L.569 J.D. [Ⓐ Latham&W.]
*PRACTICE AREAS: Communications and Media; Corporate Law.
Jacques, Stephen C. ....'72 '99 C.93 B.A L.30 J.D. [Ⓐ Sullivan&C.]
Jacques, Tammy Strange '— '96 C.497 B.A. L.1364 J.D.
419 7th Street N.W., Suite 201
Jacquez, Lynnette Conway ....'58 '83 C.589 B.A. L.602 J.D. [Ⓒ McGuiness N.&W.]
Jadallah, Maha S. '73 '98 C.187 B.A. L.221 J.D.
(adm. in MD; not adm. in DC) [Ⓒ Fulbright&J.]
*PRACTICE AREAS: International.
Jaeger, Kathleen D. .... '— '90 C.690 B.S. L.128 J.D. [Kirkpatrick&L.]
*PRACTICE AREAS: Food and Drug Law.
Jaeger, Philip W., (AV) .... '45 '75 C.188 B.S. L.128 J.D. [Jaeger&T.]
Jaeger & Teras, (AV) ....1090 Vermont Avenue N.W., Suite 350
Jaeschke, Wayne C., Jr. '65 '98 C.688 B.S. L.30 J.D.
(adm. in MD; not adm. in DC; Pat.) [Ⓐ Morrison&F.]
*PRACTICE AREAS: Patents.
Jaffe, Daniel M. ....'70 '99 C.30 B.A. L.273 J.D. [Ⓐ Slover&L.]
Jaffe, David Benjamin '65 '93 C.910 B.A. L.904 J.D.
Assoc. Dean for Student Affairs, Amer. Univ., Wash. Coll. of Law
Jaffe, David S. '58 '85 C.385 A.B. L.818 J.D.
(adm. in MA; not adm. in DC) Staff Coun., National Association of Home Builders
Jaffe, Erik S. .... '64 '92 C.197 B.A. L.178 J.D. 725 12th St., N.W.
Jaffe, Kenneth G., (AV) ....'57 '81 C.1349 B.A. L.309 J.D. [Swidler B.S.F.]
*PRACTICE AREAS: Regulatory Law; Utility Law.
Jaffe, Matthew P., (AV) .... '55 '82 C.446 B.A. L.208 J.D. [Lipstein,J.&L.]
*PRACTICE AREAS: International Trade; Customs; Corporate.
Jaffe, Matthew S. .... '61 '86 C.1044 B.A. L.273 J.D. [Ⓒ Sonosky,C.S.E.&P.]
*PRACTICE AREAS: Indians and Native Population.
Jaffe, Michael Evan, (AV) ....'42 '67 C.691 B.A. L.178 LL.B. [Arent F.K.P.&K.]
*PRACTICE AREAS: Litigation; International Arbitration; International Litigation; Construction Law.
Jaffe, Peter E. '62 '90 C.604 A.B. L.477 J.D.
(adm. in PA; not adm. in DC) 701 Penn. Ave., N.W., Ste. 900
Jaffe, Theodore .... '10 '35 C.103 Ph.B. L.309 LL.B. 2450 Va. Ave., N.W. #E316
Jaffee, Neil H. .... '48 '74 C.156 B.A. L.184 J.D. 625 Indiana Ave NW Ste 550

Jagtiani & Guttag
(See Fairfax, Virginia)

Jain, Abhi-Shék .... '68 '93 C.445 B.S. L.446 J.D. [Jones J.]
Jain, Mishrilal L., (CV) ....'43 '81 C.37 Ph.D. L.446 J.D. [Ⓒ Jones J.] (Pat.)
Jain, Samir .... '69 '95 C.813 B.S. L.309 J.D. [Ⓒ Wilmer,C.&P.]
*PRACTICE AREAS: Telecommunications Law; Electronic Commerce; Internet Law; Appellate Practice.
Jakes, John Michael, (AV) '57 '86
C.228 BSEE L.276 J.D. [Finnegan,H.F.G.&D.] (See Pat. Sect.)
*PRACTICE AREAS: Intellectual Property Litigation; Appellate Practice; Electrical Intellectual Property; Computer and Software Patents; Medical Patents.

Jakovic, Ellen M. ... '60 '85 C&L.309 A.B., J.D. [🄲 White&C.]
*PRACTICE AREAS: Antitrust.
Jakubiak, Jeffrey M. ... '71 '98 C.813 A.B. L.188 J.D. [🄰 Troutman S.]
*PRACTICE AREAS: Regulatory Affairs; Regulatory Law.
Jakubowics, Craig E.R. '52 '81 C.93 A.B. L.64 J.D.
Dir., Envir. Legal Affrs., Edison Elec. Institute
Jakubowski, Teresa L. ... '67 '93 C.221 B.A. L.276 J.D. [🄰 Epstein B.&G.]
*PRACTICE AREAS: Labor and Employment Law; Disability Law.
Jalali, Laleh ... '67 '94 C.446 B.S.M.E. L.273 J.D. [🄰 Kenyon&K.] (See Pat. Sect.)
*PRACTICE AREAS: Intellectual Property.
Jalinous, Farhad ... '66 '90 C&L.276 B.A., J.D. [🄲 Kaye S.]
*PRACTICE AREAS: International Transactions; Export Compliance; Export Regulation; National Security Law.
Jalinous, Shahrzad Heyat ... '70 '95 C&L.276 B.A., J.D. 3008 43rd St. N.W.
Jamar, Steven D. '53 '79 C.118 B.A. L.300 J.D.
Assoc. Prof. of Law & Dir. Legal Writing Prog., Howard Univ.
James, A. Everette ... '— '95 C.575 L.46 J.D. [LeBoeuf,L.G.&M.]
*PRACTICE AREAS: Insurance; Emerging Business Law; Corporate.
James, Clarence L., (AV) ... '33 '62 C.608 B.S. L.161 J.D. 1501 M St., N.W., Suite 700
James, Deborah '59 '90 C.66 B.A. L.976 J.D.
(adm. in FL; not adm. in DC) [🄰 Hogan&H.]
*PRACTICE AREAS: International Business Transactions; Corporate Law; Securities; Energy; Government Contracts.
James, Dennis, Jr., (AV) ... '45 '73 C.390 B.A. L.276 J.D. [Cameron&H.]
*PRACTICE AREAS: International Trade Law.
James, Edgar N., (AV) ... '47 '80 C.1056 B.A. L.309 J.D. [James&H.]
*PRACTICE AREAS: Litigation; Labor; Nonprofit Organizations Law.
James, Frank P. '67 '92 C.602 B.A. L.801 J.D.
(adm. in OH; not adm. in DC) 1444 Swann St. N.W.‡
James, Gerald P. '48 '83 C.870 B.S. L.273 J.D.
(adm. in VA; not adm. in DC) [🄰 Katten M.Z.]
*PRACTICE AREAS: Real Estate; Real Estate Finance.
James, Rawn M., Jr. ... '76 '01 C.976 B.A. L.228 J.D. [🄰 Sutherland A.&B.]
*PRACTICE AREAS: Litigation.
James, Raymond K. ... '34 '63 C.569 B.A. L.309 LL.B. [Coan&L.]
*PRACTICE AREAS: Housing and Urban Affairs; Real Estate; Legislative Law.
James, Robert L., (AV) ... '44 '69 C.188 A.B. L.273 J.D. [Cole,R.&B.]
*PRACTICE AREAS: Cable Television; Common Carrier; Cable Programming; Cable Franchising; Satellite Communications.
James, Sylvia F. ... '70 '96 C.881 A.B. L.228 J.D. [🄰 Scopelitis,G.L.&H.]
*PRACTICE AREAS: Employment; Labor.
James, Thomas L. ... '— '85 C.446 B.S. L.276 J.D. [Foley&L.]
*PRACTICE AREAS: Securities Law; Corporate Law.

James & Hoffman, P.C., (AV)
1101 17th Street, NW Suite 510, 20036-4704
Telephone: 202-496-0500 Fax: 202-496-0555
URL: http://www.jamhoff.com
Edgar N. James; Steven K. Hoffman; Judith A. Scott; Kathy L. Krieger; David P. Dean;—Marie Chopra; Jeffrey S. Vogt (Not admitted in DC); Jessica Rachel Arons (Not admitted in DC). Of Counsel: Mary Joyce Carlson (Not admitted in DC); Martha Walfoort; Christy Hoffman.
Civil Litigation, Labor Law, Bankruptcy, Tort, Employee Benefits, Employment Discrimination, Insurance, College and University Law and Non-Profit Organization Law.
See Professional Biographies, WASHINGTON, DISTRICT OF COLUMBIA

Jameson, Paul W., (BV) ... '51 '79 C.665 B.A. L.276 J.D. [🄲 Hale&D.]
*PRACTICE AREAS: International Trade Law.
Jamieson, Ballard, Jr. ... '46 '72 C.674 B.A. L.976 J.D. [Gardner,C.&D.]
*PRACTICE AREAS: Environmental Law; International Environmental Law.
Jamieson, Paul W. ... '69 '98 C.976 B.A. L.893 J.D. [🄰 Piper M.R.&W.]
*PRACTICE AREAS: Communications.
Jamison, Scott R. ... '60 '87 C.797 B.A. L.446 J.D. [Gordon&B.]
*PRACTICE AREAS: Government Contracts; Employee Benefits Law; Health Law; Insurance Law; Trial and Appellate Practice.
Janas, David M. ... '— '93 C.1350 B.S. L.904 J.D. 701 Pennsylvania Avenue, N.W.
Janeiro, Gina Kay ... '74 '99 C.958 B.S. L.30 J.D. 11911 Freedom Dr. (⊙Reston, VA)
Jani, Jerome J. ... '35 '70 C.128 A.B. L.273 J.D. Wash. Metro. Area Transit Authority
Janis, N. Richard, (AV) ... '46 '73 C.966 B.A. L.309 J.D. [Janis,S.&W.]
*PRACTICE AREAS: White Collar Criminal Defense; Business Crimes; Federal Grand Jury; Monetary Crimes; Litigation.

Janis, Schuelke & Wechsler, (AV)
1728 Massachusetts Avenue, N.W., 20036
Telephone: 202-861-0600 Telecopier: 202-223-7230
Email: janisschuelke@msn.com
N. Richard Janis; Henry F. Schuelke, III; Lawrence H. Wechsler; S. Robert Sutton; John W. Kern; Whitney C. Ellerman. Of Counsel: William B. Shields.
Litigation. White Collar Criminal and Civil Practice in the United States and Abroad.
See Professional Biographies, WASHINGTON, DISTRICT OF COLUMBIA

Janka, John P., (AV) ... '— '87 C.228 A.B. L.1068 J.D. [Latham&W.]
*PRACTICE AREAS: Communications and Media Law; Corporate Law; Business Law; Intellectual Property.
Jankoski, Vincent A., (BV) '50 '75 C&L.273 B.A., J.D.
Asst. Gen. Coun., Washington Metropolitan Area Transit Authority
*RESPONSIBILITIES: Civil Litigation; Legal Advisor to Transit Police.
Jankowski, James Christopher '70 '96 C.140 B.A. L.790 J.D.
Amer. Council of Life Ins.
Jankowski, T. Michael, (AV) ... '58 '83 C.95 A.B. L.273 J.D. [Rini,C.&L.]
Jankowsky, Joel, (P.C.), (AV) ... '43 '68 C&L.623 B.B.A., J.D. [Akin,G.S.H.&F.]
*PRACTICE AREAS: Public Policy.
Janney, Christopher G. ... '64 '91 C.446 B.A. L.309 J.D. [Shaw P.]
Janoski, Stephen G. ... '62 '91 C.659 B.A. L.64 J.D. [🄲 Drinker B.&R.]
Janousek, Joseph O. ... '11 '37 C.190 L.904 LL.B. P.O. Box 284
Janowitz, Kathy Palestrant ... '51 '80 C.608 B.S. L.659 J.D. 3900 Wisconsin Ave., N.W.
Jansons, Maris S. ... '— '93 C.529 B.A. L.831 J.D. Assoc. Tech. Coun., MCI WorldCom
Janss, Jennifer L. '68 '93 C.367 B.A. L.880 J.D.
(adm. in VA; not adm. in DC) [🄰 Sidley A.B.&W.]
Janzen, Bernd Gunnar '64 '97 C.83 B.S. L.273 J.D.
(adm. in NY; not adm. in DC) [🄰 Akin,G.S.H.&F.]
Jaques, Dane B. ... '58 '86 C.589 B.Sc. L.494 J.D. [Dombroff&G.]
Jarashow, Ronald H., (AV) ... '49 '75 C.264 B.A. L.128 J.D. [Franch,J.B.&S.] ⊙
*PRACTICE AREAS: Civil Litigation; Personal Injury; Corporate; Equipment Leasing; Bankruptcy.
Jarcho, Daniel G. ... '59 '84 C&L.309 B.A., J.D. [McKenna&C.]
*PRACTICE AREAS: Civil Litigation; Criminal Litigation; Appellate Litigation; Food and Drug Law; Federal Regulatory Law.
Jardot, Leo C. '53 '78 C.612 B.S. L.623 J.D.
(adm. in OK; not adm. in DC) Sr. Dir. & Coun., Govt. Rel., Amer. Home Products Corp.
Jareaux, Kelli J. ... '64 '89 C.329 B.A. L.276 J.D. 1200 New Hampshire Ave., NW

Jarrard & Richard
(See Bethesda, Maryland)

Jarrell, John W., Jr. ... '69 '95 C.705 B.A. L.273 J.D. [🄰 Mayer,B.&P.]
Jarrett, C. Douglas, (BV) ... '52 '79 C.174 B.A. L.273 J.D. [Keller&H.]
*PRACTICE AREAS: Telecommunications Law; Environmental Law; Computer Law.
Jarrett, Wayne A. '70 '97 C.579 B.S. L.602 J.D.
(adm. in MN; not adm. in DC) Hovde Financial LLC
Jarsulic, Marc ... '— '99 L.477 J.D. [🄰 Clifford C.R.&W.]
*PRACTICE AREAS: Antitrust.
Jarva-Weiss, Sandra ... '58 '83 C&L.273 B.A., J.D. [Piper M.R.&W.]
*PRACTICE AREAS: Health Care Law; Hospital Law; Corporate Law.
Jarvis, F. Wayne, Jr. '42 '67
C.264 B.A. L.884 J.D. Reg. Coun., Prudential Ins. Co. of Amer.
Jarvis, Ronald J., (AV) ... '53 '80 C.674 A.B. L.228 J.D. [🄲 Kelley D.&W.]
*PRACTICE AREAS: Telecommunications Law; Technology Law; Export Control.
Jarvis, Thomas L. '56 '86 C&L.575 B.A., J.D.
[🄲 Finnegan,H.F.G.&D.] (See Pat. Sect.)
*PRACTICE AREAS: Patent Litigation; Electrical Intellectual Property; Computer and Software Patents; Semiconductor Technology.
Jasinski, Douglas M. ... '68 '94 C&L.128 B.A., J.D. [🄰 White&C.]
Jaskiewicz, Edmund M., (AV) ... '23 '53 C.184 B.S.E. L.273 J.D. [🄲 Grove,J.&C.] (Pat.)
*PRACTICE AREAS: International Intellectual Property; Patent Licensing; Patent Prosecution; Trademark Licensing; Trademark Prosecution.
Jaskiewicz, Leonard A., (AV) ... '27 '54 C.184 B.A. L.273 J.D. [🄲 Grove,J.&C.]
Jaskot, John J. ... '54 '84 C.869 B.S. L.273 J.D. [🄲 Jones,W.W.P.C.&D.]
*PRACTICE AREAS: Government Affairs; Maritime Law.
Jatlow, David C., (AV) '47 '73 C.264 B.A. L.904 J.D.
V.P., Federal Affs., AT&T Wireless Servs., Inc.
Jatlow, Howard S., (AV) ... '49 '75 C.273 B.A. L.904 J.D. [Dickstein S.M.&O.]
*PRACTICE AREAS: Banking Law; Commercial Law; Real Estate Law; Sports Law.
Java, Jacqueline R. ... '75 '01 C.645 B.S. L.273 J.D. [🄰 Bracewell&P.]
*PRACTICE AREAS: Telecommunications; Energy.
Javits, Joshua M., (AV) ... '50 '79 C.976 B.A. L.276 J.D. [Ford&H.]
*PRACTICE AREAS: Arbitration; Collective Bargaining; Labor Relations.
Javitt, Gail H. ... '68 '95 C.178 B.A. L.309 J.D. 1201 Pennsylvania Ave.
Jawetz, Steven M. ... '56 '82 C.813 A.B. L.1066 J.D. [Beveridge&D.]
*PRACTICE AREAS: Superfund; Natural Resource Damages; Hazardous Waste.
Jay, Jeremy M. ... '53 '90 C.184 B.S. L.1209 J.D. [Leydig,V.&M.] (See Pat. Sect.)
Jay, Jonathan S., (AV) '48 '80 C.846 B.A. L.128 J.D.
Asst. & Spec. Coun. to Pres., United Food & Comercial Workers International Union
Jaye, T. Anthony "Todd" ... '70 '00 C.966 B.B.A. L.436 J.D. [🄰 Wilmer,C.&P.]
Jazzo, Frank R., (AV) ... '58 '84 C.569 B.S. L.1068 J.D. [Fletcher,H.&H.] ⊙
*PRACTICE AREAS: Mass Media Law; Satellite Communications; Broadcasting; Internet Law; International Telecommunications.
Jeanblanc, James K., (AV) ... '41 '66 C&L.339 B.S., J.D. [🄲 Grove,J.&C.]
*PRACTICE AREAS: Business Law; Corporate Law; Tax Law; Trusts and Estates.
Jeannot, Jennifer M. ... '72 '00 C.518 B.A. L.904 J.D. [🄰 Clifford C.R.&W.]
*PRACTICE AREAS: Securities Regulation; Banking Regulation; Corporate Law.
Jeffers, Nicole B. '62 '88 C.276 B.S. L.893 J.D.
Associate Litigation Counsel, MCI WorldCom
Jefferson, Samuel L., Jr ... '68 '94 C&L.276 A.B., J.D. [🄰 Dickstein S.M.&O.]
*PRACTICE AREAS: Insurance Litigation; Civil Litigation; Sports Law.
Jefferson, Timothy '55 '81 C.1019 B.A. L.178 J.D.
Sr. Assoc. Gen. Coun., Howard Univ.
Jefferson, Tricia G. '71 '98 C.945 B.A. L.902 J.D.
(adm. in MD; not adm. in DC) Atty., U.S. Comm. on Civil Rights
Jeffery, Donald D., (AV) ... '— '61 C.966 B.S. L.273 LL.B. [Foley&L.] (See Pat. Sect.)‡
Jeffords, James M. '34 '62 C.976 B.S. L.309 LL.B.
(adm. in VT; not adm. in DC) U.S. Senator
Jeffress, Dorothy Ames ... '65 '93 C.951 B.A. L.976 J.D. Asst. U.S. Atty.
Jeffress, Jonathan S. '71 '98 C.951 B.A. L.893 J.D.
(adm. in VA; not adm. in DC) [🄰 Williams&C.]
Jeffress, William H., Jr., (AV) ... '45 '71 C.902 B.A. L.976 LL.B. [Baker B.]
Jeffrey, Deborah J. ... '62 '86 C.367 B.A. L.309 J.D. [Zuckerman S.]
*PRACTICE AREAS: Complex Civil, Enforcement and Criminal Litigation; Securities Litigation; Suspension and Debarment; Legal Ethics; Lawyer Discipline.
Jeffrey, Eric C. ... '53 '78 C.188 B.A. L.659 J.D. [🄲 Shea&G.]
Jeffries, Stephen J. ... '63 '89 C&L.896 B.A., J.D. [🄰 Holland&K.]
*PRACTICE AREAS: Trademarks; Copyrights; Unfair Competition.
Jehle, Philip F. ... '23 '51 C.813 L.128 LL.B. 444 N. Capitol St.‡
Jekofsky, Milton ... '13 '37 L.537 J.D. 6307 N. Capitol St., N.E.‡

Jenkens & Gilchrist, A Professional Corporation, (AV)
1919 Pennsylvania Avenue, N.W., Suite 600, 20006-3404 ⊙
Telephone: 202-326-1500 Facsimile: 202-326-1555
Email: jenkens@jenkens.com URL: http://www.jenkens.com
Larry W. Caudle, Jr. (Not admitted in DC); Michael H. Cook; Jan S. Gilbert; Daniel J. Kraftson; Gary A. Lax; Keith W. McGlamery (Not admitted in DC); Michael F. Ruggio; Carl E. Zwisler III. Of Counsel: Scott R. Schoenfeld;—Patricia J. Atienza (Not admitted in DC); Jamila Braswell (Not admitted in DC); Damon Burrows, II; Rachel Hatfield (Not admitted in DC); John T. Kirsch; Iden Grant Martyn (Not admitted in DC); Karen McMillan (Not admitted in DC); John Brian Morrow (Not admitted in DC); Cheryl L. Mullin (Not admitted in DC); Michael Alexander Troy (Not admitted in DC).
Administrative Law, Antitrust, Aviation, Bankruptcy, Commercial Lending, Communications, Computer Law, Construction Law, Corporate, Employee Benefits (ERISA); Energy, Environmental Law, Estate Planning, Probate and Trusts, Exempt Organizations, Federal Practice, Financial Institutions, Finance, Franchise and Distribution Law, Governmental Affairs, Health Law, Hospitality (REIT), Immigration, Insurance Defense, Intellectual Property including Patent, Trademark, Tradesecret and Copyright (Prosecution, Litigation and Transactional), International Law, Internet Law, Labor and Employment Law, Land Use, Municipal Law, Litigation (Commercial, Tax and Fiduciary), Mergers and Acquisitions, Product Liability, Real Estate Services, Securities, Tax, Toxic Tort, Trade Regulation, Transportation, Unfair Competition, Venture Capital.
Austin, Texas Office: 2200 One American Center, 600 Congress Avenue. Telephone: 512-499-3800. Facsimile: 512-404-3520.
Dallas, Texas, Office: 1445 Ross Avenue, Suite 3200. Telephone: 214-855-4500. TWX: 910-861-4047. Telex: 73-2595. Facsimile: 214-855-4300. International Facsimile: 214-855-4300.
Los Angeles, California Office: Jenkens & Gilchrist, LLP, 12100 Wilshire Boulevard, 15th Floor. Telephone: 310-820-8800. Facsimile: 310-820-8859.
Chicago, Illinois Office: 225 West Washington, Suite 2600. Telephone: 312-425-3900. Facsimile: 312-425-3909.
Houston, Texas Office: 1100 Louisiana, Suite 1800. Telephone: 713-951-3300. Facsimile: 713-951-3314.
San Antonio, Texas Office: 1400 Frost Bank Tower, 100 West Houston Street. Telephone: 210-246-5000. Facsimile: 210-246-5999.
Great Neck, New York Office: Jenkens & Gilchrist Parker Chapin LLP, 175 Great Neck Road. Telephone: 516-482-4422. Facsimile: 516-482-4469.
Hackensack, New Jersey: Jenkens & Gilchrist Parker Chapin LLP, 190 Moore Street, Suite 307. Telephone: 201-883-6400. Facsimile: 201-883-6404.
New York, New York Office: Jenkens & Gilchrist Parker Chapin LLP, The Chrysler Building, 405 Lexington Avenue. Telephone: 212-704-6327. Facsimile: 212-704-6288.
See Professional Biographies, WASHINGTON, DISTRICT OF COLUMBIA

Jenkins, David M., II ... '35 '64 C.210 A.B. L.273 J.D. SmithKline Beecham Corp.
Jenkins, Edgar J. ... '20 '50 C.228 B.A. L.276 LL.B. 2100 Pennsylvania Ave., N.W.
Jenkins, Eric D. '73 '00 C.257 B.S. L.273 J.D.
(adm. in MD; not adm. in DC) [🄰 Kelley D.&W.]
*PRACTICE AREAS: Telecommunications.

Jenkins, John S. '32 '61 C.390 B.A. L.273 J.D.
(adm. in VA; not adm. in DC) Assoc. Dean, George Washington Univ. Law Sch.
Jenkins, Judy Parker . . . . . '56 '85 C.475 B.A. L.29 J.D. [[A] Dykema G.]
Jenkins, Robert K., Jr. '47 '75
C.329 B.A. L.273 J.D. Pres. & CEO, D.C. Local Develop. Corp.
Jenkins, Robert M., III, (AV) . . . . '47 '74 C.309 B.A. L.1066 J.D. [Mayer,B.&P.]
Jenkins, Susan M. . . . . '48 '77 C.331 A.B. L.178 J.D. [Sanchez]
Jenkins, Susan Raleigh . . . . '49 '81 C.823 B.A. L.273 J.D. The Bureau of Natl. Affs., Inc.
Jenkins, Theresa Y. '53 '84 C.1280 B.S. L.329 J.D.
(adm. in PA; not adm. in DC) 1311 Delaware Ave., S.W.‡
Jenkins, Thomas H., III, (AV) '51 '80
C.198 B.S. L.893 J.D. [Finnegan,H.F.G.&D.] (See Pat. Sect.)
*PRACTICE AREAS: Patent Litigation; Patent Prosecution.
Jenkins, Thomas J. . . . . '12 '39 C&L.276 A.B., J.D. 3912 Benton St., N.W.‡
Jenkins, Timothy W. . . . . '57 '85 C.856 B.A. L.945 J.D. [O'Connor&H.]
Jenks, David S. . . . . '63 '88 C.105 B.S. L.273 J.D. Avenue Settlement Corp.
Jenner, Gregory F. . . . . '53 '79 C.1056 B.S. L.569 J.D. [Venable,A.B.H.&C.]
*PRACTICE AREAS: Tax Law; Legislative Practice; Estate Planning.

Jenner & Block, LLC, (AV)
A Partnership including Professional Corporations
601 Thirteenth Street, N.W., Twelfth Floor, 20005 ⊙
Telephone: 202-639-6000 FAX: 202-639-6066 Cable Address: "Jenblock"
URL: http://www.jenner.com
Resident Partners: Jacqueline C. Bares; Steven N. Berk; Alan M. Buie; Julia M. Carpenter; Theresa Chmara; David A. Churchill; Paul W. "Whit" Cobb, Jr.; Joseph P. Covington; David W. DeBruin; Maureen F. Del Duca; Kevin C. Dwyer; Jerome L. Epstein; Ian Heath Gershengorn; David A. Handzo; Sam Hirsch; Richard C. Johnson; Jodie L. Kelley; Leslie H. Lepow; Deanne E. Maynard; Mark J. McGuire; Nory Miller; John B. Morris, Jr.; Carl S. Nadler; Thomas J. Perrelli; Susan R. Podolsky; Robert M. Portman; Mark D. Schneider; Paul M. Smith; Bruce Spiva; Donald B. Verrilli, Jr. Resident Associates: Imad D. Abyad; Erin Albritton (Not admitted in DC); Geoffrey A. Barrow; David C. Belt; Nicole G. Berner; Elizabeth E. Appel Blue; Elena N. Broder-Feldman; Elizabeth A. Cavanagh; Michael B. DeSanctis; Katherine A. Fallow; Lara M. Flint (Resident, Washington, D.C. Office); Jared O. Freedman; Marc A. Goldman; Daniel James Greiner; Matthew Hersh; William A. Hohengarten; Bobby J. Hollis, II; Marc E. Isserles (Not admitted in DC); Janis C. Kestenbaum; Jessie K. Liu; Daniel Mach; Jenny S. Martinez (Not admitted in DC); Robin M. Meriweather (Not admitted in DC); Robert Stephen Nichols; Cynthia J. Robertson (Not admitted in DC); Laura M. Scott (Not admitted in DC); Kevin M. Stack; Olivier Sylvain; James A. Trilling; J. Alex Ward; Kial S. Young.
General Practice.
Chicago, Illinois Office: One IBM Plaza. Telephone: 312-222-9350. FAX: 312-527-0484. Telex: 270469. Cable Address: "Jenblock."
Lake Forest, Illinois Office: One Westminster Place. Telephone: 847-295-9200. FAX: 847-295-7810.
Dallas, Texas Office: 1717 Main Street, Suite 3150. Telephone: 214-746-5700. FAX: 214-746-5757.
See Professional Biographies, WASHINGTON, DISTRICT OF COLUMBIA

Jenney, Frederick E. . . . . '57 '84 C.976 B.A. L.893 J.D. [Morrison&F.]
*PRACTICE AREAS: Project Development; Project Finance.
Jennings, Deborah E., (AV) '49 '74
C.446 B.A. L.276 J.D. [Piper M.R.&W.] (⊙Balt., MD)
*PRACTICE AREAS: Environmental Law; Litigation; Mergers and Acquisitions Law; Commercial Finance.
Jennings, James C. '45 '75 C.945 B.S. L.276 J.D.
Gen. Mgr. & Exec. V.P., Hill & Knowlton, Inc.
Jennings, Kelly S. . . . . '71 '96 C.207 B.A. L.273 J.D. [[A] Seyfarth S.]
*PRACTICE AREAS: Employment Law; Employment Discrimination; Affirmative Action.
Jennings, Leo J. . . . '64 '92 C.446 B.S.M.E. L.276 J.D. 1050 Connecticut Ave., N.W. (Pat.)
Jennings, Teresa L. '63 '88
C.446 B.A. L.273 J.D. Sr. Atty., Govt. Rels., Direct Selling Assn.
Jennings, Tipton D., IV, (AV) '32 '60
C.472 B.S.E. L.273 J.D. [[C] Finnegan,H.F.G.&D.] (See Pat. Sect.)
*PRACTICE AREAS: Patent Prosecution; Trademarks; Intellectual Property Licensing; Intellectual Property Litigation; International Intellectual Property.

Jenny, Brian Paul '48 '76 C&L.273 B.A., J.D.
Suite 440, 5335 Wisconsin Avenue, N.W., 20015-2030
Telephone: 202-362-2165 Facsimile: 703-771-9078
Email: ziik@visuallink.com URL: http://www.lawyers.com/bpjlaw
***PRACTICE AREAS: Probate Law; Trusts Law; Estates Law; Domestic Relations Law; Criminal Appeals.**
Probate, Trusts and Estates, Domestic Relations Law and Criminal Appeals. General Practice.
Reference: NationsBank.
See Professional Biographies, WASHINGTON, DISTRICT OF COLUMBIA

Jensen, Allen R., (AV) '50 '77
C.877 B.S.Chem. L.273 J.D. [Finnegan,H.F.G.&D.] (See Pat. Sect.)
*PRACTICE AREAS: Chemical Patent Prosecution; Intellectual Property Portfolio Management; Pharmaceutical Patent Prosecution.
Jensen, Jennifer L. '56 '86 C.914 B.A. L.329 J.D.
(adm. in PA; not adm. in DC) George Washington Univ. Medical Ctr.
Jensen, Mark . . . . '— '98 C.347 B.A. L.309 J.D. [[A] King&S.]
Jensen, Robert E., (AV) . . . . '38 '66 C.473 B.S. L.273 LL.B. [[C] Williams&J.]
Jensen, Robert N. . . . . '47 '72 C.197 A.B. L.976 J.D. [McDermott,W.&E.]
Jensen, Sten A. . . . . '64 '93 C.228 B.A. L.893 J.D. [[C] Hogan&H.]
*PRACTICE AREAS: Litigation.
Jensen, Thomas A. . . . . '62 '91 [[A] Baker&D.] (⊙Mpls., MN)
*PRACTICE AREAS: Immigration.
Jensen, Thomas C. . . . . '58 '84 C.800 B.A. L.596 J.D. [Troutman S.]
*PRACTICE AREAS: Natural Resources; Energy; Environmental Law; Federal Regulatory Policy; Public Policy Legislation.
Jeon, Tae Yeol . . . . '71 '00 C.976 B.A. L.569 J.D. [[A] McKee N.]
*PRACTICE AREAS: Taxation.
Jeong, Rosa S. '69 '95 C.188 B.S. L.273 J.D.
(adm. in MD; not adm. in DC) [[A] Dorsey&W.]
*PRACTICE AREAS: International Trade; Customs Law.
Jerison, Jonathan D. . . . . '52 '78 C.976 B.A. L.1066 J.D. [[A] Goodwin P.]
Jerman, Tom A. '55 '81 C&L.878 B.S., J.D.
(adm. in CA; not adm. in DC) [O'Melveny&M.]
*PRACTICE AREAS: Labor and Employment.
Jernberg, Dale L. . . . . '24 '50 C&L.273 J.D. [[C] Griffin,F.T.&M.] (⊙Greenbelt, MD)
*PRACTICE AREAS: Trusts and Estates; Estate Planning; Wills; Real Estate; Elder Law.

Jernberg, Dale L.
(See Greenbelt, Maryland)

Jeronimides, H. Rosemary . . . . '70 '95 C.309 B.A. L.276 J.D. [[A] Coudert B.]
Jesperson, JoAnna . . . . '50 '84 C.477 B.Mus. L.1136 J.D. [[A] Epstein B.&G.]
*PRACTICE AREAS: Medical Malpractice; Litigation; Health Insurance Defense Law.
Jessamy, Ronald C., (AV) . . . . '48 '74 C.329 B.A. L.273 J.D. [Jordan K.&J.]
Jessee, Russell D. . . . . '64 '99 C.999 B.A. L.902 J.D. [[A] Covington&B.]
Jessen, Polly B. '65 '94 C.674 A.B. L.178 J.D.
(adm. in CO; not adm. in DC) [[C] Akin,G.S.H.&F.] (⊙Denver, CO)
Jest, Joseph V. . . . . '60 '86 C.93 A.B. L.813 J.D. [[C] Sidley A.B.&W.]
Jester, Elizabeth Tacy . . . . '55 '80 C.93 B.A. L.128 J.D. 200 G St., N.E.
Jester, Mary Cynthia Atchley . . . . '— '89 C.612 B.A. L.273 J.D. [Foley&L.]
*PRACTICE AREAS: General Corporate Litigation; Health Law; Intellectual Property Litigation.

Jetton, C. Loring, Jr., (AV) . . . . '43 '69 C.309 A.B. L.178 J.D. [Wilmer,C.&P.]
*PRACTICE AREAS: Antitrust and Trade Regulation; Civil Practice.
Jew, Quana C., (AV) . . . . '— '90 C&L.966 B.A., J.D. [Arent F.K.P.&K.]
*PRACTICE AREAS: ERISA; Deferred Compensation; Employee Benefit Law; Pension and Profit-Sharing Law; COBRA.
Jeweler, Bernard P., (AV) . . . . '45 '70 C.446 B.A. L.273 J.D. [Ogletree,D.N.S.&S.]
*PRACTICE AREAS: Labor and Employment; Collective Bargaining; Labor Arbitration; Labor Litigation.
Jewell, Paula L. . . . . '43 '69 C.329 B.A. L.178 J.D. D.C. Bd. of Zoning Adjustment
Jewett, Freeborn G., Jr. . . . . '27 '54 C&L.976 A.B., LL.B. World Wildlife Fund
Jewett, Susan . . . . '— '77 C.145 A.B. L.309 J.D. [King&S.]
*PRACTICE AREAS: Tax.
Jezouit, Debra J. . . . . '64 '90 C.273 B.A. L.893 J.D. [Baker B.]
*PRACTICE AREAS: Environmental.
Jimenez, Heidi V. '57 '84 C.260 B.A. L.1206 J.D.
Gen. Coun., Pan American Health Organization/ World Health Organization
Jimenez, Philip '54 '81 C.994 B.A. L.178 J.D.
(adm. in NY; not adm. in DC) Asst. Coun., Cable One, Inc.
Jimison, John W., (AV) '46 '75 C.970 B.A. L.276 J.D.
[Berliner,C.&J.] (⊙Berkeley, CA)
*PRACTICE AREAS: State Public Utility Proceedings; Municipal Law; Natural Gas; Telecommunications Law; Federal Legislation and Regulation.
Joannides, George E. . . . . '22 '50 C.563 B.A. L.724 LL.B. 2211 Mass. Ave., N.W.
Joaquin, Alan J. . . . . '60 '86 C.676 B.A. L.128 J.D. [Drinker B.&R.]
*PRACTICE AREAS: Commercial Litigation.
Jobes, Jana D. . . . . '73 '99 C.16 B.S.E. L.861 J.D. [[A] Williams&C.] (Pat.)
*PRACTICE AREAS: Litigation; Intellectual Property.
Joel, Alexander W. . . . '64 '87 C.674 B.A. L.477 J.D. Asst. Gen. Coun., Marriott Int., Inc.
*RESPONSIBILITIES: Business; Transactional; Information Technology; E-Commerce.

Joelson, Mark R., Law Office, (AV) '34 '58 C&L.309 B.A., LL.B.
1776 K Street, N.W., Suite 300, 20006
Telephone: 202-785-4155 Fax: 202-785-4157
Email: joelsonmr@msn.com
***PRACTICE AREAS: Arbitration and Mediation; Antitrust; International Trade Law; Litigation.**
Trade Regulation, International Trade Law, Arbitration and Mediation.
See Professional Biographies, WASHINGTON, DISTRICT OF COLUMBIA

Joffe, Carol A. . . . . '50 '79 C.938 A.B. L.588 J.D. [Winston&S.]
*PRACTICE AREAS: Civil Litigation.
Joffe, Paul L., (AV) . . . . '47 '72 C.309 A.B. L.976 J.D. 1776 K St., NW
Johanson, David S. . . . . '64 '94 C.813 B.A. L.846 J.D. [[A] Stewart&S.]
*PRACTICE AREAS: International Trade; International Agricultural and Food Regulation; International Environmental; World Trade Organization; Legislative.
Johanson, Lynn H. . . . . '69 '94 C.880 B.S. L.846 J.D. [[A] Wilkinson B.K.]
*PRACTICE AREAS: Communications; Telecommunications Law; Energy; Administrative Law; Appellate Practice.
Johanson, Ralph N., Jr. . . . . '41 '67 C.976 B.A. L.178 LL.B. 1730 Q St., N.W.
Johanson Berenson, LLP . . . . 1201 Pennsylvania Ave., N.W. (⊙Napa, CA; Mc Lean, VA)
Johl, Charan J. '70 '98 C.1375 B.S. L.276 J.D.
(adm. in CA; not adm. in DC) 1615 L St., NW
John, Douglas F., (AV) . . . . '48 '74 C.103 B.A. L.846 J.D. [John&H.]
*PRACTICE AREAS: Energy Law.

John & Hengerer, (AV)
Suite 600, 1200 17th Street, N.W., 20036-3013
Telephone: 202-429-8800 Telecopier: 202-429-8805
Email: kquinn@jhenergy.com URL: http://www.jhenergy.com
Members of Firm: Douglas F. John; Edward W. Hengerer; Kevin M. Sweeney; Kim M. Clark; Gordon J. Smith. Associates: Matthew T. Rick (Not admitted in DC); Elizabeth A. Zembruski (Not admitted in DC).
Energy Law, Energy Regulation, Administrative Practice and Pipeline Law.
See Professional Biographies, WASHINGTON, DISTRICT OF COLUMBIA

Johns, Alexis D. '65 '92 C&L.813 A.B., J.D.
(adm. in CA; not adm. in DC) Atty.-Advisor
Johns, Richard F. . . . . '71 '99 C.511 B.S. L.273 J.D. [[A] Reed S.]
*PRACTICE AREAS: Litigation.
Johnsen, R. Christian . . . . '60 '85 C.893 B.S. L.861 J.D. [Jones,W.W.P.C.&D.]
*PRACTICE AREAS: Maritime Law; Government Affairs; Commercial Transactions.
Johnsen, Wayne D., (AV) . . . . '59 '88 C.1044 B.A. L.276 J.D. [Wiley R.&F.]
*PRACTICE AREAS: Communications; Business Law; Finance; Internet Law; Electronic Commerce.
Johnson, Alisa A. . . . . '62 '88 C.273 B.A. L.276 J.D. The Bureau of Natl. Affs., Inc.
Johnson, Arnold C., (AV) . . . . '25 '53 C.860 A.B. L.309 LL.B. Advsr. to U.S. Treasury
Johnson, Brad C. . . . . '49 '75 C.490 B.S. L.276 J.D. [Duane,M.&H.]
*PRACTICE AREAS: International Project Development and Finance; Governmental Relations.
Johnson, Bradley T. . . . . '52 '81 C.197 A.B. L.893 J.D. [Johnson&Assoc.]
Johnson, Brian A., (AV) . . . . '40 '67 C.228 A.B. L.273 J.D. [[C] Wiley R.&F.]
*PRACTICE AREAS: Business Law; Finance; Communications.
Johnson, Bruce C. '57 '86 C.707 B.A. L.128 J.D.
(adm. in MD; not adm. in DC) [[A] Grossberg,Y.F.&B.]
*PRACTICE AREAS: Estate Planning; Probate; Real Estate; Tax.
Johnson, C. Donald, Jr. . . . . '48 '73 C&L.280 A.B., J.D. [Patton B.]
Johnson, Carol Ann . . . . '63 '95 C.418 B.S. L.276 J.D. [[A] Shearman&S.]
*PRACTICE AREAS: International Tax.
Johnson, Carol Schanno . . . . '62 '98 C.492 B.A. L.276 J.D. [[A] Ross,D.&B.] ‡
Johnson, Chad S. . . . . '67 '94 C&L.309 A.B., J.D. [[A] Skadden,A.S.M.&F.]
*PRACTICE AREAS: Banking.
Johnson, Charles W., IV . . . . '66 '94 C.282 B.A. L.128 J.D. [[C] Akin,G.S.H.&F.]
*PRACTICE AREAS: Public Policy.
Johnson, Christopher H. . . . . '51 '79 C.674 B.A. L.569 J.D. [Arter&H.]
*PRACTICE AREAS: International Commercial; Litigation; Construction.
Johnson, D'Ana E., (AV) . . . . '47 '77 C.512 B.S. L.276 J.D. [Allen,J.A.&K.]
*PRACTICE AREAS: Products Liability; General Civil Trial; Insurance Law; Premises Liability; Insurance Defense.
Johnson, Daniel E. . . . . '58 '83 C.886 B.S. L.893 J.D. [McKenna&C.]
*PRACTICE AREAS: Litigation; Trade Secrets; Employment.
Johnson, David M. '64 '90
C&L.276 B.A., J.D. Univ. of the Dist. of Columbia Sch. of Law
Johnson, David R., (AV) . . . . '46 '71 C.861 B.A. L.893 J.D. [Gibson,D.&C.]
*PRACTICE AREAS: Government Contracts Law; Contracts; Computers and Software; White Collar Crime; Administrative Law.
Johnson, David R. . . . . '64 '89 C.893 B.A. L.945 J.D. [Vinson&E.]
*PRACTICE AREAS: Litigation.
Johnson, David R., (AV) . . . . '45 '73 C&L.976 B.A., J.D. [Wilmer,C.&P.]
*PRACTICE AREAS: Electronic Commerce.
Johnson, Deirdre G. . . . . '67 '93 C.838 B.A. L.276 J.D. 1875 Connecticut Avenue, N.W.
Johnson, Dennis R., (AV) . . . . '52 '81 C.273 B.A. L.128 J.D. [Olsson,F.&W.]
*PRACTICE AREAS: Agriculture Law; Food and Drug Law; Administrative Law.
Johnson, Dixie Lynn . . . . '57 '86 C.613 B.A. L.560 J.D. [Fried,F.H.S.&J.]
Johnson, Donald O. . . . . '54 '94 C.645 B.A. L.472 J.D. [[A] McKenna&C.]
*PRACTICE AREAS: Commercial Litigation; Insurance Litigation; Trade Secrets Litigation; Trademarks.
Johnson, Donna Maria Coles '62 '87 C.790 B.A. L.128 J.D.
(adm. in MD; not adm. in DC) [[C] Jacobs&Assoc.]
*PRACTICE AREAS: Internet Law; Telecommunications Law; Corporate Law; Real Estate.

Johnson, Douglas Louis '46 '80 C.1030 B.A. L.1209 J.D. Asst. Gen. Coun., Wshington Metropolitan Area Transit Authority
*RESPONSIBILITIES: Litigation.

Johnson, E. Michael .... '64 '91 C.511 B.S. L.494 J.D. [Sutherland A.&B.]
*PRACTICE AREAS: Mergers and Acquisitions; Insurance Mergers and Acquisitions; Joint Ventures; International Joint Ventures; Corporate Commercial Law.

Johnson, Erin Elizabeth '75 '99 C.280 B.A. L.276 J.D. (adm. in TX; not adm. in DC) [Ⓐ Gilbert H.&R.]
*PRACTICE AREAS: Commercial Litigation; Insurance Coverage.

Johnson, Everett C., Jr. ....'— '81 C.228 A.B. L.893 J.D. [Latham&W.]

Johnson, George E. ....'42 '68 C.188 B.A. L.178 J.D. [Ⓑ Dickstein S.M.&O.]
*PRACTICE AREAS: Electric Utility Regulation; Regulatory Litigation; Nuclear Energy.

Johnson, Gibbs A. .... '64 '99 C.101 B.S. L.309 J.D. [Ⓐ Clifford C.R.&W.]
*PRACTICE AREAS: International Project Finance.

Johnson, Glendon E. .... '24 '53 C.878 B.S. L.309 LL.B. 1025 Connecticut Ave., N.W.

Johnson, Glendon E., Jr. .... '51 '78 C.878 B.A. L.846 J.D. [Ⓑ Lee&S.]
*PRACTICE AREAS: Corporate; Corporate Finance; Mergers and Acquisitions.

Johnson, Glenn M. ....'70 '95 C.918 B.A. L.94 J.D. Ernst & Young

Johnson, Gordon W. '57 '88 C.1 B.S. L.990 J.D. (adm. in TX; not adm. in DC) Sr. Coun., World Bank

Johnson, H. Scott, Jr '72 '97 C.575 B.S. L.273 J.D. (adm. in VA; not adm. in DC) [Ⓐ Krooth&A.]
*PRACTICE AREAS: Employment Law; Commercial Litigation.

Johnson, Harold L., Jr. '54 '80 C&L.575 B.A., J.D. Dep. Gen. Coun., Mun. Secs. Rulemaking Bd.

Johnson, J. Ramsey, (AV) .... '45 '76 C.276 B.A. L.1162 J.D. Princ. Asst. U.S. Atty.

Johnson, J. Walker .... '53 '78 C.188 B.A. L.378 J.D. [Steptoe&J.]
*PRACTICE AREAS: Federal Tax Law; Tax Controversies; Tax Procedure; Taxation; Taxation of Individuals and Business Entities.

Johnson, James W., Jr. .... '41 '71 C.329 B.S. L.273 J.D. 1631 Jonquil St., N.W. (Pat.)

Johnson, Jared W. ....'— '93 C.285 B.A. L.276 J.D. [Ⓐ Latham&W.]
*PRACTICE AREAS: Energy; Electric Power.

Johnson, Jay S. '43 '68 C.477 B.A. L.813 J.D. (adm. in OR; not adm. in DC) [Ⓑ Ball J.]
*PRACTICE AREAS: Natural Resources; Administrative Law.

Johnson, Jeffrey L. '74 '01 C&L.101 B.A., J.D. (adm. in UT; not adm. in DC) [Ⓐ Wiley R.&F.]
*PRACTICE AREAS: Corporate Law.

Johnson, Jeffrey M. ....'54 '79 C.207 B .A. L.276 J.D. [Dickstein S.M.&O.]
*PRACTICE AREAS: Patent Litigation; Civil Litigation; Trial Practice.

Johnson, Jeffrey R. ....'66 '93 C.882 B.S. L.276 J.D. [McKee N.]
*PRACTICE AREAS: Securitization; Structured Finance; Corporate Securities.

Johnson, Jennifer Anne ....'69 '94 C.976 B.A. L.309 J.D. [Ⓐ Covington&B.]

Johnson, John Griffith, Jr., (AV) .... '50 '76 C.674 A.B. L.276 J.D. [Paul,H.J.&W.]
*PRACTICE AREAS: Federal Regulation of Broadcasting; Legal Ethics; Telecommunications Law; Commercial and Non-Commercial Television and Radiobroadcast Station Representation; Broadcast Industry Lender Representation.

Johnson, Julia Reynolds ....'63 '89 C&L.276 B.S., J.D. [Ⓐ Kirkpatrick&L.]
*PRACTICE AREAS: Insurance Coverage.

Johnson, Julie L.B. ....'69 '99 C.228 A.B. L.659 J.D. [Ⓐ Covington&B.]

Johnson, Lance G. ....'59 '87 C.350 B.S. L.273 J.D. [Roylance,A.B.&G.] (See Pat. Sect.)
*PRACTICE AREAS: Preparation; Prosecution; Litigation and Licensing of Patents and Trademarks.

Johnson, Lara '74 '01 C.945 B.A. L.893 J.D. (adm. in VA; not adm. in DC) [Ⓐ Shaw P.]

Johnson, LaShawn M. '72 '99 C.329 B.A. L.1066 J.D. (adm. in MD; not adm. in DC) [Ⓐ Hogan&H.]

Johnson, Lee Carol '61 '87 C.518 A.B. L.477 J.D. (adm. in VA; not adm. in DC) Georgetown Univ. Law Center

Johnson, Lewis M., (AV) '23 '49 C.311 A.B. L.421 LL.B. (adm. in KY; not adm. in DC) 1300 Nineteenth St., N.W., Ste. 700‡

Johnson, Lynn H. .... '47 '78 C.510 B.A. L.329 J.D. [Johnson&P.]

Johnson, M. Scott, (AV) .... '44 '69 C.88 B.A. L.228 J.D. [Gardner,C.&D.]
*PRACTICE AREAS: Communications and Media; Communications Law; FCC Regulation; Mass Media Law; Telecommunications Law.

Johnson, Margaret E. ....'66 '93 C.197 B.A. L.966 J.D. [Ⓐ Kalijarvi,C.&N.]
*PRACTICE AREAS: Employment Discrimination; Federal Employment Law; Employment Law.

Johnson, Mark D. .... '65 '93 C.105 B.A. L.30 J.D. [Ⓐ Squire,S.&D.]

Johnson, Mark W. ....'42 '67 C.399 B.A. L.966 J.D. Assoc. Gen. Coun., CBS Inc.

Johnson, Marvin J., (CV) '55 '80 C&L.972 B.S., J.D. (adm. in WY; not adm. in DC) Leg. Coun., Amer. Civil Liberties Union

Johnson, Mary L. .... '69 '97 C.674 A.B. L.228 J.D. [Ⓐ Hogan&H.]
*PRACTICE AREAS: Pharmaceutical Regulation.

Johnson, Melanye K. ....'71 '97 C.477 A.B. L.608 J.D. [Ⓐ Arent F.K.P.&K.]
*PRACTICE AREAS: Intellectual Property; Trademarks; Copyrights; Intellectual Property Litigation.

Johnson, Michael A. .... '66 '97 C.659 B.A. L.276 J.D. [Ⓐ Arnold&P.]
*PRACTICE AREAS: Civil Litigation Practice; Financial Institutions Litigation; Federal Claims; Asylum Law Practice.

Johnson, Michone Trinae ...... '71 '98 C.103 B.A. L.178 J.D. House of Rep., Jud. Comm.

Johnson, Noel Thomas .... '57 '86 C.128 B.A. L.861 J.D. Sr. Corp. Coun.

Johnson, O. Thomas, Jr., (AV) .... '46 '72 C&L.813 A.B., J.D. [Covington&B.]

Johnson, Orlan M. ....'62 '88 C.243 B.A. L.329 J.D. [Ⓑ Milbank,T.H.&M.]

Johnson, Owen M., Jr., (AV) ....'36 '64 C.197 A.B. L.309 LL.B. [Akin,G.S.H.&F.]
*PRACTICE AREAS: Antitrust and Trade Regulation.

Johnson, Pamela S. .... '58 '85 C.103 B.A. L.659 J.D. Coun., Fed. Nat. Mortgage Assn.

Johnson, Peter R. '— '99 C&L.446 B.S., J.D. (adm. in MD; not adm. in DC) [Ⓐ Dyer E.&J.]

Johnson, Philip McBride ....'38 '62 C.347 A.B. L.976 LL.B. [Ⓑ Skadden,A.S.M.&F.]

Johnson, R. Tenney, (AV) '30 '59 C.696 A.B. L.309 LL.B. Suite 800, 2121 K Street, N.W.

Johnson, Ralph H., (AV) ....'49 '75 C.1085 B.A. L.878 J.D. [Schmeltzer,A.&S.]
*PRACTICE AREAS: Litigation; Radiation Law.

Johnson, Ray A. ....'— '99 C.918 B.A. L.329 J.D. [Ⓐ Nixon P.]
*PRACTICE AREAS: Real Estate; Corporate Law; Zoning, Planning and Land Use.

Johnson, Repunzelle R. '71 '98 C.1049 B.A. L.273 J.D. (adm. in MD; not adm. in DC) Howard University Hosp.

Johnson, Richard A. .... '50 '77 C.103 A.B. L.976 J.D. [Arnold&P.]
*PRACTICE AREAS: Life Sciences; International Trade Law; Information Technology.

Johnson, Richard C., (AV) .... '37 '62 C&L.309 B.A., LL.B. [Jenner&B.]
*PRACTICE AREAS: Government Contracts Law.

Johnson, Robert Winthrop .... '46 '74 C.674 A.B. L.861 J.D. [Johnson&C.] ⊙
*PRACTICE AREAS: International Trade; International Law; Customs; Corporate; Government Relations Law.

Johnson, Roger C., (AV) ....'52 '77 C.477 B.A. L.273 J.D. [Koonz,M.J.D.&L.]

Johnson, Ronald M. ....'49 '76 C&L.378 B.A., J.D. [Akin,G.S.H.&F.]
*PRACTICE AREAS: Labor and Employment.

Johnson, Shannon M.P. ....'— '99 C.494 B.S L.945 J.D. [Ⓐ Morgan,L.&B.]

Johnson, Sharon Y. '73 '98 C.1356 B.A L.1117 J.D. (adm. in CA; not adm. in DC) [Ⓐ Shaw P.]
*PRACTICE AREAS: Financial Institution Regulation.

Johnson, Shirley Z., (AV) .... '40 '66 C.352 B.A. L.477 J.D. [Greenberg T.]

Johnson, Shubha K. ....'68 '96 C.446 B.A. L.1209 J.D. Clk., U.S. Ct of Fed. Claims

Johnson, Stephanie Armstead-Davis '72 '97 C.893 B.A. L.329 J.D. (adm. in VA; not adm. in DC) Law Clk. to Chf. Supr. J.

Johnson, Stephen D., (AV) .... '44 '76 C.911 B.A. L.273 J.D. [Luxenberg,J.&D.]
*PRACTICE AREAS: Family Law; Domestic Relations; Gay and Lesbian Family Law; Divorce; Child Custody.

Johnson, Steven R. ....'— '93 C.477 B.A. L.276 J.D. [Ⓐ Verner,L.B.M.&H.]
*PRACTICE AREAS: Environmental; Administrative.

Johnson, Stuart Fisk .... '43 '68 C.951 B.A. L.893 J.D. 406 5th St., N.W.

Johnson, Tracy L. .... '68 '97 C.264 B.A. L.276 J.D. [Ⓐ Arnold&P.]
*PRACTICE AREAS: Litigation.

Johnson, Valerie S. '61 '94 C.228 B.A. L.1490 LL.B. (adm. in NY; not adm. in DC) [Ⓐ Nixon P.]
*PRACTICE AREAS: Business Law; Mergers and Acquisitions; Technology Law.

Johnson, Vernon W., III ....'64 '89 C.228 B.A. L.273 J.D. [Jackson&C.] ⊙
*PRACTICE AREAS: Civil Litigation; Commercial Litigation; Trial Practice; Real Estate Litigation; Title Insurance Law.

Johnson, W. Stanfield, (AV) ....'38 '64 C.813 A.B. L.309 LL.B. [Crowell&M.]

Johnson, Wayne K., (AV) .... '45 '68 C.112 A.B. L.1066 J.D. [Jorden B.]
*PRACTICE AREAS: Tax; Corporate Securities; ERISA; Insurance.

Johnson & Associates, P.C. .... 1155 Connecticut Ave., N.W.

Johnson & Clifton, LLP
2600 Virginia Avenue N.W., Suite 508, 20037-1905 ⊙
Telephone: 202-337-8400 Telefax: 202-337-3462
Email: rwjohnson@compuserve.com URL: http://www.lawyers.com/johnson&rogers
Robert Winthrop Johnson; Edwina Clifton Rogers; Jeffrey James Clifton (Not admitted in DC).
International Trade, International Law, Aviation, Customs, Corporate, Legislative and Political Law, Government Relations and Health Law.
Birmingham, Alabama Office: 728 Shades Creek Parkway, Suite 100, 35209. Telephone: 205-870-9588. Fax: 205-870-7288.
See Professional Biographies, WASHINGTON, DISTRICT OF COLUMBIA

Johnson Henn, Emily ....'72 '99 C.918 B.A. L.276 J.D. [Ⓐ Covington&B.]

Johnson-Koch, LeAnn M. ....'64 '90 C.94 B.A. L.823 J.D. [Piper M.R.&W.]
*PRACTICE AREAS: Environmental Litigation; Environmental Law.

Johnson Oratokhai, Misty Y. '66 '00 C.1280 B.A. L.128 J.D. (adm. in MD; not adm. in DC) 441 4th St. N.W.

Johnson & Pavuk, (AV) .... Ste. 1500, 1413 K St., N.W.

Johnson & Roche
(See McLean, Virginia)

Johnson & Yang, P.C.
(See Wheaton, Maryland)

Johnston, Charles Richard, Jr., (AV) .... '48 '75 C.611 B.A. L.61 J.D. [Baker,D.B.&C.]
*PRACTICE AREAS: International Trade; International Transactions; Corporate; Legislative; Administrative.

Johnston, E. Ashton, (AV) ....'60 '91 C.1369 B.A. L.128 J.D. [Piper M.R.&W.]
*PRACTICE AREAS: Telecommunications Law; Business Law; Technology Law.

Johnston, Elaine L. '57 '82 C.800 A.B. L.893 J.D. Asst. Gen. Coun., Smithsonian Institution

Johnston, Gerald P. ....'37 '62 C.918 B.A. L.228 LL.B. [Ⓑ R.S.Hall,Jr.]

Johnston, James H., (AV) ....'44 '69 C.378 B.A. L.477 J.D. 1155 Connecticut Ave., N.W.

Johnston, Joseph F., Jr., (AV) ....'33 '61 C.674 B.A. L.309 LL.B. [Drinker B.&R.]
*PRACTICE AREAS: Directors & Officers Liability and Insurance Law; Professional Liability Insurance Law.

Johnston, Mark A. ....'73 '99 C.390 B.A. L.861 J.D. [Ⓐ Jordan C.&S.]
*PRACTICE AREAS: Litigation; Insurance Defense; Products Liability.

Johnston, Mark G. .... '65 '93 C.339 B.A. L.477 J.D. [Ⓐ Levine,B.B.&B.]
*PRACTICE AREAS: Telecommunications Law.

Johnston, Robert E. .... '68 '94 C.802 B.A. L.273 J.D. [Ⓐ Spriggs&H.]
*PRACTICE AREAS: Government Contracts; Banking Litigation; Complex Commercial Litigation; Insurance Coverage.

Johnston, Robert Olin, (AV) ....'46 '75 C&L.945 A.B., J.D. [Johnston&W.]

Johnston, Rod K. ....'37 '67 C.999 L.273 J.D. 1312 27th St. NW

Johnston, Thomas B. ....'54 '87 C.945 B.S. L.273 J.D. [Ⓑ McKenna&C.]
*PRACTICE AREAS: Toxic Substance Control Law; Pesticide Law; Environmental Law.

Johnston, Thomas D., (AV) ....'— '76 C.659 B.S. L.477 J.D. [Miller&C.]
*PRACTICE AREAS: Taxation; Tax Litigation; Tax Appeals; Tax Audits; Litigation.

Johnston & Westerfield, P.C, (AV) .... 3256 Prospect Street, N.W.

Johnstone, James M., (AV) '34 '60 C&L.976 B.A., LL.B.
1776 K Street, Third Floor, 20006
Telephone: 202-719-7060 Fax: 202-719-7049
Email: jmjatty@dc.infi.net URL: http://www.lawyers.com/jamesmjohnstone
***PRACTICE AREAS: Administrative Law; Antitrust and Trade Regulation; Advertising and Marketing; Arbitration; Mediation.**
Federal Practice, Civil Practice, Appellate Practice, Alternative Dispute Resolution, Antitrust and Trade Regulation, Drug and Medical Device Regulation, Advertising Law.
See Professional Biographies, WASHINGTON, DISTRICT OF COLUMBIA

Joiner, John E. .... '70 '96 C.623 B.B.A. L.208 J.D. [Ⓐ Williams&C.]
*PRACTICE AREAS: Appellate Practice; Civil Litigation; Class Action Litigation; Complex and Multi-District Litigation; Complex Commercial Litigation.

Joiner, Lisa Zeiler ....'69 '96 C.546 B.A. L.208 J.D. [Ⓐ Fulbright&J.]
*PRACTICE AREAS: Litigation; Securities; Commercial; Class Action Defense.

Jolles, Abbe ....'55 '82 C.33 B.A. L.629 J.D. 717 D St., N.W.

Jolley, Denise Hopkins ....'52 '78 C.329 B.A. L.128 J.D. 3319 14th St., N.E.

Jolly, Bruce O., Jr. .... '46 '73 C&L.575 A.B., J.D. [Shook,H.&B.]
*PRACTICE AREAS: Financial Institution Law.

Jolly, David Wilson '72 '01 C.1365 B.A. L.1209 J.D. (adm. in VA; not adm. in DC) [Ⓐ Fried,F.H.S.&J.]

Jolly, Thomas R., (P.C.), (AV) ....'43 '72 C.477 B.A. L.276 J.D. 1201 New York Ave Nw

Jonas, John F., (AV) ....'50 '76 C.156 B.A. L.188 J.D. [Patton B.]

Jonas, Theodore C. '62 '91 C&L.188 B.A., J.D. (adm. in GA; not adm. in DC) [Ⓑ Baker B.]

Jonas, W. James, III, (BV) ....'61 '87 C.902 B.A. L.846 J.D. [Loeffler,J.&T.] ⊙
*PRACTICE AREAS: Governmental Affairs Law.

Joned, Alima ....'— '89 C&L.999 LL.B., LL.B. [Ⓑ Foley,H.&E.]
*PRACTICE AREAS: International.

Jones, A. Quinn, III '51 '80 C&L.329 B.A., J.D. (adm. in FL; not adm. in DC) [Ⓑ Houston&H.]

Jones, Aidan D., (AV) '45 '75 C.918 B.A. L.276 J.D.
1818 N Street, N.W., Suite 700, 20036
Telephone: 202-293-2386 Facsimile: 202-331-9306
Email: ajones2506@aol.com URL: http://www.lawyers.com/aidanjones
Business Law, Civil Trials, Appellate Litigation, Estate Planning, Trusts and Estates, Estate and Gift Taxation, Wealth Preservation, Asset Protection, Family Business Succession, Business Formation, Closely Held Business Estate Planning, Probate, E-Commerce Law, Aviation.
See Professional Biographies, WASHINGTON, DISTRICT OF COLUMBIA

Jones, Allen, Jr., (AV) ....'30 '57 C.475 B.A. L.276 J.D. [Ⓑ Hamilton&H.]

Jones, Allison M. .... '73 '98 C.289 B.A. L.446 J.D. [Ⓐ Lukas,N.G.&S.]
*PRACTICE AREAS: Communications Law; Commercial Transactions.

Jones, Anne P. . . . . '35 '61 C&L.93 B.S., LL.B. 1275 Pennsylvania Ave. N.W.
Jones, Brian C. '56 '94 C.446 B.S.Ch.E. L.273 J.D.
[🄰 Blank R.C.&M.] (See Pat. Sect.)
*PRACTICE AREAS: Chemical Intellectual Property; Pharmaceutical Intellectual Property; Mechanical Intellectual Property; International Intellectual Property; Intellectual Property Infringement.
Jones, Charles A. . . . . '69 '94 C.893 B.A. L.276 J.D. [🄰 Ross,D.&B.]
Jones, Cherie J. '70 '97 C&L.446 B.A., J.D.
(adm. in MD; not adm. in DC) 1244 19th St., N.W.
Jones, Cheryl L., (BV) . . . . '54 '86 C.893 B.A. L.276 J.D. 1101 Connecticut Ave., N.W.
Jones, Christopher A. . . . . '72 '00 C.1369 B.S. L.893 J.D. [🄰 Ross,D.&B.]
Jones, Crystal J. '71 '98 C.1154 B.A. L.966 J.D.
(adm. in WI; not adm. in DC) [🄰 Kaye S.]
Jones, Cynthia Ellen, (BV) . . . . '64 '89 C.205 B.A. L.904 J.D. Pub. Def. Serv.
Jones, Delwen A. '68 '94 C.911 B.A. L.276 J.D.
(adm. in WA; not adm. in DC) [🄰 Gibson,D.&C.] ‡
*PRACTICE AREAS: General Litigation; Antitrust.
Jones, Donald M. '51 '78 C.867 B.S. L.569 J.D.
(adm. in MD; not adm. in DC) Antioch Sch. of Law
Jones, Erica D. . . . . '71 '98 C.188 B.S. L.1375 J.D. [🄰 Fulbright&J.]
*PRACTICE AREAS: Corporate Law; International Law.
Jones, Erika Z., (AV) . . . . '55 '80 C&L.276 A.B., J.D. [Mayer,B.&P.]
Jones, Frank P., Jr. '29 '57 C&L.273 A.B., LL.B.
V.P., Aluminum Company of America
Jones, George R. A. . . . . '58 '85 C.478 B.A. L.188 J.D. [🄲 Paul,H.J.&W.]
*PRACTICE AREAS: Real Estate Law.
Jones, George W., Jr. . . . . '53 '80 C.145 B.A. L.976 J.D. [Sidley A.B.&W.]
Jones, Harold D., Jr., (AV) '25 '56
C.277 B.E.E. L.245 LL.B. Ste. 200, 2120 L St., N.W. (Pat.)
Jones, Harry T., Jr., (AV) . . . . '53 '77 C&L.309 A.B., J.D. [Hogan&H.]
*PRACTICE AREAS: Civil Litigation; Employment Litigation; Business Litigation.
Jones, Heather A. . . . . '72 '99 C.197 A.B. L.378 J.D. [🄰 Wilmer,C.&P.]
Jones, Henry H. . . . . '26 '57 C&L.329 J.D. Prof. of Law, Howard Univ.
Jones, J. Sumner, (AV) . . . . '40 '64 C.976 A.B. L.309 LL.B. [Jones&B.]
*PRACTICE AREAS: Securities Law; Corporate Law.
Jones, James A. . . . . '50 '73 L.69 J.D. Coun., The World Bk.
Jones, James R. . . . . '39 '64 C.623 A.B. L.276 LL.B. [Manatt,P.&P.]
Jones, James W., (AV) . . . . '45 '70 C.859 B.A. L.569 J.D. APCO Assocs., Inc.
Jones, Janine L. . . . . '71 '96 C.339 B.A. L.352 J.D. [🄰 Akin,G.S.H.&F.]
*PRACTICE AREAS: Public Policy; Taxation.
Jones, Jean Marie . . . . '50 '83 C&L.446 B.S., J.D. [Epstein B.&G.]
*PRACTICE AREAS: Medical Malpractice; Litigation; Health Care Defense.
Jones, John B., Jr., (AV) . . . . '28 '53 C&L.309 A.B., LL.B. 1201 Penn. Ave., N.W.
Jones, Julia A. '71 '99 C.231 B.A. L.1119 J.D.
(adm. in MD; not adm. in DC) [🄰 Dorsey&W.]
*PRACTICE AREAS: Environmental Law; Natural Resources Law; Regulatory Agency Practice.
Jones, Kenneth P. . . . . '72 '99 C.259 B.S. L.260 J.D. [🄰 Patton B.]
Jones, Keri A. . . . . '70 '95 C.665 B.A. L.276 J.D. [🄰 Ashcraft&G.]
*PRACTICE AREAS: Medical Malpractice; Personal Injury.
Jones, Kevin D. '62 '88 C.575 B.A. L.477 J.D.
(adm. in PA; not adm. in DC) [🄲 Womble C.S.&R.]
*PRACTICE AREAS: Public Policy; Legislation; Aviation Law; Surface Transportation Law; Communications Law.
Jones, Leonade D. . . . . '47 '73 C.783 B.A. L.813 J.D. The Washington Post Co.
Jones, Lisa Michelle '66 '94 C&L.347 B.S., J.D.
(adm. in IN; not adm. in DC) Dir., Admin. Servs., Democratic Natl. Comm.
Jones, Marcia G. . . . . '54 '88 C.16 B.S. L.128 J.D. Health Policy Atty., AFSCME
Jones, Margaret F. '66 '92 C.446 B.A. L.273 J.D.
(adm. in MD; not adm. in DC) Bur. of Natl. Affs., Inc.
Jones, Maria O'Toole . . . . '66 '93 C.205 B.S. L.273 J.D. [🄲 Miller&C.]
*PRACTICE AREAS: Taxation; Federal Income Tax; Tax Controversies; Tax Exempt Organizations; Employee Benefits.
Jones, Mark M. . . . . '57 '84 C.183 B.S. L.383 J.D. [Carr G.]
*PRACTICE AREAS: Insurance Defense; Medical Malpractice.
Jones, Mary G., (AV) . . . . '20 '49 C.914 B.A. L.976 J.D. 1631 Suters Lane, N.W.‡
Jones, Megan E. '73 '99 C.576 B.A. L.575 J.D.
(adm. in NC; not adm. in DC) [🄰 Cohen,M.H.&T.]
*PRACTICE AREAS: Litigation.
Jones, Michael D. . . . . '60 '86 C.217 B.A. L.276 J.D. [Kirkland&E.]
*PRACTICE AREAS: Litigation.
Jones, Michael G. . . . . '65 '92 C.499 B.S. L.128 J.D. [🄰 Willkie F.&G.]
Jones, Michelle A. . . . . '74 '98 C.880 B.A. L.309 J.D. [🄰 Chadbourne&P.]
Jones, Miriam Hellen . . . . '49 '82 C.373 B.S. L.128 J.D. [🄰 Greenstein D.&L.]
*PRACTICE AREAS: Commercial Real Estate; Real Estate Development; Land Use; Historic Preservation; Administrative Law.
Jones, Mohamedu Fahnbulleh '54 '91 C.351 B.A. L.309 LL.M.
(adm. in NY; not adm. in DC) Natl. Prison Proj.
Jones, Norman W. . . . . '22 '58 C.754 B.S. L.273 LL.B. 6108 13th St., NW
Jones, Othello G., Jr. . . . . . '43 '69 C&L.329 B.A., J.D. 2041 Martin Luther King Ave., S.E.
Jones, Reginald E. . . . . '50 '77 C.976 B.A. L.569 J.D. [Ogletree,D.N.S.&S.]
*PRACTICE AREAS: Labor and Employment; Equal Employment Opportunity Law; Alternative Dispute Resolution.
Jones, Richard H., (AV) . . . . '30 '64 C.886 B.S. L.30 LL.B. [Baker&H.]
*PRACTICE AREAS: Business Law; Legislative Law.
Jones, Robert C. . . . . '51 '77 C.945 B.A. L.692 J.D. [Jones,D.R.&P.]
*PRACTICE AREAS: Antitrust and Trade Regulation; Business Combinations.
Jones, Robert C. . . . . '61 '86 C.886 B.A. L.500 J.D. [Patton B.]
Jones, Robert J. . . . . '48 '73 C&L.378 B.A., J.D. [Arnold&P.]
*PRACTICE AREAS: Tax Law; Federal Income Tax.
Jones, Roy Stapleton, Jr. . . . . '42 '74 C.870 B.S. L.446 J.D. [Birch,H.B.&C.]
Jones, Sarah Elizabeth . . . . '51 '79 C.797 B.A. L.1045 J.D. Natl. Assn. of Atty. Gen.
Jones, Shana C. . . . . '69 '95 C.808 B.A. L.420 J.D. 322 Cannon
Jones, Sheila D. . . . . '52 '78 C.446 B.A. L.309 J.D. [Akin,G.S.H.&F.] (⊙Denver, CO)
*PRACTICE AREAS: Environmental Law; Environmental Litigation.
Jones, Shelley E. . . . . '74 '00 C&L.893 B.A., J.D. [🄰 Akin,G.S.H.&F.]
*PRACTICE AREAS: Labor and Employment.
Jones, Stanley D. '45 '76 C.1028 A.B. L.273 J.D.
General Counsel & Vice President, Colonial Parking Inc.
Jones, Stephen A. . . . . '— '90 C.902 B.A. L.276 J.D. [King&S.]
*PRACTICE AREAS: Litigation and Trade.
Jones, Stephen C. . . . . '51 '77 C.112 B.A. L.1065 J.D. [Greenberg T.]
Jones, Stephen E. . . . . '67 '98 C.886 B.A. L.446 J.D. [🄰 Arnold&P.]
*PRACTICE AREAS: Litigation; Legislative.
Jones, Susan R . . . . '57 '84 C.1036 B.A. L.1162 J.D. Antioch Sch. of Law
Jones, Tenley M. '26 '56 C.188 A.B. L.178 LL.B.
(adm. in NY; not adm. in DC) The World Bk.
Jones, Terrence D., (AV) . . . . '39 '66 C.260 B.A. L.276 J.D. [Keller&H.]
*PRACTICE AREAS: Transportation Law; Trade Regulation Law.
Jones, Theodore Lawrence . . . . '20 '48 C&L.846 B.B.A., J.D. 1900 K St., N.W.
Jones, Theodore W. '— '98 C.880 B.A. L.802 J.D.
(adm. in CA; not adm. in DC) [🄰 Manatt,P.&P.]
Jones, Thomas . . . . '65 '93 C&L.276 B.A., J.D. [Willkie F.&G.]
Jones, Thomas L. . . . . '41 '72 C.852 B.S. L.329 J.D. [🄲 McFadden&S.]
Jones, Wanda P. '53 '79 C.925 B.S. L.575 J.D.
(adm. in NC; not adm. in DC) 1099 14th St. N.W.
Jones, William B. '28 '53 C.112 B.A. L.800 J.D. 4807 17th St., N.W.‡
Jones-Baskaran, Amy M. . . . . '59 '87 C&L.276 A.B., J.D. Amer. Intl. Legal Grp.

Jones & Blouch L.L.P., (AV)
Suite 410 East, 1025 Thomas Jefferson Street, N.W., 20007-0805
Telephone: 202-223-3500 Telecopier: 202-223-4593
Email: jb@jonesblouch.com URL: http://www.lawyers.com/jones&blouch
Members of Firm: J. Sumner Jones; John W. Blouch. Associate: Aneal Krishnamurthy. Of Counsel: William Randolph Thompson; Bruce W. Dunne.
Business Law Practice, Financial Services, Securities Law, Corporate Finance, Corporate Law, Banking Law.
Affiliated Offices: Jorden Burt LLP, Suite 400 East, 1025 Thomas Jefferson Street, Washington, D.C., 20007-0805; Suite 500, 777 Brickell Avenue, Miami, Florida, 33131-2803.
See Professional Biographies, WASHINGTON, DISTRICT OF COLUMBIA

Jones, Day, Reavis & Pogue, (AV)
51 Louisiana Avenue, N.W., 20001-2113 ⊙
Telephone: 202-879-3939 Telecopier: 202-626-1700
Email: counsel@jonesday.com URL: http://www.jonesday.com
Members of Firm in Washington, D.C.: Joseph S. Iannucci; Michael Bradfield; James T. O'Hara; J. Lawrence Manning, Jr.; Jonathan C. Rose; Sigmund T. Weiner; Andrew M. Kramer; James A. Wilderotter; Robert F. McDermott, Jr.; Joe Sims; James J. Graham; Mark K. Sisitsky; Junius C. McElveen, Jr.; Paul S. Ryerson; Tom D. Smith; Joseph M. David, Jr.; Clark Evans Downs; Willis J. Goldsmith; Kenneth J. Krupsky; Phillip A. Proger; Thomas F. Cullen, Jr.; Robert S. Waters; Richard D. Avil, Jr.; Donald B. Ayer; Marshall B. Babson; David C. Roseman; Lester W. Droller; Peter J. Romatowski; Raymond J. Wiacek; Stephen J. Brogan; Timothy J. Finn; Robert C. Jones; Gregory M. Luce; Toby G. Singer; Geoffrey S. Stewart; Teresa A. Brooks; Kathryn M. Fenton; Peter F. Garvin, III; Kevin D. McDonald; Joseph F. Winterscheid; Kenneth J. Ayres; Robert H. Klonoff; Mary Ellen Powers; Steven A. Teitelbaum; Peter J. Biersteker; Carolyn Y. Thompson; Michael A. Carvin; Christopher F. Dugan; Alison B. Marshall; Glen D. Nager; Adrian Wager-Zito; John M. Majoras; William V. O'Reilly; James D. Wareham; Michael P. Gurdak; Gregory M. Shumaker; Kevin J. McIntyre; Candace A. Ridgway; R. Christopher Cook (Not admitted in DC); James E. Gauch; Douglas J. Whipple; Edward K.M. Bilich; Gregory A. Castanias; Edwin L. Fountain; Daniel H. Bromberg; Martin V. Kirkwood; Joseph A. Goldman; Blaney Harper; Michael R. Shumaker. Consultant: Herbert J. Hansell (Not admitted in DC). Of Counsel: Karl L. Kellar; Kevyn D. Orr (Not admitted in DC); Kent L. Killelea; Jonathan M. Redgrave. Counsel: David A. Copus; Brian J. McManus; Jerome J. Zaucha; Kevin B. Byrd; Heidi Hughes Bumpers; Stephen J. Goodman; Elizabeth A. McLaughlin. Associates: Christine A. Bartlett; Mary L. Hale; Julia M. Broas; Kathleen Marie McChesney; James E. Anklam; Anthony P. Lalla; Steven J. Mintz; Kimberly A. Harb; Stephen J. Jorden; Robin L. Juni; Jesse A. Witten; Geoffrey K. Beach; Thomas M. Beck; Kristi D. Drefke; Lawrence D. Rosenberg; Peter J. Wang; Jonathan Berman; Sarah Mackey Mathias; Mary-Helen Perry; Paul R. Reichert; Lynn A. Airasian; Michael L. Kolis; Peter J. Love; Kevin C. Maclay; Sarah B. McClure; Anant S. Narayanan; Pamela Sak; Kenneth B. Driver; David H. Evans; Jacqueline M. Holmes; Julie E. McEvoy; Michael S. McFalls; Bevin M.B. Newman; Heather M. O'Shea; Russell O. Paige; Karen M. Espaldon; Michael S. Fried; Susan Q. Haines; Lisa Malloy Nardini; Laura Tuell Parcher; Stephen M. Polozie; Shelby L. Provencher; David S. Rutkowski; Aaron L. Agenbroad; T. Jeffrey Fitzgerald; Brian K. Grube; Shannon M. Kasley; John B. Kennedy; Kathleen M. Laubenstein; Joseph J. Migas; Amy E. Moorhus; Elizabeth Rees; J. Carter Andersen; Cynthia L. Bauerly; Jack W. Campbell IV; Mia F. Cohen; Joseph R. Derbis; Louis K. Fisher (Not admitted in DC); Laura Talley Geyer; Mark L. Glassman; Carey G.B. Kerney; Brian D. Lefort; Stacy R. Linden; Christopher J. Lovrien; Charles R.A. Morse (Not admitted in DC); J. Andrew Read; Melissa D. Stear; David S. Torborg (Not admitted in DC); Mark C. Cawley; Matthew S. Duchesne; Rachael Hammer; Kymberly D. Hankinson; Renee M. Howard; Jennifer A. Hunkler; Tamara Hardney Kassabian; Tashena Middleton Moore; Tracey L. Hallam Oley; Justin J. Roberts; Debra L. Satinoff; Sheila L. Shadmand; Janie C.I. Sheng; Stacie Simmons Sperry; Robin D. Stumpf (Not admitted in DC); Virginia C. Theis; Heather Guilette Walser; Geoffrey T. Wright; John L. Chaney; Jonathan F. Christian; Tiffany F. Donovan; Tyler L. Farmer (Not admitted in DC); Dominick V. Freda; Mark S. Hancock; H. Brian Holland; Matthew J. Hoefling (Not admitted in DC); Nancy M. Kim; Christopher T. Koegel; Tni M. LeBlanc; Gregory P. Luib; Angela M. Olsen; Noah D. Rubins (Not admitted in DC); Jennifer M. Schell; Ryan C. Thomas; Annie Tran; Caroline Tsai; Gitte J. Wendell (Not admitted in DC); Sara E. Young; Jody M. Gardner; Sandra Kaczmarczyk (Not admitted in DC); Tara R. Kaesebier; Laura J. Merianos; Mia C. Reynolds (Not admitted in DC); Cheryl E. Forchilli (Not admitted in DC). Senior Staff Attorneys: John P. McGrane, Jr.; Patrick L. Hubbard; Kerri S. Kuhlmann. Staff Attorneys: Anna L. Brown; Dara A. Lutz; Lee A. Friedman; William L. Kearney, Jr.
Languages: Chinese, Farsi, French, German, Hindi, Greek, Jamaican Patuis, Russian, Spanish, and Tamil.
Full-Service Civil Practice, Antitrust and Trade Regulation, Business Restructuring and Reorganization, Capital Markets, Corporate Criminal Investigations, Cross-Border Transactions, Employee Benefits, Energy, Environmental, Health and Safety, Finance, General Litigation, General Tax, Government Regulation, Health Care, Issues and Appeals, Intellectual Property, International Securities, Labor and Employment, Lending/Structured Finance, Mergers and Acquisitions, Private Capital, Product Liability and Regulation, Real Estate, Technology Transactions, Trade and Regulatory Law.
In Atlanta, Georgia: 3500 SunTrust Plaza, 303 Peachtree Street, N.E. Telephone: 404-521-3939. Telecopier: 404-581-8330.
In Brussels, Belgium: Avenue Louise 480, Louizalaan 480, 1050 Brussels. Telephone: 32-2-645-14-11. Telecopier: 32-2-645-14-45.
In Chicago, Illinois: 77 West Wacker. Telephone: 312-782-3939. Telecopier: 312-782-8585.
In Cleveland, Ohio: North Point, 901 Lakeside Avenue. Telephone: 216-586-3939. Telecopier: 216-579-0212.
In Columbus, Ohio: 1900 Huntington Center, 41 South High Street. Telephone: 614-469-3939. Telecopier: 614-461-4198.
In Dallas, Texas: 2727 North Harwood Street. Telephone: 214-220-3939. Telecopier: 214-969-5100.
In Frankfurt, Germany: Hochhaus am Park, Grüneburgweg 102, 60323 Frankfurt am Main. Telephone: 49-69-9726-3939. Telecopier: 49-69-9726-3993.
In Hong Kong, China: 31st Floor, Edinburgh Tower, The Landmark, 15 Queen's Road Central. Telephone: 852-2526-6895. Telecopier: 852-2868-5871 or 852-2868-5699.
In Houston, Texas: Chase Tower, 600 Travis Street, Suite 6500. Telephone: 832-239-3939. Telecopier: 832-239-3600.
In Irvine, California: 5 Park Plaza, Suite 1100. Telephone: 949-851-3939. Telecopier: 949-553-7539.
In London, England: Bucklersbury House, 3 Queen Victoria Street. Telephone: 44-20-7236-3939. Telecopier: 44-20-7236-1113.
In Los Angeles, California: 555 West Fifth Street, Suite 4600. Telephone: 213-489-3939. Telecopier: 213-243-2539.
In Madrid, Spain: Velázquez 51. Telephone: 34-91-520-39-39. Telecopier: 34-91-520-39-38.
In New York, New York: 599 Lexington Avenue. Telephone: 212-326-3939. Telecopier: 212-755-7306.
In Palo Alto, California: 1804 Embarcadero Road, Suite 201. Telephone: 650-739-3939. Telecopier: 650-739-3900.
In Paris, France: 120, rue du Faubourg Saint-Honoré. Telephone: 33-1-56-59-39-39. Telecopier: 33-1-56-59-39-38
In Pittsburgh, Pennsylvania: 500 Grant Street, 31st Floor. Telephone: 412-391-3939. Telecopier: 412-394-7959.
In Shanghai, China: 2805 Kerry Centre, 1515 Nanjing Road West. Telephone: 86-21-5298-6568. Telecopier: 86-21-5298-6569.
In Singapore, Singapore: 30 Cecil Street, #29-01 Prudential Tower. Telephone: 65 538 3939. Telecopier: 65 536 3939.
In Sydney, Australia: Governor Phillip Tower, Level 38, 1 Farrer Place. Telephone: 61-2-9210-6921. Telecopier: 61-2-9210-6926.
In Taipei, Taiwan: 8th Floor, 2 Tun Hwa South Road, Section 2. Telephone: (886-2) 2704-6808. Telecopier: (886-2) 2704-6791.
In Tokyo, Japan: Toranomon 45 Mori Building, 3rd Floor, 1-5, Toranomon 5-chome, Minato-ku, Tokyo 105-0001. Telephone: 81-3-3433-3939. Telecopier: 81-3-5401-2725.
See Professional Biographies, WASHINGTON, DISTRICT OF COLUMBIA

Jones Jain, L.L.P. . . . . 1990 M Street, N.W. Suite 800 (Pat.)

Jones & Lyles, L.L.C.
(See Bowie)

Jones-Sullivan, Jeanne ... '64 '91 C.446 B.A. L.276 J.D. 1701 Q St., N.W.

Jones, Tullar & Cooper, P.C.
(See Arlington, Virginia)

Jones, Waldo, Holbrook & McDonough, A Professional Corporation, (AV)
412 First Street, S.E., 20003 ⊙
Telephone: 202-484-4902 Telecopier: 202-484-0109
URL: http://www.joneswaldo.com
Of Counsel: Arthur H. Silverman.
General Practice including all Courts, Departments and Agencies on Federal Legislative Matters. Administrative, Regulatory and Communications Law.
Salt Lake City, Utah Office: 1500 Wells Fargo Plaza, 170 South Main Street. Telephone: 801-521-3200. Telecopier: 801-328-0537.
St. George, Utah Office: 301 N. 200 E., Suite 3-A. Telephone: 435-628-1627. Telecopier: 435-628-5225.
See Professional Biographies, WASHINGTON, DISTRICT OF COLUMBIA

Jones, Walker, Waechter, Poitevent, Carrère & Denègre, L.L.P., (AV)
499 South Capitol Street, S.W., Suite 600, 20003-4013 ⊙
Telephone: 202-203-1000 Telecopier: 202-203-0000
Email: info@joneswalker.com URL: http://www.joneswalker.com
Resident Partner: R. Christian Johnsen. Resident Special Counsel: John J. Jaskot; James D. Ogsbury (Not admitted in DC). Resident Of Counsel: W. Russell King.
Admiralty & Maritime; Antitrust & Trade Regulation; Appellate Litigation; Aviation; Banking; Bankruptcy, Restructuring & Creditors-Debtors Rights; Business & Commercial Litigation; Commercial Lending & Finance; Construction; Corporate & Securities; Employee Benefits, ERISA & Executive Compensation; Energy; Environmental & Toxic Torts; ERISA, Life, Health & Disability Insurance Litigation; Gaming; Government Relations; Health Care Litigation, Transactions & Regulation; Intellectual Property & E-Commerce; International; Labor Relations & Employment; Medical Professional & Hospital Liability; Mergers and Acquisitions; Products Liability; Professional Liability; Project Development & Finance; Public Finance; Real Estate: Land Use, Development & Finance; Tax (International, Federal, State & Local); Telecommunications & Utilities; Trusts, Estates & Personal Planning; Venture Capital & Emerging Companies; White Collar Crime.
Baton Rouge, Louisiana Office: 8555 United Plaza Boulevard. Telephone: 225-248-2000. Telecopier: 225-248-2010.
Lafayette, Louisiana Office: 500 Dover Boulevard, Suite 120. Telephone: 337-406-5610. Telecopier: 337-406-5620.
New Orleans, Louisiana Office: 201 St. Charles Avenue. Telephone: 504-582-8000. Telecopier: 504-582-8583.
Miami, Florida Office: Courvoisier Centre II, Suite 500, 601 Brickell Key Drive. Telephone: 305-679-5700. Telecopier: 305-679-5710.
The Woodlands, Texas Office: Waterway Plaza Two, Suite 350, 10001 Woodloch Forest Drive. Telephone: 281-296-5900. Telecopier: 281-296-5910.
See Professional Biographies, WASHINGTON, DISTRICT OF COLUMBIA

Jonson, Kenneth I. ... '43 '68 C&L.494 B.S., J.D. [Steptoe&J.]
*PRACTICE AREAS: Litigation.
Jordan, B. Delano ... '70 '99 C.886 B.S.E.E. L.945 J.D. [A Kenyon&K.] (See Pat. Sect.)
*PRACTICE AREAS: Intellectual Property.
Jordan, Daniel B., (AV) ... '25 '59 C&L.569 B.A., LL.B. 1311 Floral St., N.W.
Jordan, Harold E., (BV) ... '50 '77 C.399 B.A. L.966 J.D. [C Jordan K.&J.]
Jordan, Harry J., (AV) ... '34 '60 C.524 B.S. L.665 LL.B. [C Hamilton&H.]
*PRACTICE AREAS: Civil Litigation; Administrative Law; Transportation; Corporate; Employment Law.
Jordan, J. Phillip, (AV) ... '48 '74 C.674 A.B. L.893 J.D. [Swidler B.S.F.]
*PRACTICE AREAS: Regulatory Law; Utility Law.
Jordan, James F., (AV) ... '33 '65 C&L.276 B.S.S., J.D. [C Jordan C.&S.]
*PRACTICE AREAS: Alternative Dispute Resolution; Construction Law; Dental Malpractice Defense; Insurance Defense.
Jordan, Jeffrey E. ... '54 '79 C.311 B.A. L.30 J.D. [Arent F.K.P.&K.]
*PRACTICE AREAS: Securities Law; Securities Offering; Corporate Law; Mergers and Acquisitions.
Jordan, Jon B. ... '68 '94 C.259 B.S. L.425 J.D. [A Baker B.]
Jordan, Kevin M. '70 '96 C.754 B.S. L.862 J.D.
(adm. in VA; not adm. in DC) [A Wilkinson B.K.]
*PRACTICE AREAS: Corporate Law; Commercial Transactions; Taxation.
Jordan, Lloyd J. '55 '81 C.910 B.S. L.734 J.D.
(adm. in MO; not adm. in DC) [C Holland&K.]
*PRACTICE AREAS: Public Law; Government; Business Transactions; Regulatory; Litigation.
Jordan, Lynn M. ... '70 '95 C.645 B.S. L.862 J.D. [A Finnegan,H.F.G.&D.]
*PRACTICE AREAS: Trademarks.
Jordan, Natalia H. '66 '92 C.228 A.B. L.945 J.D.
(adm. in MD; not adm. in DC) [A Dickinson L.]
*PRACTICE AREAS: International Law; Foreign Corrupt Practices Act; Corporate Law.
Jordan, Richard E., (AV) ... '52 '77 C.276 B.A. L.128 J.D. [Hamilton&H.]
*PRACTICE AREAS: Civil Litigation; Personal Injury; Business Litigation; Employment Litigation; Professional Malpractice.
Jordan, Robert E., III, (AV) ... '36 '62 C.453 S.B. L.309 J.D. [Steptoe&J.]
*PRACTICE AREAS: Antitrust; Energy Law; Litigation; Technology.
Jordan, Vernon E., Jr., (AV) ... '35 '64 C.210 A.B. L.329 J.D. [C Akin,G.S.H.&F.]
*PRACTICE AREAS: General Practice.

Jordan Coyne & Savits, L.L.P., (AV)
1100 Connecticut Avenue, N.W., Suite 600, 20036 ⊙
Telephone: 202-296-4747 Telecopier: 202-496-2800
Email: jocs@idt.net URL: http://www.jocs-law.com
Members of Firm: Dwight D. Murray; John O. Easton; David P. Durbin; Carol Thomas Stone; John Tremain May; D. Stephenson Schwinn; David B. Stratton; John H. Carstens; Deborah Murrell Whelihan; Michael E. Reheuser. Associates: Clinton R. Shaw, Jr. (Resident, Fairfax, Virginia Office); Samantha D. Vanterpool (Resident, Fairfax, Virginia Office); Gregory Samuel McKee; Chritopher M. Coleman (Not admitted in DC); Anna M. Stafford (Resident, Fairfax, Virginia Office); Mark A. Johnston; Justin H. Cohen (Not admitted in DC); Rachel H. Bob. Of Counsel: James F. Jordan; Joel M. Savits.
Litigation Defense Practice in Civil and Criminal Cases (State and Federal) including: Appellate Practice, Casualty and Property Insurance, Products Liability, Professional Malpractice, Toxic Torts and Workers Compensation.
Representative Clients: Harleysville Mutual Insurance Co.; Travelers Insurance Co.
Rockville, Maryland Office: 33 Wood Lane. Telephone: 301-424-4161.
Baltimore, Maryland Office: 400 E. Pratt Street. Telephone: 410-625-5080.
Fairfax, Virginia Office: 10486 Armstrong Street. Telephone: 703-246-0900. Telecopier: 703-591-3673.
See Professional Biographies, WASHINGTON, DISTRICT OF COLUMBIA

Jordan Keys & Jessamy, LLP, (AV)
1400 16th Street, N.W., Suite 700 (⊙Greenbelt, MD)
Jorden, James F., (AV) ... '41 '66 C.216 B.A. L.273 LL.B. [Jorden B.] ⊙
*PRACTICE AREAS: Insurance and Securities Industry; Litigation; Corporate and Pension Litigation; Corporate Financing; Securities Law.
Jorden, Kathryn L. '68 '94 C.945 B.A. L.276 J.D.
(adm. in NY; not adm. in DC) 555 13th St., N.W.‡
Jorden, Stephen J. ... '66 '91 C.216 B.A. L.273 J.D. [A Jones,D.R.&P.]

Jorden Burt LLP, (AV)
A Partnership including a Professional Association
Suite 400 East, 1025 Thomas Jefferson Street, N.W., 20007-0805 ⊙
Telephone: 202-965-8100 Telecopier: 202-965-8104
URL: http://www.jordenusa.com
—Jerome V. Bolkcom; Joan E. Boros; Franklin G. Burt; Sheila J. Carpenter; Josephine Cicchetti; Raul A. Cuervo; Paul A. Fischer; Ann Began Furman; Steve Goldberg; Roland C. Goss; Wayne K.

(This Listing Continued)

Jorden Burt LLP (Continued)
Johnson; James F. Jorden; Stephen W. Kraus; Thomas F. Morante; Christopher S. Petito; Waldemar J. Pflepsen, Jr.; Keith J. Rudolf (Not admitted in DC); Phillip E. Stano; William Randolph Thompson;—Marie C. Baker (Not admitted in DC); Jason H. Gould; Michael C. Kentoff; William Glenn Merten; Min Sun Oh; Shaunda A. Patterson. Associates: Kristin Shepard; Benjamin L. Tompkins (Not admitted in DC); David White. Of Counsel: Denise A. Fee; Richard Karpinski; Marilyn A. Sponzo (Not admitted in DC).
General Practice.
Miami, Florida Office: 777 Brickell Avenue, Suite 500. Telephone: 305-371-2600. Telecopier: 305-372-9928.
Washington, D.C. Affiliated Office: Jones & Blouch L.L.P., 1025 Thomas Jefferson Street, N.W., Suite 405 West, Washington D.C. 20007-0805. Telephone: 202-223-3500. Telecopier: 202-223-4593.
San Francisco Affiliated Office: Fleming & Phillips LLP, 1340 Treat Boulevard, Suite 630, Walnut Creek, California 94596. Telephone: 925-296-2600. Telecopier: 925-296-2626.
See Professional Biographies, WASHINGTON, DISTRICT OF COLUMBIA

Jorgensen, Arlene A. '62 '91 C.182 B.A. L.300 J.D.
(adm. in MN; not adm. in DC) 2727 29th St., N.W.‡
Jorgensen, Jay T. '71 '98 C&L.101 B.A., J.D.
(adm. in UT; not adm. in DC) [Sidley A.B.&W.]
Jorling, James M., (BV) ... '58 '84 C.473 A.B. L.150 J.D. [Gardner,C.&D.]
*PRACTICE AREAS: Health Law; Health Care Contracts; Health Care Corporate Law; Managed Care; Disease Management.
Jose, Joseph W., Jr. ... '58 '85 C.759 B.S.W. L.1162 J.D. [A Peer&G.]
Josef, Brian M. '71 '99 C.659 B.A. L.128 J.D.
(adm. in MD; not adm. in DC) [A Cole,R.&B.]
*PRACTICE AREAS: Cable Television; Telecommunications Law; Internet Law; Federal Administrative Law; Copyrights.
Joseffer, Daryl ... '71 '96 C.813 A.B. L.309 J.D. [Kirkland&E.]
*PRACTICE AREAS: Appellate; Litigation.
Joselow, Robert B., (AV) ... '44 '69 C.569 B.A. L.273 J.D. [Pepper H.]
*PRACTICE AREAS: Real Estate Finance; Multi-Family Housing; Secondary Mortgage Market.
Joseph, Allen T., (AV) ... '41 '67 C.659 B.S. L.276 LL.B. [Joseph,M.&R.]
*PRACTICE AREAS: Corporate Law; Tax Law; Estate Planning Law; Trust Administration; Estate Administration.
Joseph, Bernard A. ... '65 '95 C.446 B.S. L.329 J.D. Corp. Coun., Marriott Intl., Inc.
*RESPONSIBILITIES: Litigation.
Joseph, Bruce G. ... '54 '79 C.659 B.S.B.A. L.309 J.D. [Wiley R.&F.]
*PRACTICE AREAS: Intellectual Property; Internet; Electronic Commerce; Food and Drug; Litigation.
Joseph, Daniel, (AV) ... '41 '67 C.178 A.B. L.309 LL.B. [Akin,G.S.H.&F.]
*PRACTICE AREAS: Litigation.
Joseph, James P. ... '62 '89 C&L.276 B.A., J.D. [Arnold&P.]
*PRACTICE AREAS: Tax.
Joseph, Jeffrey H. ... '48 '73 C.273 A.B. L.64 J.D. U.S. Chamber of Commerce
Joseph, Lawrence J. ... '60 '91 C.264 B.A. L.309 J.D. [A McKenna&C.]
*PRACTICE AREAS: Environmental; Administrative.
Joseph, Maurice '— '75
C&L.329 B.A., J.D. Dep. Gen. Coun., NEA Office of Gen. Coun.
Joseph, Michael, (AV) ... '36 '61 C.188 A.B. L.659 LL.B. [Dyer E.&J.]
*PRACTICE AREAS: Litigation; Securities; Mergers, Acquisitions and Divestitures; Capital Formation; Entrepreneurial Business Law.
Joseph, Robert G. ... '48 '75 C.838 B.A. L.608 J.D. Pres., Law Res., Inc.
Joseph, Susan E. ... '57 '84 C.682 B.S. L.276 J.D. 555 13th St., N.W.

Joseph, McDermott & Reiner, P.C., (AV)
1050 Seventeenth Street, N.W., Suite 700, 20036
Telephone: 202-331-1955 Facsimile: 202-293-2309
Allen T. Joseph; Mark T. McDermott; Robert M. Reiner; Peter J. Wiernicki;—Brian B. Schimming.
Taxation, Corporations, Real Estate, Estate Planning, Trusts, Probate, Litigation, Aviation, Administrative Law, Adoption, International Law and Domestic Relations.
See Professional Biographies, WASHINGTON, DISTRICT OF COLUMBIA

Joshi, Nandan M. ... '71 '96 C.420 B.A. L.276 J.D. [A Latham&W.]
*PRACTICE AREAS: Communications Law; Telecommunications Competition; Satellite Communications; Mass Media Law; Civil Appeals.
Jost, Barbara S., (AV) ... '51 '78 C.1044 B.A. L.276 J.D. [Huber L.&A.] ⊙
*PRACTICE AREAS: Energy Law; Public Utility Law; Natural Resources Law.
Jost, John C. ... '53 '78 C.276 B.S.F.S. L.893 J.D. [Dow,L.&A.]
Jost, Kenneth ... '48 '82 C.309 A.B. L.276 J.D. Congressional Quarterly, Inc.‡
Jost, Peter Hafner, (AV) ... '49 '77 C.575 A.B. L.893 J.D. [Dickstein S.M.&O.]
*PRACTICE AREAS: International Transactions; Commercial Law; Real Estate Law; Local, State, Federal and International Taxation Law; Federal Income Estate and Gift Taxation Law.
Jough, Katherine L. ... '71 '98 C.881 B.A. L.902 J.D. [A Counts,P.-D.&D.]
Jourdin, Willis W., Jr. ... '27 '55 C&L.813 A.B., LL.B. Dir., Intl. Negotiation Ctr.
Journey, Drexel D., (AV) ... '26 '52 C&L.966 B.B.A., LL.B. [Schiff H.&W.]
*PRACTICE AREAS: Energy Law; Corporate Finance Law.
Jowers, Kirk L. ... '67 '95 C.878 B.S. L.309 J.D. [A Caplin&D.]
*PRACTICE AREAS: Election, Campaign and Political Law.
Joy, David R. ... '64 '92 C.446 B.S. L.273 J.D. [Keller&H.]
*PRACTICE AREAS: Food and Drug Law; Environmental Law.
Joy, Michele F., (AV) '55 '83
C.118 B.A. L.30 J.D. Gen. Coun., Association of Oil Pipe Lines
Joyce, Frederick M., (AV) ... '58 '85 C.273 B.A. L.276 J.D. [Alston&B.]
*PRACTICE AREAS: Telecommunications Law; Electronic Commerce; Internet Law; Entertainment and the Arts.
Joyce, Jonathan R. '70 '97 C.1365 B.A. L.893 J.D.
(adm. in VA; not adm. in DC) 1333 New Hampshire Avenue, N.W., Suite 400
Joyce, Kathleen Marie ... '53 '97 C.363 B.S. L.180 J.D. [A Hogan&H.]
*PRACTICE AREAS: Food and Drug Law.
Joyce, Kevin Joseph ... '74 '00 C.674 A.B. L.893 J.D. [A Piper M.R.&W.]
*PRACTICE AREAS: Corporate Law.
Joyce, Leonard S., (AV) ... '31 '56 C&L.276 B.S., J.D. 5335 Wisconsin Ave. NW
Joyce, Rodney L., (AV) ... '51 '76 C&L.900 B.A., J.D. [Shook,H.&B.]
*PRACTICE AREAS: Communications Law.
Joyce, Stephanie A. ... '71 '98 C.602 B.A. L.273 J.D. [A Kelley D.&W.]
Juarez, Eduardo J. ... '62 '88 C.602 B.A. L.477 J.D. Pub. Def. Serv.
Jubin, Gregg S. ... '62 '91 C.555 B.S. L.823 J.D. [A Cadwalader,W.&T.]
Judd, Ardon B., Jr. '36 '63 C.207 B.A. L.846 LL.B.
V.P. & Coun., Dresser Industries, Inc.
Judelsohn, David Kent ... '68 '94 C.867 B.A. L.818 J.D. [A Wilkinson B.K.]
*PRACTICE AREAS: Communications Law.
Judge, Caroline Alice ... '71 '99 C.882 B.A. L.309 J.D. [A Zuckerman S.]
*PRACTICE AREAS: Litigation.
Judge, Thomas J. ... '64 '95 C.871 B.S. L.273 J.D. [A Ross,D.&B.]
Judish, Julia Eden ... '68 '97 C.821 B.A. L.309 J.D. [A Shaw P.]
Judy, Henry L. ... '— '68 C&L.276 A.B., J.D. [C Kirkpatrick&L.]
*PRACTICE AREAS: Financial Institutions Law; Business; Technology Law; Electronic Commerce; Year 2000 Computer Conversion.
Juhnke, H. Richard ... '44 '69 C.691 B.A. L.145 J.D. Gen. Atty., Sprint Corp.
Julian, Judy A. '50 '78 C.273 B.A. L.128 J.D.
Asst. Gen. Coun., MCI Communications Corporation
Juneau, Todd L. ... '66 '95 C.494 B.A. L.365 J.D. [Nath&Assoc.]
*PRACTICE AREAS: Intellectual Property Law; Patents; Trademarks; Copyrights.

Jung, David Y. '68 '93 C.111 B.S. L.339 J.D.
(adm. in IL; not adm. in DC) 1511 K St.‡
Jung, Song K. .... '65 '96 C.446 B.S.E.E. L.128 J.D. [Long A.&N.] (Pat.)
*PRACTICE AREAS: Intellectual Property.
Jung & Vassar, P.C. .... 1700 K St., N.W.
Junghans, Paula M., (AV) .... '49 '76 C.600 B.A. L.446 J.D. [Piper M.R.&W.]
*PRACTICE AREAS: Tax Litigation; White Collar Criminal Defense; Litigation.
Jungreis, Patricia O. '58 '85 C.914 B.A. L.904 J.D.
(adm. in NY; not adm. in DC) Princ. Coun., International Fin. Corp.
Juni, Robin L. .... '66 '91 C.300 B.A. L.309 J.D. [Ⓐ Jones,D.R.&P.]
Junkin, Timothy deForest, (AV) .... '51 '77 C.446 B.A. L.276 J.D. [Asbill,J.M.&B.]
*PRACTICE AREAS: Civil Litigation; Business Torts; Personal Injury; Professional Malpractice; Medical Malpractice.
Jurata, John A., Jr. '70 '01 C.884 B.A. L.1049 J.D.
(adm. in VA; not adm. in DC) [Ⓐ Heller E.W.&M.]
Jurkowski, Joseph T., Jr. '48 '75 C&L.260 B.S.B.A., J.D.
Asst. Gen. Coun., Fed. Home Loan Mtge. Corp.
Just, Marjorie .... '68 '94 C.228 A.B. L.273 J.D. [Ⓐ Witt&N.]
*PRACTICE AREAS: Family Law.
Justus, Johnny Brent '75 '00 C.945 B.S. L.309 J.D.
(adm. in VA; not adm. in DC) 1701 Pennsylvania Ave., N.W.
Juvelis, Antigone E. '64 '95 C.446 B.A. L.128 J.D.
(adm. in VA; not adm. in DC) [Ⓐ Roylance,A.B.&G.]
*PRACTICE AREAS: Trademarks; Copyrights; Entertainment Law; Multimedia Law.
Jystad, Robert '58 '96 C.112 B.A. L.1068 J.D.
(adm. in CA; not adm. in DC) [Ⓐ Cole,R.&B.] ⊙
*PRACTICE AREAS: Cable Television; Cable Franchising; Wireless Communications; Telecommunications Law; Internet Law.
Kabalkin, Barry E. .... '55 '81 C.103 A.B. L.309 J.D. 1201 Penn. Ave., N.W.
Kabat, Alan R. .... '— '98 C.911 B.S. L.276 J.D. [Ⓐ Bernabei&K.]
*PRACTICE AREAS: Civil Litigation; Civil Rights; Civil Liberties; Employment Discrimination Law.
Kabatchnick, Neil B., (AV) ..... '26 '55 C.754 B.S. L.273 J.D. 1050 Seventeenth St., N.W.
Kabel, Robert J., (AV) .... '46 '72 C.207 B.A. L.880 J.D. [Manatt,P.&P.]
Kacedon, D. Brian '75 '00 C.228 B.S.E. L.569 J.D.
(adm. in MD; not adm. in DC; See Pat. Sect.) [Ⓐ Finnegan,H.F.G.&D.]
*PRACTICE AREAS: Mechanical Patents; Patent Licensing; Patent Litigation; Patent Prosecution.
Kachouroff, Christopher I. '71 '99 L.1339 J.D.
(adm. in VA; not adm. in DC) Law Clerk, U.S. Court of Fed. Claims
Kaczmarczyk, Sandra '67 '01 C.309 B.A. L.276 J.D.
(adm. in MD; not adm. in DC) [Ⓐ Jones,D.R.&P.]
Kaczmarek, Christopher E. .... '66 '94 C.945 B.A. L.904 J.D. [Ⓐ Crowell&M.]
Kadas, Madeleine Boyer .... '67 '94 C&L.846 B.A., J.D. [Ⓐ Beveridge&D.]
*PRACTICE AREAS: International Environmental Law; Environmental Law.
Kadel, Eric J., Jr. .... '70 '00 C.945 B.A. L.893 J.D. [Ⓐ Sullivan&C.]
Kaden, Alan S. .... '56 '82 C.659 B.S. L.178 J.D. [Fried,F.H.S.&J.]
Kadzik, Peter J., (AV) .... '53 '78 C.107 B.A. L.276 J.D. [Dickstein S.M.&O.]
*PRACTICE AREAS: Antitrust Law; Legislative Practice; Litigation.
Kaercher, Kathleen A. '— '92 C.397 B.A. L.823 J.D.
(adm. in PA; not adm. in DC) [Ⓐ Blooston,M.D.D.&P.]
*PRACTICE AREAS: Telecommunications Law; FCC Licensing.
Kaesebier, Tara R. .... '73 '01 C.910 B.A. L.537 LL.M. [Ⓐ Jones,D.R.&P.]
Kafalenos, Vivian P. '56 '88 C.429 B.A. L.494 J.D.
(adm. in VA; not adm. in DC; Pat.) 1725 K St., N.W.
Kaffee, Stephen .... '47 '82 C.188 A.B. L.893 J.D. [S.Kaffee]
Kaffee, Stephen, P.C., Law Offices of .... 1920 N St., N.W., Ste. 660
Kafka, Gerald A., (AV) .... '51 '75 C.1115 B.S. L.150 J.D. [McKee N.]
*PRACTICE AREAS: Tax.
Kafker, Arlene .... '54 '79 C.1044 B.A. L.273 J.D. [Ⓒ O'Toole,R.N.&S.]
Kagan, Barbara K., (AV) .... '53 '78 C&L.188 B.A., J.D. [Ⓒ Steptoe&J.]
Kagan, Rory L. '58 '82 C.597 B.A. L.273 J.D.
(adm. in VA; not adm. in DC) Asst. Gen. Coun., Student Loan Mktg. Assn.
Kagan, Sarah A. .... '— '88 C.1036 B.A. L.273 J.D. [Banner&W.] (See Pat. Sect.)
*PRACTICE AREAS: Intellectual Property Law; Patents; Biotechnology; Pharmaceutical Intellectual Property.
Kahan, Jonathan S., (AV) .... '48 '73 C&L.273 B.A., J.D. [Hogan&H.]
*PRACTICE AREAS: Food and Drug Regulation; Food, Drug and Cosmetic Law; Drug and Medical Device Regulation.
Kahaner, Eileen L. .... '67 '96 C.604 B.A. L.273 J.D. [Ⓐ Arent F.K.P.&K.]
*PRACTICE AREAS: Health Care.
Kahl, James A. '56 '81 C.602 B.A. L.273 J.D.
Vice President & Corporate Counsel, Staffwise
Kahn, David S., (AV) .... '51 '76 C.188 A.B. L.273 J.D. [Holland&K.]
*PRACTICE AREAS: Commercial Real Estate Finance; Acquisitions and Dispositions; Loan Workouts; Commercial Leasing.
Kahn, Edwin L., (AV) .... '18 '40 C.575 A.B. L.309 LL.B. [Arent F.K.P.&K.] ‡
Kahn, Fritz R., (AV) .... '— '50 C&L.273 A.B., LL.B. [F.R.Kahn]
Kahn, Jeremy, (AV) .... '48 '74 C&L.893 B.A., J.D. [Kahn&K.]
Kahn, Linda G. .... '54 '81 C.446 B.A. L.273 J.D. The Bur. of Natl. Affs., Inc.
Kahn, Peter J., (AV) .... '51 '76 C.976 B.A. L.228 J.D. [Williams&C.]
Kahn, Sarah Elizabeth .... '64 '91 C.575 B.A. L.276 J.D. [Arnold&P.]
*PRACTICE AREAS: Corporate; Securities.
Kahn, Stephen D., (AV) .... '40 '66 C&L.831 B.S., J.D. [Arent F.K.P.&K.]
*PRACTICE AREAS: Public Finance; Real Estate Development; Structured Finance.
Kahn, Steven C. .... '42 '70 C.976 B.A. L.659 LL.B. [Ⓒ Miller,C.P.&S.]
*PRACTICE AREAS: Labor and Employment.
Kahn, Thomas S. .... '55 '85 C.860 B.A. L.276 J.D. House Budg. Committee
Kahn, Wendy L., (AV) .... '44 '73 C.477 B.A. L.569 J.D. [Zwerdling,P.L.K.T.&D.]
Kahn, William P. .... '73 '01 L.228 J.D. [Ⓐ Hogan&H.]
*PRACTICE AREAS: International Business Transactions; Corporate Law; Securities.
Kahn, Fritz R., P.C., (AV) .... 1920 N Street, N.W., 8th Floor

Kahn and Kahn, (AV)
1730 Rhode Island Avenue, N.W. Suite 810, 20036
Telephone: 202-887-0037 Fax: 202-833-1219
Email: jkahn@erols.com URL: http://www.lawyers.com/transportation
Members of Firm: S. Harrison Kahn (1911-1980); Jeremy Kahn.
Transportation Regulation and Administrative Law. Immigration, Customs and Business Law related to Transportation Law.
See Professional Biographies, WASHINGTON, DISTRICT OF COLUMBIA

Kahng, Anthony H. '62 '99 C.339 B.S. L.276 J.D.
(adm. in VA; not adm. in DC; Pat.) [Ⓐ Hale&D.]
*PRACTICE AREAS: Intellectual Property.
Kahrl, Benjamin M. '71 '97 C.112 B.A. L.659 J.D.
Suite 800, 1090 Vermont Ave., N.W.
Kail, F. Michael, (AV) .... '45 '72 C&L.976 B.A., LL.B. [Steptoe&J.]
*PRACTICE AREAS: Energy; Oil and Gas Pipelines; Litigation; Alternative Dispute Resolution.
Kain, Michael R., (P.C.) ...... '48 '74 C.871 B.S. L.284 J.D. 1601 Connecticut Ave., N.W.
Kaiser, Justine J. '74 '00 C.401 B.A. L.904 J.D.
(adm. in MD; not adm. in DC) [Ⓐ Cohen,M.H.&T.]
*PRACTICE AREAS: Civil Litigation; Antitrust.

Kaiser, Matthew H. .... '71 '99 C.30 B.A. L.945 J.D. [Ⓐ Thompson C.]
*PRACTICE AREAS: Maritime Finance; International Finance; Admiralty and Maritime.
Kaiser, Saamir '64 '91 C.273 B.A. L.477 J.D.
(adm. in MD; not adm. in DC) 1718 M Street, N.W. Suite 259
Kaiser, Steven J. .... '70 '96 C.674 B.S. L.309 J.D. [Ⓐ Cleary,G.S.&H.]
Kakarla, Vamsi K. '74 '01 C.645 B.S. L.1398 J.D.
(adm. in NY; not adm. in DC) [Ⓐ Finnegan,H.F.G.&D.]
*PRACTICE AREAS: Electrical Patent Prosecution; Electronic Patents; Patent Infringement; Patent Litigation; Patent Prosecution.
Kalantry, Sital '72 '99 C.188 B.A. L.659 J.D.
(adm. in NY; not adm. in DC) [Ⓐ O'Melveny&M.]
Kalb, Paul E., (BV) .... '58 '90 C.94 B.A. L.976 J.D. [Sidley A.B.&W.]
Kalbian, Haig V. .... '56 '85 C.692 B.A. L.602 J.D. [Kalbian H.]
*PRACTICE AREAS: Commercial Litigation; Personal Injury.

Kalbian Hagerty LLP
2001 L Street NW, Suite 600, 20036
Telephone: 202-223-5600 Fax: 202-223-6625
URL: http://www.kalbianhagerty.com
Partners: Haig V. Kalbian; James R. Hagerty. Of Counsel: Mary M. Baker; Jason Green; K. Thomas Shahriari; Alfonso Guida, Jr. (Not admitted in DC). Associates: Kimberly M. Davis; Amjad H. Atallah (Not admitted in DC); Saladin A. Aljurf (Not admitted in DC); Claire A. Wood (Not admitted in DC).
General Civil Litigation Practice before all Federal and State Courts, Administrative and Governmental Agencies. Tax Law, Business, Commercial, Corporate, International, Real Estate, Technology, and Venture Capital.
See Professional Biographies, WASHINGTON, DISTRICT OF COLUMBIA

Kalchbrenner, Paul '68 '96 C.282 B.A. L.1194 J.D.
(adm. in MD; not adm. in DC) [Ⓐ Lathrop&G.]
*PRACTICE AREAS: Environmental; Regulatory; Government Relations.
Kaleigh, James K. .... '72 '00 C.164 B.A. L.30 J.D. [Ⓐ Howrey S.A.&W.]
*PRACTICE AREAS: Antitrust.
Kalellis, Pat James '70 '97 C&L.884 B.A., J.D.
(adm. in NJ; not adm. in DC) [Ⓐ Barkats&Assoc.]
Kalen, Sam .... '58 '84 C.156 B.A. L.910 J.D. [Ⓒ Van Ness F.]
*PRACTICE AREAS: Natural Resources; Environment; Energy; Administrative Law; Constitutional Law.
Kalet, Joseph E. '51 '86 C.1044 B.A. L.273 J.D.
Assistant General Counsel, Metropolitan Washington Airports Authority
Kalicki, Jean E. .... '64 '90 C&L.309 B.A., J.D. [Ⓒ Arnold&P.]
*PRACTICE AREAS: International Arbitration; Commercial Litigation.
Kaliff, Matthew A. '65 '93 C.228 B.A. L.276 J.D.
(adm. in TX; not adm. in DC) Exec. Dir., Intl. Assn. of Jewish Lawyers & Jurists
Kalijarvi, June D. W., (AV) .... '41 '73 C.914 B.A. L.276 J.D. [Kalijarvi,C.&N.]
*PRACTICE AREAS: Labor and Employment; Civil Rights; Discrimination.

Kalijarvi, Chuzi & Newman, P.C., (AV)
Suite 1011, 1730 K Street, N.W., 20006
Telephone: 202-331-9260 FAX: 202-872-9562
Email: kcnlawyers@aol.com
June D. W. Kalijarvi; George M. Chuzi; Elizabeth L. Newman;—Margaret E. Johnson; E. Reynolds Wilson; Michelle L. Perry. Of Counsel: Francine K. Weiss; Stephen L. Spitz.
General Civil and Administrative Practice before all Courts, Agencies and Departments. Labor, Equal Opportunity, Civil Service, Contract.
See Professional Biographies, WASHINGTON, DISTRICT OF COLUMBIA

Kalik, Tracy Reichman .... '69 '96 C.1365 B.A. L.273 J.D. [Ⓐ Heideman]
*PRACTICE AREAS: Civil Litigation; Criminal Defense.
Kalin, Sara '76 '01 C&L.112 B.A., J.D.
(adm. in CA; not adm. in DC) [Ⓐ Kirkland&E.]
*PRACTICE AREAS: Corporate Law.
Kalinski, David E. .... '57 '83 C.674 A.B. L.188 J.D. Assoc. Gen. Coun., Fannie Mae
*RESPONSIBILITIES: Mortgage-Backed Securities; Affordable Housing; Multifamily Real Estate Finance.
Kalish, Paul William, (AV) .... '62 '86 C.228 B.A. L.597 J.D. [Crowell&M.]
*PRACTICE AREAS: Contract Law; Insurance Law.
Kalish, Steven J., (AV) .... '46 '74 C.454 B.A. L.659 J.D. [McCarthy,S.&H.]
*PRACTICE AREAS: Transportation Law; Energy Law.
Kalitka, John C. .... '64 '90 C.902 B.A. L.692 J.D [Ⓐ Garvey,S.&B.]
*PRACTICE AREAS: International Trade; Litigation.
Kallmer, Jonathan S. .... '72 '99 C.813 A.B. L.276 J.D. [Ⓐ Hogan&H.]
Kaloi, Kimo '68 '97 C.1356 B.A. L.101 J.D.
(adm. in UT; not adm. in DC) Insular Affrs. Legis. Staff
Kalt, Brian C. '72 '97 C.477 A.B. L.976 J.D.
(adm. in MI; not adm. in DC) [Ⓐ Sidley A.B.&W.]
Kalter, Sandra Cohen, (AV) .... '— '84 C.597 B.S.J. L.273 J.D. [Ⓒ King&S.]
*PRACTICE AREAS: Food and Drug Regulation.
Kam, Laura M '77 '01 C.893 B.A. L.273 J.D.
(adm. in VA; not adm. in DC) [Ⓐ O'Melveny&M.]
Kamarck, Lynn G., (AV) .... '53 '77 C.293 B.A. L.178 J.D. [Ⓒ Hogan&H.]
*PRACTICE AREAS: International Trade; Countervailing Duties; Antidumping; Import and Export Law; Asia Trade.
Kamenar, Paul D. .... '48 '75 C.705 B.A. L.276 J.D. Exec. Legal Dir., Wash. Legal Found.
Kamenshine, Wendy E. .... '72 '99 C.145 A.B. L.228 J.D. [Ⓐ Akin,G.S.H.&F.]
*PRACTICE AREAS: International.
Kamerow, Allan L., (AV) .... '21 '43 L.180 J.D. [Kamerow&K.] ⊙
Kamerow, Jacob A. .... '56 '81 C.893 B.A. L.276 J.D. [Kamerow&K.] ⊙
Kamerow, Stanley H., (AV) .... '17 '38 L.180 J.D. [Kamerow&K.]
Kamerow & Kamerow, P.C., (AV) .... 1025 Vermont Ave., N.W. (⊙Alexandria, VA)
Kamiat, Walter A., (AV) .... '54 '85 C.347 B.A. L.813 J.D. Assoc. Gen. Coun., AFL-CIO
Kamins, Scott V. .... '67 '92 C.94 B.A. L.446 J.D. [Krupin O.]
*PRACTICE AREAS: Labor Relations; Employment Law.
Kaminski, James A. '69 '97 C.347 B.A. L.424 J.D.
(adm. in IL; not adm. in DC) [Ⓐ Arent F.K.P.&K.]
*PRACTICE AREAS: Trade Regulation; Consumer Protection; Advertising Law.
Kaminski, Jeffri A. '68 '97
C.665 B.S.E.E. L.607 J.D. [Ⓐ Venable,A.B.H.&C.] (See Pat. Sect.)
*PRACTICE AREAS: Intellectual Property; Electrical Patent Prosecution; Technology Licensing.
Kaminski, Michael D., (BV) ... '— '87 C&L.477 B.S.E., J.D. [Foley&L.] (See Pat. Sect.)
*PRACTICE AREAS: Patent Litigation; Patent Licensing.
Kaminski, Steven H. .... '69 '99 C.273 B.A. L.128 J.D. [Koonz,M.J.D.&L.]
*PRACTICE AREAS: Consumer Class Actions; Personal Injury; Medical Malpractice; Employment Law.
Kaminsky, Glenn H. '74 '00 C.668 B.A. L.477 J.D.
(adm. in CA; not adm. in DC) [Ⓐ Akin,G.S.H.&F.]
*PRACTICE AREAS: Corporate; Project Finance.
Kammerer, Rudolph M. '69 '97 L.477 J.D.
(adm. in MD; not adm. in DC) [Ⓐ Sidley A.B.&W.]
Kamp, John F. .... '46 '80 C.602 B.A. L.862 J.D. [Ⓒ Wiley R.&F.]
*PRACTICE AREAS: Internet Law; Electronic Commerce; Privacy Law; Advertising Law.
Kampa-Kokesch, Duane M. .... '65 '99 C.492 B.E.S. L.1187 J.D. 441 4th St. N.W.
Kampelman, Max M., (AV) .... '20 '45 C&L.569 A.B., J.D. [Ⓒ Fried,F.H.S.&J.]
Kampman, John W., (BV) .... '47 '86 C.1017 B.S. L.1029 J.D. [Ⓒ Wallace K.M.&B.]
*PRACTICE AREAS: Environmental Law; Litigation.

Kanach, Jesse ... '— '99 C.893 B.A. L.276 J.D. [🄰 Dechert]
*PRACTICE AREAS: Financial Services Law; Investment Management.
Kananen, Ronald P., (AV) ... '37 '64 C&L.930 B.S.E.E., J.D. [Rader,F.&G.] (Pat.)
Kandare, Anthony W. '— '01 C.101 B.S.M.E. L.912 J.D.
(adm. in VA; not adm. in DC; See Pat. Sect.) [🄰 Banner&W.]
*PRACTICE AREAS: Intellectual Property.
Kane, Eugene I., Jr. '57 '83 C.423 B.A. L.276 J.D.
Asst. Gen. Coun., Washington Metropolitan Area Transit Authority
*RESPONSIBILITIES: Employer Liability; Workers Compensation; Labor Law.
Kane, Frances F. ... '36 '66 C.273 A.B. L.276 LL.B. 2900 Upton St., N.W.
Kane, Leo J. ... '63 '89 C&L.893 B.A., J.D. 1440 New York Ave. N.W.
Kane, Michael G. ... '66 '92 C.569 B.A. L.262 J.D. [Cashdan,G.&K.]
Kane, Pamela S. ... '68 '94 C.183 B.A. L.861 J.D. [🄰 Howrey S.A.&W.]
*PRACTICE AREAS: Antitrust; Commercial Litigation; Copyrights; Trademarks.
Kang, Gregory B. ... '67 '97 C.223 B.S.E.E. L.1338 J.D. [🄰 Arent F.K.P.&K.] (Pat.)
*PRACTICE AREAS: Intellectual Property; Patents; Trademarks; Copyrights.
Kang, Timothy ... '71 '00 C.223 B.S. L.30 J.D. [🄰 Wilmer,C.&P.]
Kanji, Riyaz A. ... '64 '91 C.309 A.B. L.976 J.D. 725 12th St., N.W.
Kanjorski, Russell P. ... '69 '97 C&L.659 B.A.B.S., J.D. [🄰 Covington&B.]
Kann, Simon ... '73 '98 C.800 B.S. L.188 J.D. [🄰 Arnold&P.]
*PRACTICE AREAS: Litigation.
Kanovitz, Michael I. '68 '94 C.1036 B.A. L.188 J.D.
(adm. in KY; not adm. in DC) [🄰 Mehri,M.&R.]
*PRACTICE AREAS: False Claims Act; Commercial Litigation; Consumer Fraud; Securities Act.
Kantarian, Harry K., (AV) ... '51 '76 C.105 B.A. L.273 J.D. [🄲 Stradley R.S.&Y.]
Kanter, Aaron ... '72 '98 C.477 B.A. L.893 J.D. [🄰 Dow,L.&A.]
Kanter, David M., (AV) ... '42 '68 C.30 B.S. L.273 J.D. [Kanter&W.]
Kanter, Jane A. ... '49 '74 C.994 B.A. L.1009 J.D. [Dechert]
*PRACTICE AREAS: Financial Services Law; Investment Management.
Kanter, Jonathan S. ... '73 '99 C.1044 B.A. L.910 J.D. [🄰 Fried,F.H.S.&J.]
*PRACTICE AREAS: Antitrust.
Kanter & Wishnow, Chartered, (AV) ... 1910 Sunderland Pl., N.W.
Kantor, Douglas S. '69 '96 C.893 B.A. L.976 J.D.
(adm. in MD; not adm. in DC) [🄰 Collier S.S.]
*PRACTICE AREAS: Government Relations; Litigation; Corporate Counseling.
Kantor, Mark A., (AV) ... '55 '80 C.800 A.B. L.477 J.D. 513 A Street, S.E.
Kantor, Michael ("Mickey"), (AV) ... '39 '68 C.880 B.A. L.276 LL.B. [Mayer,B.&P.]
Kantorczyk, Todd D. ... '70 '96 C.188 B.A. L.1068 J.D. [🄰 Gibson,D.&C.]
*PRACTICE AREAS: Environmental Law; Toxic Torts.
Kao, Florence '72 '97 C.674 B.A. L.276 J.D.
(adm. in NJ; not adm. in DC) 1050 Conn. Ave., N.W.‡
Kaplan, Alan H., (AV) ... '30 '55 C.569 A.B. L.309 J.D. [Kleinfeld,K.&B.]
*PRACTICE AREAS: Food, Drug and Cosmetic Law; Food and Drug Regulation; Drug and Medical Device Regulation; Federal Civil Litigation; Federal Administrative Law.
Kaplan, Andrew '— '00 C.945 B.A. L.880 J.D.
(adm. in VA; not adm. in DC) [🄰 King&S.]
Kaplan, Ann Leopold ... '62 '87 C.665 B.A. L.659 J.D. [Epstein B.&G.]
*PRACTICE AREAS: Health Law; Managed Care Law; E-Health.
Kaplan, David E. ... '56 '80 C.311 B.A. L.273 J.D. Pres., Strategic Realty Advisors, Inc.
Kaplan, Donald A., (AV) ... '45 '71 C.705 A.B. L.309 J.D. [Preston G.E.&R.M.]
*PRACTICE AREAS: Antitrust Law; Economic Regulation; Energy Law; Public Utility Law; Litigation.
Kaplan, Elizabeth N. ... '67 '93 C.911 B.A. L.276 J.D. [🄰 Debevoise&P.]
*PRACTICE AREAS: Corporate Law; Securities Regulation Law.
Kaplan, Gilbert B., (AV) ... '51 '77 C&L.309 A.B., J.D. [Hale&D.]
Kaplan, H. Deen ... '— '97 C.228 B.A. L.276 J.D. [🄰 Hogan&H.]
*PRACTICE AREAS: International Trade.
Kaplan, Hugh B. ... '63 '90 C.861 B.S. L.273 J.D. The Bureau of Natl. Affs., Inc.
Kaplan, Jeffrey H. ... '57 '86 C.477 A.B. L.904 J.D. 503 D St., NW
Kaplan, Joseph V., (AV) ... '53 '78 C.645 B.A. L.285 J.D. [Passman&K.]
*PRACTICE AREAS: Employment Law; Federal Civil Service; Equal Employment Opportunity Law; Labor Law; Security Clearances.
Kaplan, Kenneth P. ... '72 '97 C.454 B.A. L.30 J.D. [🄰 Akin,G.S.H.&F.]
*PRACTICE AREAS: Litigation.
Kaplan, Lawrence D. ... '62 '87 C.477 A.B. L.273 J.D. [🄰 Sidley A.B.&W.]
Kaplan, Leslie A. ... '47 '86 C.659 B.A. L.276 J.D. [Dickstein S.M.&O.]
*PRACTICE AREAS: Real Estate; Financial Institutions; Lending.
Kaplan, Marcia Press, (BV) ... '54 '79 C.184 B.A. L.1292 J.D. [Howrey S.A.&W.]
*PRACTICE AREAS: Antitrust; Complex Litigation.
Kaplan, Michael ... '60 '87 C.156 B.A. L.93 J.D. Coun., Kingdon Gould
Kaplan, Paul A., (AV) ... '51 '76 C.94 B.A. L.659 J.D. [Womble C.S.&R.]
*PRACTICE AREAS: Civil Litigation.
Kaplan, Philip S. ... '37 '63 C.184 B.A. L.1066 J.D. [Patton B.]
Kaplan, Robert A. ... '69 '98 C.228 A.B. L.910 J.D. [🄰 Ballard S.A.&I.]
*PRACTICE AREAS: Tax Law; Municipal Bonds.
Kaplan, Samuel C. ... '71 '98 C.846 B.A. L.309 J.D. [🄰 Boies,S.&F.]
*PRACTICE AREAS: General Commercial Litigation.
Kaplan, Sherwin ... '41 '66 C&L.145 B.A., J.D. [🄲 Piper M.R.&W.]
*PRACTICE AREAS: Employee Benefits.
Kaplan, Stephen H. '47 '73 C&L.309 A.B., J.D.
(adm. in OK; not adm. in DC) [Akin,G.S.H.&F.] (☉Denver, CO)
*PRACTICE AREAS: Aviation Law; Public Sector Law; Transportation Law; Public-Private Projects.
Kaplan, Steven ... '53 '78 C.1111 B.A. L.276 J.D. [Arnold&P.]
*PRACTICE AREAS: Corporate Law; Securities; Financial Institutions.
Kaplan, Steven M. ... '67 '93 C.339 B.S. L.276 J.D. [🄰 Kirkpatrick&L.]
*PRACTICE AREAS: Banks and Banking; Consumer Law; Financial Institution Law; Mortgage Banking Law.
Kaplan, Susan B. ... '53 '81 C.94 B.A. L.128 J.D. Assoc. V.P., George Washington Univ.
Kaplin, William A. '42 '68 C.696 A.B. L.188 J.D.
Prof. of Law, Catholic Univ. of Amer.
Kaplun, Paul T. ... '56 '85 C&L.276 B.S.,B.A., J.D. [Venable,A.B.H.&C.]
*PRACTICE AREAS: Corporate Law; Taxation Law; Business Law.
Kapp, Robert H., (AV) ... '34 '58 C.659 B.S. L.477 S.J.D. [Hogan&H.]
*PRACTICE AREAS: Taxation Law; Arbitration; Mediation.
Kappel, Brett G. ... '58 '90 C.1044 B.A. L.893 J.D. [Powell,G.F.&M.] (☉Reston, VA)
*PRACTICE AREAS: Internet Law; Legislative Advocacy; Aviation Law; Election Law.
Kappler, Ann M. '57 '88 C.197 A.B. L.569 J.D.
Sr. V.P. & Gen. Coun., Fannie Mae, Inc.
Kappler, Burke W. ... '73 '99 C.30 B.A. L.309 J.D. [🄰 Crowell&M.]
Karaganis, Joan J. ... '69 '95 C&L.128 B.A., J.D. [🄰 Trow&K.]
*PRACTICE AREAS: Immigration and Nationality Law.
Karalekas, S. Steven, (AV) ... '42 '70 C.871 B.S. L.345 J.D. [Karalekas&N.]
*PRACTICE AREAS: Government Relations; Legislative Law; Government Contracts.

Karalekas & Noone, (AV)
1211 Connecticut Avenue, N.W., Suite 302, 20036-2603
Telephone: 202-466-7330 Facsimile: 202-955-5879
Email: KN1211CONN@AOL.COM URL: http://www.lawyers.com/karalekas&noonelaw
S. Steven Karalekas; James A. Noone; William J. Hardy.
Administrative Law Practice. Legislative Law and Lobbying, Government Relations, Civil Litigation, White Collar Crime, Qui Tam, Whistleblower Litigation, Corporate Investigations.
See Professional Biographies, WASHINGTON, DISTRICT OF COLUMBIA

Karambelas, Nicholas G. ... '53 '80 C.867 B.A. L.262 J.D. [Sfikas,K.&A.]
Karas, Karen Simonek ... '60 '85 C.991 B.A. L.276 J.D. [Cooter,M.T.&W.]
Karas, William, (AV) ... '39 '72 C.178 B.A. L.705 J.D. [Steptoe&J.]
*PRACTICE AREAS: Aviation; Antitrust; Shipping; International Practice.
Karasek, John J. ... '62 '92 C.665 B.S. L.1187 J.D. 4555 Overlook Ave., SW
Karasik, Elizabeth A., (AV) ... '56 '81 C.976 B.A. L.94 J.D. 1718 P St.‡
Karcewski, Kimberly A. ... '71 '97 C.509 B.A. L.1187 J.D. [🄰 Morrison&F.]
*PRACTICE AREAS: Investment Management.
Kardis, Phillip John ... '61 '96 C.273 B.A. L.276 J.D. [🄰 McKee N.]
*PRACTICE AREAS: Corporate; Securities.
Karelis, Kathleen E. ... '60 '90 C.699 B.S. L.472 J.D. [Crowell&M.]
Karen, Ari ... '70 '96 C.446 B.A. L.245 J.D. [🄰 Krupin O.]
*PRACTICE AREAS: Securities Fraud; Consumer Fraud; Employment Discrimination.
Karesh, Lewis J. ... '59 '87 C.576 B.S. L.575 J.D. U.S. Dept. of Labor
Kargahi, Manijeh Nan ... '69 '98 C.339 B.A. L.146 J.D. [🄰 Wilmer,C.&P.]
Karina, Stephen J. '47 '88 C.972 B.A. L.446 J.D.
(adm. in MD; not adm. in DC) [🄲 Brickfield B.R.&S.]
Kariv, Tomer ... '61 '90 C&L.309 B.A., J.D. 1701 Pennsylvania Ave., N.W.
Karl, Darrel C. ... '60 '85 C.423 B.S. L.128 J.D. [Finnegan,H.F.G.&D.]
*PRACTICE AREAS: Intellectual Property Litigation; Mechanical Patents; Metallurgical Patents; Patent Litigation.

Karl, John F., Jr. '47 '79 C.025 B.A. L.904 J.D.
One Farragut Square, 900 17th Avenue, N.W., Suite 1250, 20006
Telephone: 202-293-3200 Fax: 202-429-1851
URL: http://www.lawyers.com/mcdonald&karl
***PRACTICE AREAS: Civil Litigation; Employment Litigation; Securities Litigation; Corporate Practice; General Practice.**
Associate: C. Michael Tarone.
Employment Discrimination, Title 7, A.D.A., Human Rights, Personal Injury, Estate Planning and Medical Malpractice.
See Professional Biographies, WASHINGTON, DISTRICT OF COLUMBIA

Karlan, Michael J. ... '68 '92 C.174 B.S. L.178 J.D. 2950 Van Ness St., N.W.
Karlin, Jeffrey L. ... '59 '89 C.112 B.A. L.30 J.D. [🄲 Schmeltzer,A.&S.]
*PRACTICE AREAS: Franchise Law; Commercial Litigation.
Karnes, Rebecca R. ... '52 '79 C.273 B.A. L.276 J.D. The Bureau of Natl. Affs., Inc.
Karns, Christopher A. ... '69 '95 C.197 A.B. L.30 J.D. [🄰 Dorsey&W.]
*PRACTICE AREAS: Federal Indian Law; Indian Gaming Law; Public Policy; Federal Administrative Law; Government Relations.
Karolick, Dawn Marie ... '63 '99 C.97 B.A. L.904 J.D. [🄰 Mayer,B.&P.]
*PRACTICE AREAS: Regulated Industries; Litigation.
Karp, Jeffrey M. ... '52 '77 C.1036 B.A. L.1162 J.D. [Swidler B.S.F.]
*PRACTICE AREAS: Telecommunications; Right of Way Easements; Environmental; Hazardous Waste.
Karp, Judith Sturtz, (AV) ... '— '82 C.188 B.A. L.245 J.D. [Kirkpatrick&L.]
*PRACTICE AREAS: Commercial Bankruptcy; Workouts; Business Transactions; Lenders Rights; Commercial Litigation.
Karp, Naomi '50 '78 C.477 A.B. L.588 J.D.
(adm. in NH; not adm. in DC) ABA
Karp, Ronald A., (AV) '45 '72 C.446 B.A. L.30 J.D.
[Karp,F.L.W.&N.] (☉Frederick, Rockville, MD)
*PRACTICE AREAS: Medical Malpractice; Commercial Litigation; Automobile Negligence; Premises Liability; Products Liability.

Karp, Frosh, Lapidus, Wigodsky & Norwind, P.A., (AV)
1133 Connecticut Avenue, Suite 250, 20036 ☉
Telephone: 202-822-3777 Fax: 202-822-9722
Email: ronk@karpfrosh.com URL: http://www.karpfrosh.com
Ronald A. Karp; Lawrence S. Lapidus; Jeffrey A. Wigodsky; Jack A. Gold; David L Lowans.
Serious Personal Injury Litigation, Commercial Litigation, Family Law, Estate Planning and Business Law.
Rockville, Maryland Office: 1370 Piccard Drive, Suite 290. 20850. Telephone: 301-948-3800. Fax: 301-948-5449.
Fairfax, Virginia Office: Karp & Kessel, 11350 Random Hill Road, Suite 700, 22030.
Bethesda, Maryland Office: Karp, Frosh, Lapidus, Wigodsky & Norwind, P.A., 7315 Wisconsin Avenue, Suite 800 West. 20814. Telephone: 301-656-2888. Fax: 301-654-7748.
Frederich, Maryland Office: 110 N. Court Street, 2nd Floor. 21701.
See Professional Biographies, WASHINGTON, DISTRICT OF COLUMBIA

Karpel, Amy Ann ... '74 C.911 B.A. L.904 J.D. [🄰 Stewart&S.]
*PRACTICE AREAS: International Trade; Antidumping; Countervailing Duties; Unfair Trade; World Trade Organization.
Karpinski, Irena I., (BV) ... '50 '75 C.706 B.A. L.831 J.D. 1330 New Hampshire N.W.
Karpinski, Richard ... '57 '85 C.446 B.A. L.128 J.D. [🄲 Jorden B.]
*PRACTICE AREAS: Litigation; Insurance Law; Aviation.
Karppi, Patricia C. ... '66 '93 C.893 B.A. L.128 J.D. [🄰 B.J.Klores&Assoc.]
*PRACTICE AREAS: Professional Negligence; Civil Practice.
Karr, John W., (AV) ... '30 '58 C.424 B.S. L.276 LL.B. [Karr&A.]
*PRACTICE AREAS: Civil, Criminal Trials; Appellate Practice.

Karr & Allison, P.C., (AV)
1920 N Street, N.W., Suite 300, 20036
Telephone: 202-331-7600 Fax: 202-293-3999 URL: http://www.karrallison.com
Email: tsallison@aol.com URL: http://www.lawyers.com/karrallison
John W. Karr; Theodore S. Allison.
Corporate, Business, Commercial Litigation, Small Business, General Counselling, Legal Ethics, Medical Ethics, Professional Ethics.
See Professional Biographies, WASHINGTON, DISTRICT OF COLUMBIA

Karron, Andrew T. ... '56 '85 C.309 A.B. L.569 J.D. [Arnold&P.]
*PRACTICE AREAS: Litigation; Accountants' Liability Law; Securities and Derivative Litigation.
Karsh, Jason D. '69 '99 C&L.101 B.S., J.D.
(adm. in UT; not adm. in DC) Atty. U.S. Postal Srv.
Karta, Glenn E. ... '57 '82 C.688 B.S. L.146 J.D. [🄲 Rothwell,F.E.&M.] (See Pat. Sect.)
*PRACTICE AREAS: Intellectual Property.
Karter, Philip ... '— '82 C.1365 B.A. L.966 J.D. [Miller&C.]
Kasanow, David ... '47 '91 C.659 B.A. L.276 J.D. [McKenna&C.]
*PRACTICE AREAS: Government Contracts.
Kaseman, A. Carl, III, (AV) ... '41 '71 C.608 B.A. L.659 J.D. [Harkins C.]
*PRACTICE AREAS: Tax Law; Business Law; Regulated Industries.
Kashatus, Jennifer Myers '72 '97 C.165 B.A. L.930 J.D.
(adm. in MD; not adm. in DC) [🄰 Kelley D.&W.]
*PRACTICE AREAS: Telecommunications.
Kashdan, Alan G., (BV) ... '53 '80 C.674 B.A. L.309 J.D. [🄲 Hughes H.&R.]
*PRACTICE AREAS: International Trade.
Kasle, Jill F. '47 '72 C.597 B.S. L.94 J.D.
(adm. in MA; not adm. in DC) George Washington Univ.
Kasley, Shannon M. ... '72 '97 C.890 B.A. L.776 J.D. [🄰 Jones,D.R.&P.]
Kasley, William L. '51 '76 C.98 B.S. L.339 J.D.
(adm. in IL; not adm. in DC) Sr. Coun., MCI Communications Corporation
Kaslow, Aaron M. ... '64 '91 C&L.976 B.A., J.D. [Muldoon M.&F.]
*PRACTICE AREAS: Financial Institutions; Mergers and Acquisitions; Securities; Corporate Law.
Kasparian, Faith D. ... '69 '98 C.999 B.M. L.228 J.D. [🄰 Covington&B.]
*PRACTICE AREAS: Communications; Intellectual Property.

Kasper, Alan J., (AV) '43 '68 C.1044 B.S.E.E. L.276 J.D. [Sughrue M.] (See Pat. Sect.)
*PRACTICE AREAS: Intellectual Property Law; Litigation.
Kass, Benny L., (AV) .... '36 '60 C.597 B.S. L.477 LL.B. [Kass&S.]
Kass, Brian L. .... '68 '95 C.174 B.S. L.208 J.D. [Kass&S.]
Kass, Colin R. .... '71 '96 C.145 B.A. L.477 J.D. [A Kirkland&E.]
*PRACTICE AREAS: Litigation.
Kass, Howard E. .... '68 '95 C.475 B.A. L.930 J.D. 1054 31st St. N.W.
Kass, Mark A. .... '60 '86 C.976 B.A. L.178 J.D. [Hogan&H.]
*PRACTICE AREAS: Technology Business Startups; Telecommunications; Israeli-Related Transactions; Corporate Contracts.
Kass & Skalet, PLLC, (AV) .... Suite 1100 1050 Seventeenth Street, N.W.
Kassabian, Tamara Hardney .... '68 '99 C.911 B.A. L.188 J.D. [A Jones,D.R.&P.]
Kassebaum, David P. .... '72 '01 C.112 B.A. L.178 J.D. [A Hogan&H.]
Kassim, Morenike S. .... '— '99 C.893 B.A. L.477 J.D. [A Latham&W.]
*PRACTICE AREAS: Corporate Law; Finance; Commercial Law; Energy; Communications and Media.
Kassoff, Eric S., (CV) .... '60 '86 C&L.94 B.S., J.D [Wilkes A.]
*PRACTICE AREAS: Real Property Valuation Litigation; Real Property Tax Law; Public Finance; Zoning; Real Estate Transactions.
Kastner, Kenneth M., (AV) .... '— '79 C&L.893 B.A., J.D. [Bryan C.]
Kastner, Samuel P., (AV) .... '54 '78 C.1044 B.S. L.276 J.D. [Holland&K.]
*PRACTICE AREAS: Business Planning; Corporate Law; Taxation Law; Estates.
Kaswell, Joel R., (AV) .... '37 '62 C.197 B.A. L.309 J.D. [Lukas,N.G.&S.]
*PRACTICE AREAS: Securities; Financial; Corporation Law.
Kaswell, Stuart J., (AV) '54 '79 C.881 A.B. L.904 J.D. Gen. Coun. & Sr. V.P., Securities Industry Assn.
*RESPONSIBILITIES: Securities; Administrative; Legislative; General Corporate.
Katcher, Dara Susan .... '73 '98 C.1349 B.A. L.262 J.D. [A Hyman,P.&M.]
*PRACTICE AREAS: Food and Drug Regulation.
Katcher, Robert A., (AV) .... '— '76 C&L.477 B.A., J.D. [McKee N.]
*PRACTICE AREAS: International Income Tax; Tax Planning; Federal Tax Controversies; Transfer Pricing; Taxation.
Katerberg, Robert J. .... '74 '98 C&L.575 B.A., J.D. [A Arnold&P.]
*PRACTICE AREAS: Antitrust and Trade Regulation.
Kathuria, Sandeep .... '74 '99 C.537 B.A. L.884 J.D. [A Hall,E.H.G.G.&N.]
*PRACTICE AREAS: Corporate Litigation; Oil and Gas Contracts; Business Torts; International Trade.

Katirai, Mahmoud '43 '84 L.273 M.C.L.
1050 17th Street, N.W., Suite 700, 20036 ⊙
Telephone: 202-659-4245 Fax: 202-463-6290
Email: mahmoudkatirai@aol.com URL: http://www.lawyers.com/mahmoudkatirai
***PRACTICE AREAS: International Law; Business Law; Iranian Law.**
General Practice of law with particular attention to Corporate Law, International Law; Serving as an Expert on Iranian Law before Courts and Arbitration Tribunals; Providing Advice on Contract, Transnational Agreements and Investment Arrangements; Iranian Business Formation; Preparing Corporate Legal Documents and Registering both Foreign and Domestic Legal Entities in Iran.
Tehran, Iran Office: Number 4 Second Street, Mir-Emad Avenue, Suite 3. Telephone: 8757887. Fax: 8743911.
See Professional Biographies, WASHINGTON, DISTRICT OF COLUMBIA

Katkin, Elizabeth L. .... '68 '95 C.976 B.A. L.178 J.D. [A Hogan&H.]
*PRACTICE AREAS: Corporate Law; Securities; International Transactions; Private Equity.
Katkish, Cynthia .... '51 '88 C.445 B.A. L.904 J.D. 601 Pennsylvania Ave., N.W.
Kato, Yoshihiro '66 '98 L.30 LL.M. (adm. in NY; not adm. in DC) [A Lepon M.W.&H.]
Kator, Irving, (AV) .... '20 '52 C.477 A.B. L.273 J.D. [C Kator,P.&W.]
*PRACTICE AREAS: Employment Law; Civil Rights; Administrative Law.
Kator, Michael J. .... '56 '81 C&L.846 B.A., J.D. [Kator,P.&W.]
*PRACTICE AREAS: Federal Civil Litigation; Federal Employment Law; U.S. Supreme Court Litigation.

Kator, Parks & Weiser, P.L.L.C., (AV)
1020 Nineteenth Street, N.W. Suite 350, 20036 ⊙
Telephone: 202-898-4800 Fax: 202-289-1389
Email: KATOR.SCOTT@EROLS.COM URL: http://www.kator-scott.com
Michael J. Kator; Jessica L. Parks (Not admitted in DC); David Weiser;—Laura A. Stefani; Cathy A. Harris (Not admitted in DC); Maia R. Caplan. Of Counsel: Irving Kator; Joseph B. Scott.
General Practice including Employment, Civil Service, Civil Rights, Civil Trial, Appellate and Administrative Practice before all Courts and Agencies.
Austin, Texas Office: 812 San Antonio Street, Suite 100, 78701. Telephone: 512-322-0600.
See Professional Biographies, WASHINGTON, DISTRICT OF COLUMBIA

Katriel, Roy A. .... '68 '98 C.472 B.S. L.30 J.D. [A Finkelstein,T.&L.]
Katskee, Richard B. .... '67 '00 C.477 A.B. L.976 J.D. [A Mayer,B.&P.]
*PRACTICE AREAS: Appellate Practice.
Katsurinis, Stephen A. .... '66 '92 C.810 B.A. L.1218 J.D. [A McGuirewoods]
*PRACTICE AREAS: Complex Commercial Litigation.
Kattan, Joseph, (BV) .... '52 '76 C.930 A.B. L.597 J.D. [Gibson,D.&C.]
*PRACTICE AREAS: Antitrust; Consumer Protection.
Kattar, Candace A. .... '53 '81 C.550 B.A. L.1162 J.D. 11 Dupont Circle, N.W., Ste. 775

Katten Muchin Zavis, (AV)
A Partnership including Professional Corporations
Katten Muchin & Zavis Established in Chicago 1974
1025 Thomas Jefferson Street, N.W., East Lobby, Suite 700, 20007-5201 ⊙
Telephone: 202-625-3500 Telecopier: 202-298-7570
URL: http://www.kmz.com
Members of Firm: Richard P. Bauer; Virginia A. Davis; Wendy L. Fields; Roger P. Furey; Christopher J. Hart; Bruce E. Kosub; S. Scott Morrison; Michael P. Murphy; Robert J. Pisani; Steven C. Schnitzer; David Schwinger; Gloria B. Solomon; Carol R. Van Cleef; Jeffrey M. Werthan; Edward E. Zughaib. Associates: Myron Paul Barlow; Jennifer S. Beer; Elise A. Cook (Not admitted in DC); Brian H. Corcoran; Sylvia D. Davis; Oonagh L. Deasy (Not admitted in DC); Katerina Greenspun (Not admitted in DC); Gerald P. James (Not admitted in DC); Richard D. Kelley (Not admitted in DC); Nicole L. Kobrine; Ann H. Larkin (Not admitted in DC); Adam V. Lichtenstein; Rori H. Malech; Christine Poulon (Not admitted in DC); Leta A. Principe; Forrest W. Reid; Eric C. Spencer (Not admitted in DC). Special Counsel: Thomas A. Brooks.
Advertising, Anti-Fraud Counseling and Litigation, Antitrust, Bankruptcy, Reorganization and Creditors' Rights, Business Litigation, Corporate, Corporate Insurance, Customs and International Trade, Employee Benefits and Executive Compensation, Entertainment, Entertainment Finance, Entertainment Litigation, Environmental, Finance and Structured Finance, Financial Institutions, Financial Markets and Products, Financial Services, Franchising, Licensing and Distribution, Governmental Affairs, Health Care, Health Care Compliance, Health Care Insolvency, Health Information and HIPPA Compliance, Intellectual Property, Intellectual Property Litigation, International Transactions and Litigation, Internet and E-Business, Investment Management, Joint Ventures, Strategic Alliances and Partnerships, Labor and Employment, Litigation and Dispute Resolution, Mergers and Acquisitions, Private Equity and Emerging Growth Companies, Product Liability, Public Finance, Publishing, Real Estate, Real Estate Development, Real Estate Finance, Real Estate Investment Fund Formation, Real Estate Litigation, Real Estate Taxation, Securities, Securities Litigation, Shopping Center and Retail Law, Sports Law and Sports Facilities, Tax Planning and Litigation, Taxation of Financial Products, Technology and New Media, Wealth Management and Planning, White Collar Criminal and Civil Litigation.
Chicago, Illinois Office: 525 West Monroe Street, Suite 1600. Telephone: 312-902-5200. Telecopier: 312-902-1061.
Los Angeles, California Office: 1999 Avenue of the Stars, Suite 1400. Telephone: 310-788-4400. Telecopier: 310-788-4471.
Palo Alto, California Office: 260 Sheridan Avenue, Suite 450. Telephone: 650-330-3650. Telecopier: 310-712-8420.
New York, New York Office: 245 Park Avenue, 39th Floor. Telephone: 212-764-6886. Telecopier: 212-382-3395.
See Professional Biographies, WASHINGTON, DISTRICT OF COLUMBIA

Katula, Sharon E. .... '64 '95 C.216 B.A. L.273 J.D. [A Stohlman,B.E.&S.]
Katz, Andrew B. .... '64 '89 C.390 A.B. L.273 J.D. [Cozen O.] (Pat.)
*PRACTICE AREAS: Trademarks; Unfair Competition; Copyrights; Computer Law; Patents.
Katz, Andrew S., (BV) ...... '52 '78 C.446 B.A. L.64 J.D. Sr. Atty., Edison Elect. Institute
Katz, Carl R. .... '67 '96 C.112 B.A. L.800 J.D. [A Collier S.S.]
*PRACTICE AREAS: Antitrust; Consumer Protection.
Katz, Daniel E. .... '68 '94 C&L.260 B.S., J.D. 1741 T St., N.W.
Katz, Daniel Franklin .... '57 '84 C.951 B.A. L.228 J.D. [Williams&C.]
*PRACTICE AREAS: Complex Litigation.
Katz, Daniel M., (AV) .... '44 '69 C.477 B.A. L.145 J.D. [Katz&R.]
Katz, David L. .... '56 '92 C.228 A.B. L.276 J.D. The Advisory Bd. Co.
Katz, David S. .... '55 '84 C.882 B.A. L.94 J.D. [Orrick,H.&S.]
Katz, Deborah J. .... '72 '97 C.228 A.B. L.880 J.D. [A Gibson,D.&C.]
*PRACTICE AREAS: Antitrust and Trade Regulation; Litigation.
Katz, Debra Susan, (AV) .... '58 '84 C.867 B.A. L.966 J.D. [Bernabei&K.]
*PRACTICE AREAS: Employment Discrimination; Whistleblower Law; Civil Rights; Civil Liberties.
Katz, Gerald I., (AV) .... '49 '75 C&L.893 B.A., J.D. [Katz&S.] ⊙
*PRACTICE AREAS: Construction Law; Public Contract Law; Fidelity and Surety Law.
Katz, Hadrian R. .... '49 '77 C&L.309 A.B., J.D. [Arnold&P.]
*PRACTICE AREAS: Litigation; Computer; Intellectual Property.
Katz, Isadore B. .... '33 '57 C.446 B.S. L.273 LL.B. 5335 Wisconsin Ave., N.W.
Katz, Jessica L. .... '66 '93 C.674 B.S.E. L.178 J.D. [Caplin&D.]
*PRACTICE AREAS: Tax Law.
Katz, John W. .... '43 '71 C.367 B.A. L.1066 J.D. Alaska Gov. Off.
Katz, Lawrence A., (AV) '53 '78 C.1044 B.A. L.276 J.D. [Venable,A.B.H.&C.] (⊙Mc Lean, VA)
*PRACTICE AREAS: Bankruptcy Law; Litigation; Commercial Law.
Katz, Lester A., (AV) .... '38 '63 C&L.94 B.S., J.D. [L.A.Katz]
Katz, Mark M. .... '57 '85 C.604 B.A. L.893 J.D. [Arent F.K.P.&K.]
*PRACTICE AREAS: Business Law; Tax Law; Real Estate.
Katz, Philip .... '59 '92 C.893 B.A. L.276 J.D. [Crowell&M.]
*PRACTICE AREAS: Drug and Medical Device Regulation; Food and Drug Regulation; Food, Drug and Cosmetic Law; Advertising and Labeling; False Advertising.
Katz, Rachel S. .... '74 '00 C.867 B.A. L.30 J.D. [A Fried,F.H.S.&J.]
*PRACTICE AREAS: Corporate Law.
Katz, Robert J., (AV) .... '39 '65 C.102 A.B. L.273 LL.B. [R.J.Katz]
Katz, Robert S. .... '— '92 C.119 B.S. L.273 J.D. [Banner&W.] (See Pat. Sect.)
*PRACTICE AREAS: Intellectual Property Law; Patents; Design Patents; Mechanical Intellectual Property.
Katz, Shlomo D. .... '65 '90 C.446 B.S. L.273 J.D. [A Epstein B.&G.]
*PRACTICE AREAS: Government Contracts Law; Wage and Hour Law.
Katz, Sumner J. .... '34 '60 C.976 B.A. L.309 LL.B. 601 Pennsylvania Ave., N.W.

Katz, Kutter, Haigler, Alderman, Bryant & Yon, Professional Association
801 Pennsylvania Avenue, N.W. Suite 750, 20004 ⊙
Telephone: 202-393-6222 Fax: 202-393-5959
URL: http://www.katzlaw.com
Of Counsel: Richard L. Spees, Jr. (Not admitted in DC).
General Civil Practice. Trial and Appellate Practice in all State and Federal Courts. Governmental, Administrative and Legislative Practice, including Insurance Regulation, Banking Regulation, Land Use and Environmental Law, Utility Regulation, Mobile Home Park Regulation, Regulated Professions, Alcoholic Beverages, Life Care, Health Care, and Public Contracts. General Corporate, Business, Real Property and Commercial Law, Mediation and Arbitration, Products Liability, Employment and Labor Law, Alternative Dispute Resolution, Mediation, Antitrust and Trade Regulation, Consumer Regulation.
Tallahassee, Florida Office: 106 East College Avenue, 12th Floor, 32301. Mailing address: P.O. Box 1877, 32302-1877. Telephone: 850-224-9634. Fax: 222-0103.
Orlando, Florida Office: 111 North Orange Avenue, Suite 900, 32801. Telephone: 407-841-7100. Fax: 407-648-0660.
Aventura, Florida Office: Suite 409, 2999 N.E. 191st Street, 33180. Telephone: 305-932-0996. Fax: 305-932-0972.
See Professional Biographies, WASHINGTON, DISTRICT OF COLUMBIA

Katz, Lester A., Chartered, (AV) .... 1155 15th Street, N.W., Suite 502

Katz, Neil B.
(See Rockville, Maryland)

Katz & Ranzman, P.C., (AV)
Suite 801, 1015 Eighteenth Street, N.W., 20036
Telephone: 202-659-4656 Fax: 202-659-3145
Email: dankatz@compuserve.com
Daniel M. Katz; Ellen G. Ranzman;—Nancy A. Donahue; Louise P. Zanar. Of Counsel: Ira M. Lechner.
Labor, ERISA, Civil Rights Law.
See Professional Biographies, WASHINGTON, DISTRICT OF COLUMBIA

Katz, Robert J., P.C., (AV) .... 1990 M Street, N.W. Suite 410

Katz & Stone, L.L.P., (AV)
1120 19th Street, N.W. 7th Floor, 20036 ⊙
Telephone: 703-761-3000 Facsimile: 703-761-6179
Email: info@katzandstone.com URL: http://www.katzandstone.com
Members of Firm: Gerald I. Katz; Mark J. Stone; Andrew N. Felice.
Construction, Public Contract, Surety and Alternative Dispute Resolution, Practice before Federal and State Courts.
Vienna, Virginia Office: Suite 600, 8230 Leesburg Pike. Telephone: 703-761-3000.
Rockville, Maryland Office: 600 East Jefferson Street, Suite 201, 20852. Telephone: 703-761-3000.
See Professional Biographies, WASHINGTON, DISTRICT OF COLUMBIA

Katzman, Scott H. .... '56 '81 C.188 B.S. L.178 J.D. [Steptoe&J.]
*PRACTICE AREAS: Business Law; Commercial Law; Corporate Transactions; Securities; Transactional Law.
Katzmann, Robert A. .... '53 '82 C.178 A.B. L.976 J.D. Brookings Institution
Kauder, Louis M., (AV) ..... '34 '62 C.823 B.A. L.976 LL.B. 601 Pennsylvania Ave., NW
Kauff, Scott E. .... '71 '96 C.188 B.A. L.659 J.D. [A McKenna&C.]
*PRACTICE AREAS: Environmental Law; Litigation; Administrative Law; Occupational Safety and Health Law.
Kauffman, Jeffrey A. .... '70 '97 C.216 B.A. L.823 J.D. [A Collier S.S.]
*PRACTICE AREAS: Antitrust; Consumer Protection.
Kauffman, Kathleen Clubb .... '54 '80 C&L.378 B.A., J.D. [A Ackerson]
*PRACTICE AREAS: Administrative Law; Litigation; Class Actions; Real Estate; Antitrust.
Kaufman, Andrea S. .... '68 '96 C.367 B.A. L.262 J.D. 1201 New York Ave., N.W.
Kaufman, Beth Shapiro .... '59 '85 C.668 B.A. L.309 J.D. [Caplin&D.]
*PRACTICE AREAS: Estate Planning.
Kaufman, Bonni Fine .... '59 '85 C.1365 B.A. L.276 J.D. 1155 21st Street, N.W.
Kaufman, Brian P. '70 '95 C.228 B.A. L.597 J.D. (adm. in MD; not adm. in DC) [A Steptoe&J.]
Kaufman, Bruce S. '63 '89 C.102 B.A. L.1009 J.D. (adm. in NJ; not adm. in DC) Legal Editor, The Bureau of Natl. Affs., Inc.
Kaufman, David J., (AV) .... '53 '77 C.339 B.A. L.276 J.D. [C Brown N.&K.]
*PRACTICE AREAS: Telecommunications.
Kaufman, Gal N. .... '66 '92 C.446 B.S. L.904 J.D. [A Patton B.]
Kaufman, George W., (AV) '38 '62 C.178 A.B. L.976 LL.B. (adm. in NY; not adm. in DC) 555 12th St., N.W.
Kaufman, Gregory S. .... '73 '98 C.473 B.A. L.537 J.D. [A Sutherland A.&B.]
*PRACTICE AREAS: Litigation.

Kaufman, Joel D., (AV) ....'52 '76 C.659 B.S.E.E. L.276 J.D. [Steptoe&J.]
*PRACTICE AREAS: International Trade Law.
Kaufman, Joshua J., (AV) ....'50 '77 C.446 B.A. L.276 J.D. [Venable,A.B.H.&C.]
*PRACTICE AREAS: Copyright Law; Trademark Law; Art Law; Entertainment Law; Computer Law.
Kaufman, Kenneth M., (AV) ....'48 '72 C.309 A.B. L.976 J.D. [Skadden,A.S.M.&F.]
Kaufman, Kenneth S., (AV) ....'57 '85 C.188 A.B. L.276 J.D. [Ⓒ Wright&T.]
*PRACTICE AREAS: Litigation; Environmental Law; Insurance Coverage.
Kaufman, Marc S. ....'62 '92 C.94 B.S.M.E. L.128 J.D. [Nixon P.] (Pat.)
*PRACTICE AREAS: Patent Law; Copyright Law; Trademark Law; Licensing.
Kaufman, Mark H. ....'49 '74 C.665 B.A. L.276 J.D. 1735 20th St., N.W.
Kaufman, Michael B. ....'67 '92 C.178 B.A. L.659 J.D. KPMG Peat Marwick
Kaufman, Steven M. ....'59 '85 C.976 B.A. L.309 J.D. [Hogan&H.]
*PRACTICE AREAS: Corporate Law; Securities Law.
Kaufman, Steven R. ....'68 '95 C.860 B.S. L.880 J.D. Sr. Atty., NASD Regulation
Kaufman, Thomas F., (AV) ....'49 '76 C.107 B.S.E.E. L.276 J.D. [Hunton&W.] (Pat.)
*PRACTICE AREAS: Finance; Real Estate; Technology; Corporate.
Kaufmann, Lynn F. ....'51 '90 C.659 A.B. L.1066 J.D. [Ⓐ Zuckerman S.]
*PRACTICE AREAS: Litigation.
Kaufmann, Michael E., (BV) ....'60 '86 C.446 B.S.B.A. L.276 J.D. [Venable,A.B.H.&C.]
*PRACTICE AREAS: Energy; Public Utility; Regulatory Litigation; Contracts.
Kaufmann, Roy L., (AV) ....'— '78 C.1044 B.A. L.273 J.D. [Ⓒ Jackson&C.]
*PRACTICE AREAS: Commercial Business; Real Estate; Title.
Kavanagh, John J., III '71 '98 C.273 B.A. L.93 J.D.
(adm. in NY; not adm. in DC) [Ⓐ Steptoe&J.]
Kavanaugh, Everett Edward, Jr. '41 '79
C.276 A.B. L.30 J.D. Pres., Cosmetic, Toiletry & Fragrance Assn.
Kavanaugh, Patrick, (AV) ....'47 '74 C.602 B.A. L.273 J.D. [Hamilton&H.]
*PRACTICE AREAS: Civil Litigation; Personal Injury; Insurance Litigation.
Kay, Amy H. '71 '01 C.188 B.S. L.597 J.D.
(adm. in NY; not adm. in DC) [Ⓐ O'Melveny&M.]
Kay, Andrew B. ....'— '97 C.188 B.A. L.477 J.D. [Ⓐ Kirkland&E.]
*PRACTICE AREAS: Litigation.
Kay, Paul Edward, (BV) ....'37 '75 C.999 B.B.A. L.569 J.D. [Kay&P.]
Kay & Povinelli, P.C., (BV) ....1010 Vermont Ave., N.W.
Kayal, Dev A. ....'63 '93 C.705 B.S.E.E. L.494 J.D. 1730 K St., N.W.
Kayan, S. Michael, (AV) ....'62 '93 C&L.893 B.A., J.D. Gen. Coun., PrimeShot Corp.
Kaye, Carole Penny '46 '98 C.569 B.S. L.30 J.D.
(adm. in MD; not adm. in DC) 1150 5th St. NW, 6th Fl.‡
Kaye, Donald Michael ....'60 '85 C.105 B.A. L.312 J.D. [Akin,G.S.H.&F.]
*PRACTICE AREAS: International Trade.
Kaye, Harvey, (AV) ....'34 '60 C.422 B.S. L.273 J.D. [Ⓒ Perkins,S.C.&C.]
*PRACTICE AREAS: Intellectual Property Law; Litigation; International Law.
Kaye, Jonathan M. ....'66 '94 C.659 B.S. L.276 J.D. [Ⓐ Slavit&G.]
Kaye, Laura K. ....'62 '93 C.309 A.B. L.597 J.D. 2737 Devonshire Pl., N.W.
Kaye, Stephen S. ....'— '79 C.165 A.B. L.904 J.D. [Ⓒ Bryan C.]
*PRACTICE AREAS: Government Contracts Law; Litigation; Corporate Investigations.

Kaye Scholer LLP, (AV)
A New York Limited Liability Partnership
McPherson Building, 901 Fifteenth Street, N.W., Suite 1100, 20005-2327 ⊙
Telephone: 202-682-3500 Facsimile: 202-682-3580
URL: http://www.kayescholer.com
Resident Partners: Sylvia M. Becker; David O. Bickart; Donald B. Cameron, Jr.; G. Christopher Griner; Ronald K. Henry; Michael P. House; Julie C. Mendoza; C. Christopher Parlin; Mark S. Popofsky; Kerry Alan Scanlon; Jason L. Shrinsky; Randall L. Speck. Special Counsel: William S. Eberle (P.A.) (Not admitted in DC); Christopher J. Kelly (Not admitted in DC); Steven L. Schwarcz (Not admitted in DC). Counsel: Christopher R. Brewster; David S. Christy Jr.; Bruce Alan Eisen; Farhad Jalinous; Raymond Paretzky; R. Will Planert; John P. Rynkiewicz (Not admitted in DC). Resident Associates: Nicole J. Becton (Not admitted in DC); Crystal J. Jones (Not admitted in DC); John R. Miles; Brady W. Mills; Allan Gary Moskowitz; T. Melindah Musa; Margaret Scicluna (Not admitted in DC); Deborah L. Wengel.
General and Administrative Practice.
New York, N.Y.: 425 Park Avenue, 10022-3598. Telephone: 212-836-8000. Telex: 234860 KAY UR. Facsimile: 212-836-8689.
Los Angeles, California: 1999 Avenue of the Stars, Suite 1600, 90067-6048. Telephone: 310-788-1000. Facsimile: 310-788-1200.
West Palm Beach, Florida Office: Phillips Point, West Tower 900, 777 South Flagler Drive, 33401-6163. Telephone: 561-802-3230. Facsimile: 561-802-3217.
Chicago, Illinois Office: 311 South Wacker Drive, 62nd Floor, 60606. Telephone: 312-583-2300. Facsimile: 312-583-2360.
Hong Kong: Suite 2006-2010, One International Finance Centre, No. 1 Harbor View Street, Central. Telephone: 011 852-28458989. Facsimile: 011 852-28452389.
Shanghai, Peoples Republic of China: Suite 1504-1506 CITIC Square, 1168 Nanjing Xi Lu, 200041. Telephone: 011 86-21 5298-4266. Facsimile: 011 86-21 5298-4277.
London, England Office: 10th Floor, 88 Wood Street, EC 2V 7RS. Telephone: 011-020-8528-1006. Fax: 011-020-8528-1174.
See Professional Biographies, WASHINGTON, DISTRICT OF COLUMBIA

Kayne, Veronica G. ....'— '81 C.659 B.A. L.884 J.D. [Wilmer,C.&P.]
*PRACTICE AREAS: Antitrust.
Kayser, Christopher J. '71 '98 C.770 B.A. L.596 J.D.
(adm. in OR; not adm. in DC) Dept. of Jus.
Kazakis, Georgia ....'66 '93 C.893 B.A. L.309 J.D. [Ⓐ Covington&B.]
*PRACTICE AREAS: Insurance; Insurance Coverage; Insurance Litigation; Litigation; Civil Litigation.
Kazaks, Julia M. ....'70 '94 C.813 B.A. L.276 J.D. [Ⓐ Skadden,A.S.M.&F.]
*PRACTICE AREAS: Tax; Tax Litigation.
Kazon, Peter M., (BV) ....'53 '78 C.860 B.A. L.831 J.D. [Mintz,L.C.F.G.&P.]
*PRACTICE AREAS: Health Law; Health Care Reform; Health Care Reimbursement; Medicare and Medicaid Reimbursement; Medicare and Medicaid Fraud and Abuse.
Kealy, Patrick J. '70 '00 C.30 B.A. L.904 J.D.
(adm. in MD; not adm. in DC) [Ⓐ Dickstein S.M.&O.]
*PRACTICE AREAS: Electric Power; Energy; Corporate Law.
Keane, James M. ....'35 '69 C.1016 B.A. L.424 J.D. Coldwell Banker Real Estate
Keane, Martin E. ....'61 '89 C.321 B.A. L.818 J.D. 1901 Pennsylvania Ave., NW
Keane, William K., (AV) ....'44 '72 C.321 A.B. L.893 J.D. [Arter&H.]
*PRACTICE AREAS: Telecommunications Law.
Kearney, Edward F. ....'31 '57 C.867 B.A. L.276 J.D. 641 Indiana Ave., N.W.
Kearney, Frank R. ....'67 '93 C.229 B.A. L.1209 J.D. [Koonz,M.J.D.&L.]
Kearney, James K. ....'— '76 C.665 B.A. L.893 J.D. [Reed S.]
*PRACTICE AREAS: Government Contracts; Export Compliance.
Kearney, John F. ....'58 '91 C.446 B.A. L.273 J.D. [Dyer E.&J.]
*PRACTICE AREAS: Securities; Mergers and Acquisitions; Capital Formation.
Kearney, Julie M. ....'67 '98 C.518 B.A. L.127 J.D. 1133 19th Street, N.W.
Kearney, Mary M. ....'54 '79 C&L.893 B.A., J.D. [Trow&K.]
*PRACTICE AREAS: Immigration and Nationality Law.
Kearney, Patrick J., (AV) ....'— '83 C.339 A.B. L.904 J.D. [Ⓒ Foley&L.]
*PRACTICE AREAS: Litigation; Debtor and Creditor Rights.
Kearney, William L., Jr. ....'70 '99 C&L.945 B.A., J.D. [Ⓢ Jones,D.R.&P.]
Kearns, Christine Nicolaides ....'60 '87 C.228 B.A. L.880 J.D. [Shaw P.]
*PRACTICE AREAS: Employment; Litigation.
Kearns, Jason ....'71 '96 C.208 B.A. L.659 J.D. [Ⓐ Wilmer,C.&P.]
Kearns, John S. ....'57 '83 C.446 B.A. L.64 J.D. 750 First St. N.E.
Keary, Ann O'Regan ....'50 '74 C.914 B.A. L.273 J.D. Assoc. Supr. Ct. J.

Keating, Geoffrey T., (AV) ....'40 '67 C.611 B.A. L.273 J.D. [Ⓒ McKenna&C.]
*PRACTICE AREAS: Construction Law; Government Contracts Law.
Keating, Kirsten E. ....'67 '94 C.165 B.A. L.150 J.D. [Ⓐ Ballard S.A.&I.]
*PRACTICE AREAS: Litigation; Employment Law.
Keating, R. Daniel ....'70 '98 C.475 B.S. L.276 J.D. [Ⓐ Hogan&H.]
Keats, John A. ....'40 '67 1742 N Street, N.W.
Kedia, Shalini K. ....'72 '99 C.36 B.A. L.1065 J.D. [Ⓐ Bonner K.T.&C.]
*PRACTICE AREAS: Litigation.
Kedian, Kathleen M. ....'— '00 C.1369 B.A. L.945 J.D. [Ⓐ Gibson,D.&C.]
Keefer, Sophie J. ....'68 '97 C.012 B.A. L.128 J.D. [Ⓐ Willkie F.&G.]
Keefer, Timothy J. ....'64 '98 C.107 B.A. L.902 J.D. [Ⓐ Covington&B.]
*PRACTICE AREAS: Election Law; Government Contracts.
Keeffe, Stephen Daniel ....'35 '63 C.273 B.A. L.880 LL.B. 1504 R St., N.W.
Keegan, Elise C. ....'67 '93 C&L.893 B.A., J.D. [Ⓐ Gibson,D.&C.]
*PRACTICE AREAS: Corporate Law; Securities.
Keegan, Timothy L. ....'49 '85 C.262 B.A. L.893 J.D. [Burzio&M.]
*PRACTICE AREAS: Federal Administrative Law; Postal Law.
Keehan, Timothy E. ....'61 '87 C&L.893 B.A., J.D. [Mayer,B.&P.]
*PRACTICE AREAS: Financial Services Law; E-Commerce.
Keeley, Margaret A. ....'68 '95 C.276 B.A. L.145 J.D. [Ⓐ Williams&C.]
*PRACTICE AREAS: Civil Litigation; Commercial Litigation; Criminal Defense; Election and Campaign Finance; First Amendment Law.
Keeley, Patrick J., (AV) '48 '75 C.276 B.S.B.A. L.262 J.D.
801 Pennsylvania Ave., N.W.
Keeling, J. Michael ....'47 '72 C.976 B.A. L.846 L.D. Pres., The ESOP Assn.
Keeling, Robert Daniel, III '74 '00 C.1369 B.A. L.893 J.D.
(adm. in VA; not adm. in DC) 1722 Eye St.
Keenan, Clifford T., (AV) ....'53 '83 C.276 A.B. L.128 J.D. Asst. U.S. Atty.
Keenan, Laurie E., (AV) ....'52 '83 C.945 A.B. L.893 J.D. [Ivins,P.&B.]
*PRACTICE AREAS: Employee Benefits; Employment Taxation; Executive Compensation; ERISA Litigation; ESOPs.
Keenan, Lisa A. '67 '92 C.30 B.A. L.276 J.D.
(adm. in PA; not adm. in DC) Smithsonian Institution
Keene, Bryan W. ....'74 '00 C&L.260 B.S., J.D. [Ⓐ Davis&H.]
*PRACTICE AREAS: Taxation Law; Insurance Law.
Keene, Jason O. '— '00 C.446 B.A. L.569 J.D.
(adm. in NY; not adm. in DC) [Ⓐ Groom]
*PRACTICE AREAS: Employee Benefits; Executive Compensation.
Keener, Allan W. '42 '75 C.550 B.A. L.94 J.D.
(adm. in NH; not adm. in DC) Electronic Warfare Assocs., Inc.
Keeney, John C., Jr., (AV) ....'51 '76 C.602 A.B. L.309 J.D. [Hogan&H.]
*PRACTICE AREAS: Civil Litigation; Federal Litigation; Professional Liability; Civil Rights; Election, Campaign and Political Law.
Keeney, Regina Markey ....'55 '81 C.276 B.S. L.309 J.D. [Metzger&M.]
Keevican, Leo A., Jr., (AV) '49 '75 C.976 B.A. L.94 J.D.
(adm. in PA; not adm. in DC) [DKW] ⊙
Kehoe, Brien E., (BV) ....'46 '73 C.903 A.B. L.1017 J.D. [Ⓒ Aitken I.B.&V.]
*PRACTICE AREAS: Marine Transportation; Administration Law.
Kehoe, Edw. T. ....'23 '50 C&L.276 B.S.S., J.D. 3712 Morrison St., N.W.
Kehoe, Patrick E. '41 '66 C.988 B.C.S. L.911 J.D.
(adm. in WA; not adm. in DC) Law Libr. & Prof. of Law, The American Univ.
Kehoe, Rebecca L. '60 '91 C.446 B.S.C.E. L.904 J.D.
(adm. in MD; not adm. in DC) [Cotten&S.]
Kehoe, Sean P. '69 '95 C.893 B.A. L.1209 J.D.
(adm. in VA; not adm. in DC) 5101 Wisconsin Ave., N.W.
Keifer, Eric M. '71 '99 C.92 B.A. L.1048 J.D.
(adm. in NY; not adm. in DC) [Ⓐ Hessel&A.]
Keil, Herbert B., (AV) ....'27 '53 C.945 B.S. L.146 J.D. [Keil&W.] (See Pat. Sect.)
*PRACTICE AREAS: Chemical Patent Law; Patent; Trademark Law; Litigation.

Keil & Weinkauf, (AV)
1101 Connecticut Avenue, N.W., 20036
Telephone: 202-659-0100 Telecopier: 202-659-0105
Members of Firm: Herbert B. Keil; Russell E. Weinkauf (Not admitted in DC); Jason D. Voight. Special Counsel: Gerald H. Bjorge; Norman G. Torchin; George F. Helfrich (Not admitted in DC); Ronald H. Smith (Not admitted in DC). Associates: Daniel S. Kim; David C. Liechty (Not admitted in DC). Of Counsel: Melvin Goldstein (Not admitted in DC). Technical and Foreign Patent Advisor: Barbara A. Schwalge.
Patent, Trademark, Copyright, Unfair Competition, Licensing and Related Antitrust Law. Litigation.
See Professional Biographies, WASHINGTON, DISTRICT OF COLUMBIA

Keiler, Alan D. ....'46 '71 C.331 B.A. L.107 J.D. 5225 Wisconsin Ave., NW
Keinan, Yoram '68 '96
(adm. in Israel; not adm. in DC) [Ⓐ Shearman&S.]
*PRACTICE AREAS: Taxation; Corporate Law.
Keiner, R. Bruce, Jr., (AV) ....'42 '68 C.216 B.A. L.893 LL.B. [Crowell&M.]
*PRACTICE AREAS: Administrative Practice; Aviation Law; Transportation Law.
Keir, David S. ....'62 '90 C.309 A.B. L.945 J.D. [Leventhal,S.&L.]
*PRACTICE AREAS: Communications Law; International and Domestic Satellite Law; Media Law.
Keiser, Matthew D. ....'72 '96 C.659 B.A. L.273 J.D. [Ⓐ Arnold&P.]
*PRACTICE AREAS: Litigation; Employment Law.
Keisler, Peter D. ....'60 '85 C&L.976 B.A., J.D. [Sidley A.B.&W.]
Keitelman, Charis R., (AV) '61 '86 C.867 B.A. L.30 J.D.
Dep. Gen. Coun., Quadrangle Development Corp.
*RESPONSIBILITIES: Commercial Real Estate (90%); General Practice (10%).
Keitelman, Jeffrey R., (AV) ....'60 '86 C.103 B.A. L.178 J.D. [Piper M.R.&W.]
*PRACTICE AREAS: Commercial Real Estate; General Business.
Keith, F. Ryan ....'74 '00 C.138 B.A. L.902 J.D. [Ⓐ Crowell&M.]
Keith, Jerry E. ....'44 '71 C.188 A.B. L.94 J.D. 1545 18th St., N.W.
Keith, Kimberly S. '70 '97 C.886 B.S. L.1209 J.D.
(adm. in MD; not adm. in DC) [Ⓐ Epstein B.&G.]
*PRACTICE AREAS: Corporate; Secured Transactions; Bankruptcy.
Keith, Pamela M. ....'— '95 C.112 A.B. L.93 J.D. [Ⓐ Morgan,L.&B.]
Keithley, Jay C. '48 '74 C.347 B.S. L.345 J.D.
(adm. in IN; not adm. in DC) V.P., External Affs., Sprint Corp.
Keithline, Jeffrey A. ....'65 '98 C.1279 B.A. L.902 J.D. [Ⓐ Keller&H.]
*PRACTICE AREAS: Food and Drug; Environmental Law.
Kelber, Steven B., (BV) ....'56 '81 C.446 B.A. L.273 J.D. [Piper M.R.&W.] (Pat.)
Kelemen, Gabor J. '30 '72 C&L.30 B.A., J.D.
(adm. in VA; not adm. in DC; See Pat. Sect.) [Venable,A.B.H.&C.]
*PRACTICE AREAS: Patent Law.
Kelety, Theresa K. ....'63 '94 C.446 B.S. L.893 J.D. [Ⓐ Shearman&S.]
*PRACTICE AREAS: Investment Company Law; Investment Management; Mutual Funds; Securities Offerings; Securities Regulation.
Kellar, Karl L. ....'54 '79 C.326 B.A. L.309 J.D. [Ⓒ Jones,D.R.&P.]
Kelleher, David L. ....'53 '85 C.93 B.S. L.930 J.D. [Arent F.K.P.&K.]
*PRACTICE AREAS: Litigation; First Amendment Litigation; Products Liability Law; Defective Products.
Kelleher, Michael F., (AV) ....'49 '75 C.602 A.B. L.276 J.D. [McDermott,W.&E.]
Kellenberg, Thomas More '57 '86 C.602 B.A. L.309 J.D.
(adm. in MA; not adm. in DC)
Coun., Govt. Affs., Univ. of Notre Dame, Washington Off.

Keller, Anson M. ....'36 '63 C.103 A.B. L.477 J.D. [Baise&M.]
*PRACTICE AREAS: Environmental Law; Litigation; First Amendment Law; Defamation.
Keller, Eric R. .... '69 '96 C.610 B.B.A. L.117 J.D. [🄰 Paul,H.J.&W.]
*PRACTICE AREAS: Employee Benefits; Executive Compensation.
Keller, L. Charles ....'67 '94 C.112 B.A. L.767 J.D. [Wilkinson B.K.]
*PRACTICE AREAS: Telecommunications Law.
Keller, Robert J., (AV) ...... '53 '79 C&L.128 B.A., J.D. [R.J.Keller] & [🄲 Shainis & P]
Keller, Roger A., Jr. '67 '92 C&L.734 B.A., J.D.
(adm. in MO; not adm. in DC) [🄰 Winston&S.]
Keller, Thomas J., (AV) ....'— '71 C.8 B.A. L.904 J.D. [Verner,L.B.M.&H.]
*PRACTICE AREAS: Communications Law; Intellectual Property Law.

Keller and Heckman LLP, (AV)
Suite 500 West, 1001 G Street, N.W., 20001 ⊙
Telephone: 202-434-4100 Cable Address: "Kelman" Telex: 49 95551 Telecopier: 202-434-4646
URL: http://www.khlaw.com
Members of Firm: Joseph E. Keller (1907-1994); Jerome H. Heckman; William H. Borghesani, Jr.; Wayne V. Black; Terrence D. Jones; Martin W. Bercovici; John S. Eldred; Richard J. Leighton; Douglas J. Behr; Michael F. Morrone; John B. (Jack) Richards; Jean M. Savigny (Resident, Brussels, Belgium Office); John B. Dubeck; Peter L. de la Cruz; Melvin S. Drozen; Lawrence P. Halprin; Ralph A. Simmons; Richard F. Mann; C. Douglas Jarrett; Sheila A. Millar; George G. Misko; Leslie T. Krasny (Resident, San Francisco, California Office); David I. Reader; David G. Sarvadi; Catherine Roemer Nielsen; Mark Mansour (Not admitted in DC); Elliot Belilos; Jean-Philippe Montfort (Not admitted in the United States; Resident, Brussels, Belgium Office); Arthur S. Garrett, III; Joan Sylvain Baughan; Martha E. Marrapese; David R. Joy; Frederick A. Stearns; Justin C. Powell. Associates: George Brent Mickum, IV; Thomas B. Magee; Lesa L. Byrum (Not admitted in DC); Negin Mohtadi; Nicole B. Donath; David J. Ettinger; John F. Foley; Thomas C. Berger; Rachida Semail (Resident, Brussels, Belgium Office); Eric C. Nastasi; John Dobinson (Resident, Brussels, Belgium Office); Manesh K. Rath; Carlos Celestino (Not admitted in DC); Lynn Loris Owens; Devon Wm. Hill (Resident, Brussels, Belgium Office); JoAnna R. Soffa (Resident, San Francisco, California Office); Jean-Cyril Walker (Not admitted in DC); Eric H. Singer; Colleen M. Evale; Pamela L. Gauthier; Susanne Valluet (Resident, Brussels, Belgium Office); Alexa Boonstra Barnett; Michael T. Novak; Karen Rothschild Cavanaugh; Natasha L. Drew (Not admitted in DC); Deborah W. Ziffer; Jeffrey A. Keithline; Frank J. Vitolo; Vanessa H. Broussard (Not admitted in DC); Jennifer B. Bennett; Caren A. Grau; Luther L. Hajek; Trent M. Doyle; Katherine Collins Lucas; Matthew T. Frekko (Not admitted in DC); Ruxandra Grigore (Resident, Brussels, Belgium Office); Kevin G. Rupy; Matthew Wright; Kevin Patrick Boot (Not admitted in DC); Sebastien Francois Louvion. Counsel: Alfred S. Regnery.
Administrative Practice before Federal Departments and Agencies of Federal, State and Foreign Governments; Representation before Congress and State Legislatures; Civil and Criminal Litigation before Federal and State Courts; Trade Associations Representation; Domestic and International Business Transactions. Food and Drug, Telecommunications, Environmental, Occupational Health and Safety, Labor and Employment, Transportation, Litigation, International Trade, Antitrust and Trade Regulation, Product Liability, Advertising and Labeling, Corporate, Contracts, Intellectual Property, Biotechnology, and Internet and E-Commerce.
San Francisco, California Office: California Street Center, 50 California Street, Suite 1500. Telephone: 415-277-5952. Telecopier: 415-439-5299.
Brussels, Belgium Office: 25 Rue Blanche B-1060. Telephone: 32 (2) 541 05 70. Telecopier: 32 (2) 541 05 80.
See Professional Biographies, WASHINGTON, DISTRICT OF COLUMBIA

Keller, Robert J., P.C., (AV)
1850 M Street N.W., Suite 240, P.O. Box 33428, 20036
Telephone: 202-223-2100 Facsimile: 202-223-2121
Email: rjk@telcomlaw.com URL: http://www.lawyres.com/keller
Robert J. Keller.
Telecommunications Law, Communications Law, Telecommunications Regulation, FCC Regulation, FCC Licensing.
See Professional Biographies, WASHINGTON, DISTRICT OF COLUMBIA

Kelley, Angela M. '63 '88 C.1209 B.A. L.273 J.D.
(adm. in VA; not adm. in DC) National Immigration Forum
Kelley, Carmen R. ....'63 '90 C.69 B.S.Ed. L.1015 J.D. [Ross,D.&B.]
Kelley, Elizabeth J. ....'— '99 C.1365 B.A. L.280 J.D. [🄰 Shaw P.]
Kelley, James A., (BV) ....'52 '79 C.682 B.A. L.1338 J.D. [Bastianelli,B.&K.]
*PRACTICE AREAS: Government Contracts; Maritime; Shipbuilding and Repair; Shipping Law; Construction Law.

Kelley, James H., (AV) '33 '57 C&L.93 A.B., J.D.
9611 Sutherland Road, 20901 ⊙
Telephone: 1-800-294-6372
Email: JHKLawFirm@aol.com
***PRACTICE AREAS: Commercial Law; Products Liability; Antitrust.**
Commercial Law, Products Liability and Antitrust.
Edgartown, Massachusetts Office: 230 Upper Main Street. P.O. Box, 1288. 02539-1288. Telephone: 508-627-7305. Fax: 508-627-7007. E-Mail: PEVKY@aol.com; JHKLawFirm@aol.com.
See Professional Biographies, WASHINGTON, DISTRICT OF COLUMBIA

Kelley, James J., II ....'47 '74 C.1126 B.A. L.902 J.D. [Morgan,L.&B.]
Kelley, Jodie L. ....'64 '93 C.645 B.S.S. L.309 J.D. [Jenner&B.]
*PRACTICE AREAS: Communications; Media; Civil Litigation; Appellate Practice.
Kelley, Katherine V. ....'55 '79 C.494 B.A. L.276 J.D. [🄰 Arent F.K.P.&K.]
*PRACTICE AREAS: Municipal Finance; Legislative Practice.
Kelley, Lara Chapman '69 '99
C.896 B.S. L.273 J.D. [🄰 Finnegan,H.F.G.&D.] (See Pat. Sect.)
*PRACTICE AREAS: Biotechnology Patent Law; Chemical Patent Law.
Kelley, Mercedes K. '73 '99 C.210 B.M. L.477 J.D.
(adm. in VA; not adm. in DC) [🄰 Collier S.S.]
*PRACTICE AREAS: Advertising Law; Marketing Law; Consumer Protection; Internet Law; Electronic Commerce.
Kelley, O'Brien '68 '95 C.473 B.A. L.608 J.D.
(adm. in NY; not adm. in DC) 1201 New York Ave., N.W.
Kelley, Richard D. '— '00 C.1369 B.A. L.273 J.D.
(adm. in VA; not adm. in DC) [🄰 Katten M.Z.]
*PRACTICE AREAS: Litigation.
Kelley, Shelby J. ....'— '99 C&L.276 B.A., J.D. [🄰 Bracewell&P.]
*PRACTICE AREAS: Litigation.
Kelley, Timothy J. ....'52 '79 C.197 B.A. L.930 J.D. [Dow,L.&A.]
Kelley, William K. '63 '90 C.436 B.A. L.309 J.D.
(adm. in OH; not adm. in DC) 1722 Eye St., N.W.

Kelley Drye & Warren LLP, (AV)
1200 19th Street, N.W., Suite 500, 20036 ⊙
Telephone: 202-955-9600 Fax: (202) 955-9792
Email: info@kelleydrye.com URL: http://www.kelleydrye.com
Partners: Robert J. Aamoth (Resident); Steven A. Augustino; Jonathan E. Canis; Thomas C. Jackson (Resident); Douglas P. Lobel (Resident); Brad E. Mutschelknaus (Resident); Aileen A. Pisciotta (Resident); J. Barton Seitz; Judith St. Ledger-Roty (Resident); Daniel M. Steinway (Resident); David L. Vaughan (Resident); Edward A. Yorkgitis, Jr. (Resident). Resident Of Counsel: James J. Freeman; Genevieve Morelli; Philip V. Permut (Resident). Resident Special Counsel: Jeffrey S. Longsworth; Enrico C. Soriano; Joseph F. Yenouskas. Senior Counsel: Ronald J. Jarvis. Resident Associates: Leila M. Baheri (Not admitted in DC); Katherine Elizabeth Barker (Not admitted in DC); John M. Brendel; Ross A. Buntrock; Adam Augustine Carter; Melissa S. Conway; Todd D. Daubert; James W. Deacon II (Not admitted in DC); Andrew M. Dunnaville (Not admitted in DC); Erin Weber Emmott; Michael C. Engel (Not admitted in DC); Michael J. Francesconi; Brett Heather Freedson; John J. Heitmann; Eric D. Jenkins (Not admitted in DC); Stephanie A. Joyce; Jennifer Myers Kashatus (Not admitted in DC); David C. Kirschner; Andrew M. Klein (Not admitted in DC); David A. Konuch; Carl F. Lettow; Nicholaus G. Leverett; Michael P. McGovern; Elizabeth S. Nicholas (Not admitted in DC); M. Nicole Oden; Neil Francis O'Donnell (Not admitted in DC); Aspasia Paroutsas (Not admitted in

(This Listing Continued)

Kelley Drye & Warren LLP (Continued)

DC); Troy D. Reynolds; Tristan B.L. Siegel; Randall W. Sifers; Erin R. Swansiger; David A. Vogel; Heather M. Wilson; Joseph D. Wilson, III; Darius B. Withers (Not admitted in DC).
Litigation, Commercial Litigation, Emerging Growth Companies, Employee Benefits, Executive Compensation, Environmental Law, Financial Institutions, Health Care, Immigration, Insurance, Intellectual Property, Technology Litigation, International Law, Labor and Employment Law, Mergers and Acquisitions, Private Clients, Products Liability, Project Finance, Infrastructure, Real Estate Law, Restructuring, Creditors Rights, Securities, Securities Industry, Securities Litigation, Telecommunications, Trade Regulation, Antitrust, White Collar Crime, Corporate Investigations, Year 2000, Y2K.
New York, N.Y. Office: 101 Park Avenue. Telephone: 212-808-7800. Fax: (212) 808-7897.
Los Angeles, California Office: 777 South Figueroa Street, Suite 2700. Telephone: 213-689-1300. Fax: (213) 688-8150.
Stamford, Connecticut Office: Two Stamford Plaza, 281 Tresser Boulevard. Telephone: 203-324-1400. Fax: (203) 327-2669; (203) 964-3188.
Parsippany, New Jersey Office: 5 Sylvan Way. Telephone: 973-539-0099. Fax: (973) 539-3167.
Chicago, Illinois Office: 303 West Madison Street, Suite 1400. Telephone: 312-346-6350. Fax: (312) 346-8982.
Vienna, Virginia Office: 8000 Towers Crescent Drive, Suite 1200. Telephone: 703-918-2300. Fax: 703-918-2450.
Brussels, Belgium Office: 106 Avenue Louise, 1050. Telephone: (011) (32-2) 646-1110. Fax: (011) (32-2) 640-0589.
Hong Kong Office: Suite 1602, Fairmont House, 8 Cotton Tree Drive. Telephone: (011) (852) 2869-0821. Fax: (011) (852) 2869-0049.
Affiliated Offices:
Jakarta, Indonesia: Soebagjo, Jatim, Djarot, Plaza DM, 17th Floor, Jalan Jend. Sudirman Kav. 25, Jakarta 12920, Indonesia. Telephone: (011) (62-21) 5229765. Fax: (011) (62-21) 5229752.
Tokyo, Japan: Yumoto & Ota, Kioi Royal Heights, 3-29, Kioi-Cho, Chiyoda-Ku, Tokyo 102, Japan. Telephone: (011) (81-3) 3234-2441. Fax: (011) (81-3) 3262-2729.
Manila, Philippines: Oporto Reyes Suarez & Associates, 2111 BSA Suites, 103 C. Palanca Street, Legaspi Village, Makati City, Metro Manila. Telephone: (011) (63-2) 888-6951; 888-6953. Fax: (011) (63-2) 888-6945. E-Mail: oporto@pacific.net.ph.
Bangkok, Thailand: Dej-Udom & Associates, Charn Issara Tower, 9th Floor, 942/142-3 Rama IV Road, Bangkok 10500 Thailand. Telephone: (011) (66-2) 233-0055. Fax: (011) (66-2) 236-6681. E-Mail: dejudom@loxinfo.co.th.
Mumbai (Bombay) India: Wakhariya & Wakhariya, 41 Bajaj Bhawan, 226 Nariman Point, Mumbai 400021. Telephone: (91-22) 281-0336; 91-22-285-9820. Fax: (91-22) 281-0337. E-Mail: shabbirw@counsellor.com.
See Professional Biographies, WASHINGTON, DISTRICT OF COLUMBIA

Kellis, Steven E. ....'65 '92 C.105 B.A. L.884 J.D. [S.E.Kellis]
*PRACTICE AREAS: Criminal Defense; Driving While Intoxicated; Driving Under the Influence; Vehicular Homicide; Drivers License Suspension.

Kellis, Steven E., P.C.
1411 K Street N.W., Suite 602, 20005
Telephone: 202-347-2000 Fax: 202-783-7114 URL: http://www.kellislaw.com
Email: kellislaw@mindspring.com URL: http://www.lawyers.com/kellislaw
New address effective October 30, 2001: 105 Lenox Way, Atlanta, Georgia, 30324.
Steven E. Kellis.
Criminal Defense, including DWI/DUI, Driving While Intoxicated, Driving While Under the Influence, Vehicular Homicide, Drivers License Suspension, Drug Crimes, Traffic Violations.
See Professional Biographies, WASHINGTON, DISTRICT OF COLUMBIA

Kellison, J. Bruce, (AV) .... '22 '48 C.692 B.A. L.273 J.D. 910 17th St., N.W.
Kellman, Harvey '62 '96 C.331 B.A. L.1019 J.D.
(adm. in NY; not adm. in DC) [🄰 Piper M.R.&W.]
*PRACTICE AREAS: Broadcasting; Internet; Wireless Communications; Multichannel Video; Information Technology.
Kellner, Leon B., (AV) .... '45 '72 C.1044 B.A. L.309 J.D. [Dickstein S.M.&O.]
*PRACTICE AREAS: Civil Litigation; Insurance Coverage Litigation.
Kellogg, Michael K., (AV) ....'54 '83 C.813 A.B. L.309 J.D. [Kellogg,H.H.T.&E.]
*PRACTICE AREAS: Telecommunications; Supreme Court and Appellate Litigation.
Kellogg, Philip L., (AV) ....'40 '68 C.339 B.S. L.575 J.D. [Kellogg,W.&L.]
*PRACTICE AREAS: Civil Litigation; Criminal; Corporate Law; Commercial Real Estate; Tax Law.

Kellogg, Huber, Hansen, Todd & Evans, P.L.L.C., (AV)
Sumner Square, 1615 M Street, N.W. Suite 400, 20036-3209
Telephone: 202-326-7900 Fax: 202-326-7999
Michael K. Kellogg; Peter W. Huber; Mark C. Hansen; K. Chris Todd; Mark L. Evans; Steven F. Benz; Neil M. Gorsuch; Geoffrey M. Klineberg; Reid M. Figel; Henk Brands; Sean A. Lev; Evan T. Leo; Antonia M. Apps; Michael J. Guzman; Aaron M. Panner; David E. Ross; Silvija A. Strikis; William J. Conyngham, Jr.; David C. Frederick;—Scott H. Angstreich; Scott K. Attaway; Joseph Solomon Hall (Not admitted in DC); Kevin B. Huff; Joseph K. Leahy; John H. Longwell; Teal E. Luthy; Jide O. Nzelibe; Eugene M. Paige (Not admitted in DC); John Christopher Rozendaal; Eli C. Schulman; David L. Schwarz; Colin S. Stretch; Leo R. Tsao. Of Counsel: Richard H. Stern; Shanlon Wu.
Telecommunications and Litigation.
See Professional Biographies, WASHINGTON, DISTRICT OF COLUMBIA

Kellogg, Saccoccia & Sigelman, (BV)
1742 N Street, N.W., 20036 ⊙
Mailing Address: P.O. Box 941668, Atlanta, Georgia 31141-0668
Telephone: 202-223-9880 Fax: 202-223-9449 URL: http://www.ksslawfirm.com
Email: webmaster@ksslawfirm.com
Members of Firm: Daniel W. Sigelman.
Personal Injury, Products Liability and Medical Malpractice.
Reference: Trust Company Bank.
Atlanta, Georgia Office: P.O. Box 941668, 31141-0668. Telephone: 770-220-2465. Telecopier: 770-220-2762.
See Professional Biographies, WASHINGTON, DISTRICT OF COLUMBIA

Kellogg, Williams & Lyons, (AV)
1275 K Street, N.W., 20005 ⊙
Telephone: 202-898-0722 Telecopier: 202-371-1257
Email: kwl@elinkisp.com
Members of Firm: Edwin A. Williams; Philip L. Kellogg; James L. Lyons.
Civil and Criminal Trial and Appellate Practice before all Courts and Agencies. Corporate, International Law, Tax Crimes, Commercial Real Estate Transactions.
Vienna, Virginia Office: 246 Maple Avenue, East. Telephone: 703-938-4875. Telecopier: 703-938-4877.
See Professional Biographies, WASHINGTON, DISTRICT OF COLUMBIA

Kelly, Biruta P. ....'53 '81 C.94 B.A. L.273 J.D. [Scribner,H.&T.]
Kelly, Bradley L., (AV) ....'53 '79 C&L.846 B.A., J.D. [Mintz,L.C.F.G.&P.]
*PRACTICE AREAS: Health Care; Litigation; White Collar.
Kelly, Brian S. '68 '93 C.280 B.B.A. L.228 J.D.
(adm. in NC; not adm. in DC) [Fenwick&W.]
*PRACTICE AREAS: Licensing and Online Commerce; Complex Transactions; Copyright Protection; Trade Secret Protection.
Kelly, Christopher ....'61 '89 C.205 B.A. L.1338 J.D. [🄲 Wiley R.&F.]
Kelly, Christopher J. '— '83 C.309 A.B. L.178 J.D.
(adm. in IL; not adm. in DC) [🄲 Kaye S.]
Kelly, David M., (AV) '57 '83
C.665 B.S. L.229 J.D. [Finnegan,H.F.G.&D.] (See Pat. Sect.)
*PRACTICE AREAS: Trademark Litigation; Trademark Prosecution; Domain Names; Trade Dress.
Kelly, Deborah P., (AV) ....'52 '88 C.882 B.S. L.904 J.D. [Dickstein S.M.&O.]
*PRACTICE AREAS: Employment Litigation; Corporate Counseling; Civil Litigation.
Kelly, Frank X., (AV) ....'48 '75 C&L.276 A.B., J.D. [Gallagher,B.&M.]
*PRACTICE AREAS: Energy Regulation; Natural Gas; Natural Gas Pipelines; Gas Utilities; Public Utility Rates.

Kelly, Harry J., (BV) .... '56 '82 C.951 B.A. L.94 J.D. [Nixon P.]
*PRACTICE AREAS: Bankruptcy; Environmental Law; Litigation; Housing.
Kelly, James D. .... '61 '89 C.1107 B.A. L.262 J.D. [Dickstein S.M.&O.]
*PRACTICE AREAS: Commercial Transactions; Real Estate; Banking and Financial Institutions.
Kelly, Jean M. .... '67 '96 C.602 B.A. L.262 J.D. [Ⓐ O'Donoghue&O.]
*PRACTICE AREAS: Labor and Employment Law; Employee Benefits.
Kelly, John G. .... '69 '95 C.886 B.S. L.446 J.D. [Ⓐ Holland&K.]
*PRACTICE AREAS: Real Estate; Real Estate Development; Real Estate Finance; Commercial Leasing.
Kelly, John M. '52 '89 C.906 B.S. L.8 J.D.
(adm. in MN; not adm. in DC) [Ⓒ Long A.&N.]
*PRACTICE AREAS: Intellectual Property.
Kelly, Kathleen P. '63 '92 C.696 B.A. L.128 J.D.
[Ⓐ O'Melveny&M.] (⊙Mc Lean, VA)
*PRACTICE AREAS: Employment Litigation; Employment Law; Labor Law.
Kelly, Kathryn ....'53 '78 C.108 B.A. L.602 J.D. Assoc. Prof. of Law, Catholic Univ.
Kelly, Kimberly A. '68 '94
C.30 B.A. L.659 J.D. Asst. Gen. Coun., Black Enter. Telev., Inc.
*RESPONSIBILITIES: Affiliate Sales Agreements; Regulatory Affairs; Lobbying; Corporate External Affairs.
Kelly, Mary Jo .... '55 '84 C.575 B.A. L.945 J.D. [Nixon P.]
*PRACTICE AREAS: Public Finance; Securities.
Kelly, Michael John, (AV) '37 '67 C.674 B.A. L.976 LL.B.
(adm. in MD; not adm. in DC) V.P., Georgetown Univ.
Kelly, Michael P. ....'74 '00 C.602 B.A. L.228 J.D. [Ⓐ Skadden,A.S.M.&F.]
Kelly, Michael S. ....'48 '75 C.276 B.A. L.273 J.D. [Morgan,L.&B.]
Kelly, Nevin J. .... '59 '84 C.674 A.B. L.813 J.D. [Hogan&H.]
*PRACTICE AREAS: Commercial Lending; Commercial Real Estate; International Real Estate; International Project Finance; Polish Commercial Transactions.
Kelly, Randall .... '70 '96 C.502 B.A. L.910 J.D. [Ⓐ Nixon P.]
*PRACTICE AREAS: Affordable Housing; Mortgage Banking; Real Estate.
Kelly, Raymond W. '41 '72 C.433 B.A. L.724 J.D.
(adm. in NY; not adm. in DC) 801 Pennsylvania Ave. N.W.
Kelly, Robert B., (AV) .... '56 '81 C&L.228 A.B., J.D. [Squire,S.&D.]
Kelly, Robert N. '52 '77 C.674 B.S.E. L.472 J.D.
[Jackson&C.] (⊙Balt., Rockville, MD)
Kelly, Susan N., (AV) .... '55 '80 C.502 A.B. L.273 J.D. [Miller,B.&O.]
*PRACTICE AREAS: Energy Law.
Kelly, Tara R. ....'— '01 C.945 B.A. L.94 J.D. [Ⓐ Morgan,L.&B.]
Kelly, Thomas J., Jr., (AV) .... '53 '81 C.397 B.S. L.128 J.D. [Venable,A.B.H.&C.]
*PRACTICE AREAS: Environmental Crimes Law; White Collar Criminal Law.
Kelly, Timothy J. .... '69 '98 C.228 A.B. L.276 J.D. [Ⓐ Arnold&P.]
*PRACTICE AREAS: Litigation.
Kelly, William C., Jr., (AV) ....'— '72 C.309 A.B. L.976 J.D. [Latham&W.]
*PRACTICE AREAS: Government; Historic Preservation; Housing Law; Nonprofit and Charitable Organizations; Real Estate.
Kelly, William G., Jr., (AV) ....'44 '71 C.276 A.B. L.597 J.D. [Kelly&W.]
*PRACTICE AREAS: Pollution; Endangered Species; Wetlands Regulation; National Environmental Policy Act; Federal Regulatory Law.
Kelly-Kobayashi, Eleanore '44 '80 C.1025 B.A. L.564 J.D.
(adm. in NY; not adm. in DC) [Ⓐ Rode&Q.] (⊙New York, NY)

Kelly & Weaver, A Professional Corporation, (AV)
Suite 700, 11 Dupont Circle, 20036
Telephone: 202-797-7100 Fax: 202-939-6969
Email: weaver@kellyweaver.com URL: http://www.lawyers.com/kelly&weaver
William G. Kelly, Jr.; Robert C. Weaver.
Environmental Regulation, Federal Grants, Federal Legislative Practice.
See Professional Biographies, WASHINGTON, DISTRICT OF COLUMBIA

Kelner, Robert K. ....'66 '98 C.674 A.B. L.893 J.D. [Ⓐ Covington&B.]
*PRACTICE AREAS: White Collar Crime; Election Law.
Kelner, Rona C. ....'71 '99 C.813 A.B. L.893 J.D. [Ⓐ Morgan,L.&B.]
Kelso, C. Kevin '54 '80 C.339 B.A. L.309 J.D.
(adm. in CA; not adm. in DC) [Fenwick&W.]
*PRACTICE AREAS: Corporate Securities; Mergers and Acquisitions.
Kelton, Erika Armitage ....'55 '87 C.1169 B.A. L.1066 J.D. [Phillips&C.]
Kemnitz, D'Arcy '63 '99 C.966 B.A. L.300 J.D.
(adm. in MD; not adm. in DC) Exec. Dir., Wildlife Advocacy Proj.‡
Kemp, Bernard W. .... '19 '49 C.329 L.1014 LL.B. 1710 9th St., N.W.
Kemp, J. Hovey, (AV) .... '53 '80 C.309 A.B. L.276 J.D. [Hogan&H.]
*PRACTICE AREAS: Corporate Law; Mergers and Acquisitions; Venture Capital Transactions.
Kemper, Ann-Kelley ....'67 '95 C.197 B.A. L.569 J.D. [Ⓐ Covington&B.]
*PRACTICE AREAS: Biotechnology; Biomedical Technology; Regulatory; Food and Drug Regulation; Privacy Law.
Kempler, Cecelia '40 '80 C.563 B.A. L.564 J.D.
[LeBoeuf,L.G.&M.] (⊙New York, NY)
*PRACTICE AREAS: Insurance Company Reorganization; Insurance Insolvencies; Market Conduct.
Kempler, David I., (AV) ....'42 '66 C.659 B.S. L.184 J.D. [Silverstein&M.]
*PRACTICE AREAS: Taxation; Business Planning; Exempt Organizations; Mergers and Acquisitions.
Kempner, Jonathan L. '51 '76
C.477 B.A. L.813 J.D. Pres., National Multi Housing Council
Kendall, David E., (AV) .... '44 '74 C.894 B.A. L.976 J.D. [Williams&C.]
Kendall, Douglas T. '64 '92 C&L.893 B.A., J.D.
Exec. Dir., Community Rights Counsel
Kendall, Joseph E. ....'57 '84 C.976 B.A. L.309 J.D. [Shaw P.]
*PRACTICE AREAS: Technology Transactions; Outsourcing Transactions; Software Development; Licensing Transactions; Systems Integration Transactions.

Kendall, Robert, Jr., Law Office of '47 '73 C.999 B.S. L.325 J.D.
1815 Pennsylvania Avenue, NW Suite 500, 20006
Telephone: 202-457-0516 Fax: 202-457-0537
Email: kendlawoffice@aol.com URL: http://www.kendalllawoffice.com
***PRACTICE AREAS: Immigration and Naturalization; Citizenship; Business Immigration; Employment Immigration; Family Immigration Law.**
Immigration and Citizenship Law.
See Professional Biographies, WASHINGTON, DISTRICT OF COLUMBIA

Kendrick, Cynthia ....'66 '91 C.484 B.A. L.309 J.D. [Spriggs&H.]
*PRACTICE AREAS: Products Liability; Toxic Torts; Litigation; Drug and Medical Device Defense.
Kendrick, Kim .... '55 '81 C.95 A.B. L.665 J.D. State Housing Auth.
Kendrick, Martha M. ....'49 '85 C.93 B.A. L.276 J.D. [Patton B.]
Kenealy, David J. .... '67 '95 C.150 B.S.M.E. L.904 J.D. [Ⓐ Morgan,L.&B.] (Pat.)
Kenefick, Paul William .... '69 '96 C&L.128 B.A., J.D. Sr. Coun., Alcatel USA
Kenehan, Edward F., Jr., (BV) '50 '79
C.277 B.S. L.30 J.D. [Sughrue M.] (See Pat. Sect.)
*PRACTICE AREAS: Intellectual Property.
Keniry, Shannon P. '70 '97 C.112 B.A. L.30 J.D.
(adm. in MD; not adm. in DC) [Ⓐ Finkelstein,T.&L.]
Keniston, Patrick J. ....'64 '91 C.860 B.A. L.208 J.D. 1225 Connecticut Ave., N.W.
Kenkel, John B., (AV) ....'23 '52 C.165 A.B. L.273 J.D. [Kenkel&Assoc.]
Kenkel, John J., (BV) .... '50 '80 C.276 B.A. L.1209 J.D. [Ⓒ deKieffer&H.]
*PRACTICE AREAS: International Trade; International Trade Regulation.
Kenkel and Associates, (AV) .... 1901 L St., N.W.

Kennedy, Altomease R., (AV) .... '49 '76 C.289 B.A. L.276 J.D. [Ⓒ Ashcraft&G.]
*PRACTICE AREAS: False Claims Act; Products Liability; Medical Malpractice.
Kennedy, Angela Sadie-Edith '— '95 C.674 B.A. L.329 J.D.
(adm. in MD; not adm. in DC) C.C. Off. of People's Counsel
Kennedy, Brian, (BV) '64 '91 C.350 B.A. L.221 J.D.
(adm. in IA; not adm. in DC) [Brown,W.G.G.B.&S.]
Kennedy, Charles H. ......'46 '76 C.259 B.A. L.145 J.D. [Morrison&F.] (⊙Mc Lean, VA)
*PRACTICE AREAS: Telecommunications; Internet Law.
Kennedy, Christopher P., (BV) ....'63 '89 C.446 B.S. L.128 J.D. [Schochor,F.&S.] ⊙
*PRACTICE AREAS: Medical Malpractice Law; Products Liability Law; Civil Litigation.
Kennedy, Colleen Mary, (AV) .... '55 '81 C.174 B.A. L.1162 J.D. Asst. U.S. Atty.
Kennedy, Ellen Swennes .... '72 '97 C.228 B.A. L.893 J.D. [Ⓐ Hogan&H.]
*PRACTICE AREAS: Litigation.
Kennedy, John B. ....'72 '97 C.674 A.B. L.945 J.D. [Ⓐ Jones,D.R.&P.]
Kennedy, Joseph B. .... '22 '48 C&L.273 A.B., J.D. Fed. Admn. Law J.‡
Kennedy, Kevin C. '51 '77 C.477 B.A. L.912 J.D.
(adm. in HI; not adm. in DC) [Ⓒ deKieffer&H.] (⊙East Lansing, MI)
Kennedy, Laura Page ....'56 '84 C.1307 B.A. L.569 J.D. [Ⓒ Bredhoff&K.]
Kennedy, Mary C., (AV) .... '58 '84 C.821 B.A. L.569 J.D. [Ⓒ Finnegan,H.F.G.&D.]
*PRACTICE AREAS: Trial Advocacy; Criminal Defense.
Kennedy, Paul J., (AV) .... '59 '85 C.165 B.A. L.902 J.D. [Littler M.]
*PRACTICE AREAS: Labor and Employment.
Kennedy, Robert M., Jr. ....'72 '97 C.93 B.A. L.893 J.D. [Ⓐ Hughes H.&R.]
*PRACTICE AREAS: Commercial Litigation.
Kennedy, William F. '18 '43 C&L.262 B.A., LL.B.
(adm. in NY; not adm. in DC) 1900 K St., N.W.‡
Kennelly, Thomas A., (AV) ....'30 '55 C.755 B.A. L.1268 LL.B. 4817 "V" St., NW‡
Kenney, Robert J., Jr., (AV) .... '48 '72 C&L.309 A.B., J.D. [Hogan&H.]
*PRACTICE AREAS: Computer Software Law; Information Technology Contracts; Federal Grants; Government Contract Fraud; Government Procurement.
Kenniston, Kristi A. ....'72 '97 C.1051 B.A. L.309 J.D. 2950 Van Ness, N.W., #416

Kenny Nachwalter Seymour Arnold Critchlow & Spector, Professional Association, (AV) BR
1201 Pennsylvania Avenue, Suite 300, 20004 ⊙
Telephone: 305-373-1000 Facsimile: 305-372-1861
Email: admin@knsacs.com URL: http://www.knsacs.com
William J. Blechman; Richard Alan Arnold (Not admitted in DC).
Complex Litigation, Antitrust Litigation, Securities Litigation, Professional Liability Litigation. Trials in all Courts.
Representative Clients: Albertson's, Inc.; American Bankers Insurance Group; Cartier, Inc.; Ethan Allen, Inc.; Federated Department Stores, Inc.; The Florida Bar; GTE Directories Corp.; Siemens Credit Corp.; GTE Florida; Columbia HCA.
Rogersville, Tennessee Office: 107 East Main Street, Suite 301. Telephone: 423-272-5300. Facsimile: 423-272-4961.
Miami, Florida Office: 1100 Miami Center, 201 South Biscayne Boulevard, 33131-4327. Telephone: 305-373-1000. Facsimile: 305-372-1861.
See Professional Biographies, WASHINGTON, DISTRICT OF COLUMBIA

Kent, Alan H. ....'46 '69 C&L.94 B.S.B.A., J.D. [Ⓒ Tighe P.A.T.]
*PRACTICE AREAS: Construction Law; Government Contracts; Commercial Litigation; Alternative Dispute Resolution.
Kent, M. Elizabeth, (BV) ....'43 '78 C.881 A.B. L.276 J.D. 601 Indiana Ave., N.W.
Kentoff, David R., (AV) .... '37 '61 C&L.597 B.S.L., LL.B. [Arnold&P.]
*PRACTICE AREAS: Products Liability; Litigation.
Kentoff, Michael C. .... '64 '96 C.30 B.A. L.904 J.D. [Ⓐ Jorden B.]
*PRACTICE AREAS: Commercial Litigation; Insurance Law; Products Liability.
Kentz, Andrew W. .... '56 '83 C&L.276 A.B., J.D. [Dewey B.]
*PRACTICE AREAS: Corporate Taxation; International Trade.
Kenworthy, Kevin L., (AV) ....'— '85 C.623 B.B.A. L.802 J.D. [Miller&C.]
*PRACTICE AREAS: Taxation; Federal Income Tax; Federal Tax Controversies; Tax Litigation; Mineral Taxation.
Kenworthy, William E., (AV) .... '33 '57 C&L.208 B.S., LL.B. 1920 N St Nw # 420

Kenyon & Kenyon, (AV) BR
1500 K Street, N.W., Suite 700, 20005 ⊙
Telephone: 202-220-4200 Fax: (202) 220-4201, Groups II & III
Resident Partners: John C. Altmiller; Edward T. Colbert; William K. Wells, Jr.; Brian S. Mudge; John W. Bateman; Douglas E. Ringel (Not admitted in DC). Resident Counsel: Michael N. Zachary. Resident Associates: Mark M. Supko; Judith L. Toffenetti; C. Kyle Musgrove; Gary S. Morris; William M. Merone; John McGroarty; Timothy M. Devlin; John R. Hutchins; Robert L. Hails, Jr.; Karen L. Feisthamel; Teresa A. Lavenue (Not admitted in DC); Bradley J. Meier; Kristina M. Castellano; Mark H. Neblett; Fred Grasso; Clint A. Gerdine (Not admitted in DC); Kenneth R. Corsello; Dan Salehi; R. Paul Zeineddin; Michael M. Shen (Not admitted in DC); T. Cy Walker; Barry S. Goldsmith; David J. Zibelli (Not admitted in DC); Ronald E. Prass, Jr.; Jennifer L. King; Sumeet Magoon (Not admitted in DC); Ronald L. Sigworth; Michael I. Angert; Julie E. Stein (Not admitted in DC); Zeba T. Ali (Not admitted in DC); Amy L. Hulina (Not admitted in DC); Michael A. Siem (Not admitted in DC); Cedric Chia Yang Tan; William E. Curry (Not admitted in DC); Thu A. Dang (Not admitted in DC); B. Delano Jordan; Laleh Jalali; David R. Schaffer (Not admitted in DC); W. David Wallace.
Intellectual Property Practice. Patents, Trademarks, Copyrights, Trade Secrets, Unfair Competition, Computer Law, Licensing and related Trade Regulation, Antitrust and International Trade Matters. Sports Marketing, Entertainment Law, Trials, Appeals and Arbitration.
New York, N.Y. Office: One Broadway, 10004. Telephone: 212-425-7200. Fax: (212) 425-5288.
Munich, Germany Office: Steinsdorfstr. 10, 80538 Munich. Telephone: 49 89 211 134-30. Fax: 49 89 21 134-49.
San Jose, California Office: Riverpark Towers, Suite 600, 333 West San Carlos Street, 95110. Telephone: 408-975-7500. Fax: (408) 975-7501.
See Professional Biographies, WASHINGTON, DISTRICT OF COLUMBIA

Keough, Christopher L. .... '64 '91 C.264 B.A. L.273 J.D. [Powers,P.S.&V.]
*PRACTICE AREAS: Health Care Law; Reimbursement; Litigation; Administrative Law.
Kerby, Charles K., III ....'53 '78 C.205 B.A. L.902 J.D. William M. Mercer, Inc.
Kerley-Schwartz, Karen '67 '92
C.893 B.A. L.273 J.D. Assoc. Gen. Coun., Natl. Geographic Soc.
*RESPONSIBILITIES: Litigation; Intellectual Property; Contracts.
Kerman, Leslie J. '58 '83 C.1036 B.A. L.276 J.D.
(adm. in MA; not adm. in DC) 1227 25th St., N.W.
Kern, Christopher O. ....'47 '81 C.197 B.A. L.273 J.D. Voice of America
Kern, John W., (AV) ....'57 '87 C.674 B.A. L.112 J.D. [Janis,S.&W.]
*PRACTICE AREAS: White Collar Criminal Defense.
Kern, John W., III ....'28 '53 C.674 B.A. L.309 LL.B. D.C. Ct. of Appls. Sr. J.
Kernan, Kevin A. .... '67 '95 C.1044 B.S. L.1338 J.D. [Ⓐ O'Brien,B.M.&S.]
*PRACTICE AREAS: Civil Litigation; Nonprofit Organizations Law.
Kernan, William Kerry .... '46 '96 5533 Hawthorne Pl., N.W.
Kerner, Herbert V. .... '69 '94 C.1228 B.A. L.425 J.D. [Ⓐ Hunton&W.] (Pat.)
*PRACTICE AREAS: Patent Prosecution; Licensing; Litigation.
Kerney, Carey G.B. ....'69 '98 C.282 B.A. L.128 J.D. [Ⓐ Jones,D.R.&P.]
Kerns, Alice Fleury '68 '97 C.893 B.A. L.128 J.D.
(adm. in MD; not adm. in DC) Law Clk., U.S. Ct. of Vet. App.
Kerns, Janis Fonda '63 '94 C.896 B.A. L.904 J.D.
(adm. in MD; not adm. in DC) [Ⓐ Morrison&F.]
*PRACTICE AREAS: Business; Investment Management; Securities.
Kerns, Michael W. .... '63 '89 C&L.845 B.A., J.D. 1025 Thomas Jefferson St., N.W.
Kerpelman, Jason Abraham .... '59 '98 C.861 B.S.E. L.64 J.D. 601 Indiana Ave., N.W.

Kerr, Don M. '36 '65 C.845 B.S.B.A. L.273 LL.B.
(adm. in DE; not adm. in DC; See Pat. Sect.) [Ⓒ Rothwell,F.E.&M.]
*PRACTICE AREAS: Intellectual Property.
Kerr, Karen A. . . . . '51 '89 C&L.446 B.A., J.D. [Ⓐ Cleary,G.S.&H.]
Kerrigan, Daniel J. '51 '78 C.276 B.S.F.S. L.724 J.D.
(adm. in CT; not adm. in DC) KGI, Inc.
Kerrigan, Kathleen M. . . . . '64 '91 C.93 B.S. L.602 J.D. [Ⓒ Baker&H.]
*PRACTICE AREAS: Federal Taxation; Health Law.
Kerrine, T. Michael '50 '75 C.1044 B.A. L.178 J.D.
Sr. Assoc. Gen. Coun., Tort Litig., National Railroad Passenger Corp. (Amtrak)
Kersey, B. Franklin . . . . '42 '73 C.832 B.S. L.329 J.D. 800 4th St., S.W.
Kersey, Laura Lynn '68 '94 C.838 B.A. L.273 J.D.
(adm. in MD; not adm. in DC) Coun., American Insurance Association
*RESPONSIBILITIES: Legislative/Regulatory; Litigation; Property Insurance; Environmental Issues.
Kershow, Michael R., (AV) . . . . '54 '81 C.165 B.A. L.276 J.D. [Ⓒ Collier S.S.]
*PRACTICE AREAS: International Trade; Customs Law; Food and Drug Regulation.
Kersting, Andrew S. . . . . '62 '87 C.800 B.A. L.174 J.D. [Ⓒ Dickstein S.M.&O.]
*PRACTICE AREAS: Communications Law.
Kertgate, Amy '67 '96 C.966 B.A. L.845 J.D.
(adm. in TX; not adm. in DC) [Ⓒ Fulbright&J.]
Kerxton, Jill K. . . . . '62 '87 C.896 B.S. L.180 J.D. [Piper M.R.&W.]
*PRACTICE AREAS: Corporate; Taxation; Insurance Law.
Kessler, Edward J., (AV) '43 '70
C&L.273 B.S.E.E., J.D. [Sterne,K.G.&F.] (See Pat. Sect.)
*PRACTICE AREAS: Intellectual Property Law.
Kessler, Judd L., (AV) . . . . '38 '63 C.604 A.B. L.309 LL.B. [Porter W.M.&A.]
*PRACTICE AREAS: International Business Transactions; Project Finance; Complex Commercial and International Arbitration; Public Contracting.
Kessler, Lorence L. . . . . '46 '74 C.216 A.B. L.273 J.D. [Ⓒ McGuiness N.&W.]
*PRACTICE AREAS: Equal Employment Opportunity Law.
Kessler, Michael L., (AV) . . . . '53 '80 C.103 B.A. L.1194 J.D. [Ⓒ Troutman S.]
*PRACTICE AREAS: Energy Law; Regulatory; Finance; Real Estate; Public Finance.
Kessler, Nicholas A. . . . . '74 '99 C.976 B.A. L.893 J.D. [Ⓐ Wiley R.&F.]
Kestenbaum, Janis C. . . . . '— '93 C.228 B.A. L.309 J.D. [Ⓐ Jenner&B.]
*PRACTICE AREAS: Litigation; Antitrust; Telecommunications Appellate.
Kestenbaum, Leon M., (AV) '41 '66 C.563 B.S. L.309 J.D.
(adm. in NY; not adm. in DC) V.P., Fed. Regulatory Affs., Sprint Corp.
Kester, John G., (AV) . . . . '38 '64 C.966 B.A. L.309 LL.B. [Williams&C.]
Ketchum, Richard G. '50 '76 C.860 B.A. L.569 J.D.
Exec. V.P. & Chf. Oper. Offr., National Assn. of Sec. Dealers
Ketchum, Ryan T. . . . . '73 '98 C&L.945 B.S., J.D. [Ⓐ Hunton&W.]
*PRACTICE AREAS: Project Development; Finance; Leasing.
Ketels, John Paul . . . . '44 '76 C.477 B.S. L.1067 J.D. [Clifford C.R.&W.]
Keteltas, Gilbert S., (BV) . . . . '64 '89 C.188 B.S. L.276 J.D. [Ⓒ Howrey S.A.&W.]
Kettaneh, Gillian M. '64 '90 C.054 B.S. L.309 J.D.
(adm. in NY; not adm. in DC) The World Bk.
Keup, Wayne A. . . . . '47 '76 C.800 B.A. L.128 J.D. [Dyer E.&J.]
*PRACTICE AREAS: Government Contracts; Litigation.
Key, Cecil E. . . . . '59 '97 C.1142 B.M. L.276 J.D. [Ⓐ Brobeck,P.&H.]
*PRACTICE AREAS: Intellectual Property.
Key, Glynn D. . . . . '64 '89 C&L.893 B.A., J.D. [Wilmer,C.&P.]
*PRACTICE AREAS: Corporate Law.
Key, Jennifer L. . . . . '64 '91 C.197 B.A. L.273 J.D. [Ⓒ Steptoe&J.]
*PRACTICE AREAS: Energy Regulation.
Key, Joseph Franklin . . . . . . '69 '99 C.884 B.E.E. L.446 J.D. [Ⓐ Fish&R.] (See Pat. Sect.)
*PRACTICE AREAS: Intellectual Property.
Keyes, J. Andrew . . . . '69 '94 C&L.893 B.A., J.D. [Ⓐ Williams&C.]
*PRACTICE AREAS: Civil Practice; Complex Commercial Litigation; Complex Litigation; Contract Litigation; Criminal Defense.
Keyes, Kevin M., (AV) . . . . '56 '83 C.97 B.S. L.930 J.D. [Fried,F.H.S.&J.]
*PRACTICE AREAS: Taxation Law.
Keys, George R., Jr. . . . . '48 '79 C.1070 B.S. L.976 J.D. [Jordan K.&J.]
Keys, John R., Jr. . . . . '48 '75 C.602 A.B. L.276 J.D. [Winston&S.]
*PRACTICE AREAS: Litigation; Antitrust Law; International Law; Government Contracts/Grants.
Keyser, David R. '51 '78 C.309 B.A. L.188 J.D.
Asst. Gen. Coun., Washington Metropolitan Area Transit Authority
*RESPONSIBILITIES: Business Law; Employment and Labor Law.
Keyser, Linda L. '65 '98 C.893 B.S.N. L.1049 J.D.
(adm. in VA; not adm. in DC) Dept. of Vet. Affs., Off. of Gen. Coun.
Khadiri, Gita . . . . '65 '90 C.893 B.A. L.904 J.D. [Ⓒ Silverstein&M.]
*PRACTICE AREAS: Taxation.
Khairallah, Daoud L. . . . . '37 '65 C.999 L.477 J.D. [Ⓒ White&C.]
*PRACTICE AREAS: Project Finance; Privatization; International Settlement of Disputes; International Investment.
Khan, Amina '68 '94 C&L.276 A.B., LL.M.
(adm. in VA; not adm. in DC) Sr. Policy Advisor, U.S Dept of Energy
Khan, Lailah N. '72 '97 C.477 B.A. L.846 J.D.
Asst. Corp. Coun., D.C. Child Supp. Enforce.
Khan-Monroe, Shela Shabana '75 '00 C.1265 B.S. L.912 J.D.
(adm. in MI; not adm. in DC) 500 E. St., S.W.
Kharasch, Robert N., (AV) . . . . '26 '52 C&L.145 Ph.B., J.D. [Ⓒ Galland,K.G.F.&S.]
Khater, Tony S. . . . . '53 '89 C.107 Ph.D. L.276 J.D. 2314 41st St., NW
Khinda, Philip S. . . . . '64 '92 C&L.178 B.A., J.D. [Ⓐ Debevoise&P.]
*PRACTICE AREAS: Securities Litigation and Enforcement Defense; Commercial Litigation; Securities Regulation.
Khoury, Lisa A. '66 '91 C&L.276 B.S.B.A., J.D.
(adm. in MA; not adm. in DC) Legal Resch. Consultant, West Publishing Corp.
Khoury, Paul F. . . . . '61 '86 C.197 B.A. L.273 J.D. [Wiley R.&F.]
*PRACTICE AREAS: Government Contracts; Litigation.
Khuri, Walid A. . . . . '68 '97 C.103 B.A. L.273 J.D. [Ⓐ Fried,F.H.S.&J.]
*PRACTICE AREAS: Corporate Law.
Kibbe, Mark William . . . . '61 '86 C.902 B.A. L.229 J.D. American Petroleum Institute
Kibria, Behnaz L. . . . . '75 '99 C.918 B.A. L.273 J.D. [Ⓐ Hogan&H.]
Kickingbird, Kirke '44 '69
C&L.623 B.A., J.D. [Ⓒ Hobbs,S.D.&W.] (⊙Oklahoma City, OK)
Kidalov, Max V. '75 '99 C&L.790 B.S., J.D.
(adm. in SC; not adm. in DC) 717 Madison Pl., NW
Kidd, Donnie L., Jr. . . . . '74 '99 C.893 B.A. L.692 J.D. [Ⓐ Squire,S.&D.]
Kiddoo, Jean L., (AV) . . . . '53 '80 C.165 B.A. L.128 J.D. [Swidler B.S.F.]
*PRACTICE AREAS: Telecommunications Law; Communications Common Carrier; FCC Regulation; Cable Communications; Wireless Communications.
Kider, Mitchel H. . . . . '56 '81 C.966 B.A. L.910 J.D. [Weiner B.S.K.]
*PRACTICE AREAS: Litigation; Mortgages; Real Estate Finance; Mortgage Banking; Mergers and Acquisitions.
Kidney, Jonathan A. '60 '00 C.160 B.S.E.E. L.1209 J.D.
(adm. in MD; not adm. in DC; Pat.) [Ⓐ Arent F.K.P.&K.]
Kidney, Michael L., (AV) . . . . '63 '90 C.976 B.A. L.477 J.D. [Hogan&H.]
*PRACTICE AREAS: Civil Litigation; Complex Litigation; Defense Litigation; Federal Civil Litigation; Federal Litigation.

Kiechel, Doane F., III, (BV) . . . . '58 '82 C.178 B.A. L.309 J.D. [Morrison&F.]
*PRACTICE AREAS: PCS and Wireless Communications; Transactional and Contract Work; Financing Law; Real Estate Law.
Kiefer, David W. '73 '98 C.390 B.A. L.273 J.D.
(adm. in NJ; not adm. in DC) [Ⓐ Shaw P.]
Kiefer, Kimberly B. . . . . '70 '96 C.966 B.A. L.276 J.D. [Ⓐ Brobeck,P.&H.]
*PRACTICE AREAS: Privacy Law; Internet Law; Digital Signatures; Export Regulation; Intellectual Property.
Kiefer, Peter H., (AV) . . . . '48 '75 C.276 B.S.F.S. L.1209 J.D. [Ogletree,D.N.S.&S.]
*PRACTICE AREAS: Management Labor Law; Employment Law.
Kiely, Bruce F., (AV) . . . . '44 '71 C.174 B.S. L.846 J.D. [Baker B.]
Kiely, Elise P.W. . . . . '68 '94 C.575 B.A. L.245 J.D. [Blumenfeld&C.]
*PRACTICE AREAS: Telecommunications; Antitrust; Legislation.
Kiern, Lawrence I. . . . . '52 '86 C.869 B.S. L.477 J.D. [Ⓒ Winston&S.]
*PRACTICE AREAS: Admiralty and Maritime Law; Environmental; Federal Legislative Practice; Oil Pollution; Regulatory.
Kiernan, David C. . . . . '58 '87 C&L.228 B.A., J.D. [Williams&C.]
*PRACTICE AREAS: Civil Practice; Commercial Litigation; Complex Litigation; Intellectual Property Litigation; Medical Malpractice.
Kiernan, Joseph W., (AV) . . . . '13 '40 C.197 B.A. L.276 LL.B. 5106 Klingle St., N.W.‡
Kiernan, Leslie Berger, (AV) . . . . '59 '86 C.103 A.B. L.276 J.D. [Zuckerman S.]
*PRACTICE AREAS: Criminal Litigation; Civil Litigation; Congressional Investigations; Government Ethics; Election Law.
Kiernan, Paul J., (AV) . . . . '58 '83 C.705 B.A. L.309 J.D. [Holland&K.]
*PRACTICE AREAS: Commercial Litigation; Real Property Litigation; Land Use Disputes; Eminent Domain; Landlord and Tenant Law.
Kiernan, Thomas M. '69 '94 C.886 B.A. L.1209 J.D.
(adm. in VA; not adm. in DC) Sr. Coun., INTELSAT

Kiersh, Steven R., (AV) '54 '80 C.94 B.A. L.1162 J.D.
Market Square, 717 D Street, N.W., Fourth Floor, 20004
Telephone: 202-347-0200 Fax: 202-835-1543
Email: stevenkiersh@prodigy.net URL: http://www.lawyers.com/stevenkiershlaw
Medical Negligence, Product Liability, Civil Litigation and Criminal Defense including Major Felonies, Drug and White Collar Crimes.
See Professional Biographies, WASHINGTON, DISTRICT OF COLUMBIA

Kiesel, Amy B. '65 '99 C.276 B.S.N. L.228 J.D.
(adm. in NY; not adm. in DC) [Ⓐ Shaw P.]
Kikel, David A., (BV) . . . . '46 '78 C.378 A.B. L.1066 J.D. [Hogan&H.]
*PRACTICE AREAS: Intellectual Property Litigation; Products Liability Defense; Drug and Medical Device Defense; Complex Civil Litigation.
Kiklis, Michael L. . . . . '62 '93 C.454 B.S.C.S. L.823 J.D. [Sonnenschein N.&R.] (Pat.)
*PRACTICE AREAS: Computer Technology; Patent Law.
Kilberg, William J., (AV) . . . . '46 '70 C.188 B.S. L.309 J.D. [Gibson,D.&C.]
*PRACTICE AREAS: Labor; Pension Plans and Employee Benefits.
Kilburn, Edwin A., (AV) '33 '58 C.906 B.A. L.569 J.D.
(adm. in NY; not adm. in DC) 2100 M St., N.W.
Kilcarr, Andrew J., (AV) . . . . '32 '60 C.433 B.S. L.276 J.D. [Ⓒ Hogan&H.]
*PRACTICE AREAS: Antitrust Law; Litigation.
Kilcoyne, Michael E. '58 '89 C.712 B.A. L.107 J.D.
(adm. in NY; not adm. in DC) 811 Vermont Ave., N.W., Rm. 653
Kilcullen, Peter M., (AV) . . . . '42 '66 C&L.893 B.A., LL.B. [Bell,B.&L.]
*PRACTICE AREAS: Alternative Dispute Resolution; Computers and Software; Contracts; Construction Law; Federal Procurement.
Kile, Bradford E., (AV) . . . . '43 '71 C.608 B.M.E. L.273 J.D. [Kile G.L.&R.P.] (Pat.)
*PRACTICE AREAS: Intellectual Property Litigation; Licensing and Procurement; Products Liability.
Kile, Mary Michelle . . . . . . '— '95 C.228 B.S.E. L.893 J.D. [Ⓒ Foley&L.] (See Pat. Sect.)
*PRACTICE AREAS: Intellectual Property.

Kile Goekjian Lerner & Reed PLLC, (AV)
1101 Pennsylvania Avenue, N.W., Suite 800, 20004 ⊙
Telephone: 202-639-1260 Fax: 202-639-1298; 202-639-1299 URL: http://www.kglrlaw.com
Email: info@kglrlaw.com URL: http://www.lawyers.com/kglr
Members of Firm: Bradford E. Kile; Samuel V. Goekjian; Charles D. Reed; Robert J. McManus; Karan Singh (Resident, New York, New York Office). Associate: Eduardo M. Silva (Not admitted in the United States). Of Counsel: Roger J. Lerner; Bruce K. Lagerman (Not admitted in DC); Raymond E. Vickery, Jr.
International Trade and Investment, Commercial Transactions, Telecommunications and Information Technology, Corporation and Securities, Banking and Real Estate Law, Patent, Trademark and Copyright Registration, Licensing and Litigation, Environmental and Natural Resources Law, Governmental Affairs and Administrative Law.
New York, New York Office: 729 Seventh Avenue, 14th Floor, 10019. Telephone: 212-921-9713. Fax: 212-921-9778.
See Professional Biographies, WASHINGTON, DISTRICT OF COLUMBIA

Kiley, Edward J., (AV) . . . . '48 '73 C.884 A.B. L.273 J.D. [Grove,J.&C.]
*PRACTICE AREAS: Transportation Safety; Cargo Claims; Hazardous Materials Transportation; Intellectual Property.
Kilgore, Peter G. '46 '73 C.966 B.S. L.879 J.D.
Senior Vice President & General Counsel, National Restaurant Association
Kilgore, Susan Cone, (BV) '63 '89 C.298 B.A. L.861 J.D.
(adm. in TX; not adm. in DC) Coun., Fed. Deposit Ins. Corp.
Killalea, David B. . . . . '63 '88 C.886 B.A. L.893 J.D. [Gilbert H.&R.]
*PRACTICE AREAS: Alternative Dispute Resolution; Commercial Litigation; Insurance Coverage Litigation.
Killefer, Campbell, (AV) . . . . '50 '77 C.813 A.B. L.1065 J.D. [Venable,A.B.H.&C.]
*PRACTICE AREAS: Litigation; Intellectual Property; Arbitration; Alternative Dispute Resolution.
Killelea, Kent L. . . . . '57 '86 C.197 A.B. L.309 J.D. [Ⓒ Jones,D.R.&P.]
Killian, Paul W., (AV) . . . . '47 '72 C.910 B.A. L.273 J.D. [Sutherland A.&B.]
*PRACTICE AREAS: Construction Law; Commercial Law; Contracts; Government Contracts; Litigation.
Killion, Christopher L. . . . . '59 '84 C.376 B.A. L.378 J.D. [Ⓐ Hogan&H.]
*PRACTICE AREAS: Litigation; Franchise and Distribution; Antitrust.
Killion, Frederick J., (AV) . . . . '53 '79 C.742 B.A. L.597 J.D. [Winston&S.]
*PRACTICE AREAS: Energy Law; Litigation.
Killough, Peter K. . . . . '60 '90 C.569 B.A. L.893 J.D. [Ⓐ Carter,L.&M.]
Kilmer, Paul F. . . . . '53 '80 C.351 B.A. L.904 J.D. [Holland&K.]
*PRACTICE AREAS: Copyrights; Trademarks; Unfair Competition; Transactional and Internet Law Issues.
Kilpatrick, Edward F. . . . . '13 '41 C.502 A.B. L.273 LL.B. 3320 P St., N.W.‡

Kilpatrick Stockton LLP, (AV)
607 14th Street, N.W., Suite 900, 20005-2018 ⊙
Telephone: 202-508-5800 Facsimile: 202-508-5858
Email: info@KilpatrickStockton.com URL: http://www.KilpatrickStockton.com
Members of Firm: Thomas K. Bick; Tess J. Ferrera; Ronald A. Feuerstein; Kenneth A. Godlewski; Stanley M. Gorinson; John C. Hardwick, Jr.; Michael A. Hordell; J. Vance Hughes; David R. Levin; Neil I. Levy; George T. Marcou; David Pickle; Ronald L. Raider; Steven J. Sacher; Charles T. Simmons; Mark D. Wincek. Counsel: Elliott H. Levitas; Devon Lee Miller. Associates: John William Ball, Jr.; Dawn-Marie Bey; Elizabeth R. Binder (Not admitted in DC); Amy E. Fortenberry; Amy D. Healy; Laura L. Hoffman; Yoncha L. Kundupoglu; Emmett H. Miller; Christopher A. Ott; Richard T. Peterson (Not admitted in DC); Robert V. Pambianco (Not admitted in DC); Lewis J. Saret; Mark L. Stember (Not admitted in DC).
General Civil, Trial and Appellate Practice. Administrative, Antitrust, Aviation, Banking, Bankruptcy, Charitable Foundations, Construction Law, Copyright, Corporations, Creditors' Rights, Employee Benefits, Entertainment, Equal Opportunity, Environmental, Estate Planning, Franchising, Health Care Law, Insurance, International, Labor, Medical Malpractice Defense, Municipal Finance,

(This Listing Continued)

Kilpatrick Stockton LLP (Continued)

Oil and Gas, Patent, Personal Injury Litigation, Probate, Products Liability Litigation, Public Utility, Real Estate, Securities, Taxation, Trademark, Trust and Unfair Competition.

Atlanta, Georgia Office: Suite 2800, 1100 Peachtree Street. Telephone: 404-815-6500. Facsimile: 404-815-6555. Telex: 54-2307.

Augusta, Georgia Office: 1400 First Union Bank Building, P.O. Box 2043, 30903-2043. Telephone: 706-724-2622. Facsimile: 706-722-0219.

Brussels, Belgium Office: Avenue Louise 149, BTE 15, 1050 Brussels. Telephone: 32-2-533-0300. Facsimile: 32-2-534-8638.

Charlotte, North Carolina Office: 301 South College Street, 28202-6001. Telephone: 704-338-5000. Facsimile: 704-338-5125.

Miami, Florida Office: First Union Financial Center, 200 South Biscayne Boulevard, Suite 2000, 33131-2310. Telephone: 786-777-8000. Facsimile: 786-777-8001.

London, England Office: 68 Pall Mall, London SW1Y 5ES. Telephone: 44-171-321-0477. Facsimile: 44-171-930-9733.

Raleigh, North Carolina Office: Suite 400, 3737 Glenwood Avenue, 27612. Telephone: 919-420-1700. Facsimile: 919-420-1800.

Reston, Virginia Office: 11130 Sunrise Valley Drive, Suite 300, 20191-4329. Telephone: 703-648-8500. Facsimile: 703-648-8501.

Stockholm, Sweden Office: Hovslagargatan 5 S-111 48. Telephone: 46-8-505-646-00. Facsimile: 46-8-505-646-99.

Winston-Salem, North Carolina Office: 1001 West Fourth Street, 27101-2400. Telephone: 336-607-7300. Facsimile: 336-607-7500.

See Professional Biographies, WASHINGTON, DISTRICT OF COLUMBIA

Kim, Albert Y. .... '71 '99 C.821 B.A. L.145 J.D. [🄰 Gibson,D.&C.]
*PRACTICE AREAS: Litigation; Antitrust; Mergers and Acquisitions.
Kim, Angela S. .... '69 '95 C.813 A.B. L.309 J.D. 725 12th St., N.W.
Kim, Brian Hong-Koo .... '69 '96 C.197 A.B. L.262 J.D. 1814 N St. N.W.
Kim, Daniel S. .... '72 '01 C.309 A.B. L.245 J.D. [🄰 Keil&W.]
*PRACTICE AREAS: Patents.
Kim, David H. .... '68 '95 C.112 B.A. L.309 J.D. 2300 N St. NW
Kim, Edward H. .... '66 '91 C.94 B.S. L.273 J.D. [🄲 Charapp,D.&W.]
*PRACTICE AREAS: Government Contracts; Business Litigation; Corporate.
Kim, Edward T. '67 '93 C.112 B.A. L.221 J.D.
(adm. in PA; not adm. in DC) V.P. & Sr. Coun., WorldSpace Corp.
Kim, Emily S. '— '96 C.112 B.A. L.273 J.D.
(adm. in MD; not adm. in DC) 1801 L St., N.W.‡
Kim, Grace W. .... '67 '96 C.112 B.A. L.30 J.D. [🄰 Collier S.S.]
*PRACTICE AREAS: International Trade; Immigration.
Kim, H. Grace .... '63 '89 C&L.276 B.S.F.S., J.D. [🄲 Silverstein&M.]
*PRACTICE AREAS: Federal Income Taxation.
Kim, Harold H. .... '70 '95 C.112 B.A. L.128 J.D. [🄰 Patton B.]
Kim, Hoyun .... '60 '87 C&L.273 B.A., J.D. [🄰 Venable,A.B.H.&C.]
*PRACTICE AREAS: Bankruptcy; Creditors Rights.
Kim, Hyun Sun '— '92 C.66 B.A. L.665 J.D.
(adm. in NJ; not adm. in DC) [🄰 Heller E.W.&M.]
Kim, Janet K. .... '69 '95 C.276 B.S. L.178 J.D. [🄰 Baker&M.]
*PRACTICE AREAS: International Trade; Administrative Law.
Kim, Joo-Mee '— '91
(adm. in Korea; not adm. in DC) [🄰 Foley&L.]
*PRACTICE AREAS: Intellectual Property; Biotechnology; Pharmaceutical; Chemical.
Kim, Judith U. .... '— '95 C&L.446 B.A., J.D. [🄰 Sterne,K.G.&F.] (See Pat. Sect.)
*PRACTICE AREAS: Intellectual Property.
Kim, Juhong '70 '00 C.216 B.A. L.1218 J.D.
(adm. in NY; not adm. in DC) [🄰 Baker&M.]
*PRACTICE AREAS: Intellectual Property Law; Administrative Law; Regulatory Law; Trade Regulations and Customs Law.
Kim, Junhee .... '66 '00 C&L.276 B.S.F.S., J.D. [🄰 Perkins C.]
*PRACTICE AREAS: International Trade; Telecommunications; Litigation.
Kim, Kathleen S. .... '74 '00 C.893 B.A. L.309 J.D. [🄰 Wiley R.&F.]
*PRACTICE AREAS: Directors and Officers Liability; Litigation.
Kim, Kay Lee '71 '99 C.165 B.A. L.446 J.D.
(adm. in MD; not adm. in DC) [🄰 Crowell&M.]
Kim, Laura M. .... '75 '01 C.976 B.A. L.309 J.D. [🄰 Covington&B.]
Kim, Mia S. '70 '96 C.104 B.A. L.273 J.D.
(adm. in PA; not adm. in DC) [🄰 Muldoon M.&F.]
Kim, Nam Eun .... '71 '99 C.178 B.A. L.276 J.D. [🄰 Dow,L.&A.]
Kim, Nancy M. .... '75 '00 C&L.276 B.S., J.D. [🄰 Jones,D.R.&P.]
Kim, Richard Y. '68 '95 C.893 B.A. L.94 J.D.
(adm. in VA; not adm. in DC) [🄰 McDermott,W.&E.]
Kim, Robert S. .... '70 '00 C.178 B.A. L.145 J.D. 1825 Eye St., N.W.
Kim, Soye .... '55 '99 C.999 B.M.M.M. L.893 J.D. [🄰 Guerrieri,E.&C.]
*PRACTICE AREAS: Litigation; Labor and Employment.
Kim, Stephanie J. .... '— '98 C.945 B.A. L.1209 J.D. [🄰 Manatt,P.&P.]
Kim, Stuart .... '66 '99 C.390 B.S. L.966 J.D. [🄰 McKenna&C.]
*PRACTICE AREAS: Food and Drug Regulation; Food, Drug, Medical Device and Cosmetic Law; Unfair Trade Practices.
Kim, Sukhan .... '49 '81 C.296 B.A. L.276 J.D. [Akin,G.S.H.&F.] (⊙Seoul, Korea)
*PRACTICE AREAS: International Trade.
Kim, Ted '70 '98 C.128 B.A. L.1017 J.D.
(adm. in MD; not adm. in DC) [🄰 Jaeger&T.]
Kim, Thomas J. .... '— '96 C.976 B.A. L.309 J.D. [🄰 Latham&W.]
*PRACTICE AREAS: Corporate; Securities Law; Entertainment Law.
Kim, Thomas T. '— '96
C.112 B.A. L.1494 J.D. Asst. Coun., Investment Company Institute
*RESPONSIBILITIES: Pensions.
Kim, Yoora .... '70 '95 C.188 B.S. L.273 J.D. [🄰 Ogletree,D.N.S.&S.]
*PRACTICE AREAS: Labor and Employment; Litigation; Employment Discrimination; Employment Litigation; Labor Law.
Kimball, Paul C., Ph.D. .... '46 '93 C.453 B.S. L.128 J.D. [🄲 Piper M.R.&W.] (Pat.)
*PRACTICE AREAS: Intellectual Property; Patent Law; Patent Interference Practice; Patent Licensing; Patent Litigation.
Kimball, Raymond J., (AV) ...... '48 '74 C.951 B.A. L.273 J.D. 3000 K St., NW, Ste. 300
Kimberling, Michael S. .... '68 '96 C.105 B.A. L.128 J.D. [🄰 Dickstein S.M.&O.]
*PRACTICE AREAS: Civil Litigation.
Kimble, James Lawson .... '45 '73 C.207 B.A. L.276 J.D. American Insurance Association
Kimble, Ronald L. '64 '01 C.446 B.S. L.273 J.D.
(adm. in MD; not adm. in DC; See Pat. Sect.) [🄰 Sughrue M.]
*PRACTICE AREAS: Intellectual Property.
Kimble, Tina Potuto .... '70 '95 C.93 B.A. L.904 J.D. [🄰 Steptoe&J.]
Kime, Barrett L., (BV) .... '56 '82 C&L.37 B.A., J.D. [Corey&K.] ⊙
Kimmel, Adele P. .... '60 '87 C&L.893 B.A., J.D. Trial Lawyers for Pub. Jus., P.C.
Kimmel, Melissa B. .... '71 '98 C.882 B.A. L.273 J.D. [🄰 Howrey S.A.&W.]
*PRACTICE AREAS: Antitrust; Commercial Litigation.
Kimmel, Michael .... '38 '68 C.674 A.B. L.273 LL.B. 2030 F St., N.W.
Kimmel, Phyllis G .... '67 '95 C.918 B.A. L.569 J.D. [🄰 Miller,B.&O.]

Kimmel, Edward M.
(See Takoma Park, Maryland)

Kimmell, Joseph W., II, (AV) '47 '72 C.228 B.A. L.477 J.D.
(adm. in IN; not adm. in DC) [Baker&D.] (⊙Fort Wayne, IN)
*PRACTICE AREAS: Corporate Law; Mergers and Acquisitions; International Transactions.
Kimmett, Charles T., Jr. .... '72 '98 C.705 B.A. L.976 J.D. [🄰 Williams&C.]
*PRACTICE AREAS: Civil Appeals; Civil Litigation; Civil Practice; Class Actions; Commercial Real Estate Litigation.
Kimmich, Joan M., (BV) .... '57 '91 C&L.273 B.A., J.D. [Stein,M.&M.]
*PRACTICE AREAS: Administrative Law; Antitrust; Trade Regulation; Civil Litigation.
Kimms, Lyle .... '— '90 C.433 B.E.M.E. L.276 J.D. [Foley&L.] (See Pat. Sect.)
*PRACTICE AREAS: Intellectual Property.
Kinashi, Sadao '50 '97 C.999 B.S. L.146 J.D.
[🄰 Armstrong,W.H.M.&N.] (See Pat. Sect.)
*PRACTICE AREAS: Intellectual Property (100%).
Kinberg, Robert, (AV) '48 '75
C.910 B.S.E.E. L.273 J.D. [Venable,A.B.H.&C.] (See Pat. Sect.)
*PRACTICE AREAS: Patent Law; Trademark Law.
Kinder, Jennifer Anne '67 '93 C.623 B.S. L.744 J.D.
(adm. in TX; not adm. in DC) Dep. Fin. Dir., Democratic National Committee
Kindler, Roger A. '50 '75 C.309 A.B. L.276 J.D.
V.P. & Gen. Coun., Humane Society of the United States (⊙Washington)
Kindler, Roger A. '50 '75 C.309 A.B. L.276 J.D.
[Madden,M.S.&R.A.K.] (⊙Washington)
King, Alethia N. .... '68 '97 C.446 B.A. L.966 J.D. [🄰 Hogan&H.]
*PRACTICE AREAS: Corporate; Securities; Public Finance.
King, Anthony F. .... '63 '89 C.894 A.B. L.309 J.D. [Wallace K.M.&B.]
*PRACTICE AREAS: Litigation; Environmental Law.
King, Barbara A. .... '39 '91 C&L.276 A.B., J.D. Georgetown Univ. Law Center
King, Carol Weld, (AV) .... '61 '86 C&L.893 B.A., J.D. [Hogan&H.]
*PRACTICE AREAS: Commercial Real Estate Law.
King, Craig S., (BV) .... '53 '81 C.101 B.A. L.276 J.D. [Arent F.K.P.&K.]
*PRACTICE AREAS: Government Contracts; Electronic Commerce; Antitrust (contractor mergers, joint ventures and teaming); Corporate Investigations; Corporate Compliance.
King, Donna D. .... '68 '99 C&L.880 B.E., J.D. [🄰 Howrey S.A.&W.] (See Pat. Sect.)
King, Douglas R. M. .... '— '94 C.685 B.A. L.904 J.D. [🄰 Feith&Z.]
King, Erika .... '68 '96 C.575 B.A. L.228 J.D. [🄰 Covington&B.]
*PRACTICE AREAS: Food and Drug Regulation; Privacy; Biomedical Technology.
King, George Jack, Jr. '53 '86 C.65 B.A. L.128 J.D.
Dir., Natl. Assn. of Criminal Defense Lawyers
King, J. Benjamin .... '68 '99 C.500 B.A. L.188 J.D. [🄰 Arnold&P.]
*PRACTICE AREAS: Litigation.
King, J. Brian .... '75 '00 C.160 B.A. L.245 J.D. [🄰 Dickstein S.M.&O.]
*PRACTICE AREAS: Securities Litigation; Antitrust.
King, Jeffrey M. .... '73 '98 C&L.477 B.A., J.D. [🄰 Akin,G.S.H.&F.]
*PRACTICE AREAS: Litigation; White Collar Crime.
King, Jeffrey W. .... '47 '77 C.1044 B.A. L.982 J.D. [King,P.&H.]
*PRACTICE AREAS: Complex Civil Litigation; Health Care Law; Government Contracts; Criminal Defense; Antitrust.
King, Jennifer L. .... '72 '99 C.273 B.S. L.276 J.D. [🄰 Kenyon&K.] (See Pat. Sect.)
*PRACTICE AREAS: Intellectual Property.
King, Joanna M. .... '61 '88 C.882 B.A. L.982 J.D. [Fontaine,S.K.&D.]
King, John A., Jr. '18 '49 C&L.309 A.B., LL.B.
(adm. in IL; not adm. in DC) Intl. Bk. for Reconstr. & Develop.
King, John W. .... '37 '72 C&L.329 B.S., J.D. 500 Indiana Ave., N.W.
King, John Wells, (AV) .... '46 '72 C&L.546 B.A., J.D. [🄲 Garvey,S.&B.]
*PRACTICE AREAS: Administrative Law; Communications Law; Media Law; Regulatory Law; Trademark Law.
King, Kevin M. .... '70 '97 C.30 B.A. L.813 J.D. [🄰 Coudert B.]
*PRACTICE AREAS: International Trade; Foreign Corrupt Practices Act; Export Regulation; Foreign Trade Sanctions; International Intellectual Property.
King, Kristin G. .... '68 '98 C.886 B.A. L.1206 J.D. [🄰 Weil,G.&M.]
*PRACTICE AREAS: Technology Law; Public Policy.
King, Lancelot A. .... '— '97 C.860 B.A. L.659 J.D. 701 Pennsylvania Avenue, N.W.
King, Leif B. .... '70 '96 C.1349 B.A. L.276 J.D. [🄰 Skadden,A.S.M.&F.]
*PRACTICE AREAS: Corporate.
King, Margaret Anne '76 '01 C.1365 B.A. L.309 J.D.
(adm. in IL; not adm. in DC) [🄰 Sutherland A.&B.]
*PRACTICE AREAS: Tax Law.
King, Marilou M., (AV) .... '48 '79 C.446 B.A. L.273 J.D. [McDermott,W.&E.]
King, Michael C. '45 '82
C.433 B.B.A. L.1209 J.D. Assoc. Prof., Northern Va. Community Coll.
King, Michael J. .... '55 '81 C.94 B.A. L.30 J.D. [🄲 Clifford C.R.&W.]
*PRACTICE AREAS: Securities Regulation and Enforcement; Corporate; Litigation.
King, Neil J., (AV) .... '45 '71 C&L.309 B.A., J.D. [Wilmer,C.&P.]
*PRACTICE AREAS: Appellate Litigation; Environmental Law; Occupational Safety and Health Law; Civil Practice; International Trade.
King, O'Neil S., (AV) .... '63 '89 C&L.569 B.A., J.D. [Jordan K.&J.]
King, Patricia A. .... '42 '69 C.938 B.A. L.309 J.D. Prof. of Law, Georgetown Univ.
King, Rachel C. '63 '90 C.788 B.A. L.588 J.D.
(adm. in AK; not adm. in DC) 122 Maryland Ave., N.E.
King, Richard C., Jr. '68 '98 C&L.846 B.A., J.D.
(adm. in TX; not adm. in DC) [🄰 Baker B.]
King, Robert A. .... '69 '99 C.870 B.S. L.128 J.D. [🄰 Brobeck,P.&H.] (Pat.)
*PRACTICE AREAS: Intellectual Property.
King, Rufus, (AV) .... '17 '44 C.674 A.B. L.976 J.D. 1101 Seventeenth St. NW
King, Rufus, III .... '42 '71 C.674 A.B. L.276 J.D. Assoc. Supr. Ct J.
King, Stacey H. .... '71 '01 C.1307 B.A. L.30 J.D. [🄰 Howrey S.A.&W.]
King, Susan J. .... '56 '86 C.822 A.B. L.273 J.D. [Koltun&K.]
*PRACTICE AREAS: Corporate Law; Mergers and Acquisitions; Business Law; Securities Law; Private Placement.
King, W. Russell .... '49 '74 C&L.280 B.B.A., J.D. [🄲 Jones,W.W.P.C.&D.]
*PRACTICE AREAS: Energy; Natural Resources; Environmental; International Law; Agricultural Law.
King, William K. '36 '62 C&L.477 B.S.E., J.D.
(adm. in IL; not adm. in DC; Pat.) Ford Motor Co.

King & Attridge
(See Rockville, Maryland)

King & King, Chartered, (AV) .... 1730 M Street, N.W. (⊙New York, NY)

King & Nordlinger, L.L.P., (AV)
5028 Wisconsin Avenue, N.W. Suite 300, 20016 ⊙
Telephone: 202-833-9310
URL: http://www.knlaw.com
Members of Firm: John J. Cooleen; Michael C. Blackstone; Michael R. McAdoo; Roger D. Luchs; Warren S. Oliveri, Jr.; Lynn Perry Parker; Kathleen Donovan Tammadge. Associate: Gina L. Marine (Not admitted in DC). Counsel: Albert B. Ellentuck.
General Practice before Federal and State Courts, Corporate and Business, Litigation, Real Estate, Personal Injury, Employment and Labor Law, Estate Planning and Probate, Condominium and Cooperative Law, Rent Control, Housing Law, Discrimination Law, Commercial Leasing and Landlord-Tenant Law.

(This Listing Continued)

King & Nordlinger, L.L.P. (Continued)

Arlington, Virginia Office: 4350 North Fairfax Drive, Suite 950. Telephone: 703-522-8084. Fax: 703-522-8108.
Gaithersburg, Maryland Office: 806 West Diamond Avenue, Fourth Floor. Telephone: 301-258-4571. Fax: 301-258-4575.

See Professional Biographies, WASHINGTON, DISTRICT OF COLUMBIA

King, Pagano & Harrison, (AV) [BR]
1730 Pennsylvania Avenue, N.W., 20006 ⊙
Telephone: 202-371-6800 Fax: 202-371-6770
URL: http://www.kph.com
Members of Firm: Jeffrey W. King; Jeffrey W. Pagano (New York and East Hampton, New York); Keith J. Harrison; James E. Kellett (Resident, New York, N.Y. Office); Steven Schaars; Jeffrey L. Poston; Ira M. Saxe (Not admitted in DC; Resident, New York, N.Y. Office); Cheryl A. Maier; Christopher Flynn. Of Counsel: Herbert I. Meyer (Resident, New York, N.Y. Office); Gary A. Stahl (Resident, New York,N.Y. Office). Associates: Trina L. Fairley; Emily B. Zuckerman (Resident, New York, N.Y. Office); Howard Schragin (Not admitted in DC); Frank M. Esposito (Not admitted in DC); Julie A. Barnes.
Complex Civil and Criminal Practice before Federal and State Courts, Domestic and International Management Labor Relations, Antitrust, Employment, Health Care, Managed Care, Government Contracts, Domestic and International Management Labor Relations and Intellectual Property Litigation.
Representative Clients: Brink's, Inc.; The Pittston Co.; BAX Global; Kaiser Permanente; Group Health Association of America; Capital Credit Corp; Systems Engineering Services Corp.; Noel Biscare.
New York, New York Office: 425 Park Avenue, 10022. Telephone: 212-223-4000. FAX: 212-223-4134.
East Hampton Office: 33 Newtown Lane, 11937. Telephone: 631-329-8466. Fax: 631-329-8436.

See Professional Biographies, WASHINGTON, DISTRICT OF COLUMBIA

King & Spalding, (AV)
1730 Pennsylvania Avenue, N.W., 20006-4706 ⊙
Telephone: 202-737-0500 FAX: 202-626-3737
URL: http://www.kslaw.com/
Resident Partners: Edward M. Basile; Andrew Berg; William Blumenthal; John M. Bray; Mark S. Brown; Glenn C. Campbell (Not admitted in DC); Robert E. Culbertson; Frederick H. Degnan; Kevin M. Dinan; Joseph W. Dorn; Michael C. Durst; David A. Gibbons; Thomas R. Graham; Sandra W. Hallmark; Theodore M. Hester; Eleanor J. Hill; Susan Jewett; Stephen A. Jones; Duane W. Layton; Jackie S. Levinson; Jane C. Luxton; Andrew C. Lynch; Michael P. Mabile; Patricia L. Maher; Todd Y. McArthur; Martin M. McNerney; James D. Miller; Eugene M. Pfeifer; James T. Phalen; Katherine L. Rhyne; Dvorah A. Richman; Grace M. Rodriguez; Joseph Sedwick Sollers III; Jeffrey S. Spigel; Kevin R. Sullivan. Resident Counsel: Sandra Cohen Kalter; Christina M. Markus; Lisa L. Poole; Harold M. Shaw; Christopher Sprigman (Not admitted in DC); William C. Talmadge (Not admitted in DC). Resident Associates: Christopher Kole Agbe-Davies (Not admitted in DC); Corey Amundson; Amy M. Angelo; Thomas D. Blanford (Not admitted in DC); Jeffrey S. Bucholtz; John R. Bunker (Not admitted in DC); Aileen Hurley Ciampa (Not admitted in DC); Michael J. Ciatti; Lisa L. Cochrane (Not admitted in DC); David A. Cohen; Susan R. Connella; Elizabeth S. Crockett; Melissa Dempsey; Alan F. Enslen; Mark Filpi; Rishona Fleishman (Not admitted in DC); Peter Carlton Fleming; John H. Fontham; Gary J. Greco (Not admitted in DC); Reuben Green (Not admitted in DC); Ann Marie Hart; Mark Jensen; Andrew Kaplan (Not admitted in DC); M. Alexander Koch; Steven L. Lane; Scott P. McClure; Andrew McCormack (Not admitted in DC); Amy B. Metzel (Not admitted in DC); M. Elizabeth Mims (Not admitted in DC); Thomas A. Monheim; Stephen A. Myrow; Kelly Nicole Reeves; Kerri L. Ruttenberg; Christine E. Savage; Anne R. Schott; John D. Shakow; Stacy S. Shibao; Jennafer Smoker; Cynthia A.M. Stroman; Jeffrey M. Telep; Dianna Thomsen; Peter M. Todaro; Elaine H. Tseng; Joseph R. Waala (Not admitted in DC); Anne K. Walsh; Kathryn E. Walsh (Not admitted in DC); David R. Weiser (Not admitted in DC); Jacqueline S. Weiss; Edward H. White; Ashley Whitesides; Craig M. Wolff; Tamara Yakimetz (Not admitted in DC).
General Practice in all State and Federal Courts, Administrative and Governmental Agencies; Antitrust; Arbitration & Mediation; Bankruptcy & Creditors Rights; Biotechnology & Pharmaceuticals; Capital Markets (Corporate Finance / Private Debt Finance / Structured Finance); Construction & Procurement; Cyberspace & Information Security; E-Commerce & Internet; Emerging Growth Companies); Employee Benefits & Executive Compensation; Energy Industries (Oil & Gas / Power); Environmental; Food, Drug & Medical Devices (Controlled Substances / Consumer Products Safety / FDA Practice / FTC Practice); Franchise & Distribution; Governmental Practice; Healthcare; Intellectual Property (Copyrights / Patents / Trademarks / Trade Secrets); International (German Practice / International Business / Islamic Finance & Investment / Latin American Practice/ Trade & Customs); International Energy; International Arbitration; International Business Law; Joint Ventures & Strategic Alliances; Labor & Employment; Licensing; Contracting & Outsourcing; Litigation (Appellate / Class Action / Commercial Litigation / Corporate Espionage & Competitive Intelligence / Environmental Tort Practice / Product Liability / Shareholders & Securities Litigation); Maritime Law; Mergers & Acquisitions; Private Equity & Investment Fund; Project & Equipment Finance; Public Finance; Real Estate; Special Matters & Government Investigations; Tax; Technology; Telecommunications; Trusts & Estates. (While every area within the Firm may not represented by lawyers resident in each of its offices - for example, the Firm's Food & Drug or Governmental lawyers are solely located in the Firm's Washington, D.C. office - lawyers throughout the entire Firm are nonetheless available to work and support relationships with Firm clients).
Atlanta, Georgia Office: 191 Peachtree Street, N.E., 30303-1763. Telephone: 404-572-4600. Fax: 404-572-5100.
New York, N.Y. Office: 1185 Avenue of the Americas, 10036-4003. Telephone: 212-556-2100. Fax: 212-556-2222.
Houston, Texas Office: 1100 Louisiana, Suite 4000, 77002-5213. Telephone: 713-751-3200. Fax: 713-751-3290.

See Professional Biographies, WASHINGTON, DISTRICT OF COLUMBIA

Kingery, William D., Jr. ....'48 '78 C.453 S.B. L.823 J.D. [Dickstein S.M.&O.]
*PRACTICE AREAS: Tax Law.
Kingham, Richard F. ....'46 '73 C.273 B.A. L.893 J.D. [Covington&B.]
Kingsley, Darius R. ....'67 '95 C.861 B.A. L.188 J.D. [[A] Sidley A.B.&W.]
Kingsley, Elizabeth J. ....'64 '93 C.604 L.276 J.D. [Harmon,C.S.&E.]
Kini, Satish M. ....'65 '93 C.165 B.A. L.178 J.D. [Wilmer,C.&P.]
*PRACTICE AREAS: Financial Institutions; Investment Management.
Kinnaird, Stephen B. ....'62 '95 C&L.976 B.A., J.D. [[A] Sidley A.B.&W.]
Kinner, Jeremy K. '— '97 C.198 B.A. L.575 J.D.
(adm. in NC; not adm. in DC) 1301 Massachusetts Ave. N.W.
Kinner, William B. ....'68 '99 C.445 B.S. L.1002 J.D. [[A] Saltman&S.]
*PRACTICE AREAS: Litigation; Government Contracts; Natural Resources Law.
Kinney, Charles L. ....'52 '79 C&L.276 B.S.F.S., J.D. [Winston&S.]
*PRACTICE AREAS: Federal Governmental Relations; Regulatory Affairs.
Kinsey, Sandra Folsom ...... '50 '80 C.245 B.A. L.280 J.D. [Hogan&H.] (⊙Miami, FL)
*PRACTICE AREAS: Securities; Corporate Law; International Capital Markets; Foreign Investment in the United States.
Kinsley, Michael E. ....'51 '78 C&L.309 A.B., J.D. New Republic, The
Kinslow, Joseph A. ....'21 '51 C.728 B.S. L.276 J.D. 3130 Wis. Ave., N.W.
Kinzelman, Gregory L. ....'67 '95 C.602 B.A. L.893 J.D. [[A] Hunton&W.]
*PRACTICE AREAS: Antitrust; Competition Law; International Trade; Litigation; Election Law.
Kipel, Alice Alexandra, (AV) ....'57 '82 C.674 A.B. L.276 J.D. [[C] Steptoe&J.]
*PRACTICE AREAS: International Trade Law; Customs Law; Import Law; Intellectual Property.
Kipps, Clarence T., Jr., (AV) ....'— '53 C.30 B.S. L.273 J.D. [Miller&C.]
*PRACTICE AREAS: Government Contracts; Government Construction Contracts; Legislative Practice; Fifth Amendment Law; Government Contract Fraud.
Kirby, Kathleen A., (AV) ....'59 '91 C.893 B.S. L.128 J.D. [[C] Wiley R.&F.]
*PRACTICE AREAS: Communications Law.
Kirby, Ky E. ....'56 '85 C&L.1209 B.S., J.D. [Swidler B.S.F.]
*PRACTICE AREAS: Civil Litigation; Telecommunications; False Advertising; Technology Litigation; Internet Law.
Kirby, Peter M. ....'45 '79 C.262 B.A. L.276 J.D. [Winston&S.]
*PRACTICE AREAS: Energy; Corporate.
Kirby, Richard A., (BV) ....'49 '74 C.401 B.S. L.128 J.D. [Dyer E.&J.]
*PRACTICE AREAS: Litigation; Alternative Dispute Resolution; Bankruptcy; Securities.

Kirby, Thomas W., (AV) ....'50 '75 C.420 B.A. L.276 J.D. [Wiley R.&F.]
*PRACTICE AREAS: Litigation; Intellectual Property; Election Law.
Kirchick, Wendy I. '60 '87 C.454 B.A. L.94 J.D.
(adm. in MA; not adm. in DC) 1050 Conn. Ave., N.W.‡
Kirchner, Paul G., (AV) '52 '78 C&L.893 B.A., J.D.
Exec. Dir. & Gen. Coun., Amer. Pilot's Assn.
Kirk, Michael W. ....'63 '89 C.276 A.B. L.597 J.D. [Cooper&K.]
*PRACTICE AREAS: Trial and Appellate Litigation; Constitutional Litigation; Administrative Litigation.
Kirk, Paul G., Jr., (AV) '38 '65 C&L.309 A.B., LL.B.
[Sullivan&W.] (⊙Boston, MA)‡
*PRACTICE AREAS: Business Law; Administrative Law; Corporate Law.
Kirk, Robert G. ....'66 '92 C.1057 B.A. L.273 J.D. [Wilkinson B.K.]
*PRACTICE AREAS: Communications; Telecommunications Law; Appellate Practice; Administrative Litigation; Internet Law.
Kirk, William A., Jr. ....'52 '83 C.821 B.A. L.276 J.D. [Thelen R.&P.]
*PRACTICE AREAS: Government Affairs.

Kirkland & Ellis, (AV) [BR]
A Partnership including Professional Corporations
655 Fifteenth Street, N.W., Suite 1200, 20005 ⊙
Telephone: 202-879-5000 Telex: 89-2320 Facsimile: 202-879-5200
URL: http://www.kirkland.com
Members of Firm: Jay I. Alexander; Eugene F. Assaf; Daniel F. Attridge; Pamela J. Auerbach; James F. Basile; Kenneth N. Bass; Michael S. Becker; Terrance L. Bessey; Steven Gill Bradbury; Paul F. Brinkman; Pat A. Cipollone; Thomas A. Clare; Andrew B. Clubok; Karen McCartan DeSantis; Maureen A. Donley-Hoopes; Edward C. Donovan; Stuart A. C. Drake; James Worth Draughn, Jr.; Michael T. Edsall; Thomas L. Evans; Robert R. Gasaway; James P. Gillespie; Mark E. Grummer; Barbara Mack Harding; Timothy S. Hardy; Mitchell F. Hertz; John S. Irving, Jr.; Michael D. Jones; Daryl Joseffer; Antony B. Klapper; Stephen D. Knight; Mark L. Kovner; Robert G. Krupka (P.C.); David L. Lambert; Brian R. Land; Christopher Landau; Neil L. Levy; Gregg F. LoCascio; Walter H. Lohmann, Jr.; Dawn Danzeisen Marchant; Robert G. Marks; Gerald F. Masoudi; Susan O'Sullivan McGuire; John Gibson Mullan; Granta Y. Nakayama; Craig S. Primis; Lewis T. Putman, Jr.; Jeffrey A. Rosen; Robert S. Ryland; David P. Sanders; Marimichael O. Skubel; Tefft W. Smith; Kenneth W. Starr; Robert Timothy Stephenson; David P. Swenson; Laurence A. Urgenson; Karen Natalie Walker; Edward W. Warren (P.C.); Kenneth G. Weigel; Steven M. Wellner; L. Mark Wine (P.C.); Thomas D. Yannucci; Mark D. Young; Marc J. Zwillinger. Of Counsel: Joseph J. DeSanctis (Not admitted in DC); Laura S. Harper; James S. Hostetler; David G. Norrell; Frederick M. Rowe; James D. Senger. Associates: Gary D. Anderson; Laura R. Bach; Reatha A. Baker; Jason Beckerman; Stacey L. Bennett; Bradford E. Biegon; Brant W. Bishop; Paul J. Bohr; Julie L. Brennan (Not admitted in DC); Jennifer R. Brosnahan; Zhonette Brown; Eugene F. Chay; David A. Codevilla; Gregory F. Corbett (Not admitted in DC); Joseph E. Culleiton; Elizabeth Lee Deeley; Daniel T. Donovan; Cara Tseng Duffield (Not admitted in DC); Susan Kathleen Fitch; Eric L. Fletcher (Not admitted in DC); David B. Florenzo; Laura Fraedrich; Christian S. Genetski; Daniel J. Gerkin; John P. Gonsoulin (Not admitted in DC); Ryan W. Goode (Not admitted in DC); Amy Marie Harvey; Robert W. Irish (Not admitted in DC); Geoffrey S. Irwin; Sara Kalin (Not admitted in DC); Colin R. Kass; Andrew B. Kay; James M. Koukios (Not admitted in DC); Anthony W. Lacosta; Tony Y. Lam; Jennifer G. Levy; Mark E. McKane; David E. Mendelson; Junaid "Jay" Munir (Not admitted in DC); Matthew E. Papez; Ashley Charles Parrish; Larissa Paule-Carres; Elizabeth S. Petrela (Not admitted in DC); David Pruitt; Karen M. Robinson; Rebecca I. Ruby; Christian C. Semonsen; Kannon K. Shanmugam; Martha Phillips Stuart; David P. Sullivan; Edwin John U; Elaine M. Walsh (Not admitted in DC); Amy C. Whitehurst (Not admitted in DC); Jeffrey Williamson (Not admitted in DC).
General Practice including Practice before United States Courts, Administrative Agencies and Departments of the Government and other Litigation.
Chicago, Illinois Office: 200 East Randolph Drive. Telephone: 312-861-2000. Telex: 25-4361.
Los Angeles, California Office: 777 South Figueroa Street. Telephone: 213-680-8400. Facsimile: 213-680-8500.
New York, New York Office: Citicorp Center, 153 East 53rd Street. Telephone: 212-446-4800. Facsimile: (212)-446-4900.
London, England Office: International Financial Centre, Old Broad Street. Telephone: 171-816-8700; New Telephone Effective April 1, 2000: 207-816-8700. Facsimile: 171-816-8800.

See Professional Biographies, WASHINGTON, DISTRICT OF COLUMBIA

Kirkpatrick, C. Kris, (AV) .... '48 '75 C&L.420 B.S., J.D. [Long] ⊙
Kirkpatrick, Douglas J. '56 '92 C.276 B.A. L.245 J.D.
(adm. in PA; not adm. in DC) Director & General Counsel, Heldref Publications
Kirkpatrick, G. Scott .... '65 '94 C.347 B.A. L.273 J.D. [[A] Ross,D.&B.]

Kirkpatrick & Lockhart LLP, (AV)
1800 Massachusetts Avenue, N.W. 2nd Floor, 20036-1800 ⊙
Telephone: 202-778-9000 Telex: 244859 Facsimile: 202-778-9100
URL: http://www.kl.com
Members of Firm: Clifford J. Alexander; Diane E. Ambler; Costas A. Avrakotos; Alan J. Berkeley; Joseph J. Brigati; Melanie Hibbs Brody; Arthur J. Brown; David T. Case; Susan M. Casey; Thomas F. Cooney, III; Arthur C. Delibert; Charles Lee Eisen; Mahlon M. Frankhauser; Elinor W. Gammon; Stephen W. Grafman; Robert C. Hacker; Barry M. Hartman; Benjamin J. Haskin; Philip H. Hecht; Dumond Peck Hill (1923-1991); Matthew L. Jacobs; Kathleen D. Jaeger; Judith Sturtz Karp; Rebecca H. Laird; Lawrence Coe Lanpher; Thomas M. Leahey; Jeffrey B. Maletta; Cary J. Meer; Gilbert C. Miller; Richard Charles Miller; Charles R. Mills; Michael J. Missal; A. Thomas Morris; R. Darrell Mounts; Bruce H. Nielson; Thomas J. Noto; Suzan Onel; Laurence E. Platt; Alan C. Porter; Theodore L. Press; Glenn R. Reichardt; Jeffrey B. Ritter; Robert H. Rosenblum; William Aubrey Schmidt; Phillip L. Schulman; Lynn A. Schweinfurth; Kevin Michael Sheys; Donald W. Smith; Ronald W. Stevens; Donald R. Stone; Ira L. Tannenbaum; Daniel J. Tobin; Stephen G. Topetzes; Robert A. Wittie; Gary L. Yingling; Robert J. Zutz. Of Counsel: Catherine S. Bardsley; George L. Christopher; Paul Gonson; Francis Thornton Greene (1908-1992); Kathy Kresch Ingber; Henry L. Judy; Dean E. Miller; Emalee G. Murphy; Charles Dirk Peterson; Leslie A. Sowle (Not admitted in DC); Dick Thornburgh. Associates: Alissa Jennifer Altongy; Mark C. Amorosi; Erin K. Ardale (Not admitted in DC); Angela Y. Ball; Ann Marie Begley; Eric Berger; Michele Levy Berlove; Emily J. Booth; Christopher J. Costello; Rebecca L. Dandeker; James E. Day; Amy S. Doig (Not admitted in DC); Christopher E. Dominguez; Eric John Edwardson; Jodi Finder; Edward Fishman; Leigh M. P. Freund; Ranji Martelli Garrett; Suzanne Fay Garwood (Not admitted in DC); Jennifer R. Gonzalez; Allison W. Harrison; Benjamin S. Hayes; Kimberley H. Haynes; Lance W. High; Michael Henry Hinckle; Shirley A. Hinton; Ronald A. Holinsky (Not admitted in DC); Sean R. Hunt; Julia Reynolds Johnson; Steven M. Kaplan; Rebecca L. Kline; Ivan B. Knauer; Kristie D. Kully; David A. Kurzweil; Alexandra C. LaFrankie; Stavroula E. Lambrakopoulos; Alicia L. Lewis (Not admitted in DC); Patricia A. Maxey (Not admitted in DC); John M. McCann (Not admitted in DC); Mignon McLemore; Ndenisarya M. Meekins (Not admitted in DC); Marc Mehrespand; Phillip A. Minnick (Not admitted in DC); Lucrecia Renea Moore; Adam C. Paul; Mark D. Perlow; Francine J. Rosenberger; Tara L. Royal; Lori L. Schneider; Tara C. Sirmans; Sheldon B. Sommer (Not admitted in DC); Tracie D. Spear; Fatima Sulaiman; Sean R. Sullivan (Not admitted in DC); Jon M. Talotta; Nicholas G. Terris; David U. Thomas; Courtney S. Thornton; Carol M. Tomaszczuk; Joseph P. Vitale; Nanci L. Weissgold; Gregory S. Wright; George J. Zornada; Rachael M. Zufall.
General Practice including Antitrust; Appellate; Banking and Financial Institutions; Bankruptcy and Business Restructurings; Construction; Corporate; Environmental; ERISA and Executive Compensation; Governmental Affairs and Legislation; Government Contracts; Insurance Coverage; International; Investment Companies and Investment Advisers; Labor and Employment; Litigation; Mergers and Acquisitions; Mortgage Banking and Consumer Finance; Product Liability and Toxic Torts; Real Estate; Securities; Securities Enforcement; Tax; Technology; Trusts and Estates; White Collar Crime and Year 2000 Computer Conversion.
Boston, Massachusetts Office: 75 State Street. Telephone: 617-261-3100. Facsimile: 617-261-3175.
Dallas, Texas Office: 3100 Bank One Center, 1717 Main Street. Telephone: 214-939-4900. Facsimile: 214-939-4949.
Harrisburg, Pennsylvania Office: Payne Shoemaker Building, 240 North Third Street. Telephone: 717-231-4500. Facsimile: 717-231-4501.
Los Angeles, California Office: 10100 Santa Monica Boulevard, Suite 700. Telephone: 310-552-5000. Facsimile: 310-552-5001.
Miami, Florida Office: Miami Center, 20th Floor, 201 South Biscayne Boulevard. Telephone: 305-539-3300. Facsimile: 305-358-7095.
Newark, New Jersey Office: The Legal Center, One Riverfront Plaza, Seventh Floor. Telephone: 973-848-4000. Facsimile: 973-848-4001.
New York, New York Office: 1251 Avenue of the Americas, 45th Floor. Telephone: 212-536-3900. Facsimile: 212-536-3901.

(This Listing Continued)

Kirkpatrick & Lockhart LLP (Continued)
Pittsburgh, Pennsylvania Office: Henry W. Oliver Building, 535 Smithfield Street. Telephone: 412-355-6500. Facsimile: 412-355-6501.
San Francisco, California Office: Four Embarcadero Center, 10th Floor. Telephone: 415-249-1000. Facsimile: 415-249-1001.
See Professional Biographies, WASHINGTON, DISTRICT OF COLUMBIA

Kirkwood, Martin V. . . . .'62 '91 C.273 B.A. L.128 J.D. [Jones,D.R.&P.]
*PRACTICE AREAS: Energy; Utility Law; Utility Mergers.
Kirmayer, Kathryn Dean . . . .'64 '89 C.951 B.A. L.902 J.D. [Crowell&M.]
Kirpalani, Rohit H. '61 '94 C.705 B.S. L.276 J.D.
(adm. in NY; not adm. in DC) 3050 K St., N.W.‡
Kirsch, Edward W. . . . . '59 '96 C.870 B.S. L.273 J.D. [Swidler B.S.F.]
*PRACTICE AREAS: Telecommunications Law; E-Commerce; Government Contracts.
Kirsch, Helen G., (AV) . . . .'— '88 C.276 A.B. L.884 J.D. [Reed S.]
*PRACTICE AREAS: Litigation.
Kirsch, John T. . . . .'64 '99 C.602 B.A. L.744 J.D. [Jenkens&G.]
*PRACTICE AREAS: Construction Law; Litigation; Government Contracts.

Kirsch, Larry H. '59 '85 C.1349 B.A. L.273 J.D.
5301 Wisconsin Avenue, NW, Suite 640, 20015
Telephone: 202-237-6600 Fax: 202-237-0258
Email: DClawyer@aol.com URL: http://www.lawyers.com/larrykirschlaw
***PRACTICE AREAS: Real Estate Law; Corporate Law; Wills; Probate Law.**
Commercial Transactions, Commercial Real Estate, Real Estate Acquisitions, Real Estate Sales, Commercial Real Estate Sales, Commercial Real Estate Development, Shopping Center Law, Commercial Leasing, Landlord and Tenant, Lease Finance, Real Estate Litigation, Complex Commercial Litigation, Settlements, Workouts, Bankruptcy, Chapter 7, 11, 13, Commercial Loans.
See Professional Biographies, WASHINGTON, DISTRICT OF COLUMBIA

Kirsch, Laurence S., (AV) . . . .'57 '82 C.659 B.A.S. L.309 J.D. [Cadwalader,W.&T.]
*PRACTICE AREAS: Environmental Law; Environmental Litigation; Environmental Bankruptcy.
Kirsch, Mark A. . . . .'58 '85 C.696 B.A. L.273 J.D. [Piper M.R.&W.]
*PRACTICE AREAS: Franchise Law; Licensing and Distribution Law; Corporate and Commercial Transactions.
Kirsch, Martin J., (AV) . . . .'26 '52 C&L.273 A.A., LL.B. 1615 M St., N.W.
Kirsch, Peter J. . . . . '58 '84 C.604 A.B. L.145 J.D. [Akin,G.S.H.&F.] (⊙Denver, CO)
*PRACTICE AREAS: Environmental Law; Land Use Law; Public Sector Law.
Kirsch, Steven A. '69 '94 C.597 B.A. L.880 J.D.
(adm. in MO; not adm. in DC) P.O. Box 14271
Kirschenbaum, Alan M. . . . .'48 '86 C.659 B.A. L.309 J.D. [Hyman,P.&M.]
Kirschner, David C. . . . .'62 '95 C.145 B.A. L.978 J.D. [Kelley D.&W.]
*PRACTICE AREAS: Telecommunications.
Kirschner, Greg J. '73 '99 C.537 B.A. L.276 J.D.
(adm. in VA; not adm. in DC) [Conlon,F.P.&P.]
*PRACTICE AREAS: Civil Rights; Class Actions.
Kirschten, Barbara L., (AV) . . . . '50 '83 C.659 B.A. L.597 J.D. [Morrison&F.]
*PRACTICE AREAS: Nonprofit Organizations; Tax Exempt Organizations.
Kirshenberg, Seth David . . . . '67 '92 C.260 B.S. L.904 J.D. [Kutak R.]
*PRACTICE AREAS: Real Estate; Environmental; Government Affairs.
Kirshner, Robert A. '55 '80 C.659 B.A. L.30 J.D.
Vice President & General Counsel, American Forest & Paper Assn.
Kirstein, David M., (AV) . . . .'46 '71 C.184 B.A. L.893 J.D. [Baker&H.]
*PRACTICE AREAS: Aviation; Administrative; Antitrust; Transportation; Commercial.
Kirtland, John C. . . . . '39 '71 C.871 B.S. L.276 J.D. [Winston&S.]
*PRACTICE AREAS: Legislative Practice; International Trade Law.
Kirtland, Matthew H. . . . .'72 '97 C.429 B.A. L.228 J.D. [Fulbright&J.]
*PRACTICE AREAS: Litigation; White Collar Crime.
Kirtley, Clyde '46 '70 C.383 B.S. L.893 J.D.
(adm. in KY; not adm. in DC) 3109 Tenneyson St., NW‡
Kisch, Lori B. '70 '97 C.1044 B.A. L.588 J.D.
(adm. in MD; not adm. in DC) [Gordon,S.W.&C.]
*PRACTICE AREAS: Civil Rights Litigation; Employment Discrimination.
Kiser, Cherie R., (AV) . . . .'58 '87 C.494 B.A. L.128 J.D. [Mintz,L.C.F.G.&P.]
*PRACTICE AREAS: Communications Law; FCC Regulation.
Kiser, John Daniel . . . .'46 '74 C.269 B.A. L.245 J.D. [Foxkiser]
Kishimoto, Yoshinari '54 '99 C&L.999 B.A., LL.B.
(adm. in NY; not adm. in DC; See Pat. Sect.) [Sughrue M.]
*PRACTICE AREAS: Patent Application; Patent Prosecution; Litigation.
Kiss, Albert J. . . . . '— '91 C.659 B.S. L.178 J.D. 1225 Connecticut Avenue, NW
Kissel, Peter C., (AV) . . . .'47 '73 C.823 B.A. L.30 J.D. [GKRSE]
*PRACTICE AREAS: Utility Regulation; Hydroelectricity; Natural Gas Regulation; Administrative Law; Appellate Practice.
Kissick, Ralph L., (AV) . . . . '40 '69 C.976 B.A. L.477 J.D. [Zuckert,S.&R.]
*PRACTICE AREAS: International Government Contracts; Federal Contracts; Aerospace Contracts; Aircraft Finance and Leasing.
Kissinger, Ashley I. . . . . '68 '96 C.813 A.B. L.846 J.D. [Levine S.&K.]
Kisslinger, Paul W. . . . .'68 '93 C.659 B.A. L.665 J.D. [Dickstein S.M.&O.]
*PRACTICE AREAS: Commercial Litigation; Employment Counseling and Litigation; Insurance Coverage Litigation.
Kit, Gordon, (BV) . . . . '54 '83 C.178 A.B. L.30 J.D. [Sughrue M.] (See Pat. Sect.)
*PRACTICE AREAS: Intellectual Property Law; Biotechnology.
Kitchen, Erik L., (AV) . . . . '54 '79 C.674 B.A. L.309 J.D. [Steptoe&J.]
*PRACTICE AREAS: Corporate Law; Government Investigations; Corporate Investigations; Foreign Corrupt Practices Act.
Kithcart, Tiffany Natasha '— '01 C.846 B.A. L.326 J.D.
(adm. in TX; not adm. in DC) [Epstein B.&G.]
Kittle, Ralph W. '20 '49 C.143 A.B. L.893 J.D.
(adm. in NY; not adm. in DC) 1155 15th St., N.W.
Kitto, Joseph L. . . . . '66 '99 C.623 B.A. L.188 J.D. [Holland&K.]
*PRACTICE AREAS: Indian Law; Public Law; Litigation.
Kittrell, Steven D., (AV) . . . . '53 '78 C.69 B.A. L.273 J.D. [McGuirewoods]
*PRACTICE AREAS: Employee Benefits; Securities Litigation; Mergers and Acquisitions; Executive Compensation.
Kittrie, Nicholas N. . . . . '28 '57 C&L.378 M.A., LL.B. Prof. of Law, Amer. Univ.
Kitzmiller, Howard L. '30 '54 C.216 A.B. L.1017 J.D.
Sr. V.P., Secy. & Dir., Washington Mgmt. Corp.

Kivitz & Liptz, LLC
(See Chevy Chase, Maryland)

Kiyonaga, Paul . . . . '63 '90 C.575 B.A. L.309 J.D. 910 17th St., N.W.
Kizer, Karen '63 '00 C.37 B.A. L.145 J.D.
(adm. in NY; not adm. in DC) [Covington&B.]
Kjeldgaard, Richard H., (AV) . . . .'52 '78 C.546 B.A. L.273 J.D. [Collier S.S.] (Pat.)
*PRACTICE AREAS: Intellectual Property Law; Patent, Trademark and Copyright Law.

K.K.M., P.A.
(See Bethesda, Maryland)

Klaassen, Mark . . . . '— '98 C.1288 B.S. L.602 J.D. [Latham&W.]
*PRACTICE AREAS: Litigation.
Klain, Ronald . . . . '61 '92 C.276 A.B. L.309 J.D. [O'Melveny&M.]
*PRACTICE AREAS: Appellate Litigation; Strategic Counseling; Government Relations.
Klamp, Carolyn . . . .'59 '86 C.893 B.A. L.309 J.D. [Dorn&K.]
Klanderman, Thomas C. '70 '98 C.1349 B.A. L.276 J.D.
(adm. in NY; not adm. in DC) [Bingham D.]
*PRACTICE AREAS: Real Estate.
Klapisch, Jutta . . . .'60 '96 L.999 [Arent F.K.P.&K.]
*PRACTICE AREAS: International; Corporate; Finance.
Klapow, Mark Andrew '74 '99 C.910 L.823
(adm. in CT; not adm. in DC) [Howrey S.A.&W.]
*PRACTICE AREAS: Commercial; Antitrust.
Klapper, Antony B. . . . . '67 '96 C.893 B.A. L.659 J.D. [Kirkland&E.]
*PRACTICE AREAS: Litigation.
Klarfeld, Peter J., (AV) . . . .'47 '73 C&L.893 B.A., J.D. [Wiley R.&F.]
*PRACTICE AREAS: Franchise; Litigation.
Klarman, Margaret A. . . . .'52 '82 C.518 A.B. L.128 J.D. [Brown,G.&J.]
Klass, Jennifer L. . . . .'— '98 C.401 B.A. L.1338 J.D. [Morgan,L.&B.]
Klass, Michelle Eileen . . . . . '66 '98 C.329 B.S. L.1364 J.D. 714 G. Street SE, Capitol Hill
Klatzkin, Josh . . . . '74 '99 C.264 B.A. L.893 J.D. [Hogan&H.]
Klauser, Arthur E. '23 '59 C.477 A.B. L.976 J.D.
Advsr./Trustee, Mitsui & Company (U.S.A.), Inc.
Klawiter, Donald C. . . . . '50 '75 C&L.659 B.A., J.D. [Morgan,L.&B.]
Klayman, Larry . . . .'51 '77 C.228 A.B. L.245 J.D. [Klayman&Assoc.] ⊙
Klayman, Robert A., (AV) . . . . '29 '54 C&L.923 B.S., LL.B. 1 Thomas Cir., N.W.
Klayman & Associates, P.C. . . . . 501 School St., S.W., Ste. 700 (⊙Miami, FL)
Kleiman, Susan Sonenshein . . . . '66 '91 C.1365 B.A. L.904 J.D. [Arent F.K.P.&K.]
*PRACTICE AREAS: Employee Benefits; Executive Compensation.
Klein, Allen J., (AV) . . . .'53 '79 C.188 B.A. L.107 J.D. [Shaw P.]
*PRACTICE AREAS: Outsourcing; Technology; Corporate.
Klein, Amy Loeserman, (AV) '36 '59
C.994 B.A. L.145 J.D. 1919 Pennsylvania Ave., N.W.
Klein, Andrew M. '67 '92 C.156 B.A. L.982 J.D.
(adm. in NJ; not adm. in DC) [Kelley D.&W.]
*PRACTICE AREAS: Telecommunications; Litigation.
Klein, Andrew M., (AV) . . . .'41 '67 C&L.145 B.A., J.D. [Schiff H.&W.]
*PRACTICE AREAS: Securities Regulation; Broker-Dealer Regulation; Investment Management.
Klein, Audrey E. . . . .'59 '91 C.831 B.S. L.276 J.D. [Hogan&H.] (Pat.)
*PRACTICE AREAS: Intellectual Property.
Klein, Carole R. . . . . '56 '91 C.276 B.S.F.S. L.893 J.D. [Morgan,L.&B.]
Klein, Charles B. . . . .'70 '95 C.893 B.A. L.1065 J.D. [Winston&S.]
Klein, David A. . . . .'68 '99 C.260 B.S.E.E. L.276 J.D. [Sughrue M.]
*PRACTICE AREAS: Intellectual Property.
Klein, David F. . . . .'63 '89 C.94 B.A. L.976 J.D. [Swidler B.S.F.]
*PRACTICE AREAS: Insurance Coverage Litigation.
Klein, Dennis S. . . . .'54 '81 C.529 B.A. L.893 J.D. [Hughes H.&R.]
*PRACTICE AREAS: Litigation; Financial Institutions.
Klein, Douglas A. . . . .'70 '96 C.1349 B.A. L.273 J.D. [Hogan&H.]
*PRACTICE AREAS: Telecommunications Regulation; International Telecommunications Law.
Klein, Frederick L., (AV) . . . .'54 '79 C.228 A.B. L.472 J.D. [Piper M.R.&W.]
*PRACTICE AREAS: Real Estate - Commercial.
Klein, Gary Ethan . . . .'49 '77 C.966 B.A. L.588 J.D. [Klein,L.&R.]
Klein, Gary J., (AV) . . . . '— '71 C.188 B.S. L.178 J.D. [Verner,L.B.M.&H.]
*PRACTICE AREAS: Legislative Law; Energy Law; Environmental Law; Infrastructure Development; Privatization Law.
Klein, Jeffrey M. . . . .'71 '97 C.976 B.A. L.309 J.D. [Shea&G.]
Klein, Jill Swerdloff '64 '91 C&L.893 B.A., J.D.
Assoc. Coun., Blue Cross & Blue Shield Assn.
Klein, Jo-Ellyn Sakowitz . . . . '72 '98 C.228 A.B. L.276 J.D. [Akin,G.S.H.&F.]
*PRACTICE AREAS: Health Care.
Klein, Kenneth . . . . '51 '77 C.205 B.A. L.280 J.D. [Cadwalader,W.&T.]
*PRACTICE AREAS: International Taxation; Tax Planning; Tax Controversies.
Klein, Kenneth . . . .'58 '91 C.930 B.S. L.117 J.D. 641 Indiana Ave. N.W.
Klein, Leonard E. '46 '72 C.569 A.B. L.309 J.D.
(adm. in NJ; not adm. in DC)
Legal Research Libr., George Washington Univ. Law School
Klein, Leslie E. . . . .'70 '98 C.347 B.A. L.30 J.D. [Sonnenschein N.&R.]
*PRACTICE AREAS: Litigation.
Klein, M. Michael . . . .'31 '58 C.705 Litt.B. L.276 J.D. 1155 15th St., N.W.
Klein, Michael E. . . . .'61 '93 C.870 B.S. L.893 J.D. [Patton B.]
Klein, Michael R., (AV) . . . . '42 '66 C&L.472 B.B.A., J.D. [Wilmer,C.&P.]
*PRACTICE AREAS: Securities; Corporate Law; Mergers, Acquisitions and Divestitures; Civil Practice.
Klein, Paul B. . . . . '58 '85 C.446 B.S. L.64 J.D. 1900 L St., N.W.
Klein, Richard W., Jr. '45 '72 C.976 B.A. L.904 J.D.
Pres., Tri-State Coml. Closings, Inc.
Klein, Roger A., (AV) . . . .'50 '75 C.910 B.A. L.276 J.D. [Howrey S.A.&W.]
*PRACTICE AREAS: Corporate Law; Real Estate Law; Commercial Law.
Klein, Saml. C. . . . .'11 '37 C.415 A.B. L.724 LL.B. 700 Seventh St., S.W.
Klein, Sean J. '70 '95 C.276 B.A./B.S. L.597 J.D.
(adm. in IL; not adm. in DC) [Piper M.R.&W.]
*PRACTICE AREAS: Securities; Venture Capital; General Corporate.
Klein, Sheldon H. . . . .'56 '80 C.477 B.A. L.273 J.D. [Arent F.K.P.&K.]
*PRACTICE AREAS: Intellectual Property; Trademarks; Copyrights; Unfair Competition; Advertising and Marketing.
Klein, Stephen A. . . . . '65 '91 C.659 B.A. L.477 J.D. [Spriggs&H.]
*PRACTICE AREAS: Insurance Coverage; Toxic Torts; Litigation.
Klein, Thomas L. . . . .'65 '96 C.893 B.S. L.896 J.D. [Arnold&P.]
*PRACTICE AREAS: Tax Law.
Klein & Cutler .1700 K. St. N.W., Suite 1004 (⊙Sherman Oaks, CA)
Klein, Landau & Romm . . . . 1725 K St., N.W.

Klein, Morris
(See Bethesda, Maryland)

Kleinfeld, Eric F. . . . .'59 '84 C.473 B.A. L.608 J.D. [Ryan,P.U.&M.]
Kleinfeld, George, (AV) . . . . '59 '84 C.276 B.S. L.659 J.D. [Clifford C.R.&W.]
*PRACTICE AREAS: Communications Law; International Trade; Investments.

Kleinfeld, Kaplan and Becker, (AV) BR
Suite 900, 1140 Nineteenth Street, N.W., 20036 ⊙
Telephone: 202-223-5120 Telecopier: 202-223-5619
Email: kkb@kkblaw.com URL: http://www.kkblaw.com
Vincent A. Kleinfeld (1907-1993). Members of Firm: Alan H. Kaplan; Thomas O. Henteleff; Richard S. Morey; Peter O. Safir; Kinsey S. Reagan; Peter R. Mathers; Bonnie A. Beavers; Daniel R. Dwyer; Glenn E. Davis; Prescott M. Lassman. Associates: Stacy L. Ehrlich; Jennifer A. Davidson; Stacey L. Valerio; Robert O. Winters (Not admitted in DC).
Practice before all Courts and Government Agencies. Regulatory and Administrative Law involving Food, Drugs, Cosmetics, Medical Devices, Dictary Supplements, Pesticides, Controlled Substances and Consumer Products.
San Francisco, California Office: One Market Street, Steuart Tower, Suite 1450. Telephone: 415-538-0014. Telecopier: 415-538-0016.
See Professional Biographies, WASHINGTON, DISTRICT OF COLUMBIA

Kleinman, Daniel R. . . . .'69 '97 C.569 B.S. L.1017 J.D. [Morgan,L.&B.]
Kleinman, Joel B., (AV) . . . .'49 '75 C.893 B.A. L.276 J.D. [Dickstein S.M.&O.]
*PRACTICE AREAS: Insurance Coverage Law; Antitrust and Trade Regulation Law; Communications Law.

Kleinman, Ronald W., (AV) .... '51 '76 C&L.276 B.S.F.S., J.D. [Greenberg T.]
Klepper, Arlene Fine .... '49 '75 C.70 B.A. L.273 J.D. [Arent F.K.P.&K.] ‡
*PRACTICE AREAS: Public Finance; Project Finance; Banking Law; Health Care.
Klepper, Martin, (AV) .... '47 '73 C.659 B.S. L.705 J.D. [Skadden,A.S.M.&F.]
Klessman, Todd B. .... '74 '99 C&L.477 B.B.A., J.D. [Ⓐ Dow,L.&A.]
Klett Rooney Lieber & Schorling, A Professional Corporation
600 Pennsylvania Ave., S.E. (⊙Wilmington, DE; Newark, Trenton, NJ; Harrisburg, Phila., Pitts., PA)
Kletzkin, Morris, (AV) .... '46 '72 C.1033 B.A. L.904 J.D. [Friedlander,M.S.K.&O.]
*PRACTICE AREAS: General Civil Litigation; Employment Litigation; Rental Vehicles Litigation; Insurance; Guaranty Fund Law.
Klevens, Shari L. .... '72 '99 C.446 B.A. L.273 J.D. [Ⓐ McKenna&C.]
*PRACTICE AREAS: Trademarks; Copyrights; Intellectual Property Litigation.
Kliefoth, Christopher .... '52 '81 C.112 B.A. L.893 J.D. [McDermott,W.&E.]
Kligman, Theodore, (AV) .... '30 '52 C.446 L.30 J.D. [Donohue,K.S.&K.]
Klimaski, James R., (AV) .... '46 '76 C.812 B.S. L.1162 J.D. [Klimaski&G.]
*PRACTICE AREAS: Employment Law; Military Law; Security Clearances; Pension Rights Law; Personal Injury.

Klimaski & Grill, P.C., (AV)
1400 K Street, N.W. Suite 1000, 20005-2409
Telephone: 202-296-5600 Fax: 202-296-5601 URL:http://www.klimaskigrill.com
Email: kgpc@igc.org URL: http://www.lawyers.com/klimaskilaw
James R. Klimaski; Andrea S. Grill. Of Counsel: Lynn I. Miller.
Military Law, Employment Law, Labor Relations, Civil Rights Law, Police Misconduct, Employment Benefits, Security Clearances, Criminal Defense, Personal Injury, Auto Accidents, Bankruptcy, Small Business and Contracts.
See Professional Biographies, WASHINGTON, DISTRICT OF COLUMBIA

Klimon, William M. .... '66 '98 C.659 B.A. L.446 [Ⓐ Caplin&D.]
*PRACTICE AREAS: Corporate; Mergers, Acquisitions and Divestitures; Financing; Franchising.
Klindera, Eve .... '74 '99 C.446 B.A. L.273 J.D. [Ⓐ Wiley R.&F.]
Kline, Andrew J., Law Offices, (AV) .... '56 '81 C.273 B.A. L.945 J.D. 1900 M St., N.W.
Kline, Lori E. .... '70 '95 C.446 B.S. L.945 J.D. [Ⓐ Shaw,B.V.&R.]
*PRACTICE AREAS: Employment Discrimination; Federal Personnel Law; Employment Law.
Kline, Rebecca L. .... '71 '98 C.951 B.A. L.477 J.D. [Ⓐ Kirkpatrick&L.]
*PRACTICE AREAS: SEC Enforcement; Securities Litigation.
Kline, Richard G., (AV) '30 '58
C.309 A.B. L.273 LL.B. 1025 Connecticut Ave., N.W. (Pat.)
Kline, Robert C., (AV) '27 '55
C.659 B.S. L.273 J.D. [Ⓒ Fitzpatrick,C.H.&S.] (See Pat. Sect.)
Kline, Sheldon M. .... '48 '87 C.454 B.A. L.1209 J.D. [Morgan,L.&B.]
Kline, Thomas R. .... '47 '76 C&L.178 A.B., J.D. [Andrews&K.]
*PRACTICE AREAS: Litigation.
Kline, Moore & Klein, Professional Association .... 910 17th St., N.W. (⊙Miami, FL)
Klineberg, Geoffrey M. .... '63 '94 C.674 A.B. L.976 J.D. [Kellogg,H.H.T.&E.]
*PRACTICE AREAS: Telecommunications; Appellate Litigation.
Kling, Kathryn Cole .... '70 '94 C.797 B.A. L.93 J.D. [Ⓐ Alston&B.]
*PRACTICE AREAS: Mergers and Acquisitions; Securities; Financial Services Law.

Klingenberg, Martin F., (AV) '42 '68 C.663 B.S. L.623 J.D.
1025 Thomas Jefferson Street, N.W. Suite 425 West, 20007
Telephone: 202-223-1066 Fax: 202-462-7450
Email: martin6@attglobal.net
***PRACTICE AREAS: International; Mergers and Acquisitions; Finance; Corporate; Antitrust.**
U.S., European and Asian Company Law, International Investment, International Commercial Negotiations.
See Professional Biographies, WASHINGTON, DISTRICT OF COLUMBIA

Klingler, Richard D. .... '61 '91 C&L.813 B.A., J.D. 1722 I St Nw
Klingsberg, Jordan Lee .... '68 '96 C.1155 B.S. L.276 J.D. [Ⓐ Steptoe&J.]
Klinke, Diane G. '53 '79 C.262 B.A. L.477 J.D.
Gen. Coun., Mun. Secs. Rulemaking Bd.
Klipper, Michael Russell .... '48 '73 C.823 B.A. L.273 J.D. [Meyer&K.]
Klise, J. Michael .... '47 '86 C&L.128 B.A., J.D. [Crowell&M.]
*PRACTICE AREAS: Administrative Law; Coal Law; Mine Safety and Health Law; Natural Resources Law.
Klock, Brian L. '67 '94 C.886 B.S.E.E. L.273 J.D.
[Fitzpatrick,C.H.&S.] (See Pat. Sect.)
Klock, Mark Steven ...... '58 '88 C.645 B.A. L.446 J.D. Assoc. Prof., George Wash. Univ.
Klohe, Trena Lee .... '— '98 C.685 B.A. L.560 J.D. [Ⓐ Latham&W.]
*PRACTICE AREAS: Health Care; Medicare and Medicaid Reimbursement; Health Care Regulation; International Law; International Human Rights.
Klonoff, Robert H., (AV) .... '55 '80 C.112 A.B. L.976 J.D. [Jones,D.R.&P.]
*PRACTICE AREAS: Litigation; Appellate Practice; U.S. Supreme Court Litigation; Class Actions.
Klopp, Brian W. .... '68 '98 C&L.608 B.A., J.D. Labor Economist, AFSCME
Klores, Bruce J., (AV) ...... '54 '81 C.1036 B.A. L.128 J.D. [B.J.Klores&Assoc.] ⊙
*PRACTICE AREAS: Civil Trials; Professional Negligence.
Klores, Noel H. .... '33 '58 C.569 A.B. L.309 LL.B. 1225 19th St., N.W.

Klores, Bruce J., & Associates, P.C., (AV)
915 Fifteenth Street, N.W. Suite 300, 20036 ⊙
Telephone: 202-628-8100 Telecopier: 202-628-1240 URL: http://www.klores.com
Email: office@klores.com URL: http://www.lawyers.com/klores
Bruce J. Klores;—Richard J. Fogelson; Lesley S. Zork; Patricia C. Karppi.
Civil Trial Practice with emphasis in Medical Negligence, Birth Trauma, Pediatric Malpractice and Professional Liability.
Arlington, Virginia Office: Suite 708, 2009 North 14th Street. Telephone: 703-527-0970. Telecopier: 703-522-1250.
See Professional Biographies, WASHINGTON, DISTRICT OF COLUMBIA

Kloze, Ida I. '06 '27 C.273 A.B. L.446 LL.B.
(adm. in MD; not adm. in DC) 4201 Cathedral Ave., N.W.‡
Klubes, Benjamin B., (AV) .... '65 '90 C.273 B.A. L.309 J.D. [Ⓒ Skadden,A.S.M.&F.]
Kluge, Robert H., III '69 '97 C.893 B.A. L.30 J.D.
(adm. in VA; not adm. in DC) [Ⓐ Akin,G.S.H.&F.]
*PRACTICE AREAS: General Litigation; Regulatory; Administrative.
Klumpp, Heléna M. .... '71 '96 C.340 B.A. L.276 J.D. [Ⓐ Chadbourne&P.]
Klupt, Mark Reid .... '67 '96 C.367 B.A. L.893 J.D. [Ⓐ Vinson&E.]
*PRACTICE AREAS: Federal Energy Regulation; Natural Gas Regulation; International Business Transactions; Project Finance; Regulatory Law.
Klur, Lawrence R. '43 '85 C.201 B.A. L.128 J.D.
(adm. in PA; not adm. in DC) 100 Independence Ave.
Klusaritz, John J. .... '57 '81 C.401 B.S. L.309 J.D. [Swidler B.S.F.]
*PRACTICE AREAS: Corporate Law; Finance; Mergers and Acquisitions.
Klyce, Michael J., Jr. .... '71 '96 C.1365 L.228 J.D. [Ⓐ Arnold&P.]
*PRACTICE AREAS: Litigation; Antitrust; Insurance.
Kmieciak, Steven J., (AV) .... '53 '79 C.602 B.A. L.446 J.D. [Seyfarth S.]
*PRACTICE AREAS: Construction Law; Government Contracts Law.
Knab, John A. .... '63 '93 C.1044 B.A. L.904 J.D. [Ⓐ Simon,T.&M.]
Knakmuhs, Heath K. .... '— '99 C.597 B.A. L.94 J.D. [Ⓐ Morgan,L.&B.]
Knapp, Aimee E. .... '74 '00 C.1369 B.S. L.180 J.D. [Ⓐ Fleischman&W.]
Knapp, Andrew B. .... '68 '98 C.183 B.A. L.276 J.D. 1100 Fifteenth Street, NW, Suite 700
Knapp, George M., (AV) .... '54 '78 C.112 B.A. L.273 J.D. [Squire,S.&D.]
*PRACTICE AREAS: Energy; Finance; International Law; Public Utilities; Privatization.
Knapp, Jeffery W., (AV) .... '47 '74 C.747 B.A. L.276 J.D. 1818 N. St., N.W.
Knapp, John J., (AV) .... '34 '62 C.433 B.S. L.262 J.D. [Powell,G.F.&M.]
*PRACTICE AREAS: Federal Housing Programs; Administrative; Corporate Lending Law.
Knapp, Sarah Leslie '70 '99 C.1169 B.A. L.276 J.D.
(adm. in CA; not adm. in DC) [Ⓐ Baach R.&L.P.]
Knapp, Thomas J., (AV) .... '52 '77 C.339 B.A. L.424 J.D. [Ⓒ Paul,H.J.&W.]
*PRACTICE AREAS: Labor and Employment; Litigation; Transportation; Executive Compensation.
Knappen, Theodore C. .... '44 '68 C&L.893 B.A., LL.B. Peyser Assocs., Inc.
Knauer, Ivan B. .... '61 '89 C.659 B.A. L.569 J.D. [Ⓐ Kirkpatrick&L.]
*PRACTICE AREAS: Securities Litigation; SEC Enforcement; NASD Arbitration; Commercial Litigation; Intellectual Property Litigation.
Knauer, Leon T., (AV) .... '32 '61 C.262 B.S. L.276 LL.B. [Wilkinson B.K.]
*PRACTICE AREAS: Telecommunications Law; International Commercial Transactions.
Knauss, Charles H. .... '55 '82 C.103 A.B. L.477 J.D. [Swidler B.S.F.]
*PRACTICE AREAS: Regulatory Law; Environmental Law; Legislative Counsel.
Knell, Gregory S. .... '69 '97 C.228 A.B. L.178 J.D. [Ⓐ Wilmer,C.&P.]
Kneller, Susan R. .... '56 '83 C.518 B.A. L.273 J.D. 2910 Garfield St., N.W.
Knepper, G. Jeffrey '44 '70 C&L.608 B.S., J.D.
(adm. in OH; not adm. in DC) Dir., Tax, Deloitte & Touche
Kneuer, John M. R. .... '— '94 C&L.128 B.A., J.D. [Ⓐ Verner,L.B.M.&H.]
*PRACTICE AREAS: Communications.
Knickerbocker, Beth D. '66 '92 C.187 B.A. L.352 J.D.
(adm. in IA; not adm. in DC) [Ⓐ Sutherland A.&B.]
*PRACTICE AREAS: Insurance Regulation; Banking Law; Broker-Dealer Registration.
Knight, George F. '43 '71 C.708 B.A. L.128 J.D.
(adm. in VA; not adm. in DC) 1231 25th St., N.W.‡
Knight, Jeffrey A. .... '71 '96 C.31 B.A. L.145 J.D. [Ⓐ Shaw P.]
Knight, Leonardo R. .... '57 '82 C.93 B.A. L.30 J.D. D.C. Pub. Def. Serv.
Knight, Michael H. .... '65 '91 C.1356 B.S. L.1209 J.D. [Collier S.S.]
*PRACTICE AREAS: Antitrust.
Knight, Patrick L. .... '45 '82 C.757 B.A. L.180 J.D. 3616 Ingomar Pl., N.W.
Knight, Paul L., (AV) .... '49 '75 C.112 A.B. L.1065 J.D. [O'Connor&H.]
*PRACTICE AREAS: White Collar Criminal Defense; Civil Litigation; Criminal Law.
Knight, Stephen D., (AV) .... '53 '78 C&L.893 B.A., J.D. [Kirkland&E.]
*PRACTICE AREAS: Government Contracts.
Knight, Thomas E. .... '70 '96 C.367 B.A. L.904 J.D. [Ⓐ Fleischman&W.]
Knight, Webster T., (BV) .... '47 '76 C.321 B.A. L.1209 J.D. 601 Indiana Ave., N.W.
Knight, Manzi, Nussbaum & LaPlaca, P.C.
(See Upper Marlboro)
Knoblock, Elizabeth M. .... '55 '79 C.362 B.A. L.276 J.D. [Ⓒ Dechert]
*PRACTICE AREAS: Financial Services Law; Investment Management; Securities Regulation; Broker-Dealer Regulation; Private Placement.
Knoeckel, Mary Ann .... '59 '91 C.312 B.B.A. L.846 J.D. [Ⓐ Venable,A.B.H.&C.]
*PRACTICE AREAS: Real Estate; Commercial Law.
Knoll, E. Joseph, (AV) .... '39 '64 C.546 B.S. L.276 J.D. [Krooth&A.]
Knopf, Norman G., (AV) .... '39 '64 C.188 A.B. L.178 LL.B. [Knopf&B.]
*PRACTICE AREAS: Litigation; Land Use and Zoning; Local Government; Antitrust and Trade Regulation.

Knopf & Brown, (AV)
1050 Seventeenth Street, N.W., Suite 1200, 20036
Telephone: 202-785-8200 Telecopier: 202-331-0174 URL: http://www.knopf-brown.com
URL: http://www.lawyers.com/knopf&brownlaw
Norman G. Knopf; David W. Brown; Barry S. Shanoff; Susan G. Goldberg.
General and Administrative Practice and Litigation, Antitrust and Trade Regulation, Environmental, Land Use and Zoning, Local Government, Energy, Trade Associations, Nonprofit Organizations, Corporate Law.
See Professional Biographies, WASHINGTON, DISTRICT OF COLUMBIA

Knorr, Gene A. .... '40 '65 C.747 B.A. L.597 J.D. V.P., Philip Morris Cos. Inc.
Knott, Scott A. .... '72 '99 C.690 B.S.B.A. L.472 J.D. [Ⓐ Baker&M.]
*PRACTICE AREAS: Tax Controversies (Corporate and International); Tax Planning and Advice (Corporate and International).
Knotts, Joseph B., Jr. .... '38 '64 C.674 A.B. L.309 LL.B. [Ⓒ Winston&S.]
*PRACTICE AREAS: Nuclear Energy Law; Energy Law; Public Utility Law.
Knowles, Gearold L. .... '46 '73 C.347 B.S. L.1119 J.D. [Schiff H.&W.]
*PRACTICE AREAS: Federal Energy Regulation; Natural Gas Regulation; Electric Power; Energy Project Development; International Telecommunications Law.
Knowles, Jeffrey D. .... '49 '76 C.178 B.A. L.564 J.D. [Venable,A.B.H.&C.]
*PRACTICE AREAS: Administrative Law; Advertising; Direct Marketing; Licensing; Contracts.
Knox, George R., Jr. .... '56 '82 C.150 B.B.A. L.744 J.D. [Maloney&K.]
Knox, Kenneth S. .... '62 '96 C.17 B.A. L.329 J.D. [Ⓢ Preston G.E.&R.M.]
*PRACTICE AREAS: Litigation.
Koback, Peter G. .... '68 '93 C.454 B.A. L.813 J.D. [Ⓐ Shaw P.]
Kobersy, Maya Renata .... '75 '99 C.477 B.A. L.309 J.D. [Ⓐ Hogan&H.]
Koblenz, Andrew D., (AV) '56 '83
C.867 B.A. L.309 J.D. Sr. Atty., Amer. Auto. Mfrs. Assn.
Kobrine, Nicole L. .... '70 '96 C.813 B.A. L.273 J.D. [Ⓐ Katten M.Z.]
*PRACTICE AREAS: Litigation.
Koch, Amy S. .... '56 '82 C.136 B.A. L.273 J.D. [Cameron M.]
*PRACTICE AREAS: Energy Competition; Energy Finance; Energy Project Development; Energy Regulation; Federal Energy Regulation.
Koch, Arthur D. '47 '73
C.823 B.A. L.273 J.D. Counsel - Food Operations, Giant Food, Inc.
Koch, David W. .... '60 '85 C.352 B.S. L.477 J.D. [Wiley R.&F.]
*PRACTICE AREAS: Franchise; Antitrust.
Koch, Elizabeth C. .... '61 '87 C.881 A.B. L.477 J.D. [Levine S.&K.]
Koch, James W. .... '64 '89 C.228 A.B. L.823 J.D. [Ⓐ Sherman,M.C.&A.]
*PRACTICE AREAS: Estate Planning; Estate Administration; Estate Litigation; Business Planning; Charitable Giving.
Koch, M. Alexander .... '— '97 C.893 B.A. L.276 J.D. [Ⓐ King&S.]
*PRACTICE AREAS: Litigation; Trade Regulation.
Koch, Robbie N. .... '— '98 C.763 B.A. L.30 J.D. [Ⓐ Reed S.]
*PRACTICE AREAS: Government Relations.
Koch, Robert J., (AV) '46 '73 C.215 B.S. L.128 J.D.
(adm. in VA; not adm. in DC; See Pat. Sect.) [Fulbright&J.]
*PRACTICE AREAS: Intellectual Property; Technology and Science; Technology Transfers.
Kochan, Donald J. '74 '00 C.932 B.A. L.188 J.D.
(adm. in NY; not adm. in DC) [Ⓐ Crowell&M.]
Kocher, Jennifer L. .... '68 '95 C.299 B.A. L.893 J.D. [Ⓐ Morgan,L.&B.]
Koches, Paul A., (AV) .... '53 '78 C.184 B.A. L.472 J.D. [Arent F.K.P.&K.]
*PRACTICE AREAS: Antitrust; Litigation; Intellectual Property; International Transactions.
Kochinke, Clemens, (AV) .... '52 '78 C.999 B.A. L.273 M.C.L. [Berliner,C.&R.]
*PRACTICE AREAS: International; Internet; Computer.
Kochman, Jane '44 '91 C.102 B.A. L.560 J.D.
(adm. in NM; not adm. in DC) ALIF
Kochman, Neal M. .... '50 '96 C.188 B.S. L.276 J.D. [Ⓐ Caplin&D.]
*PRACTICE AREAS: Tax.
Koda, Paul W. .... '63 '97 C.576 B.S. L.273 J.D. [IP S.] (Pat.)
Koegel, Christopher T. .... '74 '00 C.575 B.A. L.659 J.D. [Ⓐ Jones,D.R.&P.]

Koegel, J. William, Jr., (AV) . . . . '54 '79 C.597 B.A. L.93 J.D. [Steptoe&J.]
*PRACTICE AREAS: Business Litigation; Commercial Litigation; Intellectual Property Litigation; Securities Litigation.
Koegel, Susan . . . .'62 '88 C.473 B.A. L.846 J.D. [Ⓐ Covington&B.]
*PRACTICE AREAS: Intellectual Property; Intellectual Property Litigation; Intellectual Property Prosecution; Litigation; Civil Litigation.
Koehl, G. Matthew '67 '93 C.165 B.A. L.902 J.D.
(adm. in MD; not adm. in DC) [Ⓒ Preston G.E.&R.M.]
*PRACTICE AREAS: Government Contracts; Litigation.
Koehler, Beth A. . . . . '72 '97 C.475 B.A. L.276 J.D. [Ⓢ Ross,D.&B.]
Koehler, David K. . . . . '— '95 L.107 J.D. [Ⓐ Nixon P.] (⊙Mc Lean, VA)
*PRACTICE AREAS: Intellectual Property; Trademarks; Media Law; Litigation.
Koehler, Kristin Graham . . . .'69 '95 C.1372 B.A. L.107 J.D. [Ⓐ Sidley A.B.&W.]
Koempel, Michael L. . . . . . . '49 '75 C.276 B.S.F.S. L.128 J.D. Congressional Quarterly, Inc.
Koenig, David G. . . . . '59 '84 C.705 B.A. L.273 J.D. Texaco Inc.
Koenig, Peter J. '55 '82 C.608 B.A. L.477 J.D.
(adm. in PA; not adm. in DC) [Miller&C.]
*PRACTICE AREAS: International Trade Law; Unfair Competition Law; Customs.
Koenigs, Craig A. . . . . '63 '90 C.966 B.A. L.276 J.D. [Hall,E.H.G.G.&N.]
Koeppel, Jeffrey A., (AV) . . . .'53 '78 C.446 B.A. L.64 J.D. [Elias,M.T.&H.]
*PRACTICE AREAS: Corporate; Securities; Mergers and Acquisitions.
Koerner, William R., Jr. . . . . '43 '69 C.103 A.B. L.823 J.D. 1225 19th St., NW
Koff, Alexander . . . . '70 '97 C&L.477 B.A., J.D. [Ⓐ Powell,G.F.&M.]
*PRACTICE AREAS: International.
Koffler, Michael . . . .'71 '96 C.1349 B.A. L.659 J.D. [Ⓐ Sutherland A.&B.]
*PRACTICE AREAS: Securities; Broker-Dealer Regulation; Investment Adviser Regulation; Distribution of Investment Products; Insurance Regulation.
Koffler, Warren W., (AV) '38 '62 C.94 B.S. L.569 LL.B.
1730 K Street, N.W., Suite 304 (⊙Palm Beach Gardens, FL)
Kogelnik, Florian Alexander . . . . '67 '94 C.228 A.B. L.208 J.D. 1015 15th St., N.W.
Koger, Gregory H. '72 '99 C.446 B.S. L.180 J.D.
(adm. in MD; not adm. in DC) [Ⓐ McManus,S.A.&D.]
*PRACTICE AREAS: Commercial Litigation; Construction Law; Government Contracts.
Koger, Thomas L. '52 '88 C.610 B.B.A. L.262 J.D. Asst. Corp. Coun.
Koh, Christine E. . . . . '— '00 C.668 B.A. L.976 J.D. [Ⓐ Arnold&P.]
Kohl, Kenneth C. '59 '85 C.957 B.A. L.589 J.D.
(adm. in IL; not adm. in DC) Asst. U.S. Atty.
Kohlman, W. Gary, (AV) . . . .'46 '71 C&L.477 B.B.A., LL.B. [Bredhoff&K.]
Kohn, Adam M. '73 '99 C.659 B.S. L.978 J.D.
(adm. in NY; not adm. in DC) [Ⓐ Shaw P.]
*PRACTICE AREAS: Health Law.
Kohn, Dexter M., (AV) '21 '49
C.188 A.B. L.94 J.D. 2000 Massachusetts Ave. N.W. , 3rd Fl.
Kohn, Ellen, (AV) . . . . '54 '79 C.103 B.A. L.659 J.D. [Ⓒ Steptoe&J.]
*PRACTICE AREAS: Employee Benefits; ERISA.
Kohn, Janet Goldrich . . . .'28 '61 C.33 B.A. L.273 J.D. 3418 Reservoir Rd., N.W.
Kohn, Laurie S. '68 '96 C.309 B.A. L.276 J.D.
(adm. in MA; not adm. in DC) 3100 Connectiut Avenue N.W., Apartment 434
Kohn, Michael D., (AV) . . . .'54 '85 C.705 B.S. L.1162 J.D. [Kohn,K.&C.]
*PRACTICE AREAS: Whistleblower Litigation; Labor and Employment Law; Retaliatory Discharge; Qui Tam Litigation.
Kohn, Stephen M., (AV) . . . . '56 '85 C.94 B.S. L.588 J.D. [Kohn,K.&C.]
*PRACTICE AREAS: Whistleblower Litigation; Civil Liberties; Qui Tam Litigation; Labor and Employment.

Kohn, Kohn & Colapinto, P.C., (AV)
3233 P Street, N.W., 20007
Telephone: 202-342-6980 Fax: 202-342-6984
Email: kkc@kkc.com URL: http://www.kkc.com
Stephen M. Kohn; Michael D. Kohn; David K. Colapinto;—Mary Jane Wilmoth; Christopher J. Wesser (Not admitted in DC).
Whistleblower Litigation, Retaliatory Discharge, Civil Litigation, Nuclear Energy, Qui Tam Litigation, Privacy Law, Forensic Science, Congressional Investigations, Labor and Employment, First Amendment Law, Government Contract Fraud, Freedom of Information, False Claims Act.
See Professional Biographies, WASHINGTON, DISTRICT OF COLUMBIA

Kohutanycz, Margaret M. . . . . '56 '90 C.128 B.A. L.273 J.D. 1374 C St., N.E.
Kolar, Joseph M. . . . . '60 '85 C.352 B.B.A. L.276 J.D. [Goodwin P.]
*PRACTICE AREAS: Mortgage and Consumer Finance Regulation; Real Estate; Banking.
Kolben, Carolyn Kurtzack, (AV) . . . . '57 '82 C.228 B.A. L.469 J.D. Asst. U.S. Atty.
Kolesar, Andrew B., III . . . .'66 '91 C.188 B.A. L.602 J.D. [Ⓐ Slover&L.]
Kolick, Joseph E., Jr. . . . .'55 '79 C.659 B.A. L.276 J.D. [Dickstein S.M.&O.]
*PRACTICE AREAS: Securities Litigation; Commercial Litigation; Employment Law.
Kolis, Michael L. . . . .'65 '94 C.197 A.B. L.904 J.D. [Ⓐ Jones,D.R.&P.]
Kolker, Peter R., (AV) . . . . '42 '66 C.188 A.B. L.145 J.D. [Zuckerman S.]
*PRACTICE AREAS: Financial Litigation; White Collar Crime; Contested Trust and Estate Litigation; Domestic Relations Litigation.
Kolko, S. Joel . . . .'49 '76 C&L.94 B.A., J.D. Editorial Dir., The Bureau of Natl. Affs., Inc.
Kolman, Mark H., (AV) . . . .'46 '71 C.105 B.A. L.446 J.D. [Dickstein S.M.&O.]
*PRACTICE AREAS: General Litigation; Insurance Litigation.
Kolodny, Debra Ruth . . . . . '60 '85 C.188 B.S. L.659 J.D. Assoc., Restructuring Associates
Kolomietz, Galina V. . . . . '70 '99 C.999 B.A. L.893 J.D. [Ⓐ Steptoe&J.]
Kolson, Kenneth P., (AV) . . . . '42 '70 C.563 B.A. L.188 J.D. 50 F St., N.W.
Kolton, Barbra Marcus . . . . '71 '98 C.228 A.B. L.276 J.D. Frandata Corp.
Kolton, Jeffrey E. . . . .'59 '84 C.188 B.A. L.276 J.D. [Lewis&K.]
Koltun, Lawrence W., (AV) . . . . '50 '75 C.910 A.B. L.659 J.D. [Koltun&K.]
*PRACTICE AREAS: Securities Law; Mergers, Acquisitions and Divestitures; Business Law; International Securities; Corporate Law.

Koltun & King, P.C., (AV)
1146 19th Street, N.W. Suite 250, 20036
Telephone: 202-331-0123 Facsimile: 202-466-5011
Email: koltunlaw@koltunlaw.com URL: http://www.koltunlaw.com
Lawrence W. Koltun; Susan J. King.
Securities Offerings, Private Placements, Blue Sky Law, Corporate Finance, Health Care Finance, International Securities, Mergers and Acquisitions, Spin-Offs, Corporate Formation, Buy-Sell Agreements, Corporate Contracts, Employment Contracts, Non-Competition and Non-Solicitation Agreements.
See Professional Biographies, WASHINGTON, DISTRICT OF COLUMBIA

Komarow, Jeffrey D. . . . . '49 '75 C&L.477 A.B., J.D. [Bradley A.R.&W.]
*PRACTICE AREAS: Energy; Appellate Practice; Utility Law; Regulatory Law.
Komen, Edwin, (AV) . . . .'49 '76 C.800 B.A. L.273 J.D. [Cleary&K.] (See Pat. Sect.)
*PRACTICE AREAS: Copyright Law; Trademark Law; Unfair Competition Law.
Kominers, Odell, (AV) . . . . '13 '36 C&L.178 A.B., LL.B. 1401 New York Ave. N.W.
Komoroske, John H. . . . '49 '74 C.867 B.A. L.347 J.D. National Assn. of Sec. Dealers, Inc.
Konczal, David S. . . . .'72 '97 C.228 A.B. L.273 J.D. [Ⓐ Shaw P.]
*PRACTICE AREAS: Communications.
Kong, John P. '66 '95 C.569 B.S. L.273 J.D.
[Ⓐ Armstrong,W.H.M.&N.] (See Pat. Sect.)
*PRACTICE AREAS: Intellectual Property Law.
Konigsberg, Charles S. . . . . '58 '83 C.385 A.B. L.930 J.D. [Ungaretti&H.]
*PRACTICE AREAS: Legislative, Regulatory and Public Policy.

Konizeski, Joseph A. . . . . '67 '98 C.446 B.A. L.861 J.D. [Ⓐ Lipstein,J.&L.]
*PRACTICE AREAS: Antitrust; Intellectual Property; International Trade; Corporate Law; Litigation.
Konkel, Gerald P. '— '98 C&L.734 B.A., J.D.
(adm. in MD; not adm. in DC) [Ⓐ Morgan,L.&B.]
Konop, Ben '76 '01 C.1365 B.A. L.477 J.D.
(adm. in OH; not adm. in DC) [Ⓐ Fulbright&J.]

Konopka, Arthur F., (AV) '40 '66 C.190 B.A. L.178 J.D.
4530 Wisconsin Avenue, N.W., Suite 200, 20016
Telephone: 202-686-0600 Maryland 301-983-4040 Fax: 202-686-0896
Email: afk@relawpro.com URL: http://www.lawyers.com/konopkalaw
***PRACTICE AREAS: Real Estate; Probate.**
Associates: William J. Gessner (Not admitted in DC); William W. Waller. Of Counsel: Quinn O'Connell, Jr.
Commercial and Residential Real Estate Law, Real Estate Settlements, Real Estate Litigation (including issues involving Titles, Zoning, Tax Assessment and Performance Contracts), Landlord and Tenant Law, Shopping Center Law, Leases, Commercial Real Estate Transactions, Wills and Probate, Trusts and Estates.
See Professional Biographies, WASHINGTON, DISTRICT OF COLUMBIA

Konuch, David A. '64 '94 C.813 B.A. L.861 J.D.
[Ⓐ Kelley D.&W.] (⊙New York, NY)
*PRACTICE AREAS: Communications Law; Litigation.
Koonce, Thomas C. . . . .'71 '98 C.198 B.A. L.945 J.D. [Ⓐ Clifford C.R.&W.]
*PRACTICE AREAS: Antitrust; Litigation.
Koons, Erik T. . . . .'73 '98 C.705 B.A. L.884 J.D. [Ⓐ Howrey S.A.&W.]
*PRACTICE AREAS: Antitrust; Commercial Litigation.
Koontz, Glen Franklin . . . .'60 '87 C&L.902 B.A., J.D. [Hughes&B.]
Koonz, Joseph H., Jr., (AV) . . . . '34 '60 C.708 A.B. L.276 LL.B. [Koonz,M.J.D.&L.]

Koonz, McKenney, Johnson, DePaolis & Lightfoot, (AV) BB
Suite 500, 2020 K Street, N.W., 20006 ⊙
Telephone: 202-659-5500 Fax: 202-785-3719
Email: dc@koonz.com URL: http://www.koonz.com
Joseph H. Koonz, Jr.; Roger C. Johnson; Peter C. DePaolis (Resident at Falls Church, Virginia Office); William P. Lightfoot, Jr.; Marc Fiedler; Karen A. Crist (Resident at Falls Church, Virginia Office); Paulette E. Chapman; David M. Schloss; Keith W. Donahoe (Resident at Greenbelt, Maryland Office); William A. Musto (Resident at Falls Church, Virginia Office); Julie H. Heiden (Resident at Falls Church, Virginia Office); Harold E. Brazil; Daniel S. Kozma; Frank R. Kearney; Douglas K. Allston, Jr. (Resident at Greenbelt, Maryland Office); Steven H. Kaminski; Angelia T. Rowe (Resident at Greenbelt, Maryland Office); Jarvis F. Tait; Dora Monica Rodrigues.
Negligence, Medical Malpractice, Workers Compensation, Automobile, Torts, Products Liability, Aviation, Social Security, Federal Employers Liability Law, Industrial and Commercial Accident Liability, Aviation Accidents, Automobile and Public Transportation Accident Liability.
Greenbelt, Maryland Office: 6301 Ivy Lane, Suite 510. Telephone: 301-345-5700. Fax: 301-474-5578.
Falls Church, Virginia Office: Suite 400, George Mason Square, 103 W. Broad Street. Telephone: 703-237-9300. Fax: 703-533-5974.
See Professional Biographies, WASHINGTON, DISTRICT OF COLUMBIA

Kopel, Henry K., (AV) . . . . '56 '87 C.1036 B.A. L.659 J.D. Asst. U.S. Atty.
Kopistansky, Patrice I. '55 '81 C.276 B.A. L.178 J.D. Asst. U.S. Atty.
Kopit, Barry S. . . . .'55 '85 C.318 B.A. L.30 J.D. [Ⓐ J.S.Weiss] ⊙
*PRACTICE AREAS: Personal Injury; Commercial Litigation; General Trial Litigation.
Kopit, William G., (AV) . . . .'40 '65 C.105 B.A. L.178 J.D. [Ⓒ Epstein B.&G.]
*PRACTICE AREAS: Antitrust Law; Health Law.
Koplan, Michael S. . . . . '66 '91 C.705 B.A. L.29 J.D. [Spriggs&H.]
*PRACTICE AREAS: Construction Law; Litigation.
Kopp, Eugene P. . . . .'34 '61 C.602 B.A. L.923 J.D. [Ⓒ Ruddy&M.]
*PRACTICE AREAS: Telecommunications Law; Government Affairs; Tax Disputes.
Kopsidas, Andrew '70 '99 C.446 B.S.A.E. L.273 J.D.
(adm. in MD; not adm. in DC; See Pat. Sect.) [Ⓐ Fish&R.]
Korde, Rukesh . . . . '68 '99 C.178 A.B. L.659 J.D. [Ⓐ Covington&B.]
Kordich, Kelli A: '60 '91 C&L.744 B.A., J.D.
(adm. in TX; not adm. in DC) U.S. Dept. of Vet. Affs., Bd. of Vet. App.
Kordziel, Linda Liu . . . .'68 '93 C&L.228 B.S.E., J.D. [Fish&R.] (See Pat. Sect.)
*PRACTICE AREAS: Intellectual Property; Patents; Litigation.
Korenblatt, Jeffrey S. . . . .'69 '98 C.276 B.S. L.477 J.D [Ⓐ McKee N.]
*PRACTICE AREAS: International Taxation; Tax Planning.
Korenchuk, Keith M., (AV) '53 '78 C.228 B.A. L.893 J.D.
(adm. in WA; not adm. in DC) [Davis W.T.]
*PRACTICE AREAS: Health Care.
Korman, Paul, (AV) . . . .'48 '76 C.102 B.A. L.564 J.D. [Van Ness F.]
*PRACTICE AREAS: Administrative Litigation; Natural Gas; Energy; Federal Energy Regulation.
Korn, David E. . . . .'61 '87 C.228 B.S. L.309 J.D. [Ⓒ Arnold&P.]
*PRACTICE AREAS: Food and Drug; Intellectual Property.
Kornbau, Anne M., (AV) '44 '70
C.223 B.S.Chem. L.273 J.D. [Ⓐ Browdy&N.] (See Pat. Sect.)
*PRACTICE AREAS: Intellectual Property Law; Biotechnology Law; Pharmaceuticals; Chemistry Trademark Law.
Kornblau, David L. '61 '87 C.674 A.B. L.309 J.D.
(adm. in NY; not adm. in DC) 450 5th St.
Kornfeld, Daniel E. . . . .'72 '98 C.188 B.S. L.273 J.D. [Ⓐ Mooney,G.B.&S.]
*PRACTICE AREAS: Labor; ERISA; Multiemployer Plans; Litigation.
Kornman, Kay A. . . . . '— '84 C&L.477 B.A., J.D. Assoc. Gen. Coun., Fannie Mae
*RESPONSIBILITIES: Mortgage Finance.
Korns, John H., (AV) . . . .'45 '70 C&L.309 A.B., J.D. [Oppenheimer W.&D.]
*PRACTICE AREAS: Litigation; International Trade Regulation.
Korody, Kerry E. . . . . '73 '99 C.602 B.A. L.228 J.D. [Ⓐ Akin,G.S.H.&F.]
*PRACTICE AREAS: Labor and Employment.
Koromzay, Dennis . . . . '40 '66 C&L.976 B.A., LL.B. Intl. Bk. for Reconstr. & Develop.
Korth, Fred, (AV) . . . . '09 '35 C.846 A.B. L.273 LL.B. [Korth&K.]
Korth, Fritz-Alan, (AV) . . . . '38 '64 C.674 A.B. L.846 LL.B. [Korth&K.]
Korth & Korth, (AV) . . . . 1700 K St., N.W., Suite 501
Korwek, Edward L., (AV) . . . . '46 '79 C.1062 B.S. L.229 J.D. [Hogan&H.]
*PRACTICE AREAS: Biotechnology Law; Food and Drug Regulation; Technology and Science; Environmental Law.
Korytkowski, Susan L. . . . .'53 '81 C.230 B.A. L.575 J.D. [Ⓒ Weiner B.S.K.]
*PRACTICE AREAS: Litigation.
Korytnyk, Peter G. '68 '99 C.823 B.S.M.E. L.128 J.D.
(adm. in VA; not adm. in DC; Pat.) [Ⓐ Crowell&M.]
Koshy, Suresh . . . . '69 '97 C.454 B.S.E.E. L.94 J.D. 1133 19th St., N.W.
Kosloske, Verleah Brown, (Mrs.) . . . . '45 '75 Legal Aid Soc.
Koslowe, Mark A. '52 '77 C.978 B.A. L.262 J.D.
[Buchman&O.] (⊙Edison, NJ; New York, NY)
*PRACTICE AREAS: Alcoholic Beverage Control Law, Licensing and Regulation.
Kosma, Montgomery N. . . . . '67 '98 C.1167 B.S. L.145 J.D. [Ⓐ Gibson,D.&C.]
*PRACTICE AREAS: Antitrust and Trade Regulation; Computers and Software.
Koss, Roberta . . . .'63 '92 C.188 B.A. L.280 J.D. [Ⓐ Hughes H.&R.]
Kossak, Natalie H. '72 '98
C.999 B.A. L.1019 J.D. [Ⓐ Wilmer,C.&P.] (⊙Tysons Corner, VA)
Kostel, Claudia A. . . . . '67 '92 C.401 B.A. L.945 J.D. 103 Hart Senate Building
Kostel, Mary E. . . . . '64 '94 C.674 A.B. L.893 J.D. [Ⓐ Wilmer,C.&P.]

Kostopulos, N. Peter .... '53 '78 C&L.276 B.A., J.D. [Womble C.S.&R.]
*PRACTICE AREAS: Technology Law; International Trade; Litigation; Intellectual Property Licensing; Intellectual Property Litigation.
Kostyack, John F. .... '61 '86 C.893 B.A. L.362 J.D. 3805 Alton Place NW
Kostyu, Jennifer L. .... '75 '00 C.575 B.A. L.180 J.D. [Ⓐ Morrison&F.]
*PRACTICE AREAS: Litigation; Communications Law.
Kosub, Bruce E. .... '62 '88 C&L.846 B.B.A., J.D. [Katten M.Z.]
*PRACTICE AREAS: Commercial Finance; Real Estate.
Koszorus, Frank, Jr. ....'47 '77 C.30 B.A. L.209 J.D. [Ⓒ Collier S.S.]
*PRACTICE AREAS: Litigation; Government Relations; International.
Kotanchik, Laura B. ....'71 '00 C.914 B.A. L.145 J.D. [Ⓐ Wilmer,C.&P.]
Kotara, Gary M., (AV) .... '55 '83 C.839 B.S. L.796 J.D. [Vinson&E.]
*PRACTICE AREAS: International Business Transactions; Energy; Business Law.
Kotchen, Daniel '71 '98
C.970 B.A. L.966 J.D. [Ⓐ Skadden,A.S.M.&F.] (⊙New York, NY)
*PRACTICE AREAS: Antitrust; Litigation.
Koteen, Bernard, (AV) .... '15 '40 C.966 B.A. L.309 LL.B. [Holland&K.]
*PRACTICE AREAS: Telecommunications Law.
Kotelanski, Jorge ....'68 '96 C.228 A.B. L.569 J.D. [Ⓐ Dickstein S.M.&O.]
*PRACTICE AREAS: Litigation; Employment Law.
Kotelly, John T., (AV) ....'38 '68 C.688 B.A.E. L.276 J.D. [Dickstein S.M.&O.]
*PRACTICE AREAS: White Collar Criminal Defense Law; Civil and Criminal Litigation.
Kothari, Rupal G. .... '70 '97 C.367 B.A. L.30 J.D. [R.G.Kothari]
*PRACTICE AREAS: Immigration and Naturalization; Employment; Family Corporations.

Kothari, Rupal G., P.C., Law Office of
1900 K Street NW, Suite 1050, 20006
Telephone: 202-466-2921 Fax: 202-466-2925
Email: rgkothari@aol.com URL: http://www.rgkotharilaw.com
Rupal G. Kothari.
Litigation, Nationality Matters, Employment and Family Based Litigations.
See Professional Biographies, WASHINGTON, DISTRICT OF COLUMBIA

Kotlarsky, Mark ....'52 '85 C.367 Ph.D. L.446 J.D. [Ⓒ Dickstein S.M.&O.]
*PRACTICE AREAS: Tax Law.
Kotler, Sarah B. .... '73 '99 C.659 B.A. L.309 J.D. [Ⓐ Arnold&P.]
*PRACTICE AREAS: Litigation.
Kott, Stephen J. ....'62 '89 C&L.575 B.A., J.D. [Patton B.]
Koufos, Peter N. '69 '96 C.423 B.B.A. L.180 J.D.
(adm. in MD; not adm. in DC) [Ⓐ Goodwin P.]
Koukios, James M. '— '00 C.477 B.A. L.309 J.D.
(adm. in NY; not adm. in DC) [Ⓐ Kirkland&E.]
*PRACTICE AREAS: Litigation.
Koukoutchos, Brian Stuart, (AV) '58 '86 C.311 B.A. L.309 J.D.
(adm. in MA; not adm. in DC) [Ⓐ Cooper&K.]
*PRACTICE AREAS: Constitutional Law; Appellate Practice.
Kourtesis, Nikolaos Panagiotis '70 '97 C.30 B.A. L.1364 J.D.
(adm. in MD; not adm. in DC) [Ⓐ Robinson]
Koury, Joseph S. ....'53 '81 C.1044 B.A. L.982 J.D. [Wright&T.]
*PRACTICE AREAS: Energy.
Kouznetsov, Vladimir V. ....'71 '97 C.967 B.A. L.930 J.D. [Ⓐ Squire,S.&D.]
Kouzoukas, Demetrios '75 '00 C.273 B.A L.339 J.D
(adm. in VA; not adm. in DC) [Ⓐ Gardner,C.&D.]
Kovac, George '51 '76 C.976 B.A. L.145 J.D.
(adm. in IL; not adm. in DC) Marriott Drive
Kovach, David S. .... '58 '85 C.446 B.A. L.276 J.D. [Ⓒ O'Dea&Assoc.]
Kovach, Gerald J. '43 '74 C&L.912 B.A., J.D.
Sr. V.P., Regulatory & Pub. Policy, MCI Communications Corp.
Kovacic-Fleischer, Candace S. '47 '74
C.914 A.B. L.588 J.D. Prof. of Law, Amer. Univ. Coll. of Law
Kovacs, Karen T. ..... '— '92 C.475 B.A. L.1202 J.D. Off. of Asst. Secy, Fish & Wildlife
Kovalick, Vincent P., (BV) '61 '88
C.645 B.S.E.E. L.1209 J.D. [Finnegan,H.F.G.&D.] (See Pat. Sect.)
*PRACTICE AREAS: Patent Litigation; Patent Prosecution; Patent Licensing.
Kovarovics, Susan M. C. .... '— '96 C.222 B.A. L.276 J.D. [Ⓐ Foley&L.]
*PRACTICE AREAS: International Law; Corporate Law.
Kovey, Mark H., (AV) ....'42 '67 C.178 A.B. L.569 J.D. [Scribner,H.&T.]
Kovin, John F., (AV) ....'36 '62 C.905 B.A. L.273 LL.B. 1299 Penn. Ave., N.W.
Kovner, Mark L. .... '64 '89 C.1036 B.A. L.276 J.D. [Kirkland&E.]
*PRACTICE AREAS: Antitrust; Commercial Litigation.
Kowalski, Michael V., (AV) .... '45 '70 C.363 B.A. L.597 J.D. [Ashcraft&G.]
*PRACTICE AREAS: Workers Compensation; Social Security.
Kozloff, Jeannette Jang '71 '98 C.188 B.S. L.377 J.D.
(adm. in PA; not adm. in DC) 2401 Pennsylvania Ave., N.W.
Kozloff, Louis H. .... '71 '98 C.197 A.B. L.665 J.D. [Ⓐ McKenna&C.]
*PRACTICE AREAS: Litigation.
Kozlowski, Richard G. .... '38 '72 C.367 B.E.S. L.128 J.D. [Ⓒ Van Ness F.]
*PRACTICE AREAS: Environment; Clean Water Act.
Kozma, Daniel S., (AV) ....'50 '77 C.665 B.A. L.188 J.D. [Koonz,M.J.D.&L.]
Kozuch, Sophie A. '73 '99 C.659 B.A. L.569 J.D.
(adm. in NY; not adm. in DC) [Ⓐ Cadwalader,W.&T.]
*PRACTICE AREAS: Corporate Law.
Kozusko, Donald D. .... '— '70 C.884 B.A. L.309 J.D. [Kozusko L.H.]
*PRACTICE AREAS: Closely Held Business Taxation; Charitable Trusts; Non Profit Organization; International Estate Planning; Venture Capital.

Kozusko Lahey Harris LLP, (AV)
1666 K Street, NW, Suite 400, 20006
Telephone: 202-457-7200 Fax: 202-457-7201
URL: http://www.lawyers.com/kozlaw
Partners: Donald D. Kozusko; John H. Lahey; George N. Harris, Jr.; Miles C. Padgett; Stephen K. Vetter. Associate: Rashad Wareh. Of Counsel: Jeffrey M. Bucher.
Closely Held Business Taxation, Business Law, Venture Capital, Tax Planning, International Estate Planning, Estate Planning, Charitable Trusts and Non Profit Organizations, Trusts and Estates, Dispute Resolution, Tax Controversy, Tax Litigation.
See Professional Biographies, WASHINGTON, DISTRICT OF COLUMBIA

Krachman, Albert B. ....'56 '83 C.94 B.A. L.273 J.D. [Bracewell&P.]
*PRACTICE AREAS: Commercial Law; Litigation; Government Contracts; Construction Law; Technology.
Kracov, Daniel A. ....'63 '88 C.446 B.A. L.893 J.D. [Patton B.]
Kracov, Eric S. ....'57 '85 C.446 B.A. L.273 J.D. [Muldoon M.&F.]
*PRACTICE AREAS: Employee Benefits; Federal Taxation; ERISA; Trade Associations; Tax-Exempt Organizations.
Kraemer, Jay R. ....'48 '73 C&L.273 B.A., J.D. [Fried,F.H.S.&J.]
Kraft, Barbara, (AV) ....'47 '79 C.477 B.A. L.912 J.D. [Beins,A.&K.]
Kraftson, Daniel J., (AV) ....'51 '77 C.937 B.A. L.945 J.D. [Jenkens&G.]
*PRACTICE AREAS: Construction Law; Construction Litigation; Government Contracts.
Kragie, Scott T., (AV) ....'50 '75 C.945 B.A. L.1119 J.D. [Squire,S.&D.]
*PRACTICE AREAS: Civil; Criminal and Administrative Litigation; Health Care.
Kraham, Kevin M. ....'70 '98 C.94 B.A. L.904 J.D. [Ⓐ Ford&H.]
*PRACTICE AREAS: Labor and Employment Law; Mediation.
Krainin, Daniel M. ....'69 '97 C.918 B.A. L.893 J.D. [Ⓐ Beveridge&D.]
*PRACTICE AREAS: Environmental; Litigation.

Krakoff, David S., (AV) ....'49 '76 C.197 A.B. L.1162 J.D. [Beveridge&D.]
*PRACTICE AREAS: White Collar Criminal Defense; Civil Litigation.
Krame, Jodi Mintzer .... '56 '83 C.1365 B.A. L.273 J.D. [Ⓒ Arter&H.]
*PRACTICE AREAS: Communications; Corporate.
Kramer, Albert H., (AV) ....'40 '68 C.112 B.A. L.813 LL.B. [Dickstein S.M.&O.]
*PRACTICE AREAS: Communications Law; Administrative Law; Trade Regulation Law.
Kramer, Andrew M., (AV) ....'44 '69 C.477 B.A. L.597 J.D. [Jones,D.R.&P.]
*PRACTICE AREAS: Labor and Employment; Employment Litigation; Management Labor Law; Collective Bargaining.
Kramer, Beth M. ....'68 '95 C.659 B.A. L.276 J.D. [Ⓐ Crowell&M.]
Kramer, Brian M. .....'73 '00 C.879 B.S.M.E. L.339 J.D. Law Clk., U.S. Court of Appeals
Kramer, Bruce E. .... '63 '89 C.893 B.S.Che. L.8 J.D. [Sughrue M.] (See Pat. Sect.)
*PRACTICE AREAS: Intellectual Property Law.
Kramer, Douglas '70 '00 C.276 B.A. L.145 J.D.
(adm. in IL; not adm. in DC) [Ⓐ Covington&B.]
Kramer, Franklin D., (AV) ....'45 '71 C.976 B.A. L.309 J.D. [Shea&G.]
*PRACTICE AREAS: Corporate Law; International Trade and Transactions; Government Contracts; Commercial Law.
Kramer, George R., (AV) '58 '84 C.16 B.A. L.178 J.D.
(adm. in NY; not adm. in DC) Assoc. Gen. Coun., Securities Industry Assn.
*RESPONSIBILITIES: Securities; Broker-Dealer Regulation; Administrative Procedure.
Kramer, Gerson B. ....'25 '55 C.705 A.B. L.273 LL.B. [Braude&M.]
*PRACTICE AREAS: Federal Contracts; Litigation; Construction Law; Arbitration Mediation.
Kramer, Howard L., (AV) ....'55 '81 C&L.477 B.A., J.D. [Schiff H.&W.]
*PRACTICE AREAS: Securities; Commodities.
Kramer, Karen ....'68 '96 C.674 A.B. L.273 J.D. [Ⓐ Covington&B.]
*PRACTICE AREAS: Commercial Real Estate; Real Estate; Real Estate Leasing.
Kramer, Karen M. ....'— '95 C&L.813 B.A., J.D. [Ⓐ Baker&H.]
*PRACTICE AREAS: Media and First Amendment; Internet Law; Intellectual Property; Employment Law.
Kramer, Karen W. .... '68 '96 C.674 A.B. L.273 J.D. 1201 Penn. Ave., N.W.
Kramer, Kelly B. ....'— '98 C.945 A.B. L.659 J.D. [Ⓐ Ropes&G.]
Kramer, Kenneth S., (P.C.), (AV) '41 '67
C.966 B.S. L.309 J.D. 1001 Pennsylvania Ave. N.W.‡
Kramer, Merrill L., (P.C.), (AV) .... '54 '78 C.178 B.A. L.912 J.D. [Akin,G.S.H.&F.]
*PRACTICE AREAS: Energy.
Kramer, Noel Anketell .... '45 '72 C.881 B.A. L.477 J.D. Supr. Ct. J.
Kramer, Scott A. ....'64 '89 C.1044 B.A. L.30 J.D. [Mann B.]
Kramer, Shane N. ....'73 '99 C.893 B.A. L.902 J.D. [Ⓐ Counts,P.-D.&D.]
Kramer, Steven M. ....'60 '87 C.446 B.S. L.692 J.D. [Ⓒ Milbank,T.H.&M.]
Kramer, Theodore D., (AV) '45 '71
C.477 B.B.A. L.273 J.D. 1000 Potomac Street NW, 5th Floor
Kramer, Victor H. ....'13 '38 C.309 A.B. L.976 LL.B. 4201 Cathedral Ave., N.W.‡
Kramer, William D. ....'— '69 C.604 A.B. L.309 J.D. [Verner,L.B.M.&H.]

Kramer & Associates, P.C.
(See Arlington, Virginia)

Kramm, Deborah L. .... '54 '77 C.98 B.S. L.1202 J.D. [Holland&K.]
*PRACTICE AREAS: Trademarks; Licensing; Copyrights.

Kramon & Graham, P.A.
(See Baltimore, Maryland)

Krantz, Sheldon, (AV) .... '38 '70 C&L.546 B.S., J.D. [Piper M.R.&W.]
*PRACTICE AREAS: Business Crime Law; Criminal Trial Practice and Federal Practice; White Collar Crime.
Krantz, Stefan M. ....'67 '92 C.188 B.A. L.904 J.D. [Dickstein S.M.&O.]
*PRACTICE AREAS: Energy Law; Natural Gas Transactions; Regulatory.
Kranz, Heidi E. ....'72 '00 C&L.276 B.S., J.D. [Ⓐ Wilmer,C.&P.]
Kranz, Lisa C. Barton .... '68 '97 C.494 B.A. L.1035 J.D. 1613 Webster St. N.W.
Krash, Abe, (AV) ....'27 '50 C&L.145 A.B., J.D. [Arnold&P.]
*PRACTICE AREAS: Antitrust; Competition and Trade; Regulation; Litigation.
Kraskin, Stephen G. ....'51 '75 C.1365 B.A. L.30 J.D. 2120 L St., N.W.
Krasne, Hale Ansberry ....'55 '84 C.112 A.B. L.276 J.D. 3245 Elliott St. N.W.
Krasne, Robert M., (AV) .... '55 '83 C&L.276 A.B., J.D. [Williams&C.]
Krasnegor, Daniel G. .... '69 '93 C.910 A.B. L.245 J.D. [Ⓐ Wright,R.O.&T.]
*PRACTICE AREAS: Veteran's Benefits; Appellate Practice; Litigation; Federal Tort Claims.
Krasner, Wendy L., (AV) ....'53 '78 C.309 B.A. L.1066 J.D. [McDermott,W.&E.]
Krasnow, Erwin G., (AV) .... '— '61 C.94 B.A. L.309 J.D. [Verner,L.B.M.&H.]
*PRACTICE AREAS: Communications Law.
Kratchman, Paul M., (BV) .... '59 '87 C.30 B.A. L.1162 J.D. Asst. Corp. Coun.
Krattenmaker, Thomas G. '43 '69 C.821 B.A. L.178 J.D.
701 Pennsylvania Avenue, N.W.
Krauland, Edward J., (AV) ....'55 '80 C.674 A.B. L.477 J.D. [Steptoe&J.]
*PRACTICE AREAS: Import Relief; Export Control; International Trade and Investment Regulatory Compliance; International Government Procurement; Immigration and Nationality Law.
Krauland, Elke M. ....'71 '98 C.184 B.A. L.273 J.D. [Ⓐ Cleary,G.S.&H.]
Kraus, Anna D. ....'56 '83 C.560 B.A. L.813 J.D. [Ⓒ Covington&B.]
Kraus, Eric J. '65 '95 C.502 B.A. L.128 J.D.
(adm. in NJ; not adm. in DC; Pat.) [McDermott,W.&E.]
Kraus, Heidi L. ....'69 '97 C.645 B.S. L.273 J.D. [Ⓐ Sterne,K.G.&F.] (See Pat. Sect.)
*PRACTICE AREAS: Intellectual Property Law; Patent Prosecution; Life Sciences; Biomedical Technology; Pharmaceutical Intellectual Property.
Kraus, Kenneth, (AV) .... '42 '67 C&L.724 B.B.A., LL.B. [Ⓒ Skadden,A.S.M.&F.]
Kraus, Lawrence B. '43 '68 C&L.597 B.S.B.A., J.D.
Senior Vice President -Adminstration, U.S. Chamber of Commerce
Kraus, Rainer K., (AV) '36 '61 C&L.309 B.A., LL.B.
1150 Connecticut Ave Nw # 1000‡
Kraus, Stephen W., (BV) ....'42 '68 C.102 B.S. L.273 J.D. [Jorden B.]
*PRACTICE AREAS: Pension Plans; Employee Benefits; Insurance.
Krause, Paul D., (AV) ....'46 '72 C.1046 B.A. L.692 J.D. [Wilson,E.M.E.&D.]
*PRACTICE AREAS: Health Care; Medical Malpractice.
Krause, Thomas W. .... '61 '91 C.339 B.S. L.309 J.D. [Ⓒ Covington&B.]

Krause & Ferris
(See Annapolis, Maryland)

Kraushaar, Kevin J., (CV) '55 '81 C.477 A.B. L.215 J.D.
(adm. in MI; not adm. in DC)
VP, Dir. of Gov't Rel., Consumer Healthcare Products Association
Krauss, Gregory A. .... '62 '88 C.602 B.S.Chem.E. L.1338 J.D. [McDermott,W.&E.]
Krauss, Joseph G. .... '56 '84 C.205 B.S. L.1338 J.D. [Hogan&H.]
*PRACTICE AREAS: Antitrust Counseling; Mergers and Acquisitions; Joint Ventures; Trade Associations; Civil Investigations.

Kraut, Nina, (BV) '43 '78 C.569 B.S. L.1218 J.D.
3815 Yuma Street, N.W., 20016-2213
Telephone: 202-745-0300 Fax: 202-745-0300 * 51
Email: ninakraut@aol.com URL: http://www.lawyers.com/kraut
***PRACTICE AREAS: Federal Litigation; Constitutional Law; First Amendment Law; Civil Liberties; Civil Rights.**
Federal Litigation, Constitutional Law, First Amendment Law, Civil Liberties, Civil Rights, Discrimination, Womens Rights, U.S. Supreme Court Litigation, Complex Litigation, Public Interest Law, Civil Appeals, Freedom of Information, Freedom of Religion.
See Professional Biographies, WASHINGTON, DISTRICT OF COLUMBIA

Kraut, Richard S., (AV) .... '41 '67 C.165 B.A. L.178 LL.B. [Dilworth P.P.]

Krauthamer & Stahl, Chartered
(See Chevy Chase, Maryland)

Kravetz, Beth .... '49 '75 C.1086 B.A. L.276 J.D. 4323 Warren St., N.W.
Kravetz, Eric S., (AV) .... '47 '71 C.216 A.B. L.309 J.D. 3511 Porter St., NW
Kravetz, Paul I. .... '63 '92 C.352 B.S.E.E. L.209 J.D. [Staas&H.] (See Pat. Sect.)
*PRACTICE AREAS: Patents; Copyrights; Trademarks.
Kravitz, Carl S., (AV) .... '55 '81 C.309 A.B. L.178 J.D. [Zuckerman S.]
*PRACTICE AREAS: Civil and Criminal Litigation; Trial Practice.
Kravitz, Neal E. .... '57 '84 C.976 B.A. L.309 J.D. Supr. Ct. J.
Krawczun, Diane L. .... '67 '94 C.728 B.A. L.734 J.D. [Ⓐ Wiley R.&F.]
Krawczyk, Susan S. .... '56 '84 C.659 B.A. L.276 J.D. [Sutherland A.&B.]
*PRACTICE AREAS: Broker-Dealer Regulation; Investment Regulation; Financial Services Regulation; Insurance Regulation; Insurance Products.
Krebs, Frederick J., (AV) '49 '75 C.25 B.A. L.930 J.D.
Pres., Amer. Corp. Coun. Assn.
*RESPONSIBILITIES: Association Management (80%); Legal Issues Affecting Corporate Counsel (20%).
Krebs, Joseph M., Jr. '43 '67 C&L.734 A.B., J.D.
(adm. in MO; not adm. in DC) WRC-TV, NBC
Krebs, William F., (BV) .... '52 '77 C.645 B.A. L.276 J.D. [Galland,K.G.F.&S.]
*PRACTICE AREAS: Civil and White Collar Criminal Litigation; Appellate Litigation; Commercial Law; Admiralty Law.
Kreeger, David M. .... '72 '98 C.176 B.A. L.472 J.D. [Ⓐ Wilmer,C.&P.]
Kreig, Andrew T. '49 '91 C.188 B.A. L.145 J.D.
V.P. & Gen. Coun., Wireless Cable Assn. Intl.
Kreiger, Amy T. .... '70 '96 C.454 B.A. L.309 J.D. [Ⓐ Wilmer,C.&P.]
Krein, Benjamin Lee '74 '00 C.188 B.S. L.273 J.D.
(adm. in NY; not adm. in DC) [Ⓐ McDermott,W.&E.]
Krell, Jonathan M. .... '70 '98 C.918 B.A. L.273 J.D. [Ⓐ Akin,G.S.H.&F.]
*PRACTICE AREAS: Labor and Employment; Technology.
Krentler, Kerry A. '76 '00 C.800 B.A. L.228 J.D.
(adm. in CA; not adm. in DC) [Ⓐ O'Melveny&M.]
Kress, James G. .... '65 '90 C.446 B.S. L.276 J.D. [Howrey S.A.&W.]
*PRACTICE AREAS: Litigation; Antitrust.
Kress, Marjorie Mae .... '52 '77 C.966 B.A. L.494 J.D. ULLICO INC.
*RESPONSIBILITIES: Managed Health Care; ERISA; Regulatory Law.
Kresse, Claire E. .... '69 '97 C.276 B.A. L.228 J.D. [Ⓐ Spriggs&H.]
*PRACTICE AREAS: Construction Law; Government Contracts; Litigation.
Kresse, Joseph A. .... '65 '95 C.276 B.S.B.A. L.107 J.D. [Ⓐ Covington&B.]
Kresslein, Michael J. .... '69 '94 C.276 B.A.B.A. L.446 J.D. [Ⓐ Ludwig&R.]
*PRACTICE AREAS: Litigation; Corporate Law.
Kreutzer, Matthew J. '73 '98 C.30 B.S. L.273 J.D.
(adm. in MD; not adm. in DC) [Ⓐ Goldstein&L.]
Kriebel, Keith W. .... '58 '83 C.216 B.A. L.659 J.D. [Orrick,H.&S.]
*PRACTICE AREAS: Project Finance; Corporate Law.
Kriegel, Alan, (AV) ....'47 '77 C.705 B.A. L.276 J.D. [Skadden,A.S.M.&F.]
Krieger, Kathy L., (AV) .... '53 '78 C.976 A.B. L.569 J.D. [James&H.]
*PRACTICE AREAS: Labor Law; Employment Law.
Krieger, Roy W. '54 '83 C.273 B.A. L.30 J.D.
601 Pennsylvania Avenue, Suite 900 South
Kriesberg, Simeon M., (AV) .... '51 '77 C.309 A.B. L.976 J.D. [Mayer,B.&P.]
Krikawa, Charles, IV .... '54 '78 C.1044 B.A. L.904 J.D. 126 C St., N.W.
Krill, Edward J. .... '41 '67 C.436 A.B. L.276 J.D. [Ⓒ Carr G.]
*PRACTICE AREAS: Health Care; Employment Law; Labor Law.
Kringel, Eric '70 '96 C.546 B.A. L.904 J.D.
(adm. in MD; not adm. in DC) 1906 New Hampshire Ave., N.W.‡
Krinsky, Richard Paul ...... '— '82 C.24 B.S. L.180 J.D. [Ⓒ Barnes&T.] (See Pat. Sect.)
*PRACTICE AREAS: Patents; Trademarks; Copyrights; Aviation Law; Intellectual Property.
Kris, Jody Manier .... '68 '96 C.839 J.D. L.145 J.D. [Baker B.]
Krishnamurthy, Aneal .... '74 '99 C.347 B.A. L.273 J.D. [Ⓐ Jones&B.]
*PRACTICE AREAS: Securities Law; Corporate Law.
Kristal, Phyllis '— '00 C.453 B.S.M.E. L.818 J.D.
(adm. in MA; not adm. in DC; See Pat. Sect.) [Ⓐ Fish&R.] (ⓞBoston, MA)
*PRACTICE AREAS: Patent Law.
Kritz, David J. .... '66 '92 C.597 B.A. L.107 J.D. [Ⓐ Sutherland A.&B.]
*PRACTICE AREAS: Employee Benefits; Tax Law.
Krivit, Daniel H., (AV) .... '33 '57 C.103 B.A. L.94 J.D. [Krivit&K.]
Krivit & Krivit, P.C., (AV) .... 1220 G St. NW
Krizek, Monika Blanche .... '62 '90 C.66 B.A. L.94 J.D. 2111 Bancroft Pl. N.W.
Krncevic, Raymond .... '73 '98 C.597 B.A. L.893 J.D. [Ⓐ Hunton&W.]
Krogh, Frank W. .... '45 '71 C.103 A.B. L.976 LL.B. [Ⓒ Morrison&F.]
*PRACTICE AREAS: Telecommunications; Administrative Law.
Krol, Margaret Irene .... '47 '81 C.1044 B.A. L.128 J.D. 471 H St., N.W.
Kroll, C. Kelly .... '67 '00 C.696 B.A. L.1209 J.D. [Ⓐ Cohen M.]
*PRACTICE AREAS: Government Contracts; Commercial Law.
Kroll, Milton P., (AV) .... '14 '38 C.923 A.B. L.309 J.D. [Ⓒ Freedman,L.K.&S.]
Kromer, John P. .... '65 '93 C.602 B.A. L.893 J.D. [Goodwin P.]
*PRACTICE AREAS: Consumer Financial Services.
Kronenberg, Angie W. .... '70 '95 C.69 B.A. L.128 J.D. [Ⓐ Willkie F.&G.]
Krongold, Sheryl .... '59 '84 C.66 B.A. L.978 J.D. [Ⓐ Powell,G.F.&M.]
*PRACTICE AREAS: Litigation; Antitrust.
Kronheim, Milton S., Jr. .... '11 '37 C.367 B.A. L.276 LL.B. Sr. Assoc. Supr. Ct. J.
Kronowitz, Rachel S. .... '60 '88 C.788 B.A. L.309 J.D. [Gilbert H.&R.]
*PRACTICE AREAS: Alternative Dispute Resolution; Insurance Coverage Law.
Kronstein, Werner, (AV) .... '30 '56 C&L.276 A.B., LL.B. [Arnold&P.]
*PRACTICE AREAS: Corporate; Securities; International.
Krooth, John D. .... '39 '65 C.188 B.A. L.178 LL.B. 1700 35th St., N.W.

Krooth & Altman LLP, (AV)
Suite 400, 1850 M Street, N.W., 20036-5803 ⊙
Telephone: 202-293-8200 Telecopier: 202-872-0145, 202-775-5872
Members of Firm: David L. Krooth (1907-1978); Norman S. Altman (1912-1997); E. Joseph Knoll; Michael E. Mazer; Donald F. Libretta; Daniel Randolph Cole, Jr.; Patrick J. Clancy; James F. Perna; Harrison C. Smith; David A. Barsky; John E. Vihstadt; Bonnie Hochman Rothell; Jon I. Opert. Of Counsel: William S. Tennant; William J. Delany; Michael J. Milton; Robert J. Siciliano; Kenneth A. Lazarus; Patricia Pritt Toadvine (Not admitted in DC). Associates: H. Scott Johnson, Jr (Not admitted in DC); Roderick D. Owens; Monica E. Monroe (Not admitted in DC); Deborah A. Turner; Gordon C. F. Chin (Not admitted in DC); Amy B. Connelly (Not admitted in DC).
General, Administrative and Business Practice. Corporate, Taxation, Securities, Bond Finance, Real Estate, Health Care, Housing and Urban Development, Banking, Mortgage Banking, Creditor's Rights, Entertainment Law. Civil Litigation in all Federal and State Courts and Agencies.
See Professional Biographies, WASHINGTON, DISTRICT OF COLUMBIA

Krosin, Kenneth E., (AV) '— '72 C.674 B.S.E.E. L.273 J.D.
[Foley&L.] (See Pat. Sect.)
*PRACTICE AREAS: Intellectual Property Litigation.
Kruchko, John G., (AV) .... '48 '75 C.973 A.B. L.945 J.D. [Kruchko&F.] ⊙
Kruchko & Fries, (AV) .... 601 Pennsylvania Ave. (ⓞBalt., MD; Mc Lean, VA)
Krucoff, Neal E., (AV) .... '35 '62 C.659 A.B. L.276 LL.B. [Ⓒ Berliner,C.&R.]
*PRACTICE AREAS: Real Estate; Family; Probate; Estate Planning; Litigation.

Krudys, Kent M. .... '63 '88 C.69 B.B.A. L.1029 J.D. [Muldoon M.&F.]
*PRACTICE AREAS: Financial Institutions; Corporate Law; Banks and Banking; Securities; Bankruptcy.
Krueger, Karen .... '38 '75 C.378 B.A. L.208 J.D. 429 North St., S.W.
Krueger, Nicole V. '69 '95 C.339 B.A. L.273 J.D.
(adm. in MD; not adm. in DC) 4200 Cathedral Ave. N.W.‡
Kruger, Stuart A., (AV) .... '54 '82 C&L.893 B.S., J.D. [Womble C.S.&R.]
*PRACTICE AREAS: Real Estate.
Krugman, Gary D., (AV) '48 '73 C.1044 B.S. L.930 J.D.
[Sughrue M.] (See Pat. Sect.)
*PRACTICE AREAS: Trademark Law; Unfair Competition Law; Copyright Law.

Krukowski & Costello, S.C., (AV)
1401 Eye Street NW, Suite 1210, 20005 ⊙
Telephone: 202-898-1031 Facsimile: 202-898-1311
URL: http://www.krukowski.com
Elliot H. Shaller; Maria Pia Torretti Gekas (Not admitted in DC);—Timothy P. Blodgett (Not admitted in DC).
Representing Management in Labor and Employment Law.
Milwaukee, Wisconsin Office: 7111 West Edgerton Avenue, P.O. Box 28999, 53228-0999. Telephone: 414-423-1330. Telefax: 414-423-1694.
See Professional Biographies, WASHINGTON, DISTRICT OF COLUMBIA

Krulwich, Andrew S., (AV) .... '41 '66 C&L.178 B.A., LL.B. [Wiley R.&F.]
*PRACTICE AREAS: Food and Drug; Advertising Law; Product Safety; Litigation.
Krumholz, Marjorie F. .... '56 '81 C.696 B.A. L.273 J.D. [Thompson C.]
*PRACTICE AREAS: Maritime Finance; Corporate Finance; General Corporate.
Krupin, Jay P., (AV) .... '54 '78 C.273 B.A. L.734 J.D. [Krupin O.]
*PRACTICE AREAS: Labor Law; Employment Law.

Krupin O'Brien, (AV) BR
1156 15th Street, NW Suite 200, 20005
Telephone: 202-530-0700 Fax: 202-530-0703
Email: info@krupinobrien.com URL: http://www.krupinobrien.com
Jay P. Krupin; James J. O'Brien; Caryn G. Pass; Scott V. Kamins. Senior Associates: D. Jay Sumner; Monique A. van Stiphout;—Ari Karen; Jeffrey M. Ricapito (Not admitted in DC); Neda E. Bitar; Alison N. Davis; Daniel Feldman (Not admitted in DC); Scott A. Mirsky; Craig Symons.
Management Side Labor and Employment Law, Business Immigration, Benefits and Related Litigation.
See Professional Biographies, WASHINGTON, DISTRICT OF COLUMBIA

Krupka, Catherine M. .... '62 '95 C.767 B.S. L.94 J.D. [Ⓐ McDermott,W.&E.] (Pat.)
Krupka, Robert G., (P.C.), (AV) '49 '74
C.276 B.S. L.145 J.D. [Kirkland&E.] (Pat.) (ⓞL.A., CA; Chgo., IL)
*PRACTICE AREAS: Intellectual Property; Litigation; Advertising and Marketing; Antitrust; Trade Regulation.
Krupsaw, Fulton H. .... '18 '40 C&L.273 LL.B. 2810 Ellicott St., N.W.‡
Krupsky, Kenneth J., (AV) .... '47 '73 C&L.178 B.A., J.D. [Jones,D.R.&P.]
*PRACTICE AREAS: Taxation; International Taxation; Tax Controversies; Federal Legislative Practice.
Krus, Cynthia M. .... '62 '89 C.1365 B.A. L.861 J.D. [Sutherland A.&B.]
*PRACTICE AREAS: Securities Offerings; Securities Regulation; Mergers and Acquisitions; Corporate Governance; Financial Institutions.
Krusen, Robert P. '64 '90 C&L.446 B.A., J.D.
(adm. in MD; not adm. in DC) Public Brodcasting Corp.
Krutulis, Jay '72 '00 C.347 B.S. L.893 J.D.
(adm. in VA; not adm. in DC) [Ⓐ Alston&B.]
*PRACTICE AREAS: Technology and Science; Corporate Law; Intellectual Property.
Kruyer, Timothy A. .... '73 '98 C.475 B.A. L.1410 J.D. [Ⓐ Wilkinson B.K.]
*PRACTICE AREAS: Telecommunications Law; Communications Law; Administrative Litigation.
Krvaric, Silvio Aaron '73 '00
C.999 B.A. L.770 J.D. Assoc. Atty., Center for Individual Rights
Kubovcik, Ronald J., (AV) '44 '73
C.665 B.S.Ch.E. L.229 J.D. [Kubovcik&K.] (See Pat. Sect.)
*PRACTICE AREAS: Chemical Intellectual Property; Pharmaceutical Intellectual Property; Mechanical Intellectual Property; Trademarks; Patent Prosecution.

Kubovcik & Kubovcik, (AV)
The Farragut Building, 900 17th Street, N.W., Suite 710, 20006
Telephone: 202-887-9023 Fax: 202-887-9093
Email: KandK@kubovcik.com URL: http://www.lawyers.com/kubovciklaw
Ronald J. Kubovcik; Keiko Tanaka Kubovcik (Not admitted in the United States).
Intellectual Property Law, Chemical Intellectual Property, Pharmaceutical Intellectual Property, Mechanical Intellectual Property, Patent Interference Practice, Trademarks.
See Professional Biographies, WASHINGTON, DISTRICT OF COLUMBIA

Kuchinsky, Dori Anne '59 '85 C.881 B.A. L.724 J.D.
Sr. Litig. Coun., W. R. Grace & Co., Gov. Rel.
Kucik, George R., (AV) .... '37 '61 C.1028 B.S. L.884 LL.B. [Arent F.K.P.&K.]
*PRACTICE AREAS: Litigation; Arbitration; Trial Practice; Appellate Practice; Antitrust.
Kuckes, Niki .... '59 '87 C.188 B.A. L.976 J.D. [Baker B.]
Kuczajda, Thomas A. .... '73 '99 C.477 B.A. L.276 J.D. [Ⓐ O'Melveny&M.]
Kuder, Armin U., (AV) .... '35 '59 C.390 A.B. L.309 LL.B. [Kuder,S.&F.]
*PRACTICE AREAS: Domestic Relations Law; Estate Probate; Professional Association Law; Mental Health Law; Civil Litigation.

Kuder, Smollar & Friedman, P.C., (AV)
Suite 200, 1925 K Street, N.W., 20006 ⊙
Telephone: 202-331-7522 Fax: 202-331-0388
Email: Lawyers@ksflaw.com URL: http://www.ksflaw.com
Armin U. Kuder; Paul R. Smollar; Susan Meyers Friedman; Theresa M. Mihalik;—Andrea E. Hirsch.
General Civil Trial and Family Law Practice, Malpractice and Personal Injury, Association and Health Law, Probate and Estate Planning.
Rockville, Maryland Office: 414 Hungerford Drive, Suite 456. Telephone: 301-340-9090.
See Professional Biographies, WASHINGTON, DISTRICT OF COLUMBIA

Kudon, H. Kenneth, (AV) .... '42 '71 C.16 B.A. L.838 J.D. [Kudon]
*PRACTICE AREAS: Business Torts Litigation; Antitrust Litigation; Franchise Law; Unfair Competition Litigation; Electronic Banking.

Kudon Law Firm, (AV)
Suite 200, 2000 L Street, N.W., 20036
Telephone: 202-965-1602 Fax: 301-294-6407 Mobile: 240-472-1086
Email: kudonlaw@abanet.org URL: http://www.lawyers.com/kudonlaw
H. Kenneth Kudon.
Complex Civil Litigation, Business Torts, Anti-Trust, Unfair Competition, Class Actions, Electronic Banking and Funds Transfer Litigation.
See Professional Biographies, WASHINGTON, DISTRICT OF COLUMBIA

Kuester, Timothy J. .... '— '93 C.546 B.A. L.378 J.D. 701 Pennsylvania Avenue, N.W.
Kuhl, Eric A. .... '59 '90 C.999 B.A. L.64 J.D. [Ⓐ Williams&C.]
Kuhl, Richard S. .... '62 '88 C.932 B.A. L.477 J.D. [Jackson&C.]
*PRACTICE AREAS: Insurance Coverage; Civil Litigation.
Kuhlik, Bruce N., (AV) .... '56 '82 C&L.309 A.B., J.D. [Covington&B.]
Kuhlmann, Kerri S. .... '61 '90 C.690 B.A. L.904 J.D. [Ⓢ Jones,D.R.&P.]
Kuhn, Nancy Ortmeyer '55 '88 C.187 B.S.S. L.174 J.D.
(adm. in CO; not adm. in DC) [Ⓒ Powell,G.F.&M.]
*PRACTICE AREAS: Federal Tax; Tax Exempt Organizations; Litigation.
Kuhn, Nancy R. .... '51 '85 C.575 B.A. L.273 J.D. [Morgan,L.&B.]
Kulczak, Michael J. .... '46 '73 C.93 B.S. L.861 J.D. 1735 K St NW 12th Fl

Kulerman, Michele A. . . . . '52 '85 C.813 B.A. L.809 J.D. [🄲 Hogan&H.]
*PRACTICE AREAS: Blue Sky Law; Corporate Law; Securities.
Kulik, David J. . . . . '65 '94 C.112 B.A. L.273 J.D. [🄲 Wiley R.&F.] (Pat.)
*PRACTICE AREAS: Intellectual Property.
Kuller, Mark A., (AV) . . . . '52 '79 C.569 B.S. L.1068 J.D. [McKee N.]
*PRACTICE AREAS: Tax Planning; Tax Litigation.
Kully, Kristie D. . . . . '67 '94 C.546 B.A. L.188 J.D. [🄰 Kirkpatrick&L.]
*PRACTICE AREAS: Mortgage Banking; Consumer Finance.
Kumar, Anjali . . . . '67 '92 C.273 B.A. L.276 J.D. [🄰 Shaw,B.V.&R.]
*PRACTICE AREAS: Labor and Employment; Federal Employment Law; Employment Discrimination; Civil Litigation; Mediation.
Kumar, Johnny A. . . . . '— '93 C.846 B.S.E.E. L.1209 J.D. [Foley&L.] (See Pat. Sect.)
*PRACTICE AREAS: Intellectual Property Law; Electrical and Computer Patent Law.
Kump, Edward R., (AV) . . . . '53 '78 C&L.128 B.A., J.D. [🄲 Hamilton&H.]
*PRACTICE AREAS: Communications Law; Corporate Law; Business Law.
Kundra, Sunanda '70 '97 C.589 B.S. L.546 J.D.
(adm. in CA; not adm. in DC) [🄰 Arent F.K.P.&K.]
*PRACTICE AREAS: International Employment Contracts; International Agency and Distribution Agreements; International Licensing; International Corporate Law; Litigation.
Kundupoglu, Yoncha L. . . . . '65 '95 C.112 B.S.M.E. L.284 J.D. [🄰 Kilpatrick S.] (Pat.)
*PRACTICE AREAS: Patents; Intellectual Property; Litigation.
Kuney, David R., (AV) . . . . '45 '73 C&L.893 B.A., J.D. [Sidley A.B.&W.]
Kuney, Steven R. . . . . '48 '78 C.918 B.A. L.659 J.D. [Williams&C.]
Kunin, Christy C. . . . . '61 '93 C.67 B.A. L.128 J.D. [Blumenfeld&C.]
*PRACTICE AREAS: Telecommunications Law; Communications Law; Technology Law.
Kunitz, Norman N., (AV) '35 '61
C.223 B.S.E.E. L.273 J.D. [Venable,A.B.H.&C.] (See Pat. Sect.)
*PRACTICE AREAS: Patent Law; Trademark Law.
Kunselman, Michael '74 '00 C&L.446 B.A., J.D.
(adm. in MD; not adm. in DC) [🄰 Swidler B.S.F.]
*PRACTICE AREAS: Energy.
Kunst, Mark W. . . . . '59 '89 C.205 B.A.A.S. L.1338 J.D. [O'Donoghue&O.]
Kuntamukkala, Ajay . . . . '73 '00 C.93 B.A. L.276 J.D. [🄰 Hogan&H.]
Kuntz, Stuart M. . . . . '73 '99 C.1365 B.A. L.569 J.D. [🄰 Shaw P.]
Kunz, J. Catherine . . . . '71 '99 C.813 B.A. L.228 J.D. [🄰 Crowell&M.]
Kunz, Todd W. '65 '00 C.339 B.S. L.405 J.D.
(adm. in IL; not adm. in DC) [🄰 Nath&Assoc.]
*PRACTICE AREAS: Patents.
Kunzi, S. Gregg . . . . '54 '86 C.840 B.S. L.494 J.D. [Hogan&H.]
*PRACTICE AREAS: Government Contracts; Health Care Contracting; Federal Grants; Federal Tort Claims; Bid Protests.
Kupfer, Jeffrey F. . . . . '67 '93 C.976 B.A. L.309 J.D. 3375 Stephenson Pl. N.W.
Kupfer, Nancy S. . . . . '59 '88 C.282 B.A. L.776 J.D. Sr. Coun., Marriott Intl., Inc.
*RESPONSIBILITIES: International Hotel Development.
Kurent, Edward A., (AV) . . . . '46 '71 C.611 B.A. L.150 J.D. 1250 Eye St., NW
Kurian, Anna J. . . . . '74 '99 C.228 B.A. L.276 J.D. [🄰 Hogan&H.]
Kurland, Adam H. . . . . '57 '81 C.112 B.A. L.1068 J.D. 2900 Van Ness St., N.W.
Kurland, Norman G. '30 '60
C.184 B.A. L.145 J.D. Pres., Center for Economic & Social Justice
Kurlander, Stuart S., (AV) . . . . '— '89 C.347 B.A. L.734 J.D. [Latham&W.]
*PRACTICE AREAS: False Claims Act; Health Care Corporate Law; Health Care Mergers and Acquisitions; Health Care Regulation; Health Care Reimbursement.
Kurman, Michael J. . . . . '51 '77 C.608 B.A. L.273 J.D. [Arent F.K.P.&K.]
*PRACTICE AREAS: Energy Law; Hydroelectric Law; Indian Affairs Law; Legislative Practice; Campaign Finance Law.
Kurnick, Robert D., (AV) . . . . '52 '76 C.659 B.A. L.273 J.D. [Sherman,D.C.L.&Y.]
*PRACTICE AREAS: Labor and Employment Law; Union Labor Law.
Kurrelmeyer, Louis H., (AV) '28 '53 C&L.178 A.B., LL.B.
1133 Connecticut Ave., N.W.
Kurtis, Michael K., (AV) . . . . '53 '78 C&L.879 B.S.E.E., J.D. [Kurtis&Assoc.]
*PRACTICE AREAS: Cellular Radio; PCS; Telephone Litigation; Arbitration; Business Transactions.
Kurtis, Rhonda Pines '52 '78 C.597 B.A. L.879 J.D.
(adm. in IN; not adm. in DC) [🄰 Kurtis&Assoc.]
*PRACTICE AREAS: Corporate Law; Communications Law.

Kurtis & Associates, P.C., (AV)
1000 Potomac Street, N.W., Suite 200, 20007
Telephone: 202-328-4500 Telecopier: 202-328-1231
Email: RMcgovern@kurtispc.com URL: http://www.kurtispc.com
Michael K. Kurtis;—Rhonda Pines Kurtis (Not admitted in DC); Lisa L. Leibow; Anna E. Ward. Of Counsel: Jerome K. Blask.
Corporate, Communications and Telecommunications Law.
See Professional Biographies, WASHINGTON, DISTRICT OF COLUMBIA

Kurucza, Robert M. '48 '73 C&L.659 B.A., J.D.
(adm. in PA; not adm. in DC) [Morrison&F.]
*PRACTICE AREAS: Financial Services.
Kurz, Raymond A. . . . . '57 '81 C.1044 B.A. L.273 J.D. [Hogan&H.] (Pat.)
*PRACTICE AREAS: Intellectual Property.
Kurzman, Stephen, (AV) . . . . '32 '59 C&L.309 A.B., J.D. 3026 1/2 Q St Nw
Kurzweil, David A. . . . . '74 '00 C.945 B.A. L.692 J.D. [🄰 Kirkpatrick&L.]
*PRACTICE AREAS: Investment Management; Investment Company Law; Securities; Mutual Funds; Hedge Funds.
Kurzweil, Jeffrey . . . . '50 '75 C.228 A.B. L.880 J.D. 1620 L. St. N.W.
Kushan, Jeffrey P., (BV) . . . . '63 '92 C.945 B.S. L.273 J.D. [Powell,G.F.&M.]
*PRACTICE AREAS: Intellectual Property; International Trade; Public Policy; Government Affairs.
Kushner, Gary Jay, (AV) . . . . '50 '75 C.477 A.B. L.276 J.D. [Hogan&H.]
*PRACTICE AREAS: Food and Drug Law; Agricultural Law; Regulatory Law; Trade Association Law.
Kushner, Michael G. . . . . '52 '77 C.273 B.A. L.893 J.D. 1250 23rd Street, N.W.
Kushnick, Michael G. . . . . '33 '58 C.165 B.A. L.178 LL.B. 888 Seventeenth St., N.W.‡
Kusske, Kathryn A. . . . . '58 '86 C.276 B.S.F.S. L.30 J.D. [Mayer,B.&P.]

Kutak Rock LLP, (AV) 🄱🄱
Suite 1000, 1101 Connecticut Avenue, N.W., 20036-4374 ⊙
Telephone: 202-828-2400 Fax: 202-828-2488
URL: http://www.kutakrock.com
Members of Firm: Joseph A. Ingrisano; Mitchell J. Bragin; Jeffrey S. Jacobovitz; George R. Schlossberg; Barry P. Steinberg; Gilbert W. Boyce; Alan D. Strasser; Paul D. Borja; Alicia A. Terry; Seth David Kirshenberg. Of Counsel: Robert M. Disch; John J. Vecchione. Associates: Nancy Elizabeth Nunan; Leslie Carey (Not admitted in DC); Jennifer M. Blunt; Jorge A. del Rio.
Civil Litigation and Bankruptcy, Public Finance, Corporate and Structured Finance, Banking and Commercial Lending, Real Estate Law, Taxation Law, Health Care and Hospital Law.
Atlanta, Georgia Office: Suite 2100, 225 Peachtree Street, NE, 30303-1731. Telephone: 404-222-4600. Facsimile: 404-222-4654.
Denver, Colorado Office: Suite 2900, 717 Seventeenth Street, 80202-3329. Telephone: 303-297-2400. Facsimile: 303-292-7799.
Des Moines, Iowa Office: Suite 124, Highland Building, 4201 Westown Parkway, West Des Moines, 50266-6720. Telephone: 515-224-1266. Facsimile: 515-457-7669.
Fayetteville, Arkansas Office: 2766 Millennium Place, Highway 265 and Joyce Street, 72703-4793. Telephone: 501-973-4200. Facsimile: 501-973-0007.
Kansas City, Missouri Office: Valencia Place, Suite 200, 444 West 47th Street, 64112-1914. Telephone: 816-960-0090. Telefax: 816-960-0041.
Little Rock, Arkansas Office: Suite 1100, 425 West Capitol Avenue, 72201-3409. Telephone: 501-975-3000. Facsimile: 501-975-3001.

(This Listing Continued)

Kutak Rock LLP (Continued)
New York, New York Office: 650 Fifth Avenue, 10019-6108. Telephone: 212-713-6480. Facsimile: 212-713-6481.
Oklahoma City, Oklahoma Office: Suite 475, 6305 Waterford Boulevard, 73118-1116. Telephone: 405-848-2475. Facsimile: 405-842-5748.
Omaha, Nebraska Office: The Omaha Building, 1650 Farnam Street, 68102-2186. Telephone: 402-346-6000. Facsimile: 402-346-1148.
Scottsdale, Arizona Office: Suite 300, 8601 N. Scottsdale Road, 85253-2742. Telephone: 480-429-5000. Facsimile: 480-429-5001.
Newport Beach, California Office: Suite 450, 620 Newport Center Drive, 92660-8019. Telephone: 949-718-6700. Facsimile: 949-718-6708.
Pasadena, California Office: Suite 210, 117 East Colorado Boulevard. Telephone: 626-432-1630. Facsimile: 626-432-1614.
Richmond, Virginia Office: Bank of America Center, Suite 800, 1111 East Main Street, 23219-3103. Facsimile: 804-783-6192.
Chicago, Illinois Office: Kutak Rock Illinois LLC, One South Wacker Drive, 60606-4614. Telephone: 312-602-4100. Facsimile: 312-602-4101.
See Professional Biographies, WASHINGTON, DISTRICT OF COLUMBIA

Kutcher, Joan L. . . . . '53 '78 C.937 B.A. L.128 J.D. [🄰 Covington&B.]
*PRACTICE AREAS: Regulatory Law; Food and Drug Regulation; Litigation; Complex Litigation.
Kutler, Alison L. . . . . '71 '99 C.276 B.A. L.813 J.D. [🄰 Arent F.K.P.&K.]
*PRACTICE AREAS: Government Relations; International.
Kuwana, Eric A. . . . . '66 '91 C.145 A.B. L.378 J.D. [Patton B.]
Kuzas, Kevin J. . . . . '66 '92 C.800 B.A. L.893 J.D. [Dow,L.&A.]
Kuzmik, Anna M. . . . . '70 '95 C.212 B.A. L.309 J.D. [🄰 Sullivan&C.]
Kwan, Gregory D. '72 '00 C.446 B.A. L.893 J.D.
(adm. in MD; not adm. in DC) [🄰 Dickstein S.M.&O.]
Kwon, Samuel R. '74 '99 C.659 B.S. L.276 J.D.
(adm. in NY; not adm. in DC) [🄰 Chadbourne&P.]
Kyhos, Thomas F. . . . . '47 '74 C.210 B.A. L.128 J.D. 3528 K St., N.W.
Kyle, John W. . . . . '50 '83 C.651 B.A. L.64 J.D. [Hahn K.&H.]
Kyle, Robert D. . . . . '55 '82 C.188 B.A. L.309 J.D. [Hogan&H.]
*PRACTICE AREAS: International Trade; Legislative.
Kysela, Sussan Mahallati '66 '94 C.276 B.S.B.A. L.128 J.D.
Labor Coun., National Chamber Litig. Ctr., Inc.
Kysilka, Karin J. '— '98 C.645 B.A. L.309 J.D.
(adm. in PA; not adm. in DC) [🄰 Shaw P.]
*PRACTICE AREAS: Real Estate.
Laane, M. Sean, (AV) . . . . '61 '89 C.339 B.A. L.477 J.D. [Arnold&P.]
*PRACTICE AREAS: Products Liability; Civil Litigation.
Labaton, Stephen '61 '89 C.860 B.A. L.228 J.D.
(adm. in NY; not adm. in DC) The New York Times
LaBelle, R. Michael . . . . '54 '80 C.966 B.A. L.30 J.D. 4201 Conn. Ave., N.W.
Labgold, Marc R. '64 '95 C.569 B.A. L.273 J.D.
(adm. in GA; not adm. in DC; Pat.) [Piper M.R.&W.]
*PRACTICE AREAS: Patent Litigation; Patent Prosecution; Biotechnology Patents; Intellectual Property.
Laboe, James F. '69 '00 C.602 B.A. L.1218 J.D.
(adm. in NH; not adm. in DC) [🄰 Arent F.K.P.&K.]
*PRACTICE AREAS: OSHA; Litigation; Labor and Employment.
Laboschin, Debra M. '71 '99 C.659 B.A. L.1065 J.D.
(adm. in CA; not adm. in DC) [🄰 Patton B.]
Labovitz, Priscilla, (AV) . . . . '46 '73 C.914 B.A. L.588 J.D. 6856 Eastern Ave., N.W.
Labson, Michael Scott . . . . '67 '94 C&L.309 A.B., J.D. [🄰 Covington&B.]
Lacey, Pamela A. '55 '84 C.104 A.B. L.273 J.D.
Senior Managing Counsel, American Gas Association
Lacey, Stephen L. . . . . '67 '99 C.882 B.A. L.180 J.D. [🄰 Olsson,F.&W.]
*PRACTICE AREAS: Agriculture Law; Food and Drug Regulation; Administrative Law; Legislation.
Lachance, Andre J. '62 '88 C.367 B.A. L.273 J.D.
(adm. in VA; not adm. in DC) Coun. Regulatory, Verizon Wireless
Lachenmayr, Andrea . . . . '— '00 C.918 B.A. L.276 J.D. [🄰 Thelen R.&P.]
*PRACTICE AREAS: Business and Finance; Project and Asset Finance; General Corporate; Securities.
Lachter, Stephen H., (AV) . . . . '44 '69 C.823 A.B. L.276 J.D. [Lachter&C.]
*PRACTICE AREAS: Civil Litigation; Antitrust Law; Aviation Law; International Aviation; Administrative.

Lachter & Clements LLP, (AV)
Suite 900, 1150 Connecticut Avenue, N.W., 20036-4192
Telephone: 202-862-4321 Telecopier: 202-835-3219
Email: lachter@starpower.net URL: http://www.lawyers.com/lachterclementslaw
Stephen H. Lachter; Roxanne S. Clements.
Antitrust, Aviation Law, including International Aviation Law, Airline Regulation, Administrative Litigation, International Law, Transportation Law, Commercial Litigation.
See Professional Biographies, WASHINGTON, DISTRICT OF COLUMBIA

Laciak, Christine A. . . . . '68 '99 C.128 B.A. L.145 J.D. [🄰 Morgan,L.&B.]
Lackey, Michael E., Jr. . . . . '61 '93 C.453 B.S. L.273 J.D. [🄰 Mayer,B.&P.]
Lackritz, Marc E., (AV) . . . '46 '75 C.674 A.B. L.309 J.D. Pres., Securities Industry Assn.
Lacosta, Anthony W. . . . . '69 '99 C.950 B.A. L.1066 J.D. [🄰 Kirkland&E.]
*PRACTICE AREAS: White Collar Crime; Litigation.
Lacovara, Philip Allen, (AV) '43 '67
C.276 A.B. L.178 J.D. [Mayer,B.&P.] (⊙New York, NY)
Ladd, Christine R. . . . . '58 '86 C.976 B.A. L.569 J.D. 1350 Connecticut Ave., N.W.
Laderberg, Amy E. '74 '99 C.951 B.A. L.945 J.D.
(adm. in VA; not adm. in DC) [🄰 Crowell&M.]
LaDuca, Charles J. '74 '01 C.273 B.A. L.128 J.D.
(adm. in NY; not adm. in DC) [🄰 Cuneo]
*PRACTICE AREAS: Litigation; Torts; Consumer Law; Securities; Antitrust.
Laessig, Walter B. . . . . '41 '66 C&L.188 A.B., LL.B. 1101 Vt. Ave., N.W.
Lafaivre, Michele L. '— '99 L.446 J.D.
(adm. in MD; not adm. in DC) National Assoc. of Home Builders
LaFalce, Frank A., Jr. '54 '79 C.928 B.A.
(adm. in MD; not adm. in DC) [Gray B.&Assoc.]
Lafave, Arthur J., III, (AV) . . . . '54 '81 C.951 B.A. L.893 J.D. [Dickstein S.M.&O.]
*PRACTICE AREAS: Customs Law; International Trade Law.
LaFave, Julie A. . . . . '57 '83 C.914 B.A. L.477 J.D. 727 6th St.,S.E.
Laffert, Donald A. '64 '91 C.802 B.A. L.902 J.D.
Asst. Gen. Coun., Washington Metropolitan Area Transit Authority
*RESPONSIBILITIES: Litigation (50%); Construction Law (50%).
La Fleur, Monique J. . . . . '65 '97 C.1077 B.A. L.477 J.D. [🄰 Covington&B.]
*PRACTICE AREAS: Employee Benefits; Executive Compensation.
LaFontaine, Maribel . . . . '67 '97 C.262 B.A. L.128 J.D. [🄰 Salgado&Assoc.]
*PRACTICE AREAS: Immigration; Visas; Political Asylum; Deportation.
LaForce, Pierre J., (AV) . . . . '36 '60 C.708 A.B. L.276 J.D. [🄲 Wilkinson B.K.]
*PRACTICE AREAS: Appellate Practice; Trial Practice; Corporate; Commercial Transactions; Administrative Litigation.
LaForge, William N., (AV) . . . . '50 '75 C.206 B.A. L.500 J.D. [🄲 McGuiness N.&W.]
*PRACTICE AREAS: Legislation; Government Relations; Administrative; International Trade; Commercial Law.
LaForte, Rene M. '68 '93 C.645 B.A. L.201 J.D.
(adm. in OH; not adm. in DC) [🄰 Sutherland A.&B.]
*PRACTICE AREAS: Trademarks; Copyrights; Unfair Competition.

LaFranchi, Jane Woods '56 '82
(adm. in TX; not adm. in DC) [Strasburger&P.]
*PRACTICE AREAS: International Business Law; International Franchising; Mexico Trade.
LaFrankie, Alexandra C. .... '73 '00 C.216 B.S. L.904 J.D. [Ⓐ Kirkpatrick&L.]
*PRACTICE AREAS: Investment Management.
LaFrankie, Robert L. .... '62 '90 C.945 B.A. L.893 J.D. [Ⓐ Willkie F.&G.]
LaFuria, David A., (AV) .... '59 '85 C.831 B.A. L.128 J.D. [Lukas,N.G.&S.]
*PRACTICE AREAS: Telecommunications Law; Wireless Communications; Telecommunications Contracts.
Lagano, Rhea A. '74 '99 C.1349 B.A. L.575 J.D.
(adm. in NC; not adm. in DC) [Ⓐ Slevin&H.]
*PRACTICE AREAS: Employee Benefits.
Lagerman, Bruce K. '59 '90 C.128 B.S. L.904 J.D.
(adm. in VA; not adm. in DC; Pat.) [Ⓒ Kile G.L.&R.P.] (⊙Reston, VA)
*PRACTICE AREAS: Intellectual Property Licensing.
Lago, Victor A. '65 '93 C.165 L.902 J.D.
(adm. in WA; not adm. in DC)
Vice President-Legal Affairs, Diveo Broadband Networks, Inc.
Laguarda, Fernando R. .....'— '94 C.309 A.B. L.276 J.D. 701 Pennsylvania Avenue, N.W.
LaHaie, Gerald P. '50 '75 C.1154 B.A. L.213 J.D.
(adm. in MI; not adm. in DC) V.P., Fannie Mae
Laham, Carol A. .... '59 '85 C.914 B.A. L.569 J.D. [Wiley R.&F.]
*PRACTICE AREAS: Election Law.
Lahey, John H., (AV) .... '— '72 C.473 B.S. L.608 J.D. [Kozusko L.H.]
*PRACTICE AREAS: Taxation; International Law; Nonprofit and Charitable Organizations; Business Law; Trusts and Estates.
Lahiff, Christopher M. ......'57 '86 C.602 B.A./B.S.Ch.E L.904 J.D. [McDermott,W.&E.]
Lahlou, Shari Ross '67 '99 C.216 B.A. L.273 J.D.
(adm. in MD; not adm. in DC) [Ⓐ Crowell&M.]
Lahr, Jack L., (AV) ....'— '63 C.851 B.S.M.E. L.273 J.D. [Foley&L.] (See Pat. Sect.)
*PRACTICE AREAS: Litigation; Intellectual Property Law; Antitrust Law; Administrative Law.
Laidhold, Michael R. ....'72 '99 C.473 B.A. L.665 J.D. [Ⓐ Piper M.R.&W.]
*PRACTICE AREAS: Franchise Law; Distribution; International Law; Corporate Law.
Laing, David J. .... '59 '88 C.893 B.A. L.575 J.D. [Baker&M.]
*PRACTICE AREAS: Antitrust and Unfair Trade Practices Law; Criminal Law; Mergers and Acquisitions.
Laird, Rebecca H. .... '— '70 C.659 B.A. L.276 J.D. [Kirkpatrick&L.]
*PRACTICE AREAS: Banking Law; Thrift Institutions Law; Investment Company Law; Investment Management; Trust Law.
Lakatos, Alex .... '70 '96 C.446 B.A. L.1065 J.D. [Ⓐ Shaw P.]
Lake, F. David, Jr., (AV) .... '43 '67 C.31 B.A. L.893 LL.B. [Wilmer,C.&P.]
*PRACTICE AREAS: Taxation.
Lake, Monte B., (AV) ....'47 '73 C.169 B.A. L.464 J.D. [McGuiness N.&W.]
*PRACTICE AREAS: Agricultural Labor Law; Equal Employment Opportunity Law; Employment Law; Business Immigration Law; Government Relations.
Lake, William T., (AV) .... '43 '69 C.976 B.A. L.813 J.D. [Wilmer,C.&P.]
*PRACTICE AREAS: Communications and Media; International Law.
Lakis, Joseph S., Jr. '69 '94 C.415 L.1019 J.D.
(adm. in CT; not adm. in DC) [Ⓐ McGuiness N.&W.]
*PRACTICE AREAS: Employment Law; Equal Employment Opportunity Law; Affirmative Action Compliance.
Lakritz, Robb M. ....'72 '97 C.477 B.A. L.245 J.D. 801 Penn. Ave., NW
Lalla, Anthony P. ....'59 '89 C.1122 B.A. L.30 J.D. [Ⓐ Jones,D.R.&P.]
Lally, Carol Williams '67 '95
C.170 B.A. L.228 J.D. 555 Twelfth Street, N.W. (⊙L.A., CA)
Lalos, Peter N., (AV) .....'34 '61 C.688 B.S.M.E. L.30 LL.B. [Lalos&K.] (See Pat. Sect.)
*PRACTICE AREAS: Intellectual Property Law; Corporate Law; Litigation; Appellate Practice.

Lalos & Keegan, (AV) BR
1146 Nineteenth Street N.W., Fifth Floor, 20036-3723
Telephone: 202-887-5555 Telecopier: (202) 296-1682
Email: laloskeegan@radix.net URL: http://www.lawyers.com/lalos&keeganlaw
Members of Firm: Peter N. Lalos; Alfred A. Stadnicki (Not admitted in DC). Associates: Sterling W. Chandler (Not admitted in DC); Kenneth John Whittington (Not admitted in DC).
Intellectual Property Law including Patent, Trademark, Copyright, International Trade and Unfair Competition Law, before Federal Trial and Appeal Courts, International Trade Commission, Federal Agencies and State Trial and Appeal Courts.
See Professional Biographies, WASHINGTON, DISTRICT OF COLUMBIA

Lam, Edward W. '66 '95 C.801 B.A. L.823 J.D.
(adm. in NY; not adm. in DC) [Ⓐ Shaw P.]
*PRACTICE AREAS: Federal Income Tax.
Lam, Gregory B. '64 '91 C&L.378 B.A., J.D.
(adm. in KS; not adm. in DC) [Copilevitz&C.] ⊙
*PRACTICE AREAS: Charitable Trusts and Foundations; Non-Profit Tax Law; Charitable Giving Law; Non-Profit Organizations Law.
Lam, Ngoc H. .....'70 '95 C.645 B.S. L.30 J.D. [Ⓐ Jackson&C.] (⊙Balt., Rockville, MD)
Lam, Tony Y. .... '— '98 C.999 B.A. L.776 J.D. [Ⓐ Kirkland&E.]
*PRACTICE AREAS: Corporate; Securities.
Lamade, Lawrence L., (AV) .... '47 '75 C.674 A.B. L.276 J.D. [Akin,G.S.H.&F.]
LaMadrid, Marisol '61 '92 C.999 B.A. L.861 LL.M.
(adm. in NY; not adm. in DC) [Marty,L.&S.]

Lamb, David B., (AV) '42 '68 C.276 B.S.B.A. L.904 J.D.
1818 N Street, N.W., 7th Floor, 20036 ⊙
Telephone: 202-785-4822 Facsimile: 202-785-2210 URL: http://www.washington-office.com
Email: lambdb@wizard.net URL: http://www.lawyers.com/davidblamb
***PRACTICE AREAS: Civil Litigation; Criminal Litigation; Personal Injury Law; Divorce.**
Civil Trials, Commercial Litigation, Personal Injury, Auto Accidents, Premises Liability, Family Law, Divorce, Separation, Custody, Visitation, Marital Property, Matrimonial Law, White Collar Crime, Securities, Labor, E-Commerce Law, Internet Law, General Civil Litigation in the Federal and Local Courts of Maryland and The District of Columbia.
Rockville, Maryland Office: Suite 200, 255 North Washington Street. Telephone: 301-279-7500.
Fairfax, Virginia Office: 10511 Judicial Drive. Telephone: 703-273-3190.
See Professional Biographies, WASHINGTON, DISTRICT OF COLUMBIA

Lamb, James C. .... '65 '95 C.477 B.A. L.912 J.D. [Ⓐ Ryan,P.U.&M.]
Lamb, Lewis E., III ....'62 '93 C.276 B.A. L.575 J.D. [Ⓐ Hunton&W.]
*PRACTICE AREAS: Trademarks; Copyrights; Internet Law; Unfair Competition.
Lamb, Melissa E. ....'73 '98 C.188 B.A. L.309 J.D. [Ⓐ Fried,F.H.S.&J.]
*PRACTICE AREAS: White Collar Criminal Defense; Civil Litigation.
Lamb, Robert H. '43 '74 C.893 B.A. L.500 J.D.
(adm. in MS; not adm. in DC) [Wright&T.]
*PRACTICE AREAS: Legislative Lobbying; Regulated Industries.
Lamba, Sanjay '72 '97 C.1356 B.S. L.94 J.D.
(adm. in VA; not adm. in DC) [Ⓐ Dechert]
*PRACTICE AREAS: Financial Services Law; Investment Management.
Lamberg Kafele, Heather '72 '98 C.429 B.A. L.276 J.D.
(adm. in MD; not adm. in DC) [Ⓐ Shearman&S.]
*PRACTICE AREAS: Commercial Litigation; Antitrust Litigation; FDA Related Litigation.
Lambergman, Barry .... '59 '83 C.823 B.A. L.1068 J.D. Motorola, Inc.
Lambert, David L. .... '— '93 C.228 B.A. L.574 J.D. [Kirkland&E.]
*PRACTICE AREAS: Mergers and Acquisitions; Securities.
Lambert, David M. F., (AV) .... '25 '55 C.855 A.B. L.188 J.D. [Hewes,G.L.&D.]
Lambert, Eugene I., (AV) .... '35 '60 C.273 A.B. L.976 J.D. [Covington&B.]
Lambert, Jeremiah D., (AV) .... '34 '60 C.674 A.B. L.976 LL.B. [Shook,H.&B.]
*PRACTICE AREAS: Energy; Corporate Law.
Lambert, Paul J. .... '46 '70 C.321 A.B. L.309 J.D. [Bingham D.]
*PRACTICE AREAS: Commercial Litigation; Environmental Litigation; Administrative Litigation; Employment Litigation.
Lambert, Sanda K. .... '51 '77 C.881 B.A. L.178 J.D. 2855 Woodland Dr. N.W.
Lambert, Steven C., (AV) .... '— '75 C.228 B.A. L.276 J.D. [Foley&L.]
*PRACTICE AREAS: Litigation; Valuation Law; Government Contracts.
Lambert & Furlow, (AV) .... 1730 M. St., N.W. (⊙Chevy Chase, MD)
Lamberton, Benjamin P., (AV) ....'40 '66 C.867 B.A. L.893 LL.B. [Friedeman,I.W.&L.]
*PRACTICE AREAS: Litigation; Employment Law; Higher Education Law.
Lambiotte, Benjamin J. .... '60 '89 C.30 B.A. L.128 J.D. [Ⓒ Garvey,S.&B.]
*PRACTICE AREAS: Commercial Law; Litigation; Intellectual Property.
Lamboley, E. Gerald '15 '39 C&L.966 Ph.B., LL.B.
(adm. in WI; not adm. in DC) 21 Snows Ct., N.W.‡
Lambrakopoulos, Stavroula E. .... '62 '95 C&L.273 B.A., J.D. [Ⓐ Kirkpatrick&L.]
*PRACTICE AREAS: SEC Enforcement; Securities Litigation; Securities Arbitration; Corporate Litigation; Civil Appeals.
Lamensdorf, Rolland G., (AV) '11 '36 C.659 B.S. L.276 J.D.
5123 Linnean Ave., N.W.‡
Lamm, Carolyn B., (AV) .... '48 '73 C.107 B.S. L.472 J.D. [White&C.]
*PRACTICE AREAS: International Arbitration; International Trade; Litigation.
Lammers, Corinne A. .... '70 '96 C.30 B.A. L.228 J.D. [Ⓐ Gibson,D.&C.]
*PRACTICE AREAS: International Trade.
Lamont, Robert S., Jr. .... '73 '98 C.260 B.S. L.259 J.D. [Ⓐ Dechert]
*PRACTICE AREAS: Financial Services Law; Investment Management.
Lamothe, Kathryn Anne '73 '98 C.128 B.A. L.945 J.D.
(adm. in VA; not adm. in DC) U.S. Dept. of Transp.
Lampert, Donna N., & Associates, (AV) '57 '82
C.65 A.B. L.1068 J.D. 1750 K Street, NW
Lampley, Judith A. '53 '92 C.449 B.S. L.273 J.D.
(adm. in VA; not adm. in DC) [Ⓐ McGuiness N.&W.]
*PRACTICE AREAS: Human Resources Training; Employment Law; Equal Employment Opportunity Law.
Lan, Elizabeth .... '74 '99 C.659 B.A. L.861 J.D. U.S. Dept. of Jus.
Lanam, Linda L. '48 '75 C.347 B.S. L.1119 J.D.
(adm. in IN; not adm. in DC) V.P. & Chf. Coun., State Rel., Amer. Council of Life Ins.
Lancaster, Margaret E. ....'68 '99 C.576 B.A. L.329 J.D. [Ⓐ Skadden,A.S.M.&F.]
*PRACTICE AREAS: Communications Law.
Lance, James W. '43 '73 C&L.45 B.S.B.A., J.D.
(adm. in AR; not adm. in DC) [Ⓒ Silver,F.&T.]
*PRACTICE AREAS: Financial Institution Law.
Lancellotta, Amy B. R., (AV) '59 '84
C.645 B.A. L.273 J.D. Sr. Coun., Investment Co. Inst.
*RESPONSIBILITIES: Securities.
Lancellotta, Steven A., (AV) .... '— '82 C.690 B.A. L.273 J.D. [Manatt,P.&P.]
Lancetti, Luisa L., (AV) '54 '80
C.347 B.A. L.893 J.D. V.P., PCS Regulatory Affs., Sprint Corp.
Lanchester, Michelle .... '58 '86 C.881 B.A. L.329 J.D. P.O. Box 2191
Lancour, Anne Marie J. '60 '89 C.1031 B.A. L.1048 J.D.
(adm. in NY; not adm. in DC) ABA Ctr. on Children & the Law
Land, Brian R. .... '60 '89 C.910 B.S. L.273 J.D. [Kirkland&E.]
*PRACTICE AREAS: Environmental Law.
Land, Hans A., (AV) ....'22 '50 C.976 B.A. L.309 J.D. [Land&L.]
Land, Kelley L. ....'67 '99 C.205 B.S. L.30 J.D. Atty., U.S. Sentencing Commission
Land, Stuart J., (AV) .... '30 '54 C.823 A.B. L.309 LL.B. [Arnold&P.]
*PRACTICE AREAS: Food, Drug and Medical Device; Litigation.
Land & Lemle, (AV) .... 1775 I St., NW
Landau, Christopher ....'63 '90 C&L.309 A.B., J.D. [Kirkland&E.]
*PRACTICE AREAS: Appellate Litigation; Commercial Litigation; Products Liability.
Landau, David P. .... '55 '81 C.446 B.S. L.64 J.D. 1725 K St., N.W.

Landau, Gail B., P.C.
(See Rockville, Maryland)

Landauer, Craig L. .... '51 '85 C.893 B.A. L.64 J.D. [Ⓒ Pickard&D.]
*PRACTICE AREAS: Statutory Disqualification and other NASD Administrative Proceedings; NASD Membership and Registration Issues; Broker-Dealer Compliance.
Lander, Daryl A. .... '52 '81 C.938 B.A. L.950 J.D. [Ⓒ Crowell&M.]
Landerholm, Arthur S. .... '— '96 C.668 B.A. L.1068 J.D. [Ⓐ Latham&W.]
*PRACTICE AREAS: Communications and Media; Mergers, Acquisitions and Divestitures.
Landers, David Michael ....'62 '95 C.228 B.A. L.1209 J.D. [Ⓐ Williams&J.]
Landers, Denise '66 '96 C.914 B.A. L.94 J.D.
(adm. in MA; not adm. in DC) [Ⓐ Clifford C.R.&W.]
*PRACTICE AREAS: Securities Law.
Landesberg, Martha K. '50 '89 C.976 B.A. L.150 J.D.
(adm. in OH; not adm. in DC) [Ⓒ Dorsey&W.]
*PRACTICE AREAS: Civil Trial; Criminal Law.
Landfield, Richard, (AV) ....'41 '66 C.31 B.A. L.309 LL.B. [Berliner,C.&R.]
*PRACTICE AREAS: Corporate; International; Real Estate.
Landgraf, L. Charles .... '52 '78 C.691 B.A. L.569 J.D. [LeBoeuf,L.G.&M.]
*PRACTICE AREAS: Insurance; Legislation; Intellectual Property.
Landis, Allison F. '74 '00 C.893 B.A. L.94 J.D.
(adm. in NY; not adm. in DC) [Ⓐ Swidler B.S.F.]
*PRACTICE AREAS: Litigation.
Landman, Jessica C. .... '55 '85 C.145 B.A. L.276 J.D. Natural Res. Def. Council
Landmeier, Lisa M. ....'64 '93 C.352 B.S. L.276 J.D. [Dickinson L.]
*PRACTICE AREAS: International Law; Foreign Corrupt Practices Act; Foreign Asset Control; Export Regulations and Compliance; Corporate Law.
Landon, Matthew B. .... '71 '98 C.589 B.A. L.188 J.D. [Ⓐ Baker&M.]
*PRACTICE AREAS: Corporate and Partnership Law; Securities and Financial Products; Mergers and Acquisitions.
Landry, Brock R., (AV) ....'47 '74 C.976 B.A. L.477 J.D. [Venable,A.B.H.&C.]
*PRACTICE AREAS: Association Law; International Trade; Environmental Law; Administrative Law.
Landsman, Lisa A. '57 '89
C.918 B.A. L.1066 J.D. Asst. Gen. Coun., Smithsonian Institution
Landsman, Sheldon I., (P.C.), (AV) '42 '68
C.563 B.E.Ch.E. L.273 J.D. [Sughrue M.] (See Pat. Sect.)
*PRACTICE AREAS: Intellectual Property Law.

Landsman, Ron M., P.A.
(See Bethesda, Maryland)

Landy, Charles J., (AV) ....'44 '73 C.659 B.A. L.831 J.D. [Shaw P.]
*PRACTICE AREAS: Securities Enforcement; Securities Litigation; Corporate Securities.
Landy, Jonathan M. ....'73 '99 C.197 B.A. L.976 J.D. [Ⓐ Williams&C.]
*PRACTICE AREAS: Appellate Practice; Intellectual Property.
Lane, Andrea '— '01 C.260 B.S. L.273 J.D.
(adm. in VA; not adm. in DC) [Ⓐ Alston&B.]
*PRACTICE AREAS: International Taxation; Federal Taxation.
Lane, Brian J. '58 '83 C.900 B.A. L.904 J.D.
(adm. in MD; not adm. in DC) [Gibson,D.&C.]
*PRACTICE AREAS: Securities; Mergers, Acquisitions and Divestitures; Corporate Law.

Lane, Bruce S., (AV) .... '32 '55 C&L.309 A.B., J.D. [Nixon P.]
*PRACTICE AREAS: Tax; Real Estate; Business Law.
Lane, Carol M. ....'43 '78 C.446 B.S. L.128 J.D. 3325 Runnymede Pl., N.W.
Lane, Denise Catherine '69 '97 C.454 B.S. L.94 J.D.
(adm. in MA; not adm. in DC; See Pat. Sect.) [Ⓐ Blank R.C.&M.]
*PRACTICE AREAS: Intellectual Property Litigation; Intellectual Property Licensing; Patent Prosecution.
Lane, Erin Patten .... '75 '00 C.500 B.A L.309 J.D. [Ⓐ Paul,H.J.&W.]
*PRACTICE AREAS: Litigation.
Lane, Hite Colby .... '74 '99 C.484 B.S. L.309 J.D. [Ⓐ Wilmer,C.&P.]
Lane, John D., (AV) '21 '48 C&L.276 B.S., J.D.
1200 New Hampshire Ave., N.W., Ste. 800 (⊙Norwalk, CT)
Lane, Joseph M., (AV) '28 '57 C.124 B.S. L.273 J.D.
2600 Virginia Avenue, N.W. (Pat.)
Lane, Mark ....'27 '51 L.1009 LL.B. 105 2nd St., N.E.
Lane, Steven L. ....'— '97 C.197 B.A. L.880 J.D. [Ⓐ King&S.]
*PRACTICE AREAS: Intellectual Property.

Lane, Aitken & McCann, L.L.P.
(See Venable, Attorneys at Law, Venable, Baetjer and Howard, LLP)

Lang, Gordon L., (AV) .... '51 '76 C.477 B.A. L.309 J.D. [Nixon P.]
Lang, Jane, (AV) .... '47 '70 C.821 B.A. L.659 J.D. [Sprenger&L.]
*PRACTICE AREAS: Employment; Complex Federal Litigation; Professional and Trade Associations.
Lang, Jeffrey M., (AV) .... '42 '67 C.95 A.B. L.893 LL.B. [Wilmer,C.&P.]
*PRACTICE AREAS: International Regulatory Law; International Trade; Legislation; European Community Law.
Lang, Jessica B. '74 '00 C.893 B.A. L.145 J.D.
(adm. in MD; not adm. in DC) [Ⓐ Steptoe&J.]
Lang, Lindsey B., (AV) .... '51 '82 C.788 B.A. L.904 J.D. [Ⓐ Steptoe&J.]
Lang, Neil S., (AV) ....'— '68 C.563 B.A. L.724 J.D. [Sutherland A.&B.]
*PRACTICE AREAS: Securities; Litigation; Business Law; Legal Ethics; Professional Responsibility.
Lang, Paul R., (AV) .... '57 '83 C.174 B.A. L.273 J.D. [Dow,L.&A.]
Lang, Thomas J. ....'— '96 C.674 A.B. L.188 J.D. [Ⓐ Morgan,L.&B.]
Langan, Eugenia ....'52 '85 C.178 B.A. L.145 J.D. [Shea&G.]
*PRACTICE AREAS: Civil Litigation; Labor Law; Transportation Law.
Langan, Michael G. ....'68 '98 C.165 B.A. L.1356 J.D. [Ⓐ Piper M.R.&W.]
*PRACTICE AREAS: White Collar Crime; Civil Litigation; Criminal Litigation; Commercial Litigation.
Langbein, Stuart M. .... '65 '91 C.860 B.A. L.659 J.D. [Hogan&H.]
*PRACTICE AREAS: Health Care.
Langdon, James C., Jr., (AV) ....'45 '70 C&L.846 B.B.A., J.D. [Akin,G.S.H.&F.]
*PRACTICE AREAS: Energy; Project Finance.
Langdon, Mark Bancroft ....'69 '94 C&L.188 B.A., J.D. [Ⓐ Arent F.K.P.&K.]
*PRACTICE AREAS: Health Care Law.
Lange, Anne M. ....'49 '78 C.19 B.A. L.128 J.D. The Bureau of Natl. Affs., Inc.
Lange, Gene C., (AV) '47 '73
C.350 B.S. L.276 J.D. [Ⓒ Dickinson,M.T.&H.] (⊙Washington)
*PRACTICE AREAS: Association; Corporate; Immigration Law.
Lange, Gene C., (AV) .... '47 '73 C.350 B.S. L.276 J.D. [Luman,L.&W.] (⊙Washington)
*PRACTICE AREAS: Business Law; Commercial Law; Business Immigration Law; Trade and Professional Associations.
Lange, Lori Ann .... '66 '91 C&L.273 B.A., J.D. [Ⓐ Bastianelli,B.&K.]
*PRACTICE AREAS: Government Contracts; Construction Law; Maritime Law.
Lange, William M., (AV) '46 '75
C.347 B.A. L.273 J.D. Asst. Gen. Coun., Consumers Energy Co.
Langer, Elizabeth, (BV) ....'46 '74 C.66 B.A. L.705 J.D. 1828 L St., N.W., Ste 500
Langford, James T., (AV) '43 '74 C.262 A.B. L.245 J.D.
Intl. Union of Bricklayers & Allied Craftworkers
Langford, Joy L. ....'69 '94 C.496 B.A. L.276 J.D. [Ⓐ Chadbourne&P.]
Langhammer, Frank L. .... '44 '92 C.674 A.B. L.659 J.D. 5051 Millwood Ln. NW
Langhorne, Chiswell D., Jr., (AV) '40 '66 C&L.893 B.A., J.D.
1616 H Street, N.W., Suite 902, 20006
Telephone: 202-628-5093 Telecopier: 202-628-5932
Email: langhorc@erols.com
General Civil and Administrative Practice. Estate Planning, Probate, Natural Resources, Taxation and Trusts.
See Professional Biographies, WASHINGTON, DISTRICT OF COLUMBIA
Langley, Jason Paul .... '73 '00 C.43 B.A. L.276 J.D. [Ⓐ Dow,L.&A.]
Langley, Robert E. '22 '56 C.573 B.S. L.276 J.D.
(adm. in VA; not adm. in DC) 3901 Conn. Ave., NW‡
Langworthy, Elisabeth A. '55 '84
C.788 A.B. L.273 J.D. [Sutherland A.&B.] (See Pat. Sect.)
*PRACTICE AREAS: Trademarks; Copyrights; Intellectual Property Licensing; Intellectual Property Litigation.
Langworthy, Lucinda Minton ....'56 '81 C.105 B.A. L.273 J.D. [Ⓒ Hunton&W.]
*PRACTICE AREAS: Environmental.
Lanigan, Kevin J. .... '57 '82 C.378 B.A. L.893 J.D. [Hogan&H.]
*PRACTICE AREAS: Litigation; Administrative Law; Civil Rights; Education Law; Government.

Lankford & Coffield
(See Alexandria, Virginia)

Lannan, Kathleen A. '64 '92
C.024 B.A. L.012 LL.B. Atty., Organization of American States
Lanning, Geoffrey B. '46 '76 C.309 B.A. L.1049 J.D.
(adm. in CA; not adm. in DC) [Ⓐ White&C.]
Lanoff, Ian D., (AV) ....'42 '67 C&L.477 B.A., J.D. [Groom]
*PRACTICE AREAS: Employee Benefits; Labor and Employment; Pension and Profit Sharing; Health Care Law; ERISA.
Lanou, John H.R. ....'72 '00 C.893 B.A. L.945 J.D. [Ⓐ Collier S.S.]
*PRACTICE AREAS: Antitrust.
Lanpher, Lawrence Coe ....'— '75 C.94 B.A. L.273 J.D. [Kirkpatrick&L.]
*PRACTICE AREAS: Labor and Employment; Disabilities; Litigation; Insurance Coverage.
Lansdale, John, Jr. ....'12 '37 C.885 B.A. L.309 LL.B. 1201 Pennsylvania Ave., N.W.‡
Lansing, Brian C. ....'67 '92 C.692 B.A. L.896 J.D. [Ⓐ Arent F.K.P.&K.]
*PRACTICE AREAS: Federal Civil Litigation; State Civil Litigation.
Lanthier, Veronique .... '66 '98 C.112 B.A. L.813 J.D. [Ⓐ O'Melveny&M.]
Lantor, Todd Bradley ....'71 '96 C.477 B.A. L.94 J.D. [Ⓐ Steptoe&J.]
Lanza, Ernesto A. .... '63 '88 C.309 B.A. L.659 J.D. Mun. Sec. Rulemaking Brd.
Lanzo, Douglas J. .... '71 '98 C&L.309 B.A., J.D. [Ⓐ Vinson&E.]
*PRACTICE AREAS: Corporate Law.
La Padula, Paschal R., (BV) '24 '50
C&L.276 B.S., J.D. 311 G St., N.W. (⊙Bethesda, MD)
Lapham, Anthony A., (AV) ....'36 '62 C.976 B.A. L.276 J.D. [Ⓒ Shea&G.]
Lapiana, John K. '60 '87 C&L.1044 B.S., J.D.
(adm. in MA; not adm. in DC) Asst. Gen. Coun., Smithsonian Institution
Lapidus, Jack David ....'69 '94 C.705 B.A. [Ⓐ Macleay,L.G.&L.]
*PRACTICE AREAS: Insurance Defense.
Lapidus, Lawrence S., (AV) '45 '73
C.273 B.A. L.904 J.D. [Karp,F.L.W.&N.] (⊙Washington)
*PRACTICE AREAS: Medical Malpractice; Auto Negligence; Premises Liability; Product Liability.
Lapidus, Lawrence S., (AV) '45 '73
C.273 B.A. L.30 J.D. 1232 17th St. N.W. (⊙Washington)
Lapidus, Nancy S. ....'— '95 C.910 B.A. L.273 J.D. [Ⓐ Shaw P.]
*PRACTICE AREAS: Intellectual Property; Food and Drug Regulation.
LaPlaca, M. Michael, (AV) ....'37 '74 C.276 B.A. L.1065 J.D. [Edidin&L.]
Laponsky, Mark D. '58 '84 C.823 B.A. L.904 J.D.
The International Trade Center, 1300 Pennsylvania Avenue, NW, Suite 700, 20004
Telephone: 202-789-0990 Facsimile: 202-789-7349
Email: mdlaponsky@laponsky-law.com URL: http://www.lawyers.com/laponskylaw
***PRACTICE AREAS: Employment Law; Disabilities; Civil Rights; Education; Constitutional. Labor and Employment, Disabilities, Civil Rights, Education Law, Constitutional Law, Civil Litigation, Business Law.**
See Professional Biographies, WASHINGTON, DISTRICT OF COLUMBIA
Laporte, Gerald J.S., (AV) .... '46 '76 C.706 B.A. L.273 J.D. [Ⓒ Hogan&H.]
*PRACTICE AREAS: Securities; Debt and Equity Finance; Investment Partnerships; Public Offerings; Emerging Growth Companies.
La Puma, Christopher P. ....'69 '96 C.813 A.B. L.276 J.D. [Ⓐ McKee N.]
*PRACTICE AREAS: Federal Taxation; Tax Controversies.
Larach, Richard L. .... '62 '89 C.674 A.B. L.309 J.D. [Ⓒ Sidley A.B.&W.]
Lardent, Esther F. '47 '72 C.103 A.B. L.145 J.D.
(adm. in IL; not adm. in DC) 3761 Benton St., N.W.
Larkin, Ann H. '73 '00 C.1349 B.A. L.945 J.D.
(adm. in VA; not adm. in DC) [Ⓐ Katten M.Z.]
*PRACTICE AREAS: Business Litigation; Litigation; Alternative Dispute Resolution; Real Estate Litigation.
Larkin, John J. .... '13 '52 C.93 A.B. L.537 LL.B. Hearing Comr., Supr. Ct.
Larkins, James M., III ....'69 '95 C.627 B.S.B.A. L.190 J.D. [Ⓐ Arent F.K.P.&K.]
*PRACTICE AREAS: Securities; Financial Institutions Law; Corporate Law.
Larkins, Richard G. ....'60 '90 C.911 B.A. L.597 J.D. 1775 Pennsylvania Ave.
Laro, Marlene Ellen .... '71 '98 C.276 B.S.F.S. L.569 J.D. [Ⓐ Ivins,P.&B.]
*PRACTICE AREAS: Federal Taxation; International Taxation.
LaRocca, Anthony J., (AV) .... '55 '84 C.477 A.B. L.309 J.D. [Steptoe&J.]
*PRACTICE AREAS: Antitrust Law; International Business Law; Economic Regulation.
La Rodriguez, Jamie .... '74 '99 C.1356 B.A. L.575 J.D. 1424 16th St., N.W.

LaRoe, Winn, Moerman & Donovan, (AV) BR
3900 Highwood Court, N.W., 20007
Telephone: 202-298-8100 Telecopier: 202-298-8200
Email: p.m.donovan@worldnet.att.net
Members of Firm: Wilbur LaRoe, Jr. (1921-1957); Arthur L. Winn, Jr. (1928-1995); Paul M. Donovan. Of Counsel: Samuel H. Moerman.
Legislative Practice. Civil, Administrative and Appellate Litigation. Antitrust, Transportation, Environment, Occupational Safety and Health Law.
See Professional Biographies, WASHINGTON, DISTRICT OF COLUMBIA

Larosiliere, Jean D. ....'63 '89 C.1030 B.A. L.862 J.D. Georgetown Univ.
Laroski, Joseph A., Jr .... '71 '98 C.276 B.S.F.S. L.262 J.D. [Ⓐ Skadden,A.S.M.&F.]
Larrabee, Sylvia V. .... '59 '85 C.220 B.A. L.861 J.D. Asst. Corp. Coun.
Larroca, Jeffrey W. ....'64 '94 C.1369 B.A. L.128 J.D. [Ⓐ Ballard S.A.&I.]
*PRACTICE AREAS: Banks and Banking; Commercial Law; Insurance Defense; Labor and Employment Litigation; Age Discrimination in Employment.
Larroca, Raymond G., (AV) ....'30 '57 C&L.276 B.S.S., J.D. [Baker B.]
Larsen, Bruce Morse .... '66 '93 C.506 B.S. L.585 J.D. 1301 K Street
Larsen, Joan L. ....'68 '93 C.351 B.A. L.597 J.D. 1722 Eye St., N.W.
Larsen, Karen L. ....'48 '74 C.788 B.A. L.273 J.D. U.S. Dept. of Agri.
Larsen, Kari S. '73 '99 C.1349 B.A. L.30 J.D.
(adm. in NY; not adm. in DC) [Ⓐ McDermott,W.&E.]
Larsen, Kerry Elizabeth ....'73 '98 C.502 B.S.B.A. L.228 J.D. [Ⓐ Fulbright&J.]
*PRACTICE AREAS: Litigation.
Larsen, Paul J. '71 '97 C.309 B.A. L.880 J.D.
(adm. in GA; not adm. in DC) [Ⓐ Buchanan I.]
*PRACTICE AREAS: Food, Drug and Cosmetic Law; Sweepstakes.
Larsen, Xanthe M. ....'— '98 C&L.878 B.A., J.D. [Ⓐ Akin,G.S.H.&F.]
*PRACTICE AREAS: Corporate Law; Securities; Project Finance; Infrastructure Development.
Larson, Keith D. ....'71 '96 C.390 A.B. L.823 J.D. [Ⓐ Hogan&H.]
*PRACTICE AREAS: Project Finance; Eurobonds.
Larson, Kristin ....'58 '01 C.1051 B.A. L.273 J.D. [Ⓐ Skadden,A.S.M.&F.]
Larson, Paul Alan '71 '00 C.101 B.S. L.273 J.D.
(adm. in VA; not adm. in DC) [Ⓐ Finnegan,H.F.G.&D.]
*PRACTICE AREAS: Mechanical Patents; Medical Patents; Patent Prosecution.
Larson, Philip C., (AV) ....'46 '71 C.350 B.S. L.228 J.D. [Hogan&H.]
*PRACTICE AREAS: Antitrust and Trade Regulation; Business Torts; Litigation; Advertising and Marketing.
Larson, Raphael J.A. '72 '99 C.1056 B.S. L.276 J.D.
(adm. in MD; not adm. in DC) [Ⓐ Patton B.]
Larson, Ronald D. .... '35 '62 C.388 B.A. L.597 J.D. [Ⓒ Trainum,S.&D.]
*PRACTICE AREAS: Estate Planning; Probate.
Larson-Jackson, P.C., Law Firm of, (BV) .... 1500 K Street, N.W., Suite 900
Larson-Jackson, Steve, (BV) .....'56 '87 C.259 B.S. L.1162 J.D. [Firm of Larson-Jackson]

Larson & Taylor, PLC
(See Alexandria, Virginia)

Larue, Homer C. .... '48 '75 C.679 B.A. L.188 J.D. 2900 Van Ness St., N.W.
Lasa, Monroig & Veve .... 2121 K Street, N.W., Suite 800
Lasater, Nancy E., The Law Office of, (AV) '56 '79
C.112 B.A. L.1068 J.D. 700 Thirteenth Street, N.W. Suite 950
Lashway, David .... '71 '97 C.216 B.A. L.1194 J.D. [Ⓐ Shaw P.]
*PRACTICE AREAS: Food and Drug; Trade; Environmental.
Laskas, Karl M. '70 '99 C.665 B.a. L.893 J.D.
(adm. in OH; not adm. in DC) [Ⓐ Thompson H.]
*PRACTICE AREAS: Intellectual Property; Government Affairs; Regulations.
Lasker, Eric G. .... '65 '90 C.659 B.A. L.976 J.D. [Spriggs&H.]
*PRACTICE AREAS: Products Liability; Toxic Torts; Litigation; Drug and Medical Device Defense; Insurance Coverage.
Laskin, Sheldon H. '51 '76 C.705 A.B. L.1292 J.D.
(adm. in NJ; not adm. in DC) Multistate Tax Comm.
Lasky, Robert T. ....'42 '67 C.264 B.A. L.659 LL.B. [Ⓒ Cadwalader,W.&T.]
*PRACTICE AREAS: Securitization; Structured Finance; Mortgage Securitization; Mortgage Backed Securities.
Lasoff, Laurence J., (AV) ....'50 '82 C.178 B.A. L.273 J.D. [Collier S.S.]
*PRACTICE AREAS: International Trade; Customs Law.
Lassen, Wendy A. '68 '93 C.477 A.B. L.64 J.D.
(adm. in MD; not adm. in DC) Lexis-Nexis
Lassman, Malcolm, (P.C.), (AV) ....'38 '63 C&L.902 B.A., LL.B. [Akin,G.S.H.&F.]
*PRACTICE AREAS: General Law.
Lassman, Prescott M. .... '63 '91 C.976 B.A. L.893 J.D. [Kleinfeld,K.&B.]
*PRACTICE AREAS: Food, Drug and Cosmetic Law; Food and Drug Regulation; Drug and Medical Device Regulation; Advertising Law; Federal Civil Litigation.
Lassow, Dina R. ....'47 '73 C.681 B.A. L.976 J.D. Suite 770, 1275 K Street, N.W.
Last, David A. '73 '00 C.1036 B.A. L.276 J.D.
(adm. in MD; not adm. in DC) [Ⓐ Sutherland A.&B.]
*PRACTICE AREAS: Litigation.
Lastelic, Stephen M. ....'74 '00 C.575 B.A. L.945 J.D. [Ⓐ Long A.&N.]
*PRACTICE AREAS: Litigation.

Laster, John L., (AV) '50 '79 C.604 A.B. L.128 J.D.
1776 Massachusetts Avenue, N.W., Suite 300, 20036 ⊙
Telephone: 202-530-0850
Email: TrustToLast@prodigy.com
Trusts, Estates, Estate Planning and Elder Law.
Bethesda, Maryland Office: Telephone: 301-656-0744.
Falls Church, Virginia Office: 103 Rowell Court, Telephone: 703-538-3600. Fax: 703-538-3601.
See Professional Biographies, WASHINGTON, DISTRICT OF COLUMBIA

Lastowka, James A. . . . . '51 '76 C.823 B.A. L.276 J.D. [McDermott,W.&E.]
Latek, Kevin P. . . . . '70 '96 C.276 B.S.B.A. L.893 J.D. [Ⓐ Dow,L.&A.]
Latham, Patricia Horan, (Mrs.), (AV) . . . . . .'41 '67 C.821 B.A. L.145 J.D. [Latham&L.]
*PRACTICE AREAS: Alternative Dispute Resolution; Corporate Law; Disabilities; Employment Law.
Latham, Peter S., (AV) . . . .'40 '66 C.821 B.A. L.659 LL.B. [Latham&L.]
*PRACTICE AREAS: Government Contracts Law; Disabilities; Employment Law.
Latham, Weldon H., (AV) . . . . '47 '72 C.329 B.A. L.276 J.D. [Holland&K.]
*PRACTICE AREAS: Corporate Diversity Counseling; Government Contracts; Corporate; Government Relations; Corporate Law.

Latham & Latham, (AV)
1155 Fifteenth Street, N.W., Suite 1004, 20005
Mailing Address: P.O. Box 40157, Washington, District of Columbia 20016
Telephone: 202-223-5097 Fax: 202-223-5096
Email: plath3@his.com
Members of Firm: Peter S. Latham; Patricia Horan Latham (Mrs.).
ADR, Employment Law, Corporate and Government Contracts.

Latham & Watkins, (AV)
555 11th Street, N.W., Suite 1000, 20004-1304 ⊙
Telephone: 202-637-2200 Telecopier: 202-637-2201
URL: http://www.lw.com
Partners: Nicholas W. Allard; Jennifer C. Archie; Teresa D. Baer; James H. Barker, III; James R. Barrett; Eric L. Bernthal (Resident); Richard P. Bress; Karen Brinkmann; Richard A. Conn, Jr.; Gary M. Epstein; Roger S. Goldman; McGee Grigsby; Julia A. Hatcher; Carolyne R. Hathaway; David J. Hayes; David R. Hazelton; John J. Huber; Paul J. Hunt; John P. Janka; Everett C. Johnson, Jr. (Resident); William C. Kelly, Jr.; Stuart S. Kurlander; Daniel T. Lennon; Curtis P. Lu; Maureen E. Mahoney; Mark E. Newell; William Patrick O'Neill; Thomas L. Patten; William K. Rawson; James F. Ritter; James F. Rogers; John L. Sachs; Kenneth A. Schuhmacher; David L. Schwartz; Edward J. Shapiro; DeMaurice F. Smith; Eric A. Stern; Joseph D. Sullivan; Robert M. Sussman; Kenneth W. Weinstein; W. Harrison Wellford; Beth A. Wilkinson; E. Marcellus Williamson; Peter L. Winik; Leonard A. Zax. Of Counsel: Bruce Babbitt (Not admitted in DC); David A. Barrett; Edward Correia; David M. Leive; Esther R. Scherb; Erin M. Sweeney. Special Legal Consultant: Bettina Veronica Freire (Not admitted in DC). Associates: Joel B. Ard; Wendy Atrokhov; Seung W. Baik; Dori K. Bailey; Vicky L. Beasley; David A. Becker; Jacob D. Bernstein; David I. Brown; Ana María Cabassa (Not admitted in DC); Richard R. Cameron; George D. Cannon, Jr.; William S. Carnell; Ramona R. Carroll (Not admitted in DC); Sue J. Choi; Ann Claassen; Barton B. Clark; Cheryl Miller Coe; Marcelo N. Corpuz, III; David S. Dantzic; Nestor M. Davidson (Not admitted in DC); Kevin H. Douglas; Alexandra Felder Dufresne (Not admitted in DC); Bart S. Epstein; Adam S. Fels; Jill France; W. Andrew H. Gantt, III; Allen M. Gardner; Michael J. Gergen; Nicholas B. Gertler; Barbara M. Gibian; Brian L. Glassberg; Michael Joseph Golden; Todd S. Gordon; Jennifer L. Gowetski; Timothy W. Gregg; Raymond B. Grochowski; James R. Hanna; Claudia Hinsch (Not admitted in DC); Julie K. Hoffman; John G. Holland; Claire Holloway; Andrew D. Irwin; Benoit N. Jacqmotte; Jared W. Johnson; Nandan M. Joshi; Morenike S. Kassim; Thomas J. Kim; Mark Klaassen; Trena Lee Klohe; Arthur S. Landerholm; Matthew R. Lewis; Stephanie Szu-Ping Lim; Jeremy B. Lustman; Julia MacLaren; Chittaranjan Mallik; Geoffrey A. Manne (Not admitted in DC); John R. Manthei; Jeffrey A. Marks; Erica McFarquhar; Heather M. McPhee (Not admitted in DC); David M. McPherson; Elliott Milhollin; Andrew D. Morton; Ashlie Muss Hegerle; Laura H. Neuwirth; Claudia M. O'Brien; Lynley A. Ogilvie; Amy J. Oliver; Elizabeth R. Park; Jennifer O. Patel; C. Thomas Powell; Jamal Qaimmaqami; Abid Riaz Qureshi; Justin R. Rhoades; Kathryn H. Ruemmler; Tonya Rutherford (Not admitted in DC); Scott E. Schang; Janice M. Schneider (Not admitted in DC); Steven H. Schulman; Patrick H. Shannon; Joseph A. Simei; Andrew R. Stewart; Olivier P. Strauch (Not admitted in DC); Cassandra Sturkie; Amy Lynn Sypula; H. Barton Thomas; Joel H. Trotter; Matthew R. VanderGoot; Jennifer Van Driesen; Rachel Ward; John W. Westmoreland; Liane N. Wilson; Joel D. Wright (Not admitted in DC); Eric J. Wycoff.
Communications, Corporate, Energy, Environmental, Health Care, Government Contracts, Government Relations, Litigation, Products Liability, Project Finance, Real Estate, Securities, Taxation, White Collar Crime.
Chicago, Illinois; Costa Mesa, California; Frankfurt/Main, Germany Office- Latham & Watkins Schön Nolte; Hamburg, Germany Office- Latham & Watkins Schön Nolte; Hong Kong, China; London, England; Los Angeles, California; Menlo Park, California; Moscow, Russia; Newark, New Jersey; Newton, Massachusetts; New York, N.Y.; Paris, France; Reston, Virginia; San Diego, California; San Francisco, California; Singapore; Tokyo, Japan.
See Professional Biographies, WASHINGTON, DISTRICT OF COLUMBIA

Lathrop, Alexander J. . . . .'68 '99 C.112 B.A. L.893 J.D. [Ⓐ Swidler B.S.F.]
*PRACTICE AREAS: Litigation.

Lathrop & Gage PLLC, (AV)
Suite 800, 1200 G Street, N.W., 20005 ⊙
Telephone: 202-434-8984 Facsimile: 202-434-8992
URL: http://www.lathropgage.com
—Paul Kalchbrenner (Not admitted in DC).
General and Administrative Practice and Litigation before all Courts and Agencies. Government Contracts, International Trade and Investment Law, Environmental and Energy Law.
Kansas City, Missouri Office: Lathrop & Gage LC, 2345 Grand Boulevard, Suite 2800. Telephone: 816-292-2000. Facsimile: 816-292-2001.
Overland Park, Kansas Office: 10851 Mastin Boulevard, Building 82, Suite 1000. Telephone: 913-451-5100. Facsimile: 913-451-0875.
St. Louis, Missouri Office: Lathrop & Gage, 1010 Market Street, Suite 1300. Telephone: 314-613-2500. Facsimile: 314-613-2550.
Jefferson City, Missouri Office: Lathrop & Gage LC, 326 East Capitol. Telephone: 573-893-4336. Facsimile: 573-893-5398.
Boulder, Colorado Office: 4845 Pearl East Circle, Suite 302, 80301. Telephone: 303-449-5800. Facsimile: 303-443-6998.
Springfield, Missouri Office: 1845 S. National, P.O. Box 4288. Telephone: 417-886-2000. Facsimile: 417-886-9126.
See Professional Biographies, WASHINGTON, DISTRICT OF COLUMBIA

Latimer, Aimee D. '71 '96 C.597 B.S. L.424 J.D.
(adm. in IL; not adm. in DC) [Ⓐ Clifford C.R.&W.]
*PRACTICE AREAS: Commercial Litigation; Litigation.
Latimer, Hugh, (AV) . . . . '33 '58 C&L.309 A.B., J.D. [Wiley R.&F.]
*PRACTICE AREAS: Advertising; Internet; Electronic Commerce; Intellectual Property.
Latimer, Katharine R. . . . . '61 '86 C.143 B.A. L.276 J.D. [Spriggs&H.]
*PRACTICE AREAS: Products Liability; Toxic Torts; Litigation; Drug and Medical Device Defense; Civil Appeals.
Latimer, L. Patrice . . . . . .'53 '80 C.612 B.S. L.623 J.D. Atty., Washington Gas Light Co.
Latker, Norman J. . . . . . . '31 '56 C&L.339 B.S.C.E., J.D. [Ⓐ Browdy&N.] (See Pat. Sect.)
*PRACTICE AREAS: Intellectual Property Law; Mechanical; Electro-Mechanical; Chemistry Law; Government Patent Policy.
Latsey, Christine J. . . . .'— '78 C.860 B.S. L.276 J.D. [I.J.Fredman]
Lattal, Laura A. '74 '01 C.473 B.A. L.188 J.D.
(adm. in NY; not adm. in DC) [Ⓐ Sonnenschein N.&R.]
*PRACTICE AREAS: Litigation.
Lattimore, Rachel G. . . . .'67 '94 C.575 B.A. L.228 J.D. [Ⓐ Arent F.K.P.&K.]
*PRACTICE AREAS: Biotechnology; Environmental Law.
Latto, Lawrence J., (AV) . . . . '20 '48 C.563 B.S. L.178 LL.B. [Ⓒ Shea&G.]
*PRACTICE AREAS: Securities Law; Professional Responsibility.
Lau, Karen . . . .'— '94 C.999 L.273 J.D. 2101 L St., N.W.
Lau, Karen Y. '73 '99 C.896 B.A. L.893 J.D.
(adm. in NC; not adm. in DC) [Ⓐ Shearman&S.]
*PRACTICE AREAS: Tax.
Lau, Michael N. . . . . . . '65 '93 C.801 B.S.E.E. L.352 J.D. 1101 14th Street, NW, Suite 504
Laubenstein, Kathleen M. . . . .'70 '97 C.66 B.A. L.831 J.D. [Ⓐ Jones,D.R.&P.]
Lauber, Albert G., Jr., (AV) . . . . '50 '77 C&L.976 B.A., J.D. [Caplin&D.]
Lauderdale, Melissa L. . . . . '69 '96 C&L.846 B.A., J.D. [Ⓐ Brunenkant&H.]
*PRACTICE AREAS: Energy Law; Utility Law.
Lauerman, Colleen M. . . . .'68 '97 C&L.276 B.S., J.D. [Ⓐ Sidley A.B.&W.]
Lauerman, Thomas C. . . . . '— '75 C.976 B.A. L.893 J.D. [Foley&L.]
*PRACTICE AREAS: Securities Law; Corporate Law.
Laufman, Mark S., (BV) . . . .'54 '81 C.846 B.A. L.273 J.D. [Vinson&E.]
*PRACTICE AREAS: Energy; Project Finance and Development; Mergers, Acquisitions and Divestitures; Outsourcing; Computer Services.
Laughlin, Felix B., (AV) . . . . '42 '67 C&L.838 B.S., LL.B. [Dewey B.]
*PRACTICE AREAS: Corporate Tax.
Laughlin, Gregory H., (AV) '42 '67 C.839 B.A. L.846 LL.B.
(adm. in TX; not adm. in DC) [Ⓒ Patton B.]
Laurenza, Paul M. . . . .'48 '74 C.550 B.S. L.910 J.D. [Oppenheimer W.&D.]
*PRACTICE AREAS: Litigation.
Lauroesch, Janice Mulligan '60 '86 C.732 B.A. L.597 J.D.
National Railroad Passenger Corp. (AMTRAK)
Laursen, Francesca D. . . . .'66 '01 C.454 B.A. L.30 J.D. [Ⓐ Clifford C.R.&W.]
*PRACTICE AREAS: Project Finance; Corporate Finance; '40 Act Investment Compliance; Family Law.
Lautrup, Greer O. . . . . '63 '96 C.871 B.A. L.893 J.D. [Ⓐ Sidley A.B.&W.]
Lavallee, Fernand A. . . . .'63 '89 C.276 A.B. L.945 J.D. [Venable,A.B.H.&C.]
*PRACTICE AREAS: Government Contracts, International Commercial Transactions.
Lavallée, Peter J. '66 '94 C.178 B.A. L.861 J.D.
(adm. in NH; not adm. in DC) Comm. Dir.
Lavalleye, Marie A. . . . . '62 '90 C.188 B.A. L.94 J.D. [Ⓐ Covington&B.]
*PRACTICE AREAS: Intellectual Property; Trademarks; Unfair Competition; Copyrights.
Lavan, David J. '62 '97 C.893 B.A. L.61 J.D.
(adm. in NY; not adm. in DC) [Ⓐ Fleischman&W.]
Lavanga, Michael K. . . . .'69 '00 C.128 B.A. L.446 J.D. [Ⓐ Brickfield B.R.&S.]
*PRACTICE AREAS: Energy.
Lavelle, Joseph P., (AV) '57 '82
C.1028 B.S. L.665 J.D. [Howrey S.A.&W.] (See Pat. Sect.)
*PRACTICE AREAS: Intellectual Property; Antitrust; Complex Litigation.
Lavenue, Lionel M. . . . . '66 '92 C.880 B.A. L.904 J.D. [Ⓐ Finnegan,H.F.G.&D.]
*PRACTICE AREAS: Software Protection; Intellectual Property Litigation; Intellectual Property Portfolio Management; Computer and Software Patents; Patent Litigation.
Lavenue, Teresa A. '66 '98 C.880 B.S. L.910 J.D.
(adm. in CA; not adm. in DC; See Pat. Sect.) [Ⓐ Kenyon&K.]
*PRACTICE AREAS: Intellectual Property.
Lavergne, Edwin N., (AV) . . . . '54 '80 C.354 B.S. L.276 J.D. [Shook,H.&B.]
*PRACTICE AREAS: Advertising and Marketing; Telecommunications; Business Law.
Lavine, Henry W., (AV) . . . . '36 '61 C&L.659 B.A., J.D. [Squire,S.&D.]
*PRACTICE AREAS: Corporate; Securities; Finance.
Lavine, Irvin A., (AV) . . . '25 '50 C.128 B.A. L.273 J.D. [Nath&Assoc.] (See Pat. Sect.)‡
Law, David Bradford . . . .'50 '78 C.309 A.B. L.904 J.D. [Sherman,M.C.&A.]
*PRACTICE AREAS: Real Property; Corporate Law.
Law, Glenn . . . . '— '92 C.188 B.S.E.E. L.273 J.D. [Foley&L.] (See Pat. Sect.)
*PRACTICE AREAS: Patent Law and Litigation; Intellectual Property.
Lawch, Richard S. '53 '79 C&L.659 B.A., J.D.
(adm. in NY; not adm. in DC) V.P., Multifamily Capital Mkts., Fed. Natl. Mtge. Assn.
Lawhead, Alan . . . .'63 '93 C.800 B.A. L.276 J.D. Coun., NASD Regul., Inc.
Lawhorn, Charles A. '57 '86 C.1109 B.A. L.426 J.D.
(adm. in CA; not adm. in DC)
Sr. V.P., Legal Dir., Anti-Piracy, Recording Industry Assoc. of America, Inc.
Lawler, Gregory E. . . . .'47 '73 C.976 B.A. L.659 J.D. 1909 K St., N.W.
Lawler, Thomas M., Jr. '49 '73
C.754 B.S. L.128 J.D. Assoc. Gen. Coun., Deloitte & Touche LLP
Lawler, William E., III, (AV) . . . .'60 '85 C.602 B.A. L.276 J.D. [Vinson&E.]
*PRACTICE AREAS: Litigation.
Lawless, Bonnie J., (AV) . . . .'47 '76 L.273 J.D. [G.W.Vesper]
Lawless, Megan A. '71 '96 C.524 B.A. L.1017 J.D.
(adm. in PA; not adm. in DC) MCI WorldCom
Lawrence, Andrew M. '74 '99 C.896 B.A. L.884 J.D.
(adm. in NJ; not adm. in DC) Staff Atty., U.S. Sec. & Exch. Comm.
Lawrence, George H. '25 '57 C.612 B.S. L.796 J.D.
(adm. in TX; not adm. in DC) 1333 New Hampshire Ave., N.W.
Lawrence, Gregory K., (BV) . . . .'66 '91 C.855 B.A. L.1202 J.D. [McDermott,W.&E.]
Lawrence, J. Stephen, Jr., (AV) . . . . '49 '78 C.228 A.B. L.145 J.D. [Arnold&P.]
*PRACTICE AREAS: Government Contracts; Construction Contracts; Commercial Contracts.
Lawrence, Jeffrey F., (AV) . . . . '52 '77 C.659 B.A. L.705 J.D. [Sher&B.]
*PRACTICE AREAS: Transportation; Maritime Law; International Law; Corporate Law; Commercial Law.
Lawrence, John W. . . . .'61 '93 C.679 B.S. L.128 J.D. [Ⓒ LeBoeuf,L.G.&M.]
*PRACTICE AREAS: Nuclear Law; Energy Law; Litigation.
Lawrence, Mary Patricia '75 '00 C&L.16 B.S., J.D.
(adm. in AL; not adm. in DC) Legis. Coun.
Lawrence, Robert F. . . . .'55 '83 C.197 A.B. L.276 J.D. [Milbank,T.H.&M.]
Lawrence, Stanton T., III, (AV) '45 '73 C.172 B.S.Chem. L.273 J.D.
[Pennie&E.] (See Pat. Sect.) (⊙New York, NY)
*PRACTICE AREAS: Intellectual Property Litigation.
Lawrence, Thomas, III '51 '87 C.1044 B.A. L.1209 J.D.
(adm. in VA; not adm. in DC) [Oppenheimer W.&D.]
*PRACTICE AREAS: Transportation Law.
Laws, Tracey W. . . . .'64 '90 C.945 B.A. L.893 J.D. [Chadbourne&P.]
Lawson, A. E. . . . .'29 '58 C.665 A.B. L.309 LL.B. Intl. Brotherhood of Teamsters
Lawson, David L., (BV) . . . . '61 '91 C.623 B.S. L.145 J.D. [Sidley A.B.&W.]
Lawson, Dennis J. . . . .'66 '95 C.367 B.A. L.446 J.D. [Ⓐ Dechert]
*PRACTICE AREAS: Complex Litigation; Litigation; Complex Commercial Litigation.
Lawson, Eugene M., Jr. . . . .'47 '95 C.30 B.G.S. L.904 J.D. [Fletcher,H.&H.] ⊙
*PRACTICE AREAS: Business Law; Bankruptcy; Estate Planning; Civil Litigation.
Lawson, Grace W. . . . . '67 '91 C.846 B.B.A. L.145 J.D. [Lipstein,J.&L.]
*PRACTICE AREAS: Antitrust; Copyright & Trademark; Consumer Protection; International Trade; Corporate.
Lawson, Keith D. . . . . '57 '82 C.928 B.A. L.273 J.D. Sr. Coun., Investment Co. Inst.
*RESPONSIBILITIES: Tax.
Lawson, Kurt L.P., (BV) . . . .'58 '85 C.976 B.A. L.893 J.D. [Shaw P.]
Lawson, Lynn Michelle . . . . '63 '00 NASD Regulation, Inc.
Lawson, Marjorie M., (AV) . . . . '12 '39 C.477 A.B. L.178 J.D. 1850 M St., N.W.
Lawson, Thomas B. '56 '83
C.867 B.A. L.1019 J.D. Nat. Assn. of Escs. Dealers Regul. Inc.
Lawson, Warner, Jr. '40 '71 C&L.329 B.A., J.D.
(adm. in NY; not adm. in DC) Assoc. Dean, Howard Univ. Sch. of Law
Lawton, Bettina M., (AV) . . . .'54 '80 C.1021 B.B.A. L.276 J.D. [Dechert]
*PRACTICE AREAS: Securities Litigation; Financial Services Law; Investment Management; SEC Enforcement.

Lawton, Julie D. . . . . '— '97 C.257 B.S. L.329 J.D. [🄰 Morrison&F.]
*PRACTICE AREAS: Financial Services.

Lax, Gary A. . . . . '61 '86 C.205 B.A. L.1338 J.D. [Jenkens&G.]
*PRACTICE AREAS: Financial Institutions; Securities; Corporate Law.

Laxa, Rowena E. . . . . '59 '98 C.477 B.A. L.1209 J.D. [🄰 Cohen M.]
*PRACTICE AREAS: Employment Law; Commercial Litigation; Government Contracts.

Lay, Elizabeth A. '71 '98 C.691 B.A. L.208 J.D.
(adm. in TX; not adm. in DC) 1455 Pennsylvania Ave., N.W.‡

Lay, Tillman L., (AV) . . . . '55 '81 C.838 B.S. L.477 J.D. [🄲 Miller,C.P.&S.]
*PRACTICE AREAS: Communications Law; Appellate Practice; Antitrust Law.

Layman, William K. '60 '87 C.951 B.A. L.276 J.D. The Field School

Layne, Robert Jeffrey . . . . '68 '94 C.840 B.B.A. L.228 J.D. [🄰 Fulbright&J.]
*PRACTICE AREAS: Health Care Law; Litigation.

Layton, Duane W. . . . . '— '82 C.911 B.A. L.61 J.D. [King&S.]
*PRACTICE AREAS: Litigation; Trade.

Layton, Elisabeth . . . . '68 '98 C&L.976 B.A., J.D. [🄰 O'Melveny&M.]

Layton, Robert, (AV) '31 '56 C.477 B.A. L.976 LL.B.
(adm. in NY; not adm. in DC) [🄲 Inman D.] (⊙New York, NY)
*PRACTICE AREAS: International and Domestic Litigation; International Arbitration.

Layton, William R. . . . . '69 '98 C.612 B.A. L.273 J.D. [🄰 Wilkinson B.K.]
*PRACTICE AREAS: Telecommunications Law.

Lazarus, Arthur, Jr. (P.C.), (AV) '26 '51
C.178 B.A. L.976 LL.B. [🄲 Sonosky,C.S.E.&P.]

Lazarus, Kenneth A., (AV) . . . . '42 '67 C.201 B.A. L.602 J.D. [Lazarus&Assoc.]

Lazarus, Maggi A. . . . . '67 '93 C.893 B.A. L.861 J.D. [🄰 J.T.O'Rourke]
*PRACTICE AREAS: Legislative.

Lazarus, Mitchell, (AV) . . . . '42 '84 C.453 Ph.D. L.276 J.D. [🄲 Fletcher,H.&H.] ⊙
*PRACTICE AREAS: Communication; Communications Common Carrier; Telecommunications; High Technology; Telephone, Paging, and Cellular.

Lazarus, Richard B. . . .'— '74 C.679 B.S.M.E. L.128 J.D. [🄲 Barnes&T.] (See Pat. Sect.)
*PRACTICE AREAS: Patent Prosecution; Patents; Copyrights; Trademarks.

Lazarus, Simon, III, (AV) . . . . '41 '68 C.309 B.A. L.976 LL.B. [Powell,G.F.&M.]
*PRACTICE AREAS: Legislation; Electronic Commerce; Telecommunications; Antitrust.

Lazarus & Associates, (AV)
1850 M Street, Suite 400, 20036
Telephone: 202-457-0380 fax: 202-452-1822
Email: LazarusLaw@aol.com
Kenneth A. Lazarus.
Litigation in all courts. Legislation and Regulation. Business Counseling.
See Professional Biographies, WASHINGTON, DISTRICT OF COLUMBIA

Lazerwitz, Michael R. . . . . '58 '85 C.674 A.B. L.145 J.D. [Cleary,G.S.&H.]

Laznovsky, Frank T. . . . . '47 '76 C.415 B.A. L.365 J.D. [🄲 Franch,J.B.&S.] ⊙

Lazo, Theodore R. . . . . '67 '95 C.478 B.A. L.128 J.D. 450 Fifth St., N.W.

Lazris, Mitchell J. . . . . '66 '92 C.674 A.B. L.309 J.D. [Hogan&H.]
*PRACTICE AREAS: Litigation; Health Law.

Lazrus, Jay N. '57 '81 C&L.446 B.A., J.D.
(adm. in MD; not adm. in DC) [Myers L.T.]
*PRACTICE AREAS: Communications and Media; Business Law; Litigation.

Leader, Allison B. . . . . '68 '98 C.367 B.A. L.273 J.D. Associated Press, Attorney

Leader, Martin R., (AV) . . . . '40 '67 C.860 A.B. L.880 J.D. [Shaw P.]
*PRACTICE AREAS: Communications.

Leahey, Thomas M. . . . . '— '76 C.103 A.B. L.976 J.D. [Kirkpatrick&L.]
*PRACTICE AREAS: Financial Institutions Law; Investment Management; Corporate Law; Securities Regulation.

Leahy, David M. . . . . '58 '85 C.178 A.B. L.309 J.D. [Sullivan&W.]
*PRACTICE AREAS: Investment Company Law; Investment Adviser Law; Securities Law.

Leahy, Jeannie '59 '84 C.103 B.A. L.966 J.D.
(adm. in WI; not adm. in DC) [🄲 Ivins,P.&B.]
*PRACTICE AREAS: Pension and Profit Sharing Plans; Employee Benefits.

Leahy, Joseph K. . . . . '72 '98 C.821 B.A. L.569 J.D. [🄰 Kellogg,H.H.T.&E.]
*PRACTICE AREAS: Litigation.

Leahy, Michael H., (AV) . . . . '45 '70 C.976 B.A. L.228 J.D. [Arent F.K.P.&K.]
*PRACTICE AREAS: Real Estate.

Leahy, Susan . . . . '64 '98 C.712 B.B.A. L.128 J.D. [🄲 Powell,G.F.&M.]
*PRACTICE AREAS: Charitable Giving; Tax Exempt Organizations; Private Foundations; Public Charities.

Leaman, J. Welby . . . . '70 '00 C.1053 B.S. L.976 J.D. [🄰 Wilmer,C.&P.]

Leape, James P. . . . . '55 '80 C&L.309 A.B., J.D. Sr. V.P., World Wildlife Fund

Lear, Allen L. . . . . '43 '75 C.797 B.A. L.273 J.D. 3733 N. Hampton St. NW

Lear, Richard E., (AV) . . . . '58 '83 C.550 B.A. L.902 J.D. [Holland&K.]
*PRACTICE AREAS: Bankruptcy; Litigation; Workouts; Creditor Rights; Commercial Law.

Learn, Mark D. . . . . '60 '98 C.446 B.S. L.831 J.D. [🄰 Hogan&H.]

Learned, Kevin R. . . . . '73 '99 C.273 B.A. L.145 J.D. [🄰 Shaw P.]
*PRACTICE AREAS: Corporate; Securities.

Leary, David W. . . . . '70 '00 C.893 B.A. L.276 J.D. [🄰 Arnold&P.]
*PRACTICE AREAS: Intellectual Property; Technology Law.

Leary, Denise B. '48 '74 C.94 A.B. L.228 J.D.
(adm. in NC; not adm. in DC) Dep. Gen. Coun., National Public Radio, Inc.

Leary, Douglas J. . . . . '63 '91 C.165 B.A. L.94 J.D. [🄲 Sutherland A.&B.]
*PRACTICE AREAS: Corporate Governance; Mergers and Acquisitions; Securities Offerings.

Leary, John . . . . '49 '87 C.728 B.A. L.128 J.D. [O'Donoghue&O.]

Leason, Chris S. . . . . '63 '94 C.645 B.S. L.273 J.D. [McKenna&C.]
*PRACTICE AREAS: Environmental Law; Transportation Law; Occupational Safety and Health Law; Administrative Law.

Leavens, Amy Susan . . . . '72 '98 C.276 B.A. L.990 J.D. [🄰 Piper M.R.&W.]
*PRACTICE AREAS: Corporate and Securities Law; Venture Capital.

Leavitt, Dana Elizabeth . . . . '61 '97 445 12th St.

LeBeau, F. William . . . . '70 '95 C.893 B.S. L.309 J.D. [🄰 Hogan&H.]
*PRACTICE AREAS: FCC Licensing; FCC Regulation; Mass Media Law; Broadcast Applications; Broadcast Licensing.

LeBeau, Josephine Aiello . . . . '— '95 C.861 B.A. L.309 J.D. [🄰 Miller&C.]
*PRACTICE AREAS: Export Regulation; Import and Export Law; Foreign Trade Sanctions; International Trade; International Law.

LeBlanc, Robert E., (AV) . . . . '— '51 C.861 B.S. L.276 J.D. 600 13th St., N.W. (Pat.)

LeBlanc, Tni M. . . . . '73 '00 C.999 B.A. L.276 J.D. [🄰 Jones,D.R.&P.]

Lebo, Diane '60 '86 C&L.347 B.A., J.D.
(adm. in MD; not adm. in DC) Lead Elec. Prod. Editor, The Bureau of Natl. Affs., Inc.

LeBoeuf, Lamb, Greene & MacRae, L.L.P., (AV)
A Limited Liability Partnership including Professional Corporations
Formerly LeBoeuf, Lamb, Leiby & MacRae
1875 Connecticut Avenue, N.W., 20009 ⊙
Telephone: 202-986-8000 Facsimile: 202-986-8102 Telex: 440274
URL: http://www.llgm.com
Partners: George R. Abramowitz; Lawrence G. Acker; Dennis L. Allen; Cynthia T. Andreason; Douglas N. Beck; Samuel Behrends, IV; Michael A. Bell; D. Randall Benn; Douglas G. Bonner; David A. Colson; Elias G. Farrah; A. Everette James; Cecelia Kempler; L. Charles Landgraf; Mary A. Lopatto; Michael F. McBride; Bruce W. Neely; Brian D. O'Neill; David R. Poe; M. Kristan Rizzolo; Davis R. Robinson; Elizabeth Barry Sandza; Melvin S. Schwechter; LaJuana S. Wilcher. Of Counsel: Thomas F. Brosnan; Frank Cummings (P.C.); James P. Fama; Charles W. Havens III (P.C.); Carl D. Hobelman (P.C.); John W. Lawrence; Martin G. Malsch; Arnold W. Reitze, Jr. Counsel: Mary A. Murphy; Susan E. Seabrook; Robert W. Woody.

(This Listing Continued)

LeBoeuf, Lamb, Greene & MacRae, L.L.P. (Continued)

General Practice including Administrative, Antitrust, Copyrights, Corporate, EMF Litigation, Energy, Environmental, ERISA, Government Relations, Insurance, International Trade & Customs, Labor, Legislative, Litigation, Maritime, Municipal Bonds, Oil & Gas, Patents, Public Utilities, Reinsurance, Securities, Taxation, Telecommunications, Trademarks, Transportation, Venture Capital.
Eastern United States:
New York, N.Y. Office: 125 West 55th Street. Telephone: 212-424-8000. Facsimile: 212-424-8500. Telex: 423416 or 1561363.
Albany, New York Office: One Commerce Plaza, 99 Washington Avenue, Suite 2020. Telephone: 518-626-9000. Facsimile: 518-626-9010.
Boston, Massachusetts Office: 260 Franklin Street. Telephone: 617-439-9500. Facsimile: 617-439-0341; 439-0342.
Harrisburg, Pennsylvania Office: 200 North Third Street, Suite 300, P.O. Box 12105. Telephone: 717-232-8199. Facsimile: 717-232-8720.
Hartford, Connecticut Office: Goodwin Square, 225 Asylum Street, 13th Floor. Telephone: 860-293-3500. Facsimile: 860-293-3555.
Newark, New Jersey Office: The Legal Center, One Riverfront Plaza. Telephone: 973-643-8000. Facsimile: 973-643-6111.
Pittsburgh, Pennsylvania Office: One Gateway Center, Fort Duquesne Boulevard, Suite 1600. Telephone: 412-594-2300. Facsimile: 412-594-5237.
Western United States:
Denver, Colorado Office: 633 17th Street, Suite 2000. Telephone: 303-291-2600. Facsimile: 303-297-0422.
Los Angeles, California Office: 725 South Figueroa Street, Suite 3100. Telephone: 213-955-7300. Facsimile: 213-955-7399. Telex: 678982.
Salt Lake City, Utah Office: 1000 Kearns Building, 136 South Main Street. Telephone: 801-320-6700. Facsimile: 801-359-8256.
San Francisco, California Office: One Embarcadero Center, Suite 400. Telephone: 415-951-1100. Facsimile: 415-951-1180; 951-1181. Telex: 470167.
Southern United States:
Houston, Texas Office: 1000 Louisiana Avenue. Telephone: 713-287-2000. Facsimile: 713-287-2100.
Jacksonville, Florida Office: 50 North Laura Street, Suite 2800. Telephone: 904-354-8000. Facsimile: 904-353-1673.
European Offices:
Brussels, Belgium Office: Kunstlaan/Avenue des Arts, 19H, B-1000 Brussels, Belgium. Telephone: 011-32-2-227-0900. Facsimile: 011-32-2-227-0909.
London, England Office: LeBoeuf, Lamb, Greene & MacRae (A London Based Multinational Partnership); One Minster Court, Mincing Lane, 6th Floor, London EC3R 7AA England. Telephone: 011-44-20-7-459-5000. Facsimile: 011-44-20-7-459-5099.
Moscow, Russian Federation Office: Nikitsky Pereulok, 5 (formerly Ulitsa Belinskogo) 103473 Moscow, Russian Federation. Telephone: 011-7-095-737-5000. Facsimile: 011-7-095-737-5050.
Paris, France Office: 30, rue du Faubourg Saint-Honoré 75008 Paris, France. Telephone: 011-33-1-53-93-77-00. Facsimile: 011-33-1-42-56-08-06.
Asian Offices:
Almaty, Kazakhstan Office: Prospect Seyfullin, 531, 5th Floor, 480083, Almaty, Republic of Kazakhstan. Telephone: 011-7-3272-50-7575. Facsimile: 011-7-3272-50-7576.
Bishkek, Kyrgyz Office: Ulitsa Panfilova, 205 Bishkek, Kyrgyz Republic. Telephone: 011-996-3312-22-2994. Facsimile: 011-996-3312-66-2233.
Tashkent, Uzbekistan Office: Ulitsa Turab Tula, 1 700003 Tashkent Republic of Uzbekistan. Telephone: 011-7-3712-40-6050. Facsimile: 011-7-3712-40-6052.
African Office:
Johannesburg, South Africa Office: 11 Alice Lane, 2nd Floor, West Wing, Standard Bank Building, Sandton 2196 Johannesburg, South Africa. Telephone: 27-011-784-0233. Fax: 27-011-784-2855.
See Professional Biographies, WASHINGTON, DISTRICT OF COLUMBIA

Lebow, Edward M., (AV) . . . . '48 '74 C&L.309 B.A., J.D. [Miller T.W.&L.]
*PRACTICE AREAS: International Trade and Customs; Administrative Law; Commercial Law.

Lebowitz, Brian E., (AV) . . . . '50 '81 C.31 B.A. L.813 J.D. [🄲 Alston&B.]
*PRACTICE AREAS: Federal Income Tax; International Income Taxation; International Tax Controversies; Tax Planning; Tax Valuation.

Lechner, Ira M., (AV) . . . . '34 '58 C.682 B.A. L.976 LL.B. [🄲 Katz&R.]

Lechner, Stanley F. . . . . '49 '83 C.645 B.S. L.276 J.D. [Morgan,L.&B.]

Lechtman, Arthur Thomas . . . . '69 '95 C.112 B.A. L.990 J.D. [🄰 Wilkinson B.K.]

Lechtman, Vladimir . . . . '55 '87 L.846 J.D. [Akin,G.S.H.&F.]
*PRACTICE AREAS: Corporate Law.

Leckar, Stephen C. . . . . '48 '74 C.1059 B.S. L.228 J.D. [Butera&A.]
*PRACTICE AREAS: Federal Civil Litigation; Federal Criminal Law.

LeCraw, Linda L. . . . . '71 '97 C&L.309 A.B., J.D. [🄰 Ropes&G.]
*PRACTICE AREAS: Corporate Transactional; Biotechnology Transactional.

Ledbetter, James E. '50 '77 C&L.260 B.S., J.D.
(adm. in GA; not adm. in DC; See Pat. Sect.) [Stevens,D.M.&M.]
*PRACTICE AREAS: Patent Law; Electrical Patents; Mechanical Patents; Trademarks; Copyrights.

Leddy, Mark, (AV) . . . . '47 '71 C&L.93 B.A., J.D. [Cleary,G.S.&H.]

Ledecky, David '61 '87 C.309 B.A. L.976 J.D.
Exec. V.P. & Chf. Admin. Offr., Consolidation Capital Corp.

Leder, Paul A. . . . . '57 '81 C&L.477 B.A., J.D. [🄲 Richards S.K.&O.] ⊙

Lederer, Brian J. H., (AV) . . . . '44 '73 C.309 B.A. L.911 J.D. 3003 Van Ness St., N.W.

Lederer, Gerard L. '58 '83 C.311 B.A. L.831 J.D.
(adm. in PA; not adm. in DC) [🄲 Miller&V.]
*PRACTICE AREAS: Telecommunications Law; Private Property; Contracts/Licensing; Advocacy.

Lederman, Gordon . . . . '71 '98 C&L.309 A.B., J.D. [🄰 Arnold&P.]
*PRACTICE AREAS: Public Policy; Legislative Practice; International; Litigation; Government Contracts.

Ledig, Robert H. . . . . '58 '83 C.1044 B.A. L.273 J.D. [Fried,F.H.S.&J.]

Ledner, Sherri L., (AV) . . . . '64 '89 C.446 B.A. L.276 J.D. [🄲 Weiner B.S.K.]
*PRACTICE AREAS: Mortgage Banking Law; Consumer Finance; Regulatory Compliance.

Ledoux, Amy E. . . . . '70 '97 C.910 A.B. L.276 J.D. [🄰 Levine S.&K.]

Ledoux, Conrad C. . . . . '64 '89 C.1029 B.S. L.1040 J.D. [🄰 Spriggs&H.]
*PRACTICE AREAS: Litigation; Government Contracts; Construction Law; Insurance Coverage.

Lee, Adams C. . . . . '67 '94 C.309 A.B. L.569 J.D. [🄰 White&C.]

Lee, Andrew B. . . . . '64 '90 C.529 B.A. L.128 J.D. Ernst & Young

Lee, Anne H. . . . . '72 '00 C.477 B.A. L.659 J.D. [🄰 Gibson,D.&C.]

Lee, Carol F., (AV) . . . . '55 '82 C&L.976 B.A., J.D. V.P. & Gen. Coun., Intl. Fin. Corp.

Lee, Carolyn S. . . . . '74 '00 C.1375 B.A. L.273 J.D. [🄰 Dechert]
*PRACTICE AREAS: Financial Services Law; Investment Management.

Lee, Cary L. '71 '96 C&L.500 B.A., J.D.
(adm. in MS; not adm. in DC) Dir. of Placement, Co-Counsel

Lee, Daniel . . . . '— '99 C.1494 B.A. L.273 J.D. [🄰 Brobeck,P.&H.]
*PRACTICE AREAS: Venture Capital; Public Offerings; Emerging Growth Companies.

Lee, David B., (AV) . . . . '49 '76 C.878 B.A. L.101 J.D. [Lee&S.]
*PRACTICE AREAS: Federal Legislative Practice; Administrative Law.

Lee, David Chan . . . . '72 '99 C.575 B.A. L.245 J.D. [🄰 Pennie&E.]
*PRACTICE AREAS: Intellectual Property.

Lee, David P. '39 '65 C.602 A.B. L.276 LL.B.
Gen. Coun., National Railway Labor Conference

Lee, David S. '— '92 C.823 B.S.E.E. L.128 J.D.
(adm. in MD; not adm. in DC; See Pat. Sect.) [🄰 Banner&W.]
*PRACTICE AREAS: Intellectual Property.

Lee, Debra L., (AV) '54 '81 C.103 B.A. L.309 J.D.
Pres. & C.O.O., Black Entertainment Television, Inc.
*RESPONSIBILITIES: Communications Law; Corporate Law.

Lee, Eileen C. . . . . '72 '97 C.1375 B.A. L.904 J.D. [🄰 Holland&K.]
*PRACTICE AREAS: Commercial Real Estate.

Lee, Elizabeth C. ....'59 '85 C.604 B.A. L.276 J.D. [Womble C.S.&R.]
*PRACTICE AREAS: Business Formation and Planning; Commercial and Real Estate Transactions; Contracts; Corporate and Real Estate Finance.
Lee, F. Gordon .... '53 '78 C.835 B.S. L.273 J.D. [O'Connor&H.]
Lee, Grace M. '67 '99 C.893 B.A. L.1209 J.D.
(adm. in VA; not adm. in DC) [[A] Dillingham&M.]
*PRACTICE AREAS: Intellectual Property; Internet Law; E-Commerce; Corporate Law; Labor and Employment.
Lee, Gregory .... '48 '75 C.597 B.A. L.910 J.D. Federal Publications, Inc.
Lee, Harry, (BV) ....'60 '86 C.277 B.S. L.128 J.D. [Steptoe&J.]
*PRACTICE AREAS: Insurance Coverage; Complex Litigation; Professional Malpractice Law; Insurance Agents Errors and Omissions.
Lee, James F., Jr., (AV) ....'50 '75 C&L.823 B.A., J.D. [Lee&M.]
*PRACTICE AREAS: Business Transactions; Construction; Architects and Engineers; Commercial Litigation.
Lee, Jeanny K. ....'70 '98 C.309 B.A. L.276 J.D. [[A] Venable,A.B.H.&C.]
*PRACTICE AREAS: Corporate; Business Transactions.
Lee, Jennifer M. .... '70 '96 C.174 B.S. L.823 J.D. [[A] Morgan,L.&B.] (Pat.)
Lee, John Y. .... '28 '62 C&L.976 B.A., J.D. [[C] Gainer&R.]
Lee, Judith A. ....'62 '87 C.518 B.A. L.945 J.D. [Gibson,D.&C.]
*PRACTICE AREAS: Customs Law; International Trade Law; Export Controls; Foreign Corrupt Practices Act; Economic Sanctions and Embargoes.
Lee, Julia ....'66 '92 C.910 B.A. L.273 J.D. [[A] Clifford C.R.&W.]
*PRACTICE AREAS: Securities; Mergers and Acquisitions; Corporate Finance.
Lee, Kenneth G. ....'49 '76 C.878 B.A. L.273 J.D. [[C] Stites&H.]
Lee, Kenneth James '56 '96 C.570 B.S.C.E. L.273 J.D.
(adm. in VA; not adm. in DC) [[A] Dombroff&G.]
Lee, Lansing B., III, (AV) ....'48 '74 C.575 B.A. L.245 J.D. [[C] Patton B.]
Lee, Marie Kalamaras '73 '00 C.94 B.A. L.30 J.D.
(adm. in MD; not adm. in DC) [[A] Sutherland A.&B.]
*PRACTICE AREAS: Taxation; Employee Benefits.
Lee, Marietta S. ....'69 '95 C.276 B.A. L.128 J.D. Court TV
Lee, Matthew William '70 '96 C.890 B.A. L.1009 J.D.
[[A] Eccleston&W.] (⊙Fairfax, VA)
Lee, Michael A. ....'42 '80 C.112 B.A. L.1066 J.D. [[C] Arnold&P.]
*PRACTICE AREAS: Tax; Real Estate; Non-Profit Organizations.
Lee, Michael Quentin '62 '93
C.893 B.S.E.E. L.276 J.D. [Sterne,K.G.&F.] (See Pat. Sect.)
*PRACTICE AREAS: Intellectual Property Law.
Lee, Michael Shumway ....'71 '98 C&L.101 B.S., J.D. 1722 Eye St., N.W.
Lee, Mitchell D. ....'— '97 C&L.188 B.A., J.D. [[A] Brobeck,P.&H.]
*PRACTICE AREAS: Corporate and Securities; Venture Capital; Mergers and Acquisitions.
Lee, Nancy C. '50 '77 C.914 B.A. L.245 J.D.
Sr. V.P. & Assoc. Gen. Coun., Lab. & Emp., Marriott Intl., Inc.
Lee, Nathan Shawn '73 '98 C.112 B.A. L.966 J.D.
(adm. in WI; not adm. in DC) [[A] Bennett,T.&C.]
*PRACTICE AREAS: Food and Drug Regulation; Health Law; Medical Technology.
Lee, Patrick W., (AV) ....'37 '62 C.755 B.A. L.276 J.D. [Crowell&M.]
*PRACTICE AREAS: Litigation; Products Liability Law.
Lee, Peter M. ....'71 '98 C.165 B.A. L.228 J.D. [[A] Wilmer,C.&P.]
Lee, R. Stephen ....'55 '80 C.575 B.A. L.1048 J.D. 200 Constitution Ave., NW
Lee, Ronald D. ....'59 '86 C.674 A.B. L.976 J.D. [Arnold&P.]
*PRACTICE AREAS: Telecommunications Law; Intellectual Property; Technology Law; Privacy Law; National Security Law and Policy.
Lee, Susan C. '54 '82 C.446 B.A. L.767 J.D.
[[C] Gebhardt&Assoc.] (⊙Silver Spring, MD)
*PRACTICE AREAS: Intellectual Property; Administrative Law.
Lee, Susan G. ....'59 '88 C.893 B.A. L.178 J.D. [Arnold&P.]
*PRACTICE AREAS: Derivatives; Litigation; International Law; International Litigation; Arbitration.
Lee, Tashir J. ....'71 '97 C.188 B.S. L.659 J.D. [[A] Piper M.R.&W.]
*PRACTICE AREAS: Communications.
Lee, Tony S. ....'68 '94 C.446 B.S.E.E. L.30 J.D. [[A] Swidler B.S.F.]
*PRACTICE AREAS: Communications Law.
Lee, Yong '70 '98 C.976 B.A. L.477 J.D.
(adm. in IL; not adm. in DC) [[A] Cameron&H.]
*PRACTICE AREAS: Business Transactions; Litigation; International Trade.
Lee, Yoon-Young ....'63 '88 C.367 B.A. L.309 J.D. [Wilmer,C.&P.]
*PRACTICE AREAS: Securities; SEC Enforcement.
Lee, Yvonne O. ....'63 '89 C.329 B.A. L.276 J.D. Asst. Dist. Atty.

Lee & McShane, PC, (AV)
1211 Connecticut Avenue N.W., Suite 425, 20036
Telephone: 202-530-8100 Fax: 202-530-0402 URL: http://www.leemcshane.com
Email: jrb@lee-mcshane.com URL: http://www.lawyers.com/leeandmcshanelaw
James F. Lee, Jr.; Terrence M. McShane;—Laurence C. Fauth; Brandon M. Gladstone; Karen O. Sheehan; Eugene W. Policastri; Arthur T. K. Norris.
Architecture Law, Engineering Law, Corporate Law.
See Professional Biographies, WASHINGTON, DISTRICT OF COLUMBIA

Lee & Smith, P.C., (AV)
1101 30th Street N.W., Suite 200, 20007
Telephone: 202-293-4584 Fax: 202-293-4588
Email: davidlee@leesmithpc.com URL: http://www.lawyers.com/federalregulatorylaw
David B. Lee; C. William Smith. Of Counsel: Glendon E. Johnson, Jr.
Federal Administrative Law, Federal Regulatory Law, Legislative Lobbying, Defense Contracts, Foreign Military Sales, Army Export Controls and Regulations, High Technology Transfer, Government Affairs, Government Relations, Export Compliance, Public Land Law, Defense Department Trade Controls, Technical Assistance Agreements.
See Professional Biographies, WASHINGTON, DISTRICT OF COLUMBIA

Leeds, Henry W., (AV) ....'31 '56 C.659 B.S. L.477 J.D. [[C] Drinker B.&R.]
*PRACTICE AREAS: Trademark Law; Copyright Law.
Leeds, Sanford '64 '89 C.16 B.S. L.893 J.D.
(adm. in TX; not adm. in DC) Nat. Assoc. of Secs. Dealers Regul. Inc.
Leeper, Charles S., (AV) ....'51 '76 C.105 B.S.B.A. L.665 J.D. [Spriggs&H.]
*PRACTICE AREAS: White Collar Crime; Litigation.
Lees, Frederick J. '30 '62 C.893 B.A. L.30 J.D.
Prof., George Washington Univ. Law Sch.
Lefever, D. Michael ....'53 '79 C.216 B.A. L.94 J.D. [Covington&B.]
Leff, Elizabeth A. .....'57 '87 C.454 B.S. L.813 J.D. [Rothwell,F.E.&M.] (See Pat. Sect.)
*PRACTICE AREAS: Intellectual Property; Litigation.
Leff, Peter J. ....'71 '96 C.910 B.A. L.477 J.D. [[A] O'Donnell,S.&A.]
Leffel, Michael ....'67 '98 C.182 B.A. L.477 J.D. [[A] Wilmer,C.&P.]
Lefkowitz, Alan '70 '00 C.309 A.B. L.145 J.D.
(adm. in CA; not adm. in DC) [[A] O'Melveny&M.]
Lefkowitz, Melvin E. ....'— '73 C.446 B.A. L.273 J.D. [[C] Hogan&H.]
*PRACTICE AREAS: Tax; Business; Finance.
Lefkowitz, Michael L. ....'69 '94 C.529 B.A. L.64 J.D. [[A] Holland&K.]
*PRACTICE AREAS: Commercial Real Estate (100%).
Lefkowitz, Neil ....'53 '80 C.604 B.A. L.575 J.D. [Dickstein S.M.&O.]
*PRACTICE AREAS: Emerging Company Law; Corporate Transactions; Corporate Finance.
Lefkowitz, Paul S., (AV) '49 '74
C&L.930 B.A., J.D. [Climaco,L.P.W.&G.] (⊙Cleve., OH)
Lefkowitz, Todd ....'66 '92 C.31 B.A. L.880 J.D. Policy Dept., America Online, Inc.
Lefort, Brian D. ...'67 '98 C.454 B.S.M.E. L.818 J.D. [[A] Jones,D.R.&P.] (See Pat. Sect.)
Leftwich, J. Daniel ....'53 '89 C&L.846 B.J., J.D. [Berry&L.]
Leftwich, Norma B. ....'48 '92 C.665 B.A. L.276 J.D. Gen. Coun., Howard Univ.

Leftwich & Douglas, P.L.L.C., (AV)
Suite 600, 1401 New York Avenue, N.W., 20005
Telephone: 202-434-9100 Facsimile: 202-783-3420
URL: http://www.lawyers.com/leftwich&douglaslaw
Frederick A. Douglas; Nicholas S. Penn; Natalie O. Ludaway;—Curtis A. Boykin; Thomas D. Bridenbaugh; Charniele Herring (Not admitted in DC); Nicole C. Mason; Nat N. Polito; Malaika T. Smith; Rebecca Lynn Taylor. Of Counsel: Leonard A. Sacks.
General Practice, Commercial Litigation, Telecommunications, Government Contracts, Energy, Construction, Real Estate, Estate Planning, Divorce, Employment Law.
See Professional Biographies, WASHINGTON, DISTRICT OF COLUMBIA

Legg, JoEllen Lotvedt ....'61 '98 C.908 B.A. L.128 J.D. [[A] Fried,F.H.S.&J.]
*PRACTICE AREAS: Corporate Law; Securities.
Legg, Randy G. ....'65 '98 C.446 B.A. L.128 J.D. [[A] Dechert]
*PRACTICE AREAS: Financial Services Law; Investment Management.
Leggett, Isiah ....'— '74 C.803 B.A. L.329 J.D. 2900 Van Ness St., N.W.
Leggette, L. Poe ....'53 '78 C.860 B.A. L.893 J.D. [Fulbright&J.]
*PRACTICE AREAS: Oil and Gas Law; Litigation; Administrative Law; Public Land Law.
Legro, Stanley W., (AV) ....'— '67 C.871 B.S. L.309 J.D. [[C] Verner,L.B.M.&H.]
*PRACTICE AREAS: Environmental Law.
Lehman, Amy Elizabeth '73 '00 C.668 B.A. L.477 J.D.
(adm. in CA; not adm. in DC) [[A] Swidler B.S.F.]
*PRACTICE AREAS: Corporate Law.
Lehman, Christine E. '70 '94
C.821 B.S. L.569 J.D. [[A] Finnegan,H.F.G.&D.] (See Pat. Sect.)
*PRACTICE AREAS: Patent Litigation; Intellectual Property Litigation.
Lehman, Kenneth R. ....'59 '87 C.831 B.B.A. L.1067 J.D. [Luse L.G.P.&S.]
*PRACTICE AREAS: Securities; Corporate.
Lehmann, Richard Paul ....'66 '99 C.107 B.S. L.904 J.D. 4201 Massachusetts Ave., N.W.
Lehner, George A., (AV) ....'48 '77 C.918 B.A. L.477 J.D. [Pepper H.]
*PRACTICE AREAS: Litigation; International Dispute Resolution.
Lehner, Jonathan '70 '96 C.705 B.A. L.1292 J.D.
(adm. in MD; not adm. in DC) Walter Reed Army Med. Ctr.★
Lehner, Mary N. ....'73 '98 C.945 B.A. L.145 J.D. [[A] Vinson&E.]
*PRACTICE AREAS: Litigation.
Lehnigk, George F., (AV) ...'63 '91 C.228 B.S. L.273 J.D. [Sughrue M.] (See Pat. Sect.)
*PRACTICE AREAS: Intellectual Property Law.
Lehr, Dennis J., (AV) ....'32 '59 C.569 B.A. L.976 LL.B. [[C] Hogan&H.]
*PRACTICE AREAS: Financial Law; Banking Law; Bank Securities; Administrative Agency Practice.
Lehrenbaum, Warren U. ....'63 '89 C.1349 B.A. L.273 J.D. [Shaw P.]
Lehrfeld, William J., (AV) ....'36 '66 C.401 B.S. L.128 J.D. [[C] Powell,G.F.&M.]
*PRACTICE AREAS: Charitable Giving; Private Foundations; Public Charities; Tax Exempt Organizations Litigation.
Lehrhoff, Michael B. ....'53 '92 C.918 B.A. L.276 J.D. [[A] Epstein B.&G.]
*PRACTICE AREAS: Labor and Employment Law.
Lehrman, Margie A.S. ......'59 '87 C.449 B.A. L.61 J.D. Sr. Dir., Assn. of Trial Lawyers
Lehtman, Jeffrey A. ....'75 '00 C.880 B.A. L.477 J.D. [[A] Wilmer,C.&P.]
Lehtonen, Todd A. '64 '93 C.446 B.S. L.273 J.D.
Associate Counsel, ChamberBiz, L.L.C.
Leib, David A. ....'— '97 C.473 B.A. L.446 J.D. [[A] Manatt,P.&P.]
Leibenluft, Robert F., (AV) ....'52 '80 C.976 B.A. L.1066 J.D. [Hogan&H.]
*PRACTICE AREAS: Antitrust; Health Law.
Leibig, Michael T. ....'45 '71 C.276 B.A. L.893 J.D. [Zwerdling,P.L.K.T.&D.]
Leibman, Sara F., (AV) ....'56 '87 C.293 B.A. L.276 J.D. [Mintz,L.C.F.G.&P.]
*PRACTICE AREAS: Communications; Wireless Communications.
Leibner, Robert F., (AV) ....'53 '79 C&L.273 J.D. [Leibner&P.]
*PRACTICE AREAS: Real Estate Law; Commercial Litigation.

Leibner & Potkin, P.C., (AV)
4725 Wisconsin Avenue, N.W. Suite 250, 20016
Telephone: 202-244-0600 Fax: 202-244-8930
Email: potkin@bellatlantic.net URL: http://www.lawyers.com/leibner&potkin
Robert F. Leibner; Lane H. Potkin;—John E. Arness, II.
Real Estate Law, Residential Development, Settlements, Mortgage Leasing, Landlord and Tenant Law, Leasing, General Civil Practice, Commercial Litigation, Commercial Transactions, Business Law, Corporate Law, Small Business, Estate Planning and Trust Administration, Probate, Tax Law.
See Professional Biographies, WASHINGTON, DISTRICT OF COLUMBIA

Leibold, Arthur W., Jr., (AV) ....'31 '57 C.311 A.B. L.659 LL.B. [[C] Dechert]
*PRACTICE AREAS: Banking Law; Savings and Loan Institutions Law.
Leibold, Peter M. '63 '89 C.311 B.A. L.976 J.D.
Gen. Coun., Catholic Health Association of the U.S.
Leibow, Lisa L. ....'66 '91 C.273 B.A. L.818 J.D. [[A] Kurtis&Assoc.]
*PRACTICE AREAS: Telecommunications Law; Federal Regulatory Law.
Leibowitz, Katherine R. .....'67 '94 C.674 A.B. L.659 J.D. [[A] Hogan&H.] (⊙Phila., PA)
*PRACTICE AREAS: Intellectual Property Licensing; Internet Law; Computer and Software Law; Privacy Law; Technology Law.
Leibowitz, Lewis E., (AV) ....'47 '75 C&L.446 B.A., J.D. [Hogan&H.]
*PRACTICE AREAS: International Trade Law; Antidumping; Countervailing Duties; Safeguards; Customs Law.
Leibsohn, Seth '68 '98 C.1168 B.A. L.588 J.D.
(adm. in MA; not adm. in DC) Jewish Policy Ctr.
Leiby, Lana L. ....'73 '98 C.418 B.S. L.861 J.D. [[A] Collier S.S.]
Leichman, Sherry L., (BV) ....'54 '85 C.94 B.S. L.1162 J.D. [[A] Lewis]
*PRACTICE AREAS: Family Law.
Leidl, Richard J. ....'51 '77 C.93 B.A. L.893 J.D. [Thelen R.&P.]
*PRACTICE AREAS: Government Affairs.
Leifer, David M. '63 '88 C.276 J.D. L.990 J.D.
(adm. in CA; not adm. in DC) 1001 Pennsylvania Avenue, N.W.
Leifer, Elihu I., (AV) ....'40 '65 C.674 A.B. L.309 LL.B. [Sherman,D.C.L.&Y.]
*PRACTICE AREAS: Labor and Employment Law; Union Labor Law.
Leifer, Jacqueline C., (AV) ....'52 '77 C&L.188 B.A., J.D. [Feldesman,T.L.F.&B.]
*PRACTICE AREAS: Health Care; Corporate Litigation.
Leifer, Steven L. ....'52 '77 C.1036 A.B. L.188 J.D. [Baker B.]
Leigh, Monroe, (AV) ....'19 '47 C.301 B.A. L.893 LL.B. [Steptoe&J.]
*PRACTICE AREAS: International Law; International Trade; Administrative Law; Arbitration.
Leigh, Rebecca Kapell ....'51 '81 C.66 B.A. L.893 J.D. Mayfair Properties, Ltd.
Leighton, Adam R. ....'71 '98 C.861 B.A. L.851 J.D. [[A] Cohen&C.]
*PRACTICE AREAS: Medical Malpractice; Personal Injury.
Leighton, Richard J., (AV) ....'39 '71 C.645 B.A. L.30 J.D. [Keller&H.]
*PRACTICE AREAS: Commercial Litigation; Food, Drug, Cosmetic and Device Litigation; Trade Regulation; Labeling and Advertising; Intellectual Property.
Leiman, Joe '60 '88 C.1222 B.B.A. L.276 J.D.
(adm. in FL; not adm. in DC) 1775 Pennsylvania Ave., N.W.
Leimkuhler, Mark J. ....'60 '86 C.893 B.A. L.659 J.D. [Baach R.&L.P.]
*PRACTICE AREAS: Civil Litigation; Commercial Litigation; Insurance Coverage; Reinsurance Coverage.
Leiter, Jeffrey L. ....'53 '81 C.273 B.A. L.128 J.D. [Collier S.S.]
*PRACTICE AREAS: Energy; Petroleum Marketing; Environmental Law.

Leitz, J. Christophe ... '71 '00 C.112 B.A. L.94 J.D. [A Dechert]
*PRACTICE AREAS: Financial Services Law; Investment Management; Securities Regulation.
Leive, David M. ... '— '61 C.178 A.B. L.309 LL.B. [C Latham&W.]
Leland, Thomas D. ... '69 '98 C.174 B.A. L.1356 J.D. [A Holland&K.]
*PRACTICE AREAS: Civil Litigation; Commercial Litigation; International Litigation; Aviation.
Lemanski, Susan M. '67 '97 C.971 B.S. L.734 J.D.
(adm. in MA; not adm. in DC) 330 Independence Ave. S.W.
LeMaster, Roger Joe ... '— '70 C.383 M.A. L.472 J.D. Exec Dir, Tax Council, The
Lemble, Lisa Mae '65 '99 C.1434 B.A. L.851 J.D.
(adm. in MI; not adm. in DC) Riggs Nat'l Bank
Lemert, James E. ... '35 '61 C.679 B.S.E.E. L.273 J.D. 5524 Broad Branch Rd., N.W.
Lemke, Thomas P. ... '54 '79 C.1044 B.A. L.904 J.D. [Morgan,L.&B.]
Lemle, J. Stuart, (AV) ... '48 '74 C.188 A.B. L.309 J.D. [Land&L.]
Lemon, Chrys D., (BV) ... '57 '91 C.1070 B.S. L.612 J.D. [McIntyre]
*PRACTICE AREAS: Insurance Regulation; Corporate Organization; Environmental Regulation; Banking Law.
Lemov, Michael R., (AV) ... '35 '60 C.165 B.A. L.309 LL.B. [Winston&S.]
*PRACTICE AREAS: Product Safety; Product Recall; Warranty Law; Advertising and Marketing; Product Packaging and Labeling.
Lempert, Lawrence S. ... '50 '77 C&L.477 B.A., J.D. The Bureau of Natl. Affs., Inc.
Lempres, Michael T. ... '60 '85 C.197 A.B. L.1066 J.D. 1828 L. St., N.W.
Lenahan, John C., (AV) ... '41 '66 C.573 B.A. L.724 LL.B. [Crowell&M.]
*PRACTICE AREAS: Litigation; Intellectual Property; Employment Law; Aviation Law; Products Liability.
Lenett, Michael G. ... '62 '88 C.1036 B.A. L.276 J.D. [Cuneo]
*PRACTICE AREAS: Litigation; Torts; Consumer Law; Securities; Government Relations.
Lenhardt, Robin A. ... '67 '95 C.103 A.B. L.309 J.D. [A Wilmer,C.&P.]
Lenhart, Benedict M. ... '63 '90 C.477 B.A. L.309 J.D. [C Covington&B.]
Lenhart, J. Thomas, (P.C.), (AV) ... '46 '73 C&L.178 A.B., J.D. [Shaw P.]
*PRACTICE AREAS: Litigation; Corporate Investigations.
Lenihan, Mary Anne ... '65 '91 C.696 B.A. L.107 J.D. Federal Publications, Inc.
Lennie, Bradley T. ... '68 '95 C.966 B.A. L.30 J.D. [A Hunton&W.]
*PRACTICE AREAS: Litigation; Intellectual Property.
Lennon, Daniel T. ... '— '90 C.602 B.A. L.128 J.D. [Latham&W.]
Lennon, Duncan '21 '52 C.339 B.S. L.309 LL.B.
(adm. in IL; not adm. in DC) 888 Sixteenth St. N.W.
Lennon, Kathleen '73 '98 C.1349 B.A. L.1194 J.D.
(adm. in NY; not adm. in DC) [A Beveridge&D.]
*PRACTICE AREAS: Environmental Law; Environmental Litigation.
Lennon, Rose T. ... '52 '77 C&L.602 A.B., J.D. Atty., Washington Gas Light Co.
Lennon, Susan M. ... '63 '91 C.262 B.S. L.228 J.D. 2300 N St., N.W.
Lenser, Jeffrey M. ... '65 '91 C.945 B.A. L.846 J.D. [C Howrey S.A.&W.]
*PRACTICE AREAS: Insurance Coverage; Litigation.
Lent, Norman F. '31 '57 C.1019 B.A. L.188 LL.B.
(adm. in NY; not adm. in DC) 555 13th St., N.W.‡
Lent, Susan Heck ... '61 '86 C.1365 B.A. L.273 J.D. [C Akin,G.S.H.&F.]
*PRACTICE AREAS: Public Policy; Transportation; Infrastructure Development.
Lentchner, Cassandra F. '64 '89 C&L.705 B.A., J.D.
(adm. in NJ; not adm. in DC) [C Perkins C.]
*PRACTICE AREAS: White Collar Criminal; Political Law; Congressional Investigation; Securities.
Lentz, Sally A. ... '56 '81 C.604 B.A. L.446 J.D. The Oceanic Soc.
Lenzner, Terry F., (AV) ... '39 '66 C&L.309 B.A., LL.B. [T.F.Lenzner]
*PRACTICE AREAS: Trial Practice; Administrative; Mergers and Acquisitions; Due Diligence; Internet Investigations.

Lenzner, Terry F., P.C., (AV)
1015 Fifteenth Street, N.W., Suite 400, 20005
Telephone: 202-789-7620 Telecopier: 202-789-7740
Email: tlenzner@igint.com URL: http://www.lawyers.com/terryflenzner
Terry F. Lenzner. Of Counsel: Edward T. Ferguson, III (Not admitted in DC).
General Civil, Criminal, Administrative and Trial Practice.
See Professional Biographies, WASHINGTON, DISTRICT OF COLUMBIA

Leo, Evan T. ... '68 '94 C.112 B.A. L.273 J.D. [Kellogg,H.H.T.&E.]
*PRACTICE AREAS: Telecommunications.
Leo, Leonard A. ... '65 '90 C&L.188 A.B., J.D. Dir., The Federalist Soc.
Leon, Richard J., (AV) ... '49 '75 C.321 A.B. L.818 J.D. [Vorys,S.S.&P.]
*PRACTICE AREAS: White-Collar Criminal Defense; Congressional Investigations; Civil Trial Litigation; Environmental Litigation.
Leonard, Evita A. '63 '91 C.329 B.A. L.64 J.D.
(adm. in PA; not adm. in DC) Staff Atty., D.C. City Council
Leonard, Jane E. ... '40 '71 C.838 B.A. L.880 J.D. 4445 Lowell St., N.W.
Leonard, Jerris, (AV) ... '— '55 C&L.436 B.S.B.A., J.D. [Foley&L.]
*PRACTICE AREAS: Government Contract Law; Lobbying; State and Federal Legislative Practice; Financial Organization; Litigation.
Leonard, Patricia A. ... '62 '94 C.446 B.S. L.64 J.D. [A Arent F.K.P.&K.]
*PRACTICE AREAS: Corporate Transactions; Corporate Finance; Entertainment Transactions.
Leonard, Robert J. ... '46 '71 C.659 A.B. L.880 J.D. [Washington C.]
Leonard, Will E., (AV) ... '35 '58 C&L.861 B.A., LL.B. [Adduci,M.&S.]
*PRACTICE AREAS: International Trade; Customs Law; Government Relations.

Leonard Hurt Frost Lilly & Levin, A Professional Corporation, (AV)
1701 K Street, N.W., Suite 300, 20006-1522 ⊙
Telephone: 202-223-2500 Telecopy: 202-223-2501
Email: mfassler@leonardhurt.com URL: http://www.leonardhurt.com
Edmund B. Frost; Michael H. Levin. Of Counsel: Max A. Stolper; Pauline C. Shoback; Marsha R. Greenfield (Not admitted in DC).
General Civil Practice. Municipal Finance, Environmental Finance, Infrastructure Finance, Real Estate, General Litigation, Antitrust, Environmental Law, Bankruptcy, Creditor's Rights, Corporate, Banking, Securities, Government Contract, Legislative, Administrative, Agricultural, Business and Taxation. Alternative Dispute Resolution.
Dallas, Texas Office: 600 North Pearl, Suite 900. Telephone: 214-954-6300. Telecopy: 214-954-6386.
Austin, Texas Office: 816 Congress, Suite 1280. Telephone: 512-477-7161. Telecopy: 512-476-1676.
Houston, Texas Office: 4545 Bissonnet, Suite 131. Telephone: 713-666-6388. Telecopy: 713-666-6454.
See Professional Biographies, WASHINGTON, DISTRICT OF COLUMBIA

Leonard, Street and Deinard, Professional Association
600 Pennsylvania Avenue, N.W., Suite 900, South Building, 20004 ⊙
Telephone: 202-974-6100 Fax: 202-974-6101
Email: lsd1500@leonard.com URL: http://www.leonard.com
Steven A. Weiler; Robert Y. Hirasuna.
General Civil and Trial Practice, including Administrative Law, Advertising and Sales Promotion, Alternative Dispute Resolution, including Mediation, Antitrust, Architectural Law, Arts Law, Banking Law, Bankruptcy Litigation, Business Law, Business Succession Planning, Commercial Litigation, Communications Law, Computer Law, Condemnation and Valuation Litigation, Construction Law, Copyright and Trademark Law and Litigation, Corporations, Deceptive Trade Practices, Employment Law and Litigation, Employee Benefits, Entertainment Law, Environmental Law, Estate Planning, Family Law, Federal Indian Law, Financial Institutions Law, Financial Reorganization, Franchise Law, Governmental Relations, Health Care Law, Housing Development and Finance, Immigration Law, Income Tax Law, Insurance Disputes, Intellectual Property Law and Litigation, Labor Relations, Land Use, Internet Law, Licensing, Medical Malpractice, Mergers and Acquisitions, Multimedia Law, Online Law, Partnerships, Patent Litigation, Private and Emerging Business Law, Public Finance, Public Utility Law, Probate and Trust Administration, Product Distribution and Marketing, Products Liability and Tort Litigation, Professional Liability, Real Estate Development and Finance, Securities Law and Litigation, Shareholder Disputes, Taxable and Tax-exempt Securities, Trade Secret Law, Unfair Competition and White Collar Crime.

(This Listing Continued)

Leonard, Street and Deinard, Professional Association (Continued)
Representative Clients: Hubbard Broadcasting, Inc.; Midcontinent Media, Inc.
St. Paul, Minnesota Office: 380 St. Peter Street, Suite 500. Telephone: 651-222-7455. Fax: 651-222-7644.
Mankato, Minnesota Office: 121 East Walnut Street, P. O. Box 967. Telephone: 507-345-1179. Fax: 507-345-1182.
Washington D.C. Office: 601 Pennsylvania Avenue N.W., Suite 900, South Building.
See Professional Biographies, WASHINGTON, DISTRICT OF COLUMBIA

Leonardo, Christopher '71 '98 C.282 B.A. L.30 J.D.
(adm. in NY; not adm. in DC) [A Dickstein S.M.&O.]
*PRACTICE AREAS: Antitrust; Insurance.
Leonce, Jo An ... '69 '97 C.329 B.A. L.446 J.D. [A Arent F.K.P.&K.]
*PRACTICE AREAS: Health Care.
Leone, Frank, Jr. ... '60 '85 C&L.893 B.A., J.D. [Spriggs&H.]
*PRACTICE AREAS: Environmental Law; Litigation; Products Liability; Asbestos Defense.
Leong, Katherine K. '63 '00 C.999 B.A. L.446 J.D.
1100 Fifteenth Street, NW, Suite 700
Leotta, Michael J. ... '72 '97 C.446 B.A. L.309 J.D. [A Williams&C.]
*PRACTICE AREAS: Computer Law; Media and First Amendment; Litigation.
Lepon, Jeffrey M., (AV) ... '53 '78 C&L.309 A.B., J.D. [Lepon M.W.&H.]
Lepon McCarthy White & Holzworth, (AV) ... 1225 Nineteenth Street, N.W., Suite 600
Le Pore, John C. '64 '92 C.93 A.B. L.276 J.D.
(adm. in MD; not adm. in DC) 1333 New Hampshire Ave., N.W., Suite 400‡
Lepow, Leslie H., (AV) ... '49 '75 C.178 A.B. L.276 J.D. [Jenner&B.]
*PRACTICE AREAS: Government Contracts; Minority and Small Business Law; Government Investigations.
Lepre, Michael G., (AV) ... '63 '88 C.602 B.A. L.273 J.D. [C Shaw P.]
*PRACTICE AREAS: Energy Transactions; Energy; Public Utility Regulatory Law.

Lerch, Early & Brewer, Chartered, (AV)
1900 M Street, N.W., Suite 601, 20005 ⊙
Telephone: 202-293-5494
URL: http://www.lerchearly.com
Stanley J. Reed.
General Civil and Appellate Practice. Real Estate, Land Use, Historic Preservation and Development, Corporate and Tax, Estate Planning and Probate, Commercial, Banking, Hospital and Health Care, Domestic Relations, Community Associations, Employment and Labor Law, White Collar Criminal Defense and Criminal Trial Practice.
Bethesda, Maryland Office: 3 Bethesda Metro Center, Suite 460. Telephone: 301-986-1300. Telecopy: 301-986-0332.
Fairfax, Virginia Office: 9302 Lee Highway, Suite 1100. Telephone: 703-278-9020.
Frederick, Maryland Office: 228 West Patrick Street.
See Professional Biographies, WASHINGTON, DISTRICT OF COLUMBIA

Lerman, Steven Alman, (AV) ... '47 '72 C.659 B.S. L.273 J.D. [Leventhal,S.&L.]
*PRACTICE AREAS: Communications Law; Media Law.
Lerner, Arthur N., (AV) ... '51 '77 C.477 A.B. L.309 J.D. [Crowell&M.]
*PRACTICE AREAS: Antitrust Law; Health Care Law.
Lerner, Bruce R. ... '57 '84 C.1044 B.A. L.659 J.D. [Bredhoff&K.]
Lerner, Christopher ... '58 '85 C.012 B.A. L.273 J.D. Coun, The World Bk.
Lerner, Craig S. ... '— '95 C&L.309 A.B., J.D. 1500 K Street, N.W.
Lerner, Herbert J. ... '38 '64 C.705 B.S. L.276 J.D. Ernst & Young
Lerner, Maida Oringher ... '52 '77 C.1044 B.A. L.94 J.D. [C Hunton&W.]
*PRACTICE AREAS: Environmental.
Lerner, Matthew D. ... '60 '85 C.31 A.B. L.309 J.D. [Steptoe&J.]
*PRACTICE AREAS: Federal Tax Controversies; Tax Litigation; Criminal Taxation; Business Planning.
Lerner, Roger J., (AV) ... '54 '79 C.273 B.A. L.910 J.D. [C Kile G.L.&R.P.]
*PRACTICE AREAS: Finance; Banking; Litigation; Real Estate; Bankruptcy.
Lesch, Kenneth M. '70 '98 C.659 B.S.E.E. L.273 J.D.
(adm. in MA; not adm. in DC) [A Finnegan,H.F.G.&D.]
*PRACTICE AREAS: Electrical Patent Prosecution.
Lesch, Peter C. ... '48 '73 C.604 B.A. L.477 J.D. [Gallagher,B.&M.]
*PRACTICE AREAS: Electric Utility Regulation; Natural Gas Regulation; Independent Power; Hydroelectricity Licensing; Regulatory Agency Practice.
Lescht, Alan ... '62 '88 C.273 B.A. L.724 J.D. 1050 17th Street, N.W., Suite 220
Lese, Laurence S. ... '45 '70 C&L.188 B.A., J.D. [Duane,M.&H.]
*PRACTICE AREAS: Federal and State Securities; Mergers and Acquisitions; Corporate Law; Partnership Law.
LeSeur, John H. ... '52 '79 C.197 B.A. L.276 J.D. [Slover&L.]
Lesk, Jeffrey S., (AV) ... '54 '80 C.813 B.A. L.37 J.D. [Nixon P.]
*PRACTICE AREAS: Real Estate; Housing and Urban Development.
Leske, Brian J. ... '69 '95 C.197 B.A. L.276 J.D. [WorldCom]
Leskovsek, Andreas H. ... '65 '91 C.446 B.A. L.276 J.D. [Winston&S.]
*PRACTICE AREAS: Environmental Law.
Leskovsek, Natasha V. ... '67 '96 C.446 B.S.N. L.276 J.D. [A Heller E.W.&M.]
Lesmes, George Scott '67 '93
C.240 B.S. L.945 J.D. V.P. Dep. Gen. Coun., Fannie Mae Inc.
*RESPONSIBILITIES: Corporate; Securities.
Lesmes, Melissa Callahan ... '68 '93 C.228 A.B. L.945 J.D. [A Arent F.K.P.&K.]
*PRACTICE AREAS: Commercial Litigation; Products Liability; Insurance Coverage; Construction.
L'Esperance, John F. '68 '96 C.1330 B.S. L.1364 J.D.
(adm. in FL; not adm. in DC) [Baumann,D.&L.]
Lesse, Sylvia ... '54 '81 C.893 B.A. L.30 J.D. 2120 L St., N.W.
Lessenco, Gilbert B., (AV) ... '29 '53 C.367 B.S. L.309 LL.B. [C Thompson H.]
*PRACTICE AREAS: Consumer Product Safety Commission; Lobbying; Administration Law; Estate; Government Affairs.
Lesser, Jill A. '65 '90 C.477 B.A. L.94 J.D.
(adm. in MA; not adm. in DC) Policy Dept., America Online, Inc.
Lesser, Patricia R. ... '53 '80 C.055 L.273 J.D. [C Silverstein&M.]
*PRACTICE AREAS: International Taxation.
Lessy, Roy P., Jr., (AV) ... '44 '69 C.264 B.A. L.273 J.D. [Akin,G.S.H.&F.]
*PRACTICE AREAS: Energy; Antitrust and Trade Regulation.
Lester, Kathleen J. ... '71 '98 C.210 B.A. L.276 J.D. [A Patton B.]
Lester, Thomas Edwin ... '69 '97 2141 P Street, NW
Lestina, Matthew J. '63 '96 C.188 B.S.E.E. L.1044 J.D.
(adm. in NY; not adm. in DC; Pat.) 1522 K. St., NW, Ste. 300
Letcher, J. Clifford ... '15 '57 C.602 B.A. L.276 J.D. 1411 Montague St., N.W.
Letham, Glenn W., (AV) ... '46 '72 C.945 A.B. L.228 J.D. [Squire,S.&D.]
*PRACTICE AREAS: Energy Law; Federal Energy Regulatory Commission; Contracts; Utility Law; Antitrust.
Letson, Janet Marie "Jaye" ... '58 '89 C.112 A.B. L.976 J.D. 1722 I St., N.W.
Letteri, John C. ... '57 '87 C.882 B.A. L.128 J.D. [C Fulbright&J.]
*PRACTICE AREAS: Litigation.
Lettow, Carl F. ... '70 '95 C.945 B.A. L.896 J.D. [A Kelley D.&W.]
Lettow, Charles F., (AV) ... '41 '69 C.350 B.S.Ch.E. L.813 LL.B. [Cleary,G.S.&H.]
Lettow, Renee B. '68 '95 C.674 B.A. L.976 J.D.
Assoc. Prof. of Law, George Wash. Univ.
Letts, David S. ... '07 '41 C.641 B.A. L.273 LL.B. 4217 43rd St., N.W.‡
Letwin, Jeffrey W., (AV) ... '53 '80 C.665 B.A. L.904 J.D. [DKW] (⊙Pitts., PA)
Letzler, Kenneth A. ... '43 '68 C.178 A.B. L.309 LL.B. [Arnold&P.]
*PRACTICE AREAS: Antitrust; Litigation.
Leuba, Thomas R. ... '64 '90 C.174 B.A. L.273 J.D. [C Sullivan&C.]

Leuckel, Sarae T. ....'68 '93 C.446 B.A. L.1358 J.D. [Ⓐ Greenstein D.&L.]
*PRACTICE AREAS: Real Estate; Land Use; International Law.
Lev, Ori ....'70 '96 C.477 A.B. L.976 J.D. 901 E St. N.W.
Lev, Sean A. ....'66 '93 C.951 B.A. L.309 J.D. [Kellogg,H.H.T.&E.]
*PRACTICE AREAS: Telecommunications; Appellate Litigation; General Litigation.
Leva, Marx, (AV) ....'15 '40 C.16 B.S. L.309 LL.B. 1801 K St., N.W.
Leval, Gerard, (AV) ....'50 '76 C&L.145 B.A., J.D. [Arent F.K.P.&K.]
*PRACTICE AREAS: Business Law; International Business Law; Real Estate; Museum Law.
Levendis, George P., (AV) ....'— '74 C.976 B.A. L.893 J.D. [Patton B.]
Levendusky, David B. '46 '71 C.201 B.A. L.602 J.D.
(adm. in IN; not adm. in DC) V.P., Federal Publications, Inc.
Levene, Beth A. ....'70 '97 C.197 B.A. L.145 J.D. [Ⓐ Williams&C.]
Levenson, Alan B., (AV) ....'35 '62 C.197 A.B. L.976 LL.B. [Fulbright&J.]
*PRACTICE AREAS: Securities; Corporate Law.
Levenson, Amy B. ....'69 '97 C.446 B.A. L.273 J.D. [Ⓐ Garvey,S.&B.]
*PRACTICE AREAS: Litigation.
Levenson, Gary D. ....'64 '93 C.145 B.A. L.347 J.D. [Ⓐ Bruder,G.&M.]
*PRACTICE AREAS: Electric Utilities; Electric Cooperatives; Mergers and Acquisitions; Administrative Law.
Levenson, Rebecca J. ....'70 '95 C.103 B.A. L.893 J.D. [Ⓐ Skadden,A.S.M.&F.]
Levenson, Wendy J. ....'71 '97 C.549 B.A. L.880 J.D. [Ⓐ Arnold&P.]
*PRACTICE AREAS: Litigation; Products Liability.
Leventhal, Dinah S. ....'66 '96 C.309 A.B. L.446 J.D. [Ⓐ O'Donoghue&O.]
*PRACTICE AREAS: Labor and Employment; Employee Benefit Law.
Leventhal, Mark R. ....'69 '97 C.659 B.S. L.831 J.D. [Ⓐ Adduci,M.&S.]
*PRACTICE AREAS: International Trade; Antidumping; Unfair Competition; Trademarks.
Leventhal, Norman P., (AV) ....'43 '68 C.446 B.A. L.976 LL.B. [Leventhal,S.&L.]
*PRACTICE AREAS: Communications Law; Media Law; Intellectual Property; Internet Law.

Leventhal, Senter & Lerman, P.L.L.C., (AV)
Suite 600, 2000 K Street, N.W., 20006
Telephone: 202-429-8970 Telecopier: 202-293-7783
Email: info@lsl-law.com URL: http://www.lsl-law.com
Members of Firm: Norman P. Leventhal; Meredith S. Senter, Jr.; Steven Alman Lerman; Raul R. Rodriguez; Dennis P. Corbett; Brian M. Madden; Barbara K. Gardner; Stephen D. Baruch; Sally A. Buckman; Nancy L. Wolf; David S. Keir; Deborah R. Coleman; Howard A. Topel. Associates: Nancy A. Ory; Linda Danielle Feldmann; John D. Poutasse; Christopher J. Sova; Philip A. Bonomo; Jennifer A. Merrill. Of Counsel: Stephen Austin Hildebrandt; Beth-Sherri Akyereko; S. Jenell Trigg.
General Federal Administrative Practice including Legislative and Governmental Affairs and Federal Court Litigation, International and U.S. Communications Law (including Satellite and Space Technology), Media Contracts and Transactions, Corporate and Commercial, and Intellectual Property Law including Copyright, Trademark, Service Mark and Internet Matters and Related Litigation.
See Professional Biographies, WASHINGTON, DISTRICT OF COLUMBIA

Lever, Jack Q., Jr., (AV) ...'48 '74 C.160 B.S.M.E. L.128 J.D. [McDermott,W.&E.] (Pat.)
Leverett, Nicholaus G. ....'75 '00 C.10 B.S. L.902 J.D. [Ⓐ Kelley D.&W.]
*PRACTICE AREAS: Telecommunications.
Leverich, Bingham B., (AV) ....'37 '65 C.918 B.A. L.976 LL.B. [Covington&B.]
Leveridge, Richard J. ....'56 '81 C.676 B.A. L.276 J.D. [Dickstein S.M.&O.]
*PRACTICE AREAS: Litigation.
Leveton, Erin L. '72 '96 C.1349 B.A. L.273 J.D.
(adm. in VA; not adm. in DC) Staff Atty., Whitman-Walker Clinic Legal Services
*RESPONSIBILITIES: Disability Discrimination; Social Security; Medicare and Medicaid; Health Insurance.
Levey, Kevin S. ....'71 '98 C.30 A.B. L.904 J.D. [Ⓐ Squire,S.&D.]
Levi, Harold L., (AV) ....'47 '72 C.184 B.A. L.276 J.D. 1120 19th Street, N.W.
Levi, Joel G. ....'69 '96 C.880 B.A. L.188 J.D. [Ⓐ Swidler B.S.F.]
*PRACTICE AREAS: Litigation.
Levi, Richard H. ....'47 '78 C.918 B.A. L.904 J.D. 1824 47th Pl., N.W.‡
Levi, Zion ....'66 '96 C.262 B.A. L.1009 J.D. [Ⓐ Miller&C.]
*PRACTICE AREAS: Taxation; Tax Planning; Federal Taxation of Consolidated Group; International Taxation; Federal Tax Controversies.
Levick, Sandra K. ....'53 '81 C.659 B.A. L.588 J.D. Staff Atty. to Pub. Def.
Levie, Richard A. ....'45 '69 C.216 A.B. L.273 J.D. Supr. Ct. J.
Levien, Jason M. '71 '99 C.668 B.A. L.477 J.D.
(adm. in NJ; not adm. in DC) [Ⓐ Williams&C.]
*PRACTICE AREAS: Sports Law; Litigation.
Levien, Lawrence D., (P.C.), (AV) .....'46 '71 C.951 B.A. L.309 J.D. [Akin,G.S.H.&F.]
*PRACTICE AREAS: Labor and Employment.
Levin, Adam K. ....'72 '97 C.659 B.A. L.569 J.D. [Ⓐ Hogan&H.]
*PRACTICE AREAS: Civil Litigation; Complex Litigation; Federal Litigation; Trial Practice; Federal Civil Litigation.
Levin, Andrew S. ....'60 '94 C.951 B.A. L.309 J.D. AFL-CIO
Levin, David R., (AV) ....'47 '78 C.273 B.A. L.128 J.D. [Kilpatrick S.]
*PRACTICE AREAS: Employee Benefits; ERISA Counseling; ERISA Litigation.
Levin, Edward R., (AV) ....'43 '68 C.103 A.B. L.893 LL.B. [Schmeltzer,A.&S.]
*PRACTICE AREAS: Management Labor Law; Employment Law; Employee Benefits Law.
Levin, Harvey A., (AV) ....'48 '74 C.951 B.A. L.276 J.D. [Birch,H.B.&C.]
*PRACTICE AREAS: Commercial Litigation; Banking; Commercial Transactions; Bankruptcy.
Levin, Heather L. ....'70 '95 C.446 B.A. L.128 J.D. Gen. Coun., Koba Instit. Inc.
Levin, Jeffrey S. ....'62 '88 C.1349 B.A. L.904 J.D. [Harris E.&L.]
*PRACTICE AREAS: Customs Law; International Trade Regulation; Unfair Competition; Antitrust Law; Legislative Practice.
Levin, John S. '— '85 C.659 B.S. L.813 J.D.
(adm. in PA; not adm. in DC) [Ⓒ Miller&C.]
*PRACTICE AREAS: Taxation; Federal; International Taxation; Federal Tax Controversies.
Levin, Karen B. ....'68 '95 C.228 A.B. L.910 J.D. Lit. Atty., Paralyzed Vet. of Amer.
Levin, Michael H. ....'42 '70 C.659 B.A. L.309 J.D. [Leonard H.F.L.&L.]
*PRACTICE AREAS: Environmental; Environmental Finance; Government Relations; Administrative Law; Appellate Litigation.
Levin, Peter J., (AV) ....'42 '67 C.103 A.B. L.145 J.D. [Pierson S.&B.]
Levin, Richard F., (AV) ....'53 '79 C.645 B.S. L.273 J.D. [Grossberg,Y.F.&B.]
Levin, Steven A., (AV) '53 '80
C.918 B.A. L.564 J.D. Sr. V.P. & Gen. Coun., The Kaempfer Co.
Levin, Stuart S. '50 '75 C.645 B.A. L.30 J.D.
(adm. in VA; not adm. in DC) V.P., Commercial Settlements, Inc.

Levin, Robert N., P.C.
(See Rockville, Maryland)

Levin & Rosenstein, P.C., (AV)
1130 Seventeenth Street, N.W., Suite 314, 20036
Telephone: 202-429-1795 Fax: 202-429-9729
URL: http://www.lawyers.com/levin&rosenstein
Joseph B. Levin (1918-1985); Larry M. Rosenstein (1941-2000); Daniel N. Rosenstein; Raymond R. Mulera.
Practice before Federal Courts, Departments and Agencies and Arbitration in matters of Agricultural Insurance Law, Agriculture Law, Government Contract, and Insurance.
See Professional Biographies, WASHINGTON, DISTRICT OF COLUMBIA

Levine, Aaron M. '73 '99 C.188 B.S.Engr. L.569 J.D.
(adm. in NY; not adm. in DC) [Ⓐ Howrey S.A.&W.]
*PRACTICE AREAS: Patent Litigation.

Levine, Aaron M., & Associates, (AV) '34 '60 C.102 A.B. L.273 LL.B. BB
1320 - 19th Street, N.W., 20036
Telephone: 202-833-8040 Fax: 202-833-8046 URL: http://www.aaronlevinelaw.com
Email: aaronlevinelaw@aol.com URL: http://www.lawyers.com/aaronlevine
***PRACTICE AREAS: Medical Products Liability; Medical Malpractice; Personal Injury.**
—Brandon J. Levine; Renee L. Robinson-Meyer; Steven Jay Lewis (Not admitted in DC).
Civil Trial Practice. Personal Injury, Medical and Drug Products Liability, Medical Malpractice, LASIK Surgery Malpractice, Diethylstilbestrol (DES) Class Action, "DES" Daughter's Class Action.
See Professional Biographies, WASHINGTON, DISTRICT OF COLUMBIA

Levine, Amy L. ....'71 '98 C&L.976 B.A., J.D. [Ⓐ Covington&B.]
Levine, Arthur J., (AV) ....'36 '64 C.918 B.A. L.178 LL.B. [Ⓒ Finnegan,H.F.G.&D.]
*PRACTICE AREAS: International Copyright Law; Software Copyright; Copyright Protection.
Levine, Arthur N., (AV) ....'45 '71 C.112 B.A. L.1066 J.D. [Arnold&P.]
*PRACTICE AREAS: Food, Drug and Medical Device; Litigation.
Levine, Barry Wm., (AV) ....'42 '69 C.569 B.S. L.1066 J.D. [Dickstein S.M.&O.]
*PRACTICE AREAS: Criminal Law; Criminal Trial Practice; Civil Litigation; Intellectual Property Trial Practice.
Levine, Brandon J., (AV) ....'60 '87 C.273 B.A. L.329 J.D. [Ⓐ A.M.Levine&Assoc.]
*PRACTICE AREAS: Medical Products Liability; Medical Malpractice; Personal Injury; Drugs and Medical Devices.
Levine, David J. ....'58 '85 C.170 B.A. L.910 J.D. [McDermott,W.&E.]
Levine, David N. ....'— '98 C.367 B.A. L.659 J.D. [Ⓐ Groom]
*PRACTICE AREAS: Employee Benefits; Tax.
Levine, Ezra C., (AV) ....'44 '69 C.33 B.A. L.705 J.D. [Howrey S.A.&W.]
*PRACTICE AREAS: Antitrust; Insurance Coverage; Environmental; Litigation; Government Regulation.
Levine, Glenn S. '61 '89 C.893 B.A. L.472 J.D.
(adm. in VA; not adm. in DC) 2501 Connecticut Ave. N.W., Apt. 803
Levine, Gregory H. ....'68 '97 C.103 A.B. L.276 J.D. [Ⓐ Arnold&P.]
*PRACTICE AREAS: Food and Drug Regulation; Health Care; Litigation.
Levine, Henry D., (AV) ....'51 '77 C.976 B.A. L.309 J.D. [Levine,B.B.&B.]
*PRACTICE AREAS: Telecommunications Law; Contracts.
Levine, Howard J., (AV) ....'47 '73 C.331 B.A. L.107 J.D. [Roberts&H.]
*PRACTICE AREAS: Taxation; International Taxation; Like Kind Exchanges; Federal Tax Controversies.
Levine, Howard Warren ....'67 '93 C.228 B.A. L.276 J.D. [Ⓐ Finnegan,H.F.G.&D.]
*PRACTICE AREAS: Intellectual Property Litigation; Biotechnology.
Levine, Jason A. ....'69 '95 C.1036 B.A. L.309 J.D. [Ⓐ Covington&B.]
*PRACTICE AREAS: Litigation; Civil Litigation.
Levine, Jason E. ....'70 '98 C.1044 B.A. L.705 J.D. [Ⓐ Ice M.] (⊙Indpls., IN)
*PRACTICE AREAS: Employee Benefits.
Levine, Jay L. ....'65 '91 C.446 B.A. L.262 J.D. [Winston&S.]
Levine, Kenneth S. ....'48 '74 C.188 A.B. L.309 J.D. 1225 Eye St. N.W.
Levine, Lee, (AV) ....'54 '80 C.659 B.A. L.976 J.D. [Levine S.&K.]
Levine, Lisa L. ....'69 '94 C.659 B.A. L.904 J.D. [Ⓐ Mayer,B.&P.]
*PRACTICE AREAS: Litigation.
Levine, Marci Rose ....'70 '95 C.910 B.A. L.273 J.D. [Ⓐ Sonnenschein N.&R.]
*PRACTICE AREAS: Health Care.
Levine, Melissa B. ....'73 '98 C.30 B.A. L.276 J.D. [Ⓐ Hogan&H.]
*PRACTICE AREAS: Health Law; Health Care Fraud; Medicare Fraud and Abuse; Health Care Regulation; Privacy Law.
Levine, Melissa F. ....'72 '97 C.1365 B.A. L.273 J.D. [Ⓐ Skadden,A.S.M.&F.]
Levine, Robin P. ....'70 '98 C.446 B.S. L.180 J.D. [Ⓐ Dorsey&W.]
*PRACTICE AREAS: Corporate; Tax; Securities and Banking.
Levine, Sharron P.A. ....'58 '84 C&L.569 B.A., J.D. Assoc. Gen. Coun., Fannie Mae
*RESPONSIBILITIES: Low Income Tax Credits; DUS Large Loans; Asset Management.
Levine, Stanley A. ....'36 '61 C.645 B.A. L.831 LL.B. 3 Washington Circle, Apt. 608‡
Levine, Steven M., (AV) ....'56 '81 C.156 B.A. L.273 J.D. 2000 L St., N.W.

Levine & Associates
(See Arlington, Virginia)

Levine, Blaszak, Block & Boothby, LLP, (AV)
2001 L Street, N.W., Suite 900, 20036
Telephone: 202-857-2550 Fax: 202-223-0833
URL: http://www.LB3Law.com
Members of Firm: Henry D. Levine; James S. Blaszak; Ellen G. Block; Colleen L. Boothby; Kevin S. DiLallo; Laura F. H. McDonald; D.E. Boehling. Associates: Janine F. Goodman; Mark G. Johnston; Justin G. Castillo; Marc A. Lindsey; Andrew M. Brown; Bonnie R. Gerhardt; Stephen J. Rosen; Benjamin Huang (Not admitted in DC).
Communications, Telecommunication Regulations, Internet Law, E-Commerce Law, High Technology Law, Administrative Law, Contract Law and Litigation.
See Professional Biographies, WASHINGTON, DISTRICT OF COLUMBIA

Levine Sullivan & Koch, L.L.P., (AV) BB
1050 Seventeenth Street, N.W. Suite 800, 20036
Telephone: 202-508-1100 Facsimile: 202-861-9888
Email: info@lskslaw.com
Members of Firm: Lee Levine; Michael D. Sullivan; Elizabeth C. Koch; James E. Grossberg; Celeste Phillips (Not admitted in DC); Seth D. Berlin; Jay Ward Brown. Of Counsel: Cameron A. Stracher. Associates: Ashley I. Kissinger; Amy E. Ledoux; Audrey Billingsley; Thomas Curley.
Media, Defamation, First Amendment, Publishing and related law, Copyright, and General Civil Litigation.
See Professional Biographies, WASHINGTON, DISTRICT OF COLUMBIA

Leviner, Ron '— '00 C.659 B.A. L.178 J.D.
(adm. in NY; not adm. in DC) [Ⓐ Fried,F.H.S.&J.]
*PRACTICE AREAS: Corporate Law; Mergers and Acquisitions.
Levingston, Kirsten D. ....'66 '90 C.800 A.B. L.309 J.D. 2555 M St., N.W.
Levinson, Jackie S. ....'— '73 C.881 A.B. L.976 J.D. [King&S.]
*PRACTICE AREAS: Tax.
Levinson, Lawrence E., (AV) '— '57 C.823 B.S. L.309 LL.B.
(adm. in NY; not adm. in DC) [Verner,L.B.M.&H.]
*PRACTICE AREAS: Media; Communications; Military Base Reconversion.
Levinson, Lizbeth R. ....'56 '82 C.914 B.A. L.276 J.D. [Manatt,P.&P.]
Levinstein, Mark S. ....'58 '83 C.893 B.A. L.309 J.D. [Williams&C.]
Levit, Lawrence A., (AV) ....'45 '72 C.145 B.A. L.309 J.D. [Arent F.K.P.&K.]
*PRACTICE AREAS: Commercial and Residential Lending and Closings; Real Estate Development and/or Syndications Law; Loan Workouts; Real Estate-Commercial Law; Real Estate (Property) Law.
Levitas, Elliott H., (AV) '30 '55 C.1365 A.B. L.245 J.D.
[Ⓒ Kilpatrick S.] (⊙Atlanta, GA)
*PRACTICE AREAS: Government Contracts; Legislative; Environmental Law; Administrative Law; Constitutional Law.
Levitin, Michael J. ....'60 '87 C&L.309 A.B., J.D. [Hale&D.]
*PRACTICE AREAS: Corporate Law.
Levitine, Ilia ....'67 '96 C.296 B.S. L.902 J.D. [Ⓐ McKenna&C.]
*PRACTICE AREAS: Electricity Regulation; Gas; Public Utilities; International Law.
Levitt, Alfred P. ....'69 '95 C.999 B.F.A. L.831 J.D. [Ⓐ Boies,S.&F.]
*PRACTICE AREAS: Antitrust; Trade Regulation; Securities.
Levitt, Chet D. .....'66 '92 C.178 B.A. L.1019 J.D. 1150 Connecticut Ave., N.W., 9th Fl.
Levitt, Melinda F. ....'— '90 C.1036 B.A. L.273 J.D. [Foley&L.]
*PRACTICE AREAS: Litigation; International Trade.
Levitt, Sarah L. ....'64 '92 C.25 B.A. L.29 J.D. 1319 F Street N.W.
Levitt, Scott J. ....'70 '95 C.188 B.S. L.273 J.D. [Ⓐ Swidler B.S.F.]
*PRACTICE AREAS: Insurance Coverage Litigation; Employment Litigation.
Levy, Aaron ....'11 '40 C.563 A.B. L.145 J.D. 1875 Connecticut Ave., N.W.
Levy, Andrew D. ....'59 '98 C.1365 B.S. L.659 J.D. [Ⓐ Covington&B.]

Levy, Arnold, (AV) .... '13 '36 C.563 B.A. L.309 J.D. [C Freedman,L.K.&S.] ‡
Levy, Charles S., (AV) .... '45 '71 C.94 B.A. L.273 J.D. [Wilmer,C.&P.]
*PRACTICE AREAS: International Law.
Levy, David M., (AV) .... '54 '79 C.188 B.A. L.477 J.D. [Sidley A.B.&W.]
Levy, Fred L., (AV) .... '53 '77 C.188 B.S. L.800 J.D. [Sonnenschein N.&R.]
*PRACTICE AREAS: Corporate Law.
Levy, Frederic M., (AV) ....'53 '78 C&L.178 B.A., J.D. [McKenna&C.]
*PRACTICE AREAS: White Collar Criminal Defense Law; White Collar Fraud; Government Procurement Law; Commercial Transactions; Commercial Litigation.
Levy, Gregg H., (AV) .... '53 '77 C&L.309 A.B., J.D. [Covington&B.]
Levy, Harold A., (AV) .... '50 '74 C.385 B.A. L.276 J.D. [C Swidler B.S.F.]
*PRACTICE AREAS: Real Estate; Finance; Housing Programs.
Levy, Jack Alan .... '71 '99 C.367 B.A. L.276 J.D. [A Wilmer,C.&P.]
Levy, Jennifer G. ....'— '98 C&L.228 B.A., J.D. [A Kirkland&E.]
*PRACTICE AREAS: Litigation.
Levy, Joel H., (AV) .... '35 '60 C.197 A.B. L.309 LL.B. [Cohn&M.]
*PRACTICE AREAS: Mass Media Law; Telecommunications Law; Electronic Media Mergers and Acquisitions; Administrative Litigation.
Levy, Louis J. .... '56 '96 C.597 B.A. L.904 J.D. [A Finnegan,H.F.G.&D.]
*PRACTICE AREAS: Trademarks; Copyrights; Unfair Competition.
Levy, M. Barry, (AV) '36 '61 C.945 B.A. L.262 J.D.
(adm. in NY; not adm. in DC) [Sharretts,P.C.&B.] ⊙
*PRACTICE AREAS: Customs Law; International Trade; Imports and Exports; Antidumping; Countervailing Duties.
Levy, Marc .... '61 '86 C.1036 B.A. L.273 J.D. [C Holland&K.]
*PRACTICE AREAS: Securities; Corporate; Financial Services Law.
Levy, Mark I., (AV) ....'49 '76 C&L.976 B.A., J.D. [Howrey S.A.&W.]
*PRACTICE AREAS: Appellate and Supreme Court Litigation.
Levy, Micah A. ....'71 '98 C.454 B.A. L.94 J.D. [A Baker&M.]
*PRACTICE AREAS: Tax Planning and Advice (Corporate and International); Tax Controversies (Corporate and International); Employee Benefits; Bankruptcy, Insolvency and Reorganization.
Levy, Michael A. .... '72 '99 C.309 A.B. L.893 J.D. [A Sidley A.B.&W.]
Levy, Michael M., (AV) ....'44 '69 C.188 A.B. L.477 J.D. [Crowell&M.]
*PRACTICE AREAS: Litigation.
Levy, Michael N., (AV) ....'63 '90 C.976 B.A. L.309 J.D. [Swidler B.S.F.]
*PRACTICE AREAS: White Collar Criminal Defense; Corporate Compliance; Internal Investigations; Congressional Investigations; Governmental Investigations.
Levy, Michael R., (AV) ....'48 '74 C.976 B.A. L.309 J.D. [Covington&B.]
Levy, Michael S., (AV) ....'40 '66 C.882 B.A. L.273 J.D. [Baise&M.]
*PRACTICE AREAS: Litigation; Condominium; Real Estate; Corporate.
Levy, Neil I., (AV) .... '48 '72 C&L.659 B.S.E., J.D. [Kilpatrick S.]
*PRACTICE AREAS: Government Contracts; Real Estate; Litigation.
Levy, Neil L. .... '65 '90 C.273 B.A. L.607 J.D. [Kirkland&E.]
*PRACTICE AREAS: Energy Law and Litigation; Utility Regulatory Law.
Levy, Paul Alan .... '50 '77 C.685 B.A. L.145 J.D. Public Citizen Litig. Grp.
Levy, Robert G., (AV) '32 '60 C.197 A.B. L.893 LL.B.
(adm. in MD; not adm. in DC) [C Sutherland A.&B.]
*PRACTICE AREAS: Litigation; Civil Litigation; Intellectual Property; Trade Secrets; Antitrust.
Levy, S. David .... '37 '63 C.966 A.B. L.309 LL.B. Pres., Key Theatre Enterprises
Levy, Steven E. ....'49 '76 C&L.309 A.B., J.D. 2317 20th St., N.W.
Levy, William C. '15 '39 C.63 B.S.S. L.309 LL.B.
(adm. in NY; not adm. in DC) 2801 New Mexico Ave., N.W.‡
Levy & Grandinetti, (AV) ....Suite 1401-M 1725 K Street, N.W. (Pat.)
Lew, Darryl S. ....'64 '90 C.1113 B.A. L.178 J.D. [Hunton&W.]
*PRACTICE AREAS: Commercial Litigation; International Arbitration.
Lewandrowski, Jennifer Joy '63 '00 C.972 B.S. L.276 J.D.
(adm. in VA; not adm. in DC) Pricewaterhouse Coopers, LLP
Lewin, Nathan, (AV) ....'36 '62 C.978 B.A. L.309 J.D. [Mintz,L.C.F.G.&P.]
*PRACTICE AREAS: U.S. Supreme Court Litigation; Criminal Defense; Constitutional Litigation; Appellate Litigation; Federal Litigation.
Lewine, Alan R. .... '55 '99 C.560 B.S. L.276 J.D. [A Piper M.R.&W.]
*PRACTICE AREAS: Technology Transactions; Internet Technology; Electronic Commerce; Software Licensing; Strategic Alliances.
Lewis, Algie R. .... '21 '71 C.892 A.B. L.329 J.D. 1710 1st St., N.E.‡
Lewis, Alicia L. '72 '01 C.659 B.S. L.945 J.D.
(adm. in NY; not adm. in DC) [A Kirkpatrick&L.]
*PRACTICE AREAS: Investment Company Law; Investment Management.
Lewis, Anne M. .... '65 '95 C.890 B.A. L.893 J.D. [A Powell,G.F.&M.]
*PRACTICE AREAS: Health Care Law; Food and Drug; Legislative Law; Advocacy; Pharmacy Law.
Lewis, Carlton A. ....'58 '88 C.302 B.A. L.329 J.D. Dept. of Human Servs.
Lewis, Carrie M. '65 '91 C&L.188 B.A., J.D.
(adm. in NY; not adm. in DC) 1875 Conn. Ave., N.W.
Lewis, Cathy A., (AV) .... '46 '78 C.473 B.S. L.276 J.D. [Vinson&E.]
*PRACTICE AREAS: Litigation; Antitrust and Trade Regulation; Finance.
Lewis, Craig A. .... '62 '91 C.659 B.A. L.276 J.D. [Hogan&H.]
*PRACTICE AREAS: International Trade; Litigation.
Lewis, Cynthia A., (AV) .... '53 '78 C.945 B.A. L.309 J.D. [Beveridge&D.]
*PRACTICE AREAS: Environmental Law; Advertising and Labeling; Pesticide Regulation; International Environmental Law; Environmental Administrative Law.
Lewis, Daniel Martin, (AV) ....'44 '73 C&L.976 B.A., LL.B. [Arnold&P.]
*PRACTICE AREAS: Bankruptcy.
Lewis, David J. ....'48 '73 C&L.339 B.S., J.D. [Sidley A.B.&W.]
Lewis, David R. ....'53 '82 C.453 B.S. L.273 J.D. [Shaw P.]
*PRACTICE AREAS: Energy; Administrative; Environmental.
Lewis, Don Charles .... '— '85 C&L.845 B.A., J.D. [Verner,L.B.M.&H.]
*PRACTICE AREAS: Antitrust Law; Healthcare Law; Litigation.
Lewis, Donald W. ....'31 '57 C.994 B.A. L.1009 LL.B. 1710 Rhode Island Ave., N.W.
Lewis, Emma Kelton '67 '98 C.178 A.B. L.976 J.D.
(adm. in NY; not adm. in DC) [A Arnold&P.]
*PRACTICE AREAS: Litigation; Environmental Law.
Lewis, Emmett B., (AV) ....'— '67 C&L.228 B.A., J.D. [Miller&C.]
*PRACTICE AREAS: Federal Litigation; Tax Controversies and Litigation; Government Contract Litigation.
Lewis, Eric L. .... '57 '85 C.674 A.B. L.976 J.D. [Baach R.&L.P.]
*PRACTICE AREAS: Civil Litigation; Commercial Litigation; White Collar Crime; International Insolvency; Fraud.
Lewis, Floyd H., Jr. .... '51 '77 C.309 B.A. L.276 J.D. 2520 36th Pl., S.E.
Lewis, George William .... '52 '79 C.705 B.A. L.1292 J.D. [Jacobson,H.]
*PRACTICE AREAS: Trademark Law; Copyright Law; Internet Law.
Lewis, Glenn C., (AV) ....'52 '77 C.472 B.A. L.1209 J.D. [Lewis] (⊙Fairfax, VA)
*PRACTICE AREAS: Family Law.
Lewis, Gregory A. '59 '88 C.93 B.A. L.273 J.D.
Assoc. Gen. Coun., National Public Radio, Inc.
Lewis, Harry C. ....'26 '50 C.102 B.A. L.502 LL.B. 1030 15th St., N.W.
Lewis, James L. ....'35 '67 C.674 A.B. L.1048 LL.B. [A Levy&G.]
Lewis, James L. '49 '74 C.454 B.A. L.93 J.D.
(adm. in MA; not adm. in DC)
V.P., MCI Telecommunications Corp. (Regulatory Affairs)
Lewis, Jeffrey M., (BV) .... '46 '75 C.1044 B.A. L.904 J.D. 600 F St., N.W.
Lewis, Jennifer W. .... '70 '96 C&L.477 B.A., J.D. [A Sidley A.B.&W.]
Lewis, Joseph D., (AV) ....'— '79 C.319 B.A. L.273 J.D. [Barnes&T.] (See Pat. Sect.)
*PRACTICE AREAS: Intellectual Property; Computer Law; Trademarks; Copyrights; Technology Law.
Lewis, Karen Judd ....'57 '89 C.483 B.A. L.596 J.D. [Williams&J.]
*PRACTICE AREAS: Transportation Law; Health Law.
Lewis, Laurie D. .... '58 '83 C.339 B.S. L.30 J.D. 1001 Pennsylvania Avenue, N.W.
Lewis, Mark K., (AV) .... '65 '90 C.446 B.S. L.276 J.D. [Baker B.]
Lewis, Matthew R. ....'— '96 C.878 B.A. L.178 J.D. [A Latham&W.]
*PRACTICE AREAS: Business Arbitration; Business Litigation; Federal Civil Practice.
Lewis, Maureen A. '57 '82 C.811 B.A. L.276 J.D.
Sr. Assoc. Gen. Coun., Howard Univ.
Lewis, Meredith Kolsky ....'68 '95 C.597 B.A. L.276 J.D. [A Shearman&S.]
Lewis, Michael K. .... '43 '76 C.197 A.B. L.276 J.D. [Lichtman,T.S.&R.]
Lewis, Mose, III .... '38 '71 C.1023 B.S. L.329 J.D. [Powers&L.]
Lewis, Patricia G., (AV) .... '45 '71 C.914 B.A. L.309 J.D. [Caplin&D.]
*PRACTICE AREAS: Federal Tax Practice.
Lewis, Richard S. ....'54 '86 C.860 B.A. L.659 J.D. [Cohen,M.H.&T.]
*PRACTICE AREAS: Environmental Class Actions; Antitrust; Consumer Rights.
Lewis, Robert A. .... '65 '88 C.30 B.A. L.904 J.D. 1030 15th St., NW
Lewis, Stephen C. '73 '00 C.911 B.A. L.273 J.D.
(adm. in VA; not adm. in DC) [Margolius,M.D.R.&T.]
*PRACTICE AREAS: Estate Administration (75%); Estate Planning (10%); Tax Law (10%); Corporate Law (5%).
Lewis, Steven Jay '66 '00 C.769 B.S. L.273 J.D.
(adm. in VA; not adm. in DC) [A A.M.Levine&Assoc.]
*PRACTICE AREAS: Personal Injury; Medical Liability; Medical Malpractice.
Lewis, Stuart M., (AV) .... '45 '70 C&L.893 B.A., J.D. [Silverstein&M.]
Lewis, Suzanne Marie ....'69 '94 C.893 B.A. L.1209 J.D. [A Shapiro,L.&S.]
*PRACTICE AREAS: Labor and Employment Law; Debtor Bankruptcy; Creditor Bankruptcy; Creditor Rights; Commercial Real Estate Law.
Lewis, W. Alton .... '42 '71 C.254 B.A. L.329 J.D. 1010 Mass. Ave., N.W.
Lewis, William H., Jr., (AV) .... '42 '70 C&L.575 A.B., J.D. [Morgan,L.&B.]
Lewis, Wilma A. ....'56 '81 C.821 B.A. L.309 J.D. [Crowell&M.]
*PRACTICE AREAS: Litigation.

Lewis and Associates
(See Springfield, Virginia)

Lewis-Eng, Claudia A. '70 '96 C.329 B.A. L.904 J.D.
(adm. in CT; not adm. in DC) [A Emord&Assoc.]
*PRACTICE AREAS: Food and Drug Law; Administrative Law; Constitutional Law; False Advertising Law; General Civil Litigation.
Lewis & Kolton, PLLC .... Suite 875, 1150 18th Street, N.W.

Lewis Law Firm, The, A Professional Corporation, (AV) BB
805 15th Street, N.W. Suite 200, 20005 ⊙
Telephone: 202-408-0655 Fax: 202-408-9826
Email: glewis@lewislawfirm.com URL: http://www.lewislawfirm.com
Glenn C. Lewis;—Wendy Helene Schwartz; Daniel G. Dannenbaum; Gregory R. Nugent; Catherine M. Reese; Amy L. Hadley (Not admitted in DC); Sherry L. Leichman; Robert C. Eustice; Richard F. Gibbons, Jr.; Roberta Kathryn Henault (Not admitted in DC).
Family Law, Adoptions, Child Custody, Child Support, Divorce, Criminal Law, Business and Transaction Matters, General, Civil and Commercial Litigation, Appellate practice in State and Federal Courts.
Fairfax, Virginia Office: Suite 100, 10306 Eaton Place. Telephone: 703-691-8686.
Rockville, Maryland Office: Suite 402, 11921 Rockville Pike, 20852.
See Professional Biographies, WASHINGTON, DISTRICT OF COLUMBIA

Lewis & Munday, A Professional Corporation, (AV) BB
(Formerly Lewis, White & Clay, P.C.)
1120 Connecticut Avenue N.W., Suite 280, 20036 ⊙
Telephone: 202-835-0616 Fax: 202-833-3316
Email: KBrown@lewismunday.com URL: http://www.lewismunday.com
Karen Kendrick Brown (Resident).
Business, Banking, Bankruptcy, Casualty Insurance, Real Estate, Litigation, Civil Rights, Corporate, Life and Health Insurance, Mortgage, Municipal Bond, Municipal, Urban Affairs and Railroad Law.
Detroit, Michigan Office: 1300 First National Building, 660 Woodward Avenue. 48226-3531. Telephone: 313-961-2550. Fax: 313-961-1270.
Boston, Massachusetts Office: 101 Federal Street, Suite 1900. 02110. Telephone: 617-478-0553. Fax: 617-478-0543.
See Professional Biographies, WASHINGTON, DISTRICT OF COLUMBIA

Lewris, Basil J., (AV) '49 '77
C.563 B.S.Ch.E. L.273 J.D. [Finnegan,H.F.G.&D.] (See Pat. Sect.)
*PRACTICE AREAS: Civil Appeals; Chemical Intellectual Property; Intellectual Property Litigation; Pharmaceutical Intellectual Property; Biotechnology.

Leydig, Voit & Mayer, Ltd., (AV) BB
700 Thirteenth Street N.W., Suite 300, 20005-3960 ⊙
Telephone: 202-737-6770 Telecopier: 202-737-6776
Email: mail@leydig.com URL: http://www.leydig.com
John M. Belz (Resident); Jeffrey A. Wyand (Resident); Jeremy M. Jay (Resident);—Xavier Pillai (Not admitted in DC; Resident); Shannon D. Schemel (Not admitted in DC; Resident); Leah C. Oubre (Resident). Of Counsel: John P. Bundock, Jr. (Resident); John D. Foster (Resident).
Patent, Trademark, Copyright, Unfair Competition and Related Antitrust and International Trade Law. Trials and Appeals.
Chicago, Illinois Office: Two Prudential Plaza, Suite 4900. 180 North Stetson Avenue. Telephone: 312-616-5600. Telecopier: 312-616-5700.
Rockford, Illinois Office: 6815 Weaver Road, Suite 300. Telephone: 815-963-7661. Telecopier: 815-963-7664.
See Professional Biographies, WASHINGTON, DISTRICT OF COLUMBIA

Leyland, Nora H., (AV) ....'52 '89 C.94 B.A. L.904 J.D. [Sherman,D.C.L.&Y.]
*PRACTICE AREAS: Labor and Employment Law; Union Labor Law.
Leyrer, Colleen M. .... '65 '99 C.551 B.A. L.446 J.D. [A Henrichsen S.]
*PRACTICE AREAS: Employment Law; Civil Rights; Litigation.
Leyva, Natan J. .... '65 '00 C.309 A.B. L.976 J.D. [A Wilmer,C.&P.]
Lezell, Mark L., (AV) ....'47 '73 C.475 B.A. L.904 J.D. [Ropes&G.]
*PRACTICE AREAS: Business Law; Corporation Law; Finance, Technology and Securities.
Lhevine, Paul '67 '94 C.170 B.A. L.1194 J.D.
(adm. in CO; not adm. in DC) 502 Groff Ct., N.E.
L'Hommedieu, Samuel J., Jr. ...'25 '51 C.446 B.S. L.273 LL.B. 3946 Highwood Ct. N.W.
Li, K. Thomas .... '55 '97 C.999 B.A. L.446 J.D. [I.J.Fredman]
Li, Kening '63 '98 C.999 B.S. L.966 J.D.
(adm. in WI; not adm. in DC; Pat.) [A Pepper H.]
*PRACTICE AREAS: Intellectual Property.
Lian, Robert G., Jr. .... '68 '93 C.164 B.A. L.128 J.D. [C Akin,G.S.H.&F.]
*PRACTICE AREAS: Labor and Employment.
Liang, Angela N. .... '70 '99 C.112 B.A. L.446 J.D. P.O. Box 66738
Liao, Virginia W. .... '74 '00 C.893 B.A. L.188 J.D. [A Arnold&P.]
*PRACTICE AREAS: Corporate Law; Securities.
Liberman, Howard M., (AV) ....'46 '73 C.241 B.S. L.1009 J.D. [Arter&H.]
*PRACTICE AREAS: Communications Law; Communications Industry Transactions and Litigation.
Liberman, Susan S. .... '47 '73 C.70 B.A. L.1009 J.D. 1339 30th St., NW
Libin, Jerome B., (AV) .... '36 '61 C.597 B.S. L.477 J.D. [Sutherland A.&B.]
*PRACTICE AREAS: Federal Taxation; International Taxation; Tax Litigation.
Libow, Daryl A. ....'59 '86 C.309 A.B. L.188 J.D. [Sullivan&C.] (⊙New York, NY)
Libretta, Donald F. .... '38 '65 C.870 B.S. L.276 J.D. [Krooth&A.]

Lichtenbaum, Greta L.H. ... '65 '90 C.311 B.A. L.309 J.D. [Ⓑ Vinson&E.]
*PRACTICE AREAS: International Trade; International Law.
Lichtenbaum, Peter, (AV) ... '65 '90 C.674 B.A. L.309 J.D. [Steptoe&J.]
*PRACTICE AREAS: International Trade; International Law.
Lichtenstein, Adam V. ... '65 '91 C.1019 B.B.A. L.1187 J.D. [Ⓐ Katten M.Z.]
*PRACTICE AREAS: Criminal Law; Family Law; Labor and Employment; Civil Practice.
Lichtenstein, Elissa C. ... '54 '80 C.788 A.B. L.273 J.D. Dir. Pub. Servs., Amer. Bar Assn.
Lichtenstein, Michael J., (AV) ... '54 '88 C.1036 B.A. L.30 J.D. [Swidler B.S.F.]
*PRACTICE AREAS: Commercial Litigation; Bankruptcy; Creditors Rights.
Lichtenstein, Natalie G. ... '53 '78 C.681 A.B. L.309 J.D. The World Bk.
Lichter, Erik J. ... '72 '97 C.1365 B.A. L.446 J.D. [Ⓐ Hogan&H.]
*PRACTICE AREAS: Securities Law; Corporate Law.
Lichtman, Elliott C., (AV) ... '39 '65 C.976 A.B. L.309 LL.B. [Lichtman,T.S.&R.]
Lichtman, Trister, Singer & Ross, (AV) ... 1666 Connecticut Ave., N.W.
Lidoff, Herbert J. ... '11 '40 C.453 S.B. L.904 LL.B. 6433 31st Pl. N.W.‡
Lieb, David B. ... '70 '97 C.886 B.A. L.893 J.D. [Ⓐ Spiegel&M.]
*PRACTICE AREAS: Energy; Litigation; Utility Law.
Liebeler, Lars H. ... '62 '87 C.478 B.A. L.347 J.D. [Thaler L.] (⊙Fairfax, VA)
*PRACTICE AREAS: Civil Litigation; Employment Law; Antitrust and Trade Regulation; Construction Law.
Lieber, Gary L., (AV) ... '49 '74 C.30 B.A. L.904 J.D. [Schmeltzer,A.&S.]
*PRACTICE AREAS: Management Labor Law; Employment Law; Employee Benefits Law.
Lieber, Rachel Carlson ... '70 '95 C.884 B.A. L.276 J.D. Asst. U.S. Atty.
Lieberman, Eric N. ... '65 '91 C.309 B.A. L.228 J.D. Assoc. Coun., Washington Post Co.
Lieberman, Kathy A. ... '68 '95 C.945 B.A. L.30 J.D. 729 15th St., N.W., 2nd Fl.
Lieberman, Michael L. '56 '81 C.477 B.A. L.228 J.D.
(adm. in OH; not adm. in DC) Coun., Anti-Defamation League
Lieberman, Paul ... '42 '66 C.339 B.S. L.209 J.D. 1884 Columbia Rd., N.W.‡
Lieberman, Richard D., (AV) ... '46 '88 C.188 A.B. L.276 J.D. [McCarthy,S.&H.]
*PRACTICE AREAS: Government Contracts; Contract Fraud; Government Investigations.
Lieberman, Steven ... '59 '85 C.674 A.B. L.178 J.D. [Rothwell,F.E.&M.] (See Pat. Sect.)
*PRACTICE AREAS: Intellectual Property; Litigation; Constitutional Law.
Liebesman, Lawrence R., (BV) ... '47 '74 C.705 B.A. L.273 J.D. [Holland&K.]
*PRACTICE AREAS: Natural Resources Law; Administrative Law; Environmental Law.
Lieblich, William C. ... '42 '68 C.691 B.A. L.309 LL.B. 1054 31st Street, N.W.
Liebman, Ronald S., (AV) ... '43 '69 C.928 B.A. L.446 J.D. [Patton B.]
Liechty, David C. '69 '99 C.101 B.S. L.878 J.D.
(adm. in UT; not adm. in DC; See Pat. Sect.) [Ⓐ Keil&W.]
*PRACTICE AREAS: Chemical Patents; Biotechnology Patents.
Lieder, Michael D. ... '54 '84 C.311 B.A. L.276 J.D. [Sprenger&L.]
*PRACTICE AREAS: Employment; Civil Rights; Complex Federal Litigation.
Liedtka, Jeanne M. ... '69 '94 C&L.893 B.A., J.D. [Ⓐ Patton B.]

Lieff, Cabraser, Heimann & Bernstein, LLP, (AV)
1100 New York Avenue, N.W., Suite 1080 - West Tower, 20005-3934 ⊙
Telephone: 202-582-1000 Facsimile: 202-582-1500
Email: mail@lchb.com URL: http://www.lchb.com
Richard T. Seymour.
Practice Limited to Class Actions and Multi-Plaintiff Litigation.
New York, New York Office: 780 Third Avenue, 48th Floor, 10017-2024. Telephone: 212-355-9500. Facsimile: 212-355-9592.
San Francisco, California Office: Embarcadero Center West, 30th Floor, 275 Battery Street, 94111-3339. Telephone: 415-956-1000. Facsimile: 415-956-1008.
Boston, Massachusetts Office: 175 Federal Street, 7th Floor, 02110-1216. Telephone: 617-720-5000. Facsimile: 617-720-5015.
Nashville, Tennessee Office: 3319 West End Avenue, Suite 600, 37203-1074. Telephone: 615-313-9000. Facsimile: 615-313-9965.
See Professional Biographies, WASHINGTON, DISTRICT OF COLUMBIA

Liekweg, John A. '44 '74 C&L.446 B.A., J.D.
Assoc. Gen. Coun., U.S. Catholic Conference
Lien, R. Andrew ... '69 '99 C.1169 B.A. L.94 J.D. [Ⓐ Hunton&W.]
*PRACTICE AREAS: Project Finance; Leasing.
Lienhard, Jonathan Philip ... '72 '97 C&L.602 B.A., J.D. [Ⓐ McKenna&C.]★
*PRACTICE AREAS: Civil Litigation.
Liesemer, Jeffrey A. ... '65 '93 C.105 B.A. L.665 J.D. [Ⓐ Arnold&P.]
*PRACTICE AREAS: Bankruptcy; Civil Litigation.
Lieth, William ... '47 '80 C.415 B.A. L.273 J.D. [Ⓐ Wiley R.&F.]
Lietz, David K., (AV) ... '66 '91 C.427 B.A. L.276 J.D. [Coale C.L.M.]
*PRACTICE AREAS: Aviation; Wrongful Death; Commercial Vehicle Liability.
Lifschitz, Judah, (AV) ... '52 '77 C.978 B.A. L.273 J.D. [Shapiro,L.&S.] ⊙
*PRACTICE AREAS: Construction; Government Contracts; Business Litigation.
Liggett, Martha L. '50 '83 C.546 B.S. L.276 J.D.
1625 Massachusetts Ave., N.W. 6th Fl.
Light, Russell '— '01 C.453 B.S. L.145 J.D.
(adm. in IL; not adm. in DC) [Ⓐ Fried,F.H.S.&J.]
*PRACTICE AREAS: Tax.
Lightfoot, William P., Jr., (AV) ... '50 '77 C.329 B.A. L.910 J.D. [Koonz,M.J.D.&L.]
Lighthizer, Robert E., (AV) ... '47 '73 C&L.276 B.A., J.D. [Skadden,A.S.M.&F.]
Lightman, Stacey Ellen '74 '99 C.1128 B.S. L.1206 J.D.
(adm. in FL; not adm. in DC) 441 4th St. NW, 6th Fl.
Ligon, Anne ... '48 '90 C.890 B.A. L.1209 J.D. 955 26th St., N.W.
Liles, Detria J. ... '— '90 600 5th St. NW, Suite 2808
Liles, Robert E., II, (AV) ... '— '78 C.154 B.A. L.178 J.D. [Miller&C.]
*PRACTICE AREAS: Corporate Tax Controversies; Accounting Law; Federal Income Tax; Tax Appeals; Tax Audits.
Liles, Robert Walton '59 '93 C.797 B.A. L.796 J.D.
(adm. in TX; not adm. in DC) Exec. Off., U.S. Attys.
Lilienthal, Scott R. ... '61 '87 C.174 B.A. L.446 J.D. [Hogan&H.]
*PRACTICE AREAS: Federal Taxation; Public Finance.
Lilley, Stephanie Blessey '65 '94 C.855 B.A. L.276 J.D.
2001 Pennsylvania Avenue, N.W.
Lillywhite, Jeffery M. '— '00 C.878 B.S. L.1218 J.D.
(adm. in UT; not adm. in DC) [Ⓐ Morgan,L.&B.]
Lilyestrom, John R., (AV) ... '62 '89 C.309 B.A. L.446 J.D. [Hogan&H.]
*PRACTICE AREAS: Electric Power; Energy Contracts; Electric Utility Regulation; Public Utility Law.
Lim, Esther H. ... '— '95 C.445 B.A. L.446 J.D. [Ⓐ Finnegan,H.F.G.&D.] (See Pat. Sect.)
*PRACTICE AREAS: Intellectual Property Litigation; Computer and Software Patents; Technology Licensing; International Intellectual Property; Software Protection.
Lim, Stephanie Szu-Ping ... '— '00 C.31 B.A. L.228 J.D. [Ⓐ Latham&W.]
Limberg, Allen L. '36 '73 C.867 B.E.E. L.776 J.D.
(adm. in NJ; not adm. in DC; Pat.) Assoc. Pat. Coun., Samsung Electronics
Limprecht, Jane E. ... '54 '80 C&L.966 B.A., J.D. The Bur. of Natl. Affs., Inc.
Lin, Margaret A. ... '70 '99 C.659 B.S. L.893 J.D. [Ⓐ Steptoe&J.]
Lin, Tony ... '69 '98 C.893 B.A. L.352 J.D. [Ⓐ Shaw P.]
*PRACTICE AREAS: Communications.
Lincoln, Devon '74 '99 C.178 B.A. L.1066 J.D.
(adm. in NY; not adm. in DC) [Ⓐ Milbank,T.H.&M.]
Lincoln, Sheryl J. ... '52 '95 C.910 B.A. L.276 J.D. [Ⓐ Goldberg,G.W.&W.]
*PRACTICE AREAS: Communications and Media; Internet Law.
Lincoln-Stewart, Kimberly ... '— '90 C.302 B.A. L.329 J.D. [Ⓐ Manatt,P.&P.]

Lind, Keith D. ... '47 '85 C&L.477 B.S.N., J.D. [Ⓐ Holland&K.]
*PRACTICE AREAS: Health Law; Medicare and Medicaid Law; Legislative Practice; Regulatory Law; Business Law.
Lindburg, John A. '44 '73 C.976 B.A. L.273 J.D.
Dep. Secy. & Dep. Gen. Coun., Natl. Gallery of Art
*RESPONSIBILITIES: International Law; Administrative Law.
Linde, Selena J. ... '69 '97 C.1356 B.A. L.893 J.D. [Ⓐ Dickstein S.M.&O.]
*PRACTICE AREAS: Insurance Coverage Litigation; Civil Litigation.
Lindeman, Jeffrey A. ... '61 '92 C.923 B.A. L.276 J.D. [Morgan,L.&B.] (Pat.)
Lindemann, Albert P., Jr. ... '37 '62 C.690 B.S. L.94 LL.B. [O'Connor&H.]
*PRACTICE AREAS: Litigation; International Law; Trade Regulation.
Linden, Stacy R. ... '73 '98 C.128 B.A. L.904 J.D. [Ⓐ Jones,D.R.&P.]
Linder, Jeffrey S., (AV) ... '58 '83 C.228 A.B. L.813 J.D. [Wiley R.&F.]
*PRACTICE AREAS: Communications.
Lindholm, Douglas L. ... '58 '86 C.428 B.S. L.904 J.D. Price Waterhouse
Lindner, Russell C. ... '54 '80 C.367 B.A. L.273 J.D. Chmn., Bear Street Properties
Lindquist, Leigh Ann ... '— '98 C.788 A.B. L.273 J.D. [Ⓐ Sughrue M.] (See Pat. Sect.)
*PRACTICE AREAS: Intellectual Property.
Lindsay, G. Griffith '54 '79 C.216 B.A. L.1017 J.D.
(adm. in PA; not adm. in DC) V.P. & Mng. Tax Dir., Marriott Intl., Inc.
Lindsay, J. Wade ... '61 '88 C.311 A.B. L.245 J.D. [Wilkinson B.K.]
*PRACTICE AREAS: Communications; Telecommunications Law; Energy; Natural Resources; Administrative Litigation.
Lindsay, Joseph L. ... '67 '95 C.549 B.A. L.221 J.D. [Ⓐ McDermott,W.&E.]
Lindsay, Ronald A. ... '52 '80 C.276 A.B. L.893 J.D. [Ⓑ Seyfarth S.]
*PRACTICE AREAS: Labor Law; Employment Law; Fair Housing Law.
Lindsay, Hart, Neil & Weigler, LLP ... 1201 Pennsylvania Ave., N.W. (⊙Port., OR)
Lindsey, Marc A. ... '66 '96 C.329 B.S.E.E. L.575 J.D. [Ⓐ Levine,B.B.&B.]
*PRACTICE AREAS: Technology Law; Software Licensing; Intellectual Property Licensing; Telecommunications Law; Outsourcing.
Lindsey, Sarah C. ... '73 '98 C.475 B.A. L.904 J.D. [Ⓐ Crowell&M.]
Linehan, Kathleen Mary ... '50 '80 C.446 B.A. L.1209 J.D. V.P., Philip Morris Cos. Inc.
Ling, Ling ... '69 '98 C.999 B.A. L.575 J.D. [Ⓐ Sutherland A.&B.]
*PRACTICE AREAS: Corporate; Securities.
Liniado, Mark E. ... '68 '99 C.918 B.A. L.880 J.D. [Ⓐ Dow,L.&A.]

Liniak, Berenato, Longacre & White, LLC
(See Bethesda, Maryland)

Linick, Steve A. ... '63 '90 C&L.276 B.A., J.D. Asst. Dist. Atty.
Link, Jonathan ... '72 '98 C.339 B.S.E.E. L.1209 J.D. [Ⓐ Hunton&W.] (Pat.)
*PRACTICE AREAS: Intellectual Property Litigation; Prosecuting; Licensing.
Linkie, Matthew ... '72 '99 C.884 B.A. L.128 J.D. [Ⓐ Mann B.]
*PRACTICE AREAS: Civil Litigation; Commercial Law.

Linklaters
900 17th Street, N.W. Suite 450, 20006 ⊙
Telephone: 1-202- 296- 8337 Fax: 1-202- 296- 8454
Email: enquiries@linklaters.com URL: http://www.linklaters.com
Assistant Solicitor: Philippa Cottle (Not admitted in the United States).
OFFICES IN: Alicante, Antwerp, Bangkok, Berlin, Bratislava, Brussels, Bucharest, Budapest, Cologne, Frankfurt am Main, Hong Kong, London, Luxembourg, Madrid, Malmö, Milan, Moscow, Munich, New York, Paris, Prague, São Paulo, Shanghai, Singapore, Stockholm, Tokyo, Warsaw, Washington.
See Professional Biographies, WASHINGTON, DISTRICT OF COLUMBIA

Linney, Barbara D. ... '55 '82 C.011 B.Comm. L.024 LL.B. [Dyer E.&J.]
*PRACTICE AREAS: Securities; Mergers and Acquisitions; International Trade; Import and Export Law; Executive Employment Law.
Linowes, R. Robert, (AV) '22 '49
C.299 L.178 LL.B. [Linowes&B.] (⊙Silver Spring, MD)‡

Linowes and Blocher LLP, (AV)
Suite 302, 1150 17th Street, N.W., 20036 ⊙
Telephone: 202-293-8510 Telecopier: 202-293-8513
Email: inbox@linowes-law.com URL: http://www.linowes-law.com
Partner Emeritus: R. Robert Linowes.
Real Estate Development, Zoning and Land Use, Municipal Law, Administrative Law, Banking, Corporate, Environmental Law, Municipal Finance, Bankruptcy/Workouts, Condominium/Community Association Development, Litigation, Real Estate Finance and Taxation, Securities Law.
Representative Clients: See Silver Spring, Maryland Office.
Silver Spring, Maryland Office: Suite 1000, 1010 Wayne Avenue. Telephone: 301-588-8580. Telecopier: 301-495-9044.
Greenbelt, Maryland Office: Suite 202, 6411 Ivy Lane. Telephone: 301-982-3382. Telecopier: 301-982-0595.
Annapolis, Maryland Office: 145 Main Street. Telephone: 410-268-0881. Telecopier: 301-261-2603.
Frederick, Maryland Office: 247 West Patrick Street. Telephone: 301-695-0244. Telecopier: 301-663-6656.
Columbia, Maryland Office: Suite B215, 10015 Old Columbia Road. Telephone: 410-312-5457. Fax: 410-290-5285.
See Professional Biographies, WASHINGTON, DISTRICT OF COLUMBIA

Linowitz, Sol M. ... '13 '38 C.299 A.B. L.188 J.D. 1875 Conn. Ave. N.W.
Linton, Katherine Connor ... '61 '88 C.478 B.A. L.1068 J.D. [Crispin&B.]
*PRACTICE AREAS: Professional Liability and Insurance Law; Commercial Litigation; Communications Law.
Linzmeyer, Peter C., (AV) ... '— '68 C&L.276 B.S., J.D. [Ⓑ Foley&L.]
*PRACTICE AREAS: Joint Ventures; Licensing; Business Acquisitions; Distribution; Strategic Alliances.
Liotta, Robert Case, (AV) ... '42 '69 C.103 A.B. L.276 J.D. [Liotta,D.&E.]
*PRACTICE AREAS: Family Law; Domestic Relations; Personal Injury; Tort Law; Criminal Law.

Liotta, Dranitzke & Engel, LLP, (AV)
Suite 250, 1666 Connecticut Avenue, N.W., 20009
Telephone: 202-797-7700 Facsimile: 202-797-2354
Email: attys@ldelaw.com
Members of Firm: Alan Dranitzke; Robert Case Liotta; Diana R. Engel. Associate: Regina A. DeMeo.
General Practice, Real Estate, Domestic Relations, Litigation, Torts, Business Law, Wills and Estates, Probate, Family Law, Divorce, Criminal Law and Mediation.
See Professional Biographies, WASHINGTON, DISTRICT OF COLUMBIA

Lipinski Galland, Stephanie A. '— '89 C.1329 B.A. L.945 J.D.
(adm. in VA; not adm. in DC) [Ⓑ Holland&K.]
*PRACTICE AREAS: State Tax; Local Tax; Electronic Commerce Taxation; Canadian Goods and Service Tax.
Lipinsky de Orlov, Lino S., (AV) '58 '83
C.103 A.B. L.569 J.D. [McKenna&C.] (⊙Denver, CO)
*PRACTICE AREAS: Civil Practice; Civil Appeals; Trial Practice; Technology Law.
Lipkin, Gary D., (AV) '52 '77 C.30 B.A. L.273 J.D.
Asst. Gen. Coun., Nat. Assn. of Sec. Dealers, Inc.
Lipkin, Harriet ... '— '78 C.910 A.B. L.1162 J.D. [Verner,L.B.M.&H.]
*PRACTICE AREAS: Labor Law; Employment Law; Civil Rights Law.
Lipman, Andrew D., (AV) ... '51 '77 C.696 B.A. L.813 J.D. [Swidler B.S.F.]
*PRACTICE AREAS: Regulatory Law; Telecommunications Law; Internet Law; Transportation Law.
Lipnick, Dale Keats ... '64 '89 C.94 B.S.B.A. L.276 J.D. 4763 Indian Lane, N.W.‡
Lipp, Christopher R. '69 '98 C.886 B.S.
(adm. in VA; not adm. in DC; See Pat. Sect.) [Ⓐ Sughrue M.]
*PRACTICE AREAS: Intellectual Property.

Lipp, Mark N., (AV) . . . . '49 '74 C.446 B.A. L.64 J.D. [Shook,H.&B.]
*PRACTICE AREAS: Communications Law; Administrative Law.
Lippard, Benjamin S. '73 '98 C.684 B.A. L.893 J.D.
(adm. in VA; not adm. in DC) [Ⓐ Vinson&E.]
*PRACTICE AREAS: Administrative Law; Environmental Law.
Lippincott, Victoria L. . . . . '71 '97 C&L.500 B.P.A., J.D. [Ⓐ Collier S.S.]
Lippman, Solaman G. . . . . '12 '37 C&L.145 B.A., J.D. [Lippman&S.]
*PRACTICE AREAS: Employment Law; Arbitration.

Lippman & Semsker, PLLC, (BV)
1120 G Street, N.W., Suite 200, 20005-3801
Telephone: 202-824-8100 Fax: 202-824-8199 URL: http://www.lippmansemsker.com
Email: mail@lippmansemsker.com URL: http://www.lawyers.com/lippman&semskerlaw
Solaman G. Lippman; Richard H. Semsker. Associate: Shannon Micah Salb.
Labor and Employment, Wrongful Termination, Civil Rights, Discrimination (age, sex, race, disability), Disabilities, Retaliation, Sexual Harassment, Computers and Software, e-Commerce Law, Technology Law, Small Business Law, Corporate Law, Civil Practice, Appellate Practice.
See Professional Biographies, WASHINGTON, DISTRICT OF COLUMBIA

Lipps, Andrew L., (AV) . . . . '49 '75 C.855 B.A. L.813 J.D. 3000 K St., N.W.
Lipresti, Peter, (AV) . . . . . . '52 '77 C.1044 B.A. L.276 J.D. [Jackson&C.] (⊙Vienna, VA)
*PRACTICE AREAS: Corporate Law; Health Care; Taxation.
Lipsen, Charles B. . . . . '25 '51 C&L.966 B.S., J.D. 1826 Calvert St. N.W.
Lipsen, Zel E., (AV) . . . . . '32 '65 C.966 B.S. L.30 J.D. One Mass Avenue, N.W. Suite 330
Lipsett, Linda, (AV) . . . . '51 '77 C.112 B.A. L.273 J.D. [Bernstein&L.]
*PRACTICE AREAS: Labor Law.
Lipsey, Charles E., (AV) '50 '77
C.277 B.S.Ch.E. L.273 J.D. [Finnegan,H.F.G.&D.] (See Pat. Sect.)
*PRACTICE AREAS: Intellectual Property Litigation; Patent Infringement.
Lipsher, Robert I. . . . . '51 '77 C.156 B.A. L.184 J.D. [Luse L.G.P.&S.]
Lipshie, Jonathan W. . . . . '60 '88 C.276 B.S.F.S. L.880 J.D. [Ⓒ Arter&H.]
*PRACTICE AREAS: Litigation; Bankruptcy.
Lipshultz, Frank L., (AV) . . . . '46 '72 C.446 B.A. L.64 J.D. [Lipshultz&H.] ⊙
*PRACTICE AREAS: Labor and Employment; Employment Disabilities; Workers Compensation Defense; Workers Compensation Insurance; Employment Claims Defense.
Lipshultz, Leonard L., (AV) . . . . '22 '56 C.30 B.S. L.904 J.D. [Lipshultz&H.] ⊙
*PRACTICE AREAS: Products Liability Defense; Automotive Product Liability; Recreational Vehicles; Medical Malpractice Defense; Defense Litigation.
Lipshultz, Stanley L., (AV) . . . . '44 '71 C.910 A.B. L.30 J.D. [Ⓒ Lipshultz&H.] ⊙

Lipshultz and Hone, Chartered, (AV)
Suite 200, 2000 L Street, N.W., 20036 ⊙
Telephone: 202-872-0909
Leonard L. Lipshultz; John Llewellyn Hone; Frank L. Lipshultz; Ronald G. DeWald; Michael T. O'Bryant; Stephen S. Brown; James R. Schraf;—Victor I. Weiner (Not admitted in DC); Christopher A. Conte. Of Counsel: Stanley L. Lipshultz.
Products Liability Defense, Insurance Agents and Brokers Errors and Omissions Defense, Defense Insurance Law (including coverage opinions and analysis), Environmental, Pollution, Contamination and Toxic Tort Claims and Defense, Property Insurance Law (including Fire, Marine and Inland Marine Claims), Excess, Surplus Lines and Reinsurance Claims and Defense, Employment Law, Workers Compensation Defense, Professional Liability Defense (including medical and professional malpractice), General Civil and Criminal Trial Practice and State Courts, Corporate, Probate and Real Estate.
Silver Spring, Maryland Office: Suite 108 Montgomery Center, 8630 Fenton Street. Telephone: 301-587-8500. Fax: 301-495-9759.
See Professional Biographies, WASHINGTON, DISTRICT OF COLUMBIA

Lipsitz, Alan J. . . . '53 '84 C.454 B.A. L.209 J.D. Exec. Dir., BlueCross BlueShield Assn.
Lipson, David R. . . . . '70 '94 C.1036 B.A. L.596 J.D. [Ⓐ Morgan,L.&B.]
Lipson, Jack L., (AV) . . . . '32 '58 C.102 A.B. L.309 LL.B. [Arnold&P.]
*PRACTICE AREAS: Litigation.
Lipson, Kevin J., (AV) . . . . '55 '80 C.273 B.A. L.910 J.D. [Hogan&H.]
*PRACTICE AREAS: Energy.
Lipstein, Robert A., (AV) . . . . '54 '78 C&L.813 A.B., J.D. [Lipstein,J.&L.]
*PRACTICE AREAS: Antitrust; Trademark & Copyright; Corporate; International Trade.

Lipstein, Jaffe & Lawson L.L.P., (AV)
1900 M Street, N.W. Suite 700, 20036-3508
Telephone: 202-296-6655 Telecopier: 202-296-0848
Email: Lawinfo@LJLLaw.com URL: http://www.LJLLaw.com
Members of Firm: Robert A. Lipstein; Matthew P. Jaffe; Grace W. Lawson. Associate: Joseph A. Konizeski.
Practice before Federal and Local Courts, and Federal Agencies, specializing in counseling and litigation in the areas of Antitrust, Corporate, Consumer Protection, International Trade and Intellectual Property.
See Professional Biographies, WASHINGTON, DISTRICT OF COLUMBIA

Liptak, Charlotte S. '53 '78 C.509 B.A. L.424 J.D.
VP State Gov. Rel., Amer. Gen. Corp.
Lipton, Jane S. . . . . '49 '73 C.575 B.A. L.818 J.D. 1666 Connecticut Ave. N.W.
Lipton, Joshua . . . . '72 '99 C.31 B.A. L.477 J.D. [Ⓐ Gibson,D.&C.]
*PRACTICE AREAS: Antitrust.
Lisowski, Ronald J., Jr. . . . . '70 '97 C.339 B.A. L.904 J.D. 909 U St., N.W.
Lispcome, Marie-Claire Brown, (BV) . . . . '60 '85 C.94 B.A. L.846 J.D. [Robinson&G.]
Liss, Brian Z. . . . . '— '99 C.696 B.A. L.273 J.D. [Ⓐ Morgan,L.&B.]
Liss, Burton D . . . . '— '67 C.446 B.S. L.30 J.D. [B.D.Liss]
Liss, Franklin R. . . . . '65 '93 C.659 B.A. L.245 J.D. [Ⓐ Arnold&P.]
*PRACTICE AREAS: Antitrust.
Liss, Jeffrey F., (AV) . . . . '51 '75 C&L.477 B.A., J.D. [Piper M.R.&W.]
*PRACTICE AREAS: Litigation; Insurance Law; Environmental Law.
Liss, Marvin, (CV) '60 '86 C.1048 B.S.B.A. L.904 J.D.
(adm. in MD; not adm. in DC) 5301 Wisconsin Ave., N.W.
Liss, Burton D., P.C. . . . . 5301 Wisconsin Avenue, N.W., Suite 640
Lister, James H. . . . . '69 '94 C&L.945 B.A., J.D. [Ⓐ McGuireWoods]
*PRACTICE AREAS: Creditors Rights; Bankruptcy; Telecommunications; Commercial Litigation.
Lister, Penelope M. "Gari" . . . . '65 '92 C.914 B.A. L.273 J.D. [Morgan,L.&B.]
Litch, Christopher Scott '61 '88 C&L.446 B.A., J.D.
Gen. Coun. & Assoc. Exec. Dir., American Association of Dental Schools
Litchtman, Joanne '62 '88 C.882 B.A. L.309 J.D.
(adm. in CA; not adm. in DC) Natural Res. Def. Council
Litman, Gary V. . . . . '61 '92 C.999 M.A. L.273 J.D. U.S. Chamber of Commerce

Litman Law Offices, Ltd.
(See Arlington, Virginia)

Litmans, Murray Ian, (AV) '37 '62 C.31 B.A. L.477 J.D.
401 9th Street, N.W, Suite 900
Litow, Jason R. . . . . '75 '01 C.188 B.A. L.273 J.D. [Ⓐ Covington&B.]
Litowitz, Robert D. . . . . '56 '81 C.216 B.A. L.273 J.D. [Finnegan,H.F.G.&D.]
*PRACTICE AREAS: Trademark Litigation.
Litt, Daniel M., (AV) . . . . '52 '78 C.823 B.A. L.276 J.D. [Dickstein S.M.&O.]
*PRACTICE AREAS: Bankruptcy Law; Creditors Rights; Commercial Litigation.
Litt, David G. . . . . '62 '89 C.976 B.A. L.145 J.D. [O'Melveny&M.]
*PRACTICE AREAS: Mergers and Acquisitions; Joint Ventures; Finance; International Business Law.
Litt, Robert S., (AV) . . . . '49 '78 C.309 A.B. L.976 J.D. [Arnold&P.]
*PRACTICE AREAS: White Collar Criminal Litigation; Civil Litigation.

Littell, Richard, (AV) '31 '57 C.188 A.B. L.309 J.D.
1220 Nineteenth Street, N.W. Suite 400, 20036
Telephone: 202-466-8260 Fax: 202-293-4377
Email: littell@dgs.dgsys.com
Utility Rates, Airline Regulation, Postal Regulation, Gas Utility Regulation, Endangered Species.
See Professional Biographies, WASHINGTON, DISTRICT OF COLUMBIA

Littell, Susan A. . . . . '68 '96 C.446 B.S. L.564 J.D. [Ⓐ Dickstein S.M.&O.]
*PRACTICE AREAS: Litigation.
Little, Caroline H., (AV) '59 '86 C.918 B.A. L.569 J.D.
Chf. Oper. Affcr., Washington Post, Newsweek Interactive
Little, Fred A., (AV) . . . . '31 '58 C.293 B.A. L.309 LL.B. 2300 N St., N.W.
Little, Holly H. . . . . '69 '93 C.454 B.A. L.588 J.D. [Hand,L.P.&C.]
Little, Kara D. . . . . '73 '98 C.893 B.A. L.276 J.D. [Ⓐ Dow,L.&A.]
Little, Kathleen C., (AV) . . . . '53 '80 C.446 B.S. L.273 J.D. [Vinson&E.]
*PRACTICE AREAS: Litigation.
Little, Robert C., (BV) . . . . '51 '83 C.446 B.A. L.64 J.D. Asst. U.S. Atty.
Littlefield, Bridget E. '73 '00 C&L.446 B.A., J.D.
(adm. in MD; not adm. in DC) [Ⓐ Crowell&M.]
Littlejohn, J. Michael . . . . '— '94 C.575 B.A. L.1209 J.D. [Feith&Z.]
Littlejohn, Roy . . . . '33 '61 C&L.329 B.A., LL.B. 7080 31st St., N.W.
Littlepage, Samuel D., (AV) . . . . '47 '77 C.923 B.A. L.1209 J.D. [Dickinson W.]
*PRACTICE AREAS: Trademark Litigation; Copyright Litigation; Unfair Competition Litigation.

Littler Mendelson, A Professional Corporation, (AV)
1225 I Street, N.W., Suite 1000, 20005-3914 ⊙
Telephone: 202-842-3400 Facsimile: 202-842-0011
Email: info@littler.com URL: http://www.littler.com
Peter A. Susser; Mark A. de Bernardo; Kevin L. Wright; Joseph P. Harkins; Todd Andrew Bromberg; Annita M. Riddick; Ronald I. Tisch; Paul J. Kennedy; Jason M. Branciforte; Garen E. Dodge; Maria A. Perugini;—Nancy N. Delogu; Katherine Anne Goetzl; Janis A. Thom; Tessa J. Gelbman; Stacy Holmes Hawkins; Margarita D. Santos (Not admitted in DC); Christa Haas. Of Counsel: Joseph E. Schuler.
Offices located in: Phoenix, Arizona, California — Bakersfield, Fresno, Los Angeles, Oakland, Palm Desert, Sacramento, San Diego, San Francisco, San Jose, Santa Maria, Santa Rosa, Stockton and Walnut Creek; Denver, Colorado; Atlanta, Georgia; Chicago, Illinois; Baltimore, Maryland; Minneapolis, Minnesota; Reno and Las Vegas, Nevada (a partnership with Hicks & Walt); Newark, New Jersey; New York, New York; Columbus, Ohio; Philadelphia and Pittsburgh, Pennsylvania; Dallas and Houston, Texas; and Seattle and Yakima, Washington
See Professional Biographies, WASHINGTON, DISTRICT OF COLUMBIA

Liu, Goodwin H. '70 '98 C.813 B.S. L.976 J.D.
(adm. in CA; not adm. in DC) [Ⓐ O'Melveny&M.]
Liu, Henry . . . . '72 '97 C.446 B.S. L.273 J.D. [Ⓐ Morgan,L.&B.]
Liu, Jessie K. . . . . '73 '98 C.309 A.B. L.976 J.D. [Ⓐ Jenner&B.]
*PRACTICE AREAS: Litigation.
Livedalen, Kristi J., (BV) '65 '91 C.174 B.A. L.990 J.D.
(adm. in CA; not adm. in DC) 1120 Twentieth Street, N.W.
Lively, P. Susan . . . . '58 '90 C.420 B.S. L.861 J.D. [Ⓒ Paul,H.J.&W.]
*PRACTICE AREAS: Environmental Law; Food and Drug Law; Health Care.
Liverman, Thierry J. . . . . . . '48 '71 C.273 B.A. L.309 J.D. Pres., M. Chatel Associates, Inc.
Livingston, Catherine E. . . . . '65 '92 C&L.976 B.A., J.D. [Caplin&D.]
*PRACTICE AREAS: Tax; Non Profit Organizations.
Livingston, Donald R., (AV) . . . . '52 '77 C&L.280 A.B., J.D. [Akin,G.S.H.&F.]
*PRACTICE AREAS: Labor and Employment.
Livingston, S. William, Jr., (AV) . . . . '44 '70 C.118 B.A. L.309 J.D. [Covington&B.]
Livingstone, James D. . . . . '73 '98 C.184 B.A. L.273 J.D. [Ⓐ Cleary,G.S.&H.]
Livnat, Shmuel (Sandy) '48 '92
C.999 B.S. L.273 J.D. [Venable,A.B.H.&C.] (See Pat. Sect.)
Llaurado, Mireya A.R. . . . . '72 '98 C.112 B.A. L.276 J.D. [Ⓐ Heller E.W.&M.]
Llewellyn, Scott . . . . '68 '98 C.976 B.A. L.477 J.D. [Ⓐ Wilmer,C.&P.]

Llewellyn, Thomas Sayre, (AV) '55 '80 C.893 B.A. L.273 J.D.
5125 MacArthur Boulevard, N.W. Suite 32A, 20016
Telephone: 202-237-7291 Fax: 202-237-7884
Email: t.llewellyn@worldnet.att.net URL: http://www.lawyers.com/llewellyn
***PRACTICE AREAS: Environmental Law; Federal Administrative Law; Air Pollution; Water Pollution; Hazardous Waste.**
Environmental law and litigation practice with emphasis on agency proceedings and appellate litigation. Resource Conservation and Recovery Act (RCRA), Clean Air Act, Clean Water Act, and other environmental laws.
See Professional Biographies, WASHINGTON, DISTRICT OF COLUMBIA

Lloyd, Anna R. . . . . '53 '90 C.1280 B.B.A. L.128 J.D. 6706 14th Pl. N.W.
Lloyd, Brian D. . . . . '66 '96 C.690 B.A. L.904 J.D. [Lloyd&M.]
*PRACTICE AREAS: Personal Injury; Criminal Defense.
Lloyd, Frank W., (AV) . . . . '41 '68 C.951 B.A. L.309 LL.B. [Mintz,L.C.F.G.&P.]
*PRACTICE AREAS: Communications Law; Cable TV.
Lloyd, Henry M., (AV) . . . . '35 '73 C.188 B.A. L.276 J.D. [Ⓒ Cadeaux&T.]
*PRACTICE AREAS: Litigation; Antitrust.
Lloyd, James T. '— '67 C.375 B.A. L.802 LL.B.
Sr. V.P. & Gen. Coun., Natl. Railroad Passenger Corp. (AMTRAK)
Lloyd, Mark I. . . . . '54 '93 C.477 B.A. L.276 J.D. 1200 New Hampshire Ave., N.W.
Lloyd, Timothy A. . . . . '57 '82 C.473 B.A. L.966 J.D. [Hogan&H.]
*PRACTICE AREAS: Taxation; Corporate Law; Partnership Law; Estate Planning.

Lloyd & Marcotte, PLLC
645 Pennsylvania Avenue SE, 2nd Floor, 20003
Telephone: 202-548-0856 Fax: 202-548-2647
Email: lloyer@kreative.net URL: http://www.lawyers.com/lloyd&marcotte
David P. Marcotte; Brian D. Lloyd.
General Practice, Personal Injury, Criminal Defense, Real Estate, Social Security Disability.
See Professional Biographies, WASHINGTON, DISTRICT OF COLUMBIA

Lo, Albert . . . . '66 '97 C.420 B.S. L.146 J.D. [Ⓐ White&C.]
Lo, Josephine S. . . . . '57 '88 C.500 B.A. L.276 J.D. [Ⓒ Shaw P.]
*PRACTICE AREAS: Tax.
Lobel, Douglas P. . . . . '57 '84 C.311 B.A. L.273 J.D. [Kelley D.&W.]
*PRACTICE AREAS: Litigation; Telecommunications Law; White Collar Criminal Litigation; Business Crimes; Securities Arbitrations.
Lobel, Martin, (AV) . . . . '41 '65 C&L.94 A.B., J.D. [Lobel,N.&L.]
*PRACTICE AREAS: Entertainment and Art; Civil Litigation; U.S. Supreme Court Litigation.

Lobel, Novins & Lamont, (AV)
Suite 770, 1275 K Street, N.W., 20005
Telephone: 202-371-6626 Telecopier: 202-371-6643 URL: http://www.lnllaw.com
Email: lobel@lnllaw.com URL: http://www.lawyers.com/lobelnovinslamont
Members of Firm: William J. Lamont (1916-1994); Martin Lobel; Jack A. Blum; Lee Ellen Helfrich; Henry M. Banta. Of Counsel: Alan S. Novins; Arthur L. Fox, II; Mark Zaid.
Civil and Administrative Practice. Energy Law, Communications, Natural Resources, Public Lands Law, Taxation, International Law, Antitrust, Legal Ethics, Litigation in Federal Courts.
See Professional Biographies, WASHINGTON, DISTRICT OF COLUMBIA

Lobl, Peter W. . . . . '64 '93 C.311 B.A. L.228 J.D. 1863 California St. N.W., Ste. 4
Lobred, Thomas L. . . . . '— '69 C.446 B.A. L.597 J.D. [Ⓒ Miller] (⊙Kansas City, MO)
*PRACTICE AREAS: International Trade Law; U.S. Foreign -Trade Zones; Customs Law.

LoCascio, Gregg F. . . . . . '70 '95 C.886 B.S.M.E. L.602 J.D. [Kirkland&E.]
*PRACTICE AREAS: Intellectual Property; General Litigation.
Lock, Reinier H. J. H., (AV) . . . . '42 '73 C&L.999 B.Com., LL.B. [Ⓒ Cameron M.]
Locke, Paul A. . . . . '55 '84 C.95 A.B. L.880 J.D. 1616 P Street, N.W.
Locke, Thomas T. . . . . '60 '91 C.560 B.S.E.E. L.273 J.D. [Ross,D.&B.]
Locklin, Tracy Anderson . . . . '69 '98 C&L.893 B.A., J.D. [Ⓐ Dow,L.&A.]
Locklin-George, Barbara E. '57 '87
C.66 B.A. L.477 J.D. UMWA Health & Retirement Funds
Lockridge Grindal Nauen P.L.L.P., (AV)
601 Pennsylvania Avenue, N.W. (⊙Mpls., MN)
Lockwood, James C. '44 '74 C.506 B.S. L.823 J.D.
(adm. in NY; not adm. in DC) Contract Coun., Lockheed Martin Ims.
Lockwood, Karen M., (AV) . . . . '50 '78 C.970 B.A. L.904 J.D. [Howrey S.A.&W.]
*PRACTICE AREAS: Litigation; Arbitration; Antitrust.
Lockwood, Peter Van N., (AV) . . . . '40 '68 C&L.309 A.B., J.D. [Caplin&D.]
*PRACTICE AREAS: Civil Litigation; Corporation Law; Securities Law.
Lockyer, Charles W., Jr. . . . . '44 '96 C.262 A.B. L.276 J.D. [Ⓐ Fried,F.H.S.&J.]
*PRACTICE AREAS: Corporate; Banking Regulation; E-Commerce.
Lodde, Kelly '71 '00 L.1119 J.D.
(adm. in IN; not adm. in DC) [Ⓐ Holland&K.]
*PRACTICE AREAS: Timeshare; Resort Development.
Lodge, Deborah M. . . . . '51 '77 C.914 B.A. L.93 J.D. [Patton B.]
Loeb, Daniel E. . . . . '53 '82 C.172 B.S. L.174 J.D. [Fried,F.H.S.&J.]
Loeb, Eric H. '68 '96 C.95 B.A. L.276 J.D.
(adm. in OR; not adm. in DC) 555 13th St., N.W.‡
Loeb, G. Hamilton, (AV) . . . . '51 '79 C.893 B.A. L.309 J.D. [Paul,H.J.&W.]
*PRACTICE AREAS: Commercial Litigation; Technology Litigation; Intellectual Property Litigation; Financial Litigation; Patent Litigation.
Loeb, Laura E. . . . . '59 '84 C.339 B.S. L.813 J.D. [Hogan&H.]
*PRACTICE AREAS: Medicare and Medicaid; Regulatory Law.
Loeffler, Robert H., (AV) . . . . '43 '69 C.309 A.B. L.178 J.D. [Morrison&F.]
*PRACTICE AREAS: Alternative Dispute Resolution; Energy; Intellectual Property.
Loeffler, Thomas G., (AV) . . . . '46 '71 C&L.846 B.B.A., J.D. [Loeffler,J.&T.] ⊙
*PRACTICE AREAS: Government Affairs.

Loeffler, Jonas & Tuggey, L.L.P., (AV)
1801 K Street NW, Suite 340K, 20006-0301 ⊙
Telephone: 202-775-4430 Fax: 202-775-0836
Partners: Thomas G. Loeffler; W. James Jonas, III.
Administrative Law, Appellate Practice, Banks and Banking, Business Law, Commercial Law, Contracts, Corporate Law, Election, Campaign and Political Law, Environmental Law, Finance, Government, Health Care, Litigation, Mergers, Acquisitions and Divestures, Mortgages, Municipal Law, Probate, Real Estate, Securities, Sports Law, Wills.
San Antonio, Texas Office: One Riverwalk Place, 700 North Saint Mary's Street, Suite 800, 78205. Telephone: 210-354-4300. Fax: 210-354-4034. Email: info@ljtlaw.com.
Austin, Texas Office: 1005 Congress Avenue, Suite 330, 78701. Telephone: 512-479-6403. Fax: 512-479-8282.
See Professional Biographies, WASHINGTON, DISTRICT OF COLUMBIA

Loepere, Carol Colborn, (BV) . . . . '— '85 C.681 B.A. L.569 J.D. [Reed S.]
*PRACTICE AREAS: Health Care.
Loera, Patricia E. . . . . '67 '00 1030 15th Street Northwest, Suite 470
Loessberg, Shari . . . . '60 '88 C.276 A.B. L.846 J.D. 2300 N St., N.W.
Loevinger, Lee, (AV) . . . . '13 '36 C&L.494 B.A., J.D. [Ⓒ Hogan&H.]
*PRACTICE AREAS: Antitrust and Trade Regulation; Business Combinations; Appellate Practice.
Loewenstein, K. Karen . . . . '— '97 C.999 B.S. L.276 J.D. [Ⓐ Morgan,L.&B.] (Pat.)
Loewinger, Andrew P. . . . . '53 '84 C.170 B.A. L.276 J.D. [Buchanan I.]
*PRACTICE AREAS: Franchising; Antitrust; International Franchising; Distribution.
Loewinger, Kenneth J., (AV) . . . . '45 '71 C&L.276 B.A., J.D. [Loewinger&B.]
*PRACTICE AREAS: Real Property Law; Landlord and Tenant Law; Condominium Law; Cooperative Housing Law; Environmental Law.

Loewinger & Brand, PLLC, (AV)
471 H Street, N.W., 20001
Telephone: 202-789-2382 Fax: 202-789-0939 http://www.loewinger-brand.com
URL: http://www.lawyers.com/loewinger&brandlaw
Kenneth J. Loewinger; Michael E. Brand.
Landlord-Tenant, Commercial Real Estate Law, including matters dealing with Lead Paint and Oil Tank Storage, Arbitration and Mediation, Bankruptcy, Construction Law, and Complex Corporate and Commercial Litigation.
See Professional Biographies, WASHINGTON, DISTRICT OF COLUMBIA

Loffredo, Brian A. '74 '99 C.446 B.A. L.128 J.D.
(adm. in MD; not adm. in DC) [Ⓐ Goldstein&L.]
*PRACTICE AREAS: Employment Law; Family Law.
Lofgren, Mark L. . . . . '62 '92 C.446 B.S. L.945 J.D. [Groom]
*PRACTICE AREAS: Pension and Profit Sharing; Employee Benefits; ERISA.
Loftis, James R., III, (AV) . . . . '43 '68 C.902 A.B. L.273 J.D. [Gibson,D.&C.]
*PRACTICE AREAS: Antitrust.
Loftman, Kelli '— '97 C.755 B.A. L.300 J.D.
(adm. in MN; not adm. in DC) Cntr. for Jus. & Intl. Law
Loftus, C. Michael, (AV) . . . . '46 '73 C.1115 B.S. L.128 J.D. [Slover&L.]
Lofwall, Ian C. . . . . '73 '98 C.597 B.A. L.146 J.D. [Ⓐ McGuirewoods]
*PRACTICE AREAS: Executive Compensation; Employee Benefits.
Logan, Charles W., Jr. . . . . '61 '89 C.309 A.B. L.976 J.D. [Metzger&M.]
Logan, John S., (AV) . . . . '53 '79 C.880 B.A. L.893 J.D. [Dow,L.&A.]
Logan, Kimberly Marie Taylor . . . . '65 '91 C.1280 B.A. L.1029 J.D. 7603 Georgia Ave.
Logan, Robert Scott '62 '00 C.446 B.S. L.273 J.D.
(adm. in VA; not adm. in DC) [Ⓐ Shaw P.]
Logan, Stuart J. '59 '85 C.235 B.S. L.29 J.D.
(adm. in MD; not adm. in DC) [Ⓒ Moore&B.]
LoGerfo, Gregory D. '73 '00 C.472 B.A. L.945 J.D.
(adm. in NY; not adm. in DC) Political Officer
Logwood, Kenneth W., (AV) . . . . '48 '78 C.454 B.A. L.976 J.D. [Womble C.S.&R.]
*PRACTICE AREAS: Real Estate.
Lohmann, Walter H., Jr., (AV) . . . . '58 '83 C.188 A.B. L.273 J.D. [Kirkland&E.]
*PRACTICE AREAS: Environmental Transaction Support; Environmental Counseling.
Loiseau, Holly E. Washington . . . . '70 '95 C.893 B.A. L.273 J.D. [Ⓐ Weil,G.&M.]
Lomax, Dionne C. . . . . '70 '95 C.329 B.B.A. L.659 J.D. [Ⓐ Vinson&E.]
*PRACTICE AREAS: Litigation; Antitrust.
Lomax, Jason A. . . . . '— '98 C&L.93 B.A., J.D. [Ⓐ Morgan,L.&B.]
Lomax, Tarrant H., (AV) . . . . '46 '77 C.502 B.A. L.273 J.D. [T.H.Lomax] ⊙

Lomax, Tarrant H., Esq., P.C., (AV)
4530 Wisconsin Avenue, N.W., Suite 200, 20016 ⊙
Telephone: 202-537-7320 Fax: 202-686-0896
Email: tarrantlomax@abanet.org
Tarrant H. Lomax.
Civil and Commercial Litigation, Contracts, Construction Law, Government Contracts, Business Law, Business Formation, Corporate Law, Maritime Law, Trusts and Estates, Wills, Probate.
Annapolis, Maryland Office: 613 Third Street. Telephone: 410-267-6151.
See Professional Biographies, WASHINGTON, DISTRICT OF COLUMBIA

Lomba, Alicia D. . . . . '— '99 C.472 B.A. L.276 J.D. [Ⓐ Miller&C.]
*PRACTICE AREAS: International Law; International Trade; Foreign Asset Control; Customs Law; Export Regulation.
Lombard, Matthew Jackson . . . . '74 '00 C.165 B.A. L.273 J.D. 633 Indiana Ave., N.W.
Lombardi, Marianne Elizabeth '67 '93
C&L.823 B.A., J.D. Dep. Dir., Center for Law & Democracy
Lonardo, Joseph D., (AV) . . . . '47 '72 C.276 A.B. L.477 J.D. [Vorys,S.S.&P.]
*PRACTICE AREAS: Litigation; Environmental Law.
London, Eric D. . . . . '64 '90 C.1036 B.A. L.273 J.D. 430 S. Capitol St., S.E.
London, Lawrence Alan '61 '87 C.659 B.A. L.813 J.D.
(adm. in NY; not adm. in DC) [Ⓐ Ruben&A.]
*PRACTICE AREAS: Corporate Law; Mergers and Acquisitions; Tax Law.
London, Lisa Peller, (AV) . . . . '64 '89 C.188 B.S. L.273 J.D. [Finnegan,H.F.G.&D.]
*PRACTICE AREAS: International Trademarks; Trademark Protection; Trademark Prosecution; Trademark Litigation.
London, Mark, (AV) . . . . '52 '79 C.31 B.A. L.273 J.D. [London&M.]
*PRACTICE AREAS: Civil Litigation.
London, Ronald G. . . . . '68 '95 C.260 B.S. L.276 J.D. [Ⓐ Hogan&H.]
*PRACTICE AREAS: Communications; Telecommunications; Internet; Trademark.
London, Sheldon I. . . . . '38 '64 C.197 A.B. L.184 LL.B. 1156 15th St., N.W.

London & Mead, (AV)
1225 Nineteenth Street, Northwest Suite 320, 20036
Telephone: 202-331-3334 Fax: 202-785-4280
URL: http://www.lawyers.com/london&meadlaw
Mark London; Christopher B. Mead.
Civil and Criminal Litigation, Business Litigation, Commercial Litigation, White Collar Criminal Defense, Personal Injury, Wrongful Death, Complex Litigation, Complex and Multi-District Litigation.
See Professional Biographies, WASHINGTON, DISTRICT OF COLUMBIA

Long, Andrew K. . . . . '70 '99 C.205 B.A. L.659 J.D. [Ⓐ Wiley R.&F.]
Long, Bernard J., Jr., (AV) . . . . '40 '65 C.321 A.B. L.893 LL.B. [Dow,L.&A.]
Long, C. Thomas . . . . '42 '71 C.197 A.B. L.309 J.D. 1450 G St. N.W.‡
Long, Catherine E. . . . . '64 '95 C.893 B.A. L.94 J.D. [Ⓐ Covington&B.]
*PRACTICE AREAS: Insurance; Litigation; White Collar Crime.
Long, Charles B. . . . . '64 '94 C.808 B.A. L.425 J.D. 3050 K St., N.W.
Long, Cheryl Marie, (AV) . . . . '49 '75 C&L.276 B.S.F.S., J.D. Dir., Pub. Def. Serv.
Long, Darren E. '69 '00 C.48 B.A. L.665 J.D.
(adm. in VA; not adm. in DC) [Ⓐ Dickstein S.M.&O.]
*PRACTICE AREAS: Litigation.
Long, Gina D. '— '97 C.30 B.A. L.776 J.D.
(adm. in NJ; not adm. in DC) America's Most Wanted
Long, Joel M. . . . . '71 '98 C.174 B.A. L.273 J.D. [Ⓐ Henrichsen S.]
*PRACTICE AREAS: Construction Law; Surety Law; Commercial Law; Civil Litigation.
Long, Kerry B. . . . . '50 '81 C.165 A.B. L.188 J.D. [Fulbright&J.]
*PRACTICE AREAS: Corporate Finance; Aircraft Finance and Leasing.
Long, Kraig B. . . . . '68 '99 C.831 B.B.A. L.446 J.D. [Ⓐ Arnold&P.]
*PRACTICE AREAS: Litigation.
Long, Leonard L., Jr., (BV) . . . . '56 '83 C.511 B.A. L.329 J.D. [Long&Assoc.]
Long, Mary Beth . . . . '63 '98 C.645 B.A. L.902 J.D. [Ⓐ Williams&C.]
*PRACTICE AREAS: Litigation.
Long, Meredith N. '73 '98 C.902 B.A. L.945 J.D.
(adm. in VA; not adm. in DC) [Ⓐ Falk]
*PRACTICE AREAS: Civil Trials; Civil Appeals; Commercial Contracts; Government Contracts; Estate Administration.
Long, Rachell F. '71 '96 C.273 B.A. L.112 J.D.
(adm. in CA; not adm. in DC) 218 Rittenhouse St., N.E.
Long, Robert A., Jr . . . . '58 '87 C.575 B.A. L.976 J.D. [Covington&B.]
Long, Stuart J. . . . . '42 '68 C.321 A.B. L.273 J.D. [O'Brien&L.]
*PRACTICE AREAS: Municipal Law.
Long, Victor E., (AV) . . . . '54 '80 C.367 B.A. L.588 J.D. [Regan,H.&L.] ⊙
*PRACTICE AREAS: Medical Malpractice; Personal Injury; Construction Accidents; Wrongful Death; Automobile Injuries.

Long Aldridge & Norman LLP, (AV)
A Limited Liability Partnership including Professional Corporations
Suite 600, 701 Pennsylvania Avenue, N.W., 20004 ⊙
Telephone: 202-624-1200 FAX: 202-624-1298
Email: dc@lanlaw.com URL: http://www.lanlaw.com
Members of Firm: Philip D. Bartz (Resident); Gaspare J. Bono (Resident); Cameron Cohick (Resident); Dennis A. Davison (Resident); Gordon D. Giffin; Song K. Jung (Resident); C. Randall Nuckolls (Resident); Ian K. Portnoy (Resident); Ira S. Shapiro (Resident); Edgar H. Sims, Jr. (P.C.). Resident Associates: Katherine R. Blanchette (Not admitted in DC); Lesley E. Daigle; Donna M. Donlon; Brian E. Finch; Rebecca A. Goldman; Stephen M. Lastelic; Adrian P.J. Mollo; Anna W. Nicol; Kenneth D. Springer. Of Counsel: John M. Kelly (Not admitted in DC).
General Litigation and Appellate Practice before Federal and State Courts and Regulatory Agencies, Antitrust, Public Utilities, Natural Gas and Electric Power Regulations, Federal and State Taxation, Corporate, Commercial, Securities, Real Property, Environmental, Immigration, Government Relations, Communications, Healthcare, Financial Restructurings, Transportation Matters, Intellectual Property and Patent, International Law and Transactions, Technology, Public Finance, Sports and Entertainment Law , Estate Planning and Administration and Employee Benefits.
Atlanta, Georgia Office: Suite 5300, 303 Peachtree Street, 30308. Telephone: 404-527-4000. Telecopier: 404-527-4198.
See Professional Biographies, WASHINGTON, DISTRICT OF COLUMBIA

Long & Associates, P.C., (BV) . . . . 1818 Eleventh St., N.W.
Long Law Firm, (AV) . . . Suite 750, 801 Pennsylvania Avenue, N.W. (⊙Baton Rouge, LA)
Longacre, James B. . . . . '68 '96 C.288 B.A. L.276 J.D. [Ⓐ McDermott,W.&E.]
Longanecker, Stacey J. '65 '93
C.446 B.S.E.E. L.128 J.D. [Roylance,A.B.&G.] (See Pat. Sect.)
*PRACTICE AREAS: Patent, Trademark and Copyright Law; Electrical Patent Law; Computer Law.
Longmuir, Shelley A., (AV) '56 '84 C.103 B.A. L.569 J.D.
V.P., Governmental Affairs, United Airlines, Inc.
Longosz, Edward J., II, (AV) . . . . '55 '83 C.717 B.A. L.607 J.D. [Eckert S.C.&M.]
*PRACTICE AREAS: Product Liability; Medical Malpractice Liability; Professional Liability; Fraud, Insurance and Commercial Litigation.
Longstreet, Susan Cannon, (AV) . . . . '44 '84 C.273 B.A. L.945 J.D. [Winston&S.]
*PRACTICE AREAS: Real Estate Finance; Commercial Real Estate; Real Estate Acquisitions; Real Estate Investment Trusts; Real Property.
Longstreth, John L. . . . . '56 '82 C.311 B.A. L.309 J.D. [Preston G.E.&R.M.]
*PRACTICE AREAS: Antitrust; Aviation; Litigation.
Longsworth, Jeffrey S. . . . . '62 '91 C.31 B.A. L.128 J.D. [Ⓒ Kelley D.&W.]
*PRACTICE AREAS: Environmental Law.
Longwell, John H. . . . . '70 '00 C.893 B.A. L.280 J.D. [Ⓐ Kellogg,H.H.T.&E.]
*PRACTICE AREAS: Litigation.
Lonian, Andrea G. . . . . '72 '98 C.276 A.B. L.309 J.D. [Ⓐ Spiegel&M.]
*PRACTICE AREAS: Energy; Litigation; Communications Law.
Lookadoo, Phillip G. . . . . '53 '80 C.923 B.S. L.245 J.D. [Thelen R.&P.] (Pat.)
*PRACTICE AREAS: Infrastructure Development; Energy Marketing Transactions; Energy Regulation; Project Finance; International Transactions.
Loomis, Ralph E. '49 '79 C.273 B.A. L.904 J.D.
(adm. in IL; not adm. in DC) New England Electric Sys.
Looney, Joseph D. . . . . '71 '96 C.999 B.A. L.446 J.D. [Ⓐ Weil,G.&M.]
*PRACTICE AREAS: Consumer Finance; Banking.

Loope, Sarah J. '— '01 C.475 B.A. L.477 J.D.
(adm. in MI; not adm. in DC) [Ⓐ Manatt,P.&P.]
Loos, Dickson R., (AV) '24 '49 C.197 B.A. L.273 LL.B.
2100 Pennsylvania Ave., N.W.
Loots, James M., (AV) ... '58 '84 C.597 B.S. L.477 J.D. [Goldstein&L.]
*PRACTICE AREAS: Employment Law; Litigation; Small Business Law; Association Law; Franchise Law.
Lopardo, Robert C. ... '57 '82 C.893 B.A. L.276 J.D. MCI Telecom. Corp.
Lopatkiewicz, Stefan M., (AV) ... '48 '73 C.893 B.A. L.309 J.D. [Ⓑ Dorsey&W.]
*PRACTICE AREAS: Telecommunications; International Corporate Law; Nonprofit Organizations; Satellite Law.

Lopatto, John S., III, (AV) '51 '76 C.659 B.A. L.1017 J.D.
1800 K Street, NW Suite 300, 20006-2202
Telephone: 202-861-5800 1-800-814-3447 1-888-887-6399 Fax: 202-861-5802
Email: JLopatto3@aol.com URL: http://www.lawyers.com/lopattolaw
Automobile Crash Worthiness, Negligence, Personal Injury, Automobile Accidents, Wrongful Death, Head Trauma, Government Contracts, Professional Malpractice, Medical Malpractice, Products Liability, General Business and Commercial Litigation, Intellectual Property, Black Lung, Venture Capital. Complex Civil Litigation, Toxic Torts.
See Professional Biographies, WASHINGTON, DISTRICT OF COLUMBIA

Lopatto, Mary A. ... '54 '86 C.674 A.B. L.128 J.D. [LeBoeuf,L.G.&M.]
*PRACTICE AREAS: Reinsurance; Insurance; Litigation.
Lopes, Grace M. ... '55 '81 C.1123 B.A. L.1162 J.D. Spec. Master, Dist. Ct.
Lopez, Eugene A. '51 '78 C.999 B.A. L.724 J.D.
(adm. in NY; not adm. in DC) Asst. Gen. Coun., The Nasdaq Stock Market, Inc.
Lopez, Jeffrey J. ... '66 '96 C.770 B.A. L.276 J.D. [Ⓐ Drinker B.&R.]
Lopez, Jorge, Jr. ... '58 '84 C.128 B.A. L.309 J.D. [Akin,G.S.H.&F.]
*PRACTICE AREAS: Health Care.
Lopez, José M. ... '47 '78 C.478 B.A. L.818 J.D. Supr. Ct. J.
Lopez, Kurt E. '70 '98 C.477 B.A. L.912 J.D.
(adm. in MI; not adm. in DC) [Ⓐ Sutherland A.&B.]
*PRACTICE AREAS: Corporate Law; Securities Law.
Lopez, Margaret S. ... '62 '96 C.893 B.A. L.273 J.D. [Ⓐ Heenan,A.&R.]
*PRACTICE AREAS: Employment Law; Occupational Safety and Health Law; ERISA; Labor Law.
Lopez, Mark J. '59 '86 C.115 B.S. L.705 J.D.
(adm. in IL; not adm. in DC) The National Prison Proj.
Lopez, Richard E. '44 '85 C.768 B.A. L.329 J.D.
Dir., Substance Abuse Prog., D.C. Gen. Hosp.
Lopez, Stephen E. ... '67 '92 C&L.846 B.B.A., J.D. [Ⓐ Dow,L.&A.]
Lopina, Brian C. ... '55 '80 C.602 B.A. L.209 J.D. [Ⓑ Patton B.]
Lopp, Harriette H. ... '71 '96 C.198 B.A. L.228 J.D. [Ⓐ Hogan&H.]
*PRACTICE AREAS: Corporate Law; Securities.
Lorber, Lawrence Z., (AV) ... '47 '70 C.102 B.A. L.446 J.D. [Proskauer R.]
Lorber, Leah ... '64 '94 C&L.347 B.A., J.D. [Ⓑ Shook,H.&B.]
*PRACTICE AREAS: Torts; Insurance Litigation.
Lord, Linda L. ... '53 '84 C.446 B.S. L.128 J.D. 1201 New York Ave., N.W.
Lord, Susan M. '55 '85 C.446 B.A. L.64 J.D.
(adm. in MD; not adm. in DC) Sr. Atty., MCI Communications Corporation
Lore, Kenneth G., (AV) ... '48 '73 C.30 B.A. L.904 J.D. [Swidler B.S.F.]
*PRACTICE AREAS: Structured Finance; Real Estate; Housing; Securities.
Lorello, David S. '74 '01 C.705 B.A. L.178 J.D.
(adm. in NJ; not adm. in DC) [Ⓐ Steptoe&J.]
Lorenzo, June L. '60 '88 C.1264 B.A. L.188 J.D.
(adm. in NM; not adm. in DC) Staff Atty., Indian Law Resource Ctr.
Lorenzo, Richard M. '51 '75 C.1044 B.S. L.930 J.D.
(adm. in NY; not adm. in DC) [Huber L.&A.] ⊙
*PRACTICE AREAS: Litigation; Antitrust Law; Energy Law; Public Utility Law; Securities.
Lorenzo-Giguere, Paul Joseph '63 '91 C.999 B.S. L.1218 J.D.
(adm. in NY; not adm. in DC) 800 North Capital Street
Lorman, Alvin J., (AV) ... '45 '75 C.1353 B.A. L.893 J.D. [Mintz,L.C.F.G.&P.]
*PRACTICE AREAS: Food and Drug; Environmental; Health Care Law.
Lorndale, Robert G., Jr. ... '61 '96 C.880 B.A. L.284 J.D. [Ⓐ Dewey B.]
*PRACTICE AREAS: Taxation.
Losch, Robert E., (AV) ... '26 '53 C.436 B.S. L.276 LL.B. [R.E.Losch]

Losch, Robert E., P.C., (AV)
1716 New Hampshire Avenue, N.W., 20009-2502
Telephone: 202-296-4222 Fax: 202-745-1747
Robert E. Losch.
General Civil Practice before Federal Courts and Agencies, Administrative, Legislative, Government Contracts and Environmental Law.

Losey, Franklin W. '41 '64 C&L.150 A.B., J.D.
(adm. in OH; not adm. in DC) Gen. Coun., Brown & Co. Inc.
Losey, James A. ... '53 '90 C.604 B.A. L.813 J.D. [Skadden,A.S.M.&F.]
Loss, Lewis K. ... '58 '83 C.477 B.A. L.309 J.D. [Ross,D.&B.]
Lostumbo, Rachel '66 '98 C.72 B.A. L.276 J.D.
(adm. in MD; not adm. in DC) 1825 K St.
Lotkin, Ralph L. ... '46 '71 C.801 B.A. L.838 J.D. 201 Massachusetts Ave NE
Lotstein, Robert S., (AV) ... '61 '87 C.30 B.S.B.A. L.904 J.D. [Lotstein B.]
*PRACTICE AREAS: Mortgage Banking Law; Real Estate; Business Transactions; Commercial Litigation.

Lotstein Buckman, LLP, (AV)
5185 MacArthur Boulevard, N.W., 20016-3341
Telephone: 202-237-6000 Facsimile: 202-237-8900
Email: info@lotsteinbuckman.com URL: http://www.lotsteinbuckman.com
Steven M. Buckman; Robert S. Lotstein;—Stephanie L. Shaw; Paul A. Mondor; Anna Campo Pané; Charlotte K. Booncharoen (Not admitted in DC).
Mortgage Banking, Real Estate, Title, Condominium, Foreclosure, Business Transactions, Commercial Litigation, Probate, and Bankruptcy.
See Professional Biographies, WASHINGTON, DISTRICT OF COLUMBIA

Lotterman, Thomas R. ... '56 '83 C.674 A.B. L.477 J.D. [Swidler B.S.F.]
*PRACTICE AREAS: Environmental Law; Administrative Law; Litigation; Communications and Media; Commercial Law.
Loubier, Erin Michelle '70 '98 C.222 B.A. L.30 J.D.
Pub. Bene. Atty., Whitman-Walker Clinic Legal Servs.
*RESPONSIBILITIES: Social Security; Medicare and Medicaid.
Loughlin, Charles A. ... '67 '94 C.550 B.A. L.276 J.D. [Howrey S.A.&W.]
*PRACTICE AREAS: Antitrust; Commercial Litigation.
Loughlin, Peter J. '68 '98 C.999 B.A. L.602 J.D.
(adm. in NY; not adm. in DC) [Ⓐ Hunton&W.]★
*PRACTICE AREAS: Litigation; Intellectual Property; Antitrust.
Loughlin, Stephanie M. ... '64 '88 C.128 B.A. L.893 J.D. [Dow,L.&A.]
Loughney, Robert M. '55 '81 C.754 B.S. L.831 J.D.
(adm. in PA; not adm. in DC) [Couch W.] ⊙
*PRACTICE AREAS: Energy Law; Environmental Law.
Loughran, Alice E. ... '66 '95 C.210 B.A. L.365 J.D. [Ⓐ Steptoe&J.]
Louisell, John C., (AV) '47 '75 C.912 B.A. L.213 J.D.
(adm. in MI; not adm. in DC) 1742 N Street, N.W. (⊙Detroit, MI)
Louison, Audrey C. '58 '94 L.93 J.D.
(adm. in VA; not adm. in DC) [Ⓐ Hunton&W.] (⊙Richmond, VA)

Loulakis, Michael C., (AV) '54 '79
C.860 B.S.C.E. L.94 J.D. [Wickwire G.] (⊙Vienna, VA)
*PRACTICE AREAS: Construction Law; Project Delivery Systems; Alternative Dispute Resolution; Government Contracts; Public Contract Law.
Lourie, Vanessa Carpenter ... '53 '78 C.329 B.A. L.276 J.D. [Ⓑ V.C.Lourie]
*PRACTICE AREAS: Civil Litigation; Real Estate Law; Corporate Law; Domestic Relations; Personal Injury.

Lourie, Vanessa Carpenter, P.C.
4400 MacArthur Boulevard, NW, Suite 205, 20007-2521
Telephone: 202-342-8000 Facsimile: 202-342-9000
Email: vlourie@vclaw.zyan.net URL: http://www.lawyers.com/commercialrealestate
Counsel: Vanessa Carpenter Lourie.
Commercial and Real Estate Litigation, Commercial and Real Estate Transactions, Landlord and Tenant Law, Acquisitions, Finance Restructuring, Leasing, Contracts, Collections, Partnerships, Wills, Estates, Trusts, Personal Injury, Domestic Relations.
See Professional Biographies, WASHINGTON, DISTRICT OF COLUMBIA

Louthian, Robert C., III ... '62 '87 C.896 B.A. L.945 J.D. [McDermott,W.&E.]
Louvion, Sebastien Francois ... '74 '01 L.692 J.D. [Ⓐ Keller&H.]
*PRACTICE AREAS: Food and Drug Regulation; Intellectual Property.
Love, Andrew J. ... '72 '97 C.1349 B.A. L.276 J.D. [Ⓐ Shaw P.]
*PRACTICE AREAS: Bankruptcy; Creditors Rights; Litigation.
Love, Margaret Colgate ... '— '77 C.771 B.A. L.976 J.D. [Ⓑ Brand&F.]
*PRACTICE AREAS: Post-Conviction Remedies; Professional Conduct; Government Ethics.
Love, Peter J. ... '68 '94 C.112 B.A. L.145 J.D. [Ⓐ Jones,D.R.&P.]
Lovelady, Stephen T. ... '57 '90 C.1086 B.S.M.E. L.326 J.D. [Ⓐ Thompson H.]
*PRACTICE AREAS: Commercial Transactions; Corporate; Securities; Real Estate; Banking.
Loveland, Christopher M. ... '74 '00 C.397 B.A. L.94 J.D. [Ⓐ Schmeltzer,A.&S.]
*PRACTICE AREAS: Commercial Litigation; Franchise Law; Election and Campaign Finance.

Lovells, (AV)
401 9th Street, N.W., Suite 1150, 20004 ⊙
Telephone: +1-202 783-6144 Fax: +1 202 783-6250
Email: information@lovells.com URL: http://www.lovells.com
Resident Partner: Anne Price Fortney. Resident Lawyer: Markus B. Heyder; Julia A. Novina (Not admitted in DC); Andrew MacGregor Smith.
Concentrating in consumer financial services, privacy and federal regulatory compliance.
Alicante, Spain Office: Lovells Boesebeck Droste, Bilbao 1, 5° Piso, 03001 Alicante. Telephone: +34 96 514 41 05. Fax: +34 96 514 43 03.
Amsterdam, Netherlands Office: Frederiksplein 42, 1017 XN Amsterdam. Telephone: +31 20 55 33 600. Fax: +31 20 55 33 777.
Beijing, Republic of China Office: Suite 414 Tower B, COFCO Plaza, 8 Jianguomennei Dajie, Beijing 100005. Telephone: +86 10 6526 3490. Fax: +86 10 6526 3492.
Berlin, Germany Office: Lovells Boesebeck Droste, Schlüterstrasse 37, 10629 Berlin. Telephone: +49 30 8 89 19-0. Fax: +49 30 8 89 19-100.
Brussels, Belgium Office: Lovells Boesebeck Droste, Avenue Louise 523, Bte 24, 1050 Brussels. Telephone: +32 -2 647 06 60. Fax: +32-2 647 11 24.
Budapest, Hungary Associated Office: Squarra & Partos, Andrassy ut. 2, 1061 Budapest. Telephone: +36 1 474 2080. Fax: +36 1 474 2081.
Chicago, Illinois Office: One IBM Plaza, 330 North Wabash Avenue, Suite 1900, Chicago, IL 60611. Telephone: +1 312 832 4400. Fax: +1 312 832 4444.
Dresden, Germany Office: Lovells Boesebeck Droste, Heideparkstrasse 4, 01099 Dresden. Telephone: +49 351 829 61-0. Fax: +49 351 829 61-99.
Dusseldorf, Germany Office: Lovells Boesebeck Droste, Kennedydamm 17, 40476 Düsseldorf. Telephone: +49 211 13 68-0. Fax: +49 211 32 44 39.
Frankfurt, Germany Office: Lovells Boesebeck Droste, Darmstädter Landstrasse 125, 60598 Frankfurt am Main. Telephone: +49 69 962 36-0. Fax: +49 69 962 36-100.
Hamburg, Germany Office: Lovells Boesebeck Droste, Warburgstrasse 50, 20354 Hamburg. Telephone: +49 40 419 93-0. Fax: +49 40 419 93-200.
Ho Chi Minh City, Vietnam: 10th Floor, OSIC Building, 8 Nguyen Hue Street, District 1, Ho Chi Minh City. Telephone: +84 8 829 5100. Fax: +84 8 829 5101.
Hong Kong Office: 23rd Floor, Cheung Kong Center, 2 Queen's Road Central, Hong Kong. Telephone: +852 2219 0888. Fax: +852 2219 0222.
London, England Office: 65 Holborn Viaduct, London EC1A 2DY. Telephone: +44 20 7296 2000. Fax: +44 20 7296 2001.
Milan, Italy Office: Via F.lli Gabba 3, 20121 Milan. Telephone: +39 02 7202 521. Fax: +39 02 7202 5252.
Moscow, Russia Office: 5th Floor, Usadba Centre, 22 Voznesensky, Pereulok, Moscow 103032. Telephone: +7 095 933 3000. Fax: +7 095 933 3001.
Munich, Germany Office: Lovells Boesebeck Droste, Marstallstrasse 8, 80539 München. Telephone: +49 89 290 12-0. Fax: +49 89 290 12-222.
New York, N.Y. Office: 900 Third Avenue, 16th Floor, New York, NY 10022. Telephone: +1 212 909 0600. Fax: +1 212 909 0666.
Paris, France Office: 37 Avenue Pierre 1er de Serbie, 75008, Paris. Telephone: +33 1 53 67 47 47. Fax: +33 1 47 23 96 12.
Prague, Czech Republic Office: Slovanský dům, Na Příkopě 22, 110 00 Prague 1. Telephone: +420 2 2141 1700. Fax: +420 2 2421 0004.
Rome, Italy Office: Via Due Macelli 66, 00187 Rome. Telephone: +39 06 675 8231. Fax: +39 06 6758 2323.
Singapore Office: 80 Raffles Place #54-01 UOB Plaza 1, Singapore 048624. Telephone: +65 538 0900. Fax: +65 538 7077.
Tokyo, Japan Office: 3rd Floor, Joware Hanzomon, 2-19 Hayabusa-cho, Chiyoda-ku Tokyo 102-0092. Telephone: +81-3 3221 8511. Fax: +81-3 3221 8560.
Vienna, Austria Associated Office: Graben 29 A, 1010 Vienna. Telephone: +43 1 53 55 744. Fax: +43 1 53 50 649.
Warsaw, Poland Office: Lovells Boesebeck Droste, ul. Nowogrodzka 50, 00695 Warszawa. Telephone: +48 22 529 29 00. Fax: +48 22 529 29 01.
Zagreb, Croatia Associated Office: Mirko Bogdanović & Tin Dolički, ul. Alexandera von Humboldta 4b/III, 10000 Zagreb. Telephone: +385 1 6 15 95 95. Fax: +385 1 6 15 77 33.
Revisers of the German Law Digest for this directory
See Professional Biographies, WASHINGTON, DISTRICT OF COLUMBIA

Lovinger, Todd D. ... '66 '92 C.446 B.S. L.273 J.D. Envir. Atty., Afton Assoc., Inc.
Lovitch, Karen S. ... '— '95 C.923 B.A. L.30 J.D. 701 Pennsylvania Avenue, N.W.

Lovitky, Jeffrey A., (AV) '54 '80 C.477 B.A. L.1187 J.D.
1735 New York Avenue N.W., Suite 700, 20006
Telephone: 202-429-3393 Fascimile: 202-318-4013 URL: http://www.lawyers.com/lovitky
Email: jeff@lovitky.com URL: http://www.lovitky.com
(Board Certified Health Law Lawyer, Florida Bar Board of Legal Specialization and Education).
Health Law, Medicare Law including Reimbursement Disputes and Payment Suspensions; Fraud and Abuse; Health Privacy; Government Contracts Law.
See Professional Biographies, WASHINGTON, DISTRICT OF COLUMBIA

Lovrien, Christopher J. ... '72 '98 C.1268 B.A. L.309 J.D. [Ⓐ Jones,D.R.&P.]
Low, Lucinda A., (AV) ... '— '77 C.668 B.A. L.1068 J.D. [Miller&C.]
*PRACTICE AREAS: Business Law; Corporate Law; International Law; International Trade; Investments.
Lowans, David L '51 '97 C.276 B.S.F.S. L.229 J.D.
[Karp,F.L.W.&N.] (⊙Rockville, MD)
*PRACTICE AREAS: Corporate; Securities; Commercial Law; Real Estate.
Lowe, Allen J., (AV) ... '51 '77 C.30 B.A. L.904 J.D. [Ashcraft&G.]
*PRACTICE AREAS: Workers Compensation.
Lowe, Ira M. ... '24 '49 C.276 L.273 J.D. 2700 Q St., N.W.
Lowe, James W. ... '63 '90 C.976 B.A. L.309 J.D. [Wilmer,C.&P.]
*PRACTICE AREAS: Antitrust; EU Competition; Aviation Law; Aviation Defense; Telecommunications Law.
Lowe, Jeffrey Alan ... '65 '90 C.188 B.S. L.945 J.D. [Hogan&H.]
*PRACTICE AREAS: Corporate Law; Mergers and Acquisitions.
Lowe, John C., (AV) ... '36 '67 C.401 B.S. L.893 J.D. [Finnegan,H.F.G.&D.]
*PRACTICE AREAS: Patent Litigation; Trademark Litigation; Copyright Litigation; Trade Secrets Litigation.

Lowe, Marta T. ... '71 '96 C.911 B.A. L.145 J.D. [🄰 Shaw P.]
Lowe, Mary Baroody ... '62 '91 C.893 B.A. L.945 J.D. [🄲 Powell,G.F.&M.]
*PRACTICE AREAS: Government Contracts Law.
Lowe, Randall B., (AV) ... '48 '73 C.690 B.A. L.910 J.D. [Davis W.T.]
*PRACTICE AREAS: Communications Law.
Lowell, Abbe David, (AV) ... '52 '77 C&L.178 B.A., J.D. [Manatt,P.&P.]
Lowell, H. Bret, (AV) ... '53 '78 C.1044 B.A. L.276 J.D. [Piper M.R.&W.]
*PRACTICE AREAS: Franchising; Trade Regulation; Corporate; Trademarks.
Lowell, James R. '43 '83 C.150 B.S.M.E. L.1161 J.D.
(adm. in OH; not adm. in DC) U.S. Telephone Assn.
Lowen, Martin K. ... '64 '91 C.446 B.S. L.659 J.D. MCI Communications Corp.
Lower, Janice L., (AV) ... '53 '81 C.012 B.A. L.273 J.D. [Duncan,W.G.&P.]
*PRACTICE AREAS: Energy; Communications Law; Public Utility Law.
Lowery, Charles R., Jr. ... '54 '80 C.813 B.A. L.477 J.D. Off. of the City Admr.
Lowery, Richard C. ... '41 '67 C.198 B.A. L.893 LL.B. [Wiley R.&F.]
*PRACTICE AREAS: Antitrust; Litigation.
Lowery, Ruth Ann ... '72 '97 C.484 B.A. L.904 J.D. [🄰 Beveridge&D.]
*PRACTICE AREAS: Environmental Law; Environmental Litigation.
Lowinger, Brian Marc '70 '00 C.273 B.S. L.128 J.D.
(adm. in MA; not adm. in DC) [🄰 Arent F.K.P.&K.]
*PRACTICE AREAS: Telecommunications.
Lowman, Michael K. ... '67 '93 C.107 B.A. L.904 J.D. [🄰 Arent F.K.P.&K.]
*PRACTICE AREAS: Commercial Litigation; Securities Litigation; Shareholder Litigation; Construction; Government Contracts.
Lowrey, Carmen Guzman ... '61 '86 C&L.37 B.A., J.D. 1775 Eye St.
Lowry, Mark Alan '61 '00 C.352 B.S. L.276 J.D.
(adm. in MD; not adm. in DC) [🄰 Vinson&E.]
*PRACTICE AREAS: Biotechnology; Health Law; Intellectual Property; White Collar Crime; International Law.
Lowther, Frederick M., (AV) ... '43 '69 C.103 A.B. L.976 J.D. [Dickstein S.M.&O.]
*PRACTICE AREAS: Administrative Law; Energy Law; International Practice; Water Law.
Lowy Tinsky, Karen '74 '98 C.112 B.A. L.273 J.D.
(adm. in CA; not adm. in DC) [🄰 Hale&D.]
Loy, Frank E., (AV) '28 '53 C.112 A.B. L.309 J.D.
Pres., The German Marshall Fund of the U.S.
Loy, Jennifer G. '74 '00 C.976 B.A. L.178 J.D.
(adm. in GA; not adm. in DC) [🄰 Gibson,D.&C.]
*PRACTICE AREAS: Litigation.
Loyd, Susan Danielle ... '70 '96 C.112 B.A. L.1194 J.D. [🄰 Swidler B.S.F.]
*PRACTICE AREAS: Environmental Law.
Lu, Christopher P. ... '66 '92 C.674 A.B. L.309 J.D. Ste. 511
Lu, Curtis P. ... '— '91 C.893 B.A. L.309 J.D. [Latham&W.]
*PRACTICE AREAS: Securities Litigation; Health Care Fraud; Commercial Litigation.
Lu, Ji ... '70 '98 C.293 B.A. L.569 J.D. [🄰 Paul,W.R.W.&G.]
Luband, Charles A. ... '67 '97 C.103 B.A. L.309 J.D. [🄰 Powell,G.F.&M.]
*PRACTICE AREAS: Health Law.
Luberda, R. Alan, (AV) ... '59 '85 C.273 B.A. L.188 J.D. [🄲 Collier S.S.]
*PRACTICE AREAS: International Trade; Customs Law.
Lubin, Michael A., (AV) '49 '74 C.390 A.B. L.472 J.D.
Vice President & General Counsel, Pathnet, Inc.
Lubin, Robert ... '57 '83 C.012 B.Com. L.472 J.D. [R.Lubin] ⊙
Lubin, Robert, P.C. ... 2000 L Street, N.W. (⊙Vienna, VA)
Lubitz, David M. ... '64 '91 C.309 A.B. L.178 J.D. [🄲 Swidler B.S.F.]
*PRACTICE AREAS: Public Interest Law; Litigation.
Lubkin, Gregory P. ... '— '96 C.999 M.A. L.309 J.D. [🄰 Shearman&S.]
*PRACTICE AREAS: Taxation; Federal Income Tax; International Income Tax; International Taxation; Tax Controversies.
Lublin, Edward L., (AV) ... '40 '66 C&L.477 B.B.A., J.D. [Dyer E.&J.]
*PRACTICE AREAS: Corporate Law; Securities; Mergers and Acquisitions.
Lubrano, Michael '61 '88 C.309 A.B. L.569 J.D.
(adm. in NY; not adm. in DC) World Bank
Luby, Arthur M., (AV) ... '53 '80 C.103 B.A. L.477 J.D. [O'Donnell,S.&A.]
*PRACTICE AREAS: Labor Law; Employee Benefits Law; Transportation Law.
Lucas, Bradford '75 '01 C.893 B.A. L.1209 J.D.
(adm. in VA; not adm. in DC) [🄰 Fried,F.H.S.&J.]
*PRACTICE AREAS: Corporate; Securities.
Lucas, Katherine Collins ... '73 '00 C.893 B.A. L.276 J.D. [🄰 Keller&H.]
*PRACTICE AREAS: Telecommunications Law.
Lucas, Reginald '70 '01 C.1083 B.S. L.945 J.D.
(adm. in VA; not adm. in DC) [🄰 Sterne,K.G.&F.]
*PRACTICE AREAS: Electrical Intellectual Property.
Lucas, Richard M. ... '65 '90 C.276 B.S.B.A. L.976 J.D. [Arnold&P.]
*PRACTICE AREAS: Real Estate; Litigation; Bankruptcy.
Lucas, Steven M., (AV) ... '48 '73 C.976 B.A. L.880 J.D. 1730 K Street, N.W., Suite 304
Luce, Gregory M., (AV) ... '51 '77 C.893 B.A. L.692 J.D. [Jones,D.R.&P.]
*PRACTICE AREAS: Litigation; Health Care Litigation; Health Care Fraud; False Claims Act.
Lucey, James J. O. ... '60 '86 C.205 B.S.B.A. L.276 J.D. 1101 Pennsylvania Ave. N.W.
Lucey, Paul R. ... '60 '91 C.309 A.B. L.188 J.D. [🄰 Dickstein S.M.&O.]
*PRACTICE AREAS: Insurance Litigation; Commercial Litigation.
Luchs, Richard W., (AV) ... '51 '77 C.604 A.B. L.273 J.D. [Greenstein D.&L.]
Luchs, Roger D., (AV) ... '51 '81 C.951 B.A. L.273 J.D. [King&N.] (⊙Arlington, VA)
*PRACTICE AREAS: Real Estate; Commercial Litigation; Civil Litigation; Personal Injury; Landlord and Tenant Law.
Luchsinger, Daniel W. ... '65 '92 C.494 B.S. L.276 J.D. [Miller&C.]
*PRACTICE AREAS: Taxation; Federal Income Tax; International Taxation; Tax Planning.
Luck, Stacey Kyle '75 '00 C.645 B.A. L.280 J.D.
(adm. in MD; not adm. in DC) [🄰 Vinson&E.]
*PRACTICE AREAS: Litigation.
Luckau, Erik W. '70 '98 C.383 B.B.A. L.276 J.D.
(adm. in CA; not adm. in DC) [🄰 Shearman&S.]
Ludaway, Natalie O., (AV) ... '61 '86 C.331 B.A. L.273 J.D. [Leftwich&D.]
Luddington, Natasha R. ... '74 '99 C.347 B.S. L.273 J.D. [🄰 Fried,F.H.S.&J.]
*PRACTICE AREAS: Corporate Finance; Corporate Law.
Ludovici-Lint, Joanne ... '64 '91 C.690 B.S. L.1048 J.D. [McDermott,W.&E.]
Ludwig, James M., III ... '53 '88 C.299 B.A. L.893 J.D. [Bode&G.]
*PRACTICE AREAS: Civil Rights; Internet Litigation; Computer Litigation; Commercial Litigation; Product Liability.
Ludwig, Kenneth D., (AV) ... '50 '77 C.311 B.A. L.309 J.D. [🄲 Steptoe&J.]
Ludwig, Robert W., Jr. ... '55 '82 C.165 B.A. L.902 J.D. [Ludwig&R.]
Ludwig, Stacy M. ... '63 '88 C&L.966 B.A., J.D. Asst. U.S. Atty.
Ludwig, Steven R. ... '60 '95 C.645 B.S. L.273 J.D. [Sterne,K.G.&F.] (See Pat. Sect.)
*PRACTICE AREAS: Intellectual Property Law; Interference Law; Litigation; Trade Secrets; Alternative Dispute Resolution.

Ludwig & Robinson, P.L.L.C.
555 Eleventh Street, N.W. Suite 850, 20004-1304
Telephone: 202-289-1800 Telecopier: 202-289-1804
Email: contact@ludwigrobinson.com URL: http://www.ludwigrobinson.com
Robert W. Ludwig, Jr.; Phillip L. Robinson; Michael H. Mobbs; Salvatore Scanio. Of Counsel: Ethan S. Burger; William L. Menard;—Glenn J. Melcher; Edwin Y. Szeto; Michael J. Kresslein; Evgenia V. Sorokina (Not admitted in DC; Foreign Legal Advisor).

(This Listing Continued)

Ludwig & Robinson, P.L.L.C. (Continued)
Domestic and International Civil Practice, Litigation, Arbitration and Mediation, Administrative, Aviation, Banking, Corporate Finance and Restructuring, Commercial Law, Mergers, Acquisitions and Divestitures, Computer, Technology and Internet. Employment, Export, Customs and Trade. Insurance, Products Liability, Negligence, Securities, Trademark and Telecommunications.
Affiliated Law Firm: K ümmerlein, Simon & Partner, Rechtsanwälte, Huyssenallee 58-64, D-45128 Essen, Germany. Telephone: 011-49-201-1756-600. Telecopier: 011-49-201-1756-666. Email: zentrale@Ksup.de
See Professional Biographies, WASHINGTON, DISTRICT OF COLUMBIA

Ludwikowski, Mark R. '71 '97 C&L.128 B.A., J.D.
(adm. in MD; not adm. in DC) [🄰 Sandler,T.&R.]
*PRACTICE AREAS: International Trade; Customs Regulation; International Business Law.
Ludwiszewski, Raymond B., (AV) ... '58 '85 C.588 B.S. L.309 J.D. [Gibson,D.&C.]
*PRACTICE AREAS: Environmental Law.
Luedke, John F. C. ... '68 '95 C.197 B.A. L.966 J.D. [🄰 Covington&B.]
*PRACTICE AREAS: Regulatory Law; Food and Drug Regulation.
Luers, Margaret F., (Miss) ... '12 '35 C&L.273 B.A., LL.B. 4201 Cathedral Ave., N.W.‡
Lugo-Cox, Christina A. ... '59 '96 C.840 B.F.A. L.1280 J.D. Asst. Corp. Coun.
Lui, Bradley S. ... '64 '89 C.976 B.A. L.1066 J.D. [Morrison&F.]
*PRACTICE AREAS: Antitrust; Civil Litigation; Criminal Litigation.
Lui, Lisa '66 '94 C.188 B.S. L.823 J.D.
(adm. in NJ; not adm. in DC) Sr. Counsel, World Bank
Luib, Gregory P. ... '71 '00 C&L.893 B.A., J.D. [🄰 Jones,D.R.&P.]
Luigs, David A. ... '66 '96 C.945 B.A. L.999 J.D. [🄰 Wilmer,C.&P.]
Lukas, Russell D., (AV) ... '46 '75 C.823 B.A. L.276 J.D. [Lukas,N.G.&S.]
*PRACTICE AREAS: Telecommunications Law; Appellate Practice.

Lukas, Nace, Gutierrez & Sachs, Chartered, (AV) BB
1111 19th Street, N.W., Suite 1200, 20036
Telephone: 202-857-3500 Telecopier: 202-842-4485
Email: lmng@fcclaw.com URL: http://www.fcclaw.com
Russell D. Lukas; David L. Nace; Thomas Gutierrez; Elizabeth R. Sachs; George L. Lyon, Jr.; Joel R. Kaswell; Pamela L. Gist; David A. LaFuria. Of Counsel: John J. McAvoy; Joseph K. Hage, III (Not admitted in DC);—Marilyn Suchecki Mense; Pamela C. Gaary-Holran; B. Lynn F. Ratnavale; Todd R. Slamowitz; David M. Briglia; Allison M. Jones; Steven M. Chernoff.
Telecommunications Law, Business Organizations, Commercial Transactions and Litigation.
See Professional Biographies, WASHINGTON, DISTRICT OF COLUMBIA

Luke, Jordan, (AV) ... '44 '73 C.976 A.B. L.659 J.D. [Davis P.&W.]
Luken, Susan J. ... '63 '88 C.150 B.A. L.904 J.D. [🄰 Mayer,B.&P.]
Lukitsch, Shirley M. '50 '86 C.665 B.A. L.1066 J.D.
(adm. in IL; not adm. in DC) [Schiff H.&W.]
*PRACTICE AREAS: Corporate; Securities; Banking.
Luley, John E. ... '47 '82 C.446 B.S. L.128 J.D. Potomac Elec. Power Co.
Luman, Joseph C. ... '36 '72 C.870 B.S. L.276 J.D. [🄲 Luman,L.&W.]
*PRACTICE AREAS: Association Law; Government Law.

Luman, Lange & Wheeler, (AV)
1660 L Street, N.W., Suite 506, 20036
Telephone: 202-463-1260 Fax: 202-463-6328
Email: LLW1660@aol.com URL: http://www.lawyers.com/lumanlange&wheeler
Members of Firm: Gene C. Lange; Christopher Wheeler; John W. Thomas. Associate: Sean P. McMullen (Not admitted in DC). Of Counsel: Joseph C. Luman.
Administrative Law, Antitrust, Business Law, Commercial Law, Education, Food and Drug Litigations, Trade and Professional Associations.
See Professional Biographies, WASHINGTON, DISTRICT OF COLUMBIA

Lund, Juli Ann '72 '98 C.802 B.A. L.976 J.D.
(adm. in MN; not adm. in DC) [🄰 Williams&C.]
Lund, Ronald E., (AV) '34 '62 C.350 B.S. L.838 LL.B.
(adm. in MN; not adm. in DC; Pat.) Gen. Coun., American Red Cross
Lund, Wendell, (AV) ... '05 '38 C.57 A.B. L.276 J.D. 3346 Tennyson St., N.W.‡
Lundberg, Rolf Th., Jr., (BV) ... '59 '85 C&L.893 B.A., J.D. Marriott Dr.
Lunde, Marvin C., III ... '— '98 C.575 B.A. L.846 J.D. [🄰 Foley&L.]
*PRACTICE AREAS: Securities Law.
Lundell, Karin J. '55 '00 C.055 B.A. L.569 J.D.
(adm. in NY; not adm. in DC) [🄰 Caplin&D.]
*PRACTICE AREAS: Tax Exempt Organizations; Taxation.
Lundman, Robert J. ... '71 '99 C.951 B.A. L.477 J.D. [🄰 Covington&B.]
Lundquist, Maryellen M. ... '64 '91 C&L.276 B.S.F.S., J.D. 1301 K St. N.W., Suite 800 E.
Lundquist, Thomas R. ... '52 '77 C.867 B.S. L.309 J.D. [🄲 Crowell&M.]
*PRACTICE AREAS: Federal Administrative Law; Endangered Species; National Environmental Policy Act (NEPA); Forestry Law; Public Land Law.
Lundy, Seth H. ... '69 '96 C.31 B.A. L.273 J.D. [🄰 Fulbright&J.]
*PRACTICE AREAS: Health Care; Litigation.
Lunenfeld, Douglas L. ... '70 '97 C&L.446 B.S., J.D. Coun., INTELSAT
Lunn, Mark P. ... '62 '96 C.1161 B.S. L.128 J.D. [🄰 Coudert B.]
*PRACTICE AREAS: International Trade; Export Control.
Lunnen, Robert C. '56 '85 C.101 B.A. L.425 J.D.
(adm. in UT; not adm. in DC) 1400 New York Ave., NW
Luparello, Stephen '59 '84 C.1031 B.A. L.902 J.D.
(adm. in VA; not adm. in DC) Nasdaq Stock Market, Inc.
Lupo, Anthony V. ... '64 '92 C.1356 B.A. L.329 J.D. [Arent F.K.P.&K.]
*PRACTICE AREAS: E-Commerce; Intellectual Property; International Intellectual Property; Licensing; Distance Education.
Lupo, Raphael V., (AV) ... '41 '68 C&L.273 B.S.E.E., J.D. [McDermott,W.&E.] (Pat.)
Luque, Nancy A., (AV) ... '— '76 C.763 B.A. L.1049 J.D. [Reed S.]
*PRACTICE AREAS: Litigation; Government Contracts; Export Compliance.
Luria, Edward M., (AV) '41 '68
[Alvord&A.] & [🄲 Damico&Assoc.; Moore&B.] (⊙Wilmington, DE)
*PRACTICE AREAS: Tax Law; Estate Planning; Employee Benefits; Asset Protection.
Luria, Joan M. '66 '92 C.446 B.A. L.823 J.D.
(adm. in MD; not adm. in DC) [🄰 Friedlander,M.S.K.&O.]
*PRACTICE AREAS: Commercial Finance; Commercial Real Estate; Commercial Leasing; Business Law.
Lurie, Dawn M. ... '65 '90 C.645 B.A. L.30 J.D. [D.Lurie]
Lurie, Dawn, Law Offices of ... 1100 Connecticut Avenue N.W. Suite 800
Luse, Eric, (BV) ... '52 '78 C.976 B.A. L.904 J.D. [Luse L.G.P.&S.]
*PRACTICE AREAS: Banking and Financial Institutions; Mergers and Acquisitions; Securities; Corporate.

Luse Lehman Gorman Pomerenk & Schick, A Professional Corporation, (AV)
5335 Wisconsin Avenue, N.W. Suite 400, 20015
Telephone: 202-274-2000 Facsimile: 202-362-2902
Email: john@luselaw.com URL: http://www.luselaw.com
Eric Luse; John J. Gorman; Robert B. Pomerenk; Kenneth R. Lehman; Alan Schick; Beverly White; Robert I. Lipsher; Edward A. Quint.
Banking and Financial Institutions, Savings and Loans, Mergers and Acquisitions, Securities and Corporate Law.
See Professional Biographies, WASHINGTON, DISTRICT OF COLUMBIA

Luskey, Lane M. '67 '93 C.846 B.B.A. L.861 J.D.
(adm. in TX; not adm. in DC) 1808 Connecticut Ave., N.W.
Luskin, Robert D., (AV) ... '50 '79 C&L.309 A.B., J.D. [Patton B.]
Lustig, Steven D. ... '68 '95 C.1036 B.A. L.823 J.D. [🄰 Stevens,D.M.&M.]

Lustman, Jeremy B. ....'73 '00 C.978 B.A. L.276 J.D. [▣ Latham&W.]
*PRACTICE AREAS: Telecommunications Law; Corporate Finance; Health Care Corporate Law; Business Acquisitions; Technology Law.
Lutes, Mark E. ....'56 '84 C&L.276 B.S.F.S., J.D. [Epstein B.&G.]
*PRACTICE AREAS: Health Law; Corporate Law; Insurance Law; Antitrust Law.
Luther, Cara J. ....'45 '88 C.953 B.A. L.446 J.D. [Baum,H.A.G.&S.]
*PRACTICE AREAS: Personal Injury; Wrongful Death; Products Liability; Railroad Accidents and Injuries; Mass Disaster Litigation.
Luther, Kurt Albert '68 '97
C.37 B.S.M.E. L.36 J.D. [▣ Finnegan,H.F.G.&D.] (See Pat. Sect.)
*PRACTICE AREAS: Patent Prosecution; Patent Litigation; Mechanical Patents; Computer and Software Patents; Electro-Mechanical Patents.
Luther, Paul T. ....'— '92 C.691 B.A. L.846 J.D. [▣ Verner,L.B.M.&H.]
Luthy, Teal E. ....'69 '00 C.188 B.A. L.145 J.D. [▣ Kellogg,H.H.T.&E.]
*PRACTICE AREAS: Litigation; Telecommunications Law.
Lutjen, Karen M. ....'— '96 C.94 B.S. L.602 J.D. [▣ Verner,L.B.M.&H.]
*PRACTICE AREAS: Taxation; Corporate; International Taxation.
Lutter, Rudolph V., Jr. '32 '61 C.645 B.A. L.309 J.D.
Prof. of Law, Howard Univ. School of Communications
Lutz, Christopher T., (AV) ....'49 '75 C.674 A.B. L.309 J.D. [Steptoe&J.]
*PRACTICE AREAS: Litigation; Insurance Law; Employment Law.
Lutz, Dara A. ....'64 '95 C.273 B.A. L.904 J.D. [▣ Jones,D.R.&P.]
Lutz, Holley Thames ....'67 '94 C.890 B.A. L.500 J.D. [▣ Gardner,C.&D.]
*PRACTICE AREAS: Health Care.
Lutz, Martin T. ....'— '89 C.602 B.A. L.846 J.D. [Verner,L.B.M.&H.]
Lutz, Nancy H. ....'59 '95 C.210 B.A. L.365 J.D. [▣ Pennie&E.] (See Pat. Sect.)
*PRACTICE AREAS: Litigation; Trademark Law; Copyright Law; Unfair Competition Law; Advertising Law.
Lutz, Warren C. ... '57 '85 C.276 B.A. L.273 J.D. [Jackson&C.] (⊙Balt., Rockville, MD)
*PRACTICE AREAS: Litigation; Products Liability; Construction Litigation; Construction Arbitration; Toxic Torts.
Lutzen, Helen E. '10 '39 C&L.966 B.A., J.D.
(adm. in WI; not adm. in DC) P.O. Box 1149‡
Lutzker, Gary S. ....'52 '94 L.978 J.D. [▣ Dow,L.&A.]
Luxenberg, Deborah, (AV) ....'49 '74 C.930 B.A. L.180 J.D. [Luxenberg,J.&D.]
*PRACTICE AREAS: Family Law; Domestic Relations; Gay and Lesbian Family Law; Divorce; Child Custody.

Luxenberg, Johnson & Dickens, P.C., (AV)
1244 19th Street, N.W., 20036
Telephone: 202-265-3340 Fax: 202-265-0101
Email: counsel@luxlaw.com URL: http://www.lawyers.com/luxenbergjohnsondickens
Deborah Luxenberg; Stephen D. Johnson; Dorrance D. Dickens.
Family Law, Domestic Relations, Gay and Lesbian Family Law, Divorce, Separation, Custody Litigation, Child Support, Adoption, Prenuptial and Marital Agreements, Family Law Mediation, Spousal Abuse, Domestic Violence, Probate, Estate Planning, Family Trusts, Wills, Employment Law (Employee Representation and Advice and Counsel to Management), Employment Discrimination, Wrongful Termination, Business Law, Nonprofit Organizations Law, Chancery and Equity, Federal Civil Practice, Litigation.
See Professional Biographies, WASHINGTON, DISTRICT OF COLUMBIA

Luxton, Jane C., (AV) ....'— '76 C.309 A.B. L.188 J.D. [King&S.]
*PRACTICE AREAS: Environmental.
Luzietti-Myers, Debra L. '53 '78 C.98 B.A. L.879 J.D.
(adm. in IL; not adm. in DC) Staff Atty., Paralyzed Vet. of Amer.
Lybecker, Martin E., (AV) ....'45 '70 C&L.911 B.A., J.D. [Ropes&G.]
Lyden, Thomas J. ....'49 '79 C.494 B.A. L.1035 J.D. [McKee N.]
*PRACTICE AREAS: Tax.
Lyle, Michael '63 '88 C.696 B.A. L.930 J.D.
(adm. in IL; not adm. in DC) [▣ Weil,G.&M.]
*PRACTICE AREAS: Litigation.
Lyles, David L. ....'62 '96 C.1280 B.B.A. L.128 J.D. Asst. Gen. Coun.
Lyman, Joseph J., (AV) ....'12 '38 C.103 B.A. L.273 LL.B. 1250 24th St., NW
Lyn, Jessica Glick ....'68 '98 C.1215 B.A. L.29 J.D. [▣ Cohen,M.H.&T.]
*PRACTICE AREAS: Civil Rights; Employment Discrimination; Antitrust.
Lynam, Terence J. ....'53 '78 C.659 B.A. L.276 J.D. [Akin,G.S.H.&F.]
*PRACTICE AREAS: Litigation; White Collar Criminal Defense.
Lynch, Andrew C. ....'— '82 C&L.893 B.A., J.D. [King&S.]
*PRACTICE AREAS: Corporate; Finance.
Lynch, George F. ....'12 '41 C.321 A.B. L.276 J.D. 6229 29th St., N.W.
Lynch, James M. ....'57 '83 C&L.893 B.A., J.D. 607 14th St., N.W.
Lynch, John C., (AV) ....'52 '79 C.390 B.A. L.744 J.D. [Macleay,L.G.&L.]
*PRACTICE AREAS: Insurance Defense; ERISA; Medical and Professional Liability; Product Liability Defense.
Lynch, John E., (AV) ...... '37 '64 C.262 B.S. L.276 J.D. [Fulbright&J.] (See Pat. Sect.)
*PRACTICE AREAS: Intellectual Property.
Lynch, John J. '59 '84 C&L.724 B.A., J.D.
(adm. in NY; not adm. in DC) [▣ Dillingham&M.] ⊙
*PRACTICE AREAS: Information Technology; Intellectual Property; Business Law; Employment Law; Civil Litigation.
Lynch, Joseph E. ....'56 '85 C.188 B.A. L.893 J.D. [▣ Vinson&E.]
*PRACTICE AREAS: Health Law.
Lynch, Karina V. '73 '99 C.1019 B.A. L.904 J.D.
(adm. in CT; not adm. in DC) [▣ Williams&J.]
*PRACTICE AREAS: Health Care; Pharmacy Law; Administrative Law; Antitrust.
Lynch, Marilyn T. '70 '96 C.446 B.A. L.1049 J.D.
(adm. in MD; not adm. in DC) [▣ Dickstein S.M.&O.]
*PRACTICE AREAS: Complex Commercial Litigation; Antitrust; Alternative Dispute Resolution; Insurance Coverage Litigation.
Lynch, Mark H., (AV) ....'44 '74 C.976 B.A. L.273 J.D. [Covington&B.]
Lynch, Michael C. ....'— '83 C.951 B.A. L.276 J.D. [Reed S.]
*PRACTICE AREAS: Labor and Employment.
Lynch, Patrick Winston ....'62 '88 C.228 B.A. L.178 J.D. [Dickstein S.M.&O.]
*PRACTICE AREAS: Energy; Project Finance; International Law; Water Law.
Lynch, Richard P. '33 '62 C&L.477 A.B., J.D.
Dir., Spec. Projects Off., Amer. Bar Assn.
Lynch, Robert P. ....'58 '85 C.884 B.A. L.744 J.D. [Macleay,L.G.&L.]
*PRACTICE AREAS: Insurance Liability Defense; Automobile; Subrogation.
Lynch, Timothy G. ....'67 '97 C.696 B.A. L.276 J.D. [▣ Shea&G.]
Lynes, Timothy J., (AV) ....'59 '84 C.1030 B.A. L.285 J.D. [Rosenman&C.]
Lynham, John M., Jr., (AV) ....'52 '83 C.855 B.S. L.273 J.D. [Ross,M.&F.]
*PRACTICE AREAS: Real Estate Law; Tax Law; Estate Planning; Trust Law.
Lynn, Daniel J. ....'69 '97 C.676 B.A. L.180 J.D. [▣ Jackson&C.]
*PRACTICE AREAS: Insurance Coverage; Insurance Defense Litigation.
Lynn, David E., (AV) ....'53 '82 C.103 A.B. L.276 J.D. [Docter,D.&L.]
*PRACTICE AREAS: Bankruptcy Law; Commercial Law; Reorganization Law.
Lynn, Giannina ....'61 '90 C.66 B.A. L.276 J.D. 1008 Pennsylvania Ave., S.E.
Lynn, James T. ... '27 '51 C.930 A.B. L.309 LL.B. Sr. Advisor, Lazard Freres & Co., LLC
Lyon, Edwin L. ....'47 '76 C.804 B.S. L.910 J.D. [Cadwalader,W.&T.]
*PRACTICE AREAS: Commodities Regulation; Investment Partnerships; Securities Offerings.
Lyon, George L., Jr., (AV) ....'54 '79 C.893 B.A. L.945 J.D. [Lukas,N.G.&S.]
*PRACTICE AREAS: Communications; Civil and Appellate Litigation; Transactions.
Lyon, Mary B. ....'66 '95 C.575 B.A. L.276 J.D. American University
Lyon, Richard K., (AV) ....'12 '36 C.197 A.B. L.276 J.D. 3107 Garfield St., N.W.

Lyon & Lyon LLP
A Limited Liability Partnership including Professional Corporations
Suite 1040, 1701 Pennsylvania Avenue, N.W., 20006 ⊙
Telephone: 202-331-3600 Fax: 202-331-3301
Email: lyon@lyonlyon.com URL: http://www.lyonlyon.com
Resident Partner: James T. Carmichael (Not admitted in DC). Resident Associate: Rouget F. Henschel. Resident Of Counsel: Scott H. Blackman; Suet M. Chong.
Intellectual Property, Patents, Trademarks, Copyrights, Technology and Science, Trade Secrets, Unfair Competition, Antitrust, Biomedical Devices, Chemical Compositions, Electrical Devices, Electronic Devices, Mechanical Devices, Biotechnology, Computers and Software, Internet Law, Internet Trademark Law, Software Copyright, Software Licensing, Software Protections, Franchises and Franchising, Patent Litigation, Trademark Litigation, Copyright Litigation, Patent Prosecution, Patents Reexaminations, Patent Reissues, Patent Interferences, Patent Appeals, Trademark Prosecution, Trademark Oppositions, Trademark Appeals, Artistic Design Protections, Trade Dress Protection, International Trade Commission, Intellectual Property Licensing, Technology Transfer, Intellectual Property Audits, Intellectual Property Portfolio Management, Intellectual Property Planning, Intellectual Property Opinion Letters and Intellectual Property General Counseling.
Los Angeles, California Office: Suite 4700, 633 West Fifth Street, 90071-2066. Telephone: 213-489-1600.
Irvine, California Office: Sixth Floor, 1900 Main Street, 92614. Telephone: 949-567-2300. Fax: 949-567-6600.
San Jose (Silicon Valley), California Office: Suite 800, 333 West San Carlos Street, 95110. Telephone: 408-993-1555. Fax: 408-287-2664.
La Jolla, California Office: Suite 800, 4225 Executive Square, 92037. Telephone: 858-552-8400. Fax: 858-552-0159.
White Plains, New York Office: Suite 1500, 1 North Lexington Avenue, 10601. Telephone: 914-681-8851. Fax: 914-686-4488.
See Professional Biographies, WASHINGTON, DISTRICT OF COLUMBIA

Lyons, Clinton '40 '72 C.433 B.A. L.705 J.D.
(adm. in NJ; not adm. in DC) Exec. Dir., Natl. Legal Aid & Def. Assn.
Lyons, Dennis G., (AV) ....'31 '55 C.321 A.B. L.309 LL.B. [Arnold&P.]
*PRACTICE AREAS: Corporate; Securities; Litigation; Transportation Law.
Lyons, Ellen L. ....'60 '91 C.893 B.A. L.228 J.D. [▣ Skadden,A.S.M.&F.]
*PRACTICE AREAS: Employment Relations; Commercial Litigation; Antitrust; Futures Law.
Lyons, Ellis, (AV) ....'15 '39 C.604 A.B. L.597 J.D. 918 16th St.NW
Lyons, Gregory ....'63 '91 C.446 B.S.E.E. L.309 J.D. [Wiley R.&F.] (Pat.)
*PRACTICE AREAS: Intellectual Property; Litigation.
Lyons, James A., Jr., (AV) ....'30 '57 C.728 B.S. L.884 J.D. [▣ Coan&L.]
*PRACTICE AREAS: Real Estate; Housing and Urban Affairs; Fair Housing.
Lyons, James L., (AV) ....'37 '68 C.1115 A.B. L.276 J.D. [Kellogg,W.&L.]
*PRACTICE AREAS: Civil Litigation; Criminal; Appellate Practice.
Lyons, John F., Jr. '46 '71
C.951 B.A. L.273 J.D. Telecom. Strategy & Regul., Motorola, Inc.
Lyons, John H. ....'— '95 [▣ Skadden,A.S.M.&F.]
Lyons, Kenneth M., (AV) ....'55 '80 C.776 A.B. L.902 J.D. [Dickstein S.M.&O.]
Lyons, Mona, (AV) ....'50 '75 C.999 B.A. L.128 J.D. [Clifford,L.&G.]
*PRACTICE AREAS: Civil Litigation; Employment; Medical Malpractice; Personal Injury.
Lyons, Patrice A. ....'42 '70 C.1040 B.A. L.276 J.D. [P.Lyons]
Lyons, Stephen B. ....'50 '77 C.605 A.B. L.276 J.D. [▣ Sidley A.B.&W.]

Lyons, Patrice, Chartered, Law Offices of
910 17th Street, N.W., Suite 800, 20006
Telephone: 202-293-5990 Fax: 202-293-5121
Email: palyons@bellatlantic.net
Patrice A. Lyons.
Copyright Law, Trademark, Internet Law Issues.
Representative Client: Corporation for National Research Initiatives, Reston, Va.

Lystad, Robert D. ....'62 '90 C.597 B.S. L.145 J.D. [Baker&H.]
*PRACTICE AREAS: Litigation; First Amendment; Libel; Media Law.
Ma, Christopher Y.W. ....'50 '78 C.309 A.B. L.1066 J.D. Newsweek Magazine
Ma, Mike Yuh-hung ....'61 '90 C.999 LL.B. L.1066 J.D. WorldSpace Inc.
Maberry, Scott ....'64 '94 C.597 B.S. L.276 J.D. [▣ Weil,G.&M.]
Mabile, Michael P. ....'— '77 C&L.259 B.S., J.D. [King&S.]
*PRACTICE AREAS: Litigation and Trade.
Mabus, Raymond E., Jr., (BV) '48 '76
C.500 B.A. L.309 J.D. [▣ Baker,D.B.&C.] (⊙Jackson, MS)
*PRACTICE AREAS: International Law.
Macalester, T. Lane ....'57 '84 C.1365 B.A. L.910 J.D. [▣ Shaw P.]
*PRACTICE AREAS: Technology Law; Health Law.
Macallair, Tanya Axenson ....'75 '01 C.188 B.S. L.309 J.D. [▣ Gibson,D.&C.]
Mac Allister, Thomas W. ....'— '99 C.1369 B.S. L.273 J.D. [▣ Foley&L.]
*PRACTICE AREAS: Intellectual Property.
MacArthur, Stephen M. '35 '68 C&L.477 B.A., J.D.
(adm. in CA; not adm. in DC) Wash. Rep., Nestle USA, Inc.
Macaulay, Joan M. ....'69 '96 C.112 B.A. L.276 J.D. [▣ Skadden,A.S.M.&F.]
*PRACTICE AREAS: Litigation.
Macauley, Cherie L. ....'70 '96 C.951 B.A. L.976 J.D. [▣ Wilmer,C.&P.]
MacAvoy, Christopher J., (AV) ......'57 '82 C.309 B.A. L.276 J.D. [Howrey S.A.&W.]
*PRACTICE AREAS: Antitrust; Trade Regulation.
Macbeth, Angus, (AV) ....'42 '70 C&L.976 B.A., LL.B. [Sidley A.B.&W.]
Macbeth, JoAnn E. ....'48 '76 C.914 B.A. L.178 J.D. [Crowell&M.]
MacCleery, Laura I. '— '99 C.893 B.A. L.813 J.D.
(adm. in CO; not adm. in DC) 1844 Columbia Road, N.W., Apt. 206
Macdonald, Alan S. ....'62 '90 C.478 B.A. L.276 J.D. [Akin,G.S.H.&F.]
*PRACTICE AREAS: Litigation.
Macdonald, Alison B. '73 '01 C.104 A.B. L.477 J.D.
(adm. in VA; not adm. in DC) [▣ Shaw P.]
*PRACTICE AREAS: Litigation.
MacDonald, Andrew F. ....'48 '73 C.696 B.A. L.273 J.D. [Thelen R.&P.]
*PRACTICE AREAS: Business; Finance.
Macdonald, David R., (AV) ....'30 '55 C.188 B.S. L.477 J.D. 815 Conn. Ave., N.W.
Macdonald, Douglas W. ....'69 '97 C.550 B.A. L.1048 J.D. [▣ Webster,C.&B.]
*PRACTICE AREAS: Corporate Law; Business Law; Intellectual Property Law; Trade and Professional Associations; Nonprofit Corporations.
MacDonald, Ellen M. ....'69 '94 C.976 B.A. L.575 J.D. [▣ Chadbourne&P.]
MacDonald, Gary A. ....'58 '89 C.475 B.A. L.477 J.D. [Skadden,A.S.M.&F.]
MacDonald, John K., (AV) .....'33 '60 C.728 A.B. L.309 J.D. 1730 K St., N.W., Ste. 304
Macdonald, Margaret D. ....'69 '95 C.855 B.A. L.904 J.D. [▣ Howrey S.A.&W.]
*PRACTICE AREAS: Intellectual Property.
MacDonald, William A. ....'— '99 C.309 A.B. L.276 J.D. [▣ Miller&C.]
*PRACTICE AREAS: Corporate Taxation; Exempt Organizations; International Taxation; Tax Practice; Tax Procedure.
MacDougall, Bennett A. ....'71 '98 C.1331 B.A. L.221 J.D. [▣ Dechert]
*PRACTICE AREAS: Financial Services Law; Investment Management.
MacDougall, Gordon P. ....'30 '55 C.477 A.B. L.178 1025 Connecticut Ave., N.W.
MacDougall, Heather L. '69 '94 C.966 B.A. L.436 J.D.
(adm. in WI; not adm. in DC) [▣ McGuiness N.&W.]
*PRACTICE AREAS: Labor and Employment Law; Human Resources Compliance and Training.
MacDougall, Mark J., (AV) ....'56 '85 C.602 B.A. L.273 J.D. [Akin,G.S.H.&F.]
*PRACTICE AREAS: Litigation; White Collar Criminal Defense.
Macdowell, G. Kendrick ....'59 '90 C&L.846 B.A., J.D. [Patton B.]

Macel, Stanley C., IV ... '66 '93 C.951 B.A. L.228 J.D. 450 5th St., N.W.
MacGregor, Clark '22 '48 C.197 B.A. L.494 LL.B.
(adm. in MN; not adm. in DC) 2834 Foxhall Rd., N.W.
MacGuineas, D. Biard, (AV) ... '40 '66 C&L.309 A.B., LL.B. [Dykema G.]
*PRACTICE AREAS: Trade Regulation Law; Energy Law.
Mach, Daniel ... '70 '98 C.674 B.A. L.569 J.D. [[A] Jenner&B.]
*PRACTICE AREAS: Civil Litigation; First Amendment Law; Telecommunications Law; Antitrust Law.
Machado, John L. ... '68 '92 C.472 B.A. L.602 J.D. 305 H St., NW
Machado, Leslie P. ... '70 '97 C.262 B.A. L.107 J.D. [[A] Nixon P.]
*PRACTICE AREAS: Litigation; Media Law.
MacHarg, Jean Veeder ... '56 '81 C.914 B.A. L.145 J.D. [Patton B.]
Machen, Ronald C. ... '69 '94 C.813 A.B. L.309 J.D. [[C] Wilmer,C.&P.]
*PRACTICE AREAS: White Collar Crime; Internal Investigations; Civil Litigation; Complex Litigation.
Machi, Mark A. ... '67 '95 C.1169 B.A. L.446 J.D. [[A] Venable,A.B.H.&C.]
Machiz, Marc I. ... '52 '78 C.659 B.A. L.1066 J.D. [Cohen,M.H.&T.]
*PRACTICE AREAS: Employee Benefits; ERISA.
Machlin, Marc D., (AV) ... '57 '81 C.103 A.B. L.309 J.D. [Pepper H.]
*PRACTICE AREAS: Environmental Law; Antitrust; Public Utility Regulation.
MacIntyre, Susan A. ... '67 '96 C.321 B.A. L.273 J.D. [[A] Winston&S.]
*PRACTICE AREAS: Environmental Law.
Mack, Julia Cooper ... '20 '52 C.302 B.S. L.329 LL.B. Ct. of App. J.
Mack, Julie N. '64 '91 C&L.309 A.B., J.D.
(adm. in NY; not adm. in DC) [[A] Coudert B.]
Mack, Kenneth E. ... '62 '94 C.1307 B.A. L.588 J.D. [[A] Coudert B.]
*PRACTICE AREAS: Project Finance; Russia Trade; Oil and Gas Law; Electric Power.
Mack, Peter G., (AV) ... '— '73 C.436 B.M.E. L.273 J.D. [Foley&L.] (See Pat. Sect.)
*PRACTICE AREAS: Intellectual Property Litigation.
Mack, Susan J., (AV) ... '50 '83 C.174 B.A. L.30 J.D. [Sughrue M.] (See Pat. Sect.)
*PRACTICE AREAS: Intellectual Property Law; Biotechnology.
Mack, Timothy C. ... '46 '77 C.911 B.A. L.823 J.D. 929 Westminister Street, NW
Mackall, Laidler B., (AV) ... '16 '47 C.674 A.B. L.276 J.D. 1330 Connecticut Ave., N.W.
Mackaronis, Christopher G., (AV) ... '52 '78 C.674 B.A. L.30 J.D. [Bell,B.&L.]
*PRACTICE AREAS: Labor and Employment Law; Age Discrimination.
Mackell, Cheryl Hamer ... '48 '84 C.178 B.S. L.1026 J.D. [[C] Cohen,M.H.&T.]
*PRACTICE AREAS: Securities; Business Law; Civil Rights; Criminal Law.
Mackenzie, Elizabeth A. '72 '99 C.112 B.A. L.861 J.D.
(adm. in CA; not adm. in DC) [[A] Reed S.]
*PRACTICE AREAS: Health Care.
Mackiewicz, Edward R., (AV) ... '51 '76 C.976 B.A. L.178 J.D. [Steptoe&J.]
*PRACTICE AREAS: Employee Benefits; Employment Law; Bankruptcy Law.
Mackinnon, Allan P. ... '31 '58 C.478 B.A. L.893 LL.B. 717 D St., N.W.
Mackintosh, Brooks ... '73 '99 C.659 B.A. L.945 J.D. [[A] Covington&B.]
*PRACTICE AREAS: Litigation.
Mackler, Bruce F., (AV) ... '41 '79 C.831 B.A. L.796 J.D. [Heller E.W.&M.]
*PRACTICE AREAS: Food and Drug Regulation Law; Environmental Law; Agriculture Law.
Macklin, Jay '58 '87 C.870 B.S. L.273 J.D.
Associate Litigation Counsel, WorldCom Inc
MacLaren, Julia ... '— '00 C.276 B.A. L.893 J.D. [[A] Latham&W.]
*PRACTICE AREAS: Litigation; White Collar Crime.
Maclay, Kevin C. ... '69 '94 C.105 B.A. L.893 J.D. [[A] Jones,D.R.&P.]
MacLean, Jennifer Allison ... '71 '01 C.674 A.B. L.893 J.D. [[A] Perkins C.]

Macleay, Lynch, Gregg & Lynch, P.C., (AV)
Suite 1150, 1629 K Street, N.W., 20006
Telephone: 202-785-0123 FAX: 202-393-3390
Email: maclmac@aol.com
Donald Macleay (1908-1994); Hugh Lynch, Jr. (1913-1994); John C. Lynch; Robert P. Lynch; Robert G. McGinley; James C. Gregg;—Jack David Lapidus; Brett Schoel.
General Civil Practice in all Courts and Agencies. General Insurance Defense Practice, Subrogations, Workers Compensation, ERISA, Automobile, Medical and Professional Liability.
See Professional Biographies, WASHINGTON, DISTRICT OF COLUMBIA

Macleod, John A., (AV) ... '42 '69 C&L.602 B.B.A., J.D. [Crowell&M.]
*PRACTICE AREAS: Natural Resources Law; Mining Law; Timber Law; Environmental Law.
MacLeod, William C., (AV) ... '52 '79 C.694 B.A. L.472 J.D. [Collier S.S.]
*PRACTICE AREAS: Antitrust; Trade Regulation.
MacMeekin, Daniel H. '41 '71 C.645 B.S. L.813 J.D.
1776 Massachusetts Avenue, N.W., Suite 801
MacMichael, Shannon P. ... '70 '98 C.893 B.A. L.145 J.D. [[A] Steptoe&J.]
MacMillan, Keith Douglas '62 '00
C.205 B.A. L.273 J.D. [[A] Finnegan,H.F.G.&D.] (See Pat. Sect.)
*PRACTICE AREAS: Chemical Patent Prosecution; Patent Infringement.
Maco, Paul S. ... '52 '78 C.401 B.A. L.569 J.D. [Vinson&E.]
*PRACTICE AREAS: Public Finance Law; Securities.
Macpeak, Kathleen M. ... '— '99 C.128 B.A. L.180 J.D. [[A] Morgan,L.&B.]
MacPherson, J. Randolph ... '47 '72 C&L.770 B.S.C., J.D. [Sullivan&W.]
*PRACTICE AREAS: Government Contracts and Communications Law.
MacRae, C. Duncan ... '40 '94 C.309 A.B. L.1209 J.D. [[A] Groom]
*PRACTICE AREAS: Employee Benefits.
Macres, Philip J. ... '66 '98 C.260 B.S.B.A. L.362 J.D. [[A] Swidler B.S.F.]
*PRACTICE AREAS: Telecommunications.
Macri, Renee C. '76 '01 C.1369 B.A. L.276 J.D.
(adm. in VA; not adm. in DC) [[A] Sonnenschein N.&R.]
Macrory, Patrick F. J., (AV) ... '41 '64 C.051 B.A. L.273 LL.M. [[C] Akin,G.S.H.&F.]
*PRACTICE AREAS: International Trade.
MacVittie, Lisa A. ... '66 '93 C.945 B.A. L.276 J.D. [Sonnenschein N.&R.]
*PRACTICE AREAS: Litigation; Employment Law.
Madan, Allison A. ... '62 '90 C.754 B.S. L.128 J.D. [Slevin&H.]
*PRACTICE AREAS: Employee Benefits.
Madan, Raj ... '— '93 C.569 B.A. L.273 J.D. [McKee N.]
*PRACTICE AREAS: Taxation; Federal Tax Controversies; Tax Appeals; Tax Collection; Tax Controversies.
Madden, Brian M., (AV) ... '49 '75 C.659 B.A. L.273 J.D. [Leventhal,S.&L.]
*PRACTICE AREAS: Communications Law; Media Law.
Madden, Murdaugh Stuart, (AV) '22 '48 C.273 B.A. L.309 J.D.
V.P. & Sen. Coun., Humane Society of the United States (⊙Washington)
Madden, Murdaugh Stuart, (AV) '22 '48
C.273 B.A. L.309 J.D. [Madden,M.S.&R.A.K.] (⊙Washington)
Madden, Robert E., (AV) '43 '70 C&L.188 B.S., J.D.
[Powell,G.F.&M.] (⊙Reston, VA)
*PRACTICE AREAS: Trusts and Estates; Executive Compensation; Federal Taxation; Corporate.
Madden, Thomas J., (AV) '41 '68
C.884 B.S.E.E. L.128 J.D. [Venable,A.B.H.&C.] (See Pat. Sect.)
*PRACTICE AREAS: Government Contract Law; Intellectual Property; Legislative Practice.
Madden, Turner D. ... '52 '83 C.658 B.A. L.999 J.D. [Madden&P.]
Madden, William J., Jr., (AV) ... '39 '65 C.321 A.B. L.477 J.D. [Winston&S.]
*PRACTICE AREAS: Energy Law; Environmental Law; Public Utility Law.

Madden, Murdaugh Stuart and Roger A. Kindler, (AV)
2100 L Street, N.W., 20037
Telephone: 202-833-3360 Fax: 202-778-6126
URL: http://www.lawyers.com/madden-kindler
Murdaugh Stuart Madden; Roger A. Kindler.

(This Listing Continued)

Madden, Murdaugh Stuart and Roger A. Kindler (Continued)
Tax Exempt Organizations, Wills, Trusts and Estate Law, Wealth Preservation, Immigration Law, International Law.
See Professional Biographies, WASHINGTON, DISTRICT OF COLUMBIA

Madden & Patton, L.L.C. ... 1919 Pennsylvania Avenue, N.W., Suite 800
Maddox, John D., (AV) ... '40 '73 C.871 B.S. L.893 J.D. [Arter&H.]
Maddox, Michael Paul ... '62 '90 C.1256 B.A. L.945 J.D. [[A] Meyers&A.]
Maddox, Steven ... '65 '89 C.309 A.B. L.893 J.D. [McDermott,W.&E.]
Maddry, Tyler '66 '95 C.309 B.A. L.273 J.D.
(adm. in VA; not adm. in DC; Pat.) [[A] Hunton&W.]
*PRACTICE AREAS: Patent and Technology Licensing; Patent Prosecution; Patent Litigation.
Mader, Joyce A. ... '51 '76 C.216 B.A. L.128 J.D. [O'Donoghue&O.]
Madigan, Kimberly A. ... '56 '82 C.339 B.S. L.904 J.D. 122 C St., N.W.
Madigan, Michael J., (P.C.), (AV) ... '43 '68 C.184 B.A. L.128 J.D. [Akin,G.S.H.&F.]
*PRACTICE AREAS: Complex Litigation; White Collar Crime; Congressional Investigations; Mediation; Arbitration.
Madonick, Helene B. ... '60 '87 C.860 B.A. L.178 J.D. [Arnold&P.]
*PRACTICE AREAS: Litigation; Food and Drug.
Madrid, Linda A., (BV) '59 '85 C.36 B.A. L.276 J.D.
Managing Director, General Counsel & Secretary, CarrAmerica Realty Corporation
Madsen, Douglas L. ... '61 '91 C.101 B.A. L.309 J.D. [Orrick,H.&S.]
*PRACTICE AREAS: Corporate; Structured Finance.
Maebius, Stephen B. ... '— '94 C.188 B.A. L.273 J.D. [Foley&L.] (See Pat. Sect.)
*PRACTICE AREAS: Intellectual Property.
Maechling, Charles, Jr., (AV) ... '20 '50 C.976 B.A. L.893 J.D. 3403 Lowell St., N.W.
Maerowitz, Deena Alyssa '67 '97 C.518 A.B. L.306 J.D.
(adm. in CT; not adm. in DC) 1819 Q St.‡
Maerten, Daniel P. ... '68 '98 C.712 B.A. L.128 J.D. 1299 Pennsylvania Avenue, N.W.
Magazine & Hillman, P.C. ...
Magee, George T., (BV) ... '60 '85 C.397 B.A. L.904 J.D. [Holland&K.]
*PRACTICE AREAS: Real Estate Development Law; Finance Law.
Magee, Jamelle Thompson '68 '94 C.16 B.S. L.420 J.D.
(adm. in VA; not adm. in DC) Food Research & Action Center
Magee, James E., (AV) ... '49 '75 C.690 B.A. L.276 J.D. [Reboul,M.H.M.&K.]
*PRACTICE AREAS: Regulatory; Telecommunications and Energy; Tort Defense/Product Liability.
Magee, John B. ... '— '72 C.668 B.A. L.911 J.D. [McKee N.]
*PRACTICE AREAS: Tax Planning; Tax Controversies; Tax Litigation; International Taxation.
Magee, Lorraine M. ... '64 '90 C.999 B.S. L.276 J.D. [[C] Henrichsen S.]
*PRACTICE AREAS: Civil Litigation; Construction Law; Surety Law; Insurance.
Magee, Marybeth Brennan '74 '00 C.93 B.A. L.724 J.D.
(adm. in NY; not adm. in DC) [[A] Preston G.E.&R.M.]
Magee, Thomas B. ... '59 '91 C&L.174 B.A., J.D. [[A] Keller&H.]
*PRACTICE AREAS: Communications Law.
Magenau, Jeff L. ... '63 '96 C.94 B.A. L.30 J.D. [[A] Fried,F.H.S.&J.]
*PRACTICE AREAS: Intellectual Property; Information Technology; Internet Law; E-Commerce.
Maggio, Michael, (AV) ... '47 '78 C.831 B.A. L.1162 J.D. [Maggio&K.]
*PRACTICE AREAS: Immigration and Nationality Law.

Maggio & Kattar, P.C., (AV) [BR]
Eleven Dupont Circle, N.W., Suite 775, 20036
Telephone: 202-483-0053 FAX: 202-483-6801
Email: inquire@maggio-kattar.com URL: http://www.maggio-kattar.com
Michael Maggio;—Alison J. Brown (Not admitted in DC); Elizabeth A. Quinn (Not admitted in DC); Andres Cayetano Benach (Not admitted in DC); Shoba Sivaprasad (Not admitted in DC).
Immigration and Nationality Law. Business and Employment Immigration Law.
See Professional Biographies, WASHINGTON, DISTRICT OF COLUMBIA

Maggs, Gregory Eaton ... '64 '89 C&L.309 A.B., J.D. George Washington Univ. Law Sch.
Magid, Creighton R. '61 '87 C.674 A.B. L.477 J.D.
(adm. in IA; not adm. in DC) [Dorsey&W.]
*PRACTICE AREAS: Litigation.
Magid, Paul S. '40 '65 C.367 B.A. L.178 LL.B.
(adm. in NY; not adm. in DC) Gen. Coun., African Development Foundation
Magielnicki, Robert L. ... '47 '71 C.705 A.B. L.188 J.D. [Schnader H.S.&L.]
*PRACTICE AREAS: Antitrust Law; Commercial Law; Corporate Law; International Law; Litigation.
Magielnicki, Robert L., Jr. '70 '97 C.893 B.A. L.362 J.D.
(adm. in NY; not adm. in DC) [[A] Powell,G.F.&M.]
Maginnis, Edward J. '62 '88 C.367 B.A. L.904 J.D.
Assoc. Gen. Coun., Washington Met. Area Transit Auth.
*RESPONSIBILITIES: Real Estate; Contracts; Finance; Litigation.

Maginnis, John C., III '48 '74 C&L.477 B.B.A., J.D.
1350 Connecticut Ave., N.W., Suite 301, 20036
Telephone: 202-659-4420 Fax: 202-775-2463
Email: maginnisdclaw@msn.com
***PRACTICE AREAS: Family Law; Estate Planning; Probate; Personal Injury; Medical Malpractice.**
Family Law, Divorce, Custody, Adoption, Visitation, Marital Property, Estate Planning, Wills, Probate, Trusts, Personal Injury, Auto Accidents, Medical Malpractice, Orthopedic Malpractice, Family Business Law, Business Formation, Small Business Litigation.
See Professional Biographies, WASHINGTON, DISTRICT OF COLUMBIA

Magner, Maureen '73 '01 C.156 B.A. L.180 J.D.
(adm. in NY; not adm. in DC) [[A] Dechert]
*PRACTICE AREAS: Investment Management; Financial Services Law.
Magney, John S. ... '46 '73 C.436 A.B. L.597 J.D. [Cleary,G.S.&H.]
Magnus, John R. ... '64 '90 C.813 A.B. L.145 J.D. [Dewey B.]
*PRACTICE AREAS: Antitrust; Communications; International Trade.
Magnus, Ron L. ... '58 '84 C.623 B.A. L.329 J.D. Spec. Coun., Office of Corp. Coun.
Magnuson, Elizabeth McGoogan '70 '95 C.347 B.A. L.228 J.D.
[[A] Finnegan,H.F.G.&D.]
*PRACTICE AREAS: Trademark Litigation; Trademark Prosecution; Copyright Litigation; Internet Trademark Law.
Magnuson, Mark G. '48 '73 C.893 B.A. L.245 J.D.
V.P. & Asst. Gen. Coun., Consolidated Nat. Gas Co.
Magoon, Sanjeev '72 '97 C.276 B.S.B.A. L.893 J.D.
(adm. in NY; not adm. in DC) [[A] Shearman&S.]
*PRACTICE AREAS: Tax.
Magoon, Sumeet '71 '99 C.223 B.S.E.E. L.64 J.D.
(adm. in VA; not adm. in DC; See Pat. Sect.) [[A] Kenyon&K.]
*PRACTICE AREAS: Intellectual Property.
Magruder, Meghan H., (AV) ... '58 '83 C.1365 B.A. L.245 J.D. [Hale&D.]
*PRACTICE AREAS: Environmental Law.
Magurshak, Jeanine L. ... '70 '99 C.918 B.A. L.276 J.D. [[A] Wilmer,C.&P.]
Mahaffey, David C. ... '58 '82 C.674 A.B. L.309 J.D. [Sullivan&W.]
*PRACTICE AREAS: Business Law; Investment Companies; Financing; Securities Law.
Mahaffey, George S., Jr. '73 '00 C.446 B.A. L.64 J.D.
(adm. in MD; not adm. in DC) [[A] Eccleston&W.]
*PRACTICE AREAS: Insurance Defense; Professional Malpractice.
Mahaffey, Sylvia M., (P.C.) ... '55 '80 C.104 A.B. L.846 J.D. [Shaw P.]
*PRACTICE AREAS: Corporate Securities.
Mahaffie, Charles D., Jr., (AV) ... '31 '55 C.31 B.A. L.309 LL.B. 1752 N St., N.W.

Mahaley, Peri N. ....'55 '79 C&L.276 B.S.F.S., J.D. [Swidler B.S.F.]
*PRACTICE AREAS: Litigation; Insurance Coverage.
Mahan, Dee ....'59 '85 C.421 B.A. L.273 J.D. Health Systems Mktg. & Develop., Inc.
Mahdavi, David R., (P.C.), (BV) '62 '87 C&L.1209 B.S., J.D.
(adm. in VA; not adm. in DC) [Fracassi M.] (⊙Falls Church, VA)
Maher, Anne M. '61 '91
C.105 B.A./B.S.E.E. L.276 J.D. [Fitzpatrick,C.H.&S.] (See Pat. Sect.)
Maher, Marcus E. ....'73 '99 C.352 B.S. L.309 J.D. [Ⓐ Wiley R.&F.]
Maher, Patricia L. ....'— '82 C.103 A.B. L.276 J.D. [King&S.]
*PRACTICE AREAS: Business Litigation.
Maher, William F., Jr. ....'57 '84 C.602 B.S. L.309 J.D. [Halprin,T.G.&M.]
*PRACTICE AREAS: Telecommunications Law; Computer Law.
Mahini, Robert .... '75 '01 C.893 B.A. L.880 J.D. [Ⓐ Hogan&H.]
Mahinka, Stephen Paul, (AV) ....'49 '75 C.367 A.B. L.309 J.D. [Morgan,L.&B.]
Mahn, Terry G., (AV) ....'48 '75 C.477 B.S.S.E. L.128 J.D. [Fish&R.]
*PRACTICE AREAS: Intellectual Property; FCC Regulation; Software Copyright; Software Licensing.
Mahon, Paul A. ....'63 '87 C.597 B.A. L.276 J.D. [Mahon P.R.&F.]
Mahon Patusky Rothblatt & Fisher .... 1735 Connecticut Ave., N.W. 3rd Fl.
Mahoney, Christopher W. ....'59 '85 C.867 B.A. L.276 J.D. [Duane,M.&H.]
*PRACTICE AREAS: Complex Civil Litigation; Environmental; Toxic Tort; Mass Torts; Commercial And Business Tort Matters.
Mahoney, Colleen P., (AV) ....'57 '81 C&L.30 B.A., J.D. [Skadden,A.S.M.&F.]
Mahoney, John P. .... '68 '93 C.1107 A.B. L.180 J.D. [Ⓐ Shaw,B.V.&R.]
*PRACTICE AREAS: Federal Employment Law; Employment Law; Federal Personnel Law; Employment Discrimination; Civil Litigation.
Mahoney, Maureen E., (AV) ....'— '78 C.347 A.B. L.145 J.D. [Latham&W.]
Mahoney, William G., (AV) ....'25 '50 C&L.602 J.D. [Ⓒ Highsaw,M.&C.]
*PRACTICE AREAS: Appellate Court Practice; Supreme Court Practice; Railway Labor Act; Contract and Legislative Negotiations; Interstate Commerce Act.
Maier, Cheryl A. .... '59 '89 C.705 B.A. L.93 J.D. [King,P.&H.]
*PRACTICE AREAS: Complex Civil Litigation; Civil Law; Criminal; Appellate Practice; Employment Law.
Mailander, William S. '58 '88
C.569 B.A. L.831 J.D. Asst. Gen. Coun., Paralyzed Vet. of Amer.
Maiman, Seth E. .... '61 '85 C.1044 B.A. L.904 J.D. MCI WorldCom
Main, David C., (BV) ....'48 '77 C.210 B.A. L.276 J.D. [Shaw P.]
*PRACTICE AREAS: Health Law.
Maines, Ronald D., (AV) '56 '84 C.198 B.A. L.896 J.D.
[Maines&L.] & [Wood,M.&B.]
Maines & Loeb, PLLC, (AV) .... 1827 Jefferson Place, N.W.
Mainigi, Enu A. ....'70 '94 C.30 B.S. L.309 J.D. [Ⓐ Williams&C.]
Maiolo, Tina M. .... '71 '96 C&L.945 B.A., J.D. [Ⓐ Carr G.]
Mairs, Stephanie L. '67 '94 C.67 B.A. L.893 J.D.
(adm. in MD; not adm. in DC) 1725 Desales Street, N.W.
Maisel, Gregg .... '64 '89 C.976 B.A. L.309 J.D. Asst. U.S. Atty.
Maitha, Mutheu '73 '01 C.1369 B.A. L.188 J.D.
(adm. in NY; not adm. in DC) [Ⓐ Cleary,G.S.&H.]
Maiwurm, James J., (AV) '48 '74
C.970 B.A. L.477 J.D. [Squire,S.&D.] (⊙Tysons Corner, VA)
*PRACTICE AREAS: Business Law; Commercial Law; Joint Ventures; Mergers and Acquisitions; Securities Offerings.
Maizel, Jonathan A. '64 '88 C.555 B.A. L.705 J.D.
(adm. in NJ; not adm. in DC) [Milbank,T.H.&M.]
Majett, Nicholas A. .... '52 '85 C&L.329 B.A., J.D. Asst. Corp. Coun.
Majev, Howard R., (AV) ....'52 '78 C.367 B.A. L.446 J.D. [Winston&S.]
*PRACTICE AREAS: Real Estate.
Major, Scott J. ....'62 '92 C.602 B.B.A. L.128 J.D. [Ⓐ Cleary&K.]
*PRACTICE AREAS: Trademark Law; Unfair Competition Law; Copyright Law.
Majoras, John M., (AV) ....'61 '86 C&L.930 B.A., J.D. [Jones,D.R.&P.]
*PRACTICE AREAS: Litigation; Antitrust; Complex Business Litigation.
Majors, Jay D. ....'68 '93 C.309 A.B. L.893 J.D. [Ⓐ Fried,F.H.S.&J.]
*PRACTICE AREAS: Civil Litigation.
Majure, Kimberly T. '68 '93
C.893 B.A. L.309 J.D. [Ⓒ Skadden,A.S.M.&F.] (⊙New York, NY)
*PRACTICE AREAS: International Taxation.
Mak, Pamela J. .... '58 '84 C.831 B.A. L.884 J.D. [Danziger,M.&F.]
*PRACTICE AREAS: Business Immigration; Citizenship; Consular Law.
Makepeace, Caroline Dibona ....'62 '88 C&L.893 B.A., J.D. U.S Environmental Protection
Makins, Kelly D. ....'74 '00 C.228 A.B. L.893 J.D. [Ⓐ Skadden,A.S.M.&F.]
*PRACTICE AREAS: Corporate Law.
Makuch, Michael A. .... '58 '84 C.976 B.S. L.930 J.D. [Smith,G.&R.] (See Pat. Sect.)
*PRACTICE AREAS: Intellectual Property Law.
Malabonga, Daniel M. .... '58 '93 C&L.662 A.B., LL.B. [Ⓐ Troutman S.]
*PRACTICE AREAS: International Arbitration; International Litigation; General Practice; Philippine Law.
Malady, Brian C. .... '68 '96 C.823 B.A. L.94 J.D. [Ⓐ Fleischman&W.]
Malamuth, Eldad Z. '— '01 C.477 B.S. L.145 J.D.
(adm. in IL; not adm. in DC) [Ⓐ Mayer,B.&P.]
*PRACTICE AREAS: Litigation.
Malara, Anthony James, III '70 '96 C.276 B.A. L.128 J.D.
(adm. in MD; not adm. in DC) 4850 Conn. Ave., N.W.‡
Malasky, Alan R., (AV) ....'44 '68 C.665 B.B.A. L.273 J.D. [Seyfarth S.]
*PRACTICE AREAS: Agriculture Law; Antitrust and Trade Regulation Law; Administrative Law; Litigation.
Malech, Lloyd Alan ....'68 '94 C.705 B.A. L.273 J.D. 1015 18th St .NW
Malech, Rori H. ....'70 '96 C.94 B.A. L.273 J.D. [Ⓐ Katten M.Z.]
Malet, Philip L., (AV) ....'55 '79 C.659 B.S.E.E. L.537 J.D. [Steptoe&J.]
*PRACTICE AREAS: Administrative Law; Communications Common Carrier; Cable T.V.; Consumer Fraud Law; Satellite Communications.
Maletta, Jeffrey B., (AV) .... '— '79 C.309 B.A. L.813 J.D. [Kirkpatrick&L.]
*PRACTICE AREAS: SEC Enforcement; Securities Litigation; Corporate Litigation; Insurance Coverage.
Malhotra, Nick .... '68 '95 C.103 B.A. L.178 J.D. [Ⓐ Arnold&P.]
*PRACTICE AREAS: Litigation.
Malhotra, Shibani ....'74 '00 C.012 B.A. L.904 J.D. [Ⓐ Dickstein S.M.&O.]
*PRACTICE AREAS: Antitrust Civil Litigation; International Trade Remedies.

Malia, Gerald A., Law Offices of, (AV) '33 '59 C.749 B.S. L.276 LL.B.
1660 L Street, NW Suite 506, 20036
Telephone: 202-639-8000 Fax: 202-463-6328
URL: http://www.lawyers.com/malialaw
General Practice.
See Professional Biographies, WASHINGTON, DISTRICT OF COLUMBIA

Malik, Rajeev K. ....'73 '98 C.473 B.A. L.608 J.D. [Ⓐ White&C.]
Malitzis, John F. ....'67 '92 C.1044 B.A. L.93 J.D. Atty., NASD Regulation, Inc.
Malizia, Samuel J. .... '54 '79 C.645 B.S. L.273 J.D. [Malizia S.&F.] ⊙
*PRACTICE AREAS: Securities; Banking; Corporate; Tax.

Malizia Spidi & Fisch, PC, (AV)
1100 New York Avenue, N.W. Suite 340 West, 20005 ⊙
Telephone: 202-434-4660 Facsimile: 202-434-4661
Email: mail@malizialaw.com URL: http://www.malizialaw.com
(This Listing Continued)

Malizia Spidi & Fisch, PC (Continued)
Samuel J. Malizia; John J. Spidi; Richard Fisch; Felicia C. Battista; Daniel H. Burd;—Tiffany A. Henricks; Evan M. Seigel; Jennifer E. Martella.
Financial Institutions, Securities, Corporate, Business Start-ups, Employee Benefits, ERISA, Taxation, Business Law. Practice before Federal and State Regulatory Agencies including Securities and Exchange Commission, Office of Thrift Supervision, Federal Deposit Insurance Corporation, Office of the Comptroller of the Currency, Federal Reserve Board, Internal Revenue Service and state banking agencies.
State College, Pennsylvania Office: 637 Kennard Road, 16801. Telephone: 814-466-6625. Fax: 814-466-6703.
See Professional Biographies, WASHINGTON, DISTRICT OF COLUMBIA

Malkin, Arthur N. ....'54 '79 C.1044 B.A. L.588 J.D. [Mehri,M.&R.]
*PRACTICE AREAS: Lobbying; Governmental Relations.
Malkin, Brian J. .... '66 '91 C&L.273 B.A., J.D. [Ⓐ Hyman,P.&M.]
*PRACTICE AREAS: Food and Drug Regulation.
Malkin, Robert G. .... '70 '97 C.674 B.A. L.910 J.D. [Ⓐ Hogan&H.]
*PRACTICE AREAS: Health Law; Health Care Fraud; Health Care Compliance; Health Care Reimbursement.

Malkin, Rachel E.
(See Bethesda, Maryland)

Mallen, Richard David .... '64 '92 C.197 A.B. L.309 J.D. [Ⓐ Metzger&M.]
Mallett, Terri T. ....'— '94 C.329 B.S. L.1059 J.D. [Ⓐ Weil,G.&M.]

Malley, Keith R., P.C.
(See Arlington, Virginia)

Mallick, Earl W. '26 '50 C.597 B.S. L.309 LL.B.
(adm. in PA; not adm. in DC) U.S. Steel Corp.
Mallik, Chittaranjan .... '— '00 C.446 B.S. L.477 J.D. [Ⓐ Latham&W.]
*PRACTICE AREAS: Corporate Law.
Mallios, Dimitri P., (AV) '32 '60
C&L.273 B.A., LL.B. [Margolius,M.D.R.&T.] (⊙Largo, MD)
*PRACTICE AREAS: Liquor Licensing; Alcoholic Beverages; Hospitality Law; Business Law.
Mallonee, John E. .... '74 '99 C.264 B.A. L.575 J.D. 1901 18th St., N.W.
Mallory, C. King, III, (AV) .... '36 '61 C.976 B.A. L.861 LL.B. [Hunton&W.]
*PRACTICE AREAS: Energy; Finance.
Mallory, Lark T. ....'69 '98 C&L.608 B.S.B.A., J.D. [Ⓐ Arnold&P.]
Malloy, Eileen '55 '81 C.1214 B.A. L.904 J.D.
Sr. Legal Editor, Bur. of Natl. Affs., Inc.
Malloy, John A. ....'59 '85 C.93 B.A. L.1209 J.D. MCI Communications Corp.
Malmierca-Smith, Montserrat '67 '99 L.30 LL.M.
(adm. in NY; not adm. in DC) 2375 Pennsylvania Avenue N.W.
Malmud, Paul Edward '68 '95 C.696 B.A., L.273 J.D.
(adm. in NY; not adm. in DC) [Ⓐ McDermott,W.&E.]
Malone, Brian C. ....'65 '98 C.395 B.A. L.276 J.D. [Ⓐ Mooers&M.]
*PRACTICE AREAS: Insurance Defense; Insurance Coverage; Civil Litigation.
Malone, Harry N., III .... '52 '98 C.119 B.S. L.446 J.D. [Ⓐ Swidler B.S.F.]
*PRACTICE AREAS: Telecommunications.
Malone, Louis P., III .... '54 '80 C.475 B.A. L.213 J.D. [O'Donoghue&O.]
Malone, Patrick A., (AV) ....'51 '85 C.378 B.A. L.976 J.D. [Stein,M.&M.]
*PRACTICE AREAS: Civil Litigation; Medical Malpractice; Product Liability.
Malone, William R., (AV) ....'36 '62 C&L.309 A.B., J.D. [Miller&V.]
*PRACTICE AREAS: Administrative Agency Practice; Municipal Taxation; International Telecommunications Law; Communications Common Carrier; Broadcasting Law.
Maloney, Barry C., (AV) .... '42 '68 C.276 B.S.B.A. L.273 J.D. [Maloney&K.]
Maloney, James T., (AV) ....'53 '78 C.446 A.B. L.273 J.D. [Maloney&M.]
*PRACTICE AREAS: General Practice.
Maloney, Jennifer C. ....'66 '92 C.999 B.M. L.1048 J.D. [Ⓐ Mayer,B.&P.]
*PRACTICE AREAS: Tax Controversies.
Maloney, John P., Jr. ....'70 '96 C.882 B.S. L.896 J.D. [Ⓐ O'Melveny&M.]
Maloney, Kenneth T. ....'61 '86 C.893 B.A. L.705 J.D. [Cullen&D.]
Maloney, Lynn Duffy ....'64 '92 C.276 B.A. L.262 J.D. [Ⓒ Collier S.S.]
*PRACTICE AREAS: International Trade.
Maloney, Matthew G. .... '57 '81 C.276 B.S.F.S. L.893 J.D. [Dickstein S.M.&O.]
*PRACTICE AREAS: Securities Law; General Corporate Law.
Maloney, Matthew P. .... '62 '91 C.882 B.S. L.273 J.D. [Sherman,M.C.&A.]
*PRACTICE AREAS: Civil Litigation; Personal Injury; Medical Malpractice; Toxic Tort.
Maloney, Michael D. ....'— '88 C.692 B.A. L.273 J.D. [Ⓐ Epstein B.&G.]
*PRACTICE AREAS: Government Contracts; Litigation.
Maloney, Paul J., (AV) .... '54 '82 C.902 B.A. L.128 J.D. [Carr G.]
*PRACTICE AREAS: Professional Liability; Products Liability.
Maloney, Philip J. ....'16 '50 C.602 Ph.B. L.276 J.D. 4520 Burlington Pl., N.W.
Maloney, Regina G. .... '62 '92 C.659 B.A. L.276 J.D. [Williams&C.]
Maloney, William J. '56 '84 C.93 B.A. L.818 J.D.
(adm. in MA; not adm. in DC) [Rode&Q.] (⊙New York, NY)
Maloney & Knox, (AV) ....5225 Wisconsin Ave., N.W., Ste. 316

Maloney & Mohsen, (AV)
4201 Connecticut Avenue, Suite 404, 20008-1129
Telephone: 202-237-6800 Fax: 202-966-5270 http://www.mmlegal.com
Email: partners@mmlegal.com URL: http://www.lawyers.com/maloney&mohsen
Members of Firm: James T. Maloney; Arya A. Mohsen.
Civil Litigation Law and Litigation, Communications Law, Contracts, Labor and Employment Law, Wrongful Termination, Civil Rights, Commercial Landlord and Tenant Law, Professional Liability, Legal Ethics and Professional Responsibility, Medical Malpractice, Child Sexual Abuse Litigation, Personal Injury, Automobile Accidents and Injuries, Products Liability, Criminal Defense, White Collar Crime, Alcoholic and Beverage Control.
See Professional Biographies, WASHINGTON, DISTRICT OF COLUMBIA

Maloy, Heather C. '62 '90 C.1365 B.B.A. L.188 J.D.
(adm. in FL; not adm. in DC) Rm 3316, 1111 Constitution Ave NW
Malpede, Scott D. '61 '88
C.645 B.S.M.E. L.273 J.D. [Fitzpatrick,C.H.&S.] (See Pat. Sect.)
Malsch, Martin G. ....'42 '68 C.321 B.S. L.184 J.D. [Ⓒ LeBoeuf,L.G.&M.]
*PRACTICE AREAS: Nuclear Energy; Environmental; Administrative; Litigation.
Malson, Laurel Pyke ....'54 '80 C.918 B.A. L.309 J.D. [Crowell&M.]
Maltby, Jeremy '68 '97 C.309 A.B. L.178 J.D.
(adm. in NY; not adm. in DC) [Ⓐ O'Melveny&M.]
Malter, Barry L., (AV) .... '47 '72 C&L.260 B.A., J.D. 3000 K St., NW, Ste. 300
Maltz, David S. ....'71 '96 C.477 B.B.A. L.273 J.D. [Ⓐ Skadden,A.S.M.&F.]
Malveaux, Suzette M. .... '66 '96 C.309 A.B. L.569 J.D. [Ⓐ Cohen,M.H.&T.]
*PRACTICE AREAS: Civil Rights.
Mamlet, Alfred M., (AV) .... '59 '84 C.668 B.A. L.1066 J.D. [Steptoe&J.]
*PRACTICE AREAS: Communications Law; International Telecommunications; Computer Law.
Man, Christopher D. ....'70 '95 C.378 B.A. L.910 J.D. [Ⓐ Arnold&P.]
*PRACTICE AREAS: Environmental; Litigation.
Manasevit, Leigh M., (AV) .... '48 '75 C.178 B.A. L.184 J.D. [Brustein&M.]
*PRACTICE AREAS: Education; Civil Litigation.
Manatt, Charles T., (P.C.), (AV) .... '— '62 C.350 B.S. L.273 J.D. [Manatt,P.&P.]

Manatt, Phelps & Phillips, LLP, (AV)
A Limited Liability Partnership including Professional Corporations
1501 M Street, N.W., Suite 700, 20005-1702 ⊙
Telephone: 202-463-4300 FAX: 202-463-4394
Email: mpp@manatt.com URL: http://www.manatt.com
Members of Firm: Charles T. Manatt (P.C.); June Langston (Walton) DeHart; Michael B. Adlin; Jonathan E. Allen (Not admitted in DC); Irwin P. Altschuler; David R. Amerine; Barrie D. Berman; Jack W. Buechner; Stephen E. Coran; Donald J. Fitzgerald; Gregory A. Gehlmann; Mary Ann Gilleece; James R. Jones; Robert J. Kabel; Steven A. Lancellotta; Lizbeth R. Levinson; Abbe David Lowell; Pamela J. Marple; Marylin Jenkins Milner; Stephen L. Neal Jr.; Jeffrey S. Neeley; B. Michael Rauh; John L. Ray; Steven F. Reich; Robert J. Rini; James H. Roberts III; Stephen M. Ryan; Susan M. Schmidt; Donald S. Stein; Jessica A. Wasserman. Of Counsel: David G. O'Neil; Ronald M. Wisla. Resident Associates: Michael T. Brown; Julie A. Campbell (Not admitted in DC); Lindsey W. Cooper (Not admitted in DC); Andrew N. Gentin; Theodore W. Jones (Not admitted in DC); Stephanie J. Kim; David A. Leib; Kimberly Lincoln-Stewart; Sarah J. Loope (Not admitted in DC); Ruel B. Pile; Holly A. Roth; Sarah E. Stephens; James A. Tartal; Christine H. T. Yang; E. Lawrence Zolt.
LITIGATION: Civil Trial Practice in all Courts; Class Action Defense; Energy and Natural Resources; Entertainment; General Commercial; Health Care; Insurance; Intellectual Property; Labor and Employment; National and International Arbitration; Mediation and Preventive Law; Securities; Special Investigations and White-Collar Defense. BUSINESS, FINANCE and REAL ESTATE: Banking and Financial Services; Bankruptcy and Reorganization; Corporate Finance and Securities; Electronic Commerce and Telecommunications; Executive Compensation and Employee Benefits; Real Estate; Tax; Venture Capital and Private Equity. ENTERTAINMENT, MEDIA and INTELLECTUAL PROPERTY: Internet and New Media; Motion Picture and Television; Music; Technology. GOVERNMENT and INTERNATIONAL TRADE and POLICY: Domestic and International Government Affairs; Election and Campaign Law; Global Business Strategies; Government Contracts; International Trade and Customs; Land Use, Energy and Environmental; Latin America and China Advisory; Legislative and Regulatory Advocacy; Political, Economic and Business Risk Assessment.
Los Angeles, California Office: Trident Center, East Tower, 11355 West Olympic Boulevard. Telephone: 310-312-4000. Fax: 310-312-4224.
Palo Alto, California Office: 1001 Page Mill Road, Building 2. Telephone: 650-812-1300. Fax: 650-213-0260.
Sacramento, California Office: 1215 K Street, Suite 1900. Telephone: 916-552-2300. Fax: 916-552-2323.
Costa Mesa, California Office: 12th Floor, Center Tower, 650 Town Center Drive. Telephone: 714-371-2500. Fax: 714-371-2550.
See Professional Biographies, WASHINGTON, DISTRICT OF COLUMBIA

Manbeck, Harry F., Jr. '26 '55
C.401 B.S.E.E. L.421 LL.B. [Rothwell,F.E.&M.] (See Pat. Sect.)
Manca, Paul D. .... '68 '93 C.770 B.S. L.276 J.D. [Hogan&H.]
*PRACTICE AREAS: Commercial Law; Corporate Law; Mergers and Acquisitions; Divestitures; Securities.
Mance, Robert W., (AV) ..... '44 '71 C&L.329 B.A., J.D. 1850 M Street, N.W. Suite 280
Mancini, Mark A., (AV) .... '48 '73 C.659 A.B. L.831 J.D. [Wasserman,M.&C.]
*PRACTICE AREAS: Immigration and Nationality Law.
Mancini, Mary Ann, (AV) .... '57 '84 C.903 B.A. L.128 J.D. [Steptoe&J.]
*PRACTICE AREAS: Estate Planning; Estate & Trust Administration; Business Planning; Tax.
Mancusi, Michael Andrew '72 '97 C.893 B.S. L.692 J.D.
(adm. in VA; not adm. in DC) [Ⓐ Shaw P.]
Mandel, Carol Ruth '54 '84 C.1168 B.A. L.809 J.D.
(adm. in CO; not adm. in DC) Assoc. Prof., Georgetown U.
Mandel, Michael S., (AV) .... '49 '74 C&L.575 A.B., J.D. [Akin,G.S.H.&F.]
*PRACTICE AREAS: Real Estate; Structured Financial Transactions; Real Estate Investment Trusts.
Mandell, Paul S. .... '73 '98 C.446 B.A. L.976 J.D. 555 Twelfth Street, N.W.
Mandell, Steven J. .... '58 '83 C.692 B.A. L.128 J.D. [Piper M.R.&W.] (⊙Balt., MD)
*PRACTICE AREAS: Health Care and Hospital Law; Corporate Law; Venture Capital.
Manderscheid, David J. ...... '65 '91 C.352 B.A. L.309 J.D. Sr. Coun., Marriott Intl. Dr.
*RESPONSIBILITIES: Lodging Operations; Business; Transactional.
Mandigma, Aileen F. .... '73 '98 C.205 B.A. L.1338 J.D. 1615 H. Street, SW
Mandir, William H. .... '60 '87 C.446 B.S.E.E. L.1218 J.D. [Sughrue M.] (See Pat. Sect.)
*PRACTICE AREAS: Intellectual Property Law; Litigation.
Mandl, David J. '74 '99 C.37 B.S. L.276 J.D.
(adm. in MA; not adm. in DC) [Ⓐ Winston&S.]
*PRACTICE AREAS: Environmental.
Mandolia, Charles E. '44 '76 C.378 B.S. L.800 J.D.
Dep. Gen. Coun., Tort Claims & Litig., National Railroad Passenger Corp. (AMTRAK)
Manela, Stewart S., (AV) .... '52 '77 C.966 B.A. L.273 J.D. [Arent F.K.P.&K.]
*PRACTICE AREAS: Employment Litigation; Equal Opportunity Law; Labor Law; Occupational Safety and Health; Workers Compensation.
Manelli, Daniel J., (AV) .... '35 '62 C&L.602 B.S., LL.B. [Manelli,D.&S.]
*PRACTICE AREAS: Food, Drug and Cosmetic Law; Administrative Law; Legislative Law.

Manelli, Denison & Selter, P.L.L.C., (AV) [BB]
2000 M Street, N.W. Suite 700, 20036-3307
Telephone: 202-261-1000 Fax: 202-887-0336
URL: http://www.mdslaw.com
Daniel J. Manelli; Mary Boney Denison; Michael H. Selter; Eliot J. Halperin; Jeffrey Scott Melcher; William H. Bollman; Edward J. Stemberger; Stuart E. Benson; W. Warren Taltavull III; Leon R. Turkevich; Paul E. White, Jr.; George A. Quadrino. Of Counsel: Deana E. Rose.
Intellectual Property, Internet Law, Venture Capital.
See Professional Biographies, WASHINGTON, DISTRICT OF COLUMBIA

Maner, Forbes .... '51 '77 C.309 B.A. L.893 J.D. [Burt,M.&M.]
*PRACTICE AREAS: Litigation.
Manfred, Robert D., Jr. .... '58 '83 C.188 B.S. L.309 J.D. 1800 M St., N.W.
Mangan, John J. .... '41 '68 C&L.188 B.C.E., J.D. [Skadden,A.S.M.&F.]
Mangas, Robert .... '60 '86 C.383 B.A. L.178 J.D. [Ⓒ Dickstein S.M.&O.]
Mangefrida, David J., Jr. .... '58 '85 C.367 B.A. L.178 J.D. Ernst & Young LLP
Mangel, Douglas M. .... '60 '85 C.1365 B.A. L.276 J.D. [Drinker B.&R.]
Mangione, Peter T. .... '48 '74 C.262 B.A. L.982 J.D. 1319 F St., N.W.
Mango, Andrea R. '72 '99 C.473 B.A. L.180 J.D.
(adm. in MD; not adm. in DC) [Ⓐ Dechert]
*PRACTICE AREAS: Securities Litigation.
Mangold, Donna S. .... '56 '81 C.991 B.A. L.276 J.D. [Cooter,M.T.&W.]
Mangrum, Michelle R. .... '55 '86 C&L.502 B.S., J.D. [Shook,H.&B.]
*PRACTICE AREAS: Pharmaceutical/Medical Device Litigation.
Mangrum, Robert A., (AV) .... '41 '66 C&L.838 B.S., J.D. [Winston&S.]
*PRACTICE AREAS: Government Contract Law.
Manheim, Bruce S., Jr. .... '55 '88 C.668 B.A. L.276 J.D. [Ⓒ Bennett,T.&C.]
Mani, Lalitha '50 '86 C.999 B.A. L.930 J.D.
(adm. in OH; not adm. in DC) [Ⓐ Perkins C.]
*PRACTICE AREAS: Intellectual Property; Trademarks; Copyrights.
Manier, Jody Ann .... '68 '96 C.839 B.A. L.145 J.D. 2555 M St., N.W.
Manigo-Truell, Simone '72 '01 C.276 B.S. L.178 J.D.
(adm. in NY; not adm. in DC) [Ⓐ Covington&B.]
Maniscalco, Denise Ann '67 '92 C.846 B.A. L.425 J.D.
(adm. in TX; not adm. in DC) 1328 18th St. N.W.
Mankiewicz, Frank F. '24 '55 C&L.112 A.B., LL.B.
Vice Chmn., Hill & Knowlton, Inc.
Mankofsky, Lisa S., (AV) .... '— '86 C.1044 B.A. L.477 J.D. [Foley&L.]
*PRACTICE AREAS: Intellectual Property Litigation; Manufacturer and Distributor Relations.
Manley, Jeffrey A., (AV) .... '41 '68 C&L.309 A.B., LL.B. [Wilmer,C.&P.]
*PRACTICE AREAS: Aviation Law; Administrative Law.

Manley, Lawrence Bain .... '58 '84 C.30 B.A. L.94 J.D. 2026 32nd St. S.E.
Manley, Nena .... '50 '76 C.1169 A.B. L.1066 J.D. The World Bk.
Mann, Barbara J. .... '44 '77 C.772 B.A. L.329 J.D. Asst. Corp. Coun.
Mann, Hollye R. .... '73 '99 C.197 B.A. L.188 J.D. 2101 L Street, N.W.
Mann, Kim D., (AV) .... '40 '65 C.976 B.A. L.880 LL.B. [Shawncoulson]
Mann, Kimberly V. .... '59 '95 C.205 B.S. L.446 J.D. [Ⓐ Shaw P.]
Mann, Lawrence M., (AV) .... '40 '67 C.575 B.A. L.276 LL.B. [Alper&M.]
*PRACTICE AREAS: Railroad Safety; Personal Injury; Family Law; Civil Litigation.
Mann, Michael D. .... '53 '81 C.999 B.A. L.1162 J.D. [Richards S.K.&O.] ⊙
Mann, Neal L. '42 '76 C.446 B.S. L.276 J.D.
(adm. in IL; not adm. in DC) 909 Mass. Ave., N.E.
Mann, Phillip L., (AV) .... '— '62 C&L.846 B.B.A., LL.B. [Miller&C.]
*PRACTICE AREAS: Taxation; Business Taxation; Financial Institutions Taxation; Oil and Gas Taxation; Tax Controversies.
Mann, Richard F. .... '51 '77 C.880 A.B. L.30 J.D. [Keller&H.]
*PRACTICE AREAS: Advertising and Labeling; Federal and State Trade Regulation; Food, Drug and Device Law.
Mann, Ronald J. '61 '85 C.691 B.A. L.846 J.D.
(adm. in TX; not adm. in DC) 1827 Jeferson Pl. N.W.
Mann, William M. .... '71 '99 C.692 B.A. L.893 J.D. [Ⓐ Crowell&M.]

Mann Bracken, LLC
Suite 360 Chevy Chase Pavillion, 5335 Wisconsin Avenue, N.W., 20015 ⊙
Telephone: 202-274-2140 Facsimile: 202-686-9709
Email: skramer@mannbracken.com URL: http://www.mannbracken.com
Scott A. Kramer; Connell A. Loftus (Resident, Washington, D.C. Office);—Matthew Linkie (Resident, Washington, DC Office).
General Civil and Business Litigation, Commercial and Bankruptcy Law. Retail and Commercial Collection Law, Alimony and Child Support Collection Law, Domestic Relations and Family Law, Personal Injury Law. Trials in all State and Federal Courts.
Atlanta, Georgia Office: Suite 700 Peachtree Center International Tower, 229 Peachtree Street, N.E. Telephone: 404-586-0500. Facsimile: 404-586-0638.
See Professional Biographies, WASHINGTON, DISTRICT OF COLUMBIA

Mannava, Ashok '69 '99 C.588 B.S.E.E. L.128 J.D.
(adm. in VA; not adm. in DC) [Ⓐ Wilmer,C.&P.]
Manne, Geoffrey A. '— '00 C&L.145 A.B., J.D.
(adm. in VA; not adm. in DC) [Ⓐ Latham&W.]
*PRACTICE AREAS: Antitrust; Appellate Practice; Commercial Litigation.
Mannen, Ted R. .... '50 '75 C.801 B.A. L.597 J.D. [Ⓒ Baker&D.]
*PRACTICE AREAS: Health Care; Legislation.
Manner, Jennifer Abbe .... '64 '92 C.1044 B.A. L.564 J.D. MCI Worldcom Inc.
Mannina, George J., Jr. .... '49 '80 C.188 B.S. L.30 J.D. [O'Connor&H.]
Manning, Christopher C. S. .... '72 '97 C.623 B.A. L.902 J.D. [Ⓐ Bryan C.]
*PRACTICE AREAS: Commercial Litigation; Insurance Coverage; Environmental Litigation.
Manning, Christopher N. .... '73 '99 C.228 A.B. L.309 J.D. [Ⓐ Williams&C.]
*PRACTICE AREAS: Civil Litigation; Criminal Defense; General Practice; Media and First Amendment; Trial Practice.
Manning, Christopher Nicholas .... '73 '99 C.228 A.B. L.309 J.D. 725 12th St., N.W.
Manning, J. Lawrence, Jr. .... '43 '68 C.902 B.S. L.893 J.D. [Jones,D.R.&P.]
*PRACTICE AREAS: Mergers and Acquisitions; International Securities; Project Finance.
Manning, John J. .... '69 '99 C.813 A.B. L.276 J.D. 555 4th St. N.W.
Manning, Mary Jo .... '42 '67 C.322 B.A. L.790 J.D. [Ⓒ Wiley R.&F.]
*PRACTICE AREAS: Government Affairs; Communications Law.
Manning, Michael J., (AV) .... '44 '69 C.378 A.B. L.900 J.D. [Fulbright&J.]
*PRACTICE AREAS: Energy; Oil and Gas Law; Natural Resources; Administrative Law; Litigation.
Manning, Paul Stephen '63 '94 C.93 A.B. L.1209 J.D.
(adm. in VA; not adm. in DC) I.R.S.
Mannino, James A., (P.C.), (AV) .... '42 '68 C&L.575 A.B., J.D. [Ashcraft&G.]
*PRACTICE AREAS: Workers Compensation.
Mannion, Robert E., (AV) .... '43 '69 C.276 A.B. L.128 J.D. [Arnold&P.]
*PRACTICE AREAS: Financial Institutions; International.
Mannix, Richard J. .... '43 '84 C.749 B.S. L.1009 J.D. [Ⓒ Crowell&M.]
Manoogian, David E., (AV) .... '44 '69 C.216 B.A. L.273 J.D. [Epstein B.&G.]
*PRACTICE AREAS: Litigation; Medical Malpractice; Health Litigation.
Manor, C. Robert .... '49 '87 C.923 B.A. L.128 J.D. [Spriggs&H.]
*PRACTICE AREAS: Products Liability; Toxic Torts; Litigation; Environmental Law; Drug and Medical Device Defense.
Manos, Karen Louise, (AV) .... '59 '86 C.1070 B.S. L.228 J.D. [Howrey S.A.&W.]
*PRACTICE AREAS: Government Contracts; Commercial Litigation.
Mansbach, B. Thomas, (AV) .... '39 '64 C.976 B.A. L.309 LL.B. [Ⓒ Russin&V.]
*PRACTICE AREAS: International Investment; International Finance; Emerging Markets; Political Risk Insurance; Project Finance.
Manson, Joseph L., III, (AV) .... '— '74 C.893 B.S. L.245 J.D. [Verner,L.B.M.&H.]
*PRACTICE AREAS: Aviation Law; International Transactions; Labor Law; Litigation.
Mansour, Mark '57 '88 C&L.276 B.S.F.S., J.D.
(adm. in MI; not adm. in DC) [Keller&H.]
*PRACTICE AREAS: International Trade Regulation; Biotechnology; Food and Drug Law.
Manspeizer, David Avrum, (BV) '63 '91
C.659 B.A. L.705 J.D. [Finnegan,H.F.G.&D.] (See Pat. Sect.)
*PRACTICE AREAS: Intellectual Property Litigation; Pharmaceutical Intellectual Property; Federal Litigation; Biotechnology Patent Prosecution; Biotechnology Patents.
Mansulla, Wayne M., (AV) .... '45 '74 C.1200 A.B. L.276 J.D. [Ashcraft&G.]
*PRACTICE AREAS: Medical Malpractice; Personal Injury.
Manteria, S. William '45 '71 C&L.724 B.A., J.D.
(adm. in NY; not adm. in DC) V.P., Natl. Retail Federation
Manthei, John R. .... '— '94 C.473 B.A. L.966 J.D. [Ⓐ Latham&W.]
*PRACTICE AREAS: Food and Drug Law; Government Relations.
Manthripragada, Ranganath .... '62 '89 C&L.446 B.A., J.D. Trial Atty.
Manuel, Hilda A. '51 '87 C.112 B.A. L.560 J.D.
(adm. in AZ; not adm. in DC) [Ⓒ Steptoe&J.]
*PRACTICE AREAS: Natural Resources; Indian Law.
Manzer, Nancy L., (BV) .... '61 '89 C.309 A.B. L.188 J.D. [Ⓒ Wilmer,C.&P.]
*PRACTICE AREAS: Civil Litigation; Insurance.
Mao, Emily W. .... '66 '92 C.659 B.A. L.30 J.D. [Ⓐ Alston&B.]
*PRACTICE AREAS: ERISA; Employee Benefits Taxation.
Mao, Yibing '63 '90
(adm. in VA; not adm. in DC) Asst. Gen. Coun., Marriott Intl., Inc.
*RESPONSIBILITIES: International Lodging Development.
Mapes, William R., Jr., (AV) .... '52 '78 C.473 B.S. L.30 J.D. [Duane,M.&H.]
*PRACTICE AREAS: Energy Law; Litigation; Appellate Practice.
Maples, Timothy C. .... '69 '96 C&L.597 B.A., J.D. [Ⓐ Hogan&H.]
*PRACTICE AREAS: Corporate Law; Mergers and Acquisitions; Securities.
Marames, William E. .... '55 '81 [Arent F.K.P.&K.]
*PRACTICE AREAS: Trademark Law; Copyright Law; Electronic Commerce.
Marangi, Karen L. .... '66 '96 C&L.813 B.A., J.D. [Ⓐ Patton B.]
Marans, J. Eugene, (AV) .... '40 '66 C&L.309 A.B., LL.B. [Ⓒ Cleary,G.S.&H.]
Marantz, Wendy .... '73 '99 C.228 A.B. L.477 J.D. 111 F Street, N.W.
Marcelle, Dawn P. .... '61 '91 C.103 A.B. L.1066 J.D. 3900 Wisconsin Ave., N.W.
Marchant, Anyda .... '11 '43 C&L.537 A.B., LL.B. Intl. Bk. for Reconstr. & Develop.
Marchant, Byron F. '57 '87 C.871 B.S. L.893 J.D.
Exec. V.P. & Chf. Admin. Offr., Black Entertainment Television, Inc.

Marchant, Dawn Danzeisen ....'66 '90 C.401 B.S. L.309 J.D. [Kirkland&E.]
*PRACTICE AREAS: Commercial Litigation; Product Liability.

Marcil, Lorrie M. ....'60 '85 C.165 B.A. L.228 J.D. [Sidley A.B.&W.]

Marcin, Raymond B. '38 '64 C.999 A.B. L.262 J.D.
Prof. of Law, Catholic Univ. of Amer.

Marcolin, Carla M. ....'61 '88 C.823 B.S. L.128 J.D. [Ⓐ Dickstein S.M.&O.]
*PRACTICE AREAS: Civil Litigation; Labor and Employment.

Marcotte, David P. ....'67 '97 C.588 B.S. L.1364 J.D. [Lloyd&M.]
*PRACTICE AREAS: Personal Injury; Criminal Defense; Real Estate; Social Security Disability.

Marcotte, Eric J., (AV) ....'57 '88 C.640 B.S. L.846 J.D. [Winston&S.]
*PRACTICE AREAS: Government Contracts; Commercial Law.

Marcou, George T. ....'57 '84 C.453 B.S.M.E. L.276 J.D. [Kilpatrick S.] (Pat.)
*PRACTICE AREAS: Intellectual Property; Patents.

Marcoux, J. Michel, (AV) ....'45 '73 C.902 A.B. L.893 LL.B. [Bruder,G.&M.]
*PRACTICE AREAS: Natural Gas; Appellate Practice.

Marcson, Nicole E. '74 '00 C.228 A.B. L.880 J.D.
(adm. in VA; not adm. in DC) [Ⓐ Shaw P.]
*PRACTICE AREAS: Technology Law.

Marcus, Jeremy D. '71 '97 C.659 B.A. L.276 J.D.
(adm. in NY; not adm. in DC) [Ⓐ Blumenfeld&C.]
*PRACTICE AREAS: Communications Law; Telecommunications Law; Technology Law; Transactional Law.

Marcus, Kenneth L. ....'66 '92 C.951 B.A. L.1066 J.D. [Holland&K.]
*PRACTICE AREAS: Trial and Appellate Litigation; Financial Services Litigation; Constitutional Litigation.

Marcus, Michael S., (BV) '49 '84
C.563 B.Ch.E. L.1209 J.D. [Morgan&F.] (See Pat. Sect.)
*PRACTICE AREAS: Intellectual Property; Patents; Reexamination and Petition Practice.

Marcus, Michael S., (P.C.) ....'44 '70 C.264 A.B. L.884 J.D. [Akin,G.S.H.&F.]
*PRACTICE AREAS: Litigation.

Marcus, Mitchell Lane '63 '89 C.1365 B.B.A. L.273 J.D.
(adm. in MD; not adm. in DC) 1775 Pennsylvania Ave., N.W.

Marcus, Stephen H., (AV) ....'53 '80 C.025 B.A. L.019 LL.B. [Baach R.&L.P.]
*PRACTICE AREAS: Civil Litigation; Commercial Litigation; International Trade; Insurance Litigation; Coverage Litigation.

Marcus, Theodore C. '64 '91 C.893 B.A. L.846 J.D.
Compliance Coun., BellSouth Corp.

Marcuss, Stanley J., (AV) ....'— '69 C.855 B.A. L.309 J.D. [Bryan C.]

Marder, Mitchell S. ....'61 '86 C&L.273 B.A., J.D. [Piper M.R.&W.]
*PRACTICE AREAS: Corporate Finance; Venture Capital; Banking Law.

Mares, Jan W. '36 '64 C&L.309 B.A., LL.B.
(adm. in NY; not adm. in DC) 3228 Woodley Rd Nw

Maresca, Charles A., Jr. '53 '88 C&L.128 B.A., J.D.
(adm. in MD; not adm. in DC)
National Interreligious Serv. Bd. for Conscientious Objectors

Margand, Christopher G. ....'60 '91 C&L.276 B.S., J.D. [Ⓐ Holland&K.]
*PRACTICE AREAS: Litigation.

Marget, Jonathan P. ....'37 '65 C.309 A.B. L.30 J.D. 2401 "H" St., N.W.

Margolies, Hubert H. ....'10 '35 C&L.178 A.B., LL.B. 2800 Woodley Rd Nw # 538‡

Margolin, Andrew S. '64 '91
C.994 B.A. L.1009 J.D. Atty., The Nasdaq Stock Market, Inc.

Margolin, Elissa D. '68 '95 C.012 B.A. L.30 J.D.
(adm. in MA; not adm. in DC) Dep. Exec. Dir., League of Amer. Bicyclists

Margolis, Vicki ....'64 '89 C.473 B.S. L.446 J.D. [Venable,A.B.H.&C.] (⊙Balt., MD)
*PRACTICE AREAS: Intellectual Property Litigation; Commercial Litigation.

Margolius, Bernard, (AV) .....'13 '37 C&L.273 A.B., LL.B. 2801 N. Mexico Ave., NW‡

Margolius, Philip N., (AV) '40 '66
C.197 B.A. L.976 LL.B. [Margolius,M.D.R.&T.] (⊙Largo, MD)
*PRACTICE AREAS: Probate and Estate Planning; Real Estate; Commercial Transactions.

Margolius, Mallios, Davis, Rider & Tomar, LLP, (AV)
1828 L Street, N.W., Suite 500, 20036 ⊙
Telephone: 202-296-1000 Fax: 202-296-6400
Email: info@mmdrt.com URL: http://www.lawyers.com/mmdrt
James L. Rider; Dimitri P. Mallios; Philip N. Margolius; Richard T. Tomar; Gary A. Stein; Sharon M. Goley; Susan M. Butler; Laura G. Moldowan; Cheryl K. Graham (Not admitted in DC); Jennifer M. Barham (Not admitted in DC); Melissa Polito; Harvey J. Cohen; Stephen C. Lewis (Not admitted in DC). Largo, Maryland Office: Angelia Merritt Gates; Alyssa W. Chang. Of Counsel: Eugene G. Horowitz; Edward L. Weidenfeld.
General Civil Practice, Estate Planning and Probate, Matrimonial and Family Law, Personal Injury, Commercial and Residential Landlord and Tenant Law, Negligence and Medical Malpractice, General Civil Commercial Litigation, Real Estate Transactions, Alcoholic Beverage Law, before Courts, Agencies and Departments in the District of Columbia, Maryland and Virginia.
References: BB&T.
Largo, Maryland Office: 9200 Basil Court, Suite 300, 20774. Telephone: 301-925-4900. Fax: 301-925-9752.
Alexandria, Virginia Office: 120 South Fairfax Street, Suite 300, 22314.
See Professional Biographies, WASHINGTON, DISTRICT OF COLUMBIA

Margulies, Irving P., (AV) ....'25 '51 C&L.912 A.B., LL.B. [Margulies&W.]

Margulies, J. Richard, (AV) '45 '74
C.188 B.S. L.276 J.D. [Ⓑ Braude&M.] (⊙Rockville, MD)
*PRACTICE AREAS: Construction Law; Administrative Law; Civil Trial Practice Law.

Margulies & Wagner, P.C., (AV) .... 1200 G St., N.W.

Mariani, Patricia '55 '90 C.788 A.B. L.276 J.D.
Immigration Briefings, Federal Publications, Inc.

Mariano, Joseph N. '58 '83 C&L.445 B.S., J.D.
(adm. in MD; not adm. in DC) Senior Vice President, Direct Selling Association

Marine, Gina L. '73 '00 C.893 B.A. L.1209 J.D.
(adm. in VA; not adm. in DC) [Ⓐ King&N.] ⊙

Mariner, Rachel A. ....'67 '93 C.937 B.A. L.309 J.D. [Ⓐ Skadden,A.S.M.&F.]

Marini, Luis '75 '01 C.477 B.B.A. L.276 J.D.
(adm. in VA; not adm. in DC) [Ⓐ Shaw P.]

Marino, Frank A. ....'51 '80 C.472 B.A. L.64 J.D. [Ⓐ Piper M.R.&W.]
*PRACTICE AREAS: Real Estate; Commercial Leasing.

Marino, Keith R. ....'— '94 C&L.945 B.A., J.D. [Ⓐ Arent F.K.P.&K.]
*PRACTICE AREAS: International Trade; International Finance; Customs Law; Patent Litigation.

Marino, Robert M., (AV) ....'— '86 C.1031 B.A. L.276 J.D. [Ⓑ Reed S.]
*PRACTICE AREAS: Bankruptcy.

Marion, Eric M. ....'72 '98 C.264 B.A. L.945 J.D. [Ⓐ Elias,M.T.&H.]

Markakis, Constance ....'54 '86 C.477 B.A. L.912 J.D. [Ⓑ Bredhoff&K.]

Markarian, Gahmk S. '66 '91 C.309 A.B. L.145 J.D.
(adm. in IL; not adm. in DC) 1133 20th St., N.W.

Marketos, James L. ....'54 '80 C.674 A.B. L.569 J.D. [Berliner,C.&R.]
*PRACTICE AREAS: Litigation.

Markey, David J. '40 '67 C.928 B.S. L.446 LL.B.
(adm. in MD; not adm. in DC) V.P., Govt. Affs., BellSouth Corporation

Markey, Regina M. ....'— '94 C.184 B.A. L.128 J.D. 2800 Wisconsin Ave., NW

Markham, Allan W., (AV) ....'32 '61 C&L.575 A.B., J.D. [A.W.Markham]

Markham, Colleen L.S. ....'69 '97 C.674 A.B. L.276 J.D. [Ⓐ Ivins,P.&B.]
*PRACTICE AREAS: Trusts and Estates; Federal Taxation; Estate and Gift Taxation; Individual Taxation; Tax Exempt Organizations.

Markham, Julian E., Jr., (AV) '42 '67 C.902 B.A. L.260 J.D.
[Thompson,O.M.N.&H.] (⊙Rockville, MD; Arlington, VA)
*PRACTICE AREAS: Trusts and Estates; Estate Planning; Estate Administration; Trust Administration; Fiduciary Litigation.

Markham, Allan W., P.C., (AV) ....2733 36th St., NW

Markman, Sherwin J., (AV) ....'29 '52 C.352 A.B. L.976 LL.B. [Ⓑ Hogan&H.]
*PRACTICE AREAS: Litigation (Civil, Criminal, Commercial, Appellate).

Markoski, Joseph P. ....'48 '73 C&L.276 B.S.F.S., J.D. [Squire,S.&D.]
*PRACTICE AREAS: Telecommunications; Privatization.

Markovich, Stephen E. '51 '77
C.757 B.A. L.607 J.D. Sr. Atty., MCI Communications Corporation

Markow, Scott B. '72 '99 C.188 B.S. L.276 J.D.
(adm. in MD; not adm. in DC; See Pat. Sect.) [Ⓐ Covington&B.]
*PRACTICE AREAS: Intellectual Property; Litigation; Electronic Commerce; Food and Drug Regulation.

Markowitz, Bruce, (AV) ....'54 '83 C.696 B.A. L.904 J.D. [Swidler B.S.F.]
*PRACTICE AREAS: Corporate Transactions; Telecommunications; Banking Law; Real Estate; Bankruptcy.

Markowitz, Petrina M. ....'57 '81 C.322 B.A. L.276 J.D. [Piper M.R.&W.]

Marks, Andrew H., (AV) ....'51 '76 C.309 A.B. L.477 J.D. [Crowell&M.]
*PRACTICE AREAS: Directors and Officers Liability; Insurance Coverage; Litigation; Professional Liability Law; RICO.

Marks, Herbert E., (AV) ....'35 '64 C.477 A.B. L.976 J.D. [Squire,S.&D.]
*PRACTICE AREAS: Regulatory Affairs; Telecommunications.

Marks, Jeffrey A. ....'— '98 C.264 B.A. L.537 J.D. [Ⓐ Latham&W.]
*PRACTICE AREAS: Communications Common Carrier; Wireless Communications; Satellite Communications; Federal Civil Litigation.

Marks, Leonard H., (AV) ....'16 '38 C&L.665 A.B., LL.B. [Ⓑ Cohn&M.]

Marks, Matthew J., (AV) ....'14 '41 C.197 B.A. L.178 LL.B. 2001 L St., N.W.

Marks, Michelle S. ....'— '96 C.1168 B.A. L.446 J.D. [Ⓐ Shaw P.] (Pat.)
*PRACTICE AREAS: Intellectual Property.

Marks, Richard D., (AV) ....'44 '72 C.893 B.A. L.976 J.D. [Davis W.T.]
*PRACTICE AREAS: Computer; Telecommunications; HIPAA; First Amendment; Media.

Marks, Richard J. ....'67 '93 C.597 B.S.E.E. L.446 J.D. [Piper M.R.&W.]
*PRACTICE AREAS: Banking; Finance; Business Reorganization; Business Taxation; Business.

Marks, Robert G. ....'69 '94 C.674 A.B. L.309 J.D. [Kirkland&E.]
*PRACTICE AREAS: Corporate.

Marks, Steven M. '67 '93 C&L.228 A.B., J.D.
Sr. V.P., Dir. Bus. Affs., Recording Industry Assoc. of America, Inc.

Marks, William R. ....'61 '92 C.309 A.B. L.276 J.D. 1001 Pennsylvania Ave. N.W.

Markun, David J. '22 '48 C&L.494 B.S.L., J.D.
(adm. in MN; not adm. in DC) 4405 W St., NW‡

Markus, Christina M. ....'— '92 C.945 A.B. L.893 J.D. [Ⓑ King&S.]
*PRACTICE AREAS: Food and Drug Law.

Markus, Eric R. ....'60 '87 C&L.976 B.A., J.D. [Wilmer,C.&P.]
*PRACTICE AREAS: Corporate Law; Securities; Bankruptcy.

Marlow, William F. C., Jr. ....'44 '69 C.893 B.S. L.446 J.D. [Marlow&W.] ⊙

Marlow & Wyatt .... 6935 Wisconsin Ave. (⊙Towson, MD)

Marmelstein, Charles M., (AV) '41 '70
C.446 B.S.E.E. L.30 J.D. [Arent F.K.P.&K.] (Pat.)
*PRACTICE AREAS: Intellectual Property; Patents; Trade Secrets; Trademarks; Copyrights.

Marmon, William F., Jr. '42 '80 C.674 B.A. L.893 J.D.
Exec. Dir. & All./New Ventures, MCI WorldCom

Marmorstone, Edwin ....'18 '51 C&L.276 B.S., J.D. 4101 Cathedral Ave., N.W.‡

Marn, Stephanie L. ....'66 '95 C.311 B.A. L.813 J.D. [Ⓐ Proskauer R.]

Maroney, Terry A. '67 '99 C.604 B.A. L.569 J.D.
(adm. in NY; not adm. in DC) [Ⓐ Wilmer,C.&P.]

Marple, Pamela J. ....'64 '91 C.893 B.A. L.966 J.D. [Manatt,P.&P.]
*PRACTICE AREAS: Litigation.

Marquardt, Paul D. ....'68 '96 C.477 B.A. L.976 J.D. [Ⓐ Cleary,G.S.&H.]

Marquez, Jim J. ....'41 '73 C.560 B.A. L.900 J.D. [Ⓑ Holland&K.] (⊙Mc Lean, VA)
*PRACTICE AREAS: Transportation Law; Aviation; Motor Carrier Regulation; International Transactions.

Marquez, Joaquin A. ....'42 '67 C.659 B.S. L.677 LL.B. [Drinker B.&R.]
*PRACTICE AREAS: Corporate and Securities Law; Banking Law; Legislation Law.

Marquis, Milton A. '57 '85 C.280 A.B. L.930 J.D.
601 Thirteenth Street, NW 12th Floor

Marra, Anthony F. '41 '66
C.602 B.S. L.178 LL.B. Sr. V.P. & Dep. Gen. Coun., Fannie Mae

Marrapese, Martha E. ....'62 '92 C.882 B.S. L.128 J.D. [Keller&H.]
*PRACTICE AREAS: Environmental Law; Occupational Safety and Health Law.

Marraro, Christopher H. ....'52 '83 C.282 B.A. L.1218 J.D. [Wallace K.M.&B.]
*PRACTICE AREAS: Environmental Law; Litigation.

Marriott, Frank S. '28 '54 C.611 B.A. L.608 J.D.
(adm. in OH; not adm. in DC) 1455 Pennsylvania Ave., N.W.

Marrocco, Drew W. ....'68 '95 C.692 B.A. L.30 J.D. [Ⓐ Sonnenschein N.&R.]
*PRACTICE AREAS: Government Contracts; Litigation.

Marsala, Gina M. '69 '00 C.119 B.A. L.262 J.D.
(adm. in NY; not adm. in DC) William M. Mercer, Inc.

Marsan, William P. ....'63 '89 [Ⓐ Troutman S.]
*PRACTICE AREAS: Government Affairs; Utility Regulation; Electronic Commerce; Regulatory Law.

Marsh, David R. ....'64 '96 C.054 B.S. L.569 J.D. [Arnold&P.] (Pat.)

Marsh, Jennifer Evans '62 '99 C.446 B.S. L.884 J.D.
(adm. in MD; not adm. in DC) One Columbus Cir., NE

Marsh, Joan '62 '90 C.112 B.A. L.800 J.D.
(adm. in CA; not adm. in DC) Divn. Mgr., AT&T

Marsh, Richard E., Jr., (AV) '55 '81 C.105 B.A. L.575 J.D.
(adm. in NC; not adm. in DC) 53 D St., S.E. (⊙Charlotte, NC)

Marsh, Richard S. T., (AV) ....'22 '48 C.976 B.A. L.273 LL.B. [Ross,M.&F.]
*PRACTICE AREAS: Estate Planning; Trust and Estate Administration; Tax Law; Real Estate Law.

Marsh, Virgil H., (AV) '35 '64
C.446 B.S.Ch.E. L.276 J.D. [Fisher,C.&S.] (See Pat. Sect.)
*PRACTICE AREAS: Patent, Trademark, Copyright; Unfair Competition and related Litigation.

Marsh Fleischer & Quiggle, Chartered
(See Bethesda, Maryland)

Marshall, Alison B. ....'59 '84 C.674 A.B. L.659 J.D. [Jones,D.R.&P.]
*PRACTICE AREAS: Labor and Employment; Employment Litigation; Employment Class Actions; Title IX Discrimination.

Marshall, Catherine E. '71 '98 C.276 B.A. L.128 J.D.
(adm. in NY; not adm. in DC) [Ⓐ Shaw P.]

Marshall, David J. ....'54 '81 C.245 B.A. L.309 J.D. [Ⓑ Bernabei&K.]
*PRACTICE AREAS: Civil Rights; Class Actions; Whistleblower Law; Employment Discrimination; Civil Liberties.

Marshall, David L. ....'54 '84 C.207 B.A. L.477 J.D. [Baker&H.]
*PRACTICE AREAS: Taxation; Tax-Exempt Organizations; Employment Taxes.

Marshall, Edith S. ....'52 '77 C.309 A.B. L.477 J.D. [Ⓑ Powers,P.S.&V.]
*PRACTICE AREAS: Health Care Law; Litigation; Administrative Law; Information and Privacy; Health Insurance Portability and Accountability Act (HIPAA).

Marshall, Elizabeth A. ....'63 '90 C.223 A.B. L.893 J.D. [Ⓐ Drinker B.&R.]

Marshall, Joan E. '66 '92 C.575 B.A. L.1017 J.D.
(adm. in PA; not adm. in DC) The Nasdaq Stock Market, Inc.

Marshall, Karl N. .... '52 '77 C.329 B.A. L.800 J.D. 2000 L St., N.W.‡
Marshall, Kimberly L. ....'68 '93 C.896 B.A. L.280 J.D. 1150 Eighteenth St., N.W.
Marshall, Lynda K. .... '68 '95 C.602 B.A. L.893 J.D. [A Hogan&H.]
*PRACTICE AREAS: Antitrust.
Marshall, Penny, (AV) .... '56 '82 C.205 B.A. L.309 J.D. Fed. Pub. Def.
Marshall, Richard S. .... '53 '81 C.860 B.A. L.273 J.D. [C Silverstein&M.]
*PRACTICE AREAS: Taxation; Tax Controversies.
Marshall, Rolf .... '40 '91 C.477 B.A. L.273 J.D. [Preston G.E.&R.M.]
*PRACTICE AREAS: Maritime Law; Government Procurement; Litigation.
Marshall, Susan A., (AV) ....'45 '72 C.881 B.A. L.273 J.D. [C Fletcher,H.&H.] ⊙
*PRACTICE AREAS: Communications Law; Mass Media Law; Broadcasting Law; Communications Transactions.
Marshall, Thurgood, Jr. .... '— '82 C&L.893 B.A., J.D. [Swidler B.S.F.]
*PRACTICE AREAS: Government Affairs.
Marston, Philip M. .... '50 '76 C.216 B.A. L.893 J.D. XENERGY, INC.
Marta, Mary R. .... '— '99 C.831 B.A. L.446 J.D. [A Epstein B.&G.]
*PRACTICE AREAS: Health Law.
Martel, Jonathan S., (AV) .... '64 '89 C.197 A.B. L.976 J.D. [Arnold&P.]
*PRACTICE AREAS: Environmental; Regulatory; Litigation.
Martell, Frank J., (AV) ....'22 '50 C.197 A.B. L.276 J.D. [C Martell,D.G.&G.]
Martell, Mary, (AV) ....'56 '80 C.659 B.S. L.1292 J.D. [Martell&Assoc.]
*PRACTICE AREAS: Transactional Law; Housing and Urban Development.

Martell & Associates, (AV)
1718 Connecticut Avenue, N.W., 20009
Telephone: 202-483-3550 Telecopier: 202-483-7159
Mary Martell. Of Counsel: Roberta Beary.
Mortgage and Related Securities, Financial Institutions, Housing and Urban Development Law.
See Professional Biographies, WASHINGTON, DISTRICT OF COLUMBIA

Martell, Donnelly, Grimaldi & Gallagher, P.A., (AV)
1815 H Street, N.W., Suite 420, 20006 ⊙
Telephone: 202-293-0830 Fax: 202-452-8460
Email: d.gallagher@mdgg.com URL: http://www.mdgg.com
David F. Grimaldi; Wade J. Gallagher; Don F. Ryder, Jr.;—Nona Jean Bonanno; David Franklin Ryder; Anthony E. Grimaldi; William J. Virgulak, Jr.; Dana L. Scott, Jr. Of Counsel: Frank J. Martell; William J. Donnelly, Jr.
General and Insurance Practice, Casualty, Professional Malpractice, Products Liability, Life and Health, Aviation and Automobile Law.
Rockville, Maryland Office: 9 North Adams Street. Telephone: 301-424-1300. Fax: 301-217-9088.
Fairfax, Virginia Office: 10201 Lee Highway, Suite 490, 22030-2222. Telephone: 703-273-2811. Fax: 703-273-3208.
See Professional Biographies, WASHINGTON, DISTRICT OF COLUMBIA

Martella, Jennifer E. .... '71 '99 C.112 B.A. L.128 J.D. [A Malizia S.&F.]
*PRACTICE AREAS: Securities; Corporate; Banking.
Martello, Kendra A. '— '01 C.446 B.A. L.904 J.D.
(adm. in MD; not adm. in DC) [A Morgan,L.&B.]
Martin, David H. .... '39 '68 C.928 B.A. L.273 LL.B. [C Employment]
*PRACTICE AREAS: Federal Practice; Criminal Law; Civil Practice; Trade Association Law.
Martin, David L. .... '66 '98 C.840 B.A. L.893 J.D. [A Hogan&H.]
Martin, David L. ....'— '98 C.840 B.A. L.893 J.D. 1200 New Hampshire Ave., N.W.
Martin, Dawn V. ....'57 '82 C.66 B.A. L.569 J.D. [D.V.Martin]
Martin, Edgar H., (AV) ... '— '62 C.688 B.Met.E. L.276 LL.B. [C Morgan,L.&B.] (Pat.)
Martin, Edwin M., Jr., (AV) .... '42 '66 C&L.309 A.B., LL.B. [Piper M.R.&W.]
*PRACTICE AREAS: Securities Regulation Law; Venture Capital Law; Technology Law; Mergers and Acquisitions.
Martin, ElChino M. '61 '86 C.575 B.A. L.976 J.D.
(adm. in NC; not adm. in DC) General Counsel, AFL-CIO Housing Investment Trust
Martin, Gordon G. .... '60 '87 C&L.16 B.S., J.D. Ala. Power Co.
Martin, Guy, (AV) .... '11 '38 C.051 B.A. L.976 LL.B. [Saltzstein,R.A.&G.M.]
Martin, Guy R., (AV) ....'42 '67 C&L.174 B.A., J.D. [Perkins C.]
*PRACTICE AREAS: Natural Resource Law; Public Lands Law; Environmental Law; Energy Law; Federal Legislative Practice.
Martin, Harry C., (AV) ....'45 '73 C.893 B.A. L.273 J.D. [Fletcher,H.&H.] ⊙
*PRACTICE AREAS: Mass Media Law; Media Transactions; Broadcast Radio; Radio and Television.
Martin, Herbert J., (AV) ....'40 '71 C.262 B.A. L.128 J.D. [Crowell&M.]
*PRACTICE AREAS: Energy Law; Federal Gas Law; Interstate Commerce Law; Public Utility Law; Transportation Law.
Martin, J. T., (AV) ....'36 '65 C.880 B.Ch.E. L.893 J.D. 1521 44th Street, N.W.
Martin, James Robertson ....'63 '94 C.454 B.A. L.426 J.D. [A Dickstein S.M.&O.]
*PRACTICE AREAS: Civil Litigation; Antitrust.
Martin, James V. .... '74 '00 C.893 B.A. L.569 J.D. [A O'Melveny&M.]
*PRACTICE AREAS: Mergers and Acquisitions.
Martin, Jeffrey C. ....'53 '79 C.347 A.B. L.145 J.D. [Shea&G.]
*PRACTICE AREAS: Insurance Law; Securities; Retail Law; Complex Litigation; Government Relations.
Martin, Jeffrey N. ....'52 '78 C.399 B.A. L.309 J.D. [Hunton&W.]
*PRACTICE AREAS: Environmental.
Martin, Jenifer J. .... '— '97 C.477 B.A. L.276 J.D. [A Verner,L.B.M.&H.]
*PRACTICE AREAS: Legislative.
Martin, John C. ....'53 '79 C.972 B.S. L.276 J.D. [Patton B.]
Martin, John L. ....'37 '66 C&L.823 B.A., J.D. 2121 K St., N.W.
Martin, Joshua R. ....'72 '97 C.945 B.A. L.893 J.D. [A Fulbright&J.]
*PRACTICE AREAS: Securities Regulation; Securities Litigation.
Martin, Julie Glass ....'61 '93 C.446 B.S. L.128 J.D. [A Goldsmith]
*PRACTICE AREAS: General Practice.
Martin, Kate Abbott '52 '77 C.668 B.A. L.893 J.D.
Dir., Ctr. for Natl. Sec. Studies, ACLU
Martin, Katherine K. '75 '00 C&L.823 B.A., J.D.
(adm. in NY; not adm. in DC) [A Sullivan&C.]
Martin, Keith, (AV) ....'53 '77 C.918 B.A. L.273 J.D. [Chadbourne&P.]
Martin, Kenneth A. .... '55 '86 C.21 B.A. L.818 J.D. [Martin&A.]
*PRACTICE AREAS: Government Contracts; Complex Business Litigation; White Collar Criminal Defense; Intellectual Property Litigation; Construction Law.
Martin, Lawrence H. '— '98 C.95 B.A. L.309 J.D.
(adm. in MA; not adm. in DC) [A Foley,H.&E.]
*PRACTICE AREAS: Litigation.
Martin, Lewe B., (AV) ....'24 '52 C&L.902 B.S., LL.B. 1920 N St., N.W.
Martin, Marc S. '65 '91 C.183 B.A. L.823 J.D.
V.P., Gen. Coun. & Secy., BET.com, LLC
Martin, Mark E., (AV) .... '51 '83 C.309 A.B. L.569 J.D. [C Sidley A.B.&W.]
Martin, Middleton A. ....'43 '76 C.674 A.B. L.276 J.D. [Patton B.]
Martin, Pamela Murch ....'59 '85 C&L.276 B.A., J.D. 3900 Wisconsin Ave., N.W.
Martin, Paul '69 '00 C.999 B.A. L.569 J.D.
(adm. in NY; not adm. in DC) [A Paul,W.R.W.&G.]
*PRACTICE AREAS: Project Finance; Mergers and Acquisitions; Public Law.
Martin, Paul G. '73 '99 C.228 B.A. L.880 J.D.
(adm. in MD; not adm. in DC) [A Sidley A.B.&W.]
Martin, Peter A. ....'60 '86 C.881 A.B. L.831 J.D. [Vorys,S.S.&P.]
*PRACTICE AREAS: Antidumping; Customs Law; Export Regulation; Foreign Trade Sanctions; Import and Export Law.
Martin, Ralph Drury, (AV) ....'47 '72 C.861 B.A. L.910 J.D. [Dilworth P.P.]
*PRACTICE AREAS: Securities Law; Litigation; International.
Martin, Rebecca B. .... '72 '00 C.104 B.A. L.276 J.D. [A Dechert]
*PRACTICE AREAS: Financial Services Law; Investment Management.
Martin, Robert, (AV) ....'27 '49 C.197 A.B. L.178 LL.B. [C Simon,T.&M.]
*PRACTICE AREAS: Government Procurement; International Transactions; Mergers and Acquisitions.
Martin, Scott '74 '00 C.352 B.A. L.537 J.D.
(adm. in MD; not adm. in DC) [A Webster,F.&B.]
*PRACTICE AREAS: Bankruptcy; Employment Law.
Martin, Stephen Russell, II ....'68 '94 C.208 B.A. L.190 J.D. U.S. Attorney's Office
Martin, Thomas S., (AV) .... '46 '73 C.1113 B.A. L.145 J.D. [Shearman&S.]
Martin, William D. ....'11 '52 C.943 B.S. L.276 J.D. 4422 Eads St., N.E.‡
Martin, William R., (AV) ....'49 '76 C.329 B.A. L.150 J.D. [Dyer E.&J.]
*PRACTICE AREAS: Litigation; White Collar Defense; Criminal Litigation; Sports and Entertainment Law; Commercial Litigation.

Martin & Adams, PLLC
1730 Rhode Island Avenue, N.W. Suite 812, 20036-3114
Telephone: 202-408-1155 Fax: 202-408-7554 URL: http://www.martinadams.com
Email: info@martinadams.com URL: http://www.lawyers.com/martin&rylanderpc
Kenneth A. Martin; Jennifer Collesano Adams;—Jasen Dean Adams (Not admitted in DC).
See Professional Biographies, WASHINGTON, DISTRICT OF COLUMBIA

Martin, Dawn V., Law Offices of ....1090 Vermont Ave., N.W.

Martin, Snyder & Bernstein, P.A.
(See Baltimore, Maryland)

Martindale, Richard D. '70 '95 C.880 B.A. L.910 J.D.
(adm. in TX; not adm. in DC) [A Gilbert H.&R.]
*PRACTICE AREAS: Complex Dispute Resolution; Commercial Litigation; Insurance Litigation.
Martinez, Jenny S. '71 '99 C.976 B.A. L.309 J.D.
(adm. in VA; not adm. in DC) [A Jenner&B.]
*PRACTICE AREAS: Litigation; First Amendment Law; International Law.
Martinez, Michael L., (AV) ....'54 '79 C&L.112 A.B., J.D. [Crowell&M.]
*PRACTICE AREAS: Federal Civil Litigation; False Claims Act; Government Contract Fraud; Foreign Sovereign Immunities Act; Health Care Fraud.
Martinez, Robert J. ....'53 '79 C.674 B.S.E. L.276 J.D. [Williams&J.]
Martinez, Vincente L. .... '69 '99 C.276 B.A. L.1066 J.D. [A Patton B.]
Martocci, Joseph P., Jr. '52 '78
C.1030 B.A. L.1209 J.D. Coun., I.A.M. Natl. Pension Fund
*RESPONSIBILITIES: ERISA; ERISA Collections; Taft-Hartley Plans; Multi-Employer Benefits.
Martorana, Francis J. ....'51 '82 C.1031 B.S. L.128 J.D. [O'Donoghue&O.]
Marty, LaMadrid & Starkey ....1225 I St., N.W.
Martyn, Iden Grant '59 '84 C.381 B.A. L.1003 J.D.
(adm. in OH; not adm. in DC) [A Jenkens&G.]
*PRACTICE AREAS: Health Law; Health Care Fraud; Litigation.
Martz, Stephanie A. .... '69 '97 C.276 A.B. L.813 J.D. [A Baker B.]
Maruca, Samuel M., (AV) ....'55 '83 C.976 B.A. L.276 J.D. [Miller&C.]
*PRACTICE AREAS: Taxation; Tax Controversies; International Taxation; Tax Audits; Tax Planning.
Maruyama, Warren H., (AV) .... '55 '80 C.118 B.A. L.188 J.D. [Hogan&H.]
*PRACTICE AREAS: International Trade Law.
Marvel, L. Paige, (AV) ....'49 '74 C.600 B.A. L.446 J.D. Judge, U.S. Tax Ct.
Marvin, Barbara M.R. ....'— '95 C.1106 B.A. L.30 J.D. [A Jackson&C.] ⊙
*PRACTICE AREAS: Insurance Coverage.
Marvin, Charles R. "Rod", Jr., (BV) '53 '82 C.477 B.A. L.94 J.D.
[Venable,A.B.H.&C.]
*PRACTICE AREAS: Government Contract Law; Commercial Litigation; Computer.
Marvin, Douglas R., (AV) ....'47 '72 C.390 A.B. L.893 J.D. [Williams&C.]
Marx, Fredrick M., (AV) .... '55 '80 C.216 B.A. L.659 J.D. [Slevin&H.]
*PRACTICE AREAS: Employee Benefits.
Marx, Gary Samuel ....'54 '79 C.910 A.B. L.902 J.D. 1101 Conn. Ave., N.W.
Maryn, Michael R. ....'60 '89 C.446 B.A. L.128 J.D. [Sonnenschein N.&R.]
*PRACTICE AREAS: Employee Benefits.
Marzen, Stephen James ....'60 '85 C.665 B.A. L.309 J.D. [Shearman&S.]
Marzouk, Tobey B., (AV) .... '52 '77 C.674 A.B. L.309 J.D. [Marzouk&P.]
*PRACTICE AREAS: Computer Software Law; Technology Law; Copyrights; Trade Secrets; Trademarks.

Marzouk & Parry, (AV)
1120 Nineteenth Street, N.W., Seventh Floor, 20036
Telephone: 202-463-7293 Telecopier: 202-955-9371
Email: tmarzouk@veriomail.com URL: http://www.lawyers.com/marzouk&parrylaw
Tobey B. Marzouk; Thomas M. Parry. Of Counsel: Paul G. Gaston.
Computer and Software, Internet, Electronic Commerce, Technology Licensing, Copyrights, Trade Secrets, Trademark Law, Litigation and Cyber Law and Emerging Business Law.
See Professional Biographies, WASHINGTON, DISTRICT OF COLUMBIA

Marzulla, Brenda D. '74 '99 C.78 B.A. L.200 J.D.
(adm. in VA; not adm. in DC) Marzulla & Marzulla
Marzulla, Nancie G. .... '— '82 C.174 M.D.P.A. L.1165 J.D. [C Wewer]
Masback, Harold E., III, (AV) .... '51 '76 C.951 B.A. L.178 J.D. [C Ross,D.&B.]

Masciola, Peter R., Law Office of '57 '83 C.1200 B.A. L.1202 J.D.
601 Indiana Avenue, Suite 603, 20004
Telephone: 202-628-5680; 1-800-741-5308 Fax: 202-628-5682
Email: petermas@erols.com URL: http://www.lawyers.com/petermasciola
Medical Malpractice, Military Medical Malpractice, Military Health Care, Military Courts Martial, Military Law, Military Criminal Law, Cerebral Palsy, Catastrophic Injury, Birth Trauma, Serious Personal Injury, Airplane Crashes, Military Accidents and Tort Law.
See Professional Biographies, WASHINGTON, DISTRICT OF COLUMBIA

Mascola, Robert E. .... '64 '96 C&L.309 A.B., J.D. [A Arnold&P.]
*PRACTICE AREAS: Antitrust.
Maser, John K., III, (AV) ....'45 '73 C.645 A.B. L.276 J.D. [C Thompson H.]
*PRACTICE AREAS: Administrative Law; Transportation Law.
Mashhadi, Marjan ....'— '01 C.910 B.A. L.94 J.D. [A Morgan,L.&B.]
Masiello, Anthony R. .... '56 '87 C&L.309 A.B., J.D. [A Holland&K.]
*PRACTICE AREAS: Trademarks; Unfair Competition; Copyrights.
Mason, Cassandra D. '69 '99 C.445 B.S. L.800 J.D.
(adm. in CA; not adm. in DC) [A Conlon,F.P.&P.]
*PRACTICE AREAS: Civil Rights; Class Actions.
Mason, Charles N., Jr. .... '11 '72 C.309 B.S. L.329 J.D. P.O. Box 108‡
Mason, Cheryl L. '64 '89 C.607 B.A. L.190 J.D.
(adm. in NE; not adm. in DC) Atty., Bd. of Vet. App.
Mason, DaCosta R., (AV) ....'48 '75 C.823 B.A. L.128 J.D. 3382 Erie St., S.E.
Mason, Gary E., (AV) .... '62 '88 C.103 A.B. L.228 J.D. [Cohen,M.H.&T.]
*PRACTICE AREAS: Antitrust Class Actions; Consumer Class Actions; Environmental Class Actions.
Mason, Geoffrey Colbourne '71 '97
C.309 A.B. L.276 J.D. [A Finnegan,H.F.G.&D.] (See Pat. Sect.)
*PRACTICE AREAS: Pharmaceutical Intellectual Property; Civil Litigation; Biotechnology Patent Prosecution.
Mason, Heidi L. .....'65 '90 C.350 B.S. L.276 J.D. Center for Reproductive Law & Policy
Mason, John D. ....'69 '97 C&L.425 B.A., J.D. 1501 "M" St., N.W.
Mason, Karen E. ....'65 '94 C.95 A.B. L.124 J.D. [A Venable,A.B.H.&C.]
*PRACTICE AREAS: Real Estate; Commercial Law; Telecommunications Law.
Mason, Kent A., (AV) ....'54 '81 C.31 B.A. L.659 J.D. [Caplin&D.]
*PRACTICE AREAS: Employee Benefits Law.

Mason, Mary Anne, (BV) .... '49 '83 C.945 B.A. L.276 J.D. [Hogan&H.]
*PRACTICE AREAS: Antitrust and Trade Regulation; Energy Regulation; Mergers and Acquisitions.
Mason, Matthew Jerald '70 '00
C.101 B.S.Ch.E. L.846 J.D. [🄰 Finnegan,H.F.G.&D.] (See Pat. Sect.)
*PRACTICE AREAS: Chemical Patents; Pharmaceutical Patents.
Mason, Michael F. .... '68 '96 C.874 B.A. L.273 J.D. [🄰 Hogan&H.]
Mason, Miles S. .... '61 '86 C.918 B.A. L.276 J.D. [Shaw P.]
*PRACTICE AREAS: Communications; Corporate; Business.
Mason, Nicole C. .... '73 '98 C.105 B.A. L.273 J.D. [🄰 Leftwich&D.]
*PRACTICE AREAS: Telecommunications; Government Contracts; Government Procurement; Litigation; Criminal Law.
Mason, Paul J. .... '32 '58 C.102 B.A. L.273 J.D. [🄲 Dechert]
*PRACTICE AREAS: Financial Services Law; Financial Services Regulation; Investment Banking Law; Investment Company Law; Investment Management.
Mason, Sasha A. '— '99 C.867 B.A. L.273 J.D.
(adm. in MD; not adm. in DC) [🄰 Miller&C.]
*PRACTICE AREAS: Federal Litigation.
Mason, Thomas B., (AV) .... '56 '85 C.976 B.A. L.178 J.D. [Zuckerman S.]
*PRACTICE AREAS: White Collar Criminal Defense; Extradition; Asset Forfeitures; Attorney Discipline; Wineries and Vineyards.
Masonson, Nina .... '51 '83 C.881 B.A. L.978 J.D. 1320 19th St. N.W.
Masoudi, Gerald F. .... '— '94 C.31 B.A. L.145 J.D. [Kirkland&E.]
*PRACTICE AREAS: Commercial Litigation; Appellate Litigation.
Masri, Selwa '67 '98 C.276 B.S. L.30 J.D.
(adm. in MD; not adm. in DC) [🄰 Holland&K.]
*PRACTICE AREAS: Content Licensing; Software Distribution Contracts; Drafting Negotiations.
Massa, Cliff .... '49 '75 C.597 B.S. L.273 J.D. [Patton B.]
Massaro, John C. .... '67 '93 C.951 B.A. L.309 J.D. [Arnold&P.]
*PRACTICE AREAS: Litigation.
Massey, David A., (AV) .... '59 '84 C&L.893 B.A., J.D. [Sutherland A.&B.]
*PRACTICE AREAS: Mergers and Acquisitions; Insurance Mergers and Acquisitions; Securities Regulation; Corporate Organization; Mutual Funds.
Massey, Eugene A., (AV) .... '42 '67 C.1030 A.B. L.309 LL.B. [Arent F.K.P.&K.]
*PRACTICE AREAS: International Infrastructure Projects; Maritime; Liquified Natural Gas; Energy Law; Health (Health Care) and Hospital Law.
Massimino, Elisa Christine '60 '90
C.859 B.A. L.477 J.D. Lawyers Committee for Human Rights
Masson, George T., Jr., (AV) .... '42 '68 C.118 B.A. L.477 J.D. [Hamilton&H.]
*PRACTICE AREAS: Civil Litigation; Personal Injury; Employment Law.
Massumi, Ronald R. .... '53 '80 C.881 B.A. L.276 J.D. [🄰 Sutherland A.&B.]
*PRACTICE AREAS: Corporate Law; Securities; Business Litigation; White Collar Criminal Defense; Appellate Practice.
Masters, Gregory L., (AV) .... '64 '89 C.801 B.A. L.128 J.D. [Wiley R.&F.]
*PRACTICE AREAS: Communications; Business Law; Finance.
Masters, Joan E. '68 '96 C.178 B.A. L.30 J.D.
(adm. in MD; not adm. in DC) [🄰 Shaw P.]
*PRACTICE AREAS: Communications.
Masters, Lorelie S., (AV) .... '54 '81 C.276 A.B. L.602 J.D. [Beveridge&D.]
*PRACTICE AREAS: Litigation; Insurance Litigation; High-Technology; Health Insurance.
Masters, Robert M. ...... '63 '90 C.645 B.S.E.E. L.64 J.D. [Sughrue M.] (See Pat. Sect.)
*PRACTICE AREAS: Intellectual Property Law; Litigation.
Masterson, Brian Scott '73 '01 C.1064 B.S. L.577 J.D.
(adm. in VA; not adm. in DC) [🄰 Dechert]
*PRACTICE AREAS: Investment Management; Financial Services Law.
Mastrangelo, Jonathan M. .... '71 '96 C.1044 B.A. L.659 J.D. [🄰 Wilmer,C.&P.]
Mastriani, Louis S., (AV) .... '50 '76 C.436 B.A. L.1148 J.D. [Adduci,M.&S.]
*PRACTICE AREAS: Customs Law; International Trade Regulation; Antidumping; Customs; Intellectual Property and Unfair Competition.
Mastrosimone, Joseph P. .... '73 '98 C.696 B.A. L.273 J.D. [🄰 Crowell&M.]
Masur, Daniel A. .... '52 '77 C.436 B.A. L.276 J.D. [Mayer,B.&P.]
Masurovsky, Laura P., (AV) .... '57 '84 C.860 B.A. L.309 J.D. [🄲 Finnegan,H.F.G.&D.]
*PRACTICE AREAS: Intellectual Property Litigation.
Mataka, Geraldine R.S. .... '70 '00 C.893 B.A. L.1209 J.D. [🄰 Holland&K.]
*PRACTICE AREAS: Aircraft Finance and Leasing; Project Finance; Corporate.
Matal, Maren Lee .... '69 '97 C.36 B.S. L.145 J.D. [🄰 Wilmer,C.&P.]
Matalon, Renee R. .... '56 '81 C&L.309 A.B., J.D. [🄲 Sonenthal&O.]
*PRACTICE AREAS: Nonprofit Corporations; Litigation; Employment; Government Contracts; Federal Grants.
Mataya, James M. '45 '71 C&L.424 B.S., J.D.
(adm. in IL; not adm. in DC) Coun., America's Community Bkrs.
Matelis, Joseph James, II .... '71 '97 C.575 B.A. L.309 J.D. [🄰 Sullivan&C.]
Matelski, Wayne H., (AV) .... '48 '75 C.645 B.A. L.273 J.D. [Arent F.K.P.&K.]
*PRACTICE AREAS: Food, Drug and Cosmetic Law; International Law; Food and Drug Regulation; Drug and Medical Device Regulation; Controlled Substances Law.
Mates, Carol M. '48 '73 C.66 A.B. L.178 J.D.
(adm. in NY; not adm. in DC) Princ. Coun., International Fin. Corp.
Matheny, Richard L. .... '69 '00 C.228 B.A. L.659 J.D. [🄰 Shea&G.]
Mather, Judith A. .... '52 '77 C.573 B.A. L.276 J.D. [Dow,L.&A.]
Mathers, Peter R., (AV) .... '55 '79 C.688 B.S. L.976 J.D. [Kleinfeld,K.&B.]
*PRACTICE AREAS: Food, Drug and Cosmetic Law; Food and Drug Regulation; Drug and Medical Device Regulation; Controlled Substances Law; Advertising and Labeling.
Matheson, Anna A. '49 '80 C.1209 B.S. L.1067 J.D.
(adm. in CA; not adm. in DC) Asst. U.S. Atty.
Mathew, N. Ajoy .... '66 '96 C.118 B.A. L.276 J.D. 1776 K St., NW

Mathews, Craig, (AV) '29 '54 C&L.976 B.A., J.D.
3902 Jocelyn Street, N.W., 20015
Telephone: 202-966-8965 Fax: 202-966-8978
General Corporate, Antitrust, Environmental, Trade Associations, Federal Departmental and International Practice.
See Professional Biographies, WASHINGTON, DISTRICT OF COLUMBIA

Mathews, David P. '63 '89 C.612 B.S. L.990 J.D.
(adm. in TX; not adm. in DC) [🄰 Shearman&S.]
*PRACTICE AREAS: Business Law; Corporate Law.
Mathews, Lara Bernstein .... '69 '95 C.112 B.A. L.770 J.D. [🄰 Dyer E.&J.]
*PRACTICE AREAS: Legislative Practice; Maritime Law; Environmental Law; Transportation.
Mathews, Roberta I. .... '34 '80 C.66 A.B. L.30 J.D. 5700 26th St., N.W.
Mathews, Susan M. .... '66 '91 C.608 B.A. L.976 J.D. [🄰 Powell,G.F.&M.]
*PRACTICE AREAS: Customs; International Trade Policy and Litigation; International Law; Legislative Advocacy.
Mathewson, Laurie M. '65 '94 C.813 A.B. L.276 J.D.
(adm. in MD; not adm. in DC) 607 14th St., N.W.‡
Mathias, Richard D., (AV) .... '40 '66 C.321 B.S. L.309 LL.B. [Zuckert,S.&R.]
*PRACTICE AREAS: Airline Regulation; International Aviation.
Mathias, Sarah Mackey .... '67 '93 C.797 B.A. L.45 J.D. [🄰 Jones,D.R.&P.]
Mathiascheck, Susan .... '62 '88 C.309 A.B. L.94 J.D. [Patton B.]
Mathieu, Dickens .... '— '94 C.31 B.A. L.893 J.D. 1800 M St., NW
Mathis, Vincent W. .... '63 '89 C.692 B.A. L.893 J.D. [🄰 Shearman&S.]

Matisik, Edward N. '62 '99 C.94 B.S. L.30 J.D.
4201 Massachusetts Avenue, N.W., Suite 5047, 20016-4701
Telephone: 202-244-7611 Fax: 202-244-3544
Email: enmatisik@hotmail.com URL: http://www.stateregistrations.com
***PRACTICE AREAS: Nonprofit Organizations Law; Mental Disability Law; Education Law; Medical Malpractice.**
Nonprofit and Charitable Organizations Law, Charitable Giving, Nonprofit Tax Law, Charitable Trusts and Foundations, Public Charitites, Private Foundations, Fundraising Legal Consultation, Fundraising Licensing, Taxability Assesment of Charitable Contributions, Education Law.
See Professional Biographies, WASHINGTON, DISTRICT OF COLUMBIA

Matisoff, Robert .... '49 '74 C.309 A.B. L.273 J.D. [O'Donoghue&O.]
Matlack, Linda S. .... '46 '85 C.966 B.A. L.276 J.D. [🄲 Cleary,G.S.&H.]
Matney, William Jackson, Jr. '62 '95 C.886 B.S. L.273 J.D.
[🄰 Milbank,T.H.&M.] (Pat.)
*PRACTICE AREAS: Intellectual Property Law.
Matson, John R., III .... '69 '94 [🄰 Huber L.&A.]
*PRACTICE AREAS: Energy Law; Public Utility Law.
Matt, Peter K., (AV) .... '47 '73 C.665 B.A. L.273 J.D. [🄲 Bruder,G.&M.]
*PRACTICE AREAS: Electric Utilities; Energy; Antitrust Law; Energy Project Development.
Matta, Richard K. .... '57 '82 C.665 B.A. L.276 J.D. [Groom]
*PRACTICE AREAS: ERISA; Securities; Tax; Corporate Law.
Mattar, Mohammed y '— '78 C.999 LL.B. L.1099 LL.M.
(adm. in Egypt; not adm. in DC) Res. Assoc., Emirates Advoc. Assoc. Office
Matte, Jeanine L. .... '49 '74 C.886 B.S. L.575 J.D. [Skadden,A.S.M.&F.]
Mattei, Andrea M. '54 '83 C.518 B.A. L.446 J.D.
(adm. in MA; not adm. in DC) [Piper M.R.&W.]
*PRACTICE AREAS: Finance; Real Estate Finance; Corporate; Securities.
Matteis, August J., Jr. .... '67 '93 C.976 B.A. L.276 J.D. [🄰 Skadden,A.S.M.&F.]
Matteo, John J., (BV) .... '60 '86 C.262 B.A. L.128 J.D. [Jackson&C.] ⊙
*PRACTICE AREAS: Corporate Law; Business Law; Business Transactions; Health Law; Real Estate.
Mattheis, Peter J. .... '59 '85 C.473 B.S. L.659 J.D. [Brickfield B.R.&S.]
*PRACTICE AREAS: Energy; Energy Regulation; Public Utility Law; Energy Contracts; Legislative Practice.
Matthew, Robin J. .... '64 '91 C.302 B.A. L.329 J.D. 1849 C St. N.W.
Matthews, Barbara C. '64 '93 C.276 B.S.F.S. L.228 J.D.
(adm. in NY; not adm. in DC) The Institute of Intl. Fin., Inc.
Matthews, Carol L. B. .... '45 '71 C.477 B.A. [Holland&K.]
*PRACTICE AREAS: Trademark Law; Copyright Law.
Matthews, Carol W. .... '42 '73 C.945 B.A. L.228 J.D. 3702 Reno Rd., NW
Matthews, Claude L., Jr. '41 '86 C.329 B.S. L.276 J.D.
(adm. in PA; not adm. in DC) 2805 31st Pl., N.E.
Matthews, Elizabeth A. .... '70 '95 C.976 B.A. L.309 J.D. [🄲 Akin,G.S.H.&F.]
*PRACTICE AREAS: Labor and Employment.
Matthews, John D., (AV) ..... '32 '59 C.321 B.S. L.276 J.D. 1255 23rd St., N.W., Ste. 500
Matthews, John E. .... '64 '90 C.276 B.S.F.S. L.893 J.D. [Morgan,L.&B.]
Matthews, Katharine I. .... '57 '92 C.413 B.A. L.276 J.D. [🄰 Collier S.S.] (Pat.)
*PRACTICE AREAS: Patent; Trademark; Copyright; Litigation.
Matthews, Marsha Dula .... '58 '84 C.893 B.A. L.945 J.D. [McDermott,W.&E.]
Matthews, Martha A. .... '48 '83 C.788 A.B. L.276 J.D. The Bur. of Natl. Affs., Inc.
Matthews, Robert A. .... '48 '74 C.282 A.B. L.262 J.D. [McKenna&C.]
Matthews, Robert A., Jr. '63 '92
C.886 B.S.M.E. L.893 J.D. [🄰 Finnegan,H.F.G.&D.] (See Pat. Sect.)
*PRACTICE AREAS: Electro-Mechanical Patents; Patent Infringement; Patent Litigation.
Matthews, Timothy P. .... '— '94 C.871 B.S.M.E. L.273 J.D. [🄰 Morgan,L.&B.]
Matthews, William A. .... '31 '60 C&L.273 B.A., LL.B. 3030 Wisconsin Ave., N.W.‡
Matties, Deborah J. .... '70 '98 C.659 A.B. L.273 J.D. [🄰 Covington&B.]
Mattison, Beatrice M. .... '12 '62 C.112 B.A. L.1066 LL.B. 630 C St., S.E.‡
Mattison, Victoria .... '45 '85 C.403 B.A. L.976 J.D. 1440 New York Ave., N.W.
Mattox, Barbara Groves, (AV) '53 '78 C.283 A.B. L.923 J.D.
Sr. Tax Coun., GE Capital
Matulef, Mark L '58 '00 C.1036 B.A. L.446 J.D.
(adm. in MD; not adm. in DC) U.S. Dept. of HUD
Matuszewski, David M. .... '61 '86 C&L.477 B.B.A., J.D. [🄰 Holland&K.]
Matyas, David A. .... '68 '93 C.659 B.A. L.846 J.D. [Epstein B.&G.]
*PRACTICE AREAS: Health Law; Health Care Fraud; Medicare and Medicaid Reimbursement.
Matz, Marshall L. .... '46 '71 C.184 B.A. L.421 J.D. [Olsson,F.&W.]
*PRACTICE AREAS: Legislation; Agriculture Law; Indian Law; Trade Association Law.
Matz, Timothy B., (AV) .... '44 '70 C.893 B.A. L.273 J.D. [Elias,M.T.&H.]
Matzzie, Colette G. .... '66 '95 C.103 B.A. L.276 J.D. Public Citizen Litigation Grp.
Mauney, Duane J. .... '70 '96 C&L.575 B.A., J.D. [🄰 Arnold&P.]
*PRACTICE AREAS: Litigation; Products Liability.
Mauprivez, Bruno J. .... '51 '86 C.30 B.A. L.904 J.D. [🄲 Choné&Assoc.]
*PRACTICE AREAS: Torts; Commercial Litigation.
Maurer, Aaron P. '73 '99 C.576 B.S. L.309 J.D.
(adm. in NC; not adm. in DC) [🄰 Williams&C.]
Maurer, Eric J. .... '— '97 C.367 B.S. L.273 J.D. [🄰 Morgan,L.&B.]
Mauro, James G .... '44 '71 C.385 B.A. L.178 J.D. 1693 32nd St. N.W.
Mauro, Louis D. .... '42 '68 C&L.276 A.B., J.D. 1849 C Street NW‡

Mauro, Thomas A., & Associates '45 '73 C.667 B.S. L.276 J.D.
1050 Seventeenth Street, N.W. Suite 1200, 20036
Telephone: 202-452-9865 Fax: 202-452-0092
URL: http://www.lawyers.com/maurolaw
***PRACTICE AREAS: Intellectual Property Law.**
Complex Commercial Litigation, Patent Litigation, Intellectual Property Law, Electromechanical Patent Law, Computer and Software Patent, Patent Infringement, Trademark Law, Complex Patent Litigation.
See Professional Biographies, WASHINGTON, DISTRICT OF COLUMBIA

Mause, Philip J. .... '44 '68 C.276 A.B. L.309 J.D. [Drinker B.&R.]
*PRACTICE AREAS: Energy; Litigation; International Trade; Telecommunications Law.
Mauser, Amy J. .... '63 '89 C.518 B.A. L.904 J.D. [Boies,S.&F.]
*PRACTICE AREAS: Commercial Litigation.
Max, Kenneth A., (AV) .... '47 '77 C.831 B.A. L.276 J.D. [Wilkes A.]
*PRACTICE AREAS: Real Estate Tax Appeals; Transactional Real Estate; Estate Planning.
Maxey, Patricia A. '67 '95 C.161 B.A. L.1202 J.D.
(adm. in MA; not adm. in DC) [🄰 Kirkpatrick&L.]
*PRACTICE AREAS: Investment Management.
Maxwell, Jane B. .... '52 '84 C.103 B.A. L.30 J.D. [🄰 Sullivan&W.]
*PRACTICE AREAS: Communications Law; Securities Law; Investment Companies.
Maxwell, Melissa E. .... '72 '97 C.478 B.A. L.846 J.D. [🄰 Baker B.]
*PRACTICE AREAS: Civil Litigation (80%); Civil Appeals (20%).
Maxwell, R. Bruce .... '35 '62 C.951 B.A. L.477 J.D. 1613 35th St., N.W.
Maxwell, Rosemary .... '57 '87 C.1044 B.A. L.273 J.D. [🄲 Arnold&P.]
May, Albert E. '27 '55 C&L.276 A.B., J.D.
Exec. V.P., Council of Amer.-Flag Ship Operators
May, Colby M., (AV) '51 '80 C.362 B.A. L.1209 J.D.
(adm. in VA; not adm. in DC) [American L.&J.]
May, Edgar B. .... '29 '59 C.107 B.A. L.273 LL.B. 1155 21st St., NW
May, Eric M., (AV) .... '43 '72 C.645 B.S. L.128 J.D. [E.M.May]

May, Gregory Evers, (AV) ... '53 '78 C.945 A.B. L.309 J.D. [Freshfields B.D.]
*PRACTICE AREAS: International Taxation; Corporate Taxation.

May, John Tremain, (AV) ... '53 '79 C.119 B.S. L.276 J.D. [Jordan C.&S.]
*PRACTICE AREAS: Legal Ethics and Professional Responsibility; NASD Arbitration; Legal Malpractice Defense; Accountants Malpractice; Professional Liability Defense.

May, Kenneth ... '50 '77 C&L.128 B.A., J.D. Legal Editor, Bur. of National Affairs

May, Kerim P. ... '— '69 C.918 B.A. L.30 J.D. [🄰 Verner,L.B.M.&H.]
*PRACTICE AREAS: Energy.

May, Richard Edward, (AV) ... '46 '73 C.446 A.B. L.276 J.D. [Hunton&W.]
*PRACTICE AREAS: Taxation.

May, Timothy J., (AV) ... '32 '57 C.128 B.A. L.276 J.D. [Patton B.]

May, Timothy James '68 '98 C.966 B.S.E.E. L.1209 J.D.
(adm. in VA; not adm. in DC; See Pat. Sect.) [🄰 Finnegan,H.F.G.&D.]
*PRACTICE AREAS: Intellectual Property Litigation; Patent Prosecution.

May, Eric M., P.C., (AV) ... 1717 K Street, N.W.

Maydew, Jeffrey P. '70 '96 C.350 B.S. L.352 J.D.
(adm. in IA; not adm. in DC) [🄰 Baker&M.]
*PRACTICE AREAS: Taxation.

Mayer, Andrea Laura ... '— '95 C.446 B.A. L.273 J.D. 409 3rd St. S.W., 7th Fl.

Mayer, Charles H., (AV) ... '19 '47 C.30 B.A. L.309 LL.B. [Shapiro&M.]

Mayer, Joseph L. '33 '78 C&L.494 B.A., J.D.
Pres. & Gen. Coun., Copper & Brass Fabricators' Council, Inc.

Mayer, Lloyd H. ... '67 '94 C.813 A.B. L.976 J.D. [🄰 Caplin&D.]
*PRACTICE AREAS: Tax; Exempt Organizations.

Mayer, Neal Michael, (AV) ... '41 '67 C.385 B.A. L.276 J.D. [Hoppel,M.&C.]
*PRACTICE AREAS: Maritime Administrative Law; Transportation; International Maritime Law; Shipping Regulations.

Mayer, Robert C., (AV) ... '22 '54 C.276 B.S. L.273 LL.B. 815 15th St. N.W.

Mayer, Brown & Platt, (AV) BR
1909 K Street, N.W., 20006-1101 ⊙
Telephone: (202) 263-3000 Facsimile: (202) 263-3300 Telex: 892603 Cable: LE MAYDC
URL: http://www.mayerbrown.com
Partners: Robert E. Bloch; David I. Bloom; Kim Marie Kozaczek Boylan; Robert P. Davis; David F. Dowd; Kerry Lynn Edwards; Donald M. Falk; Richard J. Favretto; Andrew L. Frey; Kenneth S. Geller; Mark H. Gitenstein; John S. Hahn; Cameron Street Hamrick; Werner J. Hein; Charles M. Horn; Robert M. Jenkins, III; Erika Z. Jones; Michael ("Mickey") Kantor; Timothy E. Keehan; Simeon M. Kriesberg; Kathryn A. Kusske; Philip Allen Lacovara; Daniel A. Masur; James R. Mogle; Miriam R. Nemetz; Carolyn P. Osolinik; Eileen Penner; Stuart P. Pergament; Scott P. Perlman; Michael W. Punke; Mitchell D. Raup; Lee H. Rubin; Mark W. Ryan; Peter L. Scher; John P. Schmitz; Brian W. Smith; Adrian L. Steel, Jr.; John J. Sullivan; Robert H. Swart; Evan M. Tager; Charles S. Triplett; Keith J. Willner; Gary A. Winters. Senior Counsel: David B. Finnegan. Special Counsel: David Hyman; Charles Rothfeld. Counsel: Carol J. Bilzi; Brian T. Borders; Thomas B. Burnside (Not admitted in DC); Courtney A. Dinsmore (Not admitted in DC); Julian P. Gehman; Andrew J. Morris; Howard A. Parelskin; Roger W. Patrick; Linda L. Rhodes; Adam C. Sloane. Associates: Robert L. Bronston; Mary Beth Brooks (Not admitted in DC); Jay S. Brown; Craig W. Canetti; Peter C. Choharis; Steven J. Duffield (Not admitted in DC); Michael J. Farley; Gregory S. Feder; David M. Gossett; Britton B. Guerrina (Not admitted in DC); Shoufen Hu; John C. C. Hughes; Craig Isenberg; John W. Jarrell, Jr.; Dawn Marie Karolick; Richard B. Katskee; Michael E. Lackey, Jr.; Lisa L. Levine; Susan J. Luken; Eldad Z. Malamuth (Not admitted in DC); Jennifer C. Maloney; Julie K. McConnell (Not admitted in DC); Jill K. McDowell; Rita W. Morales; Scott A. Morehouse; Wendy L. Morris; J. Kevin Muldowney (Not admitted in DC); Andrew A. Nicely; Ronald D. Parisotto; Julie Anna Potts; Laura A. Reilly; Andrea Elisa Ryan; Timothy R. Ryan; Kristin Hart Smith; Lily Fu Swenson; Jeffrey P. Taft; Jodi L. Valeri; Sheila Dearybury Walcoff; Arthur C. Walker, Jr.; Christopher C. Wang; Nick S. Williams (Not admitted in DC); Joseph E. Yesutis; George E. York (Not admitted in DC).
General Practice.
Chicago, Illinois Office: 190 South LaSalle Street, 60603-3441. Telephone: (312) 782-0600. Facsimile: (312) 701-7711. Telex: 190404. Cable: LEMAY.
Berlin, Germany Office: Breite Strasse 29, Muehlendamm, 10178. Telephone: 011-49-30-2060-7710. Facsimile: 011-49-30-2060-7744.
Charlotte, North Carolina Office: 100 North Tryon Street, Suite 2400. Telephone: (704) 444-3500. Fax: (704) 377-2033.
Cologne, Germany Office: Kaiser-Wilhelm-Ring 27-29, 50672. Telephone: 011-49-221-5771-100. Facsimile: 011-49-221-5771-199.
Frankfurt/Main, Germany Office: Mayer, Brown, Platt, Gaedertz. Bockenheimer Landstraße 98-100. Telephone: 011-49-69 79 41-0. Facsimile: 011-49-69 79 41-100.
Houston, Texas Office: 700 Louisiana Street, Suite 3600, 77002-2730. Telephone: (713) 221-1651. Facsimile: (713) 224-6410. Telex: 775809. Cable: LEMAYHOU.
London, England Office: Bucklersbury House, 3 Queen Victoria Street, London, EC4N 8EL, England. Telephone: 011-44-207-246-6200. Facsimile: 011-44-207-329-4465. Telex: 8811095. Cable: LEMAYLDN.
Los Angeles, California Office: 350 South Grand Avenue, 25th Floor, 90071-1503. Telephone: (213) 229-9500. Facsimile: (213) 625-0248. Telex: 188089. Cable: LEMAYLA.
New York, New York Office: 1675 Broadway, 10019-5820. Telephone: (212) 506-2500. Facsimile: (212) 262-1910. Telex: 701842. Cable: LEMAYEN.
Representative Offices:
Ashgabat, Turkmenistan: 28 Gogal Street, 744000. Telephone: 011-99-312-355247. Facsimile: 011-99-312-510074.
Mexico City, Mexico, D.F., Independent Mexico Correspondent: Jáuregui, Navarrete, Nader y Rojas, S.C., Torre Arcos, Paseo de los Tamarindos No. 400-B. Col. Bosques de las Lomas, 05120. Telephone: 011-525-267-45-00. Facsimile: 011-525-267-45-99.
Paris, France, Independent Paris Correspondent: Lambert & Lee, 13 Avenue Hoche, 75008. Telephone: 011-33-1-53-53-43-43. Facsimile: 011-33-1-53-96-03-83.

See Professional Biographies, WASHINGTON, DISTRICT OF COLUMBIA

Mayers, Daniel K., (AV) ... '34 '60 C&L.309 A.B., LL.B. [🄲 Wilmer,C.&P.]
*PRACTICE AREAS: Antitrust; Trade Regulation.

Mayers, Joyce E. ... '51 '77 C.914 B.A. L.93 J.D. [Cullen]
*PRACTICE AREAS: Securities; Commodities; Complex Litigation; False Claims Act; Telecommunications Law.

Mayers, Oscar S., Jr. ... '54 '86 C.228 B.S. L.128 J.D. Off. of the U.S. Atty.

Mayerson, Anne Ronnel ... '62 '88 C.103 B.A. L.309 J.D. [Bredhoff&K.]

Mayerson, Marc S. ... '61 '88 C.477 A.B. L.309 J.D. [Spriggs&H.]
*PRACTICE AREAS: Insurance Coverage; Litigation.

Mayes, Jeffrey W. ... '65 '95 C&L.893 B.A., J.D. [🄰 Winston&S.]
*PRACTICE AREAS: Energy.

Mayes, Thompson M. '58 '86 C&L.575 B.A., J.D.
Assoc. Gen. Coun., National Trust for Historic Preservation

Mayet-Astorga, Juan Antonio '63 '97 C.555 B.S. L.329 J.D.
(adm. in MD; not adm. in DC) 3636 16th St. NW

Mayfield, Earl N., III ... '70 '97 C.475 B.A. L.597 J.D. 1722 Eye St., N.W.

Mayfield, Kenneth A. '50 '80 C.1142 B.A. L.744 J.D.
(adm. in TX; not adm. in DC) [🄲 O'Connor&H.]

Mayfield, Richard H., (AV) ... '21 '48 C.821 A.B. L.309 LL.B. [Craighill,M.F.C.&C.]
*PRACTICE AREAS: Estate Planning; Probate Law; Trusts.

Mayfield, Trey N. ... '— '97 C.475 B.A. L.597 J.D. [🄰 Sidley A.B.&W.]

Maynard, Deanne E. ... '65 '91 C.893 B.A. L.309 J.D. [Jenner&B.]
*PRACTICE AREAS: Civil Litigation; Appellate Practice; First Amendment Law.

Maynard, Kevin J. ... '69 '96 C.188 B.A. L.273 J.D. [🄰 Wiley R.&F.]

Mayo, Ann Perry ... '70 '96 C.321 B.A. L.146 J.D. [🄰 Wilmer,C.&P.]

Mayo, George W., Jr., (AV) ... '46 '73 C.1365 A.B. L.893 J.D. [Hogan&H.]
*PRACTICE AREAS: Insurance Coverage; Transportation; Litigation; Administrative Law.

Mayor, Heidi H. ... '62 '95 C.145 B.A. L.276 J.D. Staff Atty., S.E.C.

Mayoral, Rafael Hernandez '60 '88 L.976 J.D.
(adm. in PR; not adm. in DC) [🄲 Morrison&F.]

Mays, William J. ... '54 '80 C&L.276 B.S.F.S., J.D. [🄰 Nemirow&H.]

Maysonett, James A. ... '72 '98 C.674 A.B. L.569 J.D. [🄰 Howrey S.A.&W.]
*PRACTICE AREAS: Environmental.

Maywalt, Roxane E. ... '64 '92 C.188 B.S. L.823 J.D. [🄲 Sutherland A.&B.]
*PRACTICE AREAS: Energy; Federal Energy Regulation; Gas Utilities; Electric Utilities.

Mazard, Camelia C. ... '— '99 C.800 B.S. L.1066 J.D. [🄰 Powell,G.F.&M.]
*PRACTICE AREAS: International Trade.

Mazawey, Louis T., (AV) ... '49 '75 C.569 B.A. L.276 J.D. [Groom]
*PRACTICE AREAS: Employee Benefits; Labor and Employment; Pension and Profit Sharing; Tax Law; ERISA.

Mazer, Michael E., (AV) ... '42 '67 C.976 B.A. L.309 J.D. [Krooth&A.]

Mazer, Robert A., (AV) ... '51 '78 C.446 B.S. L.30 J.D. [Vinson&E.]
*PRACTICE AREAS: Communications Law.

Mazliah, Sandra ... '65 '93 C.994 B.A. L.276 J.D. [🄰 Passman&K.]

Mazo, Mark E., (AV) ... '50 '75 C.674 A.B. L.309 J.D. [Hogan&H.]
*PRACTICE AREAS: International Mergers and Acquisitions; International Business Law; International Joint Ventures; Foreign Investment in the U.S.; Buying and Selling of Businesses.

Mazumdar, Anandashankar ... '69 '97 C.1208 B.A. L.276 J.D. 1231 25th St., N.W.

Mazur, Kim M. '74 '98 C.1044 B.S. L.904 J.D.
(adm. in NY; not adm. in DC) [🄰 Shearman&S.]

Mazure, Kathleen L., (AV) ... '61 '85 C.477 B.A. L.945 J.D. [🄲 Duncan,W.G.&P.]
*PRACTICE AREAS: Energy Law; Public Utility Law.

Mazurek, Brian E. ... '66 '91 C.20 A.B. L.477 J.D. [🄰 Hogan&H.]
*PRACTICE AREAS: Litigation; Labor and Employment.

Mazza, George J. ... '55 '76 C.347 B.A. L.276 J.D. Coun., National Coalition Bldg. Instit.

Mazza, Pamela J., (AV) ... '58 '84 C.651 B.A. L.273 J.D. [Piliero,M.&P.] ⊙
*PRACTICE AREAS: Government Contracts; Corporate Law; Small Business Programs; Administrative Law; Indian Law.

Mazzer, Kenneth A. '47 '78 C.674 A.B. L.178 J.D.
3133 Connecticut Ave., N.W., Ste. 115

Mazzuchi, Michael A. ... '67 '92 C&L.477 B.A., J.D. [Cleary,G.S.&H.]

McAdoo, Michael R., (AV) ... '49 '75 C&L.893 B.A., J.D. [King&N.] ⊙
*PRACTICE AREAS: Trusts and Estates; Commercial Real Estate Transactions; Secured Lending.

McAdoo-Brobson, Leslie S. ... '68 '96 C.445 B.A. L.276 J.D. [🄰 Holland&K.]
*PRACTICE AREAS: White Collar Crime; Civil Litigation; Corporate Compliance.

McAfee, Laura K. '66 '91 C.118 B.A. L.846 J.D.
(adm. in MD; not adm. in DC) [🄲 Beveridge&D.]
*PRACTICE AREAS: Environmental Law; Air Pollution; Environmental Litigation; Environmental Permitting; Civil Litigation.

McAleer, Charles F. B., Jr. ... '59 '84 C&L.276 A.B., J.D. [Miller&C.]
*PRACTICE AREAS: Federal Civil Litigation; Complex Commercial Litigation; Professional Malpractice; Technology Law; Litigation.

McAleese & Associates, P.C.
(See McLean, Virginia)

McAllister, Douglas C. ... '60 '86 C.45 B.A. L.228 J.D. 1120 20th St Nw # 300

McAllister, John P. ... '51 '77 C.976 B.A. L.276 J.D. [🄲 Groom]
*PRACTICE AREAS: Employee Benefit Taxation; Employee Benefits Law; Tax Law; Civil Trial Practice; Appellate Practice.

McAllister, Singleton B. ... '52 '85 C.446 B.A. L.329 J.D. [Patton B.]

McAnaney, Kevin G., (AV) '49 '78 C.575 A.B. L.178 J.D.
Chief, Industry Guidance Branch, Health & Human Servs., Off. of Coun. to the Inspector

McAndrew, Christa Parker ... '72 '00 C.178 B.A. L.861 J.D. [🄰 Morrison&F.]
*PRACTICE AREAS: Communications Law.

McAndrew, Edward J. ... '— '95 C.1376 B.A. L.128 J.D. [🄰 Reed S.]
*PRACTICE AREAS: Litigation.

McAndrew, Mark A. ... '— '00 C.602 B.A. L.861 J.D. [🄰 Proskauer R.]

McAndrews, Roland George, Jr. '68 '98
C.884 B.M.E. L.128 J.D. [🄰 Finnegan,H.F.G.&D.] (See Pat. Sect.)
*PRACTICE AREAS: Mechanical Patents.

McArthur, Todd Y. ... '— '90 C&L.893 B.S., J.D. [King&S.]
*PRACTICE AREAS: Tax.

McArthur, Virginia A., Law Office of, (AV) '42 '75 C.105 B.A. L.276 J.D.
1101 17th Street, N.W. Suite 820, 20036
Telephone: 202-857-3434 Fax: 202-463-3060
Email: vmcarthur@mcarthurlaw.com URL: http://www.lawyers.com/mcarthurlaw
***PRACTICE AREAS: Trusts and Estates; Estate Planning; Estate Administration.**
—Ann St. Laurent.
Trusts and Estates, Estate Planning, Estate Administration, Estate and Gift Taxation.

See Professional Biographies, WASHINGTON, DISTRICT OF COLUMBIA

McAuley, James A. I., IV '68 '99
C.712 M.A./B.A. L.128 J.D. 1901 Penn. Avenue N.W., Suite 902

McAuliffe, Susan Rotatori ... '60 '88 C.183 B.A. L.178 J.D. [🄰 Hogan&H.]
*PRACTICE AREAS: Clean Water Act; Environmental Compliance; Environmental Health and Safety; Environmental Regulation; Resource Conservation and Recovery Act (RCRA).

McAuliffe, Terence R. '57 '85
C.128 B.A. L.276 J.D. Fin. Chair., Democratic Natl. Comm.

McAvoy, John J., (AV) ... '33 '58 C&L.336 B.A., LL.B. [🄲 Lukas,N.G.&S.]
*PRACTICE AREAS: Civil Litigation; Antitrust; Legal Ethics.

McBean, Simone R. '72 '00 C.597 B.S. L.262 J.D.
(adm. in NY; not adm. in DC) [🄰 Thelen R.&P.]
*PRACTICE AREAS: Mergers and Acquisitions; General Corporate; Long Term Financing/Indenture.

McBride, Andrew G. ... '60 '90 C.321 B.A. L.813 J.D. [Wiley R.&F.]
*PRACTICE AREAS: Communications; Appellate Practice; Litigation.

McBride, James W., (AV) ... '38 '63 C&L.846 B.A., LL.B. [Baker,D.B.&C.]
*PRACTICE AREAS: State and Local Tax; Tax Planning and Litigation.

McBride, Lawrence G. ... '— '74 C.813 A.B. L.1066 J.D. [Foley&L.]
*PRACTICE AREAS: Natural Resources Law; Regulatory Law.

McBride, Maurice H. '44 '75 C.101 B.A. L.273 J.D.
Secy., National Petro. Refiners Assn.

McBride, Michael F., (AV) ... '51 '76 C.959 B.S. L.956 J.D. [LeBoeuf,L.G.&M.]
*PRACTICE AREAS: Transportation; Litigation; Environmental; Utilities.

McBride, Scott D. '71 '99 C.611 B.A. L.945 J.D.
Dept. of Comm., Off. of Chf. Coun. for Input Admin.

McBride, Thaddeus R. ... '— '01 C.674 B.A. L.93 J.D. [🄰 Arnold&P.]
*PRACTICE AREAS: Litigation; International Trade.

McBride, Timothy B., (AV) ... '46 '75 C.770 B.A. L.276 J.D. [🄲 Heenan,A.&R.]
*PRACTICE AREAS: Closely Held Business; Real Estate; Taxation; Estate and Trust Planning; Wealth Management and Transfers.

McBrier, Charles R., Jr. ... '48 '76 C.880 B.A. L.1209 J.D. 1150 Connecticut Ave., N.W.

McBurney, Christian M. ... '59 '86 C.103 B.A. L.569 J.D. [Nixon P.]
*PRACTICE AREAS: Taxation; Mergers and Acquisitions.

McCabe, Brian J. ... '69 '95 C.93 B.A. L.273 J.D. [🄰 Whiteford,T.&P.]
*PRACTICE AREAS: Litigation; Community Association Law.

McCabe, John F. ... '58 '86 C.228 B.A. L.861 J.D. Asst. Corp. Coun.

McCabe, Kara E. '70 '01 C.454 B.A. L.818 J.D.
(adm. in MA; not adm. in DC) [🄰 Bingham D.]
*PRACTICE AREAS: Commercial Real Estate.

McCabe, Kevin William '70 '99
C.692 B.S. L.273 J.D. [🄰 Finnegan,H.F.G.&D.] (See Pat. Sect.)
*PRACTICE AREAS: Patent Litigation; Biotechnology Patent Prosecution.

McCadney, Jennifer E. ....'73 '01 C&L.273 B.A., J.D. [Ⓐ Collier S.S.]
*PRACTICE AREAS: International Trade.

McCafferty, Brian P. '67 '92 C&L.602 B.A., J.D.
(adm. in PA; not adm. in DC) [Ⓐ Provost&U.]
*PRACTICE AREAS: General Civil and Trial Practice; False Claims Act Litigation; Antitrust Litigation; Commercial Litigation; Employment and Labor Violations Litigation.

McCaffrey, Donna S. '— '84 C.128 B.A. L.945 J.D.
(adm. in VA; not adm. in DC)
Assoc. Gen. Coun., Litig., National Railroad Passenger Corp. (AMTRAK)

McCaffrey, John E. ....'69 '95 C.93 B.A. L.273 J.D. [Ⓐ Morrison&H.]
*PRACTICE AREAS: Energy Regulation; Electric Power; Natural Gas; Litigation.

McCaffrey, Read Kemp, (AV) ....'43 '71 C.893 B.A. L.64 J.D. [Patton B.]

McCahill, John A., (AV) '— '70 C.178 A.B. L.128 J.D. BB
2021 L Street, N.W., Suite 300, 20036
Telephone: 202-861-0070 Fax: 202-861-2939
Email: Artabane@cais.com URL: http://www.lawyers.com/mccahilllaw
(Also Of Counsel, Artabane & Belden, P.C.).
***PRACTICE AREAS: Civil Litigation; Legislative Law; Criminal Law; White Collar Crime; Personal Injury.**
White Collar Criminal Defense, Commercial Fraud, Business Crimes, Electronic Surveillance, Qui Tam, Criminal Appeals, Securities Fraud, International Criminal Defense, Export Crimes, Grand Jury Practice, Personal Injury, Civil Trial Law.
See Professional Biographies, WASHINGTON, DISTRICT OF COLUMBIA

McCain Parson, Linda Faye ...... '57 '96 C.893 B.S.N. L.838 J.D. Dept. Veterans Affairs

McCaleb, Scott M. ....'66 '91 C.103 A.B. L.276 J.D. [Wiley R.&F.]

McCall, Duke K., III ....'68 '93 C.269 B.A. L.880 J.D. [Ⓐ Swidler B.S.F.]
*PRACTICE AREAS: Environmental; Litigation.

McCall, Lee Ann Anderson ....'66 '92 C.914 B.A. L.790 J.D. [Ⓐ Sullivan&C.]

McCall, Molly A. ....'63 '98 C&L.665 B.S., J.D. [Ⓐ Sterne,K.G.&F.] (See Pat. Sect.)
*PRACTICE AREAS: Intellectual Property Law.

McCallum, Elizabeth B. ....'64 '91 C.893 B.A. L.880 J.D. [Howrey S.A.&W.]
*PRACTICE AREAS: Antitrust; Commercial Litigation.

McCally, Thomas L., (AV) .... '59 '84 C.205 B.A. L.245 J.D. [Carr G.]
*PRACTICE AREAS: Employment Law; Labor Law; Employee Benefits.

McCalmon, Brian K. ....'69 '96 C.623 B.A. L.276 J.D. [Ⓐ Preston G.E.&R.M.]
*PRACTICE AREAS: Antitrust; Litigation.

McCalmon, Julia M. ....'69 '96 C.1097 B.A. L.276 [Ⓐ Thompson H.]
*PRACTICE AREAS: Customs Law; Export Licensing; International Trade Law.

McCampbell, William A., III ....'45 '78 C.112 A.B. L.1067 J.D. [McCampbell&W.]

McCampbell & Walthall, P.C. ....1250 24th St., N.W.

McCandless, Robert C., (AV) '37 '65 C.273 B.A. L.623 J.D.
618 E Street, S.E., 20003
Telephone: 202-547-1200 Fax: 202-543-2931
URL: http://www.lawyers.com/robertcmccandless
Federal Legislative Practice, Financial and Insurance Institutions, Corporate Law, Foreign Governments and Legislative Strategies.
Reference: 1st American Bank of Washington.
See Professional Biographies, WASHINGTON, DISTRICT OF COLUMBIA

McCann, Clifton E., (AV) '50 '78
C.697 B.S. L.128 J.D. [Venable,A.B.H.&C.] (See Pat. Sect.)
*PRACTICE AREAS: Patent Litigation; Patents; Trademarks; Copyrights; New Media Law.

McCann, John M. '75 '00 C.188 B.A. L.893 J.D.
(adm. in OH; not adm. in DC) [Ⓐ Kirkpatrick&L.]
*PRACTICE AREAS: Investment Management; Corporate Law.

McCann, Joseph E. '54 '86 C.645 B.A. L.861 J.D.
(adm. in PA; not adm. in DC) 1900 E Street, NW

McCann, Robert W. .... '51 '80 C.473 A.B. L.477 J.D. [Akin,G.S.H.&F.]
*PRACTICE AREAS: Antitrust; Public Finance; Health and Hospital Law.

McCann, Sean P. ....'72 '98 C.880 B.A. L.188 J.D. [Ⓐ Wilmer,C.&P.]

McCann, Vonya B. ....'54 '80 C.112 B.A. L.1066 J.D. Sr. V.P., Sprint Corp.

McCarrick, John E. ....'— '94 C&L.276 B.S., J.D. [Ⓐ Hogan&H.]
*PRACTICE AREAS: Corporate; Private Equity.

McCarron, Stephen P., (AV) ....'51 '78 C.1150 B.A. L.128 J.D. [McCarron&D.]
*PRACTICE AREAS: Perishable Agricultural Commodities Act; Food and Agriculture.

McCarron, William, Jr. .... '66 '94 C.165 B.A. L.128 J.D. [Ⓐ Morrison&F.]
*PRACTICE AREAS: Bankruptcy; Creditors' Rights; Litigation.

McCarron & Diess, (AV)
4910 Massachusetts Avenue, N.W., Suite 18, 20016
Telephone: 202-364-0400 Fax: 202-364-2731
URL: http://www.mccarronlaw.com
Members of Firm: Stephen P. McCarron; Louis W. Diess, III (Not admitted in DC).
Perishable Agricultural Commodities Act (PACA) Law.
Reference: NationsBank.
See Professional Biographies, WASHINGTON, DISTRICT OF COLUMBIA

McCart, Alice M. '47 '93 C.378 B.A. L.46 J.D.
(adm. in IL; not adm. in DC) P.O. Box 65135

McCarter, Robert A., III .... '72 '97 C.93 B.A. L.309 J.D. [Ⓐ Arnold&P.]
*PRACTICE AREAS: Products Liability Litigation; Litigation.

McCarter, Susan A. '68 '97 C.550 B.A. L.564 J.D.
(adm. in MA; not adm. in DC) [Ⓐ Cadwalader,W.&T.]
*PRACTICE AREAS: Corporate Law.

McCarthy, Catherine ....'71 '95 C&L.051 B.A., J.D. [Ⓐ Clifford C.R.&W.]
*PRACTICE AREAS: Project Finance; Banking Law.

McCarthy, Catherine P. ...'67 '93 C.976 B.A. L.276 J.D. 1875 Connecticut Avenue, N.W.

McCarthy, Charles R., Jr., (AV) ...... '38 '66 C.1031 B.S. L.276 J.D. [◎ O'Connor&H.]

McCarthy, David J. '52 '80 C.602 B.A. L.1209 J.D.
Asst. Gen. Coun., Indianapolis Power & Light Co.

McCarthy, David J., Jr. '35 '60 C.1030 A.B. L.276 J.D.
Prof. of State & Local Govt. Law, Georgetown Univ.

McCarthy, Eric J. ....'71 '95 C.197 A.B. L.659 J.D. [Ⓐ Howrey S.A.&W.]
*PRACTICE AREAS: Antitrust; Commercial Litigation; Products Liability.

McCarthy, Helen M. ....'21 '53 C.687 A.B. L.273 J.D. 1850 M St., N.W. (Pat.)

McCarthy, Jennifer D. ....'68 '94 C.800 B.A. L.128 J.D. [Ⓐ Willkie F.&G.]

McCarthy, John E., Jr. ....'53 '89 C.698 B.S.E.S. L.128 J.D. [◎ Crowell&M.]
*PRACTICE AREAS: Information Technology; Bid Protests; Public Contract Law; Insurance Coverage; E-Commerce.

McCarthy, Kevin R., (AV) ....'46 '74 C.602 A.B. L.276 J.D. [Lepon M.W.&H.]

McCarthy, Martin L. '66 '92 C&L.190 B.A., J.D.
(adm. in MO; not adm. in DC) [Ⓐ Copilevitz&C.] ⊙
*PRACTICE AREAS: Tax Exempt Organizations; Charitable Organization Registration; Fund-Raiser Registration; Administrative Agency Practice.

McCarthy, Michael R. ....'66 '91 C.602 B.S. L.128 J.D. [Ⓐ Collier S.S.]
*PRACTICE AREAS: Litigation.

Mccarthy, Sarah E. '63 '94 C.95 B.A. L.588 J.D.
(adm. in MA; not adm. in DC)
Staff Atty., National Law Ctr. on Homelessness & Poverty

McCarthy, Thomas J. ....'69 '99 C.477 A.B. L.893 J.D. [Ⓐ Akin,G.S.H.&F.]
*PRACTICE AREAS: International Trade; Entertainment Law.

McCarthy, Sweeney & Harkaway, P.C., (AV)
2175 K Street, N.W. Suite 600, 20037
Telephone: 202-393-5710 Telecopier: 202-393-5721
Email: MSH@MSHPC.com URL: http://www.mshpc.com
Charles J. McCarthy (1907-1995); Steven J. Kalish; John M. Cutler, Jr.; Douglas M. Canter; Andrew P. Goldstein; Lawrence W. Bierlein; Richard D. Lieberman; Channing D. Strother Jr. Of Counsel: Karen R. O'Brien.
Energy, Public Utility, Transportation, Government Contracts and Administrative Practice Areas.
See Professional Biographies, WASHINGTON, DISTRICT OF COLUMBIA

McCarthy, Wilson & Ethridge
(See Rockville, Maryland)

McCartney, Noble, (AV) ....'18 '49 C.674 A.B. L.309 LL.B. 901 15th St., N.W.

McCarty, J. Laurence ...'34 '60 C.321 A.B. L.93 LL.B. V.P., Prudential Ins. Co. of Amer.

McCarty, Joyce E. ....'50 '86 C.848 B.A. L.312 J.D. [Ⓐ Cleary,G.S.&H.]

McCarty, Michael N., (AV) ....'53 '79 C.893 B.A. L.128 J.D. [Brickfield B.R.&S.]
*PRACTICE AREAS: Energy; Hydroelectricity Licensing; Natural Resources; Endangered Species; Health Care Administration.

McCarty, Philip A. ....'51 '76 C.174 B.S. L.208 J.D. [McDermott,W.&E.]

McCarty-Jones, Brendolyn R. '57 '85 C.864 B.S. L.329 J.D.
(adm. in NE; not adm. in DC) Dept. of Fin. & Rev.

McCawley, Harrison B. .... '23 '55 C.674 A.B. L.309 LL.B. [◎ Silverstein&M.]

McChesney, Kathleen Marie ....'57 '86 C.446 B.A. L.276 J.D. [Ⓐ Jones,D.R.&P.]

McChesney, Robert W., Jr., (AV) '23 '51
C.321 A.B. L.276 LL.B. [McChesney&D.] (⊙Bowie, MD)

McChesney & Dale, P.C., (AV)
1225 Connecticut Ave., Suite 300 (⊙Bowie, MD; Alexandria, VA)

McClafferty, Eric R. ....'58 '96 C.477 B.A. L.893 J.D. [Ⓐ Collier S.S.]
*PRACTICE AREAS: International Trade; Import and Export Compliance; Business Immigration; Customs; Export Controls.

McClain, Beth C. '61 '92 C.93 B.S.N. L.813 J.D.
(adm. in NJ; not adm. in DC) [Ⓐ Fried,F.H.S.&J.]
*PRACTICE AREAS: Civil False Claims Act; Health Care.

McClain, William T. '26 '58
C.383 B.S.Met.E. L.425 J.D. [◎ Finnegan,H.F.G.&D.] (See Pat. Sect.)
*PRACTICE AREAS: Chemical Intellectual Property; Intellectual Property Infringement; Intellectual Property Licensing; International Licensing; Mechanical Intellectual Property.

McClanahan, Kay M. '44 '90 C.45 B.S.E. L.1243 J.D.
(adm. in AR; not adm. in DC) 1775 K St.

McClarnon, Carol T. ....'60 '90 C.63 B.S. L.347 J.D. [◎ Sutherland A.&B.]
*PRACTICE AREAS: Employee Benefits; ERISA Compliance.

McCleary, James .... '62 '88 C.1044 B.A. L.128 J.D. U.S. Environmental Prot. Agcy.

McClelland, Jill Kleppe ....'63 '91 C.174 B.A. L.276 J.D. [Ⓐ Fleischman&W.]

McClenan, Jennifer P. .... '65 '92 C.893 B.S. L.602 J.D. [Ⓐ Shaw P.] (Pat.)

McClendon, Samuel ....'52 '80 C.477 B.A. L.273 J.D. Asst. Bar Coun., Off. of Bar Coun.

McCloskey, Maureen A. '53 '89
C.383 B.A. L.276 J.D. Dir. Advocacy, Paralyzed Vet. of Amer.

McCloskey, Robert L. ....'30 '54 C.321 A.B. L.276 LL.B. 5310 Nevada Ave., N.W.

McClure, Elizabeth J. ....'71 '99 C.1365 B.A. L.280 J.D. 2300 N St., N.W.

McClure, Helen P. ....'55 '85 C.597 B.S. L.273 J.D. [◎ Hogan&H.]
*PRACTICE AREAS: Business Law; Commercial Law; Telecommunications Contracts; Fiber Optics; Technology Contracts.

McClure, Sarah B. ....'67 '94 C.95 A.B. L.276 J.D. [Ⓐ Jones,D.R.&P.]

McClure, Scott D. .... '65 '91 C.999 B.B.A. L.228 J.D. [Hogan&H.]
*PRACTICE AREAS: Tax.

McClure, Scott P. ....'66 '94 C.556 B.A.B.S. L.352 J.D. [Ⓐ King&S.]
*PRACTICE AREAS: Litigation; Trade Regulation.

McClure, William P., (AV) .... '25 '51 C.659 B.S. L.273 J.D. [White&C.]
*PRACTICE AREAS: Taxation.

McCoin, Michael A. '— '95 C.477 B.A. L.215 J.D.
(adm. in MI; not adm. in DC) [Ⓐ Goldberg,G.W.&W.]
*PRACTICE AREAS: Communications; Media.

McColl, Diane Barber, (AV) .... '54 '84 C&L.790 B.S., J.D. [Hyman,P.&M.]

McColl, Jennifer Duncan Collier '70 '96 C.976 B.A. L.446 J.D.
(adm. in MD; not adm. in DC) Leg. Coun., Legal Action Center

McCollian, Kelly N. '75 '00 C.659 B.A. L.273 J.D.
(adm. in VA; not adm. in DC) [Ⓐ Willkie F.&G.]
*PRACTICE AREAS: Telecommunications Law.

McCombs, Harold K., Jr., (AV) '50 '75 C.477 B.A. L.273 J.D.
[◎ Dickstein S.M.&O.]
*PRACTICE AREAS: Communications Law.

McConathy, Lucinda O. ....'49 '94 C.914 A.B. L.145 J.D. [Richards S.K.&O.] ⊙

McConihe, Michael H., (AV) .... '40 '65 C.674 A.B. L.276 LL.B. [O'Brien,B.M.&S.]

McConkey, Matthew J. ....'65 '91 C.477 B.A. L.904 J.D. [◎ Coudert B.]
*PRACTICE AREAS: Customs; International Trade.

McConnell, Bradley K. ....'68 '95 C.674 A.B. L.273 J.D. [Ⓐ Piper M.R.&W.]
*PRACTICE AREAS: Business and Technology; Corporate; Venture Capital; Emerging Growth Companies.

McConnell, James F., Jr. ...'47 '76 C.363 A.B. L.30 J.D. 1130 Connecticut Ave Nw # 300

McConnell, John W., Jr. ....'21 '48 C.16 A.B. L.976 LL.B. 2000 Pennsylvania Ave., N.W.

McConnell, Julie K. '71 '97 C.896 B.A. L.30 J.D.
(adm. in PA; not adm. in DC) [Ⓐ Mayer,B.&P.]

McConnell, Mark S., (AV) .... '53 '79 C.367 B.A. L.813 J.D. [Hogan&H.]
*PRACTICE AREAS: International Law; International Trade Law.

McConnell, Nicholas S., (AV) ....'46 '72 C.95 B.A. L.273 J.D. [Jackson&C.] ⊙
*PRACTICE AREAS: Health Law; Hospital Law; Medical Malpractice; General Litigation; Corporate Law.

McConnell, Nuala ....'68 '95 C.674 A.B. L.276 J.D. [Ⓐ Sidley A.B.&W.]

McConnell, Richard L., (AV) .... '52 '78 C.838 B.A. L.893 J.D. [Wiley R.&F.]
*PRACTICE AREAS: Litigation; Insurance; Reinsurance; Environmental Law.

McConville, Frederick J. .... '— '85 C.870 B.S. L.309 J.D. [◎ Verner,L.B.M.&H.]
*PRACTICE AREAS: Corporate Transactions; Securities Transactions.

McCord, Michael A. ....'48 '75 C.347 A.B. L.309 J.D. [◎ Morgan,L.&B.]

McCormack, Andrew '— '00 C.31 B.A. L.569 J.D.
(adm. in NY; not adm. in DC) [Ⓐ King&S.]
*PRACTICE AREAS: Government Investigations.

McCormally, Timothy J. ....'52 '76 C.352 B.A. L.276 J.D. Tax Exec. Institute, Inc.

McCormick, Matthew H., (AV) ....'50 '79 C&L.629 B.S., J.D. [Reddy,B.&M.]
*PRACTICE AREAS: Communications Law; Copyright and Trademark Law.

McCormick, Patrick J., III ....'56 '85 C.1115 B.A. L.128 J.D. [Balch&B.]
*PRACTICE AREAS: Public Utility Law; Environmental Law; Legislative Practice.

McCormick, Robert S. '44 '75 C&L.273 B.S., J.D.
(adm. in MD; not adm. in DC) 2445 M St., N.W.

McCormick, Thomas C. '71 '01 C.385 B.A. L.262 J.D.
(adm. in NY; not adm. in DC) [Ⓐ Morrison&F.]
*PRACTICE AREAS: Financial Services Law; Banking Law; Legislative Practice; Regulatory Law.

McCormick, Thomas H. .... '50 '77 C.433 B.S. L.276 J.D. [Shaw P.]
*PRACTICE AREAS: Corporate Securities; Technology.

McCoy, Dennis R. '50 '88 C.477 B.S. L.1356 J.D.
(adm. in VA; not adm. in DC) Assoc. Gen. Coun., CareFirst Blue Cross Blue Shield

McCoy, Jerry J., (AV) '41 '67 C.923 B.S. L.228 LL.B.
Suite 1200 1050 Connecticut Avenue, P.O. Box 66491, 20035-6491
Telephone: 202-466-6941 Fax: 202-466-6942
Email: mccoylaw@aol.com
Charitable Giving, Charitable Trusts and Foundations, Nonprofit and Charitable Organizations, Nonprofit Tax Law.
See Professional Biographies, WASHINGTON, DISTRICT OF COLUMBIA

McCoy, John C. ....'47 '76 C.602 B.B.A. L.273 J.D. [Arent F.K.P.&K.]
*PRACTICE AREAS: Taxation Law; Business Planning Law; Tax Controversies.
McCoy, Mark B. '61 '86 C.423 B.A. L.64 J.D.
Assoc. Gen. Coun., Blue Cross & Blue Shield of Natl. Capital Area
McCoy, Neal S., (AV) .... '40 '66 C.378 A.B. L.309 LL.B. [Ⓒ Skadden,A.S.M.&F.]
McCoy, Rikki '75 '00 C.705 B.S. L.329 J.D.
(adm. in NY; not adm. in DC) [Ⓐ Paul,H.J.&W.]
*PRACTICE AREAS: Litigation.
McCray, Donyelle C. ....'74 '99 C.811 B.A. L.309 J.D. [Ⓐ Sutherland A.&B.]
*PRACTICE AREAS: Trusts and Estates.
McCray, Renee D. .... '65 '92 C.102 B.A. L.1009 J.D. 1429 G St., N.W.
McCrea, Keith R., (AV) ....'47 '73 C.401 B.S.Ch.E. L.276 J.D. [Sutherland A.&B.]
*PRACTICE AREAS: Electric Power; Energy Contracts; Energy Regulation; Federal Energy Regulation.
McCrea, Lisa ....'63 '94 C.112 B.A. L.902 J.D. [Ⓐ Dechert]
*PRACTICE AREAS: Securities Regulation; SEC Enforcement.
Mccreery, John Healy ....'68 '00 C.884 B.A. L.724 J.D. 450 Fifth St. NW
McCrickard, Keith A. ....'73 '99 C.575 B.A. L.893 J.D. [Ⓐ McDermott,W.&E.]
McCrum, R. Timothy, (AV) .... '58 '84 C.264 B.A. L.1051 J.D. [Crowell&M.]
*PRACTICE AREAS: Environmental Law; Mining and Mineral Law; Natural Resources Law.
McCrystal, Colleen B .... '68 '95 C.1107 B.A. L.30 J.D. Public Defender Service
McCue, Gregory S. .... '68 '95 C.602 B.A. L.276 J.D. [Ⓐ Steptoe&J.]
McCulloch, Anne Segrest ...'58 '85 C&L.861 B.A., J.D. Assoc. Gen. Coun., Fannie Mae
*RESPONSIBILITIES: Multifamily Housing; Finance.
McCulloch, Bruce C. ....'68 '98 C.893 B.A. L.1209 J.D. [Ⓐ Vinson&E.]
*PRACTICE AREAS: Litigation.
McCulloch, Robert F. ....'28 '56 C.103 A.B. L.893 J.D. 4800 Upton St., N.W.‡
McCullough, Edward A. ....'55 '79 C.893 B.A. L.945 J.D. [Pepper H.]
*PRACTICE AREAS: Public Finance; Municipal Bonds; Federal Taxation.
McCullough, James J., (AV) ....'47 '76 C.884 B.A. L.893 J.D. [Fried,F.H.S.&J.]
*PRACTICE AREAS: Government Contracts; Litigation.
McCullough, John A. ....'45 '71 C.674 B.A. L.976 J.D. [Ⓐ Wiley R.&F.]
McCurdy, Barbara Clarke '60 '86
C.228 B.S.M.E. L.818 J.D. [Finnegan,H.F.G.&D.] (See Pat. Sect.)
*PRACTICE AREAS: Intellectual Property Infringement; Intellectual Property Litigation; Mechanical Intellectual Property; Medical Intellectual Property; Technology Protection.
McCurdy, Gregor B. ....'36 '74 C.813 B.S. L.770 J.D. [Ⓒ Freedman,L.K.&S.]
McCutcheon, Kimberly E. '72 '98 C&L.575 B.A., J.D.
(adm. in NC; not adm. in DC) [Ⓐ Bennett,T.&C.] ‡
*PRACTICE AREAS: Food and Drug Regulation; Health Law.
McCutcheon, Nathan W. ....'65 '93 C.880 B.S.E. L.273 J.D. [Morgan,L.&B.]

McDade Warran & Zimmerman
(See Jason R. Warran, Kensington, Maryland)

McDanell, Jay '71 '00 C.861 B.A. L.276 J.D.
(adm. in VA; not adm. in DC) [Ⓢ Sutherland A.&B.]
*PRACTICE AREAS: Civil Litigation.
McDaniel, James B. ....'38 '67 C.608 B.S. L.329 LL.B. Off. of Corp. Coun.
McDaniel, John, Jr. ....'23 '52 C&L.329 A.B., LL.B. 1100 6th St.
McDaniel, S. Tovan ....'72 '97 C.910 B.A. L.228 J.D. [Ⓐ Hogan&H.]
*PRACTICE AREAS: Corporate Law; Commercial Law; Project Finance; Mergers, Acquisitions and Divestitures; Aircraft Finance and Leasing.
McDaniels, William E., (AV) ....'41 '67 C.951 B.A. L.276 J.D. [Williams&C.]
*PRACTICE AREAS: Administrative Law; Complex and Multi-District Litigation; Criminal Law; Intellectual Property; Libel, Slander and Defamation.
McDannell, Jennifer K. ....'71 '97 C.861 B.S. L.228 J.D. [Ⓐ Howrey S.A.&W.]
*PRACTICE AREAS: Commercial Litigation; Patent Litigation; Products Liability.
McDavid, J. Gary, (AV) ....'47 '73 C.608 B.A. L.276 J.D. [Dorsey&W.]
*PRACTICE AREAS: Cooperatives; Corporate Law.
McDavid, Janet L., (AV) ....'50 '75 C.597 B.A. L.276 J.D. [Hogan&H.]
*PRACTICE AREAS: Antitrust Law.
McDermid, John F., (AV) '46 '73 C.699 B.A. L.904 J.D.
Pres., COO & Gen. Coun., Intl. Bus. Govt. Counsellors, Inc.
McDermott, Brian M. ....'73 '98 C.260 B.S. L.128 J.D. [Ⓐ Swidler B.S.F.]
*PRACTICE AREAS: Telecommunications.
McDermott, Daniel J. '53 '79 C.976 B.A. L.352 J.D.
(adm. in IA; not adm. in DC) V.P., Govt. Relations, Providian Corporation
McDermott, Francis O., (AV) .... '— '60 C.190 L.904 LL.B. [Foley&L.]
*PRACTICE AREAS: Tax (Administrative) Law; Legislative Law.
McDermott, John J., (AV) ....'51 '76 C&L.276 B.A., J.D. [Hall,E.H.G.G.&N.]
*PRACTICE AREAS: Litigation; White Collar Criminal Defense; Trade Association Law.
McDermott, Kathleen, (AV) '61 '86 C.1208 B.A. L.818 J.D.
(adm. in MD; not adm. in DC) [Blank R.C.&M.]
*PRACTICE AREAS: False Claims Act; Qui Tam Litigation; Government Investigations; Health Care Fraud; Health Care Litigation.
McDermott, Kathleen E., (AV) ....'49 '75 C&L.276 B.S.F.S., J.D. [Collier S.S.]
*PRACTICE AREAS: Antitrust and Trade Regulation; Corporate Law.
McDermott, Mark T., (AV) ....'48 '74 C&L.347 B.S., J.D. [Joseph,M.&R.]
*PRACTICE AREAS: Litigation; Aviation Law; Adoption Law.
McDermott, Mary '55 '80 C.923 B.A. L.309 J.D.
(adm. in FL; not adm. in DC) 1401 H St., N.W.
McDermott, Mikaela A. '70 '99 C.309 A.B. L.893 J.D.
1333 New Hampshire Avenue, N.W., Suite 400 (⊙New York, NY)
McDermott, Patricia M. ....'71 '97 C.860 B.A. L.273 J.D. [Ⓐ Cleary,G.S.&H.]
McDermott, Robert F., Jr., (AV) ......'45 '70 C.309 A.B. L.976 LL.B. [Jones,D.R.&P.]
*PRACTICE AREAS: Litigation; Products Liability; Corporate Criminal Law.
McDermott, Will & Emery, (AV)
600 Thirteenth Street, N.W. (Pat.) (⊙Irvine, L.A., Menlo Park, CA; Miami, FL; Chgo., IL; Boston, MA; New York, NY)
McDevitt, Daune M. ....'48 '74 C.30 B.A. L.910 J.D. 5025 Upton St. N.W.
McDiarmid, Robert C., (AV) ....'37 '64 C.821 B.S. L.309 LL.B. [Spiegel&M.]
*PRACTICE AREAS: Energy; Antitrust; Litigation; Administrative Law; Utility Law.
McDonald, Bradley G., (AV) '34 '61
C.623 B.A. L.276 J.D. 900 17th Avenue, N.W., Suite 1250
McDonald, Bruce A., (AV) ....'53 '80 C.112 B.A. L.904 J.D. [Wiley R.&F.]
*PRACTICE AREAS: Intellectual Property Law; Trademarks; International Law.
McDonald, Bruce L., (AV) ....'41 '67 C&L.309 A.B., LL.B. [Wiley R.&F.]
*PRACTICE AREAS: Litigation; Privacy.
McDonald, Calonette M. ....'62 '89 C.577 B.A. L.329 J.D. Dept. of Human Servs.
McDonald, Farnese H. '60 '86 C.30 B.A. L.329 J.D.
1401 New York Ave., N, Suite 600
McDonald, John J. ....'71 '99 C.1350 B.S. L.276 J.D. [Ⓐ Hogan&H.]
*PRACTICE AREAS: Corporate Law; Private Equity; Mergers and Acquisitions.
McDonald, John K. ....'45 '73 C&L.623 B.B.A., J.D. [Jackson&K.P.]
*PRACTICE AREAS: Natural Resources; Administrative.
McDonald, John M. ....'63 '90 C.602 B.A. L.383 J.D. [Shaw P.]
McDonald, Kevin D. ....'52 '78 C.385 A.B. L.930 J.D. [Jones,D.R.&P.]
*PRACTICE AREAS: Litigation; Antitrust and Trade Regulation; Medical Antitrust.
McDonald, Laura F. H. ....'63 '88 C&L.893 B.A., J.D. [Levine,B.B.&B.]
*PRACTICE AREAS: Telecommunications Law; Technology; Civil Litigation; Alternative Dispute Resolution.
McDonald, Mary Dobson .... '53 '80 C.228 B.A. L.893 J.D. 51 Louisiana Ave. NW
McDonald, Susan ....'— '99 C.858 B.A. L.128 J.D. 701 Pennsylvania Avenue, N.W.
McDonald, Terrence F. ....'44 '75 C.683 B.A. L.744 J.D. 1706 Irving St., N.W.
McDonald, Tom, (AV) .... '54 '81 C.273 B.A. L.494 J.D. [Arter&H.] (⊙Cleve., OH)
*PRACTICE AREAS: International Law; Arbitration; Government Relations; Labor and Employment Law.
McDonnell, Ellen Kathleen ....'70 '97 C.1356 B.A. L.1355 J.D. [Ⓐ Finnegan,H.F.G.&D.]
*PRACTICE AREAS: Trademark Prosecution; Trademark Litigation; Copyright Prosecution; Copyright Litigation; International Trademarks.
McDonnell, Kathryn E. '47 '72 C.724 B.S. L.262 J.D.
Asst. Gen. Coun., MCI WorldCom
McDonnell, Mary C. ....'42 '67 C.450 B.A. L.910 J.D. 1155 Connecticut Ave., NW
McDonough, Guy M. '62 '96 C&L.174 B.A., J.D.
(adm. in CT; not adm. in DC) [Ⓐ Washington C.]
McDonough, Julia A. ....'60 '97 C.426 B.A. L.893 J.D. [Ⓐ Fried,F.H.S.&J.]
*PRACTICE AREAS: Securities Law; Corporate.
McDonough, Michael J. ....'65 '97 C.999 B.A. L.273 J.D. [Ⓐ Dechert]
*PRACTICE AREAS: Financial Services Law; Investment Management.
McDonough, Patrick John ....'51 '89 C&L.446 B.A., J.D. [Ⓒ Stewart&S.]
*PRACTICE AREAS: Civil Litigation: CIT, CAFC; Administrative Law; ITC; ITA; Customs Law.
McDonough, Robert S. ....'51 '76 C.434 B.A. L.276 J.D. [Rund&M.] ⊙
McDowell, Barbara Ann '— '87 C.935 B.S. L.273 J.D.
(adm. in VA; not adm. in DC; See Pat. Sect.) [Ⓒ Foley&L.]
*PRACTICE AREAS: Chemistry; Biotechnology; Patent Prosecution.
McDowell, Heather L. .... '65 '90 C.645 B.S. L.273 J.D. [Venable,A.B.H.&C.]
*PRACTICE AREAS: Communications Law; Advertising; Electronic Commerce.
McDowell, Jill K. ....'68 '98 C.260 B.S. L.128 J.D. [Ⓐ Mayer,B.&P.]
*PRACTICE AREAS: Litigation; Government Contracts; Regulated Industries.
McDowell, Suzanne Ross, (AV) '49 '77
C.788 A.B. L.273 J.D. Dep. Gen. Coun., Natl. Geographic Soc.
*RESPONSIBILITIES: Federal Income Tax; State and Local Tax; Publishing Law; Intellectual Property; Contracts.
McElfish, James M., Jr., (AV) '54 '79
C.216 B.A. L.976 J.D. Sr. Atty., Environmental Law Institute
*RESPONSIBILITIES: Environmental Law; Natural Resources Law.
McElhennon, Stephen H. '69 '96 C&L.262 B.A., J.D.
(adm. in NY; not adm. in DC) Assoc. Gen. Coun., Fannie Mae
*RESPONSIBILITIES: Corporate; Securities.
McElligott, Paul J., (AV) '38 '63 C.321 A.B. L.276 J.D.
Exec. Dir., North Capitol Neighborhood Develop.
McElroy, Carolyn J., (AV) '52 '81 C.550 B.A. L.446 J.D.
(adm. in MD; not adm. in DC) 701 Pennsylvania Avenue, N.W.
McElroy, Kathryn A. ....'68 '95 C.183 B.A. L.588 J.D. [Ⓐ Dechert]
*PRACTICE AREAS: Financial Services Law; Investment Management.
McElroy, Michael J. '69 '97 C.385 B.A. L.276 J.D.
(adm. in VA; not adm. in DC) [Ⓐ Orrick,H.&S.]
McElroy, Paul J. ....'63 '90 C.602 B.A. L.128 J.D. [Ⓒ Sullivan&C.]
McElveen, Junius C., Jr., (AV) ....'47 '72 C&L.893 B.A., J.D. [Jones,D.R.&P.]
*PRACTICE AREAS: Environmental Litigation; OSHA; Toxic Substance Liability.
McElwain, William G. ....'55 '82 C.976 B.A. L.309 J.D. [Hale&D.]
McEnery, Kevin P. ....'51 '77 C.103 A.B. L.893 J.D. [Ⓒ Wilmer,C.&P.]
McEnery, Rosemary H. ....'57 '83 C.840 B.A. L.846 J.D. [Howrey S.A.&W.]
*PRACTICE AREAS: Antitrust; Commercial Litigation.
McEntee, Joan M. ....'— '83 C.449 B.A. L.30 J.D. [Baker,D.B.&C.]
McErlean, Thomas P., Jr. ....'47 '73 C&L.276 A.B., J.D. 2461 Wisconsin Ave., N.W.
McEvoy, John T. '37 '61 C&L.190 A.B., LL.B.
Exec. Dir., Natl. Council of St. Housing Agcys.‡
McEvoy, Julie E. ....'68 '95 C.945 B.A. L.602 J.D. [Ⓐ Jones,D.R.&P.]
McEwen, James G. '70 '96 C.846 B.S. L.273 J.D.
(adm. in VA; not adm. in DC; See Pat. Sect.) [Ⓐ Staas&H.]
*PRACTICE AREAS: Patent Law; Trademark Law; Trade Secret; Licensing; Intellectual Property Law.
McFadden, Douglas B., (AV) ....'40 '65 C&L.150 B.S., J.D. [McFadden&S.]
McFadden, Janet R. ....'52 '98 C.93 B.A. L.846 J.D. [Ⓐ Drinker B.&R.]
McFadden, Jeffrey E. ....'57 '90 C.871 B.S. L.276 J.D. [Ⓒ Wilmer,C.&P.]
*PRACTICE AREAS: Securities Enforcement; Securities Litigation; White Collar Crime.
McFadden, W. Clark, II, (AV) ....'46 '72 C.951 B.A. L.309 J.D. [Dewey B.]
*PRACTICE AREAS: International Trade and Transactions.
McFadden & Shoreman, P.C., (AV) ....1314 19th Street, N.W.
McFalls, Michael S. ....'68 '95 C.477 B.A. L.893 J.D. [Ⓐ Jones,D.R.&P.]
McFarland, Andrew J. ....'71 '98 C.30 B.A. L.180 J.D. [Ⓐ Dickstein S.M.&O.]
*PRACTICE AREAS: Insurance Litigation.
McFarland, Elizabeth A. ....'65 '93 C.112 B.A. L.276 J.D. [Cooter,M.T.&W.]
McFarland, Eric A. '61 '89 C.1099 B.A. L.329 J.D.
(adm. in PA; not adm. in DC) D.C. Council Committee on Pub. Servs.
McFarlane, Randall H. '48 '73 C.197 A.B. L.659 J.D.
Dir., Govt. Rel., Savings & Community Bkrs. of America
McFarquhar, Erica ....'— '98 C.674 A.B. L.1049 J.D. [Ⓐ Latham&W.]
*PRACTICE AREAS: Litigation; Internet Law; Computer Fraud; Health Care Fraud.
McField, Terri L. '— '94 C.1099 B.S. L.329 J.D.
(adm. in PA; not adm. in DC) 1235 W. Street, N.E.
McGann, Kathleen ....'52 '78 C.93 B.A. L.276 J.D. International Fin. Corp.
McGarrah, Robert E., Jr. '47 '72 C.390 A.B. L.884 J.D.
Sen. Policy Analyst, Amer. Federation of State, Co. & Mun. Employees
McGarry, J. Michael, III, (AV) ....'43 '69 C.659 B.S. L.893 LL.B. [Winston&S.]
*PRACTICE AREAS: Energy Law; Administrative Law; Natural Resources Law.
McGeary, Elizabeth Anne ....'64 '91 C.856 B.A. L.893 J.D. [Dow,L.&A.]
McGee, Edith Moore '57 '99 C.269 B.A. L.1356 J.D.
(adm. in VA; not adm. in DC) [Ⓐ Piliero,M.&P.]
*PRACTICE AREAS: Employment Law; Government Contracts; Corporate Counseling.
McGee, Joyce A. '69 '99 C.999 B.A. L.1280 J.D.
Assoc. Coun., HALT - Americans for Legal Reform
McGee, Karen A. ....'— '88 C.676 B.A. L.273 J.D. [Ⓒ Barnes&T.]
*PRACTICE AREAS: Trademarks; International Trade; Intellectual Property.
McGee, Peter ....'55 '85 C.188 B.S. L.128 J.D. [Ⓐ Ostrolenk,F.G.&S.] (See Pat. Sect.)
*PRACTICE AREAS: Patent Law.
McGee, Shelly Lynn ....'— '96 C.383 B.A. L.150 J.D. [Ⓐ Hogan&H.]
*PRACTICE AREAS: Trademark; Copyright; Unfair Competition.
McGettigan, Marianne, (AV) '50 '75 C.156 B.A. L.94 J.D.
(adm. in WA; not adm. in DC) [Ⓒ Verrill&D.] (⊙Port., ME)
McGiffert, David E., (AV) '26 '53 C&L.309 A.B., J.D.
1201 Pennsylvania Ave Nw # 11
McGill, Brian Andrew ....'70 '95 C.575 B.A. L.276 J.D. [Ⓐ McDermott,W.&E.]

McGill, Brian E. '55 '81 C.117 B.A. L.276 J.D. 1353 Taylor St., N.W.
McGill, John P., Jr. . . . . '66 '99 C.692 B.A. L.276 J.D. [Ⓐ Cleary,G.S.&H.]
McGillivary, Gregory K., (AV) . . . . '57 '83 C.597 B.A. L.629 J.D. [Woodley,G.&M.]
*PRACTICE AREAS: Public Sector Labor Relations Law; Employment Discrimination Law; Fair Labor Standards Law.
McGinley, Molly M. . . . . '67 '94 C.999 B.A. L.629 J.D. 1100 New York Avenue, N.W.
McGinley, Patrick C. . . . . '51 '77 C.602 B.B.A. L.190 J.D. 1101 30th St., N.W.
McGinley, Robert G., (AV) . . . . '62 '88 C.754 B.A. L.128 J.D. [Macleay,L.G.&L.]
*PRACTICE AREAS: Insurance Defense.
McGinley, William '67 '97 C.1068 B.A. L.273 J.D.
(adm. in MD; not adm. in DC) [Ⓐ Patton B.]
McGinn, Kelly Sweeney . . . . '69 '96 C.276 B.S.F.S. L.893 J.D. [Ⓐ Harris,W.&G.]
*PRACTICE AREAS: Telecommunications.
McGinn, Stacie E. . . . . '59 '91 C.69 B.B.A. L.276 J.D. [Skadden,A.S.M.&F.]
McGinnis, Amy L. . . . . '72 '98 C.30 B.A. L.273 J.D. [Ⓐ Arnold&P.]
*PRACTICE AREAS: Litigation; Product Liability.
McGinnis, Bryan T. . . . . '49 '89 C.309 B.A. L.813 J.D. [Ⓒ Shaw P.]
*PRACTICE AREAS: Communications Transactions; Media Law.
McGinnis, Ellen Gibson . . . . '60 '86 C.976 B.A. L.569 J.D. [Haynes&B.]
McGinnis, Nicole M. . . . . '73 '98 C.170 A.B. L.145 J.D. [Ⓐ Wiley R.&F.]
McGlamery, Keith W., (AV) '47 '76 C.612 B.A. L.966 J.D.
(adm. in WI; not adm. in DC) [Jenkens&G.]
*PRACTICE AREAS: Real Estate.
McGlone, Patrick '61 '86
C.262 B.A. L.273 J.D. Assoc. Gen. Coun., U.S. Office Products Co.
*RESPONSIBILITIES: Commercial Litigation; Employment Litigation; Intellectual Property; Tort Litigation.
McGlone, William M. . . . . '— '88 C.309 A.B. L.276 J.D. [Miller&C.]
*PRACTICE AREAS: International Trade Regulation; Export Regulation; Foreign Trade Sanctions; Import and Export Law; International Trade.
McGlynn, John W. '73 '98 C.423 B.A. L.128 J.D.
(adm. in MD; not adm. in DC) [Ⓐ Venable,A.B.H.&C.]
*PRACTICE AREAS: Intellectual Property.
McGoldrick, Margaret A. . . . . '58 '84 C.20 B.A. L.309 J.D. [Ⓒ Spiegel&M.]
*PRACTICE AREAS: Administrative Law; Arbitration; Contracts; Public Utility Law; Energy.
McGolrick, Susan J. . . . . '60 '90 C.446 B.A. L.276 J.D. 1121 12th St., N.W.
McGonagle, Erin N. '65 '91
C.575 B.A. L.990 J.D. [Ⓐ Jackson&C.] (⊙Balt., Rockville, MD)
McGonigal, Kyle A. '70 '98 C.823 B.A. L.1002 J.D.
(adm. in MD; not adm. in DC) 717 D St., N.W.‡
McGonigle, Thomas J., (AV) . . . . '57 '83 C.754 B.S. L.276 J.D. [McGuirewoods]
*PRACTICE AREAS: Consumer Financial Services; Securities Compliance; Securities Litigation.
McGonnigal, Michael T. '54 '85 C.588 B.A. L.128 J.D.
Staff Atty., Columbus Community Legal Servs.
McGovern, Helen-Mary Bridget '73 '01 C.276 B.A. L.602 J.D.
(adm. in MA; not adm. in DC) [Ⓐ Brand&F.]
McGovern, John J., Jr. '55 '85
C.446 B.S. L.276 J.D. [Higgins,M.&S.] & [Ⓒ Doepken K.&W.]
McGovern, Julie S. . . . . '69 '96 C.893 B.A. L.659 J.D. [Ⓐ Reno&C.]
*PRACTICE AREAS: Real Estate Transactions; Administrative Law; Affordable Housing.
McGovern, Kathryn C. . . . . '— '99 C.945 B.S. L.861 J.D. [Ⓐ Arnold&P.]
*PRACTICE AREAS: Real Estate.
McGovern, Kristin '71 '00 C.67 B.A. L.910 J.D.
(adm. in MD; not adm. in DC) [Ⓐ Fulbright&J.]
McGovern, Michael B., (AV) . . . . '47 '73 C&L.276 A.B., J.D. [Hanson&M.]
*PRACTICE AREAS: Real Estate; Estate Planning; Trust Law; Litigation.
McGovern, Michael P. . . . . '62 '90 C.446 B.S. L.893 J.D. [Ⓐ Kelley D.&W.]
*PRACTICE AREAS: Environmental Law.
McGovern, Thomas L., III . . . . '57 '88 C.1070 B.S. L.813 J.D. [Hogan&H.]
*PRACTICE AREAS: Government; Government Contracts.
McGowan, G. Rico '67 '94 C&L.446 B.A., J.D.
(adm. in MD; not adm. in DC) Howard University
McGowan, Gerald S., (AV) . . . . '46 '75 C&L.276 B.S.B.A., J.D. U.S. Embassy
McGowan, Michael P. . . . . '64 '90 C.309 A.B. L.276 J.D. 2300 N St., N.W.
McGowan, Tracy M. . . . . '62 '90 C.367 B.A. L.597 J.D. 1722 Eye St., N.W.
McGrail, Elizabeth H. . . . . '62 '90 C.880 B.A. L.945 J.D. 1815 H St. N.W., Ste. 650
McGranahan, J. Russell . . . . '70 '96 C.128 B.A. L.976 J.D. [Ⓐ Skadden,A.S.M.&F.]
*PRACTICE AREAS: Corporate Law; Securities; Mergers and Acquisitions; Venture Capital; Banking Law.
McGrane, John D. . . . . '51 '76 C.187 B.A. L.276 J.D. [Morgan,L.&B.]
McGrane, John P., Jr. . . . . '51 '87 C.276 B.S. L.128 J.D. [Ⓢ Jones,D.R.&P.]
McGrann, Sara B. . . . . '— '43 C.273 L.180 LL.B. 4801 Conn. Ave., N.W.‡
McGrath, C. Dean, Jr. '53 '78 C.228 B.A. L.546 J.D.
(adm. in NE; not adm. in DC) American Automobile Manufacturers Association
McGrath, Dorn C., III, (BV) . . . . '— '82 C.198 A.B. L.273 J.D. [Reed S.]
*PRACTICE AREAS: Government Contracts; Export Compliance.
McGrath, Felicity A. '70 '95 C.659 B.A. L.472 J.D.
[Ⓐ Bonner K.T.&C.] (⊙Rockville, MD; Parsippany, NJ; Fairfax, VA)
*PRACTICE AREAS: Liability Litigation.
McGrath, Jerome J., (AV) . . . . '22 '51 C&L.276 B.S., LL.B. 1000 Vermont Ave., N.W.‡
McGrath, Katherine E. '52 '81 C.901 B.A. L.818 J.D.
(adm. in MA; not adm. in DC) Assoc. Gen Coun., CareFirst Blue Cross Blue Shield
McGrath, Kathryn B., (AV) . . . . '44 '69 C.518 A.B. L.276 J.D. [Morgan,L.&B.]
McGrath, Keri C. '73 '00 C.575 B.A. L.276 J.D.
(adm. in VA; not adm. in DC) [Ⓐ McDermott,W.&E.]
McGrath, Matthew J. . . . . '56 '86 C.602 B.A. L.273 J.D. [McKenna&C.]
*PRACTICE AREAS: Government Contracts; International Business Transactions; International Dispute Resolution; International Financing; Foreign Corrupt Practices Act.
McGrath, Matthew T., (AV) . . . . '54 '79 C.105 B.A. L.273 J.D. [Barnes,R.&C.]
*PRACTICE AREAS: Customs; International Trade.
McGrath, William A., (BV) . . . . '61 '91 C.802 B.F.A. L.945 J.D. [Wiley R.&F.]
*PRACTICE AREAS: Advertising; Food and Drug; Internet; Electronic Commerce; Litigation.
McGrath, William P., Jr. . . . . '61 '87 C.823 B.A. L.273 J.D. [Porter W.M.&A.]
*PRACTICE AREAS: Litigation.
McGraw, Stacey L. . . . . '68 '93 C.893 B.A. L.477 J.D. [Ross,D.&B.]
McGraw, Wendy C. . . . . '70 '94 C.1090 B.A. L.893 J.D. [Ⓐ Swidler B.S.F.]
*PRACTICE AREAS: Litigation.
McGregor, Frank '67 '00 C.329 B.A. L.180 J.D.
(adm. in NJ; not adm. in DC) 1025 Thomas Jefferson St., N.W.
McGregor, Stephen E. . . . . '49 '74 C.94 B.A. L.945 J.D. 1440 New York Ave. N.W.
McGrew, James H., (AV) . . . . '44 '74 C&L.309 B.A., J.D. [Bruder,G.&M.]
*PRACTICE AREAS: Natural Gas; Electric Utility Law; Energy Law; Appellate Practice.
McGrew, John L. . . . . '50 '81 C.197 B.A. L.893 J.D. [Ⓐ Willkie F.&G.]
McGriff, Alison J. '71 '97 C.811 B.S. L.446 J.D.
[Ⓐ Bonner K.T.&C.] (⊙Rockville, MD)
*PRACTICE AREAS: Insurance Defense; Professional Liability.
McGroarty, John . . . . '67 '97 C.659 B.S. L.276 J.D. [Ⓐ Kenyon&K.] (See Pat. Sect.)
*PRACTICE AREAS: Intellectual Property.

McGuan, Kathleen H. . . . . '— '81 C.30 B.A. L.128 J.D. [Reed S.]
*PRACTICE AREAS: Litigation.
McGuffey, Catherine P. '60 '86 C.105 B.A. L.273 J.D.
(adm. in VA; not adm. in DC) Sr. Atty., MCI WorldCom
McGuigan, J. April '54 '80 C.320 B.A. L.692 J.D.
(adm. in VA; not adm. in DC) [Klein,L.&R.]
McGuiness, Jeffrey C., (AV) . . . . '47 '79 C.675 B.A. L.904 J.D. [McGuiness N.&W.]
*PRACTICE AREAS: Employment Relations Law.

McGuiness Norris & Williams, LLP, (AV)
Suite 1200, 1015 Fifteenth Street, N.W., 20005 ⊙
Telephone: 202-789-8600 Telecopier: 202-789-1708
Email: Info@mnwlaw.net URL: http://www.mnwlaw.net
Members of Firm: Jeffrey C. McGuiness; Jeffrey A. Norris; Edward E. Potter; G. John Tysse; Monte B. Lake; Robert E. Williams; Ann Elizabeth Reesman; Daniel V. Yager; Christine M. Cooper; Mark E. Baker. Associates: Timothy J. Bartl; Judith A. Lampley (Not admitted in DC); Amy M. Habib; Joseph S. Lakis, Jr. (Not admitted in DC); Michael J. Eastman (Not admitted in DC); Rae T. Vann (Not admitted in DC); Katherine Y.K. Cheung. Of Counsel: Lorence L. Kessler; Lynnette Conway Jacquez; William N. LaForge; Heather L. MacDougall (Not admitted in DC).
Practice before the Federal Courts and Administrative Agencies. Employment, Labor, Equal Employment Opportunity, Agricultural Labor, Immigration, Federal Appellate Practice and Government Relations.
See Professional Biographies, WASHINGTON, DISTRICT OF COLUMBIA

McGuinn, John A., (AV) . . . . '34 '59 C.321 A.B. L.276 LL.B. [Ⓒ Schmeltzer,A.&S.]
*PRACTICE AREAS: Management Labor Law; Employment Law; Employee Benefits Law.
McGuinness, Charlotte M. . . . . . . '49 '99 C.1100 A.B. L.276 J.D. [Ⓐ Venable,A.B.H.&C.]
*PRACTICE AREAS: Patent Prosecution.
McGuinness, J. Michael, (BV) '57 '84 C.953 B.A. L.574 J.D.
900 Pennsylvania Avenue, N.W., Suite 700 (⊙Boston, MA; Elizabethtown, NC)
McGuinness, Sean P., (AV) . . . . '54 '81 C.860 B.S. L.276 J.D. [Swidler B.S.F.]
*PRACTICE AREAS: Corporate Law; Securities; Project Finance.
McGuire, Carrie L. '71 '00 C.692 B.A. L.273 J.D.
(adm. in VA; not adm. in DC) [Ⓐ Morrison&H.]
*PRACTICE AREAS: Bankruptcy; Communications.
McGuire, Debra A. . . . . '67 '92 C&L.276 B.S., J.D. [Ⓐ Greenberg T.]
McGuire, Edward D., Jr., (BV) '48 '73 C.893 B.S. L.945 J.D.
808 17th St., N.W., 12th Fl. (⊙Rockville, MD; Alexandria, Annandale, VA)
McGuire, Julie E., (AV) '58 '85 C.119 B.S. L.229 J.D.
(adm. in PA; not adm. in DC) [Hull M.] ⊙
*PRACTICE AREAS: Corporate Law; Business Planning; Mergers, Acquisitions and Divestitures; Taxation; International Taxation.
McGuire, Mark J., (AV) . . . . '53 '81 C.1102 B.A. L.734 J.D. [Jenner&B.]
*PRACTICE AREAS: Energy Law; Public Utility Law; Antitrust.
McGuire, Patricia A. . . . . '52 '77 C.856 B.A. L.276 J.D. Georgetown Law Ctr.
McGuire, Raymond L. '33 '60 C.496 B.A. L.500 LL.B.
Exec. V.P., Govt. Affs., BellSouth Corporation
McGuire, Susan O'Sullivan . . . . '60 '87 C.945 B.A. L.893 J.D. [Kirkland&E.]
*PRACTICE AREAS: Environmental Law; Environmental Litigation.
McGuire, W. John . . . . '57 '86 C.942 B.A. L.900 J.D. [Morgan,L.&B.]

McGuireWoods LLP, (AV) BR
Washington Square, 1050 Connecticut Avenue, N.W., Suite 1200, 20036-5317 ⊙
Telephone: 202-857-1700 Fax: 202-857-1737
Email: info@mcguirewoods.com URL: http://www.mcguirewoods.com
Members of Firm: James L. Blasiak; Mark F. Brzezinski (Not admitted in DC); Neal J. Cabral; Douglas W. Charnas; James M. Costan; Jerry A. Isenberg (Not admitted in DC); Steven D. Kittrell; Thomas J. McGonigle; David H. Pankey; James U. Troup. Retired Partner: Clifford R. Oviatt Jr. Of Counsel: Rochelle S. Hall; Anita M. Herrera (Not admitted in DC). Associates: Kathryn B. Allen (Not admitted in DC); Adrian B. Copiz (Not admitted in DC); George W. Erikson Jr.; Robert P. Howard, Jr.; Leyla Gainievna Kalniazova; Stephen A. Katsurinis; James H. Lister; Ian C. Lofwall; Amy E. Miller (Not admitted in DC); Vincent J. Miraglia (Not admitted in DC); Jennifer L. Schwitzer (Not admitted in DC); Kurt T. Slawson; Kristen I. Zarenko.
Accountants Liability, Affordable Housing and Tax Credits, Antitrust, Appellate, Asset Securitization, Automotive, Aviation Disaster Litigation, Banking, Business Acquisitions, Business Reorganizations and Divestitures, Capital Markets, Charitable Giving and Tax-Exempt Organizations, Class Action Litigation, Commercial Litigation, Complex Commercial Litigation, Construction Equipment, Construction Litigation, Consumer Financial Services, Consumer Products, Corporate Finance and Securities, Corporate Services, Creditors Rights and Bankruptcy, Distribution and Franchising, Document and Discovery Management, e-Commerce, Emerging Growth and Technology, Employee Benefits, Employment Discrimination, Energy and Utilities, Executive Compensation Arrangements, Executive Compensation Litigation, Family Businesses, Fiduciary Litigation, Financial Services, First Amendment, Government Compliance, Government Investigations, Government Relations, Health Care, Higher Education, Immigration, Insurance Coverage Litigation, Intellectual Property, Labor and Employment, Labor Management Relations, Land Use, Leasing, Litigation Management, Medical Devices, Drugs and Pharmaceuticals, Mergers and Acquisitions, Non-compete Litigation, Partnerships and Joint Ventures, Products Liability, Project Finance, Public Finance, Real Estate, REIT's and Financial Products, Resorts and Hospitality, Risk Management, Securities Compliance and Enforcement, Securities Litigation, Sports Law, State and Local Taxation, Taxation, Tax Audits; Toxic Torts, Trade Regulation, Traditional Real Estate Transactions, White Collar Crime, Wrongful Discharge.
Atlanta, Georgia Office: The Proscenium, 1170 Peachtree Street, N.E., Suite 2100, 30309-7649. Telephone: 404-443-5500. Fax: 404-443-5599.
Baltimore, Maryland Office: 7 Saint Paul Street, Suite 1000, 21202-1671. Telephone: 410-659-4400. Fax: 410-659-4599.
Charlotte, North Carolina Offices: Bank of America Plaza, 101 South Tryon Street, Suite 3700, 28280. Telephone: 704-373-8999. Fax: 704-373-8980 and Bank of America Corporate Center, Suite 2900, 100 North Tryon Street, 28202. Telephone: 704-373-8999. Fax: 704-373-8935.
Charlottesville, Virginia Office: Court Square Building, 310 Fourth Street, N.E., Suite 300, P.O. Box 1288, 22902-1288. Telephone: 804-977-2500. Fax: 804-980-2222.
Chicago, Illinois Office: 77 West Wacker Drive, Suite 4500, 60601-1635. Telephone: 312-849-3699. Fax: 312-849-3690.
Jacksonville, Florida Office: Bank of America Tower, 50 North Laura Street, 32202-3635. Telephone: 904-798-3200. Fax: 904-798-3207.
McLean, (Tysons Corner) Virginia Office: 1750 Tysons Boulevard, Suite 1800, 22102-3892. Telephone: 703-712-5000. Fax: 703-712-5050.
New York, New York Office: 9 West 57th Street, Suite 1620, 10019. Telephone: 212-548-2100. Fax: 212-548-2150.
Norfolk, Virginia Office: World Trade Center, 101 West Main Street, Suite 9000, 23510-1655. Telephone: 757-640-3700. Fax: 757-640-3701.
Pittsburgh, Pennsylvania Office: Dominion Tower, 23rd Floor, 625 Liberty Avenue, 15222. Telephone: 412-667-6000. Fax: 412-667-6050.
Richmond, Virginia Office: One James Center, 901 East Cary Street, 23219-4030. Telephone: 804-775-1000. Fax: 804-775-1061.
Almaty, Republic of Kazakhstan Office: McGuire Woods Kazakhstan LLP, Park Palace, 41 Kazibek Bi Street, 2nd Floor, 480100. Telephone: 7-3272-608-300. Fax: 7-3272-608-305.
Brussels, Belgium Office: 250 Avenue Louise, Boite 64, 1050. Telephone: 32-2-629-42-11. Fax: 32-2-629-42-22.
Revisers of the Virginia Law Digest for this Directory
See Professional Biographies, WASHINGTON, DISTRICT OF COLUMBIA

McGuirl, Marlene C. '38 '63 C.347 A.B. L.209 J.D.
Admin., Washington Metropolitan Area Transit Authority.
McGurk, Michael R., (BV) '60 '88
C.205 B.S.Ch.E. L.273 J.D. [Finnegan,H.F.G.&D.] (See Pat. Sect.)
*PRACTICE AREAS: Intellectual Property Litigation; Patent Interference Practice; Patent Licensing; Patent Prosecution.
McGwin, Madonna A. . . . . '56 '79 C.690 B.A. L.276 J.D. [Ⓒ Holland&K.]
*PRACTICE AREAS: Employment Law; Mediation; Litigation; Professional Practices.

McHale, James M., (AV) .... '46 '72 C.918 B.A. L.188 J.D. [Seyfarth S.]
*PRACTICE AREAS: Civil Litigation; Government Contracts Law; International Contracts Law; Administrative Law.
McHale, James T. .... '66 '91 C&L.790 B.S., J.D. [⊡ Morgan,L.&B.]
McHugh, James L., Jr., (AV) '37 '63 C.229 B.A. L.884 J.D.
Gen. Coun., American Psychological Association
McHugh, Matthew F. '38 '64 C.524 B.S. L.884 LL.B.
(adm. in NY; not adm. in DC) World Bank
McHugh, Richard P. ....'55 '80 C&L.276 A.B., J.D. [Dow,L.&A.]
McHugh, Ronan Joseph ....'67 '91 L.999 LL.B. [⊡ Arent F.K.P.&K.]
*PRACTICE AREAS: Construction Dispute Resolution; International Arbitration.
McIndoe, David T. '72 '98 C.197 B.A. L.902 J.D.
(adm. in VA; not adm. in DC) [⊡ Hunton&W.]
McInerny, Francis W., (AV) ....'19 '49 C.321 B.S. L.276 LL.B. [McInerny&J.]
McInerny, Julia Wernett .... '64 '93 C.446 B.S. L.64 J.D. [Coale C.L.M.]
*PRACTICE AREAS: Civil Litigation; Commercial Vehicle Liability.
McInerny & Jordan, (AV) .... 1140 Connecticut Ave., N.W.
McInnis, Daniel F. .... '67 '94 C.976 B.A. L.276 J.D. [⊡ Akin,G.S.H.&F.]
*PRACTICE AREAS: Antitrust and Trade Regulation; Litigation.
McIntire, John M. ....'63 '93 C&L.446 B.A., J.D. [⊡ O'Donoghue&O.]
McIntosh, Hugh M., (AV) '45 '73 C.497 B.S. L.893 J.D.
1455 Pennsylvania Ave., N.W.
McIntosh, Robert J. ....'22 '48 C&L.477 J.D. 1522 K St., N.W. (⊙Fort Gratiot, MI)
McIntosh, Scott A. .... '71 '98 C.112 B.A. L.276 J.D. [⊡ Hogan&H.]
*PRACTICE AREAS: Franchise Arbitration; Franchise Law; Franchise Licensing; Franchise Litigation; Franchise Termination.
McIntyre, Heather E. '71 '97 C.945 B.A. L.910 J.D.
(adm. in VA; not adm. in DC) [⊡ Ross,D.&B.]
McIntyre, James T., (AV) .... '40 '63 C&L.280 A.B., J.D. [McIntyre]
*PRACTICE AREAS: Banking Law; Corporate Organization; Federal Legislative Practice; Environmental Regulation; Trade Association Law.
McIntyre, Kevin J. ....'60 '88 C.763 A.B. L.276 J.D. [Jones,D.R.&P.]
*PRACTICE AREAS: Energy; Energy Regulation; Utility Mergers.
McIntyre, Robert V. ....'11 '45 C&L.273 A.B., J.D. 1737 H St., N.W.

McIntyre Law Firm, PLLC, (AV)
Madison Office Building, 1155 Fifteenth Street, Northwest, Suite 1101, 20005
Telephone: 202-659-3900 Fax: 202-659-5763
Email: mcintyre@mcintyrelf.com
James T. McIntyre; Chrys D. Lemon.
Banking Law, Corporate Organization, Federal Legislative Practice, Environmental Regulation, Trade Association Law and Insurance Regulation.
See Professional Biographies, WASHINGTON, DISTRICT OF COLUMBIA

McIsaac, Christopher C. ....'59 '85 C.575 B.A. L.893 J.D. [Winston&S.]
*PRACTICE AREAS: Project Finance; Corporate Finance; Banking.
McJunkin, John, (AV) ....'62 '87 C.301 B.A. L.150 J.D. [Piper M.R.&W.]
*PRACTICE AREAS: Commercial Litigation; Bankruptcy; General Business; Workouts; Telecommunications Law.
McKaig, J. Carter, (AV) ....'32 '58 C.321 A.B. L.276 LL.B. 1666 K St., N.W.‡
McKalip, Frederick D. '— '00 C&L.893 B.A., J.D.
(adm. in VA; not adm. in DC) [⊡ Arent F.K.P.&K.]
McKane, Mark E. ....'— '97 C.976 B.A. L.597 J.D. [⊡ Kirkland&E.]
*PRACTICE AREAS: Litigation.
McKay, Jack, (P.C.), (AV) ....'46 '70 C.880 B.A. L.893 J.D. [Shaw P.]
*PRACTICE AREAS: Commercial Litigation.
McKay, James C., (AV) .... '17 '46 C.188 B.S. L.276 LL.B. [⊡ Covington&B.]
McKay, James C., Jr. .... '46 '72 C.188 A.B. L.893 J.D. Asst. Corp. Coun.
McKay, Lynn K. ....'66 '91 C.945 B.A. L.347 J.D. [Schmeltzer,A.&S.]
*PRACTICE AREAS: Radiation Litigation; Oilfield NORM Defense; Civil Litigation.
McKay, Margo M. ....'46 '75 C.254 B.A. L.276 J.D. Assoc. Gen. Coun., Fannie Mae
*RESPONSIBILITIES: Employment Law.
McKay, Robert L., Jr. ....'—'98 C.101 B.A. L.178 J.D. [⊡ Piper M.R.&W.]
*PRACTICE AREAS: Venture Capital; Emerging Companies; Securities; Mergers and Acquisitions.

McKay Chadwell, P.L.L.C.
(See Seattle, Washington)

McKee, Carolyn A. '71 '98 C.309 A.B. L.597 J.D.
(adm. in MA; not adm. in DC) Trial Atty.
McKee, Christopher L. .....'— '88 C.350 B.S. L.273 J.D. [Banner&W.] (See Pat. Sect.)
*PRACTICE AREAS: Intellectual Property Law; Intellectual Property Litigation; Appellate Practice.
McKee, Gregory Samuel ....'73 '98 C.682 B.A. L.64 J.D. [⊡ Jordan C.&S.]
*PRACTICE AREAS: Litigation; Insurance Defense; Personal Injury Defense; Product Liability; Professional Liability.
McKee, William S., (AV) ....'44 '71 C.976 B.A. L.309 J.D. [McKee N.]
*PRACTICE AREAS: Taxation.

McKee Nelson LLP, (AV)
1919 M Street, N.W., Suite 800, 20036
Telephone: 202-775-1880 Fax: 202-775-8586
Email: info@mckeenelson.com URL: http://www.mckeenelson.com
J. Bradford Anwyll; John C. Arnholz; James D. Bridgeman; Rita A. Cavanagh; David J. Curtin; Jeffrey G. Davis; F. Scott Farmer; Edward E. Gainor; Joe Garcia, Jr.; Jasper A. Howard; Jeffrey R. Johnson; Gerald A. Kafka; Robert A. Katcher; Mark A. Kuller; Thomas J. Lyden; Raj Madan; John B. Magee; William S. McKee; William F. Nelson; Stephen M. Piper; R. Nicholas Singh; Richard C. Stark; Sanford W. Stark; H. John Steele; Michele E. Williams. Of Counsel: Gerald Goldman; Paul C. Hurdle, III; Timothy Sadler. Associates: A. Sonny Abbasi; Jonathan Z. Ackerman; Craig T. Beazer (Not admitted in DC); Hartman E. Blanchard, Jr.; Ronald L. Buch, Jr.; Corina R. Caplan; Nathan Elliott Clukey; Shanna Monique Cohn; Amy Kathleen Tesar Contreras; Michael J. Desmond; Sheri Dillon; John A. Galotto; Matthew Genasci; Anthony C. Green; Gwyneth E. Hambley; Tae Yeol Jeon; Phillip John Kardis; Jeffrey S. Korenblatt; Christopher P. La Puma; Christine Rushin Mistr; Peter C. Morreale; Mark David Nelson; Neeraj D. Pai (Not admitted in DC); Andrew B. Rosenstein; Cornelia Schnyder; Anita Caroline Soucy (Not admitted in DC); Joshua E. Spooner; Julie K. Weinstein (Not admitted in DC).
Taxation.
See Professional Biographies, WASHINGTON, DISTRICT OF COLUMBIA

McKeever, Joseph F., III, (AV) ....'50 '78 C&L.273 B.A., J.D. [Davis&H.]
*PRACTICE AREAS: Taxation Law; Insurance Law.
McKenna, Denis D., (BV) ....'39 '70 C.676 A.B. L.128 J.D. [Hadley&M.] ⊙
McKenna, F. Gregory, (AV) ....'52 '78 C.321 B.A. L.276 J.D. [Hall&E.] (⊙Denver, CO)
*PRACTICE AREAS: Government Contracts; Environmental Law.
McKenna, John J., Jr. '63 '91 C.708 B.A. L.180 J.D.
(adm. in MD; not adm. in DC) [McManus,S.A.&D.]
*PRACTICE AREAS: Construction Defects; Construction Claims; Insurance Coverage; Real Estate Title; Contracts.
McKenna, John P., (AV) .... '32 '59 C.397 B.S. L.659 LL.B. [Stohlman,B.E.&S.]
McKenna, Juliet J. '70 '95 C.276 B.A. L.976 J.D.
(adm. in CA; not adm. in DC) Off. of the Corp. Coun.
McKenna, Patricia A. '69 '95 C.1021 B.A. L.945 J.D.
U.S. Dept. of Jus., Envir. Enforce.
McKenna, Peter A. ..... '51 '94 C.570 B.S.E.E. L.776 J.D. [Sughrue M.] (See Pat. Sect.)
*PRACTICE AREAS: Intellectual Property Law.

McKenna & Cuneo, L.L.P., (AV)
1900 K Street, N.W., 20006 ⊙
Telephone: 202-496-7500 Telecopier: 202-496-7756
URL: http://www.mckennacuneo.com
Ashley Sellers (1902-1977); Gilbert A. Cuneo (1913-1978). Resident Partners: Jeffrey P. Altman; Ray M. Aragon; Tami Lyn Azorsky; Raymond B. Biagini; Thomas F. Burke; J. Keith Burt; Robert L. Carter, Jr.; John D. Conner (Partner Emeritus); John D. Conner, Jr.; Del Stiltner Dameron; C. Stanley Dees; Joseph F. Dennin; Alison L. Doyle; Lawrence S. Ebner; Michael L. Fayad; Peter Buck Feller; Herbert L. Fenster; T. Mark Flanagan, Jr.; Ruth S. Flynn; Stephen K. Gardner; Peter L. Gray; Kurt J. Hamrock; Jacqueline A. Henson; E. Sanderson Hoe; Michael A. Hopkins; Daniel G. Jarcho; Daniel E. Johnson; David Kasanow; Chris S. Leason; Frederic M. Levy; Lino S. Lipinsky de Orlov; Robert A. Matthews; Matthew J. McGrath; Kellie L. Newton; Charles A. O'Connor, III; Thomas C. Papson; Don J. Pelto; Larry R. Pilot; Raymond S. E. Pushkar; Frank M. Rapoport; Andrew M. Reidy; Murray D. Sacks; Michael G. Scheininger; Matthew J. Schlesinger; Jeff E. Schwartz; Catherine J. Serafin; Carol A. Smoots; Donna Lee Yesner; Charles E. Yonkers. Resident Of Counsel: Walter J. Eidson, Jr.; Lawrence M. Farrell; Stephen Mark Goldman; Thomas B. Johnston; Geoffrey T. Keating; Mary S. Webster. Resident Associates: Paul R. Almanza (Not admitted in DC); Monica A. Aquino; Michael James Bearman; Anne D. Berube; John A. Bonello; Jeffrey R. Boodman; Michael Boucher; Christopher C. Bouquet; Lora A. Brzezynski; Christina M. Carroll; Paul R. Cassell; Richard P. Castiglia, Jr.; Cass Walker Christenson; John M. Clerici; Stacey Ann Feldman; Brian T. Fisher; Michelle L. Hylton; Donald O. Johnson; Lawrence J. Joseph; Scott E. Kauff; Stuart Kim; Shari L. Klevens; Louis H. Kozloff; Ilia Levitine; Jonathan Philip Lienhard; Jane Ann Roe Neiswender; Lisa Michele Norrett; William T. O'Brien; Dana Barrie Pashkoff; Manik K. Rath; Christopher Robinson; Stephen E. Ruscus; Jason M. Silverman; Kathrin V. Smith; Jodi T. Tuer; Traci Meakem Vanek; Leah Warnick; Jason N. Workmaster (Not admitted in DC); Joanne L. Zimolzak.
General Civil, Criminal and Trial Practice in all State and Federal Courts, Federal Departments and Agencies. Government Contracts, Construction, Environmental, Food and Drug, Trade Associations; Health Care, Energy, White Collar Crime, Antitrust, International, Trade Regulation, Trademark, Estate Planning, Trust, Probate, Labor and Employment, Product Liability Litigation, Insurance Coverage and Intellectual Property.
Los Angeles, California Office: 444 South Flower Street, 90071. Telephone: 213-688-1000.
San Francisco, California Office: One Market, Steuart Street Tower, Twenty-Seventh Floor, 94105. Telephone: 415-267-4000.
Denver, Colorado Office: 370 Seventeenth Street, Suite 4800, 80203. Telephone: 303-634-4000.
San Diego, California Office: Symphony Towers, Suite 3300, 750B Street, 92101. Telephone: 619-595-5400.
Brussels, Belgium Office: 56, rue des Colonies, Box 14, B-1000. Telephone: 011-322-278-1211.
Devon, Pennsylvania Office: 28 South Waterloo Road, Suite 101. 19333. Telephone: 610-687-9750.
See Professional Biographies, WASHINGTON, DISTRICT OF COLUMBIA

McKeon, Michael J. .... '68 '97 C.184 B.S. L.273 J.D. [Fish&R.] (See Pat. Sect.)
*PRACTICE AREAS: Intellectual Property Litigation.
McKeown, James F., (AV) .... '42 '70 C.563 B.E. L.128 J.D. [Crowell&M.] (Pat.)
*PRACTICE AREAS: Patents; Trademarks; Copyrights; Trade Secrets; Litigation.
McKevitt, James D. "Mike", (AV) .... '28 '56 C.336 B.A. L.208 J.D. 1101 16th St., N.W.
McKew, Robert E., Jr. '57 '87 C.869 B.S. L.128 J.D.
Gen. Coun. & V.P., American Financial Services Association
McKey, Arthur D. ....'49 '78 C.93 B.A. L.336 J.D. [Hanson&M.]
*PRACTICE AREAS: Litigation; Antitrust; Internet Law; Media/First Amendment Law; Non-Profit Organizations.
McKie, Edward F., Jr., (AV) '— '52
C.688 B.E.E. L.276 J.D. [⊡ Banner&W.] (See Pat. Sect.)
*PRACTICE AREAS: Intellectual Property Law.
McKiernan, Thomas Edward '62 '95 C.1229 B.S.M.E. L.215 J.D.
(adm. in MI; not adm. in DC; See Pat. Sect.) [⊡ Rothwell,F.E.&M.]
*PRACTICE AREAS: Intellectual Property.
McKinley, Erica Taylor .... '— '00 C.852 B.A. L.500 J.D. [⊡ Arnold&P.]
*PRACTICE AREAS: Litigation; Product Liability.
McKinney, James D., Jr., (AV) ....'31 '58 C&L.352 B.A., LL.B. [Ross,M.&F.]
*PRACTICE AREAS: Energy Law; Utility Law; Litigation; Administrative Law.
McKinney, Linda Otani, (AV) ....'59 '88 C.101 B.A. L.276 J.D. Asst. U.S. Atty.
McKinney, Scott D. .... '71 '98 C.145 A.B. L.339 J.D. [⊡ Akin,G.S.H.&F.]
*PRACTICE AREAS: Corporate Law; Securities.
McKinnon, Mark E. '64 '90 C.145 B.A. L.128 J.D.
(adm. in MI; not adm. in DC) [⊡ Dombroff&G.]
McKnight, Beverly A. '52 '78 C.329 B.A. L.229 J.D.
(adm. in PA; not adm. in DC) 530 Whittier St., N.W.‡
McKnight, Cynthia M. ....'67 '97 C.473 B.S. L.276 J.D. [⊡ Hogan&H.]
*PRACTICE AREAS: Corporate Law.
McKnight, H. Vincent, Jr., (AV) .... '53 '79 C.103 B.A. L.659 J.D. [Ashcraft&G.]
*PRACTICE AREAS: Railroad Law; Personal Injury; Whistleblower Litigation.
McKnight, Kathy J. ....'49 '83 C.10 B.S. L.276 J.D. [Shaw P.]
McKnight, Maxwell S. '10 '37 C&L.976 A.B., J.D.
(adm. in NY; not adm. in DC) 520 N. St., S.W.‡
McKown, Jeremy K. ....'71 '99 C.354 B.S. L.823 J.D. [⊡ Wilmer,C.&P.] (Pat.)
McKoy, Letitia W. .... '70 '96 C.1378 B.A. L.180 J.D. [⊡ Fulbright&J.]
*PRACTICE AREAS: Energy.
McKoy, Linda C. ....'55 '83 C.976 B.A. L.276 J.D. 3432 34th St. N.W.
McLachlan, Brian A. .... '63 '00 C&L.911 B.A., J.D. [⊡ Williams&C.]
*PRACTICE AREAS: Litigation.
McLaren, Douglas E. .... '48 '85 C.999 B.Sc. L.309 J.D. Senior Consultant, TRW Inc.
McLaughlin, Christine ....'65 '90 C.262 B.A. L.128 J.D. [⊡ Alston&B.]
*PRACTICE AREAS: Telecommunications; Appellate Litigation.
McLaughlin, Donald W., Jr. ....'64 '96 C&L.276 B.S.F.S., J.D. [⊡ Winston&S.]
McLaughlin, Elizabeth A. ....'57 '91 C.945 B.A. L.1209 J.D. [⊡ Jones,D.R.&P.]
McLaughlin, James A. ....'73 '98 C.31 B.A. L.976 J.D. [⊡ Covington&B.]
*PRACTICE AREAS: Insurance Litigation; Civil Litigation.
McLaughlin, Matthew G. ....'72 '99 C.299 B.A. L.128 J.D. [⊡ Sutherland A.&B.]
*PRACTICE AREAS: Tax Law.
McLaughlin, Michael J. '67 '99 C.911 B.A. L.1358 J.D.
(adm. in MD; not adm. in DC) [⊡ Winston&S.]
*PRACTICE AREAS: Administrative Law; Government Relations.
McLaughlin, Nicole M. ....'64 '92 C.914 B.A. L.588 J.D. [Harmon,C.S.&E.]
McLaughlin, Robert E., (AV) ....'38 '65 C.350 B.S. L.276 J.D. [Steptoe&J.]
*PRACTICE AREAS: Business Law; Corporate; Securities; Mergers and Acquisitions; Real Estate.
McLaughlin, Ronée C. '59 '85 C.811 B.A. L.276 J.D.
National Assn. of Sec. Dealers, Inc.
McLaughlin, Thomas W. ....'47 '74 C.378 B.S. L.477 J.D. [Burzio&M.]
*PRACTICE AREAS: Federal Administrative Law; Postal Law; Aviation Regulatory Law.
McLaughlin, Veronica D. ....'68 '94 C.692 B.A. L.976 J.D. [⊡ Shaw P.]
*PRACTICE AREAS: Communications.
McLean, Donald C. ....'56 '81 C.879 B.A. L.602 J.D. [Arent F.K.P.&K.]
*PRACTICE AREAS: Litigation; Environmental Law; Toxic Tort Law.
McLean, R. Bruce, (AV) ....'46 '71 C&L.347 B.S., J.D. [Akin,G.S.H.&F.]
*PRACTICE AREAS: Litigation.
McLean, Rogelyn D. '74 '00 C.575 B.A. L.574 J.D.
(adm. in NC; not adm. in DC) [⊡ Dow,L.&A.]
McLeland, Le-Nhung '49 '83
C.1209 B.A. L.904 J.D. [⊡ Armstrong,W.H.M.&N.] (See Pat. Sect.)
McLemore, Mignon ....'65 '97 C.329 B.S. L.861 J.D. [⊡ Kirkpatrick&L.]
*PRACTICE AREAS: Securities; Broker-Dealer Regulation; Broker-Dealer Registration.
McLeod, James E. ....'53 '85 C.945 B.S. L.1194 J.D. 2424 Pennsylvania Ave., N.W.

McLeod, Linda K. ....'63 '89 C.950 B.A. L.629 J.D. [Mintz,L.C.F.G.&P.]
*PRACTICE AREAS: Intellectual Property; Trademarks; Trademark Clearance; Trademark Prosecution; Trademark Enforcement.
McLeod, Michael R. ....'41 '67 C.280 A.B. L.30 J.D. [McLeod,W.&M.]
*PRACTICE AREAS: Agricultural and Trade Association Law.

McLeod, Watkinson & Miller, (AV)
Eighth Floor, One Massachusetts Avenue, N.W., 20001
Telephone: 202-842-2345 Telecopy: 202-408-7763
URL: http://www.mwmlaw.com
Members of Firm: Michael R. McLeod; Wayne R. Watkinson; Marc Eric Miller; Richard T. Rossier; Charles A. Spitulnik. Associates: Richard E. Pasco; Alex Menendez; Paul D. Smolinsky.
Agriculture and Agribusiness, Food, Drug and Nutrition, Transportation, Litigation, Employment, Medical Malpractice, International Trade, Real Estate, Corporate and Trade Association, Administrative, Entertainment, Legislation and Government Relations.
See Professional Biographies, WASHINGTON, DISTRICT OF COLUMBIA

McLish, Thomas P. ....'64 '89 C.154 B.A. L.178 J.D. [Akin,G.S.H.&F.]
*PRACTICE AREAS: Litigation; Government Contracts; Libel, Slander and Defamation; First Amendment Law.
McLucas, William R., (AV) ....'50 '75 C.645 B.A. L.831 J.D. [Wilmer,C.&P.]
*PRACTICE AREAS: Securities; Regulatory; Litigation.
McLurkin, Wayne B. '53 '78 C.309 B.A. L.575 J.D.
(adm. in NC; not adm. in DC) 3900 Wisconsin Ave., NW
McMackin, John J., Jr. ....'52 '77 C.602 B.A. L.976 J.D. [Williams&J.]
McMahon, Linda M. ....'64 '94 C.823 B.A. L.1009 J.D. [Ⓐ Shearman&S.]

McMahon, Martin F., & Associates, (BV) '45 '70 C.563 B.B.A. L.262 J.D.
1150 Connecticut Avenue, N.W., Suite 900, 20036
Telephone: 202-862-4343 Telecopier: 202-828-4130
Email: McMahonM@I-opener.net URL: http://www.lawyers.com/martinmcmahonlaw
Business Law, Commercial Litigation, Complex Civil Trial Practice, Employment Litigation, Corporate Law, White Collar Criminal Defense, Commercial and Securities Fraud. The firm represents individuals and small to mid-size businesses throughout metro D.C., Northern Virginia and Southern Maryland.
See Professional Biographies, WASHINGTON, DISTRICT OF COLUMBIA

McMahon-Lohrer, Kathryn ....'62 '92 C.823 B.A. L.188 J.D. [Collier S.S.]
*PRACTICE AREAS: Environmental; Occupational Safety and Health; Employment Discrimination Law.
McMann, James P. ....'38 '66 C.653 B.S. L.273 LL.B. 3900 Wisconsin Ave., N.W.
McManus, Brian J., (AV) ....'42 '69 C&L.276 A.B., J.D. [Ⓒ Jones,D.R.&P.]
McManus, James T., (AV) ....'47 '75 C.808 B.S.E.E. L.273 J.D. [Wright&T.]
*PRACTICE AREAS: Energy; Regulatory Law.
McManus, Joseph A., Jr., (AV) ......'48 '72 C.321 A.B. L.228 J.D. [McManus,S.A.&D.]

McManus, Joseph M., (AV) '46 '71 C.749 B.S. L.262 J.D.
2001 L Street, N.W., Suite 400, 20036
Telephone: 202-822-8888 Fax: 202-775-9330
Email: JMM@JMMCMANUS.COM
(Also Of Counsel to Ross Marsh & Foster).
Tax Law.
See Professional Biographies, WASHINGTON, DISTRICT OF COLUMBIA

McManus, Michael G. '69 '94 C.280 B.A. L.45 J.D.
(adm. in GA; not adm. in DC; See Pat. Sect.) [Ⓐ Adduci,M.&S.]
*PRACTICE AREAS: Customs Law; International Trade Regulation; Patent Litigation.
McManus, Michael J. ....'50 '76 C.602 B.A. L.861 J.D. [Drinker B.&R.]
*PRACTICE AREAS: Litigation; Insurance Coverage Litigation.
McManus, Randolph Quaile, (AV) ....'50 '75 C.951 B.A. L.326 J.D. [Baker B.]
McManus, Robert J. ....'40 '68 C&L.976 A.B., LL.B. [Kile G.L.&R.P.]
*PRACTICE AREAS: Environmental and Natural Resources Law.

McManus, Schor, Asmar & Darden, L.L.P., (AV)
1301 Connecticut Avenue, N.W. Sixth Floor, 20036
Telephone: 202-296-9260 Fax: 202-659-3732
Email: info@msadlaw.com URL: http://www.msadlaw.com
Joseph A. McManus (1916-1995). Members of Firm: Joseph A. McManus, Jr.; Laurence Schor; Charles M. Asmar; Eric J. Darden; Susan L. Schor; Daniel K. Felsen; John J. McKenna, Jr. (Not admitted in DC). Associates: Jeremiah S. Regan; Gregory H. Koger (Not admitted in DC); John T. Bergin; William F. Gibson, II. Of Counsel: Richard W. Schwartzman; Brett L. Antonides.
Construction, Government Contracts, Commercial, Real Estate, Business, Bankruptcy, Corporate and Administrative Law.
See Professional Biographies, WASHINGTON, DISTRICT OF COLUMBIA

McMeley, Christin S. '70 '95 C.804 B.A. L.862 J.D.
(adm. in OK; not adm. in DC) [Ⓐ Cole,R.&B.]
*PRACTICE AREAS: Satellite Communications; Communications Law; Litigation; Satellite and Cable Programming.
McMichael, James D. ....'56 '82 C.420 B.A. L.846 J.D. [Ⓐ Shapiro,L.&S.]
*PRACTICE AREAS: Construction Litigation; Government Contracts; Business Litigation.
McMickle, John '68 '95 C.838 B.A. L.30 J.D.
(adm. in VA; not adm. in DC) [Ⓐ Winston&S.]
McMillan, Ann C. ....'59 '84 C.893 B.A. L.1068 J.D. [Ⓒ Caplin&D.]
*PRACTICE AREAS: Securities (10%); Corporate (90%).
McMillan, Charlene H. ....'71 '00 C.976 B.A. L.94 J.D. 950 H St. N.W.
McMillan, James G. ....'59 '85 C.893 B.A. L.309 J.D. [Hogan&H.]
*PRACTICE AREAS: Corporate Commercial Law; Securities Regulation; Federal Legislative Practice.
McMillan, Karen '75 '01 C.165 B.A. L.276 J.D.
(adm. in VA; not adm. in DC) [Ⓐ Jenkens&G.]
*PRACTICE AREAS: Litigation.
McMillan, Karen Hess ....'61 '87 C.945 B.A. L.893 J.D. [Ⓒ Shearman&S.]
McMillan, Richard, Jr., (AV) ....'44 '72 C.674 B.A. L.494 J.D. [Crowell&M.]
*PRACTICE AREAS: Litigation.
McMillen, Julia ....'68 '99 C.475 B.A. L.734 J.D. [Ⓐ Proskauer R.]
McMinn, Donald R. ....'64 '91 C.821 B.A. L.569 J.D. [Spriggs&H.]
*PRACTICE AREAS: Insurance Coverage; Litigation.
McMorrow, Robert G., (P.C.), (AV) '30 '57
C.999 B.S. L.276 LL.B. [Ⓒ Sughrue M.] (See Pat. Sect.)
*PRACTICE AREAS: Intellectual Property Law; Trademark Law.
McMullen, Sean P. '65 '90 C.309 A.B. L.945 J.D.
(adm. in VA; not adm. in DC) [Ⓐ Luman,L.&W.]
*PRACTICE AREAS: Civil Litigation; Employment; Business Law; Creditor Rights; Bankruptcy.
McNabb, Stephen M., (AV) ....'56 '82 C.309 A.B. L.276 J.D. [Fulbright&J.]
*PRACTICE AREAS: White Collar Crime; Civil Practice Litigation; Appellate Practice.
McNally, Amy S. ....'74 '99 C.221 B.A. L.378 J.D. [Ⓐ Arent F.K.P.&K.]
*PRACTICE AREAS: Corporate Transaction; Corporate Finance; Real Estate.
McNally, John M. ....'51 '76 C.659 B.A. L.276 J.D. [Hawkins,D.&W.]
McNamara, Brian J., (AV) '— '86 C.433 B.E.E. L.446 J.D.
[Foley&L.] (See Pat. Sect.) (⊙Annapolis, MD)
*PRACTICE AREAS: Electronics; Intellectual Property.
McNamara, Douglas J. '70 '96 C.1044 B.A. L.569 J.D.
(adm. in NY; not adm. in DC) [Ⓐ Cohen,M.H.&T.]
*PRACTICE AREAS: Mass Tort; Consumer Protection.
McNamara, Ellen M., (AV) ....'50 '75 C.705 B.A. L.893 J.D. [Steptoe&J.]
*PRACTICE AREAS: Antitrust; Government Procurement.
McNamara, Jacqueline Mohyla '63 '94 C.705 B.A. L.446 J.D.
(adm. in MD; not adm. in DC) Assoc. Editor, Environmental Law Institute

McNamara, John ....'59 '86 C.205 B.S. L.228 J.D. 1440 New York Ave. N.W.
McNamara, Michael T. ....'69 '96 C.228 A.B. L.309 J.D. [Ⓐ Arent F.K.P.&K.]
*PRACTICE AREAS: Electronic Commerce; Election, Campaign and Political Law; Administrative Law; Public Policy; Trade and Professional Associations.
McNamara, Stephen H. ....'43 '67 C&L.893 B.A., J.D. [Hyman,P.&M.]

McNamee, Hosea, Jernigan & Kim, P.A.
(See Greenbelt, Maryland)

McNary, Gene, (AV) ....'35 '60 C&L.347 B.S., J.D. [McNary,M.&S.]
*PRACTICE AREAS: Immigration Law.

McNary, Morris & Smalley, (AV)
1712 New Hampshire Avenue N.W., 20009
Telephone: 202-265-7200 Fax: 202-265-7530 URL: http://www.visalink.com
Email: MMS@visalink.com URL: http://www.lawyers.com/mcnarymorris&smalley
Members of Firm: Gene McNary; David M. Morris (Not admitted in DC). Associate: Nicole Hughes (Not admitted in DC). Of Counsel: Charles W. Pley (Not admitted in DC); Frederick R. Troncone.
Immigration, Nationality Law, Consular Law, Administrative Law, Business Immigration, Information Technology, Computer Technology.
See Professional Biographies, WASHINGTON, DISTRICT OF COLUMBIA

McNasby, Jennifer D. ....'71 '96 C.575 B.A. L.93 J.D. [Ⓐ Ropes&G.]
McNeely, Kevin J. ....'63 '92 C.971 B.S. L.1202 J.D. [Ⓐ Fish&R.] (See Pat. Sect.)
*PRACTICE AREAS: Patent Prosecution; Telecommunications Law; Regulatory; Internet Law; Intellectual Property.
McNeely, Michael D. ....'45 '76 C.688 B.S. L.950 J.D. [Ⓒ Blumenfeld&C.]
*PRACTICE AREAS: Antitrust Litigation and Counseling; Telecommunications Law; Civil Litigation; Administrative Litigation.

McNees Wallace & Nurick LLC
1200 G Street, N.W., Suite 800, 20005 ⊙
Telephone: 202-434-8991 Fax: 202-347-0988
Email: info@mwn.com URL: http://www.mwn.com
Resident Associate: Robert A. Weishaar, Jr. (Not admitted in DC).
General Civil Practice. Administrative, Antitrust, Bankruptcy, Corporate, Banking and Finance, ERISA, Tax, Probate, Labor and Employment, Litigation, Real Estate, Securities, Municipal Bonds, Public Utilities, Intellectual Property, Health Care, Environmental, Automotive, Transportation, Trademark, Copyright, Computer, Franchise and Unfair Competition Law.
Harrisburg, Pennsylvania Office: 100 Pine Street, P.O. Box 1166, 17108. Telephone: 717-232-8000. Fax: 717-237-5300.
Columbus, Ohio Office: 21 East State Street, 17th Floor, 43215. Telephone: 614-469-8000. Fax: 614-469-4653.
Hazleton, Pennsylvania Office: 1 South Church Street, Suite 302, 18201. Telephone: 570-455-8300. Fax: 570-455-8390.
See Professional Biographies, WASHINGTON, DISTRICT OF COLUMBIA

McNeil, Chris E., Jr., (BV) '48 '79
C&L.813 B.A., J.S.D. Rep. & Coun., Mashantucket Pequot Tribe
McNeil, Daniel James ....'71 '97 C.475 B.A. L.276 J.D. [Ⓐ O'Donoghue&O.]
*PRACTICE AREAS: Labor and Employment Law; ERISA.
McNeil, J. E. ....'51 '79 C.691 B.A. L.326 J.D. [McNeil&R.]
McNeil & Ricks, P.C. .... 4614 Wisconsin Ave., N.W.
McNeill, Rebecca '70 '97 C.604 B.A. L.276 J.D.
[Ⓐ Finnegan,H.F.G.&D.] (See Pat. Sect.)
*PRACTICE AREAS: Biotechnology Patent Prosecution; International Intellectual Property.
McNeilly, R. Scott ....'60 '88 C.165 B.A. L.588 J.D. Wash. Legal Clinic for the Homeless
McNemar, Georgia '33 '56 C&L.896 B.S., LL.B.
(adm. in NC; not adm. in DC) 216 6th St., S.E.‡
McNerney, Martin M. ....'— '80 C.301 B.A. L.893 J.D. [King&S.]
*PRACTICE AREAS: Litigation and Trade.
McNicholas, Edward R. ....'69 '96 C.674 A.B. L.309 J.D. [Ⓐ Sidley A.B.&W.]

McNiel, Dale E. '48 '76 C.352 B.A. L.145 J.D.
1776 Eye Street, N.W. Ninth Floor, 20006
Telephone: 202-756-1368 Fax: 202-756-1501
Email: dalemcniel@aol.com URL: http://www.lawyers.com/dalemcniel
***PRACTICE AREAS: International Trade; Administrative Law; Agriculture.**
Agriculture Law, International Law, International Trade Law, International Agriculture Law.
See Professional Biographies, WASHINGTON, DISTRICT OF COLUMBIA

McNiven, Melissa H. ....'66 '91 C.861 B.A. L.904 J.D. [Ⓐ Baach R.&L.P.]
*PRACTICE AREAS: Litigation.
McNulty, Christopher M. ....'55 '81 C.823 B.S. L.365 J.D. [King&K.] ⊙
McNulty, James F. M. '24 '53 C&L.262 B.S., J.D.
(adm. in NY; not adm. in DC) Union Labor Life Ins. Co.
McNulty, Maura S. '65 '91 C.228 B.A. L.262 J.D.
(adm. in MA; not adm. in DC) U.S. Secs. & Exch. Comm.
McNulty, Paul E., (AV) ....'30 '57 C&L.273 B.A., J.D. [King&K.]
McNulty, Paul J. '58 '83 C.294 B.A. L.117 J.D.
(adm. in PA; not adm. in DC) 2300 N St., N.W.‡
McNulty, Robert H. '40 '66 C.112 B.S. L.1066 LL.B.
(adm. in CA; not adm. in DC) Pres., Partners for Livable Communities
McNulty, Tamara M. ....'67 '95 C&L.966 B.A., J.D. [Ⓐ Thompson H.]
*PRACTICE AREAS: Construction Litigation; Commercial Litigation.
McNutt, Geoffrey M. '— '95 C.945 B.A. L.1209 J.D.
(adm. in VA; not adm. in DC) [Ⓐ Foley&L.]
*PRACTICE AREAS: Trademark Law; Copyright.
McPhee, Gillian ....'72 '97 C.976 B.A. L.846 J.D. [Ⓐ Gibson,D.&C.]
*PRACTICE AREAS: Corporate Law; Securities.
McPhee, Heather M. '— '00 C.674 A.B. L.145 J.D.
(adm. in VA; not adm. in DC) [Ⓐ Latham&W.]
McPherson, David J. ....'59 '85 C.264 B.A. L.273 J.D. [Morgan,L.&B.]
McPherson, David M. ....'— '94 C.454 B.S. L.94 J.D. [Ⓐ Latham&W.]
McPherson, Harry, (AV) ....'— '56 C.797 B.A. L.846 LL.B. [Verner,L.B.M.&H.]
*PRACTICE AREAS: Legislative Law; Regulatory Law.
McPherson, Lawrence G. ....'49 '81 C&L.150 B.A., J.D. Law Clk., Supr. Ct.
McPherson, Patrick Dennis '63 '95 C.871 B.S. L.128 J.D.
(adm. in MD; not adm. in DC; Pat.) [Ⓒ Carter,L.&M.]
*PRACTICE AREAS: Intellectual Property; Litigation.
McPhie, Iain R. ....'70 '00 C.276 B.S.F.S. L.945 J.D. [Ⓐ Squire,S.&D.]
McPhillips, Carolyn M. '— '00 C&L.575 B.S., J.D.
(adm. in VA; not adm. in DC) [Ⓐ Dechert]
*PRACTICE AREAS: Financial Services Law; Investment Management.
McPoland, Paula A. ....'54 '83 C.518 A.B. L.180 J.D. 3621 Newark St., N.W.

McQuade & Hite, P.L.L.C.
(See Alexandria, Virginia)

McQuinn, Urenthea ....'— '73 C&L.329 B.A., J.D. Asst. Corp. Coun.
McQuiston, Cathie J. '71 '97 C.935 B.A. L.30 J.D.
(adm. in MD; not adm. in DC) Atty., AFGE Fair Practices Dept.
McRae, Cori Fisher '— '95 C.309 A.B. L.262 J.D.
(adm. in NJ; not adm. in DC) [Ⓐ Epstein B.&G.]
*PRACTICE AREAS: Health Law.
McRae, David K. ....'62 '94 C.188 A.B. L.446 J.D. [Ⓐ Griffin,F.T.&M.]
*PRACTICE AREAS: Corporate Law; Civil Practice; Real Estate; Administrative Law.

McReynolds, Mary A., (AV) .... '46 '71 C.518 A.B. L.276 J.D. [M.A.McReynolds]
*PRACTICE AREAS: Communications Law; Complex Civil Litigation.

McReynolds, Mary A., P.C., (AV)
Suite 300, 1701 Pennsylvania Avenue, N.W., 20006
Telephone: 202-835-7455 Telecopier: 202-296-8791
Email: marymcreynolds@aol.com URL: http://www.lawyers.com/maryamcreynolds
Mary A. McReynolds.
The Firm specializes in complex Commercial and Government Civil Litigation, Civil Appellate Practice and Communications Law (including Broadcast and Common Carrier Regulation).
See Professional Biographies, WASHINGTON, DISTRICT OF COLUMBIA

McShane, Terrence M., (BV) .... '50 '84 C&L.276 B.S., J.D. [Lee&M.]
*PRACTICE AREAS: Construction; Architects and Engineers; Products Liability; Real Estate.
McSpadden, Stephen R. '47 '72 C.112 B.A. L.1066 J.D.
Gen. Coun., Natl. Assn. of Police Organizations, Inc.
McTaggart, Kelli C. .... '70 '99 C&L.276 A.B., J.D. [Ⓐ Baker B.]
McTaggart, Timothy R., (BV) .... '60 '85 C&L.309 A.B., J.D. [Nixon P.]
*PRACTICE AREAS: Banks and Banking; Corporate; Legislative.
McTigue, Kevin D. '65 '92 C&L.276 B.A., J.D.
(adm. in NY; not adm. in DC) Inter-American Develop. Bk.
McVerry, Judith '51 '84 C.831 B.A. L.1209 J.D.
(adm. in VA; not adm. in DC) Assoc. Litig. Coun., MCI WorldCom
McVey, Thomas B. .... '54 '80 C.178 B.A. L.276 J.D. [Williams M.]
*PRACTICE AREAS: International Business; Corporate Law; Finance Law; Banking Law.
McWhinney, Christopher .... '— '00 C.945 B.S. L.472 J.D. [Ⓐ Wilmer,C.&P.] (Pat.)
McWhite, Melinda Falgout '51 '77
C.418 B.A. L.861 J.D. MCI Communications Corporation
McWilliams, Karen Turner .... '— '92 C.893 B.S. L.1209 J.D. [Verner,L.B.M.&H.]
*PRACTICE AREAS: Employment Law; Labor Law.
McWilliams, O'Kelly E., III '68 '93
C.889 B.S.B.A. L.1356 J.D. [Ⓐ Pepper H.] (⊙Tysons Corner, VA)
*PRACTICE AREAS: Labor and Employment; Business Litigation; Commercial Litigation.
McZier, Ruby B. .... '40 '65 C.824 A.B. L.329 J.D. 1420 N St. N.W.
Meacham, Jeannette C. .... '72 '98 C.93 B.A. L.945 J.D. [Ⓐ Venable,A.B.H.&C.]
*PRACTICE AREAS: Corporate Finance; Securities; Corporate.
Mead, Christopher B., (AV) .... '59 '85 C&L.976 B.A., J.D. [London&M.]
*PRACTICE AREAS: Civil Litigation; White Collar Criminal Litigation.
Mead, David A. .... '44 '70 C.477 A.B. L.309 J.D. Sr. Coun., The World Bk.
Mead, Gilbert D. .... '30 '91 C.976 B.S. L.446 J.D. 2700 Virginia Ave., N.W.
Meade, Christopher J. '68 '97 C.674 A.B. L.569 J.D.
(adm. in NY; not adm. in DC) [Ⓐ Wilmer,C.&P.]
Meade, David E. .... '34 '62 C.951 B.A. L.893 LL.B. [Ⓒ Foxkiser]
Meade, John P. '37 '62 C.436 B.S. L.276 LL.B.
1919 Pennsylvania Ave., N.W., Suite 800
Meade, Kenneth R. .... '61 '85 C.477 A.B. L.273 J.D. [Hale&D.]
*PRACTICE AREAS: Environmental Law.
Meade, Kris David .... '65 '90 C.477 B.A. L.273 J.D. [Crowell&M.]
*PRACTICE AREAS: Labor and Employment.
Meadors, C. Brian .... '— '99 C.477 B.S.E. L.276 J.D. [Ⓐ Morgan,L.&B.]
Meadors, Erika Esterbrook .... '74 '99 C.228 B.A. L.309 J.D. [Ⓐ Akin,G.S.H.&F.]
*PRACTICE AREAS: Litigation; Immigration.
Meagher, Niall P. .... '65 '88 L.058 LL.B. [Powell,G.F.&M.]
*PRACTICE AREAS: International Trade Law.
Meaney, Donald C. .... '31 '63 C.205 B.S. L.30 J.D. 802 D St., N.E.
Meaney, Francis X., (AV) '33 '60
C.602 A.B. L.309 LL.B. [Mintz,L.C.F.G.&P.] (⊙Boston, MA)
*PRACTICE AREAS: Financial Services Law; Federal and State Relations Law; Health Care.
Means, Thomas C., (AV) .... '47 '78 C.197 A.B. L.273 J.D. [Crowell&M.]
*PRACTICE AREAS: Natural Resources Law; Mining or Mineral Law; Mine Safety and Health Law; Environmental Law; Administrative Law.
Meckley, John E., III '70 '96 C.216 B.A. L.273 J.D.
(adm. in PA; not adm. in DC) 1440 N.Y. Ave., NW
Medaglia, M. Elizabeth, (AV) .... '47 '72 C.822 B.A. L.893 J.D. [Jackson&C.] ⊙
*PRACTICE AREAS: Civil Litigation; Insurance Coverage Litigation.

Medalie, Richard J., (AV) '29 '58 C.494 B.A. L.309 J.D.
1750 K Street, N.W., Suite 1200, 20006-2303
Telephone: 202-659-0880 Telefax: 202-659-5618
Email: rmedalie@worldnet.att.net
Corporate, Commercial and Complex Litigation, Commercial Arbitration and Mediation, Domestic and International Estate Plannings, Wills and Trusts, Charitable Trusts and Foundations, Family Wealth Transfer.
See Professional Biographies, WASHINGTON, DISTRICT OF COLUMBIA

Medalie, Susan D. .... '38 '87 C.771 B.A. L.904 J.D. Pres., Medalie Consultants
Medina, Monica P. '62 '86
C.276 B.A. L.178 J.D. [Heller E.W.&M.] (⊙Gaithersburg, MD)
*PRACTICE AREAS: Environmental; Government Affairs; Litigation.
Medine, David .... '53 '78 C.1307 B.A. L.145 J.D. [Hogan&H.]
*PRACTICE AREAS: Privacy Law; Financial Services Law; Consumer Protection; Advertising Law; Internet Law.
Medler, Teresa Uliva .... '62 '98 C.158 B.S.M.E. L.273 J.D. [Ⓐ Sterne,K.G.&F.]
*PRACTICE AREAS: Patent Litigation; Patent Prosecution; Mechanical Patents; Design Patents; Coatings Technology.
Medlock, Nina L. .... '— '80 C.217 B.S. L.273 J.D. [Banner&W.] (See Pat. Sect.)
*PRACTICE AREAS: Intellectual Property Law; Patents; Electrical Intellectual Property; Computer and Software Patents.
Medway, Leah E. .... '69 '96 C.860 B.A. L.893 J.D. [Ⓐ Vinson&E.]
*PRACTICE AREAS: Business Law; Commercial Law; Corporate Law; International Business Transactions; Telecommunications Law.
Medway, Richard A. .... '67 '92 C.966 B.A. L.180 J.D. [Powell,G.F.&M.]
*PRACTICE AREAS: Bankruptcy; Commercial Litigation.
Meeds, Lloyd .... '27 '58 C.999 L.285 LL.B. [Ⓒ Preston G.E.&R.M.]
*PRACTICE AREAS: Legislative Advocacy; Procedures of the House of Representatives.
Meegan, Molly A. .... '66 '92 C.188 B.S. L.273 J.D. [Ⓒ Skadden,A.S.M.&F.]
Meehan, Andrew C., (BV) .... '62 '87 C.893 B.A. L.902 J.D. 1120-20th St., N.W.
Meehan, Edward J. .... '54 '85 C.93 B.A. L.273 J.D. [Skadden,A.S.M.&F.]
Meehan, Thomas P., (AV) .... '40 '65 C.478 B.A. L.228 LL.B. [Ⓒ Sherman,M.C.&A.]
Meeker, Courtney Beth .... '75 '00 C.893 B.S. L.273 J.D. [Ⓐ Finnegan,H.F.G.&D.]
Meeker, Frederic M. .... '— '92 C.1356 B.S. L.1209 J.D. [Banner&W.] (See Pat. Sect.)
*PRACTICE AREAS: Intellectual Property Law; Patents; Intellectual Property Litigation; International Trade; Electrical Intellectual Property.
Meeker, Leonard C. .... '16 '40 C.31 B.A. L.309 LL.B. 3000 Chain Bridge Rd., N.W.‡
Meekins, C. Martin '71 '97 C&L.846 B.A., J.D.
(adm. in TX; not adm. in DC) [Ⓐ Covington&B.]
Meekins, Ndenisarya M. '72 '00 C.024 B.A. L.276 J.D.
(adm. in MD; not adm. in DC) [Ⓐ Kirkpatrick&L.]
*PRACTICE AREAS: Investment Management; Investment Company Law; Mutual Funds.
Meeks, J. Marcus '72 '00 C.611 B.A. L.1365 J.D.
(adm. in VA; not adm. in DC) [Ⓐ Arent F.K.P.&K.]
*PRACTICE AREAS: Litigation.

Meenan, John M. '50 '76 C.321 B.A. L.770 J.D.
(adm. in CA; not adm. in DC)
Sr. V.P.- Industry Policy, Air Transport Association of America
Meer, Cary J. .... '— '83 C.659 B.S. L.309 J.D. [Kirkpatrick&L.]
*PRACTICE AREAS: Securities Offerings; Securities Regulation; Commodities Regulation; Investment Partnerships; Private Placement.
Meggesto, James T. .... '71 '98 C.1044 B.S. L.982 J.D. [Ⓐ Sonosky,C.S.E.&P.]
Megregian, Scott S. .... '65 '91 C.893 B.A. L.309 J.D. [McDermott,W.&E.]
Mehle, Roger W. '41 '77 C.871 B.S. L.262 J.D.
Exec. Dir., Fed. Retire. Thrift Invest. Bd.
Mehler, Charles V., III '69 '96 C.705 B.A. L.902 J.D.
(adm. in VA; not adm. in DC) [Ⓐ Dickstein S.M.&O.]
*PRACTICE AREAS: Litigation.
Mehra, Ajay '70 '96 C.882 B.A. L.823 J.D.
(adm. in NJ; not adm. in DC) [Ⓐ Shearman&S.]
Mehrespand, Marc .... '73 '98 C.1356 B.A. L.273 J.D. [Ⓐ Kirkpatrick&L.]
*PRACTICE AREAS: Corporate; Securities; 1940 Act; Investment Management; Private Equity.
Mehri, Cyrus, (AV) .... '61 '88 C.308 B.A. L.188 J.D. [Mehri,M.&R.] ⊙
*PRACTICE AREAS: Employment Discrimination; False Claims Act; Consumer Fraud; Securities Fraud; Employee Stock Ownership Plans.

Mehri, Malkin & Ross, PLLC, (AV)
2120 L Street, NW, Suite 400, 20037 ⊙
Telephone: 202-822-5100 Fax: 202-822-4997
Email: mmr@findjustice.com URL: http://www.lawyers.com/mm&rlaw
Cyrus Mehri; Arthur N. Malkin; Donald K. Ross;—Pamela Coukos; Michael I. Kanovitz (Not admitted in DC); Gouri Bhat. Of Counsel: Bradley Scott Weiss.
Complex and Multi-District Litigation, Class Actions, Commercial Fraud, Employment Discrimination, Consumer Fraud, Antitrust, Securities Fraud, Qui Tam Litigation, Consumer Protection, Civil Rights, Employee Stock Ownership.
See Professional Biographies, WASHINGTON, DISTRICT OF COLUMBIA

Mehta, Amit P. .... '71 '97 C.276 B.A. L.893 J.D. [Ⓐ Zuckerman S.]
*PRACTICE AREAS: Litigation.
Mehta, Dipali B. .... '70 '95 C.1030 B.A. L.184 J.D. [Ⓐ Cleary,G.S.&H.]
Mehta, Mainak Himanshu .... '70 '99 C.893 B.S. L.1209 J.D. [Ⓐ Sughrue M.]
*PRACTICE AREAS: Intellectual Property.
Mehta, Pinak A. .... '39 '77 C.999 B.S. L.537 J.D. 907 Barry Pl., N.W.
Mehta, Prakash H. .... '69 '94 C&L.276 B.S.F.S., J.D. [Ⓐ Clifford C.R.&W.]
*PRACTICE AREAS: International; Corporate Transactional; Private Equity.
Meiburger, George J., (AV) .... '21 '52 C.734 A.B. L.276 LL.B. [Ⓒ Gallagher,B.&M.]
*PRACTICE AREAS: Energy; Utility Contracts.
Meier, Bradley J. .... '73 '99 C.902 B.S. L.602 J.D. [Ⓐ Kenyon&K.] (See Pat. Sect.)
*PRACTICE AREAS: Intellectual Property.
Meier, Joan S. '57 '83 C.309 A.B. L.145 J.D.
Prof. of Clinical Law, George Washington Univ. Natl. Law Ctr. Community Legal Clinics
Meier, Mike .... '64 '94 C.999 M.A. L.276 J.D. Intl. Law Grp., PLLC
Meiers, Donald H. .... '58 '87 C.216 B.A. L.188 J.D. [Holland&K.]
*PRACTICE AREAS: Securities Law; Mergers and Acquisitions; General Corporate Law.
Meigel, Robin L. .... '54 '88 C.104 A.B. L.1009 J.D. U.S.D.A. Rural Utilities Serv.
Meighan, Katherine Wells .... '70 '95 C.945 B.A. L.893 J.D. [Ⓐ Clifford C.R.&W.]
*PRACTICE AREAS: Corporate; Banking; International Law.
Meigher, Eugene J., (AV) .... '37 '64 C&L.734 A.B., LL.B. [Arent F.K.P.&K.]
*PRACTICE AREAS: Antitrust Law; Criminal Antitrust; Complex and Multi-District Litigation; Joint Ventures Law; Business Combinations.
Meigher, Eva L. '34 '66 C.668 B.A. L.1066 J.D.
(adm. in CA; not adm. in DC) The World Bk.
Meigs, Arthur V. .... '12 '39 C.674 A.B. L.309 LL.B. 3224 Cathedral Ave., N.W.‡
Meija, Ilze Ingrida '72 '00 C&L.475 B.A., J.D.
(adm. in MI; not adm. in DC) U.S. Dept. of Labor
Meikle, Kristin L. .... '67 '95 C.260 B.A. L.276 J.D. [Ⓐ Chadbourne&P.]
Meindertsma, Donn C. .... '62 '87 C.114 B.A. L.477 J.D. [Winston&S.]
*PRACTICE AREAS: Labor and Employment Law; Employment Litigation; Whistleblower Litigation.
Meinrath, John C. '47 '73 C.902 B.A. L.846 J.D.
(adm. in TX; not adm. in DC) MCI Communications Corporation
Meisburg, Ronald E. .... '47 '74 C.122 B.A. L.421 J.D. [Heenan,A.&R.]
*PRACTICE AREAS: Labor and Employment Law; Labor Arbitration; Employment Dispute Resolution; Litigation; International Labor Law.
Meise, Ashley Anne .... '68 '98 C.881 B.A. L.276 J.D. [Ⓐ Clifford C.R.&W.]
*PRACTICE AREAS: Securities; Cross Border Finance; Mergers and Acquisitions; Emerging Markets; General Corporate Practice.
Meisel, Pamela G. .... '68 '95 C.188 B.A. L.178 J.D. [Ⓐ Cleary,G.S.&H.]
Meiser, Margaret A. .... '60 '90 C.976 B.A. L.309 J.D. [Ⓒ Spiegel&M.]
*PRACTICE AREAS: Energy; Environmental Law; Public Interest Law.
Meiser, Robert N., (AV) .... '35 '59 C.347 A.B. L.1119 LL.B. 1718 M St., N.W.
Meisner, Matthew .... '— '95 C.454 B.B.A. L.273 J.D. [Ⓐ Arnold&P.]
Meisner, Stefan M. .... '68 '99 C.454 B.A. L.30 J.D. [Ⓐ McDermott,W.&E.]
Meissnerpritchard, Janet Edna '66 '97 C.128 B.A. L.569 J.D.
(adm. in NY; not adm. in DC) 204 11th St. NE
Meister, Brenda G. '— '88 L.1209 J.D.
(adm. in PA; not adm. in DC) [Verner,L.B.M.&H.]
*PRACTICE AREAS: Legislative Practice; International Tax Policy.
Melamed, A. Douglas .... '45 '70 C.976 B.A. L.309 J.D. [Wilmer,C.&P.]
*PRACTICE AREAS: Antitrust.
Melamed, Carol D., (AV) '46 '74
C.103 A.B. L.128 J.D. V.P. Govt. Affs., Washington Post, The
Melander, Deneen J. .... '60 '87 C.188 B.S.E.E. L.273 J.D. [Fried,F.H.S.&J.]
Melbye, Donald A. '28 '53 L.174 LL.B.
(adm. in CO; not adm. in DC) 2440 Virginia Ave., N.W.
Melcher, Douglas C. .... '69 '00 C.823 B.S. L.273 J.D. [Ⓐ Paul,W.R.W.&G.]
*PRACTICE AREAS: Communications.
Melcher, Glenn J. .... '60 '87 C.446 B.A. L.128 J.D. [Ⓐ Ludwig&R.]
*PRACTICE AREAS: Complex Litigation; Tax Controversies; International Law.
Melcher, Jeffrey Scott .... '61 '91 C.957 B.S. L.436 J.D. [Manelli,D.&S.]
*PRACTICE AREAS: Patent Litigation; Patent Prosecution; Patent Infringement; Intellectual Property.
Melincoff, David R., (AV) .... '32 '61 C.95 A.B. L.93 LL.B. [O'Connor&H.]
Mell, Paula I. .... '51 '77 C.1130 B.A. L.902 J.D. 2031 Florida Ave.,NW
Mellor, Gwen E. '71 '00 C.216 B.A. L.326 J.D.
(adm. in TX; not adm. in DC) 1001 G. St., N.W.
Mellow, Juliet '56 '88 C.1349 B.A. L.273 J.D.
Staff Coun., International Union of Bricklayers and Allied Craftsmen
Melnik, Karen L. .... '66 '91 C.477 B.A. L.904 J.D. 555 4th St. N.W.
Melnyk, Markian M. .... '63 '90 C.994 B.A. L.107 J.D. 1875 Connecticut Avenue, N.W.
Meloy, Brian M. '73 '98 C&L.352 B.A., J.D.
(adm. in MN; not adm. in DC) 1140 19th St., N.W.
Melrod, Daniel .... '58 '87 C.276 B.A. L.904 J.D. 1990 M St.
Melrod, Leonard S., (AV) .... '17 '42 C.705 L.273 LL.B. 1050 Conn. Ave., N.W.

Melser, Allen S., (AV) '46 '72 C.659 B.S.E.E. L.276 J.D. [Jacobson,H.] (See Pat. Sect.)
*PRACTICE AREAS: Intellectual Property; Electrical Patents; Computer and Software Patents; Multimedia Law.
Melton, Carol A. ....'54 '81 C.896 B.A. L.904 J.D. 800 Connecticut Ave., N.W.
Melton, Lawrence C. ....'48 '76 C.861 B.A. L.902 J.D. [Bastianelli,B.&K.]
*PRACTICE AREAS: Government Contracts; Litigation.
Meltzer, David B. ....'60 '86 C.659 B.A. L.273 J.D. V.P. & Gen. Coun., INTELSAT
Meltzer, Richard ....'47 '75 C.696 A.B. L.597 J.D. [Washington C.]
Meltzer, Ronald I., (AV) ....'48 '90 C.610 B.A. L.107 J.D. [[C] Wilmer,C.&P.]
*PRACTICE AREAS: International Trade; International Aviation.
Melvin, Donald J. ....'34 '62 C.754 B.S. L.128 LL.B. 4641 Green Pl., N.W.
Membrino, Joseph R., Jr., (AV) ......'46 '72 C.276 A.B. L.93 J.D. [Hall,E.H.G.G.&N.]
*PRACTICE AREAS: Administrative Law; Indians and Native Populations; Natural Resources.
Memmer, Donald N. ....'31 '61 C.972 L.861 LL.B. 1120 20th St Nw # 300
Menard, Arthur P., (AV) '38 '65 C.321 B.S. L.93 LL.B. (adm. in MA; not adm. in DC) [[C] Menard,M.&W.] ⊙
*PRACTICE AREAS: Labor Relations; Employment Discrimination; Wage-Hour; Wrongful Discharge.
Menard, William L. ....'60 '92 C.951 B.A. L.276 J.D. [[C] Ludwig&R.]
*PRACTICE AREAS: Corporate Law; International Law; Business Transactions; International Contracts; Foreign Corrupt Practices Act.

Menard, Murphy & Walsh LLP
Farragut Park, 910 17th Street, NW, Suite 800, 20006 ⊙
Telephone: 202-293-3500 Telecopier: 202-293-3596
Email: mmw@mmwlaw.com URL: http://mmwlaw.com
Of Counsel: Arthur P. Menard (Not admitted in DC).
Civil Litigation, Management Labor, Employment Law, Corporate Intellectual Property, Finance and Real Estate, Construction and Environmental Law, Eminent Domain, Tax Abatement, Discrimination, Wrongful Discharge, Wage-Hour, Higher Education Law, Domestic Relations.
Boston, Massachusetts Office: 60 State Street, 34th Floor, 02109. Telephone: 617-832-2500. Telecopier: 617-832-2550.
See Professional Biographies, WASHINGTON, DISTRICT OF COLUMBIA

Menasco, Patrick S. ....'69 '95 C&L.861 B.A., J.D. [[A] Steptoe&J.]
Mencher, Bruce S. ....'35 '60 C&L.273 B.A., J.D. Sr. Supr. Ct. J.
Menconi, Christopher Dennis ....'— '94 C&L.128 B.A., J.D. [[A] Morgan,L.&B.]
Mendales, Richard E. ....'50 '82 C.145 A.B. L.976 J.D. [[C] Crowell&M.]
*PRACTICE AREAS: Corporate; Bankruptcy Reorganization; Professional Responsibility; Structured Finance; International Business Transactions.
Mendel, David S. ....'— '98 C.103 A.B. L.477 J.D. [[A] Wilmer,C.&P.]
Mendelsohn, Allan I., (AV) '32 '55 C&L.339 S.B., LL.B. 1233 - 20th Street, N.W., Suite 800
Mendelsohn, Bruce S., (AV) ....'52 '77 C&L.446 B.S., J.D. [Akin,G.S.H.&F.]
*PRACTICE AREAS: Corporate and Securities Law.
Mendelsohn, Craig B., M.D. '54 '94 C.1365 B.A. L.276 J.D. Sr. Coun., American National Red Cross
*RESPONSIBILITIES: Food and Drug; Medical Device.
Mendelsohn, Martin, (AV) ....'— '67 C.102 B.A. L.273 LL.B. [Verner,L.B.M.&H.]
*PRACTICE AREAS: International Law; Legislative Law.
Mendelson, David E. ....'71 '97 C.446 B.A. L.904 J.D. [[A] Kirkland&E.]
*PRACTICE AREAS: Litigation.
Mendelson, Joseph, III '66 '91 C.165 B.A. L.273 J.D. Int'l Ctr. for Technology Assessment
Mendelson, Sondra Tova ....'74 '98 C.645 B.A. L.665 J.D. [[A] McDermott,W.&E.]
Mendenhall, Greggory B., (AV) '45 '72 C.101 B.A. L.273 J.D. [Schnader H.S.&L.] (⊙New York, NY)
*PRACTICE AREAS: International Maritime; Marine Finance and Contracts; Corporate Law; Finance; Internet Law.
Mendenhall, James E. ....'67 '93 C.602 B.A. L.309 J.D. [Powell,G.F.&M.]
*PRACTICE AREAS: International Trade; International Arbitration.
Mendonca, Sonia '70 '96 L.904 LL.M. (adm. in NY; not adm. in DC) 1875 Connecticut Avenue, N.W.
Mendoza, Jocelyn Christine '74 '99 C.93 B.A. L.904 J.D. (adm. in MA; not adm. in DC) 1155 21st St., N.W.
Mendoza, Julie C., (AV) ....'55 '81 C.860 B.A. L.145 J.D. [Kaye S.]
*PRACTICE AREAS: International Trade.
Mendoza Bourelly, Cristina ....'66 '92 C.228 B.A. L.597 J.D. [[C] Wilmer,C.&P.]
*PRACTICE AREAS: Corporate Transactions; Project Finance; Privatization; Technology Law; Venture Capital.
Menendez, Alex ....'66 '92 C.674 B.A. L.273 J.D. [[A] McLeod,W.&M.]
*PRACTICE AREAS: Commercial Litigation; Corporate Law; Employment Law; Medical Malpractice; Transportation Law.
Menge, Eric E. '72 '97 C.260 B.S. L.128 J.D. (adm. in MD; not adm. in DC) Indendent Telephone and Telecommunications alliance
Menkel-Meadow, Carrie J. '49 '74 C.66 A.B. L.659 J.D. Prof. of Law, Georgetown University Law Center
Menkes, Brian J. ....'62 '90 C.829 B.S. L.1048 J.D. [[C] Wilmer,C.&P.]
*PRACTICE AREAS: Tax; Corporate Transactions; Venture Capital.
Menotti, David E., (AV) ....'42 '67 C.823 A.B. L.659 J.D. [Shaw P.]
*PRACTICE AREAS: Environmental Law.
Mense, Marilyn Suchecki ....'64 '92 C.454 B.A. L.273 J.D. [[A] Lukas,N.G.&S.]
*PRACTICE AREAS: Telecommunications Law; FCC Regulation; FCC Licensing.
Menter, Joshua L., (AV) ....'50 '75 C.867 B.A. L.569 J.D. [Miller,B.&O.]
*PRACTICE AREAS: Natural Gas Regulation; Electric Power; Energy Contracts.
Mentz, J. Roger, (AV) ....'42 '67 C.674 B.S.E. L.893 LL.B. [White&C.]
*PRACTICE AREAS: Taxation.
Merber, Selig S., (AV) '48 '75 C.688 B.S. L.276 J.D. Coun., Intl. Trade Regul. & Sourcing, General Electric Co.
Merbeth, Russell C. '59 '90 C&L.846 B.S., J.D. Assoc. V.P., Legal & Regul. Affs., WinStar Telecommunications, Inc.
Mercurio, James P., (AV) ....'40 '64 C&L.602 A.B., LL.B. [Arent F.K.P.&K.]
*PRACTICE AREAS: Litigation; Alternative Dispute Resolution; Legal Ethics and Discipline Law.
Meredith, Pamela L. '56 '89 L.999 J.D. (adm. in NY; not adm. in DC) [[C] Zuckert,S.&R.]
*PRACTICE AREAS: Aerospace Law; Aerospace Contracts; Space Law.
Merelman, Jack M. ....'27 '52 C&L.446 A.B., LL.B. Dep. Dir. of Natl. Affairs
Mergele, Cary W. ....'68 '94 C&L.878 B.S., J.D. [Hughes&B.]
Merianos, Laura J. ....'75 '01 C.893 B.A. L.904 J.D. [[A] Jones,D.R.&P.]
Meriweather, Robin M. '74 '98 C.477 B.A. L.976 J.D. (adm. in IL; not adm. in DC) [[A] Jenner&B.]
*PRACTICE AREAS: Litigation.
Merkel, William G. ....'65 '98 C.367 B.A. L.178 J.D. 1776 K St. NW
Merkle, Patrick G. ....'56 '83 C.184 B.A. L.276 J.D. [P.G.Merkle]
Merkle, Patrick G., PLLC .... 1750 K Street, Suite 325
Merklinger, James Anthony '65 '94 C.968 B.A. L.790 J.D. Mng. Atty., Amer. Corp. Coun. Assoc.
*RESPONSIBILITIES: General Corporate; Nonprofits; Issues affecting in-house practice of law.
Merley, Mark R. ....'58 '83 C.659 B.A.B.S. L.309 J.D. [Arnold&P.]
*PRACTICE AREAS: Antitrust; Litigation.
Merlin, Paul ....'34 '58 C&L.309 A.B., LL.B. Chief Adm. Law J.‡
Mernick, George H., III, (AV) ....'52 '79 C.696 A.B. L.276 J.D. [Hogan&H.]
*PRACTICE AREAS: Federal Litigation; Trial Practice; Securities Litigation; Corporate Litigation.
Meron, Daniel ....'65 '93 C&L.309 A.B., J.D. [[A] Sidley A.B.&W.]
Merone, William M. '69 '95 C.800 B.S.B.A. L.893 J.D. [[A] Kenyon&K.] (See Pat. Sect.)
*PRACTICE AREAS: Intellectual Property.
Meros, Alicia A. ....'73 '98 C.880 B.E. L.273 J.D. [[A] Swidler B.S.F.] (Pat.)
*PRACTICE AREAS: Intellectual Property; Patents; Trademarks; Copyrights; Trade Secrets.
Merrigan, Edward L., (AV) ....'21 '47 C.861 L.425 J.D. 1776 Eye St., N.W.
Merrigan, John A., (AV) ....'— '73 C.276 A.B. L.425 J.D. [Verner,L.B.M.&H.]
*PRACTICE AREAS: Regulatory and Legislative Law.
Merrill, Jennifer A. ....'70 '00 C.839 B.A. L.846 J.D. [[A] Leventhal,S.&L.]
*PRACTICE AREAS: Broadcast Media Law; Intellectual Property.
Merrill, Richard A. ....'37 '64 C&L.178 A.B., LL.B. [[C] Covington&B.]
Merriman, Richard M., (AV) '27 '56 C.436 B.S.E.E. L.273 J.D. 701 Pennsylvania Ave., N.W.
Merritt, Elizabeth Sherrill '55 '80 C.483 B.A. L.309 J.D. Assoc. Gen. Coun., National Trust for Historic Preservation
Merritt, Kristin C. '73 '99 C.932 B.A. L.424 J.D. (adm. in MD; not adm. in DC) Off. of the Comptr. of the Currency Enforce.
Merski, Kira A. ....'— '97 C.347 B.A. L.276 J.D. [[A] Paul,W.R.W.&G.]
Merson, Gary N. '72 '98 C.880 B.A. L.861 J.D. (adm. in MA; not adm. in DC) [[C] Fragomen,D.B.&L.]
Merten, William Glenn ....'72 '97 C.692 B.A. L.273 J.D. [[A] Jorden B.]
*PRACTICE AREAS: Litigation; Insurance Law; Labor and Employment Law.
Mertens, William J. ....'48 '75 C.976 B.A. L.276 J.D. [[C] Asbill,J.M.&B.]
*PRACTICE AREAS: Civil and Criminal Litigation; Commercial Litigation; Business Litigation; Torts Litigation; Contract Litigation.
Meshulam, Deborah R. ....'56 '82 C.893 B.A. L.178 J.D. [Piper M.R.&W.]
*PRACTICE AREAS: Securities Litigation; Business Litigation; Mergers and Acquisitions Litigation; Financial Litigation; Accounting Litigation.
Mesirow, Harold E., (AV) ....'32 '57 C&L.273 A.B., LL.B. [Robins,K.M.&C.]
*PRACTICE AREAS: Transportation Law; Administrative Law; Federal Government; Environmental Law; Maritime Law.
Mesirow, John B., (AV) ....'62 '91 C.473 B.A. L.273 J.D. [Mesirow&S.]
Mesirow & Stravitz, PLLC, (AV) .... 2015 R. St., Ste. 300
Mesnard, James M. ....'53 '86 C.885 B.A. L.446 J.D. [[A] Seyfarth S.]
*PRACTICE AREAS: Litigation.
Messenger, Harold W. '35 '64 C.623 B.B.A. L.273 J.D. (adm. in OK; not adm. in DC) The World Bk.
Messenger, Jay N. ....'67 '98 C&L.831 B.A., J.D. 1775 Eye Street, N.W.
Messina, Michael A., (AV) '60 '88 C.672 B.M.E. L.188 J.D. (adm. in NY; not adm. in DC; Pat.) [McDermott,W.&E.]
Messina, Raymond A. .....'45 '71 C&L.262 B.A., J.D. Princ., Govt. Rel., Morgan Stanley
Messineo, Carl L. ....'67 '95 C.119 B.S. L.659 J.D. 1901 Pennsylvania Ave., N.W.
Messinger, Michael V. ....'63 '95 C.228 B.S. L.276 J.D. [[A] Sterne,K.G.&F.]
*PRACTICE AREAS: Intellectual Property.
Mestre, Alvaro J. ....'70 '95 C.260 B.A. L.276 J.D. [[A] Squire,S.&D.]
Meszoly, Peter T., (AV) ....'— '71 C.401 A.B. L.228 J.D. [Holland&K.]
*PRACTICE AREAS: Commercial Real Estate; Multi-Family Housing.
Meta, Jean D. '74 '00 C.30 B.A. L.665 J.D. (adm. in MD; not adm. in DC) [[A] Chavers]
*PRACTICE AREAS: Intellectual Property; Internet Law; Business Organization; Entertainment and the Arts; Sports Law.
Metalitz, Steven J. ....'51 '78 C.145 B.A. L.276 J.D. [Smith&M.]
*PRACTICE AREAS: Copyrights; Trademarks; Privacy Law; Electronic Commerce; Government.
Metallo, Virginia R. ....'57 '88 C.216 B.A. L.128 J.D. [Howrey S.A.&W.]
*PRACTICE AREAS: Antitrust; Trade Regulation.
Metcalf, J. Todd '70 '97 C.838 B.A. L.910 J.D. (adm. in NY; not adm. in DC) [[A] Vinson&E.]
*PRACTICE AREAS: Business Law; International Business Transactions; Telecommunications Law; Project Finance; Internet Law.
Metheny, Earl L., (P.C.) ....'51 '78 C.685 B.A. L.569 J.D. 1111 14th St., N.W.
Metlin, Elaine, (BV) ....'51 '85 C.665 B.A. L.893 J.D. [Dickstein S.M.&O.]
*PRACTICE AREAS: White Collar Criminal Defense; Antitrust; Health Care; Civil Litigation.
Metro, Joseph W., (BV) ....'— '89 C.216 B.A. L.273 J.D. [Reed S.]
*PRACTICE AREAS: Health Care.
Metzel, Amy B. '— '96 C.309 A.B. L.945 J.D. (adm. in VA; not adm. in DC) [[A] King&S.]
Metzenthin, George A. ....'69 '95 C&L.930 B.S.E.E., J.D. [Cahn&S.] (See Pat. Sect.)
*PRACTICE AREAS: Intellectual Property Law.
Metzger, David P., (AV) ....'48 '74 C&L.966 B.A., J.D. [Holland&K.]
*PRACTICE AREAS: Government Contracts Law; Litigation.
Metzger, Elisa D. ....'62 '87 C&L.879 B.S., J.D. [[A] Morrison&F.]
*PRACTICE AREAS: Investment Management; Investments; Broker-Dealer Regulation.
Metzger, Michael J. ....'60 '85 C.477 B.B.A. L.879 J.D. [Rosenman&C.]
*PRACTICE AREAS: Finance; Securities; Banks and Banking.
Metzger, Raphael ....'— '95 C.477 A.B. L.276 J.D. Gen. Coun., MSD, Inc.
Metzger, Richard, Jr. ....'49 '77 C.951 B.A. L.276 J.D. [Metzger&M.]
Metzger, Hollis, Gordon & Alprin .... 1275 K St., N.W.
Metzger & Milkman .... 1909 K St., NW
Metzler, Cynthia A. ....'48 '74 C.602 B.A. L.347 J.D. [[C] Pepper H.]
*PRACTICE AREAS: Employment; Labor.
Meuser, Robert L. ....'55 '80 C.273 B.A. L.276 J.D. 3834 T St Nw
Mew, Caroline Marie ....'73 '99 C&L.575 B.A., J.D. [[A] Fulbright&J.]
*PRACTICE AREAS: Litigation.
Mexic, Darryl, (P.C.), (AV) '40 '66 C.277 B.E.E. L.276 J.D. [Sughrue M.] (See Pat. Sect.)
*PRACTICE AREAS: Intellectual Property Law.
Meyer, Aileen ....'48 '81 C.788 A.B. L.1009 J.D. [[C] Pillsbury W.]
*PRACTICE AREAS: Environmental Law; Antitrust.
Meyer, Christopher W. ....'71 '98 C.859 B.A. L.902 J.D. [[A] Skadden,A.S.M.&F.]
*PRACTICE AREAS: Antitrust and Trade Regulation.
Meyer, Daniel P. '65 '97 C.188 B.A. L.347 J.D. Coun., Public Employees for Environmental Responsibility
Meyer, David Lawrence ....'61 '87 C.31 B.A. L.976 J.D. [Covington&B.]
Meyer, Dennis I., (AV) ....'35 '60 C.201 B.S. L.276 J.D. [Baker&M.]
*PRACTICE AREAS: Tax Controversies (Corporate and International); Tax Planning and Advice (Corporate and International).
Meyer, Jerald L. '— '98 C.477 B.S. L.1218 J.D. (adm. in VA; not adm. in DC; See Pat. Sect.) [[A] Nath&Assoc.]
Meyer, John J., (AV) ....'49 '79 C.674 A.B. L.966 J.D. [Arent F.K.P.&K.]
*PRACTICE AREAS: Health Law.
Meyer, Jonathan E. ....'65 '93 C.309 A.B. L.178 J.D. Dept. Asst. Atty. Gen.

Meyer, Lawrence G., (AV) '40 '65 C.475 B.A. L.477 J.D.
1735 New York Avenue, Suite 700, 20006-5209
Telephone: 202-661-3910 Fax: 202-331-1024
Email: larry@lawlgm.com
***PRACTICE AREAS: Antitrust Law; Trade Regulations Law; Unfair Competition Law; Food, Drug and Cosmetic Law; Litigation.**

(This Listing Continued)

Meyer, Lawrence G. (Continued)
Antitrust Law, Trade Regulations Law, Unfair Competition Law, Food, Drug and Cosmetic Law, Litigation.
See Professional Biographies, WASHINGTON, DISTRICT OF COLUMBIA

Meyer, Lindsay Beardsworth .... '61 '87 C.184 B.S. L.273 J.D. [Venable,A.B.H.&C.]
*PRACTICE AREAS: International Trade; International Transactional Law.
Meyer, Maureen A. '72 '97 C.884 B.A. L.30 J.D.
(adm. in MD; not adm. in DC) Street Law Inc.‡
Meyer, Michael A. .... '65 '93 C&L.276 B.S., J.D. Goldman, Sachs & Co.
Meyer, Natalie K. .... '70 '99 C.88 B.A. L.893 J.D. [[A] Brobeck,P.&H.]
*PRACTICE AREAS: Technology Law; Intellectual Property; Corporate Law.
Meyer, Nicole M. '73 '98 C.31 B.A. L.904 J.D.
(adm. in VA; not adm. in DC; See Pat. Sect.) [[A] Dickinson W.]
*PRACTICE AREAS: Trademark Litigation and Prosecution; Copyright Litigation and Prosecution.
Meyer, Paul A. .... '57 '83 C.665 B.A. L.930 J.D. Coun., Watson Wyatt Worldwide
Meyer, Richard S., (AV) .... '60 '88 C.186 B.E. L.276 J.D. [Morgan,L.&B.] (Pat.)
*PRACTICE AREAS: Intellectual Property Law; Patents; Litigation.
Meyer, Robert J. .... '— '85 C.94 B.A. L.893 J.D. [Foley&L.]
*PRACTICE AREAS: White Collar Criminal Defense; Government Enforcement; Compliance.
Meyer, Roberta B. '53 '79 C.861 B.A. L.692 J.D.
(adm. in VA; not adm. in DC) Coun., Amer. Council of Life Ins.
Meyer, Tracy Anette .... '70 '96 C.173 B.A. L.904 J.D. [[A] Sherman,M.C.&A.]
*PRACTICE AREAS: Family Law.

Meyer & Klipper, PLLC
923 Fifteenth Street, N.W., 5th Floor, 20005
Telephone: 202-637-0850 Fax: 202-637-0851
Email: meyerklipper@mindspring.com URL: http://www.lawyers.com/meyer&klipperlaw
Christopher A. Meyer (1946-1999); Michael Russell Klipper; Christopher A. Mohr. Of Counsel: Robert A. Gorman (Not admitted in DC).
Domestic and International Copyright Issues, Trademark Law, Constitutional and Legislative Law Practice.
See Professional Biographies, WASHINGTON, DISTRICT OF COLUMBIA

Meyer, Suozzi, English & Klein, P.C., (AV)
Suite 600, 1300 Connecticut Avenue, N.W., 20036 ⊙
Telephone: 202-955-6340 Telecopier: 202-223-0358
Email: meyersuozzi@msek.com
Harold Ickes (Not admitted in DC).
General Practice before all State and Federal Courts. Appellate and Trial Practice, Antitrust, Banking, Commercial, Corporate, Criminal, Elder Law, Election Law, Governmental Relations, Labor and Employment, Land Use and Environment, Legal, Medical and Professional Liability, Lobbying, Medical and Health Care, Municipal and Public Finance, Personal Injury, Probate, Real Estate, Tax Certiorari, Condemnation and Zoning Law, and Trusts, Estates and Estate Planning.
Mineola, New York Office: 1505 Kellum Place, 11501. Telephone: 516-741-6565; 212-227-5511. Cable Address: Islandlaw New York. Telecopier: 516-741-6706. Email: meyersuozzi@msek.com.
Albany, New York Office: One Commerce Plaza, 12260. Telephone: 518-465-5551. Telecopier: 518-465-2033. Email: meyersuozzi@msek.com.
New York, N.Y. Office: 1350 Broadway, Suite 501, 10018. Telephone: 212-239-4999. Telecopier: 212-239-1311. Email: meyersuozzi@msek.com.
See Professional Biographies, WASHINGTON, DISTRICT OF COLUMBIA

Meyers, Erik J. .... '49 '75 C.276 B.S.F.S. L.262 J.D. Environmental Law Institute
*RESPONSIBILITIES: Environmental Law; Corporate Law; Taxation Law.
Meyers, James E. .... '47 '77 C.472 B.A. L.1209 J.D. 1633 Connecticut Ave., NW
Meyers, Kenneth John, (AV) '40 '71
C.474 B.S. L.276 J.D. [Finnegan,H.F.G.&D.] (See Pat. Sect.)
*PRACTICE AREAS: Pharmaceutical Patents; Biotechnology Patents.
Meyers, N. Marshall, (AV) ....'38 '65 C.311 B.A. L.659 LL.B. [Meyers&A.]
Meyers, Tedson J., (AV) .... '28 '53 C.569 A.B. L.309 J.D. [Coudert B.]
*PRACTICE AREAS: Telecommunications; Aerospace.
Meyers & Alterman, (AV) .... 1220 19th Street, N.W., Suite 400
Meyhardie, E. Jane .... '60 '86 C.682 B.A. L.893 J.D. 1775 Pennsylvania Ave., N.W.
Meyrowitz, Martin L., (P.C.) .... '55 '80 C.446 B.S. L.472 J.D. [Silver,F.&T.]
*PRACTICE AREAS: Financial Institutions; Securities Law; Mergers and Acquisitions; Financial Institutions; Corporate Law.
Mezey, Marc L. .... '73 '00 C.367 B.A. L.178 J.D. [[A] Cleary,G.S.&H.]
Mezey, Naomi Jewel '66 '96 C.918 B.A. L.813 J.D.
Assoc. Prof. of Law, Georgetown Univ. Law Ctr.
Mezines, Basil J., (AV) ....'24 '48 C&L.273 B.A., LL.B. [Stein,M.&M.]
*PRACTICE AREAS: Antitrust; Trade Regulation.
Mezzetti, Lisa M. .... '56 '82 C.1200 B.A. L.128 J.D. [Cohen,M.H.&T.]
*PRACTICE AREAS: Complex Commercial Litigation; Complex and Multi-District Litigation; Securities Arbitration; Securities Class Actions.
Miano, Andrea S. .... '65 '90 C&L.276 B.A., J.D. [[A] Dewey B.]
*PRACTICE AREAS: Telecommunications (100%).
Miano, Anne M. .... '53 '79 C.4 B.A. L.724 J.D. [[C] Patton B.]
Michael, Helen Katherine ....'59 '88 C.1307 B.A. L.575 J.D. [Howrey S.A.&W.]
*PRACTICE AREAS: Antitrust Law; Complex Litigation; Class Action Litigation; Insurance Coverage Litigation; Products Liability.
Michael, Jeanette Ann '50 '77 C.706 A.B. L.273
Gen. Coun., D.C. Lottery & Charitable Games Bd.
Michael, Marc Zaki '73 '98 C&L.128 B.A., J.D.
(adm. in MD; not adm. in DC) [[A] Winston&S.]
*PRACTICE AREAS: Litigation.
Michael, Rebecca J. .... '67 '93 C.327 B.A. L.880 J.D. 1875 Connecticut Avenue, N.W.
Michaels, Anthony L. .... '70 '95 C.886 B.S. L.945 J.D. [[A] Beveridge&D.]
*PRACTICE AREAS: Environmental Law; Litigation.
Michaels, Jacqueline '75 '00 C.976 B.A. L.178 J.D.
(adm. in MD; not adm. in DC) [[A] Steptoe&J.]
Michaels, Joel L., (AV) ....'50 '75 C.273 B.A. L.30 J.D. [McDermott,W.&E.]
Michaels, Louis P. ......'30 '59 C.103 B.A. L.276 LL.B. Intl. Bk. for Reconstr. & Develop.
Michaelson, Martin, (AV) .... '43 '68 C.145 B.A. L.93 J.D. [Hogan&H.]
*PRACTICE AREAS: Administrative Law; Business Law; Education Law; Government; Labor and Employment.
Michaelson, Michael Gary ....'47 '85 C.367 A.B. L.309 J.D. [[C] Covington&B.]
Michal, James R., (AV) '47 '73
C.177 A.B. L.276 J.D. [Jackson&C.] (⊙Balt., Rockville, MD)
*PRACTICE AREAS: Wills; Trust and Probate Law; International Business; Real Estate Law; Zoning, Planning and Land Use.
Michalopoulos, Pantelis .... '63 '90 C.999 B.S. L.659 LL.M. [Steptoe&J.]
*PRACTICE AREAS: Communications Law; Transportation Law; Regulatory Law; International Practice.
Michel, Christian C. '70 '99 C.390 B.S.E.E. L.884 J.D.
(adm. in PA; not adm. in DC; See Pat. Sect.) [[A] Roylance,A.B.&G.]
*PRACTICE AREAS: Electrical Patent Law; Trademark; Computer Law.
Michel, Laurie L. .... '53 '79 C.788 A.B. L.273 J.D. Merck & Co. Inc.
Michel, Mary Patricia, (AV) .... '50 '82 C&L.276 B.S., J.D. [[C] Sutherland A.&B.]
*PRACTICE AREAS: International Trade; International Law; Corporate; Litigation.
Michel, Scott D. ....'55 '81 C.597 B.S. L.893 J.D. [Caplin&D.]
*PRACTICE AREAS: Criminal Litigation; Tax Litigation.
Michels, Dina L. ....'61 '87 C.309 A.B. L.276 J.D. [Ropes&G.]

Michelsohn, Arie M. '62 '99 C.178 B.A. L.273
(adm. in NY; not adm. in DC; See Pat. Sect.) [[A] Finnegan,H.F.G.&D.]
*PRACTICE AREAS: Intellectual Property Litigation; Intellectual Property Portfolio Management; Biotechnology Patents; Chemistry; Life Sciences.
Michelson, Robert '40 '68 C.178 A.B. L.705 J.D.
(adm. in NJ; not adm. in DC) MCI Telecom. Corp.
Michetti, Michael L., Jr. '71 '98 C.477 B.A. L.128 J.D.
(adm. in MD; not adm. in DC) [[A] S.G.DeNigris]
Mickey, Anne E., (AV) .... '51 '76 C.788 B.A. L.273 J.D. [Sher&B.]
*PRACTICE AREAS: Transportation; Corporate Law; Commercial Law; Maritime Law.
Mickey, Paul F., Jr., (AV) .... '49 '74 C.674 A.B. L.893 J.D. [Shaw P.]
*PRACTICE AREAS: Labor and Employment Law; Transportation; Appellate Litigation.
Micklos, Jeffrey G. '— '94 C.884 B.A. L.128 J.D.
(adm. in PA; not adm. in DC) [[C] Foley&L.]
*PRACTICE AREAS: Health Care; Litigation.
Mickney, Marcus R. '69 '00 C.886 BSAE L.1209 J.D.
(adm. in VA; not adm. in DC; See Pat. Sect.) [[A] Roylance,A.B.&G.]
*PRACTICE AREAS: Patents; Trademarks; Copyrights.
Mickum, George Brent, IV .... '54 '84 C.273 B.A. L.1356 J.D. [[A] Keller&H.]
*PRACTICE AREAS: Litigation; Advertising Law; Federal Practice; Criminal Law.
Middleton, John H. .... '10 '40 C.878 B.S. L.904 J.D. 7800 Moorland Ln.‡
Middleton, John Howard, II .... '66 '93 C.682 B.A. L.1228 J.D. 1629 K St., N.W.
Middleton, Margaret E.K. ....'67 '93 C&L.93 B.A., J.D. [[A] Hogan&H.]
*PRACTICE AREAS: Civil Litigation; Franchises and Franchising.
Midlen Law Center
(See Chevy Chase, Maryland)
Midler, Robert A. '52 '80 C.473 B.A. L.1003 J.D.
Natl. Tax Dept., Ernst & Young, LLP
Mierzewski, Michael B. .... '51 '80 C.128 B.A. L.329 J.D. [Arnold&P.]
*PRACTICE AREAS: Financial Institutions.
Mietus, John R., Jr., (BV) ....'— '90 C.446 B.A. L.276 J.D. [Verner,L.B.M.&H.]
*PRACTICE AREAS: Aviation Law; Transportation Law.
Migas, Joseph J. .... '66 '97 C.966 B.B.A. L.276 J.D. [[A] Jones,D.R.&P.]
Migdail, Evan M., (AV) ....'54 '79 C.659 B.A. L.884 J.D. [Verner,L.B.M.&H.]
*PRACTICE AREAS: Federal Tax; Nonprofit and Charitable Organizations; Legislative; Political Law.
Migdal, Nelson F., (AV) ....'53 '79 C.1019 B.A. L.982 J.D. [Holland&K.]
Mihalik, Theresa M., (AV) ....'63 '87 C.754 B.A. L.180 J.D. [Kuder,S.&F.]
*PRACTICE AREAS: Domestic Relations Law.
Mika, Sarah Fitzgerald ....'58 '83 C.645 B.S. L.128 J.D. Assoc. Gen. Coun., AARP
*RESPONSIBILITIES: Non-Profit; Marketing and Advertising; Consumer Law.
Mikael, Sahlu .... '58 '89 L.880 J.D. 1012 14th St., NW
Mikkelson, Katherine Z. ....'65 '91 C.608 B.A. L.128 J.D. Asst. Dir. Amer. Bar Assn.
Miko, Kathleen M., (AV) ....'55 '80 C.555 B.A. L.776 J.D. 1133 Connecticut Ave.
Mikolop, Todd S. '75 '00 C.999 B.A. L.1194 J.D.
(adm. in MA; not adm. in DC) Maritime & Int'l Law Off.
Mikula, Thomas J. ....'59 '84 C.602 B.A. L.273 J.D. [Shea&G.]
*PRACTICE AREAS: Products Liability; Insurance; Environmental Law; Labor Law.
Milano, James M. .... '60 '89 C&L.420 B.A., J.D. [[C] Weiner B.S.K.]
*PRACTICE AREAS: Mortgage Banking Law; Consumer Credit; Regulatory Compliance; Real Estate; Financial Institutions.

Milbank, Tweed, Hadley & McCloy LLP, (AV) [BB]
International Square Building, Suite 1100, 1825 Eye Street, N.W., 20006 ⊙
Telephone: 202-835-7500 Fax: 202-835-7586
Email: postmaster@milbank.com URL: http://www.milbank.com
Partners: Winthrop N. Brown; Glenn S. Gerstell; Robert F. Lawrence; Jonathan A. Maizel (Not admitted in DC); Michael D. Nolan; John E. Shockey; Richard C. Tufaro; William E. Wallace, III; William H. Webster. Of Counsel: Orlan M. Johnson; Steven M. Kramer. Associates: David S. Cohen; Nicholas DeCarlo; David L. Elmont (Not admitted in DC); Perry Hicks (Not admitted in DC); Kathryn E. Hoff-Patrinos; Michael H. Jacobs; Devon Lincoln (Not admitted in DC); William Jackson Matney, Jr.; Dara A. Panahy; Franceska O. Schroeder; Carla J. Urquhart; Debra Alligood White (Not admitted in DC); Naomi Wilkinson; Elizabeth A. Zelinka.
General Practice.
New York, New York Offices: 1 Chase Manhattan Plaza, 10005-1413. Telephone: 212-530-5000. Fax: 212-530-5219. ABA/net: MilbankNY.
Midtown Office: 375 Park Avenue, Suite 3601, 10152.
Los Angeles, California Office: 601 South Figueroa Street, 90017. Telephone: 213-892-4000. Fax: 213-629-5063.
Palo Alto, California Office: 630 Hansen Way, 94304-1022. Telephone: 650-739-7000. Fax: 650-739-7100.
Frankfurt am Main, Germany Office: Frankfurter Welle, An Der Welle 4, 60422. Telephone: 011-49-69-7593-7170. Fax: 011-49-69-7593-8303.
Tokyo, Japan Office: Fukoku Seimei Building, 2-2, Uchisaiwai-cho 2-Chome, Chiyoda-ku, Tokyo 100-0011, Japan. Telephone: 011-81-3-3504-1050. Telephone: 011-81-3-3504-1050. Fax: 011-81-3-3595-2790, 011-81-3-3595-2840.
London, England Office: Dashwood House, 69 Old Broad Street, London, EC2M 1QS. Telephone: 44-207-448-3000. Fax: 44-207-448-3029.
Hong Kong: 3007 Alexandra House, 16 Chater Road. Telephone: 852-2971-4888. Fax: 852-2840-0792, 852-2854-9046.
Singapore Office: 14-00 Caltex House, 30 Raffles Place, 048622. Telephone: 65-428-2400. Fax: 65-428-2500.
See Professional Biographies, WASHINGTON, DISTRICT OF COLUMBIA

Milbauer, Jean R. '61 '89 C.273 B.A. L.978 J.D.
Assoc. Gen. Coun., Dir., Royalty Admin., Recording Industry Assoc. of America, Inc.
Milbourne, W. Robertson, Jr. '72 '00 C.197 A.B. L.228 J.D.
(adm. in NY; not adm. in DC) [[A] Chadbourne&P.]
Milch, Thomas H., (AV) .... '50 '76 C&L.976 B.A., J.D. [Arnold&P.]
*PRACTICE AREAS: Environmental Law.
Milem, Anne L. ....'70 '95 C.845 B.A. L.276 J.D. [[A] Arent F.K.P.&K.]
*PRACTICE AREAS: Civil Litigation; Employment Litigation; Construction Litigation; Business Torts; Civil Appeals.
Miles, David Michael .... '54 '79 C.156 B.A. L.273 J.D. [Sidley A.B.&W.]
Miles, John J., (AV) .... '46 '73 C.886 B.S. L.902 J.D. [Ober,K.G.&S.]
Miles, John R. ....'39 '85 C.473 B.A. L.276 J.D. [[A] Kaye S.]
*PRACTICE AREAS: Environmental Law; Litigation.
Miles, John S., (AV) ....'45 '73 C.321 B.A. L.276 J.D. [W.J.Olson] ⊙
*PRACTICE AREAS: Business Law; Non-Profit Tax Law; Postal Law; Election Law; Civil Litigation.
Miles, Kathleen ....'57 '83 C.681 A.B. L.893 J.D. Assoc. Gen. Coun., Fannie Mae
*RESPONSIBILITIES: Securitizations; Mortgage-Backed Securities; International Project Finance; Public Finance.
Miles, Michael R., (AV) .... '50 '78 C.610 B.S. L.608 J.D. [Sutherland A.&B.]
*PRACTICE AREAS: Corporate Taxation; Corporate Tax Planning; Federal Income Tax; Federal Tax Controversies; Leasing.
Miles, Susan P. .... '52 '89 C.994 B.S. L.180 J.D. Off. of Thrift Supvr.

Miles & Stockbridge P.C., (AV)
1140 Connecticut Avenue, N.W., Suite 1212, 20036-4001 ⊙
Telephone: 202-737-9600 Facsimile: 202-737-0097
URL: http://www.milesstockbridge.com
Samuel A. Bleicher; Richard D. Bennett.
General Practice.
Baltimore, Maryland Office: 10 Light Street, Telephone: 410-727-6464. Facsimile: 410-385-3700.
Cambridge, Maryland Office: 300 Academy Street. Telephone: 410-228-4545. Facsimile: 410-228-5652.

(This Listing Continued)

Miles & Stockbridge P.C. (Continued)
Columbia, Maryland Office: 9881 Broken Land Parkway, Suite 400, Telephone: 410-381-6000. Facsimile: 410-381-6430.
Easton, Maryland Office: 101 Bay Street. Telephone: 410-822-5280. Facsimile: 410-822-5450.
Frederick, Maryland Office: 30 West Patrick Street. Telephone: 301-662-5155. Facsimile: 301-662-3647.
McLean, Virginia Office: 1751 Pinnacle Drive, Suite 500. Telephone: 703-903-9000. Facsimile: 703-610-8686.
Rockville, Maryland Office: 22 West Jefferson Street. Telephone: 301-762-1600. Facsimile: 301-762-0363.
Towson, Maryland Office: 600 Washington Avenue, Suite 300. Telephone: 410-821-6565. Facsimile: 410-823-8123.
See Professional Biographies, WASHINGTON, DISTRICT OF COLUMBIA

Milhollin, Elliott .... '— '99 C.477 B.A. L.966 J.D. [A] Latham&W.]
*PRACTICE AREAS: Appellate Practice; Regulatory Law; Environmental Law.
Miliauskas, Bradley R. .... '70 '97 C.945 B.A. L.893 J.D. [[A] Swidler B.S.F.]
*PRACTICE AREAS: Energy.
Milin, Katherine S. .... '70 '99 C.1369 B.B.A. L.1209 J.D. [[A] Sutherland A.&B.]
*PRACTICE AREAS: Corporate Law; Securities.
Miljanic, Kathy Marlo .... '62 '92 C.1349 B.A. L.659 J.D. [[A] Hogan&H.]
*PRACTICE AREAS: Aviation and Aerospace; Aviation Regulation; Airport Regulation; Aeronautical Regulation; Airport Law.
Milkman, Ruth .... '59 '86 C.309 B.A. L.477 J.D. [Metzger&M.]
Millar, Joel .... '71 '99 C.260 B.A. L.659 J.D. [[A] Wilmer,C.&P.]
Millar, Sheila A. .... '53 '80 C.104 B.A. L.904 J.D. [Keller&H.]
*PRACTICE AREAS: E-Commerce; Privacy Law; Environmental Law; Trade Regulation Law; Trademark Law.
Millard, Kendall .... '68 '99 L.347 J.D. [[A] Arnold&P.]
*PRACTICE AREAS: Antitrust Litigation; Litigation.

Millen, White, Zelano & Branigan, P.C.
(See Arlington, Virginia)

Miller, Adelaide M. .... '37 '73 C&L.273 A.B., J.D. 1050 17th St. N.W.
Miller, Amy E. '68 '99 C.945 B.A. L.1509 J.D.
(adm. in GA; not adm. in DC) [[A] McGuirewoods]
*PRACTICE AREAS: Labor Management Relations; Employment Discrimination.
Miller, Amy L. '71 '96 C&L.692 B.S., J.D.
(adm. in VA; not adm. in DC; Pat.) [[A] Piper M.R.&W.]
*PRACTICE AREAS: Intellectual Property; Patent Prosecution; Domestic and Foreign Prosecution; Biochemical Patents; Chemical Patents.
Miller, Amy T. '61 '91 C.276 B.S. L.128 J.D.
(adm. in PA; not adm. in DC) National Conference of Catholic Bishops
Miller, Amy Wilsey .... '— '99 C.612 B.A. L.276 J.D. [[A] Foley&L.]
*PRACTICE AREAS: Litigation.
Miller, Andrew J. '72 '99 C.188 B.S. L.228 J.D.
(adm. in PA; not adm. in DC) [[A] Vinson&E.]
*PRACTICE AREAS: Business Law; International Law.
Miller, Andrew P., (AV) .... '32 '60 C.674 A.B. L.893 LL.B. [Dickstein S.M.&O.]
*PRACTICE AREAS: Litigation; Government Affairs.
Miller, Anja '74 '01 C.813 B.A. L.309 J.D.
(adm. in NY; not adm. in DC) [[A] Wilmer,C.&P.]
Miller, Ann M. .... '74 '00 C.788 B.A. L.37 J.D. [[A] Sullivan&C.]
Miller, Barbara R., (AV) .... '53 '79 C.976 B.A. L.813 J.D. [Reuss&M.]
Miller, Barry P. .... '61 '87 C&L.16 B.S., J.D. [Wilkinson B.K.]
*PRACTICE AREAS: Intellectual Property Law; Privacy Law; Computer and Internet Law; Broadcasting Law; Telecommunications Law.
Miller, Betsy '74 '99 C.197 A.B. L.309 J.D.
(adm. in MA; not adm. in DC) 1120 G St. N.W.
Miller, Binny .... '56 '85 C.118 B.A. L.145 J.D. Prof., Amer. Univ. Wash. Coll. of Law
Miller, Brett I. .... '64 '95 C.1365 B.A. L.893 J.D. [[A] Morgan,L.&B.]
Miller, Carla .... '73 '99 C.659 B.S. L.245 J.D. [[A] Thompson C.]
*PRACTICE AREAS: Litigation; Transportation; International Trade.
Miller, Charles A., (AV) .... '35 '60 C.112 A.B. L.1066 LL.B. [Covington&B.]
Miller, Charles L., Jr. .... '52 '87 C.918 B.A. L.1066 J.D. [[A] Dickstein S.M.&O.]
*PRACTICE AREAS: Civil and Environmental Litigation.
Miller, Christopher G. '64 '92 C.951 B.A. L.477 J.D.
(adm. in MD; not adm. in DC) 1350 I St., N.W., Suite 700
Miller, Craig D .... '71 '97 C.347 B.A. L.273 J.D. [[A] Cohen&C.]
*PRACTICE AREAS: Personal Injury; Medical Malpractice; Products Liability; Class Actions.
Miller, Daryl Anne .... '44 '79 C&L.329 B.S., J.D. Sr. Assoc. Gen. Coun., Howard Univ.
Miller, David L., (AV) .... '41 '68 C&L.477 A.B., LL.B. [Arter&H.]
Miller, Dean E. .... '— '60 C.221 B.A. L.309 LL.B. [[C] Kirkpatrick&L.]
*PRACTICE AREAS: Financial Institutions Law.
Miller, Deborah .... '65 '92 C.446 B.S. L.893 J.D. [[C] Fried,F.H.S.&J.] (Pat.)
*PRACTICE AREAS: Patents; Licensing; Intellectual Property; Corporate Law.
Miller, Devon Lee .... '53 '85 C.976 B.A. L.276 J.D. [[C] Kilpatrick S.]
*PRACTICE AREAS: Employee Benefits.
Miller, Donald '45 '72 C.216 A.B. L.188 J.D.
(adm. in PA; not adm. in DC) Sr. Coun., American National Red Cross
*RESPONSIBILITIES: Real Estate; Taxation; Employee Benefits; ERISA.
Miller, Edward Clifford '59 '86 C.706 B.A. L.564 J.D.
(adm. in NY; not adm. in DC) Nat'l Assn. of Realtors
Miller, Emily A. .... '71 '97 C.477 B.A. L.273 J.D. [[A] Hogan&H.]
*PRACTICE AREAS: Financial Institutions Law.
Miller, Emmett H. .... '68 '94 C&L.880 B.A., J.D. [[A] Kilpatrick S.]
*PRACTICE AREAS: Government Contracts; Commercial Litigation.
Miller, Eugene P. .... '37 '62 C.893 B.A. L.309 J.D. [Preston G.E.&R.M.]
*PRACTICE AREAS: Maritime and Shipping Regulation Law; Corporate Finance Law.
Miller, Evan, (AV) .... '56 '82 C.178 B.A. L.276 J.D. [Hogan&H.]
*PRACTICE AREAS: Employee Benefits.
Miller, Frances J. .... '50 '96 C.569 B.A. L.1356 J.D. [[A] Dickstein S.M.&O.]
*PRACTICE AREAS: Complex Dispute Resolution; Real Estate; Finance.
Miller, Frederick L., Jr., (AV) .... '43 '68 C.976 B.A. L.276 J.D. [[C] Duncan,W.G.&P.]
*PRACTICE AREAS: Natural Resources; Energy; Civil Litigation.
Miller, G. Daniel, (AV) '49 '74 C&L.880 B.A., J.D.
(adm. in TX; not adm. in DC) [Ice M.] (⊙Indpls., IN)
*PRACTICE AREAS: Employee Benefits Law; Federal Government Affairs.
Miller, Gail Suzanne .... '65 '91 C.184 B.S. L.904 J.D. Asst. Corp. Coun., D.C.
Miller, George W., (AV) .... '41 '66 C.674 B.A. L.309 LL.B. [Hogan&H.]
*PRACTICE AREAS: Litigation; Appellate Practice; Natural Resources; Environmental Law; Government Contracts.
Miller, Gerie A. .... '74 '99 C.30 B.A. L.904 J.D. [[A] Cole,R.&B.]
*PRACTICE AREAS: Telecommunications Law; Cable Communications; Administrative Law.
Miller, Gilbert C. .... '— '63 C.309 B.A. L.477 J.D. [Kirkpatrick&L.]
*PRACTICE AREAS: SEC Enforcement; Securities Litigation; Appellate Practice.
Miller, Glenn S. .... '67 '92 C.420 B.S. L.309 J.D. [Swidler B.S.F.]
*PRACTICE AREAS: Taxation.
Miller, Gordon L. '53 '80 C.813 A.B. L.145 J.D.
(adm. in TX; not adm. in DC) [[C] Hogan&H.]
*PRACTICE AREAS: Banking Regulation; Mergers and Acquisitions; Electronic Commerce.

Miller, H. Todd, (AV) .... '47 '71 C.107 B.A. L.228 J.D. [Hogan&H.]
*PRACTICE AREAS: Federal Income Tax; International Income Tax; Tax Controversies; Corporate Taxation.
Miller, Heather Leigh '70 '97 C.112 B.A. L.893 J.D.
Asst.Gen.Coun., Air Transport Assoc.of Amer.
*RESPONSIBILITIES: General Corporate; International Law.
Miller, Henry B. .... '51 '77 C.247 B.A. L.276 J.D. [Burt,M.&M.]
*PRACTICE AREAS: Tax Planning; Tax Controversy; Litigation.
Miller, Herbert D., Jr., (AV) '41 '66
C.976 B.A. L.893 LL.B. 1150 Connecticut Ave Nw # 1000‡
Miller, Herbert J., Jr., (AV) .... '24 '49 C&L.273 B.A., LL.B. [Baker B.]
Miller, J. Russell .... '66 '96 C&L.911 B.A., J.D. [[A] Orrick,H.&S.]
Miller, James D. .... '— '75 C.1275 B.A. L.976 J.D. [King&S.]
*PRACTICE AREAS: Litigation and Trade.
Miller, James Forrest .... '52 '78 C.197 B.A. L.178 J.D. [Hunton&W.]
*PRACTICE AREAS: Governmental Affairs.
Miller, James Robert, (AV) '26 '49 C&L.273 A.A., J.D.
(adm. in MD; not adm. in DC) [[C] Brault,G.S.&B.] (⊙Rockville, MD)
*PRACTICE AREAS: Personal Injury; Criminal Defense; Civil Litigation; Probate.
Miller, Jeffrey A. .... '74 '99 C.529 B.A. L.446 J.D. 1000 Independence Ave. S.W.
Miller, Jennifer Tetenbaum .... '— '00 C.518 B.A. L.276 J.D. [[A] Morgan,L.&B.]
Miller, Jerrold D., (AV) .... '42 '72 C.453 B.S. L.30 J.D. [Miller&M.]
Miller, Jessica D. .... '68 '96 C.178 B.A. L.276 J.D. [[A] O'Melveny&M.]
*PRACTICE AREAS: Litigation; Administrative Law.
Miller, John C. H., Jr., (AV) '44 '69
C.228 B.A. L.16 J.D. [Miller,H.S.O.&B.] (⊙Mobile, AL)
*PRACTICE AREAS: Bank Regulatory Law; Corporate Law; Financial Institutions; Mergers and Acquisitions; Complex Financial Institution Litigation.
Miller, John M. .... '37 '64 C.228 A.B. L.896 LL.B. [[C] Anderson&G.]
Miller, John T., (AV) '35 '65
C.835 B.A.Chem. L.273 J.D. [[C] Wenderoth,L.&P.] (See Pat. Sect.)
*PRACTICE AREAS: Patents; Chemical Patents; Pharmaceutical Patents; Interference Practice.

Miller, John T., Jr., (AV) '22 '49 C.156 A.B. L.276 J.D.
1001 Connecticut Avenue, N.W., 20036
Telephone: 202-331-1630 Fax: 202-331-3806
Email: jtmillerjr@erols.com
***PRACTICE AREAS: Federal Administrative Law; Energy Regulation.**
Practice before Federal Courts and Federal Administrative Agencies.
See Professional Biographies, WASHINGTON, DISTRICT OF COLUMBIA

Miller, Joseph F. '60 '90 C.999 B.S. L.564 J.D.
(adm. in NJ; not adm. in DC) [[A] Weil,G.&M.]
*PRACTICE AREAS: Real Estate.
Miller, Joseph S. '67 '95 C.724 B.A. L.597 J.D.
(adm. in MD; not adm. in DC) [[A] Sidley A.B.&W.]
Miller, Judith A. .... '50 '77 C.72 B.A. L.976 J.D. [Williams&C.]
*PRACTICE AREAS: Aerospace Technology; Antitrust; Complex Business Litigation; Computer Security; Constitutional Law.
Miller, Juliane C. .... '66 '92 C.1044 B.A. L.607 J.D. [Carter&C.] ⊙
*PRACTICE AREAS: Health Care Litigation; ERISA; Disabilities.
Miller, Juliane C. '66 '92 C.1044 B.A. L.607 J.D.
900 Seventeenth Street, N.W., Suite 900 (⊙Wash., DC; Alexandria, VA)
Miller, Julie Simon .... '67 '93 C.881 B.A. L.273 J.D. [[C] Covington&B.]
Miller, Karen J. .... '55 '87 C.273 B.B.A. L.276 J.D. [[A] Jordan K.&J.]
Miller, Karin M. '— '01 C&L.477 B.A., J.D.
(adm. in MD; not adm. in DC) [[A] Piper M.R.&W.]
*PRACTICE AREAS: Franchise Law.
Miller, Kevin M. .... '66 '96 C.886 B.A. L.128 J.D. [[A] Willkie F.&G.]
Miller, Kyle Vandeusen '74 '99 C.823 B.S. L.273 J.D.
(adm. in VA; not adm. in DC) Inspector Gen. Off., Dept. of Transportation
Miller, Laura Ariane .... '54 '88 C.477 B.A. L.976 J.D. [Nixon P.]
*PRACTICE AREAS: Litigation; Affordable Housing; Environmental Law; White Collar Crime.
Miller, Laura C. '72 '00 C.893 B.A. L.1209 J.D.
(adm. in UT; not adm. in DC) [[A] Howrey S.A.&W.]
*PRACTICE AREAS: Intellectual Property.
Miller, Lawrence A., (AV) .... '36 '60 C&L.665 A.B., LL.B. [Grossberg,Y.F.&B.]
Miller, Lawrence A. .... '46 '76 C.597 B.A. L.976 J.D. [Sidley A.B.&W.]
Miller, Lawrence M., (AV) .... '46 '73 C.216 A.B. L.273 J.D. [Schwartz,W.&M.]
Miller, Leonard A. .... '42 '67 C.1036 A.B. L.309 J.D. [Swidler B.S.F.]
*PRACTICE AREAS: Environmental Law; Pesticide Regulation; Water Pollution; Insurance Coverage.
Miller, Linda J. '56 '86 C.705 B.A. L.276 J.D.
Dep. Gen. Coun., Universal Service Admin. Co.
Miller, Lisa M. R. .... '66 '97 C.881 B.A. L.180 J.D. [[A] Dickstein S.M.&O.]
*PRACTICE AREAS: Civil Litigation.
Miller, Lynn I. .... '49 '77 C.788 B.A. L.904 J.D. [[C] Klimaski&G.]
*PRACTICE AREAS: Employment Law; Police Misconduct; Pension Rights Law; Civil Rights.
Miller, Marc E. .... '69 '95 C.976 B.A. L.273 J.D. [[A] Holland&K.]
*PRACTICE AREAS: Civil Litigation; Commercial Litigation; Real Estate Litigation.
Miller, Marc Eric, (AV) .... '47 '73 C.674 A.B. L.309 J.D. [McLeod,W.&M.]
*PRACTICE AREAS: Government Ethics; Corporate; Entertainment Law.
Miller, Margaret L. .... '64 '90 C.910 B.S. L.878 J.D. [Dow,L.&A.]
Miller, Mark A. .... '64 '99 C.880 B.A. L.276 J.D. [[A] Baker B.]
Miller, Mark Allison '64 '99 C.880 B.A. L.276 J.D.
(adm. in VA; not adm. in DC) 2555 M Street N.W.
Miller, Mark Edwin .... '60 '93 C.25 B.S. L.796 J.D. [[A] Greenberg T.]
Miller, Marshall Lee, (AV) .... '42 '71 C.309 B.A. L.976 J.D. [Baise&M.]
*PRACTICE AREAS: Environmental Law; International Law.
Miller, Marshall V., (AV) .... '— '71 C.502 B.A. L.893 J.D. [Miller] ⊙
*PRACTICE AREAS: International Trade Law; U.S. Foreign -Trade Zone Law; Customs Law; Government Relations Law.
Miller, Michael R. '46 '80 C.683 B.A. L.128 J.D.
(adm. in VA; not adm. in DC) 1220 19th St., N.W.
Miller, Michael Reed .... '44 '74 C.81 B.A. L.564 J.D. 1220 19th Street Nw, Suite 400
Miller, Mishelle C. .... '66 '91 C.38 B.S. L.880 J.D. Thompson Publishing Grp.
Miller, Montserrat C. .... '69 '97 C.1356 B.A. L.30 J.D. [[A] Pederson&F.]
Miller, N. Barr, (AV) .... '07 '38 C.504 B.S. L.597 J.D. 1801 K St., N.W.
Miller, Nicholas P., (AV) .... '44 '73 C&L.911 B.A., J.D. [Miller&V.]
*PRACTICE AREAS: International Joint Ventures; Privatization; Communications Law; Media Law; Cable Franchising.
Miller, Nory .... '— '89 C.821 B.A. L.178 J.D. [Jenner&B.]
*PRACTICE AREAS: First Amendment; Intellectual Property; Civil Litigation; Appellate Practice.
Miller, Paul J. .... '63 '93 C.1031 B.A. L.107 J.D. [[A] Ballard S.A.&I.]
*PRACTICE AREAS: Real Estate; Business; General Practice.
Miller, Paul M. '71 '98 C.575 B.S.B.A. L.823 J.D.
(adm. in VA; not adm. in DC) 1200 G St., N.W.
Miller, Paul M. .... '71 '98 C.575 B.S.B.A. L.823 J.D. [[A] Seward&K.]
*PRACTICE AREAS: Securities.
Miller, R. Charles .... '57 '86 C.309 B.A. L.659 J.D. [Shearman&S.]
Miller, Randall K. .... '63 '96 C.645 B.A. L.273 J.D. [[A] Arnold&P.]
*PRACTICE AREAS: Litigation; Constitutional Law.

Miller, Reed, (AV) . . . . '18 '41 C&L.923 A.B., LL.B. 555 12th St., N.W.
Miller, Richard Charles . . . . '— '86 C.309 B.A. L.659 J.D. [Kirkpatrick&L.]
*PRACTICE AREAS: Investment Company Law; Securities Regulation; Corporate Finance.
Miller, Richard W., Jr. . . . . '49 '78 C.25 B.A. L.276 J.D. 2000 M St. N.W.
Miller, Stephanie Gale . . . . '58 '85 C.1365 B.A. L.245 J.D. Asst. U.S. Atty.
Miller, Steven L. '64 '90 C.645 B.A. L.904 J.D.
(adm. in PA; not adm. in DC) [Ⓐ Dickstein S.M.&O.]★
*PRACTICE AREAS: Energy.
Miller, Thomas P. . . . . '64 '90 C.610 B.A. L.607 J.D. [Richter,M.&F.]
Miller, Victor J. . . . . '66 '93 C.976 B.A. L.945 J.D. [Howrey S.A.&W.]
*PRACTICE AREAS: Antitrust; Commercial Litigation; Products Liability.
Miller, W. Todd . . . . '60 '86 C.893 B.A. L.477 J.D. [Baker&M.P.]
Miller, Warren L., (AV) . . . . '44 '69 C.30 B.A. L.273 J.D. [W.L.Miller]
Miller, William L. . . . . '60 '92 C.951 B.A. L.588 J.D. [Ⓐ Goldstein&Assoc.]
*PRACTICE AREAS: Energy; Environmental Law; Litigation.
Miller, William T., (AV) . . . . '41 '66 C.674 A.B. L.893 LL.B. [Miller,B.&O.]
*PRACTICE AREAS: Electric Power; Electric Utilities; Municipal Utility Law; Natural Gas; Electric Cooperative Law.

Miller, Balis & O'Neil, P.C., (AV)
1140 Nineteenth Street, N.W. Suite 700, 20036
Telephone: 202-296-2960 Fax: 202-296-0166
URL: http://www.mbolaw.com
William T. Miller; Stanley W. Balis; Robert A. O'Neil; James R. Choukas-Bradley; John Michael Adragna; James H. Byrd; John P. Gregg; Sean T. Beeny; Susan N. Kelly; Randolph Lee Elliott; Joshua L. Menter; Benjamin L. Willey. Counsel: Linda K. Browning (Not admitted in DC); Milton J. Grossman; Mary A. Hekman;—Lisa M. Ochsenhirt (Not admitted in DC); Craig W. Silverstein; Phyllis G Kimmel.
Practice before Federal and State Regulatory Agencies, State and Federal Courts and Congress. Energy, Environmental, General Administrative Law, Governmental Affairs, Hydroelectric Licensing, International, Litigation, Maritime, Military, and Public Utilities.
See Professional Biographies, WASHINGTON, DISTRICT OF COLUMBIA

Miller, Canfield, Paddock and Stone, P.L.C. BB
A Professional Limited Liability Company
Founded in 1852 by Sidney Davy Miller
1900 K Street, N.W., Suite 1150, 20006 ⊙
Telephone: 202-429-5575 Fax: 202-331-1118
URL: http://www.millercanfield.com
Principals of Firm: John O. Renken (Not admitted in DC); Richard A. Walawender (Not admitted in DC). Of Counsel/Senior Counsel: Tillman L. Lay; David H. Jacobs; Randall E. Robertson; Cer Gladwyn Goins (Not admitted in DC); Steven C. Kahn.
Accounting Litigation, Administrative, Admiralty/Maritime, Antidumping, Antitrust, Appellate Practice, Banking, Bankruptcy & Reorganization, Commercial Transactions, Computer, Condemnation, Condominiums & Cooperatives, Construction Litigation, Corporate, Domestic Relations, Education, Emerging Business, Environmental, Estate Planning & Administration, Foundations & Nonprofit Organizations, Franchising, Health Care & Hospital, Immigration, Insurance, Intellectual Property, International Law, International Trade & Customs, Labor & Employment, Libel & Slander Litigation, Licensing & High Technology, Litigation & Alternative Dispute Resolution, Litigation Management, Mergers & Acquisitions, Municipal & School Finance & Bond Counsel, Nuclear Power Plant Litigation, Oil & Gas, Pension, Profit-Sharing & Employee Benefits, Product Liability Consulting & Defense, Professional Malpractice Consulting & Defense, Public Law, Real Estate Development & Investment, Securities (Corporate & Municipal), Securities Litigation, State, Finance & Bond Counsel, Taxation, Tax-Exempt Financing, Telecommunications, Toxic Torts Litigation, Transportation, Utilities, Zoning.
Detroit, Michigan Office: 150 West Jefferson, Suite 2500, 48226-4415. Telephone: 313-963-6420. Fax: 313-496-7500. Cable Address: "Stem Detroit."
Ann Arbor, Michigan Office: 101 North Main Street, 7th Floor, 48104-1400. Telephone: 734-663-2445. Fax: 734-747-7147.
Grand Rapids, Michigan Office: 99 Monroe, N.W., Suite 1200, 49503-2639. Telephone: 616-454-8656. Fax: 616-776-6322.
Howell, Michigan Office: 121 South Barnard Street, Suite 7, 48843-2305. Telephone: 517-546-7600. Fax: 517-546-6974.
Kalamazoo, Michigan Office: 444 West Michigan Avenue, 49007-3751. Telephone: 616-381-7030. Fax: 616-382-0244.
Lansing, Michigan Office: Suite 900, One Michigan Avenue, 48933-1609. Telephone: 517-487-2070. Fax: 517-374-6304.
Monroe, Michigan Office: 214 East Elm Avenue, Suite 100, 48162-2682. Telephone: 734-243-2000. Fax: 734-243-0901.
Troy, Michigan Office: 840 West Long Lake Road, Suite 200, 48098-6358. Telephone: 248-879-2000. Fax: 248-879-2001.
Pensacola, Florida Office: 25 West Cedar Street, Suite 500, 32501. Telephone: 850-469-1088. Fax: 850-432-0677.
New York, New York Office: 1450 Broadway, 41st Floor, 10018. Telephone: 212-704-4400. Fax: 212-704-4410.
Gdynia, Poland Office: ul. Batorego 28-32, 81-366. Telephone: 011 (48-58) 782-0200. Fax: 011 (48-58) 782-0201.
Warsaw, Poland Office: ul. Nowogrodzka 11, 5th Floor, 00-513. Telephone: 011 (48-22) 529-0200. Fax: 011 (48-22) 529-0201.
Katowice, Poland Office: ul. Francuska 35/37, 40-027. Telephone: 011 (48-32) 757-2414. Fax: 011 (48-32) 757-2483.
Revisers of the Michigan Law Digest for this Directory
See Professional Biographies, WASHINGTON, DISTRICT OF COLUMBIA

Miller & Chevalier, Chartered, (AV)
Established 1920
655 Fifteenth Street, N.W., Suite 900, 20005-5701
Telephone: 202-626-5800 Fax: 202-628-0858
Email: inquiries@milchev.com URL: http://www.millerchevalier.com
Members: Stuart Chevalier (1879-1956); Robert Netherland Miller (1879-1968); Richard H. Abbey (Not admitted in DC); James B. Altman; John D. Bates; Dennis P. Bedell; James A. Bensfield; Leonard Bickwit, Jr.; David B. Blair; Michael D. Campbell; Jay L. Carlson; Catherine L. Creech; David B. Cubeta; Joel Davidow; F. Amanda DeBusk; Peter D. Ehrenhaft; F. David Foster; Lawrence B. Gibbs; Robert E. Herzstein; Alan I. Horowitz; Peter B. Hutt II; Thomas D. Johnston; Kevin L. Kenworthy; Philip Karter; Clarence T. Kipps, Jr.; Peter J. Koenig (Not admitted in DC); Emmett B. Lewis; Robert E. Liles, II; Lucinda A. Low; Daniel W. Luchsinger; Phillip L. Mann; Samuel M. Maruca; Charles F. B. McAleer, Jr.; William M. McGlone; Robert L. Moore, II; Homer E. Moyer, Jr.; Matthew M. Nolan; Herbert Odell (Not admitted in DC); Lynda Troutman O'Sullivan; C. Frederick Oliphant III; Jean A. Pawlow; Scott E. Pickens; John Lloyd Rice; Frederick H. Robinson; Steven M. Rosenthal; Hal S. Shapiro; Anthony F. Shelley; Serena Gray Simons; Sturgis M. Sobin; Mary Lou Soller; Patricia J. Sweeney; Anthony J. Trenga; Joel C. Weiss (Not admitted in DC); Alexander Zakupowsky, Jr.; David W. Zimmerman (Not admitted in DC). Of Counsel: Charles T. Akre; John C. Chiu (Not admitted in DC); Terry Bancroft Dowd; A. John Gabig; Philip S. Neal; David W. Richmond; Numa L. Smith, Jr. Counsel: Kathryn Cameron Atkinson; Michael T. Brady; Paul Cherecwich, Jr.; Mitchell W. Dale; John E. Davis; Janet A. Forest; David R. Hamill (Not admitted in DC); George A. Hani; Mark van Dyke Holmes; Maria O'Toole Jones; John S. Levin (Not admitted in DC); Joel W. Rogers; Jeri Kaylene Somers. Senior Associates: Josephine Aiello LeBeau; Marjorie A. Burnett; Michael L. Burton; Anne E. Collier; Jeannette Dayan (Not admitted in DC); Jacqueline de Gramont; Patrick P. de Gravelles; Adam P. Feinberg; Myles S. Getlan; Shane T. Hamilton; Brian A. Hill; Zion Levi; Sarah M. Nappi; Robin H. Villanueva. Associates: Charles F. Abernathy (Not admitted in DC); Tamara W. Ashford (Not admitted in DC); Thomas E. Coony; Leonard Jon Cooperman; Charles F. De Jager; William C. Elwell (Not admitted in DC); Jeanne K. Falstrom (Not admitted in DC); Kimberly R. Heifetz; Alicia D. Lomba; William A. MacDonald; Sasha A. Mason (Not admitted in DC); Sydney H. Mintzer; Ragan G. Reeves; Matthew Reinhard (Not admitted in DC); Elizabeth Robitschek; David A. Roman; Kara N. Schmidt; Kristen Smith; Duncan N. Stevens; James G. Tillen; Christine S. Trafford (Not admitted in DC); Adam B. Walker; Jeffrey C. Walker; Lori B. Wittlin. Foreign Consultant: Jose De Reyes (Not admitted in DC).
Taxation: Federal Taxation, International Taxation, Tax Planning, Tax Litigation, Tax Appeals, Tax Audits, Tax Controversies, Federal Tax Legislation. Government Contracts: Bid Protests, Government Contract Fraud, Government Procurement, Public Contract Law, False Claims Act, Qui Tam Litigation, Legislative Practice, Information Technology Contracts, Government Construction Con-

(This Listing Continued)

Miller & Chevalier, Chartered (Continued)
tracts, Health Care Contracts, Health Care Fraud, Health Care Litigation, Health Insurance, Managed Care, and Medicare Fraud and Abuse. Litigation: Federal Litigation, Complex Litigation, Complex Commercial Litigation, RICO, White Collar Crime, Administrative Litigation, Antitrust, Patent Litigation, Federal Administrative Law, Trial Practice and U.S. Supreme Court Litigation. International Trade: International Law, International Trade Regulation, International Dispute Resolution, International Intellectual Property, Foreign Corrupt Practices Act, North American Free Trade Agreement, Import and Export Law, and Foreign Trade Sanctions.
See Professional Biographies, WASHINGTON, DISTRICT OF COLUMBIA

Miller & Company P.C., (AV) BB
1825 I Street, N.W., Suite 400, 20006 ⊙
Telephone: 202-429-2017 Fax: 202-659-6848
Email: intllaw@millerco.com URL: http://www.millerco.com
Marshall V. Miller. Of Counsel: Thomas L. Lobred.
International Trade, Customs and Foreign-Trade Zone Law.
Kansas City, Missouri Office: 4929 Main Street, 64112. Telephone: 816-561-4999. Fax: 816-561-5999.
New York, N.Y. Office: 51st Floor, 233 Broadway, 10279. Telephone: 212-608-2707. Fax: 212-513-7206.
See Professional Biographies, WASHINGTON, DISTRICT OF COLUMBIA

Miller, Hamilton, Snider, Odom & Bridgeman, L.L.C., (AV)
Suite 200, 1925 K Street, N.W., 20006 ⊙
Telephone: 202-429-9223 Telecopier: 202-331-0388
Members of Firm: Lester M. Bridgeman; Palmer C. Hamilton (Not admitted in DC); John C. H. Miller, Jr.; Ronald A. Snider (Not admitted in DC). Of Counsel: Lewis G. Odom, Jr.
Administrative, Admiralty, Antitrust, Aviation, Banking, Bank Regulation, Corporations, Energy, ERISA, Litigation, Securities, Taxation, Transportation and International Trade.
Mobile, Alabama Office: Miller, Hamilton, Snider & Odom, L.L.C., 254-256 State Street. P.O. Box 46. Telephone: 251-432-1414. Telecopier: 251-433-4106.
Montgomery, Alabama Office: Miller, Hamilton, Snider & Odom, L.L.C., Suite 305, One Commerce Street. Telephone: 334-834-5550. Telecopier: 334-265-4533.
See Professional Biographies, WASHINGTON, DISTRICT OF COLUMBIA

Miller & Miller, P.C., (AV) . . . . 1990 M St., N.W.

Miller Thomson Wickens & Lebow LLP, (AV) BB
Suite 610, 1919 Pennsylvania Avenue, N.W., 20006 ⊙
Telephone: 202-775-2400 Telecopier: 202-331-7538
Email: Washington@millerthomson.com
Members of Firm: William E. Wickens; Edward M. Lebow. Of Counsel: Joseph S. Hoover, Jr.; Beverly D. Ross.
Commercial Litigation in all Federal Courts. International Trade and Customs. Administrative Practice before Federal Agencies.
Edmonton, Alberta Office: Miller Thomson, Suite 2700 Commerce Place, 10155 102nd Street, Edmonton, Alberta, T5J 4G8. Telephone: 780-429-1751. Fax: 780-424-5866.
Toronto, Ontario Office: Miller Thomson, 20 Queen Street West, Suite 2500, Toronto, Ontario, M5H 3S1. Telephone: 416-595-8500. Fax: 416-595-8695.
York Region, Ontario Office: Miller Thomson, 60 Columbia Way, Suite 600, Markham, Ontario, L3R 0C9. Telephone: 905-415-6700. Fax: 905-415-6777.
Calgary, Alberta Office: Miller Thomson, 3000, 700 - 9th Avenue S.W., Calgary, Alberta, T2P 3V4. Telephone: 403-298-2400. Fax: 403-262-0007.
Law Firm Affiliations/Associations:
Priel, Stevenson, Hood & Thornton, Saskatoon, Saskatchewan
McCarter Grespan Robson Beynon - Kitchener, Ontario
Azevedo Sette Advogados - Sao Paulo and Belo Horizonte, Brazil, South America
Estudio Faraggi, Sateler & CIA - Santiago, Chile
Davies Arnold Cooper - London, England (Offices also in Manchester, Brussels, Vienna, Zurich, Madrid and Hong Kong)
Schürmann & Partners - Germany (Offices in Frankfurt, Berlin, Bonn, Dresden, Leipzig, Munich, Brussels, Milan, New York, Paris and Prague)

CONTACT: JOHN A. PETERS. Telephone: 403-298-2434. E-mail: jpeters@millerthomson.ca.
See Professional Biographies, WASHINGTON, DISTRICT OF COLUMBIA

Miller & Van Eaton, P.L.L.C., (AV) BB
1155 Connecticut Avenue, N.W., Suite 1000, 20036-4320 ⊙
Telephone: 202-785-0600 Fax: 202-785-1234
Email: info2@millervaneaton.com URL: http://www.millervaneaton.com
Nicholas P. Miller; Joseph Van Eaton; William R. Malone; Frederick E. Ellrod III; Matthew C. Ames; William L. Lowery (Resident, San Francisco, California Office). Of Counsel: James R. Hobson; Gerard L. Lederer (Not admitted in DC). Associates: Marci Lynn Frischkorn (Not admitted in DC); Mitsuko R. Herrera (Not admitted in DC); Kenneth A. Brunetti (Resident, San Francisco, California Office); Holly Lynn Saurer (Not admitted in DC).
Administrative, Business, Legislative and Litigation Practice in Telecommunications including: Cable Television and Electronic Media (franchise renewal, rate regulation, transfers, municipal system ownership, and public, educational and government (PEG) services), Telephone, Common Carrier and Wireless Services, Broadcasting, Satellite and New Technology Licensing, Consumer Protection and Fair Competition, Financing and Joint Ventures, and Privatization. Additional specialties include First Amendment, Constitutional Law, Intellectual Property Law, Public Utilities Law, Real Estate Law, State Tax Law, Transportation Law and Bankruptcy Law.
San Francisco, California Office: 400 Montgomery Street, Suite 501, 94104. Telephone: 415-477-3650. Fax: 415-477-3652.
See Professional Biographies, WASHINGTON, DISTRICT OF COLUMBIA

Miller, Warren L., P.C., (AV) . . . . 2300 N Street, N.W.
Millhauser, Marguerite S., (AV) . . . . '53 '77 C&L.446 B.S., J.D. 1614 20th St., N.W.
Millian, John C. . . . . '58 '84 C.1375 B.A. L.976 J.D. [Gibson,D.&C.]
*PRACTICE AREAS: Complex and Multi-District Litigation; Class Actions; Securities; Banking.
Millian, Kathleen L. '60 '86 C.188 B.S. L.813 J.D. 1121 12th St., N.W.
Milligan, David H. '74 '99 C.546 B.S. L.273 J.D.
(adm. in VA; not adm. in DC) [Ⓐ Hunton&W.]
*PRACTICE AREAS: Patent Prosecution.
Milligan, Susan . . . . '58 '85 C.216 B.A. L.904 J.D. N.Y. Stock Exchange
Milliken, Stephen . . . . '51 '78 C.309 B.A. L.1162 J.D. Supr. J.
Millman, Diane S. . . . . '55 '81 C.264 B.A. L.309 J.D. [Powers,P.S.&V.]
*PRACTICE AREAS: Health Law.
Millonig, Robert C. . . . . '61 '94 C.433 B.S. L.273 J.D. [Ⓐ Sterne,K.G.&F.]
*PRACTICE AREAS: Intellectual Property Law.
Mills, Brady W. . . . . '— '98 C.445 B.S. L.276 J.D. [Ⓐ Kaye S.]
*PRACTICE AREAS: International Trade; Litigation.
Mills, Charles R. . . . . '— '77 C.605 B.A. L.276 J.D. [Kirkpatrick&L.]
*PRACTICE AREAS: Securities Litigation; SEC Enforcement; Securities Arbitration; Securities Regulation; Commodities Regulation.
Mills, Christopher A. . . . . '43 '68 C.31 B.A. L.477 J.D. [Slover&L.]
Mills, David E., (AV) . . . . '60 '86 C.1036 B.A. L.228 J.D. [Dow,L.&A.]
Mills, J. Kevin . . . . '66 '93 C.309 A.B. L.145 J.D. [Ⓐ Dow,L.&A.]
Mills, John L. '26 '49 C.1365 A.B. L.245 LL.B.
(adm. in GA; not adm. in DC) 5844 Eastern Ave., NE‡
Mills, Laurin H. . . . . '57 '89 C.446 B.S. L.276 J.D. [Nixon P.]
*PRACTICE AREAS: Litigation; White Collar Crime; Intellectual Property Litigation; Internet and Media Law.
Mills, Sherylle '69 '95 C.999 B.M. L.1066 J.D.
(adm. in CA; not adm. in DC) Smithsonian Institution
Mills, Thomas L. . . . . '48 '75 C.869 B.S. L.273 J.D. [Winston&S.]
*PRACTICE AREAS: Health Care; Maritime Law.
Mills, Timothy B. . . . . '51 '86 C.112 B.A. L.1065 J.D. [Patton B.]

Mills, Wilfred T., Jr. '57 '83 C.1102 B.A. L.884 J.D.
(adm. in PA; not adm. in DC)
Assoc. Gen. Coun., Tort Claims and Lit., National Railroad Passenger Corp. (AMTRAK)
Millstein, Larry S. ....'50 '94 C.563 B.S. L.1356 J.D. 3050 K St., NW (Pat.)
Milner, Claire A. '70 '97 C.105 B.A. L.128 J.D.
(adm. in CA; not adm. in DC) [Ⓐ Brustein&M.]
*PRACTICE AREAS: Education Law; Federal Legislative Practice; Government Relations.
Milner, Jean A. '67 '96 C&L.999 B.A., J.D.
(adm. in NY; not adm. in DC) [Ⓐ Baker&M.]
*PRACTICE AREAS: Corporate and Partnership Law; Securities and Financial Products.
Milner, Marylin Jenkins, (AV) ....'50 '79 C.914 B.A. L.426 J.D. [Manatt,P.&P.]
Milon, Patricia A. .... '63 '88 C.197 A.B. L.880 J.D. V.P., Dep. Gen. Coun., Fannie Mae
*RESPONSIBILITIES: Financial Institutions (Regulatory and Legislative).
Milone, Richard D., Jr. ....'65 '92 C.602 B.A. L.276 J.D. [Gilbert H.&R.]
*PRACTICE AREAS: Insurance Coverage; Antitrust; Commercial Litigation.
Milstein, Elliott S. ....'44 '69 C.1033 B.A. L.184 J.D. Dean, Wash. Coll. Law
Milstein, Herbert E., (AV) ....'36 '61 C.309 A.B. L.178 LL.B. [Cohen,M.H.&T.]
*PRACTICE AREAS: Complex and Multi-District Litigation; Securities Fraud Class Actions; Securities Litigation.
Miltenberg, Ned I. .....'50 '86 C.188 B.A. L.477 J.D. Assoc. of Trial Lawyers of America
Milton, Michael J. ....'37 '64 C&L.309 B.A., LL.B. [Ⓒ Krooth&A.]
Mims, Buffy Joann ....'68 '99 C.831 B.A. L.276 J.D. 555 12th Street, NW
Mims, Jerry '62 '90 C.475 B.A. L.276 J.D.
Asst. Gen. Coun., United Mine Workers of Amer. Health & Retirement Funds
Mims, M. Elizabeth '— '98 C.790 B.A. L.880
(adm. in GA; not adm. in DC) [Ⓐ King&S.]
Min, Byung Joon ....'71 '98 C&L.893 B.S., J.D. [Ⓐ Akin,G.S.H.&F.]
Mincavage, Karen M. .... '67 '92 C.477 B.S. L.575 J.D. [Ⓒ Wilmer,C.&P.]
*PRACTICE AREAS: Securities Law.
Mincberg, Elliot M., (AV) '52 '77
C.597 B.A. L.309 J.D. Legal Dir., People for the American Way
Miner, Michael R. ....'73 '98 C.477 B.A. L.273 J.D. [Ⓐ Spriggs&H.]
*PRACTICE AREAS: Government Contracts; Federal Claims; Litigation.
Minesinger, Kenneth M. ....'65 '91 C.446 B.A. L.273 J.D. [Morrison&F.]
*PRACTICE AREAS: Energy Regulation; Natural Gas Pipelines; Antitrust.
Minikes, Stephan M., (AV) ....'38 '65 C.188 B.S. L.976 J.D. [Thelen R.&P.]
*PRACTICE AREAS: Administrative Law; Government Contract Law; International Trade Law; Legislative Practice.
Mink, Jennifer J. ....'71 '96 C.1356 B.S. L.893 J.D. [Ⓐ Clifford C.R.&W.]
*PRACTICE AREAS: Corporate.
Minkoff, Jon F. ... '72 '99 C.293 B.A. L.1194 J.D. 4545 Connecticut Avenue NW, Apt. 30
Minnick, Phillip A. '71 '00 C.446 B.A. L.273 J.D.
(adm. in NJ; not adm. in DC) [Ⓐ Kirkpatrick&L.]
*PRACTICE AREAS: Investment Company Law; Investment Management; Securities.
Minogue, James S., III '54 '80 C.1031 B.A. L.178 J.D.
Assoc. Gen. Coun., Watson Wyatt Worldwide
Minor, Edward T. ....'29 '63 C.976 A.B. L.326 LL.B. 115 5th St., N.E.‡
Minor, William H. ....'— '95 C.860 B.A. L.178 J.D. [Ⓐ Verner,L.B.M.&H.]
*PRACTICE AREAS: Legislative; Federal Matters; Political Law.
Minshew, Nicholas C. '— '00 C.289 B.A. L.30 J.D.
(adm. in MD; not adm. in DC) [Ⓐ Morgan,L.&B.]
Minsker, Helen Hill, (AV) '— '88 C.881 A.B. L.273 J.D.
[Banner&W.] (See Pat. Sect.)
*PRACTICE AREAS: Intellectual Property Law; Trademarks; Copyrights; Intellectual Property Litigation.
Minsker, Martin D., (AV) ....'42 '69 C.188 B.S. L.309 J.D. [Baker B.]
Minsky, Kevin D. ....'69 '98 C.911 B.A. L.823 J.D. [Ⓒ Swidler B.S.F.]
*PRACTICE AREAS: Telecommunications; Internet Law.
Minton, David ....'34 '62 C.586 B.A. L.846 LL.B. 1211 Connecticut Ave.
Mintz, Alan L., (AV) ....'49 '74 C.477 B.A. L.976 J.D. [Van Ness F.]
*PRACTICE AREAS: Public Lands; Alaska Natives; Energy; Natural Resources.
Mintz, Herbert H., (AV) '46 '72
C.186 B.Ch.E. L.273 J.D. [Finnegan,H.F.G.&D.] (See Pat. Sect.)
*PRACTICE AREAS: Patent Interference Practice; Patent Litigation.
Mintz, M. J., (AV) ....'40 '69 C&L.831 B.S., J.D. [Dickstein S.M.&O.]
*PRACTICE AREAS: Employee Benefit Law; ERISA; Tax Controversies Law; Business Planning.
Mintz, Michael J. ....'60 '86 C&L.893 B.S., J.D. 1133 19th St. N.W.
Mintz, Seymour S., (AV) ....'12 '36 C&L.273 A.B., J.D. [Ⓒ Hogan&H.]
*PRACTICE AREAS: Taxation Law.
Mintz, Steven J. ....'62 '89 C.674 A.B. L.309 J.D. [Ⓐ Jones,D.R.&P.]

Mintz, Levin, Cohn, Ferris, Glovsky and Popeo, P.C., (AV) BR
701 Pennsylvania Avenue, N.W., 20004-2608 ⊙
Telephone: 202-434-7300 Fax: 202-434-7400 Internet: Each Attorney's Internet Address takes the following form: first initial, last name @mintz.com (e.g., rmintz@mintz.com)
URL: http://www.mintz.com
Francis X. Meaney; Charles D. Ferris; Nathan Lewin; William C. Brashares; Frank W. Lloyd; Raymond D. Cotton; Harvey I. Saferstein; Hope S. Foster; Thomas M. Antone, IV; Bruce D. Sokler; Alvin J. Lorman; James L. Casserly; Benjamin J. Griffin; Peter M. Kazon; Charles Alan Samuels; Howard J. Symons; Bradley L. Kelly; Russell H. Fox; David N. Baumann; Richard M. Graf; Susan W. Berson (Not admitted in DC); Christopher J. Harvie; Susan L. Burke; Cherie R. Kiser; Sara F. Leibman; William A. Davis; Erin M. Falk (Not admitted in DC); Linda K. McLeod; Michael H. Pryor; Laura J. Oberbroeckling; James J. Valentino.
Administrative, Antitrust and Trade, Banking, Business Law, Cable Programming, Class Actions, College and University Law, Communications, Copyright Litigation, Copyrights, Corporate Law, Environmental, FCC Regulation, Federal Education Grants, Federal Practice, Finance, Food and Drug, Government, Health Care, Health Care Fraud, Health Care Legislation, Health Care Mergers and Acquisitions, Health Care Reimbursement, Intellectual Property, International, Internet Law, Investments, Legislation, Litigation, Medicare and Medicaid Reimbursement, Mergers and Acquisitions, Municipal Bonds, Real Estate, Regulatory Law, Satellite Communications, Securities, Technology Business Startups, Technology Finance, Telecommunications, Telemedicine, Trademarks, Venture Capital, Wireless Communications.
Boston, Massachusetts Office: One Financial Center. Telephone: 617-542-6000. Fax: 617-542-2241.
New York, N.Y. Office: Chrysler Center, 666 Third Avenue. Telephone: 212-935-3000. Fax: 212-983-3115.
New Haven, Connecticut Office: 157 Church Street. Telephone: 203-777-8200. Fax: 203-777-7111.
Reston, Virginia Office: One Fountain Square, 11911 Freedom Drive. Telephone: 703-464-4800. Fax: 703-464-4895.
See Professional Biographies, WASHINGTON, DISTRICT OF COLUMBIA

Mintzer, Erica S. ....'68 '93 C.860 B.A. L.659 J.D. [Ⓐ Hogan&H.]
*PRACTICE AREAS: Antitrust.
Mintzer, Sydney H. ....'69 '98 C.112 L.569 J.D. [Ⓐ Miller&C.]
*PRACTICE AREAS: International Trade; Antidumping; Export Regulation; Foreign Asset Control; Customs Law.
Minutoli, Gianni ....'66 '98 C.1350 B.E.E.E. L.724 J.D. [Ⓐ Dickstein S.M.&O.]
*PRACTICE AREAS: Intellectual Property.
Mion, John H., (P.C.), (AV) '31 '58
C.705 B.S.E.E. L.273 J.D. [Sughrue M.] (See Pat. Sect.)
*PRACTICE AREAS: Intellectual Property Law.
Miossi, William G. ....'59 '85 C&L.276 B.S., J.D. [Winston&S.] (⊙Chgo., IL)
*PRACTICE AREAS: Labor and Employment.
Mir, Aimen '74 '00 C&L.276 B.S.F.S., J.D.
(adm. in VA; not adm. in DC) [Ⓐ Hale&D.]
Mirabelli, Mario V., (AV) ....'39 '66 C.276 B.A. L.904 J.D. [Patton B.]
Miraglia, Vincent J. '69 '95 C.818 B.A. L.128 J.D.
(adm. in GA; not adm. in DC) [Ⓐ McGuirewoods]
*PRACTICE AREAS: Employment Discrimination; Labor-Management Relations.
Miranda, Anthony L. ....'74 '00 C.911 B.A. L.94 J.D. [Ⓐ Hogan&H.]
Miranda, Carlos Ortiz '54 '83 C.677 B.A. L.1162 J.D.
Assoc. Gen. Coun., U.S. Catholic Conference
Mirbagheri, Ladan .... '62 '86 C.643 B.A. L.665 J.D. 1700 K St. N.W., Suite 903
Mirbagheri-Smith, Ladan ....'62 '87 C.643 B.A. L.665 J.D. [Carliner,R.&M.]
*PRACTICE AREAS: Immigration Law; Visas.
Mireles, Christina M. ....'71 '00 C.860 B.A. L.597 J.D. [Ⓐ Crowell&M.]
Mirengoff, Paul E. ....'49 '75 C.197 B.A. L.813 J.D. [Ⓒ Akin,G.S.H.&F.]
*PRACTICE AREAS: Labor and Employment; Litigation; Telecommunications.
Mirkow, Frank J. '65 '01 C.446 B.A. L.188 J.D.
(adm. in NY; not adm. in DC) [Ⓐ Shaw P.]
*PRACTICE AREAS: Corporate Law; International Trade.
Miron, George, (AV) ....'— '57 C.691 A.B. L.145 J.D. [Feith&Z.] (⊙Jerusalem, Israel)
Mirsky, Jonathan B. ....'68 '95 C.867 B.A. L.976 J.D. [Harris,W.&G.]
*PRACTICE AREAS: Communications.
Mirsky, Scott A. ....'72 '97 C.30 B.A. L.64 J.D. [Ⓐ Krupin O.]
*PRACTICE AREAS: Labor and Employment.
MirVahabi, Farin ....'44 '89 L.564 J.S.D. 1730 K St., N.W.
Mishalanie, Sonja A. '72 '00 C.188 B.S. L.446 J.D.
(adm. in VA; not adm. in DC) [Ⓐ Whiteford,T.&P.]
*PRACTICE AREAS: Civil Litigation; Condominium Association Law; Environmental Law.
Mishkin, Andrew E. ....'47 '75 C.309 A.B. L.276 J.D. [Duane,M.&H.]
*PRACTICE AREAS: Environmental Law; Real Estate Law; Regulatory Law; Commercial Law; Transactional Matters.
Mishkin, Barbara F., (AV) ....'36 '82 C.518 A.B. L.30 J.D. [Hogan&H.]
*PRACTICE AREAS: Administrative Agency Practice; Administrative Hearings and Appeals; Federal Administrative Law; False Claims Act; Federal Grants.
Misko, George G., (BV) ....'55 '80 C&L.128 B.A., J.D. [Keller&H.]
*PRACTICE AREAS: Food and Drug Law; Environmental Law; Trade Regulation Law.
Miskovsky, Milan C., (AV) '26 '57
C.477 B.S. L.273 LL.B. 5500 Chevy Chase Pkwy. N.W.
Missal, Michael J. ....'— '82 C.902 B.S. L.128 J.D. [Kirkpatrick&L.]
*PRACTICE AREAS: SEC Enforcement; Blue Sky Law; Broker-Dealer Regulation; Self Regulatory Agency Investment; Securities Arbitration.
Missing, John B. ....'56 '82 C&L.188 A.B., J.D. [Brobeck,P.&H.]
*PRACTICE AREAS: Securities Litigation; Commercial Litigation.
Mister, Steven M. '64 '89 C.445 B.S. L.945 J.D.
Assoc. Gen. Coun., Consumer Healthcare Products Association
Mistr, Christine Rushin ....'71 '98 C.692 B.S. L.893 J.D. [Ⓐ McKee N.]
*PRACTICE AREAS: Federal Taxation.
Mital, Manish K. ....'76 '00 C.453 S.B. L.309 J.D. [Ⓐ Williams&C.]
*PRACTICE AREAS: Litigation.
Mitchell, Allison ....'62 '91 C.788 A.B. L.477 J.D. Aspen Systems Corp.
Mitchell, Anne M. '— '85 C.999 B.L.Sc.
(adm. in NY; not adm. in DC) [Mitchell&D.]
*PRACTICE AREAS: Immigration Law; Visas; International Law.
Mitchell, Brent M. ....'69 '98 C.659 B.A. L.309 J.D. [Ⓐ Hale&D.]
*PRACTICE AREAS: Litigation.
Mitchell, Carol A., (AV) ....'57 '83 C.881 A.B. L.945 J.D. [Ⓒ Steptoe&J.]
*PRACTICE AREAS: International Trade and Customs Law.
Mitchell, Celeste Elizabeth '71 '99
C.155 B.A. L.1158 J.D. Sr. Assoc., PricewaterhouseCooper LLP
Mitchell, Charles P. '57 '86 C.939 A.B. L.309 J.D.
(adm. in OR; not adm. in DC) Center for Science in the Pub. Interest
Mitchell, Charles William '59 '94
C.870 B.S. L.1338 J.D. 3726 Connecticut Avenue, NW Apt. 504
Mitchell, Christopher H. ....'62 '88 C.309 B.A. L.276 J.D. [Stein,M.&M.]
Mitchell, Cleta Deatherage Mitchell, (AV) ......'— '76 C&L.623 B.A., J.D. [Foley&L.]
*PRACTICE AREAS: Public Affairs; Constitutional Law; Election, Campaign and Political Law.
Mitchell, David Cary ....'— '94 C.197 A.B. L.823 J.D. [Ⓐ Blooston,M.D.D.&P.]
*PRACTICE AREAS: Telecommunications; FCC Licensing; FCC Regulation; PCS.
Mitchell, Donald B., Jr. ....'54 '81 C.276 B.A. L.273 J.D. [Arent F.K.P.&K.]
*PRACTICE AREAS: Environmental Law; Hazardous Materials Law; Litigation; Toxic Torts.
Mitchell, Douglas B. ....'46 '72 C.546 B.S. L.273 J.D. [Bassman,M.&A.]
Mitchell, Douglas F. ....'48 '74 C.259 B.S. L.362 J.D. 5302 Colorado Ave NW
Mitchell, Elizabeth L. '71 '99 C.575 B.S. L.309 J.D.
(adm. in MA; not adm. in DC) [Ⓐ Wilmer,C.&P.]
Mitchell, George J., (AV) '— '60
C.95 B.A. L.276 J.D. [Ⓒ Verner,L.B.M.&H.] (⊙Port., ME)
Mitchell, George W. ....'35 '62 C&L.329 A.B., LL.B. Assoc. J., Supr. Ct. D.C.
Mitchell, Gerald L., (AV) ....'57 '85 C.976 B.A. L.145 J.D. [Arent F.K.P.&K.]
*PRACTICE AREAS: Commercial Real Estate; Commercial Real Estate Acquisitions; Commercial Real Estate Development; Commercial Real Estate Finance; Finance.
Mitchell, Gerard E., (AV) .... '44 '69 C.276 A.B. L.893 LL.B. [Stein,M.&M.]
*PRACTICE AREAS: Medical Malpractice; Personal Injury; Wrongful Death.
Mitchell, Glenn A., (AV) ....'36 '61 C.893 B.A. L.276 LL.B. [Stein,M.&M.]
*PRACTICE AREAS: Civil Litigation; Administrative Litigation; Antitrust; Trade Regulation.
Mitchell, Grant E. ....'— '65 C.1044 B.S. L.861 J.D. [Ⓒ Reed S.]
*PRACTICE AREAS: Financial Services.
Mitchell, James A. ....'12 '56 C.403 B.S. L.347 2816 Ga. Ave., N.W.
Mitchell, James K. ....'43 '71 C.188 B.S. L.336 J.D. [Thelen R.&P.]
*PRACTICE AREAS: Business; Finance.
Mitchell, Jeffrey A. ....'68 '96 C.597 B.A. L.209 J.D. [Ⓐ Sidley A.B.&W.]
Mitchell, Jeffrey A. ....'— '97 C.911 B.A. L.276 J.D. [Ⓐ Swidler B.S.F.]
*PRACTICE AREAS: Federal Civil Litigation; Administrative Litigation; Telecommunications.
Mitchell, John A. ....'40 '66 C.1115 B.A. L.276 J.D. 1400 Independence Avenue
Mitchell, John T. ....'52 '88 C.276 B.A. L.421 J.D. [Seyfarth S.]
*PRACTICE AREAS: First Amendment Law; Legislative Practice; Franchise and Distributorship Litigation; Trade Associations; Antitrust.
Mitchell, Larry H. ....'49 '74 C.390 A.B. L.276 J.D. [Ⓒ Schmeltzer,A.&S.]
*PRACTICE AREAS: Civil Litigation; Franchise Litigation.
Mitchell, Mary T. ....'69 '99 C.95 A.B. L.477 J.D. [Ⓐ Steptoe&J.]
Mitchell, Michael Hoyt ....'61 '87 C.1021 B.S. L.276 J.D. [Orrick,H.&S.]
Mitchell, Roy S., (AV) ....'34 '59 C.188 B.S. L.273 J.D. 1800 M St., NW
Mitchell, Samuel A. ....'65 '91 C.92 B.S. L.208 J.D. [Scribner,H.&T.]
Mitchell, Shelby F., (AV) ....'40 '82 C&L.446 B.S., J.D. [Baker&H.]
*PRACTICE AREAS: Family Law; Commercial Litigation; Trial.
Mitchell, T. L. .... '56 '87 C.1123 B.A. L.1162 J.D. 1730 K N.W., Suite 304
Mitchell, Thomas W. ....'63 '89 C.893 B.A. L.276 J.D. [Collier S.S.]
*PRACTICE AREAS: Litigation; Telecommunications.
Mitchell, William Gray, Jr. '69 '96 C&L.575 B.A., J.D.
(adm. in NC; not adm. in DC) [Ⓐ Counts,P.-D.&D.]

Mitchell and Dunn
818 18th Street, N.W., 20006
Telephone: 202-296-6844 Fax: 202-296-6855

(This Listing Continued)

Mitchell and Dunn (Continued)

Members of Firm: Anne M. Mitchell (Not admitted in DC); Thomas F. Dunn. Of Counsel: Robert F. Condon.
Immigration and Nationality and International Law, Criminal and Personal Injury Practice before Government Agencies. Trial, Appellate and Supreme Court Practice.

See Professional Biographies, WASHINGTON, DISTRICT OF COLUMBIA

Mitchell-Rankin, Zinora .... '56 '79 C.811 B.A. L.273 J.D. Supr. Ct. J.
Mitek, Mark M. .... '57 '86 C.879 B.A. L.1162 J.D. [Kass&S.]
Mitnick, Marcia R. .... '52 '82 C.966 B.A. L.276 J.D. [[C] Steptoe&J.]
*PRACTICE AREAS: Corporate; Securities; Technology Licensing.
Mittelberger, Ralph A., (AV) ... '45 '75 C.453 B.S. L.276 J.D. [Fish&R.] (See Pat. Sect.)
*PRACTICE AREAS: Intellectual Property; Litigation; International Trade Commission.
Mittendorff, Robert E. .... '46 '71 C.893 B.A.E. L.309 J.D. P.O. Box 70759
Mitterhoff, Daniel J. .... '62 '88 C.787 B.A. L.904 J.D. 1730 "K" St., N.W.
Mittler, Austin S., (AV) .... '39 '63 C.197 B.A. L.569 LL.B. [Hogan&H.]
*PRACTICE AREAS: Civil Litigation; White Collar Criminal Defense; Equine Law.
Mitzner, Ira R., (AV) .... '47 '73 C.103 B.A. L.276 LL.B. [Dickstein S.M.&O.]
*PRACTICE AREAS: ERISA; Labor (Employees) Law; Litigation.
Mixter, Christian J. .... '53 '78 C.608 B.A. L.228 J.D. [Morgan,L.&B.]
Mize, Gregory E. .... '46 '74 C.424 A.B. L.276 J.D. Supr. Ct. J.
Mizrack, Richard, (AV) .... '42 '67 C.145 B.A. L.178 J.D. [Mizrack&G.] ⊙
*PRACTICE AREAS: Corporate Law; Business Law; Mergers and Acquisitions Law; Transnational Business Law; Technology Transfers Law.

Mizrack & Gantt, (AV)
Suite 850, 555 11th Street, N.W., 20004-1304 ⊙
Telephone: 202-628-1717 Fax: 202-628-1919 Email: jbgantt@attglobal.net
Email: johngantt@aol.com
Members of Firm: Richard Mizrack; John B. Gantt.
Civil and Commercial Laws, Regulations and Policies related to Outer Space, International Trade and Commercial Matters, Public International Law, Commercial Law, Corporate Law, Business Law, Mergers and Acquisitions Law, Transactional Business Law, Technology Transfers Law and Trade Matters.
New York, New York Office: Park Avenue Tower, 31st Floor, 65 East 55th Street, 10022. Telephone: 212-418-0638. Fax: 212-308-5856.

See Professional Biographies, WASHINGTON, DISTRICT OF COLUMBIA

Mizroch, John F. '48 '75 C.893 B.A. L.945 J.D.
Exec. Dir., Environmental Export Council
Mizusawa, Bert K. .... '57 '90 C.870 B.S. L.309 J.D. 1701 Pennsylvania Ave., N.W.
Mlyniec, Wallace .... '45 '70 C.597 B.S. L.276 J.D. 600 New Jersey Ave.
Moates, G. Paul, (AV) .... '47 '75 C.31 B.A. L.145 J.D. [Sidley A.B.&W.]
Mobbs, Michael H. .... '48 '74 C.976 B.A. L.145 J.D. [Ludwig&R.]
*PRACTICE AREAS: International; Commercial Transactions; Corporate; Securities.
Mobedshahi, Katayoun .... '72 '97 C.347 B.S. L.74 J.D. 10 G St., N.E.
Mobley, Erika '68 '95 C.976 B.A. L.276 J.D.
(adm. in NJ; not adm. in DC) 1020 19th St., N.W.
Mode, Paul J., Jr., (AV) .... '38 '68 C.188 B.M.E. L.309 LL.B. [Wilmer,C.&P.]
*PRACTICE AREAS: Civil Practice.
Modell, Edward G., (AV) .... '46 '74 C.976 B.A. L.893 J.D. [[C] Dickstein S.M.&O.]
*PRACTICE AREAS: Administrative Law; Litigation; State and Federal Grants Law.
Modhera, Gazal Gulam-Mohmed '73 '98
C.276 B.A. L.904 J.D. Equal Employment Opportunity Comm.
Modhera, Prufesh R. .... '— '99 C.705 B.A. L.904 J.D. [[A] Morgan,L.&B.]
Modi, David T. '54 '80 C.352 B.A. L.575 J.D.
(adm. in PA; not adm. in DC) Sr. Dir., Georgia-Pacific Corporation
Modrall, James R. '58 '87 C.813 B.A.S. L.477 J.D.
(adm. in NY; not adm. in DC) [Cleary,G.S.&H.]
Moeiny, Nadá Melissa '75 '00 C.1375 B.A. L.174 J.D.
(adm. in CO; not adm. in DC) [[A] Schmeltzer,A.&S.]
*PRACTICE AREAS: Labor and Employment.
Moeller, Elizabeth C. .... '70 '96 C.112 B.A. L.1068 J.D. [[A] Patton B.]
Moeller, James W., (BV) .... '58 '85 C.393 B.A. L.309 J.D. [Brunenkant&H.]
*PRACTICE AREAS: Energy Law; Environmental Law; Utility Law.
Moeller, Jeffrey E. .... '63 '88 C.645 B.A. L.276 J.D. [Ivins,P.&B.]
*PRACTICE AREAS: Business Taxation; Corporate Taxation; Federal Tax; Partnerships.
Moerman, Samuel H., (AV) .... '13 '34 L.273 J.D. [[C] LaRoe,W.M.&D.]
Moetell, Michael C. .... '61 '85 C.884 B.S. L.309 J.D. [Shaw P.]
*PRACTICE AREAS: Commercial Tax.
Moffatt, J. Curtis, (AV) .... '51 '77 C.228 B.A. L.575 J.D. [Van Ness F.]
*PRACTICE AREAS: Administrative Law; Energy; Natural Gas; Petroleum.
Moffitt, William B., (AV) '49 '75 C.623 B.A. L.904 J.D.
(adm. in VA; not adm. in DC) [Asbill,J.M.&B.]
*PRACTICE AREAS: Criminal Law; Civil Litigation; Constitutional Law; Appellate Litigation; Drugs and Narcotics.
Moga, Thomas T. .... '57 '85 C.477 B.A. L.734 J.D. [Powell,G.F.&M.] (Pat.)
*PRACTICE AREAS: Intellectual Property; International Business Law.
Mogel, William A., (AV) .... '42 '67 C.319 B.A. L.659 LL.B. [Squire,S.&D.]
*PRACTICE AREAS: Energy.
Moghadam, Sara Z. '— '98 C.105 B.A. L.446 J.D.
(adm. in MD; not adm. in DC) [[A] Piper M.R.&W.]
*PRACTICE AREAS: Business Litigation; Securities Litigation.
Mogilnicki, Eric J., (AV) .... '60 '86 C&L.976 B.A., J.D. [Wilmer,C.&P.]
*PRACTICE AREAS: Civil Practice; Securities; Litigation; Banking.
Mogin, Paul .... '56 '81 C.674 B.A. L.309 J.D. [Williams&C.]
*PRACTICE AREAS: Appellate Practice; Civil Litigation; Class Actions; Criminal Appeals; U.S. Supreme Court Litigation.
Mogle, James R. .... '44 '74 C.597 B.S. L.904 J.D. [Mayer,B.&P.]
Mohanty, Nihar R. .... '67 '92 C.446 B.A. L.339 J.D. [Vorys,S.S.&P.]
Mohler, Paul B. '— '93 C.763 A.B. L.1209 J.D.
(adm. in VA; not adm. in DC) [[C] Heller E.W.&M.]
Mohler, Shaun C. .... '67 '95 C.893 B.A. L.30 J.D. [[A] Brickfield B.R.&S.]
*PRACTICE AREAS: Energy; Litigation.
Mohr, Andrew J. .... '54 '80 C.860 B.A. L.273 J.D. [Cohen M.]
*PRACTICE AREAS: Corporate Law; Business Law; Computers and Software Contracts; Government Contracts; Commercial Law.
Mohr, Brian C. .... '49 '79 C.1044 B.A. L.1040 J.D. [[C] Skadden,A.S.M.&F.]
Mohr, Christopher A. .... '69 '96 C.311 B.A. L.128 J.D [Meyer&K.]
*PRACTICE AREAS: Copyrights; Electronic Commerce; Trademarks; Unfair Competition.
Mohrman-Gillis, Marilyn, (AV) '49 '79 C.741 B.A. L.128 J.D.
V.P., Policy & Legal Affs., Association of American Public Television Stations
Mohsen, Arya A. .... '68 '94 C.95 A.B. L.823 J.D. [Maloney&M.]
Mohtadi, Negin .... '67 '92 C.477 B.A. L.215 J.D. [[A] Keller&H.]
*PRACTICE AREAS: Environmental Law; Transactional Law; International Law.
Moir, Brian R., (AV) .... '45 '73 C.641 B.A. L.208 J.D. [Moir&H.]
*PRACTICE AREAS: Telecommunications Law; Communications Law; Antitrust Law; Administrative Law; International Law.

Moir & Hardman, (AV) [BB]
1015 18th Street, NW, Suite 800, 20036-5204
Telephone: 202-872-8680 Fax: 202-872-8698
Brian R. Moir; Kenneth E. Hardman.

(This Listing Continued)

Moir & Hardman (Continued)

Telecommunications and Information Services Law, Communication, Antitrust and Trade Regulation Law, Corporate and Commercial Litigation, Practice Before Administrative Agencies, Federal Courts and Legislative Bodies.

See Professional Biographies, WASHINGTON, DISTRICT OF COLUMBIA

Mok, Arthur C. .... '71 '97 C.178 A.B. L.273 J.D. [[A] Hogan&H.]
*PRACTICE AREAS: Corporate; Securities; Private Equity; Emerging Company Transactions.
Mola, Elena C. '61 '90 C.469 B.A. L.276 J.D.
(adm. in FL; not adm. in DC) 1440 New York Ave., N.W.
Moldowan, Laura G. .... '64 '94 C.886 B.S. L.260 J.D. [Margolius,M.D.R.&T.]
*PRACTICE AREAS: Estate Planning; Estate Administration; Business Planning.
Molenkamp, Jack A., (AV) .... '52 '79 C.475 B.A. L.477 J.D. [Hunton&W.]
*PRACTICE AREAS: Corporate Law; Securities; Project Finance.
Molina, Joseph C. '48 '73 C&L.37 B.A., J.D.
(adm. in AZ; not adm. in DC) 1126 E. Capitol St.‡
Moll, Peter E., (AV) .... '49 '75 C&L.93 B.A., J.D. [Howrey S.A.&W.]
*PRACTICE AREAS: Antitrust; Complex Litigation; Litigation.
Mollen, Neal D. .... '56 '85 C.1090 B.S. L.692 J.D. [Paul,H.J.&W.]
*PRACTICE AREAS: Appellate Practice; Labor Law; Employment Law; Litigation; Reductions in Force.
Moller, Mark K. '71 '99 C.228 B.A. L.145 J.D.
(adm. in VA; not adm. in DC) [[A] Gibson,D.&C.]
Mollison, Richard M. .... '44 '69 C&L.629 B.A., J.D. [Shook,H.&B.]
*PRACTICE AREAS: Products Liability.
Mollo, Adrian P.J. .... '74 '99 C.956 B.A. L.790 J.D. [[A] Long A.&N.]
*PRACTICE AREAS: Information Technology; Corporate; Litigation.
Molloy, J. Brian, (AV) .... '43 '71 C.433 B.C.E. L.276 J.D. [Piper M.R.&W.]
*PRACTICE AREAS: Environmental Law.
Molloy, James Dennis .... '43 '83 C.524 B.S. L.1162 J.D. [Hanson&M.]
*PRACTICE AREAS: Corporate Law; Commercial Law; Insurance and Reinsurance; Antitrust; Trusts.
Molm, John R. .... '47 '73 C.579 B.A. L.276 J.D. [Troutman S.]
*PRACTICE AREAS: Energy Law and Hydropower Compliance and Licensing; Environmental Law; Railroad Transportation; Water Rights; Transportation.
Molnar, Jennifer Barbee '72 '01 C.112 B.A. L.1049 J.D.
(adm. in CA; not adm. in DC) [[A] Baker&M.]
*PRACTICE AREAS: Tax Planning and Advice (Corporate and International); Tax Controversies (Corporate and International); Estate and Personal Tax Planning.
Molofsky, Robert A. '50 '78 C.188 B.S. L.30 J.D.
Amalgamated Transit Union, AFL-CIO
Molot, David S. .... '69 '98 C.976 B.A. L.273 J.D. [[A] Wilmer,C.&P.]
Molster, Charles B., III .... '56 '84 C.893 B.A. L.692 J.D. [Winston&S.]
*PRACTICE AREAS: Commercial Litigation; Business Litigation; Employment Defense; Antitrust Litigation; Patent Litigation.
Mon, Gonzalo E. .... '73 '00 C.1376 B.A. L.273 J.D. [[A] Collier S.S.]
*PRACTICE AREAS: Promotion Law; Advertising Law.
Monaco, Cynthia M. '65 '91 C&L.309 B.A., J.D.
(adm. in MA; not adm. in DC) 1301 K Street, NW, Suite 800 East
Monaco, Stephanie M. .... '57 '82 C.446 B.A. L.64 J.D. [Morgan,L.&B.]
Monagan, John S., (AV) .... '11 '38 C.197 A.B. L.309 J.D. 3043 W. Lane Keys, N.W.‡
Monahan, Mary E. .... '64 '91 C.276 A.B. L.273 J.D. [[C] Sutherland A.&B.]
*PRACTICE AREAS: Federal Income Tax Litigation; Federal Income Tax Controversy.
Monahan, Sharon O'Malley '57 '83 C.881 B.A. L.1048 J.D.
(adm. in MA; not adm. in DC) [Fleischman&W.]
Monderer, Howard, (AV) .... '27 '49 C.563 B.S. L.309 LL.B. N.B.C.
Mondor, Paul A. .... '57 '89 C&L.128 B.A., J.D. [[A] Lotstein B.]
*PRACTICE AREAS: Mortgage Banking Law.
Mong, Keith A. .... '62 '87 C.446 B.A. L.128 J.D. [Silverstein&M.]
*PRACTICE AREAS: Employee Benefits; Executive Compensation; Federal Taxation; ERISA.
Mongia, Nisha '69 '95 C.696 B.A. L.273 J.D.
(adm. in MA; not adm. in DC) Nat. Broadcasting Co., Inc.
Monheim, Thomas A. .... '— '92 C.659 B.A. L.1068 J.D. [[A] King&S.]
*PRACTICE AREAS: Litigation; Trade Regulation.
Monica, John C., Jr. .... '64 '91 C.597 B.A. L.273 J.D. [[A] Shook,H.&B.]
Monk, Brandy Clark '74 '00 C.260 B.A. L.608 J.D.
(adm. in FL; not adm. in DC) U.S. Air Force JAG
Monk, Carl C. '42 '71 C.612 B.A. L.329 J.D.
Exec. V.P. & Exec. Dir., Assn. of Amer. Law School
Monroe, David K. .... '50 '81 C.1044 B.S. L.309 J.D. [Galland,K.G.F.&S.]
Monroe, James B. '63 '91 C.910 B.S. L.273 J.D.
[Finnegan,H.F.G.&D.] (See Pat. Sect.)
*PRACTICE AREAS: Chemical Intellectual Property; Intellectual Property Litigation; Intellectual Property Portfolio Management; Pharmaceutical Intellectual Property; Patent Litigation.
Monroe, Monica E. '74 '99 C.94 B.A. L.273 J.D.
(adm. in MD; not adm. in DC) [[A] Krooth&A.]
*PRACTICE AREAS: Employment Law; Commercial Litigation.
Monroe, Raymond F., (AV) .... '55 '80 C.319 B.A. L.228 J.D. [Crowell&M.]
*PRACTICE AREAS: Government Contract Law; Business Crimes Law.
Monroig, Antonio .... '44 '69 C.677 B.A. L.1087 J.D. [Lasa,M.&V.]
Monsanto, Lisa-Marie C. '65 '97 C.012 B.A. L.178 J.D.
(adm. in NY; not adm. in DC) [[A] Shaw P.]
Monsees, Paul R., (AV) .... '— '82 C.390 B.A. L.128 J.D. [Foley&L.]
*PRACTICE AREAS: Commercial Litigation; Employment.
Monsey, Christopher A. '66 '97 C.640 B.S. L.615 J.D.
(adm. in MD; not adm. in DC) [[A] Dickstein S.M.&O.]
*PRACTICE AREAS: Intellectual Property.
Montague, R. Latane, IV .... '70 '98 C&L.893 B.A., J.D. [[A] Hogan&H.]
*PRACTICE AREAS: Environmental; Transportation.
Montano, Kevin E. ... '60 '86 C.823 B.A. L.276 J.D. Asst. Gen. Coun., Marriott Intl., Inc.
*RESPONSIBILITIES: Environmental Law; Real Estate Development.
Montano, Mark J. .... '72 '98 C.228 B.A. L.659 J.D. [[A] Arnold&P.]

Monteau, Peebles & Crowell, LLP, (AV)
511 C Street, N.E., 20002 ⊙
Telephone: 202-543-5000 Fax: 202-543-7716
Email: ndnlaw@ndnlaw.com URL: http://www.ndnlaw.com
Michael J. Anderson. Associate: Loretta A. Tuell (Not admitted in DC).
Federal Indian Law, Indian Economic Development, Indian Child Welfare Act, Indian Gaming Law, Indian Land Law, Indian Water Claims, Tribal Taxation, Civil Litigation, Appellate Practice, and Administrative Law.
Omaha, Nebraska Office: 12100 West Center Road, Suite 202, 68144. Telephone: 402-333-4053. Fax: 402-333-4761. E-Mail: ndnlaw@ndnlaw.com
Sacramento, California Office: 1001 Second Street, 95814. Telephone: 916-441-2700. Fax: 916-441-2067. E-Mail: ndnlaw@ndnlaw.com
Kirkland, Washington Office: 1670 10th Street West, 98033. Telephone: 425-828-9070. Fax: 425-828-8978. E-Mail: ndnlaw@ndnlaw.com
Kalispell, Montana Office: 235 Wild Rose Trail, 59901. Telephone: 406-755-3544. Fax: 406-755-3546. E-Mail: hmonteau@ndnlaw.com

See Professional Biographies, WASHINGTON, DISTRICT OF COLUMBIA

Montebello, Mary A. .... '60 '85 C&L.383 B.A., J.D. [[A] Smith,G.&R.] (See Pat. Sect.)
*PRACTICE AREAS: Patents.
Montero, Francisco R. .... '60 '87 C.477 B.A. L.273 J.D. [Shaw P.]

Montgomery, Bruce L., (AV) .... '35 '60 C.691 B.A. L.976 LL.B. [Arnold&P.]
*PRACTICE AREAS: Antitrust; Litigation.
Montgomery, Charles R. '34 '61 C&L.893 B.A., LL.B.
V.P., Koones & Montgomery, Inc.
Montgomery, George Cranwell .... '44 '76 C.893 B.A. L.880 J.D. [Baker,D.B.&C.]
*PRACTICE AREAS: International Law; Corporate Law.
Montgomery, James T., Jr. ....'— '81 C.511 A.B. L.276 J.D. [Foley,H.&E.]
*PRACTICE AREAS: Taxation.
Montgomery, John B. ....'48 '73 C.871 B.S. L.502 J.D. [Tighe P.A.T.]
*PRACTICE AREAS: Business Acquisitions and Technology Law; Government Relations; Legislation; Military Base Closures & Development.
Montgomery, John H. ..... '40 '68 C.674 A.B. L.276 J.D. 1200 New Hampshire Ave. NW
Montgomery, M. Katherine ....'74 '00 C.425 B.A. L.276 J.D. [Ⓐ Chadbourne&P.]
Montgomery, Robert E., Jr., (AV) ... '39 '70 C.870 B.S. L.1066 J.D. [Paul,W.R.W.&G.]
*PRACTICE AREAS: International Trade and Arbitration; Intellectual Property; Antitrust; Energy.
Monthy, Jeremy Todd .... '73 '00 C.976 B.A. L.846 J.D. [Ⓐ Hogan&H.]
*PRACTICE AREAS: Litigation.
Montoya, Mauro A., Jr. ...... '58 '85 C.556 B.A. L.273 J.D. Whitman-Walker Clinic, Inc.
Monts, William L., III .... '61 '89 C.976 B.A. L.790 J.D. [Hogan&H.]
*PRACTICE AREAS: Antitrust; Litigation.
Monville, Mary K., (CV) '66 '92 C.475 B.A. L.208 J.D.
(adm. in SC; not adm. in DC) [Ⓐ Wickwire G.] (⊙Madison, WI)
*PRACTICE AREAS: Construction Litigation; Insurance Defense.
Moodee, Valaree M. ..... '56 '85 C.415 B.A. L.1009 J.D. Assoc. Gen. Coun., Fannie Mae
*RESPONSIBILITIES: Employment Law.
Moody, Randall J., (BV) '43 '91 C.190 B.A. L.546 J.D.
(adm. in NE; not adm. in DC) 4404 Burlington Pl., N.W.
Moody, T. Rush, Jr., (AV) .... '30 '56 C&L.846 B.B.A., LL.B. 1701 Penns. Ave., N.W.
Mooers, Donald L. .... '60 '87 C.228 B.A. L.273 J.D. [Ⓑ Trow&K.]
*PRACTICE AREAS: Immigration and Naturalization.
Mooers, Edwin A., Jr. ....'16 '42 C.273 L.904 J.D. 5005 Belt Rd., N.W.‡
Mooers, Thomas R., (AV) .... '59 '89 C.999 B.F.A. L.64 J.D. [Mooers&M.]
*PRACTICE AREAS: Insurance Defense; Insurance Coverage; Medical Malpractice; Construction Litigation; Civil Litigation.

Mooers & Mount, PLLC, (AV)
1730 M Street, N.W., Suite 905, 20036
Telephone: 202-955-6227 Fax: 202-955-1149
URL: http://www.lawyers.com/mooers_law
Thomas R. Mooers;—Rocco C. Nunzio; Brian C. Malone.
Insurance Defense, Auto Negligence Defense, Premises and Products Liability Defense, Workers Compensation Defense. Commercial Litigation, Complex Multijurisdictional Litigation, Civil Trial, Medical Malpractice.
See Professional Biographies, WASHINGTON, DISTRICT OF COLUMBIA

Moog, Audrey Elaine .... '66 '00 C.569 B.A. L.180 J.D. [Ⓐ Hogan&H.]
Moon, H. Paul '71 '99 C.1400 B.A. L.910 J.D.
Federal Communications Commission, Common Carrier Bureau
Moon, Jeffrey Hunter '53 '78 C.478 B.A. L.930 J.D.
Solicitor, U.S. Catholic Conference
Mooney, John R. .... '56 '82 C.945 B.A. L.128 J.D. [Mooney,G.B.&S.]
*PRACTICE AREAS: Labor Law; Litigation; Constitutional Law; RICO; Union Organization.
Mooney, Joshua A. .... '71 '00 C.423 B.A. L.276 J.D. [Ⓐ Ross,D.&B.]
Mooney, Marilyn, (AV) ....'52 '77 C&L.659 B.A., J.D. [Fulbright&J.]
*PRACTICE AREAS: Mergers and Acquisitions; Joint Ventures; Business Divestitures; Securities Offerings; Securities Regulation.

Mooney, Green, Baker & Saindon, P.C., (AV)
1920 L Street, N.W., Suite 400, 20036
Telephone: 202-783-0010 Telecopier: 202-783-6088
Email: pgseen@mooneygreen.com URL: http://www.mooneygreen.com
John R. Mooney; Paul A. Green; Marilyn L. Baker; Elizabeth A. Saindon;—Mark J. Murphy; Daniel E. Kornfeld; Douglas L. Parker. Special Counsel: Robert H. Stropp, Jr.
Labor Law, Public Sector Labor Relations, Labor Arbitration and Litigation, Collective Bargaining, Employee Benefits, ERISA, Multiemployer Pensions and Benefits, Taft-Hartley Plans, Qualified Pension Plans, Public Employee Retirement, Employee Relations, Equal Opportunity Law, Bankruptcy Law, RICO, Antitrust and General Civil Litigation.
See Professional Biographies, WASHINGTON, DISTRICT OF COLUMBIA

Moor, Karl R. '56 '86 C.9 B.A. L.276 J.D.
(adm. in AL; not adm. in DC) V.P. & Assoc. Gen. Coun., Southern Co.
Moore, Amy N., (AV) ....'53 '84 C.518 A.B. L.893 J.D. [Covington&B.]
Moore, Angela M. '64 '94 C.30 B.S. L.93 J.D.
(adm. in OH; not adm. in DC) [Ⓐ Winston&S.]
*PRACTICE AREAS: Corporate Law; Securities Law.
Moore, Beverly C., Jr., P.C., (AV) .... '45 '71 C.575 B.A. L.309 J.D. [Moore&B.]
Moore, Bryan J. '74 '00 C.16 B.A. L.861 J.D.
(adm. in MD; not adm. in DC) [Ⓐ Beveridge&D.]
*PRACTICE AREAS: Environmental Law; Pesticide Regulation.
Moore, Christopher D. ....'66 '91 C.853 B.A. L.383 J.D. Atty., Sprint Corp.
Moore, Clarence W. .... '12 '35 C&L.477 A.B., J.D. [Kline,M.&K.]
Moore, Dennis M. '51 '76 C.645 B.A. L.273 J.D.
Sr. Assoc. Gen. Coun., Litig., National Railroad Passenger Corp. (AMTRAK)
Moore, Donald R. .... '14 '50 C.902 A.B. L.276 J.D. 3316 Legation St., N.W.‡
Moore, Eugene H. '47 '72 C&L.69 B.A., J.D.
(adm. in TX; not adm. in DC) [Ⓑ Stewart&S.]
*PRACTICE AREAS: Corporate (organization and governance); Commercial Transactions (U.S. and international); Mergers and Acquisitions; Litigation Management.
Moore, Gregory F. .... '60 '96 C.426 B.A. L.1358 J.D. [Ⓐ O'Donoghue&O.]
*PRACTICE AREAS: Employee Benefits; Labor and Employment.
Moore, Jacqueline J., (BV) ....'41 '76 C.1298 L.329 J.D. 7605 14th St., N.W.
Moore, Jean S., (AV) .... '47 '72 C&L.608 B.A., J.D. [Hogan&H.]
*PRACTICE AREAS: Litigation; Arbitration; Financial Fraud; Securities Fraud; Civil Litigation.
Moore, Jerry A., III, (AV) .... '46 '75 C.494 B.A. L.276 J.D. [Arter&H.]
*PRACTICE AREAS: Real Estate and Zoning Law; Municipal; Litigation; Employment Discrimination Defense.
Moore, John L., Jr. ....'60 '86 C.276 B.A. L.273 J.D. [Ⓑ Piper M.R.&W.]
*PRACTICE AREAS: Customs Law; Insurance Law.
Moore, Jonathon R., (AV) .... '47 '75 C.951 B.A. L.273 J.D. [Moore&B.]
Moore, Julia M. ....'68 '96 C.30 B.A. L.893 J.D. [Ⓐ Swidler B.S.F.]
*PRACTICE AREAS: Energy.
Moore, Lucrecia Renea .... '70 '95 C.575 B.A. L.436 J.D. [Ⓐ Kirkpatrick&L.]
*PRACTICE AREAS: Financial Institutions Law.
Moore, Margaret A., (AV) ....'55 '80 C.216 B.A. L.273 J.D. [Van Ness F.]
*PRACTICE AREAS: Electric Power; Federal Energy Regulation; Energy Contracts; Utility Acquisitions.
Moore, Matthew J. ....'68 '96 C&L.823 B.S., J.D. [Ⓐ Howrey S.A.&W.] (See Pat. Sect.)
*PRACTICE AREAS: Patent Litigation; Patent Prosecution; Copyright; Trademark; Licensing.
Moore, Miriam R. '75 '99 C.281 B.A. L.273 J.D.
Legal Policy Analyst, Family Research Council
Moore, Nancy J. .... '49 '75 C&L.846 B.A., J.D. 804 Somerset Pl., NW
Moore, Patrick L. '49 '78 C.424 B.A. L.365 J.D.
(adm. in IL; not adm. in DC) 5505 Connecticut Ave., N.W.

Moore, Ralph J., Jr., (AV) '32 '61
C.976 B.A. L.1066 LL.B. [Shea&G.] (⊙Chevy Chase, MD)
*PRACTICE AREAS: Labor; Employment Law; Transportation Law; Trusts and Estates.
Moore, Richard T. ....'58 '86 C.347 B.A. L.1119 J.D. P.O. Box 76365
Moore, Robert James .....'57 '87 C.112 A.B. L.770 J.D. Wash. Rep. of the Gov. of Calif.
Moore, Robert L., II, (AV) ....'— '64 C.198 B.A. L.893 LL.B. [Miller&C.]
*PRACTICE AREAS: Taxation; Federal Tax Controversies; Tax Appeals; Tax Audits; Tax Controversies.
Moore, Robert T. ....'37 '63 C.228 B.A. L.846 LL.B. 233 Kentucky Ave., S.E.‡
Moore, Susan A. '62 '97 C.477 B.A. L.128 J.D.
(adm. in VA; not adm. in DC) [Ⓐ Van Ness F.]
*PRACTICE AREAS: Natural Gas; Hydroelectricity; Indian Law.
Moore, Tashena Middleton ....'70 '99 C.976 B.A. L.276 J.D. [Ⓐ Jones,D.R.&P.]
Moore, William ....'63 '99 C.893 B.A. L.500 J.D. 1901 18th St., N.W.
Moore, William S., (AV) ....'44 '72 C.339 B.A. L.477 J.D. [Shea&G.]
*PRACTICE AREAS: Estate Planning; Trusts and Estates; Litigation.
Moore & Brown, (AV) .... 4900 Massachusetts Ave. N.W. (⊙Winston-Salem, NC)

Moore & Bruce, LLP, (AV)
1072 Thomas Jefferson Street, N.W., 20007 ⊙
Telephone: 202-965-5300 Facsimile: 202-965-7745
URL: http://www.lawyers.com/moore&brucellp
Charles M. Bruce; Jonathon R. Moore. Of Counsel: Michael C. Durney; William Morris; Edward M. Luria (Resident, Wilmington, Delaware Office).
Taxation, Corporate and Commercial Law, International Trade and Customs Law, Trusts and Estates, Civil and Criminal Tax Litigation.
Wilmington, Delaware Office: 2 East 7th Street, Suite 302. Telephone: 302-655-0582. Fax: 302-655-9321.
London, England Office: 43 Upper Grosvenor Street. Telephone: 011-44-207-493-4840. Fax: 011-44-207-493-4299.
See Professional Biographies, WASHINGTON, DISTRICT OF COLUMBIA

Moore Hamrick, Mary '57 '87 C.228 B.A. L.575 J.D.
(adm. in NC; not adm. in DC) V.P., New York Life Ins. Co.
Moorehead, Donald V., (AV) ....'43 '68 C.893 B.A. L.273 J.D. [Patton B.]
Moorehead, Rebecca C. ....'75 '98 C.69 B.A. L.902 J.D. [Ⓐ Brunenkant&H.]
*PRACTICE AREAS: Energy.
Moorhead, Eileen M. ....'— '95 [Ⓐ Troutman S.]
*PRACTICE AREAS: Federal Regulatory Policy; Environmental Law; Natural Resources.
Moorhead, Joanna L. ....'49 '79 C.228 B.A. L.128 J.D. 60 Mass. Ave., N.E.
Moorhouse, Richard L., (AV) ....'— '82 C.454 B.A. L.818 J.D. [Reed S.]
*PRACTICE AREAS: Government Contracts; Export Compliance.
Moorhus, Amy E. ....'67 '97 C.705 B.A. L.262 J.D. [Ⓐ Jones,D.R.&P.]
Moorman, Thomas J. ....'58 '84 C.1208 B.A. L.128 J.D. 2120 L St., N.W.
Moosally, Frederick Peter, III '69 '98 C.1369 B.S. L.128 J.D.
(adm. in MD; not adm. in DC) Off. of Corp. Coun. Legal Div.
Moot, John S., (AV) ....'61 '88 C.732 B.A. L.30 J.D. [Skadden,A.S.M.&F.]
Morales, Alberto J. '52 '78 C.659 B.A. L.884 J.D.
(adm. in PA; not adm. in DC) Marriott Dr.
Morales, Manar Sweillam ....'71 '97 C.188 B.S. L.128 J.D. [Woodley,G.&M.]
*PRACTICE AREAS: Labor and Employment Law; Fair Labor Standards Law; Public Sector Labor Relations.
Morales, Rita W. ....'61 '92 C.235 B.A. L.329 J.D. [Ⓐ Mayer,B.&P.]
Moran, Anne E., (AV) .... '— '78 C.914 B.A. L.309 J.D. [Steptoe&J.]
*PRACTICE AREAS: Tax; Employee Benefits.
Moran, Charles A., (BV) ....'40 '68 C.276 A.B. L.228 J.D. 6600 5th St Nw
Moran, F. Thomas, (AV) ....'45 '73 C.103 A.B. L.30 J.D. [Wilkinson B.K.]
*PRACTICE AREAS: Communications; Commercial Transactions; Telecommunications Law; Tax Law.
Moran, Janet Fitzpatrick ....'63 '91 C.1369 B.A. L.276 J.D. [Ⓐ Patton B.]
Moran, John P., (AV) .... '52 '83 C.884 B.E. L.128 J.D. [Ⓑ Swidler B.S.F.] (Pat.)
*PRACTICE AREAS: Intellectual Property; Patents; Trademarks; Copyrights; Trade Secrets.
Moran, John T. ....'60 '89 C.31 B.A. L.1356 J.D. 1815 19th St., N.W.
Moran, Karen M. .... '63 '88 C.1365 B.A. L.228 J.D. [Ⓑ Fulbright&J.]
*PRACTICE AREAS: Employment Discrimination; Appellate Practice.
Moran, Maria Celeste '71 '01 C.821 B.A. L.477 J.D.
(adm. in MD; not adm. in DC) [Ⓐ Cole,R.&B.]
*PRACTICE AREAS: Cable TV; Litigation; Antitrust; Internet Law.
Moran, Mark A. ....'55 '87 C&L.477 B.S., J.D. [Steptoe&J.]
*PRACTICE AREAS: International Law; International Trade; International Arbitration.
Moran, Michael John '53 '95 C&L.37 B.S., J.D.
(adm. in AZ; not adm. in DC; See Pat. Sect.) [Ⓐ Rothwell,F.E.&M.]
*PRACTICE AREAS: Intellectual Property.
Moran, Nancy Lee ....'45 '83 C.128 B.A. L.30 J.D. P.O. Box 262‡
Moran, Patrick J., (AV) ...'49 '73 C.602 A.B. L.276 J.D. 1818 N St., N.W. (⊙Hous., TX)
Moran, Thomas Paul '61 '90 C.588 B.S. L.128 J.D.
(adm. in MA; not adm. in DC) Atty., Nat. Assn. of Sec. Dealers, Inc.
Moran, Timothy J. '67 '93
C&L.893 B.A., J.D. [Ⓑ Skadden,A.S.M.&F.] (⊙New York, NY)
Moran, William J. '— '99 C.602 B.A. L.893 J.D.
(adm. in VA; not adm. in DC) [Ⓐ White&C.]
Morante, Thomas F., (AV) ....'51 '77 C.867 B.A. L.30 J.D. [Jorden B.] ⊙
*PRACTICE AREAS: International Financial Services; Securities; Corporate; Insurance Regulation; Insurance Products.
Morchower, Adrian L., (AV) ....'30 '65 C.823 B.A. L.705 J.D. [Ⓑ Morgan,L.&B.]
Mordi, Francisca N. ....'66 '97 C.999 B.A. L.1202 J.D. [Ⓐ J.O.Iweanoge]
Mordkofsky, Harold, (AV) .....'— '63 C.563 B.E.E. L.446 LL.B. [Blooston,M.D.D.&P.]
*PRACTICE AREAS: Telecommunications Law; Cellular Radio; FCC Licensing; FCC Regulation.
More, John H. .... '42 '79 C.976 B.A. L.309 J.D. [Rogers&M.]
Moreau, Lucien E. '35 '67 C.178 L.309 LL.B.
(adm. in MA; not adm. in DC) Intl. Bk. for Reconstr. & Develop.
Morehouse, Scott A. ....'67 '93 C.454 B.A. L.276 J.D. [Ⓐ Mayer,B.&P.]
*PRACTICE AREAS: Real Estate; Finance.
Morel, William R. ....'42 '67 C&L.923 B.S., J.D. Asst. Corp. Coun.
Moreland, Joseph A. '36 '61 C&L.923 B.S., LL.B.
(adm. in WV; not adm. in DC) Dir., Off. of Civil Defense
Morell, Karalee C. ....'73 '99 C.184 B.A. L.188 J.D. [Ⓐ Wiley R.&F.]
Morell, Karl '48 '76 C.30 B.S. L.425 J.D.
(adm. in MD; not adm. in DC) [Ⓑ Ball J.]
*PRACTICE AREAS: Transportation Law; Administrative Law; Commercial Transactions; Government Affairs.
Morell, Rafael E. ....'73 '99 C.1044 B.A. L.188 J.D. [Ⓐ Ogletree,D.N.S.&S.]
*PRACTICE AREAS: Labor and Employment.
Morella, Anthony C., (AV) .... '30 '59 C.94 A.B. L.30 J.D. Prof of Law, Amer. Univ.
Morelli, Genevieve ....'56 '81 C.569 B.A. L.273 J.D. [Ⓑ Kelley D.&W.]
*PRACTICE AREAS: Telecommunications.
Morelli, Lisa Ann ....'67 '94 C.884 B.S. L.128 J.D. Ste. 1140, 1875 Ct Ave., NW
Morelli, Mark S. '69 '96 C.103 B.A. L.976 J.D.
(adm. in IL; not adm. in DC) [Ⓐ Wilmer,C.&P.]
Moreno, Jeffrey O., (BV) ....'66 '91 C.1236 B.S. L.276 J.D. [Thompson H.]
*PRACTICE AREAS: Communications; Transportation; Administrative Law.
Moretz-Edmisten, Jane ....'38 '67 C.575 B.A. L.273 J.D. [J. Mortez-Edmisten&Assoc.]
Moretz-Edmisten, Jane, P.A., & Associates ....4530 Wisconsin Avenue

Morey, Richard S., (AV) .... '38 '66 C.659 B.S. L.178 J.D. [Kleinfeld,K.&B.]
*PRACTICE AREAS: Food, Drug and Cosmetic Law; Food and Drug Regulation; Drug and Medical Device Regulation; Controlled Substances Law; Advertising Law.
Morey, Thomas C. .... '71 '97 C.674 A.B. L.228 J.D. [Ⓐ Hogan&H.]
Morgan, D. Scott '51 '76 C.575 B.A. L.1017 J.D.
(adm. in PA; not adm. in DC)
Assoc. Gen. Coun., Tort Litig., Natl. Railroad Passenger Corp. (AMTRAK)
Morgan, Daniel L., (AV) ....'52 '77 C.860 B.A. L.184 J.D. [Venable,A.B.H.&C.]
*PRACTICE AREAS: Employee Benefits Law; Employment Law; Corporate Law.
Morgan, Devin S. .... '74 '99 C.197 B.A. L.1218 J.D. [Ⓐ Hunton&W.] (Pat.)
*PRACTICE AREAS: Intellectual Property.
Morgan, Donald L., (AV) .... '34 '62 C&L.309 A.B., LL.B. [Cleary,G.S.&H.]
Morgan, Frank H. ....'73 '98 C.884 B.A. L.180 J.D. [Ⓐ White&C.]
Morgan, Gerald D., Jr., (AV) .... '37 '66 C.31 B.A. L.178 LL.B. [Pillsbury W.]
*PRACTICE AREAS: Construction Law; Real Estate; Project Development.
Morgan, Helen L. '50 '75 C.665 B.A. L.273 J.D.
Assoc. Gen. Coun., Intl. Union of Oper. Engrs.
Morgan, Janice R. .... '58 '83 C.518 B.A. L.276 J.D. Migrant Legal Action Program
Morgan, Mark S. '56 '90 C.454 B.A. L.1194 J.D.
Exec. Dir. & Chf. Coun., Petroleum Transp. & Storage Assn.
Morgan, Peter W., (AV) ....'51 '78 C.198 A.B. L.893 J.D. [Dickstein S.M.&O.]
*PRACTICE AREAS: Alternative Dispute Resolution; Litigation; Government Ethics; Governmental Affairs.
Morgan, Thomas D. '42 '65 C.597 B.A. L.145 J.D.
(adm. in IL; not adm. in DC) Prof. of Law, George Washington Univ.
Morgan, W. Edward ....'23 '45 C&L.37 LL.B. Prof., Univ. of Antioch School of Law

Morgan & Finnegan, L.L.P., (AV) BB
A Registered Liability Partnership
1775 Eye Street, N.W., 4th Floor, 20006 ⊙
Telephone: 202-857-7887 Facsimile: 202-857-7929
URL: http://www.MorganFinnegan.com
Resident Partners: Michael S. Marcus; John E. Hoel (Not admitted in DC). Counsel: Joseph C. Redmond, Jr. Associates: James Hwa (Not admitted in DC); Peter Zura (Not admitted in DC); Keats A. Quinalty (Not admitted in DC); Gregory Perrone; Kenneth P. Waszkiewicz.
Patent and Technology-related law, Trademark, Copyright, Trade Secret and Unfair Competition, Licensing and Related Antitrust, Trade Regulation, Environmental and Food and Drug Law. International Trade Law. Trials and Appeals. Arbitration.
New York, N.Y. Office: 345 Park Avenue, 10154. Telephone: 212-758-4800. Cable Address: "Findurpine". Facsimile: (212) 751-6849. Telex: ITT 421792.
See Professional Biographies, WASHINGTON, DISTRICT OF COLUMBIA

Morgan, Lewis & Bockius LLP, (AV)
1800 M Street, N.W., 20036-5869 ⊙
Telephone: 202-467-7000 Fax: 202-467-7176
Email: postmaster@morganlewis.com URL: http://www.morganlewis.com
Members of Firm in Washington: John Quarles; Charles P. O'Connor; John H. Shenefield; Caswell O. Hobbs, III; Ralph N. Albright, Jr.; William L. Gardner; James A. Glasgow; Kathryn B. McGrath (Resident); Gary G. Quintiere; Harry A. Rissetto; Thomas F. Williamson; Charles I. Cohen; George L. Edgar; William H. Lewis, Jr.; Alvin H. Gutterman; Peter E. Halle; Linda L. Griggs; James J. Kelley, II; Kenneth A. Rubin; Michael Berenson; Gary S. Smuckler; Harry W. Burton; Kathleen W. Collins; Kevin P. Gallen; Roberta L. Halladay; Michael S. Kelly; Donald C. Klawiter; Stephen Paul Mahinka; Floyd L. Norton, IV; Robert A. Dufek; Celia Roady; Joseph E. Santucci, Jr.; Thomas A. Schmutz; George G. Yearsich; Peter Buscemi; Michael F. Healy; John D. McGrane; Michael W. Steinberg; Howard T. Weir, III; Robert J. Gaybrick; Mark N. Bravin; Steven P. Frantz; Jay M. Gutierrez; Thomas P. Lemke; Arthur B. Axelson; Michael F. Clayton; Donald L. Havermann; Thomas E. Reinert, Jr.; Donald J. Silverman; Kathryn L. Gleason; Charles C. Thebaud, Jr.; Francis L. Casey; Reid G. Adler; Grace E. Speights; Scott A. Stempel; D. Michael Underhill; Thomas S. Harman; Stanley F. Lechner; Robert S. Schlossberg; Sandra J.P. Dennis; Stephanie M. Monaco; Donna K. Thiel; Anthony C. Roth; David J. McPherson; Ron N. Dreben; James R. Sims III; Richard S. Meyer; Kathleen M. Sanzo; Steven W. Stone; Jonathan M. Rich; Gregory L. Needles; Mark A. Srere; Mark D. Fitterman; Nancy R. Kuhn; Mary Ann K. Huntington; John E. Matthews; John F. Ring; David A. Sirignano; Lawrence P. Stadulis; Paul Huey-Burns; Christian J. Mixter; Willard K. Tom; Gregory P. Asciolla; M. Elizabeth Bierman; Peter M. Boyle; Karen A. Butcher; Brad Fagg; Carole R. Klein; Jeffrey A. Lindeman; Penelope M. "Gari" Lister; Nathan W. McCutcheon; Nancy L. Rowe; John G. Smith; John H. Williamson; John D. Zele; Christopher L. White; Michael R. Dzwonczyk; Lynn E. Eccleston; Michele Van Patten Frank; R. Tyler Goodwyn, IV; Michael C. Griffen; Sheldon M. Kline; W. John McGuire; Paul J. Zaffuts. Counsel: Sheldon S. Cohen; Richard C. Hotvedt; Adrian L. Morchower; E. Carl Uehlein, Jr. Special Counsel in Washington: Edgar H. Martin; Mona C. Zeiberg. Of Counsel in Washington: William E. Baer, Jr.; Christopher J. Barr; John Mills Barr; Mary Jane Boswell; Joseph Brooks; John E. Daniel; Jack P. Drogin (Not admitted in DC); Barbara A. Friedman; Margery Sinder Friedman; L. Denise Galambos; Angela C. Goelzer; Alissa A. Horvitz; Richard F. Jackson; Michael A. McCord; David M. Morris; Thomas J. O'Brien; Monica L. Parry; Daryl M. Shapiro; Don Wallace, Jr.; Elizabeth Weimar; Robert B. Wiggins; Kenneth D. Woodrow; Phillip C. Zane. Associates in Washington: John V. Ayanian; Maya J. Bermingham; Jessica R. Bernanke; Paul M. Bessette; Dorothy J. Black; Jeffrey C. Blockinger; Christine E. Bloomquist; Travis P. Boozer (Not admitted in DC); George Borovas; Anne Brafford; Donald E. Broadfield, Jr.; Adrienne A. Brown; Boyd J. Brown, II; James A. Budinetz; Vu Bui; Gregory W. Camet; Daniel S. Carlineo; Meredith A. Carlo; G. Scott Carter; Terra E. Castaldi; Maria D. Castner (Not admitted in DC); Lisa Ann Chaikin; A. C. Brooke Clagett; Thomas P. Conaghan; Patrick D. Conner; Amy J. Conway; Leslie Sperling Cruz; Patrick M. Curran, Jr.; Rachel B. Damelin; F. Nikki Davis (Not admitted in DC); Ann K. Derstine (Not admitted in DC); Rani E. Doyle; Susan S. Dunne; Magda El Guindi-Rosenbaum; Salman H. Elmi; Donald E. English, Jr.; J. Clayton Everett, Jr.; Robert C. Farley, Jr. (Not admitted in DC); Barbara M. Flaherty; Colin T. Flynn; John M. Ford; Stephanie M. Foster; Paul A. Fournier; Mary J. Frank; Douglas J. Free (Not admitted in DC); Jonathan C. Fritts; Lawrence S. Ganslaw; Cynthia M. Gayton (Not admitted in DC); Latrice A. George; Lance E. Gibbons; Mark A. Goodin; Gayle Grabow-Wallace; Lia Silva Grassl (Not admitted in DC); Lora M. Green (Not admitted in DC); Charles P. Groppe; Frederick J. Hamble; Jacquenette M. Helmes (Not admitted in DC); Robert P. Henley (Not admitted in DC); Lisa D. Herbst; Jason I. Hewitt; David M. Hibey; Robert J. Hollingshead; Rhonda C. Holmes; Martha J. Hopkins; Katharine B. Houlihan; Joseph R. House; Rima Idzelis (Not admitted in DC); Tomer J. Inbar; Shannon M.P. Johnson; Pamela M. Keith; Tara R. Kelly; Rona C. Kelner; David J. Kenealy; Jennifer L. Klass; Daniel R. Kleinman; Heath K. Knakmuhs; Jennifer L. Kocher; Gerald P. Konkel (Not admitted in DC); Christine A. Laciak; Thomas J. Lang; Jennifer M. Lee; Jeffery M. Lillywhite (Not admitted in DC); David R. Lipson; Brian Z. Liss; Henry Liu; K. Karen Loewenstein; Jason A. Lomax; Kathleen M. Macpeak; Kendra A. Martello (Not admitted in DC); Marjan Mashhadi; Timothy P. Matthews; Eric J. Maurer; James T. McHale; C. Brian Meadors; Christopher Dennis Menconi; Brett I. Miller; Jennifer Tetenbaum Miller; Nicholas C. Minshew (Not admitted in DC); Prufesh R. Modhera; Phoebe Mounts, Ph.D.; Nathan J. Muyskens; Arlene P. Neal; Thomas E. Nelson; Corinne A. Niosi; Regina A. O'Brien (Not admitted in DC); Lisa Erin O'Donald; Shana E. Ommaya; Danielle Helen Paradine; Collin W. Park; Allison L. Parlin; Ross H. Parr; Ralph A. Phillips (Not admitted in DC); Amy E. Pocino; Alex S. Polonsky; Anita B. Polott; Crane M. Pomerantz; Brian M. Privor; Laurel E. Queeno; Liza M. Ray; James L. Reed; Tara Lee Reinhart; Corinne Ann Richardson (Not admitted in DC); Jeffrey L. Riley; Jonathan G. Rose; Scott D. Sadler; Julian F. Saenz (Not admitted in DC); Matthew O. Schad (Not admitted in DC); Alex M. Schnell; Todd A. Schroeder; Laine M. Schwartz; Amaal A.D. Scroggins (Not admitted in DC); Sangita A. Shah; Barbara Ann Shirley; Robert Smyth, Ph.D.; Yiota G. Souras; Denise L. Speas; Stephen M. Spina; Goran P. Stojkovich; Victoria L. Strohmeyer (Not admitted in DC); Michael Strong; Richard A. Sugarman; Charles Swinburn; Khoi Ta (Not admitted in DC); Gregory R. Talbot; Todd P. Taylor; John F. Terzaken, III; Angela F. Thornhill; Jeffrey N. Townes; John C. Truong; Michael S. Tuscan; Erich E. Veitenheimer, III; Anthony J. Verducci; Mary D. Walsh; Emil P. Wang (Not admitted in DC); Carolyn O. Ward; Joseph E. Washington; Andrea J. Weinstein; Robyn B. Weiss; Gregory F. Wells (Not admitted in DC); Pamela R. Williams (Not admitted in DC); Timothy J. Wolf.
Acquisitions and Mergers, Antitrust, Banking, Bankruptcy, Civil Litigation, Construction, Corporate, Elections and Campaign Financing, Employee Benefits and Pensions, Environmental, Estate Planning, Government Regulation, Health and Biotechnology, Immigration, Intellectual Property, Insurance, International Law, Investment Management and Financial Services, Labor and Employment, Legislative, Litigation, Municipal Finance, Natural Resources, Non-Profit Organizations, Partnerships, Patent Litigation, Personal Injury, Personal Law and Probate, Product Liability, Public Utilities, Real Estate, Savings and Loan, Securities Offerings, Trademarks and Copyrights, Taxation and White Collar Defense.

(This Listing Continued)

Morgan, Lewis & Bockius LLP (Continued)
Philadelphia, Pennsylvania Office: 1701 Market Street, 19103-2921. Telephone: 215-963-5000. Fax: 215-963-5299.
New York, New York Office: 101 Park Avenue, 10178-0060. Telephone: 212-309-6000. Fax: 212-309-6273.
Los Angeles, California Office: 300 South Grand Avenue, 22nd Floor, 90071-3132. Telephone: 213-612-2500. Fax: 213-612-2554.
Miami, Florida Office: 5300 First Union Financial Center, 200 South Biscayne Boulevard, 33131-2339. Telephone: 305-579-0300. Fax: 305-579-0321.
Harrisburg, Pennsylvania Office: One Commerce Square, 417 Walnut Street, 17101-1904. Telephone: 717-237-4000. Fax: 717-237-4004.
Pittsburgh, Pennsylvania Office: One Oxford Centre, 301 Grant Street, 32nd Floor, 15219-6401. Telephone: 412-560-3300. Fax: 412-560-3399.
Princeton, New Jersey Office: 502 Carnegie Center, 08540-6241. Telephone: 609-919-6600. Fax: 609-919-6639.
Northern Virginia Office: 1600 Tysons Boulevard, McLean, Virginia 22102-4824. Telephone: 703-918-1000. Fax: 703-918-1999.
London, England Office: Morgan, Lewis & Bockius, 2 Gresham Street, London EC2V 7PE. Telephone: 44-207-710-5500. Fax: 44-207-710-5600.
Frankfurt, Germany Office: Guiollettstraße 54, 60325 Frankfurt am Main. Telephone: (49-69) 71 40 07-0. Fax: (49-69) 71 40 07-10.
Brussels, Belgium Office: Morgan, Lewis & Bockius, 7 Rue Guimard, B-1040. Telephone: 32-2/507.75.00. Fax: 32-2/507.75.55.
Tokyo, Japan Office: Yurakucho Denki Building S-556, 7-1 Yurakucho 1-chome, Chiyoda-ku, Tokyo 100-0006. Telephone: (81-3) 5219-2500. Fax: (81-3) 5219-2501.
See Professional Biographies, WASHINGTON, DISTRICT OF COLUMBIA

Morgans, Gary A., (AV) .... '53 '78 C.855 B.A. L.276 J.D. [Steptoe&J.]
*PRACTICE AREAS: Energy Regulation; Electric Utility Law.
Morganti, Andrew J. '72 '98 C.477 B.A. L.213 J.D.
(adm. in MI; not adm. in DC) 1050 30th St., N.W.
Morgenstern, Michael S., (AV) '52 '80 C.608 B.A. L.30 J.D.
[M.S.Morgenstern&Assoc.] (⊙Frederick, Rockville, MD)
Morgenstern, Michael S., & Associates, P.C., (AV)
601 Pennsylvania Ave., N.W. (⊙Frederick, Rockville, MD; Fairfax, VA)
Moriarty, James F., (AV) .... '57 '82 C.705 B.A. L.128 J.D. [Fleischman&W.]
Moriarty, John B., Jr. ....'67 '94 C.893 B.A. L.280 J.D. [Ⓐ Epstein B.&G.]
*PRACTICE AREAS: Health Law; Government Investigations; Fraud and Abuse; Health Litigation.
Morillo, Juan P. '— '98 C.472 B.A. L.276 J.D.
(adm. in FL; not adm. in DC) [Ⓐ Sidley A.B.&W.]
Morin, Charles H., (AV) .... '22 '48 C.309 B.S. L.94 LL.B. [Ⓒ Dickstein S.M.&O.]
*PRACTICE AREAS: Casinos and Gambling; Client Counseling; Banking; Legal Ethics and Professional Responsibility; Money Management.
Morin, Heather ....'70 '94 C.453 B.S. L.446 J.D. [Ⓐ Fish&R.]
*PRACTICE AREAS: Intellectual Property: Patents; Patent Prosecution; Patent Litigation.
Morin, Michael A. '70 '95
C.679 B.S.I.E. L.273 J.D. [Ⓐ Finnegan,H.F.G.&D.] (See Pat. Sect.)
*PRACTICE AREAS: Intellectual Property Litigation; Technology Licensing; Civil Appeals.
Moring, Frederick, (AV) '35 '61 C.886 B.S. L.273 J.D.
1001 Pennsylvania Avenue, N.W.‡
Morisi, Andrea '61 '89 C.93 B.S. L.273 J.D.
(adm. in MA; not adm. in DC) Sr. Coun., American National Red Cross
*RESPONSIBILITIES: Corporate Compliance; Trademark/Intellectual Property; Contracts.
Morita, Susan T. .... '60 '88 C.813 B.A. L.309 J.D. [Arnold&P.]
*PRACTICE AREAS: International Trade; Corporate Transactions.
Morlan, William E. ....'67 '99 C.1038 B.S. L.30 J.D. [Ⓐ Alston&B.]
*PRACTICE AREAS: Financial Services Law; Mergers and Acquisitions; Technology Law.
Morley, Dean R., IV .... '66 '91 C.228 B.A. L.280 J.D. [Ⓐ Ivins,P.&B.]
*PRACTICE AREAS: Employee Benefits; Pensions; Executive Compensation; Employment Tax.
Morley, Guy A. ....'59 '88 C.1371 B.A. L.893 J.D. [Winston&S.]
*PRACTICE AREAS: Project Finance; Corporate Law; Energy Law.
Morley, Matt T. .... '56 '83 C.165 B.A. L.976 J.D. [Fried,F.H.S.&J.]

Morley Caskin
(See Cameron McKenna LLP)

Mormino, Anthony J. '— '94 C.35 B.A. L.30 J.D.
(adm. in AZ; not adm. in DC) Asst. Gen. Coun., Reins. Assn. of America
Morreale, Peter C. ....'69 '94 C.276 B.A. L.262 J.D. [Ⓐ McKee N.]
*PRACTICE AREAS: Securitization; Structured Finance.
Morrell, Amber ....'75 '01 C.276 B.S.F.S. L.228 J.D. [Ⓐ Wilmer,C.&P.]
Morrell, Kay Allan ....'56 '84 C&L.101 B.A., J.D. 1101 30th St., N.W.
Morris, A. Thomas .... '— '89 C.276 B.S.B.A. L.228 J.D. [Kirkpatrick&L.]
*PRACTICE AREAS: Environmental Insurance Coverage; Labor and Employment.
Morris, Andrew J. ....'58 '86 C&L.893 B.S., J.D. [Ⓒ Mayer,B.&P.]
Morris, Carolyn E. ....'73 '98 C.103 A.B. L.893 J.D. [Ⓐ Finnegan,H.F.G.&D.]
*PRACTICE AREAS: Trademark Prosecution; Trademark Litigation.
Morris, Cynthia J. ....'52 '81 C.1078 B.A. L.446 J.D. [Piper M.R.&W.]
*PRACTICE AREAS: Environmental Law; Environmental Litigation; Commercial Litigation; Insurance Coverage.
Morris, David M. '67 '92 C.107 B.A. L.201 J.D.
(adm. in MA; not adm. in DC) [McNary,M.&S.]
*PRACTICE AREAS: Immigration Law; Litigation.
Morris, David M. ....'— '89 C.1090 B.A. L.893 J.D. [Ⓒ Morgan,L.&B.]
Morris, Douglas Wayne .... '55 '87 C.475 B.S. L.796 J.D. Amer. Petro. Institute
Morris, Frank C., Jr., (AV) .... '— '73 C.597 B.S. L.893 J.D. [Epstein B.&G.]
*PRACTICE AREAS: Litigation; Labor Law; Employment Law.
Morris, Gary S. ....'61 '96 C.688 B.S. L.276 J.D. [Ⓐ Kenyon&K.] (See Pat. Sect.)
*PRACTICE AREAS: Intellectual Property.
Morris, Helen '63 '92 C.058 B.A./M.A. L.569 J.D.
(adm. in NY; not adm. in DC) Staff Atty., Catholic Legal Immigration Network
Morris, Henry, Jr., (AV) ....'56 '83 C&L.178 B.A., J.D. [Arent F.K.P.&K.]
*PRACTICE AREAS: Employment Law; Labor Law; Employee Benefits Law.
Morris, Herbert E. '26 '53 C&L.976 B.A., LL.B.
(adm. in CT; not adm. in DC) 6200 32nd Place, N.W.‡
Morris, John B., Jr. ....'58 '87 C&L.976 B.A., J.D. [Jenner&B.]
*PRACTICE AREAS: Civil and Appellate Litigation; Technology Law; Internet Law; First Amendment Law.
Morris, Jon Paul .... '58 '95 C.749 B.S. L.276 J.D. [Ⓐ Patton B.]
Morris, Paul M. '65 '95
C.665 B.A. L.188 J.D. Sr. Couns., U.S., Dep. of Justice, Policy Dep.
Morris, Robert B. ....'31 '55 C&L.276 B.S., J.D. V.P., Marriott Intl. Corp.
Morris, Roy R., (AV) .... '52 '76 C.902 A.B. L.276 J.D. [Carr,M.&G.]
*PRACTICE AREAS: Business Law; Corporate Law; Estate Planning.
Morris, W. Davis, III ....'59 '91 C.311 B.A. L.1017 J.D. 1003 K St., N.W.
Morris, Wendy L. .... '67 '92 C.273 B.A. L.904 J.D. [Ⓐ Mayer,B.&P.]
Morris, William, (AV) ....'— '66 C.705 A.B. L.276 J.D. [Ⓒ Moore&B.]

Morris, Manning & Martin, LLP, (AV)
The Colorado Building, 1341 G Street, N.W., Suite 610, 20005 ⊙
Telephone: 202-408-5153 Fax: 202-408-5146
URL: http://www.mmmlaw.com
Member of Firm: Thomas A. Player (Not admitted in DC). Counsel: S. Roy Woodall, Jr.; Robert H. Myers, Jr. (Resident); L. Chris Petersen (Not admitted in DC).

(This Listing Continued)

Morris, Manning & Martin, LLP (Continued)

General Commercial Practice including Practice in all Courts. Administrative Law and Litigation, Antitrust, Asset Based Lending, Banking Regulation and RTC, Bankruptcy and Creditor's Rights, Bond Financing, Business Litigation, Real Estate Lending, Real Estate Transactions, Construction Law, Corporate, Employment Law, Environmental Law, ERISA and Employee Benefits, Government Guaranteed Lending, Governmental Relations, Healthcare, Insurance, Insurance Regulatory, International, Liquidation and Rehabilitation of Insurers and Reinsurers, Leasing, Patent, Partnership, Residential Real Estate, Securities, Taxation, Technology and Intellectual Property, Title Insurance, Trusts and Estates.

Atlanta (Buckhead) Office: 1600 Atlanta Financial Center, 3343 Peachtree Road, N.E., Atlanta, Georgia, 30326. Telephone: 404-233-7000.

Atlanta (Northside) Office: Suite 150, 5775-B Peachtree Dunwoody Road, Atlanta, Georgia, 30342. Telephone: 404-255-6900.

Gwinnett County Office: 2180 Satellite Boulevard, Suite 180, Duluth, Georgia, 30097. Telephone: 678-987-2800. Fax: 678-417-0056.

Forsyth County Office: 307 Atlanta Highway, Cumming, Georgia, 30040. Telephone: 770-781-3000. Fax: 770-781-3007.

Charlotte, North Carolina Office: 600 Fairview Road, Suite 1125, 28210. Telephone: 704-554-7070. Fax: 704-556-9554.

See Professional Biographies, WASHINGTON, DISTRICT OF COLUMBIA

Morrisey, Patrick J. ... '67 '92 C&L.705 B.A., J.D. 1050 Conn. Ave., N.W.

Morrison, Alan B. ... '38 '67 C.976 B.A. L.309 LL.B. Public Citizen Litig. Grp.

Morrison, Alexia, (AV) ... '48 '73 C.705 B.A. L.273 J.D. 3000 K St., N.W.

Morrison, Brian S. '74 '99 C.1036 B.A. L.309 J.D.
(adm. in MA; not adm. in DC) [A Williams&C.]

Morrison, Faye ... '67 '94 C.475 B.A. L.912 J.D. Analyst, General Instrument Corp.

Morrison, Jill C. '70 '95 C.705 B.A. L.976 J.D.
(adm. in PA; not adm. in DC) National Women's Law Ctr.

Morrison, Kent R., (AV) ... '44 '69 C.691 B.A. L.976 LL.B. [Crowell&M.]
*PRACTICE AREAS: Public Contract Law; Litigation; Criminal Law.

Morrison, Linda G. ... '67 '92 C&L.880 B.S., J.D. [A Skadden,A.S.M.&F.]
*PRACTICE AREAS: Communications.

Morrison, Roger A. ... '42 '66 C.367 B.A. L.178 J.D. 3754 McKinley St., N.W.

Morrison, S. Scott, (AV) ... '54 '79 C&L.813 A.B., J.D. [Katten M.Z.]
*PRACTICE AREAS: Complex Litigation; Defense Litigation; Civil Trial; Construction Law.

Morrison, Samuel M., Jr., (AV) ... '39 '78 C.834 B.S.C.E. L.1045 J.D. [Braude&M.]
*PRACTICE AREAS: Construction Law; Administrative Law; Civil Trial Practice Law.

Morrison, Trevor '71 '01 C.05 B.A. L.178 J.D.
(adm. in MD; not adm. in DC) [A Wilmer,C.&P.]

Morrison, Truman A., III ... '43 '70 C.72 B.A. L.966 J.D. Supr. Ct. J.

Morrison, Valerie P., (AV) '58 '85
C&L.273 B.A., J.D. [Gold M.&L.] (⊙Tysons Corner, VA)
*PRACTICE AREAS: Bankruptcy; Creditors' Rights; Foreclosure; Litigation; Banking Law.

Morrison & Foerster LLP, (AV)
2000 Pennsylvania Avenue, N.W., Suite 5500, 20006-1888 ⊙
Telephone: 202-887-1500 Facsimile: 202-887-0763
URL: http://www.mofo.com
Members of Firm: Lee S. Adams; Marco E. Adelfio (Resident); Jonathan Band (Resident); Barry E. Bretschneider (Resident); Alex Chartove; Steven G. Cravath (Resident); L. Richard Fischer (Resident); William D. Freedman; Randolph M. Goodman; Louis Gurman; Kenneth W. Irvin; Frederick E. Jenney; Charles H. Kennedy; Doane F. Kiechel, III; Robert M. Kurucza (Not admitted in DC; Resident); Robert H. Loeffler (Resident); Bradley S. Lui (Resident); Kenneth M. Minesinger; W. Stephen Smith (Resident); Nicholas J. Spiliotes (Resident); Margaret L. Tobey (Resident); Cheryl A. Tritt (Resident); Thomas J. Umberg (Not admitted in DC; Irvine, California and Washington, D.C. Offices); Barbara S. Wellbery. Resident Of Counsel: Linda A. Arnsbarger; Panagiotis C. Bayz; Jonathan F. Cayne; Leonard N. Chanin; Peter J. Davis; Drew S. Days, III (Not admitted in DC); Morris F. DeFeo, Jr.; Oliver I. Ireland (Not admitted in DC); Barbara L. Kirschten; Frank W. Krogh; Rafael Hernandez Mayoral (Not admitted in DC); Joan E. Neal; Bryan A. Schwartz; Eileen M. Smiley (Not admitted in DC); Edward J. Twomey; Katherine C. Zeitlin. Resident Associates: Jonathan Bockman; Allison G. Bothell; Tyler S. Brown; Michael Dashefsky (Not admitted in DC); Raj S. Davé; Krista DeLargy (Not admitted in DC); Tina F. Hofmann; Rachel Howell (Not admitted in DC); Melissa L. Ivers; Wayne C. Jaeschke, Jr. (Not admitted in DC); Kimberly A. Karcewski; Janis Fonda Kerns (Not admitted in DC); Jennifer L. Kostyu; Julie D. Lawton; Christa Parker McAndrew; William McCarron, Jr.; Thomas C. McCormick (Not admitted in DC); Elisa D. Metzger; Samantha J. Pelosi; Lois K. Perrin (Not admitted in DC); Barry I. Pershkow (Not admitted in DC); Obrea O. Poindexter (Not admitted in DC); Nadja S. Sodos-Wallace; Andrew N. Spivak; Kevin R. Spivak; Navid J. Tofigh; Michelle A. Wakino (Not admitted in DC); Victoria Y. Wei; Gang Xu; John R. Zitko.
Other offices located in: San Francisco, Los Angeles, New York, London, Brussels, Beijing, Hong Kong, Singapore, Tokyo, Irvine, San Diego, Sacramento, Palo Alto, Walnut Creek, Denver, Northern Virginia (McLean) and Century City.

See Professional Biographies, WASHINGTON, DISTRICT OF COLUMBIA

Morrison & Hecker L.L.P., (AV)
1150 Eighteenth Street, N.W., Suite 800, 20036-3816 ⊙
Telephone: 202-785-9100 Telefax: 202-785-9163
Email: POSTMASTER@moheck.com URL: http://www.moheck.com
Retired Partner: Richard A. Solomon (1917—);—Harvey L. Reiter; David D'Alessandro (Not admitted in DC); Janet M. Nesse; Steven K. White; Michael E. Tucci; Kelly A. Daly; Marc E. Albert; Darrell W. Clark; Glen L. Ortman;—John E. McCaffrey; Lawrence P. Block; Gregory O. Olaniran; Robert L. Eskay, Jr. (Not admitted in DC); Carrie L. McGuire (Not admitted in DC); Katherine M. Sutcliffe Becker (Not admitted in DC); Marie Denyse Zosa; Adrienne E. Clair.
Civil Practice, Litigation, Banks and Banking, Commercial Law, Bankruptcy, Public Utility Law, Environmental Law, Administrative, International, Commercial Litigation.
Kansas City, Missouri Office: 2600 Grand Avenue, 64108-4606. Telephone: 816-691-2600. Telefax: 816-474-4208.
Overland Park, Kansas Office: Corporate Woods, Building 9 Suite 450, 9200 Indian Creek Parkway, 66210-2008. Telephone: 816-691-2600. Telefax: 913-451-6352.
Wichita, Kansas Office: 600 Commerce Bank Center, 150 North Main Street, 67202-1320. Telephone: 316-265-8800. Telefax: 316-265-1349.
Phoenix, Arizona Office: 1850 North Central Avenue, Suite 2100, 85004-4584. Telephone: 602-279-1600. Telefax: 602-240-6925.

See Professional Biographies, WASHINGTON, DISTRICT OF COLUMBIA

Morrison & Reynolds, (AV) ... 1110 Vermont Avenue, N.W. (⊙Alexandria, VA)

Morrissey, Paul D. ... '50 '78 C.276 B.A. L.1149 J.D. [Morrissey B.]

Morrissey Brothers, P.C. ... 3003 M Street N.W., Suite 2 (⊙Bowie, MD)

Morrone, Michael F., (AV) ... '46 '75 C.165 B.A. L.276 J.D. [Keller&H.]
*PRACTICE AREAS: Telecommunications Law; Transportation Law.

Morrow, John Brian '64 '97 C.112 B.S. L.352 J.D.
(adm. in CA; not adm. in DC) [A Jenkens&G.]
*PRACTICE AREAS: Construction Law.

Morrow, Kenneth R., (AV) ... '58 '90 C&L.446 B.S., J.D. [Dickstein S.M.&O.]
*PRACTICE AREAS: Corporations; Mergers and Acquisitions; Securities; Business Law.

Morrow, William S., Jr. '52 '86 C.446 B.S. L.276 J.D.
Gen. Coun., Washington Metropolitan Area Transit Commission

Morse, Charles R.A. '70 '98 C.02 B.A. L.309 J.D.
(adm. in NY; not adm. in DC) [A Jones,D.R.&P.]

Morse, Jeffrey A. ... '62 '99 C.959 B.A. L.436 J.D. [A Zuckert,S.&R.]
*PRACTICE AREAS: Taxation; Employee Benefits.

Morse, Lewis F., (AV) ... '48 '75 C.188 B.S. L.273 J.D. [Greenstein D.&L.]

Morse, M. Howard, (AV) ... '59 '84 C.197 A.B. L.309 J.D. [Drinker B.&R.]
*PRACTICE AREAS: Antitrust Law.

Morse, Robert G. ... '68 '96 C.813 A.B. L.273 J.D. [A Wilkinson B.K.]
*PRACTICE AREAS: Telecommunications Law; Administrative Law.

Mort, Susan A. ... '71 '97 C.188 B.A. L.823 J.D. [A Fleischman&W.]

Mortenson, R. Stan, (AV) ... '45 '72 C.610 B.A. L.477 J.D. [Baker B.]

Mortimer, Harold E. ... '28 '56 C.728 A.B. L.276 J.D. 1275 K St., N.W.‡

Morton, Andrew D. ... '— '00 C.446 B.A. L.659 J.D. [A Latham&W.]
*PRACTICE AREAS: Government Relations; Telecommunications Law; Health Care.

Morton, Karen G. '68 '94 C.228 B.A. L.893 J.D.
(adm. in FL; not adm. in DC) 1701 Penn. Ave., N.W.‡

Morton, Laura S. '66 '95 C.575 B.A. L.273 J.D.
(adm. in GA; not adm. in DC) [A Fulbright&J.]
*PRACTICE AREAS: Litigation; Appellate Practice; Administrative Law; Oil and Gas Law; Business Immigration.

Morton, Thomas D. ... '59 '85 C.433 B.S. L.188 J.D. [Shaw P.]
*PRACTICE AREAS: Partnership Taxation; Affordable Housing; Equipment Leasing.

Morvillo, Richard J., (AV) ... '48 '75 C.165 A.B. L.262 J.D. [Crowell&M.]
*PRACTICE AREAS: SEC Enforcement Law; Litigation; White Collar Criminal Defense Law.

Moser, Peirce R. '67 '01 C.1077 B.S. L.893 J.D.
(adm. in CA; not adm. in DC) [A Wilmer,C.&P.]

Moses, Alfred H., (AV) ... '29 '56 C.197 B.A. L.276 LL.B. [C Covington&B.]

Moses, Debra G. '57 '84 C.188 B.S. L.273 J.D.
(adm. in MD; not adm. in DC) Boston Properties, Inc.

Moses, Michael F. '56 '83
C.602 B.A. L.502 J.D. Asst. Gen. Coun., U.S. Catholic Conference

Moses & Aiken
(See Rockville, Maryland)

Mosher, Ellsworth H., (AV) '10 '39
C.823 B.S. L.273 LL.B. P.O. Box 1400 K St., NW (Pat.)

Moskowitz, Allan Gary, (AV) ... '48 '73 C.831 B.A. L.276 J.D. [A Kaye S.]
*PRACTICE AREAS: Communications Law; Telecommunications Law; Internet Law.

Moskowitz, Danielle K. ... '68 '95 C.012 B.Sc. L.665 J.D. [S Gibson,D.&C.]
*PRACTICE AREAS: Antitrust and Trade Regulation.

Moskowitz, James N. ... '66 '96 C.945 B.S. L.276 J.D. [A Swidler B.S.F.]
*PRACTICE AREAS: Telecommunications.

Moskowitz, Marc S., (BV) ... '55 '81 C.1365 B.A. L.128 J.D. 1828 L St., N.W.

Moskowitz, Saul L., (AV) ... '54 '79 C.696 B.A. L.575 J.D. [Dean B.&M.]

Moskowitz, Simor L. ... '47 '72 C&L.273 B.A., J.D. [Jacobson,H.]
*PRACTICE AREAS: Intellectual Property Law; Trademarks; Copyrights; Trade Regulation.

Mosley, Audrey Byrd '52 '77 C.48 B.A. L.309 J.D.
Assoc. Gen. Coun., National Academy of Sciences

Moss, Allen J. '64 '97 C.871 B.S. L.36 J.D.
(adm. in AZ; not adm. in DC; See Pat. Sect.) [A Finnegan,H.F.G.&D.]
*PRACTICE AREAS: Patent Litigation; Electrical Patent Prosecution; Software Patent Prosecution; Mechanical Patent Prosecution.

Moss, Anne E. ... '52 '83 C.145 B.A. L.846 J.D. 1244 19th St., N.W.

Moss, Deborah A. ... '65 '91 C.674 A.B. L.276 J.D. Sr. Atty., Consumers Energy Co.

Moss, Nicole Jo ... '— '00 L.309 J.D. [A Covington&B.]

Moss, Randolph D. ... '61 '87 C.299 A.B. L.976 J.D. [Wilmer,C.&P.]
*PRACTICE AREAS: Constitutional Law; Administrative Law; Complex Civil Litigation.

Moss, Robert E. '40 '66 C.169 B.A. L.1066 J.D.
V.P., Amer. Automotive Manufacturers Assn.

Moss, Robert James ... '69 '94 C.477 B.A. L.273 J.D. [A Dickstein S.M.&O.]
*PRACTICE AREAS: Government Contracts Litigation; Information Technology Contracts.

Mossberg, Christer L. ... '45 '88 C.67 B.A. L.1066 J.D. [C Sutherland A.&B.]
*PRACTICE AREAS: International Law; International Trade; Litigation; Corporate Law.

Mostoff, Allan S., (AV) ... '32 '58 C.188 B.S. L.564 LL.B. [Dechert]
*PRACTICE AREAS: Investment Management; Financial Services Law; Securities Law; Corporate Law.

Motley, Thomas J. ... '54 '81 C.178 B.A. L.309 J.D. Asst. U.S. Atty.

Mott, Andrew H. '41 '66 C.309 A.B. L.477 J.D.
(adm. in MI; not adm. in DC) Exec. Dir., Center for Community Change

Mott, John G. ... '29 '58 C.674 A.B. L.309 LL.B. 3406 Lowell St., N.W.‡

Mott, W. Gregory ... '62 '92 C&L.276 B.S., J.D. [A Heenan,A.&R.]
*PRACTICE AREAS: Labor Law; Coal Mining; Health Benefits; Administrative Hearings and Appeals; Federal Civil Litigation.

Mottley, Darrell Gilbert '— '00 C.886 B.S.E.S.M. L.273 J.D.
(adm. in VA; not adm. in DC; See Pat. Sect.) [A Banner&W.]
*PRACTICE AREAS: Intellectual Property; Design Patents; Mechanical Intellectual Property; Computer and Software Patents; Electrical Intellectual Property.

Moulds, Elizabeth G. '73 '99 C.339 B.A. L.93 J.D.
(adm. in IL; not adm. in DC) [A Ballard S.A.&I.]
*PRACTICE AREAS: Commercial Litigation; Employment Litigation.

Moulton, Barbara '59 '89 C.1107 B.A. L.276 J.D.
(adm. in MA; not adm. in DC) Georgetown Univ. Law Ctr.

Moultrie, H. Carl, III '77 '01 C.188 B.S. L.276 J.D.
(adm. in VA; not adm. in DC) [A Shaw P.]

Mount, Clifton Merritt, (BV) ... '61 '88 C.207 B.A. L.896 J.D. [A Bode&G.]
*PRACTICE AREAS: Insurance Litigation; Professional Malpractice; Workers' Compensation Defense; Construction Litigation; Civil Litigation.

Mounteer, Thomas R. ... '61 '86 C.867 B.A. L.273 J.D. [Paul,H.J.&W.]
*PRACTICE AREAS: Environmental Law.

Mounts, Lynda S., (AV) ... '46 '73 C.563 B.A. L.174 J.D. Sr. Coun., American Ins. Assn.
*RESPONSIBILITIES: Regulatory Law; Administrative Law; Litigation.

Mounts, Phoebe, Ph.D. ... '— '99 C.665 B.S. L.276 J.D. [A Morgan,L.&B.]

Mounts, R. Darrell ... '— '88 C.901 B.A. L.945 J.D. [Kirkpatrick&L.]
*PRACTICE AREAS: Investment Company Law; Investment Management; Investment Regulation; Mutual Funds; Securities Regulation.

Moustafa, Hoda Atia ... '72 '98 C.446 B.S. L.276 J.D. [A Clifford C.R.&W.]
*PRACTICE AREAS: Project Finance.

Moustakas, John ... '64 '92 C.94 B.A. L.188 J.D. [Shea&G.]
*PRACTICE AREAS: Complex Civil Litigation; White Collar Criminal Defense.

Mouysset, Isabelle ... '59 '90 L.923 J.D. The World Bk.

Movshin, Lawrence J., (AV) ... '49 '74 C.705 B.A. L.273 J.D. [Wilkinson B.K.]
*PRACTICE AREAS: Communications; Telecommunications Law; Corporate; Commercial Transactions; International Telecommunications.

Mow, Laura C., (AV) ... '57 '82 C.914 B.A. L.930 J.D. [Gardner,C.&D.]
*PRACTICE AREAS: Communications and Media; FCC Regulation; Radio Common Carrier; Telecommunications Contracts; Wireless Communications.

Mowatt, Frederick W. '15 '42 C.197 A.B. L.94 LL.B.
(adm. in MA; not adm. in DC) Asst. V.P., Fed. Natl. Mtge. Assn.

Mowry, Kristin H. ... '70 '99 C.145 B.A. L.276 J.D. [A O'Melveny&M.]

Moy, John P. ... '72 '99 C.1375 B.S. L.569 J.D. [A Venable,A.B.H.&C.]
*PRACTICE AREAS: Intellectual Property Litigation.

Moyd, Olinda ... '59 '88 C.999 B.S. L.608 J.D. Staff Atty., Pub. Def. Serv.

Moyer, Homer E., Jr., (AV) ... '— '67 C.1365 B.A. L.976 LL.B. [Miller&C.]
*PRACTICE AREAS: International Trade Regulation; Foreign Corrupt Practices Act; North American Free Trade Agreement; International Dispute Resolution; International Trade.

Moyer, Shannon M. ... '75 '00 C.823 B.A. L.537 J.D. [A Zuckert,S.&R.]

Mrava, Susan Lynn S. '65 '96 C.1369 B.B.A. L.945 J.D.
(adm. in VA; not adm. in DC) Tax Atty., Ernst & Young L.L.P.

Mrizek, Richard J. '71 '96 C.597 B.A. L.477 J.D.
1333 New Hampshire Avenue, N.W., Suite 400

Mroczka, Victor . . . . '71 '00 C.276 B.S.F.S. L.30 J.D. [[A] Dorsey&W.]
*PRACTICE AREAS: Customs Law; Antidumping; Export Controls.
Mros, Don J. . . . . '51 '84 C&L.502 B.A., J.D. [[C] Chadbourne&P.]
Mrose, James E. . . . . '64 '89 C.309 S.B.E.E. L.94 J.D. [[C] Fish&R.] (See Pat. Sect.)
*PRACTICE AREAS: Intellectual Property; Patents.
Mucchetti, Peter J. . . . . '68 '97 C.976 B.A. L.309 J.D. [[A] Wilmer,C.&P.]
Muchnikoff, Dave M., (P.C.) . . . . '58 '86 C.276 B.S.B.A. L.904 J.D. [Silver,F.&T.]
*PRACTICE AREAS: Securities Law; Financial Institutions Law; Corporate Finance Law.
Muckenfuss, Cantwell Faulkner, III, (AV) '45 '73
C.880 B.A. L.976 J.D. [Gibson,D.&C.]
*PRACTICE AREAS: Financial Institutions Law and Regulation; Legislative and Public Policy Matters; Mergers and Acquisitions.

Mudd, Richard J. '41 '72 C&L.273 B.A., J.D.
2319 Pennsylvania Avenue, S.E., 20020
Telephone: 703-360-0941 Fax: 703-360-8770
Email: rich3333@erols.com URL: http://www.lawyers.com/richardmudd
***PRACTICE AREAS: Civil Trial Practice; Medical Malpractice; Professional Malpractice; Personal Injury; Probate Litigation.**
Civil Trial Practice, Medical Malpractice, Professional Malpractice, Personal Injury, Probate Litigation, Real Estate Litigation, Estate Planning and Administration.
See Professional Biographies, WASHINGTON, DISTRICT OF COLUMBIA

Mudge, Amy Ralph . . . . '69 '96 C.788 B.A. L.188 J.D. [[A] Arnold&P.]
*PRACTICE AREAS: Antitrust; Trade Regulation; Litigation.
Mudge, Brian S. . . . . '56 '91 C&L.659 B.S., J.D. [Kenyon&K.] (See Pat. Sect.)
*PRACTICE AREAS: Intellectual Property.
Mudge, Wilson D. . . . . '68 '96 C.475 B.A. L.904 J.D. [[A] Arnold&P.]
*PRACTICE AREAS: Antitrust and Trade Regulation; Litigation.
Muellenberg, Kurt W. '32 '61 C&L.446 B.A., LL.B. 1300 I St., N.W.
Mueller, Michael J. . . . . '60 '86 C&L.477 A.B., J.D. [Akin,G.S.H.&F.]
*PRACTICE AREAS: Litigation.
Mueller, Robert S., III, (AV) . . . . '44 '74 C.674 B.A. L.893 J.D. U.S. Atty's. Off.
Mueller, Ronald O. . . . . '60 '87 C.880 B.A. L.178 J.D. [Gibson,D.&C.]
*PRACTICE AREAS: Securities; Corporate Disclosure and Proxy Regulation; Executive Compensation.
Mueller, Thomas . . . . '65 '90 [Wilmer,C.&P.]
*PRACTICE AREAS: EU Competition; Antitrust.
Mugavero, Patricia S. . . . . '62 '91 C.705 B.A. L.904 J.D. [[A] Goodwin P.]
Muhammad, Natasha T. . . . . '74 '99 C.329 B.A. L.309 J.D. [[A] Hogan&H.]
*PRACTICE AREAS: Health Law.
Muhlendorf, Kevin Brian . . . . '73 '98 C.893 B.A. L.945 J.D. [[A] Steptoe&J.]
Muir, J. Dapray, (AV) . . . . '36 '64 C.951 A.B. L.893 J.D. [Ruddy&M.]
*PRACTICE AREAS: Corporate Law; Securities Law; Mergers and Acquisitions.
Muir, John D., Jr. . . . . '67 '96 C.880 B.A. L.1009 J.D. [[A] Piper M.R.&W.]
*PRACTICE AREAS: Commercial Real Estate.
Muir, Patrick D. '67 '96
C.886 B.S.E.E. L.1356 J.D. Coun., Samsung Electronics America (Pat.)
*RESPONSIBILITIES: Patent (100%).
Mulcahy, Daniel J., (AV) . . . . '46 '72 C.823 A.B. L.893 J.D. [Cadwalader,W.&T.]
*PRACTICE AREAS: Federal Income Tax; Leveraged Leasing; Aircraft Financing and Leasing.
Mulcahy, Edwin C., Jr. '40 '66 C.910 B.S.E.E. L.276 J.D.
Dep. Gen. Coun., Pharmaceutical Resch. & Manufacturers of Amer.
Muldoon, Joseph A., III, (BV) '55 '89 C.37 B.S. L.276 J.D.
1299 Pennsylvania Ave., N.W.
Muldoon, Joseph A., Jr., (AV) . . . . '31 '57 C&L.276 B.S., LL.B. [Muldoon M.&F.]
*PRACTICE AREAS: Legislative Practice; Congressional; Federal Government; Finance; Savings and Loan.

Muldoon Murphy & Faucette LLP, (AV) [BR]
5101 Wisconsin Avenue, N.W., 20016
Telephone: 202-362-0840 Telecopier: 202-966-9409; 202-363-5068
Email: counsel@mmf-law.com URL: http://www.mmf-law.com
Members of Firm: Joseph A. Muldoon, Jr.; George W. Murphy, Jr.; Douglas P. Faucette; John R. Hall; Thomas J. Haggerty (Not admitted in DC); Joseph P. Daly; Lori M. Beresford; Christina M. Gattuso; Lawrence M. F. Spaccasi (Not admitted in DC); Paul M. Aguggia; Eric S. Kracov; Victor L. Cangelosi; Aaron M. Kaslow; Kent M. Krudys; Thomas P. Hutton. Associates: Scott A. Brown (Not admitted in DC); Suzanne A. Walker; Mia S. Kim (Not admitted in DC); Michael B. Woodard (Not admitted in DC); Roy E. Brownell, II; Jon C. Findlay, Jr. (Not admitted in DC). Of Counsel: Leslie Ann Murphy; Arthur D. Perschetz (Not admitted in DC).
Practice before Federal and State Regulatory Agencies. Savings and Loan, Corporation, Banking, Securities and Administrative Law, Employee Benefits, Taxation, representation of Nonprofit and Charitable Organizations.
See Professional Biographies, WASHINGTON, DISTRICT OF COLUMBIA

Muldowney, J. Kevin '64 '01 C.999 B.S. L.1209 J.D.
(adm. in VA; not adm. in DC) [[A] Mayer,B.&P.]
Mulera, Raymond R. . . . . '65 '91 C.602 B.A. L.180 J.D. [Levin&R.]
*PRACTICE AREAS: Agricultural Law; Insurance; Government Contracts; Litigation.
Mulford, Brian . . . . '73 '99 C.696 B.A. L.893 J.D. [[A] Nixon P.]
*PRACTICE AREAS: Corporate Law.
Mullady, Raymond G., Jr. . . . . '57 '83 C&L.446 B.S., J.D. [Piper M.R.&W.]
*PRACTICE AREAS: Litigation; Products Liability Law; Food and Drug; Libel and Slander Law.
Mullan, John Gibson . . . . '53 '83 C.659 B.A. L.893 J.D. [Kirkland&E.]
*PRACTICE AREAS: Administrative Law; Environmental Law-Air Pollution Regulation; Appellate Litigation; Regulatory Litigation.
Mullen, Clair X., Jr., (BV) '33 '60
C.757 B.S. L.665 LL.B. [Finnegan,H.F.G.&D.] (See Pat. Sect.)
*PRACTICE AREAS: International Patent Prosecution; Metallurgical Patents; Patent Licensing; Patent Prosecution.
Mullen, Daniel A. . . . . '67 '94 C.860 B.A. L.978 J.D. [[A] McDermott,W.&E.]
Mullen, John E. . . . . '38 '64 C.966 B.S. L.309 LL.B. [[C] Fredrikson&B.]
*PRACTICE AREAS: International Finance; International Law; Federal Administrative Law.
Mullen, Kevin P. . . . . '61 '88 C&L.893 B.A., J.D. [Piper M.R.&W.]
*PRACTICE AREAS: Government Contracts; Construction Law.
Mullen, Lauren C. . . . . '66 '92 C.178 A.B. L.145 J.D. [[A] Orrick,H.&S.]
Mullenholz, John, (P.C.), (AV) . . . . '42 '67 C.93 A.B. L.276 J.D. [Mullenholz,B.&B.]
Mullenholz, Brimsek & Belair, (AV) . . . . . 1150 Connecticut Avenue, Northwest, Suite 700
Mullens, Richard A., (AV) . . . . '18 '42 C&L.972 B.A., LL.B. [[C] Silverstein&M.]
Muller, Clifford E., (AV) . . . . '56 '81 C.105 B.S.B.A. L.273 J.D. [Sutherland A.&B.]
*PRACTICE AREAS: International Taxation; Federal Taxation.
Muller, Scott W., (AV) . . . . '50 '77 C.674 B.A. L.276 J.D. [Davis P.&W.]
Mullick, Sanjay Jose . . . . '69 '98 C&L.276 B.S.F.S., J.D. [[A] Shaw P.]
Mullin, Cheryl L. '67 '95 C.831 B.A. L.1338 J.D.
(adm. in NJ; not adm. in DC) [[A] Jenkens&G.]
*PRACTICE AREAS: Franchise Law; Distribution; Intellectual Property; Antitrust; Commercial Law.
Mullin, Elizabeth D. . . . . '56 '85 C.518 B.A. L.569 J.D. Environmental Law Inst.
Mullin, Eugene F., (AV) . . . . '25 '50 C.103 A.B. L.273 LL.B. [Mullin,R.E.&T.]
Mullin, Rhyne, Emmons and Topel, Professional Corporation, (AV)
1225 Connecticut Ave., N.W.
Mullings, Lorraine T. '— '00 C.276 B.A. L.273 J.D.
(adm. in CT; not adm. in DC) [[A] Reed S.]
*PRACTICE AREAS: Government Contracts; Export Compliance.
Mullins, P. Todd . . . . '64 '89 C.923 B.S. L.273 J.D. [Howrey S.A.&W.]
*PRACTICE AREAS: Commercial Litigation; Antitrust.

Mullins, William A., (BV) . . . . '61 '88 C&L.174 B.A., J.D. [Troutman S.]
*PRACTICE AREAS: Transportation; Administrative Law; Government Relations; Antitrust.
Mulvihill, Donald J., (AV) . . . . '31 '57 C.602 A.B. L.262 LL.B. [Cahill G.&R.]
Mulville, Kathleen T. '71 '99 C.893 B.S.C.E. L.945 J.D.
(adm. in VA; not adm. in DC) [[A] Brickfield B.R.&S.]
*PRACTICE AREAS: Energy Law.
Muncy, Curtis L. . . . . '54 '80 C.763 A.B. L.990 J.D. Price Waterhouse
Mundle, Winfred R. . . . . '30 '60 C.329 B.A. L.276 J.D. 6401 16th St., N.W.
Mundt, Michelle Marie . . . .'— '95 C.228 B.A. L.276 J.D. 701 Pennsylvania Avenue, N.W.
Munir, Junaid "Jay" '76 '01 C.976 B.A. L.309 J.D.
(adm. in FL; not adm. in DC) [[A] Kirkland&E.]
*PRACTICE AREAS: Litigation.
Munk, Jeffrey W. . . . . '61 '88 C.210 B.M. L.823 J.D. [Hogan&H.]
*PRACTICE AREAS: Tax Legislative Practice; Energy Legislative Practice; Transportation Legislative Practice; Appropriations; Legislative Practice.
Munro, Alan B. '58 '84 C.893 B.S. L.902 J.D.
(adm. in NY; not adm. in DC) Arthur Anderson LLP‡
Munro, Donald J. . . . . '69 '96 C.367 B.A. L.893 J.D. [[A] Shea&G.]
Munsat, Susan Chertkof . . . . '60 '91 C&L.659 B.A., J.D. [Lichtman,T.S.&R.]
Muntzing, L. Manning, (AV) . . . . '34 '60 C.575 A.B. L.309 LL.B. 1800 M St., N.W.‡
Muoio, Ann WrayJohnson '72 '98 C.674 A.B. L.893 J.D.
(adm. in VA; not adm. in DC) U.S. Dept. of Jus.
Muoio, Ralph A., (AV) . . . . '32 '62 C.659 B.S. Econ. L.309 LL.B. [Caplin&D.]
*PRACTICE AREAS: Federal Tax Litigation.
Muoio, Ralph M. . . . . '67 '97 C.178 B.A. L.893 J.D. [[A] Covington&B.]
*PRACTICE AREAS: Insurance.
Murad, Gregory M., (AV) '48 '75 C.1031 B.A. L.128 J.D.
Assoc. Gen. Coun., Medlantic Healthcare Group
Muratori, Francesca '57 '00 C.472 B.A. L.276 J.D.
(adm. in MD; not adm. in DC) [[A] Dow,L.&A.]
Murchison, David C., (AV) . . . . '23 '49 C&L.273 LL.B. [Howrey S.A.&W.]
Murchison, Pete M., (BV) . . . . '45 '80 C.846 B.A. L.1209 J.D. [O'Connell&Assoc.]
*PRACTICE AREAS: Litigation; Family Law.
Murck, William W. . . . . '35 '73 C.103 B.A. L.128 J.D. 5431 41st Pl., N.W.
Murdock, Eric J. . . . . '60 '85 C.674 A.B. L.228 J.D. [Hunton&W.]
*PRACTICE AREAS: Environmental Law; Litigation.
Murdock, J. E., III, (AV) . . . . '47 '73 C.674 A.B. L.178 J.D. [Shaw P.]
*PRACTICE AREAS: Transportation Law; Aviation Law; Administrative Law; Lobbying; Environmental Law.
Murdock, John . . . . '72 '99 C.846 B.A. L.329 J.D. 2451 18th St., NW
Murdock, John M. . . . . '— '86 C.951 B.A. L.880 J.D. [Epstein B.&G.]
*PRACTICE AREAS: Litigation.
Murdy, Heidi E. . . . . '75 '01 C.229 B.A. L.976 J.D. [[A] Williams&C.]
*PRACTICE AREAS: Litigation.

Murphey, Michael R., (AV) '47 '73 C.473 B.A. L.273 J.D.
Suite 202, 1320 19th Street, N.W., 20036
Telephone: 202-659-8611 Fax: 202-659-8612
Email: murpheyusa@aol.com URL: http://www.lawyers.com/murpheylaw
Bankruptcy, Bankruptcy Chapter 7, Bankruptcy Chapter 13 and Bankruptcy Chapter 11, Debtor and Creditor, Consumer Rights, Commercial Bankruptcy, Probate Litigation, Wills, Trust Law, Estate Administration, Inheritance, Probate Taxation, Small Business Law, Business Successions, Business Reorganization, Incorporation, Family Business Law, Family Law.
See Professional Biographies, WASHINGTON, DISTRICT OF COLUMBIA

Murphy, Anne Marie . . . . '61 '00 C.999 B.S. L.1338 J.D. [[A] Hyman,P.&M.]
*PRACTICE AREAS: Food and Drug Law.
Murphy, Barbara A., (AV) '57 '82
C.197 B.A. L.273 J.D. [Adduci,M.&S.] (See Pat. Sect.)
*PRACTICE AREAS: Antidumping; International Trade Regulation; Unfair Competition; Intellectual Property.
Murphy, Betty Southard, (AV) . . . . '— '58 C.608 B.A. L.30 J.D. [Baker&H.]
*PRACTICE AREAS: Employment Law; Administrative Law; International Law.
Murphy, Brian P., (AV) . . . . '43 '69 C.276 A.B. L.128 J.D. [Griffin,F.T.&M.]
*PRACTICE AREAS: Corporate Law; Civil Practice; Real Estate; International Law; Business Law.
Murphy, C. Westbrook, (AV) . . . . '40 '66 C.228 A.B. L.976 LL.B. Price Waterhouse
Murphy, Celeste M. . . . . '71 '97 C.569 B.A. L.107 J.D. Atty. Advsr.
Murphy, Christopher P. . . . . '61 '94 C.816 B.E. L.347 J.D. [[C] Shook,H.&B.]
*PRACTICE AREAS: Patent, Trademark, Copyright and Trade Secret Litigation; Intellectual Property Counseling.
Murphy, David M. . . . . '61 '86 [Grunfeld,D.L.&K.] (⊙New York, NY)
*PRACTICE AREAS: Customs; International Business Transactions; Trade Regulation; Foreign Trade Zones; International Sanctions Programs (OFAC).
Murphy, Elizabeth Kondonijakos . . . . '71 '97 C.70 B.A. L.831 J.D. [[A] Epstein B.&G.]
*PRACTICE AREAS: Health Law.
Murphy, Emalee G., (AV) . . . . '— '80 C.604 A.B. L.904 J.D. [[C] Kirkpatrick&L.]
*PRACTICE AREAS: Food and Drug Regulation; Medical Devices; Alternative Health Care Products; Personal Care Products; Animal Drug Regulation.
Murphy, George R., (AV) '37 '64 C&L.128 A.B., LL.B.
Gen. Coun., United Food & Comercial Workers International Union
Murphy, George W., Jr., (AV) . . . . '29 '54 C&L.276 B.S., LL.B. [Muldoon M.&F.]
*PRACTICE AREAS: Financial Institutions; Mergers and Acquisitions; Regulation; Savings and Loan; Savings and Loan Regulation.
Murphy, Jack W., (AV) . . . . '58 '84 C.1044 B.A. L.93 J.D. [Dechert]
*PRACTICE AREAS: Investment Management; Financial Services Law; Securities; Corporate Law.
Murphy, James J. . . . . '66 '94 C.321 A.B. L.128 J.D. [[C] Akin,G.S.H.&F.]
*PRACTICE AREAS: Labor and Employment.
Murphy, James J. . . . . '— '58 C&L.734 B.S., LL.B. [[C] Bryan C.]
*PRACTICE AREAS: Litigation; Administrative Practice; Legislation.
Murphy, James P., (AV) . . . '44 '69 C.602 A.B. L.477 J.D. [Squire,S.&D.] (⊙Cleve., OH)
*PRACTICE AREAS: Litigation.
Murphy, Jane C. . . . . '53 '78 C.93 B.A. L.107 J.D. Georgetown Univ. Law Ctr.
Murphy, Jerome A. . . . . '63 '92 C.276 B.A. L.446 J.D. [[A] Crowell&M.]
Murphy, John C., Jr., (AV) . . . . '45 '72 C.276 A.B. L.659 J.D. [Cleary,G.S.&H.]
Murphy, John G., Jr. . . . . '37 '62 C.309 A.B. L.276 J.D. 2119 R St., N.W.

Murphy, Jos. Dinsmore, (AV) '33 '62 C&L.309 A.B., LL.B.
5015 Lowell Street, N.W., 20016
Telephone: 202-237-1633 Fax: 202-537-5571
General Civil Practice before all Courts, Departments and Agencies. Administrative Law, Labor and Employment Law, Personal Injury. Litigation.

Murphy, Joseph A., (AV) '34 '63 C.276 B.S. L.213 J.D.
(adm. in MI; not adm. in DC) 1310 G St., N.W., 9th Fl.‡
Murphy, Keith R. '— '00 C.645 B.S. L.273 J.D.
(adm. in VA; not adm. in DC) [[A] Wilkinson B.K.]
*PRACTICE AREAS: Communications Law.
Murphy, Kevin M., (AV) . . . . '59 '84 C.602 B.B.A. L.128 J.D. [Carr G.] ⊙
*PRACTICE AREAS: Products Liability; Intellectual Property; Professional Liability.
Murphy, Kevin W. '68 '93 C&L.347 B.A., J.D.
(adm. in IN; not adm. in DC) Dep. Coun., Republican Natl. Comm.
Murphy, Leslie Ann . . . . '45 '82 C.323 B.A. L.259 J.D. [[C] Muldoon M.&F.]
*PRACTICE AREAS: Securities; Capital Formation; Corporate Law; Business Law; Financial Institutions.

Murphy, Lisa T. '67 '93
C.629 B.S. L.188 J.D. Assoc. Coun., BlueCross BlueShield Assn.
Murphy, Mara Walker . . . . '70 '96 C.170 B.A. L.893 J.D. [Ⓐ Williams&C.]
Murphy, Marcia Gaughan '49 '75 C.788 A.B. L.602 J.D.
(adm. in OH; not adm. in DC) Prof., The Amer. Univ., Wash. Coll. of Law
Murphy, Mark J. . . . . '68 '96 C.321 B.A. L.1009 J.D. [Ⓐ Mooney,G.B.&S.]
Murphy, Mary A. . . . .'64 '89 C.937 B.A. L.273 [Ⓒ LeBoeuf,L.G.&M.]
*PRACTICE AREAS: Energy; Utilities.
Murphy, Michael C. '73 '00 C.821 B.A. L.904 J.D.
Staff Atty., International Brotherhood of Teamsters
Murphy, Michael E. . . . . '71 '97 C.321 B.A. L.659 J.D. [Ⓐ Baker&M.]
*PRACTICE AREAS: Litigation; Regulatory Law; International Trade Regulation; Trade Regulations and Customs Law; Federal Administrative Law.
Murphy, Michael J. . . . . '63 '89 C.390 A.B. L.128 J.D. [Ogletree,D.N.S.&S.]
*PRACTICE AREAS: Labor and Employment; Employment Litigation; Equal Employment Opportunity Law; Employment Contracts; Fair Labor Standards.
Murphy, Michael K. . . . . '71 '99 C.276 B.S. L.893 J.D. [Ⓐ Gibson,D.&C.]
*PRACTICE AREAS: Government Contracts; Environmental Law.
Murphy, Michael P. . . . .'54 '81 C.103 A.B. L.262 J.D. [Katten M.Z.]
*PRACTICE AREAS: Structured Finance; Public Finance.
Murphy, Michael T., (BV) '58 '83
C.446 B.A. L.64 J.D. [Roylance,A.B.&G.] (See Pat. Sect.)
*PRACTICE AREAS: Patents; Trademarks; Copyright Law; Litigation; Unfair Competition Law.
Murphy, Michele Harrington . . . . '68 '93 C.886 B.A. L.575 J.D. [Ⓒ Akin,G.S.H.&F.]
*PRACTICE AREAS: Labor and Employment.
Murphy, Mona M. . . . .'— '80 C.94 Ed.M. L.818 J.D. [Ⓐ Feith&Z.]
Murphy, Paul N., (AV) . . . . '44 '73 C.902 A.B. L.893 J.D. [Tighe P.A.T.]
*PRACTICE AREAS: Tax and Securities Enforcement; Complex Civil and Criminal Litigation.
Murphy, Peter P. . . . . '65 '90 C.276 B.S. L.477 J.D. [Gibson,D.&C.]
*PRACTICE AREAS: Environmental.

Murphy, Pierre E., Law Offices of, (AV) '56 '79 C.999 L.966 J.D.
2445 M Street, N.W., Suite 260, 20037
Telephone: 202-872-1679 Fax: 202-872-1725
Email: pmurphy@lopmurphy.com
***PRACTICE AREAS: Aviation Law; Regulatory Law; Commercial Law; International Law.**
Associate: Andrea Ruiz (Not admitted in DC).
Aviation, Regulatory and Commercial Law. International Law. Travel Law.
See Professional Biographies, WASHINGTON, DISTRICT OF COLUMBIA

Murphy, Rebecca L. . . . . '73 '00 C.223 B.S. L.128 J.D. [Ⓐ Bennet&B.]
*PRACTICE AREAS: Communications Law.
Murphy, Richard G., Jr., (AV) '48 '73 C.103 A.B. L.880 J.D.
(adm. in GA; not adm. in DC) [Sutherland A.&B.]
*PRACTICE AREAS: Bankruptcy; Commercial Litigation; Banks and Banking.
Murphy, Robert B. . . . .'56 '83 C.602 B.A. L.884 J.D. [Piper M.R.&W.]
*PRACTICE AREAS: Finance; Corporate Law; Securities.
Murphy, Sean P. . . . .'63 '90 C&L.276 B.S.F.S., J.D. [Ⓒ Patton B.]
Murphy, Starr L. '56 '81 C.1111 B.A. L.910 J.D.
(adm. in MO; not adm. in DC) 2300 40th St., N.W.‡
Murphy, Stephen P. . . . .'— '76 C.93 A.B. L.128 J.D. [Reed S.]
*PRACTICE AREAS: Litigation.
Murphy, Tecla A. . . . . '64 '89 C.339 B.A. L.145 J.D. [Ⓒ Akin,G.S.H.&F.]
*PRACTICE AREAS: Health Care Law; Corporate Transactional.
Murphy, Ted J. . . . .'71 '96 C.1044 B.A. L.893 J.D. [Ⓐ Hunton&W.]
*PRACTICE AREAS: Energy Regulation.
Murphy, Terence, (AV) . . . .'37 '67 C.309 A.B. L.477 J.D. [Ⓒ Murphy E.W.]
*PRACTICE AREAS: Export Compliance; Intellectual Property; Administrative Law.
Murphy, Thomas Francis . . . . '71 '96 C.1369 B.S. L.280 J.D. [Ⓐ Friedlander,M.S.K.&O.]
*PRACTICE AREAS: Civil Litigation; Commercial Leasing; Business Law.

Murphy Ellis Weber, (AV) BB
818 Connecticut Avenue, N.W., Suite 700, 20006-2702
Telephone: 202-833-9211 Fax: 202-833-6570 URL: http://www.MurphyEllisWeber.com
Email: mew@MurphyEllisWeber.com
Members of Firm: Courtenay Ellis; Charles A. Weber. Senior Counsel: Terence Murphy.
International Business Law, Litigation, Administrative Law and Government Relations, Export Controls. Defense Trade/Technology Transfer, Encryption, Economic Sanctions, E-Commerce/Telecommunications, Intellectual Property Law, Antitrust and Trade Regulation.
Representative Clients: Allergan; American Association of Exporters and Importers; American Express; British-American Business Association; Carl Zeiss Jena; Embraer; Malta Financial Services Centre; Nokia; OneTravel.com.
Associated Offices: Fact Law Group (Helsinki & Washington) and Kiskalt, Dielmann & Schoenberger (Frankfurt).
See Professional Biographies, WASHINGTON, DISTRICT OF COLUMBIA

Murray, Andrew H. . . . . '74 '99 C.273 B.A. L.276 J.D. [Ⓐ Hunton&W.]
*PRACTICE AREAS: Project Finance; Lease Finance.
Murray, Brian L., Jr. '66 '91 C.108 B.A. L.477 J.D.
(adm. in MI; not adm. in DC) 1301 K Street, NW, Suite 800 East
Murray, Daniel H. . . . .'— '70 C.415 B.A. L.262 J.D. [Bigham E.J.&H.]
*PRACTICE AREAS: State Government Law; Federal Government Law; Business Development.
Murray, David P. . . . . '60 '85 C.999 B.A. L.276 J.D. [Willkie F.&G.]
Murray, David T. . . . .'61 '98 C.1356 B.A. L.201 J.D. 444 N. Capitol St., N.W.
Murray, Dwight D., (AV) . . . .'44 '76 C.974 B.A. L.276 J.D. [Jordan C.&S.]
*PRACTICE AREAS: Litigation; Defense Litigation; U.S. Supreme Court Litigation; Hospital Law; Legal Ethics and Professional Responsibility.
Murray, Edward R. . . . .'70 '00 C.886 B.A. L.273 J.D. [Ⓐ Crowell&M.]
Murray, Frank S. . . . .'70 '95 C.976 B.A. L.893 J.D. 1200 New Hampshire Ave., N.W.
Murray, Fred F., (AV) . . . . '50 '75 C.691 B.A. L.846 J.D. P.O. Box 774
Murray, Frederick Franklin '50 '87
C.691 B.A. L.846 J.D. Natl. Foreign Trade Council, Inc.
Murray, James E. . . . . '55 '84 C&L.229 B.A., J.D. Natl. Assoc. for Home Care
Murray, James V., III '42 '67 C.276 A.B. L.262 J.D.
(adm. in NY; not adm. in DC) Union Carbide Corp.
Murray, Kerry E. . . . .'64 '91 C.228 A.B. L.276 J.D. Dir., Intl. Reg. Affs., MCI WorldCom
Murray, Lisa A. . . . .'67 '97 C.604 B.A. L.477 J.D. [Ⓐ Gibson,D.&C.]
*PRACTICE AREAS: International Trade; Litigation.
Murray, Milissa A. . . . . '58 '87 C.445 B.S. L.64 J.D. [Ⓒ Swidler B.S.F.]
*PRACTICE AREAS: Environmental Litigation; Environmental Enforcement; Commercial Litigation; Bankruptcy; Business Reorganization.
Murray, Nancy A. . . . .'55 '79 C.354 B.A. L.201 J.D. [Ⓒ Patton B.]
Murray, Robert B., (AV) . . . '35 '67 C.502 B.S.Ch.E. L.904 J.D. [Arent F.K.P.&K.] (Pat.)
*PRACTICE AREAS: Intellectual Property; Patents; Technology Law; Chemical Patents; Medical Patents.
Murray, Scott B. . . . . '68 '94 C.674 B.S.E. L.1292 J.D. [Ⓐ Clifford C.R.&W.]
*PRACTICE AREAS: Antitrust and Trade Regulation.
Murray, Teresa White . . . . '72 '98 C.329 B.A. L.273 J.D. [Ⓐ O'Donoghue&O.]
*PRACTICE AREAS: Labor and Employment Law; EEO; Employee Benefits.
Murray, William R., Jr. '49 '75 C&L.276 A.B., J.D.
Nat. Res. Coun., American Forest & Paper Assn.
Murray, William R., Jr. . . . .'59 '84 C.1021 B.A. L.276 J.D. [Williams&C.]
Murray, Purcell & Crump, PLLC . . . . .1822 11th St., NW
Murrell, Travis A. . . . . '42 '76 C&L.276 B.S.L., J.D. [Murrell&B.]
*PRACTICE AREAS: Special Education.

Murrell & Brown
1401 I Street N.W. Suite 250, 20005
Telephone: 202-289-9001 Fax: 202-289-9094
Email: ATTYTRAV@aol.com
Members of Firm: Travis A. Murrell; James E. Brown. Associates: Domiento C.R. Hill (Not admitted in DC).
Special Education Law, Disability Rights, Psychological Evaluation, Individual Education Programs.
See Professional Biographies, WASHINGTON, DISTRICT OF COLUMBIA

Murry, Harold D., Jr., (AV) . . . . '43 '68 C&L.623 B.A., J.D. [Baker B.]
Murtha, Frank F. '38 '64 C.884 A.B. L.178 J.D.
(adm. in NY; not adm. in DC) [Ⓒ Collier S.S.]
Musa, T. Melindah . . . .'74 '99 C.112 B.A. L.309 J.D. [Ⓐ Kaye S.]
*PRACTICE AREAS: Litigation; Campaign Finance and Regulatory Work.
Muse, Robert F., (AV) . . . .'47 '73 C.93 B.S. L.276 J.D. [Stein,M.&M.]
Museles, Scott D. . . . .'— '92 C.260 B.S. L.128 J.D. 1800 M St., N.W.
Museles, Steven A. . . .'63 '88 C.893 B.A. L.276 J.D. General Counsel, CapitalSource LLC
Musella, Joseph L. . . . . '73 '99 C.273 B.B.A. L.1209 J.D. [Ⓐ Clifford C.R.&W.]
*PRACTICE AREAS: Banking Law; Corporate Law; Securities.
Musgrove, C. Kyle . . . .'70 '96 C.861 B.S. L.1128 J.D. [Ⓐ Kenyon&K.] (See Pat. Sect.)
*PRACTICE AREAS: Intellectual Property.
Muskin, Jonathan H. '67 '96 C.861 B.S. L.1000 J.D.
(adm. in NJ; not adm. in DC; See Pat. Sect.) [Ⓐ Staas&H.]
*PRACTICE AREAS: Intellectual Property Law; Patents; Trademarks; Copyright Law.
Musonye-Smith, Rose '58 '86 C.411 B.A. L.329 J.D.
Legal Counsel to Comm. on Educ. & Libraries
Muss Hegerle, Ashlie . . . .'— '95 C.188 B.A. L.569 J.D. [Ⓐ Latham&W.]
*PRACTICE AREAS: Commercial Financing; Secured Transactions; Mergers and Acquisitions Finance.
Musslewhite, Lon E., (AV) . . . . '50 '84 C.658 B.S. L.904 J.D. [Williams&C.]
Mutryn, William J., (AV) . . . . '48 '75 C.930 B.S. L.273 J.D. [Holland&K.]
*PRACTICE AREAS: Corporate Law; Securities; Mergers and Acquisitions; Health Care Law; Finance Law.
Mutschelknaus, Brad E. . . . .'54 '80 C.182 B.A. L.276 J.D. [Kelley D.&W.]
*PRACTICE AREAS: Communications; Antitrust and Trade Regulation; Litigation; Corporate Law.
Muys, Jerome C., (AV) . . . . '32 '57 C.674 A.B. L.813 LL.B. [Muys&Assoc.]
Muys, Jerome C., Jr., (AV) . . . .'54 '79 C.575 B.A. L.273 J.D. [Swidler B.S.F.]
*PRACTICE AREAS: Environmental Compliance; Groundwater Contamination; Hazardous Waste; Property Remediation; Superfund.
Muys & Associates, (AV) . . . . 1575 Eye St., N.W.
Muyskens, Nathan J. . . . .'— '95 C.893 B.A. L.378 J.D. [Ⓐ Morgan,L.&B.]
Myers, Christopher A., (AV) . . . .'49 '77 C.385 B.A. L.128 J.D. [Holland&K.]
*PRACTICE AREAS: Complex Civil and Criminal Litigation; White Collar Criminal Defense and Compliance Programs; Health Care.
Myers, David '65 '91 C.350 B.S. L.352 J.D.
(adm. in MN; not adm. in DC) [Ⓐ Fried,F.H.S.&J.]
*PRACTICE AREAS: Antitrust.
Myers, Donald Bruce, Jr. '71 '97
C&L.893 B.A., J.D. Staff Atty., Environmental Law Institute
*RESPONSIBILITIES: Environmental Law.
Myers, Donald J., (AV) . . . .'— '68 C.563 B.A. L.188 J.D. [Reed S.]
*PRACTICE AREAS: Employee Benefits.
Myers, George C., Jr., (AV) '38 '73 C.871 B.S. L.93 J.D.
(adm. in MA; not adm. in DC; See Pat. Sect.) [Ⓒ Blank R.C.&M.]
*PRACTICE AREAS: Patent Litigation; Patent Prosecution; Patent Licensing.
Myers, Gordon I. '59 '88 C&L.813 A.B., J.D.
(adm. in NY; not adm. in DC) Atty., Intl. Fin. Corp.
Myers, James E. . . . .'— '99 C.228 B.A. L.477 J.D. [Ⓐ Shaw P.]
Myers, James Ernest, Jr. . . . .'71 '99 C.228 A.B. L.477 J.D. 2300 N St., NW
Myers, Matthew L., (AV) '47 '75 C.860 B.A. L.477 J.D.
President, National Center for Tobacco-Free Kids
Myers, Michael J. '68 '94
C.188 B.S. L.1194 J.D. 1050 Connecticut Ave., N.W., Suite 1100
Myers, Polly A. . . . .'62 '88 C.608 B.A. L.276 J.D. [Ⓐ Howrey S.A.&W.]
*PRACTICE AREAS: Litigation; Antitrust.
Myers, Richard S., (AV) . . . .'58 '84 C.339 B.A. L.904 J.D. [Myers L.T.]
*PRACTICE AREAS: Cellular Communications; FCC Licensing; Federal Litigation.
Myers, Robert H., Jr., (AV) . . . .'47 '72 C.674 A.B. L.893 J.D. [Ⓒ Morris,M.&M.]
*PRACTICE AREAS: Insurance Regulation; General Corporate; Antitrust; Trade Association Law.
Myers, Stephanie A. '73 '98 C.381 B.A. L.851 J.D.
Assoc. Coun., Comm. on Agriculture
Myers, Thomas '67 '93 C.436 B.A. L.215 J.D.
(adm. in MI; not adm. in DC) [Ⓐ Jones J.]
Myers, William G., III '55 '81 C.945 A.B. L.208 J.D.
Office of the Solicitor, U.S. Department of the Interior, MS 6352-M1B
Myers-Kerbal, Elisabeth R. . . . .'63 '93 C.331 B.A. L.904 J.D. [Ⓐ Shook,H.&B.]

Myers Lazrus Technology Law Group, (AV)
1990 M Street, NW, Suite 200, 20036
Telephone: 202-296-0626 Fax: 202-296-1680 URL: http://www.lawyers.com/myerskeller
URL: http://www.myerslazrus.com
Richard S. Myers; Jay N. Lazrus (Not admitted in DC).
Telecommunications Law (Broadcast, Common Carrier, Cellular Radio, Satellite, MDS, and Private Radio). Litigation Practice before the Federal Communications Commission and Federal Courts.
See Professional Biographies, WASHINGTON, DISTRICT OF COLUMBIA

Myers-Payne, Sean Christopher '67 '01 C.611 B.A. L.1209 J.D.
(adm. in VA; not adm. in DC; See Pat. Sect.) [Ⓐ Finnegan,H.F.G.&D.]
*PRACTICE AREAS: Patent Prosecution; Biochemical Patents; Pharmaceutical Patents; Biotechnology Patents; Chemical Patents.
Myerson, Paul E. . . . .'21 '49 C&L.966 Ph.B., J.D. 3001 Veazey Ter., N.W.
Myhre, William N. . . . . '49 '76 C.813 B.A. L.659 J.D. [Preston G.E.&R.M.]
*PRACTICE AREAS: Maritime.
Myron, Jennifer L. . . . . '72 '98 C.216 B.A. L.1017 J.D. [Ⓐ Arent F.K.P.&K.]
*PRACTICE AREAS: Trademarks; Advertising Law; Copyright; Electronic Commerce.
Myrow, Stephen A. . . . .'— '96 C.165 B.A. L.276 J.D. [Ⓐ King&S.]
Mysliwiec, Stephen R., (AV) . . . .'48 '76 C.602 B.A. L.976 J.D. [Piper M.R.&W.]
*PRACTICE AREAS: Construction Law; Insurance Law; Litigation.
Naas, Lindsay R. '58 '87 C.492 B.F.A. L.494 J.D.
(adm. in MN; not adm. in DC) 1250 I St Nw # 1000
Nabatoff, Ross A., (AV) . . . .'58 '84 C.228 B.A. L.910 J.D. [Brand&F.]
*PRACTICE AREAS: Criminal Litigation; Civil Litigation; Federal Employment Litigation.
Nabors, Theresa K. . . . .'71 '96 C.602 B.A. L.575 J.D. [Ⓐ Hogan&H.]
*PRACTICE AREAS: Tax Controversies; Litigation.
Nace, Barry J., (AV) . . . .'44 '70 C.216 B.S. L.1017 J.D. [Paulson&N.] ⊙
*PRACTICE AREAS: Medical Malpractice; Products Liability; Wrongful Death; Automobile.
Nace, David L., (AV) . . . . '49 '76 C.1108 B.S. L.30 J.D. [Lukas,N.G.&S.]
*PRACTICE AREAS: Telecommunications Law; FCC Regulation; Business Transfers.
Nace, Eleanor, (AV) . . . . '46 '75 C.706 B.A. L.273 J.D. [Lichtman,T.S.&R.]
Nachmann, John D. '67 '92 C.94 B.A. L.228 J.D.
(adm. in MA; not adm. in DC) The Nasdaq Stock Market, Inc.

Nacht, Lori N. .... '74 '99 C.273 B.A. L.1365 J.D. [Ⓐ Gebhardt&Assoc.]
*PRACTICE AREAS: Employment Law; Employment Discrimination; Disability Retirement; Civil Rights; Federal Civil Practice.
Nack, Emily A. .... '66 '92 C.890 B.A. L.180 J.D. [Ⓐ Eckert S.C.&M.]
*PRACTICE AREAS: Litigation.
Nacke, Philip A., (AV) .... '— '73 C.838 A.B. L.276 J.D. [Foley&L.]
*PRACTICE AREAS: Litigation; Valuation Law; Natural Resources Law; Government Contracts Law.
Nadeau, Elizabeth A. '59 '86 C.976 B.A. L.477 J.D.
Associate General Counsel, International Union of Operating Engineers
*RESPONSIBILITIES: Labor Law; Administrative Law.
Nadel, Michael S. .... '74 '99 C.659 B.A. L.273 J.D. [Ⓐ McDermott,W.&E.]

Naditch, Ronald M., P.A.
(See Annapolis, Maryland)

Nadler, Carl S., (AV) .... '55 '83 C.33 B.A. L.910 J.D. [Jenner&B.]
*PRACTICE AREAS: Civil Litigation; Antitrust Law; Intellectual Property; Telecommunications Law.
Nadler, David M. .... '56 '81 C.102 B.A. L.831 J.D. [Dickstein S.M.&O.]
*PRACTICE AREAS: Computer Technology Law; Intellectual Property; Government Contracts.
Nadler, Jonathan Jacob .... '56 '90 C.881 A.B. L.178 J.D. [Squire,S.&D.]
*PRACTICE AREAS: Federal Regulatory; Telecommunications; Antitrust; Competition.
Naegele, Kurt D. '69 '96 C.112 B.A. L.990 J.D.
(adm. in CA; not adm. in DC) 1201 Pennsylvania Ave.
Naegele, Timothy D., & Associates, (AV) '41 '66 C.112 A.B. L.1066 LL.B.
1201 Pennsylvania Avenue, N.W. (⊙Malibu, CA)
Naegle, LaDawn .... '— '84 C.1049 B.A. L.273 J.D. [Bryan C.]
*PRACTICE AREAS: Corporate Law; Securities Regulation Law; Technology.
Naeve, Clifford M., (AV) ....'47 '84 C.846 B.S.M.E. L.276 J.D. [Skadden,A.S.M.&F.]
Naftalin, Alan Y., (AV) .... '26 '52 C&L.976 B.A., LL.B. [Holland&K.]
*PRACTICE AREAS: Telecommunication Law.
Naftalin, Charles R., (AV) .... '58 '85 C.604 A.B. L.1358 J.D. [Holland&K.]
*PRACTICE AREAS: Telecommunications Law.
Naftzger, J. Christopher .... '67 '95 C.301 B.A. L.950 J.D. [Ⓐ Dyer E.&J.]
*PRACTICE AREAS: Administrative Law; Corporate Finance; Corporate Reorganization.
Nagel, John C. .... '70 '96 C.197 B.A. L.228 J.D. [Ⓐ Wilmer,C.&P.]
Nagel, Stephanie L. '70 '98 C.197 B.A. L.861 J.D.
(adm. in DE; not adm. in DC) [Ⓐ McDermott,W.&E.]
Nagel, Trevor W. .... '51 '86 C.145 B.A. L.309 J.D. [Shaw P.]
*PRACTICE AREAS: Information Technology; Telecommunications; Intellectual Property; Infrastructure Development; International.
Nagel, Walter ....'57 '84 C&L.705 B.A., J.D. Tax Dept., MCI Communications Corp.
Nagelhout, Mary .... '62 '88 C.273 B.A. L.537 J.D. 955 26th St., N.W.
Nager, Glen D., (AV) .... '58 '85 C.846 B.B.A. L.813 J.D. [Jones,D.R.&P.]
*PRACTICE AREAS: Litigation; Appellate Practice; U.S. Supreme Court Litigation; Employment Litigation.
Nagle, Paul J. '74 '99 C.446 B.A. L.127 J.D.
(adm. in MD; not adm. in DC) [Ⓐ Wilkinson B.K.]
*PRACTICE AREAS: Telecommunications Law; Internet Law.
Nagrotsky, Stephen A. .... '51 '78 C.188 B.S. L.569 J.D. Airline Pilots Assn.
Nahra, Kirk J. .... '62 '87 C.276 B.A. L.309 J.D. [Wiley R.&F.]
*PRACTICE AREAS: Insurance Fraud; Privacy; Compliance Programs.
Nahra, Margit H., (AV) .... '62 '89 C.276 B.S.F.S. L.893 J.D. [Ⓒ Crowell&M.]
*PRACTICE AREAS: Litigation; Health Care Law.
Naimon, Jeffrey P. .... '63 '91 C.976 B.A. L.893 J.D. [Goodwin P.]
*PRACTICE AREAS: Mortgages; Consumer Finance; Regulatory Law; Legislative Practice.
Nairn, John W., (AV) ...... '20 '50 C.659 B.S.E. L.276 J.D. 4301 Connecticut Ave., N.W.
Nakahata, John T. .... '61 '86 C.918 B.A. L.309 J.D. [Harris,W.&G.]
*PRACTICE AREAS: Communications Law; Antitrust; Legislative Practice.
Nakamura, Dean H. '52 '93 C.312 B.S. L.273 J.D.
[Roylance,A.B.&G.] (See Pat. Sect.)
*PRACTICE AREAS: Intellectual Property Law; Biotechnology.
Nakamura, Hope G. .... '60 '86 C.813 B.A. L.1068 J.D. ACLU
Nakamura, Kent Y. ....'51 '77 C.312 A.B. L.477 J.D. Gen. Atty., Sprint Corp.
Nakayama, Granta Y. .... '58 '94 C.453 S.B. L.1209 J.D. [Kirkland&E.]
*PRACTICE AREAS: Environmental Law; Intellectual Property.
Nakhleh, William '— '99 C.30 B.S. L.273 J.D.
(adm. in VA; not adm. in DC; See Pat. Sect.) [Ⓐ Finnegan,H.F.G.&D.]
*PRACTICE AREAS: Chemical Intellectual Property; Pharmaceutical Intellectual Property.
Nakhuda, Carol M. '67 '94 C.289 B.A. L.64 J.D.
(adm. in MD; not adm. in DC)
Assoc. Gen. Coun., Blue Cross & Blue Shield of Natl. Capital Area
Nalda, Carlos M. .... '66 '93 C.30 B.A. L.273 J.D. [Ⓐ Dow,L.&A.]
Nall, David A. .... '51 '85 C.893 B.A. L.128 J.D. [Squire,S.&D.]
*PRACTICE AREAS: Telecommunications; Regulatory Affairs.
Nalls, Charles H. .... '56 '83 C.210 B.A. L.276 J.D. [Ⓒ deKieffer&H.] (Pat.)
*PRACTICE AREAS: Intellectual Property Litigation; International Trade; Trademarks; Trademark Licensing; Commercial Law.
Nam, Ki W. '62 '95 C.893 B.A. L.904 J.D.
(adm. in VA; not adm. in DC) [Cotten&S.]
Namian, Michael D. .... '65 '93 C.165 B.A. L.861 J.D. [Ⓐ Dean B.&M.]
Namiki, James .... '58 '00 C.911 B.S. L.823 J.D. [Ⓐ Hogan&H.]
*PRACTICE AREAS: Patent Prosecution; Patent Litigation; Trademarks.
Nammo, Laura D. .... '68 '95 C.576 B.S. L.273 J.D. [Ⓐ Piper M.R.&W.] (Pat.)
*PRACTICE AREAS: Intellectual Property; Patent Prosecution; Patent Litigation; Opinion Work; Client Counseling.
Namorato, Cono R., (AV) .... '42 '68 C.1041 B.B.A. L.1009 J.D. [Caplin&D.]
*PRACTICE AREAS: Criminal Litigation.
Namrow, Eric S. .... '67 '96 C.105 B.A. L.446 J.D. [Ⓐ Venable,A.B.H.&C.]
*PRACTICE AREAS: Intellectual Property Litigation.
Nankin, Kenneth S. .... '63 '88 C.902 B.A. L.309 J.D. 1133 Connecticut Avenue N.W.
Nannes, Michael E., (AV) .... '53 '77 C.477 B.B.A. L.276 J.D. [Dickstein S.M.&O.]
*PRACTICE AREAS: Energy Law; Construction Law; Arbitration Law.
Nantz, John .... '48 '81 C.30 B.A. L.276 J.D. 5700 Nevada Ave., N.W.
Napier, John L., (AV) .... '47 '72 C.198 A.B. L.790 J.D. [Ⓒ Winston&S.]
*PRACTICE AREAS: Federal Legislative; Regulatory; Governmental Law; Government Affairs; Lobbying.
Napier, Stephanie L. .... '71 '97 C.477 B.A. L.276 J.D. [Ⓐ Groom]
*PRACTICE AREAS: Employee Benefits; ERISA; Health Care Law.
Napoli, Eric Louis '72 '99
(adm. in NY; not adm. in DC) [Ⓐ Hopp&Assoc.]
*PRACTICE AREAS: International Law; Environmental Law; Environmental Regulation.
Nappi, Sarah M. .... '— '93 C.188 B.A. L.276 J.D. [Ⓐ Miller&C.]
*PRACTICE AREAS: Customs; International Trade.
Naqvi, Syeda B. '66 '97 C.999 B.A. L.128 J.D.
[Ⓐ Jackson&C.] (⊙Balt., Rockville, MD)
*PRACTICE AREAS: Litigation; Commercial Law; Construction Law; Business Law; Zoning, Planning and Land Use.
Narayanan, Anant S. '59 '94
C.999 B.Tech. L.273 J.D. [Ⓐ Jones,D.R.&P.] (See Pat. Sect.)
Nardi, Nicholas A. .... '72 '98 C.860 B.A. L.596 J.D. [Ⓐ Epstein B.&G.]
*PRACTICE AREAS: Government Contracts and Technology; Health.

Nardi, Scott Bergan .... '73 '99 C.972 B.S. L.494 J.D. [Ⓐ Skadden,A.S.M.&F.]
*PRACTICE AREAS: International Trade.
Nardini, Gregory G. .... '75 '01 C&L.339 A.B., J.D. [Ⓐ Clifford C.R.&W.]
*PRACTICE AREAS: Corporate Law.
Nardini, Lisa Malloy ....'64 '96 C.893 B.A. L.904 J.D. [Ⓐ Jones,D.R.&P.]
Nardone, S. Nicole '70 '97 C.1113 B.A. L.767 J.D.
(adm. in CA; not adm. in DC) [Ⓐ Gordon,S.W.&C.]
*PRACTICE AREAS: Civil Rights Litigation; Employment Discrimination.
Nardotti, Michael J., Jr. .... '47 '77 C.870 B.S. L.262 J.D. [Patton B.]
Nargiso, John S. .... '74 '00 C.705 B.A. L.273 J.D. [Ⓐ Fried,F.H.S.&J.]
*PRACTICE AREAS: Corporate Finance; Real Estate.
Narkin, Stephen J. .... '54 '78 C.659 B.A. L.813 J.D. 1440 New York Ave. NW
Narrow, S. Lee, (AV) .... '42 '68 C.966 B.A. L.276 J.D. [Arnold&P.]
*PRACTICE AREAS: Real Estate; Corporate; Finance.
Naseman, David M., (AV) '48 '76 C.94 B.A. L.861 J.D.
(adm. in NY; not adm. in DC) [Blumenfeld&C.]
Nash, Andrea '61 '87 C.846 B.B.A. L.802 J.D.
(adm. in TX; not adm. in DC) Fed. Aviation Admn.
Nash, Bernard, (AV) .... '42 '66 C.563 B.B.A. L.1009 J.D. [Dickstein S.M.&O.]
*PRACTICE AREAS: Antitrust; Complex Litigation; Alternative Dispute Resolution; State Government Law; Public Policy.
Nash, Daniel L. .... '54 '83 C.1044 B.S. L.1065 J.D. [Akin,G.S.H.&F.]
*PRACTICE AREAS: Labor and Employment.
Nash, James P. .... '25 '51 C&L.276 A.B., J.D. 3617 Quesada St., N.W.‡
Nash, John F., Jr. .... '46 '80 C.112 A.B. L.276 J.D. Coun., Milliken & Co.
Nash, Ralph C., Jr. '28 '58 C.674 A.B. L.273 J.D.
Prof. of Law, Emeritus, George Washington Univ.
Nash, Stuart G. .... '65 '92 C.228 A.B. L.309 J.D. 725 12th St., N.W.
Nash, Warren J. ....'52 '78 C&L.190 B.A., J.D. 441 4th St., N.W.
Nash, William L., III '72 '00 C.880 B.A. L.273 J.D.
(adm. in VA; not adm. in DC) [Ⓐ Patton B.]
Nasir, Jamil E. .... '55 '83 C&L.477 B.G.S., J.D. [Ⓒ Swidler B.S.F.]
*PRACTICE AREAS: Public Utilities; General Litigation; Environmental.
Nason, David G. .... '70 '95 C.30 B.S.B.A. L.904 J.D. [Ⓐ Covington&B.]
Nassab, Rebecca ....'69 '95 C.659 B.S. L.273 J.D. [Ⓐ Arnold&P.]
*PRACTICE AREAS: Intellectual Property; Technology Law.
Nassau, Stephen M., (AV) .... '40 '64 C.103 A.B. L.178 J.D. [O'Toole,R.N.&S.]

Nasseri, Kurosh, Law Offices of '59 '86 C.30 B.A. L.276 J.D.
3207-A M St., NW, 3rd Floor, 20007
Telephone: 202-457-0808 Fax: 202-457-0909
Email: mail@kurosh.net URL: http://www.kurosh.net
***PRACTICE AREAS: Entertainment Law; Contracts.**
—Terrie M. Bjorklund, Ms.
Entertainment Law, Licensing, Publishing, Entertainment Business Counselling, Electronic Music, International Licensing, Contract Licensing.
See Professional Biographies, WASHINGTON, DISTRICT OF COLUMBIA

Nassikas, John N., III, (AV) ....'59 '84 C.976 B.A. L.893 J.D. [Arent F.K.P.&K.]
*PRACTICE AREAS: White Collar Crime; Litigation; Criminal Law; Health Care Fraud; Criminal Litigation.
Nastasi, Eric C. .... '70 '94 C.446 B.A. L.1003 J.D. [Ⓐ Keller&H.]
*PRACTICE AREAS: Telecommunications Law; Corporate Law; Transactional Law; Mergers and Acquisitions.
Natale, Kenneth E. .... '52 '77 C.602 B.A. L.273 J.D. [Ⓒ Akin,G.S.H.&F.]
*PRACTICE AREAS: Project Finance; Energy; Corporate; International.
Natalie, Ronald B., (AV) ....'— '62 C.860 A.B. L.273 J.D. [Verner,L.B.M.&H.]
*PRACTICE AREAS: Labor Law; Employment Law.
Nateman, Gary M. .... '38 '66 C.610 B.S.C. L.273 LL.B. [Ⓒ Shook,H.&B.]
*PRACTICE AREAS: Alcoholic Beverages.
Nath, Gary M., (AV) ..... '44 '75 C.693 B.S. L.30 J.D. [Nath&Assoc.] (See Pat. Sect.) ⊙
*PRACTICE AREAS: Patent and Trademark Prosecution and Litigation; Trade Secrets; Licensing; Acquisitions, Divestitures and Mergers; Joint Ventures.

Nath & Associates, PLLC, (AV) BR
1030 15th Street, N.W. 6th Floor, 20005 ⊙
Telephone: 202-775-8383 or 202-775-9393 Facsimile: 202-775-8396 or 202-882-9409
Email: IP@NATHLAW.COM URL: http://www.NATHLAW.COM
Members of Firm: Gary M. Nath; Harold L. Novick; Todd L. Juneau; Ross A. Epstein (Not admitted in DC). Associates: Michelle L. Hartland (Not admitted in DC); Lee C. Heiman (Not admitted in DC); Jerald L. Meyer (Not admitted in DC); Marvin C. Berkowitz (Not admitted in DC); Tanya E. Harkins (Not admitted in DC); Joshua L. Goldberg (Not admitted in DC); Todd W. Kunz (Not admitted in DC); Joseph K. Hemby Jr. (Not admitted in DC). Retired: Irvin A. Lavine; Donald M. Sandler (Not admitted in DC).
Patent, Trademark, Copyright, Licensing Litigation, International Patents, General Counsel Services. San Diego, California Office: 110 West C Street, Suite 1300, 92101. Telephone: 619-645-5290. Facsimile: 619-645-5289.
See Professional Biographies, WASHINGTON, DISTRICT OF COLUMBIA

Nathan, Bonnie Dunninger .... '68 '97 C.477 B.A. L.276 J.D. [Ⓐ Williams&C.]
*PRACTICE AREAS: Employment Discrimination; Litigation.
Nathan, Hans A., (AV) .... '13 '45 C.999 L.273 J.D. 1920 N St., N.W.
Nathan, Irvin B., (AV) .... '43 '69 C.367 B.A. L.178 LL.B. [Arnold&P.]
*PRACTICE AREAS: White Collar Crime Defense; Corporate Civil Litigation; Antitrust; Securities; Civil RICO.
Nathan, Nancy B. .... '46 '77 C.518 A.B. L.734 J.D. NBC, Inc.‡
Nathani, Nina Glickman .... '60 '86 C.976 B.A. L.893 J.D. [Ⓒ Sonenthal&O.]
*PRACTICE AREAS: Government Procurement; Non-Profit Organizations Law; Litigation; Intellectual Property.
Nathanson, James E. .... '32 '59 C.309 A.B. L.273 LL.B. 3900-A Watson Pl., N.W.
Nathanson, Kirsten L. ....'70 '98 C.659 B.A. L.273 J.D. [Ⓐ Crowell&M.]
Natiello, Christian .... '73 '00 C.105 B.A. L.124 J.D. [Ⓐ Dechert]
*PRACTICE AREAS: Litigation; Products Liability.
Naughten, Christopher F. '59 '88 C.423 B.A. L.180 J.D.
(adm. in MD; not adm. in DC) Univ. Title
Naughton, Ronald F. '34 '67 C.651 B.S. L.229 J.D.
(adm. in PA; not adm. in DC; See Pat. Sect.) [Ⓒ Armstrong,W.H.M.&N.]
Nauheim, Stephen A., (P.C.), (AV) .... '42 '68 C.575 B.S. L.276 J.D. Price Waterhouse
Navarrete, Andres L. .... '65 '93 C.945 B.A. L.93 J.D. 1800 M St., NW
Navarro, Bruce C. ....'54 '80 C.228 B.A. L.347 J.D. 1742 N St., N.W.
Navarro-Bowman, Chandri .... '64 '93 C.945 B.A. L.30 J.D. [Sandler,T.&R.]
*PRACTICE AREAS: International Trade; Customs Law; International Law.
Nawabi, Mariam A. .... '73 '99 C.1356 B.A. L.276 J.D. [Ⓐ Dechert]
*PRACTICE AREAS: Litigation.
Nazario, Edwin Javiel ....'73 '98 C.575 B.A. L.178 J.D. [Ⓐ Skadden,A.S.M.&F.]
*PRACTICE AREAS: Project Finance.
Nead, John E. .... '— '26 C.273 A.B. L.999 LL.B. 3533 Ordway St., N.W.‡
Nead, Lena C. .... '— '39 C&L.799 B.C.S., LL.B. 3533 Ordway St.
Neaher, Edward R. '12 '43 C.602 A.B. L.262 LL.B.
(adm. in NY; not adm. in DC) 4000 Mass. Ave., N.W.‡
Neaher, Edward R., Jr. ....'58 '85 C.951 L.188 J.D. [White&C.]
*PRACTICE AREAS: Project Finance; International Private Equity; Capital Markets; Venture Capital.
Neal, Anne deHayden '55 '81
C&L.309 A.B., J.D. V.P. & Gen. Coun., Natl. Alumni Forum

Neal, Arlene P. .... '67 '98 C.1177 B.S. L.1202 J.D. [A] Morgan,L.&B.] (Pat.)
Neal, Chellis E. .... '57 '90 C.446 B.A. L.64 J.D. [A] Venable,A.B.H.&C.] (See Pat. Sect.)
Neal, Daria E. '74 '99 C.302 B.A. L.1068 J.D.
(adm. in CA; not adm. in DC) [A] Jackson L.S.&K.]
*PRACTICE AREAS: Employment Litigation.
Neal, Guy S. .... '67 '93 C.945 B.A. L.276 J.D. [A] Sidley A.B.&W.]
Neal, Joan E. .... '63 '89 C.477 B.A. L.976 J.D. [C] Morrison&F.]
Neal, Peyton R., Jr. .... '39 '67 C.576 B.S. L.575 LL.B. 1738 Irving St., N.W.
Neal, Philip S., (AV) ....'— '59 C.174 B.A. L.273 J.D. [C] Miller&C.]
Neal, Sean M. .... '74 '99 C.813 B.A. L.276 J.D. [A] Duncan,W.G.&P.]
*PRACTICE AREAS: Energy Law; Environmental Law.
Neal, Stephen L., Jr. .... '67 '93 C.228 A.B. L.575 J.D. [Manatt,P.&P.]
Nealon, F. Joseph, (AV) .... '49 '74 C&L.276 A.B., J.D. [Ballard S.A.&I.]
*PRACTICE AREAS: Commercial Law; Insurance Defense; Labor and Employment; Litigation; Fidelity and Surety.
Nealon, Stephen W., (AV) .... '46 '74 C.401 B.S. L.846 J.D. [Hamilton&H.]
*PRACTICE AREAS: Estate Planning; Probate; Real Estate; Business Law.

Nealon & Moran, LLP
(See Alexandria, Virginia)

Nebeker, W. Mark, (AV) .... '59 '84 C.893 B.A. L.904 J.D. Asst. U.S. Atty.
Neblett, Mark H. .... '58 '94 C.339 B.S. L.276 J.D. [A] Kenyon&K.] (See Pat. Sect.)
*PRACTICE AREAS: Intellectual Property.
Nedelkoff, Rebecca R. '64 '91 C.93 B.A. L.818 J.D.
(adm. in PA; not adm. in DC) 111 Mass. Ave., N.W.
Needle, Barbara Wachter .... '62 '87 C.446 B.S. L.273 J.D. [Robins,K.M.&C.]
*PRACTICE AREAS: Real Estate Law; Corporate Law; Commercial Real Estate Development; Commercial Real Estate Finance; Business Law.
Needles, Gregory L. .... '60 '87 C&L.260 B.S.A.C., J.D. [Morgan,L.&B.]
Neeley, Jeffrey S., (BV) .... '53 '79 C.597 B.A. L.273 J.D. [Manatt,P.&P.]
Neely, Bruce W., (AV) .... '48 '79 C.970 B.A. L.665 J.D. [LeBoeuf,L.G.&M.]
*PRACTICE AREAS: Utilities.
Neely, John S., (AV) .... '62 '88 C.354 B.S. L.1017 J.D. [A] Miller&M.]
Neff, Christyne L., (AV) '60 '90 C.390 B.A. L.446 J.D.
(adm. in MD; not adm. in DC) Asst. Gen. Coun., USCW
Neff, William L., (AV) .... '47 '75 C.502 A.B. L.309 J.D. [Hogan&H.]
*PRACTICE AREAS: Employee Benefits; Taxation; Tax Law; Deferred Compensation; Public Employee Retirement.
Negroni, Andrea Lee, (AV) .... '53 '82 C.1365 B.A. L.178 J.D. [Goodwin P.]
*PRACTICE AREAS: Regulatory Law; Administrative Law; Mortgage Banking Law; Real Estate.
Nehrer, Roger A. .... '63 '93 C.659 B.A. L.273 J.D. 1200 23rd St. N.W.
Neidle, Alan F. '29 '56 C.976 B.A. L.477 J.D.
(adm. in MO; not adm. in DC) 2129 Florida Ave., N.W.‡
Neil, Rhonda L., (BV) .... '63 '88 C.787 B.A. L.904 J.D. [Brown N.&K.]
*PRACTICE AREAS: Telecommunications.
Neils, Paul F. .... '59 '89 C.475 B.S.M.E. L.128 J.D. [Sughrue M.] (See Pat. Sect.)
*PRACTICE AREAS: Intellectual Property Law.
Neilson, Christopher J. '60 '00 C.1059 B.A. L.276 J.D.
(adm. in OR; not adm. in DC) Dept. of Agriculture
Neilson, Michael R. .... '60 '86 C.128 A.B. L.893 J.D. [C] Beveridge&D.]
*PRACTICE AREAS: Biotechnology; Chemical Regulation; Chemical Products Liability.
Neilson, Mikol S. B. .... '— '78 C&L.770 B.S., J.D. [C] Verner,L.B.M.&H.]
*PRACTICE AREAS: Federal and State Taxation.
Neily, Clark M., III '68 '94 C&L.846 B.A., J.D.
(adm. in TX; not adm. in DC) Staff Atty., Institute for Just.
Neimark, Sheridan, (AV) .... '35 '62 C.119 B.S. L.273 J.D. [Browdy&N.] (See Pat. Sect.)
*PRACTICE AREAS: Patent Opinions; Patent Prosecution; Pharmaceuticals and Pesticides; Chemistry; Plastics and Moldings.
Neimeyer, Paul Craig ...... '65 '91 C.229 B.A. L.665 J.D. 2100 Pennsylvania Ave., N.W.
Neiswender, Jane Ann Roe .... '71 '99 C.674 A.B. L.127 J.D. [A] McKenna&C.]
*PRACTICE AREAS: Litigation.
Nejaime, Nadia B. .... '67 '94 C.30 B.A. L.273 J.D. [A] Shaw P.]
*PRACTICE AREAS: Technology and Science; Contracts.
Neller, Kristen '68 '93
(adm. in IL; not adm. in DC) 1775 Pennsylvania Ave.
Nellis, Joseph L. .... '16 '41 C&L.597 B.S., J.D. 3539 Albemarle St., N.W.‡
Nellor, Susan A. .... '49 '78 C&L.190 B.A., J.D. Asst. U.S. Atty.‡
Nelms, Laura Diane '64 '98 C.1288 B.A. L.930 J.D.
(adm. in MD; not adm. in DC) 2401 Calvert St. N.W.
Nelsen, Michelle Lynn '70 '94 C&L.221 B.A., J.D.
(adm. in CO; not adm. in DC) 811 Vermont Ave
Nelson, Charles D. .... '35 '61 C&L.329 LL.B. 3723 S. Dakota Ave., N.E.
Nelson, Charles E. '30 '57
C&L.309 A.B., LL.B. Exec. Vice President, U.S. Institute of Peace
Nelson, Daniel W. .... '68 '94 C.165 B.A. L.477 J.D. [A] Gibson,D.&C.]
*PRACTICE AREAS: Litigation; General Litigation; Appellate Practice.
Nelson, David D. '71 '97 C.893 B.A. L.188 J.D.
(adm. in NY; not adm. in DC; Pat.) [A] Hogan&H.]
*PRACTICE AREAS: Patents.
Nelson, David P. '58 '86 C.45 B.S.B.A. L.1243 J.D.
(adm. in AR; not adm. in DC) Asst., V.P., Commercial Settlements, Inc.
Nelson, Douglas T., (BV) '46 '80 C.705 A.B. L.178 J.D.
(adm. in NJ; not adm. in DC) Sr. V.P. & Gen. Coun., American Crop Protection Assoc.
*RESPONSIBILITIES: General Corporate; Antitrust; Environmental Law.
Nelson, Hedy L. .... '59 '85 C.1349 B.S. L.273 J.D. [Golden&N.] ⊙
*PRACTICE AREAS: Corporate Law; Business Law; Commercial Law; Finance; Contracts.
Nelson, Howard L., (BV) ..... '55 '81 C.107 B.S.B.A. L.30 J.D. Sr. Coun., El Paso Corp.
Nelson, Jeffrey C. .... '72 '97 C&L.477 B.S., J.D. [A] Hogan&H.]
*PRACTICE AREAS: Environmental Law.
Nelson, Joseph B. .... '65 '92 C.336 B.A. L.128 J.D. [C] Van Ness F.]
*PRACTICE AREAS: Natural Resources; Water; Energy.
Nelson, Mark David .... '74 '00 C.16 B.A. L.813 J.D. [A] McKee N.]
*PRACTICE AREAS: Tax Litigation.
Nelson, Mark W. .... '67 '93 C.188 B.S. L.309 J.D. [A] Cleary,G.S.&H.]
Nelson, Maureen .... '55 '81 C.30 B.A. L.904 J.D. [C] Skadden,A.S.M.&F.]
Nelson, Nancy Jo .... '55 '85 C.608 B.A. L.273 J.D. [Bracewell&P.]
*PRACTICE AREAS: Project Finance; Export Finance; Loan Facilities; Letters of Credit; Structured Finance.
Nelson, Norman E. '37 '66 C.57 A.B. L.339 LL.B.
(adm. in IL; not adm. in DC) Prog. Dir., Federal Publications, Inc.
Nelson, Regina A. '68 '95 C.1192 B.A. L.93 J.B.
Corp. Coun., Marriott International, Inc.
*RESPONSIBILITIES: Real Estate; Development.
Nelson, Robert A., Jr., (AV) .... '46 '73 C.276 B.S. L.893 J.D. [Stoel R.]
*PRACTICE AREAS: Energy Law; Energy Regulation; Energy Transactions; Litigation; Appellate.
Nelson, Robert L. ...... '31 '60 C.67 B.A. L.276 J.D. Gen. Coun., Paralyzed Vet. of Amer.
Nelson, Sabrina A. .... '71 '96 C.197 B.A. L.188 J.D. [A] Dickstein S.M.&O.]
*PRACTICE AREAS: Civil Litigation.
Nelson, Sharon T. .... '47 '72 C&L.800 B.S., J.D. 3622 Jocelyn St., N.W.
Nelson, Thomas E. .... '— '94 C.645 B.S.E.E. L.823 J.D. [A] Morgan,L.&B.] (Pat.)

Nelson, William F., (AV) .... '47 '72 C.497 B.S. L.893 J.D. [McKee N.]
*PRACTICE AREAS: Taxation.

Nelson, Marilyn E.
(See Bethesda, Maryland)

Nelson & Nelson LLP
(See Bethesda, Maryland)

Nemec, Emil '67 '94
(adm. in NY; not adm. in DC) [A] White&C.]
Nemeroff, Michael A., (AV) .... '46 '72 C.145 B.A. L.178 J.D. [Sidley A.B.&W.]
Nemeroff, Scott M. .... '59 '85 C.276 B.A. L.446 J.D. [Nixon P.]
*PRACTICE AREAS: Securities; Corporate Law; Affordable Housing.
Nemetz, Miriam R. .... '63 '90 C&L.309 B.A., J.D. [Mayer,B.&P.]
Nemiroff, Elisa A. .... '74 '99 C.401 B.S. L.537 J.D. [A] Collier S.S.]
*PRACTICE AREAS: Advertising; Privacy.
Nemirow, Samuel B., (AV) .... '40 '66 C.184 B.A. L.94 LL.B. [Nemirow&H.]
Nemirow & Hu, PC, (AV) .... 1101 Connecticut Avenue, N.W. Suite 900
Nepveu, Julie '— '92 C.882 B.A. L.1294 J.D.
(adm. in VA; not adm. in DC) Atty., Lawyers Comm. for Civil Rights Under Law
*RESPONSIBILITIES: Housing and Community Development.
Nesbitt, Katherine .... '72 '01 C&L.228 A.B., J.D. [A] Crowell&M.]
Nesbitt, La Fonte, (AV) .... '58 '88 C.1369 B.S. L.893 J.D. [Holland&K.]
*PRACTICE AREAS: Multifamily Housing Finance and Development; Commercial Real Estate Finance and Development; Community Development; Military Housing; Privatization.
Nesbitt, Leroy, (AV) .... '34 '60 C.26 B.S. L.329 LL.B. Assoc. Gen. Coun., Howard Univ.
Nesbitt, William T. '71 '98 C.1275 B.A. L.64 J.D.
(adm. in MD; not adm. in DC) [A] Ruben&A.]
Ness, Andrew David .... '52 '77 C.813 B.S. L.309 J.D. [Thelen R.&P.]
*PRACTICE AREAS: Construction Law; Government Contracts.
Nesse, Janet M., (AV) .... '58 '81 C.976 B.A. L.945 J.D. [Morrison&H.]
*PRACTICE AREAS: Bankruptcy; Commercial Law; Government Contracts; Litigation.
Nester, Brian R. '66 '97 C.831 B.A. L.273 J.D.
(adm. in DE; not adm. in DC) [A] Fish&R.]
*PRACTICE AREAS: Intellectual Property Law.
Neth, Joann M. ..... '59 '89 C.104 A.B. L.893 J.D. [Finnegan,H.F.G.&D.] (See Pat. Sect.)
*PRACTICE AREAS: Chemical Intellectual Property; Chemical Patents; Patent Infringement; Patent Licensing; Patent Litigation.
Nethercutt, Mary Beth '51 '83 C.790 B.A. L.285 J.D.
(adm. in WA; not adm. in DC) U.S. Senate - Committee on Appropriations
Nettleford, Leslie A. .... '— '95 C.905 B.A. L.276 J.D. [Kass&S.]
Nettler, Richard B., (AV) .... '52 '77 C.273 B.A. L.284 J.D. [Robins,K.M.&C.]
*PRACTICE AREAS: Litigation; Land Use Law; Zoning Law; Administrative Law; Government Contracts.
Neuchterlein, Jeffrey D. .... '57 '87 C&L.893 B.A., J.D. 1775 Pennsylvania Ave., N.W.
Neufeld, Michael '72 '00 C.259 B.A. L.910 J.D.
(adm. in MD; not adm. in DC) [A] Rogers&M.]
Neuman, Arthur E., (BV) '26 '55 C.836 B.S. L.273 LL.B.
3201 New Mexico Ave., N.W.
Neuman, Barry S., (AV) .... '49 '75 C.696 B.A. L.1066 J.D. [B.S.Neuman]
*PRACTICE AREAS: Environmental Law; Complex Litigation; Administrative Law; Trade Association Law.
Neuman, David A. .... '73 '99 C.477 B.A. L.273 J.D. [A] Fried,F.H.S.&J.]
*PRACTICE AREAS: Corporate Securities.
Neuman, Reed W. .... '52 '77 C.207 B.A. L.930 J.D. [Howrey S.A.&W.]
*PRACTICE AREAS: Environmental; Complex Litigation; Administrative.
Neuman, Robert H. '36 '62
C&L.309 A.B., LL.B. 1050 Connecticut Ave., N.W., Suite 1100

Neuman, Barry S., P.L.L.C., (AV)
1752 N Street, N.W., Suite 800, 20036
Telephone: 202-466-2886 Fax: 202-887-8044
Email: bneuman@neumanpllc.com URL: http://www.lawyers.com/neumanlaw
Barry S. Neuman.
Environmental Law.
See Professional Biographies, WASHINGTON, DISTRICT OF COLUMBIA

Neumann, Kent S. .... '71 '99 C.112 B.A. L.861 J.D. [A] Ritter E.&N.]
*PRACTICE AREAS: Public Finance Law; Housing.
Neun, Kristin M. .... '63 '93 C.216 B.A. L.904 J.D. [A] Hessel&A.]
Neuner, Tillman H. ..... '27 '53 C.976 B.A. L.276 J.D. Intl. Bk. for Reconstr. & Develop.
Neuwirth, Laura H. .... '— '93 C.188 B.A. L.976 J.D. [A] Latham&W.]
*PRACTICE AREAS: Environmental Administrative Law; Product Safety.

Neville, Peterson LLP, (AV)
1233 20th Street, N.W., Suite 500, 20036 ⊙
Telephone: 202-861-2959 Fax: 202-861-2924
Email: info@npwtradelaw.com URL: http://www.npwtradelaw.com
George Thompson. Of Counsel: Michael K. Tomenga; Lawrence J. Bogard; John A. Detzner (Resident). Associate: Julia S. Padierna-Peralta (Not admitted in DC).
Customs, International Trade, Antitrust, Trade Regulation, Trade Association, Franchise, Government Contract Litigation, International Commercial Law, Administrative and Admiralty Law. Litigation in all Courts. Federal Practice.
New York, N.Y. Office: Neville, Peterson & Williams, 80 Broad Street, 10004. Telephone: 212-635-2730. Facsimile: (212) 635-2734. Internet: info@npwtradelaw.com
See Professional Biographies, WASHINGTON, DISTRICT OF COLUMBIA

Nevin, Heather L. '71 '00 C.951 B.A. L.145 J.D.
(adm. in IL; not adm. in DC) [A] Covington&B.]
Nevins, J. Patrick .... '67 '92 C.893 B.A. L.276 J.D. [Hogan&H.]
*PRACTICE AREAS: Energy Law; Natural Resources; Utility Law.
Nevins, Louis H. .... '38 '63 C&L.659 B.S., LL.B. Pres., Western League of Svgs. Inst.
Newberg, Brad .... '72 '97 C&L.659 B.A., J.D. [A] Arnold&P.]
*PRACTICE AREAS: Intellectual Property Litigation.
Newberger, Stuart H., (AV) .... '53 '80 C.273 B.A. L.276 J.D. [Crowell&M.]
*PRACTICE AREAS: Trial Practice/Litigation; Appellate Practice; Constitutional Law; Insurance Coverage; Environmental Law.
Newberry, Edward J. .... '62 '89 C.1209 B.A. L.276 J.D. [Patton B.]
Newberry, Jennifer Ann .... '72 '97 C.839 B.A. L.1356 J.D. [S] Reboul,M.H.M.&K.]
*PRACTICE AREAS: Regulatory; Telecommunications and Energy.
Newborn, Steven A., (AV) .... '46 '75 C.1353 B.A. L.724 J.D. [Clifford C.R.&W.]
*PRACTICE AREAS: Antitrust; Litigation; International Law.
Newby, Narda M. .... '69 '95 C.273 B.B.A. L.659 J.D. [A] J.H.Olender&Assoc.]
*PRACTICE AREAS: Medical Malpractice; Personal Injury; Products Liability.
Newcomb, Megan E. .... '75 '99 C.260 B.A. L.259 J.D. 1000 Connecticut Ave., N.W.
Newell, Gary J., (AV) .... '53 '78 C.103 A.B. L.659 J.D. [Spiegel&M.]
*PRACTICE AREAS: Energy; Utility Law; Alternative Dispute Resolution; Nuclear Power; Natural Gas.
Newell, Hal H. .... '17 '47 C.197 B.A. L.930 1629 K St., N.W.
Newell, Mark E. .... '— '83 C.20 A.B. L.309 J.D. [Latham&W.]
*PRACTICE AREAS: Insurance Coverage; Civil Litigation; Commercial Litigation.
Newkirk, Nancy W., (AV) .... '43 '69 C.999 B.A. L.569 J.D. 607 14th St., N.W.
Newland, Benjamin R. '66 '97 C.178 B.A. L.145 J.D.
(adm. in GA; not adm. in DC) 2000 Penn. Ave., N.W.‡

Newland, James R., Jr. '65 '98 C.886 B.A. L.665 J.D.
(adm. in VA; not adm. in DC) [🄰 Arent F.K.P.&K.]
*PRACTICE AREAS: Construction Litigation; Construction Contracts; Construction Claims; Arbitration; Commercial Law.
Newlon, Jeanne Louise .... '70 '96 C.260 B.S.B.A. L.273 J.D. [🄰 Venable,A.B.H.&C.]
*PRACTICE AREAS: Estate Planning; Tax.
Newman, Amy B. .... '71 '00 C.860 B.A. L.30 J.D. [🄰 Crowell&M.]
Newman, Bevin M.B. .... '70 '95 C.453 S.B. L.178 J.D. [🄰 Jones,D.R.&P.]
Newman, Cynthia D. '22 '44 C.788 L.893 LL.B.
(adm. in VA; not adm. in DC) Pres., Waters Travel Serv.
Newman, Elizabeth L., (AV) .... '48 '73 C.787 B.A. L.276 J.D. [Kalijarvi,C.&N.]
*PRACTICE AREAS: Labor and Employment; Discrimination; Security Clearances Law.
Newman, Jay S., (AV) .... '65 '90 C.1036 B.A. L.659 J.D. [Shook,H.&B.]
*PRACTICE AREAS: Communications Law; Advertising; Promotions Law; E-Commerce.
Newman, Jeffrey S. .... '— '94 C.696 B.A. L.930 J.D. [© Foley&L.]
*PRACTICE AREAS: Government Contracts; Litigation.
Newman, Jonathan D. .... '67 '94 C.299 B.A. L.446 J.D. [Sherman,D.C.L.&Y.]
*PRACTICE AREAS: Labor and Employment Law; Union Labor Law.
Newman, Karen Faye '76 '01 C.367 B.A. L.659 J.D.
(adm. in VA; not adm. in DC) [🄰 Shaw P.]
Newman, Karol Lyn, (AV) .... '49 '73 C&L.446 B.A., J.D. [Hogan&H.]
*PRACTICE AREAS: Energy.
Newman, Kimberly A. .... '61 '89 C&L.893 B.A., J.D. [Hunton&W.]
*PRACTICE AREAS: Antitrust; Telecommunications; Litigation.
Newman, Mark M., (AV) '— '62 C.33 B.S. L.904 LL.B.
[© Barnes&T.] (See Pat. Sect.)
*PRACTICE AREAS: Patents; Trademarks; Copyrights.
Newman, Richard A., (AV) .... '57 '80 C.569 B.A. L.930 J.D. [Arent F.K.P.&K.]
*PRACTICE AREAS: Municipal Bonds; Commercial Real Estate; Nonprofit Tax Law; Tax Exempt Organizations.
Newman, Robert S. .... '70 '97 C.103 B.A. L.569 J.D. [🄰 Covington&B.]
Newman, Stanley L. .... '34 '59 C.855 B.A. L.178 LL.B. 1401 16th St.
Newman, Thomas P. '68 '96 C.062 B.C.L. L.309 LL.M.
(adm. in NY; not adm. in DC) [🄰 Alston&B.]
*PRACTICE AREAS: International Trade.
Newman, Winn I. .... '24 '49 C&L.966 LL.B. 3001 Veazey Terrace N.W., Apt. 402

Newman & McIntosh
(See Bethesda, Maryland)

Newmann, David .... '67 '93 C.347 B.A. L.477 J.D. [Hogan&H.] (©Phila., PA)
*PRACTICE AREAS: Civil Litigation.
Newmyer, Tara L. .... '70 '98 C.705 B.S. L.893 J.D. [🄰 Dickstein S.M.&O.]
*PRACTICE AREAS: Litigation; Government Contracts.
Newquist, Brian J. .... '71 '00 C.494 B.A. L.477 J.D. [🄰 Steptoe&J.]
Newsom, Elizabeth W. .... '65 '92 C.659 B.A. L.273 J.D. [🄰 Crowell&M.]
Newsome, Larry D. '52 '78 C&L.329 B.A., J.D.
Assoc. Gen. Coun., UMWA Health & Retirement Funds
Newton, Kellie L. .... '59 '84 C.216 B.A. L.117 J.D. [McKenna&C.]
*PRACTICE AREAS: Corporate; Business.
Newton, Nell J. .... '44 '77 C.112 B.A. L.1065 J.D. Prof., Catholic Univ. Law School
Neylon, Lyn B. .... '55 '88 C.1016 B.G.S. L.1065 J.D. Street Law, Inc.
Nezer, Melanie R. .... '68 '93 C.477 B.A. L.93 J.D. 1717 Massachusetts Ave., Ste. 200
Ngau, Timothy A. .... '53 '80 C.976 B.A. L.94 J.D. [Swidler B.S.F.]
*PRACTICE AREAS: Commercial Litigation; Antitrust; Electric Utility; Regulated Industries.
Ngo, Viet H. .... '70 '95 C.886 B.S.E.E. L.893 J.D. [🄰 Steptoe&J.]
Nguyen, Jeannie H. .... '74 '99 C.893 B.A. L.902 J.D. [🄰 Arnold&P.]
*PRACTICE AREAS: Corporate Law; Securities.
Nguyen, Loan K.P. .... '73 '98 C&L.446 B.A., J.D. 1200 Pennsylvania Ave., N.W.
Nguyen, Son B. .... '68 '99 C.120 B.A. L.446 J.D. [🄰 Arnold&P.]
*PRACTICE AREAS: Antitrust; Competition and Trade; Regulation; Environmental Law.
Nguyenduy, Elise Tuong-Vi '56 '83 C.914 B.A. L.659 J.D.
(adm. in MA; not adm. in DC) 1200 18th St., N.W.‡
Nibley, Stuart B., (AV) .... '53 '79 C&L.902 B.A., J.D. [Seyfarth S.]
*PRACTICE AREAS: Government Contracts Law; Construction Contracts Law; Administrative Law.
Niblock, John F. '59 '94 C.198 B.A. L.1068 J.D.
(adm. in CA; not adm. in DC) [🄰 O'Melveny&M.]
Niccolini, Cristina G. '72 '98 C.188 B.A. L.477 J.D.
(adm. in MI; not adm. in DC) [🄰 Venable,A.B.H.&C.]
*PRACTICE AREAS: Litigation.
Nice, Amy Marmer, (AV) .... '62 '87 C.861 B.A. L.273 J.D. [© Dickstein S.M.&O.]
*PRACTICE AREAS: Immigration Law.
Nicely, Andrew A. .... '67 '97 C.67 B.A. L.659 J.D. [🄰 Mayer,B.&P.]
*PRACTICE AREAS: Commercial Litigation; Labor and Employment; Appellate Practice.
Nicely, Matthew R. .... '64 '91 C.604 B.A. L.904 J.D. [🄰 Willkie F.&G.]
Nicholas, Elizabeth S. '72 '99 C.260 B.S. L.861 J.D.
(adm. in NY; not adm. in DC) [🄰 Kelley D.&W.]
*PRACTICE AREAS: Environmental Law.
Nicholas, Jon S. .... '64 '89 C.900 B.B.A. L.145 J.D. [Dilworth P.P.]
Nicholas, Patricia E. '54 '79 C.4 B.A. L.588 J.D.
(adm. in MA; not adm. in DC) D.C. Gen. Hosp.
Nicholas, Robert B., (AV) .... '44 '69 C.732 B.A. L.94 J.D. [McDermott,W.&E.]
Nicholas, Stefan C. '68 '98 C.276 B.A. L.893 J.D.
(adm. in NY; not adm. in DC) [🄰 Shaw P.]
*PRACTICE AREAS: Corporate; Banking Law; Technology Law.
Nichols, Carl John .... '70 '98 C.197 B.A. L.145 J.D. [🄰 Boies,S.&F.]
*PRACTICE AREAS: Complex Commercial Litigation; International Arbitration.
Nichols, Joel A. .... '72 '00 C.1 B.A. L.1365 J.D. [🄰 Wilmer,C.&P.]
Nichols, Robert Stephen .... '— '94 C.35 B.S.B.A. L.36 J.D. [🄰 Jenner&B.]
*PRACTICE AREAS: Arbitration; Government Contracts Litigation and Counseling; Government Relations.
Nichols, Sara S. '61 '88 C.685 B.A. L.107 J.D.
George Washington Univ. Natl. Law Ctr.
Nicholson, Christine '52 '77
C.197 A.B. L.309 J.D. Asst. Gen. Coun., Smithsonian Institution
Nicholson, Cynthia K. .... '59 '91 C.1288 B.S. L.276 J.D. [Hale&D.] (Pat.)
*PRACTICE AREAS: Intellectual Property.
Nicholson, E. Bruce '49 '77 C.597 B.A. L.339 J.D.
(adm. in OH; not adm. in DC) Leg. Coun., Govt. Affs., Amer. Bar Assn.
Nicholson, Gregory M. '60 '87 C.445 B.S. L.446 J.D.
(adm. in MD; not adm. in DC) Atty., MCI WorldCom
Nicholson, Jeanmarie LoCoco, (AV) '58 '81 C&L.425 B.A., J.D.
[© Sherman,M.C.&A.]
*PRACTICE AREAS: Family Law; Civil Litigation.
Nicholson, John D., (AV) '52 '85 C&L.623 B.B.A., J.D.
(adm. in TX; not adm. in DC) Assoc. Gen. Coun., Fannie Mae
*RESPONSIBILITIES: Real Estate Law; Multi Family Mortgage Lending.
Nicholson, John Leslie '— '96 C.951 B.A. L.880 J.D.
(adm. in MD; not adm. in DC) [🄰 Shaw P.]
Nicholson, Kristin E. '69 '98 C.30 B.A. L.904 J.D.
(adm. in MD; not adm. in DC) Riggs Bk. NA

Nickel, Carol K., (AV) .... '43 '68 C.914 B.A. L.273 J.D. [Ivins,P.&B.]
*PRACTICE AREAS: Federal Tax; Estate and Gift Taxation; Individual Tax; Tax Exempt Organizations.
Nickel, David F. '75 '00 C.674 B.A. L.273 J.D.
(adm. in MD; not adm. in DC) [🄰 Adduci,M.&S.]
*PRACTICE AREAS: Intellectual Property; International Trade Regulation; Litigation.
Nickel, Henry V., (AV) .... '43 '68 C.893 A.B. L.273 J.D. [Hunton&W.]
*PRACTICE AREAS: Environmental.
Nickel, Leslie A. .... '56 '94 C.1349 B.A. L.893 J.D. [🄰 Arnold&P.]
*PRACTICE AREAS: Federal and State Legislation; Election and Campaign Finance Law; Lobbying; Government Ethics.
Nickerson, Joshua B. .... '69 '98 C.276 B.A. L.893 J.D. [🄰 Skadden,A.S.M.&F.]
Nickerson, William W. .... '44 '80 C.454 B.A. L.818 J.D. [© O'Connor&H.]
Nickler, Patrick A. '74 '99 C.264 B.A. L.93 J.D.
(adm. in PA; not adm. in DC) [🄰 Buchanan I.]
*PRACTICE AREAS: Real Estate.
Nickles, Peter J., (AV) .... '38 '64 C.674 B.A. L.309 LL.B. [Covington&B.]
Nicol, Anna W. .... '69 '98 C.94 B.A. L.276 J.D. [🄰 Long A.&N.] (Pat.)
*PRACTICE AREAS: Litigation.
Nicol, Jesse A. .... '69 '00 C.112 B.A. L.276 J.D. [🄰 Paul,W.R.W.&G.]
*PRACTICE AREAS: Corporate Law; International Trade; Project Finance.
Nicolas, Stephanie .... '72 '00 C.103 B.A. L.276 J.D. [🄰 Wilmer,C.&P.]
Nicoli, David Paul .... '57 '84 C.494 B.A. L.904 J.D. 1341 G Street Nw
Nicoll, David L. '50 '83 C.918 B.A. L.128 J.D.
Assoc. Gen. Coun., National Cable Television Assn.
Nicoson, William J. .... '32 '60 C.674 A.B. L.309 LL.B. 1155 Conn. Ave., NW
Nido, Luis M. .... '48 '80 C.870 B.S. L.276 J.D. [Bracewell&P.]
*PRACTICE AREAS: Environmental Law; Environmental Liability; Environmental Litigation; Mergers and Acquisitions; Superfund.
Niebler, Andrew K. .... '67 '98 C.674 A.B. L.276 J.D. [🄰 Cleary,G.S.&H.]
Niebylski, Charles D. '60 '00 C.602 B.S. L.128 J.D.
(adm. in MD; not adm. in DC; See Pat. Sect.) [🄰 Finnegan,H.F.G.&D.]
*PRACTICE AREAS: Chemical Patent Prosecution; Pharmaceutical Intellectual Property; Intellectual Property Portfolio Management.

Niedermayer, Roy I.
(See Bethesda, Maryland)

Nields, Annamaria Locsin '73 '00 C.165 B.A. L.1209 J.D.
(adm. in VA; not adm. in DC) [🄰 Akin,G.S.H.&F.]
*PRACTICE AREAS: Labor and Employment.
Nields, John W., Jr., (AV) .... '42 '69 C.976 B.A. L.659 LL.B. [Howrey S.A.&W.]
*PRACTICE AREAS: White Collar Criminal Defense; Intellectual Property.
Nielsen, Catherine Roemer, (BV) .... '62 '85 C.16 B.A. L.893 J.D. [Keller&H.]
*PRACTICE AREAS: Food and Drug Law; Environmental Law.
Nielsen, Mark C. '71 '97 C.347 B.A. L.107 J.D.
(adm. in NY; not adm. in DC) [Feder,S.C.&B.]
*PRACTICE AREAS: Employee Benefits; ERISA; Health Care; Antitrust.
Nielsen, Vicki M. '74 '00 C.856 B.A. L.273 J.D.
(adm. in NY; not adm. in DC) [🄰 McDermott,W.&E.]
Nielson, Bruce H. .... '— '87 C.101 B.S. L.309 J.D. [Kirkpatrick&L.]
*PRACTICE AREAS: Information Technology Contracts; Information Technology Licensing; Computer Contracts; Software Licensing.
Niemeyer, Elizabeth Ann '72 '00 C.104 A.B. L.846 J.D.
(adm. in VA; not adm. in DC) [🄰 Finnegan,H.F.G.&D.]
*PRACTICE AREAS: Patent Litigation; Patent Prosecution; Electrical Patent Prosecution; Semiconductor Technology.
Nietert, Robyn G., (AV) .... '53 '80 C&L.273 B.A., J.D. [Brown N.&K.]
*PRACTICE AREAS: Telecommunications.
Nieva, Jocelyn C. '60 '97 C.273 B.A. L.904 J.D.
(adm. in MD; not adm. in DC) [🄰 Powell,G.F.&M.]
*PRACTICE AREAS: Health Care.
Nifong, William R. .... '66 '01 C&L.228 B.A., J.D. [🄰 Wilmer,C.&P.]
Nigro, Bernard A., Jr., (BV) .... '60 '86 C.276 A.B. L.273 J.D. [Fried,F.H.S.&J.]
*PRACTICE AREAS: Antitrust and Trade Regulation; Criminal Defense; Franchising and Distribution Law.
Nikaido, David T., (AV) .... '34 '63 C.174 B.A. L.208 J.D. [Rader,F.&G.] (Pat.)
*PRACTICE AREAS: U.S./Japan Negotiations; Patent Licensing.
Niklas, Cynthia A., (AV) .... '48 '74 C.665 B.A. L.30 J.D. 4545 42nd St., N.W
Niles, Stephen D., (AV) .... '61 '87 C.264 B.A. L.904 J.D. [Holland&K.]
*PRACTICE AREAS: Housing Development; Housing Finance; Mortgage Banking; Commercial Real Estate.
Niles-Spencer, Sharon L. .... '— '91 [🄰 Skadden,A.S.M.&F.]
Nilles, Kathleen M., (AV) .... '51 '85 C.770 B.A. L.893 J.D. [Gardner,C.&D.]
*PRACTICE AREAS: Taxation; Nonprofit and Charitable Organization; Health Care; Health Care Taxation; Indian and Native Populations.
Nilsson, Michael D. .... '70 '97 C.112 B.A. L.276 J.D. 531 Hart Bldg.
Ninomiya, Roland B. '62 '97 C.478 B.A. L.1209 J.D.
(adm. in VA; not adm. in DC) [🄰 Schmeltzer,A.&S.]
*PRACTICE AREAS: Litigation; Franchise Law.
Niosi, Corinne A. .... '70 '96 C.1030 B.A. L.128 J.D. [🄰 Morgan,L.&B.]
Nirenberg, Darryl D. .... '59 '87 C.165 B.A. L.273 J.D. [Patton B.]
Nirenstein, Marcia R. .... '56 '80 C.30 B.A. L.276 J.D. [Skadden,A.S.M.&F.]
Nirmel, Chittaranjan N., (AV) .... '38 '76 C.054 B.Sc. L.569 J.D. [© Jones J.] (Pat.)
Nisenson, Aaron .... '63 '90 C.1044 B.A. L.93 J.D. [Henrichsen S.]
*PRACTICE AREAS: Employment Law; Labor Law; Products Liability; Class Actions; Litigation.
Nix, Clayton J. .... '68 '94 C.846 B.A. L.930 J.D. [🄰 Epstein B.&G.]
*PRACTICE AREAS: Health Law.
Nixon, Duncan A. '47 '76 C.1044 B.A. L.724 J.D.
(adm. in NY; not adm. in DC) [Sharretts,P.C.&B.]
*PRACTICE AREAS: Customs Law; International Trade; Imports and Exports; Antidumping; Countervailing Duties.
Nixon, E. Carrie .... '— '00 C.1369 B.S. L.893 J.D. 701 Pennsylvania Avenue, N.W.
Nixon, William F. .... '66 '98 C.885 B.S. L.201 J.D. [🄰 Hogan&H.] (Pat.)
*PRACTICE AREAS: Intellectual Property.

Nixon Peabody LLP, (AV)
401 9th Street, N.W., Suite 900, 20004-2128 ⊙
Telephone: 202-585-8000 Fax: 202-585-8080
Email: nixonpeabody@nixonpeabody.com URL: http://www.nixonpeabody.com
Partners: Veronica M. Ahern; William S. Andrews; Leslie P. Arrington; Gary A. Band; Edward C. Berkowitz; Robert C. Bernius; Robert L. Bodansky; John M. Bradham; William F. Causey; J. William Codinha (P.C.); Jeff M. Cohen; Susan O. Cunningham; Robert L. Daileader, Jr.; George L. Daves; Charles L. Edson; Robert P. Fletcher; Richard S. Goldstein; Raymond J. Gustini; Kenneth G. Hance, Jr.; John C. Hayes, Jr.; Marc S. Kaufman; Harry J. Kelly; Mary Jo Kelly; Bruce S. Lane; Gordon L. Lang; Jeffrey S. Lesk; Christian M. McBurney; Timothy R. McTaggart; Laura Ariane Miller; Laurin H. Mills; Scott M. Nemeroff; John C. Partigan; Barry J. Pollack; Richard M. Price; Mitchell H. Rapaport (Not admitted in DC); Robert F. Reklaitis; Joseph H. Reynolds; Edward M. Rogers; Ruth Borsuk Rosenberg; Kenneth H. Silverberg; John Stuart Smith; Herbert F. Stevens; Kathleen F. Sullivan; Monica Hilton Sussman; Kendal Tyre, Jr.; Gary L. Valby; G. Joseph Votava, Jr.; Marie Johnson Wadler; Stephen J. Wallace; Elizabeth Ward Whittle; Justine E. Wilcox; Debra D. Yogodzinski. Counsel: Richard P. Stanton. Associates: Elizabeth A. Allen; Hollis Bryan Brewer III; Tracy L. Bruehs; Molly R. Bryson; Margaret J. Chriss; Louis E. Dolan, Jr.; Susan E. Eggers; Mark M. Foster; Monica O. Frazer; Ray A. Johnson; Valerie S. Johnson (Not admitted in DC); Randall Kelly; David K. Koehler; Leslie P. Machado; Brian Mulford; Andrew S. Potts; Michael H. Reardon

(This Listing Continued)

Nixon Peabody LLP (Continued)

(Not admitted in DC); Anthony D. Ruvolo; David F. Schon; Scott D. Sergio; Lamont H. Silas; Julia A. Solo (Not admitted in DC); Sarah A. Stone; Dwayne M. Toliver; Lydia P.A. Turnipseed; Susan L. Wilder.
Rochester, New York Office: Clinton Square. Telephone: 716-263-1000. Fax: 716-263-1600.
New York, N.Y. Office: 437 Madison Avenue. Telephone: 212-940-3000. Fax: 212-940-3111.
Albany, New York Office: Omni Plaza, 30 South Pearl Street. Telephone: 518-427-2650. Fax: 518-427-2666.
Garden City, New York Office: 990 Stewart Avenue. Telephone: 516-832-7500. Fax: 516-832-7555.
Buffalo, New York Office: 1600 Main Place Tower. Telephone: 716-853-8100. Fax: 716-853-8109.
Hartford, Connecticut Office: City Place, 185 Asylum Street. Telephone: 860-275-6820. Fax: 860-275-6821.
Boston, Massachusetts Office: 101 Federal Street. Telephone: 617-345-1000. Fax: 617-345-1300.
Manchester, New Hampshire Office: 889 Elm Street. Telephone: 603-628-4000. Fax: 603-628-4040.
Providence, Rhode Island Office: One Citizens Plaza. Telephone: 401-454-1000. Fax: 401-454-1030.
McLean, Virginia Office: 8180 Greensboro Drive, Suite 800. Telephone: 703-790-9110. Telecopier: 703-883-0370.
Costa Mesa, California Office: 600 Anton Boulevard, Suite 1600, 92626. Telephone: 714-241-0101. Fax: 714-241-0105.
San Francisco, California Office: Two Embarcadero Center, Suite 2700, 94111-3996. Telephone: 415-984-8200. Fax: 415-984-8300.

See Professional Biographies, WASHINGTON, DISTRICT OF COLUMBIA

Nixon & Vanderhye P.C.
(See Arlington, Virginia)

Nizzardini, Richard J. . . . . '68 '93 C.1365 B.A. L.880 J.D. 2300 N St., N.W.
Noah, Jennifer L. . . . . '73 '99 C.1372 B.S. L.107 J.D. [Ⓐ Thompson H.]
*PRACTICE AREAS: Government Affairs; Regulations.
Noble, John H. . . . . '31 '55 C.604 B.A. L.309 LL.B. 1250 24th St., NW‡
Nocjar, Aaron P. . . . . . . '73 '99 C.602 B.A. L.930 J.D. [Ⓐ Steptoe&J.]
Noel, Elizabeth A. . . . . . . '50 '76 C.262 B.A. L.276 J.D. Off. of the People's Coun.
Noffsinger, Zachary N. '72 '99 C&L.228 B.A., J.D.
(adm. in NY; not adm. in DC) [Ⓐ Piper M.R.&W.]
*PRACTICE AREAS: Corporate Law; Business; Technology; Venture Capital; Emerging Companies.
Nogueira, Ricardo '70 '96 C.390 B.A. L.997
(adm. in NJ; not adm. in DC) [Ⓐ Van Ness F.]
*PRACTICE AREAS: International Transactions; Energy; Climate Change; Mergers and Acquisitions.
Noh, Solomon J. . . . . . . '74 '01 C.674 A.B. L.309 J.D. [Ⓐ Steptoe&J.]
Nojeim, Gregory T. . . . . . '59 '85 C.696 B.A. L.893 J.D. Legislative Counsel, ACLU
Nolan, Catherine R., (AV) . . . . . '— '88 C.129 B.A. L.904 J.D. 800 Conn. Ave., N.W.
Nolan, J. Thomas . . . . . . '— '95 C.696 B.A. L.276 J.D. [Ⓐ Shook,H.&B.]
Nolan, James G., (AV) . . . . . . '43 '72 C.276 A.B. L.273 J.D. [Witt&N.] ⊙
*PRACTICE AREAS: Family Law.
Nolan, Janet S. . . . . . . '64 '89 C&L.893 B.A., J.D. [Ⓒ Fulbright&J.]
*PRACTICE AREAS: Health Care; Litigation.
Nolan, John E., (AV) . . . . . . '27 '55 C.871 B.S. L.276 LL.B. [Steptoe&J.]
Nolan, Laurence . . . . . . '— '74 C.329 B.S. L.477 J.D. 2900 Van Ness St., N.W.
Nolan, Matthew M., (AV) . . . . . . '58 '86 C.860 B.A. L.276 J.D. [Miller&C.]
*PRACTICE AREAS: Antidumping; Countervailing Duty; Customs Law; Export Compliance; Export Regulation.
Nolan, Michael D. . . . . . . '65 '92 C.309 A.B. L.145 J.D. [Milbank,T.H.&M.]
Nolan, Stuart W., Jr. '68 '99 C.30 B.A. L.128 J.D.
(adm. in VA; not adm. in DC) [Wood,M.&B.]
*PRACTICE AREAS: Communications Law.
Nolan, Walker F., Jr. '43 '71 C.896 B.A. L.575 J.D.
818 Connecticut Ave. NW, Suite 1100
Nolton, Jeffrey, (BV) '39 '70
C.350 B.S.I.E. L.276 J.D. 2033 K Street, N.W., Suite 800 (Pat.)‡
Noon, Susan M. . . . . . . '53 '91 C.112 B.A. L.128 J.D. ULLICO INC.
*RESPONSIBILITIES: Litigation; Group Life and Health Insurance.
Noonan, Edward R. . . . . . . '51 '76 C.103 A.B. L.273 J.D. [Eckert S.C.&M.]
*PRACTICE AREAS: Labor and Employment Law.
Noonan, Elizabeth A. '64 '91 C.103 A.B. L.910 J.D.
(adm. in MO; not adm. in DC) 1615 L St., N.W.‡
Noonan, Linda . . . . . . '51 '77 C.30 B.A. L.904 J.D. [Ⓒ Gibson,D.&C.]
*PRACTICE AREAS: Money Laundering.
Noonan, Nancy A. . . . . . . '68 '96 C.692 B.A. L.823 J.D. [Ⓐ Arent F.K.P.&K.]
*PRACTICE AREAS: International Trade; Customs.
Noonberg, Lewis A., (AV) . . . . . '38 '62 C.197 A.B. L.446 LL.B. [Piper M.R.&W.]
*PRACTICE AREAS: Antitrust; Trade Regulation Law; Litigation.
Noone, James A. . . . . . . '44 '85 C.754 B.A. L.30 J.D. [Karalekas&N.]
*PRACTICE AREAS: Government Relations; Legislative Law; Government Contracts.
Noone, Mary-Ellen . . . . . . '69 '98 C.273 B.A. L.64 J.D. [Ⓐ Berliner,C.&R.]
*PRACTICE AREAS: Litigation; Corporate.
Norberg, Charles Robert, (AV) . . . . . '12 '40 C.188 B.S. L.309 LL.B. 1819 H St., N.W.‡
Norcross, David A., (AV) '37 '61
C.205 B.A. L.659 LL.B. [Blank R.C.&M.] (⊙Trenton, NJ)
*PRACTICE AREAS: Federal Government Law; Federal Legislative Practice; Government Affairs; Government Relations; State Government Law.
Nordberg, Carl A., Jr., (AV) . . . . '35 '60 C.477 A.B. L.273 LL.B. [Ⓒ McDermott,W.&E.]
Nordeng, Amy E. . . . . . . '70 '01 C.604 B.A. L.477 J.D. [Ⓐ Powers,P.S.&V.]
*PRACTICE AREAS: Health Care; Privacy Law; Education Law; Administrative Law.
Nordhaus, Robert R., (AV) . . . . . '37 '63 C.813 B.A. L.976 LL.B. [Van Ness F.]
*PRACTICE AREAS: Energy; Environment.

Nordhaus, Haltom, Taylor, Taradash & Bladh, LLP, (AV)
816 Connecticut Avenue, N.W., Suite 300, 20006 ⊙
Telephone: 202-530-1270 Telecopier: 202-530-1920
Jill Elise Grant.
Indian Affairs, Litigation, Energy, Oil and Gas, Water, Environmental Law, Natural Resources, Commercial Transactions, State and Tribal Taxation, Business and General Civil Practice.
Albuquerque, New Mexico Office: 500 Marquette Avenue, N.W., Suite 1050. Telephone: 505-243-4275. Telecopier: 505-243-4464.
Santa Fe, New Mexico Office: 200 West De Vargas, Suite 9. Telephone: 505-982-3622. Telecopier: 505-982-1827.

See Professional Biographies, WASHINGTON, DISTRICT OF COLUMBIA

Nordlinger, Bernard I., (AV) '09 '32 C&L.273 A.B., J.D.
3101 New Mexico Ave., N.W.‡
Nordlinger, Dean S. '69 '00 C.477 B.A. L.276 J.D.
(adm. in VA; not adm. in DC) [Ⓐ Brobeck,P.&H.]
*PRACTICE AREAS: Business and Technology Transactions.
Nordstrom, Paul E., (AV) . . . . . '— '82 C.478 B.A. L.569 J.D. [Verner,L.B.M.&H.]
*PRACTICE AREAS: Public Utility Law; Administrative Law.
Nordwind, William R. '67 '96 C.602 B.A. L.273 J.D.
(adm. in MD; not adm. in DC) 1919 Pennsylvania Ave., N.W., Suite 800
Noreika, Keith A. . . . . . . '72 '97 C.659 B.S.B.A. L.309 J.D. [Ⓐ Covington&B.]
Norman, David L. . . . . . . '24 '57 C.112 A.B. L.1066 LL.B. Ret. Supr. Ct. J.‡
Norman, Donna . . . . . . '66 '92 C.966 B.A. L.276 J.D. [Ⓐ Arnold&P.]
*PRACTICE AREAS: Intellectual Property; Antitrust; Commercial Litigation.
Norman, Jane Carol . . . . . . '51 '75 C.112 B.A. L.426 J.D. [Bond,C.&N.]
Norman, W. Caffey, III, (AV) . . . . . '53 '77 C.16 B.A. L.893 J.D. [Patton B.]
Norrell, David G. . . . . . . '53 '80 C.259 B.A. L.893 J.D. [Ⓒ Kirkland&E.]
*PRACTICE AREAS: International Law; International Trade Regulation; International Acquisitions and Investment; Worldwide Litigation.
Norrett, Lisa Michele . . . . . . '73 '98 C.945 B.A. L.893 J.D. [Ⓐ McKenna&C.]
*PRACTICE AREAS: Products Liability Litigation; Civil Litigation.
Norris, Arthur T. K. . . . . . . '64 '91 C.813 A.B. L.228 J.D. [Ⓐ Lee&M.]
*PRACTICE AREAS: Civil Litigation; Construction Law; Architects and Engineers; Real Estate; Title Insurance.
Norris, Jeffrey A., (AV) . . . . . '45 '70 C.105 A.B. L.188 J.D. [McGuiness N.&W.] ⊙
*PRACTICE AREAS: Labor Relations Law; Equal Employment Opportunity Law.
Norris, Jerome J. '38 '71 C.329 B.S. L.64 J.D.
(adm. in NY; not adm. in DC) 1919 Pennsylvania Ave.
Norris, Jon W. . . . . . . '61 '90 C.446 B.S. L.443 J.D. Pub. Def. Serv.
Norris, R. Wade '47 '74 C&L.228 B.A., J.D.
(adm. in GA; not adm. in DC) [Ritter E.&N.]
*PRACTICE AREAS: Public Finance Law; Housing.
Norris, Walter F. . . . . . . '30 '56 C.934 A.B. L.273 LL.B. 1215 17th St., N.W.
Northam, Frank M. . . . . . . '46 '74 C.976 B.A. L.345 J.D. [Webster,C.&B.]
*PRACTICE AREAS: Taxation; Trade and Professional Associations; Nonprofit and Charitable Organizations; Antitrust and Trade Regulation; Litigation.
Northern, Christina '56 '84 C.910 B.A. L.1162 J.D.
(adm. in MD; not adm. in DC) 1113 R St., N.W.
Northrop, Carl W., (AV) . . . . . '50 '76 C.477 B.B.A. L.276 J.D. [Paul,H.J.&W.]
*PRACTICE AREAS: Wireless Telecommunications Industry; Radio Paging (common and private carrier); Cellular Telephones (MSA, RSA and unserved area licensees); Specialized Mobile Radio (standard and enhanced); Personal Communications Service (wideband PCS and narrowband PCS).
Norton, Eleanor Holmes . . . . . . '37 '64 C.33 B.A. L.976 J.D. (M.C.)
Norton, Floyd L., IV, (AV) . . . . . '50 '75 C&L.893 B.A., J.D. [Morgan,L.&B.]
Norton, Gerald P., (AV) . . . . . '40 '64 C.674 A.B. L.178 LL.B. [Harkins C.]
*PRACTICE AREAS: Litigation; Appellate Practice; Administrative Law; Antitrust; Employment Law.
Norton, Helen L. '63 '89 C.813 B.A. L.1066 J.D.
(adm. in CA; not adm. in DC) Women's Legal Def. Fund
Norton, Lisa K. . . . . . . '68 '94 C&L.101 B.S., J.D. [Ⓐ Piper M.R.&W.] (Pat.)
*PRACTICE AREAS: Intellectual Property.
Norton, Randell Hunt, (AV) '48 '73 C&L.893 B.A., J.D.
[Thompson,O.M.N.&H.] (⊙Rockville, MD; Arlington, VA)
*PRACTICE AREAS: Insurance Coverage; Construction Liability; Arbitration; Personal Injury; Products Liability.
Norwalk, Leslie V. . . . . . . '— '96 C.914 B.S. L.1209 J.D. [Ⓐ Epstein B.&G.]
*PRACTICE AREAS: Health Law.
Nosal, Chester W. . . . . . '44 '70 C.209 B.S.C. L.276 J.D. 1133 Connecticut Avenue, N.W.
Noskow, Alan M. . . . . . . '75 '00 C.696 B.A. L.472 J.D. [Ⓐ Piper M.R.&W.]
*PRACTICE AREAS: Bankruptcy; Business Reorganization; Creditors Rights; Finance; Financial Services Law.
Noss, David B. '57 '96 C.446 B.A. L.273 J.D.
(adm. in MD; not adm. in DC) Sr. Legal Editor, Bur. of Natl. Affs.‡

Nossaman, Guthner, Knox & Elliott, LLP, (AV)
c/o French & Company The Homer Building, Suite 370-S, 601 13th Street, N.W., 20005 ⊙
Telephone: 202-783-7272
Of Counsel: Warren G. Elliott; Murray Zweben.
Legislative Law. General Civil Practice, including Administrative and Regulatory, Antitrust, Trade Regulation and Unfair Competition, Appellate Practice, Bankruptcy and Creditors Rights, Business and Corporate, Communications, Construction and Construction Litigation, Eminent Domain, Environmental, Estate Planning, Probate and Trusts, Financial Institutions, Franchise, Hazardous Waste, Health Care, Health Maintenance Organizations and Medical Groups, Infrastructure, Insurance Coverage, Land Use, Legislative Advocacy, Litigation, Natural Resources, Oil and Gas, Physician and Professional Licensure and Discipline, Labor and Employment Counseling and Litigation, Municipal and Public Agency Law, Public Finance, Public Utility Regulation, Real Estate, Tax, Transportation, Securities, Sports, Water Rights, White Collar Criminal Defense.
Los Angeles, California Office: Thirty-First Floor, Union Bank Square, 445 South Figueroa Street. Telephone: 213-612-7800.
San Francisco, California Office: Thirty-Fourth Floor, 50 California Street. Telephone: 415-398-3600.
Orange County, California Office: Suite 1800, 18101 Von Karman Avenue, Irvine, California. Telephone: 714-833-7800.
Sacramento, California Office: Suite 1000, 915 L Street. Telephone: 916-442-8888.

See Professional Biographies, WASHINGTON, DISTRICT OF COLUMBIA

Notarius, Joyce M., (AV) . . . . . '50 '75 C.966 B.A. L.1119 J.D. [Cadeaux&T.]
*PRACTICE AREAS: Personal Injury; Medical Malpractice; Products Liability.
Notigan, Robert . . . . . . '72 '98 C.645 B.A. L.273 J.D. [Ⓐ Jackson&C.]
*PRACTICE AREAS: Corporate Securities; Real Estate; Litigation.
Noto, Aldo . . . . . . '64 '90 C.1044 B.S.E.E. L.273 J.D. [Dorsey&W.] (Pat.)
*PRACTICE AREAS: Patent Law, Other Intellectual Property Law; Computer Law; Litigation; Patent Licensing; Electronic Patents.
Noto, Anne Doris . . . . . . '58 '86 C.188 B.A. L.273 J.D. [Sonosky,C.S.E.&P.]
Noto, Mario T., (AV) . . . . . '17 '40 C.724 L.262 LL.B. [Noto&O.]
*PRACTICE AREAS: International Law; Immigration Law.
Noto, Thomas J. . . . . . . '— '86 C.156 B.A. L.128 J.D. [Kirkpatrick&L.]
*PRACTICE AREAS: Consumer Banking; Fair Lending; Truth in Lending; Consumer Credit Compliance; Lender Regulation.

Noto & Oswald, P.C., (AV)
1850 M Street, NW Suite 920, 20036
Telephone: 202-331-2883 Fax: 202-261-2835
Email: rscottoswald@compuserve.com URL: http://www.lawyers.com/noto&oswald
Mario T. Noto; Robert L. Oswald; Danielle L. C. Beach (Not admitted in DC); R. Scott Oswald.
Civil and Criminal Trial Practice before all Courts and International Practice, Legislative Practice, Immigration Law, Business Immigration, Employment Visas, Religious Visas, Deportation, Political Asylum, Refugee Law, Civil Service, Commercial Transactions, Corporate Law.

See Professional Biographies, WASHINGTON, DISTRICT OF COLUMBIA

Novack, Laura A. . . . . . . '60 '86 C.705 B.A. L.569 J.D. [Ⓐ Dechert]
*PRACTICE AREAS: Financial Services Law; Investment Management.
Novak, Alan R. . . . . . . '34 '65 C&L.976 B.A., LL.B. 3000 K St., N.W.
Novak, Sheila R. . . . . . . '69 '96 C&L.945 B.A., J.D. [Ⓐ Sutherland A.&B.]
*PRACTICE AREAS: Real Estate.
Novello, David P. . . . . . . '57 '85 C.197 B.A. L.178 J.D. [D.Novello]
*PRACTICE AREAS: Environmental Law; Clean Air Act; Environmental Litigation; Environmental Compliance; Environmental Permitting.

Novello, David, LLC, Law Offices of
1752 N Street NW, Suite 800, 20036
Telephone: 202-857-9708 Fax: 202-887-8044
Email: dnovello@novellolaw.com URL: http://www.novellolaw.com
David P. Novello.
Environmental Law, Clean Air Act, Environmental Litigation, Environmental Compliance, Environmental Permitting, Environmental Regulation, Environmental Legislative Practice, Administrative Law, Appellate Litigation.

See Professional Biographies, WASHINGTON, DISTRICT OF COLUMBIA

Novick, Amy R. '56 '84 C.156 B.A. L.1162 J.D.
Assoc. Dir., Amer. Immigration Lawyers Assn.
Novick, Harold L., (AV) . . '42 '73 C.473 B.A. L.273 J.D. [Nath&Assoc.] (See Pat. Sect.)
*PRACTICE AREAS: Electro-Mechanical Patents; Prosecution; Intellectual Property Licensing; Trademark Prosecution; Copyright Prosecution.

Novick, Robert T. .... '58 '84 C.105 B.A. L.30 J.D. [Wilmer,C.&P.]
*PRACTICE AREAS: International Trade and Business Law; International Investments Law; International Law; Customs.
Novina, Julia A. '70 '88 C.183 B.A. L.276 J.D.
(adm. in MD; not adm. in DC) [Ⓐ Lovells]
*PRACTICE AREAS: Consumer Financial Services; Privacy Law; Federal Regulatory Compliance.
Novins, Alan S., (AV) .... '37 '64 C.309 A.B. L.178 J.D. [Ⓒ Lobel,N.&L.]
*PRACTICE AREAS: Legal Ethics; Civil Litigation.
Novitt, Anita D. '57 '00 C.571 M.S. L.776 J.D.
(adm. in NJ; not adm. in DC) [Ⓐ Foxkiser]
Nowak, G. Philip, (AV) .... '44 '70 C.976 B.A. L.880 J.D. [Sidley A.B.&W.]
Nowell, Courtney Collins .... '71 '96 C.914 B.A. L.945 J.D. [Ⓐ Patton B.]
Nowezki, Diana P. '62 '87
C.713 B.A. L.1202 J.D. Deloitte & Touche, LLP (⊙New York, NY)
Nowlin, Warren E. .... '56 '84 C.893 B.S. L.902 J.D. [Williams M.]
*PRACTICE AREAS: Corporate; Securities; Mergers and Acquisitions; Banking; Venture Capital.
Noyes, John P., (AV) '51 '89 C.94 A.B. L.818 J.D.
[Ⓒ Bonner K.T.&C.] (⊙Boston, MA)
*PRACTICE AREAS: Trial Practice; Appellate Practice; Product Liability; General Liability; Insurance Law.
Nucci, Gregory B., (AV) ... '55 '80 C.602 B.B.A. L.276 J.D. 1301 K St. N.W., Ste. 800 E.
Nucci, Katherine S. .... '51 '81 C.893 B.A. L.128 J.D. [Thompson C.]
*PRACTICE AREAS: Government Contract Law.
Nuckolls, C. Randall, (AV) .... '52 '77 C&L.280 B.S.A., J.D. [Long A.&N.]
*PRACTICE AREAS: Legislation; Regulations.
Nudelman, Noel J. .... '67 '93 C.94 B.A. L.1009 J.D. [Heideman]
*PRACTICE AREAS: Civil Litigation; Criminal Defense; Corporate; International Trade; Corporate Transactions.
Nuechterlein, Jonathan .... '64 '94 C&L.976 B.A., J.D. [Wilmer,C.&P.]
*PRACTICE AREAS: Telecommunications Law; Appellate Practice.
Nüesch, Pablo O. .... '65 '97 C.1210 B.S. L.790 J.D. [Ⓐ Spiegel&M.]
*PRACTICE AREAS: Aviation Law; Airport Law; Civil Litigation.
Nugent, Gregory R. .... '62 '89 C.93 B.A. L.818 J.D. [Ⓐ Lewis] (⊙Rockville, MD)
*PRACTICE AREAS: Family Law; Criminal Law; Civil Litigation.
Nugent, Victoria S. '69 '99 C.918 B.A. L.276 J.D.
(adm. in MD; not adm. in DC) [Ⓐ Cohen,M.H.&T.]
*PRACTICE AREAS: Consumer Law; Antitrust.
Nuland, Anthony C. J., (AV) .... '43 '69 C.674 A.B. L.569 J.D. [Seward&K.]
*PRACTICE AREAS: Investment Companies; Brokers and Dealers; Corporations; Securities; Banking.
Numrych, David C. .... '64 '90 C.339 B.A. L.146 J.D. [Ⓐ Bonner K.T.&C.]
*PRACTICE AREAS: Corporate Defense; Insurance Defense; Employer Liability; Personal Injury; Insurance Coverage Disputes.
Nunan, Nancy Elizabeth .... '63 '93 C.188 B.A. L.276 J.D. [Ⓐ Kutak R.]
*PRACTICE AREAS: Employment Law; White Collar Crime; Securities; Civil Litigation.
Nunzio, Nicholas S. .... '29 '60 C&L.273 B.A., LL.B. Sr. Supr. Ct. J.
Nunzio, Nicholas S., Jr., (AV) .... '54 '81 C.273 B.A. L.64 J.D. [Ⓐ Cadeaux&T.]
Nunzio, Rocco C., (BV) .... '56 '82 C.273 B.A. L.64 J.D. [Ⓐ Mooers&M.]
*PRACTICE AREAS: Insurance Defense; Premises Liability Defense; Products Liability Defense; Insurance Coverage Litigation; Civil Litigation.
Nurick, Lester .... '14 '37 C.563 B.S.S. L.1009 LL.B. [Ⓒ Wilmer,C.&P.]
*PRACTICE AREAS: International Law; Arbitration; Project Finance.
Nurmi, Thomas D. .... '45 '72 C.473 B.A. L.893 J.D. 5301 Wisconsin Ave., N.W.
Nuschler, Robin M. .... '63 '87 C&L.861 B.A., J.D. [Akin,G.S.H.&F.]
*PRACTICE AREAS: Energy.
Nusel, Rami '59 '89 L.999 LL.B.
(adm. in NY; not adm. in DC) [Ⓐ R.M.Price] (⊙Tel Aviv, Israel)
Nussbaum, Harold J., (AV) .... '21 '53 C.188 L.904 J.D. 4000 Albemarle St., N.W.
Nussbaum, Michael, (AV) .... '35 '62 C.1019 A.B. L.145 J.D. [Ropes&G.]
Nussbaum, William D., (AV) .... '53 '77 C.94 B.S. L.30 J.D. [Hogan&H.]
*PRACTICE AREAS: Civil Litigation; White Collar Criminal Litigation; Civil Rights Defense; College and University Law; School Tenure.

Nussbaum & Wald
(See Baach Robinson & Lewis PLLC)

Nussdorf, Melanie F., (AV) .... '49 '73 C.659 B.A. L.569 J.D. [Steptoe&J.]
*PRACTICE AREAS: ERISA; Labor Law.
Nutall, Dexter U. .... '— '96 C.524 B.S. L.329 J.D. [Ⓐ Reed S.]
*PRACTICE AREAS: Litigation.
Nuterangelo, Brian .... '68 '93 C.94 B.S.B.A. L.904 J.D. [Ⓐ Wiley R.&F.]
Nuxoll, Dennis R. .... '73 '98 C.228 B.A. L.575 J.D. [Ⓐ Stewart&S.]
*PRACTICE AREAS: International Trade; Antidumping; Countervailing Duties; Administrative Law; Unfair Competition.
Nyborg, Philip S. .... '45 '75 C.112 A.B. L.477 J.D. MCI Telecom. Corp.
Nyland, Margaret D. .... '60 '92 C.893 B.A. L.1209 J.D. 2120 L St., N.W.
Nyquist, Polly A. '69 '97 C.228 A.B. L.309 J.D.
(adm. in NY; not adm. in DC) 1050 Conn. Ave., N.W.‡
Nzelibe, Jide O. .... '70 '98 C.722 B.A. L.976 J.D. [Ⓐ Kellogg,H.H.T.&E.]
*PRACTICE AREAS: Telecommunications; Litigation.
O, Ki .... '— '01 C.165 B.S. L.537 J.D. [Ⓐ Arnold&P.]
*PRACTICE AREAS: Intellectual Property; Technology Law; Litigation.
Oakes, Andra N. .... '46 '71 C.104 A.B. L.145 J.D. Prog. Dir., Emeritus Found.
Oakley, Robert L. '45 '77 C&L.188 B.A., J.D.
(adm. in NY; not adm. in DC) Dir., Law Libr., Georgetown Univ. Law Ctr.
Oas, Julia A. .... '61 '86 C.477 B.A. L.966 J.D. [Ⓒ Baker&H.]
*PRACTICE AREAS: Trade Regulation; Consumer Law; Litigation; Advertising Law.
Obebe, Oluwasegun G. '52 '90 C&L.329 B.A., J.D.
(adm. in PA; not adm. in DC) 1923 Vermont Ave., N.W.
Ober, David .... '— '91 C.861 B.A. L.30 J.D. [Ⓒ Reed S.]
*PRACTICE AREAS: Litigation.

Ober, Kaler, Grimes & Shriver, A Professional Corporation, (AV)
Suite 500, 1401 H Street, N.W., 20005-2110 ⊙
Telephone: 202-408-8400 Facsimile: 202-408-0640
Email: info@ober.com URL: http://www.ober.com
Lawrence D. Hollman; Stephen L. Parker; Paul M. Vincent; Harry R. Silver; John J. Miles; Patrick K. O'Hare; John S. Graham III; Robert L. Ash; Martha Purcell Rogers; John N. Rodock; Thomas K. Hyatt; Leon Rodriguez (Not admitted in DC); E. John Steren; Edwin G. Davila-Bloise; Nikolaus F. Schandlbauer;—Harold G. Belkowitz. Of Counsel: James R. Worsley, Jr.; Carlyle C. Ring, Jr.
Admiralty, Shipping and Transportation, Business and Corporate, Commercial Financing, Construction, Creditors' Rights Workouts, and Bankruptcy, Employee Benefits, Employment and Labor Matters, Equipment Finance, Estates and Trusts, Financial Institution/Regulatory, Health Law, Intellectual Property, Litigation, Real Estate, Tax, and White-Collar Criminal Defense.
Baltimore, Maryland Office: 120 East Baltimore Street. Telephone: 410-685-1120. Facsimile: 410-547-0699.
Falls Church, Virginia Office: 254 North Washington Street. Telephone: 703-237-0126. Facsimile: 703-237-2644.
See Professional Biographies, WASHINGTON, DISTRICT OF COLUMBIA

Oberbroeckling, Laura J. .... '67 '92 C.352 B.A. L.309 J.D. [Mintz,L.C.F.G.&P.]
*PRACTICE AREAS: Health Care; Litigation.
Oberdorfer, Carol B. '45 '81
C.966 B.A. L.326 J.D. Legal Editor, The Bureau of Natl. Affs., Inc.
Oberdorfer, John L., (AV) .... '44 '69 C.197 A.B. L.976 LL.B. [Patton B.]
Obergh & Berlin .... 1424 K St., NW
Oblich, David '48 '73 C&L.665 B.A., J.D.
(adm. in PA; not adm. in DC) U.S. Dept. of Agric.

Oblon, Spivak, McClelland, Maier & Neustadt, P.C.
(See Arlington, Virginia)

Oboz, Kim M. .... '45 '73 C&L.831 B.A., J.D. AT&T
Oboz, M. Kenneth '44 '72 C.674 B.A. L.831 J.D.
(adm. in PA; not adm. in DC) V.P., Prudential Ins. Co. of Amer.
O'Brien, Alice .... '65 '95 C.976 B.A. L.276 J.D. [Ⓐ Bredhoff&K.]
O'Brien, Andrea I. .... '60 '85 C.602 B.A. L.276 J.D. [Venable,A.B.H.&C.]
*PRACTICE AREAS: Employee Benefits; Employment Law; Corporate Law.
O'Brien, Anne J., (AV) .... '45 '88 C.560 B.A. L.29 J.D. [Arnold&P.]
*PRACTICE AREAS: Estate Planning; Probate; Charitable Planning; Estate and Trust Administration.
O'Brien, Anthony A. '— '56 C&L.273 B.M.E., J.D.
1000 Connecticut Ave., N.W. (Pat.)
O'Brien, Anthony N. .... '62 '89 C&L.309 A.B., J.D. Federal Document Clearing Hs., Inc.
O'Brien, Claudia M. .... '— '94 C.976 B.A. L.276 J.D. [Ⓐ Latham&W.]
*PRACTICE AREAS: Environmental Law.
O'Brien, Coleman C. '47 '74 C&L.602 A.B., J.D.
(adm. in VA; not adm. in DC) Pres., Coley O'Brien & Assocs.
O'Brien, David W. .... '50 '75 C.602 B.A. L.276 J.D. [Crowell&M.]
*PRACTICE AREAS: Criminal Law; Litigation; Surety and Fidelity Bond Law; Construction Law.
O'Brien, Edward L. .... '45 '73 C.893 B.A. L.276 J.D. Exec. Dir., Street Law, Inc.‡
O'Brien, Elizabeth A. .... '70 '98 C&L.477 B.A., J.D. [Ⓐ Williams&C.]
*PRACTICE AREAS: Civil Litigation; Criminal Defense; General Practice; Trial Practice.
O'Brien, James D., (AV) ...... '26 '60 C.276 B.S. L.273 LL.B. 3346 Tennyson St., N.W.‡
O'Brien, James J. .... '57 '87 C.1046 B.S. L.128 J.D. [Krupin O.]
*PRACTICE AREAS: Employment Law; Immigration Law.
O'Brien, John J. .... '59 '85 C.893 B.S. L.945 J.D. [Ⓒ Cohen M.]
*PRACTICE AREAS: Government Contracts Law; Litigation; Business Law.
O'Brien, Karen R. .... '62 '87 C.573 B.B.A. L.1194 J.D. [Ⓒ McCarthy,S.&H.]
*PRACTICE AREAS: Government Contracts.
O'Brien, Keith G. .... '37 '63 C&L.800 B.A., LL.B. [Rea,C.&A.]
*PRACTICE AREAS: Administrative Law; Interstate Commerce; Transportation; Railroads.
O'Brien, Kevin '54 '84 C.276 B.A. L.767 J.D.
(adm. in CA; not adm. in DC) [Thelen R.&P.]
*PRACTICE AREAS: Construction Law; Environmental Litigation; General Commercial Litigation.
O'Brien, Kevin M. .... '56 '83 C.667 B.S.Ch.E. L.424 J.D. [Baker&M.]
O'Brien, Kevin P., (AV) .... '51 '76 C&L.276 A.B., J.D. [Ivins,P.&B.]
*PRACTICE AREAS: Employee Benefits; Employment Taxation; Executive Compensation; ERISA Litigation; ESOPs.
O'Brien, Kevin P. '49 '80
C.107 B.S. L.1209 J.D. Sr. V.P., The Riggs Natl. Bk. of Wash., D.C.
O'Brien, Lawrence F., III, (AV) .... '45 '73 C.309 B.A. L.178 J.D. 1350 Eye St Nw
O'Brien, Michelle '70 '99 C.851 B.A. L.273 J.D.
(adm. in MD; not adm. in DC) [Ⓐ Finnegan,H.F.G.&D.]
*PRACTICE AREAS: Chemical Intellectual Property.
O'Brien, Patrick D. '45 '97 C.885 B.S. L.1209 J.D.
[Ⓐ Sterne,K.G.&F.] (See Pat. Sect.)
*PRACTICE AREAS: Intellectual Property Law.
O'Brien, Paul L., (AV) .... '26 '53 C.918 B.A. L.893 LL.B. [Ⓒ O'Brien,B.M.&S.]
O'Brien, Raymond C. .... '44 '69 C.397 A.B. L.893 LL.B. Prof. of Law, Catholic Univ.
O'Brien, Regina A. '— '99 C.1356 B.A. L.276 J.D.
(adm. in VA; not adm. in DC) [Ⓐ Morgan,L.&B.]
O'Brien, Stephen J. .... '46 '75 C.276 A.B. L.128 J.D. [O'Brien&L.] (⊙Fairfax, VA)
*PRACTICE AREAS: Alcoholic Beverage Licensing; Liquor Licensing; Commercial Litigation; Business Planning; Municipal Law.
O'Brien, Thomas J. .... '47 '84 C.321 A.B. L.273 J.D. [Ⓒ Morgan,L.&B.]
O'Brien, Timothy A., III '45 '76 C.475 B.A. L.425 J.D.
Law Correspondent, ABC News
O'Brien, William R., (AV) .... '44 '69 C.321 A.B. L.276 J.D. [Howrey S.A.&W.]
*PRACTICE AREAS: Antitrust; Complex Litigation; Insurance Coverage.
O'Brien, William T. .... '64 '94 C.94 B.S. L.128 J.D. [Ⓐ McKenna&C.]
*PRACTICE AREAS: Litigation.

O'Brien, Butler, McConihe & Schaefer, PLLC, (AV)
Suite 1000 Brawner Building, 888 Seventeenth Street, N.W., 20006-3967
Telephone: 202-298-6161 Fax: 202-293-1640
Email: schae001@winstarmail.com
Members of Firm: William J. Butler, Jr.; Michael H. McConihe; Jerome C. Schaefer (Resident); Steven P. Benson. Associates: A. Statton Hammock, Jr.; Mark B. Sandground, Jr. (Not admitted in DC); Stephen M. Schaefer; Kevin A. Kernan. Of Counsel: Harry Teter; Paul L. O'Brien.
General Civil Practice before the Courts of the District of Columbia, Maryland, Virginia and before the Federal Departments and Commissions. Civil Litigation, Non-Profit Organizations Law, Association Law, Insurance Law, Health Care Law, Estates and Trusts.
See Professional Biographies, WASHINGTON, DISTRICT OF COLUMBIA

O'Brien & Long
Suite 208, 2600 Virginia Avenue, N.W., 20037
Telephone: 202-625-7700 Fax: 202-625-7706
URL: http://www.lawyers.com/obrienandlong
Stephen J. O'Brien; Stuart J. Long; Michael D. Fonseca; Barbara Lee Smith.
Alcoholic Beverage Licensing, Liquor Licensing, Municipal Law, Commercial Litigation, Business Planning.
See Professional Biographies, WASHINGTON, DISTRICT OF COLUMBIA

O'Bryan, Stacey H .... '71 '97 C&L.893 B.A., J.D. U.S. Dept. of Jus.
O'Bryant, Michael T., (AV) .... '46 '71 C.712 B.A. L.128 J.D. [Lipshultz&H.] ⊙
*PRACTICE AREAS: Insurance Defense; Automobile Insurance Defense; Wrongful Death; Insurance Arbitration; Psychological Injuries.
O'Bryon, Laurie E. .... '60 '89 C.282 B.A. L.94 J.D. Jesuit Refugee Serv.
O'Bryon, Maureen, (AV) .... '46 '75 C.352 B.A. L.276 J.D. [Hogan&H.]
*PRACTICE AREAS: Antitrust and Trade Regulation; Complex Litigation and Multi-District Litigation; Antitrust Class Actions; Litigation.
Obuchowski, Janice I. .... '51 '76 C.914 B.A. L.276 J.D. [Ⓒ Halprin,T.G.&M.]
*PRACTICE AREAS: Communications Law; International Law.
Ocasal, Christopher '66 '93 C.724 B.A. L.273 J.D.
(adm. in VA; not adm. in DC) 815 Conn. Ave., N.W.‡
Ochoa, Joan T. '55 '92 C.446 B.S. L.64 J.D.
Staff Coun., National Association of Home Builders
Ochs, Joan G., (AV) .... '56 '81 C.597 B.A. L.273 J.D. [Ⓒ Arnold&P.]
*PRACTICE AREAS: Government Contracts.
Ochs, Justin '72 '00 C.188 B.A. L.893 J.D.
(adm. in NY; not adm. in DC) [Ⓐ Wilmer,C.&P.]

Ochs, Laurance J., (AV) '44 '70 C.107 B.A. L.329 J.D.
1748 N Street, N.W., 20036
Telephone: 202-331-9009 Facsimile: 202-785-0066
Email: llochs@aol.com URL: http://www.lawyers.com/llochs
General Practice. Litigation, Counseling, Commercial, Computer, Corporate, Intellectual Property Rights, E-Commerce Law, Internet Law.
See Professional Biographies, WASHINGTON, DISTRICT OF COLUMBIA

Ochs, Michelle ....'73 '98 C&L.597 B.S., J.D. [A Sonnenschein N.&R.]
*PRACTICE AREAS: Labor and Employment; Litigation.
Ochsenhirt, Frederick D. '68 '94 C.8 B.A. L.945 J.D.
(adm. in VA; not adm. in DC) 2101 L. Street
Ochsenhirt, Lisa M. '68 '94 C.893 B.A. L.945 J.D.
(adm. in VA; not adm. in DC) [A Miller,B.&O.]
Ochsman, Jeffrey W., (AV) ......'52 '77 C.945 B.A. L.30 J.D. [Friedlander,M.S.K.&O.]
*PRACTICE AREAS: Workers Compensation Law; Personal Injury Law; Insurance Defense Law.
Ochsman, Joanne '55 '83 C.575 B.A. L.276 J.D.
V.P. & Dep. Gen. Coun., Allbritton Communications Company
O'Connell, Andrew J. ....'65 '98 C.1044 B.A. L.564 J.D. [A Skadden,A.S.M.&F.]
*PRACTICE AREAS: Litigation.
O'Connell, Edward J. .... '56 '83 C.976 B.A. L.276 J.D. [Dow,L.&A.]
O'Connell, James J., Jr. ....'69 '99 C.119 B.S. L.1365 J.D. [A Shearman&S.]
O'Connell, James R. .... '43 '68 C.446 B.A. L.276 J.D. [O'Donoghue&O.]
O'Connell, John W., (AV) ....'21 '60 C&L.276 B.S.F.S., J.D. [O'Connell&G.]
*PRACTICE AREAS: International Law.
O'Connell, K. Michael .... '50 '84 C.1176 B.A. L.128 J.D. 3050 K St., N.W.
O'Connell, Marjorie A., (AV) ....'48 '73 C.128 B.A. L.276 J.D. [O'Connell&Assoc.]
*PRACTICE AREAS: Family Law; Taxation; Divorce Taxation; Estate and Gift Taxation; Estate Planning.
O'Connell, Maureen Ann ....'58 '86 C&L.352 B.A., J.D. News Corp.
O'Connell, Peter D., (AV) ....'33 '59 C&L.276 B.S., J.D. [C Wiley R.&F.]
*PRACTICE AREAS: Communications Law.
O'Connell, Quinn, Jr. .... '52 '96 C.686 B.S. L.30 J.D. [C A.F.Konopka]
*PRACTICE AREAS: Real Estate; Probate; Litigation; Criminal Defense.
O'Connell, Thomas J. '48 '86
C.454 B.S. L.904 J.D. [Fitzpatrick,C.H.&S.] (See Pat. Sect.)

O'Connell & Associates, (AV)
1730 Rhode Island Avenue, N.W. Suite 809, 20036
Telephone: 202-466-8200 Fax: 202-466-4663
Email: maoc@oconnell-associates.com URL: http://www.lawyers.com/oconnell&associates
Marjorie A. O'Connell; Pete M. Murchison. Associate: Jessica Adler.
Tax, Family Law, Estate Planning, and Employee Benefits.
See Professional Biographies, WASHINGTON, DISTRICT OF COLUMBIA

O'Connell & Glock, P.C., (AV)
1100 Connecticut Avenue, N.W. 9th Floor, 20036-4114
Telephone: 202-293-7909 Telecopier: 202-293-7907
URL: http://www.lawyers.com/oconnell&glock
John W. O'Connell; Earl F. Glock.
General Practice. Real Estate, Commercial Law, Corporate, Small Business Law, Taxation and International.
See Professional Biographies, WASHINGTON, DISTRICT OF COLUMBIA

O'Connell & O'Connell
(See Rockville, Maryland)

O'Connor, Charles A., III, (AV) .... '42 '67 C.309 A.B. L.276 J.D. [McKenna&C.]
*PRACTICE AREAS: Environmental Regulation; Chemical Regulation.
O'Connor, Charles P., (AV) .... '40 '66 C.321 B.S. L.93 LL.B. [Morgan,L.&B.]
O'Connor, Christine ....'— '89 C.276 B.A. L.602 J.D. [A Thelen R.&P.]
*PRACTICE AREAS: Construction.
O'Connor, David A. ....'69 '98 C.259 B.A. L.1009 J.D. [A Holland&K.]
*PRACTICE AREAS: Telecommunications; International; Administrative.
O'Connor, Eileen C. ....'17 '41 C.715 A.B. L.273 J.D. 1 Scott Circle, N.W.‡
O'Connor, Heather Shanan '70 '96 C.205 B.A. L.446 J.D.
(adm. in MD; not adm. in DC) [A Eccleston&W.]
O'Connor, James E. (Jim) '47 '73
C.156 B.A. L.93 J.D. Tax Coun., America's Community Bnkrs.
O'Connor, John F., Jr. .... '66 '95 C.696 B.A. L.446 J.D. [A Steptoe&J.]
O'Connor, John J., III, (AV) '— '53
C&L.813 A.B., LL.B. [C Bryan C.] (⊙Phoenix, AZ)
*PRACTICE AREAS: Litigation; Corporate Law.
O'Connor, John M. ....'29 '60 C.754 B.S. L.276 LL.B. 3422 Quebec St., N.W.‡
O'Connor, Karen P. '52 '78 C&L.107 B.A., J.D.
(adm. in GA; not adm. in DC) American Univ.
O'Connor, Mary Kathleen ....'66 '92 C.259 B.A. L.94 J.D. [A Hughes H.&R.]
O'Connor, Michael F. ....'64 '94 C.893 B.A. L.309 J.D. [A Williams&C.]
*PRACTICE AREAS: Business Law; Corporate Law; Mergers, Acquisitions and Divestitures.
O'Connor, Nancy Morrison, (AV) .... '51 '77 C.282 B.A. L.602 J.D. [Bracewell&P.]
*PRACTICE AREAS: Labor and Employment; Civil Litigation.
O'Connor, Patrick J. '73 '00 C.692 B.A. L.276 J.D.
(adm. in VA; not adm. in DC) [A Blumenfeld&C.]
*PRACTICE AREAS: Telecommunications Law; Antitrust Law; International Law; Corporate Law.
O'Connor, Patrick J., (AV) ....'20 '45 C.190 Ph.B. L.494 LL.B. [O'Connor&H.]
O'Connor, Stephen J., (P.C.) .... '59 '85 C.1369 B.B.A. L.273 J.D. [Tobin,O.&E.]
*PRACTICE AREAS: Transaction; Tax; Business; Corporate; Exempt Securities.
O'Connor, Steven P. '60 '96
C.705 B.A. L.893 J.D. [A Finnegan,H.F.G.&D.] (See Pat. Sect.)
*PRACTICE AREAS: Pharmaceutical Intellectual Property; Biomedical Technology; Microbiology; Biochemical Patents; Biotechnology Patents.
O'Connor, Victoria A. ....'72 '99 C.273 B.A. L.538 J.D. [A Sutherland A.&B.]
*PRACTICE AREAS: Corporate Taxation; International Taxation; Tax Controversies.

O'Connor, Brian M.
(See Reston)

O'Connor & Hannan, L.L.P., (AV) BR
Suite 500, 1666 K Street, N.W., 20006 ⊙
Telephone: 202-887-1400 Telecopy: 202-466-2198
Email: oh@oconnorhannan.com URL: http://www.oconnorhannan.com
Members of Firm: Patrick J. O'Connor; Joe A. Walters (Civil Trial Specialist Certified by the Civil Litigation Section, Minnesota State Bar Association); David R. Melincoff; F. Gordon Lee; George J. Mannina, Jr.; Robert M. Adler; Timothy W. Jenkins; Stephen N. Shulman; James W. Symington; Larry Pressler; J. Craig Potter; Christina W. Fleps; Gary C. Adler; John M. Himmelberg; Roy C. Coffee III (Not admitted in DC); Kurt E. Blase; Edward A. Beck III; Albert P. Lindemann, Jr.; Jed L. Babbin; Sharon L. Babbin; Emil Hirsch; Frederick T. Dombo III; Paul L. Knight; Michael J. Wing (Not admitted in DC); D. Lee Antton. Non-Attorney Member: Thomas J. Corcoran. Associate: James P. Ryan (Not admitted in DC). Of Counsel: Kenneth A. Mayfield (Not admitted in DC); Charles R. McCarthy, Jr.; William W. Nickerson; Stephen M. Soble; Thomas J. Schneider.
General Practice before United States Courts, Administrative Agencies, Government Departments and the Congress. Environmental and Natural Resources, Associations, White Collar Crime, Employment, Corporate, Health, Communications, Taxation, Probate. Customs, Immigration Law, Export Control, and International Trade.
Vienna, Virginia Office: 8300 Boone Boulevard, Suite 554. Telephone: 703-714-6670. Fax: 703-848-4586.
Madrid, Spain Office: Velázquez 21-4°. Telephone: +(011) 34-91-575-0944; +(011) 34-91-357-2251. Fax: +(011) 34-91-577-0822.
See Professional Biographies, WASHINGTON, DISTRICT OF COLUMBIA

O'Conor, Jerry R., (AV) ....'51 '77 C&L.446 B.A., J.D. [Venable,A.B.H.&C.]
*PRACTICE AREAS: Commercial; Real Estate; Environmental Law.
Oday, Larry A., (AV) ....'47 '73 C.124 B.A. L.338 J.D. [Vinson&E.]
*PRACTICE AREAS: Health Law; Legislative Practice; Medicare and Medicaid; Hospital Law.

Oddo, Danielle R. ....'73 '99 C&L.93 B.A., J.D. [A Howrey S.A.&W.]
*PRACTICE AREAS: Commercial Litigation; Antitrust Litigation.
O'Dea, James L., III, (AV) ....'45 '73 C.321 B.A. L.818 J.D. [O'Dea&Assoc.]
O'Dea & Associates, (AV) .... Ste. 1000, 1111 14th St. N.W.
Odedra, Dhiren R. '71 '98 C.959 B.S. L.831 J.D.
[A Wenderoth,L.&P.] (See Pat. Sect.)
*PRACTICE AREAS: Patent Law; Electrical Patents; Computer and Software Patents; Patent Prosecution.
Odedra, Kaushal R. '69 '95 C.494 B.S. L.436 J.D.
[A Wenderoth,L.&P.] (See Pat. Sect.)
*PRACTICE AREAS: Trademark and Copyright Law.
Odell, Herbert, (AV) '— '63 C.659 B.S. L.472 LL.B.
(adm. in FL; not adm. in DC) [Miller&C.]
Odell, Jonathan C. ....'64 '95 C.188 B.S.S. L.472 J.D. [A Dickstein S.M.&O.]
*PRACTICE AREAS: Mergers and Acquisitions; Corporate; Venture Capital; Securities.
Odell, Turner R., Jr. '— '90 C.188 B.S. L.1292 J.D.
(adm. in NY; not adm. in DC) Environmental Law Institute
*RESPONSIBILITIES: Environmental Law.
Oden, Kiyo D. .... '71 '96 C.329 B.A. L.273 J.D. [A Fried]
Oden, M. Nicole ....'70 '99 C.1111 B.A. L.276 J.D. [A Kelley D.&W.]
*PRACTICE AREAS: Telecommunications.
Odintz, Joshua D. ....'70 '95 C.112 B.A. L.61 J.D. 600 13th Street, N.W.
Odle, Bob Glen, (AV) ....'37 '66 C&L.846 B.A., LL.B. [Hogan&H.]
*PRACTICE AREAS: Commercial Law; Corporate Law.
Odle, Robert C., Jr., (AV) ....'44 '69 C.912 B.A. L.213 J.D. [Weil,G.&M.]
*PRACTICE AREAS: Administrative Law; Energy Law; Environmental Law; Government Law; International Law.
Odom, Lewis G., Jr. ....'26 '49 C.861 L.16 LL.B. [C Miller,H.S.O.&B.] ⊙
*PRACTICE AREAS: Banking Law; Corporate Law; Securities Law.
Odom, Thomas H., (AV) .... '62 '88 C.705 B.A. L.659 J.D. [C Arter&H.]
*PRACTICE AREAS: Appellate Litigation; Administrative Law; Federalism; Constitutional Law; Legal Ethics and Discipline.
O'Donald, Lisa Erin ....'70 '96 C.884 B.A. L.945 J.D. [A Morgan,L.&B.]
O'Donnell, Earle H., (AV) ....'49 '75 C.853 B.A. L.273 J.D. [Dewey B.]
*PRACTICE AREAS: Energy.
O'Donnell, Jeffrey M. '58 '88 C.473 B.S. L.309 J.D.
(adm. in IL; not adm. in DC) 815 Conn. Ave., N.W.‡
O'Donnell, John Jude, (AV) '32 '56
C.884 A.B. L.276 J.D. [Thompson,O.M.N.&H.] (⊙Rockville, MD)
*PRACTICE AREAS: General Practice; Alternative Dispute Resolution; Medical Malpractice; Professional Liability; Estate Litigation.
O'Donnell, Neil Francis '69 '96 C.276 A.B. L.575 J.D.
(adm. in CO; not adm. in DC) [A Kelley D.&W.]
*PRACTICE AREAS: Corporate Finance; Project Finance.
O'Donnell, Patrick ....'67 '97 C.659 B.A. L.276 [A Harris,W.&G.]
*PRACTICE AREAS: Criminal Law; Litigation; Civil Litigation.
O'Donnell, Patrick E., (AV) ...... '37 '62 C.276 B.A. L.904 LL.B. [Venable,A.B.H.&C.]
O'Donnell, Terrence, (AV) '44 '71
C.1070 B.S. L.276 J.D. [Williams&C.] (⊙Providence, RI)
*PRACTICE AREAS: Administrative Law; Business Law; Government Contracts; Litigation; Products Liability.
O'Donnell, Thomas J. '67 '96 C.300 B.A. L.329 J.D.
(adm. in MD; not adm. in DC) CEO, DFinteractive
O'Donnell, Thomas P. ....'59 '92 C.976 B.A. L.846 J.D. [C Patton B.]

O'Donnell, Schwartz & Anderson, P.C., (AV)
1300 L Street, N.W. Suite 1200, 20005
Telephone: 202-898-1707 FAX: 202-682-9276
John F. O'Donnell (1907-1993); Darryl J. Anderson; Martin R. Ganzglass; Lee W. Jackson; Arthur M. Luby; Anton G. Hajjar; Susan L. Catler; Richard S. Edelman;—Peter J. Leff; Melinda K. Holmes; Murshed Zaheed (Not admitted in DC); Daniel B. Smith (Not admitted in DC). Of Counsel: Asher W. Schwartz.
Labor Relations Law, Aviation and Railroad Law, Employee Benefits, Civil Rights and Torts.
Other Washington, D.C. Office: Suite 707, 1900 L Street, N.W., 20036. Telephone: 202-898-1824. Fax: 202-429-8928.
See Professional Biographies, WASHINGTON, DISTRICT OF COLUMBIA

O'Donoghue & O'Donoghue, (AV)
4748 Wisconsin Avenue, N.W., 20016 ⊙
Telephone: 202-362-0041 Telecopier: 202-362-2640
Members of Firm: Martin F. O'Donoghue (1903-1973); Patrick C. O'Donoghue (1930-1979); Joseph P. Boyle (1954-1998); Donald J. Capuano; James R. O'Connell; Robert Matisoff; Joyce A. Mader; Sally M. Tedrow; Brian A. Powers; John L. Bohman; Francis J. Martorana; Nicholas R. Femia; Ellen O. Boardman; Charles W. Gilligan; Louis P. Malone III; Mary Capuano Feller; John Leary; John R. Harney; R. Richard Hopp; Gerard M. Waites (Not admitted in DC); Mark W. Kunst; Robert P. Curley (Not admitted in DC). Associates: Daniel James McNeil; Teresa White Murray; Dinah S. Leventhal; Jean M. Kelly; Keith R. Bolek; Gregory F. Moore; David D. Capuano (Not admitted in DC); Todd Bitner Castleton; John M. McIntire. Of Counsel: Phyllis C. Borzi.
General Practice, Labor Law and Employee Benefits Law.
Philadelphia, Pennsylvania Office: Constitution Place, Suite 515, 325 Chestnut Street. Telephone: 215-629-4970. Telecopier: 215-629-4996.
See Professional Biographies, WASHINGTON, DISTRICT OF COLUMBIA

O'Duden, Gregory, (AV) '51 '78 C.262 B.A. L.273 J.D.
Gen. Coun., National Treasury Employees Union
Odujinrin, Dami Y. '75 '99 C.999 LL.B. L.309 LL.M.
(adm. in NY; not adm. in DC) [A Bailey]
*PRACTICE AREAS: Commercial Real Estate; Beverage Alcohol Control.
O'Dwyer, Jeffrey S. ....'67 '93 C.674 A.B. L.188 J.D. [A Hogan&H.]
Oehmann, Andrew F., Jr., (AV) ....'41 '68 C.321 B.S. L.276 J.D. 3026 44th Pl., N.W.
Offutt, James R. ....'39 '67 C.502 B.J. L.276 J.D. 1100 New York Ave NW‡
O'Flaherty, Michael J. .... '56 '87 C.597 B.S. L.424 J.D. [Olsson,F.&W.]
*PRACTICE AREAS: Food and Drug Law; Trademark Law; Customs Law.
O'Flaherty, Neil F., (AV) ....'65 '90 C.602 B.A. L.424 J.D. [Olsson,F.&W.]
*PRACTICE AREAS: Medical Device Law; Food and Drug Law.
O'Flanagan, Jennie ....'71 '99 C.1236 B.A. L.976 J.D. [A Wilmer,C.&P.]
Ogden, David W. ....'53 '83 C.659 B.A. L.309 J.D. [Wilmer,C.&P.]
*PRACTICE AREAS: Civil and Appellate Litigation; Administrative and Constitutional Law; Media and First Amendment Law; Association Law.
Ogene, Chidi J. '68 '99 L.276 J.D.
(adm. in NY; not adm. in DC) [A Sullivan&C.]
Ogg, Joelle Kay ....'72 '97 C.914 B.A. L.273 J.D. [A Williams M.]
*PRACTICE AREAS: Energy Law.
Ogg, Randell C., (AV) ....'52 '77 C&L.347 B.A., J.D. [Sherman,M.C.&A.]
*PRACTICE AREAS: Civil Litigation; Personal Injury.
Ogilby, Remsen B., (AV) ......'17 '48 C.309 A.B. L.273 LL.B. 888 Seventeenth St., N.W.
Ogilvie, Lynley A. ....'— '95 C.309 B.A. L.893 J.D. [A Latham&W.]
*PRACTICE AREAS: International Finance.
Ogilvy, J. P. '45 '73 C.1056 B.A. L.1051 J.D.
Assoc. Prof. of Law, Catholic Univ. of Amer.
Ogletree, Benjamin R. '71 '99 C.140 B.A. L.128 J.D.
(adm. in MD; not adm. in DC) [A Dickstein S.M.&O.]
*PRACTICE AREAS: Securities Litigation.

Ogletree, Deakins, Nash, Smoak & Stewart, P.C., (AV) BR
Fifth Floor, 2400 N Street, N.W., 20037 ⊙
Telephone: 202-887-0855 Facsimile: 202-887-0866
Email: Washington@odnss.com URL: http://www.ogletreedeakins.com
J. Frank Ogletree, Jr. (1930-1985); Peter G. Nash (1937-1993); Dixie L. Atwater (1948-1992); John A. Penello (1909-1998); Peter H. Kiefer; David S. Fortney; Harold P. Coxson, Jr.; Bernard P. Jeweler; Michael J. Murphy; Burton J. Fishman; J. Robert Brame, III (Not admitted in DC); Reginald E. Jones; Steven R. Semler;—Yoora Kim; Consuela A. Pinto; Rafael E. Morell. Of Counsel: Stanley R. Strauss.
Labor Relations, Employment, Employee Benefits, Occupational Safety and Health, Environmental, Construction and Immigration Law, Legislation. Civil Litigation in all State and Federal Courts and before Administrative Agencies.
Atlanta, Georgia Office: 600 Peachtree Street, N.E., Suite 2100. Telephone: 404-881-1300.
Birmingham, Alabama Office: 1900 SouthTrust Tower, 420 North 20th Street. Telephone: 205-328-1900.
Charleston, South Carolina Office: 134 Meeting Street, Suite 500, P.O. Box 1808. Telephone: 843-853-1300.
Chicago, Illinois Office: Twenty-Fifth Floor, Two First National Plaza, 20 South Clark Street. Telephone: 312-558-1220.
Columbia, South Carolina Office: 1501 Main Street, Suite 600, P.O. Box 11206. Telephone: 803-252-1300.
Dallas, Texas Office: 700 Preston Commons, 8117 Preston Road. Telephone: 214-987-3800.
Greenville, South Carolina Office: The Ogletree Building, 300 North Main Street, P.O. Box 2757. Telephone: 864-271-1300.
Houston, Texas Office: One Allen Center, 500 Dallas Street, Suite 3000. Telephone: 713-655-0855.
Indianapolis, Indiana Office: Suite 2300, One Indiana Square. Telephone: 317-916-1300.
Nashville, Tennessee Office: SunTrust Center, Suite 800, 424 Church Street. Telephone: 615-254-1900.
Raleigh, North Carolina Office: 2301 Sugar Bush Road, P.O. Box 31608. Telephone: 919-787-9700.
San Antonio, Texas Office: 100 West Houston Street, Suite 1700. Telephone: 210-354-1300.
St. Thomas, U.S. Virgin Islands Office: The Tunick Building, 1336 Beltjen Road, Suite 202. Telephone: 340-714-1235.
See Professional Biographies, WASHINGTON, DISTRICT OF COLUMBIA

Ogolo, Chidi A ....'56 '86 C.494 B.S. L.329 J.D. 733 15th St., N.W.
O'Grady, Kristin Moody '66 '94 C.629 B.A. L.560 J.D.
Asst. Chf. Coun., American Public Transit Assn.
O'Grady, Liam '50 '77 C.264 B.A. L.1209 J.D.
(adm. in VA; not adm. in DC) [Finnegan,H.F.G.&D.]
*PRACTICE AREAS: Patent Infringement; Trademark Infringement.
O'Grady, Michael J. '70 '97 C.93 B.A. L.1194 J.D.
(adm. in VT; not adm. in DC) Staff Atty., Environmental Law Institute
Ogren, Robert W., (AV) ....'37 '63 C.918 A.B. L.145 J.D. 1200 19th St.
Ogsbury, James D. '59 '86 C.309 A.B. L.36 J.D.
(adm. in AZ; not adm. in DC) [C Jones,W.W.P.C.&D.]
*PRACTICE AREAS: Government Relations.
Oh, Hyun S. '70 '98 C.575 B.A. L.245 J.D.
(adm. in MD; not adm. in DC) [A Pepper H.]
*PRACTICE AREAS: Intellectual Property.
Oh, Min Sun ....'65 '96 C.401 B.S. L.128 J.D. [A Jorden B.]
*PRACTICE AREAS: Securities Law; Mutual Funds; Insurance Products.
O'Hanlon, Sean P. '71 '01 C.277 B.M.E. L.1209 J.D.
(adm. in VA; not adm. in DC; Pat.) [A Swidler B.S.F.]
*PRACTICE AREAS: Intellectual Property.
O'Hara, Christopher C. ....'67 '93 C.659 B.A. L.446 J.D. [A Dickstein S.M.&O.]
*PRACTICE AREAS: Administrative; Energy; Litigation.
O'Hara, James T., (AV) ....'36 '62 C.1113 B.S. L.128 LL.B. [Jones,D.R.&P.]
*PRACTICE AREAS: Taxation; Corporate Tax Planning.
O'Hare, Patrick K., (AV) ....'46 '73 C.103 B.A. L.813 J.D. [Ober,K.G.&S.]
Ohlrich, Roger C., (AV) ....'38 '65 C&L.477 B.B.A., J.D. [Gardner,O.&V.]
Ohly, Frederick C. '43 '69 C.951 B.A. L.813 J.D.
Sr. Assoc. Gen. Coun., Corp. Affs., National Railroad Passenger Corp. (AMTRAK)
Ohm, Angela June '69 '95 C.45 B.A. L.569 J.D.
(adm. in AR; not adm. in DC) 2346 Raybum
O'Hop, Paul A., Jr. ....'62 '89 C&L.602 B.A., J.D. [Squire,S.&D.]
*PRACTICE AREAS: International Corporate; International Finance.
Ohri, Shaila Lakhani ....'72 '97 C.30 B.A. L.273 J.D. [A Dyer E.&J.]
*PRACTICE AREAS: Corporate Law; International Business Law.
O'Keefe, Daniel F., Jr., (AV) '36 '60
C&L.893 B.A., LL.B. 1150 Connecticut Ave. N.W., 12th Fl.‡
O'Keefe, Michael K. ....'63 '93 C.602 B.A. L.30 J.D. 1919 Pennsylvania Ave., N.W.
O'Keefe, Patrick K., (BV) ....'59 '85 C.188 B.S. L.659 J.D. 1900 K Street, N.W.
O'Keeffe, Carol B. '47 '78 C.267 B.A. L.280 J.D.
Prin. Dep. Gen. Coun., Washington Metropolitan Area Transit Authority
*RESPONSIBILITIES: Government Contracts; Labor and Employment - Public Sector; Eminent Domain; Real Estate; Environmental Law.
Okuliar, Alexander Paul '73 '99 C.659 B.S.B.A. L.880 J.D.
(adm. in TX; not adm. in DC) [A Vinson&E.]
*PRACTICE AREAS: Securities; Mergers, Acquisitions and Divestitures; Corporate Law.
Olafson, Meredith K. '75 '00 C.597 B.A. L.276 J.D.
(adm. in CA; not adm. in DC) [A Sonnenschein N.&R.]
*PRACTICE AREAS: Litigation; Labor and Employment.
Olafson, Vickie R ....'53 '87 C.446 B.A. L.179 J.D. Atty., NASD Regulation, Inc.
Olaniran, Gregory O. ....'61 '95 C.512 B.S. L.273 J.D. [A Morrison&H.]
*PRACTICE AREAS: Copyright; Communications; Energy; Business Law.
Olcott, Bruce A. ....'61 '95 C.768 B.A. L.178 J.D. [A Squire,S.&D.]
Oldaker, William C., (AV) ....'41 '66 C&L.352 B.S., LL.B. [Oldaker&B.]

Oldaker & Biden, LLP, (AV)
818 Connecticut Avenue, N.W. Suite 1100, 20006
Telephone: 202-728-1010 Facsimile: 202-728-4044
Email: rhb@aldaker-biden.com URL: http://www.oldaker-biden.com
William C. Oldaker; R. Hunter Biden (Not admitted in DC).
Federal Administrative and Legislative Practice, Elections, Campaign Finance, Lobbying Disclosures and Ethics, Transportation, Communications, Internet Law, Intellectual Property.
See Professional Biographies, WASHINGTON, DISTRICT OF COLUMBIA

Olderman, Neil S. ....'63 '90 C.347 B.A. L.128 J.D. [Akin,G.S.H.&F.]
*PRACTICE AREAS: Health Care Transactions; Health Care Corporate Law.
Oldham, James C. '40 '65 C.228 B.S. L.813 LL.B.
(adm. in CO; not adm. in DC) Prof. of Law, Georgetown Univ. Law Ctr.
Oldham, Judith L., (AV) ....'42 '81 C.477 B.A. L.276 [Collier S.S.]
*PRACTICE AREAS: Advertising; Trade and Professional Associations.
O'Leary, Howard E., Jr., (AV) ....'38 '64 C&L.477 B.A., J.D. [Dykema G.]
*PRACTICE AREAS: Litigation; Business Crimes Law.
O'Leary, Patrick B. '71 '97 C.433 B.A. L.904 J.D.
(adm. in MD; not adm. in DC) Assoc. Tech. Coun., MCI WorldCom
O'leary, Patrick James ....'74 '99 C.659 B.A. L.861 J.D. 450 Fifth NW
O'Leary, Timothy J., Jr. ....'48 '76 C.454 B.A. L.1292 J.D. 1101 17th St., N.W.
O'Leary, Trystan Phifer ....'73 '00 C.478 B.A. L.352 J.D. [A Dorsey&W.]
Oleck, Adrienne ....'59 '85 C.103 B.A. L.260 J.D. Amer. Assn. of Ret. Persons
Olender, Jack H., (AV) ....'35 '61 C&L.665 A.B., J.D. [J.H.Olender&Assoc.]
*PRACTICE AREAS: Malpractice; Products Liability; Personal Injury.

Olender, Jack H., and Associates, P.C., (AV) BR
888 17th Street, N.W., 4th Floor, 20006
Telephone: 202-879-7777 Fax: 202-393-2245 URL: http://www.olender.com
Email: jhopc@olender.com URL: http://www.lawyers.com/olenderlaw
Jack H. Olender;—Harlow R. Case; Sandra H. Robinson; Kim Keenan Solomon; Melissa Rhea; Karen E. Evans; Elizabeth Jesukiewicz Frey; Narda M. Newby. Of Counsel: Robert S. Chabon (Not admitted in DC).
Malpractice Law, Personal Injury, General Negligence Trials and Appeals, Products Liability.
See Professional Biographies, WASHINGTON, DISTRICT OF COLUMBIA

Oler, Harriet L. B. ....'— '66 C.216 A.B. L.659 LL.B. 101 Independence Avenue‡
Oleson, Nathan J. ....'73 '99 C.30 B.A. L.276 J.D. [A Akin,G.S.H.&F.]
*PRACTICE AREAS: Labor and Employment.
Olexy, Peter D., (P.C.), (AV) '43 '68
C.645 B.S.Ch.E. L.273 J.D. [Sughrue M.] (See Pat. Sect.)
*PRACTICE AREAS: Intellectual Property Law.
Oley, Tracey L. Hallam ....'74 '99 C&L.945 A.B., J.D. [A Jones,D.R.&P.]
Oleynik, Ronald A. ....'60 '90 C.184 B.A. L.273 J.D. [Holland&K.]
*PRACTICE AREAS: International Trade; Customs; Export Controls.
Olifer, Edward G. '68 '93 C.886 B.A. L.1356 J.D.
(adm. in VA; not adm. in DC) 5101 Wisconsin Ave.,N.W.

Oliff & Berridge, PLC
(See Alexandria, Virginia)

Oliner, Joyce L. ....'57 '84 C.050 B.A. L.966 J.D. [Shaw P.]
*PRACTICE AREAS: Employment.
Oliphant, C. Frederick, III, (AV) ....'— '75 C.575 A.B. L.477 J.D. [Miller&C.]
*PRACTICE AREAS: Employee Benefits; Qualified Retirement Plans; Executive Compensation; Fringe Benefits; Employment Tax.
Oliveira, Nelson R. '62 '92 C.95 B.A. L.93 J.D.
(adm. in NY; not adm. in DC) [C Wilmer,C.&P.]
*PRACTICE AREAS: Business Transactions; Corporate Finance; Project Finance.
Oliver, Amy J. ....'— '00 C.878 B.S. L.309 J.D. [A Latham&W.]
*PRACTICE AREAS: Litigation; Labor and Employment.
Oliver, Brenda J. ....'73 '99 C.1375 B.A. L.945 J.D. [C Fulbright&J.]
*PRACTICE AREAS: Immigration Law.
Oliver, Daniel '39 '67 C.309 B.A. L.262 LL.B.
(adm. in NY; not adm. in DC) [C Aitken I.B.&V.]
Oliver, Eric ....'65 '93 C.223 B.S.E.E. L.273 J.D. [Dickstein S.M.&O.] (Pat.)
*PRACTICE AREAS: Intellectual Property.
Oliver, Joseph M., Jr., (AV) ....'46 '70 C.893 B.A. L.280 J.D. [C Crowell&M.]
*PRACTICE AREAS: Energy Law; Public Utility Law.
Oliver, Justin J. '72 '97 C.856 B.S. L.904 J.D.
(adm. in VA; not adm. in DC; See Pat. Sect.) [A Fitzpatrick,C.H.&S.]
Oliver, Linda L., (AV) ....'53 '80 C.976 B.A. L.276 J.D. [Hogan&H.]
*PRACTICE AREAS: Telecommunications Law; Cable TV; FCC and State Regulation; Wireless Communications.
Oliver, Mary Ann, (AV) ....'48 '73 C.454 B.A. L.93 J.D. [Oliver&O.]
Oliver, Richard A., (AV) ....'47 '73 C.197 B.A. L.93 J.D. [Oliver&O.]
Oliver, Teel '36 '74 C.699 B.A. L.776 J.D.
(adm. in NJ; not adm. in DC) V.P., Govt. Rel., Merck & Co., Inc.‡
Oliver Jr., David M. '73 '98 C&L.420 B.S., J.D.
(adm. in LA; not adm. in DC) [A Burt,M.&M.]
*PRACTICE AREAS: Federal Taxation; International Taxation; Tax Controversies.

Oliver & Oliver, P.C., (AV)
Suite 800, 1090 Vermont Avenue, N.W., 20005
Telephone: 202-371-5656 Telecopier: 202-289-8113
Richard A. Oliver; Mary Ann Oliver.
General and Administrative Practice before Federal and State Courts, Departments and Agencies, including Energy, Business and Public Utility Law. Legislative Practice.
See Professional Biographies, WASHINGTON, DISTRICT OF COLUMBIA

Oliveri, Warren S., Jr., (AV) ....'47 '74 C&L.276 B.S.F.S., J.D. [King&N.] ⊙
*PRACTICE AREAS: Commercial Leasing; Real Estate.
Olmer, Jody R. ....'50 '89 C.862 A.B. L.276 J.D. U.S. Chamber of Com.
Olmstead, Cecil J. ....'20 '50 C&L.280 B.A., LL.B. [C Steptoe&J.]
*PRACTICE AREAS: International Law; European Community Law; Law of the Sea; Economics Sanctions.
Olmsted, Matthew L. ....'70 '97 C.112 B.A. L.1068 J.D. [A O'Melveny&M.]
O'Loughlin, John B., Jr. ....'61 '96 C.445 B.S. L.446 J.D. [A Weil,G.&M.]
*PRACTICE AREAS: Environmental Law; OSHA; Product Safety.
Olsen, Angela M. ....'68 '00 C.299 A.B. L.904 J.D. [A Jones,D.R.&P.]
Olsen, Eric N. '61 '89 C&L.494 B.A., J.D.
(adm. in MN; not adm. in DC) [C Patton B.]
Olsen, Erika Ellen '74 '00 C.976 B.A. L.902 J.D.
(adm. in VA; not adm. in DC) [A McDermott,W.&E.]
Olsen, George G., (AV) ....'50 '75 C.708 B.A. L.273 J.D. [Williams&J.]
*PRACTICE AREAS: Health Care; Pharmaceuticals; Managed Care; Medicare and Medicaid; Administrative Litigation.
Olsen, Matthew G. ....'62 '88 C.893 B.A. L.309 J.D. Asst. U.S. Atty.
Olsen, Michelle ....'71 '97 C&L.101 B.A., J.D. 1700 G. St., N.W., 3rd Fl.
Olsen, Roger M., Law Offices of, (AV) '— '69 C.112 A.B. L.1066 J.D.
1201 Connecticut Avenue, Suite 600, 20036
Telephone: 202-887-6820 Fax: 202-887-9073
Federal and State Taxation Law, Civil and Criminal Tax Litigation.
See Professional Biographies, WASHINGTON, DISTRICT OF COLUMBIA
Olsen, Troy L. ....'68 '98 C.878 B.S. L.273 J.D. [A Skadden,A.S.M.&F.]
*PRACTICE AREAS: Federal Taxation.
Olsen, Warren E., (AV) '46 '75
C.563 B.E. Mech. L.276 J.D. [Fitzpatrick,C.H.&S.] (See Pat. Sect.)
Olshonsky, Michael A. ....'44 '69 C.188 A.B. L.904 J.D. 1625 K. St. NW
Olson, Barbara K. '55 '89 C.1268 B.A. L.978 J.D.
(adm. in MD; not adm. in DC) [Balch&B.]
*PRACTICE AREAS: Legislative Practice; Public Policy Law; Litigation; Regulatory.
Olson, Benjamin K. '74 '01 C.861 B.A. L.276 J.D.
(adm. in VA; not adm. in DC) [A Hogan&H.]
Olson, Beth J., (BV) ....'60 '93 C.932 B.S. L.851 J.D. 1111 19th St., NW
Olson, Bradley J. ....'57 '94 C.829 B.A. L.1218 J.D. [A Robins,K.M.&C.] (Pat.)
*PRACTICE AREAS: Intellectual Property.
Olson, Brian R. '48 '76 C.598 B.S. L.1294 J.D.
(adm. in ME; not adm. in DC) 1642 Jonquil St. NW‡
Olson, Erik D. ....'58 '84 C.178 B.A. L.893 J.D. Sr. Atty., Natural Res. Def. Council
Olson, James W., (AV) ....'47 '73 C.112 A.B. L.976 J.D. [Howrey S.A.&W.]
*PRACTICE AREAS: Antitrust; Telecommunications; Computer Law.
Olson, Jeffrey H., (AV) ....'50 '75 C.967 B.A. L.1003 J.D. [C Paul,W.R.W.&G.]
*PRACTICE AREAS: Communications.
Olson, John F., (AV) ....'39 '65 C.1375 A.B. L.309 LL.B. [Gibson,D.&C.]
*PRACTICE AREAS: Securities Law and Litigation; Mergers and Acquisitions; General Corporate Law; Administrative Law.
Olson, Kathryn E. '66 '94 C.659 B.A. L.1066 J.D.
(adm. in CA; not adm. in DC) [A Arnold&P.]

Olson, Kelly A. '73 '99 C.958 B.S. L.823 J.D.
(adm. in WI; not adm. in DC) [Swidler B.S.F.]
*PRACTICE AREAS: Telecommunications Law.
Olson, Theodore B. ...... '40 '66 C.169 B.A. L.1066 LL.B. [Gibson,D.&C.]
*PRACTICE AREAS: Constitutional Law; Appellate Litigation; Commercial Law; Administrative Law; First Amendment Litigation.
Olson, Thomas P., (AV) ...... '53 '84 C.477 B.A. L.309 J.D. [Wilmer,C.&P.]
*PRACTICE AREAS: Civil Practice; Intellectual Property.
Olson, William J., (AV) '49 '76
C.103 A.B. L.692 J.D. [W.J.Olson] & [Gilman & Assoc.] ⊙
*PRACTICE AREAS: Business Law; Non-Profit Tax Law; Postal Law; Election Law; Civil Litigation.

Olson, William J., P.C., (AV)
600 Pennsylvania Avenue, SE, Suite 410, 20003-4303 ⊙
Telephone: 202-547-9080 Fax: 202-547-8944
Email: wjo@mindspring.com URL: http://www.lawandfreedom.com
William J. Olson; John S. Miles. Of Counsel: Herbert W. Titus (Not admitted in DC).
General Civil Practice, Business Law, Nonprofit Tax, Postal Law, Constitutional Law, Election Law, Civil Litigation, Tax Litigation, Appellate Practice
McLean, Virginia Office: 8180 Greensboro Drive, Suite 1070. Telephone: 703-356-5070. Fax: 703-356-5085.

See Professional Biographies, MCLEAN, VIRGINIA

Olsson, Philip C., (AV) ...... '39 '65 C&L.309 A.B., LL.B. [Olsson,F.&W.]
*PRACTICE AREAS: Agriculture Law; Food and Drug Law; International Trade Law.

Olsson, Frank and Weeda, P.C., (AV)
Suite 400, 1400 Sixteenth Street, N.W., 20036
Telephone: 202-789-1212 Telecopier: 202-234-3550
Email: info@ofwlaw.com URL: http://www.ofwlaw.com
Principals: Philip C. Olsson; Richard L. Frank; David F. Weeda; Dennis R. Johnson; Arthur Y. Tsien; John W. Bode (Not admitted in DC); Stephen D. Terman; Marshall L. Matz; Michael J. O'Flaherty; David L. Durkin; Neil F. O'Flaherty; Pamela J. Furman. Of Counsel: Jur T. Strobos; Jacqueline H. Eagle; Kenneth D. Ackerman; Mark L. Itzkoff. Senior Attorney: Richard D. Siegel. Associates: Tish Eggleston Pahl; Brett T. Schwemer; Karen R. Harned; Robert A. Hahn; Naomi Joy Levan Halpern; Stephen L. Lacey; Jan M. Brunner (Not admitted in DC); Susan Page Grymes; Sharon D. Brooks; Ryan W. Stroschein (Not admitted in DC); Evan Phelps (Not admitted in DC).
General Administrative and Trade Regulation Practice. Agriculture, Food and Drug, International Trade, Litigation and Legislation.

See Professional Biographies, WASHINGTON, DISTRICT OF COLUMBIA

Olszowy, Colleen Rachel ...... '67 '91 C.10 B.A. L.178 J.D. 1625 Mass. Ave., N.W.
O'Malley, Grace D. ...... '71 '98 C.93 B.A. L.127 J.D. 4000 Tunlaw Rd., NW
Oman, Ralph, (AV) ...... '40 '73 C.299 A.B. L.276 J.D. [Dechert] (See Pat. Sect.)
*PRACTICE AREAS: Intellectual Property.
O'Mara, James D. ...... '28 '53 C&L.145 A.B., J.D. 1616 18th St., N.W.
O'Meara, John J. '40 '71 C.436 A.B. L.208 J.D.
(adm. in CO; not adm. in DC) Gen. Coun., Fed. Retire. Thrift. Invest. Bd.

O'Melveny & Myers LLP, (AV)
555 13th Street, NW, 20004-1109 ⊙
Telephone: 202-383-5300 Facsimile: 202-383-5414 Cable: MOMSWSH Telex: 89622
Email: omminfo@omm.com URL: http://www.omm.com
Chairman: Arthur B. Culvahouse, Jr. Partners: Kermit W. Almstedt; Brian C. Anderson; David T. Beddow; John H. Beisner; Donald T. Bliss, Jr.; Brian D. Boyle; Nadia St. George Burgard; Walter E. Dellinger (Not admitted in DC); Robert N. Eccles; Cliff H. Fonstein; Stephen J. Harburg; Bruce A. Hiler; Gary N. Horlick; Tom A. Jerman (Not admitted in DC); Ronald Klain; David G. Litt; Richard G. Parker; David G. Pommerening; Ira H. Raphaelson; Robert A. Rizzi; William H. Satchell; Carl R. Schenker, Jr.; Henry C. Thumann (Not admitted in DC); Debra A. Valentine; Karen Mary Wahle. Senior Counsellor: William T. Coleman, Jr. Senior Counsel: Joel S. Burton. Of Counsel: Susan S. Richardson. Special Counsel: Evelyn Becker; Peggy Ann Clarke; Teresa E. Dawson; Suzanne Rich Folsom; Neil K. Gilman; Pamela A. Harris; Lynn E. Parseghian; Patrick Robert Rizzi; Ian Simmons; Gary S. Tell; Gregg H. Vicinanza. Associates: David Applebaum; Elizabeth H. Baird; Shannon M. Barrett (Not admitted in DC); Jeremy B. Bash (Not admitted in DC); Sean G. Blackman (Not admitted in DC); K. Lee Blalack II; Benjamin G. Bradshaw; Brian P. Brooks; William T. Buffaloe (Not admitted in DC); Nathan Garrett Bush (Not admitted in DC); Danielle L. Cannata (Not admitted in DC); Charles F. Connolly; John J. Donoghue (Not admitted in DC); Richard J. Dyer; Leslie A. Fahrenkopf (Not admitted in DC); Daniel E. Farrington; Rebecca H. Farrington; Theodore H. Frank; Richard D. Gardner (Not admitted in DC); Paul G. Griffin; CarrieLyn D. Guymon; Jonathan Hacker; Katharine B. Hazlett; Paul Horwitz; Benjamin R. Jacewicz; Sital Kalantry (Not admitted in DC); Laura M Kam (Not admitted in DC); Amy H. Kay (Not admitted in DC); Kathleen P. Kelly; Kerry A. Krentler (Not admitted in DC); Thomas A. Kuczajda; Veronique Lanthier; Elisabeth Layton; Alan Lefkowitz (Not admitted in DC); Goodwin H. Liu (Not admitted in DC); John P. Maloney, Jr.; Jeremy Maltby (Not admitted in DC); James V. Martin (Also at New York, NY Office); Jessica D. Miller; Kristin H. Mowry; John F. Niblock (Not admitted in DC); Matthew L. Olmsted; Shannon M. Pazur (Not admitted in DC); K. David Phan (Not admitted in DC); Gregory Y. Porter; Kelly Riordan; Rachel A. Shapiro (Not admitted in DC); Matthew M. Shors (Not admitted in DC); Srikanth Srinivasan (Not admitted in DC); Robert Stern (Not admitted in DC); William J. Stuckwisch; Morgen A. Sullivan (Not admitted in DC); Scott A. Thompson (Not admitted in DC); Andrew J. Trask; Darren S. Tucker; Andrew J. Varner; Joshua Waldman (Not admitted in DC); Robert E. Winter; Andrea Worden; Garrett Wotkyns (Not admitted in DC).
General Civil Litigation, Appellate Practice, and Criminal Trials Practice in all State and Federal Courts. Administrative; Antitrust; Banking; Bankruptcy; Commercial; Communications; Construction; Corporation and Corporate Financing; Environmental; Immigration and Naturalization; Insurance Coverage Defense; Intellectual Property; Internet Law; International Business; Labor and Employment; Employment Benefits; Media and Entertainment; Municipal, Municipal Zoning and Municipal Finance; Natural Resources; Oil and Gas; Patent, Trademark, Copyright and Unfair Competition; Probate, Trusts and Estate Planning; Public Utilities; Real Estate; Securities; Telecommunications; and Tax Law.
Los Angeles, CA Office: 400 South Hope Street, 90071-2899. Cable: MOMS. Telex: 674122. Tel: 213-430-6000. Fax: 213-430-6407. E-mail: omminfo@omm.com.
Century City, CA Office: 1999 Avenue of the Stars, Los Angeles, 90067-6035. Telex: 674097. Tel: 310-553-6700. Fax: 310-246-6779.
Irvine, CA Office: 114 Pacifica, Suite 100, 92618-3318. Tel: 949-737-2900. Fax: 949-737-2300.
Newport Beach, CA Office: 610 Newport Center Drive, 92660-6429. Telex: 4722088. Tel: 949-760-9600. Fax: 949-823-6994.
Menlo Park, CA Office: 990 Marsh Road, 94025-1949. Telephone: 650-473-2600. Facsimile: 650-473-2601.
San Francisco, CA Office: Embarcadero Center West, 275 Battery Street, 94111-3305. Tel: 415-984-8700. Fax: 415-984-8701.
New York, NY Office: Citigroup Center, 153 East 53rd Street, 10022-4611. Telex: 129165. Tel: 212-326-2000. Fax: 212-326-2061.
McLean, VA Office: 1650 Tysons Boulevard, 22102. Tel: 703-287-2400. Fax: 703-287-2404.
London Office: O'Melveny & Myers, 3 Finsbury Square, London, EC2A 1LA, England. Tel: 44-20-7256-8451. Fax 44-20-7638-8205.
Tokyo Office: Akasaka Twin Tower, East 14F, 2-17-22, Akasaka, Minato-ku, Tokyo 107-0052, Japan. Tel: 81-3-5562-2800. Fax: 81-3-5575-3840.
Hong Kong Office: O'Melveny & Myers, Suite 1905, Tower Two, Lippo Centre, 89 Queensway, Central, Hong Kong. Tel: 852-2523-8266. Fax: 852-2522-1760.
Shanghai Office: Kerry Centre, 20F, 1515 Nanjing Road West, Shanghai, 200040 People's Republic of China. Tel: 86-21-5298-5600. Fax: 86-21-5298-5500.

See Professional Biographies, WASHINGTON, DISTRICT OF COLUMBIA

Omlie, Lynne J. '52 '79 C.494 B.A. L.273 J.D.
Gen. Coun., Distilled Spirits Council of the U.S.A.
Ommaya, Shana E. ...... '67 '93 C.29 B.A. L.128 J.D. [Morgan,L.&B.]
Omwenga, Samuel N. ...... '64 '98 C.446 B.A. L.1292 J.D. 1730 K St., N.W.
Oncu, Melike S. ...... '71 '96 C.390 B.A. L.273 J.D. [Swidler B.S.F.]
Ondeck, Christopher E. ...... '70 '96 C&L.893 B.A., J.D. [McDermott,W.&E.]
önder, Ayla '— '69
(adm. in Turkey; not adm. in DC) [D.L.Simon]

Ondrasik, Paul J., Jr., (AV) ...... '50 '76 C.674 A.B. L.893 J.D. [Steptoe&J.]
O'Neal, John F. ...... '37 '62 C&L.69 B.B.A., LL.B. 1455 Pennsylvania Ave., N.W.
O'Neil, Carol Q. '47 '88 C.706 B.A. L.276 J.D.
(adm. in PA; not adm. in DC) Asst. Dean, Georgetown Univ. Law Ctr.
O'Neil, David G., (AV) ...... '— '87 C.823 B.A. L.904 J.D. [Manatt,P.&P.]
O'Neil, Michael J. ...... '46 '71 C.321 A.B. L.276 J.D. [Preston G.E.&R.M.]
O'Neil, Nancy Doerr, (AV) .... '57 '82 C.893 B.S. L.276 J.D. [Hogan&H.] (⊙Balt., MD)
*PRACTICE AREAS: Taxation.
O'Neil, Robert A. ...... '46 '71 C&L.93 B.A., J.D. [Miller,B.&O.]
*PRACTICE AREAS: Energy Contracts; Energy Project Development; Project Finance; Electric Utilities.
O'Neil, Thomas F., III, (AV) '57 '82
C.197 A.B. L.276 J.D. Chief Litigation Counsel, MCI WorldCom
O'Neil, William T. ...... '63 '90 C.602 B.A. L.228 J.D. [Swidler B.S.F.]
*PRACTICE AREAS: Litigation.
O'Neill, Brian D., (AV) ...... '46 '71 C&L.259 B.A., J.D. [LeBoeuf,L.G.&M.]
*PRACTICE AREAS: Energy Regulation; Administrative Litigation.
O'Neill, Christopher R., (AV) ...... '49 '77 C.93 B.S. L.276 J.D. [O'Neill,A.&C.]
O'Neill, Edward S., (AV) ...... '31 '61 C&L.128 A.B., LL.B. [Fletcher,H.&H.] ⊙
*PRACTICE AREAS: Communications Law.
O'Neill, Hugh, (AV) ...... '40 '68 C.728 B.S. L.884 J.D. Coun., Jefferson Waterman Intl.
O'Neill, J. Timothy '54 '80
C.276 B.S.F.S. L.309 J.D. 1919 Pennsylvania Ave., N.W., Suite 800
O'Neill, James Richard ...... '50 '75 C&L.802 B.B.A., J.D. [Dickstein S.M.&O.]
*PRACTICE AREAS: Taxation; Trusts and Estates; Probate; Real Estate; Corporate Law.
O'Neill, John H., Jr. (P.C.) ...... '46 '76 C.871 B.S. L.976 J.D. [Shaw P.]
*PRACTICE AREAS: Energy; Nuclear Energy; Electric Utility; International Energy Transactions.
O'Neill, John J., Jr. '71 '00 C.787 B.A. L.276 J.D.
(adm. in MA; not adm. in DC) [Davis&H.]
*PRACTICE AREAS: Taxation Law; Pension Law; Employee Benefits Law.
O'Neill, Kathleen S. '71 '98 C.659 B.A. L.861 J.D.
(adm. in PA; not adm. in DC) [Drinker B.&R.]
O'Neill, Kevin M. '69 '99 C.823 B.A. L.945 J.D.
(adm. in VA; not adm. in DC) [Patton B.]
O'Neill, MaryEllen ...... '64 '87 C.477 B.A. L.128 J.D. Atty., Washington Gas Light Co.
*RESPONSIBILITIES: Litigation; Information Technology; Contracts.
O'Neill, Philip L. ...... '52 '77 C.145 A.B. L.276 J.D. [Jacobson,H.]
*PRACTICE AREAS: Trademarks; Copyrights; Antitrust and Trade Regulation; Litigation.
O'Neill, Sean Michael ...... '69 '95 C.602 B.A. L.273 J.D. U.S. Dept. of Justice
O'Neill, William Patrick ...... '— '76 C.378 B.A. L.477 J.D. [Latham&W.]
*PRACTICE AREAS: Mergers, Acquisitions and Divestitures; Securities.
O'Neill, Athy & Casey, P.C., (AV) ...... 1310 19th St., N.W.
Onel, Suzan ...... '— '90 C.659 B.A. L.893 J.D. [Kirkpatrick&L.]
Ongman, John Will, (AV) ...... '51 '76 C.679 B.S. L.597 J.D. [Pepper H.]
*PRACTICE AREAS: Antitrust; Economic Regulatory Law; Technology and Science.
Onley, Douglas S. ...... '64 '96 C.893 B.A. L.945 J.D. [Howrey S.A.&W.]
*PRACTICE AREAS: Antitrust Litigation; Commercial Litigation.
Onorato, Joanna R. ...... '71 '98 C.855 B.A. L.904 J.D. [Henrichsen S.]
*PRACTICE AREAS: Construction Law; Surety Law; Employment Law; Civil Litigation.
Ontell, David J. ...... '46 '73 C.705 B.A. L.273 J.D. 5712 Nebraska Ave., N.W.
Oosterhuis, Paul W., (AV) ...... '46 '73 C.103 B.A. L.309 J.D. [Skadden,A.S.M.&F.]
Oparil, Richard J., (AV) ...... '60 '86 C.823 B.A. L.930 J.D. [Piper M.R.&W.]
*PRACTICE AREAS: White Collar Crime; Complex Litigation; Civil Litigation; Patent Litigation.
Opert, Jon I. ...... '63 '89 C.401 B.S. L.273 J.D. [Krooth&A.]
*PRACTICE AREAS: Real Estate Transactions.
Oppenheim, Daniel P. ...... '28 '62 C.311 B.A. L.976 LL.B. 500 23rd St., N.W.
Oppenheim, Matthew J. '67 '93 C.966 B.A. L.188 J.D.
V.P. Civil Litig., Recording Industry Assoc. of America, Inc.
Oppenheimer, James Chadwick ...... '68 '97 C.855 B.A. L.145 J.D. [Shea&G.]
Oppenheimer, Jerry L., (AV) ...... '37 '61 C.575 B.S. L.893 LL.B. 1909 K Street, N.W.‡
Oppenheimer, Nanette L. '57 '81 C&L.446 B.A., J.D.
(adm. in MD; not adm. in DC) MCI Telecom. Corp.
Oppenheimer, Peter H. ...... '64 '92 C&L.976 B.A., J.D. 4390 Ben Franklin Sta.

Oppenheimer Wolff & Donnelly LLP, (AV)
1620 L Street, N.W. Suite 600, 20036 ⊙
Telephone: 202-312-8000 FAX: 202-312-8100 For attorney e-mails use: First initial of first name, last name, firm name, e.g., bkeil@oppenheimer.com
Email: info@oppenheimer.com URL: http://www.oppenheimer.com
Resident Partners: Harry W. Cladouhos; John H. Korns; Paul M. Laurenza; Thomas Lawrence, III (Not admitted in DC); Brian R. Coleman (Not admitted in DC). Resident Associates: Daphne L. Burton (Not admitted in DC); Chad Smith (Not admitted in DC); David Bogart Dort; Ronald S. Grubb, Jr.
International Trade and Corporate Law, Taxation, Government Contracts, Environmental Law, Litigation, Immigration, Agency and Regulatory Law.
Minneapolis, Minnesota Office: 3300 Plaza VII, 45 South Seventh Street, 55402. Telephone: 612-607-7000. FAX: 612-607-7100.
Brussels, Belgium Office: Avenue Louise 240, Box 5, 1050. Telephone: 32-2-626-0500. FAX: 32-2-626-0510.
Newport Beach, California Office: 840 Newport Center Drive, Suite 700, 92660. Telephone: 949-823-6000. FAX: 949-823-6100.
New York, N.Y. Office: The Chrysler East Building, Suite 1900, 666 Third Avenue, 10017. Telephone: 212-884-4500. FAX: 212-884-4600.
Paris, France Office: 35 Boulevard des Capucines, 75002. Telephone: (33/1) 53 45 40 00. FAX: (33/1) 53 45 40 10.
Los Angeles, California Office: 2029 Century Park East, Suite 3800, 90067. Telephone: 310-788-5000. FAX: 310-788-5100.
Palo Alto, California Office: 1400 Page Mill Road, 94304. Telephone: 650-320-4000. FAX: 650-320-4100.

See Professional Biographies, WASHINGTON, DISTRICT OF COLUMBIA

Oram, George E., Jr., (AV) '47 '78 C.205 B.Ch.E. L.128 J.D.
[Arent F.K.P.&K.] (Pat.)
*PRACTICE AREAS: Mechanical Intellectual Property; Intellectual Property Infringement; International Intellectual Property.
Orange, Vincent B. ...... '57 '83 C.169 B.S. L.329 J.D. 4101 S Dakota Ave Ne‡
Orban, Frank A., III '44 '68
C.309 B.A. L.659 LL.B. [deKieffer&H.] (⊙Belgrade, Yugoslavia)
*PRACTICE AREAS: International Transactions; Foreign Investment; Customs Law; Export Compliance; International Arbitration.
Ordway, John A., Jr., (AV) ...... '56 '86 C.309 A.B. L.273 J.D. [Berliner,C.&R.]
*PRACTICE AREAS: Government Procurement; Export Control; Criminal Defense; Litigation.
Ordynsky, Eugenia ...... '60 '95 C.1375 B.A. L.64 J.D. [Arent F.K.P.&K.]
*PRACTICE AREAS: Immigration Law.
O'Reilley, D. Patrick, (AV) '43 '75
C.871 B.S. L.273 J.D. [Finnegan,H.F.G.&D.] (See Pat. Sect.)
*PRACTICE AREAS: Intellectual Property Infringement; Intellectual Property Licensing; Intellectual Property Litigation; International Licensing; Mechanical Intellectual Property.
O'Reilly, James Francis ...... '70 '97 C.976 B.A. L.309 J.D. [Wilmer,C.&P.]
O'Reilly, Juliana Schulte '64 '89 C.893 B.A. L.273 J.D.
Assoc. Gen. Coun., Fannie Mae
*RESPONSIBILITIES: Regulatory, Legislative and Financial Institution Law.
O'Reilly, Paul J. '60 '86 C.94 B.A. L.1162 J.D.
(adm. in PA; not adm. in DC) [O'Reilly&M.] ⊙

O'Reilly, William V. .... '58 '86 C&L.893 B.A., J.D. [Jones,D.R.&P.]
*PRACTICE AREAS: Litigation; Complex Commercial Litigation; Corporate Investigations; Antitrust.
O'Reilly & Mark, P.C.
1742 New Hampshire Avenue, N.W. (⊙Bethesda, MD; Alexandria, VA)
Oremland, Annalisa '64 '89 C.860 B.A. L.767 J.D.
(adm. in CA; not adm. in DC) 3801 Connecticut Ave., N.W.‡
Orenberg, Allen H., (AV) ....'54 '82 C.446 B.A. L.796 J.D. [Dilworth P.P.]
*PRACTICE AREAS: Criminal Law; Corporate Litigation; Securities.
Orenstein, Harry C. ......'50 '82 C.30 B.A. L.893 J.D. Senior Counsel, Xerox Corporation
Orenstein, Leo F., (AV) .... '— '80 C.976 B.A. L.309 J.D. [Ⓒ Foley&L.]
*PRACTICE AREAS: Litigation; Securities Regulation; SEC and SRO Enforcement.
Orentlicher, Diane .... '— '81 C.976 B.A. L.178 J.D. Prof. of Law, American Univ.
Orfanedes, Paul J. ....'64 '90 C.339 B.A. L.904 J.D. [Ⓐ Klayman&Assoc.]
Orfield, Daniel G. ....'65 '92 C.103 A.B. L.569 J.D. 1025 Conn. Ave., N.W.
Orin, Rhonda D., (BV) ....'57 '85 C.659 B.A. L.569 J.D. [Anderson K.&O.]
*PRACTICE AREAS: Insurance Litigation; General Litigation.
O'Riordan, Martin J. '59 '85 C.676 B.A. L.94 J.D.
(adm. in MA; not adm. in DC) [Ⓒ Silver,F.&T.]
*PRACTICE AREAS: Banking; Corporate Law; Derivative Products.
Orlin, David P. W. ....'67 '99 C.103 A.B. L.276 J.D. [Ⓐ Covington&B.]
Orloff, Leslye E. '56 '82 C.1036 B.A. L.1068 J.D.
Dir., Prog. Develop., Ayuda Clinica Legal Latina
Orlove, Brett D. ....'66 '91 C.659 B.A. L.273 J.D. [Grossberg,Y.F.&B.]
Orlow, Lisa H. '65 '91 C.223 B.S. L.831 J.D.
(adm. in VA; not adm. in DC) Sr. Acct. Rep., LEXIS-NEXIS
Ormond, John E., Jr. ....'41 '75 C.321 A.B. L.362 J.D. Board of Vet. App.
Ornelas, Christopher D. ....'68 '01 C.893 B.A. L.904 J.D. [Ⓐ Wilkinson B.K.]
*PRACTICE AREAS: Mass Media Law; Telecommunications Law; Trademarks; Corporate Transactions; Commercial Transactions.
Ornstein, Stephen F. J. ....'63 '89 C.103 A.B. L.178 J.D. [Thacher P.&W.]
*PRACTICE AREAS: Real Estate Law; Consumer Compliance Law.

O'Rourke, John T., Law Offices of, (AV) '49 '81 C&L.276 A.B., J.D.
801 Pennsylvania Avenue, N.W. Fifth Floor, 20004
Telephone: 202-662-4720 Fax: 202-662-4748
***PRACTICE AREAS: Legislative; Banking; Securities; Telecommunications; International Trade and Transactions.**
Associate: Maggi A. Lazarus.
General Practice, Banking and Financial Institutions, Legislative, Tax, Telecommunications, International Transactions and International Trade.
See Professional Biographies, WASHINGTON, DISTRICT OF COLUMBIA

O'Rourke, Lawrence M. ....'38 '70 C.884 A.B. L.276 J.D. Nat. Press Bldg.
O'Rourke, Michael S., (AV) '42 '73 C.205 B.A. L.724 J.D.
[Rode&Q.] (⊙New York, NY)
O'Rourke, Thomas J., (AV) '46 '73
C.651 B.S. L.602 J.D. [Ⓒ Shaw,B.V.&R.] (⊙Rockville, MD)
*PRACTICE AREAS: Estate Planning; Probate; Taxation Law; Associations Law; Corporate Law.
O'Rourke, Timothy J., (AV) ....'56 '81 C&L.893 B.A., J.D. [Dow,L.&A.]
O'Rourke & Cundra, (AV) ....818 18th N.W. Street, Suite 800 (⊙Chgo., IL)
Orquiza, Dana Denise M. '71 '01 C.276 B.S.N. L.180 J.D.
(adm. in MD; not adm. in DC) [Ⓐ Bonner K.T.&C.]
*PRACTICE AREAS: Liability.
Orr, Allen, Jr. ....'73 '99 C.511 B.A. L.329 J.D. [Ⓐ Baker&M.]
*PRACTICE AREAS: Immigration Law; Administrative Law; Construction Law.
Orr, Bette M., (BV) ....'43 '89 C.1295 B.A. L.976 J.D. [Gilbert H.&R.]
*PRACTICE AREAS: Alternative Dispute Resolution; Insurance.
Orr, Kevyn D. '58 '84 C&L.477 B.A., J.D.
(adm. in FL; not adm. in DC) [Ⓒ Jones,D.R.&P.]

Orrick, Herrington & Sutcliffe LLP, (AV)
Washington Harbour, 3050 K Street, N.W., 20036 ⊙
Telephone: 202-339-8400 Telecopier: 202-339-8500
URL: http://www.orrick.com
Resident Partners: Cameron L. Cowan; Felicia B. Graham; Michael D. Hornstein; Thomas J. Horton; David S. Katz; Keith W. Kriebel; Douglas L. Madsen; Michael Hoyt Mitchell; Edwin G. Oswald (Not admitted in DC); Diana Weiss (Not admitted in DC). Resident Of Counsel: Michele E. Beasley; Jonathan W. Haddon; Dianne L. Stoddard; Sandra E. Trimble; Patricia R. Zeigler. Resident Associates: Reagen Beck; Mark S. Dola; Kyle W. Drefke (Not admitted in DC); Johanna Eadie (Not admitted in DC); Wells Engledow; Craig Fishman; Michael H. Freedman; Shazmah Hakim (Not admitted in DC); Michael J. McElroy (Not admitted in DC); J. Russell Miller; Lauren C. Mullen; Mark R. Riccardi; Hina Shaikh (Not admitted in DC); Scott A. Stengel; Barbara Stettner; Michael R. Trocchio (Not admitted in DC); Kenneth J. Yellen (Not admitted in DC). London, England Members of the Firm: R. Michael Bacon; Martin Stewart-Smith; Paul S. Stock; Paul Weiffenbach. Los Angeles, California Members of Firm: Alan G. Benjamin; J. Keith Biancamano; William W. Bothwell; Lori A. Bowman; Eugene Carron; Gerald L. Chaleff; Blase P. Dillingham; Greg Harrington; W. Douglas Kari; Linda S. Koffman; Michael A. McAndrews; Richard C. Mendelson; Mary H. Neale; William W. Oxley; Gary D. Samson; Larry D. Sobel; Paul A. Webber; Bradley S. White; Neal L. Wolf. Menlo Park, California Members of Firm: William L. Anthony; W. Reece Bader; Scott D. Blickenstaff; Brian C. Burr; William Sloan Coats; Peter Cohn; Scott D. Elliott; Vickie L. Feeman; Robert E. Freitas; G. Hopkins Guy, III; Lynne C. Hermle; Craig R. Kaufman; Amy Landers; Geoffrey P. Leonard; Christopher R. Ottenweller; Robert S. Shwarts; Gary E. Weiss; Eric L. Wesenberg; Thomas H. Zellerbach. New York, New York Members of Firm: Peter A. Bicks; Charles W. Bradley; Bradford S. Breen; Mary Rose Brusewitz; Peter Bucci; Fred C. Byers, Jr.; William R. Campbell; James J. Capra, Jr.; Michael B. Carlinsky; Richard Chirls; J. Peter Coll, Jr.; Jeffrey A. Conciatori; Peter J. Connors; Robert A. Cote; Katharine I. Crost; Duncan Darrow; Michael Delikat; Edward M. DeSear; Laurie Dix; Lauren Elliot; Joseph Evall; Rubi Finkelstein; Robert A. Fippinger; Lawrence B. Fisher; Stephen G. Foresta; Charles W. Gerdts, III; Lawrence B. Goodwin; F. Susan Gottlieb; Arnold Gulkowitz; Eileen B. Heitzler; Robert M. Isackson; David R. Jewell; Mitchell S. Kaplan; John J. Keohane; Alan M. Knoll; Martin H. Levenglick; Herbert J. Levine; Carl F. Lyon, Jr.; John A. MacKerron; Joseph E. Maloney; Richard W. Mark; Daniel Mathews; Lorraine S. McGowen; Michael R. Meyers; Robert B. Michel; Sam Scott Miller; Christopher J. Moore; Barbara Moses; P. Quinn Moss; James J. Murtha; David Nirenberg; Perry A. Pappas; Anthony Princi; Joshua E. Raff; Clayton Reynolds; Jill L. Rosenberg; Ira G. Rosenstein; Al B. Sawyers; Stephen K. Sawyier; Albert Simons, III; Louis H. Singer; Elaine F. Stein; James L. Stengel; Daniel J. Thomasch; Michael Voldstad; L. Mark Weeks; Robert S. Whitman; Neil T. Wolk. Sacramento, California Members of Firm: Norman C. Hile; Perry E. Israel; Cynthia J. Larsen; Marc A. Levinson; Timothy J. Long; Virginia C. Magan; Iain Mickle; John R. Myers; Thomas J. Welsh. San Francisco, California Members of Firm: William F. Alderman; David T. Alexander; Denise Alter; Ralph H. Baxter, Jr.; Elaine R. Bayus; Daniel R. Bedford; William D. Berry; Paul C. Borden; Fred A. Brown; Colman J. Burke; Charles C. Cardall; Thomas Y. Coleman; Mary A. Collins; Dean E. Criddle; Roger L. Davis; Ana Marie Del Rio; Stanley J. Dirks; William M. Doyle; Raymond G. Ellis; Robert P. Feyer; Grant Finlayson; Carlo S. Fowler; Kathy Woeber Gardner; Richard A. Gilbert; Robert J. Gloistein; Richard Grey; Richard D. Harroch; John M. Hartenstein; Dolph M. Hellman; Gary A. Herrmann; Richard I. Hiscocks; Leslie P. Jay; Lawrence T. Kane; John H. Knox; Mark R. Levie; Michael H. Liever; Peter Lillevand; Sean A. Lincoln; Gary Louie; Joseph M. Malkin; Steven C. Malvey; Dora Mao; Jesse W. Markham; Thomas C. Mitchell; William G. Murray; Noel W. Nellis; Jonathan M. Ocker; Tracy Preston; M. J. Pritchett; Greg R. Riddle; Marie B. Riehle; William L. Riley; Peter E. Root; William R. Sawyers; Paul J. Sax; John F. Seegal; Gary R. Siniscalco; Richard V. Smith; Stephen A. Spitz; Alan Talkington; James V. Telfer; Ralph C. Walker; Jeffrey S. White; Kenneth G. Whyburn; Jeffrey D. Wohl; George G. Wolf; Cameron W. Wolfe Jr.; George A. Yuhas. Singapore Members of Firm: Marie-Anne Jacoba Birken; Bruce R. Schulberg. Tokyo Member of Firm: Howard M. Goldwasser; Christopher Lewis; Dennis P. Martin. Seattle, Washington Members of Firm: Keith C. Cochran; Stephen M. Graham; Scott J. Moore.
General Practice, including Corporate and Municipal Finance, Domestic and International Commercial Law, Banking and Commercial Finance, Project Finance, Structured Finance, Mergers and Acquisitions, Commercial Litigation, Insurance, Insurance Insolvency, White Collar Criminal De-

(This Listing Continued)

Orrick, Herrington & Sutcliffe LLP (Continued)

fense, Tax, Employee Benefits and Personal Estates, Antitrust, Distribution, and Trade Regulation, Intellectual Property, Real Estate, Environmental and Energy and Labor and Employment Law and Bankruptcy.
San Francisco, California Office: Old Federal Reserve Bank Building, 400 Sansome Street. Telephone: 415-392-1122. Telecopier: 415-773-5759.
Los Angeles, California Office: 777 South Figueroa Street. Telephone: 213-629-2020. Telecopier: 213-612-2499.
New York, New York Office: 666 Fifth Avenue. Telephone: 212-506-5000. Telecopier: 212-506-5151.
Sacramento, California Office: 400 Capitol Mall. Telephone: 916-447-9200. Telecopier: 916-329-4900.
Menlo Park, California Office: 1020 Marsh Road. Telephone: 650-614-7400. Fax: 650-614-7401.
Singapore Office: 10 Collyer Quay, #23-08 Ocean Building, Singapore. Telephone: 011-65-538-6116, Telecopier: 011-65-538-0606.
Tokyo, Japan Office: 11th Floor, Main Tower, Akasaka Twin Towers, 17-22 Akasaka 2-Chome, Minato-Ku. Telephone: 011-81-3-3224-2900. Telecopier: 011-81-3-3224-2901.
London, England Office: 1st Floor, 4 Broadgate, London EC2M 2DA. Telephone: 011-44-20-7638-1584. Telecopier: 011-44-20-7628-0078.
Seattle, Washington Office: 719 Second Avenue, Suite 900. Telephone: 206-839-4300. Fax: 206-839-4301.
See Professional Biographies, WASHINGTON, DISTRICT OF COLUMBIA

Orseck, Gary A. ....'63 '89 C.103 B.A. L.813 J.D. [Robbins,R.E.O.&U.]
Orta, David M. ....'69 '94 C.861 B.A. L.362 J.D. [Ⓐ Arnold&P.]
*PRACTICE AREAS: Products Liability Litigation; Complex Commercial Litigation; Employment Litigation.
Ortins, J. Bradley ....'51 '85 C.454 B.A. L.128 J.D. 1601 Conn. Ave., N.W.
Ortiz, Manuel A. ....'73 '99 C&L.378 B.A., J.D. [Ⓐ Greenberg T.]
Ortman, David B., (AV) ....'23 '52 C&L.178 B.A., LL.B. 61 G St., S.W.
Ortman, Glen L., (AV) ....'— '72 C.95 B.A. L.208 J.D. [Morrison&H.]
*PRACTICE AREAS: Energy Law.

Ortman, Love & Huckabay
(See Bethesda, Maryland)

Orudjev, F. Alec '74 '99 C.576 B.A. L.823 J.D.
(adm. in NY; not adm. in DC) [Ⓐ De Martino F.R.&V.] ⊙
*PRACTICE AREAS: Securities; Corporate Law; Mergers and Acquisitions.
Orvis, Douglas D., II ....'71 '96 C.347 B.A. L.1065 J.D. [Ⓐ Swidler B.S.F.]
*PRACTICE AREAS: Telecommunications; International.
Ory, Nancy A. ....'63 '94 C.645 B.A. L.273 J.D. [Ⓐ Leventhal,S.&L.]
*PRACTICE AREAS: Communications Law; Media Law.
Osborn, L. John, (AV) .... '48 '74 C&L.93 A.B., J.D. [Ⓒ Sonnenschein N.&R.]
*PRACTICE AREAS: Transportation; Economic Regulatory Law; Antitrust.
Osborne, James C., Jr. .... '55 '84 C.296 B.A. L.273 J.D. [Ⓒ Akin,G.S.H.&F.]
*PRACTICE AREAS: Litigation.
Osborne, Leutrell M. C., II .... '60 '89 C.893 B.A. L.1065 J.D. Off. of U.S. Atty.
Osborne, William W., Jr., (AV) .... '48 '75 C.951 B.A. L.128 J.D. [Osborne]
*PRACTICE AREAS: Labor and Employment Law; Pension Plans; Equal Employment Opportunity Law; Bankruptcy Law.
Osborne, Woodley B., (AV) ....'38 '65 C.855 B.A. L.569 J.D. [Osborne&D.]
*PRACTICE AREAS: Litigation; Civil Rights; Labor and Employment.

Osborne and Deutsch, (AV)
Suite 550, 1666 Connecticut Avenue, N.W., 20009
Telephone: 202-728-0820 Fax: 202-234-1270
URL: http://www.lawyers.com/osborne&deutsch
Woodley B. Osborne; Morris H. Deutsch.
General Practice, Specializing in Immigration and Nationality Law, Civil Litigation, Labor and Employment, Domestic Relations Mediation.
See Professional Biographies, WASHINGTON, DISTRICT OF COLUMBIA

Osborne Law Offices, P.C., (AV)
4301 Connecticut Avenue, NW Suite 108, 20008
Telephone: 202-243-3200 Fax: 202-243-3207
Email: Lawfirm@OsborneLaw.com
William W. Osborne, Jr.;—Jason J. Valtos (Not admitted in DC).
General Civil Litigation, Labor, Pension and Employee Relations Law, Equal Opportunity Law and Bankruptcy Law.
See Professional Biographies, WASHINGTON, DISTRICT OF COLUMBIA

Osburn, C. Dixon .... '64 '94 C.813 A.B. L.276 J.D. ServiceMembers Legal Def. Network.
Osenga, Kristen Rae Jakobsen '72 '00
C.352 B.S.E. L.339 J.D. [Ⓐ Finnegan,H.F.G.&D.] (See Pat. Sect.)
Oser, Aaron M. .... '61 '90 C.1044 B.A. L.724 J.D. [Shaw P.]
Osha, J. Frank, (AV) ..... '39 '66 C.453 B.S. L.309 LL.B. [Sughrue M.] (See Pat. Sect.)
*PRACTICE AREAS: Intellectual Property Law.
O'Shea, Heather M. .... '70 '95 C.840 B.S. L.425 J.D. [Ⓐ Jones,D.R.&P.]
O'Shea, Michael A. .... '61 '88 C.597 B.S. L.262 J.D. [Clifford C.R.&W.] (Pat.)
*PRACTICE AREAS: Civil Trial Practice; Patents; Copyrights; Trademarks.
O'Shea, Timothy P. '63 '95 C.976 B.A. L.262 J.D.
(adm. in NY; not adm. in DC) [Holland&K.]
*PRACTICE AREAS: Corporate; Finance.
Oshinsky, Jerold, (AV) ....'42 '68 C.102 B.A. L.178 LL.B. [Dickstein S.M.&O.]
*PRACTICE AREAS: Insurance Litigation; Commercial Litigation.
Oshman, Michele T. '58 '86 C.445 B.A. L.64 J.D.
(adm. in MD; not adm. in DC) [Ⓐ Bonner K.T.&C.]
*PRACTICE AREAS: Insurance Coverage Litigation; Litigation.
Oshtry, Daniel I. '59 '86 C.1307 B.A. L.1162 J.D.
(adm. in PA; not adm. in DC) 1828 Irving St Nw
Osnos, David M., (AV) ....'32 '56 C&L.309 A.B., J.D. [Arent F.K.P.&K.]
*PRACTICE AREAS: Real Estate-Commercial Law; Taxation Law; Sports Law; Securities; Estate Planning.
Osolinik, Carolyn P. .... '52 '77 C.412 B.S. L.273 J.D. [Mayer,B.&P.]
Osseiran, Nina M. '— '00 C.30 B.A. L.770 J.D.
(adm. in CA; not adm. in DC) [Ⓒ Foley&L.]
*PRACTICE AREAS: Intellectual Property; Patents; Trademarks.
Ossola, Charles D., (AV) .... '53 '78 C.951 B.A. L.884 J.D. [Arnold&P.]
*PRACTICE AREAS: Intellectual Property Litigation; Patent Litigation; Trademark Litigation; Copyright Litigation; Unfair Competition Litigation.
Oster, Steven M. .... '58 '83 C.1044 B.A. L.178 J.D. [Steptoe&J.]
*PRACTICE AREAS: Administrative Law; Alternative Dispute Resolution; Business Transactions; Civil Litigation; Environmental, Natural Resources and Health and Safety.
Osterhaus, Kristina R. .... '73 '98 C.896 B.A. L.145 J.D. [Ⓐ Wiley R.&F.]
Osterhaus, Timothy D. ....'71 '98 C.387 B.A. L.893 J.D. [Ⓐ Arent F.K.P.&K.]
*PRACTICE AREAS: International Trade; Antidumping; Customs Law.
Osterhout, David E., (BV) .... '39 '83 C.197 B.A. L.494 J.D. 2606 36th Pl., N.W.
Osterman, R. Dennis, (AV) ....'47 '77 C.294 B.S. L.30 J.D. [R.D.Osterman]
*PRACTICE AREAS: Employment Law; Litigation; Medical Malpractice Law; White Collar; Criminal Defense.

Osterman, R. Dennis, PLLC, Law Offices of, (AV)
1901 Pennsylvania Avenue, Suite 1005, 20006
Telephone: 202-861-4297 Fax: 202-463-2039
Email: rdostermanpllc@aol.com
R. Dennis Osterman.

(This Listing Continued)

Osterman, R. Dennis, PLLC, Law Offices of (Continued)
Compensation and Insurance Benefits, Sex Discrimination, Wrongful Termination, Race Discrimination, Employment Law, Litigation Medical Malpractice Law, Personal Injury, Automobile Accidents, Wrongful Death, White Collar Crime, Federal Criminal Law, Criminal Defense, Assaults, Felonies.
See Professional Biographies, WASHINGTON, DISTRICT OF COLUMBIA

Ostmann, James Buckley ....'44 '70 C&L.276 B.S., J.D. 2461 Wisconsin Ave., N.W.
Ostoyich, Joseph A. ....'66 '92 C.188 B.A. L.145 J.D. [Howrey S.A.&W.]
*PRACTICE AREAS: Antitrust Law; Commercial Litigation.
Ostroff, Joseph S. ......'72 '97 C.188 B.S. L.273 J.D. [Ⓐ Sterne,K.G.&F.] (See Pat. Sect.)
*PRACTICE AREAS: Patents; Chemical Patents; Biotechnology Patents; Patent Interference Practice; Pharmaceutical Patents.

Ostrolenk, Faber, Gerb & Soffen, LLP, (AV)
1725 K Street NW, 20006 ⊙
Telephone: 202-457-7785 Fax: 202-429-8919
Email: email@ostrolenk.com
Stephen A. Soffen. Associates: Peter McGee; Ellen S. Tao. Of Counsel: Leon Zitver.
Patent, Trademark, Copyright and Unfair Competition.
New York, New York Office: 1180 Avenue of the Americas. 10036. Telephone: 212-382-0700. Facsimile: 212-382-0888.
See Professional Biographies, WASHINGTON, DISTRICT OF COLUMBIA

Ostrov, Jerome ....'42 '67 C.94 B.S.B.A. L.982 J.D. [Friedlander,M.S.K.&O.]
*PRACTICE AREAS: Tax; Estate Planning; Commercial Law; Appellate Practice.
Ostrowski, Stacy H. '70 '97
(adm. in VA; not adm. in DC) [Ⓐ Sullivan&W.]
*PRACTICE AREAS: Securities Law; Investment Company Law; Government Contracts.
Ostrowsky, Lenore S. ....'48 '75 C.339 B.A. L.846 J.D. [Greenberg T.]
O'Sullivan, John B. ....'43 '74 C.674 B.A. L.569 J.D. [Chadbourne&P.]
O'Sullivan, Judith R. ....'42 '96 C.521 B.A. L.276 J.D. 600 E Street, NW
O'Sullivan, Julie R. '59 '85
C.813 A.B. L.188 J.D. Prof. of Law, Georgetown Univ. Law Ctr.
O'Sullivan, Lynda Troutman, (AV) ....'52 '78 C.30 B.A. L.276 J.D. [Miller&C.]
*PRACTICE AREAS: Government Contracts; Health Care Contracts; Federal Litigation; Alternative Dispute Resolution.
Osuna, Juan P. '62 '90 C.273 B.A. L.904 J.D.
(adm. in PA; not adm. in DC) Federal Publications, Inc.
*RESPONSIBILITIES: Immigration Law.
Oswald, Edwin G., (AV) '59 '89 C&L.724 B.S., J.D.
(adm. in NY; not adm. in DC) [Orrick,H.&S.]
*PRACTICE AREAS: Tax Law; Tax Exempt Bonds.
Oswald, R. Scott ....'67 '97 C.893 B.A. L.329 J.D. [Employment] & [Noto&O.]
*PRACTICE AREAS: Labor and Employment; Immigration Law; Corporate Law.
Oswald, Robert L., (AV) ....'37 '81 C.446 B.A. L.273 J.D. [Noto&O.]
*PRACTICE AREAS: Immigration Law.
Otis, Laura A. ....'— '98 C.276 B.S.F.S. L.30 J.D. [Ⓐ Rosenman&C.]
O'Toole, Francis J., (AV) ....'44 '70 C.309 A.B. L.1294 J.D. [Sidley A.B.&W.]
O'Toole, Jeffrey B., (AV) ....'49 '76 C.184 B.S. L.1162 J.D. [O'Toole,R.N.&S.]
O'Toole, Kevin M. ....'67 '92 C.378 B.A. L.659 J.D. [McDermott,W.&E.]
O'Toole, Rothwell, Nassau & Steinbach, (AV) .... 1700 K Street, N.W., Suite 700
Ott, Christopher A. .... '— '99 C.140 B.A. L.734 J.D. [Ⓐ Kilpatrick S.]
*PRACTICE AREAS: Intellectual Property Litigation.
Ott, Keith C. '64 '95 C.378 B.S.B.A. L.862 J.D.
(adm. in KS; not adm. in DC) [Ⓐ Counts,P.-D.&D.]
Ottaviano, Deanne M. ....'64 '92 C.94 B.A. L.276 J.D. [Arent F.K.P.&K.]
*PRACTICE AREAS: Insurance Coverage; Clean Air Act; Emerging Business Law; Electronic Commerce; Trade Association Law.
Ottenberg, Lee I. ....'47 '73 C.597 B.A. L.273 J.D. V.P., Ottenberg's Bakery
Ottenstein, Thomas R. '29 '54 C.823 A.B. L.276 J.D.
(adm. in MD; not adm. in DC) 5203 MacArthur Terr., N.W.‡
Ottinger, Gregg D., (AV) ....'50 '80 C.894 B.A. L.276 J.D. [Duncan&A.]
*PRACTICE AREAS: Administrative Law; Contracts; Natural Resources; Public Utilities.
Ottinger, Lawrence S. '60 '88
C.112 B.A. L.813 J.D. Sr. Staff Atty., People for the American Way
Oubre, Leah C. ....'75 '00 C.420 B.S. L.1509 J.D. [Ⓐ Leydig,V.&M.] (See Pat. Sect.)
Oulahan, Courts, (AV) ....'20 '48 C.311 B.S. L.976 J.D. 1730 K St., N.W.
Outman, William D., II, (AV) ....'40 '66 C.902 B.S. L.276 J.D. [Baker&M.]
*PRACTICE AREAS: Trade Regulations and Customs Law; Litigation; Appellate Practice.
Ovedovitz, David M. '— '99 C.867 B.S. L.1209 J.D.
(adm. in VA; not adm. in DC) [Ⓐ Wenderoth,L.&P.]
*PRACTICE AREAS: Patents.
Overall, Scott C. ....'56 '84 C.103 A.B. L.904 J.D. [Sonenthal&O.]
*PRACTICE AREAS: Government Procurement; International Government Contracts; Federal Grants; International Construction Law; International Contracts.
Overman, Dean L. ....'43 '69 C.323 A.B. L.1066 J.D. [Winston&S.]
*PRACTICE AREAS: General Corporate.
Oviatt, Clifford R., Jr., (AV) ....'26 '54 C.918 B.A. L.188 LL.B. [McGuirewoods] ‡
*PRACTICE AREAS: Labor Management Relations.
Owczarski, John W. ....'62 '88 C.659 B.S. L.178 J.D. [Ⓐ White&C.]
Owczarski, Karen Estilo '63 '89 C.66 B.A. L.569 J.D.
(adm. in NY; not adm. in DC) Staff Atty.
Owen, Stephen F., Jr., (AV) '34 '62
C.454 B.S.E.E. L.188 J.D. 5335 Wisconsin Ave. Ste. 920
Owens, André E. ....'63 '88 C.676 B.S. L.309 J.D. [Schiff H.&W.]
*PRACTICE AREAS: Securities Regulation; Broker-Dealer Regulation.
Owens, Carrie Lee ....'75 '00 C.886 B.A. L.309 J.D. [Ⓐ Willkie F.&G.]
*PRACTICE AREAS: International Trade.
Owens, Jonathan M. ....'42 '74 C.1280 B.D. L.329 J.D. 129 Thomas St., N.W.
Owens, Joseph H. '40 '63 C&L.790 B.A., LL.B.
(adm. in SC; not adm. in DC) Exec. Dir. & Gen. Coun., Council of State Administrators
Owens, Joseph H., Jr. '37 '63 C&L.790 B.A., J.D.
(adm. in SC; not adm. in DC) P.O. Box 3776
Owens, Kerry H. '63 '94 C.966 B.S. L.273 J.D.
(adm. in MD; not adm. in DC; Pat.) [Ⓐ Hunton&W.]
*PRACTICE AREAS: Patents; Trademarks; Trade Secrets; Copyrights.
Owens, Kevin Mitchel '53 '86 C&L.64 B.S., J.D.
(adm. in MD; not adm. in DC) 1225 Conn. Ave., N.W.
Owens, Lynn Loris ....'61 '95 C.178 B.A. L.659 J.D. [Ⓐ Keller&H.]
*PRACTICE AREAS: Commercial Litigation; Unfair Trade Practices; Products Liability; Toxic Torts.
Owens, Marcus Sherman '49 '74 C.259 B.A. L.228 J.D.
(adm. in FL; not adm. in DC) [Caplin&D.]
*PRACTICE AREAS: Federal Taxation; Tax Exempt Organizations.
Owens, Philip W. ....'59 '93 C.846 B.S. L.276 J.D. Sr. Coun., Marriott Intl., Inc.
*RESPONSIBILITIES: Commercial Contracts; Construction Law; Development Law.
Owens, Roderick D. ....'72 '98 C.446 B.A. L.861 J.D. [Ⓐ Krooth&A.]
*PRACTICE AREAS: Real Estate Finance; Corporate Law.
Owens, William H., Jr. ....'45 '75 C.502 B.A. L.30 J.D. 1111 14th St., N.W.
Oxenford, David D., (AV) ....'54 '80 C.945 B.A. L.245 J.D. [Shaw P.]
*PRACTICE AREAS: Communications; Intellectual Property; Internet and World Wide Web.

Oxfeld, Eric J. '51 '76 C.976 B.A. L.273 J.D.
Pres., UWC-Strategic Servs. on Unemp. & Wkrs. Comp.
Oyewole, G. Godwin, (BV) '42 '81 C.1373 B.A. L.276 J.D.
601 Pennsylvania Ave., N.W.
Oyler, Gregory K., (AV) ....'53 '78 C.674 A.B. L.276 J.D. [Scribner,H.&T.]
Ozeck, Samuel Adam ....'74 '99 C.945 B.A. L.309 J.D. [Ⓐ Venable,A.B.H.&C.]
*PRACTICE AREAS: Banking Law; Corporate Finance.
Ozgu, Murat ....'69 '97 C.401 B.S.M.E. L.1187 J.D. [Ⓐ Arent F.K.P.&K.] (Pat.)
*PRACTICE AREAS: Intellectual Property (100%); Electrical Intellectual Property; Intellectual Property Infringement; International Intellectual Property; Mechanical Intellectual Property.
Ozlu, John A. ....'55 '86 C.597 B.A. L.767 J.D. Pres., Turo Corp.
Pabis, Ronald J. '66 '94 C.319 B.S. L.982 J.D.
(adm. in FL; not adm. in DC) [Ⓐ McDermott,W.&E.]
Pablo, Jeanette M. ....'59 '89 C.893 B.A. L.276 J.D. Tenn. Valley Auth.
Pace, Regina Famiglietti ....'70 '94 C&L.893 B.A., J.D. [Ⓐ Fleischman&W.]
Pace and Rose, (AV) .... 1912 Sunderland Pl., N.W. (⊙L.A., CA; Paris, France)
Pacella, Mark A. ....'65 '95 C.688 B.S. L.273 J.D. [Ⓐ Wiley R.&F.] (Pat.)
Pacious, James M. '70 '95 C.228 B.A. L.884 J.D.
(adm. in PA; not adm. in DC) [Ⓐ Collier S.S.]
*PRACTICE AREAS: Trademarks.
Package, Anne M. ....'69 '95 C.659 B.A. L.477 J.D. [Ⓐ Arnold&P.]
*PRACTICE AREAS: Litigation.
Packman, Mark A., (AV) ....'55 '80 C.674 A.B. L.276 J.D. [Gilbert H.&R.]
*PRACTICE AREAS: Election Law; Litigation; RICO; Securities Law; White Collar Criminal Defense.
Padgett, Miles C. ....'— '94 C.188 B.A. L.880 J.D. [Kozusko L.H.]
*PRACTICE AREAS: Closely Held Business Taxation; Business Law; Charitable Trusts and Foundations; Nonprofit Organizations; International Estate Planning.
Padierna-Peralta, Julia S. '65 '00 C.276 B.S.F.S. L.904 J.D.
(adm. in FL; not adm. in DC) [Ⓐ Neville,P.] ⊙
*PRACTICE AREAS: Mexico Trade; Customs Law; Regulatory Law; Trade Law; International Trade Law.
Pafford, Abram J. ....'72 '00 C.999 B.S. L.273 J.D. [Ⓐ Fried,F.H.S.&J.]
*PRACTICE AREAS: White Collar Crime; Commercial Litigation; Government Contracts.
Page, Reid A. '75 '00 C.469 B.A. L.276 J.D.
(adm. in VA; not adm. in DC) [Ⓐ Piper M.R.&W.]
*PRACTICE AREAS: Litigation.
Page, Rodney F., (AV) ....'— '71 C.383 B.A. L.309 J.D. [Bryan C.]
*PRACTICE AREAS: Commercial Litigation; Appellate Practice.
Pages, Krista L. ....'63 '89 C.732 B.A. L.904 J.D. [© Winston&S.]
Paglin, Max D. '14 '39 C.563 B.S.S. L.178 LL.B.
Exec. Dir., Golden Jubilee Comm. on Telecommunications
Pagotto, Kim K.S. '73 '00 C&L.477 B.A., J.D.
(adm. in MI; not adm. in DC) [Ⓐ Piper M.R.&W.]
*PRACTICE AREAS: Real Estate.
Pahl, Tish Eggleston ....'61 '88 C&L.597 B.S., J.D. [Ⓐ Olsson,F.&W.]
*PRACTICE AREAS: Food and Drug Law; Dietary Supplements; Advertising; Litigation.
Pai, Neeraj D. '74 '00 C.884 B.S. L.309 J.D.
(adm. in PA; not adm. in DC) [Ⓐ McKee N.]
*PRACTICE AREAS: Tax Litigation.
Paige, Eugene M. '73 '99 C.691 B.A. L.309 J.D.
(adm. in CA; not adm. in DC) [Ⓐ Kellogg,H.H.T.&E.]
*PRACTICE AREAS: Litigation.
Paige, John Patrick '51 '81 C.276 B.S. L.1234 J.D.
(adm. in GA; not adm. in DC) Universal Media Inc.
Paige, L. Stanley ....'28 '54 C&L.329 A.B., LL.B. V.P., Post-Newsweek Stations, Inc.
Paige, Michael, (AV) ....'41 '67 C.309 B.A. L.893 LL.B. [© Jackson&C.]
*PRACTICE AREAS: Corporate Law; Securities; International Transactions.
Paige, Russell O. ....'59 '95 C.688 B.S.M.E. L.846 J.D. [Ⓐ Jones,D.R.&P.]
Paikin, Jonathan E. ....'71 '97 C.367 B.A. L.659 J.D. [Ⓐ Wilmer,C.&P.]
Paine, Cynthia Langelier '62 '99 C.588 B.S. L.276 J.D.
(adm. in VA; not adm. in DC) [Ⓐ Goulston&S.]
*PRACTICE AREAS: Corporate; Real Estate.
Painter, Michelle Billand '70 '95 C&L.893 B.A., J.D.
(adm. in VA; not adm. in DC) Coun., MCI WorldCom
Paisner, Richard D. ....'49 '75 C&L.309 A.B., J.D. 600 New Hampshire Ave., N.W.‡
Pak, Song A. ....'70 '99 C.990 B.A. L.30 J.D. [Ⓐ Thacher P.&W.]
*PRACTICE AREAS: Securities; Corporate Law; Financial Institutions Law.
Pak, Song H. '69 '94 C.802 B.A. L.846 J.D.
(adm. in TX; not adm. in DC) [Ⓐ Piper M.R.&W.]
*PRACTICE AREAS: Business; Technology; Venture Capital; Emerging Growth Companies.
Palacios, Alejandro J. ....'54 '82 C.31 B.A. L.904 J.D. U.S. Comm. for UNICEF
Paladini, Vincent M. '— '97 C.705 B.A. L.94 J.D.
(adm. in NJ; not adm. in DC) [Ⓐ Piper M.R.&W.]
*PRACTICE AREAS: Communications Law; Federal Regulatory Law; Administrative Law; International Trade.
Palan, Perry, (AV) ....'— '70 C.910 B.S.E.E. L.273 J.D. [Barnes&T.] (See Pat. Sect.)
*PRACTICE AREAS: Patents; Trademarks; Copyrights; Technology Licensing; Technology Transfers.
Palansky, IJay ....'72 '96 C.028 B.A. L.309 J.D. [Ⓐ Wilmer,C.&P.]
Palchick, Mark J., (AV) ....'50 '75 C.473 B.A. L.1017 J.D. [Holland&K.]
*PRACTICE AREAS: Communications and Media; Cable Communications Law.
Palermo, Nancy M. '67 '97 C.692 B.A. L.128 J.D.
(adm. in MD; not adm. in DC) Garrison & Sisson, Inc.
Palk, Jeffrey R. ....'69 '95 C.309 A.B. L.276 J.D. 3050 K St., N.W.
Palko, Monica J. ....'65 '91 C.315 B.A. L.273 J.D. 2000 K St Nw # 500
Pallesen, Kathleen Spethman '66 '91 C.714 B.A. L.546 J.D.
(adm. in NE; not adm. in DC) Seabury & Smith
Palma, José A. ....'68 '94 L.999 J.D. [Swidler B.S.F.]
*PRACTICE AREAS: Telecommunications; Transactional; International; Government Affairs.
Palmer, Alan K., (AV) ....'41 '70 C.197 A.B. L.309 J.D. [Holland&K.]
*PRACTICE AREAS: Litigation; Antitrust; Consumer Protection; Federal Indian Law.
Palmer, Alicia J. ....'67 '95 C.651 B.S. L.904 J.D. [Ⓐ Crowell&M.]
Palmer, Allan, (AV) ....'36 '62 C.102 B.A. L.1009 LL.B. 1707 N St., N.W.
Palmer, Christopher E. ....'60 '86 C.723 B.A. L.276 J.D. [Shea&G.]
*PRACTICE AREAS: Securities; Insurance; Litigation.
Palmer, David B. ....'46 '76 C.260 B.A. L.823 J.D. [Akin,G.S.H.&F.]
*PRACTICE AREAS: Health Care.
Palmer, Debra Ann, (AV) ....'62 '87 C.860 B.A. L.930 J.D. [Ⓐ Schiff H.&W.]
*PRACTICE AREAS: Federal Energy Regulation; Electric Power.
Palmer, Karla L. ....'65 '92 C.945 B.A. L.692 J.D. [McDermott,W.&E.]
Palmer, Michael T. ....'65 '93 C.420 B.G.S. L.424 J.D. [Ⓐ Patton B.]
Palmer, Ronald Joseph '59 '86 C.845 B.A. L.846 J.D.
(adm. in TX; not adm. in DC) 2101 Constitution Ave. N.W.
Palmer, Shaun M. '74 '01 C.893 B.A. L.309 J.D.
(adm. in NY; not adm. in DC) [Ⓐ Covington&B.]
Palmer, Stephen C. ....'49 '78 C.367 B.A. L.823 J.D. [Swidler B.S.F.]
*PRACTICE AREAS: Energy Law; Antitrust Law.
Palmeter, N. David, (AV) ....'38 '63 C.823 A.B. L.145 J.D. [Powell,G.F.&M.]
*PRACTICE AREAS: International Trade Law.

Pambianco, Robert V. '— '98 C.397 B.A. L.127 J.D.
(adm. in MD; not adm. in DC) [Ⓐ Kilpatrick S.]
*PRACTICE AREAS: Antitrust.
Pan, Eric J. .... '72 '99 C&L.309 A.B., J.D. [Ⓐ Covington&B.]
Pan, Susan Perng .... '69 '95 C.893 B.S.E.E. L.273 J.D. [Sughrue M.] (See Pat. Sect.)
*PRACTICE AREAS: Intellectual Property Law.
Panagakos, Elaine A. .... '62 '88 C.976 B.A. L.228 J.D. [Ⓐ Ackerson]
*PRACTICE AREAS: Commercial Litigation; Class Actions; Franchise Litigation.
Panagopoulos, Constantinos G. .... '66 '88 C.69 B.A. L.273 J.D. [Ballard S.A.&I.]
*PRACTICE AREAS: Commercial Litigation; Employment Law; Insurance Defense; Fidelity and Surety.
Panahy, Dara A. .... '70 '98 C.893 B.A. L.904 J.D. [Ⓐ Milbank,T.H.&M.]
*PRACTICE AREAS: Space Law; Communications Law; Corporate; Capital Markets.
Panarites, Peter E., (AV) .... '— '59 C.188 B.S. L.276 J.D. [Ⓒ Foley&L.]
*PRACTICE AREAS: Securities Law; Corporate Law.
Pancholy, Sona Navin '71 '95 C&L.94 B.A., J.D.
Assoc Coun., Intl. Mun. Lawyers Assoc.
Pancost, Karen B. ... '49 '76 C.477 A.B. L.228 J.D. Sr. Atty., Washington Gas Light Co.
Pande, Nalini K. .... '— '97 C.674 A.B. L.309 J.D. [Ⓐ Foley&L.]
*PRACTICE AREAS: Health Law; Regulatory Law.
Pandohie-Johnson, Lisa P. '73 '00 C.976 B.A. L.276 J.D.
(adm. in MD; not adm. in DC) [Ⓐ Sonnenschein N.&R.]
*PRACTICE AREAS: Patent Litigation; Litigation.
Pané, Anna Campo .... '70 '97 C.1113 B.A. L.94 J.D. [Ⓐ Lotstein B.]
*PRACTICE AREAS: Mortgage Banking Law.
Pangas, Harry S. '71 '97 C.823 B.S. L.861 J.D.
(adm. in NY; not adm. in DC) [Ⓐ Dow,L.&A.]

Pangia, Michael J., Law Offices of, (AV) '42 '67 C.1027 B.S. L.724 J.D. BR
1717 N Street, N.W., 20036
Telephone: 202-955-6450 Fax: 202-955-9444
Email: Michael.Pangia@Verizon.Net URL: http://www.lawyers.com/aviation
***PRACTICE AREAS: Aviation Accidents; Aviation Injuries; Aviation Torts; Helicopter Litigation; Marine Law.**
Aviation, Automobile, Maritime, Railroad and Transportation Litigation, Medical Malpractice, Product Liability, Negligence, Civil and Administrative Trials and Appeals in all Courts including Multi-National and Multi-District Tort Disasters, U.S. and Foreign Personal Injuries and Wrongful Deaths.
See Professional Biographies, WASHINGTON, DISTRICT OF COLUMBIA

Panigrahi, Julie J. '72 '00 C.367 B.A. L.659 J.D.
(adm. in NY; not adm. in DC) [Ⓐ Fried,F.H.S.&J.]
*PRACTICE AREAS: Corporate Law.
Panitch, Gerson S. '63 '88 C&L.966 B.S.I.E., J.D.
[Finnegan,H.F.G.&D.] (See Pat. Sect.)
*PRACTICE AREAS: Intellectual Property Portfolio Management; Medical Patents; Patent Litigation; Patent Protection.
Pankau, Anne Frances ....'— '80 C.912 B.A. L.477 J.D. Assoc. Gen. Coun., Fannie Mae
*RESPONSIBILITIES: Executive and Employee Benefits.
Pankey, David H. .... '52 '76 C.692 B.A. L.976 J.D. [McGuirewoods]
*PRACTICE AREAS: Securities Litigation; Corporate Finance; Securities; Energy; Utility Law.
Pankratz, Jeffrey R. .... '60 '91 C.1074 B.S. L.1119 J.D. [Ⓐ Venable,A.B.H.&C.]
*PRACTICE AREAS: Affordable Housing; Community Development; Business Law; Tax Law; Real Estate.
Pannell, Susan J. .... '55 '87 C.454 B.A. L.276 J.D. 1133 21st St Nw # 450
Panner, Aaron M. .... '65 '95 C.976 B.S. L.309 J.D. [Kellogg,H.H.T.&E.]
*PRACTICE AREAS: Telecommunications; Litigation.
Panopoulos, Frank .... '57 '92 C.433 B.A. L.178 J.D. [Ⓐ White&C.]
Pantaleo, Peter S. .... '— '76 C.964 B.S. L.585 J.D. [Verner,L.B.M.&H.]
*PRACTICE AREAS: Labor Law; Employment Law; Civil Rights.
Pantano, Paul J., Jr., (AV) .... '55 '80 C.855 B.A. L.228 J.D. [McDermott,W.&E.]
Pantelis, Irene N. '70 '97 C.446 B.A. L.276 J.D.
Asst. Coun., National Treasury Employees Union
Pantzer, Daniel .... '72 '98 C.553 B.A. L.1292 J.D. Legal Asst. Atty.
Panzer, David S. '73 '98 C.674 A.B. L.273 J.D.
(adm. in VA; not adm. in DC) 900 Seventeenth Street, N.W., Suite 900
Paoletta, Patricia J. .... '62 '88 C.93 B.A. L.276 J.D. [Wiley R.&F.]
*PRACTICE AREAS: International Telecommunications Law; Trade Policy; Government Relations.
Paolino, Catherine I. '70 '96 C.551 B.A. L.184 J.D.
(adm. in MA; not adm. in DC) Assoc. Coun., American Ins. Assn.
*RESPONSIBILITIES: Insurance; Legislative and Regulatory Drafting; Litigation.
Papadopoulos, Mark E. .... '73 '99 C.311 B.A. L.188 J.D. [Ⓐ Gibson,D.&C.]
*PRACTICE AREAS: Litigation; Appellate Practice; Constitutional Law.
Papandrea, John F. .... '72 '98 C.145 B.A. L.976 J.D. [Ⓐ Wiley R.&F.]
Papandrea, Mary-Rose .... '70 '95 C.976 B.A. L.145 J.D. [Ⓐ Williams&C.]
Papavizas, Constantine G. .... '57 '84 C.276 B.A. L.273 J.D. [Winston&S.]
*PRACTICE AREAS: Health Care; Maritime Law; Securities.
Pape, Stuart M., (AV) .... '48 '73 C&L.893 B.A., J.D. [Patton B.]
Paper, Lewis J., (AV) .... '46 '71 C.477 B.A. L.309 J.D. [Dickstein S.M.&O.]
*PRACTICE AREAS: Communications Law; Litigation; Government Relations Law.
Papez, Matthew E. .... '74 '99 C.549 B.S. L.309 J.D. [Ⓐ Kirkland&E.]
*PRACTICE AREAS: Litigation.
Papiewski, Suzanne M. ....'60 '91 C.339 B.A. L.276 J.D. Assoc. Gen. Coun., Fannie Mae
*RESPONSIBILITIES: Federal Taxation; Financial Transactions; Financial Products.
Papkin, Robert D., (AV) .... '33 '57 C&L.309 A.B., LL.B. [Squire,S.&D.]
*PRACTICE AREAS: Regulatory Affairs; Aviation.
Pappas, George F., (AV) '50 '76 C&L.446 B.A., J.D.
[Venable,A.B.H.&C.] (⊙Balt., MD)
*PRACTICE AREAS: Intellectual Property and Technology Related Litigation and Counseling; Litigation.
Pappas, Michael D. .... '70 '95 C.276 B.A. L.446 J.D. [Ⓐ Dechert]
*PRACTICE AREAS: Financial Services Law; Investment Management.
Papson, Thomas C., (AV) .... '51 '77 C.659 B.A. L.276 J.D. [McKenna&C.]
*PRACTICE AREAS: Commercial Litigation; Government Contract Litigation; Administrative.
Paquinelli, Emily .... '— '01 C.216 B.A. L.273 J.D. [Ⓐ Arnold&P.]
Paracuellos, Amanda J. .... '71 '96 C.477 A.B. L.352 J.D. [Ⓐ Arnold&P.]
*PRACTICE AREAS: Corporate Law; Securities.
Paradine, Danielle Helen ....'— '98 C.347 B.A. L.273 J.D. [Ⓐ Morgan,L.&B.]
Paradise, Theodore Joseph '74 '00 C.336 B.A. L.276 J.D.
(adm. in VA; not adm. in DC) [Ⓐ Swidler B.S.F.]
*PRACTICE AREAS: Energy Law.
Paradiso, Joseph C., (AV) '50 '78
C.30 B.A. L.1209 J.D. [Paradiso,D.T.&O.] (⊙Bethesda, MD)
*PRACTICE AREAS: Family Law; Civil Litigation; Mediation.

Paradiso, Dack, Taub & Oler, P.C., (AV)
Sixth Floor, 1201 Connecticut Avenue, N.W., 20036 ⊙
Telephone: 301-986-7900
Joseph C. Paradiso; Leonard J. Dack; Robin B. Taub.
Family Law, Domestic Relations, Divorce, Custody, Marital Property, Adoption, Domestic Violence, Visitation, Marital Agreements, Separation Agreements, Name Changes, Paternity, Alimony, Arbitration and Mediation, Negligence, Personal Injury.
Bethesda, Maryland Office: Suite 640, 3 Bethesda Metro Center. Telephone: 301-986-7900. Fax: 301-986-4001.
Vienna, Virginia Office: Suite 540, 8045 Leesburg Pike. Telephone: 703-917-9030. Fax: 703-917-9060.
See Professional Biographies, WASHINGTON, DISTRICT OF COLUMBIA

Parascandola, Christina Bechak ....'— '00 C.30 B.A. L.904 J.D. [Ⓐ Collier S.S.]
*PRACTICE AREAS: Administrative Law; Environmental Law.
Parcher, Laura Tuell ....'69 '96 C.1356 B.A. L.276 J.D. [Ⓐ Jones,D.R.&P.]
Parchment, Monica Charisse ..... '70 '96 C.524 B.A. L.273 J.D. [Ⓐ Venable,A.B.H.&C.]
*PRACTICE AREAS: Government Contracts; Technology Law; Civil Litigation.
Pardee, Katherine '55 '97 C.446 B.A. L.128
(adm. in MD; not adm. in DC) Coun., American Academy of Actuaries
Pardo, Jason A. ...'70 '95 C.93 B.S. L.128 J.D. [Ⓐ Jackson&C.] (⊙Balt., Rockville, MD)
*PRACTICE AREAS: Business Litigation; Commercial Litigation; Health Care Litigation.
Pardo, Mark E. '66 '94
(adm. in NY; not adm. in DC) [Ⓐ Grunfeld,D.L.&K.]
Pardo, Michelle Ciszak ....'70 '97 C.423 B.A. L.128 J.D. [Ⓐ Fulbright&J.]
*PRACTICE AREAS: Litigation.
Parelskin, Howard A., (AV) .... '52 '77 C.659 B.S. L.813 J.D. [Ⓒ Mayer,B.&P.]
*PRACTICE AREAS: Real Estate Transactions; Real Estate Finance.
Parent, Heather L. '75 '01 C.820 B.S. L.1194 J.D.
(adm. in MA; not adm. in DC) [Ⓐ Bonner K.T.&C.]
*PRACTICE AREAS: Insurance Defense; Environmental Law.
Paretzky, Raymond .... '62 '90 C.994 B.A. L.976 J.D. [Ⓒ Kaye S.]
*PRACTICE AREAS: International Trade.
Parfitt, Michelle A., (AV) ....'54 '81 C.588 B.S. L.1019 J.D. [Ashcraft&G.]
*PRACTICE AREAS: Pharmaceutical & Medical Device Litigation; Products Liability; Medical Malpractice.
Pargament, Jeffrey J., (BV) .... '57 '84 C.188 B.S. L.273 J.D. [Piliero,M.&P.] ⊙
*PRACTICE AREAS: Labor and Employment; Civil Litigation; Trade and Professional Associations.
Parham, Monica G. ....'68 '93 C.575 B.A. L.976 J.D. [Ⓒ Crowell&M.]
Pari, Joseph M. .... '62 '87 C.676 B.S. L.93 J.D. [Dewey B.]
*PRACTICE AREAS: Corporate Taxation.
Parikh, Pooja Seth '73 '00 C.012 B.A. L.276 J.D.
Staff Atty./Dep. Dir. India Prog., Environmental Law Institute
*RESPONSIBILITIES: Developing India Program; Judicial Training Workshops in India.
Parini, Michael J. ....'74 '00 C&L.276 B.A., J.D. [Ⓐ Akin,G.S.H.&F.]
*PRACTICE AREAS: Health Care.
Pariser, Daniel S. .... '73 '99 C.659 B.A. L.309 J.D. [Ⓐ Arnold&P.]
*PRACTICE AREAS: Products Liability Litigation.
Pariser, Jeffrey D. .... '65 '93 C.893 B.A. L.569 J.D. [Hogan&H.]
*PRACTICE AREAS: Litigation.
Parisi, Barbara E. .... '72 '97 C&L.893 B.A., J.D. [Ⓐ Thompson H.]
*PRACTICE AREAS: Consumer Product Safety.
Parisi, Gregory F. .... '— '00 C.692 B.A. L.276 J.D. [Ⓐ Hogan&H.]
Parisotto, Ronald D. ....'64 '98 C.038 B.Math. L.823 J.D. [Ⓐ Mayer,B.&P.]
Parizek, George B. ....'68 '94 C.645 B.A. L.284 J.D. [Ⓐ Fried,F.H.S.&J.]
*PRACTICE AREAS: Corporate Law; Securities.
Park, Alexander J. .... '71 '96 C&L.273 B.A.A., J.D. [Ⓐ Hogan&H.]
*PRACTICE AREAS: Capital Markets; Private Equity; Mergers and Acquisitions; General Corporate Law; Securities.
Park, Collin W. ....'— '97 C&L.893 B.E., J.D. [Ⓐ Morgan,L.&B.] (Pat.)
Park, Elizabeth R. .... '— '00 C.860 B.S. L.273 J.D. [Ⓐ Latham&W.]
Park, Hae-Chan '62 '92 L.999 LL.B.
(adm. in NY; not adm. in DC) [Ⓐ Howrey S.A.&W.]
*PRACTICE AREAS: Intellectual Property Law; International Trade Law.
Park, Hong J. '73 '00 C.976 B.A. L.178 J.D.
(adm. in MD; not adm. in DC) [Ⓐ Preston G.E.&R.M.]
*PRACTICE AREAS: Antitrust; Litigation.
Park, Howard F. '58 '87 C.72 B.A. L.966 J.D.
(adm. in WI; not adm. in DC) Grassroots Results
Park, J. David .... '71 '97 C.860 B.A. L.94 J.D. [Ⓐ Akin,G.S.H.&F.]
*PRACTICE AREAS: International Trade.
Park, Jaemin '64 '92 C.112 B.S. L.692 J.D.
(adm. in MD; not adm. in DC) [Akin,G.S.H.&F.]
Park, Richard C. .... '70 '97 C.188 J.D. L.588 J.D. [Ⓐ Fried,F.H.S.&J.]
*PRACTICE AREAS: Antitrust; Telecommunications.
Park-Suk, Hae .... '70 '97 C.893 B.A. L.1209 J.D. [Ⓐ Cleary&K.]
*PRACTICE AREAS: Trademarks; Unfair Competition Law; Copyrights.
Parker, Bryan D. '68 '93 C.861 B.A. L.276 J.D.
(adm. in VA; not adm. in DC) [Ⓐ Shawncoulson]
Parker, Craig W. '49 '80 C.378 B.S. L.128 J.D.
(adm. in MD; not adm. in DC) Gen. Coun., Catholic Univ. of Amer.
Parker, Darrel S. ....'46 '75 [Roundtree,H.&P.]
Parker, David Patton ....'49 '74 C.797 B.A. L.893 J.D. [Dickstein S.M.&O.]
*PRACTICE AREAS: Finance; Venture Capital; Business Transactions; Corporate; Creditors Rights.
Parker, Douglas L. .... '42 '68 C.813 A.B. L.309 J.D. Dir., Institute for Pub. Representation
Parker, Douglas L. .... '69 '97 C.1369 B.A. L.893 J.D. [Ⓐ Mooney,G.B.&S.]
*PRACTICE AREAS: Labor; Labor Arbitration; Litigation; Labor Strikes.
Parker, E. Stuart .... '73 '00 C.16 B.A. L.276 J.D. [Ⓐ Wilmer,C.&P.]
Parker, Elissa A. '46 '70 C.119 B.A. L.665 J.D.
(adm. in PA; not adm. in DC)
Dir., Resch., Policy & Training, Enviromental Law Institute
*RESPONSIBILITIES: U.S. and International Law and Policy.
Parker, Kimberly .... '70 '98 C.674 A.B. L.309 J.D. [Ⓐ Wilmer,C.&P.]
Parker, Phillip D., (AV) .... '47 '75 C.385 A.B. L.893 J.D. [Ⓒ Debevoise&P.]
*PRACTICE AREAS: Securities Regulation and Enforcement; Broker-Dealer Regulation; Securities Litigation; Corporate Investigations.
Parker, Richard G. .... '48 '74 C.112 A.B. L.1494 J.D. [O'Melveny&M.]
*PRACTICE AREAS: Litigation.
Parker, Robert P. .... '60 '84 C.367 B.A. L.659 J.D. [Paul,W.R.W.&G.]
*PRACTICE AREAS: Litigation; International Trade; Federal Administrative Law.
Parker, Stephen L. .... '42 '67 C.31 B.A. L.178 LL.B. [Ober,K.G.&S.]
Parker, Steven C. ....'59 '95 C.1356 B.A. L.976 J.D. [Ⓐ Fried,F.H.S.&J.]
*PRACTICE AREAS: Litigation.
Parker, Tamara R. .... '58 '93 C.1208 B.A. L.976 J.D. [Ⓐ Wallace K.M.&B.]
*PRACTICE AREAS: Civil Litigation; Products Liability; Toxic Torts.
Parkinson, James T. '68 '99 C.282 B.A. L.30 J.D.
(adm. in CA; not adm. in DC) [Ⓐ Beveridge&D.]
*PRACTICE AREAS: Environmental Law; White Collar Crime.
Parks, Edward B., II .... '71 '95 C.999 B.A. L.893 J.D. [Ⓐ Hogan&H.]
*PRACTICE AREAS: Insurance Coverage Litigation; Bankruptcy Litigation.
Parks, Jeanus B., Jr. ....'29 '56 C&L.329 LL.B. Prof. of Law, Emeritus, Howard Univ.
Parks, Jessica L. '53 '80 C.861 B.A. L.838 J.D.
(adm. in NC; not adm. in DC) [Kator,P.&W.]
*PRACTICE AREAS: Federal Employment Law; Whistleblower Litigation; Federal Government Law.
Parks, M. Elizabeth '74 '00
C.1105 B.A. L.846 J.D. 1050 Connecticut Avenue, N.W., Suite 1200
Parks, Russell W., Jr. .... '47 '73 C.855 B.A. L.228 J.D. [Akin,G.S.H.&F.]
*PRACTICE AREAS: Corporate Law.
Parlin, Allison L. ....'69 '95 C.860 B.A. L.659 J.D. [Ⓐ Morgan,L.&B.]
Parlin, C. Christopher, (AV) ....'49 '75 C.976 B.A. L.904 J.D. [Kaye S.]
*PRACTICE AREAS: International Trade.
Parmet, Jeff C. '46 '77 C.188 B.A. L.767 J.D.
(adm. in CA; not adm. in DC) Ptnr., PricewaterhouseCoopers

Parmet, Suzanne ... '65 '92 C.893 B.S. L.659 J.D. 2100 Pennsylvania Ave., N.W.
Parmley, Bruce E., (AV) ... '48 '76 C.610 B.S.C. L.128 J.D. [Hogan&H.]
*PRACTICE AREAS: Commercial Real Estate Law; Commercial Law; Business Law; Leases and Leasing; Real Estate.
Paroutsas, Aspasia '73 '00 C.569 B.A. L.128 J.D.
(adm. in MD; not adm. in DC) [Ⓐ Kelley D.&W.]
*PRACTICE AREAS: Telecommunications.
Parr, D. David, Jr. ... '67 '00 C.692 B.A. L.893 J.D. [Ⓐ Cadwalader,W.&T.]
*PRACTICE AREAS: Real Estate; Public Finance; Securitization.
Parr, Heather Stacey '73 '99 C.260 B.A. L.945 J.D.
(adm. in DE; not adm. in DC) [Ⓐ Sutherland A.&B.]
*PRACTICE AREAS: Corporate Litigation.
Parr, Ross H. ... '72 '99 C.475 B.A. L.945 J.D. [Ⓐ Morgan,L.&B.]
Parris, Lisa Silverman '58 '85 C.696 B.A. L.273 J.D.
(adm. in MD; not adm. in DC) MCI Communications Corp.
Parris, Stanford E. ... '29 '58 C.339 B.S. L.273 J.D. [Ⓒ Dickstein S.M.&O.]
*PRACTICE AREAS: Government; Legislative Law.
Parrish, Ashley Charles ... '72 '98 C.911 B.A. L.145 J.D. [Ⓐ Kirkland&E.]
*PRACTICE AREAS: Litigation; Appellate Practice.
Parrish, Sharon L., (CV) '56 '85 C.172 B.S.B.A. L.326 J.D.
(adm. in TX; not adm. in DC) Asst. Gen. Couns., INTELSAT
Parrish-Dixon, Kenya ... '66 '96 C.1286 B.A. L.945 J.D. [Ⓐ Epstein B.&G.]
*PRACTICE AREAS: Health Care Litigation; Government Contract and Technology Litigation.

Parrott Firm, The
(See Annapolis, Maryland)

Parry, John '48 '75 C.393 B.A. L.910 J.D.
(adm. in NY; not adm. in DC) Dir., Staff, Amer. Bar Assn.
Parry, John T. ... '64 '91 C.674 A.B. L.309 J.D. 725 12th St., N.W.
Parry, Monica L. ... '58 '96 C.436 B.A. L.945 J.D. [Ⓒ Morgan,L.&B.]
Parry, Thomas M. ... '52 '83 C.170 B.A. L.276 J.D. [Marzouk&P.]
*PRACTICE AREAS: Computer Software Law; Software Copyright; Trademark Infringement; Business Law.
Parry and Romani Associates, Inc. ... 233 Constitution Ave., N.E.
Parsazad, Mandana ... '63 '92 C.454 B.A. L.861 J.D. [Ⓐ Baker&H.]
*PRACTICE AREAS: Tax Law; International Taxation.
Parseghian, Lynn E. ... '65 '92 C.659 B.A. L.145 J.D. [Ⓒ O'Melveny&M.]
*PRACTICE AREAS: Litigation; Administrative Law.
Parsky, Laura Haas ... '69 '95 C.976 B.A. L.1066 J.D. [Ⓐ Williams&C.]
Parsons, Barry M. ... '65 '95 C.1113 B.S. L.1209 J.D. [Ⓐ Crowell&M.]
Parsons, Charles C. ... '40 '67 C.846 B.S.M.E. L.30 J.D. [C.C.P.Chrtd.&Assoc.] (Pat.)
Parsons, Mark L. '69 '01 C.611 B.A. L.273 J.D.
(adm. in NY; not adm. in DC) [Ⓐ Thompson C.]
*PRACTICE AREAS: International Trade; Utility Law; Postal Law.
Parsons, Charles C., Chrtd. & Associates ... 126 C St., N.W. (Pat.)
Partawi, Suhail '67 '00 C.823 B.S. L.477 J.D.
(adm. in NY; not adm. in DC) [Ⓐ Baker B.]
Partigan, John C., (BV) ... '59 '86 C.950 B.S. L.982 J.D. [Nixon P.]
*PRACTICE AREAS: Business Law; Securities; Mergers and Acquisitions; Telecommunications Law.
Partridge, Anthony ... '29 '57 C&L.309 A.B., LL.B. 5901 32nd St., N.W.‡
Partridge, B. Waring, III ... '44 '81 C.976 B.A. L.128 J.D. [Partridge] ‡
Partridge Group, The, Chartered ... 4935 Quebec St., N.W.
Parver, Alan K. ... '51 '77 C.30 B.A. L.188 J.D. [Powell,G.F.&M.]
*PRACTICE AREAS: Health Care Law; Governmental Relations Law.
Parver, Corrine Propas, (AV) ... '44 '83 C.012 B.P.T. L.904 J.D. [Dickstein S.M.&O.]
*PRACTICE AREAS: Health Care; Administrative Government Relations.
Pascal, Paul L., (AV) ... '37 '66 C.446 B.A. L.273 LL.B. [Pascal&W.]
*PRACTICE AREAS: Lobbying; Labor; Employment; Alcoholic Beverage Control.
Pascal, Robert Frederick '68 '94 C.692 B.A. L.201 J.D.
(adm. in VA; not adm. in DC) 3 Washington Circle‡

Pascal & Weiss, P.C., (AV)
1008 Pennsylvania Avenue, S.E., 20003
Telephone: 202-544-2200 Fax: 202-544-5839
Email: pascalweis@aol.com
Paul L. Pascal; Anton M. Weiss; Kathleen I. Andrews.
General and Civil Litigation. Bankruptcy, Commercial, Corporate, Creditors Rights, Banking, Landlord and Tenant and Real Estate Law, City and Government Regulations, Labor and Employment, Alcoholic Beverage Control, Personal Injury.
See Professional Biographies, WASHINGTON, DISTRICT OF COLUMBIA

Paschal, Evangeline C. ... '70 '95 C.813 B.A. L.846 J.D. [Ⓒ Akin,G.S.H.&F.]
*PRACTICE AREAS: Litigation.
Paschal, Richard A. ... '65 '00 C.575 A.B. L.893 J.D. [Ⓐ Shea&G.]
Paschall, Samuel S. ... '55 '81 C.893 B.A. L.309 J.D. Asst. Dean, Howard Univ.
Pasco, Richard E. ... '55 '83 C.911 B.S. L.546 J.D. [Ⓐ McLeod,W.&M.]
*PRACTICE AREAS: Legislative Practice; Food and Agriculture Law.
Pasekoff, Marc Eric ... '67 '92 C.893 B.A. L.260 J.D. [Ⓐ Bode&G.]
*PRACTICE AREAS: Civil Litigation; Commercial Litigation.
Pashkoff, Dana Barrie ... '72 '97 C.446 B.A. L.273 J.D. [Ⓐ McKenna&C.]
*PRACTICE AREAS: Government Contracts; Information Security; Privacy.
Pashkoff, Lionel E., (AV) ... '43 '68 C.446 B.A. L.273 J.D. [Ⓒ Proskauer R.]
Pashkoff, Paul H. ... '72 '97 C.477 B.A. L.273 J.D. [Ⓐ Fried,F.H.S.&J.]
*PRACTICE AREAS: Securities Law.
Pass, Caryn G. ... '59 '85 C.446 B.S. L.930 J.D. [Krupin O.]
*PRACTICE AREAS: Labor Law; Employment Law.
Passaic, Joseph G., Jr. ... '53 '79 C.645 B.A. L.205 J.D. [Patton B.]
Passananti, Mari J. '73 '99 C.690 B.A. L.276 J.D.
(adm. in VA; not adm. in DC) Suite 900
Passman, Edward H., (AV) ... '39 '68 C.1040 B.B.A. L.309 J.D. [Passman&K.]
*PRACTICE AREAS: Federal Employment Law; Federal Civil Service; Equal Employment Opportunity Law; Labor Law; Retirement.

Passman & Kaplan, PC, (AV)
1090 Vermont Avenue, N.W., Suite 500, 20005
Telephone: 202-789-0100 Fax: 202-789-0101
Email: inquiry@passmanandkaplan.com URL: http://www.lawyers.com/passman&kaplan
Edward H. Passman; Joseph V. Kaplan; James M. Eisenmann. Senior Associates: Kristin D. Alden; Sandra Mazliah. Associates: Tanisha M. Cole; Daniel A. Perez (Not admitted in DC).
Federal Government Civil Service Law, D.C. Civil Service, Civil Rights, Employment Law, Employee Benefits, Labor Law, Unfair Labor Practices, Wrongful Termination, Age Discrimination, Sexual Harassment, Wage and Hour Law, Security Clearances, Family and Medical Leave Act, congressional Accountability Act, Personnel Policies, Grievances, Disability Discrimination, Employment Contracts, Executive Compensation, ERISA, Health Benefits, Retirement Benefits.
See Professional Biographies, WASHINGTON, DISTRICT OF COLUMBIA

Pasternak, Arthur David ... '58 '83 C.103 B.A. L.976 J.D. [Gibson,D.&C.]
Pastor, Nakita M. '— '00 C.94 B.A. L.30 J.D.
(adm. in MD; not adm. in DC) [Ⓐ Goodwin P.]
Pate, Michael L., (AV) ... '51 '76 C.847 B.S. L.846 J.D. [Bracewell&P.]
*PRACTICE AREAS: Federal and State Taxation; Energy; Environmental; Legislation.
Patek, Jewell '71 '97 C.934 B.A. L.502 J.D.
(adm. in MO; not adm. in DC) 1407 Consworth HOB

Patel, Aarti J. ... '74 '98 C.362 B.B.A. L.1365 J.D. [Ⓐ Hogan&H.]
*PRACTICE AREAS: Securities; Mergers, Acquisitions and Divestitures; Corporate Law.
Patel, Jennifer O. ... '— '99 C.877 B.A. L.276 J.D. [Ⓐ Latham&W.]
Patel, Nikesh R. ... '71 '96 C.259 B.S. L.276 J.D. [Ⓐ Baker B.]
Patenaude, Craig W. '59 '87 C.103 B.A. L.770 J.D.
(adm. in CA; not adm. in DC) ULLICO Inc.
*RESPONSIBILITIES: Employment; Employee Benefits; ERISA; Labor; Corporate.
Pater, Matthew A. ... '72 '97 C.692 B.S. L.472 J.D. [Ⓐ Swidler B.S.F.]
*PRACTICE AREAS: Intellectual Property.
Patera Sterling, Lisa M. ... '67 '98 C.546 B.A. L.128 J.D. [Ⓐ Garvey,S.&B.]
*PRACTICE AREAS: Communications Law; Media Law; Administrative Law; Trademark and Copyright Law; Internet Law.
Pathak, Ajay S. ... '— '93 C.607 B.S. L.161 J.D. [Ⓐ Banner&W.] (See Pat. Sect.)
*PRACTICE AREAS: Intellectual Property Law; Patents; Biotechnology; Pharmaceutical Intellectual Property; Chemical Intellectual Property.
Patin, Douglas L., (BV) ... '54 '79 C.962 B.A. L.273 J.D. [Spriggs&H.]
*PRACTICE AREAS: Construction Law; Litigation.
Patrich, Kenneth D., (AV) ... '51 '81 C.999 B.A. L.276 J.D. [Wilkinson B.K.]
*PRACTICE AREAS: Telecommunications Law; Administrative Law.
Patrick, Roger W. ... '59 '84 C.119 B.S. L.976 J.D. [Ⓒ Mayer,B.&P.]
*PRACTICE AREAS: Environmental Law.
Patrick, Scott S. ... '63 '96 C.834 B.S.E.E. L.893 J.D. [Ⓐ Dow,L.&A.]

Patrick Henry Cappell & Lewis, LLP
(See Alexandria, Virginia)

Patrizia, Charles A. ... '50 '76 C.575 A.B. L.976 J.D. [Paul,H.J.&W.]
*PRACTICE AREAS: Environmental and Energy Law; Federal and State Regulatory and Permitting Requirements; Electric Utilities; International Trade and Regulation; Commercial Litigation.
Patt, Jacqueline Levasseur ... '71 '99 C&L.446 B.S., J.D. [Ⓐ Venable,A.B.H.&C.]
*PRACTICE AREAS: Trademark Prosecution; Intellectual Property Litigation.
Patten, Thomas L., (AV) ... '— '69 C&L.502 B.S., J.D. [Latham&W.]
*PRACTICE AREAS: Arbitration; Qui Tam Litigation; Public Contract Law; Complex Litigation; White Collar Criminal Defense.
Patterson, A. Krisan '73 '01 C.788 B.A. L.846 J.D.
(adm. in AK; not adm. in DC) [Ⓐ Wilmer,C.&P.]
Patterson, Donald J., Jr. ... '57 '82 C.945 B.A. L.477 J.D. [Beveridge&D.]
*PRACTICE AREAS: Environmental Law; Litigation.
Patterson, Donna E., (AV) ... '49 '81 C&L.976 B.A., J.D. [Arnold&P.]
*PRACTICE AREAS: Antitrust; Competition and Trade; Regulation; Litigation; National Security Law and Policy.
Patterson, Elizabeth H. '45 '74 C.242 A.B. L.128 J.D.
Assoc. Prof. & Assoc. Dean, Georgetown Univ. Law Ctr.
Patterson, Errol R. ... '53 '84 C.679 B.S.M.E. L.276 J.D. [Ⓒ Steptoe&J.]
Patterson, Herbert W. ... '22 '50 C.1027 B.S. L.982 LL.B. 1300 I St., N.W. (Pat.)
Patterson, J. Steven ... '65 '90 C.45 B.S. L.902 J.D. [Akin,G.S.H.&F.]
*PRACTICE AREAS: Corporate Law; Securities.
Patterson, Justin P. '39 '65 C.347 B.S. L.1119 J.D.
(adm. in IN; not adm. in DC) 1849 C Street NW‡
Patterson, Kendrick '66 '96
C.277 B.S.I.E. L.273 J.D. [Ⓐ Sterne,K.G.&F.] (See Pat. Sect.)
*PRACTICE AREAS: Patent; Intellectual Property.
Patterson, Laird D. '42 '67 C.228 A.B. L.659 LL.B.
(adm. in PA; not adm. in DC) Coun., Bethlehem Steel Corp.
Patterson, Lowell H., III ... '59 '98 C.301 B.A. L.692 J.D. [Ⓐ Seyfarth S.]
*PRACTICE AREAS: Creditors Rights; Bankruptcy; Commercial Law.
Patterson, N. Paul '39 '82 C.06 M.S. L.893 J.D.
(adm. in VA; not adm. in DC) Asst. U.S. Atty.
Patterson, Robert B. ... '46 '71 C.502 A.B. L.309 J.D. [Ⓐ Barkats&Assoc.]
Patterson, Roger J. ... '56 '83 C.494 B.E.S. L.145 J.D. [Ⓒ Wilmer,C.&P.]
*PRACTICE AREAS: Corporate Law; Securities.
Patterson, Shaunda A. ... '74 '98 C.302 B.A. L.273 J.D. [Ⓐ Jorden B.]
*PRACTICE AREAS: Litigation; Insurance; Civil Practice.

Pattishall, McAuliffe, Newbury, Hilliard & Geraldson
(See Alexandria, Virginia)

Patton, Douglas J. ... '40 '70 C&L.352 B.A., J.D. [Ⓒ Holland&K.]
*PRACTICE AREAS: Legislative; Land Use; Securitization; Elections.
Patton, Frances A. ... '17 '40 C.363 L.180 LL.B. 3725 Macomb St., N.W.‡
Patton, George Thomas, Jr., (AV) ... '61 '87 C.894 A.B. L.1119 J.D. [Bose M.&E.] ⊙
*PRACTICE AREAS: Litigation; Appellate Practice.
Patton, James R., Jr., (AV) ... '28 '51 C.575 A.B. L.309 J.D. [Patton B.]
Patton, Michael F. '47 '74 C&L.446 B.A., J.D.
(adm. in NY; not adm. in DC) Ernst & Young
Patton, Thomas Earl, (AV) ... '40 '66 C&L.128 A.B., LL.B. [Tighe P.A.T.]
*PRACTICE AREAS: Corporate Law; Finance; Securities; Complex Civil and Criminal Litigation.

Patton Boggs LLP, (AV) BR
2550 M Street, N.W., Suite 500, 20037-1350 ⊙
Telephone: 202-457-6000 Telecopier: 202-457-6315
Email: info@pattonboggs.com URL: http://www.pattonboggs.com
Members of Firm: James R. Patton, Jr.; George Blow (Retired); Joseph L. Brand; Thomas Hale Boggs, Jr.; Timothy J. May; Elliot H. Cole; J. Gordon Arbuckle; David C. Todd; Richard Alan Earle; David B. Robinson; John H. Vogel; Allan Abbot Tuttle; John L. Oberdorfer; Timothy A. Vanderver, Jr.; Middleton A. Martin; Garret G. Rasmussen; James B. Christian, Jr.; David E. Dunn, III; Ronald S. Liebman; J. Kirk Wade; Stuart M. Pape; Steven M. Schneebaum; Cliff Massa III; Shaoul Aslan; Donald V. Moorehead; Frank R. Samolis; George M. Borababy; Jeffrey T. Smith; Katharine R. Boyce; George J. Schutzer; Scott N. Stone; John F. Jonas; Duane Alan Siler; Russell V. Randle; Jean Veeder MacHarg; Dean M. Dilley; John C. Martin; Deborah M. Lodge; Mitchell R. Berger; Donald H. Pearlman; Jeffrey L. Turner; Charles E. Talisman; W. Caffey Norman III; Paul A. J. Wilson; Mary Elizabeth Bosco; Read Kemp McCaffrey; Ross E. Eichberg; Geoffrey G. Davis; Martha M. Kendrick; Kenneth A. Grigg, Jr.; Michael A. Curto; James A. Reeder; Philip S. Kaplan; Daniel E. Waltz; John F. Fithian; Timothy B. Mills; Benjamin L. Ginsberg; Henry Chajet; Mark N. Savit; Robert S. Brams; David J. Farber; Daniel A. Kracov; Benjamin G. Chew; Robert C. Jones; Richard M. Stolbach; Paul C. Besozzi; Stephen Diaz Gavin; J. Jeffrey Craven; Joseph E. Schmitz; Penelope S. Farthing; Edward J. Newberry; Michael J. Schaengold; John J. Deschauer, Jr.; Michael J. Nardotti, Jr.; G. Kendrick Macdowell; Darryl D. Nirenberg; Mary M. Sjoquist; Joseph G. Passaic, Jr.; Florence Weatherly Prioleau; Timothy A. Chorba; Lanny J. Davis; Jonathan R. Yarowsky; Joseph V. Colaianni; Michael T. Platt; George P. Levendis; Sally D. Garr; Stephen J. Kott; William E. Slade; Eric A. Kuwana; Peter D. Robertson; Susan B. Bastress; Susan Mathiascheck; Robert D. Luskin; Douglas C. Proxmire; Stephen H. Sherman; Denise A. Vanison; Jamie S. Gardner; Joseph S. Trapasso; Mark D. Cowan; Leslie T. Thornton; John W. Schryber; C. Donald Johnson, Jr.; Daniel R. Addison; Philip A. Bangert; Philip G. Feigen; Rodney A. Grandon; Robert A. Hager; Clayton Lee Hough; Aubrey A. Rothrock, III; Paul D. Rubin; Anne Slaughter Andrew; V. Heather Sibbison; Rodney E. Slater (Not admitted in DC); Mario V. Mirabelli; Laurence E. Harris (Not admitted in DC); Singleton B. McAllister; Robert J. Horn (Not admitted in DC); Ira Fishman. Associates: Elizabeth E. Ring; Edward S. Wisneski (Not admitted in DC); Jeanne M. Liedtka; Thomas C. Downs; Michael T. Wood; Janet Fitzpatrick Moran; Harold H. Kim; Jon Paul Morris; Elizabeth C. Moeller; Willa B. Perlmutter; Sean Patrick Clancy; Andrew M. Rosenberg; Amy C. Davine; Stephen S. (Todd) Anderson, Jr.; Jennifer J. Spokes; John Spitaleri Shaw; Michael T. Palmer; Michele J. Bianco; Marcus E. Rosenlehner (Not Admitted in the United States) (Foreign Associate); Bing Xu; Laurence E. Stein (Not admitted in DC); Jay L. Eizenstat (Not admitted in DC); Andrew M. Friedman; Amy B. Chasanov (Not admitted in DC); Lisa A. Hunt; Alyssa T. Senzel; Lisa Lavelle Burke; Robert K. Tompkins; Jennifer A. Goldstein; Michael Bloomquist; Andrew Zimmitti; William McGinley (Not admitted in DC); Christopher Hellmich (Not admitted in DC); Karen L. Marangi; David M. Tafuri; Jonathan C. Pavony; Stephanie J. Peters; Matthew F. Stowe (Not admitted in DC); Patrick J. Slevin; Alexandra V. Butler; Courtney Collins Nowell; Crystal Gothard; J. Yost Conner, Jr.; Vincente L. Martinez; Gal N. Kaufman; Michael

(This Listing Continued)

Patton Boggs LLP (Continued)

Guiffre; Matthew D. Cutts (Not admitted in DC); Daniel R. Volkmuth (Not admitted in DC); Michael E. Klein; Uzoamaka S. Emeka; J. Alexander Hershey; Lisa M. Dwyer; Debra M. Laboschin (Not admitted in DC); Raphael J.A. Larson (Not admitted in DC); R. Brian Hendrix; Shannon W. Conway (Not admitted in DC); Robyn M. Underwood; Matthew E. Paul; Ugo Colella; Babak Bagheri; Michael Gold (Not admitted in DC); William L. Nash, III (Not admitted in DC); Marek Drell Gootman (Not admitted in DC); John A. Rosans (Not admitted in DC); Jonathan Edgar (Not admitted in DC); Donald M. Deng (Not admitted in DC); Darren P. Riley (Not admitted in DC); Key Reid (Not admitted in DC); Kevin M. O'Neill (Not admitted in DC); Kathryn W. Hambrick (Not admitted in DC); Kathleen J. Lester; Julie K. Stapel; Benjamin Wood (Not admitted in DC); Kenneth P. Jones; Gordon F. Peery; David J. Weiler; Catherine Sun (Not admitted in DC). Foreign Associate: Wang Zhang (Not admitted in the United States). Of Counsel: John C. Camp; Gregory H. Laughlin (Not admitted in DC); Thomas P. O'Donnell; Anne M. Miano; Graham G. Wisner; Brian C. Lopina; Lansing B. Lee, III; Gregory S. Walden; Thomas L. Siebert; Sean P. Murphy; John D. Austin, Jr.; Nancy A. Murray; Eric N. Olsen (Not admitted in DC); Parker E. Brugge. Public Service Counsel: Melanie K. Gerber.
Languages: Farsi, French, German, Italian, Spanish, Arabic, Indonesian, Portuguese, Persian.
General Practice. Administrative Law, Antitrust and Economic Regulation, Business Law, Construction Law, Environment and Natural Resources, Government Contracts, Health and Consumer Safety, International, Legislative Advocacy, Litigation, Tax, Transportation and Energy.
Anchorage, Alaska Office: Suite 504, 1031 W. Fourth Avenue, 99501. Telephone: 907-277-4900. Facsimile: 907-277-4117.
Louisville, Colorado Office: Suite 200, 867 Coal Creek Circle, 80027. Telephone: 303-379-1100. Facsimile: 303-379-1155.
Dallas, Texas Office: 2001 Ross Avenue, Suite 3000, 75201-2774. Telephone: 214-758-1500. Facsimile: 214-758-1550.
Denver, Colorado Office: Suite 1900, 1660 Lincoln Street, 80264. Telephone: 303-830-1776. Facsimile: 303-894-9239.
McLean, Virginia Office: 8484 Westpark Drive, Suite 900, 22102. Telephone: 703-744-8000. Facsimile: 703-744-8001.

See Professional Biographies, WASHINGTON, DISTRICT OF COLUMBIA

Patusky, Christopher ....'63 '88 C.597 B.A. L.309 J.D. [Mahon P.R.&F.]
Paugh, Wayne Bruce '69 '00
C.1111 B.S.B.A. L.1209 J.D. Intellectual Prop. Owners Assoc.
Pauker, Molly, (AV) '50 '77 C.681 B.A. L.309 J.D.
V.P., Corp. & Legal Affs., Fox Television Stations, Inc.
Paul, Adam C. ....'72 '97 C.1369 B.A. L.128 J.D. [🄰 Kirkpatrick&L.]
*PRACTICE AREAS: Bankruptcy Litigation; Bankruptcy Reorganization; Commercial Litigation; Civil Litigation.
Paul, C. Robert '55 '81 C.659 B.A. L.569 J.D.
(adm. in NY; not adm. in DC) [McDermott,W.&E.]
Paul, George L. ....'67 '93 C.497 B.A. L.309 J.D. [🄰 White&C.]
Paul, John C., (AV) '54 '79 C.103 A.B. L.930 J.D.
[Finnegan,H.F.G.&D.] (See Pat. Sect.)
*PRACTICE AREAS: Intellectual Property Portfolio Management; Intellectual Property Licensing; Patent Litigation; Patent Prosecution.
Paul, Marc A. ....'— '95 C.188 B.A. L.659 J.D. [🄰 Steptoe&J.]
Paul, Marc R. ....'60 '86 C&L.309 A.B., J.D. [Baker&M.]
*PRACTICE AREAS: Corporate Financings (Public and Private); Mergers and Acquisitions; Bank Lending and Other Extensions of Credit (General); Corporate and Partnership Law; Information Technology/Telecommunications.
Paul, Matthew E. ....'65 '93 C.918 B.A. L.893 J.D. [🄰 Patton B.]
Paul, Nancy E. Furman ....'69 '96 C.976 B.A. L.309 J.D. [🄰 Wilmer,C.&P.]
Paul, Robert D. ....'41 '68 C.93 B.A. L.309 LL.B. [White&C.]
*PRACTICE AREAS: Antitrust; Litigation.
Paul, Robert E., (AV) ....'45 '71 C.930 B.A. L.273 J.D. [Zwerdling,P.L.K.T.&D.]
Paul, Scott D. '65 '98 C.184 B.S. L.259 J.D.
(adm. in FL; not adm. in DC; Pat.) [🄰 McDermott,W.&E.]
Paul, William M., (AV) ....'51 '78 C.367 B.A. L.477 J.D. [Covington&B.]

Paul, Hastings, Janofsky & Walker LLP, (AV) 🄱🅁
A Limited Liability Partnership including Professional Corporations
1299 Pennsylvania Avenue, N.W., 20004-2400 ⊙
Telephone: 202-508-9500 Fax: 202-508-9700
URL: http://www.paulhastings.com
Members of Firm: E. Lawrence Barcella, Jr.; Kirby D. Behre; Barbara Berish Brown; William D. DeGrandis; R. Bruce Dickson; E. Donald Elliott; Ralph B. Everett; Scott M. Flicker; John J. Gallagher; Jon A. Geier; Judith Richards Hope; John Griffith Johnson, Jr.; G. Hamilton Loeb; Neal D. Mollen; Thomas R. Mounteer; Carl W. Northrop; Charles A. Patrizia; Bruce D. Ryan; Kenneth M. Willner. Of Counsel: David D. Burns; Claudia Treadwell Callaway; Michelle Weisberg Cohen; Christopher A. Cole; Edwin I. Colodny; Wendell M. Faria; Intra L. Germanis; George R. A. Jones; Thomas J. Knapp; P. Susan Lively; Robert S. Plotkin; Joseph Mark Poerio; Margaret H. Spurlin; Mark A. Stachiw; Gregory R. Watchman; Jenny C. Wu; Gerald H. Yamada. Associates: Quisaira Y. Almanzar; Kathrine L. Calderazzi; Christopher T. Cloutier (Not admitted in DC); Dianne C. Coombs; Christine M. Crowe; Behnam Dayanim; Diana L. Embrey; Judith A. Farrand; Rachel Gagnebin (Not admitted in DC); Lauren T. Hollander (Not admitted in DC); Jennifer L. Hong; Patricia E. Hurt (Not admitted in DC); A. Jeff Ifrah; John P. Isa; Eric R. Keller; Erin Patten Lane; Rikki McCoy (Not admitted in DC); Jennifer Levy Rappaport (Not admitted in DC); Lisa K. Rushton; William P. Scharfenberg; Melissa Cales Schwartz (Not admitted in DC); Anna Lincoln Spradlin; Jocelyn M. Sturdivant; Stephen A. Weisbrod.
Aircraft Finance Practice, Asia-Pacific, Banking and Financial Services, Computer Law, Creditor's Rights and Bankruptcy, Customs, International Trade and Export Control, Emerging Growth and Technology, Energy, Federal Legislative, Healthcare, International Energy/Utility/Infrastructure, International Trade, Internet and Electronic Commerce, Investment Management, Japan Practice for United States-Based Clients, Latin America, Lease and Asset-Based Finance, Mergers and Acquisitions, Project and Infrastructure Finance, Structured Finance and Asset Securitization, Telecommunications and Media, Timber, Paper and Packaging, Trade Regulation and Proprietary Rights, Year 2000, Employee Benefits, Executive Practice, Immigration, Railroad Labor and Employment Law, Accountant's Liability, Alternative Dispute Resolution (ADR), Antidumping, Countervailing Duty and Related Trade Proceedings, Antitrust Litigation and Government Enforcement, Appellate, Entertainment, Environmental, Government Contracts, Insurance Coverage, Intellectual Property, Technology Licensing and Litigation, Trade Secret, Patent Litigation, Securities and Corporate Finance Litigation, White Collar Corporate Criminal Defense, Affordable Housing, Land Use, Real Estate Acquisition and Disposition, Resort, Restaurant and Recreation, Retail Leasing, International Tax and Tax Litigation.
Atlanta, Georgia Office: 24th Floor, 600 Peachtree Street, N.E. Telephone: 404-815-2400.
Los Angeles, California Office: 555 South Flower Street. Telephone: 213-683-6000.
New York, New York Office: 399 Park Avenue. Telephone: 212-318-6000 and 75 East 55th Street. Telephone: 212-318-6000.
Orange County, California Office: 695 Town Center Drive, Costa Mesa. Telephone: 714-668-6200.
San Francisco, California Office: 345 California Street. Telephone: 415-835-1600.
Stamford, Connecticut Office: 1055 Washington Boulevard. Telephone: 203-961-7400.
Tokyo, Japan Office: 27F Ark Mori Building, 12-32, Minato-Ku, Akasaka 1-Chome, P.O. Box 577 . Telephone: (03) 3586-4711.
London, England Office: Tower 42, 25 Old Broad Street. Telephone: +44 (0) 20 7562-4000.

See Professional Biographies, WASHINGTON, DISTRICT OF COLUMBIA

Paul, Weiss, Rifkind, Wharton & Garrison, (AV) 🄱🅁
1615 L Street, NW Suite 1300, 20036-5694 ⊙
Telephone: 202-223-7300 TDD 202-223-7490 Facsimile: 202-223-7420
Email: mailbox@paulweiss.com URL: http://www.paulweiss.com
Resident Partners: Terence J. Fortune; Robert E. Montgomery, Jr.; Robert P. Parker; Warren B. Rudman; Dale M. Sarro; Phillip L. Spector; Stuart G. Steingold. Counsel: Richard S. Elliott; Carl W. Hampe; Jeffrey H. Olson; Laura B. Sherman. Resident Associates: Patrick S. Campbell; Matthew Chavez; Diane C. Gaylor; Gaela K. Gehring-Flores; Ji Lu; Paul Martin (Not admitted in DC); Douglas C. Melcher; Kira A. Merski; Jesse A. Nicol; Kathleen McAuliffe Smith; Matthew H. Wheelock.
International Trade Policy and Regulation, Telecommunications, Multimedia, Computer Law, Internal Corporate Investigations, International and Domestic Project Finance, Corporate and Aircraft

(This Listing Continued)

Paul, Weiss, Rifkind, Wharton & Garrison (Continued)

Finance, Leasing and Federal Administrative, Legislative and Litigation Matters. Foreign Investment, Government Procurement, Antitrust, Energy, Appellate, Education and Civil Rights Law, Intellectual Property.
New York, N.Y. Office: 1285 Avenue of the Americas, 10019-6064. Telephones: 212-373-3000, TDD 212-373-2000. Facsimile: 212-757-3990.
Paris, France Office: 62, rue du Faubourg Saint-Honor é, 75008. Telephone: (33-1) 53.43.14.14. Facsimile: (33-1) 53.43.00.23.
Tokyo, Japan Office: Fukoku Seimei Building, 2-2 Uchisaiwaicho 2-chome, Chiyoda-ku, Tokyo 100-0011, Japan. Telephone: (81-3) 3597-8101. Facsimile: (81-3)3597-8120.
Beijing, China Office: 2918 China World Tower II, No.1 Jianguomenwai Dajie, 100004. Telephone: (86-10) 6505-6822. Facsimile: (86-10) 6505-6830.
Hong Kong, China Office: 12th Floor, Hong Kong Club Building, 3A Chater Road, Central Hong Kong. Telephone: (011-852) 2536-9933. Facsimile: 011 (852) 2536-9622.

See Professional Biographies, WASHINGTON, DISTRICT OF COLUMBIA

Paulding, Mark ....'72 '98 C.674 A.B. L.309 J.D. [🄰 Hogan&H.]
*PRACTICE AREAS: Antitrust; Litigation.
Paule-Carres, Larissa ....'71 '99 C.207 B.A. L.978 J.D. [🄰 Kirkland&E.]
*PRACTICE AREAS: Litigation.
Pauling, Theresa A. ....'57 '91 C.823 B.A. L.994 J.D. U.S. Sentencing Comm.
Paull, Joseph, (BV) ....'19 '51 C.390 A.B. L.537 J.D. 4827 Nebraska Ave., N.W.‡
Paulsen, Margaret E.M. '65 '98 C.918 B.A. L.273 J.D.
(adm. in NY; not adm. in DC) [🄰 Davis P.&W.]
Paulsen, Peter W. ....'60 '94 C.855 B.A. L.309 J.D. [🄲 Crowell&M.]

Paulson & Nace, (AV) 🄱🅁
1814 N Street, N.W., 20036-2404 ⊙
Telephone: 202-463-1999 Fax: 202-223-6824
Email: p&n@lawtort.com URL: http://www.lawyers.com/lawtort
Members of Firm: Richard S. Paulson (1928-1986); Barry J. Nace. Associate: Barry W. Walker (Not admitted in DC).
Negligence, Medical Malpractice, Legal Malpractice, Product Liability and Insurance Law. Trials, Administrative Law. Appellate Advocacy.
Martinsburg, West Virginia Office: 1444 Edwin Miller Boulevard, P.O. Box 1938, 25402. Telephone: 888-529-2628.

See Professional Biographies, WASHINGTON, DISTRICT OF COLUMBIA

Pavageau, Laurent C. ....'70 '96 C&L.228 B.A., J.D. [🄲 Akin,G.S.H.&F.]
*PRACTICE AREAS: Corporate Law.
Pavco, Lucille A. '60 '85 C.728 B.S. L.276 J.D.
Assoc. Gen. Coun., National Public Radio, Inc.
Pave, Margo ....'65 '97 C.976 B.A. L.597 J.D. 1025 Connecticut Ave., N.W.
Pavel, Mary J. ....'65 '92 C.197 B.A. L.911 J.D. [Sonosky,C.S.E.&P.]
Pavelko, Thomas P. '49 '80
C.570 B.S.ChE L.1209 J.D. [Stevens,D.M.&M.] (See Pat. Sect.)
*PRACTICE AREAS: Chemical Patents; Mechanical Patents; Biotechnology Patents.
Pavia, Francisco J. ....'64 '91 C.674 A.B. L.309 J.D. [🄲 Winston&S.]
Pavlick, John J., Jr., (AV) ....'48 '78 C.870 B.S. L.659 J.D. [Venable,A.B.H.&C.]
*PRACTICE AREAS: Government Contracts; Regulatory Law and Compliance; Internal Investigations; Freedom of Information Act; Civil Fraud.
Pavlick, Stephen ....'53 '77 C&L.692 B.S.B.A., J.D. [McDermott,W.&E.]
Pavony, Jonathan C. ....'71 '97 C.260 B.S. L.128 J.D. [🄰 Patton B.]
Pavuk, Matthew A., (AV) ....'54 '80 C.604 B.A. L.276 J.D. [Johnson&P.]
Pawlik, David H. ....'— '92 [🄰 Skadden,A.S.M.&F.]
Pawlow, Jean A. ....'— '89 C.112 B.S. L.309 J.D. [Miller&C.]
*PRACTICE AREAS: Taxation; Tax Controversies; Tax Litigation; Accounting Law; International Taxation.
Pawluk, Michael C. ....'73 '99 C.276 B.S.F.S. L.893 J.D. [🄰 Sutherland A.&B.]
*PRACTICE AREAS: Securities Regulation; Private Placement; Public Offerings; Securities Registration; Mergers and Acquisitions.
Pax, Thomas J. ....'58 '87 C.309 A.L.B. L.93 J.D. [Shaw P.]
*PRACTICE AREAS: Financial Institutions Law.
Paxson, Stacy L. ....'67 '94 C.205 B.S.B.A. L.128 J.D. [🄰 Fried,F.H.S.&J.]
*PRACTICE AREAS: SEC Enforcement; Broker-Dealer Regulation.
Paykel, Neela A. ....'68 '93 C.340 B.A. L.273 J.D. [🄰 Gardner,C.&D.]
*PRACTICE AREAS: Managed Care; Health Law.
Payne, Jacqueline Kathleen ......'72 '97 C.339 B.S. L.477 J.D. Legal Def. of Edu. Fund
Payne, Kenneth E., (AV) '36 '65
C.378 B.S. L.30 J.D. [🄲 Finnegan,H.F.G.&D.] (See Pat. Sect.)
*PRACTICE AREAS: Intellectual Property Litigation; Patent Infringement; Technology Transfers; International Intellectual Property; Mechanical Intellectual Property.
Payne, Patricia L. ....'54 '80 C.477 A.B. L.276 J.D. [Payne&Assoc.]
*PRACTICE AREAS: Finance; Securities Law; Corporate Law; Business Law; Labor and Employment.
Payne, Phillis, (AV) ....'48 '74 C.577 B.A. L.228 J.D. [Connerton&P.]
Payne, Stephen R. '59 '88 C.478 B.A. L.188 J.D.
(adm. in NY; not adm. in DC) [🄰 White&C.]

Payne & Associates
1250 24th Street, N.W., Suite 300, 20037
Telephone: 202-835-1610 Fax: 202-835-1697
Email: Paynelegal@aol.com
Patricia L. Payne.
General Business Law practice including Corporate Transactions, Contracts, Franchising, Licensing, Trademarks, Business Torts, Civil Litigation, Finance, State and Federal Securities Law, Estate Planning and Administration, Labor, Employment.

See Professional Biographies, WASHINGTON, DISTRICT OF COLUMBIA

Paytas, Antoinette D. ....'59 '97 C&L.446 B.S., J.D. [🄰 Thomsen&B.] ⊙
*PRACTICE AREAS: Corporate Law; International Trade; Export Regulation; Business Law.
Payton, John, (AV) ....'46 '77 C.668 B.A. L.309 J.D. [Wilmer,C.&P.]
*PRACTICE AREAS: Civil Practice; Civil Rights.
Payton, Willis C. ....'23 '51 C.574 L.1014 LL.B. 2139 Branch Ave., S.E.
Paz-Soldan, Carlos M. ....'67 '94 C.605 B.A. L.273 J.D. [🄰 Schmeltzer,A.&S.]
*PRACTICE AREAS: Legislative Practice; Natural Resources; Municipal Law.
Pazienza, Marc V. '69 '96 C.216 B.A. L.128 J.D.
(adm. in MD; not adm. in DC) Sr. V.P. & Gen. Coun., Uniglobe Travel
Pazur, Shannon M. '72 '01 C.228 B.A. L.893 J.D.
(adm. in VA; not adm. in DC) [🄰 O'Melveny&M.]
Peacock, Stuart L. ....'62 '87 C.1169 B.A. L.1065 J.D. [Bonner K.T.&C.]
*PRACTICE AREAS: Insurance Coverage Disputes; Commercial Litigation.

Pearce, C. Jack, (AV) '34 '62 C.69 B.A. L.802 LL.B.
1730 K Street, N.W., Suite 304, 20006-3802
Telephone: 202-785-0048 Facsimile: 202-331-3759
Email: washlaw@erols.com
Administrative, Antitrust, Regulatory, Transportation and Corporation.

Pearl, Frank H., (AV) ....'43 '69 C&L.30 B.A., J.D. Pres., Perseus, Inc.
Pearl, Marc A. ....'50 '79 C.930 B.A. L.245 J.D. [Shaw P.]
Pearl, Sara L. '58 '84 C.165 B.A. L.94 J.D.
(adm. in NY; not adm. in DC) Assoc. Gen. Coun., Kaplan Educational Centers, Inc.
Pearlberg, Felicia S. ....'69 '95 C&L.659 B.A., J.D. 1625 Massachusetts Ave.
Pearle, Lynn K., (AV) ....'43 '75 C.788 B.A. L.93 J.D. [Arent F.K.P.&K.]
*PRACTICE AREAS: Estate Planning; Probate Law; Charitable Trusts and Foundations; Taxation (Local, Personal Property, State, Federal, or International) Law; Federal Income, Estate and Gift Taxation Law.

Pearlman, Donald H. ....'35 '60 C.309 A.B. L.976 J.D. [Patton B.]
Pearlman, Jeffrey ....'71 '99 C.910 B.A. L.273 J.D. [Ⓐ Ropes&G.]
*PRACTICE AREAS: Litigation.
Pearlman, Joel '44 '79 C.453 B.S. L.446 J.D.
(adm. in MD; not adm. in DC) [Ⓒ Cole,R.&B.]
Pearlman, Ronald A., (AV) '40 '65 C&L.597 B.A., J.D.
Prof., Georgetown Univ. Law Ctr.
Pearlman, Sandra L. ....'63 '91 C.1145 B.S. L.904 J.D. [Winston&S.]
*PRACTICE AREAS: Labor and Employment; Affirmative Action; Employment Discrimination; Equal Employment Opportunity Law; Fair Employment Practices.
Pearlman, Steven W. ....'66 '92 C.228 B.A. L.477 J.D. 2300 N St. NW

Pearlstein, Paul D., & Associates, (AV) '38 '62 C.659 A.B. L.893 LL.B.
1730 Rhode Island Avenue, N.W., Suite 505, 20036
Telephone: 202-223-5848 Fax: 202-223-8737
Email: merraul@aol.com URL: http://www.pearlstein-law.com
***PRACTICE AREAS: Real Estate; Bankruptcy; Trials; Estate Planning.**
Of Counsel: Alan H. Yamamoto.
Real Estate, Bankruptcy, Estate Planning, Probate, Litigation and Appeals.
See Professional Biographies, WASHINGTON, DISTRICT OF COLUMBIA

Pearsall, Elizabeth ....'64 '94 C.674 B.A. L.846 J.D. [Ⓐ Covington&B.]
Pearson, Gordon ....'61 '95 C.691 B.S. L.178 J.D. [Ⓒ Wilmer,C.&P.]
Pearson, Marilyn A. ....'51 '76 C&L.494 B.A., J.D. [Ⓒ Verner,L.B.M.&H.]
*PRACTICE AREAS: Labor and Employment.
Pearson, Rebecca E. ....'64 '89 C.228 A.B. L.575 J.D. [Ⓒ Venable,A.B.H.&C.]
*PRACTICE AREAS: Public Contract Law.
Pearson, Victoria N. '72 '97 C.574 B.A. L.893 J.D.
(adm. in NC; not adm. in DC) Ct. of App.
Pease, Gregory R. '48 '74 C.602 B.A. L.1119 J.D.
(adm. in IN; not adm. in DC) The Bureau of Natl. Affs., Inc.
Peca, John A., (AV) '52 '77 C.363 B.S. L.930 J.D.
[Climaco,L.P.W.&G.] (⊙Cleve., OH)
Pecau, William G., (AV) '51 '77 C.797 B.A. L.880 J.D.
(adm. in NY; not adm. in DC) [Pennie&E.]
*PRACTICE AREAS: Intellectual Property; Intellectual Property Litigation.
Pechacek, Clarence G., (AV) ....'10 '36 C.350 L.276 LL.B. 3410 Macomb St., N.W.‡
Peck, Alison E. '70 '97 C.108 B.A. L.976 J.D.
(adm. in IN; not adm. in DC) [Ⓐ Boies,S.&F.]
*PRACTICE AREAS: Commercial Litigation; Arbitration; International Arbitration.
Peck, James R. '64 '00 C.112 B.A. L.945 J.D.
(adm. in VA; not adm. in DC) [Ⓐ Pepper H.]
*PRACTICE AREAS: Mortgage Finance; Real Estate; Housing Law.
Peck, Karen L. ....'63 '91 C.259 B.A. L.145 J.D. 725 12th St. N.W.
Peck, Robert S., (AV) ....'53 '79 C.273 B.A. L.161 J.D. 1050 31st St., N.W.
Peckarsky, Peter '47 '77 C.453 B.S.E.E. L.930 J.D.
[Ⓒ Stevens,D.M.&M.] (See Pat. Sect.)
*PRACTICE AREAS: Intellectual Property; Complex Litigation; Antitrust; Corporate Law; Fraud.
Peckham, Rufus W., Jr. ....'28 '58 C.30 B.S. L.904 LL.B. 2501 Q St., N.W.‡
Peckinpaugh, Tim L. ....'59 '86 C.154 B.A. L.276 J.D. [Preston G.E.&R.M.]
*PRACTICE AREAS: Energy Law; Nuclear Power; Environmental Law; Hazardous Waste Cleanup; Legislative Law.
Pedas, George Theodore ....'61 '96 C.1044 B.S. L.273 J.D. 4018 Brandywine St. NW
Pedas, Joanna M. ....'65 '90 C.228 B.A. L.273 J.D. 4018 Brandywine St. NW
Pedersen, Nils E. '60 '89 C.454 B.S.M.E. L.1209 J.D.
[Wenderoth,L.&P.] (See Pat. Sect.)
*PRACTICE AREAS: Mechanical Patents; Electrical Patents; Prosecution; Licensing.
Pederson, Jan M., (P.C.), (AV) ....'49 '75 C.911 B.A. L.329 J.D. [Pederson&F.]
*PRACTICE AREAS: Immigration and Naturalization.
Pederson, Leonard C., Jr., (AV) ....'49 '75 C.911 B.A. L.276 J.D. [Schulze&P.]

Pederson & Freedman, L.L.P., (AV)
A Registered Limited Liability Partnership of Professional Corporations
2001 L Street, N.W., Suite 601, 20036-4910
Telephone: 202-785-1960 Telecopier: 202-785-3815 URL: http://www.ilw.com/pederson
URL: http://www.lawyers.com/dcimmigrationlaw
Jan M. Pederson (P.C.); Roberta Freedman (P.C.). Senior Associate: Montserrat C. Miller.
Languages: Spanish, Chinese, Korean, Bulgarian, French, Russian, Arabic and Portuguese.
Immigration and Nationality Law. Visas for Business and High Tech Professionals, Foreign Health Care Workers, and for J-1 Physicians, Consular Visa Processing at American Embassies and Counsular Posts. Permanent Residency.
See Professional Biographies, WASHINGTON, DISTRICT OF COLUMBIA

Peek, Harold B. ....'34 '73 C.97 B.S. L.30 J.D. 624 A St Se
Peek, Jeffrey L. ....'64 '91 C.445 B.S. L.446 J.D. [Ⓐ T.C.Cardaro&Assoc.] ⊙
Peele, B. Thomas, III ....'47 '83 C.893 B.A. L.309 J.D. [Baker&M.]
*PRACTICE AREAS: Trade Regulations and Customs Law; Litigation; Arbitration and Dispute Resolution; Administrative Law; China Trade.
Peele, Jo Anne ....'— '84 C.221 B.A. L.352 J.D. [Ⓒ Bryan C.]
*PRACTICE AREAS: Litigation; International.
Peer & Gan LLP, (AV) ....1140 Connecticut Ave., N.W.
Peery, Donna R. S. ....'63 '94 C.1 B.B.A. L.845 J.D. [Ⓐ Tobin,O.&E.]
*PRACTICE AREAS: Federal Litigation; Commercial Litigation; Civil Litigation.
Peery, Gordon F. ....'67 '96 C.800 B.A. L.880 J.D. [Ⓐ Patton B.]
Peet, Richard C. ....'— '94 C.311 B.S. L.128 J.D. [Foley&L.] (See Pat. Sect.)
*PRACTICE AREAS: Patents; Trademarks; Licensing; Litigation.
Pegg, William D. '67 '98 C.705 B.S.M.E. L.146 J.D.
(adm. in MD; not adm. in DC; Pat.) [Ⓐ McDermott,W.&E.]
Pehrson, Gordon O., (AV) ....'43 '68 C.945 A.B. L.477 J.D. [Pehrson&Assoc.]

Pehrson & Associates, P.L.L.C., (AV)
4517 Foxhall Crescent, 20006
Telephone: 202-298-5614 Fax: 202-298-9292
Email: gopehrson@aol.com URL: http://www.lawyers.com/pehrson
Gordon O. Pehrson.
Tax Law, Tax Controversies, Tax Planning, Life Insurance, Insurance Companies, Mergers and Acquisitions
See Professional Biographies, WASHINGTON, DISTRICT OF COLUMBIA

Peil, Michael A. ......'73 '98 C.896 B.A. L.188 J.D. Exec. Dir., Inter'l Law Student Assoc.
Peirce, John C., (AV) ....'53 '80 C.976 B.A. L.188 J.D. [Howrey S.A.&W.]
*PRACTICE AREAS: Antitrust; Complex Litigation; Insurance Coverage; Electric Utilities; International Trade Law.
Peisert, Marc O. '72 '00
(adm. in NY; not adm. in DC) [Ⓐ Piper M.R.&W.]
*PRACTICE AREAS: Corporate Law; Venture Capital; Mergers and Acquisitions.
Pelak, Steven W. ....'60 '85 C.373 B.A. L.477 J.D. Asst. Dep. Atty.
Pelavin, Mark J. '61 '91 C.1036 B.A. L.276 J.D.
(adm. in MD; not adm. in DC) Assoc. Dir., VAHL Religious Action Ctr.
Pelesh, Mark L., (AV) ....'53 '78 C.813 A.B. L.976 J.D. [Drinker B.&R.]
*PRACTICE AREAS: Litigation; Education; Administrative Law.
Pelican, Joseph P. ....'60 '85 C.688 B.S. L.178 J.D. [Ⓒ Bingham D.]
*PRACTICE AREAS: Commercial Finance; Corporate Law; Workouts.
Pelkey, Bruce A. ....'54 '82 C.36 B.S. L.990 J.D. 1026 16th St. N.W.

Pelkey, John M., (AV) ....'50 '75 C&L.276 B.S.F.S., J.D. [Ⓒ Garvey,S.&B.]
*PRACTICE AREAS: Communications Law; First Amendment Law; Radio Law; Telecommunications Law; Telephone, Paging and Cellular Law.
Pell, Nancy L., (BV) ....'65 '93 C.893 B.A. L.692 J.D. [Ⓐ Fulbright&J.]
*PRACTICE AREAS: Administrative and Judicial Litigation; Energy; Natural Resources; Government Contracts.

Pellegrin, John D., P.C.
(See Burke, Virginia)

Pellegrini, Carl J. .....'60 '92 C.436 B.S.E.E. L.966 J.D. [Ⓐ Sughrue M.] (See Pat. Sect.)
*PRACTICE AREAS: Intellectual Property Prosecution; Intellectual Property Litigation.
Pelletier, Angela M. ....'— '98 C.623 B.A. L.659 J.D. [Ⓐ Wallace K.M.&B.]
*PRACTICE AREAS: Litigation; Environmental Law; Intellectual Property.
Pelletreau, Robert H. ....'35 '62 C.976 B.A. L.309 LL.B. [Afridi,A.&P.] (⊙Washington)
Pelletreau, Robert H. '35 '62 C.976 B.A. L.309 LL.B.
[Ⓒ Baker B.] & [Afridi,A.&P.] (⊙Washington)
Pelley, Douglas S. ....'70 '96 C.54 B.S. L.188 J.D. [Ⓐ Arnold&P.]
*PRACTICE AREAS: Employee Benefits; Taxation.
Pellow, Wendy Marie '69 '94 C.378 B.A. L.30 J.D.
Leg. Coun., National Association of Insurance Commissioners
Pelosi, Samantha J. ....'71 '98 C.228 B.A. L.893 J.D. [Ⓐ Morrison&F.]
*PRACTICE AREAS: Project Finance; Export Compliance; Corporate Law.
Pelto, Don J., (BV) ....'60 '85 C.446 B.S. L.64 J.D. [McKenna&C.] (Pat.)
*PRACTICE AREAS: Intellectual Property; Biotechnology Patents; Pharmaceutical Patents; Patent Procurement; Patent Litigation.
Pelton, Valerie J. '64 '96 C.880 B.A. L.1148 J.D.
(adm. in VA; not adm. in DC) [Ⓐ De Martino F.R.&V.]
*PRACTICE AREAS: Securities; Mergers and Acquisitions; Corporate Law; Aviation Law.
Peltzman, Lee J., (AV) ....'48 '73 C.831 B.A. L.178 J.D. [Shainis&P.]
*PRACTICE AREAS: Communications Law; Corporate Law; Appellate Practice.
Pelz, Richard K. ....'23 '50 C.597 L.145 J.D. Suite 800, 1615 M St., N.W.
Pemberton, Alan A., (AV) ....'52 '82 C.145 B.A. L.477 J.D. [Ⓒ Covington&B.]
Pemberton, Elizabeth Nelson, (BV) '42 '82
C.597 B.A. L.33 J.D. 801 Pennsylvania Ave., N.W.
Pemberton, James A., (AV) ....'39 '63 C&L.502 A.B., J.D. [King&K.]
Pemberton, John L. '68 '94 C.802 B.A. L.190 J.D.
(adm. in NE; not adm. in DC) 1301 Pennsylvania Ave., N.W.
Pembroke, James D., (AV) ....'48 '75 C.446 B.A. L.276 J.D. [Duncan,W.G.&P.]
*PRACTICE AREAS: Public Utility Law; Antitrust; Energy.
Peña, Bert R. ....'49 '74 C.999 B.A. L.744 J.D. [Hogan&H.]
*PRACTICE AREAS: Legislative; Regulatory Law; International Trade; Agriculture; Tax.
Pence, Brenda J., (BV) '62 '88
C.37 B.A. L.597 J.D. 103 Hart Senate Building, U.S. Senate
Pence, Mary S., (AV) ....'45 '84 C.477 B.S. L.273 J.D. [Feldesman,T.L.F.&B.]
*PRACTICE AREAS: Family Law; Matrimonial Law.
Pender, Robert B., Jr. ....'53 '83 C.478 B.A. L.276 J.D. [Hogan&H.]
*PRACTICE AREAS: Corporate Finance; Project Finance; International Transactions; Mergers and Acquisitions.
Pendergast, William F., (AV) ....'46 '73 C.1044 B.A. L.982 J.D. [Dickinson L.]
*PRACTICE AREAS: White Collar Criminal Law; Complex Business Litigation; Defense Contract Fraud; False Claims Act; Foreign Corrupt Practices Act.
Pendergast, William R., (AV) ......'31 '57 C.698 B.S. L.502 J.D. 1050 Conn. Ave., N.W.
Pendergrass, Alphonso W. ....'29 '59 C&L.789 A.B., LL.B. 666 11th St., N.W.
Pendergrass, John A. '54 '79 C.475 B.S. L.930 J.D.
(adm. in OH; not adm. in DC) Sr. Atty., Environmental Law Institute
*RESPONSIBILITIES: Judicial Education; Environmental Law.
Pendleton, Constance M. ....'70 '98 C.66 B.A. L.893 J.D. [Ⓐ Davis W.T.]
*PRACTICE AREAS: Litigation; First Amendment Law.
Pendleton, Edmund, (AV) ....'22 '48 C.659 B.S. L.276 J.D. 1700 K St., N.W.
Pendleton, Elisabeth M. '41 '68
C.788 B.A. L.309 J.D. Sr. Coun., Intl. Bk. for Reconstr. & Develop.
Pendry, Reita P. ....'45 '73 C.680 A.B. L.575 J.D. Chf. Asst. Fed. Def.
Penman, Janis M. ....'72 '98 C.788 B.A. L.273 J.D. [Ⓐ Baker&H.]
*PRACTICE AREAS: Securities; Corporate Law.
Penn, Nicholas S. ....'59 '87 C&L.276 B.A., J.D. [Leftwich&D.]
Penna, Richard A., (AV) ....'46 '71 C.712 B.S. L.128 J.D. [Van Ness F.]
*PRACTICE AREAS: Clean Air Act; Environmental.
Penner, Eileen ....'63 '89 C.1375 A.B. L.309 J.D. [Mayer,B.&P.]

Pennie & Edmonds LLP, (AV)
1667 K Street, N.W., 20006 ⊙
Telephone: 202-496-4400 Facsimile: 202-496-4444
Email: pennie@info.pennie.com URL: http://www.pennie.com
John C. Pennie (1858-1921); Dean S. Edmonds (1879-1972). Partners: Stanton T. Lawrence, III; Paul J. Zegger (Not admitted in DC); Marcia H. Sundeen; Todd A. Wagner (Not admitted in DC); William G. Pecau (Not admitted in DC). Associates: Nanda K. Alapati; Carl P. Bretscher; Greg P. Roggin; Eric J. Fues; George A. Willinghan, III (Not admitted in DC); Gregory J. Gonsalves (Not admitted in DC); Christopher G. Hayden (Not admitted in DC); Nancy H. Lutz; Max Bachrach (Not admitted in DC); Paul E. Dietze; Serge Sira; Gary Zhang (Not admitted in DC); Seth Alain Watkins; David Chan Lee; Karen G. Horowitz (Not admitted in DC).
Intellectual Property and Technology Litigation including Patent, Trademark, Trade Secrets, Copyright and Unfair Competition Causes, Environmental Law, Communications Law and Related Government Agency Proceedings, Licensing, Arbitration and International Trade Matters. Trials and Appeals in all Federal and State Courts.
New York, New York Office: 1155 Avenue of the Americas. Telephone: 212-790-9090. Facsimile: (212) 869-9741, (212) 869-8864.
Palo Alto, California Office: 3300 Hillview Avenue. Telephone: 650-493-4935. Facsimile: 650-493-5556.
See Professional Biographies, WASHINGTON, DISTRICT OF COLUMBIA

Penniman, William H., (AV) ....'48 '74 C.25 A.B. L.276 J.D. [Ⓒ Sutherland A.&B.]
*PRACTICE AREAS: Energy; Electric Power; Energy Contracts; Regulatory Law; Natural Resources.
Penning, Ann Cooper, Mrs. ....'22 '56 C&L.477 A.B., LL.B. 149 D St., S.E.‡
Pennington, Brenda K. '62 '87 C.329 B.A. L.446 J.D.
(adm. in MD; not adm. in DC) 1250 Connecticut Ave., N.W.
Pennington, Edward A. ....'56 '84 C.923 B.S. L.1209 J.D. [Swidler B.S.F.] (Pat.)
*PRACTICE AREAS: Patent Litigation; Patent Prosecution; Trademark Litigation; Trademark Prosecution.
Pennington, J. Gordon ....'53 '78 C.138 A.B. L.923 J.D. Sr. Coun., El Paso Corp.
Pennington, Jennifer B. ....'66 '93 C.30 B.A. L.692 J.D. [Ⓐ Feldesman,T.L.F.&B.]
*PRACTICE AREAS: Federal Grants Law; Special Education Law; Disability Rights.
Penz, Janet A. ....'48 '88 C.454 B.A. L.128 J.D. Sr. Atty., Washington Gas Light Co.
*RESPONSIBILITIES: Taxation; Employee Benefits.
Pépin, François J. '52 '75 L.018 LL.M.
(adm. in QU; not adm. in DC) Dep. Project Dir., Capital Mkt. Develop. Proj.‡
Pepper, Amelia S. ....'62 '87 C.298 B.A. L.623 J.D. Legal Aid Soc.
Pepper, Vincent A., (AV) ....'27 '51 C.911 B.S. L.276 J.D. [Pepper&C.]
*PRACTICE AREAS: Communications and Media; Broadcast Television; International Telecommunications Law; Telecommunications Contracts.

Pepper & Corazzini, L.L.P., (AV)
1776 K Street, N.W. Suite 200, 20006
Telephone: 202-296-0600 Telecopier: 202-296-5572
Email: pepcor@commlaw.com URL: http://www.commlaw.com

(This Listing Continued)

Pepper & Corazzini, L.L.P. (Continued)

Members of Firm: Vincent A. Pepper; Robert D. L'Heureux (1912-1969); Robert F. Corazzini; Frederick W. Ford (1909-1986); Peter Gutmann; John F. Garziglia; Gregg P. Skall; Howard J. Barr. Associates: Suzanne Spink Goodwyn; Patricia M. Chuh; Joan D. Stewart; Mark Eric Blacknell (Not admitted in DC).
Communications Law, International Telecommunications, Radio, Television, CATV, MMDS, CLEC, ITFS Satellite and Microwave, Mobile Radio, Internet Law, General Practice before Federal Courts and Administrative Agencies.

See Professional Biographies, WASHINGTON, DISTRICT OF COLUMBIA

Pepper Hamilton LLP, (AV) BR
Hamilton Square, 600 Fourteenth Street, N.W., 20005-2004 ⊙
Telephone: 202-220-1200 Telecopy: 202-220-1665
Email: phinfo@pepperlaw.com URL: http://www.pepperlaw.com
Partners: George A. Lehner (Chair, Washington Office Management Committee); Charles H. Carpenter; Gregory C. Dorris; K. Stewart Evans, Jr.; Steven J. Fox; Donald H. Green; Robert B. Joselow; Marc D. Machlin; Edward A. McCullough; John Will Ongman; Daniel I. Prywes; Richard A. Rossman (Not admitted in DC); Sheldon L. Schreiberg; Michael B. Staebler (Not admitted in DC); Martin D. Teckler; Stephen M. Truitt; William J. Walsh; David A. Wormser. Of Counsel: Cynthia A. Metzler. Associates: Edward M. Andries; Christine Waldmann Carmody; Dennis P. Cawley (Not admitted in DC); Scott E. Fireison; Kening Li (Not admitted in DC); O'Kelly E. McWilliams, III; Hyun S. Oh (Not admitted in DC); James R. Peck (Not admitted in DC); Corinne M. Pouliquen; Elizabeth D. Rodriguez; Dawn M. Sims (Not admitted in DC); Jeffrey S. Tibbals; Edna Vassilovski; Rachel H. Wilson (Not admitted in DC).
General Practice.
Philadelphia, Pennsylvania Office: 3000 Two Logan Square, Eighteenth and Arch Streets, 19103-2799. Telephone: 215-981-4000. Fax: 215-981-4750.
Detroit, Michigan Office: 100 Renaissance Center, 36th Floor, 48243-1157. Telephone: 313-259-7110. Fax: 313-259-7926.
New York, New York Office: 1180 Avenue of the Americas, 14th Floor, 10036-8401. Telephone: 212-899-5090. Fax: 212-899-5091.
Pittsburgh, Pennsylvania Office: 500 Grant Street, 50th Floor, 15219-2502. Telephone: 412-454-5000. Fax: 412-281-0717.
Berwyn, Pennsylvania Office: 1235 Westlakes Drive, Suite 400, 19312-2401. Telephone: 610-640-7800. Fax: 610-640-7835.
Cherry Hill, New Jersey Office: LibertyView Building, Suite 420, 457 Haddonfield Road, 08002-2220. Telephone: 856-910-7200. Fax: 856-665-7743.
Harrisburg, Pennsylvania Office: 200 One Keystone Plaza, North Front and Market Streets, P.O. Box 1181, 17108-1181. Telephone: 717-255-1155. Fax: 717-238-0575.
Princeton, New Jersey Office: 300 Alexander Park, 08543-5276. Telephone: 609-452-0808. Fax: 609-452-1147.
Tysons Corner, Virginia Office: 8280 Greensboro Drive, Suite 800, 22102-3807. Telephone: 703-748-3900. Fax: 703-356-0005.
Wilmington, Delaware Office: 1201 Market Street, Suite 1600, P.O. Box 1709, 19899-1709. Telephone: 302-777-6500. Fax: 302-656-8865.

See Professional Biographies, WASHINGTON, DISTRICT OF COLUMBIA

Pera, Lonnie Anne .... '59 '90 C.105 B.A. L.128 J.D. [Zuckert,S.&R.]
*PRACTICE AREAS: Airline Regulation; Aviation Law; International Aviation Law; International Trade.
Peragallo, Alane A. .... '62 '96 C.968 B.A. L.30 J.D. [A Feldesman,T.L.F.&B.]
*PRACTICE AREAS: Family Law; Civil Litigation; Criminal Law.

Perazich, John, (AV) '41 '67 C.604 A.B. L.273 J.D.
1701 Q Street, N.W., 20009-2455
Telephone: 202-986-7500 Facsimile: 202-986-2386
URL: http://www.lawyers.com/perazichlaw
General Civil and Criminal Litigation Practice before Federal and State Courts. Family Law.

See Professional Biographies, WASHINGTON, DISTRICT OF COLUMBIA

Perdue, David K. '51 '79 C.668 B.A. L.228 J.D.
Assoc. Gen. Coun. & Corp. Secy., American Institute of Architects, The
Perdue, Wendy Collins .... '53 '79 C.914 B.A. L.228 J.D. Prof. of Law, Georgetown Univ.
Peregoy, Robert M. '47 '84 C.506 Ed.D. L.1066 J.D.
(adm. in CO; not adm. in DC) 1712 N St., N.W.
Pereles, Susan M. '66 '91 C.659 B.A. L.178 J.D.
(adm. in NJ; not adm. in DC) 1050 Conn. Ave., N.W.‡
Peretti, Brian J. ....'67 '92 C.693 L.904 J.D. [A Shook,H.&B.]
Perez, Antonio F. .... '58 '86 C.309 A.B. L.178 J.D. Catholic Univ.
Perez, Benjamin ....'47 '77 C&L.188 B.S., J.D. Owner, ABACUS Comm. Co.
Perez, Daniel A. '74 '00 C.1175 B.A. L.273 J.D.
(adm. in FL; not adm. in DC) [A Passman&K.]
*PRACTICE AREAS: Employment Law; Federal Civil Service; Equal Employment Opportunity Law; Labor Law.
Perez, Joseph M. ....'50 '93 C.966 B.A. L.1209 J.D. Legis. Analyst, Dept. of Labor
Perez, Ruth .... '68 '94 C.1222 B.Acct. L.188 J.D. 1301 K Street, N.W.
Perez-Pineiro, Rafael '72 '01
(adm. in FL; not adm. in DC) [A Blank R.C.&M.]
*PRACTICE AREAS: Intellectual Property.
Pergament, Stuart P. .... '42 '80 C.1044 B.S.E. L.262 J.D. [Mayer,B.&P.]
Pergola, Michael P. .... '52 '86 C.659 B.A. L.188 J.D. 2445 M St., N.W.
Pergolizzi, Frank J., (AV) ....'59 '84 C.884 B.A. L.896 J.D. [Slover&L.]
Perini, Victor J., Jr. '23 '50 C&L.477 A.B., J.D.
(adm. in MI; not adm. in DC) Highway Users Fed.
Perka, Daniel J. ....'52 '78 C.674 A.B. L.228 J.D. [C Swidler B.S.F.]
*PRACTICE AREAS: Telecommunications; Cable Television; Real Estate.
Perkins, Andrew H. .... '47 '76 C.732 B.A. L.273 J.D. NASD Regulation, Inc.
Perkins, Jennifer S. ....'— '86 C.311 B.A. L.276 J.D. [Arnold&P.]
*PRACTICE AREAS: Real Estate.
Perkins, Martha L. '51 '91 C.1128 B.A. L.356 J.D.
(adm. in MS; not adm. in DC) Asst. Gen. Coun., American Insurance Association
*RESPONSIBILITIES: Draft and Analyze Fidelity and Surety Legislation; Draft Educational Materials; Testify Before Legislative Committees; Fidelity and Surety.
Perkins, Nancy L. .... '56 '88 C&L.309 A.B., J.D. [C Arnold&P.]
*PRACTICE AREAS: International; Litigation; Legislative.
Perkins, Samuel T., (AV) .... '46 '75 C.103 A.B. L.976 J.D. [Steptoe&J.]
*PRACTICE AREAS: Oil and Gas Law; Energy Law; Environmental Regulation; Contract Law.
Perkins, Victoria J., (P.C.), (AV) ....'45 '76 C.705 B.A. L.309 J.D. [Shaw P.]
*PRACTICE AREAS: Real Estate; Corporate; Commercial Finance.

Perkins Coie LLP, (AV) BR
607 Fourteenth Street, N.W., 20005 ⊙
Telephone: 202-628-6600 Facsimile: 202-434-1690
Email: perkins@perkinscoie.com URL: http://www.perkinscoie.com
Partners: Robert F. Bauer; Donald C. Baur; Allen Cannon III; Richard B. Clifford, Jr.; Judith L. Corley; Lee P. Curtis; John M. Devaney; Jeffrey N. Eisenstein (Not admitted in DC); Donald J. Friedman; Mary Rose Hughes; Guy R. Martin; Barry J. Reingold; Kara M. Sacilotto; Yoshihiro Saito; Benjamin S. Sharp; Thomas V. Vakerics; Martin P. Willard; Jeffrey A. Wool (Not admitted in DC). Of Counsel: Margot F. Bester; Wilford H. "Buzz" Fawcett (Also at Boise, Idaho Office); Cassandra F. Lentchner (Not admitted in DC); Helen P. Starr; Ellen L. Weintraub; Lis Wiehl (Not admitted in DC; Also at Seattle, Washington Office); Sloane Anders Wildman. Resident Associates: Kelly A. Cameron; Donald J. Carney; Alyssa Chumnanvech; John F. Clark (Not admitted in DC); James F. Cobb, Jr. (Not admitted in DC); Suzette W. Derrevere; Marc E. Elias; Rebecca H. Gordon (Not admitted in DC); Junhee Kim; Jennifer Allison MacLean; Lalitha Mani (Not admitted in DC); Jason C. Rylander (Not admitted in DC); Brian G. Svoboda; Mark T. Wasden; W. Hartmann Young.
Trial and Appellate Practice, Congressional and Administrative Representation, Government Ethics, Election, Campaign Finance and Lobbying Law, International Trade Law, Aircraft Finance and Leasing, Non-Profit Tax Law, Electronic Commerce, Telecommunications Law, Securities Law,

(This Listing Continued)

Perkins Coie LLP (Continued)

Antitrust, Government Contracts, Environmental, Energy and Natural Resources, International Commercial Transactions, White Collar Crime, Employment Law, Product Liability and Intellectual Property Law.
Anchorage, Alaska Office: 1029 West Third Avenue, Suite 300, 99501-1981. Telephone: 907-279-8561. Facsimile: 907-276-3108.
Menlo Park, California Office: 101 Jefferson Drive, 94025-1114. Telephone: 650-838-4300. Facsimile: 650-838-4350.
San Francisco, California Office: 180 Townsend Street, 3rd Floor, 94107-1909. Telephone: 415-344-7000. Facsimile: 415-344-7050.
Santa Monica, California Office: 1620 26th Street, Sixth Floor, 90404. Telephone: 310-788-9900. Facsimile: 310-788-3399.
Denver, Colorado Office: 1899 Wynkoop, Suite 700, 80202-1043. Telephone: 303-291-2300. Facsimile: 303-291-2400.
Boise, Idaho Office: 251 East Front Street, Suite 400, 83702-7310. Telephone: 208-343-3434. Facsimile: 208-343-3232.
Portland, Oregon Office: 1211 Southwest Fifth Avenue, Suite 1500, 97204-3715. Telephone: 503-727-2000. Facsimile: 503-727-2222.
Bellevue, Washington Office: One Bellevue Center, Suite 1800, 411 - 108th Avenue N.E., 98004-5584. Telephone: 425-453-6980. Facsimile: 425-453-7350.
Olympia, Washington Office: 1110 Capitol Way South, Suite 405, 98501-2251. Telephone: 360-956-3300. Facsimile: 360-956-1208.
Seattle, Washington Office: 1201 Third Avenue, Suite 4800, 98101-3099. Telephone: 206-583-8888. Facsimile: 206-583-8500.
Spokane, Washington Office: North 221 Wall Street, Suite 600, 99201-0826. Telephone: 509-624-2212. Facsimile: 509-458-3399.
Beijing, R.O.C. Office: 1018, Tower 2, China World Trade Center, 1 Jianguomenwai Avenue. 100004. Telephone: 86 10 6505-6399. Facsimile: 86 10 6505-6390.
Hong Kong Office: 17/F, Standard Charter Bank Building, 4 Des Voeux Road Central. Telephone: 852-2878-1177. Facsimile: 852-2524-9988.
Revisers of the Washington Law Digest for this Directory

See Professional Biographies, WASHINGTON, DISTRICT OF COLUMBIA

Perkins, Smith, Cohen & Crowe, LLP, (AV)
1001 Pennsylvania Avenue, N.W., Suite 450N, 20004 ⊙
Telephone: 202-789-8787 Fax: 202-789-4242
Email: dcoffice@pscboston.com URL: http://www.pscboston.com
Partner: Robert B. Crowe (P.C.). Of Counsel: Harvey Kaye (Resident); Charles D. Ablard (Resident).
General Practice, Litigation (All Courts and Agencies), Antitrust, Banking and Finance, Bankruptcy, Biotechnology, Commercial, Computer Law, Copyright, Corporate, Criminal Defense, Domestic Relations, Employment Law, Entertainment, Environmental, Estate Planning, Exempt Organizations, Government Contracts (Federal and State), Government Relations, Immigration, Insurance, Intellectual Property, International Business, Investor Fraud, Patent, Probate, Publishing, Real Estate, Scientific Misconduct, Securities, Taxation, Technology, Telecommunications and Electronic Commerce, Trademark, Trusts and Estates.
Boston, Massachusetts Office: Perkins, Smith & Cohen, LLP, One Beacon Street, 02108. Telephone: 617-854-4000. Fax: 617-854-4040. E-Mail: psc@pscboston.com.
Providence, Rhode Island Office: Tillinghast Licht Perkins Smith & Cohen, LLP, Ten Weybosset Street, 02903. Telephone: 401-456-1200. Fax: 401-456-1210. Email: tlsprov@tlslaw.com.

See Professional Biographies, WASHINGTON, DISTRICT OF COLUMBIA

Perl, Margaret G. ....'75 '00 C.36 B.A. L.276 J.D. [A Bryan C.]
Perle, Linda E. ....'47 '72 C.659 A.B. L.309 J.D. Ctr. for Law & Soc. Policy
Perlik, William R., (AV) ....'25 '52 C.604 B.A. L.976 LL.B. 950 Penn. Ave.,NW
Perlis, Mark L., (AV) ....'52 '78 C.976 B.A. L.309 J.D. [C Dickstein S.M.&O.]
*PRACTICE AREAS: Energy; Taxation.
Perlman, Adam L. .... '72 '97 C.860 B.A. L.659 J.D. [A Williams&C.]
*PRACTICE AREAS: Civil Practice; Commercial Litigation; Libel and Slander; Litigation; Media and First Amendment.
Perlman, Matthew S., (AV) ....'36 '60 C.103 A.B. L.309 LL.B. [Arent F.K.P.&K.]
*PRACTICE AREAS: Construction Law; Government Contracts.
Perlman, Ronald S., (AV) .... '48 '72 C.102 B.A. L.93 J.D. [Zuckert,S.&R.]
*PRACTICE AREAS: Government Contracts.
Perlman, Scott P. .... '60 '87 C.659 B.A. L.309 J.D. [Mayer,B.&P.]
*PRACTICE AREAS: Antitrust; Hart-Scott-Rodino; Litigation.
Perlman, T. S. L., (AV) ....'25 '50 C.674 A.B. L.309 LL.B. 1000 Sixteenth St., N.W.
Perlmutter, Willa B. ....'58 '83 C.518 B.A. L.184 J.D. [A Patton B.]
Perlow, Mark D. ....'64 '91 C.112 A.B. L.976 J.D. [A Kirkpatrick&L.]
*PRACTICE AREAS: Investment Management; Securities; Electronic Commerce; Broker-Dealer Regulation.
Perlstein, William J., (AV) ....'50 '74 C.867 B.A. L.976 J.D. [Wilmer,C.&P.]
*PRACTICE AREAS: Bankruptcy; Civil Practice.
Perman, Corey M. ....'73 '99 C.597 B.S. L.910 J.D. [A Epstein B.&G.]
*PRACTICE AREAS: Health Law; Litigation.
Permut, David L. ....'68 '93 C.197 A.B. L.893 J.D. [Goodwin P.]
*PRACTICE AREAS: Mortgage Banking Law; Antitrust; Class Action Defense.
Permut, Jacob ....'10 '34 C&L.273 A.B., LL.B. 3701 International Dr.
Permut, Philip V., (AV) ....'43 '68 C.611 A.B. L.94 J.D. [C Kelley D.&W.]
*PRACTICE AREAS: Communications; Administrative Law; Litigation.
Perna, James F. ....'47 '76 C.188 A.B. L.1066 J.D. [Krooth&A.]
Perot, Sczerina A. ....'68 '96 C.178 B.A. L.276 J.D. Washington Legal Clinic
Perrelli, Thomas J. .... '66 '91 C.103 A.B. L.309 J.D. [Jenner&B.]
*PRACTICE AREAS: Litigation; Public Policy.
Perrin, Lois K. '71 '96 C.36 B.A./B.S. L.800 J.D.
(adm. in CA; not adm. in DC) [A Morrison&F.]
Perrin, Richard P. .... '46 '74 C.97 B.S. L.564 J.D. [C Dickstein S.M.&O.]
Perrine, James B. ....'70 '95 C.16 B.S. L.976 LL.M. [A Covington&B.]
Perron, Jeannie M. .....'57 '85 C.679 B.S. L.273 J.D. [A Covington&B.] (See Pat. Sect.)
*PRACTICE AREAS: Regulatory Law; Food and Drug Regulation; Regulatory Offences.
Perrone, Gregory ....'67 '97 C.690 B.S.E.E. L.383 J.D. [A Morgan&F.]
*PRACTICE AREAS: Intellectual Property.
Perry, Anne B., (BV) ....'64 '89 C.216 B.A. L.273 J.D. [C Fried,F.H.S.&J.]
*PRACTICE AREAS: Government Contracts Litigation; Civil Litigation.
Perry, B. Dwight, (AV) .... '33 '64 C.623 B.A. L.276 J.D. [Dow,L.&A.]
Perry, Christopher D. ....'65 '97 C.886 B.S. L.930 J.D. [A Thompson H.]
*PRACTICE AREAS: Customs Law; Import and Export Law; International Trade; Transportation; Construction.
Perry, David L. .... '64 '89 C.25 B.A. L.659 J.D. 2001 K Street, N.W.
Perry, Douglas E., (CV) ....'62 '88 C.385 A.B. L.188 J.D. [Fried,F.H.S.&J.]
*PRACTICE AREAS: Government Contracts; Litigation; Export Compliance.
Perry, John W. .... '25 '52 C&L.477 B.S.E., J.D. [Perry&P.]
Perry, Kenneth M. ....'63 '89 C.893 B.A. L.276 J.D. Assoc. Gen. Coun., Fannie Mae
*RESPONSIBILITIES: Securitization; Mortgage-Backed Securities; Mortgage Finance.
Perry, Mary-Helen ....'67 '93 C.914 B.A. L.1066 J.D. [A Jones,D.R.&P.]
Perry, Michelle L. ....'67 '97 C.8 B.A. L.273 J.D. [A Kalijarvi,C.&N.]
*PRACTICE AREAS: Labor and Employment; Civil Rights; Federal Employment Law.
Perry, Robert X., Jr., (AV) ....'32 '59 C.321 A.B. L.276 LL.B. 1666 K St., N.W.
Perry, Rotraud M., (Mrs.) ....'27 '54 C.104 A.B. L.477 LL.B. [Perry&P.]
Perry, Scott M. ....'72 '97 C.705 B.S. L.128 J.D. [A Piper M.R.&W.]
*PRACTICE AREAS: Litigation; Telecommunications; Internet.
Perry, Suzanne B. ....'72 '99 C.188 B.A. L.976 J.D. [A Cleary,G.S.&H.]
Perry, Suzanne M., (AV) '46 '70
C.813 B.A. L.976 LL.B. 1200 New Hampshire Ave., N.W.

Perry, William E., (AV) ... '49 '78 C.610 B.A. L.178 J.D. [Ⓒ Garvey,S.&B.]
*PRACTICE AREAS: International Trade and Investment Law; Customs and Antidumping Law; Intellectual Property Law.
Perry, William K. ... '54 '84 C&L.477 A.B., J.D. [Chadbourne&P.]
Perry, William R. ... '53 '78 C.103 A.B. L.276 J.D. [Sonosky,C.S.E.&P.]
Perry, Wm. D., (AV) ... '31 '62 C.674 A.B. L.273 LL.B. S.C. Johnson & Son, Inc.
Perry & Perry ... 3511 Idaho Ave., N.W. (⊙Storm Lake, IA)
Perschetz, Arthur D. '43 '69 C&L.823 B.A., J.D.
(adm. in NY; not adm. in DC) [Ⓒ Muldoon M.&F.]
*PRACTICE AREAS: Insurance Regulation; Corporate.
Persechino, Nancy M. ... '54 '81 C&L.145 B.A., J.D. [Bingham D.]
*PRACTICE AREAS: Energy; Corporate; Finance.
Persh, Barry ... '74 '99 C.228 A.B. L.893 J.D. [Ⓐ Dow,L.&A.]
Pershkow, Barry I. '66 '93 C.228 B.A. L.861 J.D.
(adm. in PA; not adm. in DC) [Ⓐ Morrison&F.]
*PRACTICE AREAS: Investment Management; Financial Services.
Persian, Eric M., (BV) '59 '84 C.446 B.A. L.1209 J.D.
[Doherty,S.&P.] (⊙Bethesda, MD; Fairfax, VA)
*PRACTICE AREAS: Civil Litigation; Criminal Law; Traffic Law.
Person, John C. ... '52 '83 C&L.477 B.S.C.E., J.D. [Person&C.]
Person & Craver LLP ... 1133 Connecticut Avenue, N.W. Suite 1000
Persons, Oscar N., (AV) '39 '67 C.277 B.I.E. L.245 J.D.
(adm. in GA; not adm. in DC) [Alston&B.] (⊙Atlanta, GA)
*PRACTICE AREAS: Securities Fraud Class Actions; Complex Litigation; Business Torts; Federal Legislative Matters.

Pertierra, José , (AV) '51 '84 C.426 B.A. L.273 J.D.
1010 Vermont Avenue, N.W. Suite 620, 20005
Telephone: 202-783-6666 FAX: 202-347-1925
Email: josepertierra@aol.com URL: http://www.lawyers.com/pertierra
Immigration Law, Civil Litigation, International Human Rights Law. Business Visas, Business Immigration.
See Professional Biographies, WASHINGTON, DISTRICT OF COLUMBIA

Perugini, Maria A. ... '68 '93 C.676 B.A. L.128 J.D. [Littler M.]
*PRACTICE AREAS: Labor and Employment; Litigation.
Pestone, Wayne ... '66 '92 C.881 B.A. L.276 J.D. [Ⓒ Bingham D.]
Petalas, Daniel A. ... '69 '99 C.1077 B.A. L.846 J.D. [Ⓐ Vinson&E.]
*PRACTICE AREAS: Litigation; Media Law; Libel, Slander and Defamation; Products Liability; Torts.
Petcove, Debra L. ... '64 '89 C.659 B.A. L.276 J.D. [Ⓐ Slevin&H.]
*PRACTICE AREAS: Employee Benefits.
Peter, David L. '66 '97 C.273 B.B.A. L.1209 J.D.
(adm. in VA; not adm. in DC) V.P.-CFO, Republic Properties Corp.
Peter, Phillips S. '— '59 C&L.893 B.A., J.D.
(adm. in CA; not adm. in DC) [Ⓒ Reed S.]
*PRACTICE AREAS: Government Relations.
Peterman, Scott D. ... '51 '97 C.646 B.A. L.276 J.D. [Ⓐ Hogan&H.]
*PRACTICE AREAS: Private Equity; Telecoms and High-Tech Transactions; Securities.
Peters, Ann Marie H. ... '49 '76 C.856 A.B. L.128 J.D. [Ⓐ Ballard S.A.&I.]
*PRACTICE AREAS: Real Estate; Commercial Real Estate Finance.
Peters, Aulana L., (AV) '41 '74 C.562 B.A. L.800 J.D.
(adm. in CA; not adm. in DC) [Ⓒ Gibson,D.&C.]
*PRACTICE AREAS: Securities Litigation; Securities Law; SEC Regulatory Matters; Accountant's Liability; Commercial Litigation.
Peters, Diana L.S. '37 '80 C.66 B.A. L.262 J.D.
(adm. in MI; not adm. in DC) 1350 Conn. Ave.
Peters, Eugene F. ... '29 '60 C.276 A.B. L.128 LL.B. [Burwell,P.&H.]
Peters, F. Whitten ... '46 '78 C&L.309 B.A., J.D. [Williams&C.]
*PRACTICE AREAS: Aviation and Aerospace; Civil Practice; Computers and Software; Criminal Law; Government.
Peters, Jeffrey S. ... '70 '96 C.1036 B.A. L.659 J.D. [Arent F.K.P.&K.]
*PRACTICE AREAS: Health Care.
Peters, Julie M. '73 '01 C.276 B.A. L.659 J.D.
(adm. in VA; not adm. in DC) 901 15th Street, N.W.
Peters, M. Elizabeth ... '65 '91 C.228 B.A. L.178 J.D. [Hogan&H.]
*PRACTICE AREAS: International Trade; Immigration Law.
Peters, Mary I. ... '69 '98 C.477 A.B. L.893 J.D. [Ⓐ Zuckerman S.]
*PRACTICE AREAS: Civil Litigation; Criminal Law.
Peters, Richard L. '28 '62 C.128 B.E.E. L.276 J.D.
Chmn. of the Bd., Lamb Seal & Stencil Co., Inc.
Peters, Rise J. ... '61 '87 C.945 B.A. L.309 J.D. [Spiegel&M.]
*PRACTICE AREAS: Aviation Law; Airport Law; Airport Regulation; International Aviation Law; Transportation.
Peters, Stephanie J. ... '64 '91 C.608 B.A. L.276 J.D. [Ⓐ Patton B.]
Petersberger, Ralph I., (AV) ... '33 '58 C&L.309 A.B., LL.B. 1850 K St., N.W.
Petersen, Christian C.D. ... '69 '98 C.112 B.A. L.94 J.D. [Ⓐ Wilmer,C.&P.]
Petersen, Erik Anders ... '71 '96 C&L.893 B.A., J.D. [Ⓐ Shaw P.]
*PRACTICE AREAS: Intellectual Property; Licensing; Trademarks; Copyrights; Licensing.
Petersen, L. Chris '56 '84 C.910 B.A. L.276 J.D.
(adm. in VA; not adm. in DC) [Ⓒ Morris,M.&M.] (⊙Atlanta, GA)
*PRACTICE AREAS: Insurance Regulation; Health Care.
Petersen, Matthew S. ... '— '99 C.101 B.A. L.893 J.D. [Ⓐ Wiley R.&F.]
Petersen, Rafe ... '70 '97 C.319 B.A. L.273 J.D. [Ⓐ Holland&K.]
*PRACTICE AREAS: Environmental.
Petersen, Susan M. '58 '97 C.959 B.A. L.180 J.D.
(adm. in MD; not adm. in DC) [Ⓐ Clifford C.R.&W.]
*PRACTICE AREAS: Securities.
Peterson, Bruce D. ... '56 '82 C.1106 B.A. L.602 J.D. [Hunton&W.]
*PRACTICE AREAS: Project Finance.
Peterson, Cathleen P. ... '64 '91 C.878 B.A. L.659 J.D. [Ⓒ Wilmer,C.&P.]
*PRACTICE AREAS: Aviation Defense; Government Contracts; Administrative Law.
Peterson, Charles Dirk ... '— '90 C.862 B.A. L.910 J.D. [Ⓒ Kirkpatrick&L.]
*PRACTICE AREAS: Securities; Corporate.
Peterson, Charles H. ... '38 '74 C.871 B.S. L.813 J.D. [Shaw P.]
Peterson, Charles W., Jr. '50 '91 C.910 B.S.E.E. L.273 J.D.
(adm. in NY; not adm. in DC; Pat.) [Fitch,E.T.&F.]
Peterson, Dan M. ... '51 '78 C.352 B.A. L.309 J.D. [Fulbright&J.]
*PRACTICE AREAS: Health Care; Litigation.
Peterson, Frank K. ... '43 '81 C.871 B.S. L.276 J.D. [Holland&K.]
*PRACTICE AREAS: Government Contracts; Telecommunications; Information Technology.
Peterson, Jaqualin Friend ... '66 '92 C&L.878 B.S., J.D. [Ⓐ Shaw P.]
*PRACTICE AREAS: Communications.
Peterson, Kathleen A. ... '75 '00 C.1372 B.A. L.94 J.D. [Ⓐ Epstein B.&G.]
*PRACTICE AREAS: Health Law.
Peterson, Laura Bennett '51 '83 C.674 A.B. L.813 J.D.
(adm. in NY; not adm. in DC) 700 New Hampshire Ave.
Peterson, Matthew D. ... '68 '94 C.30 B.A. L.569 J.D. [Foxkiser]
*PRACTICE AREAS: Food and Drug Regulation; Health Law; Litigation.
Peterson, Richard T. '54 '95 C.178 B.S. L.276 J.D.
(adm. in VA; not adm. in DC; Pat.) [Ⓐ Kilpatrick S.]
*PRACTICE AREAS: Intellectual Property Litigation.
Peterson, Robert A. ... '52 '84 C&L.309 A.B., J.D. MCI Communications Corp.
Peterson, Stephen L., (AV) '44 '74
C.768 B.S. L.117 J.D. [Finnegan,H.F.G.&D.] (See Pat. Sect.)
*PRACTICE AREAS: Patent Prosecution; Patent Litigation; Trade Secrets.
Peterson, Thomas L. ... '47 '85 C.980 B.S. L.1003 J.D. [Banner&W.] (See Pat. Sect.)
*PRACTICE AREAS: Intellectual Property Law; Patents; Intellectual Property Licensing; Patent Prosecution; Computer and Software Patents.
Peterson, Timothy P. ... '69 '99 C.473 A.B. L.276 J.D. [Ⓐ Clifford C.R.&W.]
*PRACTICE AREAS: Securities; Securities Litigation; White Collar Crime.
Peterson, Todd D. '51 '76 C.103 A.B. L.477 J.D.
Prof. of Law, George Washington Univ.
Peterson, Woody N., (AV) ... '48 '77 C&L.309 A.B., J.D. [Dickstein S.M.&O.]
*PRACTICE AREAS: Litigation; Civil Litigation; Appellate Practice; Employee Rights.
Peterson & Basha, PLC, (AV) ... 1825 I Street, N.W., Suite 400 (⊙Vienna, VA)
Petesch, Peter J. ... '60 '85 C.477 A.B. L.276 J.D. [Ford&H.]
*PRACTICE AREAS: Discrimination; Employment Termination; Executive Employment Law; Labor Relations; Disability and Workplace Harassment Law.
Petito, Christopher S. ... '55 '82 C&L.976 B.A., J.D. [Jorden B.]
*PRACTICE AREAS: Securities Law; Insurance; Securities Regulation.
Petitpas, Michael R. '73 '01 C.309 A.B. L.178 J.D.
(adm. in NY; not adm. in DC) [Ⓐ Skadden,A.S.M.&F.]
*PRACTICE AREAS: Tax Law.
Petkovich, Michael N. ... '52 '79 C.454 B.S. L.879 J.D. [Jackson L.S.&K.]
Petralia, Joseph '53 '84 C.728 A.B. L.276 J.D.
Assoc. Gen. Coun., Blue Cross & Blue Shield of Natl. Capital Area
Petramalo, Frank, Jr., (AV) ... '43 '69 C.602 A.B. L.276 J.D. [Gordon&B.]
*PRACTICE AREAS: Labor and Employment; Trial Practice; Appellate Practice.
Petras, Mary M. ... '65 '90 C.665 B.A. L.276 J.D. 504 7th Street, S.E.
Petrash, Jeffrey M., (AV) ... '48 '74 C&L.477 A.B., J.D. American Gas Assoc.
Petrela, Elizabeth S. '— '00 C.188 B.S. L.309 J.D.
(adm. in NV; not adm. in DC) [Ⓐ Kirkland&E.]
*PRACTICE AREAS: Appellate Litigation.
Petren, Carol Ann '52 '77 C.93 B.A. L.502 J.D.
(adm. in MO; not adm. in DC) [Wilson,E.M.E.&D.]
*PRACTICE AREAS: Health Care; Medical Malpractice.
Petricone, Michael D. '64 '89 C.860 B.A. L.276 J.D.
(adm. in MD; not adm. in DC) 1101 17th., N.W.
Petrilla, Antony R. ... '71 '95 C.893 B.A. L.309 J.D. Reg. Coun., Covad Comms. Co.
Petrilla, Shannan Stamper ... '72 '97 C.853 B.A. L.309 J.D. [Ⓐ Sutherland A.&B.]
*PRACTICE AREAS: International Taxation; Corporate Taxation; Partnership Taxation.
Petrillo, Joseph J., (AV) ... '48 '73 C&L.276 B.S.F.S., J.D. [Petrillo&P.]
*PRACTICE AREAS: Government Contracts; Bid Protests; Federal Contracts; Information Technology Contracts; Health Care.

Petrillo & Powell, P.L.L.C., (AV)
1101 15th Street, N.W., Suite 605, 20005-2207
Telephone: 202-887-4848 Fax: 202-887-1121
URL: http://www.petrillopowell.com
Joseph J. Petrillo; Karen D. Powell.
Administrative, Litigation and Legislative Practice including Government Contracts, International Trade and Information Law.
See Professional Biographies, WASHINGTON, DISTRICT OF COLUMBIA

Petro, Caroline E. ... '64 '89 C.674 A.B. L.477 J.D. [Piper M.R.&W.]
*PRACTICE AREAS: Commercial Litigation; Employment; Bankruptcy.
Petro, Gina M. ... '75 '99 C.893 B.A. L.477 J.D. [Ⓐ Winston&S.]
Petro, Lee G. ... '70 '97 C.475 B.A. L.128 J.D. [Ⓐ Gardner,C.&D.]
*PRACTICE AREAS: Telecommunications Law; Broadcast Regulation; Wireless Regulation; Telecommunications Transactions; Intellectual Property.
Petroni, Alyson M. '73 '00 C.276 B.S.B.A. L.893 J.D.
(adm. in NY; not adm. in DC) [Ⓐ Dewey B.]
*PRACTICE AREAS: Tax Law.
Petrosinelli, Joseph G. ... '66 '91 C.103 A.B. L.276 J.D. [Williams&C.]
*PRACTICE AREAS: Criminal Defense; Grand Jury Practice; Litigation; Products Liability.
Petruzzelli, Julie A. '57 '83 C.103 Sc.B. L.893 J.D.
[Venable,A.B.H.&C.] (See Pat. Sect.)
*PRACTICE AREAS: Intellectual Property; Complex Civil Litigation.
Petsonk, Carol A. '57 '85 C.170 B.A. L.309 J.D.
(adm. in MA; not adm. in DC) 1875 Connecticut Ave. NW.
Pettit, Mitchell S. '54 '79 C&L.378 B.A., J.D.
(adm. in KS; not adm. in DC) 1133 Connecticut Ave.
Pettit, Robert L., (AV) ... '52 '77 C.502 B.A. L.228 J.D. [Wiley R.&F.]
*PRACTICE AREAS: Communications.
Pettus, Carla G. '59 '84 C.1305 B.S.B.A. L.64 J.D.
(adm. in MD; not adm. in DC) Assoc., Pepco Holdings, Inc.
Petty, Charles W., Jr., (AV) ... '38 '64 C.937 B.S. L.228 LL.B. [Ross&H.]
*PRACTICE AREAS: Corporate Law; Finance; Insurance Regulation; Financial Services Law; Nonprofit and Charitable Organizations.
Petty, Michael D. ... '54 '87 C&L.575 B.A., J.D. [Bennett,T.&C.]
*PRACTICE AREAS: Food and Drug Regulation.
Petty, Thomas R. ... '57 '83 C.93 A.B. L.902 J.D. [Ⓒ Shaw P.]
Pew, James S. ... '62 '90 C.813 B.A. L.659 J.D. Earthjustice Legal Def. Fund
Peyser, Lilyanna L. ... '73 '99 C.893 B.A. L.309 J.D. [Ⓐ Shaw P.]
*PRACTICE AREAS: Corporate Law; Securities; Mergers and Acquisitions.
Peyser, Theodore D., (AV) ... '29 '55 C.674 B.A. L.976 LL.B. [Ⓒ Roberts&H.]
*PRACTICE AREAS: Taxation; Tax Litigation.
Pfadenhauer, Glenn J. ... '59 '87 C.945 B.B.A. L.276 J.D. [Williams&C.]
*PRACTICE AREAS: Commercial Litigation; Criminal Law; Patent Litigation.
Pfaehler, Kenneth J. ... '61 '89 C.893 B.A. L.178 J.D. [Sonnenschein N.&R.]
*PRACTICE AREAS: Litigation; Insurance.
Pfau, Sandra K. ... '62 '88 C.476 B.S. L.273 J.D. 1730 Massachusetts Ave., NW
Pfeifer, Eugene M., (AV) ... '— '67 C.103 B.A. L.276 J.D. [King&S.]
*PRACTICE AREAS: Food and Drug Regulation.
Pfeifer, Michael George ... '46 '75 C.976 A.B. L.188 J.D. 1225 Connecticut Ave. NW
Pfeiffer, Margaret K., (AV) ... '44 '74 C.228 B.A. L.705 J.D. [Sullivan&C.]
Pfeiffer, Paul N. ... '16 '41 C.976 A.B. L.309 LL.B. 2013 H St., N.W.
Pfeiffer, Steven B., (AV) ... '47 '76 C.918 B.A. L.976 J.D. [Fulbright&J.]
*PRACTICE AREAS: Corporate Law; Commercial Law; International Law; Energy Law.
Pfenninger, Lisa M. ... '68 '95 C.259 B.S. L.276 J.D. 1200 New Hampshire Ave., N.W.
Pfizenmayer, Rickard F. ... '44 '69 C.228 A.B. L.477 J.D. [Ⓒ Wallace K.M.&B.]
*PRACTICE AREAS: Corporate Law; Employment Law; Antitrust; Environmental Law.
Pflepsen, Waldemar J., Jr. ... '51 '77 C.475 B.A. L.904 J.D. [Jorden B.]
*PRACTICE AREAS: Litigation; Insurance and Securities; ERISA.
Pfohl, Peter A. ... '67 '97 C.602 B.A. L.180 J.D. [Ⓐ Slover&L.]
Pfotenhauer, Jeanette '47 '79
C.1058 B.A. L.911 J.D. Assoc. Gen. Coun., U.S. Chamber of Com.
Pfunder, Malcolm R., (AV) ... '44 '71 C.309 A.B. L.976 J.D. [Ⓒ Gibson,D.&C.]
*PRACTICE AREAS: Antitrust and Trade Regulation; Mergers, Acquisitions and Divestitures; Hart-Scott-Rodino Act.
Phalen, James T., (AV) ... '— '91 C.321 A.B. L.597 J.D. [King&S.]
*PRACTICE AREAS: Litigation; Trade Regulation.
Phan, K. David '— '01 C.228 B.A. L.276 J.D.
(adm. in NY; not adm. in DC) [Ⓐ O'Melveny&M.]

Phelan, Brian P., (AV) .... '48 '73 C&L.276 A.B., J.D. [Conlon,F.P.&P.]
*PRACTICE AREAS: Commercial Litigation; Personal Injury Law; Family Law; Estate Planning; Real Estate Law.
Phelps, Evan '65 '01 C.859 B.A. L.1209 J.D.
(adm. in VA; not adm. in DC) [A] Olsson,F.&W.]
*PRACTICE AREAS: Food and Drug Law; Medical Device Law; Litigation.
Phelps, James R., (AV) .... '38 '62 C&L.150 A.B., LL.B. [Hyman,P.&M.]
Phelps, N. Nelson .... '63 '91 C.446 B.S. L.61 J.D. First American Title Insurance Co.
Philbin, Stephanie .... '70 '97 C.321 B.A. L.276 J.D. [A] Hale&D.]
*PRACTICE AREAS: Food, Drug and Cosmetic Law.
Philion, Norman J., III .... '46 '76 C.347 A.B. L.228 J.D. 1920 N Street, N.W.‡
Philips, A. Merrill '63 '90 C.575 B.A. L.893 J.D.
(adm. in VA; not adm. in DC) 1050 Conn. Ave., N.W.‡
Philips, Merrill .... '— '90 C.575 B.A. L.893 J.D. The Wallace Law Registry
Phillip, Monya A. .... '70 '99 C.205 B.A. L.446 J.D. [A] Crowell&M.]
Phillipps, Stephanie M., (AV) .... '52 '77 C.681 B.A. L.309 J.D. [Arnold&P.]
*PRACTICE AREAS: Telecommunications Law; Communications Law; Real Estate.
Phillips, Amy K. .... '69 '98 C.575 B.S.B.A. L.276 J.D. [A] Arnold&P.]
*PRACTICE AREAS: Litigation.
Phillips, Arden T. .... '— '98 C.178 B.A. L.228 J.D. [A] Foley&L.]
*PRACTICE AREAS: Business Law; Mergers and Acquisitions.
Phillips, Bryan R. '62 '99 C.128 B.Arch. L.1209 J.D.
(adm. in VA; not adm. in DC) [A] Holland&K.]
*PRACTICE AREAS: Construction Litigation; Government Contracts; Construction Law.
Phillips, Carter G., (AV) .... '52 '77 C.608 B.A. L.597 J.D. [Sidley A.B.&W.]
Phillips, Celeste '53 '81 C.112 A.B. L.1065 J.D.
(adm. in CA; not adm. in DC) [Levine S.&K.]

Phillips, Cyrus E., IV '44 '68 C.339 B.A. L.945 J.D.
Suite 660 1828 L Street, N.W., 20036-5104
Telephone: 202-466-7008 Fax: 202-822-6665 URL: http://www.procurement-lawyer.com
Email: lawyer@procurement-lawyer.com URL: http://www.lawyers.com/procurementlawyer
***PRACTICE AREAS: Government Contracts; Federal Procurement; Computers and Software; Federal Civil Practice.**
Government Contracts, Federal Contracts, Bid Protests, Government Procurement, Computer Contracts, Computer and Software Law, Information Technology, Contracts, Internet Law, e-Commerce, Federal Procurement, Emerging Business Law.
See Professional Biographies, WASHINGTON, DISTRICT OF COLUMBIA

Phillips, Daniel P. .... '69 '98 C.311 B.A. L.893 J.D. [A] Skadden,A.S.M.&F.]
Phillips, Douglas E., (AV) .... '55 '81 C.674 A.B. L.569 J.D. [C] Covington&B.]
Phillips, E. Louise R. .... '50 '86 C.1287 B.A. L.678 J.D. Asst. Corp. Coun., D.C.
Phillips, Eric .... '65 '96 C.604 B.A. L.477 J.D. [A] Covington&B.]
Phillips, Gary L. .... '55 '80 C.228 B.A. L.976 J.D. Dir. of LEgal Affs., Ameritech
Phillips, Gregory James .... '70 '98 C.674 A.B. L.893 J.D. [A] Shaw P.]
Phillips, John R. .... '42 '70 C.602 A.B. L.1066 J.D. [Phillips&C.]
*PRACTICE AREAS: False Claims; Qui Tam.
Phillips, Laura Hathaway, (AV) .... '58 '86 C.856 B.A. L.904 J.D. [Dow,L.&A.]
Phillips, Lisa N. '64 '01 C.645 B.S. L.1209 J.D.
(adm. in PA; not adm. in DC; See Pat. Sect.) [A] Rothwell,F.E.&M.]
*PRACTICE AREAS: Patent Prosecution; Patent Litigation.
Phillips, Mary V., (BV) .... '52 '89 C&L.30 B.S., J.D. Corp. Coun.
Phillips, Ralph A. '— '00 C.645 B.S. L.659 J.D.
(adm. in PA; not adm. in DC) [A] Morgan,L.&B.]
Phillips, Rosalind Ann '41 '69 C&L.502 A.B., J.D.
(adm. in MO; not adm. in DC) Corp. Secy., GEICO Corp.
Phillips, Steven R. .... '— '88 C&L.1228 B.A., J.D. [Verner,L.B.M.&H.]
*PRACTICE AREAS: Legislative; International Trade; Communications.
Phillips, Susan .... '68 '95 C.313 B.S. L.472 J.D. [A] Jackson&C.]
*PRACTICE AREAS: Litigation.
Phillips, Victoria A. .... '69 '98 C.604 B.A. L.273 J.D. 2243 40th Street, N.W.
Phillips, William D. .... '53 '86 C.249 B.S. L.276 J.D. [Ryan,P.U.&M.]

Phillips & Cohen LLP
2000 Massachusetts Avenue, N.W., 1st Floor, 20036 ⊙
Telephone: 202-833-4567 Facsimile: 202-833-1815 URL: http://www.phillipsandcohen.com
URL: http://www.whistleblowers.com
John R. Phillips; Mary Louise Cohen; Peter Wilson Chatfield; Erika Armitage Kelton; Stephen L. Meagher (Resident, San Francisco Office); Eric R. Havian (Resident, San Francisco Office). Associates: Bonny Harbinger; Mary A. Inman (Resident, San Francisco Office). Of Counsel: Gerald M. Stern; Lisa Foster (Resident, San Diego Office).
San Diego, California Office: 705 12th Avenue. Telephone 619-231-6655. Facsimile: 619-231-9777.
Web Site: http://www.whistleblowers.com; http://www.phillipsandcohen.com.
San Francisco, California Office: 131 Steuart Street, Suite 501. Telephone: 415-836-9000. Facsimile: 415-836-9001.
See Professional Biographies, WASHINGTON, DISTRICT OF COLUMBIA

Philp, Mary Susan .... '54 '79 C.430 B.S. L.228 J.D. [Powers,P.S.&V.]
*PRACTICE AREAS: Health Care Law; Hospital Law; Antitrust Law; Medical-Legal Law.
Philson-Skalski, Rita Anne '48 '85 C.446 B.A. L.329 J.D.
(adm. in PA; not adm. in DC) P.O. Box 29419‡
Phipps, James D. .... '64 '96 C&L.101 B.A., J.D. [A] Wiley R.&F.]
Phyo, Eugene Cho (Max) '71 '97
C.188 B.A. L.588 J.D. National Assn. of Securities Dealers
Phythyon, Daniel B., (AV) .... '56 '81 C.935 B.A. L.188 J.D. [C] Wilmer,C.&P.]
*PRACTICE AREAS: Communications and Media; Electronic Commerce; Legislative Practice.
Picard, B. Donovan .... '— '76 C&L.893 B.A., J.D. [Verner,L.B.M.&H.]
Piché, Dianne Marie '56 '86 C.1044 B.A. L.128 J.D.
(adm. in MD; not adm. in DC) 2000 M St., N.W.
Pickard, Daniel B. .... '67 '95 C.645 B.A. L.284 J.D. [A] Wiley R.&F.]
Pickard, Lee A., (AV) .... '38 '63 C.165 A.B. L.309 LL.B. [Pickard&D.]

Pickard and Djinis LLP, (AV)
1990 M Street, N.W., 20036
Telephone: 202-223-4418 Telecopier: 202-331-3813
Email: pickdjin@aol.com
Members of Firm: Lee A. Pickard; Anthony W. Djinis; Mari-Anne Pisarri; Paul J. Bazil. Of Counsel: Craig L. Landauer. Associate: William D. Edick.
Securities, Corporate, Litigation, Arbitration and Banking.
See Professional Biographies, WASHINGTON, DISTRICT OF COLUMBIA

Pickens, Scott E. .... '— '81 C&L.188 B.S., J.D. [Miller&C.]
*PRACTICE AREAS: Government Contracts; Information Technology Contracts; Intellectual Property; Government Contract Fraud; Bid Protests.
Pickering, John H., (AV) .... '16 '41 C&L.477 A.B., J.D. [C] Wilmer,C.&P.]
*PRACTICE AREAS: Civil Practice; Energy; Business Law; Natural Resources.
Pickett, J. Michael .... '65 '89 C.210 B.A. L.910 J.D. [Bingham D.]
*PRACTICE AREAS: Commercial Real Estate.
Pickle, David .... '62 '91 C.118 B.A. L.378 J.D. [Kilpatrick S.]
*PRACTICE AREAS: Employee Benefits; Labor and Employment.
Pickup, James A. .... '— '97 L.276 J.D. [A] Verner,L.B.M.&H.]
*PRACTICE AREAS: Legislative Practice; Federal Practice.

Piczak, C. Todd '71 '01 C.893 B.A. L.665 J.D.
(adm. in VA; not adm. in DC) [A] Dickstein S.M.&O.]
*PRACTICE AREAS: Energy.
Pidgeon, Tina M. .... '68 '94 C.602 B.A. L.893 J.D. [A] Drinker B.&R.]
Pierce, John P., (AV) '58 '85 C.679 B.S. L.846 J.D.
(adm. in CA; not adm. in DC) [C] Dickstein S.M.&O.]
*PRACTICE AREAS: Litigation.
Pierce, Kenneth J. .... '56 '86 C.882 B.A. L.188 J.D. [Willkie F.&G.]
Pierce, Robert J. .... '25 '80 C.477 B.A. L.1162 J.D. 4101 Cathedral Ave., NW, Apt. 505‡
Piercy, Glenn T. '45 '74 C.228 B.A. L.930 J.D.
(adm. in OH; not adm. in DC) 4401-A Conn. Ave. NW
Pierson, Kit A. .... '57 '85 C.429 B.A. L.477 J.D. [Heller E.W.&M.]
*PRACTICE AREAS: Media Law; Association Law; Civil Litigation.
Pierson, Stuart F., (AV) .... '43 '69 C.319 B.A. L.228 J.D. [Troutman S.]
*PRACTICE AREAS: Qui Tam Litigation; Grand Jury Practice; White Collar Crime; Insurance Defense.
Pierson, W. DeVier, (AV) .... '31 '57 C&L.623 A.B., LL.B. [Pierson S.&B.]
Pierson Semmes and Bemis, (AV) .... 1054 31st Street, N.W.
Pies, Roger A., (AV) .... '42 '67 C.188 L.107 LL.B. [Baker&H.]
*PRACTICE AREAS: Tax.
Pietrowski, Robert F., Jr. .... '45 '74 C.813 B.S. L.893 J.D. [Coudert B.]
*PRACTICE AREAS: International Arbitration.
Pignatelli, Melissa L. .... '74 '99 [A] Troutman S.]
*PRACTICE AREAS: Energy; Administrative Law; Legislative Practice; Environmental Law; Regulatory Law.
Pihlstrom, Mark D. .... '70 '97 C.118 B.A. L.904 J.D. [A] Fleischman&W.]
Pike, Andrew D. '50 '76 C.821 B.A. L.659 J.D.
Assoc. Prof., Wash. Coll. of Law, Amer. Univ.
Pike, Mary Carolyn '50 '82 C&L.16 B.S., J.D.
(adm. in AL; not adm. in DC) Assn. of Trial Lawyers of Amer.
Pikofsky, Sara Rachel '70 '98 C.012 B.A. L.178 J.D.
U.S. Dept. of Labor, Off .of Solr., Plan Benefits Sec. Div.
Pikrallidas, Susan Gustafson '51 '89 C.297 B.A. L.276 J.D.
(adm. in VA; not adm. in DC) V. P., AAA
Pilch, Gennady .... '63 '88 C.472 B.A. L.976 J.D. World Bank
Pilchen, Saul M. .... '57 '83 C.477 B.A. L.276 J.D. [Skadden,A.S.M.&F.]
Pilcher, John H. '52 '79 C.1320 B.A. L.190 J.D.
Asst. Gen. Coun., Nat. Assn. of Sec. Dealers, Inc.
Pilcher, Walter Todd '66 '95 C.245 B.A. L.910 J.D.
Staff Atty., Whitman-Walker Clinic Legal Servs.
*RESPONSIBILITIES: Immigration and Naturalization; Debtors Rights; Health Insurance.
Pile, Ruel B. .... '— '91 C.1048 B.A. L.818 J.D. [A] Manatt,P.&P.]
Pilecki, Paul S., (P.C.), (AV) .... '50 '78 C.726 A.B. L.831 J.D. [Shaw P.]
*PRACTICE AREAS: Banking.
Pilgrim, Lily T. '28 '60 C.569 L.1202 J.D.
(adm. in MA; not adm. in DC) 1420 N St., N.W.‡
Pilgrim, Michelle A. .... '69 '97 C&L.446 B.A., J.D. [A] Conlon,F.P.&P.]
*PRACTICE AREAS: Civil Rights; Class Actions.
Pilgrim, Shirleen M. .... '70 '95 C.665 B.A. L.446 J.D. American Bar Assoc.

Piliero, Mazza & Pargament, PLLC, (AV)
Farragut Square, 888 Seventeenth Street, N.W., Suite 1100, 20006 ⊙
Telephone: 202-857-1000 Fax: 202-857-0200
Email: pmp@pmplawfirm.com URL: http://www.pmplawfirm.com
Members of Firm: Daniel J. Piliero II (1942-1990); Pamela J. Mazza; Jeffrey J. Pargament; Andrew P. Hallowell; Antonio R. Franco; Philip M. Dearborn III. Associates: Frank C. Gulin; Judith M. Barger; Joseph J. Summerill IV; Edith Moore McGee (Not admitted in DC).
General Civil and Appellate Practice in all State and Federal Courts. Governmental Departments and Federal Agencies, Government Contracts, Administrative Law, Corporate Counseling, Commercial Transactions, Employment Law, Government Relations, Trade Associations and Native American Law.
Representative Clients: American Production and Inventory Control Society (APICS); RMS Technologies, Inc.; City of Portsmouth, N.H.; Shady Grove Adventist Hospital; Advanced Sciences, Inc.; Latin American Management Association (LAMA); Adventist HealthCare, Inc.
New York, N.Y. Office: 292 Madison Avenue, 10017. Telephone: 212-213-8200.
See Professional Biographies, WASHINGTON, DISTRICT OF COLUMBIA

Pillai, Xavier '52 '94 C.930 Ph.D. L.146 J.D.
(adm. in IL; not adm. in DC; See Pat. Sect.) [A] Leydig,V.&M.]
Pillard, Cornelia T. L. .... '61 '89 C.976 B.A. L.309 J.D. Georgetown Univ. Law Ctr.
Pillette, John '66 '99 C.1320 B.A. L.446 J.D.
(adm. in MD; not adm. in DC) [A] Moore&B.]
Pillion, Kevin P. .... '62 '90 C.751 B.S. L.276 J.D. 4410 Massachusetts Ave. N.W.
Pillow, Roger F. '57 '81 C.43 B.S. L.45 J.D.
(adm. in AR; not adm. in DC) Arthur Andersen LLP
Pillsbury, L. Harrison '43 '70 C.976 B.A. L.273 J.D.
(adm. in MN; not adm. in DC) 4900 Man Ave.‡

Pillsbury Winthrop LLP, (AV) [BB]
1133 Connecticut Avenue, N.W., 20036 ⊙
Telephone: 202-775-9800 Fax: 202-833-8491
URL: http://www.pillsburywinthrop.com
Members of Firm: Isaac D. Benkin; Terry Calvani (Also at San Francisco, California Office); Donald A. Carr; John E. Gillick; Jay L. Halpern; Gerald D. Morgan, Jr.; Roxane A. Polidora (Not admitted in DC); Kenneth P. Quinn (Not admitted in DC); Joshua I. Romanow; Raymond L. Sweigart (Also at McLean, Virginia Office); Mary Ann Walker; Christopher R. Wall. Counsel: Robert Reed Gray; Aileen Meyer; Peter S. Watson (Not admitted in DC; Resident, Other Washington, D.C. Office). Senior Attorneys: Henry J. Daley; Thomas P. Hilliard; William L. Thomas. Associates: Sophy Chen; Cecil S. Chung; Thomas M. deButts; William H. Espinosa; James L. Gallagher; David M. Hernandez; Christopher M. Heywood; Paul W. Terry; Jiyul Yoo.
General Practice with an emphasis on Administrative, Admiralty and Maritime, Alternative Dispute Resolution, Antitrust and Trade Regulation, Appellate Practice, Art, Aviation and Aerospace, Bankruptcy, Banking, Biotechnology, Business, Civil, Class Actions, Commerce & Technology, Commercial, Communications and Media, Complex and Multi-District Litigation, Construction, Contracts, Corporate, Creditor's Rights, E-Commerce, Emerging Companies, Employee Benefits, Energy, Environmental, Equipment Finance and Leasing, Executive Compensation, Finance, Guardianship and Conservatorship, Health Care and Hospital, International, International Trade, Internet, Labor and Employment, Leases and Leasing, Licensing, Life Sciences, Litigation, Medicare and Medicaid, Mergers, Acquisitions and Divestitures, Natural Resources, Nonprofit and Charitable Organizations, Partnership, Patents, Planning and Land Use, Political, Probate, Products Liability, Project Finance, Real Estate, Regulatory, RICO, Securities, Taxation, Torts, Toxic Torts, Trademark, Trust and Estates, Utility, White Collar Crime, Wills and Zoning Law.
San Francisco, California Office: 50 Fremont Street, 94105-2228. Telephone: 415-983-1000. Fax: 415-983-1200.
New York, New York Office: One Battery Park Plaza, 10004-1490. Telephone: 212-858-1000. Fax: 212-858-1500.
Los Angeles, California Office: 725 South Figueroa Street, Suite 2800, 90017-5406. Telephone: 213-488-7100. Fax: 213-629-1033.
Other Los Angeles, California Office: Century City, 10100 Santa Monica Boulevard, Suite 2300.
Orange County, California Office: 650 Town Center Drive, Seventh Floor, Costa Mesa, California 92626-7122. Telephone: 714-436-6800. Fax: 714-436-2800.
McLean, Virginia Office: 1600 Tysons Boulevard, 22102. Telephone: 703-905-2000. Fax: 703-905-2500.
Palm Beach, Florida Office: 125 Worth Avenue, 33480. Telephone: 561-655-7297. Fax: 561-833-6726.
Sacramento, California Office: 400 Capitol Mall, Suite 1700, 95814-4419. Telephone: 916-329-4700. Fax: 916-441-3583.

(This Listing Continued)

Pillsbury Winthrop LLP (Continued)

San Diego, California Office: 101 West Broadway, Suite 1800, 92101-8219. Telephone: 619-234-5000. Fax: 619-236-1995.
Other San Diego, California Office: 11975 El Camino Real, Suite 200, 92130-5000. Telephone: 619-234-5000. Fax: 858-509-4010.
Silicon Valley, California Office: 2550 Hanover Street, Palo Alto, California 94304-1115. Telephone: 650-233-4500. Fax: 650-233-4545.
Stamford, Connecticut Office: Financial Centre, 695 East Main Street, 06904-6760. Telephone: 203-348-2300. Fax: 203-965-8226.
London, England Office: 54 Lombard Street, EC3V 9DH. Telephone: +44-171-648-9200. Fax: +44-171-283-1656.
Sydney, Australia Office: Level 10, 7 Macquarie Place, NSW2000. Telephone: +612-8214-2200. Fax: 612-8214-2211.
Tokyo, Japan Office: Fuerte Kojimachi Building, 5th Floor, 1-7-25 Kojimachi, Chiyoda-ku, 102-0083. Telephone: +011-81-3-5226-7260. Fax: +011-81-3-5226-7261.
Other Tokyo, Japan Office: 6 Gaikokuho Jimu Bengoshi Jimusho, Fifth Floor, Samon Eleven Building, 3-1, Samon-cho, Shinjuku-ku, 160. Telephone: +813-3354-3531. Fax: +813-3354-3534.
Hong Kong, China Office: 2504-6 Asia Pacific Finance Tower, Citibank Plaza, 3 Garden Road, Central Hong Kong. Telephone: +852-2530-3400. Fax: +852-2530-3355.
Singapore Office: 6 Battery Road #38-01B, 049909. Telephone: +65-227-4700. Fax: +65-227-4711.

See Professional Biographies, WASHINGTON, DISTRICT OF COLUMBIA

Pilot, Larry R. .... '40 '67 C.912 B.S. L.128 J.D. [McKenna&C.]
Pilsk, W. Eric .... '60 '88 C.918 B.A. L.880 J.D. [Ⓒ Akin,G.S.H.&F.]
Pimentel, Frank T. .... '— '95 C&L.602 B.A., J.D. [Ⓐ Reed S.]
*PRACTICE AREAS: Litigation; Criminal Law.
Pinco, Robert G., (AV) .... '44 '69 C.184 B.S.Ph. L.276 J.D. [Buchanan I.]
*PRACTICE AREAS: Food, Drug and Cosmetic Law.
Pinegar, Daniel G. ....'76 '01 C&L.352 B.A., J.D. 1464 Rhode Island Avenue NW #400
Pingel, Luke C. '70 '98 C.629 B.A. L.770 J.D.
(adm. in CA; not adm. in DC) [Ⓐ Artabane&B.]
*PRACTICE AREAS: Civil Litigation; Workers' Compensation; Employment Law.
Pinkerton, Brooke A. '63 '91
C.112 B.A L.128 J.D. [Thompson,O.M.N.&H.] (⊙Rockville, MD)
*PRACTICE AREAS: Employment; Premises Liability; Insurance Defense; Personal Injury; Nursing Home Litigation.
Pinkney, India J. '73 '99 C&L.893 B.A., J.D.
(adm. in NC; not adm. in DC) [Ⓐ Baker&H.]
*PRACTICE AREAS: International; Employment.
Pinkowski & Associates
(See Fairfax, Virginia)
Pinnell, Maria Carmen S. '74 '00 C.276 B.A. L.30 J.D.
(adm. in MD; not adm. in DC) 1350 Connecticut Ave., N.W.
Pinto, Consuela A. ....'70 '95 C.94 B.S. L.823 J.D. [Ⓐ Ogletree,D.N.S.&S.]
*PRACTICE AREAS: Labor and Employment; Litigation; Employment Discrimination; Employment Litigation; Labor Law.
Pinto, Earl G. .... '71 '01 C.188 B.S. L.945 J.D. [Ⓐ Bryan C.]
Pinto, Edward J. '49 '74 C.339 B.A. L.1119 J.D.
(adm. in MI; not adm. in DC) Federal Natl. Mtge. Assn.
Pintro Armstrong, Linda M. '61 '84 C.823 B.A. L.273 J.D.
(adm. in PA; not adm. in DC) MCI Communications Corporation
Pinzel, Bonnie J. '— '81 C.966 B.A. L.276 J.D.
(adm. in NY; not adm. in DC) Assoc. Gen. Coun., Fannie Mae
*RESPONSIBILITIES: Securities; Municipal Finance; Corporate.
Piorkowski, Joseph D., Jr. ....'56 '88 C.1019 B.A. L.276 J.D. [Shook,H.&B.]
Piper, Endi N. '71 '99 C&L.893 B.A, J.D.
(adm. in NY; not adm. in DC) Prod. Coun., Black Entertainment Television, Inc.
*RESPONSIBILITIES: Entertainment Law.
Piper, Stephen M. ....'56 '81 C.198 B.A. L.902 J.D. [McKee N.]
*PRACTICE AREAS: Securities; Mergers and Acquisitions; Transactions; Corporate Law; Corporate Finance.

Piper Marbury Rudnick & Wolfe LLP, (AV) BR
1200 Nineteenth Street, N.W., 20036-2430 ⊙
Telephone: 202-861-3900 FAX: 202-223-2085
Email: info@piperrudnick.com URL: http://www.piperrudnick.com
Members of Firm: Perry C. Ausbrook; David H. Bamberger; William D. Blakely; Gary P. Blitz; Benjamin S. Boyd; Daniel J. Carrigan; Emilio W. Cividanes; David Clarke, Jr.; Philip L. Cohan; John E. Corette, III; Jay A. Epstien; Steven B. Feirman; Jay Gary Finkelstein; David J. Fisher (Not admitted in DC); Ann K. Ford; Mary E. Gately; Leonard L. Gordon; Douglas H. Green; James J. Halpert (Resident); Thomas L. Hanley; Larry D. Harris; Barry M. Heller; Adam S. Hoffinger; E. Leslie Hoffman III (Not admitted in DC); Deborah J. Israel; Sandra Jarva-Weiss; Deborah E. Jennings; LeAnn M. Johnson-Koch; E. Ashton Johnston; Paula M. Junghans; Jeffrey R. Keitelman; Steven B. Kelber; Jill K. Kerxton; Mark A. Kirsch; Frederick L. Klein; Sheldon Krantz; Marc R. Labgold (Not admitted in DC); Jeffrey F. Liss; H. Bret Lowell; Steven J. Mandell; Mitchell S. Marder; Petrina M. Markowitz; Richard J. Marks; Edwin M. Martin, Jr.; Andrea M. Mattei (Not admitted in DC); John McJunkin; Deborah R. Meshulam; Cynthia J. Morris; Raymond G. Mullady, Jr.; Kevin P. Mullen; Robert B. Murphy; Stephen R. Mysliwiec; Lewis A. Noonberg; Richard J. Oparil; Caroline E. Petro; Lee J. Plave; Ronald L. Plesser; James P. Rathvon; Richard P. Rector; Anthony H. Rickert; Robert A. Salerno; Jerold I. Schneider; Theodore D. Segal; Earl J. Silbert; Gregory A. Smith; Nancy A. Spangler; Kenneth G. Starling; Ernest M. Stern (Resident); Jane Kwok Ping Tam; Mark J. Tauber; John M. Tifford; Carl L. Vacketta; Charles B. Wayne; William R. Weissman; John T. Westermeier, Jr.; Thomas C. Wheeler; Anthony L. Young; Philip F. Zeidman. Of Counsel: Lucinda J. Bach; Kevin M. Bell (Not admitted in DC); Charles A. Berardesco; Wib Chesser; F. Martin Dajani; Elizabeth R. Dewey; Cary M. Feldman; Daniel S. Goldberg; Robert M. Hall; Sherwin Kaplan; Paul C. Kimball, Ph.D.; John L. Moore, Jr.; Sheila Stark. Partner Emeritus: Toni K. Allen; Nathan B. Feinstein; J. Brian Molloy. Resident Associates: Allison Leslie Alexander; Regina B. Amolsch; J. Darrel Barros; Alisa M. Bergman; Christopher J. Blagg; R. Timothy Bryan; Jim Carlson (Not admitted in DC); Mark Wayne Carmean; Emily S. Chen (Not admitted in DC); Khari M. Clay (Not admitted in DC); Sulee J. Clay; Scott P. Collins; William J. Crowley; Mary Jane DeWeese; Amy L. DuVall; John J. Dwyer; Teresa E. Dykes; Kesha D. Evans; Erik M. Feig; Marjorie P. Fisher (Not admitted in DC); Brandon M. Fitzgerald; Bridget M. Fitzpatrick (Not admitted in DC); David E. Fletcher (Not admitted in DC); Steven E. Friedman; Lorrie A. Giventer; Kelly D. Goldstein (Not admitted in DC); Keara M. Gordon; Steven J. Groseclose; Carol Guy-Jackson; Alfred M. Haas; James B. Hallmark; Heather D. Hamilton; Jeffrey J. Heins; James M. Heintz; Cathy A. Hinger; Daniel M. Horrigan; Tami J. Howie (Not admitted in DC); Charles M. Inokon; Paul W. Jamieson; Kevin Joseph Joyce; Harvey Kellman (Not admitted in DC); Sean J. Klein (Not admitted in DC); Michael R. Laidhold; Michael G. Langan; Amy Susan Leavens; Tashir J. Lee; Alan R. Lewine; Frank A. Marino; Bradley K. McConnell; Robert L. McKay, Jr.; Amy L. Miller (Not admitted in DC); Karin M. Miller (Not admitted in DC); Sara Z. Moghadam (Not admitted in DC); John D. Muir, Jr.; Laura D. Nammo; Zachary N. Noffsinger (Not admitted in DC); Lisa K. Norton; Alan M. Noskow; Reid A. Page (Not admitted in DC); Kim K.S. Pagotto (Not admitted in DC); Song H. Pak (Not admitted in DC); Vincent M. Paladini (Not admitted in DC); Marc O. Peisert (Not admitted in DC); Scott M. Perry; Susan H. Pope; Andrew M. Price; Tilghman Earle Price; John M. Purcell; Deepika Reddy (Not admitted in DC); Adam D. Resnick; William F. Reynolds, Jr.; Susan B. Ross; Louis J. Rouleau (Not admitted in DC); David M. Rubenstein; Edward S. Scheideman (Not admitted in DC); Mark I. Schwartz; Reed P. Sexter; Emily C. Sexton; Anoop G. Shroff; Cristen E. Sikes (Not admitted in DC); Joseph E. Springsteen; Amy L. Schaner Stanley (Not admitted in DC); James Michael Sullivan; Patrice J. Harris Talbott (Not admitted in DC); Rachel Tausend (Not admitted in DC); Lisa R. Trovato; Kenneth Y. Turnbull; Joshua Udler; Anne Magee Vaughan (Not admitted in DC); Kenneth K. D. Vu (Not admitted in DC); Janice L. Weiner; Gregory A. Werkheiser; Robin A. Williams.
Advertising, Promotion and Trade Practices, Antitrust, Bankruptcy and Business Reorganization, Biotechnology, Business Tax, Class Action Litigation, Communications, Construction, Corporate and Securities, Domain Names, ERISA and Employee Benefits, Electronic Commerce and Privacy, Energy and Public Utilities, Environmental, Finance, Financial Services, Franchise and Distribution, Franchise Litigation, Gaming Law, Government Contracts, Health Care, Information Technology, Insurance and Reinsurance, Intellectual Property, International Transactions, Labor and Employment Law, Land Use and Development, Leasing, Life Sciences, Litigation, Lodging and Timeshare, Medical

(This Listing Continued)

Piper Marbury Rudnick & Wolfe LLP (Continued)

Malpractice Defense, Mergers and Acquisitions, Multi-Family Housing, Patent Litigation, Patent Prosecution; Pesticide, Private Client Services (Estates and Trusts), Product Liability and Toxic Torts, Professional Liability, Project Finance, Public Finance, REIT and Real Estate Securitizations, Real Estate, Real Estate Finance, Secured Lending, Securities Litigation, Sports Facilities Development, State Legislation and Public Policy, Venture Capital and Emerging Companies, White Collar.
Chicago, Illinois Office: Piper Marbury Rudnick & Wolfe, 203 North La Salle Street, Suite 1800, 60601-1293. Telephone: 312-368-4000. Telecopier: 312-236-7516. Telex: 754347.
Tampa, Florida Office: 101 East Kennedy Boulevard, Suite 2001, 33602-5149. Telephone: 813-229-2111. Telecopier: 813-229-1447.
Baltimore, Maryland Office: 6225 Smith Avenue, 21209-3600. Telephone: 410-580-3000. FAX: 410-580-3001.
Other Baltimore, Maryland Office: 111 South Calvert Street, Suite 1950, 21202-6174. Telephone: 410-580-3000. FAX: 410-580-3665.
Dallas, Texas Office: 1717 Main Street, Suite 4600, 75201-2605. Telephone: 214-743-4500. FAX: 214-743-4545.
New York, N.Y. Office: 1251 Avenue of the Americas, 10020-1104. Telephone: 212-835-6000. FAX: 212-835-6001.
Philadelphia, Pennsylvania Office: 3400 Two Logan Square, 18th & Arch Streets, 19103-2762. Telephone: 215-656-3300. FAX: 215-656-3301.
Princeton, New Jersey Office: 116 Village Boulevard, Suite 200, Princeton Forrestal Village, 08540. Telephone: 609-951-2252. FAX: 609-951-2216.
Easton, Maryland Office: Piper Marbury Rudnick & Wolfe LLP, 117 Bay Street, 21601-2703. Telephone: 410-820-4460. FAX: 410-820-4463.
Reston, Virginia Office: 1775 Wiehle Avenue, Suite 400, 20190. Telephone: 703-773-4000. FAX: 703-773-5000.
Los Angeles, California Office: 9255 Sunset Boulevard, Suite 710, 90069-3309. Telephone: 310-288-8110. FAX: 310-288-8111.

See Professional Biographies, WASHINGTON, DISTRICT OF COLUMBIA

Pipestem, Wilson K. .... '69 '96 C.612 B.A. L.813 J.D. 3000 K St., NW, Ste. 300
Piquado, Paul D.A. '— '99 C.951 B.A. L.569 J.D.
(adm. in MA; not adm. in DC) [Ⓐ Powell,G.F.&M.]
*PRACTICE AREAS: International; Litigation.
Piranian, Heidi '75 '00 C.674 B.A. L.309 J.D.
(adm. in PA; not adm. in DC) [Ⓐ Crowell&M.]
Pires, Alexander J., Jr., (AV) .... '47 '73 C.94 B.S.B.A. L.273 J.D. [Conlon,F.P.&P.]
*PRACTICE AREAS: Agricultural Law; Civil Rights; Litigation.
Pirri, Kathleen S. ....'58 '86 C.437 B.S. L.851 J.D. [Ⓐ Wright,R.O.&T.]
*PRACTICE AREAS: Commercial Litigation; Employment Litigation.
Pisa-Relli, John C. .... '— '93 C.397 B.A. L.1338 J.D. [Ⓐ Foley&L.]
*PRACTICE AREAS: International Trade; Foreign Asset Control; International Trade Regulation; International Corporate Law; Antiboycott Compliance.
Pisani, Robert J. ....'52 '79 C.861 B.A. L.30 J.D. [Katten M.Z.]
*PRACTICE AREAS: Customs Law; International Trade.
Pisarri, Mari-Anne .... '56 '81 C.732 B.A. L.188 J.D. [Pickard&D.]
Pisciotta, Aileen A. ....'51 '83 C.659 B.A. L.276 J.D. [Kelley D.&W.]
*PRACTICE AREAS: International Communications Law; Administrative Law; Communications Law; Finance.
Pishva, Reza '— '01 C.597 B.A. L.904 J.D.
(adm. in NY; not adm. in DC) [Ⓐ Dechert]
*PRACTICE AREAS: Financial Services Law; Investment Management.
Pita, Howard (Skip) K. '66 '92 C.846 B.A. L.802 J.D.
(adm. in TX; not adm. in DC) Central Amer. Refugee Ctr.
Pitcher, David M., (AV) ..... '45 '71 C.477 B.S.E. L.823 J.D. [Staas&H.] (See Pat. Sect.)
*PRACTICE AREAS: Intellectual Property Law; Patent, Trademark, Copyright and Unfair Competition.
Pitler, Steven P. ....'52 '79 C.207 B.A. L.276 J.D. Sr. Coun., Motorola, Inc.
Pitofsky, Robert .... '29 '56 C.569 B.A. L.178 LL.B. [Ⓒ Arnold&P.]
*PRACTICE AREAS: Antitrust; Competition and Trade; Regulation; Privacy; National Security Law and Policy.
Pittle, Herbert .... '10 '37 C&L.273 A.B., LL.B. 4449 Warren St., N.W.
Pittman, Edward L. ....'56 '84 C&L.260 B.A., J.D. [Ⓒ Thelen R.&P.]
*PRACTICE AREAS: Business; Finance.
Pittman, Jonathan Hale ....'63 '91 C.881 B.A. L.880 J.D. [Ⓒ Crowell&M.]
Pittman, Steuart L., (P.C.), (AV) ....'19 '48 C&L.976 B.A., J.D. [Ⓒ Shaw P.]
*PRACTICE AREAS: International Transactions; Banking.
Pitts, George R., (AV) ....'50 '83 C.821 B.A. L.893 J.D. [Dickstein S.M.&O.]
*PRACTICE AREAS: Bankruptcy; Commercial Litigation.
Pitts, James T. .... '49 '73 C.315 B.A. L.45 J.D. [Winston&S.]
*PRACTICE AREAS: Transportation Law; Banking Law; Securities Regulation Law; Litigation.
Pitts, Patrice M. ....'57 '85 C.674 A.B. L.976 J.D. [Ⓐ Sutherland A.&B.]
*PRACTICE AREAS: Insurance Products; Investment Company Act; Securities Regulation.
Pitts, Vaden S., (AV) .... '24 '52 C.682 L.537 LL.B. 1513 P St., N.W.
Pivec, Mary E., (AV) ....'49 '81 C.445 B.A. L.446 J.D. [Greenberg T.]
Pizzarello, Annalisa .... '66 '93 C.103 B.A. L.145 J.D. [Ⓐ Arnold&P.]
*PRACTICE AREAS: Food and Drug Law.
Pizzirusso, James '75 '01 C.838 B.A. L.276 J.D.
(adm. in VA; not adm. in DC) [Ⓐ Cohen,M.H.&T.]
*PRACTICE AREAS: Mass Torts; Consumer; Environmental.
Plagata-Neubauer, Christine M. '69 '94 C.945 B.A. L.904 J.D.
(adm. in VA; not adm. in DC) [Ⓐ Brustein&M.]
*PRACTICE AREAS: Education Law; Administrative Law; Civil Rights.
Plaine, Daniel J., (AV) ....'43 '70 C.951 B.A. L.976 J.D. [Gibson,D.&C.]
*PRACTICE AREAS: International Trade; International Law; Antitrust and Trade Regulations; International Transactions.
Plaine, Lloyd Leva, (AV) ....'47 '75 C.659 B.A. L.276 J.D. [Sutherland A.&B.]
*PRACTICE AREAS: Estate and Gift Taxation; Trusts and Estates Taxation; Generation Skipping Tax; Transfer Tax; Business Estate Planning.
Plaisted, G. Laurence ....'71 '96 C&L.378 B.S., J.D. [Ⓐ Hogan&H.]
*PRACTICE AREAS: Business Law; Corporate Law; Securities.
Planert, R. Will ....'62 '87 C.945 A.B. L.477 J.D. [Ⓒ Kaye S.]
*PRACTICE AREAS: International Trade.
Planning, Anne K., (AV) ....'60 '88 C.350 B.A. L.273 J.D. [Shaw P.]
*PRACTICE AREAS: Real Estate.
Planning, Mark D. '61 '98 C.973 B.S. L.1209 J.D.
(adm. in NJ; not adm. in DC) [Ⓐ Ryan,P.U.&M.]
Plant, Ian .... '— '97 L.477 J.D. [Ⓐ Arnold&P.]
*PRACTICE AREAS: Antitrust.
Plantamura, Mary Lawless ....'60 '85 C.321 B.A. L.273 J.D. [Ⓒ Davis W.T.]
*PRACTICE AREAS: Communications; Broadcast Station Transfers; Federal Communication Commission Compliance.
Planzos, Sotiris A. (Ted) ....'57 '83 C.1139 B.A. L.1188 J.D. [Ⓒ Troutman S.]
*PRACTICE AREAS: Complex Litigation; White Collar Criminal Defense; Securities; White Collar Crime.
Platner, Michael L. '56 '82 C.612 B.S. L.846 J.D.
(adm. in TX; not adm. in DC) Rep., Amer. Petroleum Instit.
Platt, Henry A. ....'64 '89 C.188 B.A. L.1068 J.D. [Schmeltzer,A.&S.]
*PRACTICE AREAS: Management Labor Law; Employment Law.
Platt, Laurence E. .... '— '82 C.665 B.A. L.273 J.D. [Kirkpatrick&L.]
*PRACTICE AREAS: Housing Law; Banks and Banking; Business Law; Finance; Consumer Law.
Platt, Leslie A., (AV) .... '44 '70 C.273 B.A. L.569 J.D. 1776 K St. NW, Fl. 4
Platt, Leslie A. .... '67 '95 C.20 B.A. L.945 J.D. [Ⓐ Wiley R.&F.]
Platt, Michael T., (AV) ....'35 '61 C.688 B.E.E. L.273 J.D. [Patton B.] (Pat.)
Platt, Robert C. ....'51 '77 C&L.188 A.B., J.D. [Ⓒ Cameron M.]
*PRACTICE AREAS: Energy Law; Administrative Law.

Platzer, William J. ....'33 '62 C&L.494 B.S.L., J.D. Univ. of Dist. of Columbia

Plave, Lee J. ....'58 '84 C.156 B.A. L.564 J.D. [Piper M.R.&W.]
*PRACTICE AREAS: Franchising; Trade Regulation; Technology Licensing.

Plave, Mitchell E. F. ....'61 '86 C.918 B.A. L.30 J.D. Coun., F.D.I.C.

Player, Thomas A., (AV) '40 '65 C.269 B.A. L.893 LL.B. (adm. in SC; not adm. in DC) [Morris,M.&M.] (⊙Atlanta, GA)
*PRACTICE AREAS: Corporate Law; Insurance; Reinsurance; Insurance Rehabilitation and Liquidation; Insurance Mergers and Acquisitions.

Player, William E. ....'51 '82 C.454 B.S. L.93 J.D. [Jacobson,H.] (See Pat. Sect.)
*PRACTICE AREAS: Intellectual Property Law; Biotechnology Patents; Chemical Patents.

Plaza, Ann M. ....'67 '93 C.378 B.S. L.276 J.D. [🄰 Collier S.S.]

Pledger & Feord P.L.C.
(See McLean, Virginia)

Plegge, Lisa Doussard ....'58 '83 C.383 B.A. L.608 J.D. 3000 K St.

Pleshaw, Robert J. ....'33 '62 C.823 A.B. L.94 J.D. 1111 14th St., N.W.

Plesser, Ronald L., (AV) ....'45 '71 C&L.273 B.A., J.D. [Piper M.R.&W.]
*PRACTICE AREAS: Information and Privacy (33%); Communications Law (33%); Intellectual Property Law (33%).

Plevin, Mark D., (AV) ....'57 '81 C.1044 B.A. L.893 J.D. [Crowell&M.]
*PRACTICE AREAS: Litigation; Insurance Coverage; RICO.

Pley, Charles W. '59 '85 L.035 LL.B. (adm. in NY; not adm. in DC) [🄲 McNary,M.&S.] (⊙Mississauga, ON)
*PRACTICE AREAS: Business Immigration; International Immigration; Related Matters.

Plitsch, Jennifer ....'71 '96 C.222 B.A. L.309 J.D. [🄰 Covington&B.]
*PRACTICE AREAS: Civil Litigation; Antitrust.

Plotkin, Mark E., (AV) ....'61 '87 C.976 B.A. L.309 J.D. [Covington&B.]

Plotkin, Robert S., (AV) ....'46 '71 C&L.150 B.A., J.D. [🄲 Paul,H.J.&W.]
*PRACTICE AREAS: White Collar Defense; Securities Enforcement; Health Care Fraud; Complex Federal Civil and Criminal Litigation; Fraud.

Plotnick, Michael ....'72 '97 C.860 B.A. L.273 J.D. [🄰 Wilmer,C.&P.]

Plotz, Thomas J., (BV) ....'53 '78 C.178 B.A. L.569 J.D. [🄲 Shaw P.]
*PRACTICE AREAS: Securities Offerings; Corporate Financing Law.

Plubell, Ann Marie ....'50 '76 C.107 B.A. L.276 J.D. 3429 Quebec St., N.W.

Plumer, Mark J. ....'61 '87 C.264 B.A. L.273 J.D. [Swidler B.S.F.]
*PRACTICE AREAS: Insurance Coverage.

Plump, Andrew R. ....'53 '78 C.1044 B.A. L.659 J.D. [Zuckert,S.&R.]
*PRACTICE AREAS: Commercial Litigation; Civil Litigation; Employment Litigation; Federal Contracts; Transportation Regulation.

Poag, Mary Woodson (Molly) ....'61 '86 C.140 B.A. L.790 J.D. [🄲 Steptoe&J.]
*PRACTICE AREAS: Litigation; Environmental Insurance Litigation.

Poche, Thomas F. ....'63 '95 C.659 B.A. L.94 J.D. [🄰 Connolly B.L.&H.] ⊙

Pocino, Amy E. ....'— '99 C.93 B.A. L.1292 J.D. [🄰 Morgan,L.&B.]

Podesta, Mary S. ....'44 '76 C.788 A.B. L.276 J.D. Sr. Coun., Investment Co. Inst.
*RESPONSIBILITIES: International.

Podgore, John Eric '70 '98 C.674 A.B. L.228 J.D. (adm. in NY; not adm. in DC) [🄰 White&C.]
*PRACTICE AREAS: Corporate Law.

Podgorsky, Arnold B., (AV) ....'51 '75 C.24 B.A. L.823 J.D. [Wright&T.]
*PRACTICE AREAS: Litigation; Energy Contracts.

Podolsky, Susan R. ....'59 '87 C.197 A.B. L.893 [Jenner&B.]
*PRACTICE AREAS: Civil Litigation; Commercial Litigation.

Podryhula, Oleh '52 '81 C.1156 B.A. L.1209 J.D. (adm. in VA; not adm. in DC) 1413 K St., N.W.

Podurgiel, Debra A. '72 '99 C.797 B.A. L.790 J.D. (adm. in SC; not adm. in DC) Legal & Regulatory Advisor, Nat. Assoc. of Indep. Schools

Poe, David R., (AV) ....'48 '75 C.502 B.S.M.E. L.228 J.D. [LeBoeuf,L.G.&M.]
*PRACTICE AREAS: Communications; Utilities.

Poe, L. Harvey, Jr., (AV) '16 '40 C&L.893 B.S., J.D.
Suite 514, 2600 Virginia Avenue, N.W., 20037 ⊙
Telephone: 202-337-3080 Facsimile: 202-337-1185
Email: LHPOE@AOL.COM
General Practice before Federal and Local Courts, Governmental Departments and Regulatory Agencies, Aviation, Banking, Corporation, Financing, International Business and Finance, Education, Real Estate and Investments Law, Aviation Aerospace Law, International Law.
See Professional Biographies, WASHINGTON, DISTRICT OF COLUMBIA

Poe, Paul A. '69 '95 C.1299 B.A. L.1161 J.D. (adm. in OH; not adm. in DC) 1627 Eye St., N.W.

Poerio, Joseph Mark ....'58 '85 C.893 B.A. L.188 J.D. [🄲 Paul,H.J.&W.]
*PRACTICE AREAS: Executive Compensation; Employee Benefits; ERISA.

Poffenberger, Clara M. ....'64 '90 C.886 B.A. L.904 J.D. [🄰 Baker B.]

Pogoda, Darren E. ....'74 '00 C.1376 B.A. L.128 J.D. [🄰 Arter&H.]
*PRACTICE AREAS: Intellectual Property.

Pohl, Mark R. '54 '80 C.1044 B.A. L.273 J.D. Assoc. Gen. Coun., Washington Metropolitan Area Transit Authority
*RESPONSIBILITIES: Pension Law; Employee Benefits Law; Taxation Law; Disability Rights Law.

Pohoryles, Louis, (AV) ....'37 '64 C.563 B.B.A. L.273 J.D. 1920 N. St., N.W.‡

Poindexter, Obrea O. '68 '94 C.329 B.A. L.276 J.D. (adm. in PA; not adm. in DC) [🄰 Morrison&F.]

Poindexter, Thomas C. ....'55 '90 C.679 B.S. L.1209 J.D. [Winston&S.]
*PRACTICE AREAS: Administrative Law; Nuclear Energy Law.

Poirier, Mary Ann ....'70 '96 C.201 B.C.M.E. L.880 J.D. [🄰 Baker B.]

Poisson, David E. ....'51 '79 C.454 B.A.M.Ed. L.37 J.D. National Educ. Assn.

Polach, Patricia, (BV) ....'54 '85 C.475 B.A. L.477 J.D. [🄲 Bredhoff&K.]

Polacheck, Laura R. ....'59 '84 C.966 B.A. L.273 J.D. Center for Auto Safety

Polacheck, Lori Jean '62 '89 C.477 B.A. L.145 J.D. (adm. in IL; not adm. in DC) [🄰 Bode&G.]
*PRACTICE AREAS: Litigation.

Polatnick, Eden M. '72 '98 C.183 B.A. L.30 J.D. (adm. in NJ; not adm. in DC) [🄰 Dickstein S.M.&O.]
*PRACTICE AREAS: Legislative and Governmental Affairs.

Poldy, Megan Rae '65 '90 C.240 B.A. L.945 J.D. Assoc. Gen. Coun., Northwest Airlines, Inc.

Polebaum, Elliot E., (AV) ....'50 '78 C.478 A.B. L.569 J.D. [Fried,F.H.S.&J.]
*PRACTICE AREAS: International Arbitration; Commercial Litigation; Intellectual Property Litigation.

Policastri, Eugene W. ....'61 '89 C.165 B.A. L.861 J.D. [🄰 Lee&M.]
*PRACTICE AREAS: Construction Litigation; Architects and Engineers; Commercial Litigation; Maritime Law.

Policy, Vincent Mark J. ....'48 '74 C.446 B.A. L.276 J.D. [Greenstein D.&L.]

Polidora, Roxane A. '60 '88 C.112 B.A. L.1065 J.D. (adm. in CA; not adm. in DC) [Pillsbury W.]
*PRACTICE AREAS: Class Actions; Antitrust; Unfair Competition; Litigation.

Polin, Eva ....'56 '81 C.367 B.A. L.276 J.D. Asst. U. S. Atty.

Poliner, Elizabeth S. ....'60 '88 C.95 B.A. L.893 J.D. [🄰 Baise&M.]
*PRACTICE AREAS: Environmental Law; Administrative Law.

Poliner, Michael C. ....'— '80 C&L.893 B.A., J.D. [Feith&Z.] (⊙Jerusalem, Israel)

Poling, William Compton, Jr ....'69 '95 C.160 B.A. L.930 J.D. [🄰 Powell,G.F.&M.]
*PRACTICE AREAS: Litigation; Corporate Transactions.

Polino, Teresa M. ....'52 '78 C.1044 B.A. L.276 J.D. [Sandler,T.&R.]
*PRACTICE AREAS: Customs Law; International Trade Law; Administrative Agency Practice.

Polito, Melissa ....'69 '95 C.611 B.A. L.273 J.D. [Margolius,M.D.R.&T.]
*PRACTICE AREAS: Litigation; Family Law.

Polito, Nat N. ....'69 '95 C.276 A.B. L.273 J.D. [🄰 Leftwich&D.]
*PRACTICE AREAS: Medical Negligence; Personal Injury; Domestic Relations; Real Property.

Polivy, Gail L. '47 '77 C.930 B.A. L.128 J.D. Assoc. Gen. Coun., Legal Compl., Verizon Communications

Polivy, Margaret (Margot), (AV) ....'38 '65 C.331 A.B. L.569 LL.B. [Renouf&P.]

Polk, C. Edward, Jr. '67 '99 C.446 B.S. L.273 J.D. (adm. in VA; not adm. in DC; See Pat. Sect.) [🄰 Covington&B.]
*PRACTICE AREAS: Intellectual Property; Patents.

Polk, John W. ....'43 '72 C.105 B.A. L.276 J.D. [🄲 Baker&M.]
*PRACTICE AREAS: Litigation; Public Contracts and Utilities; Product Liability Law; Intellectual Property Law; Regulatory Law.

Polk, Loretta P. ....'55 '81 Assoc. Gen. Coun., National Cable Television Assn.

Pollack, Barry J., (AV) ....'64 '91 C.347 B.S. L.276 J.D. [Nixon P.]
*PRACTICE AREAS: White Collar Criminal Defense; Civil Litigation.

Pollack, Catherine Evans ....'61 '91 C.945 B.A. L.1209 J.D. [🄲 Fried,F.H.S.&J.]
*PRACTICE AREAS: Government Contracts; Litigation.

Pollack, Irving M. ....'18 '42 C.102 B.A. L.1009 LL.B. [Dilworth P.P.]

Pollack, Kenneth L. ....'67 '95 C.860 B.A. L.880 J.D. [🄰 Arnold&P.]
*PRACTICE AREAS: Real Estate; Health Care; Litigation.

Pollack, Michael J. ....'63 '88 C&L.273 B.A., J.D. [Arter&H.]
*PRACTICE AREAS: Product Liability; Personal Injury Litigation; Commercial Litigation; Intellectual Property Litigation.

Pollak, Cary D. ....'45 '71 C.477 B.A. L.276 J.D. Off. of the Corp. Coun.

Pollak, Michele C. ....'55 '81 C.914 A.B. L.597 J.D. Amer. Assoc. of Ret. Persons

Pollak, Roger ....'59 '91 C.112 B.S. L.976 J.D. [Bredhoff&K.]

Pollak, Stephen J., (AV) ....'28 '56 C.197 A.B. L.976 LL.B. [Shea&G.]
*PRACTICE AREAS: Civil Litigation; Trial Practice; Appellate Practice; ERISA; Labor Law.

Pollak, Tom '59 '93 C.1044 B.A. L.276 J.D. (adm. in MD; not adm. in DC) 1826 6th St. NW, 12th Fl.‡

Pollard, Randle B. ....'63 '89 C.302 B.S. L.276 J.D. Asst. Corp. Coun.

Pollock, Robert A. '62 '99 C.976 B.S. L.273 J.D. [🄰 Finnegan,H.F.G.&D.] (See Pat. Sect.)
*PRACTICE AREAS: Genetics; Immunology; Biotechnology Patent Prosecution; Biotechnology Patents; Molecular Biology Patents.

Pollock, Stacy J. ....'69 '95 C.1296 B.A. L.273 J.D. [🄰 Arnold&P.]
*PRACTICE AREAS: Litigation.

Polmer, Henry M. ....'45 '71 C.910 A.B. L.273 J.D. General Counsel, Mondex USA

Polon, Ira H., (AV) ....'43 '68 C.401 B.A. L.178 LL.B. [Dickstein S.M.&O.]
*PRACTICE AREAS: Mergers, Acquisitions and Divestitures Law; Business Law; Corporate Law; Finance Law.

Polonsky, Alex S. ....'— '99 C.918 B.S. L.1194 J.D. [🄰 Morgan,L.&B.]

Polott, Anita B. ....'— '96 C.910 B.A. L.904 J.D. [🄰 Morgan,L.&B.]

Polowy, Carolyn I. '44 '71 C.999 B.A. L.966 J.D. Gen. Coun., Natl. Assn. of Soc. Wkrs.

Polozie, Katarina K. '72 '98 C.914 B.A. L.597 J.D. (adm. in NY; not adm. in DC) [🄰 McDermott,W.&E.]

Polozie, Stephen M. ....'65 '96 C.012 B.S. L.597 J.D. [🄰 Jones,D.R.&P.]

Pomerantz, Crane M. ....'71 '96 C.477 B.A. L.94 J.D. [🄰 Morgan,L.&B.]

Pomeranz, John Putnam '63 '95 C.918 B.A. L.800 J.D. Staff Atty., Harrison Inst., Georgetown Univ.

Pomeranz, Morton ....'22 '48 C&L.178 A.B., J.D. 601 13th St. N.W.

Pomeranz, William E. ....'60 '98 C.311 B.A. L.30 J.D. [🄰 Williams M.]
*PRACTICE AREAS: International Law; Commercial Law; E-Commerce; Corporate; Russian Law.

Pomerenk, Robert B. ....'58 '84 C.276 B.S.F.S. L.893 J.D. [Luse L.G.P.&S.]
*PRACTICE AREAS: Corporate Finance; Securities; Financial Institutions.

Pomeroy, Harlan, (AV) ....'23 '49 C.976 B.S. L.309 LL.B. [Baker&H.]
*PRACTICE AREAS: Tax Law; Personal Planning Law.

Pomeroy, John H. ....'48 '79 C.1070 B.S. L.309 J.D. [Dow,L.&A.]

Pommer, Virginia Rowan ....'66 '93 C.93 B.A. L.128 J.D. 1732 Church St., N.W.

Pommerening, David G. ....'60 '86 C.228 A.B. L.893 J.D. [O'Melveny&M.]
*PRACTICE AREAS: Corporate Law; Corporate Transactions.

Pommert, G. Steven '56 '81 C&L.608 B.A., J.D. (adm. in OH; not adm. in DC) Asst. Reg. Mgr., West Publishing Corp.

Pompeo, Michael R. ....'63 '94 C.870 B.S. L.309 J.D. 725 12th St., N.W.

Pomper, Brian ....'70 '96 C.453 B.S. L.188 J.D. [🄰 Skadden,A.S.M.&F.]
*PRACTICE AREAS: International Trade.

Pomper, David E. ....'62 '89 C.821 B.A. L.659 J.D. [Spiegel&M.]
*PRACTICE AREAS: Antitrust; Aviation Law; Energy; Environmental Law; Regulatory Law.

Pomper, Stephen E. ....'65 '94 C.309 A.B. L.976 J.D. [🄰 Cleary,G.S.&H.]

Poms, Douglas L. ....'63 '94 C&L.893 B.S., J.D. [🄰 Dewey B.]
*PRACTICE AREAS: Tax.

Ponder, Gwendolyn K. ....'72 '01 C.112 B.A. L.276 J.D. [🄰 Wilmer,C.&P.]

Ponds, Billy L., (AV) ....'57 '84 C.790 B.A. L.329 J.D. [Ponds]

Ponds, Navron ......'48 '74 C&L.309 A.B., J.D. 1700 K St. N.W., 903, Commerce Bldg.

Ponds Law Firm, The, (AV) ....1000 Potomac Street, N.W., Suite 302

Pongrace, Donald R. ....'57 '85 C.67 B.A. L.904 J.D. [Akin,G.S.H.&F.]
*PRACTICE AREAS: International Government Relations; Public Policy; Africa Trade; China Trade; Latin America Trade.

Ponomarenko, Xenia M. '66 '91 C.831 B.A. L.128 J.D. (adm. in NJ; not adm. in DC) Asst. Dir., Ukrainian Natl. Assn.

Ponticelli, Barry A. ....'46 '73 C.676 B.A. L.128 J.D. Bureau of Natl. Affs.

Poole, Brooke D. '73 '98 C.1375 A.B. L.273 J.D. (adm. in MD; not adm. in DC) [🄰 Winston&S.]
*PRACTICE AREAS: Nuclear Energy.

Poole, Lisa L. ....'— '89 C.477 A.B. L.228 J.D. [🄲 King&S.]
*PRACTICE AREAS: Tax.

Poole, R. Edward ....'69 '95 C.145 B.A. L.904 J.D. [🄰 Dickstein S.M.&O.]
*PRACTICE AREAS: Insurance Litigation.

Poon, Torsdon D. '68 '95 C.1021 B.A. L.30 J.D. (adm. in MD; not adm. in DC) Ernst & Young LLP - Natl. Tax

Pope, Douglas V. '45 '70 C.231 A.B. L.446 J.D. Corp. Secy. Atty., Washington Gas Light Co.

Pope, Susan H. ....'66 '96 C.575 B.A. L.1209 J.D. [🄰 Piper M.R.&W.]
*PRACTICE AREAS: Antitrust and Trade Regulation.

Popejoy, Linda B. ....'67 '94 C.188 B.S. L.309 J.D. [🄰 Dorsey&W.]
*PRACTICE AREAS: Commercial Litigation.

Poper, Lauren Beth '69 '97 C.128 B.A. L.477 J.D. (adm. in NY; not adm. in DC) Sec. & Exch. Comm.

Popkin, Richard A., (AV) ....'49 '75 C.273 B.A. L.472 J.D. [Swidler B.S.F.]
*PRACTICE AREAS: International Law; Trade Regulation Law; Export Regulation; Foreign Trade Sanctions; World Trade Organization.

Popma, Scott J. ....'73 '99 C&L.477 B.S., J.D. [🄰 Finnegan,H.F.G.&D.]
*PRACTICE AREAS: Genetics; Immunology; Biotechnology Patent Prosecution; Patent Litigation; Pharmaceutical Patents.

Popofsky, Mark S. ....'67 '94 C.103 A.B. L.309 J.D. [Kaye S.]
*PRACTICE AREAS: Antitrust and Trade Regulation; Intellectual Property; E-Commerce; Mergers and Acquisitions; Litigation.
Popp, Karen A. ....'58 '87 C.1128 B.A. L.575 J.D. [Sidley A.B.&W.]
Poppalardo, Judith C. '56 '86 C&L.1029 B.S., J.D.
(adm. in VA; not adm. in DC) Asst. Gen. Coun., Securities Industry Assn.
*RESPONSIBILITIES: Securities; Broker-Dealer Regulation; Broker-Dealer Operations; Arbitration.
Pordy, David A., (AV) '50 '75 C.645 B.A. L.273 J.D.
[Shulman,R.G.P.&E.] (⊙Rockville, MD; Mc Lean, VA)
Porges, Amelia ....'— '80 C.188 A.B. L.309 J.D. [Powell,G.F.&M.]
*PRACTICE AREAS: World Trade Organization; International Trade; International Investment; International Arbitration.
Porritt, Nicholas ....'68 '91 C.999 L.L.B. L.145 L.L.M. [Arnold&P.]
*PRACTICE AREAS: Litigation.
Port, Joseph C., Jr. ....'60 '88 C.165 B.A. L.276 J.D. [Sidley A.B.&W.]
Porta, Earnest W., Jr. '64 '92 C&L.276 B.S., J.D.
(adm. in VA; not adm. in DC) Off. of Spons. Prog., Georgetown Univ.
Porta, Libretta A. ....'72 '98 C.645 B.S. L.30 J.D. [Steptoe&J.]
Porter, Alan C. ....'— '76 C.401 B.A. L.930 J.D. [Kirkpatrick&L.]
*PRACTICE AREAS: Investment Company Law; Investment Management; Securities Regulation.
Porter, Carson P. ....'45 '71 C&L.383 B.A., J.D. [Arent F.K.P.&K.]
*PRACTICE AREAS: Health Care; Litigation.
Porter, Daniel L. ....'60 '85 C.178 B.A. L.188 J.D. [Willkie F.&G.]
Porter, Gregory Y. ....'61 '96 C.454 B.A. L.800 J.D. [O'Melveny&M.]
Porter, Jennifer M. ....'48 '84 C.1382 B.A. L.273 J.D. [Coates,D.&G.]
*PRACTICE AREAS: Corporate Law; Environmental Law; Occupational Safety and Health Law; Administrative Law; Association Law.
Porter, John E., (AV) '35 '61 C.597 B.S.B.A. L.477 J.D.
(adm. in IL; not adm. in DC) [Hogan&H.]
*PRACTICE AREAS: Health Law; Legislative; Education Law.
Porter, Lane .... '39 '64 C&L.893 B.S., LL.B. 4007 Connecticut Ave., N.W.
Porter, Richard H., (AV) ....'42 '68 C&L.276 B.S.B.A., J.D. [Steptoe&J.]
*PRACTICE AREAS: Complex Civil Litigation; Reinsurance; Antitrust Law; Internal Corporate Investigations.
Porter, Stephen J. '58 '93 C.477 A.B. L.276 J.D.
(adm. in PA; not adm. in DC) 1615 L St., N.W.‡
Porter, Stephen W., (AV) .... '39 '66 C&L.966 B.B.A., J.D. [Arnold&P.]
*PRACTICE AREAS: Real Estate; Corporate; Securities.
Porter, Veronica A. ....'58 '86 C.597 B.A. L.477 J.D. Asst. Corp. Coun.
Porter, W. Lane .... '39 '64 C&L.893 B.S., LL.B. 4007 Connecticut Ave., N.W.
Porter, William G., Jr., (AV) ....'23 '49 C.112 L.608 LL.B. 1233 20th St., N.W.

Porter Wright Morris & Arthur LLP, (AV)
1919 Pennsylvania Avenue, N.W. Suite 500, 20006-3434 ⊙
Telephone: 202-778-3000; (800-456-7962) Fax: 202-778-3063
Email: washington@porterwright.com URL: http://www.porterwright.com
Members of Firm: David L. Douglass; Alison MacDonald Duncan; E. Jay Finkel; Leslie Alan Glick; Thomas O. Gorman; Judd L. Kessler; William P. McGrath, Jr.; W. Scott Simmer; Mitchell A. Stearn. Resident Associates: David Timothy Fischer; Kevin M. Grace (Not admitted in DC); John E. Hedstrom; Catherine L. Hess; Jennifer J. Illingworth (Not admitted in DC); Thomas J. Poulin (Not admitted in DC); Robert T. Rhoad; Heather J. Stewart; Renata S. Vasconcellos (Not admitted in DC); Jason E. Woehrmyer (Not admitted in DC).
Alternative Dispute Resolution, Business and Corporate, Construction, Employee Benefits, Energy and Utilities, Environment, Federal Contracting and Procurement, Financial Institutions, General Practice, Governmental Affairs, Health Care, Insurance, Intellectual Property, International Business, Labor and Employment, Litigation, Public Law, Public Finance, Real Estate, Securities, Taxation, Technology, Trusts and Estates.
Columbus, Ohio Office: 41 South High Street, 43215-6194. Telephones: 614-227-2000; (800-533-2794). Fax: 614-227-2100. Internet: columbia@porterwright.com.
Dayton, Ohio Office: One Dayton Centre, One South Main Street, Suite 1600, 45402-2028. Telephones: 937-449-6810; (800-533-4434). Fax: 937-449-6820. Internet: dayton@porterwright. com.
Cincinnati, Ohio Office: 250 E. Fifth Street, Suite 2200, 45202-4199. Telephones: 513-381-4700; (800-582-5813). Fax: 513-421-0991. Internet: cincinnati@porterwright.com.
Cleveland, Ohio Office: 925 Euclid Avenue, Suite 1700, 44115-1483. Telephones: 216-443-9000; (800-824-1980). Fax: 216-443-9011. Internet: cleveland@porterwright.com.
Naples, Florida Office: 5801 Pelican Bay Boulevard, Suite 300, 34108-2709. Telephones: 941-593-2900; (800-876-7962). Fax: 941-593-2990. Internet: naples@porterwright.com.
See Professional Biographies, WASHINGTON, DISTRICT OF COLUMBIA

Portman, Robert M. ....'59 '86 C.597 B.A. L.309 J.D. [Jenner&B.]
*PRACTICE AREAS: Health Care; Trade Associations.
Portnoy, Aryeh S. ....'73 '99 C.178 B.A. L.569 J.D. [Crowell&M.]
Portnoy, Elliott I. ....'65 '92 C.823 B.A. L.309 J.D. [Arent F.K.P.&K.]
*PRACTICE AREAS: Legislative Practice; Education Law; Special Education; Campaign Ethics; Election and Campaign Finance.
Portnoy, Ian K., (AV) ....'43 '69 C.477 B.A. L.884 J.D. [Long A.&N.]
*PRACTICE AREAS: Real Estate; Intellectual Property Transactions.
Portnoy, James S. ....'60 '89 C.659 B.A. L.477 J.D. [Covington&B.]
Portnoy, Michael S. ....'— '98 C.103 B.A. L.94 J.D. [Epstein B.&G.]
*PRACTICE AREAS: Health Law.
Posner, Ethan M. ....'62 '90 C.918 B.A. L.477 J.D. [Covington&B.]
Posner, Morton J. ...... '67 '92 C.813 B.A. L.30 J.D. Gen. Coun., Allegiance Telecom, Inc.
Posner, Theodore R. .... '68 '96 C.674 A.B. L.976 J.D. 254 Dirksen SOB
Posorske, Laurence H. ....'48 '92 C.966 B.A. L.276 J.D. [Brobeck,P.&H.] (Pat.)
Possessky, Edward F. '32 '64
C.119 B.S.E.E. L.229 LL.B. 1300 I St., N.W., Suite 700 (Pat.)
Possick, Howard B. ....'48 '76 C.188 B.A. L.473 J.D. [Arent F.K.P.&K.]
*PRACTICE AREAS: Business Law; Corporate Law; Securities Law; Transactions; Litigation.
Post, Michael L. .... '69 '99 C.112 B.A. L.273 J.D. 1722 Eye Street, NW, 6th Floor
Post-Garza, Betsy ....'76 '00 C.779 B.S. L.1209 J.D. 1150 18th St., N.W.
Postar, Adeen J. '55 '80 C&L.910 A.B., J.D.
(adm. in RI; not adm. in DC) 600 New Hampshire Ave., N.W., 11th Fl.
Postar, Michael R. ....'54 '79 C.273 B.A. L.910 J.D. [Duncan,W.G.&P.]
*PRACTICE AREAS: Energy; Communications Law.
Postol, Lawrence P., (AV) ....'51 '76 C&L.188 B.S., J.D. [Seyfarth S.]
*PRACTICE AREAS: Labor and Employment Law; Environmental Litigation; Worker's Compensation Law.
Poston, Bradford R. '71 '98 C.154 B.A. L.37 J.D.
(adm. in AZ; not adm. in DC) 1111 Constitution Avenue, N.W.
Poston, Jeffrey L. ....'61 '88 C.692 B.A. L.276 J.D. [King,P.&H.]
*PRACTICE AREAS: Complex Civil Litigation; Criminal Litigation; Health Care Law; Employment Law; Government Contracts.
Posz, David G., Law Office of '66 '92
C.277 B.E.E. L.347 J.D. 2000 L Street N.W. Suite 200 (Pat.)
Potenza, Joseph M., (AV) '— '75
C.999 B.S.E.E. L.276 J.D. [Banner&W.] (See Pat. Sect.)
*PRACTICE AREAS: Intellectual Property Law; Patents; Copyrights; Intellectual Property Litigation; Intellectual Property Licensing.
Potkin, Lane H., (AV) ....'54 '78 C&L.273 B.A., J.D. [Leibner&P.]
*PRACTICE AREAS: Real Estate Law; Business Law; Trusts and Estates; Probate; Commercial Law.
Pott, Claudia Anne ....'49 '85 C.477 A.B. L.273 J.D. [Sherman,M.C.&A.]
*PRACTICE AREAS: Family Law; Estate Planning.
Potter, Caryl A., III, (AV) ....'47 '78 C.813 B.A. L.502 J.D. [Sonnenschein N.&R.]
*PRACTICE AREAS: Government Contract Law; Commercial Litigation.

Potter, Clarissa C. '61 '90 C.473 A.B. L.976 J.D.
(adm. in NY; not adm. in DC) Georgetown Univ. Law Ctr.
Potter, Edward E., (BV) .... '46 '79 C.475 B.A. L.904 J.D. [McGuiness N.&W.] ⊙
*PRACTICE AREAS: International Labor Law; Labor Relations Law; Employment Law.
Potter, J. Craig ....'43 '73 C.339 A.B. L.972 J.D. [O'Connor&H.]
*PRACTICE AREAS: Natural Resources Law; Environmental Law.
Potter, Jonathan ....'63 '89 C.696 B.A. L.569 J.D. 1615 L St., N.W.
Potter, Kathy ....'— '95 C.276 B.A. L.1209 J.D. [Epstein B.&G.]
*PRACTICE AREAS: Health Law; Litigation; ERISA Litigation.
Potter, Patrick John ....'64 '89 C.475 B.A. L.477 J.D. [Shaw P.]
Potter, Robert A. '60 '87 C&L.276 A.B., J.D.
(adm. in PA; not adm. in DC) 1440 New York Ave. N.W
Potter, Sara E. .... '43 '74 C.732 B.A. L.588 J.D. National Educ. Assn.
Potter, Trevor, (AV) ....'55 '83 C.309 A.B. L.893 J.D. [Caplin&D.]
*PRACTICE AREAS: Election, Campaign and Political Law.
Potts, Andrew S. ....'67 '93 C&L.347 B.A., J.D. [Nixon P.]
*PRACTICE AREAS: Real Estate; Affordable Housing; Tax; Historic Preservation.
Potts, Julie Anna ....'69 '97 C&L.104 A.B., J.D. [Mayer,B.&P.]
*PRACTICE AREAS: Environmental Law; Litigation.
Potts, Ramsay D., (P.C.), (AV) ....'16 '48 C.575 B.S. L.309 J.D. [Shaw P.]
*PRACTICE AREAS: Transportation; Aviation; Government; Legislation; Commercial.
Potts-Dupre, David H. ....'54 '83 C.112 B.S. L.1067 J.D. [Counts,P.-D.&D.]
Poulin, Thomas J. '60 '88 C.608 B.A. L.431 J.D.
(adm. in ME; not adm. in DC) [Porter W.M.&A.]
Pouliquen, Corinne M. ....'65 '93 C.446 B.S. L.1170 J.D. [Pepper H.] (Pat.)
*PRACTICE AREAS: Patents; Intellectual Property.
Poulon, Christine '68 '99 C.881 B.A. L.904 J.D.
(adm. in MD; not adm. in DC) [Katten M.Z.]
Poulson, Zoe S. ....'74 '98 C.896 B.A. L.309 J.D. [Williams&C.]
*PRACTICE AREAS: Litigation.
Poutasse, John D. ....'64 '95 C.165 B.A. L.273 J.D. [Leventhal,S.&L.]
*PRACTICE AREAS: Communications Law; Media Law.
Povich, David, (AV) ....'35 '62 C.976 B.A. L.178 LL.B. [Williams&C.]
Povich, Douglas L. '60 '86 C.867 B.A. L.276 J.D.
[Squire,S.&D.] (⊙Tysons Corner, VA)
*PRACTICE AREAS: Technology Law; Telecommunications; Wireless Communications.
Povinelli, Lawrence ....'62 '91 C.475 B.A. L.1209 J.D. [Kay&P.]
Powell, C. Thomas ....'— '99 C&L.575 A.B., J.D. [Latham&W.]
*PRACTICE AREAS: Environmental Law; Litigation.
Powell, Cameron C. .... '67 '92 C.174 B.S. L.309 J.D. 3000 K St., N.W., Suite 500
Powell, David W., (AV) ....'57 '82 C.802 B.B.A. L.846 J.D. [Groom]
*PRACTICE AREAS: Employee Benefits Law; Tax Law; ERISA.
Powell, Gwendolyn A. ....'66 '91 C.243 B.A. L.1066 J.D. Marriott Drive
Powell, Ida A. ....'44 '78 C.940 B.A. L.846 J.D. Asst. Corp. Coun.
Powell, Jerome, (AV) ....'21 '49 C&L.276 A.B., J.D. 1301 K St., N.W.
Powell, Justin C. ....'43 '96 C.119 B.S. L.1209 J.D. [Keller&H.]
*PRACTICE AREAS: Domestic and International Chemical Control Law; Chemical Regulation; Chemical Nomenclature.
Powell, Karen D. ....'61 '89 C.112 B.A. L.93 J.D. [Petrillo&P.]
*PRACTICE AREAS: Public Contract Law; Alternative Dispute Resolution; International Government Contracts; International Trade; Intellectual Property.
Powell, Marjorie E. '42 '85 C.67 B.A. L.477 J.D.
Asst. Gen. Coun., Pharmaceutical Research & Mnfct. of America
Powell, Raymond H. J., Jr. '52 '88 C.152 B.S.E.E. L.273 J.D.
(adm. in VA; not adm. in DC; See Pat. Sect.) [Adduci,M.&S.] (⊙Arlington, VA)
*PRACTICE AREAS: Patent Law.
Powell, V. Elizabeth '61 '00 C.478 B.A. L.902 J.D.
(adm. in MD; not adm. in DC) [Shaw P.]
*PRACTICE AREAS: Financial Institutions Law.
Powell, William E., III ....'59 '93 C.839 B.A. L.94 J.D. [Dickstein S.M.&O.] (Pat.)
*PRACTICE AREAS: Intellectual Property; Patent Prosecution; Trademark Prosecution; Copyright Prosecution; Copyright Litigation.

Powell, Goldstein, Frazer & Murphy LLP, (AV)
6th Floor, 1001 Pennsylvania Avenue, N.W., 20004 ⊙
Telephone: 202-347-0066 Fax: 202-624-7222
URL: http://www.pgfm.com
Resident Members: Jessica C. Abrahams; J. Gail Bancroft; Richard M. Belanger; Joseph M. Berl; Jerome A. Breed; Ralph J. Caccia; Kelly Cameron; Anne B. Camper; Michael H. Chanin; William C. Crenshaw; Butler C. Derrick, Jr.; Robert W. Doyle, Jr.; William Gerald Driggers; Neil R. Ellis; Michael E. Fine; Lawrence R. Fullerton; Larry S. Gage; Ronald S. Gart; Elizabeth Cole Hafner; David C. Hammond; Harry Huge; Brenda A. Jacobs; Brett G. Kappel; John J. Knapp; Jeffrey P. Kushan; Simon Lazarus, III; Robert E. Madden; Niall P. Meagher; Richard A. Medway; James E. Mendenhall; Thomas T. Moga; N. David Palmeter; Alan K. Parver; Daniel M. Price; Charles H. Roistacher; Leonard J. Rubin; Allen S. Rugg; Michael I. Sanders; Peter W. Segal; W. Bruce Shirk; Andrew W. Shoyer; Steven K. Stranne; Andrew J. Strenio, Jr.; Robert Torresen, Jr.; Mark Traphagen; Colin W. Uckert; William H.E. von Oehsen; Lawrence R. Walders; Richard C. Wilder (Not admitted in DC). Of Counsel: Andrew I. Gavil; David Ginsburg; Amber Wong Hsu; Nancy Ortmeyer Kuhn (Not admitted in DC); Susan Leahy; William J. Lehrfeld; Amelia Porges; G. Lee Skillington; David W. Woodward. Counsel: Susan A. Cobb; Charlotte Collins (Not admitted in DC); Barbara D.A. Eyman; Robert N. Falk; Michael J. Grace; Mary Baroody Lowe. Resident Associates: Jill M. Abrams; Andre Barlow (Not admitted in DC); Marinn F. Carlson; June Casalmir (Not admitted in DC); Robert G. Coberly; Lisa Ann Crosby; Maria T. DiGiulian (Not admitted in DC); Christa L. Dommers (Not admitted in DC); Lorenzo F. Exposito; Leigh Fraiser; Robert L. Galbreath; Diane Greenlee; Jennifer L. Haworth (Not admitted in DC); Robin Heimann-McGhee; Kyra Fischbeck Howell (Not admitted in DC); Thomas E.M. Hutton (Not admitted in DC); Alexander Koff; Sheryl Krongold; Anne M. Lewis; Charles A. Luband; Robert L. Magielnicki, Jr. (Not admitted in DC); Susan M. Mathews; Camelia C. Mazard; Jocelyn C. Nieva (Not admitted in DC); Paul D.A. Piquado (Not admitted in DC); William Compton Poling, Jr; David C. Quam; J. Christopher Rodgers (Not admitted in DC); Donna Marie Rodney; Stephen R. Smith; David A. Steffes (Not admitted in DC); Bart T. Valad; Adam W. Walsh; Cynthia Y. Wong (Not admitted in DC); Anie Elizabeth Wulkan. Foreign Counsel: Stanimir A. Alexandrov; Lauro Locks (Not admitted in the United States); Maurits J.F. Lugard. Foreign Associate: Patricio Grané Labat (Not admitted in the United States).
Administrative Advocacy, Antitrust and Trade Regulation, Banking, Litigation, Corporate Finance and Securities, Employee Benefits, Executive Compensation, Environmental, Estate Planning, Financial Institutions, Lending and Securitization, Government Contracts and Construction Litigation, Healthcare, Immigration, Intellectual Property and Technology, International Business, International Trade, Labor and Employment, Legislative and Public Policy Advocacy, Litigation, Mergers and Acquisitions, Public Finance, Real Estate and Housing, Securities, Secured Transactions, Tax, Technology Litigation, Trade Associations, Software, Trademarks, Patents and Copyrights, White Collar Crime, Workouts, Bankruptcy and Insolvency, Y2K.
Atlanta, Georgia Office: Sixteenth Floor, 191 Peachtree Street, N.E., 30303. Telephone: 404-572-6600. Fax: 404-572-6999.
Reston, Virginia Office: Suite 1375, 11951 Freedom Drive, 20190. Telephone: 703-251-4828.
Geneva, Switzerland Office: Sixth Floor, Rue de Lausanne 139, 1202 Geneva. Telephone: +41-22-908 25 25.
See Professional Biographies, WASHINGTON, DISTRICT OF COLUMBIA

Powell-Woodson, Dorthula H. .... '56 '82 C.892 B.A. L.692 J.D. [Wiley R.&F.]
*PRACTICE AREAS: Health Care; Government Contracts; Privacy Law.
Power, Richard J. ....'51 '79 C.94 B.S. L.1202 J.D. 1825 I St., N.W.
Power, Susan H. '48 '74 C.207 B.A. L.273 J.D.
Assoc. Gen. Coun., Potomac Electric Power Company

Power, Tracy J. ....'56 '81 C&L.276 B.A., J.D. [Power&P.] ⊙
*PRACTICE AREAS: Federal Taxation; State Taxation; Taxation Law; Corporate Taxation; Business Law.

Power & Power, (AV)
4721 MacArthur Boulevard, 20007 ⊙
Telephone: 202-659-9061
Email: tpower@erols.com
Tracy J. Power.
Practice before Federal and State Courts, Agencies and Departments. Labor and Employment, Wage and Hour, Tax, Tax Litigation.
Arlington, Virginia Office: Courthouse Plaza, Suite 1107, 2300 Clarendon Boulevard. Telephone: 703-841-1330. Facsimile: 703-841-1822. E-Mail: power@erols.com.
See Professional Biographies, WASHINGTON, DISTRICT OF COLUMBIA

Powers, Brian A., (AV) .... '50 '77 C.1044 B.A. L.575 J.D. [O'Donoghue&O.]
Powers, David N. ....'56 '82 C.674 A.B. L.893 J.D. [Baker B.]
Powers, Galen D., (AV) ....'36 '62 C&L.477 A.B., LL.B. [Powers,P.S.&V.]
*PRACTICE AREAS: Health Care Law; Hospital Law; Corporate Law; Joint Ventures Law.
Powers, Joan S., (AV) ...... '53 '78 C.103 A.B. L.659 J.D. Sr. Coun., Intl. Monetary Fund
Powers, Mary Ellen ....'55 '80 C.604 A.B. L.893 J.D. [Jones,D.R.&P.]
*PRACTICE AREAS: Litigation; Complex Business Litigation; Corporate Investigations; RICO.
Powers, N. Thompson, (AV) ..... '29 '54 C.228 B.A. L.309 LL.B. 1330 Conn. Ave., N.W.
Powers, Peter G., (AV) '30 '59 C.051 B.A. L.309 LL.B.
(adm. in MA; not adm. in DC) Gen. Coun., Smithsonian Instit.
Powers, Richard E., Jr. ....'52 '77 C.285 B.S. L.602 J.D. [Dorsey&W.]
*PRACTICE AREAS: Energy; Administrative; Public Utility; Legislative Practice; International.
Powers, Thomas P., (AV) ....'34 '65 C.107 B.A. L.273 LL.B. [Powers&L.]
Powers & Lewis, (AV) ....4201 Connecticut Ave., N.W.

Powers, Pyles, Sutter & Verville, P.C., (AV) BB
Twelfth Floor, 1875 Eye Street, N.W., 20006-5409
Telephone: 202-466-6550 Fax: 202-785-1756
Email: ppsv@ppsv.com URL: http://www.ppsv.com
Galen D. Powers; James C. Pyles; Ronald N. Sutter; Richard E. Verville; Mary Susan Philp; Robert J. Saner, II; Stanley A. Freeman; Peter W. Thomas; Thomas Hylden; Christopher L. Keough; Harold Damelin; Joel M. Hamme; Joel M. Rudnick; Diane S. Millman;—Marla P. Spindel; C. Anthony Russo; Adam H. Greene (Not admitted in DC); Amy E. Nordeng; Justin R. Hunter (Not admitted in DC). Of Counsel: Rebecca L. Burke; Donald W. Aaronson; D. Benson Tesdahl; Edith S. Marshall; Sherry Mastrostefano Gray.
Health Care and Hospital Law, Education Law, Antitrust, Taxation and Corporate Law, Litigation, Legislative Law.
See Professional Biographies, WASHINGTON, DISTRICT OF COLUMBIA

Poynor, Daniel J. ....'69 '95 C.937 B.A. L.893 J.D. [Ⓐ Steptoe&J.]
Pozen, Sharis Arnold, (BV) .... '64 '89 C.183 B.A. L.910 J.D. [Hogan&H.]
*PRACTICE AREAS: Antitrust and Trade Regulation; Litigation.
Pozen, Thorn L. ....'65 '98 L.904 J.D. [Ⓐ Arnold&P.]
*PRACTICE AREAS: Government Contracts; Public Policy.
Poznick, Jill L. ....'67 '92 C.477 B.A. L.30 J.D. 10 G St., N.E.
Prabhu, Jay V. .... '70 '96 C&L.309 B.A., J.D. [Ⓐ Wilmer,C.&P.]
Prada, Vincent F., (AV) ....'56 '82 C.951 B.A. L.145 J.D. [Sidley A.B.&W.]
Prado, Marta Maria ....'74 '99 C&L.276 B.A., J.D. [Ⓐ Stewart&S.]
*PRACTICE AREAS: International Trade; Antidumping; Countervailing Duties; World Trade Organization.
Prager, Lutz Alexander ....'32 '58 C.311 B.A. L.976 LL.B. Asst. Dep. Corp. Coun.
Prakash, Ambari ....'70 '97 C.882 B.A. L.276 J.D. [Ⓐ Thelen R.&P.]
*PRACTICE AREAS: Corporate Law; Project and Asset Finance.
Prall, Willow J. ....'65 '94 C.446 B.A. L.273 J.D. [Ⓐ De Carlo,C.&S.]
Prame, Christine Liverzani ....'67 '92 C.321 B.A. L.724 J.D. [Ⓐ Sidley A.B.&W.]
Prame, Michael J. ....'68 '94 C.1031 B.S. L.276 J.D. [Ⓐ Groom]
Prass, Ronald E., Jr. .... '63 '96 C.871 B.S. L.30 J.D. [Ⓐ Kenyon&K.] (See Pat. Sect.)
*PRACTICE AREAS: Intellectual Property.
Prasse, Barbara J. '72 '00 C.1090 B.S. L.1209 J.D.
(adm. in VA; not adm. in DC) [Ⓐ Friedlander,M.S.K.&O.]
*PRACTICE AREAS: Civil Litigation; Insurance Defense; Workers Compensation.
Pratt, Darren G. '69 '95 C&L.893 B.S., J.D.
(adm. in MD; not adm. in DC) 815 Conn. Ave., N.W.‡

Pratt, Elina Hum '56 '83 C.188 A.B. L.276 J.D.
1120 G Street N.W., Suite 200, 20005
Telephone: 202-347-3773; 877-460-6372 Fax: 202-347-3861 URL: www.prattlaw.com
Email: epratt@prattlaw.com URL: http://www.lawyers.com/prattlaw
***PRACTICE AREAS: Taxation Law; Trusts and Estates; Probate; Income Tax; Estate and Gift Taxation.**
Cantonese and Chinese
Taxation, Trusts and Estates, Wills, Probate, Income Tax, Estates, Gift Taxation, International Taxation, Corporate Taxation and Business Planning.
See Professional Biographies, WASHINGTON, DISTRICT OF COLUMBIA

Pratt, Richard J. ....'65 '91 C.228 A.B. L.659 J.D. [Ross,D.&B.]
Pratt, William H. .... '54 '88 C.1102 B.S. L.30 J.D. [Finnegan,H.F.G.&D.]
*PRACTICE AREAS: Intellectual Property Arbitration; Intellectual Property Licensing; International Intellectual Property; International Licensing; Technology Licensing.
Pravlik, Carolyn Smith ....'55 '80 C.600 B.A. L.128 J.D. [Terris,P.&W.]
Preheim, Elissa J. ....'71 '96 C.597 B.A. L.347 J.D. [Ⓐ Arnold&P.]
*PRACTICE AREAS: Litigation; Intellectual Property.
Preis, John Frederick '71 '00 C.188 B.S. L.880 J.D.
(adm. in VA; not adm. in DC) 1310 E St. NE
Preiss, Jeremy O. ....'62 '90 C.367 B.A. L.659 J.D. 1722 Eye St., N.W.
Preiss, Valerie G. ....'65 '89 C.839 B.A. L.273 J.D. [Ⓐ Carr G.]
Preminger, Clifford J., (BV) ...'52 '76 C.823 A.B. L.930 J.D. 5335 Wisconsin Ave., N.W.
Prendergast, John A. ....'— '85 C.423 B.A. L.276 J.D. [Blooston,M.D.D.&P.]
*PRACTICE AREAS: Telecommunications Law; FCC Licensing; FCC Regulation; PCS.
Prensky, David N. ....'52 '77 C.966 B.A. L.276 J.D. [Chasen&C.]
Press, Daniel S. ....'43 '69 C.178 B.A. L.976 LL.B. [Van Ness F.]
*PRACTICE AREAS: Indian Law; Indian Economic Development.
Press, Michelle Lynn ....'71 '97 C.273 B.A. L.930 J.D. [Press&P.]
Press, Morton H., (AV) ....'41 '66 C&L.273 B.A., J.D. [Press&P.]
Press, Theodore L., (AV) ....'— '68 C.188 A.B. L.178 J.D. [Kirkpatrick&L.]
*PRACTICE AREAS: Federal Income Tax; Corporate Tax Planning; Partnership Taxation; Investment Partnerships; Business Trusts.
Press & Press, PLLC, (AV) ....2150 Wisconsin Avenue, N.W.
Pressel, Wayne M. .... '47 '72 C.299 A.B. L.94 J.D. National Legal Aid & Def. Assn.
Pressey, Montia Givens .... '66 '92 C.893 B.A. L.276 J.D. [Ⓐ Finnegan,H.F.G.&D.]
*PRACTICE AREAS: Trademarks.
Pressler, James W., Jr., (AV) ....'48 '74 C.884 A.B. L.818 J.D. [Riselli&P.]
Pressler, Larry ....'42 '72 C.793 B.A. L.309 J.D. [O'Connor&H.]
*PRACTICE AREAS: Telcom; Corporate Law; International Law.
Pressley, John F., Jr. ....'49 '84 C.329 B.S.E.E. L.273 J.D. 7600 Georgia Ave., N.W.
Preston, Richard McKim, (AV) ....'47 '76 C&L.902 B.A., J.D. [Seyfarth S.]
*PRACTICE AREAS: Construction Contracts Law; Government Contracts Law; International Contracts Law.
Preston, Stephen W. ....'57 '83 C.976 B.A. L.309 J.D. [Wilmer,C.&P.]
*PRACTICE AREAS: Appellate Litigation; Civil Litigation; Defense and Aerospace; False Claims Act and Qui Tam; Foreign Corrupt Practices Act.

Preston Gates Ellis & Rouvelas Meeds LLP, (AV)
1735 New York Avenue, N.W. Suite 500, 20006-5209 ⊙
Telephone: 202-628-1700 Facsimile: 202-331-1024
Email: info@prestongates.com URL: http://www.prestongates.com
Resident Partners: Jonathan Blank; Pamela Jeanne Garvie; Susan B. Geiger; Bruce J. Heiman; Christopher S. Huther; Glenn F. Ivey; Donald A. Kaplan; John L. Longstreth; Rolf Marshall; Eugene P. Miller; William N. Myhre; Michael J. O'Neil; Tim L. Peckinpaugh; Emanuel L. Rouvelas; Mark H. Ruge (Not admitted in DC); Melanie Sabo; William A. Shook; Martin L. Stern; Lisa Helpert Tucker (Not admitted in DC); James R. Weiss. Resident Associates: Julie J. Crain; Kelley Patrick Doran; Lisa L. Friedlander; Caryn Blythe Houck (Not admitted in DC); Kristie Jackson (Not admitted in DC); Marybeth Brennan Magee (Not admitted in DC); Brian K. McCalmon; Hong J. Park (Not admitted in DC); Daniel Ritter (Not admitted in DC); Jorge Romero; Daniel A. Silien; W. David Thomas; Megan H. Troy (Not admitted in DC). Of Counsel: John A. Bastek (Not admitted in DC); Arthur Dimopoulos; Elizabeth Wallace Fleming; Harrison D. Hutson; G. Matthew Koehl (Not admitted in DC); Lloyd Meeds; Sandra E. Rizzo; Steven Richards Valentine. Staff Attorney: David M. Gilmore; Kenneth S. Knox.
Federal Legislative, Administrative and Litigation Practice. Transportation, Telecommunications, Fisheries, Reinsurance and Insurance, High Technology, Antitrust, International Trade, Tax Policy, Forest Products and Natural Resources, Government Contract Law and Federal Procurement Policy, Environmental, Energy and Native American Issues.
Anchorage, Alaska Office: Preston Gates & Ellis LLP, 420 L Street, Suite 400, 99501-1937. Telephone: 907-276-1969. Facsimile: 907-276-1365.
Coeur d'Alene, Idaho Office: Preston Gates & Ellis LLP, 1200 Ironwood Drive, Suite 315, 83814. Telephone: 208-667-1839. Facsimile: 208-765-2494.
Irvine, California Office: Preston Gates & Ellis LLP, Four Park Plaza, Suite 1900, 92614-5925. Telephone: 949-253-0900. Facsimile: 949-253-0902.
Los Angeles, California Office: Preston Gates & Ellis LLP, 725 South Figueroa Street, Suite 2100, 90017. Telephone: 213-624-2395. Facsimile: 213-624-5924.
Palo Alto, California Office: Preston Gates & Ellis LLP, 100 Hamilton Avenue, Suite 100, 94301-1656. Telephone: 650-325-8088. Fax: 650-325-8388.
Portland, Oregon Office: Preston Gates & Ellis LLP, 222 S.W. Columbia Street, 1400 KOIN Tower, 97201-6632. Telephone: 503-228-3200. Facsimile: 503-248-9085.
San Francisco, California Office: Preston Gates & Ellis LLP, One Maritime Plaza, Suite 2400, 94111. Telephone: 415-788-8822. Facsimile: 415-788-8819.
Seattle, Washington Office: Preston Gates & Ellis LLP, 701 Fifth Avenue, Suite 5000, 98104-7078. Telephone: 206-623-7580. Facsimile: 206-623-7022.
Spokane, Washington Office: Preston Gates & Ellis LLP, 601 West Riverside Drive, Suite 1400, 99201-0636. Telephone: 509-624-2100. Facsimile: 509-456-0146.
Hong Kong Office: Preston Gates & Ellis LLP, 1001 Hutchison House, 10 Harcourt Road. Telephone: 852-2511-5100. Facsimile: 852-2511-9515.
See Professional Biographies, WASHINGTON, DISTRICT OF COLUMBIA

Pretty, William '— '98 C.1042 B.A. L.999 LL.B.
(adm. in AZ; not adm. in DC) 400 Second St., S.W.
Prettyman, E. Barrett, Jr., (AV) .... '25 '54 C.976 B.A. L.893 LL.B. [Hogan&H.]
*PRACTICE AREAS: Administrative Law; Appellate Practice; Civil Appeals.
Pretzat, Mark F. .... '56 '82 C.276 A.B. L.724 J.D. [Duane,M.&H.]
*PRACTICE AREAS: Financial Institutions Law; Corporate Law.
Prewitt, Jean M. ......'48 '75 C.681 A.B. L.276 J.D. Jr. V.P. & CFO, Podesta Assocs., Inc.
Prezioso, Giovanni P., (AV) ....'57 '82 C&L.309 A.B., J.D. [Cleary,G.S.&H.]
Prezis, Samuel B. ....'17 '47 L.537 LL.B. 4858 Albemarle St., N.W.‡
Price, Alan H., (BV) .... '59 '84 C.1044 B.A. L.273 J.D. [Wiley R.&F.]
*PRACTICE AREAS: International Trade.
Price, Andrew Douglas ....'69 '96 C.880 B.A. L.802 J.D. [Ⓐ Venable,A.B.H.&C.]
*PRACTICE AREAS: Trademarks.
Price, Andrew M. ....'— '95 C.174 B.S.B.A. L.1209 J.D. [Ⓐ Piper M.R.&W.]
*PRACTICE AREAS: Government Contracts.
Price, D. Douglas, (AV) ....'43 '68 C.502 B.S.Ch.E. L.273 J.D. [Ⓒ Steptoe&J.] (Pat.)
*PRACTICE AREAS: Intellectual Property Law; Chemical Patents; Mechanical Patents; Interference Law.
Price, Daniel M., (BV) .... '55 '81 C.311 B.A. L.309 J.D. [Powell,G.F.&M.]
*PRACTICE AREAS: International Business Transactions; International Arbitration.
Price, David E. '64 '96 C.446 B.A. L.1364 J.D.
(adm. in MD; not adm. in DC) [Ⓐ R.M.Price]
Price, Griffith B., Jr., (AV) ...... '42 '67 C.309 A.B. L.569 LL.B. [Finnegan,H.F.G.&D.]
*PRACTICE AREAS: Trade Secrets; Domain Name Infringement; Internet Trademark Law; Intellectual Property Litigation; Patent Litigation.
Price, Irene, (AV) ....'48 '78 C.911 B.A. L.273 J.D. [McDermott,W.&E.]
Price, Joseph H., (AV) .... '39 '64 C.16 A.B. L.309 LL.B. [Gibson,D.&C.]
*PRACTICE AREAS: International Trade; International Business Transactions; International Arbitrations; Customs and Administrative Law.
Price, Joseph R. ....'71 '96 C.945 B.A. L.893 J.D. [Ⓐ Arent F.K.P.&K.]
*PRACTICE AREAS: White Collar Crime; Criminal Defense; Civil Litigation; Employment Litigation.
Price, Lee '50 '77 C.813 B.A. L.477 J.D.
(adm. in MI; not adm. in DC) Intl. Union, UAW
Price, Lisa A. ....'64 '93 C&L.893 B.A., J.D. [Ⓐ Arnold&P.]
*PRACTICE AREAS: Litigation.
Price, Lori Hamilton .... '62 '93 C&L.446 B.A., J.D. [Ⓐ Wilmer,C.&P.]
Price, Natalie S. '65 '93 C.797 B.A. L.1015 J.D.
(adm. in TN; not adm. in DC) 3050 K St., N.W.
Price, R. Edward ....'69 '95 C.454 B.A. L.273 J.D. [Ⓐ Vinson&E.]
*PRACTICE AREAS: Telecommunications Law; Communications and Media; Regulatory Law; Administrative Law; Appellate Practice.
Price, Richard M., (AV) .... '64 '88 C&L.273 B.A., J.D. [Nixon P.]
*PRACTICE AREAS: Litigation; Housing; Community Development; Administrative Law; Commercial Real Estate.
Price, Robert L., (AV) ....'35 '65 C.516 B.S. L.273 J.D. [McDermott,W.&E.] (Pat.)
Price, Robert M., Law Offices of, (AV) '38 '63
C.790 A.B. L.273 J.D. 1915 Eye Street, N.W. Suite 500
Price, Seth J. ....'69 '96 C.659 B.A. L.273 J.D. 3000 K St., N.W.
Price, Stephen J. .... '59 '91 C.216 B.A. L.420 J.D. Atty., Washington Gas Light Co.
*RESPONSIBILITIES: Litigation.
Price, Tilghman Earle .... '66 '95 C.893 B.A. L.64 LL.D. [Ⓐ Piper M.R.&W.]
*PRACTICE AREAS: Real Estate Development; Finance; Securities.
Price, William C. '48 '77 C.103 A.B. L.818 J.D.
(adm. in MA; not adm. in DC) American Insurance Association
Price-Wright, Shanna N. '71 '00
C.446 B.S. L.180 J.D. Consultant, Pricewaterhouse Coopers LLP
Prichard, Daniel D. '74 '00 C.1365 B.S. L.893 J.D.
(adm. in VA; not adm. in DC) [Ⓐ Dow,L.&A.]
Pries, Stephanie M. ....'69 '98 C.674 A.B. L.770 J.D. [Ⓐ Brobeck,P.&H.]
*PRACTICE AREAS: Corporate Law; Securities.
Priesing, Dana ....'57 '84 C.75 B.A. L.276 J.D. 733 15th St., N.W.
Priest, Alan G. ....'52 '79 C.1044 B.A. L.273 J.D. [Ropes&G.]
Priester, Benjamin J. '74 '99 C.309 A.B. L.228 J.D.
(adm. in CT; not adm. in DC) [Ⓐ Ropes&G.]
Prieto, Mariana '— '96
(adm. in NY; not adm. in DC) [Ⓐ Foley,H.&E.]
*PRACTICE AREAS: International Business Transactions; Securities Regulation.
Primis, Craig S. ....'69 '96 C.103 A.B. L.309 J.D. [Kirkland&E.]
*PRACTICE AREAS: Litigation.
Primosch, Robert D., (AV) ....'61 '87 C&L.276 B.A., J.D. [Wilkinson B.K.]
*PRACTICE AREAS: Communications; Telecommunications Law; Corporate; Commercial Transactions; Appellate Practice.

Prince, Allison C., (AV) .... '58 '84 C.105 B.A. L.128 J.D. [Ⓒ Shaw P.]
*PRACTICE AREAS: Real Estate; Zoning, Planning and Land Use; Municipal Law.
Prince, Carolyn A. .... '— '97 C.1042 B.A. L.904 J.D. [Ⓐ Garvey,S.&B.]
*PRACTICE AREAS: Litigation; Government Contracts; Corporate Law.
Prince, Edward M., (AV) .... '37 '62 C.976 B.S. L.893 LL.B. [Ⓒ Alston&B.] (Pat.)
*PRACTICE AREAS: Trademarks.
Principe, Leta A. .... '71 '99 C.918 B.A. L.276 J.D. [Ⓐ Katten M.Z.]
*PRACTICE AREAS: Commercial Real Estate Transactions.
Pringle, Shawn R. '70 '96 C.260 B.S. L.569 J.D.
(adm. in FL; not adm. in DC) 2100 Pennsylvania Ave., N.W.
Prioleau, Florence Weatherly, (AV) .... '52 '79 C.289 B.A. L.276 J.D. [Patton B.]
Pritchard, Erik .... '71 '99 C.112 B.A. L.893 J.D. [Ⓐ Ross,D.&B.]
Pritchard, Therese D. '53 '78 C.104 A.B. L.93 J.D.
(adm. in MA; not adm. in DC) [Bryan C.]
*PRACTICE AREAS: Banking Securities.
Pritchard-Kelly, Ruth .... '61 '96 C&L.446 B.A., J.D. [Ⓐ Swidler B.S.F.]
*PRACTICE AREAS: Telecommunications.
Pritchett, Daniel M., III .... '28 '67 C.512 B.S. L.275 J.D. 4200 19th St., NE‡
Pritchett, Diane P. .... '67 '94 C&L.502 B.S., J.D. [Ⓐ Hamilton&H.]
*PRACTICE AREAS: Civil Litigation; Employment Law; Education Law; Corporate Law.
Pritchett, Scott M. .... '57 '93 C.184 B.S. L.228 J.D. [Ⓐ Holland&K.]
*PRACTICE AREAS: Health Care; Regulatory and Civil/Criminal Fraud Defense; Corporate.
Pritzker, Malcolm L., (AV) '35 '68
C.645 B.A. L.831 J.D. 5301 Wisconsin Avenue, N.W., Suite 610
Privor, Brian M. .... '— '00 C.861 B.A. L.309 J.D. [Ⓐ Morgan,L.&B.]
Procter, Ben R. .... '53 '92 C.840 B.A. L.276 J.D. Procter & Co.
Proctor, Deidra Nicole '72 '00 C.512 B.A. L.276 J.D.
(adm. in MD; not adm. in DC) [Ⓐ Swidler B.S.F.]
*PRACTICE AREAS: Insurance Litigation; Litigation.
Proctor, John P., (AV) .... '42 '68 C.674 B.A. L.659 LL.B. [Winston&S.]
*PRACTICE AREAS: Environmental Law; Energy Law.
Proctor, Shemin V. .... '65 '91 C.681 B.A. L.309 J.D. [Andrews&K.]
*PRACTICE AREAS: Energy Law.
Profaizer, Joseph R. .... '67 '93 C&L.846 B.A., J.D. [Ⓒ Wilmer,C.&P.]
*PRACTICE AREAS: Litigation; Arbitration; International Law.
Profeta, Laura .... '58 '85 C.174 B.A. L.861 J.D. Inter-Amer. Develop. Bk.
Proger, Phillip A., (AV) .... '48 '73 C&L.446 B.A., J.D. [Jones,D.R.&P.]
*PRACTICE AREAS: Antitrust; Antitrust Class Actions; Business Combinations; International Antitrust.
Prokop, Christopher J. .... '73 '99 C.659 B.A. L.309 J.D. [Ⓐ Covington&B.]
Prokop, John A., Jr. .... '35 '67 C&L.273 A.B., J.D. 1133 15th St., N.W.
Propst, Stephen F. .... '70 '98 C.674 B.A. L.893 J.D. [Ⓐ Hogan&H.]
Prosen, Lawrence M. .... '70 '97 C.446 B.S. L.128 J.D. [Ⓐ Bell,B.&L.]
*PRACTICE AREAS: Construction Litigation; Government Contracts Law; Architects and Engineers Errors and Omissions; Civil Practice; Real Estate.

Proskauer Rose LLP, (AV) BR
1233 Twentieth Street, N.W. Suite 800, 20036-2396 ⊙
Telephone: 202-416-6800 FAX: 202-416-6899
URL: http://www.proskauer.com
Members of Firm: Jon A. Baumgarten; Mark J. Biros; Joseph E. Casson; Warren L. Dennis; Malcolm J. Harkins, III; Lawrence Z. Lorber; Richard H. Rowe; Christopher Wolf. Washington, D.C. Senior Counsel: Thomas H. Brock; Alec W. Farr; James P. Holloway; Lionel E. Pashkoff; Stephen D. Solomon; Susan A. Turner. Washington, D.C. Associates: Margaret J. Babb; Christine D. Bachman; Anita M. Bahauddin (Not admitted in DC); Richard S. Basile (Not admitted in DC); Bruce E. Boyden; Susan Brinkerhoff; Amy J. Dilcher (Not admitted in DC); Brian Elsbernd; Amybeth Garcia-Bokor; Stephanie L. Marn; Mark A. McAndrew; Julia McMillen; Richard E. Ramsay; Cheralyn E. Schessler; Megan H. Tinker; Andrew L. Wexton.
General Practice.
New York, New York Office: 1585 Broadway. Telephone: 212-969-3000. Fax: 212-969-2900.
Los Angeles, California Office: 2049 Century Park East, Suite 3200. Telephone: 310-557-2900. Fax: 310-557-2193.
Boca Raton, Florida Office: One Boca Place, Suite 340 West, 2255 Glades Road. Telephone: 407-241-7400. Fax: 561-241-7145.
Newark, New Jersey Office: One Newark Center. Telephone: 973-274-3200. Fax: 973-274-3299.
Paris, France Office: Proskauer Rose, 68, rue du Faubourg Saint-Honoré. Telephone: +33-1-53-05-60-00. Fax: +33-1-53-05-60-05.

See Professional Biographies, WASHINGTON, DISTRICT OF COLUMBIA

Prothro, Gwendolyn .... '72 '96 C.674 A.B. L.309 J.D. [Ⓐ Steptoe&J.]
Proto, Neil T., (BV) .... '— '73 C.1102 B.A. L.273 J.D. [Verner,L.B.M.&H.]
*PRACTICE AREAS: Environmental; Administrative; Urban Development; Litigation.
Proujansky, Adam .... '63 '89 C.188 A.B. L.309 J.D. [Dickstein S.M.&O.]
*PRACTICE AREAS: Criminal and Civil Litigation.
Proulx, Dana K. '51 '82 C.103 A.B. L.273 J.D.
(adm. in MD; not adm. in DC) Asst. V.P. & Ins. Law Compliance Offr., GEICO Corp.
Provencher, Shelby L. .... '69 '96 C.882 B.A. L.128 J.D. [Ⓐ Jones,D.R.&P.]
Provencio, Carlos E. .... '68 '96 C.821 B.A. L.734 J.D. [Ⓐ Clifford C.R.&W.]
*PRACTICE AREAS: Antitrust; Commercial Litigation; Securities Litigation; Corporate Compliance; White Collar.

Provost & Umphrey Law Firm, L.L.P.
Suite 410, 1155 15th Street, N.W., 20005 ⊙
Telephone: 202-466-0900 Fax: 202-637-2977
Email: provost@erols.com URL: http://www.provostumphrey.com
Member of Firm: Reuben A. Guttman (Manager, Washington, D.C. Office). Associates: Brian P. McCafferty (Not admitted in DC); Traci L. Buschner; Katherine B. Bornstein (Not admitted in DC). General Civil and Trial Practice. False Claims Act Litigation, Antitrust Litigation, Securities Litigation, Commercial Litigation, Employment and Labor Litigation, Environmental Litigation, First Amendment Litigation and Civil Rights Litigation.
Port Arthur, Texas Office: 2901 Turtle Creek Drive, Suite 250, 77643. Telephone: 409-721-6260. Fax: 409-721-9579.
Beaumont, Texas Office: 490 Park Street, 77701. Telephone: 409-838-8821. Fax: 409-813-8655.
Nashville, Tennessee Office: 3343 Perimeter Hill, Suite 110. Telephone: 615-242-0199. Fax: 615-256-5922.
Albuquerque, New Mexico Office: 9621 Fourth Street NW. Telephone: 505-792-8500. Fax: 505-792-8700.
Denver, Colorado Office: 4155 East Jewell Avenue, Suite 707. Telephone: 303-756-3335. Fax: 303-756-9334.
Little Rock, Arkansas Office: 124 West Capitol Avenue, Suite 1805. Telephone: 501-374-3655. Fax: 501-374-4279.
Atlanta, Georgia Office: 181 14th Street, N.E., Suite 425. Telephone: 404-876-8100; 1-800-340-7862.
Friendswood, Texas Office: 211 East Parkwood, Suite 2017, 77546. Telephone: 281-992-1550. Fax: 281-992-2617.

See Professional Biographies, WASHINGTON, DISTRICT OF COLUMBIA

Proxmire, Douglas C. .... '61 '87 C.896 B.A. L.276 J.D. [Patton B.]
Prud'homme, Gerard J. .... '49 '86 C.367 B.A. L.446 J.D. [Hogan&H.]
*PRACTICE AREAS: Regulatory Law; Food, Drug and Cosmetic Law; Drug and Medical Device Regulation; Food and Drug Regulation.
Pruitt, David .... '70 '99 C&L.602 B.B.A., J.D. [Ⓐ Kirkland&E.]
*PRACTICE AREAS: Civil Litigation.
Pruitt, James C. .... '50 '75 C.880 B.A. L.861 J.D. V.P., Fed. Govt. Affs., Texaco Inc.
Pruitt, Jana Lee, (AV) .... '55 '81 C.383 B.A. L.421 J.D. [Baker&D.]
*PRACTICE AREAS: Insurance; Legislative and Regulatory.
Pruitt, Kristin L. .... '71 '96 C.602 B.A. L.930 J.D. [Ⓐ Skadden,A.S.M.&F.]
*PRACTICE AREAS: Mergers and Acquisitions; Corporate Finance.

Pruthy, Suresh, & Associates, Law Offices of '57 '89
C.999 B.A. L.329 M.C.J. 2120 L Street, NW, Suite 210
Pruzan, Jerry Z. '38 '61 C.339 B.A. L.145 J.D.
(adm. in IL; not adm. in DC) ARCO
Pryce, Jeffrey F. .... '60 '93 C.918 B.A. L.976 J.D. [Ⓒ Steptoe&J.]
*PRACTICE AREAS: International Law; Electronic Commerce.
Pryor, Michael H. .... '53 '89 C.907 B.S. L.276 J.D. [Mintz,L.C.F.G.&P.]
*PRACTICE AREAS: Communications Law; Policy and Regulation.
Pryor, William C. .... '32 '59 C.197 A.B. L.276 J.D. Sr. Assoc. J., D.C. Ct. of App.
Prywes, Daniel I. .... '57 '80 C&L.659 B.A., J.D. [Pepper H.]
*PRACTICE AREAS: Commercial Litigation; Regulatory Law.
Przypyszny, John R. .... '65 '90 C&L.276 A.B., J.D. [Ⓒ Drinker B.&R.]
Psyhogeos, Nicholas J. '67 '93 C.93 B.A. L.818 J.D.
(adm. in MA; not adm. in DC) Corp. Atty., Microsoft Corp.
Pucciariello, Nona S. '64 '90 C.846 B.B.A. L.845 J.D.
(adm. in TX; not adm. in DC) [Ⓐ Cameron M.]
*PRACTICE AREAS: Energy; Project Finance.
Puckett, Craig L. '65 '99 C.112 B.S. L.1218 J.D.
(adm. in VA; not adm. in DC) [Ⓐ Brobeck,P.&H.]
*PRACTICE AREAS: Intellectual Property.
Puentes, Jacqueline P. '74 '01 C.31 B.A. L.880 J.D.
(adm. in VA; not adm. in DC) [Ⓐ Womble C.S.&R.]
*PRACTICE AREAS: Banking, Finance and Property.
Pugh, Daniel W. .... '66 '94 C.453 S.B. L.446 J.D. [Ⓒ Davis W.T.]
Pugh, Keith E., Jr., (AV) .... '37 '62 C.675 L.800 J.D. [Howrey S.A.&W.]
*PRACTICE AREAS: Antitrust; Complex Commercial Litigation.
Pugh, Martha Groves .... '64 '93 C.923 B.S.B.A. L.284 J.D. [McDermott,W.&E.]
Pujo, Leslie Johnson .... '65 '97 C.857 B.A. L.273 J.D. [Ⓐ Wiley R.&F.]
Pump, Ronald E. .... '42 '74 C.276 A.B. L.904 J.D. AT&T
Punke, Michael W. .... '— '89 C.273 B.A. L.188 J.D. [Mayer,B.&P.]
*PRACTICE AREAS: International Law.
Pupkin, Barry A., (AV) .... '50 '76 C.763 A.B. L.813 J.D. [Squire,S.&D.]
*PRACTICE AREAS: Regulatory Affairs; Antitrust and Trade Regulation.
Purcell, John M. .... '— '00 C.966 B.A. L.276 J.D. [Ⓐ Piper M.R.&W.]
*PRACTICE AREAS: Corporate Law; Securities; Mergers and Acquisitions; Venture Capital; Emerging Growth Companies.
Purcell, Michael Sean .... '67 '92 C.30 B.A. L.128 J.D. [Vorys,S.S.&P.]
*PRACTICE AREAS: Corporate Law; International Law.
Purdie, Denise W. '50 '83 C.329 B.A. L.823 J.D.
(adm. in NY; not adm. in DC) Howard University Law Sch.
Purdy, Donald A., Jr. .... '51 '76 C.945 B.A. L.893 J.D. Chief Deputy, Gen. Coun.
Puretz, Jeffrey S. .... '53 '81 C.446 B.A. L.128 J.D. [Dechert]
*PRACTICE AREAS: Corporate Securities Law; Investment Management Law; Insurance Law; Financial Services Law.
Puri, Nicole D. .... '72 '00 C.966 B.B.A. L.1356 J.D. Sr. Proj. Mang./Staff Atty.
Purvis, Jennifer A. .... '68 '95 C.860 B.A. L.276 J.D. [Ⓐ Hogan&H.]
*PRACTICE AREAS: Communications.
Pusey, William A., (AV) .... '36 '63 C.674 A.B. L.893 J.D. [Ⓒ Hunton&W.]
*PRACTICE AREAS: Corporate; Securities.
Pushkar, Raymond S. E., (AV) .... '38 '63 C&L.436 A.B., J.D. [McKenna&C.]
*PRACTICE AREAS: Government Contracts Litigation; Commercial Contracts Litigation; Electronic Commerce; Litigation; International Contracts.
Puth, Jonathan C. .... '58 '92 C.174 B.A. L.276 J.D. [Ⓐ Webster,F.&B.]
*PRACTICE AREAS: Employment Law; Labor Law; Personal Injury; Litigation.
Putman, Lewis T., Jr. .... '61 '94 C.171 B.S. L.339 J.D. [Kirkland&E.]
*PRACTICE AREAS: Environmental Law; Natural Resources Law; Environmental Transaction Support.
Putnam, Earle W. '28 '58 C.197 A.B. L.273 J.D.
Gen. Coun., Amalgamated Transit Union, AFL-CIO
Putnam, John E. .... '— '93 C.951 B.A. L.145 J.D. [Ⓒ Akin,G.S.H.&F.] (⊙Denver, CO)
Pyle, Howard, III .... '40 '67 C.674 A.B. L.893 J.D. Houston Industries, Inc.
Pyle, Jennifer M. .... '65 '93 C.309 B.A. L.588 J.D. Pub. Def.
Pyles, James C., (AV) .... '45 '72 C.893 B.A. L.838 LL.B. [Powers,P.S.&V.]
*PRACTICE AREAS: Health Care Law; Hospital Law; Litigation; Administrative Law.
Pysher, Shannon M. .... '69 '97 C.309 B.A. L.893 J.D. [Ⓐ Shaw P.]
*PRACTICE AREAS: Technology Transactions; Health Law.
Qaimmaqami, Jamal .... '— '00 C.30 B.A. L.1494 J.D. [Ⓐ Latham&W.]
Quadrino, George A. .... '45 '71 C.455 B.S. L.276 J.D. [Manelli,D.&S.]
*PRACTICE AREAS: Maritime Law; Administrative Law; Transportation Regulation.

Quagliano & Seeger, (AV)
3243 P Street, N.W., 20007
Telephone: 202-822-8838 Fax: 202-822-6982
Email: info@quagseeg.com
Julie Quagliano Westemeier; Stephen M. Seeger; James J. Faughnan. Associate: Nicola Y. Whiteman; Seth Adam Robbins. Of Counsel: Alton K. Burton.
Commercial Litigation, Construction Law, Government Contracts, Bankruptcy and Creditors' Rights.

See Professional Biographies, WASHINGTON, DISTRICT OF COLUMBIA

Quale, John C., (AV) .... '46 '71 C&L.309 A.B., J.D. [Skadden,A.S.M.&F.]
Qualiana, Mary K. .... '59 '85 C.475 B.A. L.273 J.D. [Dow,L.&A.]
Quam, David C. .... '68 '93 C.228 B.A. L.880 J.D. [Ⓐ Powell,G.F.&M.]
*PRACTICE AREAS: Government Relations; Intellectual Property; International Business.
Quamme, Steven J. .... '60 '86 C&L.597 B.A., J.D. 5126 Tilden St., N.W.‡
Quan, Ducchi T. .... '74 '99 C.1505 B.A. L.597 J.D. [Ⓐ Fried,F.H.S.&J.]
*PRACTICE AREAS: Corporate Law.
Quander, Rohulamin .... '43 '74 C&L.329 B.A., J.D. Dept. of Consumer & Reg. Affs.
Quarles, Eloise .... '— '95 C.423 B.A. L.446 J.D. [Ⓐ Wilmer,C.&P.]
Quarles, James L., III, (AV) .... '46 '74 C.207 B.S. L.309 J.D. [Hale&D.]
*PRACTICE AREAS: Litigation.
Quarles, John, (AV) .... '35 '80 C.976 B.A. L.309 LL.B. [Morgan,L.&B.]
Quarles, Steven P., (AV) .... '42 '80 C.674 A.B. L.976 J.D. [Crowell&M.]
*PRACTICE AREAS: Natural Resources Law; Forestry Law; Mineral Law; Environmental Law; Energy Law.
Quarterman, Cynthia L., (BV) .... '61 '87 C.597 B.S.I.E. L.178 J.D. [Steptoe&J.]
*PRACTICE AREAS: Energy; Natural Resources; Environmental Law; Transportation; Administrative Law.
Quartner, Andrew A. '53 '78 C.976 B.A. L.178 J.D.
(adm. in MD; not adm, in DC) Cellport
Quashie, René Y. .... '66 '97 C.36 B.S. L.273 J.D. [Ⓐ Fulbright&J.]
*PRACTICE AREAS: Health Care.
Quatrini, Phillip A. .... '61 '94 C.645 B.S. L.128 J.D. [Ⓐ Bryan C.]
*PRACTICE AREAS: Transactions; Corporate Finance; Securities Regulation.
Quattrone, Robyn C. .... '73 '98 C.659 B.A. L.569 J.D. [Ⓐ Skadden,A.S.M.&F.]
*PRACTICE AREAS: Litigation.
Quattrucci, Ellen M. .... '69 '98 C.93 B.A. L.276 J.D. [Ⓐ Goodwin P.]
Queen, Elliott J. '57 '85 C&L.329 B.A., J.D.
(adm. in PA; not adm. in DC) 500 11th St., N.E.
Queen, Evelyn E. Crawford .... '45 '76 C&L.329 B.S., J.D. Assoc. J., Supr. Ct.
Queen, Thomas W., (AV) .... '49 '76 C.976 B.A. L.309 J.D. [Wiley R.&F.]
*PRACTICE AREAS: Intellectual Property; Franchise; Litigation; Antitrust.
Queeno, Laurel E. .... '70 '95 C.475 B.A. L.477 J.D. [Ⓐ Morgan,L.&B.]

Quesnel, Karen Marie ... '62 '87 C.562 B.A. L.273 J.D. 601 "D" St., N.W.
Quianzon, Raymond J. '— '98 C.30 B.S. L.904 J.D.
(adm. in VA; not adm. in DC) [[A] Fletcher,H.&H.] ⊙
*PRACTICE AREAS: Federal Income Tax; Federal Excise Tax; Business Law; Telecommunications Law.
Quick, Helen E. ... '67 '91 C&L.893 B.A., J.D. [[C] Epstein B.&G.]
*PRACTICE AREAS: Corporate Law.
Quick, Margaret E. ... '50 '77 C&L.574 B.S.C., J.D. 816 Wheeler Hill Dr., S.E.
Quigley, David H. ... '73 '99 C.188 B.S. L.309 J.D. [[A] Akin,G.S.H.&F.]
*PRACTICE AREAS: Environmental Land Use; Project Finance.
Quigley, Gary P., (AV) ... '37 '66 C.696 A.B. L.823 LL.B. [[C] Sidley A.B.&W.]
Quigley, L. Matthew ... '65 '96 C&L.228 B.A., J.D. [[A] Steptoe&J.]
Quigley, Michael, (AV) ... '57 '83 C.112 A.B. L.990 J.D. [Akin,G.S.H.&F.]
*PRACTICE AREAS: Taxation Litigation.
Quill, Edward S., Jr. ... '66 '95 C.67 B.A. L.208 J.D. [[A] Swidler B.S.F.]
*PRACTICE AREAS: Telecommunications; Transactional.
Quill, Terry F. ... '54 '88 C.912 B.S. L.477 J.D. [Duane,M.&H.]
*PRACTICE AREAS: Environmental Law; Toxic Substances.
Quillen, Cecil D., Jr. '37 '62 C.886 B.S.Ch.E. L.893 LL.B.
(adm. in VA; not adm. in DC; Pat.) Sr. Advsr., Putman, Hayes & Bartlett, Inc.
Quillian, Harry W. ... '38 '69 C.197 A.B. L.273 J.D. 5321 Broad Branch Rd., N.W.‡
Quillin, George E., (AV) '— '84 C.870 B.S. L.790 J.D.
(adm. in SC; not adm. in DC; See Pat. Sect.) [Foley&L.]
*PRACTICE AREAS: Intellectual Property Law.
Quin, Whayne S., (AV) ... '37 '64 C.880 B.A. L.893 LL.B. [Holland&K.]
*PRACTICE AREAS: Real Estate; Zoning, Planning and Land Use; Municipal Law; Historic Preservation; Environmental Law.
Quinalty, Keats A. '71 '96 C.502 B.S.M.E. L.900 J.D.
(adm. in KS; not adm. in DC) [[A] Morgan&F.]
*PRACTICE AREAS: Intellectual Property.
Quinn, Brian C. '65 '98 C&L.128 B.A., J.D.
(adm. in MD; not adm. in DC) [[A] Tighe P.A.T.]
*PRACTICE AREAS: Corporate Law; Securities; Complex Civil and Criminal Litigation; Computer and Software; Information Technology.
Quinn, Brian F. ... '61 '89 C&L.107 B.A., J.D. [[A] De Carlo,C.&S.]
Quinn, Dennis J. ... '63 '88 C.555 B.A. L.273 J.D. [[A] Carr G.]
Quinn, Elizabeth A. '66 '93 C.945 B.A. L.273 J.D.
(adm. in VA; not adm. in DC) [[A] Maggio&K.]
*PRACTICE AREAS: Immigration and Nationality Law.
Quinn, Harold P., Jr. '55 '80 C.207 B.A. L.896 J.D.
Sr. V.P., Gen. Coun. & Secy., National Mining Association
Quinn, John D. ... '51 '77 C.884 B.S. L.665 J.D. [Claxton,S.&Q.]
*PRACTICE AREAS: Commercial Litigation; Employment Law; Telecommunications Law; Business Law.
Quinn, John H., Jr., (AV) ... '36 '61 C.806 B.A. L.893 J.D. [Quinn,R.&G.]
*PRACTICE AREAS: Business Law; Corporate Law; Estate Planning; Fiduciary Law; Elder Law.
Quinn, Kathleen T. ... '50 '87 C&L.262 B.A., J.D. 600 F St., N.W.
Quinn, Kenneth P., (AV) '60 '85 C.589 B.S. L.209 J.D.
(adm. in IL; not adm. in DC) [Pillsbury W.]
*PRACTICE AREAS: Aviation Law; Transportation; Antitrust.
Quinn, Linda C., (AV) '48 '73 C.518 B.A. L.276 J.D.
[Shearman&S.] (⊙New York, NY)
Quinn, Michael J. ... '58 '86 C.299 A.B. L.659 J.D. [Berry&L.]
Quinn, Paul S., (AV) ... '34 '61 C.676 A.B. L.276 J.D. [Bingham D.]
*PRACTICE AREAS: Legislative Practice; Financial Institutions; Telecommunications; International Business.
Quinn, Robert W., Jr. '60 '88 C.339 B.A. L.209 J.D.
(adm. in IL; not adm. in DC) Senior Attorney, AT&T Corp.
Quinn, Terence P., (AV) ... '39 '70 C.350 B.S. L.30 J.D. [Steptoe&J.]
*PRACTICE AREAS: Securities; Securities Offerings; Corporate Law; Acquisitions, Divestitures and Mergers Finance.
Quinn, Thomas D., Jr., (AV) ... '30 '56 C.466 L.273 J.D. [[C] Hamilton&H.]
*PRACTICE AREAS: Civil Litigation; Education Law; Employment Law.
Quinn, Thomas H., (AV) ... '37 '63 C.676 A.B. L.276 LL.B. [Venable,A.B.H.&C.]
Quinn-Barabanov, Jennifer ... '68 '95 C.976 B.A. L.276 J.D. [[A] Steptoe&J.]

Quinn, Racusin & Gazzola, Chartered, (AV) [BB]
1400 K Street, N.W. Suite 1010, 20005-2403
Telephone: 202-842-9300 Facsimile: 202-682-0148 URL: http://www.qrg-law.com
Email: qrg@qrg-law.com URL: http://www.lawyers.com/quinnracusin&gazzola
Aaron J. Racusin (1915-1998); John H. Quinn, Jr.; Robert A. Gazzola. Associate: Mark R. Galbraith (Not admitted in DC).
General, Corporate, Business and Administrative Practice, Securities, Tax, Estate Planning and Administration, Elder Law.
See Professional Biographies, WASHINGTON, DISTRICT OF COLUMBIA

Quint, Arnold H., (AV) ... '42 '67 C.311 B.A. L.976 LL.B. [Hunton&W.]
*PRACTICE AREAS: Energy.
Quint, Edward A. ... '69 '95 C.228 B.A. L.880 J.D. [Luse L.G.P.&S.]
*PRACTICE AREAS: Corporate Financing Law; Financial Institutions Law; Securities.
Quinter, Neil F. '62 '88 C.165 A.B. L.309 J.D.
(adm. in MD; not adm. in DC) [McDermott,W.&E.]
Quintiere, Gary G., (AV) ... '44 '69 C.390 A.B. L.273 J.D. [Morgan,L.&B.]
Quintos, Mel R. '56 '86 C.1044 B.E. L.608 J.D.
[Armstrong,W.H.M.&N.] (See Pat. Sect.)
Quirk, Ronald E., Jr. ... '58 '94 C.1356 B.A. L.128 J.D. [[A] Alston&B.]
*PRACTICE AREAS: Telecommunications Law; Administrative Law.
Quirk, Rory F., (BV) ... '43 '80 C&L.276 A.B., J.D. [[A] Dewey B.]
*PRACTICE AREAS: International Trade.
Quirk, Sherry A., (AV) ... '— '82 C.518 A.B. L.904 J.D. [Verner,L.B.M.&H.]
*PRACTICE AREAS: Energy Law; Legislative Law.
Quiroga, Lorraine ... '— '00 C.259 B.S. L.904 J.D. [[A] Verner,L.B.M.&H.]
*PRACTICE AREAS: Legislative; Trade.
Qureshi, Abid Riaz ... '— '97 C.188 B.A. L.309 J.D. [[A] Latham&W.]
*PRACTICE AREAS: Technology Law; Internet Litigation.
Raasch, Robert Lee '69 '94 C.612 B.S. L.910 J.D.
(adm. in OK; not adm. in DC) Keane, Inc.
Rabecs, Robert N. ... '64 '90 C.754 B.A. L.276 J.D. [[C] Hogan&H.]
*PRACTICE AREAS: Health Care.
Rabekoff, Elise J., (AV) '59 '86 C.674 A.B. L.976 J.D.
V.P., Gen. Coun. & Secy., Quadrangle Development Corp.
*RESPONSIBILITIES: Closely Held Corporations (50%); Commercial Real Estate (35%); General Practice (15%).
Rabena, John F. ... '65 '94 C.870 B.S.E.E. L.64 J.D. [Sughrue M.] (See Pat. Sect.)
*PRACTICE AREAS: Intellectual Property Law; Litigation.
Raber, Stephen D. ... '59 '85 C.112 A.B. L.893 J.D. [Williams&C.]
Rabie, Aseel M. ... '71 '98 C&L.309 B.A., J.D. Coun., INTELSAT

Rabil, Louis, (AV) '30 '57 C.575 B.S. L.276 J.D.
Suite 700, 1700 K Street, N.W., 20006
Telephone: 202-466-4944 Fax: 202-223-3260
Email: lrabil@aol.com
***PRACTICE AREAS: Corporate; Business Litigation; Civil Litigation; Appellate Practice; General Practice.**

(This Listing Continued)

Rabil, Louis (Continued)

General Practice in all Courts and before Federal and Local Governmental Departments. Corporation Law, Real Estate, Personal Injury, Probate, Employment Law, Business Litigation and Commercial Transactions, Appellate Practice.
See Professional Biographies, WASHINGTON, DISTRICT OF COLUMBIA

Rabin, Raymond ... '17 '57 L.180 LL.B. 815 15th St., N.W.
Rabinovitz, Bruce H., (AV) ... '45 '71 C.910 B.A. L.273 J.D. [Wilmer,C.&P.]
*PRACTICE AREAS: Transportation Law; Asset Based Financing Law; Administrative Law.
Rabinowitz, Julie M. '57 '83 C&L.352 B.A., J.D.
Sr. Dir. & Coun., Govt. Rel., American Home Prod.
Rabinowitz, Mitchell L. ... '67 '93 C.659 B.A., B.S. L.309 J.D. [[A] Cleary,G.S.&H.]
Raburn, Janice K. ... '58 '89 C.69 B.A. L.273 J.D. Sr. Atty, American Petroleum Institute
Racca, Andrew William ... '73 '99 C.1021 B.A. L.180 J.D. [[A] Steptoe&J.]
Race, Dennis M. ... '47 '73 C.251 B.A. L.930 J.D. [Akin,G.S.H.&F.]
*PRACTICE AREAS: Litigation.
Racich, Christopher J. '71 '98 C.188 B.A. L.904 J.D.
Dir., High Tech Investigations, Kroll Assocs.‡
Racicot, Marc, (AV) '48 '73 C.120 B.A. L.508 J.D.
(adm. in MT; not adm. in DC) [Bracewell&P.]
*PRACTICE AREAS: Government Relations and Strategy; Public Policy.
Racicot, Timothy John ... '74 '00 C.120 B.A. L.602 J.D. [[A] Steptoe&J.]
Racilla, Brian T. '73 '99 C.228 B.S.E. L.276 J.D.
(adm. in VA; not adm. in DC) [[A] Fish&R.]
*PRACTICE AREAS: Intellectual Property.
Racin, John P., (AV) ... '48 '77 C.923 B.A. L.1162 J.D. [Weissbrodt&R.]
*PRACTICE AREAS: Litigation; Civil Rights Law; Fair Employment Law.
Racine, Richard B., (AV) '56 '81
C.276 B.S. L.930 J.D. [Finnegan,H.F.G.&D.] (See Pat. Sect.)
*PRACTICE AREAS: Patent Litigation; Pharmaceutical Patents; Chemical Patents.
Raciti, Eric P. ... '66 '95 C.886 B.S. L.128 J.D. [[A] Finnegan,H.F.G.&D.] (See Pat. Sect.)
*PRACTICE AREAS: Intellectual Property Procurement; International Intellectual Property; Electro-Mechanical Patents; Medical Patents; Patent Litigation.
Racunas, Robert V. '71 '96 C.665 B.S. L.273 J.D.
(adm. in VA; not adm. in DC; See Pat. Sect.) [[A] Fish&R.]
Radack, Jesselyn A. ... '70 '96 C.103 A.B. L.976 J.D. Legal Advisor
Radanovic, Lawrence R., (AV) ... '38 '67 C&L.128 B.C.E., LL.B. [Dykema G.] (Pat.)
*PRACTICE AREAS: Mechanical Patents; Patent Law; Trademarks; Licensing; Litigation.
Raddatz, Mark R. ... '70 '97 C.37 B.A. L.436 J.D. [Raddatz]
Raddatz Law Firm, PLLC ... 2131 K Street NW, Suite 710
Rademacher, Jason E. ... '72 '00 C.665 B.A L.966 J.D. [[A] Dow,L.&A.]
Rader, Robert M. ... '46 '72 C.390 A.B. L.188 J.D. [Winston&S.]
*PRACTICE AREAS: Commercial Litigation; Energy Litigation; Environmental Litigation.

Rader, Fishman & Grauer PLLC, (AV) [BB]
1233 20th Street, Suite 501, 20036 ⊙
Telephone: 202-955-3750 Fax: 202-955-3751
Email: info@raderfishman.com URL: http://www.raderfishman.com
Ronald P. Kananen; Yoichiro Yamaguchi; Ellen A. Efros; David T. Nikaido. Associate: Robert S. Green; Brian Keith Dutton; David K. Benson (Not admitted in DC); Carl Schaukowitch. Of Counsel: Paul W. Fish.
Patent, Trademark, Copyright, Computer Law, Unfair Competition, Trial and Appellate Practice.
Bloomfield Hills, Michigan Office: 39533 Woodward, Suite 140, 48304. Telephone: 248-594-0600. Fax: 248-594-0610.
Englewood, Colorado Office: 383 Inverness Drive South, Suite 140, 80112. Telephone: 303-991-1200. Fax: 303-991-1210.
Salt Lake City, Utah Office: 10653 S. River Front Parkway, Suite 150, South Jordan, 84095. Telephone: 801-572-0185. Fax: 801-572-7666.
See Professional Biographies, WASHINGTON, DISTRICT OF COLUMBIA

Radford, Bruce W. ... '50 '75 C.893 B.A. L.896 J.D. 3601 Connecticut Ave., N.W.‡
Radich, Miriam J. '73 '96 L.999 LL.B.
(adm. in NY; not adm. in DC) [[A] Shearman&S.]
Radomsky, Leon ... '69 '99 C.178 B.S. L.1209 J.D. [[A] Foley&L.]
*PRACTICE AREAS: Patent Law; Intellectual Property.
Radowitz, Melvin ... '45 '77 C.831 A.B. L.1009 J.D. AARP
*RESPONSIBILITIES: Commercial Contracts; Labor; Leases; Tax-Exempt Organization.
Radsan, A. John ... '62 '88 C.228 A.B. L.309 J.D. [[C] Afridi,A.&P.] & [[C] Baker B.]
Radway, Theodore L. ... '71 '99 C.1036 B.A. L.276 J.D. [[A] Dow,L.&A.]
Rafey, Judd A. ... '67 '92 C.156 B.A. L.30 J.D. 5039 Connecticut Ave., N.W.
Raffaniello, Patrick J. ... '55 '83 C.30 B.A. L.904 J.D. 3050 K St.

Rafferty, Catherine Mary, Law Offices of '66 '91 C.145 B.A. L.128 J.D.
4801 Yuma Street NW, 20016
Telephone: 202-244-0608 Fax: 202-244-2967
Email: c-rafferty-11@alumni.uchicago.edu URL: http://www.lawyers.com/rafferty
***PRACTICE AREAS: Trusts and Estates; Probate; Estate Planning; Wills; Living Wills.**
Estate Planning and Probate Administration with special emphasis on Estate Taxation and Collateral Estate Planning Matters.
See Professional Biographies, WASHINGTON, DISTRICT OF COLUMBIA

Rafferty, James G. ... '51 '85 C.103 A.B. L.276 J.D. [Harkins C.]
*PRACTICE AREAS: Tax Law; Business Law; Economic Regulation.
Rafferty, John M. ... '72 '97 C.36 B.A. L.569 J.D. [[A] Hogan&H.]
*PRACTICE AREAS: Corporate Law; Securities.
Rafferty, Michael G. ... '69 '98 C.446 B.S. L.30 J.D. [[A] Arent F.K.P.&K.]
*PRACTICE AREAS: Municipal Finance; Project Finance; Real Estate.
Raffman, Mark S. ... '60 '86 C.951 B.A. L.309 J.D. [Shea&G.]
*PRACTICE AREAS: Civil Litigation; Arbitration; Environmental; Labor.
Rafkin, Jodi B., (Ms.) '57 '83 C.783 B.A. L.770 J.D.
(adm. in CA; not adm. in DC) 3133 Conn. Ave., NW‡
Rafter, John A., (AV) ... '26 '52 C.698 B.S. L.276 J.D. 1255 23rd St., N.W., Ste. 500‡
Ragland, Gerald F., Jr., (BV) ... '41 '75 C.889 B.S. L.831 J.D. [Carter&C.] ⊙
*PRACTICE AREAS: Gneral Tort liability; Professional Liability; Medical Malpractice; Civil Trials; Civil Appeals.
Ragosta, John A., (AV) ... '60 '84 C.294 B.S. L.893 J.D. [Dewey B.]
*PRACTICE AREAS: International Trade.
Ragovis, George ... '31 '78 C.277 B.S. L.276 J.D. Dir., MCI Communications Corporation
Ragsdale, Jeffrey R. ... '55 '80 C.924 B.A. L.150 J.D. Asst. U.S. Atty.
Ragsdale, Mary C. ... '65 '95 C&L.893 B.A., J.D. [[A] Sidley A.B.&W.]
Rah, John S. '68 '93 C.569 B.A. L.276 J.D.
(adm. in MD; not adm. in DC) [[A] Epstein B.&G.]
*PRACTICE AREAS: Health Law.
Rahal, Linda A. ... '64 '93 C.860 B.A. L.904 J.D. [Trow&K.]
*PRACTICE AREAS: Immigration and Nationality Law.
Raher, Patrick M., (AV) ... '47 '72 C.602 B.B.A. L.276 J.D. [Hogan&H.]
*PRACTICE AREAS: Clean Air Act; Environmental Compliance; Environmental Criminal Defense; Environmental Dispute Resolution; Environmental Due Diligence.
Rahilly, Lyn Michele ... '70 '95 C.890 B.A. L.273 J.D. Atty./Adv.
Raibman, Michael D. ... '71 '96 C.910 A.B. L.659 J.D. [[A] Arnold&P.]
*PRACTICE AREAS: Litigation; Food Products Liability; Drug and Medical Device Litigation; Regulatory.
Raider, Ronald L. ... '60 '86 C.1044 B.A. L.273 J.D. [Kilpatrick S.]
Raij, Irwin Perry ... '— '95 C.472 B.B.A. L.910 J.D. [[A] Foley&L.]
*PRACTICE AREAS: Public Affairs; Regulatory Law.

Raikin, Steven G. . . . . '49 '80 C.966 B.A. L.1066 J.D. [© Kass&S.]
Railsback, Thomas F. . . . . '32 '57 C.293 B.A. L.597 J.D. [© Holland&K.]
*PRACTICE AREAS: Federal Legislative; Patent; Copyright; Trademark; Telecommunications.
Raim, David M., (AV) . . . . '53 '79 C.976 B.A. L.659 J.D. [Chadbourne&P.]
Rainbolt, John V., II . . . . '39 '64 C&L.623 B.A., LL.B. [Rainbolt]
Rainbolt Law Office . . . . 1200 G Street, N.W. Suite 800
Rainey, J. Scott '63 '93 C.869 B.S. L.911 J.D.
(adm. in WA; not adm. in DC) Dep. Dir., Amer. Pilot's Assn.
Raish, Leonard R., (AV) . . . . '18 '51 C&L.276 B.S.F.S., J.D. [Fletcher,H.&H.]
*PRACTICE AREAS: Telecommunications; International Telecommunications.
Rakestraw, Ann H. . . . . '70 '95 C&L.893 B.A., J.D. [Ⓐ Williams&C.]
Raksphal, Anirma '69 '93 C.446 B.S.E.E. L.276 J.D.
2100 Pennsylvania Ave., N.W. (Pat.)
Ralls, Mary Ann, (AV) . . . . '60 '89 C.893 B.A. L.180 J.D. [© Duane,M.&H.]
*PRACTICE AREAS: Energy Law; Regulatory Law; Transactions; Public Utility.
Ralph, Regan Elisabeth '65 '94 C.309 B.A. L.976 J.D.
(adm. in MD; not adm. in DC)
Washington Dir., Human Rights Watch/Women's Rights Proj.
Ralston, David T., Jr., (AV) . . . . '— '80 C&L.276 B.S., J.D. [Foley&L.]
*PRACTICE AREAS: Civil Practice; White Collar; Criminal Litigation; Government Contract Law; Airport Regulation.
Raman, Anand S. . . . . '68 '97 C.145 A.B. L.976 J.D. [Ⓐ Skadden,A.S.M.&F.]
*PRACTICE AREAS: Criminal Litigation; Civil Litigation.
Ramanathan, Subhasri '69 '94 C.705 B.A. L.1292 J.D.
(adm. in PA; not adm. in DC) American Bar. Assoc.
Rambo, Frank W. '69 '01 C.797 B.S. L.569 J.D.
(adm. in NY; not adm. in DC) [Ⓐ Baker B.]
Ramey, Carl R., (AV) . . . . '41 '68 C.434 A.B. L.273 LL.B. [Wiley R.&F.]
*PRACTICE AREAS: Communications.
Ramirez, Anthony M. '59 '85 C.423 B.A. L.846 J.D.
(adm. in TX; not adm. in DC) Legal Services Corp.
Ramirez, Martin F. . . . . '— '97 C.813 B.A. L.178 J.D. [Ⓐ Wilmer,C.&P.]
Ramirez, Ted L., (BV) '52 '77 C.999 B.A. L.608 J.D.
(adm. in OH; not adm. in DC) [Arter&H.] (⊙Columbus, Dayton, OH)
Ramonas, George A. . . . . '47 '75 C.436 B.A. L.930 J.D. The Advocacy Grp.
Ramos, Jeneen '72 '00 C.1175 B.A. L.329 J.D.
(adm. in NY; not adm. in DC) [Ⓐ Clifford C.R.&W.]
*PRACTICE AREAS: Litigation.
Ramos, Louis . . . . '73 '98 C.188 B.A. L.659 J.D. [Ⓐ Fried,F.H.S.&J.]
*PRACTICE AREAS: Litigation.
Rampilla, Narayana R. '54 '91 L.280 J.D.
(adm. in GA; not adm. in DC) 1860 Clydesdale Pl., N.W.‡
Rampy, Matthew C. . . . . '71 '96 C.477 B.A. L.1049 J.D. [Ⓐ Shaw P.]
*PRACTICE AREAS: Corporate; Mergers and Acquisitions; Technology Law.
Ramsay, James B., (AV) '55 '85 C.496 B.S. L.420 J.D.
Gen. Coun., Natl. Assn. of Reg. Utility Commissioners
Ramsay, Richard E. . . . . '63 '90 C.69 B.A. L.221 J.D. [Ⓐ Proskauer R.]
Ramsey, Elizabeth A. '58 '84 C.692 B.A. L.30 J.D.
(adm. in NY; not adm. in DC) National Assn. of Manufacturers
Ramsey, Patricia . . . . '54 '81 C&L.477 B.A., J.D. Acting Gen. Coun.
Ramsingh, Omyra M. . . . . '70 '96 C.260 B.S. L.178 J.D. [Ⓐ Hogan&H.]
*PRACTICE AREAS: Corporate; Securities; Private Equity.
Randall, Albert B. . . . . '48 '74 C&L.446 B.S., J.D. [© Baker,D.B.&C.]
*PRACTICE AREAS: Aviation; Legislation; Administrative Law.
Randall, Deborah A., (AV) . . . . '47 '76 C.681 A.B. L.178 J.D. [Arent F.K.P.&K.]
*PRACTICE AREAS: Health and Hospital Law; Medicare; Certificates of Need; Health Care Contracts; Health Care Facility Licensing.
Randall, Donald A., (AV) . . . . '33 '54 C&L.469 J.D. [D.A.Randall]
Randall, James D., Jr., (AV) '46 '77
C.329 B.A. L.276 J.D. Supervisory Asst. Corp. Coun., D.C.
Randall, Donald A., Law Offices of, (AV) . . . . 321 D. St., N. E.
Randle, Russell V., (AV) . . . . '55 '80 C.674 A.B. L.976 J.D. [Patton B.]
Randolph, Jerome C., (AV) '48 '78 C.973 B.A. L.145 J.D.
(adm. in OH; not adm. in DC) [Gilbert H.&R.]
*PRACTICE AREAS: Litigation; Insurance Coverage.
Raney, William E. '70 '95 C.502 B.A. L.893 J.D.
(adm. in MO; not adm. in DC) [Ⓐ Copilevitz&C.] ⊙
*PRACTICE AREAS: Constitutional Law; Tax Exempt Organizations; Civil Litigation; Telemarketing Law; Administrative Agency Practice.
Range, John Jay . . . . '55 '80 C.477 A.B. L.575 J.D. [Hunton&W.]
*PRACTICE AREAS: Litigation.
Ranowsky, Kathleen L., (BV) '51 '83 C.645 B.S. L.1049 J.D.
Assoc. Gen. Coun., Corp. Affs., National Railroad Passenger Corp. (AMTRAK)
Ransom, David D. '61 '92 C.352 B.A. L.1035 J.D.
(adm. in MN; not adm. in DC) Mgr., Editorial Servs., Assn. of Trial Lawyers of Amer.
Ranzman, Ellen G. . . . . '47 '80 C.363 B.A. L.128 J.D. [Katz&R.]
Raofield, Jason C. . . . . '71 '98 C.823 B.A. L.93 J.D. [Ⓐ Howrey S.A.&W.]
*PRACTICE AREAS: Antitrust; Commercial Litigation.
Rapaport, Marc A. . . . . '67 '92 C.569 B.A. L.276 J.D. [Shaffer,R.&S.] ⊙
Rapaport, Mitchell H. '58 '83 C.1019 B.B.A. L.273 J.D.
(adm. in NY; not adm. in DC) [Nixon P.]
*PRACTICE AREAS: Public Finance.
Raphael, Aaron M. '73 '99
C.477 B.S. L.245 J.D. [Ⓐ Finnegan,H.F.G.&D.] (See Pat. Sect.)
*PRACTICE AREAS: Patent Law.
Raphaelson, Ira H., (AV) . . . . '53 '77 C&L.597 B.A., J.D. [O'Melveny&M.]
*PRACTICE AREAS: Complex Litigation; Corporate Compliance and Special Investigations; Antitrust; White Collar Defense; Health Care.
Rapoport, Frank M., (AV) '50 '76 C.659 B.A. L.831 J.D.
[McKenna&C.] (⊙Devon, PA)
*PRACTICE AREAS: Government Contracts; Public Health Law; Health Care Fraud.
Raposo, Cynthia A. . . . . . . '54 '85 C.242 B.A. L.64 J.D. Assoc. Lit. Coun., MCI WorldCom
Rappaport, Jennifer Levy '— '99 C.103 A.B. L.569 J.D.
(adm. in PA; not adm. in DC) [Ⓐ Paul,H.J.&W.]
*PRACTICE AREAS: Employment Law.
Rappaport, Kim . . . . '— '00 C.188 B.Arch. L.30 J.D. [Ⓐ Arnold&P.]
*PRACTICE AREAS: Litigation.
Rapping, Jonathan A. . . . . '66 '95 C.145 B.A. L.273 J.D. Pub. Def. Serv.
Rappoport, Joel E. . . . . '58 '85 C.197 A.B. L.94 J.D. [Stradley R.S.&Y.]
Rappoport, Stephen S. . . . . . '42 '67 C.604 A.B. L.569 LL.B. The Bureau of Natl. Affs., Inc.
Raptis, Stephen T. . . . . '69 '95 C&L.923 B.A., J.D. [Ⓐ Swidler B.S.F.]
Rasenberger, Raymond J., (AV) . . . . '27 '57 C.197 A.B. L.273 J.D. [© Zuckert,S.&R.]
*PRACTICE AREAS: Mediation; Arbitration.
Rasevic, Kimberly Dopkin . . . . '66 '91 C.174 B.A. L.228 J.D. [© Dechert]
*PRACTICE AREAS: Securities; Financial Services Law; Investment Management.
Raskin, David B., (BV) . . . . '54 '79 C.659 B.A. L.276 J.D. [Steptoe&J.]
Raskin, Jamin Ben . . . . '62 '87 C&L.309 B.A., J.D. Prof. of Law, American Univ.
Rasmussen, Garret G., (AV) . . . . '49 '74 C.197 A.B. L.309 J.D. [Patton B.]
Rasmussen, Jane Lemley . . . . '67 '93 C&L.893 B.A., J.D. [© Thaler L.]
*PRACTICE AREAS: Litigation; Employment Law.
Rasmussen, Jeffery P. '54 '80 C.723 B.A. L.734 J.D.
(adm. in MN; not adm. in DC) Asst. Tax Coun., Tax Executives Inst., Inc.
Rasmussen, Thomas M. '47 '72 C.1058 B.A. L.879 J.D.
(adm. in WA; not adm. in DC) Dir. of Progs. & Opers., IONA Sr. Servs.
Rassman, Franz R. . . . . '57 '82 C.205 B.S. L.30 J.D. [Akin,G.S.H.&F.]
*PRACTICE AREAS: Real Estate; Real Estate Finance.
Rath, Francis S., (AV) . . . . '55 '80 C.918 B.A. L.276 J.D. [© Squire,S.&D.]
*PRACTICE AREAS: Eastern Europe; International Corporate.
Rath, Manesh K. . . . . '69 '95 C.886 B.S. L.945 J.D. [Ⓐ Keller&H.]
*PRACTICE AREAS: Employment and Labor Law; OSHA; Litigation.
Rath, Manik K. . . . . '69 '94 C&L.893 B.A., J.D. [Ⓐ McKenna&C.]
*PRACTICE AREAS: Labor and Employment Law; Business Litigation.
Rathbun, Douglas B. . . . . '71 '01 C.425 B.A.Mus. L.846 Trial Atty.
Rathbun, Robert G. '53 '82 C.1154 B.S. L.215 J.D.
(adm. in MI; not adm. in DC) [Cozen O.]
*PRACTICE AREAS: Corporate Law; International Business; Mergers and Acquisitions.
Rathvon, James P. . . . . '51 '82 C.860 B.S. L.273 J.D. [Piper M.R.&W.]
*PRACTICE AREAS: Environmental; Commercial Litigation.
Ratino, John M., (AV) . . . . '56 '85 C.446 B.S. L.128 J.D. [Hunton&W.]
*PRACTICE AREAS: Corporate Finance; Real Estate.
Ratnavale, B. Lynn F. . . . . '67 '93 C.93 B.A. L.128 J.D. [Ⓐ Lukas,N.G.&S.]
*PRACTICE AREAS: Wireless Communications; FCC Regulation; FCC Licensing; Cable TV.
Ratner, Brian A. . . . . '74 '00 C.347 B.A. L.665 J.D. [Ⓐ Cohen,M.H.&T.]
*PRACTICE AREAS: Litigation; Antitrust.
Rattley, Donna C. . . . . '61 '91 C.1036 B.A. L.276 J.D. [Cole,R.&B.]
*PRACTICE AREAS: Cable Communications; Cable Franchising Law; Telecommunications Law; Telecommunications Legislation; Telecommunications Competition.
Rattner, David L. . . . '64 '89 C.276 B.A. L.665 J.D. Assco. Comm. Coun., MCI WorldCom
Rau, Charles W. '37 '62 C&L.879 A.B., J.D.
(adm. in IN; not adm. in DC) V.P., Tax Dept., MCI Communications Corp.
Rau, Lee A., (AV) . . . . '— '66 C.494 B.S.B. L.1068 J.D. [© Reed S.]
*PRACTICE AREAS: Antitrust; Litigation.
Rauch, T. Stewart '67 '95 C.478 B.A. L.893 J.D.
(adm. in VA; not adm. in DC) [Ⓐ Sperduto]
*PRACTICE AREAS: Complex Commercial Litigation; Litigation; Employment Law; Real Estate Litigation; Government Contracts.
Rauchholz, William F. '— '92 C.477 B.S.E. L.1356 J.D.
[© Banner&W.] (See Pat. Sect.)
*PRACTICE AREAS: Intellectual Property; Patents; Chemical Intellectual Property.
Rauh, B. Michael, (AV) . . . . '36 '61 C.477 A.B. L.893 LL.B. [Manatt,P.&P.]
Rauh, Carl S., (AV) . . . . '40 '66 C.178 A.B. L.659 LL.B. [Skadden,A.S.M.&F.]
Raul, Alan Charles, (AV) . . . . '54 '82 C.309 A.B. L.976 J.D. [Sidley A.B.&W.]
Raum, Violet G. '12 '37 C.914 B.A. L.800 LL.B.
(adm. in CA; not adm. in DC) 2622 31st St., N.W.‡
Raup, Mitchell D. . . . . '59 '83 C.145 B.A. L.228 J.D. [Mayer,B.&P.]
Rausch, Siobhan C. . . . . '70 '97 C&L.128 B.A., J.D. [Ⓐ Hogan&H.]
*PRACTICE AREAS: Tax.
Rauser, Paul C. . . . . '— '98 C.918 B.A. L.976 J.D. [Ⓐ Williams&C.]
*PRACTICE AREAS: White Collar Criminal Law; Civil Litigation.
Raval, M. Isabelle '68 '95 C.1369 B.A. L.823 J.D.
Asst. Gen. Coun., Natl. Gallery of Art
Ravdin, Linda J., (AV) . . . . '48 '74 C.608 B.A. L.273 J.D. [Ravdin&W.]
*PRACTICE AREAS: Domestic Relations; Trusts and Estates; Civil Litigation.

Ravdin & Wofford, A Professional Corporation, (AV)
1700 K Street, N.W., Suite 650, 20006
Telephone: 202-429-5551 Fax: 202-429-5553
URL: http://www.lawyers.com/ravdin-wofford
Linda J. Ravdin; Cindy Lynn Wofford;—Kelly J. Capps.
Family Law, Trusts and Estates, Divorce Taxation. Practicing in District of Columbia, Maryland, Virginia and Texas.

See Professional Biographies, WASHINGTON, DISTRICT OF COLUMBIA

Raven-Hansen, Peter . . . . . '46 '74 C&L.309 B.A., J.D. Prof. of Law, George Wash. Univ.
Ravin, Idan A. . . . . '70 '96 C.446 B.S. L.61 J.D. [Ⓐ Shearman&S.]
*PRACTICE AREAS: Capital Markets; Corporate Finance.
Ravin, Sean A. . . . . '68 '94 C.112 B.A. L.800 J.D. 1429 G St. N.W.
Ravitch, Michael D. . . . . '67 '95 C.645 B.S. L.273 J.D. [Ⓐ Grossberg,Y.F.&B.]
Ravitz, James R. . . . . '70 '98 C.1036 B.A. L.94 J.D. [Ⓐ Arent F.K.P.&K.]
*PRACTICE AREAS: Food and Drug; Intellectual Property.
Rawert, Jennifer R. '67 '98 C.602 B.B.A. L.4210 J.D.
(adm. in KY; not adm. in DC) [Ⓐ Sutherland A.&B.]
*PRACTICE AREAS: Business Law; Securities; Mergers and Acquisitions; Taxation.
Rawicz, Leonard . . . . '31 '60 C.184 B.S.E.E. L.273 J.D. [© Skadden,A.S.M.&F.]
Rawlings, Dwayne S. '69 '97 C.103 A.B. L.276 J.D.
(adm. in MD; not adm. in DC)
Atty.- Advsr., D.C. Lottery & Charitable Games Control Bd.
Rawlins, Andrew E. . . . . '— '92 C.645 B.S.I.E. L.30 J.D. [Foley&L.]
*PRACTICE AREAS: Intellectual Property.
Rawls, Charles R. '57 '82 C.576 B.A. L.1228 J.D.
(adm. in NC; not adm. in DC) Gen. Coun. U.S. Dept. of Agric.
Rawls, W. Lee . . . . '44 '77 C.674 B.A. L.273 J.D. 801 Pennsylvania Ave., N.W.
Rawson, Robert J., (AV) . . . . '14 '39 L.128 LL.B. 2600 Virginia Ave. N.W.
Rawson, William K. . . . . '— '80 C.31 B.A. L.813 J.D. [Latham&W.]
Ray, Andrew M. . . . . '66 '93 C.276 A.B. L.228 J.D. [Swidler B.S.F.]
*PRACTICE AREAS: Corporate Law; Securities Law; Venture Capital; Information Technology; Telecommunications.
Ray, Charles A., Jr., (AV) '52 '78 C.311 B.A. L.575 J.D.
1625 K Street, N.W., Suite 400
Ray, John L., (AV) . . . . '43 '75 C&L.273 B.A., J.D. [Manatt,P.&P.]
Ray, Larry E. '52 '77 C.532 B.A. L.117 J.D.
(adm. in OH; not adm. in DC) 613 Rhode Island Ave. N.W.
Ray, Liza M. . . . . '— '00 C.472 B.A. L.128 J.D. [Ⓐ Morgan,L.&B.]
Ray, Mary Beth Pendley '60 '86 C.880 B.A. L.420 J.D.
(adm. in LA; not adm. in DC) Sr. Atty., MCI Communications Corporation
Ray, Michael B. . . . . '64 '90 C.550 B.S.E.E. L.1218 J.D. [Sterne,K.G.&F.] (See Pat. Sect.)
*PRACTICE AREAS: Intellectual Property Law.
Raymond, Robert . . . . '62 '89 C.262 B.A. L.1029 J.D. Assoc. Gen. Coun., USDOJ/INS
Raynes, Evan A. . . . . '59 '93 C.477 B.G.S. L.273 J.D. [Ⓐ Finnegan,H.F.G.&D.]
*PRACTICE AREAS: Trademarks; Copyrights; Unfair Competition; Intellectual Property Litigation.
Raynsford, Kathleen J. . . . . . . '55 '81 C.112 B.A. L.800 J.D. 60 Massachusetts Ave., N.E.‡
Raz, Lawrence W. '52 '77 C.597 B.A. L.178 J.D.
V.P. & Assoc. Dir. Legal Affs., Riggs Bk. N.A.
Razi, Benjamin J. '75 '01 C.262 B.A. L.30 J.D
(adm. in MD; not adm. in DC) [Ⓐ Covington&B.]
Razzano, Frank C., (AV) '48 '73 C.734 B.A. L.276 J.D.
(adm. in NY; not adm. in DC) [Dickstein S.M.&O.]
*PRACTICE AREAS: Broker Dealer Securities; White Collar Criminal Defense Litigation.

Rea, Bryce, Jr., (AV) ....'18 '41 C&L.902 B.A., LL.B. [Rea,C.&A.]
*PRACTICE AREAS: Administrative Law; Interstate Commerce; Transportation.

Rea, Cross & Auchincloss, (AV)
1707 L Street, N.W., Suite 570, 20036
Telephone: 202-785-3700 Fax: 202-659-4934
Email: RCALaw@Erols.com
Members of Firm: Edgar Watkins (1903-1959); Bryce Rea, Jr.; Donald E. Cross (1923-1986); Thomas M. Auchincloss, Jr.; Leo C. Franey; Brian L. Troiano; Keith G. O'Brien; John D. Heffner.
General and Administrative Law. Practice before all Courts and Federal Administrative Agencies. Interstate Commerce, Trucking, Railroad, Maritime, Government Contracts and Claims, Antitrust Law.
See Professional Biographies, WASHINGTON, DISTRICT OF COLUMBIA

Read, Charles C., (AV) ....'49 '75 C.309 A.B. L.1068 J.D. [Steptoe&J.]
*PRACTICE AREAS: Public Utility Law; Telecommunications Law; Energy Law; Business Litigation.
Read, J. Andrew ....'59 '98 C.893 B.S. L.1209 J.D. [Ⓐ Jones,D.R.&P.]
Read, Tod W. ....'59 '88 C.293 B.A. L.259 J.D. [Ⓒ Bonner K.T.&C.]
*PRACTICE AREAS: Environmental Law; Toxic Torts; Insurance Defense.
Reade, Claire E. ....'52 '80 C.918 B.A. L.309 J.D. [Arnold&P.]
*PRACTICE AREAS: International.
Reade, Steven G. ....'56 '83 C.813 B.A. L.659 J.D. [Arnold&P.]
*PRACTICE AREAS: Litigation; Employment Law.
Reader, David I., (AV) ....'58 '83 C.1044 B.S. L.809 J.D. [Keller&H.]
*PRACTICE AREAS: Business Planning; Business Organization; Corporate Law; Transactional Law; Mergers and Acquisitions.
Ready, William J. '43 '69 C&L.575 B.S., J.D.
(adm. in NC; not adm. in DC) Bank of America
Reagan, Kinsey S., (AV) ....'50 '75 C.688 B.S. L.309 J.D. [Kleinfeld,K.&B.]
*PRACTICE AREAS: Food, Drug and Cosmetic Law; Drug and Medical Device Regulation; Controlled Substance Law; Animal Drug Regulation; Food Labeling and Inspection.
Reams, David A. '58 '84 C.475 B.S. L.851 J.D.
(adm. in OH; not adm. in DC) 654 6th St., N.E.‡
Reardon, John '66 '94 C.94 B.A. L.178 J.D.
General Counsel, Mobex Communications, Inc.
Reardon, Leigh A. '57 '82 C.318 B.A. L.608 J.D.
(adm. in OH; not adm. in DC) 1099 14th St., N.W.
Reardon, Michael H. '50 '77 C.276 B.S.F.S. L.818 J.D.
(adm. in MA; not adm. in DC) [Ⓐ Nixon P.]
*PRACTICE AREAS: Real Estate; Affordable Housing.
Reasoner, C. Dean, (AV) ......'17 '42 C.352 B.S. L.273 J.D. 888 17th St. N.W., Ste. 800‡

Reaves, John Daniel, (AV) '39 '65 C.10 B.S. L.893 LL.B.
1225 19th Street N.W., Suite 450, 20036
Telephone: 202-296-4950 Fax: 202-296-4951
Email: jdreavesoffice@yahoo.com URL: http://www.lawyers.com/johndanielreaves
***PRACTICE AREAS: Antitrust; Trade Regulation Law.**
Business Counselling, E-Commerce Law, Internet Law, Trade Association Law, Emerging Business Law, Antitrust Regulation, Trade Regulation, Unfair Trade, Consumer Protection, Regulatory Law, Federal Trade Commission, Corporate Law, Small Business Law, Emerging Growth Law, Strategic Alliances, Complex Litigation.
See Professional Biographies, WASHINGTON, DISTRICT OF COLUMBIA

Reaves, Kelvin L. ....'74 '00 C.446 B.A. L.30 J.D. [Ⓐ Bennet&B.]
*PRACTICE AREAS: Communications Law.
Reavis, Donyale Y. Hooper '70 '01 C.94 B.A. L.659 J.D.
(adm. in NJ; not adm. in DC) [Ⓐ Fried,F.H.S.&J.]
*PRACTICE AREAS: Intellectual Property; E-Commerce; Corporate Law.
Reback, Joyce E. ....'48 '76 C.103 B.A. L.273 J.D. Intl. Monetary Fund

Reboul, MacMurray, Hewitt, Maynard & Kristol, (AV)
Suite 406, 1111 Nineteenth Street, N.W., 20036 ⊙
Telephone: 202-429-0004 Telecopier: 202-429-8743; 202-296-0627
Email: lawyers@reboul.com URL: http://www.reboul.com
Resident Partner: James E. Magee. Resident Associate: Kristie S. Hassett. Staff Attorneys: Jennifer Ann Newberry; Bernard M. Schulte.
General Practice. Corporate, Corporate Finance/Securities, Mergers and Acquisitions, Venture Capital/Buyouts, Start-Ups, International, Banking, Litigation, Commercial Litigation, Bankruptcy, Reorganization and Restructuring, ERISA, Telecommunications, Product Liability Defense, Labor/Employment, Alternative Dispute Resolution, Criminal Defense and Tax.
New York, N.Y. Office: 45 Rockefeller Plaza, 10111. Telephone: 212-841-5700.
See Professional Biographies, WASHINGTON, DISTRICT OF COLUMBIA

Rechsteiner, Vera Ann '57 '85 C.276 B.S.F.S. L.273 J.D.
(adm. in MD; not adm. in DC) [Coudert B.]
*PRACTICE AREAS: International Business Transactions; Project Finance; Energy; International Taxation.
Recht, Stacey A. '73 '00 C.1365 B.A. L.659 J.D.
(adm. in MD; not adm. in DC) [Ⓐ Akin,G.S.H.&F.]
*PRACTICE AREAS: Labor and Employment.
Recinto, Jose R., Jr. '41 '75 C&L.999 A.B., LL.B.
(adm. in VA; not adm. in DC) Legal Editor, The Bur. of Natl. Affs., Inc.
Recio, Carlos M. ....'52 '77 C.776 B.A. L.276 J.D. [Ⓒ Davis&C.]
*PRACTICE AREAS: Immigration and Naturalization; Complex Litigation; Commercial Law.
Recio, Irene M. '68 '97 C&L.472 B.S., J.D.
(adm. in FL; not adm. in DC) [Ⓐ Baker&M.]
*PRACTICE AREAS: Immigration Law.
Record, Warren A. '71 '96 C.806 B.A. L.356 J.D.
(adm. in MS; not adm. in DC) 716 Sicard St., S.E.★
Rector, Richard P., (AV) ....'59 '87 C&L.446 B.A., J.D. [Piper M.R.&W.]
*PRACTICE AREAS: Government Contracts.
Reddan, Colleen M. ....'74 '99 C.945 B.A. L.228 J.D. [Ⓐ Bryan C.]
Reddick, Kimberly N. '70 '96 C.197 B.A. L.273 J.D.
(adm. in NJ; not adm. in DC) [Ⓐ Sterne,K.G.&F.]
*PRACTICE AREAS: Trademarks; Patents; Copyrights.
Redding, J. Christopher, (AV) ....'52 '79 C.228 B.A. L.862 J.D. [Dow,L.&A.]
Reddy, Deepika '74 '01 C.860 B.A. L.94 J.D.
(adm. in MA; not adm. in DC) [Ⓐ Piper M.R.&W.]
*PRACTICE AREAS: Litigation; Intellectual Property.
Reddy, Richard L. '46 '79 C.602 B.B.A. L.851 J.D.
(adm. in PA; not adm. in DC) Sr. Legal Coun., Parsons Transp. Grp.

Reddy, Begley & McCormick, LLP, (AV)
2175 K Street, N.W., Suite 350, 20037-1803
Telephone: 202-659-5700 Facsimile: 202-659-5711
Email: rbm@rbmfcclaw.com URL: http://www.lawyers.com/rbmfcclaw
Members of Firm: Dennis F. Begley; Matthew H. McCormick.
Communications, Administrative, Copyright and Trademark Law, Broadcasting Law, Satellite Communications, FCC Regulations, FCC Licensing, Broadcast Station Transfers, Music Licensing.
See Professional Biographies, WASHINGTON, DISTRICT OF COLUMBIA

Redente, Gary E. ....'58 '00 C.331 B.A. L.94 J.D. [Ⓐ Steptoe&J.]
Redgrave, Jonathan M. ....'66 '91 C.602 B.A. L.494 J.D. [Ⓒ Jones,D.R.&P.]
Redinger, Craig T. ....'51 '77 C.893 B.A. L.999 [Fulbright&J.]
*PRACTICE AREAS: International Law; Corporate Law; Mergers, Acquisitions and Divestitures.
Redman, Lipman, (AV) ....'18 '42 C&L.659 A.B., LL.B. 1050 Conn. Ave., N.W.
Redmond, Gregory M. '67 '93 C.93 B.A. L.818 J.D.
Counsel, Metropolitan Life Insurance Company
Redmond, Joseph C., Jr. '24 '55 C.860 B.E.E. L.273 J.D.
[Ⓒ Morgan&F.] (See Pat. Sect.)
*PRACTICE AREAS: Patents; Copyright; Trademarks; Intellectual Property Law.
Redmond, Thomas Eugene '53 '87 C.500 B.A. L.329 J.D.
(adm. in TX; not adm. in DC) Pub. Serv. Comm.
Rednik, Debra H. ....'73 '98 C.910 A.B. L.273 J.D. [Ⓐ Dickstein S.M.&O.]
*PRACTICE AREAS: Energy Law.
Redpath, Peter K. ....'73 '00 C.1105 B.A. L.69 J.D. 1015 18th St. N.W.
Redway, Linn Kaiser ....'60 '86 C.695 B.A. L.273 J.D. [Ⓐ Crowell&M.]
Reed, Aaron J. ....'71 '96 C.860 B.A. L.260 J.D. [Ⓐ Akin,G.S.H.&F.]
*PRACTICE AREAS: Labor and Employment.
Reed, Barry S. ....'44 '81 C.911 B.A. L.128 J.D. [Swartz&R.]
Reed, Benjamin B. ....'73 '99 C.790 B.A.S. L.893 J.D. [Ⓐ Wiley R.&F.]
Reed, Charles D. ....'35 '67 C.691 B.A. L.796 [Kile G.L.&R.P.]
*PRACTICE AREAS: Corporate Law; Securities; Banking Law; Real Estate.
Reed, Dena C. ....'60 '85 C.856 B.S. L.329 J.D. Asst. Corp. Coun.
Reed, James L. ....'— '99 C.94 B.S. L.30 J.D. [Ⓐ Morgan,L.&B.]
Reed, James W. ....'50 '99 C.477 A.B. L.276 J.D. [Ⓐ Sonnenschein N.&R.]
*PRACTICE AREAS: International Trade Regulation.
Reed, Johana A. ....'59 '97 C.1090 B.S. L.276 J.D. [Ⓐ Venable,A.B.H.&C.]
*PRACTICE AREAS: Government Contracts; Corporate.
Reed, Kevin F., (AV) ....'48 '73 C.321 B.A. L.276 J.D. [Dow,L.&A.]
Reed, Michael P. ....'71 '00 C.033 B.A. L.94 LL.M. [Ⓐ Alston&B.]
*PRACTICE AREAS: Financial Services Law; Technology Law.
Reed, Natalie L. ....'69 '97 C.383 B.A. L.276 J.D. [Ⓐ Hale&D.]
*PRACTICE AREAS: Real Estate.
Reed, Rebecca R. ....'70 '96 C.477 B.A. L.273 J.D. [Ⓐ Davis W.T.]
*PRACTICE AREAS: Communications Law; Information Technology.
Reed, Stanley J., (AV) '51 '77 C.1036 B.A. L.477 J.D.
[Lerch,E.&B.] (⊙Bethesda, MD)
*PRACTICE AREAS: White Collar Criminal Defense; Complex Commercial Litigation; Civil Litigation; Health Care Litigation; Professional Ethics and Responsibility Law.
Reed, Steven, (AV) ....'52 '80 C&L.309 B.A., J.D. [Steptoe&J.]
*PRACTICE AREAS: Administrative Law; Energy Law; Natural Resources; Transportation; Oil and Gas Law.
Reed, Tamara Cain, (AV) '58 '83 C.758 B.A. L.259 J.D.
(adm. in FL; not adm. in DC) Assoc. Coun., Investment Co. Inst.
*RESPONSIBILITIES: Securities; State Investments; Investment Advisers.
Reed, Wendy N. '67 '92 C.893 B.A. L.945 J.D.
(adm. in VA; not adm. in DC) [Wright&T.]
*PRACTICE AREAS: Energy.
Reed, William F., (AV) ....'31 '55 C.860 B.A. L.276 LL.B. 1700 K St., N.W.

Reed Smith LLP, (AV)
Suite 1100 - East Tower, 1301 K Street, N.W., 20005-3317 ⊙
Telephone: 202-414-9200 FAX: 202-414-9299
Email: reedsmith@reedsmith.com URL: http://www.reedsmith.com
Members of Firm: Kevin R. Barry; A. Scott Bolden; Elizabeth B. Carder; Bernard J. Casey; Donald O. Clark; George R. Clark; Francis P. Dicello; Eric A. Dubelier; David C. Evans; Donald A. Farmer Jr.; Thomas C. Fox; Judith L. Harris; Henry A. Hart; Gordon W. Hatheway, Jr.; Robert J. Hill; James K. Kearney; Helen G. Kirsch; Carol Colborn Loepere; Nancy A. Luque; Michael C. Lynch; Dorn C. McGrath III; Kathleen H. McGuan; Joseph W. Metro; Richard L. Moorhouse; Stephen P. Murphy; Donald J. Myers; Joseph A. Rieser, Jr.; Christopher L. Rissetto; Gordon B. Schatz; Marc J. Scheineson; C. Stevens Seale; Olivia Shay-Byrne; Douglas K. Spaulding; Eugene Tillman. Counsel: Kenneth S. Barr; Linda A. Baumann; John A. Beck; Amy B. Bergner; Mary E. Buckles; Robert D. Clark; William R. Cowden; José A. Fuentes; Robert H. Jackson; Robert M. Marino; Grant E. Mitchell; David Ober; Phillips S. Peter (Not admitted in DC); Lee A. Rau; Michael B. Richman; Henry Sanchez, Jr. (Not admitted in DC); Ann E. Schmitt; Stephen M. Sorett; John H. Sterne, Jr.; Patricia H. Wittie. Associates: SueLyn Smith Athey (Not admitted in DC); Brad P. Bender (Not admitted in DC); Jacqueline E. Bennett (Not admitted in DC); David J. Bloch; Danielle R. Cesarano; Jiwen Chen (Not admitted in DC); Daniel A. Cody; Gail L. Daubert (Not admitted in DC); Bridnetta D. Edwards; Kurt D. Ferstl (Not admitted in DC); Philip J. Fick; Kelly Call Griffith (Not admitted in DC); Scot T. Hasselman; Jason M. Healy; David T. Hickey (Not admitted in DC); Andrew L. Hurst; Richard F. Johns; Robbie N. Koch; Elizabeth A. Mackenzie (Not admitted in DC); Edward J. McAndrew; Lorraine T. Mullings (Not admitted in DC); Dexter U. Nutall; Frank T. Pimentel; James P. Schulz; Tamara V. Scoville; Evan D. Selig (Not admitted in DC); Donna M. Sheinbach (Not admitted in DC); David L. Tanenholz (Not admitted in DC); Nigel L. Wilkinson (Not admitted in DC); Jarrell E. Williamson (Not admitted in DC).
Antitrust and Trade Regulation, Asbestos, Bank Regulatory, Bankruptcy, China/Asia, Communications, Construction, Consumer Financial Services, Corporate and Securities, E-Commerce, Eminent Domain/Condemnation, Employee Benefits, Employment Discrimination Litigation, Employment Law, Energy and Natural Resources, Environmental, Equipment Leasing, Family Business, Financial Services, Financial Services Insurance, Financial Services Litigation, First Amendment, Food, Drug & Device, Franchise, Government Contracts & Export Compliance, Government Relations, Health Care, Higher Education, Immigration, Information Technology, Insurance, Insurance Coverage, Intellectual Property, International, Land Use, Litigation, Media and Entertainment, Mergers and Acquisitions, Non-Profit Organizations, Product Liability, Professional Liability, Project Finance, Public Finance, Real Estate, Restrictive Covenants/Trade Secrets, Satellite Transactions, Tax, Technology, Telecommunications, Tissue Engineering and Biomedical Applications, Trusts & Estates, Venture, White Collar Crime, Year 2000.
Pittsburgh, Pennsylvania Office: 435 Sixth Avenue, 15219-1886. Telephone: 412-288-3131. FAX: 412-288-3063.
Philadelphia, Pennsylvania Office: 2500 One Liberty Place, 19103-7301. Telephone: 215-851-8100. FAX: 215-851-1420.
Harrisburg, Pennsylvania Office: 213 Market Street, 17101-2132. Telephone: 717-234-5988. FAX: 717-236-3777.
Princeton, New Jersey Office: 136 Main Street, Suite 250, 08540-5799. Telephone: 609-987-0050. FAX: 609-951-0824.
New York, N.Y. Office: 375 Park Avenue, 17th Floor, 10152. Telephone: 212-521-5400. FAX: 212-521-5450.
Newark, New Jersey Office: The Legal Center, One Riverfront Plaza, First Floor, 07102-5400. Telephone: 973-621-3200. FAX: 973-621-3199.
Wilmington, Delaware Office: 1201 Market Street, Suite 1500, 19801. Telephone: 302-778-7500. FAX: 302-778-7575.
McLean, Virginia Office: Suite 1100, 8251 Greensboro Drive, 22102-3844. Telephone: 703-734-4600. FAX: 703-734-4699.
Falls Church, Virginia Office: Suite 1400, 3110 Fairview Park Drive, 22042. Telephone: 703-641-4200. FAX: 703-641-4340.
Leesburg, Virginia Office: 44084 Riverside Parkway, Suite 300. 20176. Telephone: 703-729-8500. Metro: 703-478-1992. FAX: 703-478-8003.
Richmond, Virginia Office: Riverfront Plaza, West Tower, 901 East Byrd Street, Suite 1700, 23219-4069. Telephone: 804-344-3400. FAX: 804-344-3410.
London, England Office: Reed Smith Warner Cranston, Pickfords Wharf, Clink Street, SE1 9DG. Telephone: +44-20-7403-2900. FAX: +44-20-7403-4221.
Coventry, England Office: Reed Smith Warner Cranston, Park House, Station Square, CV1 2FL. Telephone: +44 24 7629 3000. FAX: +44 24 7629 3030. DX: 11203 Coventry 1.
See Professional Biographies, WASHINGTON, DISTRICT OF COLUMBIA

Reeder, James A. ....'33 '60 C.902 B.A. L.846 LL.B. [Patton B.]
Reeder, Joe R., (AV) ....'47 '76 C.870 B.S. L.846 J.D. [Greenberg T.]
Reems, Thomas B. '68 '99 C.902 B.A. L.893 J.D.
(adm. in FL; not adm. in DC) 1875 Connecticut Avenue, N.W.
Rees, David Charles ....'54 '93 C.722 B.A. L.30 J.D. 700 5th St., N.W.
Rees, Elizabeth ....'72 '97 C.896 B.A. L.1365 J.D. [Ⓐ Jones,D.R.&P.]

Rees, Jonathan T. .... '63 '91 C.103 A.B. L.893 J.D. [Hogan&H.]
*PRACTICE AREAS: Labor and Employment; Litigation.
Rees, Thomas S. .... '49 '79 C.945 B.A. L.976 J.D. Asst. U.S. Atty.

Rees, Broome & Diaz, P.C.
(See Vienna, Virginia)

Reese, Catherine M. .... '63 '98 C.446 B.A. L.180 J.D. [🄰 Lewis] (⊙Fairfax, VA)
*PRACTICE AREAS: Family Law.
Reese, Evan .... '71 '00 C.165 B.A. L.861 J.D. [🄰 Van Ness F.]
*PRACTICE AREAS: Energy; Oil and Gas Law; Oil and Gas Pipelines.
Reese, Rex E. '59 '85 C.258 B.S. L.862 J.D.
(adm. in PA; not adm. in DC) [🄲 Galland,K.G.F.&S.]
*PRACTICE AREAS: Asset-based and Project Finance; Aerospace and Aviation; Domestic and International Taxation; Corporate Transactions; Commercial Transactions.
Reesman, Ann Elizabeth, (AV) .... '56 '81 C.665 B.A. L.1017 J.D. [McGuiness N.&W.]
*PRACTICE AREAS: Employment Law; Federal Appellate Practice.
Reesman, David A. .... '64 '92 C.651 B.A. L.201 J.D. Marriott Intl., Inc.
Reeves, David C. .... '55 '80 [🄰 Troutman S.]
*PRACTICE AREAS: Transportation Regulation; Transportation; Corporate Law.
Reeves, Kelly Nicole .... '71 '99 C.576 B.A. L.446 J.D. [🄰 King&S.]
*PRACTICE AREAS: Food and Drug Regulations.
Reeves, Marsha Y. .... '71 '94 C.273 B.A. L.309 J.D. Assoc. Gen. Coun., Fannie Mae
*RESPONSIBILITIES: Intellectual Property; Technology Law.
Reeves, Ragan G. .... '— '97 C&L.846 B.B.A., J.D. [🄰 Miller&C.]
*PRACTICE AREAS: Taxation; Technology and Science; Aeronautical Technology; International Taxation; Tax Credits.
Reff, Alisa H. .... '61 '88 C.30 B.A. L.276 J.D. [🄲 Swidler B.S.F.]
*PRACTICE AREAS: Employment Litigation; Equal Employment Opportunity Law; Fair Labor Standards; Family and Medical Leave Act; Sexual Harassment.
Regal, Sally A., (AV) .... '53 '79 C&L.276 B.A., J.D. [🄲 Baach R.&L.P.]
*PRACTICE AREAS: Civil Litigation.
Regalado, Eloisa .... '52 '78 C.705 A.B. L.1292 J.D. AT&T
Regan, Christopher F. .... '65 '91 C.1044 B.S. L.477 J.D. [Beveridge&D.]
*PRACTICE AREAS: White Collar Criminal Defense; Environmental Law.
Regan, Elizabeth G. '62 '91 C.674 A.B. L.893 J.D.
(adm. in NJ; not adm. in DC) Sr. Coun., Marriott Intl., Inc.
*RESPONSIBILITIES: Intellectual Property.
Regan, James J., (AV) .... '51 '76 C&L.276 B.A., J.D. [Crowell&M.]
*PRACTICE AREAS: Government Contracts Law.
Regan, Jeremiah S. .... '66 '96 C.446 B.A. L.127 J.D. [🄰 McManus,S.A.&D.]
*PRACTICE AREAS: Government Contracts; Construction Litigation.
Regan, Karen Anne .... '— '99 C.855 B.A. L.575 J.D. [🄰 Verner,L.B.M.&H.]
*PRACTICE AREAS: Legislative.
Regan, Laura Partee .... '71 '97 C&L.477 B.B.A., J.D. [🄰 Skadden,A.S.M.&F.]
*PRACTICE AREAS: Tax.
Regan, Patrick M., (AV) .... '55 '80 C.299 B.A. L.128 J.D. [Regan,H.&L.] ⊙
*PRACTICE AREAS: Medical Malpractice; Product Liability; Personal Injury; Wrongful Death; Construction Accidents.
Regan, Paul K. .... '48 '77 C.1036 B.A. L.276 J.D. [Regan]
Regan, Theresa M. '67 '97 C.378 B.A. L.910 J.D.
(adm. in MO; not adm. in DC) [🄰 Weil,G.&M.]
*PRACTICE AREAS: Securities; Corporate Law.
Regan Associates, Chartered .... 1003 K St., N.W.

Regan, Halperin & Long, P.L.L.C., (AV)
Presidential Plaza, 900 Nineteenth Street, N.W., Suite 200, 20006 ⊙
Telephone: 202-463-3030 Fax: 202-463-0667
Email: rhllaw.com URL: http://www.rhllaw.com
Patrick M. Regan; Jonathan E. Halperin; Victor E. Long; Salvatore J. Zambri;—Karen M. Doherty; Thanos Basdekis; Thomas P. Silis (Not admitted in DC).
Negligence, Medical Malpractice, Product Liability, Automobile Torts, Aviation Accidents, Construction Site Accidents, Industrial and Commercial Liability, Public Transportation Accidents Liability, Tap Water Scald Cases, Elevator and Escalator Accidents, Defective Consumer Product's Claims, Contingency Commercial Litigation, Bad Faith Claims and Private Sector Workers' Compensation.
Fairfax, Virginia Office: Suite 140, 10680 Main Street, 22030. Telephone: 703-549-9663.
See Professional Biographies, WASHINGTON, DISTRICT OF COLUMBIA

Regas, Beth H. .... '65 '95 C.882 B.A. L.1194 J.D. [🄰 Hunton&W.]
Regnery, Alfred S. .... '42 '71 C.72 B.A. L.966 J.D. [🄲 Keller&H.]
*PRACTICE AREAS: Publishing; Direct Marketing; International Trade.
Reheuser, Michael E., (AV) '61 '86
C.401 B.S. L.128 J.D. [Jordan C.&S.] (⊙Fairfax, VA)
*PRACTICE AREAS: Tort Defense; Premises Liability Defense; Construction Law; Military Law; Toxic Tort Defense.
Rehm, John B., (AV) .... '30 '55 C.309 A.B. L.178 LL.B. [Dorsey&W.]
Reich, Steven F. .... '61 '87 C&L.178 B.A., J.D. [Manatt,P.&P.]
Reichardt, Glenn R. .... '— '77 C.228 A.B. L.309 J.D. [Kirkpatrick&L.]
*PRACTICE AREAS: SEC Enforcement; Antitrust and Trade Regulation; International Trade; Federal Civil Litigation; Alternative Dispute Resolution.
Reichart, Stuart R. .... '24 '48 C.836 L.1009 LL.B. 1001 Pa. Ave., N.W., Ste. 800
Reicher, Terri L. '61 '86 C.378 B.A. L.945 J.D.
Assistant General Counsel, National Association of Securities Dealers
Reichert, Paul R. .... '68 '93 C.299 A.B. L.273 J.D. [🄰 Jones,D.R.&P.]
Reichertz, Peter S., (AV) .... '50 '76 C.103 A.B. L.273 J.D. [Arent F.K.P.&K.]
*PRACTICE AREAS: Animal Drug Regulation; Administrative Law; Administrative Adjudications; Administrative Agency Practice; Administrative Hearings and Appeals.
Reichler, Paul S., (AV) .... '— '73 C.860 B.A. L.309 J.D. [Foley,H.&E.]
*PRACTICE AREAS: International Arbitration; Litigation; International Business Law; Government Affairs; Lobbying.
Reichs, Kerry E. '70 '00 C.604 B.A. L.228 J.D.
(adm. in NC; not adm. in DC) [🄰 Arent F.K.P.&K.]
*PRACTICE AREAS: Internet Law; Electronic Commerce; Intellectual Property; Advertising; Contests and Sweepstakes.
Reid, Allison Hope '67 '97 C.1138 B.B.A. L.262 J.D.
(adm. in NY; not adm. in DC) NASD Regulation, Inc.
Reid, Forrest W. .... '60 '94 C&L.846 B.B.A., J.D. [🄰 Katten M.Z.]
*PRACTICE AREAS: Real Estate; Commercial Leasing; Banking and Financial Institutions; Retailing.
Reid, George B., Jr. .... '48 '75 C.976 B.A. L.309 J.D. 1201 Penn. Ave., N.W.
Reid, Inez Smith .... '37 '63 C.860 B.A. L.976 LL.B. 500 Indiana Ave., N.W.
Reid, James S. .... '15 '51 C.188 A.B. L.273 J.D. 2500 Va. Ave., N.W.
Reid, Key '74 '99 C.893 B.A. L.1209 J.D.
(adm. in NV; not adm. in DC) [🄰 Patton B.]
Reid, Robert Newton .... '08 '30 C&L.145 Ph.B., J.D. 1135 16th St., N.W.‡
Reid, Thomas R., III .... '44 '76 C.674 A.B. L.273 J.D. 1150 15th St., N.W.
Reid, Victor L. .... '56 '86 C.511 B.A. L.329 J.D. [🄲 Arnold&P.]
*PRACTICE AREAS: Corporate; Private Equity; Securities; Commercial Practice.
Reider, Alan E., (AV) .... '49 '75 C.103 A.B. L.94 J.D. [Arent F.K.P.&K.]
*PRACTICE AREAS: Health Care Law; Health Care Fraud; Health Care Reimbursement; Physician Contracts; Physician Licensing.
Reidy, Andrew M. .... '62 '87 C.93 B.A. L.273 J.D. [McKenna&C.]
*PRACTICE AREAS: Commercial Litigation; Insurance Recovery Litigation; Directors and Officers Insurance Coverage; Fidelity Bond Litigation.
Reif, Robert D. .... '52 '77 C.205 B.A. L.128 J.D. [Epstein B.&G.]
*PRACTICE AREAS: Health Law; Corporate Law.
Reif, Timothy M., (AV) .... '59 '86 C.674 A.B. L.178 J.D. 1775 Pennsylvania Ave., N.W.
Reif, Wanda J., (AV) .... '46 '72 C&L.477 A.B., J.D. 2141 P Street, N.W.
Reifel, Charles M., (AV) .... '46 '74 C.197 A.B. L.273 J.D. [Bastianelli,B.&K.]
*PRACTICE AREAS: Government Contracts; Construction Law.
Reiff, Neil P. .... '68 '93 C.1349 B.A. L.273 J.D. [Sandler,R.&Y.]
*PRACTICE AREAS: Election, Campaign and Political Law; Election and Campaign Finance.
Reifman, Suzanne D. .... '67 '98 C.860 B.A. L.273 J.D. [🄰 Vinson&E.]
*PRACTICE AREAS: Litigation.
Reik, Jennifer '— '00 C.929 B.A. L.1338 J.D.
(adm. in MD; not adm. in DC) [🄰 Seward&K.]
*PRACTICE AREAS: Securities.
Reilly, James T., (AV) .... '23 '52 C&L.276 B.S.S., LL.B. [Comstock&R.]
Reilly, John R., (AV) .... '28 '55 C&L.352 B.A., J.D. [🄲 Baker&M.]
*PRACTICE AREAS: Antitrust Law; Mergers and Acquisitions; U.S. Trade.
Reilly, Kevin Michael '52 '91
C.446 B.A. L.276 J.D. 3601 Connecticut Avenue, NW, Suite 206
Reilly, Laura A. .... '70 '95 C.390 B.A. L.273 J.D. [🄰 Mayer,B.&P.]
*PRACTICE AREAS: Real Estate.
Reilly, Matthew J. '66 '95 C.164 B.A. L.276 J.D.
(adm. in MA; not adm. in DC) 607 14th St., N.W.‡
Reilly, Patrick W. .... '— '86 C.93 B.A. L.893 J.D. [🄲 Foley&L.]
*PRACTICE AREAS: Regulatory; Surface Transportation.
Reilly, Peter R. '39 '70 C.602 A.B. L.276 J.D.
Sr. Assoc. Gen. Coun., Tort Litig., National Railroad Passenger Corp. (AMTRAK)
Reilly, Sean M. '— '93 C.692 B.S. L.602 J.D.
(adm. in VA; not adm. in DC) [🄰 Shook,H.&B.]
Reimer, Daniel S. '70 '95 C.260 B.A. L.1165 J.D.
(adm. in CO; not adm. in DC) [🄰 Akin,G.S.H.&F.] (⊙Denver, CO)
Rein, Bert W., (AV) .... '41 '64 C.31 B.A. L.309 LL.B. [Wiley R.&F.]
*PRACTICE AREAS: Litigation; Antitrust; International.
Reiner, Alyssa L. .... '72 '99 C.188 B.A. L.276 J.D. [Pepco,H.]
Reiner, Burton J. .... '28 '53 C&L.276 B.S., J.D. 401 M St., S.W.‡
Reiner, Robert M., (AV) .... '52 '76 C.659 B.S. L.273 J.D. [Joseph,M.&R.]
*PRACTICE AREAS: Tax Law; Estate Planning; Estate Administration; Closely Held Corporations.
Reinert, Thomas E., Jr. .... '54 '80 C&L.309 B.A., J.D. [Morgan,L.&B.]
Reingold, Barry J. .... '51 '77 C.31 B.A. L.273 J.D. [Perkins C.]
*PRACTICE AREAS: Civil Litigation; Antitrust and Consumer Protection Litigation; Litigation; Federal Trade Commission; Internet Law.
Reinhard, Matthew '74 '01 C.170 B.A. L.352 J.D.
(adm. in VA; not adm. in DC) [🄰 Miller&C.]
*PRACTICE AREAS: Commercial Litigation; Government Contracts.
Reinhart, Tara Lee .... '— '94 C.575 B.A. L.128 J.D. [🄰 Morgan,L.&B.]
Reinke, Fred W. .... '61 '88 C.747 B.A. L.178 J.D. [🄲 Clifford C.R.&W.]
Reis, Harold F., (AV) .... '16 '41 C.563 B.S.S. L.178 LL.B. 1800 M St., N.W.
Reischel, Charles L., (AV) .... '43 '69 C&L.309 A.B., J.D. Dep. Corp. Coun.
Reisenfeld, Kenneth B., (AV) .... '53 '79 C.604 B.A. L.309 J.D. [Haynes&B.]
*PRACTICE AREAS: International Trade; Customs; International Arbitration.
Reiser, Bert C., (BV) .... '63 '90 C.132 B.A. L.30 J.D. [Howrey S.A.&W.]
*PRACTICE AREAS: International Trade; Section 337.
Reiser, David A. .... '56 '82 C&L.976 B.A., J.D. [🄲 Zuckerman S.]
Reiskin, Terri Steinhaus .... '59 '84 C.674 A.B. L.309 J.D. [Hogan&H.]
*PRACTICE AREAS: Automotive Products Liability; Drug and Medical Device Defense; Products Liability Defense; Complex Litigation; Class Action Defense.
Reiss, Kenneth M. '65 '92 C.228 B.S. L.893 J.D.
Assoc. Litigation Coun., WorldCom, Inc.
Reiss, Rena Hozore '59 '86 C.674 A.B. L.309 J.D.
Sr. Coun., Marriott International, Inc.
Reister, Andrea G. .... '57 '93 C.911 B.S. L.1209 J.D. [🄲 Covington&B.] (See Pat. Sect.)
Reiter, Harvey L., (AV) .... '50 '75 C.475 B.A. L.94 J.D. [Morrison&H.]
*PRACTICE AREAS: Federal Energy Regulation; Energy Marketing; Appellate; Telecommunications Law; Litigation.
Reiter, Scott Lev-Benjamin .... '74 '99 C.367 B.A. L.276 J.D. Fed. Trade Comm.
Reitner & Stuart .... 1730 K Street, N.W., Suite 1100 (⊙San Luis Obispo, CA)
Reitze, Arnold W., Jr. .... '38 '71 C.1046 B.A. L.705 LL.B. [🄲 LeBoeuf,L.G.&M.]
*PRACTICE AREAS: Environmental Law.
Reklaitis, Robert F., (AV) .... '53 '78 C.403 B.A. L.893 J.D. [Nixon P.]
*PRACTICE AREAS: Litigation; Antitrust; Insurance; Securities; Telecommunications Law.
Relle, Brian M. '56 '85 C.688 B.S. L.1002 J.D.
Attorney & Vice President, Hill International, Inc.
Relyea, Richard J., III '40 '67 C.309 A.B. L.188 LL.B.
(adm. in NY; not adm. in DC) Med. Claims Atty., Walter Reed Army Med. Ctr.
Remeikis, Albert A. '42 '68 C.1122 B.S. L.276 J.D.
(adm. in NY; not adm. in DC) Pricewaterhouse Coopers LLP
Remes, David H., (AV) .... '54 '83 C.178 B.A. L.309 J.D. [Covington&B.]
Remes, Robert A., (AV) .... '48 '73 C.188 B.S. L.94 J.D. [Carliner,R.&M.]
*PRACTICE AREAS: Immigration and Naturalization; Visas; Political Asylum.
Remington, Kristi L. '70 '95 C.207 B.A. L.30 J.D.
(adm. in MD; not adm. in DC) [🄰 Balch&B.]
*PRACTICE AREAS: Legislative Practice; Energy.
Remington, Michael J., (AV) .... '45 '73 C&L.966 B.S., J.D. [Drinker B.&R.]
*PRACTICE AREAS: Intellectual Property; General Lobbying.
Remy, Donald Michael .... '67 '91 C.420 B.A. L.329 J.D. V.P., Fannie Mae
*RESPONSIBILITIES: Litigation; Employment Law; Antitrust; Contracts.
Remy, John M. .... '71 '97 C.597 B.S. L.477 J.D. [🄰 Akin,G.S.H.&F.]
*PRACTICE AREAS: Labor and Employment.
Renaud, D. Mark .... '72 '00 C.976 B.A. L.893 J.D. [🄰 Wiley R.&F.]
Renberg, Dan H. '64 '90 C.674 A.B. L.894 J.D.
(adm. in VA; not adm. in DC) Director, Export-Import Bank of the U.S.
Renfro, William L. '45 '73 C.688 B.S. L.184 J.D.
(adm. in CT; not adm. in DC) Policy Analysis Co., Inc.
Renfroe, Diane L .... '47 '77 C.914 B.A. L.93 J.D. Arthur Andersen LLP
Renigar, James A. "Del" .... '70 '96 C.228 A.B. L.477 J.D. [🄰 Steptoe&J.]
Renken, John O. '65 '90 C.212 B.A. L.1119 J.D.
(adm. in MI; not adm. in DC) [Miller,C.P.&S.] (⊙Ann Arbor, MI)
*PRACTICE AREAS: Municipal Finance or Bond Law; Real Estate Finance; Housing Finance; Health Care Finance; Project Finance.
Renkey, Albert Zuard '58 '86
C.893 B.A. L.976 J.D. Assoc. Gen. Coun., Ernst & Young LLP
Renneisen, John D. .... '64 '93 C.951 B.A. L.228 J.D. [🄰 Dewey B.]
Renner, Curtis S. .... '58 '88 C.918 B.A. L.309 J.D. [Watson&R.]
*PRACTICE AREAS: Trials and Litigation; Scientific Trials; Medical Causation; Cancer & Carcinogenesis; Toxic Torts.
Renner, W. Karl '69 '99 C.446 B.S.E.E. L.273 J.D.
(adm. in VA; not adm. in DC; See Pat. Sect.) [🄰 Fish&R.]
Rennert, Jamie Palter .... '— '92 C.477 A.B. L.659 J.D. [Foley&L.]
*PRACTICE AREAS: Transportation; Administrative Law.
Reno, Lee P. .... '40 '70 C.932 B.S. L.329 J.D. [Reno&C.]
*PRACTICE AREAS: Affordable Housing; Real Estate Finance Transactions; General Corporate; Nonprofit Organizations; Captive Insurance Company Regulation.

Reno & Cavanaugh, PLLC, (AV)
Suite 900 1250 Eye Street, N.W., 20005-3922
Telephone: 202-783-2800 Fax: 202-783-0550
URL: http://www.renocavanaugh.com
Members of Firm: Lee P. Reno; Megan Glasheen; Sharon Wilson Géno. Associates: Julie S. McGovern; Robert A. Graham; Sharon M. Weathers (Not admitted in DC); Tiffani K. Whittaker. Of Counsel: Gordon Cavanaugh.
Affordable Housing and Real Estate Transactions, Public Housing, Community Development, Legislation, Administrative Law, Nonprofit Organizations, Captive Insurance, and Litigation.
See Professional Biographies, WASHINGTON, DISTRICT OF COLUMBIA

Renouf, Katrina, (AV) .... '38 '63 C.881 A.B. L.309 LL.B. [Renouf&P.]
Renouf & Polivy, (AV) ....1532 16th St., N.W.
Rent A Lawyer - By The Day, (BV) .... 2147 O Street, N.W., Suite 306
Renton, Susan L. .... '60 '89 C.802 B.A. L.940 J.D. [Ⓐ Sandler,T.&R.]
*PRACTICE AREAS: Trade Regulation; Customs; Export Regulation.
Renuart, Elizabeth A., (BV) '52 '77 C.1031 B.A. L.128 J.D.
(adm. in MD; not adm. in DC) National Consumer Law Ctr.
Renzi, Anthony J., Jr. .... '64 '89 C.1044 B.S. L.904 J.D. [Clifford C.R.&W.]
Repass, David Michael .... '46 '70 C&L.362 B.A., J.D. Price Waterhouse
Repetto, Augusto .... '64 '95 [Ⓒ Wilmer,C.&P.]
Repka, David A. .... '57 '81 C.597 B.A. L.276 J.D. [Winston&S.]
*PRACTICE AREAS: Nuclear Energy; Nuclear Waste; Administrative Agency Practice; Administrative Hearings and Appeals.
Repp, Marissa G., (AV) .... '56 '84 C.1044 B.A. L.276 J.D. [Hogan&H.]
*PRACTICE AREAS: Communications Law; Commercial Transactions; FCC Regulation; Broadcast Regulations; Broadcast Station Transfers.
Repp, Sheldon D. .... '47 '75 C.103 A.B. L.107 J.D. Gen. Coun., NCHELP
Repper, George R. '54 '82 C.1044 B.S. L.982 J.D.
[Rothwell,F.E.&M.] (See Pat. Sect.)
Resnick, Adam D. .... '71 '98 C.823 B.A. L.64 J.D. [Ⓐ Piper M.R.&W.]
*PRACTICE AREAS: Intellectual Property Law; Electronic Commerce.
Resnick, Murray I., (BV) '36 '62 C&L.446 B.A., LL.B.
[Resnick,A.&S.] (⊙Balt., MD)
Resnick, Richard M., (AV) .... '51 '76 C.188 B.S. L.273 J.D. [Sherman,D.C.L.&Y.]
*PRACTICE AREAS: Labor and Employment Law; Union Labor Law.

Resnick, Abraham & Schwartzman, L.L.C., (BV)
Suite 304, 1730 K Street, N.W., 20006 ⊙
Telephone: 201-452-1411
URL: http://www.ra-atty.com
Murray I. Resnick; Philip Abraham.
Commercial and Collection Law. Admiralty, Personal Injury, Immigration, Naturalization, Bankruptcy Law.
Baltimore, Maryland Office: One East Franklin Street, 21202. Telephone: 410-539-6087.
Fairfax, Virginia Office: 12600 Fair Lakes Circle, Suite 220. Telephone: 703-818-0223.
Syosset, New York Office: 485 Underhill Boulevard, Suite 302. Telephone: 515-364-5300
Wilmington, Delaware Office: 100 East 14th Street. Telephone: 302-655-1943.
Glen Mills, Pennsylvania Office: 30 Regency Plaza. Telephone: 610-358-9600.
Burlington, New Jersey Office: 505 High Street, P.O. Box 1427. Telephone: 609-386-1911.
Roswell, Georgia Office: 1265 Minihinette Drive, Suite 150, P.O. Box 1870. Telephone: 770-840-8482.
Los Angeles, California Office: 2049 Century Park East, Suite 460. Telephone: 310-557-2599.
Deerfield Beach, Florida Office: 1701 West Hillsboro Boulevard, Suite 303. Telephone: 954-480-6220.
Charlotte, North Carolina Office: 1721 Norland Road. Telephone: 704-535-8440.
Cary, North Carolina Office: 140 Preston Executive Drive. Telephone: 919-781-1880.
See Professional Biographies, WASHINGTON, DISTRICT OF COLUMBIA

Resolution Law Group, P.C.
5335 Wisconsin Avenue, N.W., Suite 305, 20015 ⊙
Telephone: 202-686-4844 Fax: 202-686-4843
Email: firm@reslawgrp.com URL: http://www.reslawgrp.com
Michael D. Goodstein;—Deanna J. Chang.
Civil Litigation, Insurance Coverage, Insurance Bad Faith Litigation, Environmental Law, Environmental Litigation, Toxic Torts Litigation, Securities Litigation and Arbitration.
Lafayette, California Office: 3717 Mt. Diablo Boulevard, Suite 200, 94549. Telephone: 925-284-0840. Fax: 925-284-0870. Email: firm@reslawgrp.com. URL: http://ww.,reslawgrp.com
See Professional Biographies, WASHINGTON, DISTRICT OF COLUMBIA

Respess, Thomas S., III '52 '91
C.277 B.S. L.1209 J.D. Sr. Manager, PricewaterhouseCoopers
Restrepo, Daniel A. .... '71 '99 C.893 B.A. L.659 J.D. [Ⓐ Williams&C.]
*PRACTICE AREAS: Litigation.
Restrepo, Monica '72 '96
(adm. in Colomb; not adm. in DC) [Ⓐ Coudert B.]
*PRACTICE AREAS: Global Project Finance.
Retchin, Judith E. .... '52 '78 C.273 B.A. L.128 J.D. Supr. Ct. J.
Rettew, Douglas A. .... '70 '95 C.477 B.A. L.273 J.D. [Ⓐ Finnegan,H.F.G.&D.]
*PRACTICE AREAS: Trademark Litigation; Copyright Protection; Trademark Licensing; Trademark Protection; International Intellectual Property.
Retureta, Manuel J. .... '61 '91 C.112 B.A. L.128 J.D. Jud. Clk.
Reuben, Todd H. .... '61 '89 C.1365 B.B.A. L.273 J.D. [Venable,A.B.H.&C.]
*PRACTICE AREAS: Tax Law; Business Planning Law; Partnership Law; Business Transaction Law.

Reuss & Miller, (AV)
1130 17th Street, N.W., Suite 400, 20036
Telephone: 202-778-1166
Christopher M. Reuss (1943-1986); Barbara R. Miller.
Probate, Estate Planning and Administration, Conservatorships, Guardianships and Elder Law.

Reuther, Alan V. .... '49 '77 C&L.477 B.A., J.D. Legis. Dir., UAW
Revaz, Cris R. .... '59 '88 C.183 B.A. L.128 J.D. [Ⓒ Hale&D.]
*PRACTICE AREAS: International Trade.
Revell, Mary N. '49 '78
C.882 B.A. L.665 J.D. Asst. Gen. Coun., Nasdaq Stock Market, Inc.
Reves, Jerry T. '68 '99 C.1142 B.A. L.1363 J.D.
(adm. in TX; not adm. in DC) 1710 Rhode Island Ave. NW, 10th Floor
Rexinger, Allan R. .... '46 '75 C.473 B.S. L.879 J.D. 717 A St., S.E.
Rexinger, Allen Robert .... '46 '75 717 A St., S.E.
Reyes, Ana L. '74 '01 C.853 B.A. L.309 J.D.
(adm. in NY; not adm. in DC) [Ⓐ Williams&C.]
Reyes, Arcadio J. '58 '90 C.178 B.A. L.564 J.D.
1150 Connecticut Avenue, N.W., Ninth Floor
Reyes, Thomas J. '62 '98 C.454 B.S. L.94 J.D.
(adm. in MA; not adm. in DC) [Ⓐ Sutherland A.&B.]
*PRACTICE AREAS: Corporate Law.
Reyna, Jimmie V., (AV) .... '52 '79 C.696 B.A. L.560 J.D. [Williams M.]
*PRACTICE AREAS: International Trade; International Trade Regulations; International Trade Agreements; Import and Export Law; Antidumping.
Reyna, Ruben F. '72 '97 C.276 B.A. L.477 J.D.
(adm. in MD; not adm. in DC) [Ⓐ Wallace K.M.&B.]
*PRACTICE AREAS: Litigation.
Reyner, William S., Jr., (AV) .... '45 '70 C&L.976 B.A., LL.B. [Ⓒ Hogan&H.]
*PRACTICE AREAS: Communications Law; Commercial Transactions; Sports and Entertainment Law.
Reynolds, Christopher S. '74 '99 C&L.276 B.A., J.D.
(adm. in MD; not adm. in DC) [Ⓐ Holland&K.]
*PRACTICE AREAS: Real Estate Finance; Commercial Leasing; Real Estate Acquisitions.
Reynolds, Donald B., Jr., (AV) .... '54 '79 C.299 B.A. L.276 J.D. [Silverstein&M.]
*PRACTICE AREAS: Federal Tax; Real Estate; Business Transactions.
Reynolds, Hal F. .... '27 '57 C.951 A.B. L.309 LL.B. The World Bk.
Reynolds, John B., III, (AV) .... '56 '82 C.951 B.A. L.976 J.D. [Wiley R.&F.]
*PRACTICE AREAS: International Trade; Internet; Electronic Commerce.
Reynolds, Joseph H. .... '46 '77 C.401 B.A. L.982 J.D. [Nixon P.]
*PRACTICE AREAS: Corporate Finance; Mergers and Acquisitions.
Reynolds, Kristina Astrid .... '73 '98 C.896 B.A. L.145 J.D. 1776 "K" St., N.W.
Reynolds, MaryJane, (AV) .... '46 '71 C&L.966 B.A., J.D. [Morrison&R.]
Reynolds, Max M. .... '70 '96 C.245 B.A. L.893 J.D. [Ⓐ Shaw P.]
Reynolds, Mia C. '75 '01 C.309 B.A. L.904 J.D.
(adm. in MA; not adm. in DC) [Ⓐ Jones,D.R.&P.]
Reynolds, Nicholas S., (AV) .... '44 '71 C.1028 B.S. L.273 J.D. [Winston&S.]
*PRACTICE AREAS: Energy Law; Public Utility Law; Nuclear Energy; Electric Power; Energy Acquisitions.
Reynolds, Sung Park .... '52 '79 C.228 B.S. L.276 J.D. [Ⓒ Holland&K.]
*PRACTICE AREAS: Land Sales Regulation; Real Estate Law; Resort Timeshares.
Reynolds, Tina D. .... '70 '95 C.30 B.A. L.575 J.D. [Ⓐ Dickstein S.M.&O.]
*PRACTICE AREAS: Government Contracts; Litigation; Regulatory Law; White Collar Crime.
Reynolds, Tina R. .... '70 '96 C.945 B.A. L.724 J.D. [Ⓐ Shaw P.]
*PRACTICE AREAS: Litigation; Corporate; Business.
Reynolds, Troy D. .... '67 '92 C&L.383 B.A., J.D. [Ⓐ Kelley D.&W.]
*PRACTICE AREAS: Business Law; Commercial Law; Intellectual Property Law; Contracts; Corporate.
Reynolds, William Bradford, (AV) '42 '68 C.976 B.A. L.880 S.J.D.
[Howrey S.A.&W.]
*PRACTICE AREAS: Antitrust Litigation (Trial Court); Commercial Litigation (Trial Court); Federal Appellate Practice.
Reynolds, William F., Jr. .... '62 '95 C.352 B.S. L.309 J.D. [Ⓐ Piper M.R.&W.]
*PRACTICE AREAS: Corporate Financing Law; Mergers and Acquisitions.
Reynolds-Amuso, Jessica K. '72 '98 C.104 B.A. L.982 J.D.
(adm. in MA; not adm. in DC) Staff Atty., NASD Dispute Resolution, Inc.
Rezneck, Daniel A., (AV) '35 '59 C&L.309 B.A., LL.B.
D.C. Fin. Responsibility & Mgmt. Assistance Auth.
Reznick, Robert P. .... '54 '79 C.1167 B.S. L.309 J.D. [Hughes H.&R.]
*PRACTICE AREAS: Litigation; Antitrust; Government Contracts.
Reznik, Bruce A. .... '52 '84 C.273 B.A. L.280 J.D. 2020 Pennsylvania Ave., N.W.
Rezvani, Tracy D. '71 '96 C.446 B.S. L.273 J.D.
(adm. in MD; not adm. in DC) [Ⓐ Finkelstein,T.&L.]
Rhea, Melissa .... '57 '82 C.910 A.B. L.904 J.D. [Ⓐ J.H.Olender&Assoc.]
*PRACTICE AREAS: Medical Malpractice; Personal Injury.
Rhees, Carol A., (AV) .... '51 '77 C.188 A.B. L.893 J.D. [Ⓒ Steptoe&J.]
*PRACTICE AREAS: Estate Planning.
Rhilinger, James E. .... '70 '97 C.1145 B.S. L.128 J.D. [Ⓐ Fried,F.H.S.&J.]
*PRACTICE AREAS: Antitrust.
Rhinelander, John B., (P.C.), (AV) .... '33 '64 C.976 B.A. L.893 LL.B. [Ⓒ Shaw P.]
*PRACTICE AREAS: Government; Health Care.
Rhoad, Robert T. .... '67 '94 C.882 B.A. L.1194 J.D. [Ⓐ Porter W.M.&A.]
*PRACTICE AREAS: Complex Litigation; Health Care Fraud; White Collar Crime.
Rhoades, Justin R. .... '— '00 C.668 B.A. L.309 J.D. [Ⓐ Latham&W.]
*PRACTICE AREAS: Business Litigation; Antitrust; Intellectual Property Litigation.
Rhoads, Carrie Aleen .... '72 '98 C.528 B.A. L.276 J.D. [Ⓐ Steptoe&J.]
Rhoads, Philip S. .... '49 '80 C.273 B.A. L.383 J.D. 504 A St. S.E.
Rhodes, Jeffrey .... '67 '95 C.30 B.A. L.904 J.D. [Ⓐ Dickstein S.M.&O.]
*PRACTICE AREAS: Bankruptcy; Creditors Rights; Commercial Litigation.
Rhodes, John J. .... '16 '42 C.375 B.S. L.309 LL.B. [Ⓒ Hunton&W.]
*PRACTICE AREAS: Energy.
Rhodes, John J., III .... '— '68 C.976 B.A. L.37 J.D. [Ⓒ Hunton&W.]
*PRACTICE AREAS: Environmental; Natural Resources; Federal Legislative Practice.
Rhodes, Linda L. .... '62 '87 C.945 B.B.A. L.893 J.D. [Ⓒ Mayer,B.&P.]
Rhodes, Paul M., (AV) .... '08 '39 L.273 J.D. 4530 Wisconsin Ave., N.W., Ste. 200
Rhodes, Robert L., Jr., (AV) .... '47 '72 C.1365 B.A. L.893 J.D. [Holland&K.]
*PRACTICE AREAS: Environmental Law.
Rhodes, Sylvia A. .... '67 '99 C.766 B.A. L.112 J.D. [Ⓐ Bryan C.]
*PRACTICE AREAS: International Trade.
Rhyne, Katherine L., (AV) .... '— '80 C&L.893 B.A., J.D. [King&S.]
*PRACTICE AREAS: Environmental.

Rhyne, Sidney White, (AV) '31 '55 C.695 A.B. L.659 LL.B.
3250 Arcadia Place, N.W., 20015-2330
Telephone: 202-244-6248 Fax: 202-244-4279
Email: swrhyne@abanet.org
Communications Law, Broadcasting Law, Estate Administration.
See Professional Biographies, WASHINGTON, DISTRICT OF COLUMBIA

Ricapito, Jeffrey M. '73 '98 C.645 B.S. L.1019 J.D.
(adm. in CT; not adm. in DC) [Ⓐ Krupin O.]
Ricard, Kathryn A. '65 '93 C.893 B.S. L.273 J.D.
Assoc. Coun., Investment Co. Institute
*RESPONSIBILITIES: ERISA.
Ricardo, Mark E. .... '69 '99 C.896 B.A. L.823 J.D. [Ⓐ Akin,G.S.H.&F.]
*PRACTICE AREAS: Commercial Real Estate; Federal Taxation; State Taxation; Local Taxation.
Riccardi, Jennifer Danner .... '69 '94 C.262 B.A. L.273 J.D. [Ⓐ Dewey B.]
*PRACTICE AREAS: International Trade; Litigation.
Riccardi, Mark R. .... '69 '94 C.165 A.B. L.276 J.D. [Ⓐ Orrick,H.&S.]
Ricci, Adrian J., (AV) .... '48 '73 C.886 B.A. L.273 [Shiffman&R.]
Rice, Annemarie Brennan .... '62 '97 C.690 B.A. L.1194 J.D. [Ⓐ Schmeltzer,A.&S.]
*PRACTICE AREAS: Business Law; Business Transactions; Commercial Litigation.
Rice, Daryl L. '66 '98 C.112 B.A. L.902 J.D.
(adm. in CA; not adm. in DC) [Ⓐ McDermott,W.&E.]
Rice, Donnellda L. .... '56 '81 C.411 B.S. L.329 J.D. [Ⓒ Graves&H.]
Rice, Fred J., Jr. .... '21 '50 C.128 B.A. L.180 LL.B. 51 Louisiana Ave., N.W.
Rice, John Lloyd .... '— '65 C.962 B.S. L.309 LL.B. [Miller&C.]
*PRACTICE AREAS: Government Contracts; Government Agency Practice; Contract Litigation; Administrative Litigation; Federal Administrative Law.
Rice, Paul Jackson .... '38 '62 C&L.502 A.B., J.D. [Arent F.K.P.&K.]
*PRACTICE AREAS: Motor Vehicle Safety Law; Automobile Law; Transportation Law; Hazardous Materials Transportation; Motor Carrier Law.
Rice, Richard A., Jr. .... '68 '94 C.280 B.A. L.602 J.D. [Ⓐ Hunton&W.]
*PRACTICE AREAS: White Collar Criminal Defense; Commercial Litigation; Products Liability.
Rice, Robert R. '34 '63 C.282 A.B. L.1017 LL.B.
(adm. in PA; not adm. in DC) 700 13th St., N.W.
Rice, William E. .... '55 '95 C.401 B.S.C.E. L.208 J.D. [Ⓐ Dewey B.]
*PRACTICE AREAS: Energy.
Rich, Bruce M. .... '47 '82 C.976 B.A. L.659 J.D. Natural Res. Def. Council
Rich, Edward Jeffrey, (BV) .... '56 '89 C.145 B.A. L.276 J.D. 1801 K Street, N.W.
Rich, J. Curtis '64 '95 C.939 B.A. L.508 J.D.
(adm. in MT; not adm. in DC) [Ⓒ Van Ness F.]
*PRACTICE AREAS: Energy; Natural Resources; Environment; Public Lands; Taxation.
Rich, James E., Jr. '51 '77 C.473 B.A. L.150 J.D.
(adm. in VA; not adm. in DC) Coun., Shell Oil Co.
Rich, John Townsend, (AV) .... '43 '70 C.309 A.B. L.976 LL.B. [Shea&G.]
*PRACTICE AREAS: Civil Litigation; Appeals; Administrative Law; Antitrust; Transportation.

Rich, Jonathan M. .... '59 '85 C.674 A.B. L.178 J.D. [Morgan,L.&B.]
Rich, Norman J. '— '92 C.30 B.A. L.831 J.D.
(adm. in PA; not adm. in DC) [🄰 Foley&L.]
*PRACTICE AREAS: Intellectual Property; Trademarks; Copyrights.
Rich, Randall S., (AV) .... '55 '80 C.1036 B.A. L.910 J.D. [Bracewell&P.]
*PRACTICE AREAS: Oil and Gas Pipelines; Public Utility Regulation; Energy Regulation; Electric Power.
Rich, Sally K. .... '48 '80 C.895 B.A. L.273 J.D. 60 Mass. Ave., N.E.

Rich Greenberg Rosenthal & Costle, LLP
(See Alexandria, Virginia)

Rich and Henderson, P.C.
(See Annapolis, Maryland)

Richard, Diana Gale .... '53 '88 C.9 B.S. L.446 J.D. [🄲 Gibson,D.&C.]
*PRACTICE AREAS: Government Contracts; Computers and Software.
Richard, Eric L. '49 '76 C.674 A.B. L.309 J.D.
Executive Vice President & General Counsel, Credit Union National Association and Affiliates
Richard, Kerry McLain '65 '90 C.208 B.A. L.94 J.D.
[🄲 Tobin,O.&E.] (⊙Bethesda, MD)
*PRACTICE AREAS: Management Labor Law; Employment Law; Business Immigration; Corporate Law; Commercial Litigation.
Richards, Douglas A. '58 '84 C.8 B.S. L.7 J.D.
(adm. in OH; not adm. in DC) Sr. Coun., MCI WorldCom
Richards, Edward I. .... '72 '00 C.95 B.A. L.446 J.D. [🄰 Howrey S.A.&W.]
*PRACTICE AREAS: Antitrust.
Richards, Femi S. '71 '97 C.454 B.A. L.184 J.D.
(adm. in CT; not adm. in DC) [🄰 Holland&K.]
*PRACTICE AREAS: Corporate Diversity Counseling; Government Relations.
Richards, Glenn S. .... '61 '86 C.923 B.S. L.564 J.D. [Shaw P.]
*PRACTICE AREAS: Communications.
Richards, John A. ...... '58 '93 C.1138 B.A. L.276 J.D. Assoc. Gen. Coun., Fannie Mae
*RESPONSIBILITIES: Intellectual Property and Technology Law.
Richards, John B. (Jack), (AV) .... '66 '97 C.645 B.A. L.1017 J.D. [Keller&H.]
*PRACTICE AREAS: Telecommunications Law.
Richards, John Thorpe, Jr., (AV) .... '60 '87 C.732 B.A. L.893 J.D. [Trout&R.] ⊙
*PRACTICE AREAS: Commercial Litigation; Criminal Litigation.
Richards, Michael .... '58 '00 C.156 B.A. L.276 [🄰 Shaw P.]
Richards, Neil Michael '72 '97 C.273 B.A. L.893 J.D.
(adm. in VA; not adm. in DC) [🄰 Wilmer,C.&P.]
Richards, Patricia McCloskey '51 '85
C.605 A.B. L.1017 J.D. Mgr. Govtl. Affrs., USX Corp.
Richards, Richard .... '32 '60 C.999 L.878 J.D. 1025 Thomas Jefferson St., N.W.
Richards, Suzanne V., (AV) .... '27 '58 C&L.273 A.B., J.D. 1701 K St., N.W.

Richards Spears Kibbe & Orbe
1775 Eye Street, N.W., 20006-2401 ⊙
Telephone: 202-261-2960 Fax: 202-261-2999
Email: info@rsko.com
Members of Firm: Michael D. Mann; Lucinda O. McConathy. Of Counsel: Paul A. Leder.
New York City, New York Office: One Chase Manhattan Plaza, 10005-1413. Telephone: 212-530-1800. Fax: 212-530-1801.
See Professional Biographies, WASHINGTON, DISTRICT OF COLUMBIA

Richardson, Ann B. ....'40 '88 C.276 B.A. L.273 J.D. David A. Clarke School of Law
Richardson, Charles T., (AV) .... '47 '72 C.347 A.B. L.477 J.D. [Baker&D.]
*PRACTICE AREAS: Insurance Regulation; Insurance Insolvency.
Richardson, Christine Mary '71 '98 C.107 B.A. L.180 J.D.
(adm. in NJ; not adm. in DC) 450 Fifth Street, N.W.
Richardson, Corinne Ann '— '98 C.674 A.B. L.276 J.D.
(adm. in NY; not adm. in DC) [🄰 Morgan,L.&B.]
Richardson, Greg D. '55 '81 C.965 B.A. L.966 J.D.
(adm. in WI; not adm. in DC) Natl. Dir. for Policy Develop., Justice Fellowship
Richardson, Henry J., III '41 '68 C.33 A.B. L.976 LL.B.
(adm. in IN; not adm. in DC) 2812 Adams Mill Rd.‡
Richardson, John, Jr. '21 '50 C&L.309 A.B., J.D.
(adm. in NY; not adm. in DC) Georgetown Univ.
Richardson, John L., (AV) .... '40 '67 C.477 B.A. L.893 J.D. [Crispin&B.]
*PRACTICE AREAS: Corporate Law; Government; Transportation; International Commercial Law.
Richardson, Julia R., (AV) .... '46 '71 C&L.477 A.B., J.D. [Van Ness F.]
*PRACTICE AREAS: Energy; Natural Gas; Electric Power; International Energy.
Richardson, Maureen M. '74 '00 C.188 B.S. L.276 J.D.
(adm. in NY; not adm. in DC) [🄰 Dow,L.&A.]
Richardson, P. David, II .... '48 '80 C.893 B.A. L.309 J.D. [Sidley A.B.&W.]
Richardson, Steven '48 '73 C.347 B.A. L.1119 J.D.
(adm. in IN; not adm. in DC) [Van Ness F.]
*PRACTICE AREAS: Natural Resources; Energy; Native American.
Richardson, Susan S. .... '46 '81 C.788 B.A. L.1066 J.D. [🄲 O'Melveny&M.]
*PRACTICE AREAS: Corporate Law; Banking; Project Finance; Mergers and Acquisitions.
Richardson, Thomas W. .... '63 '90 C.882 B.A. L.705 J.D. [Arnold&P.]
*PRACTICE AREAS: Trusts and Estates; Tax; International.
Richardson, Warren S. ...... '23 '54 C.696 A.B. L.180 LL.B. 325 Pennsylvania Ave., S.E.
Richardson, William R., Jr., (AV) .... '52 '77 C.674 A.B. L.893 J.D. [Wilmer,C.&P.]
*PRACTICE AREAS: Communications and Media.
Richart, Christie L. .... '72 '98 C.339 B.A. L.902 J.D. [🄰 Brunenkant&H.]
*PRACTICE AREAS: Energy Law; Utility Law.
Richeimer, Gabriela A. .... '72 '97 C.415 B.A. L.904 J.D. [🄰 Ross,D.&B.]
Richer, Diane Shapiro, (AV) .... '59 '85 C.659 B.A. L.276 J.D. [Shaw P.]
*PRACTICE AREAS: Commercial Real Estate.
Richichi, Thomas .... '53 '78 C.502 B.A. L.276 J.D. [Beveridge&D.]
*PRACTICE AREAS: Litigation; Environmental Law; Aviation Law; International Environmental Law.
Richie, Scott A. ....'52 '90 C.957 B.A. L.1035 J.D. [🄲 Andrews&K.]
*PRACTICE AREAS: Civil Litigation; Antitrust; Intellectual Property; Political Asylum.
Richman, Dvorah A., (AV) .... '— '83 C.36 B.S. L.128 J.D. [King&S.]
*PRACTICE AREAS: Food and Drug Regulation.
Richman, Gerald L. .... '53 '79 C.705 B.A. L.276 J.D. [🄰 Skadden,A.S.M.&F.]
*PRACTICE AREAS: Energy.
Richman, Jeff .... '65 '95 C&L.659 B.S.E., J.D. [🄰 Arnold&P.]
*PRACTICE AREAS: Legislative.
Richman, Michael B. ....'— '88 C.674 A.B. L.178 J.D. [🄲 Reed S.]
*PRACTICE AREAS: Employee Benefits.
Richman, Monica Blair ....'— '95 C.273 B.A. L.245 J.D. 1300 I St., N.W., Suite 700
Richman, Todd M. .... '70 '97 C.478 L.276 [🄰 Ropes&G.]
Richmond, David W., (AV) ....'— '36 L.273 LL.B. [🄲 Miller&C.]
Richmond, Garth D. .... '— '97 C&L.352 B.S., J.D. [🄰 Foley&L.]
*PRACTICE AREAS: Energy Law; Nuclear Energy.
Richmond, Judith Klein '53 '78 C.1350 B.A. L.273 J.D.
Assoc. Gen. Coun., U.S. Chamber of Commerce

Richowsky, John C.
(See Friendship, Maryland)

Richter, Melvin, (AV) .... '16 '40 C&L.309 A.B., J.D. 1200 G St., N.W.‡

Richter, Paul S., (P.C.), (AV) .... '46 '71 C.453 B.S. L.273 J.D. [Richter,M.&F.] (Pat.)

Richter, Miller & Finn, (AV)
A Partnership including Professional Corporations
1815 H Street, N.W., Suite 410, 20006
Telephone: 202-467-6200 Fax: 202-293-4395 Email: info@rlaw.com
URL: http://www.rlaw.com/rmf
Paul S. Richter (P.C.); Thomas P. Miller; Kelley A. Finn (P.A.) (Not admitted in DC); John M. Widder.
Litigation, Administrative and Transactional Practice including Business, Taxation, Intellectual Property, Corporate, International Business, Government Contract, Business Crimes Law, and Estate Planning.
See Professional Biographies, WASHINGTON, DISTRICT OF COLUMBIA

Rick, Matthew T. '74 '99 C.475 B.A. L.273 J.D.
(adm. in VA; not adm. in DC) [🄰 John&H.]
*PRACTICE AREAS: Energy Law.
Rickard, Stephen A. ....'56 '84 C.5 B.A. L.976 J.D. 1367 Connecticut Ave., N.W.
Rickert, Anthony H. .... '55 '82 C.446 B.A. L.276 J.D. [Piper M.R.&W.]
*PRACTICE AREAS: Business Law; Commercial Law; Corporate Financing Law; Health Care.
Rickman, Tamara Schiebel, (AV) '58 '87
C.276 B.S.F.S. L.128 J.D. [Venable,A.B.H.&C.]
*PRACTICE AREAS: Real Estate; Commercial Transactions.

Ridberg, Press & Sherbill, LLP
(See Bethesda, Maryland)

Riddick, Annita M. .... '61 '92 C.329 B.A. L.228 J.D. [Littler M.]
*PRACTICE AREAS: Labor and Employment.

Riddick, Johnny M., & Associates '56 '83 C.1296 B.A. L.1162 J.D.
505 Capitol Court N.E., Suite 100, 20002
Telephone: 202-371-1933 Fax: 202-371-8332
Email: jriddick@bellatlantic.net URL: http://www.lawyers.com/johnnyriddicklaw
Associates: Sharon R. Herron (Not admitted in DC); Jasmin A. Dabney.
Family Law, Divorce, Custody, Visitation, Marital Property, Separation Agreements, Pre-nuptial Agreements, Family Mediation, Personal Injury, Auto Accidents, Medical Negligence, Wrongful Death, Premises Liability, Employment Discrimination, Small Business Law, Minority Business Law, Corporate, Commercial Litigation.
See Professional Biographies, WASHINGTON, DISTRICT OF COLUMBIA

Riddick, Stephen A. '63 '88 C.893 B.A. L.575 J.D.
(adm. in MD; not adm. in DC) [Brobeck,P.&H.]
*PRACTICE AREAS: Corporate Finance; Mergers and Acquisitions.
Riddle, Clarine Nardi '49 '74 C.347 A.B. L.1119 J.D.
Sr. V.P. & Gen. Coun., Govt. Affs., National Multi Housing Council
Rider, James L., (AV) '42 '66
C.390 B.A. L.262 J.D. [Margolius,M.D.R.&T.] (⊙Alexandria, VA)
*PRACTICE AREAS: Family Law; Mediation.
Rider, Robert E., Jr. .... '63 '88 C&L.893 B.A., J.D. [Jackson&C.] ⊙
*PRACTICE AREAS: Insurance Coverage Litigation.
Ridge, Janet Durholz .... '60 '96 C.724 B.A. L.188 J.D. [🄲 Wilmer,C.&P.]
Ridgway, Candace A. .... '53 '88 C.36 B.A. L.188 J.D. [Jones,D.R.&P.]
*PRACTICE AREAS: Taxation; Corporate Tax Planning; Tax Controversies.
Ridings, Donald J., Jr. .... '68 '99 C.309 A.B. L.273 J.D. [🄰 Covington&B.]
*PRACTICE AREAS: International Law; Private International Law; Litigation; Complex Litigation; International Civil Litigation.
Ridings, Donald J., Jr. ...... '68 '99 C.309 B.A. L.273 J.D. 1201 Pennsylvania Ave., N.W.
Ridley, Andrew E. .... '50 '75 C.201 B.A. L.280 J.D. Asst. Corp. Coun., D.C.
Riebling, Peter J. .... '65 '92 C.112 B.A. L.809 J.D. [Arter&H.]
*PRACTICE AREAS: Trademarks; Copyright; Software Licensing; Trade Secrets.
Riedel, Amanda Lynn '75 '00 C&L.893 B.A., J.D.
(adm. in VA; not adm. in DC) [🄰 Vinson&E.] (⊙Hous., TX)
*PRACTICE AREAS: Litigation.
Riederer von Paar, Max '63 '97
(adm. in NY; not adm. in DC) [Dilworth P.P.]
*PRACTICE AREAS: International Estate Planning; Computer Law; Internet Law; International Business Law; Corporate Law.
Riedy, James A. .... '52 '77 C.375 B.S. L.378 J.D. [McDermott,W.&E.]
Riedy, Marian K. .... '55 '82 C.378 B.A. L.309 J.D. [🄰 Sperduto]
*PRACTICE AREAS: Complex Commercial Litigation; High-Tech Business Litigation; Dispute Resolution; Intellectual Property.
Riedy, Mark J., (AV) .... '53 '80 C.477 B.A. L.276 J.D. [Thelen R.&P.]
*PRACTICE AREAS: Energy; Communications Law; Information Technology; International Trade; Project Finance.
Rieffel, Alaire Bretz '45 '69 C.788 A.B. L.94 J.D.
Dir., Sect. of Intl. Law & Practice, Amer. Bar Assn.
Riegel, Quentin, (AV) '51 '78 C.918 B.A. L.276 J.D.
Deputy General Counsel, National Association of Manufacturers
Rient, Peter F. .... '38 '64 C&L.309 B.A., LL.B. [Gainer&R.]
Rierson, Autumn L. '72 '00 C.575 B.A. L.280 J.D.
Assist. Gen. Coun., National Trust for Historic Preservation
Riesenberg, Thomas L. '52 '81
C.604 B.A. L.569 J.D. Assoc. Gen. Coun., Ernst & Young LLP
Rieser, Joseph A., Jr., (AV) ....'— '74 C.674 A.B. L.309 J.D. [Reed S.]
*PRACTICE AREAS: Tax.
Rieveschl, David C. .... '68 '98 C.228 B.A. L.861 J.D. [🄰 Williams&C.]
*PRACTICE AREAS: Business Law; Corporate Law; Finance; Mergers, Acquisitions and Divestitures; Securities.
Riewe, Julie M. .... '70 '00 C&L.228 A.B., J.D. [🄰 Wilmer,C.&P.]
Rifkin, Marjorie L. .... '52 '90 C.331 M.S. L.178 J.D. University Legal Services
Rifkin, Robert W. .... '47 '73 C.823 B.A. L.276 J.D. [🄲 Obergh&B.]
Rifkind, Amy B. .... '67 '94 C&L.976 B.A., J.D. [🄰 Arnold&P.]
*PRACTICE AREAS: Real Estate.
Rifkind, David F. .... '67 '95 C.1365 B.A. L.276 J.D. [🄰 Steptoe&J.]
Rifkind, Marc H. .... '63 '87 C.94 B.A. L.477 J.D. [Slevin&H.]
*PRACTICE AREAS: Employee Benefits.
Rigaux, Stephanie A. .... '65 '90 C.645 B.A. L.904 J.D. [Arent F.K.P.&K.]
*PRACTICE AREAS: Litigation.
Rigler, Douglas V., (AV) .... '34 '63 C.871 B.S. L.273 J.D. [🄲 Andrews&K.]
*PRACTICE AREAS: Commercial Litigation; Antitrust Litigation; Intellectual Property; Complex Multi-district Litigation; International.
Rigsby, Anna E. Blackburne '61 '88 C.228 B.A. L.329 J.D.
Spec. Coun., Corp. Coun. of the District of Columbia
Riley, Charles J., Jr. .... '10 '55 C.276 L.904 LL.B. 3457 Eads St., N.E.
Riley, Claire Margaret '61 '86 C.966 B.A. L.1162 J.D.
(adm. in PA; not adm. in DC) Center for Study of Responsive Law
Riley, Daniel J., (AV) .... '47 '72 C&L.846 B.A., J.D. [Baker B.]
Riley, Darren P. '72 '00 C.910 B.A. L.329 J.D.
(adm. in MD; not adm. in DC) [🄰 Patton B.]
Riley, James P., (AV) .... '40 '64 C.107 B.S. L.228 LL.B. [Fletcher,H.&H.] ⊙
*PRACTICE AREAS: Communications Law; Broadcasting Law; Communications Transactions.
Riley, Jeffrey L. .... '67 '96 C&L.273 B.A., J.D. [🄰 Morgan,L.&B.]
Riley, Kimberly A. '69 '95 C.945 B.A. L.128 J.D.
(adm. in VA; not adm. in DC) 1401 H St., N.W.‡

Riley, Margaret ....'— '00 C.1371 B.A. L.1522 J.D. [Ⓐ Dechert]
*PRACTICE AREAS: Financial Services Law; Investment Management.
Riley, Patricia A., (AV) .... '44 '80 C.24 B.A. L.904 J.D. Asst. U.S. Atty.
Riley, Patrick J. '51 '78 C.436 B.A. L.276 J.D.
Coun., Sheet Metal Workers' Intl. Assoc.
Riley, Richard F., Jr., (AV) .... '— '83 C.976 B.A. L.228 J.D. [Foley&L.]
*PRACTICE AREAS: Taxation Law; Transportation Law.
Riley, Robert F. .... '57 '85 C.734 B.A. L.930 J.D. [Williams M.]
*PRACTICE AREAS: Energy; Legislative Practice; Regulatory Law.
Riley, Sandra A. ....'59 '93 C.222 B.A. L.629 J.D. [Ⓐ Arent F.K.P.&K.]
*PRACTICE AREAS: Intellectual Property; Trademarks.
Riley, Susan L. ....'53 '78 C.918 B.A. L.276 J.D. Howard Univ.
Riley, Thomas A., III '65 '92 C.276 B.A. L.884 J.D.
(adm. in PA; not adm. in DC) 3044 R. St. N.W. 2‡
Riley, Vincent J. '28 '61 C.705 B.A. L.276 J.D.
(adm. in VA; not adm. in DC) Intl. Bk. for Reconstr. & Develop.

Riley Roumell & Connolly, P.C., (AV)
1707 N Street, N.W., 20036 ⊙
Telephone: 202-331-0660 Telefax: 202-223-4884
Email: rrlaw@tir.com URL: http://www.rrc-law.com
Michael J. Connolly (Not admitted in DC); Marc K. Shaye (Not admitted in DC); Clifford J. Scharman (Resident).
General Practice, Trials and Appeals in State and Federal Courts and Administrative Agencies, Arbitration, Labor and Employment Relations Law and Litigation in the Private and Public Sectors, Employment Discrimination, Corporate, Taxation, Commercial/Business Litigation, Environmental Law, Natural Resources, Occupational Safety and Health, Product Liability, Real Estate, Estate Planning, Probate, Civil Rights, Domestic Relations, Family Law, Education and School Law, Workers' Compensation, Health Care Law, Construction Law, Banking Law, Admiralty and Maritime Law, Trademark Law and Entertainment Law.
Representative Clients: National Tech Team, Inc.; Chrysler Financial Corp.; Blue Cross Blue Shield of Michigan; The Accident Fund Company; Federal National Mortgage Assn.; Federal Home Loan Mortgage Corp.; Community Bank of Dearborn; Dearborn Federal Credit Union; County of Wayne; Board of Education of the City of Detroit.
Detroit, Michigan Office: 7th Floor Ford Building, 48226. Telephone: 313-962-8255. Fax: 313-962-2937.
Harbor Springs, Michigan Office: 151 East Bay Street, 49740. Telephone: 231-526-2300. Fax: 231-526-6787.
See Professional Biographies, WASHINGTON, DISTRICT OF COLUMBIA

Rill, James F., (AV) .... '33 '59 C.197 A.B. L.309 LL.B. [Howrey S.A.&W.]
*PRACTICE AREAS: Antitrust; Trade Regulation.
Rinaldi, Steven D. '60 '88 C.207 B.A. L.930 J.D.
(adm. in PA; not adm. in DC) Assoc. Gen. Coun., American Bankers Association
*RESPONSIBILITIES: Contracts (25%); Franchise (25%); Trademark (20%); Copyright (15%); International (10%).
Rindler, Richard M., (AV) ....'44 '69 C.012 B.A. L.276 J.D. [Swidler B.S.F.]
*PRACTICE AREAS: Telecommunications; Regulated Industries; Antitrust.
Rindner, Marc E. '— '97 C.205 B.A. L.30 J.D.
(adm. in MD; not adm. in DC) 3000 K St., N.W.‡
Rinehart, Tara '65 '94 C.923 B.A. L.128 J.D.
(adm. in VA; not adm. in DC) 1800 M St. N.W.
Rines, David D. '68 '99 C.489 B.F.A. L.276 J.D.
(adm. in MD; not adm. in DC) [Ⓐ Swidler B.S.F.]
*PRACTICE AREAS: Telecommunications; International Law.
Ring, Carlyle C., Jr., (AV) .... '31 '56 C.299 B.A. L.228 LL.B. [Ⓒ Ober,K.G.&S.]
Ring, Elizabeth E. ....'67 '92 C.893 B.A. L.846 J.D. [Ⓐ Patton B.]
Ring, John F. ....'63 '89 C&L.128 B.A., J.D. [Morgan,L.&B.]
Ring, Kathleen Murphy .... '47 '81 C.1115 B.A. L.128 J.D. [Ⓐ Comey B.&L.]
Ring, Kevin A. '70 '96 C.823 B.A. L.128 J.D.
(adm. in MD; not adm. in DC) [Greenberg T.]
Ring, Sanford B., (BV) ....'61 '90 C.475 B.A. L.128 J.D. [Ⓒ Dykema G.]
*PRACTICE AREAS: Government; International Trade.
Ringel, Douglas E. '66 '93 C.188 B.S. L.477 J.D.
(adm. in NY; not adm. in DC; See Pat. Sect.) [Kenyon&K.]
*PRACTICE AREAS: Intellectual Property.
Ringell, Richard H. '45 '69 C.473 B.A. L.30 J.D.
(adm. in MD; not adm. in DC) 4434 Lowell St. N.W.‡
Ringo, Alexea L. ....'72 '00 C.112 B.A. L.262 J.D. 555 12th Street
Ringwood, Irene L. .... '58 '84 C.906 B.A. L.285 J.D. [Ball J.]
*PRACTICE AREAS: Government Relations Law; International Trade Law.
Rini, Robert J., (AV) ....'— '86 C.1044 B.A. L.128 J.D. [Manatt,P.&P.]
Rini, Coran & Lancellotta, P.C., (AV) ....1350 Connecticut Avenue, N.W., Suite 900
Rinkerman, Gary J. ....'55 '80 C.705 B.A. L.276 J.D. 1050 Connecticut Ave., N.W.
Rinn, Christine Clements ....'62 '87 C.273 B.A. L.904 J.D. [McDermott,W.&E.]
Rinzel, Daniel F. '42 '68 C.436 B.A. L.966 J.D.
888 16th Street, N.W. Suite 700 (⊙Fairfax, VA)
Rinzler, Kenneth .... '55 '79 C.276 A.B. L.776 J.D. 3229-B Sutton Pl., N.W.
Riordan, Kelly ....'67 '99 C.597 B.S. L.893 J.D. [Ⓐ O'Melveny&M.]
Riordan, Kevin J. .... '47 '72 C.454 B.S. L.818 J.D. General Electric Co.
Ripley, Richard A., (AV) ....'60 '86 C.608 B.A. L.273 J.D. [Howrey S.A.&W.]
*PRACTICE AREAS: Antitrust; Complex Litigation; White Collar Criminal Defense.
Rippel, Brian B. '65 '91 C.420 B.A. L.425 J.D.
(adm. in LA; not adm. in DC) 810 Vermont Avenue, N.W.
Rippeon, Benjamin H. .... '74 '00 C.902 B.S. L.276 J.D. [Ⓐ Gibson,D.&C.]
Rippey, Edward Holden .... '65 '95 C&L.309 A.B., J.D. [Ⓐ Covington&B.]
*PRACTICE AREAS: Commercial Litigation; Environmental Litigation; Litigation; Civil Litigation; Federal Litigation.
Ripy, Thomas B. '38 '74 C.853 B.A. L.836 J.D.
(adm. in TN; not adm. in DC) 101 Independence Ave‡
Ririe, Verna B. .... '65 '94 C&L.101 B.A., J.D. [Ⓐ Dombroff&G.]
Riselli, Michael J., (AV) ....'46 '72 C.860 A.B. L.818 J.D. [Riselli&P.]
Riselli & Pressler, P.C., (AV) ....21 Dupont Circle, N.W. Suite 600
Rishe, Melvin ....'40 '67 C.1016 B.S.B.A. L.209 J.D. [Sidley A.B.&W.]
Risk, Sharon C. ....'19 '51 C.674 B.A. L.976 J.D. V.P., Johnston, Lemon & Co., Inc.
Risoleo, Robert Samuel '58 '84 C&L.976 B.A., J.D.
(adm. in NY; not adm. in DC) [Sullivan&C.]
Rissetto, Christopher L., (AV) ....'— '73 C.766 B.A. L.966 J.D. [Reed S.]
*PRACTICE AREAS: Government Contracts; Export Compliance.
Rissetto, Harry A., (AV) ....'43 '69 C.1030 A.B. L.276 J.D. [Morgan,L.&B.]
Ristau, Bruno A., (AV) .... '29 '58 C&L.930 B.B.A., J.D. [B.A.Ristau]
*PRACTICE AREAS: Foreign Sovereign Immunities Act; Transnational Litigation; International Arbitration; Diplomatic and Consular Immunities.

Ristau, Bruno A., P.L.L.C., Law Offices of, (AV)
4500 Foxhall Crescent, N.W., 20007
Telephone: 202-965-3810 Fax: 202-965-3811
Email: baristau@aol.com

(This Listing Continued)

Ristau, Bruno A., P.L.L.C., Law Offices of (Continued)
Bruno A. Ristau.
Transactional Litigation, International Arbitration.

Ritchie, John A. '48 '79 C.674 B.A. L.818 J.D.
1320 19th Street, N.W., Suite 202, 20036
Telephone: 202-887-9690 Fax: 202-659-8612
Email: jritch8@aol.com
***PRACTICE AREAS: Business Law; Intellectual Property; Estate Planning; Business Immigration Law.**
General Civil and Trial Practice in all Courts. Business Planning and Counseling; Copyright, Trademark, Trade Secrets, Internet Law, Tax-Exempt Organizations, Estate Planning and Probate Law, Business Immigration Law.
See Professional Biographies, WASHINGTON, DISTRICT OF COLUMBIA

Rittenberg, Andrew ....'70 '99 C.976 B.A. L.145 J.D. [Ⓐ Covington&B.]
Rittenberg, Traci '73 '01 C.385 B.A. L.273 J.D.
(adm. in VA; not adm. in DC) [Ⓐ Sonnenschein N.&R.]
*PRACTICE AREAS: Corporate Law.
Ritter, C. Willis, (AV) ....'40 '65 C.188 A.B. L.893 J.D. [Ritter E.&N.]
*PRACTICE AREAS: Public Finance Law; Federal Income Taxation; Housing.
Ritter, Curtis A. ....'47 '76 C.446 B.S. L.273 J.D. [Dow,L.&A.]
Ritter, Daniel '66 '92 C.31 B.A. L.976 J.D.
(adm. in NY; not adm. in DC) [Ⓐ Preston G.E.&R.M.]
*PRACTICE AREAS: Policy; Government Relations.
Ritter, James F. ....'— '86 C.197 A.B. L.893 J.D. [Latham&W.]
*PRACTICE AREAS: Finance; Corporate Law; Business Law; Mergers, Acquisitions and Divestitures; Debtor and Creditor.
Ritter, Jeffrey B., (BV) .... '— '79 C.608 B.A. L.228 J.D. [Kirkpatrick&L.]
*PRACTICE AREAS: Electronic Commerce; Information and Privacy; Mergers and Acquisitions; Commercial Law; International Trade.
Ritter, Stephanie M. '60 '90 C.645 B.S. L.1280 J.D.
(adm. in PA; not adm. in DC) Dir., Community Servs.

Ritter Eichner & Norris, PLLC, (AV)
The Jefferson Building, 1225 19th Street, N.W., 7th Floor, 20036
Telephone: 202-973-0100 Fax: 202-296-6990
Members of Firm: C. Willis Ritter; Richard A. Eichner; R. Wade Norris (Not admitted in DC). Associates: Matthew J. Bissonette; Robert A. Wrzosek; Kent S. Neumann; Ryan L. George.
Public Finance Law. Federal Income Taxation. Housing, Non-Profit Organizations.
See Professional Biographies, WASHINGTON, DISTRICT OF COLUMBIA

Ritts, Frederick H., (AV) ....'39 '71 C.228 B.S. L.280 J.D. [Brickfield B.R.&S.]
*PRACTICE AREAS: Energy; Energy Regulation; Energy Finance; Energy Contracts; Legislative Practice.
Ritts, Leslie S., (BV) ....'55 '80 C.674 A.B. L.945 J.D. [Hogan&H.]
*PRACTICE AREAS: Clean Air Act; Environmental Compliance; Environmental Litigation; Environmental Regulation; Wetlands Regulation.

Ritzert & Leyton, P.C.
(See Fairfax, Virginia)

Riva, Monica Anne .... '66 '97 C.692 B.S.B.A. L.1209 J.D. [Ⓐ Finnegan,H.F.G.&D.]
*PRACTICE AREAS: Trademark Infringement; Trademark Litigation; Trademark Prosecution; Trademark Protection; Trademark Registration.
Rivard, Paul M. ....'— '98 C.158 B.S. L.128 J.D. [Ⓐ Banner&W.] (See Pat. Sect.)
*PRACTICE AREAS: Intellectual Property Law; Patents; Chemical Intellectual Property; Pharmaceutical Intellectual Property.
Rivera, Henry M., (AV) ....'46 '73 C&L.560 B.A., J.D. [Shook,H.&B.]
*PRACTICE AREAS: Communications Law; Corporate Law; Commercial Law.
Rivera, Michael J. ....'66 '92 C.724 B.S. L.659 J.D. [Fried,F.H.S.&J.]
*PRACTICE AREAS: Securities Regulation and Compliance; Securities Enforcement; Corporate.
Rivero, David R. '55 '80
C.276 B.S.F.S. L.178 J.D. Sr. Coun., Intl. Bk. for Reconstr. & Develop.
Rivers, Richard R., (P.C.), (AV) ..... '42 '75 C.861 B.A. L.128 J.D. 1600 Avon Pl., N.W.
Rivkin, David B. ....'56 '85 C.276 B.S.F.S. L.178 J.D. [Baker&H.]
*PRACTICE AREAS: Administrative Law; Environmental; Energy; International Law; Litigation.
Rivkin, Steven R., (AV) .... '37 '63 C&L.309 A.B., LL.B. 1401 New York Ave., N.W.
Rivlin, Lewis A., (AV) .... '29 '57 C.821 B.A. L.309 J.D. [L.A.Rivlin]
Rivlin, Lewis A., P.C., Law Offices of, (AV) .... 8th Floor, 2300 M Street, N.W.
Rizek, Christopher S., (AV) .... '56 '83 C.197 A.B. L.276 J.D. [Caplin&D.]
*PRACTICE AREAS: Taxation; Litigation.
Rizzi, Margaret Rhinelander .... '65 '94 C.813 A.B. L.893 J.D. [Ⓐ Hogan&H.]
Rizzi, Patrick Robert ....'68 '93 C.276 B.S.B.A. L.569 J.D. [Ⓒ O'Melveny&M.]
*PRACTICE AREAS: Aviation Regulation; Class Action Defense; Commercial Litigation.
Rizzi, Robert A. ....'49 '78 C.674 A.B. L.309 J.D. [O'Melveny&M.] (⊙Menlo Park, CA)
*PRACTICE AREAS: Tax Law.
Rizzo, James G. ....'62 '90 C.276 A.B. L.262 J.D. [McDermott,W.&E.]
Rizzo, Sandra E. .... '68 '92 C.273 B.A. L.945 J.D. [Ⓒ Preston G.E.&R.M.]
*PRACTICE AREAS: Energy; Administrative Litigation.
Rizzolo, M. Kristan ....'66 '91 C&L.273 B.A., J.D. [LeBoeuf,L.G.&M.]
*PRACTICE AREAS: Tax.
Roady, Celia, (AV) ....'51 '76 C&L.228 A.B., J.D. [Morgan,L.&B.]
Roady, Stephen E., (AV) ....'49 '76 C.198 A.B. L.228 J.D. 3000 K St., N.W.
Robb, Charles S. ....'39 '73 C.966 B.B.A. L.893 J.D. U.S. Sen.
Robbett, Kenneth G. ....'58 '84 C.276 A.B. L.262 J.D. [Smith&D.]
Robbins, Alan I., (AV) ....'53 '78 C.1044 B.A. L.273 J.D. [GKRSE]
*PRACTICE AREAS: Electric Utilities; Electric Power; Municipal Law; Utilities; Electric Utility Regulation.
Robbins, Christopher L. .... '72 '97 C.674 A.B. L.880 J.D. [Ⓐ Wiley R.&F.]
Robbins, David H. .... '53 '93 C.831 B.B.A. L.273 J.D. [Duane,M.&H.]
*PRACTICE AREAS: Health Care Fraud; Health Care Litigation; Regulation; Medicare Reimbursement Appeals; "Stark" Rules.
Robbins, Debra M. ....'59 '84 C.497 B.S. L.356 J.D. [Ⓒ Dyer E.&J.]
Robbins, Hugh R. ....'13 '42 L.178 LL.B. 100 Varnum St., N.E.‡
Robbins, Ira P. '49 '74
C.659 A.B. L.309 J.D. Prof., Washington Coll. of Law, Amer. Univ.
Robbins, Lawrence S., (AV) ....'52 '80 C.976 B.A. L.309 J.D. [Robbins,R.E.O.&U.]
Robbins, Lori A. '74 '99 C.346 B.S. L.1119 J.D.
(adm. in IN; not adm. in DC) 1875 Connecticut Avenue, N.W.
Robbins, Robert B., (P.C.), (AV) ....'51 '75 C.188 A.B. L.309 J.D. [Shaw P.]
*PRACTICE AREAS: Corporate Securities.
Robbins, Seth Adam .... '74 '00 C.820 B.S. L.1209 J.D. [Ⓐ Quagliano&S.]
*PRACTICE AREAS: Construction Law; Government Contracts; Bankruptcy; Civil Litigation.
Robbins, Thomas D. '70 '00 C.446 B.S.E.E. L.128 J.D.
(adm. in MD; not adm. in DC; See Pat. Sect.) [Ⓐ Wenderoth,L.&P.]
*PRACTICE AREAS: Mechanical Patent Prosecution; Electrical Patent Prosecution.

Robbins, Russell, Englert, Orseck & Untereiner LLP, (AV)
1801 K Street, N.W., Suite 411, 20006
Telephone: 202-775-4500 Fax: 202-775-4510
URL: http://www.robbinsrussell.com
Lawrence S. Robbins; Donald J. Russell (Not admitted in DC); Roy T. Englert, Jr.; Gary A. Orseck; Alan E. Untereiner. Counsel: Arnon D. Siegel. Associates: Kathryn Schaefer Zecca; Sherri Lynn Wolson (Not admitted in DC).

(This Listing Continued)

Robbins, Russell, Englert, Orseck & Untereiner LLP (Continued)

Antitrust, Civil Trial Practice, Criminal Trial Practice, Appellate Litigation, Telecommunications Litigation, Administrative Law.

See Professional Biographies, WASHINGTON, DISTRICT OF COLUMBIA

Roberge, Thomas C., Jr. .... '74 '99 C&L.276 A.B., J.D. [[A] Sutherland A.&B.]
*PRACTICE AREAS: Tax Law.
Roberson, Sam H. .... '58 '84 C.280 B.B.A. L.469 J.D. [Sherman,M.C.&A.]
*PRACTICE AREAS: Employee Benefits; Corporate Law; Tax Planning; Estate Planning.
Roberti, Christopher D. .... '71 '99 C.339 A.B. L.597 J.D. [[A] Clifford C.R.&W.]
*PRACTICE AREAS: Corporate; International Private Equity; International Mergers and Acquisitions; Securities.
Roberts, Amy T., (BV) .... '64 '91 C.999 B.A. L.64 J.D. MMI Cos., Inc.
Roberts, Beth L. .... '66 '94 C.659 B.S. L.846 J.D. [[C] Hogan&H.]
*PRACTICE AREAS: Health Care.
Roberts, Caprice L. .... '72 '98 C.806 B.A. L.902 J.D. [[A] Skadden,A.S.M.&F.]
*PRACTICE AREAS: Litigation.
Roberts, James H., III, (AV) .... '49 '74 C.602 A.B. L.734 J.D. [Manatt,P.&P.]
Roberts, James J. .... '61 '90 C.1048 B.A. L.276 J.D. 17 14th St. S.E.
Roberts, Jane Sullivan .... '54 '86 C.321 A.B. L.276 J.D. [Shaw P.]
*PRACTICE AREAS: Technology Transactions.
Roberts, Jared I., (AV) '46 '74 C.674 B.A. L.893 J.D.
Sr. Assoc. Gen. Coun., Envir. & Corp. Affs., National Railroad Passenger Corp. (AMTRAK)
Roberts, John G., Jr., (AV) .... '55 '81 C&L.309 A.B., J.D. [Hogan&H.]
*PRACTICE AREAS: U.S. Supreme Court Litigation; Appellate Practice; Federal Litigation.
Roberts, John T., (AV) .... '35 '61 C.453 B.S. L.893 LL.B. 1825 Eye St. (Pat.)
Roberts, Justin J. .... '72 '99 C&L.846 B.A., J.D. [[A] Jones,D.R.&P.]
Roberts, Lawrence, (AV) .... '56 '81 C.893 B.A. L.276 J.D. [Skadden,A.S.M.&F.]
Roberts, Maurice A. '10 '32 C&L.705 LL.B.
(adm. in NJ; not adm. in DC) Editor in Chf., Federal Publications, Inc.
*RESPONSIBILITIES: Immigration and Naturalization.
Roberts, Michael G. .... '56 '83 C.475 B.A. L.30 J.D. [Thompson C.]
*PRACTICE AREAS: Admiralty and Maritime Law; Legislative Practice; Transportation.
Roberts, Michael J., (AV) .... '— '66 C.228 A.B. L.904 J.D. [Verner,L.B.M.&H.]
*PRACTICE AREAS: Aviation Law; Administrative Law; Legislative Law.
Roberts, Michele A. .... '56 '80 C.918 B.A. L.1066 J.D. 504 7th St Se
Roberts, Michelle C. .... '69 '01 C.821 B.A. L.893 J.D. [[A] Dechert]
*PRACTICE AREAS: Financial Services Law; Investment Management.
Roberts, Neil E. .... '42 '67 C.446 B.S.E.E. L.273 LL.B. 3050 K St., N.W.
Roberts, Richard L., (AV) .... '62 '88 C.445 B.S. L.446 J.D. [Steptoe&J.]
*PRACTICE AREAS: Energy; Antitrust Law; Litigation.
Roberts, Richard M., (AV) .... '20 '44 C&L.273 LL.B. 888 16th St., N.W.
Roberts, Richard Y. .... '51 '76 C.10 B.S.E.E. L.16 J.D. [[C] Thelen R.&P.]
*PRACTICE AREAS: Business; Finance.
Roberts, Simon D. '68 '91 C&L.999 B.Sc.
(adm. in NY; not adm. in DC; See Pat. Sect.) [[A] Fitzpatrick,C.H.&S.]
Roberts, Thomas C. '54 '79 C.791 B.S. L.878 J.D.
(adm. in AK; not adm. in DC) [Van Ness F.]
*PRACTICE AREAS: Environment; Energy; Natural Resources; Alaska Natives; Public Policy.
Roberts, William A., III .... '47 '76 C.1255 B.A. L.352 J.D. [Wiley R.&F.]
*PRACTICE AREAS: Government Contracts.

Roberts & Holland LLP, (AV)
2175 K Street, N.W. Suite 800, 20037-1827 ⊙
Telephone: 202-293-3400 Telecopier: 202-293-0479
Email: rhtax.com URL: http://www.robertsandholland.com
Resident Partner: Howard J. Levine. Of Counsel: Louis Tiger, Jr.; Theodore D. Peyser;—David A. Weintraub.
Federal, State and International Tax Practice, Related Litigation in Federal and State Courts, Estate Planning, Trusts, Probate, Employee Benefits, Executive Compensation and International Business
New York, N.Y. Office: Worldwide Plaza, 825 Eighth Avenue. Telephone: 212-903-8700.
See Professional Biographies, WASHINGTON, DISTRICT OF COLUMBIA

Roberts & Hundertmark, LLP
(See Chevy Chase, Maryland)

Roberts & Wood
(See Riverdale, Maryland)

Robertson, Charles J. '34 '65 C.893 B.A. L.273 J.D.
Dep. Dir., National Museum of American Art, Smithsonian Institution
Robertson, Colleen R. .... '67 '91 C.10 B.A. L.178 J.D. [[A] Slevin&H.]
*PRACTICE AREAS: Employee Benefits; Taxation.
Robertson, Cynthia J. '68 '98 C.880 B.A. L.339 J.D.
(adm. in IL; not adm. in DC) [[A] Jenner&B.]
*PRACTICE AREAS: General Litigation.
Robertson, Diane E., Ph.D. .... '63 '99 C.518 B.A. L.276 J.D. [Foxkiser]
*PRACTICE AREAS: Food and Drug Regulation; Legislation.
Robertson, Donald B., (AV) .... '31 '59 C.604 B.A. L.178 LL.B. [Ross,M.&F.]
*PRACTICE AREAS: Estate Planning; Estate and Trust Administration; Taxation Law; Election Law; Real Estate Law.
Robertson, Irving J., Jr. ...... '39 '78 C.325 B.B.A. L.128 J.D. 1801 Clydesdale Pl., N.W.
Robertson, Jeffrey F. .... '68 '96 C.838 B.A. L.178 J.D. [[C] Crowell&M.]
*PRACTICE AREAS: SEC Enforcement; Securities Litigation; Broker-Dealer Arbitration; Securities Class Actions; NASD Arbitration.
Robertson, Mark J. .... '71 '99 C.301 B.A. L.893 J.D. [[A] Hogan&H.]
*PRACTICE AREAS: Corporate Law; Securities.
Robertson, Peter D. .... '55 '87 C.623 B.A. L.276 J.D. [Patton B.]
Robertson, Randall E. .... '53 '78 C&L.575 B.S., J.D. [[C] Miller,C.P.&S.] (⊙Detroit, MI)
*PRACTICE AREAS: Employment Litigation; Labor.
Robertson, Robert A. '60 '87 C.154 B.A. L.1068 J.D.
(adm. in CA; not adm. in DC) [[C] Dechert]
*PRACTICE AREAS: Securities Law; Litigation; Financial Services Law; Investment Management.
Robertson, Scott L. .... '57 '87 C.103 B.A. L.94 J.D. [Hunton&W.]
*PRACTICE AREAS: Intellectual Property; Patent; Antitrust; Commercial Litigation.
Robertson, Stephen C. .... '61 '99 C&L.945 B.A., J.D. [[A] Willkie F.&G.]
*PRACTICE AREAS: Litigation.

Robertson, Monagle & Eastaugh, A Professional Corporation
(See Arlington, Virginia)

Robin-Vergeer, Bonnie I. '65 '90
C.276 A.B. L.813 J.D. Staff Atty., Public Citizen Litig. Grp.
Robins, Eric P. '74 '99 C.893 L.1209 J.D.
(adm. in VA; not adm. in DC; See Pat. Sect.) [[C] Stevens,D.M.&M.]
*PRACTICE AREAS: Patents; Trademarks; Copyright.
Robins, Lena .... '69 '95 C.165 B.A. L.446 J.D. [[A] Epstein B.&G.]
*PRACTICE AREAS: Health Law.
Robins, Philip L. .... '37 '61 C&L.472 B.B.A., J.D. [[C] Adduci,M.&S.]
*PRACTICE AREAS: Customs; International Trade Regulation.

Robins, Kaplan, Miller & Ciresi L.L.P., (AV)
Suite 1200, 1801 K Street, N.W., 20006 ⊙
Telephone: 202-775-0725 Fax: 202-223-8604
URL: http://www.rkmc.com

(This Listing Continued)

Robins, Kaplan, Miller & Ciresi L.L.P. (Continued)

Partners: Stacy E. Costello; Brian R. Dinning; Sharon Cummings Giles; Robert E. Falb; Charles A. Hunnicutt; Eric S. Jackson; Harold E. Mesirow; Richard B. Nettler; Keith R. Styles; Dirk D. Thomas; Barbara Wachter Needle. Associates: G. Brent Connor; B. Gerard Cordelli; David L. Finch; Bradley J. Olson; Jeannine Rustad Zigner; Matthew J. Thomas (Not admitted in DC). Of Counsel: Jeffrey J. Downey.
Trials and Appeals in all Federal and State Courts. Administrative, Antitrust, Appellate, Banking, Bankruptcy and Reorganization, Construction, Communications, Corporate, Employment and Employee Benefits, Environmental, Estate Planning and Probate, Franchising, Finance, Health, Insurance Law, Intellectual Property, International Litigation and Trade, Medical Malpractice, Personal Injury, Products Liability, Real Estate, Securities, Tax, Transportation.
Atlanta, Georgia Office: 2600 One Atlanta Plaza, 950 East Paces Ferry Road NE. Telephone: 404-233-1114. Fax: 404-233-1267.
Boston, Massachusetts Office: 111 Huntington Avenue, Suite 1300. Telephone: 617-267-2300. Fax: 617-267-8288.
Costa Mesa, California Office: 600 Anton Boulevard, Suite 1600. Telephone: 714-540-6200. Fax: 714-545-6915.
Los Angeles, California Office: 2049 Century Park East, Suite 3700. Telephone: 310-552-0130. Fax: 310-229-5800.
Minneapolis, Minnesota Office: 2800 LaSalle Plaza, 800 LaSalle Avenue. Telephone: 612-349-8500. Fax: 612-339-4181.
Naples, Florida Office: Suite 201, 711 5th Avenue South. Telephone: 941-430-7070. Fax: 941-213-1970.
See Professional Biographies, WASHINGTON, DISTRICT OF COLUMBIA

Robinson, Alan B. .... '61 '91 C.893 B.A. L.446 J.D. [[A] Jordan K.&J.] ⊙
Robinson, Armand I. .... '24 '52 C.223 B.S. L.273 LL.B. 1725 K St., N.W.
Robinson, Barry K., (AV) '45 '71 C.645 B.A. L.569 J.D.
Sr. V.P., Dir. Bus. Affs., Recording Industry Assoc. of America, Inc.
Robinson, Bryant, III, (BV) .... '64 '91 C.860 B.A. L.893 J.D. [[A] Schnader H.S.&L.]
*PRACTICE AREAS: Corporate; Commercial Transactions; Real Estate Transactions.
Robinson, Christopher .... '73 '00 C.1372 B.S. L.602 J.D. [[A] McKenna&C.]
*PRACTICE AREAS: Corporate Law; Immigration Law; Health Care.
Robinson, David, Jr. '28 '56 C.685 B.A. L.178 LL.B.
Prof. of Law, George Wash. Univ.
Robinson, David B., (AV) .... '43 '70 C.299 B.A. L.976 J.D. [Patton B.]
Robinson, Davis R., (AV) .... '40 '68 C.976 B.A. L.309 LL.B. [LeBoeuf,L.G.&M.]
*PRACTICE AREAS: International; Corporate.
Robinson, Douglas G., (AV) .... '43 '69 C.911 B.A. L.273 J.D. [Skadden,A.S.M.&F.]
Robinson, Douglas W. ..... '— '86 C.688 B.S. L.978 J.D. [[C] Banner&W.] (See Pat. Sect.)
*PRACTICE AREAS: Patent; Trademark; Copyright and Unfair Competition Law.
Robinson, Erika L. .... '67 '95 C.309 A.B. L.276 J.D. [[C] Wilmer,C.&P.]
Robinson, Frederick, (AV) .... '57 '82 C&L.228 A.B., J.D. [Fulbright&J.]
*PRACTICE AREAS: Federal Criminal Law; False Claims Act; Business Crimes; Government Investigations; Health Care Fraud.
Robinson, Frederick H., (AV) .... '— '73 C.188 B.A. L.893 J.D. [Miller&C.]
*PRACTICE AREAS: Taxation; Health Insurance; Tax Litigation; Federal Tax Controversies.
Robinson, Harriet A. .... '62 '87 C.145 B.A. L.976 J.D. 601 13th St., N.W.
Robinson, Jason F. '71 '99 C.902 B.A. L.813 J.D.
(adm. in MD; not adm. in DC) [[A] Covington&B.]
Robinson, Jeffrey D., (AV) .... '58 '83 C.390 A.B. L.976 J.D. [Baach R.&L.P.]
*PRACTICE AREAS: Civil Litigation; Commercial Litigation; White Collar Crime; Government Relations; Employment.
Robinson, Karen M. .... '72 '98 C.276 B.S.F.S. L.846 J.D. [[A] Kirkland&E.]
*PRACTICE AREAS: Litigation.
Robinson, Keith T. .... '65 '92 C.893 B.A. L.575 J.D. [Dechert]
*PRACTICE AREAS: Securities Regulation; Financial Services Law; Investment Management.
Robinson, Kenneth G., Jr., (AV) .... '45 '69 C&L.575 A.B., J.D. Two Lafayette Ctr.
Robinson, Kenneth Michael, (AV) .... '43 '68 C&L.790 A.B., J.D. [Robinson]
Robinson, Lisa M. .... '69 '94 C&L.309 A.B., J.D. [[A] Ivins,P.&B.]
*PRACTICE AREAS: Employee Benefits; Executive Compensation; Federal Taxation; Corporate Taxation.
Robinson, Perry D. .... '53 '87 C.886 B.S. L.64 J.D. [Ballard S.A.&I.]
*PRACTICE AREAS: Business Law; Energy; Project Finance.
Robinson, Phillip L. .... '47 '86 C.940 B.A. L.273 J.D. [Ludwig&R.]
*PRACTICE AREAS: Banking Law; Corporate; Mergers and Acquisitions; International Business Law; Offshore Trusts.
Robinson, Ralph D. '52 '92
C&L.1209 B.S., J.D. 1090 Vermont Ave., NW (⊙Herndon, VA)
Robinson, Reginald L. '55 '83 C.329 B.A. L.659 J.D.
(adm. in NY; not adm. in DC) 2900 Van Ness St., N.W.

Robinson, Ronda '57 '90 C.329 B.A. L.472 J.D.
631 Constitution Avenue, N.E., Suite 3, 20002-6082
Telephone: 202-547-5699 Fax: 202-332-0503
Email: rrr.entlaw@prodigy.net
***PRACTICE AREAS: Entertainment Law; Communications Law.**
Communications and Media Law, Broadcast Licensing, Radio, Broadcast Station Transfers, FCC Licensing and Regulation, Wireless Communications, Telecommunications, Information Technology Licensing, Internet Licensing, Software Licensing, Broadcast Property Acquisition, Music Law, Video Law, Multimedia Law, Music Copyright and Publishing, Entertainment Litigation, Contracts.
See Professional Biographies, WASHINGTON, DISTRICT OF COLUMBIA

Robinson, Sandra H., (AV) ...... '51 '83 C.604 B.A. L.128 J.D. [[A] J.H.Olender&Assoc.]
*PRACTICE AREAS: Medical Malpractice; Personal Injury; Products Liability.
Robinson, Sara A. '— '00 C.602 B.A. L.145 J.D.
(adm. in IL; not adm. in DC) [[A] Verner,L.B.M.&H.]
*PRACTICE AREAS: International.
Robinson, Stacy R. .... '68 '94 C.477 B.A. L.245 J.D. [[A] Skadden,A.S.M.&F.]
*PRACTICE AREAS: Public Policy; Communications Law.
Robinson, Stephanie L. '65 '95 C.103 B.A. L.930 J.D.
Lawyers Comm. for Human Rights
Robinson, Steven N. .... '50 '84 C.103 A.B. L.180 J.D. [Hogan&H.]
*PRACTICE AREAS: Corporate Law; Securities.
Robinson, Theodore W. '22 '60 C.285 A.B. L.981 LL.B.
(adm. in MT; not adm. in DC) 837 Crittenden St., N.E.‡
Robinson, William C.E. '57 '84 C&L.329 B.A., J.D.
Sr. Assoc. Gen. Coun., Howard Univ.
Robinson, William H., Jr., (AV) '43 '74 C&L.880 B.A., J.D.
(adm. in VA; not adm. in DC) [Wright,R.O.&T.] (⊙Richmond, VA)
*PRACTICE AREAS: Trials; Product Liability Defense Litigation; Complex and Multi-District Defense Litigation.
Robinson, William L. '41 '66 C.604 B.A. L.178 LL.B.
Dean, Univ. of Dist. of Columbia
Robinson, Wm. A. .... '16 '52 C.922 B.S. L.276 J.D. 2920 Military Rd., N.W.‡
Robinson and Geraldo, A Professional Corporation, (AV)
1316 Pennsylvania Ave., S.E. (⊙Carlisle, Harrisburg, PA)
Robinson Kourtesis, Cameron '70 '98 C.645 B.A. L.1364 J.D.
(adm. in NJ; not adm. in DC) [[A] Robinson]
Robinson Law Firm, The, (AV) .... 717 D Street, N.W., 4th Floor
Robinson-Meyer, Renee L. ..... '64 '95 C.229 B.S.N. L.276 J.D. [[A] A.M.Levine&Assoc.]
*PRACTICE AREAS: Medical Malpractice; Products Liability.
Robison, Samuel K. '64 '96
C.679 B.S.C.N.E. L.146 J.D. [[A] Wickwire G.] (⊙Vienna, VA)
*PRACTICE AREAS: Construction Law.

Robitaille, Lynn '74 '00 C.454 B.A L.276 J.D.
(adm. in MD; not adm. in DC) [A Coudert B.]
*PRACTICE AREAS: Telecommunications Law; Latin America Trade.
Robitschek, Elizabeth .... '71 '00 C.259 B.S. L.276 J.D. [A Miller&C.]
*PRACTICE AREAS: Taxation.
Robling, Kenneth C. .... '69 '96 C.610 B.S.J. L.1003 J.D. Pub. Def.
Roby, David A., Jr. .... '68 '93 C.259 B.S. L.280 J.D. [A Sutherland A.&B.]
*PRACTICE AREAS: Federal Income Tax; Corporate Income Tax; Partnership Taxation; Tax Planning; Federal Tax Controversies.
Roby, Loretta Jo .... '63 '90 C.744 B.B.A. L.846 J.D. [© Weil,G.&M.]
*PRACTICE AREAS: Tax Law.
Roby, Rebecca '72 '98 C.518 B.A. L.910 J.D.
(adm. in VA; not adm. in DC) [A Dorsey&W.]
*PRACTICE AREAS: Trademark Prosecution; Trademark Litigation.
Rocap, James E., III, (AV) .... '50 '75 C.602 B.A. L.276 J.D. [Baker B.]
Roccograndi, Anthony J., (AV) .... '35 '68 C.563 B.S. L.569 J.D. [Sonnenreich&R.]
Rocha, Nancy Gast '42 '85 C.999 B.A. L.769 J.D.
(adm. in CA; not adm. in DC) 2301 Connecticut Ave., N.W.
Roche, Jerome J. .... '70 '97 C.679 B.S. L.477 J.D. [A Wilmer,C.&P.]
Roche, Kevin T. '70 '00 C.890 B.A. L.128 J.D.
(adm. in NY; not adm. in DC) [A Clifford C.R.&W.]
*PRACTICE AREAS: Financial Services Law; Technology and Science.
Roche, Paul G. .... '60 '89 C.184 B.A. L.276 J.D. [A Wiley R.&F.]
Rochon, Mark, (AV) .... '57 '83 C.932 B.S. L.813 J.D. 504 7th St., S.E.
Rock, Patrick C. .... '59 '84 C.602 B.A. L.128 J.D. [Gardner,C.&D.]
*PRACTICE AREAS: Energy; Federal Energy Regulation; International Energy Law; Environmental Law; International Drug Regulatory Affairs.
Rockefeller, Edwin S., (AV) .... '27 '51 C&L.976 B.A., LL.B. [© Schiff H.&W.]
Rockelli, Patrick M. '53 '80
C.444 B.A. L.862 J.D. Sen. V.P., Congressional Quarterly, Inc.
Rockler, Walter J., (AV) .... '20 '46 C.145 A.B. L.309 LL.B. [Arnold&P.]
*PRACTICE AREAS: Federal Tax; International.
Rockoff, Jennifer M. .... '73 '01 C.674 B.A. L.893 J.D. [A Wilmer,C.&P.]
Rockwell, Sarah M., (AV) '58 '85 C.813 B.A. L.94 J.D.
(adm. in CO; not adm. in DC) [Akin,G.S.H.&F.] (⊙Denver, CO)
*PRACTICE AREAS: Land Use; Environmental; Real Estate.
Rocque, René L. .... '75 '00 C&L.309 A.B., J.D. [A Fried,F.H.S.&J.]
*PRACTICE AREAS: General Litigation.

Rocque, Vincent J., (AV) '45 '71 C.276 A.B. L.178 J.D.
Suite 400, 1155 Connecticut Avenue, N.W., 20036
Telephone: 202-429-6659 Telecopy: 202-872-1575
Email: vinrocque@aol.com
Federal Regulatory Law and Enforcement, International Business Transactions, Corporate Investigations, Legislation, Import and Export Law, Foreign Trade Sanctions, Antiboycott Compliance.
See Professional Biographies, WASHINGTON, DISTRICT OF COLUMBIA

Roda, Anthony J. .... '61 '90 C.446 B.A. L.128 J.D. [Williams&J.]
*PRACTICE AREAS: Intellectual Property; Bankruptcy; Antitrust; Trade; Taxation.
Roddy, Carol L. '54 '79 C&L.45 B.A., J.D.
(adm. in AR; not adm. in DC) Sr. Prog. Advsr., Off. of Surgeon Gen.
Rode, John S., (AV) ...... '39 '66 C.674 B.A. L.569 LL.B. [Rode&Q.] (⊙New York, NY)
Rode & Qualey, (AV) .... 1742 N Street (⊙New York, NY; Karachi, Pakistan)
Roderick, Kristine D. .... '73 '98 C.184 B.A. L.1048 J.D. 555 12th St., Ste. 254
Rodgers, C.W. (Quincy) '42 '69
C&L.976 B.A., J.D. V.P., Govt. Affs., General Instrument Corp.
Rodgers, Dennis C. .... '62 '89 C.431 B.S. L.273 J.D. [Smith,G.&R.] (See Pat. Sect.)
*PRACTICE AREAS: Intellectual Property Law; Patent Prosecution; International Patent Prosecution.
Rodgers, J. Christopher '67 '94 C.446 B.S. L.273 J.D.
(adm. in MD; not adm. in DC) [A Powell,G.F.&M.]
*PRACTICE AREAS: Corporate Finance; Real Estate.
Rodgers, Peter H., (AV) .... '48 '73 C.976 B.A. L.813 J.D. [Sutherland A.&B.]
*PRACTICE AREAS: Energy; Environmental Law; Commodities; Commercial Law.
Rodgers, Richard R. .... '69 '00 C.976 B.A. L.178 J.D. [A Arnold&P.]
*PRACTICE AREAS: Corporate Law; Securities; Real Estate.
Rodgers, William J., (AV) '43 '68 C.188 B.S. L.262 J.D.
(adm. in NY; not adm. in DC) [Collier S.S.]
*PRACTICE AREAS: Labor and Employment Law.
Rodin, Richard S., (AV) .... '38 '63 C&L.178 B.A., LL.B. [Hogan&H.]
*PRACTICE AREAS: Communications and Media; Broadcast Radio; Broadcast Regulation; Broadcast Television; FCC Regulation.
Rodin, W. Victor '10 '34 C.831 A.B. L.309 J.D.
(adm. in PA; not adm. in DC) 5032 Fulton St., N.W.‡
Rodney, Donna Marie .... '66 '92 C.329 B.A. L.1066 J.D. [A Powell,G.F.&M.]
*PRACTICE AREAS: Housing Law; Real Estate Law.
Rodock, John N. .... '56 '82 C.602 B.B.A. L.893 J.D. [Ober,K.G.&S.]
Rodrigues, Dora Monica .... '71 '01 C.30 B.A. L.362 J.D. [Koonz,M.J.D.&L.]
*PRACTICE AREAS: Personal Injury; Medical Malpractice; Workers Compensation.
Rodrigues, Robert W. .... '49 '78 C.36 B.A. L.602 J.D. Sr. Lit. Coun., MCI WorldCom
Rodriguez, Agnes Milagros '61 '98
C.845 B.B.A. L.273 J.D. Asst. Corp. Coun., Off. of the Corp. Coun.
Rodriguez, Cara L. .... '75 '01 C.273 B.A. L.904 J.D. 401 9th St., N.W., Ste. 1000
Rodriguez, Carlos, (AV) .... '41 '75 C.846 B.A. L.776 J.D. [Rodriguez O.F.G.&W.]
*PRACTICE AREAS: Transportation; Admiralty Law; Regulatory Law; Maritime Law; International Commercial Transactions.
Rodriguez, Elizabeth D. .... '67 '94 C.976 B.A. L.477 J.D. [A Pepper H.]
*PRACTICE AREAS: Intellectual Property; Corporate Law; Securities.
Rodriguez, Grace M. .... '— '87 C.309 B.A. L.178 J.D. [King&S.]
*PRACTICE AREAS: Special Matters/Government Investigations.
Rodriguez, Janice M. .... '— '99 C.446 B.S. L.276 J.D. [A Arnold&P.]
*PRACTICE AREAS: Civil Litigation.
Rodriguez, Leon '— '89 C.103 B.A. L.93 J.D.
(adm. in NY; not adm. in DC) [Ober,K.G.&S.]
Rodriguez, Raul R., (AV) .... '48 '74 C.1111 B.A. L.259 J.D. [Leventhal,S.&L.]
*PRACTICE AREAS: Communications Law; Media Law.
Rodriguez-Creus, Yira '65 '88 L.999 J.D.
(adm. in NY; not adm. in DC) [A Coudert B.]
*PRACTICE AREAS: Project Finance; International Commercial Law; Corporate; Telecommunications.
Rodriguez Harrison, Belinda '71 '01 C.656 B.S. L.30 J.D.
(adm. in MD; not adm. in DC) [A Cullen]
*PRACTICE AREAS: Transportation; Bankruptcy; First Amendment Law.

Rodriguez O'Donnell Fuerst Gonzalez & Williams, (AV) BR
1710 Rhode Island Avenue, N.W. Tenth Floor, 20036-3007 ⊙
Telephone: 202-293-3300 Facsimile: 202-293-3307 URL: http://www.rofgw.com
Email: rodriguez@rofgw.com URL: http://www.lawyers.com/transportationlaw
Carlos Rodriguez; Thomas J. O'Donnell (Resident, Chicago, Illinois Office); Mitchell S. Fuerst (Not admitted in DC); Henry P. Gonzalez (Not admitted in DC); R. Kevin Williams (Not admitted in DC;, Resident, Chicago, Illinois Office). Associates: Kevin L. Kelly (Not admitted in DC; Resident, Chicago, Illinois Office); Lara A. Rutenberg-Austrins (Not admitted in DC; Resident, Chicago, Illinois Office); Ellen C. Smith (Not admitted in DC; Resident, Chicago, Illinois Office). Of Counsel: Todd C. Fineberg; Michael A. Johnson (Not admitted in DC; Resident, Chicago, Illinois Office); Donald W. Lewis.

(This Listing Continued)

Rodriguez O'Donnell Fuerst Gonzalez & Williams (Continued)
International Transportation, Trade, Customs, Maritime, Commercial Transactions Law, Government Relations, Tax and Tax Litigation.
Chicago, Illinois Office: 20 North Wacker Drive, Suite 1416, 60606. Telephone: 312-372-7000. Fax: 312-372-1719.
Miami, Florida Office: 1200 Brickell Avenue, 33131. Telephone: 305-350-5690. Fax: 305-371-8989.
New York, New York Office: 61 Broadway, 10006. Telephone: 212-344-6600. Fax: 212-509-4066.
See Professional Biographies, WASHINGTON, DISTRICT OF COLUMBIA

Rodriquez, Miguel E. .... '72 '99 C&L.659 B.A., J.D. [A Crowell&M.]
Roe, Christopher P. .... '64 '89 C.276 B.A. L.966 J.D. 1130 Conn. Ave., N.W.
Roe, Richard L. ...... '46 '77 C.976 B.A. L.1294 J.D. Prof., Georgetown Univ. Law Center

Roeder and Associates, P.C.
(See McLean, Virginia)

Roegner, Nicholas M. .... '67 '97 C.178 B.A. L.945 J.D. [A Clifford C.R.&W.]
*PRACTICE AREAS: International Capital Markets; International Trade.
Roellke, Jon Randall .... '59 '87 C.766 B.A. L.93 J.D. [Clifford C.R.&W.]
*PRACTICE AREAS: Antitrust; Intellectual Property; Commercial Litigation.
Roesel, Richard '44 '69 C.743 B.A. L.245 J.D.
Asst. Gen. Coun., United Food & Comercial Workers International Union
Roessel, Faith R. '56 '82 C.1262 B.A. L.560 J.D.
(adm. in NM; not adm. in DC) 1662 Hobart St., N.W.‡
Rogan, James E. '57 '84 C.1375 B.A. L.1068 J.D.
(adm. in CA; not adm. in DC) [Venable,A.B.H.&C.]
Rogan, Michael P., (AV) .... '48 '74 C.604 B.A. L.184 J.D. [Skadden,A.S.M.&F.]
Rogers, Alec D. '68 '93 C.475 B.A. L.477 J.D.
(adm. in MI; not adm. in DC) Perm. Subcommittee on Invest., U.S. Senate
Rogers, Amy Smith '72 '99 C.299 B.A. L.588 J.D.
(adm. in MD; not adm. in DC) Kohn, Kohn & Colapinto, PC
Rogers, Arthur P. .... '35 '60 C.1057 B.S. L.818 J.D. [Whiteford,T.&P.]
*PRACTICE AREAS: Corporate Law; Labor and Employment; Alternative Dispute Resolution; Mediation.
Rogers, C. Bryant, (BV) '48 '78 C.497 B.A. L.309 J.D.
(adm. in NM; not adm. in DC) [© Hobbs,S.D.&W.] (⊙Santa Fe, NM)
Rogers, Christian E., Jr. ...... '15 '52 C.420 B.S. L.276 LL.B. 820 Constitution Ave., N.E.
Rogers, David E. .... '60 '85 C.258 B.S. L.30 J.D. [McDermott,W.&E.]
Rogers, Donald R., (AV) '46 '70
C.331 B.S. L.276 J.D. [Shulman,R.G.P.&E.] (⊙Rockville, MD)
Rogers, Edward M. .... '60 '87 C&L.893 B.A., J.D. [Nixon P.]
*PRACTICE AREAS: Real Estate; Real Estate Leasing; Real Estate Finance.
Rogers, Edward M., Jr. .... '58 '85 L.16 J.D. [© Balch&B.]
*PRACTICE AREAS: Government Law; Legislative Practice.
Rogers, Edwina Clifton .... '64 '91 C.16 B.S. L.128 J.D. [Johnson&C.]
*PRACTICE AREAS: Legislation; Administrative Law; Political Law; International Law.
Rogers, Ellen Sheriff .... '57 '82 C.518 A.B. L.597 J.D. Potomac Electric Power Company
Rogers, George C. .... '57 '91 C.188 B.A. L.178 J.D. Inter-Amer. Develop. Bk.
Rogers, George M., Jr. (P.C.), (AV) .... '33 '59 C.674 A.B. L.893 LL.B. [© Shaw P.]
*PRACTICE AREAS: Corporate Securities; Tax; Real Estate.
Rogers, James A. .... '38 '63 C.724 B.A. L.893 LL.B. United Parcel Service
Rogers, James F., (AV) .... '— '81 C.976 B.A. L.178 J.D. [Latham&W.]
*PRACTICE AREAS: Corporate Law; Communications and Media.
Rogers, Joel W. .... '— '92 C.893 B.A. L.128 J.D. [© Miller&C.]
*PRACTICE AREAS: Customs; International Trade; Export Control; Intellectual Property.
Rogers, Joyce A. '— '00 C.951 B.A. L.659
(adm. in MD; not adm. in DC) [A Verner,L.B.M.&H.]
*PRACTICE AREAS: Federal Affairs.
Rogers, L. Lawton, III, (AV) '36 '67 C.790 B.S.E.E. L.276 J.D.
[© Carter,L.&M.] (Pat.)
*PRACTICE AREAS: Intellectual Property; Litigation.
Rogers, Martha Purcell, (AV) .... '44 '77 C.846 B.A. L.273 J.D. [Ober,K.G.&S.]
Rogers, Melissa '66 '92 C.69 B.A. L.659 J.D.
Assoc. Gen. Coun., Baptist Joint Commission on Public Affairs
Rogers, Melissa B. '66 '91 C.319 B.A. L.1066 J.D.
Assoc. Gen. Coun., Labor & Employ., National Railroad Passenger Corp. (AMTRAK)
Rogers, Michelle Proctor '69 '96 C.811 B.S. L.446 J.D.
(adm. in MD; not adm. in DC) Sr. Prod. Coun., Black Entertainment Television, Inc.
Rogers, Paul G., (AV) .... '21 '48 C&L.260 B.A., J.D. [Hogan&H.]
*PRACTICE AREAS: Corporate Law; Health Law; Environmental Law; Legislative Law.
Rogers, Paul V., (AV) .... '57 '85 C.951 B.A. L.276 J.D. [Covington&B.]
Rogers, Reginald J. .... '54 '83 C.454 B.A. L.1162 J.D. [R.J.Rogers]
Rogers, Richard B. .... '73 '98 C.893 B.A. L.228 J.D. [A McDermott,W.&E.]

Rogers, Stephen C., (AV) '41 '69 C.309 A.B. L.276 J.D.
Suite 200, 1120 G Street, N.W., 20005-3801
Telephone: 202-737-0629 Fax: 202-737-0920
Email: SRogersLaw@aol.com URL: http://www.lawyers.com/stephencrogers
Transportation, Railroad Law, Arbitration, Contracts, Arbitration and Interstate Commerce.
See Professional Biographies, WASHINGTON, DISTRICT OF COLUMBIA

Rogers, W. Sherman .... '51 '77 C.999 B.A. L.329 J.D. 2900 Van Ness St., N.W.
Rogers, William D., (AV) .... '27 '53 C.674 A.B. L.976 LL.B. [Arnold&P.]
*PRACTICE AREAS: International.
Rogers, William G. '62 '92
C.446 B.S. L.1338 J.D. Dep. Exec. Offr., The Dist. of Col. Cts.

Rogers & Killeen
(See Carter Ledyard & Milburn)

Rogers & More, PLLC .... 1510 H Street, N.W., Suite 950
Rogers, Reginald J., P.C. .... P.O. Box 77741
Roggensack, Margaret E., (AV) .... '54 '84 C.118 B.A. L.273 J.D. [© Hogan&H.]
*PRACTICE AREAS: International Government Relations; Legislative Practice; International Trade Regulation; Latin America Trade; Customs Law.
Roggeveen, Dirk Gardiner '56 '86 C.112 B.A. L.30 J.D.
(adm. in MA; not adm. in DC) Sr. Litig. Atty., Institute for Jus.
Roggin, Greg P. .... '69 '94 C.477 B.A. L.910 J.D. [A Pennie&E.] (See Pat. Sect.)
*PRACTICE AREAS: Patent Litigation; Intellectual Property Licensing; Intellectual Property Litigation.
Roh, Charles E., Jr., (AV) .... '47 '73 C.674 B.A. L.309 J.D. [Weil,G.&M.]
*PRACTICE AREAS: International Trade and Investment; Public Policy.
Rohal, Brian J. .... '74 '00 C.602 B.A. L.228 J.D. [A Gibson,D.&C.]
*PRACTICE AREAS: International Trade.
Rohde, Clifford Chance .... '65 '96 C.188 B.A. L.273 J.D. [Terris,P.&W.]
Rohde, Wayne R. .... '62 '89 C.393 B.A. L.276 J.D. [A Sher&B.]
*PRACTICE AREAS: Transportation; Maritime Law; Administrative Law; Antitrust.
Rohe, Charles A. .... '48 '90 C.208 B.A. L.190 J.D. [© Swidler B.S.F.]
*PRACTICE AREAS: Telecommunications; Right of Way; Commercial Leasing.
Rohrbach, Peter A., (AV) .... '53 '79 C.976 B.A. L.813 J.D. [Hogan&H.]
*PRACTICE AREAS: Telecommunications Law; Satellite Communications; Broadcasting Law; International Communications Law; Internet Law.
Roig, Julia A. '70 '97 C.941 B.A. L.273 J.D.
(adm. in MD; not adm. in DC) 1730 M. Street, N.W. Suite 300

Roistacher, Charles H., (AV) . . . . '43 '68 C.893 B.A. L.472 J.D. [Powell,G.F.&M.]
*PRACTICE AREAS: White Collar Crime; Congressional Investigations; Internal Corporate Investigations; Government Enforcement Litigation; Complex Civil Litigation.
Roiter, Eric D., (AV) . . . . '48 '73 C.690 B.A. L.276 J.D. 555 13th St., N.W.
Roland, Josh L. . . . . '69 '96 C.103 B.A. L.273 J.D. [Ⓐ Wilmer,C.&P.]
Rolfe, Jonathan P. '72 '98 C&L.494 B.A., J.D.
(adm. in MD; not adm. in DC) [Ⓐ Guerrieri,E.&C.]
Roll, David L., (AV) . . . . '40 '65 C.31 B.A. L.477 J.D. [Ⓒ Steptoe&J.]
*PRACTICE AREAS: Antitrust and Trade Regulation; Civil Trials; Complex Litigation; Energy Law; Government Regulation.
Roller, Moffett B., (AV) . . . . '51 '76 C.886 B.S. L.893 J.D. [Roller&B.]
*PRACTICE AREAS: Airline Regulation; International Aviation Law; Air Cargo; Aviation Tax; Aircraft Finance and Leasing.

Roller & Bauer, PLLC, (AV)
1020 Nineteenth Street, N.W. Suite 400, 20036
Telephone: 202-331-3300 Fax: 202-331-3322
Email: airlaw@rollerbauer.com URL: http://www.lawyers.com/roller&bauerairlaw
Members of Firm: Moffett B. Roller; Lee Anthony Bauer.
Aviation Regulation, Federal Aviation Licenses, (Dept. of Transportation (DOT), Federal Aviation Administration (FAA), Customs, Immigration (INS), Agriculture (APHIS), etc.), International Aviation Law, Airline Contracts, Aviation Tax (Property, Excise Tax, User Fees, etc.), Aircraft Financing and Leasing, Aircraft Sales, Aircraft Title, Aviation Litigation, Aviation-related Trademark and Copyright.
See Professional Biographies, WASHINGTON, DISTRICT OF COLUMBIA

Rollins, Jamie T. . . . . '71 '96 C.228 A.B. L.276 J.D. 3000 K St., N.W.
Rollins, Victoria Radd . . . . '57 '85 C&L.309 A.B., J.D. [Williams&C.]
*PRACTICE AREAS: Complex Litigation; Federal Civil Litigation; Media and First Amendment; Media Libel.
Rolph, Katherine A. . . . . '65 '94 C&L.893 B.A., J.D. [Ⓐ Swidler B.S.F.]
*PRACTICE AREAS: Telecommunications.
Romain, Alex G. . . . . '70 '97 C.976 B.A. L.477 J.D. [Ⓐ Williams&C.]
Romaine, Ama B. . . . . '72 '00 C.035 B.A. L.329 J.D. [Ⓐ White&C.]
Romaine, Christopher D. . . . . '72 '98 C.103 A.B. L.659 J.D. [Ⓐ Dow,L.&A.]
Roman, David A. . . . . '75 '00 C.118 B.A. L.188 J.D. [Ⓐ Miller&C.]
*PRACTICE AREAS: Taxation.
Roman, Neil K. . . . . '58 '86 C.95 A.B. L.309 J.D. [Covington&B.]
Roman, Steven John, (AV) . . . . '56 '80 C.893 B.A. L.976 J.D. [Ⓒ Dickstein S.M.&O.]
*PRACTICE AREAS: Commercial Litigation; Complex Civil Litigation; Criminal Law.
Roman, Tracy A. . . . . '65 '92 C&L.893 B.A., J.D. [Ⓒ Crowell&M.]
*PRACTICE AREAS: Antitrust; Commercial Litigation; Class Action Defense; Aviation Products Liability.
Romaneski, Mark '53 '82 C.870 B.S. L.93 J.D.
(adm. in MA; not adm. in DC) 2200 Army Pentagon★
Romano, John-Alex . . . . '73 '00 C&L.276 B.S.F.S., J.D. [Ⓐ Wilmer,C.&P.]
Romano, Salvatore A., (AV) . . . . '40 '65 C&L.724 B.A., LL.B. [Seyfarth S.]
*PRACTICE AREAS: Litigation.
Romanow, Joshua I. . . . . '64 '92 C.1036 B.A. L.861 J.D. [Pillsbury W.]
*PRACTICE AREAS: Aviation Law; Travel Law; Advertising Law; Media Law; Maritime Law.
Romansky, Michael A., (AV) . . . . '52 '77 C.597 B.S.S. L.273 J.D. [McDermott,W.&E.]
Romanzo, Cara . . . . '70 '98 C.696 B.A. L.276 J.D. [Ⓐ Dickstein S.M.&O.]
*PRACTICE AREAS: Energy; Environmental; Administrative; Family Law; Corporate.
Romary, John M., (AV) '47 '73
C.401 B.S.E.E. L.276 J.D. [Finnegan,H.F.G.&D.] (See Pat. Sect.)
*PRACTICE AREAS: Patent Litigation; Patent Prosecution; Patent Licensing.
Romatowski, Peter J., (AV) . . . . '50 '76 C.309 A.B. L.276 J.D. [Jones,D.R.&P.]
*PRACTICE AREAS: Litigation; White Collar Crime; Government Procurement; SEC Enforcement.
Rome, Eric M., (AV) . . . . '57 '82 C.107 B.A. L.1162 J.D. [Eisen&R.]
Romeo, Peter J., (AV) . . . . '42 '68 C.276 B.S.B.A. L.273 J.D. [Hogan&H.]
*PRACTICE AREAS: Securities.
Romero, Jorge . . . . '54 '84 C&L.178 B.A., J.D. [Ⓐ Preston G.E.&R.M.]
*PRACTICE AREAS: Corporate; Finance; International Project Finance; International Investments; Maritime and Shipping Regulation Law.
Romero, Mario S. . . . . '20 '50 C.178 L.273 LL.B. 818 18th St., N.W.
Romero, Tobin J. . . . . '71 '98 C&L.276 B.A., J.D. [Ⓐ Williams&C.]
*PRACTICE AREAS: Criminal Law; Litigation; White Collar Crime.
Romero-Ostolaza, Richard Thomas '61 '97
C.178 B.A. L.1398 J.D. 1300 Pennsylvania Ave., N.W.
Romhilt, Dean A. . . . . '— '99 C.228 B.A. L.893 J.D. [Ⓐ Hogan&H.]
Romm, Barry M. . . . . '57 '81 C&L.273 B.A., J.D. [Klein,L.&R.]
Romm, David C. . . . . '48 '77 C.446 B.A. L.608 J.D. [Winston&S.]
*PRACTICE AREAS: Surety; Construction; Government Contracts; Civil Litigation.
Rommel, John M., (AV) '25 '54 C.30 B.A. L.904 J.D.
1025 Connecticut Ave., N.W. (Pat.)
Romney, Brenda '62 '90 C.188 B.A. L.813 J.D.
(adm. in CA; not adm. in DC) Staff Atty., Ctr. for Reproductive Law & Policy
Romney, Norman D. . . . . '51 '89 C.329 B.S.C.E. L.128 J.D. Hill International, Inc.
Ronis, Catherine Kane . . . . '64 '91 C.321 B.A. L.823 J.D. [Wilmer,C.&P.]
*PRACTICE AREAS: Communications Law; Telecommunications Law.
Ronnell, Anne J. '62 '88 C.103 A.B. L.309 J.D.
(adm. in CA; not adm. in DC) 1700 Penn Ave., N.W.
Rons, Pamela A. . . . . '55 '80 C.210 B.A. L.1119 J.D. [Ⓢ Winston&S.]
*PRACTICE AREAS: Civil Litigation; Criminal Litigation; Securities Arbitration.
Rood, L. Eden '74 '00 C.893 B.A. L.273 J.D.
(adm. in MD; not adm. in DC) [Ⓐ Andrews&K.]
*PRACTICE AREAS: Litigation.
Rooks, James E., Jr. '45 '74 C.197 A.B. L.94 J.D.
Asst. Gen. Coun., Association of Trial Lawyers of America
Rooney, John T. . . . . '52 '86 C.30 B.A. L.284 J.D. Staff Atty., Office of Bar Coun.
Roosevelt, Kermit, Jr., (AV) . . . . '38 '67 C.309 A.B. L.178 LL.B. 5052 Macomb St., N.W.
Roots, John C. . . . . '43 '74 C&L.802 B.B.A., J.D. 122 C Street, NW

Roper & Quigg
(See Arlington, Virginia)

Ropes & Gray, (AV) BR
One Franklin Square, 1301 K Street, NW, Suite 800 East, 20005-3333 ⊙
Telephone: 202-626-3900 Telecopy: 202-626-3961
Email: postmaster@ropesgray.com URL: http://www.ropesgray.com
Resident Members: Michael Nussbaum; Thomas M. Susman; Russell A. Gaudreau, Jr.; Martin E. Lybecker; Samuel J. Buffone; Mark L. Lezell; Colburn T. Cherney; J. Daniel Berry; Mark A. Greenwood; James M. Spears; David O. Stewart; Alan G. Priest; Peter M. Brody; Gregory J. Glover; Thomas B. Smith; Kathleen Marie Delaney; Dina L. Michels. Resident Associates: J. Steven Baughman; Alyssa Albertelli; Jennifer D. McNasby; David J. Baum; Kelly B. Kramer; Todd M. Richman; Linda L. LeCraw; Benjamin J. Priester (Not admitted in DC); Ashley N. Bailey; Patricia L. Block (Not admitted in DC); Amy Sobba Diaz (Not admitted in DC); Jeffrey Pearlman.
Antitrust, Banking, Bankruptcy and Creditors' Rights, Corporate, Employee Benefits, Environmental, Financial Institutions, Government Contracts, Legislative and Regulatory, Litigation and Appeals in all Courts, Securities, Taxation, Healthcare, Intellectual Property Information, Privacy.
Boston, Massachusetts Office: One International Place. Telephone: 617-951-7000. Fax: 617-951-7050.
Providence, Rhode Island Office: 30 Kennedy Plaza. Telephone: 401-455-4400. Fax: 401-455-4401.
New York, New York Office: 885 Third Avenue, Suite 3200. Telephone: 646-840-6800. Fax: 646-840-6850.
See Professional Biographies, WASHINGTON, DISTRICT OF COLUMBIA

Rorer, Kathryn E. . . . . '67 '93 C&L.309 B.A., J.D. [Sullivan&C.]
Rosa, Andrew K. . . . . '63 '94 C.911 B.A. L.477 J.D. 607 14th St., N.W.
Rosans, John A. '75 '00 C.188 B.A. L.477 J.D.
(adm. in VA; not adm. in DC) [Ⓐ Patton B.]
Rosaya, Lisa Weiss . . . . '70 '97 C.94 B.A. L.1049 J.D. [Ⓐ Coudert B.]
Roschwalb, Jerold '35 '66 C.102 B.A. L.276 LL.B.
National Association of State University and Land-Grant Colleges
Roscoe, Jerry P. '53 '82 C.165 A.B. L.128 J.D. 1666 Conn. Ave., N.W.
Roscoe, Lisa Le Grow '58 '91 C&L.802 B.B.A., J.D.
Assoc. Litig. Coun., MCI WorldCom
Rose, A. Hewitt, (AV) . . . . '51 '81 C&L.575 B.A., J.D. [Brickfield B.R.&S.]
*PRACTICE AREAS: Public Utility Law; Energy; Antitrust; Administrative Law; Litigation.
Rose, Andrea D. . . . . '65 '96 C.659 B.S.N. L.831 J.D. [Ⓐ Spriggs&H.]
*PRACTICE AREAS: Products Liability; Toxic Torts; Drug and Medical Device Defense; Litigation.
Rose, Charles P., Jr. '42 '69 C&L.228 A.B., J.D.
(adm. in NY; not adm. in DC) 4001 Nebraska Ave., N.W.‡
Rose, David L., (AV) . . . . '31 '56 C&L.309 A.B., LL.B. [Rose&R.]
*PRACTICE AREAS: Equal Employment Opportunity Law; Appellate Litigation.
Rose, Deana E. . . . . '51 '76 C.383 B.A. L.421 J.D. [Ⓒ Manelli,D.&S.]
*PRACTICE AREAS: Administrative Law; Admiralty and Maritime Law; Transportation Law; Litigation.
Rose, Henry . . . . '27 '51 C&L.107 B.A., J.D. [Ⓒ Ice M.] (⊙Indpls., IN)
*PRACTICE AREAS: Employee Benefits.
Rose, James M., Jr. . . . . '27 '55 C.674 A.B. L.309 LL.B. 4913 Rodman St., N.W.
Rose, Jonathan C., (AV) . . . . '41 '68 C.976 B.A. L.309 LL.B. [Jones,D.R.&P.]
*PRACTICE AREAS: International Trade; Federal Legislative Practice.
Rose, Jonathan G. . . . . '63 '92 C.928 B.A. L.128 J.D. [Ⓐ Morgan,L.&B.]
Rose, Joshua N., (AV) . . . . '62 '87 C.910 A.B. L.575 J.D. [Rose&R.]
*PRACTICE AREAS: Environmental Litigation; Environmental Cost Recovery; Water Quality; Civil Rights; Employment Litigation.
Rose, Lewis . . . . '57 '82 C&L.107 B.A., J.D. [Collier S.S.]
*PRACTICE AREAS: Advertising Law; Consumer Law; Consumer Credit Law; Unfair Trade Practice; Internet Law.

Rose & Rose, (AV)
1320 19th Street NW, Suite 601, 20036
Telephone: 202-331-8557 Fax: 202-331-0996 URL: http://www.lawyers.com/rose&rose
URL: http://www.rose&rose.com
David L. Rose; Joshua N. Rose; David M. Wachtel. Associate: Linda Y. Sroufe.
Employment Discrimination, Employment Law, Civil Rights Litigation, Environmental Law, Superfund and Hazardous Waste Issues, Administrative Law, Civil Litigation.
See Professional Biographies, WASHINGTON, DISTRICT OF COLUMBIA

Roselló, Luis R. . . . . '— '99 C.602 B.A. L.276 J.D. [Ⓐ Steptoe&J.]
Roseman, David C. . . . . '48 '75 C.188 B.A. L.904 J.D. [Jones,D.R.&P.]
*PRACTICE AREAS: Bankruptcy; Creditors Rights; Corporate Trusts; Commercial Transactions; Real Estate Workouts.
Roseman, Robert D., (AV) . . . . '47 '72 C.94 B.A. L.273 J.D. [Williams M.]
*PRACTICE AREAS: Real Estate; Finance; Business; Corporate Transactional.
Rosemond, Ernest E. '58 '92
C.477 B.A. L.276 J.D. Natl. Alliance of Black Sch. Educators
Rosen, Bruce G. . . . . '66 '92 C&L.831 B.B.A., J.D. [Ⓒ Akin,G.S.H.&F.]
*PRACTICE AREAS: Commercial Real Estate; Real Estate Finance.
Rosen, Charlotte Rothenberg . . . . '60 '86 C&L.273 B.A., J.D. [Ⓒ Dickstein S.M.&O.]
*PRACTICE AREAS: Government Contracts; Technology Transactions.
Rosen, David L., (BV) . . . . '55 '91 C.184 B.S. L.180 J.D. [McDermott,W.&E.]
Rosen, Elisa P. . . . . '68 '93 C.659 B.A. L.273 J.D. [Ⓐ Dow,L.&A.]
Rosen, Jeffrey A., (AV) . . . . '58 '82 C.597 B.A. L.309 J.D. [Kirkland&E.]
*PRACTICE AREAS: Commercial Litigation; Class Actions; Antitrust.
Rosen, Jeffrey B., (BV) '56 '82 C.309 B.A. L.569 J.D.
(adm. in NY; not adm. in DC) [Arent F.K.P.&K.]
*PRACTICE AREAS: Real Estate; Project Finance; Public Service Concessions.
Rosen, Jeffrey M. '64 '92 C.309 A.B. L.976 J.D.
Legal Affairs Editor, New Republic, The
Rosen, Jeffrey S., (AV) '46 '71
C&L.178 B.A., J.D. [De Martino F.R.&V.] (⊙New York, NY)
*PRACTICE AREAS: Commodities Law; Securities Law; Alternative Dispute Resolution; Litigation.
Rosen, Lisa Alpert, (AV) . . . . '58 '83 C.1019 B.A. L.976 J.D. [Sutherland A.&B.]
*PRACTICE AREAS: Real Estate; Real Estate Finance; Real Estate Restructuring; Real Estate Bankruptcy; Real Estate Acquisitions.
Rosen, Mark A. '45 '71 C.421 B.A. L.273 J.D. 4701 Connecticut Ave.
Rosen, Perry M. . . . . . . '55 '81 C.1044 B.A. L.336 J.D. [Akin,G.S.H.&F.] (⊙Denver, CO)
*PRACTICE AREAS: Environmental Litigation; Land Use; Project Litigation; Commercial Litigation.
Rosen, Phillip A. '48 '84 C.882 B.A. L.1209 J.D.
Assoc. Gen. Coun., Nat. Assn. of Sec. Dealers, Inc.
Rosen, Richard L., (AV) . . . . '50 '75 C.453 S.B. L.724 J.D. [Arnold&P.]
*PRACTICE AREAS: Antitrust; Communications; Litigation.
Rosen, Robert M. '37 '60 C.563 B.B.A. L.1009 LL.B.
(adm. in NY; not adm. in DC) 1225 Connecticut Ave., N.W.‡
Rosen, Sol . . . . '36 '64 C.477 B.A. L.178 LL.B. 717 D St., N.W., 4th Fl.
Rosen, Stephen J. . . . . '62 '93 C.674 B.A. L.273 J.D. [Ⓐ Levine,B.B.&B.]
*PRACTICE AREAS: Communications Law.
Rosen, Steven . . . . '70 '98 C.276 B.A. L.273 J.D. [Ⓐ Wilmer,C.&P.]

Rosen & De Martino
(See De Martino Finkelstein Rosen & Virga)

Rosen, Harold, Law Office of
(See Potomac, Maryland)

Rosenau, Kenneth H., (AV) . . . . '55 '80 C.273 B.A. L.30 J.D. [Rosenau&R.]
Rosenau, Susan Hansen . . . . '63 '89 C.881 A.B. L.94 J.D. [Rosenau&R.]
Rosenau & Rosenau, (AV) . . . . 1424 16th St., N.W., Ste. 502
Rosenbaum, Daniel B., (AV) . . . . '44 '69 C.563 B.B.A. L.813 J.D. [Caplin&D.]
*PRACTICE AREAS: Federal Tax Practice; Tax Controversies; Corporate Tax Planning; Employment Tax.
Rosenbaum, Jessica T. . . . . '70 '96 C.674 B.A. L.309 J.D. 666 11th St., N.W.
Rosenbaum, Robert D., (AV) . . . . '43 '68 C.659 B.S. L.178 LL.B. [Arnold&P.]
*PRACTICE AREAS: Corporate; Securities; Litigation.
Rosenbaum, Sidney Jerome, IV . . . '72 '98 C.886 B.S. L.692 J.D. [Ⓐ Grossberg,Y.F.&B.]
*PRACTICE AREAS: Construction; Government Contracts; Real Estate; International; Commercial Litigation.
Rosenbaum, Steven J. . . . . '55 '80 C.846 B.A. L.309 J.D. [Covington&B.]
Rosenberg, Andrew M. . . . . '68 '97 C.31 B.A. L.893 J.D. [Ⓐ Patton B.]
Rosenberg, Craig M. . . . . '62 '87 C.339 B.A. L.273 J.D. 101 Constitution Ave., N.W.
Rosenberg, David A. . . . . '58 '86 C.354 B.A. L.64 J.D. [Ford&H.]
*PRACTICE AREAS: Employment Litigation; Employment Termination; Discrimination; Sexual Harassment Law; Commercial Litigation.
Rosenberg, Heidi Elisabeth . . . . '— '99 C&L.309 A.B., J.D. [Ⓐ Foley&L.]
*PRACTICE AREAS: Intellectual Property Litigation.
Rosenberg, Kermit A., (AV) . . . . '45 '74 C.608 B.S. L.276 J.D. [Tighe P.A.T.]
*PRACTICE AREAS: Bankruptcy; Insolvency.
Rosenberg, Lawrence D. . . . . '67 '92 C.188 B.A. L.659 J.D. [Ⓐ Jones,D.R.&P.]

Rosenberg, Leonard L., (AV) '46 '71 C.994 B.A. L.273 J.D.
[Sandler,T.&R.] (⊙L.A., San Fran., CA; Miami, FL; Chgo., IL; New York, NY; Hous., TX)
*PRACTICE AREAS: Customs Law; Trade Regulation Law; International Law.

Rosenberg, Marvin, (AV) '36 '61
C.1062 B.S.B.A. L.276 J.D. [Holland&K.] (⊙Arlington, VA)
*PRACTICE AREAS: Communications Law.

Rosenberg, Michael T. ... '63 '91 C.183 B.A. L.904 J.D. [Ⓐ P.Stein]

Rosenberg, Rebecca I. '— '92 C.104 A.B. L.309 J.D.
(adm. in PA; not adm. in DC) [Ⓒ Caplin&D.]
*PRACTICE AREAS: International Tax; General Tax.

Rosenberg, Robert D. ... '56 '82 C.103 A.B. L.309 J.D. [Slover&L.]

Rosenberg, Ronald Micah '72 '99 C.846 B.A. L.893 J.D.
(adm. in FL; not adm. in DC) US DOJ/INS

Rosenberg, Ruth Borsuk, (AV) ... '35 '64 C.705 A.B. L.659 J.D. [Nixon P.]
*PRACTICE AREAS: Leases and Leasing; Real Estate; Zoning, Planning and Land Use.

Rosenberg, Meryl Berger
(See Potomac, Maryland)

Rosenberger, Francine J. ... '67 '95 C.372 B.A. L.128 J.D. [Ⓐ Kirkpatrick&L.]
*PRACTICE AREAS: Investment Company Law; Investment Management; Investment Regulation; Mutual Funds.

Rosenblat, Alan ... '26 '55 C&L.145 B.A., J.D. [Ⓒ Dechert]
*PRACTICE AREAS: Investment Management; Financial Services Law.

Rosenblatt, Gregg H. '— '99 C.896 B.S. L.1209 J.D.
(adm. in MD; not adm. in DC) [Ⓐ Foley&L.]
*PRACTICE AREAS: Patent Prosecution; Patent Applications; Patent Litigation; Licensing; Intellectual Property Agreements.

Rosenblatt, Howard T. ... '61 '86 C.880 B.A. L.228 J.D. [Howrey S.A.&W.]
*PRACTICE AREAS: Antitrust; Commercial Litigation.

Rosenblatt, Marni K. ... '70 '99 C.1044 B.S. L.472 J.D. [Ⓐ Baker&M.]
*PRACTICE AREAS: Taxation.

Rosenblatt, Peter R., (AV) ... '33 '59 C&L.976 B.A., LL.B. [Heller&R.]
*PRACTICE AREAS: International Transactions; Federal Government Law.

Rosenbloom, H. David, (AV) ... '41 '67 C.674 A.B. L.309 J.D. [Caplin&D.]
*PRACTICE AREAS: Federal Tax Practice.

Rosenbloom, Joel, (AV) ... '30 '54 C.339 B.A. L.347 J.D. [Ⓒ Wilmer,C.&P.]
*PRACTICE AREAS: Communications Law; Mass Media Law.

Rosenblum, Elyse '66 '94 C.951 B.A. L.846 J.D.
(adm. in PA; not adm. in DC) 555 13th St., N.W.‡

Rosenblum, Jeff '72 '99 C.446 B.A. L.424 J.D.
(adm. in IL; not adm. in DC) [Ⓐ Arent F.K.P.&K.]
*PRACTICE AREAS: Commercial Litigation.

Rosenblum, Mark C. '54 '80 C.446 B.A. L.477 J.D.
(adm. in NY; not adm. in DC) V.P., AT&T

Rosenblum, Robert H. ... '— '87 C.1349 B.A. L.276 J.D. [Kirkpatrick&L.]
*PRACTICE AREAS: Investment Partnerships; Financial Services Regulation; Broker-Dealer Regulation; Investment Regulation; Private Placements.

Rosenfeld, Dana B. ... '59 '85 C.446 B.A. L.904 J.D. [Ⓒ Bryan C.]
*PRACTICE AREAS: Advertising Law; Consumer Protection; Privacy Law.

Rosenfeld, Douglas E. ... '58 '87 C.867 B.A. L.904 J.D. 1912 Sunderland Pl., N.W.

Rosenfeld, Evan L. ... '66 '91 C.309 A.B. L.659 J.D. [Ⓐ Hogan&H.] (Pat.)
*PRACTICE AREAS: Food and Drug Regulation; Food and Medical Device Regulation.

Rosenfeld, Nancy J. ... '64 '92 C.659 B.A. L.262 J.D. [Ⓐ Coudert B.]

Rosenfield, Harry N., (AV) ... '11 '34 C.563 B.A. L.178 LL.B. 3749 Chesapeake St., NW

Rosenhauer, James J., (AV) ... '42 '68 C.128 A.B. L.976 LL.B. [Hogan&H.]
*PRACTICE AREAS: International Finance; Mergers, Acquisitions and Divestitures; Project Finance; Corporate Law; Commercial Real Estate.

Rosenman, Louis ... '27 '55 C.102 B.A. L.273 J.D. 1725 DeSales St., N.W.

Rosenman & Colin LLP, (AV)
805 15th Street, N.W., 9th Floor, 20005-2212 ⊙
Telephone: 202-216-4600 Facsimile: (202) 216-4700
URL: http://www.rosenman.com
Resident Partners: Howard J. Braun; Richard A. Gross; Timothy J. Lynes; Michael J. Metzger.
Special Counsel: Michael Dean Gaffney; Shelley Sadowsky (Not admitted in DC); Lee Warner Shubert; Sandra L. Spalletta. Resident Associates: Laura A. Otis.
General Practice.
New York, N.Y. Office: 575 Madison Avenue, 10022. Telephone: 212-940-8800. Facsimiles: (212) 940-8776; (212) 935-0679. Website: http://www.rosenman.com.
Newark, New Jersey Office: Suite 2600, 1 Gateway Center, 07102-5397. Telephone: 973-645-0572. Facsimile: 973-645-0573.
Charlotte, North Carolina Office: 401 South Tryon Street, Suite 2600, 28202-1935. Telephone: 704-444-2000. Facsimile: 704-444-2060.
See Professional Biographies, WASHINGTON, DISTRICT OF COLUMBIA

Rosenow, Scott Edward ... '61 '88 C&L.494 B.A., J.D. [Ⓒ Stein S.S.&O.]
*PRACTICE AREAS: Customs Law; International Trade Law.

Rosenstein, Andrew B. ... '72 '98 C.477 B.B.A. L.273 J.D. [Ⓐ McKee N.]
*PRACTICE AREAS: Securities; Venture Capital; Mergers and Acquisitions; Corporate.

Rosenstein, Daniel N., (AV) ... '66 '91 C.575 A.B. L.128 J.D. [Levin&R.]
*PRACTICE AREAS: Agricultural Law; Government Contracts; Insurance; Administrative Law.

Rosenstein, Mace J., (AV) ... '53 '84 C.309 B.A. L.145 J.D. [Hogan&H.]
*PRACTICE AREAS: Communications and Media; Broadcast Regulation; Broadcast Station Transfers; Public Broadcasting; Telecommunications Regulation.

Rosenstock, Howard J., (AV) ... '54 '80 C.446 B.A. L.276 J.D. [Hogan&H.]
*PRACTICE AREAS: Real Estate; Finance.

Rosenthal, Barry P., (AV) ... '48 '74 C.696 B.A. L.659 J.D. [Bingham D.]
*PRACTICE AREAS: Commercial Real Estate; Real Estate Finance; Corporate Law.

Rosenthal, Brian '78 '01 C.028 B.Sc. L.188 J.D.
(adm. in NY; not adm. in DC) [Ⓐ Howrey S.A.&W.]

Rosenthal, Chandra Triplett '68 '94 C.174 B.A. L.596 J.D.
Assoc., Defenders of Wildlife

Rosenthal, Douglas E., (AV) ... '40 '68 C&L.976 A.B., LL.B. [Sonnenschein N.&R.]

Rosenthal, Eric David '63 '93 C.145 B.A. L.276 J.D.
(adm. in NY; not adm. in DC) Mental Disab. Rights Intl.

Rosenthal, Herbert A., (AV) ... '41 '66 C.976 A.B. L.893 LL.B. [H.A.Rosenthal]

Rosenthal, Ilene G., (AV) '52 '83
C.918 B.A. L.276 J.D. Gen. Coun., Software Publishers Assocs.

Rosenthal, J. W., (AV) ... '19 '43 C.563 B.S. L.309 J.D. 1250 Connecticut Ave., N.W.

Rosenthal, James M. ... '71 '96 C.668 B.A. L.477 J.D. [Ⓐ Arnold&P.]
*PRACTICE AREAS: Litigation.

Rosenthal, Jay A. ... '57 '85 C.30 B.A. L.1162 J.D. [Berliner,C.&R.]
*PRACTICE AREAS: Entertainment; Intellectual Property; Internet Law; Copyright and Trademark.

Rosenthal, Jessica N. ... '74 '99 C.860 B.A. L.273 J.D. [Ⓐ Wiley R.&F.]

Rosenthal, John J. ... '62 '89 C.367 B.A. L.893 J.D. [Howrey S.A.&W.]
*PRACTICE AREAS: Antitrust Law; Complex Commercial Litigation; Franchise Litigation.

Rosenthal, Karen A. ... '64 '93 C.1369 B.A. L.893 J.D. [Ⓐ Crowell&M.]

Rosenthal, Linda K. ... '61 '87 C&L.893 B.A., J.D. [Ⓒ Dyer E.&J.]
*PRACTICE AREAS: Securities; Mergers, Acquisitions and Divestitures; Corporate Law.

Rosenthal, Michael L. ... '68 '94 C.188 B.S. L.309 J.D. [Ⓐ Covington&B.]

Rosenthal, Oren ... '71 '96 C.597 B.S. L.477 J.D. [Ⓐ Wiley R.&F.]

Rosenthal, Paul C., (AV) ... '50 '76 C.112 A.B. L.1067 J.D. [Collier S.S.]
*PRACTICE AREAS: International Trade.

Rosenthal, Roger C. '50 '76 C.976 B.A. L.276 J.D.
Exec. Dir., Migrant Legal Action Prog.

Rosenthal, Samuel ... '50 '76 C&L.188 B.S., J.D. [Curtis,M.C.&M.]
*PRACTICE AREAS: Civil Litigation; International Litigation.

Rosenthal, Steven M. ... '57 '85 C.112 A.B. L.1066 J.D. [Miller&C.]
*PRACTICE AREAS: Tax Law.

Rosenthal, Steven S., (AV) ... '49 '74 C.197 A.B. L.309 J.D. [Holland&K.]
*PRACTICE AREAS: Trial and Appellate Litigation; Administrative Law; Financial Institutions.

Rosenthal, Stuart P. '57 '85 C.475 B.A. L.976 J.D.
Pres., Senior Beacon of Greater Washington, Inc.

Rosenthal, Herbert A., Chartered, (AV) ... 1050 Seventeenth Street, N.W., Suite 1200

Rosenzweig, Paul S. ... '59 '87 C.311 B.A. L.145 J.D. [Rosenzweig]
*PRACTICE AREAS: Appellate Practice; Legal Ethics; Environmental Criminal Law; Federal Criminal Law; Federal Civil Litigation.

Rosenzweig, Sidney A. ... '72 '98 C.103 B.S. L.659 J.D. [Ⓐ Arnold&P.]
*PRACTICE AREAS: Intellectual Property; Technology Law.

Rosenzweig Law Office, L.L.P.
516 C Street Northeast, Suite 300, 20002
Telephone: 202-543-9370 Fax: 202-543-9372 URL: http://www.rosenzweiglaw.com
Email: psr@rosenzweiglaw.com URL: http://www.lawyers.com/rosenzweiglawoffice
Paul S. Rosenzweig.
Supreme Court and Federal Appeals, White Collar Crimes, Grand Jury Practice, Legal Ethics, Legal and Professional Malpractice, Administrative Law, Legislative Practice, Environmental Law and Environmental Criminal Defense.
See Professional Biographies, WASHINGTON, DISTRICT OF COLUMBIA

Rosette, Kristina ... '66 '95 C.276 B.S.F.S. L.280 J.D. [Ⓐ Covington&B.]
*PRACTICE AREAS: Communications and Media; Domain Name Infringement; Internet Law; Trademarks; Trademark Protection.

Rosic, Edward A., Jr. '57 '83
C.216 B.A. L.188 J.D. V.P. & Asst. Gen. Coun., Marriott Intl., Inc.
*RESPONSIBILITIES: Employee Benefits; Executive Compensation.

Rosini, Matthew M. ... '72 '97 C&L.93 B.S., J.D. [Ⓐ Brobeck,P.&H.]

Rosinski, Douglas J. '59 '97 C.696 B.S. L.790 J.D.
(adm. in SC; not adm. in DC) [Ⓐ Shaw P.]
*PRACTICE AREAS: Energy Law.

Rosman, Adam L. ... '65 '96 C.867 B.A.P.S. L.813 J.D. Asst. U.S. Atty.

Rosman, Michael E. ... '59 '85 C.696 B.A. L.976 J.D. Gen. Coun., Ctr. for Indiv. Rights

Rosner, Abraham J. ... '56 '88 C.276 B.S. L.1209 J.D. [Sughrue M.] (See Pat. Sect.)
*PRACTICE AREAS: Intellectual Property Law.

Ross, Beverly D. ... '46 '74 C.569 B.A. L.276 J.D. [Ⓒ Miller T.W.&L.]
*PRACTICE AREAS: International Banking; International Trade and Finance; Maritime Law.

Ross, Bradford, (AV) ... '12 '36 C.893 L.273 LL.B. 1401 "H" St. N.W.

Ross, Brendan J. ... '67 '93 C.813 A.B. L.228 J.D. Sr. Coun., Marriott International
*RESPONSIBILITIES: International Business; Corporate Transactions; Financing.

Ross, David E. ... '71 '95 C.367 B.A. L.178 J.D. [Kellogg,H.H.T.&E.]
*PRACTICE AREAS: Litigation.

Ross, David G. '71 '97 C.390 B.A. L.30 J.D.
(adm. in NJ; not adm. in DC) [Ⓐ Goldstein&L.] ⊙
*PRACTICE AREAS: Franchise Law.

Ross, David M. ... '68 '98 C.928 B.A. L.273 J.D. 1875 Connecticut Avenue, N.W.

Ross, Deborah Komins ... '71 '96 C&L.276 B.S.F.S., J.D. Corp. Coun., Marriott Int., Inc.
*RESPONSIBILITIES: Hotel and Resort Law; Corporate Law.

Ross, Donald K. ... '47 '70 C.262 B.A. L.569 J.D. [Mehri,M.&R.]
*PRACTICE AREAS: Lobbying; Governmental Relations.

Ross, Edward D., Jr. ... '45 '70 C.755 B.A. L.276 J.D. [Ⓒ Skadden,A.S.M.&F.]

Ross, Edwin G. '21 '51 C.178 B.S. L.569 J.D.
(adm. in NY; not adm. in DC) 3003 Van Ness St., N.W.

Ross, Elisabeth Hewitt, (AV) ... '52 '78 C.103 B.A. L.588 J.D. [Birch,H.B.&C.]
*PRACTICE AREAS: Communications; Public Utilities; Administrative; Energy; Legislative.

Ross, Gail E. ... '55 '80 C.860 B.A. L.276 J.D. [Lichtman,T.S.&R.]

Ross, John J., (AV) ... '29 '56 C.885 B.S. L.276 LL.B. [Ⓒ Hogan&H.]
*PRACTICE AREAS: Labor Law.

Ross, John S., III ... '57 '83 C.976 A.B. L.893 J.D. [Ⓒ Silverstein&M.]
*PRACTICE AREAS: Federal and State Taxation; Tax Controversies; Real Estate.

Ross, Lawrence J., (AV) ... '39 '66 C.597 B.S. L.477 J.D. [Ross]

Ross, Matthew E. ... '71 '97 C.367 B.A. L.1009 J.D. [Ⓐ Cameron M.]
*PRACTICE AREAS: Energy Law; Public Utilities Law; Corporate Law; International Law.

Ross, Meredith J. '71 '98 C.860 B.A. L.93 J.D.
(adm. in MA; not adm. in DC) [Ⓐ Dickstein S.M.&O.]
*PRACTICE AREAS: Corporate Law.

Ross, Michael K. ... '67 '93 C.668 B.A. L.477 J.D. Sr. Coun., Marriott International, Inc.
*RESPONSIBILITIES: Hotel and Resort Law.

Ross, Michele D. ... '56 '83 C.30 B.A. L.1065 J.D. [Shaw P.]
*PRACTICE AREAS: Corporate Finance; Securities.

Ross, Peter D., (AV) ... '61 '86 C.813 A.B. L.309 J.D. [Wiley R.&F.]
*PRACTICE AREAS: Internet; Electronic Commerce; Communications.

Ross, Renee S. ... '50 '76 C.30 B.A. L.904 J.D. 4854 Reservoir Rd. NW

Ross, Riley Henderson, III ... '71 '99 C.889 B.S. L.893 J.D. [Ⓐ Williams&C.]
*PRACTICE AREAS: Litigation.

Ross, Ronald R. ... '60 '86 C.976 B.A. L.309 J.D. [Troutman S.]
*PRACTICE AREAS: Project Finance; Privatizations; Acquisitions; Corporate; Public Finance.

Ross, Simone ... '66 '93 C.813 A.B. L.276 J.D. [Ⓐ Covington&B.]

Ross, Stanford G., (AV) ... '31 '57 C.910 B.A. L.309 J.D. [Arnold&P.]
*PRACTICE AREAS: Tax; Administrative Law.

Ross, Steven J., (AV) ... '56 '82 C.1044 B.A. L.326 J.D. [Steptoe&J.]
*PRACTICE AREAS: Energy; Litigation.

Ross, Steven R., (AV) ... '51 '76 C.264 B.A. L.273 J.D. [Akin,G.S.H.&F.]
*PRACTICE AREAS: Public Policy; White Collar Criminal Defense.

Ross, Stuart Philip, (AV) ... '40 '67 C&L.273 A.B., LL.B. [Ross,D.&B.]

Ross, Susan B. ... '60 '94 C.228 B.S.E. L.36 J.D. [Ⓐ Piper M.R.&W.]
*PRACTICE AREAS: Information Technology; Venture Capital; Emerging Growth Companies.

Ross, Terence P. ... '58 '83 C.813 A.B. L.893 J.D. [Gibson,D.&C.]
*PRACTICE AREAS: Technical Litigation; Intellectual Property Litigation; Communications and Media Law; Computers and Software Law.

Ross, Valerie Ellen ... '66 '93 C.475 B.S. L.145 J.D. [Shea&G.]
*PRACTICE AREAS: Civil Litigation; Environmental Law; Professional Practices.

Ross, Dixon & Bell, L.L.P., (AV) BB
2001 K Street, N.W., 20006-1040 ⊙
Telephone: 202-662-2000 Fax: 202-662-2190
Email: info@rdblaw.com URL: http://www.rdblaw.com
Partners: Leslie S. Ahari; Daniel Aronowitz; Alec M. Barinholtz (Resident, Irvine, California); Roy Morrow Bell (Irvine and San Diego, California); Charles T. Blair; Eileen King Bower (Resident, Chicago, Illinois); William H. Briggs, Jr.; Wallace A. Christensen; Gary V. Dixon; John W. Duchelle; David R. Dwares; Barbara E. Etkind; Elizabeth Sarah Gere; John R. Gerstein; David M. Gische; Charles I. Hadden; Sean M. Hanifin; Van E. Haynie (Resident, San Diego, California); Merril Jay Hirsh; Timothy P. Irving (Irvine and San Diego, California); Carmen R. Kelley; Thomas T. Locke; Lewis K. Loss; Stacey L. McGraw; Terrence R. McInnis (Irvine and San Diego, California); Fletcher W. Paddison (Resident, San Diego, California); Robert M. Pozin (Irvine and San Diego, California); Richard J. Pratt; Rebecca L. Ross (Resident, Chicago, Illinois); Stuart Philip Ross; Cathy Ann Simon;

(This Listing Continued)

Ross, Dixon & Bell, L.L.P. (Continued)

Richard A. Simpson; James W. Stubblefield (Resident, San Diego, California); Van A. Tengberg (Resident, San Diego, California); Peter G. Thompson; Michael P. Tone (Resident, Chicago, Illinois); Karen Hahn Ventrell; Michael J. Whitton (Resident, San Diego, California); Solomon Louis Wisenberg. Of Counsel: Michael G. Bruton (Resident, Chicago, Illinois); Clinton E. Cameron (Resident, Chicago, Illinois); Hallie Miller Fahey (Resident, Chicago, Illinois); Michele L. Lynch (Resident, Irvine, California); Harold E. Masback, III; James T. Waring (Resident, San Diego, California). Associates: Calandra A. Almond (Not admitted in DC); Christopher P. "Hawk" Barry (Resident, San Diego, California); Kimberly E. Blair (Resident, Chicago, Illinois); Julie L. Burgener (Resident, Chicago, Illinois); Sheila R. Caudle (Not admitted in DC); Patricia E. Charles (Resident, Chicago, Illinois); Jodi L. Cleesattle; Daniel J. Cross (Resident, San Diego, California); Jacqueline K. Cuncannan; James J. Dalessio (Resident, San Diego, California); J. Kirk Donnelly (Resident, Irvine, California); Benjamin C. Eggert; Vicki Bajefsky Fishman; Monique M. Fuentes (Resident, Irvine, California); Jennifer L. Gates (Not admitted in DC); Stephen M. Hall; David A. Harrington; Jason S. Hartley (Resident, San Diego, California); Carol Schanno Johnson; Charles A. Jones; Christopher A. Jones; Thomas J. Judge; Kevin Fomasi Kieffer (Resident, Irvine, California); G. Scott Kirkpatrick; Peter D. Lindau (Resident, Chicago, Illinois); Jason M. Lindner (Resident, San Diego, California); Jennifer Mathis (Resident, Irvine, California); Heather E. McIntyre (Not admitted in DC); Joshua A. Mooney; Kim S. Orbeck (Resident, Irvine, California); Erik Pritchard; Sasha L. Ransom (Resident, Irvine, California); Paul A. Rauner (Resident, Chicago, Illinois Office); Gabriela A. Richeimer; Stacey Engelbrecht Rufe; Amy K. Savage; Stephanie T. Schmelz; Pragna Soni; Cathlene A. Tharp; Scott E. Turner (Not admitted in DC; Resident, Chicago, Illinois); Paul C. Vitrano; Christopher L. Walters (Resident, San Diego, California); Jeffrey J. Ward; Julia C. Weissman (Resident, Irvine, California); Jon R. Williams (Resident, San Diego, California); Laura Cohen Zimmitti. Staff Attorneys: Jo Ann Abramson; Sharon Lynn Gibson; Marcus B. Holladay; Becki Fomasi Kieffer (Resident, Irvine, California); Beth A. Koehler; Jenni R. Wallace.

General Trial and Appellate Practice before State and Federal Courts, Insurance Coverage Litigation and Counseling, Directors and Officers Liability, Professional Liability, Environmental/Mass Tort Coverage, White Collar Criminal Defense, Antitrust.

Irvine, California Office: 5 Park Plaza, Suite 1200, 92614. Telephone: 949-622-2700. Fax: 949-622-2739.

San Diego, California Office: 550 West B Street, Suite 400, 92101-3538. Telephone: 619-235-4040. Fax: 619-231-8796.

Chicago, Illinois Office: 3 First National Plaza, 70 West Madison Street, Suite 525, 60602-4261. Telephone: 312-759-1920. Fax: 312-759-1939.

See Professional Biographies, WASHINGTON, DISTRICT OF COLUMBIA

Ross & Hardies, (AV)
A Partnership including Professional Corporations
888 - 16th Street, N.W., 20006-4103 ⊙
Telephone: 202-296-8600 Fax: 202-296-8791
Email: marketing@rosshardies.com URL: http://www.rosshardies.com
Resident Partners: John R. Fornaciari; Charles W. Petty, Jr.; James A. Stenger. Of Counsel: Paula DiMeo Grant.
General Practice before all Courts, Departments and Administrative Agencies. Antitrust and Litigation, Communications and Telecommunications, Corporate, Customs and International Trade, Employment and Labor Law, Banking, Insurance and Financial Services, Health Care, Housing, Immigration, Securities, Taxation, White Collar Criminal Defense and Technology and eCommerce.
Chicago, Illinois Office: Suite 2500, 150 North Michigan Avenue. Telephone: 312-558-1000. Fax: 312-750-8600.
New York, N.Y. Office: 65 East 55th Street. Telephone: 212-421-5555. Fax: 212-421-5682.

See Professional Biographies, WASHINGTON, DISTRICT OF COLUMBIA

Ross Legal Group, P.C., (AV) .... 1700 K Street, N.W., Suite 1100

Ross, Marsh & Foster, (AV)
2001 "L" Street, N.W. Suite 400, 20036
Telephone: 202-822-8888 Fax: 202-775-9330
Email: rmfmarsh@aol.com
Members of Firm: Bernard A. Foster, Jr. (1909-1968); Richard S. T. Marsh; James D. McKinney, Jr.; Bernard A. Foster, III; John M. Lynham, Jr.; Donald B. Robertson; John Mourer Bixler; William E. Davis; Raymond L. Gooch. Of Counsel: Joseph M. McManus.
General Civil Practice. Corporate, Administrative, Health Care, Energy, Real Estate, Probate, Tax, Exempt Organizations and Litigation.

See Professional Biographies, WASHINGTON, DISTRICT OF COLUMBIA

Rosselli Del Turco, William D. '68 '99 C.856 B.A. L.1194 J.D.
(adm. in MD; not adm. in DC) 4540 MacArthur Blvd., Ste. 205

Rosser, Adam J. .... '71 '00 C.93 B.A. L.276 J.D. [Ⓐ Hunton&W.]
*PRACTICE AREAS: Immigration; Nationality.

Rosser, Matthew C. .... '65 '90 C.188 B.A. L.477 J.D. Assoc. Gen. Coun., AARP
*RESPONSIBILITIES: Internet Law; Technology Law; Corporate Law; Intellectual Property.

Rossetti, John J., Jr. .... '64 '92 C.1041 B.A. L.128 J.D. [Riselli&P.]

Rossi, James A. .... '36 '69 C.645 B.S.I.E. L.569 J.D. [Ⓒ Skadden,A.S.M.&F.]

Rossi, Matthew A. .... '64 '94 C.1031 B.A. L.188 J.D. [Ⓒ Akin,G.S.H.&F.]
*PRACTICE AREAS: Litigation.

Rossides, Eugene T., (AV) .... '27 '53 C&L.178 A.B., J.D. 607 14th St., N.W.

Rossier, Richard T., (AV) .... '54 '79 C.477 B.A. L.276 J.D. [McLeod,W.&M.]
*PRACTICE AREAS: Civil Litigation; Commercial Law; Real Estate Law.

Rossman, Kenneth F., IV .... '68 '96 C.893 B.A. L.1209 J.D. [Ⓐ Boies,S.&F.]
*PRACTICE AREAS: Complex Commercial Litigation; Antitrust.

Rossman, Richard A., (AV) '39 '64 C&L.477 A.B., J.D.
(adm. in MI; not adm. in DC) [Pepper H.] (⊙Detroit, MI)
*PRACTICE AREAS: Commercial Litigation; White Collar Crime.

Rossotti, Barbara M., (P.C.), (AV) .... '40 '64 C.518 B.A. L.309 LL.B. [Shaw P.]
*PRACTICE AREAS: Corporate; Technology; International Transactions.

Rost, Catherine Haley, (BV) '59 '85 C.197 B.A. L.273 J.D.
1050 17th St. NW, Ste. 1100

Rost, Rynthia Manning '55 '80
C.254 B.A. L.1119 J.D. Vice President Public Affairs, GEICO Corp.

Rostow, Victoria P. .... '56 '85 C&L.976 B.A., J.D. [Ⓒ Gibson,D.&C.]
*PRACTICE AREAS: Banks and Banking; Government.

Rostron, Allen K. '68 '95 C.893 B.A. L.976 J.D.
(adm. in NY; not adm. in DC) Center to Prevent Handgun Violence

Rotberg, Eugene H. .... '30 '54 C.831 B.S. L.659 LL.B. The World Bk.

Rotella, Robert F. '41 '68
C.569 B.E.E. L.273 J.D. [Ⓒ Finnegan,H.F.G.&D.] (See Pat. Sect.)
*PRACTICE AREAS: Intellectual Property.

Roth, Alan J., (AV) .... '33 '58 C&L.309 A.B., LL.B. [Spiegel&M.]
*PRACTICE AREAS: Administrative Law; Energy; Natural Gas; Natural Gas Regulation; Utility Law.

Roth, Andrew D. .... '61 '88 C.188 B.S. L.477 J.D. [Bredhoff&K.]

Roth, Anthony C. .... '57 '83 C.288 B.A. L.602 J.D. [Morgan,L.&B.]

Roth, Aviva M. '74 '98 C.994 B.A. L.1398 J.D.
(adm. in NJ; not adm. in DC) [Ⓐ Hawkins,D.&W.]

Roth, Christopher B. .... '— '99 C.679 B.S. L.494 J.D. [Ⓐ Banner&W.] (See Pat. Sect.)
*PRACTICE AREAS: Intellectual Property Law; Intellectual Property Litigation; Chemical Intellectual Property; Patent Prosecution.

Roth, Daniel S. .... '57 '85 C.1350 B.A. L.904 J.D. 4530 Wisconsin Ave Nw # 200

Roth, Debra L. '— '86 C.1375 B.A. L.112 J.D.
(adm. in CA; not adm. in DC) [Ⓒ Berliner,C.&J.]

Roth, Debra L. .... '62 '89 C.94 B.A. L.30 J.D. [Shaw,B.V.&R.]
*PRACTICE AREAS: Employment Law; Litigation.

Roth, Evan J. .... '60 '86 C.860 B.A. L.276 J.D. 725 12th St. NW

Roth, Gabrielle S. .... '64 '90 C.696 B.A. L.273 J.D. [Dickstein S.M.&O.]
*PRACTICE AREAS: Trademark and Copyright Prosecution; Intellectual Property Litigation; Unfair Competition Litigation.

Roth, Holly A. .... '— '95 C.773 B.A. L.904 J.D. [Ⓐ Manatt,P.&P.]

Roth, Leo A., Jr., (AV) .... '42 '68 C.896 B.A. L.30 J.D. [Brault,G.S.&B.] ⊙
*PRACTICE AREAS: General Civil Litigation; Personal Injury; Professional Malpractice.

Roth, Pamela H. '61 '85 C.401 B.A. L.273 J.D.
601 Pennsylvania Avenue N.W., Suite 900 South PMB 263

Roth, Patricia O. .... '42 '87 C&L.276 B.S., J.D. Prof. of Law, D.C. Sch. of Law.

Roth, Randall D. '— '96 C.1044 B.A. L.659 J.D.
(adm. in NY; not adm. in DC) [Ⓐ Wiley R.&F.]
*PRACTICE AREAS: Litigation; Insurance Law.

Roth, Robert L. .... '54 '82 C.401 B.A. L.823 J.D. [Crowell&M.]
*PRACTICE AREAS: Health Care; Health Insurance; Employee Benefits; Legislation; Litigation.

Roth, Stephen E., (AV) .... '51 '78 C.602 A.B. L.976 J.D. [Sutherland A.&B.]
*PRACTICE AREAS: Investment Management; Insurance Regulation; Securities Regulation; Mutual Funds; Insurance Products.

Roth, Steven M., (AV) .... '42 '68 C.645 B.A. L.228 LL.B. P.O. Box 57160

Rothandler, Stephen M. .... '68 '93 C.1349 B.A. L.30 J.D. [C.C.P.Chrtd.&Assoc.]

Rothberg, Michael D. .... '69 '94 C.910 B.A. L.309 J.D. [Ⓐ Dow,L.&A.]

Rothblatt, Martine A. .... '54 '81 C.112 B.A. L.1068 J.D. [Mahon P.R.&F.]

Rothell, Bonnie Hochman, (BV) .... '63 '88 C.1036 B.A. L.472 J.D. [Krooth&A.]
*PRACTICE AREAS: Litigation; Employment Law; Alternative Dispute Resolution.

Rothenberg, Pamela V. .... '58 '84 C.860 B.A. L.597 J.D. [Womble C.S.&R.]
*PRACTICE AREAS: Business Formation and Planning; Commercial and Real Estate Transactions; Real Estate and Technology; Contracts; Leasing.

Rothfarb, Lauren ....'59 '85 C.112 B.A. L.1065 J.D. Intl. Union of Elec. Wkrs., AFL-CIO

Rothfeld, Charles, (AV) .... '56 '82 C.188 A.B. L.145 J.D. [Ⓒ Mayer,B.&P.]

Rothman, Larry P. .... '52 '79 C.309 A.B. L.94 J.D. 4120 Harrison St., N.W.

Rothman, Michael S. .... '70 '99 C.1365 B.A. L.446 J.D. [Ⓐ Arent F.K.P.&K.]
*PRACTICE AREAS: Commercial Litigation; Intellectual Property Litigation; Electronic Commerce.

Rothman, Stuart, (AV) .... '14 '37 C&L.494 B.S., LL.B. 607 14th St., N.W.

Rothman, Yeeleng '53 '84 C.821 B.A. L.893 J.D.
Lead Coun., Commercial Restructuring, INTELSAT

Rothrock, Aubrey A., III .... '68 '93 C&L.575 B.A., J.D. [Patton B.]

Rothrock, Jerry E., (AV) .... '45 '75 C.691 B.A. L.309 J.D. [Akin,G.S.H.&F.]
*PRACTICE AREAS: Energy.

Rothschild-Seidel, Aleen ....'52 '77 C.860 B.A. L.280 J.D. 3201 New Mexico Ave., N.W.

Rothstein, Amy L. '63 '87 C.1365 B.A. L.245 J.D.
Sr. Coun., Corp. Affs., Philip Morris Mgmt. Corp.

Rothstein, Julius .... '— '93 C.893 B.A. L.945 J.D. Asst. U.S. Atty.

Rothstein, Paul F. '— '61
C&L.597 B,S.L., LL.B. Prof. of Law, Georgetown Univ. Law Ctr.

Rothstein, Paul M. .... '— '90 C.976 B.A. L.813 J.D. [Ⓒ Fried,F.H.S.&J.]
*PRACTICE AREAS: Technology Transactions; Internet Transactions; Intellectual Property.

Rothwarf, Marta .... '57 '90 425 I St. N.W.

Rothwell, David J., (AV) .... '47 '78 C.188 B.A. L.1162 J.D. [O'Toole,R.N.&S.]

Rothwell, G. Franklin, (AV) '28 '56
C.502 B.S.M.E. L.273 J.D. [Rothwell,F.E.&M.] (See Pat. Sect.)
*PRACTICE AREAS: Intellectual Property.

Rothwell, Robert J. '66 '94 C.1369 B.B.A. L.128 J.D.
(adm. in VA; not adm. in DC) [Ⓐ Vinson&E.]
*PRACTICE AREAS: Litigation.

Rothwell, Suzanne E. .... '45 '81 C.273 B.B.A. L.537 J.D. [Ⓒ Skadden,A.S.M.&F.]

Rothwell, Figg, Ernst & Manbeck, A Professional Corporation, (AV) BB
Suite 701 East Tower, 555 Thirteenth Street, N.W., 20004 ⊙
Telephone: 202-783-6040 Facsimile: 202-783-6031
Email: info@rothwellfigg.com URL: http://www.rothwellfigg.com
G. Franklin Rothwell; E. Anthony Figg; Barbara G. Ernst; Harry F. Manbeck, Jr.; George R. Repper; Steven Lieberman; Vincent M. DeLuca; Joseph A. Hynds; Robert J. Jondle (Resident, Omaha, Nebraska Office); Elizabeth A. Leff;—Martha Cassidy; Gregg L. Jansen (Not admitted in DC; Resident, Omaha, Nebraska Office); Nancy T. Morris (Not admitted in DC; Resident, Omaha, Nebraska Office); Lisa A. Fahien Uldrich (Not admitted in DC; Resident, Omaha, Nebraska Office); Robert H. Cameron; Richard Wydeven; Thomas Edward McKiernan (Not admitted in DC); Jason M. Shapiro (Not admitted in DC); Michael John Moran (Not admitted in DC); Anne M. Sterba; Lisa N. Phillips (Not admitted in DC); Leigh M. Zanowski (Not admitted in DC); C. Nichole Gifford (Not admitted in DC). Of Counsel: Don M. Kerr (Not admitted in DC); Jeffrey L. Ihnen; Glenn E. Karta; Mark I. Bowditch; Minaksi Bhatt; Michael G. Sullivan.
Intellectual Property Law, Practice and Related Litigation, including Patent, Trademark, Copyright, Unfair Competition, Trade Secrets, Licensing and Related Antitrust Law. Defamation Law and other First Amendment Issues.
Omaha, Nebraska Office: 13906 Gold Circle, Suite 204, 68144. Telephone: 402-333-1550. Fax: 402-333-1510.

See Professional Biographies, WASHINGTON, DISTRICT OF COLUMBIA

Rottenberg, Julie B. .... '68 '94 C.763 A.B. L.273 J.D. [Arnold&P.]
*PRACTICE AREAS: Litigation.

Rotwein, Jos., (AV) .... '20 '41 C.846 L.910 LL.B. 1500 Mass. Ave., N.W.

Rouleau, Louis J. '— '97 C.184 B.A. L.30 J.D.
(adm. in MD; not adm. in DC) [Ⓐ Piper M.R.&W.]
*PRACTICE AREAS: Litigation.

Roundtree, Dovey J., (Mrs.) .... '14 '51 C.811 A.B. L.329 LL.B. [Roundtree,H.&P.]

Roundtree, Hunter & Parker, (BV) ....1822 11th St., N.W.

Rounsaville, John, Jr., (AV) .... '44 '73 C.846 A.B. L.309 J.D. [Wilmer,C.&P.]
*PRACTICE AREAS: Civil Practice; Criminal Practice; International Law; Antitrust and Trade Regulation.

Rouse, William M. '39 '64 C.496 B.S. L.500 LL.B.
(adm. in MS; not adm. in DC) 401 M St., N.E.‡

Roush, Corey W. .... '72 '97 C.880 B.A. L.276 J.D. [Ⓐ Hogan&H.]
*PRACTICE AREAS: Antitrust and Trade Regulation; Consumer Law; Privacy Law; Internet Law; Unfair Competition.

Rouson, Brigette M. .... '57 '83 C.329 B.A. L.276 J.D. 2311 N Capitol St NE

Roussel, Robert Walter .... '16 '54 C.999 B.A. L.1009 J.D. 1730 K St., N.W.

Rousselot, Peter F., (AV) .... '42 '67 C.976 B.A. L.309 LL.B. Union Pacific Corp.

Routh, Steven J. .... '57 '83 C.659 B.A. L.309 J.D. [Hogan&H.]
*PRACTICE AREAS: Litigation; Complex Litigation; Intellectual Property Litigation; Trial Practice; Education Law.

Routhier, Vincent M. '63 '97 C.012 B.A. L.014 LL.B.
(adm. in NY; not adm. in DC) 818 Connecticut Avenue, N.W., Suite 700

Rouvelas, Emanuel L., (AV) .... '44 '68 C.911 B.A. L.309 J.D. [Preston G.E.&R.M.]
*PRACTICE AREAS: Governmental Relations Law; Maritime; Transportation.

Rouvelas, Mary P. '— '96 C.914 B.A. L.893 J.D.
Legislative Counsel, American Cancer Society, Inc.

Rovner, Gary S. .... '— '95 C.197 B.A. L.273 J.D. [Ⓐ Foley&L.]
*PRACTICE AREAS: Environmental Law; Patent Litigation; Trademark Litigation.

Rowan, Carl T., Jr., (AV) .... '52 '79 C.156 B.A. L.276 J.D. [Rowan&G.]

Rowan, Grant K. .... '68 '94 C.446 B.S.E.E. L.273 J.D. [Sughrue M.]
*PRACTICE AREAS: Intellectual Property Law; Litigation.

Rowan, J. Patrick, (BV) .... '64 '89 C.197 B.A. L.893 J.D. Asst. U.S. Atty.

Rowan & Grody, (AV) .... 3251-C Sutton Place, N.W.

Rowat, Malcolm '45 '91 C.012 B.A. L.276 J.D.
(adm. in NY; not adm. in DC) World Bank

Rowden, Marcus A. .... '28 '53 C&L.477 A.B., J.D. [Ⓒ Fried,F.H.S.&J.]

Rowe, Eric C., (BV) .... '58 '83 C.404 A.B. L.575 J.D. [Greenberg T.]

Rowe, Evelyn F., (CV) .... '47 '84 C.890 B.A. L.276 J.D. 1514 17th St., N.W.

Rowe, Frederick M., (AV) . . . . '25 '52 C.563 B.B.A. L.976 LL.B. [Ⓒ Kirkland&E.]
*PRACTICE AREAS: Antitrust; Commercial Litigation; Legislative; International Antitrust and Trade Regulation.
Rowe, James H., III, (AV) . . . . '51 '80 C.309 A.B. L.276 J.D. CLS & Assocs., Inc.
Rowe, Nancy L. . . . . '64 '92 C.105 B.A. L.128 J.D. [Morgan,L.&B.]
Rowe, Richard H., (AV) . . . . '37 '65 C.67 A.B. L.309 J.D. [Proskauer R.]
Rowe, Robert G., III . . . '54 '79 C.95 A.B. L.94 J.D. Independent Bankers Assoc. of Amer.
Rowell, Andrew M. . . . . '73 '99 C.228 B.A. L.893 J.D. [Ⓐ Hogan&H.]
*PRACTICE AREAS: Estate Planning; Corporate Tax.
Roy, Michael L. . . . . '58 '85 C.197 B.A. L.93 J.D. [Hobbs,S.D.&W.]
Royal, Tara L. . . . . '71 '00 C.881 B.A. L.128 J.D. [Ⓐ Kirkpatrick&L.]
*PRACTICE AREAS: Investment Company Law; Investment Management; Investment Regulation; Mutual Funds.
Royal, Vaughn W., (AV) . . . . . . '52 '77 C.373 B.A. L.477 J.D. 5335 Wisconsin Ave., N.W.
Royalty, Phillip G. . . . . '51 '77 C&L.383 B.S., J.D. Ernst & Young

Royce, Sylvia, Law Offices of '45 '77 C.860 B.S. L.1162 J.D.
5505 Connecticut Avenue, NW, Suite 243, 20015
Telephone: 202-362-3445 Fax: 202-686-4271
Email: sylvia_royce@hotmail.com URL: http://www.lawyers.com/sylviaroyce
***PRACTICE AREAS: International Treaty Law; International Criminal Law; International Child Abduction; Post-Conviction Remedies.**
International Prisoner Transfer, Prisoner Exchange, Hague Convention, Proceedings, International Child Abduction, Post Conviction Remedies, Expungement of Records, International Post Conviction Remedies.
See Professional Biographies, WASHINGTON, DISTRICT OF COLUMBIA

Roylance, Abrams, Berdo & Goodman, L.L.P., (AV) BR
1300 19th Street, N.W., Suite 600, 20036-1649
Telephone: 202-659-9076 Facsimile: 202-659-9344
Email: RABG@roylance.com URL: http://www.roylance.com
D. C. Roylance (1920-1995); David S. Abrams; Robert H. Berdo; Alfred N. Goodman; Mark S. Bicks; Richard A. Flynt; John E. Holmes; Michael T. Murphy; Lance G. Johnson; Dean H. Nakamura; Stacey J. Longanecker; Joseph J. Buczynski; Garrett V. Davis. Associates: Antigone E. Juvelis (Not admitted in DC); Tara Laster Hoffman (Not admitted in DC); Jeffrey J. Howell (Not admitted in DC); Aisha Ahmad (Not admitted in DC); Marcus R. Mickney (Not admitted in DC); Christian C. Michel (Not admitted in DC); Mark V. Sparacino (Not admitted in DC); Mark W. Hrozenchik.
Patent, Trademark, Copyright and Unfair Competition Law. International Patent and Trademark Practice. Litigation in all Federal Courts.
See Professional Biographies, WASHINGTON, DISTRICT OF COLUMBIA

Royster, Linda L. . . . . '47 '79 C.890 B.A. L.692 J.D. D.C. Housing Auth.
Rozendaal, John Christopher . . . . '67 '97 C&L.846 B.A., J.D. [Ⓐ Kellogg,H.H.T.&E.]
*PRACTICE AREAS: Litigation; Telecommunications.
Ruane, Michael J., (AV) . . . . '46 '73 C.754 B.A. L.273 J.D. [Holland&K.]
*PRACTICE AREAS: Commercial Real Estate Financing; Commercial Real Estate Sales; Leasing; Hotel Management; Hotel Development.
Rubel, Eric A. . . . . '60 '85 C.478 B.A. L.273 J.D. [Arnold&P.]
*PRACTICE AREAS: Product Safety; Regulatory Law; Products Liability Litigation; Litigation.
Ruben, Robert L. . . . . '62 '86 C.893 B.A. L.1017 J.D. [Ruben&A.]
*PRACTICE AREAS: Securities Law; Corporate Finance; Securities Fraud.

Ruben & Aronson, LLP
3299 K Street, Suite 403, 20036
Telephone: 202-965-3600 Fax: 202-965-3700
Email: laronson@randalaw.com URL: http://www.lawyers.com/rubenandaronsonlaw
Robert L. Ruben; Louis M. Aronson. Associates: Lawrence Alan London (Not admitted in DC); William T. Nesbitt (Not admitted in DC). Of Counsel: Edward A. Friedman (Not admitted in DC); Marshall F. Berman.
Corporate Law, Commercial Transactions, Securities Law, Mergers and Acquisitions, Real Estate, Tax, Labor and Employment, Business Law, Small Business Law, Emerging Business Law, Business Formation.
See Professional Biographies, WASHINGTON, DISTRICT OF COLUMBIA

Rubenfeld, Eric P. . . . . '70 '96 C.112 B.A. L.309 J.D. [Ⓐ Fried,F.H.S.&J.]
*PRACTICE AREAS: Structured Finance.
Rubenstein, David M. . . . . '72 '97 C.245 B.A. L.228 J.D. [Ⓐ Piper M.R.&W.]
*PRACTICE AREAS: Corporate Law.
Rubenstein, David M. '67 '96 C.94 B.S. L.30 J.D.
Asst. Corp. Coun., DC Off. of the Corp. Coun.
Rubenstein, David M., P.C., (AV) . . . . '49 '74 C.228 B.A. L.145 J.D. 2300 N St., N.W.
Rubenstein, Herbert R., (AV) . . . . '53 '82 C.902 B.A. L.276 J.D. [Coroneos&R.]
Rubenstein, Hy David . . . . '56 '80 C.1139 B.A. L.1009 J.D. [Ⓢ Hale&D.]
*PRACTICE AREAS: Antitrust.
Rubenstein, Leonard S. '49 '75 C.918 B.A. L.309 J.D.
Exec. Dir., Bazelon Ctr. for Mental Health Law
Rubenstein, Leslie R. '74 '99 C.1365 B.A. L.245 J.D.
(adm. in GA; not adm. in DC) I.R.S.
Rubin, Andrew Ellis, (BV) . . . . '49 '74 C.605 B.A. L.813 J.D. 1701 Q St., N.W.
Rubin, Blake D., (AV) . . . . '55 '80 C.311 B.A. L.659 J.D. [Arnold&P.]
*PRACTICE AREAS: Federal Taxation; Real Estate Taxation; Partnership Taxation.
Rubin, Brad A. '73 '99 C.910 A.B. L.276 J.D.
(adm. in PA; not adm. in DC) 1875 Connecticut Avenue, N.W.
Rubin, Brian L. . . . . '62 '87 C.659 B.S. L.228 J.D. NASDAQ Stock Market, Inc.
Rubin, Corey A. . . . . '69 '97 C.1060 B.A. L.1355 J.D. [Ⓐ Brand&F.]
*PRACTICE AREAS: Election and Campaign Finance; White Collar Crime; Administrative Law.
Rubin, David B., (BV) . . . . '60 '85 C.103 A.B. L.94 J.D. [Ⓒ Swidler B.S.F.]
*PRACTICE AREAS: Energy Regulation; Federal Energy Regulation.
Rubin, Eric H. . . . . '66 '91 C.861 B.S.M. L.904 J.D. Tax Mgmt., Inc.
Rubin, Eric M., (P.C.), (AV) . . . . '43 '67 C.273 B.A. L.705 J.D. [Rubin,W.D.H.&C.]
*PRACTICE AREAS: Outdoor Advertising Law; Media; Advertising; Trade Regulation; Sports.
Rubin, Gary I. . . . . '46 '84 C.1019 B.A. L.128 J.D. [Spriggs&H.]
*PRACTICE AREAS: Toxic Torts; Litigation; Drug and Medical Device Defense; Environmental Law.
Rubin, Howard R. . . . . '69 '96 C.472 B.A. L.228 J.D. [Ⓐ Shea&G.]
Rubin, Jenny R. '74 '00 C.801 B.A. L.276 J.D.
(adm. in XX; not adm. in DC) 555 13th St., NW
Rubin, Kenneth A., (AV) . . . . '47 '74 C&L.188 B.S., J.D. [Morgan,L.&B.]
Rubin, Kerry Pyle . . . . '71 '97 C.105 B.A. L.94 J.D. [Ⓐ Hale&D.]
*PRACTICE AREAS: Litigation.
Rubin, Lee H. . . . . '63 '89 C.228 B.A. L.813 J.D. [Mayer,B.&P.]
Rubin, Leonard J., (AV) . . . . '41 '68 C.1019 B.A. L.30 J.D. [Powell,G.F.&M.]
*PRACTICE AREAS: Financial Institution Regulation; Corporate; Nonprofit Organizations.
Rubin, Michael A. . . . . '73 '99 C.31 B.A. L.976 J.D. [Ⓐ Arnold&P.]
*PRACTICE AREAS: Litigation; Products Liability; Pro Bono.
Rubin, Nancy G. . . . . '61 '86 C.309 A.B. L.477 J.D. [Ⓒ Skadden,A.S.M.&F.]
Rubin, Paul D. . . . . '67 '92 C&L.659 B.S., J.D. [Patton B.]
Rubin, Peter J. . . . . '62 '88 C.976 B.A. L.309 J.D. Assoc. Prof. of Law, Georgetown Univ.
Rubin, Rochelle E. . . . . '72 '00 C.472 B.A. L.569 J.D. [Ⓐ Covington&B.]
Rubin, Seymour J., (AV) '14 '39 C.477 B.A. L.309 LL.B.
2223 Massachusetts Ave., N.W.

Rubin & Rubin, P.C.
(See Silver Spring, Maryland)

Rubin, Winston, Diercks, Harris & Cooke, L.L.P., (AV)
A Limited Liability Partnership including a Professional Corporation
1155 Connecticut Avenue, N.W., Sixth Floor, 20036
Telephone: 202-861-0870 Telecopier: 202-429-0657
Email: administrator@rwdhc.com URL: http://www.rwdhc.com
Eric M. Rubin (P.C.); James L. Winston; Walter E. Diercks; Jeffrey Harris; Frederick D. Cooke, Jr.; Steven J. Stone. Associates: Paul M. Breakman.
Litigation before Federal and State Courts. Practice before United States Courts, Governmental Departments and Agencies. Civil and White Collar Criminal Litigation. Trade Regulation, Communications, Media, Land Use and Zoning, Advertising and Franchise Regulation, Corporate, Banking, Construction, Government Contract, Public Utility, Legislative and Sports Law Practice.
See Professional Biographies, WASHINGTON, DISTRICT OF COLUMBIA

Rubinger, James C., (AV) . . . . '55 '80 C.103 B.A. L.273 J.D. [Wiley R.&F.]
*PRACTICE AREAS: Franchise; Litigation; Intellectual Property; Antitrust.
Rubino, Richard D. . . . . '— '85 C.1083 B.A. L.616 J.D. [Blooston,M.D.D.&P.]
*PRACTICE AREAS: Telecommunications Law; FCC Licensing; FCC Regulation.
Rubinoff, Edward L., (P.C.), (AV) . . . . . '50 '75 C.659 B.A. L.273 J.D. [Akin,G.S.H.&F.]
*PRACTICE AREAS: International Trade; Technology.
Rubins, Noah D. '71 '00 C.103 A.B. L.309 J.D.
(adm. in NY; not adm. in DC) [Ⓐ Jones,D.R.&P.]
Rubinson, Gene Z. '42 '71 C.563 B.E.E. L.904 J.D.
(adm. in MD; not adm. in DC; Pat.) [McDermott,W.&E.]
Rubinstein, Joel S., (AV) . . . . '48 '73 C&L.339 B.A., J.D. [Bell,B.&L.]
*PRACTICE AREAS: Construction Law; Litigation; Government Contracts Law.
Rubio, Miguel Eugenio . . . . '62 '89 C&L.276 B.S.F.S., J.D. [Ⓒ Holland&K.]
*PRACTICE AREAS: Project Finance; Privatization; International Finance; International Business Transactions.
Rubman, Gary '74 '00 C.453 B.S. L.273 J.D.
(adm. in NY; not adm. in DC) [Ⓐ Covington&B.]
Ruby, Joseph L., (AV) . . . . '55 '85 C.685 B.A. L.976 J.D. [Baach R.&L.P.]
*PRACTICE AREAS: Civil Litigation; Commercial Litigation; Insurance Coverage; Bad Faith Disputes.
Ruby, Rebecca I. . . . . '74 '99 C.103 A.B. L.276 J.D. [Ⓐ Kirkland&E.]
*PRACTICE AREAS: Litigation.
Ruch, Joseph J., Jr., (BV) '48 '75 C.223 B.S. L.273 J.D.
(adm. in VA; not adm. in DC; See Pat. Sect.) [Sughrue M.]
*PRACTICE AREAS: Intellectual Property Law.
Rucker, William Randolph (Randy) '72 '00 C.16 B.S. L.365 J.D.
(adm. in IL; not adm. in DC) [Ⓐ Baker&M.]
*PRACTICE AREAS: Trade Regulations and Customs Law.
Ruckert, Edward M., (AV) . . . . '50 '76 C.276 B.A. L.851 J.D. [McDermott,W.&E.]
Ruda, Richard . . . . '50 '80 C.976 B.A. L.309 J.D. Chief Coun., State & Local Legal Ctr.
Ruddy, Frank . . . . . . '37 '67 C.321 A.B. L.424 LL.B. [Ruddy&M.] & [Ⓒ Claxton,S.&Q.]
*PRACTICE AREAS: Environmental Law; Energy Law; International Law.

Ruddy & Muir, LLP, (AV)
1730 K Street, N.W. Suite 304, 20006
Telephone: 202-835-0055 Fax: 202-337-6459
URL: http://www.lawyers.com/ruddy&muir
Frank Ruddy; J. Dapray Muir. Of Counsel: Eugene P. Kopp; Thomas P. Gross.
Energy Law, International Law, Corporate Law and Securities Law, Telecommunications Law, Environmental Law, Litigation.
See Professional Biographies, WASHINGTON, DISTRICT OF COLUMBIA

Rudebusch, Thomas L., (AV) . . . . '56 '86 C.959 B.A. L.966 J.D. [Duncan,W.G.&P.]
*PRACTICE AREAS: Energy; Administrative Law.
Rudge, Andrew W. . . . . '72 '98 C.228 A.B. L.893 J.D. [Ⓐ Williams&C.]
Rudin, David M. . . . . '71 '98 C.112 B.A. L.94 J.D. [Ⓐ Dow,L.&A.]
Rudman, Warren B., (AV) . . . . '30 '60 C.823 B.S. L.1149 LL.B [Paul,W.R.W.&G.] ⊙
Rudnick, Amy G., (AV) . . . . '54 '80 C.813 B.A. L.273 J.D. [Gibson,D.&C.]
*PRACTICE AREAS: White Collar Crime; Financial Institutions.
Rudnick, Joel M. . . . . '66 '91 C.569 B.A. L.276 J.D. [Powers,P.S.&V.]
*PRACTICE AREAS: Education Law; Administrative Law; Litigation.
Rudnick, Robert A., (AV) . . . . '48 '73 C.164 B.A. L.188 J.D. [Shearman&S.]
Rudolf, Keith J. '51 '79 C.162 B.A. L.597 J.D.
(adm. in IL; not adm. in DC) [Jorden B.]
*PRACTICE AREAS: Investment Management; Securities; Corporate.
Rudolph, Barbara R. . . . . '59 '94 C.823 B.S. L.273 J.D. [Ⓐ Finnegan,H.F.G.&D.]
*PRACTICE AREAS: Intellectual Property Litigation; Pharmaceutical Patents; Patent Infringement; Patent Prosecution.
Rudolph, Gary Allen '65 '97 C.260 B.S.B.A. L.128 J.D.
(adm. in VA; not adm. in DC) 450 5th St., N.W.
Rudolph, John B. . . . . '48 '74 C.893 B.A. L.623 J.D. [Hall,E.H.G.G.&N.]
Rudy, Beverly J., (BV) . . . . '54 '81 C.860 B.A. L.273 J.D. [Sutherland A.&B.]
*PRACTICE AREAS: Foreign Trade Sanctions; Petroleum Trading; Petroleum Contracts; Excise Tax; Energy.
Rudy, Tony C. '66 '95 C.454 B.B.A. L.1209 J.D.
(adm. in VA; not adm. in DC) [Greenberg T.]
Ruemmler, Kathryn H. . . . . '— '98 C.911 B.A. L.276 J.D. [Ⓐ Latham&W.]
*PRACTICE AREAS: Criminal Litigation; Civil Litigation.
Rufe, Stacey Engelbrecht . . . . '71 '98 C&L.276 A.B., J.D. [Ⓐ Ross,D.&B.]
Ruffin, Thomas T., Jr. . . . . '56 '83 C.329 B.A. L.273 J.D. 153 Galveston Place, SW
Rufkahr, Michael J. . . . . '53 '80 C&L.477 A.B., J.D. [Arnold&P.]
*PRACTICE AREAS: Taxation.
Ruge, Mark H. '58 '93 C.591 B.A. L.276 J.D.
(adm. in VA; not adm. in DC) [Preston G.E.&R.M.]
*PRACTICE AREAS: Federal Practice; Policy; Maritime Law; Tax; Health Care.
Rugg, Allen S., (AV) . . . . . . '49 '75 C&L.273 B.A., J.D. [Powell,G.F.&M.] (⊙Reston, VA)
*PRACTICE AREAS: Civil Litigation; Business Litigation.
Ruggeri, James P. . . . . '65 '91 C.165 B.A. L.880 J.D. [Hogan&H.]
Ruggiero, Jennifer Gulbrandsen '— '99
C.703 B.A. L.309 J.D. 701 Pennsylvania Avenue, N.W.
Ruggio, Michael F. . . . . '56 '82 C.569 B.S. L.665 J.D. [Jenkens&G.]
*PRACTICE AREAS: Health Law.
Ruiz, Andrea '67 '00
(adm. in NY; not adm. in DC) [Ⓐ P.E.Murphy]
*PRACTICE AREAS: Aviation Law; International Law.
Ruiz, Jennifer '68 '92 C&L.472 B.A., J.D.
Sr. Assoc. Coun., United Mine Workers of Amer. Health & Retirement Funds
Ruiz, Vanessa . . . . '50 '75 C.914 B.A. L.276 J.D. Ct. of Appls.
Ruiz de Gamboa, Isabel P. '72 '97 C.886 B.S. L.273 J.D.
(adm. in VA; not adm. in DC) [Ⓐ Greenstein D.&L.]
*PRACTICE AREAS: Commercial Real Estate; Real Estate Finance; Commercial Leasing; Financial Institutions Law.
Ruiz-de-Velasco, Jorge L. . . . . '61 '88 C.309 A.B. L.1066 J.D. P.O. Box 18553
Rukuba-Ngaiza, Nightingale T '60 '92 L.999 LL.B.
(adm. in NY; not adm. in DC) World Bank
Rule, Charles F. (Rick), (AV) . . . . '55 '83 C.880 B.A. L.145 J.D. [Fried,F.H.S.&J.]
*PRACTICE AREAS: Antitrust; Competition Law; International Antitrust.
Rumeld, Harvey David '56 '81
C.1044 B.A. L.659 J.D. Assoc. Litig. Coun., MCI WorldCom
Rummel, Jeffrey E. . . . . '67 '91 C.705 B.A. L.273 J.D. 1915 Eye St.,N.W.
Rumph, Charles W. '32 '64 C.326 B.S. L.1066 LL.B. 3328 N St., N.W.

Rumsfeld, Kurt T. .... '63 '93 C.951 B.A. L.588 J.D. [Woodley,G.&M.]
*PRACTICE AREAS: Labor and Employment Law; Fair Labor Standards Law; Public Sector Labor Relations Law.
Rund, Grayce Karole .... '47 '86 C.112 B.A. L.209 J.D. [Rund&M.] ⊙
Rund & McDonough, L.L.P. ....1155 Connecticut Ave., N.W. (⊙Alexandria, VA)
Rundlet, Peter '65 '95 C.103 B.A. L.659 J.D.
(adm. in CA; not adm. in DC) [Ⓐ Skadden,A.S.M.&F.]
*PRACTICE AREAS: Political Law.
Rupp, John Peter, (AV) '44 '72 C.352 B.A. L.976 J.D.
[Covington&B.] (⊙Paris, France)
Rupp, Megan E. '69 '97 C&L.276 B.S.F.S., J.D.
Asst. Coun., The Washington Post Co.
Ruppert, Christine A. Schnabel '65 '94
C.951 B.A. L.477 J.D. Sr. Coun., Marriott International, Inc.
*RESPONSIBILITIES: Labor and Employment.
Rupy, Kevin G. .... '68 '01 C.262 B.A. L.904 J.D. [Ⓐ Keller&H.]
*PRACTICE AREAS: Telecommunications Law; Business Transactions.
Rusch, Wayne H., (AV) .... '45 '70 C&L.966 B.B.A., J.D. [Berliner,C.&R.]
*PRACTICE AREAS: International; Corporate; Commercial Transactions.
Ruschke, David P. .... '63 '97 C.494 B.S. L.276 J.D. [Ⓐ Covington&B.]
*PRACTICE AREAS: Litigation; Intellectual Property.
Ruscus, Stephen E. .... '64 '91 C.575 B.A. L.128 J.D. [Ⓐ McKenna&C.]
*PRACTICE AREAS: Government Contracts; Litigation; Health Care Fraud; Medicaid/VA Compliance Pricing.
Rush, Michael J., (AV) '54 '79 C.918 B.A. L.273 J.D.
Assoc. Gen. Coun., Assn. of Amer. Railroads
Rushforth, Brent N. .... '41 '70 C.813 B.A. L.1066 J.D. [Heller E.W.&M.]
*PRACTICE AREAS: Civil Litigation; Antitrust Law; Cable Television and Telecommunications Law.
Rushing, Charles Colin .... '72 '99 C.1369 B.A. L.893 J.D. [Ⓐ Wilmer,C.&P.]
Rushton, Lisa K. .... '67 '94 C.105 B.A. L.861 J.D. [Ⓐ Paul,H.J.&W.]
*PRACTICE AREAS: Litigation; Environmental.
Ruskin, Andrew '65 '97 C.918 B.A. L.930 J.D.
(adm. in NY; not adm. in DC) [Ⓐ Vinson&E.]
*PRACTICE AREAS: Health Law; Medicare and Medicaid; Hospital Law; Corporate Law.
Russell, Angela W. .... '64 '89 C.319 B.A. L.446 J.D. [Ⓐ Carr G.]
Russell, Donald J. '52 '77 C.546 B.A. L.309 J.D.
(adm. in MA; not adm. in DC) [Robbins,R.E.O.&U.]
Russell, Harold S. '35 '62 C.976 B.A. L.145 J.D.
(adm. in PA; not adm. in DC) V.P., Govt. Affs., FMC Corp.‡
Russell, James M., (AV) .... '24 '58 C&L.273 A.B., J.D. 1815 Pennsylvania Ave. NW
Russell, Jeffrey P., (BV) '56 '81 C&L.446 B.A., J.D.
Hearing Examiner, Office of Hearing & Adjudications
Russell, Reed L. .... '69 '99 C.896 B.S. L.128 J.D. [Ⓐ Akin,G.S.H.&F.]
Russell, Ronald G. .... '33 '62 C.813 B.A. L.309 LL.B. 805 15th St., N.W.
Russell, Scott D. .... '71 '99 C.945 B.A. L.1209 J.D. [Ⓐ Howrey S.A.&W.]
*PRACTICE AREAS: Antitrust.
Russell, Susan B. '45 '80 C.477 A.B. L.128 J.D.
(adm. in VA; not adm. in DC) Sr. Atty., Consolidated Nat. Gas Co.
Russell-Albach, Cynthia L. '69 '96 C.176 B.A. L.896 J.D.
(adm. in NC; not adm. in DC) The Appleseed Found.
Russell-Einhorn, Malcolm L. '56 '84 C.976 B.A. L.309 J.D.
Amer. Bar Assn., Central & E. European Law Institute

Russian-Ukrainian Legal Group, P.A.
1200 19th Street, N.W., Suite 201, 20036
Telephone: 202-822-1620 Fax: 202-822-1622
Email: general@rulg.com URL: http://www.rulg.com
Russian-Ukrainian Legal Group: Senior Counsel and President: Irina Paliashvili. Senior Counsel: Richard H. Smith, III. Of Counsel: Professor Levan Alexidze; Ethan S. Burger; Galina Dmitrieva; Evgeny A. Danilov; (Professor) Igor Lukashuk. Ukrainian Legal Group: Senior Counsel: Victor Kovalenko; Tamara Lukanina; Alexander Padalka. Counsel: Vyacheslav Novak. Of Counsel: Pytor M. Bogdanovitch; Sergei Denisenko.
Corporate, commercial, oil and gas, customs and administrative law, intellectual and industrial property practice, telecommunications, energy, commercial litigation in the Russian Federation and Ukraine. International Arbitration and Mediation.
With affiliated offices in Moscow, Russia and Kiev, Ukraine.
See Professional Biographies, WASHINGTON, DISTRICT OF COLUMBIA

Russin & Vecchi L.L.P.
International Legal Counsellors
815 Connecticut Avenue, N.W. Suite 650, 20006 ⊙
Telephone: 202-822-6100 Fax: 202-822-6101
Email: lawyers@russinvecchi.com URL: http://www.russinvecchi.com
Members of Firm: Jonathan Russin (Resident, Moscow Office); William R. White; Irina Paliashvili. Of Counsel: Ethan S. Burger; B. Thomas Mansbach.
General Practice, including International Business and Trade, Foreign Investment and Finance, Transaction Structuring, Corporate Law and Taxation, Foreign Joint Ventures and Branch Operations, Agencies and Distributorships, Export Finance, Civil Litigation and Arbitration, International Programs of Educational Organizations and Religious Institutions.
Bangkok, Thailand Office: International Legal Counsellors Thailand, Ltd., Sathorn City Tower, 175 South Sathorn Road, 18th Floor, 10120. Telephone: 662-679-6005; 662-679-6015. Fax: 662-679-6041, 662-679-6042. e-mail: ilct@mozart.inet.co.th.
Hanoi, Vietnam Office: Russin & Vecchi, L.L.C., Hanoi Central Office Building, 44B Ly Thuong Kiet Street, 11/F. Telephone: (84-4) 825-1700. Fax: (84-4) 825-1742. e-mail: rusvechn@hn.vnn.vn.
Ho Chi Minh City, S.R. Vietnam Office: Russin & Vecchi, L.L.C., 8 Nguyen Hue Boulevard, 15th Floor, Q1. Telephone: (84-8) 8243-026/243-114. Fax: (84-8) 8243-113. e-mail: rusvec@hcm.vnn.vn.
Moscow, Russia Office: Russin & Vecchi L.L.C., Ulitsa Bolshaya Ordynka, 60/2, Moscow 109017. Telephone: 7-095-959-1288/1294. Fax: 7-095-959-1290. e-mail: lawyers@russinvecchi.ru.
New York, New York Office: Russin, Vecchi & Berg L.L.P., 15th Floor, 605 Third Avenue, 10158. Telephone: 212-490-6644. Fax: 212-490-1809. e-mail: lawyers@rvbnewyork.com.
Puerto Plata, Dominican Republic Office: Russin Vecchi & Heredia Bonetti L.L.P., Plaza Turisol Local #11A. Telephone: 809-586-5535. Fax: 809-586-5861. e-mail: rmedina@rvhb.com.
Yuzhno-Sakhalinsk, Russia Office: Russin & Vecchi L.L.C., 32 Kommunisticheski Pr. 693000. Telephone: 7-4242-726-786/87. Fax: 7-4242-726-758. e-mail: russinvecchi@snc.ru.
Santo Domingo, Dominican Republic Office: Russin Vecchi & Heredia Bonetti L.L.P., Edificio Monte Mirador, Calle El Recodo No 2, Tercer Piso, Ensanche Bella Vista, Apartado Postal 425. Telephone: 809-535-9511. Fax: 809-535-6649. e-mail: rvhb@rvhb.com.
Taipei, Taiwan Office: Russin & Vecchi, Bank Tower 9th Floor, 205 Tun Hwa N. Road. Telephone: (886-2) 2712-8956. Fax: (886-2) 2713-4711. e-mail: rusvectp@ms2.hinet.net.
Vladivostok, Russia Office: Russin & Vecchi L.L.C., Sukhanova Street, 3A, 690091. Telephone: 7-4232-260-465; 261-015. Fax: 7-4232-226-505. e-mail: russinvecchi@stl.ru.
Yangon, Myanmar Office: Russin & Vecchi, Ltd., 8C Bogyoke Museum Rd., Bahan Township. Mailing Address: Box No. 729 G.P.O., Yangon, Myanmar. Telephone (951) 541794/540995. Fax: (951) 548835. e-mail: burmalaw@mptmail.net.mm
See Professional Biographies, WASHINGTON, DISTRICT OF COLUMBIA

Russo, C. Anthony .... '— '99 C.260 B.A. L.273 J.D. [Ⓐ Powers,P.S.&V.]
*PRACTICE AREAS: Health Care Law; Administrative Law; Corporate Law; Litigation.
Russo, Kathleen M. .... '54 '79 C.30 B.S. L.276 J.D. [Hughes H.&R.]
*PRACTICE AREAS: Corporate; Securities; Financial Services.
Russo, Martha L. '72 '00 C.861 B.A. L.846 J.D.
(adm. in TX; not adm. in DC) [Ⓐ Hogan&H.]
*PRACTICE AREAS: Litigation.
Russo, Roy R., (AV) .... '36 '59 C.178 B.A. L.823 LL.B. [Cohn&M.]
*PRACTICE AREAS: Communications Law.
Rust-Tierney, Diann .... '55 '82 C.970 B.A. L.446 J.D. 122 Maryland Ave. N.E.

Rustum, Michael J., (BV) .... '64 '89 C.1044 B.A. L.823 J.D. [Ⓒ Dickstein S.M.&O.]
*PRACTICE AREAS: Energy Law.
Rutenberg, Alan D. .... '— '94 C.853 B.A. L.309 J.D. [Ⓒ Foley&L.]
*PRACTICE AREAS: Antitrust; Regulatory; Commercial Litigation.
Ruthenberg, Kirk R. .... '52 '79 C.339 B.A. L.276 J.D. [Sonnenschein N.&R.]
*PRACTICE AREAS: Commercial Litigation; Intellectual Property.
Rutherford, Alanna '75 '01 C.276 B.S.P.S. L.178 J.D.
(adm. in NY; not adm. in DC) [Ⓐ Boies,S.&F.]
*PRACTICE AREAS: Antitrust; Commercial Litigation; Telecommunications Law.
Rutherford, Tonya '— '97 C.367 B.A. L.273 J.D.
(adm. in GA; not adm. in DC) [Ⓐ Latham&W.]
*PRACTICE AREAS: Communications Common Carrier.
Rutkowski, David S. .... '71 '96 C.813 A.B. L.602 J.D. [Ⓐ Jones,D.R.&P.]
Rutkowski, Joanne C. .... '57 '83 C.21 B.S. L.309 J.D. [Baker B.]
*PRACTICE AREAS: Utility; Regulatory; Mergers and Acquisitions.
Rutledge, E. Preston .... '54 '84 C.336 B.S. L.273 J.D. [Ⓒ Silver,F.&T.]
Rutledge, Peter B. '70 '00 C.309 B.A. L.145 J.D.
(adm. in MD; not adm. in DC) [Ⓐ Wilmer,C.&P.]
Rutngamlug, W. Ray .... '73 '00 C.276 B.S.F.S. L.188 J.D. [Ⓐ Swidler B.S.F.]
*PRACTICE AREAS: Telecommunications.
Rutstein, David W. .... '— '69 C.659 B.A. L.273 J.D. [Ⓒ Venable,A.B.H.&C.]
Rutten, Timothy M. .... '— '92 C.628 B.S. L.950 J.D. [Ⓐ Verner,L.B.M.&H.]
*PRACTICE AREAS: Legislative; Federal Affairs.
Ruttenberg, Charles B., (AV) .... '— '49 C.893 B.A. L.659 LL.B. [Arent F.K.P.&K.]
*PRACTICE AREAS: Antitrust; Entertainment Law; Intellectual Property; Copyrights; Trademark Law.
Ruttenberg, Hattie '65 '92
C.674 B.A. L.976 J.D. Asst. Ge. Coun., Children's Defense Fund
Ruttenberg, Kerri L. .... '— '99 C.30 B.A. L.537 J.D. [Ⓐ King&S.]
Ruttinger, George D., (AV) .... '48 '74 C&L.477 A.B., J.D. [Crowell&M.]
*PRACTICE AREAS: Litigation; Government (or Public) Contract Law; Contract Law; Construction Law.
Ruvolo, Anthony D., (BV) .... '60 '87 C.659 B.A. L.276 J.D. [Ⓐ Nixon P.]
*PRACTICE AREAS: Affordable Housing; Real Estate.
Ruyak, Robert F., (AV) .... '49 '74 C.1062 B.A. L.276 J.D. [Howrey S.A.&W.]
*PRACTICE AREAS: Antitrust; Patent Litigation; Trademark Litigation; Trade Secrets; Copyright Litigation.
Ryan, Amy F. .... '66 '99 C.893 B.A. L.276 J.D. [Ⓐ Arnold&P.]
*PRACTICE AREAS: Intellectual Property.
Ryan, Andrea Elisa .... '75 '01 C.446 B.A. L.276 J.D. [Ⓐ Mayer,B.&P.]
*PRACTICE AREAS: Litigation.
Ryan, Bruce D., (BV) .... '52 '79 C.347 A.B. L.273 J.D. [Paul,H.J.&W.]
*PRACTICE AREAS: Antitrust; Communications Transactions, Regulation and Litigation.
Ryan, Charles W., III .... '61 '87 C.1021 B.A. L.990 J.D. [Ⓐ Dombroff&G.]
Ryan, Cheryl Feik .... '62 '88 C.518 A.B. L.228 J.D. [Van Ness F.]
*PRACTICE AREAS: Energy; Electric Utilities; Administrative Litigation.
Ryan, Christine C. .... '49 '83 C.702 B.A. L.276 J.D. [Brickfield B.R.&S.]
Ryan, Denise M. '58 '94 C&L.128 B.A., J.D.
(adm. in MD; not adm. in DC) Law Editor, Legal Times
Ryan, Edward A., (AV) '53 '78 C&L.659 B.A., J.D.
Sr. V.P. & Assoc. Gen. Coun., Lodging, Marriott International
*RESPONSIBILITIES: Lodging Development and Operations; Corporate Transactions.
Ryan, Elizabeth .... '59 '86 C.321 B.A. L.128 J.D. Neighborhood Legal Servs. Prog.
Ryan, Frederick J., Jr. '55 '80
C&L.800 B.A., J.D. Vice Chmn., Allbritton Communications Co.
Ryan, James P. '65 '97 C.1175 B.A. L.472 J.D.
(adm. in FL; not adm. in DC) [Ⓐ O'Connor&H.]
*PRACTICE AREAS: Intellectual Property Litigation; Commercial Litigation; Bankruptcy; Trademarks; Copyrights.
Ryan, James P. A. .... '64 '90 C.197 A.B. L.145 J.D. [Ⓐ Covington&B.]
Ryan, Jane I., (AV) .... '52 '82 C.1044 B.A. L.273 J.D. [Steptoe&J.]
*PRACTICE AREAS: Energy; Litigation.
Ryan, Jay T. .... '66 '91 C.696 B.A. L.209 J.D. [Ⓒ Van Ness F.]
*PRACTICE AREAS: Energy; Environment; Government Relations.
Ryan, Jerry W., (AV) .... '28 '52 C&L.477 A.B., J.D. 1001 Penn. Ave., N.W.
Ryan, John M. .... '61 '93 C.966 B.A. L.276 J.D. [Ⓐ Weil,G.&M.]
Ryan, John W. .... '57 '86 C.105 B.A. L.273 J.D. [Wilmer,C.&P.] (Pat.)
*PRACTICE AREAS: Intellectual Property Licensing; Patent Infringement Opinions; Patent Litigation.
Ryan, Joseph, (AV) '42 '68 C.911 B.A. L.178 LL.B.
Exec. V.P. & Gen. Coun., Marriott Intl., Inc. (⊙Atlanta, GA)
*RESPONSIBILITIES: Corporate.
Ryan, Joy-Elan M. '61 '96 C.103 B.A. L.472 J.D.
Legis. Dir. & Coun., Health Ins. Assn. of America
Ryan, Kathleen M. .... '71 '96 C&L.309 A.B., J.D. [Ⓐ Williams&C.]
*PRACTICE AREAS: Corporate Law; Media Law; Publishing Law.
Ryan, Kenneth E. .... '63 '88 C.93 B.A. L.273 J.D. [Ⓒ Drinker B.&R.]
*PRACTICE AREAS: Insurance Law; Civil Litigation.
Ryan, Kevin D. '70 '98 C.732 B.A. L.128 J.D.
(adm. in MA; not adm. in DC) [Ⓐ Schiff H.&W.]
Ryan, Mark W. .... '55 '81 C.823 B.A. L.228 J.D. [Mayer,B.&P.]
Ryan, Michael .... '71 '00 C.659 B.A. L.893 J.D. [Ⓐ Wilmer,C.&P.]
Ryan, Michael J., Jr. '63 '91 C.884 B.S. L.128 J.D.
(adm. in MD; not adm. in DC) NASDAQ Stock Market, Inc.
Ryan, Stephen M., (AV) .... '55 '80 C.188 B.S. L.602 J.D. [Manatt,P.&P.]
Ryan, Terrance L., (AV) '47 '76 C&L.851 B.A., J.D.
(adm. in OH; not adm. in DC) [Shanahan] ⊙
*PRACTICE AREAS: Civil Litigation; Labor (Management) Law; Employment Discrimination; Collective Bargaining.
Ryan, Thomas M. .... '48 '75 C.602 B.A. L.276 J.D. [Ryan,P.U.&M.]
Ryan, Timothy R. .... '70 '97 C.1369 B.S. L.893 J.D. [Ⓐ Mayer,B.&P.]
*PRACTICE AREAS: Finance; Corporate Law; Technology Law.
Ryan, Phillips, Utrecht & MacKinnon, (BV) ....1133 Connecticut Avenue, N.W., Suite 300
Rybeck, Richard S. '56 '88 C.311 B.A. L.904 J.D.
Legislative Asst., Council of the D.C.
Ryberg, Paul, Jr. .... '52 '77 C.942 B.A. L.309 J.D. [Ryberg&S.]

Ryberg & Smith, LLP
Canal Square, 1054 31st Street, N.W., 20007
Telephone: 202-333-4000 Fax: 202-965-3445
Paul Ryberg, Jr.; David F. B. Smith.
Federal Legislative and Regulatory Practice focusing on International Trade, Federal Regulation of Real Estate Services and Native American Law, Commercial Litigation, and Commercial Transactions.
See Professional Biographies, WASHINGTON, DISTRICT OF COLUMBIA

Ryder, David Franklin, (BV) '60 '86
C.282 B.A. L.904 J.D. [Ⓐ Martell,D.G.&G.] (⊙Rockville, MD)
Ryder, Don F., Jr., (AV) '32 '59
C.282 A.B. L.276 J.D. [Martell,D.G.&G.] (⊙Rockville, MD)
Rydzewski, Leo G. .... '68 '97 C.276 B.A. L.259 J.D. [Ⓐ Holland&K.]
*PRACTICE AREAS: Litigation.

Ryerson, Paul S., (AV) ....'46 '72 C.918 B.A. L.178 J.D. [Jones,D.R.&P.]
*PRACTICE AREAS: Environmental Law; Environmental Insurance Coverage; Products Liability; Toxic Torts.
Rygiel, Mark W. '73 '00 C.602 B.S.M.E. L.273 J.D.
(adm. in PA; not adm. in DC; Pat.) [[A] Collier S.S.]
*PRACTICE AREAS: Intellectual Property; Patents; Trademarks; Copyrights.
Ryland, Barbara H. ....'60 '88 C.893 B.A. L.228 J.D. [[C] Crowell&M.]
*PRACTICE AREAS: Health Care Law.
Ryland, Robert S., (AV) .... '60 '88 C.821 B.A. L.145 J.D. [Kirkland&E.]
*PRACTICE AREAS: Government Contracts; Health Care Law; White Collar Defense.
Rylander, Jason C. '71 '00 C.188 B.A. L.945 J.D.
(adm. in VA; not adm. in DC) [[A] Perkins C.]
*PRACTICE AREAS: Campaign Ethics; Business Law; White Collar Crime; Natural Resources; Environmental Law.
Rynkiewicz, John P. '56 '81 C.1113 B.A. L.1017 J.D.
(adm. in PA; not adm. in DC) [[C] Kaye S.]
*PRACTICE AREAS: Trademarks; Intellectual Property; Electronic Commerce; Internet.
Saad, Martin L. .... '70 '96 C&L.477 B.A., J.D. [[A] Venable,A.B.H.&C.]
*PRACTICE AREAS: Internet Law; Advertising Law; Sweepstakes; Intellectual Property; Litigation.
Saadat, Mahshid '57 '97 C.768 B.S.E.E. L.904 J.D.
(adm. in VA; not adm. in DC; Pat.) [[A] McDermott,W.&E.]
Saadeh, Catherine M. ....'69 '94 C.273 B.A. L.309 J.D. [[C] Wilmer,C.&P.]
*PRACTICE AREAS: Securities.
Saari, David J. ....'34 '62 C&L.494 B.A., LL.B. Amer. Univ.
Saas, Richard T., (AV) ....'63 '88 C.1204 B.S. L.838 J.D. [Steptoe&J.]
*PRACTICE AREAS: Energy; Natural Resources; Utility Law.
Saba, Joseph P. ....'47 '76 C.1113 B.A. L.976 J.D. The World Bk.
Sabagh, Denyse, (AV) ....'48 '77 C.446 B.A. L.1209 J.D. [Duane,M.&H.]
*PRACTICE AREAS: Immigration and Nationality Law; Immigration Litigation.
Sabatino, Charles P. '50 '78 C.188 A.B. L.276 J.D.
Asst. Dir., Comm. on Legal Probs. of the Elderly, Amer. Bar Assn.
Saber, Charles W. ....'54 '79 C.454 B.A. L.276 J.D. [Dickstein S.M.&O.]
*PRACTICE AREAS: Patent, Trademark and Copyright Law; Litigation.
Sabo, Melanie ....'59 '91 C.94 B.S. L.477 J.D. [Preston G.E.&R.M.]
*PRACTICE AREAS: Antitrust; Litigation.
Sabrin, Amy R. ....'51 '86 C.914 B.A. L.273 J.D. [Skadden,A.S.M.&F.]
Saccoccio, Louis J. '54 '82 C.871 B.S. L.309 J.D.
General Counsel, American Association of Health Plans
Sachdev, Amit K. '68 '94 C.119 B.S. L.245 J.D.
(adm. in GA; not adm. in DC) 1301 K St. N.W., Suite 800 E.
Sacher, Steven J., (AV) ....'42 '68 C.966 B.S. L.145 J.D. [Kilpatrick S.]
*PRACTICE AREAS: ERISA; Employee Benefits; Federal Regulatory; Legislative Practice.
Sachs, Elizabeth R., (AV) ....'49 '80 C.702 B.A. L.904 J.D. [Lukas,N.G.&S.]
*PRACTICE AREAS: Telecommunications Law; FCC Regulation; Business Transfers.
Sachs, Heather Berner ....'74 '99 C.659 B.A. L.178 J.D. [[A] Dow,L.&A.]
Sachs, John L., (AV) ....'— '80 C.976 B.A. L.309 J.D. [Latham&W.]
*PRACTICE AREAS: Energy; Energy Project Development; Infrastructure Development; Project Finance.
Sachs, Stephen H., (AV) ....'34 '60 C.311 A.B. L.976 LL.B. [[C] Wilmer,C.&P.]
*PRACTICE AREAS: Civil Practice; Criminal Law; White Collar Crime.
Sachs, Susan Valerie ....'60 '87 C&L.945 B.A., J.D. [[A] Cohn&M.]
*PRACTICE AREAS: Communications Law; Cable TV; Mass Media Law.
Sachse, Harry R., (AV) ....'34 '57 C&L.420 B.A., LL.B. [Sonosky,C.S.E.&P.]
Sacilotto, Kara M. ....'64 '90 C&L.893 B.A., J.D. [Perkins C.]
*PRACTICE AREAS: Telecommunications Law; Civil Litigation; Commercial Litigation.
Sackey, Michael A. ....'— '99 L.902 J.D. [[A] Arnold&P.]
Sackler, Arthur B. ....'50 '74 C&L.823 B.A., J.D. 800 Connecticut Ave., N.W.
Sacks, David A., (AV) ....'— '67 C.64 B.S. L.276 J.D. [Foley&L.]
*PRACTICE AREAS: Federal Taxation Law; Corporate Law.
Sacks, Leonard A., (AV) ....'46 '71 C.401 B.A. L.273 J.D. [[C] Leftwich&D.]
*PRACTICE AREAS: Construction Law.
Sacks, Murray D., (BV) ....'61 '86 C.910 B.S. L.273 J.D. [McKenna&C.]
*PRACTICE AREAS: Insurance Litigation; Commercial Litigation.
Sacks, Rand Evan ....'71 '97 C.1365 B.A. L.659 J.D. Corp. Coun., SFX Sports Grp.
Sacks, Stephen M., (AV) ....'42 '66 C.188 B.S. L.309 LL.B. [Arnold&P.]
*PRACTICE AREAS: Litigation.

Sacks & Chapin, P.C., (AV)
748 Executive Building, 1030 Fifteenth Street, N.W., 20005
Telephone: 202-659-1200 Fax: 202-659-1029
Email: schapinpc@aol.com
Fred C. Sacks (1913-1990); Peter A. Chapin.
Litigation Practice. Personal Injury, Family and Corporate Law.
See Professional Biographies, WASHINGTON, DISTRICT OF COLUMBIA

SáCouto, Susana L. .... '68 '98 C.103 B.A. L.588 J.D. Natl. Assn. for Pub. Interest Law
Sadel, Steven A. ....'52 '77 C.1365 B.A. L.472 J.D. [[C] Holland&K.]
*PRACTICE AREAS: Retail Real Estate; Real Estate.
Sadick, Craig S. '59 '88 C.112 B.A. L.1065 J.D.
Sr. Dir., Govt. Rel., National Assn. of Wholesaler-Distributors
Sadik-Khan, Janette '60 '90 C.605 B.A. L.178 J.D.
(adm. in NY; not adm. in DC) Dep. Admr., Fed. Transit Admn.
Sadler, Constance A. ....'55 '80 C.546 B.A. L.309 J.D. [Sidley A.B.&W.]
Sadler, Scott D. ....'73 '99 C.446 B.A. L.329 J.D. [[A] Morgan,L.&B.]
Sadler, Timothy ....'49 '75 C.951 B.S. L.276 J.D. [[C] McKee N.]
*PRACTICE AREAS: Securities.
Sadow, Michael S., (P.C.) ....'62 '89 C.529 A.B. L.904 J.D. [Silver,F.&T.]
*PRACTICE AREAS: Securities; Corporate Law; Financial Institutions.
Sadowski, James D. ....'65 '92 C.273 B.A. L.180 J.D. [[A] Greenstein D.&L.]
Sadowsky, Shelley, (AV) '52 '84 C.273 B.A. L.446 J.D.
(adm. in MD; not adm. in DC) [[C] Rosenman&C.]
*PRACTICE AREAS: Telecommunications.
Sadur, Marvin P., (AV) ....'22 '49 C&L.273 A.B., J.D. 1615 L St., N.W.
Saenz, Almira P. '76 '01 C.691 B.A. L.893 J.D.
(adm. in VA; not adm. in DC) [[A] Baker B.]
Saenz, Julian F. '— '99 C.976 B.A. L.276 J.D.
(adm. in MD; not adm. in DC) [[A] Morgan,L.&B.]
Safavian, David H. ....'67 '93 C.734 B.A. L.213 J.D. Janus-Merritt Strategies, L.L.C.
Saferstein, Harvey I., (AV) ....'43 '69 C.112 B.A. L.309 LL.B. [Mintz,L.C.F.G.&P.]
*PRACTICE AREAS: Antitrust; Intellectual Property; Litigation.
Saffern, David H. ....'49 '75 C.903 B.A. L.276 J.D. [Bode&G.]
*PRACTICE AREAS: Real Property Tax and Assessment Appeals; Eminent Domain; Litigation.
Safford, Carrie M. ....'72 '99 C.696 B.S. L.1040 J.D. [[A] Dickstein S.M.&O.]
*PRACTICE AREAS: Energy Law.
Safir, Peter O., (AV) ....'45 '73 C.674 A.B. L.976 J.D. [Kleinfeld,K.&B.]
*PRACTICE AREAS: Food, Drug and Cosmetic Law; Drug and Medical Device Regulation; Advertising Law; Federal Civil Litigation; Corporate Investigations.
Sage, Marcia '— '78 C.112 B.A. L.1137 J.D.
(adm. in CA; not adm. in DC) Assoc. Coun., Martin E. Segal Co.
Sager, Steven R. ....'— '94 C.999 B.S. L.1439 J.D. [[C] Hughes&B.]
Sagers, Christopher L. ....'70 '98 C.352 B.A. L.477 J.D. [[A] Shea&G.]

Sagner, Robert-Paul '72 '01 C&L.178 B.A., J.D.
(adm. in NY; not adm. in DC) [[A] Wilmer,C.&P.]
Sahota, Saryad S. '— '93 C.188 B.S. L.1292 J.D.
(adm. in NY; not adm. in DC) [[A] R.E.Bushnell]
Sahr, David R. ....'53 '82 C&L.276 B.S.F.S., J.D. [Shaw P.]
*PRACTICE AREAS: International; Banking; Financial Services.
Sahr, Evelyn D. .... '58 '83 C.575 B.A. L.273 J.D. [[C] Condon&F.]
Saia, Doreen Unis '66 '94 C.951 B.A. L.902 J.D.
(adm. in NY; not adm. in DC) [Couch W.] ⊙
*PRACTICE AREAS: Energy Law; Construction Law; Commercial Litigation; Appellate Practice.
Saidman, Perry J., (AV) '45 '73
C&L.273 B.S.E.E., J.D. [S.DesignLaw] (See Pat. Sect.) ⊙
*PRACTICE AREAS: Intellectual Property; Design Patents; Design Law; Trade Dress; Artistic Property.

SAIDMAN DesignLaw Group, (AV)
1201 Connecticut Avenue, Suite 750, 20036 ⊙
Telephone: 202-223-0800 Fax: 202-223-6607
Email: Group@designlaw.com
Perry J. Saidman.
Industrial Designs, Design Protection, Industrial Design Law, Industrial Design Registrations, Design Patents, Design Law, Design Law Expert, Design Law Consulting, Design Patent Prosecution, Design Patent Infringement, Trade Dress, Product Configurations, Trademark Law, Trademark Infringement, Trademark Registration, Unfair Competition Law, Intellectual Property, Patent Protection, Royalty Agreements, Licensing Agreements, Expert Witness, Design Copyrights, Designer Agreements, Hague Agreement, Utility Patents, PCT Applications, Utility Patent Infringement, Copyright Law, Copyright Registration, Mediation.
Representative Clients: Imperial Schrade Corp.; Toyota; Boston Acoustics; The Burdick Group; Design Ideas, Ltd.; Virginia Plastics Co.; Panasonic.
Silver Spring, Maryland Office: 1110 Bonifant Street, Suite 510, 20910. Telephone: 301-585-8601. Fax: 301-585-0138.
See Professional Biographies, WASHINGTON, DISTRICT OF COLUMBIA

Sailer, Francis J., (AV) ....'53 '78 C&L.436 B.A., J.D. [Dickstein S.M.&O.]
*PRACTICE AREAS: Customs Law; Import and Export Law; International Law; International Sales; Trade Regulation Law.
Sailer, Henry P., (AV) ....'29 '57 C.674 A.B. L.309 LL.B. 1201 Pennsylvania Ave., N.W.
Saindon, Elizabeth A. ....'67 '91 C.260 B.S. L.30 J.D. [Mooney,G.B.&S.]
*PRACTICE AREAS: ERISA; Employee Benefits; ERISA Collections; Taft-Hartley Plans; Litigation.
St. Jean, Deborah ....'57 '87 C.999 B.A. L.1162 J.D. [[A] Coale C.L.M.]
*PRACTICE AREAS: Products Liability; Criminal Law.
St. John, James B., III .... '66 '98 C.902 B.A. L.861 J.D. [[A] Charapp,D.&W.]
*PRACTICE AREAS: Civil Litigation; Corporate Law.
St. John, Kevin M. '74 '00 C.966 B.S. L.145 J.D.
(adm. in VA; not adm. in DC) [[A] Gibson,D.&C.]
St. Landau, Norm D. .... '56 '80 C.605 A.B. L.1162 J.D. [Drinker B.&R.]
*PRACTICE AREAS: Intellectual Property Law; Advertising Law; Entertainment Law.
St. Laurent, Ann ....'44 '90 C.788 B.A. L.861 J.D. [[A] V.A.McArthur]
*PRACTICE AREAS: Trusts and Estate; Estate Planning; Estate Administration.
St. Ledger-Roty, Judith, (AV) ....'52 '79 C.1175 B.A. L.161 J.D. [Kelley D.&W.]
*PRACTICE AREAS: Telecommunications Law; Commercial Law.
St. Martin, Andrée M. ....'58 '83 C.812 B.A. L.309 J.D. [Groom]
*PRACTICE AREAS: Employee Benefits; Pension and Profit Sharing; ERISA.
St. Paul, Roland .... '62 '93 C.999 B.Sc. L.893 J.D. [[A] Dechert]
*PRACTICE AREAS: Securities; Corporate Law; Financial Services Law; Investment Management.
St. Vincent, Roger L. ....'50 '93 C.182 B.M. L.904 J.D. [[A] Dewey B.]
*PRACTICE AREAS: Energy (100%).
Sait, Mohammed F. .... '39 '73 C.905 B.A. L.329 J.D. 1226 11th St., N.W.
Saito, Yoshihiro, (AV) ....'41 '81 C.999 B.A. L.904 J.D. [Perkins C.]
*PRACTICE AREAS: International Trade; International Business Law; Import and Export Law.
Sak, Pamela ....'64 '94 C.675 B.A. L.273 J.D. [[A] Jones,D.R.&P.]
Sakhleh, John I. ....'73 '99 C.446 B.S.A. L.273 J.D. [[A] Dechert]
*PRACTICE AREAS: Financial Services Law; Investment Management; Securities Regulation.
Saks, Lisa J. ....'56 '85 C.604 B.A. L.273 J.D. [Howrey S.A.&W.]
*PRACTICE AREAS: Antitrust; Complex Litigation.
Salaman, Alban, (AV) ....'49 '74 C.659 B.A. L.831 J.D. [Holland&K.]
*PRACTICE AREAS: Estate Planning; Estate Administration; Employee Benefits; Tax.
Salamandrakis, Vasilios .... '74 '00 C.1213 B.S. L.273 J.D. [[A] Bryan C.]
Salamon, Beata Z. '65 '97 C.276 L.999 J.D.
(adm. in NY; not adm. in DC) 1050 Connecticut Ave., N.W.
Salans, Laurence E. .... '60 '87 C.37 B.S.B.A. L.273 J.D. [Sherman,M.C.&A.]
*PRACTICE AREAS: Estate Planning; Estate Administration; Estate Litigation; Charitable Giving; Business Planning.
Salario, Samuel J., Jr. ....'70 '96 C.30 B.A. L.260 J.D. [[A] Wilmer,C.&P.]
Salb, Brian M. '75 '00 C.93 B.A. L.228 J.D.
(adm. in CA; not adm. in DC) [[A] Dow,L.&A.]
Salb, Shannon Micah .... '69 '95 C.184 B.A. L.245 J.D. [[A] Lippman&S.]
*PRACTICE AREAS: Employment Law; Business Litigation; Technology Law; Civil Litigation; Appellate Practice.
Salcido, Robert ....'62 '89 C.154 B.A. L.309 J.D. [Akin,G.S.H.&F.]
*PRACTICE AREAS: Health Care.
Saldana, Anthony ....'69 '96 C.309 A.B. L.976 J.D. [[A] Skadden,A.S.M.&F.]
*PRACTICE AREAS: Corporate.
Sale, Stephen, (AV) ....'52 '77 C.1105 B.A. L.276 J.D. [Claxton,S.&Q.]
*PRACTICE AREAS: Telecommunications Law; Government Contracts; Energy; Corporate Law.
Salehi, Dan ....'67 '99 C.1074 B.S. L.1218 J.D. [[A] Kenyon&K.] (See Pat. Sect.)
*PRACTICE AREAS: Intellectual Property.
Salem, George R., (AV) .... '53 '78 C.1365 B.A. L.245 J.D. [Akin,G.S.H.&F.]
*PRACTICE AREAS: Labor and Employment; Middle East.
Salem, Richard J., (AV) ....'47 '72 C.1126 A.B. L.228 J.D. [Salem S.] (⊙Tampa, FL)
Salem Saxon, P.A., (AV) .... 1730 K. Street N.W. (⊙Orlando, Tallahassee, Tampa, FL)
Salen, Kenneth Harry '64 '00 C.446 B.S. L.1209 J.D.
(adm. in VA; not adm. in DC; See Pat. Sect.) [[A] Armstrong,W.H.M.&N.]
*PRACTICE AREAS: Intellectual Property; Patents.
Salerno, Robert A., (AV) ....'61 '90 C.103 B.A. L.893 J.D. [Piper M.R.&W.]
*PRACTICE AREAS: Commercial Civil Litigation; White Collar Criminal Litigation.
Salgado, Elizabeth M. R. .... '66 '98 C.347 B.A. L.893 J.D. [[A] Dow,L.&A.]
Salgado, Luis F., (AV) .... '48 '80 C.453 B.S. L.276 J.D. [Salgado&Assoc.]
*PRACTICE AREAS: Immigration Law; Visas; Political Asylum; Deportation; Consular Law.
Salgado, R. Anthony ....'62 '87 C&L.893 B.A., J.D. [Dyer E.&J.]
*PRACTICE AREAS: Corporate Law; International Business Law; Maritime Law; Ship Finance; Charter Parties.

Salgado & Associates, (AV)
1220 L Street, N.W., Suite 540, 20005-4018
Telephone: 202-408-1800 Fax: 202-898-0566
Email: salgadolf@aol.com URL: http://www.for-a-visa.com
Luis F. Salgado. Associates: Maribel LaFontaine; Juan Carlos Freire (Not admitted in DC).
Business Immigration, Deportation, Family Immigration, Religious Visas, Political Asylum, Consular Law, Immigration and Discrimination, Employment Visas and Nationality Law.
See Professional Biographies, WASHINGTON, DISTRICT OF COLUMBIA

Saliba, Raja N. .... '66 '97 C.999 B.S. L.273 J.D. [[A] Sughrue M.] (See Pat. Sect.)
*PRACTICE AREAS: Patent Litigation; Patent Prosecution.

Salinas, Norberto Perez .... '75 '00 C.894 A.B. L.477 J.D. [Ⓐ A.Banov&Assoc.]
*PRACTICE AREAS: Retaliatory Discharge; Employment Discrimination; Equal Employment Opportunity Law; Title VII Discrimination; Employment Law.

Salky, Steven M., (AV) .... '54 '82 C.855 B.A. L.976 J.D. [Zuckerman S.]
*PRACTICE AREAS: Criminal and Civil Litigation; Complex Litigation; Criminal Law; Grand Jury Proceedings.

Salles, James E. .... '60 '87 C.367 B.A. L.245 J.D. [Caplin&D.]
*PRACTICE AREAS: Taxation Law.

Salmon, John J., (AV) .... '48 '75 C.276 A.B. L.273 J.D. [Dewey B.]
*PRACTICE AREAS: Tax.

Salmon, Sheila C. .... '63 '88 C.886 B.S. L.904 J.D. [Ⓐ Coan&L.]
*PRACTICE AREAS: Housing and Urban Development; Fair Housing; Real Estate; Probate.

Salmons, Brent T. '73 '99 C.804 B.S. L.276 J.D.
(adm. in MO; not adm. in DC) [Ⓐ Swidler B.S.F.]
*PRACTICE AREAS: Corporate; Mergers and Acquisitions; Securities.

Salmons, David B. '68 '98 C.101 B.A. L.145 J.D.
(adm. in GA; not adm. in DC) [Ⓐ Gibson,D.&C.]
*PRACTICE AREAS: Appellate Practice; Litigation.

Salomon, Kenneth D., (AV) .... '45 '70 C.860 B.A. L.273 J.D. [Dow,L.&A.]

Salonen, Eric P., (AV) .... '59 '85 C.276 B.S.F.S. L.659 J.D. [Ⓒ Stewart&S.]
*PRACTICE AREAS: International Trade; Antidumping; Countervailing Duty and Subsidy; Section 337 Unfair Import Investigations; Safeguards.

Salow, Heidi Pearlman ....'69 '95 C.012 B.A. L.64 J.D. [Ⓐ Cole,R.&B.]
*PRACTICE AREAS: Communications and Media; Intellectual Property; Computers and Software.

Salsbury, Michael H., (AV) '49 '75
C.197 B.A. L.893 J.D. Exec. V.P. & Gen. Coun., MCI WorldCom

Salter, Christopher M. ....'67 '95 C.1369 B.B.A. L.1209 J.D. [Ⓐ Fried,F.H.S.&J.]
*PRACTICE AREAS: Securities Regulation; Securities Enforcement.

Saltman, Alan I., (AV) .... '48 '73 C.588 A.B. L.93 J.D. [Saltman&S.]
*PRACTICE AREAS: Government Contract Law; Timber and Logging; Litigation.

Saltman & Stevens, P.C., (AV)
1801 K Street, N.W. Suite M-110, 20006
Telephone: 202-452-2140 Fax: 202-775-8217
Alan I. Saltman; Gary G. Stevens; Ruth G. Tiger; Kevin Garden; Richard W. Goeken;—William B. Kinner.
Practice before Administrative Agencies and Federal Courts, Government Contract, Timber and Logging, Construction, Antitrust, Environmental, Corporate and Commercial Law, Business.
See Professional Biographies, WASHINGTON, DISTRICT OF COLUMBIA

Saltsman, Richard H., (AV) ....'48 '73 C.674 B.A. L.273 J.D. [Howrey S.A.&W.]
*PRACTICE AREAS: Commercial Litigation; White Collar Criminal Defense.

Saltzberg, Anne L. ....'74 '99 C.763 B.A. L.809 J.D. [Ⓐ Coburn&S.]
*PRACTICE AREAS: Criminal Defense; Civil Litigation.

Saltzman, David S. .... '65 '91 C.945 A.B. L.902 J.D. 1010 Vermont Ave., N.W.

Saltzstein, Robert A., (AV) .... '12 '48 C.477 A.B. L.273 J.D. [Saltzstein,R.A.&G.M.]

Saltzstein, Robert A. and Guy Martin, Law Office of, (AV) ....1725 De Sales St., N.W.

Saluja, Amit ....'71 '97 C&L.273 B.S., J.D. [Ⓐ Hogan&H.]
*PRACTICE AREAS: Corporate Law; Securities; Mergers and Acquisitions; Finance.

Salus, Stanley M., (AV) '44 '69 C.861 B.B.A. L.30 J.D.
[Wickwire G.] (⊙Vienna, VA)
*PRACTICE AREAS: Bankruptcy; Reorganization; Commercial Law.

Salus, Therese I. ....'56 '86 C.788 A.B. L.30 J.D. U.S. Gen. Serv. Adm.

Salvatore, Vincent D., Jr. ....'54 '80 C.197 B.A. L.309 J.D. [Winston&S.]
*PRACTICE AREAS: International Project Finance; Infrastructure Development; Asset Based Finance; Foreign Corrupt Practices Act.

Salwin, Marjorie B. '48 '87 C.112 A.B. L.273 J.D.
(adm. in PA; not adm. in DC) 4401A Connecticut Ave., N.W.

Salzman, Amelia Stuart '58 '86 C.103 B.A. L.569 J.D.
(adm. in NY; not adm. in DC) 1532 Otis St., N.E.‡

Samaraweera, Rohan J., (AV) .... '51 '79 C&L.93 B.S., J.D. 1150 Connecticut Ave., N.W.

Samarias, Joseph J. ....'71 '97 C.880 B.A. L.910 J.D. [Ⓐ Wilmer,C.&P.]

Samet, Andrew James ....'57 '83 C.976 B.A. L.276 J.D. [Ⓒ Sandler,T.&R.]
*PRACTICE AREAS: International Trade; International Labor Law.

Samolis, Frank R., (AV) ....'51 '76 C&L.276 B.S.F.S., J.D. [Patton B.]

Samorajczyk, Stanley J., (AV) .... '42 '68 C.276 A.B. L.128 J.D. [Akin,G.S.H.&F.]
*PRACTICE AREAS: Business Reorganization; International Insolvency; International Bankruptcy; Commercial Insolvency.

Sampson, Erie F. ... '60 '85 C.910 B.A. L.273 J.D. Gen. Coun., State Dept. of Pub. Works

Sampson, Keith T. ....'61 '88 C.183 B.A. L.273 J.D. [Crowell&M.]
*PRACTICE AREAS: Electricity and Natural Gas Law; Public Utility; Administrative Law.

Sampson, Michael H. ....'74 '00 C.893 B.A. L.145 J.D. [Ⓐ Bredhoff&K.]

Sampson, Michael P. ....'40 '66 C&L.188 B.S., J.D. Prof. of Tax., The Amer. Univ.

Sampson, Sherri A. Braden ....'69 '95 C.228 B.A. L.911 J.D. [Ⓐ Hogan&H.]
*PRACTICE AREAS: Corporate; Securities.

Sams, James F., (AV) '32 '57 C.597 B.S. L.477 J.D.
Pres. & Gen. Coun., Amer. Development Servs. Corp.

Samuel, Wendy B. ....'50 '76 C.659 B.A. L.976 J.D. Assoc. Gen. Coun., Fannie Mae

Samuels, Charles Alan, (AV) .... '54 '78 C&L.893 B.A., LL.B. [Mintz,L.C.F.G.&P.]
*PRACTICE AREAS: Federal Legislation and Regulation; Natural Resources; Antitrust Law.

Samuels, Frederick N. '63 '90 C.446 B.S.E.G. L.273 J.D.
[Cahn&S.] (See Pat. Sect.) ⊙
*PRACTICE AREAS: Intellectual Property Law.

Samuels, Joel ....'72 '00 C.674 B.A. L.477 J.D. [Ⓐ Covington&B.]
*PRACTICE AREAS: International Law; Litigation.

Sanchez, Ernest T., (AV) ....'48 '74 C.1012 B.S. L.276 J.D. [Sanchez]

Sanchez, Henry, Jr. '— '84 C.1214 B.A. L.705 J.D.
(adm. in PA; not adm. in DC) [Ⓒ Reed S.] (⊙Washington)
*PRACTICE AREAS: Corporate Law.

Sanchez, Peter B. '71 '00 C.102 B.A. L.801 J.D.
(adm. in NY; not adm. in DC) [Ⓐ Fleischman&W.]

Sanchez Law Firm, (AV) .... 2000 L St., N.W.

Sand, Fred W. ....'47 '91 C.966 B.A. L.884 Small Bus. Admn.

Sandalls, Helen M. .... '45 '87 C.914 B.A. L.36 J.D. 3604 Macomb St., N.W.

Sandercock, Colin G., (AV) ......'— '84 C.509 B.S. L.128 J.D. [Heller E.W.&M.] (Pat.)
*PRACTICE AREAS: Intellectual Property Law; Patent Law.

Sanders, David P. .... '60 '87 C.477 B.A. L.208 J.D. [Kirkland&E.]
*PRACTICE AREAS: Customs Law; International Trade.

Sanders, David Seth .... '— '96 C.477 B.A. L.276 J.D. [Ⓐ Foley&L.]
*PRACTICE AREAS: Corporate Law; Mergers and Acquisitions; Securities.

Sanders, John M. '54 '80 C.339 B.S. L.1000 J.D.
(adm. in IL; not adm. in DC) [Ⓐ Sughrue M.] ⊙
*PRACTICE AREAS: Intellectual Property.

Sanders, Michael I., (AV) ....'38 '64 C&L.569 B.S., LL.B. [Powell,G.F.&M.]
*PRACTICE AREAS: Taxation Law; Real Estate Law.

Sanders, Neal A. ....'52 '80 C.4 B.B.A. L.809 J.D. 2550 M St., N.W. (⊙Butler, PA)

Sanders, Susan L., (AV) .... '48 '79 C.112 B.A. L.273 J.D. [Farha&S.]

Sanders & Sanders
(See Upper Marlboro, Maryland)

Sanders, Schnabel & Brandenburg, P.C., (AV)
Suite 900, 900 Seventeenth Street, N.W., 20006-2501
Telephone: 202-638-2241 Telecopier: 202-293-3419
Email: ssb@ssblegal.com URL: http://www.ssblegal.com
John A. Sanders (1924-1998); Dan S. Brandenburg; David Weingarten; Cheryl Risley Hughes;—Stacey A. Bradford; Joanne G. Jacobson; Susan Yoder Torres; Lincoln Weed. Of Counsel: Robert V. Schnabel; William H. Bradford, Jr.; Carol V. Calhoun.
Pension and Profit Sharing, Employee Benefits, Taxation, Corporate Law, Professional Corporations, Tax Exempt Organizations, Employment Law (Management), Estate Planning, Trusts, Probate, Litigation and Administrative Law.
See Professional Biographies, WASHINGTON, DISTRICT OF COLUMBIA

Sandground, Mark B., Jr. '60 '85 C.813 B.A. L.893 J.D.
(adm. in VA; not adm. in DC) [Ⓐ O'Brien,B.M.&S.]
*PRACTICE AREAS: Nonprofit Organizations Law; Corporate Law; Real Estate; Restaurant Law; Civil Litigation.

Sandground Barondess West & New, P.C.
(See Vienna, Virginia)

Sandler, Andrew L. ....'56 '83 C.867 B.A. L.659 J.D. [Skadden,A.S.M.&F.]

Sandler, Donald M., (AV) '27 '57 C.367 B.E. L.64 LL.B.
(adm. in MD; not adm. in DC; See Pat. Sect.) [Nath&Assoc.] ‡

Sandler, Gilbert Lee, (AV) '44 '69 C.197 A.B. L.569 J.D.
(adm. in FL; not adm. in DC) [Sandler,T.&R.] (⊙L.A., San Fran., CA; Miami, FL; Chgo., IL; New York, NY; Hous., TX)
*PRACTICE AREAS: Customs Law; International Trade Law; Intellectual Property Law.

Sandler, Joseph E. ....'53 '78 C&L.309 A.B., J.D. [Sandler,R.&Y.]
*PRACTICE AREAS: Election, Campaign and Political Law; Nonprofit and Charitable Organizations; Nonprofit Tax Law; Election and Campaign Finance; Commercial Law.

Sandler, Richard A. '65 '95 C.880 B.A. L.339 J.D.
Fair Housing Council of Greater Wash.

Sandler, Reiff & Young, P.C., (AV)
50 E Street, S.E., Suite 300, 20003
Telephone: 202-479-1111 Fax: 202-479-1115
Email: sandler@sandlerreiff.com URL: http://www.sandlerreiff.com
Joseph E. Sandler; Neil P. Reiff; John Hardin Young.
Election, Campaign and Political Law, Nonprofit and Charitable Organizations, Nonprofit Tax Law, Government Law, Commercial Law and Litigation.
See Professional Biographies, WASHINGTON, DISTRICT OF COLUMBIA

Sandler, Travis & Rosenberg, P.A., (AV)
1300 Pennsylvania Avenue, Suite 400, 20004 ⊙
Telephone: 202-216-9307 Fax: 202-842-2247
Email: info@strtrade.com URL: http://www.strtrade.com
Gilbert Lee Sandler (Not admitted in DC); Thomas G. Travis; Leonard L. Rosenberg; Ronald W. Gerdes; Teresa M. Polino; Peggy Louie Chaplin; Philip S. Gallas; Chandri Navarro-Bowman;—David E. Cohen; Mark R. Ludwikowski (Not admitted in DC); Susan L. Renton. Of Counsel: Paul G. Giguere; Andrew James Samet.
Customs Law, International Trade and Transportation Law. International Corporate, Copyright and Trademark Law. Trial, Appellate, Federal and Administrative Practice. Immigration and Nationality Law. International Labor Law, NAFTA, Government Relations, Trade Negotiations, International Trade Policy, Intellectual Property, Import and Export Law, Foreign Trade Sanctions, Shipping Law, Surety.
Miami, Florida Office: The Waterford, 5200 Blue Lagoon Drive, Suite 600, 33126-2022. Telephone: 305-267-9200. Fax: 305-267-5155.
New York, New York Office: 551 Fifth Avenue, Suite 614, 10176. Telephone: 212-883-1300. Fax: 212-883-0068.
Baltimore, Maryland Office: 111 South Calvert Street, Suite 2700, 21202. Telephone: 410-385-5208. Fax: 410-837-2441.
San Francisco, California Office: Sandler, Travis & Rosenberg and Glad & Ferguson, P.C., 1 Sutter Street, 10th Floor, 94014. Telephone: 415-986-1088. Fax: 415-986-2271.
Chicago, Illinois Office: Sandler, Travis & Rosenberg LLC, 200 West Madison Street, Suite 2670, 60606. Telephone: 312-236-6555. Telecopier: 312-236-6568.
Houston, Texas Office: 440 Louisiana, Suite 900, 77002. Telephone: 713-236-7715. Fax: 713-236-7768.
Los Angeles, California Office: Sandler, Travis & Rosenberg and Glad & Ferguson, P.C., 5230 Pacific Concourse Drive, Suite 200, 90045. Telephone: 310-643-4494. Telecopier: 310-643-4493.
See Professional Biographies, WASHINGTON, DISTRICT OF COLUMBIA

Sandman, James J., (AV) .... '51 '76 C.93 A.B. L.659 J.D. [Arnold&P.]
*PRACTICE AREAS: Litigation; Products Liability.

Sandman, Jeffrey M. '56 '86 C.994 B.A. L.276 J.D.
Exec. V.P. & Gen. Coun., Kamber Group, The

Sandor, Lawrence P. ....'62 '87 C.94 B.S. L.245 J.D. [Ⓒ Dickstein S.M.&O.]
*PRACTICE AREAS: Securities Compliance and Enforcement; Securities; Securities Arbitration; Securities Mediation; Broker Dealer.

Sandri, Joseph M., Jr. '63 '91 C.446 B.S. L.128 J.D.
V.P. & Regul. Coun., WinStar Telecommunications, Inc.

Sandstrom, Mark Roy, (AV) ....'42 '69 C&L.477 B.A., J.D. [Thompson H.]
*PRACTICE AREAS: International Trade Law; Customs Law; International Business Law; Government Affairs; Regulatory Law.

Sandza, Elizabeth Barry, (AV) ....'51 '79 C.494 B.S. L.831 J.D. [LeBoeuf,L.G.&M.]
*PRACTICE AREAS: Insurance; Litigation.

Saner, Robert J., II, (AV) .... '47 '73 C.674 A.B. L.309 J.D. [Powers,P.S.&V.]
*PRACTICE AREAS: Health Care Law; Environmental Law.

Sanford, Bruce W., (AV) ....'45 '70 C.299 A.B. L.569 J.D. [Baker&H.]
*PRACTICE AREAS: Business Litigation; First Amendment/Libel Law.

Sanford, David W. .... '57 '97 C.881 A.B. L.813 J.D. [Ⓐ Gordon,S.W.&C.]
*PRACTICE AREAS: Civil Rights; Employment Litigation; Appellate Practice.

Sanford, Jeannine C. ....'64 '90 C&L.608 B.A., J.D. Neighborhood Legal Servs. Prog.

San Martin, David R. ....'— '97 C.613 B.S. L.623 J.D. [Ⓐ Hogan&H.]
*PRACTICE AREAS: Intellectual Property; Bioscience Transactions; International High Technology; Entertainment.

Sannes, Victor E. '51 '78 C.491 B.A. L.494 J.D.
(adm. in MN; not adm. in DC) CPT Corp.

Sano, Curtis L. ....'66 '93 C.976 B.A. L.1066 J.D. [Ⓐ Holland&K.]
*PRACTICE AREAS: Real Estate Purchase and Sale; Real Estate Finance; Retail Development and Leasing; Office Development and Leasing; Affordable Housing.

Sanok, Jeffrey D. ....'62 '88 C.602 B.S.E.E. L.276 J.D. [Crowell&M.] (Pat.)
*PRACTICE AREAS: Litigation; Patents; Trademarks; Copyrights; Trade Secrets.

Santa, Donald F., Jr. ....'58 '83 C.228 A.B. L.178 J.D. [Troutman S.]
*PRACTICE AREAS: Energy Marketing; Regulatory; Public Policy Legislation.

Santarelli, Donald E., (AV) .... '37 '62 C.524 A.B. L.893 LL.B. [Bell,B.&L.]
*PRACTICE AREAS: Legislative; Transportation.

Santiago, Simon J. ...... '71 '96 C.339 B.A. L.904 J.D. [Ⓐ Wickwire G.] (⊙Vienna, VA)
*PRACTICE AREAS: Construction Law; Public Contract Law.

Santorelli, Albert J., (AV) '38 '64
C.688 B.S.E.E. L.276 LL.B. [Finnegan,H.F.G.&D.] (See Pat. Sect.)
*PRACTICE AREAS: Patent Litigation; Patents; Patent Interference Practice; Patent Infringement.

Santos, Christa '69 '99 C.156 B.A. L.102 J.D.
(adm. in MA; not adm. in DC) 1875 Connecticut Avenue, N.W.

Santos, Margarita D. '70 '97 C.273 B.A. L.1003 J.D.
(adm. in OH; not adm. in DC) [Ⓐ Littler M.]
*PRACTICE AREAS: Employment Litigation; Employment Counseling; Labor Law; Immigration Law.

Santos-Caballero, Lillian ....'38 '83 C.102 B.A. L.1162 J.D. 900 S St., N.W.

Santucci, Joseph E., Jr. ....'50 '76 C.602 B.A. L.128 J.D. [Morgan,L.&B.]

Sanz-Rexach, Gabriel R. ... '68 '94 C.276 B.S.F.S. L.893 J.D. [Ⓐ Willkie F.&G.]
Sanzo, Kathleen M. ... '57 '82 C.228 A.B. L.245 J.D. [Morgan,L.&B.]
Saperstein, Jonathan ... '46 '80 C.165 B.A. L.276 J.D. 60 Mass. Ave., N.E.
Saphire, Daniel '57 '81 C.1349 B.A. L.273 J.D.
Gen. Atty., Association of American Railroads
Sapin, David R. ... '66 '94 C.846 B.B.A. L.273 J.D. Price Waterhouse
Sapir, Genevieve D. ... '72 '97 C.30 B.A. L.273 J.D. [Ⓐ Cole,R.&B.]
*PRACTICE AREAS: Telecommunications Law; Cable TV; Administrative Law; Litigation.
Sapir, Judith S. '44 '86 C.823 B.A. L.273 J.D.
Vice President & General Counsel, APCO Worldwide
Sapiro, Todd S. ... '67 '92 C.477 B.A. L.30 J.D. [Ⓐ Friedlander,M.S.K.&O.]
*PRACTICE AREAS: Workers Compensation; Personal Injury; Products Liability; Insurance Defense; Civil Litigation.
Saporito, Gina M. ... '72 '98 C.30 B.A. L.904 J.D. [Ⓐ Baach R.&L.P.]
*PRACTICE AREAS: Civil Litigation; Employment Law.
Sapper, Arthur G., (AV) ... '50 '75 C.1044 B.A. L.276 J.D. [McDermott,W.&E.]
Saran, Atul ... '73 '99 C.813 B.S. L.339 J.D. [Ⓐ Hogan&H.]
*PRACTICE AREAS: Business Law; Corporate Law; Computers and Software; Biotechnology; Investments.
Saran, Roopal Mehta ... '72 '98 C.813 B.A. L.339 J.D. First Book
Sarbacher, Harold J. ... '29 '58 C.870 B.Sc. L.276 J.D. 2700 Virginia Ave.
Sarchio, Christina Guerola ... '69 '95 C.188 B.A. L.273 J.D. [Ⓐ Howrey S.A.&W.]
*PRACTICE AREAS: Commercial Litigation; White Collar.
Sardella, William J. '59 '97 C.870 B.S. L.823 J.D.
(adm. in NY; not adm. in DC) Corp. Coun., Marriott Intl., Inc.
*RESPONSIBILITIES: Marriott Distribution Services; Commercial Transactions; Real Estate; General Corporate.
Saret, Lewis J. ... '59 '90 C.1061 B.B.A. L.273 J.D. [Ⓐ Kilpatrick S.]
*PRACTICE AREAS: Tax; Estate Planning.
Sargent, Mary Randolph ... '71 '99 C.105 B.A. L.276 J.D. [Ⓐ Cadwalader,W.&T.]
Sarkis, Paul A. '67 '94 C.645 B.A. L.607 J.D.
(adm. in MD; not adm. in DC) Editor, Bureau of National Affairs, Inc., The
Sarraille, William A., (BV) ... '63 '89 C.976 B.A. L.309 J.D. [Arent F.K.P.&K.]
*PRACTICE AREAS: Civil Litigation; Health Care; White Collar Criminal Defense; Health Care Legislation.
Sarro, Dale M. ... '56 '85 C.31 A.B. L.309 J.D. [Paul,W.R.W.&G.]
*PRACTICE AREAS: International and Domestic Project Finance; Telecommunications; Corporate Finance.
Sarsfield, James B., (AV) ... '49 '74 C.276 A.B. L.128 J.D. [Hamilton&H.]
*PRACTICE AREAS: Civil Litigation; Personal Injury; Employment Law; Education Law.
Sartori, Michael A. '— '98
C.602 B.S.E.E. L.276 J.D. [Ⓒ Venable,A.B.H.&C.] (See Pat. Sect.)
*PRACTICE AREAS: Intellectual Property.
Sarvadi, David G. ... '47 '86 C.645 B.S.B.A. L.1209 J.D. [Keller&H.]
*PRACTICE AREAS: Environmental Law; Occupational Health and Safety Law; Pesticides; Hazardous Materials; Transportation.
Sarver, Marnie K., (AV) ... '46 '80 C.207 B.A. L.226 J.D. [Ⓒ Wiley R.&F.]
*PRACTICE AREAS: Communications Law.
Sasinowski, Frank J. ... '53 '82 C.188 B.S. L.276 J.D. [Hyman,P.&M.]
Sasse, Daniel A. ... '72 '97 C.879 B.A. L.245 J.D. [Ⓐ Crowell&M.]
Satagaj, John S. ... '52 '77 C.860 B.A. L.184 J.D. 1156 15th St., N.W.
Satchell, William H. '53 '79 C.112 A.B. L.800 J.D.
[O'Melveny&M.] (⊙New York, NY)
*PRACTICE AREAS: Banking.
Satinoff, Debra L. ... '73 '99 C.910 B.A. L.904 J.D. [Ⓐ Jones,D.R.&P.]
Satola, David E. '60 '86 C.367 B.A. L.966 J.D.
(adm. in WI; not adm. in DC) The World Bank
Satten, Kenneth E., (AV) ... '55 '79 C.1044 B.A. L.273 J.D. [Wilkinson B.K.]
*PRACTICE AREAS: Communications Law; Administrative Law; Corporate Law; Commercial Transactions.
Satterfield, L. Kendall ... '59 '84 C.607 B.S. L.245 J.D. [Finkelstein,T.&L.]
Satterfield, Lee A., (AV) ... '33 '63 C&L.329 A.B., LL.B. [Ⓒ Whiteford,T.&P.]
*PRACTICE AREAS: Communications Law; Regulatory Law; Government Affairs; Corporate Law.
Satterfield, Pamela S. ... '62 '89 C.118 B.A. L.128 J.D. Asst. U.S. Atty.
Satterthwaite, Janet F. ... '60 '86 C.976 B.A. L.893 J.D. [Venable,A.B.H.&C.]
*PRACTICE AREAS: Trademark Prosecution; Trademark Counseling; Trademark Litigation; Licensing; Internet Law.
Sauber, Pamela G., (BV) ... '60 '85 C.893 B.A. L.692 J.D. 2020 K St., 7th Fl.
Sauber, Richard A., (AV) ... '50 '77 C.976 B.A. L.569 J.D. [Fried,F.H.S.&J.]
Sauc, Jacqueline Marie, (AV) ... '— '75 C.518 B.A. L.276 J.D. [Foley&L.]
*PRACTICE AREAS: Health Law; Antitrust Law; Corporate Law; Litigation.
Sauer, Edward W., (AV) ... '49 '75 C&L.276 B.S.F.S., J.D. [Squire,S.&D.]
*PRACTICE AREAS: Aviation; Practice before U.S. Department of Transportation.
Saul, Lewis J. ... '49 '80 C.1123 B.A. L.1209 J.D. [L.J.Saul]
Saul, Lewis J., P.C. ... 5335 Wisconsin Ave., N.W.
Sauls, Daniel C. ... '54 '80 C&L.893 B.A., J.D. [Steptoe&J.]
*PRACTICE AREAS: Government Contracts; Health Care; Litigation; Construction Law; Insurance Coverage.
Saunders, Andrea Dawn '67 '93 C.999 B.S. L.64 J.D.
(adm. in MD; not adm. in DC)
Legis. Specialist, American Association of Retired Persons
Saunders, Margot Freeman '53 '78 C.1036 B.A. L.575 J.D.
(adm. in NC; not adm. in DC) National Consumer Law Ctr.
Saunders, Mary Jane ... '56 '82 C.886 B.A. L.469 J.D. [Venable,A.B.H.&C.]
*PRACTICE AREAS: Intellectual Property; Technology; Employment; Litigation.
Saunders, Nathan H. ... '72 '00 C.197 A.B. L.228 J.D. [Ⓐ Hogan&H.]
Saunders, Sanford M., Jr. ... '58 '83 C.367 B.A. L.276 J.D. [Akin,G.S.H.&F.]
*PRACTICE AREAS: Litigation; Technology Law.
Saunders, William Lee, Jr. '53 '81
C.575 B.A. L.309 J.D. Prof. of Law, Catholic Univ. of America

Saunders & Schmieler, P.C., (AV)
1050 17th Street, N.W. Suite 600, 20036 ⊙
Telephone: 202-833-2999
Email: schmielj@sslawfirm.com URL: http://www.sslawfirm.com
Member of Firm: Jeffrey R. Schmieler.
General Civil, Trial and Appellate Practice in all Courts, Insurance Defense, Trial and Litigation, Insurance Coverage, Self-Insurance Defense, Liability Defense Litigation, Intellectual Property Law, Products Liability Defense, Premises Liability Defense, Construction Liability Defense, Personal Injury Defense, Civil Rights Litigation, Discrimination Claims, Errors and Omissions, Professional Malpractice Defense, Advice and Consultation, Insurance Risk Management, Corporate Law, Commercial Litigation, Environmental Law, Toxic Tort Defense, Personal Injury Defense, Real Estate Law, Advertising Injury Defense, Labor Relations, Workers' Compensation, Mass Tort and Litigation Defense.
Silver Spring, Maryland Office: 8737 Colesville Rd., Suite L-200. Telephone: 301-588-7717. Facsimile: 301-588-5073.
Baltimore, Maryland Office: Suite 2700, 111 South Calvert Street. Telephone: 410-235-7558.
Arlington, Virginia Office: 2111 Wilson Boulevard, Suite 700. Telephone: 703-243-1100.
See Professional Biographies, WASHINGTON, DISTRICT OF COLUMBIA

Saurer, Holly Lynn '72 '00 C.823 B.S. L.904 J.D.
(adm. in MD; not adm. in DC) [Ⓐ Miller&V.]
*PRACTICE AREAS: Telecommunications Law; Cable TV; Cable Franchising; Local Government Law.
Sausser, Gail D. '52 '99 C.999 B.A. L.904 J.D.
(adm. in MD; not adm. in DC) [Ⓐ Vinson&E.]
*PRACTICE AREAS: Medicare and Medicaid Reimbursement; Medicare Fraud and Abuse; Privacy Law.
Sauter, Donna M. '67 '00 C.990 B.A. L.128 J.D.
(adm. in VA; not adm. in DC) [Ⓐ McDermott,W.&E.]
Sautter, Willis N. '70 '01 C.976 B.A. L.145 J.D.
(adm. in NY; not adm. in DC) [Ⓐ Williams&C.]
Savage, Amy K. ... '70 '00 C.1012 B.A. L.276 J.D. [Ⓐ Ross,D.&B.]
Savage, Carroll J., (AV) ... '34 '64 C.797 B.A. L.309 J.D. [Ivins,P.&B.]
*PRACTICE AREAS: Employee Benefits; Employment Taxation; Executive Compensation; ERISA Litigation; ESOPs.
Savage, Christine E. ... '— '99 C.477 B.A. L.128 J.D. [Ⓐ King&S.]
Savage, Christopher W., (BV) ... '56 '80 C&L.309 A.B., J.D. [Cole,R.&B.]
*PRACTICE AREAS: Telecommunications Regulation; Wireless Communications; Internet Law; Telecommunications Competition; New Media Law.
Savage, Joseph P. ... '60 '87 C.893 B.A. L.1065 J.D. 1401 H St., N.W.
Savage, Justin A. ... '72 '97 C.1089 B.A. L.893 J.D. [Ⓐ Beveridge&D.]
*PRACTICE AREAS: Environmental Law; Litigation.
Savage, Malcolm Brooks, Jr. ... '57 '83 C&L.945 A.B., J.D. [Abed&S.]
Savage, Stephen J., (BV) '49 '75 C.446 B.A. L.64 J.D.
Dept. Head - Labor Rel., Washington Gas Light Co.
Savarese, Ralph J., (AV) ... '36 '62 C.1041 B.B.A. L.477 LL.B. [Howrey S.A.&W.]
*PRACTICE AREAS: Antitrust Law; Complex Commercial Litigation.
Savarino, William F. ... '58 '83 C.446 B.S. L.421 J.D. [Cohen M.]
*PRACTICE AREAS: Litigation; Government Contracts; Business Law; Computers and Software.
Saveth, Henry ... '46 '77 C.966 B.A. L.1009 J.D. William M. Mercer, Inc.
Savir, Mika Z. '57 '82 C&L.575 B.A., J.D.
(adm. in NC; not adm. in DC) 445 12th St., S.W.
Savit, Mark N., (AV) ... '49 '76 C.800 B.A. L.276 J.D. [Patton B.]
Savits, Joel M., (AV) '35 '60
C.319 B.A. L.276 J.D. [Ⓒ Jordan C.&S.] (⊙Balt., Rockville, MD)
*PRACTICE AREAS: Legal Malpractice Defense; Medical Malpractice Defense; Professional Liability Defense; Alternative Dispute Resolution.
Savitsky, Gerald S. '49 '73 C&L.309 A.B., J.D.
Vice President and Associate Director, Riggs Bk. N.A.
Savitt, Gary ... '— '99 C.871 B.S.A.E. L.904 J.D. [Ⓐ Fish&R.] (See Pat. Sect.)
*PRACTICE AREAS: Intellectual Property.
Savitt, Lisa J., (AV) ... '56 '82 C.273 B.A. L.564 J.D. [Ⓒ Blank R.C.&M.]
*PRACTICE AREAS: Aviation Liability; Aviation Litigation; Products Liability; International Commercial Litigation; Employment Law.
Savoy, Eric J. ... '71 '96 C.1155 B.S. L.1202 J.D. 555 12th St., N.W.
Saxe, Bernhard D., (AV) ... '— '81 C.367 B.A. L.273 J.D. [Foley&L.] (See Pat. Sect.)
*PRACTICE AREAS: U.S. and Foreign Chemical, Pharmaceutical; Biotechnological Patent, Licensing and Litigation; Trademarks; Technology Transfers.
Saxena, Nisha ... '75 '01 C.494 B.S. L.537 J.D. [Ⓐ Zuckert,S.&R.]
Saxenian, James R. ... '65 '90 C.1044 B.S. L.273 J.D. [Dow,L.&A.]
Saxon, Janet D. ... '27 '52 C.881 A.B. L.477 LL.B. The Dunham Gallery
Saxon, Sean G. '65 '97 C&L.836 B.A., J.D.
(adm. in TN; not adm. in DC) [Ⓐ Winston&S.]
Saxon, Stephen M. ... '51 '79 C.165 A.B. L.276 J.D. [Groom]
*PRACTICE AREAS: Business Law; Employee Benefits; Health Care; Tax; Labor and Employment.
Saybolt, David P. '63 '99 C.31 B.A. L.276 J.D.
(adm. in VA; not adm. in DC) Asst. U.S. Atty.
Sayler, Robert N., (AV) ... '40 '65 C.813 A.B. L.309 LL.B. [Covington&B.]
Sayles, Crystal D. ... '54 '98 C.367 M.S.C.S. L.904 J.D. [Ⓐ Sterne,K.G.&F.]
*PRACTICE AREAS: Intellectual Property.
Sayles, Eric Howell ... '42 '68 C&L.260 B.A., J.D. 2015 R St., N.W.
Sayles, Julia L. ... '40 '66 C.239 A.B. L.575 LL.B. Chf., Fin. Sect., Off. of Corp. Coun.
Saylor, Alice C., (AV) '48 '76 C.145 B.A. L.190 J.D.
V.P. & Gen Coun., Amer. Short Line & Reg. R.R. Assn.
Saylor, David J., (AV) ... '45 '71 C.951 A.B. L.309 J.D. [Hogan&H.]
*PRACTICE AREAS: Communications and Media; Antitrust and Trade Regulation.
Sayre, Claudia G. ... '63 '88 C.976 B.A. L.569 J.D. 2824 Northampton St., N.W.
Sayre, David A. ... '48 '74 C.216 B.A. L.273 J.D. The Bureau of Natl. Affs., Inc.
Sayre, Robert M. '24 '56 C.950 A.B. L.273 J.D.
Asst. Secy. for Mgmt., Organ. of Amer. States
Scala, Keith B. '75 '00 C.188 B.S. L.365 J.D.
(adm. in IL; not adm. in DC; See Pat. Sect.) [Ⓐ Sughrue M.]
*PRACTICE AREAS: Patents.
Scallet, Edward A., (AV) ... '50 '75 C.309 A.B. L.910 J.D. [Groom]
*PRACTICE AREAS: Employee Benefits; Litigation.
Scanio, Salvatore ... '65 '92 C&L.861 B.A., J.D. [Ludwig&R.]
*PRACTICE AREAS: Complex Litigation; Banking Law; Corporate Law.
Scanlan, James P. ... '45 '69 C.363 A.B. L.309 J.D. [Ⓒ Akin,G.S.H.&F.]
*PRACTICE AREAS: Labor and Employment.
Scanlon, Kerry Alan ... '51 '77 C.309 A.B. L.1162 J.D. [Kaye S.]
*PRACTICE AREAS: Civil Rights; Employment Discrimination.
Scanlon, Michael J. ... '70 '97 C.478 B.A. L.276 J.D. [Ⓐ Gibson,D.&C.]
Scanlon, Patrick M., (AV) '40 '68 C.260 B.A. L.362 J.D.
Gen. Coun., Communications Workers of America
Scanlon, Tara A. ... '66 '91 C.299 B.A. L.659 J.D. [Holland&K.]
*PRACTICE AREAS: Commercial Real Estate; Business Law.
Scarborough, Ryan T. ... '71 '98 C.228 A.B. L.309 J.D. [Ⓐ Williams&C.]
*PRACTICE AREAS: Litigation.
Scardino, Kimberly A. ... '69 '96 C.30 B.A. L.276 J.D. Assoc. Coun., WorldCom
Scarlett, Thomas ... '43 '69 C.178 B.A. L.976 LL.B. [Hyman,P.&M.]
Scarrow, James W. ... '61 '90 C.197 B.A. L.893 J.D. [Ⓐ Chadbourne&P.]
Scavazzo, Stephen D. ... '54 '80 C.433 B.S.C.E. L.128 J.D. 1704 Lamdn St., N.W.
Schaars, Steven ... '45 '70 C&L.966 B.S., J.D. [King,P.&H.]
*PRACTICE AREAS: Criminal Law; Complex and Multi-District Litigation; Health Care; RICO.
Schaberg, Richard A. ... '59 '85 C.105 B.A. L.273 J.D. [Thacher P.&W.]
*PRACTICE AREAS: Corporate and Financial Institutions; Securities; Mergers and Acquisitions.
Schachte, William L., Jr., (BV) ... '40 '73 C.160 B.A. L.790 J.D. [Ⓒ Dyer E.&J.]
*PRACTICE AREAS: Government Contracts; Defense Contracts; Government.
Schad, Matthew O. '— '98 C.31 B.A. L.896 J.D.
(adm. in VA; not adm. in DC) [Ⓐ Morgan,L.&B.]
Schad, Steven P. ... '— '87 C.474 B.S.C.E. L.1209 J.D. [Banner&W.] (See Pat. Sect.)
*PRACTICE AREAS: Intellectual Property Law; Patents; Intellectual Property Licensing; Mechanical Intellectual Property.
Schaecher, Gina L., (BV) ... '65 '94 C.627 B.S.B.A. L.546 J.D. [Ⓒ Halloran&S.]
*PRACTICE AREAS: Commercial Litigation; Construction Law; Government Contracts.
Schaefer, Alexander H. ... '73 '98 C.188 B.A. L.1209 J.D. [Ⓐ Sonnenschein N.&R.]
*PRACTICE AREAS: International Trade; Customs.
Schaefer, Caroline ... '— '97 C.788 B.A. L.904 J.D. [Ⓐ Dechert]
*PRACTICE AREAS: Securities; Financial Services Law; Investment Management; Corporate Law.
Schaefer, Jerome C., (AV) ... '46 '72 C.363 B.A. L.128 J.D. [O'Brien,B.M.&S.]
*PRACTICE AREAS: Tort Defense; Indemnity; Nonprofit Organizations Law; Civil Rights Defense; Media and First Amendment.

Schaefer, Kelsey '72 '00 C.999 B.A. L.94 J.D.
(adm. in MA; not adm. in DC) [Ⓐ Hughes H.&R.]
*PRACTICE AREAS: Litigation.
Schaefer, Mark .... '68 '95 C.1044 B.A. L.273 J.D. 1614 20th St., N.W.
Schaefer, Stephen M. .... '74 '99 C&L.884 B.A., J.D. [Ⓐ O'Brien,B.M.&S.]
*PRACTICE AREAS: Media and First Amendment; Nonprofit Organizations Law; Corporate Law; Civil Litigation.
Schaefer Zecca, Kathryn ...... '69 '95 C.276 B.S.F.S. L.145 J.D. [Ⓐ Robbins,R.E.O.&U.]
Schaefermeier, Martin .... '— '90 L.999 J.D. [Ⓖ Verner,L.B.M.&H.]
Schaeffer, Alan J. .... '60 '89 C.188 B.S. L.659 J.D. [McDermott,W.&E.]
Schaeffer, Judith E., (AV) '52 '79 C.674 A.B. L.976 J.D.
Dep. Legal Dir., People for the American Way
Schaefgen, John R., Jr. .... '48 '78 C&L.276 B.S., J.D. [Ⓖ Thelen R.&P.]
*PRACTICE AREAS: Infrastructure Development; Project Finance.
Schaengold, Michael J. .... '59 '86 C.216 B.A. L.893 J.D. [Patton B.]
Schaerr, Gene C. .... '57 '87 C.101 B.A. L.976 J.D. [Sidley A.B.&W.]
Schafer, Carolyn .... '68 '96 C.884 B.A. L.128 J.D. [Ⓐ Dow,L.&A.]
Schafer, John H., (AV) .... '26 '55 C.951 A.B. L.893 LL.B. [Ⓖ Covington&B.]
Schafer, Judy D. '50 '86 C.423 B.A. L.276 J.D.
(adm. in PA; not adm. in DC) Vet. Admn. Med. Ctr.
Schafer, Todd D. .... '62 '90 C.881 B.A. L.309 J.D. [Hogan&H.]
*PRACTICE AREAS: International Corporate Law; International Financial Transactions and Restructurings; International Regulatory Law; International Arbitration.
Schaffer, Arthur D. .... '17 '43 C.102 B.A. L.276 J.D. 1220 19th St Nw # 400
Schaffer, David R. '58 '97 C.945 B.A. L.128 J.D.
(adm. in VA; not adm. in DC; See Pat. Sect.) [Ⓐ Kenyon&K.]
*PRACTICE AREAS: Intellectual Property.
Schaffer, Gregory Paul .... '63 '88 C.273 B.A. L.800 J.D. 1501 M St., N.W., Suite 700
Schaffer, Mark L., (P.C.), (AV) .... '45 '72 C.94 A.B. L.276 J.D. [Ashcraft&G.]
*PRACTICE AREAS: Workers Compensation.
Schaffer, Steven C., (AV) .... '51 '76 C.966 B.A. L.273 J.D. [Schwartz,W.&M.]
*PRACTICE AREAS: Communications Law; Telecommunications Law; Copyright and Trademark Law; Broadcast Production and Distribution Law.
Schafrick, Frederick C., (AV) .... '48 '73 C&L.477 A.B., J.D. [Shea&G.]
*PRACTICE AREAS: Appellate Practice; Aviation; Product Liability; Administrative.
Schagrin, Roger B., (AV) .... '57 '81 C.976 B.A. L.893 J.D. [Schagrin]
*PRACTICE AREAS: International Trade; Legislative Law.

Schagrin Associates, (AV)
1100 Fifteenth Street, NW Suite 700, 20005
Telephone: 202-223-1700 Fax: 202-429-2522
Email: schagrin@erols.com
Member of Firm: Roger B. Schagrin.
International Trade Practice before the Civil Courts, Government Departments and Congressional Committees. International Corporate and Customs Law. Antitrust, Administrative and Civil Litigation Law.
See Professional Biographies, WASHINGTON, DISTRICT OF COLUMBIA

Schakel, Linda B. .... '48 '86 C.350 B.S. L.276 J.D. [Ballard S.A.&I.]
*PRACTICE AREAS: Municipal Bonds Taxation; Project Finance.
Schaller, James P., (AV) .... '40 '69 C.1113 B.A. L.273 J.D. [Jackson&C.] ⊙
*PRACTICE AREAS: Insurance Coverage Litigation; Environmental; Hazardous Waste; Toxic Torts; Professional Liability Litigation.
Schaller, Madeleine B. .... '42 '70 C.473 B.A. L.273 J.D. [Ⓖ Baker&H.]
*PRACTICE AREAS: Contract Law; Administrative Law; Real Estate Transactions.
Schamel, Mark E. .... '73 '99 C.1381 B.S. L.94 J.D. [Ⓐ Coburn&S.]
*PRACTICE AREAS: Criminal Litigation; Civil Litigation.
Schamest, Joanne .... '53 '81 C.94 B.A. L.273 J.D. 1301 20th St., N.W.
Schandlbauer, Nikolaus F., (AV) .... '64 '90 C.893 B.A. L.1017 J.D. [Ober,K.G.&S.]
Schane, Demian Asa .... '71 '98 C.197 B.A. L.945 J.D. 1121 12th St., NW
Schaner, Kenneth I. .... '41 '66 C&L.339 B.S., J.D. [Swidler B.S.F.]
*PRACTICE AREAS: Corporate Law; Tax Exempt Organizations; Taxation Law.
Schang, Scott E. .... '— '94 C.976 B.A. L.276 J.D. [Ⓐ Latham&W.]
*PRACTICE AREAS: Environmental Law.
Schaper, Vincent D. '65 '99 C.446 B.S./B.A. L.273 J.D.
(adm. in MD; not adm. in DC) [Ⓐ Goodwin P.]
Schapira, Joel Richard .... '49 '93 C.277 B.M.E. L.1356 J.D. 625 Indiana Ave., N.W.
Schapiro, Mary L. .... '55 '80 C.264 B.A. L.273 J.D. Nasdaq Stock Market, Inc.
Schapiro, Robert A. .... '62 '90 C&L.976 B.A., J.D. 1722 Eye St., N.W.
Scharfenberg, William P. .... '67 '96 C.674 A.B. L.1356 J.D. [Ⓐ Paul,H.J.&W.]
*PRACTICE AREAS: Energy Law.
Scharff, Jeffrey S. .... '57 '84 C.1349 B.A. L.575 J.D. [Swidler B.S.F.]
*PRACTICE AREAS: Real Estate; Structured Finance.
Scharman, Clifford J. .... '55 '80 C.188 B.S. L.477 J.D. [Riley R.&C.]
*PRACTICE AREAS: Labor and Employment.
Schattenfield, Thomas, (AV) .... '26 '55 C.477 A.B. L.930 LL.B. [Arent F.K.P.&K.]
*PRACTICE AREAS: Communications Law; Trial Practice; Broadcast Transactions.
Schatz, Gordon B., (BV) .... '— '80 C.311 B.A. L.831 J.D. [Reed S.]
*PRACTICE AREAS: Health Care.
Schatz, Thomas A. .... '53 '77 C.1349 B.A. L.273 J.D. Citizens Against Govt. Waste
Schatzow, Michael, (AV) '49 '73
C.930 A.B. L.145 J.D. [Venable,A.B.H.&C.] (⊙Balt., MD)
*PRACTICE AREAS: Criminal Law; Litigation; Professional Discipline.
Schaufelberger, Thomas S., (AV) .... '55 '81 C.886 B.S. L.276 J.D. [Wright,R.O.&T.]
*PRACTICE AREAS: Insurance Coverage; Commercial and Environmental Litigation.
Schaukowitch, Carl .... '51 '80 C.645 B.S. L.208 J.D. [Ⓐ Rader,F.&G.] (Pat.)
*PRACTICE AREAS: Patents.
Schaumber, Peter Carey, (AV) '42 '69
C&L.276 B.S.B.A., J.D. Exec. Dir., CLA Ctr. for Litig. Alternatives
Schaumberg, Tom M., (AV) .... '38 '64 C.976 B.A. L.309 LL.B. [Adduci,M.&S.]
*PRACTICE AREAS: International Trade; Intellectual Property Litigation.
Schechter, Mark C., (AV) .... '51 '78 C.645 B.A. L.1162 J.D. [Howrey S.A.&W.]
*PRACTICE AREAS: Antitrust.
Schechter, Roger E. '53 '77 C.273 B.A. L.309 J.D.
(adm. in NY; not adm. in DC) Prof. of Law, George Wash. Univ. Law Sch.
Schechter, Ronald A. .... '50 '76 C.823 B.A. L.276 J.D. [Arnold&P.]
*PRACTICE AREAS: Government Contracts; Litigation; Intellectual Property.
Schechter, Susan '61 '89 C.910 B.A. L.665 J.D.
(adm. in PA; not adm. in DC) National Assn. for Pub. Interest Law
Schectel, Lori H. '74 '99 C.1365 B.A. L.446 J.D.
(adm. in MD; not adm. in DC) [Ⓐ Bracewell&P.]
*PRACTICE AREAS: Environmental Law.
Schecter, Michael D. '64 '94 C.67 B.A. L.188 J.D.
(adm. in NY; not adm. in DC) Sr. Coun., Marriott Intl., Inc.
*RESPONSIBILITIES: Finance; Mergers and Acquisitions; Private Equity Investments.
Scheer, Craig M. .... '70 '95 C.823 B.A. L.273 J.D. [Ⓐ Silver,F.&T.]
*PRACTICE AREAS: Financial Institutions Law; Securities Law.
Schehl, Joanne, (AV) .... '54 '84 C&L.893 B.A., J.D. [Arent F.K.P.&K.]
*PRACTICE AREAS: Finance; Real Estate; Business Law.
Scheib, John .... '71 '97 C.893 B.A. L.884 J.D. [Ⓐ Covington&B.]

Scheideman, Edward S. '— '98 C.319 B.A. L.910 J.D.
(adm. in MD; not adm. in DC) [Ⓐ Piper M.R.&W.]
*PRACTICE AREAS: Antitrust and Trade Regulation.
Scheiner, Arthur, (AV) .... '17 '40 C.569 B.A. L.178 LL.B. 2100 Pennsylvania Ave. N.W.
Scheineson, Cathy Zeman .... '57 '87 C.788 A.B. L.273 J.D. [McDermott,W.&E.]
Scheineson, Marc J., (AV) .... '— '80 C&L.150 B.A., J.D. [Reed S.]
*PRACTICE AREAS: Health Care; Food, Drug and Cosmetic Law.
Scheininger, Michael G., (AV) .... '47 '72 C.264 B.A. L.659 J.D. [McKenna&C.]
*PRACTICE AREAS: Civil Litigation; White Collar Criminal Defense Law; General Liability.
Schell, Jennifer M. .... '74 '00 C&L.602 B.A., J.D. [Ⓐ Jones,D.R.&P.]
Schellie, Peter D. .... '45 '70 C.347 A.B. L.477 J.D. [Bingham D.]
*PRACTICE AREAS: Commercial Finance; Project Finance; Workouts; Bankruptcy.
Scheltema, James R. J. '60 '89 C.446 B.A. L.30 J.D.
(adm. in MD; not adm. in DC) [Ⓖ Cole,R.&B.]
Schember, Daniel M. .... '49 '74 C.309 A.B. L.477 J.D. 1666 Connecticut Ave., N.W.
Schemel, Shannon D. '73 '00 C.790 B.S. L.273 J.D.
(adm. in VA; not adm. in DC; See Pat. Sect.) [Ⓐ Leydig,V.&M.]
Schendt, Thomas G. '58 '85 C&L.436 B.A., J.D.
(adm. in WI; not adm. in DC) [Alston&B.]
*PRACTICE AREAS: Taxation; Employee Benefits.
Schenendorf, Jack Lee '44 '75 C.867 B.S. L.276 J.D.
(adm. in MD; not adm. in DC) [Ⓖ Covington&B.]
Schenker, Carl R., Jr., (AV) .... '49 '74 C&L.813 B.A., J.D. [O'Melveny&M.]
*PRACTICE AREAS: Civil Practice; Appellate Practice.
Schenker, Catherine .... '71 '99 C.976 B.A. L.569 J.D. [Ⓐ Hogan&H.]
Schenof, Barry R., (AV) .... '45 '73 C.273 B.A. L.309 J.D. 2300 N. St., N.W.
Scher, Gerald, (AV) .... '32 '58 C&L.966 B.B.A., LL.B. 3222 Klingle Rd., N.W.
Scher, Peter L. .... '61 '88 C.30 B.A. L.904 J.D. [Mayer,B.&P.]
Scherb, Esther R. .... '— '87 C.102 B.S. L.692 J.D. [Ⓖ Latham&W.]
*PRACTICE AREAS: Health Law; Medicare and Medicaid Reimbursement; Federal Administrative Law.
Scherer, Jonathan L. .... '54 '82 C.24 B.S. L.1040 J.D. [Jacobson,H.] (See Pat. Sect.)
*PRACTICE AREAS: Intellectual Property Law; Electrical Patents; Mechanical Patents.
Scherman, William S., (AV) .... '58 '84 C.273 B.A. L.421 J.D. [Skadden,A.S.M.&F.]
Scherr, Jason R. .... '72 '98 C.659 B.A. L.446 J.D. [Ⓐ Swidler B.S.F.]
*PRACTICE AREAS: Commercial Litigation.
Scherr, S. Jacob '48 '74 C.918 B.A. L.446 J.D.
Sr. Staff Atty., Natural Res. Def. Council
Schertler, David, (AV) .... '55 '82 C.31 B.A. L.893 J.D. [Coburn&S.]
*PRACTICE AREAS: Criminal Litigation; Civil Litigation.
Schessler, Cheralyn E. .... '46 '92 C.845 B.A. L.128 J.D. [Ⓐ Proskauer R.]
Scheuerman, Paul T. .... '52 '77 C.602 B.S. L.362 J.D. 1722 I St.
Scheuerman, Sheila B. .... '— '97 C.321 B.A. L.910 J.D. [Ⓐ Arnold&P.]
Scheuermann, John E., (AV) .... '45 '73 C.745 B.A. L.276 J.D. 700 E St., S.E.
Schick, Alan .... '59 '84 C.1044 B.A. L.818 J.D. [Luse L.G.P.&S.]
*PRACTICE AREAS: Corporate Law; Securities Law; Mergers and Acquisitions; Financial Institutions.
Schick, Sharon Hyman .... '58 '84 C.1044 B.A. L.1019 J.D. [Ⓖ Steptoe&J.]
*PRACTICE AREAS: Intellectual Property.
Schief, William R. '32 '61 C.146 A.B. L.276 LL.B.
Dir., Reg. Attys. & Anti Fraud Unit, National Assn. of Sec. Dealers, Inc.
Schiff, Edward F., (AV) .... '44 '69 C.645 B.A. L.902 LL.B. [Schnader H.S.&L.]
*PRACTICE AREAS: Corporate Transactions; Real Estate Finance; Debt Restructuring.
Schiff, Janis B., (BV) .... '58 '83 C.1036 B.A. L.818 J.D. [Holland&K.]
*PRACTICE AREAS: Real Estate; Leasing; Commercial Law.
Schiff, Richard B. '44 '69 C.477 B.A. L.273 J.D.
(adm. in VA; not adm. in DC) Sr. Atty., National Indian Gaming Comm.
Schiff, Robert F. .... '57 '87 C.103 A.B. L.477 J.D. Public Citizen's Congress Watch

Schiff Hardin & Waite, (AV) BR
A Partnership including Professional Corporations
Founded 1864
1101 Connecticut Avenue, N.W., 20036 ⊙
Telephone: 202-778-6400 Facsimile: 202-778-6460
Email: attorneys@schiffhardin.com URL: http://www.schiffhardin.com
Resident Partners: Barbara K. Heffernan; Andrew M. Klein; Gearold L. Knowles; Howard L. Kramer; Shirley M. Lukitsch (Not admitted in DC); André E. Owens. Special Partner: Drexel D. Journey. Resident Of Counsel: John W. Glendening, Jr.; Edwin S. Rockefeller. Resident Associates: Debra Ann Palmer; James L. Eastman; Kevin D. Ryan (Not admitted in DC).
General Practice.
Chicago, Illinois Office: 6600 Sears Tower, 60606-6473. Telephone: 312-258-5500. Facsimile: 312-258-5600. TWX: 910-221-2463.
Merrillville, Indiana Office: 8585 Broadway, Suite 842, 46410. Telephone: 219-738-3820. Facsimile: 219-738-3826.
New York, New York Office: 150 East 52nd Street, Suite 2700, 10022. Telephone: 212-753-5000. Facsimile: 212-753-5044.
Dublin, Ireland Office: The Enterprise Building, 5 Harbourmaster Place, International Financial Services Centre. Telephone: +353-1-670-2980. Facsimile: +353-1-670-2988.
See Professional Biographies, WASHINGTON, DISTRICT OF COLUMBIA

Schiffbauer, William G. '54 '79 C.627 B.S. L.190 J.D.
Suite 700, North Tower, 1300 Pennsylvania Ave., N.W., 20004-3002
Telephone: 202-204-3030 Fax: 202-789-7349
Email: wgslaw@erols.com URL: http://www.lawyers.com/healthcareregulation
Health Care Regulation, Health Maintenance Organizations, Managed Care, Health Care Contracts, Health Care Fraud, Health Insurance Defense, Alternative Health Care Delivery Systems, Patients Rights, Government Relations, State Legislative Practice, COBRA, ERISA, Health Benefits.
See Professional Biographies, WASHINGTON, DISTRICT OF COLUMBIA

Schiffman, Howard, (AV) .... '51 '78 C.165 B.A. L.262 J.D. [Dickstein S.M.&O.]
*PRACTICE AREAS: Securities Litigation; Litigation; Criminal Law.
Schiffrin, Jon .... '71 '96 C.260 B.S. L.472 J.D. [Ⓐ Howrey S.A.&W.]

Schildhaus, Aaron '43 '69 C.882 B.A. L.30 J.D.
1101 New Hampshire Avenue, N.W., 20037
Telephone: 202-775-4570 Fax: 202-887-1912 URL: http://www.lawyers.com/aaronschildhaus
Email: schildhaus@aol.com URL: http://www.schildhaus.com
Business and Corporate Law, Contracts, Joint Ventures, Foreign Corrupt Practices Act, International Financial Transactions, Aviation Law, Aerospace Law, Privatization, Export Controls, International Trade, International Commercial Law, Dispute Resolution, International: Non Governmental Organizations (NGO'S), Non Profit Organizations, Europe, Africa, Asia, EU, Russia, China, India.
See Professional Biographies, WASHINGTON, DISTRICT OF COLUMBIA

Schildhause, Sol, (AV) .... '17 '41 C.563 B.S.S. L.309 J.D. 1801 K St., N.W.‡
Schildkraut, Marc G., (AV) .... '51 '77 C&L.178 B.A., J.D. [Howrey S.A.&W.]
*PRACTICE AREAS: Antitrust Law.
Schildkraut, Peter J. .... '68 '97 C&L.309 A.B., J.D. [Ⓐ Arnold&P.]
*PRACTICE AREAS: Telecommunications; Communications Law.
Schill, Charles F., (AV) ...... '— '73 C.1031 B.S. L.117 J.D. [Foley&L.] (See Pat. Sect.)
*PRACTICE AREAS: International Trade Regulation; Intellectual Property; Litigation; Patents; Trademarks.
Schiller, Jonathan D., (AV) .... '46 '73 C&L.178 B.A., J.D. [Boies,S.&F.]
*PRACTICE AREAS: Litigation; Civil Litigation; Criminal Defense; International Arbitration.
Schiller, Patricia .... '13 '38 C.999 B.S. L.1009 LL.B. 3401 38th St., N.W.
Schimming, Brian B. .... '66 '92 C.446 B.S. L.273 J.D. [Ⓐ Joseph,M.&R.]
*PRACTICE AREAS: Trusts and Estates; Tax Law; Corporate Law.
Schindler, Christopher A. .... '65 '94 C.880 B.A. L.273 J.D. [Ⓐ Hogan&H.]

Schink, Laura A. ....'72 '99 C.347 B.A. L.823 J.D. [Ⓐ Wilkinson B.K.]
*PRACTICE AREAS: Telecommunications.
Schipma, Scott A.........................'67 '93 C.999 B.A. L.209 J.D. [Ⓐ Winston&S.]
Schlachter, Krisanne ....'75 '00 C.602 B.B.A. L.893 J.D. [Ⓐ Wilmer,C.&P.]
Schlactus, Glenn '68 '00 C&L.276 A.B., J.D.
(adm. in CA; not adm. in DC) [Ⓐ Gilbert H.&R.]
*PRACTICE AREAS: Litigation; Insurance Coverage.
Schlager, Ivan A. '61 '89 C.597 B.A. L.276 J.D.
(adm. in CA; not adm. in DC) [Ⓒ Skadden,A.S.M.&F.]
Schlanger, Michael A., (AV) ....'43 '70 C.178 A.B. L.273 J.D. [Sonnenschein N.&R.]
*PRACTICE AREAS: Litigation; RICO; Securities; Antitrust and Trade Regulation.
Schlanger, Phoebe '62 '89 C.696 B.A. L.904 J.D.
Envir. Coun., National Association of Home Builders
Schlefer, Mark P., (AV) ....'22 '49 C&L.309 S.B., LL.B. 1000 Sixteenth Street, N.W.
Schleifman, Paul S., (BV) ....'54 '82 C.1044 B.S. L.1209 J.D. [Shook,H.&B.]
*PRACTICE AREAS: Commercial Litigation; Antitrust Litigation; Complex Litigation; Insurance Coverage Litigation.
Schlesinger, M. Jean ....'64 '89 C.30 B.S. L.597 J.D. [Steptoe&J.]
*PRACTICE AREAS: Surety Law; Litigation; Government Contracts.
Schlesinger, Matthew J., (BV) ....'63 '89 C.30 B.A. L.597 J.D. [McKenna&C.]
*PRACTICE AREAS: Insurance Coverage; Complex Commercial Litigation.
Schlesinger, Michael A. ....'58 '85 C.401 B.S. L.94 J.D. [Venable,A.B.H.&C.]
*PRACTICE AREAS: Business Law; Mergers and Acquisitions; Real Estate.
Schlesinger, Michael N. ....'67 '96 C.604 A.B. L.178 J.D [Ⓐ Smith&M.]
*PRACTICE AREAS: Copyrights; Trademarks; International Trade.
Schlesinger, Victoria A. ... '68 '95 C.354 B.S. L.904 J.D. 1200 New Hampshire Ave., NW
Schlosberg, Hubert M., (AV) '31 '58
C.823 A.B. L.276 LL.B. 2000 Massachusetts Ave., N.W., 3rd Fl.
Schlosberg, Jason '75 '00 C.1365 B.A L.29 J.D.
(adm. in VA; not adm. in DC) [Ⓐ Gardner,C.&D.]
*PRACTICE AREAS: Technology Law; Telecommunications Law; Internet Law.
Schloss, David M., (AV) ....'63 '88 C.860 B.A. L.273 J.D. [Koonz,M.J.D.&L.]
Schloss, Laura G.........................'72 '99 C.674 B.A. L.30 J.D. [Ⓐ Cole,R.&B.]
*PRACTICE AREAS: Cable Television; Telecommunications Law; Administrative Law; Litigation.
Schlossberg, George R.......................'52 '77 C.1044 B.A. L.1202 J.D. [Kutak R.]
*PRACTICE AREAS: Construction Law; Military Base Closures.
Schlossberg, Robert S. ....'57 '83 C.264 B.A. L.273 J.D. [Morgan,L.&B.]
Schlossberg, Stephen I. ....'21 '57 C&L.893 B.S., LL.B. Dir., Intl. Labor Organization
Schlosser, Jennifer E. '75 '01 C.823 B.A. L.273 J.D.
(adm. in VA; not adm. in DC) [Ⓐ Crowell&M.]
Schlozman, Bradley J. ....'71 '96 C.659 B.A. L.273 J.D. [Ⓐ Howrey S.A.&W.]
*PRACTICE AREAS: Litigation; Appellate Litigation.
Schmedes, Susan M. ....'54 '79 C&L.705 B.A., J.D. Amer. Petroleum Instit. - OGC
Schmeltzer, Edward, (AV) ....'23 '54 C.331 B.A. L.273 J.D. [Ⓒ Schmeltzer,A.&S.]
*PRACTICE AREAS: Maritime Law; Aviation Law.
Schmeltzer, Kathryn R., (AV) ....'46 '74 C.788 A.B. L.893 J.D. [Shaw P.]
*PRACTICE AREAS: Communications.

Schmeltzer, Aptaker & Shepard, P.C., (AV) BR
The Watergate, Suite 1000, 2600 Virginia Avenue, N.W., 20037-1922 ⊙
Telephone: 202-333-8800 Cable Address: "Ship"Telex: 440517 Facsimile: 202-337-6065
Email: sas@saslaw.com URL: http://www.saspc.com
Ira M. Shepard; J. Thomas Esslinger; Paul M. Heylman; Ralph H. Johnson; Gary L. Lieber; Edward R. Levin; Robert L. Zisk; Robert L. Duston; Leon B. Taranto; Mark I. Gruhin; J. Anthony Smith; Henry A. Platt; Lynn K. McKay; Michael C. White; Anessa Abrams; David Worthen; Katherine Brewer;—Carlos M. Paz-Soldan; Linda G. Hill; Annemarie Brennan Rice; Roland B. Ninomiya (Not admitted in DC); Stephen J. Vaughan; Elizabeth Thomas (Not admitted in DC); Matthew I. Van Horn; Craig M. Cibak; Rebecca A. Hirselj (Not admitted in DC); Gregory Zini (Not admitted in DC); Michael C. Griffin; Nadá Melissa Moeiny (Not admitted in DC); Christopher M. Loveland; Christopher J. Wallace (Not admitted in DC); Timothy H. Goodman. Counsel: John A. McGuinn; Edward Schmeltzer; Edward Aptaker; Stephen Horn; Denise Bonn; Daniel P. Ben-Zvi (Resident, Los Angeles, California Office); Martin Jay Gaynes; Larry H. Mitchell; Jeffrey L. Karlin; Eric L. Yaffe; Tèrese M. Connerton; David L. Smith.
Labor and Employment Law, Franchise, Maritime, Equal Employment Opportunity, Civil Litigation, Employee Benefits, Health Care, Business and Transactional Law, Legislative Law, Municipal, Natural Resources, Antitrust and Corporate Law.
Los Angeles, California Office: 10880 Wilshire Boulevard, Suite 2070, 90024-4121. Telephone: 310-234-5688. FAX: 310-234-5699.
See Professional Biographies, WASHINGTON, DISTRICT OF COLUMBIA

Schmelz, Stephanie T....................'68 '96 C.311 B.A. L.477 J.D. [Ⓐ Ross,D.&B.]
Schmertz, John R., Jr. .....'29 '57 C.321 A.B. L.276 J.D. Prof. of Law, Georgetown Univ.
Schmidt, Gregory M., (AV) ....'50 '76 C.821 B.A. L.813 J.D. LTN Television Co.
Schmidt, Jeffrey A. ....'68 '97 C.107 B.S. L.128 J.D. [Ⓐ Sughrue M.] (See Pat. Sect.)
Schmidt, Kara N. ....'72 '99 C.145 B.A. L.276 J.D. [Ⓐ Miller&C.]
*PRACTICE AREAS: Qui Tam Litigation; Federal Litigation.
Schmidt, Lauren Elizabeth '75 '01 C.945 B.A. L.477 J.D.
(adm. in CA; not adm. in DC) [Ⓐ Gibson,D.&C.]
*PRACTICE AREAS: Environmental Law; Litigation.
Schmidt, Marsha Kostura ....'59 '84 C.665 B.A. L.273 J.D. [Hobbs,S.D.&W.]
Schmidt, Patrick L. ....'56 '86 C.309 B.A. L.276 J.D. [Winston&S.]
*PRACTICE AREAS: Federal Legislative; International.
Schmidt, Paul W. ....'70 '99 C.05 B.A. L.569 J.D. [Ⓐ Covington&B.]
*PRACTICE AREAS: Litigation.
Schmidt, Richard D. '51 '85 C.485 B.A. L.1218 J.D.
(adm. in NY; not adm. in DC) [Venable,A.B.H.&C.]
*PRACTICE AREAS: Intellectual Property.
Schmidt, Richard M., Jr., (AV) ....'24 '48 C&L.208 A.B., J.D. [Ⓒ Cohn&M.]
*PRACTICE AREAS: First Amendment Law; Trade Association Law; Legislative Law.
Schmidt, Ronald A. ....'65 '95 C.412 B.A. L.546 J.D. [Shaffer,R.&S.]
*PRACTICE AREAS: Labor and Employment; Class Actions; Commercial Litigation.
Schmidt, Rosemarie '59 '88
C.1021 B.A. L.276 J.D. Sr. Coun., Marriott International, Inc.
*RESPONSIBILITIES: Construction Law; Commercial Law; Contracts.
Schmidt, Susan M...........................'57 '83 C.966 B.A. L.94 J.D. [Manatt,P.&P.]
Schmidt, William A., Jr. '39 '68 C.381 B.S.B.A. L.161 J.D.
(adm. in OH; not adm. in DC) Gen. Coun., Universities Reseach Association, Inc.
Schmidt, William Aubrey, (AV) .... '— '73 C&L.893 B.A., J.D. [Kirkpatrick&L.]
Schmidt, William C., (AV) ....'48 '74 C&L.893 B.S., J.D. [Hogan&H.]
*PRACTICE AREAS: Employee Benefits; Taxation; Federal Income Tax; Executive Compensation; Tax Exempt Organizations.
Schmidt, William H., Jr. ....'72 '97 C.222 B.A. L.273 J.D. [Ⓐ Chadbourne&P.]
Schmidtlein, Elizabeth A. ....'68 '94 C.575 B.A. L.128 J.D. 1730 Pennsylvania Ave., N.W.
Schmidtlein, John E. ....'66 '93 C.103 A.B. L.276 J.D. [Williams&C.]
*PRACTICE AREAS: Antitrust and Trade Regulation; Class Actions; Complex and Multi-District Litigation; General Practice; Litigation.
Schmiedigen, George A.......................'06 '45 C.999 B.A. L.309 LL.B. 733-15th St., N.W.
Schmieler, Jeffrey R., (AV) ....'42 '67 C&L.446 B.S., J.D. [Saunders&S.] ⊙
*PRACTICE AREAS: Insurance Defense; Environmental Law; Products Liability; Medical Malpractice; Construction Accident Liability Defense.
Schmitt, Ann E., (AV) .... '— '81 C.527 B.S. L.30 J.D. [Ⓒ Reed S.]
*PRACTICE AREAS: Bankruptcy.

Schmitt, Catherine E. ....'64 '99 C.446 B.S. L.221 J.D. [Ⓐ Tobin,O.&E.]
*PRACTICE AREAS: Real Estate.
Schmitz, John P. ....'55 '85 C.276 B.A. L.813 J.D. [Mayer,B.&P.]
Schmitz, Joseph E. ....'56 '88 C.871 B.S. L.813 J.D. [Patton B.]
Schmoyer, Craig W. '45 '00 C.679 B.S.E.E. L.809 J.D.
(adm. in CA; not adm. in DC) [Ⓐ Sughrue M.] ⊙
Schmulewitz-Getlan, Leah ....'71 '96 C.367 B.A. L.665 J.D. [Ⓐ Weiner B.S.K.]
*PRACTICE AREAS: Litigation.
Schmutz, Thomas A., (AV) ....'48 '76 C.1046 B.A. L.902 J.D. [Morgan,L.&B.]
Schnabel, Robert V., (AV) ....'31 '55 C&L.893 B.A., LL.B. [Ⓒ Sanders,S.&B.]
*PRACTICE AREAS: Real Estate Law; Taxation; Corporate Law; Estates.
Schnabolk, Andra E. '74 '01 C.188 B.S. L.276 J.D.
(adm. in NY; not adm. in DC) [Ⓐ Dickstein S.M.&O.]
*PRACTICE AREAS: Energy and Regulatory.

Schnader Harrison Segal & Lewis LLP, (AV)
11th Floor East 1300 I Street, N.W., 20005-3314 ⊙
Telephone: 202-216-4200 Fax: 202-775-8741
URL: http://www.schnader.com
Partners of the Firm in Washington, D.C.: Robert L. Magielnicki; Greggory B. Mendenhall; Edward F. Schiff. Counsel to the Firm in Washington, D.C.: M. Roy Goldberg; Jonathan M. Stern. Retired Member of the Firm in Washington, D.C.: Paul G. Dembling. Associates in Washington, D.C.: Bryant Robinson, III; Ki Jun Sung; Steven B. Weinberg (Not admitted in DC); Gordon S. Woodward.
Administrative, Antitrust and Trade Regulation, Aviation and Aerospace, Appellate Practice, Business, Commercial Law, Constitutional Law, Contracts, Corporate Law, Government Contracts, Government, Health and Hospital Law, Intellectual Property, International Law, International Trade, Labor and Employment, Insurance, Litigation, Media Law, Mergers and Acquisitions, Personal Injury, Products Liability, Real Estate, Securities, Technology and Science.
Philadelphia, Pennsylvania Office: Suite 3600, 1600 Market Street. Telephone: 215-751-2000. Fax: 215-751-2205.
Other Philadelphia, Pennsylvania Office: Suite 3800, 1735 Market Street, 19103-7598.
New York, N.Y. Office: 140 Broadway, Suite 3100. Telephone: 212-973-8000. Fax: 212-972-8798.
San Francisco, California Office: 601 California Street, 12th Floor. Telephone: 415-364-6700. Fax: 415-364-6785.
Harrisburg, Pennsylvania Office: Suite 700, 30 North Third Street. Telephone: 717-231-4000. Fax: 717-231-4012.
Norristown, Pennsylvania Office: Suite 901, One Montgomery Plaza. Telephone: 610-277-7700. Fax: 610-277-3211.
Pittsburgh, Pennsylvania Office: Suite 2700, Fifth Avenue Place, 120 Fifth Avenue. Telephone: 412-577-5200. Fax: 412-765-3858.
Canonsburg (Southpointe), Pennsylvania Office: Suite 200, Summit Corporate Center, Southpointe Commercial Park, 1001 Corporate Drive, 15317. Telephone: 724-873-2870. Fax: 724-743-2901.
Cherry Hill, New Jersey Office: Suite 200, Woodland Falls Corporate Park, 220 Lake Drive East. Telephone: 856-482-5222. Fax: 856-482-6980.
Atlanta, Georgia Office: Suite 2800, SunTrust Plaza, 303 Peachtree Street, N.E. Telephone: 404-215-8100. Fax: 404-223-5164.
Boston, Massachusetts: Schnader Harrison Goldstein & Manello, 265 Franklin Street. Telephone: 617-946-8000. Fax: 617-946-8100.
See Professional Biographies, WASHINGTON, DISTRICT OF COLUMBIA

Schneck, Melanie Jane ....'75 '99 C.674 A.B. L.309 J.D. [Ⓐ Steptoe&J.]
Schneebaum, Steven M., (AV) ....'48 '78 C.976 B.A. L.273 M.C.L. [Patton B.]
Schneider, Alison M. '65 '90 C.659 B.A. L.309 J.D.
(adm. in PA; not adm. in DC) 1726 19th St., N.W.‡
Schneider, Andy ....'48 '75 C.674 A.B. L.659 J.D. [Ⓒ Berliner,C.&J.]
*PRACTICE AREAS: Health Policy; Federal and State Legislation.
Schneider, Charles A., (AV) '45 '75 C.880 B.A. L.1015 J.D.
4616 Butterworth Pl., N.W.
Schneider, Cheryl Lynn .... '61 '87 C.475 B.A. L.30 J.D. [Telecom]
Schneider, Cynthia G. ...... '47 '72 C.959 B.A. L.966 J.D. Migrant Legal Action Program
Schneider, Ellen J., (AV) ....'48 '77 C.569 B.A. L.1009 J.D. [Ⓒ Skadden,A.S.M.&F.]
Schneider, Jan ....'47 '74 C.103 B.A. L.976 J.D. 1133 Connecticut Ave.
Schneider, Janice M. '— '92 C.472 B.S. L.1051 J.D.
(adm. in MD; not adm. in DC) [Ⓐ Latham&W.]
*PRACTICE AREAS: Natural Resources; Environmental Law; Indians and Native Populations; Administrative Law; Energy.
Schneider, Jerold I., (AV) .....'42 '70 C.570 B.S.E.E. L.273 J.D. [Piper M.R.&W.] (Pat.)
*PRACTICE AREAS: Intellectual Property Law; Patent; Trademark; Copyright; Internet Law.
Schneider, Jessica R. '74 '99 C.813 B.A. L.276 J.D.
(adm. in VA; not adm. in DC) [Ⓐ Seyfarth S.]
*PRACTICE AREAS: Labor and Employment.
Schneider, Jonathan D., (AV) '56 '82 C.165 B.A. L.982 J.D.
(adm. in NY; not adm. in DC) [Huber L.&A.]
*PRACTICE AREAS: Administrative Law; Energy Law; Communications Law; Public Utility Law.
Schneider, Lawrence A., (AV) .... '49 '75 C.976 B.A. L.309 J.D. [Arnold&P.]
*PRACTICE AREAS: International; Litigation.
Schneider, Leslie Jay, (AV) ....'46 '71 C.446 B.S. L.276 J.D. [Ivins,P.&B.]
*PRACTICE AREAS: Accounting; Audits; Inventory Taxation.
Schneider, Lori L. ....'70 '96 C.93 B.A. L.665 J.D. [Ⓐ Kirkpatrick&L.]
*PRACTICE AREAS: Investment Company Law; Investment Management; Investment Regulation; Mutual Funds.
Schneider, Mark D., (AV) .... '54 '84 C.821 B.A. L.178 J.D. [Jenner&B.]
*PRACTICE AREAS: Litigation; Appellate Practice; Supreme Court Practice; Media and First Amendment; Telecommunications Law.
Schneider, Matthew J. .... '73 '00 C.475 B.A. L.477 J.D. [Ⓐ Wiley R.&F.]
Schneider, Matthew R. ....'48 '76 C.188 B.A. L.128 J.D. [Garvey,S.&B.]
*PRACTICE AREAS: Administrative Law; FIFRA; Trade Association Law; Environmental Law; Consumer Product Regulation.
Schneider, Norman G. .... '57 '87 C.659 B.A. L.276 J.D. 1025 Vermont Ave., N.W.
Schneider, Pauline A., (AV) ....'43 '78 C.1116 B.A. L.976 J.D. [Hunton&W.]
*PRACTICE AREAS: Public Finance; Government Relations.
Schneider, Stephen J. ...... '59 '89 C.629 B.S. L.596 J.D. Amer. Israel Pub. Affs. Comm.
Schneider, Susann Sharon '54 '94
C.651 B.A. L.229 J.D. Gen. Coun., U.S. Postal Inspection Serv.
Schneider, Thomas J. ....'51 '80 C&L.309 A.B., J.D. [Ⓒ O'Connor&H.]
Schneiderman, Daniel ....'71 '96 C&L.178 B.A., J.D. [Ⓐ Skadden,A.S.M.&F.]
*PRACTICE AREAS: International Trade.
Schneiderman, Martin D., (AV) .... '42 '67 C.156 A.B. L.178 LL.B. [Steptoe&J.]
*PRACTICE AREAS: Labor and Employment; Government Contracts; Litigation; Transportation.
Schneiders, Anne E. ....'38 '94 C.726 B.A. L.128 J.D. 2828 Wisconsin Ave., N.W.
Schnell, Alex M. .... '— '94 C.94 B.S. L.846 J.D. [Ⓐ Morgan,L.&B.]
Schneller, Marina V., (AV) '43 '72
C.788 A.B. L.30 J.D. [Venable,A.B.H.&C.] (See Pat. Sect.)
*PRACTICE AREAS: Intellectual Property.
Schnitzer, Maxine C. '59 '85 C.1156 B.S. L.1029 J.D.
VP & Director of Finance & Legal Affairs, Washington Opera
Schnitzer, Steven C. ....'62 '88 C.446 B.A. L.1325 J.D. [Katten M.Z.]
*PRACTICE AREAS: Corporate Law; Finance; Structured Finance; Joint Ventures; Strategic Alliances.
Schnorrenberg, David M. ....'63 '90 C.575 B.A. L.178 J.D. [Crowell&M.]
*PRACTICE AREAS: Civil Litigation; Complex and Multi-District Litigation; Antitrust; Securities Litigation; Products Liability.
Schnose, Paul A. ....'67 '96 C.792 B.S. L.846 J.D. 1200 G St., N.W.
Schnyder, Cornelia ....'71 '97 C.1038 B.S. L.260 J.D. [Ⓐ McKee N.]
*PRACTICE AREAS: Taxation.

Schochet, K. Barry, (BV) ....'47 '73 C.575 A.B. L.245 J.D. [K.B.Schochet]
Schochet, K. Barry, P.C., (BV) .... 1301 Pennsylvania Ave., Ste. 500
Schochor, Jonathan, (AV) .... '46 '71 C.645 B.A. L.904 J.D. [Schochor,F.&S.] ⊙
*PRACTICE AREAS: Medical Malpractice Law; Products Liability Law; Civil Litigation.

Schochor, Federico and Staton, P.A., (AV)
10 G Street, N.E., Suite 650, 20002 ⊙
Telephone: 202-408-3300 Toll Free: 888-234-0001
URL: http://www.sfspa.com
Jonathan Schochor; Philip C. Federico; Kerry D. Staton; Christopher P. Kennedy.
Medical Malpractice, General, Negligence, Products Liability, Personal Injury Law, Lead Paint Poisoning and Civil Trial.
Baltimore, Maryland Office: The Paulton, 1211 St. Paul Street, 21202. Telephone: 410-234-1000. Fax: 410-234-1010.
See Professional Biographies, WASHINGTON, DISTRICT OF COLUMBIA

Schoeberlein, Adam Matthew '72 '01 C.893 B.A. L.276 J.D.
(adm. in VA; not adm. in DC) [Ⓐ Dechert]
*PRACTICE AREAS: Securities Litigation; SEC Enforcement.
Schoeffler, Andrew P. .... '72 '98 C.608 B.A. L.276 J.D. [Ⓐ Covington&B.]
Schoel, Brett .... '71 '99 C.446 B.A. L.273 J.D. [Ⓐ Macleay,L.G.&L.]
Schoenfeld, Henry .... '40 '67 C&L.178 A.B., LL.B. 601 Indiana Ave., N.W.
Schoenfeld, Scott R., (AV) .... '36 '65 C&L.309 A.B., LL.B. [Ⓒ Jenkens&G.]
*PRACTICE AREAS: Government (Public) Contract Law; Litigation; Regulatory Law.
Schoettle, Ferdinand P. '33 '62 C.674 A.B. L.309 LL.B.
(adm. in PA; not adm. in DC) 3104 Dumbarton Ave., N.W.
Schofield, Mary Anne '— '98 C.667 B.S. L.262 J.D.
(adm. in NY; not adm. in DC; See Pat. Sect.) [Ⓐ Fulbright&J.]
*PRACTICE AREAS: Intellectual Property; Patent Prosecution.
Schomer, Morton W., (AV) .... '28 '53 C&L.569 B.A., LL.B. [Ⓒ Hessel&A.]
Schomig, Jeffrey P. .... '70 '97 C.30 B.A. L.692 J.D. 2445 M Street, N.W.
Schon, David F. .... '66 '92 C.477 B.A. L.912 J.D. [Ⓐ Nixon P.]
*PRACTICE AREAS: Real Estate; Affordable Housing; Partnership Law; Corporate Law.
Schooler, Michael S., (AV) '47 '75 C.309 A.B. L.145 J.D.
Dep. Gen. Coun., National Cable Television Assn.
Schools, Shelly W. '72 '97 C&L.500 B.B.A., J.D.
(adm. in MS; not adm. in DC) 122 Scherz Blvd.★
Schooner, Heidi M. .... '60 '85 C.228 A.B. L.276 J.D. Asst. Prof., Catholic Univ. of Amer.
Schopf, Joshua N. '72 '98 C.367 B.A. L.178 J.D.
(adm. in MD; not adm. in DC) [Ⓐ Sidley A.B.&W.]
Schopf, Simeon M. .... '— '96 C.367 B.A. L.178 J.D. 701 Pennsylvania Avenue, N.W.
Schor, Laurence, (AV) .... '42 '66 C.802 B.B.A. L.846 J.D. [McManus,S.A.&D.]
*PRACTICE AREAS: Government Contracts; Construction Law.
Schor, Susan L., (AV) .... '43 '77 C.861 B.A. L.128 J.D. [McManus,S.A.&D.]
*PRACTICE AREAS: Commercial Leasing and Litigation; Government Contracts; Civil Litigation.
Schornstein, Sherri L. .... '59 '83 C.352 B.B.A. L.61 J.D. Spec. Asst. U.S. Atty.
Schorr, David K. '59 '89 C.604 B.A. L.976 J.D.
(adm. in NY; not adm. in DC) Sr. Program Offr., World Wildlife Fund
Schoshinski, Robert S. .... '31 '58 C.602 B.S. L.276 J.D. Prof. of Law, Georgetown Univ.
Schotland, Roy A. '33 '64 C.178 A.B. L.309 J.D.
(adm. in NY; not adm. in DC) Georgetown Univ. Law Ctr.
Schotland, Sara D., (AV) .... '48 '72 C.681 A.B. L.276 J.D. [Cleary,G.S.&H.]
Schott, Anne R. .... '— '98 C.309 A.B. L.893 J.D. [Ⓐ King&S.]
*PRACTICE AREAS: Federal Criminal Law; Grand Jury Practice; Congressional Investigations; Government Investigation; Civil Litigation.
Schott, Stephen C. .... '35 '61 C.262 B.S. L.309 LL.B. 1747 Pennsylvania Ave., N.W.
Schottland, Rachel '— '01 C.188 B.S. L.880 J.D.
(adm. in NY; not adm. in DC) [Ⓐ Verner,L.B.M.&H.]
*PRACTICE AREAS: Labor and Employment Law.
Schrader, Wayne A., (AV) .... '50 '75 C.800 B.A. L.1068 J.D. [Gibson,D.&C.]
*PRACTICE AREAS: Insurance Coverage; Bad Faith/Insurer Conduct; Employment; Litigation.
Schraf, James R., (BV) .... '60 '85 C.524 B.S. L.30 J.D. [Lipshultz&H.] ⊙
*PRACTICE AREAS: Commercial Defense; Commercial Torts; Uniform Commercial Code; Negotiable Instruments; Construction Surety Bonds.
Schrag, Philip G. .... '43 '67 C.309 A.B. L.976 LL.B. Prof. of Law, Georgetown Univ.
Schrage, Steven P. '— '95 C.228 B.A. L.477 J.D.
(adm. in GA; not adm. in DC) 1050 Conn. Ave., N.W.‡
Schragin, Howard '70 '98 C.966 B.S. L.262 J.D.
(adm. in NY; not adm. in DC) [Ⓐ King,P.&H.]
*PRACTICE AREAS: Employment Discrimination; Labor Law; Employee Benefits.
Schram, Steven H., (AV) .... '53 '79 C.659 B.S. L.276 J.D. [Shapiro,L.&S.]
*PRACTICE AREAS: Business Law; Commercial Finance; Commercial Transactions; Technology Licensing; Corporate Law.

Schraub & Company, Chtd., A Prof. Law Corp.
(See McLean, Virginia)

Schreiber, Rudolf L. .... '56 '95 C.930 B.A. L.1280 J.D. 1400 C St., N.E.
Schreiber, Scott B., (AV) .... '48 '73 C.67 B.A. L.178 J.D. [Arnold&P.]
*PRACTICE AREAS: Financial Institutions; Litigation; Professional Liability; Insurance Coverage.
Schreiberg, Sheldon L., (AV) .... '42 '74 C.494 B.A. L.309 J.D. [Pepper H.]
*PRACTICE AREAS: Real Estate; Affordable Housing; Project Finance.
Schreibman, Julian D. '72 '98 C&L.976 B.A., J.D.
(adm. in NY; not adm. in DC) 815 Conn. Ave., N.W.‡
Schreiner, Stephen T. '64 '97 C.886 B.S.E.E. L.276 J.D.
(adm. in VA; not adm. in DC; Pat.) [Ⓐ Hunton&W.]
*PRACTICE AREAS: Patent; Trade Secret; Copyright.
Schrier, Michael J. .... '68 '93 C.188 B.A. L.273 J.D. [Ⓐ Bell,B.&L.]
*PRACTICE AREAS: Litigation; Employment Law.
Schrode, Kristi Elaine .... '68 '95 C.112 B.S. L.326 J.D. [Ⓐ Bennett,T.&C.]
*PRACTICE AREAS: Food and Drug Regulation; Health Law.
Schroeder, Franceska O. .... '63 '92 C.860 B.A. L.904 J.D. [Ⓐ Milbank,T.H.&M.]
Schroeder, Julie A. .... '72 '97 C.264 B.A. L.904 J.D. [Ⓐ Baach R.&L.P.]
*PRACTICE AREAS: Civil Litigation; Commercial Litigation; Insurance.
Schroeder, Roland G. .... '64 '91 C.401 B.S. L.276 J.D. [Ⓐ Shearman&S.]
Schroeder, Todd A. .... '— '00 C.10 B.S. L.16 J.D. [Ⓐ Morgan,L.&B.]
Schroeder, William B. .... '70 '97 C.264 B.A. L.904 J.D. [Ⓐ Carr G.]
*PRACTICE AREAS: Medical Malpractice; Professional Liability; Insurance Defense.
Schroer, Sharon M. .... '56 '85 C.893 B.A. L.477 J.D. [Ⓒ Baach R.&L.P.]
*PRACTICE AREAS: Commercial Litigation; Insurance Coverage Litigation.
Schropp, James H., (AV) .... '43 '73 C.692 B.A. L.276 J.D. [Fried,F.H.S.&J.]
Schryber, John W. .... '57 '84 C.260 B.S. L.564 J.D. [Patton B.]
Schryver, David G. .... '38 '63 C.712 B.A. L.276 LL.B. [Ⓐ Condon&F.]
Schubert, Richard F. '36 '62 C.236 B.A. L.976 LL.B.
(adm. in PA; not adm. in DC) 1155 Connecticut Ave., N.W.‡
Schuchat, Michael A., (AV) .... '24 '50 C.976 B.E. L.276 LL.B. 1818 N St., N.W.‡
Schueler, Jeffrey John .... '63 '92 C.473 B.S. L.1035 J.D. 810 Vermont Ave.
Schuelke, Henry F., III, (AV) .... '42 '68 C.749 A.B. L.884 J.D. [Janis,S.&W.]
*PRACTICE AREAS: White Collar Criminal Defense; Business Crimes; International Criminal Law; Federal Grand Jury; Monetary Crimes.

Schuette, James M., and Associates, (AV) '31 '55 C&L.276 B.S., J.D.
1111 19th Street, N.W., Suite 209, 20036
Telephone: 301-948-5555; 202-955-5581 Fax: 202-659-1610
***PRACTICE AREAS: Defective Products; Product Liability Law; Negligence Law.**
—James M. Schuette, Jr.
Negligence Law, Product Liability, Personal Injury, Automobile Accidents.
Reference: The Palmer National Bank, Washington, D.C.
See Professional Biographies, WASHINGTON, DISTRICT OF COLUMBIA

Schuette, James M., Jr. .... '60 '88 C.423 B.A. L.200 J.D. [Ⓐ J.M.Schuette&Assoc.]
*PRACTICE AREAS: Defective Products; Products Liability Law; Negligence Law.
Schuhmacher, Kenneth A. .... '65 '92 C.197 A.B. L.477 J.D. [Latham&W.]
*PRACTICE AREAS: Project Finance.
Schulder, Elliott, (AV) .... '47 '74 C.976 B.A. L.569 J.D. [Ⓒ Covington&B.]
Schuler, Joseph E., (AV) .... '54 '79 C.446 B.A. L.276 J.D. [Barrett&S.] (⊙Washington)
Schuler, Joseph E., (AV) ... '54 '79 C.446 B.A. L.276 J.D. [Ⓒ Littler M.] (⊙Washington)
*PRACTICE AREAS: Labor and Employment; Litigation.
Schuler, Lynda .... '62 '89 C.691 B.A. L.477 J.D. [Williams&C.]
*PRACTICE AREAS: Civil Practice; Estate Litigation; Fiduciary Litigation; Legal Malpractice; Litigation.
Schull, Deborah J. .... '56 '95 C.999 B.A. L.564 J.D. U.S. Immigration Services
Schulman, Eli C. .... '70 '98 C.178 B.A. L.309 J.D. [Ⓐ Kellogg,H.H.T.&E.]
*PRACTICE AREAS: Litigation.
Schulman, Joseph R. .... '70 '96 C.48 B.A. L.575 J.D. 1500 K St., N.W.
Schulman, Margaret B. .... '18 '59 C&L.273 B.A., LL.B. 3208 Ellicott St., N.W.
Schulman, Phillip L., (AV) .... '— '75 C&L.588 B.A., J.D. [Kirkpatrick&L.]
*PRACTICE AREAS: Administrative Law; Finance; Housing Law; Real Estate; Regulatory Law.
Schulman, Robert M., (BV) .... '58 '83 C.705 B.S. L.29 J.D. [Hunton&W.] (Pat.)
Schulman, Steven H. .... '— '94 C.1036 B.A. L.597 J.D. [Ⓐ Latham&W.]
*PRACTICE AREAS: Litigation; Antitrust; White Collar Criminal Defense; Pro Bono Immigration Law; Communications Law.
Schulte, Bernard M. .... '62 '87 C.105 B.A. L.608 J.D. [Ⓢ Reboul,M.H.M.&K.]
*PRACTICE AREAS: Regulatory; Telecommunications and Energy; Tort Defense/Product Liability.
Schulte, Valerie, (AV) '46 '76 C.112 B.A. L.273 J.D.
Dep. Gen. Coun., National Association of Broadcasters
*RESPONSIBILITIES: Communications Law and Policy; Digital Television; Advertising/Commercial Speech Law; Communications Technology; Antitrust.
Schultis, Lawrence A. .... '— '92 C&L.273 B.B.A., J.D. [Shaw P.]
Schultz, Carol Regina '56 '80 C.339 B.S. L.1068 J.D.
(adm. in CA; not adm. in DC) MCI Telecommunications Corp. (Regulatory Affairs)
Schultz, Daniel E., (AV) .... '41 '67 C.694 A.B. L.597 J.D. [Schultz&T.]
Schultz, James C. .... '34 '62 C.546 B.S. L.273 J.D. 50 F St., N.W.
Schultz, Nancy S. '33 '80 C.188 B.A. L.229 J.D.
1350 Pennsylvania Ave Nw, Room 320
Schultz, Robert .... '54 '80 C.30 B.S. L.446 J.D. [Ⓐ Akman&Assoc.] (⊙Lutherville, MD)
Schultz, William B. .... '48 '75 C.976 B.A. L.893 J.D. [Zuckerman S.]
*PRACTICE AREAS: Food and Drug Regulation; Appellate Practice; Civil Litigation.

Schultz & Trombly, PLLC, (AV)
Suite 1250, 1050 17th Street, N.W., 20036-5510
Telephone: 202-887-5000 Fax: 202-457-0343 URL: http://www.injurycases.com
Email: trombly@erols.com URL: http://www.lawyers.com/injurycases
Daniel E. Schultz; Kenneth M. Trombly.
Plaintiffs Trial Practice. Personal Injury, Automobile Accidents and Injuries, Wrongful Death, Negligence, Premises Liability, Product Liability, Medical Malpractice, Police Misconduct, Civil Rights.
See Professional Biographies, WASHINGTON, DISTRICT OF COLUMBIA

Schulwolf, Andrew B. .... '68 '93 C.893 B.A. L.472 J.D. 3 Bethesda Metro Ctr.
Schulz, James P. .... '— '96 C.259 B.A. L.128 J.D. [Ⓐ Reed S.]
*PRACTICE AREAS: Communications; Satellite Communications; Telecommunications.
Schulz, Jennifer L. .... '72 '98 C.898 B.A. L.352 J.D. Zacchaeus Free Leg. Clinic
Schulze, Charles H., (BV) .... '36 '67 C.30 B.A. L.904 J.D. [Schulze&P.]
Schulze & Pederson, P.C., (AV) .... 5039 Conn. Ave., N.W.
Schumacher, David K. .... '64 '89 C.893 B.A. L.273 J.D. [Chadbourne&P.]
Schunck, Michael J. .... '67 '00 C.689 B.A. L.569 J.D. [Ⓐ Swidler B.S.F.]
*PRACTICE AREAS: Telecommunications; Internet; Antitrust; Privacy.
Schupak, Sidney .... '67 '91 C.994 B.A. L.904 J.D. [Ashcraft&G.]
*PRACTICE AREAS: Products Liability; Personal Injury; Medical Malpractice.
Schur, David T. '74 '00 C.860 B.A. L.94 J.D.
(adm. in NY; not adm. in DC) [Ⓐ Dickstein S.M.&O.]
*PRACTICE AREAS: Securities Litigation.
Schuster, Michael .... '50 '75 C.755 B.A. L.602 J.D. AARP
*RESPONSIBILITIES: Social Security; Nursing Homes; Class Action Litigation; Health Care.
Schutzer, George J. .... '55 '80 C.951 B.A. L.976 J.D. [Patton B.]
Schwaab, Richard L., (AV) '— '71
C.966 B.S.Ch.E. L.273 J.D. [Foley&L.] (See Pat. Sect.) (⊙Milw., WI)
*PRACTICE AREAS: Intellectual Property Law.

Schwabe, Williamson & Wyatt
A Partnership including Professional Corporations
600 Thirteenth Street, N.W. Suite 790, 20005 ⊙
Telephone: 202-628-6870 Fax: 202-628-7804
Email: info@schwabe.com URL: http://www.schwabe.com
Resident Shareholder: Martin B. Gold.
Administrative Hearings and Appeals, Federal Administrative Law, Government Relations, Health Care Legislation, Health Care Reform, Health Care Regulation.
Portland, Oregon Office: Suites 1600-1900 Pacwest Center, 1211 S.W. Fifth Avenue. Telephone: 503-222-9981. Fax: 503-796-2900.
Bend, Oregon Office: 600 S.W. Columbia, Suite 3210, 97702. Telephone: 541-330-0904. Fax: 541-330-1153.
Seattle, Washington Office: U.S. Bank Centre, Suite 3500, 1420 Fifth Avenue. Telephone: 206-622-1711. Fax: 206-292-0460.
Vancouver, Washington Office: Suite 410, Main Place Building, 1111 Main Street. Telephone: 360-694-7551; 696-0241.
See Professional Biographies, WASHINGTON, DISTRICT OF COLUMBIA

Schwalb, Brian L. .... '67 '92 C.228 A.B. L.309 J.D. [Schwalb,D.&S.]
*PRACTICE AREAS: Commercial Litigation.
Schwalb, Burton A., (AV) .... '36 '60 C&L.309 A.B., LL.B. [Schwalb,D.&S.]
*PRACTICE AREAS: Commercial Litigation.
Schwalb, Eric J. '75 '01 C.734 B.A. L.276 J.D.
(adm. in IL; not adm. in DC) [Ⓐ Goldberg,G.W.&W.]
*PRACTICE AREAS: Communications; Media; Internet.

Schwalb, Donnenfeld & Schwalb, A Professional Corporation, (AV)
1155 21st Street, N.W., Suite 210, 20036
Telephone: 202-965-7910 202-337-0676 URL: http://www.schwalblaw.com
URL: http://www.lawyers.com/schwalblaw
Burton A. Schwalb; Brian L. Schwalb. Associate: David N. Geier. Senior Counsel: Charles R. Donnenfeld.
Federal, State and Administrative Trial Practice, Appellate Practice, Commercial. Tax, Securities, Real Estate, Regulatory, Insurance Coverage, Government Contracts, Zoning, Business Litigation, Arbitration and Mediation.
See Professional Biographies, WASHINGTON, DISTRICT OF COLUMBIA

Schwaninger, Robert H., Jr. ....'52 '82 C&L.502 B.J., J.D. [Schwaninger&Assoc.]
*PRACTICE AREAS: Communications; Contracts; Administrative Law.

Schwaninger & Associates, P.C
1331 H Street, N.W., Suite 500, 20005
Telephone: 202-347-8580 Facsimile: 202-347-8607
Email: rschwaninger@sa-lawyer.net URL: http://www.lawyers.com/schwaningerandassociates
Robert H. Schwaninger, Jr.
Communications, Transactional, Contract, Valuation of Telecommunications Properties, Commercial Litigation, Federal Appellate, Business Formation, Federal Communications, Intellectual Property, Small Business Law.
See Professional Biographies, WASHINGTON, DISTRICT OF COLUMBIA

Schwarcz, Steven L., (AV) '49 '75 C.569 B.S. L.178 J.D.
(adm. in NY; not adm. in DC) [Ⓒ Kaye S.]
*PRACTICE AREAS: Asset Securitization; Structured Finance; Bankruptcy and Corporate Reorganization; Commercial Finance; Banking.
Schwartz, Adam J. ....'73 '99 C.881 B.A. L.273 J.D. [Ⓐ Wilmer,C.&P.]
Schwartz, Arthur, (AV) '— '63 C.350 B.S.I.E. L.273 J.D.
[Foley&L.] (See Pat. Sect.)‡
*PRACTICE AREAS: Intellectual Property Law.
Schwartz, Asher W., (AV) '11 '35
C.951 A.B. L.309 LL.B. [Ⓒ O'Donnell,S.&A.] (⊙New York, NY)
Schwartz, Bryan A. ....'60 '88 C.103 B.A. L.813 J.D. [Ⓒ Morrison&F.]
Schwartz, Christopher "Kip", (AV) ....'53 '80 C.299 B.A. L.564 J.D. [Holland&K.]
*PRACTICE AREAS: Litigation; Intellectual Property; Employment Law.
Schwartz, Daniel C., (AV) ....'43 '69 C.813 A.B. L.273 J.D. [Bryan C.]
*PRACTICE AREAS: White Collar Criminal Defense; Trade Regulation; Antitrust Law.
Schwartz, David Craig '71 '96 C.1044 B.A. L.273 J.D.
(adm. in MD; not adm. in DC) 1001 26th St., N.W.‡
Schwartz, David L., (AV) ....'— '89 C.95 A.B. L.904 J.D. [Latham&W.]
*PRACTICE AREAS: Electric Power; Energy Regulation; Energy Contracts.
Schwartz, David M., (AV) ....'30 '58 C.197 B.A. L.276 J.D. 1025 Conn. Ave., N.W.
Schwartz, David M. ....'62 '92 C.846 B.A. L.309 J.D. [Thompson C.]
*PRACTICE AREAS: International Trade; Commercial Litigation; Immigration.
Schwartz, Edward B., (BV) ....'57 '85 C.299 B.A. L.93 J.D. [Howrey S.A.&W.]
*PRACTICE AREAS: Antitrust Litigation; Commercial Litigation.
Schwartz, Eric J. ....'57 '85 C.367 B.A. L.30 J.D. [Smith&M.]
*PRACTICE AREAS: Copyrights; Trademarks; Electronic Commerce; Government.
Schwartz, Erich T. ....'58 '83 C.446 B.A. L.273 J.D. [Ⓒ Skadden,A.S.M.&F.]
Schwartz, Gilbert T., (AV) ....'46 '74 C&L.831 B.B.A., J.D. [Schwartz&B.]
*PRACTICE AREAS: Banking; Financial Services.

Schwartz, Gregory J. '58 '86 C.446 B.A. L.180 J.D.
International Square, 1825 I Street, N.W., Suite 400, 20006
Telephone: 202-429-2094 Fax: 202-429-2094
Email: gsesquire@aol.com
United States and International Private Investments, Offshore Investment, Offshore Finance, Private Finance, International Business Law, Venture Capital, Mergers and Acquisitions.
REPRESENTATIVE CLIENTS: Accredited and Sophiscated Investors (U.S. & International).
See Professional Biographies, WASHINGTON, DISTRICT OF COLUMBIA

Schwartz, Howard S. ....'37 '64 C.472 B.B.A. L.273 LL.M. Asst. Corp. Coun., D.C.
Schwartz, Jason C. ....'72 '99 C.537 B.A. L.276 J.D. [Ⓐ Gibson,D.&C.]
*PRACTICE AREAS: Labor and Employment; Litigation.
Schwartz, Jeff E. ....'58 '93 C.870 B.S. L.276 J.D. [McKenna&C.] (Pat.)
*PRACTICE AREAS: Patent Law; Patent Licensing; Mechanical Intellectual Property; Medical Intellectual Property; Aerospace Intellectual Property.
Schwartz, Jennifer '72 '99 C.197 A.B. L.569 J.D.
(adm. in NY; not adm. in DC) [Ⓐ Covington&B.]
Schwartz, Jennifer Kane ....'71 '99 C.119 B.S. L.273 J.D. [Ⓐ Crowell&M.]
Schwartz, Joel D. ....'62 '90 C.264 M.A. L.569 J.D. [Ⓐ Zuckerman S.]
*PRACTICE AREAS: Criminal Litigation; Civil Litigation.
Schwartz, Jordana G. ....'64 '92 C.145 B.A. L.262 J.D. [Ⓒ Shaw P.]
Schwartz, Joshua I. '51 '77 C.309 A.B. L.188 J.D.
Prof. of Law, George Washington Natl. Law Ctr.
Schwartz, Karen K. ....'43 '75 C.681 A.B. L.976 J.D. [Ⓐ Arnold&P.]
*PRACTICE AREAS: Trusts and Estates; Wills.
Schwartz, Keith M. ....'59 '85 C.1040 B.A. L.823 J.D. [Ⓒ Dewey B.]
*PRACTICE AREAS: Project Finance; Real Estate.
Schwartz, Kenneth L. ....'65 '92 C.659 B.A. L.273 J.D. [Arnold&P.]
*PRACTICE AREAS: Corporate; Securities; Real Estate.
Schwartz, Laine M. ....'— '01 C.846 B.A. L.280 J.D. [Ⓐ Morgan,L.&B.]
Schwartz, Lara Hope ....'71 '99 C.103 A.B. L.309 J.D. [Ⓐ Gilbert H.&R.]
*PRACTICE AREAS: Litigation; Insurance Coverage.
Schwartz, Louis, (AV) ....'18 '47 C.102 A.B. L.273 LL.B. [Ⓒ Schwartz,W.&M.] ‡
*PRACTICE AREAS: Communications Law; Telecommunications Law; Copyright and Trademark Law; Broadcast Production and Distribution Law.
Schwartz, Mark I. ....'63 '96 C.012 B.S. L.086 J.D. [Ⓐ Piper M.R.&W.]
*PRACTICE AREAS: Venture Capital; High Technology; Emerging Business Law.
Schwartz, Melissa Cales '70 '96 C.945 B.A. L.245 J.D.
(adm. in GA; not adm. in DC) [Ⓐ Paul,H.J.&W.]
*PRACTICE AREAS: Corporate; Corporate Finance.
Schwartz, Michael A. ....'56 '95 C.111 B.S.E.E. L.273 J.D. [Ⓐ Swidler B.S.F.] (Pat.)
*PRACTICE AREAS: Patent; Intellectual Property.
Schwartz, Philip M. ....'64 '89 C.1119 B.S. L.273 J.D. [Carr,M.&G.]
*PRACTICE AREAS: Labor and Employment; Civil Litigation; Corporate Law; Real Estate Finance.
Schwartz, Phillip L. '41 '74 C.696 B.S. L.262 J.D.
(adm. in NY; not adm. in DC)
V.P., Fin. & Assoc. Gen. Coun., American Insurance Association
*RESPONSIBILITIES: Insurance; Accounting; Finance; Securities; Insurance Regulation.
Schwartz, Rachael E. ....'57 '81 C.367 B.A. L.276 J.D. [Baker&M.]
*PRACTICE AREAS: Communications and Media Law; Corporate and Partnership Law.
Schwartz, Richard E., (AV) ....'48 '73 C.976 B.A. L.477 J.D. [Crowell&M.]
*PRACTICE AREAS: Environmental Law; Toxic Torts; Water Quality Law.
Schwartz, Richard L. ....'50 '83 C.902 B.A. L.896 J.D. [Ⓐ Dombroff&G.]
Schwartz, Robert S., (AV) ....'49 '74 C.188 B.A. L.659 J.D. [McDermott,W.&E.]
Schwartz, Roger A. ....'44 '70 C.184 B.A. L.276 J.D. [Feldesman,T.L.F.&B.]
*PRACTICE AREAS: Health Care Law.
Schwartz, Steven J. '54 '81 C&L.446 B.A., J.D.
Gen. Coun., CFO, Blake Construction Co.
Schwartz, Teresa M. '43 '71 C.813 A.B. L.273 J.D.
Prof. of Law, George Washington Univ. Law Sch.
Schwartz, Victor E., (AV) ....'40 '65 C.94 A.B. L.178 LL.B. [Shook,H.&B.]
*PRACTICE AREAS: Torts; Products Liability; Insurance; Legislative Practice; Public Policy.
Schwartz, Wendy Helene ....'54 '90 C.999 B.A. L.904 J.D. [Ⓐ Lewis] ⊙
*PRACTICE AREAS: Family Law; Criminal Law.

Schwartz & Ballen, (AV)
Suite 500, 1990 M Street, N.W., 20036-3418
Telephone: 202-776-0700 Fax: 202-776-0720
URL: http://www.schwartzandballen.com
Members of Firm: Gilbert T. Schwartz; Robert G. Ballen; Thomas A. Fox. Associate: Brandon M. Dell'Aglio (Not admitted in DC).

(This Listing Continued)

Schwartz & Ballen (Continued)
Banking, Financial Services, E-Commerce and Payments Law.
See Professional Biographies, WASHINGTON, DISTRICT OF COLUMBIA

Schwartz, Woods & Miller, (AV)
Suite 300 The Dupont Circle Building, 1350 Connecticut Avenue, N.W., 20036-1717
Telephone: 202-833-1700 Cable Address: "SWMLAW" Telecopier: 202-833-2351
Email: watts@swmlaw.com
Of Counsel: Louis Schwartz (Retired); Robert A. Woods. Members of Firm: Lawrence M. Miller; Steven C. Schaffer; Malcolm G. Stevenson. Counsel: Camille M. Cunningham; Mark B. Weinberg (P.C.).
Communications, Telecommunications Law (Radio, Television, Common Carrier, Private Radio). Copyright and Trademark Law. Broadcast Program Production and Distribution Law. Practice before the Federal Courts and Administrative Agencies.
See Professional Biographies, WASHINGTON, DISTRICT OF COLUMBIA

Schwartzman, Andrew Jay '46 '72
C&L.659 A.B., J.D. Pres. & Exec. Dir., Media Access Proj.
Schwartzman, Richard W., (AV) '45 '69 C.644 B.A. L.1202 J.D.
[Ⓒ McManus,S.A.&D.]
*PRACTICE AREAS: Construction Law; Government Contracts; Surety Law; Litigation.
Schwarz, Benjamin K. ....'12 '37 C&L.273 A.B., LL.B. 3850 Tunlaw Rd., N.W.‡
Schwarz, Carl W., (AV) ....'36 '62 C.188 B.C.E. L.273 J.D. [McDermott,W.&E.]
Schwarz, David L. ....'71 '00 C&L.309 A.B., J.D. [Ⓐ Kellogg,H.H.T.&E.]
*PRACTICE AREAS: Telecommunications.
Schwarz, Deborah Glass ....'50 '79 C.577 B.A. L.896 J.D. Sr. Labor Rel. Offr.
Schwarz, Jeffrey A. ....'69 '94 C.893 B.A. L.309 J.D. [Ⓐ Spiegel&M.]
*PRACTICE AREAS: Litigation; Energy; Aviation Law.
Schwarz, Melvin A. ....'50 '75 C.367 B.A. L.145 J.D. [Dechert]
*PRACTICE AREAS: Antitrust and Competition Law; Intellectual Property; Securities Fraud; International Arbitration.
Schwechter, Melvin S., (AV) ......'47 '75 C.999 B.J.Ed. L.569 J.D. [LeBoeuf,L.G.&M.]
*PRACTICE AREAS: International.
Schweinfurth, Lynn A. ....'— '91 C.188 B.S. L.94 J.D. [Kirkpatrick&L.]
*PRACTICE AREAS: Investment Company Law; Investment Management; Investment Regulation; Mutual Funds.
Schweitzer, Felicia Goldberg ....'70 '95 C.659 B.A. L.273 J.D. [Ⓐ Crowell&M.]
Schweitzer, Frank J. ....'68 '94 C.1030 B.A. L.117 J.D. [Ⓐ White&C.]
Schweitzer, James J., (AV) ....'47 '73 C.976 B.A. L.893 J.D. [Cuneo]
*PRACTICE AREAS: Government Relations.
Schweitzer, Richard P. ....'57 '81 C&L.383 B.A., J.D. [Zuckert,S.&R.]
*PRACTICE AREAS: Regulated Industries; Interstate Tax; State Taxation; Interstate Commerce; Motor Carrier Law.
Schweitzer, William H., (AV) ....'44 '70 C.855 B.A. L.276 J.D. [Baker&H.]
*PRACTICE AREAS: Litigation; Election Law.
Schwemer, Brett T. ....'67 '92 C.1369 B.B.A. L.607 J.D. [Ⓐ Olsson,F.&W.]
*PRACTICE AREAS: Agriculture Law; Food and Drug Law; Litigation.
Schwentker, Donald M. ....'34 '61 C&L.150 M.E., J.D. 1913 Eye St., N.W.
Schwer, Jeremy R. ....'73 '98 C.896 B.A. L.128 J.D. [Ⓐ Akin,G.S.H.&F.]
Schwinger, David, (AV) ....'56 '82 C.659 B.S. L.273 J.D. [Katten M.Z.]
*PRACTICE AREAS: Real Estate and Finance.
Schwinn, D. Stephenson, (AV) '56 '81
C.1044 B.A. L.276 J.D. [Jordan C.&S.] (⊙Balt., Rockville, MD)
*PRACTICE AREAS: Premises Liability; Personal Injury; Workers Compensation; Environmental Insurance Coverage; Construction Law.
Schwitzer, Jennifer L. '73 '98 C.162 B.A. L.862 J.D.
(adm. in OK; not adm. in DC) [Ⓐ McGuirewoods]
*PRACTICE AREAS: Energy Law; Utility Law.
Sciara, Nicolle '74 '99 C.846 B.A. L.659 J.D.
(adm. in TX; not adm. in DC) [Ⓐ Gibson,D.&C.]
Sciaroni, Robert J., (AV) ....'45 '76 C.767 B.A. L.1065 J.D. [Bell,B.&L.]
*PRACTICE AREAS: Construction Law; Government Contracts Law; Surety Law.
Sciarrino, Dawn M. ....'63 '91 C.354 B.A. L.128 J.D. [Ⓒ Shaw P.]
*PRACTICE AREAS: Communications.
Scicluna, Margaret '69 '98 C.569 B.A. L.94 J.D.
(adm. in NY; not adm. in DC) [Ⓐ Kaye S.]
*PRACTICE AREAS: International Trade; World Trade Organization; Litigation.

Scopelitis, Garvin, Light & Hanson, P.C.
1500 "K" Street, N.W., Suite 910, 20005-1209 ⊙
Telephone: 202-783-9222 Fax: 202-783-9230
Email: washingtondc@scopelitis.com URL: http://www.scopelitis.com
Daniel R. Barney; Laurie T. Baulig (Resident). Associate: Sylvia F. James (Resident).
General Civil Practice. Litigation in all State and Federal Courts, including Appellate Practice, Transportation, Motor Carrier, Corporate, Administrative, Antitrust and Trade Regulation, Business, Insurance Defense, Negligence, Labor and Employment, Environmental, Workers Compensation, Probate and Estate Planning and Public Utility Law.
Indianapolis, Indiana Office: 10 West Market Street, Suite 1500. Telephone: 312-637-1777. Fax: 317-687-2414.
Chicago, Illinois Office: 120 South LaSalle Street, Suite 1700. 60603-3419. Telephone: 312-422-1200. Fax: 312-422-1224.
See Professional Biographies, WASHINGTON, DISTRICT OF COLUMBIA

Scorce, John M. '35 '62 C.262 B.S. L.724 J.D.
Sr. Regul. Coun., MCI Telecommunications Corp. (Regulatory Affairs)
Scott, Dana L., Jr., (BV) ....'51 '78 C.893 B.A. L.1209 J.D. [Ⓐ Martell,D.G.&G.] ⊙
*PRACTICE AREAS: Automobile Liability; Civil Practice; Personal Injury Litigation; Commercial Liability; Defense Litigation.
Scott, Gregory M. ....'60 '93 C.170 B.A. L.904 J.D. [Collier S.S.]
*PRACTICE AREAS: Legislative; Administrative.
Scott, Hugh N. '28 '54 C.674 A.B. L.309 LL.B.
(adm. in PA; not adm. in DC) Intl. Bk. for Reconstr. & Develop.
Scott, Isabelle ....'40 '92 L.128 J.D. [Ⓐ Shaw P.]
Scott, James E. ....'47 '73 C.276 B.S.F.S. L.477 J.D. [Venable,A.B.H.&C.]
*PRACTICE AREAS: Banking; Finance; Regulatory Law.
Scott, James J. '23 '52 C&L.16 B.S., LL.B.
(adm. in AL; not adm. in DC) 1344 4th St. S.W.‡
Scott, Jodi K. ....'72 '98 C.221 B.S. L.128 J.D. [Ⓐ Hogan&H.]
*PRACTICE AREAS: Federal Food and Drug Law.
Scott, John T., III, (AV) '53 '78 C.674 A.B. L.893 J.D.
V.P. & Dep. Gen. Coun.-Regulatory, Verizon Wireless
Scott, Jonathan P. ....'69 '95 C.94 B.S. L.904 J.D. [Ⓐ Fried,F.H.S.&J.]
*PRACTICE AREAS: SEC Enforcement; Securities Regulation; Securities Litigation.
Scott, Joseph B., (AV) ....'43 '70 C.1375 A.B. L.112 J.D. [Ⓒ Kator,P.&W.]
Scott, Judith A., (AV) ....'49 '75 C.914 B.A. L.588 J.D. [James&H.]
*PRACTICE AREAS: Labor Law; Employment Law.
Scott, Kelleen McGinnis ....'70 '98 C.276 B.A. L.273 J.D. [Ⓐ Hogan&H.]
*PRACTICE AREAS: Federal Election Law; Securities Fraud; Securities Litigation; Corporate Litigation.
Scott, Laura M. '— '93 C.1356 B.A. L.329 J.D.
(adm. in VA; not adm. in DC) [Ⓐ Jenner&B.]
*PRACTICE AREAS: Antitrust; Trade Regulation.
Scott, Laurence T., (AV) '28 '56
C.573 B.S. L.273 LL.B. [Ⓒ Brault,G.S,&B.] (⊙Rockville, MD)
*PRACTICE AREAS: Medical Malpractice Law.

Scott, Lela R. ....'— '00 C.276 B.S.F.S. L.893 J.D. [Ⓐ Verner,L.B.M.&H.]
*PRACTICE AREAS: International Law; Export Controls.
Scott, Marcela Villalta ....'73 '99 C.347 B.A. L.276 J.D. [Ⓐ Squire,S.&D.]
Scott, Michael, (AV) ......'30 '59 C.188 B.A. L.477 J.D. Amer. Soc. of Anesthesiologists
Scott, Patrick F. .....'69 '96 C.436 B.A. L.589 J.D. U.S. Securities and Exchange Comm.
Scott, Robert G., Jr. ....'61 '87 C.1369 B.A. L.945 J.D. [Cole,R.&B.]
*PRACTICE AREAS: FCC Regulation; Cable TV; Cable Franchising; Internet Law; Telecommunications Competition.
Scott, Stephanie Leigh '69 '95 C.893 B.A. L.273 J.D.
Legal Editor, Amer. Immigration Lawyers Assn.
Scott, Sterling C. ....'55 '85 C.1100 B.A. L.209 J.D. [Ⓒ Haas&N.]
Scott, Thomas J., Jr., (AV) ....'43 '74 C.976 B.E. L.880 J.D. [Hunton&W.] (Pat.)
*PRACTICE AREAS: Intellectual Property; Patent.
Scott, Thomas P., III ....'58 '83 C.198 B.A. L.280 J.D. [Ⓒ Weadon&Assoc.]
*PRACTICE AREAS: International Trade and Transactions; Customs Law; Export Compliance; Export Regulation; Foreign Trade Sanctions.
Scott, William W., (AV) ....'37 '65 C.103 A.B. L.276 LL.B. [Collier S.S.]
Scoutt, Jerrold, Jr., (AV) ....'22 '49 C.118 A.B. L.309 LL.B. [Ⓒ Zuckert,S.&R.]
Scoville, Tamara V. ....'— '94 C.282 B.A. L.128 J.D. [Ⓐ Reed S.]
*PRACTICE AREAS: Health Care.
Scribner, John E. ....'64 '92 C.934 B.A. L.623 J.D. [Clifford C.R.&W.]
*PRACTICE AREAS: Antitrust.

Scribner, Hall & Thompson, LLP, (AV)
1875 I Street, N.W. Suite 1050, 20006
Telephone: 202-331-8585 Telecopier: 202-331-2032
Email: lawfirm@scribnerhall.com URL: http://www.scribnerhall.com
Fred C. Scribner, Jr. (1908-1994); Leonard W. Hall (1900-1979). Members of Firm: Thomas C. Thompson, Jr.; Mark H. Kovey; Stephen P. Dicke; Peter H. Winslow; Susan J. Hotine; Biruta P. Kelly; Gregory K. Oyler; Lori J. Brown; Thomas D. Sykes; Samuel A. Mitchell. Of Counsel: G. Norris Watson (Not admitted in DC).
Federal Tax Practice before Government Departments and Courts.
See Professional Biographies, WASHINGTON, DISTRICT OF COLUMBIA

Scroggins, Amaal A.D. '— '00 C.811 B.A. L.910 J.D.
(adm. in MD; not adm. in DC) [Ⓐ Morgan,L.&B.]

Scull, David L.
(See Bethesda, Maryland)

Scullin, Robert P. ....'44 '74 C.276 L.128 J.D. 1730 K St., N.W.
Scully, Elizabeth A. '— '97 C.884 B.A. L.608 J.D.
(adm. in OH; not adm. in DC) [Ⓐ Baker&H.]
Scully, Katharine W. '66 '93 C.309 B.A. L.813 J.D.
Assoc. Coun., Washington Post, Newsweek Interactive
Scully, Raymond F. ....'29 '57 C&L.262 A.B., LL.B. 2700 Virginia Ave., N.W.
Seabrook, Susan E. ....'60 '86 C.174 B.A. L.285 J.D. [Ⓒ LeBoeuf,L.G.&M.]
Seal, Brian Sherwood ....'69 '01 C.893 B.A. L.16 J.D. [Ⓐ Howrey S.A.&W.]
*PRACTICE AREAS: Intellectual Property Litigation.
Seale, C. Stevens ....'53 '87 C&L.500 B.A., J.D. [Reed S.]
*PRACTICE AREAS: Government Relations.
Sealls, Kenneth E. ....'59 '85 C.401 B.A. L.329 J.D. 1625 K St., N.W.
Seals, William E., Jr. ....'44 '76 C&L.659 A.B., J.D. 1730 K St. N.W.
Seam, Sumeet ....'74 '99 C.273 B.A. L.178 J.D. [Ⓐ Hogan&H.]
Seaman, Julie M. '71 '99 C.518 A.B. L.602 J.D.
(adm. in NY; not adm. in DC) [Ⓐ Finnegan,H.F.G.&D.]
*PRACTICE AREAS: Intellectual Property Procurement; Chemical Patents.
Seaman, Michael P. ....'73 '00 C.602 B.A. L.228 J.D. [Ⓐ Akin,G.S.H.&F.]
*PRACTICE AREAS: Corporate.
Seamon, Julie P. ....'74 '99 C.945 B.A. L.904 J.D. [Ⓐ Dickstein S.M.&O.]
*PRACTICE AREAS: Corporate.
Seamon, Theodore I., (AV) ....'13 '37 C.67 B.A. L.276 LL.B. [Ⓒ Hewes,G.L.&D.]
Seanor, Stacey '68 '97 C.846 B.A. L.45 J.D.
(adm. in AR; not adm. in DC) 2720 Wisc. Ave., N.W.‡
Searchinger, Timothy D. '60 '87 C.31 B.A. L.976 J.D.
(adm. in PA; not adm. in DC) Environmental Defense Fund
Searcy, Lori J. ....'— '00 C.446 B.S. L.276 J.D. [Ⓐ Hogan&H.]
Sears, Edward B. '64 '93 C.197 B.A. L.184 J.D.
(adm. in CT; not adm. in DC) Sr. Assoc. Editor, Environmental Law Institute
Sears, John P., (AV) ....'40 '63 C.602 B.S. L.276 J.D. [Firm of J.P.Sears] ‡
Sears, Mary Helen, (AV) .....'— '60 C.188 A.B. L.273 J.D. [M.H.Sears] (See Pat. Sect.)
*PRACTICE AREAS: Intellectual Property; Patents; Trademarks; Copyrights; Trade Secrets.
Sears, John P., Law Firm of, (AV) .... 2021 K St., NW

Sears, M.H., The, Law Firm, Chartered, (AV) BB
910 Seventeenth Street, N.W., Suite 800, 20006
Telephone: 202-463-3892 Facsimile: 202-463-4852 URL: http://www.searshahn.com
Email: mhsears@mhsears.com URL: http://www.lawyers.com/mhsearslaw
Members of Firm: Mary Helen Sears.
Litigation, Counseling and Procurement of Rights in all areas of Intellectual Property, including Patents, Trademarks, Copyrights, Trade Secrets and general Unfair Competition matters.
See Professional Biographies, WASHINGTON, DISTRICT OF COLUMBIA

Seas, Robert J., Jr. (P.C.), (AV) '32 '62
C.119 B.S.E.E. L.273 LL.B. [Sughrue M.] (See Pat. Sect.)
*PRACTICE AREAS: Intellectual Property Law.
Seaton, Elizabeth A. ....'63 '94 C.273 L.904 J.D. 1407 S. St., N.W.
Sechler, Philip A. ....'63 '90 C.645 B.S. L.276 J.D. [Williams&C.]
*PRACTICE AREAS: Administrative Law; Commercial Law; Constitutional Law; Consumer Law; Food, Drug and Cosmetic Law.
Seckel, Nicolas E. '67 '96 L.999 J.D.
(adm. in NY; not adm. in DC; See Pat. Sect.) [Ⓐ Armstrong,W.H.M.&N.]
*PRACTICE AREAS: Intellectual Property (100%).
Secrest, Jonathan D. .....'67 '00 C.31 B.A. L.597 J.D. Fed. Communications Commission
Secrest, Lawrence W., III, (AV) ....'42 '68 C.30 B.A. L.273 J.D. [Wiley R.&F.]
*PRACTICE AREAS: Communications.
Seder, Arthur R., Jr. '20 '48 C&L.597 B.S.L., LL.B.
(adm. in IL; not adm. in DC) 700 13th St., NW
Sedgewick, Michelle L. ....'63 '91 C.860 B.A. L.945 J.D. 800 K. St. N.W.
Seebald, Craig P. ....'67 '92 C.264 B.A. L.273 J.D. [McDermott,W.&E.]
Seeber, Joseph G. ....'41 '75 C.870 B.S. L.276 J.D. [Ⓐ R.E.Bushnell] (Pat.)
Seeger, Charles M., III, (BV) '48 '77
C.367 B.A. L.128 J.D. Sr. V.P. & Coun., Chicago Mercantile Exch.
Seeger, Edwin H., (AV) .....'30 '57 C.367 B.A. L.276 J.D. 2121 K Street, NW, Suite 700
Seeger, Stephen M., (AV) ....'63 '90 C.401 B.A. L.273 J.D. [Quagliano&S.]
*PRACTICE AREAS: Government Contracts; Construction Law; Civil Litigation.
Seery, Catherine S. ....'65 '96 C.276 B.S. L.904 J.D. [Ⓐ Hogan&H.]
*PRACTICE AREAS: Health Care Corporate Law; Health Law.
Seewald, Scott E. ....'71 '98 C.659 B.A. L.228 J.D. [Ⓐ Akin,G.S.H.&F.]
*PRACTICE AREAS: Litigation.
Seewald, Stacey Wruble ....'71 '96 C.659 B.S./B.A. L.276 J.D. [Ⓐ Akin,G.S.H.&F.]
*PRACTICE AREAS: Corporate Law; Securities.

Sega, A. Christopher '54 '91
C.197 A.B. L.128 J.D. [Venable,A.B.H.&C.] (ⓞRockville, MD)
*PRACTICE AREAS: Trusts and Estates; Tax Law; Business Planning.
Segal, Allen D. '70 '99 C.156 B.A. L.904 J.D.
(adm. in MA; not adm. in DC) Spec. Asst. Legislation, Natl. Assoc. of Letter Carriers
Segal, Deborah G., (AV) ....'57 '83 C.860 B.A. L.94 J.D. [Ⓒ Friedlander,M.S.K.&O.]
*PRACTICE AREAS: Commercial Finance; Commercial Real Estate; Commercial Leasing; Business Law.
Segal, Donald E. ....'47 '72 C.1036 B.A. L.93 J.D. [Buchanan I.]
*PRACTICE AREAS: Food, Drug and Cosmetic Law; Regulatory Law; Biotechnology; Administrative Law.
Segal, Julie Ann ....'66 '91 C.910 A.B. L.823 J.D. 1255 23rd St Nw # 500
Segal, Peter W., (AV) ....'43 '69 C.860 A.B. L.94 J.D. [Powell,G.F.&M.]
*PRACTICE AREAS: Real Estate Development and Financing Law; Corporate Law; Mortgage Banking Law; Commercial Leasing Law; Housing and Urban Development.
Segal, Scott H. ....'64 '89 C.1365 B.A. L.846 J.D. [Bracewell&P.]
*PRACTICE AREAS: Trade; Legislation; Energy; Environmental.
Segal, Theodore D. ....'55 '85 C.228 B.A. L.276 J.D. [Piper M.R.&W.] (ⓞBalt., MD)
*PRACTICE AREAS: Corporate and Securities; Venture Capital; Health Care; Life Sciences; Biotechnology.
Segall, Harold L. ....'58 '85 C.976 B.A. L.145 J.D. [Beveridge&D.]
*PRACTICE AREAS: Environmental Litigation; Commercial Litigation; Environmental Real Estate; Alternative Dispute Resolution.
Segall, Wynn H. ....'60 '90 C.659 A.B. L.145 J.D. [Ⓒ Akin,G.S.H.&F.]
*PRACTICE AREAS: International Government Relations; International Trade; Technology.
Segar, Susan Pecoraro ....'67 '93 C&L.420 B.S., J.D. [Ⓐ Burt,M.&M.]
*PRACTICE AREAS: Federal Taxation; International Taxation; Tax Controversies.
Segel, Eric W., (AV) '51 '76 C.446 B.A. L.1209 J.D.
1828 L. St., N.W. (ⓞRockville, MD)
Seidel, Stuart P. ....'45 '70 C.331 B.A. L.1009 J.D. [Baker&M.]
*PRACTICE AREAS: Trade Regulations and Customs Law.
Seidelson, David E. '29 '56 C&L.665 B.A., LL.B.
(adm. in PA; not adm. in DC) Prof. of Law, Geo. Wash. Univ.
Seiden, Elliott M. ....'45 '71 C&L.569 B.A., J.D. Northwest Airlines, Inc.
Seiden, Matthew J. ....'48 '86 C.309 B.A. L.446 J.D. [Arnold&P.]
*PRACTICE AREAS: Intellectual Property; Computer Law; Internet Law; International Trade; International Transactions.
Seidl, Sarah Curtis ....'66 '91 C.446 B.A. L.1128 J.D. Sr. Coun., Marriot Intl., Inc.
*RESPONSIBILITIES: Employee Benefits; Executive Compensation.
Seidman, David ....'72 '97 C.659 B.A. L.910 J.D. [Ⓐ Thompson C.]
*PRACTICE AREAS: Transportation; Aviation; Maritime Law.
Seidman, L. William ....'21 '49 C.197 A.B. L.309 LL.B. Chm., FDIC,

Seidman & Associates, P.C.
(See Vienna, Virginia)

Seifman, Richard M. '40 '66 C.477 B.A. L.178 J.D.
(adm. in NY; not adm. in DC) 6443 Western Ave., N.W.
Seigel, Evan M. ....'68 '93 C.347 B.S. L.229 J.D. [Ⓐ Malizia S.&F.]
*PRACTICE AREAS: Securities; Banking; Corporate; Tax; Employee Benefits.
Seiger, Jonathan '57 '00 C.966 B.A. L.276 J.D.
(adm. in RI; not adm. in DC) [Ⓐ White&C.]
*PRACTICE AREAS: International Trade Law; Corporate Law.
Seitz, J. Barton ....'59 '87 C.945 A.B. L.273 J.D. [Kelley D.&W.]
*PRACTICE AREAS: Environmental Law; Environmental Litigation.
Seitz, Virginia A. ....'56 '85 C.228 B.A. L.107 J.D. [Sidley A.B.&W.]
Seiver, John D., (AV) ....'53 '79 C.893 B.A. L.94 J.D. [Cole,R.&B.]
*PRACTICE AREAS: Communications Law; Telecommunications Competition; Video Competition; Telecommunications Regulation; Satellite Communications.
Seka, Peter M. ....'— '93 C.999 B.M. L.1048 J.D. [Ⓐ Skadden,A.S.M.&F.]
*PRACTICE AREAS: Taxation.
Sekowski, Karen Ann '75 '00 C.165 B.A. L.128 J.D.
(adm. in MD; not adm. in DC) [Ⓐ Stevens,D.M.&M.]
*PRACTICE AREAS: Intellectual Property; Trademark Litigation; Unfair Competition; Copyrights; Litigation.
Selby, Thomas H. L. ....'67 '99 C.145 B.A. L.846 J.D. [Ⓐ Williams&C.]
*PRACTICE AREAS: Litigation; Criminal; Civil.
Selden, Jack W., (AV) '55 '81 C.893 B.A. L.16 J.D.
(adm. in AL; not adm. in DC) [Bradley A.R.&W.] (ⓞBirm., AL)
*PRACTICE AREAS: Litigation; Health Care Fraud; White Collar Criminal Defense; Governmental Affairs.
Seldon, Robert C. ....'52 '76 C.910 A.B. L.276 J.D. 1319 F St. N.W.
Seletzky, Dimitri ....'69 '98 C.722 B.A. L.64 J.D. [Ⓢ Fulbright&J.]
*PRACTICE AREAS: Administrative Law; Energy Law; Litigation.
Seley, Peter E. ....'68 '93 C.674 A.B. L.188 J.D. [Ⓐ Gibson,D.&C.]
*PRACTICE AREAS: Environmental; Toxic Tort.
Self, Laurie C. ....'64 '92 C.228 A.B. L.893 J.D. [Covington&B.]
Selfe, Roger L. ....'48 '73 C.610 B.A. L.608 J.D. [Bingham D.]
Selfon, Bruce I., (BV) ....'47 '72 C.930 B.A. L.276 J.D. [Cotten&S.]
Selig, Evan D. '72 '99 C.165 B.A. L.273 J.D.
(adm. in MD; not adm. in DC) [Ⓐ Reed S.]
Sellars, David Troy '69 '97 C.645 B.S. L.362 J.D.
(adm. in FL; not adm. in DC) Jus. Dept.
Sellers, Joseph M., (AV) ....'53 '80 C.103 A.B. L.930 J.D. [Cohen,M.H.&T.]
*PRACTICE AREAS: Civil Rights; Employment Law.
Sellinger, David E., (AV) ....'49 '77 C.309 B.A. L.569 J.D. [Venable,A.B.H.&C.]
*PRACTICE AREAS: Complex Civil Litigation; Commercial Litigation; White Collar Criminal Defense.
Selman, John B., (AV) '31 '57 C&L.846 B.B.A., LL.B.
(adm. in TX; not adm. in DC) [Ⓒ Silver,F.&T.] (ⓞAustin, TX)
*PRACTICE AREAS: Financial Institutions; Corporate Financing; Mergers and Acquisitions.
Selman, Thomas M. '58 '84 C.691 B.A. L.846 J.D.
(adm. in TX; not adm. in DC) Investment Co. Inst.
Selter, Michael H., (AV) ....'49 '75 C.103 A.B. L.659 J.D. [Manelli,D.&S.]
*PRACTICE AREAS: Litigation; Appellate Practice; Intellectual Property Litigation.

Seltzer, Diane A., The Law Firm of '67 '91 C.860 B.A. L.30 J.D.
1730 K Street, Northwest Suite 1107, 20006
Telephone: 202-331-3338 Fax: 202-298-9194
Email: diseltz@erols.com
Labor and Employment, Civil Rights, Discrimination, Litigation.
See Professional Biographies, WASHINGTON, DISTRICT OF COLUMBIA

Seltzer, E. Manning ....'12 '38 C.884 B.S. L.309 J.D. 1301 K Street, N.W.‡
Seltzer, Tammy ....'63 '96 C.188 B.S. L.904 J.D. 1101 15th St., N.W.
Selvaggio, Andrea W. ....'49 '78 C.1373 B.S. L.276 J.D. Dept. of Labor
Semel, Elisabeth, (AV) '50 '75 C.65 B.A. L.1067 J.D.
(adm. in CA; not adm. in DC) Dir., Amer. Bar Assn. Death Penalty Representation Proj.
Semilof, Bonnie J. ....'61 '86 C.273 B.A.P.I. L.276 J.D. [Spriggs&H.]
*PRACTICE AREAS: Product Liability; Toxic Torts; Litigation; Drug and Medical Device Defense.
Semko, Jennifer Ancona '73 '98 C.276 B.S.F.S. L.861 J.D.
(adm. in LA; not adm. in DC) [Ⓐ Baker&M.]
*PRACTICE AREAS: Litigation; Arbitration and Dispute Resolution; Appellate Practice.
Semler, Steven R. ....'45 '71 C.331 B.A. L.273 J.D. [Ogletree,D.N.S.&S.]
*PRACTICE AREAS: Labor Law; Employment Discrimination Law; OSHA.

Semmes, Bowen & Semmes, A Professional Corporation, (AV)
Suite 1100 1001 Connecticut Avenue, N.W., 20036 ⊙
Telephone: 202-822-8250 Facsimile: 202-822-8258
Email: semmes@mail.semmes.com URL: http://www.semmes.com
Principals: Alan N. Gamse; Thomas G. Hagerty; Jonathan R. Topazian; R. Michael Haynes. Of Counsel: Richard H. Gimer.
General Practice. Litigation in all Courts and Tribunals. Alternative Dispute Resolutions. Representation in all aspects of Corporate and Partnership Planning and Transactions. Specialties include Administrative Law, Admiralty and Maritime, Antitrust, Banking, Bankruptcy and Creditors' Rights, Commercial and Consumer Lending, Construction, Consumer Product Safety, Corporate, Criminal, Environmental, Estate Planning and Probate, Family Law, Government Contracts and Regulation, Health Care, Immigration, Insurance, Intellectual Property (Copyrights, Trademarks), International Trade and Business, Labor Relations and Employment, Legislative, Mergers and Acquisitions, Pension and Profit Sharing, Product Liability, Professional Malpractice, Real Estate, Securities, Small Business Investment Companies, Taxation, Toxic Torts, Venture Capital, Workers' Compensation and Zoning.
Baltimore, Maryland Office: 250 West Pratt Street, 16th Floor. Telephone: 410-539-5040.
Hagerstown, Maryland Office: 322 East Antietam Street. Telephone: 301-739-4558.
Salisbury, Maryland Office: 231 West Main Street. Telephone: 410-749-1710.
McLean, Virginia Office: Suite 410, 6862 Elm Street. Telephone: 703-760-9473.
See Professional Biographies, WASHINGTON, DISTRICT OF COLUMBIA

Semmes, John Gibson
(See Potomac, Maryland)

Semo, Joseph, (AV) .... '51 '76 C.659 B.S. L.273 J.D. [Feder,S.C.&B.]
*PRACTICE AREAS: Multi-Employer Benefits; Executive Compensation; Pension Plans; Health Care; Fiduciary Defense Litigation.
Semo, Judith J. .... '52 '77 C.103 B.A. L.537 J.D. [C Squire,S.&D.]
*PRACTICE AREAS: Health Care; Professional Associations; Legislation.
Semonsen, Christian C. .... '65 '99 C.112 B.A. L.273 J.D. [A Kirkland&E.]
*PRACTICE AREAS: Environmental Law.
Semsker, Richard H., (BV) .... '60 '87 C.823 B.A. L.1338 J.D. [Lippman&S.]
*PRACTICE AREAS: Employment Law; Business Litigation; Technology Law; Civil Litigation; Appellate Practice.
Senatore, E. Taylor '72 '99 C.472 B.B.A. L.128 J.D.
(adm. in MD; not adm. in DC) [Dobin&S.]
*PRACTICE AREAS: Elder Law; Estate Planning; Estates; Trusts; Probate.
Senchak, Marlisa L. '56 '84 C.705 B.A. L.776 J.D.
(adm. in NJ; not adm. in DC) 3900 Wisconsin Ave., N.W.
Sendar, Michael D. .... '46 '73 C.696 B.A. L.477 J.D. 1032 33rd St., N.W.
Sendek, Kristine L. .... '68 '97 C.477 B.A. L.128 J.D. [A Dyer E.&J.]
*PRACTICE AREAS: Complex Litigation; Civil Litigation; Commercial Litigation.
Senft, William W. '60 '88 C.893 B.S. L.902 J.D.
(adm. in MD; not adm. in DC) 2300 N. St., N.W.‡
Senftle, Patrick G. .... '60 '87 C.910 B.A. L.734 J.D. 1225 Eye St., N.W.
Senger, James D., (AV) .... '56 '81 C.197 A.B. L.976 J.D. [C Kirkland&E.]
*PRACTICE AREAS: Energy.
SenGupta, P. Moni .... '66 '92 C.119 B.S. L.608 J.D. [A Arnold&P.]
*PRACTICE AREAS: Financial Institutions; Litigation; Securities Regulation.
Senhauser, William B. '62 '89 C.197 A.B. L.880 J.D.
(adm. in IL; not adm. in DC) V.P. Dep. Gen. Coun., Fannie Mae Inc.
*RESPONSIBILITIES: Fair Housing; Fair Lending and Compliance.
Senior, Christopher Glenn '66 '92 C.94 B.A. L.1019 J.D.
(adm. in MA; not adm. in DC)
Dir. of Legal Servs., National Association of Home Builders
Sensenbrenner, Eric B. .... '71 '96 C.183 B.A. L.209 J.D. [A Skadden,A.S.M.&F.]
Sensiba, Charles R. '71 '99 C.878 B.S. L.174 J.D.
(adm. in CO; not adm. in DC) [A Van Ness F.]
*PRACTICE AREAS: Energy; Natural Resources; Environmental.
Senter, Meredith S., Jr., (AV) .... '53 '78 C.228 B.A. L.276 J.D. [Leventhal,S.&L.]
*PRACTICE AREAS: Communications Law; Media Law.
Senzel, Alyssa T. .... '68 '95 C.659 B.A. L.893 J.D. [A Patton B.]
Sepanik, Michael J. '73 '99 C.145 B.A. L.245 J.D.
(adm. in MD; not adm. in DC) [A Carr G.]
*PRACTICE AREAS: Product Liability; Antitrust; Business Tort; Employment Law; Professional Liability.
Serafin, Catherine J., (AV) .... '61 '86 C.1113 B.A. L.884 J.D. [McKenna&C.]
*PRACTICE AREAS: Insurance Coverage Litigation.
Serfaty, Alicia Myara '64 '89 C.012 B.A. L.276 J.D.
Sr. Dep. Gen. Coun., Natl. Railroad Passenger Corp. (AMTRAK)
Sergio, Scott D. .... '70 '99 C.692 B.A. L.831 J.D. [A Nixon P.]
*PRACTICE AREAS: Real Estate; Syndication; Affordable Housing.
Serling, Susan H., (AV) .... '51 '77 C.910 B.A. L.178 J.D. [Steptoe&J.]
*PRACTICE AREAS: Federal Income Taxation Law; Tax Controversies; Tax Procedure; Taxation of Individuals and Business Entities; Federal Tax Law.
Sernoff, Louis R. .... '40 '66 C&L.659 B.A., LL.B. [Baker&H.]
*PRACTICE AREAS: Litigation; Trade Regulation.
Serpico, Vincent '66 '97 C.569 B.S. L.178 J.D.
(adm. in NY; not adm. in DC) [A Clifford C.R.&W.]
*PRACTICE AREAS: Technology; Internet Law.
Serron, Eric G. .... '57 '85 C&L.966 B.A., J.D. [C Steptoe&J.]
*PRACTICE AREAS: Employee Benefits.
Serumgard, John R. '44 '69 C&L.276 A.B., J.D.
Exec. V.P., Rubber Manufacturers Assoc.
Session, Warner H. .....'55 '85 C.813 B.A. L.276 J.D. [W.H.Session] & [C D.M.Temple]
Session, Warner H., P.C. .... 1150 Connecticut Avenue, Northwest, Suite 900
Settanni, Andrea M. .... '70 '95 C.93 B.A. L.128 J.D. [A Bracewell&P.]
*PRACTICE AREAS: Regulatory Law; Utility Law; Energy Law.
Settlemyer, Carl H., III .... '64 '94 C.446 B.A. L.276 J.D. 1000 Vermont Ave., N.W.
Sever, Frank, Jr. .... '39 '81 C.665 B.S.Ch.E. L.1209 J.D. [C Stevens,D.M.&M.]
*PRACTICE AREAS: Intellectual Property.
Seward, John R. .... '72 '99 C.880 B.A. L.802 J.D. [A Shearman&S.]

Seward & Kissel LLP, (AV) BR
(Smith & Martin 1890)
1200 G Street, N.W. Suite 350, 20005 ⊙
Telephone: 202-737-8833 Cable Address: "Sewkis New York" Telex: 23-9046; 62-0982 Facsimile: 202-737-5184
URL: http://www.sewkis.com
Resident Partners: Anthony C. J. Nuland; Paul T. Clark. Resident Counsel: Kathleen K. Clarke; Kevin M. Broadwater. Resident Associates: Andrew C. Baek; Paul M. Miller; Nora L. Sheehan; Jennifer Reik (Not admitted in DC).
General Practice including Corporate Finance and Capital Markets, Investment Management, Litigation, Real Estate, Tax and Employee Benefits, Individual Client Matters, Legislative and Regulatory Representation.
New York, New York Office: One Battery Park Plaza. Telephone: 212-574-1200. Facsimile: 212-480-8421.
See Professional Biographies, WASHINGTON, DISTRICT OF COLUMBIA

Sewell, Harry B., Jr., Attorney At Law, Chartered
(See Kensington, Maryland)

Sexter, Reed P. .... '67 '92 C.477 B.A. L.1019 J.D. [A Piper M.R.&W.]
*PRACTICE AREAS: Real Estate; Bankruptcy.
Sexton, Emily C. .... '74 '99 C.339 B.A. L.309 J.D. [A Piper M.R.&W.]
*PRACTICE AREAS: Intellectual Property.

Seyfang, Matthew G. '62 '90 C.851 B.A. L.608 J.D.
(adm. in NY; not adm. in DC) 2130 P St., N.W.‡

Seyfarth Shaw, (AV)
815 Connecticut Avenue, N.W., 20006-4004 ⊙
Telephone: 202-463-2400 Facsimile: 202-828-5393
Email: mailbox@seyfarth.com URL: http://www.seyfarth.com
Partners: Donald M. Barnes; Anita Barondes; Susan Carol Benner; Steven L. Briggerman; Peter Chatilovicz; Kevin P. Connelly; Joseph R. Damato; Joseph J. Dyer (Not admitted in DC); Sara Beiro Farabow; Martin J. Golub; Bennett D. Greenberg; Karla Grossenbacher; Abbey Gail Hairston; Michael B. Hubbard; Steven J. Kmieciak; Alan R. Malasky; James M. McHale; John T. Mitchell; Stuart B. Nibley; Lawrence P. Postol; Richard McKim Preston; Salvatore A. Romano; Donald L. Rosenthal (1950-2001); Fredric S. Singerman; Michael A. Viccora; Christopher A. Weals; William Karl Wilburn. Of Counsel: Grace A. Bateman; Nathaniel H. Goodrich; Russell H. Gore; Ronald A. Lindsay. Resident Associates: Raymond C. Baldwin (Not admitted in DC); David A. Blake (Not admitted in DC); Anne D. Bolling; Paul R. Brockmeyer (Not admitted in DC); David Michael Burns (Not admitted in DC); Susan Jeanblanc Cohen; Emily R. Friedman (Not admitted in DC); Suzanne Harness (Not admitted in DC); Howard C.M. Hobbs (Not admitted in DC); Jeffrey M. Hummel; Kelly S. Jennings; James M. Mesnard; Lowell H. Patterson, III; Jessica R. Schneider (Not admitted in DC); Mark Stevenson; Charles Frederick Walters.
Labor and Employment Law, Employee Benefits, Employment Discrimination, Employment-at-Will, Health Care, Occupational, Safety and Health, Worker's Compensation. Government Contracts. White-Collar Criminal. Litigation, Administrative Law, Business Contract Disputes, Construction, Corporations and Partnerships, General Tort, Insurance, Intellectual Property, Product Liability, Professional Liability, Securities and Commodities. Corporate, Acquisitions, Antitrust, Bankruptcy and Creditors' Rights, Commercial and Financial Transactions, Contracts, Divestitures, Joint Ventures, Mergers, Real Estate, Tax Law, Trust and Probate. Environmental, Safety and Health.
Chicago, Illinois Office: 55 E. Monroe Street, Suite 4200. Telephone: 312-346-8000. Facsimile: 312-269-8869.
Los Angeles, California Office: 2029 Century Park East. Telephone: 310-277-7200. Facsimile: 310-201-5219.
New York, N.Y. Office: 1270 Avenue of the Americas, Suite 2500. Telephone: 212-218-5500. Facsimile: 212-218-5526.
San Francisco, California Office: Suite 2900, 101 California Street. Telephone: 415-397-2823. Facsimile: 415-397-8549.
Sacramento, California Office: 400 Capitol Mall, Suite 2350. Telephone: 916-448-0159. Facsimile: 916-558-4839.
Houston, Texas Office: 700 Louisiana Street, Suite 3850. Telephone: 713-225-2300. Facsimile: 713-225-2340.
Atlanta, Georgia Office: 1545 Peachtree Street, N.E., One Peachtree Pointe, Suite 700. Telephone: 404-885-1500. Facsimile: 404-892-7056.
Boston, Massachusetts Office: Two Seaport Lane, Suite 300. Telephone: 617-946-4800. Facsimile: 617-946-4801.
Brussels, Belgium Office: Avenue Louise 500, Box 8. Telephone: (32) (2) 647.60.25. Fax: (32) (20 640.70.71.
See Professional Biographies, WASHINGTON, DISTRICT OF COLUMBIA

Seymon-Hirsch, Barbara N., (AV) .... '53 '78 C.881 B.A. L.61 J.D. [Davis&H.]
*PRACTICE AREAS: Taxation Law; Pensions Law; Employee Benefits Law; Insurance Law; Employment Tax Law.
Seymour, J. Gordon .... '67 '95 C.976 B.A. L.145 J.D. 725 12th St., N.W.
Seymour, Richard T., (AV) .... '42 '68 C.1121 A.B. L.309 LL.B. [Lieff,C.H.&B.]
Sfikas, Perry .... '55 '89 C.273 B.A. L.1002 J.D. [Sfikas,K.&A.] (⊙Balt., MD)
Sfikas, Karambelas & Akaras, LLP
1201 Pennsylvania Avenue, N.W. Suite 300 (⊙Balt., MD; New York, NY)
Shachter, Rachel '— '01 C.945 B.A. L.893 J.D.
(adm. in VA; not adm. in DC) [A Wilmer,C.&P.]
Shack, Thomas G., Jr., (AV) .... '33 '58 C&L.93 B.S., J.D. [T.G.Shack,Jr.]
*PRACTICE AREAS: International Trade; Commercial Transactions; Arbitration; Communications.

Shack, Thomas G., Jr., P.C., (AV)
1150 Connecticut Avenue, N.W., Suite 900, 20036
Telephone: 202-293-5900 Telecopier: 202-659-3493
URL: http://www.lawyers.com/thomasshacklaw
Thomas G. Shack, Jr.
General Litigation Practice before all Courts, Departments, Commissions and Federal Agencies. Specializing in International Trade and Commercial Transactions, International Arbitration and in all areas of Telecommunications.
See Professional Biographies, WASHINGTON, DISTRICT OF COLUMBIA

Shacter, Michael H., (AV) .... '47 '83 C.273 B.A. L.276 J.D. 1776 K St.NW
Shadmand, Sheila L. .... '73 '99 C.890 B.A. L.893 J.D. [A Jones,D.R.&P.]
Shadoan, George W., (AV) .... '33 '60 C&L.383 B.S., LL.B. [Shadoan&M.] ⊙
Shadoan and Michael, LLP, (AV) .... 4443 29th St. (⊙Rockville, MD)
Shadyac, Richard C., Jr., (AV) ... '57 '82 C.436 B.A. L.424 J.D. [Feldesman,T.L.F.&B.]
*PRACTICE AREAS: Domestic Relations; Litigation; Civil; Criminal; Personal Injury.
Shafer, Edward M. .... '16 '49 C.604 A.B. L.309 J.D. 1417 36th St., N.W.‡
Shaffer, David J., (BV) .... '58 '84 C.967 B.A. L.813 J.D. [Shaffer,R.&S.]
*PRACTICE AREAS: Labor and Employment Law.
Shaffer, David S. .... '67 '96 C.966 B.A. L.904 J.D. [A Andrews&K.]
*PRACTICE AREAS: Energy Law.
Shaffer, Erin E. ..... '58 '92 C.911 B.A. L.184 J.D. Coun. Fed. Corp. Affs., Intl. Paper Co.
Shaffer, Gary L. '49 '79 C&L.665 B.S.Che., J.D.
[Venable,A.B.H.&C.] (See Pat. Sect.)
*PRACTICE AREAS: Patent Litigation; Patent Prosecution; Biotechnology; Pharmaceuticals; Medical Devices.
Shaffer, Mark L. .... '47 '73 C.112 B.A. L.1066 J.D. [Baise&M.]
*PRACTICE AREAS: Civil Trial Practice; Administrative Law; Corporations; Intellectual Property; Employment.
Shaffer, Robert Frederic .... '70 '00 C.276 B.A. L.1209 J.D. [A Finnegan,H.F.G.&D.]
*PRACTICE AREAS: Biochemical Technology; Intellectual Property Arbitration; Intellectual Property Infringement; Intellectual Property Portfolio Management; Patent Litigation.

Shaffer, Rapaport & Schmidt, L.L.P., (BV)
1225 I Street N.W., Suite 500, 20005 ⊙
Telephone: 202-789-8188 Fax: 202-312-2203
David J. Shaffer; Marc A. Rapaport; Ronald A. Schmidt.
Labor and Employment Law, Commercial Litigation, Matrimonial Law, Personal Injury, Social Security Law, Medical Malpractice.
New York, NY Office: 1501 Broadway, 31st Floor, 10036. Telephone: 212-382-1600. Fax: 212-382-0920.
Jersey City, NJ Office: 574 Newark Avenue, Suite 211, 07306. Telephone: 201-418-4888. Fax: 212-382-0920.
See Professional Biographies, WASHINGTON, DISTRICT OF COLUMBIA

Shafferman, Howard H., (AV) .... '54 '78 C.674 A.B. L.893 J.D. [Ballard S.A.&I.]
*PRACTICE AREAS: Energy Regulation; Project Finance; Natural Resources; Cogeneration; Electric Power.
Shaffert, Kurt .... '29 '63 C.563 B.Ch.E. L.569 LL.B. 1401 H Street NW‡
Shafner, Jonathan L. .... '57 '85 C.184 B.A. L.1048 J.D. Coun., GEICO Corp.
Shafran, Nina .... '— '91 C.104 B.A. L.273 J.D. [A Dow,L.&A.]
Shah, Alpita A. '70 '96 C.339 B.A. L.976 J.D.
(adm. in IL; not adm. in DC) U.S. Dept. of Treasury, Legal Div., Hons. Program
Shah, Amee A. .... '72 '99 C.1519 B.S. L.276 J.D. [A Holland&K.]
*PRACTICE AREAS: Employment; Commercial Litigation.
Shah, Ami P. '67 '95 C.912 B.S.E.C.E. L.161 J.D.
(adm. in MD; not adm. in DC; Pat.) [A Dorsey&W.]
*PRACTICE AREAS: Electrical Intellectual Property; Electronic Intellectual Property; Intellectual Property Litigation; Mechanical Intellectual Property; Computer and Software Patents.

Shah, Amish M. .... '71 '99 C.446 B.S. L.273 J.D. [A Sutherland A.&B.]
*PRACTICE AREAS: Federal Taxation; International Taxation; Tax Controversies.
Shah, Ankur D. .... '— '97 C.645 B.S. L.273 J.D. [A Foley&L.] (See Pat. Sect.)
*PRACTICE AREAS: Intellectual Property.
Shah, Rajat R. .... '71 '97 C.282 B.A. L.880 J.D. [A Akin,G.S.H.&F.]
*PRACTICE AREAS: Corporate Law; Securities; Project Finance.
Shah, Sangita A. .... '— '01 C.1090 B.A. L.329 J.D. [A Morgan,L.&B.]
Shahan, Bridget .... '63 '93 C&L.128 B.S., J.D. [A Cameron M.]
*PRACTICE AREAS: Energy Law.
Shaheen, David T. .... '54 '85 C.602 B.A. L.537 J.D. [Babirak,A.V.&S.]
Shaheen, Frederick F. .... '53 '93 C.823 A.B. L.273 J.D. [Howrey S.A.&W.]
*PRACTICE AREAS: International Commercial Law; Foreign Military Sales; Export Regulation.
Shaheen, Randal M. .... '60 '85 C.105 B.A. L.309 J.D. [C Arnold&P.]
*PRACTICE AREAS: Antitrust; Consumer Protection.
Shahida, Stephen K. .... '67 '96 C.1356 B.S.E.E. L.276 J.D. [A McDermott,W.&E.]
Shahriari, K. Thomas .... '57 '83 C.1044 B.A. L.30 J.D. [A Kalbian H.]
*PRACTICE AREAS: Litigation; Insurance.
Shaikh, Hina '72 '99 C&L.861 B.A., J.D.
(adm. in NY; not adm. in DC) [A Orrick,H.&S.]
Shail, Scott A. .... '71 '99 C.34 B.S. L.64 J.D. [A Hogan&H.]
Shaines, Marsha Sue '52 '77
C.788 A.B. L.94 J.D. Dep. Gen. Coun., Smithsonian Institution
Shainis, Aaron, (AV) .... '48 '73 C.608 B.A. L.838 J.D. [Shainis&P.]
*PRACTICE AREAS: Communications Law; Corporate Law; Appellate Practice; Telecommunications.

Shainis & Peltzman, Chartered, (AV)
1850 M Street, N.W., Suite 240, 20036
Telephone: 202-293-0011 Fax: 202-293-0810
Email: shainis-peltzman@s-plaw.com URL: http://www.lawyers.com/s&plaw
Aaron Shainis; Lee J. Peltzman. Of Counsel: William H. DuRoss, III; Robert J. Keller.
Telecommunications Law, Communications Law, Telecommunications Regulation, FCC Regulation, FCC Licensing.
See Professional Biographies, WASHINGTON, DISTRICT OF COLUMBIA

Shakow, John D. .... '69 '97 C.821 B.A. L.893 J.D. [A King&S.]
*PRACTICE AREAS: Litigation; Trade Regulation.
Shakow, Susannah .... '— '98 C.198 B.A. L.893 J.D. [A Verner,L.B.M.&H.]
*PRACTICE AREAS: Legislative; Health Care Law.
Shakow, Thomas E. .... '72 '98 C&L.976 B.A., J.D. [A Williams&C.]
Shalaby, Mark A. .... '73 '99 C.813 B.A. L.276 J.D. [A White&C.]
Shaller, Elliot H. .... '52 '77 C.102 B.A. L.273 J.D. [Krukowski&C.]
*PRACTICE AREAS: Labor and Employment Law.
Shambon, Leonard M., (AV) .... '45 '73 C.976 B.A. L.659 J.D. [C Wilmer,C.&P.]
*PRACTICE AREAS: International Trade.
Shamraj, Larissa A. .... '73 '99 C.914 B.A. L.309 J.D. [A Spiegel&M.]
*PRACTICE AREAS: Energy.
Shanahan, J. Kearney, (AV) .... '44 '72 C.674 A.B. L.276 J.D. [Shanahan] ⊙
Shanahan, James R., Jr. .... '53 '83 C.602 B.B.A. L.809 J.D. Price Waterhouse
Shanahan, Michelle M., (AV) '66 '91 C.884 B.A. L.659 J.D.
Asst. Gen. Coun., National Public Radio, Inc.

Shanahan Law Firm, The, LLC, (AV)
Suite 510 1725 K Street N.W., 20006 ⊙
Telephone: 202-785-2940 Fax: 202-785-2941
Terrance L. Ryan (Not admitted in DC); J. Kearney Shanahan.
Business, Litigation and Transactional Practice, Acquisitions and Divestitures, Antitrust, Banks and Banking, Business Law, Civil Litigation, Collective Bargaining, Commercial Law, Computers and Software, Construction Law, Contracts, Corporate Law, Entertainment Law, Environmental Law, Finance, Intellectual Property, Investments, Labor and Employment, Leases and Leasing, Mergers, Mortgages, Partnership Law, Real Estate, Securities, Taxation, Technology, Trusts and Estates, and Venture Capital.
Cleveland, Ohio Office: 1750 Huntington Building, 925 Euclid Avenue, 44115-1483. Telephone: 216-363-1700. Fax: 216-363-1096.
See Professional Biographies, WASHINGTON, DISTRICT OF COLUMBIA

Shane, Jeffrey N., (AV) .... '41 '67 C.674 A.B. L.178 LL.B. [Hogan&H.]
*PRACTICE AREAS: Aviation; Commercial Space Transportation; Administrative Law.
Shane, John R. .... '62 '88 C.105 B.A. L.276 J.D. [Wiley R.&F.]
*PRACTICE AREAS: International Trade.
Shang, Wendy Wan-Long '68 '94 C&L.893 B.A., J.D.
(adm. in VA; not adm. in DC) American Bar Assoc.
Shanker, Vijay ....'72 '99 C.228 B.A. L.893 J.D. [A Covington&B.]
Shankman, Bernard, (BV) .... '08 '37 L.94 LL.B. 1300 L St., NW
Shanks, Hershel, (AV) .... '30 '56 C.311 B.A. L.309 LL.B. 5208 38th St., N.W.‡

Shanks & Herbert
(See Alexandria, Virginia)

Shanley and Baker, (AV)
Georgetown Building, Suite 235, 2233 Wisconsin Avenue, N.W., 20007
Telephone: 202-333-5800 Facsimile: 202-333-5803
Members of Firm: James J. Shanley (1906-1995); Raymond N. Baker.
Intellectual Property, Patent, Trademark and Copyright Law.
See Professional Biographies, WASHINGTON, DISTRICT OF COLUMBIA

Shanmugam, Kannon K. .... '72 '01 C&L.309 A.B., J.D. [A Kirkland&E.]
*PRACTICE AREAS: Appellate Litigation; Commercial Litigation; Arbitration; Antitrust; Competition.
Shannon, James W., Jr. '63 '93 C.112 B.A. L.309 J.D.
(adm. in VA; not adm. in DC) 725 12th St., N.W.
Shannon, John P., Jr. '46 '75
C.215 B.M.E. L.273 J.D. [Venable,A.B.H.&C.] (See Pat. Sect.)
*PRACTICE AREAS: Intellectual Property; Patents; Mechanical Patents; International Patents; Trademarks.
Shannon, Laura Delong '61 '87 C.1369 B.A. L.1209 J.D.
(adm. in VA; not adm. in DC) 111 Mass. Ave., N.W.
Shannon, Patrick H. .... '— '99 L.893 J.D. [A Latham&W.]
*PRACTICE AREAS: Corporate Law; Communications Law.
Shannon, Thomas F., (AV) .... '27 '53 C.95 A.B. L.893 LL.B. [C Collier S.S.]
*PRACTICE AREAS: International Trade.
Shanoff, Barry S. .... '43 '68 C&L.597 B.S., J.D. [Knopf&B.]
*PRACTICE AREAS: Environmental Law; Local Government Law; Solid Waste.
Shapar, Howard K. .... '23 '51 C.31 B.A. L.976 J.D. 2300 N. St. NW
Shapiro, Alison J. '72 '99 C.861 B.S. L.30 J.D.
(adm. in VA; not adm. in DC) [A Fletcher,H.&H.] ⊙
*PRACTICE AREAS: Communications Law; Mass Media Law; Telecommunications Regulation Law; Satellite Communications Law; Intellectual Property Law.
Shapiro, Claire L. .... '53 '80 C.477 A.B. L.276 J.D. [Cullen]
*PRACTICE AREAS: Transportation Law; Class Actions; Litigation; Insurance Coverage; Insurance Litigation.
Shapiro, Daryl M. .... '63 '91 C.831 B.B.A. L.472 J.D. [C Morgan,L.&B.]
Shapiro, David H. .... '49 '74 C.30 B.A. L.930 J.D. [Swick&S.]
Shapiro, David I., (AV) .... '28 '49 C.966 L.1009 LL.B. [C Dickstein S.M.&O.]
*PRACTICE AREAS: Alternative Dispute Resolution.
Shapiro, David T. .... '56 '98 C.696 B.A. L.273 J.D. 700 13th St., N.W.
Shapiro, David T. '— '97 C.855 B.A. L.184 J.D.
(adm. in CT; not adm. in DC) 701 Pennsylvania Avenue, N.W.
Shapiro, Edward J. .... '— '81 C.674 A.B. L.309 J.D. [Latham&W.]
Shapiro, Ellen Louise .... '50 '93 C.454 B.S. L.276 J.D. American Auto Mfg. Assoc.
Shapiro, George H., (AV) .... '36 '60 C&L.309 B.A., LL.B. 1050 Conn. Ave., N.W.
Shapiro, Hal S. .... '66 '92 C&L.178 B.A., J.D. [Miller&C.]
*PRACTICE AREAS: International Trade; International Trade Agreements; Import and Export Law; Foreign Trade Sanctions; Federal Litigation.
Shapiro, Harold P. '12 '37 C&L.976 B.A., LL.B.
(adm. in CT; not adm. in DC) 4629 Chesapeake, N.W.‡
Shapiro, Howard E., (AV) .... '26 '55 C.339 B.Sc. L.178 LL.B. [Van Ness F.]
*PRACTICE AREAS: Appellate Practice; Energy; Antitrust; Regulated Industries; Federal Administrative Law.
Shapiro, Howard M., (AV) .... '60 '86 C.951 B.A. L.976 J.D. [Wilmer,C.&P.]
*PRACTICE AREAS: Criminal Law; Internal Investigations; White Collar Crime; Civil Practice.
Shapiro, Howard S. .... '55 '81 C&L.259 B.A., J.D. [C Bennet&B.]
*PRACTICE AREAS: Communications Law.
Shapiro, Ira S., (AV) .... '47 '73 C.1036 B.A. L.659 J.D. [Long A.&N.]
*PRACTICE AREAS: Government Relations; Public Policy; International Trade and Customs.
Shapiro, Jason M. '64 '94 C.367 B.S. L.64 J.D.
(adm. in MD; not adm. in DC; See Pat. Sect.) [A Rothwell,F.E.&M.]
*PRACTICE AREAS: Intellectual Property.
Shapiro, Jeffrey K. .... '61 '86 C.103 A.B. L.309 J.D. [Hogan&H.]
*PRACTICE AREAS: Food, Drug and Cosmetic Law; Drug and Medical Device Regulation.
Shapiro, Joel M. '68 '94 C.188 A.B. L.1068 J.D.
(adm. in CA; not adm. in DC) 1615 L St., N.W.‡
Shapiro, Judith A. .... '52 '83 C.299 B.A. L.276 J.D. [Hobbs,S.D.&W.]
Shapiro, Larry E., (AV) .... '47 '73 C.446 B.S. L.276 J.D. [McDermott,W.&E.]
Shapiro, Linda J., (AV) ... '52 '77 C.860 B.S. L.273 J.D. [A Jacobson,H.] (See Pat. Sect.)
*PRACTICE AREAS: Intellectual Property Law; Mechanical Patents; Computer and Software Patents.
Shapiro, Marc H. ..... '50 '75 C.575 A.B. L.893 J.D. [A Hyman,P.&M.] (⊙Durham, NC)
*PRACTICE AREAS: Food and Drug Law.
Shapiro, Neil K. .... '60 '86 C.976 B.A. L.813 J.D. [A Baker&M.]
*PRACTICE AREAS: Litigation; Arbitration and Dispute Resolution; Criminal Law.
Shapiro, Rachel A. '71 '99 C.659 B.A. L.569 J.D.
(adm. in NY; not adm. in DC) [A O'Melveny&M.]
Shapiro, Randy L. '64 '90 C.860 B.A. L.94 J.D.
(adm. in NY; not adm. in DC) Asst. Coun., Newsweek
Shapiro, Robert A. .... '61 '97 C.183 B.A. L.188 J.D. [Barnes,R.&C.]
*PRACTICE AREAS: Customs; International Trade.
Shapiro, Robert B. .... '49 '74 C.608 B.S. L.823 J.D. [Bernstein] ⊙
*PRACTICE AREAS: Insurance Regulation; Financial Guaranty Insurance; Reinsurance; International Insurance; Fidelity and Surety.
Shapiro, Robert F. .... '51 '76 C.855 B.A. L.273 J.D. [Chadbourne&P.]
Shapiro, Robert L. .... '62 '87 C.659 B.A. L.145 J.D. [Spriggs&H.]
*PRACTICE AREAS: Government Contracts; Banking Litigation; Litigation; Federal Claims.
Shapiro, Ronald E. ...... '53 '78 C.367 B.A. L.446 J.D. [Vorys,S.S.&P.] (See Pat. Sect.)
Shapiro, Ronald S., (AV) .... '47 '73 C.446 B.S. L.273 J.D. [Shapiro,L.&S.]
*PRACTICE AREAS: Real Estate; General Business Law; Finance; Creditors Rights.
Shapiro, Stephen Brett, (AV) .... '62 '87 C.446 B.A. L.273 J.D. [Holland&K.]
*PRACTICE AREAS: Government Contracts; Construction Law; Litigation.
Shapiro, Tamar '— '00 C&L.309 A.B., J.D.
(adm. in PA; not adm. in DC) [A Hogan&H.]
Shapiro, William Dana .... '46 '72 C.951 B.A. L.893 J.D. [Potomac C.I.]

Shapiro, Lifschitz and Schram, P.C., (AV) BR
The Evening Star Building, 1101 Pennsylvania Avenue N.W. Suite 1050, 20004 ⊙
Telephone: 202-347-4111 Facsimile: 202-347-8341
URL: http://www.slslaw.com
Ronald S. Shapiro; Judah Lifschitz; Steven H. Schram;—Robert A. Foster; Randal W. Wax; James D. McMichael; Thomas R. Bartman; Jonathan A. Beldon; Helmut E. Gerlach; Suzanne Marie Lewis.
Business, Corporate, Real Estate, Litigation, Commercial Transactions, Arbitration, Mediation and Alternative Dispute Resolution, Construction, Government Contracts, Creditors Rights and Remedies, Technology Licensing, Civil Fraud, Appellate Practice, Taxation, Estate Planning.
Greenbelt, Maryland Office: 6411 Ivy Lane, Suite 116, 20770. Telephone: 202-347-4111. Facsimile: 202-347-8341.
See Professional Biographies, WASHINGTON, DISTRICT OF COLUMBIA

Shapiro & Mayer, (AV) .... 1001 Connecticut Ave., N.W.

Shapiro and Olander
(See Shapiro Sher & Guinot, P.A.)

Shapiro Sher & Guinot, P.A.
(Formerly known as Shapiro and Olander)
1800 K Street, N.W., Suite 716, 20006 ⊙
Telephone: 202-331-0200 FAX: 202-331-7457
Email: lg@shapirosher.com URL: http://www.shapirosher.com
Partner: Luis Guinot, Jr. Resident Members, Baltimore, Maryland Office: Charles S. Fax; Joel I. Sher; William E. Carlson; Lonnie M. Ritzer; Sheryl N. Stephenson.
Administrative Law, Alternative Dispute Resolution, Arbitration, Asset Based Finance, Banking, Bankruptcy, Bankruptcy Chapter 7, Bankruptcy Chapter 11, Bankruptcy Litigation, Bankruptcy Reorganization, Biotechnology, Blue Sky Law, Business Law, Civil Litigation, Civil Rights Litigation, Commercial Bankruptcy, Commercial Insolvency, Commercial Law, Commercial Leasing, Commercial Litigation, Commercial Real Estate, Commercial Transactions, Commercial Workouts, Complex Commercial Litigation, Complex Litigation, Computer Law, Computer Software Law, Computers and Software, Contracts, Copyrights, Corporate Law, Creditor Bankruptcy, Creditors Rights, Creditors Rights in Bankruptcy, Debtor Bankruptcy, Debtor and Creditor, Debtor and Creditor Remedies, Debtor and Creditor Reorganization, Debtor and Creditor Rights, Debtor Rights, Defense Litigation, Employment Litigation, Federal Civil Litigation, Federal Litigation, Finance, Financial Institution Regulation, Financial Institutions Law, Franchises and Franchising, Franchise Law, Fraudulent Conveyance, Government Relations, Initial Public Offerings, Intellectual Property, International Commercial Law, International Law, International Trade, Internet Law, Internet Trademark Law, Land Development, Land Use, Liquidations, Litigation, Mediation, Mergers and Acquisitions, Municipal Bonds, Municipal Civil Rights, Municipal Corporation Law, Municipal Defense, Municipal Finance, Municipal Law, Municipal Liability, Out of Court Debt Restructuring, Pre-Bankruptcy Workouts, Products Liability, Products Liability Defense, Public Offerings, Real Estate, Real Estate Development, Real Estate Finance, Real Estate Secured Lending, Receiverships, Retail Financing, Secured Creditors Rights, Securities, Securities Regulation, Software Copyright, Start-Up Organization and Financing, Taxation, Technology Transfer, Trademarks, Trial Practice, Venture Capital, Workouts, U.S. Supreme Court Litigation, Uniform Commercial Code, Unsecured Creditors Rights, Zoning.
Baltimore, Maryland Office: Suite 2000, 36 South Charles Street, 21201. Telephone: 410-385-0202. Fax: 410-539-7611.
See Professional Biographies, WASHINGTON, DISTRICT OF COLUMBIA

Sharara, Norma M. '63 '94 C.30 B.A. L.446 J.D.
(adm. in MD; not adm. in DC) [A Silverstein&M.]
*PRACTICE AREAS: Employee Benefits; Executive Compensation.
Sharkey, Edward E. .... '68 '93 C.976 B.A. L.893 J.D. [A Dickstein S.M.&O.]
*PRACTICE AREAS: Commercial Litigation; Securities Litigation.
Sharkey, Michael T. .... '69 '94 C&L.976 B.A., J.D. [A Dickstein S.M.&O.]
*PRACTICE AREAS: General Litigation; Insurance Litigation.
Sharlitt, Joseph H., (AV) .... '24 '50 C&L.309 A.B., J.D. 1899 L St Nw # 500
Sharma, Onkar N. '47 '75 C&L.999 B.Com., LL.B.
Asst. Gen. Coun., Wash. Metro Area Transit Auth.

Sharma, Parmanand "Anand" K. '71 '98
C.446 B.S.M.E. L.564 J.D. [Ⓐ Finnegan,H.F.G.&D.] (See Pat. Sect.)
*PRACTICE AREAS: Intellectual Property Litigation; Patent Prosecution; Intellectual Property Portfolio Management.

Sharma, Sarah M. '73 '01 C.30 B.A. L.861 J.D.
(adm. in NY; not adm. in DC) [Ⓐ Sher&B.]
*PRACTICE AREAS: Transportation; Maritime Law; Corporate Law; Commercial Law.

Sharo, David P. .... '56 '94 C.645 B.S. L.30 J.D. 1875 Connecticut Avenue, N.W.

Sharp, Benjamin S., (AV) .... '44 '73 C.390 B.A. L.581 J.D. [Perkins C.]
*PRACTICE AREAS: Antitrust Law; Civil Litigation; Federal Criminal Law; Federal Trade Commission.

Sharp, Ira H. '43 '68 C.910 A.B. L.178 LL.B.
CEO & General Counsel, Alderson Reporting Company, Inc.

Sharp, Thomas E. .... '72 '98 C.567 B.A. L.976 J.D. [Ⓐ Wilmer,C.&P.]

Sharpe, David J. ...... '30 '55 C.575 A.B. L.309 LL.B. Prof. of Law, George Wash. Univ.

Sharpe, Kieran '51 '79 C.21 B.A. L.904 J.D.
(adm. in PA; not adm. in DC) [Ⓒ Aitken I.B.&V.]

Sharretts, Paley, Carter & Blauvelt, P.C., (AV)
Suite 725, 1707 L Street, N.W., 20036 ⊙
Telephone: 202-223-4433 Cable Address: "Customlex" Washington Fax: 202-659-3904
Email: 102160.3466@compuserve.com URL: http://www.sharretts-paley.com/index.htm
M. Barry Levy (Not admitted in DC); Gail T. Cumins (Not admitted in DC); Duncan A. Nixon (Not admitted in DC; Resident); Beatrice A. Brickell (Resident).
Customs Law, International Trade, Imports and Exports, Anti-Dumping and Countervailing Duties.
New York, N.Y. Office: 75 Broad Street, 26th Floor. Telephone: 212-425-0055.

See Professional Biographies, WASHINGTON, DISTRICT OF COLUMBIA

Shattuck, Cathie A. .... '45 '70 C&L.546 B.A., J.D. [Ⓒ Epstein B.&G.]

Shatynski, Patricia Ann '62 '99
C.570 B.S.Ch.E. L.1338 J.D. [Ⓐ Finnegan,H.F.G.&D.] (See Pat. Sect.)
*PRACTICE AREAS: Chemical Patent Prosecution; Pharmaceutical Patent Prosecution; Chemicals; Organic Chemistry; Semiconductor Technology.

Shatzer, Larry L., II .... '— '87 C.1064 B.A. L.276 J.D. [Foley&L.]
*PRACTICE AREAS: Intellectual Property Litigation; International Trade; Trademarks; Antidumping.

Shaughnessy, Brian W., (AV) .... '38 '68 C.659 B.A. L.705 J.D. [Shaughnessy,V.&G.]

Shaughnessy, Robert J. .... '61 '88 C.674 A.B. L.893 J.D. [Williams&C.]

Shaughnessy, Volzer & Gagner, P.C., (AV) .... 1155 Fifteenth Street, N.W., Suite 502

Shavitz, Ian A. ...... '71 '96 C.446 B.A. L.1040 J.D. 1333 New Hampshire Avenue, N.W.

Shavitz, Jeannine R. '69 '95 C.884 B.A. L.1040 J.D.
(adm. in NJ; not adm. in DC) [Ⓐ Counts,P.-D.&D.]

Shaw, Anthony W., (AV) .... '54 '81 C.188 B.A. L.276 J.D. [Brobeck,P.&H.] (Pat.)

Shaw, Arnold F., (AV) .... '10 '33 C&L.597 B.S.L. [Donohue,K.S.&K.]

Shaw, Brackley, (AV) .... '13 '39 C&L.477 A.B., J.D. 2801 New Mexico Ave. N.W.‡

Shaw, Elizabeth (Nena) C. .... '70 '99 C.477 B.S. L.228 J.D. [Ⓐ Hunton&W.]
*PRACTICE AREAS: Environmental Law.

Shaw, Frank C. .... '63 '89 C.309 A.B. L.477 J.D. [Ⓒ Skadden,A.S.M.&F.]

Shaw, G. Jerry, Jr., (AV) .... '40 '70 C.285 B.B.A. L.744 J.D. [Shaw,B.V.&R.]
*PRACTICE AREAS: Administrative Law; Legislative Law; Association Law; Employment Law.

Shaw, Gordon M. '37 '62 C&L.145 A.B., J.D.
(adm. in IL; not adm. in DC) 2510 Virginia Ave., N.W.‡

Shaw, Harold M. .... '— '79 C.216 A.B. L.276 J.D. [Ⓒ King&S.]
*PRACTICE AREAS: Environmental.

Shaw, John Spitaleri .... '69 '95 C.823 B.S. L.128 J.D. [Ⓐ Patton B.]

Shaw, Kevin G. .... '74 '99 C.659 B.A. L.273 J.D. [Ⓐ Hogan&H.]
*PRACTICE AREAS: Intellectual Property; Patents; Computer and Software Patents.

Shaw, Marilyn Tebor, (AV) '54 '80
C.188 A.B. L.1044 J.D. Assoc. Gen. Coun., Natl. Gallery of Art

Shaw, Peg, (BV) .... '41 '79 C.94 B.A. L.904 J.D. [Rent]

Shaw, Robert E. .... '57 '84 C&L.705 B.A., J.D. [Ⓒ Covington&B.]

Shaw, Ruth C., (AV) .... '47 '73 C.66 A.B. L.273 J.D. [Ⓐ Silverstein&M.]
*PRACTICE AREAS: Trusts and Estates.

Shaw, Sarah E. .... '72 '97 C.477 B.A. L.273 J.D. [Ⓐ Shaw P.]
*PRACTICE AREAS: Real Estate; Zoning, Planning and Land Use; Municipal Law.

Shaw, Stephanie L. .... '68 '96 C.264 B.A. L.128 J.D. [Ⓐ Lotstein B.]
*PRACTICE AREAS: Mortgage Banking Law; Real Estate.

Shaw, Bransford, Veilleux & Roth, A Professional Corporation, (AV) BR
1100 Connecticut Avenue, N.W., Suite 900, 20036-4101
Telephone: 202-463-8400 Telecopier: 202-833-8082
Email: sbvr@shawbransford.com URL: http://www.shawbransford.com
G. Jerry Shaw, Jr.†; William L. Bransford; Diana J. Veilleux; Debra L. Roth;—Lori E. Kline; Bernard E. Doyle; John P. Mahoney; Anjali Kumar; Janice A. Simons; Anthony Vergnetti. Of Counsel: Thomas J. O'Rourke.
Administrative, Associations, Legislative, Litigation, Corporation, Taxation, Estate Planning, Probate, Employment Law, EEO and Federal Personnel Law.
†Professional Corporation

See Professional Biographies, WASHINGTON, DISTRICT OF COLUMBIA

Shaw Pittman LLP, (AV)
A Limited Liability Partnership Including Professional Corporations
2300 N Street, N.W., 20037 ⊙
Telephone: 202-663-8000 Cable Address: "Shawlaw" Telex: 89-2693 (Shawlaw Wsh) Telecopier: 202-663-8007
Email: postmaster@sppt.com URL: http://www.shawpittman.com
Members of Firm: George F. Trowbridge (1919-1989); James L. Alberg; Walter J. Andrews (Resident, McLean, Virginia Office); Scott A. Anenberg (P.C.); Dean D. Aulick (P.C.); Aslan Baghdadi (Resident, McLean, Virginia Office); Deborah Brand Baum; Thomas A. Baxter (P.C.); Stephan E. Becker; Michael D. Bednarek (Resident, McLean, Virginia Office); Lon A. Berk (Resident, McLean, Virginia Office); Charles G. Berry (Resident, New York, N.Y. Office); Robert Bishop (Resident, London, England Office); Ernest L. Blake, Jr. (P.C.); James A. Blalock III; Brian M. Blum; Eileen L. Brownell (P.C.); Denise R. Cade; Cecelia A. Calaby; John L. Carr, Jr.; Kenneth A. Caruso (Resident, New York, N.Y. Office); Thomas J. Catliota; Craig E. Chason (Resident, McLean, Virginia Office); Howard L. Clemons (Resident, McLean, Virginia Office); Marc R. Cohen; Robert E. Cohn; H. Guy Collier; Alan S. Cooper; B. Scott Custer, Jr.; David J. Cynamon (P.C.); Thomas J. Delaney; Craig A. de Ridder; Robert M. Di Giovanni (Resident, Los Angeles, California Office); Marie N. Doland; Richard C. Donaldson (Not admitted in DC; Resident); Mario F. Dottori; Maureen Ellen Dwyer; John Engel (P.C.); Gregory S. Feis; Phil T. Feola; Charles S. Fiedler (Resident, Los Angeles, California Office); Eric T. Fingerhut (Resident, McLean, Virginia Office); David G. Fiske; Lauren Lynch Flick; Scott R. Flick; Bruce M. Fried; Paul A. Gaukler; Gregory M. Giammittorio (Resident, McLean, Virginia Office); Jefferson C. Glassie; Barry H. Gottfried; Lawrence J. Gotts (Resident, McLean, Virginia Office); Edmund D. Graff; R. Timothy Hanlon (P.C.); Edward J. Hansen (Resident, New York, N.Y. Office); Elisabeth J. Harper (Resident, McLean, Virginia Office); John S. Harper (Resident, McLean, Virginia Office); Clifford M. Harrington; Ellen K. Harrison; Sheila McC. Harvey; Robert E. Hasty; Devon Elizabeth Hewitt (Resident, McLean, Virginia Office); J. Patrick Hickey (P.C.); Thomas C. Hill (P.C.); Christopher Holder (Resident, London, England Office); Jeffrey D. Hutchings; Stephen B. Huttler (P.C.); Rebecca L. Jackson; Bruce D. Jacobs; Jerald A. Jacobs; Christopher G. Janney; John E. Jensen (Resident, McLean, Virginia Office); Christine Nicolaides Kearns; Joseph E. Kendall; Allen J. Klein; Eric A. Klein (Resident, Los Angeles, California Office); Thomas J. Knox (Resident, McLean, Virginia Office); M. David Krohn; Charles J. Landy; Kurt L.P. Lawson; Martin R. Leader; Warren U. Lehrenbaum; J. Thomas Lenhart (P.C.); David R. Lewis; Jack L. Lewis (Resident, McLean, Virginia Office); Robert Y. Lewis (Resident, New York, N.Y. Office); Sylvia M. Mahaffey (P.C.); David C. Main; Clara Ruyan Martin (Resident, Los Angeles, California Office); Miles S. Mason; Jennifer Lynn Mattingly (Resident, London, England Office); Alistair Maughan (Resident, London, England Office); Thomas H. McCormick; John M. McDonald; Jack McKay (P.C.); Kathy J. McKnight; Steven L. Meltzer (P.C.) (Senior Partner, McLean, Virginia Office); David E. Menotti; Paul F. Mickey, Jr.; David L. Miller (P.C.) (Resident, McLean, Virginia Office); Michael C. Moetell; Francisco R. Montero; Thomas D. Morton; Andrew C. Moyle (Resident, London, England Office); J. E. Murdock

(This Listing Continued)

Shaw Pittman LLP (Continued)

III; Michael T. Murphy (Resident, Los Angeles, California Office); Trevor W. Nagel; Joyce L. Oliner; John H. O'Neill, Jr. (P.C.); Aaron M. Oser; David D. Oxenford; Thomas J. Pax; Marc A. Pearl; Victoria J. Perkins (P.C.); William J. Peters (Resident, Los Angeles, California Office); Charles H. Peterson; Paul S. Pilecki (P.C.); Anne K. Planning; Patrick John Potter; Glenn S. Richards; Diane Shapiro Richer; Robert B. Robbins (P.C.); Jane Sullivan Roberts; Michele D. Ross; Barbara M. Rossotti (P.C.); Gary D. Roth (Resident, New York, N.Y. Office); David R. Sahr; Kathryn R. Schmeltzer; Lawrence A. Schultis; Charles Severs (Resident, London, England Office); Jay E. Silberg (P.C.); Lynn A. Soukup (P.C.); Debbie Beecher Spartin (P.C.); Thomas J. Spulak; Akiba Stern (Resident, New York, N.Y. Office); Elizabeth Espin Stern; Charles B. Temkin (P.C.); Alexander D. Tomaszczuk (Resident, McLean, Virginia Office); Matias F. Travieso-Diaz (P.C.); Andrew M. Tucker (Resident, McLean, Virginia Office); Timothy Hansen Watkins; Gadi Weinreich; Robert N. Weinstock; Sheldon J. Weisel (P.C.); Wendelin A. White; Milton B. Whitfield; James H. Wilkins, Jr.; Frank Winston, Jr. (Resident, McLean, Virginia Office); D. Craig Wolff; Andrew L. Woods; Jeffery L. Yablon (P.C.); Lawrence T. Yanowitch (Resident, McLean, Virginia Office); Gino Zaccardelli (Also at McLean, Virginia Office); Robert E. Zahler (P.C.); Richard R. Zaragoza. Senior Counsel: Richard S. Beatty; Nathaniel P. Breed, Jr. (P.C.); Gerald Charnoff (P.C.); Mary Jane Dodson; Ben C. Fisher; Ellen Canan Grady (Resident, McLean, Virginia Office); Steuart L. Pittman (P.C.); Ramsay D. Potts (P.C.); John B. Rhinelander (P.C.); George M. Rogers, Jr. (P.C.); Leslie Srager (Resident, New York, N.Y. Office). Counsel: Scott E. Barat (Resident, McLean, Virginia Office); Maureen Byrne Beahn (Resident, McLean, Virginia Office); Mindy Buren; Lisa M. Byington; Graeme A. Chambers (Resident, New York, N.Y. Office); Alvin Dunn; Lori Vaughn Ebersohl (Resident, McLean, Virginia Office); John C. Eichenberger; John T. Epting; Nancy A. Fischer; Jennifer A. Giblin; Cynthia D. Greer; James M. Grosser; David S. Houston (Resident, McLean, Virginia Office); Sheryl R. Israel; Marvin R. Lange; Michael G. Lepre; Josephine S. Lo; Charles B. Lobsenz (Resident, McLean, Virginia Office); T. Lane Macalester; Bryan T. McGinnis; John J. Molloy, III (Resident, Los Angeles, California Office); Thomas R. Petty; Thomas J. Plotz; Allison C. Prince; Elizabeth M. Roesel (Resident, McLean, Virginia Office); Jordana G. Schwartz; Dawn M. Sciarrino; Greg Short (Resident, Los Angeles, California Office); John C. Simons (Resident, New York, N.Y. Office); Danielle R. Srour; Michele N. Tanaka; Beth Mezoff Wilson (Resident, Los Angeles, California Office); Carroll John Yung; Maryelena Zaccardelli; Janice Helen Ziegler. Associates: Matthew A. Anzaldi; Thomas E. Arend, Jr.; Steven P. Arnheim (Resident, McLean, Virginia Office); Rainey L. Astin; Gerard M. Babendreier (Not admitted in DC); Eric M. Baim (Not admitted in DC); Susan E. Baldwin (Not admitted in DC); Thomas J. Ball, Jr. (Resident, McLean, Virginia Office); Laurie G. Ballenger; D. Sean Barnett (Not admitted in DC); John L. Barton (Not admitted in DC); Margaret M. Bateman (Resident, New York, N.Y. Office); Bart E. Beals (Not admitted in DC); Beverly A. Boban (Resident, New York, N.Y. Office); James P. Bobotek (Resident, McLean, Virginia Office); Brian R. Bodor; Susan J. Borschel (Resident, McLean, Virginia Office); Lauren W. Bright; Joseph S. Brown (Not admitted in DC); Leslie S. Brown (Resident, McLean, Virginia Office); M. Scott Brown (Resident, McLean, Virginia Office); Stephenie L. Brown (Resident, New York, N.Y. Office); Christian A. Buerger; Ann Marie Burke; Michele M. Burris (Resident, McLean, Virginia Office); Robert W. Busby Jr. (Resident, McLean, Virginia Office); Daisy M. Bygrave (Not admitted in DC); Colette M. Capretz; Christina M. Carlson (Resident, Los Angeles, California Office); Lee C. Carter; Dava Casoni; Gina M. Cavalier (Not admitted in DC); G. A. "Jay" Chadwick, IV; Indra Sehdev Chalk (Not admitted in DC); David J. Charles (Resident, McLean, Virginia Office); Albert S. Cho; Jack Y. Chu (Resident, McLean, Virginia Office); Poh C. Chua (Resident, McLean, Virginia Office); Paul A. Cicelski; Karen L. Cipriani; Kevin E. Colangelo (Resident, New York, N.Y. Office); Damon D. Colbert (Not admitted in DC); Michael K. Colby (Resident, McLean, Virginia Office); Kristen M. Colston; Cheryl R. Covello; Christopher A. Crouch; Kimberly A. Crowder; Brooke Daniels (Not admitted in DC); Brad M. Dashoff (Not admitted in DC); Richard J. Davis (Resident, McLean, Virginia Office); Benjamin Masur Dean; Bianca M. DeGaudenzi (Resident, New York, N.Y. Office); Sean Dennison (Not admitted in DC); Roux De Villiers (Resident, London, England Office); Elizabeth J. Dillon (Resident, McLean, Virginia Office); Brooke Amy Dombek (Not admitted in DC); Mildred Domenech (Not admitted in DC); Jeanne M. Moore Duross; Jesse Eggert (Not admitted in DC); Julie Ehinger (Resident, McLean, Virginia Office); Lawrence D. Eisen (Resident, McLean, Virginia Office); Joseph A. Eisert (Resident, McLean, Virginia Office); Sheila T. Evans; Alejandro Ferrate; Thomas P. FitzGerald (Resident, McLean, Virginia Office); Joshua D. Fitzhugh; Lauren L. Francis; Peter G. Freeman; Norman J. Fry; Rudy Fuentes (Not admitted in DC); Jonathan W. Gannon (Not admitted in DC); Craig H. Garnett (Resident, New York, N.Y. Office); Tammy Gershoni (Not admitted in DC); Jennifer G. Glass; Amy Goldfrank (Not admitted in DC); Christine M. Gollatz; Ronald B. Graber; Edward J. Grass (Resident, McLean, Virginia Office); Eric M. Green (Not admitted in DC); Kevin Green (Resident, London, England Office); Andrew B. Greenfield; Jeffrey B. Grill; Allison S. Groff (Resident, McLean, Virginia Office); Luke Grubb (Resident, London, England Office); Robert Haemer (Not admitted in DC); Susan M. Hafeli; Alexander Hamilton (Resident, London, England Office); Atina S. Harley-Boyce; Elizabeth A. Harris; Michael L. Hentrel; Rita M. Herscovici (Resident, Los Angeles, California Office); Elisabeth M. Hertzberg (Not admitted in DC); Wayne G. Hess (Not admitted in DC; Resident, McLean, Virginia Office); Anthony S. Higgins; Brendan Holland; M. Jennifer Hopeman (Not admitted in DC); William L. Horton, Jr.; Shantelle Denise Hughes; Michelle M. Huhnke (Resident, McLean, Virginia Office); Sol L. Irvine (Resident, New York, N.Y. Office); David C. Isaacson (Resident, McLean, Virginia Office); D. David Jackson (Resident, New York, N.Y. Office); Paul E. Janaskie (Resident, McLean, Virginia Office); Helen Jerry (Resident, London, England Office); Lara Johnson (Not admitted in DC); Sharon Y. Johnson (Not admitted in DC); Julia Eden Judish; Niki A. Kaplan; Charles W. Katz (Resident, McLean, Virginia Office); Elizabeth J. Kelley; Alisa C. Key (Resident, McLean, Virginia Office); David W. Kiefer (Not admitted in DC); Amy B. Kiesel (Not admitted in DC); Jeffrey A. Knight; Peter G. Koback; Mark R. Koehn (Resident, McLean, Virginia Office); Adam M. Kohn (Not admitted in DC); David S. Konczal; Joshua B. Konvisser (Resident, New York, N.Y. Office); Keith R. Kost (Resident, McLean, Virginia Office); Lindsay B. Krause (Resident, McLean, Virginia Office); Cynthia R. Krips (Resident, McLean, Virginia Office); Stuart M. Kuntz; Karin J. Kysilka (Not admitted in DC); Alex Lakatos; Edward W. Lam (Not admitted in DC); Nancy S. Lapidus; David Lashway; Kevin R. Learned; Brian K. Lee (Resident, McLean, Virginia Office); Michael S. Lee (Resident, McLean, Virginia Office); Andrea Lisa Leeb (Resident, Los Angeles, California Office); Katherine Leh (Resident, Los Angeles, California Office); Michael S. Levine (Resident, McLean, Virginia Office); Timothy J. Levy (Resident, McLean, Virginia Office); Tony Lin; Robert Scott Logan (Not admitted in DC); Eric R. LoPresti (Resident, McLean, Virginia Office); Andrew J. Love; Marta T. Lowe; Alison B. Macdonald (Not admitted in DC); John P. Malloy (Resident, McLean, Virginia Office); Michael Andrew Mancusi (Not admitted in DC); Kimberly V. Mann; Nicole E. Marcson (Not admitted in DC); Luis Marini (Not admitted in DC); C. Todd Marks (Resident, McLean, Virginia Office); Michelle S. Marks; Catherine E. Marshall (Not admitted in DC); Mary Martin (Not admitted in DC; Resident, McLean, Virginia Office); Joan E. Masters (Not admitted in DC); Daniel Max (Resident, McLean, Virginia Office); Jennifer P. McClenan; James T. McCormick (Resident, McLean, Virginia Office); Veronica D. McLaughlin; Samantha Miller (Resident, McLean, Virginia Office); Frank J. Mirkow (Not admitted in DC); Lisa-Marie C. Monsanto (Not admitted in DC); H. Carl Moultrie, III (Not admitted in DC); Sanjay Jose Mullick; James E. Myers; Anthony Nagle (Resident, London, England Office); Nadia B. Nejaime; Karen Faye Newman (Not admitted in DC); Stefan C. Nicholas (Not admitted in DC); John Leslie Nicholson (Not admitted in DC); Vipul N. Nishawala (Resident, New York, N.Y. Office); Michael A. Oblon (Resident, McLean, Virginia Office); Barbara J. O'Connell (Resident, McLean, Virginia Office); David B. Oshinsky (Resident, Los Angeles, California Office); Erik Anders Petersen; Jaqualin Friend Peterson; Lilyanna L. Peyser; Gregory James Phillips; V. Elizabeth Powell (Not admitted in DC); Tiffany L. Powers (Resident, McLean, Virginia Office); Alicia A. Prather (Resident, McLean, Virginia Office); Dennis E. Pryba II (Resident, McLean, Virginia Office); Gennet Purcell (Resident, McLean, Virginia Office); Shannon M. Pysher; Matthew C. Rampy; Max M. Reynolds; Tina R. Reynolds; Michael Richards; Douglas J. Rosinski (Not admitted in DC); James M. Ross (Resident, McLean, Virginia Office); Joseph M. Ryan (Resident, McLean, Virginia Office); V. Ann Sandor (Resident, McLean, Virginia Office); Stacy A. Schultz (Resident, Los Angeles, California Office); Wendy B. Schreckinger (Resident, New York, N.Y. Office); Isabelle Scott; Sarah E. Shaw; Patrick J. Shea (Resident, McLean, Virginia Office); Robert Putman Sherley; William A. Shreiner, Jr. (Resident, McLean, Virginia Office); Eric J. Shufflebarger (Not admitted in DC); Rebecca L. Shwayder (Resident, McLean, Virginia Office); Jared R. Silverman (Not admitted in DC); Erica Sapper Simpson (Not admitted in DC); P.L. Skip Singleton, Jr.; David Skinner (Resident, London, England Office); Caroline C. Smith; Rachel E. Smith (Resident, McLean, Virginia Office); Craig A. Sperling (Resident, McLean, Virginia Office); Michael A. Spielman; Matthew L. Steimel (Resident, Los Angeles, California Office); Katherine Tong-Shin Suh; Sean M. Sullivan (Not admitted in DC); Amy D. Tichenor (Resident, Los Angeles, California Office); Melda A. Tisoglu (Resident, N.Y., N.Y. Office); Lisa J. Tomasetti (Resident, McLean, Virginia Office); Richard F. Trimber (Not admitted in DC); Paul A Tummonds, Jr; Joanna S. Valdes (Resident, McLean, Virginia Office); Lee Van Blerkom; Amy Van De Kerckhove; Alexander M.R. Van der Bellen; Erik J. Velapoldi (Resident, McLean, Virginia Office); Colleen Kotyk Vossler (Not admitted in DC); Wanji Walcott; Tom Chia-Kai Wang (Not admitted in DC); Jeffrey I. Wasserman (Resident, New York, N.Y. Office); Meredith R. Weinberg (Not admitted in DC); Jeremiah Wolsk; Tim Wright (Resident, London, England Office); Yuchong C. Yi (Not admitted in DC); Sylvia S. Yu (Not admitted in DC); Restituto E. Yuson, III (Resident, New York, NY Office); John A. Zaloom (Resident, New York, NY Office); Jon T. Zeidler; Jason M. Zuckerman.

(This Listing Continued)

Shaw Pittman LLP (Continued)

General Federal, Corporate, Commercial, Administrative, International Practice, Litigation, Technology Transactions, Real Estate, Securities, Tax, Financial Institutions, Communications (including broadcast, common carrier, cellular telephone, paging, cable, satellite and business radio), Entertainment, Copyright, Intellectual Property and Trademark Law.
McLean, Virginia Office: 1650 Tysons Boulevard. Telephone: 703-770-7900. Telecopier: 703-821-2397.
New York, N.Y. Office: 335 Madison Avenue. Telephone: 212-603-6800. Facsimile: 212-603-6801.
Los Angeles, California Office: 2029 Century Park East. Telephone: 310-551-4500. Facsimile: 310-551-4501.
London, England Office: Regis House, 45 King Street. Telephone: 011-44-171-337-9400. Fax: 011-44-171-337-9401.

See Professional Biographies, WASHINGTON, DISTRICT OF COLUMBIA

Shawe & Rosenthal, LLP
(See Baltimore, Maryland)

Shawn, William H., (AV) '47 '73
C&L.273 B.A., J.D. [Shawncoulson] (⊙Newport Beach, CA)

ShawnCoulson, L.L.P., (AV)
1850 M Street, N.W., Suite 2000 (⊙L.A., Newport Beach, San Diego, San Fran., CA)

Shay, Albert W. . . . . '59 '87 C.446 B.A. L.734 J.D. [Sonnenschein N.&R.]
*PRACTICE AREAS: Health Care; Administrative Law; Hospitals.

Shay, Mary C. . . . . '62 '87 C.893 B.A. L.276 J.D. MCI Communications Corp.

Shay, William Dixon, III . . . . '71 '98 C.105 B.A. L.30 J.D. [Ⓐ Akin,G.S.H.&F.]
*PRACTICE AREAS: Corporate Law.

Shay-Byrne, Olivia, (BV) . . . . . '— '82 C.95 B.A. L.851 J.D. [Reed S.] (⊙Washington)
*PRACTICE AREAS: Real Estate.

Shaye, Marc K., (AV) '42 '69
(adm. in MI; not adm. in DC) [Riley R.&C.]
*PRACTICE AREAS: Environmental Law; Natural Resources; Occupational Safety and Health; Entertainment Law.

Shayne, Adam M. . . . . '65 '91 C.976 B.A. L.477 J.D. Sr. Coun., World Bank, The

Shea, Diane S. '— '89 C.347 B.S. L.345 J.D.
(adm. in IN; not adm. in DC) Assoc. Legis. Dir., Natl. Assn. of Cos.

Shea, James L., (AV) '52 '77 C.674 A.B. L.893 J.D.
[Venable,A.B.H.&C.] (⊙Balt., MD)
*PRACTICE AREAS: Federal Civil Practice; Products Liability; Litigation; Banking and Commercial Litigation; Construction Litigation.

Shea, Kathleen H. . . . . '35 '57 C.942 A.B. L.569 J.D. 1800 M St., N.W.

Shea, Lance L., (AV) '59 '89 C.37 B.S. L.763 J.D.
(adm. in TX; not adm. in DC) [Fulbright&J.]
*PRACTICE AREAS: Toxic Torts; Environmental Law.

Shea, Lauren E., (AV) . . . . '58 '87 C.1248 B.S. L.563 J.D. [Sherman,M.C.&A.]
*PRACTICE AREAS: Family Law.

Shea, Michael J., (AV) . . . . '31 '58 C&L.276 A.B., J.D. [Sutherland A.&B.]
*PRACTICE AREAS: Litigation; Government Contracts; Construction Law.

Shea, Richard C., (AV) . . . . '52 '85 C.31 A.B. L.893 J.D. [Covington&B.]

Shea, Timothy B. . . . . '48 '73 C.321 B.A. L.602 J.D. [Nemirow&H.]

Shea, Timothy J., Jr. '66 '95 C.902 B.S. L.146 J.D.
[Ⓐ Sterne,K.G.&F.] (See Pat. Sect.)
*PRACTICE AREAS: Intellectual Property; Biotechnology; Patent Prosecution; Licensing.

Shea & Gardner, (AV)
1800 Massachusetts Avenue, N.W., 20036
Telephone: 202-828-2000 Fax: 202-828-2195
URL: http://www.sheagardner.com
Members of Firm: Francis M. Shea (1905-1989); Robert T. Basseches; Benjamin W. Boley; Ralph J. Moore, Jr.; Martin J. Flynn; Stephen J. Pollak; David Booth Beers; John D. Aldock; William S. Moore; John Townsend Rich; James R. Bieke; William F. Sheehan; R. James Woolsey; Frederick C. Schafrick; David B. Cook; Franklin D. Kramer; Patrick M. Hanlon; Timothy K. Shuba; Michael S. Giannotto; Jeffrey C. Martin; William R. Hanlon; Elizabeth Runyan Geise; Collette C. Goodman; Laura S. Wertheimer; Richard M. Wyner; Thomas J. Mikula; Eugenia Langan; Nancy B. Stone; Christopher E. Palmer; Mark S. Raffman; Valerie Ellen Ross; Michael K. Isenman; John Moustakas. Senior Counsel: Warner W. Gardner; Lawrence J. Latto. Of Counsel: Richard T. Conway; William H. Dempsey; Anthony A. Lapham; Eric C. Jeffrey. Associates: Heather H. Anderson; Reena N. Glazer; Donald J. Munro; Howard R. Rubin; Timothy G. Lynch; Matthew M. Hoffman; James Chadwick Oppenheimer; Jeffrey M. Klein; Christopher L. Sagers; Jill Ilan Berger Inbar; M. David Dobbins; Lisa M. Harrison; Adam Michael Chud; Michele L. Svonkin; Elena A. Baylis; Ross E. Davies; Richard A. Paschal; Richard L. Matheny.
Admiralty and Maritime Law, Antitrust and Trade Regulation, Aviation and Aerospace, Bankruptcy, Banks and Banking, Business Law, Civil Rights, Class Actions, Communications and Media, Constitutional Law, Corporate Law, Employee Benefits, Environment Law, Finance, General Practice, Government Contracts, Insurance Regulation, Intellectual Property, International Trade, Investments, Labor and Employment, Legal Ethics and Professional Responsibility, Natural Resources, Nonprofit and Charitable Organizations, Occupational Safety and Health, Products Liability, Professional Liability, Railroad Law, Regulatory Law, Securities, Taxation, Toxic Torts, Transportation, Trusts and Estates, Utility Law and White Collar Crime.

See Professional Biographies, WASHINGTON, DISTRICT OF COLUMBIA

Sheaks, Chantel . . . . '71 '96 C.683 B.A. L.588 J.D. [Ⓐ Venable,A.B.H.&C.]
*PRACTICE AREAS: Employee Benefits.

Shean, Owen J., (AV) . . . . . '56 '82 C&L.893 B.A., J.D. [Wickwire G.] (⊙Vienna, VA)
*PRACTICE AREAS: Commercial and Construction Litigation.

Shearman & Sterling, (AV) 🅱🅱
801 Pennsylvania Avenue, N.W., Suite 900, 20004-2604 ⊙
Telephone: (202) 508-8000 Fax: (202) 508-8100
URL: http://www.shearman.com
Resident Partners: Thomas S. Martin (Managing Partner); Abigail Arms; Laurence M. Bambino (Not admitted in DC); Roger J. Baneman (Not admitted in DC); Barry P. Barbash; Robert A. Bergquist; Jonathan L. Greenblatt; Stephen James Marzen; R. Charles Miller; Linda C. Quinn; Robert A. Rudnick; Michael Bradley Shulman; Frank R. Strong; Steven C. Sunshine; B. John Williams, Jr.; Thomas B. Wilner; Jeffrey M. Winton. Of Counsel: Edward Bransilver. Counsel: Wendy E. Ackerman; Karen Hess McMillan; Emanuel D. Strauss; Anthony A. Vertuno; James F. Warren. Resident Associates: B. Kurt Baca (Not admitted in DC); Perry S. Bechky; Dominique C. Fuentes; Richard J. Gagnon, Jr.; Craig J. Gibian (Not admitted in DC); Caryn Glasser (Not admitted in DC); Merrill C. Godfrey; Michael E. Hatchett (Not admitted in DC); Jane G. Heinrichs; Carol Ann Johnson; Yoram Keinan (Not admitted in DC); Theresa K. Kelety; Heather Lamberg Kafele (Not admitted in DC); Karen Y. Lau (Not admitted in DC); Meredith Kolsky Lewis; Gregory P. Lubkin; Erik W. Luckau (Not admitted in DC); Anne MacGregor; Linda M. McMahon; Sanjeev Magoon (Not admitted in DC); David P. Mathews (Not admitted in DC); Vincent W. Mathis; Kim M. Mazur (Not admitted in DC); Ajay Mehra (Not admitted in DC); James J. O'Connell, Jr.; Miriam J. Radich (Not admitted in DC); Idan A. Ravin; Roland G. Schroeder; John R. Seward; Steven M. Simpson; Suzanne Miller Trinh (Not admitted in DC); Gabriela Maria Vallejo (Not admitted in DC); Charles V. Webb; Sam J. Yoon (Not admitted in DC).
General Practice.
New York, N.Y. Office: 599 Lexington Avenue, New York, New York, 10022-6069. Telephone: (212) 848-4000. Telex: 667290. Num Lau. Fax: (212) 848-7179.
Abu Dhabi, United Arab Emirates Office: Butti Al Otaiba Building, 13th Floor, Suite 1301-1302, Sheikh Khalifa Street, P.O. Box 2948. Telephone: (971-2) 6274477. Fax: (971-2) 6268933.
Beijing, People's Republic of China Office: Suite 2318, China World Tower II, 1 Jianguomenwai Dajie, Chaoyang District, 100004 Beijing. Telephone: (86-10) 6505-3399. Fax: (86-10) 6505-1818.
Brussels, Belgium Office: Avenue des Artes 53, 1000 Bruxelles. Telephone: (32 02) 500-9800. Fax: (32 02) 500-9801.
Düsseldorf, Federal Republic of Germany Office: Breite Strasse 69, 40213 Düsseldorf. Telephone: (49 211) 178 88-0. Fax: (49 211) 178 88-88.
Frankfurt, Federal Republic of Germany Office: Gervinusstrasse 17, 60322 Frankfurt am Main. Telephone: ++49 69 9711 1000. Fax: ++49 69 9711 1100.

(This Listing Continued)

Shearman & Sterling (Continued)

Hong Kong Office: 12/F Gloucester Tower, The Landmark, 11 Pedder Street, Central. Telephone: (852) 2978-8000. Fax: (852) 2978-8099.
London, England Office: Broadgate West, 9 Appold Street, London EC2A 2AP. Telephone: 44-20-7655-5000. Fax: 44-20-7655-5500.
Mannheim, Federal Republic of Germany Office: Otto-Beck-Strasse 42, 68165 Mannheim. Telephone: 49 621-4257-0. Fax: 49 621-4257-280.
Menlo Park, California Office: 1080 Marsh Road, 94025-1022. Telephone: (650) 838-3600. Fax: (650) 838-3699.
Munich, Federal Republic of Germany Office: Oberanger 28, 80331 München. Telephone: (49 089) 23888-200. Fax: (49 089) 23888-201.
Paris, France Office: 114, avenue des Champs-Elysées, 75008. Telephone: (33-1) 53-89-7000. Fax: (33-1) 53-89-7070.
San Francisco, California Office: 555 California Street, 94104-1522. Telephone: (415) 616-1100. Fax: (415) 616-1199.
Singapore Office: Shearman & Sterling Stamford, 6 Battery Road #19-02. Singapore 049909. Telephone: (65) 230-3800. Fax: (65) 230-3899.
Tokyo, Japan Office: Fukoku Seimei Building, 5th Floor 2-2-2, Uchisaiwaicho, Chiyoda-ku, Tokyo 100-0011. Japan. Telephone: (81 3) 5251-1601. Fax: (81 3) 5251-1602.
Toronto, Ontario, Canada Office: Commerce Court West, Suite 4405, P.O. Box 247, M5L 1E8. Telephone: (416) 360-8484. Fax: (416) 360-2958.

See Professional Biographies, WASHINGTON, DISTRICT OF COLUMBIA

Sheehan, Bernard F., Jr. . . . . '66 '00 C.188 B.A. L.276 J.D. [Ⓐ Dickstein S.M.&O.]
*PRACTICE AREAS: Litigation.

Sheehan, Catherine F. . . . . '67 '96 C.914 B.A. L.93 J.D. Asst. U.S. Atty.

Sheehan, Karen O. . . . . '66 '95 C.105 B.A. L.273 J.D. [Ⓐ Lee&M.]
*PRACTICE AREAS: Business Transactions; Construction Litigation; Commercial Litigation.

Sheehan, Kenneth J. '65 '92
C.1350 B.S.E.E. L.724 J.D. 1050 Connecticut Ave., N.W. (Pat.)

Sheehan, Margaret A. . . . . '59 '88 C.228 A.B. L.276 J.D. [Alston&B.]
*PRACTICE AREAS: Investment Management (30%); Broker-Dealer Regulation (30%); Investment Company Law (20%); Electronic Commerce (18%); Insurance Products (2%).

Sheehan, Nora L. . . . . '65 '93 C.890 B.A. L.128 J.D. [Ⓐ Seward&K.]
*PRACTICE AREAS: Mutual Funds; Investment Regulation; Securities Regulation.

Sheehan, Sue Bak . . . . '63 '89 C.999 B.A. L.276 J.D. [Ⓐ Skadden,A.S.M.&F.]

Sheehan, William F., (AV) . . . . '47 '73 C.976 B.A. L.659 J.D. [Shea&G.]
*PRACTICE AREAS: Complex Business Litigation; Mass Torts; Appellate Practice.

Sheehy, Donald J. '31 '69 C.676 B.A. L.128 J.D.
Chief Admin. Law J., Dept. of Cons. & Reg. Affrs.

Sheehy, Fairlea . . . . '50 '78 C.914 A.B. L.309 J.D. [Ⓐ Covington&B.]
*PRACTICE AREAS: Corporate Taxation; E-Commerce; Technology Law.

Sheehy, Terrence C., (AV) . . . . . . '37 '63 C.686 B.S. L.276 LL.B. [Ⓖ Howrey S.A.&W.]
*PRACTICE AREAS: Antitrust; Litigation.

Sheeline, Paul C. . . . . '21 '49 C&L.309 B.S., J.D. 901 15th St., N.W.

Sheers, Nathan C. . . . . '65 '92 C.923 B.A. L.178 J.D. [Ⓐ Sidley A.B.&W.]

Sheesley, James P., II '73 '99 C.425 B.A. L.188 J.D.
(adm. in NY; not adm. in DC) [Ⓐ Hale&D.]
*PRACTICE AREAS: Real Estate; Corporate; Banking Law; Finance.

Sheffield, Allie Johnson . . . . '50 '70 C.575 A.B. L.1162 J.D. [Ⓖ Garfinkle&Assoc.]

Sheffield, Malvern J., Jr., (AV) . . . . '30 '54 C&L.893 B.S., LL.B. 1050 Conn. Ave., N.W.‡

Sheikerz, Mehdi D. '65 '96 C.886 B.S. L.1218 J.D.
(adm. in FL; not adm. in DC; See Pat. Sect.) [Ⓐ Staas&H.]
*PRACTICE AREAS: Intellectual Property; Patents; Licensing; Trademarks; Copyrights.

Sheinbach, Donna M. '72 '01 C.473 B.A. L.127 J.D.
(adm. in PA; not adm. in DC) [Ⓐ Reed S.]

Shelburne, Patrice A. . . . . '65 '99 C.914 B.A. L.276 J.D. [Ⓐ Zuckerman S.]
*PRACTICE AREAS: Litigation.

Shelburne, Patricia A. '65 '98 C.914 B.A. L.276 J.D.
1201 Connecticut Ave. N.W. # 600

Sheldon, Elizabeth Torrant . . . . '66 '96 C.170 B.A. L.966 J.D. [Ⓐ Baach R.&L.P.]
*PRACTICE AREAS: Civil Litigation; Commercial Litigation.

Sheldon, Karin P. . . . . '44 '71 C.881 A.B. L.911 J.D. Pres., The Wilderness Soc.

Sheldon, Stuart A., (AV) . . . . '48 '74 C.367 B.A. L.659 J.D. [Dow,L.&A.]

Shellaway, Justin M. '75 '00 C.659 B.A. L.976 J.D.
(adm. in TX; not adm. in DC) [Ⓐ Vinson&E.] (⊙Hous., TX)
*PRACTICE AREAS: Litigation.

Shelley, Anthony F. . . . . '— '88 C.116 B.A. L.309 J.D. [Miller&C.]
*PRACTICE AREAS: Federal Litigation; Employee Benefits and ERISA; Health Care.

Shelley, Herbert C., (AV) . . . . '47 '73 C.178 B.A. L.880 J.D. [Steptoe&J.]
*PRACTICE AREAS: International Trade Law; Import and Export Law.

Shelton, April Everette . . . . '71 '97 C&L.575 B.A., J.D. [Ⓐ Dickstein S.M.&O.]
*PRACTICE AREAS: Corporate; Mergers and Acquisitions; Securities.

Shelton, Deborah M. . . . . '60 '98 C&L.446 B.S., J.D. [Ⓐ Arent F.K.P.&K.]
*PRACTICE AREAS: Food and Drug Law; Intellectual Property; Electronic Commerce; Trademarks.

Shelton, Jerome H. . . . . '43 '77 C.512 B.S. L.273 J.D. 1730 "K" ST., NW

Shelton, Julia B. . . . . '68 '97 C.999 B.A. L.880 J.D. [Ⓐ Williams&C.]

Shelton, Mark S. . . . . '67 '92 C.378 B.A. L.893 J.D. [Wilmer,C.&P.]
*PRACTICE AREAS: Securities Law; Broker-Dealer Regulation.

Shelton, Morgan Wayne '— '99 C.888 B.S. L.469 J.D.
(adm. in GA; not adm. in DC) [Ⓐ Foley&L.]
*PRACTICE AREAS: Electronic Business; Information Technology.

Shen, Michael M. '73 '98 C.477 B.S.Ch.E. L.276 J.D.
(adm. in NY; not adm. in DC; See Pat. Sect.) [Ⓐ Kenyon&K.]
*PRACTICE AREAS: Intellectual Property.

Shenefield, John H., (AV) . . . . '39 '66 C&L.309 A.B., LL.B. [Morgan,L.&B.]

Sheng, Janie C.I. . . . . '70 '99 C.446 B.A. L.276 J.D. [Ⓐ Jones,D.R.&P.]

Shenk, Christopher T. . . . . '70 '99 C.367 B.A. L.575 J.D. [Ⓐ Sidley A.B.&W.]

Shepard, Fern L. . . . . '60 '85 C&L.112 B.A., J.D. Sierra Club Legal Def. Fund

Shepard, Ira M., (AV) . . . . '47 '72 C&L.188 B.S., J.D. [Schmeltzer,A.&S.]
*PRACTICE AREAS: Management Labor Law; Employment Law; Employee Benefits Law.

Shepard, Julian L., (AV) . . . . '— '84 C.347 B.S. L.1119 J.D. [Venable,A.B.H.&C.]
*PRACTICE AREAS: Telecommunications Law; Communications; Mergers and Acquisitions; Information Technology; Internet Law.

Shepard, Kristin . . . . '75 '00 C&L.910 B.A., J.D. [Ⓐ Jorden B.]
*PRACTICE AREAS: Litigation; Insurance.

Shepard, Scott A. . . . . '73 '00 C.692 B.A. L.893 J.D. [Ⓐ Wilmer,C.&P.]

Shepherd, James A. '61 '95 C.928 B.A. L.347 J.D.
(adm. in VA; not adm. in DC) [Ⓐ Wilmer,C.&P.]

Shepler, Donald C. . . . . '48 '73 C&L.208 B.A., J.D. 2000 M St. N.W.

Sheppard, Cara E. . . . . '71 '98 C.1372 B.A. L.128 J.D. [Ⓐ Fleischman&W.]

Sheppard, Edward J., IV, (AV) . . . . '41 '69 C.674 A.B. L.893 LL.B. [Thompson C.]
*PRACTICE AREAS: Maritime Law; Transportation Law; International.

Sheppard, Hale E. '70 '99 C&L.378 B.S., JD.
(adm. in FL; not adm. in DC) [Ⓐ Haynes&B.]
*PRACTICE AREAS: International Law; Trade Regulation; Customs Law.

Sheppard, Michael B. . . . . '39 '65 C.269 B.A. L.309 LL.B. [Ⓖ Simon,T.&M.]
*PRACTICE AREAS: Corporate Law; Government Contracts.

Sher, Lawrence S. . . . . '64 '90 C.454 B.A. L.30 J.D. [Dyer E.&J.]
*PRACTICE AREAS: Corporate Law; Securities; Litigation.

Sher, Paul D. '50 '78
(adm. in TN; not adm. in DC) [Ⓖ Klayman&Assoc.] (⊙London, England)

Sher, Stanley O., (AV) ....'35 '59 C.966 B.S. L.309 LL.B. [Sher&B.]
*PRACTICE AREAS: Transportation; Litigation; Antitrust; Maritime Law.
Sher, Tara A. .... '66 '92 C.276 B.A. L.893 J.D. 1250 I St Nw # 1000

Sher & Blackwell LLP, (AV)
1850 M Street, N.W., Suite 900, 20036-5820
Telephone: 202-463-2500 Facsimile: 202-463-4950
URL: http://www.sherblackwell.com
Mark W. Atwood; Robert J. Blackwell; John W. Butler; Earl W. Comstock (Not admitted in DC); Marc J. Fink; Jeffrey F. Lawrence; Anne E. Mickey; Stanley O. Sher; David F. Smith; Paul M. Tschirhart;—Wayne R. Rohde; Heather Spring; Antilla E. Trotter, III; Sarah M. Sharma (Not admitted in DC).
Administrative, Antitrust, Commercial, Corporate, Environmental, Government Contracts, Government Relations, International, Legislative, Litigation, Marine Resources, Maritime, Telecommunications, Transportation.
See Professional Biographies, WASHINGTON, DISTRICT OF COLUMBIA

Sheridan, Edwin A., (AV) '35 '64
C.923 B.S.B.A. L.30 J.D. [Doherty,S.&P.] (⊙Fairfax, VA)
*PRACTICE AREAS: Civil Practice; Personal Injury Litigation.
Sherley, Robert Putman ....'66 '92 C.446 B.A. L.188 J.D. [[A] Shaw P.]
Sherman, Andrew J. ....'61 '87 C.446 B.A. L.30 J.D. [McDermott,W.&E.]
Sherman, Cary Howard, (AV) ....'48 '71 C.188 A.B. L.309 J.D. RIAA
Sherman, Charles W., Jr. ....'45 '83 C.259 B.A. L.1066 J.D. [Groom]
*PRACTICE AREAS: Employee Benefits; Pension and Profit Sharing; Tax Law; ERISA.
Sherman, Elizabeth Jorgenson '61 '89 C.293 B.A. L.93 J.D.
(adm. in MA; not adm. in DC) Georgtown University Law Center
Sherman, Gerald H., (AV) .... '32 '59 C.563 B.B.A. L.309 LL.B. [Silverstein&M.]
*PRACTICE AREAS: Taxation.
Sherman, Ira, (AV) .... '45 '74 C.1044 B.S. L.107 J.D. [Chaikin&S.] ⊙
*PRACTICE AREAS: Wrongful Death; Medical Malpractice; Auto Negligence; Products Liability; Serious Personal Injury.
Sherman, Jeffrey M., (AV) .... '58 '81 C.563 B.A. L.273 J.D. [O'Rourke&C.]
Sherman, Jonathan .... '63 '92 C.696 B.A. L.813 J.D. [[A] Boies,S.&F.]
Sherman, Laura B. .... '51 '86 C.188 B.A. L.276 J.D. [[C] Paul,W.R.W.&G.]
*PRACTICE AREAS: Communications Law; International Trade Law; Corporate Law.
Sherman, Lawrence J., (AV) ....'42 '67 C.665 B.A. L.477 J.D. 1400 K St., NW
Sherman, Michael D., (BV) ....'50 '75 C.976 A.B. L.893 J.D. [Collier S.S.]
Sherman, Michael Lauren '74 '01 C.30 B.A. L.880 J.D.
(adm. in MD; not adm. in DC) [[A] Dechert]
*PRACTICE AREAS: Investment Management; Financial Services Law.
Sherman, Peter R., (AV) ....'39 '65 C.347 B.S. L.276 LL.B. [Sherman,M.C.&A.]
*PRACTICE AREAS: Family Law.
Sherman, Roger C. ....'66 '95 C.31 B.A. L.309 J.D. Sr. Atty., Sprint Spectrum L.P.
Sherman, Stephen A. '53 '79 C.161 B.B.A. L.930 J.D.
(adm. in OH; not adm. in DC) 2939 Van Ness St., N.W.‡
Sherman, Stephen H. ....'61 '86 C.223 B.S. L.1017 J.D. [Patton B.]

Sherman, Dunn, Cohen, Leifer & Yellig, P.C., (AV)
Suite 801, 1125 Fifteenth Street, N.W., 20005
Telephone: 202-785-9300 Fax: 202-775-1950
Email: shermandunn@shermandunn.com
Louis Sherman (1912-1996); Thomas X. Dunn (1911-1991); Laurence J. Cohen; Elihu I. Leifer; Terry R. Yellig; Richard M. Resnick; Robert D. Kurnick; Victoria L. Bor; Nora H. Leyland; Martin J. Crane; Sue D. Gunter; Jonathan D. Newman.
Labor and Employment Law, Occupational Safety and Health Law, Pensions and Trusts.
See Professional Biographies, WASHINGTON, DISTRICT OF COLUMBIA

Sherman, Meehan, Curtin & Ain, A Professional Corporation, (AV)
Suite 600, 1900 M Street, NW, 20036-3565
Telephone: 202-530-3300 Facsimile: 202-530-4411
Email: info@smcalaw.com URL: http://www.smcalaw.com
Peter R. Sherman; Michael F. Curtin; Sanford K. Ain; Thomas E. Dunigan; David Bradford Law; Randell C. Ogg; Faith D. Dornbrand; Mark S. Carlin; Claudia Anne Pott; Sam H. Roberson; Douglas E. Fierberg; Laurence E. Salans; Lauren E. Shea; Matthew P. Maloney. Of Counsel: Thomas P. Meehan; Jeanmarie LoCoco Nicholson;—Nancy L. Walsh; Anne Marie Jackson; James W. Koch; Darryl Alan Feldman; Tracy Anette Meyer; Jason A. Dzubow.
See Professional Biographies, WASHINGTON, DISTRICT OF COLUMBIA

Sherrod-Ali, Gilda, (BV) ....'50 '83 C.107 B.S. L.1292 J.D. 234 Warren St., N.E.
Sherwood, David D. '71 '99 C.176 B.A. L.309 J.D.
(adm. in CA; not adm. in DC) [[A] Ivins,P.&B.]
*PRACTICE AREAS: Taxation.
Sherzer, Harvey G., (AV) ....'44 '70 C.831 B.A. L.273 J.D. [Howrey S.A.&W.]
*PRACTICE AREAS: Government Contracts Law.
Shewman, Christi ....'69 '00 C.133 B.A. L.1209 J.D. [[A] Willkie F.&G.]
Sheybani, Kathryn M. '51 '84 C.429 B.A. L.184 J.D.
(adm. in CT; not adm. in DC) 2008 1/2 R St. N.W.
Sheys, Kevin Michael, (AV) .... '— '87 C.297 B.A. L.494 J.D. [Kirkpatrick&L.]
*PRACTICE AREAS: Transportation.
Shibao, Stacy S. .... '— '95 C&L.276 B.A., J.D. [[A] King&S.]
*PRACTICE AREAS: Corporate.
Shichman, Robin Remis ....'— '96 C.867 B.A. L.128 J.D. [[A] Verner,L.B.M.&H.]
*PRACTICE AREAS: Energy Law.
Shields, Carrington, (AV) ...'— '51 C.683 A.B. L.904 LL.B. 3732 Chesapeake St., N.W.‡
Shields, Peter D., (AV) .... '62 '88 C.1044 B.A. L.823 J.D. [Wiley R.&F.]
*PRACTICE AREAS: Communications.
Shields, Robyn ....'53 '98 C.569 B.A. L.982 J.D. [[A] Clifford C.R.&W.]
*PRACTICE AREAS: International Banking Law; Corporate.
Shields, William B., (AV) ....'49 '74 C.433 B.A. L.569 J.D. [[C] Janis,S.&W.]
*PRACTICE AREAS: Criminal Defense; Civil Litigation.
Shiffman, Paul, (AV) .... '37 '62 C.893 L.904 LL.B. [Shiffman&R.]
Shiffman & Ricci, P.C., (AV) ....1700 Pennsylvania Ave., N.W. Suite 560
Shiker, Brian L. .... '73 '98 C.145 B.A. L.880 J.D. [[A] Hogan&H.]
*PRACTICE AREAS: Employee Benefits; ERISA.
Shiker, Christine Moseley '72 '97 C&L.945 B.A., J.D.
(adm. in TX; not adm. in DC) [[A] Holland&K.]
*PRACTICE AREAS: Zoning; Land Use.
Shimamoto, Sean M. ....'67 '97 C.112 B.A. L.629 J.D. [[A] Skadden,A.S.M.&F.]
*PRACTICE AREAS: Taxation.
Shimazaki, J. John ..... '59 '88 C.1074 B.S. L.101 J.D. [[C] Dickinson W.] (See Pat. Sect.)
*PRACTICE AREAS: Patent Law; Trademark Law; Licensing.
Shimkin, Thomas K.E. ....'63 '93 C.860 B.A. L.276 J.D. [Fontaine,S.K.&D.]
Shine, Edith S. '62 '93 C.66 B.A. L.1059 J.D.
(adm. in GA; not adm. in DC) Asst. Gen. Coun., National Trust for Historic Preservation
Shingleton, A. Bradley '53 '82
C.216 B.A. L.228 J.D. Legal Coun., Deutsche Telekom, Inc.
Shinjyu Global IP Counselors, LLP .... 1233 20th St., N.W. (Pat.)
Shipley, Howard N. ....'— '96 C.886 B.S. L.1209 J.D. [[A] Foley&L.] (See Pat. Sect.)
*PRACTICE AREAS: Intellectual Property.
Shipman, Richard E. '29 '55 C&L.602 B.S., J.D.
(adm. in IL; not adm. in DC) 12 5th St., N.E.‡
Shipp, Wallace E., Jr. .... '47 '73 C.630 B.A. L.904 J.D. Dep. Bar Coun.

Shirk, W. Bruce, (AV) .... '40 '69 C&L.309 B.A., J.D. [Powell,G.F.&M.]
*PRACTICE AREAS: Health Care; Government Contract; Construction Contracts; Administrative Law.
Shirley, Barbara Ann .... '— '96 C.886 B.S. L.273 J.D. [[A] Morgan,L.&B.]
Shniderman, Harry L., (AV) '16 '41
C.477 B.A. L.309 LL.B. 1201 Pennsylvania Ave., N.W.
Shoaff, John Paul .... '69 '00 C.602 B.B.A. L.446 J.D. 1200 Pennsylvania Ave.
Shoback, Pauline C. .... '55 '84 C.788 B.A. L.893 J.D. [[C] Leonard H.F.L.&L.]
*PRACTICE AREAS: Corporate Law; Securities.
Shockey, John E. ....'42 '67 C&L.326 B.B.A., J.D. [Milbank,T.H.&M.]
Shoneman, Charles H., (AV) .... '47 '73 C.228 B.A. L.273 J.D. [Bracewell&P.]
*PRACTICE AREAS: Electric Power; Energy Regulation; Oil and Gas Pipelines; Regulated Industries; Public Utility Regulation.
Shonkwiler, Tatjana M. .... '64 '89 C.025 B.A. L.309 J.D. [Duncan,W.G.&P.]
*PRACTICE AREAS: Public Utility Law; Communications Law; Environmental Law.
Shook, Langley R., (AV) ....'47 '74 C&L.477 A.B., J.D. 1501 K Street N.W.
Shook, William A. .... '52 '86 C.101 B.A. L.273 J.D. [Preston G.E.&R.M.]
*PRACTICE AREAS: Governmental Contract Law; Procurement Policy.

Shook, Hardy & Bacon L.L.P., (AV)
Hamilton Square, 600 14th Street, N.W., Suite 800, 20005-2004 ⊙
Telephone: 202-783-8400 Facsimile: 202-783-4211
URL: http://www.shb.com
Partners: Mark A. Behrens; Keith T. Borman; Barkley Clark; William F. Demarest, Jr.; Barry P. Golob; Peter W. Gowdey; Thomas A. Hart, Jr.; Bruce O. Jolly, Jr.; Rodney L. Joyce; Jeremiah D. Lambert; Edwin N. Lavergne; Mark N. Lipp; Michelle R. Mangrum; Richard M. Mollison; Jay S. Newman; Joseph D. Piorkowski, Jr.; Henry M. Rivera; Paul S. Schleifman; Victor E. Schwartz; Jacolyn A. Simmons; Larry S. Solomon; D. Edward Wilson, Jr.; Robert J. Woody. Of Counsel: Peter S. Glaser; Robert M. Gurss; Leah Lorber; Christopher P. Murphy; Gary M. Nateman; Ramsey L. Woodworth. Associates: Phillip R. Anderson; Peter D. Bernstein; Curtis D. Blanc; Tamara Y. Brown; Janine A. Carlan; Edgar Class III; John P. Foley; John K. Hsu (Not admitted in DC); John C. Monica, Jr.; Elisabeth R. Myers-Kerbal; J. Thomas Nolan; Brian J. Peretti; Sean M. Reilly (Not admitted in DC); Cary Silverman (Not admitted in DC); Rochelle M. Tedesco (Not admitted in DC). Staff Attorney: John C. Coots.
Acquisitions, Administration, Agriculture, Antitrust, Banking and Commercial Law, Bankruptcy and Creditor's Rights, Broadcasting, Communications, Compensation Planning, Construction Law, Copyright, Corporate, Employment Rights, Energy, Environmental, ERISA, Estate Planning, Federal Communications Commission Issues, Federal Trade Commission Issues, Financial Institution Regulation, Franchise and Professional Corporation Law, General Civil, Trial and Appellate Practice, Health Law, Intellectual Property, International, Labor and Employment, Libel, Mergers and Acquisitions, Municipal, Negligence, Patent, Probate, Products Liability, Real Estate, Restructuring and Reorganization, Securities, Syndications, Taxation, Technology Law, Trade Secret Law, Trademark, Unfair Competition and Workers Compensation Litigation.
Kansas City, Missouri Office: One Kansas City Place, 1200 Main Street, 64105-2118. Telephone: 816-474-6550. Facsimile: 816-421-5547.
Overland Park, Kansas Office: 84 Corporate Woods, 10801 Mastin, Suite 1000, 66210-1671. Telephone: 913-451-6060. Facsimile: 913-451-8879.
Houston, Texas Office: Chase Tower, 600 Travis Street, Suite 1600, 77002-2911. Telephone: 713-227-8008. Facsimile: 713-227-9508.
Miami, Florida Office: Miami Center, Suite 2400, 201 South Biscayne Boulevard, 33131-4332. Telephone: 305-358-5171. Facsimile: 305-358-7470.
Tampa, Florida Office: 100 North Tampa Street, Suite 2900, 33602-5810. Telephone: 813-202-7100. Facsimile: 813-221-8837.
San Francisco, California Office: 333 Bush Street, 94104-2828. Telephone: 415-544-1900. Facsimile: 415-391-0281.
London, England Office: 25 Cannon Street, EC4M 5SE. Telephone: 011-44-02-07-332 4500. Facsimile: 011-44-02-07-332 4501.
Geneva, Switzerland Office: 118, rue du Rhône, 1204. Telephone: 011-41-22-787-2000. Facsimile: 011-41-22-786-5008.
See Professional Biographies, WASHINGTON, DISTRICT OF COLUMBIA

Shopfner, David R. '59 '87 C.16 B.S. L.861 J.D.
(adm. in LA; not adm. in DC) Associate Litigation Counsel, MCI WorldCom
Shor, Michael L. ....'50 '87 C.575 B.A. L.564 J.D. [[C] Swidler B.S.F.]
*PRACTICE AREAS: Telecommunications; Litigation; Debtor-Creditor.
Shor, Michael T. .... '58 '83 C.197 A.B. L.309 J.D. [Arnold&P.]
*PRACTICE AREAS: International Trade.
Shore, Linda K. .... '59 '84 C.94 B.A. L.477 J.D. [Silverstein&M.]
*PRACTICE AREAS: Employee Benefits Law; Securities.
Shore, Richard D. .... '61 '88 C.446 B.A. L.178 J.D. [Gilbert H.&R.]
*PRACTICE AREAS: Insurance Coverage; Alternative Dispute Resolution; Election Law; International Trade.
Shore, Stacy '71 '99 C.1036 B.A. L.831 J.D.
(adm. in PA; not adm. in DC) [[A] Fragomen,D.B.&L.]
Shoreman, John M. ....'58 '86 C.454 L.823 J.D. [McFadden&S.]
Shores, Laura S., (AV) ....'64 '88 C.788 A.B. L.145 J.D. [Howrey S.A.&W.]
*PRACTICE AREAS: White Collar Criminal Defense; Litigation.
Shorey, Clyde E., Jr., (AV) '22 '50 C.976 A.B. L.178 LL.B.
3033 W. Lane Keys, N.W.‡
Shors, Matthew M. '71 '00 C.477 B.A. L.813 J.D.
(adm. in MN; not adm. in DC) [[A] O'Melveny&M.]
Short, Larri A. .... '47 '92 C.477 B.S. L.575 J.D. [Arent F.K.P.&K.]
*PRACTICE AREAS: Medicare and Medicaid; Health Care; Pharmacy Law; Fraud and Compliance.
Short, Laurence A., (AV) ....'29 '58 C.734 B.S. L.276 LL.B. 1330 Conn. Ave., N.W.
Shorter, John A. ....'27 '54 C.329 A.B. L.276 J.D. 1440 New York Ave., N.W.
Shortill, Kevin ....'63 '89 C.910 A.B. L.477 J.D. [[C] Covington&B.]
Shostak, S. Richard, (AV) ....'31 '56 C.112 A.B. L.1066 J.D. [Stein S.S.&O.] ⊙
*PRACTICE AREAS: Customs Law; International Trade Law.
Showen, James E. .... '53 '79 C.228 A.B. L.923 J.D. [Hogan&H.]
*PRACTICE AREAS: Partnership Law; Securities Law; Corporate Law.
Shoyer, Andrew W., (AV) .... '60 '86 C.659 B.A. L.276 J.D. [Powell,G.F.&M.]
*PRACTICE AREAS: International Trade and Investment Law; International Dispute Settlement.
Shrinsky, Jason L., (AV) ....'37 '63 C.665 B.A. L.273 J.D. [Kaye S.]
*PRACTICE AREAS: Sports Law; Mergers and Acquisitions; Telecommunications Law; Communications Law.
Shriver, Robert H., III '71 '97 C.886 B.A. L.273 J.D.
Asst. Coun., National Treasury Employees Union
Shriver, Sargent .... '15 '41 C&L.976 B.A., LL.B. [[C] Fried,F.H.S.&J.]
Shroff, Anoop G. ....'69 '95 C.188 A.B. L.659 J.D. [[A] Piper M.R.&W.]
*PRACTICE AREAS: Corporate; Securities; Mergers and Acquisitions; Venture Capital.
Shtasel, Sana F. '51 '76 C.188 B.A. L.569 J.D.
Dir., Policy & Legislation, Ctr. for Reproductive Law & Policy‡
Shuba, Timothy K. ....'49 '77 C.198 A.B. L.659 J.D. [Shea&G.]
*PRACTICE AREAS: Energy Law; Commercial Law.
Shubert, Lee Warner, (AV) ....'45 '73 C.473 A.B. L.1340 J.D. [[C] Rosenman&C.]
*PRACTICE AREAS: Administrative Law; Business Law; Communications Law; Covenants Not To Compete; Entertainment Law.
Shue, Robert B. '56 '84 C.321 B.A. L.1209 J.D.
(adm. in VA; not adm. in DC) Princ., Spaulding & Slye
Shufflebarger, Carrie A. '74 '99 C.853 B.A. L.228 J.D.
(adm. in VA; not adm. in DC) [[A] McDermott,W.&E.]
Shufflebarger, Eric J. '75 '00 C.853 B.A. L.575 J.D.
(adm. in VA; not adm. in DC) [[A] Shaw P.]
*PRACTICE AREAS: Corporate Law; Securities.
Shugarman, Keith D., (AV) .... '64 '88 C.787 B.A. L.188 J.D. [Goodwin P.]
*PRACTICE AREAS: Antitrust; Trade Regulation.

Shukis, Anne K. '73 '00 C.890 B.A. L.1209 J.D.
(adm. in VA; not adm. in DC) [Ⓐ Squire,S.&D.]
Shull, Joe A., (AV) . . . . '45 '69 C&L.846 B.B.A., J.D. [Venable,A.B.H.&C.]
*PRACTICE AREAS: Corporate; Securities; Commercial; Creditors' Rights; Partnership Law.
Shulman, Beth '49 '74 C.112 B.A. L.276 J.D.
Intl. V.P., United Food & Comercial Workers International Union
Shulman, Bruce N., (AV) . . . . '48 '75 C.273 B.A. L.904 J.D. [Stein S.S.&O.]
*PRACTICE AREAS: Customs Law; International Trade Law; Export Licensing.
Shulman, Daniel Jay '73 '99 C.30 B.A. L.910 J.D.
(adm. in MD; not adm. in DC) 3701 Connecticut Ave. N.W.
Shulman, David L. '67 '95 C&L.494 B.A., J.D.
(adm. in MN; not adm. in DC) [Ⓐ Sprenger&L.] ⊙
*PRACTICE AREAS: Civil Rights; Commercial Litigation; Antitrust; Class Actions; Employment Law.
Shulman, Jerry L., (AV) . . . . '46 '72 C.976 B.A. L.309 J.D. [Williams&C.]
Shulman, Lawrence A., (AV) '42 '67 C&L.276 A.B., J.D.
[Shulman,R.G.P.&E.] (⊙Greenbelt, Rockville, MD)
Shulman, Martin, (AV) '45 '70 C.178 A.B. L.309 J.D.
Assoc. Gen. Coun., Washington Met. Area Transit Auth.
*RESPONSIBILITIES: Real Property.
Shulman, Michael Bradley '68 '94
C.145 B.A. L.880 J.D. [Shearman&S.] (⊙New York, NY)
Shulman, Robert H., (AV) . . . . '53 '79 C.188 B.A. L.861 J.D. [Howrey S.A.&W.]
*PRACTICE AREAS: Insurance Coverage; Complex Litigation; Litigation.
Shulman, Stephen N., (AV) . . . . '33 '58 C.309 A.B. L.976 LL.B. [O'Connor&H.]
*PRACTICE AREAS: Litigation; Associations; Employment Law.

Shulman, Rogers, Gandal, Pordy & Ecker, P.A., (AV)
West Tower, Suite 500, 1100 New York Avenue, N.W., 20005-3934 ⊙
Telephone: 202-872-0400
Email: lawfirm@srgpe.com URL: http://www.shulmanrogers.com
Lawrence A. Shulman; Donald R. Rogers; Larry N. Gandal; David A. Pordy.
General Practice including Trial and Administrative practice before U.S. Courts and State Courts, Government Departments, Commissions and Federal Agencies. Antitrust, Banking, Bankruptcy, Civil Rights, Commercial Law, Commercial Litigation and Commercial Transactions, Construction, Corporate, Disabilities, Employment, Entertainment, Environmental, Estate Planning and Administration, Family Law, Federal Tort Claims Act, Franchising, Government Contracts, Health Care, Hotels, Housing and Urban Development, Immigration, Insurance, Intellectual Property, International, Interstate Land Sales, Landlord/Tenant, Leasing, Media, Medical Malpractice, Mergers and Acquisitions, Mortgage banking, Municipal Finance, Pension Plans, Partnerships, Personal Injury, Professional Liability, Real Estate, Reorganizations, Securities, Shopping Center, Taxation and Zoning, Tax Exempt Bond Financing, Telecommunications.
Rockville, Maryland Office: 11921 Rockville Pike. Telephone: 301-230-5200. Telecopier: 301-230-2891.
McLean, Virginia Office: 8180 Greensboro Drive, Suite 750. Telephone: 703-684-5200.
Greenbelt, Maryland Office: 6404 Ivy Lane, Suite 718. Telephone: 301-699-9883.
See Professional Biographies, WASHINGTON, DISTRICT OF COLUMBIA

Shumaker, Gregory M. . . . . '62 '87 C.103 Sc.B. L.602 J.D. [Jones,D.R.&P.]
*PRACTICE AREAS: Litigation; Complex Business Litigation.
Shumaker, Michael R. . . . . '66 '92 C.390 A.B. L.602 J.D. [Jones,D.R.&P.]
*PRACTICE AREAS: Litigation; Products Liability; Corporate Investigations.
Shuman, Jerome . . . . '39 '64 C&L.329 B.A., LL.B. Prof. of Law, Howard Univ.
Shupe, Harry G. . . . . '29 '53 C.216 A.B. L.446 LL.B. 321 D St., N.E.
Shur, Luba . . . . '71 '97 C&L.893 B.A., J.D. [Ⓐ Williams&C.]
*PRACTICE AREAS: Litigation.
Shuren, Allison Weber . . . . '64 '98 C.461 B.S.N. L.477 J.D. [Ⓐ Arent F.K.P.&K.]
*PRACTICE AREAS: Health Law; Medicare and Medicaid; Fraud; Compliance; Government Relations.
Shuster, Robert L. . . . '65 '92 C.645 B.S. L.1017 J.D. [Ⓒ Klett R.L.&S.] (⊙Harrisburg, PA)
Sibarium, Michael L., (AV) . . . . '59 '85 C.184 B.A. L.273 J.D. [Winston&S.]
*PRACTICE AREAS: Litigation; Antitrust Law; E-Commerce; Trade Regulation Law; Trade and Professional Associations.
Sibbison, V. Heather . . . . '61 '89 C.860 B.A. L.178 J.D. [Patton B.]
Sibears, Daniel M. '52 '78 C.1154 B.A. L.213 J.D.
(adm. in MI; not adm. in DC) Dir., National Assn. of Sec. Dealers, Inc.
Sichel, Lucien J. '13 '40 C&L.976 B.A., LL.B.
(adm. in NY; not adm. in DC) 175 R St., N.E.‡
Siciliano, Robert J., (AV) . . . . '41 '67 C.776 B.S. L.128 J.D. [Ⓒ Krooth&A.]
*PRACTICE AREAS: Estate Administration; Real Estate; Tax Audit.
Sidamon-Eristoff, Simon . . . . '58 '85 C.674 A.B. L.178 J.D. Gen. Coun., Amer. Farmland
Siddall, David R. . . . . '— '77 C.412 B.A. L.273 J.D. [Verner,L.B.M.&H.]
*PRACTICE AREAS: Communications; High Technology.
Siddiqui, Muddassir Husain '48 '83 L.309 LL.M.
(adm. in NY; not adm. in DC) Legal Advsr., Royal Embassy of Saudi Arabia
Sidell, Gary M. . . . . '49 '77 C.473 A.B. L.93 J.D. 1717 Massachusetts Ave., N.W.
Sidley Austin Brown & Wood, (AV)
1722 Eye Street, N.W. (⊙L.A., San Fran., CA; Chgo., IL; New York, NY; Dallas, TX; Seattle, WA)
Sidman, Lawrence R., (AV) . . . . '— '73 C.31 A.B. L.93 J.D. [Verner,L.B.M.&H.]
*PRACTICE AREAS: Legislative Law; Communications Law; Government Contracts Law.
Sidman, Mark H., (AV) . . . . '56 '80 C.319 B.A. L.665 J.D. [Weiner B.S.K.]
*PRACTICE AREAS: Transportation; Mergers and Acquisitions; Asset Sales; Regulatory Compliance; Federal Taxation.
Siebel, Brian J. . . . . '56 '91 C.907 B.A. L.30 J.D. 1250 Eye Street, NW, Suite 802
Siebert, Thomas L. . . . . '46 '74 C&L.276 A.B., J.D. [Ⓒ Patton B.]
Siedlecki, Christina M. Saarlas . . . . '61 '95 C.446 B.S. L.128 J.D. 1255 23rd St., N.W.
Siegel, Allan M. . . . . '69 '94 C&L.273 B.B.A., J.D. [Ⓐ Chaikin&S.]
*PRACTICE AREAS: Medical Malpractice; Auto Negligence; Wrongful Death; Premises Liability; Product Liability.
Siegel, Allen G., (AV) . . . . '34 '60 C.563 L.228 LL.B. [Arent F.K.P.&K.]
*PRACTICE AREAS: Labor and Employment; Collective Bargaining; Employment Discrimination Law; Alternative Dispute Resolution; Arbitration Law.
Siegel, Arnon D. . . . . '63 '90 C.103 A.B. L.976 J.D. [Ⓒ Robbins,R.E.O.&U.]
Siegel, David B., (AV) . . . . '53 '79 C&L.659 B.A., J.D. [Crowell&M.]
Siegel, Deborah E. . . . . '59 '88 C.860 B.A. L.273 J.D. 700 19th Street Nw
Siegel, Eric L. . . . . '64 '90 C.860 B.A. L.112 J.D. [Henrichsen S.]
*PRACTICE AREAS: Civil Rights; Disability Rights; Constitutional Law; Commercial Torts; Litigation.
Siegel, Gary, (AV) . . . . '42 '74 C.871 B.S. L.128 J.D. [Bromberg,R.&S.] ⊙
Siegel, Kenneth E. '— '72 C.229 B.S.B.A. L.831 J.D.
(adm. in PA; not adm. in DC) [Ⓐ Strasburger&P.]
*PRACTICE AREAS: Transportation; Federal Legislative Practice.
Siegel, Neil B., (AV) . . . . '42 '67 C.339 B.S. L.597 J.D. [Sughrue M.] (See Pat. Sect.)
*PRACTICE AREAS: Intellectual Property Law; Litigation.
Siegel, Richard D. . . . . '39 '65 C.659 A.B. L.309 J.D. [Ⓐ Olsson,F.&W.]
*PRACTICE AREAS: Agriculture Law; Food and Drug Regulation; Medical Law; Legislative Practice; Forestry Law.
Siegel, Ronald A., (AV) . . . . '40 '65 C&L.477 B.A., J.D. [Cohn&M.]
*PRACTICE AREAS: Communications Law; Cable Television; Mass Media and New Technologies.
Siegel, Stephanie . . . . '59 '85 C.696 B.A. L.904 J.D. [Ⓐ Collier S.S.]
*PRACTICE AREAS: Occupational Safety and Health; Environmental Law.
Siegel, Tristan B.L. . . . . '66 '96 C.573 B.A. L.893 J.D. [Ⓐ Kelley D.&W.]
*PRACTICE AREAS: Litigation.
Siegelbaum, Jonathan H. '73 '00 C.951 B.A. L.893 J.D.
(adm. in VA; not adm. in DC) [Ⓐ Wilmer,C.&P.]

Siegler, Douglas L., (AV) . . . . '61 '86 C.674 B.A. L.228 J.D. [Sutherland A.&B.]
*PRACTICE AREAS: Estate and Gift Taxation; Fiduciary Income Tax; Generation Skipping Tax.
Siegler, Ellen . . . . '— '75 C.966 B.A. L.184 J.D. [Ⓒ Hogan&H.]
*PRACTICE AREAS: Clean Air Act; Clean Water Act.

Siegler, Ira S., (AV) '28 '51 C.674 B.A. L.309 LL.B.
1616 H Street, N.W., Suite 900, 20006
Telephone: 202-737-0220 Telecopier: 202-347-2075
Email: ira_s_siegler@prodigy.net
Estate Planning, Taxation, Trusts, Estates, Wills and Probate Law.
See Professional Biographies, WASHINGTON, DISTRICT OF COLUMBIA

Siegner, A. Wes, Jr. . . . . '52 '87 C.103 B.A. L.188 J.D. [Hyman,P.&M.]
Siekman, Michael T. '67 '95
C.67 B.S. L.94 J.D. [Ⓐ Finnegan,H.F.G.&D.] (See Pat. Sect.)
*PRACTICE AREAS: Pharmaceutical Patent Prosecution; Patent Litigation; Intellectual Property Portfolio Management; Patent Interference Practice.
Siem, Michael A. '73 '01 C.46 B.S. L.477 J.D.
(adm. in NY; not adm. in DC; See Pat. Sect.) [Ⓐ Kenyon&K.]
*PRACTICE AREAS: Intellectual Property.
Sieradzki, David L., (AV) . . . . '62 '89 C.112 B.A. L.976 J.D. [Hogan&H.]
*PRACTICE AREAS: Communications.
Sierck, Alexander W., (AV) . . . . '40 '65 C&L.893 B.A., LL.B. [Cameron&H.]
*PRACTICE AREAS: International Trade Law; Antitrust Law; Federal Regulatory Law.
Sierra, Gretchen T. '72 '00 C&L.352 B.A., J.D.
(adm. in IL; not adm. in DC) [Ⓐ Skadden,A.S.M.&F.]
Siesser, Steven C. '51 '76 C.569 B.A. L.724 J.D.
Asst. V.P., National Assoc. Life Underwriters
Sieving, Charles E. . . . . '72 '99 C.207 B.A. L.150 J.D. [Ⓐ Hogan&H.]
Sifers, Randall W. . . . . '57 '97 C.502 B.S.B.A. L.347 J.D. [Ⓐ Kelley D.&W.]
*PRACTICE AREAS: Telecommunications.
Siffermann, Mary M. . . . . '65 '94 C.746 B.A. L.146 J.D. [Ⓐ Gordon&B.]
*PRACTICE AREAS: Employment Law; Employee Benefits Law; Health Law; Insurance Law; Trial and Appellate Practice.
Sigall, Jule L. . . . . '68 '96 C.228 A.B. L.128 J.D. [Ⓐ Arnold&P.]
*PRACTICE AREAS: Intellectual Property.
Sigel, Carin J. . . . . '59 '86 C.659 B.A. L.94 J.D. [Gardner,C.&D.]
*PRACTICE AREAS: Medicare; Health Care.
Sigelman, Daniel W., (BV) . . . . '49 '80 C.197 A.B. L.1066 J.D. [Kellogg,S.&S.] ⊙
*PRACTICE AREAS: Torts; Personal Injury; Toxic Torts; Pharmaceutical Law; Medical Device Litigation.
Signorille, Mary Ellen, (AV) '52 '77 C.107 B.A. L.128 J.D.
Legal Proj. Coord., American Assn. of Ret. Persons
Sigsbee, Cheryl Ann . . . . '58 '85 C.999 B.A. L.845 J.D. 1077 30th St., NW
Sigworth, Ronald L. '64 '97 C.893 B.S.M.E. L.128 J.D.
[Ⓐ Kenyon&K.] (See Pat. Sect.)
*PRACTICE AREAS: Intellectual Property.
Sikes, Cristen E. '73 '99 C.276 B.A. L.945 J.D.
(adm. in MD; not adm. in DC) [Ⓐ Piper M.R.&W.]
Sikes, Lucinda A. . . . . '61 '89 C.112 A.B. L.309 J.D. 1600 20th St. N.W.
Sikora, Clifford S. '62 '89 C.188 B.S. L.201 J.D.
(adm. in PA; not adm. in DC) [Troutman S.]
*PRACTICE AREAS: Electric Utility Regulation; Independent Power Production; Public Policy; Legislation; Regulatory Policy.
Sikorski, Gerald E., (AV) . . . . '48 '74 C&L.494 B.A., J.D. (M.C.) [Holland&K.]
*PRACTICE AREAS: Public Law; Intellectual Property; Indian Law.
Sikorski, Kerri R. . . . . '74 '00 C.884 B.S. L.309 J.D. [Ⓐ Hogan&H.]
Silard, Stephen A. . . . . . '38 '64 C&L.309 B.A., LL.B. Asst. Gen. Coun., World Bank, The
Silas, Lamont H. . . . . '67 '95 C.1101 B.A. L.276 J.D. [Ⓐ Nixon P.]
*PRACTICE AREAS: Public Finance; Tax.
Silber, Jonathan S. '47 '79 C.563 B.A. L.1209 J.D.
Assistant VP & Assistant General Counsel, GEICO Corp.

Silber, Richard F., (AV) '52 '81 C.72 B.S. L.1218 J.D. BR
3221 M Street, N.W., 20007
Telephone: 202-338-0687 Fax: 202-333-0858
Email: info@injury-law1.com URL: http://www.lawyers.com/richardsilberlaw
Personal Injury Law, Automobile Accidents and Injuries, Liability, Product Liability, Premises Liability, Medical and Professional Malpractice, Construction Accidents, Wrongful Death, Nursing Home Negligence, Obstetric Malpractice, Pediatric Malpractice, Lead Poisoning, Head Trauma, Spinal Cord Injuries, Baycol Drug Usage, Drowning, Swimming Accidents.
See Professional Biographies, WASHINGTON, DISTRICT OF COLUMBIA

Silberbogen, Rebecca E. . . . . '74 '99 C.692 B.A. L.945 J.D. [Ⓐ Arent F.K.P.&K.]
*PRACTICE AREAS: Insurance Litigation; Environmental Litigation.
Silberg, Jay E., (P.C.), (AV) . . . . '41 '66 C.31 B.A. L.309 J.D. [Shaw P.]
*PRACTICE AREAS: Energy; Nuclear; Litigation; Administrative.
Silbergeld, Alan Mark '40 '66 C.347 A.B. L.910 J.D.
(adm. in MO; not adm. in DC) Consumers Union of U.S., Inc.
Silbermann, James M. '— '96 C.446 B.S.Ch.E. L.128 J.D.
[Ⓐ Foley&L.] (See Pat. Sect.)
*PRACTICE AREAS: Intellectual Property; Patent Law.
Silbert, Earl J., (AV) . . . . '36 '60 C&L.309 A.B., LL.B. [Piper M.R.&W.]
*PRACTICE AREAS: Corporate Litigation; White Collar Crime Defense; Legal Ethics Advice, Discipline and Malpractice; Securities Enforcement; Tax.
Silby, D. Wayne . . . . '48 '75 C.659 B.S. L.276 J.D. 1715 18th St. N.W.
Silcox, Clark R. . . . . '53 '78 C.112 B.A. L.273 J.D. [Ⓒ Bode&G.]
*PRACTICE AREAS: Antitrust and Trade Regulation.
Silecchia, Lucia Ann '67 '90 C.994 B.A. L.976 J.D.
Asst. Prof. of Law, The Catholic Univ. of Amer.
Siler, Duane Alan . . . . '49 '78 C.174 B.A. L.1066 J.D. [Patton B.]
Siler, J. Bernard . . . . '51 '80 C.201 B.A. L.150 J.D. Pros., D.C. Corp. Coun.
Silfen, Thomas E., (AV) . . . . '42 '67 C&L.477 B.A., J.D. [Ⓒ Arnold&P.]
*PRACTICE AREAS: Litigation; Products Liability.
Silien, Daniel A. . . . . '70 '97 C.30 B.A. L.569 J.D. [Ⓐ Preston G.E.&R.M.]
*PRACTICE AREAS: Litigation; Technology and Science; Antitrust.
Silis, Thomas P. '69 '00 C.273 B.A. L.564 J.D.
(adm. in NY; not adm. in DC) [Ⓐ Regan,H.&L.]
*PRACTICE AREAS: Personal Injury; Medical Malpractice; Premises Liability; Products Liability.
Silk, James J. '47 '89 C.477 A.B. L.976 J.D.
Dir., Robert F. Kennedy Memorial Ctr. for Human Rights
Sill, William J., (AV) . . . . '53 '78 C&L.831 B.A., J.D. [Wilkinson B.K.]
*PRACTICE AREAS: Telecommunications Law; Commercial Transactions.
Silliman, Craig L. . . . . '67 '94 C.575 B.A. L.893 J.D. 3050 K St., N.W.
Sills, Richard P., (AV) . . . . '45 '70 C&L.659 B.A., LL.B. [Holland&K.]
*PRACTICE AREAS: Trusts and Estates; Tax Law; Business Law; Exempt Organizations.
Silva, Alejandro . . . . '63 '88 [Ⓒ Chadbourne&P.]
Silva, Elizabeth J. . . . . '68 '00 C.858 B.A. L.276 J.D. [Ⓐ Hogan&H.]
*PRACTICE AREAS: Corporate Law.
Silva, Fabio Roman . . . . '69 '99 C.112 B.A. L.813 J.D. [Ⓐ Arnold&P.]
*PRACTICE AREAS: Consumer Product Safety; Civil Litigation; Intellectual Property Transactions.
Silva, Theodore S., Jr. . . . . '58 '86 C.602 B.A. L.1209 J.D. [Holland&K.]
*PRACTICE AREAS: Commercial Real Estate Law; Corporation Law.
Silva, William D., (AV) . . . . '43 '69 C.705 B.A. L.184 J.D. 5335 Wisconsin Ave., NW

Silveira, Maria De Fatima '62 '92
C&L.472 B.A., J.D. Assoc. Coun. for Latin America, Worldcom
Silver, Daniel B., (AV) ....'41 '68 C.112 B.A. L.309 LL.B. [🄲 Cleary,G.S.&H.]
Silver, David .... '31 '59 C.563 B.A. L.309 LL.B. Pres., ICI Mutual Ins. Co.‡
Silver, David C., (AV) .... '59 '88 C.401 B.S. L.276 J.D. [Holland&K.]
*PRACTICE AREAS: Commercial Transactions; Real Estate Law; Corporate Law.
Silver, Harry R., (AV) .... '46 '72 C.831 B.A. L.178 J.D. [Ober,K.G.&S.]
Silver, Howard S. ....'59 '85 C.659 B.S. Ec. L.276 J.D. [Hogan&H.]
*PRACTICE AREAS: Nonprofit and Charitable Organizations; Tax-Exempt Organizations; Nonprofit Tax Law; Public Charities; Private Foundations.
Silver, Joel Z., (AV) .... '46 '71 C.569 B.A. L.273 J.D. [Silver&S.]
*PRACTICE AREAS: Real Estate Law; Corporate Law; Business Law.
Silver, Leslie Carter .... '49 '75 C.881 A.B. L.273 J.D. [Silver&S.]
*PRACTICE AREAS: Real Estate Law; Corporate Law; Business Law.
Silver, Rugenia ....'50 '80 C.831 B.A. L.273 J.D. Assoc. Gen. Coun., Fannie Mae
*RESPONSIBILITIES: Single Family Business; Product Development; Legislative Practice; Regulatory Law.
Silver, Sidney J., **(P.C.)**, (AV) ....'34 '62 C.401 B.S. L.276 J.D. [Silver,F.&T.]
*PRACTICE AREAS: Taxation; Corporate and Partnership; Mergers, Acquisitions and Reorganizations; Real Estate Leasing; Estate and Gift Tax.
Silver, Stephen M. ....'74 '99 C.178 B.A. L.276 J.D. [🄰 Baker B.]

Silver, Freedman & Taff, L.L.P., (AV)
A Partnership including Professional Corporations
1100 New York Avenue, N.W., Suite 700, 20005-3934
Telephone: 202-414-6100 Telecopier: 202-682-0354
URL: http://www.sftlaw.com
Members of Firm: Sidney J. Silver (P.C.); Robert L. Freedman (P.C.); Barry P. Taff (P.C.); James S. Fleischer (P.C.); Martin L. Meyrowitz (P.C.); Dave M. Muchnikoff (P.C.); Steven M. Abramson (P.C.); Brian L. Alpert (P.C.); Michael S. Sadow (P.C.); Nancy M. Stiles (P.C.); Beth A. Freedman. Associates: Craig M. Scheer; Agata Szypszak (Not admitted in DC). Of Counsel: John F. Breyer, Jr. (Also Member, Breyer & Associates, P.C.); Lawrence J. Eisenberg; John B. Selman (Not admitted in DC); James W. Lance (Not admitted in DC); Martin J. O'Riordan (Not admitted in DC); E. Preston Rutledge.
Practice before Federal and State Regulatory Agencies, including Securities and Exchange Commission, Office of Thrift Supervision, Office of the Comptroller of the Currency, Federal Reserve Board, Federal Deposit Insurance Corporation, National Credit Union Administration and the Internal Revenue Service Emphasis on Banking, Corporate, Securities, Employee Benefits, Taxation, Syndication, Business, Trial and Appellate Court Practice.
See Professional Biographies, WASHINGTON, DISTRICT OF COLUMBIA

Silver & Silver, P.C., (AV)
1612 K Street, NW, Suite 1204, 20006-2802
Telephone: 202-861-1200 Fax: 202-861-1268
Email: silverpc@aol.com URL: http://www.lawyers.com/silverpc
Joel Z. Silver; Leslie Carter Silver.
Real Estate, Corporate and Business Planning and Transactions.
See Professional Biographies, WASHINGTON, DISTRICT OF COLUMBIA

Silverberg, James Lorin ....'55 '81 C.1044 B.A. L.273 J.D. [Silverberg&W.]
Silverberg, Kenneth H., (AV) ....'46 '73 C.477 B.A. L.276 J.D. [Nixon P.]
*PRACTICE AREAS: Business; Nonprofit and Charitable Organizations; Tax Law; Litigation; Trusts and Estates.
Silverberg, Kristen L. ....'70 '96 C.309 B.A. L.846 J.D. 725 12th St., N.W.
Silverberg, Margaret ....'46 '84 C.145 B.A. L.273 J.D. 4705 29th Pl. NW
Silverberg, Robert P., (AV) ....'45 '71 C.861 B.B.A. L.273 J.D. [Silverberg,G.&B.]
*PRACTICE AREAS: Air Transportation Law; Commercial Transportation Law; International Air Law.
Silverberg, Steven J. ....'56 '84 C.1044 B.A. L.30 J.D. 1629 K St., N.W.

Silverberg, Goldman and Bikoff, L.L.P., (AV)
Suite 120, 1101 Thirtieth Street, N.W., 20007
Telephone: 202-944-3300 Telecopier: 202-944-3306
URL: http://www.lawyers.com/bagileosilverberg&goldman
Robert P. Silverberg; Michael F. Goldman; James L. Bikoff; David I. Wilson;—Michael W. Ambrose, Jr.; David K. Heasley.
Aviation, Commercial Transportation Law, Administrative Law, Antitrust, International Trade, Customs, Litigation, Import and Export Control, Intellectual Property, including Trademarks, Copyrights and Trade Secrets, Internet and Technology Law.
See Professional Biographies, WASHINGTON, DISTRICT OF COLUMBIA

Silverberg & Wade .... 1625 Massachusetts Ave., NW
Silverman, Alan H. '54 '81 C.299 B.A. L.659 J.D.
V.P., Gen. Coun. & Dir., Admin., Cable One, Inc.
Silverman, Alexei M. ....'70 '96 C.691 B.A. L.309 J.D. [🄰 Covington&B.]
Silverman, Arthur H. '39 '63
C.659 B.S. L.188 J.D. [🄲 Jones,W.H.&M.] (⊙Salt Lake City, UT)
*PRACTICE AREAS: Government Relations.
Silverman, Carl S., (AV) ....'46 '71 C.205 B.A. L.276 J.D. [Hodes,U.P.&K.]
*PRACTICE AREAS: Labor and Employment; Employment Litigation; Trade Association Law.
Silverman, Cary '75 '00 C.1372 B.S. L.273 J.D.
(adm. in MD; not adm. in DC) [🄰 Shook,H.&B.]
Silverman, David M., (AV) .... '50 '80 C.1275 B.A. L.597 J.D. [Cole,R.&B.]
*PRACTICE AREAS: Intellectual Property Law, including Trademark and Copyright Registration; Licensing and Litigation; Broadcast and Cable Regulatory and Transactional Matters.
Silverman, Donald J. ....'55 '80 C&L.665 B.A., J.D. [Morgan,L.&B.]
Silverman, Jared R. '71 '97 C.477 B.A. L.659 J.D.
(adm. in IL; not adm. in DC) [🄰 Shaw P.]
*PRACTICE AREAS: Litigation.
Silverman, Jason M. .... '72 '00 C.1365 B.A. L.597 J.D. [🄰 McKenna&C.]
*PRACTICE AREAS: Litigation.
Silverman, Mark J., (AV) ....'45 '71 C.347 B.S. L.818 J.D. [Steptoe&J.]
*PRACTICE AREAS: Taxation Law; Federal Income Estate and Gift Taxation Law; Taxation of Individuals and Business Entities Law.
Silverman, Michael R. ....'47 '73 C.823 B.A. L.276 J.D. [🄲 Clifford C.R.&W.]
*PRACTICE AREAS: International Project Finance; International Investment; International Commercial Law.
Silverman, Noah J. ...... '68 '93 C.674 A.B. L.659 J.D. Sr. Coun., Marriott International
*RESPONSIBILITIES: Lodging Franchise Development and Operations.
Silverman, Richard S., (AV) .... '43 '68 C&L.705 B.A., J.D. [Hogan&H.]
*PRACTICE AREAS: Agricultural Law; Food, Drug and Cosmetic Law; Food Labeling and Inspection; Food Processing; Food and Drug Regulation.
Silverman, Scott D. '58 '84 C.994 B.A. L.1398 J.D.
(adm. in NY; not adm. in DC) [🄲 Sutherland A.&B.]
*PRACTICE AREAS: Mergers and Acquisitions; Insurance Regulation.
Silverman, William, (AV) ....'45 '69 C.659 B.A. L.145 J.D. [Hunton&W.]
*PRACTICE AREAS: International Trade.

Silversmith, Gary J., Law Offices of '56 '81 C.174 B.S. L.276 J.D.
The Watergate, 2600 Virginia Avenue, N.W., Suite 606, 20037
Telephone: 202-337-7300 Fax: 202-429-5290
Email: nebagamon@aol.com URL: http://www.lawofficesofgaryjsilversmith.com
Toxic Torts, Asbestos Law, Lead Paint Poisoning, Mold, Environmental Law, Collections.
Newark, Deleware Office: 131 Continental Drive, Suite 108. 19713. Telephone: 302-368-3100. Fax: 302-368-2255.
See Professional Biographies, WASHINGTON, DISTRICT OF COLUMBIA
Silversmith, Jol A. .... '72 '98 C&L.309 A.B., J.D. [🄰 Zuckert,S.&R.]

Silverstein, Craig W. ....'72 '98 C.30 B.A. L.665 J.D. [🄰 Miller,B.&O.]
Silverstein, Leonard L., (AV) .... '22 '49 C.976 A.B. L.309 LL.B. [Silverstein&M.]
Silverstein, Scott E. ....'72 '99 C.188 B.S. L.569 J.D. [🄰 Gibson,D.&C.]

Silverstein and Mullens, (AV) 🄱🅁
A Division of Buchanan Ingersoll
1776 K Street, N.W., Suite 800, 20006 ⊙
Telephone: 202-452-7900 Telecopier: 202-452-7989
Email: info@silmul.bipc.com URL: http://www.silmul.bipc.com
Members of Firm: Leonard L. Silverstein; Gerald H. Sherman; Stuart M. Lewis; Ronald D. Abramson; John P. Warner; Donald B. Reynolds, Jr.; David I. Kempler; David H. Dickieson; James J. Freedman; Aen W. Webster; Louis H. Diamond; Linda K. Shore; Gary K. Bahena; Keith A. Mong. Counsel: Deborah M. Beers; Carmen Irizarry-Díaz; H. Grace Kim. Special Tax Counsel: Patricia R. Lesser; John S. Ross, III; Richard S. Marshall; Carol P. Tello; Gita Khadiri. Associates: Ruth C. Shaw; Norma M. Sharara (Not admitted in DC); Laura A. Baek. Of Counsel: Richard A. Mullens; Harrison B. McCawley.
Federal Taxation, International Taxation, Commercial Real Estate, Legislative Matters, Corporate Law, Litigation, Bankruptcy, Municipal Finance, Estate Planning, Partnerships, Pension and Retirement Planning, Charitable Giving and Tax-exempt Organizations.
Pittsburgh, Pennsylvania Office: Buchanan Ingersoll, One Oxford Centre, 301 Grant Street, 20th Floor. Telephone: 412-562-8800.
Philadelphia, Pennsylvania Office: Buchanan Ingersoll, Eleven Penn Center, 14th Floor, 1835 Market Street. Telephone: 215-665-8700.
Bryn Mawr, Pennsylvania Office: Buchanan Ingersoll, 937 East Haverford Road, Suite 201. Telephone: 610-581-7004.
Harrisburg, Pennsylvania Office: Buchanan Ingersoll, One South Market Square, 213 Market Street, 3rd Floor. Telephone: 717-237-4800.
Tampa, Florida Office: Buchanan Ingersoll, SunTrust Financial Centre, 401 East Jackson Street, Suite 2500. Telephone: 813-222-8180.
Aventura, Florida Office: Buchanan Ingersoll, One Turnberry Place, 19495 Biscayne Boulevard, Suite 606. Telephone: 305-933-5600.
Miami, Florida Office: Buchanan Ingersoll, Bank of America Tower, 100 S.E. Second Street, Suite 2100. Telephone: 305-347-4080.
Princeton, New Jersey Office: Buchanan Ingersoll, 700 Alexander Park, Suite 300. Telephone: 609-987-6800.
Buffalo, New York Office: Buchanan Ingersoll, 268 Main Street, Suite 201. Telephone: 716-853-2330.
New York, New York Office: Buchanan Ingersoll, 140 Broadway, 35th Floor. Telephone: 646-458-2340.
McLean, Virginia Office: Buchanan Ingersoll, 8280 Greensboro Drive, Suite 601. Telephone: 703-749-6060.
London, England Office: Buchanan Ingersoll, Tower 42, International Financial Centre, Old Broad Street, EC2N 1HQ. Telephone: 44-171-629-7343.
Dublin, Ireland Office: Buchanan Ingersoll, Level 1, 4 Custom House Plaza, IFSC, Dublin 1. Telephone: 011-353-1611-7266. Fax: 3531-836-9305.
See Professional Biographies, WASHINGTON, DISTRICT OF COLUMBIA

Silverthorne, Katherine Andrea '68 '97
C.1169 B.A. L.882 J.D. U.S. Public Interest Research Group
Silvester, L. V., III .... '49 '86 C.399 B.A. L.1187 J.D. V.P., First Union National Bank
Sim, John .... '74 '00 C.659 B.A. L.30 J.D. [🄰 Akin,G.S.H.&F.]
*PRACTICE AREAS: International Trade; Corporate Law.
Simchak, Matthew S., (AV) .... '47 '73 C.855 B.A. L.893 J.D. [Wiley R.&F.]
*PRACTICE AREAS: Government Contracts.
Simei, Joseph A. .... '65 '98 C.871 B.S. L.597 J.D. [🄰 Latham&W.]
*PRACTICE AREAS: Mergers and Acquisitions.
Simeone, Thomas J., (BV) ....'64 '91 C.823 B.S. L.178 J.D. [Cohen&C.]
*PRACTICE AREAS: Personal Injury; Medical Malpractice; Product Liability.
Simeone, Timothy J. .... '68 '95 C.309 A.B. L.145 J.D. [🄰 Harris,W.&G.]
*PRACTICE AREAS: Appellate Practice; Administrative Law; Telecommunications Law; Litigation.
Simkin, Michele M. ....'— '93 C.966 B.S. L.273 J.D. [Foley&L.]
*PRACTICE AREAS: Intellectual Property; Biotechnology; Pharmaceutical.
Simkins, Christopher P. .... '70 '97 C&L.101 B.A., J.D. [🄰 Wilmer,C.&P.]
Simmer, W. Scott, (BV) ....'51 '85 C.187 B.A. L.352 J.D. [Porter W.M.&A.]
*PRACTICE AREAS: Health Care; Health Care Fraud; ERISA; Employee Benefits; Litigation.
Simmonds, Denise A. ....'65 '95 C.94 B.A. L.276 J.D. [🄰 Skadden,A.S.M.&F.]
Simmons, Barry E. '58 '94
C.454 B.B.A. L.273 J.D. Assoc. Coun., Investment Co. Institute
*RESPONSIBILITIES: Securities; Financial Regulation.
Simmons, Charles T. ....'54 '91 C.1033 B.S. L.184 J.D. [Kilpatrick S.]
*PRACTICE AREAS: Environmental.
Simmons, G. Lindsay, (AV) .... '49 '74 C.119 B.A. L.930 J.D. [Jackson&K.P.]
*PRACTICE AREAS: Litigation; Government Contracts; Safety and Health.
Simmons, Ian .... '63 '92 C.012 B.A. L.659 J.D. [🄲 O'Melveny&M.]
Simmons, Jack M., III ....'46 '76 C&L.174 B.A., J.D. 3952 Garrison, N.W.
Simmons, Jacolyn A., (AV) ....'54 '82 C.30 B.A. L.329 J.D. [Shook,H.&B.]
*PRACTICE AREAS: Energy Law; Environmental Law.
Simmons, Melanie A. ....'67 '98 C.15 B.S. L.273 J.D. [🄰 Hogan&H.]
*PRACTICE AREAS: Corporate Law; Securities.
Simmons, Omari S. '74 '99 C.896 B.A. L.659 J.D.
(adm. in MD; not adm. in DC) [🄰 Wilmer,C.&P.]
Simmons, Ralph A. ....'52 '77 C.674 A.B. L.693 J.D. [Keller&H.]
*PRACTICE AREAS: Food and Drug Law; Trade Regulation Law.
Simmons, S. Jnatel .... '72 '97 C.95 A.B. L.659 J.D. [🄰 Arnold&P.]
*PRACTICE AREAS: Litigation.
Simms, Larry L., (AV) .... '44 '74 C.197 A.B. L.94 J.D. [Gibson,D.&C.]
*PRACTICE AREAS: Appellate Litigation; Constitutional Litigation; Insurance Law (International and Domestic); Chinese Law; International Arbitration.
Simoes, James R. '72 '98 C.94 B.S. L.273 J.D.
(adm. in VA; not adm. in DC) [🄰 Hunton&W.]
Simon, Barry S., (AV) .... '49 '76 C&L.309 B.A., J.D. [Williams&C.]
*PRACTICE AREAS: Appellate Practice; Criminal Law; Litigation; Qui Tam Litigation; White Collar Crime.
Simon, Cathy Ann, (AV) .... '50 '76 C.860 B.A. L.273 J.D. [Ross,D.&B.]
Simon, Cynthia W. .... '49 '80 C.659 B.A. L.976 J.D. Georgetown Univ. Law Ctr.
Simon, Daniel A. '63 '95 C.976 B.A. L.659 J.D.
(adm. in NY; not adm. in DC) Staff Atty., People for the American Way
Simon, Daniel R. '71 '99 C.228 B.A. L.575 J.D.
(adm. in NC; not adm. in DC) [🄰 Sutherland A.&B.]
*PRACTICE AREAS: Energy; Commodities.

Simon, David L., Law Offices of '47 '77 C.722 B.A. L.446 J.D.
Suite 412, 1000 Connecticut Avenue, NW, 20006
Telephone: 202-481-9000 Fax: 202-481-9010 URL: http://www.dlsimon.com
Email: dlsimon@dlsimon.com URL: http://www.lawyers.com/davidsimonlaw
***PRACTICE AREAS: International Trade Law; Customs Law.**
—Ayla önder (Not admitted in DC).
International Trade Law, Antidumping, Asia Trade, Customs Law, Countervailing Duties, Import and Export Law, Middle East Trade, Foreign Trade Sanctions, Pacific Rim Trade.
See Professional Biographies, WASHINGTON, DISTRICT OF COLUMBIA

Simon, Donald J. ....'53 '78 C&L.309 B.A., J.D. [🄰 Sonosky,C.S.E.&P.]
Simon, Elizabeth Treubert ....'68 '99 C.659 B.A. L.982 J.D. [Vorys,S.S.&P.]
*PRACTICE AREAS: Litigation; Professional Liability.
Simon, Jean-Marie ...... '54 '92 C.276 B.S. L.309 J.D. Pan American Health Organization
Simon, Jeremy S. .... '69 '94 C&L.228 B.A., J.D. [🄲 Wilmer,C.&P.]

Simon, Joel N., (AV) ... '36 '60 C.339 B.S. L.477 J.D. [Arent F.K.P.&K.]
*PRACTICE AREAS: Real Estate-Commercial Law; Real Estate (Property) Law; Real Estate Development and/or Syndications Law; Taxation.
Simon, Jonathan D. ... '70 '98 C.188 B.A. L.273 J.D. [Ⓐ Van Ness F.]
*PRACTICE AREAS: Natural Resources; Energy; Environment.
Simon, Julie ... '54 '78 C.112 B.A. L.284 J.D. 1401 H Street, N.W., Suite 760
Simon, Karla W. '47 '72 C.926 B.A. L.228 J.D.
(adm. in NC; not adm. in DC) Prof., Catholic Univ. Sch. of Law
Simon, Kenneth M., (AV) ... '52 '77 C.665 B.A. L.276 J.D. [Dickstein S.M.&O.]
*PRACTICE AREAS: Project Finance; Energy Law; Cogeneration Law; International Law.
Simon, Kimberly A. ... '74 '99 C.188 B.A. L.273 J.D. 1801 L St., N.W.
Simon, Lennox J. '52 '85 L.1162 J.D.
(adm. in IA; not adm. in DC) 4945 11th St., N.W.‡
Simon, Marcus B. ... '70 '99 C.569 B.A. L.904 J.D. Trial Coun.
Simon, Roger N. ... '65 '93 C.860 B.A. L.276 J.D. [Ⓐ Weil,G.&M.]
*PRACTICE AREAS: Real Estate Finance; Mortgage Securitization; Loans.
Simon, Ronald ... '47 '73 C&L.309 A.B., J.D. [Simon&Assoc.]
*PRACTICE AREAS: Environmental Law.
Simon, Stephen A. '66 '94 C.309 B.A. L.569 J.D.
(adm. in NY; not adm. in DC) 818 Connecticut Ave., N.W., Suite 700
Simon, Tamara M. '71 '97 C.339 B.A. L.352 J.D.
(adm. in IL; not adm. in DC) William M. Mercer, Inc.
Simon, William, (AV) ... '12 '35 C.999 L.146 LL.B. [Howrey S.A.&W.]
Simon, William D. ... '47 '79 C&L.976 B.A., J.D. [Simon,T.&M.]
*PRACTICE AREAS: Corporate Law; Business Transactions; Mergers, Acquisitions and Divestitures; Taxation.

Simon & Associates
1742 N Street, N.W., 20036
Telephone: 202-429-0094 Fax: 202-429-0075
Email: ron@lawtort.com URL: http://www.lawyers.com/ronaldsimonlaw
Ronald Simon.
Toxic Torts, Environmental Law, Class Actions, Environmental Diseases, Contamination, Groundwater Contamination, Nuclear Waste, Federal Insecticide, Fungicide and Rodenticide Act (FIFRA).
See Professional Biographies, WASHINGTON, DISTRICT OF COLUMBIA

Simon, Turnbull & Martin, Chartered, (AV) BB
2000 Pennsylvania Avenue, N.W., Suite 4600, 20006-1812
Telephone: 202-785-2202 Fax: 202-785-2273
Email: info@stmlaw.com
William D. Simon; Lowell D. Turnbull; Jeffrey L. Squires;—John A. Knab. Of Counsel: Robert Martin; Michael B. Sheppard.
Corporate Mergers and Acquisitions, Financial Transactions, Tax Law, Government Contract Law, Federal Regulatory Practice, Export Controls, Copyright, Trademark, Franchise, and Commercial and Corporate Litigation.
See Professional Biographies, WASHINGTON, DISTRICT OF COLUMBIA

Simonds, Albert R., Jr. ... '43 '69 C.575 A.B. L.659 J.D. [Bruder,G.&M.] ‡
*PRACTICE AREAS: Electric Utility; Appellate Practice.
Simonds, Jerome H., (AV) ... '18 '41 C&L.209 LL.B. [Ⓒ Freedman,L.K.&S.] ‡
Simonetti, Katherine '65 '91
C.569 B.A. L.178 J.D. Sr. Coun., American National Red Cross
*RESPONSIBILITIES: Corporate; International; Non-Profit.
Simons, Barbara M. '29 '53 C&L.477 A.B., J.D.
(adm. in NY; not adm. in DC) [Simons&S.]
Simons, Janice A. ... '68 '95 C.915 B.A. L.904 J.D. [Ⓐ Shaw,B.V.&R.]
*PRACTICE AREAS: Employment.
Simons, Lawrence B. ... '24 '49 C.228 L.178 J.D. 1001 Pennsylvania Ave.
Simons, Morton L. '28 '53 C&L.477 A.B., J.D.
(adm. in NY; not adm. in DC) [Simons&S.]
Simons, Serena Gray ... '50 '84 C&L.228 B.A., J.D. [Miller&C.]
*PRACTICE AREAS: ERISA; Executive Compensation; Health Benefits; Qualified Retirement Plans.
Simons & Simons ... 5025 Linnean Ave., N.W.
Simonsen, Jan E. ... '60 '88 C.588 B.S. L.1194 J.D. [Carr G.]
*PRACTICE AREAS: Litigation; Products Liability.
Simonyi, Juli Z. ... '71 '97 C.401 B.A. L.776 J.D. [Ⓐ Eccleston&W.]
*PRACTICE AREAS: Litigation; Insurance Defense.
Simowitz, Lee H., (AV) ... '46 '73 C.309 B.A. L.976 J.D. [Baker&H.]
*PRACTICE AREAS: Litigation; Antitrust and Trade Regulation.
Simpich, Frederick, (AV) ... '31 '61 C&L.813 A.B., LL.B. [Cameron&H.]
*PRACTICE AREAS: International Business Law; Commercial Real Estate; Insurance; Reinsurance; Nonprofit Organizations Law.
Simpkins, John L. ... '70 '00 C.309 A.B. L.228 J.D. [Ⓐ Baach R.&L.P.]
Simpkins, Mary N. ... '56 '81 C.880 B.S. L.893 J.D. 450 5th St., N.W., Rm. 10108
Simpson, Alan K., (AV) '31 '58 C&L.972 B.S., J.D.
(adm. in WY; not adm. in DC) [Burg S.E.H.&J.] (⊙Englewood, CO)
Simpson, Amy E. '74 '00 C.336 B.S. L.1218 J.D.
(adm. in UT; not adm. in DC) [Ⓐ Sughrue M.]
*PRACTICE AREAS: Patent Prosecution; Patent Litigation.
Simpson, Angela M. '72 '00 C.446 B.A. L.880 J.D.
(adm. in NY; not adm. in DC) [Ⓐ Squire,S.&D.]
Simpson, C. Kristopher ... '72 '97 C.446 B.S. L.273 J.D. [Ⓐ Holland&K.]
*PRACTICE AREAS: Corporate Law; Health Care Law.
Simpson, Charles J., Jr. ... '51 '79 C.860 B.A. L.276 J.D. [Zuckert,S.&R.]
*PRACTICE AREAS: Antitrust; Aviation Law; Commercial Litigation; International Law.
Simpson, D. Brian ... '72 '99 C.651 B.A. L.201 J.D. Ben Franklin Station
Simpson, Deborah ... '65 '95 C.222 B.A. L.564 J.D. Institute for Jus.
Simpson, Erica Sapper '75 '00 C.59 B.A. L.30 J.D.
(adm. in MD; not adm. in DC) [Ⓐ Shaw P.]
*PRACTICE AREAS: Litigation.
Simpson, James D. ... '28 '52 C&L.494 B.S.L., LL.B. 4200 Massachusetts Ave., N.W.‡
Simpson, John M., (AV) ... '50 '79 C.309 A.B. L.178 J.D. [Fulbright&J.]
*PRACTICE AREAS: Federal Administrative Law; Arbitration; Commercial Litigation; College and University Law; Employment Litigation.
Simpson, Michael D. '50 '75
C.198 B.A. L.280 J.D. Asst. Gen. Coun., NEA Office of Gen. Coun.
Simpson, Richard A. ... '52 '78 C.918 B.A. L.575 J.D. [Ross,D.&B.]
Simpson, Steven M. ... '64 '96 C.222 B.A. L.564 J.D. [Ⓐ Shearman&S.]
*PRACTICE AREAS: Litigation.

Simpson, Gary Howard
(See Bethesda, Maryland)

Sims, Dawn M. '70 '96 C&L.329 E.E., J.D.
(adm. in MD; not adm. in DC) [Ⓐ Pepper H.]
*PRACTICE AREAS: Intellectual Property; Patents.
Sims, Edgar H., Jr. (P.C.), (AV) ... '41 '65 C.108 A.B. L.228 LL.B. [Long A.&N.] ⊙
*PRACTICE AREAS: Banks; Banking; Finance; Government Affairs; Municipal Law.
Sims, James R., III ... '60 '86 C.323 B.A. L.273 J.D. [Morgan,L.&B.]
Sims, Joe, (AV) ... '44 '70 C&L.36 B.S., J.D. [Jones,D.R.&P.]
*PRACTICE AREAS: Antitrust and Trade Regulation; Business Combinations; Telecommunications Competition; Internet Law.
Sims, Nathaniel '42 '92 C.378 B.S. L.276 J.D.
(adm. in PA; not adm. in DC) 1912 Spruce Dr. NW

Sims, Roberta Willis '54 '81 C.302 B.A. L.276 J.D.
V.P. & Corp. Rel., Washington Gas Light Co.
Sims, Savalle C. ... '70 '95 C.823 B.S. L.602 J.D. [Ⓐ Arent F.K.P.&K.]
*PRACTICE AREAS: Domestic Relations; Civil Litigation.
Sims-Taylor, Lynne '— '95 C.228 B.A. L.608 J.D.
(adm. in NY; not adm. in DC) 5301 Wisconsin Ave. NW, Ste. 740
Sinai, Tom K. '71 '00 C.445 B.S. L.285 J.D.
(adm. in MD; not adm. in DC) [Ⓐ Technology]
Sinclair, Howard V. ... '52 '78 C.696 B.A. L.273 J.D. [Arent F.K.P.&K.]
*PRACTICE AREAS: Litigation; Commercial Transactions.
Sinder, Scott ... '63 '89 C&L.477 A.B., J.D. [Collier S.S.]
*PRACTICE AREAS: Litigation; Government Relations; Trade Association Law; Election Law.
Sinderbrand, Paul J., (AV) ... '53 '79 C.178 B.A. L.276 J.D. [Wilkinson B.K.]
*PRACTICE AREAS: Communications; Telecommunications Law; Corporate; Commercial Transactions; Appellate Practice.
Sindler, Michael H. ... '43 '68 C&L.276 B.S.F.S., J.D. 4548 Linnean Ave., N.W.
Sindt, Robert H. ... '50 '75 C&L.546 B.S., J.D. 1850 M St., N.W.
Sinel, Norman M., (AV) ... '41 '67 C.976 B.A. L.813 LL.B. [Arnold&P.]
*PRACTICE AREAS: Telecommunications.
Singer, Bonnie J. ... '56 '82 C.112 B.A. L.276 J.D. 1666 Connecticut Ave., N.W.
Singer, Craig D. ... '67 '94 C.918 B.A. L.145 J.D. [Ⓐ Williams&C.]
*PRACTICE AREAS: Appellate Practice; Civil Practice; Constitutional Law; Criminal Law; Litigation.
Singer, Daniel M., (AV) ... '30 '56 C.821 B.A. L.976 LL.B. [Ⓒ Fried,F.H.S.&J.]
Singer, Eric H. ... '61 '97 C.178 B.A. L.1356 J.D. [Ⓐ Keller&H.]
*PRACTICE AREAS: Litigation; Product Safety.
Singer, Erika K. ... '70 '94 C.475 B.A. L.145 J.D. [Ⓒ Wilmer,C.&P.]
Singer, Joel ... '50 '78 L.999 LL.B. [Sidley A.B.&W.]
Singer, Leonard H. '58 '84 C.1044 B.A. L.107 J.D.
(adm. in NY; not adm. in DC) [Couch W.] ⊙
*PRACTICE AREAS: Energy Law; Telecommunications Law; Commercial Litigation.
Singer, Linda R., (AV) ... '41 '68 C.681 A.B. L.273 J.D. [Lichtman,T.S.&R.]
Singer, Nancy, (AV) '48 '76 C.188 B.S. L.569 J.D.
Spec. Coun., Health Industry Manufacturers Association
Singer, Nancy L. ... '53 '77 C.1155 B.S.B.A. L.831 J.D. [Ⓒ Stier,A.&M.] ⊙
*PRACTICE AREAS: Internal Investigations; Complex Litigation.
Singer, Norman H., (P.C.), (AV) ... '45 '71 C.732 A.B. L.902 J.D. [Singer&Assoc.]
Singer, Richard M. ... '46 '72 C&L.659 B.A., J.D. [Drinker B.&R.]
*PRACTICE AREAS: Telecommunications Law; Regulatory Law.
Singer, Saul J. ... '51 '90 C.102 L.446 J.D. [Bode&G.]
*PRACTICE AREAS: Litigation; Civil Litigation; Professional Discipline.
Singer, Terry E. ... '54 '94 C.104 A.B. L.273 J.D. [Ⓒ Duncan,W.G.&P.]
*PRACTICE AREAS: Energy.
Singer, Toby G., (AV) ... '52 '77 C.918 B.A. L.276 J.D. [Jones,D.R.&P.]
*PRACTICE AREAS: Antitrust and Trade Regulation; Business Combinations.
Singer & Associates, A Professional Corporation, (AV) ... 1730 K Street N.W. Suite 304
Singerman, Fredric S., (AV) ... '59 '82 C.150 B.A. L.145 J.D. [Seyfarth S.]
*PRACTICE AREAS: Employee Benefits Law; ERISA Litigation.
Singh, Jagpreet ... '70 '95 C.692 B.S. L.884 J.D. [Ⓐ Venable,A.B.H.&C.]
*PRACTICE AREAS: Corporate; Securities; Corporate Finance.
Singh, R. Nicholas ... '59 '91 C.118 B.A. L.904 J.D. [McKee N.]
*PRACTICE AREAS: Corporate; Securities.
Singh, Ranjeev ... '— '99 C.999 B.S. L.846 J.D. [Ⓐ Finnegan,H.F.G.&D.]
*PRACTICE AREAS: Intellectual Property Portfolio Management; Computer and Software Patents; Electrical Patent Prosecution; Electronic Patents; Patent Litigation.
Singiser, Dana E. ... '70 '99 C.103 B.A. L.276 J.D. [Ⓐ Akin,G.S.H.&F.]
*PRACTICE AREAS: Public Law and Policy; Legislative.
Single, William, IV '64 '90 C.367 B.A. L.446 J.D.
(adm. in MD; not adm. in DC) MCI
Singleton, Harry M. ... '49 '75 C.367 B.A. L.976 J.D. 2121 K Street, N.W.
Singleton, Kristi ... '74 '99 C.1356 B.A. L.893 J.D. [Ⓐ Dickstein S.M.&O.]
*PRACTICE AREAS: Contracts; Labor and Employment.
Singleton, Paul L., Jr. ... '59 '99 C.500 B.A. L.1218 J.D. Shaw Pittman
Singleton, P.L. Skip, Jr. ... '59 '99 C.500 B.A. L.1218 J.D. [Ⓐ Shaw P.]
Singleton, Sarah P. ... '74 '00 C.477 B.A. L.245 J.D. [Ⓐ Arter&H.]
*PRACTICE AREAS: Real Estate.
Singley, Mark A. ... '61 '87 C.945 B.A. L.813 J.D. [Singley&B.]
*PRACTICE AREAS: Antitrust; Trade Regulation; Telecommunications Law.

Singley & Beal, P.L.L.C.
1730 Rhode Island Avenue, N.W., Suite 806, 20036
Telephone: 202-463-3090 Fax: 202-463-3095
URL: http://www.lawyers.com/singley&beallaw
Mark A. Singley; W. Ashby Beal, Jr.
Antitrust and Trade Regulation, Telecommunications Law.
See Professional Biographies, WASHINGTON, DISTRICT OF COLUMBIA

Sinha, Pankaj K. ... '64 '90 C.178 A.B. L.276 J.D. [Skadden,A.S.M.&F.]
Sinick, Marshall Sanford, (AV) ... '42 '68 C.94 B.A. L.1119 J.D. [Squire,S.&D.]
*PRACTICE AREAS: Business Counseling; Litigation; Regulatory Affairs; Aviation.
Sinkfield, Richard H., III ... '69 '94 C.276 B.S.F.S. L.309 J.D. [Ⓐ Sidley A.B.&W.]
Sinn, Leroy G. ... '25 '56 C.879 A.B. L.345 J.D. 1850 M St., N.W. (Pat.)
Sinowitz, Betty E. ... '— '89 C.994 B.A. L.1234 J.D. 4200 Cathedral Ave. NW
Sinrod & Tash ... 2201 Wisconsin Ave., N.W.
Sipe, Samuel M., Jr., (AV) ... '45 '78 C.674 A.B. L.976 J.D. [Steptoe&J.]
*PRACTICE AREAS: Antitrust Law; Railway/Railroad Law; Regulatory Law; Commercial Arbitration.
Sipes, Christopher N. ... '65 '92 C&L.309 A.B., J.D. [Covington&B.] (See Pat. Sect.)
Sipes, Grail Peyton Walsh ... '63 '95 C.976 B.A. L.309 J.D. [Ⓐ Covington&B.]
Sipple, John M., Jr., (AV) ... '46 '73 C.665 B.A. L.446 J.D. [Ⓒ Clifford C.R.&W.]
*PRACTICE AREAS: Antitrust; HSR Premerger Notification; International Merger Notification.
Sira, Serge ... '61 '99 C.025 Ph.D. L.446 J.D. [Ⓐ Pennie&E.] (See Pat. Sect.)
*PRACTICE AREAS: Intellectual Property.
Siracusa, Richard A., (BV) '42 '75 C.884 B.S. L.564 J.D.
5425 Connecticut Ave., N.W. (⊙New York, NY)
Sirignano, David A. ... '53 '79 C.433 B.A. L.982 J.D. [Morgan,L.&B.]
Sirmans, Tara C. ... '68 '95 C.259 B.S. L.1158 J.D. [Ⓐ Kirkpatrick&L.]
*PRACTICE AREAS: Taxation.
Sirulnik, Eric S. ... '44 '69 C.264 B.A. L.94 J.D. Assoc. Prof. of Law, G. Wash. Univ.
Sisitsky, Mark K. ... '45 '71 C.197 B.A. L.477 J.D. [Jones,D.R.&P.]
*PRACTICE AREAS: Structured Finance; Derivative Products.
Sisk, Marcus W., Jr., (AV) ... '40 '65 C.813 B.A. L.309 LL.B. [Ⓒ Bastianelli,B.&K.]
Sisson, Edward H. ... '55 '92 C.453 B.S. L.276 J.D. [Arnold&P.]
*PRACTICE AREAS: Litigation; Government Contracts.
Sisti, Thomas R. ... '58 '85 C.188 B.S. L.564 J.D. AT&T
*RESPONSIBILITIES: Federal Procurement Law; Commercial Transactions; Appropriations Law; Advocacy Support.
Sistrunk, Karen R. ... '59 '84 C.1350 B.A. L.1009 J.D. Regulatory Atty., Sprint Corp.
Sitchman, Barton ... '48 '75 National Vets. Legal Servs. Program
Sitnick, Joseph ... '14 '35 L.537 J.D. Hearing Comr., Supr. Ct.
Sitomer, David J. ... '47 '75 C.273 B.A. L.1065 J.D. 1614 Kilbourne Pl., N.W.

Sivaprasad, Shoba '75 '00 C.347 B.A. L.276 J.D.
(adm. in MD; not adm. in DC) [Ⓐ Maggio&K.]
*PRACTICE AREAS: Immigration Law; Nationality Law.
Sivon, James C., (AV) . . . . '51 '82 C.207 B.A. L.276 J.D. [Barnett&S.]
*PRACTICE AREAS: Banking Law; Financial Institutions.
Sizer, Henry S. . . . . '33 '59 C&L.976 B.A., LL.B. Amer. Foreign Serv. Assn.
Sjoberg, William C. . . . . '60 '91 C.846 B.A. L.845 J.D. 1875 Connecticut Avenue, N.W.
Sjoquist, Mary M. . . . . '— '82 C.038 B.A. L.128 J.D. [Patton B.]
Skacel, Patrick T. '65 '01 C.21 B.S. L.262 J.D.
(adm. in NY; not adm. in DC; Pat.) [Ⓐ Dickstein S.M.&O.]
*PRACTICE AREAS: Intellectual Property.

Skadden, Arps, Slate, Meagher & Flom LLP, (AV)
1440 New York Avenue, N.W., 20005 ⊙
Telephone: 202-371-7000 Fax: 202-393-5760
URL: http://www.skadden.com
Partners: Lynn R. Coleman; Leslie J. Goldman; Douglas G. Robinson; C. Benjamin Crisman, Jr.; Michael P. Rogan; Robert E. Lighthizer; Fred T. Goldberg, Jr.; Ronald C. Barusch; Stephen W. Hamilton; William J. Sweet, Jr.; Erica A. Ward; Glenn J. Berger; Clifford M. Naeve; Martin Klepper; Paul W. Oosterhuis; Richard L. Brusca; Marcia R. Nirenstein; Robert S. Bennett; Janet L. Goetz; Alan Kriegel; Jeanine L. Matte; Carl S. Rauh; John J. Mangan; William S. Scherman; Albert H. Turkus; Kenneth Berlin; Mitchell S. Ettinger; Kenneth A. Gross; James V. Alpi; C. Kevin Barnette; Jeffrey S. Christie; Andrew L. Sandler; John C. Quale; John N. Estes, III; Clifford R. Gross; Edward J. Meehan; Pankaj K. Sinha; Colleen P. Mahoney; Lance T. Brasher; James A. Losey; Gary A. MacDonald; Stacie E. McGinn; John S. Moot; Saul M. Pilchen; Kenneth W. Gideon; Kenneth M. Kaufman; James C. Hecht; Amy R. Sabrin; Lawrence Roberts. Of Counsel: Curtis H. Barnette; Samuel H. Gillespie, III (Not admitted in DC); Philip McBride Johnson; Neal S. McCoy; Mary Lou Steptoe. Counsel: John A. Amodeo; Jody J. Brewster; June Broadstone; Gerard A. Clark; Arthur A. Cohen; Roseann M. Cutrone; Mark C. Del Bianco; Mona E. Ehlenberger; Henry C. Eisenberg; Carl R. Erdmann; Matthew W. S. Estes; Cheryl M. Foley (Not admitted in DC); James A. Frazer; Don Joaquin Frost, Jr.; David J. Hill; Richard A. Hindman; Ki P. Hong; Jerry L. Jackson; Benjamin B. Klubes; Kimberly T. Majure; Molly A. Meegan; Brian C. Mohr; Timothy J. Moran; Maureen Nelson; Leonard Rawicz; James A. Rossi; Suzanne E. Rothwell; Nancy G. Rubin; Ivan A. Schlager (Not admitted in DC); Ellen J. Schneider; Erich T. Schwartz; Frank C. Shaw; Matthew A. Stevens; Douglas W. Swalina (Not admitted in DC); Charles F. Walker. Special Counsel: Kenneth Kraus; Edward D. Ross, Jr. Associates: Eric S. Adams (Not admitted in DC); Worth S. Anderson; Katherine D. Ashley; Bonnie J. Austin; Kathryn K. Baran; Joseph L. Barloon; Kathleen L. Barron; John M. Beahn; Galen D. Bellamy (Not admitted in DC); Michael R. Bergmann; Glen S. Bernstein; Kurt W. Bilas; Sherri L. Booye; Jamie L. Boucher; Jennifer P. Brovey; Raina E. Brubaker; Eric M. Burt; Lily A. Camet; C. Grace Campbell; David E. Carney; Richard G. Castanon (Not admitted in DC); Judith A. Center; Douglas M. Chapin, Jr. (Not admitted in DC); Steven J. Cleveland (Not admitted in DC); Jodi B. Cohen (Not admitted in DC); Victor A. Contract; Deborah E. Cooper; Jill A. Cramer; Michael J. Deltergo; Gary DiBianco; Erik H. Elsea; William M. Emnett; Nicole A. Epstein (Not admitted in DC); Benga Farina; Mary Margaret Farren; Cristina M. L. Ferreira; Marc S. Gerber; Jeffrey D. Gerrish; Marc J. Gerson; Thomas A. Gilson; Holly A. Gimbel; Jeffrey A. Goldberg; Melissa M. Goldstein; David J. Goldstone; Armando Gomez; Louis D. Greenstein; Carolyn N. Guthrie; Kevin Hahm; Catharine A. Hartzenbusch; Robert John Hellewell; Babak Hoghooghi; William R. Hollaway; Jessica A. Hough; Chad S. Johnson; Julia M. Kazaks; Michael P. Kelly; Leif B. King; Daniel Kotchen; Margaret E. Lancaster; Joseph A. Laroski, Jr; Kristin Larson; Rebecca J. Levenson; Melissa F. Levine; Ellen L. Lyons; John H. Lyons; Joan M. Macaulay; Kelly D. Makins; David S. Maltz; Rachel A. Mariner; August J. Matteis, Jr.; J. Russell McGranahan; Christopher W. Meyer; Linda G. Morrison; Scott Bergan Nardi; Edwin Javiel Nazario; Joshua B. Nickerson; Sharon L. Niles-Spencer; Andrew J. O'Connell; Troy L. Olsen; David H. Pawlik; Michael R. Petitpas (Not admitted in DC); Daniel P. Phillips; Brian Pomper; Kristin L. Pruitt; Robyn C. Quattrone; Anand S. Raman; Laura Partee Regan; Gerald L. Richman; Caprice L. Roberts; Stacy R. Robinson; Peter Rundlet (Not admitted in DC); Anthony Saldana; Daniel Schneiderman; Peter M. Seka; Eric B. Sensenbrenner; Sue Bak Sheehan; Sean M. Shimamoto; Gretchen T. Sierra (Not admitted in DC); Denise A. Simmonds; Mary L. Smith (Not admitted in DC); Jennifer L. Spaziano; Ralph L. Stengren; Jamison B. Taylor; Mark B. Teerink; Jamie R. Towey (Not admitted in DC); Robert D. Tronnes (Not admitted in DC); Malcolm J. Tuesley; Christopher J. Ulery; Stephen P. Vaughn; Jennifer K. Walter; Robert W. Warnement; Brian D. Weimer; Andrew E. Weis; Paul Franklin Wight; Donna L. Wilson; Harry M. Wingo, Jr.; Andrew McCanse Wright (Not admitted in DC); Michelle A. Zamarin.
General Practice.
Firm/Affiliate Offices:
New York, New York: Four Times Square, 10036. Telephone: 212-735-3000. Fax: 212-735-2000.
Boston, Massachusetts: One Beacon Street, 02108. Telephone: 617-573-4800. Fax: 617-573-4822.
Wilmington, Delaware: One Rodney Square, P.O. Box 636, 19899. Telephone: 302-651-3000. Fax: 302-651-3001.
Los Angeles, California: 300 South Grand Avenue, 90071. Telephone: 213-687-5000. Fax: 213-687-5600.
Chicago, Illinois: Skadden, Arps, Slate, Meagher & Flom (Illinois), 333 West Wacker Drive, 60606. Telephone: 312-407-0700. Fax: 312-407-0411.
San Francisco, California: Four Embarcadero Center, 94111. Telephone: 415-984-6400. Fax: 415-984-2698.
Houston, Texas: 1600 Smith Street, Suite 4400, 77002. Telephone: 713-655-5100. Fax: 713-655-5200.
Newark, New Jersey: One Newark Center, 07102. Telephone: 973-639-6800. Fax: 973-639-6858.
Palo Alto, California: 525 University Avenue, Suite 1100, 94301. Telephone: 650-470-4500. Fax: 650-470-4570.
Reston, Virginia: 11911 Freedom Drive, Suite 550, 20190. Telephone: 703-796-2345. Fax: 703-796-2344.
Tokyo, Japan: ATT Main Tower 12F, 2-17-22, Akasaka, Minato-ku, 107-0052. Telephone: 011-813-3568-2600. Fax: 011-813-3568-2626.
London, England: One Canada Square, Canary Wharf, E14 5DS. Telephone: 011-44-20-7519-7000. Fax: 011-44-20-7519-7070.
Hong Kong, China: 30/F Tower Two, Lippo Centre, 89 Queensway, Central. Telephone: 011-852-2820-0700. Fax: 011-852-2820-0727.
Sydney, New South Wales 2000, Australia: Skadden, Arps, Slate, Meagher & Flom (International), Level 13, 131 Macquarie Street. Telephone: 011-61-2-9253-6000. Fax: 011-61-2-9253-6044.
Toronto, Ontario, Canada: Suite 1820, North Tower, P.O. Box 189, Royal Bank Plaza, M5J 2J4. Telephone: 416-777-4700. Fax: 416-777-4747.
Brussels, Belgium: 523 avenue Louise, Box 30, 1050. Telephone: 011-32-2-639-0300. Fax: 011-32-2-639-0339.
Frankfurt am Main, Germany: MesseTurm, 27th Floor, 60308. Telephone: 011-49-69-742200. Fax: 011-49-69-74220300.
Paris, France: 68, rue du Faubourg Saint-Honoré, 75008. Telephone: 011-331-55-27-11-00. Fax: 011-331-55-27-11-99.
Beijing, China: East Wing Office, Level 4, China World Trade Center, No. 1, Jian Guo Men Wai Avenue, 100004. Telephone: 011-86-10-6505-5511. Fax: 011-86-10-6505-5522.
Moscow, Russia: Degtyarniy Pereulok 4, Building 1, 103009. Telephone: 011-7-501-797-4600. Fax: 011-7-501-797-4601.
Singapore, Singapore: Skadden, Arps, Slate, Meagher & Flom (International), 9 Temasek Boulevard, Suite 29-01, Suntec Tower Two, 038989. Telephone: 011-65-434-2900. Fax: 011-65-434-2988.
See Professional Biographies, WASHINGTON, DISTRICT OF COLUMBIA

Skaggs, David E. . . . . '43 '68 C.918 B.A. L.976 LL.B. [© Hogan&H.] (⊙Denver, CO)
*PRACTICE AREAS: Legislative; Government Relations; Nonprofit and Charitable Organizations.
Skalaban, Paula Primost . . . . '72 '97 C.659 B.A. L.309 J.D. [Ⓐ Hogan&H.]
*PRACTICE AREAS: Insurance Coverage Litigation; Litigation.
Skalaban, Peter J., Jr. . . . . '69 '94 C.659 B.A. L.273 J.D. [Ⓐ Spriggs&H.]
*PRACTICE AREAS: Government Contracts; Construction Law; Litigation.
Skalet, Steven A., (AV) . . . . '46 '72 C.696 B.A. L.659 J.D. [Kass&S.]
Skall, Gregg P., (AV) . . . . '44 '69 C.608 B.S. L.150 J.D. [Pepper&C.]
*PRACTICE AREAS: International Telecommunications Law; Communications Common Carrier; Broadcast Radio; Telecommunications Licensing; Telecommunications Regulation.
Skancke, Nancy J., (AV) . . . . '50 '75 C.679 B.S. L.273 J.D. [GKRSE]
*PRACTICE AREAS: Energy Law; Commercial Law; Natural Gas Regulations; Hydroelectric Licensing; Public Utilities Regulation.
Skeen, Joseph Ike '66 '96 C.904 LL.M. L.055 J.D.
(adm. in NY; not adm. in DC) 1730 K. St. N.W.

Skelly, Paul C., (AV) . . . . '53 '79 C&L.893 B.A., J.D. [Hogan&H.]
*PRACTICE AREAS: Employment Law; Litigation.
Skelton, Meghan S. '70 '95 C.228 A.B. L.945 J.D.
(adm. in VA; not adm. in DC) [Ⓐ Vinson&E.]
Skene, G. Neil, Jr. '51 '77 C.880 B.A. L.469 J.D.
(adm. in GA; not adm. in DC) Congressional Quarterly, Inc.
Skerpon, Joseph M. . . . . '— '82 C.674 B.S.E. L.107 J.D. [Banner&W.] (See Pat. Sect.)
*PRACTICE AREAS: Intellectual Property Law; Patents; Biotechnology; Pharmaceutical Intellectual Property; Chemical Intellectual Property.
Skidmore, Matthew L. . . . . '71 '00 C.878 B.A. L.659 J.D. [Ⓐ Fried,F.H.S.&J.]
*PRACTICE AREAS: Corporate Law.
Skiles, James H., (AV) '44 '69 C.197 A.B. L.276 J.D.
V.P. & Gen. Coun., Grocery Manufacturers of America
Skillington, G. Lee . . . . '50 '81 C.645 B.S. L.273 J.D. [© Powell,G.F.&M.]
*PRACTICE AREAS: Intellectual Property.
Skilton, John S., (AV) . . . '— '69 C&L.966 B.A., J.D. [Heller E.W.&M.] (⊙Madison, WI)
*PRACTICE AREAS: Commercial and Intellectual Property Litigation.
Skilton, Thomas E. . . . . '66 '93 C.197 B.A. L.188 J.D. [Ⓐ Squire,S.&D.]
Skinner, Darren C. . . . . '65 '95 L.999 LL.B. [Ⓐ Arnold&P.]
*PRACTICE AREAS: International; Corporate.
Skinner, Laurence E., (BV) '56 '84 C.945 B.B.A. L.692 J.D.
(adm. in VA; not adm. in DC) [Hunton&W.]
*PRACTICE AREAS: Energy; Project Finance and Development.
Skinner, Raquel Cheatham . . . . '71 '98 C.811 B.A. L.659 J.D. [Ⓐ Womble C.S.&R.]
*PRACTICE AREAS: Real Estate.
Skinner, William P., (AV) . . . . '51 '76 C&L.309 B.A., J.D. [Covington&B.]
Skitol, Robert A., (AV) . . . . '46 '70 C.319 B.A. L.569 J.D. [Drinker B.&R.]
*PRACTICE AREAS: Antitrust; Litigation.
Skladany, Barney J., Jr. . . . . '45 '70 C.705 B.A. L.273 J.D. [Akin,G.S.H.&F.]
*PRACTICE AREAS: Public Policy.
Skladany, Linda Arey . . . . '44 '77 C.945 B.A. L.692 J.D. [Ⓐ Parry&R.]
Sklar, Morton H. . . . '40 '64 C.569 A.B. L.976 LL.B. Catholic Univ. of Amer. Law School
Sklover, Beverly Jacks Schwarz '47 '85 C.576 B.A. L.128 J.D.
4504 Albemarle St., N.W.
Skolnick, Cory J. '75 '00 C.674 A.B. L.228 J.D.
(adm. in VA; not adm. in DC) [Ⓐ Gibson,D.&C.]
Skowronek, Andrew Dieter . . . . '71 '98 C.951 B.A. L.273 J.D. [Ⓐ Fried,F.H.S.&J.]
*PRACTICE AREAS: Civil Fraud; Commercial Litigation.
Skubel, Marimichael O. . . . . '55 '79 C.651 B.A. L.128 J.D. [Kirkland&E.]
*PRACTICE AREAS: Antitrust.
Skucas, Ruta Kalvaitis . . . . '71 '98 C.93 B.A. L.94 J.D. [Ⓐ White&C.]
Skwierawski, Audrey '67 '92 C.597 B.S. L.276 J.D.
(adm. in WI; not adm. in DC) 1300 L St., N.W.
Slade, Kenneth H. . . . . '55 '79 C.674 A.B. L.178 J.D. [Hale&D.]
*PRACTICE AREAS: Corporate Law.
Slade, Shelley R. . . . . '58 '85 C.674 B.A. L.813 J.D. [Vogel&S.]
*PRACTICE AREAS: False Claims Act; Litigation; Health Care Fraud; Health Care Compliance.
Slade, William E. . . . . '59 '84 C.732 B.A. L.1194 J.D. [Patton B.]
Slaight, Joanne D., (AV) . . . . '53 '80 C.1044 B.A. L.128 J.D. 305 H St., N.W.
Slaiman, Gary D. . . . . '56 '81 C&L.893 B.A., J.D. [Swidler B.S.F.]
*PRACTICE AREAS: Antitrust Law; Governmental Affairs; Communications and Media; Intellectual Property.
Slamowitz, Todd R. . . . . '66 '94 C.966 B.S. L.128 J.D. [Ⓐ Lukas,N.G.&S.]
*PRACTICE AREAS: FCC Regulation; FCC Licensing; Telecommunications Law.
Slater, Marcus B., Jr., (AV) . . . . '39 '69 C.228 B.A. L.30 J.D. [Slater&Z.]
*PRACTICE AREAS: Government Contracts; Shipbuilding Contracts; Litigation; Complex Commercial Litigation; Maritime.
Slater, Matthew D. . . . . '57 '84 C.309 A.B. L.145 J.D. [Cleary,G.S.&H.]
Slater, Rodney E. '55 '80 C.476 B.S. L.45 J.D.
(adm. in AR; not adm. in DC) [Patton B.]
Slater, Valerie A., (AV) . . . . '52 '77 C.25 B.A. L.128 J.D. [Akin,G.S.H.&F.]
*PRACTICE AREAS: International Trade.

Slater & Zeien, L.L.P., (AV)
1030 Fifteenth Street, N.W., Suite 300, 20005
Telephone: 202-467-5900 Fax: 202-467-4045
Marcus B. Slater, Jr.; Jennifer J. Zeien. Of Counsel: Leonard Egan; Frederick C. Williams.
Government Contracts, Government Procurement, International Government Contracts, Federal Contracts, Shipbuilding and Repair, Maritime Contracts, Shipyard Litigation, Complex Commercial Litigation, Maritime and Shipping Regulation Law, Ship Financing, Environmental Law, Transportation Law, Intellectual Property.
See Professional Biographies, WASHINGTON, DISTRICT OF COLUMBIA

Slattery, Jim . . . . '48 '75 C&L.900 B.S., J.D. [Wiley R.&F.]
*PRACTICE AREAS: Government Affairs; International Trade; Energy.
Slattery, Michael J. . . . . '67 '99 C.128 B.M.E. L.273 J.D. [Ⓐ Dickstein S.M.&O.]
*PRACTICE AREAS: Government Contracts.
Slattery, Richard G. '58 '85 C.821 B.A. L.893 J.D.
Sr. Assoc. Gen. Coun., Litig., National Railroad Passenger Corp. (AMTRAK)
Slattery, Thomas K. . . . . '55 '89 C.1070 B.S. L.273 J.D. [Arter&H.]
Slaughter, James B., (AV) . . . . '60 '87 C.976 B.A. L.178 J.D. [Beveridge&D.]
*PRACTICE AREAS: Environmental Litigation; Toxic Tort; Superfund; Civil Litigation; Criminal Defense.
Slaughter, Kenneth S. . . . . '51 '76 C.103 A.B. L.276 J.D. [Venable,A.B.H.&C.]
*PRACTICE AREAS: State Government Law; Local Government Law; Corporate Law; Health Care; Hospital Law.
Slaughter, Ruth N. . . . . '11 '41 L.904 LL.B. 5206 Manning Pl., N.W.‡
Slavit, Howard G., (AV) . . . . '46 '73 C.860 B.A. L.273 J.D. [Slavit&G.]

Slavit & Gill, P.C., (AV)
1025 Thomas Jefferson Street, N.W. Suite 425 West, 20007
Telephone: 202-342-1402 Telecopier: 202-342-8387
Email: OFFICE@SLAVITGILL.COM
Howard G. Slavit; Robert C. Gill, II;—Jonathan M. Kaye; H. David Starr; Melissa A. Zeller (Not admitted in DC); Kristie G. Haynes.
Commercial Litigation and Arbitration, Corporate, Commercial Transactions, Distribution and Marketing, Technology, Media, Trademark and Copyright, Aviation, Real Estate, Government Contracts and Practice before the U.S. Departments of Transportation, Treasury and Commerce, Federal Aviation Administration, Patent and Trademark Office, Copyright Office, General Accounting Office and other departments and agencies.
See Professional Biographies, WASHINGTON, DISTRICT OF COLUMBIA

Slawson, Kurt T. . . . . '66 '94 C.293 B.A. L.477 J.D. [Ⓐ McGuirewoods]
*PRACTICE AREAS: Employee Benefits; Executive Compensation.
Slear, James D. . . . . '57 '92 C.249 B.A. L.276 J.D. [Ⓐ Gibson,D.&C.]
*PRACTICE AREAS: Litigation; Government Contracts; Antitrust.
Slease, Clyde H., III . . . . '44 '69 C.228 A.B. L.665 J.D. [DKW] (⊙Pitts., PA)
Slee, Malcolm C. . . . . '72 '99 C.860 B.A. L.276 J.D. [Ⓐ Slevin&H.]
*PRACTICE AREAS: Employee Benefits.
Slevin, Barry S., (AV) . . . . '51 '75 C.823 A.B. L.1009 J.D. [Slevin&H.]
*PRACTICE AREAS: Employee Benefits.
Slevin, Patrick J. . . . . '61 '88 C&L.276 A.B., J.D. [Ⓐ Patton B.]

Slevin & Hart, P.C., (AV) **BB**
1625 Massachusetts Avenue, N.W., Suite 450, 20036
Telephone: 202-797-8700 Fax: 202-234-8231
Email: slevinhart.com
Barry S. Slevin; Thomas J. Hart; Fredrick M. Marx; Jeffrey S. Endick; Marc H. Rifkind; Sharon McNeilly Goodman; Allison A. Madan;—Beth A. Bangert (Not admitted in DC); Lynn A. Bowers; Rhea A. Lagano (Not admitted in DC); Debra L. Petcove; Colleen R. Robertson; Malcolm C. Slee; Laura Barton Stack; Sarah E. Suhre; Marc A. Tenenbaum; Jennifer C. Wiseman.
Employee Benefits Law and Litigation.
See Professional Biographies, WASHINGTON, DISTRICT OF COLUMBIA

Slipakoff, Pam Faith .... '74 '99 C.860 B.A. L.273 J.D. The Fed. Communications Comm.
Sliter, Charles E. .... '49 '74 C.602 B.A. L.276 J.D. [Ⓒ Venable,A.B.H.&C.]
*PRACTICE AREAS: Hotel and Resort Law; Corporate Transactions; Commercial Finance; Financial Institution Regulation.
Sloame, Stuart C. .... '39 '64 C&L.178 B.A., LL.B. 4508 28th St., N.W.
Sloan, Amy E. .... '64 '93 C.846 B.A. L.273 J.D. Assoc. Prof., George Washington Univ.
Sloan, Catherine R. ..... '56 '82 C.262 B.A. L.276 J.D. V.P., Congressional Rel., Comptel
Sloan, E. Ned .... '35 '72 C.980 B.A. L.128 J.D. [Sloan&Assoc.]
Sloan, Edith .... '38 '74 [Ⓐ Sloan&Assoc.]
Sloan, Laurie Anne '75 '01 C.228 A.B. L.276 J.D.
(adm. in VA; not adm. in DC) 1440 New York Avenue
Sloan, Leonard A., (AV) .... '40 '68 C.30 B.S. L.273 J.D. [Friedlander,M.S.K.&O.]
*PRACTICE AREAS: Banking; Real Estate; Commercial Law; Corporate Law.
Sloan, Michael C. .... '65 '95 C.976 B.A. L.966 J.D. [Ⓐ Swidler B.S.F.]
*PRACTICE AREAS: Telecommunications Litigation.
Sloan, Richard S. .... '52 '76 C&L.608 B.A., J.D. Pres., Challenge Amer., Inc.
Sloan, Robert V., (P.C.), (AV) '33 '64 C.1031 B.S. L.64 LL.B.
(adm. in MD; not adm. in DC; See Pat. Sect.) [Sughrue M.]
*PRACTICE AREAS: Intellectual Property Law.
Sloan & Associates, P.C. .... 7600 Georgia Ave., N.W.
Sloane, Adam C. .... '58 '93 C.311 B.A. L.477 J.D. [Ⓒ Mayer,B.&P.]
Slobasky, Michael R., (AV) '45 '72
C.912 B.S.E.E. L.273 J.D. [Jacobson,H.] (See Pat. Sect.)
*PRACTICE AREAS: Intellectual Property Law; Electrical Patents; Mechanical Patents.
Slobodin, Alan M. '57 '84 C.831 B.B.A. L.273 J.D.
Pres. & Gen. Coun., Legal Studies Div., Washington Legal Found.
Slocombe, Walter B. .... '41 '70 C.674 A.B. L.309 LL.B. [Caplin&D.]
*PRACTICE AREAS: Civil Litigation; Tax Exempt Organizations.
Slomowitz, Alan .... '51 '80 C.966 B.A. L.1019 J.D. [Greenberg T.]
Sloniewsky, Andrew J. .... '65 '91 C.722 B.A. L.145 J.D. [Ⓐ Steptoe&J.]
Slovak, Dorothy C. .... '58 '00 C.397 B.S. L.128 J.D. [Ⓐ Holland&K.]
*PRACTICE AREAS: Litigation; Government Contracts.
Slover, William L., (AV) .... '37 '62 C.976 A.B. L.178 LL.B. [Slover&L.]

Slover & Loftus, (AV)
1224 Seventeenth Street, N.W., 20036
Telephone: 202-347-7170 Telecopier: 202-347-3619
Email: info@sloverandloftus.com URL: http://www.sloverandloftus.com
William L. Slover; C. Michael Loftus; Donald G. Avery; John H. LeSeur; Kelvin J. Dowd; Robert D. Rosenberg; Christopher A. Mills; Frank J. Pergolizzi;—Andrew B. Kolesar III; Peter A. Pfohl; Daniel M. Jaffe; Karen Hassell Herren.
Administrative Law. Practice before Federal and State Courts, Commissions, Departments and Agencies. Commercial Arbitration, Transportation, Utility, Energy, Trade Regulation, Commercial Contracts, Government Contracts and Legislative Law.
See Professional Biographies, WASHINGTON, DISTRICT OF COLUMBIA

Slowinski, Richard L. .... '65 '91 C.105 B.A. L.128 J.D. [Baker&M.]
*PRACTICE AREAS: Tax Controversies (Corporate and International); Tax Planning and Advice (Corporate and International).
Smail, David W. .... '65 '91 C.429 B.A. L.309 J.D. [Hogan&H.]
*PRACTICE AREAS: Commercial Law.
Small, Daniel A. .... '59 '87 C.165 B.A. L.904 J.D. [Cohen,M.H.&T.]
*PRACTICE AREAS: Antitrust; Class Actions; Complex and Multi-District Litigation.
Small, Joseph T., Jr., (AV) .... '47 '75 C.902 B.A. L.893 J.D. [Fulbright&J.]
*PRACTICE AREAS: White Collar Crime; General Litigation; Export Regulation; Administrative Law.
Small, Michael E., (AV) .... '54 '79 C.893 B.S. L.1162 J.D. [Wright&T.]
*PRACTICE AREAS: Energy.
Smalley, Ruth '15 '46 C.347 A.B. L.1119 J.D.
(adm. in IN; not adm. in DC) 5361 Sherier Pl., N.W.‡
Smelkinson, Lynn M. '— '82 C.273 B.S. L.767 J.D.
Assoc. Gen. Coun., Corp. Affrs., National Railroad Passenger Corp. (AMTRAK)
Smetana & Avakian
1919 Pennsylvania Ave., N.W. (⊙Chgo., IL; North Springfield, VA)
Smethurst, Ryan S. '71 '99 C.188 B.A. L.1209 J.D.
(adm. in MD; not adm. in DC) [Ⓐ McDermott,W.&E.]
Smilack, Stanley .... '48 '74 C.453 S.B. L.477 J.D. [Ⓒ Steptoe&J.]
*PRACTICE AREAS: Taxation.
Smiley, Eileen M. '59 '89 C.855 B.A. L.1067 J.D.
(adm. in CA; not adm. in DC) [Ⓒ Morrison&F.]
*PRACTICE AREAS: Investment Management.
Smiley, Stafford, (AV) .... '48 '76 C.976 B.A. L.309 J.D. [Caplin&D.]
*PRACTICE AREAS: Federal Tax Practice; Estate Planning.
Smith, Abbe .... '56 '89 C.976 B.A. L.569 J.D. Prof. of Law, Georgetown Univ.
Smith, Andrew MacGregor .... '65 '94 C.951 B.A. L.945 J.D. [Ⓐ Lovells]
*PRACTICE AREAS: Consumer Financial Services; Privacy Law; Federal Regulatory Compliance.
Smith, Anne D. .... '50 '76 C.823 B.A. L.276 J.D. [Ⓒ White&C.]
*PRACTICE AREAS: Federal Administrative Law; Civil Litigation; Foreign Sovereign Immunities Act; International Arbitration.
Smith, Barbara Lee .... '44 '85 C&L.329 B.A., J.D. [O'Brien&L.]
*PRACTICE AREAS: Civil (General Civil) Law; Landlord and Tenant Law; Domestic Law; Probate; Divorce.
Smith, Bernard L. .... '69 '94 C.823 B.S.CE L.273 J.D. [Ⓐ Holland&K.]
*PRACTICE AREAS: Commercial Real Estate Development; Hotel and Resort Development; Condominium Development; Timeshare Development; Finance.
Smith, Bradley P. .... '70 '98 C.691 B.A. L.976 J.D. [Ⓐ Sullivan&C.]
Smith, Brenda Denise '74 '99 C.78 B.A. L.200 J.D.
(adm. in VA; not adm. in DC) 1350 Connecticut Ave.
Smith, Brenda V. .... '59 '85 C.811 B.A. Sr. Coun., National Women's Law Center
Smith, Brian W. .... '47 '72 C&L.724 B.A., J.D. [Mayer,B.&P.]
Smith, C. William .... '42 '75 L.30 J.D. [Lee&S.]
*PRACTICE AREAS: Federal Legislative Practice; Administrative Law.
Smith, Carey W. .... '69 '96 C.31 A.B. L.976 J.D. [Ⓐ Arnold&P.]
*PRACTICE AREAS: Tax; Real Estate.
Smith, Carl M. .... '48 '74 C.893 B.A. L.276 J.D. [Higgins,M.&S.]
Smith, Caroline C. .... '69 '97 C.902 B.S. L.30 J.D. [Ⓐ Shaw P.]
Smith, Carrie L. ...'68 '93 C.740 B.A. L.284 J.D. [Ⓐ Dillon,H.&L.] (⊙Stuttgart, Germany)
Smith, Chad '67 '96 C.494 B.S. L.1018 J.D.
(adm. in MN; not adm. in DC) [Ⓐ Oppenheimer W.&D.]
*PRACTICE AREAS: Intellectual Property.
Smith, Charles D., IV '41 '73 C.604 A.B. L.94 J.D.
(adm. in MA; not adm. in DC) Institute of Peace
Smith, Charles R. .... '48 '74 C.273 B.A. L.802 J.D. 1428 Webster St., N.W.

Smith, Chesterfield, (AV) '17 '48 C&L.260 J.D.
2100 Pennsylvania Ave., N.W. (⊙Miami, FL)
Smith, Christopher, (AV) .... '47 '72 C.894 A.B. L.378 J.D. [Arent F.K.P.&K.]
*PRACTICE AREAS: Administrative Law; Commercial Law; Antitrust; Trade Regulation; Environmental Law.
Smith, Christopher '76 '01 C.309 A.B. L.276 J.D.
(adm. in VA; not adm. in DC) [Ⓐ Dechert]
*PRACTICE AREAS: Investment Management; Financial Services Law.
Smith, Christopher D. '76 '01 C.309 A.B. L.276 J.D.
(adm. in VA; not adm. in DC) 1775 Eye St. N.W.
Smith, Clarence A. .... '21 '62 C&L.329 LL.B. 1807 Potomac Ave., S.E.‡
Smith, Colby A. .... '56 '88 C.878 B.S. L.178 J.D. [Debevoise&P.]
*PRACTICE AREAS: Securities Law; Federal and State Election Law; Intellectual Property Litigation.
Smith, Corinne E. .... '55 '87 C.788 B.A. L.93 J.D. Housing Investment Trust
Smith, D. Jacques .... '66 '91 C.425 B.A. L.420 J.D. [Ⓐ Arent F.K.P.&K.]
*PRACTICE AREAS: Complex Commercial Litigation; Intellectual Property; Health Care Fraud Litigation; White Collar Litigation; Military Law.
Smith, Daniel B. '72 '01 C.367 B.A. L.276 J.D.
(adm. in MD; not adm. in DC) [Ⓐ O'Donnell,S.&A.]
Smith, Daniel C. .... '45 '74 C.668 B.A. L.309 J.D. V.P. & Dep. Gen. Coun., Fannie Mae
*RESPONSIBILITIES: Mortgage Finance.
Smith, Daniel C. .... '36 '66 C.37 B.S. L.30 J.D. 1815 H St. N.W., Ste. 1001
Smith, Darlene H. '70 '97 C.893 B.A. L.823 J.D.
(adm. in MD; not adm. in DC) [Ⓐ Ford&H.]
*PRACTICE AREAS: Employment Law; Employment Litigation; Labor Law.
Smith, David C., Jr. .... '59 '87 C.732 B.A. L.276 J.D. [Ⓒ Collier S.S.]
*PRACTICE AREAS: International Trade Law; Customs Law.
Smith, David F. .... '53 '81 C.288 B.A. L.273 J.D. [Sher&B.]
*PRACTICE AREAS: Transportation; Litigation; Administrative Law; Maritime Law.
Smith, David F. B. .... '52 '77 C&L.276 B.S.F.S., J.D. [Ryberg&S.]
Smith, David L. .... '60 '88 C.216 B.A. L.94 J.D. [Ⓒ Schmeltzer,A.&S.]
*PRACTICE AREAS: Franchise Law; Employment Litigation; White Collar Defense.
Smith, Delbert D. .... '40 '69 C&L.959 B.S., J.D. [Dorsey&W.]
*PRACTICE AREAS: Telecommunications Law; International Law; Space Law; Satellite Law.
Smith, DeMaurice F., (AV) .... '— '89 C.130 B.S. L.893 J.D. [Latham&W.]
*PRACTICE AREAS: White Collar Criminal Defense; Computer Crime; Trial Practice; Litigation; Grand Jury Practice.
Smith, Derek C. '62 '88 C&L.893 B.A., J.D.
(adm. in VA; not adm. in DC) 1875 Connecticut Avenue, N.W.
Smith, Diann L. '63 '91 C.473 B.A. L.276 J.D.
(adm. in NY; not adm. in DC) 122 C. St., N.W.
Smith, Donald H. .... '60 '85 C.347 B.A. L.597 J.D. [Ⓒ Sidley A.B.&W.]
Smith, Donald S. .... '28 '55 C.390 A.B. L.262 LL.B. Supr. Ct. J.
Smith, Donald W., (AV) .... '— '78 C.976 B.A. L.893 J.D. [Kirkpatrick&L.]
*PRACTICE AREAS: Banking Regulation; Securities Regulation; Investment Company Law; Export Regulation.
Smith, Douglas W. .... '59 '87 C.453 S.B. L.976 J.D. [Van Ness F.]
Smith, Duncan C., III, (AV) .... '47 '76 C.222 B.A. L.945 J.D. [Dyer E.&J.]
*PRACTICE AREAS: Legislative Practice; Lobbying; Regulatory Law.
Smith, Dwight C., III .... '55 '82 C&L.976 B.A., J.D. [Ⓒ Alston&B.]
*PRACTICE AREAS: Banking; Electronic Banking; Privacy; Bank Mergers and Acquisitions; Bank Holding Company Regulation.
Smith, Edward J., Jr. .... '40 '66 C.309 B.A. L.446 J.D. [Ⓒ Bell,B.&L.]
Smith, Eleanor H. .... '60 '88 C.575 B.A. L.178 J.D. [Zuckerman S.]
*PRACTICE AREAS: Civil and Criminal Litigation; Administrative Law; Freedom of Information; Privacy Law; Native American Law.
Smith, Ellen Resnick ..... '70 '97 C.860 B.S. L.1209 J.D. [Ⓐ Sughrue M.] (See Pat. Sect.)
Smith, Eric H. .... '43 '69 C.813 A.B. L.1066 J.D. [Smith&M.]
*PRACTICE AREAS: Copyrights; Entertainment and the Arts; Electronic Commerce; International Trade.
Smith, Eugene T., (BV) .... '30 '60 C&L.45 B.S.L., LL.B. 715 G St., S.E.
Smith, Francis S. .... '48 '73 C.367 B.A. L.276 J.D. Gen. Coun., Howard Univ.
Smith, Frank .... '07 '43 C.273 A.B. L.276 J.D. 5334 32nd St., N.W.‡
Smith, G. Nelson, III '61 '86 C.329 B.A. L.893 J.D.
(adm. in VA; not adm. in DC) [Smith C.]
*PRACTICE AREAS: Environmental.
Smith, Gare A. .... '— '85 C.367 B.A. L.477 J.D. [Ⓒ Foley,H.&E.]
*PRACTICE AREAS: International; Corporate Social Responsibility; Legislative.
Smith, Gary J., (AV) .... '51 '76 C.154 B.A. L.309 J.D. [Beveridge&D.]
*PRACTICE AREAS: Environmental Law; Litigation.

Smith, Geoffrey R. W. '45 '71 C&L.813 B.A., J.D.
1350 I Street, NW, Suite 900, 20005-7202
Telephone: 202-625-1224 Fax: 202-333-1637
Email: grwslawyer@aol.com URL: http://www.lawyers.com/geoffreysmithlaw
***PRACTICE AREAS: Complex Litigation.**
Complex Litigation.
See Professional Biographies, WASHINGTON, DISTRICT OF COLUMBIA

Smith, George C. '45 '74
C.645 B.A. L.228 J.D. Assoc. Gen. Coun., Wash. Legal Foundation
Smith, George P., II '39 '65 C.347 B.S. L.1119 J.D.
Prof. of Law, Catholic Univ. of Amer.
Smith, Gina S. '74 '99 C.967 B.A. L.608 J.D.
(adm. in OH; not adm. in DC) 1800 Mass. Ave., N.W.‡
Smith, Gordon J., (AV) .... '63 '88 C.880 B.A. L.273 J.D. [John&H.]
*PRACTICE AREAS: Energy Law.
Smith, Gregory A., (AV) .... '47 '72 C.473 A.B. L.893 J.D. [Piper M.R.&W.]
*PRACTICE AREAS: Government Contracts.
Smith, Gregory A. .... '60 '87 C.976 B.A. L.188 J.D. 1840 Biltmore St. N.W.
Smith, Gregory Dean '69 '95 C.300 B.A. L.276 J.D.
(adm. in MD; not adm. in DC) American Legis. Exch. Council
Smith, Gregory K. '65 '93 C&L.276 A.B., J.D.
(adm. in IL; not adm. in DC) [Ⓐ Winston&S.]
Smith, Gregory Stuart '59 '86 C.896 B.A. L.575 J.D.
(adm. in GA; not adm. in DC) [Ⓒ Sutherland A.&B.]
*PRACTICE AREAS: Litigation; White Collar Crime; Criminal Law; Appellate Practice.
Smith, Guy C. .... '62 '88 C.473 B.A. L.30 J.D. 1775 Pennsylvania Ave., N.W.
Smith, Harrison C. .... '54 '79 C.188 B.S. L.228 J.D. [Krooth&A.] ⊙
Smith, Herbert G., II .... '58 '84 C&L.902 B.A., J.D. [Venable,A.B.H.&C.]
*PRACTICE AREAS: Commercial Litigation; Construction Litigation; Product Liability Litigation.
Smith, Holly H. .... '57 '82 C.276 B.A. L.128 J.D. [Ⓒ Sutherland A.&B.]
*PRACTICE AREAS: Securities; Broker-Dealer Regulation.
Smith, Holly Rachel .... '73 '99 C.174 B.A. L.629 J.D. [Ⓐ Davis W.T.]
*PRACTICE AREAS: Telecommunications; Technology; Government Regulation.
Smith, J. Anthony, (BV) .... '42 '71 C&L.188 B.S., J.D. [Schmeltzer,A.&S.]
*PRACTICE AREAS: International Business Law; Public Policy; Natural Resources; Municipal; Civil Litigation.
Smith, J. Clay, Jr. ...... '42 '67 C.190 B.A. L.329 J.D. Prof., Howard Univ. School of Law
Smith, James Hiner .... '60 '99 C&L.575 B.A., J.D. 111 F. St., NW
Smith, James O. .... '69 '97 C&L.228 A.B., J.D. [Ⓐ Hogan&H.]
*PRACTICE AREAS: Corporate.

Smith, Janene M. .... '65 '96 C.659 B.S. L.1338 J.D. [🄰 Dechert]
*PRACTICE AREAS: Financial Services Law; Investment Management.
Smith, Jason D. ....'72 '98 C.1349 B.A. L.273 J.D. [🄰 Howrey S.A.&W.]
*PRACTICE AREAS: Antitrust; Commercial Litigation.
Smith, Jay T. .... '60 '88 C&L.309 A.B., J.D. [Covington&B.]
Smith, Jeffrey H. ....'44 '71 C.870 B.S. L.477 J.D. [Arnold&P.]
*PRACTICE AREAS: Legislative; International.
Smith, Jeffrey M. .... '72 '99 C.659 B.S. L.228 J.D. [🄰 Williams&C.]
*PRACTICE AREAS: Litigation.
Smith, Jeffrey T. ....'53 '79 C.31 B.A. L.813 J.D. [Patton B.]
Smith, Jennifer G. '72 '98 C.259 B.A. L.262 J.D.
(adm. in NY; not adm. in DC) [🄰 Drinker B.&R.]
Smith, John G. ....'63 '91 C.436 B.S.E.E. L.273 J.D. [Morgan,L.&B.] (Pat.)
Smith, John Stuart, (AV) ....'43 '68 C&L.309 A.B., LL.B. [Nixon P.] (⊙Roch., NY)
*PRACTICE AREAS: Antitrust Law; Litigation.
Smith, John Thomas, II .... '43 '68 C&L.976 B.A., J.D. [Covington&B.]
Smith, Jonathan M., (AV) '58 '84 C.431 B.A. L.1162 J.D.
Exec. Dir., D.C. Prisoners' Legal Servs. Proj., Inc.
Smith, Joseph A., Jr. '49 '75 C.198 A.B. L.893 J.D.
(adm. in NY; not adm. in DC) [🄲 Thacher P.&W.]
*PRACTICE AREAS: Corporate Law; Financial Institutions Law.
Smith, Joseph P., III ....'43 '69 C.884 B.S. L.945 J.D. [🄲 Inman D.]
*PRACTICE AREAS: International Criminal Law and Procedures; Legal Due Diligence; Freedom of Information Privacy Act.
Smith, Kathleen McAuliffe .... '70 '97 C&L.734 B.A., J.D. [🄰 Paul,W.R.W.&G.]
Smith, Kathrin V. .... '74 '99 C.1507 B.S. L.665 J.D. [🄰 McKenna&C.]
*PRACTICE AREAS: Insurance Litigation.
Smith, Keith J. .... '55 '87 C.1044 B.A. L.1162 J.D. Land Research Grp.
Smith, Kevin G., (AV) .... '53 '80 C.1203 B.A. L.1234 J.D. [Sughrue M.]
*PRACTICE AREAS: Trademark Law.
Smith, Kevin J. .... '54 '82 C&L.734 A.B., J.D. [🄲 Holland&K.]
*PRACTICE AREAS: Real Estate; Commercial Leasing; Commercial Finance; Real Estate Development.
Smith, Kimberlee Nichole '73 '98 C.945 B.A. L.276 J.D.
(adm. in IL; not adm. in DC) 1815 Pennsylvania Ave.
Smith, Kimberly J. ....'62 '87 C.945 B.A. L.309 J.D. [Sutherland A.&B.]
*PRACTICE AREAS: Insurance Products; Mutual Funds; Securities Regulation.
Smith, Kirk Callan ....'46 '78 C.1060 B.A. L.329 J.D. 1717 Mass. Ave., N.W.
Smith, Kristen ....'— '95 C.128 B.A. L.823 J.D. [🄰 Miller&C.]
*PRACTICE AREAS: International Trade; Customs.
Smith, Kristin Hart .... '69 '94 C.645 B.S. L.1065 J.D. [🄰 Mayer,B.&P.]
Smith, Kristin L. .... '72 '99 C.108 B.S. L.345 J.D. [🄰 Blumenfeld&C.]
*PRACTICE AREAS: Communications Law; Technology Law.
Smith, Lawrence S. .....'18 '49 C.260 A.B. L.273 LL.B. 2122 Massachusetts Ave., N.W.‡
Smith, Leonard, Jr. '61 '95
C.871 B.S. L.276 J.D. [🄰 Finnegan,H.F.G.&D.] (See Pat. Sect.)
*PRACTICE AREAS: Computer and Software Patents; Computer Architecture Patents; Biotechnology Patent Prosecution; Biotechnology Patents; Patent Litigation.
Smith, Leslie C. .... '44 '75 C.822 B.A. L.893 J.D. 3000 K St. N.W.
Smith, Lolita D. '71 '96 C.861 B.A. L.846 J.D.
Staff Coun., Cellular Telecommunication Indus. Assn.
Smith, Malaika T. .... '71 '96 C.659 B.A. L.273 J.D. [🄰 Leftwich&D.]
*PRACTICE AREAS: Family Law; Estate Litigation; Probate; General Practice.
Smith, Marcus H. '60 '91 C.72 B.A. L.508 J.D.
(adm. in MT; not adm. in DC) Legis. Dir. & Gen. Coun., U.S. Senate
Smith, Mary L. '— '91 C.424 B.S. L.145 J.D.
(adm. in IL; not adm. in DC) [🄰 Skadden,A.S.M.&F.]
Smith, Mary Lou .... '56 '81 C.475 B.A. L.659 J.D. [Howe,A.&S.]
Smith, Masha ....'75 '01 C.999 B.A. L.188 J.D. [🄰 Cleary,G.S.&H.]
Smith, Michael R., (AV) .... '53 '80 C.861 B.A. L.813 J.D. [Zuckerman S.]
*PRACTICE AREAS: Civil Trial; Criminal Trial; Litigation; Trial Practice.
Smith, Nancy C. .... '49 '75 C.112 A.B. L.1067 J.D. Off. of Corp. Coun.
Smith, Nicole A. .... '66 '99 C.465 B.A. L.276 J.D. [🄰 Akin,G.S.H.&F.]
*PRACTICE AREAS: Labor and Employment.
Smith, Numa L., Jr., (AV) ....'— '42 C.269 A.B. L.228 LL.B. [🄲 Miller&C.]
Smith, Patrick J. ....'51 '81 C&L.309 A.B., J.D. [Ivins,P.&B.]
*PRACTICE AREAS: Accounting; Inventory Taxation.
Smith, Paul M. ....'55 '81 C.31 B.A. L.976 J.D. [Jenner&B.]
*PRACTICE AREAS: Civil and Appellate Litigation; Media and First Amendment Law; Election Law; Antitrust.
Smith, R. Evan '41 '67 C.821 B.A. L.128 LL.B.
(adm. in NY; not adm. in DC) [🄲 Boros&G.]
*PRACTICE AREAS: Aircraft Finance Law; Equipment and Project Finance Law; General Corporate Law.
Smith, R. Michael .... '48 '75 C.165 B.A. L.145 J.D. [🄲 Dechert]
*PRACTICE AREAS: Labor and Employment; Employment Litigation.
Smith, Ralph M. ....'48 '83 1775 Eye Street, Northwest
Smith, Richard H., (AV) '37 '65
C.401 B.S.I.E. L.273 J.D. [Finnegan,H.F.G.&D.] (See Pat. Sect.)
*PRACTICE AREAS: Patent Prosecution; Patent Litigation; Patent Licensing; Computer and Software Patents.
Smith, Richard H., III .... '69 '94 C.945 B.A. L.64 J.D. [🄲 Russian-Ukrainian]
*PRACTICE AREAS: Corporate Law; International Business Law; Labor Law; Data Protection; Intellectual Property.
Smith, Richard W. ....'71 '99 C.880 B.A. L.902 J.D. [🄰 Covington&B.]
Smith, Robert A., (AV) ....'54 '79 C&L.128 B.A., J.D. [Wiley R.&F.]
*PRACTICE AREAS: Franchise, Licensing and Distribution.
Smith, Robert J. '52 '92 C.423 B.A. L.446 J.D.
(adm. in MD; not adm. in DC) [🄰 Dechert]
*PRACTICE AREAS: Securities; Litigation; Bank Broker/Dealer.
Smith, Robert R., (BV) ....'50 '75 C.575 B.A. L.446 J.D. [Franch,J.B.&S.] ⊙
*PRACTICE AREAS: Civil Litigation; Personal Injury; Insurance Defense; Lead Paint; Equipment Leasing.
Smith, Ronald H. '38 '76 C.966 B.S. L.446 J.D.
(adm. in MD; not adm. in DC; See Pat. Sect.) [🄲 Keil&W.]
*PRACTICE AREAS: Patents.
Smith, Russell L. .... '46 '72 C.880 B.A. L.280 J.D. [🄲 Willkie F.&G.]
Smith, S. Amelia '63 '98 C.846 B.A. L.128 J.D.
(adm. in VA; not adm. in DC) Corp. Coun., Conservation International
Smith, Sherrese M. ....'71 '96 C.790 B.S. L.597 J.D. [🄰 Arnold&P.]
*PRACTICE AREAS: Intellectual Property; Technology Law.
Smith, Stephen F. '67 '95 C.197 B.A. L.893 J.D.
(adm. in VA; not adm. in DC) [🄰 Sidley A.B.&W.]
Smith, Stephen R. .... '69 '94 C.884 B.A. L.273 J.D. [🄰 Powell,G.F.&M.]
*PRACTICE AREAS: Litigation.
Smith, Stuart R. .... '49 '87 C.30 B.A. L.904 J.D. 1224 Underwood St., NW
Smith, Sydney M. .... '52 '87 C.112 B.A. L.273 J.D. [🅂 Gibson,D.&C.]
*PRACTICE AREAS: Antitrust.
Smith, Tefft W., (AV) .... '46 '71 C.103 B.A. L.145 J.D. [Kirkland&E.]
*PRACTICE AREAS: Competition and Antitrust Law; Sales of Business Disputes; Distribution Litigation.
Smith, Thomas B. ....'54 '86 C.216 B.A. L.276 J.D. [Ropes&G.]
*PRACTICE AREAS: Communications; Trade Regulation; First Amendment; Privacy Law.

Smith, Thomas C. '46 '72 C.443 B.S. L.446 J.D.
Dir., Crim. Jus. Sect., Amer. Bar Assn.
Smith, Thomas Peter, Jr. ....'66 '98 C.871 B.S.M.E. L.276 J.D. [🄰 Fried,F.H.S.&J.]
*PRACTICE AREAS: Corporate Law.
Smith, Timothy C. ... '68 '93 C.629 B.S. L.284 J.D. [Dillon,H.&L.] (⊙Stuttgart, Germany)
Smith, Timothy Martin '71 '98 C.477 B.A. L.861 J.D.
(adm. in NY; not adm. in DC) [🄰 Howrey S.A.&W.]
*PRACTICE AREAS: Antitrust.
Smith, Tom D., (AV) ....'47 '72 C.586 B.A. L.276 J.D. [Jones,D.R.&P.]
*PRACTICE AREAS: Antitrust and Trade Regulation; Premerger Notification; Business Combinations.
Smith, Tracy A. Heinzman ....'64 '92 C.1044 B.A. L.893 J.D. [Howrey S.A.&W.]
*PRACTICE AREAS: Environmental.
Smith, Turner T., Jr., (AV) .... '40 '68 C.674 B.A. L.309 LL.B. [Hunton&W.]
*PRACTICE AREAS: Environmental; International Criminal Law.
Smith, Victor H. ....'69 '96 C.821 B.A. L.904 J.D. [🄰 Boros&G.]
*PRACTICE AREAS: Aviation Law.
Smith, W. Mark, (AV) ....'55 '81 C.378 B.A. L.188 J.D. [Sutherland A.&B.]
*PRACTICE AREAS: Employee Benefits; Insurance; Taxation.
Smith, W. N. Harrell, IV, (AV) .... '38 '66 C.951 B.A. L.309 LL.B. [Gardner,C.&D.]
*PRACTICE AREAS: Administrative Law; International Trade; International Dispute Resolution; Regulatory Law.
Smith, W. Stephen, (AV) .... '56 '83 C.597 B.A. L.145 J.D. [Morrison&F.]
*PRACTICE AREAS: Antitrust; Administrative Law.
Smith, Walter J., Jr., (AV) '36 '66
C.299 A.B. L.178 LL.B. 1850 M Street, NW Suite 280 (⊙Balt., MD)
Smith, William C. '33 '61 C.309 A.B. L.659 LL.B.
(adm. in PA; not adm. in DC) 3436 17th St., NW‡
Smith, William E. '66 '92 C.475 B.A. L.477 J.D.
Assoc. Lit. Coun., MCI Worldcom, Inc.
Smith, William Joseph H., (AV) '36 '63
C.228 A.B. L.145 J.D. 1775 Pennsylvania Ave., N.W.
Smith, Wm. Randolph, (AV) ....'51 '76 C.861 B.A. L.813 J.D. [Crowell&M.]
*PRACTICE AREAS: Antitrust Law; Unfair Trade Practices; Consumer Law.
Smith & Associates .... 1225 I Street, NW, Suite 500

Smith Cooper, LLP
1029 Vermont Avenue, N.W., Suite 300, 20005-3517
Telephone: 202-789-8700 Fax: 202-789-8775
URL: http://www.lawyers.com/smithcooper
G. Nelson Smith, III (Not admitted in DC); Lawrence N. Cooper;—Kimberly C. Ayers; Marcus Antoine Clifton (Not admitted in DC); Damien V. Alexander. Of Counsel: Michael S. Steele (Not admitted in DC).
Complex-Multi District Litigation, Commercial Litigation, Business Law, Environmental Law, Products Liability, Toxic Torts, Civil Trials, Corporate Transactions, Finance, Taxation, Entertainment Law, Entertainment Acquisition, Development, Production and Distribution, Television and Motion Picture Programming and Development Legal Issues.
See Professional Biographies, WASHINGTON, DISTRICT OF COLUMBIA

Smith & Downey, A Professional Association
1110 Vermont Avenue, N.W., Suite 400 (⊙Balt., MD; Hauppauge, NY)

Smith, Gambrell & Russell, LLP, (AV)
Suite 800, 1850 M Street, N.W., 20036 ⊙
Telephone: 202-263-4300 Telecopier: 202-263-4329
Partners: Andrew B. Beveridge (1915-1972); Joseph A. DeGrandi (1927-1999); Dennis O. Doherty (Not admitted in DC); Robert G. Weilacher; Frederick F. Calvetti; Michael A. Makuch; Dennis C. Rodgers. Associates: Michael K. Carrier; Brandon Boss (Not admitted in DC); Scott D. Woldow; Patrick R. Delaney; Mary A. Montebello. Counsel: Jacob S. Frenkel (Not admitted in DC).
Patent, Trademark, Copyright, Antitrust, Unfair Competition and Trade Regulation Law. Practice before Federal Courts and Government Departments.
Atlanta, Georgia Office: Suite 3100, Promenade II, 1230 Peachtree Street, N.E. Telephone: 404-815-3500. Fax: 404-815-3509.
Jacksonville, Florida Office: Bank of America Tower, 50 North Laura Street, Suite 2200. Telephone: 904-598-6100. Fax: 904-598-6300.
See Professional Biographies, WASHINGTON, DISTRICT OF COLUMBIA

Smith-Hill, Gloria F. .... '52 '76 C.1015 B.A. L.494 J.D. [G.F.Smith-Hill]
Smith-Hill, Gloria F., Law Offices of ....700 13th St. NW, Suite 950

Smith & Metalitz, L.L.P.
1747 Pennsylvania Avenue, N.W., Suite 825, 20006-4604
Telephone: 202-833-4198 Fax: 202-872-0546
Email: info@smimetlaw.com URL: http://www.smimetlaw.com
Eric H. Smith; Steven J. Metalitz; Eric J. Schwartz; Maria S. Strong;—Michael N. Schlesinger.
Copyrights, Trademarks, Entertainment Law, Electronic Commerce.
See Professional Biographies, WASHINGTON, DISTRICT OF COLUMBIA

Smith, Pachter, McWhorter & Allen, P.L.C.
(See Vienna, Virginia)

Smitherman, Geralyn G. .... '68 '94 C.228 B.A. L.813 J.D. 1201 Penn. Ave., N.W.
Smithwick, Gary S., (AV) ....'46 '71 C.576 B.S. L.896 J.D. [Smithwick&B.]
*PRACTICE AREAS: Administrative; Communications; Radio and TV.

Smithwick & Belendiuk, P.C., (AV)
5028 Wisconsin Avenue, N.W. Suite 301, 20016
Telephone: 202-363-4050 Telecopier: 202-363-4266 URL: http://www.lawyers.com/smithwick&belendiuk
Email: fcclaw@fccworld.com URL: http://www.fccworld.com
Gary S. Smithwick; Arthur V. Belendiuk. Of Counsel: James K. Edmundson; William M. Barnard; Ellen Mandell Edmundson.
Practice before the Federal Courts and Administrative Agencies. Communications, Radio, Television, Cable and Common Carrier.
See Professional Biographies, WASHINGTON, DISTRICT OF COLUMBIA

Smoker, Jennafer .... '— '99 C.665 B.A. L.276 J.D. [🄰 King&S.]
*PRACTICE AREAS: Tax.

Smolen Plevy
(See Vienna, Virginia)

Smoler, Barry M. .... '40 '66 C.976 B.A. L.309 J.D. [🄲 Spiegel&M.]
*PRACTICE AREAS: Hydroelectricity Licensing.
Smolinsky, Paul D. ....'67 '96 C.118 B.A. L.273 J.D. [🄰 McLeod,W.&M.]
Smollar, Paul R., (AV) ....'44 '69 C.178 A.B. L.597 J.D. [Kuder,S.&F.]
*PRACTICE AREAS: Domestic Relations Law; Personal Injury Law; General Civil Litigation.
Smoots, Carol A., (AV) .... '— '78 C.909 B.A. L.950 J.D. [McKenna&C.]
*PRACTICE AREAS: Energy Law; Administrative Law; International Law.
Smothergill, Polly B. .... '75 '01 C.477 B.A. L.309 J.D. [🄰 Wilmer,C.&P.]
Smoyer, Divonne .... '70 '96 C.788 A.B. L.309 J.D. [🄰 Gilbert H.&R.]
*PRACTICE AREAS: Alternative Dispute Resolution; Litigation; Insurance.
Smtih, Justin P. '— '00 C.311 B.A. L.569 J.D.
(adm. in NY; not adm. in DC) Fuchsberg Fellow, Public Citizen Litigation Group
Smuck, John C., (AV) ....'37 '62 C.893 B.A. L.309 J.D. [Cross,M.S.&H.]
*PRACTICE AREAS: Estate Planning Law; Trusts Law; Tax Law.
Smuckler, Gary S. ....'49 '74 C.477 B.A. L.912 J.D. [Morgan,L.&B.]
Smurzynski, Kenneth C. .... '66 '92 C.103 A.B. L.276 J.D. [Williams&C.]
*PRACTICE AREAS: Commercial Litigation; Litigation; Real Estate Litigation.

Smutny, Abby Cohen ....'64 '91 C.881 A.B. L.145 J.D. [White&C.]
*PRACTICE AREAS: International Arbitration; International Dispute Resolution; International Investment.
Smutny, David F. ....'65 '90 C.958 B.A. L.145 J.D. [Ⓒ Heller E.W.&M.]
Smyth, David D., III '70 '00 C.198 A.B. L.575 J.D.
(adm. in NC; not adm. in DC) [Ⓐ Steptoe&J.]
Smyth, Robert, Ph.D. ....'— '00 C.823 B.S. L.831 J.D. [Ⓐ Morgan,L.&B.]
Smythe, Marianne K., (AV) ....'42 '74 C.105 B.S. L.577 J.D. [Wilmer,C.&P.]
*PRACTICE AREAS: Securities Law; Corporate Law; Investments.
Snape, William J., III '64 '90
C.112 B.A. L.273 J.D. V.P., Law & Litig., Defenders of Wildlife
Snapp, Sandra ....'65 '95 C.972 B.S. L.1187 J.D. [Ⓐ Dykema G.]
Snarr, Michael S. '— '01 C.878 B.A. L.276 J.D.
(adm. in NY; not adm. in DC) [Vorys,S.S.&P.]
Snead, O. Carter, IV ....'72 '99 C.722 B.A. L.276 J.D. [Ⓐ Wilmer,C.&P.]
Sneed, James H., (AV) ....'47 '72 C&L.623 B.A., J.D. [McDermott,W.&E.]
Sneed, Letta F. ....'71 '97 C.674 A.B. L.569 J.D. [Ⓐ Wallace K.M.&B.]
*PRACTICE AREAS: Commercial Litigation.
Sneed, Maree F. ....'48 '83 C.623 B.A. L.276 J.D. [Hogan&H.]
*PRACTICE AREAS: Education Law; Civil Litigation; Appellate Litigation.
Snellings, E. Frank, (BV) '49 '75 C.1080 B.A. L.420 J.D.
(adm. in LA; not adm. in DC) 634 A St. S.E.
Snider, Ronald A., (AV) '48 '73 C&L.16 B.A., J.D.
(adm. in AL; not adm. in DC) [Miller,H.S.O.&B.] (⊙Mobile, AL)
*PRACTICE AREAS: Banking Law; Corporate Law; Merger and Acquisition.
Snider, Ronald R., (AV) '37 '65
C.679 B.S.E.E. L.477 J.D. [Snider&Assoc.] (See Pat. Sect.)
*PRACTICE AREAS: Litigation; Licensing Law; Intellectual Property Law.
Snider, Steven S., (AV) ....'56 '80 C.188 A.B. L.145 J.D. [Hale&D.]
*PRACTICE AREAS: Corporate Law.
Snider, Thomas R. '— '01 C.602 B.A. L.309 J.D.
(adm. in MA; not adm. in DC) [Ⓐ Verner,L.B.M.&H.]
*PRACTICE AREAS: International Commerce; Litigation; Legislative Practice.

Snider & Associates, (AV)
1054 31st Street, N.W., Suite 400, 20007
Telephone: 202-347-2600 Fax: 202-347-7870
Email: sniderpatent@yahoo.com URL: http://www.lawyers.com/snider&assoclaw
Ronald R. Snider.
Intellectual Property Law, Patents, Trademarks, Copyrights, Government Contracts.
See Professional Biographies, WASHINGTON, DISTRICT OF COLUMBIA

Snodgrass, Francis R. ....'39 '64 C.674 A.B. L.309 LL.B. [Arter&H.]
Snodgrass, John Charles '68 '98 C.893 B.A. L.945 J.D.
(adm. in NY; not adm. in DC) [Ⓐ Dickstein S.M.&O.]
*PRACTICE AREAS: Intellectual Property.
Snow, Mary Ann ....'50 '84 C.477 A.B. L.128 J.D. U.S. Attys. Off.
Snow, Rebecca ....'60 '86 C.101 B.S. L.309 J.D. [Covington&B.]
Snowdon, Richard W., III, (AV) .... '43 '68 C.823 B.S. L.273 J.D. [Trainum,S.&D.]
*PRACTICE AREAS: Trusts and Estates; Nonprofit and Charitable Organizations; Taxation; Probate.
Snuggs, M. Ann ....'37 '80 C.10 B.S. L.128 J.D. 2802 Devonshir Pl., N.W.
Snyder, Brad M. '72 '01 C.228 A.B. L.976 J.D.
(adm. in MD; not adm. in DC) [Ⓐ Williams&C.]
Snyder, Brett A. .... '— '99 C.453 B.S. L.276 J.D. 1875 Connecticut Avenue, N.W.
Snyder, Daniel C. '57 '93 C.923 B.A. L.276 J.D.
(adm. in VA; not adm. in DC) Atty., MCI WorldCom
Snyder, David F. '51 '76 C.216 B.A. L.273 J.D.
Asst. Gen. Coun., American Insurance Association
*RESPONSIBILITIES: Automobile Insurance; Highway Safety; Legislative/Regulatory; Litigation.
Snyder, Frances E. ....'— '92 C.923 B.S. L.276 J.D. Sr. Coun., Marriott Intl., Inc.
*RESPONSIBILITIES: Employee Benefits; Executive Compensation.
Snyder, Hillary L. ....'59 '87 C.659 B.A. L.569 J.D. [Ⓒ Howrey S.A.&W.] ‡
Snyder, Jeffrey L., (AV) ....'57 '84 C.30 B.A. L.904 J.D. [Sonnenschein N.&R.]
*PRACTICE AREAS: International Trade.
Snyder, John Beaumont, III .....'75 '00 C.560 B.A. L.228 J.D. U.S. dept. of Jus., Tax Div.
Snyder, Lynn Shapiro, (AV) ....'56 '79 C.264 B.A. L.273 J.D. [Epstein B.&G.]
*PRACTICE AREAS: Health Law; Hospital Law; Health Care Fraud; Medicare and Medicaid Reimbursement; Pharmaceutical Health Regulatory Law.
Snyder, Margaret R. ....'48 '77 C&L.838 B.A., J.D. 4052 Chancery Ct., N.W.
Snyder, Patricia N. ....'53 '78 C.401 B.A. L.910 J.D. [Thompson C.]
*PRACTICE AREAS: Aviation and Aerospace; Transportation; Environmental.
Snyder, Sharon A. ....'— '88 C.966 B.A. L.260 J.D. [Cohen,M.H.&T.]
*PRACTICE AREAS: Antitrust; Antitrust Class Actions; Securities Fraud Class Actions.
Snyder, Todd D. ....'63 '94 C&L.446 B.A., J.D. [Ⓒ Dyer E.&J.]
*PRACTICE AREAS: Corporate Law; Finance; Securities; Mergers, Acquisitions and Divestitures; International Commercial Finance.

Snyder, Slutkin & Lodowski
(See Baltimore, Maryland)

Soba, George H. ....'56 '81 C.264 B.A. L.851 J.D. Deloitte & Touche
Sobel, David L. ....'54 '80 C.477 B.A. L.260 J.D. 3600 Quesada St., N.W.
Sobel, Marc A., (AV) ..... '58 '85 C&L.276 A.B., J.D. Gen. Coun., JM Zell Partners, Ltd.
Sobelsohn, David C. '53 '78 C.145 B.A. L.94 J.D.
(adm. in CA; not adm. in DC) Human Rights Campaign Fund
Sobin, Darrin P. ....'65 '94 C.273 B.A. L.1364 J.D. [Ⓐ Bode&G.]
*PRACTICE AREAS: Intellectual Property; Internet Law; Contracts; Litigation; Appellate Practice.
Sobin, Sturgis M., (AV) ....'55 '83 C.309 B.A. L.30 J.D. [Miller&C.]
*PRACTICE AREAS: International Trade Law; Antitrust; Unfair Competition Law; Intellectual Property Licensing; Intellectual Property Litigation.
Soble, Stephen M. ....'51 '78 C.823 B.A. L.309 J.D. [Ⓒ O'Connor&H.]
*PRACTICE AREAS: International Infrastructure Development; International Project Finance; International Government Relations.
Sobo, Diana Michelle '69 '98 C.472 B.S. L.260 J.D.
(adm. in FL; not adm. in DC) [Ⓐ Browdy&N.]
*PRACTICE AREAS: Trademarks; Copyrights; Unfair Competition; Intellectual Property; Entertainment Law.
Socarras, Michael P. ....'61 '88 C.1036 B.A. L.976 J.D. [Greenberg T.]
Socha, Kenneth M., (AV) ....'46 '73 C.602 B.A. L.228 J.D. 1627 I St., N.W.
Socie, David G. .... '68 '99 C.107 B.A. L.724 J.D. [Ⓐ Akin,G.S.H.&F.]
*PRACTICE AREAS: Labor and Employment Law.
Socknat, John D. ....'68 '95 C.1369 B.A. L.180 J.D. [Ⓐ Weiner B.S.K.]
*PRACTICE AREAS: Mortgage Banking; Consumer Credit; Regulatory Compliance; Financial Institutions.
Sodos-Wallace, Nadja S. .... '68 '93 C.454 B.A. L.276 J.D. [Ⓐ Morrison&F.]
*PRACTICE AREAS: Communications Law.
Soegeng, Jemy '68 '98 C.1075 B.S. L.629 J.D.
[Ⓐ Finnegan,H.F.G.&D.] (See Pat. Sect.)
*PRACTICE AREAS: Intellectual Property Portfolio Management; Mechanical Patents; Medical Patents; International Patent Prosecution.
Soffen, Stephen A., (AV) '56 '83
C.188 B.S.E.E. L.818 J.D. [Ostrolenk,F.G.&S.] (See Pat. Sect.)
*PRACTICE AREAS: Patent; Trademark; Copyright; Unfair Competition.
Sohn, Gigi B. ....'61 '87 C.94 B.S. L.659 J.D. Dep. Dir., Media Access Proj.
Sohn, Hyung .... '62 '00 C.119 B.S.E.E. L.1356 J.D. [Ⓐ Wilmer,C.&P.]
Sohn, Michael N., (AV) ....'40 '64 C.178 A.B. L.309 LL.B. [Arnold&P.]
*PRACTICE AREAS: Antitrust; Trade Regulation.
Sokal, Allen M., (AV) '46 '73
C.659 B.S.Ch.E. L.276 J.D. [Finnegan,H.F.G.&D.] (See Pat. Sect.)
*PRACTICE AREAS: Intellectual Property Rights; Chemical Patents; Patent Litigation; Patent Prosecution; Pharmaceutical Patents.
Sokler, Bruce D., (AV) ....'49 '75 C.674 A.B. L.276 J.D. [Mintz,L.C.F.G.&P.]
*PRACTICE AREAS: Antitrust Law; Communications Law; Copyright Litigation.
Sokohl, Robert E. ....'65 '91 C.823 B.S.C.E. L.904 J.D. [Sterne,K.G.&F.] (See Pat. Sect.)
*PRACTICE AREAS: Intellectual Property Law.
Sokolov, Dan S. .... '— '95 C.976 B.A. L.1066 J.D. 725 12th St., N.W.
Sokolove, Roxane N., (AV) ....'55 '79 C.30 B.A. L.64 J.D. [Akin,G.S.H.&F.]
*PRACTICE AREAS: Labor and Employment Litigation.
Sokolow, Jonathan '59 '85 C.477 B.A. L.1009 J.D.
Asst. Gen. Coun., UMWA Health & Retirement Funds
Soldo, Linda J. ....'50 '81 C.706 A.B. L.128 J.D. [Cleary,G.S.&H.]
Solen, Donna ....'72 '97 C.259 B.S. L.260 J.D. [Ⓐ Cohen,M.H.&T.]
*PRACTICE AREAS: Health Care; Consumer Fraud; Products Liability; Antitrust; Environmental.
Solender, Michael S. .... '64 '90 C.178 A.B. L.976 J.D. Gen. Coun. [Ⓐ Arnold&P.]
Soler, Lawrence Alan ....'68 '96 C.156 B.A. L.273 J.D. Amer. Univ.
Sollee, William L., (AV) ....'42 '66 C&L.260 B.S.B.A., J.D. [Ivins,P.&B.]
*PRACTICE AREAS: Employee Benefits; Employment Taxation; Executive Compensation; ERISA Litigation; ESOPs.
Soller, Mary Lou, (AV) ....'— '77 C.914 B.A. L.813 J.D. [Miller&C.]
*PRACTICE AREAS: Criminal Law; Litigation; Government Contracts; Health Care.
Sollers, Joseph Sedwick, III, (AV) ....'— '83 C.674 A.B. L.446 J.D. [King&S.]
*PRACTICE AREAS: Special Matters/Government Investigations.
Solnik, Bernard A. ....'65 '92 C.228 A.B. L.659 J.D. 2000 K St., N.W., Suite 600
Solo, Julia A. '— '96 C.477 B.A. L.567 J.D.
(adm. in NY; not adm. in DC) [Ⓐ Nixon P.] (⊙New York, NY)
*PRACTICE AREAS: Syndication; Affordable Housing; Real Estate.
Solodky, Howard N. ....'51 '77 C.156 B.A. L.107 J.D. [Womble C.S.&R.]
*PRACTICE AREAS: Taxation; Municipal Finance; Corporate Law.
Solomon, Barbara Davis, (BV) '— '83
C.112 A.B. L.767 J.D. 1775 Pennsylvania Ave., NW
Solomon, Gloria B. ....'56 '81 C.860 B.A. L.309 J.D. [Katten M.Z.]
*PRACTICE AREAS: Commercial Litigation; Appellate Litigation.
Solomon, Henry A., (AV) ....'39 '63 C&L.477 B.A., LL.B. [Ⓒ Garvey,S.&B.]
*PRACTICE AREAS: Communications and Media; Business Law; Administrative Law; Corporate Law; Mergers and Acquisitions.
Solomon, Kim Keenan, (AV) '62 '88 C.276 B.S.F.S. L.893 J.D.
[Ⓐ J.H.Olender&Assoc.]
*PRACTICE AREAS: Medical Malpractice; Personal Injury; Complex Civil Litigation.
Solomon, Larry S., (AV) ....'49 '75 C.273 B.A. L.93 J.D. [Shook,H.&B.]
*PRACTICE AREAS: Telecommunications Law; Litigation.
Solomon, Richard A., (AV) .... '17 '42 C.309 A.B. L.976 LL.B. [Morrison&H.] ‡
Solomon, Robin M. ....'71 '97 C.999 A.B. L.309 J.D. [Ⓐ Ivins,P.&B.]
*PRACTICE AREAS: Tax; Employee Benefits.
Solomon, Sirak ....'70 '98 C.1059 B.S. L.329 J.D. [Ⓐ Arnold&P.]
*PRACTICE AREAS: Corporate Law; Securities.
Solomon, Stephen D. ....'56 '86 C.1349 B.A. L.564 J.D. [Ⓒ Proskauer R.]
Soltis, Ann M. ....'69 '95 C&L.602 B.A., J.D. 1722 Eye St., N.W.
Soltis, Cassandra A. ....'— '95 C&L.608 B.A., J.D. [Ⓐ Hyman,P.&M.]
*PRACTICE AREAS: Food and Drug Regulation.
Soltis, Debra ....'66 '91 C.229 N.S. L.276 J.D. 910 17th, N.W.
Soltys, Darlene M. ....'65 '90 C.446 B.A. L.276 J.D. Asst. Corp. Coun.
Somech, Dennis A. '74 '00 C.1365 B.A. L.273 J.D.
(adm. in VA; not adm. in DC) [Ⓐ Tighe P.A.T.]
*PRACTICE AREAS: Complex Litigation; Civil Litigation; White Collar Crime; Government Contracts; Internet Law.
Somer-Greif, Penny ....'70 '96 C.1349 B.S. L.904 J.D. [Ⓐ Arnold&P.]
*PRACTICE AREAS: Corporate Law; Securities.
Somers, Jeri Kaylene ....'— '86 C.1209 B.A. L.904 J.D. [Ⓒ Miller&C.]
*PRACTICE AREAS: Government Contracts; Litigation.
Sommer, Christine J. '71 '00 C&L.190 B.A., J.D.
(adm. in NY; not adm. in DC) [Ⓐ Baker&M.P.]
*PRACTICE AREAS: Antitrust; Litigation.
Sommer, Gerald I. '44 '70 C.30 B.A. L.273 J.D.
Admin. Coun., Service Employees Intl. Union
Sommer, Michael C. '53 '83
C.1211 B.A. L.602 J.D. Prin. Consult., Pricewaterhouse Coopers LLP
Sommer, Sheldon B. '68 '00 C.574 B.B.A. L.309 J.D.
(adm. in VA; not adm. in DC) [Ⓐ Kirkpatrick&L.]
*PRACTICE AREAS: Insurance Coverage.
Sommers, Daniel S. ....'60 '86 C.867 B.A. L.273 J.D. [Cohen,M.H.&T.]
*PRACTICE AREAS: Securities Litigation; Class Actions.
Sommers, Mark, (AV) ....'56 '82 C.611 B.A. L.589 J.D. [Finnegan,H.F.G.&D.]
*PRACTICE AREAS: Domain Name Infringement; Internet Trademark Law; Trade Dress; Trademark Infringement; Trademark Litigation.
Somson, Barbara C. ....'48 '75 C.94 B.A. L.128 J.D. 1757 North Street N.W.‡
Son, Anthony H. ....'— '97 C.446 B.S. L.978 J.D. [Ⓐ Foley&L.] (See Pat. Sect.)
*PRACTICE AREAS: Intellectual Property; Litigation.
Sonde, Theodore, (AV) ....'40 '64 C.563 B.A. L.569 LL.B. [Dechert]
*PRACTICE AREAS: Securities Regulation Law; Litigation; International Finance Law; White Collar Defense Law.
Sonenthal, Robert B. ....'49 '80 C.309 B.A. L.659 J.D. [Sonenthal&O.]
*PRACTICE AREAS: Nonprofit Corporations; Corporate Governance; Government Contracts and Grants; Renewable Energy; Civil Litigation.

Sonenthal & Overall, PC
1120 19th Street N.W., Suite 460, 20036
Telephone: 202-785-0227 Fax: 202-785-5904; Email: rsonenthal@psiwash.org
Email: soverall@psiwash.org URL: http://www.lawyers.com/soverall
Scott C. Overall; Robert B. Sonenthal. Of Counsel: Renee R. Matalon; Nina Glickman Nathani; Tamera A. Fillinger (Not admitted in DC).
Government Contracts, Federal Grants, Nonprofit Organizations Law, Corporate Governance; International Government Contracts, Renewable Energy, Civil Litigation.
See Professional Biographies, WASHINGTON, DISTRICT OF COLUMBIA

Song, Yisun ....'72 '00 C.446 B.S.E.E. L.273 J.D. [Ⓐ Hunton&W.] (Pat.)
*PRACTICE AREAS: Patents.
Songer, Michael J. ....'64 '90 C.602 B.S.M.E. L.228 J.D. [Arnold&P.] (Pat.)
*PRACTICE AREAS: Intellectual Property.
Soni, Pragna ....'70 '97 C.165 B.A. L.352 J.D. [Ⓐ Ross,D.&B.]
Sonnenreich, Michael R., (AV) ....'38 '65 C.966 A.B. L.309 J.D. [Sonnenreich&R.]
Sonnenreich & Roccograndi, (AV) ....2600 Virginia Avenue, N.W.

Sonnenschein Nath & Rosenthal, (AV) BB
1301 K Street, N.W. Suite 600 East Tower, 20005 ⊙
Telephone: 202-408-6400 Fax: 202-408-6399
URL: http://www.sonnenschein.com

(This Listing Continued)

Sonnenschein Nath & Rosenthal (Continued)

Resident Partners: Amy L. Bess; John J. Calkins; Todd R. Eskelsen; Elizabeth A. Ferrell; D. Andrew Floam (Not admitted in DC); Frances J. Henderson; Joseph P. Hornyak; Michael L. Kiklis; Fred L. Levy; Lisa A. MacVittie; Michael R. Maryn; Kenneth J. Pfaehler; Caryl A. Potter, III; Douglas E. Rosenthal; Kirk R. Ruthenberg; Michael A. Schlanger; Albert W. Shay; Jeffrey L. Snyder; Ronald E. Stauffer; Evelyn M. Suarez; Louis L.S. Tao; Jerome P. Weiss (Deceased, 1934-1996). Resident Of Counsel: L. John Osborn; Jean C. Edwards. Resident Associates: Daniel D. Barnowski; Imanta M. Bergmanis; Anne M. Bertsch; William E. Copley, III; Hilary Duke; Kerri B. Gannon (Not admitted in DC); Catherine B. Gardner; Lori E. Graham; Allyson B. Handler; Raymond J. Ho; Leslie E. Klein; Laura A. Lattal (Not admitted in DC); Marci Rose Levine; Renee C. Macri (Not admitted in DC); Drew W. Marrocco; Michelle Ochs; Meredith K. Olafson (Not admitted in DC); Lisa P. Pandohie-Johnson (Not admitted in DC); James W. Reed; Traci Rittenberg (Not admitted in DC); Alexander H. Schaefer; Sameer Upadhya (Not admitted in DC); Alison B. Wilson (Not admitted in DC).
General Practice.
Chicago, Illinois Office: Suite 8000 Sears Tower, 233 South Wacker Drive. Telephone: 312-876-8000. Cable Address: "Sonberk". Telex: 25-3526. Facsimile: 312-876-7934.
New York, N.Y. Office: 1221 Avenue of the Americas. Telephone: 212-768-6700. Facsimile: 212-768-6800.
San Francisco, California Office: 685 Market Street, 6th Floor. Telephone: 415-882-5000. Facsimile: 415-543-5472.
Los Angeles, California Office: 601 South Figueroa Street, Suite 1500. Telephone: 213-623-9300. Facsimile: 213-623-9924.
St. Louis, Missouri Office: One Metropolitan Square, Suite 3000. Telephone: 314-241-1800. Facsimile: 314-259-5959.
Kansas City, Missouri Office: Suite 1100, 4520 Main Street, 64111. Telephone: 816-460-2400. Facsimile: 816-531-7545.
West Palm Beach, Florida Office: Phillips Point, West Tower, 777 South Flagler Drive, Suite 1102. Telephone: 561-833-2410. Facsimile: 561-833-8387.

See Professional Biographies, WASHINGTON, DISTRICT OF COLUMBIA

Sonosky, Chambers, Sachse, Endreson & Perry, (AV)
Suite 1000, 1250 Eye Street, N.W., 20005 ⊙
Telephone: 202-682-0240 Telecopier: 202-682-0249
Resident Partners: Marvin J. Sonosky (1909-1997); Reid Peyton Chambers; Harry R. Sachse; Douglas B. L. Endreson; William R. Perry; Lloyd Benton Miller (Resident, Anchorage, Alaska Office); Anne Doris Noto; Mary J. Pavel. Resident of Counsel: Arthur Lazarus, Jr. (P.C.); Matthew S. Jaffe. Resident Associates: James T. Meggesto; James E. Glaze (Not admitted in DC); Donald J. Simon.
General Trial, Administrative and Legislative Practice, Indian and Alaska Native Affairs, Public Land and Natural Resource Law, Energy, Constitutional Litigation, Election and Campaign Finance Law.
Anchorage, Alaska Office: Sonosky, Chambers, Sachse, Miller & Munson. Suite 700, 900 West Fifth Avenue. Telephone: 907-258-6377. Telecopier: 907-272-8332.
Juneau, Alaska Office: Sonosky, Chambers, Sachse, Miller & Munson. 318 Fourth Street. Telephone 907-586-5880. Telecopier: 907-586-5883.
San Diego, California Office: Symphony Towers, 750 B Street, Suite 3300, 92101. Telephone: 619-595-8070. Fax: 619-595-8077.
Albuquerque, NM office: Sonosky, Chambers, Sachse, Endreson & Perry. 501 Tijeras Avenue, NW, Suite 200, 87102. Telephone: 505-247-0147.

See Professional Biographies, WASHINGTON, DISTRICT OF COLUMBIA

Sonu, Andrew Chanho '46 '87
C.112 B.S.E.E. L.1338 J.D. [Finnegan,H.F.G.&D.] (See Pat. Sect.)
*PRACTICE AREAS: Intellectual Property Litigation; Intellectual Property Licensing; Intellectual Property Arbitration; Technology Transfer; Patent Prosecution.

Sopchick, Michael K. .... '61 '98 C.884 B.A. L.128 J.D. [Ⓐ Sullivan&C.]

Sorcher, Alan E., (BV) '58 '84
C.659 B.A. L.94 J.D. Asst. Gen. Coun., Securities Industry Assn.
*RESPONSIBILITIES: Securities; Banking; Administrative Procedure.

Sorensen, Carlie B. ....'52 '79 C.966 B.A. L.273 J.D. 4009 Highwood Ct., NW‡

Sorenson, Arne M. .... '58 '83 C.427 B.A. L.494 J.D. Marriott Dr.

Sorett, Stephen M. ....'49 '76 C.976 B.A. L.537 J.D. [Ⓒ Reed S.]
*PRACTICE AREAS: Government Contracts; Export Compliance.

Soriano, Enrico C. ....'58 '91 C.999 B.A. L.831 J.D. [Ⓒ Kelley D.&W.]
*PRACTICE AREAS: Communications Law; Litigation.

Sorini, Marc E. ....'66 '94 C.401 B.A. L.276 J.D. [McDermott,W.&E.]

Sorkin, Stuart H., P.C. ....'54 '81 C.30 B.S.B.A. L.472 J.D. [Ⓒ Hewes,G.L.&D.]

Sorokina, Evgenia V. '71 '99 C&L.999 J.D.
(adm. in Russia; not adm. in DC) [Ⓐ Ludwig&R.]
*PRACTICE AREAS: Russian Civil Law; International Law.

Soschin, Alan B., (AV) '47 '73 C.401 B.A. L.276 J.D.
400 Seventh Street, N.W., Suite 400, 20004
Telephone: 202-638-4264 Fax: 202-628-0249
Email: cardshp@aol.com
***PRACTICE AREAS: Family Law; Criminal Law; Personal Injury.**
Family Law, Divorce, Custody, Visitations, Marital Property, Support, Pre-Nuptial Agreements, Family Mediation, Post-Divorce Modification, Criminal Defense, Traffic Violations, DWI, Drug Crimes, Business Fraud, White Collar Crimes, Homicide, Felonies, Misdemeanors, Automobile Accidents, Wrongful Death, Personal Injury.

See Professional Biographies, WASHINGTON, DISTRICT OF COLUMBIA

Sossamon, Melinda A. .... '70 '00 C.623 B.A. L.276 J.D. [Ⓐ Hogan&H.]

Sostowski, Lorraine .... '53 '77 C.860 A.B. L.309 J.D. [Hogan&H.]
*PRACTICE AREAS: Electronic Intellectual Property; Emerging Companies; Corporate Contracts; Corporate Finance; Mergers and Acquisitions.

Sotir, Lisa M. '66 '92 C.188 B.A. L.273 J.D.
(adm. in NY; not adm. in DC) 1899 L Street NW

Sotsky, Lester .... '54 '79 C.1036 B.A. L.976 J.D. [Arnold&P.]
*PRACTICE AREAS: Environmental; Litigation.

Sottile, James, IV ....'60 '86 C.260 B.S. L.276 J.D. [Baach R.&L.P.]
*PRACTICE AREAS: Civil Litigation; Commercial Litigation; Professional Malpractice; Securities; Commercial Fraud.

Soucy, Anita Caroline '73 '99 C.938 B.A. L.280 J.D.
(adm. in VA; not adm. in DC) [Ⓐ McKee N.]
*PRACTICE AREAS: Taxation; Tax Litigation.

Souders, David M. ....'55 '85 C.321 B.A. L.910 J.D. [Ⓒ Weiner B.S.K.]
*PRACTICE AREAS: Litigation; Regulatory Compliance; Administrative Law.

Souk, Fred S., (AV) ....'43 '75 C.453 B.S. L.273 J.D. [Crowell&M.]
*PRACTICE AREAS: Products Liability Law; Tort Law; Construction Law; Contract Law; Litigation.

Soukenik, John P., Jr. '51 '76 C.381 B.A. L.128 J.D.
(adm. in OH; not adm. in DC) [Elias,M.T.&H.]

Soukup, Lynn A., (P.C.) ....'56 '81 C.105 B.A. L.276 J.D. [Shaw P.]
*PRACTICE AREAS: Corporate; Structured Finance; Asset Securitization; Commercial Finance; Securities.

Soulanille, Nicole D. '63 '88 C.668 B.A. L.1068 J.D.
(adm. in CA; not adm. in DC) 811 Vermont Avenue, NW

Soulen, Allison Rutland ....'60 '90 C.1365 B.A. L.976 J.D. Neighborhood Legal Servs.

Soundararajan, Srinivasan '68 '96 C.688 B.S. L.309 J.D.
(adm. in NY; not adm. in DC) The Advisory Board Co.

Souras, Yiota G. ....'— '00 C.367 B.A. L.262 J.D. [Ⓐ Morgan,L.&B.]

Sousa, Edward Ramos '— '87 C.1036 B.A. L.659 J.D.
(adm. in NJ; not adm. in DC)
[Ⓒ Wolf,A.&C.] (⊙New York, NY; Bonao, Dominican Republic)
*PRACTICE AREAS: International Business Law; International Investment; International Banking Law; International Economic Development; Artistic Property.

Southall, David M. .... '42 '80 C.259 B.A. L.446 J.D. [Ⓒ Wiley R.&F.]
*PRACTICE AREAS: Government Contracts; Business Law.

Southard, C. Dennis, IV ....'61 '89 C.477 B.A. L.823 J.D. [Ⓐ Holland&K.]
*PRACTICE AREAS: Civil Litigation.

Southard, David N. ....'70 '99 C.1369 B.S. L.30 J.D. [Ⓐ Weil,G.&M.]
*PRACTICE AREAS: Litigation; Regulatory Law.

Southfield, Julie A. ....'72 '00 C.679 B.A. L.273 J.D. [Ⓐ Cleary,G.S.&H.]

Sova, Christopher J. ....'62 '96 C.776 M.B.A. L.705 J.D. [Ⓐ Leventhal,S.&L.]
*PRACTICE AREAS: Communications Law; Commercial Transactions; Corporate Law; Commercial Law.

Sowle, Leslie A. '— '90 C.682 B.A. L.597 J.D.
(adm. in IL; not adm. in DC) [Ⓒ Kirkpatrick&L.]
*PRACTICE AREAS: Intellectual Property; Technology Law.

Soyars-Berman, Julia A. '65 '90
C&L.823 B.A., J.D. Sr. Coun., American National Red Cross
*RESPONSIBILITIES: Contracts.

Sozan, Michael L. .... '69 '94 C.945 B.A. L.273 J.D. [Ⓐ Arnold&P.]
*PRACTICE AREAS: Telecommunications Law.

Spaccasi, Lawrence M. F. '62 '88 C&L.107 B.A., J.D.
(adm. in NY; not adm. in DC) [Muldoon M.&F.]
*PRACTICE AREAS: Finance; Banks and Banking; Corporate Law; Securities; Securities and Exchange Commission Regulation.

Spacek, Eric A. ....'66 '91 C.1305 B.A. L.904 J.D. [Ⓒ Bonner K.T.&C.] (⊙Fairfax, VA)
*PRACTICE AREAS: Civil Liability; Defense Litigation; Insurance Defense; Professional Liability Defense Law.

Spackman, Paul '70 '99 C.30 B.A. L.904 J.D.
(adm. in VA; not adm. in DC) [Ⓐ Dickstein S.M.&O.]
*PRACTICE AREAS: Insurance Coverage Litigation.

Spada, Teresa D. ....'53 '84 C.37 B.A. L.30 J.D. Supr. Ct.

Spade, Gina M. .... '69 '96 C.942 B.A. L.276 J.D. [Ⓐ Hogan&H.]
*PRACTICE AREAS: Communications and Media; Telecommunications; Internet; Regulatory Law; Corporate Law.

Spaeder, Roger C., (AV) ....'43 '71 C.97 B.S. L.273 J.D. [Zuckerman S.]
*PRACTICE AREAS: Complex Criminal and Civil Litigation.

Spaeth, Earl C. '20 '62 C.604 B.A. L.273 LL.B.
(adm. in VA; not adm. in DC) 1233 20th St., N.W. (⊙Kalamazoo, MI)

Spaeth, Jonathan S., (BV) .... '59 '84 C.477 B.A. L.893 J.D. [Akin,G.S.H.&F.]
*PRACTICE AREAS: Litigation.

Spaeth, Melvin, (AV) .... '26 '52 C&L.145 A.B., J.D. [Ⓒ Arnold&P.]
*PRACTICE AREAS: Litigation; Products Liability; Antitrust.

Spafford, Michael L., (AV) ....'58 '84 C.1349 B.A. L.228 J.D. [Swidler B.S.F.]
*PRACTICE AREAS: Professional Liability; SEC Enforcement; Commercial Litigation; Government Investigations; White Collar Fraud.

Spagnoletti, Robert James ....'62 '88 C.390 B.A. L.276 J.D. Asst. U.S. Atty.

Spahn, Stephanie C. '56 '81 C.589 B.A. L.352 J.D.
(adm. in IA; not adm. in DC) Natl. Def. Univ.

Spak, Gregory J. ....'62 '87 C&L.276 B.S.F.S., J.D. [White&C.]

Spak, Walter J. ....'51 '78 C.602 B.A. L.276 J.D. [White&C.]
*PRACTICE AREAS: International Trade Regulation.

Spalding, Todd N. '— '01 C.101 B.S. L.945 J.D.
(adm. in VA; not adm. in DC) [Ⓐ Foley&L.]
*PRACTICE AREAS: Intellectual Property; Biotechnology.

Spalletta, Sandra L. ....'54 '80 C.216 B.A. L.309 J.D. [Ⓒ Rosenman&C.]
*PRACTICE AREAS: Corporate Law; Real Estate Law.

Spangler, David C. '61 '95 C.473 A.B. L.273 J.D.
VP-Int'l & Asst. Gen. Coun., Consumer Healthcare Products Association

Spangler, Nancy A. .....'63 '89 C.350 B.A. L.893 J.D. [Piper M.R.&W.] (⊙Reston, VA)
*PRACTICE AREAS: Venture Capital; Emerging Growth Companies; Corporate Finance and Securities Law.

Spann, Girardeau A. ..... '48 '75 C.674 A.B. L.309 J.D. Prof., Georgetown Univ. Law Ctr.

Sparacino, Mark V. '64 '96 C.645 B.S. L.174 J.D.
(adm. in CO; not adm. in DC) [Ⓐ Roylance,A.B.&G.]
*PRACTICE AREAS: Trademarks; Copyrights.

Sparagna, Giovanna T., (AV) ....'54 '80 C.1214 B.A. L.823 J.D. [Sutherland A.&B.]
*PRACTICE AREAS: Corporate Reorganization; International Corporate Taxation; International Mergers and Acquisitions; International Taxation; Tax Controversies.

Sparks, Randy C., Jr. '71 '96 C.893 B.A. L.945 J.D.
(adm. in VA; not adm. in DC) [Ⓐ Ford&H.]
*PRACTICE AREAS: Labor and Employment Law; Insurance Coverage.

Sparlin, Derry Dean, Jr. ....'57 '86 C.128 B.A. L.945 J.D. [Ⓒ Gibson,D.&C.]
*PRACTICE AREAS: Labor and Employment; Employee Benefits.

Sparling, Richard P., (AV) ....'63 '91 C.273 B.A. L.276 J.D. [Ⓐ Swidler B.S.F.]
*PRACTICE AREAS: Energy.

Spartin, Debbie Beecher, (P.C.) ....'62 '87 C.893 B.A. L.309 J.D. [Shaw P.]
*PRACTICE AREAS: Commercial Real Estate.

Spataro, Carl L., Jr. '59 '96 C.871 B.S. L.813 J.D.
(adm. in CA; not adm. in DC) [Ⓐ Covington&B.]
*PRACTICE AREAS: Corporate Finance; Securities.

Spath, Gregg A. ....'52 '78 C.696 B.A. L.1202 J.D. [Ⓐ Swidler B.S.F.]
*PRACTICE AREAS: Telecommunications; E-Commerce; Software Licensing; Intellectual Property; Real Estate.

Spaulding, Douglas K., (AV) ....'— '77 C.436 B.A. L.893 J.D. [Reed S.]
*PRACTICE AREAS: Litigation.

Spaziano, Jennifer L. ....'71 '95 C.93 A.B. L.990 J.D. [Ⓐ Skadden,A.S.M.&F.]
*PRACTICE AREAS: Litigation.

Spear, Tracie D. .... '71 '98 C.893 B.A. L.128 J.D. [Ⓐ Kirkpatrick&L.]
*PRACTICE AREAS: Transportation Law; Corporate Law.

Spearing, Mary C., (BV) ....'51 '77 C.881 A.B. L.262 J.D. [Baker B.]

Spears, Byron P., Jr. ....'47 '88 C.446 B.A. L.904 J.D. [Butler&S.]

Spears, James M. ....'52 '78 C.845 B.B.A. L.846 J.D. [Ropes&G.]
*PRACTICE AREAS: Litigation; Administrative Law; Antitrust and Trade Regulation; International Law.

Speas, Denise L. ....'— '92 C.190 B.S. L.208 J.D. [Ⓐ Morgan,L.&B.]

Specht, Jalena G. '72 '00 C.339 B.S. L.276 J.D.
(adm. in VA; not adm. in DC) [Ⓐ Covington&B.]
*PRACTICE AREAS: Food and Drug Regulation; Information Technology.

Speck, Randall L., (AV) ....'46 '77 C.1 B.A. L.309 J.D. [Kaye S.]
*PRACTICE AREAS: Litigation, International Arbitration.

Spector, Barry S., (AV) .... '51 '76 C.696 B.A. L.273 J.D. [Wright&T.]
*PRACTICE AREAS: Energy; Electric Utilities.

Spector, Jeremy D. ....'70 '97 C.976 B.A. L.477 J.D. [Ⓐ Covington&B.]
*PRACTICE AREAS: Taxation; Audits; Federal Income Tax; Sales and Use Tax; Tax Planning.

Spector, Mark A. '55 '88 C.454 B.S. L.1202 J.D.
(adm. in MA; not adm. in DC) [Ⓒ R.E.Bushnell]

Spector, Phillip L., (AV) ....'50 '76 C.112 B.A. L.309 J.D. [Paul,W.R.W.&G.] ⊙
*PRACTICE AREAS: Communications and Media; Internet Law; Computers and Software.

Speed-Bost, Regina Y. '— '90 C.197 A.B. L.276 J.D.
(adm. in MD; not adm. in DC) [Ⓒ Verner,L.B.M.&H.]
*PRACTICE AREAS: Energy Regulatory Law; Administrative Law.

Spees, Richard L., Jr. '54 '79 C.112 B.A. L.276 J.D.
(adm. in CA; not adm. in DC) [Ⓒ Katz,K.H.A.B.&Y.]
*PRACTICE AREAS: Federal Government Law; International Trade; Transportation; Local Government Law.

Speidel, Richard Henry, (AV) '20 '50 C.309 A.B. L.178 J.D.
1819 H Street, N.W., 20006
Telephone: 202-293-1455 Fax: 202-828-1057
Practice before the United States and Local Courts and Government Departments. Probate, Government Contract and International Law. Arbitration, Family Law and Trusts and Estates.
Reference: Riggs National Bank, Washington, D. C.
See Professional Biographies, WASHINGTON, DISTRICT OF COLUMBIA

Speights, Grace E., (AV) ....'57 '82 C.659 B.A. L.273 J.D. [Morgan,L.&B.]
Speights, Nathaniel H., (AV) ....'49 '76 C.970 B.A. L.472 J.D. 1819 H St. N.W.
Spekter, Michael L. ....'49 '75 C.884 B.A. L.831 J.D. 1090 Vermont Ave., N.W.
Spenard, David A. '56 '93 C.589 B.S.E.E. L.851 J.D.
(adm. in OH; not adm. in DC; Pat.) [McDermott,W.&E.]
Spence, Lee H., (AV) ....'42 '69 C.103 B.A. L.228 J.D. [Ⓒ Baker&M.]
*PRACTICE AREAS: Tax Planning and Advice.
Spencer, Anna L. ....'69 '95 C.797 B.A. L.880 J.D. [Ⓐ Arent F.K.P.&K.]
*PRACTICE AREAS: Health Care Fraud; Health Care Regulation; Information and Privacy; Health Care Reimbursement; Health Care Legislation.
Spencer, Brad W., (AV) ....'57 '83 C.188 B.S. L.228 J.D. [Gordon&B.]
*PRACTICE AREAS: Labor Law; Employee Benefits; Health Law; Commercial Law; Insurance.
Spencer, Eric C. '63 '92 C.1505 B.S.M.E. L.1325 J.D.
(adm. in NY; not adm. in DC; Pat.) [Ⓐ Katten M.Z.]
*PRACTICE AREAS: Patents; Intellectual Property; Computer Law.
Spencer, George H., (AV) '28 '52
C.976 B.E. L.188 J.D. [Venable,A.B.H.&C.] (See Pat. Sect.)
*PRACTICE AREAS: Intellectual Property Law; Patent Law; Trademark Law; Litigation.
Spencer, Margaret S. ....'60 '86 C.674 A.B. L.813 J.D. Pres., Spencer Consulting
Spencer, Robert L. ....'37 '91 C.445 B.S. L.446 J.D. [Ⓒ Hogan&H.]
*PRACTICE AREAS: Drug and Medical Device Regulation.
Spencer, William Gregory ....'54 '80 C&L.574 B.S., J.D. Asst. Fed. Pub. Def.

Spencer & Frank
(See Venable, Attorneys at Law, Venable, Baetjer and Howard, LLP)

Spencer, Graham & Holderman, (AV)
2000 Massachusetts Avenue, N.W., 20036-1022
Telephone: 202-785-1220 Facsimile: 202-785-1807
Email: SGHLaw@aol.com
Members of Firm: Samuel Spencer (1910-1997); Donald K. Graham; Richard A. Holderman; Patrick J. Howley; R. Scott Gardner.
Probate, Trust, Estate Planning, Corporate and Tax Law and General Practice.
See Professional Biographies, WASHINGTON, DISTRICT OF COLUMBIA

Sperduto, Kim Hoyt, (AV) ....'53 '80 C.880 B.A. L.228 J.D. [Sperduto]
*PRACTICE AREAS: Financial Services Litigation; Real Estate Litigation; Insurance Coverage; Environmental Litigation; Intellectual Property.

Sperduto Law Firm, The, P.L.C., (AV)
2021 L Street N.W. Second Floor, 20036
Telephone: 202-408-8900 Fax: 202-408-8910 URL: http://www.sperdutolaw.com
Email: ksperduto@sperdutolaw.com URL: http://www.lawyers.com/sperdutolawfirm
Kim Hoyt Sperduto;—Marian K. Riedy; John E. Howell; T. Stewart Rauch (Not admitted in DC); Michael J. Wade (Not admitted in DC).
Complex Commercial Litigation including Financial Services, Shareholder, Real Estate, Environmental, Intellectual Property, Government Contracts, Employment, Insurance Coverage, Construction, and Sports Law.
See Professional Biographies, WASHINGTON, DISTRICT OF COLUMBIA

Spergel, Barry A. ....'52 '78 C.918 B.A. L.976 J.D. Sr. Coun., World Wildlife Fund
Sperling, Aliza '74 '01 C.66 B.A. L.569 J.D.
(adm. in MA; not adm. in DC) [Ⓐ Cleary,G.S.&H.]
Sperry, Stacie Simmons ....'74 '99 C.612 B.S. L.276 J.D. [Ⓐ Jones,D.R.&P.]
Speser, Philip ....'51 '81 L.107 J.D. Federation of Amer. Scientists
Spicer, Ibn D. ....'68 '95 C.832 B.S. L.329 J.D. 1900 W Place N.E.
Spidi, John J., (AV) ....'57 '82 C.588 B.A. L.1202 J.D. [Malizia S.&F.]
*PRACTICE AREAS: Securities; Corporate; Banking.
Spiegel, Daniel L. ....'45 '80 C.910 B.A. L.276 J.D. [Akin,G.S.H.&F.]
*PRACTICE AREAS: International Trade; Public Policy.
Spiegel, Leslie H. '71 '00 C.893 B.A. L.446 J.D.
(adm. in MD; not adm. in DC) [Ⓐ Dickstein S.M.&O.]
*PRACTICE AREAS: Complex Dispute Resolution.

Spiegel & McDiarmid, (AV)
1350 New York Avenue, N.W., 20005-4798
Telephone: 202-879-4000 Facsimile: 202-393-2866
Email: info@spiegelmcd.com URL: http://www.spiegelmcd.com
Members of Firm: George Spiegel (1919-1997); Robert C. McDiarmid; Robert A. Jablon; James N. Horwood; Alan J. Roth; Frances E. Francis; Daniel I. Davidson; Thomas C. Trauger; John J. Corbett, Jr.; Cynthia Schneider Bogorad; Gary J. Newell; Scott H. Strauss; Ben Finkelstein; Lisa G. Dowden; Rise J. Peters; Peter J. Hopkins; David E. Pomper; William S. Huang. Of Counsel: Lee C. White; Sandra J. Strebel; Margaret A. McGoldrick; P. Daniel Bruner; Barry M. Smoler; Margaret A. Meiser. Associates: Matthew W. Ward; Jeffrey A. Schwarz; David B. Lieb; Pablo O. Nüesch; Andrea G. Lonian; Larissa A. Shamraj; Tracy E. Connor (Not admitted in DC).
Energy, Administrative, Airports and Aviation, Antitrust, Appellate, Communications and Media, Environmental, Federal Legislative, Government Affairs, Hydroelectricity, Litigation, Municipal Infrastructure, Natural Resources, Public Utility, Qui Tam, Regulatory and Transportation Law before Federal and State Courts, Agencies and Congress.
See Professional Biographies, WASHINGTON, DISTRICT OF COLUMBIA

Spielberg, Anne ....'60 '86 C.604 A.B. L.477 J.D. [Harmon,C.S.&E.]
Spielman, Michael A. ....'70 '96 C.910 B.A. L.930 J.D. [Ⓐ Shaw P.]
*PRACTICE AREAS: Taxation; Corporate; Business.
Spies, Charles R. '72 '98 C.477 B.A. L.276 J.D.
(adm. in VA; not adm. in DC) Dep. Coun.
Spiezio, Julie ....'59 '84 C.436 B.A. L.734 J.D. Amer. Council of Life Ins.
Spiezio, Nicholas J. ....'41 '69 C.103 B.A. L.276 J.D. [Ⓐ Hurwitz&A.]
Spigel, Jeffrey S. ....'67 '92 C.1365 B.A. L.472 J.D. [King&S.]
*PRACTICE AREAS: Litigation; Trade Regulation.
Spiliotes, Nicholas J. ....'55 '86 C.951 B.A. L.178 J.D. [Morrison&F.]
*PRACTICE AREAS: Project Finance; Corporate Finance; International.
Spillan, Lawrence Michael, (AV) ....'43 '82 C.446 B.A. L.1234 J.D. 503 D St., NW
Spillman, C. Fairley ....'59 '84 C.228 B.A. L.309 J.D. [Akin,G.S.H.&F.]
*PRACTICE AREAS: Litigation.
Spina, John J. ....'71 '99 C.555 B.A. L.575 J.D. [Ⓐ Davis&H.]
*PRACTICE AREAS: Taxation Law; Insurance Law.
Spina, Stephen M. ....'— '96 C.93 B.A. L.861 J.D. [Ⓐ Morgan,L.&B.]
Spindel, Marla P. ....'68 '93 C.188 B.A. L.273 J.D. [Ⓐ Powers,P.S.&V.]
*PRACTICE AREAS: Health Care Law; Fraud; Managed Care; Administrative Law; Corporate Law.
Spingarn, Jerome H. ....'14 '40 C.197 A.B. L.178 J.D. 1409 29th St., N.W.
Spingler, Frank J., Jr. '44 '72 C.712 B.A. L.276 J.D.
Sr. V.P., Real Estate, Potomac Capital Investment Corporation
*RESPONSIBILITIES: Real Estate Law.
Spinner, Joseph J. '52 '77
C.401 B.A. L.276 J.D. Dep. Gen. Coun., Inter-Amer. Develop. Bk.
Spirer, Julian H., (AV) ....'47 '72 C.674 A.B. L.309 J.D. [Spirer&G.] ⊙
*PRACTICE AREAS: Corporate; Tax Exempt Organizations; International Law; Civil Litigation; Immigration Law.

Spirer & Goldberg, P.C., (AV)
927 Fifteenth Street, N.W., Third Floor, 20005 ⊙
Telephone: 202-628-2900 Telecopier: 202-628-4608 URL: http://www.spirerandgoldberg.com
Email: FGoldberg@spirerandGoldberg.com URL: http://www.lawyers.com/spirergoldberglaw
Julian H. Spirer; Fred B. Goldberg. Of Counsel: Hans Ulfson Andersen.
General Corporate, Non-Profit Organizations, Family Law, Personal Injury, Medical Malpractice, Professional Malpractice, International, Immigration, Estate Planning, Employment Law, Wrongful Death.
Rockville, Maryland Office: 20 Courthouse Square, Suite 210, 20850. Telephone: 301-570-0343.
See Professional Biographies, WASHINGTON, DISTRICT OF COLUMBIA

Spitalney, Leslie S. ....'67 '92 C.893 B.A. L.273 J.D. [Ⓐ Holland&K.]
*PRACTICE AREAS: Intellectual Property; Litigation.
Spitulnik, Charles A., (AV) ....'51 '79 C.604 A.B. L.893 J.D. [McLeod,W.&M.]
*PRACTICE AREAS: Transportation Law; Labor Law; Administrative Law; Corporate Law.
Spitz, Jerry David ....'61 '87 C.205 B.S.B.A. L.273 J.D. [Ⓐ Ashcraft&G.]
*PRACTICE AREAS: Personal Injury.
Spitz, Stephen L. ....'47 '72 C.477 A.B. L.145 J.D. [Ⓒ Kalijarvi,C.&N.]
*PRACTICE AREAS: Civil Rights; Labor and Employment; Discrimination.
Spitzer, Arthur B., (AV) '49 '75 C.188 B.S. L.976 J.D.
Legal Dir., ACLU of the National Capital Area
Spiva, Bruce ....'66 '93 C.976 B.A. L.309 J.D. [Jenner&B.]
*PRACTICE AREAS: Litigation; Antitrust; Trade Regulation; Class Action Litigation; Media and First Amendment.
Spivack, Peter S. ....'63 '88 C.813 B.A. L.1068 J.D. [Hogan&H.]
*PRACTICE AREAS: White Collar Criminal; False Claims Act; Civil Litigation.
Spivack, Stephen R., (AV) ....'46 '72 C.831 B.A. L.273 J.D. [Spriggs&H.]
*PRACTICE AREAS: White Collar Crime; Litigation.
Spivak, Andrew N. ....'73 '98 C.696 B.A. L.64 J.D. [Ⓐ Morrison&F.]
*PRACTICE AREAS: Intellectual Property.
Spivak, Kevin R. ....'69 '97 C.273 B.S.Comp.E. L.30 J.D. [Ⓐ Morrison&F.] (Pat.)
*PRACTICE AREAS: Intellectual Property.
Spivak, Marjorie Giller ....'63 '87 C.30 B.A. L.128 J.D. [Bennet&B.]
*PRACTICE AREAS: Communications Law.
Spivak, Mark R. ....'58 '83 C.529 B.A. L.276 J.D. [Vinson&E.]
*PRACTICE AREAS: Project Finance; Energy.
Spivey, Michael O., (AV) ....'55 '88 C.88 B.A. L.276 J.D. [Ⓒ C.L.Burgess]
*PRACTICE AREAS: Healthcare.
Splitt, David A. '45 '71 C.886 B.A. L.904 J.D.
Gen. Coun., University of the District of Columbia
Spohr, David William '69 '97 C.95 A.B. L.893 J.D.
(adm. in WA; not adm. in DC) U.S. Dept. of Jus.
Spokes, Jennifer J. ....'70 '98 C.228 A.B. L.94 J.D. [Ⓐ Patton B.]
Sponzo, Marilyn A. '53 '87 C.788 B.A. L.184 J.D.
(adm. in MA; not adm. in DC) [Ⓒ Jorden B.]
*PRACTICE AREAS: Insurance; Securities.
Spooner, Eric P. ....'65 '92 C.103 A.B. L.309 J.D. [Ⓐ White&C.]
Spooner, Joshua E. ....'72 '00 C.273 B.A. L.431 J.D. [Ⓐ McKee N.]
*PRACTICE AREAS: Securitization.
Spooner, Nancy Killien ....'66 '93 C&L.945 B.A., J.D. [Swidler B.S.F.]
*PRACTICE AREAS: Telecommunications Law.
Sporkin, Stanley ....'32 '58 C.645 B.A. L.976 LL.B. [Weil,G.&M.]
Spotts, David A. ....'57 '88 C.201 B.S. L.813 J.D. Sr. Atty., NASD Regulation, Inc.
Spracker, Stanley M., (BV) ....'52 '80 C.966 B.A. L.145 J.D. [Weil,G.&M.]
*PRACTICE AREAS: Environmental Law; Health and Safety Law; EPA; OSHA.
Spradlin, Anna Lincoln ....'71 '97 C.475 B.A. L.477 J.D. [Ⓐ Paul,H.J.&W.]
*PRACTICE AREAS: Employment Law.
Spragens, Janet R. ....'43 '68 C.914 B.A. L.273 J.D. Amer. Univ.
Sprague, E. Sue ....'— '80 C.846 B.A. L.276 J.D. Assoc. Gen. Coun., Fannie Mae
*RESPONSIBILITIES: Business; Mortgage Finance; Securities.
Sprague, Mary Gabrielle ....'57 '84 C.309 A.B. L.976 J.D. [Arnold&P.]
*PRACTICE AREAS: Environmental; Indian Law; Civil Litigation.
Sprague, Morgain Mary '72 '00 C.383 B.A. L.150 J.D.
(adm. in VA; not adm. in DC) Litig. Atty., Paralyzed Veterans of America
Sprague, Sharon A., (AV) ....'55 '82 C.813 A.B. L.1066 J.D. Asst. U.S. Atty.
Spranger, Susan G. '55 '84 C&L.201 B.S., J.D.
(adm. in VA; not adm. in DC) West Publishing Corp.
Spreadbury, Andrew W. ....'67 '95 C.976 B.A. L.893 J.D. KPMG
Sprenger, Kyle Micah '74 '99 C.260 B.S. L.575 J.D.
(adm. in NC; not adm. in DC) DynCorp
Sprenger, Paul C., (AV) ....'40 '65 C&L.477 B.B.A., J.D. [Sprenger&L.]
*PRACTICE AREAS: Employment; Complex Federal Litigation.
Sprenger, Steven M. ....'62 '88 C.293 B.A. L.352 J.D. [Sprenger&L.]
*PRACTICE AREAS: Employment Law; Civil Rights; Complex Federal Litigation.

Sprenger & Lang, PLLC, (AV) BR
1614 Twentieth Street, N.W., 20009 ⊙
Telephone: 202-265-8010 Fax: 202-332-6652
URL: http://www.sprengerlang.com
Members of Firm: Jane Lang; Paul C. Sprenger; Michael D. Lieder; Lawrence P. Schaefer (Not admitted in DC; Resident, Minneapolis, Minnesota Office); Steven M. Sprenger; Daniel Wolf; Susan E. Stokes (Not admitted in DC; Resident, Minneapolis, Minnesota Office); Susan M. Coler (Not admitted in DC; Resident, Minneapolis, Minnesota Office);—Cynthia J. Totten (Not admitted in DC); Lisa C. Stratton (Resident, Minneapolis, Minnesota Office); David L. Shulman (Not admitted in DC); Sara Madsen (Not admitted in DC; Resident, Minneapolis, Minnesota Office). Of Counsel: Mara R. Thompson (Not admitted in DC; Resident, Minneapolis, Minnesota Office); Teresa K. Patton (Not admitted in DC; Resident, Minneapolis, Minnesota Office).
Employment Litigation, Professional and Trade Associations, Civil Rights, Complex Federal Litigation.
Minneapolis, Minnesota Office: Sprenger & Lang, PLLC, 325 Ridgewood Avenue. Telephone: 612-871-8910. Fax: 612-871-9270.
See Professional Biographies, WASHINGTON, DISTRICT OF COLUMBIA

Spriggs, Karyl Terese '63 '88 C.103 A.B. L.893 J.D.
Assoc. Dir., Legal Servs. Programs, Whitman-Walker Clinic Legal Servs.
*RESPONSIBILITIES: Social Security; Estate Planning for the Disabled; Disability Discrimination; Debtors Rights.
Spriggs, William J., (AV) ....'39 '64 C.1 B.A. L.900 J.D. [Spriggs&H.]
*PRACTICE AREAS: Government Contracts; Government Procurement; Litigation.

Spriggs & Hollingsworth, (AV)
1350 I Street, N.W., Suite 900, 20005
Telephone: 202-898-5800 Telecopier: 202-682-1639
Email: Postmaster@spriggs.com URL: http://www.spriggs.com
Members of Firm: William J. Spriggs; Joe G. Hollingsworth; Catherine R. Baumer; Edward J. Beder, Jr.; Bruce J. Berger; Neil S. Bromberg; Martin C. Calhoun; William J. Cople III; Donald W. Fowler; Patrick R. Harkins; Cynthia Kendrick; Stephen A. Klein; Michael S. Koplan; Eric G. Lasker; Katharine R. Latimer; Charles S. Leeper; Frank Leone, Jr.; C. Robert Manor; Marc S. Mayerson; Donald R. McMinn; Douglas L. Patin; Gary I. Rubin; Bonnie J. Semilof; Robert L. Shapiro; Stephen R. Spivack; Rosemary Stewart; Jerry Stouck; Robert J. Symon; Paul V. Waters; Rebecca A. Womeldorf. Of Counsel: Julie A. Blum; Conrad J. Jacoby. Associates: Shawn D. Bryant; William S. D. Cravens (Not admitted in DC); Jean M. Cunningham; Christopher G. Cwalina; Monica A. Freas; Eric A. Frechtel (Not admitted in DC); Glenn S. Greene; Kirby T. Griffis; Vivek Hatti (Not admitted in DC); Robert E. Johnston; Claire E. Kresse; Conrad C. Ledoux; Michael R. Miner; Andrea D. Rose; Peter J. Skalaban Jr.; Scott S. Thomas.

(This Listing Continued)

Spriggs & Hollingsworth (Continued)

Specializing in: Antitrust, Asbestos Defense, Banking Litigation, Civil Appeals, Complex Commercial Litigation, Construction Law, Drug and Medical Device Defense; Employment Law, Environmental Law, Federal Claims, Government Contracts, Government Procurement, Insurance Coverage, International Arbitration, Litigation, Products Liability, Toxic Torts and White Collar Crime.

See Professional Biographies, WASHINGTON, DISTRICT OF COLUMBIA

Sprigman, Christopher '— '95 C.659 B.A. L.145 J.D. (adm. in NY; not adm. in DC) [Ⓒ King&S.]
*PRACTICE AREAS: Litigation; Trade Regulation.

Spring, Heather .... '71 '97 C.1044 B.A. L.904 J.D. [Ⓐ Sher&B.]
*PRACTICE AREAS: Transportation; Maritime Law; Litigation; Administrative Law; Government Contracts.

Spring, Margaret F. .... '60 '93 C.197 B.A. L.228 J.D. 1722 I St., N.W.

Springer, David E. .... '53 '79 C.228 A.B. L.904 J.D. [Venable,A.B.H.&C.]
*PRACTICE AREAS: Legislative.

Springer, James vanR., (AV) .... '34 '62 C&L.309 A.B., LL.B. [Dickstein S.M.&O.]
*PRACTICE AREAS: Antitrust Law; Appellate Practice; Federal Practice.

Springer, Kenneth D. .... '60 '94 C.277 B.E.E. L.276 J.D. [Ⓐ Long A.&N.] (Pat.)
*PRACTICE AREAS: Patents, Trademark, Copyright.

Springer, Rebecca L. .... '71 '99 C.910 B.A. L.228 J.D. [Ⓐ Crowell&M.]

Springfield, Craig R. .... '64 '90 C.1175 B.S.B.A. L.260 J.D. [Davis&H.]
*PRACTICE AREAS: Taxation Law; Insurance Law.

Springmann, J. Michael .... '45 '98 C.276 B.F.S. L.30 J.D. 4619 Yuma St., N.W.

Springsteen, George S. '58 '84 C.197 A.B. L.930 J.D. Chf. Coun., International Fin. Corp.

Springsteen, Joseph E. .... '— '00 C.575 B.A. L.30 J.D. [Ⓐ Piper M.R.&W.]
*PRACTICE AREAS: Franchise Law; Distribution.

Spulak, Thomas J. .... '56 '82 C.472 B.A. L.259 J.D. [Shaw P.]

Spurlin, Margaret H. .... '47 '79 C.788 B.A. L.823 J.D. [Ⓒ Paul,H.J.&W.]
*PRACTICE AREAS: Labor Law; Airline Labor Law; Railway Labor Law; Labor Issues Relating to Corporate Mergers/Restructurings/Bankruptcies; Formation of Non-union Subsidiaries and Double-breasted Operations.

Spyropoulos, George E. .... '26 '53 C.790 A.B. L.276 J.D. 4639 Van Ness St., N.W.‡

Squire, Daniel H. .... '54 '80 C.976 B.A. L.309 J.D. [Wilmer,C.&P.]
*PRACTICE AREAS: Civil Practice; Environmental Law; Financial Institutions; Litigation.

Squire, Sanders & Dempsey L.L.P., (AV) BB
1201 Pennsylvania Avenue, N.W., P.O. Box 407, 20044-0407 ⊙
Telephone: 202-626-6600 Fax: 202-626-6780
URL: http://www.ssd.com
Partners: John H. C. Barron Jr.; Timothy W. Bergin; Sam Black; Ann R. Brashear; A. Randolph Bregman; Alan L. Briggs; Donald T. Bucklin; John A. Burlingame; Sarah C. Carey; James V. Dick; Charles F. Donley II; Charles Friedlander; Edward A. Geltman; Coralyn Goode; Lisa G. Henneberry; John C. Henry Jr.; John A. Howell; Robert B. Kelly; George M. Knapp; Scott T. Kragie; Henry W. Lavine; Glenn W. Letham; James J. Maiwurm; Joseph P. Markoski; Herbert E. Marks; William A. Mogel; James P. Murphy; Jonathan Jacob Nadler; David A. Nall; Paul A. O'Hop Jr.; Robert D. Papkin; Douglas L. Povich; Barry A. Pupkin; Edward W. Sauer; Marshall Sanford Sinick; Ritchie T. Thomas; Nancy A. White; Robert I. White; Glenn M. Young. Of Counsel: Francis S. Rath; Judith J. Semo; Louis Stokes. Associates: Amy L. Brown; Elizabeth C. Collins; Amy L. Easton; Amy L. Friedman; Christopher H. Gordon; Mark D. Johnson; Donnie L. Kidd, Jr.; Vladimir V. Kouznetsov; Kevin S. Levey; Susan L. Maslen (Not admitted in the United States); Iain R. McPhie; Alvaro J. Mestre; Bruce A. Olcott; Marcela Villalta Scott; Anne K. Shukis (Not admitted in DC); Angela M. Simpson (Not admitted in DC); Thomas E. Skilton; James P. Wehner.
General and International Practice.
U.S. Offices: Cincinnati, Cleveland, Columbus, Houston, Jacksonville, Los Angeles, Miami, New York, Palo Alto, Phoenix, San Francisco, Tampa, Tysons Corner.
European Offices: Bratislava, Brussels, Budapest, Kyiv, London, Madrid, Milan, Moscow, Prague.
Asian Offices: Almaty, Beijing, Hong Kong, Taipei, Tokyo.

See Professional Biographies, WASHINGTON, DISTRICT OF COLUMBIA

Squires, Jeffrey L., (AV) .... '46 '73 C.910 B.A. L.966 J.D. [Simon,T.&M.]
*PRACTICE AREAS: Commercial Litigation; Corporate Litigation; Information Technology; Copyrights; Trademarks.

Srere, Mark A. .... '59 '86 C.685 B.A. L.846 J.D. [Morgan,L.&B.]

Srinivasan, Srikanth '67 '99 C&L.813 B.A., J.D. (adm. in CA; not adm. in DC) [Ⓐ O'Melveny&M.]

Sroufe, Linda Y. .... '51 '86 C.597 B.A. L.273 J.D. [Ⓐ Rose&R.]
*PRACTICE AREAS: Employment Litigation.

Srour, Danielle R. .... '57 '82 C.518 A.B. L.659 J.D. [Ⓒ Shaw P.]
*PRACTICE AREAS: Securities; Corporate.

Staas, H. J., (AV) .... '38 '64 C.401 B.S. L.276 LL.B. [Staas&H.] (See Pat. Sect.)
*PRACTICE AREAS: Intellectual Property Law; Patent, Trademark, Copyright and Unfair Competition.

Staas & Halsey LLP, (AV)
700 Eleventh Street, N.W., Suite 500, 20001
Telephone: 202-434-1500 Facsimile: 202-434-1501
Email: info@s-n-h.com URL: http://www.staasandhalsey.com
Members of Firm: H. J. Staas; James D. Halsey, Jr.; David M. Pitcher; John C. Garvey; J. Randall Beckers; William F. Herbert; Richard A. Gollhofer; Mark J. Henry; Paul I. Kravetz; Gene M. Garner, II; Michael D. Stein. Associates. Jonathan H. Muskin (Not admitted in DC); Stephen T. Boughner (Not admitted in DC); Christine J. Gilsdorf; Mehdi D. Sheikerz (Not admitted in DC); John H. Stowe (Not admitted in DC); James G. McEwen (Not admitted in DC); Michael John Badagliacca (Not admitted in DC); Alicia M. Choi (Not admitted in DC); Heath E. Wells (Not admitted in DC); James T. Strom (Not admitted in DC); Eric Berkowitz (Not admitted in DC).
Patent, Trademark, Copyright, Unfair Competition and Computer Law. International Patent and Trademark Practice. Practice before Federal Courts and Administrative Agencies.

See Professional Biographies, WASHINGTON, DISTRICT OF COLUMBIA

Stabbe, Mitchell H., (AV) .... '55 '80 C.696 B.A. L.145 J.D. [Dow,L.&A.]

Stachiw, Mark A. .... '61 '85 C&L.112 A.B., J.D. [Ⓒ Paul,H.J.&W.]
*PRACTICE AREAS: Telecommunications Law; Corporate; Interconnection Regulatory.

Stack, Kevin M. .... '68 '00 C.103 A.B. L.976 J.D. [Ⓐ Jenner&B.]
*PRACTICE AREAS: Litigation.

Stack, Laura Barton .... '68 '96 C.1169 B.A. L.1065 J.D. [Ⓐ Slevin&H.]
*PRACTICE AREAS: Employee Benefits.

Stack, Robert B. .... '55 '87 C.1044 B.A. L.276 J.D. [Wilmer,C.&P.]
*PRACTICE AREAS: Taxation; Civil Practice.

Stade, Nancy K. .... '65 '95 C&L.178 A.B., J.D. [Ⓐ Hale&D.]
*PRACTICE AREAS: Food and Drug Regulation.

Stadler, Frances M., (BV) '58 '85 C.896 B.A. L.893 J.D. Dep. Sr. Coun., Investment Co. Inst.
*RESPONSIBILITIES: Securities.

Stadnicki, Alfred A. '50 '78 C.422 B.S.C.E. L.1048 J.D. (adm. in MA; not adm. in DC; See Pat. Sect.) [Lalos&K.]

Stadulis, Lawrence P. .... '64 '90 C&L.93 B.A., J.D. [Morgan,L.&B.]

Staebler, Michael B., (AV) '43 '69 C.309 B.A. L.477 J.D. (adm. in MI; not adm. in DC) [Pepper H.] (⊙Detroit, MI)
*PRACTICE AREAS: Business Acquisitions; Securities; Venture Capital.

Stafford, James L., (BV) ...... '36 '62 C.254 A.B. L.329 LL.B. 4308 Georgia Ave., N.W.

Stahl, Howard H., (AV) .... '48 '73 C.140 B.S. L.276 J.D. [Steptoe&J.]
*PRACTICE AREAS: Commercial Litigation.

Stahl, Lawrence A., (AV) '54 '79 C.94 A.B. L.273 J.D. [Fitzpatrick,C.H.&S.] (See Pat. Sect.)

Stahlman, Kimberly J. .... '68 '98 C.30 B.S.B.A. L.309 J.D. [Ⓐ Hogan&H.]
*PRACTICE AREAS: Employee Benefits; Taxation.

Staley, Mary J. R. .... '71 '97 C.321 B.A. L.128 J.D. [Ⓐ Steptoe&J.]

Staley, Mary Tuck .... '57 '83 C.385 B.A. L.30 J.D. [Ⓒ Collier S.S.]
*PRACTICE AREAS: International Trade Law.

Staley, Timothy W. .... '72 '97 C.363 B.A. L.128 J.D. [Ⓐ Wiley R.&F.]
*PRACTICE AREAS: Government Contracts; Litigation; Business Counseling.

Stallard, Kenneth G., (AV) '63 '88 C.886 B.A. L.902 J.D. [Thompson,O.M.N.&H.] (⊙Arlington, VA)
*PRACTICE AREAS: Small Corporations; Construction Defects; Commercial Leasing; Contract Litigation; Personal Injury.

Stallings, William S. '45 '81 C&L.705 B.A., J.D. (adm. in MD; not adm. in DC) MCI Telecom. Corp.

Stamoulas, Maria A. .... '63 '89 C.945 B.A. L.309 J.D. [Facer&S.]

Stamper, Ryan J. '75 '00 C.893 B.S. L.273 J.D. (adm. in VA; not adm. in DC) [Ⓐ Sterne,K.G.&F.]
*PRACTICE AREAS: Intellectual Property.

Stanceu, Timothy Charles .... '51 '80 C.165 A.B. L.276 J.D. [Hogan&H.]
*PRACTICE AREAS: Customs Law; Foreign Trade Sanctions; International Trade Regulation; North American Free Trade Agreement; U.S. Foreign Trade Zones.

Stancil, Mark T. '74 '99 C&L.893 B.A., J.D. (adm. in VA; not adm. in DC) [Ⓐ Baker B.]

Stanco, Eric R. .... '62 '89 C.259 B.A. L.818 J.D. [E.R.Stanco&Assoc.]

Stanco, Eric R., & Associates ....126 C Street, NW

Standish, Daniel J. .... '60 '86 C.95 A.B. L.145 J.D. [Wiley R.&F.]
*PRACTICE AREAS: Insurance; Litigation.

Stanford, Robert J., (AV) ....'29 '55 C&L.276 B.S., J.D. 1700 K St., N.W., Ste. 700

Stang, David P., P.C. .... '39 '70 C.645 B.A. L.273 J.D. 2019 Park Rd., NW

Stanislawczyk, Marc A. .... '— '97 C.659 B.A. L.128 J.D. [Ⓐ Arnold&P.]
*PRACTICE AREAS: Government Contracts; Litigation; Health Care and Pharmaceutical; Fraud, Abuse and Compliance.

Stanislawski, Howard J. .... '49 '86 C.012 B.A. L.93 J.D. [Sidley A.B.&W.]

Stanley, Amy L. Schaner '68 '96 C.95 B.A. L.904 J.D. (adm. in MD; not adm. in DC) [Ⓐ Piper M.R.&W.]
*PRACTICE AREAS: Environmental; Litigation.

Stanley, David W. .... '44 '72 C&L.893 B.A., J.D. [Cuneo]
*PRACTICE AREAS: Litigation.

Stanley, Earl R, (AV) .... '21 '49 C.381 B.S. L.273 J.D. 1735 New York Ave., N.W.‡

Stanley, Gary L. .... '53 '78 C.1365 B.A. L.309 J.D. [Ⓒ Shawncoulson]

Stanley, John P. .... '68 '96 C.309 B.A. L.477 J.D. 1776 K St., N.W.

Stanley, Joseph W. .... '13 '47 C.309 A.B. L.818 LL.B. 4600 Reservoir Rd.‡

Stanley, Karlyn D. .... '53 '83 C.477 B.A. L.128 J.D. [Cole,R.&B.]
*PRACTICE AREAS: Telecommunications; Telecommunications Competition; Internet Law; International Telecommunications.

Stanley, Mari R. '52 '85 C.999 B.A. L.64 J.D. (adm. in MD; not adm. in DC) Gen. Coun. Off., Assoc. Gen. Coun.

Stanley, Nancy E. '43 '71 C.388 B.A. L.273 J.D. Dir. Dispute Resolution Prog., U.S. Cts.

Stanley, Neil A. ......'67 '92 C.896 B.A. L.260 J.D. Asst. Corp. Coun., Offc. Corp. Coun.

Stanley, Tamar C. .... '70 '94 C.164 B.A. L.893 J.D. [Ⓐ Baker B.]

Stano, Phillip E. .... '53 '78 C&L.16 B.A., J.D. [Jorden B.]
*PRACTICE AREAS: Class Action Litigation; Insurance Law; Regulatory Law.

Stansbury, Claude B. .... '65 '91 C.276 B.S.F.S. L.1066 J.D. [Freshfields B.D.]
*PRACTICE AREAS: Tax.

Stansbury, Philip R., (AV) '31 '56 C.311 A.B. L.309 J.D. 1201 Pennsylvania Ave., N.W.

Stansbury, Todd M., (AV) .... '62 '90 C.839 B.S. L.904 J.D. [Wiley R.&F.]
*PRACTICE AREAS: Communications; Business Law; Finance.

Stansbury, Wanda R. '56 '00 C.514 B.S. L.178 J.D. (adm. in NY; not adm. in DC) [Ⓐ Arent F.K.P.&K.]

Stansel, James C. .... '70 '98 C.101 B.S. L.976 J.D. 1722 Eye St.

Stanton, James V. .... '32 '61 C.201 L.1003 LL.B. 1310 19th St., N.W.

Stanton, John F. .... '71 '97 C.197 B.A. L.276 J.D. [Ⓐ Howrey S.A.&W.]
*PRACTICE AREAS: Commercial Litigation; Appellate Advocacy; Insurance Coverage.

Stanton, John Maloney '63 '89 C.861 B.A. L.276 J.D. Coun. & Envir. Comm. Dir., Natl. Conference of State Legis.

Stanton, John S. .... '54 '79 C.112 A.B. L.309 J.D. [Hogan&H.]
*PRACTICE AREAS: Legislative Practice; Taxation; Public Pension Plans.

Stanton, Richard P. .... '64 '90 C.93 B.A. L.276 J.D. [Ⓒ Nixon P.]
*PRACTICE AREAS: Government Relations; Intellectual Property Law.

Stanton, Thomas R. '60 '88 C.101 B.A. L.273 J.D. (adm. in MI; not adm. in DC) Sr. Coun., Marriott Intl., Inc.
*RESPONSIBILITIES: Litigation.

Stapel, Julie K. .... '70 '96 C.477 B.A. L.347 J.D. [Ⓐ Patton B.]

Staple, Gregory C. .... '53 '78 C.696 B.A. L.477 J.D. [Vinson&E.]
*PRACTICE AREAS: Telecommunications Law; Communications and Media; Commercial Law.

Stapleton, Thomas L. .... '34 '59 C.102 B.A. L.659 LL.B. [Ⓒ Davis&H.]
*PRACTICE AREAS: Taxation Law; Insurance Law; Legislative Practice; Tax Litigation.

Starek, Roscoe B., III ....'47 '73 C.823 A.B. L.30 J.D. Sr. V.P., Direct Mktg. Assoc.

Stark, Nathan J. ....'20 '49 C.1027 B.S. L.146 J.D. 1401 New York Ave. NW

Stark, Richard C., (AV) .... '— '76 C&L.880 B.A., J.D. [McKee N.]
*PRACTICE AREAS: Taxation; Federal Taxation; Federal Income Tax; Federal Tax Controversies; Tax Litigation.

Stark, Roger D. .... '55 '85 C.994 B.A. L.880 J.D. [Coudert B.]
*PRACTICE AREAS: Business Transactions; Financial Transactions; Energy; Infrastructure; International Law.

Stark, Sanford W. .... '66 '91 C.976 B.A. L.228 J.D. [McKee N.]
*PRACTICE AREAS: Tax Litigation; Litigation; Federal Tax Controversies.

Stark, Sheila .... '64 '88 C.945 B.A. L.273 J.D. [Ⓒ Piper M.R.&W.]
*PRACTICE AREAS: Government Contracts; Litigation Counseling; Contract Law.

Starke, Jane Sutter, (AV) .... '56 '82 C.183 B.A. L.1019 J.D. [Thompson C.]
*PRACTICE AREAS: Transportation; Legislative Law.

Starke, R. Penfield .... '56 '82 C.882 B.A. L.221 J.D. 3103 Garfield St., N.W.

Starkey, Sheila T. '67 '95 C.107 B.A. L.494 J.D. (adm. in MN; not adm. in DC) [Marty,L.&S.]

Starling, Kenneth G., (AV) .... '48 '73 C.575 A.B. L.228 J.D. [Piper M.R.&W.]
*PRACTICE AREAS: Antitrust; Litigation; Mergers and Acquisitions.

Starnes, Thomas E., (AV) .... '57 '83 C.431 B.A. L.273 J.D. [Ⓒ Andrews&K.]
*PRACTICE AREAS: Church and State; Ecclesiastical Law; Federal Civil Litigation; Environmental Litigation; First Amendment Law.

Starobin, A. Fred, (BV) .... '25 '56 C.446 B.S.E.E. L.273 J.D. 419 7th St., N.W. (Pat.)

Starr, David A. .... '58 '81 C.472 A.B. L.910 J.D. [Williams&J.]

Starr, Dawn E. .... '54 '81 C.401 B.A. L.930 J.D. [Ⓒ Akin,G.S.H.&F.]
*PRACTICE AREAS: Labor and Employment.

Starr, H. David .... '72 '98 C.446 B.A. L.273 J.D. [Ⓐ Slavit&G.]

Starr, Helen P. .... '47 '79 C.643 B.A. L.276 J.D. [Ⓒ Perkins C.]
*PRACTICE AREAS: Corporate Law; Executive Compensation; Nonprofit Associations; Mergers and Acquisitions.

Starr, Judson W., (AV) '45 '75 C.901 B.A. L.276 J.D. [Venable,A.B.H.&C.] (⊙Balt., MD)
*PRACTICE AREAS: Environmental Law; Environmental Crimes; Litigation; Government and Special Investigations Law; Criminal Law.

Starr, Kenneth W., (AV) .... '46 '73 C.273 A.B. L.228 J.D. [Kirkland&E.]
*PRACTICE AREAS: Appellate Litigation; Commercial Litigation; Antitrust Law.
Starrett, Sarah J. .... '58 '92 C.917 B.A. L.276 J.D. [Beins,A.&K.]
Statland, Edward M., (AV) .... '32 '59 C&L.273 B.A., J.D. [Statland&B.]
*PRACTICE AREAS: Commercial Law; Broker-Dealer Arbitration; Arbitration; Estate Planning; Estate Administration.

Statland & Buckley, P.C., (AV)
1828 L Street, N.W., Suite 660, 20036-5112
Telephone: 202-296-0555 Fax: 202-296-9434
Email: lawyers@statbuck.com
Edward M. Statland; David W. Buckley.
General Civil, Litigation, Commercial, Corporate, Real Estate, Construction, Negligence, Family and Creditor's Rights.
See Professional Biographies, WASHINGTON, DISTRICT OF COLUMBIA

Statman, Alan J., (AV) .... '53 '78 C.628 B.S. L.823 J.D. [Wright&T.]
*PRACTICE AREAS: Energy.
Staton, Kerry D., (AV) .... '54 '80 C.604 B.A. L.446 J.D. [Schochor,F.&S.] ⊙
*PRACTICE AREAS: Medical Malpractice Law; Products Liability Law; Civil Litigation.
Staton, Robert V., (AV) ....'36 '63 C.575 A.B. L.273 J.D. 1920 N. St., N.W.‡
Staub, Phillip T. '66 '92 C.645 B.A. L.273 J.D.
Asst. Gen. Coun., Washington Metropolitan Area Transit Authority
*RESPONSIBILITIES: Government Contracts; Litigation; Construction Law; Administrative Law.
Staudinger, Deborah Kim .... '55 '98 C.874 B.A. L.862 J.D. [🄰 Hogan&H.]
*PRACTICE AREAS: Energy; Commercial.
Stauffer, Ronald E. .... '49 '73 C.453 S.B. L.309 J.D. [Sonnenschein N.&R.]
*PRACTICE AREAS: Employee Benefits Law; Executive Compensation Law.
Stawasz, Michael J. '71 '97 C.197 A.B. L.276 J.D.
(adm. in MA; not adm. in DC) [🄰 Dow,L.&A.]
Stayin, Randolph J. ....'— '67 C.197 A.B. L.150 J.D. [Barnes&T.]
*PRACTICE AREAS: Antidumping; Countervailing Duties; Customs Law; Export Regulation; World Trade Organization.
Steadman, Charles W., (AV) ....'14 '39 C.546 A.B. L.309 J.D. 1730 K St., N.W.
Steadman, Dawn L. '73 '00 C&L.101 B.A., J.D.
(adm. in AZ; not adm. in DC) 625 Indiana Ave. N.W., Ste. 900
Stear, Melissa D. ....'73 '98 C.228 B.A. L.273 J.D. [🄰 Jones,D.R.&P.]
Stearn, Mitchell A. .... '58 '85 C&L.273 B.A., J.D. [Porter W.M.&A.]
*PRACTICE AREAS: Complex Litigation; Insurance; Environmental; Professional Liability; Mass Torts.
Stearns, Christopher T. '64 '89 C.951 B.A. L.188 J.D.
(adm. in NJ; not adm. in DC) [Hobbs,S.D.&W.] ‡
Stearns, Frederick A. ....'66 '93 C.188 B.S. L.273 J.D. [Keller&H.]
*PRACTICE AREAS: Food and Drug Law.
Stearns, James C. ....'50 '77 C.197 A.B. L.276 J.D. [Halloran&S.]
*PRACTICE AREAS: Administrative; Government Contracts; International Trade.
Stearns, Laurie ....'54 '93 C.399 B.A. L.1066 J.D. Asst Gen Coun.
Stebbins, Joshua R. ....'70 '98 C.367 B.A. L.569 J.D. [🄰 Wilmer,C.&P.]
Steed, James A. ....'44 '83 C.1365 B.A. L.30 J.D. 1616 16th St. N.W.
Steel, Adrian L., Jr. ....'50 '75 C.502 A.B. L.477 J.D. [Mayer,B.&P.]
Steel, Laura Nachowitz '56 '82 C.66 B.A. L.273 J.D.
[Wilson,E.M.E.&D.] (⊙Balt., MD)
*PRACTICE AREAS: Insurance Defense Law; Professional Malpractice Law; Psychotherapy Law; Fire Litigation; Police Civil Liability.
Steele, Charles J., (AV) '30 '54 C&L.276 A.B., J.D.
Blue Cross & Blue Shield of Natl. Capital Area
Steele, Charles N. ....'39 '66 C&L.309 A.B., LL.B. Conservation Intl.
Steele, Douglas L., (AV) .... '64 '90 C&L.823 B.S., J.D. [Woodley,G.&M.]
*PRACTICE AREAS: Labor and Employment Law; Fair Labor Standards Law.
Steele, H. John ....'55 '81 C.258 B.S. L.260 J.D. [McKee N.]
*PRACTICE AREAS: Securitization; Structured Finance; Corporate; Securities.
Steele, James P. .... '64 '92 C.205 B.A. L.128 J.D. [🄰 Carr G.]
Steele, Michael S. '58 '92 C.367 B.A. L.276 J.D.
(adm. in PA; not adm. in DC) [🄲 Smith C.]
Steele, Shari .. '59 '90 C&L.1338 B.A., J.D. Dir., Legal Servs., Electronic Frontier Found.
Steen, Ellen B. ....'66 '91 C.861 B.A. L.575 J.D. [🄲 Crowell&M.]
*PRACTICE AREAS: Environmental Law; Clean Water Act; Hazardous Materials and Substances.
Steers, Terry .... '74 '99 C.276 L.910 J.D. U.S. Dept. of State
Stefani, Laura A. ....'69 '97 C.399 B.A. L.273 J.D. [🄰 Kator,P.&W.]
*PRACTICE AREAS: Employment Law; Civil Litigation.
Stefanowicz, Elizabeth W. '60 '88 C.518 B.A. L.273 J.D.
(adm. in MA; not adm. in DC) Sr. Atty., THe Nasdaq Stock Market, Inc.
Steffan, John D. ....'46 '79 C.553 B.A. L.838 J.D. [Steffan&Assoc.] ⊙
Steffan & Associates .... 1620 L St., N.W. (⊙Fairfax, VA)
Steffe, Eric K. ....'64 '94 C.280 B.S. L.1209 J.D. [Sterne,K.G.&F.] (See Pat. Sect.)
*PRACTICE AREAS: Intellectual Property; Patent Licensing; Patent Infringement; Biochemical Patents; Biotechnology Patents.
Steffes, David A. '— '98 C.958 B.S. L.966 J.D.
(adm. in VA; not adm. in DC; Pat.) [🄰 Powell,G.F.&M.]
*PRACTICE AREAS: Patents; Intellectual Property; Technology Transfers; Technology Licensing.
Steffes, Larry R. '56 '83 C.436 B.A. L.966 J.D.
Dep. Gen. Coun., Corp. Affs., National Railroad Passenger Corp. (AMTRAK)
Stegeby, E. Kenneth .... '66 '00 C.1222 B.A. L.101 J.D. [🄰 Wiley R.&F.]
Stegemann, Traci J. ....'61 '86 C.951 B.A. L.276 J.D. 2300 N St., N.W.
Steggerda, Todd R. .... '65 '98 C.871 B.S. L.352 J.D. [🄰 Wilmer,C.&P.]
Stegmaier, Gerard M. .... '70 '00 C.1356 B.A. L.1209 J.D. [🄰 Wiley R.&F.]
*PRACTICE AREAS: Internet Law; E-Commerce; Business Law; Finance; Intellectual Property.
Steifel, Alysa M. ....'73 '99 C.205 B.A. L.884 J.D. Federal Trade Comm.
Steimel, Walter E., Jr. .... '56 '81 C.840 B.B.A. L.846 J.D. [Greenberg T.] (Pat.)
Steimer, Natacha D. ....'70 '95 C.30 B.A. L.273 J.D. [🄰 Wilmer,C.&P.]
Stein, Alisa Naomi '75 '00 C.477 B.A. L.276 J.D.
(adm. in VA; not adm. in DC) [🄰 Sutherland A.&B.]
*PRACTICE AREAS: Energy; Commodities.
Stein, Allan J. '50 '75 C.107 B.A. L.276 J.D.
V.P. & Asst. Gen. Coun., American Insurance Association
*RESPONSIBILITIES: Federal and State Insurance; Lobbying; Legislative/Regulatory; Litigation.
Stein, Barry G. .... '44 '70 C.831 A.B. L.273 J.D. [Deso,T.&S.]
Stein, Carolyn Israel '65 '91
C.823 B.S. L.273 J.D. [🄲 Bonner K.T.&C.] (⊙Rockville, MD)
*PRACTICE AREAS: Medical Malpractice; Construction Litigation; Product Liability; Premises Liability; Personal Injury.
Stein, Cheryl D. ....'53 '78 C&L.976 B.A., J.D. 705 8th St., S.E.
Stein, Donald S. ....'53 '81 C.273 B.A. L.904 J.D. [Manatt,P.&P.]
Stein, Gary A., (AV) '48 '80
C&L.276 B.S.F.S., J.D. [Margolius,M.D.R.&T.] (⊙Largo, MD)
*PRACTICE AREAS: Personal Injury; Negligence; Medical Malpractice.
Stein, Jacob A., (AV) .... '25 '48 C&L.273 LL.B. [Stein,M.&M.]
Stein, Julie E. '71 '00 C.453 B.S. L.273 J.D.
(adm. in CA; not adm. in DC; See Pat. Sect.) [🄰 Kenyon&K.]
*PRACTICE AREAS: Intellectual Property.
Stein, Kara M. ....'64 '92 C&L.976 B.A., J.D. 444 Russell Senate Off. Bldg.

Stein, Laurence E. '55 '93 C.1083 B.S.E.E. L.1209 J.D.
(adm. in VA; not adm. in DC) [🄰 Patton B.]
Stein, Linda S. .... '58 '83 C.914 B.A. L.309 J.D. [Steptoe&J.]
*PRACTICE AREAS: Civil Litigation; Railroads; Energy; Environmental Litigation.
Stein, Michael D. ....'65 '92 C.30 B.S.E.E. L.659 J.D. [Staas&H.] (See Pat. Sect.)
*PRACTICE AREAS: Intellectual Property Law; Patent, Trademark and Copyright Law.
Stein, Michael H., (AV) .... '42 '71 C.821 B.A. L.178 LL.B. [🄲 Dewey B.]
*PRACTICE AREAS: International Trade.
Stein, Michael J. '54 '86 C.951 B.A. L.861 J.D.
(adm. in VA; not adm. in DC) Asst. Gen. Coun., Marriott Intl., Inc.
Stein, Michael J. .... '65 '96 C.401 B.A. L.276 J.D. V.P., Govt. Rel., Morgan Stanley
Stein, Philip, Law Office of '36 '66
C.30 B.A. L.904 J.D. 1140 Connecticut Avenue, N.W., Suite 1202

Stein, Robert E., Law Office of, (AV) '39 '64 C.1036 B.A. L.178 LL.B.
4945 Brandywine Street, N.W., 20016
Telephone: 202-686-9090 Fax: 202-686-9098
Email: resteinlaw@aol.com
Health Care Law, Mediation, Arbitration and Dispute Resolution, Employment and Disability Law.
See Professional Biographies, WASHINGTON, DISTRICT OF COLUMBIA

Stein, Stuart G. .... '60 '85 C.273 B.B.A. L.893 J.D. [Hogan&H.]
*PRACTICE AREAS: Bank Holding Company Law; Bank Mergers and Acquisitions; Electronic Banking; Thrift Institutions Law; Corporate Law.
Stein, William R. ....'52 '78 C&L.178 A.B., J.D. [Hughes H.&R.]
*PRACTICE AREAS: Appeals; Litigation; Regulatory and Legislative Matters.

Stein, Mitchell & Mezines, (AV)
1100 Connecticut Avenue, N.W., Suite 1100, 20036
Telephone: 202-737-7777
Email: jstein@steinmitchell.com URL: http://www.steinmitchell.com
Members of Firm: Jacob A. Stein; Glenn A. Mitchell; Basil J. Mezines; Gerard E. Mitchell; Robert F. Muse; David U. Fierst; Richard A. Bussey; Patrick A. Malone; Robert L. Bredhoff; Laurie A. Amell; Christopher H. Mitchell; Andrew Michael Beato; William F. Burton; Joan M. Kimmich. Of Counsel: George A. Fisher.
General, Civil, Criminal and Administrative Practice before Federal and Local Courts, Agencies and Departments.
See Professional Biographies, WASHINGTON, DISTRICT OF COLUMBIA

Stein Shostak Shostak & O'Hara, A Professional Corporation, (AV)
Suite 807, 1620 L Street, N.W., 20036-5605 ⊙
Telephone: 202-223-6270 Telecopier: 202-659-4237
Email: tradelaw@steinshostak.com
S. Richard Shostak; Joseph P. Cox; Bruce N. Shulman (Resident); David R. Stepp. Of Counsel: Scott Edward Rosenow.
Customs and International Trade Law. Practice before Federal Administrative Agencies. Trials and Appeals.
Los Angeles, California Office: 515 South Figueroa Street, Suite 1200. Telephone: 213-486-0010. Fax: 213-486-0011.
San Diego, California Office: 2675 Customhouse Court, Suite B. Telephone: 619-661-6317. Fax: 619-661-1448.
See Professional Biographies, WASHINGTON, DISTRICT OF COLUMBIA

Steinbach, Brian W. ....'53 '78 C.918 B.A. L.893 J.D. [🄰 Epstein B.&G.]
*PRACTICE AREAS: Labor and Employment Law.
Steinbach, Mark H., (P.C.), (AV) .... '49 '74 C.930 B.A. L.128 J.D. [O'Toole,R.N.&S.]
Steinbach, Sheldon E., (AV) '41 '67 C.367 B.A. L.178 LL.B.
V.P. & Gen. Coun., American Council on Education
Steinbach, Steven A. .... '56 '82 C.309 A.B. L.976 J.D. [Williams&C.]
*PRACTICE AREAS: Appellate Practice; Computers and Software; Criminal Law; Litigation; White Collar Crimes.
Steinberg, Barry P. .... '41 '66 C&L.692 B.A., J.D. [Kutak R.]
*PRACTICE AREAS: Environmental; Military Personnel; Municipal.
Steinberg, Michael A. '65 '90 C.602 B.S. L.945 J.D.
(adm. in VA; not adm. in DC; Pat.) [🄰 Arent F.K.P.&K.]
*PRACTICE AREAS: Trademarks.
Steinberg, Michael W., (BV) ....'52 '77 C.976 B.A. L.659 J.D. [Morgan,L.&B.]
Steinberg, Steven P. .... '68 '93 C.188 B.S. L.273 J.D. [🄰 Dyer E.&J.]
*PRACTICE AREAS: Employment Law; Litigation.
Steinberger, David P. .... '70 '98 C.282 B.S. L.1040 J.D. [🄰 Vinson&E.]
*PRACTICE AREAS: Environmental Law; Administrative Law.
Steinberger, John C. ....'— '88 C.150 B.A. L.309 J.D. [🄰 Ablondi,F.S.&D.]
Steinborn, Steven B. ....'62 '87 C.475 B.S. L.477 J.D. [Hogan&H.]
*PRACTICE AREAS: Food and Agriculture; Food and Drug Regulation; Trade Regulation Law.
Steinbrecher, Bradley K. .... '67 '95 C.1053 B.S. L.659 J.D. [🄰 Buchanan I.]
*PRACTICE AREAS: International Franchising; Franchising.
Steindler, Thomas P. ....'55 '85 C.339 B.A. L.273 J.D. [McDermott,W.&E.]
Steiner, Arthur J. '38 '71 C.569 B.S. L.904 J.D.
(adm. in NY; not adm. in DC; Pat.) [McDermott,W.&E.]
Steingold, Stuart G. .... '45 '71 C.674 A.B. L.309 J.D. [Paul,W.R.W.&G.]
*PRACTICE AREAS: International and Domestic Project Finance; International and Domestic Aircraft Finance; Corporate Finance; Leasing.
Steinhardt, Ralph G., III '54 '80 C.95 B.A. L.309 J.D.
Prof., Natl. Law Ctr., George Washington Univ.
Steinhorn, Allan W., (BV) '55 '85
C.446 B.G.S. L.64 J.D. [🄲 Swartz&R.] (⊙Beltsville, MD)
Steinman, Melissa Landau ....'68 '93 C.178 A.B. L.309 J.D. [🄰 Venable,A.B.H.&C.]
*PRACTICE AREAS: Antitrust and Distribution; Regulatory; Technology Law; Electronic Commerce; Litigation.
Steinman, William B. Fenning ....'68 '93 C.882 B.A. L.309 J.D. [🄰 Winston&S.]
Steinmetz, Calvin, (AV) ....'52 '77 C.696 B.A. L.273 J.D. [Steinmetz,W.&M.]
Steinmetz, Weinberg & Moats, (AV) ....2141 P St., NW
Steinway, Daniel M., (BV) .... '50 '76 C.477 B.S.E. L.273 J.D. [Kelley D.&W.]
*PRACTICE AREAS: Environmental Law; Administrative Law; Litigation.
Steinwurtzel, Richard A., (AV) '50 '75
C.867 B.A. L.273 J.D. [Fried,F.H.S.&J.] (⊙New York, NY)
Steinwurtzel, Robert N., (AV) ....'53 '78 C.264 B.A. L.273 J.D. [Swidler B.S.F.]
*PRACTICE AREAS: Environmental Law; Litigation; OSHA Law.
Stekler, Beth A. ....'67 '92 C.188 B.A. L.976 J.D. [🄲 Wilmer,C.&P.]
*PRACTICE AREAS: Broker-Dealer Compliance; Investment Management; Securities Law.
Stelacone, Jay A. '64 '93
C.645 B.S.A.E. L.546 J.D. [🄰 Finnegan,H.F.G.&D.] (See Pat. Sect.)
*PRACTICE AREAS: Patent Litigation; Patent Infringement; Patent Interference Practice.
Stelck, Jane E., (AV) .... '46 '78 C.339 B.A. L.30 J.D. [🄲 Heller E.W.&M.]
*PRACTICE AREAS: Energy Law.
Stelzig, Tim .... '66 '99 C.923 B.A. L.659 J.D. [🄰 Arnold&P.]
Stember, Mark L. '68 '96 C.492 B.S. L.300 J.D.
(adm. in IA; not adm. in DC) [🄰 Kilpatrick S.]
*PRACTICE AREAS: Employee Benefits; Executive Compensation.
Stemberger, Edward J. .... '63 '91 C.201 B.M.E. L.1003 J.D. [Manelli,D.&S.]
*PRACTICE AREAS: Intellectual Property; Patent Prosecution; Design Patents.
Stempel, Karen Ostrow '56 '82
C.659 B.A. L.273 J.D. 1050 Connecticut Ave., N.W., Suite 1100
Stempel, Scott A. ....'57 '82 C.597 B.A. L.273 J.D. [Morgan,L.&B.]
Stempler, David S., (P.C.) ..... '47 '73 C.319 B.A. L.276 J.D. 5335 Wisconsin Ave., N.W.

Stencel, Debra N. '55 '83 C.172 B.S. L.823 J.D.
Sr. V.P & Gen. Coun., N.A., U.S. Off. Prod., Co.
Stenerson, Todd M. . . . . '69 '94 C.999 B.B.A. L.602 J.D. [Akin,G.S.H.&F.]
*PRACTICE AREAS: Complex Litigation; Commercial Litigation; Intellectual Property Litigation; Alternative Dispute Resolution.
Stengel, Scott A. . . . . '71 '96 C&L.602 B.A., J.D. [Orrick,H.&S.]
*PRACTICE AREAS: Bankruptcy; Commercial Law; Structured Finance.
Stenger, Daniel F. . . . . '55 '80 C.679 B.S. L.273 J.D. [Ballard S.A.&I.]
*PRACTICE AREAS: Business Law; Energy; Project Finance.
Stenger, Frank W. . . . . '45 '73 C&L.846 B.A., J.D. 2144 California St., N.W.
Stenger, James A. . . . . '52 '78 C.999 L.276 J.D. [Ross&H.]
*PRACTICE AREAS: Communications and Media; Intellectual Property; Litigation; Mergers, Acquisitions and Divestitures; Real Estate.
Stenger, Jenny Lynn Hebert . . . . '63 '90 C.1210 B.S.B.A. L.29 J.D. 1003 K St., N.W.
Stengren, Ralph L. . . . . '63 '97 C.722 B.A. L.569 J.D. [Skadden,A.S.M.&F.]
*PRACTICE AREAS: Energy; Project Finance.
Stennes, Matthew L. . . . . '72 '99 C.747 B.A. L.309 J.D. [Steptoe&J.]
Stepan, Gregg K. . . . . '71 '99 C.101 B.A. L.273 J.D. [Duane,M.&H.]
*PRACTICE AREAS: Corporate Law; Energy; Securities Law; International Trade Law.
Stephanos, Ann M. '67 '98 C.884 B.S. L.64 J.D.
(adm. in MD; not adm. in DC) 401 M St., S.W.
Stephen, Christopher T. . . . . '74 '99 C.93 B.A. L.128 J.D. [Baker&H.]
*PRACTICE AREAS: Legislative Practice; Health Care; Medicare; Tax.
Stephens, Andrew R. '57 '92
C.1349 B.A. L.813 J.D. Pres., People for Common Sense Court
Stephens, Jacqueline . . . . '— '98 C.800 B.S. L.893 J.D. [Fried,F.H.S.&J.]
*PRACTICE AREAS: Litigation; Internal Investigations.
Stephens, Sarah E. . . . . '— '93 C.674 A.B. L.273 J.D. [Manatt,P.&P.]
Stephens, William T., (AV) . . . . '22 '50 C&L.273 A.B., J.D. [Stephens] ⊙

Stephens Law Firm, PLLC, (AV)
1029 Vermont Avenue, N.W., Suite 400, 20005 ⊙
Telephone: 202-331-8200
Members of Firm: William T. Stephens; Michael A. Williams; Neil E. Graham (Not admitted in DC). Nonprofit and Tax Exempt Organizations, Business, Corporate, Associations, Administrative and Federal Legislative Practice, Contracts, Commercial Law, General, Securities Law, Antitrust.
McLean, Virginia Office: 1800 Old Meadow Road. P.O. Box 1096. Telephone: 703-821-8700. Facsimile: 703-827-7761. Email: stelawfirm@aol.com
See Professional Biographies, WASHINGTON, DISTRICT OF COLUMBIA

Stephenson, Andrew W., (AV) . . . . '50 '76 C.651 B.A. L.276 J.D. [Holland&K.]
*PRACTICE AREAS: Construction Law; Government Contracts; Labor Law.
Stephenson, Charles R. '66 '93 C&L.861 B.A., J.D.
(adm. in LA; not adm. in DC) Intl. Equity Partners
Stephenson, Robert Timothy . . . . '56 '90 C.623 B.A. L.276 J.D. [Kirkland&E.]
*PRACTICE AREAS: Employment Relations; Labor Relations.
Stepp, David R. . . . . '61 '86 C.228 A.B. L.280 J.D. [Stein S.S.&O.] (⊙L.A., CA)
*PRACTICE AREAS: Customs Law; International Trade Law.
Steptoe, Mary Lou . . . . '49 '74 C.605 B.A. L.893 J.D. [Skadden,A.S.M.&F.]

Steptoe & Johnson LLP, (AV) BR
1330 Connecticut Avenue, N.W., 20036 ⊙
Telephone: 202-429-3000 Fax: 202-429-3902 Cable Address: "Stepjohn"
Email: kreddy@steptoe.com URL: http://www.steptoe.com
Members: Calvin H. Cobb, Jr.; Monroe Leigh; Richard P. Taylor; John E. Nolan; Robert D. Wallick; James P. Holden; Betty Jo Christian; Robert E. Jordan III; Matthew J. Zinn; Richard H. Weise; Robert E. McLaughlin; James T. Halverson; Martin D. Schneiderman; Richard O. Cunningham; Richard H. Porter; Sheldon E. Hochberg; Kenneth I. Jonson; J. A. Bouknight, Jr.; Ronald S. Cooper; Terence P. Quinn; Roger E. Warin; F. Michael Kail; Mark J. Silverman; William Karas; John T. Collins; Steven H. Brose; Robert W. Fleishman; Howard H. Stahl; W. George Grandison; Arthur L. Bailey; Herbert C. Shelley; Edmund W. Burke; Morgan D. Hodgson; Douglas G. Green; Ellen d'Alelio; Mark F. Horning; Christopher T. Lutz; Samuel T. Perkins; Ellen M. McNamara; Paul J. Ondrasik, Jr.; Tom Collier; Reid H. Weingarten; Charles C. Read; Stewart A. Baker; Charles G. Cole; Susan H. Serling; Joel D. Kaufman; Filiberto Agusti; Thomas P. Barletta; Timothy M. Walsh; Peter L. Wellington; Olin L. Wethington; Daryl A. (Sandy) Chamblee; Anthony C. Epstein; Stephen A. Fennell; Seth Goldberg; Samuel M. Sipe, Jr.; Gary A. Morgans; Anne E. Moran; J. William Koegel, Jr.; Steven Reed; Daniel C. Sauls; David B. Raskin; Melanie F. Nussdorf; Philip L. Malet; Antonia B. Ianniello; Edward J. Krauland; J. Walker Johnson; Erik L. Kitchen; Mark P. Fitzsimmons; Scott H. Katzman; Kevin Gover; Steven J. Ross; Jane I. Ryan; Jerald S. Howe Jr.; Virginia L. White-Mahaffey; David H. Coburn; Anthony J. LaRocca; Alfred M. Mamlet; Steven K. Davidson; Harry Lee; Mark A. Moran; Thomas M. Barba; William T. Hassler; Linda S. Stein; Cynthia L. Quarterman; Richard L. Roberts; Mark J. Hulkower; Mary Ann Mancini; Pantelis Michalopoulos; Steven J. Barber; Stuart T. F. Huang; M. Jean Schlesinger; Edward R. Mackiewicz; Steven B. Teplinsky; Peter Lichtenbaum; Caroline Gaudet; Matthew D. Lerner; Eric C. Emerson; Savery M. Gradoville; Kenneth P. Ewing; Christopher C. Tai; Richard T. Saas; Steven M. Oster. Of Counsel: Cecil J. Olmstead; Richard Diamond; Kenneth D. Ludwig; Richard A. Whiting; Stanley Smilack; William K. Condrell; Sara Beth Watson; Carol A. Mitchell; Scott A. Harman; Joseph E. Stubbs; Errol R. Patterson; Ellen Kohn; John J. Duffy; James M. Talens; Mary Woodson (Molly) Poag; Carolyn Doozan Clayton; Alice Alexandra Kipel; Thomas J. Trendl; John L. Jacobus; Jennifer L. Key; Douglas L. Hilleboe; Jeffrey F. Pryce; Carol A. Rhees; Maureen O'Keefe Ward; David L. Roll; Frederick J. Horne; Eric G. Serron; D. Douglas Price. Special Counsel: Susan G. Blumenthal; David A. Clark (Not admitted in DC); John Flyger; Hilda A. Manuel (Not admitted in DC); Marcia R. Mitnick; Sharon Hyman Schick; Scott D. Watkins (Public Service Counsel); Barbara K. Kagan; Matthew Frumin. Associates: Benjamin R. Achenbach, Jr.; Aaron M. Altschuler; James C. Bailey; Robert A. Bailey (Not admitted in DC); Alexandra E. P. Baj; Jean Male Baxley; Bruce C. Bishop; Michael A. Bishop; Mark A. Black (Not admitted in DC); Amber Blaha; Rhonda M. Bolton; Yves Botteman (Not admitted in the United States); Stacey M. Brandenburg; Stephen C. Bullock; Jeffrey Scot Burk; George R. Calhoun, V; Stephanie Morris Carmody; Heather Doherty Clark; Gordon M. Clay; Carlynne S. Cockrum; Shannen W. Coffin; March Dolan Coleman (Not admitted in DC); Thomas M. Contois; Troy Cribb (Trade Counsel); Jody Allen Cummings (Not admitted in DC); Evangeline de Gracia (Not admitted in DC); Johnna Brooke Dumler; Elizabeth Johnson Dunaway (Not admitted in DC); L. Benjamin Ederington; Jason H. Ehrenberg; James G. Ennis; Wm. Fletcher Fairey; Edward L. Froelich; Brooke L. Gaede; Kimberly A. Gates; Gary C. Geating; Susan Gihring; Tara R. Gingerich; Catherine M. Giovannoni; José Ramón González-Magaz; Carol R. Gosain; Kathleen M. Graber; Sean C. Griffin; Susan Harthill; Brian M. Heberlig; Andrew J. Hefty (Not admitted in DC); Caroline J. Heller (Not admitted in DC); Leslie R. Hoffman; Ryan Block Hotchkiss; Timothy K. Howard; Paul R. Hurst; Julie M. Jackson; Brian P. Kaufman (Not admitted in DC); John J. Kavanagh, III (Not admitted in DC); Tina Potuto Kimble; Jordan Lee Klingsberg; Galina V. Kolomietz; Stéphane Lagonico (Not admitted in the United States); Jessica B. Lang (Not admitted in DC); Lindsey B. Lang; Todd Bradley Lantor; Margaret A. Lin; David S. Lorello (Not admitted in DC); Alice E. Loughran; Shannon P. MacMichael; Gregory S. McCue; Patrick S. Menasco; Jacqueline Michaels (Not admitted in DC); Mary T. Mitchell; Kevin Brian Muhlendorf; Brian J. Newquist; Viet H. Ngo; Aaron P. Nocjar; Solomon J. Noh; John F. O'Connor Jr.; Marc A. Paul; Libretta A. Porta; Daniel J. Poynor; Gwendolyn Prothro; L. Matthew Quigley; Jennifer Quinn-Barabanov; Andrew William Racca; Timothy John Racicot; Gary E. Redente; James A. "Del" Renigar; Carrie Aleen Rhoads; David F. Rifkind; Luis R. Roselló; Melanie Jane Schneck; Andrew J. Sloniewsky; David D. Smyth, III (Not admitted in DC); Mary J. R. Staley; Matthew L. Stennes; Ellen Hochstedler Steury; Lesley Stone; David N. Tanenbaum; Cynthia L. Taub; Stephanie A. Taylor; Brian J. Telpner; Shaun Leland Terrill; Lynn Ann Trujillo (Not admitted in DC); Jamie D. Underwood; Richard R. Verma; Julie A. S. Vinyard; Richard M. Wartchow (Not admitted in DC); Andrew J. Weinstein; Ripple L. Weistling; Gayle Weiswasser; Greg R. Yates; Matthew Yeo; Lisa M. Zarlenga.
General Practice. Air and Surface Transportation, Alternative Dispute Resolution, Antitrust, Arbitration, Bankruptcy and Creditors Rights, Commercial Litigation, Corporate, Criminal Defense, Employment, Environment and Land Use, ERISA and Employee Benefits, Financial Services, Food and Drug, Government Contracts, Indian Affairs, Intellectual Property, Insurance Coverage Litigation, Insurance Law and Regulation, International Law, International Trade, Labor Standards, Legislative Advocacy, Oil Pipelines and Natural Gas Regulation, Products Liability, Real Estate,

(This Listing Continued)

Steptoe & Johnson LLP (Continued)
Reinsurance, Securities and SEC Enforcement, Space Commercialization, Tax, Technology and Electric Power, Telecommunications (domestic and international), Toxic Torts, Transactions, Trusts and Estates, Utility Finance.
Phoenix, Arizona Office: Collier Center, 201 East Washington Street, #1600, 85004. Telephone: 602-257-5200. Fax: 602-257-5299.
Los Angeles, California Office: 633 West Fifth Street, Suite 700, 90071. Telephone: 213-439-9400. Fax: 213-439-9599.
London, England Office: Steptoe & Johnson Rakisons, Clements House, 14/18 Gresham Street, EC2V 7JE. Telephone: +44 (0)20 7367 8000. Fax: +44 (0)20 7367 8001.
See Professional Biographies, WASHINGTON, DISTRICT OF COLUMBIA

Sterba, Anne M. . . . . '73 '98 C.935 B.A. L.1209 [Rothwell,F.E.&M.] (See Pat. Sect.)
Sterbenz, Jolanta . . . . '61 '93 C.999 M.A. L.659 J.D. [Hogan&H.]
*PRACTICE AREAS: Energy Regulation; Natural Gas; Electric Power.
Steren, E. John . . . . '64 '89 C.446 B.A. L.276 J.D. [Ober,K.G.&S.]
Sterling, Gabriel Stephen, III . . . . '72 '98 C.309 A.B. L.276 J.D. [Hogan&H.]
*PRACTICE AREAS: Energy.
Sterling, Mark A. . . . . '54 '79 C&L.477 B.A., J.D. [Hogan&H.] (⊙Miami, FL)
*PRACTICE AREAS: Health Care; Mergers and Acquisitions; Government Regulation; Corporate.
Sterling, Scott Andrew, (AV) . . . . '55 '81 C.910 A.B. L.273 J.D. [Holland&K.]
*PRACTICE AREAS: Commercial Real Estate Acquisition, Development and Finance; Affordable Multifamily Housing.
Stern, Bruce L. . . . . '64 '90 C.112 B.A. L.94 J.D. 2001 M St. N.W.
Stern, David '59 '85 C.867 B.A. L.276 J.D.
Exec. Dir., National Assn. for Pub. Interest Law
Stern, Elizabeth Espin . . . . '61 '86 C&L.893 B.A., J.D. [Shaw P.]
*PRACTICE AREAS: Business Immigration.
Stern, Eric A. . . . . '— '85 C.197 A.B. L.309 J.D. [Latham&W.]
Stern, Ernest M. . . . . '50 '75 C.95 A.B. L.276 J.D. [Piper M.R.&W.]
*PRACTICE AREAS: Corporate Law; Securities.
Stern, Gerald M. . . . . '37 '61 C.659 B.S. L.309 LL.B. [Phillips&C.]
*PRACTICE AREAS: False Claims Act; Qui Tam Litigation.
Stern, Jeffrey B., (AV) . . . . '50 '76 C.855 B.A. L.273 J.D. [Holland&K.]
*PRACTICE AREAS: Real Estate Law; Financial Institutions Law; Resort Timeshares; Hotel and Resort Development; Hotel and Resort Law.
Stern, Jeremy H. . . . . '59 '88 C.477 B.A. L.276 J.D. [Cole,R.&B.] ⊙
*PRACTICE AREAS: Cable Television; Telecommunications Regulation; Wireless Communications; Internet Law; Legislative Practice.
Stern, Jill Abeshouse, (AV) . . . . . . '53 '78 C.788 B.A. L.273 J.D. 4840 Glenbrook Rd., NW
Stern, Jonathan L. . . . . '57 '83 C.299 B.A. L.569 J.D. [Arnold&P.]
*PRACTICE AREAS: Complex Civil Litigation; Complex Criminal Litigation.
Stern, Jonathan M. . . . . '59 '87 C.1333 B.S. L.904 J.D. [Schnader H.S.&L.]
*PRACTICE AREAS: Civil Litigation; Aviation Litigation; Insurance Coverage; Insurance Litigation.
Stern, Kevin E. . . . . '68 '95 C.597 B.A. L.1065 J.D. [Greenberg T.]
Stern, Lowell R. . . . . '63 '91 C.918 B.A. L.893 J.D. [Hogan&H.]
*PRACTICE AREAS: Antitrust and Trade Litigation; Civil Litigation; Franchise Litigation.
Stern, Lynne '65 '91 C.705 B.A. L.1202 J.D.
(adm. in NY; not adm. in DC) Assn. of Trial Lawyers of Amer.
Stern, Margo BeVier . . . . '— '79 C.675 B.A. L.904 J.D. [Ballard S.A.&I.]
*PRACTICE AREAS: Municipal Finance; Real Estate; Housing Law; Affordable Housing; Low Income Housing.
Stern, Martin L., (AV) . . . . '57 '84 C.696 B.A. L.276 J.D. [Preston G.E.&R.M.]
*PRACTICE AREAS: Telecommunications; Information Technology; Competition.
Stern, Marvin R., (AV) '35 '63
C.223 B.S.Ch.E. L.273 J.D. [Jacobson,H.] (See Pat. Sect.)
*PRACTICE AREAS: Intellectual Property Law; Chemical Patents; Mechanical Patents; Trademarks.
Stern, Richard H., (AV) '31 '59
C.178 B.S.E.E. L.976 LL.B. [Kellogg,H.H.T.&E.] (Pat.)
*PRACTICE AREAS: Copyrights; Computer Software Law; Intellectual Property; Antitrust.
Stern, Richard S., (AV) '49 '75
C.966 B.S. L.893 J.D. 419 7th St., N.W. (⊙Rockville, MD)
Stern, Robert '69 '00 C&L.705 B.A., J.D.
(adm. in NY; not adm. in DC) [O'Melveny&M.]
Stern, Ronald A., (AV) '50 '75 C.103 A.B. L.309 J.D.
V.P & Sr. Coun., Antitrust, General Electric Co.
Stern, Samuel A., (AV) . . . . '29 '52 C.659 A.B. L.309 LL.B. [Hills&S.]
*PRACTICE AREAS: Project Finance; Investment and Trade with Emerging and Transitional Economies; International Commercial Arbitration.
Stern, Todd D. . . . . '51 '77 C.197 B.A. L.309 J.D. [Wilmer,C.&P.]
*PRACTICE AREAS: Strategic Alliances; Congressional Investigations; Government Relations.
Stern-Bird, Margaret . . . . '65 '93 C&L.276 B.S., J.D. 1775 Pennsylvania Ave., N.W.

Sternberg, Richard S., (AV) '55 '83 C.659 B.A. L.276 J.D. BR
Madison Office Building, Suite 502, 1155 Fifteenth Street, N.W., 20005 ⊙
Telephone: 202-638-2300 Telecopier: 202-371-9046 Sternberg@WashingtonLawGroup.com
Email: Richard@SternbergLaw.Net URL: http://www.SternbergLaw.Net
General Civil Litigation, Business and Corporate Practice, Employment, Labor, and Civil Rights, Commercial Tenant Litigation, Personal Injury Litigation, Wills and Probate, Estates, Commercial Law.
Potomac, Maryland Office: 9620 Trailridge Terrace, 20854. Telephone: 301-340-2848.

Sterne, John H., Jr. . . . . '— '93 C.1083 B.A. L.902 J.D. [Reed S.]
*PRACTICE AREAS: Government Relations.
Sterne, Robert Greene, (AV) '51 '77
C.860 B.S.E.E. L.446 J.D. [Sterne,K.G.&F.] (See Pat. Sect.)
*PRACTICE AREAS: Intellectual Property Law.

Sterne, Kessler, Goldstein & Fox P.L.L.C., (AV)
1100 New York Avenue N.W., 20005
Telephone: 202-371-2600 Fax: 202-371-2540
URL: http://www.skgf.com
Directors of Firm: Robert Greene Sterne; Edward J. Kessler; Jorge A. Goldstein; David K.S. Cornwell; Robert W. Esmond; Tracy-Gene Graveline Durkin; Michele A. Cimbala; Michael B. Ray; Robert E. Sokohl; Eric K. Steffe; Michael Quentin Lee; Steven R. Ludwig; Linda E. Alcorn; John M. Covert. Senior Counsel: Samuel L. Fox;—Robert C. Millonig; Michael V. Messinger; Judith U. Kim; Timothy J. Shea, Jr.; Patrick E. Garrett; Jeffrey T. Helvey (Not admitted in DC); Heidi L. Kraus; Patrick D. O'Brien; Lawrence B. Bugaisky; Crystal D. Sayles; Edward W. Yee; Albert L. Ferro (Not admitted in DC); Donald R. Banowit; Peter A. Jackman; Molly A. McCall; Teresa Uliva Medler; Jeffrey S. Weaver; William Brian Edge (Not admitted in DC); Kendrick Patterson; Donald J. Featherstone; Vincent L. Capuano; John A. Harroun (Not admitted in DC); Albert J. Fasulo, II (Not admitted in DC); Eldora Ellison Floyd (Not admitted in DC); Thomas C. Fiala; Brian J. Del Buono (Not admitted in DC); Virgil Lee Beaston (Not admitted in DC); Ryan J. Stamper (Not admitted in DC); Reginald Lucas (Not admitted in DC); Theodore A. Wood; Elizabeth J. Haanes; Kimberly N. Reddick (Not admitted in DC); Bruce Edward Chalker; Joseph S. Ostroff.
Patent, Trademark, Copyright, Unfair Competition, Computer, Electronics, Biotechnology, Chemical, Interference, Alternative Dispute Resolution, Mechanical, Industrial Design, Internet, Related Litigation and Licensing.
See Professional Biographies, WASHINGTON, DISTRICT OF COLUMBIA

Sternfels, Urvan Ruiz '40 '72 C.502 B.A. L.276 J.D.
Pres. & Gen. Coun., National Petro. Refiners Assn.
Sterrett, Samuel B., (AV) . . . . '22 '50 C.31 A.B. L.893 LL.B. [Vinson&E.]
*PRACTICE AREAS: Litigation; Taxation; International Taxation.

Sterrett, Samuel B., Jr., (AV) .... '— '88 C.31 B.A. L.893 J.D. [Foley&L.]
*PRACTICE AREAS: Federal and State Tax Law; Corporate; Technology Licensing; Technology Transactions.
Stertzer, Annette L. ....'59 '85 C.36 B.S. L.37 J.D. Admr., Security Tr. Co., N.A.
Stetler, C. Joseph .... '17 '41 C.273 L.128 LL.B. 700 Thirteenth St., N.W., Ste. 1200
Stetson, Catherine E. .... '69 '94 C.228 A.B. L.893 J.D. [A Hogan&H.]
*PRACTICE AREAS: Litigation.
Stettner, Barbara .... '62 '96 C.112 B.A L.1117 J.D. [A Orrick,H.&S.]
Steuart, George C., (AV) '24 '53 C.1365 A.B. L.309 LL.B.
1025 Connecticut Ave., N.W.
Steury, Ellen Hochstedler .... '52 '96 C.347 A.B. L.966 J.D. [A Steptoe&J.]
Steven, Lee A. .... '62 '98 C.937 B.S. L.893 J.D. [A White&C.]
Stevens, Clifford E., Jr. ....'— '91 C.602 B.A. L.178 J.D. [C Verner,L.B.M.&H.]
*PRACTICE AREAS: International Commerce; Litigation.
Stevens, Dian Patricia '72 '00 C.777 B.A. L.273 J.D.
(adm. in MD; not adm. in DC) [A Weiner B.S.K.]
*PRACTICE AREAS: Corporate Law.
Stevens, Douglas R., (BV) ....'50 '80 C.309 B.A. L.276 J.D. 3158 O St., N.W.
Stevens, Duncan N. ....'75 '01 C.821 B.A. L.597 J.D. [A Miller&C.]
*PRACTICE AREAS: Government Contracts; Litigation.
Stevens, Gary G., (AV) .... '45 '73 C.262 B.A. L.477 J.D. [Saltman&S.]
*PRACTICE AREAS: Government Contract Law; Timber and Logging; Construction Law; Antitrust Law; Natural Resources.
Stevens, Herbert F., (AV) .... '48 '75 C.453 S.B. L.128 J.D. [Nixon P.]
*PRACTICE AREAS: Tax; Real Estate; Syndication; Housing Law.
Stevens, Mary E. G. .... '65 '92 C.846 B.A. L.128 J.D. Amer. Council of Life Ins.
Stevens, Matthew A. ....'64 '90 C.378 B.A. L.309 J.D. [C Skadden,A.S.M.&F.]
Stevens, Michael L. ....'59 '84 C.165 B.A. L.659 J.D. [Arent F.K.P.&K.]
*PRACTICE AREAS: Labor and Employment Law; Collective Bargaining; Employer Rights; Employment Contracts; Employment Discrimination.
Stevens, Paul Schott ....'52 '79 C.976 B.A. L.893 J.D. [Dechert]
*PRACTICE AREAS: Securities; Financial Services Regulation; Investment Management.
Stevens, Richard W. ....'55 '88 C.112 B.A. L.1049 J.D. [C Swick&S.]
Stevens, Ronald W., (AV) ....'— '73 C.118 B.A. L.893 J.D. [Kirkpatrick&L.]
*PRACTICE AREAS: Banking Litigation; Directors and Officers Liability; Securities Fraud Class Actions; Complex Litigation; Trial Practice.
Stevens, Sandra Tvarian .... '73 '97 C.30 B.A. L.904 J.D. [A Wiley R.&F.]
Stevens, Sarah '61 '86 C.298 B.A. L.861 J.D.
(adm. in LA; not adm. in DC) Mng. Editor, The Bureau of Natl. Affs., Inc.

Stevens, Davis, Miller & Mosher, L.L.P.
1615 L Street, N.W. Suite 850, 20036
Telephone: 202-408-5100; 202-785-0100 Fax: 202-408-5200; 202-408-5088
Email: sdmm@stevensdavis.com URL: http://www.stevensdavis.com
Members of Firm: James E. Ledbetter (Not admitted in DC); Thomas P. Pavelko; Anthony P. Venturino; Barth X. de Rosa. Of Counsel: Peter Peckarsky; Christopher M. Collins (Not admitted in DC); Frank Sever, Jr.; Ruth Mae Finch (Not admitted in DC); Clifford L. Tager (Not admitted in DC); Eric P. Robins (Not admitted in DC); David E. Herron II (Not admitted in DC). Associates: Steven D. Lustig; Noreen O'Hara Welch (Not admitted in DC); Scott W. Goode (Not admitted in DC); Karen Ann Sekowski (Not admitted in DC).
Domestic and International Practice in the field of Intellectual Property Law, concentrating on: Patents, Trademarks, Copyrights and Trade Secrets. Patent, Trademark, Copyright and Unfair Competition Litigation before Federal and State Courts. Specialized Practice in Patent Interference Proceedings before the Board of Appeals and Patent Interferences and Practice before the Trademark Trial and Appeal Board. Intellectual Property Licensing. Computer and High-Technology Law. Biotechnology Law. Food and Drug Administration Law. Anti-Counterfeiting Enforcement Efforts before the U.S. Customs Service and Federal Courts. Due Diligence Practice emphasizing Intellectual Property in the context of Corporate Acquisitions, Audits, Mergers, Corporate Financing and Initial Public Offerings.
References will be provided upon request.
See Professional Biographies, WASHINGTON, DISTRICT OF COLUMBIA

Stevenson, Eric ....'26 '51 C&L.976 B.A., LL.B. Comm. on Mental Health
Stevenson, Hugh O. ....'45 '75 C.112 A.B. L.904 J.D. Hearing Comr., Supr. Ct.
Stevenson, Lisa J. ....'70 '97 C.31 B.A. L.477 J.D. [A Covington&B.]
Stevenson, Malcolm G., (AV) ....'53 '80 C.112 B.A. L.273 J.D. [Schwartz,W.&M.]
*PRACTICE AREAS: Communications Law; Telecommunications Law; Copyright and Trademark Law; Broadcast Production and Distribution Law.
Stevenson, Mark ....'68 '99 C.276 B.S.F.S. L.30 J.D. [A Seyfarth S.]
*PRACTICE AREAS: Employee Benefits.
Stevenson, Virginia Leggett ....'70 '96 C.945 B.A. L.902 J.D. 1722 Eye St., NW
Stewart, Andrew R. ....'— '98 C.228 B.A. L.893 J.D. [A Latham&W.]
*PRACTICE AREAS: Environmental Law.
Stewart, Anthony L. ....'49 '75 C&L.329 B.A., J.D. Neighborhood Legal Servs. Prog.
Stewart, Charles V. ....'41 '85 C.311 B.A. L.228 J.D. [C Akin,G.S.H.&F.]
*PRACTICE AREAS: ERISA.
Stewart, Coke Morgan ....'— '97 C.228 B.A. L.893 J.D. [A Howrey S.A.&W.]
*PRACTICE AREAS: Commercial Litigation.
Stewart, Corey A. ....'68 '97 C.276 B.S. L.1035 J.D. [A Gardner,C.&D.]
Stewart, Damien G. ....'70 '97 C.273 B.A. L.893 J.D. [A Holland&K.] ‡
*PRACTICE AREAS: Employment and Labor Law (100%).
Stewart, David '— '00 C.902 B.A. L.893 J.D.
(adm. in AL; not adm. in DC) [A Bradley A.R.&W.] (⊙Birm., Montgomery, AL)
*PRACTICE AREAS: Government Affairs; Election Law; Campaign Law; Political Law; Litigation.
Stewart, David '— '00 C.902 B.A. L.893 J.D.
801 Pennsylvania Avenue, NW, Suite 230
Stewart, David L. '42 '74 C.1097 B.S. L.273 J.D.
(adm. in VA; not adm. in DC; Pat.) [McDermott,W.&E.]
Stewart, David O., (AV) ....'51 '80 C&L.976 B.A., J.D. [Ropes&G.]
*PRACTICE AREAS: Complex Litigation; White Collar Crime; Appellate Practice; Supreme Court Litigation.
Stewart, Dawn C. ......'63 '87 C.903 B.A. L.902 J.D. [Henrichsen S.] (⊙Alexandria, VA)
*PRACTICE AREAS: Insurance Law; Civil Litigation; Construction Law; Surety Law; Creditors Rights.
Stewart, Elizabeth A. '54 '79 C&L.420 B.A., J.D.
(adm. in LA; not adm. in DC) Dep. Gen. Coun.
Stewart, G. Cope, III, (AV) '41 '66 C.911 B.A. L.273 J.D.
Sr. V.P. & Dep. Gen. Coun., Corp. Affs., Marriott Intl., Inc.
*RESPONSIBILITIES: Securities Offerings Law; Corporate Law; Mergers and Acquisitions; Real Estate Development Law.
Stewart, Geoffrey S., (AV) ....'51 '77 C.103 A.B. L.309 J.D. [Jones,D.R.&P.]
*PRACTICE AREAS: Litigation; Complex Commercial Litigation; White Collar Crime; Internet Law.
Stewart, Heather J. ....'71 '96 C.602 B.S. L.477 J.D. [A Porter W.M.&A.]
*PRACTICE AREAS: Health Care Fraud.
Stewart, James C. '43 '74 C.446 B.S. L.64 J.D.
(adm. in MD; not adm. in DC) Auditor Gen., Wash. Metro. Area Transit Auth.
Stewart, James C. ....'51 '79 C.475 B.A. L.128 J.D. [Stradley R.S.&Y.]
Stewart, James K. ....'43 '69 C.339 B.S. L.945 J.D. [C Akin,G.S.H.&F.]
*PRACTICE AREAS: Government Contracts Law; Construction Litigation.
Stewart, Jan C. ....'58 '88 C.338 B.A. L.339 J.D. [McDermott,W.&E.]
Stewart, Jelahn '68 '94 C.800 B.A. L.30 J.D.
(adm. in VA; not adm. in DC) Asst. U.S. Atty.
Stewart, Joan D. ....'72 '99 C.1356 B.A. L.30 J.D. [A Pepper&C.]
*PRACTICE AREAS: Communications.

Stewart, John I., Jr., (AV) ....'50 '75 C.893 B.A. L.145 J.D. [Crowell&M.]
*PRACTICE AREAS: Litigation; Communications Law; Copyright Law; Insurance Coverage.
Stewart, Martina M. '72 '97 C.976 B.A. L.309 J.D.
(adm. in CA; not adm. in DC) [A Heller E.W.&M.]
Stewart, N. Simone '66 '91 C.273 L.831 J.D.
(adm. in PA; not adm. in DC) Atty., The Nasdaq Stock Market, Inc.
Stewart, Perry P. ....'44 '75 C.410 B.S. L.178 J.D. 7711 12th St., N.W.
Stewart, Rosemary, (AV) .... '49 '75 C.607 B.A. L.276 J.D. [Spriggs&H.]
*PRACTICE AREAS: Government Contracts; Banking Litigation; Civil Litigation.
Stewart, Terence P., (AV) ....'48 '79 C.321 B.A. L.276 J.D. [Stewart&S.]
*PRACTICE AREAS: Antidumping; Countervailing Duties; Safeguard/Escape Clause; International Trade Regulation; International Trade.

Stewart and Stewart, (AV) BB
Suite 200, 2100 M Street, N.W., 20037-1207
Telephone: 202-785-4185 Telecopier: 202-466-1286; 466-1287; 466-1288
Email: general@stewartlaw.com URL: http://www.stewartlaw.com
Eugene L. Stewart, Founder (1920-1998). Members of Firm: Terence P. Stewart; Wesley K. Caine; William A. Fennell; Geert De Prest; Alan M. Dunn. Associates: David S. Johanson; Dennis R. Nuxoll; Marta Maria Prado; Amy Ann Karpel. Of Counsel: Bernard Spinoit (Not admitted in the United States); Lane Steven Hurewitz; Patrick John McDonough; Amy S. Dwyer; Eric P. Salonen; James R. Holbein; Eugene H. Moore (Not admitted in DC).
International Trade Law and Policy, including Administrative and Judicial Proceedings and Dispute Settlement on Import and Export Activity. Advice and Lobbying on Multilateral, Plurilateral and Bilateral Trade Agreements and Negotiations, International Dispute Settlement Proceedings on Trade Agreement Issues, Customs Law Representation and Advocacy, International Transaction Law, Investment Law, Competition Law and Corporate Law.
Charleroi, Belgium Correspondent Office: Boulevard Dewandre 13, B6000 Charleroi. Telephone: 011-32-7-132-5131. Fax: 011-32-7-132-3526. Email: spinoit.wese@brutele.be
Moscow, Russia Representative Office: Leninskiy Prospect, Dom 42, Corpus 1, Suite 1562, Moscow 117119. Telephone: 011-7-095-938-7775. Fax: 011-7-095-938-7388. Email: stewart@pol.ru
Kiev, Ukraine Representative Office: 15/35 Kreshehatik Street, Kiev 252001 Ukraine. Telephone: 011-380-44-228-3857. Fax: 011-380-44-228-3113. Email: stewartlaw@mail.ru
See Professional Biographies, WASHINGTON, DISTRICT OF COLUMBIA

Steyer, Richard Alan, (AV) .... '51 '77 C.910 A.B. L.273 J.D. [Howe,A.&S.]
*PRACTICE AREAS: Labor and Employment Law; Nonprofit Associations; Trade Regulation; Legislative.
Stichman, Bennett Coyne '67 '99 C.170 B.A. L.273 J.D.
(adm. in MD; not adm. in DC) 1825 I Street, N.W. Suite 400
Stickles, Milton J., Jr. ....'28 '52 C&L.911 B.A., J.D. 1333 New Hampshire Ave.
Stickman, Jon R. '72 '97 C.800 B.A. L.861 J.D.
(adm. in CA; not adm. in DC) [A Duncan&A.]
*PRACTICE AREAS: Energy Law; Electric Utility; Antitrust; Securities Litigation; International Law.
Stief, Gerard J. '51 '76 C&L.128 B.A., J.D.
Assoc. Gen. Coun., Washington Metropolitan Area Transit Authority
*RESPONSIBILITIES: Litigation.
Stiegel, Lori A. ....'57 '82 C.260 B.A. L.273 J.D. Assoc. Staff Dir., Amer. Bar Assn.
Stier, Max .... '65 '93 C.976 B.A. L.813 J.D. 725 12th St., N.W.

Stier, Anderson & Malone, LLC
2175 K Street, NW, Suite 320, 20037-1809 ⊙
Telephone: 202-659-0303 Fax: 202-659-5968
Email: stierdc@aol.com URL: http://www.stier.com
Resident Partners: Howard T. Anderson; Paul F. Colarulli. Associate: Susan J. Charen. Of Counsel: Nancy L. Singer.
Special Counsel Investigations, Corporate Compliance Monituring, Complex Litigation, Employment Relations, Sexual Harassment Investigations, Appellate and Administrative Practice.
Skillman, New Jersey Office: 30 Vreeland Dr., 08558. Telephone: 609-597-6466. Fax: 609-497-2909.
See Professional Biographies, WASHINGTON, DISTRICT OF COLUMBIA

Stiffler, George W., (AV) ....'55 '81 C.945 B.A. L.273 J.D. [Bastianelli,B.&K.]
*PRACTICE AREAS: Government Contracts; Shipbuilding and Repair; Construction Law; Maritime.
Stiles, Nancy M., (P.C.) ....'49 '78 C.66 A.B. L.273 J.D. [Silver,F.&T.]
*PRACTICE AREAS: Regulation of Financial Institutions; Federal Regulatory Law.
Still, Edward, (AV) ....'46 '71 C&L.16 B.A., J.D. [C Dickstein S.M.&O.]
*PRACTICE AREAS: Voting Rights; Elections; Redistricting.
Stillman, Bradley C. '66 '91 C.339 B.S. L.209 J.D.
Legis. Coun., Consumer Federation of America
Stimson, Thomas M. ....'73 '98 C.350 B.A. L.893 J.D. [A Winston&S.]
*PRACTICE AREAS: Litigation; Antitrust.
Stinchfield, John E., (AV) '— '74
C.918 B.A. L.1065 J.D. General Counsel, Donohoe Companies Inc.
Stine, David Paul '71 '97 C.645 B.A. L.273 J.D.
(adm. in MD; not adm. in DC) 3121 Adams Mill Rd., N.W.‡
Stinemetz, Danielle K. '74 '00 C.36 B.S. L.823 J.D.
(adm. in IL; not adm. in DC) [A Cadwalader,W.&T.]
*PRACTICE AREAS: Corporate Law.
Stiner, John E. ....'52 '82 C.183 B.A. L.306 J.D. 1919 Penn. Ave., N.W., Suite 850
Stinger, Kenneth F. '41 '66
C.705 B.A. L.273 LL.B. Dir., Govt. Affs., Amer. Trucking Assn.
Stinson, John Mccollum, III ....'— '73 1667 K St., N.W., Ste. 460
Stirling, E. Tillman, (AV) .... '27 '54 C&L.273 B.S., J.D. [Hamilton&H.]
*PRACTICE AREAS: Estate Planning; Probate; Trusts.
Stites & Harbison, PLLC
1200 G St., N.W. (⊙Atlanta, GA; Jeffersonville, IN; Frankfort, Hyden, Lexington, Louisville, KY; Nashville, TN)
Stock, Stuart C., (AV) .... '46 '71 C.679 B.S. L.309 J.D. [Covington&B.]
Stockdale, Bruce R. .... '33 '75 C.276 B.S. L.64 LL.B. 3401 Prospect St., N.W.
Stockman, Jeanne W. .... '69 '94 C.893 B.S.E.E. L.692 J.D. [A Swidler B.S.F.]
*PRACTICE AREAS: Telecommunications.
Stoddard, Dianne L., (AV) ....'46 '75 C.546 B.A. L.190 J.D. [C Orrick,H.&S.]
*PRACTICE AREAS: Municipal Law; Public Finance; Structured Finance.
Stoel, Thomas B., Jr. ....'41 '66 C.674 A.B. L.309 LL.B. Natural Res. Def. Council

Stoel Rives LLP, (AV)
Suite 810, 1275 K Street, N.W., 20005-4006 ⊙
Telephone: 202-347-7744 Facsimile: 202-347-7750
URL: http://www.stoel.com/
Resident Partner: Robert A. Nelson, Jr.
Administrative and Legislative Practice before Federal Agencies and U.S. Congress. Practice before Federal Energy Regulatory Commission. General Practice and Litigation in Oregon and Washington State Courts and Federal Courts. Energy Law, Public Utilities, Natural Resources and Environmental Law.
Portland, Oregon Office: Suite 2600, 900 S.W. Fifth Avenue. Telephone 503-224-3380.
Vancouver, Washington Office: Suite 725, 805 Broadway. Telephone: 360-699-5900.
Seattle, Washington Office: Suite 3600, One Union Square, 600 University. Telephone: 206-624-0900.
Boise, Idaho Office: Suite 1900, 101 S. Capitol Boulevard. Telephone: 208-389-9000.
Salt Lake City, Utah Office: Suite 1100, One Utah Center, 201 South Main Street. Telephone: 801-328-3131.
San Francisco California Office: 111 Sutter Street, Suite 700. Telephone: 415-617-8900.
Sacramento, California Office: 770 L Street, Suite 990. Telephone: 916-447-0700.
Tahoe City, California Office: 3000 N. Lake Boulevard, Suite 1, P.O. Box 7336. Telephone: 530-583-2116.
See Professional Biographies, WASHINGTON, DISTRICT OF COLUMBIA

Stoeppelwerth, Ali M. .... '63 '90 C&L.813 B.A., J.D. [Wilmer,C.&P.]
*PRACTICE AREAS: Antitrust; EU Competition; Media Law; Electronic Commerce.

Stoer, Eric F., (AV) .... '— '69 C&L.446 B.A., J.D. [Bryan C.]
*PRACTICE AREAS: International Business; Licensing; Antitrust.
Stohlman, Beuchert, Egan & Smith, Chartered, (AV) .... 1775 Pennsylvania Ave., N.W.
Stoia, Daniela ....'75 '98 C.475 B.A. L.880 J.D. [Ⓐ Davis&H.]
*PRACTICE AREAS: Taxation Law.
Stojic, Steve, (AV) ....'56 '80 C&L.477 B.A., J.D. [Gallagher,B.&M.]
*PRACTICE AREAS: Federal Energy Regulation; Natural Gas; Natural Gas Pipelines; Gas Utilities; Public Utility Rates.
Stojkov, Dusko J. '69 '97 C.476 B.S. L.912 J.D.
(adm. in MI; not adm. in DC) Sr. Assoc., Ernst & Young LLP - Natl. Tax
Stojkovich, Goran P. ....'65 '97 C.339 B.S. L.146 J.D. [Ⓐ Morgan,L.&B.]
Stokes, Christopher S., (AV) ....'61 '89 C.902 B.S. L.276 J.D. [Ⓒ Hogan&H.]
*PRACTICE AREAS: International Trade.
Stokes, Louis, (AV) ....'25 '53 C.930 L.1003 LL.B. [Ⓒ Squire,S.&D.] (⊙Cleve., OH)
Stokes, Sean A. ....'64 '90 C.207 B.A. L.273 J.D. [B.Herbst]
*PRACTICE AREAS: Telecommunications Competition; Telecommunications Regulation; Cable Franchising; Cable TV; Wireless Communications.
Stolbach, Richard M. ....'52 '76 C.860 B.A. L.273 J.D. [Patton B.]
Stole, Einar '64 '00 C.911 B.S. L.446 J.D.
(adm. in MD; not adm. in DC; See Pat. Sect.) [Ⓐ Fulbright&J.]
*PRACTICE AREAS: Intellectual Property; Patents.
Stolee, Anne M., (AV) ....'59 '84 C.976 B.A. L.228 J.D. [Baker,D.B.&C.]
*PRACTICE AREAS: State and Local Tax; Federal Trial and Appellate Litigation.
Stoll, Kara Farnandez '68 '97
C.477 B.S.E.E. L.276 J.D. [Ⓐ Finnegan,H.F.G.&D.] (See Pat. Sect.)
*PRACTICE AREAS: Intellectual Property Litigation; Electrical Patent Prosecution.
Stoll, Richard G., (AV) .... '— '71 C.934 B.A. L.276 J.D. [Foley&L.]
*PRACTICE AREAS: Environmental Law.
Stoller, Kenneth A. '67 '97 C.1036 B.A. L.260 J.D.
(adm. in FL; not adm. in DC) Coun., American Ins. Assn.
*RESPONSIBILITIES: Legislative/Regulatory; Workers Compensation; Occupational Safety and Health; Litigation.
Stoller, Stacy Robbin ....'69 '98 C.674 A.B. L.477 J.D. 1701 Pennsylvania Ave., NW
Stollman, Thomas F. ....'65 '96 C.034 B.A. L.1018 J.D. [Ⓐ D.J.Hudson,III]
*PRACTICE AREAS: Securities Law; Corporate Law; Litigation.
Stoloff, Neil H. ....'53 '79 C.475 B.S. L.276 J.D. National Indian Gaming Comm.
Stolove, Evan S. ....'68 '94 C.477 A.B. L.446 J.D. [Ⓐ Arent F.K.P.&K.]
*PRACTICE AREAS: Appellate Litigation; Commercial Litigation.
Stolper, Max A., (AV) ....'24 '53 C&L.309 A.B., LL.B. [Ⓒ Leonard H.F.L.&L.]
*PRACTICE AREAS: Securities; Corporate Law; Investment Law.
Stoltz, Gerald D. ....'48 '74 C.951 B.A. L.273 J.D. [Thompson C.]
*PRACTICE AREAS: Maritime Finance; International Finance Law; Project Finance.
Stone, Carol Thomas, (AV) '54 '80
C.269 B.A. L.273 J.D. [Jordan C.&S.] (⊙Fairfax, VA)
*PRACTICE AREAS: Legal Malpractice Defense; Accountants Malpractice; Professional Liability Defense; Insurance Coverage; Commercial Litigation.
Stone, Daniel B. ....'55 '79 C.918 B.A. L.309 J.D. [Ivins,P.&B.]
*PRACTICE AREAS: Pensions; Employee Benefits; Employment Taxation; ERISA Litigation; ESOPs.
Stone, David E. '59 '85 C.589 B.S. L.365 J.D.
(adm. in IL; not adm. in DC) [Ⓒ Freedman,L.K.&S.] ⊙
Stone, Donald R., (AV) ....'— '63 C&L.966 B.S., J.D. [Kirkpatrick&L.]
*PRACTICE AREAS: Food, Drug and Medical Device Law; Products Liability.
Stone, Elaine Wintroub ....'53 '80 C.66 B.A. L.569 J.D. [Ⓒ Covington&B.]
Stone, Garrett A., (AV) ....'58 '82 C.48 B.A. L.575 J.D. [Brickfield B.R.&S.]
Stone, James R. '63 '92 C.94 B.S. L.178 J.D.
(adm. in MA; not adm. in DC) 655 15th St., N.W., Suite 1200
Stone, Jonathan R. ....'50 '89 C.454 B.S. L.273 J.D. [Ⓐ Cadwalader,W.&T.]
*PRACTICE AREAS: Environmental Law.
Stone, Lea Ann P. ....'64 '90 C.339 B.S. L.477 J.D 2300 N St., N.W.
Stone, Lesley ....'74 '99 C.1369 B.S. L.309 J.D. [Ⓐ Steptoe&J.]
Stone, Mark J., (AV) ....'52 '80 C.674 B.S.E. L.276 J.D. [Katz&S.] ⊙
*PRACTICE AREAS: Construction Law; Public Contract Law.
Stone, Nancy B. ....'59 '86 C.821 B.A. L.659 J.D. [Shea&G.]
*PRACTICE AREAS: Civil Litigation; Products Liability.
Stone, Paul F. ....'71 '00 C.112 B.A. L.659 J.D. [Ⓐ White&C.]
Stone, Sarah A. ....'56 '82 C.276 B.S.F.S. L.893 J.D. [Ⓐ Nixon P.]
*PRACTICE AREAS: Tax Credits; Syndication; Affordable Housing; Bankruptcy; Workouts.
Stone, Scott N. ....'52 '79 C&L.976 B.A., J.D. [Patton B.]
Stone, Steven J. ....'60 '86 C.273 B.A. L.128 J.D. [Rubin,W.D.H.&C.]
*PRACTICE AREAS: Communications; Corporate Law; Real Estate; Litigation.
Stone, Steven W. ....'60 '88 C.67 B.A. L.273 J.D. [Morgan,L.&B.]
Stoner, James R., (AV) ....'27 '52 C.264 B.S. L.273 LL.B. 1825 K. Street
Stonerock, Jeffrey A. ....'57 '84 C.870 B.S. L.228 J.D. [Baker B.]
Storch, Laurence, (AV) ....'50 '74 C.453 S.B. L.309 J.D. [Dilworth P.P.]
Storch, Stephen E. '45 '71 C.30 B.A. L.273 J.D.
V.P.; Govt. Affs., Commodity Exchange, Inc.
Storch Amini & Munves, P.C., (AV)
1201 Pennsylvania Avenue N.W. Suite300 (⊙South River, NJ; Mineola, New York, NY)
Storch & Brenner LLP
(See Dilworth Paxson PLLC)
Stormont, Charles Alan '76 '01 C.198 B.S. L.893 J.D.
(adm. in VA; not adm. in DC) [Ⓐ Vinson&E.] (⊙Hous., TX)
Storms, John Edward, Jr., P.A.
(See Wheaton, Maryland)
Storzer, Roman P. ....'72 '96 C.019 B.Comm. L.273 J.D. Beckett Fund, The
Stosser, Michael A., (AV) ....'52 '79 C.1097 B.A. L.809 J.D. [Heller E.W.&M.]
*PRACTICE AREAS: Energy Law.
Stouck, Jerry, (AV) ....'55 '81 C.918 B.A. L.569 J.D. [Spriggs&H.]
*PRACTICE AREAS: Government Contracts; Banking Litigation; Complex Commercial Litigation; Federal Claims.
Stough, John T., Jr., (AV) ....'44 '74 C.309 B.A. L.846 J.D. [Hogan&H.]
*PRACTICE AREAS: Administrative Law; Energy; Regulatory Law; Utility Law.
Stout, Laura P. ....'70 '99 C.674 B.A. L.309 J.D. [Ⓐ Williams&C.]
Stout, Lynn A. ....'57 '83 C.674 A.B. L.976 J.D. Prof., Georgetown Univ. Law Ctr.
Stout, Thomas A., Jr. ....'50 '75 C.367 B.A. L.446 J.D. 1455 Penn. Ave., N.W.
Stowe, John H. '39 '71 C.277 B.E.E. L.347 J.D.
(adm. in IN; not adm. in DC; See Pat. Sect.) [Ⓐ Staas&H.]
Stowe, Matthew F. '72 '99 C.197 A.B. L.309 J.D.
(adm. in TX; not adm. in DC) [Ⓐ Patton B.]
Stowe, Susan E. ....'58 '96 C.893 B.A. L.1209 J.D. [Ⓐ Caldwell]
Stowell, Alan M. '48 '73 C.350 B.S. L.352 J.D.
(adm. in IA; not adm. in DC) Bur. of Natl. Affs.
Stracher, Cameron A. ....'61 '88 C.31 B.A. L.309 J.D. [Ⓒ Levine S.&K.]
Stradley Ronon Stevens & Young, LLP
1220 19th Street, N.W. Suite 700 (⊙Wilmington, DE; Cherry Hill, NJ; Malvern, Phila., PA)
Strand, Joan H. '50 '76 C&L.273 B.A., J.D.
Prof. of Law, George Wash. Univ. Natl. Law Ctr.
Strand, Stratton C. ....'66 '93 C.197 B.A. L.112 J.D. 441 Fourth St., N.W.
Strange, Luther J., III, (AV) '53 '79 C&L.861 B.A., J.D.
[Bradley A.R.&W.] (⊙Birm., Huntsville, Montgomery, AL)
*PRACTICE AREAS: Governmental.
Stranne, Steven K. ....'64 '94 C.228 B.S.E. L.309 J.D. [Powell,G.F.&M.]
*PRACTICE AREAS: Health Care.
Stras, Marcela B., (BV) ....'51 '80 C.966 B.A. L.472 J.D. [Thompson C.]
*PRACTICE AREAS: International Trade Law; Immigration Law; Customs Law.

Strasburger & Price, L.L.P., (AV)
A Partnership including Professional Corporations
1101 Pennsylvania Avenue N.W., 7th Floor, 20004 ⊙
Telephone: 202-756-2260 Fax: 202-756-7511
URL: http://www.strasburger.com
Member of Firm: Mark J. Andrews; Jane Woods LaFranchi (Not admitted in DC). Of Counsel: Kenneth E. Siegel (Not admitted in DC).
Antitrust and Trade Regulation, Antitrust Class Actions, Appellate Practice, Bankruptcy, Workouts, Business Litigation, Commercial Litigation, Banking Litigation, Commercial Loans, Business Law, Commercial Law, Construction Law, Securities, Drug and Medical Device Defense, Environmental Law, Superfund, Toxic Torts, Nuclear Energy, Oil and Gas Law, Estate and Gift Taxation, Trusts and Estates Taxation, Wills, Fidelity and Surety, Finance, Franchises and Franchising, International Franchising, Franchise Law, Governmental Law, Local Government Law, County Government Law, Health Care, Health Law, Health Care Litigation, Managed Care, Medical Law, Nursing Home Litigation, Insurance, Insurance Defense, Commercial Insurance Defense, Insurance Bad Faith Defense, Insurance Coverage Defense, Insurance Reinsurance, Risk Management, Intellectual Property, Intellectual Property Licensing, Intellectual Property Litigation, New Media Law, Patent Litigation, Patent Licensing, Trademarks, Copyrights, International Law, International Trade, Labor and Employment, Employment Law, Personal Injury, Products Liability, Products Liability Defense, Mass Torts, Professional Liability, Real Estate, Zoning, Planning and Land Use, Taxation, International Taxation, Tax Controversies, Income Tax, White Collar Crime, Transportation, International Transportation Law.
Dallas, Texas Office: 901 Main Street, Suite 4300. Telephone: 214-651-4300. Fax: 214-651-4330.
Austin, Texas Office: 600 Congress Avenue, Suite 2600. Telephone: 512-499-3600. Fax: 512-499-3660.
Houston, Texas Office: 1301 N. McKinney Street, Suite 3200. Telephone: 713-951-5600. Fax: 713-951-5660.
San Antonio, Texas Office: Bank of America Plaza, 300 Convent Street, Suite 900. Telephone: 210-250-6000. Fax: 210-250-6100.
Mexico City Office: Strasburger & Price, S.C., Montes Urales 632, Piso 3, Lomas de Chapultepec, 11000 Mexico D.F. Telephone: 525-202-7665. Fax: 525-202-2367.
See Professional Biographies, WASHINGTON, DISTRICT OF COLUMBIA

Strasser, Alan D., (AV) ....'52 '77 C.976 B.A. L.309 J.D. [Kutak R.]
*PRACTICE AREAS: Criminal Defense, Employment Law.
Stratton, David B. '55 '80
C.976 B.A. L.184 J.D. [Jordan C.&S.] (⊙Balt., Rockville, MD)
*PRACTICE AREAS: Appellate Practice; Insurance Defense; Insurance Coverage; Professional Liability Defense; Civil Litigation.
Stratton, Kathleen M., (AV) ....'59 '84 C.323 B.A. L.1119 J.D. [Ⓒ Crowell&M.]
*PRACTICE AREAS: Health and Hospital Law; Fraud and Abuse; Administrative Law.
Strauch, Olivier P. '— '00 C.309 A.B. L.276 J.D.
(adm. in MD; not adm. in DC) [Ⓐ Latham&W.]
*PRACTICE AREAS: Communications Law; Civil Litigation.
Straus, David R., (AV) ....'45 '70 C.197 A.B. L.659 J.D. [Thompson C.]
*PRACTICE AREAS: Administrative; Postal; Utility.
Straus, Jerry C., (AV) ....'37 '61 C&L.178 A.B., LL.B. [Hobbs,S.D.&W.]
Strausman, Jack E. '61 '85 C.1044 B.A. L.273 J.D.
Asst. Gen. Coun., Potomac Electric Power Company
Strauss, Emanuel D. ....'60 '86 C&L.188 B.A., J.D. [Ⓒ Shearman&S.]
*PRACTICE AREAS: Corporate; Securities.
Strauss, Francine Rachelle ....'59 '89 C.445 B.S. L.446 J.D. 2440 Virginia Ave., N.W.
Strauss, Michael J. ....'54 '87 C.1044 B.A. L.273 J.D. [Ⓒ Fulbright&J.] (See Pat. Sect.)
*PRACTICE AREAS: Litigation; Antitrust; Intellectual Property; Patent.
Strauss, Pamela S. ....'66 '94 C.659 B.A. L.904 J.D. [Ⓐ Willkie F.&G.]
*PRACTICE AREAS: Telecommunications.
Strauss, Robert S., (AV) ......'18 '41 C&L.846 LL.B. [Akin,G.S.H.&F.] (⊙Dallas, TX)
*PRACTICE AREAS: General Practice.
Strauss, Scott H., (AV) ....'56 '81 C.188 B.S. L.659 J.D. [Spiegel&M.]
*PRACTICE AREAS: Administrative Law; Energy; Telecommunications Law.
Strauss, Stanley R. ....'15 '41 C.951 B.A. L.178 LL.B. [Ⓒ Ogletree,D.N.S.&S.]
*PRACTICE AREAS: Labor and Employment; National Labor Relations Act; Management Labor Law; Appellate Practice.
Strauss, William L. ....'51 '98 C.165 B.A. L.659 J.D. [Ⓐ Finnegan,H.F.G.&D.]
*PRACTICE AREAS: Intellectual Property Litigation.
Stravitz, Eric N. ....'66 '92 C.1044 B.A. L.273 J.D. [Mesirow&S.]
Straw, Charles A. '51 '76 C.970 B.A. L.276 J.D.
(adm. in MD; not adm. in DC) MCI Telecom. Corp.
Strebel, Sandra J., (AV) ....'38 '62 C.188 A.B. L.228 LL.B. [Ⓒ Spiegel&M.]
*PRACTICE AREAS: Administrative Hearings and Appeals; Alternative Dispute Resolution; Environmental Law; Public Utility Law; Appellate Practice.
Street, David P. ....'45 '76 C.228 B.A. L.276 J.D. [Galland,K.G.F.&S.]
Street, Mathew H. '48 '82 C.30 B.A. L.273 J.D.
Assoc. Gen. Coun., American Bankers Association
*RESPONSIBILITIES: State Banking Law (75%); Advice to In-House Enterprises (25%).
Streeter, Lucille Anderson .....'45 '73 C.788 B.A. L.846 J.D. 5255 Partridge Lane, N.W.‡
Streeter, Richard H., (AV) ....'— '70 C&L.846 B.A., J.D. [Barnes&T.]
*PRACTICE AREAS: International Trade; Freight Loss and Damage; Hazardous Materials and Substances; Customs Law; Railroad Law.
Strella, Paul V. ....'58 '82 C.945 B.A. L.145 J.D. William M. Mercer, Inc.
Strench, Bibb Lamar ....'62 '88 C.880 B.A. L.893 J.D. [Ⓒ Stradley R.S.&Y.]
Strenio, Andrew J., Jr., (AV) ....'52 '80 C.674 A.B. L.309 J.D. [Powell,G.F.&M.]
*PRACTICE AREAS: Antitrust; Intellectual Property.
Stretch, Colin S. ....'69 '99 C.197 A.B. L.309 J.D. [Ⓐ Kellogg,H.H.T.&E.]
*PRACTICE AREAS: Telecommunications; Litigation.
Strick, Nancy L. '— '98 C&L.347 B.A., J.D.
(adm. in IL; not adm. in DC) [Ⓐ Greenberg T.]
Strickland, David L. .....'68 '93 C.597 B.S. L.309 J.D. Assoc. of Trial Lawyers of Amer.
Strickland, Sidney L., Jr. '50 '77 C.112 B.S. L.1067 J.D.
Assoc. Gen. Coun., Burlington Northern and Santa Fe Railway Company
Strickland, Wesley L. '67 '98 C.446 B.S. L.972 J.D.
(adm. in VA; not adm. in DC; Pat.) [Ⓐ McDermott,W.&E.]
Strickler, J. Sloane '69 '01 C.112 B.A. L.273 J.D.
(adm. in NY; not adm. in DC) [Ⓐ Weil,G.&M.]
*PRACTICE AREAS: International Trade.
Strickler, Mitchell L. ....'31 '61 C.197 A.B. L.976 LL.B. 3803 Gramercy St., N.W.‡
Strikis, Silvija A. ....'62 '95 C.446 B.S. L.276 J.D. [Kellogg,H.H.T.&E.]
*PRACTICE AREAS: Telecommunications; Litigation.
Strimel, Mary N. ....'71 '94 C.910 A.B. L.309 J.D. [Ⓐ Cohen,M.H.&T.]
*PRACTICE AREAS: Antitrust; Environmental Law.
Stringer, John D. '17 '41 C.976 L.748 LL.B.
(adm. in MN; not adm. in DC) 3126 38th St., N.W.‡
Stringham, Bart '53 '89 C.446 B.A. L.64 J.D.
Assoc. Gen. Coun., National Association of Broadcasters
*RESPONSIBILITIES: Contracts; Corporate Law; Labor and Employment.
Strobel, Gil M. ....'67 '92 C.477 B.A. L.145 J.D. [Ⓐ Metzger&M.]

Strobos, Jur T. .... '52 '88 C.367 B.A. L.659 J.D. [© Olsson,F.&W.]
*PRACTICE AREAS: Food and Drug Law; Health Law; Patent Litigation.
Strochak, Adam P. ....'65 '93 C.882 B.A. L.273 J.D. [Ⓐ Weil,G.&M.]
Strohmeyer, Victoria L. '— '00 C.446 B.A. L.276 J.D.
(adm. in MD; not adm. in DC) [Ⓐ Morgan,L.&B.]
Strom, Cordia A. '58 '84 C.679 B.S. L.472 J.D.
Exec. Dir., The Immigration Reform Law Institute
Strom, James T. '67 '00 C.446 B.S. L.836 J.D.
(adm. in MD; not adm. in DC) [Ⓐ Staas&H.]
*PRACTICE AREAS: Intellectual Property.
Strom, Kathy Silberthau ....'56 '82 C.309 A.B. L.569 J.D. [Ⓐ Cahill G.&R.]
Stroman, Cynthia A.M. ....'64 '94 C.188 B.S. L.477 J.D. [Ⓐ King&S.]
Stromberg, Clifford D., (AV) ....'49 '75 C.976 B.A. L.309 J.D. [Hogan&H.]
*PRACTICE AREAS: Health Care; Corporate Law; Mergers, Acquisitions and Divestitures; Antitrust and Trade Regulation; Trade Association Law.
Stromberg, Robert E. .... '09 '35 C.1279 M.C.S. L.799 LL.M. 6138 31st Pl. N.W.‡
Stromseth, Jane E. '56 '88 C.821 B.A. L.976 J.D.
(adm. in PA; not adm. in DC) Assoc. Prof. of Law, Georgetown Univ.
Strong, Angela J. '67 '99 C&L.546 B.A., J.D.
(adm. in NE; not adm. in DC) Stateside Assocs.
Strong, Carter ....'47 '72 C.354 B.A. L.472 J.D. [Arent F.K.P.&K.]
*PRACTICE AREAS: Mergers and Acquisitions; Securities Offerings; Corporate Law; Finance.
Strong, Frank R. ....'64 '90 C.118 B.A. L.36 J.D. [Shearman&S.]
Strong, Maria S. ....'63 '90 C.112 B.A. L.273 J.D. [Smith&M.]
*PRACTICE AREAS: Copyrights; International Trade.
Strong, Michael ....'— '00 C.112 B.S., B.A. L.424 J.D. [Ⓐ Morgan,L.&B.]
Strong, Rachel Lisa ....'69 '94 C.446 B.A. L.273 J.D. [© Howrey S.A.&W.]
*PRACTICE AREAS: Public Service Counsel.
Strongin, Seymour '30 '60 C.823 B.A. L.1009 LL.B.
(adm. in NY; not adm. in DC) 2141 Wyoming Ave. NW‡
Stropp, Robert H., Jr., (AV) .... '47 '75 C.446 B.A. L.192 J.D. [© Mooney,G.B.&S.]
Stroschein, Ryan W. '70 '00 C.791 B.A. L.627 J.D.
(adm. in SD; not adm. in DC) [Ⓐ Olsson,F.&W.]
*PRACTICE AREAS: Agricultural Law; Indian Law; Forestry Law.
Strother, Channing D., Jr., (AV) ....'52 '77 C&L.893 B.A., J.D. [McCarthy,S.&H.]
*PRACTICE AREAS: Energy Law; Public Utility Law; Antitrust Law.
Stroud, Geraldine G. ....'42 '72 C.777 B.A. L.665 J.D. Gen. Coun., Group Health Assn.
Stroud, Terri Diane ....'70 '99 C.575 B.A. L.276 J.D. Staff Atty.
Stroup, Richard Lee, (AV) '48 '76
C.607 B.S.ME L.893 J.D. [Finnegan,H.F.G.&D.] (See Pat. Sect.)
*PRACTICE AREAS: Intellectual Property Litigation; Mechanical Intellectual Property; Civil Litigation; Technology Licensing; Trademarks.
Strumberger, Gregg ....'70 '99 C.476 B.S. L.94 J.D. [Ⓐ Swidler B.S.F.]
*PRACTICE AREAS: Telecommunications; Antitrust.
Strunck, Thomas F. ...'22 '50 C.1191 B.E. L.424 J.D. National Railway Labor Conference
Strupp, Werner ....'25 '56 C&L.273 A.B., J.D. [Sinrod&T.]
Strzalka, Philip R. '71 '98 C.339 B.S. L.146 J.D.
(adm. in IL; not adm. in DC) [Ⓐ Dow,L.&A.]
Stuart, David M. ....'67 '95 C.918 B.A. L.569 J.D. U.S. Sec. and Exch. Comm.
Stuart, James R., III ....'61 '86 C.119 B.S. L.309 J.D. [Crowell&M.]
*PRACTICE AREAS: Corporate Law; Business Law; Securities Finance; Venture Capital; Commercial Contracts.
Stuart, John F. ....'47 '72 C&L.767 B.A., J.D. [Reitner&S.]
Stuart, Martha Phillips ....'71 '96 C.339 B.A. L.734 J.D. [Ⓐ Kirkland&E.]
*PRACTICE AREAS: Corporate Law; Mergers and Acquisitions; Private Equity; Venture Capital.

Stuart, Pamela B., (AV) '49 '74 C.518 A.B. L.477 J.D.
1101 Connecticut Avenue, N.W., Suite 1000, 20036
Telephone: 202-835-2200 Facsimile: 202-835-2202 URL: http://www.stuart-law.com
Email: pamstuart@aol.com URL: http://www.lawyers.com/pamelastuartlaw
Of Counsel: Kathleen E. Voelker.
Litigation, White Collar Criminal Defense, Labor and Employment, Employment Discrimination, Disability Discrimination, Commercial Law, International Law including Extradition and Immigration, Security Clearances, Congressional Investigations, Business Law, Health Law, Antitrust and Trade Regulation, Copyright and Trademark, Medical Malpractice, Wills, Trusts and Estates, Real Estate, Products Liability and Personal Injury, Estate Planning, Family Law.
See Professional Biographies, WASHINGTON, DISTRICT OF COLUMBIA

Stubbs, Joseph E., (AV) ....'45 '80 C.475 B.S. L.273 J.D. [© Steptoe&J.]
*PRACTICE AREAS: Energy Law; Regulatory Law.
Stuckwisch, William J. ....'69 '96 C&L.893 B.A., J.D. [Ⓐ O'Melveny&M.]
Studley, Janet R., (AV) ....'50 '76 C.242 B.A. L.260 J.D. [Holland&K.]
*PRACTICE AREAS: Federal Legislative Practice; Administrative Law.
Stukes, Anne W. '69 '97 C&L.575 B.A., J.D.
(adm. in GA; not adm. in DC) [Ⓐ Winston&S.]
*PRACTICE AREAS: Litigation.
Stultz, Cheryl A. '59 '85 C.602 B.A. L.128 J.D.
Assoc. Gen. Coun., Corp. Affs., Natl. Railroad Passenger Corp. (AMTRAK)
Stumberg, Robert K. '50 '75
C.429 B.A. L.276 J.D. Prof. of Law, Georgetown Univ. Law Ctr.
Stumpf, Mark H., (AV) ....'47 '73 C&L.309 A.B., J.D. [Arnold&P.]
*PRACTICE AREAS: International; Corporate; Securities.
Stumpf, Robin D. '71 '99 C.602 B.A. L.893 J.D.
(adm. in IL; not adm. in DC) [Ⓐ Jones,D.R.&P.]
Stuntz, Linda Gillespie, (AV) '54 '79 C.967 B.A. L.309 J.D.
1201 Pennylvania Ave., NW
Stup, Carolyn K. '68 '97 C.446 B.A. L.94 J.D.
(adm. in MD; not adm. in DC) Reg. Coun., Teligent, Inc.
Stup, Robert E. ....'— '95 C.446 B.S. L.188 J.D. 701 Pennsylvania Avenue, N.W.
Stupar, Branko, (AV) ....'22 '51 C.532 B.A. L.904 LL.B. [Faulkner,S.&S.]
Sturc, John H., (AV) ....'50 '75 C.188 A.B. L.309 J.D. [Gibson,D.&C.]
*PRACTICE AREAS: Securities; Civil and Criminal Litigation.
Sturdevant, Patricia, (AV) '42 '72 C.112 B.A. L.1068 J.D.
(adm. in CA; not adm. in DC) [Natl. C.A.&Assoc.]
Sturdivant, Jocelyn M. ....'66 '94 C.103 B.A. L.309 J.D. [Ⓐ Paul,H.J.&W.]
Sturgell, Robert A. ....'59 '94 C.871 B.S. L.893 J.D. United Airlines
Sturkie, Cassandra ....'— '00 C.790 B.Ar.Sc. L.228 J.D. [Ⓐ Latham&W.]
*PRACTICE AREAS: Administrative Litigation; Environmental Law; Political Asylum; Zoning, Planning and Land Use.
Sturm, Joy E. ....'67 '95 C.659 B.A. L.273 J.D. [Ⓐ Hogan&H.]
*PRACTICE AREAS: Government Contracts; Health Care Contracting; International Contracts.
Sturm, Michael L. ....'62 '87 C.945 B.A. L.309 J.D. [Wiley R.&F.]
*PRACTICE AREAS: Litigation; Intellectual Property; Franchise.
Sturm, Michael O., (AV) '43 '73 C.350 B.S. L.1128 J.D.
(adm. in VA; not adm. in DC; See Pat. Sect.) [Henderson&S.] ⊙
Sturm, Sharon Louise '60 '88 C.446 B.A. L.128 J.D.
(adm. in NY; not adm. in DC) NASD Regul., Inc.

Sturtevant, Albert D., (AV) '42 '67 C&L.976 B.A., LL.B.
888 Seventeenth Street, N.W., Suite 1000, 20006-3967
Telephone: 202-298-6161 Fax: 202-293-1640
***PRACTICE AREAS: Business Law; Corporate Law; Securities; International Investment; Probate.**

(This Listing Continued)

Sturtevant, Albert D. (Continued)

Sturtevant, Leslie Anne ....'— '99 C.103 A.B. L.477 J.D. [Ⓐ Wilmer,C.&P.]
Styles, Keith R., (AV) ....'57 '83 C.976 B.A. L.276 J.D. [Robins,K.M.&C.]
*PRACTICE AREAS: Business and Large Project Financing; Mergers and Acquisitions; Technology Law; General Business Counseling.
Su, Tricia Chwenchii ....'72 '99 C.339 B.S. L.569 J.D. [Ⓐ Fried,F.H.S.&J.]
*PRACTICE AREAS: Tax; Corporate.
Suagee, Dean B. ....'50 '78 C.37 B.A. L.577 J.D. [© Hobbs,S.D.&W.]
Suarez, Evelyn M., (BV) ....'52 '79 C.705 B.A. L.276 J.D. [Sonnenschein N.&R.]
*PRACTICE AREAS: Customs Law; International Trade.
Suarez, Pedro F. '64 '00 C.1070 B.S.E.E. L.273 J.D.
(adm. in CA; not adm. in DC; See Pat. Sect.) [Ⓐ Finnegan,H.F.G.&D.]
*PRACTICE AREAS: Software Protection; Intellectual Property Infringement; Intellectual Property Litigation; Electrical Patent Prosecution; Electronic Patents.
Subramanian, Chid ....'61 '97 C.8 M.S.Ch.E. L.276 J.D. [Ⓐ Sughrue M.] (See Pat. Sect.)
Suchman, Bonnie A. ....'58 '83 C.65 B.A. L.273 J.D. [© Troutman S.]
*PRACTICE AREAS: Energy; Utility Law; Regulatory Law.
Sudhakara, Meena ....'53 '86 C&L.999 B.Sc., J.D. Asst. Corp. Coun.
Sudol, Eric W. ....'64 '93 C.273 B.S. L.1280 J.D. 942 24th St., N.W.
Sudow, Ellen L. ....'46 '77 C.183 A.B. L.1162 J.D. Prof., Antioch Law School
Sudow, William E., (AV) ....'45 '70 C.976 B.A. L.659 J.D. [Sidley A.B.&W.]
Sue, Norman, Jr. '49 '75 C.747 B.A. L.838 J.D.
Assoc. Gen. Coun., Nat. Assn. of Sec. Dealers, Inc.
Suffoletta, Mary C. '58 '93
C.446 B.S. L.146 J.D. Bd. of Vet. App., U.S. Dept. of Vet. Affs.
Sugameli, Glenn P. '54 '79 C.674 A.B. L.893 J.D.
Sr. Legislative Coun., Earthjustice Legal Defense Fund
Sugarman, Halye ....'75 '01 C.260 B.A. L.273 J.D. [Ⓐ Collier S.S.]
*PRACTICE AREAS: Litigation.
Sugarman, Richard A. ....'— '01 C.454 B.A. L.273 J.D. [Ⓐ Morgan,L.&B.]
Sugarman, Robert J., (AV) '38 '64 C.103 A.B. L.309 LL.B.
3251 Prospect St., NW (⊙Doylestown, Phila., PA)

Sughrue Mion, PLLC, (AV) BR
A Professional Limited Liability Company including Professional Corporations
Suite 800, 2100 Pennsylvania Avenue, N.W., 20037-3213 ⊙
Telephone: 202-293-7060 Facsimile: 202-293-7860
Email: sughrue@sughrue.com URL: http://www.sughrue.com
Members of Firm: Richard C. Sughrue (1921-2000); John H. Mion (P.C.); Robert J. Seas, Jr. (P.C.); Darryl Mexic (P.C.); Robert V. Sloan (P.C.) (Not admitted in DC); Peter D. Olexy (P.C.); J. Frank Osha; Louis Gubinsky (P.C.); Neil B. Siegel; David J. Cushing; Cynthia Clarke Weber; John R. Inge; Joseph J. Ruch, Jr. (Not admitted in DC); Sheldon I. Landsman (P.C.); Richard C. Turner; Howard L. Bernstein (P.C.); Alan J. Kasper; Kenneth J. Burchfiel; Gordon Kit; Susan J. Mack; Frank L. Bernstein; Mark Boland; William H. Mandir; Gary D. Krugman; Brian W. Hannon; Abraham J. Rosner; Bruce E. Kramer; Paul F. Neils; Brett S. Sylvester; Robert M. Masters; William Mack Webner; George F. Lehnigk; John T. Callahan; Steven M. Gruskin; Peter A. McKenna; Edward F. Kenehan, Jr.; John F. Rabena; Grant K. Rowan; Susan Perng Pan; Kevin G. Smith; Jody Haller Drake. Associates: Lee C. Wright; Stanislav Torgovitsky; Carl J. Pellegrini; Kelly G. Hyndman; Ellen Resnick Smith; Raja N. Saliba; H. Ray Heflin (Not admitted in DC); Chid Subramanian; Jeffrey A. Schmidt; Paul J. Wilson; Eric P. Halber; Christopher R. Lipp (Not admitted in DC); Kevin M. Barner (Not admitted in DC); Leigh Ann Lindquist; John W. Bain; David A. Klein; L. Raul Tamayo; Keiko K. Takagi (Not admitted in DC); Drew Hissong, Ph.D.; Paul M. Higgins; Mainak Himanshu Mehta; Craig W. Schmoyer (Not admitted in DC); Amy E. Simpson (Not admitted in DC); Keith B. Scala (Not admitted in DC); Terrance Jay Wikberg (Not admitted in DC); Mark R. Woodall; Ronald L. Kimble (Not admitted in DC); Cameron W. Beddard (Not admitted in DC); Timothy P. Cremen (Not admitted in DC); Michael J. Whitehead; Daniel V. Williams; Jennifer M. Hayes; William K. Yee (Not admitted in DC); John M. Sanders (Not admitted in DC); Yoshinari Kishimoto (Not admitted in DC); David A. Sumy; John M. Bird (Not admitted in DC); George Brieger (Not admitted in DC). Senior Counsel: Robert G. McMorrow (P.C.).
Patent, Trademark, Copyright, Unfair Competition Law. Practice before the Federal Courts and Administrative Agencies. Antitrust, International Trade Regulation, International Patent and Trademark Law.
Tokyo, Japan Office: Toei Nishi Shimbashi Building, Suite 4F, 13-5 Nishi Shimbashi 1-Chome 105. Telephone: (03) 3 503-3760.
Menlo Park, California Office: 1010 El Camino Real, Suite 360. Telephone: 650-325-5800. Facsimile: 650-325-6606.
See Professional Biographies, WASHINGTON, DISTRICT OF COLUMBIA

Sugiyama, George Y. ....'49 '76 C.221 B.A. L.446 J.D. [Dorsey&W.]
*PRACTICE AREAS: Environmental Law; Regulatory Agency Practice; Federal Administrative Law.
Suh, Ann Sungmie ....'41 '81 C&L.494 M.A., J.D. 601 Penn. Ave.,N.W.
Suh, Katherine Tong-Shin ....'72 '99 C.893 B.A. L.902 J.D. [Ⓐ Shaw P.]
*PRACTICE AREAS: Communications.
Suhre, Sarah E. ....'76 '00 C.446 B.A. L.276 J.D. [Ⓐ Slevin&H.]
*PRACTICE AREAS: Employee Benefits.
Suk, Steve C. ....'69 '97 C.1356 B.A. L.128 J.D. [Ⓐ Arnold&P.]
*PRACTICE AREAS: Corporate Law; Securities; Financial Institutions.
Sukduang, Sanya ...'73 '99 C.93 B.S. L.30 J.D. [Ⓐ Finnegan,H.F.G.&D.] (See Pat. Sect.)
*PRACTICE AREAS: Patent Litigation; Patent Interference Practice; Chemical Patent Prosecution; Biotechnology Patent Prosecution.
Sulaiman, Fatima ....'71 '97 C.890 B.A. L.884 J.D. [Ⓐ Kirkpatrick&L.]
*PRACTICE AREAS: Investment Management; Securities Law; Investment Company Law; Mutual Funds.
Sulik, William P. '59 '86 C.1369 B.S. L.1339 J.D.
(adm. in VA; not adm. in DC) Legal Servs. Corp.
Sullivan, A. Michael, Jr. '42 '66 C.708 A.B. L.128 LL.B.
(adm. in RI; not adm. in DC) Pres., Michael Sullivan, Inc.
Sullivan, Anne H. ....'74 '99 C.296 B.S. L.64 J.D. [Ⓐ Wilkinson B.K.]
*PRACTICE AREAS: Telecommunications Law.
Sullivan, Brendan V., Jr., (AV) ....'42 '67 C&L.276 A.B., J.D. [Williams&C.]
Sullivan, Caleb W., (BV) ....'58 '85 C.293 A.B. L.284 J.D. [Ⓐ White&C.]
Sullivan, Catherine D. ......'69 '95 C.94 B.A. L.208 J.D. Bureau of Natl. Affairs, Inc., The
Sullivan, Courtney Ann ....'71 '98 C.602 B.A. L.494 J.D. [Ⓐ Arent F.K.P.&K.]
*PRACTICE AREAS: Litigation.
Sullivan, David P. ....'71 '00 C.659 B.A. L.904 J.D. [Ⓐ Kirkland&E.]
*PRACTICE AREAS: Commercial Litigation.
Sullivan, Dennis C. ....'59 '85 C.276 B.S. L.128 J.D. [Sullivan&C.]
Sullivan, Diane M., (AV) ....'43 '69 C&L.273 A.B., J.D. Asst. U.S. Atty.
Sullivan, James Michael ....'70 '98 C.321 B.A. L.128 J.D. [Ⓐ Piper M.R.&W.]
*PRACTICE AREAS: Commercial Litigation; White Collar Litigation.
Sullivan, Jennifer A. '51 '76
C.1036 B.A. L.309 J.D. Dep. Gen. Coun., International Fin. Corp.
Sullivan, John J. ....'59 '87 C.103 A.B. L.178 J.D. [Mayer,B.&P.]
Sullivan, John J. '53 '79 C.102 B.A. L.273 J.D.
Assoc. Gen. Coun., Potomac Electric Power Company
Sullivan, John Louis '70 '97 C.477 A.B. L.569 J.D.
(adm. in NY; not adm. in DC) Sec. & Exch. Comm.
Sullivan, Joseph D. ....'— '85 C&L.276 B.A., J.D. [Latham&W.]
Sullivan, Julia E., (AV) ....'63 '88 C.839 B.A. L.904 J.D. [Sidley A.B.&W.]
Sullivan, Kathleen F. ....'49 '81 C.93 B.A. L.128 J.D. [Nixon P.]
*PRACTICE AREAS: Taxation; Real Estate; Partnerships.
Sullivan, Kevin R., (AV) ....'— '75 C.1062 B.A. L.128 J.D. [King&S.]
*PRACTICE AREAS: Litigation and Trade.

Sullivan, Mary Anne .... '51 '76 C.262 B.A. L.976 J.D. [Hogan&H.]
*PRACTICE AREAS: Energy; Nuclear Energy; Federal Lands; Environmental Law; Global Climate Change.
Sullivan, Michael D., (AV) .... '55 '80 C.608 B.A. L.276 J.D. [Levine S.&K.]
Sullivan, Michael Deuel, (AV) .... '52 '78 C.910 A.B. L.128 J.D. [Wilkinson B.K.]
*PRACTICE AREAS: Administrative Litigation; Appellate Practice; Communications; Telecommunications Law; Information Technology.
Sullivan, Michael G. '63 '91 C.1119 B.S. L.64 J.D. [Ⓒ Rothwell,F.E.&M.] (See Pat. Sect.)
*PRACTICE AREAS: Intellectual Property.
Sullivan, Morgen A. '74 '99 C.197 B.A. L.228 J.D. (adm. in CA; not adm. in DC) [Ⓐ O'Melveny&M.]
Sullivan, Neal E. .... '60 '90 C.1200 B.A. L.818 J.D. [Bingham D.]
*PRACTICE AREAS: Securities Litigation; Broker-Dealer; Investment Adviser Regulation; Market Regulation.
Sullivan, Paul E. '— '79 C.770 B.S. L.990 J.D. (adm. in CA; not adm. in DC) [Foley&L.]
*PRACTICE AREAS: Public Affairs.
Sullivan, Raymond F., Jr., (AV) .... '49 '76 C&L.446 B.A., J.D. [Ⓐ Willkie F.&G.]
Sullivan, Russell W. ...'61 '88 C.69 B.B.A. L.846 J.D. Legis. Dir.; U.S. Sen. Bob Graham
Sullivan, Sean M. '76 '01 C.472 B.S. L.30 J.D. (adm. in VA; not adm. in DC) [Ⓐ Shaw P.]
Sullivan, Sean R. '71 '96 C.401 B.A. L.665 J.D. (adm. in PA; not adm. in DC) [Ⓐ Kirkpatrick&L.]
*PRACTICE AREAS: Antitrust; Civil Litigation; Insurance Coverage; Products Liability Defense; Class Action Defense.
Sullivan, Stephen P. .... '70 '99 C.587 B.A. L.902 J.D. [Ⓐ McDermott,W.&E.]
Sullivan, T. J., (AV) .... '53 '85 C.759 B.A. L.273 J.D. [Gardner,C.&D.]
*PRACTICE AREAS: Health Care; Taxation.
Sullivan, Terry L. .... '61 '95 C.911 B.A. L.273 J.D. [Ⓐ Howrey S.A.&W.]
*PRACTICE AREAS: Antitrust Litigation; Commercial Litigation.
Sullivan, Theodore M. '66 '97 C.1356 B.S. L.146 J.D. (adm. in IL; not adm. in DC) [Ⓐ Buchanan I.]
*PRACTICE AREAS: Food, Drug and Cosmetic Law.
Sullivan, Timothy, (AV) .... '48 '75 C.477 B.A. L.276 J.D. [Thompson C.]
*PRACTICE AREAS: Government Contract Law.

Sullivan & Cromwell, (AV)
1701 Pennsylvania Avenue, N.W., 20006-5805 ⊙
Telephone: 202-956-7500 Telecopier: 202-293-6330
URL: http://www.sullcrom.com
Partners in Washington, D.C.: H. Rodgin Cohen (Not admitted in DC); Robert H. Craft, Jr.; Daryl A. Libow; Margaret K. Pfeiffer; Robert Samuel Risoleo (Not admitted in DC); Kathryn E. Rorer; Dennis C. Sullivan; Edwin D. Williamson. Of Counsel in Washington, D.C.: Janet Thiele Geldzahler. Special Counsel in Washington, D.C.: Stephen C. Connor (Not admitted in DC); Thomas R. Leuba; Paul J. McElroy. Associates in Washington, D.C.: Christine Ayotte-Brennan; Toryah S. Cameron; John E. Capps (Not admitted in DC); Rita M. Carrier; Robert E. Chandler (Not admitted in DC); Jennifer E. Cook; Geoffrey P. Eaton (Not admitted in DC); Bruce Fein; Alexander D. Fine (Not admitted in DC); Jacqueline Suzanne Hackett (Not admitted in DC); Thomas F. Hancock; Stephen C. Jacques; Eric J. Kadel, Jr.; Anna M. Kuzmik; Katherine K. Martin (Not admitted in DC); Joseph James Matelis, II; Lee Ann Anderson McCall; Ann M. Miller; Chidi J. Ogene (Not admitted in DC); Bradley P. Smith; Michael K. Sopchick; Veronique K. Waites; Joy Marzilli Willing; Christopher M. Zochowski.
General Practice.
New York City Office: 125 Broad Street, 10004-2498. Telephone: 212-558-4000. Telex: 62694. Telecopier: 212-558-3588.
Los Angeles, California Office: 1888 Century Park East, 90067-1725. Telephone: 310-712-6600. Telecopier: 310-712-8800.
Palo Alto, California Office: 1870 Embarcadero Road, 94303-3308. Telephone: 650-461-5600. Telecopier: 650-461-5700.
Paris Office: 8, place Vendôme, 75001 Paris, France. Telephone: (011)(331) 44 50 60 00. Telecopier: (011)(331) 44 50 60 60.
London Office: St. Olave's House, 9a Ironmonger Lane, London EC2V 8EY, England. Telephone: (011)(44207) 710 6500. Telecopier: (011)(44207) 710 6565.
Melbourne Office: 101 Collins Street, Melbourne 3000, Australia. Telephone: (011)(613) 9635-1500. Telecopier: (011)(613) 9654-2422.
Tokyo Office: Otemachi First Square East Tower 16F, 5-1, Otemachi 1-chome, Chiyoda-ku, Tokyo 100-0004, Japan. Telephone: (011)(813) 3213-6140. Telecopier: (011)(813) 3213-6470.
Hong Kong Office: 28th Floor, Nine Queen's Road, Central, Hong Kong. Telephone: (011)(852) 2826-8688. Telecopier: (011)(852) 2522-2280.
Frankfurt Office: Neue Mainzer Strasse 52, 60311 Frankfurt am Main, Germany. Telephone: (011)(4969) 7191 26-0. Telecopier: (011)(4969) 7191 26-10.
Beijing Office: The Beijing Representative Office of Sullivan & Cromwell, Suite 501, China World Trade Center Tower 1, No. 1 Jianguo Menwai Avenue, Beijing 100004, P.R.C. Telephone: (011)(86) 10 6505 6120. Telecopier: (011)(86) 10 6505 6136.
Sydney Office: Level 34, The Chifley Tower, 2 Chifley Square, Sydney, NSW 2000, Australia. Telephone: (001) 61-2 8227-6700. Telecopier: (001) 61-2 8227-6750.
See Professional Biographies, WASHINGTON, DISTRICT OF COLUMBIA

Sullivan Law Group .... 1200 G Street, NW, Suite 800 (⊙Phoenix, AZ)

Sullivan & Worcester LLP, (AV)
1025 Connecticut Avenue, N.W., 20036 ⊙
Telephone: 202-775-8190 Telecopier: 202-293-2275
URL: http://www.sandw.com
Resident Partners: John A. Dudley; Robert N. Hickey; J. Randolph MacPherson; David M. Leahy; David C. Mahaffey. Retired Partner: Paul G. Kirk, Jr. Associates: Jane B. Maxwell; Stacy H. Ostrowski (Not admitted in DC); Christine S. Boehm. Staff Attorney: John L. Chilton (Not admitted in DC).
Corporate and Administrative Law Practice before all Federal Departments and Agencies. Securities, Investment Companies, Banking, International Trade, Communications, High Technology, Municipal, Government Contracts and Federal Legislative Practice, ERISA, Real Estate Investment Trusts, Leasing, Mergers and Acquisitions, Closely-held Businesses, Debt/Equity Financing, Asset-Based Lending, Commercial Transactions, Private Placements, Public Offerings, Venture Capital Investments and SEC: Regulatory Compliance, Land Use and High Technology Law.
The firm also has offices at: One Post Office Square, Boston, Massachusetts, 02109. Telephone: 617-338-2800; 565 Fifth Avenue, New York, New York, 10017. Telephone: 212-486-8200; 292 Madison Avenue, New York, New York 10017-6307. Telephone: 212-213-8200.
See Professional Biographies, WASHINGTON, DISTRICT OF COLUMBIA

Sultan, Ilana Z. .... '67 '94 C.178 B.A. L.145 J.D. [Ⓐ Beveridge&D.]
*PRACTICE AREAS: White Collar Criminal Defense; Environmental Law.
Sulzer, Stephen L. .... '55 '80 C.597 B.A. L.245 J.D. [Dickinson W.]
*PRACTICE AREAS: Patent and Intellectual Property Litigation; Intellectual Property Licensing; Antitrust Litigation and Counseling; ITC Section 337 Litigation.
Summerill, Joseph J., IV .... '66 '93 C.164 B.A. L.1218 J.D. [Ⓐ Piliero,M.&P.]
*PRACTICE AREAS: Government Contracts; Corrections Law; Corporate Law; Intellectual Property; Civil Litigation.
Summers, Erica L. .... '52 '77 C.976 B.A. L.659 J.D. [Ⓒ Ice M.] (⊙Indpls., IN)
*PRACTICE AREAS: Employee Benefits Law.
Sumner, Bret A. .... '70 '98 C.1369 B.S. L.180 J.D. [Ⓐ Fulbright&J.]
*PRACTICE AREAS: Energy; Project Finance.
Sumner, D. Jay .... '71 '98 C.806 B.A. L.838 J.D. [Ⓐ Krupin O.]
*PRACTICE AREAS: Labor Law; Employment Law.
Sumpter, Corinne J. .... '73 '99 C.112 B.A. L.813 J.D. 111 F St., NW
Sumy, David A. .... '63 '98 C.1293 B.Mus. L.365 J.D. [Ⓐ Sughrue M.]
*PRACTICE AREAS: Patent Law.
Sun, Alexander K. .... '69 '96 C&L.276 B.S., J.D. [Ⓐ Wiley R.&F.]
Sun, Catherine '73 '98 C.1356 B.A. L.30 J.D. (adm. in NY; not adm. in DC) [Ⓐ Patton B.]
Sundback, Mark F., (AV) .... '56 '81 C.216 B.A. L.178 J.D. [Andrews&K.]
*PRACTICE AREAS: Energy Regulation; Natural Gas Pipelines; Electric Utilities; Oil and Gas Pipelines.
Sundburg, Alan Dean .... '61 '87 C.299 A.B. L.945 J.D. [Friedlander,M.S.K.&O.]
*PRACTICE AREAS: Workers Compensation Law; Insurance Defense Law.
Sundby, Suzannah K. '72 '99 C.959 B.S. L.1218 J.D. (adm. in CA; not adm. in DC; See Pat. Sect.) [Ⓐ Jacobson,H.]
*PRACTICE AREAS: Biotechnology Patents; Chemical Patents; Pharmaceutical Patents; Medical Patents; Patent Applications.
Sundeen, Marcia H., (AV) .... '54 '81 C.436 B.S. L.930 J.D. [Pennie&E.] (See Pat. Sect.)
*PRACTICE AREAS: Intellectual Property; Intellectual Property Litigation; International Trade.
Sunderdick, Vincent J., (BV) '47 '78 C.502 B.S.E.E. L.276 J.D. (adm. in MI; not adm. in DC; Pat.) [Ⓒ Crowell&M.]
*PRACTICE AREAS: Patent Law.
Sunderland, Philip G. .... '45 '72 C.197 B.A. L.813 J.D. 1121 12th St., N.W.
Sundermeyer, Michael S., (AV) .... '51 '76 C.378 B.A. L.893 J.D. [Williams&C.]
*PRACTICE AREAS: Commercial Litigation; Complex Litigation; Federal Administrative Law; Judicial Review; Legal Ethics.
Sung, Ki Jun .... '67 '93 C.188 B.A. L.893 J.D. [Ⓐ Schnader H.S.&L.]
*PRACTICE AREAS: Commercial Litigation; Products Liability; Construction Law; Real Estate.
Sunshine, Steven C. .... '59 '85 C.103 B.A. L.93 J.D. [Shearman&S.]
Super, David A. .... '64 '91 C&L.446 B.S., J.D. [Baker B.]
Super, David A. '59 '83 C.674 A.B. L.309 J.D. (adm. in MI; not adm. in DC) 1875 Conn. Ave., N.W.
Supik, Frank J. .... '69 '94 C.446 B.S. L.276 J.D. 1400 L Street, N.W.
Supko, Mark M. .... '63 '94 C.754 B.S. L.276 J.D. [Ⓐ Kenyon&K.] (See Pat. Sect.)
*PRACTICE AREAS: Intellectual Property.
Suri, Sharan K. .... '73 '98 C&L.477 B.A., J.D. [Ⓐ Fried,F.H.S.&J.]
*PRACTICE AREAS: Litigation.
Suringa, Dirk J. .... '70 '97 C.674 A.B. L.309 J.D. Tres. Dept.
Suringa, Kimberly Stallings .... '70 '96 C.893 B.A. L.309 J.D. [Ⓐ Akin,G.S.H.&F.]
*PRACTICE AREAS: Health Care.
Surrisi, Cynthia M. '— '82 C.585 B.A. L.1035 J.D. (adm. in MN; not adm. in DC) [Verner,L.B.M.&H.]
*PRACTICE AREAS: Labor and Employment; Aviation Law; Administrative Law; Contracts.
Suski, Amy .... '70 '98 C.914 B.A. L.893 J.D. [Ⓐ Arter&H.]
*PRACTICE AREAS: Business Litigation; Products Liability.
Suski, David A. .... '71 '98 C.128 B.A.M.A. L.893 J.D. [Ⓐ Hale&D.]
*PRACTICE AREAS: Food and Drug Regulation.
Susman, Thomas M., (AV) .... '43 '67 C.976 B.A. L.846 J.D. [Ropes&G.]
Susser, Peter A. .... '55 '79 C.188 B.S. L.945 J.D. [Littler M.]
*PRACTICE AREAS: Labor and Employment; Occupational Safety and Health Law.
Sussman, Bernard J. .... '47 '79 C.128 L.30 J.D. Law Libr., U.S. Ct. of Vet. App.
Sussman, Edward C. .... '48 '73 C.188 B.S. L.273 J.D. 601 Pennsylvania Ave., N.W.
Sussman, Monica Hilton, (AV) .... '52 '77 C.823 B.A. L.1019 J.D. [Nixon P.]
*PRACTICE AREAS: Real Estate; Affordable Housing; Real Estate Finance; Legislation; Corporate.
Sussman, Robert M., (AV) .... '— '74 C&L.976 B.A., LL.B. [Latham&W.]
*PRACTICE AREAS: Environmental; Air Quality; Chemical Regulation; Superfund.
Susswein, Steven A. '69 '96 C.477 B.A. L.273 J.D. (adm. in MI; not adm. in DC) [Ⓐ Howrey S.A.&W.]
*PRACTICE AREAS: Commercial Litigation.
Suter, Eric .... '67 '99 C&L.174 B.A., J.D. [Ⓐ Arnold&P.]
*PRACTICE AREAS: Litigation.

Sutherland Asbill & Brennan LLP, (AV)
1275 Pennsylvania Avenue, N.W., 20004-2415 ⊙
Telephone: 202-383-0100 Cable Address: "Sutab Wash" Telex: 89-501 Facsimile: 202-637-3593
Email: info@sablaw.com URL: http://www.sablaw.com
Members of the Firm in Washington, D.C.: William A. Sutherland (1896-1987); Mac Asbill, Sr. (1893-1992); Joseph B. Brennan (1903-1991); Mac Asbill, Jr. (1922-1992).
Eric A. Arnold; Frederick R. Bellamy; Herbert N. Beller; Steven B. Boehm; George H. Bostick; James Randall Buchanan; James M. Bushee; James M. Cain; Nicholas T. Christakos; Lovida H. Coleman, Jr.; James D. Darrow; Warren N. Davis; Jacob Dweck; Paul F. Forshay; Hamilton P. Fox, III; Thomas A. Gick; David S. Goldstein; Francis M. Gregory, Jr. (1941-1993); Edward J. Grenier, Jr.; James V. Heffernan; James L. Henderson, III (Not admitted in DC); Mark D. Herlach; Mark D. Jackson; Paul D. Jacokes; E. Michael Johnson; Paul W. Killian; Susan S. Krawczyk; Cynthia M. Krus; Neil S. Lang; Elisabeth A. Langworthy; Jerome B. Libin; David A. Massey; Keith R. McCrea; Michael R. Miles; Clifford E. Muller; Richard G. Murphy, Jr. (Not admitted in DC); Lloyd Leva Plaine; Peter H. Rodgers; Lisa Alpert Rosen; Stephen E. Roth; Beverly J. Rudy; Michael J. Shea; Douglas L. Siegler; Kimberly J. Smith; W. Mark Smith; Giovanna T. Sparagna; Steuart H. Thomsen; F. Brook Voght; William J. Walderman; Carol A. Weiser; Dena Eve Wiggins; Mary Jane Wilson-Bilik; Katherine P. Yarbrough; H. Karl Zeswitz, Jr. Of Counsel: Jack H. Blaine; William S. Corey; Joel E. Hoffman; Robert G. Levy (Not admitted in DC); William H. Penniman; Holly H. Smith. Counsel: Thomas E. Bisset; James J. Briody; Charles M. Flickinger (Not admitted in DC); Anne W. Geldon; Nancy L. Hankin; Lori E. Harwell; Ian A. Herbert (Not admitted in DC); Douglas J. Leary; Roxane E. Maywalt; Carol T. McClarnon; Mary Patricia Michel; Mary E. Monahan; Christer L. Mossberg; Scott D. Silverman (Not admitted in DC); Gregory Stuart Smith (Not admitted in DC); Lewis S. Wiener; Catherine S. Wooledge. Associates of the Firm in Washington, D.C.: James A. Baldwin (Not admitted in DC); Lloyd F. Bernard; Thomas Robinson Bundy, III (Not admitted in DC); Ronesha A. Butler; Ann B. Cammack; Robert S. Chase, II; Eric Ciccoretti (Not admitted in DC); Adam Cohen; Margaret M. Connell (Not admitted in DC); Kathleen M. Devereaux (Not admitted in DC); Marshall O. Donley, III (Not admitted in DC); Pamela K. Ellis; John J. Fahey; Blair E. Flynn (Not admitted in DC); Daniel E. Frank; Kirstin E. Gibbs; Danielle Giroux; Elisabeth Grano; Bryan M. Haynes; John E. Hinding; Rebecca L. Hirsch; John L. Hynes; Rawn M. James, Jr.; Gregory S. Kaufman; Margaret Anne King (Not admitted in DC); Beth D. Knickerbocker (Not admitted in DC); Michael Koffler; David J. Kritz; Rene M. LaForte (Not admitted in DC); David A. Last (Not admitted in DC); Marie Kalamaras Lee (Not admitted in DC); Ling Ling; Kurt E. Lopez (Not admitted in DC); Ronald R. Massumi; Donyelle C. McCray; Jay McDanell (Not admitted in DC); Matthew G. McLaughlin; Katherine S. Milin; Sheila R. Novak; Victoria A. O'Connor; Heather Stacey Parr (Not admitted in DC); Michael C. Pawluk; Shannan Stamper Petrilla; Patrice M. Pitts; Jennifer R. Rawert (Not admitted in DC); Thomas J. Reyes (Not admitted in DC); Thomas C. Roberge, Jr.; David A. Roby, Jr.; Amish M. Shah; Daniel R. Simon (Not admitted in DC); Alisa Naomi Stein (Not admitted in DC); Christopher F. Tate; Mary E. Thornton; Thomas M. Tracy (Not admitted in DC); Paul B. Turner; Gail L. Westover; Wendy Ann Wilkenfeld; Charles J. Zangara (Not admitted in DC).
General Practice. Trial and Appellate Practice in all Courts. Federal and State Tax, Antitrust and Trade Regulation, Securities, Arbitration, Energy, Environmental, Public Utility and Administrative Law, Corporate, Communications, Food and Drug Law, Financial Services, International, Employee Benefits, Estate Planning, Trusts, Probate, Government Contracts, Real Property, Patent, Copyright and Trademark Law, Legislative, Federal and State Insurance Company Practice, Construction Law.
Atlanta, Georgia Office: 999 Peachtree Street, N.E., 30309-3996. Telephone: 404-853-8000.
New York, N.Y. Office: 350 Park Avenue, 25th Floor, 10022. Telephone: 212-655-3883.
Austin, Texas Office: 701 Brazos Street, Suite 1040, 78701-2559. Telephone: 512-478-1665.
Tallahassee, Florida Office: 2282 Killearn Center Boulevard, 32308-3561. Telephone: 850-894-0015.
See Professional Biographies, WASHINGTON, DISTRICT OF COLUMBIA

Sutter, Ronald N., (AV) .... '47 '75 C.770 B.A. L.1066 J.D. [Powers,P.S.&V.]
*PRACTICE AREAS: Health Care Law; Hospital Law; Litigation; Administrative Law.
Sutter & Enslein .... 1738 Wisconsin Ave., N.W.
Sutton, Alan B.T. '70 '96 C.846 B.S. L.326 J.D. (adm. in TX; not adm. in DC) [Ⓐ Howrey S.A.&W.]
*PRACTICE AREAS: Government Contracts; Export Regulation.
Sutton, George Michael '57 '92 C.877 B.S. L.273 J.D. (adm. in VA; not adm. in DC) World Wildlife Fund
Sutton, Kathryn M. .... '64 '88 C.645 B.A. L.276 J.D. [Winston&S.]
*PRACTICE AREAS: Nuclear Energy Law.

Sutton, Michelle R. .... '71 '97 C.845 B.A. L.904 J.D. 1900 L St., N.W.
Sutton, Nathan P. '73 '01 C.576 B.S. L.145 J.D.
(adm. in CA; not adm. in DC) [Ⓐ Williams&C.]
*PRACTICE AREAS: Intellectual Property; Antitrust; Litigation.
Sutton, S. Robert, (AV) .... '55 '80 C.597 B.A. L.813 J.D. [Janis,S.&W.]
*PRACTICE AREAS: White Collar Criminal Defense; Business Crimes.
Svoboda, Brian G. .... '67 '94 C.546 B.A. L.893 J.D. [Ⓐ Perkins C.]
*PRACTICE AREAS: Election Law; Administrative Law; Litigation.
Svonkin, Michele L. .... '71 '99 C.1036 B.A. L.188 J.D. [Ⓐ Shea&G.]
Swails, J. Edward '57 '83 C.493 B.A. L.477 J.D.
(adm. in PA; not adm. in DC) Ernst & Young
Swain, Frank S. .... '51 '76 C.165 B.A. L.276 J.D. [Baker&D.]
*PRACTICE AREAS: Health Care Law; Financial Services Regulation; Government Privatization and Contracts.
Swalina, Douglas W. '68 '98 C.886 B.S. L.362 J.D.
(adm. in FL; not adm. in DC) [Ⓒ Skadden,A.S.M.&F.]
*PRACTICE AREAS: Litigation.
Swaminathan, Gopal ....'— '95 C.918 B.A. L.1009 J.D. [Ⓐ Verner,L.B.M.&H.]
*PRACTICE AREAS: Energy Law; Corporate Law.
Swan, Jennifer S. '— '01 C&L.665 B.A., J.D.
(adm. in VA; not adm. in DC; See Pat. Sect.) [Ⓐ Finnegan,H.F.G.&D.]
*PRACTICE AREAS: Biochemical Technology; Intellectual Property Litigation; Pharmaceutical Intellectual Property.
Swankin, David A. .... '34 '62 C.1036 B.A. L.273 J.D. [Swankin&T.]
Swankin & Turner .... Suite 330, 1400 16th Street, NW
Swann, Cynthia G. .... '61 '92 C.1044 B.S. L.276 J.D. [Ⓐ Weiner B.S.K.]
*PRACTICE AREAS: Litigation.
Swansiger, Erin R. .... '67 '95 C.446 B.A. L.128 J.D. [Ⓐ Kelley D.&W.]
*PRACTICE AREAS: Telecommunications Law.
Swanson, Edrei G. .... '71 '99 C.1059 B.S. L.329 J.D. [Ⓐ McDermott,W.&E.]
Swanson, M. Anne, (AV) .... '54 '81 C.923 B.S.J. L.976 J.D. [Dow,L.&A.]
Swanstrom, Deborah A., (AV) .... '— '88 C.492 B.A. L.273 J.D. [Verner,L.B.M.&H.]
*PRACTICE AREAS: Energy Law; Administrative and Appellate Litigation.
Swanz, Sarah P. .... '71 '98 C.478 B.A. L.228 J.D. [Ⓐ Bryan C.]
*PRACTICE AREAS: Securities Regulation; Litigation.
Swanzey, Genine C. .... '73 '00 C.321 B.A. L.276 J.D. [Ⓐ Foxkiser]
*PRACTICE AREAS: Food and Drug Regulation; Health Law.
Swart, Robert H. .... '46 '70 C&L.477 A.B., J.D. [Mayer,B.&P.]
Swartz, Dean E., (AV) .... '49 '74 C.813 A.B. L.851 J.D. [Swartz&R.]
Swartz, Sheila J. Dombal .... '70 '97 C.602 B.B.A. L.904 J.D. [Ⓐ Thacher P.&W.]

Swartz & Reed, (AV) BV
1825 Jefferson Place, 20036
Telephone: 202-429-0429
Email: swartzreed@earthlink.net URL: http://www.lawyers.com/visas
Members of Firm: Dean E. Swartz; Barry S. Reed. Associate: Timothy A. Wray. Of Counsel: Allan W. Steinhorn; John A. Blazer.
Personal Injury, Product Liability and Medical Negligence Litigation.
See Professional Biographies, WASHINGTON, DISTRICT OF COLUMBIA

Swayze, John M. .... '12 '38 C&L.273 A.B., LL.B. 4505 46th St., N.W.‡
Sweeney, Erin M., (AV) .... '— '89 C.610 B.S./B.A. L.30 J.D. [Ⓒ Latham&W.]
*PRACTICE AREAS: ERISA Compliance; ERISA Litigation; Executive Compensation; Health Benefits; Pension and Profit Sharing Plans.
Sweeney, Kevin M., (AV) .... '56 '82 C.945 B.A. L.273 J.D. [John&H.]
*PRACTICE AREAS: Energy Law.
Sweeney, Mary Katherine (Katie) '65 '91 C.945 B.A. L.1356 J.D.
(adm. in VA; not adm. in DC) Assoc. Gen. Coun., National Mining Association
Sweeney, Patricia J. .... '— '80 C.477 B.A. L.94 J.D. [Miller&C.]
*PRACTICE AREAS: Taxation; Federal Tax Controversies; Federal Taxation; Nonprofit Tax Law; Natural Resources.
Sweeney, Philip J., III .... '44 '69 C.945 A.B. L.904 J.D. [Hamilton&H.]
*PRACTICE AREAS: Taxation; Exempt Organizations; Estate Planning; Corporate; Business Law.
Sweeney, Sean M. '74 '99 C.893 B.A. L.896 J.D.
(adm. in MD; not adm. in DC) 555 12th Street, N.W.
Sweet, Mark D. '66 '99 C.945 B.S. L.180 J.D.
[Ⓐ Finnegan,H.F.G.&D.] (See Pat. Sect.)
*PRACTICE AREAS: Chemical Intellectual Property; Patent Prosecution.
Sweet, William J., Jr., (AV) .... '51 '78 C.105 B.A. L.276 J.D. [Skadden,A.S.M.&F.]
Swegman, George E. .... '48 '75 C.645 B.A. L.128 J.D. [Ashcraft&G.]
*PRACTICE AREAS: Workers Compensation; Personal Injury.
Sweigart, Raymond L. '47 '73 C.1024 B.A. L.150 J.D.
[Pillsbury W.] (⊙Mc Lean, VA)
*PRACTICE AREAS: Intellectual Property; Complex and Multi-District Litigation; Commercial Law; Technology and Science; Creditors Rights.
Swendiman, Alan R., (AV) '47 '73
C.575 A.B. L.276 J.D. [Jackson&C.] (⊙Balt., Rockville, MD)
*PRACTICE AREAS: Estate Planning; Estate Administration; Nonprofit Organizations Law; Tax Exempt Organizations; Business Law.
Swenson, C. David, (AV) .... '51 '78 C&L.500 B.A., J.D. [Baker&M.]
*PRACTICE AREAS: Tax Controversies (Corporate and International); Tax Planning and Advice (Corporate and International).
Swenson, David P. .... '67 '94 C.93 B.A. L.494 J.D. [Kirkland&E.]
*PRACTICE AREAS: Intellectual Property; Litigation; Appellate Practice.
Swenson, George W., Jr. '33 '92 C.812 B.S. L.273 J.D.
[Vorys,S.S.&P.] (See Pat. Sect.)
Swenson, Lily Fu .... '69 '94 C.966 B.A. L.494 J.D. [Ⓐ Mayer,B.&P.]
*PRACTICE AREAS: Trial Practice; Appellate Practice; Antitrust; White Collar Crime.
Swers, Andrew T. .... '72 '97 C.367 B.A. L.178 J.D. [Ⓐ Akin,G.S.H.&F.]
Swett, Trevor W., III, (AV) .... '53 '82 C.976 B.A. L.893 J.D. [Caplin&D.]
*PRACTICE AREAS: Commercial Litigation; Tax Litigation.
Swick, Richard L., (AV) .... '47 '74 C.870 B.S. L.446 J.D. [Swick&S.] (⊙Bowie, MD)
Swick & Shapiro, P.C., (AV) .... 1225 Eye Street, N.W., Suite 1290
Swidler, Joseph C., (AV) .... '07 '30 C.339 L.145 J.D. 3000 K St., N.W.

Swidler Berlin Shereff Friedman, LLP, (AV)
3000 K Street, N.W., Suite 300, 20007 ⊙
Telephone: 202-424-7500 Facsimile: 202-424-7643
URL: http://www.swidlaw.com
Steven J. Agresta; Bernard P. Bell; Thomas A. Belles; Edward Berlin; Russell M. Blau; Eric J. Branfman; David J. Butler; Keith N. Cole; Paul T. Denis; Barry B. Direnfeld; Helen E. Disenhaus; Susan E. Duvall; Laurence J. Eisenstein; John R. Ferguson; Warren Anthony Fitch; Brian W. Fitzgerald; Roger Frankel; Harold P. Goldfield; James Hamilton; Gerald S. Hartman; James J. Hoecker; Gregory W. Homer; Robert D. Jacobs; Kenneth G. Jaffe; J. Phillip Jordan; Jeffrey M. Karp; Jean L. Kiddoo; Ky E. Kirby; David F. Klein; John J. Klusaritz; Charles H. Knauss; Michael N. Levy; Michael J. Lichtenstein; Andrew D. Lipman; Kenneth G. Lore; Thomas R. Lotterman; Peri N. Mahaley; Bruce Markowitz; Thurgood Marshall, Jr.; Sean P. McGuinness; Glenn S. Miller; Leonard A. Miller; Jerome C. Muys, Jr.; Timothy A. Ngau; José A. Palma; Stephen C. Palmer; Edward A. Pennington; Mark J. Plumer; Richard A. Popkin; Andrew M. Ray; Richard M. Rindler; Kenneth I. Schaner; Jeffrey S. Scharff; Gary D. Slaiman; Michael L. Spafford; Nancy Killien Spooner; Robert N. Steinwurtzel; Mary A. Wallace; Catherine Wang; Priscilla Anne Whitehead; Michael B. Wigmore; Richard H. Wyron. Senior Of Counsel: Lester S. Hyman. Counsel: Suzan F. Charlton; Robin F. Cohn; Lynn Monk Gallagher; William B. Glew, Jr.; George I. Gordon; David M. Lubitz; Milissa A. Murray; Jamil E. Nasir; William T. O'Neil; Alisa H. Reff; David B. Rubin; C. Joel Van Over; Michael E. Ward;

(This Listing Continued)

Swidler Berlin Shereff Friedman, LLP (Continued)
Tacie H. Yoon. Of Counsel: Peter Barnes; Daniel Eric Cohen; Colleen Covell; Rebecca P. Dick; L. Elise Dieterich; Patrick J. Donovan; William L. Fishman; Eric J. Franklin; Eliot J. Greenwald; Marvin T. Griff; Harold A. Levy; John P. Moran; Daniel J. Perka; Charles A. Rohe; Michael L. Shor; Troy F. Tanner; Julie A. Weisman; Phyllis A. Whitten; Patrick J. Whittle; Robert V. Zener. Associates: Daniel Abraham (Not admitted in DC); Sean A. Atkins; Harisha J. Bastiampillai; Robert C. Bertin (Not admitted in DC); Rebecca A. Blackmer; Joshua M. Bobeck; Jessica Y. Brewster; Rebecca S. Briggs (Not admitted in DC); Christopher James Carney; Amy K. Carpenter-Holmes; Melanie K. Carr (Not admitted in DC); Melissa R. Castro; Maria L. Cattafesta; Grace R. Chiu; Zenas J. Choi (Not admitted in DC); Aristotelis A. Chronis (Not admitted in DC); Kathy L. Cooper; Wendy M. Creeden; Frank M. Dale, Jr.; Kristine DeBry; James T. DeLorenzo; Ronald W. Del Sesto Jr.; Benjamin D. Diamond; Michael P. Donahue; Ofer Elitzur (Not admitted in DC); Christine F. Ericson; Michael D. Farber; Michael K. Federman; Brett P. Ferenchak; James Ferguson; Tamar E. Finn; Michael W. Fleming; Laura A. Ford; Sandra Franco (Not admitted in DC); Paul D. Frangie (Not admitted in DC); Jonathan S. Frankel; Brian G. Friel; Paul O. Gagnier, Jr.; Gary G. Gallant, Jr.; Mara Glaser; Brooke Deratany Goldfarb; Jeffrey M. Goodman (Not admitted in DC); Kathleen L. Greenan; Jonathan P. Guy; Paul B. Hudson; Chadwick A. Jackson (Not admitted in DC); Edward W. Kirsch; Michael Kunselman (Not admitted in DC); Allison F. Landis (Not admitted in DC); Alexander J. Lathrop; Tony S. Lee; Amy Elizabeth Lehman (Not admitted in DC); Joel G. Levi; Scott J. Levitt; Susan Danielle Loyd; Philip J. Macres; Harry N. Malone III; Duke K. McCall, III; Brian M. McDermott; Wendy C. McGraw; Alicia A. Meros; Kevin D. Minsky; Bradley R. Miliauskas; Jeffrey A. Mitchell; Julia M. Moore; James N. Moskowitz; Sean P. O'Hanlon (Not admitted in DC); Kelly A. Olson (Not admitted in DC); Melike S. Oncu; Douglas D. Orvis II; Theodore Joseph Paradise (Not admitted in DC); Matthew A. Pater; Ruth Pritchard-Kelly; Deidra Nicole Proctor (Not admitted in DC); Edward S. Quill, Jr.; Stephen T. Raptis; David D. Rines (Not admitted in DC); Katherine A. Rolph; W. Ray Rutngamlug; Brent T. Salmons (Not admitted in DC); Jason R. Scherr; Michael J. Schunck; Michael A. Schwartz; Michael C. Sloan; Richard P. Sparling; Gregg A. Spath; Jeanne W. Stockman; Gregg Strumberger; Steven J. Tave; Kathryn Rae Taylor; David Tiger; Andrew Topps, IV (Not admitted in DC); Thomas Silvio Valente (Not admitted in DC); Michael A. Valerio; David J. Walker; Edie Walters; Eric C. Wang; Ranan Z. Well; William Banks Wilhelm, Jr.; Jason M. Yanowitz.
Litigation, Insurance Coverage, Employment Law, Telecommunications, Energy, Corporate, Bankruptcy, Creditor's Rights, Antitrust and Trade Regulation, Government Affairs, Environmental, Tax, ERISA, Real Estate, Structured Finance, Intellectual Property, International Trade.
New York, N.Y. Office: The Chrysler Building, 405 Lexington Avenue. Telephone: 212-973-0111. Fax: 212-891-9598.
See Professional Biographies, WASHINGTON, DISTRICT OF COLUMBIA

Swift, Byron '53 '78 C.813 B.A. L.178 J.D.
Dir., Energy & Innovation Ctr., Environmental Law Institute
Swift, Carolyn J.A., (AV) '53 '80
C.165 B.A. L.188 J.D. V.P. & Dep. Gen. Coun., Fannie Mae
*RESPONSIBILITIES: Tax.
Swift, Peter J. '45 '71 C&L.309 A.B., J.D.
(adm. in NY; not adm. in DC) Asst. Gen. Coun., Marriott Intl., Inc.
Swift, Richard F., (AV) .... '35 '63 C.602 B.S. L.276 J.D. 2175 K St., N.W.
Swiger, Michael A., (AV) .... '55 '82 C.385 A.B. L.976 J.D. [Van Ness F.]
*PRACTICE AREAS: Energy; Natural Resources; Administrative Law; Hydroelectricity; Environmental Law.
Swinburn, Charles .... '— '93 C.674 B.A. L.659 J.D. [Ⓐ Morgan,L.&B.]
Swindler, John R., (AV) .... '25 '51 C.893 B.M.E. L.276 LL.B. 2360 Mass. Ave., N.W.‡
Swirski, Alan J. J. .... '63 '88 C.93 B.A. L.276 J.D. [Ⓒ Ivins,P.&B.]
*PRACTICE AREAS: Corporate Taxation; Tax Litigation.
Swirsky, Keith G., (AV) .... '59 '84 C.188 B.S. L.276 J.D. [Galland,K.G.F.&S.]
*PRACTICE AREAS: Aviation Law; Federal and State Tax and FAA Planning; Aircraft Acquisitions, Sales and Operations; Aircraft Tax-Free Exchanges.
Swisher, Anthony W. .... '68 '95 C.893 B.A. L.273 J.D. [Ⓒ Akin,G.S.H.&F.]
*PRACTICE AREAS: Antitrust and Trade Regulation; Litigation.

Swiss, Marsha E., (AV) '40 '66 C.821 B.A. L.309 LL.B.
1735 20th Street, N.W., 20009
Telephone: 202-986-5555 Fax: 202-462-0379
Email: betwixt@compuserve.com URL: http://www.lawyers.com/swisslaw
Estate Planning, Probate, Fiduciary Law and General Civil Litigation.
See Professional Biographies, WASHINGTON, DISTRICT OF COLUMBIA

Switkay, Henry M. .... '25 '51 C.659 A.B. L.309 LL.B. The Legal Aid Soc. of D.C.‡
Switzer, Michael D. .... '68 '96 C.867 B.S.E.E. L.904 J.D. [Ⓐ McDermott,W.&E.] (Pat.)
Sydnor, Thomas D., II .... '65 '94 C.608 B.A. L.228 J.D. [Ⓒ Arnold&P.]
*PRACTICE AREAS: Products Liability; Administrative Law.
Syed, Mohammad A. '74 '01 C.696 B.A. L.273 J.D.
(adm. in NY; not adm. in DC) [Ⓐ Ashcraft&G.]
*PRACTICE AREAS: Products Liability; Medical Malpractice.
Sykes, Christine E. '62 '92 C.645 B.A. L.831 J.D.
(adm. in PA; not adm. in DC) Asst. U.S. Atty.
Sykes, Ronald G. '48 '85 C.215 B.B.A. L.213 J.D.
Sr. Washington Rep., General Motors Corporation
Sykes, Thomas D. .... '54 '79 C.957 B.A. L.608 J.D. [Scribner,H.&T.]
Sylla, Jean-Marie, Jr. '68 '99
C&L.446 B.A., J.D. [Ⓐ Bonner K.T.&C.] (⊙Rockville, MD)
*PRACTICE AREAS: Business Litigation; Insurance Coverage; Insurance Liability; Products Liability.
Sylvain, Olivier .... '— '00 C.951 B.A. L.276 J.D. [Ⓐ Jenner&B.]
Sylvester, Brett S. .... '62 '87 C.188 B.S. L.365 J.D. [Sughrue M.] (See Pat. Sect.)
*PRACTICE AREAS: Intellectual Property Law.
Sylvia, Lisa Marie .... '64 '90 C.93 A.B. L.276 J.D. 701 Pennsylvania Avenue, N.W.

Sylvia, Timothy J.
(See Columbia, Maryland)

Symczak, Paul E. '50 '75 C.665 B.A. L.273 J.D.
Sr. V.P., Corp. Affs. & Secy., Corporation for Pub. Bdcstg.
Symington, James W., (AV) .... '27 '54 C.976 B.A. L.178 LL.B. [O'Connor&H.]
Symon, Robert J. .... '66 '92 C.901 B.A. L.64 J.D. [Spriggs&H.]
*PRACTICE AREAS: Government Contracts; Construction Law; Litigation.
Symons, Craig .... '75 '00 C.451 B.A. L.273 J.D. [Ⓐ Krupin O.]
*PRACTICE AREAS: Business Immigration.
Symons, Howard J., (AV) .... '53 '79 C.976 B.A. L.309 J.D. [Mintz,L.C.F.G.&P.]
*PRACTICE AREAS: Telecommunications Law; Cable TV; Wireless Communications; FCC Regulation.
Sypula, Amy Lynn .... '75 '00 C&L.145 B.A., J.D. [Ⓐ Latham&W.]
*PRACTICE AREAS: Environmental Law.
Szabo, Laura J. V. .... '64 '91 C.1211 B.S. L.273 J.D. [Ⓒ Dickstein S.M.&O.]
*PRACTICE AREAS: Energy Law; Domestic and International Energy Project Development.
Szabo, Robert G., (AV) .... '47 '72 C&L.420 B.S., J.D. [Van Ness F.]
*PRACTICE AREAS: Environmental Law; Natural Resources; Government.
Szeto, Edwin Y. .... '71 '96 C.1369 B.B.A. L.692 J.D. [Ⓐ Ludwig&R.]
*PRACTICE AREAS: Commercial Litigation; Corporate Law; Commercial Law; Customs and International Trade; Electronic Commerce.
Szilagyi, Catherine A. .... '66 '98 C.649 B.A. L.276 J.D. Asst. U.S. Atty.
Szmuszkovicz, Kathryn E., (AV) .... '55 '84 C.373 B.A. L.477 J.D. [Beveridge&D.]
*PRACTICE AREAS: Biotechnology; Pesticide, Seed and Food Regulation; Alternative Dispute Resolution; Commercial Law.
Szukelewicz, Michael E. .... '59 '86 C.886 B.A. L.61 J.D. 3534 Quesada St., N.W.★
Szybala, René L. .... '52 '77 C.1044 B.A. L.823 J.D. Legal Servs. Corp.
Szybillo, Victoria M. '76 '01 C.273 B.B.A. L.180 J.D.
(adm. in MD; not adm. in DC) [Ⓐ Dechert]
*PRACTICE AREAS: Investment Management; Financial Services Law.

Szymanski, Patrick J., (AV) ....'49 '76 C&L.912 B.A., J.D. [Baptiste&W.]
*PRACTICE AREAS: Labor Law; Employment Law; ERISA; Federal Civil Litigation; Appellate Litigation.
Szypszak, Agata '74 '01 C.94 B.S.B.A. L.276 J.D.
(adm. in MA; not adm. in DC) [[A] Silver,F.&T.]
*PRACTICE AREAS: Securities; Corporate; Financial Institutions Law.
Ta, Khoi '— '01 C.886 B.S. L.1209 J.D.
(adm. in VA; not adm. in DC) [[A] Morgan,L.&B.]
Tabach, Kenneth B. ....'57 '82 C.446 B.S. L.692 J.D. [Elias,M.T.&H.]
Tabachnik, Andrew D. '68 '94 C.999 B.A.
(adm. in NY; not adm. in DC) 1776 K St., N.W.
Tabah, Agnes ....'59 '85 C.478 B.A. L.273 J.D. Atty., National Geographic Society
*RESPONSIBILITIES: Contracts; Intellectual Property.
Tabor, John K., (AV) ....'21 '51 C.976 B.A. L.309 LL.B. 1616 34th St.,NW‡
Tackett-Hunt, Cristy '67 '97 C.352 B.A. L.589 J.D.
(adm. in IL; not adm. in DC) Corp. Tax Consultant, Ernst & Young LLP - Natl. Tax
Tafara, Ethiopis '64 '95 C.674 A.B. L.276 J.D.
(adm. in NY; not adm. in DC) U.S. Comm. Futures Trading Com.
Tafe, Elizabeth Marie '63 '98 C.309 B.A. L.597 J.D.
(adm. in MA; not adm. in DC) Nat. Labor Relations Board
Taff, Barry P., (P.C.), (AV) ....'45 '72 C.446 B.A. L.904 J.D. [Silver,F.&T.]
*PRACTICE AREAS: Corporate; Corporate and Financial Institutions Taxation; Mergers, Acquisitions and Reorganizations; Business and Real Estate Debt Restructuring.
Taft, Jeffrey P. ....'67 '93 C.861 B.A. L.665 J.D. [[A] Mayer,B.&P.]
*PRACTICE AREAS: Bank Regulatory; Consumer Financial Services; Privacy Law.
Tafuri, David M. ....'70 '96 C.1365 B.A. L.276 J.D. [[A] Patton B.]
Tag, Howard M. '49 '80 C.1044 B.S. L.724 J.D.
(adm. in NY; not adm. in DC) [Tag&Assoc.]
Tag & Associates, P.C. ....1250 24th St., N.W., Suite 300
Tager, Clifford L., (CV) '— '87 C.161 B.E.E. L.273 J.D.
(adm. in PA; not adm. in DC; See Pat. Sect.) [[C] Stevens,D.M.&M.]
*PRACTICE AREAS: Intellectual Property (100%); Patents; Trademarks; Copyrights; Trade Secrets.
Tager, Evan M. ....'60 '86 C.674 A.B. L.813 J.D. [Mayer,B.&P.]
*PRACTICE AREAS: Appellate Litigation; Constitutional Law.
Taglieri, James W., (AV) ....'50 '75 C.276 B.S.F.S. L.904 J.D. [Cadeaux&T.]
*PRACTICE AREAS: Personal Injury; Medical Malpractice; Nursing Home Liability; Products Liability; Workers Compensation.
Tahernia, Susan ....'64 '90 C.862 B.A. L.276 J.D. [[A] Thelen R.&P.]
*PRACTICE AREAS: Labor and Employment.
Tahsuda, John '66 '94 C.612 B.S. L.188 J.D.
(adm. in CO; not adm. in DC) [[A] Hobbs,S.D.&W.]
Tai, Christopher C. ....'60 '87 C.112 B.A. L.976 J.D. [Steptoe&J.]
*PRACTICE AREAS: Telecommunications; Commercial Transactions; Corporate; Corporate Finance; Joint Ventures.
Tait, Edward T., (AV) ....'20 '49 C&L.665 A.B., J.D. 1301 K St., N.W.
Tait, Jarvis F. ....'72 '99 C.602 B.B.A. L.229 J.D. [Koonz,M.J.D.&L.]
*PRACTICE AREAS: Personal Injury.
Taitsman, Julie K. '73 '98 C.103 B.A. L.309 J.D.
(adm. in MA; not adm. in DC) 555 12th St., N.W.
Takagi, Keiko K. '74 '99 C.880 B.S. L.424 J.D.
(adm. in IL; not adm. in DC) [[A] Sughrue M.]
*PRACTICE AREAS: Intellectual Property Law.
Talbert, Angelia C. '70 '96 C.444 B.A. L.128 J.D.
(adm. in MD; not adm. in DC) Law Clk., Ct. of App.
Talbert, Jeffrey D. ....'75 '00 C.373 B.A. L.477 J.D. [[A] White&C.]
Talbert, Robin J. ....'51 '80 C.575 B.A. L.910 J.D. Amer. Assoc. of Ret. Persons
Talbot, Gregory R. ....'68 '98 C.602 B.A. L.128 J.D. [[A] Morgan,L.&B.]
Talbot, Jill S. '64 '89 C.25 B.S. L.902 J.D.
(adm. in MD; not adm. in DC) Exec. Editor, Thompson Publishing Grp.
Talbot, Maurice P., Jr. '38 '72 C.454 B.S.E.E. L.818 J.D.
Exec. Dir.- Fed. Regulatory, BellSouth Corporation
Talbott, Kirk L. ....'55 '87 C.976 B.A. L.276 J.D. World Resources Institute
Talbott, Patrice J. Harris '70 '95 C.813 A.B. L.276 J.D.
(adm. in MD; not adm. in DC) [[A] Piper M.R.&W.]
Talcott, Jonathan H. ....'62 '89 C.575 B.A. L.893 J.D. [Alston&B.]
*PRACTICE AREAS: Technology Law; Securities; Financial Services Law; International.
Talens, James M. ....'46 '75 C.659 B.S.E.E. L.631 J.D. [[C] Steptoe&J.]
*PRACTICE AREAS: Telecommunications; Communications; Wireless Communications; Satellite Communications.
Talieh, Koorosh ....'60 '88 C.31 B.A. L.276 J.D. [Howrey S.A.&W.]
*PRACTICE AREAS: General Litigation; Insurance Litigation.
Talisman, Charles E. ....'57 '82 C.228 B.A. L.813 J.D. [Patton B.]
Talisman, Harold L., (AV) ....'28 '53 C&L.608 B.S., J.D. [[C] Wright&T.]
*PRACTICE AREAS: Energy.
Talkovsky, Steven H. ....'54 '77 C.569 B.A. L.94 J.D. AT&T
*RESPONSIBILITIES: Government Contracts; International Procurement; Information Technology; Commercial Transactions.
Tallent, Stephen E., (AV) ....'37 '63 C.813 A.B. L.145 J.D. [[C] Gibson,D.&C.]
*PRACTICE AREAS: Labor; Employee Benefits; Employment and Discrimination Litigation; International Labor Law.
Talley, Martha J. ....'50 '75 C.680 A.B. L.1066 J.D. [Dewey B.]
*PRACTICE AREAS: Litigation.
Talmadge, William C. '— '68 C.575 A.B. L.280 J.D.
(adm. in GA; not adm. in DC) [[C] King&S.]
*PRACTICE AREAS: Governmental Law.
Talotta, Jon M. ....'66 '99 C.645 B.A. L.893 J.D. [[A] Kirkpatrick&L.]
*PRACTICE AREAS: Litigation; Insurance Coverage.
Taltavull, W. Warren, III, (AV) ... '43 '71 C.128 B.A. L.273 J.D. [Manelli,D.&S.] (Pat.)
Tam, Jane Kwok Ping ....'65 '90 L.982 J.D. [Piper M.R.&W.]
*PRACTICE AREAS: Corporate; Securities; Venture Capital.
Tamayo, L. Raul ....'73 '99 C.260 B.S.Ch.E. L.276 J.D. [[A] Sughrue M.]
*PRACTICE AREAS: Intellectual Property Law.
Tamburo, Esther G. ....'68 '97 L.659 J.D. [[A] Akin,G.S.H.&F.]
*PRACTICE AREAS: Labor and Employment.
Tamburo, Salvatore P. '68 '99 C.667 B.S.E.E. L.724 J.D.
[[A] Dickstein S.M.&O.] (Pat.)
*PRACTICE AREAS: Intellectual Property.
Tammadge, Kathleen Donovan '65 '91
C.1044 B.A. L.276 J.D. [King&N.] (⊙Arlington, VA)
*PRACTICE AREAS: Commercial Real Estate Transactions; Landlord and Tenant Law.
Tan, Carol B. ....'71 '95 C.1142 B.B.A. L.802 J.D. Tax Mgr., KPMG Peat Marwick‡
Tan, Cedric Chia Yang ....'73 '97 C.02 B.Sc. L.861 J.D. [[A] Kenyon&K.]
*PRACTICE AREAS: Intellectual Property.
Tan, Michael W. '64 '89 C.228 B.S. L.902 J.D.
(adm. in MD; not adm. in DC) Asst. Dir., Georgetown Univ. Law Ctr.
Tanaka, John Kevin '66 '00 C.1110 B.A. L.36 J.D.
(adm. in NM; not adm. in DC) 1849 C St., N.W.
Tanaka, Michele N. ....'55 '83 C.674 A.B. L.276 J.D. [[C] Shaw P.]
*PRACTICE AREAS: International Trade; Intellectual Property; Corporate; Transactional; Litigation.
Tanaka, Vanessa G. '69 '00 C.94 B.A. L.966 J.D.
(adm. in IL; not adm. in DC) [[A] McDermott,W.&E.]
Tanenbaum, David N. ....'67 '94 C.881 B.A. L.930 J.D. [[A] Steptoe&J.]
Tanenbaum, Larry E. ....'51 '76 C.446 B.A. L.64 J.D. [Akin,G.S.H.&F.]
*PRACTICE AREAS: Litigation; Technology.

Tanenberg, Ellyn R. '49 '92 C.339 B.S. L.904 J.D.
1201 Pennsylvania Avenue NW, Suite 300, 20004 ⊙
Telephone: 202-387-7747 Fax: 301-649-5895
Email: tanenberg@taxlawyer-cpa.com URL: http://www.lawyers.com/tanenberglaw
***PRACTICE AREAS: Taxation; Income Tax; Estate and Gift Taxation; Wills; Probate. Taxation, Federal Estate and Gift Taxation, Federal Tax Controversies, Income Tax, Individual Taxation, International Income Tax, International Tax Controversies, International Taxation, Small Business Taxation, Divorce Taxation, Wills, Probate, Business Immigration Taxation.**
Bethesda, Maryland Office: 7272 Wisconsin Avenue, Suite 300. 20814. Telephone: 301-907-0019.
See Professional Biographies, WASHINGTON, DISTRICT OF COLUMBIA

Tanenhaus, Marta I. ....'56 '91 C.1044 B.A. L.1066 J.D. [[A] Hogan&H.]
*PRACTICE AREAS: Civil Litigation; Transportation.
Tanenholz, David L. '72 '00 C.446 B.S. L.537 J.D.
(adm. in MD; not adm. in DC) [[A] Reed S.]
Tang, Chad Y. ....'73 '98 C.103 A.B. L.659 J.D. [[A] Covington&B.]
Tanguay, Donna M., (AV) ....'56 '87 C&L.128 B.A., J.D. [McDermott,W.&E.]
Tanis, Paul Jeffrey ....'65 '96 C.477 A.B. L.273 J.D. 2100 L Street N.W.
Tank, Margo H.K. ....'63 '92 C.882 B.A. L.221 J.D. [Goodwin P.]
*PRACTICE AREAS: Consumer Financial Services.
Tankel, Adam B. ....'65 '97 C.659 B.A.,B.S. L.893 J.D. [[A] Hogan&H.]
*PRACTICE AREAS: Corporate Law; Private Equity.
Tankel, Jerome K. ....'35 '64 C.339 B.A. L.309 J.D. [[C] Barkats&Assoc.]
Tankersley, Michael E. '60 '86
C.945 B.A. L.309 J.D. Staff Atty., Public Citizen Litig. Grp.
Tannenbaum, Ira L., (AV) ....'— '68 C.103 A.B. L.477 J.D. [Kirkpatrick&L.]
*PRACTICE AREAS: Thrift Institution Regulation; Banking Regulation; International Banking Law.
Tannenwald, Peter, (AV) ....'43 '68 C.103 A.B. L.309 LL.B. [Irwin,C.&T.]
Tanner, Christopher Mark '— '98
C.1086 B.S.E.E. L.260 J.D. [[A] Dickstein S.M.&O.] (Pat.)
Tanner, James L., Jr. ....'68 '93 C.575 B.A. L.145 J.D. [[A] Williams&C.]
*PRACTICE AREAS: Corporate Law; Securities; Sports Law.
Tanner, Jeanne M. '58 '97
C.453 B.S.M.E. L.1209 J.D. [[A] Finnegan,H.F.G.&D.] (See Pat. Sect.)
*PRACTICE AREAS: Intellectual Property Litigation; Mechanical Intellectual Property; Mechanical Patents.
Tanner, Troy F. ....'63 '88 C.101 B.A. L.273 J.D. [[C] Swidler B.S.F.]
*PRACTICE AREAS: Telecommunications; International.

Tansey, James J., (AV) '44 '69 C.951 A.B. L.94 J.D.
2823 29th Street, N.W., 20008
Telephone: 202-232-8557 Fax: 202-232-8549
Commercial Litigation. Construction Law, Government Contract, Surety Law, Mechanics Lien Law.
See Professional Biographies, WASHINGTON, DISTRICT OF COLUMBIA

Tansill, Frederick R., (AV) .... '14 '40 C&L.276 B.S.S., J.D. 3001 Veazey Terr., NW‡
Tansill, Frederick J., & Associates, LLC
(See McLean, Virginia)
Tantum, Amanda L. '75 '00 C.362 B.S. L.893 J.D.
(adm. in VA; not adm. in DC) [[A] Wilmer,C.&P.]
Tanyi, Gerald B. '63 '95 C.999 D.E.A. L.976 J.S.D.
(adm. in NY; not adm. in DC) 2121 Pennsylvania Ave., N.W.
Tao, Ellen S. ......'69 '95 C.910 B.S. L.30 J.D. [[A] Ostrolenk,F.G.&S.] (See Pat. Sect.) ⊙
*PRACTICE AREAS: Patent Prosecution.
Tao, Josephine J. '66 '98 C.273 B.B.A. L.1209 J.D.
Securities Exchange Commission, Market Regul. Div.
Tao, Louis L.S. ....'42 '75 C.999 B.A. L.309 LL.B. [Sonnenschein N.&R.]
Tapley, Kate ....'58 '97 C.914 B.A. L.178 J.D. [[A] Dickstein S.M.&O.]
Tarantino, Arthur E. ....'12 '42 C.871 L.446 LL.B. 1815 H St. N.W.
Tarantino, Joseph Burke ....'64 '93 C.93 B.A. L.273 J.D. 1230 23rd St., N.W.
Taranto, Leon B. ....'51 '76 C.861 B.A. L.245 J.D. [Schmeltzer,A.&S.]
*PRACTICE AREAS: Radiation; Toxic Tort; Environmental Contamination; Workers Compensation Litigation.
Taranto, Richard G., (AV) ....'57 '82 C.668 B.A. L.976 J.D. [Farr&T.]
*PRACTICE AREAS: Appellate Practice; Telecommunications; Antitrust.
Tarantowicz, Laurie A. '62 '89
C.1350 B.A. L.276 J.D. Assoc. Coun., Legal Services Corporation
Tarasevich, Deborah A. ....'58 '91 C.732 B.A. L.276 J.D. 401 9th Street N.w.
Tardiff, Darrell L. '70 '00 C.420 B.A. L.425 J.D.
(adm. in LA; not adm. in DC) Law Clerk
Tarkenton, Jeffrey L., (AV) ....'56 '81 C&L.945 B.A., J.D. [Womble C.S.&R.]
*PRACTICE AREAS: Bankruptcy; Civil Litigation.
Tarnoff, David L. ....'60 '88 C.188 B.S. L.128 J.D. [Shinjyu] (Pat.)
Tarnow, Jonathan D. ....'71 '97 C&L.273 B.A., J.D. [[A] Brustein&M.]
*PRACTICE AREAS: Administrative Law; Education Law; Civil Litigation.
Tarone, C. Michael ....'45 '71 C&L.276 B.S.B.A., J.D. [[A] J.F.Karl,Jr.]
*PRACTICE AREAS: Maritime Law; International Law; Automobile Liability; Negligence; Insurance.
Tarr, David R. ....'37 '74 C.477 B.A. L.30 J.D. Congressional Quarterly, Inc.
Tarris, Virginia M. .....'50 '77 C.289 B.A. L.276 J.D. Mng. Tax Dir., Marriott Intl., Inc.
Tartal, James A. ....'— '97 C.367 B.S. L.93 J.D. [[A] Manatt,P.&P.]
Tarter, Ulysses S. '16 '50 C.302 B.S. L.1003 LL.B.
(adm. in OH; not adm. in DC) 240 M St., S.W.‡
Tash, Hymen ....'09 '43 C&L.799 B.C.S., LL.B. [Sinrod&T.] ‡
Tasker, Joseph, Jr., (AV) .... '50 '75 C.623 B.A. L.273 J.D. 5059 Glenrock Terrace N.W.
Taskier, Paul R., (AV) ....'55 '83 C.860 B.A. L.276 J.D. [Dickstein S.M.&O.]
*PRACTICE AREAS: Insurance Coverage Litigation; Commercial Litigation; Civil Litigation.
Taslitz, Andrew E. .... '56 '81 C.994 B.A. L.659 J.D. 2900 Van Ness St., N.W.
Tasman, Sharon L. ....'65 '92 C&L.446 B.S., J.D [[A] Hogan&H.]
*PRACTICE AREAS: Computer and Software Law; Internet Law; E-Commerce Law; Technology Licensing; Intellectual Property.
Tassey, Jeffrey A. ....'53 '80 C.970 B.A. L.910 J.D. [Williams&J.]
*PRACTICE AREAS: Legislative Practice; Financial Services Law; Bankruptcy.
Tassi, Julie A. ....'58 '89 C.30 B.A. L.273 J.D. [Fulbright&J.]
*PRACTICE AREAS: Real Estate.
Tate, Christopher F. ....'64 '97 C.893 B.A. L.1209 J.D. [[A] Sutherland A.&B.]
*PRACTICE AREAS: Tax Law; Estate and Gift Taxation.
Tate, Rodger L., (AV) ....'47 '75 C.150 B.S.Ch.E. L.276 J.D. [Brobeck,P.&H.] (Pat.)
*PRACTICE AREAS: Intellectual Property.
Tatelbaum, Mark F. ....'67 '92 C.696 B.A. L.93 J.D. [[A] Arent F.K.P.&K.]
*PRACTICE AREAS: Health Care; Health Care Fraud.
Tatge, David B., (AV) ....'56 '86 C.945 B.B.A. L.273 J.D. [Epstein B.&G.]
*PRACTICE AREAS: Creditors' Rights Law; Bankruptcy Law; Commercial Litigation; Business Transactions; Health Law.
Tatum, L. Kay, (AV) ....'51 '80 C.861 B.A. L.326 J.D. [Wiley R.&F.]
*PRACTICE AREAS: Business Law; Finance.
Taub, Andrew L. ....'44 '91 C.994 B.A. L.150 J.D. U.S. Dept. Jus.

Taub, Cynthia L. ... '65 '93 C.1375 B.A. L.1066 J.D. [Ⓐ Steptoe&J.]
Taub, Kathy S. ... '55 '80 C.228 B.A. L.446 J.D. [Arent F.K.P.&K.]
*PRACTICE AREAS: Construction Law.
Taub, Robin B., (AV) '59 '83 C&L.228 A.B., J.D. [Paradiso,D.T.&O.] (⊙Bethesda, MD)
*PRACTICE AREAS: Family Law.
Taub, Steven P. ... '62 '88 C.659 B.S.E. L.276 J.D. [Ⓒ Crowell&M.]
Tauber, Mark J., (AV) ... '49 '73 C.477 B.A. L.273 J.D. [Piper M.R.&W.]
*PRACTICE AREAS: Communications Law; Copyright Law; Trademark Law.
Taurman, John D., (AV) ... '46 '71 C.228 A.B. L.309 J.D. [Vinson&E.]
*PRACTICE AREAS: Litigation; Complex and Multi-District Litigation; International Arbitration; Contracts; Antitrust and Trade Regulation.
Tausend, Rachel '— '01 C.95 B.A. L.477 J.D. (adm. in VA; not adm. in DC) [Ⓐ Piper M.R.&W.]
*PRACTICE AREAS: Litigation.
Tavares, Lisa Ann '68 '96 C.811 B.A. L.93 J.D. (adm. in MA; not adm. in DC) [Ⓐ Venable,A.B.H.&C.]
*PRACTICE AREAS: Employee Benefits; ERISA; Tax.
Tave, Steven J. ... '75 '00 C.597 B.A. L.893 J.D. [Ⓐ Swidler B.S.F.]
*PRACTICE AREAS: Litigation.
Tavel, Bruce '69 '94 C.966 B.A. L.1009 J.D. (adm. in NJ; not adm. in DC) [Ⓐ McDermott,W.&E.]
Tayler, C. William, (AV) ... '23 '49 C.696 A.B. L.309 J.D. [Ⓒ Whiteford,T.&P.]
*PRACTICE AREAS: Condominium Law; Cooperative Association Law; Education Law; Litigation.
Taylor, Bruce Clark Ragan ... '50 '82 C&L.838 B.A., J.D. Fed. Dist. Ins. Corp.
Taylor, Charles A., III '43 '68 C.682 B.A. L.790 J.D. Asst. V.P., Govt. Rel, Natl. Assn. of Independent Insurers
Taylor, Cheri M., (AV) '48 '86 C.10 B.S. L.1209 J.D. [Finnegan,H.F.G.&D.] (See Pat. Sect.)
*PRACTICE AREAS: Biotechnology; Pharmaceuticals; Chemical Patents; Cosmetics; International Trade.
Taylor, David J. ... '43 '69 C.59 B.A. L.276 J.D. [Tighe P.A.T.]
*PRACTICE AREAS: Complex Civil Litigation; Government Contracts; Nonprofit Organizations Law.
Taylor, David S. ... '68 '93 C.446 B.S. L.273 J.D. [Ⓐ Sullivan]
Taylor, Durward M., (BV) ... '36 '64 C&L.329 B.A., LL.B. [Taylor&O.]
Taylor, Elizabeth G., (AV) ... '54 '84 C.575 B.A. L.893 J.D. [Ⓒ Zuckerman S.]
*PRACTICE AREAS: Criminal Litigation.
Taylor, F. Alvin ... '— '99 C.10 B.S.C.E. L.276 J.D. [Ⓐ Venable,A.B.H.&C.]
*PRACTICE AREAS: Energy; Environmental Law.
Taylor, Harriett R. ... '32 '55 C.102 A.B. L.178 LL.B. Assoc. Supr. Ct. J.
Taylor, James, Jr. ... '42 '73 C.797 A.B. L.276 J.D. [Adduci,M.&S.]
*PRACTICE AREAS: International Transactions; International Trade; Customs; Government Relations.
Taylor, Jamison B. ... '67 '97 C.597 B.S. L.145 J.D. [Ⓐ Skadden,A.S.M.&F.]
*PRACTICE AREAS: International Trade; Litigation.
Taylor, Jean G. ... '27 '67 C.822 A.B. L.273 LL.B. 4000 Massachusetts Ave., N.W.‡
Taylor, John L. ... '45 '79 L.309 LL.M. The World Bk.
Taylor, Joy ... '64 '93 C&L.326 B.S., J.D. [Ⓐ Arnold&P.]
*PRACTICE AREAS: Federal Taxation.
Taylor, Kathryn Rae ... '64 '94 C.893 B.A. L.309 J.D. [Ⓐ Swidler B.S.F.]
Taylor, Kim Antoinette ... '55 '81 C.103 A.B. L.976 J.D. Dir., Pub. Def. Serv.
Taylor, LaShanda D. ... '74 '99 C.811 B.A. L.564 J.D. The Children's Law Center, Inc.
Taylor, Mark D. ... '58 '91 C.1193 B.A. L.878 J.D. [Ⓒ Akin,G.S.H.&F.]
*PRACTICE AREAS: Financial Restructuring.
Taylor, Michael A., (AV) ... '— '64 C.216 B.A. L.904 J.D. [Ⓒ Verner,L.B.M.&H.]
*PRACTICE AREAS: Labor Law; Employment Law.
Taylor, Nancy E., (AV) ... '— '88 C.878 B.S. L.128 J.D. [Greenberg T.]
Taylor, Peggy E. '74 '00 C.893 B.A. L.276 J.D. (adm. in VA; not adm. in DC) [Ⓐ Carter&C.] ⊙
*PRACTICE AREAS: Insurance Defense; Health Law; Medical Malpractice; Federal Litigation.
Taylor, Peggy E. '74 '00 C.893 B.A. L.276 J.D. (adm. in VA; not adm. in DC) 900 Seventeenth Street, N.W., Suite 900 (⊙Wash., DC; Alexandria, VA)
Taylor, Peter V., (AV) ... '55 '80 C.1144 B.A. L.966 J.D. Asst. U.S. Atty.
Taylor, R. Eric '58 '84 C.896 B.A. L.192 J.D. (adm. in VA; not adm. in DC) Coml. & Indus. Coun., Chicago Title Ins. Co.
Taylor, Ralph A., Jr., (AV) ... '48 '75 C.674 B.S.E. L.893 J.D. [Dorsey&W.]
*PRACTICE AREAS: Intellectual Property; Commercial Litigation.
Taylor, Ramsey R. ... '71 '97 C&L.945 B.A., J.D. [Ⓐ Baker B.]
Taylor, R.C. "Russ", III ... '— '96 C&L.1356 B.A., J.D. 701 Pennsylvania Avenue, N.W.
Taylor, Rebecca Lynn ... '68 '95 C.446 B.A. L.273 J.D. [Ⓐ Leftwich&D.]
*PRACTICE AREAS: Employment Law; Estate Litigation; Contracts; Domestic Relations.
Taylor, Rex '57 '83 L.45 LL.M. (adm. in AR; not adm. in DC) Coun. Compliance & Enfor Sec., FDIC
Taylor, Richard P., (AV) ... '28 '52 C&L.893 B.A., LL.B. [Steptoe&J.]
*PRACTICE AREAS: Administrative Law; Airport Law; Aviation Law; Transportation Law; Urban, State and Local Government Law.
Taylor, Robert Preston, Jr ... '51 '98 C.839 B.A. L.362 J.D. 1500 K Street N.W., Ste 200
Taylor, Robin M. ... '62 '86 C&L.575 B.S.B.A., J.D. 3050 K St., N.W.
Taylor, Ruthie L. '35 '68 C.1010 B.S. L.329 J.D. (adm. in TN; not adm. in DC) Dir., Nat. Bar Assn. & E.E.O. Loan Fund Proj.
Taylor, Sarah E. ... '57 '89 C.966 B.S. L.273 J.D. [Ⓒ Covington&B.]
Taylor, Sharon L. ... '54 '89 C.446 B.S. L.128 J.D. [Ⓒ Arnold&P.]
*PRACTICE AREAS: Energy; Government Contracts.
Taylor, Stephanie A. ... '73 '99 C.299 B.A. L.982 J.D. [Ⓐ Steptoe&J.]
Taylor, Stuart S., Jr. '48 '78 C.674 A.B. L.309 J.D. Sr. Writer, American Lawyer Media, L.P. and Legal Times
Taylor, Tamika L. '73 '00 C.790 B.A. L.329 J.D. (adm. in MD; not adm. in DC) [Ⓐ Thompson,O.M.N.&H.]
*PRACTICE AREAS: Employment Law; Insurance Defense; Personal Injury; Civil Litigation; Insurance Coverage.
Taylor, Thomas C. '60 '92 C.1070 B.S. L.1209 J.D. (adm. in VA; not adm. in DC) Jud. Law Clk., U.S. Ct. of Vet. Appeals
Taylor, Todd P. ... '— '00 C.602 B.S. L.30 J.D. [Ⓐ Morgan,L.&B.]
Taylor, Trent ... '73 '99 C.806 B.A. L.309 J.D. [Ⓐ Arnold&P.]
*PRACTICE AREAS: Litigation; Products Liability.
Taylor, Vannie, III ... '43 '77 C.369 B.A. L.107 J.D. 1225 Eye St., N.W.
Taylor, W. R. Duke '58 '84 C&L.8 B.S.M.E., J.D. [Harness,D.&P.] (See Pat. Sect.) (⊙Troy, MI)
*PRACTICE AREAS: Patent, Trademark and Intellectual Property.
Taylor, William L. ... '31 '55 C.102 B.A. L.976 LL.B. 2000 M St., NW
Taylor, William W., III, (AV) ... '44 '69 C.575 A.B. L.976 LL.B. [Zuckerman S.]
*PRACTICE AREAS: Criminal and Civil Litigation; Commercial Litigation; Native American Civil Rights; Election Law.
Taylor & Overby, (BV) ... 5911 3rd St., N.E.
Teague, Michael L., (AV) ... '48 '76 C&L.893 B.S.N.E., J.D. [Hunton&W.]
*PRACTICE AREAS: Environmental.
Teague, Randal C., (AV) ... '44 '72 C.30 B.A. L.273 J.D. [Vorys,S.S.&P.]
*PRACTICE AREAS: International Business; Legislative Practice; Taxation; International Taxation; Federal Taxation.

Technology Law Group, L.L.C., (AV)
5335 Wisconsin Avenue, N.W. Suite 440, 20015
Telephone: 202-895-1707 Fax: 202-244-8257
Email: mail@tlgdc.com URL: http://www.tlgdc.com
Neil S. Ende. Associate: Alexandre B. Bouton; Tom K. Sinai (Not admitted in DC).
Telecommunications, Litigation, Commercial Law, Regulatory Issues, Transactional Law.
See Professional Biographies, WASHINGTON, DISTRICT OF COLUMBIA

Teckler, Martin D. ... '46 '72 C.94 B.A. L.273 J.D. [Pepper H.]
*PRACTICE AREAS: Venture Capital; Small Business Law; Securities.
Tedards, William P., Jr. '42 '67 C&L.902 A.B., LL.B. 412 1st St., S.E., Suite 1, Lobby Level
Tedesco, Rochelle M. '75 '01 C.323 B.A. L.477 J.D. (adm. in MA; not adm. in DC) [Ⓐ Shook,H.&B.]
Tedhams, David ... '63 '95 C.112 B.A. L.831 J.D. Staff Atty., Ct. of App.
Tedrow, Sally M. ... '47 '77 C.914 B.A. L.128 J.D. [O'Donoghue&O.]
Teel, Keith A. ... '56 '81 C.902 B.S. L.893 J.D. [Covington&B.] (See Pat. Sect.)
Teeples, David ... '69 '97 C.623 B.A. L.575 J.D. [Ⓐ Elias,M.T.&H.]
Teerink, Mark B. ... '66 '97 C.898 B.A. L.352 J.D. [Ⓐ Skadden,A.S.M.&F.]
Tegtmeyer, Rene D., (AV) ... '34 '63 C.910 B.S. L.273 J.D. [Ⓒ Fish&R.] (See Pat. Sect.)
*PRACTICE AREAS: Intellectual Property; Patents; Litigation.
Tehrani, Farinaz S. ... '66 '91 C.860 B.A. L.276 J.D. [Ⓐ Hogan&H.]
*PRACTICE AREAS: Corporate Law; Securities.
Teich, Joan F. ... '61 '86 C.1036 B.A. L.273 J.D. 10 E St., S.E.
Teichler, Stephen L., (AV) ... '52 '77 C&L.893 B.A., J.D. [Duane,M.&H.]
*PRACTICE AREAS: Energy Law and Litigation.
Teimourian, Sheila M. '60 '87 C&L.276 B.S.F.S., J.D. Assoc. Gen. Coun., Fannie Mae
*RESPONSIBILITIES: E-Commerce; Mortgage Finance.
Teir, Robert ... '61 '86 C.273 B.A. L.276 J.D. Center for Community Interest
Teitelbaum, David ... '61 '86 C.31 B.A. L.813 J.D. [Sidley A.B.&W.]

Teitelbaum, George A., (BV) '43 '83 C.667 B.S.E.E. L.30 J.D.
1629 K Street N.W., Suite 802, 20006
Telephone: 202-783-7177 Fax: 202-775-7465 Email: georget@clark.net URL: http://www.arrowweb.com/gilt
URL: http://www.lawyers.com/lawyergeorge
Probate, Wills, Trusts and Estates, Estate Planning, Asset Protection, Conservatorship, Guardianship, Bankruptcy, Consumer Bankruptcy, Chapter 7 and 13, Business Law, Corporate Law, Divorce, Separation Agreements, Child Support, Child Custody, Adoption, Family Law, Landlord and Tenant Law, Civil Litigation, Negligence, Auto Accidents, Personal Injury.
See Professional Biographies, WASHINGTON, DISTRICT OF COLUMBIA

Teitelbaum, Steven A., (AV) ... '56 '80 C&L.178 A.B., J.D. [Jones,D.R.&P.]
*PRACTICE AREAS: Commercial Real Estate; Real Estate Finance; Hotel and Resort Development; Leasing.
Telecki, Nicole ... '71 '97 C.674 B.A. L.94 J.D. [Ⓐ Wilmer,C.&P.]
Telecom Legal Services ... 1776 I Street, N.W., 9th Floor
Telep, Jeffrey M. ... '— '90 C.1175 B.A. L.260 J.D. [Ⓐ King&S.]
*PRACTICE AREAS: Litigation; Trade Regulation.
Tell, Gary S. ... '67 '92 C.103 A.B. L.145 J.D. [Ⓒ O'Melveny&M.]
*PRACTICE AREAS: Employee Benefits; Litigation.
Tello, Carol P. ... '46 '81 C.945 B.A. L.446 J.D. [Ⓒ Silverstein&M.]
*PRACTICE AREAS: International Taxation.
Tello, James W. ... '41 '69 C.690 B.S.M.E. L.94 J.D. 1776 I Street, N.W., 9th Floor
Telpner, Brian J. ... '69 '97 C.228 A.B. L.276 J.D. [Ⓐ Steptoe&J.]
Temchine, Daly D. E., (AV) ... '— '69 C.178 A.B. L.705 J.D. [Epstein B.&G.]
*PRACTICE AREAS: Health Care Litigation; ERISA Litigation; Fraud and Abuse.
Temkin, Charles B., (P.C.), (AV) ... '48 '73 C.178 B.A. L.309 J.D. [Shaw P.]
*PRACTICE AREAS: Tax.
Temkin, Susan O'Hearn, (AV) ... '— '79 C.184 B.A. L.1048 J.D. [Verner,L.B.M.&H.]
*PRACTICE AREAS: Tax Law; Transactional Law.
Temko, Francine S., (AV) ... '22 '47 C.66 A.B. L.178 LL.B. 666 11 St., N.W.‡
Temko, Stanley L., (AV) ... '20 '43 C&L.178 A.B., LL.B. [Ⓒ Covington&B.]
Temple, Bonnie S., (AV) ... '41 '75 C.681 B.A. L.276 J.D. [Ⓒ Bingham D.]
*PRACTICE AREAS: Corporate Law; Finance; Real Estate.
Temple, C. Brooke, III '71 '96 C.659 B.A. L.228 J.D. (adm. in CA; not adm. in DC) 2001 Penn. Ave., N.W.
Temple, Donald M. ... '53 '78 C.329 B.A. L.770 J.D. [D.M.Temple]
Temple, Karyn Annise '72 '98 C.477 B.A. L.178 J.D. Dept. of Jus., Civil Div., Fed. Prog. Branch
Temple, Ralph J., (AV) ... '32 '57 C.472 B.B.A. L.309 LL.B. 3036 44th St Nw
Temple, Riley K., (AV) ... '49 '75 C.390 A.B. L.276 J.D. [Halprin,T.G.&M.]
*PRACTICE AREAS: Legislative Law; Telecommunications Law.
Temple, Donald M., P.C. ... 1200 G Street, N.W., Suite 370
Templeton, Bruce A., (AV) ... '53 '81 C&L.477 A.B., J.D. [Andrews&K.]
*PRACTICE AREAS: Energy; General Corporate; International Trade.
Tendler, Paul M. ... '43 '80 C.994 B.A. L.329 J.D. [Tendler&B.]
Tendler & Biggins, Chartered, (AV) ... 1090 Vermont Ave., N.W.
Tenenbaum, Ellen S. ... '58 '90 C.446 B.A. L.893 J.D. [McDermott,W.&E.]
Tenenbaum, Jeffrey S. ... '68 '96 C.659 B.A. L.128 J.D. [Ⓒ Venable,A.B.H.&C.]
*PRACTICE AREAS: Trade and Professional Association Law.
Tenenbaum, Marc A. ... '62 '89 C.477 A.B. L.608 J.D. [Ⓐ Slevin&H.]
*PRACTICE AREAS: Employee Benefits Litigation.

Tenenbaum & Saas, P.C.
(See Bethesda, Maryland)

TenHoor, Stuart J., (BV) '54 '80 C.27 B.A. L.945 J.D. (adm. in VA; not adm. in DC) 1730 Rhode Island Ave.
Tennant, William S., (AV) ... '31 '56 C.294 A.B. L.597 J.D. [Ⓒ Krooth&A.]
Tenney, Frederic T. '— '00 C&L.228 B.S.E., J.D. (adm. in VA; not adm. in DC) [Ⓐ Foley&L.]
*PRACTICE AREAS: Patent Prosecution; Patent Litigation.
Tennis, William J. '54 '82 C.309 B.A. L.569 J.D. (adm. in NY; not adm. in DC) Marriott Drive
Teplinsky, Steven B. ... '58 '83 C.477 A.B. L.145 J.D. [Steptoe&J.]
*PRACTICE AREAS: Federal Income Tax.
Teplitz, Steven N. ... '65 '91 C.164 B.A. L.273 J.D. Policy Dept., America Online, Inc.
Tepper, Cary S. ... '57 '85 C.1019 B.A. L.30 J.D. [Booth,F.I.&T.]
Tepper, Gary C., (AV) ... '53 '81 C.1036 B.A. L.976 J.D. [Arent F.K.P.&K.]
*PRACTICE AREAS: Franchise Litigation; Financial Institutions Litigation; Real Estate Litigation.
Teras, Christopher A., (AV) ... '49 '74 C.477 A.B. L.284 J.D. [Jaeger&T.]
Terbush, Theron L. ... '12 '40 C.446 B.S. L.273 LL.B. 3218 Stephenson Pl., N.W.
Terhune, Henry A. ... '57 '87 C.1044 B.A. L.273 J.D. [Akin,G.S.H.&F.]
*PRACTICE AREAS: Public Policy.
Terhune, Karen L. ... '63 '93 C.696 B.A. L.128 J.D. 700 East St., S.E.
Terio, B. Cheryl ... '44 '84 C.446 B.A. L.1209 J.D. [Ⓒ Ballard S.A.&I.]
*PRACTICE AREAS: Construction Contracts; Construction and Design Law.
Terman, Stephen D., (AV) ... '51 '76 C&L.446 B.S., J.D. [Olsson,F.&W.]
*PRACTICE AREAS: Medical Device Law; Litigation; Food and Drug Law.

Terr, Leonard B., (AV) .... '46 '75 C.397 A.B. L.188 J.D. [Baker&M.]
*PRACTICE AREAS: Tax Controversies (Corporate and International); Tax Planning and Advice (Corporate and International).

Terrell, Andrew J., (BV) ....'62 '89 C.745 B.A. L.1209 J.D. [Whiteford,T.&P.]
*PRACTICE AREAS: Litigation; Construction Law; Insurance Defense; Condominium Law.

Terrell-Collier, Tanya N. '69 '98 C.446 B.A. L.273 J.D.
(adm. in MD; not adm. in DC) Asst. Dir., American Bar Association

Terrill, Damon A. ....'69 '00 C.352 B.A. L.569 J.D. [Ⓐ Clifford C.R.&W.]
*PRACTICE AREAS: International Dispute Resolution; International Arbitration; International Litigation; Telecommunications Regulation; Data Privacy Regulation.

Terrill, Shaun Leland .... '72 '97 C.367 B.A. L.273 J.D. [Ⓐ Steptoe&J.]

Terris, Bruce J., (AV) .... '33 '57 C&L.309 A.B., LL.B. [Terris,P.&W.]

Terris, Nicholas G..................... '71 '98 C.893 B.A. L.309 J.D. [Ⓐ Kirkpatrick&L.]
*PRACTICE AREAS: Litigation; Securities; Investment Company Law; Investment Management; Mutual Funds.

Terris, Pravlik and Wagner, (AV) ....1121 12th St., N.W.

Terry, Alicia A. ....'53 '88 C.329 B.M.E. L.276 J.D. [Kutak R.]
*PRACTICE AREAS: Public Finance Law; Asset-Backed Structured Finance Law.

Terry, John A. ....'33 '60 C.976 B.A. L.276 J.D. Ct. App. J.

Terry, Joseph M. .... '74 '01 C.597 B.A. L.145 J.D. [Ⓐ Williams&C.]

Terry, Paul W. ....'63 '91 C.93 B.A. L.273 J.D. [Ⓐ Pillsbury W.]
*PRACTICE AREAS: Environmental Law; Internet Law; Litigation.

Terry, Wendy Anderson .... '67 '92 C.788 B.A. L.893 J.D. [Ⓒ Hale&D.]
*PRACTICE AREAS: Litigation.

Terwilliger, George J., III, (AV) ....'50 '78 C.776 B.A. L.1162 J.D. [White&C.]
*PRACTICE AREAS: Government Investigations; Complex Litigation; Health Care Fraud; Election Law; Voting Rights.

Terzaken, Ann Marie '73 '98
C.30 B.A. L.273 J.D. [Ⓐ Jackson&C.] (⊙Balt., Rockville, MD)
*PRACTICE AREAS: Health Care Litigation; Hospital Liability Defense; General Litigation; Commercial Litigation.

Terzaken, John F., III .... '— '00 C.30 B.A. L.893 J.D. [Ⓐ Morgan,L.&B.]

Terzian, Tamar V. '— '99 C.188 B.A. L.94 J.D.
(adm. in MA; not adm. in DC) 701 Pennsylvania Avenue, N.W.

Tesdahl, D. Benson ....'52 '84 C.870 B.S. L.629 J.D. [Ⓒ Powers,P.S.&V.]
*PRACTICE AREAS: Tax Exempt Organizations; Health Care Law; Corporate Law.

Tesler, Shana E. '— '00 C.1036 B.A. L.978 J.D.
(adm. in NY; not adm. in DC) [Ⓐ Greenberg T.]

Teslik, Sarah A. B. .... '53 '83 C.939 B.A. L.276 J.D. 1730 Rhode Island Ave., N.W.

Teslik, W. Randolph, (P.C.), (AV) ..... '49 '76 C.228 A.B. L.904 J.D. [Akin,G.S.H.&F.]
*PRACTICE AREAS: Litigation.

Tessier, Margaret C. ....'48 '77 C.976 B.A. L.276 J.D. 1450 T St., N.W.

Testoni, Maureen ....'— '97 C.145 B.A. L.273 J.D. [Ⓐ Weil,G.&M.]

Teter, Harry ....'40 '66 C.902 B.A. L.276 J.D. [Ⓒ O'Brien,B.M.&S.]

Tetrault, Charles D., (AV) .... '50 '75 C.188 B.S. L.273 J.D. [Vinson&E.]
*PRACTICE AREAS: Litigation; Energy; White Collar Crime.

Tetro, Valerie L......................'60 '86 C.183 B.A. L.904 J.D. [Ⓐ Whiteford,T.&P.]
*PRACTICE AREAS: Insurance Defense Litigation; Medical Malpractice; Appellate Practice; Insurance Coverage.

Teuwen, Elizabeth '71 '99 C.321 B.A. L.276 J.D.
(adm. in MA; not adm. in DC) [Ⓐ GKRSE]
*PRACTICE AREAS: Energy; Administrative Law.

Thacher Proffitt & Wood, (AV)
1700 Pennsylvania Avenue, N.W., 20006 ⊙
Telephone: 202-347-8400 Facsimile: 202-626-1930
Email: firm@tpwlaw.com URL: http://www.tpwlaw.com
Members of Firm: V. Gerard Comizio; Stephen F. J. Ornstein; Richard A. Schaberg. Counsel: Joseph A. Smith, Jr. (Not admitted in DC). Associates: Kara L. Bue (Not admitted in DC); Christian H. Chandler (Not admitted in DC); Matthew Dyckman (Not admitted in DC); Jeffrey L. Hare (Not admitted in DC); Song A. Pak; Sheila J. Dombal Swartz; Matthew S. Yoon (Not admitted in DC).
Admiralty and Maritime, Banking, Bankruptcy, Corporate, Employee Benefits, Insurance, Intellectual Property, Litigation, Mergers and Acquisitions, Real Estate, Securitization, Tax, Technology and Science, Transportation, Wills and Probate.
Offices:
New York, N.Y.: 11 West 42nd Street. Telephone: 212-789-1200. Facsimile: 212-789-3500.
White Plains, N.Y.: 50 Main Street. Telephone: 914-421-4100. Facsimile: 914-421-4150/4151.
Jersey City, N.J.: One Exchange Place. Telephone: 201-369-3280. Facsimile: 201-369-3290/4151.
Affiliated Office:
México City, Mexico: Avenida Paseo de la Reforma No. 2620 - Piso 4, Colonia Lomas Altas, 11950 México, D.F. Telephone: +(52) (5) 257-2940. Facsimile: +(52) (5) 257-2950.

See Professional Biographies, WASHINGTON, DISTRICT OF COLUMBIA

Thackery, Joseph C. ....'14 '49 C.434 B.A. L.228 LL.B. 4201 Harrison St., N.W.‡

Thaler, Paul S. ....'61 '87 C.881 A.B. L.276 J.D. [Thaler L.] (⊙Fairfax, VA)
*PRACTICE AREAS: Civil Litigation; Business Law; Employment Law; Family Law; Alternative Dispute Resolution.

Thaler Liebeler, LLP
1919 Pennsylvania Avenue N.W., Suite 200, 20006 ⊙
Telephone: 202-466-4110 Fax: 202-466-2693
URL: http://www.lawyers.com/thaler&liebelerlaw
Paul S. Thaler; Lars H. Liebeler. Of Counsel: Lilliam Machado (Resident, Chevy Chase, Maryland Office); Jane Lemley Rasmussen; Cathleen Schmidt Gormley (Resident, Fairfax, VA Office);—Lauren A. Greenberg.
Civil Litigation, Labor and Employment, Business Law, Antitrust and Trade Regulation, Construction Law, Contracts, Alternative Dispute Resolution, Corporate.
Chevy Chase, Maryland Office: 8555 Connecticut Avenue, Suite 201, 20815. Telephone: 301-941-8081. Fax: 301-941-8082.
Fairfax, Virginia Office: 9691-A Main Street. Telephone: 703-978-9883. Fax: 703-978-9055.

See Professional Biographies, WASHINGTON, DISTRICT OF COLUMBIA

Thao, Le Chi .... '43 '81 C.367 M.A. L.273 M.C.L. 1090 Vermont Avenue, N.W.

Tharp, Cathlene A. .... '69 '97 C.473 B.Phil. L.494 J.D. [Ⓐ Ross,D.&B.]

Thebaud, Charles C., Jr. ....'52 '81 C.870 B.S. L.1017 J.D. [Morgan,L.&B.]

Theberge, John E. ....'44 '83 C.745 B.A. L.276 J.D. [Holland&K.]
*PRACTICE AREAS: Federal Taxation; Public Finance.

Theis, Virginia C. ....'73 '99 C.893 B.A. L.273 J.D. [Ⓐ Jones,D.R.&P.]

Theisen, Mary Carol '64 '93 C&L.966 B.A., J.D.
c/o ABA/CEELI, 740 15th Street NW, Suite 800

Thelen Reid & Priest LLP, (AV) Ⓑ
Market Square, 701 Pennsylvania Avenue, N.W., 20004-2608 ⊙
Telephone: 202-508-4000 Facsimile: 202-508-4321
URL: http://www.thelenreid.com
Daniel M. Berman; Howard A. Cooper; Benjamin I. Delancy (Not admitted in DC); Deborah A. DeMasi; Charles M. English, Jr.; Mark Fox Evens; Lee M. Goodwin; Robert T. Hall, III; David E. Jacobson; William A. Kirk, Jr.; Richard J. Leidl; Phillip G. Lookadoo; Andrew F. MacDonald; Stephan M. Minikes; James K. Mitchell; Andrew David Ness; Kevin O'Brien (Not admitted in DC); Mark J. Riedy; Richard Y. Roberts; Kenneth B. Weiner. Of Counsel: Raymond F. Dacek; William A. DeVan (Not admitted in DC); Keith S. Fischler; Steven S. Honigman; Edward L. Pittman; John R. Schaefgen, Jr.; Johannes W. Williams. Resident Associates: Amy B. Comer (Not admitted in DC); Michelle R. Depuy; Jeffrey R. Gans; Nicholas C. Geale; Andrea Lachenmayr; Simone R. McBean (Not admitted in DC); Christine O'Connor; Ambari Prakash; Susan Tahernia (Resident, McLean, Virginia Office); Mary Margaret Utterback; Todd Jason Wagnon; Aliya Wong (Not admitted in DC); Wendy M. Yoviene.

(This Listing Continued)

Thelen Reid & Priest LLP (Continued)

General and International Practice. Antitrust and Trade Regulations, Bankruptcy, Business Litigation, Commercial Finance, Construction, Corporate, Environmental, Equipment Leasing, Franchising, Government Contracts, Insurance, Intellectual Property, Labor and Employment Relations, Mining, Project Finance, Real Estate and Land Use, Securities, Tax Benefits, Trusts and Estates, Technology Law, Tort Law, Energy, Utility, Entertainment, International, Internet, Telecommunications and Year 2000 Law.
San Francisco, California Office: 101 Second Street, Suite 1800. Telephone: 415-371-1200. Fax: 415-371-1211.
Los Angeles, California Office: 34th Floor, 333 South Grand Avenue. Telephone: 213-621-9800. Fax: 213-623-4742.
Silicon Valley/San Jose, California Office: 17th Floor, 333 West San Carlos Street. Telephone: 408-292-5800. Fax: 408-287-8040.
New York, New York Office: 40 West 57th Street. Telephone: 212-603-2000. Fax: 212-603-2001.
Morristown, New Jersey Office: 65 Madison Avenue, Suite 100. Telephone: 973-644-3400. Fax: 973-644-3159.

See Professional Biographies, WASHINGTON, DISTRICT OF COLUMBIA

Theodore, Carol N., (AV) '43 '77 C.518 A.B. L.976 J.D.
Assoc. Gen. Coun., Fannie Mae
*RESPONSIBILITIES: Multi-Family Transactions.

Theroux, Eugene, (AV) .... '38 '69 C.672 B.I.D. L.276 J.D. [Baker&M.]

Thesz, J. Michael, Jr. ....'43 '74 C.602 B.S.E.E. L.276 J.D. [Ⓒ Hogan&H.]
*PRACTICE AREAS: Computer and Software Patents; Electrical Patent Prosecution; Electrical Patents; Electro-Mechanical Patents; Electronic Patents.

Thiel, Donna K., (AV) ....'57 '82 C.222 B.A. L.94 J.D. [Morgan,L.&B.]

Thieman, Peter P. ....'68 '94 C.893 B.A. L.146 J.D. [Ⓐ White&C.]

Thies, Roger C. ....'44 '69 C.894 A.B. L.145 J.D. [Hyman,P.&M.]

Thiessen, Jacob G. '63 '98 C.145 A.B. L.276 J.D.
(adm. in MD; not adm. in DC) [Ⓐ Goodwin P.]

Thom, Janis A. ....'72 '99 C.446 B.S. L.659 J.D. [Ⓐ Littler M.]
*PRACTICE AREAS: Labor and Employment.

Thomas, Andrew E.......................'63 '89 C&L.790 B.S., J.D. [Ⓐ Willkie F.&G.]

Thomas, Bertrand S. ....'53 '80 C&L.329 B.A., J.D. Spec. Asst. Clk., Supr. Ct.

Thomas, Charles B. .... '48 '75 C.103 A.B. L.276 J.D. [Deso,T.&S.]

Thomas, David U. ....'64 '89 C.309 A.B. L.893 J.D. [Ⓐ Kirkpatrick&L.]
*PRACTICE AREAS: Investment Company Law; Investment Management; Hedge Funds; Mutual Funds; Securities Law.

Thomas, Dirk D., (BV) ...... '59 '86 C.446 B.S.M.E. L.273 J.D. [Robins,K.M.&C.] (Pat.)
*PRACTICE AREAS: Intellectual Property.

Thomas, Elizabeth '72 '98 C.188 B.A. L.1375 J.D.
(adm. in FL; not adm. in DC) [Ⓐ Schmeltzer,A.&S.]
*PRACTICE AREAS: Labor and Employment Litigation.

Thomas, Gordon M. .... '51 '80 C.296 B.A. L.128 J.D. Dir., Govt. Affs., Textron Inc.

Thomas, H. Barton ....'— '98 C.699 A.B. L.1051 J.D. [Ⓐ Latham&W.]
*PRACTICE AREAS: Tax Controversies; Tax Planning; Civil Litigation.

Thomas, Herbert ... '57 '91 C.164 B.A. L.893 J.D. [Ⓒ Debevoise&P.] (⊙New York, NY)
*PRACTICE AREAS: General Litigation; Securities Litigation; Insurance Litigation and Regulation.

Thomas, Jeane A...........................'64 '89 C.608 B.A. L.276 J.D. [Crowell&M.]

Thomas, Joel T. '43 '70 C.855 B.A. L.608 J.D.
Gen. Coun., National Wildlife Federation

Thomas, John Davidson ....'61 '90 C.188 A.B. L.94 J.D. [Cole,R.&B.]
*PRACTICE AREAS: Telecommunications Regulation; Telecommunications Competition; Cable Television; Pole Attachments; Satellite Communications.

Thomas, John W. '49 '71
C.350 B.S. L.273 J.D. [Luman,L.&W.] & [Ⓒ Dickinson,M.T.&H.]
*PRACTICE AREAS: Food and Drug Law; Government Relations; Business Law; Trade and Professional Associations.

Thomas, L. Jackson, II .... '47 '76 C.411 B.A. L.30 J.D. Asst. U.S. Atty.

Thomas, Mary Lucinda '52 '82 C.273 B.A. L.276 J.D.
(adm. in VA; not adm. in DC) Kent & O'Connor, Inc.

Thomas, Matthew J. '68 '92 C&L.893 B.A., J.D.
(adm. in VA; not adm. in DC) [Ⓐ Robins,K.M.&C.]
*PRACTICE AREAS: Administrative Law; Government-Federal; Transportation Law; International Trade.

Thomas, Nancie A. .... '63 '88 C&L.477 B.A., J.D. Gen. Coun., Conservation Intl.

Thomas, Paul M. ....'48 '75 C.393 A.B. L.309 J.D. [Holland&K.]
*PRACTICE AREAS: Employment Law; Corporate Diversity Counseling; Litigation.

Thomas, Peter W. .... '64 '90 C.93 B.A. L.276 J.D. [Powers,P.S.&V.]
*PRACTICE AREAS: Health Care Law and Legislation; Disability and Rehabilitation; Americans with Disabilities Act.

Thomas, R. G. '59 '86 C.893 B.A. L.692 J.D.
Mng. Editor & Gen. Coun., Congressional Digest Corporation

Thomas, R. Keith .... '44 '69 C&L.880 B.A., J.D. 950 Pennsylvania Avenue, NW‡

Thomas, Ritchie T., (AV) ....'36 '64 C.188 B.A. L.930 J.D. [Squire,S.&D.]
*PRACTICE AREAS: International Trade; International Transactions; Regulatory Affairs; Copyright.

Thomas, Robert W. ....'14 '40 C.446 A.B. L.276 J.D. 3262 N St., NW‡

Thomas, Ryan C. ....'75 '00 C.611 B.A. L.893 J.D. [Ⓐ Jones,D.R.&P.]

Thomas, S. Pamela ....'55 '89 C.555 B.A. L.705 J.D. Pub. Def. Serv.

Thomas, Scott S...........................'67 '96 C&L.101 B.A., J.D. [Ⓐ Spriggs&H.]
*PRACTICE AREAS: Products Liability; Toxic Torts Litigation; Drug and Medical Device Defense.

Thomas, W. David .... '72 '98 C.216 B.A. L.446 J.D. [Ⓐ Preston G.E.&R.M.]
*PRACTICE AREAS: Legislative; Regulatory; Environmental; Transportation.

Thomas, W. Todd '65 '93
C.260 B.A. L.976 J.D. [Boies,S.&F.] (⊙Palm Beach Gardens, FL)
*PRACTICE AREAS: Litigation; International Arbitration.

Thomas, William L.......................'63 '90 C.747 B.A. L.276 J.D. [Ⓐ Pillsbury W.]
*PRACTICE AREAS: Environmental Law; Litigation; International Law.

Thomas & Libowitz, P.A.
(See Baltimore, Maryland)

Thomases, Susan P., (AV) '44 '78 C.183 B.A. L.178 J.D.
(adm. in NY; not adm. in DC) 1155 21st St., N.W.‡

Thomason and Hessmer, LLC
(See Bethesda, Maryland)

Thomasson, Denise Ann '66 '99 C.8 B.A. L.904 J.D.
(adm. in NY; not adm. in DC) [Ⓐ Danziger,M.&F.]
*PRACTICE AREAS: Business Immigration; Citizenship; Consular Law.

Thompson, Andrew M. ....'59 '93 C.273 B.A. L.1280 J.D. Neighborhood Legal Servs.

Thompson, Anthony, (AV) ....'49 '76 C.309 A.B. L.1162 J.D. [Zuckerman S.]
*PRACTICE AREAS: Business Law; International Transactions; Real Estate; Corporate Law; Finance.

Thompson, Brent T. '62 '90 C.911 B.A. L.1209 J.D.
(adm. in VA; not adm. in DC)
Dir., Corp. Fin. & Mgmt., National Assn. of Manufacturers

Thompson, Cametra ....'73 '99 C.813 B.A. L.309 J.D. [Ⓐ Covington&B.]
*PRACTICE AREAS: Corporate Law.

Thompson, Carolyn Y., (AV) ....'43 '81 C.880 B.A. L.893 J.D. [Jones,D.R.&P.]
*PRACTICE AREAS: Energy; Federal Energy Regulation; Utility Rates.

Thompson, Charles C. '65 '98 C.59 B.A. L.802 J.D.
(adm. in NY; not adm. in DC) [Ⓐ Dewey B.]
*PRACTICE AREAS: Corporate Taxation (50%); International Taxation (50%).

Thompson, Chet M. ....'68 '93 C.93 B.A. L.128 J.D. [Collier S.S.]
*PRACTICE AREAS: Environmental Law; Litigation.
Thompson, Daniel R., (AV) ....'29 '61 C.994 B.A. L.276 LL.B. [D.R.Thompson]
Thompson, David H. ....'68 '95 C&L.309 A.B., J.D. [Cooper&K.]
Thompson, Dionne '67 '94 C.309 B.A. L.893 J.D.
(adm. in PA; not adm. in DC) [Ⓐ Troutman S.]
*PRACTICE AREAS: Federal Regulatory; Public Law; Regulatory Law.
Thompson, Douglas G., Jr., (AV) .... '44 '70 C&L.813 A.B., J.D. [Finkelstein,T.&L.]
Thompson, Duane K. .... '58 '84 C.659 B.A. L.976 J.D. [Baach R.&L.P.]
*PRACTICE AREAS: Insurance Coverage Litigation; Civil Litigation; Intellectual Property; Communications.
Thompson, Dudley E., Jr. .... '48 '80 C.197 B.A. L.30 J.D. [Klein&C.]
Thompson, Gary, (BV) .... '65 '90 C.276 B.A. L.705 J.D. [Gilbert H.&R.]
*PRACTICE AREAS: Commercial Litigation; Insurance Coverage; Antitrust.
Thompson, George .... '56 '82 C.1044 B.S. L.188 J.D. [Neville,P.]
*PRACTICE AREAS: International Trade; Administrative Practice; Litigation.
Thompson, Grant P...... '40 '68 C.668 B.A. L.976 LL.B. Exec. V.P., The Wilderness Soc.
Thompson, Kathleen O'Flaherty '48 '77 C.945 A.B. L.276 J.D.
Coun. & Sr. V.P., Credit Union National Association
Thompson, Kerri E. ....'69 '94 C.881 B.A. L.861 J.D. Off. of Corp. Coun.
Thompson, Leslie A. '68 '00 C.16 B.S. L.893 J.D.
(adm. in AL; not adm. in DC) [Ⓐ McDermott,W.&E.]
Thompson, Lonna M. '53 '84 C.400 B.A. L.276 J.D.
Dir., Legal Affs., Association of American Public Television Stations
Thompson, Marcia K. '69 '98 C.475 B.A. L.1209 J.D.
(adm. in VA; not adm. in DC) 1150 18th Street North West, # 600
Thompson, Michael J. .... '55 '81 C.608 B.S.B.A. L.273 J.D. [Wright&T.]
*PRACTICE AREAS: Energy Regulation; Communications; Common Carrier Law.
Thompson, Patricia S. '53 '91 C.959 B.S.N. L.64 J.D.
(adm. in MD; not adm. in DC) 555 13th St., N.W.‡
Thompson, Peter G. .... '54 '79 C&L.910 A.B., J.D. [Ross,D.&B.]
Thompson, Peter J. .... '62 '90 C&L.128 B.A., J.D. [Ⓐ Andrews&K.]
*PRACTICE AREAS: Federal Energy Regulation; Energy Regulation.
Thompson, Phyllis D. .... '52 '81 C&L.273 B.A., J.D. [Covington&B.]
Thompson, Scott A., (CV) '57 '82 C.112 A.B. L.464 J.D.
(adm. in CA; not adm. in DC) [Ⓐ O'Melveny&M.] (⊙L.A., CA)
Thompson, Stacey Walsh ....'70 '98 C.454 B.A. L.273 J.D. [Ⓐ Brickfield B.R.&S.]
*PRACTICE AREAS: Energy; Litigation.
Thompson, T. Scott .... '66 '93 C.260 B.A. L.273 J.D. [Cole,R.&B.]
*PRACTICE AREAS: Telecommunications Competition; Cable Television Law; Telecommunications Law; Commercial Litigation.
Thompson, Terri A. '— '94 C.329 B.S. L.1059 J.D.
D.C. Dept. of Human Servs., Dep. Gen. Coun.
Thompson, Thomas C., Jr., (AV) ......'26 '50 C.659 B.S. L.273 LL.B. [Scribner,H.&T.]
Thompson, William R. .... '12 '41 L.537 J.D. 733 15th St., N.W.‡
Thompson, William Randolph, (AV) '46 '74
C.309 A.B. L.276 J.D. [Jorden B.] & [Ⓒ Jones & Blouch L.L.P.]
*PRACTICE AREAS: Securities Law; Mutual Funds; Insurance Products.
Thompson, William W., II, (AV) '47 '74 C.31 B.A. L.178 J.D.
[Zwerdling,P.L.K.T.&D.]
Thompson, Wm. S. .... '11 '42 C.329 B.S. L.1014 LL.B. Ret. Supr. Ct. J.

Thompson Coburn LLP, (AV)
1909 K Street, N.W., 6th Floor, 20006-1101 ⊙
Telephone: 202-585-6900 Telecopier: 202-585-6969 for attorney email use: first initial of first name, last name@thompsoncoburn.com e.g. aallred@thompsoncoburn.com
Email: info@thompsoncoburn.com URL: http://www.thompsoncoburn.com
Members of Firm: Anthony A. Anderson; Richard K. Bank; Murray J. Belman; Bonnie S. Blair; R. Lawrence Coughlin; Warren L. Dean, Jr.; Edward J. Gill, Jr.; Michael A. Greenspan; Marjorie F. Krumholz; Katherine S. Nucci; Michael G. Roberts; David M. Schwartz; Edward J. Sheppard, IV; Patricia N. Snyder; Jane Sutter Starke; Gerald D. Stoltz; Marcela B. Stras; David R. Straus; Timothy Sullivan; G. Kent Woodman. Of Counsel: Milton D. Andrews. Associates: Eileen P. Brown; Gabriela Carias-Troconis (Not admitted in DC); Jacqueline T. Colclough; Matthew H. Kaiser; Carla Miller; Mark L. Parsons (Not admitted in DC); David Seidman.
Admiralty, Antitrust, Business Immigration, Commercial Finance, Corporate, Government Contracts, International Trade and Transactions, Litigation, Maritime, Mass Transit, Postal, Transportation, Utilities.
Representative Clients: American Municipal Power-Ohio, Inc.; Appleton Papers, Inc.; Cold Finished Steel Bar Institute; GATX Capital Corporation; Riso, Inc.; Shell Bermuda (Overseas) Limited; Venepal, S.A.C.A.; World Bank.
St. Louis, Missouri Office: One Firstar Plaza. Telephone: 314-552-6000. Telecopier: 314-552-7000.
Belleville, Illinois Office: 525 West Main Street. Telephone: 618-277-4700. Telecopier: 618-236-3434.
See Professional Biographies, WASHINGTON, DISTRICT OF COLUMBIA

Thompson, Daniel R., P.C., (AV) .... 1620 I St., N.W.

Thompson Hine LLP, (AV)
1920 N Street, N.W., Suite 800, 20036-1600 ⊙
Telephone: 202-331-8800 Fax: 202-331-8330 Telex: 904173 Cable Address: "Caglaw"
Email: Attorneys@ThompsonHine.com URL: http://www.ThompsonHine.com
Amos Burt Thompson (1871-1965); Charles P. Hine (1877-1942); Walter L. Flory (1880-1951); David J. Hooker (Managing Partner); Patricia Mann Smitson (Partner-in-Charge, Cincinnati); Paul N. Harris (Partner-in-Charge, Cleveland); Thomas J. Bonasera (Partner-in-Charge, Columbus); Joseph M. Rigot (Partner-in-Charge, Dayton); David H. Baker (Partner-in-Charge, Washington, D.C.).
Members of Firm: David H. Baker (Partner-in-Charge, Washington, D.C.); Karyn A. Booth; Irving P. Cohen (Resident); Nicholas J. DiMichael; Charles L. Freed; Barry A. Friedman (Resident); Frederick B. Gibbon; Peter A. Greene; Jeffrey O. Moreno; Mark Roy Sandstrom; Daniel E. Toomey; Thomas W. Wilcox; Frederic L. Wood. Associates: Frank S. Baldino; Carolina Coll (Not admitted in DC); Scott A. Harvey; Michael H. Higgins; Karl M. Laskas (Not admitted in DC); Stephen T. Lovelady; Julia M. McCalmon; Tamara M. McNulty; Jennifer L. Noah; Barbara E. Parisi; Christopher D. Perry; Angela M. Varner. Senior Attorney: Amy G. Davies. Of Counsel: Gilbert B. Lessenco (Resident); John K. Maser III. Staff Attorney: Patricia W. S. Douglas.
Administrative Law, Admiralty and Maritime Law, Agency and Distributorships, Antitrust and Trade Regulation, Aviation and Aerospace, Bankruptcy, Banks and Banking, Biotechnology, Business Law, Business Litigation, Business Regulation, Business Transactions, Closely Held Business Law, Joint Ventures, Class Actions, Commercial Law, Commercial Real Estate, Communications and Media, FCC Regulation, Computers and Software, Construction Law, Contracts, Copyrights, Corporate Law, Corporate Finance, Corporate Litigation, Corporate Tax Controversies, Debtor and Creditor, Employee Benefits, ERISA, Energy, Energy Regulation, Environmental Law, Finance, Commercial Finance, Franchises and Franchising, General Practice, Government, False Claims Act, Qui Tam Litigation, Government Contracts, Health Care, Insurance Coverage, Insurance Regulation, Intellectual Property, International Law, International Trade, Internet Law, Labor and Employment, Litigation, Complex Litigation, Medicare Fraud and Abuse, Mergers, Acquisitions and Divestitures, Natural Resources, Nonprofit and Charitable Organizations, Occupational Safety and Health, OSHA, Partnership Law, Patents, Probate, Products Liability, Product Safety, Professional Liability, Public Finance, Railroad Law, Real Estate, Regulatory Law, Drug and Medical Device Regulation, Food and Drug Regulation, International Regulatory Law, Regulated Industries, Securities, Initial Public Offerings, Public Offerings, Taxation, Tax Controversies, Toxic Torts, Trade Secrets, Trademarks, Transportation, Trusts and Estates, Unfair Competition, Utility Law, White Collar Crime, Zoning, Planning and Land Use.
Cleveland, Ohio Office: 3900 Key Center, 127 Public Square, 44114-1216. Telephone: 216-566-5500. Fax: 216-566-5800. Email: Attorneys@ThompsonHine.com.
Cincinnati, Ohio Office: 312 Walnut Street, 14th Floor, 45202-4029. Telephone: 513-352-6700. Fax: 513-241-4771. Email: Attorneys@ThompsonHine.com.
Columbus, Ohio Office: One Columbus, 10 West Broad Street, 43215-3435. Telephone: 614-469-3200. Fax: 614-469-3361. Email: Attorneys@ThompsonHine.com.

(This Listing Continued)

Thompson Hine LLP (Continued)
Dayton, Ohio Office: 2000 Courthouse Plaza, N.E., 10 West Second Street, 45402-1706. Telephone: 937-443-6600. Fax: 937-443-6637, 937-443-6635. Email: Attorneys@ThompsonHine.com.
Brussels, Belgium Office: Place J. Jacobs 5, 1000 Brussels, Belgium, Telephone: 011 (32-2) 514-5400. Fax: 011 (32-2) 514-2932. Email: Attorneys@ThompsonHine.com.
See Professional Biographies, WASHINGTON, DISTRICT OF COLUMBIA

Thompson, O'Donnell, Markham, Norton & Hannon, (AV) BB
The Southern Building, 805 Fifteenth Street, N.W., Suite 705, 20005
Telephone: 202-289-1133 Facsimile: 202-289-0275
John Jude O'Donnell; Julian E. Markham, Jr.; Randell Hunt Norton; James W. Greene; J. Michael Hannon; Kenneth G. Stallard; Brooke A. Pinkerton. Associates: Matthew W. Carlson; Michele L. Bulger; Tamika L. Taylor (Not admitted in DC). Of Counsel: James F. Bromley.
Torts, Surety and Fidelity Law. Insurance, Government Contract Claims in Courts and Departments. Trials and Appeals, Federal, District of Columbia, Maryland and Virginia Courts. Estate Planning, Wills, Trusts, Probate and Taxation, Criminal Defense.
Representative Clients: CNA Insurance Companies; Washington Mutual Investors Fund; Allfirst Trust Company, N.A.; Bernard F. Locraft, Civil Engineers, Washington, D. C.
Reference: Allfirst Bank.
See Professional Biographies, WASHINGTON, DISTRICT OF COLUMBIA

Thompson & Waldron
(See Alexandria, Virginia)

Thomsen, Dianna .... '63 '97 C.881 B.A. L.770 J.D. [Ⓐ King&S.]
*PRACTICE AREAS: Food and Drug Regulation.
Thomsen, Roszel C., II, (AV) ....'58 '85 C.309 B.A. L.30 J.D. [Thomsen&B.] ⊙
*PRACTICE AREAS: Corporate Law; International Trade; Export Regulation; Business Law; Government Contracts.
Thomsen, Steuart H. .... '54 '79 C&L.309 A.B., J.D. [Sutherland A.&B.]
*PRACTICE AREAS: Civil Litigation; ERISA; Insurance Litigation; Intellectual Property Litigation; Tax Litigation.

Thomsen and Burke, LLP, (AV) BB
Suite 500, 1225 Eye Street, N.W., 20005 ⊙
Telephone: 202-682-4741 Fax: 202-547-3713
URL: http://www.t-b.com
Roszel C. Thomsen, II;—Antoinette D. Paytas.
Federal Taxation and Estate Planning. Corporation, Probate and Trust Law, International Trade Law and Government Contracts.
Baltimore, Maryland Office: Suite 400, One North Charles Street, 21201. Telephone: 410-539-2595. FAX: 410-783-0710.
See Professional Biographies, WASHINGTON, DISTRICT OF COLUMBIA

Thomson, Christopher C. .... '66 '91 C.228 A.B. L.477 J.D. 1741 T St. N.W.
Thomson, Kathryn B. .... '64 '90 C.339 B.A. L.659 J.D. [Sidley A.B.&W.]
Thomson, William, (AV) .... '08 '37 L.799 LL.B. 2604 31st St., N.W.‡
Thorgeirsson, Sif ....'71 '98 C.012 B.A. L.273 J.D. [Ⓐ Troutman S.]
*PRACTICE AREAS: Project Development; Project Finance; International Law; Corporate Law; Finance.
Thornburgh, Dick, (AV) '— '57
C.976 B.Eng. L.665 LL.B. [Ⓒ Kirkpatrick&L.] (⊙Harrisburg, PA)
*PRACTICE AREAS: Economic Development; Corporate Investigations; Federal Criminal Law; Americans with Disabilities Act; Government Relations.
Thorne, James L. .... '44 '75 C.845 B.A. L.326 J.D. [Hewes,G.L.&D.]
Thornell, Richard P. ....'36 '74 C.254 B.A. L.976 J.D. Prof. of Law, Howard Univ.
Thornhill, Angela F. ....'— '96 C.1070 B.S. L.945 J.D. [Ⓐ Morgan,L.&B.]
Thornton, Cleveland .... '46 '71 C&L.16 B.A., J.D. 15 2nd St., NE
Thornton, Courtney S. .... '47 '88 C.104 A.B. L.904 J.D. [Ⓐ Kirkpatrick&L.]
*PRACTICE AREAS: Investment Company Law; Investment Management; Mutual Funds.
Thornton, Josephine Cockrell ....'22 '69 C.914 B.A. L.276 J.D. 2700 Virginia Ave. N. W.
Thornton, Justin Allen, (AV) .... '50 '77 C.575 B.A. L.790 J.D. [J.Thornton]
Thornton, Leslie T. ....'58 '83 C.659 B.A. L.276 J.D. [Patton B.]
Thornton, Mary E. ....'69 '95 C.838 B.S. L.575 J.D. [Ⓐ Sutherland A.&B.]
*PRACTICE AREAS: Investment Company Law; Securities Regulation; Broker-Dealer Regulation; Insurance Products; Mutual Funds.
Thornton, Sean M. ....'73 '97 C.309 A.B. L.276 J.D. [Ⓐ Willkie F.&G.]
Thornton, Tracey E. '— '83 C.329 B.A. L.1292 J.D.
(adm. in PA; not adm. in DC) 1210 Longworth Bldg.

Thornton, Justin, Law Offices of, (AV)
1615 L Street, N.W., Suite 1200, 20036
Telephone: 202-778-0559 Telecopier: 202-530-0625
Email: jat@thorntonlaw.com URL: http://www.lawyers.com/thorntonlaw
Justin Allen Thornton.
White Collar Crime with emphasis on Tax Fraud, Financial Crimes, Health Care Fraud and Abuse, and Corporate Compliance.
See Professional Biographies, WASHINGTON, DISTRICT OF COLUMBIA

Thorpe, Jane Kang ....'57 '82 C.273 B.A. L.276 J.D. [Ⓐ Sidley A.B.&W.]
Thorpe, Leslie Burris ....'73 '99 C.1365 B.A. L.734 J.D. [Ⓐ Epstein B.&G.]
*PRACTICE AREAS: Health.
Thorson, Rodney O. ....'32 '61 C&L.339 B.A., LL.B. 1440 NY Ave., N.W.
Thrasher, Michael A., (AV) ....'45 '70 C.228 B.A. L.575 J.D. [Ⓒ Groom]
*PRACTICE AREAS: Employee Benefits; Exempt Organizations; ERISA.
Threatt, Glennon F., Jr. ....'57 '84 C.674 B.A. L.329 J.D. 1424 16th St. N.W.
Thronson, Mark J. .... '59 '89 C.961 B.S. L.273 J.D. [Dickstein S.M.&O.] (Pat.)
*PRACTICE AREAS: Intellectual Property; Patent Law.
Thumann, Henry C., (AV) '35 '61 C.339 B.A. L.309 LL.B.
(adm. in CA; not adm. in DC) [O'Melveny&M.] (⊙L.A., CA)
*PRACTICE AREAS: General Business Litigation; Antitrust; Securities.
Thurston, Cathy ....'60 '88 C.811 B.A. L.329 J.D. Atty., Sprint Corp.
Tiao, Paul M. .... '— '96 C.453 S.B. L.178 J.D. [Ⓐ Wilmer,C.&P.]
Tibbals, Jeffrey S. .... '73 '99 C.902 B.A. L.861 J.D. [Ⓐ Pepper H.]
*PRACTICE AREAS: Commercial Litigation.
Tibbels, C. Jeffrey .... '71 '99 C.918 B.A. L.904 J.D. [Ⓐ Hogan&H.]
Tibbs, Thurlow E. .... '21 '52 C&L.329 A.B., LL.B. 1910 Vermont Ave., N.W.
Tidler, Cynthia E. .... '— '97 C.446 B.A. L.309 J.D. [Ⓐ Foley&L.]
*PRACTICE AREAS: Litigation; Compliance; Counseling; Government Enforcement.
Tiedemann, Charles Welch, (AV) ....'56 '81 C.602 A.B. L.128 J.D. [Holland&K.]
*PRACTICE AREAS: Commercial Real Estate Law; Commercial Finance; Workouts.
Tieder, John B., Jr., (AV) '46 '71
C.367 A.B. L.30 J.D. [Watt,T.H.&F.] (⊙Mc Lean, VA)
*PRACTICE AREAS: International Construction; Construction; Government Contracts.
Tiedrich, Lee J. '66 '91 C.228 B.S.E. L.659 J.D.
[Covington&B.] (See Pat. Sect.) (⊙San Fran., CA)
Tiernan, Raymond A. ....'50 '76 C.103 A.B. L.128 J.D. [Elias,M.T.&H.]
Tierney, J. Brian ...... '36 '64 C.120 B.A. L.285 LL.B. US Embassy Pretoria Dpt. of State
Tierney, John L., (AV) .... '32 '59 C.749 B.S. L.276 LL.B. 2175 K St., N.W.
Tierney, Julia C. ....'76 '00 C.367 B.A. L.276 J.D. [Ⓐ Buc&B.]
Tievsky, Seth H. ....'50 '75 C.696 B.A. L.1068 J.D. 1225 connecticut Ave. N.W.
Tifford, John M., (AV) ....'42 '65 C.563 B.A. L.188 LL.B. [Piper M.R.&W.]
*PRACTICE AREAS: Franchising; Licensing; Distribution; Consumer Protection; Advertising Law.
Tigar, Jane .... '55 '96 C.976 B.A. L.178 J.D. [Tigar]
Tigar, Michael E., (AV) .... '41 '67 C.1375 B.A. L.1066 J.D. [Tigar]
Tigar Law Firm, The, (AV) .... 1155 Connecticut Ave., N.W., Suite 500

Tiger, David . . . . '65 '92 C&L.446 B.A., J.D. [🄰 Swidler B.S.F.]
*PRACTICE AREAS: Real Estate; Structured Finance.
Tiger, Louis, Jr., (AV) . . . . '31 '58 C&L.309 A.B., LL.B. [🄲 Roberts&H.]
*PRACTICE AREAS: Taxation; Corporate Taxation.
Tiger, Ruth G. . . . . '58 '85 C.216 B.A. L.904 J.D. [Saltman&S.]
*PRACTICE AREAS: Government Contracts; Timber and Logging; Litigation.
Tighe, Alfred Joseph, Jr. . . . . . '25 '54 C.93 A.B. L.276 J.D. 5247 Wisconsin Ave., N.W.
Tighe, Kevin P., (P.C.) . . . . '44 '69 C.708 B.A. L.128 J.D. [Tighe P.A.T.]
*PRACTICE AREAS: Administrative Law; Regulatory Law; Commercial Law; Corporate Law; Business Law.

Tighe Patton Armstrong Teasdale, P.L.L.C., (AV)
A Professional Limited Liability Company
1747 Pennsylvania Avenue, N.W. Suite 300, 20006-4604
Telephone: 202-454-2800 Facsimile: 202-454-2805
URL: http://www.tighepatton.com
Kevin P. Tighe (P.C.); Thomas Earl Patton; Paul N. Murphy; Walter G. Birkel; Brent S. Franzel; Carol Elder Bruce; Kermit A. Rosenberg; John B. Montgomery; Richard H. Gordin; Patrick B. Fazzone; David J. Taylor;—Brian C. Quinn (Not admitted in DC); Joseph G. Cosby; Dennis A. Somech (Not admitted in DC). Of Counsel: Alan H. Kent.
Complex Civil and Criminal Litigation, Government Contracts, Congressional and Federal Agency Representation, International Representation, Administrative and Trade Association Law, Antitrust, Tax and Securities Enforcement, Business Law, Construction Law.
See Professional Biographies, WASHINGTON, DISTRICT OF COLUMBIA

Tignor, Jeffrey H. . . . . '74 '99 C.309 A.B. L.228 J.D. [🄰 Dickstein S.M.&O.] (Pat.)
*PRACTICE AREAS: Telecommunications.
Tignor, Robert S. . . . . '44 '69 C.329 B.A. L.273 J.D. Assoc. J., Supr. Ct.
Tillen, James G. . . . . '— '99 C.184 B.A. L.273 J.D. [🄰 Miller&C.]
*PRACTICE AREAS: Federal Litigation; International Litigation.
Tillinghast, Pamela . . . . '61 '90 C.104 B.A. L.94 J.D. 555 13th St., N.W.
Tillman, Eugene, (AV) . . . . '— '76 C.112 B.A. L.1068 J.D. [Reed S.]
*PRACTICE AREAS: Health Care.
Tillotson, David, Law Office of, (AV) '43 '67
C.145 B.A. L.976 J.D. 4606 Charleston Terr., N.W.
Tillotson, Frank A. '65 '96 C.1044 B.S. L.280 J.D.
(adm. in GA; not adm. in DC) [Butera&A.]
*PRACTICE AREAS: Government Relations.
Tillou, Patrick A. '75 '00 C.228 A.B. L.477 J.D.
(adm. in VI; not adm. in DC) [🄰 Cleary,G.S.&H.]
Timbie, Richard E., (AV) . . . . '46 '73 C&L.813 B.S., J.D. [Caplin&D.]
*PRACTICE AREAS: Tax; International Taxation; Litigation.
Timmeny, Wallace L., (AV) . . . . '37 '65 C.1030 B.B.A. L.569 LL.B. [Dechert]
*PRACTICE AREAS: Securities Regulation; Investment Management; Financial Services Law.
Timmerman, Jerianne '61 '89 C.934 B.A. L.477 J.D.
Assoc. Gen. Coun., National Association of Broadcasters
*RESPONSIBILITIES: Communications Law; Broadcast Regulation; Mass Media Law; First Amendment Law.
Timmons, John '55 '81 C.20 B.A. L.902 J.D.
(adm. in VA; not adm. in DC) 1620 L St., N.W.
Timmons, Richard C. . . . . '15 '44 L.180 LL.B. 2939 Van Ness St., N.W.
Ting, Henry P. . . . . '69 '97 C.103 Sc.B. L.188 J.D. [🄰 Covington&B.] (See Pat. Sect.)
Tinker, Megan H. . . . . '— '99 C.692 B.A. L.904 J.D. [🄰 Proskauer R.]
Tinker, Susanne C. '70 '01 C.446 B.S.M.E. L.276 J.D.
(adm. in VA; not adm. in DC; See Pat. Sect.) [🄰 Finnegan,H.F.G.&D.]
*PRACTICE AREAS: Mechanical Patents; Medical Patents; Patent Prosecution; Medical Technology.
Tinnes, Christy A. '69 '98 C&L.790 B.S., J.D.
(adm. in SC; not adm. in DC) [🄰 Groom]
*PRACTICE AREAS: Employee Benefits.
Tippet, Sarah E. . . . . '74 '98 C.893 B.A. L.306 J.D. [🄰 Holland&K.]
*PRACTICE AREAS: Real Estate Law.
Tirana, Bardyl R., (AV) '37 '62
C.674 A.B. L.178 LL.B. 3550 Tilden Street, N.W. (⊙New York, NY)
Tisch, Ronald I., (AV) . . . . '44 '69 C.102 B.A. L.273 J.D. [Littler M.]
*PRACTICE AREAS: Labor and Employment.
Tisi, Christopher V., (BV) . . . . '60 '86 C.1044 B.A. L.896 J.D. [Ashcraft&G.]
*PRACTICE AREAS: Products Liability; Personal Injury; Diet Drug Litigation; Pharmacy Law.
Tisinger, Tina S. . . . . '53 '88 C.1356 B.S. L.1209 J.D. [Bastianelli,B.&K.]
*PRACTICE AREAS: Construction Law; Government Contracts; Civil Litigation.
Titlebaum, Joseph M. '63 '91 C.178 A.B. L.309 J.D.
(adm. in MA; not adm. in DC) [XM S.R.]
Tittsworth, David G. '53 '78 C&L.378 B.A., J.D.
(adm. in KS; not adm. in DC) Investment Counsel Assn. of Amer.
Titus, Herbert W. '37 '62 C.629 B.A. L.309 J.D.
(adm. in OR; not adm. in DC) [🄲 W.J.Olson] ⊙
*PRACTICE AREAS: Constitutional Law; Employment Discrimination; Election Law; Campaign Finance; General Practice.
Titus, Marlana K. . . . . . '66 '91 C.576 B.S. L.446 J.D. 1100 New York Ave., N.W., 9th Fl.
Tiu, James F. . . . . '66 '92 C.973 B.S. L.150 J.D. 521 8th St. N.E.
Toadvine, Patricia Pritt '58 '85 C.260 B.A. L.362 J.D.
(adm. in MD; not adm. in DC) [🄲 Krooth&A.]
*PRACTICE AREAS: Multi-Family Housing; Health Care Facility Regulation; Mortgage Finance.
Tobe, Roslyn T. '59 '86
C.823 B.A. L.365 J.D. Navy Lit. Off., Off. of the Gen Coun. (Pat.)
Tobenkin, David N. . . . . '66 '98 C.1375 B.A. L.800 J.D. [🄰 Cole,R.&B.]
*PRACTICE AREAS: Telecommunications Law; Cable TV; Broadcast Television; Intellectual Property.
Tobey, Margaret L., (AV) . . . . '49 '80 C&L.352 B.A., J.D. [Morrison&F.]
*PRACTICE AREAS: Communications and Media.
Tobias, Michael H. . . . . '56 '93 C.453 B.S. L.276 J.D. 700 Thirteenth St. N.W. (Pat.)
Tobin, Charles D. . . . . '62 '89 C&L.260 B.S., J.D. [Holland&K.]
Tobin, Charles Michael, (AV) . . . . '— '68 C.94 A.B. L.126 J.D. [Foley&L.]
*PRACTICE AREAS: Litigation; Commercial Law; Trade Regulation.
Tobin, Christopher M. '64 '93 C&L.884 B.S.E.E., J.D.
(adm. in PA; not adm. in DC) [🄰 Fenwick&W.]
*PRACTICE AREAS: Patent Law; Intellectual Property.
Tobin, Daniel J. . . . . '— '91 C.176 B.A. L.446 J.D. [Kirkpatrick&L.]
*PRACTICE AREAS: Civil Litigation; Commercial Litigation; Employment Litigation.
Tobin, David C., (P.C.), (AV) . . . . . . '59 '84 C.935 B.A. L.273 J.D. [Tobin,O.&E.]
*PRACTICE AREAS: Civil Litigation; Criminal Litigation; Administrative Law; White Collar Crime.
Tobin, Donald A., (AV) . . . . '47 '73 C.321 A.B. L.93 J.D. [Bastianelli,B.&K.]
*PRACTICE AREAS: Government Contracts; Construction Law.
Tobin, Francine Norz '64 '90
C.262 B.S. L.178 J.D. Asst. Gen. Coun., NASD Regulation, Inc.
Tobin, Lorretta K. '59 '87 C.1369 B.A. L.190 J.D.
(adm. in VA; not adm. in DC) [Brown N.&K.]
*PRACTICE AREAS: Telecommunications.
Tobin, Maurice B. . . . . '33 '59 C.711 B.S. L.378 LL.B. 1850 K St., N.W.
Tobin, Robert W. . . . . '27 '53 C&L.276 B.S.S., LL.B. 3015 Cambridge Pl., N.W.
Tobin, Timothy '69 '01 C.475 B.A. L.1209 J.D.
(adm. in VA; not adm. in DC) [🄰 Cole,R.&B.]
*PRACTICE AREAS: Cable TV; Telecommunications Law; Internet Law; Intellectual Property.

Tobin, O'Connor & Ewing, (AV)
A Partnership of Professional Corporations
5335 Wisconsin Avenue, N.W., Suite 700, 20015 ⊙
Telephone: 202-362-5900 Fax: 202-362-5901
URL: http://www.dstlaw.com
Members of Firm: David C. Tobin (P.C.); Stephen J. O'Connor (P.C.); Todd Ewing (P.C.). Associates: John M. Tran (Not admitted in DC; Resident, Alexandria, Virginia Office); David A. Conforti; Donna R. S. Peery; Catherine E. Schmitt; Anthony M. Black. Of Counsel: Kerry McLain Richard.
Litigation, Trial Practice, Criminal Defense, Tax, Business, Transactional Matters, Corporate, Exempt Securities, Environmental, Government Contracts, Computer, Estate Planning, Probate Law, Real Estate.
Alexandria, Virginia Office: 908 King Street, Suite 200. Telephone: 703-836-7071. Fax: 703-836-7099.
See Professional Biographies, WASHINGTON, DISTRICT OF COLUMBIA

Tockman, Albert, (AV) . . . . '27 '61 C.563 B.S. L.446 J.D. 1725 K St. (Pat.)
Todaro, Peter M. . . . . '70 '96 C&L.893 B.A., J.D. [🄰 King&S.]
*PRACTICE AREAS: Litigation; Trade Regulation.
Todd, David C., (AV) . . . . '36 '62 C.429 B.A. L.477 LL.B. [Patton B.]
Todd, Glenn D. '69 '96 L.117 J.D.
(adm. in OH; not adm. in DC) KPMG Peat Marwick
Todd, K. Chris . . . . '46 '72 C.845 B.A. L.846 J.D. [Kellogg,H.H.T.&E.]
*PRACTICE AREAS: Litigation.
Todd, Michael C. . . . . '65 '91 C.103 B.A. L.472 J.D. [🄲 Brobeck,P.&H.]
*PRACTICE AREAS: Corporate Law; Securities; Mergers and Acquisitions; Venture Capital; Finance.
Toensing, Brady C. . . . . '67 '96 C&L.276 A.B., J.D. [🄰 diGenova&T.]
Toensing, Victoria, (AV) . . . . '41 '75 C.347 B.S. L.215 J.D. [diGenova&T.]
Toffenetti, Judith L. . . . . . . '53 '94 C.66 B.A. L.273 J.D. [🄰 Kenyon&K.] (See Pat. Sect.)
*PRACTICE AREAS: Intellectual Property.
Tofigh, Navid J. . . . . '72 '97 C.770 B.S.C. L.802 J.D. [🄰 Morrison&F.]
*PRACTICE AREAS: Securities; Business Law; Investment Management.
Toikka, Richard S. '44 '88 C.309 A.B. L.276 J.D.
Assoc. Gen. Coun., Berman & Company
Toledo, Alison . . . . '69 '94 C.178 B.A. L.276 J.D. U.S. Sec. & Exchange Comm.
Toledo-Rivera, Félix '52 '86
C.677 B.A. L.276 J.D. Staff Atty., Ayuda Clinica Legal Latina
Tolford, John C. . . . . '32 '61 C.477 B.A. L.273 LL.B. 3900 Cathedral Ave., N.W.‡
Tolhurst-Lapp, Kimberly A. . . . . '70 '96 C.893 B.A. L.945 J.D. [🄰 Crowell&M.]
Toliver, Dwayne M. . . . . '58 '95 C.397 B.S. L.180 J.D. [🄰 Nixon P.]
*PRACTICE AREAS: Commercial Real Estate; Nonprofit and Charitable Organizations; Leases and Leasing.
Toliver, Karen Bland . . . . '67 '94 C.893 B.A. L.904 J.D. [🄲 Akin,G.S.H.&F.]
*PRACTICE AREAS: International Trade.
Toll, Joshua C. . . . . '71 '97 C.188 B.A. L.309 J.D. [🄰 Akin,G.S.H.&F.]
*PRACTICE AREAS: Litigation.
Toll, Martha A. . . . . '57 '83 C.976 B.A. L.94 J.D. 3930 Mckinley St. N.W.
Toll, Steven J., (AV) . . . . '50 '75 C.659 B.S. L.276 J.D. [Cohen,M.H.&T.]
*PRACTICE AREAS: Products Liability Class Actions; Securities Fraud Class Actions.
Tollefson, Brian A. '69 '98 C.886 B.S.E.E. L.446 J.D.
(adm. in MD; not adm. in DC) [🄰 Arent F.K.P.&K.]
*PRACTICE AREAS: Intellectual Property; Computer Law; Internet Law; Patents.
Tollett, Kenneth S., Sr. '31 '55 C&L.145 A.B., J.D.
(adm. in IL; not adm. in DC) Howard Univ.
Tollin, L. Andrew, (AV) . . . . '50 '76 C&L.273 B.A., J.D. [Wilkinson B.K.]
*PRACTICE AREAS: Communications; Telecommunications Law; Administrative Litigation; Appellate Practice.
Tolmachoff, Innokenty, Jr. '38 '81 C.1150 B.A. L.276 J.D.
1010 Rhode Island Ave., N.E.
Tom, Willard K. . . . . '52 '79 C&L.309 B.A., J.D. [Morgan,L.&B.]
Tomalty, Sarah E. . . . . '69 '94 C.197 B.A. L.128 J.D. NGC Corp. (⊙Hous., TX)
Tomar, Richard T., (AV) '45 '71
C.178 B.A. L.659 J.D. [Margolius,M.D.R.&T.] (⊙Largo, MD)
*PRACTICE AREAS: Litigation; Family Law.
Tomasek, Bryan J., (AV) . . . . '50 '76 C.339 B.A. L.276 J.D. [Arnold&P.]
*PRACTICE AREAS: Taxation; Partnership Law; Joint Ventures; Limited Liability Company Law; Real Estate Investment Trusts.
Tomaselli, Michael V. . . . . '47 '74 C.708 B.A. L.818 J.D. Asst. U.S. Atty.
Tomasevich, Jeffery A. . . . . '63 '89 C.188 B.S. L.569 J.D. [Holland&K.]
*PRACTICE AREAS: Litigation; Administrative Law; Administrative Litigation; Airport Law.
Tomaszczuk, Carol M. . . . . '58 '85 C.840 B.A. L.502 J.D. [🄰 Kirkpatrick&L.]
*PRACTICE AREAS: Mortgage Banking Law; Real Estate; Consumer Law; Banks and Banking; Commercial Real Estate.
Tomenga, Michael K., (AV) . . . . '53 '78 C.732 B.A. L.128 J.D. [🄲 Neville,P.]
*PRACTICE AREAS: Customs Law; International Trade Law.
Tomilson, Robert W. . . . . '— '01 C.550 B.A. L.910 J.D. [🄰 Bryan C.]
Tompa, Peter K., (AV) . . . . '60 '87 C.276 B.S.F.S. L.30 J.D. [McDermott,W.&E.]
Tompert, James E. . . . . '54 '81 C.228 B.A. L.477 J.D. [Cooter,M.T.&W.]
Tompkins, Benjamin L. '74 '00 C.990 B.A. L.273 J.D.
(adm. in MO; not adm. in DC) [🄰 Jorden B.]
*PRACTICE AREAS: Litigation.
Tompkins, Charles E. . . . . '70 '98 C.165 B.A. L.893 J.D. [🄰 Cohen,M.H.&T.]
*PRACTICE AREAS: Civil Litigation; Antitrust.
Tompkins, Joseph B., Jr., (AV) . . . . '50 '75 C.902 B.A. L.309 J.D. [Sidley A.B.&W.]
Tompkins, Robert K. . . . . '68 '94 C&L.902 B.A., J.D. [🄰 Patton B.]
Toomey, A. Katherine . . . . '65 '91 C.910 A.B. L.976 J.D. [Baach R.&L.P.]
*PRACTICE AREAS: Commercial Litigation; RICO Litigation; International Insolvency; Financial Fraud.
Toomey, Daniel E., (AV) . . . . '— '68 C.749 B.A. L.276 J.D. [Thompson H.]
*PRACTICE AREAS: Construction; Surety; Competition; Government Contracts; Commercial Litigation.
Topazian, Jonathan R. . . . . '61 '91 C.829 B.A. L.30 J.D. [Semmes,B.&S.]
*PRACTICE AREAS: Employment Law; Complex Litigation; Labor.
Topel, Howard A., (AV) . . . . '48 '73 C&L.659 B.A., J.D. [Leventhal,S.&L.]
Topelius, Kathleen E., (AV) . . . . '— '78 C.184 B.A. L.128 J.D. [Bryan C.]
*PRACTICE AREAS: Banking; International Banking; Financial Institutions; Mergers and Acquisitions; Administrative Law.
Topetzes, Stephen G. . . . . '— '88 C.494 B.A. L.276 J.D. [Kirkpatrick&L.]
*PRACTICE AREAS: Civil Litigation; SEC Enforcement; Trial Practice; Securities Arbitration; Securities Class Actions.
Topmiller, Joseph E. '74 '99 C.201 B.S. L.228 J.D.
(adm. in VA; not adm. in DC) [🄰 Covington&B.]
Topol, Allan J., (AV) . . . . '41 '66 C.119 B.S. L.976 LL.B. [Covington&B.] (See Pat. Sect.)
Toppelberg, Alan S., & Associates, (CV) '45 '75
C.871 B.S. L.229 J.D. 1444 N Street, N.W. (Pat.)
Topping, Gloria W. . . . . '63 '88 C.228 A.B. L.800 J.D. 50 F St., N.W.
Topping, John C., Jr., (AV) . . . . '43 '67 C.197 A.B. L.976 J.D. Climate Institute
Topping, Mara E. R. . . . . '59 '99 C.188 B.A. L.276 J.D. [🄰 White&C.]
Topps, Andrew, IV '71 '97 C.893 B.A. L.276 J.D.
(adm. in MD; not adm. in DC) [🄰 Swidler B.S.F.]
*PRACTICE AREAS: Antitrust.
Topps, Margaret M. '51 '77 C.386 B.A. L.260 J.D.
Dep. Gen. Coun., UMWA Health & Retirement Funds
Torborg, David S. '72 '98 C.473 B.S. L.608 J.D.
(adm. in OH; not adm. in DC) [🄰 Jones,D.R.&P.]

Torchin, Norman G. .... '29 '61 C&L.273 B.S., LL.B. [🄲 Keil&W.] (See Pat. Sect.)
*PRACTICE AREAS: Patents; Trademark Law.
Torgerson, William T. '44 '73 C.674 A.B. L.446 J.D.
Senior Vice President and General Counsel, Potomac Electric Power Company
Torgovitsky, Stanislav ...... '67 '96 C&L.273 B.A., J.D. [🄰 Sughrue M.] (See Pat. Sect.)
*PRACTICE AREAS: Intellectual Property.
Tormey, John R. R. .... '68 '96 C.1239 B.A. L.273 J.D. [🄰 Chadbourne&P.]
Tornatore, Tonia June '68 '98 C.1369 B.B.A. L.229 J.D.
(adm. in PA; not adm. in DC) 1100 "L" St., N.W.
Toro, Emin '74 '01 C.999 B.A. L.575 J.D.
(adm. in NY; not adm. in DC) [🄰 Covington&B.]
Torrente, Josephine M. .... '66 '97 C.930 B.S. L.831 J.D. [🄰 Hyman,P.&M.]
*PRACTICE AREAS: Food and Drug Law.
Torres, Blanca E. ... '47 '92 C.905 B.A. L.276 J.D. Admin. Law J., Off. of Employee App.
Torres, Jasmin Marie ....'— '00 C.1373 B.A. L.1364 5100 Connecticut Ave.
Torres, Luis F. .... '72 '98 C.276 B.S.F.S. L.273 J.D. [🄰 Chadbourne&P.]
Torres, Susan Yoder .... '62 '90 C.893 B.A. L.1209 J.D. [🄰 Sanders,S.&B.]
*PRACTICE AREAS: Business Law; Corporate Law; Estate Planning; Fiduciary Law; Probate Law.
Torres-Ramos, Antonia .... '60 '88 C.788 B.A. L.93 J.D. Off. of the Corp. Coun.
Torresan Wilson, Luiza '71 '96 L.999 LL.B.
(adm. in NY; not adm. in DC) [🄰 Cameron&H.] ⊙
*PRACTICE AREAS: Project Finance; Litigation; International Trade.
Torresen, Robert, Jr. .... '57 '83 C.323 B.A. L.273 J.D. [Powell,G.F.&M.]
*PRACTICE AREAS: International Trade; Customs Law; Export Control Law.
Torretti Gekas, Maria Pia '59 '95 C.914 B.A. L.276 J.D.
(adm. in VA; not adm. in DC) [Krukowski&C.]
*PRACTICE AREAS: Labor and Employment Law; Transportation; Drug Testing; Immigration.
Torrez, P. Andrew '73 '97 C.273 B.A. L.309 J.D.
(adm. in MD; not adm. in DC) [🄰 Covington&B.]
Tosini, Stephen C. .... '— '00 C.446 B.S. L.472 J.D. [🄰 Wiley R.&F.]
Tostrud, Jon Anders '69 '94 C.747 B.A. L.1035 J.D.
(adm. in MN; not adm. in DC) [🄲 Cuneo]
*PRACTICE AREAS: Civil Rights; Class Actions; Wage and Hour Law; Antitrust Class Actions; Securities Class Actions.
Totaro, John Burt, Jr. .... '68 '94 C.385 A.B. L.999 J.D. [🄰 Harris E.&L.]
*PRACTICE AREAS: International Trade Regulation; Customs Law.
Toth, Richard J. .... '46 '74 C.611 B.A. L.30 J.D. 4821 43rd St., N.W.
Totten, Cynthia J. '72 '98 C.914 B.A. L.309 J.D.
(adm. in CA; not adm. in DC) [🄰 Sprenger&L.]
*PRACTICE AREAS: Employment Law; Civil Rights; Complex Federal Litigation.

Toulouse, Paul M., (BV) '49 '75 C.1030 A.B. L.276 J.D.
503 D Street, N.W., 20001
Telephone: 202-347-4020 Telecopier: 202-347-1942
Email: PMToulouse@aol.com URL: http://www.lawyers.com/toulouselaw
***PRACTICE AREAS: Personal Injury; Professional Malpractice; Probate; Family Law; Real Estate.**
Civil Litigation with Special Emphasis in the Areas of Personal Injury including Professional Negligence, Medical Malpractice, Vehicular Liability, General Personal Injury Claims and Worker's Compensation, District of Columbia Consumer Protection Procedures Act Law, Probate Litigation, Real Estate Litigation, Bankruptcy Litigation, Divorce and Separation, Estate Planning and Administration.
See Professional Biographies, WASHINGTON, DISTRICT OF COLUMBIA

Tourish, Thomas J., Jr., (AV) .... '48 '75 C.884 B,A. L.276 J.D. Dep. Chf., U.S. Atty. Off.
Tourtellotte, James R., (AV) ....'35 '59 C.612 B.A. L.623 J.D. 2100 Pennsylvania Ave.
Tower, Eric S. ....'— '93 C.597 B.A. L.966 J.D. 701 Pennsylvania Avenue, N.W.

Towey, David P., (AV) '49 '75 C.415 B.A. L.309 J.D.
1914 Sunderland Place, N.W., 20036
Telephone: 202-452-9886 Facsimile: 202-452-9896
Email: dpt@sprynet.com URL: http://www.lawyers.com/davidtowey
White Collar Criminal Defense and Civil Litigation with emphasis on Federal Criminal Law, Grand Jury Practice, Corporate Investigations, Trial Practice, Criminal Appeals, Government Contract Fraud, Criminal Antitrust, RICO, Federal Civil Litigation, Securities Fraud, Governments Contracts, False Claims Act, Qui Tam Litigation, Civil Fraud, Libel, Slander and Defamation and Gaming Law.
See Professional Biographies, WASHINGTON, DISTRICT OF COLUMBIA

Towey, Jamie R. '— '99 C.659 B.A. L.276 J.D.
(adm. in VA; not adm. in DC) [🄰 Skadden,A.S.M.&F.]
*PRACTICE AREAS: Antitrust.
Townes, Jeffrey N. .... '— '00 C.105 B.S. L.1209 J.D. [🄰 Morgan,L.&B.] (Pat.)
Townsend, Donald E. ....'34 '64 C.502 B.S.C.E. L.273 J.D. [Townsend&B.] (Pat.)
Townsend, John M., (AV) ....'47 '72 C&L.976 B.A., J.D. [Hughes H.&R.]
*PRACTICE AREAS: Litigation; Antitrust; Arbitration.
Townsend, Rachel H. '69 '00
C.860 B.S. L.276 J.D. [🄰 Finnegan,H.F.G.&D.] (See Pat. Sect.)
Townsend & Banta ....1225 Eye St., N.W. (Pat.)
Toy, Charles D. '55 '81 C&L.309 B.A., J.D.
(adm. in NY; not adm. in DC) [Wilmer,C.&P.]
*PRACTICE AREAS: Business Transactions; Corporate Finance; Project Finance.
Tracey, Peter L., (BV) ....'60 '89 C.976 B.A. L.1017 J.D. [Howrey S.A.&W.]
*PRACTICE AREAS: Insurance Coverage Litigation; Commercial Litigation.
Trachtenberg, Stephen J. '37 '64 C.178 B.A. L.976 LL.B.
(adm. in NY; not adm. in DC) Pres. & Prof., The George Washington Univ.
Tracy, Thomas M. '70 '96 C.1350 B.A. L.477 J.D.
(adm. in NY; not adm. in DC) [🄰 Sutherland A.&B.]
*PRACTICE AREAS: Real Estate; Litigation.
Trafford, Christine S. '72 '98 C.1365 B.S. L.128 J.D.
(adm. in VA; not adm. in DC) [🄰 Miller&C.]
*PRACTICE AREAS: Government Contracts.
Trafford, Sherry .... '68 '96 C.347 B.A. L.976 J.D. 1101 15th St., N.W.
Trager, Michael D., (AV) ....'59 '85 C.918 B.A. L.94 J.D. [Fulbright&J.]
*PRACTICE AREAS: Securities Regulation; Securities Litigation; Corporate Law.
Trainer, Corina M. '56 '90 C.161 B.A. L.273 J.D.
Asst. Gen. Coun., UMWA Health & Retirement Funds
Trainer, Laurie Jo ....'56 '82 C.276 B.A. L.893 J.D. 1200 New Hampshire Ave., N.W.
Trainer, Ryan, (AV) ....'56 '81 C.174 B.A. L.273 J.D. [Clifford C.R.&W.]
*PRACTICE AREAS: International Trade Regulation and Policy.
Trainer, Timothy P. '53 '87
C.381 B.A. L.161 J.D. Pres., Intl. AntiCounterfeiting Coalition, Inc.
Trainor, Daniel Sean ..... '72 '98 C.475 B.S.M.E. L.273 J.D. [🄰 McDermott,W.&E.] (Pat.)
Trainor, Larisa Avner ....'70 '98 C.1044 B.S. L.273 J.D. [🄰 Fried,F.H.S.&J.]
*PRACTICE AREAS: Corporate Law; Securities.
Trainum, Charles A., Jr. ....'41 '66 C.886 B.S. L.893 LL.B. [Trainum,S.&D.]
*PRACTICE AREAS: Real Estate; Corporate Laws; Alcoholic Beverages; Trusts and Estates.

Trainum, Snowdon & Deane, P.C., (AV)
1317 F Street, NW, Suite 350, 20004
Telephone: 202-783-5488 Facsimile: 202-783-5502
URL: http://www.lawyers.com/trainumsnowdon&deane
John Russell Deane III; Richard W. Snowdon III; Charles A. Trainum, Jr. Of Counsel: Thomas A. Frazier, Jr.; Ronald D. Larson; Rayburn Hanzlik.

(This Listing Continued)

Trainum, Snowdon & Deane, P.C. (Continued)
General Practice before all U.S. Courts, Departments and Agencies, Real Estate, Taxation, Corporate Law, Legislative Practice, Estate Planning, Litigation, Environmental and Energy Law.
See Professional Biographies, WASHINGTON, DISTRICT OF COLUMBIA
Trambley, C. Anthony .... '— '95 C.112 B.A. L.1194 J.D. [🄰 Foley&L.]
*PRACTICE AREAS: Litigation.
Tramhel, Jeannette M. '58 '95 C.02 B.Sc. L.019 LL.B.
(adm. in NY; not adm. in DC) Organization of Amer. States
Tran, Annie .... '72 '00 C.93 B.A. L.128 J.D. [🄰 Jones,D.R.&P.]
Tran, Hoanh Dinh '52 '84 L.436 J.D.
(adm. in WI; not adm. in DC) MCI Communications Corporation
Trangsrud, Roger H. '50 '75 C.118 B.A. L.145 J.D.
Prof. & Assoc. Dean, George Washington Univ. Law Sch.
Trapasso, Joseph S. ....'65 '91 C.183 B.A. L.659 J.D. [Patton B.]
Traphagen, Mark .... '59 '85 C.201 B.A. L.208 J.D. [Powell,G.F.&M.]
*PRACTICE AREAS: Intellectual Property; Copyright; Trademark; Electronic Commerce; New Media.
Trask, Andrew J. ....'71 '98 C&L.145 B.A., J.D. [🄰 O'Melveny&M.]
Trattles, Gloria Martinez ....'67 '94 C.178 B.A. L.569 J.D. [🄰 Crowell&M.]
Trattner, Stephen M., (AV) ....'45 '71 C.347 B.S. L.1119 J.D. [🄲 Lewis&K.]
Trauben, Bruce K. .... '54 '92 C.381 B.S. [🄰 Dorsey&W.] (Pat.)
*PRACTICE AREAS: Technology and Science; Environmental; Insurance Coverage; Litigation.
Trauger, Thomas C. ....'51 '77 C.910 B.S.E.E. L.309 J.D. [Spiegel&M.]
*PRACTICE AREAS: Energy; Alternative Dispute Resolution; Litigation; Antitrust; Agricultural Law.
Travers, Naomi S. '66 '93 C.329 B.A. L.446 J.D.
Asst. Gen. Coun., Black Entertainment Television, Inc.
*RESPONSIBILITIES: Corporate Law; Publishing; Internet; Intellectual Property.
Travieso-Diaz, Matias F., (P.C.), (AV) ....'43 '76 C.472 B.S. L.178 J.D. [Shaw P.]
*PRACTICE AREAS: Energy; Litigation; International; Cuba.
Travis, Edmunds, Jr., (AV) '26 '51 C&L.846 B.A., J.D.
(adm. in TX; not adm. in DC) Suite 750, 1310 G Street, N.W.
Travis, Thomas G. '47 '72 C.674 A.B. L.178 J.D.
[Sandler,T.&R.] (⊙L.A., San Fran., CA; Miami, FL; Chgo., IL; New York, NY; Hous., TX)
*PRACTICE AREAS: Customs Law; International Trade Law.
Traylor, Patrick D. .... '69 '94 C.839 B.A. L.796 J.D. [🄰 Hogan&H.]
*PRACTICE AREAS: Environmental.
Treacy, Vincent E. .... '42 '72 C.93 A.B. L.273 J.D. 5143 Yuma St. N.W.
Treanor, Gerard, (AV) ....'43 '69 C.321 A.B. L.128 J.D. [Venable,A.B.H.&C.]
*PRACTICE AREAS: Criminal Litigation; Commercial Litigation; Appeals.
Treanor, Richard B. .... '31 '56 C.321 A.B. L.309 J.D. 613 4th Pl. S.W.
Treanor, Timothy Charles '51 '77 C.602 B.A. L.107 J.D.
(adm. in NY; not adm. in DC) U.S. Small Bus. Admin.
Trebach, Barry D., (AV) '54 '81
C.881 B.A. L.1162 J.D. [Bonner K.T.&C.] (⊙Rockville, MD)
*PRACTICE AREAS: Alternative Dispute Resolution; Medical Malpractice; Personal Injury; Product Liability; Torts.
Trebilcock, Christopher M. '74 '01 C.27 B.A. L.896 J.D.
(adm. in MI; not adm. in DC) Off. of Admin. Law J., Assoc. Chief J. Thomas Burke
Tredick, Peter W., (AV) ......'40 '65 C.674 B.A. L.309 J.D. [🄲 Hogan&H.] (⊙L.A., CA)
*PRACTICE AREAS: Equal Employment Opportunity Law; Management Labor Law; Employment Litigation.
Treene, Eric W. ..... '65 '93 C.31 B.A. L.309 J.D. The Becket Fund for Religious Liberty
Trees, Linda C. ....'62 '92 C.788 A.B. L.945 J.D. [🄰 Hunton&W.]
Tremaine, Degas G. '63 '92 C.569 B.A. L.276 J.D.
(adm. in PA; not adm. in DC) 1014 E. Capitol St. SE
Tremols, Joaquin A. .... '58 '95 C.205 B.A. L.273 J.D. USDA Rural Housing Serv.
Trendl, Thomas J. .... '63 '88 C.340 B.A. L.801 J.D. [🄲 Steptoe&J.]
*PRACTICE AREAS: International Trade Law; Import and Export Law; Customs Law.
Trenga, Anthony J., (AV) ....'49 '74 C.674 A.B. L.893 J.D. [Miller&C.]
*PRACTICE AREAS: Complex Commercial Litigation; Trial Practice; Professional Liability; Securities Litigation.
Trenor, John A. .... '69 '96 C.188 B.A. L.674 J.D. [🄰 Wilmer,C.&P.]

Trevelline, Michael J. '61 '87 C.801 B.A. L.420 J.D.
601 Pennsylvania Avenue, N.W. Suite 900 South, 20004-2601
Telephone: 202-737-1139 Outside D.C. Metropolitan Area: 1-800-587-1700 Fax: 202-783-3423
Email: MJTrevelline@cs.com
***PRACTICE AREAS: Small Business; General Practice; Securities Arbitration; Political Asylum; Trade Regulation.**
Business Law and Commercial Litigation with special emphasis in the areas of Small Business Formation and Venture Capital, Investor Responsibility, International Trade, Securities Arbitration, Political Asylum.
See Professional Biographies, WASHINGTON, DISTRICT OF COLUMBIA

Trew, Heather M. .... '— '01 C.813 B.A. L.477 J.D. [🄰 Foley&L.]
*PRACTICE AREAS: Litigation.
Tribulski, Jennifer H. '— '93 C.156 B.A. L.1252 J.D.
(adm. in CT; not adm. in DC) [🄰 Verner,L.B.M.&H.]
*PRACTICE AREAS: Energy; Environmental.
Trice, Ronald David .... '67 '01 C.475 B.S.E.E. L.1218 J.D. [🄰 Baker&M.] (Pat.)
*PRACTICE AREAS: Intellectual Property Law; Litigation.
Trice Beil, Sheila '49 '74 C.914 B.A. L.309 J.D.
(adm. in MA; not adm. in DC) [🄲 Coates,D.&G.]
*PRACTICE AREAS: Education Law; General.
Trier, Dana L., (AV) .... '48 '75 C.347 A.B. L.477 J.D. [Davis P.&W.]
*PRACTICE AREAS: Tax Law.
Trigg, S. Jenell .... '57 '97 C.598 B.S. L.128 J.D. [🄲 Leventhal,S.&L.]
Trilling, Helen R., (AV) .... '50 '77 C.681 A.B. L.309 J.D. [Hogan&H.]
*PRACTICE AREAS: Health Law; Health Care Compliance; Health Care Regulation; Health Care Reimbursement; Medicare and Medicaid Reimbursement.
Trilling, James A. .... '72 '99 C.347 B.A. L.309 J.D. [🄰 Jenner&B.]
*PRACTICE AREAS: Civil Litigation.
Trimber, Richard F. '69 '98 C.1356 B.A. L.128 J.D
(adm. in MD; not adm. in DC) [🄰 Shaw P.]
*PRACTICE AREAS: Asset Securitization; Private Placements; Corporate; Mergers and Acquisitions.
Trimble, Sandra E. ....'52 '89 C.172 B.A. L.276 J.D. [🄲 Orrick,H.&S.]
*PRACTICE AREAS: Corporate; Structured Finance.
Trimble, Stephen A., (AV) ....'33 '61 C.575 A.B. L.276 LL.B. [🄲 Hamilton&H.]
*PRACTICE AREAS: Appellate Practice; Civil Litigation; Personal Injury.
Trimble, Thomas B. ....'59 '88 C.105 B.A. L.904 J.D. [Akin,G.S.H.&F.]
Trimboli, Thomas A. .... '47 '74 C.724 B.S. L.276 J.D. Dep. Gen. Coun., Howard Univ.
Trimmer, Joy L. '70 '95 C.346 B.S. L.1119 J.D.
(adm. in IN; not adm. in DC) Amer. Medical Assn.
Trinder, Rachel B., (AV) ....'55 '79 C.051 L.893 LL.M. [Zuckert,S.&R.]
*PRACTICE AREAS: Aviation Law; Airport Regulation; Employment Claims; Aerospace Law; Commercial Litigation.
Trinh, Suzanne Miller '69 '98 C.518 B.A. L.276 J.D.
(adm. in VA; not adm. in DC) [🄰 Shearman&S.]
Triplett, Charles S. .... '48 '75 C.698 B.S. L.502 J.D. [Mayer,B.&P.]
*PRACTICE AREAS: International Taxation; Tax Controversies.
Trister, Michael B., (AV) ....'41 '68 C.674 A.B. L.976 LL.B. [Lichtman,T.S.&R.]

Tritt, Cheryl A., (AV) .... '47 '76 C.546 B.S. L.597 J.D. [Morrison&F.]
*PRACTICE AREAS: Telecommunications; Multimedia and Information Technology.
Trocchio, Michael R. '71 '98 C.276 B.A. L.724 J.D.
(adm. in NY; not adm. in DC) [Ⓐ Orrick,H.&S.]
Troiano, Brian L., (AV) .... '48 '73 C.610 B.B.A. L.838 J.D. [Rea,C.&A.]
*PRACTICE AREAS: Administrative Law; Interstate Commerce; Transportation; Freight Loss and Damage; Government Contracts.
Troike, Robert L. .... '36 '64 C.1027 B.S. L.1002 LL.B. [Ⓒ Baker B.] (See Pat. Sect.)
Troilo, Louis M. .... '67 '98 C.645 B.S. L.128 J.D. [Ⓐ Finnegan,H.F.G.&D.]
*PRACTICE AREAS: Chemical Patents; Medical Patents; Metallurgical Patents; Patent Litigation; Patent Prosecution.
Tromble, Katherine R. .... '72 '99 C.276 B.A. L.880 J.D. [Ⓐ Williams&C.]
Trombly, Kenneth M., (AV) ....'49 '73 C.273 A.B. L.128 J.D. [Schultz&T.]
Troncone, Frederick R. ....'57 '82 C.645 B.A. L.851 J.D. [Troncone&Assoc.]
*PRACTICE AREAS: Business Immigration; Consular Law; Visas; Investor Visas; Family Immigration Law.

Troncone & Associates, Law Offices of
666 Eleventh Street, NW, Suite 315, 20001
Telephone: 202-232-5100 Telecopier: 202-232-6140 URL: http://www.us-visas.net
Email: frtusa@starpower.net URL: http://www.lawyers.com/usvisalaw
Frederick R. Troncone.
Business Immigration, Investment-Based Visas, Consular Law, and Visas.
See Professional Biographies, WASHINGTON, DISTRICT OF COLUMBIA

Tronnes, Robert D. '75 '00 C.112 B.A. L.273 J.D.
(adm. in CA; not adm. in DC) [Ⓐ Skadden,A.S.M.&F.]
*PRACTICE AREAS: Litigation.
Troobnick, Mark Nathan ....'— '88 C.1044 B.S. L.446 J.D. [American L.&J.]
Trooboff, Peter D., (AV) ....'42 '68 C.178 A.B. L.309 LL.B. [Covington&B.]
Trosten, Leonard M., (AV) .....'32 '55 C&L.178 A.B., J.D. 1875 Connecticut Ave., N.W.
Trotter, Antilla E., III .... '61 '01 C.329 B.A. L.128 J.D. [Ⓐ Sher&B.]
*PRACTICE AREAS: Telecommunications Law; Government Relations; Health Care; Animal Welfare; Transportation.
Trotter, Daphne ....'62 '91 C.276 A.B. L.904 J.D. [McDermott,W.&E.]
Trotter, Jack T. ....'26 '52 C.846 B.A. L.326 1100 Connecticut Ave., N.W.
Trotter, Joel H. .... '71 '95 C&L.893 B.A., J.D. [Ⓐ Latham&W.]
*PRACTICE AREAS: Corporate Law.
Trotter, Julia Anne '57 '83 C.820 B.A. L.945 J.D.
General Counsel, Vietnam Veterans of America Foundation
Trotter, Kenneth B. .... '66 '93 C.1335 B.A. L.880 J.D. [Ⓐ Dickstein S.M.&O.]
*PRACTICE AREAS: Civil Litigation; Insurance Coverage.
Troup, James U. .... '58 '85 C.276 B.S. L.893 J.D. [McGuirewoods]
*PRACTICE AREAS: Telecommunications; Media.
Trout, Robert P., (AV) ....'48 '73 C.902 B.A. L.893 J.D. [Trout&R.] ⊙
*PRACTICE AREAS: Commercial Litigation; White Collar Criminal Defense and Enforcement.

Trout & Richards, P.L.L.C., (AV) BB
1100 Connecticut Avenue, N.W., Suite 730, 20036 ⊙
Telephone: 202-463-1920 Fax: 202-463-1925
Email: trlaw@troutrichards.com URL: http://www.troutrichards.com
Robert P. Trout; John Thorpe Richards, Jr.; Amy Berman Jackson;—Patricia E. Connelly.
Trial and appellate practice, with particular emphasis on complex commercial litigation, white collar criminal defense and the defense of agency enforcement actions.
Alexandria, Virginia Office: 301 North Pitt Street, 22314. Telephone: 703-519-8840.
See Professional Biographies, WASHINGTON, DISTRICT OF COLUMBIA

Troutman Sanders LLP, (AV)
A Partnership including Professional Corporations
401 Ninth Street, N.W., Suite 1000, 20004-2134 ⊙
Telephone: 202-274-2950 Fax: 202-274-2994
URL: http://www.troutmansanders.com
Members of Firm: C. Jonathan Benner; Todd R. Coles; M. Lisanne Crowley; Kevin C. Fitzgerald; Benjamin Lee Israel; Thomas C. Jensen; John R. Molm; William A. Mullins; Stuart F. Pierson; Ronald R. Ross; Donald F. Santa, Jr.; Clifford S. Sikora (Not admitted in DC); Roger D. Williams. Associates: Elizabeth Anne Bell (Not admitted in DC); Sandra L. Brown; Virginia A. Brunelli (Not admitted in DC); Antoine P. Cobb; Amie V. Colby; William R. Derasmo (Not admitted in DC); Ilana R. Fisher; Jeffrey M. Jakubiak; Daniel M. Malabonga; William P. Marsan; Eileen M. Moorhead; Melissa L. Pignatelli; David C. Reeves; R. Michael Sweeney (Not admitted in DC; Resident); Dionne Thompson (Not admitted in DC); Sif Thorgeirsson; Charles A. Zdebski. Of Counsel: James C. Beh (Resident); Sean T. Connaughton; Robert G. Dreher; Mary Clare Fitzgerald; Leonard L. Fleisig; Thomas J. Healey, Jr. (Not admitted in DC); Michael L. Kessler; Sotiris A. (Ted) Planzos; Bonnie A. Suchman.
Communications, Corporate, Energy, Environment, Federal Regulatory, Intellectual Property, Legislation, Litigation, Transportation.
Atlanta, Georgia Office: Bank of America Plaza, 600 Peachtree Street, N.W., Suite 5200. Telephone: 404-885-3000. Facsimile: 404-885-3900.
Other Atlanta Offices at: 999 Peachtree Street, Suite 750, 30309. Telephone: 404-885-3651, Facsimile: 404-885-3652.
Hong Kong Office: Suite 3503A Two Exchange Square, 8 Connaught Place, Central, Hong Kong. Telephone: 852-2533-7888. Facsimile: 852-2533-7898.
London, England Office: 10th Floor, Dashwood House, 69 Old Broad Street, EC2N1QS. Phone: (207) 065-2600. Fax: (207) 065-2777.
Richmond, Virginia Office: Troutman Sanders Mays & Valentine, 1111 East Main Street, P.O. Box 1122, 23218-1122. Telephone: 804-697-1200. Facsimile: 804-697-1339.
West End Office: Troutman Sanders Mays & Valentine, 500 Libbie Avenue, Suite 2A, Richmond, 23226. Telephone: 804-697-1200. Facsimile: 804-288-8366.
Norfolk, Virginia Office: Troutman Sanders Mays & Valentine, 999 Waterside Drive, P.O. Box 3670, 23514-3670. Telephone: 757-687-7700. Facsimile: 757-687-7701.
Tysons Corner, Virginia Office: Troutman Sanders Mays & Valentine, 1660 International Drive, Suite 600, McLean, 22102. Telephone: 703-734-4334. Facsimile: 703-734-4340.
Virginia Beach, Virginia Office: Troutman Sanders Mays & Valentine, 4425 Corporation Lane, Suite 420, P.O. Box 61185, 23466-1185. Telephone: 757-687-7500. Facsimile: 757-687-7510.
See Professional Biographies, WASHINGTON, DISTRICT OF COLUMBIA

Trovato, Lisa R. ....'71 '97 C.188 B.S. L.477 J.D. [Ⓐ Piper M.R.&W.]
*PRACTICE AREAS: Intellectual Property.
Trow, Stephen C., (AV) .... '51 '78 C.1164 B.A. L.188 J.D. [Trow&K.]
*PRACTICE AREAS: Immigration and Nationality Law.

Trow & Kearney, P.C., (AV)
Suite 440 5335 Wisconsin Avenue, N.W., 20015-2003
Telephone: 202-537-4830 Fax: 202-537-4831
Email: mailbox@tk-law.com
Stephen C. Trow; Mary M. Kearney; Linda A. Rahal;—Cynthia B. Hemphill; Joan J. Karaganis; Norma Briscoe Hoffpauir. Of Counsel: Donald L. Mooers.
Immigration and Nationality Law.
See Professional Biographies, WASHINGTON, DISTRICT OF COLUMBIA

Troy, Megan H. '71 '97 C.112 B.A. L.276 J.D.
(adm. in CA; not adm. in DC) [Ⓐ Preston G.E.&R.M.]
*PRACTICE AREAS: Telecommunications Law; Federal Policy.
Troy, Michael Alexander '71 '97 C.93 B.A. L.904 J.D.
(adm. in MD; not adm. in DC) [Ⓐ Jenkens&G.]
*PRACTICE AREAS: Securities; Corporate; Financial Institutions.
Troyer, Thomas A., (AV) .... '33 '58 C.309 A.B. L.477 J.D. [Caplin&D.]
*PRACTICE AREAS: Federal Tax Practice; Tax Exempt Organizations; Charitable Foundations; Public Charities; Charitable Giving.

Trpis, Martin .... '57 '87 C.446 B.A. L.893 J.D. [Ashcraft&G.]
*PRACTICE AREAS: Medical Malpractice; Personal Injury.
Trubatch, Sheldon L. ....'— '78 C.667 B.S. L.178 J.D. [Foley&L.]
*PRACTICE AREAS: Nuclear Law; Administrative Law.
Truhe, Joseph V., Jr., (AV) ......'53 '77 C.976 B.A. L.893 J.D. 111 Michigan Ave., N.W.
Truitt, Stephen M., (AV) .... '39 '66 C.309 A.B. L.976 LL.B. [Pepper H.]
*PRACTICE AREAS: Litigation.
Trujillo, Bernard Roberts '66 '93 C.674 A.B. L.976 J.D.
(adm. in PA; not adm. in DC) 2445 M St., N.W.‡
Trujillo, Lynn Ann '72 '01 C.197 B.A. L.560 J.D.
(adm. in NM; not adm. in DC) [Ⓐ Steptoe&J.]
Trulove, Jodi .... '71 '96 C&L.276 B.S.B.A., J.D. [Ⓐ Dickstein S.M.&O.]
*PRACTICE AREAS: White Collar Criminal Defense; Civil Litigation.
Trumka, Richard L. '49 '74 C.645 B.S. L.884 J.D.
Intl. Pres., United Mine Wkrs. of Amer.
Truong, John C. ....'— '99 C.800 B.A. L.30 J.D. [Ⓐ Morgan,L.&B.]
Truong, To-Quyen ....'65 '89 C&L.976 B.A., J.D. [Ⓒ Dow,L.&A.]
Truslow, Frederic J., (AV) ....'39 '64 C.976 B.A. L.309 LL.B. 1627 I St., N.W.
Tsacoumis, Stephanie .... '56 '81 C.945 B.A. L.893 J.D. [Gibson,D.&C.]
*PRACTICE AREAS: Securities; Corporations; Mergers, Acquisitions and Divestitures; Venture Capital; Financial Services Law.
Tsaganos, Vasiliki B. ....'65 '90 C.30 B.A. L.597 J.D. [Fried,F.H.S.&J.]
*PRACTICE AREAS: Corporate; Securities.
Tsai, Caroline ....'69 '00 C.477 B.A. L.904 J.D. [Ⓐ Jones,D.R.&P.]
Tsai, Winston Wen-Hsiung ....'34 '71 C.999 B.A. L.128 J.D. 5032 River Rd.
Tsao, Leo R. .... '70 '99 C.705 B.A. L.188 J.D. [Ⓐ Kellogg,H.H.T.&E.]
*PRACTICE AREAS: Telecommunications; Litigation.
Tschirhart, Paul M. ....'40 '68 C.602 B.S. L.912 J.D. [Sher&B.]
*PRACTICE AREAS: Administrative Law; Aviation Law; Corporate Law; Commercial Law; Litigation.
Tseng, Elaine H. ....'71 '96 C.188 L.309 J.D. [Ⓐ King&S.]
Tsien, Arthur Y., (AV) .... '49 '78 C.860 B.S. L.911 J.D. [Olsson,F.&W.]
*PRACTICE AREAS: Food and Drug Law; Litigation.
Tsilas, Vicky ....'68 '93 C.104 B.A. L.262 J.D. [Ⓐ Ballard S.A.&I.]
*PRACTICE AREAS: Taxation; Federal Income Tax.
Tsirigotis, Petros L. .... '68 '98 C.94 B.A. L.180 J.D. [Ⓐ Dechert]
*PRACTICE AREAS: Securities Regulation; Financial Services Law; Investment Management.
Tsiros, Alexandra A. '72 '98 C.608 B.A. L.228 J.D.
(adm. in MD; not adm. in DC) 200 Constitution Ave.
Tsoudis, Nicholas '70 '97 C.569 B.S. L.861 J.D.
(adm. in NY; not adm. in DC) [Ⓐ Arent F.K.P.&K.]
Tsui, Susan '— '86 C.30 B.A. L.276 J.D.
Exec. Coun., National Air Traffic Controllers Assn. (AFL-CIO)
Tu-Sekine, Anthony '61 '97 C.1109 B.A. L.309 J.D.
(adm. in MA; not adm. in DC) [Ⓐ Goodwin P.]
Tucci, Michael E. .... '57 '85 C&L.838 B.A., J.D. [Morrison&H.]
*PRACTICE AREAS: Mortgage and Commercial Banking Law and Litigation; Complex Commercial Litigation; Professional Liability; Federal Regulation.
Tuck, Chanda '69 '95 C.329 B.B.A. L.588 J.D.
(adm. in MA; not adm. in DC) Coun., Rep. Edolphus Towns, U.S. House of Rep.
Tucker, Darren S. .... '72 '98 C.945 B.A. L.659 J.D. [Ⓐ O'Melveny&M.]
Tucker, Douglas A. ....'66 '96 C.871 B.S. L.893 J.D. [Ⓐ Holland&K.]
*PRACTICE AREAS: Trial and Appellate Litigation.
Tucker, Eric E. ....'69 '95 C.282 B.A. L.446 J.D. [Ⓐ Venable,A.B.H.&C.]
*PRACTICE AREAS: Corporate; Securities.
Tucker, J. Scott '50 '79 C.209 B.A. L.347 J.D.
(adm. in IN; not adm. in DC) William M. Mercer, Inc.
Tucker, James R., Jr. .... '69 '97 C.902 B.A. L.469 J.D. [Ⓐ Akin,G.S.H.&F.]
*PRACTICE AREAS: Public Policy.
Tucker, Kimberly J., (AV) '59 '85 C.259 B.S. L.893 J.D.
(adm. in FL; not adm. in DC) [Ⓒ Boies,S.&F.]
*PRACTICE AREAS: Litigation; Constitutional Law.
Tucker, Lisa Helpert '63 '91 C.228 A.B. L.310 J.D.
(adm. in WA; not adm. in DC) [Preston G.E.&R.M.]
*PRACTICE AREAS: Litigation; Energy; Transportation.
Tucker, Louise L.M. '46 '71 C.174 B.A. L.273 J.D.
Sr. Coun., Telcordia Technologies (⊙Morristown, NJ)
Tucker, Marc B., (BV) .... '50 '77 C.855 B.A. L.178 J.D. [Baker&M.]
*PRACTICE AREAS: Litigation; Appellate Practice; Corporate and Partnership Law; Criminal Law; Insurance Law.
Tucker, Marna S., (AV) .... '41 '66 C.846 B.S. L.276 LL.B. [Feldesman,T.L.F.&B.]
*PRACTICE AREAS: Family Law; Domestic Relations; Trial Practice.
Tucker, Seth A., (AV) ....'62 '88 C&L.309 A.B., J.D. [Covington&B.]
Tucker, Stefan F., (AV) .... '38 '64 C&L.477 B.B.A., J.D. [Venable,A.B.H.&C.]
*PRACTICE AREAS: Tax Law; Business Law; Real Estate; Partnerships; Estate Planning.

Tucker, Flyer
(See Venable, Attorneys at Law, Venable, Baetjer and Howard, LLP)

Tuckett, Ernest A., III ....'70 '96 C&L.276 B.A., J.D. [Ⓐ Arent F.K.P.&K.]
*PRACTICE AREAS: Labor and Employment; Litigation; Civil Rights.
Tuckfelt, Jeffrey C. ....'49 '74 C.665 B.A. L.273 J.D. [Ⓒ Obergh&B.]
Tuell, Loretta A. '— '93 C.906 B.A. L.1494 J.D.
(adm. in CA; not adm. in DC) [Ⓐ Monteau,P.&C.]
*PRACTICE AREAS: Indian Law; Administrative Law; Federal Legislative Practice.
Tuer, Jodi T. .... '66 '94 C.012 B.A. L.904 J.D. [Ⓐ McKenna&C.]
*PRACTICE AREAS: Insurance Recovery; Commercial Litigation.
Tuesley, Malcolm J. ....'74 '00 C.347 B.S. L.1119 J.D. [Ⓐ Skadden,A.S.M.&F.]
*PRACTICE AREAS: Communications Law.
Tufaro, Richard C., (AV) ....'44 '69 C.197 A.B. L.309 LL.B. [Milbank,T.H.&M.]
Tuite, James P., (AV) .... '— '73 C.228 A.B. L.846 J.D. [Akin,G.S.H.&F.]
*PRACTICE AREAS: Complex Litigation; Trial Practice; Appellate Practice; Energy; Antitrust.
Tulumello, Andrew S. .... '70 '98 C&L.309 A.B., J.D. [Ⓐ Gibson,D.&C.]
*PRACTICE AREAS: Litigation.
Tummonds, Paul A, Jr ....'70 '95 C.477 B.A. L.912 J.D. [Ⓐ Shaw P.]
*PRACTICE AREAS: Real Estate; Zoning, Planning and Land Use; Municipal Law.
Tunick, Jennifer A. ....'71 '99 C.276 B.A. L.30 J.D. [Ⓐ Howrey S.A.&W.]
*PRACTICE AREAS: Antitrust.
Tunnell, Shawna R. .... '65 '92 C.378 B.A. L.569 J.D. [Hogan&H.]
*PRACTICE AREAS: Transactional Tax.
Tuohey, Mark H., III, (AV) ....'46 '73 C.712 B.A. L.262 J.D. [Vinson&E.]
*PRACTICE AREAS: Litigation; White Collar Crime; Complex and Multi-District Litigation; Alternative Dispute Resolution.
Turbitt, Clifford J. .... '— '99 C.659 B.S. L.262 J.D. [Ⓐ Dechert] (⊙New York, NY)
*PRACTICE AREAS: Investment Management; Financial Services Law.
Turco, Mark A. ....'50 '82 C.178 A.B. L.276 J.D. [Beveridge&D.] (⊙Balt., MD)
*PRACTICE AREAS: Environmental Law; Litigation.
Turk, David Matthew '73 '00 C.339 B.A. L.893 J.D.
(adm. in VA; not adm. in DC) 530 Senate Hart Off. Bldg.
Turk, Randall J., (AV) ....'50 '81 C.674 B.A. L.276 J.D. [Baker B.]
*PRACTICE AREAS: Business Crimes; White Collar Crime; Government Investigations; Complex and Multi-District Litigation; First Amendment.

Turkevich, Leon R. ....'62 '91 C.446 B.S.E.E. L.273 J.D. [Manelli,D.&S.] (Pat.)
*PRACTICE AREAS: Patent Law.
Turkewitz, Neil '58 '86 C.012 B.A. L.904 J.D.
Exec. V.P., Int'l, Recording Industry Assoc. of America, Inc.
Turkus, Albert H., (AV) ....'45 '71 C.659 B.S. L.309 J.D. [Skadden,A.S.M.&F.]
Turley, Jonathan R '61 '87 C.145 B.A. L.597 J.D.
Prof. of Law, George Wash. Univ. Natl. Law Ctr.
Turley, Patrick W.D. ....'61 '87 C.165 B.A. L.128 J.D. [Dechert]
*PRACTICE AREAS: Financial Services Law; Investment Management.
Turnage, Fred D., (AV) ....'20 '48 C&L.896 A.B., LL.B. [Ⓒ Cleary,G.S.&H.]
Turnbull, Albert W. ....'63 '88 C.299 A.B. L.893 J.D. [Hogan&H.]
*PRACTICE AREAS: Corporate Litigation; Securities Litigation; Securities Class Actions; Shareholder Derivative Actions; Legal Ethics.
Turnbull, Bruce H., (AV) ....'51 '76 C.188 B.A. L.273 J.D. [Weil,G.&M.]
*PRACTICE AREAS: International Trade; Intellectual Property Policy; Telecommunications.
Turnbull, Kenneth Y. ....'69 '99 C.722 B.A. L.446 J.D. [Ⓐ Piper M.R.&W.]
*PRACTICE AREAS: Litigation; Products Liability.
Turnbull, Lowell D., (AV) ....'47 '73 C&L.309 B.A., J.D. [Simon,T.&M.]
*PRACTICE AREAS: Corporate Law; Mergers and Acquisitions; Government Procurement.
Turner, Andrew J. ....'66 '92 C.1086 B.B.A. L.923 J.D. [Ⓐ Hunton&W.]
*PRACTICE AREAS: Environmental Law; Administrative Law; Litigation.
Turner, Deborah A. ....'72 '00 C.1365 B.A. L.30 J.D. [Ⓐ Krooth&A.]
*PRACTICE AREAS: Real Estate; Commercial Litigation; Employment Litigation.
Turner, James E., (AV) ...... '52 '78 C.31 A.B. L.30 J.D. 1717 K Street, N.W., Suite 1107
Turner, James S. ....'40 '69 C&L.608 B.A., J.D. [Swankin&T.]
Turner, Jeffrey L. ....'55 '82 C.861 B.A. L.276 J.D. [Patton B.]
Turner, John H. '55 '81 C.16 B.S. L.880 J.D.
(adm. in TN; not adm. in DC) V.P., Envirnmental Law Inst.
*RESPONSIBILITIES: Environmental Law; Natural Resources Law; Toxic Tort Law; Land Use Law.
Turner, Joshua S. ....'73 '99 C&L.477 B.A., J.D. [Ⓐ Wiley R.&F.]
Turner, Kevin F. '64 '98 C.688 B.S. L.1209
(adm. in VA; not adm. in DC; Pat.) [Ⓐ Arent F.K.P.&K.]
*PRACTICE AREAS: Intellectual Property; Patents.
Turner, Leslie M., (BV) ....'57 '86 C.569 B.S. L.276 J.D. [Akin,G.S.H.&F.]
*PRACTICE AREAS: Litigation.
Turner, Paul B. ....'67 '96 C.145 A.B. L.893 J.D. [Ⓐ Sutherland A.&B.]
*PRACTICE AREAS: Energy; Federal Energy Regulation; Sales and Use Tax; Energy Regulation.
Turner, Phyllis M. '49 '76 C.112 B.A. L.1066 J.D.
(adm. in CA; not adm. in DC) 1121 Constitutional Ave. N.E.‡
Turner, Richard C. ....'55 '81 C.688 B.S. L.273 J.D. [Sughrue M.] (See Pat. Sect.)
*PRACTICE AREAS: Patent Law; Intellectual Property Law; Trade Regulation Law; Unfair Competition Law.
Turner, Rodney W. ....'66 '93 C.893 B.A. L.1356 J.D. NASD Regul.
Turner, Samuel D. ....'47 '76 C.880 B.A. L.893 J.D. [Bennett,T.&C.]
Turner, Scott E. '68 '95 C.37 B.A. L.597 J.D.
(adm. in IL; not adm. in DC) [Ⓐ Ross,D.&B.] (⊙Chgo., IL)
Turner, Shadey K. '72 '99 C.302 B.S. L.64 J.D.
(adm. in MD; not adm. in DC) 3900 Wisconsin Ave.
Turner, Susan A. ....'55 '90 C.273 B.S. L.128 J.D. [Ⓒ Proskauer R.]
*PRACTICE AREAS: Health Care Law.
Turnipseed, Lydia P.A. ....'69 '96 C.880 B.A. L.276 J.D. [Ⓐ Nixon P.]
*PRACTICE AREAS: Litigation; White Collar Crime; Insurance Law.
Turnipseed, Terry L. .... '64 '96 C.497 B.S. L.276 J.D. [Ⓐ Covington&B.]
*PRACTICE AREAS: Wealth Management and Estate Planning; Trust and Estate Administration.
Turow, Stuart A. ....'60 '86 C.205 B.S. L.1029 J.D. [Wilkes A.]
*PRACTICE AREAS: Real Property Tax and Assessment Law; Condemnation and Zoning Law.
Turrentine, J. Drake, (AV) '42 '72 C.659 A.B. L.976 J.D.
Vice President General Counsel, Special Olympics, Inc.
Turza, Dale C., (AV) ....'49 '78 C.183 B.A. L.276 J.D. [Clifford C.R.&W.]
Turza, Peter H., (AV) ....'49 '75 C.976 B.A. L.276 J.D. [Gibson,D.&C.]
*PRACTICE AREAS: Employee Benefits; Labor; Tax; Health Services.
Tuscan, Michael S. ....'— '99 C.121 B.S. L.276 J.D. [Ⓐ Morgan,L.&B.]
Tushin, Richard H., (AV) ....'46 '73 C.188 B.S. L.276 J.D. [Dykema G.] (Pat.)
*PRACTICE AREAS: Intellectual Property; Chemical Intellectual Property; Mechanical Intellectual Property.
Tuttle, Allan Abbot, (AV) ....'39 '66 C&L.976 B.A., LL.B. [Patton B.]
Tuttle, Jonathan R. ....'67 '92 C.945 B.A. L.309 J.D. [Debevoise&P.]
*PRACTICE AREAS: Securities Litigation; Securities Enforcement Defense; Commercial Litigation.
Tuttle, Lois M. '72 '97 C.1349 B.A. L.904 J.D.
(adm. in MD; not adm. in DC) Staff Atty., Natl. Vet. Legal Servs. Prog.
Tuttle, Robin E. ....'— '95 C.682 B.A. L.1209 J.D. 701 Pennsylvania Avenue, N.W.
Tuttle, Taylor & Heron, (AV) .... 1025 Thomas Jefferson Street, N.W. (⊙L.A., CA)
Twedt, Thomas D. ....'63 '92 C.586 B.A. L.326 J.D. [Dow,L.&A.]
Twitchell, Karen R. '51 '87 C.546 B.A. L.793 J.D.
Mng. Tax Dir, Resch. & Plnng., Marriott Intl., Inc.
*RESPONSIBILITIES: Tax; International Tax.
Twomey, Edward J., (AV) ....'47 '74 C.494 B.S. L.276 J.D. [Ⓒ Morrison&F.]
*PRACTICE AREAS: Litigation; Electric Utilities; Antitrust; Oil and Gas Law.
Tycko, Jonathan K. ....'68 '93 C.367 B.A. L.178 J.D. [Ⓐ Gibson,D.&C.]
*PRACTICE AREAS: Litigation; Media Law.
Tydings, Joseph D., (AV) ....'28 '52 C&L.446 B.A., LL.B. [Ⓒ Dickstein S.M.&O.]
Tyle, Craig S., (AV) '60 '88 C.821 B.A. L.309 J.D.
(adm. in NY; not adm. in DC) Gen. Coun., Investment Co. Inst.
*RESPONSIBILITIES: Securities; Financial Regulation; Tax; Pension; International.
Tyler, Robert ....'— '99 C.1375 B.A. L.569 J.D. [Ⓐ Hogan&H.]
*PRACTICE AREAS: Private Equity.
Tyler, Thomas Loy '65 '94 C.352 B.A. L.276 J.D.
(adm. in VA; not adm. in DC) Inst. of Scrap Recycl. Indust.

Tyler, Bartl, Burke & Gorman, P.L.C.
(See Alexandria, Virginia)

Tynan, Natalie S. ....'— '99 C.390 B.A. L.180 J.D. [Ⓐ Hogan&H.]
Tyndall, William F. ....'55 '82 C.813 A.B. L.1065 J.D. 901 15th St., N.W.
Tyre, Kendal, Jr. ....'67 '93 C.103 B.A. L.494 J.D. [Nixon P.]
*PRACTICE AREAS: Business; Energy Finance; Project Finance Law.
Tyson, Tina R. ....'71 '96 L.893 J.D. [Ⓐ Bryan C.]
*PRACTICE AREAS: Litigation; International; Dispute Resolution.
Tysse, G. John ....'46 '73 C.323 B.A. L.608 J.D. [McGuiness N.&W.]
*PRACTICE AREAS: Employment Law.
U, Edwin John ....'73 '98 C&L.309 B.A., J.D. [Ⓐ Kirkland&E.]
*PRACTICE AREAS: Litigation.
Uchendu, Vincent C. ....'62 '90 C.045 B.A. L.329 J.D. 666 11th St., N.W.
Uckert, Colin W., (AV) '61 '86 C.29 B.A. L.945 J.D.
[Powell,G.F.&M.] (⊙Reston, VA)
*PRACTICE AREAS: Real Estate; Banking; Workouts and Foreclosures.
Udell, Nancy A. ....'61 '96 C.262 B.A. L.976 J.D. [Ⓐ Covington&B.]
Udler, Joshua ....'— '00 C.1349 B.A. L.446 J.D. [Ⓐ Piper M.R.&W.]
Udoff, Michael D. '44 '70 C.588 A.B. L.276 J.D.
(adm. in NY; not adm. in DC) Assoc. Gen. Coun., Securities Industry Assn.
*RESPONSIBILITIES: Corporate; Regulatory Advocacy.

Udupa, Vaishali '74 '01 C.893 B.S. L.30 J.D.
(adm. in VA; not adm. in DC) 1667 K St., N.W.
Uehlein, E. Carl, Jr. ....'41 '65 C.821 B.A. L.94 LL.B. [Ⓒ Morgan,L.&B.]
Ufford, Roberta J. ....'60 '94 C.289 B.A. L.273 J.D. [Groom]
*PRACTICE AREAS: Employee Benefits; ERISA; Securities; Pension and Profit Sharing.
Ugast, Frederick B. ....'23 '50 C.128 B.A. L.309 LL.B. Ret. Supr. Ct. Chief J.
Ugolini, Francesca ....'76 '00 C.446 B.S. L.893 J.D. [Ⓐ Akin,G.S.H.&F.]
*PRACTICE AREAS: Tax.
Ugoretz, Mark J. .... '40 '67 C&L.966 B.S., J.D. Pres., The ERISA Indus. Comm.
Uhlmann, Michael M., (AV) ....'39 '66 C.976 B.A. L.893 LL.B. 1015 15th St., N.W.
Uhrig, Paul L. ....'62 '86 C.602 B.A. L.30 J.D. [Akin,G.S.H.&F.]
*PRACTICE AREAS: Health Care; Corporate Planning; Mergers and Acquisitions.
Uitz, Ronald A. ....'64 '89 C.659 B.A. L.276 J.D. 1730 K St., N.W., Ste. 304
Ulery, Christopher J. ....'71 '97 C.381 B.A. L.608 J.D. [Ⓐ Skadden,A.S.M.&F.]
Ullberg, Alan D. '33 '61
C.685 B.A. L.309 J.D. Assoc. Gen. Coun., Smithsonian Institution‡
Ulman, Craig H., (AV) ....'51 '77 C&L.309 B.A., J.D. [Hogan&H.]
*PRACTICE AREAS: Bankruptcy; ATM Networks; Uniform Commercial Code; Creditors Rights; Structured Finance.
Umana, John, (AV) '47 '77 C.433 B.A. L.477 J.D.
1150 Connecticut Avenue, Ninth Floor
Umayam, Michael Arthur '74 '01 C.945 B.A. L.128 J.D.
(adm. in VA; not adm. in DC) [Ⓐ Fried,F.H.S.&J.]
*PRACTICE AREAS: Litigation.
Umberg, Thomas J., (AV) '55 '80 C.112 B.A. L.1065 J.D.
(adm. in CA; not adm. in DC) [Morrison&F.] (⊙Irvine, CA)
*PRACTICE AREAS: Federal Legislative Practice; State Legislative Practice; Regulatory Law; Project Development; International Project Development.
Umeda, Sayuri '63 '98 C.276 L.999 LL.B.
(adm. in NY; not adm. in DC) Shinjyu Global
Umin, Steven M., (AV) ....'39 '65 C&L.976 B.A., LL.B. [Williams&C.]
*PRACTICE AREAS: Administrative Agency Practice; Administrative Hearings and Appeals; Appellate Practice; Arbitration; Art Fraud.
Underhill, D. Michael ....'58 '82 C.119 B.S. L.228 J.D. [Morgan,L.&B.]
Underhill, David L. '60 '86 C.165 B.A. L.184 J.D.
(adm. in CT; not adm. in DC) 815 Conn. Ave., N.W.‡
Underhill, Kathryn A. ....'59 '84 C.472 B.A. L.228 J.D. [Ⓒ Crowell&M.]
*PRACTICE AREAS: Litigation; Insurance Law.
Underhill, William Amory, (AV) '10 '36
C&L.362 LL.D. 3900 Watson Pl., NW (⊙De Land, FL)
Underhill, Wingate E. ....'09 '36 C.575 B.S. L.273 J.D. 4509 Burlington Pl., N.W.
Underwald, Suzanne M. .... '70 '95 C.705 B.A. L.276 J.D. [Ⓐ Dow,L.&A.]
Underwood, Adam C. '— '99 C.1222 B.S.E.E. L.260 J.D.
(adm. in FL; not adm. in DC; Pat.) [Ⓐ Baker&M.]
*PRACTICE AREAS: Intellectual Property.
Underwood, Jamie D. ....'72 '98 C.339 B.A. L.904 J.D. [Ⓐ Steptoe&J.]
Underwood, Robyn M. ....'58 '89 C.808 B.A. L.420 J.D. [Ⓐ Patton B.]
Underwood, Sean E. ....'66 '93 C.577 B.A. L.128 J.D. [Ⓐ A.S.Toppelberg&Assoc.]
Underwood, Thomas C. '36 '62 C.165 A.B. L.800 LL.B.
(adm. in CA; not adm. in DC) Marriott Dr.
Ungar, Robert J. ....'42 '68 C.724 B.A. L.276 J.D. [Ⓒ Fish&R.]
*PRACTICE AREAS: Telecommunications; FCC Regulation.

Ungaretti & Harris, (AV)
1500 K Street, N.W., Suite 250, 20005-1714 ⊙
Telephone: 202-639-7500 Fax: 202-639-7505
Email: info@uhlaw.com URL: http://www.uhlaw.com
Partners: Joseph A. Cari, Jr. (Not admitted in DC); Edward P. Faberman; Charles S. Konigsberg (Resident). Associates: Page C. Faulk (Not admitted in DC; Resident); Michelle M. Faust (Not admitted in DC; Resident).
General Practice, including Business and Corporate, Financial Services and Securities, Litigation and Appeals, Real Estate, Health Care, Information Technology, Public Finance, Legislative and Regulatory Affairs, Labor and Employment, Employee Benefits, Taxation, Affordable Housing, Environmental, Bankruptcy and Creditors' Rights, Estates and Trusts, Gaming Law, Intellectual Property and Patent Litigation, Class Actions and Securities Arbitration.
Chicago, Illinois Office: 3500 Three First National Plaza. Telephone: 312-977-4400. FAX: 312-977-4405.
See Professional Biographies, WASHINGTON, DISTRICT OF COLUMBIA

Unger, Peter V.B., (AV) ....'57 '84 C.472 B.A. L.150 J.D. [Fulbright&J.]
*PRACTICE AREAS: Corporate Law; Litigation.
Ungerman, Mark E., (AV) '59 '88
C.1044 B.S.E.E. L.273 J.D. [Fulbright&J.] (See Pat. Sect.)
*PRACTICE AREAS: Intellectual Property; Technology and Science Transfers; Patents; Trademarks; Computer and Software Patents.
Ungvarsky, Ann M. ....'74 '00 C.339 B.S. L.893 J.D. [Ⓐ Hogan&H.]
Ungvarsky, Edward John ....'68 '93 C.918 B.A. L.976 J.D. Pub. Def. Off.
Untereiner, Alan E., (AV) ....'60 '90 C.309 A.B. L.976 J.D. [Robbins,R.E.O.&U.]
Upadhya, Sameer '75 '00 C.1365 B.S. L.276 J.D.
(adm. in MD; not adm. in DC) [Ⓐ Sonnenschein N.&R.]
*PRACTICE AREAS: Corporate.
Uram, Charlotte ....'48 '73 C.150 B.A. L.597 J.D. 1722 Eye St., N.W.
Urban, Michael A. '57 '83 C.105 B.A. L.276 J.D.
(adm. in NY; not adm. in DC) Pricewaterhouse Coopers LLP
Urban, Theodore W. '50 '74 C.188 B.S. L.128 J.D.
(adm. in MD; not adm. in DC) General Counsel, Ferris Baker Watts Inc.
Urbanczyk, Stephen L., (AV) ....'49 '74 C.321 B.A. L.813 J.D. [Williams&C.]
*PRACTICE AREAS: Civil Practice; Litigation; Mass Torts; Medical Malpractice; Products Liability.
Urgenson, Laurence A., (AV) ....'47 '76 C.563 B.B.A. L.1009 J.D. [Kirkland&E.]
*PRACTICE AREAS: White Collar Crime; Commercial Litigation.
Urquhart, Carla J. ....'— '96 C.1090 B.S. L.902 J.D. [Ⓐ Milbank,T.H.&M.]
Urwitz, Jay P., (AV) ....'49 '76 C.1044 B.A. L.309 J.D. [Hale&D.]
*PRACTICE AREAS: Government Relations Law.
Uscher, Ronald H. ....'48 '73 C.1044 B.A. L.273 J.D. [Bastianelli,B.&K.]
*PRACTICE AREAS: Government Contracts; Energy Law.
Uslander, Gerald L. '38 '65 C.118 B.A. L.365 J.D.
(adm. in IL; not adm. in DC) 1255 23rd St. NW
Utrecht, Carolyn ....'52 '79 C.976 B.A. L.276 J.D. [Ryan,P.U.&M.]
Utterback, Mary Margaret ....'63 '91 C.012 B.A. L.446 J.D. [Ⓐ Thelen R.&P.]
*PRACTICE AREAS: Commercial Litigation; Intellectual Property; Health Care; Trade Regulation.
Uttrich, Donald L., (BV) ....'63 '89 C.930 B.A. L.276 J.D. [Jackson&C.]
*PRACTICE AREAS: Insurance Law; Environmental Law; Toxic Substances Law.
Vachon, Genelle Tanos '63 '88 C.1222 B.A. L.472 J.D.
(adm. in FL; not adm. in DC) USCG 2100 2nd St., S.W.
Vacketta, Carl L., (AV) ....'41 '65 C&L.339 B.S., J.D. [Piper M.R.&W.]
*PRACTICE AREAS: Contract Law; Government Contracts.
Vadon, Marilyn C. ....'68 '93 C.184 B.S. L.1338 J.D. [Ⓒ Akin,G.S.H.&F.]
*PRACTICE AREAS: Corporate; Health Care Law; Business Transactions.
Vagins, Deborah J. ....'69 '96 C.821 B.A. L.904 J.D. [Ⓐ Cohen,M.H.&T.]
*PRACTICE AREAS: Civil Rights; Employment Discrimination Litigation.
Vagle, Steven E. ....'45 '78 C.793 B.A. L.564 J.D. 3730 48th St., N.W.

Vagley, Robert E. '40 '77 C.645 B.S. L.276 J.D. Pres., Amer. Ins. Assn.
Vail, John '53 '79 C.145 A.B. L.880 J.D. Assoc. of Trial Lawyers of America
Vaillancourt, George H. '14 '38 L.904 LL.B. 3850 Tunlaw Rd., N.W.‡
Vakerics, Thomas V., (AV) '44 '68 C.97 B.A. L.273 J.D. [Perkins C.]
*PRACTICE AREAS: Antitrust Law; International Trade Law.
Valad, Bart T. '— '98 C.30 B.S. L.1209 J.D. [Ⓐ Powell,G.F.&M.]
*PRACTICE AREAS: Antitrust; Litigation.
Valby, Gary L. '48 '74 C.478 B.A. L.569 J.D. [Nixon P.]
*PRACTICE AREAS: Energy Finance; Project Finance.
Valder, Joseph B., (AV) '45 '71 C.177 B.A. L.276 J.D. Asst. U.S. Atty.
Valdez, Marlana R. '54 '79 C&L.846 B.S., J.D. George Washington Univ., Law Ctr.
Valenstein, Carl A. '57 '83 C.976 B.A. L.477 J.D. [Arent F.K.P.&K.]
*PRACTICE AREAS: Project Finance; Infrastructure Development; International Business (or Trade or Finance) Law; Import and Export Law; Maritime Law.
Valenstein, Jill M. '60 '95 C.241 B.S. L.64 J.D. [Ⓐ Cole,R.&B.]
*PRACTICE AREAS: Telecommunications Law; Cable TV; Litigation.
Valente, Thomas Silvio '76 '01 C.128 B.A. L.893 J.D. (adm. in VT; not adm. in DC) [Ⓐ Swidler B.S.F.]
*PRACTICE AREAS: Government Affairs.
Valentine, Debra A. '53 '80 C.674 A.B. L.976 J.D. [O'Melveny&M.]
*PRACTICE AREAS: Litigation; Antitrust and Trade Regulation.
Valentine, John A. '70 '98 C.95 A.B. L.659 J.D. [Ⓐ Wilmer,C.&P.]
Valentine, Steven Richards '56 '83 C.347 B.G.S. L.345 J.D. [Ⓒ Preston G.E.&R.M.]
*PRACTICE AREAS: Federal Legislative Practice; Federal Regulatory Law.
Valentine, Teresa E. '62 '88 C.128 B.A. L.273 J.D. ULLICO Inc.
*RESPONSIBILITIES: Corporate Law; Corporate Compliance; Litigation; Regulatory.
Valentino, James J. '63 '92 C&L.276 B.S., B.S. [Mintz,L.C.F.G.&P.]
*PRACTICE AREAS: Communications; Internet Law.
Valer, Robert D. '50 '86 C.999 B.S. L.276 J.D. [Ⓒ Groom]
*PRACTICE AREAS: Employee Benefits; ERISA; Tax Law.
Valeri, Jodi L. '70 '96 C.260 B.S. L.276 J.D. [Ⓐ Mayer,B.&P.]
Valerio, Michael A. '68 '93 C.367 B.A. L.128 J.D. [Ⓐ Swidler B.S.F.]
*PRACTICE AREAS: Litigation.
Valerio, Stacey L. '70 '96 C.659 B.A. L.273 J.D. [Ⓐ Kleinfeld,K.&B.]
*PRACTICE AREAS: Food, Drug and Cosmetic Law; Drug and Medical Device Regulation; Advertising Law; Civil Litigation.
Valette, Paul Andrew '46 '97 C.475 B.A. L.276 J.D. 441 4th St., N.W.
Valiant, Carrie, (AV) '56 '83 C.1044 B.A. L.273 J.D. [Epstein B.&G.]
*PRACTICE AREAS: Health; Health Care Fraud; Medicare-Medicaid Reimbursement.
Valinoti, Elizabeth H. '69 '97 C.280 A.B.J. L.128 J.D. (adm. in IL; not adm. in DC) Fed. Communications Comm.
Valle, Gabriel B. '70 '98 C.1019 B.S. L.30 J.D. (adm. in NY; not adm. in DC) [Ⓐ Dickstein S.M.&O.]
*PRACTICE AREAS: Corporate.
Vallejo, Gabriela Maria '71 '98 C.352 B.A. L.966 J.D. (adm. in WI; not adm. in DC) [Ⓐ Shearman&S.]
*PRACTICE AREAS: Antitrust.
Vallender, Charles F., III '39 '72 C&L.976 B.A., LL.B. 4000 Mass. Ave., N.W.
Valliere, Barbara '59 '87 C.103 A.B. L.818 J.D. U.S. Attorney's Off.
Valltos, Jessica A. '71 '97 C.886 B.S. L.8 J.D. [Ⓐ Greenberg T.]
Valtos, Jason J. '74 '99 C.645 B.S. L.1338 J.D. (adm. in WA; not adm. in DC) [Ⓐ Osborne]
*PRACTICE AREAS: Union Labor Law; Litigation.
Van Alstyne, Debra Manning '51 '77 C.112 B.S. L.1068 J.D. Assoc. Gen. Coun., Fannie Mae
*RESPONSIBILITIES: Multi-Family Transactions; Finance; Securitization; Electronic Commerce Law.
VanArsdale, Christopher J. '67 '97 C.309 A.B. L.188 J.D. [Ⓐ Akin,G.S.H.&F.]
*PRACTICE AREAS: Environmental Law; Environmental Litigation.
Van Arsdall, Michael G. '70 '99 C.690 B.A. L.128 J.D. [Ⓐ Crowell&M.]
Van Beek, John P., (AV) '53 '79 C.188 B.A. L.273 J.D. [Young,G.&V.] ⊙
*PRACTICE AREAS: Civil Litigation; Creditor's Rights; Bankruptcy; Secured Transactions; Contracts.
Van Bergh, Mark, (AV) '56 '81 C.823 B.A. L.273 J.D. [Ⓒ Arter&H.]
*PRACTICE AREAS: Communications.
Van Blerkom, Lee '70 '96 C.31 B.A. L.893 J.D. [Ⓐ Shaw P.]
Van Brunt, Kirk '58 '85 C.594 B.A. L.309 J.D. [Davis&H.]
*PRACTICE AREAS: Taxation Law.
Van Buren, Lynn M. '— '97 C.746 B.A. L.966 J.D. [Ⓐ Verner,L.B.M.&H.]
Vance, Andrew Joseph '72 '98 C&L.477 B.S.E., J.D. [Ⓐ Finnegan,H.F.G.&D.]
*PRACTICE AREAS: Intellectual Property Rights.
Vance, John T. '21 '50 C.508 B.A. L.273 LL.B. 3286 M St., N.W.‡
Vance, Scott W. '69 '92 C.309 B.A. L.893 J.D. (adm. in VA; not adm. in DC) Ernst & Young
Van Cleef, Carol R. '56 '85 C.276 B.S.F.S. L.904 J.D. [Katten M.Z.]
*PRACTICE AREAS: Internet and E-Commerce; Financial Institutions Law; Legislation.
Van Cleve, George, (AV) '52 '77 C.145 B.A. L.309 J.D. [VanCleve&E.]

Van Cleve & Eder, (AV)
1155 Connecticut Avenue, N.W., Suite 300, 20036
Telephone: 202-467-8022 Fax: 202-887-9144
Email: gvclaw@erols.com
George Van Cleve; Elliot D. Eder.
Civil Litigation, including Patent Licensing, Copyright and Trademark Licensing, Contract, Fraud, Antitrust, Class Action, Civil Rights, Employment and other Complex Litigation and Appeals; Specialty Risk Insurance Matters. Environmental Law, Corporate Investigations, Government Contracts, Intellectual Property.
See Professional Biographies, WASHINGTON, DISTRICT OF COLUMBIA

Van Croft, Keith H. '65 '97 C.446 B.A. L.128 J.D. 1120 Connecticut Ave., N.W.
Van De Kerckhove, Amy '73 '99 C.602 B.A. L.276 J.D. [Ⓐ Shaw P.]
*PRACTICE AREAS: Communications.
Van Demark, Dale C. '70 '97 C.1044 B.A. L.1040 J.D. [Ⓐ Venable,A.B.H.&C.]
*PRACTICE AREAS: Business Law; Corporate Law; Taxation.
Van der Bellen, Alexander M.R. '66 '94 C.299 A.B. L.861 J.D. [Ⓐ Shaw P.]
Vanderbilt, Tanya B. '66 '91 C.821 B.A. L.659 J.D. [Ⓐ Epstein B.&G.]
*PRACTICE AREAS: Antitrust Law; Health Law.
VanderGoot, Matthew R. '71 '00 C.602 B.A. L.477 J.D. [Ⓐ Latham&W.]
*PRACTICE AREAS: Corporate Law; Communications and Media.
Vander Jagt, Guy '31 '61 C.323 B.A. L.477 J.D. (adm. in MI; not adm. in DC) [Ⓒ Baise&M.]
*PRACTICE AREAS: Tax Law; Legislative Practice; Litigation.
Vander Lugt, Robert D. '65 '92 C.1288 B.A. L.893 J.D. [Ⓒ Vinson&E.]
*PRACTICE AREAS: Litigation; International Trade; Government Contracts; International Law; Aviation and Aerospace.
Vander Schaaf, Lyle B. '62 '88 C.352 B.A. L.904 J.D. [Ⓐ White&C.]
Vanderstar, John, (AV) '33 '61 C.674 B.S.E. L.309 J.D. [Covington&B.]
Vanderver, Timothy A., Jr., (AV) '44 '69 C.902 B.A. L.309 J.D. [Patton B.]
Van Doren, Charles N. '24 '49 C.309 B.A. L.178 LL.B. (adm. in NY; not adm. in DC) 4541 Lowell St., N.W.
Van Driesen, Jennifer '69 '97 C.228 B.A. L.276 J.D. [Ⓐ Latham&W.]
*PRACTICE AREAS: Secured Financing.
Van Dyke, Raymond '57 '90 C.577 B.S. L.575 J.D. (adm. in NJ; not adm. in DC; Pat.) [Dorsey&W.]
*PRACTICE AREAS: Intellectual Property; Intellectual Property Litigation; Licensing; Opinion; E-Commerce Law.
Van Eaton, Joseph, (AV) '53 '79 C.823 B.A. L.659 J.D. [Miller&V.]
*PRACTICE AREAS: Communications Law; Cable Franchising; Telecommunications Law; First Amendment Law; Electric Power.
Vanek, Traci Meakem '70 '97 C.945 B.S. L.94 J.D. [Ⓐ McKenna&C.]
*PRACTICE AREAS: Environmental Litigation; Products Liability; Appellate Practice; White Collar Crime Litigation.
Van Engen, Kurt E. '64 '98 C.30 B.A. L.904 J.D. [Ⓐ Ballard S.A.&I.]
*PRACTICE AREAS: Real Estate; Asset Finance; Real Property Finance.
Van Gelder, Barbara, (AV) '50 '76 C.94 B.A. L.245 J.D. [Wiley R.&F.]
*PRACTICE AREAS: Litigation; White Collar Crime; Government Contracts; Telecommunications; Labor and Employment.
Vangsnes, Peter J. '55 '80 C.103 B.A. L.188 J.D. [Ashcraft&G.]
*PRACTICE AREAS: Toxic Torts; Products Liability; Personal Injury.
Van Hollen, Christopher, Jr. '59 '91 C.821 B.A. L.276 J.D. [Arent F.K.P.&K.]
*PRACTICE AREAS: Litigation.
Van Hook, Matthew B. '50 '75 C.276 A.B. L.477 J.D. Dep. Gen. Coun., Pharmaceutical Research & Mnfct. of America
Van Hook, Paul R. '60 '86 C.880 B.S. L.228 J.D. Assoc. Gen. Coun., Fannie Mae
*RESPONSIBILITIES: Securitization; Capital Markets Transactions.
Van Horn, Charles E. '42 '68 C.401 B.S.Ch.E. L.30 J.D. [Finnegan,H.F.G.&D.] (See Pat. Sect.)
*PRACTICE AREAS: Patents.
Van Horn, Matthew I. '71 '99 C.301 B.A. L.862 J.D. [Ⓐ Schmeltzer,A.&S.]
*PRACTICE AREAS: Civil Litigation; Commercial Litigation; Franchise Law.
van Horne, Jon W. '45 '71 C.243 B.A. L.309 J.D. [Greenberg T.]
Vanison, Denise A. '66 '92 C.893 B.A. L.276 J.D. [Patton B.]
Van Kirk, Darcy Lynn '71 '98 C.902 B.A. L.228 J.D. [Ⓐ Wilmer,C.&P.]
*PRACTICE AREAS: Corporate Securities.
Van Kirk, Robert A. '65 '91 C.602 B.A. L.228 J.D. [Williams&C.]
*PRACTICE AREAS: Administrative Law; Commercial Law; Federal Government Law; First Amendment Law.
VanLandingham, Mark D., (BV) '60 '86 C.620 B.A. L.623 J.D. (adm. in OK; not adm. in DC) Mgr., Fed. Rel., Kerr-McGee Corp.
Vann, Adam '73 '98 C.976 B.A. L.575 J.D. [Ⓐ Dickstein S.M.&O.]
*PRACTICE AREAS: Energy Law.
Vann, Rae T. '68 '94 C.119 B.S. L.306 J.D. (adm. in CT; not adm. in DC) [Ⓐ McGuiness N.&W.]
*PRACTICE AREAS: Employment.
Van Nelson, Patricia L. '49 '84 C.1044 B.A. L.30 J.D. Dep. Prog. Mgr., Roy F. Weston, Inc.

Van Ness Feldman, A Professional Corporation, (AV)
Seventh Floor, 1050 Thomas Jefferson Street, N.W., 20007-3877 ⊙
Telephone: 202-298-1800 Fax: 202-338-2416
Email: vnf@vnf.com URL: http://www.vnf.com
Howard J. Feldman; William J. Van Ness, Jr. (Resident, Seattle, Washington Office); Ben Yamagata; Robert G. Szabo; Alan L. Mintz; Robert R. Nordhaus; Gary D. Bachman; Margaret A. Moore; J. Curtis Moffatt; Richard A. Agnew (Resident, Seattle, Washington Office); Howard E. Shapiro; Michael A. Swiger; Daniel S. Press; Julia R. Richardson; Richard A. Penna; Mitchell H. Bernstein; John H. Burnes, Jr.; Stephen C. Fotis; Thomas C. Roberts (Not admitted in DC); John J. Buchovecky; David P. Yaffe; Cheryl Feik Ryan; Theresa I. Zolet; Paul Korman; Patricia Fry Godley; Pamela J. Anderson; Steven Richardson (Not admitted in DC); Douglas W. Smith. Of Counsel: Howard S. Bleichfeld; Shippen Howe; Richard G. Kozlowski; Sam Kalen; Malcolm C. McLellan (Resident, Seattle, Washington Office); J. Curtis Rich (Not admitted in DC); Joseph B. Nelson; Jay T. Ryan;—Susan A. Moore (Not admitted in DC); Britt S. Fleming; Jaeleen Kookesh Araujo; Jonathan D. Simon; Angela M. Addison (Not admitted in DC); Janet L. Woodka (Not admitted in DC); Andrew B. Art; Charles R. Sensiba (Not admitted in DC); Kyle W. Danish; Brian M. Zimmet (Not admitted in DC); Kevin W. Flynn (Not admitted in DC); Nick Goldstein (Not admitted in DC); Ricardo Nogueira (Not admitted in DC); Evan Reese; Vincenzo Franco.
Energy, Environmental Law, Natural Resources, Federal Legislative Practice, Natural Gas, Electric Power, Electric Utilities, Energy Regulation, Hydroelectricity, International Energy Law, Public Land Law, Land Reclamation, Oil and Gas Law, Water Law, Endangered Species Act, Clean Water Act, Clean Air Act, Alaska Native Law, Indian Law, Taxation, Transportation, Administrative Law, Administrative Litigation.
Seattle, Washington Office: 821 Second Avenue, Suite 2000. Telephone: 206-623-9372. Fax: 206-623-4986.
See Professional Biographies, WASHINGTON, DISTRICT OF COLUMBIA

Vannier, Ariel, (AV) '60 '84 C.367 B.A. L.902 J.D. [Ⓒ Venable,A.B.H.&C.] (⊙Balt., MD)
*PRACTICE AREAS: Corporate; Securities Regulation; Corporate Finance.
Van Ourkerk, Calvin Fred, Jr. '55 '00 C.276 M.A. L.767 J.D. 1000 Connecticut Ave., N.W.
Van Over, C. Joel '48 '83 C.174 B.A. L.93 J.D. [Ⓒ Swidler B.S.F.]
*PRACTICE AREAS: Intellectual Property; Commercial Litigation; Antitrust Counseling and Litigation; Government Contracting.
Van Pee, Kristina M. '59 '87 L.999 J.D. (adm. in VA; not adm. in DC) 815 Conn. Ave., N.W.‡
Van Puymbroeck, Rudolf V. '45 '76 C.999 L.276 J.D. Sr. Coun., The World Bk.
Van Scoyoc, Harry Stewart '47 '74 C.401 B.S.Ch.E. L.446 J.D. VanScoyoc Assoc., Inc.
Van Slooten, Heather J. '52 '87 C.30 B.A. L.893 J.D. (adm. in NY; not adm. in DC) [Ⓐ White&C.]
VanSlyke Zornada, Doretha M. '— '94 C.938 B.A. L.904 J.D. Asst. Coun., Invst. Co. Instit.
*RESPONSIBILITIES: Securities.
van Stiphout, Monique A. '70 '98 C&L.276 B.S.F.S., J.D. [Ⓐ Krupin O.]
*PRACTICE AREAS: Immigration (100%).
Vanstory, Patricia Ann Ades '70 '97 C.575 B.A. L.94 J.D. [Ⓐ Hyman,P.&M.]
Van Voorhees, Robert F., (AV) '— '72 C.273 B.A. L.893 J.D. [Bryan C.]
*PRACTICE AREAS: Environmental Law; Occupational Safety and Health Law; Administrative Law; Litigation.
Van Voorhis, Lee K. '67 '97 C.976 B.A. L.188 J.D. [Ⓐ Clifford C.R.&W.]
*PRACTICE AREAS: Antitrust.
Van Wazer, Thomas P. '60 '89 C.659 B.S. L.276 J.D. [Sidley A.B.&W.]
Vanzego, Raymond J., Jr. '67 '99 C.329 B.A. L.64 J.D. (adm. in MD; not adm. in DC) ULLICO Inc.
*RESPONSIBILITIES: Corporate Law; Regulatory Law; Litigation; Financial Services Law.
Varcoe, Frederick Turner, Jr. '44 '98 C.484 B.S. L.575 J.D. (adm. in NC; not adm. in DC) 1100 New York Ave., N.W., 9th Fl.
Vardaman, John W., (AV) '40 '67 C.902 A.B. L.309 LL.B. [Williams&C.]
*PRACTICE AREAS: Complex Litigation; Mass Torts; Products Liability Defense.
Varela, Manuel S. '72 '97 C.309 A.B. L.276 J.D. [Ⓐ Baach R.&L.P.]
*PRACTICE AREAS: Litigation; Insurance Litigation; Toxic Torts.
Vargo, John E., (AV) '49 '77 C.30 B.A. L.904 J.D. Coun., Comm. on Standards of Official Conduct
Varholy, Stephen F. '70 '00 C.790 B.A. L.128 J.D. (adm. in VA; not adm. in DC) [Ⓐ Charapp,D.&W.]
*PRACTICE AREAS: Civil Litigation; Corporate Law; Employment Law.
Varley, Douglas N. '61 '94 C&L.893 B.A., J.D. [Caplin&D.]
*PRACTICE AREAS: Tax Exempt Organizations.

Varley, J. David '64 '96 C.923 B.A. L.37 J.D
(adm. in WA; not adm. in DC) 950 L'Enfant Plaza, SW, 5th Fl.

Varma, Anurag . . . . . . '72 '98 C.02 B.A. L.208 J.D. [Ⓐ Conlon,F.P.&P.]
*PRACTICE AREAS: Civil Rights; Class Actions; Government Relations.

Varma, Asim . . . . . . '64 '88 C.477 B.S. L.309 J.D. [Arnold&P.]
*PRACTICE AREAS: Antitrust; Intellectual Property; Litigation.

Varner, Andrew J. '71 '98 C.477 B.A. L.145 J.D.
[Ⓐ O'Melveny&M.] (⊙Mc Lean, VA)

Varner, Angela M. . . . . . . '— '99 C.477 B.A. L.329 J.D. [Ⓐ Thompson H.]
*PRACTICE AREAS: Personal and Succession Planning; Corporate Law; Securities.

Varner, Robert Glenn, Jr. '47 '74 C.260 B.A. L.362 J.D.
901 15th Street, N.W., Suite 700, 20005-2327
Telephone: 202-371-6273 Fax: 202-371-6279
Email: rgv74@aol.com URL: http://www.lawyers.com/varnerlaw
***PRACTICE AREAS: Local Government Law; Environmental Law; International Law.**
Local Government, Environmental, International, Telecommunications, Project Finance.
See Professional Biographies, WASHINGTON, DISTRICT OF COLUMBIA

Varney, Andrew P. . . . . . . '62 '87 C.478 A.B. L.309 J.D. [Fried,F.H.S.&J.]

Varney, Christine A., (AV) . . . . . . '55 '86 C.1044 B.A. L.276 J.D. [Hogan&H.]
*PRACTICE AREAS: Internet Law; Antitrust Law; Consumer Protection.

Varnum, Robert V. . . . . . . '46 '73 C.613 B.A. L.276 J.D. 4801 Massachusetts Ave Nw

Varon, Jay N., (AV) . . . . . . '— '75 C.659 B.S. L.813 J.D. [Foley&L.]
*PRACTICE AREAS: Litigation; Antitrust Law; RESPA.

Varona, Anthony E. '67 '92 C&L.93 A.B., J.D.
General Counsel & Legal Director, Human Rights Campaign

Varrone, Edward G., Law Office of, (AV) '53 '78 C.30 B.A. L.273 J.D.
910 17th Street, N.W. Suite 800, 20006
Telephone: 202-861-3150 Fax: 202-861-3152
URL: http://www.lawyers.com/varronelaw
Wills, Trusts and Estates, Elder Law, Family Law, Civil Litigation.
See Professional Biographies, WASHINGTON, DISTRICT OF COLUMBIA

Vartanian, Thomas P., (AV) . . . . . . '49 '77 C.999 B.A. L.1009 J.D. [Fried,F.H.S.&J.]

Vasapoli, Joseph V., (BV) . . . . . . '52 '77 C.276 A.B. L.945 J.D. [Ryan,P.U.&M.]

Vasconcellos, Renata S. '70 '92 L.999 J.D.
(adm. in Brazil; not adm. in DC) [Ⓐ Porter W.M.&A.]
*PRACTICE AREAS: Federal Practice; International Trade; Customs Law; Import and Export Law; Antidumping.

Vasile, James B., (AV) . . . . . . '44 '75 C.705 B.A. L.276 J.D. [Davis W.T.]
*PRACTICE AREAS: Energy; Environmental; Natural Resources; Utilities.

Vaskov, Stephen G. . . . . . . '58 '85 C.659 B.A. L.904 J.D. [Ⓒ Hogan&H.]
*PRACTICE AREAS: Federal Civil Practice; International Arbitration; Complex Litigation; Antitrust Litigation; Contract Litigation.

Vasquez, Francis A., Jr. . . . . . . '64 '92 C.111 B.S. L.276 J.D. [Ⓐ White&C.]

•Vasquez, Juan F., A Prof. Corp., (BV) '48 '77 C.846 B.S.B.A. L.326 J.D.
(adm. in TX; not adm. in DC) P.O. Box 1847‡

Vassar, Thomas W. '55 '83 C.446 B.A. L.30 J.D.
[Jung&V.] (⊙Kailua-Kona, HI; Arlington, VA)

Vassilovski, Edna . . . . . . '65 '95 C.813 B.S. L.178 J.D. [Ⓐ Pepper H.] (Pat.)
*PRACTICE AREAS: Intellectual Property; Chemical Patents; Patent Prosecution.

Vasta, Jennifer M. . . . . . . '73 '98 C.1375 B.A. L.273 J.D. [Ⓐ Howrey S.A.&W.]
*PRACTICE AREAS: Antitrust.

Vatis, Michael A. . . . . . . '63 '89 C.674 A.B. L.309 J.D. [Ⓒ Fried,F.H.S.&J.]
*PRACTICE AREAS: Internet Law; E-Commerce; Privacy Law; Litigation.

Vattikuti, Shreekant . . . . . . '73 '98 C.569 B.S. L.575 J.D. Inter'l Trade Commission

Vaughan, Anne Magee '67 '97 C.309 A.B. L.893 J.D.
(adm. in LA; not adm. in DC) [Ⓐ Piper M.R.&W.]
*PRACTICE AREAS: Corporate; Securities; Finance.

Vaughan, David A. . . . . . . '65 '91 C.97 B.A. L.276 J.D. [Dechert]
*PRACTICE AREAS: Financial Services Law; Investment Management.

Vaughan, David L. . . . . . . '46 '72 C.497 B.A. L.228 J.D. [Kelley D.&W.]
*PRACTICE AREAS: Administrative Law; Aviation Law; International Law; Government Procurement.

Vaughan, Patricia Magee '44 '73
C.856 B.A. L.276 J.D. Gen. Coun., National Soft Drink Assn.

Vaughan, Stephen J. . . . . . . '73 '98 C.608 B.S. L.128 J.D. [Ⓐ Schmeltzer,A.&S.]
*PRACTICE AREAS: Commercial Litigation; Franchise Law; Corporate Transactions.

Vaughan, Tena E. '69 '98 C.145 B.A. L.904 J.D.
(adm. in MA; not adm. in DC) 3000k St., NW, Ste. 300

Vaughn, Christine L., (AV) . . . . . . '49 '75 C.705 B.A. L.276 J.D. [Vinson&E.]
*PRACTICE AREAS: Taxation; Legislative Practice.

Vaughn, Stephen P. . . . . . . '66 '91 C.880 B.A. L.976 J.D. [Ⓐ Skadden,A.S.M.&F.]

Vawter, Alison Boothby '65 '98 C.927 B.A. L.180 J.D.
(adm. in MD; not adm. in DC) 800 Independence Ave. SW

Vayra, Fabricio '74 '00 C.1356 B.S L.1209 J.D.
(adm. in VA; not adm. in DC) [Ⓐ Arent F.K.P.&K.]
*PRACTICE AREAS: Electronic Commerce; Business Transactions; Intellectual Property.

Veach, Julie A. . . . . . . '70 '97 C.679 B.A. L.1119 J.D. 445 12th Street, S.W.

Vecchione, John J. . . . . . . '64 '90 C.299 B.A. L.273 J.D. [Ⓒ Kutak R.]
*PRACTICE AREAS: Commercial Litigation; Employment Law; Corporate Law.

Veillette, James P. . . . . . . '58 '88 C&L.276 B.S.F.S., J.D. Assoc. Gen. Coun., Fannie Mae
*RESPONSIBILITIES: Technology Transactions.

Veilleux, Diana J. . . . . . . '58 '86 C.94 B.S. L.276 J.D. [Shaw,B.V.&R.]
*PRACTICE AREAS: Federal Employment Law; Employment Law; Litigation.

Veitenheimer, Erich E., III . . . . . . '52 '99 C.906 B.S. L.276 J.D. [Ⓐ Morgan,L.&B.] (Pat.)

Velarde, A.H., & Associates, P.C.
(See McLean, Virginia)

Velasquez, R. Jay . . . . . . '60 '86 C&L.846 B.B.A., J.D. 1155 21st St. NW, 3rd Fl.

Vélez, Carlos '60 '85 C.276 B.S. L.818 J.D.
(adm. in MA; not adm. in DC) 2401 Pennsylvania Ave., N.W.

Velji, Noorali A. . . . . . . '31 '59 C.999 L.276 LL.M. 1819 H St., N.W.

Vellos, Diana Louise . . . . . . '72 '97 C.429 B.A. L.904 J.D. 1666 Connecticut Ave., N.W.

Velvel, Douglas R. . . . . . . '65 '95 C.1036 B.A. L.209 J.D. 716 Sicard St., Ste. 111

Venable, Attorneys At Law, Venable, Baetjer, Howard & Civiletti, LLP, (AV) BB
A Partnership including Professional Corporations
Suite 1000, 1201 New York Avenue, N.W., 20005 ⊙
Telephone: 202-962-4800 Fax: 202-962-8300
URL: http://www.venable.com
Members of Firm: A. Hope Adams; David G. Adams; Andrew C. Aitken; Richard L. Aitken; Robert G. Ames; James K. Archibald; Maurice Baskin; Kenneth C. Bass, III; John B. Beaty; Lawrence B. Bernard; Connie N. Bertram; Joseph G. Block; Robert J. Bolger, Jr.; Neal D. Borden (Not admitted in DC); James R. Burdett; Anthony M. Carey (Not admitted in DC); Wallace E. Christner; Arthur E. Cirulnick; Benjamin R. Civiletti (P.C.); Roger A. Colaizzi; Kevin B. Collins; Bryson L. Cook (P.C.) (Not admitted in DC); William P. Cook; John F. Cooney; Thomas J. Cooper; William D. Coston; Carla Draluck Craft; Donald P. Creston; Peter J. Curtin; Paul A. Debolt; Jeffrey A. Dunn; Susan T. Edlavitch; Craig A. Emden; Anita J. Finkelstein; Michael R. Flyer; Robert J. Frank; Ronald R. Glancz; Edward F. Glynn, Jr.; David W. Goewey; Michael A. Gollin; Robert Gene Gottlieb; Jan K. Guben (Not admitted in DC); Gary D. Hailey; Mark B. Harrison; Gregory B. Hauptman; Peter E. Heyward; Gary M. Hnath; Kenneth R. Hoffman; Kenneth G. Hurwitz; Gregory F. Jenner; Paul T. Kaplun; Lawrence A. Katz (Resident); Joshua J. Kaufman; Michael E. Kaufmann; Gabor J. Kelemen (Not admitted in DC); Thomas J. Kelly, Jr.; Campbell Killefer; Robert Kinberg; Jeffrey D. Knowles;

(This Listing Continued)

Venable, Attorneys At Law, Venable, Baetjer, Howard & Civiletti, LLP (Continued)
Norman N. Kunitz; Brock R. Landry; Fernand A. Lavallee; Shmuel (Sandy) Livnat; Thomas J. Madden; Vicki Margolis; Charles R. "Rod" Marvin, Jr.; Clifton E. McCann; Heather L. McDowell; Lindsay Beardsworth Meyer; Daniel L. Morgan; Andrea I. O'Brien; Jerry R. O'Conor; Patrick E. O'Donnell; George F. Pappas; John J. Pavlick, Jr.; Julie A. Petruzzelli; Thomas H. Quinn; Todd H. Reuben; Tamara Schiebel Rickman; James E. Rogan (Not admitted in DC); Janet F. Satterthwaite; Mary Jane Saunders; Michael Schatzow; Michael A. Schlesinger; Richard D. Schmidt (Not admitted in DC); Marina V. Schneller; James E. Scott; A. Christopher Sega; David E. Sellinger; Gary L. Shaffer; John P. Shannon, Jr.; James L. Shea; Julian L. Shepard; Joe A. Shull; Kenneth S. Slaughter; Herbert G. Smith, II; George H. Spencer; David E. Springer; Judson W. Starr; Gerard Treanor; Stefan F. Tucker; Ian D. Volner; Martha Jo Wagner; Barbara L. Waite; Ashley J. Wells; Judith L. Wheat; N. Frank Wiggins; Thomas G. Wiseman; Allen Wood. Of Counsel: Ralph P. Albrecht; Robert S. Babayi; Fei-Fei Chao; Paul F. Daebeler; David G. Dickman; Robert C. Harmala; Frank Horton; Erik V. Huey; Rebecca E. Pearson; David W. Rutstein; Michael A. Sartori; Charles E. Sliter; Jeffrey S. Tenenbaum; Ariel Vannier; Catherine M. Voorhees. Associates: Chad C. Anderson (Not admitted in DC); Theodore W. Atkinson; Harry I. Atlas; Marcia A. Auberger; Purvi Badiani; Gregory S. Braker; Rita L. Brickman; Jennifer J. Bruton; Frank A. Ciatto; Rosemary E. Dailey; Molly A. Delea (Not admitted in DC); W. Patrick Doherty (Not admitted in DC); Kathleen S. Dolan; Richard F. Ensor (Not admitted in DC); Patricia A. Exposito; Danielle Fagre (Not admitted in DC); David M. Farnum (Not admitted in DC); Rachel L. Finkle (Not admitted in DC); Brian L. Flack; Darryl L. Franklin; Christopher E. Gatewood (Not admitted in DC); Jason L. Goldblatt; Rebecca L. Goldsmith; Keith G. Haddaway; John F. Henault, Jr. (Not admitted in DC); Linda A. Hildreth; Tonya D. Horton (Not admitted in DC); Brian M. Hudson; Baris H. Ipeker; Davida H. Isaacs; Jeffri A. Kaminski; Hoyun Kim; Mary Ann Knoeckel; Jeanny K. Lee; Mark A. Machi; Karen E. Mason; John W. McGlynn (Not admitted in DC); Charlotte M. McGuinness; Jeannette C. Meacham; John P. Moy; Eric S. Namrow; Chellis E. Neal; Jeanne Louise Newlon; Cristina G. Niccolini (Not admitted in DC); Samuel Adam Ozeck; Jeffrey R. Pankratz; Monica Charisse Parchment; Jacqueline Levasseur Patt; Andrew Douglas Price; Johana A. Reed; Martin L. Saad; Chantel Sheaks; Jagpreet Singh; Melissa Landau Steinman; Lisa Ann Tavares (Not admitted in DC); F. Alvin Taylor; Eric E. Tucker; Dale C. Van Demark; Russell J. E. Verby (Not admitted in DC); Gregory L. Waddoups; William C. Waller; Margaret T. Watkins; Robin Waugh-Farretta; Eric J. Weierstall; Alan D. Wilbur (Not admitted in DC); Yvette D. Williams (Not admitted in DC); Kristin K. Woody; Damon W. D. Wright; Gilda M. Zimmet; Linda J. Zirkelbach.
General Practice. Administrative; Antitrusts; Appellate; Banking; Bankruptcy and Creditor's Rights; Communications; Consumer Financial Services; Construction Litigation; Corporate; Corporate Finance and Securities; Electronic Marketing and Distribution; Employee Benefits; Environmental; Estates and Trusts; Government Contracts; Health Care; Immigration; Information Law; Insurance Defense and Coverage; Intellectual Property; International; Labor and Employment; Legislative and Regulatory; Litigation; Civil, Commercial and Criminal; Products Liability Litigation; Public Finance; Real Estate Development and Financing; Taxation; Tax Controversies Litigation; Technology.
Baltimore, Maryland Office: Venable, Baetjer and Howard LLP, 1800 Mercantile Bank & Trust Building, 2 Hopkins Plaza. Telephone: 410-244-7400. Fax: 410-244-7742.
McLean, Virginia Office: Venable, Baetjer and Howard LLP, Suite 400, 2010 Corporate Ridge. Telephone: 703-760-1600. Fax: 703-821-8949.
Rockville, Maryland Office: Venable, Baetjer and Howard LLP, Suite 500, One Church Street, P. O. Box 1906. Telephone: 301-217-5600. Fax: 301-217-5617.
Towson, Maryland Office: Venable, Baetjer and Howard LLP, 210 Allegheny Avenue, P. O. Box 5517. Telephone: 410-494-6200. Fax: 410-821-0147.
Revisers of the Maryland Law Digest for this Directory.
See Professional Biographies, WASHINGTON, DISTRICT OF COLUMBIA

Vendt, Eric A. . . . . . . '69 '95 C.105 B.S. L.904 J.D. [Ⓐ Whiteford,T.&P.]
*PRACTICE AREAS: Business Law; Taxation and Estate Planning; Technology; Copyright Law.

Vent, H. Henning . . . . . . '48 '75 C.976 A.B. L.446 J.D. Asst. Corp. Coun.

Ventrell, Karen Hahn . . . . . . '58 '84 C.705 B.A. L.904 J.D. [Ross,D.&B.]

Ventrell-Monsees, Cathy '58 '83
C.705 B.A. L.30 J.D. Mng. Atty., Amer. Assn. of Ret. Persons

Ventriglia, Denis L., (P.C.) '55 '83
C.273 B.A. L.128 J.D. 1750 K St., N.W. (⊙Wilmington, NC)

Venturino, Anthony P. '56 '87
C.433 B.Ch.E. L.273 J.D. [Stevens,D.M.&M.] (See Pat. Sect.)
*PRACTICE AREAS: Patent Law; Trademark Law; Licensing; Litigation.

Venus, Shirin '74 '99 C.1365 B.A. L.260 J.D.
(adm. in FL; not adm. in DC) US Envir. Protec. Agcy.

Verby, Russell J. E. '68 '94 C.431 B.S. L.1048 J.D.
(adm. in PA; not adm. in DC) [Ⓐ Venable,A.B.H.&C.]
*PRACTICE AREAS: Civil Litigation; Criminal Litigation.

Vercelli, Patricia N. '63 '98 C.1356 B.A. L.30 J.D.
(adm. in MD; not adm. in DC) [Ⓐ Drinker B.&R.]

Verdier, Stephen J., (AV) '50 '76
C.30 B.A. L.128 J.D. Legis. Coun., America's Community Bkrs.

Verducci, Anthony J. . . . . . . '58 '90 C.871 B.S. L.776 J.D. [Ⓐ Morgan,L.&B.]

Vergeer, Vytas Varekojis '65 '93 C.446 B.A. L.128 J.D.
Dir., Gov. Relations/Staff Atty., National Housing Law Project

Vergnetti, Anthony . . . . . . '67 '95 C.36 B.A. L.1338 J.D. [Ⓐ Shaw,B.V.&R.]
*PRACTICE AREAS: Employment Law; Litigation; Federal Employment Law.

Verma, Richard R. . . . . . . '68 '93 C.401 B.S. L.30 J.D. [Ⓐ Steptoe&J.]

Vermillion, Lois J., (AV) . . . . . . '45 '77 C.30 B.A. L.1209 J.D. [Ⓒ Friedlander,M.S.K.&O.]
*PRACTICE AREAS: Commercial Transactional Real Estate; Leasing.

Vermont, Samson '68 '94 C.806 B.A. L.280 J.D.
(adm. in GA; not adm. in DC; Pat.) [Ⓐ Hunton&W.]
*PRACTICE AREAS: Patents.

Vermylen, Robert T.C. . . . . . . '72 '00 C&L.276 B.S., J.D. [Ⓐ Collier S.S.]
*PRACTICE AREAS: International Trade; Antitrust.

Verner, James M., (AV) . . . . . . '— '37 C&L.575 A.B., LL.B. [Verner,L.B.M.&H.]
*PRACTICE AREAS: Aviation Law.

Verner, Liipfert, Bernhard, McPherson and Hand, Chartered, (AV) BB
901 15th Street, N.W., 20005-2301 ⊙
Telephone: 202-371-6000 Cable Address: "Verlip" Fax: 202-371-6279
Email: verner.com URL: http://www.verner.com
Michael D. Berg; Berl Bernhard; Matthew C. Bernstein; James J. Blanchard; R. Stuart Broom; Hopewell H. Darneille, III; Andrew D. Eskin; William C. Evans; J. Cathy Fogel; Harold I. Freilich; Andrea Jill Grant; Marla Grossman; Douglas W. Hall; Lloyd N. Hand; Alan N. Hernandez; Thomas M. Ingoldsby; Thomas J. Keller; Gary J. Klein; William D. Kramer; Erwin G. Krasnow; Lawrence E. Levinson (Not admitted in DC); Don Charles Lewis; Harriet Lipkin; Martin T. Lutz; Joseph L. Manson, III; Harry McPherson; Karen Turner McWilliams; Brenda G. Meister (Not admitted in DC); Martin Mendelsohn; John A. Merrigan; John R. Mietus, Jr.; Evan M. Migdail; Gary C. Moss (Resident, Las Vegas, Nevada Office); Ronald B. Natalie; Paul E. Nordstrom; Peter S. Pantaleo; Steven R. Phillips; B. Donovan Picard; Neil T. Proto; Sherry A. Quirk; Michael J. Roberts; David R. Siddall; Lawrence R. Sidman; Cynthia M. Surrisi (Not admitted in DC); Deborah A. Swanstrom; Susan O'Hearn Temkin; James M. Verner (Emeritus); Clinton A. Vince; Linda M. Weinberg; Eric T. Werner; William A. Zeitler; John H. Zentay. Special Counsel: Robert J. Dole (Not admitted in DC); George J. Mitchell; W. DeVier Pierson. Senior Counsel: Alvaro Cifuentes de Castro. Of Counsel: Gregg S. Avitabile; Howell E. Begle, Jr.; Douglas Knox Bemis, Jr.; Leonard Garment; Philip R. Hochberg; James K. Jackson; David B. Jacobsohn; Joanna S. Kishner (See listing for Las Vegas, Nevada Office); Stanley W. Legro; Paul T. Luther; Frederick J. McConville; Mikol S. B. Neilson; Marilyn A. Pearson; Martin Schaefermeier; Regina Y. Speed-Bost (Not admitted in DC); Clifford E. Stevens, Jr.; Michael A. Taylor; Celeste M. Wasielewski;—Kelli A. Andrews; Hever M. Bascon, Jr. (Not admitted in DC); Virginia R. Boggs; Jessie Marie Brooks; Jamie E. Brown; Justin M. Cawley; Dylan Cors; Virginia C. Dailey (Not admitted in DC); Patricia A. Deem; Lawrence Duncan, III; David A. Fitzgerald; Neil Fried; Carmody Ann Gaba (Not admitted in DC); Emma F. Hand (Not admitted in DC); Noelle Montano Hawley; Steven R. Johnson; Brian P. Kalmaer (Resident, Las Vegas, Nevada Office); John M. R. Kneuer; Karen M. Lutjen; Jenifer J. Martin; Kerim P. May; William H. Minor; James A. Pickup; Lorraine Quiroga; Karen Anne Regan; Sara A. Robinson (Not admitted in DC); Joyce A. Rogers (Not admitted in DC); Timothy M. Rutten; Rachel Schottland (Not admitted in DC); Lela R. Scott; Susannah Shakow; Robin Remis Shichman; Thomas R. Snider (Not admitted in DC);

(This Listing Continued)

Verner, Liipfert, Bernhard, McPherson and Hand, Chartered (Continued)

Gopal Swaminathan; Jennifer H. Tribulski (Not admitted in DC); Lynn M. Van Buren; Orlando E. Vidal; Janet Baker Walker; Linda J. Willard. Principals: Suzanne D. Cartwright (Director of Urban Development); Denis J. Dwyer (Director of Legislative and Federal Affairs); Rosemary B. Freeman (Director of Public Affairs); Vicki Hart (Director of Legislative and Federal Affairs); David A. Weiss (Director of Trade Policy).

Administrative Law, Alternative Dispute Resolution, Antitrust and Trade Regulation, Aviation and Aerospace, Bankruptcy, Business Law, Casinos and Gambling, Civil Practice, Civil Rights, Class Actions, Commercial Law, Communications and Media, Constitutional Law, Contracts, Corporate Law, Criminal Law, Debtor and Creditor, Election, Campaign and Political Law, Energy, Entertainment and the Arts, Environmental Law, Federal Practice, Finance, Financial Restructuring, General Practice, Government, Government Contracts, Health Care, Hospital Law, Indians and Native Populations, Insurance, International Law, International Trade, Investments, Internet Ventures, Labor and Employment, Legal Ethics and Professional Responsibility, Legislative Practice, Litigation, Media Law, Mergers, Acquisitions and Divestitures, Municipal Law, Natural Resources, Nonprofit and Charitable Organizations, Privatizations, Public Finance, Railroad Law, Real Estate, Regulatory Law, Resorts and Leisure, Securities, Sports Law, Taxation, Technology and Science, Trademarks, Transportation, Urban Development, Utility Law, White Collar Crime, Workouts.

Las Vegas, Nevada Affiliate Office: Gary C. Moss, Hughes Center, 3960 Howard Hughes Parkway, Suite 400, 89109. Telephone: 702-737-3433. Facsimile: 702-737-1612.

See Professional Biographies, WASHINGTON, DISTRICT OF COLUMBIA

Vernick, Michael J. .... '69 '97 C.860 B.A. L.1209 J.D. [Ⓐ Hogan&H.]
Veron, Enid L. .... '41 '79 C.102 B.A. L.893 J.D. [Bingham D.]
*PRACTICE AREAS: Project and Structured Finance; Energy.
Veron, Gary L. .... '68 '94 C.886 B.S. L.893 J.D. [Ⓐ Dickstein S.M.&O.] (Pat.)
*PRACTICE AREAS: Intellectual Property.
Verrill, Charles Owen, Jr., (AV) .... '37 '62 C.860 A.B. L.228 J.D. [Wiley R.&F.]
*PRACTICE AREAS: International Trade; Mediation; Arbitration.
Verrill & Dana, (AV)
400 N. Capitol Street, Suite 585 (⊙Westwood, KS; Augusta, Kennebunk, Port., ME)
Verrilli, Donald B., Jr., (AV) .... '57 '87 C.976 B.A. L.178 J.D. [Jenner&B.]
*PRACTICE AREAS: Civil and Appellate Litigation; Telecommunications Law; Media and First Amendment Law; Election Law.
Verstandig, John D. .... '47 '74 C&L.659 B.S., J.D. 4850 Conn. Ave., N.W.
Ver Steeg, John C. .... '47 '75 C.309 A.B. L.813 J.D. 2022 Columbia Rd., NW
Verstegen, Anne-Marie .... '46 '80 C.846 B.J. L.273 J.D. [Verstegen&F.] ⊙
Verstegen & Fobe ..... 1815 Pennsylvania Avenue, N.W. Suite 900 (⊙Chevy Chase, MD)
Vertuno, Anthony A. .... '36 '61 C.742 B.A. L.597 J.D. [Ⓒ Shearman&S.]
*PRACTICE AREAS: Securities; Financial Services Law.
Verveer, Philip L., (AV) .... '44 '69 C.276 B.S.F.S. L.145 J.D. [Willkie F.&G.]
Verville, Richard E., (AV) .... '39 '65 C.951 B.A. L.178 LL.B. [Powers,P.S.&V.]
*PRACTICE AREAS: Health Care Law; Legislative Law.
Vesper, Gerald W., Law Office of, (AV) '32 '64
C.30 B.A. L.904 J.D. 1101 17th Street, N.W. Suite 820
Vestal, Katharine T. .... '72 '97 C.500 B.A. L.904 J.D. [Ⓐ Hogan&H.]
Veta, D. Jean, (AV) .... '54 '81 C.298 B.A. L.861 J.D. [Covington&B.]
Vetrano, Donna '— '01 C.1019 B.A. L.861 J.D.
(adm. in NY; not adm. in DC) [Ⓐ White&C.]
*PRACTICE AREAS: Litigation; Intellectual Property.
Vetter, Charles T., Jr. .... '22 '54 C.299 A.B. L.537 LL.B. 2123 Leroy Pl., NW‡
Vetter, Stephen K. .... '— '91 C&L.112 B.S., J.D. [Kozusko L.H.]
*PRACTICE AREAS: Taxation; Venture Capital; Private Business; Nonprofit Organizations; Estate Planning.
Veve, Michael E. .... '48 '73 C.477 B.A. L.677 LL.B. [Lasa,M.&V.]
Veytsman, Peter A. ..... '68 '00 C.705 B.S.M.E. L.831 J.D. [Ⓐ Dickstein S.M.&O.] (Pat.)
*PRACTICE AREAS: Intellectual Property.
Viccora, Michael A. .... '63 '90 C.197 B.A. L.273 J.D. [Seyfarth S.]
*PRACTICE AREAS: Labor and Employment Law.
Vice, Daniel R. .... '72 '98 C.30 B.A. L.569 J.D. Center to Prevent Handgun Violence
Vicinanza, Gregg H. .... '65 '92 C.705 B.A. L.569 J.D. [Ⓒ O'Melveny&M.]
*PRACTICE AREAS: Litigation; Antitrust and Trade Regulation.
Vickery, Ann Morgan, (AV) .... '44 '78 C.438 A.B. L.276 J.D. [Hogan&H.]
*PRACTICE AREAS: Health Care Legislation; Health Care Reform; Health Care Regulation; Medicare and Medicaid.
Vickery, Raymond E., Jr., (AV) .... '42 '68 C.228 A.B. L.309 LL.B. [Ⓒ Kile G.L.&R.P.]
*PRACTICE AREAS: International Trade and Transactions; Government Relations.
Vickery, Thomas E. '49 '79 C.871 B.S. L.446 J.D.
(adm. in MD; not adm. in DC) V.P. & Asst. Gen. Coun., Marriott Intl., Inc.
Victor, Aurore Y. .... '75 '00 C.976 B.A. L.309 J.D [Ⓐ Akin,G.S.H.&F.]
Victorino, Louis D. .... '45 '71 C.813 B.A. L.1068 J.D. [Ⓒ Fried,F.H.S.&J.] (⊙L.A., CA)
Victory, Kathleen, (AV) .... '58 '86 C.276 B.A. L.904 J.D. [Fletcher,H.&H.] ⊙
*PRACTICE AREAS: Telecommunications Law; Corporate Law; Transactional; Communications Law; FCC Licensing.
Vidal, Norma Jean .... '64 '99 C.1356 B.A. L.802 J.D. [Ⓐ Duncan&A.]
*PRACTICE AREAS: Electric Power; Energy Regulation; Utility Law.
Vidal, Orlando E. .... '— '91 C.311 B.A. L.94 J.D. [Ⓐ Verner,L.B.M.&H.]
*PRACTICE AREAS: Civil Litigation; White Collar Criminal Defense; International.
Vidal-Cordero, David .... '55 '82 C&L.677 B.A., J.D. [Arent F.K.P.&K.]
*PRACTICE AREAS: International Project Finance; International Telecommunications; Privatizations; Corporate Law; International Business Transactions.
Vierbuchen, Margaret M. .... '67 '97 C.475 B.A. L.276 J.D. [Ⓐ Howrey S.A.&W.]
*PRACTICE AREAS: Commercial Litigation; Antitrust.
Vieth, G. Duane, (AV) .... '23 '49 C&L.352 A.B., J.D. [Arnold&P.]
*PRACTICE AREAS: Litigation.
Vietzke, Lance L. .... '65 '94 C.494 B.S.E.E. L.1035 J.D. [Dorsey&W.] (Pat.)
*PRACTICE AREAS: Intellectual Property.
Vieux, Hardy '71 '99 C.228 A.B. L.477 J.D.
(adm. in NY; not adm. in DC) 716 Sicard Sreet, S.E.
Vignola, David E. '72 '00 C.273 B.A. L.472 J.D.
Atty./Advisor, Commodity Futures Trading Commission
Vihstadt, John E. .... '52 '77 C&L.546 B.A., J.D. [Krooth&A.]
*PRACTICE AREAS: Mortgage Financing; Housing and Urban Development; Legislation.
Vikander, Laura A. .... '56 '83 C.228 B.A. L.893 J.D. [Ⓒ Dickstein S.M.&O.]
*PRACTICE AREAS: Civil Litigation; Alternative Dispute Resolution; Insurance Litigation.
Vikmanis, Valda Maija '68 '98 C&L.494 B.A., J.D.
(adm. in MN; not adm. in DC) Legal Recruiter, Cares@Law
Viles, Thomas C. .... '— '88 C.309 A.B. L.569 J.D. [Ⓐ Williams&C.]
Villa, John K., (AV) .... '48 '73 C.228 A.B. L.477 J.D. [Williams&C.]
*PRACTICE AREAS: Administrative Litigation; Bank Fraud; Corporate Investigations; Corporate Litigation; Directors and Officers Insurance Coverage.
Villacorta, Gilberto M. '57 '92
C.705 B.A. L.262 J.D. 1025 Thomas Jefferson St., N.W. (Pat.)
Villafranco, John E. .... '62 '91 C.896 B.A. L.128 J.D. [Collier S.S.]
*PRACTICE AREAS: Antitrust; Trade Regulation; Electronic Commerce; Advertising Law.
Villanueva, Robin H. .... '60 '96 C.331 B.A. L.273 J.D. [Ⓐ Miller&C.]
*PRACTICE AREAS: ERISA; Retirement Benefit Plans; Health Benefits; Deferred Compensation; Employee Benefit Taxation.
Villet, Jeffrey M. .... '57 '83 C.502 B.A. L.273 J.D. 4301 Mass. Ave., N.W.
Vince, Clinton A., (AV) .... '— '75 C.855 A.B. L.276 J.D. [Verner,L.B.M.&H.]
*PRACTICE AREAS: Energy Law; International Commercial Law; General Litigation.

Vincent, Alexander Craig .... '65 '98 C.604 B.A. L.128 J.D. [Ⓐ Berliner,C.&R.]
*PRACTICE AREAS: Complex Civil Litigation; White Collar Criminal Litigation; Corporate; Real Estate; Debtor and Creditor Collections.
Vincent, O. Kevin .... '62 '86 C&L.16 B.S., J.D. [Ⓒ Baker B.]
Vincent, Paul M., (AV) .... '44 '70 C.309 B.A. L.893 J.D. [Ober,K.G.&S.]
Vine, Howard A. .... '54 '79 C.30 B.A. L.1209 J.D. [Greenberg T.]
Vine, John M., (AV) .... '44 '70 C.31 A.B. L.309 J.D. [Covington&B.]

Vinson & Elkins L.L.P., (AV) BR

A Registered Limited Liability Partnership

The Willard Office Building, 1455 Pennsylvania Avenue, N.W., 20004-1008 ⊙

Telephone: 202-639-6500 Fax: 202-639-6604

URL: http://www.velaw.com

Resident Partners: Michael A. Andrews; David T. Andril; Stephen Angle; Alden L. Atkins; Dennis M. Barry; C. Michael Buxton; Michael R. Charness; David B. Cohen; Christopher P. B. Erckert; Ky P. Ewing, Jr.; Tegan M. Flynn; Catherine S. Gallagher; Kevin A. Gaynor; Jay H. Hebert (Not admitted in DC); Michael J. Henke; George C. Hopkins; Neil W. Imus; David R. Johnson; Gary M. Kotara; Mark S. Laufman; William E. Lawler, III; Cathy A. Lewis; Kathleen C. Little; Paul S. Maco; Robert A. Mazer; Larry A. Oday; Mark R. Spivak; Gregory C. Staple; John D. Taurman; Charles D. Tetrault; Mark H. Tuohey, III; Christine L. Vaughn; Adam Wenner; Anita Rutkowski Wilson; Paul L. Yde. Resident Of Counsel: Donna J. Bobbish; Becky M. Bruner; Debra J. Duncan; Greta L.H. Lichtenbaum; Joseph E. Lynch; Samuel B. Sterrett; Robert D. Vander Lugt. Resident Associates: Virginia Navarrete Brooks; Melissa K. Cantrell; Christopher K. Carr; Mikeal M. Clayton; Christopher M. Dawe (Not admitted in DC); John S. Decker; Benjamin Erulkar; Alexander M. Evans (Not admitted in DC); James R. Farnsworth; John M. Faust; Judith M. Feldt (Not admitted in DC); E. Malia Godfrey; David K. Godschalk; Jennifer Monday Goldman (Not admitted in DC); Melissa R.H. Hall; Karl Kiffin Hennessee (Not admitted in DC); Helen M. Hight (Not admitted in DC); Joseph E. Hunsader (Not admitted in DC); Mark Reid Klupt; Douglas J. Lanzo; Mary N. Lehner; Benjamin S. Lippard (Not admitted in DC); Dionne C. Lomax; Mark Alan Lowry (Not admitted in DC); Stacey Kyle Luck (Not admitted in DC); Bruce C. McCulloch; Leah E. Medway; J. Todd Metcalf (Not admitted in DC); Andrew J. Miller (Not admitted in DC); Alexander Paul Okuliar (Not admitted in DC); Daniel A. Petalas; R. Edward Price; Suzanne D. Reifman; Amanda Lynn Riedel (Not admitted in DC); Robert J. Rothwell (Not admitted in DC); Andrew Ruskin (Not admitted in DC); Gail D. Sausser (Not admitted in DC); Justin M. Shellaway (Not admitted in DC); Meghan S. Skelton (Not admitted in DC); David P. Steinberger; Charles Alan Stormont (Not admitted in DC); Sara C. Weinberg; James M. Wilson (Not admitted in DC).

General Civil and Trial Practice. Admiralty, Antitrust, Aviation, Banking, Corporation, Environmental, Insurance, International, Labor, Municipal, Oil and Gas, Patent, Real Estate, Taxation, Trademark and Copyright, Trust and Utility Law.

Austin, Texas Office: One American Center Suite 2700, 600 Congress Avenue, Austin, Texas, 78701-3200. Telephone: 512-542-8400. Fax: 512-542-8612.

Beijing, China Office: 20/F, Beijing Silver Tower, No. 2, Dong San Huan Bei Lu, Chaoyang District, 100027. Telephone: +86-10-6410-6300. Fax: +86-10-6410-6360.

Dallas, Texas Office: 3700 Trammell Crow Center, 2001 Ross Avenue, Dallas, Texas, 75201-2975. Telephone: 214-220-7700. Fax: 214-220-7716.

Houston, Texas Office: 2300 First City Tower, 1001 Fannin, Houston, Texas, 77002-6760. Telephone: 713-758-2222. Fax: 713-758-2346.

London, England Office: City Point, 33rd Floor, 1 Ropemaker Street, London EC2Y 9UE, England. Telephone: (44-20) 7065-6000. Fax: (44-20) 7065-6001.

Moscow, Russia Office: 16 Ulitsa Spiridonovka, Second Floor, 103001 Moscow, Russia. Telephone: (7-095) 956-1995. Local Fax: (7-095) 956-1996. U.S. Satellite Fax: (212) 803-0142.

New York, N.Y. Office: 666 Fifth Avenue, 26th Floor, New York, N.Y., 10103-0040. Telephone: 917-206-8000. Fax: 917-206-8100.

Singapore Office: 6 Battery Road, #39-01, Singapore, 049909. Telephone: (65) 536-8300. Fax: (65) 536-8311. Avenue, N.W., Washington, D.C., 20004-1008.

See Professional Biographies, WASHINGTON, DISTRICT OF COLUMBIA

Vinyard, Julie A. S. .... '71 '97 C.1369 B.S. L.893 J.D. [Ⓐ Steptoe&J.]
Vinyard, Walter Darnall, (AV) .... '43 '69 C.945 A.B. L.178 LL.B. [Vinyard&Assoc.]
Vinyard & Associates, (AV) .... 555 13th Street, N.W.
Virgulak, William J., Jr., (AV) '52 '77
C.676 B.A. L.1209 J.D. [Ⓐ Martell,D.G.&G.] (⊙Fairfax, VA)
*PRACTICE AREAS: Civil Practice; Personal Injury Litigation; Defense Litigation; Automobile Liability; Products Liability.
Virk, Devki K. .... '68 '96 C.145 A.B. L.339 J.D. [Ⓐ Bredhoff&K.]
Virnstein, Jill C. '67 '95 C.282 B.A. L.818 J.D.
(adm. in MD; not adm. in DC) Mgr., Pub. Affs., United Parcel Service
Virtue, Melodie A., (AV) .... '57 '82 C.273 B.A. L.904 J.D. [Ⓒ Garvey,S.&B.]
*PRACTICE AREAS: Radio Law; Television Law; Communications Law; Telecommunications Law; Entertainment Law.
Virtue, Paul W. .... '55 '82 C&L.923 B.S., J.D. [Ⓒ Hogan&H.]
*PRACTICE AREAS: Immigration.
Viscovich, David M. .... '70 '98 C.945 B.A. L.276 J.D. [Ⓐ Coudert B.]
*PRACTICE AREAS: Corporate; Securities; Telecommunications.
Vishab, Stefanie '72 '98 C.105 B.A. L.831 J.D.
(adm. in PA; not adm. in DC) 1150 18th St., N.W.
Visser, Robert P. .... '— '67 C.563 B.S. L.273 J.D. [Ⓒ Bryan C.]
*PRACTICE AREAS: International Investment; International Finance; International Trade; International Corporate; Corporate.
Vitale, Joseph P. .... '71 '98 C.321 A.B. L.276 J.D. [Ⓐ Kirkpatrick&L.]
*PRACTICE AREAS: Financial Institutions; Litigation; Corporate; Securities.
Vitale, Matthew J. .... '69 '96 C.446 B.A. L.904 J.D. [Ⓐ Coudert B.]
*PRACTICE AREAS: Telecommunications Law.
Vitan, Emily C. '75 '00 C&L.893 B.A., J.D.
(adm. in VA; not adm. in DC) [Ⓐ Hogan&H.]
Vitelli, Mary Louise '62 '88 C.93 B.A. L.724 J.D.
(adm. in CT; not adm. in DC) AEAI
Vitolo, Frank J. .... '73 '98 C.93 B.A. L.273 J.D. [Ⓐ Keller&H.]
*PRACTICE AREAS: Commercial Litigation; Intellectual Property Litigation; General Litigation.
Vitrano, Paul C. .... '69 '95 C.884 B.A. L.273 J.D. [Ⓐ Ross,D.&B.]
Vitt, A. Francis, Jr., (AV) '38 '64 C&L.276 A.B., J.D.
[Altmann&V.] (⊙Arlington, VA)
Vizzini, Charles S. .... '37 '60 C.102 B.A. L.178 LL.B. 2025 I St., N.W. (⊙Brooklyn, NY)
Vladeck, David C. .... '51 '77 C.569 B.A. L.178 J.D. Dir., Public Citizen Litig. Grp.
Vlossak, Frank C. '67 '99 C.299 B.A. L.1209 J.D.
(adm. in VA; not adm. in DC) [Ⓐ Williams&J.]
*PRACTICE AREAS: Legislative Practice; Energy; Environmental Law; Transportation.
Vodra, William W., (AV) .... '43 '68 C.970 B.A. L.178 J.D. [Arnold&P.]
*PRACTICE AREAS: Food and Drug; Products Liability.
Voegele, Royal J. '26 '50 C.494 B.S. L.966 LL.B.
(adm. in WI; not adm. in DC) 1711 Mass. Ave.‡
Voegtli, Naomi Abe .... '64 '98 C.846 B.S. L.309 J.D. [Ⓐ Hogan&H.] (Pat.)
*PRACTICE AREAS: Patent Litigation; Patent Prosecution; Patent Licensing; Computer Software Patents; Computer Architecture Patents.
Voelker, Kathleen E., (AV) .... '47 '77 C.1059 A.B. L.383 J.D. [Ⓒ P.B.Stuart]
*PRACTICE AREAS: Litigation; White Collar Criminal Defense; Health Law; Mediation; Employment Discrimination.
Vogel, Alexander N. .... '70 '97 C.112 B.A. L.273 J.D. 1776 K St., N.W.
Vogel, Christina M. '67 '99 C.223 B.S. L.896 J.D.
(adm. in VA; not adm. in DC) Manager, Pricewaterhouse Coopers LLP
Vogel, David A. .... '66 '92 C.477 B.S.E. L.813 J.D. [Ⓐ Kelley D.&W.]
*PRACTICE AREAS: Litigation; Government Contracts; Intellectual Property.
Vogel, Frederick W.B., (AV) '51 '77 C.575 A.B. L.893 J.D.
(adm. in VA; not adm. in DC)
Sr. V.P. & Assoc. Gen. Coun., Int. Lodging, Marriott Intl., Inc.

Vogel, John H., (AV) ....'44 '70 C.674 A.B. L.477 J.D. [Patton B.]
Vogel, Kenneth Alan, (BV) .... '57 '87 C.228 A.B. L.30 J.D. [Bar-Adon&V.]
Vogel, Ralph H. '24 '54
C.309 B.S. L.273 LL.B. Staff Dir., Fulbright Prog., U.S. Info. Agcy.
Vogel, Robert L., (AV) .... '58 '86 C.31 B.A. L.818 J.D. [Vogel&S.]
*PRACTICE AREAS: False Claims Act; Qui Tam Litigation; Health Care Fraud; Health Care Litigation.

Vogel & Slade, L.L.P., (AV)
1225 Nineteenth Street, N.W. Suite 300, 20036
Telephone: 202-223-4711 Fax: 202-223-4714 URL: http://www.lawyers.com/vogel&slade Email: robvogel@wizard.net
Email: ssladeesq@aol.com URL: http://www.fraudbuster.com
Robert L. Vogel; Shelley R. Slade.
Qui Tam Litigation, False Claims Act, Complex Multi-District Litigation, Trial Practice, White Collar Crimes, Health Care Fraud.
See Professional Biographies, WASHINGTON, DISTRICT OF COLUMBIA

Voght, F. Brook, (AV) .... '— '71 C.16 B.S. L.260 J.D. [Sutherland A.&B.]
*PRACTICE AREAS: Tax Litigation; Tax Appeals; Tax Audits; International Taxation; Taxation.
Vogler, Theresa M. .... '57 '83 C.881 A.B. L.273 J.D. 1666 K St., N.W.‡
Vogt, Carl W., (AV) ....'36 '65 C.951 B.A. L.846 LL.B. [Fulbright&J.]
*PRACTICE AREAS: Alternative Dispute Resolution; Administrative Law.
Vogt, Gregory J., (AV) .... '54 '79 C.378 B.A. L.597 J.D. [Wiley R.&F.]
*PRACTICE AREAS: Communications.
Vogt, Jeffrey S. '71 '00 C.473 B.A. L.188 J.D.
(adm. in NY; not adm. in DC) [Ⓐ James&H.]
*PRACTICE AREAS: Labor Law; Employment Law; International Law.
Voight, Jason D. ....'68 '96 C.188 B.S. L.846 J.D. [Keil&W.] (See Pat. Sect.)
*PRACTICE AREAS: Patents; Trademark Law; Litigation.
Vold, Kevin L. .... '71 '96 C.813 A.B. L.597 J.D. [Ⓐ Hogan&H.]
Vold, Tara M. ....'71 '96 C.197 B.A. L.597 J.D. [Ⓐ Howrey S.A.&W.]
*PRACTICE AREAS: Trademarks; Litigation.
Volentine, Richard J., Jr. '55 '80 C.812 B.S. L.16 J.D.
(adm. in AL; not adm. in DC) Assoc. Gen. Coun, Fannie Mae
*RESPONSIBILITIES: Mortgage Banking Law; Mortgage Finance; Real Estate.
Volin, Richard M. ....'69 '96 C.477 B.A. L.273 J.D. [Ⓐ Finkelstein,T.&L.]
Volkmuth, Daniel R. '68 '97 C.1213 B.S. L.145 J.D.
(adm. in OH; not adm. in DC) [Ⓐ Patton B.]
Volkov, Michael L., (AV) .... '57 '82 C.659 B.S.B.A. L.276 J.D. U.S. Atty. Off.
Volland, Debra R. ....'73 '99 C.197 B.A. L.309 J.D. [Ⓐ Covington&B.]
*PRACTICE AREAS: Antitrust; Litigation.
Vollmann, Alan P., (AV) ....'48 '80 C.112 B.A. L.128 J.D. [Holland&K.]
*PRACTICE AREAS: Commercial Real Estate; Finance.
Vollmer, Andrew N., (AV) ....'53 '78 C.473 B.A. L.893 J.D. [Wilmer,C.&P.]
*PRACTICE AREAS: International Law; Securities.
Vollmers, Kristin J. .... '70 '97 C.585 B.A. L.494 J.D. [Ⓐ Akin,G.S.H.&F.]
*PRACTICE AREAS: Litigation; Health Care.
Volner, Ian D., (AV) ....'40 '67 C.165 B.A. L.178 LL.B. [Venable,A.B.H.&C.]
*PRACTICE AREAS: Mass Media; Direct Marketing; Telecommunications; Legislative Practice.
Volpano, Linda '63 '89 C.966 B.A. L.94 J.D.
(adm. in NY; not adm. in DC) Assoc. Gen. Coun., Kaplan Educational Centers, Inc.
Volpe, Frank R. ....'62 '94 C.1356 B.A. L.904 J.D. [Ⓐ Sidley A.B.&W.]
Volpe, Joseph, Jr., (AV) ....'13 '40 C&L.571 LL.B. 918 16th St.NW
Voltmer, Ralph C., Jr. ....'60 '88 C.938 B.A. L.276 J.D. [Covington&B.]

Voltz, William R., (AV) '36 '62 C.1031 B.S. L.276 J.D.
2120 L Street, N.W., Suite 700, 20037
Telephone: 202-293-2131 Fax: 202-293-0947
***PRACTICE AREAS: Civil Litigation; Medical Malpractice; Legal Malpractice; Personal Injury; Trusts and Estates.**
General and Administrative Practice including Trials in all Courts, Medical Malpractice, Legal Malpractice, Corporate Law, Business Law, Probate Law, Trusts and Estates, Financial Planning, Wealth Preservation.
See Professional Biographies, WASHINGTON, DISTRICT OF COLUMBIA

Volzer, Harvey J., (BV) .... '50 '74 C.276 B.S.F.S. L.229 J.D. [Shaughnessy,V.&G.]
vom Eigen, Robert P., (AV) ....'— '71 C.918 B.A. L.1066 J.D. [Foley&L.]
*PRACTICE AREAS: Transportation Law; Administrative; Legislative Advocacy.
Von Bargen, Patrick '48 '74 C&L.813 B.A., J.D.
(adm. in CA; not adm. in DC) 1217 Massachusetts Ave., S.E.
von Conrad, Gunter, (AV) .... '34 '65 C.999 L.273 M.C.L. [Ⓒ Barnes,R.&C.]
*PRACTICE AREAS: Customs; International Trade.
Von Flatern, Jan K. ....'49 '76 C.19 B.A. L.1162 J.D. [Ⓐ Dombroff&G.]
von Luttichau, Ann H. ......'44 '82 C.999 B.A. L.128 J.D. 2801 New Mexico Ave., N.W.
von Oehsen, William H.E., (BV) ....'58 '88 C.674 A.B. L.276 J.D. [Powell,G.F.&M.]
*PRACTICE AREAS: Food and Drug Law; Health Care; Managed Care.
Von Ohsen, William H. E. '58 '89 C.674 A.B. L.276 J.D.
1001 Pennsylvania Ave., N.W.
Von-Pervieux, Claudia A. ....'68 '93 C.1158 B.A. L.29 J.D. [Ⓐ Sidley A.B.&W.]
Von Salzen, Eric, (AV) .... '43 '68 C.309 B.A. L.178 LL.B. [Hogan&H.]
*PRACTICE AREAS: Appellate Practice; Eminent Domain; Litigation; Real Estate; Transportation.
von Schriltz, Karl ....'70 '98 C.311 B.A. L.145 J.D. [Ⓐ Willkie F.&G.]
Voorhees, Catherine M. '60 '88
C.390 B.S.E.E. L.1209 J.D. [Ⓒ Venable,A.B.H.&C.] (See Pat. Sect.)
*PRACTICE AREAS: Patents; Trademarks; Copyrights.
Voorhees, Theodore, Jr., (AV) ....'49 '75 C.309 B.A. L.128 J.D. [Covington&B.]
Vorkink, Andrew N. ..... '47 '73 C.976 B.A. L.309 J.D. Intl. Bk. for Reconstr. & Develop.
Vorrasi, Nicole M. '72 '98 C.319 B.A. L.180 J.D.
(adm. in NY; not adm. in DC) [Ⓐ Dickstein S.M.&O.]
*PRACTICE AREAS: Taxation.

Vorys, Sater, Seymour and Pease LLP, (AV) BB
11th Floor, 1828 L Street, N.W., 20036-5109 ⊙
Telephone: 202-467-8800 Telex: 440693 Telecopier: 202-467-8900
URL: http://www.vssp.com
Joseph D. Lonardo; James K. Alford; Cory M. Amron; Steven R. Becker; Thomas H. Bentz, Jr.; Thomas R. Boland; Cathy A. Braxton; Pamela A. Bresnahan; Jean-Marc Brun; James M. Burns; Karen E. Christian (Not admitted in DC); Warren W. Glick; Elizabeth Toni Guarino; Richard J. Leon; Peter A. Martin; Nihar R. Mohanty; Michael Sean Purcell; Ronald E. Shapiro; Elizabeth Treubert Simon; Michael S. Snarr (Not admitted in DC); George W. Swenson, Jr.; Randal C. Teague; John W. Wilmer, Jr.; Reid M. Wilson (Not admitted in DC).
Commercial Litigation, Copyright/Patent/Trademark, Federal Legislative, Government Contracts, Intellectual Property, Customs, International Trade, Export Control, International, Congressional Investigations, White Collar Defense.
Columbus, Ohio Office: 52 East Gay Street, P.O. Box 1008, 43216-1008. Telephone: 614-464-6400. Telex: 241348. Telecopier: 614-464-6350.
Cleveland, Ohio Office: 2100 One Cleveland Center, 1375 East Ninth Street, 44114-1724. Telephone: 216-479-6100. Telecopier: 216-479-6060.
Cincinnati, Ohio Office: Suite 2100, 221 East Fourth Street, P.O. Box 0236, 45201-0236. Telephone: 513-723-4000. Telecopier: 513-723-4056.
Alexandria, Virginia Office: 277 South Washington Street, Suite 310, 22314. Telephone: 703-837-6999. Facsimile: 703-549-4492.
See Professional Biographies, WASHINGTON, DISTRICT OF COLUMBIA

Voss, Susan Lee, (AV) ....'32 '84 C.1356 B.A. L.276 J.D. [Holland&K.]
*PRACTICE AREAS: Real Estate Law; Financial Institutions Law; Timesharing; Resort Development; Golf Clubs.
Vossler, Colleen Kotyk '71 '98 C.309 A.B. L.945 J.D.
(adm. in MD; not adm. in DC) [Ⓐ Shaw P.]
Votava, G. Joseph, Jr., (AV) '54 '81 C.1021 B.B.A. L.201 J.D.
[Nixon P.] (⊙Roch., NY)
*PRACTICE AREAS: Employee Benefits; Investments; Taxation; Trusts and Estates.
Votaw, James G. ....'— '90 C.216 B.A. L.128 J.D. [Hale&D.]
*PRACTICE AREAS: Environmental.
Vovakis, Lewis H. ....'34 '64 C.659 A.B. L.1017 J.D. 2545 Waterside Dr., N.W.
Voyard, Ernest Sylvain, Jr. .... '75 '00 C.228 A.B. L.309 J.D. [Ⓐ Akin,G.S.H.&F.]
Vretenarova, Petia '73 '01 C.30 B.A. L.823 J.D.
(adm. in NY; not adm. in DC) [Ⓐ Cleary,G.S.&H.]
Vroomán, Edward A. '39 '64 C.688 B.Mgt.Eng. L.228 J.D.
(adm. in NY; not adm. in DC) [Aitken I.B.&V.] (⊙White Plains, NY)
Vu, Kenneth K. D. '66 '96 C.886 B.S.E.E. L.273 J.D.
(adm. in IL; not adm. in DC; Pat.) [Ⓐ Piper M.R.&W.]
*PRACTICE AREAS: Intellectual Property.
Vujic, Tatiana '72 '00 C.976 B.A. L.273 J.D.
(adm. in VA; not adm. in DC) 1722 Eye St., N.W.
Vukowich, William T. ....'43 '69 C.347 A.B. L.1066 J.D. Georgetown Univ. Law Ctr.
Waala, Joseph R. '72 '99 C.999 B.S. L.276 J.D.
(adm. in OH; not adm. in DC) [Ⓐ King&S.]
*PRACTICE AREAS: Tax.
Wachen, David S. ....'64 '93 C.197 A.B. L.659 J.D. [Baker&H.]
*PRACTICE AREAS: First Amendment; Media Law; General Litigation.
Wachen, Kimberly A. ....'— '93 C.228 B.A. L.659 J.D. [Arent F.K.P.&K.]
*PRACTICE AREAS: Corporate; Electronic Commerce; Real Estate.
Wachtel, Bonnie K. '55 '82 C.145 B.A. L.893 J.D.
V.P. & Gen. Coun., Wachtel & Company, Inc.
Wachtel, David M., (AV) ....'62 '90 C.910 B.A. L.846 J.D. [Rose&R.]
*PRACTICE AREAS: Employment Discrimination; Americans with Disabilities Act; Federal Employment Law; Employment Contracts; FOIA & Privacy Act.
Wackerle, Rex Brian .... '57 '87 C.36 B.S. L.990 J.D. V.P., Bank of America
Waddell, Julie A. .... '59 '84 C.373 B.A. L.477 J.D. [Ⓒ Harkins C.]
*PRACTICE AREAS: Regulated Industries; Administrative Law; Antitrust; Litigation.
Waddell, Karen T. '56 '81 C.420 B.A. L.945 J.D.
(adm. in WV; not adm. in DC) Coun., Consolidated Nat. Gas Serv. Co.
Waddington, Richard F. .... '63 '97 C.454 B.S. L.904 J.D. [Ⓐ Willkie F.&G.]
*PRACTICE AREAS: Environmental.
Waddoups, Gregory L. ....'67 '94 C.877 B.A. L.878 J.D. [Ⓐ Venable,A.B.H.&C.]
*PRACTICE AREAS: Commercial Litigation; Arbitration; Products Liability.
Wade, J. Kirk, (AV) ....'45 '73 C.802 B.A. L.273 J.D. [Patton B.]
Wade, Michael J. '68 '01 C.902 B.A. L.1209 J.D.
(adm. in VA; not adm. in DC) [Ⓐ Sperduto]
*PRACTICE AREAS: Complex Commercial Litigation; Bankruptcy; Construction Law; Environmental Litigation; Real Estate Litigation.
Wade, Robert ....'36 '68 C&L.273 A.B., J.D. [Silverberg&W.]
Wade, Stephanie Karen ....'55 '81 C.575 B.A. L.280 J.D. [Dickstein S.M.&O.]
*PRACTICE AREAS: Intellectual Property.
Wadler, Linda A. ... '63 '88 C.339 B.S. L.477 J.D. [Finnegan,H.F.G.&D.] (See Pat. Sect.)
*PRACTICE AREAS: Patent Litigation; Patent Prosecution.
Wadler, Marie Johnson ....'63 '88 C.228 A.B. L.245 J.D. [Nixon P.]
*PRACTICE AREAS: Real Estate Law; Finance Law; Commercial Leasing; Real Estate Syndication.
Wadley, Daniel J. ....'73 '00 C.101 B.S. L.276 J.D. [Ⓐ Wiley R.&F.]
Wadlow, R. Clark, (AV) ....'46 '71 C.197 A.B. L.309 J.D. [Sidley A.B.&W.]
Wadrzyk, Mark Edward '68 '98 C.597 B.S.E.E. L.146 J.D.
(adm. in IL; not adm. in DC; See Pat. Sect.) [Ⓐ Fish&R.]
*PRACTICE AREAS: Patent Law; Intellectual Property; Patent Prosecution; Patent Litigation.
Wadsworth, Jeffrey A. ....'72 '99 C.945 B.A. L.273 J.D. [Ⓐ Gibson,D.&C.]
*PRACTICE AREAS: Appellate Practice; General Litigation.
Wadyka, Christina S. .... '62 '87 C.788 B.A. L.245 J.D. [Ⓒ Dow,L.&A.]
Wadzinski, Kevin J. .... '66 '93 C&L.966 B.A., J.D. [Dorsey&W.]
*PRACTICE AREAS: Federal Indian Law; Employment Law; Tribal Law; State-Tribal Relations; Tribal Taxation.
Wager, Joseph S., (AV) ....'39 '66 C.390 B.A. L.276 J.D. [Haas&N.]
Wager-Zito, Adrian ....'60 '85 C.1044 B.A. L.273 J.D. [Jones,D.R.&P.]
*PRACTICE AREAS: Litigation; Complex Business Litigation; Securities Class Actions.
Waggoner, Daniel, (AV) .....'52 '79 C.860 B.A. L.976 J.D. [Davis W.T.] (⊙Seattle, WA)
*PRACTICE AREAS: Communications; Media; Antitrust Regulation; Litigation.
Waghorn, Andrew J. '65 '90 C&L.128 B.A., J.D.
(adm. in NY; not adm. in DC) [Ⓐ Carr G.]
*PRACTICE AREAS: Medical Malpractice Defense.
Wagman, Robert J., Jr. ....'68 '00 C.446 B.S. L.30 J.D. [Ⓐ Arnold&P.]
*PRACTICE AREAS: Government Contracts.
Wagner, Annice McBryde .... '37 '63 Chief App. Ct. J.
Wagner, Brenda Carol ....'51 '77 C&L.574 B.S., J.D. [Wagner&Assoc.]
*PRACTICE AREAS: Probate; Real Estate; Bankruptcy.
Wagner, C. Elizabeth '49 '89 C&L.846 B.B.A., J.D.
Dir., Price Waterhouse Coopers, LLP
Wagner, David W. '64 '99 C.645 B.S. L.30 J.D.
(adm. in MD; not adm. in DC) [Ⓐ Beveridge&D.]
*PRACTICE AREAS: International Environmental; Environmental Litigation.
Wagner, Erin Gibson ....'74 '00 C.473 B.A. L.124 J.D. [Ⓐ Dechert]
*PRACTICE AREAS: Financial Services Law; Investment Management.
Wagner, Fred R. ....'62 '87 C.860 B.A. L.893 J.D. [Beveridge&D.]
*PRACTICE AREAS: Litigation; Environmental Law.
Wagner, James R. ....'66 '92 C.94 B.A. L.276 J.D. [Ⓒ Howrey S.A.&W.]
*PRACTICE AREAS: Insurance; Commercial Disputes.
Wagner, Jennifer Dine ....'66 '96 C.27 B.A. L.128 J.D. [Ⓐ Fletcher,H.&H.] ⊙
*PRACTICE AREAS: Radio and Television Broadcast Law; FCC Licensing and Regulation; Cable Television Regulation; Native American Broadcast and Telecommunications; Civil Litigation.
Wagner, John P. '58 '89 C.165 B.A. L.273 J.D.
(adm. in VA; not adm. in DC) American Petroleum Institute
Wagner, Marilyn G. '36 '61 C.188 B.A. L.178 LL.B.
(adm. in CO; not adm. in DC) [Margulies&W.]
Wagner, Martha Jo ....'51 '82 C.446 B.A. L.276 J.D. [Venable,A.B.H.&C.]
*PRACTICE AREAS: Employee Benefits; ERISA Litigation.
Wagner, Matthew C. ....'70 '96 C.696 B.A. L.1048 J.D. 1633 Connecticut Ave.
Wagner, Patricia M. ....'— '00 C.378 B.A. L.734 J.D. [Ⓐ Epstein B.&G.]
*PRACTICE AREAS: Health Care.
Wagner, Roger B. ....'54 '82 C.976 B.A. L.893 J.D. [Coudert B.]
*PRACTICE AREAS: Corporate Law; Project Finance; Energy; Privatization.
Wagner, Stephen H. .... '63 '00 C.602 B.A. L.276 J.D. [Ⓐ Baker&M.]
*PRACTICE AREAS: Corporate and Partnership Law; Mergers and Acquisitions; Derivatives/Financial Products; Corporate Financings (Public and Private); Major Projects.
Wagner, Steven E. ....'72 '98 C.276 B.A. L.659 J.D. [Ⓐ Chadbourne&P.]

Wagner, Todd A. '66 '91 C.629 B.A. L.982 J.D.
(adm. in NY; not adm. in DC; See Pat. Sect.) [Pennie&E.]
*PRACTICE AREAS: Intellectual Property; Litigation.

Wagner & Associates
733 Fifteenth Street, N.W., Suite 908, 20005-2112
Telephone: 202-638-2222 Fax: 202-638-1838
Email: attywagner@msn.com URL: http://www.lawyers.com/wagnerlaw
Brenda Carol Wagner.
Trusts and Estates, Estate Litigation, Financial Planning, Family Wealth Transfer, Retirement Planning, Contested Wills, Inheritance, Probate, Missing Heir Searches, Wills, Small Business Law, Family Business Successions, Business Organization, Business Planning, Minority Business Law, Asset Protection, Bankruptcy Chapter 7, Bankruptcy Chapter 11, Bankruptcy Chapter 13, Civil Practice, Administrative Law, Regulatory Law.
See Professional Biographies, WASHINGTON, DISTRICT OF COLUMBIA

Wagnon, Todd Jason . . . . '73 '98 C.276 B.S. L.273 J.D. [Ⓐ Thelen R.&P.]
*PRACTICE AREAS: Construction.
Wahl, Barbara S., (AV) . . . .'53 '79 C.446 B.A. L.823 J.D. [Arent F.K.P.&K.]
*PRACTICE AREAS: Litigation.
Wahle, Karen Mary . . . .'59 '92 C.339 B.S. L.813 J.D. [O'Melveny&M.]
Waid, Gerald L. . . . . '55 '90 C.10 B.A. L.846 J.D. [Ⓒ Zuckert,S.&R.]
*PRACTICE AREAS: Aircraft Finance and Leasing; International Finance.
Waikart, Douglas O., (AV) . . . . '53 '78 C.446 B.A. L.273 J.D. [Wright&T.]
*PRACTICE AREAS: Energy.
Wainstein, Kenneth L., (AV) . . . . '62 '88 C.893 B.A. L.112 J.D. Fed. Pros.
Waite, Barbara L., (AV) . . . .'52 '84 C.836 B.A. L.276 J.D. [Venable,A.B.H.&C.]
*PRACTICE AREAS: Intellectual Property Law.
Waite, Frederick P., (AV) . . . .'45 '72 C.674 A.B. L.309 J.D. [Holland&K.]
*PRACTICE AREAS: International Trade Law; Customs Law; International Transactions.
Waite, G. Graham '25 '50 C&L.966 B.S., LL.B.
(adm. in WI; not adm. in DC) Catholic Univ. of Amer.
Waite, Jason M. '73 '98 C.478 B.A. L.245 J.D.
(adm. in GA; not adm. in DC) [Ⓐ Alston&B.]
*PRACTICE AREAS: Administrative Law; Customs Law; International Trade Regulation.
Waites, Gerard M. '59 '89 C.1296 B.A. L.64 J.D.
(adm. in PA; not adm. in DC) [O'Donoghue&O.]
Waites, Veronique K. . . . .'73 '98 C.012 B.A. L.893 J.D. [Ⓐ Sullivan&C.]
Waits, John A., II, (AV) . . . .'47 '78 C.500 B.A. L.569 J.D. [Winston&S.]
*PRACTICE AREAS: Legislative Practice; Administrative/Regulatory Law; Agriculture; Economic Development; Trade.
Waitzkin, Michael B., (AV) . . . . '49 '74 C.893 B.A. L.813 J.D. [Foxkiser]
Wakelyn, Catherine Carl, (AV) . . . .'42 '78 C.691 B.A. L.128 J.D. [Ⓒ Duane,M.&H.]
*PRACTICE AREAS: Energy Regulatory Law; Administrative Law.
Wakin, Alysa Beth '68 '95 C.569 B.A. L.884 J.D.
(adm. in CT; not adm. in DC) [Ⓐ Wiley R.&F.]
Wakino, Michelle A. '60 '89 C.1109 B.A. L.426 J.D.
(adm. in CA; not adm. in DC) [Ⓐ Morrison&F.] (⊙Irvine, CA; Mc Lean, VA)
Walawender, Richard A. '60 '86 C&L.477 B.A., J.D.
(adm. in MI; not adm. in DC) [Miller,C.P.&S.] (⊙Detroit, MI; Gdynia, Poland)
*PRACTICE AREAS: Business Law; Finance (Public and Project Financings); International Corporate Law; Automotive Industry; Real Estate Development.
Walcoff, Sheila Dearybury . . . .'69 '93 C.999 B.A. L.276 J.D. [Ⓐ Mayer,B.&P.]
*PRACTICE AREAS: Government Relations.
Wald, Douglas L., (AV) . . . . '54 '79 C&L.309 A.B., J.D. [Arnold&P.]
*PRACTICE AREAS: Litigation; Antitrust.
Wald, Robert L., (AV) . . . .'26 '51 C.309 A.B. L.976 LL.B. [Ⓒ Baach R.&L.P.]
*PRACTICE AREAS: Antitrust; Trade Regulation; Government Regulation; Business Mergers; Business Acquisitions.
Walden, Gregory S. . . . . '55 '81 C.902 B.A. L.1049 J.D. [Ⓒ Patton B.]
Walderman, William J. . . . .'46 '74 C.309 A.B. L.966 J.D. [Sutherland A.&B.]
*PRACTICE AREAS: ERISA Compliance; Insurance Products; Federal Income Tax.
Walders, Lawrence R., (AV) . . . . '35 '60 C.477 B.A. L.309 LL.B. [Powell,G.F.&M.]
*PRACTICE AREAS: International Trade Law.
Waldman, Brian P. . . . . '64 '92 C.145 A.B. L.1068 J.D. [Arent F.K.P.&K.]
*PRACTICE AREAS: Food, Drug, Cosmetic and Device Law; Advertising and Marketing.
Waldman, Daniel . . . . '55 '82 C.309 B.A. L.178 J.D. [Arnold&P.]
*PRACTICE AREAS: Derivatives; Litigation.
Waldman, Joshua '70 '00 C.659 B.A. L.178 J.D.
(adm. in MD; not adm. in DC) [Ⓐ O'Melveny&M.]
Waldman, Michael Alan '60 '87 C.178 B.A. L.569 J.D.
(adm. in NY; not adm. in DC) Dir. of Speech Writing, The White House
Waldman, Michael L. . . . . '60 '87 C&L.309 A.B., J.D. [Fried,F.H.S.&J.]
Waldman, Robert J., (AV) . . . . '47 '72 C.228 A.B. L.309 J.D. [Hogan&H.]
*PRACTICE AREAS: Business Law; Corporate Finance; Corporate Law; Securities Law; International Law.
Waldon, Samuel J. . . . .'67 '92 C.886 B.A. L.846 J.D. [Ⓐ Baker B.]
Waldron, Gerard J., (AV) . . . .'60 '90 C.893 B.A. L.228 J.D. [Covington&B.]
Waldron, Jonathan K. . . . . '49 '81 C.869 B.S. L.472 J.D. [Dyer E.&J.]
*PRACTICE AREAS: Environmental Law; Maritime Law; International Law; Pollution.
Waldron, Michael S. . . . .'70 '95 C.390 B.A. L.128 J.D. [Ⓐ Weiner B.S.K.]
*PRACTICE AREAS: Mortgage Banking; Real Estate Finance; Regulatory Compliance.
Waldruff, C. Tucker '72 '01 C.893 B.A. L.309 J.D.
(adm. in VA; not adm. in DC) [Ⓐ Fried,F.H.S.&J.]
*PRACTICE AREAS: Corporate.
Walfoort, Martha . . . .'49 '80 C.685 B.A. L.659 J.D. [Ⓒ James&H.]
Walitt, Angela J. . . . .'69 '96 C.976 B.A. L.846 J.D. 1875 Connecticut Avenue, N.W.
Walke, John D. . . . .'67 '93 C.228 A.B. L.309 J.D. Dir. Clean Air Progs.
Walker, Adam B. . . . .'71 '99 C.597 B.A. L.276 J.D. [Ⓐ Miller&C.]
*PRACTICE AREAS: Civil Litigation; Employee Benefits Litigation; Employment Law.
Walker, Anne McBride . . . . '66 '91 C.893 B.A. L.276 J.D. [Ⓐ Arnold&P.]
*PRACTICE AREAS: Litigation; Products Liability.
Walker, Arthur C., Jr. . . . . '71 '97 C&L.276 B.S.B.A., J.D. [Ⓐ Mayer,B.&P.]
Walker, Barry W. '69 '99 C.88 B.A. L.192 J.D.
(adm. in AL; not adm. in DC) [Ⓐ Paulson&N.]
Walker, C. Heather . . . . '74 '00 C.260 B.A. L.276 J.D. [Ⓐ Wiley R.&F.]
Walker, Charles F. . . . .'57 '85 C.94 B.A. L.569 J.D. [Ⓒ Skadden,A.S.M.&F.]
Walker, Charlton C. . . . . '69 '95 C.606 B.A. L.228 J.D. [Ⓐ Bracewell&P.]
*PRACTICE AREAS: Government Contracts; Litigation.
Walker, Cheryl J. . . . . '64 '92 C.1229 B.S.E.E. L.273 J.D. [Brunenkant&H.]
*PRACTICE AREAS: Energy Law; Utility Law.
Walker, David J. . . . .'61 '87 C.820 B.A. L.904 J.D. [Ⓐ Swidler B.S.F.]
*PRACTICE AREAS: Telecommunications.
Walker, Hans, Jr. . . . . '26 '60 L.585 LL.B. [Hobbs,S.D.&W.]
Walker, J. Brent '50 '76 C.260 B.A. L.362 J.D.
Gen. Coun., Baptist Joint Commission on Public Affairs
Walker, James F. . . . .'26 '58 C.302 B.S. L.273 LL.B. 3650 Camden St., S.E.‡
Walker, Janet Baker . . . .'— '97 C.951 B.A. L.893 J.D. [Ⓐ Verner,L.B.M.&H.]
*PRACTICE AREAS: Corporate; Finance; Technology.
Walker, Jean-Cyril '62 '96 C&L.446 B.A., J.D.
(adm. in MD; not adm. in DC) [Ⓐ Keller&H.]
*PRACTICE AREAS: Environmental Law.

Walker, Jeffrey C. . . . .'72 '98 C.107 B.A. L.273 J.D. [Ⓐ Miller&C.]
*PRACTICE AREAS: Government Contracts; Federal Litigation; Qui Tam Litigation.
Walker, John M. '56 '82 C.276 B.A. L.309 J.D.
Assoc. Gen. Coun. & Dep. Head of Litig., Verizon Communications
Walker, Karen Natalie . . . .'61 '87 C.95 B.A. L.309 J.D. [Kirkland&E.]
*PRACTICE AREAS: Commercial Litigation; Antitrust; Product Liability; Healthcare; Intellectual Property.
Walker, Mary Ann, (AV) . . . .'53 '79 C.893 B.A. L.692 J.D. [Pillsbury W.]
*PRACTICE AREAS: Federal and State Energy and Utility Regulatory Matters.
Walker, Mary Oates . . . .'67 '96 C&L.329 B.A., J.D. [Ⓐ Wiley R.&F.]
Walker, Samuel D., (AV) . . . . '58 '84 C.228 A.B. L.309 J.D. [Wiley R.&F.]
*PRACTICE AREAS: Employment; Education; Litigation.
Walker, Suzanne A. . . . . '65 '97 C.30 B.S. L.1019 J.D. [Ⓐ Muldoon M.&F.]
*PRACTICE AREAS: Employee Benefits; Securities; Corporate Law.
Walker, T. Cy . . . . '61 '92 C.1229 B.S.E.E. L.273 J.D. [Ⓐ Kenyon&K.]
*PRACTICE AREAS: Intellectual Property.

Walker, Robert B.
(See Herndon, Virginia)

Wall, Christopher D. '69 '97 C&L.101 B.A., J.D.
(adm. in UT; not adm. in DC) 600 Thirteenth Street NW
Wall, Christopher R., (AV) . . . .'52 '80 C.976 B.A. L.893 J.D. [Pillsbury W.]
*PRACTICE AREAS: International Trade; International Law.
Wall, Mary E. . . . . '54 '86 C.454 B.S. L.273 J.D. [Winston&S.]
*PRACTICE AREAS: Environmental Law; Environmental Compliance; Environmental Due Diligence; Environmental Insurance; Environmental Lender Liability.
Wall, Thomas H., (AV) . . . . '20 '49 C.573 B.S. L.276 J.D. 1225 23rd St., N.W.
Wall, Thomas Sterling '67 '00 C.1128 L.1340 J.D.
(adm. in NC; not adm. in DC) Dept. of Jus.
Wallace, Anne . . . .'48 '73 C.262 B.A. L.94 J.D. [Ⓒ Alston&B.]
*PRACTICE AREAS: Privacy Law; Consumer Banking; Banking Regulation; Electronic Banking.
Wallace, Christopher J. '70 '98 C.165 B.A. L.1040 J.D.
(adm. in NY; not adm. in DC) [Ⓐ Schmeltzer,A.&S.]
*PRACTICE AREAS: Litigation.
Wallace, Don, Jr. . . . .'32 '57 C.976 B.A. L.309 LL.B. [Ⓒ Morgan,L.&B.]
Wallace, George J. . . . .'42 '67 C.976 B.A. L.893 LL.B. [Eckert S.C.&M.]
*PRACTICE AREAS: Real Estate Law; Bankruptcy; Consumer Regulatory Agencies.
Wallace, Hank . . . . '46 '71 C.705 B.A. L.178 J.D. 3001 Veazey Ter., N.W.
Wallace, James H., Jr., (AV) . . . . '41 '67 C.790 B.S.E.E. L.276 J.D. [Wiley R.&F.] (Pat.)
*PRACTICE AREAS: Litigation; Intellectual Property; Patents.
Wallace, Jenni R. . . . . '69 '93 C.10 B.A. L.930 J.D. [Ⓢ Ross,D.&B.]
Wallace, Mary A. . . . .'— '89 C.1030 B.A. L.273 J.D. [Swidler B.S.F.]
*PRACTICE AREAS: Mergers, Acquisitions and Divestitures; Corporate Finance.
Wallace, Richard E., Jr. . . . .'54 '82 C.454 B.A. L.309 J.D. [Wallace K.M.&B.]
*PRACTICE AREAS: Litigation; Arbitration.
Wallace, Richard G. '57 '85 C.112 A.B. L.1066 J.D.
(adm. in CA; not adm. in DC) NASDAQ Stock Market, Inc.
Wallace, Robert B., (AV) . . . . '44 '70 C&L.273 B.A., J.D. [Wilson,E.M.E.&D.]
*PRACTICE AREAS: Insurance; Litigation; Construction Law; Corporate Law; Securities.
Wallace, Sidney A. . . . .'27 '69 C.869 B.S. L.273 J.D. [Ⓒ Dyer E.&J.]
*PRACTICE AREAS: Maritime Law; Maritime Regulation; Marine Environmental Law; International Law; United Nations Law.
Wallace, Stephen J. . . . .'57 '85 C.262 B.A. L.1019 J.D. [Nixon P.]
*PRACTICE AREAS: Federal Legislation; Housing and Urban Development; Real Estate Finance.
Wallace, W. David . . . .'68 '96 C.188 B.A. L.930 J.D. [Ⓐ Kenyon&K.] (See Pat. Sect.)
*PRACTICE AREAS: Intellectual Property.
Wallace, William D., (AV) . . . .'50 '87 C.674 A.B. L.260 J.D. [Crowell&M.]
*PRACTICE AREAS: FCC Regulation; Satellite Communications; Wireless Cable.
Wallace, William E., III, (AV) . . . .'53 '79 C.93 B.A. L.472 J.D. [Milbank,T.H.&M.]
*PRACTICE AREAS: Antitrust; Complex Litigation; Intellectual Property.
Wallace, William L. '48 '81 C.999 B.A. L.665 J.D.
(adm. in PA; not adm. in DC) Assoc. Gen. Coun., Natl. Geographic Soc.
*RESPONSIBILITIES: Contracts; Entertainment Law; Intellectual Property; Media Law; Labor Law.

Wallace King Marraro & Branson, PLLC, (AV)
1050 Thomas Jefferson Street, N.W., 20007
Telephone: 202-204-1000 Fax: 202-204-1001
URL: http://www.wallaceking.com
Richard E. Wallace, Jr.; Anthony F. King; Christopher H. Marraro; David J. Branson; Julie Ronder Domike. Counsel: Peter C. Condron; David M. Dorsen; William F. Hughes; John W. Kampman; Rickard F. Pfizenmayer;—Steven C. Dubuc; Letta F. Sneed; Angela M. Pelletier; Tamara R. Parker; Ruben F. Reyna (Not admitted in DC); Susan V. Watson; Alec Zacaroli; Sean R. Ward (Not admitted in DC).
Complex Commercial Litigation, Alternative Dispute Resolution, International Arbitration, Environmental Law and Litigation, Insurance Coverage.
See Professional Biographies, WASHINGTON, DISTRICT OF COLUMBIA

Wallach, Jason D. . . . .'68 '96 C.318 B.A. L.273 J.D. [Ⓐ Gilbert H.&R.]
*PRACTICE AREAS: Litigation; Insurance.
Wallach, Paul G., (AV) . . . .'47 '73 C.705 B.A. L.893 J.D. [Hale&D.]
*PRACTICE AREAS: Environmental Law.
Wallach, Ryan G. '68 '98 C.170 B.A. L.273 J.D.
(adm. in MD; not adm. in DC) [Ⓐ Willkie F.&G.]
*PRACTICE AREAS: Communications Law; Litigation.
Wallenberg, David O. '57 '90 C&L.793 B.S., J.D.
(adm. in SD; not adm. in DC) Sr. Staff Assoc., STAPPA ALAPCO
Wallenstein, Stephen M. '48 '76
C.188 B.A. L.976 J.D. 818 Connecticut Ave., N.W., Suite 700
Waller, Carolyn . . . .'37 '78 C.105 A.B. L.1162 J.D. 1666 Conn. Ave., NW
Waller, John A. . . . .'40 '71 C&L.329 B.A., J.D. 3130 Cherry Rd. N.E.
Waller, Virginia Maxwell . . . . '68 '93 C.112 B.A. L.1066 J.D. JM Zell Partners, Ltd.
Waller, William C. . . . .'69 '95 C.165 A.B. L.309 J.D. [Ⓐ Venable,A.B.H.&C.]
*PRACTICE AREAS: Food and Drug; Advertising; Government; Legislative Practice; Regulatory.
Waller, William W. . . . .'52 '95 C.205 B.A. L.30 J.D. [Ⓐ A.F.Konopka]
*PRACTICE AREAS: Real Estate; Litigation; Probate.
Walli, Karl T. '56 '82 C.838 B.A. L.575 J.D.
(adm. in VA; not adm. in DC) [Weil,G.&M.]
Wallick, Robert D., (AV) . . . .'26 '55 C.401 B.S.E. L.273 LL.B. [Steptoe&J.]
*PRACTICE AREAS: Commercial Law; Construction Law; Contract Law; Government Contract Law; International Sales.
Wallin, Stephen R. . . . .'58 '83 C.529 A.B. L.273 J.D. 1717 Columbia Rd., N.W.
Wallington, James F. . . . .'53 '80 C&L.923 A.B., J.D. [Baptiste&W.]
*PRACTICE AREAS: Labor Relations Law.
Wallison, Frieda K., (AV) . . . . '43 '67 C.788 A.B. L.309 LL.B. 1450 G St. N.W.‡
Wallison, Peter J., (AV) . . . .'41 '67 C&L.309 B.A., LL.B. [Ⓒ Gibson,D.&C.]
*PRACTICE AREAS: Banking Law and Regulation; Corporate Transactions; Securities and Financial Services Law.
Walloch, Heather M. '71 '96 C.678 B.A. L.629 J.D.
(adm. in OR; not adm. in DC) [Ⓐ Sidley A.B.&W.]
Walser, Heather Guilette . . . .'74 '99 C&L.602 B.A., J.D. [Ⓐ Jones,D.R.&P.]
Walsh, Adam W. . . . .'72 '97 C.602 B.A. L.945 J.D. [Ⓐ Powell,G.F.&M.]
*PRACTICE AREAS: Corporate; Real Estate; Banking.

Walsh, Anne K. ... '— '97 C&L.945 B.A., J.D. [🄰 King&S.]
*PRACTICE AREAS: Environmental.
Walsh, Carla Perantoni ... '54 '85 C.276 B.A. L.128 J.D. [🄲 Dickstein S.M.&O.]
*PRACTICE AREAS: Labor and Employment Law.
Walsh, Charles S., (AV) ... '42 '68 C.446 B.A. L.273 J.D. [Fleischman&W.]
Walsh, Elaine M. '— '96 C.260 B.A. L.910 J.D.
(adm. in MO; not adm. in DC) [🄰 Kirkland&E.]
*PRACTICE AREAS: Energy.
Walsh, James T. ... '49 '76 C.321 A.B. L.276 J.D. [🄲 Arnold&P.]
*PRACTICE AREAS: Intellectual Property; Trademarks; Unfair Competition.
Walsh, John M. '22 '49 C.178 A.B. L.982 J.D.
(adm. in NY; not adm. in DC) Corp. V.P., AT&T
Walsh, Kathryn E. '— '00 C.178 B.A. L.659 J.D.
(adm. in MD; not adm. in DC) [🄰 King&S.]
*PRACTICE AREAS: Litigation; Trade Law.
Walsh, Linda L. ... '60 '87 C.184 B.A. L.823 J.D. [🄲 Hunton&W.]
*PRACTICE AREAS: Public Utility Regulation; Electric Industry Restructuring.
Walsh, Mary D. ... '— '99 C.1375 B.A. L.273 J.D. [🄰 Morgan,L.&B.]
Walsh, Nancy L. ... '63 '88 C.602 B.A. L.893 J.D. [🄰 Sherman,M.C.&A.]
*PRACTICE AREAS: Business Law; Real Estate; Corporate Law.
Walsh, Patricia J. ... '65 '97 C.518 B.A. L.976 J.D. [🄰 Cleary,G.S.&H.]
Walsh, Timothy M., (AV) ... '52 '77 C.813 A.B. L.976 J.D. [Steptoe&J.]
Walsh, William C., (AV) ... '48 '76 C.397 B.A. L.1162 J.D. [Bisceglie&W.]
*PRACTICE AREAS: Constitutional Law; International Human Rights; Freedom of Information Act; Litigation.
Walsh, William J., (AV) ... '46 '78 C.433 B.S. L.273 J.D. [Pepper H.]
*PRACTICE AREAS: Superfund; Environmental Administrative Law; Environmental Litigation.
Walter, Elisse B. '50 '75 C.976 B.A. L.309 J.D.
Chf. Oper. Offr. & Exec. V.P., NASD Regulation, Inc.
Walter, Geo. R. ... '19 '47 C.273 A.B. L.309 LL.B. 4210 43rd St., N.W.‡
Walter, Jennifer K. ... '55 '81 C.950 B.S. L.273 J.D. [🄰 Skadden,A.S.M.&F.]
Walter, Nicole R. ... '74 '00 C.575 B.S.P.H. L.273 J.D. [🄰 Wilmer,C.&P.]
Walter, Steven ... '75 '00 C.188 B.S. L.273 J.D. [🄰 Dickstein S.M.&O.]
*PRACTICE AREAS: Corporate; Finance.
Walters, Charles Frederick ... '63 '94 C.025 B.S.C. L.128 J.D. [🄰 Seyfarth S.]
*PRACTICE AREAS: Labor Law; Employment Law.
Walters, Edie ... '73 '99 C.273 B.A. L.1341 J.D. [🄰 Swidler B.S.F.]
*PRACTICE AREAS: Bankruptcy; Litigation.
Walters, Gregory A. ... '67 '96 C.475 B.S.E.E. L.213 J.D. [🄰 Fish&R.] (See Pat. Sect.)
*PRACTICE AREAS: Patents; Trademarks; Intellectual Property; Copyrights; Computer Law.
Walters, Joe A., (AV) ... '20 '47 C&L.494 B.S.L., LL.B. [O'Connor&H.]
Walters, Mary F. ... '70 '97 C.839 B.A. L.846 J.D. [🄰 Clifford C.R.&W.]
*PRACTICE AREAS: Commercial Litigation; Antitrust Litigation; Intellectual Property Litigation.
Walters, Natalie Stoney ... '70 '95 C.699 A.B. L.276 J.D. [🄰 Arent F.K.P.&K.]
*PRACTICE AREAS: Government Contracts; Litigation; Construction.
Walther, Katherine A. ... '70 '99 C.902 B.A. L.893 J.D. [🄰 Dickstein S.M.&O.]
*PRACTICE AREAS: Securities Litigation; Products Liability; Antitrust.
Walther, Pamela D. ... '55 '86 C.392 B.A. L.902 J.D. [McDermott,W.&E.]
Walton, Garry L., (BV) '54 '80 C&L.477 B.A., J.D.
(adm. in MI; not adm. in DC) [🄰 Inman D.] ⊙
*PRACTICE AREAS: Commercial Transactions; Real Estate Acquisitions; Business Formation.
Walton, Jessica S. ... '62 '93 C.683 B.A. L.128 J.D. [🄰 Feldesman,T.L.F.&B.]
*PRACTICE AREAS: Health Care Law.
Walton, Linda M. ... '61 '88 C.378 B.A.B.S. L.309 J.D. Center for Auto Safety
Walton, Reggie Barnett ... '49 '74 C.922 B.A. L.30 J.D. Supr. Ct. J.
Waltz, Daniel E. ... '57 '86 C.112 B.A. L.1066 J.D. [Patton B.]
Walutes, Ronald L., Jr. ... '61 '86 C.164 B.A. L.893 J.D. Asst. U.S. Atty.‡
Wamsley, Herbert C. '42 '70 C.923 B.S.E.E. L.276 J.D.
Executive Director & Counsel, Intellectual Property Owners Association
Wan, Bonnie B. ... '45 '70 C&L.276 B.A., J.D. V.P., Kimberly-Clark Corporation
Wancjer, Hershel A. '73 '00 C.477 B.A. L.124 J.D.
(adm. in MI; not adm. in DC) [🄰 Boies,S.&F.]
*PRACTICE AREAS: Antitrust; Complex Litigation.
Wander, Elyse G. ... '48 '74 C&L.30 B.S., J.D. 60 Massachusetts Ave., NE
Wanerman, Robert E. ... '57 '86 C.145 A.B. L.564 J.D. [🄰 Arent F.K.P.&K.]
*PRACTICE AREAS: Health Care; Administrative.
Wang, Catherine ... '59 '86 C.1350 B.A. L.276 J.D. [Swidler B.S.F.]
*PRACTICE AREAS: Regulatory Law; Telecommunications Law; Technology Law.
Wang, Christopher C. ... '73 '98 C.976 B.A. L.145 J.D. [🄰 Mayer,B.&P.]
Wang, Emil P. '— '01 C.367 B.A. L.446 J.D.
(adm. in MD; not adm. in DC) [🄰 Morgan,L.&B.]
Wang, Eric C. ... '69 '93 C&L.245 B.A., J.D. [🄰 Swidler B.S.F.]
*PRACTICE AREAS: Domestic Taxation; International Taxation.
Wang, Josephine '53 '79 C.331 B.A. L.276 J.D.
Sr. Assoc. Gen. Coun., Securities Investor Protec. Corp.
Wang, Peggy Yu Ping ... '72 '00 C.477 B.A. L.228 J.D. [🄰 Hogan&H.]
*PRACTICE AREAS: Corporate Law.
Wang, Peter J. ... '69 '92 C.674 A.B. L.1066 J.D. [🄰 Jones,D.R.&P.]
Wang, Tom Chia-Kai '75 '01 C.790 B.A. L.893 J.D.
(adm. in VA; not adm. in DC) [🄰 Shaw P.]
Wang, Weimin '55 '88 C.999 B.A. L.276 J.D.
Embassy of the People's Republic of China in the U.S.
Wang, Xianping '— '91 C.999 LL.B. L.228 J.D.
(adm. in VA; not adm. in DC) 1054 31st St. N.W.
Wang, Yan '67 '01 L.260 J.D.
(adm. in MD; not adm. in DC) [🄰 Fulbright&J.]
Wanger, Betsy K., (AV) ... '63 '89 C.309 B.A. L.976 J.D. 725 12th St., N.W.
Wannisky, William M., (AV) '48 '75
C.645 B.S. L.276 J.D. [Fitzpatrick,C.H.&S.] (See Pat. Sect.)
War, Steven '57 '00 C.893 B.S.A.E. L.276 J.D.
(adm. in VA; not adm. in DC) [🄰 Fulbright&J.]
*PRACTICE AREAS: Intellectual Property; Alternative Dispute Resolution.
Warchot, Louis P., (BV) '47 '73 C.112 A.B. L.1066 J.D.
(adm. in CA; not adm. in DC)
Sr. V.P.-Law & Gen. Coun., Association of American Railroads
Ward, Amy Barton '73 '99 C.856 B.A. L.128 J.D.
2000 Pennsylvania Avenue, N.W., Suite 5500
Ward, Anna E. ... '67 '00 C.30 B.A. L.1209 J.D. [🄰 Kurtis&Assoc.]
*PRACTICE AREAS: Telecommunications Law (100%).
Ward, Bradford L., (AV) ... '57 '84 C.629 B.S. L.30 J.D. [🄲 Dewey B.]
*PRACTICE AREAS: International Trade.
Ward, Carolyn O. ... '— '95 C.228 B.A. L.904 J.D. [🄰 Morgan,L.&B.]
Ward, Carolyn Osteen ... '67 '93 C.228 B.A. L.30 J.D. 1800 M St., N.W.
Ward, Ellen Brewster ... '49 '76 C.118 B.A. L.276 J.D. 4913 47th St., N.W.
Ward, Erica A., (AV) ... '50 '76 C.813 B.A. L.477 J.D. [Skadden,A.S.M.&F.]
Ward, J. Alex ... '67 '92 C.228 B.A. L.309 J.D. [🄰 Jenner&B.]
*PRACTICE AREAS: Litigation.
Ward, Jeffrey J. ... '70 '97 C.857 B.A. L.273 J.D. [🄰 Ross,D.&B.]
Ward, Joe H., Jr. ... '30 '64 C.840 B.S. L.802 J.D. P.O. Box 77247
Ward, John D. ... '52 '77 C.197 A.B. L.178 J.D. [Dow,L.&A.]
Ward, John F., (AV) ... '42 '68 C.446 B.S. L.273 J.D. [Ward&K.] ⊙
Ward, Liliana Estevez ... '68 '93 C.945 B.A. L.1509 J.D. [🄰 Fletcher,H.&H.] ⊙
*PRACTICE AREAS: Civil Litigation; Communications Law; Internet Law; Business Law.
Ward, Lisa '63 '90 C.1099 B.A. L.861 J.D.
(adm. in MS; not adm. in DC) Suite 1011, 1730 K St., N.W.
Ward, Matthew W. ... '69 '94 C.30 B.A. L.893 J.D. [🄰 Spiegel&M.]
*PRACTICE AREAS: Environmental Law; Energy; Government Affairs; Regulatory Law; Clean Air.
Ward, Maureen O'Keefe ... '45 '79 C.734 B.A. L.145 J.D. [🄲 Steptoe&J.]
*PRACTICE AREAS: Copyright; Computer Law; Technology Transfer; Trade Regulation Law; Trade Secrets Law.
Ward, Michael E. ... '46 '74 C.197 A.B. L.813 J.D. [🄲 Swidler B.S.F.]
Ward, Nicholas D., (AV) ... '41 '67 C.178 B.A. L.276 LL.B. [Friedeman,I.W.&L.]
*PRACTICE AREAS: Estate Planning Law; Estate Administration; Trusts Law; Fiduciary Law; Bankruptcy.
Ward, Philip J., (AV) ... '49 '74 C.813 A.B. L.309 J.D. [Williams&C.]
Ward, Rachel ... '72 '98 C&L.893 B.A., J.D. [🄰 Latham&W.]
*PRACTICE AREAS: Mergers, Acquisitions and Divestitures; Corporate Finance.
Ward, Sean R. '71 '98 C.893 B.A. L.180 J.D.
(adm. in VA; not adm. in DC) [🄰 Wallace K.M.&B.]
*PRACTICE AREAS: Environmental Litigation.
Ward, Thomas G. ... '71 '97 C.222 B.A. L.178 J.D. [🄰 Williams&C.]
*PRACTICE AREAS: Intellectual Property; Litigation.
Ward, Thomas J., (AV) ... '39 '66 C.1030 B.S.S. L.602 LL.B. [Ward&Assoc.]
Ward & Associates, (AV) ... 2020 N St., N.W.
Ward & Klein, Chartered, (AV)
5028 Wisconsin Ave., Ste. 300 (⊙Gaithersburg, Greenbelt, MD; Arlington, VA)
Wardell, Robert J. ... '18 '49 C.602 A.B. L.178 LL.B. 3001 Veazey Tr., NW‡
Warden, Irving D., Jr. '46 '76 C&L.623 B.B.A., J.D.
Assoc. Gen. Coun., American Bankers Association
*RESPONSIBILITIES: Administrative Law (40%); Appellate and Amicus Curiae Litigation (10%); Corporate (30%); Insurance (20%).
Warden, Michael D. ... '60 '88 C.893 B.A. L.276 J.D. [Sidley A.B.&W.]
Wareh, Rashad ... '— '97 C.30 B.A. L.228 J.D. [🄰 Kozusko L.H.]
*PRACTICE AREAS: Closely Held Business Taxation; Tax Planning; International Estate Planning; Estate Planning; Venture Capital.
Wareham, James D. ... '60 '86 C.339 B.S. L.597 J.D. [Jones,D.R.&P.]
*PRACTICE AREAS: Litigation; Complex Business Litigation; Corporate Investigations.
Warin, F. Joseph, (AV) ... '50 '75 C.190 B.A. L.276 J.D. [Gibson,D.&C.]
*PRACTICE AREAS: Antitrust; Securities and White Collar Crime Litigation.
Warin, Roger E., (AV) ... '45 '70 C.190 A.B. L.276 J.D. [Steptoe&J.]
*PRACTICE AREAS: Litigation; Legal Malpractice; Professional Liability; Federal Election Law; Intellectual Property Law.
Warnement, Robert W. ... '64 '95 C.602 B.S.M.E. L.904 J.D. [🄰 Skadden,A.S.M.&F.]
Warnement, Thalia V. ... '67 '93 C.893 B.A. L.945 J.D. [🄰 Finnegan,H.F.G.&D.]
*PRACTICE AREAS: Chemical Patent Prosecution; Patent Infringement; Patent Interference Practice.
Warner, Brainard H., III, (AV) '25 '50 C.976 B.E. L.273 J.D.
888 Seventeenth St., N.W.
Warner, John P. ... '49 '78 C.273 B.A. L.1066 J.D. [Silverstein&M.]
*PRACTICE AREAS: Federal Income Taxation; Taxation of International Transactions; Transfer Pricing; Mediation of Tax Disputes.
Warner, Margaret H., (AV) ... '56 '81 C.732 A.B. L.602 J.D. [McDermott,W.&E.]
Warner, Seth M. ... '68 '94 C.860 B.A. L.904 J.D. [🄰 Fleischman&W.]
Warner, Steven E. '59 '88
C.1213 B.S.M.E. L.273 J.D. [Fitzpatrick,C.H.&S.] (See Pat. Sect.)
Warner, Te Mika S. '77 '01 C.724 B.A. L.309 J.D.
(adm. in NY; not adm. in DC) [🄰 Hogan&H.]
Warnick, Leah ... '75 '00 C.945 B.A. L.893 J.D. [🄰 McKenna&C.]
*PRACTICE AREAS: Environmental Law; Environmental Litigation.
Warnkle, Paul C. ... '20 '48 C.976 A.B. L.178 J.D. 1299 Pennsylvania Ave., N.W.
Warren, Charles F. ... '26 '55 C&L.575 B.S., LL.B. 1100 Connecticut Ave., N.W.
Warren, Charles L., (AV) ... '49 '74 C.910 B.S. L.846 J.D. [Akin,G.S.H.&F.]
*PRACTICE AREAS: Labor and Employment.
Warren, Edward W., (P.C.), (AV) ... '44 '69 C.976 B.A. L.145 J.D. [Kirkland&E.]
*PRACTICE AREAS: Appellate Litigation; Administrative; Constitutional Law.
Warren, James F. ... '56 '90 C.050 B.A. L.309 J.D. [🄲 Shearman&S.]
*PRACTICE AREAS: Federal Income Tax.
Warren, Mark E. ... '63 '90 C&L.276 B.S.B.A., J.D. 1722 Eye St., N.W.
Warren, Robert C., Jr. '60 '87 C&L.329 B.A., J.D.
Coun., Comm. on Govt. Oper., Coun. Dist. of Col.
Warren, Robert P. '46 '73 C.318 B.A. L.880 J.D.
(adm. in NY; not adm. in DC)
Sr. V.P., Gen. Coun. & Secy., Air Transport Association of America
Warren, Wendy Barrett ... '66 '95 C&L.893 B.A., J.D. [🄰 Baker B.]
*PRACTICE AREAS: Energy; Project Finance.
Warshaw, Melvin ... '20 '48 C.1134 B.S. L.569 J.D. Sr. U.S. Admistrative Law Judge
Warshawsky, Daniel A. '58 '86 C.696 B.A. L.273 J.D.
(adm. in NY; not adm. in DC) 600 New Jersey Ave., N.W.‡
Warshawsky, Steven M. ... '66 '97 C.674 A.B. L.276 J.D. [🄰 Covington&B.]
*PRACTICE AREAS: Litigation; Labor and Employment.
Wartchow, Richard M. '67 '99 C.801 B.A. L.910 J.D.
(adm. in NY; not adm. in DC) [🄰 Steptoe&J.]
Wasden, Mark T. ... '66 '93 C.101 B.A. L.273 J.D. [🄰 Perkins C.]
*PRACTICE AREAS: International Trade.
Waserstein, Aida, (AV) ... '48 '73 C.104 B.A. L.659 J.D. 1402 William Penn Ln.
Washburn, Alan V. ... '35 '60 C.1100 A.B. L.145 J.D. 3427 O St., N.W.
Washington, Barbara C. ... '— '76 C.705 B.A. L.1292 J.D. 4417 46th St., N.W.
Washington, Christine Quickenden ... '69 '99 C.276 B.S.F.S. L.30 J.D. [🄰 Wiley R.&F.]
Washington, Eric T. ... '53 '79 C.860 B.A. L.178 J.D. D.C. Supr. Ct.
Washington, Eunice Harris '66 '92 C.446 B.S. L.276 J.D.
Assoc. Gen. Coun., Service Employees Intl. Union
Washington, George L., Jr. ... '65 '94 C.674 A.B. L.1066 J.D. [🄰 Covington&B.]
*PRACTICE AREAS: Labor and Employment; Insurance; Sports; Civil Litigation.
Washington, Geovette E. ... '67 '92 C.917 A.B. L.228 J.D. [Baach R.&L.P.]
*PRACTICE AREAS: Civil Litigation; Commercial Litigation; Insurance; Employment.
Washington, Imoti M. '71 '99 C.811 B.A. L.446 J.D.
(adm. in MD; not adm. in DC) National Assoc. for Public Interest Law
Washington, John A., Jr. ... '59 '90 C.797 B.A. L.128 J.D. [🄰 Ballard S.A.&I.]
*PRACTICE AREAS: Public Finance.
Washington, Joseph E. ... '— '00 C.152 B.A. L.128 J.D. [🄰 Morgan,L.&B.]
Washington, Russell C. ... '34 '78 C.922 B.A. L.574 J.D. 7546 Alaska Ave., N.W.
Washington, Walter E. ... '15 '48 C&L.329 A.B., J.D. 408 "T" St. NW
Washington Counsel, P.C., (AV) ... 1150 17th St., N.W.
Wasielewski, Celeste M. ... '— '88 C.477 B.A. L.273 J.D. [🄲 Verner,L.B.M.&H.]
*PRACTICE AREAS: Labor and Employment Law.
Wasilewski, Vincent T. ... '22 '50 C&L.339 A.B., J.D. 1255 23rd St., N.W., Ste. 500

Wasko, Lawrence D., (AV) '32 '64 C.1044 A.B. L.276 LL.B.
Suite 900 1150 Connecticut Avenue, N.W., 20036
Telephone: 202-862-4370 Fax: 202-331-0599
Email: ldwasko@erols.com URL: http://www.lawyers.com/waskolaw
***PRACTICE AREAS: Aviation Law; International Trade.**
Associate: Jacquelyn N. Gluck (Not admitted in DC).
Aviation Law, Aircraft Finance and Leasing, Contracts, Letters of Credit, Aviation Insurance, Aeronautical Regulation, Aircraft Sales, Airport Finance and Development, International Aviation Law.
See Professional Biographies, WASHINGTON, DISTRICT OF COLUMBIA

Wasserman, Ivan J. . . . .'67 '93 C.881 B.A. L.273 J.D. [Ⓐ Arent F.K.P.&K.]
*PRACTICE AREAS: Drug and Medical Device Regulation; Food, Drug and Cosmetic Law; Product Safety; Advertising and Labeling; Alcoholic Beverage Control.
Wasserman, Jessica A. . . . .'59 '85 C.722 B.A. L.477 J.D. [Manatt,P.&P.]

Wasserman, Michael F. '65 '93 C.918 B.A. L.494 J.D.
800 Seventh Street, N.W., Suite 201, 20001-3718
Telephone: 202-842-3290 Facsimile: 202-842-2385
Email: mfw@law.com
Trial Practice, Appellate Practice, Complex and Multi-District Litigation, Contract Litigation, Corporate Law, Business Litigation, Employment Litigation, Libel, Slander and Defamation, Real Estate Litigation, U.S. Supreme Court Litigation, Legal Ethics, Landlord and Tenant Law, Leasing, Small Business Law, Products Liability Defense.
See Professional Biographies, WASHINGTON, DISTRICT OF COLUMBIA

Wasserman, Mancini & Chang, (AV) BB
1915 Eye Street, N.W., Suite 400, 20006
Telephone: 202-783-8905 Fax: 202-333-1688
URL: http://www.lawyers.com/wassermanmancini&chang
Members of Firm: Jack Wasserman (1913-1980); Mark A. Mancini; Sam Hsien-Cheng Chang. Associates: Richard W. Chang; Robin L. Williamson (Not admitted in DC); Tamara Y. Dowton (Not admitted in DC).
Immigration and Nationality and International Law. Practice before Government Agencies. Trial, Appellate and Supreme Court Practice. Business Immigration.
Reference: First American Bank, Washington, D.C.
See Professional Biographies, WASHINGTON, DISTRICT OF COLUMBIA

Wassermann, Marc D. . . . . '62 '87 C.659 B.S.Ec. L.309 J.D. [Sidley A.B.&W.]
Wasserstein, Jeffrey N. . . . .'71 '97 C&L.178 B.A., J.D. [Ⓐ Hyman,P.&M.]
*PRACTICE AREAS: Food and Drug Regulation; Health Care.
Wasserstrom, Richard S. '44 '68 C.475 B.A. L.477 J.D.
Envir. Coun., American Forest & Paper Assn.
Wasserstrom, Silas J., (AV) . . . . '42 '68 C.31 B.A. L.976 LL.B. 1303 Floral St., NW
Wasylik, Dineen Pashoukos . . . .'72 '99 C.188 B.S. L.276 J.D. [Ⓐ Wiley R.&F.]
Waszkiewicz, Kenneth P. '63 '98
C.446 B.S.C.S. L.64 J.D. [Ⓐ Morgan&F.] (See Pat. Sect.)
*PRACTICE AREAS: Intellectual Property; Patents.
Watchman, Gregory R. . . . . '59 '86 C.951 B.A. L.188 J.D. [Ⓒ Paul,H.J.&W.]
*PRACTICE AREAS: Labor Law; Employment Law; OSHA; Title VII; ADEA.

Waterman, Bradley S. '49 '77 C.367 B.A. L.692
Suite 1040, East Tower, 1301 K Street, N.W., 20005
Telephone: 202-682-1616 Fax: 202-682-2232
Email: BSW1040@aol.com
Civil and Criminal Tax Controversies, Federal Income Tax Planning.
See Professional Biographies, WASHINGTON, DISTRICT OF COLUMBIA

Waters, Edward T. . . . . '61 '88 C.910 B.A. L.893 J.D. [Feldesman,T.L.F.&B.]
*PRACTICE AREAS: Federal Grants; Federal Contracts; Health Care Law; Corporate Litigation.
Waters, Jennifer N., (AV) . . . .'51 '77 C.681 B.A. L.309 J.D. [Crowell&M.]
*PRACTICE AREAS: Energy Law; Public Utility Law; Oil and Gas Law; Appellate Practice.
Waters, Paul V. . . . . '55 '83 C.128 B.M.E. L.180 J.D. [Spriggs&H.]
*PRACTICE AREAS: Construction Law; Litigation.
Waters, Robert J., (AV) . . . .'55 '86 C.350 B.A. L.276 J.D. [Arent F.K.P.&K.]
*PRACTICE AREAS: Health (Health Care) and Hospital Law; Legislative Government Regulations; Telemedicine.
Waters, Robert S., (BV) . . . . '45 '74 C.871 B.S. L.893 J.D. [Jones,D.R.&P.]
*PRACTICE AREAS: Energy; Federal Energy Regulation; Utility Law.
Waters, Timothy J., (AV) . . . . '43 '68 C.767 B.S. L.273 J.D. [McDermott,W.&E.]
Watiker, Jeffrey A. . . . . .'58 '86 C.453 S.B. L.309 J.D. In-Hse. Coun., Citicorp Wash., Inc.
Watkin, Virginia G., (AV) . . . .'25 '49 C.914 A.B. L.178 LL.B. 1201 Penn. Ave., N.W.
Watkins, Angela N. . . . .'68 '95 C.813 B.A. L.1066 J.D. 1776 K St., NW
Watkins, Charles M. . . . .'54 '81 C.264 A.B. L.1017 J.D. [Ⓐ Webster,C.&B.]
*PRACTICE AREAS: Trade and Professional Associations; Tax Exempt Organizations; Employee Benefits; Employment Taxation.
Watkins, John B., V . . . .'56 '81 C.367 B.A. L.477 J.D. [Wilmer,C.&P.] (⊙Balt., MD)
*PRACTICE AREAS: Corporate Law; Securities Law.
Watkins, Kennedy C. . . . .'11 '36 C&L.273 A.B., LL.B. 3610 Mass. Ave., N.W.
Watkins, Margaret T. . . . .'67 '98 C.367 B.A. L.276 J.D. [Ⓐ Venable,A.B.H.&C.]
*PRACTICE AREAS: Litigation.
Watkins, McNeill, II, (AV) . . . .'49 '76 C.674 A.B. L.260 J.D. 1209 C St., S.E.‡
Watkins, Robert P., (AV) . . . . '37 '66 C.309 A.B. L.178 LL.B. [Williams&C.]
*PRACTICE AREAS: Bid Protests; Civil Rights; Civil Litigation; Class Actions; Class Action Defense.
Watkins, Scott D. . . . .'67 '93 C.178 B.S. L.273 J.D. [Ⓒ Steptoe&J.] (Pat.)
*PRACTICE AREAS: Intellectual Property.
Watkins, Seth Alain . . . . '70 '99 C&L.228 B.S.E., J.D. [Ⓐ Pennie&E.]
*PRACTICE AREAS: Intellectual Property.
Watkins, Timothy Hansen, (BV) . . . .'58 '86 C&L.276 B.S.F.S., J.D. [Shaw P.]
*PRACTICE AREAS: Commercial Real Estate; Corporate Lending.
Watkins, Todd R. '65 '94 C.309 A.B. L.477 J.D.
(adm. in CA; not adm. in DC) Assoc. Gen. Coun., Fannie Mae
*RESPONSIBILITIES: Multifamily.
Watkinson, Wayne R. . . . .'56 '83 C.1290 B.A. L.329 J.D. [McLeod,W.&M.]
*PRACTICE AREAS: Agricultural and Trade Association Law; Marketing Issues.
Watkiss, Jeffrey D., (AV) . . . . '54 '80 C.813 A.B. L.878 J.D. [Bracewell&P.]
*PRACTICE AREAS: Energy and Environmental.
Watsky, Stephen, (BV) . . . . '52 '76 C.273 B.A. L.190 J.D. 1275 K St.,N.W.
Watson, Felicia K. . . . .'— '96 C.988 B.S. L.285 J.D. [Ⓐ Cole,R.&B.]
*PRACTICE AREAS: Commercial Litigation; Communications Law; Cable Communications.
Watson, G. Norris '31 '57 C.692 B.A. L.893 LL.B.
(adm. in VA; not adm. in DC) [Ⓒ Scribner,H.&T.]
Watson, Keith S., (AV) . . . . '42 '68 C.855 B.A. L.309 J.D. [Wiley R.&F.]
*PRACTICE AREAS: Insurance; Litigation.
Watson, Kelli '71 '99 C.741 B.S. L.209 J.D.
(adm. in VA; not adm. in DC; Pat.) [McDermott,W.&E.]
Watson, Lee Ann '52 '76 C.347 B.S. L.910 J.D.
(adm. in IL; not adm. in DC) 950 Pennsylvania Avenue NW
Watson, Matthew S. . . . .'41 '65 C.367 B.A. L.569 LL.B. Admin. Law J.
Watson, Michael C. . . . . '65 '99 C.184 B.A. L.180 J.D. 1119 12th St., N.W.
Watson, Peter S. '53 '79 L.999
(adm. in CA; not adm. in DC) [Ⓒ Pillsbury W.]
Watson, Sara Beth . . . .'57 '85 C.840 B.S. L.802 J.D. [Ⓒ Steptoe&J.]
*PRACTICE AREAS: Chemical Regulation Law; Environmental Law; Food, Drug and Cosmetic Law; Hazardous Waste Law; OCC Safety and Health.

Watson, Shaundra L. . . . . '74 '99 C.329 B.A. L.893 J.D. [Ⓐ Hogan&H.]
Watson, Susan L. '— '00 C.59 B.A. L.846 J.D.
(adm. in TX; not adm. in DC) [Ⓐ Dyer E.&J.]
Watson, Susan V. . . . .'68 '97 C.446 B.S. L.276 J.D. [Ⓐ Wallace K.M.&B.]
Watson, Theresa L. '45 '73
C.329 B.A. L.273 J.D. Pres., Amer. League of Financial Institutions
Watson, Thomas C., (AV) . . . .'45 '72 C.1015 B.S. L.910 J.D. [Watson&R.]
*PRACTICE AREAS: Trials; Medical and Cancer Causation; Technology and Science Law.

Watson Cole Grindle Watson, P.L.L.C.
(See Dykema Gossett PLLC)

Watson & Renner, (AV)
1919 M Street, N.W., Suite 400, 20036-3307
Telephone: 202-737-6300 Fax: 202-737-7611
Email: WR@W-R.com URL: http://www.lawyers.com/watson&rennerlaw
Thomas C. Watson; Curtis S. Renner;—Nicholas Wyckoff Woodfield.
State and Federal Court Trials, Regulatory Trials, Proceedings, Small Business, General Counselling, Personal Injury Claims, Medical Causation, Cancer Causation, Toxic Torts, Electric and Magnetic Fields, Chemical and Physical Exposures, Microwave Communication, Transmission Line Siting, Surgeons' Liability, Products Liability, Intellectual Property Litigation.
See Professional Biographies, WASHINGTON, DISTRICT OF COLUMBIA

Watt, Tieder, Hoffar & Fitzgerald, L.L.P., (AV) BB
601 Pennsylvania Avenue, N.W., Suite 900, 20004 ⊙
Telephone: 703-749-1000 Telecopier: 703-893-8029
Email: contactus@wthf.com URL: http://www.wthf.com
Firm Member: John B. Tieder, Jr.
Construction, Government Contracts, Suretyship, International Business, Admiralty/Maritime and Real Estate Law.
McLean Virginia Office: 7929 Westpark Drive, Suite 400, Telephone: 703-749-1000. Telecopier: 703-893-8029.
Irvine California Office: 3 Park Plaza, Suite 1500. Telephone: 949-852-6700.
Affiliated Frankfurt, Germany Office: Heiermann Franke Knipp, Kettenhofweg 126, D-603325 Frankfurt, Germany. Telephone: 011 49 69 975 82 20.
Affiliated Florence, Italy Office: Roberto Tassi & Associates: Via Dei Della Robbia n. 68, 50132, Florence, Italy. Telephone: 011 39 55 500 1448.
See Professional Biographies, WASHINGTON, DISTRICT OF COLUMBIA

Watters, Keith W., (AV) . . . . '54 '80 C.354 B.S. L.276 J.D. 1700 K St., NW
Watts, Bradford K. '— '99 C.101 B.A. L.276 J.D.
(adm. in MA; not adm. in DC) [Ⓐ Crowell&M.]
Watts, Charles R. '62 '90
C.205 B.S.M.E. L.1209 J.D. [Wenderoth,L.&P.] (See Pat. Sect.)
*PRACTICE AREAS: Mechanical Patents; Electrical Patents; Patent Applications; Prosecution; Licensing.
Watts, Raymond D. . . . .'24 '54 C.33 B.A. L.276 J.D. 1804 T St.
Watts, Wilbert H., Jr. . . . .'74 '99 C.276 A.B. L.309 J.D. [Ⓐ Cleary,G.S.&H.]
Waugh-Farretta, Robin . . . . '— '99 C.724 B.A. L.262 J.D. [Ⓐ Venable,A.B.H.&C.]
*PRACTICE AREAS: Corporate.
Wax, Randal W. . . . . '59 '84 C.453 B.S. L.276 J.D. [Ⓐ Shapiro,L.&S.]
*PRACTICE AREAS: Government Contracts; Construction Claims and Disputes; Commercial Litigation.
Waxman, Allen P., (AV) . . . . '62 '87 C,197 B.A. L.309 J.D. [Williams&C.]
*PRACTICE AREAS: Litigation; Medical Malpractice; Personal Injury; Products Liability; Torts.
Waxman, J. Mark, (AV) '— '73 C.112 B.A. L.1066 J.D.
(adm. in CA; not adm. in DC) [Foley&L.] (⊙L.A., CA)
*PRACTICE AREAS: Commercial Litigation; Health Care; Administrative Law; Antitrust and Trade Regulation.
Waxman, Seth P. . . . . '51 '77 C.309 A.B. L.976 J.D. [Wilmer,C.&P.]
*PRACTICE AREAS: Supreme Court Litigation; Appellate Practice; Complex Litigation; Criminal Law; Constitutional Law.
Way, Kashi '71 '99 C.800 B.A. L.893 J.D.
(adm. in CA; not adm. in DC) [Ⓐ Covington&B.]
Wayne, Charles B. . . . .'51 '76 C.918 B.A. L.575 J.D. [Piper M.R.&W.]
*PRACTICE AREAS: Commercial Litigation; Employment and Employee Benefits Litigation; White Collar Criminal Litigation.
Weadon, Donald Alford, Jr., (AV) . . . .'45 '76 C.188 B.A. L.1065 J.D. [Weadon&Assoc.]
*PRACTICE AREAS: Export Compliance; Export Regulation; Foreign Trade Sanctions; Foreign Asset Control; Customs Compliance.

Weadon & Associates, (AV) BB
3338 N Street, N.W., 20007
Telephone: 202-965-4100 Fax: 202-965-4252
Email: weadonassociates@aol.com
Donald Alford Weadon, Jr. Counsel: Thomas P. Scott, III.
International Trade, International Transactions, International Trade Regulation, High Technology Law, Export Control, Customs, Intellectual Property, Ethical Business Practices, Logistics and Dispute Resolution.
See Professional Biographies, WASHINGTON, DISTRICT OF COLUMBIA

Weals, Christopher A., (BV) . . . .'59 '85 C.207 B.A. L.597 J.D. [Seyfarth S.]
*PRACTICE AREAS: Labor and Employment; ERISA Litigation; Immigration.
Wear, Terrance J. . . . . '— '75 C.1182 A.B. L.352 J.D. 888 16th St., N.W.
Wears, Bradley E., II . . . .'69 '94 C.930 B.A. L.273 J.D. 4101 Reservoir Rd., N.W.
Weathers, Sharon M. '— '88 C.379 B.A. L.352 J.D.
(adm. in IL; not adm. in DC) [Ⓐ Reno&C.]
*PRACTICE AREAS: Real Estate Transactions; Affordable Housing; Corporate Transactional.
Weaver, Jeffrey S. '66 '98 C.339 B.S.E.E. L.446 J.D.
[Ⓐ Sterne,K.G.&F.] (See Pat. Sect.)
*PRACTICE AREAS: Intellectual Property.
Weaver, Robert C. . . . .'43 '69 C&L.546 B.A., J.D. [Kelly&W.]
*PRACTICE AREAS: Water Quality; Water Pollution; Clean Water Act; Federal Grants; Environmental Law.
Weaver, Robert W. . . . . '51 '83 C&L.893 B.A., J.D. [Ⓒ Davis P.&W.]
Weaver, S. Elizabeth, (AV) . . . .'54 '79 C.821 A.B. L.851 J.D. [Ⓒ Ballard S.A.&I.]
*PRACTICE AREAS: Real Estate Development Law; Financing Law; Housing and Urban Development Law.
Weaver, Warren, Jr. . . . .'23 '59 C.31 A.B. L.982 LL.B. 1521 31st St., NW‡
Webb, Beth L. . . . .'58 '85 C.575 B.A. L.190 J.D. [Dickstein S.M.&O.]
*PRACTICE AREAS: Energy Law.
Webb, Charles V. . . . .'71 '98 C.30 B.A. L.273 J.D. [Ⓐ Shearman&S.]
Webber, A. Duane . . . .'59 '85 C.375 B.A.B.S. L.276 J.D. [Baker&M.]
*PRACTICE AREAS: Tax Controversies (Corporate and International); Tax Planning and Advice (Corporate and International).
Webber, Christine E. . . . . '67 '91 C.309 A.B. L.477 J.D. [Ⓐ Cohen,M.H.&T.]
*PRACTICE AREAS: Employment Discrimination.
Webber, Paul R., III . . . .'34 '58 C&L.789 A.B., J.D. Supr. Ct. J.
Webber, Richard J., (AV) . . . .'48 '74 C.674 B.A. L.477 J.D. [Arent F.K.P.&K.]
*PRACTICE AREAS: Government Contracts; Litigation; Construction Law; Government Procurement.
Webber, William L. . . . .'53 '81 C.976 B.A. L.228 J.D. [Howrey S.A.&W.]
*PRACTICE AREAS: Advertising; Antitrust; Appellate Practice; Litigation; White Collar Criminal Defense.
Weber, Becky Bentson '60 '84 C.69 B.A. L.378 J.D.
(adm. in KS; not adm. in DC) Peyser Assocs., Inc.
Weber, Brian J. . . . .'59 '87 C&L.145 B.A., J.D. [Ⓐ Crowell&M.]
Weber, Charles A. . . . .'59 '85 C.477 A.B. L.352 J.D. [Murphy E.W.]
*PRACTICE AREAS: Export Compliance; E-Commerce; International Business Law; Corporate.

Weber, Cynthia Clarke, (AV) '51 '76
C.914 B.A. L.128 J.D. [Sughrue M.] (See Pat. Sect.)
*PRACTICE AREAS: Litigation; Trademark Law; Unfair Competition Law; Copyright Law.
Weber, George L., (AV) .... '44 '71 C.793 B.A. L.273 J.D. [Weber&Assoc.]
Weber, John H., (AV) '50 '82 C.801 B.A. L.589 J.D.
1050 Connecticut Ave., N.W. (Pat.)
Weber, William R. .... '43 '68 C&L.477 A.B., J.D. 50 F St NW Ste 900

Weber & Associates, P.C., (AV)
1730 K Street, N.W., Suite 304, 20006
Telephone: 202-628-0200 Fax: 202-628-0021
Email: glweber44@aol.com
George L. Weber.
Energy, Environmental and Appellate Practice. Energy Regulatory, Litigation Practice before the F.E.R.C. and the E.P.A.
See Professional Biographies, WASHINGTON, DISTRICT OF COLUMBIA

Webne, Ronald L., (AV) '47 '72 C.473 B.A. L.273 J.D.
1701 Q Street, N.W., 20009
Telephone: 202-518-0418 Fax: 202-518-0318
Email: RWebne@aol.com URL: http://www.lawyers.com/webnelaw
***PRACTICE AREAS: General Practice; General Civil Litigation; Corporate Litigation; Landlord and Tenant Law; Corporate Law.**
General Litigation, specializing in Commercial, Tort, Landlord and Tenant, and other Real Estate Related Matters; General Corporate and Business Law.
See Professional Biographies, WASHINGTON, DISTRICT OF COLUMBIA

Webner, Corinne Palmer '41 '80 C.8 B.A. L.1209 J.D.
(adm. in VA; not adm. in DC) 1237 30th St., N.W.
Webner, William Mack, (AV) ....'41 '68 C&L.8 B.S., J.D. [Sughrue M.] (See Pat. Sect.)
*PRACTICE AREAS: Litigation; Trademark, Copyright and Unfair Competition Law; Trade Secret Law; Licensing.
Webster, Aen W., (AV) .... '57 '88 C.976 B.A. L.813 J.D. [Silverstein&M.]
Webster, David N., (AV) .... '34 '58 C.676 A.B. L.276 J.D. [Caplin&D.]
*PRACTICE AREAS: Airplane Crash Litigation; Arbitration; Breach of Contract; Business Torts; Class Actions.
Webster, Hugh K. .... '61 '86 C.478 B.A. L.228 J.D. [Webster,C.&B.]
*PRACTICE AREAS: Trade and Professional Associations; Nonprofit and Charitable Organizations.
Webster, Joseph H. .... '68 '95 C.679 B.A. L.273 J.D. [Ⓐ Hobbs,S.D.&W.]
Webster, Mary S. .... '60 '92 C.966 B.S. L.30 J.D. [Ⓒ McKenna&C.] (Pat.)
*PRACTICE AREAS: Intellectual Property.
Webster, R. Kenly, (AV) ....'33 '61 C.674 A.B. L.893 LL.B. [R.K.Webster]
*PRACTICE AREAS: Litigation; Criminal Law; Business Law.
Webster, Timothy Kenly '64 '91 C.118 B.A. L.893 J.D.
(adm. in VA; not adm. in DC) [Ⓐ Sidley A.B.&W.]
Webster, Wendell W., (AV) ....'50 '76 C.94 B.S. L.329 J.D. [Webster,F.&B.]
*PRACTICE AREAS: Public Utilities; Bankruptcy; Commercial Law.
Webster, William H., (AV) ....'24 '49 C.31 B.A. L.910 J.D. [Milbank,T.H.&M.]

Webster, Chamberlain & Bean, (AV) BB
Suite 1000, 1747 Pennsylvania Avenue, N.W., 20006
Telephone: 202-785-9500 Fax: 202-835-0243
Members of Firm: Arthur L. Herold; Alan P. Dye; Edward D. Coleman; Frank M. Northam; John W. Hazard, Jr.; Hugh K. Webster; David P. Goch. Associates: Charles M. Watkins; Douglas W. Macdonald; Heidi K. Abegg. Of Counsel: J. Coleman Bean (Retired); Charles E. Chamberlain; Kent Masterson Brown (Not admitted in DC); James Bopp, Jr. (Not admitted in DC).
General and Administrative Practice before all Federal Courts, Departments and Agencies. Corporation, Tax, Antitrust, Trade Regulation, Labor, Environmental, Intellectual Property, Contract and Non-Profit Organization Law.
See Professional Biographies, WASHINGTON, DISTRICT OF COLUMBIA

Webster, Fredrickson & Brackshaw, (AV) BB
Suite 300, 1819 H Street, N.W., 20006
Telephone: 202-659-8510 Telecopier: 202-659-4082
Email: firm@wf82.com
Members of Firm: Wendell W. Webster; Bruce A. Fredrickson; Susan L. Brackshaw; Linda M. Correia. Associates: Jonathan C. Puth; Jeffrey E. Fallon; Scott Martin (Not admitted in DC).
General Civil, Appellate and Administrative Practice. Public Utility, Business, Taxation, Real Estate, Bankruptcy, Commercial Litigation, Labor, Employment and Personal Injury Law.
See Professional Biographies, WASHINGTON, DISTRICT OF COLUMBIA

Webster, R. Kenly, P.C., (AV)
1201 Connecticut Avenue N.W., Sixth Floor, 20036
Telephone: 202-822-3628 Fax: 202-659-0084
Email: kenlywebster@usa.net URL: http://www.lawyers.com/rkenlywebster
R. Kenly Webster.
Litigation, Criminal Law and Business Law.
See Professional Biographies, WASHINGTON, DISTRICT OF COLUMBIA

Wechsler, Burton D. ....'24 '50 C.477 B.A. L.309 LL.B. Prof. of Law, Amer. Univ.
Wechsler, Lawrence H., (AV) .... '45 '71 C.645 B.S. L.273 J.D. [Janis,S.&W.]
*PRACTICE AREAS: White Collar Criminal Defense; International Criminal Law.

Wechsler, Selzer & Gurvitch, Chartered
(See Bethesda, Maryland)

Weckstein, Kenneth B., (AV) ....'52 '76 C.30 B.A. L.273 J.D. [Epstein B.&G.]
*PRACTICE AREAS: Government Contracts Law; Litigation; Construction Law; Trade Secrets Law.
Weed, Lincoln ....'54 '80 C.299 A.B. L.94 J.D. [Ⓐ Sanders,S.&B.]
*PRACTICE AREAS: Health Care; Employee Benefits.
Weeda, David F., (AV) ....'48 '76 C.1158 B.A. L.425 J.D. [Olsson,F.&W.]
*PRACTICE AREAS: Food and Drug Law; Litigation; White Collar Criminal Defense.
Weeke, Helle R. ....'64 '92 L.999 [Ⓐ Weil,G.&M.]
*PRACTICE AREAS: International Trade.
Wegener, Mark D., (AV) ....'48 '74 C.132 B.A. L.705 J.D. [Howrey S.A.&W.]
*PRACTICE AREAS: Antitrust; Commercial Law; Complex Litigation; Government Regulation; Litigation.
Wegman, Richard A., (AV) .... '38 '65 C.103 A.B. L.309 J.D. [Garvey,S.&B.]
*PRACTICE AREAS: Administrative Law; Environmental Law; Legislative Process.
Wegner, Harold C., (AV) .....'43 '69 C.597 B.A. L.276 J.D. [Foley&L.] (See Pat. Sect.)
*PRACTICE AREAS: Intellectual Property; Intellectual Property Asset Management.
Wehner, James P. ....'67 '95 C&L.276 B.A., J.D. [Ⓐ Squire,S.&D.]

Wehner & York, (AV) BB
1029 Vermont Avenue, N.W. Suite 300, 20005 ⊙
Telephone: 202-543-2700 Facsimile: 202-543-2023
Email: mmyork@worldnet.att.net URL: http://www.lawyers.com/w&ylaw
Members of Firm: Stephen V. Wehner (1954-2000); Michael M. York.
Litigation including Commercial, White Collar, Media Law with special emphasis in the areas of Libel, Slander, First Amendment and Copyright Infringement.
Reston, Virginia Office: 11860 Sunrise Valley Drive, Suite 100, 20191. Telephone: 703-476-8300. Fax: 703-476-8300.
See Professional Biographies, WASHINGTON, DISTRICT OF COLUMBIA

Wei, Richard ....'70 '98 C.446 B.S. L.575 J.D. [Ⓐ Dechert]
*PRACTICE AREAS: Securities Litigation.
Wei, Victoria Y. .... '72 '96 C.309 A.B. L.597 J.D. [Ⓐ Morrison&F.]
Weich, Cecile C. '34 '59
C.563 A.B. L.1009 LL.B. 701 Pennsylvania Ave., N.W. (⊙Bronx, NY)
Weich, Ronald H. .... '59 '84 C.178 B.A. L.976 J.D. [Zuckerman S.]
*PRACTICE AREAS: Government Relations; Congressional Investigations; Criminal and Civil Litigation.
Weichlein, Peter M. '68 '98 C.645 B.A. L.180 J.D.
(adm. in MD; not adm. in DC) Legis. Atty.
Weidenfeld, Edward L., (AV) '43 '68 C.966 B.S. L.178 J.D.
[Ⓒ Margolius,M.D.R.&T.]
*PRACTICE AREAS: Estate Planning; Business Planning; Trust Administration; Estate Administration; Corporate Transactions.
Weidman, Linda Mar ......'58 '84 C.309 B.A. L.597 J.D. Sr. Coun., Marriott Intl., Corp.
*RESPONSIBILITIES: International Development.
Weierstall, Eric J. ...'— '99 C&L.823 B.S., J.D. [Ⓐ Venable,A.B.H.&C.] (See Pat. Sect.)
*PRACTICE AREAS: Patents.
Weigel, Kenneth G., (AV) .... '54 '79 C.477 B.A. L.273 J.D. [Kirkland&E.]
*PRACTICE AREAS: International Law; Customs Law; International Trade Law.
Weil, Frank A., (AV) '31 '56 C&L.309 A.B., LL.B.
(adm. in NY; not adm. in DC) 1300 19th St., N.W. (⊙New York, NY)
Weil, John A. .... '16 '39 C&L.273 LL.B. 2801 Quebec St., N.W.
Weil, Robert J. .... '54 '80 C.728 B.A. L.128 J.D. [Howe,A.&S.]
*PRACTICE AREAS: Civil Litigation; Insurance Law; Legislative Practice; Association Law.
Weil, Russell T., (AV) ...... '26 '52 C&L.309 A.B., LL.B. 1660 L Street, N.W. Suite 506
Weil, Sherrill Lang '54 '89 C.128 B.A. L.276 J.D.
(adm. in PA; not adm. in DC) Dir., Develop., Georgetown Univ.
Weil, Stephan G. ....'49 '82 C.293 B.S. L.145 J.D. [Dickstein S.M.&O.]
*PRACTICE AREAS: Insurance Litigation; Commercial Litigation.
Weil, Stephen E. '28 '56 C.103 A.B. L.178 LL.B.
(adm. in NY; not adm. in DC) Ctr. for Museum Studies

Weil, Gotshal & Manges LLP, (AV)
A Limited Liability Partnership including Professional Corporations
1615 L Street, N.W. Suite 700, 20036 ⊙
Telephone: 202-682-7000 Telecopier: 202-857-0939; 857-0940 Telex: 440045
URL: http://www.weil.com
Partners: M. Jean Anderson; Richard Ben-Veniste; David R. Berz; W. Michael Bond; David I. Bower; Annemargaret Connolly; Carolyn M. DuPuy; E. Michael Flanagan; David A. Hickerson; David B. Hird; Peter D. Isakoff; Robert C. Odle, Jr.; Charles E. Roh, Jr.; Stanley Sporkin; Stanley M. Spracker; Bruce H. Turnbull; Karl T. Walli (Not admitted in DC); Walter E. Zalenski. Counsel: Gregory Husisian; Michael Lyle (Not admitted in DC); Loretta Jo Roby. Resident Associates: Sandra M. Aistars (Not admitted in DC); Todd W. Betke; Gregg S. Buksbaum; Christopher T. Cardinale (Not admitted in DC); Jeffrey L. Cimbalo (Not admitted in DC); Amy T. Dixon; Connie M. Ericson (Not admitted in DC); Lisa R. Fine (Not admitted in DC); Melanie A. Frank (Not admitted in DC); Peter M. Friedman (Not admitted in DC); Jacqueline M. Gordon; Joanne M. Guerrera; Jahna M. Hartwig (Not admitted in DC); George J. Hazel; P.J. Himelfarb; Timothy Hruby; Christine P. Hsu; Kristin G. King; Holly E. Washington Loiseau; Joseph D. Looney; Scott Maberry; Terri T. Mallett; Joseph F. Miller (Not admitted in DC); John B. O'Loughlin, Jr.; Theresa M. Regan (Not admitted in DC); John M. Ryan; Roger N. Simon; David N. Southard; J. Sloane Strickler (Not admitted in DC); Adam P. Strochak; Maureen Testoni; Helle R. Weeke; Larry I. Willis; Vincent S. Wong (Not admitted in DC).
Advertising, Antitrust/Competition Law, Art, Auditing and Accounting Litigation, Aviation, Banking and Financial Services, Bankruptcy, Biotechnology, Business and Securities, Business Finance and Restructuring, Capital Markets, Civil RICO, Class Actions, Consumer Finance, Corporate, Corporate Governance, Criminal (white collar crime), Crisis Management, Cross-Border Transactions, Debt and Equity Offerings, Derivatives, Emerging Companies, Employee Benefits, Energy, Entertainment, Environmental, Executive Compensation, Financial Services, First Amendment, Franchising, Fringe Benefits, Government Investigations, Health Care, Insurance, Intellectual Property, International, International Dispute Resolution, International Trade, Internet, Joint Ventures, Labor and Employment, Lending, Litigation, Media and Communications, Mergers and Acquisitions, Oil and Gas, Patent, Pension Funds, Private Equity, Pro Bono, Product Liability, Project Finance, Property and Finance, Public Finance, Public Policy, Real Estate, Restructurings, RICO, SEC Enforcement, Securities Offerings, Sports, Structured Alliances, Structured Finance, Tax, Technology, Telecommunications, Toxic Torts, Trade Practices and Regulatory Law, Trade Secret Litigation, Trusts and Estates, Venture Capital, Workouts.
New York, N.Y. Office: 767 Fifth Avenue. Telephone: 212-310-8000. Cable Address: "Wegoma". Telex: 424281; 423144. Telecopier: 212-310-8007.
Dallas, Texas Office: 100 Crescent Court, Suite 1300. Telephone: 214-746-7700. Fax: 214-746-7777.
Houston, Texas Office: 700 Louisiana Street, Suite 1600. Telephone: 713-546-5000. Telecopier: 713-224-9511.
Redwood Shores, California Silicon Valley Office: 201 Redwood Shores Parkway, Telephone: 650-802-3000. Telecopier: 650-802-3100.
Miami, Florida Office: 701 Brickell Avenue, Suite 2100. Telephone: 305-577-3100. Telecopier: 305-374-7159.
Brussels, Belgium Office: 81 avenue Louise, Box 9-10, 1050 Brussels. Telephone: 011-32-2-543-7460. Telecopier: 011-32-2-543-7489.
Budapest, Hungary Office: Bank Center, Granite Tower, H-1944 Budapest. Telephone: 011-36-1-302-9100. Fax: 011-36-1-302-9110.
London, England Office: The Helicon, One South Place, London EC2M 2WG. Telephone: 011-44-207-903-1000. Telecopier: 011-44-207-903-0990.
Prague, Czech Republic Office: Charles Bridge Center, Krizovnicke nam. 1, 110 00 Prague 1, Czech Republic. Telephone: 011-420-2-2140-7300. Telecopier: 011-420-2-2140-7310.
Warsaw, Poland Office: Warsaw Financial Center, ul.Emilii Plater 53 00-113 Warsaw. Telephone: 011-48-22-520-4000. Telecopier: 011-48-22-520-4001.
Frankfurt am Main, Germany Office: Main Tower, Box 19, 31st Floor, Neue Mainzer Strasse 52-58, 60311 Frankfurt am Main. Telephone: 49 69 21659 600. Facsimile: 49 69 21659 699.
See Professional Biographies, WASHINGTON, DISTRICT OF COLUMBIA

Weilacher, Robert G., (AV) '34 '61
C.178 B.S. L.273 LL.B. [Smith,G.&R.] (See Pat. Sect.)
*PRACTICE AREAS: Intellectual Property Law.
Weiler, David J. ....'65 '90 C.446 B.A. L.276 J.D. [Ⓐ Patton B.]
Weiler, Steven A. ....'57 '86 C&L.585 B.A., J.D. [Leonard,S.&D.]
*PRACTICE AREAS: Regulated Industries.
Weill, James D. '45 '69 C.188 B.A. L.569 J.D.
(adm. in NY; not adm. in DC) Gen. Coun., Children's Def. Fund
Weimar, Elizabeth ....'57 '86 C.276 B.S. L.128 J.D. [Ⓒ Morgan,L.&B.]
Weimer, Beth E. '52 '83 C.750 B.A. L.128 J.D.
Sr. V.P., Nat. Assn. Of Sec. Dealers, Inc.
Weimer, Brian D. ....'65 '96 C.145 B.A. L.276 J.D. [Ⓐ Skadden,A.S.M.&F.]
*PRACTICE AREAS: Communications; Corporate.
Weinberg, David B., (AV) ....'48 '73 C.976 B.A. L.659 J.D. [Howrey S.A.&W.]
Weinberg, Donald C., (BV) ....'49 '77 C.1044 B.A. L.1209 J.D. [Ⓐ Dombroff&G.]
Weinberg, Jonathan D. ....'— '92 C.966 B.A. L.128 J.D. [Ⓐ Epstein B.&G.]
*PRACTICE AREAS: Health Law.
Weinberg, Joshua D. .... '72 '98 C.659 B.A. L.178 J.D. [Ⓐ Wilmer,C.&P.]
Weinberg, Larry P. ....'45 '71 C&L.477 B.A., J.D. 1101 17th St., N.W.
Weinberg, Linda M. ....'— '87 C.112 B.A. L.426 J.D. [Verner,L.B.M.&H.]
*PRACTICE AREAS: Customs; Export Control; International Trade.
Weinberg, Mark B., (P.C.), (AV) '46 '71
C.36 B.A. L.145 J.D. [Ⓒ Schwartz,W.&M.] (⊙Rockville, MD)
Weinberg, Meredith R. '76 '01 C.228 A.B. L.276 J.D.
(adm. in VA; not adm. in DC) [Ⓐ Shaw P.]
Weinberg, Robert, (AV) .... '49 '75 C.72 B.A. L.659 J.D. [Duncan,W.G.&P.]
*PRACTICE AREAS: Administrative Law; Public Utility Law; Energy.
Weinberg, Robert L., (AV) ....'31 '60 C&L.976 B.A., LL.B. 725 12th St., N.W.
Weinberg, Robert M., (AV) .... '42 '69 C&L.477 B.A., J.D. [Bredhoff&K.]
Weinberg, Sara C. ....'73 '98 C.1349 B.A. L.94 J.D. [Ⓐ Vinson&E.]
*PRACTICE AREAS: Energy; Utility Law; Federal Energy Regulation; Regulatory Law; Mergers, Acquisitions and Divestitures.
Weinberg, Steven ....'52 '77 C.107 B.A. L.273 J.D. [Steinmetz,W.&M.]

Weinberg, Steven B. '64 '00 C.880 B.A. L.128 J.D.
(adm. in CA; not adm. in DC) [Ⓐ Schnader H.S.&L.]
*PRACTICE AREAS: Litigation.
Weinberger, Caspar W. ....'17 '46 C&L.309 A.B., J.D. Chmn., Forbes, Inc.
Weinberger, Mark Alan .... '61 '87 C.1365 B.A. L.930 J.D. [Washington C.]
Weinberger, Mel S., (AV) ....'56 '81 C.696 B.A. L.276 J.D. [Holland&K.]
*PRACTICE AREAS: Resort Timeshares; Hotel Development; Community Development; Finance; Real Estate Law.
Weinblatt, Amy J. ....'62 '88 C.659 B.A. L.273 J.D. Asst. Corp. Coun., D.C.
Weiner, Allan J., (AV) ....'48 '73 C.477 B.B.A. L.608 J.D. [Collier S.S.]
*PRACTICE AREAS: Federal Income Tax; Business Transactions.
Weiner, Andrew M. ....'74 '99 C.446 B.A. L.893 J.D. [Ⓐ Dickstein S.M.&O.]
*PRACTICE AREAS: Litigation; Insurance.
Weiner, George J. .... '49 '75 C.93 B.A. L.904 J.D. 600 New Hampshire Ave, N.W.
Weiner, Harvey E., (AV) ....'44 '69 C.994 B.A. L.569 J.D. [Weiner B.S.K.]
*PRACTICE AREAS: Mortgages; Real Estate Finance; Mortgage Banking; Mergers and Acquisitions; Asset Sales.
Weiner, Heather L. '68 '94 C&L.260 B.S., J.D.
(adm. in FL; not adm. in DC) Sr. Legis. Coun., Earthjustice Legal Defense Fund
Weiner, Janice L. ....'73 '97 C.276 A.B. L.309 J.D. [Ⓐ Piper M.R.&W.]
*PRACTICE AREAS: Pharmaceutical Products Liability Litigation; Health Care; Food and Drug Regulation.
Weiner, Karin E. ....'— '98 C.976 B.A. L.597 J.D. [Ⓐ Fried,F.H.S.&J.]
*PRACTICE AREAS: Corporate Law.
Weiner, Kenneth B. ....'54 '86 C.930 B.S.C.E. L.564 J.D. [Thelen R.&P.]
*PRACTICE AREAS: Project Finance; Asset Based Finance; Franchise Law.
Weiner, Richard L.A. ....'59 '87 C.309 A.B. L.178 J.D. [Hogan&H.]
*PRACTICE AREAS: European Union Law; International Trade Law; International Arbitration; Aviation Law.
Weiner, Robert N., (AV) ....'52 '79 C.674 A.B. L.976 J.D. [Arnold&P.]
*PRACTICE AREAS: Commercial Litigation; Criminal Litigation; Products Liability.
Weiner, Sigmund T., (AV) .... '42 '68 C.870 B.S. L.846 LL.B. [Jones,D.R.&P.]
*PRACTICE AREAS: Real Estate Development; Real Estate Leasing; Real Estate Finance; Real Estate Workouts.
Weiner, Victor I., (BV) '53 '78 C.446 B.A. L.64 J.D.
(adm. in MD; not adm. in DC) [Ⓐ Lipshultz&H.] ⊙
*PRACTICE AREAS: Appellate Practice; Products Liability; Insurance Law; Intellectual Property; Civil Appeals.

Weiner Brodsky Sidman Kider PC, (AV) BR
1300 Nineteenth Street, N.W., Fifth Floor, 20036
Telephone: 202-628-2000 Telecopier: 202-628-2011
Email: info@wbsk.com URL: http://www.wbsk.com
Richard J. Andreano, Jr.; James A. Brodsky; Jo A. DeRoche; Cynthia L. Gilman; Don J. Halpern; Mitchel H. Kider; Mark H. Sidman; Harvey E. Weiner. Of Counsel: Donald C. Brown Jr.; Susan L. Korytkowski; Sherri L. Ledner; James M. Milano; David M. Souders;—Andrew N. Cline (Not admitted in DC); Troy W. Garris; Karen Ruth Gustavson; Suzanne De Armond Mucchetti; Leah Schmulewitz-Getlan; John D. Socknat; Dian Patricia Stevens (Not admitted in DC); Cynthia G. Swann; Michael S. Waldron; Rose-Michele Weinryb.
General Administrative, Corporate, Legislative and Litigation Practice. Finance, Housing, Mortgage Banking, Consumer Credit and Regulatory Compliance, Real Estate, Transportation, Mergers and Acquisitions and Financial Institutions.
See Professional Biographies, WASHINGTON, DISTRICT OF COLUMBIA

Weinerman, Lloyd M., (AV) ....'40 '73 C.94 A.B. L.64 J.D. [Ⓒ Crowell&M.]
*PRACTICE AREAS: Government Contracts; Health Care.
Weingardt, Brent, (AV) ....'57 '82 C.659 B.A. L.273 J.D. [Bennet&B.]
*PRACTICE AREAS: Communications Law.
Weingarten, David, (AV) ....'51 '75 C.966 B.A. L.145 J.D. [Sanders,S.&B.]
*PRACTICE AREAS: Employee Benefits.
Weingarten, Joel C. .... '47 '73 C.1349 B.A. L.339 J.D. 1616 H St., N.W.
Weingarten, Reid H., (AV) ....'50 '75 C.188 B.S. L.1017 J.D. [Steptoe&J.]
*PRACTICE AREAS: Criminal Law; Grand Jury Proceedings; Litigation; Professional Ethics and Discipline Law; Appellate Practice.
Weinkauf, Russell E. '23 '51 C&L.966 B.S., LL.B.
(adm. in WI; not adm. in DC; See Pat. Sect.) [Keil&W.]
*PRACTICE AREAS: Patent; Trademark Law.
Weinman, Howard M., (AV) ....'47 '73 C.178 B.A. L.309 J.D. [Crowell&M.]
*PRACTICE AREAS: Taxation Law.
Weinmann, Eric ....'13 '57 C&L.178 M.A., LL.B. 3244 Nebraska Ave., N.W.‡
Weinreich, Gadi ....'62 '87 C.103 A.B. L.309 J.D. [Shaw P.]
*PRACTICE AREAS: Health Law; Health Care Regulation; Health Care Fraud and Abuse; Health Care Compliance; Health Care Litigation.
Weinrich, Harold R. ....'46 '72 C.1019 B.A. L.1009 J.D. [Jackson L.S.&K.]
Weinrieb, Jonathan Michael ....'72 '99 C.910 B.A. L.273 J.D. [Ⓐ Howrey S.A.&W.]
*PRACTICE AREAS: Insurance Coverage; Products Liability.
Weinryb, Rose-Michele ....'71 '96 C.390 B.A. L.30 J.D. [Ⓐ Weiner B.S.K.]
*PRACTICE AREAS: Transportation; Regulatory Compliance; Mergers and Acquisitions; Asset Sales; Federal Taxation.
Weinsheimer, G. Bradley, (AV) ....'63 '89 C.436 B.A. L.893 J.D. Asst. U.S. Atty.
Weinstein, Andrea J. ....'73 '98 C.910 B.A. L.30 J.D. [Ⓐ Morgan,L.&B.]
Weinstein, Andrew J. ....'69 '95 C.846 B.B.A. L.30 J.D. [Ⓐ Steptoe&J.]
Weinstein, Bonnie H. ....'55 '84 C.102 B.A. L.145 J.D. 2130 P St., N.W.
Weinstein, Daniel A. '57 '92 C.37 B.S. L.846 J.D.
(adm. in TX; not adm. in DC) 450 5th St., N.W.‡
Weinstein, Harris, (AV) ....'35 '62 C.453 S.B. L.178 LL.B. [Covington&B.]
Weinstein, Julie K. '75 '00 C.477 B.B.A. L.273 J.D.
(adm. in PA; not adm. in DC) [Ⓐ McKee N.]
*PRACTICE AREAS: Securitization; Structured Finance; General Corporate; Mergers and Acquisitions.
Weinstein, Kathleen M. ....'60 '90 C.428 B.A. L.904 J.D. [Hale&D.]
*PRACTICE AREAS: Real Estate.
Weinstein, Kenneth W., (AV) .... '— '73 C.563 B.E.E. L.276 J.D. [Latham&W.]
*PRACTICE AREAS: Environmental Litigation; Pesticide Regulation; Toxic Substance Regulation.
Weinstein, Laura D. '63 '91 C.31 B.A. L.569 J.D.
(adm. in NY; not adm. in DC) Assoc. Gen. Coun., Kaplan Educational Centers, Inc.
Weinstein, Marc K. '— '99 C.645 B.S.E.E. L.276 J.D.
(adm. in VA; not adm. in DC; See Pat. Sect.) [Ⓐ Foley&L.]
*PRACTICE AREAS: Intellectual Property; Software Patents; Computer and Software Patents; Electronic Patents.
Weinstein, Martin J., (AV) .... '— '85 C.197 B.A. L.893 J.D. [Foley&L.]
*PRACTICE AREAS: International Business Law; Foreign Corrupt Practices Act; Criminal Law; Government Investigations.
Weinstein, Richard A. ....'47 '73 C.1029 B.S. L.30 J.D. 728 5th St., N.E.
Weinstein, Richard S., (AV) '25 '49 C&L.260 J.D.
(adm. in CT; not adm. in DC) [Ⓒ Holland&K.]
*PRACTICE AREAS: Alternative Dispute Resolution; Probate; Estate Planning; Business Law.
Weinstein, Steven M. ....'67 '93 C.188 B.S. L.178 J.D. [Ⓐ Dickstein S.M.&O.]
*PRACTICE AREAS: Corporate Law, Mergers, Acquisitions, Divestitures; Corporate Finance.
Weinstock, Jeffrey C. '63 '91 C.881 B.A. L.94 J.D.
Managing Director, Law Registry, Inc.
Weinstock, Robert N., (AV) .... '46 '71 C&L.659 B.S., J.D. [Shaw P.]
*PRACTICE AREAS: Commercial Real Estate.

Weinstock, Friedman & Friedman, P.A., (AV)
1413 K St., N.W., Ste., 1500 (⊙Balt., MD; York, PA; Fairfax, VA)
Weintraub, David A. ....'54 '94 C.107 B.S. L.982 J.D. [Ⓐ Roberts&H.]
*PRACTICE AREAS: Taxation.
Weintraub, Ellen L. ....'57 '85 C.976 B.A. L.309 J.D. [Ⓒ Perkins C.]
*PRACTICE AREAS: Government Ethics; Lobbying Regulation; Election and Campaign Finance; Congressional Investigations.
Weir, Bruce Eric ....'56 '97 C.763 A.B. L.1194 J.D. 910 17th Street, N.W., Suite 800
Weir, Howard T., III, (AV) ....'49 '77 C.112 A.B. L.16 J.D. [Morgan,L.&B.]
Weis, Andrew E. ....'67 '96 C&L.813 A.B., J.D. [Ⓐ Skadden,A.S.M.&F.]
Weisbaum, Steven M. ....'64 '91 C.319 B.S. L.94 J.D. [Weisbaum]
*PRACTICE AREAS: Railroad Safety Law; Federal Employers Liability Act (FELA); Trade Association Law; Commercial Contacts; Labor and Employment Law.

Weisbaum Law Firm, The
1850 M Street, N.W., Suite 250, 20036
Telephone: 202-293-2299 Toll free: 1-866-293-5351 Fax: 202-293-1788
Email: weisbaum@earthlink.net URL: http://www.lawyers.com/weisbaumlawfirm
Steven M. Weisbaum.
See Professional Biographies, WASHINGTON, DISTRICT OF COLUMBIA

Weisbrod, Stephen A. ....'65 '92 C.477 B.A. L.309 J.D. [Ⓐ Paul,H.J.&W.]
*PRACTICE AREAS: Litigation; Criminal Defense; Government Investigations; Bankruptcy.
Weise, Craig Harrison ....'71 '97 C.682 B.A. L.893 J.D. [Ⓐ Sidley A.B.&W.]
Weise, Richard H. ....'35 '62 C.210 B.A. L.209 J.D. [Steptoe&J.]
*PRACTICE AREAS: Alternative Dispute Resolution; International; Litigation.
Weisel, Sheldon J., (P.C.), (AV) .... '45 '70 C.112 B.A. L.1068 J.D. [Shaw P.]
*PRACTICE AREAS: Commercial Real Estate.
Weisenfeld, Lorin S. '41 '68
C.299 B.A. L.309 LL.B. Multilateral Investment Gaurantee Agcy.
Weiser, Carol A. ....'52 '85 C.318 B.A. L.831 J.D. [Sutherland A.&B.]
*PRACTICE AREAS: Qualified Retirement Plans; Non-Qualified Benefits; ERISA; Flexible Benefit Plans; Fringe Benefits.
Weiser, David, (AV) ....'60 '89 C.846 B.A. L.976 J.D. [Kator,P.&W.] ⊙
*PRACTICE AREAS: Federal Employment Law; Civil Rights.
Weiser, David R. '— '98 C.679 B.A. L.228 J.D.
(adm. in VA; not adm. in DC) [Ⓐ King&S.]
*PRACTICE AREAS: Commercial Litigation.
Weisgall, Jonathan M., (AV) .... '49 '74 C.178 B.A. L.813 LL.B. [J.M.Weisgall]

Weisgall, Jonathan M., Chartered, (AV)
1200 New Hampshire Avenue, NW Suite 300, 20036
Telephone: 202-828-1378 Facsimile: 202-828-1380
Email: JWeisgall@aol.com
Jonathan M. Weisgall.
General Federal and Legislative Practice. Administrative, Energy and Natural Resources Law, Electric Power, Energy Power, Energy Project Development, Energy Regulation, Independent Power. Federal and U.S. Claims Court Litigation.
See Professional Biographies, WASHINGTON, DISTRICT OF COLUMBIA

Weishaar, Robert A., Jr. '69 '95 C.30 B.A. L.276 J.D.
(adm. in PA; not adm. in DC) [Ⓐ McNees W.&N.]
*PRACTICE AREAS: Utility Law; Energy Law; Regulatory Law.
Weisman, Julie A. ....'53 '82 C.228 B.A. L.245 J.D. [Ⓒ Swidler B.S.F.]
*PRACTICE AREAS: Environmental Litigation.
Weisman, Robin Mahler .... '68 '97 C.385 B.A. L.30 J.D. [Ⓐ Akin,G.S.H.&F.]
*PRACTICE AREAS: Public Law and Policy.
Weiss, Anton M., (AV) ....'42 '68 C.1044 B.A. L.276 J.D. [Pascal&W.]
*PRACTICE AREAS: Commercial Litigation; Commercial Collections; Creditors Rights; Probate.
Weiss, Brad D., (AV) '55 '82 C.273 B.A. L.1209 J.D.
[Charapp,D.&W.] (⊙Bethesda, MD; Vienna, VA)
*PRACTICE AREAS: Corporate and Commercial Transactions; Complex Litigation; Employment and Discrimination Litigation; Aviation Transactions.
Weiss, Bradley Scott ....'54 '88 C.424 B.A. L.46 J.D. [Ⓒ Mehri,M.&R.]
*PRACTICE AREAS: Qui Tam Litigation; Whistleblower Litigation; Wrongful Termination; Government Contract Fraud; Health Care Fraud.
Weiss, Deirdre D. K. ....'57 '83 C.75 B.A. L.276 J.D. 5327 42nd Pl., N.W.
Weiss, Diana '66 '92 C.608 B.A. L.188 J.D.
(adm. in NY; not adm. in DC) [Orrick,H.&S.]
Weiss, Erica H., (AV) ....'64 '89 C&L.659 B.S., J.D. [Bingham D.]
*PRACTICE AREAS: Commercial Real Estate; Real Estate Finance; Workouts.
Weiss, Francine K., (AV) ....'49 '75 C.112 B.A. L.426 LL.B. [Ⓒ Kalijarvi,C.&N.]
*PRACTICE AREAS: Labor and Employment; Discrimination.
Weiss, Harry J., (AV) .... '52 '77 C.367 A.B. L.94 J.D. [Wilmer,C.&P.]
*PRACTICE AREAS: Securities; Regulatory Law; Litigation.
Weiss, Howard M., (AV) ....'51 '75 C&L.273 B.A., J.D. [Fletcher,H.&H.] ⊙
*PRACTICE AREAS: FCC Regulation; Mass Media Law; Communications Law; Broadcast Licensing; Commercial Contracts.
Weiss, Jacqueline S. ....'— '96 C.178 A.B. L.945 J.D. [Ⓐ King&S.]
*PRACTICE AREAS: Litigation; Trade Regulation.
Weiss, James R., (AV) .... '49 '74 C.597 B.A. L.128 J.D. [Preston G.E.&R.M.]
Weiss, Jay S., (AV) .... '40 '67 C.446 A.B. L.329 J.D. [J.S.Weiss]
*PRACTICE AREAS: Personal Injury; Commercial Litigation; General Trial Litigation.
Weiss, Joel C. '— '79 C.102 B.S. L.1009 J.D.
(adm. in NY; not adm. in DC) [Miller&C.]
Weiss, Leesa N. ....'56 '87 C.446 B.A. L.128 J.D. [Ⓐ Jacobson,H.]
*PRACTICE AREAS: Intellectual Property Law; Trademarks.
Weiss, Mark A., (AV) ....'37 '61 C.178 A.B. L.309 LL.B. [Covington&B.]
Weiss, Michael A., (AV) '48 '73 C.901 A.B. L.880 J.D.
(adm. in PA; not adm. in DC) [DKW] (⊙Southfield, MI; Harrisburg, Pitts., PA)
Weiss, Nancy E. '65 '92 C.659 B.S. L.477 J.D.
Gen. Coun., Inst. of Museum and Library Servs.
Weiss, Robyn B. ....'— '98 C.188 B.S. L.273 J.D. [Ⓐ Morgan,L.&B.]
Weiss, Shirley H. ...... '37 '82 C.705 B.A. L.904 J.D. National Assn. of Sec. Dealers, Inc.
Weiss, Stanley, (AV) ....'32 '55 C.569 B.S. L.976 J.D. 825 8th St.
Weiss, Stephen J., (AV) ....'38 '63 C.994 B.S. L.188 LL.B. [Holland&K.]
*PRACTICE AREAS: Corporate Law; Securities Law; Insurance Law.

Weiss, Jay S., P.C., Law Offices, (AV)
1828 L Street, N.W., Suite 902, 20036 ⊙
Telephone: 202-872-1545 Fax: 202-296-0568
URL: http://www.lawyers.com/jaysweiss
Jay S. Weiss;—Barry S. Kopit.
Civil Trial Practice in District of Columbia and Maryland, Personal Injury, Automobile Injuries, Premises Liability, Security Liability, Commercial Transactions, General Trial Litigation.
Rockville, Maryland Office: One Central Plaza, Suite 802, 11300 Rockville Pike 20852. Telephone: 301-770-9440. FAX: 301-770-5217
See Professional Biographies, WASHINGTON, DISTRICT OF COLUMBIA

Weissbrodt, Abe W., (AV) .... '13 '40 C.563 A.B. L.178 LL.B. [Weissbrodt&R.]
*PRACTICE AREAS: Civil Rights; Fair Employment Law; Federal Indian Law.
Weissbrodt, I. S., (AV) ....'10 '34 C.563 A.B. L.178 LL.B. 1614 20th St., N.W.

Weissbrodt & Racin, (AV)
1721 Lamont Street, 20010
Telephone: 202-265-2516 Fax: 202-483-7895
Email: awjrlaw@erols.com URL: http://www.lawyers.com/weissbrodt&racin
Members of Firm: Abe W. Weissbrodt; John P. Racin.
Representing American Tribes, Civil Rights Litigation and Corporate Law.
See Professional Biographies, WASHINGTON, DISTRICT OF COLUMBIA

Weissgold, Nanci L. . . . . '67 '92 C.454 B.A. L.904 J.D. [Ⓐ Kirkpatrick&L.]
*PRACTICE AREAS: Mortgage Banking; Banks and Banking; Consumer Law; Real Estate.
Weisshaar, Mark G. . . . . '50 '78 C.976 B.A. L.273 J.D. [Hunton&W.]
*PRACTICE AREAS: Environmental; Government Contracts.
Weissman, Andrew B., (AV) . . . . '49 '74 C.696 A.B. L.309 J.D. [Wilmer,C.&P.]
*PRACTICE AREAS: Securities; White Collar Crime; RICO; Civil Practice; Criminal Practice.
Weissman, Jill A. '69 '94 C.66 B.A. L.904 J.D. Dept. of the Treasury
Weissman, Peter S. '66 '96 C.1350 B.E. L.273 J.D.
[Ⓐ Blank R.C.&M.] (See Pat. Sect.)
*PRACTICE AREAS: Intellectual Property Law; Electrical Patents; Mechanical Patents; Trademarks; Fastener Quality Act.
Weissman, Stephen . . . . '69 '91 C.860 B.A. L.659 J.D. [Ⓐ Howrey S.A.&W.]
*PRACTICE AREAS: Antitrust; Litigation.
Weissman, William R., (AV) . . . . '40 '65 C&L.178 B.A., J.D. [Piper M.R.&W.]
*PRACTICE AREAS: Environmental Law; Administrative Law; Appellate Litigation.
Weistling, Ripple L. . . . . '71 '99 C.1036 B.A. L.276 J.D. [Ⓐ Steptoe&J.]
Weiswasser, Elizabeth Stotland '66 '92 C.597 B.A. L.145 J.D.
(adm. in IL; not adm. in DC) [Covington&B.]
Weiswasser, Gayle . . . . '69 '96 C.103 A.B. L.309 J.D. [Ⓐ Steptoe&J.]
Weiswasser, Stephen A., (AV) . . . . '40 '67 C.912 B.A. L.309 J.D. [Covington&B.]
Weitz, Alan S., (AV) . . . . '45 '71 C.659 B.S. L.309 J.D. [Greenstein D.&L.]
*PRACTICE AREAS: Employment Law; Mediation; Litigation.
Weitzel, Daniel P., (AV) . . . . '56 '81 C.363 B.S. L.276 J.D. [Duane,M.&H.]
*PRACTICE AREAS: Banking Law; Corporate Law; Securities; Executive Compensation; Employee Benefits.
Weitzner, Michael '73 '00 C.260 B.A. L.273 J.D.
(adm. in VA; not adm. in DC) 2401 Calvert St., N.W.
Weitzner, Richard A. . . . . '61 '86 C&L.273 B.A., J.D. The George Washington Univ.
Welch, James A., (AV) . . . . '31 '59 C.602 A.B. L.276 LL.B. 1301 K St.‡
Welch, Kathleen A. '59 '92 C.732 B.A. L.107 J.D.
(adm. in NY; not adm. in DC) Exec. Dir., Natl. Assn. Pub. Int. Law
Welch, Noreen O'Hara '— '99 C.102 B.S. L.446 J.D.
(adm. in MD; not adm. in DC) [Ⓐ Stevens,D.M.&M.]
Welch, Rachel '70 '00 C.915 B.A. L.893 J.D.
(adm. in MD; not adm. in DC) [Ⓐ Covington&B.]
Welch, Timothy E. . . . . . . '— '85 C.454 B.A. L.128 J.D. 1330 New Hampshire Ave., N.W.
Welch, Bryant L., & Associates
(See Potomac, MD)
Well, Ranan Z. . . . . '72 '99 C.978 B.A. L.94 J.D. [Ⓐ Swidler B.S.F.]
*PRACTICE AREAS: Corporate; Securities; Bankruptcy.
Wellbery, Barbara S. . . . . '48 '78 C.1044 B.A. L.813 J.D. [Morrison&F.]
*PRACTICE AREAS: Financial Services Law; Communications Law.
Wellen, Robert H., (AV) . . . . '46 '71 C&L.976 B.A., J.D. [Ivins,P.&B.]
*PRACTICE AREAS: Business Taxation; Corporate Taxation; Federal Tax.
Weller, Janet L. . . . . '53 '78 C.681 B.A. L.477 J.D. [Cleary,G.S.&H.]
Weller, Mark W. '58 '83 C.347 B.A. L.1119 J.D.
(adm. in IN; not adm. in DC) [Baker&D.]
*PRACTICE AREAS: Federal Legislative Practice; Regulatory Law; Health Care.
Weller, O. Julia, (AV) . . . . '49 '74 C&L.012 B.A., LL.B. [Ⓒ Hunton&W.]
*PRACTICE AREAS: Energy; International; Regulatory Reform; Privatization; Project Finance.
Welles, Martin R. '65 '98 C.999 B.A. L.425 J.D.
(adm. in LA; not adm. in DC) P.O. Box 2489
Wellford, Hill B., III . . . . '70 '95 C.197 B.A. L.893 J.D. [Ⓐ Gibson,D.&C.]
*PRACTICE AREAS: Intellectual Property; Litigation.
Wellford, W. Harrison, (AV) . . . . '— '77 C.198 B.A. L.276 J.D. [Latham&W.]
Wellington, Daniel L. . . . . '45 '79 C.128 B.A. L.273 J.D. [Fulbright&J.]
*PRACTICE AREAS: Antitrust and Trade Regulation.
Wellington, Peter L., (AV) . . . . '50 '78 C.309 A.B. L.145 J.D. [Steptoe&J.]
*PRACTICE AREAS: Government Contract Law; Litigation.
Wellman, Mark S. '59 '87 C.608 B.A. L.209 J.D.
(adm. in OH; not adm. in DC) 1203 Longworth
Wellner, Steven M. . . . . '59 '85 C.893 B.A. L.477 J.D. [Kirkland&E.]
*PRACTICE AREAS: Environmental Law.
Wells, Ashley J. . . . . '43 '80 C&L.770 B.S., J.D. [Venable,A.B.H.&C.] (See Pat. Sect.)
*PRACTICE AREAS: Intellectual Property Law; Patents.
Wells, Gerald C. . . . . '68 '94 C.446 B.A. L.945 J.D. Sr. Corp. Coun., US Off. Prod. Co.
*RESPONSIBILITIES: Corporate Law.
Wells, Gregory F. '— '01 C.112 B.A. L.276 J.D.
(adm. in CA; not adm. in DC) [Ⓐ Morgan,L.&B.]
Wells, Heath E. '69 '98 C.885 B.S.C.E. L.904 J.D.
(adm. in VA; not adm. in DC; See Pat. Sect.) [Ⓐ Staas&H.]
*PRACTICE AREAS: Intellectual Property; Trademarks; Copyrights; Patents.
Wells, Kristin D. '66 '99 C.103 A.B. L.178 J.D.
(adm. in MD; not adm. in DC) [Ⓐ White&C.]
Wells, Patrick J. '61 '99 C.436 B.S. L.30 J.D.
(adm. in NY; not adm. in DC) [Ⓐ Connolly B.L.&H.] ⊙
Wells, Stephen E., (AV) . . . . '47 '75 C.446 B.S. L.276 J.D. [McDermott,W.&E.]
Wells, Thomas C. '57 '91 C.16 B.S. L.128 J.D.
Exec. Dir., Consortium for Child Welfare
Wells, William K., Jr., (AV) '43 '74 C.886 B.S. L.893 J.D.
[Kenyon&K.] (See Pat. Sect.)
*PRACTICE AREAS: Intellectual Property.
Wells, Gregory K., & Associates, P.A.
(See Largo, Maryland)
Welsh, Gary M. . . . . '47 '72 C&L.309 B.A., J.D. Price Waterhouse
Welsh, Roger M. . . . . '57 '91 C.801 B.S.E. L.1148 J.D. Judge Advocate
Welsh & Katz, Ltd.
(See Chicago, Illinois)
Welsh & Katz, Ltd.
(See Arlington, Virginia)
Wencl, Annette M. '64 '91 C.958 B.S. L.300 J.D.
(adm. in PA; not adm. in DC) Dir., State Affs., Assn. of Trial Lawyers of America
Wendel, Edward P. '41 '67 C.102 B.A. L.188 LL.B.
Asst. Gen. Coun., United Food & Comercial Workers International Union
Wendell, Gitte J. '74 '00 C.473 B.S. L.930 J.D.
(adm. in OH; not adm. in DC) [Ⓐ Jones,D.R.&P.]
Wenderoth, Stephen J. . . . . '60 '89 C.264 B.A. L.1040 J.D. [Ⓐ Hunton&W.]
*PRACTICE AREAS: Environmental Law; Government Contracts.
Wenderoth, Lind & Ponack, L.L.P., (AV)
2033 K Street, N.W., Suite 800 (See Pat. Sect.)

Wengel, Deborah L. . . . . '69 '96 C.188 B.A. L.1209 J.D. [Ⓐ Kaye S.]
*PRACTICE AREAS: International Trade; Customs.
Wenk, Christopher J. '73 '01 C.945 B.A. L.813 J.D.
(adm. in VA; not adm. in DC) [Ⓐ Covington&B.]
Wenner, Adam, (AV) . . . . '50 '76 C.118 B.A. L.472 LL.B. [Vinson&E.]
*PRACTICE AREAS: Administrative Law; Federal Energy Regulation.
Wenner, Charles R., (AV) . . . . '47 '74 C.140 B.A. L.183 J.D. [Fulbright&J.]
*PRACTICE AREAS: Securities.
Wentworth, Michael J '— '87 C.182 B.A. L.494 J.D.
(adm. in MN; not adm. in DC) [Ⓐ Dickstein S.M.&O.]
*PRACTICE AREAS: Energy; Military Justice.
Wenzler, Mark A. '63 '88
C.676 B.A. L.823 J.D. Envir. Coun., National Environmental Trust
Werbel, Evan Jeffrey . . . . '65 '94 C.861 B.A. L.276 J.D. [Ⓐ Howrey S.A.&W.]
*PRACTICE AREAS: Antitrust; Commercial Litigation; White Collar Criminal Defense.
Werdig, Robert M., Jr., (BV) . . . . '32 '64 C.560 B.S. L.273 LL.B. 715 8th St., S.E.
Werkheiser, Gregory A. . . . . '73 '00 C.945 B.A. L.893 J.D. [Ⓐ Piper M.R.&W.]
*PRACTICE AREAS: Litigation.
Werner, Eric T., (BV) . . . . '— '90 C.473 B.S. L.128 J.D. [Verner,L.B.M.&H.]
*PRACTICE AREAS: Mass Media; Telecommunications; Litigation.
Werner, Jack, (AV) . . . . '14 '38 C&L.494 B.A., J.D. 1200 G. St., N.W.‡
Werner, Mary Ann . . . '54 '88 C.140 B.A. L.273 J.D. V.P. & Coun., Washinton Post, The

Werner, Ralph, (AV) '35 '60 C.569 B.A. L.309 LL.B.
Hamilton Square, 600 Fourteenth Street, N.W. Sixth Floor, 20005
Telephone: 202-628-6550 Fax: 202-628-6554
Email: rwlegal@aol.com URL: http://www.lawyers.com/ralphwerner
***PRACTICE AREAS: Real Estate; Corporate Law; Litigation.**
Commercial Real Estate, Commercial Law, Landlord and Tenant Law, Leasing, Corporate Law, Securities, Complex Commercial Litigation, Commercial Bankruptcy.
See Professional Biographies, WASHINGTON, DISTRICT OF COLUMBIA

Werner, Teresa S. '70 '95 C.610 B.B.A. L.128 J.D.
(adm. in NJ; not adm. in DC) [Ⓐ Willkie F.&G.]
*PRACTICE AREAS: Communications.
Werntz, Heidi Marie . . . . '— '93 C.103 A.B. L.180 J.D. [Ⓒ Huber L.&A.]
*PRACTICE AREAS: Energy Law; Public Utility Law.
Werthan, Jeffrey M. . . . . '54 '79 C.860 B.A. L.94 J.D. [Katten M.Z.]
*PRACTICE AREAS: Banking Law; Securities Law.
Wertheim, Ronald P. . . . . '33 '58 C&L.659 B.S., J.D. Sr. J., Supr. Ct.
Wertheimer, Laura S. . . . . '55 '82 C.976 B.A. L.178 J.D. [Shea&G.]
*PRACTICE AREAS: Civil Practice; Legal Ethics and Professional Responsibility; Products Liability.
Werther, Barbara G. . . . . '53 '79 C.659 B.A. L.273 J.D. [Arent F.K.P.&K.]
*PRACTICE AREAS: Construction Litigation; Governmental Contracts; Litigation.
Wertzberger, Marsha C., (AV) . . . . '40 '76 C.378 B.A. L.276 J.D. [Arent F.K.P.&K.]
*PRACTICE AREAS: Administrative Law; Food and Drug; Advertising.
Wesser, Christopher J. '69 '99 C.1031 B.A. L.945 J.D.
(adm. in VA; not adm. in DC) [Ⓐ Kohn,K.&C.]
*PRACTICE AREAS: Whistleblower Litigation.
West, Edward S., (AV) . . . . '57 '84 C.976 B.A. L.276 J.D. [Ⓒ Covington&B.]
West, John M. . . . . '46 '89 C.237 B.A. L.477 J.D. [Bredhoff&K.]
West, Joseph D., (AV) . . . . '49 '77 C.884 B.C.E. L.273 J.D. [Arnold&P.]
*PRACTICE AREAS: Government Contracts; Construction Contracts; Contract Dispute Resolution; Commercial Litigation.
West, Matthew T. . . . . '71 '97 C.475 B.A. L.477 J.D. [Ⓐ Baker B.]
West, Ruth Clarke '28 '76 C.823 A.B. L.900 J.D.
Sr. Legal Editor, The Bureau of Natl. Affs., Inc.
West, Togo D., Jr., (AV) . . . . '42 '68 C&L.329 B.S.E.E., J.D. [Ⓒ Covington&B.]
West, William K., Jr., (AV) '37 '62
C&L.228 B.S.M.E., LL.B. [Howrey S.A.&W.] (See Pat. Sect.)
*PRACTICE AREAS: Patent; Trade-dress; Antitrust; Complex Litigation.
West & Feinberg, P.C.
(See Bethesda, Maryland)
Westbrook, Reeves C., (AV) . . . . '49 '75 C.880 B.A. L.976 J.D. [Covington&B.]
Westemeier, Julie Quagliano, (AV) . . . . '59 '85 C.602 B.B.A. L.276 J.D. [Quagliano&S.]
*PRACTICE AREAS: Commercial Law; Civil Litigation; Bankruptcy.
Wester, John F. . . . . '58 '86 C.893 B.A. L.1068 J.D. [Ⓒ Sidley A.B.&W.]
Westerfield, Mark G., (AV) . . . . '57 '85 C.63 B.A. L.273 J.D. [Johnston&W.]
Westerlund, Robert A. '56 '80 C&L.861 J.D.
[Ⓒ Adduci,M.&S.] (See Pat. Sect.) (⊙Arlington, VA)
*PRACTICE AREAS: Patent Procurement; Patent Licensing; Litigation.
Westerman, Arnold R., (AV) . . . . '38 '66 C.446 A.B. L.273 J.D. [Arent F.K.P.&K.]
*PRACTICE AREAS: Corporate Financing Law; Corporate Restructuring Law; Securities Law; Banking; Savings and Thrift Institutions Law.
Westerman, William F., (BV) '52 '79
C.675 B.S. L.862 J.D. [Armstrong,W.H.M.&N.] (See Pat. Sect.)
Westermeier, John T., Jr., (AV) . . . . '41 '74 C.870 B.S. L.904 J.D. [Piper M.R.&W.]
*PRACTICE AREAS: Computer Law; Litigation; Intellectual Property; Corporate.
Westfahl, Scott A. . . . . '63 '88 C.197 A.B. L.309 J.D. 3000 K St., N.W., Suite 500
Westfall, Elizabeth S. '68 '97 C.118 B.A. L.309 J.D.
Wash. Lawyers' Comm. for Civil Rights & Urban Affairs
Westfall, Susan Whelan . . . . '56 '88 C&L.347 B.A., J.D. [Cole,R.&B.]
*PRACTICE AREAS: Telecommunications; Cable Franchising Law; Equal Employment Opportunity Law; State and Local Regulatory Matters.
Westmoreland, John W. . . . . '72 '98 C&L.502 B.S., J.D. [Ⓐ Latham&W.]
*PRACTICE AREAS: Taxation.
Westover, Gail L. . . . . '68 '97 C.188 B.S. L.276 J.D. [Ⓐ Sutherland A.&B.]
*PRACTICE AREAS: Litigation.
Wethington, Olin L., (AV) . . . . '48 '77 C.659 B.A. L.309 J.D. [Steptoe&J.]
*PRACTICE AREAS: International Business Law; Trade Regulation.
Wetmore, William F., Jr., (AV) . . . . '21 '49 C&L.273 LL.B. 1301 K St., N.W.
Wetterer, Thomas W. . . . . . '59 '90 C.446 B.S. L.276 J.D. Staff Attorney, Greenpeace, Inc.
Wetterhahn, Mark J. . . . . '44 '72 C.994 B.A. L.904 J.D. [Winston&S.]
*PRACTICE AREAS: Atomic (Nuclear) Law; Energy Law; Nuclear Waste.
Wetzel, Leo E. '59 '83 C&L.128 B.A., J.D.
Coun., Amalgamated Transit Union, AFL-CIO
Wewer, William, (AV) . . . . '47 '77 C.668 B.A. L.273 J.D. [Wewer] ⊙
Wewer Law Firm, (AV) . . . . 1825 I Street, N.W., Suite 400 (⊙San Fran., CA; Helena, MT)
Wexler, Liza Anne '74 '98 C.401 B.A. L.448 J.D.
(adm. in MD; not adm. in DC) Legal Analyst, Amer. Assoc. of Health Plans
Wexton, Andrew L. . . . . '68 '96 C.976 B.A. L.569 J.D. [Ⓐ Proskauer R.]
*PRACTICE AREAS: Litigation.
Weyback, Mary Patricia . . . . '61 '89 C.893 B.A. L.276 J.D. [Ⓐ Drinker B.&R.]
Weymouth, Lucy C. . . . . '59 '85 C.976 B.A. L.880 J.D. Student Loan Marketing Assn.
Weymouth, T. Clark . . . . '57 '84 C.197 A.B. L.597 J.D. [Hogan&H.]
*PRACTICE AREAS: International Trade; Immigration.
Whalen, Curtis E. '47 '73 C.273 B.A. L.904 J.D.
V.P., Govt. Affs., Transco Energy Co.
Whalen, Mary Kate . . . . '62 '91 C.164 B.A. L.818 J.D. [Ⓒ Hyman,P.&M.]
*PRACTICE AREAS: Food and Drug Regulation; Administrative Law; Litigation.

Whalen, Michael P. '63 '99 C.823 B.A. L.273 J.D.
(adm. in VA; not adm. in DC) [Ⓐ Goodwin P.]
Whalen, Teresa, (BV) .... '58 '83 C.201 B.S. L.1048 J.D. 2031 Florida Ave., N.W.
Whalen, Thomas J. ....'38 '64 C.749 A.B. L.276 LL.B. [Condon&F.]
Whalley Buono, Elizabeth A. '66 '00 C.93 B.S.N. L.1209 J.D.
(adm. in VA; not adm. in DC) [Ⓐ Wiley R.&F.]
*PRACTICE AREAS: Health Care; FDA; Insurance; HIPAA Privacy and Fraud; Government Contracts.
Wharton, Ellan K. ......'49 '77 C.205 B.A. L.884 J.D. Sen. Washing. Coun., Du Pont Co.
Wharton, Leslie, (AV) ....'51 '84 C.94 B.A. L.309 J.D. [Arnold&P.]
*PRACTICE AREAS: Litigation; Product Liability Law.

Wharton Levin Ehrmantraut Klein & Nash, A Professional Association
(See Annapolis, Maryland)

Wheat, Judith L., (AV) ....'61 '89 C&L.276 B.S.F.S., J.D. [Venable,A.B.H.&C.]
*PRACTICE AREAS: Criminal Litigation; Civil Litigation.
Wheeler, Anne M. ("Nancy"), (BV) ......'54 '81 C.128 B.A. L.273 J.D. [Ⓒ Crowell&M.]
*PRACTICE AREAS: Health and Hospital Law; Mental Health Law; Malpractice Law.
Wheeler, Asher L. '19 '45 C.280 A.B. L.309 LL.B.
1522 Wisconsin Ave., N.W., 2nd Fl.‡
Wheeler, Charles W. '45 '70 C&L.966 B.S., J.D.
(adm. in WI; not adm. in DC) [Alston&B.]
*PRACTICE AREAS: Federal Taxation; International Taxation; Banks and Banking.
Wheeler, Christopher '57 '83
C.597 B.A. L.30 J.D. [Ⓒ Dickinson,M.T.&H.] (⊙Washington)
*PRACTICE AREAS: Commercial Litigation; Government Contracts; Administrative Law; Creditor Bankruptcy Law; Collections.
Wheeler, Christopher ..... '57 '83 C.597 B.A. L.30 J.D. [Luman,L.&W.] (⊙Washington)
*PRACTICE AREAS: Litigation; Government Contracts; Administrative Law; Creditor Bankruptcy Law.
Wheeler, David E. '67 '94 C.112 B.A. L.37 J.D.
(adm. in CA; not adm. in DC)
V.P. & Assoc. Gen. Coun., Antitrust, Verizon Communications
Wheeler, Douglas P., (AV) ...'42 '66 C.299 A.B. L.228 LL.B. [Hogan&H.] (⊙L.A., CA)
*PRACTICE AREAS: Natural Resources; Land Use; Environmental Regulation.
Wheeler, Edwin M. ....'26 '55 C&L.900 A.B., LL.B. Pres., The Fertilizer Inst.
Wheeler, George Y., III, (AV) ....'41 '67 C.674 A.B. L.477 LL.B. [Holland&K.]
*PRACTICE AREAS: Telecommunication Law.
Wheeler, Thomas C., (AV) ....'48 '73 C.282 B.A. L.276 J.D. [Piper M.R.&W.]
*PRACTICE AREAS: Government Contracts.
Wheeler, Trayne S. ....'— '01 C.145 A.B. L.94 J.D. [Ⓐ Dechert]
*PRACTICE AREAS: Financial Services Law; Investment Management.
Wheelock, Matthew H. ....'70 '99 C.951 B.A. L.813 J.D. [Ⓐ Paul,W.R.W.&G.]
*PRACTICE AREAS: International Trade; Project Finance; Telecommunications; Government Regulation.
Whelan, Chas. M. ....'26 '54 C.999 A.B. L.276 J.D. Georgetown Law Sch.
Whelan, M. Edward, III '60 '85 C&L.309 A.B., J.D.
(adm. in CA; not adm. in DC) 1850 M St., N.W.
Whelchel-Mathews, Leslie ....'49 '86 C.273 B.A. L.30 J.D. Editor, Bur. of Natl. Affs.
Whelihan, Deborah Murrell, (AV) '60 '86
C.216 B.A. L.902 J.D. [Jordan C.&S.] (⊙Rockville, MD)
*PRACTICE AREAS: Professional Liability Defense; Legal Ethics; Commercial Law; Financial Institutions Law; Lender Liability.
Whipple, Douglas J. '57 '89
C.569 B.A. L.276 J.D. [Jones,D.R.&P.] (⊙Budapest, Hungary)
*PRACTICE AREAS: Mergers and Acquisitions; Cross Border Investment; Software Licensing; Technology Contracts.
Whisenant, Lori A. ....'69 '98 C.1274 B.S. L.623 J.D. PricewaterhouseCoopers LLP
Whisenhunt, Carolyn, (BV) '54 '79
C.623 B.A. L.846 J.D. Staff Atty., American Forest & Paper Assn.
Whisonant, Alicia L. '67 '97 C.30 B.A. L.425 J.D.
(adm. in LA; not adm. in DC) 3163 Hawthorne Dr., N.E.‡
Whitaker, A. Duncan, (AV) ....'32 '57 C.976 B.A. L.477 J.D. [Howrey S.A.&W.]
*PRACTICE AREAS: Antitrust Law; Complex Litigation; Commercial Law.
Whitaker, Alexander Wilson, (AV) ......'40 '73 C.870 B.S. L.273 J.D. [Heggestad&W.]
Whitaker, Mark L. ....'58 '90 C.588 B.S. L.276 J.D. [Ⓒ Howrey S.A.&W.]
*PRACTICE AREAS: Litigation.
Whitaker, R. David, (BV) '58 '83 C.475 B.A. L.339 J.D.
(adm. in OK; not adm. in DC) [Ⓒ Goodwin P.]
White, Algird F., Jr., (AV) '47 '73 C.165 A.B. L.94 J.D.
(adm. in NY; not adm. in DC) [Couch W.] ⊙
*PRACTICE AREAS: Antitrust; Energy Law.
White, Bernard S., (AV) ....'18 '40 C.546 A.B. L.273 LL.M. 2025 Eye St., N.W.
White, Beverly ....'54 '84 C.326 B.S. L.273 J.D. [Luse L.G.P.&S.]
*PRACTICE AREAS: Employee Benefits; Taxation; Executive Compensation; Business Planning and Transactions; Tax-Exempt Organizations.
White, Christopher L. ....'63 '89 C.896 B.A. L.128 J.D. [Morgan,L.&B.]
White, David ....'64 '97 C.575 B.A. L.902 J.D. [Ⓐ Jorden B.]
*PRACTICE AREAS: Commercial Litigation; Appellate Practice; Federal Jurisdiction; Labor and Employment.
White, Deborah R. '63 '92
C.918 B.A. L.30 J.D. Regulatory Coun., Food Marketing Institute
White, Debra Alligood '60 '93 C.309 A.B. L.1068 J.D.
(adm. in CA; not adm. in DC) [Ⓐ Milbank,T.H.&M.]
*PRACTICE AREAS: Mergers, Acquisitions and Divestitures; Securities.
White, Edward E. .... '47 '88 C.136 B.A. L.276 J.D. Asst. Corp. Coun.
White, Edward H. ....'— '97 C.602 B.A. L.228 J.D. [Ⓐ King&S.]
*PRACTICE AREAS: Litigation; Trade Regulation.
White, Erica Denise '73 '98 C.329 B.A. L.823 J.D.
(adm. in MD; not adm. in DC) [Ⓐ Smith&Assoc.]
White, Frank A. .... '47 '71 C.228 B.A. L.184 J.D. Organization Resource Counselors
White, George M. ....'20 '61 C.453 B.S.M.S. L.930 J.D. 1201 Conn. Ave., N.W.
White, Grady Lee .....'63 '93 C.597 B.S. L.1068 J.D. [Ⓐ Covington&B.] (See Pat. Sect.)
White, Heather Brandeis '— '99 C.893 B.A. L.838 J.D.
(adm. in TN; not adm. in DC) [Environmental W.]
White, James P., (AV) ....'54 '85 C.276 B.S. L.30 J.D. [Ⓒ Fulbright&J.]
*PRACTICE AREAS: Energy; Administrative Law.
White, Jeffrey L. ....'72 '97 C.228 B.A. L.893 J.D. [Ⓐ Covington&B.]
White, Jeffrey Robert .....'51 '77 C.381 B.A. L.276 J.D. Assn. of Trial Lawyers of Amer.
White, Lee C., (AV) ....'23 '50 C&L.546 B.S.E.E., LL.B. [Ⓒ Spiegel&M.]
*PRACTICE AREAS: Environmental Law; Energy.
White, Lesyllee Maurelia '62 '89 C&L.329 B.A., J.D.
(adm. in VA; not adm. in DC) 1717 K St. N.W.
White, Marc A., (AV) ....'21 '49 C.309 A.B. L.893 LL.B. 1815 H St.
White, Matthew K. '71 '97 C.880 B.A. L.861 J.D.
(adm. in TN; not adm. in DC) [Ⓐ McDermott,W.&E.]
White, Melvin ....'59 '87 C.511 B.A. L.893 J.D. [McDermott,W.&E.]
White, Michael C. ....'44 '86 C.1209 B.S. L.128 J.D. [Schmeltzer,A.&S.]
*PRACTICE AREAS: Environmental Law; Radiation Litigation.
White, Michael D. .... '52 '82 C.893 B.S. L.838 J.D. [Ⓒ Blank R.C.&M.] (See Pat. Sect.)
*PRACTICE AREAS: Patent Litigation; Patent Validity and Infringement Opinions; Mechanical Intellectual Property; Electro-Mechanical Patents; Mechanical Patent Prosecution.

White, Nancy A. ....'56 '81 C&L.352 B.A., J.D. [Squire,S.&D.]
*PRACTICE AREAS: Energy.
White, Neil R. '70 '95 C.588 B.S. L.64 J.D.
(adm. in MD; not adm. in DC) [Ⓐ Blank R.C.&M.]
*PRACTICE AREAS: Complex Litigation; Civil Litigation; Commercial Litigation; White Collar Criminal Defense; Bankruptcy Litigation.
White, Paul E., Jr. ....'49 '83 C.446 B.S. L.818 J.D. [Manelli,D.&S.] (Pat.)
*PRACTICE AREAS: Patent Procurement; Intellectual Property; Patents; Management Labor Law; Commercial.
White, Raymond A. ....'60 '89 C&L.276 B.A., J.D. Sr. Coun., CBS Corp.
White, Richard C. ....'66 '95 C.264 B.A. L.180 J.D. 666 Penn. Ave., N.W.
White, Robert I., (AV) ....'51 '77 C.311 B.A. L.273 J.D. [Squire,S.&D.]
*PRACTICE AREAS: Administrative Law; Appellate Practice; International Contracts; Energy Contracts; Federal Energy Law.
White, Scott B. ....'51 '77 C.674 A.B. L.178 J.D. Legal Fin. Adviser, The World Bk.
White, Steven K. ....'53 '82 C.352 B.A. L.276 J.D. [Morrison&H.]
*PRACTICE AREAS: Litigation; Banking Law; Professional Liability.
White, Wendelin A., (AV) ....'52 '81 C.822 B.A. L.472 J.D. [Shaw P.]
*PRACTICE AREAS: Commercial Real Estate.
White, William Douglas, (AV) ....'45 '72 C.259 B.A. L.893 J.D. [Lepon M.W.&H.]
White, William E. '66 '91 C.93 B.A. L.990 J.D.
(adm. in CA; not adm. in DC) [Ⓒ Wilmer,C.&P.]
*PRACTICE AREAS: Securities Law.
White, William H., Jr. '69 '96
C.276 B.A. L.472 J.D. [Ⓐ Bonner K.T.&C.] (⊙Parsippany, NJ)
*PRACTICE AREAS: Insurance Coverage Litigation; Excess and Reinsurance; Commercial Litigation; Contracts; Commercial Torts.
White, William R. ....'41 '67 C&L.608 B.S., J.D. [Russin&V.]
*PRACTICE AREAS: International Business Law; Corporate Commercial Law; International Joint Ventures; Offshore Corporations; Computer Law.

White & Case, (AV) BB
Limited Liability Partnership
601 Thirteenth Street, NW, Suite 600 South, 20005-3807 ⊙
Telephone: 202-626-3600 Facsimile: 202-639-9355
URL: http://www.whitecase.com
Partners: David A. Balto; Linda E. Carlisle; William J. Clinton; Christopher F. Corr; Christopher M. Curran; Bruce N. Davis; Victor J. DeSantis; J. Mark Gidley; David A. Hildebrandt; David P. Houlihan; David W. Hunt; Carolyn B. Lamm; J. Roger Mentz; Edward R. Neaher, Jr.; Robert D. Paul; Abby Cohen Smutny; Gregory J. Spak; Walter J. Spak; George J. Terwilliger III. Partner Of Counsel: William P. McClure. Special Counsel: Charles N. Brower; Horacio A. Grigera Naon (Not admitted in DC). Counsel: Robert J. Bittman; Ellen M. Jakovic; Daoud L. Khairallah; Anne D. Smith; Laura M. Wilson. Associates: Ariana Almajan; Jocelyn A. Aqua; Karie J. Barwind; Vincent Bowen; Patrick J. Browne, Jr.; Richard J. Burke; Peter J. Carney; Daniel S. Chen (Not admitted in DC); Elizabeth L. Cheney; Gustav Chiarello; Eileen M. Cole; Jaime M. Crowe; Nicole Erb; Robert G. Gosselink; Eric Grannon; Yue Guan (Not admitted in DC); R. Shawn Gunnarson (Not admitted in DC); Gregg A. Hand; Karen Hanrahan; Laurie A. Hartman; Paul G. Hegland; Eckhard R. Hellbeck; Douglas M. Jasinski; Geoffrey B. Lanning (Not admitted in DC); Adams C. Lee; Albert Lo; Rajeev K. Malik; William J. Moran (Not admitted in DC); Frank H. Morgan; Emil Nemec (Not admitted in DC); John W. Owczarski; Frank Panopoulos; George L. Paul; Stephen R. Payne (Not admitted in DC); John Eric Podgore (Not admitted in DC); Ama B. Romaine; Frank J. Schweitzer; Jonathan Seiger (Not admitted in DC); Mark A. Shalaby; Ruta Kalvaitis Skucas; Eric P. Spooner; Lee A. Steven; Paul F. Stone; Caleb W. Sullivan; Jeffrey D. Talbert; Peter P. Thieman; Mara E. R. Topping; Lyle B. Vander Schaaf; Heather J. Van Slooten (Not admitted in DC); Francis A. Vasquez, Jr.; Donna Vetrano (Not admitted in DC); Kristin D. Wells (Not admitted in DC); Kristina Zissis.
General Practice.
Los Angeles, California: Telephone: 213-620-7700. Facsimile: 213-687-0758; 213-452-2330; 213-452-2331.
Palo Alto, California: Telephone: 650-213-0300. Facsimile: 650-213-8158.
San Francisco, California: Telephone: 415-544-1100. Facsimile: 415-544-0202.
Miami, Florida: Telephone: 305-371-2700. Facsimile: 305-358-5744; 305-358-5766.
New York, New York: Telephone: 212-819-8200. Facsimile: 212-354-8113.
Berlin, Germany: White & Case, Feddersen. Telephone: (49-30) 880 911-0. Facsimile: (49-30) 880 911-297.
Bratislava, Slovakia: White & Case, Feddersen. Telephone: (421-7) 5441-5100. Facsimile: (421-7) 5441-6100.
Brussels, Belgium: Telephone: (32-2) 219-16-20. Facsimile: (32-2) 219-16-26.
Budapest, Hungary: Réczicza Law Firm White & Case. Telephone: (36-1) 488-5200. Facsimile: (36-1) 488-5299.
Dresden, Germany: White & Case, Feddersen. Telephone: (49-351) 8 02 02 77. Facsimile: (49-351) 8 02 02 79.
Dusseldorf, Germany: White & Case, Feddersen. Telephone: (49-211) 4 91 95-0. Facsimile: (49-211) 49 19 51 00.
Frankfurt, Germany: White & Case, Feddersen. Telephone: (49-69) 2 99 94-0. Facsimile: (49-69) 28 26 15.
Hamburg, Germany: White & Case, Feddersen. Telephone: (49-40) 3 50 05-0. Facsimile: (49-40) 35 00 51 11.
Helsinki, Finland: Asianajotoimisto White & Case Oy. Telephone: (358-9) 228-641. Facsimile: (358-9) 228-64228.
Istanbul, Turkey: White & Case Müşavirlik Ltd. Şti. Telephone: (90-212) 275-75-33. Facsimile: (90-212) 275-75-43.
London, England: Telephone: (44-20) 7600-7300. Facsimile: (44-20) 7600-7030.
Milan, Italy: White & Case, Varrenti e Associati. Telephone: (39-02) 7600-2930. Facsimile: (39-02) 7600-2936.
Moscow, Russia: Telephone: (7-095) 787-3000. Facsimile: (7-095) 787-3001.
Paris, France: Telephone: (33-1) 55-04-15-15. Facsimile: (33-1) 55-04-15-16.
Prague, Czech Republic: White & Case, Feddersen. Telephone: (420-2) 24 81-08 08; 24 81-17 96; 24 10 80 00. Facsimile: (420-2) 24 81-03 30; 24 81-02 52; 24 10 81 00.
Rome, Italy: White & Case, Varrenti e Associati. Telephone: (39-06) 420-0871. Facsimile: (39-06) 4200-8758.
Stockholm, Sweden: White & Case Advokat AB. Telephone: (46-8) 506-323-00. Facsimile: (46-8) 611-21-22.
Warsaw, Poland: White & Case, Warsaw. Telephone: (48-22) 625-33-33; (48-22) 622-67-67; (43-89) 12-19-06. Facsimile: (48-22) 628-22-28.
Johannesburg, Republic of South Africa: Telephone: 27 (11) 884-7689. Facsimile: 27 (11) 884-7229.
Almaty, Kazakhstan: Telephone: (7-3272) 50-74-91. Facsimile: (7-3272) 50-74-93.
Ankara, Turkey: White & Case Müşavirlik Ltd. Şti. Telephone: (90-312) 442-5680. Facsimile: (90-312) 442-5691/4.
Bangkok, Thailand: White & Case (Thailand) Limited. Telephone: (662) 656-1721 to 32. Facsimile: (662) 656-1733/34.
Beijing, China: Colin Ng & Partners, Beijing China. Telephone: (86-10) 6539-1230. Facsimile: (86-10) 6539-1280.
Bombay/Mumbai, India: Liaison Office, (91-22) 282-6300/01/02/03. Facsimile: (91-22) 282-6305.
Hanoi, Vietnam: Telephone: (84-4) 934-5410/5411. Facsimile: (84-4) 934-5412.
Ho Chi Minh City, Vietnam: Telephone: (84-8) 821-0888. Facsimile: (84-8) 823-6902.
Hong Kong: White & Case, Solicitors. Telephone: (852) 2822-8700. Facsimile: (852) 2845-9070.
Shanghai, China: Telephone: (86-21) 6321-2200. Facsimile: (86-21) 6323-9252.
Singapore, Republic of Singapore: White & Case, Colin Ng & Partners. Telephone: (65) 225-6000. Facsimile: (65) 225-6009.
Tokyo, Japan: White & Case, LLP - Kandabashi Law Offices (Registered Association). Telephone: (81-3) 3259-0200. Facsimile: (81-3) 3259-0150.
Manama, Bahrain: Telephone: (973) 538-600. Facsimile: (973) 532-342.
Jeddah, Saudi Arabia: Law Office of Hassan Mahassni, Telephone: (966-2) 665-4353. Facsimile: (966-2) 669-2996.
Riyadh, Saudi Arabia: Law Office of Hassan Mahassni, Telephone: (966-1) 464-4006. Facsimile: (966-1) 465-1348.
Mexico City, Mexico: White & Case, S.C. Telephone: (52) 5-540-9600. Facsimile: (52) 5-540-9699.
São Paulo, SP, Brazil: Telephone: (55-11) 3171-0011. Facsimile: (55-11) 3171-0041.
Associated Law Firm(s):

(This Listing Continued)

White & Case (Continued)

Bombay/Mumbai, India: India Law Services (ILS). Telephones: (91-22) 284-1995; (91-22) 284-1847. Facsimile: (91-22) 285-0824.
New Delhi, India: India Law Services (ILS). Telephone: (91-11) 607-1602/3/4. Facsimile: (91-11) 608-8860.
Jakarta, Indonesia: Ali Budiardjo, Nugroho, Reksodiputro, Counsellors at Law. Telephone: (62-21) 250-5125. Facsimile: (62-21) 250-5392; 250-5646.

See Professional Biographies, WASHINGTON, DISTRICT OF COLUMBIA

White-Mahaffey, Virginia L., (AV) .... '58 '83 C.573 B.A. L.309 J.D. [Steptoe&J.]
*PRACTICE AREAS: Appellate Practice; Environmental Insurance Coverage; Civil Litigation; Insurance Coverage.

Whiteaker, Gregory W. .... '62 '87 C.45 B.A. L.228 J.D. [Bennet&B.]
*PRACTICE AREAS: Communications Law.

Whitebread, Joseph B., Jr. .... '47 '77 C.273 B.A. L.893 J.D. [Holland&K.]
*PRACTICE AREAS: Business Planning; Corporate; Tax Law; Estates; Partnership and Limited Liability Company Law.

Whiteford, Taylor & Preston L.L.P., (AV)
1025 Connecticut Avenue, N.W., 20036-5405 ⊙
Telephone: 202-659-6800 Fax: 202-331-0573
Email: wt&pllp@wtplaw.com URL: http://www.wtplaw.com
Partners: Glenn R. Bonard; Joseph D. Douglass; Julianne Erin Dymowski; John J. Hathway; Kenneth J. Ingram; Arthur P. Rogers; Andrew J. Terrell. Resident Of Counsel: Catherine D. Bertram; Edward S. Cogen; Lee A. Satterfield; C. William Tayler. Associates: Crystal S. Deese; Jane Saindon Dudley; Jennifer S. Jackman; Brian J. McCabe; Sonja A. Mishalanie (Not admitted in DC); Valerie L. Tetro; Eric A. Vendt.
Administrative Law, Admiralty and Maritime Law, Advertising and Marketing, Aged and Aging, Agency and Distributorships, Antitrust and Trade Regulation, Appellate Practice, Bankruptcy, Banking and Finance, Biotechnology, Business Law, Chancery and Equity, Civil Practice, Civil Rights, Class Action Defense, Collections, Commercial Law, Commercial Real Estate, Communications and Media, Computers and Software, Constitutional Law, Construction Law, Consumer Law, Contracts, Copyrights, Corporate Law, Debtor and Creditor, Disabilities, Education Law, Election, Campaign and Political Law, Eminent Domain, Employee Benefits, Energy, Environmental Law, Equipment Finance and Leasing, Fidelity and Surety, Finance, Franchises and Franchising, General Practice, Government, Government Contracts, Guardianship and Conservatorship, Health and Hospital, Housing Law, Immigration and Naturalization, Insurance, Insurance Defense, Intellectual Property, International Law, International Trade, Investments, Labor and Employment, Law Enforcement, Leases and Leasing, Legal Ethics and Professional Responsibility, Libel, Slander and Defamation, Litigation, Media Law, Medical Malpractice, Medicare and Medicaid, Mergers, Acquisition and Divestitures, Mortgages, Municipal Law, Natural Resources, Negligence, Nonprofit and Charitable Organizations, Occupational Safety and Health, Partnership Law, Patents, Personal Injury, Premise Liability, Privacy Law, Probate, Products Liability, Professional Liability, Property Law, Public Finance, Railroad Law, Real Estate, Regulatory Law, RICO, Securities, Taxation, Technology and Science, Torts, Toxic Torts, Trade Secrets, Trademarks, Transportation, Trusts and Estates, Unfair Competition, White Collar Crime, Wills, Workers Compensation, Zoning, Planning and Land Use.
Baltimore, Maryland Office: 7 Saint Paul Street. Telephone: 410-347-8700. Fax: 410-752-7092.
Towson, Maryland Office: 210 West Pennsylvania Avenue. Telephone: 410-832-2000. Fax: 410-832-2015.
Columbia, Maryland Office: 10440 Little Patuxent Parkway. Telephone: 410-884-0700. Fax: 410-884-0719.
Alexandria, Virginia Office: 1317 King Street. Telephone: 703-836-5742. Fax: 703-836-0265.

See Professional Biographies, WASHINGTON, DISTRICT OF COLUMBIA

Whitehead, Damon P. .... '67 '96 C.945 A.B. L.276 J.D. Earthjustice LDF
Whitehead, H. Allen .... '47 '73 C&L.446 B.S., J.D. 5335 Wisconsin Ave., N.W.
Whitehead, Jonathan '68 '96 C.910 B.A. L.30 J.D.
Assoc. Anti-Piracy Coun., Recording Industry Assoc. of America, Inc.

Whitehead, Michael J. '74 '01
C.608 B.S.E.E L.1218 J.D. [Ⓐ Sughrue M.] (See Pat. Sect.)
*PRACTICE AREAS: Patent Law.

Whitehead, Priscilla Anne .... '60 '87 C&L.276 B.S.L.A., J.D. [Swidler B.S.F.]
*PRACTICE AREAS: Telecommunication; International.

Whitehead, Thomas J. ..... '27 '56 C.676 B.A. L.276 J.D. 4981 Massachusetts Ave., N.W.
Whitehorn, Carol R. .... '50 '79 C.454 B.S. L.208 J.D. 5812 32nd St., N.W.

Whitehorn, Maria A. '72 '99 C.951 B.A. L.893 J.D.
(adm. in VA; not adm. in DC) [Ⓐ Holland&K.]
*PRACTICE AREAS: Litigation; Antitrust; Employment.

Whitehouse, Theodore C., (AV) .... '54 '79 C.893 B.A. L.276 J.D. [Willkie F.&G.]

Whitehurst, Amy C. '76 '01 C.228 B.A. L.309 J.D.
(adm. in NC; not adm. in DC) [Ⓐ Kirkland&E.]
*PRACTICE AREAS: Corporate.

Whiteman, Nicola Y. .... '73 '00 C.276 B.A. L.884 J.D. [Ⓐ Quagliano&S.]
*PRACTICE AREAS: Civil Litigation; Commercial Law.

Whitener, Mark D. '57 '83 C.910 A.B. L.145 J.D.
Antitrust Coun., General Electric Co.

Whitesides, Ashley .... '72 '98 C.259 B.S. L.276 J.D. [Ⓐ King&S.]
*PRACTICE AREAS: Food and Drug Regulation.

Whitestone, David C. '69 '99 C.1356 B.A. L.1209 J.D.
(adm. in VA; not adm. in DC) [Ⓐ Holland&K.]
*PRACTICE AREAS: Transportation; Public Infrastructure; Government Relations.

Whiteway, Andrea Macintosh .... '67 '92 C.188 B.A. L.446 J.D. [Ⓐ Arnold&P.]
Whitfield, Fred A. .... '58 '89 C.1228 B.B.A. L.574 J.D. 601 F St. N.W.

Whitfield, Milton B. .... '51 '79 C.893 B.S. L.276 J.D. [Shaw P.]
*PRACTICE AREAS: Administrative Law; Customs Law; Energy Law; Environmental Law; Technology Outsourcing.

Whiting, Richard A., (AV) .... '22 '50 C.197 A.B. L.976 LL.B. [Ⓒ Steptoe&J.]
*PRACTICE AREAS: Antitrust Law; Litigation; Trade Regulation Law.

Whitman, Stephen V. R. '47 '75 C.309 B.A. L.893 J.D.
Vice President & General Counsel, Hagler Bailly, Inc.

Whitney, John A., (AV) .... '32 '56 C.951 B.A. L.309 J.D. [Dilworth P.P.]
*PRACTICE AREAS: Government Contract Law; Surety Law; Construction Law; Probate Law.

Whitney & Bogris, LLP
(See Towson, Maryland)

Whitt, Richard S. '62 '88 C.1369 B.S. L.276 J.D.
Dir., Fed. Affs., LDDS WorldCom, Inc.

Whittaker, John Albert, IV .... '50 '76 C.911 B.A. L.770 J.D. [Winston&S.]
*PRACTICE AREAS: Federal Energy Regulation; Hydroelectricity Licensing; Hydroelectricity; Environmental Administrative Law; Administrative Agency Practice.

Whittaker, Shawn Charles '74 '99
C.420 B.A. L.30 J.D. 1901 Pennsylvania Avenue, NW, Suite 1007

Whittaker, Tiffani K. .... '73 '98 C.659 B.A. L.276 J.D. [Ⓐ Reno&C.]
*PRACTICE AREAS: Affordable Housing; Real Estate; Structured Finance.

Whitten, Jamie L. .... '42 '69 C.446 B.A. L.362 J.D. [Whitten&D.]

Whitten, Phyllis A., (AV) .... '55 '80 C.112 B.A. L.1065 J.D. [Ⓒ Swidler B.S.F.]
*PRACTICE AREAS: Telecommunications.

Whitten & Diamond .... 1725 Desales St., N.W.

Whittier, Holly A. .... '72 '99 C.445 B.S. L.1002 J.D. [Ⓐ Feldesman,T.L.F.&B.]
*PRACTICE AREAS: Domestic Relations.

Whittington, Kenneth John '70 '00 C.173 B.A. L.790 J.D.
(adm. in SC; not adm. in DC) [Ⓐ Lalos&K.] ‡
*PRACTICE AREAS: Intellectual Property.

Whittle, Elizabeth Ward, (AV) .... '64 '90 C.165 A.B. L.904 J.D. [Nixon P.]
*PRACTICE AREAS: Energy; Project Finance.

Whittle, James J., (AV) .... '63 '90 C.1044 B.S. L.30 J.D. [Cullen]
*PRACTICE AREAS: Insurance Coverage; Insurance Litigation; Civil Litigation; Complex Litigation; Class Actions.

Whittle, Patrick J., (AV) .... '57 '81 C.309 A.B. L.880 J.D. [Ⓒ Swidler B.S.F.]
*PRACTICE AREAS: Telecommunications.

Whittlesey, Dennis J., (AV) .... '42 '68 C.623 B.A. L.276 J.D. [Ⓒ Jackson&K.P.]
*PRACTICE AREAS: Gaming Law; Indian Law; Litigation; Environmental Law.

Wiacek, Raymond J., (AV) .... '50 '76 C.976 B.A. L.309 J.D. [Jones,D.R.&P.]
*PRACTICE AREAS: Taxation; International Taxation; International Finance; Transfer Pricing.

Wial, Howard J .... '60 '99 C.477 A.B. L.976 J.D. U.S. Gen Acctg. Off.

Wicht, Jennifer G. .... '70 '99 C.311 B.A. L.276 J.D. [Ⓐ Williams&C.]

Wick, Robert .... '65 '94 C.197 A.B. L.309 J.D. [Covington&B.]

Wick, Ronald F. .... '64 '92 C.188 A.B. L.276 J.D. [Baker&H.]

Wickens, William E., (AV) .... '39 '64 C.210 B.A. L.477 J.D. [Miller T.W.&L.]
*PRACTICE AREAS: Commercial Law; Litigation; Administrative Law.

Wickett, James '67 '98 C.861 B.A. L.273 J.D.
(adm. in VA; not adm. in DC) [Ⓐ Dewey B.]
*PRACTICE AREAS: Legislative Practice (50%); Tax Law (50%).

Wickouski, M. Stephanie, (AV) ...... '— '79 C.945 A.B. L.1218 J.D. [Arent F.K.P.&K.]
*PRACTICE AREAS: Bankruptcy.

Wicks, Carol I. '44 '79 C.884 B.A. L.1338 J.D.
(adm. in PA; not adm. in DC) [Ⓐ Fulbright&J.]
*PRACTICE AREAS: Intellectual Property.

Wicks, Glenn P. .... '66 '91 C&L.273 B.A., J.D. [Wicks]
*PRACTICE AREAS: Aviation; International; Transportation; Regulatory.

Wicks, Jenifer .... '69 '99 L.276 J.D. Pub. Def. Off.

Wicks Group, The, PLLC
1101 17th Street, Suite 604, 20036
Telephone: 202-457-7790 Fax: 202-457-7799
Email: TheWicksGroup@aol.com
Glenn P. Wicks.
Aviation, International, Commercial Transportation and Regulatory Law.

See Professional Biographies, WASHINGTON, DISTRICT OF COLUMBIA

Wickwire, Jon M., (AV) ... '44 '68 C.446 B.A. L.276 J.D. [Wickwire G.] (⊙Vienna, VA)
*PRACTICE AREAS: Construction; Public Contract; Fidelity and Surety; General Corporate Law.

Wickwire Gavin, P.C., (AV)
Two Lafayette Centre, Suite 450, 1133-21st Street, N.W., 20036-3002 ⊙
Telephone: 202-887-5200 Telecopier: 202-223-0120
URL: http://www.wickwire.com
Jon M. Wickwire; Donald G. Gavin; Robert J. Smith (Madison, Wisconsin); Michael C. Loulakis; Stanley M. Salus; Brian W. Mullins (Madison, Wisconsin); Jeffrey G. Gilmore; Owen J. Shean; Stephen B. Hurlbut; Hugh N. Anderson (Madison, Wisconsin); David P. Hendel; David P. Dapper (Los Angeles, California); Edward G. Gallagher; William B. Fisher; Shannon J. Briglia; Carl A. Sinderbrand (Madison, Wisconsin); Michael A. Gatje; Stephen J. Densmore (Los Angeles, California); Mark R. Berry (Vienna, Virginia); Mark J. Groff (Vienna, Virginia); Daniel J. Donohue; Roger P. Heyman (Los Angeles, California); Jodi M. Lewis (Los Angeles, California); Claude P. Goddard, Jr.;—Brian P. Waagner (Vienna, Virginia); Elizabeth M. Lascheid (Los Angeles, California); Simon J. Santiago; Samuel K. Robison; Kayhan M. Fatemi (Los Angeles, California); Julia Ann Bitner (Vienna, Virginia); Hal J. Perloff (Vienna, Virginia); Robert H. Shaffer, Jr. (Los Angeles, California); Mary K. Monville (Not admitted in DC); Louis J. Dennis (Los Angeles, California); Lauren P. McLaughlin (Vienna, Virginia); Scott B. Hillman (Vienna, Virginia). Of Counsel: J. Kent Holland, Jr.
Construction, Government and Public Contracts, Fidelity and Surety, Federal Grant, Environmental, Bankruptcy, Corporate, and Commercial Law.
Vienna, Virginia Office: Wickwire Gavin, P.C., International Gateway, 8100 Boone Boulevard, Suite 700. Telephone: 703-790-8750. Fax: 703-448-1801.
Madison, Wisconsin Office: Wickwire Gavin, P.C., Suite 800, 22 East Mifflin Street, P.O. Box 1683. Telephone: 608-257-2029. Telecopier: 608-257-2029.
Los Angeles, California, Office: Wickwire Gavin LLP, 38th Floor, 725 South Figueroa Street. Telephone: 213-688-9500. Telecopier: 213-627-6342.

See Professional Biographies, WASHINGTON, DISTRICT OF COLUMBIA

Widder, John M., (AV) .... '52 '78 C.966 B.A. L.813 J.D. [Richter,M.&F.]
Widman, Chas L., (AV) .... '24 '50 C&L.273 LL.B. 2000 L St., N.W.

Widnell, Nicholas A. .... '70 '99 C.145 B.A. L.1209 J.D. [Ⓐ Collier S.S.]
*PRACTICE AREAS: Antitrust.

Wiegand, Barry .... '54 '90 C&L.276 B.S.F.S., J.D. Asst. U.S. Atty.

Wiegand, Christy C. .... '— '01 C.674 A.B. L.188 J.D. [Ⓐ Arnold&P.]

Wiegard, Michael A. .... '48 '80 C.273 B.A. L.276 J.D. [Eckert S.C.&M.]
*PRACTICE AREAS: Environmental Law; Product Safety Regulation Litigation.

Wiegmann, R. Hackney .... '64 '89 C.228 B.A. L.309 J.D. [Williams&C.]

Wiehl, Lis, (AV) '61 '87 C.66 A.B. L.309 J.D.
(adm. in WA; not adm. in DC) [Ⓒ Perkins C.] (⊙Seattle, WA)
*PRACTICE AREAS: Complex Litigation; Criminal Law; Ethics; Corporate Compliance.

Wielgus, Thomas M. .... '67 '95 C.1048 B.S.B.A. L.1187 J.D. Ctr. for Indiv. Rights

Wiench, Todd E. .... '73 '98 C.436 B.A. L.221 J.D. [Ⓐ Wilmer,C.&P.]

Wiener, Jonathan L., (AV) .... '55 '80 C.183 B.A. L.309 J.D. [Goldberg,G.W.&W.]
*PRACTICE AREAS: Communications and Media.

Wiener, Lewis S., (AV) .... '62 '88 C.1044 B.A. L.904 J.D. [Ⓒ Sutherland A.&B.]
*PRACTICE AREAS: Litigation; Construction; Surety; Taking/Inverse Condemnation.

Wiener, Robin Kim '63 '94 C.659 B.S.E. L.276 J.D.
Instit. of Scrap Recycling Industries

Wiernicki, Peter J. .... '61 '87 C.105 B.A. L.64 J.D. [Joseph,M.&R.]
*PRACTICE AREAS: Litigation; Aviation Law; Adoption Law; Assisted Reproductive Technologies; Education Law.

Wierzynski, Barbara B. '45 '77 C.706 B.A. L.209 J.D.
Exec. V.P. & Gen. Coun., Futures Industry Association

Wiesenfelder, Leslie H., (AV) .... '45 '71 C.188 B.A. L.823 J.D. [Dow,L.&A.]

Wiesner, Philip J. '44 '71 C.776 B.S. L.178 J.D.
(adm. in PA; not adm. in DC) KPMG Peat Marwick

Wigger, John H. D. .... '15 '40 C.152 A.B. L.276 J.D. 1135 16th St., N.W.‡

Wiggin, Deborah M. .... '69 '94 C.914 B.A. L.309 J.D. [Hale&D.]

Wiggins, A. Lynne .... '59 '93 C.10 B.S. L.192 J.D. Asst. Chief Litig. Coun.‡

Wiggins, Dena Eve .... '55 '88 C.692 B.A. L.276 J.D. [Sutherland A.&B.]
*PRACTICE AREAS: Energy.

Wiggins, Letitia .... '70 '96 C.1378 B.A. L.128 J.D. Off. of People's Coun.
Wiggins, Mason E., Jr. .... '57 '86 C&L.128 B.A., J.D. 415 5th St. SE

Wiggins, N. Frank, (AV) .... '47 '74 C.350 B.S. L.477 J.D. [Venable,A.B.H.&C.]
*PRACTICE AREAS: Litigation; Administrative Law.

Wiggins, Robert B. .... '61 '86 C&L.575 B.S., J.D. [Ⓒ Morgan,L.&B.]

Wight, David L .... '71 '97 C.627 B.S. L.101 J.D. 810 Vermont Ave. NW (011B)

Wight, Paul Franklin .... '70 '98 C.101 B.A. L.178 J.D. [Ⓐ Skadden,A.S.M.&F.]
*PRACTICE AREAS: Energy; Regulatory; Litigation.

Wigman, Victor M., (AV) '40 '67
C.223 B.S.M.E. L.659 J.D. [Blank R.C.&M.] (See Pat. Sect.)
*PRACTICE AREAS: Intellectual Property Infringement; International Licensing; Mechanical Patents; Metallurgical Patents; Patent Infringement.

Wigmore, Michael B. .... '62 '91 C.1027 B.S. L.273 J.D. [Swidler B.S.F.]
*PRACTICE AREAS: Environmental Law; Government Affairs.

Wigodsky, Jeffrey A., (AV) .... '59 '85 C.260 B.S. L.1338 J.D. [Karp,F.L.W.&N.]
*PRACTICE AREAS: Auto Negligence; Premises Liability; Products Liability.

Wikberg, Terrance Jay '70 '00 C.1333 B.S.A.E. L.446 J.D.
(adm. in MD; not adm. in DC; See Pat. Sect.) [Ⓐ Sughrue M.]
*PRACTICE AREAS: Patents.
Wike, Donald D., (BV) ... '30 '66 C&L.30 B.A., J.D. 1636 Bladensburg Rd., N.E.
Wilan, Jonathan Michael '72 '97 C.446 B.A. L.309 J.D.
1875 Connecticut Avenue, N.W.
Wilber, Christopher A. ... '72 '99 C.473 B.S. L.276 J.D. [Ⓐ Wilmer,C.&P.]
Wilbert, Randall E., II '72 '98 C.197 B.A. L.276 J.D.
(adm. in NY; not adm. in DC) 555 13th St., N.W.‡
Wilbon, Joan M., (AV) ... '49 '74 C.569 B.A. L.273 J.D. 1120 Connecticut Ave. NW
Wilbourn, Beverly J. ... '53 '87 C.608 B.S. L.276 J.D. 3900 Wisconsin Ave., N.W.
Wilbur, Alan D. '74 '00 C.475 B.A. L.945 J.D.
(adm. in VA; not adm. in DC) [Ⓐ Venable,A.B.H.&C.]
*PRACTICE AREAS: Commercial Litigation.
Wilbur, Alan Dwight '74 '00 C.475 B.A. L.945 J.D.
(adm. in VA; not adm. in DC) 1201 New York Ave., N.W.
Wilburn, Nadine Chandler ... '67 '92 C.699 A.B. L.329 J.D. Asst. Corp. Coun.
Wilburn, William Karl, (AV) ... '48 '78 C.367 B.A. L.64 J.D. [Seyfarth S.]
*PRACTICE AREAS: Construction Law; Litigation; International Practice.
Wilcher, LaJuana S. ... '54 '80 C.929 B.S. L.1340 J.D. [LeBoeuf,L.G.&M.]
*PRACTICE AREAS: Environmental Law and Litigation; Administrative and Regulatory Law.
Wilcox, Dennis R., (AV) '51 '77
C.608 B.A. L.930 J.D. [Climaco,L.P.W.&G.] (⊙Cleve., OH)
Wilcox, James B., Jr., (AV) ... '49 '74 C.659 B.A. L.276 J.D. [Hall,E.H.G.G.&N.]
*PRACTICE AREAS: Civil Litigation; Complex Litigation; Energy.
Wilcox, Justine E., (AV) ... '49 '78 C.289 B.A. L.818 J.D. [Nixon P.]
*PRACTICE AREAS: Real Estate; Real Estate Finance; Syndication; Housing Law.
Wilcox, Leslie C. '45 '69 C&L.800 A.B., J.D.
(adm. in CA; not adm. in DC) Off. of Govt. Ethics
Wilcox, Thomas D. ... '31 '59 C.401 B.S. L.276 J.D. [T.D.Wilcox]
Wilcox, Thomas W. ... '58 '87 C.877 B.S. L.1209 J.D. [Thompson H.]
*PRACTICE AREAS: Transportation; Electric Utility Regulation; Environmental Law; Natural Resources; Government Affairs and Regulations.
Wilcox, Thomas D., P.C. ... 2011 Eye St., N.W.
Wild, David Daniel ... '55 '81 C.446 B.A. L.1066 J.D. [Dow,L.&A.]
Wilder, Marcy J. ... '63 '89 C.867 B.A. L.813 J.D. [Hogan&H.]
*PRACTICE AREAS: Health Privacy; Federal Regulatory Law; Medical Research.
Wilder, Richard C. '55 '84 C.911 B.S.M.E. L.1218 J.D.
(adm. in NH; not adm. in DC; Pat.) [Powell,G.F.&M.]
*PRACTICE AREAS: Intellectual Property; International Trade; International Business Law.
Wilder, Roland P., Jr., (AV) ... '40 '67 C.901 B.A. L.880 J.D. [Baptiste&W.]
*PRACTICE AREAS: Labor Relations Law; Federal Civil Litigation; ERISA; Civil Rights Law.
Wilder, Susan L. ... '67 '92 C.659 B.A. L.273 J.D. [Ⓐ Nixon P.]
*PRACTICE AREAS: Affordable Housing; Community Development; Real Estate; Syndication; Public Finance Law.
Wilder, William R. ... '68 '93 C.866 B.A. L.945 J.D. [Baptiste&W.]
*PRACTICE AREAS: Labor Relations; Federal Litigation; Employment Law; Civil Litigation.
Wilderotter, James A. ... '44 '69 C.276 A.B. L.339 J.D. [Jones,D.R.&P.]
*PRACTICE AREAS: International Trade; Administrative Law.
Wildman, Sloane Anders ... '65 '91 C.197 A.B. L.893 J.D. [Ⓒ Perkins C.]
*PRACTICE AREAS: Environmental Law.
Wildrick, Kathryn P. '74 '00 C.674 A.B. L.273 J.D.
(adm. in NY; not adm. in DC) [Ⓐ Wilkinson B.K.]
*PRACTICE AREAS: Telecommunications.
Wildstein, Michelle R. '71 '99 C.367 B.A. L.128 J.D.
(adm. in GA; not adm. in DC) [Ⓐ Hunton&W.]
Wileman, Leslie Meek ... '— '98 C.881 B.A. L.616 J.D. 1341 G Street, NW
Wiley, La' Vern D. ... '58 '83 C.355 B.A. L.803 J.D. [Ⓐ Eaton&M.] ⊙
*PRACTICE AREAS: Personal Injury; Medical Malpractice; Products Liability.
Wiley, Richard E., (AV) ... '34 '58 C&L.597 B.S., J.D. [Wiley R.&F.]
*PRACTICE AREAS: Communications.

Wiley Rein & Fielding LLP, (AV) BR
1776 K Street, N.W., 20006-2304 ⊙
Telephone: 202-719-7000 Facsimile: 202-719-7049
URL: http://www.wrf.com
Members of Firm: Richard E. Wiley; Bert W. Rein; Fred F. Fielding; Thomas W. Brunner; James H. Wallace, Jr.; Charles Owen Verrill, Jr.; Rand L. Allen (Resident, McLean, Virginia Office); R. Michael Senkowski (Resident, McLean, Virginia Office); Andrew S. Krulwich; Lawrence W. Secrest, III; Richard J. Bodorff; Laura A. Foggan; Jeffrey S. Linder; Jan Witold Baran; William A. Roberts, III; John B. Wyss; Richard L. McConnell; Bruce L. McDonald; Peter J. Klarfeld; Matthew S. Simchak; Carl R. Ramey; Philip J. Davis; James R. W. Bayes; Robert J. Butler; Bruce G. Joseph; Thomas W. Kirby; J. Timothy Hobbs; Robert L. Pettit; Jim Slattery; Keith S. Watson; Arthur I. Cantor; Robert A. Smith; Samuel D. Walker; Peter D. Ross; L. Kay Tatum; Thomas W. Queen; Peter D. Shields; Andrew G. McBride; William B. Baker; Alan H. Price; Gregory J. Vogt; Edwin O. Bailey; David E. Hilliard; John B. Reynolds, III; Daniel J. Standish; James T. Bruce, III; John A. Hodges; Jerry V. Haines; John L. Bartlett; Richard C. Lowery; Barbara Van Gelder; Hugh Latimer; John E. Fiorini, III; James C. Rubinger; Donna Coleman Gregg; Paul F. Khoury; Carol A. Laham; Eileen P. Bradner; Kirk J. Nahra; Michael L. Sturm; Dominic T. Bodensteiner; Kathryn Bucher; Dorthula H. Powell-Woodson; Theodore A. Howard; Richard A. Ifft; Gregory P. Cirillo (Resident, McLean, Virginia Office); Daniel B. Hassett (Resident, McLean, Virginia Office); John R. Shane; Eric W. DeSilva; Wayne D. Johnsen; Floyd B. Chapman; Patricia J. Paoletta; Dale E. Hausman; Todd M. Stansbury; Gregory L. Masters; David W. Koch; Bruce A. McDonald; Rosemary C. Harold; Gregory Lyons; William A. McGrath; John C. Yang; Mary E. Borja; John M. Burgett; Tanja E. Hens; Scott M. McCaleb; Suzanne Yelen. Of Counsel: Robert E. Boone, Jr.; Tyrone Brown; Stuart F. Carwile; Christine E. Connelly; Kurt E. DeSoto; Elizabeth Ann Eastwood; Carl R. Frank; John F. Kamp; Stephen D. Halliday; Phillip H. Harrington; Brian A. Johnson; Christopher Kelly; Kathleen A. Kirby; David J. Kulik; Mary Jo Manning; Peter D. O'Connell; Marnie K. Sarver; David M. Southall. Associates: Karyn K. Ablin; Robin C. Adams (Not admitted in DC); Thomas W. Antonucci; Scott E. Bain; Danielle E. Berry; Erika C. Birg (Not admitted in DC); Seth J. Blonder (Not admitted in DC); Michelle E. Boardman; Timothy C. Brightbill; Dorann Bunkin; Caleb P. Burns; Jennifer E. Chung; Donald E. Clark, Jr.; William J. Colwell; M. Evan Corcoran; Jason P. Cronic; Marjorie J. Dickman; Heather O. Dixon; Susan D. Drake; Brook A. Edinger; Marisa Gallehr Faunce; Leslie D. Fetter; Meredith Fuchs; Thomas S. Garrett; Bradley K. Gillen (Not admitted in DC); Elizabeth E. Goldin; Rebecca P. Goodheart; Christopher Hale; Martha E. Heller; Evan S. Henschel (Not admitted in DC); Jennifer D. Hindin; Kimberly Hrabosky; Jennifer S. Huber; Erica R. Jacobson; Mel R. Jiganti (Resident, McLean, Virginia Office); Jeffrey L. Johnson (Not admitted in DC); Nicholas A. Kessler; Kathleen S. Kim; Eve Klindera; Diane L. Krawczun; Eric W. Leonard (Resident, McLean, Virginia Office); William Lieth; Andrew K. Long; Marcus E. Maher; Kevin J. Maynard; John A. McCullough; Nicole M. McGinnis; Christopher M. Mills (Resident, McLean, Virginia Office); Karalee C. Morell; Brian Nuterangelo; Kristina R. Osterhaus; Mark A. Pacella; John F. Papandrea; Matthew S. Petersen; James D. Phipps; Daniel B. Pickard; Leslie A. Platt; Leslie Johnson Pujo; Benjamin B. Reed; D. Mark Renaud; Christopher L. Robbins; Paul G. Roche; Jessica N. Rosenthal; Oren Rosenthal; Randall D. Roth (Not admitted in DC); Matthew J. Schneider; Timothy W. Staley; E. Kenneth Stegeby; Gerard M. Stegmaier; Sandra Tvarian Stevens; Alexander K. Sun; Stephen C. Tosini; Joshua S. Turner; Daniel J. Wadley; Alysa Beth Wakin (Not admitted in DC); C. Heather Walker; Mary Oates Walker; Christine Quickenden Washington; Dineen Pashoukos Wasylik; Elizabeth A. Whalley Buono (Not admitted in DC); Amy E. Worlton; Derek A. Yeo.
General Practice, Advertising, Antitrust, Appellate, Aviation, Broadcasting, Business and Finance, Communications, Copyright, E-Commerce, Education, Election Law and Government Ethics, Employment and Labor, Energy, Food and Drug, Franchise, Government Affairs, Government Contracts, Health Care, Insurance, Intellectual Property, International Trade, Internet and E-Commerce, Legislative, Litigation, Mass Media, Patent, Privacy, Public Policy, Regulatory, Technology, Telecommunications, Trademark, White Collar Defense, Wireless.

(This Listing Continued)

Wiley Rein & Fielding LLP (Continued)
McLean, Virginia Office: 7925 Jones Branch Drive, Suite 6200. Telephone: 703-905-2800. URL: http://www.wrf.com.
See Professional Biographies, WASHINGTON, DISTRICT OF COLUMBIA
Wilhelm, William Banks, Jr. ... '68 '93 C.321 A.B. L.128 J.D. [Ⓐ Swidler B.S.F.]
*PRACTICE AREAS: Electronic Commerce; Telecommunications; Corporate Law.
Wilhelmy, John N. ... '58 '88 C.973 B.A. L.904 J.D. Assoc. Gen. Coun., Fannie Mae
*RESPONSIBILITIES: Electronic Commerce; Technology Law; Intellectual Property; Corporate Law.
Wilhite, Samuel E. ... '42 '68 C.976 B.A. L.813 LL.B. 325 Pennsylvania Ave., S.E.
Wilk, Adam R. ... '63 '88 C.1044 B.A. L.273 J.D. [Carr,M.&G.] ⊙
*PRACTICE AREAS: Civil Litigation; Commercial Law; Commercial Collections; Debtor and Creditor; Mortgage Foreclosure.
Wilkenfeld, Ari M. ... '70 '98 C.823 B.A. L.659 J.D. [Ⓐ Bernabei&K.]
*PRACTICE AREAS: Employment Discrimination; Whistleblower Litigation; Civil Rights; Civil Liberties.
Wilkenfeld, Wendy Ann ... '74 '98 C.228 A.B. L.309 J.D. [Ⓐ Sutherland A.&B.]
*PRACTICE AREAS: Estate and Gift Taxation; Trust and Estate; Federal Taxation.
Wilkerson, Carl B. '52 '78 C.446 B.S. L.128 J.D.
Assoc. Gen. Coun., Amer. Council of Life Ins.

Wilkes Artis, Chartered, (AV)
(Formerly Wilkes, Artis, Hederick & Lane)
Suite 400, 1150 18th Street, N.W., 20036-3841
Telephone: 202-457-7800
URL: http://www.wilkesartis.com
James C. Wilkes (1899-1968); James E. Artis (1907-1978); Charles A. Camalier, III; Ilene Baxt Boorman; Stanley J. Fineman; David A. Fuss; Eric S. Kassoff; Kenneth A. Max; Stuart A. Turow; Matthew G. Ahrens.
Real Estate Tax, Assessment and Condemnation, Transactional Real Estate.
See Professional Biographies, WASHINGTON, DISTRICT OF COLUMBIA

Wilkes, Artis, Hedrick & Lane
(See Wilkes Artis, Chartered)
Wilkins, Alisa A. ... '66 '95 C.347 B.A. L.30 J.D. 1666 Connecticut Ave., N.W., Ste. 225
Wilkins, James H., Jr., (AV) ... '45 '72 C.45 B.A. L.846 J.D. [Shaw P.]
*PRACTICE AREAS: Corporate Transactions; Outsourcing; Technology Transactions; Strategic Alliances; Electronic Commerce Transactions.
Wilkins, Jon Sharp '70 '96 C.197 B.A. L.976 J.D.
(adm. in MD; not adm. in DC) McKinsey & Co.
Wilkins, Richard G., (AV) ... '52 '80 C&L.101 B.A., J.D. [Maines&L.]
Wilkins, Robert L. ... '63 '90 C.701 B.S. L.309 J.D. Pub. Defender Serv.
Wilkins, Thomas H. ... '49 '88 C.697 B.A. L.128 J.D. U.S. Park Police
Wilkins, William J., (AV) ... '52 '77 C.976 B.A. L.309 J.D. [Wilmer,C.&P.]
*PRACTICE AREAS: Taxation.
Wilkinson, Beth A. ... '— '88 C.674 A.B. L.893 J.D. [Latham&W.]
*PRACTICE AREAS: White Collar Crime; Civil Litigation.
Wilkinson, Constance A. ... '60 '85 C.178 B.A. L.273 J.D. [Ⓐ Epstein B.&G.]
*PRACTICE AREAS: Government Contracts Law; Health Law.
Wilkinson, Eric Richard ... '67 '98 C.477 B.A. L.1194 J.D. Atty., U.S. E.P.A.
Wilkinson, Hugh T. ... '56 '81 C&L.276 A.B., J.D. [Elias,M.T.&H.]
Wilkinson, Laura A. ... '60 '87 C.659 B.A. L.188 J.D. [Clifford C.R.&W.]
*PRACTICE AREAS: Antitrust; Litigation.
Wilkinson, Naomi ... '71 '97 C.276 B.S. L.893 J.D. [Ⓐ Milbank,T.H.&M.]
Wilkinson, Nigel L. '64 '01 C.1209 B.A. L.128 J.D.
(adm. in VA; not adm. in DC) [Ⓐ Reed S.]
*PRACTICE AREAS: Labor and Employment.
Wilkinson, Roger W. '— '98 C.112 B.A. L.818 J.D.
(adm. in MA; not adm. in DC) U.S. Dept. of Labor, Offc. of Solicitor

Wilkinson Barker Knauer, LLP, (AV)
2300 N Street, N.W., Suite 700, 20037
Telephone: 202-783-4141 Fax: 202-833-2360; 783-5851
Email: info@wbklaw.com URL: http://www.wbklaw.com
Members of Firm: Glen A. Wilkinson (1911-1985); Robert W. Barker (1919-1987); Rosel H. Hyde (1900-1992); Leon T. Knauer; L. Andrew Tollin (Managing Partner); Kenneth E. Satten; Michael Deuel Sullivan; Kathryn A. Zachem; F. Thomas Moran; Paul J. Sinderbrand; Kenneth D. Patrich; Lawrence J. Movshin; Linda M. Wellstein (Resident, Caracas, Venezuela Office); William J. Sill; Jonathan V. Cohen; Robert D. Primosch; Timothy J. Cooney; Robert G. Kirk; J. Wade Lindsay; Carolyn W. Groves; Barry P. Miller; Craig Edward Gilmore; L. Charles Keller. Of Counsel: Pierre J. LaForce. Associates: Georgina L.O. Feigen (Not admitted in DC); José Andrés Romero Angrisano (Resident, Caracas, Venezuela Office); David Kent Judelsohn; Lynn H. Johanson; Jeffrey Scott Cohen; Camille Hansen; Paige K. Fronabarger; Arthur Thomas Lechtman; Vladimir J. Falcón (Resident, Caracas, Venezuela Office); Robert G. Morse; Brian W. Higgins; Catherine Curran Butcher; Kevin M. Jordan (Not admitted in DC); William R. Layton; Timothy A. Kruyer; Paul J. Nagle (Not admitted in DC); Laura A. Schink; Anne H. Sullivan; Christopher G. Ernst (Not admitted in DC); Keith R. Murphy (Not admitted in DC); Kathryn P. Wildrick (Not admitted in DC); Zachary Andrews Zehner (Not admitted in DC); Christopher D. Ornelas.
Administrative and Regulatory Practice before Federal Agencies, Legislative Practice before Congress, and Trial and Appellate Practice before Federal Courts. Practice sectors include: Communications and Telecommunications, Corporate and Commercial Transactions, Information Technology, Intellectual Property, International Telecommunications, Trade and Investment, Legislation and Litigation.
See Professional Biographies, WASHINGTON, DISTRICT OF COLUMBIA

Wilkof, Richard B. '51 '83
C.861 B.A. L.273 J.D. Staff Coun., NEA Office of Gen. Coun.
Wilkof, Sandra G.
(See Bethesda, Maryland)
Wilkozek, Shari L. '71 '98 C.328 B.A. L.146 J.D.
(adm. in IL; not adm. in DC) [Ⓐ Fleischman&W.]
Wilks, Zach '74 '00 C.475 B.A. L.178 J.D.
(adm. in MD; not adm. in DC) [Ⓐ Winston&S.]
*PRACTICE AREAS: Corporate; Legislative and Regulatory.
Will, Robert P., (AV) ... '31 '61 C.426 A.B. L.800 J.D. 1015 18th St., N.W.
Willard, Linda J. ... '— '94 C&L.276 A.B., J.D. [Ⓐ Verner,L.B.M.&H.]
Willard, Martin P. ... '55 '87 C.276 A.B. L.893 J.D. [Perkins C.]
*PRACTICE AREAS: Government Contract Law; Commercial Litigation.

Willard, Daniel S., P.C.
(See Rockville)
Willcox, Breckinridge L., (AV) ... '44 '69 C.976 B.A. L.228 J.D. [Arent F.K.P.&K.]
*PRACTICE AREAS: Litigation; White Collar; Criminal Defense; Environmental Law Enforcement.
Willcox, William H., (AV) ... '33 '59 C.976 B.A. L.309 LL.B. 1301 K St., N.W.
Willey, Benjamin L. ... '49 '76 C.444 B.A. L.446 J.D. [Miller,B.&O.]
*PRACTICE AREAS: Military Law; Federal Administrative Law; Federal Civil Practice; Admiralty Law; Maritime Commercial Law.
Willey, James A., (AV) ... '06 '30 L.537 LL.B. [Willey&C.] ‡
*PRACTICE AREAS: Probate; Estates; Probate Administration.

Willey and Crooks, (AV)
1616 H Street, N.W., 20006-4985
Telephone: 202-628-2477 Fax: 202-347-3422
Email: esqjcb@aol.com
James A. Crooks (1911-1982); James A. Willey (Retired); James C. Beadles.
General Civil Practice. Probate, Thrift Institutions.
See Professional Biographies, WASHINGTON, DISTRICT OF COLUMBIA

Williams, Andrea D. '56 '92 C.30 B.A. L.329 J.D.
Asst. Gen. Coun., Cellular Telecommunication Indus. Assn.
Williams, Angela F. ....'— '88 C.893 B.A. L.846 J.D. [🄲 Bryan C.]
*PRACTICE AREAS: White Collar Crime; Securities; Nonprofit Organizations Law.
Williams, B. John, Jr., (AV) ....'49 '75 C&L.273 B.A., J.D. [Shearman&S.]
Williams, Carolyn H., (AV) ....'50 '78 C.399 B.A. L.976 J.D. [Williams&C.]
*PRACTICE AREAS: Commercial Litigation; Complex and Multi-District Litigation; Complex Litigation; Environmental Litigation; Federal Civil Practice.
Williams, Charles E. ....'20 '52 C&L.329 A.B., LL.B. 1329 Shepherd St., N.W.
Williams, Daniel V. '71 '01 C.1213 B.S.M.E. L.1218 J.D.
[🄰 Sughrue M.] (See Pat. Sect.)
*PRACTICE AREAS: Intellectual Property.
Williams, David F., (AV) .... '52 '79 C.976 B.A. L.893 J.D. [Cadwalader,W.&T.]
*PRACTICE AREAS: Complex Commercial Litigation; Environmental Litigation; Bankruptcy Litigation.
Williams, David Huntington, (AV) ....'46 '73 C.309 A.B. L.813 J.D. [Williams&E.] ⊙
Williams, Edwin A., (AV) ....'40 '66 C.612 B.A. L.273 J.D. [Kellogg,W.&L.] ⊙
*PRACTICE AREAS: Civil Litigation; Criminal; Appellate Practice.
Williams, Elizabeth Z. '65 '91 C.941 B.A. L.228 J.D.
(adm. in VT; not adm. in DC) 3307 M St., N.W.
Williams, Erica Y. .... '73 '98 C&L.893 B.A., J.D. [🄰 Arnold&P.]
*PRACTICE AREAS: Litigation.
Williams, Frederick C. '— '74 C.93 B.S. L.477 J.D.
[Williams&Assoc.] & [🄲 Slater & Z.] (See Pat. Sect.)
Williams, Garrett V. .... '69 '95 C.1365 B.A. L.273 J.D. [🄰 Chaikin&S.]
*PRACTICE AREAS: Personal Injury; Employment Discrimination; Premises Liability; Medical Malpractice; Products Liability.
Williams, George H., Jr., (AV) ....'47 '76 C.893 B.A. L.64 J.D. [Cameron M.]
*PRACTICE AREAS: Energy Law; Public Utilities Law; Administrative Law; Appellate Practice.
Williams, Gregory M. ....'68 '97 C.059 B.A. L.893 J.D. [🄰 Covington&B.]
*PRACTICE AREAS: Commercial Litigation; International Litigation; International Arbitration.
Williams, Harvey S. .... '53 '80 C.893 B.A. L.945 J.D. 1701 Q Street N.W.
Williams, J. D., (AV) ....'37 '62 C.623 B.B.A. L.273 J.D. [Williams&J.]
*PRACTICE AREAS: Federal Legislative and Policy Matters.
Williams, James V., III .... '70 '95 C.276 B.S.F.S. L.896 J.D. [Williams&A.] ⊙
Williams, Jarrett ....'68 '95 C&L.309 B.A., J.D. [🄰 Covington&B.]
Williams, Joan Chalmers ...'52 '80 C.976 B.A. L.309 J.D. Prof. of Law, Amer. University
Williams, Johannes W. ....'57 '85 C.63 B.A. L.276 J.D. [🄲 Thelen R.&P.]
*PRACTICE AREAS: Energy; Electric Industry Structure; Federal and State Regulation; Electric Utilities.
Williams, John B., (AV) ....'52 '78 C.299 A.B. L.128 J.D. [Collier S.S.]
*PRACTICE AREAS: Litigation.
Williams, John C., (AV) ....'37 '63 C&L.623 B.S., LL.B. 888 NW 17th St.
Williams, John P., (AV) ....'49 '80 C.309 A.B. L.569 J.D. [Duncan&A.]
*PRACTICE AREAS: Finance; Electric Power Joint Ventures; Contracts; Electric Utility Regulation; International Law.
Williams, Julia B. .... '41 '75 C.831 B.A. L.569 J.D. 1819 L St. N.W.
Williams, Karen Hastie, (AV) ....'44 '73 C.67 B.A. L.128 J.D. [Crowell&M.]
*PRACTICE AREAS: Administrative Law; Public Contract Law; Legal Ethics and Discipline Law.
Williams, Kathleen M. ....'52 '80 C.659 B.A. L.273 J.D. [🄲 Epstein B.&G.]
*PRACTICE AREAS: Labor Law; Employment Law.
Williams, Kathy S. '53 '91 C.1280 B.A. L.276 J.D.
Hearings and App. Exam., Dept. of Employ. Servs.
Williams, Lani L. '69 '96 C.118 B.A. L.245 J.D.
(adm. in GA; not adm. in DC) Assoc. Coun., Int'l Municipal Lawyers Assoc.
Williams, Larry C., (AV) ....'31 '60 C&L.329 B.A., LL.B. 666 11th St.
Williams, Manley ....'64 '93 C.813 B.A. L.309 J.D. [🄲 Wilmer,C.&P.]
*PRACTICE AREAS: Financial Institutions.
Williams, Marc J. ....'69 '96 C.228 B.A. L.329 J.D. 4912 New Hampshire Ave., N.W.
Williams, Marcus P. ....'59 '89 C.797 B.A. L.893 J.D. Coun., Gov. Progs., IBM Corp.
Williams, Mark C. ....'63 '91 C.178 B.A. L.564 J.D. [🄲 Bingham D.]
*PRACTICE AREAS: Energy; Utility Law; Corporate; Project Finance; Federal Administrative Law.
Williams, Mary C. '57 '98 C.803 B.A. L.1206 J.D.
(adm. in FL; not adm. in DC) 666 11th Street N.W., Suite 410
Williams, Mary Newcomer ....'70 '97 C.976 B.A. L.228 J.D. [🄰 Covington&B.]
Williams, Maureen H. .... '66 '97 C.856 B.A. L.30 J.D. International Fin. Corp.
Williams, Michael A. .... '52 '80 C.494 B.A. L.1035 J.D. [Stephens] ⊙
Williams, Michael Cunningham .... '59 '84 C&L.893 B.A., J.D. [Hogan&H.]
*PRACTICE AREAS: Corporate Law; Securities Law; Life Sciences Law.
Williams, Michele E. ....'61 '91 C&L.276 B.S.F.S., J.D. [McKee N.]
*PRACTICE AREAS: Corporate Finance; Real Estate Finance; Project Finance; Asset Protection.
Williams, Nick S. '65 '99 C.1356 B.A. L.893 J.D.
(adm. in NY; not adm. in DC) [🄰 Mayer,B.&P.]
*PRACTICE AREAS: Civil Litigation; Securities Litigation; Professional Liability.
Williams, Pamela R. '— '98 C.893 B.A. L.273 J.D.
(adm. in MD; not adm. in DC) [🄰 Morgan,L.&B.]
Williams, Paul R. ....'65 '91 C.112 A.B. L.813 J.D. [🄲 McDermott,W.&E.]
Williams, Petur S. ....'48 '77 C.273 A.B. L.1162 J.D. Asst. U.S. Atty.
Williams, Robert E., (AV) ....'42 '67 C.72 B.A. L.339 J.D. [McGuiness N.&W.]
*PRACTICE AREAS: Labor Relations Law; Equal Employment Opportunity Law; Federal Appellate Practice.
Williams, Robin A. .... '68 '94 C.94 B.S. L.818 J.D. [🄰 Piper M.R.&W.]
*PRACTICE AREAS: Business; Technology; Venture Capital; Emerging Growth Companies.
Williams, Roderick B. .... '— '92 C.165 B.A. L.273 J.D. [🄰 Foley&L.]
*PRACTICE AREAS: Civil Litigation; Government Contract Law; Bankruptcy.
Williams, Roger D. ....'57 '91 C.880 B.E. L.16 J.D. [Troutman S.] (⊙Atlanta, GA)
*PRACTICE AREAS: Project Development; Project Finance; Oil and Gas.
Williams, Shirley M. ....'42 '83 C.659 B.A. L.1162 J.D. Neighborhood Legal Servs. Prog.
Williams, Susan G. '63 '89 C.103 A.B. L.813 J.D.
(adm. in CA; not adm. in DC) 4427 Westover Pl. N.W.
Williams, T. Raymond, (AV) .... '40 '64 C&L.16 B.S., J.D. [McDermott,W.&E.]
Williams, Ted J. ....'46 '87 C.30 B.S. L.64 J.D. 1200 G St. N.W.
Williams, Thomas C. ....'26 '58 C&L.276 B.S.S., J.D. 1111 19th St., N.W.
Williams, Verna '60 '88 C.276 B.S. L.309 J.D.
Sr. Coun., National Women's Law Center
Williams, Wade S. ....'41 '78 C.797 B.A. L.273 J.D. Deloitte & Touche
Williams, Wendy W., (AV) '44 '70 C.112 B.A. L.1066 J.D.
Georgetown Univ. Law Ctr.
Williams, Wesley S., Jr., (AV) ....'42 '69 C&L.309 B.A., J.D. [Covington&B.]
Williams, William A., (AV) ....'49 '77 C.1209 B.S. L.893 J.D. [Fulbright&J.]
*PRACTICE AREAS: Energy.
Williams, Yvette D. '68 '00 C.674 A.B. L.446 J.D.
(adm. in MD; not adm. in DC) [🄰 Venable,A.B.H.&C.]
*PRACTICE AREAS: Environmental Law; Energy; State Government; Local Government Law; Administrative Law.
Williams, Yvonne L. '38 '80 C.66 B.A. L.276 J.D.
Natl. Dir., Pub. Policy & Internal Affs., Academy for Educational Develop.
Williams & Asby, PLLC ....1250 24th St. NW, Suite 300 (⊙New Bern, NC)

Williams & Associates
1030 Fifteenth Street., N.W. Suite 300, 20005-1501
Telephone: 202-842-0431 Fax: 202-467-4045
Email: fcw@bellatlantic.net URL: http://www.lawyers.com/dc-patentlaw
Frederick C. Williams. Of Counsel: Jennifer J. Zeien; James L. Lewis.
Patent Prosecution, Patent Portfolio and Infringement Analysis, with special emphasis in the areas of Medical and Surgical Devices and Digital Signal Processing; Government Contract Claim Preparation and Prosecution.
See Professional Biographies, WASHINGTON, DISTRICT OF COLUMBIA

Williams-Bibbs, Mialeeka C. '73 '99 C.329 B.S. L.273 J.D.
(adm. in VA; not adm. in DC; Pat.) [🄰 Dickstein S.M.&O.]
*PRACTICE AREAS: Patents; Trademarks; Licensing; Copyright.

Williams & Connolly LLP, (AV) BB
725 Twelfth Street, N.W., 20005-5901
Telephone: 202-434-5000 Fax: 202-434-5029
Members of Firm: Edward Bennett Williams (1920-1988); Paul R. Connolly (1922-1978); David Povich; Steven M. Umin; John W. Vardaman; Paul Martin Wolff; J. Alan Galbraith; John G. Kester; William E. McDaniels; Brendan V. Sullivan, Jr.; Aubrey M. Daniel, III; Richard M. Cooper; Gerald A. Feffer; Robert P. Watkins; Jerry L. Shulman; Lewis H. Ferguson, III; Robert B. Barnett; David E. Kendall; Gregory B. Craig; John J. Buckley, Jr.; Terrence O'Donnell; John K. Villa; Barry S. Simon; Kevin T. Baine; Stephen L. Urbanczyk; Philip J. Ward; F. Whitten Peters; James A. Bruton, III; Peter J. Kahn; Judith A. Miller; Lon S. Babby; Michael S. Sundermeyer; James T. Fuller, III; Douglas R. Marvin; Bruce R. Genderson; Carolyn H. Williams; Frank Lane Heard III; Steven R. Kuney; Gerson A. Zweifach; Paul Mogin; Howard W. Gutman; Steven A. Steinbach; Mark S. Levinstein; Mary Greer Clark; Victoria Radd Rollins; Daniel Franklin Katz; Robert M. Krasne; Kathleen L. Beggs; William R. Murray, Jr.; Eva Petko Esber; Stephen D. Raber; David C. Kiernan; Lon E. Musslewhite; Heidi K. Hubbard; Glenn J. Pfadenhauer; George A. Borden; Robert J. Shaughnessy; Jonathan P. Graham; Allen P. Waxman; David S. Blatt; Ari S. Zymelman; Regina G. Maloney; Dane H. Butswinkas; Laurie S. Fulton; Dennis M. Black; Philip A. Sechler; Lynda Schuler; Paul K. Dueffert; R. Hackney Wiegmann; Robert M. Cary; Kevin M. Hodges; David M. Zinn; Joseph G. Petrosinelli; Steven M. Farina; Kevin M. Downey; Thomas G. Hentoff; Kumiki Gibson; Paul B. Gaffney; Emmet T. Flood; Robert A. Van Kirk; Marcie R. Ziegler; Kenneth C. Smurzynski; John E. Schmidtlein;—Eric A. Kuhl; Sharon L. Davis; Matthew J. Herrington; Suzanne H. Woods; Craig D. Singer; James L. Tanner, Jr.; Kathleen Quimby Garcia; J. Andrew Keyes; Nicole Chapin Duke; Julia B. Shelton; Gilbert O. Greenman; Maurita Elaine Horn; Enu A. Mainigi; Michael F. O'Connor; Thomas C. Viles; Oliver Garcia; Paul T. Hourihan; Paul C. Rauser; William J. Bachman; Margaret A. Keeley; Ann H. Rakestraw; James Gibson; Mary-Rose Papandrea; Gabriel E. Gore (Not admitted in DC); Edward J. Bennett; Kathleen M. Ryan; Mara Walker Murphy; Tobin J. Romero; Beth A. Levene; Glen Donath; Lisa M. Duggan; Thomas G. Ward; William T. Burke; Laura Haas Parsky; John E. Joiner; David S. Ardia; Luba Shur; Helen I. Dooley; Nicholas J. Boyle (Not admitted in DC); Bonnie Dunninger Nathan; Charles T. Kimmett, Jr.; Adam L. Perlman; Michael J. Leotta; Russell D. Covey; Andrew W. Rudge; Deneen C. Howell; Matthew S. Amatruda; Jason M. Levien (Not admitted in DC); David H. Angeli; David C. Rieveschl; Alex G. Romain; David A. Forkner; Francis M. Hamilton III; Elizabeth A. O'Brien; Laura P. Stout; Stephen A. Beck; Jonathan M. Landy; Christopher N. Manning; Jeffrey M. Smith; Stacey Dansky; Thomas E. Shakow; Gregory M. Gilchrist; Ryan T. Scarborough; William G. Childs; Jennifer G. Wicht; Zoe S. Poulson; Stephen D. Andrews; Jonathan S. Jeffress (Not admitted in DC); Mary Beth Long; Bradley J. Bondi; Janet C. Fisher; Juli Ann Lund (Not admitted in DC); Katherine P. Chiarello (Not admitted in DC); Thomas H. L. Selby; Leonard D. Brown, Jr.; Brian A. McLachlan; Kevin Hardy; Riley Henderson Ross III; Gabriel Feldman (Not admitted in DC); Edward Coleman Barnidge, III; Jana D. Jobes; Joseph M. Terry; Christine M. Cabezas-Gansler; Brian S. Morrison (Not admitted in DC); Katherine R. Tromble; Daniel A. Restrepo; Willis N. Sautter (Not admitted in DC); Christina P. Giffin (Not admitted in DC); Brian J. Buckelew; Michaela Allbee (Not admitted in DC); Aaron P. Maurer (Not admitted in DC); Brad M. Snyder (Not admitted in DC); Manish K. Mital; Nathan P. Sutton (Not admitted in DC); Ana L. Reyes (Not admitted in DC); Heidi E. Murdy; Shana LaVerne Fulton (Not admitted in DC). Of Counsel: Vincent J. Fuller; Raymond W. Bergan; Jeremiah C. Collins; Lyman G. Friedman. Counsel: Daniel J. Hurson.
Practice in Federal Courts and before Federal Departments and Agencies.
See Professional Biographies, WASHINGTON, DISTRICT OF COLUMBIA

Williams & Eoannou, P.C., (AV) .... 202 G Street, Northeast (⊙Rockville, MD)

Williams & Jensen, A Professional Corporation, (AV) BB
1155 - 21st Street, N.W., Suite 300, 3 Lafayette Centre, 20036
Telephone: 202-659-8201 Facsimile: 202-659-5249
Email: fd@wms-jen.com
George D. Baker; Philip E. Bechtel; Barbara Wixon Bonfiglio; William B. Canfield, III; Bertram W. Carp; David E. Franasiak; Robert E. Glennon, Jr.; J. Steven Hart; Carole L. Kuebler (1948-1979); Karen Judd Lewis; Robert J. Martinez; John J. McMackin, Jr.; George G. Olsen; Anthony J. Roda; David A. Starr; Jeffrey A. Tassey; J. D. Williams;—Tracy Doherty Taylor; David Michael Landers; Karina V. Lynch (Not admitted in DC); Frank C. Vlossak (Not admitted in DC). Of Counsel: Robert E. Jensen.
Federal Policy Practice. Congressional, Executive Branch and Administrative Representation, Constitutional and Statutory Construction and Contract Litigation, General Commercial Representation.
See Professional Biographies, WASHINGTON, DISTRICT OF COLUMBIA

Williams Mullen, (AV)
1666 K Street, NW Suite 1200, 20006 ⊙
Telephone: 202-833-9200 Fax: 202-293-5939
URL: http://www.williamsmullen.com
Lewis C. Williams (1875-1959); James Mullen; James R. Cannon, Jr.; Stuart G. Christian (1883-1967); Francis T. Coleman; Michael R. Geroe; Thomas B. McVey; Warren E. Nowlin; Jimmie V. Reyna; Robert F. Riley; Robert D. Roseman;—Julia K. Bailey; Karen A. Doner; Joelle Kay Ogg; William E. Pomeranz.
Antitrust, Business Law, Commercial Banking and Finance, Communications, Creditor's Rights and Bankruptcy, E-Commerce, Employee Benefits, Energy, Environmental, Estate Planning and Administration, Franchise, Government Contracts, Governmental Affairs, Health Care, Immigration, International, Labor and Employment, Litigation, Maritime, Mergers and Acquisitions, Mortgage Banking, Real Estate, Securities, Tax, and Technology and Intellectual Property.
Richmond Office: Two James Center, 1021 East Cary Street. P.O. Box 1320, 23218-1320. Telephone: 804-643-1991. Fax: 804-783-6507.
Charlottesville, Virginia Office: Enterprise Center, 401 East Market Street, Suite 101, 22902-5264. Telephone: 434-851-5700. Fax: 434-783-6507. Fax within area: 434-817-0977.
London, England Office: 2 Old Garden House, The Lanterns, Bridge Lane, London SW 11 3AD. Telephone: (011-44-71) 223-2765. Fax: (011-44-71) 350-0156.
Newport News Office: Harbor Bank Center, Suite 210, One Old Oyster Point Road, 23602-7119. Telephone: 757-249-5100. Fax: 757-249-5109.
Northern Virginia Office: 8270 Greensboro Drive, Suite 700, McLean, Virginia, 22102. Telephone: 703-760-5200. Fax: 804-783-6568. Fax within area: 703-748-0244.
Virginia Beach Office: One Columbus Center, Suite 900, 23462-6762. Telephone: 757-499-8800. Fax: 757-473-0395.
Detroit, Michigan Office: 11th Floor Buhl Building, 535 Griswold Street, 48226-3681. Telephone: 313-962-0643. Fax: 313-962-0688.
Ann Arbor, Michigan Office: 300 North Fifth Avenue, Suite 230, 48104. Telephone: 734-213-2700. Fax: 734-213-6832.
Bloomfield Hills, Michigan Office: 33 Bloomfield Hills Parkway, Suite 100, 48304. Telephone: 248-642-4345. Fax: 248-642-2005.
See Professional Biographies, WASHINGTON, DISTRICT OF COLUMBIA

Williams, Peter C.
(See Alexandria, Virginia)

Williams-Stander, Manley '64 '93 C.813 B.A. L.309 J.D.
(adm. in NY; not adm. in DC) 2445 M st., N.W.
Williamson, Brandi M. '69 '00 C.1151 B.S. L.575 J.D.
(adm. in NC; not adm. in DC) 2099 Pennsylvania Avenue, N.W., Suite 100
Williamson, David M. (Max) ....'65 '97 C.976 B.A. L.1194 J.D. [🄰 Beveridge&D.]
*PRACTICE AREAS: Environmental Compliance; Environmental Litigation; Environmental Land Use and Transportation Planning; Appellate Practice.
Williamson, Donald T. ....'50 '78 C.299 B.A. L.188 J.D. Amer. Univ.

Williamson, E. Marcellus ....'62 '89 C.821 B.A. L.569 J.D. [Latham&W.]
*PRACTICE AREAS: Antitrust; Civil Litigation; EU Competition.
Williamson, Edwin D., (AV) '39 '65
C.797 B.A. L.569 J.D. [Sullivan&C.] (⊙New York, NY)
Williamson, J. Paul, (AV) '48 '73
C.679 B.S.A.E. L.339 J.D. [Howrey S.A.&W.] (See Pat. Sect.)
*PRACTICE AREAS: Trademarks; International Trademarks; Trademark Litigation; Trademark Prosecution; Trademark Protection.
Williamson, Jarrell E. '71 '00 C&L.846 B.A., J.D.
(adm. in TX; not adm. in DC) [A Reed S.]
*PRACTICE AREAS: Government Relations.
Williamson, Jeffrey '74 '00 C.276 B.A. L.477 J.D.
(adm. in FL; not adm. in DC) [A Kirkland&E.]
*PRACTICE AREAS: Energy Law.
Williamson, John H. ....'63 '90 C.674 A.B. L.846 J.D. [Morgan,L.&B.]
Williamson, Mark A. '62 '90
C.223 B.S.M.E. L.276 J.D. [Fitzpatrick,C.H.&S.] (See Pat. Sect.)
Williamson, Richard F., (AV) ....'50 '75 C&L.893 B.A., J.D. [Winston&S.]
*PRACTICE AREAS: Commercial Real Estate; Corporate Finance.
Williamson, Robin L. '73 '99 C.902 B.A. L.327 J.D.
(adm. in VA; not adm. in DC) [A Wasserman,M.&C.]
*PRACTICE AREAS: Immigration and Naturalization.
Williamson, Thomas F., (AV) ....'40 '69 C.976 B.A. L.273 J.D. [Morgan,L.&B.]
Williamson, Thomas S., Jr., (AV) ....'46 '75 C.309 B.A. L.1066 J.D. [Covington&B.]
Willing, Joy Marzilli ....'64 '97 C.276 B.S. L.30 J.D. [A Sullivan&C.]
Willinghan, George A., III '65 '97 C.301 B.S. L.276 J.D.
(adm. in VA; not adm. in DC; See Pat. Sect.) [A Pennie&E.]
*PRACTICE AREAS: Intellectual Property; Patent Prosecution; Patent Litigation.
Willis, F. Michael ....'64 '98 C.945 B.A. L.276 J.D. [A Hobbs,S.D.&W.]
Willis, Kerri M. '70 '99 C.679 B.A. L.276 J.D.
(adm. in CT; not adm. in DC) [A Baker&D.]
*PRACTICE AREAS: Financial Services.
Willis, Larry I. ....'67 '96 C.352 B.A. [A Weil,G.&M.]
*PRACTICE AREAS: Public Policy; Transportation; Communications Law; Technology Law; E-Commerce.
Willis, Mark S. ....'60 '90 C.101 B.A. L.990 J.D. [Cohen,M.H.&T.]
*PRACTICE AREAS: Securities Litigation; Securities Fraud Class Actions; Civil Litigation.
Willis, Robert M. ....'43 '72 C&L.329 B.A., J.D. 2121 "K" St., N.W., Suite 700
Willis, Stacey A. ....'71 '99 C.36 B.S. L.475 J.D. 10 G St.
Willis, Thomas Edward, II '72 '97 C.893 B.A. L.629 J.D.
(adm. in VA; not adm. in DC) [A Baker&M.]
*PRACTICE AREAS: Litigation; Tax Planning and Advice (Corporate and International).

Willkie Farr & Gallagher, (AV) BR
Three Lafayette Centre, 1155 21st Street, N.W., 20036-3384 ⊙
Telephone: 202-328-8000 Fax: 202-887-8979
Resident Members: William H. Barringer; Stephen R. Bell; Sue D. Blumenfeld; Francis M. Buono; Kevin B. Clark; Christopher A. Dunn; James P. Durling; Michael H. Hammer; Thomas Jones; David P. Murray; Kenneth J. Pierce; Daniel L. Porter; Philip L. Verveer; Theodore C. Whitehouse. Resident Counsel: Russell L. Smith. Retired Counsel: Brian Conboy; Noel Hemmendinger. Resident Associates: James M. Assey, Jr.; Miriam A. Bishop; Randy Branitsky; A. Renée Callahan; Lucy G. Carlson; Kasey Chappelle (Not admitted in DC); Carolyn W. Conkling; Gregory K. Conway; Joseph G. Davis; David M. Don; Demetrios Eleftheriou; Julia K. Eppard; Jonathan A. Friedman; Jeneba Jalloh Ghatt; Kurt Hague (Not admitted in DC); D. Gunnar Halley; Michael G. Jones; Sophie J. Keefer; Angie W. Kronenberg; Robert L. LaFrankie; Jennifer D. McCarthy; Kelly N. McCollian (Not admitted in DC); John L. McGrew; Kevin M. Miller; Matthew R. Nicely; Carrie Lee Owens; Stephen C. Robertson; Gabriel R. Sanz-Rexach; Christi Shewman; Pamela S. Strauss; Raymond F. Sullivan, Jr.; Andrew E. Thomas; Sean M. Thornton; Karl von Schriltz; Richard F. Waddington; Ryan G. Wallach (Not admitted in DC); Teresa S. Werner (Not admitted in DC).
General Practice.
New York, N.Y. Office: Willkie Farr & Gallagher, The Equitable Center, 787 Seventh Avenue, 10019-6099. Telephone: 212-728-8000. Fax: 212-728-8111.
Washington, D.C. Office: Willkie Farr & Gallagher, Three Lafayette Centre, 1155 21st Street, N.W., 20036-3384. Telephone: 202-328-8000. Fax: 202-887-8979; 202-331-8187.
Paris, France Office: Willkie Farr & Gallagher, 21-23 rue de la Ville l'Evêque, 75008. Telephone: 011-33-1-53-43-45-00. Fax: 011-33-1-40-06-96-06.
London, England Office: Willkie Farr & Gallagher, 35 Wilson Street, EC2M 2SJ. Telephone: 011-44-171-696-9060. Fax: 011-44-171-417-9191.
Frankfurt, Germany Office: Willkie Farr & Gallagher, Senckenberganlage 16, D-60325, Frankfurt am Main. Telephone: +49 69 79302 0. Fax: +49 69 79302 222.
Milan, Italy Office: Studio Legale Delfino & Associati - Willkie Farr & Gallagher, Via Michele Barozzi, 2, 20122. Telephone: 001 39 02 76363 1. Fax: 011 39 02 76363 636.
Rome, Italy Office: Studio Legale Delfino & Associati - Willkie Farr & Gallagher, Via di Ripetta, 142, 00186. Telephone: +39 06 68 63 64 03. Fax: +39 06 68 63 63 63.

See Professional Biographies, WASHINGTON, DISTRICT OF COLUMBIA

Willmore, Robert L., (AV) ....'55 '81 C.453 B.S. L.976 J.D. [Crowell&M.]
*PRACTICE AREAS: Insurance Coverage Law; Products Liability Law; Toxic Torts.
Willmore, Steven P. '66 '00 C.886 B.S.E.E. L.945 J.D.
(adm. in NY; not adm. in DC) [A Hogan&H.]
*PRACTICE AREAS: Intellectual Property.
Willmott, Jonathan P. ....'65 '92 C.1044 B.A. L.1009 J.D. 601 Indiana Ave. NW, Ste. 601
Willner, Keith J., (AV) ....'59 '84 C&L.893 B.A., J.D. [Mayer,B.&P.]
Willner, Kenneth M. ....'62 '87 C&L.893 B.A., J.D. [Paul,H.J.&W.]
*PRACTICE AREAS: Employment Law and Litigation; Employment Discrimination; Labor Law; Wrongful Discharge; Discrimination.
Willott, Christopher '70 '00 C.118 B.A. L.276 J.D.
(adm. in NY; not adm. in DC) [A Clifford C.R.&W.]
*PRACTICE AREAS: Project Finance.
Willoughby, Bruce L. ....'63 '91 C.1288 B.A. L.1339 J.D. [A Robinson&G.]
Wills, Susan E. ....'48 '78 C&L.472 B.A., J.D. Natl. Conference of Catholic Bishops
Wilmarth, Arthur E., Jr., (AV) '51 '75 C.976 B.A. L.309 J.D.
Assoc. Prof. of Law, Geo. Washington Univ Law School (⊙Lancaster, PA)
Wilmer, John W., Jr. ....'48 '75 C.674 A.B. L.276 J.D. [Vorys,S.S.&P.]
*PRACTICE AREAS: Federal Civil Litigation; Environmental Law; Appellate Practice; Occupational Safety and Health Law.

Wilmer, Cutler & Pickering, (AV) BR
2445 M Street, N.W., 20037-1420 ⊙
Telephone: 202-663-6000 Fax: 202-663-6363
Email: Law@Wilmer.Com URL: http://www.wilmer.com
Richard H. Wilmer (1892-1976); J. Roger Wollenberg (1919-2000). Partners: Louis R. Cohen; Michael R. Klein; F. David Lake, Jr.; Jeffrey M. Lang; Paul J. Mode, Jr.; Stephen F. Black; C. Boyden Gray; Ronald J. Greene; Charles S. Stark (Resident, European Office, Brussels, Belgium); Gary D. Wilson; C. Loring Jetton, Jr.; William T. Lake; Jeffrey A. Manley; C. Thomas Hicks, III (Resident, Northern Virginia Office); Neil J. King; Dieter G. F. Lange (Not admitted in DC; Resident, European Office, London, England); Charles S. Levy; Robert B. McCaw (Resident, New York Office); A. Douglas Melamed; Richard W. Cass; Bruce H. Rabinovitz; A. Stephen Hut, Jr.; David R. Johnson; Mark Pollak (Not admitted in DC; Resident, Baltimore, Maryland Office); John Rounsaville, Jr.; Roger M. Witten; Robert C. Cassidy, Jr.; John D. Greenwald (Not admitted in DC); John H. Harwood II; Mary Carolyn Cox; Christopher R. Lipsett (Resident, New York Office); William J. Perlstein; Marianne K. Smythe; Andrew B. Weissman; Ambassador Charlene Barshefsky (Senior International Partner); Lynn Bregman; William R. McLucas; Stephen P. Doyle; William R. Richardson, Jr.; Kurt L. Schmoke (Resident, Baltimore, Maryland Office); Harry J. Weiss; Brandon Becker; Russell J. Bruemmer; Bruce E. Coolidge; Juanita A. Crowley; John Payton; Todd D. Stern; Seth P. Waxman; William J. Wilkins; Andrew N. Vollmer; Thomas W. White (Resident, Northern Virginia Office); Matthias

(This Listing Continued)

Wilmer, Cutler & Pickering (Continued)

Wissmann (Not admitted in DC; Resident, European Office, Berlin, Germany); Bruce M. Berman; Thomas F. Connell; Charles E. Davidow; Terrill A. Hyde; Duane D. Morse (Resident, Northern Virginia Office); Dr. Andreas Weitbrecht (Not admitted in DC) (Resident, European Offices, Berlin, Germany and Brussels, Belgium); Robert B. Bell; Kathryn C. Brown (Not admitted in DC); John H. Ratliff (Not admitted in DC; Resident, European Office, Brussels, Belgium); Daniel H. Squire; Charles D. Toy (Not admitted in DC); Peter K. Vigeland (Resident, New York Office); Gary B. Born (European Office, London, England); Veronica G. Kayne; David W. Ogden; John B. Watkins V; Philip D. Anker; Joseph K. Brenner; Carol Clayton; Meredith B. Cross; Thomas P. Olson; Patrick J. Carome; Andrew D. Kaizer (Not admitted in DC; Resident, New York Office); Robert T. Novick; Stephen W. Preston; Dr. Roland Steinmeyer (Not admitted in DC) (Resident, European Office, Berlin, Germany); William A. Wilson III (Not admitted in DC); Sheila C. Cheston; David P. Donovan (Resident, Northern Virginia Office); Paul A. von Hehn (Not admitted in DC; Resident, European Office, Brussels, Belgium); Marc C. Hansen (Not admitted in DC; Resident, European Offices, Brussels, Belgium and London, England); Andrew K. Parnell (Resident, European Office, London, England); John W. Ryan; Howard M. Shapiro; Roger W. Yoerges; Mark D. Cahn; Eric R. Markus; Randolph D. Moss; Jorge E. Alers; J. Beckwith Burr; Mark A. Dewire; Paul A. Engelmayer (Resident, New York Office); Simon Firth (Not admitted in the United States); Eric J. Mogilnicki; Robert B. Stack; Lewis J. Liman (Not admitted in DC; Resident, New York Office); R. Scott Kilgore (Also at Northern Virginia Office); Thomas E.D. Millspaugh (Not admitted in DC; Resident, Baltimore, Maryland Office); Yoon-Young Lee; James R. Wrathall; Gail C. Bernstein; Steven F. Cherry (Resident, Northern Virginia Office); Susan P. Crawford; Robert F. Hoyt; Dr. Natalie Lübben (Not admitted in DC) (Resident, European Office, Berlin, Germany); Lynn R. Charytan; Michael R. Holter (Not admitted in DC; Resident, European Office, London, England); Thomas Mueller (Also at European Office, Brussels, Belgium); Jonathan Nuechterlein; Catherine Kane Ronis; Christian L. Duvernoy (Resident, European Office, Brussels, Belgium); James W. Lowe; Ali M. Stoeppelwerth; James E. Anderson; Gregorio B. Cater (Also Resident, European Office, London, England); Erik H. Corwin; Denise Esposito; Andrew N. Goldman (Resident, New York Office); Soo J. Yim; Brigida Benitez; Stuart F. Delery; Jennifer M. Drogula; Craig T. Goldblatt; John J. Kallaugher (Not admitted in DC; Resident, European Office, London, England); Glynn D. Key; Satish M. Kini; Mark S. Shelton. Senior Counsel: Lloyd N. Cutler; John H. Pickering. Counsel: Lester Nurick; Leonard M. Shambon; Victoria E. Schonfeld (Resident, New York Office); William J. Flanagan; Carol H. Fishman; Joseph E. Killory, Jr. (Resident, Northern Virginia Office); Christopher J. Herrling; Roger J. Patterson; Daniel B. Phythyon; Matthew A. Chambers; Enrique Gomez-Pinzon; Joanne F. Catanese (Not admitted in DC; Resident, Baltimore, Maryland Office); Robert G. Bagnall; Jean-Michel Coumes (Not admitted in DC; Resident, European Office, Brussels, Belgium); Brent J. Gurney; James H. Mann (Resident, New York Office); Nancy L. Manzer; Jutta von Falkenhausen (Not admitted in DC; Resident, European Office, Berlin, Germany); Leon B. Greenfield; Ronald I. Meltzer; Martin Seyfarth (Not admitted in DC; Resident, European Office, Berlin, Germany); Eric J. Mahr (Resident, European Office, Brussels, Belgium); Jeffrey E. McFadden; Brian J. Menkes; Nelson R. Oliveira (Not admitted in DC); Jill Reynolds Seidman (Resident, Baltimore, Maryland Office); David R. Lurie (Not admitted in DC; Resident, New York Office); Bruce H. Newman (Resident, New York Office); Cathleen P. Peterson; William E. White (Not admitted in DC); Cristina Mendoza Bourelly; Steven P. Finizio (Resident, European Office, London, England); Fraser L. Hunter, Jr. (Resident, New York Office); Karen M. Mincavage; Jean Paul M. Poitras (Not admitted in DC; Resident, European Office, Brussels, Belgium); Jeffrey A. Roth (Resident, New York Office); Beth A. Stekler; Manley Williams; J. Barclay Collins, III; Douglas J. Davison; Jeffrey A. Roth (Resident, New York Office); Colleen Doherty-Minicozzi; Sara E. Emley; Augusto Repetto; Jolie F. Zimmerman; Van W. Ellis; Gregory J. Ewald (Resident, Northern Virginia Office); Jonathan J. Frankel; Samir Jain; Andrew J. Lorentz (Resident, European Office, Brussels, Belgium); Ronald C. Machen; Gordon Pearson; Janet Durholz Ridge; Erika L. Robinson; Sven B. Völcker (Not admitted in DC; Resident, European Office, Brussels, Belgium); Adam M. Abensohn (Resident, New York Office); Franca Harris Gutierrez; Kevin P. McEnery; Joseph R. Profaizer; Catherine M. Saadeh; Jeremy S. Simon; Erika K. Singer; Joern Becker (Resident European Office, Berlin, Germany). Of Counsel: James S. Campbell; Michael L. Burack; Joel Rosenbloom; Daniel K. Mayers; Stephen H. Sachs; Dennis M. Flannery. Associates: Cathy Haesang Ahn (Not admitted in DC); Maya Alexandri; Fiona Huang Anderson; Ylenia Ariano (Resident, Brussels, Belgium Office); Timothy B. Atkins; Stephanie Avakian (Resident, New York Office); David J. Aveni; Jeffrey D. Ayer; R. Kevin Bailey; Carol J. Banta; Cynthia Baraban; Ursula C. Bass; Lauralyn Elizabeth Beattie; Beth Biedronski; Mark Bieter (Not admitted in DC); Laura Blood; Christopher P. Bowers; David K. Bowsher; Joshua T. Brady; Clifton L. Brinson; Jérôme Broche (Not admitted in DC; Resident, European Office, Brussels, Belgium); Sam Broderick-Sokol; Reed Michael Brodsky; Brant K. Brown; Christopher T. Bruneau; Patricia M. Byrne; Antonio Capobianco (Resident, European Office, Brussels, Belgium); Megan L. Carlyle; Kevin M. Carroll; Linda Bray Chanow; Steve Charnovitz; Anderson Chen; Mark Chenoweth (Not admitted in DC); Gregory Scott Chernack; Cynthia H. Clark; C. Russell Clause; Melanie D. Coates; Linda Coffin; Giles T. Cohen; Paul W. Connell; Bryan N. Corbett; Lowry A. Crook; Andrew J. Currie; Christopher R.L. Davies; Melissa Hall Davis (Not admitted in DC); Joshua C. Delaney; Ricardo R. Delfin; Yolanda M. Demianczuk; Elizabeth K. Derbes; Arlo Devlin-Brown (Not admitted in DC); Kyle De Young; Flavia Distefano (Not admitted in DC; Resident, European Office, Brussels, Belgium); Allison Drimmer (Not admitted in DC); Daniel F. Duchovny; N. Jeremi Duru; Paul R. Eckert; Knight Elsberry; Lara A. Englund; Gail Susan Ennis; Dr. Björn Fasterling (Resident, European Office, Berlin, Germany); Laura E. Fein; Deborah M. Field; Luis A. Feldstein-Soto; Lynn M. Fischer; John C. Ford (Not admitted in DC); Susan D. Franck; James W. Frost; Ellen K. Fulton; Daniel M. Gallagher, Jr.; Eric S. Galler; Paramita Ghosh; Joshua S. Goldwert; Gayton P. Gomez (Not admitted in DC; Resident, New York Office); Michael E. Gordon; Terry Gray; Maura E. Griffin; Jennifer E. Grishkin; Peter Grundberg (Resident, European Office, London, England); Gerd Axel Gutermuth (Not admitted in DC; Resident, European Office, Brussels, Belgium); Patrick Gutierrez; Cora Tung Han; Russell P. Hanser; Anne Harkavy; Wilhelm M.A. Hartung (Not admitted in DC; Resident, European Office, London, England; also at Berlin, Germany Office); David Heffernan; Stephen R. Heifetz; Jan C. Heithecker (Resident, European Office, Brussels, Belgium); Andrew M. Herman; Rachael Hill; Darrin Hostetler; Eric J. Hougen; Sabrina Houlton; Matthew Huggins; Steven E. Hugie; Kate Hutchins (Not admitted in DC); Jeffrey S. Hydrick; T. Anthony "Todd" Jaye; Heather A. Jones; Timothy Kang; Dr. Jörg Karenfort (Not admitted in DC) (Resident, European Office, Berlin, Germany); Manijeh Nan Kargahi; Jason Kearns; Rachael D. Kent (Resident, European Office, London, England); Gregory S. Knell; Natalie H. Kossak (Also at Northern Virginia Office); Mary E. Kostel; Laura B. Kotanchik; Heidi E. Kranz; David M. Kreeger; Amy T. Kreiger; Sophie Jane Lamb (Not admitted in DC; Resident, European Office, London, England); Hite Colby Lane; J. Welby Leaman; Christian Leathley (Resident, European Office, London, England); Peter M. Lee; Michael Leffel; Jeffrey A. Lehtman; Robin A. Lenhardt; Jack Alan Levy; Natan J. Leyva; Scott Llewellyn; David A. Luigs; David Lynn (Resident, Baltimore, Maryland Office); Cherie L. Macauley; Jeanine L. Magurshak; Ashok Mannava (Not admitted in DC); Terry A. Maroney (Not admitted in DC); Moris Mashali (Resident, European Office, London, England); Jonathan M. Mastrangelo; Maren Lee Matal; Ann Perry Mayo; Sean P. McCann; Jeremy K. McKown; Christopher McWhinney; Christopher J. Meade (Not admitted in DC); Wendy Meharg (Not admitted in DC; Resident, European Office, London, England); David S. Mendel; Wendy Jane Miles (Not admitted in DC; Resident, European Office, London, England); Joel Millar; Anja Miller (Not admitted in DC); Joseph C. Minko (Resident, Baltimore, Maryland Office); Elizabeth L. Mitchell (Not admitted in DC); David S. Molot; Sophie Moonen (Not admitted in DC; Resident, European Office, Brussels, Belgium); Mark S. Morelli (Not admitted in DC); Amber Morrell; Trevor Morrison (Not admitted in DC); Peirce R. Moser (Not admitted in DC); Peter J. Mucchetti; Sean Mulcahy (Resident, Baltimore, Maryland Office); John C. Nagel; Joel A. Nichols; Stephanie Nicolas; William R. Nifong; Justin Ochs (Not admitted in DC); Jennie O'Flanagan; Stefan Ohlhoff (Not admitted in DC); Dennis W. O'Neill (Resident, Northern Virginia Office); James Francis O'Reilly; Jonathan E. Paikin; IJay Palansky; E. Stuart Parker; Kimberly Parker; A. Krisan Patterson (Not admitted in DC); Nancy E. Furman Paul; Christian C.D. Petersen; John V. H. Pierce (Not admitted in DC; Resident, New York Office); Michael Plotnick; Gwendolyn K. Ponder; Jay V. Prabhu; Matthew P. Previn (Resident, New York Office); Lori Hamilton Price; Eloise Quarles; Martin F. Ramirez; David Alfred John Ramm (Resident, European Office, London, England); Arun Rattan (Not admitted in DC; Resident, European Office, Brussels, Belgium); Matthew McDavid Reed (Resident, Baltimore, Maryland Office); Neil Michael Richards (Not admitted in DC); Julie M. Riewe; Jerome J. Roche; Jennifer M. Rockoff; Josh L. Roland; John-Alex Romano; Jorian Rose (Resident, New York Office); Steven Rosen; Charles Colin Rushing; Peter B. Rutledge (Not admitted in DC); Michael Ryan; Robert-Paul Sagner (Not admitted in DC); Samuel J. Salario, Jr.; Joseph J. Samarias; Alec J. Scheiner (Resident, New York Office); Krisanne Schlachter; Hartmut Schneider (Resident, European Office, Berlin, Germany); Ruediger Schuett (Resident, European Office, Berlin, Germany); Adam J. Schwartz; Franz T. Schwarz (Not admitted in DC; Resident, European Office, London, England); Rachel Shachter (Not admitted in DC); Omar Shah (Resident, European Office, London, England); Thomas E. Sharp; Scott A. Shepard; James A. Shepherd (Not admitted in DC); Jonathan H. Siegelbaum (Not admitted in DC); Christopher P. Simkins; Omari S. Simmons (Not admitted in DC); Polly B. Smothergill; O. Carter Snead, IV; Hyung Sohn; Joshua R. Stebbins; Todd R. Steggerda; Natacha D. Steimer; Leslie Anne Sturtevant; Amanda L. Tantum (Not admitted in DC); David Taylor (Resident, European Office, London, England); Nicole Telecki; Paul M. Tiao; John A. Trenor; John A. Valentine; Darcy Lynn Van Kirk; Esmée Gräfin Von Der Groeben (Not admitted in DC; Resident, European Office, Berlin, Germany); Dierdre von

(This Listing Continued)

Wilmer, Cutler & Pickering (Continued)

Dornum (Resident, New York Office); Philipp Freiherr Von Hoyenberg (Not admitted in DC; Resident European Office, Berlin, Germany); Kerrie A. Walsh (Not admitted in DC; Resident, European Office, London, England); Nicole R. Walter; Deirdre Waters (Not admitted in DC; Resident, European Office, Brussels, Belgium); Joshua D. Weinberg; Todd E. Wiench; Christopher A. Wilber; Roger S. Wise; Isha Rauchle Youhas (Not admitted in DC); Tamara Zieschang (Resident, European Office, Berlin, Germany); Dörte Zimmermann (Not admitted in DC; Resident, European Office, Berlin, Germany); Todd Zubler.

Administrative Law, Alternative Dispute Resolution, Antitrust and Trade Regulation, Appellate Practice, Aviation and Aerospace, Bankruptcy, Banks and Banking, Broker-Dealer Regulation, Business Law, Civil Practice, Communications and Media, Computer and Software, Constitutional Law, Consumer Law, Corporate Investigations, Corporate Law, Criminal Law, Election, Campaign and Political Law, Electronic Commerce, Employee Benefits, Energy, Environmental Law, EU Competition, Finance, Financial Institutions Law, General Practice, Government Contracts, Government, Insurance, Intellectual Property, International Dispute Resolution, International Trade, International Law, Investments, Latin America Trade, Litigation, Mass Media Law, Mergers, Acquisitions and Divestitures, Natural Resources, Occupational Safety and Health, Products Liability, Regulatory Law, RICO, Securities, Taxation, Telecommunications Law, Toxic Torts, Transportation and White Collar Crime.

Baltimore, Maryland Office: 100 Light Street, 21202. Telephone: 410-986-2800. Fax: 410-986-2828.
New York, New York Office: 520 Madison Avenue, 10022. Telephone: 212-230-8800. Fax: 212-230-8888.
Northern Virginia Office: 1600 Tysons Boulevard, 10th Floor, Tysons Corner, VA 22102. Telephone: 703-251-9700. Fax: 703-251-9797.
European Offices:
4 Carlton Gardens, London, SW1Y 5AA, England. Telephone: +44 (20) 7872 1000. Fax: +44 (20) 7839 3537.
Rue de la Loi 15#, B-1040 Brussels, Belgium. Telephone: +32 (2) 285 49 00. Fax: +32 (2) 285 49 49.
Friedrichstrasse 95, D-10117 Berlin, Germany. Telephone: +49 (30) 20 22 64 00. Fax: +49 (30) 20 22 65 00.

See Professional Biographies, WASHINGTON, DISTRICT OF COLUMBIA

Wilmot, David W., (AV) .... '44 '73 C.45 B.A. L.276 J.D. [Harmon,W.&B.]
*PRACTICE AREAS: Lobbying; General Corporate Law.
Wilmoth, Mary Jane .... '69 '94 C.1209 B.A. L.1218 J.D. [🄰 Kohn,K.&C.]
Wilner, John R., (AV) .... '— '66 C.659 B.S. L.276 LL.B. [Bryan C.]
*PRACTICE AREAS: Communications Law.
Wilner, Morton H., (AV) '08 '33 C.659 B.S.Ec. L.276 LL.B.
2701 Chesapeake St., N.W.‡
Wilner, Thomas B., (AV) .... '44 '69 C.976 B.A. L.659 LL.B. [Shearman&S.]
Wilson, Adam Daley .... '71 '99 C.659 B.A. L.813 J.D. [🄰 Crowell&M.]
Wilson, Alison B. '74 '00 C.893 B.A. L.273 J.D.
(adm. in VA; not adm. in DC) [🄰 Sonnenschein N.&R.]
Wilson, Anita Rutkowski .... '65 '91 C.945 B.S. L.893 J.D. [Vinson&E.]
*PRACTICE AREAS: Administrative Law; Federal Energy Regulation.
Wilson, Benjamin F. .... '51 '76 C.197 A.B. L.309 J.D. [Beveridge&D.]
*PRACTICE AREAS: Commercial Litigation; Environmental Law.
Wilson, Bruce Sandness .... '59 '88 C&L.893 B.A., J.D. [Covington&B.]
Wilson, D. Edward, Jr. .... '51 '76 C.893 B.A. L.276 J.D. [Shook,H.&B.]
*PRACTICE AREAS: U.S. and International Regulatory and Corporate.
Wilson, David A. .... '57 '88 C.309 A.B. L.276 J.D. [Hale&D.]
*PRACTICE AREAS: Litigation.
Wilson, David G., (AV) .... '41 '66 C.674 A.B. L.309 LL.B. [🄲 O'Neill,A.&C.]
Wilson, David I., (AV) .... '41 '68 C.801 B.A. L.273 J.D. [Silverberg,G.&B.]
*PRACTICE AREAS: Intellectual Property Law; Customs and Trade; Antitrust Law.
Wilson, Diane K. .... '44 '81 C.813 A.B. L.273 J.D. 4636 30th St., N.W.‡
Wilson, Donald L. .... '33 '94 C.30 B.A. L.1280 J.D. 1522 K St., N.W.
Wilson, Donna L. .... '65 '96 C.273 B.A. L.893 J.D. [🄰 Skadden,A.S.M.&F.]
Wilson, Dorothy Roth ...... '15 '39 C.477 B.A. L.273 LL.B. 1000 Connecticut Ave., N.W.
Wilson, Douglas C. .... '61 '87 C.L.787 B.A. L.30 J.D. 335 9th St., SE
Wilson, E. Reynolds .... '72 '98 C&L.893 B.A., J.D. [🄰 Kalijarvi,C.&N.]
*PRACTICE AREAS: Employment Law; Federal Employment Law; Employment Discrimination.
Wilson, Edward C., Jr. .... '65 '90 C.198 A.B. L.893 J.D. [Hogan&H.]
*PRACTICE AREAS: Drug and Medical Device Regulation.
Wilson, Edward Reynolds '72 '98 C&L.893 B.A., J.D.
(adm. in VA; not adm. in DC) 1730 K St., N.W.
Wilson, Gary D., (AV) .... '43 '70 C&L.813 B.A., LL.B. [Wilmer,C.&P.]
*PRACTICE AREAS: Civil Practice; Patents; Antitrust and Trade Regulation; Natural Resources.
Wilson, Gordon '34 '62 C.674 B.A. L.477 LL.B.
(adm. in IL; not adm. in DC) V.P., First Amer. Bk., N.A.
Wilson, Gordon C. .... '68 '96 C.945 B.A. L.893 J.D. [🄰 Hogan&H.]
*PRACTICE AREAS: Secured Finance; International Finance; Asset Sales.
Wilson, Heather M. .... '70 '98 C.966 B.A. L.1329 J.D. [🄰 Kelley D.&W.]
*PRACTICE AREAS: Telecommunications; International Telecommunications.
Wilson, J. Randolph .... '22 '50 C.886 B.S. L.178 LL.B. [🄲 Covington&B.]
Wilson, James I. .... '42 '69 C&L.472 B.A., J.D. Asst. Gen. Coun., Smithsonian Institution
Wilson, James M. '71 '99 C.902 B.A. L.893 J.D.
(adm. in SC; not adm. in DC) [🄰 Vinson&E.]
Wilson, James T. '68 '99 C.645 B.S.E.E. L.904 J.D.
(adm. in VA; not adm. in DC; See Pat. Sect.) [🄰 Finnegan,H.F.G.&D.]
*PRACTICE AREAS: Patent Prosecution; Patent Litigation; Patent Infringement; Intellectual Property Portfolio Management.
Wilson, Joseph D., III .... '68 '99 C&L.276 B.S.F.S., J.D. [🄰 Kelley D.&W.]
*PRACTICE AREAS: Litigation.
Wilson, Laura M. .... '59 '87 C&L.966 B.A., J.D. [🄲 White&C.]
Wilson, L.H. (Leonard H.) '50 '76 C.499 B.S. L.986 J.D.
(adm. in MO; not adm. in DC) Assoc. Gen. Coun., American Bankers Association
*RESPONSIBILITIES: Uniform Commercial Code; Electronic Banking; Payment Systems Law.
Wilson, Liane N. .... '71 '99 C.262 B.A. L.1040 J.D. [🄰 Latham&W.]
*PRACTICE AREAS: Corporate Practice; Mergers and Acquisitions; Securities.
Wilson, Linda J. .... '61 '86 C&L.896 B.A., J.D. 2300 N St., N.W.
Wilson, Mark F. .... '61 '89 C.262 B.A. L.128 J.D. 501 3rd St., N.W.
Wilson, Mark V. '63 '93 C.1215 B.A. L.896 J.D.
(adm. in NY; not adm. in DC) [🄰 Collier S.S.]
*PRACTICE AREAS: Corporate; Securities.
Wilson, Mary Larkin .... '54 '81 C.881 B.A. L.1162 J.D. 1812 Kenyon St., N.W.
Wilson, Michael J. .... '64 '89 C.473 B.A. L.128 J.D. [🄰 Zevnik H.]
*PRACTICE AREAS: Litigation; Insurance; Environmental.
Wilson, Nancy B. '71 '98 C.276 B.A. L.30 J.D.
(adm. in NY; not adm. in DC) [🄰 Hewes,G.L.&D.]
Wilson, Paul A. J. .... '49 '83 C.454 B.A. L.893 J.D. [Patton B.]
Wilson, Paul J. .... '61 '98 C.474 B.S.E.E. L.64 J.D. [🄰 Sughrue M.] (See Pat. Sect.)
*PRACTICE AREAS: Electronics; Computers and Software; Intellectual Property.
Wilson, R. Merinda .... '52 '76 C.659 B.A. L.309 J.D. [Sidley A.B.&W.]
Wilson, Rachel H. '71 '98 C.893 J.D. L.302 B.A.
(adm. in CT; not adm. in DC) [🄰 Pepper H.]
Wilson, Ramsey J. .... '72 '98 C.477 B.B.A. L.276 J.D. [🄰 Howrey S.A.&W.]
*PRACTICE AREAS: Antitrust; Competition.
Wilson, Reid M. '70 '97 C.790 B.A. L.273 J.D.
(adm. in VA; not adm. in DC) [Vorys,S.S.&P.]
*PRACTICE AREAS: Trademarks; Licensing; Unfair Competition.

Wilson, Richard J. '43 '72 C.210 B.A. L.339 J.D.
Prof., The American Univ., Wash. Coll. of Law
Wilson, Robert Dale .... '52 '78 C&L.790 B.A., J.D. 1155 15th St., N.W.
Wilson, S. Bruce, (AV) .... '48 '87 C.813 B.A. L.273 J.D. [Akin,G.S.H.&F.]
*PRACTICE AREAS: International Trade; Public Law and Policy.
Wilson, Thomas E., (AV) .... '42 '68 C&L.276 A.B., J.D. [🄲 Berliner,C.&R.]
*PRACTICE AREAS: Litigation; White Collar Criminal.
Wilson, Thomas W., (AV) .... '11 '38 C.446 B.S. L.276 J.D. 1255 23rd St., N.W.
Wilson, Walter A. I., (AV) .... '43 '68 C.478 A.B. L.904 J.D. [Bell,B.&L.]
*PRACTICE AREAS: Alternative Dispute Resolution; Computers and Software; Government Contracts; Construction Law; Civil Litigation.
Wilson, Whitney .... '69 '94 C.951 B.A. L.569 J.D. [🄰 Bryan C.]
*PRACTICE AREAS: Patent, Trademark and Copyright Law; Litigation.
Wilson, William A., III '56 '83 C.976 B.A. L.569 J.D.
(adm. in CT; not adm. in DC) [Wilmer,C.&P.]
*PRACTICE AREAS: Finance; Corporate Law; International Law; Venture Capital.
Wilson-Bilik, Mary Jane .... '50 '90 C.562 B.A. L.276 J.D. [Sutherland A.&B.]
*PRACTICE AREAS: Investment Company Law; Insurance Products; Mutual Funds; Securities Regulation; Insurance Regulation.

Wilson, Elser, Moskowitz, Edelman & Dicker LLP, (AV)
The Colorado Building, Fifth Floor, 1341 "G" Street, N.W., 20005 ⊙
Telephone: 202-626-7660 Telex: 89453. Facsimile: 202-628-3606
URL: HTTP://WWW.WEMED.COM
Resident Partners: Paul D. Krause; Carol Ann Petren (Not admitted in DC); Robert B. Wallace; Laura Nachowitz Steel.
New York, N.Y., Los Angeles, California, San Diego, California, San Francisco, California, Newark, New Jersey, Philadelphia, Pennsylvania, Baltimore, Maryland, Miami, Florida, Chicago, Illinois, White Plains, New York, Dallas, Texas, Houston, Texas, Albany, New York, Garden City, New York, Boston, Massachusetts, London, England.
Affiliates: Paris, France: HPMBC, Munich, Germany: Bach, Langheid Dallmayr, Cologne, Germany: Bach, Langheid Dallmayr, Frankfurt/Main, Germany: Bach, Langheid Dallmayr, Berlin, Germany: Bach, Langheid Dallmayr.

See Professional Biographies, WASHINGTON, DISTRICT OF COLUMBIA

Wiltsek, Gena E. '73 '01 C.976 B.A. L.477 J.D.
(adm. in NY; not adm. in DC) [🄰 Bernabei&K.]
*PRACTICE AREAS: Employment Discrimination; Civil Rights; Civil Liberties; Whistleblower Law.
Wiltshire, William M., (AV) .... '62 '88 C.674 A.B. L.893 J.D. [Harris,W.&G.]
*PRACTICE AREAS: Communications; Media Law; Litigation; Commercial Law.
Wiltsie, Ronald J., II .... '58 '89 C&L.893 B.S., J.D. [Hogan&H.]
*PRACTICE AREAS: Civil Litigation.
Wiltsie, Susan Frier .... '62 '89 C.945 B.A. L.896 J.D. [🄲 Hunton&W.]
*PRACTICE AREAS: Labor and Employment.
Wimbish, Robert A. .... '68 '93 C&L.276 B.A., J.D. [🄰 Harkins C.]
*PRACTICE AREAS: Administrative Law; Interstate Commerce; Transportation; Railroads.
Wimmer, Kurt A. .... '59 '87 C.502 B.J. L.823 J.D. [Covington&B.]
Winarsky, Lewis I. .... '47 '72 C.72 B.A. L.930 J.D. Atty., Washington Gas Light Co.
Winburne, Blake H. .... '67 '96 C.846 B.B.A. L.1209 J.D. [🄰 Hunton&W.]
*PRACTICE AREAS: Project Finance; Leasing.
Wincek, Mark D. .... '50 '77 C&L.93 B.A., J.D. [Kilpatrick S.]
*PRACTICE AREAS: Employee Benefits; Executive Compensation.
Windley, David W. .... '37 '77 C.575 A.B. L.904 J.D. 305 H St., N.W.
Windsor, George H., (AV) .... '18 '41 C.67 A.B. L.309 LL.B. [Cobb,H.H.&W.]
Wine, Bradley D. .... '70 '95 C.30 B.A. L.1194 J.D. [🄰 Dickstein S.M.&O.]
*PRACTICE AREAS: Government Contracts Litigation; Regulatory Law.
Wine, L. Mark, (P.C.), (AV) .... '45 '70 C.893 B.A. L.145 J.D. [Kirkland&E.]
*PRACTICE AREAS: Environmental Law and Hazardous Waste Liability and Compliance; Private Environmental Litigation; Air Pollution Regulation and Enforcement; Toxic Substance Regulation; Litigation and Counseling.
Winer, Jonathan M. .... '54 '81 C.976 B.A. L.569 J.D. [🄲 Alston&B.]
*PRACTICE AREAS: Privacy Law; Electronic Commerce; Banking Law; New Media Law; Government Relations.
Winer, Kenneth B., (AV) .... '— '81 C.659 B.S. L.309 J.D. [Foley&L.]
*PRACTICE AREAS: SEC Enforcement; Securities Litigation; Internal Investigations; FCPA Compliance.
Winer, Samuel J. .... '— '74 C.918 B.A. L.94 J.D. [Foley&L.]
*PRACTICE AREAS: Business Law; Broker-Dealer.
Wines, James M. .... '70 '97 C.577 B.A. L.575 J.D. [🄰 Dickstein S.M.&O.]
*PRACTICE AREAS: Securities Litigation; Business Crimes.
Winfield, Susan R. Holmes .... '48 '76 C.659 B.A. L.93 J.D. Asso. J., Supr. Ct. of D.C.
Wing, Michael J. '59 '00 C.174 B.A. L.796 J.D.
(adm. in TX; not adm. in DC) [O'Connor&H.]
*PRACTICE AREAS: Corporate Law; Commercial Transactions; Mergers and Acquisitions; International Business Law; Privatization.
Wingo, Harry M., Jr. .... '66 '99 C.871 B.S. L.976 J.D. [🄰 Skadden,A.S.M.&F.]
Winik, Peter L. .... '— '80 C&L.813 A.B., J.D. [Latham&W.]
*PRACTICE AREAS: Complex and Multi-District Litigation; Class Action Defense; Product Safety; Product Recall; Antidumping.
Winkelman, Scott L. .... '62 '87 C.477 B.A. L.309 J.D. [Crowell&M.]
Winland, Thomas W., (AV) '49 '74
C.608 B.S. L.228 J.D. [Finnegan,H.F.G.&D.] (See Pat. Sect.)
*PRACTICE AREAS: Intellectual Property Litigation; Intellectual Property Arbitration; Intellectual Property Licensing; Proprietary Rights.
Winn, Allan R., (AV) .... '44 '69 C.696 A.B. L.188 J.D. [Ballard S.A.&I.]
*PRACTICE AREAS: Real Estate; Finance Law; Housing and Urban Development Law; Commercial Real Estate; Commercial Real Estate Finance.
Winn, James M., Jr '— '98 C.1059 B.S. L.1356 J.D.
(adm. in VA; not adm. in DC) [🄰 Smith&D.]
Winnik, Joel S., (AV) .... '49 '74 C.966 B.A. L.910 J.D. [Hogan&H.]
*PRACTICE AREAS: Telecommunications Law; International Trade Law.
Winslow, Peter H. .... '50 '75 C.860 B.A. L.930 J.D. [Scribner,H.&T.]
Winstead, David L. .... '47 '87 C.207 B.A. L.128 J.D. [Holland&K.]
*PRACTICE AREAS: Land Use; Municipal Law; Transportation; Public Law; Legislative Practice.

Winstead Sechrest & Minick P.C., (AV)
Suite 1200, 1666 K Street, NW, 20006 ⊙
Telephone: 202-293-8130 Fax: 202-872-1431
URL: http://www.winstead.com
Daniel H. Branch.
General Business Practice: Aviation, Bankruptcy and Reorganization, Cable and Communications, Construction, Corporate, Emerging Business, Eminent Domain, Employee Benefits, Energy, Environmental, Estate Planning, Financial Institutions, Government Relations, Healthcare, Insurance, Intellectual Property, International, Labor and Employment, Legislative Relations, Litigation, Mergers and Acquisitions, Probate, Public Finance, Public Law, Public/Administrative, Real Estate, Securities, Sports and Entertainment, Surety, Taxation, Transportation and Zoning.
Dallas, Texas Office: 5400 Renaissance Tower, 1201 Elm Street. Telephone: 214-745-5400. Telex: 73-0051. Fax: 214-745-5390.
Houston, Texas Office: 2400 Bank One Center, 910 Travis Street. Telephone: 713-650-8400. Telex: 73-0051. Fax: 713-650-2400.
Austin, Texas Office: Suite 800, 100 Congress Avenue. Telephone: 512-474-4330. Telex: 73-0051. Fax: 512-370-2850.
Fort Worth, Texas Office: Suite 1100, 777 Main Street. Telephone: 817-420-8200. Fax: 817-420-8201.
The Woodlands, Texas Office: 10077 Grogan's Mill Road, Suite 475. Telephone: 281-367-2222. Fax: 281-363-0660.

(This Listing Continued)

Winstead Sechrest & Minick P.C. (Continued)

Mexico, D.F., Mexico Office: Winstead y Rivera, S.C., Av. Insurgentes Sur 1685, Piso 13-04, Torre Diamante, Colonia Guadalupe Inn, Delegacion Alvaro Obregon, 01020, Mexico, D.F., Mexico. Telephone: (011-525) 5661-3025. Fax: (011-525) 5661-3033.

See Professional Biographies, WASHINGTON, DISTRICT OF COLUMBIA

Winston, Elizabeth I. .... '73 '97 C.453 S.B. L.893 J.D. [[A] Covington&B.]
Winston, James L., (AV) ....'47 '73 C.659 B.S.E.E. L.309 J.D. [Rubin,W.D.H.&C.]
*PRACTICE AREAS: Communications; Legislative; Public Utility.
Winston, R. Whitney .... '— '99 C.453 S.B. L.1209 J.D. [[A] Fish&R.] (See Pat. Sect.)
*PRACTICE AREAS: Intellectual Property; Litigation.

Winston & Strawn, (AV) [BB]
1400 L Street, N.W., 20005-3502 ⊙
Telephone: 202-371-5700 Telecopier: 202-371-5950
Email: postmaster@winston.com URL: http://www.winston.com
Members of Firm: Norman R. Vander Clute (1932-2001); J. Michael McGarry, III (Resident); Nicholas S. Reynolds (Resident); Dean L. Overman (Resident); Donald K. Dankner (Resident); William J. Madden, Jr. (Resident); John P. Proctor (Resident); Edward F. Gerwin, Jr. (Resident); John R. Keys, Jr. (Resident); Leonard W. Belter (Resident); Thomas M. Buchanan (Resident); Peter N. Hiebert (Resident); Eric L. Hirschhorn (Resident); Frederick J. Killion (Resident); John C. Kirtland (Resident); Michael R. Lemov (Resident); Robert M. Rader (Resident); Mark J. Wetterhahn (Resident); David A. Repka (Resident); John A. Waits, II (Resident); James H. Burnley IV (Resident); Benjamin P. Fishburne, III (Resident); Barry J. Hart (Resident); Charles L. Kinney (Resident); James R. Curtiss (Resident); Robert A. Mangrum (Resident); William G. Miossi; James T. Pitts (Resident); John Albert Whittaker, IV (Resident); Timothy M. Broas (Resident); Gordon Alan Coffee (Resident); Richard A. Hibey (Resident); Christopher C. McIsaac (Resident); Eric W. Bloom (Resident); Michael L. Sibarium (Resident); Thomas L. Mills (Resident); Constantine G. Papavizas (Resident); Jeffrey G. Berman (Resident); Edmund D. Cooke, Jr. (Resident); Peter M. Kirby (Resident); John Fehrenbach (Resident); William N. Hall (Resident); William A. Anderson, II (Resident); Patrick L. Schmidt (Resident); Guy A. Morley (Resident); Joan B. Tucker Fife (Resident); Kathryn M. Sutton (Resident); Carol A. Joffe (Resident); Charles B. Molster, III (Resident); Eric J. Marcotte; Donn C. Meindertsma (Resident); Thomas C. Poindexter (Resident); Vincent D. Salvatore, Jr. (Resident); Robert Linn Draper (Resident); Mary E. Wall (Resident); David C. Romm (Resident); Garry R. Boehlert (Not admitted in DC; Resident); Michael K. Atkinson (Resident); Faton A. Bacaj (Resident); F. Stanley Echols (Resident); Sandra L. Pearlman (Resident); Raymond B. Wuslich (Resident); Richard F. Williamson (Resident); Susan Cannon Longstreet (Resident); William A. Horin; Robert A. Berger (Resident); Gerald P. Farano (Resident); Andreas H. Leskovsek (Resident); Jay L. Levine (Resident); Peter M. D'Ambrosio (Not admitted in DC; Resident); Thomas Galli; Howard R. Majev; Allan A. Fanucci (Also at New York, New York). Of Counsel: John L. Napier (Resident); Joseph B. Knotts, Jr. (Resident); Lawrence I. Kiern (Resident); Francisco J. Pavia (Resident); Krista L. Pages (Resident); Beryl F. Anthony, Jr. (Not admitted in DC; Resident). Senior Attorneys: Anne W. Cottingham. Associates: John R. Ates; Timothy Ayers (Not admitted in DC); Lori A. Bean; Dennis W. Bishop (Not admitted in DC); H. Allen Black III (Not admitted in DC); Patricia L. Campbell; Laura E. Chenoweth (Not admitted in DC); M. Carter DeLorme; Jeanne M. Dennis; Michael Thomas Dyson; Paul S. Ebert; Donald P. Ferraro; Carey W. Fleming; Erika M. Fleming (Not admitted in DC); Bryant E. Gardner; Marion Kristal Goldberg; Douglas N. Greenburg; Robert T. Hall (Not admitted in DC); Cynthia L. Hansen (Not admitted in DC); Sunshine Hernandez (Not admitted in DC); Roger A. Keller, Jr. (Not admitted in DC); Charles B. Klein; Susan A. MacIntyre; David J. Mandl (Not admitted in DC); Jeffrey W. Mayes; Donald W. McLaughlin, Jr.; Michael J. McLaughlin (Not admitted in DC); John McMickle (Not admitted in DC); Marc Zaki Michael (Not admitted in DC); Angela M. Moore (Not admitted in DC); Gina M. Petro; Brooke D. Poole (Not admitted in DC); Sean G. Saxon (Not admitted in DC); Scott A. Schipma; Gregory K. Smith (Not admitted in DC); William B. Fenning Steinman; Thomas M. Stimson; Anne W. Stukes (Not admitted in DC); Zach Wilks (Not admitted in DC); Jeffrey A. Wolfson. Staff Attorneys: Pamela A. Rons.
Alternative Dispute Resolution, Antitrust, Asset Securitization, Banking, Bankruptcy, Workouts and Financial Restructurings, Commercial Lending, Contracts, Corporate, Corporate Finance, E-Commerce, Employee Benefits and Executive Compensation, Energy, Environmental Law, Healthcare, Immigration, Intellectual Property, International, Labor and Employment Relations, Lease Finance, Litigation, Maritime, Mergers and Acquisitions, Product Liability, Project Finance, Public Finance, Real Estate, Securities, State and Federal Governmental Relations and Regulatory Affairs, Tax, Technology, Transportation, Trusts and Estates and White Collar Criminal Defense.
Chicago, Illinois Office: 35 West Wacker Drive, 60601. Telephone: 315-558-5600. Facsimile: 312-558-5700.
New York, N.Y. Office: 200 Park Avenue, 10166-4193. Telephone: 212-294-6700. Telecopier: 212-294-4700.
Los Angeles, California Office: 444 South Flower, 10th Floor, 90071-2911. Telephone: 213-615-1700.
Geneva, Switzerland Office: 43 Rue du Rhone, 1204. Telephone: +41-22 317 75 75. Fax: +41-22 317 75 00
Paris, France Office: 21 Avenue Victor Hugo. 75116. Telephone: 331-5364- 8282. Fax: 331-5364-8220.

See Professional Biographies, WASHINGTON, DISTRICT OF COLUMBIA

Winter, Anne V., (BV) '52 '82 C.806 B.A. L.838 J.D.
(adm. in MS; not adm. in DC) [[A] Baker,D.B.&C.] (⊙Jackson, MS)
*PRACTICE AREAS: Commercial Litigation.
Winter, Charles M. '48 '91 C.734 B.A. L.276 J.D.
(adm. in MD; not adm. in DC) 4548 Linnean Ave., N.W.
Winter, David A. .... '67 '93 C.178 B.A. L.477 J.D. [Hogan&H.]
*PRACTICE AREAS: Taxation.
Winter, Douglas E., (AV) .... '— '75 C.339 B.S. L.309 J.D. [[C] Bryan C.]
*PRACTICE AREAS: Litigation; Products Liability; Aviation Law; Entertainment Law.
Winter, Robert E. .... '65 '97 C.846 B.A. L.276 J.D. [[A] O'Melveny&M.]
Winter, Robert H., (AV) .... '41 '67 C.178 A.B. L.309 LL.B. [Arnold&P.]
*PRACTICE AREAS: Corporate; Securities; International.
Winterfeldt, Brian J. .... '72 '00 C.1365 B.A. L.276 J.D. [[A] Dow,L.&A.]
Winters, Christopher .... '72 '97 C.589 B.A. L.309 J.D. [[A] Arnold&P.]
*PRACTICE AREAS: Intellectual Property Litigation; Litigation.
Winters, Gary A. .... '63 '92 C.597 B.A. L.276 J.D. [Mayer,B.&P.]
*PRACTICE AREAS: Antitrust; Commercial Litigation.
Winters, Robert O. '67 '00 C.311 B.S. L.893 J.D.
(adm. in VA; not adm. in DC) [[A] Kleinfeld,K.&B.]
*PRACTICE AREAS: Food, Drug and Cosmetic Law; Food and Drug Regulation; Drug and Medical Device Regulation; Food Labeling and Inspection; Advertising Law.
Winterscheid, Joseph F., (AV) .... '53 '78 C&L.602 B.A., J.D. [Jones,D.R.&P.]
*PRACTICE AREAS: Antitrust and Trade Regulation; EU Competition; International Antitrust.
Winthrop, Pamela G. .... '56 '82 C.914 B.A. L.273 J.D. [Hogan&H.]
*PRACTICE AREAS: Corporate Finance; Project Finance.
Winton, Gregory S., (BV) ....'64 '91 C.1192 B.S. L.1325 J.D. [[C] Boros&G.]
*PRACTICE AREAS: Aviation; Civil Litigation; Personal Injury; Wrongful Death; Product Liability.
Winton, Jeffrey M. ....'61 '85 C.674 A.B. L.309 J.D. [Shearman&S.]
Wintrol, John P., (AV) ....'41 '69 C.698 B.A. L.276 J.D. [McDermott,W.&E.]
Wiorski, Robert H. '47 '72
C.602 A.B. L.424 J.D. Corp. Coun., America's Community Bkrs.
Wipper, Janette L. '— '99 C.846 B.A. L.1194 J.D.
(adm. in TX; not adm. in DC) Lawyers Comm. for Civil Rights Under Law
*RESPONSIBILITIES: Environmental Justice.
Wirick, Elizabeth ....'— '99 C.309 B.A. L.276 J.D. [[A] Arnold&P.]
*PRACTICE AREAS: Financial Institutions Law; Public Policy and Legislative.
Wirsing, Richard M. ....'55 '97 L.273 J.D. [[A] McDermott,W.&E.]
Wirtz, Cecelia E. .... '49 '75 C.329 B.A. L.309 J.D. 1218 Girard St., N.W.
Wirtz, W. Willard ....'12 '39 C.72 A.B. L.309 LL.B. 1211 Connecticut Ave., N.W.
Wise, Brian J. '74 '00 C.228 B.A. L.893 J.D.
(adm. in VA; not adm. in DC) [[A] Epstein B.&G.]
Wise, Edward J. '46 '74 C.910 B.S. L.128 J.D.
(adm. in VA; not adm. in DC; Pat.) [McDermott,W.&E.]
Wise, Joan S. .... '41 '84 C&L.276 B.A., J.D. Gen. Coun., AARP
*RESPONSIBILITIES: Non-Profit; Corporate.

Wise, Mark, (BV) '56 '84 C.688 B.S. L.1040 J.D.
(adm. in NY; not adm. in DC) [[A] Ford&H.]
*PRACTICE AREAS: Labor and Employment.
Wise, Richard G., (AV) ....'44 '70 C.763 B.A. L.1068 J.D. [Greenstein D.&L.]
Wise, Roger S. ....'69 '97 C.976 B.A. L.309 J.D. [[A] Wilmer,C.&P.]
Wiseberg, Stanley Carl '48 '74 C.831 B.A. L.818 J.D.
(adm. in MA; not adm. in DC) KPMG
Wiseman, Alan M., (AV) ....'44 '68 C.367 B.A. L.276 J.D. [Howrey S.A.&W.]
*PRACTICE AREAS: Antitrust; Appellate Practice; Commercial Law; Complex Litigation; Litigation.
Wiseman, Jennifer C. .... '68 '93 C.976 B.A. L.902 J.D. [[A] Slevin&H.]
*PRACTICE AREAS: Employee Benefits.
Wiseman, Kenneth L. .... '49 '77 C.966 B.A. L.128 J.D. [Andrews&K.]
*PRACTICE AREAS: Energy Regulation; Natural Gas Pipelines; Electric Utilities; Oil and Gas Pipelines.
Wiseman, Thomas G. '47 '84 C.415 B.S. L.64 J.D.
[Venable,A.B.H.&C.] (See Pat. Sect.)
*PRACTICE AREAS: Patent Prosecution.
Wisenberg, Solomon Louis .... '54 '80 C.910 A.B. L.846 J.D. [Ross,D.&B.]
Wishnow, Steven M. ....'51 '76 C&L.446 B.A., J.D. [Kanter&W.]
Wishod, Steven H. .... '65 '00 C.319 B.A. L.273 J.D. [[A] Feldesman,T.L.F.&B.]
*PRACTICE AREAS: Federal Grants; Government Contracts; Military Law; Civil Litigation.
Wisla, Ronald M. ....'57 '83 C.1044 B.A. L.273 J.D. [[C] Manatt,P.&P.]
Wisner, Graham G. ....'50 '81 C.33 B.A. L.276 J.D. [[C] Patton B.]
Wisner, Wilford L. ... '34 '62 C.679 B.S.E.E. L.309 J.D. 1300 I St, N.W., Suite 700 (Pat.)
Wisneski, Edward S. '68 '94 C.205 B.A. L.446 J.D.
(adm. in MD; not adm. in DC) [[A] Patton B.]
Wisor, Ronald L., Jr. ....'64 '93 C.188 B.A. L.94 J.D. [[A] Arent F.K.P.&K.]
*PRACTICE AREAS: Health Law; Health Care Fraud; Health Care Regulation; Health Care Reimbursement.
Wiss, Marcia A., (AV) ....'47 '73 C&L.276 B.S.F.S., J.D. [Hogan&H.]
*PRACTICE AREAS: International Project Finance; International Business Law; Aircraft Finance and Leasing; Corporate Law.
Witeck, Christopher M. .... '71 '98 C.893 B.A. L.276 J.D. [[A] Goodwin P.]
Withers, Darius B, '69 '94 C.893 B.A. L.273 J.D.
(adm. in MD; not adm. in DC) [[A] Kelley D.&W.]
*PRACTICE AREAS: Communications; Administrative Law.

Witherspoon, John F., (AV) '33 '65 C.234 B.S. L.276 J.D.
Suite 500, 815 Connecticut Avenue, N.W., 20006-4004
Telephone: 202-835-3700 Facsimile: 202-293-2902
Email: jfw@witherspoonlaw.com
***PRACTICE AREAS: Patent Law.**
Patent, Trademark and Copyright Law.

See Professional Biographies, WASHINGTON, DISTRICT OF COLUMBIA

Withycombe, Kent T., (AV) ....'61 '89 C.178 B.A. L.569 J.D. [Dickstein S.M.&O.]
*PRACTICE AREAS: General Litigation; Insurance Litigation.
Witiw, Eric P. '63 '88 C.705 B.A. L.564 J.D.
(adm. in NY; not adm. in DC) U.S. Dept. of Justice, Tax Division
Witkowski, Wayne C. ....'46 '72 C&L.477 B.S., J.D. Off. of Corp. Coun. of D.C.
Witmer, Rachel S. '58 '87 C.945 B.A. L.893 J.D.
(adm. in NY; not adm. in DC) Bur. of National Affairs‡
Witmer, Steven H. .... '64 '90 C.400 B.A. L.309 J.D. [Ivins,P.&B.]
*PRACTICE AREAS: Employee Benefits; Employment Taxation; Executive Compensation; ERISA Litigation; ESOPs.
Witt, Hal, (AV) .... '36 '59 C&L.145 B.A., J.D. [Witt&N.]
*PRACTICE AREAS: Family Law.

Witt & Nolan LLP, (AV)
Suite 600, 1140 Connecticut Avenue, N.W., 20036 ⊙
Telephone: 202-296-3333 Telecopier: 202-296-0416
Members of Firm: Hal Witt; James G. Nolan. Associate: Marjorie Just.
Family Law, General Litigation.
Chevy Chase, Maryland Office: Suite 801, 5530 Wisconsin Avenue. Telephone: 202-296-3333.

See Professional Biographies, WASHINGTON, DISTRICT OF COLUMBIA

Witten, Jesse A. ....'65 '91 C.674 A.B. L.309 J.D. [[A] Jones,D.R.&P.]
Witten, Roger M., (AV) ....'46 '73 C.197 A.B. L.309 J.D. [Wilmer,C.&P.]
*PRACTICE AREAS: Civil Litigation; Foreign Corrupt Practices Act; International Dispute Resolution; Internal Corporate Investigations; White Collar Crime.
Witten Rose, Tracey ....'62 '89 C.446 B.A. L.329 J.D. D.C. Off. of Zoning
Wittenborn, John L. ....'49 '74 C.1070 B.S. L.1119 J.D. [Collier S.S.]
*PRACTICE AREAS: Environmental Law and Litigation.
Wittenstein, David J., (AV) .... '56 '81 C.311 B.A. L.228 J.D. [Dow,L.&A.]
Witter, Ray Christian .... '69 '95 C.1356 B.S. L.1209 J.D. [[A] Goodwin P.]
Wittie, Patricia H., (AV) .... '50 '77 C.910 B.A. L.273 J.D. [[C] Reed S.]
*PRACTICE AREAS: Government Contracts; Export Compliance.
Wittie, Robert A. ....'— '70 C.477 A.B. L.309 J.D. [Kirkpatrick&L.]
*PRACTICE AREAS: Investment Management; Mutual Funds; Electronic Commerce; Privacy; Uniform Commercial Code.
Wittlin, Lori B. ....'74 '98 C.575 B.A. L.245 J.D. [[A] Miller&C.]
*PRACTICE AREAS: Federal Tax Controversies; Corporate Taxation; International Taxation.
Wixon, Henry N. ....'54 '86 C.446 B.S. L.273 J.D. [Hale&D.] (Pat.)
*PRACTICE AREAS: Intellectual Property Law.
Wochok, Thomas M., (AV)....................'49 '75 C.128 B.A. L.851 J.D. [[A] Cadeaux&T.]
*PRACTICE AREAS: Personal Injury; Medical Malpractice; Products Liability; Premises Liability; Construction Liability.
Wodka, Nancy A. .... '52 '84 C.156 B.A. L.273 J.D. [Bracewell&P.]
*PRACTICE AREAS: Asset Based Finance; Construction Law; Energy Project Development; Energy Acquisitions; Energy Finance.
Woehrmyer, Jason E. '72 '99 C.150 B.B.A. L.276 J.D.
(adm. in MD; not adm. in DC) [[A] Porter W.M.&A.]
*PRACTICE AREAS: Corporate Law; Mergers and Acquisitions.
Wofford, Cindy Lynn, (AV) .... '52 '78 C.814 B.A. L.846 J.D. [Ravdin&W.]
*PRACTICE AREAS: Trusts and Estates; Divorce Taxation; Domestic Relations.
Wohl, Patricia J. ....'59 '90 C.228 A.B. L.902 J.D. [[A] Elias,M.T.&H.]
Wohlsifer, William .... '54 '96 C.1175 B.A. L.1158 J.D. [W.R.Wohlsifer]
Wohlsifer, William R., P.A. .... 1730 K St., Ste. 304
Wohlstetter, Alan F., (AV) ....'— '49 C.563 A.B. L.309 LL.B. [Denning&W.]
*PRACTICE AREAS: Transportation Law; Government Contracts; Maritime Law; Trademark Law.
Wojcik, Walter W., Jr. '71 '97 C.372 B.A. L.665 J.D.
(adm. in PA; not adm. in DC) Labor Rel. Spec.
Wolcott, Jonathan F. ....'69 '96 C.31 B.A. L.893 J.D. [McDermott,W.&E.]
Woldow, Scott D. .... '71 '97 C.1019 B.A. L.30 J.D. [[A] Smith,G.&R.]
*PRACTICE AREAS: Intellectual Property; Litigation; Antitrust.
Wolf, Christopher .... '54 '80 C.95 A.B. L.902 J.D. [Proskauer R.]
Wolf, Daniel .... '60 '87 C.597 B.A. L.477 J.D. [Sprenger&L.]
*PRACTICE AREAS: Employment Law; Civil Rights; Human Rights; Complex Federal Litigation.
Wolf, Donald M. ....'44 '78 C.556 B.S. L.309 J.D. V.P., Holladay Corp.
Wolf, Jason E. '73 '00 C.378 B.A. L.629 J.D.
(adm. in OR; not adm. in DC) Staff Attorney
Wolf, Justin R., (AV) ....'11 '36 C.309 A.B. L.546 J.D. 2700 Calvert St., N.W.‡
Wolf, Kevin J. ....'— '92 C.502 B.A. L.494 J.D. [Bryan C.]
*PRACTICE AREAS: International Trade; Corporate Investigations; White Collar Criminal Defense.

Wolf, Mark C. .... '52 '77 C.800 A.B. L.616 J.D. Tax Law Editor, Tax Mgmt., Inc.
Wolf, Matthew M. .... '68 '94 C.976 B.A. L.893 J.D. [A Howrey S.A.&W.]
*PRACTICE AREAS: Corporate Litigation; Intellectual Property.
Wolf, Maurice, (AV) '31 '62 C.112 B.A. L.178 LL.B. [Wolf,A.&C.] (⊙New York, NY)
*PRACTICE AREAS: International Business Transactions; International Joint Ventures; International Telecommunications; Latin American and Caribbean Transactions; Foreign Investment Law.

Wolf, Michael '48 '73 C.188 A.B. L.569 J.D.
1015 Eighteenth Street, N.W., Suite 801, 20036
Telephone: 202-659-4656 Fax: 202-659-3145
***PRACTICE AREAS: ERISA; Commercial Litigation; Alternative Dispute Resolution; Arbitration; Mediation.**

Wolf, Nancy L., (AV) .... '52 '80 C.788 B.A. L.273 J.D. [Leventhal,S.&L.]
*PRACTICE AREAS: Communications Law; Media Law.
Wolf, Peter H. .... '35 '62 C.188 L.309 LL.B. Sr. Supr. Ct. J.
Wolf, Sarah M. .... '74 '99 C.445 B.S. L.472 J.D. [A Arent F.K.P.&K.]
*PRACTICE AREAS: Marketing Law; E-commerce; Intellectual Property.
Wolf, Timothy J. .... '65 '97 C.871 B.S. L.180 J.D. [A Morgan,L.&B.]
Wolf, William B., Jr., (AV) .... '27 '51 C.674 A.B. L.976 LL.B. [Wolf&W.]

Wolf, Arnold & Cardoso, P.C., (AV) BB
1801 K Street, N.W. Suite 203L, 20006
Telephone: 202-857-0585 Facsimile: 202-293-2068
Email: wac@interlawyers.com URL: http://www.interlawyers.com
Elting Arnold (1912-1988); Maurice Wolf; Dennis A. Foster; Carlos E. Cardoso; Lawrence I. Knoll (Not admitted in DC); Gilberto Arango. Of Counsel: Edward Ramos Sousa (Not admitted in DC).
International Business, Joint Ventures and other Trans-National Transactions, International Telecommunications, International Investments, International Arbitration, Representation before the World Bank, IFC, Inter-American Development Bank, EXIM Bank, OPIC, other U.S. and Foreign Governmental Agencies, North America Free Trade Agreement, GATT and World Trade Organization, U.S.T.R. Advisors on Laws of Europe, the Middle East, Argentina, Brazil, Colombia and other Latin American and Caribbean Countries. Foreign Investment Law, International Commercial Contracts, International Corporate Finance. Latin America Trade and Finance. Privatization, International Intellectual Property, Internet Law.
New York, N.Y. Office: Wolf, Arnold & Knoll, P.C., 590 Madison Avenue. Telephone: 212-521-4410. Fax: 212-465-9104.
Rio de Janeiro, Brazil Office: Cardoso, Rocha, Trindale & Lara Resende.
Bogota, Colombia Office: Arango, Nieto, Calderon & Asociados.
Caribbean Office: Dunn, Cox, Orett and Ashenheim, Kingston, Jamaica.
Other Associated offices also throughout Latin America, the Caribbean, Asia and the South Pacific.
See Professional Biographies, WASHINGTON, DISTRICT OF COLUMBIA

Wolf-Rodda, Howard A. ....'— '94 C.30 B.A. L.446 J.D. [A Epstein B.&G.]
*PRACTICE AREAS: Government Contracts; Commercial Litigation; Insurance Coverage Law.

Wolf & Wolf, (AV)
Suite 1210, 1001 Connecticut Avenue, N.W., 20036
Telephone: 202-296-3300 Fax: 202-296-3303
Email: BigBad@AYA.Yale.edu
Members of Firm: Alexander Wolf (1866-1930); William B. Wolf, Sr. (1905-1992); William B. Wolf, Jr.
General Practice.
See Professional Biographies, WASHINGTON, DISTRICT OF COLUMBIA

Wolfe, Charles R., Jr., (AV) '52 '78 C.401 B.S.Ch.E. L.276 J.D. [Blank R.C.&M.] (See Pat. Sect.) (⊙Phila., PA)
*PRACTICE AREAS: Patent Law; Trademark Law; Unfair Competition Law; Patent Litigation; Copyright Law.
Wolfe, Eugene .... '50 '77 C.329 B.A. L.128 J.D. U.S. Postal Rate Comm.
Wolfe, Kirsten A. .... '64 '90 C.1174 B.M. L.276 J.D. [C Clifford C.R.&W.]
*PRACTICE AREAS: Antitrust; Consumer Protection.
Wolff, Alan Wm., (AV) .... '42 '66 C.309 A.B. L.178 LL.B. [Dewey B.]
*PRACTICE AREAS: International Trade; Investment Law; Business Law.
Wolff, Bruce S., (AV) '43 '69 C.31 B.A. L.309 LL.B. [C Hogan&H.] (⊙New York, NY)
*PRACTICE AREAS: Health Care Mergers and Acquisitions; Managed Care; Health Care Contracts; Health Care Reform; Nonprofit Organizations Law.
Wolff, Craig M. .... '69 '96 C.309 B.A. L.893 J.D. [A King&S.]
*PRACTICE AREAS: Federal Criminal Law; Grand Jury Practice; Congressional Investigations; Government Investigation; Civil Litigation.
Wolff, D. Craig ....'54 '87 C.508 B.A. L.276 J.D. [Shaw P.]
*PRACTICE AREAS: Technology Law; Technology Contracts; Outsourcing; Computer; Software.
Wolff, Elroy H., (AV) ....'35 '63 C&L.178 A.B., LL.B. [Sidley A.B.&W.]
Wolff, Evan .... '70 '00 C&L.446 B.S., J.D. Tech. Coun., Environmental Protection Inter'l
Wolff, Kevin J. .... '53 '78 C.207 B.A. L.880 J.D. [A Hogan&H.]
Wolff, Marshall S., (AV) .... '48 '76 C.309 A.B. L.976 J.D. [Zuckerman S.]
*PRACTICE AREAS: Business Law; Real Estate; Finance; Workouts; Bankruptcy.
Wolff, Paul Martin, (AV) .... '41 '68 C.966 B.A. L.309 LL.B. [Williams&C.]
*PRACTICE AREAS: Arbitration; Banking Litigation; Business Litigation; Business Mediation; Civil Practice.
Wolff, Samuel .... '56 '82 C.103 A.B. L.276 J.D. [Akin,G.S.H.&F.]
*PRACTICE AREAS: Corporate Law; Securities.
Wolffe, Franklin D., (AV) '— '59 C.446 B.S.Ch.E. L.273 J.D. [C Banner&W.] (See Pat. Sect.)
*PRACTICE AREAS: Intellectual Property Law; Patents; Intellectual Property Licensing; Chemical Intellectual Property.
Wolffe, Susan A., (AV) '— '90 C.893 B.S.Ch.E. L.1209 J.D. [Banner&W.] (See Pat. Sect.)
*PRACTICE AREAS: Intellectual Property Law; Patents; Intellectual Property Licensing; Chemical Intellectual Property; Pharmaceutical Intellectual Property.
Wolfman, Andrea L. ....'69 '94 C.446 B.A. L.1338 J.D. [Riselli&P.]
Wolfman, Brian S. .... '56 '85 C.659 B.A. L.309 J.D. Public Citizen Litig. Grp.
Wolfson, Jeffrey A. ....'70 '95 C.103 Sc.B. L.273 J.D. [A Winston&S.] (Pat.)
*PRACTICE AREAS: Intellectual Property.
Wolfson, Joel Rothstein, (AV) .... '55 '80 C.966 B.S. L.188 J.D. [Blank R.C.&M.]
*PRACTICE AREAS: Computers and Software; Intellectual Property; Contracts; Commercial Law; Technology and Science.
Wolin, Jonathan S. .... '61 '89 C.446 B.S. L.128 J.D. 700 Penn. Ave., N.W., Ste. 900
Wolk, Lawrence J. .... '49 '75 C.367 B.A. L.569 J.D. [Holland&K.]
*PRACTICE AREAS: Commercial Real Estate Financing; Disposition; Leasing; Loan Workouts; Multi-Asset Sales.
Wolk, Michael D. '— '84 C.446 B.A. L.1187 J.D. (adm. in MI; not adm. in DC) [Foley&L.]
*PRACTICE AREAS: Business Law; SEC Compliance.
Wolk, Stuart R. ....'38 '61 C.994 B.A. L.1009 J.D. 3201 New Mexico Ave., N.W.
Wolly, Michael S., (AV) .... '47 '73 C&L.273 B.A., J.D. 1025 Connecticut Ave. N.W.
Wolman, Jay M. .... '76 '01 C.188 B.S. L.276 J.D. 1666 Connecticut Ave., N.W.,
Wolod, Kimberly E. .... '66 '91 C.446 B.A. L.893 J.D. 1200 19th St Nw # 800
Woloshin, Douglas, (AV) ....'48 '73 C.884 B.S. L.276 J.D. [Duane,M.&H.]
*PRACTICE AREAS: Corporate Law; Taxation.
Wolsk, Jeremiah ....'68 '96 C.367 B.A. L.910 J.D. [A Shaw P.]
Wolski, Victor J. '62 '92 C.659 B.A.B.S. L.893 J.D. (adm. in CA; not adm. in DC) [A Cooper&K.]
*PRACTICE AREAS: Constitutional Litigation (8); Trial Practice; Appellate Practice; Land Use; Administrative Law (5).

Wolson, Joshua D. '74 '99 C.659 B.A. L.309 J.D. (adm. in PA; not adm. in DC) [A Covington&B.]
*PRACTICE AREAS: Litigation; Sports Law; Antitrust; Intellectual Property.
Wolson, Sherri Lynn '70 '98 C&L.813 A.B., J.D. (adm. in IL; not adm. in DC) [A Robbins,R.E.O.&U.]

Womble Carlyle Sandridge & Rice, (AV)
Suite 700, 1401 Eye Street, 20005 ⊙
Telephone: 202-857-4400 Telecopier: 202-467-6910
Email: lawyers@wcsr.com URL: http://www.wcsr.com
Resident Members: Erik D. Bolog; Desmond D. Connall, Jr.; W. Andrew Copenhaver (Not admitted in DC); Richard G. David; Taina E. M. Edlund; Diane J. Fuchs; John D. Hagner; Paul A. Kaplan; N. Peter Kostopulos; Stuart A. Kruger; Elizabeth C. Lee; Kenneth W. Logwood; Pamela V. Rothenberg; Howard N. Solodky; Jeffrey L. Tarkenton; Stanley J. Wrobel. Associates: Christopher D. Bell; Gina M. Boscarino; Grace Cavelli; Sabrina Ciccarello (Not admitted in DC); J. David Folds; James W. Gladstone; Jacqueline P. Puentes (Not admitted in DC); Raquel Cheatham Skinner. Of Counsel: Philip J. Berkowitz; P. Terrence Gaffney; Kevin D. Jones (Not admitted in DC).
General Civil Practice, Trial and Appellate Litigation. Administrative, Antitrust, Aviation, Banking, Bankruptcy and Creditor's Rights, Bond Financing, Civil Rights, Commercial, Construction, Consumer Lending, Corporate, E-Commerce, Employee Benefits, Environmental, Estate Planning, Family, Government Relations, Health Care, Insurance, Intellectual Property, International, Labor and Employment, Municipal, Negligence, Probate, Product Liability, Real Estate, Retirement Plans, Securities, Taxation, Toxic Tort, Wills and Trusts Law.
Winston-Salem, North Carolina Office: 200 West Second Street, P.O. Drawer 84. Telephone: 336-721-3600. Fax: 336-721-3660. New Address Effective March, 2002: One West Fourth Street, 27101.
Charlotte, North Carolina Office: 3300 One First Union Center, 301 South College Street. Telephone: 704-331-4900. Fax: 704-331-4955.
Raleigh, North Carolina Office: 2100 First Union Capitol Center, 150 Fayetteville Street Mall, P.O. Box 831. Telephone: 919-755-2100. Fax: 919-755-2150.
Research Triangle Park, North Carolina Office: 2530 Meridian Parkway, Suite 400 (Durham), 27713. Telephone: 919-484-2300. Fax: 919-484-2340.
Greensboro, North Carolina Office: 300 North Greene Street. Telephone: 336-574-8030. Fax: 336-574-4520.
Atlanta, Georgia Office: One Atlantic Center, 1201 West Peachtree Street, Suite 3500. Telephone: 404-872-7000. Fax: 404-888-7490.
Other Atlanta, Georgia Office: Suite 404, 2296 Henderson Mill Road, N.E. Telephone: 770-492-9030. Fax: 770-492-9609.
Greenville, South Carolina Office: 700 Poinsett Plaza, 104 South Main Street, P.O. Box 10208. Telephone: 864-255-5400. Fax: 864-255-5440.
McLean, Virginia Office: 6862 Elm Street, Eighth Floor. Telephone: 703-790-3310. Facsimile: 703-790-2623 (7th Floor); 703-394-2205 (3rd Floor); 703-288-0622 (8th Floor).
See Professional Biographies, WASHINGTON, DISTRICT OF COLUMBIA

Womeldorf, Rebecca A. .... '66 '92 C.806 B.A. L.902 J.D. [Spriggs&H.]
*PRACTICE AREAS: Litigation; Drug and Medical Device Defense; Complex Commercial Litigation; Civil Appeals; Employment Law.
Wone, Robert E. ....'74 '00 C.945 A.B. L.659 J.D. [A Covington&B.]
*PRACTICE AREAS: Labor and Employment; Employment Law; Employment Litigation.
Wong, Aliya '72 '98 C.976 B.A. L.569 J.D. (adm. in NY; not adm. in DC) [A Thelen R.&P.]
*PRACTICE AREAS: Employee Benefits; Taxation.
Wong, Carole R.G. '68 '95 C.112 B.A. L.276 J.D. (adm. in CA; not adm. in DC) 1050 Conn. Ave., N.W.‡
Wong, Cynthia Y. '69 '95 C.569 B.A. L.705 J.D. (adm. in NY; not adm. in DC) [A Powell,G.F.&M.]
Wong, Vincent S. '70 '97 C.1138 B.B.A. L.1009 J.D. (adm. in NY; not adm. in DC) [A Weil,G.&M.]
*PRACTICE AREAS: Corporate Law.
Wong, Wing .... '23 '49 C&L.273 LL.B. 3408 Wisconsin Ave., N.W.
Wood, Allen ....'45 '75 C.59 B.A. L.30 J.D. [Venable,A.B.H.&C.] (See Pat. Sect.)
*PRACTICE AREAS: Intellectual Property Law; Patent Law.
Wood, Allison D. .... '67 '98 C.1077 B.S. L.273 J.D. [A Hunton&W.]
*PRACTICE AREAS: Environmental Law.
Wood, Barry D., (AV) .... '48 '77 C&L.101 B.S., J.D. [Wood,M.&B.]
*PRACTICE AREAS: Contracts; Communications Law.
Wood, Benjamin '72 '01 C.976 B.A L.893 J.D. (adm. in MD; not adm. in DC) [A Patton B.]
Wood, Bruce C. '49 '78 C.273 B.A. L.1209 J.D. Asst. Gen. Coun., American Insurance Association
*RESPONSIBILITIES: Workers Compensation Law.
Wood, Christopher G. .... '59 '85 C.893 B.A. L.276 J.D. [Fleischman&W.]
Wood, Christopher H. ....'68 '94 C.902 B.A. L.945 J.D. [C Crowell&M.]
Wood, Claire A. '76 '01 (adm. in NY; not adm. in DC) [A Kalbian H.]
*PRACTICE AREAS: Litigation.
Wood, Florence A. .... '48 '73 C.94 B.A. L.93 J.D. [Hawkins,D.&W.]
Wood, Frederic L., (AV) ....'45 '70 C.659 A.B. L.273 J.D. [Thompson H.]
*PRACTICE AREAS: Appellate Practice; Administrative Law; Transportation; Taxation and Employee Benefits; Estate Planning Law.
Wood, Gillian C. .... '— '99 [A Arnold&P.]
Wood, John Christopher '68 '98 C.691 B.S.B.A. L.846 J.D. (adm. in TX; not adm. in DC) [A Gibson,D.&C.]
*PRACTICE AREAS: International Trade; Intellectual Property; Antitrust.
Wood, Michael T. ....'67 '96 C.882 B.A. L.904 J.D. [A Patton B.]
Wood, Russell G., Jr. ....'68 '99 C.1369 B.A. L.273 J.D. [A Hunton&W.]
*PRACTICE AREAS: Project Finance; Corporate Law; Energy Law.
Wood, Theodore A. .... '59 '99 C.1378 B.S.E.E. L.201 J.D. [A Sterne,K.G.&F.]
*PRACTICE AREAS: Intellectual Property; Patents.
Wood, Wheaton B. '55 '82 C.855 B.A. L.823 J.D. (adm. in NY; not adm. in DC) 3508 Woodley Rd., NW‡

Wood, Dawson & Hellman
(See Hawkins, Delafield & Wood, New York, New York)
Wood-Dorsey, Deborah '53 '87 C.483 B.A. L.329 J.D. Fed. Legis. Coun., Wash. Off. for the City of L.A.

Wood, Maines & Brown, Chartered, (AV)
1827 Jefferson Place, N.W., 20036
Telephone: 202-293-5333 Fax: 202-293-9811
Email: wmb@wmblaw.org
Barry D. Wood; Ronald D. Maines; Paul H. Brown; Stuart W. Nolan, Jr. (Not admitted in DC).
Telecommunications Law emphasizing FCC Issues.
See Professional Biographies, WASHINGTON, DISTRICT OF COLUMBIA

Woodall, Judy Lynn ....'56 '88 C.262 B.A. L.329 J.D. 1003 K St. N.W., 3rd Fl.
Woodall, Mark R. .... '66 '99 C.886 B.S. L.1209 J.D. [A Sughrue M.] (See Pat. Sect.)
*PRACTICE AREAS: Intellectual Property.
Woodall, S. Roy, Jr. ... '36 '62 C&L.383 B.A., LL.B. [C Morris,M.&M.] (⊙Atlanta, GA)
*PRACTICE AREAS: Insurance; Finance; Mergers and Acquisitions; Regulatory Law.
Woodard, Michael B. '71 '99 C.893 B.A. L.1209 J.D. (adm. in VA; not adm. in DC) [A Muldoon M.&F.]
*PRACTICE AREAS: Corporate; Securities.
Woodbridge, Maria Lucia '51 '81 C.112 B.A. L.276 J.D. Resch. Atty., MCI Communications Corporation
Woodbury, Ellen H. '47 '81 C.681 B.A. L.569 J.D. (adm. in NY; not adm. in DC) [Chadbourne&P.]

Woodbury, Jennifer S. ....'71 '96 C.801 B.A. L.734 J.D. [A] Arent F.K.P.&K.]
*PRACTICE AREAS: Government Relations.
Wooden, Sean .... '71 '97 C.188 B.S.E.E. L.1292 J.D. [A] Dorsey&W.] (Pat.)
*PRACTICE AREAS: Intellectual Property; Patent Prosecution; International Patents; Computer and Software Patents; Internet Patents.
Woodfield, Nicholas Wyckoff .... '68 '95 C.902 B.A. L.192 J.D. [A] Watson&R.]
*PRACTICE AREAS: Trial Practice; Litigation; Medical Causation; Cancer and Carcinogenesis; Toxic Torts.
Woodka, Janet L. '64 '92 C.93 B.A. L.861 J.D.
(adm. in LA; not adm. in DC) [A] Van Ness F.]
*PRACTICE AREAS: Environmental Compliance; Permitting; Litigation.
Woodley, Thomas A., (AV) ....'47 '72 C.285 A.B. L.276 J.D. [Woodley,G.&M.]
*PRACTICE AREAS: Public Sector Labor Relations Law; Railway Labor Act Law; Fair Labor Standards Law; Constitutional Law; Employment Discrimination Law.

Woodley, Genser & McGillivary, (AV)
Suite 400, 1125 15th Street, N.W., 20005
Telephone: 202-833-8855 Fax: 202-452-1090
Email: info@wgm.laborlaw.com URL: http://www.wgmlaborlaw.com
Members of Firm: Thomas A. Woodley; Erick J. Genser; Gregory K. McGillivary; Douglas L. Steele; Kurt T. Rumsfeld; Molly Ann Elkin; Manar Sweillam Morales; Denise M. Dunkin.
Labor and Administrative Law. Practice before all Federal Courts, Departments and Agencies.
General Counsel for: International Association of Fire Fighters; American Train Dispatchers Assn.; International Brotherhood of Firemen & Oilers and Fund Counsel for its National Pension, Staff Union Pension and Health and Welfare Plans.
Representative Clients: Brotherhood Railway Carmen of the United States & Canada; International Brotherhood of Electrical Workers; International Association of Machinists and Aerospace Workers.
See Professional Biographies, WASHINGTON, DISTRICT OF COLUMBIA

Woodman, G. Kent ....'49 '74 C.612 B.A. L.880 J.D. [Thompson C.]
*PRACTICE AREAS: Transportation.
Woodrow, Kenneth D. ....'66 '91 C.893 B.A. L.902 J.D. [C] Morgan,L.&B.]
Woodrum, John R. ....'47 '74 C.309 B.A. L.800 J.D. [Heenan,A.&R.]
*PRACTICE AREAS: Coal Law; ERISA; Labor Law.
Woods, Andrew L. ....'62 '90 C.576 B.A. L.575 J.D. [Shaw P.]
Woods, John W., Jr. ......'68 '95 C.164 B.A. L.893 J.D. 1875 Connecticut Avenue, N.W.
Woods, Michele J. .... '62 '90 C.674 A.B. L.228 J.D. [C] Arnold&P.]
*PRACTICE AREAS: Intellectual Property; Technology Law.
Woods, Rebecca ....'72 '00 C&L.608 B.A., J.D. [A] Covington&B.]
Woods, Robert A., (AV) .... '31 '58 C&L.309 B.A., J.D. [C] Schwartz,W.&M.]
*PRACTICE AREAS: Communications Law; Telecommunications Law; Copyright and Trademark Law; Broadcast Production and Distribution Law.
Woods, Suzanne H. ....'66 '95 C.976 B.A. L.813 J.D. [A] Williams&C.]
Woods, Therese Marie .... '64 '90 C&L.262 B.S., J.D. [C] Collier S.S.]
*PRACTICE AREAS: Securities; Financial Services; Corporate.
Woods, Timothy O'Connel '56 '84 C.910 B.A. L.734 J.D.
(adm. in MO; not adm. in DC) P.O. Box 77064‡
Woods-Podwal, Stef '73 '00 C.914 B.A. L.30 J.D.
(adm. in MD; not adm. in DC) 2121 K St. N.W.
Woodside, Blair C., III, (AV) '45 '79
C.381 B.S.Ed. L.128 J.D. [Arent F.K.P.&K.] (⊙Alexandria, VA)
*PRACTICE AREAS: Commercial Real Estate; Finance.
Woodson, Roderic L., (AV) ....'47 '73 C.645 B.A. L.329 J.D. [C] Holland&K.]
*PRACTICE AREAS: Legislative Practice (40%); Administrative Law (30%); Public Finance (5%); Corporate Finance (5%); Public Utility Regulation (20%).
Woodward, David W. ....'64 '92 C.886 B.S. L.273 J.D. [C] Powell,G.F.&M.] (Pat.)
*PRACTICE AREAS: Patents; Intellectual Property.
Woodward, Gordon S. .... '68 '95 C.494 B.A. L.273 J.D. [A] Schnader H.S.&L.]
*PRACTICE AREAS: Civil Litigation; Products Liability; Aviation Law; Construction Law; Premises Liability.
Woodward, Pat Munroe, Jr., (AV) ....'62 '91 C.198 B.A. L.1209 J.D. [Dyer E.&J.]
*PRACTICE AREAS: White Collar Criminal Defense; Corporate Investigations; Corporate Compliance; Civil Litigation; Appellate Litigation.
Woodworth, Fred L., (AV) ....'40 '66 C.31 A.B. L.477 J.D. [Dykema G.]
*PRACTICE AREAS: Antitrust Law; Trade Regulation Law.
Woodworth, Ramsey L., (AV) ....'41 '67 C.103 A.B. L.823 LL.B. [C] Shook,H.&B.]
*PRACTICE AREAS: Telecommunications Law; Technology Law.
Woody, Kristin K. ....'71 '97 C.228 B.A. L.276 J.D. [A] Venable,A.B.H.&C.]
*PRACTICE AREAS: International; Food and Drug Regulation.
Woody, Robert J., (AV) .... '44 '69 C&L.378 B.A., J.D. [Shook,H.&B.]
*PRACTICE AREAS: Energy; Corporate Law.
Woody, Robert W. ....'59 '92 C.1369 B.S. L.128 J.D. [C] LeBoeuf,L.G.&M.]
*PRACTICE AREAS: Insurance; Government Relations.
Woofter, Perry W. '— '53 C&L.923 A.B., LL.B.
(adm. in WV; not adm. in DC) [Blooston,M.D.D.&P.]
*PRACTICE AREAS: Telecommunications Law; International Transactions; Federal Legislative Practice; Energy; International Project Finance.
Wool, Jeffrey A. '63 '88 C.259 B.A. L.178 J.D.
(adm. in WA; not adm. in DC) [Perkins C.]
*PRACTICE AREAS: International Commercial Law; International Business Law; Financial Transactions; Aircraft Finance; Project Finance.
Wooledge, Catherine S. ....'42 '89 C.679 B.A. L.945 J.D. [C] Sutherland A.&B.]
*PRACTICE AREAS: Corporate; Securities; Investment Company Law; Investment Management; Securities Regulation.
Woolley, Linda A. ....'54 '97 C.299 B.A. L.30 J.D. LegisLaw
Woolsey, R. James, (AV) ....'41 '69 C.813 B.A. L.976 LL.B. [Shea&G.]
*PRACTICE AREAS: International Arbitration; Mediation; Commercial Law.
Wooten, Holloway ....'36 '65 C.944 B.A. L.325 J.D. 1320 Hemlock St., N.W.
Word, Thomas Scott, III, (BV) '61 '87
C.893 B.A. L.192 J.D. 816 Connecticut Avenue, NW, Ninth Floor
Worden, Andrea .... '64 '97 C.976 B.A. L.813 J.D. [A] O'Melveny&M.]
Work, Charles R., (AV) ....'40 '65 C.918 B.A. L.145 J.D. [McDermott,W.&E.]
Work, Peter B., (AV) ....'39 '65 C.209 A.B. L.145 J.D. [Crowell&M.]
Workman, Lawrence K., Jr. ....'69 '00 C.152 B.S.E.E. L.893 J.D. [A] Dow,L.&A.]
Workmaster, Jason N. '— '00 C.260 B.A. L.1339 J.D.
(adm. in VA; not adm. in DC) [A] McKenna&C.]
*PRACTICE AREAS: Contracts; Technology Law.
Worlton, Amy E. .... '71 '00 C.101 B.A. L.569 J.D. [A] Wiley R.&F.]
Wormser, David A., (AV) '55 '80
C.473 B.S. L.608 J.D. [Pepper H.] (⊙Tysons Corner, VA)
*PRACTICE AREAS: Corporate Law; Computer Law; Intellectual Property.
Worrall, Robert Jones .... '63 '93 C.36 B.S.E.E. L.1218 J.D. [C] Arnold&P.] (Pat.)
*PRACTICE AREAS: Intellectual Property; Antitrust.
Worsley, James R., Jr., (AV) ....'24 '49 C.232 B.S. L.309 LL.B. [C] Ober,K.G.&S.]
Wortham, Leah ....'48 '73 C.429 B.A. L.309 J.D. Assoc. Prof. of Law, Catholic Univ.
Worthen, David ....'63 '88 C&L.823 B.A., J.D. [Schmeltzer,A.&S.]
*PRACTICE AREAS: Franchise Law; Civil Litigation.
Worthington, John R. '30 '55 C&L.477 B.A., J.D.
(adm. in IL; not adm. in DC) Sr. V.P. & Gen. Coun., MCI Communications Corp.
Worthington, Katherine A. ....'51 '85 C.446 B.S. L.128 J.D. Asst. U.S. Atty.
Worthington, Raymond L. '15 '62
C.446 B.S. L.273 LL.B. Intl. Bk. for Reconstr. & Develop.

Worthington, Robert F., Jr., (AV) '31 '57 C&L.838 J.D.
[Baker,D.B.&C.] (⊙Knoxville, Nashville, TN)
*PRACTICE AREAS: Business Law; Corporate Law; Government Relations; Public Utility Law.
Worthy, Patricia M. ....'44 '70 C.994 L.329 J.D. 2900 Van Ness St., N.W.
Woscoboinik, Michael L. ....'50 '78 C.861 B.A. L.273 J.D. 5713 Sherrier Pl. N.W.
Wotkyns, Garrett '74 '00 C.691 B.A. L.145 J.D.
(adm. in TX; not adm. in DC) [A] O'Melveny&M.]
Wozniak, Robert J., Jr. '66 '00 C.477 B.A. L.212 J.D.
(adm. in MI; not adm. in DC) [A] Cohen,M.H.&T.]
*PRACTICE AREAS: Antitrust.
Wrathall, James R. ....'62 '87 C.861 B.S.M. L.276 J.D. [Wilmer,C.&P.]
*PRACTICE AREAS: Civil Practice; Appellate Practice; Information and Privacy; Bankruptcy; Environmental Law.
Wray, Robert T., (AV) .... '35 '60 C.424 B.S. L.477 J.D. [Holland&K.]
*PRACTICE AREAS: International Business Law; Aircraft Finance and Leasing; Project Finance; Transportation; Infrastructure.
Wray, Timothy A. .... '49 '00 C.870 B.S. L.1209 J.D. [A] Swartz&R.]
Wrenn, Kelly Mitchell, (AV) ....'58 '84 C.896 B.A. L.902 J.D. [Ballard S.A.&I.]
*PRACTICE AREAS: Business Law; Finance; Health Care Finance; Real Estate; Debtor and Creditor.
Wright, Andrew McCanse '73 '00 C.902 B.A. L.893 J.D.
(adm. in MD; not adm. in DC) [A] Skadden,A.S.M.&F.]
*PRACTICE AREAS: Litigation; Criminal Law.
Wright, Anne Harvey '50 '83 C.562 B.A. L.276 J.D.
Assoc. Gen. Coun., Natl. Assn. of Sec. Dealers, Inc.
Wright, B. Bryan, Jr. ....'42 '70 C.575 A.B. L.893 LL.B. Fiduciary Tr. Intl.
Wright, Bradley C. .....'— '94 C.453 B.S.E.E. L.1209 J.D. [Banner&W.] (See Pat. Sect.)
*PRACTICE AREAS: Intellectual Property Law; Patents; Appellate Practice; Electrical Intellectual Property; Computer and Software Patents.
Wright, Christopher J. .... '52 '82 C.309 A.B. L.813 J.D. [Harris,W.&G.]
*PRACTICE AREAS: Appellate Practice; Telecommunications; Administrative.
Wright, Cynthia G., (BV) ....'60 '85 C.645 B.A. L.990 J.D. Asst. U.S. Atty.
Wright, Damon W. D. ....'71 '96 C.1369 B.S. L.1209 J.D. [A] Venable,A.B.H.&C.]
*PRACTICE AREAS: Complex Commercial Litigation; Criminal Litigation; Constitutional Litigation.
Wright, Donald Lewis, (BV) .... '49 '75 C.475 A.B. L.273 J.D. 1990 18th St., N.W.
Wright, Geoffrey T. ....'73 '99 C.902 B.A. L.472 J.D. [A] Jones,D.R.&P.]
Wright, Gregory S. ....'68 '94 C.228 A.B. L.276 J.D. [A] Kirkpatrick&L.]
*PRACTICE AREAS: Insurance Coverage; Insurance Insolvency; Civil Litigation.
Wright, Henrietta ....'57 '86 C&L.976 B.A., J.D. [C] Goldberg,G.W.&W.]
*PRACTICE AREAS: Communications and Media.
Wright, James R. ....'44 '73 C.608 B.S. L.273 J.D. National Academy of Sciences
Wright, Jay Kelly, (AV) .... '43 '75 C.197 A.B. L.309 J.D. [Arnold&P.]
*PRACTICE AREAS: Securities; Professional Liability; Business; Constitutional Litigation; Administrative Litigation.
Wright, Joel D. '72 '99 C.101 B.A. L.569 J.D.
(adm. in NY; not adm. in DC) [A] Latham&W.]
*PRACTICE AREAS: Project Finance; Energy Project Development; Finance; Infrastructure Development; Independent Power.
Wright, John W. '19 '50 C.966 L.472 LL.B.
(adm. in FL; not adm. in DC) 3755 Jennifer St., N.W.‡
Wright, Kevin L. .... '62 '87 C.309 A.B. L.893 J.D. [Littler M.]
*PRACTICE AREAS: Labor and Employment; Employee Benefits.
Wright, Lee C. .... '61 '96 C.446 B.S. L.1209 J.D. [A] Sughrue M.] (See Pat. Sect.)
*PRACTICE AREAS: Intellectual Property.
Wright, Lori ....'68 '96 C.164 B.A. L.30 J.D. WorldCom, Inc.
Wright, Matthew ....'75 '01 C.674 A.B. L.93 J.D. [A] Keller&H.]
*PRACTICE AREAS: Commercial Litigation; Trademark Litigation; Intellectual Property; Environmental Litigation.
Wright, Minturn T., IV ....'58 '87 C.976 B.S. L.800 J.D. 21534 Kalorama Station
Wright, Rebecca ....'48 '79 C.881 B.A. L.276 J.D. [Dickstein S.M.&O.]
*PRACTICE AREAS: Corporate Law; Finance Law; Securities Law; Project Finance Law.
Wright, Roberta Y. ....'46 '75 C.254 B.A. L.477 J.D. [Graves&H.]
Wright, Romney ....'43 '80 C.112 B.A. L.990 J.D. [R.Wright] ⊙
Wright, Samuel H. '46 '72 C.867 A.B. L.446 J.D.
(adm. in MD; not adm. in DC) V.P. & Gen. Coun., Cendant Corp.
Wright, Shawn M. ....'68 '95 C.329 B.A L.770 J.D. [A] Dyer E.&J.]
*PRACTICE AREAS: White Collar Criminal Defense; Civil Litigation; Administrative Law; Criminal Law.
Wright, Shawn W. ....'69 '99 C.329 B.A. L.770 J.D. 1501 M Street, N.W., Suite 700
Wright, Teresa Burke ....'64 '89 C.529 B.A. L.309 J.D. 1156 15th St., N.W.
Wright, William H., (AV) '43 '70
C&L.128 B.S.M.E., J.D. [Henderson&S.] (See Pat. Sect.)

Wright, Daniel J.
(See Rockville, Maryland)

Wright, Robinson, Osthimer & Tatum, (AV)
Suite 920 5335 Wisconsin Avenue, N.W., 20015 ⊙
Telephone: 202-244-4668 Telefax: 202-244-5135
URL: http://www.wrightrobinson.com
Principals: William H. Robinson, Jr. (Not admitted in DC; Also at Richmond, Virginia Office); Thomas S. Schaufelberger; Paul A. Fitzsimmons; Terrence M.R. Zic. Associates: Daniel G. Krasnegor; Kathleen S. Pirri; Christopher A. Glaser; Jeremy C. Chou.
General Civil and Trial Practice. Products Liability, Construction, Corporate, Insurance and Environmental Law.
Richmond, Virginia Office: Suite 400, 411 East Franklin Street. Telephone: 804-783-1100.
Los Angeles, California Office: Suite 1800, 888 South Figueroa Street. Telephone: 213-488-0503. Telex: 213-624-3755.
San Francisco, California Office: Suite 1800, 44 Montgomery Street. Telephone: 415-391-7111.
See Professional Biographies, WASHINGTON, DISTRICT OF COLUMBIA

Wright, Romney, P.C., Law Offices of
1730 K. St., N.W. (⊙Chincoteague, Vienna, VA)

Wright & Talisman, P.C., (AV)
1200 G Street, N.W., Suite 600, 20005-3802
Telephone: 202-393-1200 Fax: 202-393-1240
Email: mail@wrightlaw.com URL: http://www.wrightlaw.com
Harry S. Littman (1906-1982); Dale A. Wright (1927-1989); Gregory Grady; James T. McManus; Alan J. Statman; Douglas O. Waikart; Michael E. Small; Michael J. Thompson; Joseph S. Koury; Jeffrey G. DiSciullo; Arnold B. Podgorsky; Barry S. Spector; Robert H. Lamb (Not admitted in DC); Paul M. Flynn; Scott M. DuBoff; Carrie L. Bumgarner; Wendy N. Reed (Not admitted in DC);—David S. Berman; Deborah C. Brentani. Of Counsel: Harold L. Talisman; Robert H. Benna; Kenneth S. Kaufman.
Practice before Federal and State Regulatory Agencies, Departments, Legislatures and Courts. Energy, Communications, Environmental, Construction, Project Finance, International, Labor, Corporate and Insurance Law, Commercial Litigation and Government Relations.
See Professional Biographies, WASHINGTON, DISTRICT OF COLUMBIA

Wrist, Christopher Philip '58 '85
C.174 B.S. L.208 J.D. [A] Fitzpatrick,C.H.&S.] (See Pat. Sect.)
Wrobel, Stanley J., (AV) ....'51 '75 C&L.145 B.S., J.D. [Womble C.S.&R.]
*PRACTICE AREAS: Real Estate; Corporate Law.
Wroblewski, Jonathan J. '61 '86
C.228 A.B. L.813 J.D. Dep. Gen. Coun., U.S. Sentencing Comm.
Wrona, James S. '66 '93
C.1326 B.A. L.607 J.D. Off. of Gen. Coun., NASD Regulation Inc.

Wrubel, Wende A. .... '64 '89 C.966 B.A. L.904 J.D. 1301 Constitution Ave., N.W.
Wrzosek, Robert A. .... '72 '97 C.354 B.A./B.S. L.228 J.D. [Ⓐ Ritter E.&N.]
*PRACTICE AREAS: Public Finance Law; Tax.
Wu, David, (AV) ....'55 '85 C.813 B.S. L.976 J.D. 1023 U.S. Capitol
Wu, Frances K. ....'70 '96 C.112 B.A. L.94 J.D. [Ⓐ Hyman,P.&M.]
Wu, Frank H. .... '67 '92 C.367 B.A. L.477 J.D. 2900 Van Ness St., N.W.
Wu, Jenny C. .... '67 '92 C.674 A.B. L.893 J.D. [Ⓒ Paul,H.J.&W.]
Wu, Portia Yu-Jung .... '70 '99 C&L.976 B.A., J.D. [Ⓐ Bredhoff&K.]
Wu, Shanlon .... '59 '90 C.881 A.B. L.276 J.D. [Ⓒ Kellogg,H.H.T.&E.]
*PRACTICE AREAS: Litigation.
Wu, Theodore W. ....'36 '69 C.871 B.S. L.94 J.D. 1050 17th St., N.W.
Wulf, Matthew ... '71 '98 C.94 B.S.B.A. L.128 J.D. Legal Coun., Reins. Assn. of America
Wulff, Erik B. .... '52 '76 C.347 B.S. L.1119 J.D. [Hogan&H.]
*PRACTICE AREAS: Franchise Law.
Wulkan, Anie Elizabeth .... '— '99 C&L.276 B.A., J.D. [Ⓐ Powell,G.F.&M.]
*PRACTICE AREAS: White Collar Criminal Defense.
Wulkan, Donna L. .... '48 '83 C.665 B.A. L.1162 J.D. Antioch School of Law
Wulsin, Lucien, Jr. '45 '70 C.855 B.A. L.893 J.D.
(adm. in CA; not adm. in DC) [Ⓒ Berliner,C.&J.] (⊙Santa Monica, CA)
Wunderli, John P. .... '67 '95 C.878 B.A. L.309 J.D. [Ⓐ Heller E.W.&M.]
Wuslich, Raymond B. .... '59 '88 C.665 B.A. L.904 J.D. [Winston&S.]
*PRACTICE AREAS: Energy Law; Litigation.
Wyand, Jeffrey A. ..... '42 '77 C.401 B.S.E.E. L.446 J.D. [Leydig,V.&M.] (See Pat. Sect.)
Wyatt, Jami .... '75 '01 C.500 B.A. L.893 J.D. [Ⓐ Bryan C.]
Wyatt, Michael K. .... '45 '73 C.674 A.B. L.309 J.D. [Hogan&H.]
*PRACTICE AREAS: Small Business Investment Companies; Private Equity; Labor and Employment.
Wyatt, Richard L., Jr. (P.C.) .... '53 '79 C.10 B.A. L.245 J.D. [Akin,G.S.H.&F.]
*PRACTICE AREAS: Labor and Employment.
Wyatt, Sherri Lynn ...... '60 '85 C.103 B.A. L.329 J.D. 1155 Connecticut Ave., Ste. 500‡
Wycoff, Eric J. .... '74 '99 C.985 B.A. L.602 J.D. [Ⓐ Latham&W.]
Wyden, Ronald L. '49 '75 C.813 A.B. L.629 J.D.
(adm. in IA; not adm. in DC) (M.C.)
Wydeven, Richard '63 '94
C.966 B.S.E.M. L.846 J.D. [Ⓐ Rothwell,F.E.&M.] (See Pat. Sect.)
*PRACTICE AREAS: Intellectual Property.
Wydra, Heather A. '68 '96 C.860 B.S. L.262 J.D.
Trial Atty., Dept. of Justice, Disab. Rights Div.
Wyland, Darryl L. .... '31 '59 C.629 B.S. L.276 J.D. 1440 N.Y. Ave. NW
Wyler, Marcus R. .... '61 '91 C.188 B.A. L.665 J.D. [Dyer E.&J.]
*PRACTICE AREAS: Corporate Law; Intellectual Property; International Investments; Joint Ventures; International Business Law.
Wylie, Ronald J. ....'35 '64 C.243 B.A. L.477 LL.B. [Harriman,J.&W.] ⊙
Wymard, Josh T. '67 '92 C.311 B.A. L.665 J.D.
(adm. in PA; not adm. in DC) Atty., The NASDAQ Stock Market, Inc.
Wyner, Richard M. .... '57 '83 C&L.309 B.A., J.D. [Shea&G.]
*PRACTICE AREAS: Civil Litigation; Insurance Law; Environmental Law.
Wynkoop, Todd A. .... '— '95 C.262 B.A. L.276 J.D. [Ⓐ Arnold&P.]
*PRACTICE AREAS: Litigation.
Wynn, Nicole .... '69 '97 C.976 B.A. L.145 J.D. [Ⓐ Dow,L.&A.]
Wynn, Patricia .... '45 '71 C.681 A.B. L.976 J.D. Assoc. Supr. Ct. J.
Wynns, L. Pat, (AV) '47 '78 C.575 A.B. L.30 J.D.
Assoc. Gen. Coun. for Appl. Litig., National Treasury Employees Union
Wyron, Richard H., (AV) .... '54 '80 C&L.893 B.A., J.D. [Swidler B.S.F.]
*PRACTICE AREAS: Bankruptcy Reorganization; Creditors Rights; Workouts; Commercial Transactions; Insurance Insolvency.
Wysong, Wendy L. .... '59 '86 C.546 B.A. L.893 J.D. Asst. U. S. Atty.
Wyss, John B. ....'47 '72 C.813 B.S. L.976 J.D. [Wiley R.&F.]
*PRACTICE AREAS: Antitrust; Litigation; Insurance; Intellectual Property.
Xenopoulos, Damon E. .... '61 '88 C.999 B.A. L.569 LL.M. [Brickfield B.R.&S.]
*PRACTICE AREAS: Administrative Law; Business Law; Commercial Law; Contracts; Energy.
Xu, Bing ....'65 '99 C.999 B.A. L.128 J.D. [Ⓐ Patton B.]
Xu, Gang .... '67 '95 L.94 J.D. [Ⓐ Morrison&F.]
*PRACTICE AREAS: Corporate; Commercial Law; Project Finance.
Yablon, Alexis .... '73 '98 C.94 B.S. L.910 J.D. Exec. Dir., Multi-State Filer Project
Yablon, Jeffery L., (P.C.), (AV) ....'48 '74 C.966 B.A. L.813 J.D. [Shaw P.]
*PRACTICE AREAS: Taxation.
Yablonski, Joseph A., (AV) ....'41 '66 C.757 B.A. L.665 LL.B. [Yablonski,B.&E.]
Yablonski, Both & Edelman, (AV) ....Suite 800, 1140 Connecticut Avenue, N.W.
Yacura, Mark M., (AV) .... '49 '85 C.665 B.A. L.904 J.D. [Buchanan I.]
*PRACTICE AREAS: Food, Drug and Cosmetic Law; Corporate Transactions; Trade Law.
Yaeger, Diane L., (AV) '49 '75 C.706 A.B. L.262 J.D.
(adm. in NY; not adm. in DC) 4994 Glenbrook Rd., N.W.
Yaffe, David P., (AV) ....'52 '77 C.367 B.A. L.273 J.D. [Van Ness F.]
*PRACTICE AREAS: Energy; Contracts; Administrative Law; Electric Utilities; Public Utilities.
Yaffe, Eric L., (AV) ....'60 '86 C.604 B.A. L.145 J.D. [Ⓒ Schmeltzer,A.&S.]
*PRACTICE AREAS: Civil Litigation; White Collar Criminal Defense; Franchise Law; Election and Campaign Finance Law.
Yager, Daniel V. .... '50 '76 C.546 B.S. L.770 J.D. [McGuiness N.&W.]
*PRACTICE AREAS: Employment Law and Legislation.
Yahner, Ann C. .... '49 '79 C.914 B.A. L.309 J.D. [Cohen,M.H.&T.]
*PRACTICE AREAS: Antitrust Class Actions; Price-Fixing; Federal Litigation.
Yakimetz, Tamara '— '99 C.112 B.A. L.30 J.D.
(adm. in MD; not adm. in DC) [Ⓐ King&S.]
Yamada, Gerald H. .... '44 '74 C.112 B.A. L.273 J.D. [Ⓒ Paul,H.J.&W.]
*PRACTICE AREAS: Environmental Law; Federal Procurement Law; Administrative Law; Regulatory Law; Public Safety.
Yamagata, Ben, (AV) ....'47 '73 C.309 B.A. L.273 J.D. [Van Ness F.]
*PRACTICE AREAS: Energy; Government Relations; Federal Legislative Practice; Technology Transfers; Transportation.
Yamaguchi, Yoichiro ....'— '94 C.999 LL.B. L.273 LL.M. [Rader,F.&G.]
*PRACTICE AREAS: Intellectual Property Law.
Yamamoto, Alan H., (AV) '45 '73 C.112 B.S. L.930 J.D.
[Ⓒ P.D.Pearlstein&Assoc.] (⊙Alexandria, VA)
*PRACTICE AREAS: Criminal Defense; Trials; Appeals; Business Law; Corporate Law.
Yampolsky, Harvey A., (AV) ....'45 '71 C.696 A.B. L.145 J.D. [Arent F.K.P.&K.]
*PRACTICE AREAS: Health Care Fraud; Health Care Reimbursement.
Yamuder, Sheryl Ann '66 '94 C.94 B.A. L.978 J.D.
Assoc. Gen. Coun., National Geographic Society
*RESPONSIBILITIES: Entertainment Law; Contracts; Intellectual Property; Media Law.
Yanakakis, Sotirios Basil ....'67 '94 C.699 B.A. L.93 J.D. [Ⓐ Ashcraft&G.]
*PRACTICE AREAS: Diet Drug Litigation; Products Liability.
Yancer, Laura C. '72 '99 C.97 B.A. L.608 J.D.
(adm. in MD; not adm. in DC) Pres. Management Intern/Dept. Defence/Dept. of Just.
Yancey, Thomas H. .... '55 '80 C.902 B.S. L.893 J.D. [Sidley A.B.&W.]
Yang, Christine H. T. ....'— '97 C.477 A.B. L.339 J.D. [Ⓐ Manatt,P.&P.]
Yang, John C. .... '68 '92 C.910 A.B. L.273 J.D. [Wiley R.&F.]
Yang, Phoebe L. '69 '97 C.893 B.A. L.813 J.D.
(adm. in CA; not adm. in DC) 555 13th St., N.W.‡

Yanni, Palma R., (AV) '55 '79 C.518 A.B. L.597 J.D. BB
2612 P Street, N.W., 20007
Telephone: 202-338-1995 Fax: 202-338-1994 URL: http://www.palma-yanni.com
Email: palma-yanni@mindspring.com URL: http://www.lawyers.com/yannilaw
***PRACTICE AREAS: Immigration and Nationality Law.**
Immigration Law and International Business Matters.
See Professional Biographies, WASHINGTON, DISTRICT OF COLUMBIA

Yannucci, Thomas D., (AV) ....'50 '77 C&L.602 A.B., J.D. [Kirkland&E.]
*PRACTICE AREAS: Commercial Litigation; Antitrust; Defamation; Intellectual Property.
Yanoff, Amy J. .... '73 '98 C.103 A.B. L.477 J.D. [Ⓐ Arnold&P.]
*PRACTICE AREAS: Litigation.
Yanowitz, Jason M. .... '69 '00 C.446 B.S. L.61 J.D. [Ⓐ Swidler B.S.F.]
*PRACTICE AREAS: Telecommunications Law; Antitrust Law.
Yap, Maureen C. '— '00 C.477 B.A. L.276 J.D.
(adm. in VA; not adm. in DC) [Ⓐ Goodwin P.]
Yarbrough, Katherine P. .... '47 '87 C.339 B.S. L.1209 J.D. [Sutherland A.&B.]
*PRACTICE AREAS: Energy; Federal Energy Regulation.
Yarmolinsky, Adam, (AV) ..... '22 '49 C.309 A.B. L.976 LL.B. 1401 New York Ave. NW
Yarnell, Scott F. '69 '97 C.233 B.S. L.273 J.D.
(adm. in MD; not adm. in DC; Pat.) [Ⓐ Hunton&W.]
*PRACTICE AREAS: Patents.
Yarowsky, Jonathan R., (AV) .... '49 '79 C.477 A.B. L.1068 J.D. [Patton B.]
Yarrington, Hugh J. .... '42 '67 C.682 B.A. L.273 LL.B. 1817 19th St., N.W.
Yates, Anne Winfield ....'63 '89 C&L.575 B.S., J.D. 1155 Connecticut Avenue, N.W.
Yates, Edward E. '59 '88 C.112 B.A. L.1049 J.D.
(adm. in CA; not adm. in DC) Council on Envir. Quality
Yates, Greg R. ....'57 '89 C&L.16 B.A., J.D. [Ⓐ Steptoe&J.]
Yates, Valerie ....'68 '93 C&L.309 A.B., J.D. [Ⓐ Metzger&M.]
Yazbeck, Eleanor .... '43 '69 C.808 B.A. L.861 J.D. Prof., Urban Law Inst.
Yde, Paul L., (AV) .... '59 '85 C.966 B.S. L.378 J.D. [Vinson&E.]
*PRACTICE AREAS: Litigation; Antitrust and Trade Regulation; Unfair Competition.
Yeager, Frederick G. '38 '64 C.793 B.S. L.273 LL.B.
(adm. in IA; not adm. in DC) ABA/Ceeli
Yeargin, D. Grayson '74 '00 C.999 B.A. L.276 J.D.
(adm. in NY; not adm. in DC) [Ⓐ Covington&B.]
Yearsich, George G. ....'50 '76 C.108 B.A. L.309 J.D. [Morgan,L.&B.]
Yee, Edward W. ...... '57 '98 C.976 B.A. L.446 J.D. [Ⓐ Sterne,K.G.&F.] (See Pat. Sect.)
*PRACTICE AREAS: Patents.
Yee, Wendell '47 '78 C.312 B.A. L.424 J.D.
(adm. in IL; not adm. in DC) The Bureau of Natl. Affs., Inc.
Yee, William K. '— '00 C.112 B.S. L.770 J.D.
(adm. in CA; not adm. in DC) [Ⓐ Sughrue M.] ⊙
*PRACTICE AREAS: Patent Law.
Yeh, Grace Sing-Fein .... '71 '97 C&L.309 A.B., J.D. [Ⓐ Hogan&H.]
*PRACTICE AREAS: Securities Law; Mergers and Acquisitions; Corporate Law.
Yeh, Jenny Wu .... '74 '99 L.112 J.D. [Ⓐ Hogan&H.]
*PRACTICE AREAS: Corporate; Real Estate.
Yeh, Lucinda T. '71 '98 C.976 B.A. L.893 J.D.
(adm. in MD; not adm. in DC) [Ⓐ Hogan&H.]
Yeh, Luke J. ....'69 '97 C.350 B.S.C.E. L.352 J.D. [Ⓐ Hale&D.] (Pat.)
*PRACTICE AREAS: Intellectual Property.
Yeh, Michael D. ....'71 '98 C.188 B.S. L.494 J.D. [Ⓐ Arnold&P.]
*PRACTICE AREAS: Antitrust; Litigation.
Yelen, Suzanne ....'68 '93 C&L.976 B.A., J.D. [Wiley R.&F.]
Yellen, Kenneth J. '69 '96 C.112 B.A. L.94 J.D.
(adm. in NY; not adm. in DC) [Ⓐ Orrick,H.&S.]
*PRACTICE AREAS: Structured Finance.
Yellig, Terry R., (AV) ....'46 '73 C.30 B.A. L.665 J.D. [Sherman,D.C.L.&Y.]
*PRACTICE AREAS: Labor and Employment Law; Union Labor Law.
Yelverton, Ann-Kelley .... '67 '95 C.197 B.A. L.569 J.D. 1201 Penn. Ave., N.W.
Yelverton, Stephen Thomas, (AV) '47 '73
C&L.575 A.B., J.D. 601 Pennsylvania Ave, N.W., Ste 900 S.
Yenouskas, Joseph F. ....'60 '87 C.276 B.A. L.273 J.D. [Ⓒ Kelley D.&W.]
*PRACTICE AREAS: Litigation.
Yeo, Derek A. .... '66 '98 C.050 B.A. L.945 J.D. [Ⓐ Wiley R.&F.]
Yeo, Matthew .... '67 '95 C.103 A.B. L.309 J.D. [Ⓐ Steptoe&J.]
Yerxa, Rufus, (AV) ....'51 '76 Assoc. Gen. Coun.-Biotech Acceptance, Monsanto Co.
Yesner, Donna Lee, (AV) .... '50 '83 C.560 B.A. L.128 J.D. [McKenna&C.]
*PRACTICE AREAS: Public Health Law; Government Procurement.
Yesutis, Joseph E. .... '66 '94 C.309 A.B. L.861 J.D. [Ⓐ Mayer,B.&P.]
Yette, Frederick W., (AV) .... '59 '84 C.302 B.A. L.309 J.D. Asst. U.S. Atty. for D.C.
Yeutter, Clayton K., (AV) ....'30 '63 C&L.546 B.S., J.D. [Ⓒ Hogan&H.]
*PRACTICE AREAS: International Trade; Business Law.
Yi, Yuchong C. '70 '96 C.31 B.A. L.893 J.D.
(adm. in IL; not adm. in DC) [Ⓐ Shaw P.]
*PRACTICE AREAS: Real Estate.
Yim, Jeannie ......'66 '92 C.976 B.A. L.145 J.D. Asso. Litigation Coun., MCI WorldCom
Yim, Millicent C. '64 '90 C.112 B.A. L.309 J.D.
(adm. in CA; not adm. in DC) 1140 19th St NW # 900
Yim, Soo J. .... '66 '93 C&L.309 A.B., J.D. [Wilmer,C.&P.]
*PRACTICE AREAS: Broker-Dealer Regulation; Electronic Commerce; Financial Institutions Law; Investment Management; SEC Enforcement.
Yim, Susan S. ....'69 '96 C.788 B.A. L.861 J.D. [Ⓐ Ballard S.A.&I.]
*PRACTICE AREAS: Business Law; Energy; Project Finance.
Yingling, Edward L., (AV) ...... '49 '73 C.674 A.B. L.813 LL.B. 1120 Conn. Ave., N.W.
Yingling, Gary L. .... '— '68 C.575 B.S. L.245 J.D. [Kirkpatrick&L.]
*PRACTICE AREAS: Food and Drug Regulation.
Yingling, Monique E. .... '51 '77 C.881 A.B. L.838 J.D. [Zuckert,S.&R.]
*PRACTICE AREAS: Federal Tax Controversies; Federal Taxation; Income Tax; Tax Controversies; Tax Exempt Organizations.
Yingst, Robert A., (BV) ....'43 '73 C.905 B.A. L.329 J.D. [Boothby&Y.] ⊙
Yoch, Michael J. '70 '98 C&L.846 B.A., J.D.
(adm. in TX; not adm. in DC) 1868 Columbia Rd., N.W.
Yoches, E. Robert, (AV) '53 '80
C.174 B.S.E.E. L.659 J.D. [Finnegan,H.F.G.&D.] (See Pat. Sect.)
*PRACTICE AREAS: Information Technology Licensing; Software Copyright; Software Licensing; Software Protection; Intellectual Property Litigation.
Yodaiken, Ruth '— '99 C.66 B.A. L.588 J.D.
(adm. in MD; not adm. in DC) 701 Pennsylvania Avenue, N.W.
Yodice, John S., (AV) ....'32 '59 C.102 A.B. L.273 J.D. [Yodice]
Yodice, Kathleen Ann .... '60 '86 C.443 B.A. L.446 J.D. 500 E St., S.W.
Yodice Associates, (AV) ....500 E St., S.W.
Yoerges, Roger W. .... '58 '86 C.260 B.A. L.362 J.D. [Wilmer,C.&P.]
*PRACTICE AREAS: Products Liability; Civil Practice; Food, Drug and Cosmetics Regulation.
Yogodzinski, Debra D., (AV) .... '53 '78 C.645 B.A. L.128 J.D. [Nixon P.]
*PRACTICE AREAS: Real Estate; Real Estate Finance.
Yohannan, David R. .... '66 '94 C.645 B.Sc. L.1209 J.D. [Ⓐ Collier S.S.] (Pat.)
*PRACTICE AREAS: Patent, Trademark and Copyright; Litigation.

Yohay, Stephen C., (AV) '46 '71 C.867 B.A. L.276 J.D. [Arent F.K.P.&K.]
*PRACTICE AREAS: Occupational Safety and Health; Labor and Employment.
Yonkers, Charles E., (AV) '40 '66 C.976 A.B. L.309 J.D. [McKenna&C.]
Yoo, Anthony S. '68 '92 C&L.893 B.A., J.D. [🄰 Covington&B.] (See Pat. Sect.)
Yoo, Jiyul '65 '97 C.999 B.A. L.880 J.D. [🄰 Pillsbury W.]
*PRACTICE AREAS: International Trade; Corporate.
Yood, Andrew C. '47 '77
C.838 B.S. L.1048 J.D. Dir., Taxation, American Petroleum Institute
Yoon, Matthew S. '72 '99 C.1044 B.A. L.904 J.D.
(adm. in NY; not adm. in DC) [🄰 Thacher P.&W.]
Yoon, Pyong W. '63 '99 C.223 B.S.M.E. L.831 J.D. [🄰 Fried,F.H.S.&J.] (Pat.)
*PRACTICE AREAS: Intellectual Property; Patents; Corporate Law.
Yoon, Sam J. '71 '99 C.178 B.A. L.880 J.D.
(adm. in TX; not adm. in DC) [🄰 Shearman&S.]
*PRACTICE AREAS: International Trade; Customs.
Yoon, Tacie H. '61 '87 C.276 B.A. L.93 J.D. [🄲 Swidler B.S.F.]
*PRACTICE AREAS: Civil Litigation; Complex Litigation.
Yoon, Tae-Sik '67 '94 C.367 B.A. 725 12th St., N.W.
York, George E. '72 '01 C.103 B.A. L.178 J.D.
(adm. in IL; not adm. in DC) [🄰 Mayer,B.&P.]
*PRACTICE AREAS: International Trade; Government.
York, Michael M., (AV) '53 '79 C.383 B.A. L.575 J.D. [Wehner&Y.] ⊙
*PRACTICE AREAS: Media Law; Civil Litigation; Criminal Defense.
Yorkgitis, Edward A., Jr. '61 '87 C.674 A.B. L.309 J.D. [Kelley D.&W.]
*PRACTICE AREAS: Telecommunications Law.
Yoshida, Naoki '68 '98 C.705 B.S.M.E. L.823 J.D. [🄰 Finnegan,H.F.G.&D.]
*PRACTICE AREAS: Intellectual Property; Litigation; Patents; Intellectual Property Portfolio Management.
Yoskowitz, Irving B., (AV) '45 '70 C.563 B.B.A. L.309 J.D. [🄲 Crowell&M.]
Youhas, Isha Rauchle '75 '00 C.477 B.S. L.228 J.D.
(adm. in VA; not adm. in DC) [🄰 Wilmer,C.&P.]
Young, Andrew B. '68 '96 C.893 B.A. L.309 J.D. [🄰 Dewey B.]
*PRACTICE AREAS: Energy; Telecommunications Law.
Young, Anthony L., (AV) '44 '73 C.800 A.B. L.276 J.D. [Piper M.R.&W.]
*PRACTICE AREAS: Food and Drug Law; Environmental Law; Toxics Law; Litigation.
Young, Barbara Jeanne '60 '92 C.140 B.S. L.276 J.D.
(adm. in VA; not adm. in DC) 1666 K St., N.W.‡
Young, Becki L. '71 '99 C.659 B.A. L.276 J.D. [🄰 Dickstein S.M.&O.]
*PRACTICE AREAS: Immigration.
Young, Bernard J. '34 '73 C.976 B.A. L.128 J.D. 4545 42nd St., N.W.
Young, Craig B., (AV) '49 '83 C.30 B.A. L.1209 J.D. [🄲 Andrews&K.]
*PRACTICE AREAS: Commercial Litigation; Bankruptcy Litigation; Fraudulent Conveyance; Business Litigation; Federal Civil Practice.
Young, Duane K. '64 '95 C.502 B.S. L.273 J.D. 2300 N. St. NW
Young, Genevieve M. '63 '89 C.914 B.A. L.276 J.D.
(adm. in VA; not adm. in DC) 1200 18th St., N.W.‡
Young, Glenn M. '48 '75 C.608 B.A. L.309 J.D. [Squire,S.&D.]
*PRACTICE AREAS: Litigation.
Young, H. Alan, (AV) '37 '64 C.165 B.A. L.1017 LL.B. [Young,G.&V.] ⊙
*PRACTICE AREAS: Non Profit and Charitable Organizations; Civil Litigation; Business Law; Real Estate Law.
Young, James P. '65 '93 C.260 B.A. L.145 J.D. [🄰 Sidley A.B.&W.]
Young, Joanne W. '49 '75 C.918 B.A. L.276 J.D. [Baker&H.]
*PRACTICE AREAS: Transportation Law; International Law; Litigation; Administrative Law.
Young, John A. '16 '40 C.714 A.B. L.846 2000 M St.‡
Young, John Hardin, (AV) '48 '73 C.165 A.B. L.893 J.D. [Sandler,R.&Y.]
*PRACTICE AREAS: Litigation; Administrative Law; Antitrust Law; Technology Law; Business Law.
Young, Kelly Richard '68 '99 C.893 B.A. L.813 J.D. 1450 G St., NW, Ste. 445
Young, Kial S. '— '96 C.976 B.A. L.813 J.D. [🄰 Jenner&B.]
Young, Kimberly '66 '93 C.923 B.A. L.893 J.D. [🄰 Holland&K.]
*PRACTICE AREAS: International Trade; Customs Law.
Young, Mark D. '52 '77 C.860 B.A. L.276 J.D. [Kirkland&E.]
*PRACTICE AREAS: Securities; Derivatives Law; Banking; Legislative.
Young, Nancy N. '64 '90
C.945 B.A. L.309 J.D. Asst. Gen Coun., Air Trans.Assoc. of Amer.
*RESPONSIBILITIES: Environmental Law.
Young, Pamela M. '55 '80 C.188 A.B. L.569 J.D.
Asst. Gen. Coun., American Insurance Association
*RESPONSIBILITIES: Medical Malpractice Insurance; Liability Insurance; Legislative/Regulatory; Litigation.
Young, Patricia N. '51 '76
C.788 B.A. L.276 J.D. Sr. Atty., MCI Communications Corporation
Young, Richard E., (AV) '48 '79 C&L.893 B.A., J.D. [🄲 Sidley A.B.&W.]
Young, Sara E. '73 '00 C.174 B.A. L.904 J.D. [🄰 Jones,D.R.&P.]
Young, W. Hartmann '67 '96 C.945 B.A. L.1209 J.D. [🄰 Perkins C.]
*PRACTICE AREAS: Government Contracts; Litigation.
Young, W. Randolph, Law Offices of, (AV) '30 '66
C.692 B.A. L.273 LL.B. 1050 17th St., N.W.
Young, William F., (AV) '48 '77 C.893 B.A. L.309 J.D. [Hunton&W.]
*PRACTICE AREAS: Antitrust; Energy.

Young, Goldman & Van Beek, A Professional Corporation, (AV)
Suite 800, 2000 L Street N.W., 20036 ⊙
Telephone: 703-684-3260
H. Alan Young; Neil D. Goldman; John P. Van Beek.
Civil Litigation, Commercial Leasing, Commercial Loans, Telecommunications, Creditor's Rights, Bankruptcy, Real Estate Development, Business Law, Employment, Non-Profit Corporations, and Motor Sports Law.
Alexandria, Virginia Office: 510 King Street, Suite 416. Telephone: 703-684-3260. Facsimile: 703-548-4742.
See Professional Biographies, WASHINGTON, DISTRICT OF COLUMBIA

Young & Valkenet, L.L.C.
(See Baltimore, Maryland)

Youngers, Lisa R. '67 '95 C.966 B.A. L.1035 J.D.
Atty., MCI Telecommunications Corp. (Regulatory Affairs)
Yoviene, Wendy M. '70 '98 C&L.893 B.A., J.D. [🄰 Thelen R.&P.]
*PRACTICE AREAS: Government Affairs.
Yu, Hui '67 '98 C.999 B.A. L.352 J.D. [🄰 Dewey B.]
*PRACTICE AREAS: International Trade.
Yu, Sylvia S. '71 '00 C.976 B.A. L.309 J.D.
(adm. in MA; not adm. in DC) [🄰 Shaw P.]
Yu, Ted '74 '00 C.188 B.A. L.273 J.D.
(adm. in NY; not adm. in DC) 450 Fifth St., NW
Yudin, David E. '43 '70 C.665 B.A. L.276 J.D. 1301 Pennsylvania Ave Nw, Suite 404
Yuen, Barry C. '58 '90 C&L.273 B.B.A., J.D.
(adm. in MD; not adm. in DC) Intl. Monetary Fund
Yuffee, Michael A. '— '94 C.94 B.A. L.910 J.D. [🄰 McDermott,W.&E.]
Yun, John '70 '01 C.446 B.S. L.273 J.D.
(adm. in NY; not adm. in DC) [🄰 Blank R.C.&M.]
*PRACTICE AREAS: Intellectual Property.

Yung, Carroll John, (AV) '56 '82 C.453 S.B. L.188 J.D. [🄲 Shaw P.]
*PRACTICE AREAS: Communications.
Yurek, Stephen R. '62 '87 C.723 B.S. L.1018 J.D.
(adm. in MN; not adm. in DC) [🄲 Coates,D.&G.]
*PRACTICE AREAS: Education Law; Association Law; Corporate Law; Administrative Law; Energy Law.
Yurkanin, Michael, Jr '68 '97 C.880 B.A. L.69 J.D.
Trial Atty., U.S. Dept. Just., Tax Div.
Yurow, John J., (AV) '31 '58 C&L.273 B.A., J.D. [Arent F.K.P.&K.]
*PRACTICE AREAS: Taxation Law; Taxpayer Representation Law; Tax Controversies Law; Partnership Law; Corporate Law.
Zacaroli, Alec '69 '99 C.273 B.A. L.30 J.D. [🄰 Wallace K.M.&B.]
*PRACTICE AREAS: Environmental Law; Litigation.
Zaccardelli, Gino '61 '86 C.93 B.A. L.276 J.D. [Shaw P.] (⊙Mc Lean, VA)
*PRACTICE AREAS: Trusts; Estates.
Zaccardelli, Maryelena '63 '88 C.347 B.S. L.477 J.D. [🄲 Shaw P.]
Zacharia, John H. '— '95 C&L.893 B.A., J.D. [🄰 Howrey S.A.&W.]
*PRACTICE AREAS: Complex Litigation; International Arbitration and Litigation; Insurance Coverage; Antitrust; Intellectual Property.
Zachary, Michael N. '56 '84 C.178 A.B. L.309 J.D. [🄲 Kenyon&K.]
*PRACTICE AREAS: Intellectual Property.
Zachem, Kathryn A., (AV) '58 '85 C.273 B.A. L.1209 J.D. [Wilkinson B.K.]
*PRACTICE AREAS: Communications; Telecommunications Law; Administrative Law.
Zackula, Sharon K. '54 '81 C.910 A.B. L.209 J.D. Sr. Atty., NASD Regulation, Inc.
Zafarnia, Babak '73 '00 C.880 B.S. L.1356 J.D.
(adm. in MD; not adm. in DC) 215 Pennsylvania Ave. SE
Zaffuts, Paul J. '60 '92 C.688 B.S. L.188 J.D. [Morgan,L.&B.]
Zagaris, Bruce, (AV) '47 '73 C&L.273 B.A., J.D. [Berliner,C.&R.]
*PRACTICE AREAS: International; Tax; Criminal.
Zahedi, Nancy S. '59 '00 C.813 B.A. L.276 J.D. Solr. Off., Dept. of Interior
Zaheed, Murshed '73 '99 C.1494 B.A. L.94 J.D.
(adm. in MA; not adm. in DC) [🄰 O'Donnell,S.&A.]
Zahler, Robert E., (P.C.) '50 '75 C.453 S.B. L.309 J.D. [Shaw P.]
*PRACTICE AREAS: Outsourcing; Technology Licensing; Technology Transactions; Corporate.
Zaid, Mark '67 '92 C.696 B.A. L.982 J.D. [🄲 Lobel,N.&L.]
*PRACTICE AREAS: International; National Security; Freedom of Information.
Zakheim, Marcie H. '61 '98 C.566 B.S. L.273 J.D. [🄰 Feldesman,T.L.F.&B.]
*PRACTICE AREAS: Health Care Law; Corporate Law; Nonprofit Organizations Law.
Zakupowsky, Alexander, Jr., (AV) '— '73 C&L.276 B.S.B.A., J.D. [Miller&C.]
*PRACTICE AREAS: Taxation; Tax Litigation.
Zalenski, Walter E. '— '84 C&L.273 B.A., J.D. [Weil,G.&M.]
*PRACTICE AREAS: Banking.

Zall, Barnaby W.
(See Rockville, Maryland)

Zama, Nunotte '60 '95 C.454 B.S. L.472 J.D.
(adm. in MA; not adm. in DC) Coun., Organization of Amer. States
Zamarin, Michelle A. '73 '99 C.264 B.A. L.94 J.D. [🄰 Skadden,A.S.M.&F.]
*PRACTICE AREAS: Litigation.
Zambri, Salvatore J. '67 '92 C.945 B.A. L.273 J.D. [Regan,H.&L.] ⊙
*PRACTICE AREAS: Personal Injury; Medical Malpractice; Private Sector Worker's Compensation; Wrongful Death; Automobile Torts.
Zambrowicz, Kevin A. '70 '95 C&L.128 B.A., J.D. [🄰 Arnold&P.]
*PRACTICE AREAS: Financial Institutions; Corporate; Securities.
Zamoff, Mitchell E. '67 '92 C&L.893 B.A., J.D. [🄲 Hogan&H.]
*PRACTICE AREAS: Civil Litigation; Complex Litigation; Federal Criminal Law; Grand Jury Practice; Insurance Coverage.
Zampogna, Christopher A. '67 '94 C&L.602 B.A., J.D. 1700 K Street, N.W.
Zanar, Louise P. '56 '86 C.788 B.A. L.273 J.D. [🄰 Katz&R.]
Zanardi, David G. '70 '98 C.886 B.A. L.1206 J.D.
(adm. in FL; not adm. in DC) [🄰 Baise&M.]
*PRACTICE AREAS: Commercial Transactions; International Commercial Law.
Zane, Phillip C., (AV) '61 '91 C.668 B.A. L.569 J.D. [🄲 Morgan,L.&B.]
Zanga, Catherine A. '73 '99 C&L.893 B.A., J.D. Office of Special Coun.
Zangara, Charles J. '65 '00 C.705 B.A. L.569 J.D.
(adm. in NY; not adm. in DC) [🄰 Sutherland A.&B.]
*PRACTICE AREAS: Corporate Law.
Zanowski, Leigh M. '69 '00 C.699 A.B. L.128 J.D.
(adm. in MD; not adm. in DC; See Pat. Sect.) [🄰 Rothwell,F.E.&M.]
*PRACTICE AREAS: Pharmaceutical Patent Litigation; Biotechnology Patent Prosecution.
Zappala, Lori A. '63 '89 C.699 B.A. L.276 J.D. 1440 New York Ave. N.W.
Zapruder, Henry G., (AV) '38 '62 C.623 B.B.A. L.309 LL.B. [Baker&H.]
*PRACTICE AREAS: Tax.
Zaragoza, Richard R., (AV) '44 '69 C.276 A.B. L.93 J.D. [Shaw P.]
*PRACTICE AREAS: Communications.
Zarenko, Kristen I. '74 '99 C&L.276 B.S.B.A., J.D. [🄰 McGuirewoods]
*PRACTICE AREAS: Corporate Finance; Securities; Mergers and Acquisitions.
Zarin, Donald '49 '76 C.276 B.S. L.273 J.D. [Dechert]
*PRACTICE AREAS: International Trade; Transactional.
Zarlenga, Carmine R. '59 '84 C.608 B.A. L.150 J.D. [Howrey S.A.&W.]
*PRACTICE AREAS: Antitrust; Commercial Litigation; Franchise Law.
Zarlenga, Lisa M. '69 '94 C&L.608 B.S., J.D. [🄰 Steptoe&J.]
Zarro, Janice A. '47 '74 C.705 B.A. L.146 J.D.
(adm. in PA; not adm. in DC) V.P., Govt Affs.-Worldwide, Mallinckrodt Inc.
Zasada, John Robert '68 '95 C.174 B.A. L.882 J.D.
(adm. in ND; not adm. in DC)
Assoc. Dir. Regulatory Compliance, National Assn. of Fed. Credit Unions
Zatz, Clifford J. '54 '79 C.94 B.A. L.228 J.D. [Akin,G.S.H.&F.]
*PRACTICE AREAS: Litigation.
Zaucha, Jerome J. '52 '77 C.602 A.B. L.976 J.D. [🄲 Jones,D.R.&P.]
Zausner, L. Andrew, (AV) '49 '75 C.94 B.A. L.659 J.D. [Dickstein S.M.&O.]
*PRACTICE AREAS: Government; Legislative; Energy Law.
Zavareei, Hassan A. '69 '96 C.228 B.A. L.1066 J.D. [🄰 Gibson,D.&C.]
*PRACTICE AREAS: Commercial Litigation; Litigation; International Law.
Zax, Helen Kemp '52 '80 C.197 A.B. L.276 J.D. Georgetown Univ.
Zax, Leonard A., (AV) '78 C.145 A.B. L.309 J.D. [Latham&W.]
Zdebski, Charles A. '66 '94 C.309 A.B. L.273 J.D. [🄰 Troutman S.]
*PRACTICE AREAS: Business Litigation; Complex Litigation; Employment Litigation; Litigation; Complex and Multi-District Litigation.
Zebrowski, Christine C. '66 '93
C&L.276 B.A., J.D. Assoc. Gen. Coun., Natl. Geographic Soc.
*RESPONSIBILITIES: Employment Counseling and Litigation; Contracts; Internet Law; Intellectual Property.
Zegger, Paul J. '59 '87 C.454 B.S.Ch.E. L.982 J.D.
(adm. in CT; not adm. in DC; See Pat. Sect.) [Pennie&E.]
*PRACTICE AREAS: Intellectual Property; Intellectual Property Litigation.
Zehner, Zachary Andrews '73 '00 C.855 B.A. L.904 J.D.
(adm. in VA; not adm. in DC) [🄰 Wilkinson B.K.]
*PRACTICE AREAS: Telecommunications Law.
Zeiberg, Mona C. '61 '91 C.30 B.A. L.245 J.D. [🄲 Morgan,L.&B.]
Zeichner, Lee M. '61 '88 C.260 B.A. L.276 J.D. LegalNet Works Inc.

Zeidler, Jon T. .... '62 '98 C.1307 B.A. L.276 J.D. [[A] Shaw P.]
*PRACTICE AREAS: Real Estate.
Zeidman, Philip F., (AV) .... '34 '58 C.976 B.A. L.309 LL.B. [Piper M.R.&W.]
*PRACTICE AREAS: Antitrust; Franchise and Distribution Law; International Franchising; Trade Regulation; International Law.
Zeien, Jennifer J. .... '57 '92 C.860 B.S.E.M. L.273 J.D. [Slater&Z.]
*PRACTICE AREAS: Maritime and Shipping Regulation Law; Transportation Law; Procurement Law; Government Contracts; Environmental Law.
Zeien, Jennifer J. .... '57 '92 1000 Sixteenth St., N.W., Suite 701
Zeifang, Donald P., (AV) '36 '65
C.602 B.A. L.276 J.D. 1050 Connecticut Ave., N.W., Suite 1100
Zeifman, Jerome M. '25 '58
C.309 A.B. L.569 LL.B. 1919 Pennsylvania Ave., N.W., Suite 800
Zeiger, David L. .... '43 '85 C.197 B.A. L.329 J.D. 1232 17th St., N.W.
Zeigler, Luther .... '58 '85 C.604 A.B. L.813 J.D. [Crowell&M.]
*PRACTICE AREAS: Litigation; Appellate Practice.
Zeigler, Patricia R. .... '57 '83 C.604 B.A. L.767 J.D. [[C] Orrick,H.&S.]
Zeineddin, R. Paul .... '66 '98 C.610 B.S. L.273 J.D. [[A] Kenyon&K.]
*PRACTICE AREAS: Intellectual Property.
Zeitler, Wilhelm A. .... '44 '69 C.276 B.F.S. L.893 J.D 901 15th St N.W.
Zeitler, William A., (AV) .... '— '69 C.276 B.S.F.S. L.893 J.D. [Verner,L.B.M.&H.]
*PRACTICE AREAS: International Trade Law; Customs Law.
Zeitlin, Katherine C. .... '57 '85 C.681 A.B. L.145 J.D. [[C] Morrison&F.]
*PRACTICE AREAS: Energy.
Zeitlin, Kim A., (AV) .... '45 '71 C.696 A.B. L.145 J.D. [Zeitlin]
Zeitlin Law Firm, The, (AV) .... 5335 Wisconsin Avenue, N.W., Suite 440
Zeldin, Michael F. .... '51 '76 C.1044 B.A. L.273 J.D. 3131 Tennyson Street, NW
Zele, John D. .... '66 '93 C.674 B.S.E.E. L.273 J.D. [Morgan,L.&B.] (Pat.)
Zelenko, Benjamin L. .... '33 '58 C.674 A.B. L.309 LL.B. [Baach R.&L.P.]
*PRACTICE AREAS: Copyright; Defamation; Corporate; Labor Law; Federal Regulatory.
Zelenske, Ethel '52 '77 C.546 B.A. L.831 J.D.
(adm. in PA; not adm. in DC) Natl. Sr. Citizens Law Ctr.
Zelikson, Alexander .... '73 '98 C.423 B.A. L.273 J.D. [[A] Collier S.S.]
*PRACTICE AREAS: Corporate Law; Real Estate Law.
Zelinka, Elizabeth A. .... '68 '95 C.1369 B.A. L.276 J.D. [[A] Milbank,T.H.&M.]
Zell, L. Marc .... '— '77 C.674 A.B. L.446 J.D. [Feith&Z.] (⊙Jerusalem, Israel)
Zeller, Melissa A. '70 '98 C.550 B.A. L.1209 J.D.
(adm. in VA; not adm. in DC) [[A] Slavit&G.]
Zellner, Natalie '68 '98 C.893 B.A. L.1059 J.D.
(adm. in GA; not adm. in DC) The Trust for America's Health
Zelnick, Robert W. .... '65 '90 C.390 A.B. L.273 J.D. [McDermott,W.&E.] (Pat.)
Zembruski, Elizabeth A. '75 '01 C.1019 B.A. L.276 J.D.
(adm. in NY; not adm. in DC) [[A] John&H.]
*PRACTICE AREAS: Energy.
Zempolich, Stephen J. .... '63 '92 C.228 A.B. L.276 J.D. [[C] Hogan&H.]
*PRACTICE AREAS: Corporate Law; Commercial Law; Health Care Law.
Zener, Robert V., (AV) .... '35 '59 C&L.145 A.B., J.D. [[C] Swidler B.S.F.]
*PRACTICE AREAS: Environment; Litigation.
Zengerle, Lynda S., (AV) .... '44 '73 C.788 B.A. L.477 J.D. [Baker&M.]
*PRACTICE AREAS: Immigration and Naturalization Law.
Zenick, Elliott .... '72 '98 C&L.575 B.A., J.D. [[A] Arnold&P.]
*PRACTICE AREAS: Environmental.
Zenker, Jennifer A. .... '71 '99 C.966 B.A. L.273 J.D. [[A] Howrey S.A.&W.]
*PRACTICE AREAS: Commercial Litigation; Antitrust Litigation.
Zenner, Walter F. .... '52 '91 C.397 B.A. L.1209 J.D. [Arnold&P.]
*PRACTICE AREAS: Government Contracts.
Zeno, Thomas E., (AV) .... '52 '79 C.973 A.B. L.276 J.D. Asst. U.S. Atty.
Zentay, John H., (AV) .... '— '58 C&L.309 A.B., LL.B. [Verner,L.B.M.&H.]
*PRACTICE AREAS: Legislative Law; Energy Law.

Zentz, Carl E., P.A.
(See Fort Washington, Maryland)

Zern, Peter .... '73 '98 C.197 A.B. L.276 J.D. [[A] Covington&B.]
Zerzan, Gregory PJ .... '70 '96 C&L.950 B.A., J.D. 1775 Eye Street, N.W.
Zeswitz, H. Karl, Jr. .... '53 '81 C.645 B.S. L.276 J.D. [Sutherland A.&B.]
*PRACTICE AREAS: Tax Law; Federal Tax Planning; Corporate Taxation; Federal Tax Controversies; State Taxation.
Zeugin, Lee B. .... '52 '80 C.378 B.S.Ch.E. L.477 J.D. [Hunton&W.]
*PRACTICE AREAS: Environmental.
Zevnik, Paul Anton, (AV) .... '50 '77 C&L.309 A.B., J.D. [Zevnik H.]
*PRACTICE AREAS: Insurance Coverage; Environmental Law; Toxic Tort Litigation; Broadcasting and Media Transactions.

Zevnik Horton LLP, (AV) [BB]
The Warner Building, 1299 Pennsylvania Avenue, N.W. Ninth Floor, 20004 ⊙
Telephone: 202-824-0950 Facsimile: 202-824-0955
Email: law@zevnik.com URL: http://www.zevnik.com
Paul Anton Zevnik; Michel Yves Horton (Resident, Los Angeles, California Office); John D. Shugrue (Not admitted in DC; Resident, Chicago, Illinois Office); Charles J. Malaret (Not admitted in DC; Resident, Los Angeles, California Office); Michael John Miguel (Resident, Boston, Massachusetts Office); Patrick Michael McGovern (Resident, Los Angeles, California Office). Special Partners: Leon G. Krasinski (Not admitted in DC; Resident, Roseland, New Jersey Office); Thomas James Wingard (Not admitted in DC; Resident, Los Angeles, California Office);—Michael J. Wilson; Gregory M. Cork; Yolanda C. Griffin.
Commercial Litigation, Environmental Law, Insurance Coverage, Toxic Tort Litigation, International Law, Transactions involving corporate tax, securities, media and broadcasting, broker-dealer and real estate advice and representation. Practice before State and Federal Courts and Administrative Tribunals, including the National Association of Securities Dealers, Inc., the New York Stock Exchange and the Securities Exchange Commission.
Boston, Massachusetts Office: One International Place, Fourteenth Floor. Telephone: 617-790-2970. Facsimile: 617-790-2910.
San Francisco, California Office: 225 Bush Street, Seventeenth Floor. Telephone: 415-364-6300. Facsimile: 415-364-6333.
Los Angeles, California Office: 333 South Grand Avenue, Twenty First Floor. Telephone: 213-437-5200. Facsimile: 213-437-5222.
Chicago, Illinois Office: Zevnik Horton, 77 West Wacker Drive, Thirty Third Floor. Telephone: 312-977-2500. Facsimile: 312-977-2560.
London, England Office: 4 Kings Bench Walk, Temple, London EC4Y 7DL. Telephone: 207-822-8822. Facsimile: 207-822-8844.
Roseland, New Jersey: 103 Eisenhower Parkway, First Floor. Telephone: 973-618-5300. Facsimile: 973-618-5333.
Philadelphia, Pennsylvania Office: 620 Chestnut Street, Tenth Floor. Telephone: 215-440-8450. Facsimile: 215-440-8459.
See Professional Biographies, WASHINGTON, DISTRICT OF COLUMBIA

Zezulin, Lena S., (AV) .... '55 '79 C&L.309 B.A., J.D. [[C] Cameron M.]
*PRACTICE AREAS: Employee Benefit Law; Employment Law; Non-Profit Organizations; International Law; Civil Litigation.
Zhang, Gary '62 '99 L.276 J.D.
(adm. in VA; not adm. in DC) [[A] Pennie&E.]
*PRACTICE AREAS: Intellectual Property.
Zhao, Xiaohua .... '56 '92 C.999 B.A. L.879 J.D. [Holland&K.]
*PRACTICE AREAS: International Commercial Transactions; Corporate; Joint Ventures; Project Finance; Telecommunications.
Zhao, Yueyao (George) .... '64 '99 C.999 B.A. L.107 J.D. [[A] Dechert]
*PRACTICE AREAS: Financial Services Law; Investment Management; Securities; Corporate Law; Contracts.
Ziai, Fatemeh .... '64 '91 C.103 B.A. L.309 J.D. Human Rights Watch
Zibelli, David J. '61 '93 C.94 B.S.E.E. L.1170 J.D.
(adm. in VA; not adm. in DC; See Pat. Sect.) [[A] Kenyon&K.]
*PRACTICE AREAS: Intellectual Property.
Zic, Terrence M.R. .... '61 '89 C.423 B.A. L.276 J.D. [Wright,R.O.&T.]
*PRACTICE AREAS: Product Liability Defense; General Civil Litigation.
Zidlicky, Paul J. .... '66 '94 C.103 B.S. L.273 J.D. [[A] Sidley A.B.&W.]
Ziebarth, Anne Magill '62 '91 C.732 B.A. L.569 J.D.
(adm. in MA; not adm. in DC) Alliance to End Childhood Lead Poisoning
Ziegler, Cheryl L. '61 '86 C.367 B.A. L.477 J.D.
Dir., Housing, Lawyers Comm. for Civil Rights Under Law
*RESPONSIBILITIES: Civil Rights Litigation; Community Development.
Ziegler, Janice Helen .... '62 '87 C.188 B.S. L.309 J.D. [[C] Shaw P.]
Ziegler, Marcie R. .... '67 '92 C.674 A.B. L.976 J.D. [Williams&C.]
*PRACTICE AREAS: Civil Appeals; Criminal Appeals; Federal Civil Practice; Legal Malpractice; Medical Malpractice.
Zielezienski, J. Stephen '64 '89 C&L.176 B.A., J.D.
Asst. Gen. Coun., American Insurance Association
*RESPONSIBILITIES: Insurance; Trade Association; Antitrust; Appellate Litigation; Legislative and Regulatory Drafting.
Zielinski, Charles A., (AV) '44 '70 C.1031 B.A. L.107 J.D.
(adm. in NY; not adm. in DC) [Bell,B.&L.]
*PRACTICE AREAS: Communications; Energy and Environmental Law; Antitrust.
Ziems, Robert F., (AV) '29 '58
C.474 B.S. L.273 LL.B. [[C] Finnegan,H.F.G.&D.] (See Pat. Sect.)
*PRACTICE AREAS: Mechanical Patents; Mechanical Intellectual Property.
Zieve, Allison M. .... '64 '89 C.103 A.B. L.976 J.D. Staff Atty., Public Citizen Litig. Grp.
Ziff, Sheila N. .... '— '50 C.331 A.B. L.976 LL.B. 3820 Garfield St., N.W.
Ziffer, Deborah W. .... '69 '98 C.1329 B.S. L.30 J.D. [[A] Keller&H.]
*PRACTICE AREAS: Food and Drug.
Zigner, Jeannine Rustad .... '69 '95 C.1134 B.S. L.128 J.D. [[A] Robins,K.M.&C.]
*PRACTICE AREAS: Real Estate.
Zills, Gregory Aaron .... '71 '96 C.1038 B.S. L.575 J.D. U.S. Dept. Vet. Affairs
Zimberg, Leslie C. .... '61 '85 C.860 B.A. L.309 J.D. [Potomac C.I.]
Zimmer, Michael J., (AV) .... '49 '75 C.676 B.A. L.446 J.D. [Baker&M.]
*PRACTICE AREAS: Infrastructure Development; Project Finance.
Zimmer, Richard A. '44 '71 C&L.976 B.A., J.D.
(adm. in NY; not adm. in DC) [[C] Gibson,D.&C.]
*PRACTICE AREAS: Government; Corporate Law.
Zimmerman, David W. '— '87 C&L.846 B.B.A., J.D.
(adm. in NY; not adm. in DC) [Miller&C.]
*PRACTICE AREAS: Taxation.
Zimmerman, Edwin M., (AV) .... '24 '49 C&L.178 A.B., LL.B. [[C] Covington&B.]
Zimmerman, Eric .... '67 '98 C.1365 B.A. L.1209 J.D. [[A] McDermott,W.&E.]
Zimmerman, Jeff, (AV) .... '— '73 C.31 A.B. L.273 J.D. [Foley&L.]
*PRACTICE AREAS: Regulatory Law; Environmental Law; OSHA; Environmental Litigation; Real Estate.
Zimmerman, Jolie F. .... '67 '93 C.813 A.B. L.276 J.D. [[C] Wilmer,C.&P.]
*PRACTICE AREAS: Securities Law.
Zimmerman, Lawrence T., (AV) .... '34 '59 C&L.976 B.A., LL.B. 1800 Mass. Ave., NW
Zimmerman, M. Paul .... '34 '59 C.197 B.A. L.976 LL.B. 1001 Conn. Ave., N.W.
Zimmerman, Sarah J. .... '67 '96 C.659 B.A. L.273 J.D. [[A] Crowell&M.]
Zimmerman, Scott M. .... '62 '92 C.188 B.A. L.945 J.D. [Zuckert,S.&R.]
Zimmerman, Stephen H., (BV) '47 '72 C.848 B.A. L.608 J.D.
(adm. in OH; not adm. in DC) [Dykema G.]
*PRACTICE AREAS: Legislative Practice; Insurance Law.
Zimmermann, Stephen S. .... '62 '87 C.893 B.A. L.245 J.D. Sr. Counsel, The World Bank
Zimmet, Brian M. '69 '95 C.696 B.A. L.893 J.D.
(adm. in MD; not adm. in DC) [[A] Van Ness F.]
*PRACTICE AREAS: Energy; Electric Power.
Zimmet, Gilda M. '71 '97 C.659 B.A. L.276 J.D.
[[A] Venable,A.B.H.&C.] (⊙Balt., MD)
*PRACTICE AREAS: Trusts and Estates.
Zimmet, Sheila Cohen, (AV) '49 '75
C&L.276 B.S.N., J.D. Assoc. Coun., Georgetown Univ. Med. Ctr.
Zimmitti, Andrew .... '69 '95 C.145 B.A. L.276 J.D. [[A] Patton B.]
Zimmitti, Laura Cohen .... '69 '94 C.165 B.A. L.276 J.D. [[A] Ross,D.&B.]
Zimolzak, Joanne L. .... '68 '94 C.446 B.A. L.276 J.D. [[A] McKenna&C.]
Zingone, Gerald .... '60 '85 C.276 B.S.F.S. L.659 J.D. [Arent F.K.P.&K.]
*PRACTICE AREAS: Litigation; Antitrust.
Zini, Gregory '71 '98 C.107 B.A. L.862 J.D.
(adm. in NY; not adm. in DC) [[A] Schmeltzer,A.&S.]
*PRACTICE AREAS: Commercial Litigation; Franchise Law.
Zinkgraf, Gary M. .... '— '88 C&L.966 B.A., J.D. [Foley&L.]
*PRACTICE AREAS: Litigation; Patent Litigation; Transportation.
Zinn, David M. .... '64 '90 C.103 A.B. L.309 J.D. [Williams&C.]
Zinn, Matthew J., (AV) .... '36 '62 C.659 B.S. Econ. L.309 LL.B. [Steptoe&J.]
*PRACTICE AREAS: Taxation Law, Federal Income Estate and Gift Taxation Law; Taxation of Individuals and Business Entities Law; Tax Controversies.
Zins, Jacqueline E., (AV) .... '53 '78 C.674 B.A. L.976 J.D. [[C] Feinberg]
*PRACTICE AREAS: Mediation.
Zinsser, August, III .... '41 '67 C.478 A.B. L.276 J.D. Exec. V.P., First Amer. Bk., N.A.
Ziperman, Philip D. .... '65 '90 C.454 B.A. L.904 J.D. 915 15th St Nw # 3
Zipp, Joel F., (AV) .... '48 '75 C.966 B.S. L.390 J.D. [Cameron M.]
*PRACTICE AREAS: Energy; Public Utilities; Energy Project Development; North American Energy Trade; Administrative Law.
Zipursky, Diane '57 '82 C.813 B.A. L.273 J.D.
V.P., Washington Law & Policy, National Broadcasting Co.
Zirkelbach, Linda J. .... '73 '99 C.477 B.A. L.30 J.D. [[A] Venable,A.B.H.&C.]
*PRACTICE AREAS: Intellectual Property Litigation; Trademarks; Copyrights; Patents; Internet Law.
Zischkau, Jonathan D. '57 '83
C.119 B.S. L.602 J.D. Admin. Law J., DC Contract App. Bd.
Zisk, Robert L. .... '57 '83 C.188 B.S. L.228 J.D. [Schmeltzer,A.&S.]
*PRACTICE AREAS: Civil Litigation; Franchise Law.
Zissis, Kristina .... '66 '94 C.367 B.A. L.30 J.D. [[A] White&C.]
Zitko, John R. .... '66 '97 C.112 B.A. L.477 J.D. [[A] Morrison&F.]
*PRACTICE AREAS: Project Finance; Corporate Finance; International Law.
Zitlau, Warren A. .... '68 '94 C.205 B.Ch.E. L.94 J.D. [[A] Crowell&M.] (Pat.)
Zitver, Leon .... '13 '42 C.563 B.S. L.273 J.D. [[C] Ostrolenk,F.G.&S.] (See Pat. Sect.) ⊙
*PRACTICE AREAS: Patent Law.
Zlotnick, S. S. .... '13 '36 C.273 A.B. L.309 LL.B. 1616 H St., N.W.
Zobair, Talha A., (Mr.) '68 '95 C.454 B.A. L.1194 J.D.
(adm. in MI; not adm. in DC) Consultant, Price Waterhouse LLP.
Zochowski, Christopher M. .... '71 '97 C.276 B.A. L.273 J.D. [[A] Sullivan&C.]
Zoellick, Robert B., (AV) .... '53 '81 C.821 B.A. L.309 J.D. 3900 Wisconsin Ave., N.W.
Zolet, Theresa I., (AV) .... '62 '88 C.289 B.A. L.446 J.D. [Van Ness F.]
*PRACTICE AREAS: Natural Gas; Federal Energy Regulation; Administrative Law; Energy.

Zolt, E. Lawrence ....'— '86 C.473 B.A. L.446 J.D. [Ⓐ Manatt,P.&P.]
Zook, David R. '58 '86 C.575 B.A. L.209 J.D.
(adm. in IN; not adm. in DC) [Baker&D.]
*PRACTICE AREAS: Government Relations; Education; Health Care.
Zorc, Joseph M. .... '39 '64 C.767 B.A. L.276 J.D. 5910 16th St., N.W.
Zork, Lesley S., (BV) .... '58 '88 C.54 B.S. L.1162 J.D. [Ⓐ B.J.Klores&Assoc.]
*PRACTICE AREAS: Civil Trials; Medical Malpractice Law.
Zornada, George J. .... '64 '90 C.694 A.B. L.910 J.D. [Ⓐ Kirkpatrick&L.]
*PRACTICE AREAS: Investment Management; Mutual Funds; Securities.
Zorthian, Barry '20 '53 C.976 B.A. L.569 LL.B.
(adm. in NY; not adm. in DC) 2111 Wilson Blvd.‡
Zosa, Marie Denyse ....'71 '99 C.273 B.A. L.904 J.D. [Ⓐ Morrison&H.]
*PRACTICE AREAS: Litigation; Energy; Foreclosures.
Zotter, Bruce C., (AV) '42 '75
C.454 B.S.M.E. L.273 J.D. [Finnegan,H.F.G.&D.] (See Pat. Sect.)
*PRACTICE AREAS: Patent Litigation.
Zottola, Armand J. .... '— '97 C.105 B.A. L.180 J.D. [Ⓐ Brobeck,P.&H.]
*PRACTICE AREAS: Intellectual Property (Copyright and Trademark); E-Commerce; Computer and Software; Information Technology.
Zouaoui, Jamil ....'64 '90 C.970 B.A. L.93 J.D. [Bauer&Z.] ⊙
*PRACTICE AREAS: International Commercial Law; Alternative Dispute Resolution; Project Finance; Corporate Law.
Zubler, Todd ....'70 '96 C.910 A.B. L.309 J.D. [Ⓐ Wilmer,C.&P.]
Zubrow, Luize ...... '47 '72 C&L.174 B.A., J.D. Prof. of Law, George Washington Univ.
Zucker, Jill M. .... '— '90 C.705 B.S. L.893 J.D. [Ⓒ Bryan C.]
*PRACTICE AREAS: Environmental Law; Consumer Product Safety; Transportation; Regulatory Law.
Zucker, Jonathan S., (AV) .... '55 '85 C.33 B.A. L.1162 J.D. 601 Indiana Ave. NW
Zucker, Stephanie L. '74 '99 C.880 B.A. L.846 J.D.
(adm. in TX; not adm. in DC) [Ⓐ Baker B.]
Zuckerman, Alan S. '32 '59 C.339 B.S. L.930 LL.B.
(adm. in OH; not adm. in DC) 441 G Street, NW
Zuckerman, Gerald M. '40 '64 C.415 B.A. L.1009 LL.B.
(adm. in NY; not adm. in DC) ABACUS Comm. Co.
Zuckerman, Jason M. ....'74 '00 C.276 B.A. L.893 J.D. [Ⓐ Shaw P.]
*PRACTICE AREAS: Government Investigations; Employment Law; Commercial Litigation; Insurance Coverage Litigation.
Zuckerman, Jeffrey I., (AV) .... '50 '73 C.563 B.A. L.976 J.D. [Curtis,M.C.&M.]
*PRACTICE AREAS: Civil Litigation; Antitrust and Trade Regulation; Employment Law.
Zuckerman, Roger E., (AV) .... '42 '68 C.966 B.S. L.309 LL.B. [Zuckerman S.]
*PRACTICE AREAS: Complex Civil and Criminal Litigation.

Zuckerman Spaeder LLP, (AV)
1201 Connecticut Avenue, N.W., Suite 1200, 20036-2638 ⊙
Telephone: 202-778-1800 Fax: 202-822-8106
Email: counsel@zuckerman.com
Members of Firm: Roger E. Zuckerman; Mark W. Foster; Roger C. Spaeder; Bruce Goldstein; William W. Taylor, III; Peter R. Kolker; John F. Evans (1941-1988); Michael R. Smith; Herbert Better (Resident, Baltimore, Maryland Office); Ronald B. Ravikoff (Resident, Miami, Florida Office); Michael S. Pasano (Miami and Ft. Lauderdale, Florida Offices); Anthony Thompson; Nelson C. Cohen; Steven M. Salky; Marshall S. Wolff; Morris Weinberg, Jr. (Resident, Tampa, Florida Office); Blair G. Brown; Martin S. Himeles, Jr. (Resident, Baltimore, Maryland Office); Edward J. M. Little (Resident, New York, N.Y. Office); Thomas J. Meeks (Resident, Miami, Florida Office); Graeme W. Bush; Carl S. Kravitz; Deborah J. Jeffrey; Thomas B. Mason; Leslie Berger Kiernan; Cyril V. Smith (Resident, Baltimore, Maryland Office); Stephen J. Bronis (Resident, Miami, Florida Office); Ronald H. Weich; Eleanor H. Smith; Lisa A. Cahill (Resident, New York, N.Y. Office); Jennifer Rae Coberly (Resident, Miami, Florida Office); Norman L. Eisen; David H. Brody; William B. Fleming (Resident, New York, N.Y. Office); Thomas G. Macauley (Resident, Wilmington, Delaware Office); William B. Schultz. Counsel: Elizabeth G. Taylor; Lee Fugate (Resident, Tampa, Florida Office); Martin I. Kalish (Miami and Ft. Lauderdale, Florida Offices); Sally J. McKee (Miami and Ft. Lauderdale, Florida Offices); David A. Reiser. Associates: Virginia Whitehill Guldi; Lynn F. Kaufmann; Deborah S. Richardson (Resident, Baltimore, Maryland Office); Patrice A. Shelburne; Kristen M. Flynn; Carlos T. Angulo; Joel D. Schwartz; Amit P. Mehta; Caroline Alice Judge; Alexandra Foster; Mary I. Peters; David W. Hotes; Cynthia L. Tippett (Resident, Baltimore, Maryland Office).
Litigation (Civil, White Collar Criminal), Bankruptcy and Workouts, Taxation, Real Estate, Partnership, Corporate, Commercial and Health Care law.
Reference: Sovran Bank/DC National.
Miami, Florida Office: 201 South Biscayne Boulevard, Suite 900. Telephones: 305-358-5000; Broward County: 305-523-0277. Fax: 305-579-9749.
Ft. Lauderdale, Florida Office: One East Broward Boulevard, Suite 700. Telephone: 954-356-0463. Fax: 954-356-0406.
Baltimore, Maryland Office: Suite 2440, 100 East Pratt Street. Telephone: 410-332-0444. Fax: 410-659-0436.
Tampa, Florida Office: 401 East Jackson Street, Suite 2525. Telephone: 813-221-1010. Fax: 813-223-7961.
New York, N.Y. Office: 1114 Avenue of the Americas, 27th Floor, Grace Building. Telephone: 212-479-6500. Fax: 212-479-6512.
Wilmington, Delaware Office: One Commerce Center, 1201 Orange Street, Suite 650, Post Office Box 1028. Telephone: 302-427-0400. Fax: 302-427-8242.
See Professional Biographies, WASHINGTON, DISTRICT OF COLUMBIA

Zuckert, Scoutt & Rasenberger, L.L.P., (AV)
888 Seventeenth Street, N.W., 20006-3309
Telephone: 202-298-8660 Telecopier: 202-342-0683
URL: http://www.zsrlaw.com
Members of Firm: Eugene M. Zuckert (1911-2000); Richard A. Allen; Malcolm L. Benge; James A. Calderwood; William H. Callaway, Jr.; Frank J. Costello; James A. Harris; Ralph L. Kissick; Richard D. Mathias; Lonnie Anne Pera; Ronald S. Perlman; Andrew R. Plump; Richard P. Schweitzer; Charles J. Simpson, Jr.; Rachel B. Trinder; Monique E. Yingling; Scott M. Zimmerman. Of Counsel: Denise A. Daniels; James L. Devall; Pamela L. Meredith (Not admitted in DC); Raymond J. Rasenberger; Jerrold Scoutt, Jr.; Gerald L. Waid. Associates: Patricia E. Bruce; Robert A. DeHaan; Jeffrey A. Morse; Shannon M. Moyer; Nisha Saxena; Jol A. Silversmith.
Languages: English, French, Norwegian and Spanish.
Civil and Administrative Litigation Practice. General Practice with emphasis on International Business, Domestic and International Aviation, Surface Transportation, Antitrust, Taxation, Government Contracts, Asset-based Transactions, Labor and Employee Benefits, Bankruptcy, Immigration. Legislative Practice.
See Professional Biographies, WASHINGTON, DISTRICT OF COLUMBIA

Zuckman, Harvey L. ....'34 '60 C.800 A.B. L.569 LL.B. Catholic Univ. of Amer.
Zufall, Rachael M. ....'73 '98 C.367 B.A. L.569 J.D. [Ⓐ Kirkpatrick&L.]
*PRACTICE AREAS: Investment Management; Mutual Funds; Securities.
Zughaib, Edward E., (AV) ....'58 '86 C.165 B.A. L.823 J.D. [Katten M.Z.]
*PRACTICE AREAS: Real Estate.
Zukerberg, Paul H. ....'57 '85 C.299 B.A. L.30 J.D. 1790 Lanier Pl Nw
Zumas, Nicholas H., (AV) ....'30 '56 C.878 B.A. L.276 J.D. 1140 Connecticut Ave., N.W.
Zura, Peter '67 '97 C.1154 B.S.E.E. L.475 J.D.
(adm. in MI; not adm. in DC) [Ⓐ Morgan&F.]
*PRACTICE AREAS: Intellectual Property.
Zusman, Lynne K., (AV) .... '39 '64 C.104 A.B. L.976 LL.B. [L.K.Zusman&Assoc.]

Zusman, Lynne K., & Associates, P.C., (AV)
1818 N Street, NW Suite 701, 20036
Telephone: 202-659-1971 Fax: 202-659-0454
URL: http://www.lawyers.com/lynnezusmanlaw
Lynne K. Zusman. Of Counsel: Richard D. Glovsky.
Federal Regulatory Law, Administrative Litigation, Governmental Law, Whistleblower Litigation, Employment Law, White Collar Criminal Defense, Inspector General Investigations, Business Fraud, Contract Disputes, Executive Compensation, Wrongful Termination, Corporate Investigations, Congressional Investigations.
See Professional Biographies, WASHINGTON, DISTRICT OF COLUMBIA

Zutz, Robert J. .... '— '77 C.860 B.A. L.569 J.D. [Kirkpatrick&L.]
*PRACTICE AREAS: Investment Company Law; Investment Management; Investment Regulation; Mutual Funds; Broker-Dealer Regulation.
Zweben, Murray, (AV) ....'30 '59 C.1044 B.S. L.273 LL.B. [Ⓒ Nossaman,G.K.&E.]
*PRACTICE AREAS: Legislative Law.
Zweifach, Gerson A., (AV) ....'53 '80 C.103 A.B. L.976 J.D. [Williams&C.]
Zwerdling, Paul, Leibig, Kahn, Thompson & Driesen, P.C., (AV)
1025 Conn. Ave., N.W., Suite 307

Zwerling & Kemler, P.C.
(See Alexandria, Virginia)

Zwicker, Glen M. ....'71 '99 C&L.276 B.A., J.D. [Ⓐ Clifford C.R.&W.]
*PRACTICE AREAS: Corporate; International.
Zwillinger, Marc J. .... '69 '94 C.860 B.A. L.309 J.D. [Kirkland&E.]
*PRACTICE AREAS: Cyber Law; Information Technology; White Collar Crime; Litigation.
Zwisler, Carl E., III, (AV) ....'48 '73 C.602 A.B. L.209 J.D. [Jenkens&G.]
*PRACTICE AREAS: Franchise Law; Distribution Law; Antitrust Law; Trademark Law; Healthcare Law.
Zwisler, Margaret M., (AV) ....'49 '76 C.741 B.A. L.273 J.D. [Howrey S.A.&W.]
*PRACTICE AREAS: Antitrust; Complex Litigation; Government Regulation.
Zyblut, Chester A., (AV) ....'23 '53 C.209 A.B. L.273 LL.B. 2350 King Pl., N.W.‡
Zymelman, Ari S., (AV) ....'63 '89 C.976 B.A. L.145 J.D. [Williams&C.]
Zywan, Darin A. ....'71 '98 C.886 B.S. L.1209 J.D. 1666 K St., N.W.‡

ENGLISH LAWYERS RESIDENT IN WASHINGTON

Freshfields Bruckhaus Deringer
1300 I Street, NW, 12th Floor East, 20005-3314 ⊙
Telephone: 202-969-4500; 202-777-4500 Fax: 202-969-4555; 202-777-4555
Email: email@freshfields.com URL: http://www.freshfields.com
Partners: Ellen L. Hayes (Not admitted in DC); Thomas P. Hechl (Not admitted in DC); Gregory Evers May; Claude B. Stansbury.
Competition and Trade; Corporate; Dispute Resolution; Employment, Pensions and Benefits; Finance; Intellectual Property; Real Estate; Tax.
Freshfields Bruckhaus Deringer offices in: Amsterdam, Bangkok, Barcelona, Beijing, Berlin, Bratislava, Brussels, Budapest, Cologne, Düsseldorf, Frankfurt, Hamburg, Hanoi, Ho Chi Minh City, Hong Kong, London, Madrid, Milan, Moscow, Munich, New York, Paris, Prague, Rome, ★Shanghai, Singapore, Tokyo, Vienna, Washington.
★associate office.
See Professional Biographies, LONDON, ENGLAND

DISTRICT OF COLUMBIA — U. S. GOVERNMENT LAWYERS

CONTENTS

ADVISORY COUNCIL ON HISTORIC PRESERVATION

John M. Fowler, *General Counsel*

Fowler, John M. .... '45 '71 C.674 A.B. L.976 LL.B. Gen. Coun.
Marques, Javier E. .... '69 '96 (MD) C.602 B.A. L.273 J.D. Asst. Gen. Coun.

AGENCY FOR INTERNATIONAL DEVELOPMENT

(Vacant), *General Counsel*

OFFICE OF THE GENERAL COUNSEL

Barrington, Belinda K. .... '51 '76 (AZ) C.813 B.A. L.976 J.D.
Bereschak, Ann Marie .... '65 '94 C.645 B.S. L.1338 J.D.
Buser, Stephanie L. .... '57 '87 C.443 B.S. L.1209 J.D.
Diamond, Dennis .... '50 '79 C.436 B.A. L.1162 J.D.
Ferrao, Joaquin Emilio .... '72 '98 (FL) C.1222 B.A. L.260 J.D.
Fittipaldi, Mark F. .... '50 '83 C.976 B.A. L.228 J.D.
Gardner, John S. .... '62 '99 C&L.309 A.B., J.D.
Gressett, Donald F. .... '68 '93 C.236 B.A. L.30 J.D.
Grossi-Perone, Diane A. .... '62 '87 C.264 B.A. L.273 J.D.
Haiman, Arnold J. .... '46 '71 C.563 B.A. L.569 J.D.
Herscowitz, Andrew M. .... '70 '96 C&L.276 B.S.F.S., J.D.
Hsieh, Eileen .... '56 '86 C.976 B.A. L.597 J.D.
Hunter, Karen R. .... '— '93 C.811 B.A. L.309 J.D.
Kitay, Michael G. .... '40 '67 C.732 A.B. L.893 LL.B.
Kleinjan, Mary A. .... '48 '77 (NY) C.881 A.B. L.569 J.D.
Lester, Robert M. .... '47 '74 (VA) C.273 B.A. L.893 J.D.
Luten, Drew W., III .... '54 '79 (MO) C.947 B.A. L.309 J.D.
Marburg-Goodman, Jeffrey .... '57 '86 (NY) C.31 B.A. L.309 J.D.
Miller, Jan W. .... '46 '71 (VA) C&L.273 B.S.F.S., J.D.
Neiss, Dahlia I. .... '67 '93 C.208 B.A. L.273 J.D.
Pascocello, Susan Keller .... '64 '90 C.893 B.A. L.276 J.D.
Patterson, Jerome A. .... '46 '72 C.178 B.S. L.276 J.D.
Peters, James M. .... '60 '87 (IL) C&L.339 B.A., J.D.
Posey, Tyler S. .... '51 '77 C.103 A.B. L.861 J.D.
Powell, Tonia Jones .... '64 '90 C.329 B.A. L.945 J.D.
Scales, John K. .... '37 '62 C.951 B.A. L.188 LL.B.
Sosebee, Carl R. .... '48 '79 C.446 B.A. L.1162 J.D.
Tazewell, Littleton .... '59 '92 C.886 B.A. L.945 J.D.
Williams, Michael J. .... '47 '76 (NY) C.475 B.A. L.477 J.D.
Winter, Gary M. .... '46 '72 C.477 B.A. L.569 J.D.

OTHER OFFICES OF A.I.D.

Brown, Clifford H. .... '49 '76 (CA) C.939 B.A. L.1068 J.D.
Burns, John J. .... '49 '76 (PA) C.569 A.B. L.878 J.D.
Dailey, Thomas Arthur .... '55 '84 C&L.276 A.B., J.D.
Dumas, Claudia J. .... '59 '85 (MA) C.914 A.B. L.188 J.D.
Geiger, Thomas L. .... '42 '67 C.806 B.A. L.910 J.D.
Hendrix, Steven E. .... '62 '87 C.121 B.A. L.966 J.D.
Hyman, Gerald F. .... '42 '86 C.145 A.B. L.893 J.D.
Knott, Jay L. .... '60 '85 (PA) C.976 B.A. L.659 J.D.
Kotz, H. David .... '66 '91 C.446 B.A. L.188 J.D.
Lecce, Gail M. .... '52 '76 (HI) C.645 B.A. L.309 J.D.
Moore, Vicki L. .... '57 '85 (CA) C.112 B.A. L.309 J.D.
Perkins, Robert S. .... '35 '64 C.260 B.A. L.273 LL.B.
Rhodes, William S. .... '44 '75 C.605 B.A. L.1066 J.D.
Turner, Karen D. .... '55 '82 C.597 B.A. L.309 J.D.
Vance, Anthony N. .... '55 '82 (MA) C&L.309 B.A., J.D.
Vandenassem, Christian W., Jr. .... '63 '98 C.1046 B.S. L.446 J.D.
Velazquez, Marta R. .... '57 '83 C.674 B.A. L.276 J.D.
Ward, Mark S. .... '55 '82 C.112 A.B. L.1066 J.D.

LEGAL ADVISERS-OVERSEAS

Adams, D. Annette .... '49 '76 (MI) C.66 A.B. L.880 J.D.
Allen, Stephen C. .... '47 '76 C.197 B.A. L.178 J.D.
Doswell, Karen J. .... '67 '92 C&L.276 B.S., J.D.
Doyle, Justin E. .... '35 '63 (CA) C.696 B.A. L.188 LL.B.
Fickenscher, Karl W. .... '60 '89 C.446 B.A. L.309 J.D.
Freeman, Natalie J. .... '62 '89 C.30 B.S. L.659 J.D.
Godette, Michelle A.M. .... '63 '89 C.329 B.A. L.30 J.D.
Groarke, John P. .... '57 '89 C.569 B.A. L.659 J.D.
Hadley, Beverly A. .... '60 '84 C.659 B.A. L.276 J.D.
Harden, R. David .... '62 '95 (NY) C.264 B.A. L.276 J.D.
Jaruzelski, Janina A. .... '58 '86 C.674 A.B. L.659 J.D.
Johnson, Pauline G. .... '37 '72 C.1097 B.A. L.1068 J.D.
McGhie, Teresa L. .... '56 '92 C.877 B.S. L.904 J.D.
Newton, Alexander D. .... '44 '73 (NY) C.103 A.B. L.228 J.D.
Niemeyer, John R. .... '60 '91 (WA) C.172 B.A. L.276 J.D.
Parker, Joakim E. .... '— '94 (CA) C.813 B.A. L.1065 J.D.
Power, John R. .... '50 '77 C.454 B.A. L.309 J.D.
Rakas, Rosemary T. .... '57 '84 C.473 B.A. L.273 J.D.
Riedler, Tim C. .... '55 '82 (CA) C.178 B.A. L.976 J.D.
Robinson, Kim L. .... '65 '96 (CA) C.331 B.A. L.309 J.D.
Shapiro, Pat R. .... '56 '84 (NY) C&L.976 B.A., J.D.
Smith, Monica .... '69 '98 (NY) C.659 B.A. L.309 J.D.
Sullivan, Peter W. .... '59 '85 C.197 B.A. L.309 J.D.
Weisenfeld, Paul E. .... '63 '88 C.994 B.A. L.309 J.D.

ARCHITECT OF THE CAPITOL

Charles K. Tyler, *General Counsel*

Cox, Margaret P. .... '52 '79 (PA) C&L.329 B.A., J.D.
Dolan, William T. K. .... '51 '79 C.188 B.A. L.276 J.D. Legal Coun.
Tyler, Charles K. .... '45 '75 C.884 B.A. L.276 J.D. Gen. Coun.

CHIEF EMPLOYMENT COUNSEL

Martinez, Edgard .... '40 '71 (PR) C&L.677 B.B.A., J.D.
Mulshine, Kevin .... '52 '81 C.705 A.B. L.329 J.D. Chief Employ. Coun.
Tyler, Peggy L.B. .... '48 '83 C.72 B.A. L.823 J.D.

CENTRAL INTELLIGENCE AGENCY

Robert M. McNamara, Jr., *General Counsel*

OFFICE OF THE GENERAL COUNSEL

Benjamin, Thomas J. .... '55 '80 C.602 B.A. L.339 J.D. Dep. Gen. Coun.
McNamara, Robert M., Jr. .... '44 '74 C.363 A.B. L.276 J.D. Gen. Coun.
Rizzo, John A. .... '47 '73 C.103 A.B. L.273 J.D. Sr. Dep. Gen. Coun.
Sadoff, David A. .... '61 '95 C.197 A.B. L.276 J.D.

OFFICE OF THE EXECUTIVE DIRECTOR

Holmes, David P. .... '37 '74 (CO) C.860 B.A. L.945 J.D.

COMMISSION ON CIVIL RIGHTS

(Vacant), *General Counsel*

OFFICE OF THE GENERAL COUNSEL

Briggett, Marlissa S. .... '66 '92 C.309 A.B. L.93 J.D.
Brown, Erik S. .... '55 '89 C.293 A.B. L.494 J.D.
Monroig, Emma .... '44 '69 (PR) C.706 B.A. L.677 J.D.
Reid, Deborah A. .... '— '93 (MD) C&L.705 B.A., J.D.
Reilly, Peter R. .... '65 '94 C.674 B.A. L.309 J.D.
Yob, Lillian Moyano .... '67 '91 (OK) C.623 B.A. L.602 J.D.

COMMITTEE FOR PURCHASE FROM PEOPLE WHO ARE BLIND OR SEVERELY DISABLED

G. John Heyer, *General Counsel*

Heyer, G. John .... '45 '83 C.694 A.B. L.276 J.D. Gen. Coun.

COMMODITY FUTURES TRADING COMMISSION

(Vacant), *General Counsel*

OFFICE OF THE GENERAL COUNSEL

Blase, Marcia K. .... '54 '87 (GA) C.910 A.B. L.469 J.D.
Carley, James L. .... '62 '96 C.1356 B.S. L.1209 J.D.
Case, Edson G., Jr. .... '53 '78 C&L.276 B.A., J.D.
Clement, Gloria Peele .... '68 '93 (PA) C.188 B.S. L.150 J.D.
Cornell, Susan R. .... '58 '83 (PA) C.901 B.A. L.823 J.D.
Dinh, Thuy Tu Bich .... '62 '88 (PA) C&L.893 B.A., J.D.
Donovan, Eileen A. .... '72 '97 (PA) C.602 B.B.A. L.273 J.D.
Erickson, Thomas J. .... '61 '87 C.56 B.A. L.793 J.D.
Fox, Elizabeth L. R. .... '59 '88 C.645 B.A. L.273 J.D.
Garawski, Michael J. .... '70 '95 C.93 B.S. L.273 J.D.
Godel, C. Maria Dill .... '— '86 (VA) C.320 B.A. L.692 J.D.
Hammar, Julian E. .... '69 '97 C.976 B.A. L.228 J.D.
Hardman, Harold L. .... '53 '78 C.94 B.A. L.276 J.D.
Hitti, Ghassan A. .... '74 '01 C.276 B.S. L.124 J.D.
Johnson, Vincent B. .... '70 '97 C.976 B.A. L.569 J.D.
Lavik, A. Roy .... '36 '60 (TN) C&L.145 B.A., J.D.
Liebman, William S. .... '46 '75 C.994 B.A. L.1019 J.D.
Lymn, Merry .... '46 '75 C.494 B.A. L.050 LL.B.
Manharot, Kirk T. .... '59 '85 C&L.276 B.S., J.D.
Manley, Joan Marie .... '63 '88 (FL) C.473 B.S. L.260 J.D.
Markman, Natalie A. .... '— '94 L.276 J.D.
Mays, Glynn L. .... '45 '73 C.299 B.A. L.930 J.D.
McDonough, Kathleen A. .... '52 '82 (KY) C.1041 B.A. L.383 J.D.
Merrill, David R. .... '49 '75 C.184 B.A. L.276 J.D.
Mihans, Stephen F. .... '48 '79 C.575 B.A. L.273 J.D.
Nathan, Susan W.P. .... '45 '74 C.392 L.276 J.D.
Remy, Christine Patterson .... '70 '96 C.705 B.S. L.276 J.D.
Richards, Laura M. .... '50 '83 C.597 B.S. L.329 J.D.
Rozenberg, Bella L. .... '70 '00 L.904 J.D.
Scott, Gail B. .... '53 '82 C.860 B.S. L.30 J.D.
Sudik, Gabrielle A. .... '74 '00 C.30 B.A. L.228 J.D.
White, Martin B. .... '49 '74 C.178 A.B. L.477 J.D.
Wilder, George G. .... '55 '81 (IL) C.894 B.A. L.879 J.D.
Wright, Charles F. .... '58 '89 C&L.893 B.A., J.D.
Yanofsky, Nancy E. .... '53 '78 C.860 B.A. L.94 J.D.
Zwirb, Robert S. .... '49 '74 C.112 B.A. L.1068 J.D.

EXECUTIVE STAFF

Batts, Dorothy .... '— '77 (WI) C.959 B.A. L.966 J.D.
Hamilton, Madge M. .... '55 '90 (MI) C.477 B.A. L.1187 J.D.
Heitman, Donald H. .... '46 '71 C.276 B.A. L.273 J.D.
Leslie, J. Douglass .... '48 '79 C.696 A.B. L.30 J.D.
Saler, Anthony David .... '68 '93 C&L.276 B.S., J.D.
Schroeder, Megan DeLamar .... '64 '92 C.813 B.A. L.45 J.D.
Yochum, Stacy Dean .... '51 '76 C.339 B.A. L.276 J.D.

DIVISION OF ECONOMIC ANALYSIS

Architzel, Paul M. .... '53 '78 C.1044 B.A. L.537 J.D.

DIVISION OF ENFORCEMENT

Headquarters

Arbit, Terry S. .... '58 '83 (IL) C.659 B.A. L.145 J.D.
Bovee, Susan B. .... '52 '79 C.881 A.B. L.273 J.D.
Campbell, Lael E. .... '72 '98 C.216 B.A. L.902 J.D.
Capell, Heather .... '70 '98 (NY) C.999 B.A. L.846 J.D.
Cave, Keith Michael .... '67 '94 C.728 B.A. L.446 J.D.
Cela, Phyllis J. .... '51 '77 C.860 B.A. L.93 J.D.
Dunfee, John W. .... '71 '97 C.659 B.A. L.477 J.D.
Elkan, Matthew J. .... '52 '85 C.262 B.A. L.276 J.D.
Foelber, Richard P. .... '54 '78 (IL) C&L.879 B.A., J.D.
Friesen, Lloyd E. .... '45 '74 (NY) C.83 B.A. L.546 J.D.
Garcia, James Anthony .... '70 '96 C.112 B.A. L.976 J.D.
Glaser, Richard A. .... '61 '91 (NY) C.478 B.A. L.30 J.D.

COMMODITY FUTURES TRADING COMMISSION (Continued)

Haas, Peter M. . . . '55 '81 C.860 B.A. L.128 J.D.
Hamra, Jacqueline K. . . . '70 '96 (MO) C.806 B.A. L.502 J.D.
Hayeck, Paul G. . . . '64 '89 (MA) C.321 B.A. L.94 J.D.
Hoar, William O. . . . '42 '71 C&L.174 B.A., J.D.
Humenik, Stephen Michael . . . '74 '99 (MD) C.645 B.A. L.128 J.D.
Kelly, Thomas J. . . . '— '84 C.184 B.A. L.1292 J.D.
Lee, Michael T. . . . '70 '97 C.273 B.B.A. L.1009 J.D.
Lowe, Gretchen L. . . . '62 '87 C.696 B.A. L.659 J.D.
McGonagle, Vincent A. . . . '63 '88 C.397 B.A. L.990 J.D.
Morris, Leanna L. . . . '71 '96 (MD) C.689 B.A. L.30 J.D.
Norton, Lawrence H. . . . '58 '83 (MD) C&L.446 B.A., J.D.
Poplawski, Katrina L. . . . '72 '00 C.216 B.A. L.904 J.D.
Reed, David A. . . . '46 '72 C.273 B.A. L.893 J.D.
Reiley, Julie L. . . . '63 '89 C.668 B.A. L.976 J.D.
Riccobene, Edward J. . . . '64 '90 (CT) C.478 B.A. L.861 J.D.
Shakabpa, W. Derek . . . '67 '92 C.776 B.A. L.276 J.D.
Solinsky, Michael W. . . . '56 '86 C.1349 B.A. L.30 J.D.
Vargyas, Joseph F. . . . '46 '71 (OH) C.276 A.B. L.659 J.D.
Wagner, Richard B. . . . '47 '73 C.696 B.A. L.178 J.D.
Woods, Wendy . . . '60 '87 (PA) L.910 J.D.

Eastern Regional Office

Acevedo, David . . . '62 '89 (NY) C.1505 B.A. L.93 J.D.
Brennan, Elizabeth C. . . . '65 '93 (NY) C.93 B.S. L.262 J.D.
Cooper, Karl D. . . . '58 '89 C.178 A.B. L.893 J.D.
Cunningham, Andrew . . . '63 '91 C.93 B.A. L.823 J.D.
Hickson, Lenel, Jr. . . . '55 '81 C.178 B.A. L.309 J.D.
Kang, Christina J. . . . '72 '99 C.659 B.A. L.94 J.D.
MacGregor, David W. . . . '57 '82 C.228 A.B. L.597 J.D.
Morgenstern, Beth R. . . . '55 '80 (NY) C.914 B.A. L.94 J.D.
Obie, Stephen J. . . . '66 '92 C.222 B.A. L.107 J.D.
Peng, Linda Y. . . . '54 '89 (NY) C.477 B.A. L.262 J.D.
Ringer, Steven . . . '61 '87 C.102 B.A. L.1009 J.D.
Rosenberg, Joseph . . . '53 '81 (NY) C.183 B.A. L.978 J.D.
Roth, Karin N. . . . '69 '97 (NJ) C.910 B.S. L.262 J.D.
Sgro, Charles J. . . . '64 '89 C.555 B.S. L.776 J.D.
Sultan, Manal . . . '67 '96 (NY) C.1394 B.A. L.262 J.D.
Velasquez, John Richard, Jr. . . . '73 '00 C.112 A.B. L.273 J.D.

Western Regional Office

Miller, Jay M. . . . '67 '93 C.477 B.A. L.1068 J.D.
Morganstern, Myrna D. . . . '46 '76 (CA) C.549 B.A. L.494 J.D.
Traeger, Louis V. . . . '42 '66 (CA) C.112 B.A. L.1068 J.D.
Wise, John T. . . . '44 '79 (CA) C.103 A.B. L.800 J.D.
Yoshimura, Edwin J. . . . '49 '79 (CA) C.1042 B.A. L.1137 J.D.

Chicago Regional Office

Arnold, Camille M. . . . '67 '93 (NY) C.107 B.A. L.477 J.D.
Bretscher, Mark Howard . . . '56 '87 (IL) C.879 B.A. L.146 J.D.
Gould, Ava M. . . . '51 '86 (IL) C.1183 B.A. L.1000 J.D.
Gradman, Susan J. . . . '69 '94 (IL) C.1036 B.A. L.347 J.D.
Greenwald, Robert J. . . . '45 '73 (IL) C&L.597 B.S., J.D.
Hollinger, Rosemary Soffel . . . '53 '79 (IL) C.424 A.B. L.276 J.D.
Janulis, William P. . . . '51 '76 (IL) C.209 B.A. L.339 J.D.
Padove, Susan B. . . . '56 '80 (IL) C.209 B.S. L.146 J.D.
Romaniuk, Diane M. . . . '50 '75 (IL) C&L.209 B.A., J.D.
Streit, Elizabeth M. . . . '59 '84 (IL) C.339 B.S. L.145 J.D.
Terrell, David A. . . . '51 '87 (IL) C.347 B.A. L.146 J.D.
Williamson, Scott R. . . . '58 '85 (IL) C.976 B.A. L.145 J.D.
Winters, Rocell J. . . . '69 '97 C.357 B.A. L.221 J.D.

DIVISION OF TRADING AND MARKETS

Adriance, Riva Spear . . . '— '96 C.75 B.A. L.329 J.D.
Andresen, Duane C. . . . '48 '82 (NJ) C.790 A.B. L.1292 J.D.
Chapin, Andrew V. . . . '72 '97 (VA) C.945 B.B.A. L.1356 J.D.
Cummings, Christopher Ward . . . '52 '77 C&L.560 B.S., J.D.
Dietz, Phyllis P. . . . '54 '85 C.446 B.A. L.276 J.D.
Dow, De'Ana H. . . . '56 '83 C.999 B.S. L.276 J.D.
Elliott, Susan A. . . . '48 '75 C.681 B.A. L.94 J.D.
Gold, Barbara Stern . . . '47 '74 (OH) C.608 B.S. L.161 J.D.
Gregory, Lois Jane . . . '60 '85 C.544 B.S.B.A. L.190 J.D.
Kaczensky, Tobey W. . . . '44 '69 C.309 A.B. L.273 J.D.
Lawton, John C. . . . '54 '79 C.602 B.A. L.276 J.D.
Marlow, Joshua R. . . . '73 '99 (NY) C.477 A.B. L.893 J.D.
Patent, Lawrence B. . . . '52 '77 C.951 B.A. L.276 J.D.
Piracci, Michael A. . . . '73 '00 C.107 B.A. L.1019 J.D.
Sanders, Clarence R., Jr. . . . '47 '89 (VA) C.801 B.A. L.1209 J.D.
Schroeder, Helene D. . . . '59 '86 (NY) C.724 B.S. L.1009 J.D.
Seifert, Alan L. . . . '48 '73 C.107 B.A. L.150 J.D.
Smith, Thomas J. . . . '62 '92 C.433 B.S. L.1209 J.D.
Taylor, David . . . '48 '89 (MN) C.174 D.Mus. L.502 J.D.
Van Wagner, David P. . . . '57 '85 (VA) C.696 B.A. L.945 J.D.
Walek, Kevin P. . . . '54 '85 (VA) C.1044 B.A. L.1209 J.D.
Wasserman, Robert B. . . . '61 '89 C&L.659 B.S., J.D.

OFFICE OF PROCEEDINGS

Levine, Bruce C. . . . '49 '76 C.95 A.B. L.145 J.D.
Maillie, Joel R. . . . '56 '81 (KS) C.378 B.A. L.477 J.D.
McGuire, Philip V. . . . '53 '83 C.597 B.A. L.30 J.D.
Painter, George H. . . . '26 '57 C&L.502 B.S., LL.B.

CONGRESS

HOUSE OF REPRESENTATIVES

COMMITTEE ON DISTRICT OF COLUMBIA

Barthwell, Jack C., III . . . '50 '76 C.855 B.A. L.477 J.D.
Hall, Daniel . . . '51 '76 C.197 A.B. L.309 J.D.
Hogan, John E. . . . '26 '57 C.494 B.A. L.273 LL.B.
MacIver, Dale . . . '23 '50 (MN) C&L.494 B.B.A., J.D.

COMMITTEE ON POST OFFICE & CIVIL SERVICE

Blair, Dan G. . . . '59 '84 C&L.502 B.J., J.D.
Breitenberg, John F. . . . '48 '73 C.446 B.A. L.276 J.D.
Lopatin, Alan G. . . . '56 '81 C.976 B.A. L.30 J.D.
Martiny, John H. . . . '15 '43 C.712 B.A. L.273 LL.B.
O'Doherty, Kieran . . . '26 '57 (NY) C.563 A.B. L.178 LL.B.
Thompson, Herman G. . . . '30 '69 C.307 B.A. L.329 J.D.
Tillet, Rebecca . . . '62 '87 (VA) C.575 B.A. L.309 J.D.

COMMITTEE ON ARMED SERVICES

Fraser, Mary Ellen . . . '65 '91 (MD) C.93 B.S. L.128 J.D.

COMMITTEE ON GOVERNMENT REFORM

Billingsley, M. Scott . . . '70 '98 (CO) C.170 B.A. L.128 J.D.
Bowman, Thomas G. . . . '46 '79 (MA) C.846 B.A. L.1048 J.D. Sr. Coun.
Callender, John F., Jr. . . . '72 '97 (FL) C.228 B.A. L.260 J.D.
Carrillo, Pablo E. . . . '69 '97 C&L.861 B.A., J.D.
Chretien, Marc A. . . . '54 '88 (NH) C.276 A.B. L.1218 J.D. Sr. Coun.
Hollis, Andre Dale . . . '66 '92 C.674 A.B. L.893 J.D.
Kass, David A. . . . '71 '95 C&L.228 A.B., J.D. Dep. Coun.
Reed, Kimberly Ann . . . '71 '97 C.924 B.S. L.923 J.D.
Wilson, James C. . . . '59 '90 C.976 B.A. L.178 J.D. Chf. Coun.

COMMITTEE ON HOUSE ADMINISTRATION

Brown, Melanie . . . '— '99 (MD) C&L.36 B.S., J.D.
Buhler, Roman P. . . . '49 '82 (CA) C.813 A.B. L.800 J.D.
Hay, Frederick B. . . . '68 '97 (WA) C.800 B.A. L.190 J.D.
Howell, Charles T. . . . '44 '74 C.659 B.A. L.30 J.D.
Kelliher, John . . . '68 '96 C.674 B.A. L.94 J.D.
Miller, Stephen G. . . . '— '00 (MD) C.94 B.A. L.1019 J.D.

COMMITTEE ON THE JUDICIARY

Apelbaum, Perry H. . . . '58 '84 C.477 B.G.S. L.309 J.D.
Clanton, Bradley S. . . . '69 '96 C.500 B.A. L.356 J.D.
Cleaver, Cathleen A. . . . '64 '90 C.1111 B.A. L.276 J.D. Chf. Coun.
Dudas, Jonathan W. . . . '68 '93 (IL) C.339 B.S. L.145 J.D. Dep. Gen. Coun.
Filkins, Rick E. . . . '59 '87 (FL) C.1175 B.A. L.260 J.D.
Fishman, George M. . . . '62 '89 (IL) C.339 B.A. L.477 J.D.
Flam, Cori . . . '70 '95 C.309 A.B. L.178 J.D.
Freeman, Daniel M. . . . '46 '72 C.910 A.B. L.178 J.D.
Garg, Sampak P. . . . '72 '97 (CA) C.112 B.A. L.273 J.D.
Garlock, Kirsti Talikka . . . '66 '91 (OH) C.97 B.A. L.851 J.D.
Garlock, Vincent E. . . . '65 '91 (OH) C.608 B.A. L.851 J.D.
Gibson, Joseph H. . . . '61 '87 C&L.976 B.A., J.D.
Glazier, Stan Mitchell . . . '66 '91 C.597 B.S. L.880 J.D.
Jensen-Conklin, Susan A. . . . '55 '85 (NY) C&L.569 B.A., J.D.
Laman, Debra K. . . . '70 '96 (IA) C.112 B.A. L.221 J.D.
Moore, Stephanie Y. . . . '— '86 (PA) C.604 B.A. L.309 J.D. Gen. Coun.
Moschella, William E. . . . '68 '96 (VA) C.893 B.A. L.1209 J.D. Chf. Coun.
Pinkos, Stephen M. . . . '70 '95 (VA) C.473 B.A. L.209 J.D.
Ryder, Samara Tia . . . '71 '97 (MI) C.112 B.A. L.477 J.D.
Schmitt, Glenn R. . . . '61 '86 (OH) C.346 B.S. L.602 J.D. Chf. Coun.
Taylor, Paul Brian . . . '69 '94 C.976 B.A. L.309 J.D.
Vogel, Jonathan A. . . . '70 '95 (GA) C.882 B.A. L.245 J.D.
Wilon, Jim Y. . . . '63 '93 (NY) C.311 B.A. L.309 J.D.

COMMITTEE ON RESOURCES

Freemyer, Allen D. . . . '63 '89 C.877 B.S. L.878 J.D. Chf. of Staff
Olsen, Michael D. . . . '70 '98 C&L.101 B.A., J.D.
Peterson, Steven T. . . . '63 '90 C.877 B.A. L.878 J.D. Dep. Chf. Coun.
Pittman, Lisa Etta . . . '59 '84 C&L.260 B.A., J.D. Dep. Chf. Coun.

COMMITTEE ON SCIENCE

Beringer, Barry C. . . . '46 '72 (PA) C.216 B.A. L.30 J.D. Chf. Coun.
Geesey, Scott E. . . . '62 '95 (MD) C.658 B.A. L.201 J.D. Asst. Gen. Coun.
Harrington, Mark E. . . . '— '93 (MA) C.93 B.A. L.818 J.D.
Sokul, Elizabeth M. . . . '65 '91 C.446 B.A. L.128 J.D.

COMMITTEE ON WAYS & MEANS

Clark, James D. . . . '— '80 C.101 B.A. L.893 J.D. Chf. Tax Coun.
Hanford, Timothy L. . . . '55 '80 C.813 B.S. L.309 J.D.
Harrington, John L. . . . '62 '87 C.260 B.S. L.178 J.D.
Mays, Janice . . . '51 '75 (GA) C.917 A.B. L.280 J.D.
Sheiner, Jonathan R. . . . '50 '75 C.273 B.A. L.569 J.D.
Vance, Beth Kuntz . . . '53 '78 C&L.260 B.A., J.D.
Winters, Brigen Lee . . . '69 '94 C.1369 B.B.A. L.893 J.D.

COMMITTEE ON VETERANS AFFAIRS

Ryan, Patrick E. . . . '52 '78 C.446 B.A. L.276 J.D.
Smith, Kingston E. . . . '46 '77 (VA) C.228 B.A. L.692 J.D.

OFFICE OF LAW REVISION COUNSEL

Director, Jerald J. . . . '43 '67 (PA) C.823 B.A. L.831 J.D. Dep. Coun.
LeFevre, Peter G. . . . '51 '77 C.118 B.A. L.30 J.D.
Lindsey, Derrick L. . . . '66 '97 C.421 B.A. L.128 J.D.
Miller, John R. . . . '46 '72 (VA) C.150 B.A. L.273 J.D. Law Revision Coun.
Mulligan, Edward T. . . . '60 '88 (NY) C.724 B.A. L.569 J.D.
Seep, Ralph V. . . . '52 '78 (NY) C.602 B.A. L.228 J.D.
Simpson, Richard B. . . . '50 '80 C&L.446 B.A., J.D.
Sukol, Robert M. . . . '51 '95 (VA) C.831 B.A. L.1292 J.D.
Yee, Deborah Z. . . . '53 '83 C.823 B.S. L.276 J.D.

OFFICE OF PARLIAMENTARIAN

Duncan, Thomas G. . . . '52 '78 C.945 A.B. L.893 J.D. Dep. Parliamentarian
Johnson, Charles W. . . . '39 '65 C.31 A.B. L.893 LL.B. Parliamentarian
Lauer, Ethan Breneman . . . '72 '99 (WI) C.966 B.A. L.494 J.D. Asst. Parliamentarian
McCartin, Muftiah M. . . . '55 '90 (PA) C.1183 B.A. L.276 J.D. Asst. Parliamentarian
Sullivan, John V. . . . '52 '77 (IN) C.1070 B.S. L.1119 J.D. Dep. Parliamentarian
Wickham, Thomas J., Jr. . . . '68 '94 (IA) C&L.352 B.A., J.D. Asst. Parliamentarian

OFFICE OF LEGISLATIVE COUNSEL

Ballou, E. Wade, Jr. . . . '57 '83 (VA) C.886 B.S. L.893 J.D. Asst. Coun.
Barrow, M. Pope, Jr. . . . '42 '68 C.976 B.A. L.309 J.D. Legis. Coun.

Bellis, M. Douglass '47 '71 (NC) C.188 B.A. L.228 J.D. Dep. Legis. Coun.
Brown, Timothy D. '50 '79 C.399 B.A. L.1119 J.D. Asst. Coun.
Burke, Warren Porteus '— '98 (LA) C.846 B.A. L.861 J.D. Asst. Coun.
Callen, Paul C. '62 '87 (MI) C.293 B.A. L.477 J.D. Asst. Coun.
Chriss, Sherry L. '55 '83 (WI) C.1119 B.A. L.966 J.D. Asst. Coun.
Christup, Henry Wyatt '75 '00 C.497 B.B.A. L.976 J.D.
Cope, Steven A. '48 '74 (MD) C.145 B.A. L.976 J.D. Sr. Coun.
Cover, Robert W., II '50 '75 (VA) C.645 B.A. L.893 J.D. Asst. Coun.
Daly, Lisa M. '— '93 (MD) C&L.446 B.A., J.D. Asst. Coun.
Dorsey, Tobias A. '67 '93 (MA) C.188 B.A. L.1068 J.D.
Fleishman, Susan E. '61 '87 (MA) C.659 B.A. L.276 J.D. Asst. Coun.
Forstater, Ira B. '55 '80 C.311 B.A. L.659 J.D. Asst. Coun.
Gallagher, Rosemary '54 '89 C.205 B.A. L.796 J.D. Asst. Coun.
Goodloe, Peter M. '56 '85 (TN) C.88 B.S. L.880 J.D. Asst. Coun.
Grimm, Stanley B. '49 '75 (ND) C.273 B.A. L.145 J.D. Asst. Coun.
Grossman, Edward G. '49 '76 C.453 B.S. L.976 J.D. Asst. Coun.
Grossman, James D. '57 '85 (NY) C.860 B.S. L.145 J.D. Asst. Coun.
Haensel, Curt C. '60 '87 (WI) C&L.966 B.A., J.D. Asst. Coun.
Hamilton, Mark G. '71 '97 (WA) C&L.94 B.A., J.D. Asst. Coun.
Harmann, Jean L. '45 '75 (WI) C&L.966 B.S., J.D. Asst. Coun.
Haywood, Yvonne S. '53 '79 C.518 B.A. L.976 J.D. Asst. Legis. Coun.
Johnston, Lawrence A. '51 '76 C.602 B.A. L.597 J.D. Asst. Coun.
Jones, Jacqueline A. '67 '93 C.184 B.A. L.309 J.D. Asst. Coun.
Kostka, Gregory M. '58 '84 (WI) C&L.966 B.S., J.D. Asst. Coun.
Leong, Edward '53 '78 C.976 B.A. L.659 J.D. Asst. Coun.
Mendelsohn, H. David '48 '75 (NC) C&L.575 B.S., J.D. Asst. Coun.
Poisson, Pierre Charles '60 '95 (MD) C.478 B.A. L.217 J.D. Asst. Coun.
Savage, Harry A. '57 '85 C.477 B.A. L.861 J.D. Asst. Coun.
Strokoff, Sandra L. '50 '75 C&L.659 B.A., J.D. Asst. Coun.
Synnes, Mark A. '65 '90 (WI) C&L.966 B.A., J.D. Asst. Coun.
Weinhagen, Robert F., Jr. '45 '70 C.494 A.B. L.309 J.D. Sr. Coun.
Wert, James M. '48 '80 C.655 B.A. L.94 J.D. Asst. Coun.
Wofsy, Noah L. '61 '87 C.475 B.A. L.800 J.D. Asst. Coun.
Young, Brady J. '74 '00 C.101 B.A. L.276 J.D.

COMMITTEE LEGAL PERSONNEL

Baker, Andrew W. '61 '87 (GA) C.893 B.A. L.280 J.D. Com. on Agriculture
Baker, Donald M. '25 '57 (MI) C&L.477 A.B., LL.B. Com. on Education & Labor
Bloss-Baum, Linda '69 '98 C.30 B.A. L.128 J.D. Com. on Commerce
Chabot, Elliot C. '55 '80 C.446 B.A. L.273 J.D. Sr. Systems Analyst
Clark, Fred J. '57 '89 C.1074 B.S. L.276 J.D. Com. on Agriculture
Connolly, David A., Jr. '50 '75 C.262 B.A. L.1009 J.D. Com. on Educ. & Labor
Davis, Joseph R. '43 '67 C&L.16 B.S., LL.B. Com. on Appropriations
Davis, Mark J. '48 '73 C.20 B.A. L.276 J.D. House Standards of Official Conduct
Farmer, Suzanne F. '46 '81 C&L.259 B.A., J.D. Cong. Arts Caucus
Frandsen, Richard A. '44 '69 C&L.339 B.A., J.D. Com. on Interstate & Foreign Comm.
Frank, David L. '63 '88 C.659 B.A. L.309 J.D. Com. on Education & Labor
Fuller, Lauren Lea '52 '77 C&L.623 B.A., J.D. Com. on Educ. & Labor
Griffin, J. Timothy '68 '94 (LA) C.315 B.A. L.861 J.D. Govt. Reform & Oversight Com.
Grumbles, Benjamin H. '60 '86 (MD) C.896 B.A. L.245 J.D. Com. on Pub. Works & Transp.
Heymsfeld, David A. '38 '64 C.178 B.A. L.309 LL.B. Com. on Public Works
Johnson, Cheryl Lynn '60 '88 C.352 B.S. L.329 J.D. Com. on House Admin.
Johnson, Virginia Hurt '58 '86 C.228 B.A. L.896 J.D. Com. on Ethics
Kaplan, Randall J. '— '93 (OH) C.966 B.A. L.179 J.D. Com. on Gov. Reform and Oversight
Kuo, Ellen '67 '92 (VA) C.945 B.A. L.692 J.D. Com. on Banking
Lee, Charles F. '43 '67 C&L.896 B.A., J.D. Com. on House Adm.
Levin, Andrew S. '62 '95 (VA) C.441 B.S. L.438 J.D.
Leyden, Andrew Parker '66 '97 (IL) C.339 B.A. L.602 J.D. Com. on Comm.
Markus, Gloria E. '69 '99 C&L.150 B.A., J.D. Com. on Govt. Reform
Meyers, Robert J. '54 '79 C.732 B.A. L.273 J.D. Republican Resch. Com.
Petrich, Jeffrey P. '56 '84 C.197 B.A. L.1119 J.D. Com. on Interior & Insular Affairs
Phalen, James R. '37 '62 (IL) C.363 B.S. L.597 J.D. Select Com. on Small Bus.
Reich, David J. '54 '91 C.1169 B.A. L.276 J.D. Com. on the Budget
Safavian, Jennifer M. '70 '94 C.734 B.S.B.A. L.213 J.D. Com. on Govt. Reform & Oversight
Scammel, H. Glenn '48 '73 (TX) C.976 B.A. L.309 J.D. Com. on Tran. & Infrastructure
Schooler, David R. '51 '76 C.951 B.A. L.309 J.D. Com. on Interstate & Foreign Commerce
Seiger, Ryan Christopher '71 '99 (MD) C.180 B.A. L.659 J.D. Comm. on Transp. and Infrastructure
Sheridan, Sue D. '54 '80 (MA) C.228 B.A. L.880 J.D. Com. on Energy & Comm.
Weinberg, Hillel '52 '85 C.107 B.A. L.893 J.D. Com. on Intl. Relations
Wheat, John Marc '64 '96 (VA) C.339 A.B. Com. on Commerce
Yeager, Michael J. '65 '94 C.67 B.A. L.446 J.D. Com. on Govt. Reform & Oversight

CONGRESSIONAL ASSISTANTS

Agrast, Mark D. '56 '86 C.930 B.A. L.976 J.D. Sr. Legis. Asst. to M.C.
Allin, Keri A. '70 '95 (SC) C.395 B.S. L.1040 J.D. Legis. Coun. to M.C.
Alman, Lee J. '71 '96 (NC) C&L.575 B.A., J.D. Asst. to M.C.
Anaya, William B. '71 '97 (MI) C.477 B.A. L.602 J.D. Legis. Asst. to M.C.
Anderson, Douglas C. '67 '92 (AZ) C&L.145 A.B., J.D. Asst. to M.C.
Bauleke, Howard P. '59 '85 C.378 B.A. L.276 J.D. Legis. Asst. to M.C.
Bottegal, Jennifer J. '70 '98 (AL) C.88 B.A. L.16 J.D. Legis. Asst. to M.C.
Bouker, Jon S., Jr. '70 '95 C&L.276 A.B., J.D. Legis. Asst. to M.C.
Calvelli, John F. '63 '90 C&L.262 B.A., J.D. Admin. Asst. to M.C.
Colton, Kimberly H. '71 '95 (MD) C.1236 B.A. L.904 J.D. Legis. Asst. to M.C.
Corcoran, Matthew E. '64 '91 (VA) C.674 A.B. L.276 J.D. Asst. to M.C.
Donesa, Christopher A. '66 '92 C.276 A.B. L.228 J.D. Legis. Coun. to M.C.
Feather, Karen M. '62 '91 (PA) C.860 B.S. L.276 J.D. Admin. Asst. to M.C.
Flanders, David A. '53 '88 C.112 B.A. L.30 J.D. Admin. Asst. to M.C.
Forrest, Jeffrey William '71 '96 (VA) C.1349 B.A. L.273 J.D. Legis. Coun. to M.C.
Gordon, Robert M. '66 '90 C.112 B.A. L.276 J.D. Coun. to M.C.
Harrison, Michael L. '59 '85 (MO) C.862 B.A. L.910 J.D. Legis. Asst. to M.C.
Henderson, Wallace J. '44 '73 C.1089 L.420 J.D. Asst. to M.C.
Hope, Karin Marie '67 '94 (MN) C.1144 B.A. L.276 J.D. Legis. Coun. to M.C.
Horn, Joseph Peter '60 '88 L.1363 J.D.
Horne, Eleas '71 '98 (UT) C&L.878 B.S., J.D.
Keck, Kenneth '66 '96 C.362 B.A. L.1338 J.D. Legis. Asst. to M.C.
Lynch, Michael E. '48 '77 (MA) C.602 A.B. L.94 J.D. Legis. Asst. to M.C.
Maggi, Philip J. '69 '98 C.588 B.S. L.365 J.D. Coun. to M.C.
Magill, John P. '51 '78 (TN) C&L.838 B.A., J.D. Coun. to M.C.
Maloney, Andrew K. '69 '96 C.682 B.A. L.128 J.D. Legis. Asst. to M.C.
Martin, Cynthia Anita-Reddick '63 '96 (VA) C.699 B.A. L.260 J.D. Legis. Coun. to M.C.
Marty, Kenneth '41 '67 C.602 A.B. L.677 LL.B. Legal Coun. to M.C.
McKenna, Raymond J. '57 '83 C.724 B.A. L.273 J.D. Off. of the Chief Admin. Officer
McKenzie, Jeffrey Thomas '68 '94 (TN) C.838 B.S. L.845 J.D. Legis. Coun. to M.C.
McKenzie, Mary C. '68 '92 (MO) C&L.734 B.S., J.D. Legis. Coun. to M.C.
Mendelsohn, Jeffrey R. '62 '88 C&L.309 A.B., J.D. Asst. to M.C.
Metz, Craig Huseman '55 '87 C.838 B.A. L.836 J.D. Chief of Staff to M.C.
Norton, William G. '51 '79 (VA) C.276 B.A. L.945 J.D. Legis. Coun. to M.C.
Pate, Barbara A. Linch '52 '78 C&L.846 B.A., J.D. Legis. Coun. to M.C.
Pollard, John J., III '46 '73 (MO) C&L.502 A.B., J.D. Admin. Asst. to M.C.
Rossi, William H. '50 '75 C.260 B.S. L.285 J.D. Legis. Asst. to M.C.
Schoonmaker, Jan '46 '74 C.853 B.A. L.861 J.D. Legis. Asst. to M.C.
Schwadron, Steven C. '55 '86 (MA) C.103 A.B. L.276 J.D. Chief of Staff to M.C.
Shevlin, George F., IV '61 '89 (MD) C.602 B.A. L.64 J.D. Projects Dir. to M.C.
Simon, David A. '49 '75 C.112 B.A. L.1068 J.D. Legis. Asst. to M. C.
Simpson, Shelley '49 '88 (MI) C.545 B.S. L.213 J.D. Legis. Dir. to M.C.
Sirh, Michael Helbert Peter '68 '96 C.1209 B.A. L.61 J.D. Coun. to M.C.
Skelton, Ike, Jr. '31 '56 (MO) C&L.502 A.B., LL.B. Legis. Asst. to M.C.
Smith, Timothy E. '52 '79 C.259 B.A. L.904 J.D. Asst. to M.C.
Stern, Michael '60 '85 C.311 B.A. L.145 J.D. House Off. of the Gen. Coun.
Szemraj, Roger Raymond '53 '82 C&L.276 B.S.F.S., J.D. Legis. Asst. to M.C.
Tamargo, Mauricio J. '— '90 (FL) C.472 B.A. L.192 J.D. Legis. Coun. to M.C.
Taylor, Gordon M. '68 '94 C.1365 B.A. L.273 J.D. Legis. Coun. to M.C.
Turner, James H., Jr. '46 '75 C.935 B.S. L.276 J.D. Legis. Asst. to M.C.
Van Der Meid, Theodore J. '57 '84 (NY) C.1106 B.A. L.823 J.D. Wednesday Group
Whatley, Thomas L. '53 '77 (TX) C&L.846 B.A., J.D. Legis. Aide to M.C.
Wojtasik, Catherine D. '68 '94 (MA) C.184 B.A. L.1292 J.D. Legis. Dir. to M. C.
Zeppelin, Deron E. '67 '96 C&L.500 B.B.A., J.D. Legis. Dir. to M.C.

EMPLOYMENT COUNSEL

Botvin, Victoria L. '69 '95 C.477 B.A. L.831 J.D. Assoc. Coun., U.S. House of Rep.
Ferguson, Gloria Lett '55 '79 C.1044 B.A. L.273 J.D.
Herrera, Frederick M. '62 '88 C.698 B.A. L.665 J.D.
Poll, Jeffrey C. '49 '76 C.188 B.S. L.564 J.D.
Rogers, Ann R. '66 '92 C.228 B.A. L.945 J.D.

UNITED STATES SENATE

James W. Fransen, *Legislative Counsel*
(Vacant), *Legal Counsel*

OFFICE OF THE LEGISLATIVE COUNSEL

Armstrong, Charles E. '60 '87 (OR) C.103 A.B. L.477 J.D. Asst. Coun.
Ayoud, Laura M. '62 '87 C.645 B.A. L.276 J.D. Asst. Coun.
Baird, William R. '61 '86 (IL) C.338 B.S. L.365 J.D. Asst. Coun.
Bentz, Janell K. '67 '96 (WA) C.747 B.S.W. L.629 J.D. Asst. Coun.
Chan, Darcie E. '74 '98 C.347 B.A. L.1002 J.D. Asst. Coun.
Coe, Anthony C. '55 '81 (MD) C.446 B.A. L.128 J.D. Sr. Coun.
Craighill, Polly W. '41 '67 C.822 A.B. L.273 LL.B. Asst. Coun.
Delacy, Christopher '72 '99 (VA) C.893 B.A. L.945 J.D. Legis. Coun.
Endicott, Gary L. '53 '80 C&L.966 B.A., J.D. Sr. Coun.
Ernst, Ruth A. '63 '87 C.518 A.B. L.145 J.D. Asst. Coun.
Flory, Heather '— '00 C.893 B.A. L.838 J.D. Asst. Coun.
Fransen, James W. '49 '75 (WI) C&L.966 B.A., J.D. Legis. Coun.
Gaynor, Amy E. '74 '00 C.128 B.A. L.982 J.D. Staff Atty.
Goetcheus, John A. '67 '93 C&L.128 B.A., J.D. Asst. Coun.
Jensen, William F., III '51 '78 C.893 B.A. L.365 J.D. Sr. Coun.
Johnson, Janine L. '66 '90 C&L.309 A.B., J.D. Asst. Coun.
King, Elizabeth Aldridge '61 '89 (MD) C.228 B.A. L.904 J.D. Asst. Coun.
Mathiesen, Mark J. '50 '75 C.945 B.A. L.880 J.D. Asst. Coun.
Rynearson, Arthur J. '49 '76 C.299 A.B. L.188 J.D. Deputy Legis. Coun.
Scott, Gregory A. '49 '75 C.198 B.A. L.880 J.D. Sr. Coun.
Scott, James G. '71 '98 (MD) C.1369 B.S. L.128 J.D. Asst. Coun.
Trushel, Timothy D. '50 '76 C.923 B.A. L.178 J.D. Asst. Coun.

OFFICE OF SENATE LEGAL COUNSEL

Bryan, Patricia M. '55 '80 C.282 B.A. L.309 J.D.
Frankel, Morgan J. '55 '80 C.821 B.A. L.976 J.D.

OFFICE OF SENATE CHIEF COUNSEL FOR EMPLOYMENT

Hyman, Toby R. '49 '75 (NY) C.681 A.B. L.309 J.D.
Kresslein, Charles H., Jr. '32 '61 C.423 L.64 LL.B.
Manning, Jean M. '50 '84 (CA) C&L.339 B.A., J.D. Chief Coun.
Rogers, Robert L. '74 '99 C.846 B.A. L.309 J.D.
Watkins, Erica A. '71 '97 C.264 B.A. L.273 J.D.

COMMITTEE LEGAL PERSONNEL

Alexander, Paul '42 '68 C.608 B.A. L.276 J.D. Com. on Veterans Affairs
Alt, Konrad S. '60 '88 (AK) C.685 B.A. L.309 J.D. Com. on Banking, Housing and Urban Affairs
Altmeyer, Thomas H. '47 '75 C.602 B.B.A. L.425 J.D. Com. on Labor & Human Resources
Andrews, Jackson M., IV '46 '73 (KY) C.885 B.A. L.421 J.D. Com. on Labor & Public Welfare
Apol, David J. '56 '82 C.937 B.A. L.477 J.D. Com. on Ethics
Appelbaum, Judith C. '52 '78 C.659 B.A. L.813 J.D. Com. on Judiciary
Asquith, Marcia E. '65 '90 (VA) C.612 B.A. L.945 J.D. Com. on Agric.
Atcheson, Marcia N. '32 '75 (IN) C.788 A.B. L.345 J.D. Com. on Judiciary
Baird, Victor McEver '43 '74 (GA) C&L.280 B.S., J.D. Com. on Ethics
Ball, John W., III '55 '80 (AR) C.315 B.A. L.45 J.D. Com. on Small Bus.
Bamberger, Lori E. '63 '90 C.197 B.A. L.976 J.D. Com. on Housing & Urban Affairs
Bang-Jensen, Nina '55 '83 C.674 B.A. L.276 J.D. Com. on Govt. Affairs
Barnes, Alison Patrucco '58 '86 (FL) C&L.260 B.A., J.D. Spec. Com. on Aging
Barnes, Melody C. '64 '90 C.575 B.A. L.477 J.D. Com. on Judiciary
Barnes, Reginald W. '19 '49 (AL) C&L.16 LL.B. Com. on Banking & Currency
Beirne, James P. '48 '73 C.299 A.B. L.276 J.D. Com. on Int. & Insular Affairs
Belferman, John M. '55 '80 C.674 A.B. L.880 J.D. Com. on Govt. Affairs
Bell, Dexter L. '53 '80 (UT) L.878 J.D. Com. on Banking, Housing & Urban Affairs
Berkovitz, Dan M. '56 '82 C.674 A.B. L.1065 J.D. Com. on Envir. & Pub. Works
Biel, Eric R. '59 '85 C.367 B.A. L.976 J.D. Com. on Finance
Boley, Kenneth R. '65 '92 C.31 B.A. L.276 J.D. Com. on Govt. Affairs

UNITED STATES SENATE (Continued)

Bowman, Gail E. .... '52 '77 C.352 B.A. L.309 J.D. Com. on Judiciary
Brennan, Thomas C. .... '35 '60 C.776 A.B. L.276 J.D. Com. on Judiciary
Brooks, David .... '61 '87 (AZ) C&L.37 B.S., J.D. Com. on Energy & Nat. Resources
Brown, James Albert .... '62 '88 C.880 B.A. L.910 J.D. Com. on Govt. Affairs
Brudney, James J. .... '50 '81 C.31 B.A. L.976 J.D. Com. on Labor & Human Res.
Buechler, Elizabeth M. .... '57 '84 (CA) C.1042 B.S. L.990 J.D. Com. on Veterans Affairs
Burke, Dennis K. .... '62 '88 C.276 B.A. L.37 J.D. Com. on Judiciary
Buttrey, William D. .... '45 '73 C.834 B.S. L.836 J.D. Com. on Commerce
Buzhardt, Joseph R., III .... '50 '81 (SC) C.968 B.A. L.1209 J.D. Com. on Vet. Affairs
Calloway, James R. .... '28 '65 C&L.273 A.B., LL.B. Com. on Appropriations
Campbell, W. Douglas ... '48 '76 (FL) C&L.101 B.A., J.D. Com. on Labor & Human Res.
Canton, Gregory S. .... '61 '85 C&L.477 B.A., J.D. Com. on Govt. Affairs
Cantrel, Francis J., Jr. .... '55 '85 (PA) C.1030 B.A. L.1209 J.D. Com. on Finance
Carnell, Richard S. .... '53 '82 (CA) C.976 B.A. L.309 J.D. Com. on Banking
Carroll, Charles T., Jr. ..... '47 '83 C.728 B.S. L.1209 J.D. Com. on Labor & Human Res.
Chase, Gary M. .... '45 '76 C.102 B.A. L.276 J.D. Select Com. on Intelligence
Chavers, Kevin G. '63 '88 (NY)
C.893 B.S. L.309 J.D. Com. on Banking, Housing & Urban Affairs
Chesson, John B., III ..... '47 '74 (VA) C.893 B.A. L.945 J.D. Com. on Gov't. Operations
Chumbris, Peter N. .... '14 '38 C.446 A.B. L.276 J.D. Com. on Judiciary
Clancy, Martin J. .... '19 '43 (WI) C&L.436 Ph.B., LL.B. Republican Calendar Com.
Clanton, Doris M. .... '51 '78 (OH) C.832 B.S. L.608 J.D. Com. on Govt. Affairs
Clark, H. Westley .... '46 '82 C.912 B.A. L.309 J.D. Com. on Labor & Human Resources
Coffin, Tristram J. .... '63 '90 (VT) C.918 B.A. L.178 J.D. Com. on Judiciary
Collins, Thos. B. .... '15 '46 C.215 Ph.B. L.276 J.D. Com. on Judiciary
Collis, Conway H. .... '48 '75 C.605 B.A. L.813 J.D. Com. on Labor & Pub. Welfare
Cooper, James W. .... '64 '89 C.790 B.A. L.245 J.D. Com. on Judiciary
Cowen, James S. .... '52 '78 (MD) C.645 B.A. L.128 J.D. Com. on Govt. Affairs
Cowper, Gail Millar .... '55 '81 C.1044 B.A. L.107 J.D. Com. on Budget
Cubie, James M. .... '46 '75 C.236 B.A. L.446 J.D. Com. on Appropriations
Cudlipp, Katherine Y. .... '43 '76 C.683 A.B. L.276 J.D. Com. on Envir. & Pub. Works
Culver, Ray C., III .... '56 '81 (AR) C.420 B.A. L.45 J.D. Com. on Small Bus.
Dahlen, Peter Rolf .... '67 '96 C&L.128 B.A., J.D. Com. on Judiciary Counsel
D'Amato, Charles R., Jr. .... '42 '82 C.188 A.B. L.276 J.D. Democratic Policy Com.
Dauster, William G. .... '57 '85 C.800 B.A. L.178 J.D. Com. on the Budget
Davidson, James H. .... '42 '69 (MO) C&L.502 B.A., J.D. Com. on Govt. Operations
DeBobes, Richard D. .... '38 '62 (NY) C.276 A.B. L.262 LL.B. Com. on Armed Servs.
Dettelbach, Brian Andrew .... '56 '87 (VA) C.276 B.S. L.1209 J.D. Com. on Govt. Affairs
Dinsmore, F. Clement '43 '68
C.674 A.B. L.477 J.D. Com. on Banking, Housing & Urban Affs.
Disler, Mark R. .... '52 '77 C.674 A.B. L.659 J.D. Com. on Judiciary
Docherty, John F. .... '56 '86 C&L.494 B.A., J.D. Spec. Com. on Aging
Dunn, Christopher J. .... '52 '82 (IL) C.339 B.A. L.209 J.D. Com. on Judiciary
Dunn, Loretta L. .... '55 '79 C&L.383 B.A., J.D. Com. on Comm., Science & Transp.
Edelman, Alan I. .... '58 '83 C.188 B.A. L.94 J.D. Com. on Govt. Affairs
Edie, John A. .... '44 '70 C.674 A.B. L.1066 J.D. Com. on Aging
Erbs, Laura A. .... '60 '86 (MO) C.1182 B.A. L.910 J.D. Com. on Aging
Ferguson, Emmet M. .... '18 '41 C&L.362 LL.B. Demo. Policy Com.
Fisher, Douglas B. .... '57 '86 (WA) C.911 B.A. L.950 J.D. Com. on Finance
Fisk, Daniel Ward .... '57 '96 C.862 B.S. L.276 J.D. Com. on Foreign Rel.
Fountain, Galen L. .... '51 '90 (AR) C.942 B.A. L.1242 J.D. Com. on Small Bus.
Fox, Cheryl A. .... '64 '91 (MD) C.228 B.A. L.659 J.D. Com. on Banking
Frohlicher, Jean S. .... '39 '66 C.681 A.B. L.276 J.D. Com. on Labor & Public Welfare
Fulton, Robert E. .... '31 '64 (MD) C.398 A.B. L.30 LL.B. Com. on the Budget
Funke, Karl A. .... '50 '76 C.136 B.S. L.1162 J.D. Select Com. on Indian Affairs
Gerson, Matthew T. .... '58 '85 C.860 B.A. L.276 J.D. Com. on Judiciary
Gill, Kennie Lee .... '55 '87 (KY) C.383 B.A. L.276 J.D. Com. on Rules & Admin.
Ginsburg, Scott K. .... '52 '78 C.273 B.A. L.276 J.D. Com. on Human Resources
Glaser, Keith R. '55 '81 (OH) C.150 B.A. L.309 J.D.
Com. on Environment & Pub. Works
Grant, Harriet .... '61 '86 C.893 B.A. L.575 J.D. Com. on Judiciary
Grant, Jodi .... '68 '94 C.976 B.A. L.309 J.D. Dem. Steer. & Coord. Com.
Gray, David Edman .... '69 '99 C.976 B.A. L.597 J.D. Com. on Govt. Affairs
Guerney, Janis .... '56 '85 C.645 B.A. L.976 J.D. Com. on Finance
Gunn, Thomas M. .... '43 '67 (MO) C&L.734 B.A., J.D. Com. on Appropriations
Guttman, Robert M. '28 '61 C.309 A.B. L.273 LL.B.
Com. on Labor & Human Resources
Haden, Ed R. .... '62 '94 (AL) C.16 B.S. L.902 J.D. Com. on Judiciary
Hageman, Hans E. .... '58 '84 (NY) C.674 B.A. L.178 J.D. Com. on Judiciary
Halamandaris, Val J. .... '42 '70 C&L.273 A.B., J.D. Special Com. on Aging
Hantman, David S. .... '69 '95 (MD) C.178 B.A. L.262 J.D. Com. on Judiciary
Haralson, Shannon L. '63 '91
C.692 B.A. L.128 J.D. Com. on Nat. Sec. & Milit./Comm. Concerns
Hardy, Johanna Lynn .... '72 '98 (PA) C.453 B.S. L.276 J.D. Com. on Govt. Affairs
Harris, Richard M. .... '44 '73 C.923 B.S. L.575 J.D. Com. on Public Works
Hartsfield, J. Andrew, IV .... '55 '80 (NC) C.575 B.A. L.896 J.D. Com. on Judiciary
Harvey, D. Michael '34 '63 (VA)
C.696 B.A. L.276 J.D. Com. on Interior & Insular Affairs
Hayes, Holidae H. .... '63 '89 (KY) C&L.383 B.S., J.D. Com. on Banking
Hirshland, Michael J. .... '66 '96 (MD) C.309 A.B. L.893 J.D. Com. on Judiciary
Hoff, Patricia M. .... '52 '77 (CA) C.1044 B.A. L.1049 J.D. Com. on Judiciary
Hogan, Cynthia Claire .... '57 '85 C.604 B.A. L.893 J.D. Com. on Judiciary
Holcomb, Richard D. .... '52 '79 C.301 B.A. L.692 J.D. Com. on Judiciary
Holleyman, Robert W., II .... '55 '79 (LA) C.859 B.A. L.420 J.D. Com. on Commerce
Howard, Ann Gill .... '63 '90 (TX) C&L.846 B.A., J.D. Com. on Judiciary
Howell, Beryl A. .... '56 '84 C.104 B.A. L.178 J.D. Com. on Judiciary
Hulse, Carole D. .... '47 '79 (AZ) C.878 B.A. L.36 J.D. Com. on Finance
Humphreys, Robert R. '38 '65 C.911 B.A. L.273 LL.B.
Com. on Labor & Public Welfare
Johnson, David L. .... '52 '80 C&L.309 B.A., J.D. Com. on Foreign Relations
Johnson, Richard E. .... '36 '62 C.145 B.A. L.976 LL.B. Com. on Labor & Publ. Wlfr.
Johnson, Stephanie '58 '89 (PA)
C.446 B.A. L.64 J.D. Com. on Labor & Human Resources
Jordan, Carolyn D. '41 '66
C.254 B.A. L.329 LL.B. Com. on Banking, Housing & Urban Affairs
Jordan, Wm. H., Jr. .... '29 '52 C.198 L.280 LL.B. Com. on Appropriations
Jourdan, Carolyn .... '55 '81 (TN) C&L.838 B.S., J.D. Com. on Govt. Affairs
Joyce, H. Sherman .... '59 '87 (VA) C.674 A.B. L.128 J.D. Com. on Comm.
Kamarck, Jonathan D. '52 '84 C.966 B.A. L.260 J.D.
Com. on Housing & Urban Affairs
Katz, Bruce Jonathan .... '59 '86 (NY) C.103 B.A. L.976 J.D. Com. on Banking
Katzman, Julie E. .... '62 '91 (NY) C.976 B.A. L.178 J.D. Com. on Judiciary
Keefe, Thomas P., Jr. .... '48 '74 (WA) C.735 B.A. L.128 J.D. Com. on Commerce
Kelly, Kevin F. .... '58 '90 (PA) C.999 B.A. L.276 J.D. Com. on Appropriations
Kern, Charles E., II .... '34 '63 C.674 B.A. L.976 LL.B. Com. on Judiciary
Kindermann, Anna L. .... '62 '91 C.183 B.A. L.910 J.D. Special Com. on Aging
King, Bruce Warren .... '58 '83 C.861 B.A. L.813 J.D. Com. on Judiciary
Klingenstein, Andrew D. .... '57 '85 C.976 B.A. L.893 J.D. Select Com. on Indian Affairs
Knell, Gary E. .... '54 '78 (CA) C.112 B.A. L.426 J.D. Com. on Judiciary
Koetz, Maureen T. '57 '85 (NY) C.30 B.A. L.904 J.D.
Com. on Energy & Nat. Resources
Kohashi, Stephen H. .... '49 '81 C.312 B.A. L.276 J.D. Com. on Appropriations
Kuhn, Rocky L. .... '57 '82 C.976 B.A. L.30 J.D. Com. on Appropriations
Landy, Kevin J. .... '66 '93 C.31 B.A. L.976 J.D. Com. on Govt. Affairs
Lantos, Yvonne K. .... '55 '77 C.976 B.A. L.1065 J.D. Com. on Judiciary
Lee, Clendon H., Jr. .... '50 '76 C.797 B.A. L.902 J.D. Select Com. on Ethics
Lee, Eric H. M. .... '44 '69 C.674 A.B. L.309 J.D. Com. on Commerce
Lehrich, Deborah C. .... '67 '94 (PA) C.1349 B.A. L.30 J.D. Com. on Govt. Affairs
Leibowitz, Jonathan D. .... '— '85 C.966 B.A. L.569 J.D. Com. on Judiciary
Levin, Stephen .... '55 '85 C.367 B.A. L.30 J.D. Com. on Govt. Affairs
Levine, Peter K. .... '57 '83 C&L.309 A.B., J.D. Com. on Govt. Affairs
Lewis, William A., Jr. .... '46 '72 (PA) C.820 B.A. L.94 J.D. Com. on Judiciary
Lisker, Joel S. .... '37 '70 C.659 B.S. L.831 J.D. Com. on Judiciary
Loesch, Harrison '16 '39 (CO) C.170 B.A. L.976 LL.B.
Com. on Interior & Insular Affairs
Maas, Fredric J. .... '57 '83 C.319 B.A. L.823 J.D. Nat. Republican Sen. Comm.
Magida, Lenore R. .... '50 '78 C.1036 B.A. L.569 J.D. Com. on Govt. Affairs
Mahsetky, Michael D. '47 '88 (PA)
C.1142 B.A. L.1162 J.D. Select Com. on Indian Affairs
Martin, Aurene M. .... '65 '93 (WI) C&L.966 B.A., J.D. Select Com. on Indian Affairs
Martin, Dana R. .... '47 '75 C.112 B.A. L.990 J.D. Com. on Govt. Operations
Martinez, Susanne ... '45 '71 (CA) C.112 B.A. L.1065 J.D. Com. on Labor & Human Res.
McClellan, Edgar D. .... '55 '85 C&L.347 B.S., J.D. Com. on Finance
McCoy, Matthew J. .... '58 '87 (AZ) C&L.37 B.A., J.D. Com. on Judiciary
McDermott, Albert L. .... '23 '50 C.93 A.B. L.276 LL.B. Com. on Rules
McFadden, William C., II .... '46 '72 C.951 B.A. L.309 J.D. Com. on Armed Servs.
McGovern, James F. .... '46 '79 C.871 B.S. L.276 J.D. Com. on Armed Servs.
McGuiness, Kevin S. .... '52 '81 C.112 B.A. L.273 J.D. Com. on Labor & Human Res.
McHugh, Stephen J. .... '64 '92 (AZ) C.112 A.B. L.174 J.D. Select Com. on Indian Affairs
McKean, David .... '56 '87 C.309 B.A. L.228 J.D. Com. on Govt. Affairs
McNerney, Patricia .... '68 '95 (VA) C.93 B.A. L.902 J.D. Com. on Foreign Rel.
Melton, Pamela Rogers .... '51 '78 (VA) C.6 B.A. L.902 J.D. Com. on Judiciary
Menghetti, Linda C. .... '63 '90 C.645 B.A. L.1066 J.D. Com. on Finance
Miller, Jeffrey A. .... '70 '95 C.659 B.A. L.145 J.D. Com. on Judiciary
Miller, Mary Ellen .... '27 '73 C.454 A.B. L.276 J.D. Com. on Labor & Public Welfare
Miranda, Thomas B. '— '78 (MA) C.1275 A.B. L.94 J.D.
Com. on Labor & Human Res.
Monahan, John .... '61 '87 C&L.276 B.A., J.D. Special Com. on Aging
Monroe, Stephanie J. .... '58 '89 C.446 B.A. L.64 J.D. Com. on Labor & Human Res.
Moorehead, Paul G. .... '63 '89 C.205 B.A. L.831 J.D. Select Com. on Indian Affairs
Mulloy, Patrick A. .... '41 '72 C.1113 B.A. L.273 J.D. Com. on Banking
Nagao, Alvin T. .... '53 '82 C&L.312 B.A., J.D. Com. on Labor & Human Res.
Nappi, Douglas R. .... '62 '89 C.264 B.A. L.273 J.D. Com. on Banking
Neece, Allen W., Jr. .... '41 '67 C.335 B.A. L.273 LL.B. Com. on Small Bus.
Nobleman, Eli E. .... '16 '40 (NY) C&L.569 B.A., LL.B. Com. on Govt. Operations
Noe, Paul R. .... '62 '90 C.951 B.A. L.276 J.D. Com. on Govt. Affairs
O'Neal, Dudley L., Jr. '23 '50 (AL)
C&L.16 A.B., LL.B. Com. on Banking, Housing & Urban Affairs
Oscherwitz, Thomas J. .... '67 '94 C.813 B.A. L.1066 J.D. Com. on Judiciary
Pappas, Matthew J. .... '63 '88 C.16 B.S. L.902 J.D. Com. on Judiciary
Paradise, Stephen J. '33 '59 (NY)
C.390 B.A. L.569 LL.B. Com. on Banking, Housing & Urban Affairs
Parker, Terri Kay .... '52 '78 (MI) C.475 B.A. L.215 J.D. Com. on Labor & Human Res.
Parrish, Max R. .... '40 '70 (AR) C.838 A.B. L.45 J.D. Com. on Judiciary
Patch, Renn M. .... '50 '77 (MN) C.494 B.A. L.300 J.D. Com. on Judiciary
Patlis, Jason M. .... '63 '93 C.311 B.A. L.188 J.D. Com. on Envir. & Pub. Works
Paull, Ira ...... '51 '80 C&L.260 B.S.B.A., J.D. Com. on Banking, Housing & Urban Affs.
Paull, Lindy L. .... '48 '80 C.1222 B.B.A. L.260 J.D. Com. on Finance
Payne, Mary Penelope .... '57 '82 C.352 B.A. L.273 J.D. Com. on Budget
Pearson, Mary F. .... '53 '80 (MD) C.210 B.A. L.64 J.D. Com. on Finance
Peck, Keenen .... '60 '88 (WI) C&L.966 B.A., J.D. Com. on Judiciary
Polk, Franklin G. .... '40 '65 C.973 A.B. L.309 LL.B. Com. on Govt. Affairs
Pope, Edward C. .... '57 '84 C.276 B.S. L.30 J.D. Com. on Small Bus.
Prater, Mark A. .... '59 '84 (OR) C.1056 B.S. L.950 J.D. Com. on Finance
Pugash, James Z. .... '51 '78 C.976 B.A. L.309 J.D. Com. on Energy & Nat. Res.
Pujol, Maurice P. .... '24 '56 C&L.425 B.B.A., J.D. Com. on Appropriations
Raffel, Keith .... '51 '78 C&L.309 A.B., J.D. Select Com. on Intelligence
Rechtschaffen, Joyce .... '55 '78 C.674 A.B. L.309 J.D. Com. on Govt. Affairs
Rector, John M. .... '43 '70 (CA) C.112 A.B. L.1066 J.D. Com. on Judiciary
Rehnquist, Janet .... '57 '85 C&L.893 B.A., J.D. Com. on Govt. Affairs
Reznick, Scott M. '46 '73 (IL)
C.1036 A.B. L.145 J.D. Com. on Banking, Housing & Urban Affairs
Rixey, John F., Jr. .... '53 '85 (MD) C.1083 B.A. L.273 J.D. Com. on Rules
Roberts, William J. .... '56 '81 C.976 B.A. L.145 J.D. Democratic Sen. Campaign Com.
Robnett, Harriet L. .... '21 '61 C.502 B.J. L.910 J.D. Com. on Rules
Rollins, Thomas M. .... '55 '84 (TX) C.276 B.A. L.309 J.D. Com. on Labor & Human Res.
Rose, Carl P. .... '29 '56 C&L.228 A.B., LL.B. Com. on Agric. & Forestry
Rosenberger, Francis C. .... '15 '39 (VA) C.893 L.537 LL.B. Com. on Judiciary
Rosier, Theresa H .... '72 '99 (AZ) C.174 B.A. L.36 J.D. Select Com. on Indian Affairs
Ross, Lisa A. .... '59 '86 C.1044 B.S. L.276 J.D. Com. on Labor & Human Resources
Ross, Stephen F. .... '55 '79 C.112 A.B. L.1066 J.D. Com. on Judiciary
Rother, John C. .... '47 '75 C.604 A.B. L.659 J.D. Com. on Human Resources
Rowny, Michael J. .... '50 '77 C.453 B.S. L.276 J.D. Com. on Finance
Roy, Denise D. .... '59 '87 (GA) C.494 B.A. L.976 J.D. Com. on Finance
Schneider, Mark B. .... '45 '78 C.800 B.A. L.273 J.D. Select Com. on Intelligence
Schwantes, Jonathan R. .... '72 '97 (WI) C.494 B.A. L.966 J.D. Com. on Judiciary
Schwartz, Herman .... '31 '57 C&L.309 A.B., J.D. Com. on Judiciary
Scott, Samuel J. .... '10 '42 (IL) C.801 B.Ed. L.339 LL.B. Com. on Judiciary
Seat, Keith L. .... '58 '83 C.947 B.A. L.986 J.D. Com. on Judiciary
Shahinian, Dean V. '53 '78 (VA)
C.976 B.S. L.893 J.D. Com. on Banking, Housing & Urban Affs.
Shaw, Frederic E., Jr '50 '92 (NH)
C.550 B.A. L.178 J.D. Com. on Labor & Human Resources
Shimberg, Steven J. .... '53 '78 C.1044 B.A. L.228 J.D. Com. on Environ.
Shriver, Garner E. .... '12 '40 (KS) C.942 B.A. L.900 LL.B. Com. on Veterans' Affairs
Siegel, Gerald W. .... '17 '48 C.352 B.A. L.976 LL.B. Com. on Rules & Admin.

Silverstein, Robert '14 '53 L.472 LL.B. Com. on Presidential Campaign Activities
Smith, Chester H. '19 '54 (NV) C&L.273 A.B., LL.B. Com. on Small Bus.
Smith, Glenn C. '53 '78 C.273 B.A. L.569 J.D. Com. on Govt. Affairs
Snider, L. Britt '45 '69 C.198 A.B. L.893 LL.B. Select Com. on Intelligence
Snyder, Loyal T. R. '38 '70 C&L.911 B.A., J.D. Com. on Commerce
Sousa, John L. '38 '64 (RI) C.94 B.A. L.273 LL.B. Com. on Rules & Admin.
Southwell, Brian C. '46 '73 (ND) C&L.494 B.A., J.D. Com. on Judiciary
Spector, Leonard S. '45 '74 C.951 B.A. L.976 J.D. Com. on Govt. Affairs
Spira, Herbert L. '32 '58 C.867 A.B. L.309 LL.B. Select Com. on Small Bus.
Steinberg, James B. '53 '79 C.309 A.B. L.976 J.D. Com. on Labor & Human Rel.
Stern, Craig A. '54 '78 C.976 B.A. L.893 J.D. Com. on Judiciary
Stirling, Deborah Jane '47 '75 (SC) C&L.790 B.A., J.D. Com. on Commerce
Stockett, Peter M., Jr. '32 '60 (MS) C.902 B.A. L.500 LL.B. Com. on Judiciary
Strassburger, Raymond L. '46 '73
C.262 A.B. L.228 J.D. Com. on Comm., Science and Transp.
Stucky, Scott W. '48 '73 C.942 B.A. L.309 J.D. Com. on Armed Servs.
Sullivan, Peter M. '45 '70 C&L.276 A.B., J.D. Com. on Govt. Affairs
Tijerina, Kathryn Harris '50 '77 C.309 B.A. L.813 J.D. Com. on Indian Affairs
Tucker, Patrick A. '47 '72 (VA) C.886 B.S. L.273 J.D. Com. on Armed Servs.
Valentine, C. Braxton, Jr. '24 '52 C&L.893 B.A., LL.B. Select Com. on Ethics
Van Cleave, Michelle Kim '53 '79 C&L.800 B.A., J.D. Com. on Judiciary
Velasquez, Jay '60 '86 C&L.846 B.B.A., J.D. Natl. Republican Senatorial Com.
Wallace, Cheryl Y. '55 '83 (MD) C.914 B.A. L.30 J.D. Com. on Commerce
Wallace, Henry S. '51 '78 (PA) C.311 B.A. L.884 J.D. Com. on Judiciary
Werner, David L. '59 '86 (PA)
C.352 B.A. L.976 J.D. Com. on Agric., Nutrition & Forestry
Werner, Michael Jay '61 '86 (VA) C.477 B.A. L.273 J.D. Special Com. on Aging
Wexler, Stephen J. '35 '63 C.690 B.S. L.276 J.D. Com. on Labor & Publ. Wlfr.
White, Ward H. '40 '65 (KS) C.30 B.A. L.188 LL.B. Com. on Commerce
Whitehorn, Samuel E. '53 '79 (CO)
C&L.208 B.A. Com. on Commerce, Science & Transp.
Williams, Richard S. '63 '88 (AL) C.339 B.A. L.16 J.D. Com. on Judiciary
Wolf, Mitchell Craig '62 '87 (MD) C.216 B.A. L.64 J.D. Com. on Judiciary
Woodcock, Elizabeth C. '53 '88 (ME) C.95 B.A. L.1294 J.D. Com. on Govt. Affairs
Wooten, Terry L. '54 '80 (SC) C&L.790 B.A., J.D. Com. on Judiciary
Yin, George K. '49 '77 C.477 B.A. L.273 J.D. Com. on Finance
Zapple, Nicholas '14 '42 (NJ) L.997 LL.B. Com. on Commerce

SENATORIAL ASSISTANTS

Aldrete, Cristobal P. '24 '51 (TX) C.846 L.796 LL.B. Exec. Asst. to Sen.
Allen, Steven J. '56 '80 (AL) C.12 B.A. L.192 J.D. Press Secy. to Sen.
Altman, Nancy J. '50 '74 C.681 A.B. L.659 J.D. Asst. to Sen.
Amitay, Morris J. '36 '62 (VA) C.178 A.B. L.309 LL.B. Legis. Asst. to Sen.
Anderson, Tobyn J. '57 '83 C&L.585 B.S., J.D. Legis. Asst. to Sen.
Ashby, Mark J. '61 '87 (LA) C&L.420 B.S., J.D. Legis. Asst. to Sen.
Atkins, Charles N., II '52 '79 C.329 B.A. L.309 J.D. Legis. Coun. to Sen.
Atwater, Todd K. '66 '91 (SC) C.968 B.S. L.790 J.D. Staff Asst. to Sen.
Babb, James H. '57 '84 (GA) C.406 B.A. L.790 J.D. Legis. Dir. to Sen.
Bailey, Stephen R. '50 '80 (MD) C.602 B.A. L.64 J.D. Spec. Coun. to Sen.
Ballance, Frank C. '39 '67 C.228 B.A. L.976 LL.B. Asst. to Sen.
Banks, Robert C., Jr. '42 '71 (AR) C&L.45 B.A., J.D. Asst. to Sen.
Bennett, Crystal '72 '99 (MD) C&L.575 B.S.B.A., J.D. Legis. Asst. to Sen.
Billings, Anne E. '61 '91 (MO) C.1288 B.S. L.502 J.D. Legis. Asst. to Sen.
Billy, Carrie L. '61 '86 (AZ) C.37 B.A. L.276 J.D. Asst. to Sen.
Bischoff, Carol Ann '60 '88 C.94 B.S. L.893 J.D. Legis. Coun. to Sen.
Bishop, Earle J. '21 '50 (VT) C.478 A.B. L.94 LL.B. Coun. to Sen.
Blattner, Jeffrey H. '54 '81 C.659 B.A. L.309 J.D. Asst. to Sen.
Bock, Paul S. '64 '91 C.276 B.A L.597 J.D. Chief of Staff to Sen.
Bode, Denise Anne '54 '82 (OK) C.623 B.A. L.1209 J.D. Legal Coun. to Sen.
Bonvillian, William B. '47 '75 C&L.178 B.A., J.D. Legis. Dir. to Sen.
Bosse, Linda '68 '94 C&L.494 B.A., J.D. Legis. Asst. to Sen.
Boyd, Krista Ann '74 '99 (MD) C.259 B.S. L.245 J.D. Legis. Asst. to Sen.
Brown, Max J. '65 '92 (OH) C.273 B.A. L.1003 J.D. Legis. Asst. to Sen.
Bruns, Kevin T. '57 '83 C.188 B.S. L.30 J.D. Asst. to Sen.
Buehlmann, Eric D. '68 '95 (MD) C.401 B.S. L.30 J.D. Legis. Coun. to Sen.
Bueno, Irene B. '63 '88 C.112 A.B. L.1065 J.D. Legis. Asst. to Sen.
Buxton, Anne P. '44 '72 (LA) C.681 B.A. L.976 J.D. Legis. Asst. to Sen.
Caldwell, Barry H. '60 '86 C.197 A.B. L.276 J.D. Asst. to Sen.
Carothers, Wm. A., Jr. '35 '61 C.976 B.A. L.846 LL.B. Spec. Coun. to Sen.
Carson, John K. '61 '87 (CO) C&L.174 B.A., J.D. Asst. to Sen.
Carty, James P. '38 '65 (MA) C.676 A.B. L.94 LL.B. Legis. Asst. to Sen.
Claassen, Anne-Kathryn '68 '94 (NM) C.859 B.A. L.560 J.D. Asst. to Sen.
Clark, Carla E. '67 '92 (MS) C.71 B.A. L.500 J.D. Legis. Asst. to Sen.
Cleland, Bartlett D. '68 '94 (MO) C.357 B.A. L.734 J.D. Legis. Aide to Sen.
Cochrane, William M. '17 '41 (NC) C&L.575 B.A., LL.B. Admin. Asst. to Sen.
Colbert, David M. '50 '78 C.602 B.A. L.276 J.D. Asst. Parliamentarian
Connelly, John C. '71 '96 C.276 B.A. L.150 J.D. Legis. Aide to Sen.
Conwell, Edward L., III '56 '95 C.282 B.A. L.1194 J.D. Legis. Asst. to Sen.
Cooper, J. Ashley '72 '97 (SC) C.160 B.A. L.790 J.D. Legis. Dir. to Sen.
Corbett, William L. '45 '71 (WY) C&L.972 B.S., J.D. Legis. Asst. to Sen.
Cowles, C. Deming, IV '46 '71 C.390 B.A. L.893 J.D. Legis. Aide to Sen.
Crawford, Franklin J. '27 '75 C.608 B.A. L.273 J.D. Legis. Asst. to Sen.
Cresswell, William E. '26 '48 (MS) C&L.500 LL.B. Admin. Asst. to Sen.
Davis-Watters, Patricia A. '59 '84 C.1099 B.A. L.861 J.D. Legis. Coun. to Sen.
DeLeon, Patrick H. '43 '81 (HI) C.31 B.A. L.180 J.D. Exec. Asst. to Sen.
delSobral, Julia '69 '95 C.867 B.A. L.184 J.D. Legis. Correspondent for Sen.
Dicks, Norman D. '40 '68 C&L.911 B.A., J.D. Legis. Asst. to Sen.
Donley, Owen J. '24 '51 (SD) C.602 A.B. L.793 LL.B. Legis. Asst. to Sen.
Due, Mary Jane C. '22 '56 L.878 J.D. Asst. to Sen.
Edwards, John Charles '60 '88 (AR) C.44 B.S. L.1243 J.D. Admin. Aide to Sen.
Emrich, Andrew C. '71 '96 (CO) C.999 B.A. L.972 J.D. Legis. Coun. to Sen.
Epstein, Michael T. '37 '61 (MA) C.103 B.A. L.94 J.D. Asst. to Sen.
Ermoyan, Eugenie '30 '64 (IL) C.1016 L.365 LL.B. Spec. Asst. to Sen.
Feller, Millicent A. '48 '81 C.190 A.B. L.276 J.D. Admin. Asst. to Sen.
Field, A. Searle, II '44 '72 (CT) C.674 A.B.Econ. L.273 J.D. Legis. Asst. to Sen.
Finkler, Kira L. '66 '93 (MD) C.37 B.A. L.30 J.D. Asst. to Sen.
Fisher, Mary M. '64 '91 C.602 B.B.A. L.30 J.D. Legis. Aide to Sen.
Fleming, Jonathan W. '34 '66 C.976 B.A. L.178 LL.B. Asst. to Sen.
Forman, Jonathan B. '52 '78 C.597 B.A. L.477 J.D. Legis. Asst. to Sen.
Frame, Bruce C. '42 '77 (MD) C.205 B.A. L.64 J.D. Asst. to Sen.
Gauche, Jerry N. '48 '74 C&L.629 B.S., J.D. Legis. Asst. to Sen.
Gerard, Joe G. '39 '75 (AR) C.315 L.45 J.D. Spec. Asst. to Sen.
Gernhardt, Rebecca C. '54 '81 C.210 B.A. L.128 J.D. Asst. to Sen.
Giglio, John D. '56 '86 C.367 B.A. L.659 J.D. Asst. to Sen.
Gilchrist, Gretchen C. '67 '91 (PA) C.302 B.S. L.1338 J.D. Legis. Asst. to Sen.
Goold, Linda '46 '77 C&L.101 B.A., J.D. Legis. Asst. to Sen.
Greenlaw, Denise M. '52 '78 (UT) C&L.878 B.A., J.D. Legis. Asst. to Sen.
Grill, Philip M. '47 '73 C&L.446 B.S., J.D. Legis. Aide to Sen.
Grimley, Michael J. '64 '94 C.426 B.A. L.1049 J.D. Admin. Asst. to Sen.
Gross, Brian J. '59 '90 (PA) C.839 B.A. L.276 J.D. Coun. to Sen.
Gustitus, Linda J. '47 '75 (IL) C.604 B.A. L.912 J.D. Legis. Asst. to Sen.
Hall, Robert Price, III '60 '85 (GA) C&L.280 A.B., J.D. Asst. to Sen.
Halverson, Mark B. '55 '81 C.350 B.S. L.352 J.D. Asst. to Sen.
Hamm, John W. '45 '71 (VA) C.207 B.A. L.273 J.D. Legis. Asst. to Sen.
Hardiman, Morgan P. '50 '77 (NY) C.93 B.A. L.569 J.D. Asst. to Sen.
Hayes, Dwight George '45 '82 (SC) C&L.790 B.S., J.D. Leg. Asst. to Sen.
Henderson, Frances '17 '54 C.66 B.A. L.705 LL.B. Admin. Asst. to Sen.
Hepler, Robert W. '48 '76 C.228 B.A. L.309 J.D. Legis. Asst. to Sen.
Hicks, James Virgil, Jr. '58 '83 (SC) C&L.790 B.S., J.D. Asst. to Sen.
Hill, James P. '50 '75 (MI) C.475 B.A. L.477 J.D. Legis. Asst. to Sen.
Howell, Hubert W. '40 '80 (GA) C.1059 B.S. L.969 J.D. Chief of Staff to Sen.
Irizarry, Steven E. '68 '94 (AZ) C.276 B.A. L.36 J.D. Coun. to Sen.
Jacobson, J. Douglas '61 '87 (TX) C.846 B.A. L.744 J.D. Legis. Asst. to Sen.
Jeka, Mary R. '54 '83 (MA) C&L.93 B.A., J.D. Legis. Aide to Sen.
Jenkins, Eugene A., Jr. '28 '51 (MD) C&L.273 B.S., LL.B. Admin. Asst. to Sen.
Jennison, John C., III '48 '75 (FL) C.893 B.S. L.362 J.D. Asst. to Sen.
Julyan, David S. '50 '80 (MD) C.33 B.A. L.276 J.D. Legis. Dir. for Sen.
Kelly, Hugh J. '37 '62 C.494 A.B. L.178 LL.B. Admin. Asst. to Sen.
Kidd, Doug '51 '77 (GA) C&L.280 A.B., J.D. Legis. Coun. to Sen.
Knutson, Karen Yetka '67 '96 (VA) C.17 B.A. L.896 J.D. Legis. Asst. to Sen.
Koonce, Wayne A. '49 '79 C.339 B.A. L.309 J.D. Legis. Dir. to Sen.
Kreseski, Steven L. '57 '83 (MD) C.282 B.A. L.64 J.D. Asst. to Sen.
Landavazo, Christine M. '67 '97 (NM) C.770 B.S.C. L.560 J.D. Legis. Asst. to Sen.
Larkin, Barbara Mills '51 '77 C.157 B.A. L.352 J.D. Admin. Asst. to Sen.
Lawson, Richard C. '47 '75 (GA) C.945 B.A. L.245 J.D. Admin. Asst. to Sen.
Lesesne, Joab M., III '64 '91 C.88 B.A. L.790 J.D. Chief of Staff to Sen.
Levin, Jonathan C. '53 '78 (PA) C.103 B.A. L.178 J.D. Legis. Asst. to Sen.
Levin, Neil D. '54 '82 C.390 A.B. L.1019 J.D. Asst. to Sen.
Lin, Kenneth '70 '96 C.477 A.B. L.823 J.D. Legis. Asst. to Sen.
Little, John Meighan '72 '97 (AL) C.802 B.A. L.192 J.D. Coun. to Sen.
Love, Jon B. '43 '70 (MS) C.500 B.B.A. L.356 J.D. Legis. Asst. to Sen.
Ludlam, Charles E. '45 '72 (CA) C.813 B.A. L.477 J.D. Coun. to Sen.
Madsen, Ronald E. '28 '55 C.101 B.S. L.273 J.D. State Dir. to Sen.
Mahony, Emon A., Jr. '41 '65 (AR) C&L.861 B.A., J.D. Legal Asst. to Sen.
Marks, Kathryn Jay '71 '00 (IL) C.296 B.S. L.30 J.D. Legis. Asst. to Sen.
Marshall, Angela Jolene '69 '97 (MT) C.1235 B.S.Ed. L.508 J.D. Legis. Coun. to Sen.
Matthews, Jason D. '70 '95 (IL) C.684 B.A. L.801 J.D. Dir. to Sen.
McArthur, Alan D. '21 '51 (NE) C.546 L.180 LL.B. Exec. Asst. to Sen.
McConnell, Joel C., Jr. '49 '74 (NC) C&L.896 B.A., J.D. Legis. Aide to Sen.
McCornack, Hannah S. '45 '71 C.518 B.A. L.128 J.D. Spec. Asst. to Sen.
McIntyre, Linda '64 '89 C.477 B.A. L.94 J.D. Legis. Asst. to Sen.
McLean, Christopher A. '58 '82 C&L.190 B.S., J.D. Legis. Asst. to Sen.
McMonigle, Joseph P. '66 '98 (PA) C.1113 B.A. L.1338 J.D. Gen. Coun. to Sen.
McMurray, Claudia Anne '58 '85 C.788 A.B. L.276 J.D. Asst. to Sen.
McNitt, Townsend L. '67 '93 (VA) C.999 B.A. L.602 J.D. Chief of Staff to Sen.
Mercer, Lee W. '43 '71 (NH) C.197 B.A. L.94 J.D. Asst. to Sen.
Miles, Dudley D. '25 '53 (WY) C&L.972 B.S., LL.B. Research Asst. to Sen.
Miller, Kimberly D. '66 '95 C.914 B.A. L.94 J.D. Legis. Asst. to Sen.
Miller, Pamela E. '47 '75 C.420 B.A. L.273 J.D. Legis. Asst. to Sen.
Moffet, Michael C. '50 '75 C&L.378 B.S., J.D. Admin. Asst. to Sen.
Morris, Martin W. '56 '81 C.228 A.B. L.192 J.D. Asst. to Sen.
Moseman, John H. '47 '72 C&L.546 B.A., J.D. Legis. Dir. to Sen.
Motley, Joel W., III '52 '79 (NY) C&L.309 A.B., J.D. Asst. to Sen.
Mueller, Melissa A. '65 '91 (TX) C&L.846 B.B.A., J.D. Legis. Coun. to Sen.
Mulinex, Joy A. '72 '98 (OH) C.473 B.A. L.629 J.D. Coun. to Sen.
Mulvey, Timothy P. '57 '85 (NY) C.1044 B.A. L.823 J.D. Asst. to Sen.
Murdock, Patricia Collins '60 '86 (MD) C.611 B.A. L.880 J.D. Legis. Coun. to Sen.
Myrick, Gary '67 '96 C.431 B.A. L.30 J.D. Asst. to Sen.
Nirenberg, Lori Hecht '61 '90 C.298 B.A. L.273 J.D. Legis. Coun. to Sen.
Norden, Donald J. '53 '78 (NE) C&L.546 B.A., J.D. Legis. Asst. to Sen.
Nordquist, Myron H. '40 '70 C.628 B.S. L.1188 J.D. Coun. to Sen.
O'Connor, George C., Jr. '50 '80 (VA) C.262 B.A. L.1209 J.D. Coun. to Sen.
Ohlemiller, Marcia L. '48 '84 C.879 B.A. L.596 J.D. Legis. Asst. to Sen.
Oliphant, Lincoln C. '48 '75 (UT) C&L.878 B.S., J.D. Legis. Asst. to Sen.
O'Neal, Joanne P. '31 '57 C.1369 B.S. L.273 LL.B. Asst. to Sen.
Ostrovsky, Eric '50 '82 C.930 B.A. L.284 J.D. Legis. Asst. to Sen.
Otis, Lee S. Liberman '56 '85 C.976 B.A. L.145 J.D. Coun. to Sen.
Owen, D. Robert '69 '94 (NE) C&L.546 B.A., J.D. Sen. Coun. to Sen.
Owen, Daryl H. '56 '81 (LA) C.420 B.A. L.276 J.D. Legis. Asst. to Sen.
Parker, W. Carey '34 '67 C.674 B.S.E. L.309 LL.B. Asst. to Sen.
Parson, Linda K. '53 '87 (TN) C.806 B.A. L.329 J.D. Legis. Coun. to Sen.
Patack, Melissa B. '56 '82 (NY) C.188 B.S. L.94 J.D. Asst. to Sen.
Patterson, Mark A. '61 '90 C.1044 B.A. L.128 J.D. Legis. Dir. to Sen.
Pearce, Krisann A. '65 '96 (KS) C&L.378 B.S., J.D. Coun. to Sen.
Pence, Randall G. '57 '86 C&L.546 B.A., J.D. Legis. Dir. to Sen.
Perotti, Candida F. '64 '89 C.518 B.A. L.273 J.D. Coun. to Sen.
Phillips, George L. '49 '73 (MS) C.499 B.S. L.500 J.D. Special Coun. to Sen.
Potter, Mary L. '58 '84 (NC) C.522 B.A. L.1228 J.D. Legis. Asst. to Sen.
Pritts, George W., Jr. '29 '64 C.223 B.S. L.831 LL.B. Legis. Coun. to Sen.
Reid, Warren F. '29 '61 (WA) C&L.911 B.A., J.D. Resch. Asst. to Sen.
Roberts, Brooke M. '54 '80 (IN) C.108 B.A. L.1119 J.D. Leg. Dir. to Sen.
Roberts-Malamis, Rebecca '62 '89 (VA) C.923 B.A. L.904 J.D. Legis. Asst. to Sen.
Rolfstad, John '58 '85 (ND) C.358 B.A. L.585 J.D. Legis. Asst. to Sen.
Rosen, Burt E. '49 '73 C&L.790 B.A., J.D. Legis. Asst. to Sen.
Rosen, Dean A. '65 '90 C.94 B.S. L.823 J.D. Legal Asst. to Sen.
Ross, Deborah Hardin '59 '83 (FL) C.228 A.B. L.259 J.D. Legis. Asst. to Sen.
Rothschild, Gregg A. '65 '93 C.1044 B.A. L.273 J.D. Legis. Dir. to Sen.
Routson, Samuel J. '49 '80 (ID) C.336 B.S. L.101 J.D. Legis. Dir. to Sen.
Russell, Michael J. '58 '84 C.282 B.A. L.880 J.D. Coun. to Sen.
Russert, Timothy J. '50 '77 C.363 B.A. L.161 J.D. Spec. Asst. to Sen.
Ruth, Frederick A. '39 '72 C.663 A.B. L.623 J.D. Asst. to Sen.
Sarvis, Aubrey L. '44 '76 C&L.30 B.A., J.D. Legis. Coun. to Sen.
Scarborough, Keith A. '53 '78 (NE) C&L.546 B.A., J.D. Legis. Asst. to Sen.
Schmidt, Derek L. '68 '96 C.378 B.S. L.276 J.D. Legis. Coun. to Sen.
Schnacke, J. Gregory '58 '85 (OK) C.378 B.S. L.862 J.D. Admin. Asst. to Sen.
Scholes, Dallas J. '68 '96 (VA) C.101 B.A. L.273 J.D. Coun. to Sen.
Seidel, Rebecca S. '67 '93 C.602 B.A. L.201 J.D. Coun. to Sen.
Shade, Cynthia S. '56 '83 C.276 B.A. L.128 J.D. Legis. Asst. to Sen.

UNITED STATES SENATE (Continued)

Sherman, Jo A. '50 '81 (WY) C.1219 B.S.E. L.972 J.D. Legis. Asst. to Sen.
Sigler, David Andrew '73 '98 (AL) C.276 B.A. L.192 J.D. Coun. to Sen.
Smith, Elizabeth D. '68 '94 C.228 B.A. L.893 J.D. Chf. Coun. to Sen.
Spaulding, Suzanne E. '57 '81 C&L.893 B.A., J.D. Legis. Coun. to Sen.
Spils, Carol A. '65 '92 (AK) C.602 B.A. L.1049 J.D. Legis. Asst. to Sen.
Stansel, Mary E. '45 '75 C.155 B.A. L.280 J.D. Legis. Asst. to Sen.
Steer, John R. '49 '79 (SC) C.160 B.S. L.790 J.D. Legis. Asst. to Sen.
Stein, Joshua H. '66 '95 (NC) C.197 B.A. L.309 J.D. Dep. Chief of Staff
Stoddard, Gordon P. '55 '85 C&L.276 A.B., J.D. Asst. to Sen.
Strottman, Kathleen A. '72 '99 (CA) C.321 B.A. L.1148 J.D. Legis. Asst. to Sen.
Tanielian, Matthew J. '— '96 (MI) C.94 B.A. L.30 J.D. Legis. Asst. to Sen.
Tenpenny, Chad D. '72 '97 (KS) C&L.378 B.A., J.D. Coun. to Sen.
Thompson, Sarah A. '49 '80 (GA) C.1365 B.A. L.245 J.D. Legis. Asst. to Sen.
Thompson, V. Bruce '47 '74 (OK) C.659 B.S. L.862 J.D. Asst. to Sen.
Thomson, Barbara Ellen '55 '84 (MN) C.585 B.S. L.276 J.D. Legis. Asst. to Sen.
Tobias, Damon P. '55 '88 (PA) C.560 M.B.A. L.128 J.D. Spec. Coun. to Sen.
Turner, Donnice M. '69 '99 (GA) C.811 B.A. L.329 J.D. Coun. to Sen.
Turner, Robert A. '53 '80 (WA) C.285 B.B.A. L.276 J.D. Legis. Asst. to Sen.
Ufholz, Philip J. '47 '73 C.861 B.A. L.276 J.D. Legis. Asst. to Sen.
Urban, David J. '64 '94 (PA) C.870 B.S. L.831 J.D. Chief of Staff to Sen.
van der Voort, Thomas L. '35 '60 (MA) C.674 B.A. L.309 LL.B. Legis. Asst. to Sen.
Van Heuvelen, Robert I. '50 '79 C.429 B.A. L.273 J.D. Chief of Staff to Sen.
Velde, Richard W. '31 '61 C.98 B.S. L.273 LL.B. Consultant to Sen.
Vodra, Richard E. '48 '72 C.970 B.A. L.976 J.D. Legis. Asst. to Sen.
Walls, Thomas F. '60 '88 (NY) C&L.893 B.A., J.D. Legis. Dir. to Sen.
Washburn, Barbara J. '42 '75 C.228 A.B. L.276 J.D. Asst. to Sen.
Waters, Charles L. '45 '72 (OK) C.616 B.A. L.862 J.D. Legis. Asst. to Sen.
Weiss, Shelby '67 '92 (TX) C.112 B.A. L.802 J.D. Legis. Asst. to Sen.
Widener, Carla M. '64 '91 (PA) C.72 B.A. L.910 J.D. Legis. Aide to Sen.
Wilkie, Robert L., Jr. '62 '90 (PA) C.896 B.A. L.425 J.D. Legis. Asst. to Sen.
Wolfson, Roger S. '67 '92 C.881 B.A. L.659 J.D. Legis. Asst. to Sen.
Yianilos, Christopher J. '72 '97 (VA) C.886 B.A. L.902 J.D. Legis. Coun. to Sen.
Ziglar, James W., Sr. '45 '72 C&L.273 B.A., J.D.

JOINT COMMITTEES AND COMMISSIONS

Allen, Sandra Mills '46 '76 C.105 B.A. L.831 J.D. Com. on Taxation
Arnold, Lincoln '10 '33 C&L.494 LL.B. Com. on Int. Rev. Tax.
Billinger, James L. '32 '64 C.686 B.S. L.208 J.D. Com. on Int. Rev. Tax.
Conklin, Charles R. '20 '51 (CO) C&L.309 B.A., J.D. Com. on Public Land Law Review
Ford, Roland W. '27 '66 (MD) C.472 M.B.A. L.446 LL.B. Com. on Taxation
Gotwald, Robert Caldwell '50 '76 C.604 A.B. L.150 J.D. Com. on Taxation
Johnson, Randall E. '46 '74 C.429 B.A. L.494 J.D. Fed. Election Comm.
Jones, Sara C. '59 '87 C.383 B.A. L.228 J.D. Com. on Printing
Juzenas, Walter E. '68 '95 (MD) C.966 B.S. L.273 J.D. Com. on Agriculture Nutrition & Forestry
Kavjian, Judy L. '62 '91 (PA) C.945 B.B.A. L.659 J.D. Com. on Taxation
Kies, Kenneth J. '52 '77 C.610 B.A. L.608 J.D. Com. on Taxation
Krumbhaar, George D. '36 '66 C.309 B.A. L.178 LL.B. Economic Com.
Levinson, Peter J. '43 '71 (HI) C.1036 A.B. L.309 J.D. Select Com. on Immig. & Refugee Policy
Mann, Roberta F. '60 '87 C&L.35 B.S., J.D. Com. on Taxation
McDaniel, Alysa M. '61 '88 C.976 B.A. L.276 J.D. Com. on Taxation
Merrick, Samuel V. '14 '42 C&L.659 A.B., LL.B. Com. on Congressional Operations
Miller, Mary C. '46 '77 C.770 B.A. L.30 J.D. Economic Com.
Nega, Joseph W. '60 '84 (IL) C&L.209 B.S.C., J.D. Com. on Taxation
Oleszewski, Richard '50 '81 C.674 A.B. L.904 J.D. Com. on Printing
Pena, Humberto R. '49 '74 C.1219 B.A. L.744 J.D. Com. on Agriculture
Price, James L. '50 '78 (MI) C.813 B.A. L.477 J.D. Economic Com.
Rock, Cecily W. '54 '80 (NY) C.674 B.A. L.893 J.D. Com. on Taxation
Shaviro, Daniel N. '57 '81 C.674 A.B. L.976 J.D. Com. on Finance
Smith, Carolyn E. '56 '82 (CA) C.112 B.A. L.1066 J.D. Com. on Taxation
Taylor, Peter S. '37 '63 C.900 A.B. L.273 LL.B. Amer. Indian Policy Review Comm.
Thomas, Melvin C., Jr. '44 '70 C.264 B.A. L.597 J.D. Com. on Taxation
Wallick, Ruth Brewer '22 '78 C.930 B.S. L.128 J.D. Com. on Banking, Fin. & Urban Affairs
Warren, Harold J. '16 '38 (GA) C&L.280 LL.B. Com. on Defense Production
Wold, Barry L. '52 '80 C&L.188 A.B., J.D. Com. on Taxation

CONSUMER PRODUCT SAFETY COMMISSION

(Vacant), *General Counsel*

OFFICE OF THE GENERAL COUNSEL

Allen, Richard W. '34 '63 C.723 B.A. L.276 LL.B.
Goldstein, Leonard H. '41 '66 C.472 B.B.A. L.30 J.D.
Hampshire, Melissa V. '61 '87 (VA) C&L.1209 B.S., J.D.
Jennings, Daniel L. '39 '73 C.512 B.A. L.329 J.D.
Kerwin, Harriet '55 '80 C.477 B.A. L.588 J.D.
Lemberg, D. Stephen '35 '73 C.867 B.S. L.1049 J.D.
Lowell, Martin F. '45 '82 C.188 B.S. L.276 J.D.
Noonan, Robert T. '38 '63 (OH) C.973 A.B. L.150 J.D.
Pollitzer, Patricia M. '60 '86 C.881 B.A. L.273 J.D.
Rosenthal, Joseph F. '28 '69 (NY) C.31 A.B. L.178 LL.B.
Shakin, Alan C. '47 '73 C.1036 A.B. L.659 J.D.

OFFICE OF EXECUTIVE DIRECTOR

Gilbert, Pamela '58 '85 C.860 B.A. L.569 J.D. Exec. Dir.

OFFICE OF COMPLIANCE

Gidding, Michael J. '47 '77 C&L.446 B.A., J.D.
Kacoyanis, Dennis C. '53 '79 (MA) C.588 B.A. L.209 J.D.
Kennedy, Patricia E. '72 '98 (MD) C.205 B.A. L.1194 J.D.
Lewis, Deborah J. '62 '89 C.674 B.A. L.569 J.D.
Mitchell, Belinda Bell '57 '98 (MD) C.446 B.S. L.1002 J.D.
Moore, William J., Jr. '51 '76 C&L.30 B.A., J.D.
Murawski, Anthony W. '65 '98 (MD) C.1090 B.A. L.30 J.D.
Noble, Laura E. Washburn '63 '92 (PA) C.446 B.S. L.900 J.D.
Orlove, Deborah S. '63 '91 C.025 B.Sc. L.273 J.D.
Plank, Margaret H. '57 '85 (MO) C.976 B.A. L.178 J.D.
Popkin, Seth B. '60 '86 C.1349 B.A. L.904 J.D.
Schoem, Alan H. '46 '73 C.446 B.A. L.30 J.D.
Stone, Eric L. '52 '77 C.264 B.A. L.904 J.D.
Tarnoff, Howard N. '71 '95 C.347 B.S. L.273 J.D.
Williams, Jimmie L., Jr. '62 '89 C.112 B.S. L.941 J.D.
Yelenik, Ronald G. '41 '66 C.4 B.A. L.1009 LL.B.

CHAIRMANS OFFICE

Sanders, Walt A. '50 '85 (VA) C.112 A.B. L.904 Counselor to Chmn.

COMMISSIONERS OFFICE

Gougisha, Michael '53 '92 (LA) C.217 B.A. L.861 J.D.
Moore, Thomas H. '37 '74 C.1038 B.S. L.260 J.D. Comr.
Weller, Pamela L. '48 '75 C.446 B.A. L.276 J.D.
Wilson, Dennis B. '54 '79 C&L.352 B.A., J.D.

CORPORATION FOR NATIONAL AND COMMUNITY SERVICE

(Vacant), *General Counsel*

OFFICE OF THE GENERAL COUNSEL

Bryant, Thomas L. '49 '74 (MS) C.499 B.S. L.500 J.D.
Dupré, Suzanne '41 '66 C.424 B.S. L.276 J.D.
Goren, Nicola O. '66 '92 C.1036 B.A. L.188 J.D.
Minor, Wilsie Y. '50 '77 (VA) C.681 B.A. L.976 J.D.
Rapp, Britanya E. '52 '79 (VA) C.347 B.A. L.692 J.D.
Trinity, Frank R. '63 '88 C.674 A.B. L.976 J.D.

EQUAL OPPORTUNITY STAFF

Voss, Nancy Bea '50 '81 C.55 B.A. L.273 J.D.

OFFICE OF THE INSPECTOR GENERAL

Bathen, Terry E. '46 '79 C.770 B.A. L.276 J.D.
Mulloy, Vincent A. '60 '87 C&L.45 B.A., J.D.

DEPARTMENT OF AGRICULTURE

Charles R. Rawls, *General Counsel*

OFFICE OF THE GENERAL COUNSEL

Allaben, Elizabeth A. '57 '82 C&L.477 B.S., J.D.
Andrews, James E. '40 '69 (IA) C.350 B.S. L.352 J.D.
Azeredo, Ruth Ann G. '60 '91 (NC) C.319 B.A. L.574 J.D.
Beaton, Brigette J. '68 '98 (LA) C.9 B.B.A. L.803 J.D.
Berry, Albert T. '46 '71 C&L.420 B.A., J.D.
Bishop, Rachel H. '63 '89 (VA) C.381 B.S. L.356 J.D.
Bolinger, Darlene M. '60 '86 (NC) C.575 B.A. L.574 J.D.
Bonner, Peter T. '58 '85 (NY) C.103 A.B. L.178 J.D.
Brady, Terence M. '48 '73 (MD) C.446 B.A. L.178 J.D.
Breinholt, Margaret M. '34 '72 C&L.378 B.A., J.D.
Bundy, Thomas E. '45 '70 (VA) C.645 B.A. L.893 J.D.
Butler, Gary W. '41 '71 (MA) C.659 A.B. L.94 J.D.
Carrington, Karen M. '71 '99 C.597 B.A. L.273 J.D.
Carroll, Colleen Anne '55 '87 (CA) C.112 B.A. L.426 J.D.
Clover, Frank H. '38 '62 C.845 B.A. L.846 LL.B.
Cohen, Kenneth E. '45 '70 (VA) C.823 B.A. L.276 J.D.
Conway, Thomas V. '45 '71 C&L.793 B.A., J.D.
Cooper, Gregory '47 '73 (NY) C&L.262 B.A., J.D.
Cooper, Norman G. '42 '68 C.152 B.A. L.228 J.D.
Cordova, Marion T. '57 '95 C.446 B.A. L.276 J.D.
Crummer, Frank E., Jr. '44 '73 (PA) C&L.229 B.S.B.A., J.D.
Deskins, Sharlene A. '— '89 (MI) C&L.477 A.B., J.D.
Deutsch, Nathaniel M. '52 '79 (NY) C.696 B.A. L.273 J.D.
DeWitte, Vincent L. '60 '85 (AZ) C.35 B.S. L.37 J.D.
Ertman, Robert A. '46 '79 (IL) C.378 B.A. L.209 J.D.
Flynn, M. Bradley '53 '85 (TX) C.477 B.A. L.326 J.D.
Fox, Thomas R. '60 '88 C.878 B.S. L.904 J.D.
Fox-Samson, Connie L. '54 '89 C.835 B.S. L.352 J.D.
Gippert, Michael J. '47 '73 (AZ) C.475 B.S. L.37 J.D.
Golden, John T. '41 '66 C.776 A.B. L.188 J.D.
Good, Barbara S. '49 '75 (KY) C&L.383 B.A., J.D.
Grahn, David P. '59 '86 (MN) C.118 B.A. L.494 J.D.
Groesbeck, Alan D. '53 '80 C&L.101 J.D.
Grundeman, Arnold James '36 '69 (KS) C.378 B.A. L.900 J.D.
Guillou, Kathryn '59 '83 (CA) C.112 B.S. L.1065 J.D.
Gurwitz, Michael D. '63 '91 (NY) C.1036 B.A. L.107 J.D.
Gutteridge, Georgann '50 '75 C.645 B.A. L.884 J.D.
Harris, David H. '56 '81 (NC) C.574 B.A. L.575 J.D.
Harris, Helen C. '51 '76 (NE) C.686 B.A. L.190 J.D.
Heckman, Annejanette K. '73 '98 (OH) C.201 B.A. L.602 J.D.
Herndon, Rick D. '62 '89 (MS) C&L.500 B.A., J.D.
Hill, Ronald W. '44 '70 (KS) C.378 B.A. L.900 J.D.
Hobbie, Mary Kyle '52 '78 C.198 B.A. L.893 J.D.
Holt, James D. '50 '90 (TN) C.143 B.A. L.838 J.D.
Hornstein, Ellen Ruth '59 '86 C.860 B.A. L.276 J.D.
Hughes, Lawrence D. '29 '53 (WI) C&L.436 J.D.
Hylton, Daniel N. '69 '95 (VA) C.198 A.B. L.880 J.D.
Jackson, Terrence G. '49 '75 C.893 B.A. L.902 J.D.
Jay, Gippert Michael '47 '73 (AZ) C.475 B.S. L.37 J.D.
John, Wendy M. '48 '74 (TX) C.788 B.A. L.846 J.D.
Jones, Lori Polin '64 '90 (IN) C.347 B.S. L.352 J.D.
Jones, Lorna Jacqueline '68 '99 (MD) C.035 B.A. L.329 J.D.
Kahn, Jeffrey H. '54 '80 C.918 B.A. L.30 J.D.
Kao, Nancy S. '66 '92 C.112 B.S. L.309 J.D.
Kelly, James M. '39 '64 C.602 B.A. L.893 LL.B.
Kelly, Michael W. '44 '73 (MA) C.918 B.A. L.94 J.D.
Kelly, Sean P. '69 '96 (MD) C.273 B.A. L.260 J.D.
Koch, John B. '50 '77 (WV) C&L.923 B.S., J.D.
Kreitzberg, Leonard R. '47 '74 (NY) C.273 B.A. L.107 J.D.
Lagomarcino, Leslie K. '60 '90 (IA) C.945 B.A. L.352 J.D.
Lawrence, Richard M. '60 '90 (FL) C&L.472 B.B.A., J.D.
Leland, Arlean '— '80 C.103 B.A. L.273 J.D.
Linden, Ralph A. '57 '82 (NE) C.546 B.A. L.602 J.D.
Loizeaux, Paul C. '46 '72 C.112 A.B. L.1068 J.D.

MacHare, Peter '54 '81 C.902 B.A. L.128 J.D.
Maher, Maureen T. '56 '81 C.321 A.B. L.659 J.D.
Martin, Frank, Jr. '57 '90 (OK) C.724 B.S. L.862 J.D.
McAmis, Donald M. '48 '74 C.197 A.B. L.880 J.D.
McCavitt, Mary Jane '— '86 C.93 B.A. L.945 J.D.
McWhirter, Jay D. '65 '90 (FL) C&L.260 B.A., J.D.
Meckus, Kevin F. '51 '78 C.276 B.S.F.S. L.982 J.D.
Montoya, David F. '47 '95 (NM) C.446 B.A. L.560 J.D.
Morgan, Rita '45 '88 (VA) C.840 B.A. L.1209 J.D.
Mulach, Ronald W. '62 '90 (GA) C.339 B.S. L.280 J.D.
O'Brien, Maureen A. '69 '95 C.882 B.A. L.262 J.D.
Olson, Eric C. '59 '89 C.228 B.S. L.893 J.D.
Paul, Eric '43 '72 (CO) C.895 B.S. L.776 J.D.
Poling, Jan Wade '56 '81 (AL) C.10 B.S. L.16 J.D.
Rawls, Charles R. '57 '82 (NC) C.576 B.A. L.1228 J.D. Gen. Coun.
Reilly, Stephen M. '49 '92 C.953 B.S. L.575 J.D.
Reuben, Harold J. '44 '70 (NY) C&L.823 B.A., J.D.
Ristino, Laurie Ann '66 '92 (PA) C.477 B.A. L.352 J.D.
Rosen, Charlene A. '47 '74 C.783 B.A. L.1202 J.D.
Ruttenberg, Pilar '67 '92 (VA) C.012 B.A. L.910 J.D.
Safian, Janet H. '62 '87 (VA) C.893 B.A. L.902 J.D.
Samofal, Alexander W. '41 '72 C.184 B.S. L.560 J.D.
Sculley, Jeffrey S. '64 '92 (IL) C.98 B.A. L.339 J.D.
Settle, Jane H. '49 '90 (MN) C.886 B.S. L.494 J.D.
Shelton, Daniel R. '52 '94 (VA) C.259 B.S. L.1209 J.D.
Shelton, Stuart L. '49 '75 (NC) C.198 B.A. L.575 J.D.
Silverstein, M. Howard '36 '65 C.588 B.S.Ch.E. L.273 LL.B.
Snow, James B. '48 '74 C&L.339 A.B., J.D.
Southers, Philip L. '57 '82 (VA) C.885 B.A. L.893 J.D.
Stanton, Andrew Y. '50 '75 (VA) C.1044 B.A. L.904 J.D.
Stevens, Garrett B. '47 '73 C.207 B.A. L.273 J.D.
Temme-Dietz, Teresa '65 '90 C.375 B.A. L.378 J.D.
Tichenor, Patricia E. '70 '96 C.1019 B.A. L.30 J.D.
Tracy, Donald A. '48 '73 C.966 B.A. L.178 J.D.
Trost, Tami '68 '94 C.659 B.A. L.30 J.D.
Vail, Jeffrey T. '63 '91 (WI) C.30 B.A. L.966 J.D.
Vail, Kenneth H. '40 '69 C.260 B.A. L.362 J.D.
Vos, John P. '65 '91 C.114 B.A. L.352 J.D.
Walsh, Thomas M. '44 '74 C&L.94 A.B., J.D.
Westerlage, Electra '67 '92 (TX) C.691 B.A. L.326 J.D.
White, Sharmian L. '68 '96 (NY) C.309 A.B. L.846 J.D.
Whitten, George S. '40 '64 (MS) C.496 B.A. L.500 J.D.
Young, L. Benjamin, Jr. '64 '91 (VA) C&L.893 B.A., J.D.

OFFICE OF ADMINISTRATIVE LAW JUDGES

Bernstein, Edwin S. '30 '55 C.659 B.A. L.178 LL.B.
Pollack, Howard A. '46 '72 C&L.446 B.A., J.D.

AGRICULTURAL COOPERATIVE SERVICE

Frederick, Donald A. '45 '70 C.72 B.A. L.228 J.D.

AGRICULTURAL RESEARCH SERVICE

Connor, Margaret '41 '75 (CA) C.494 B.S. L.767 J.D.
Gonzales, Thomas L. '54 '84 C.31 B.A. L.276 J.D.
Steiner, Frank G. '36 '90 (VA) C.724 B.A. L.1209 J.D.

FARM SERVICE AGENCY

Boileau, Raymond G. '41 '91 (MD) C.446 B.A. L.64 J.D.
Chott, John W., Jr. '45 '82 C.367 B.A. L.276 J.D.
Day, H. Talmage, Jr. '42 '85 (VA) C.188 A.B. L.659 J.D.
Dent, Walter J. '39 '66 C.311 B.A. L.325 J.D.
Donaldson, Kathleen A. '54 '85 (VA) C.706 B.A. L.1209 J.D.
DuVarney, Andrée A., (Ms.) '58 '85 (VA) C.893 B.A. L.1209 J.D.
Goldman, Linda kay '59 '88 (VA) C.827 B.A. L.1209 J.D.
Harris, Thomas F., III '51 '82 C.602 B.A. L.262 J.D.
Hicks, Vicki J. '55 '81 C.663 B.S. L.623 J.D.
Kalil, Thomas F. '53 '83 (MD) C.446 B.S. L.64 J.D.
Kean, Jeffrey P '45 '70 (MO) C&L.502 B.S.B.A.
Lauer, Kurt A. '57 '92 (VA) C.945 B.A. L.893 J.D.
Race, Annette S. '52 '85 C.575 B.A. L.1209 J.D.
Roney, Paula B. '58 '85 (VA) C.893 B.S. L.1209 J.D.

ANIMAL AND PLANT HEALTH INSPECTION SERVICE

Barnet, Elna K. '50 '78 (VA) C.75 B.A. L.273 J.D.
Chamberlain, Nancy E. '47 '79 (MS) C.90 B.A. L.500 J.D.
Lidsky, Michael A. '48 '76 C.112 B.A. L.61 J.D.
Medley, Terry L. '51 '78 (VA) C.31 B.A. L.893 J.D.
Psaltis, Edmond G. '29 '60 (MD) C.999 B.S. L.276 J.D.
Tang, Frank Y. '44 '90 C.188 A.B. L.823 J.D.

ECONOMIC RESEARCH SERVICE

DeBraal, J. Peter '40 '65 (WI) C&L.966 B.A., J.D.

GRAIN INSPECTION PACKERS AND STOCKYARDS ADMINISTRATION

Gross, Harold M. '35 '62 C&L.813 B.A., J.D.

FOOD AND CONSUMER SERVICE

Hendez, Ana Maria '69 '96 (VA) C.473 B.S. L.904 J.D.
Renaud, Pedro J. '28 '53 (FL) L.999
Tropp, Laurence H. '49 '76 (FL) C&L.260 B.A., J.D.

FOOD SAFETY AND INSPECTION SERVICE

Dailey, William F. '37 '63 C.913 B.A. L.705 LL.B.
Levine, Victoria A. '63 '91 C.705 B.A. L.1292 J.D.
Liepold, Alfred J. '32 '73 C.10 D.V.M. L.30 J.D.
Neibrief, Judith A. '46 '74 C.477 A.B. L.309 J.D.
Stafko, Ralph E. '46 '74 (MI) C.475 B.F.A. L.912 J.D.
Stratmoen, Sally O. '45 '75 C.326 B.S. L.900 J.D.
Vitiello, Daniel J. '44 '70 C.321 A.B. L.128 J.D.

FOREIGN AGRICULTURAL SERVICE

Brosch, Kevin J. '48 '81 C.945 A.B. L.128 J.D.
Hegwood, David B. '59 '83 (GA) C.502 B.S. L.280 J.D.
Miranda, John A. '44 '76 (VA) C.93 B.S. L.276 J.D.
Perkel, Ronald D. '60 '87 (WI) C.174 B.S. L.966 J.D.
Wagner, Lynnett M. '63 '91 (IL) C.546 B.S.C. L.276 J.D.
Winski, John B. '66 '92 (MD) C&L.37 B.A., J.D.

FOREST SERVICE

Maxwell, Hugh D., III '50 '92 (GA) C.259 B.A. L.1059 J.D.
McDonald, James Gregory '45 '96 (VA) C.679 B.S. L.1209 J.D.
Towns, Eleanor S. '43 '83 (CO) C.339 A.B. L.208 J.D.

OFFICE OF BUDGET AND PROGRAM ANALYSIS

Clayton, Diane M. '74 '99 C.401 B.A. L.30 J.D.
Dewhurst, Stephen B. '42 '67 C&L.273 B.A., J.D.

OFFICE OF INSPECTOR GENERAL

Allen, Richard F. '44 '69 (IN) C.347 B.A. L.1119 J.D.
Gallo, Katherine R. '61 '88 (OH) C.201 B.A. L.608 J.D.
Martin, Thomas M. '47 '88 C.1044 B.S. L.1325 J.D.
Rush, Jeffrey, Jr. '46 '90 C.60 B.M. L.1209 J.D.
Thomas, Glen S. '70 '99 C.37 B.A. L.144 J.D. Prog. Analyst

OFFICE OF THE JUDICIAL OFFICER

Jenson, William G. '47 '75 (MA) C.319 B.A. L.818 J.D.
Stewart, Michael J. '48 '73 C.790 B.A. L.228 J.D.

OFFICE OF CIVIL RIGHTS ENFORCEMENT

Beaumont, Thomas M. '48 '77 (MD) C&L.128 B.A., J.D.
Knishkowy, Jeffrey A. '59 '85 C.976 B.A. L.94 J.D.

BOARD OF CONTRACT APPEALS

Doherty, Sean '36 '68 C.184 B.S. L.836 J.D.
Eaton, Marilynn M. '29 '76 C.597 B.S. L.273 J.D.
Gish, Elden M. '31 '61 (OR) C.1163 B.A. L.950 J.D.
Houry, Edward '37 '67 (OH) C&L.1003 B.M.E., J.D.
Seto, Robert M.M. '36 '68 C&L.734 B.S., J.D.
Shager, Merrie C. '46 '86 C.966 B.A. L.273 J.D.

RURAL UTILITIES SERVICE

Kumor, Kenneth M. '45 '77 C.453 B.S. L.1068 J.D.
Miller, Bruce '55 '82 C.276 A.B. L.607 J.D.

DEPARTMENT OF THE AIR FORCE

(Vacant), *General Counsel*

OFFICE OF THE GENERAL COUNSEL

Anderson, William H. '62 '88 (PA) C.860 B.S. L.665 J.D.
At Lee, W. Kipling, Jr. '46 '77 (TX) C.503 B.A. L.846 J.D. Dep. Gen. Coun.
Bachman, Marcia '53 '78 (TN) C&L.838 B.A., J.D.
Bourne, Brian D. '58 '83 (IL) C.589 B.A. L.146 J.D.
Bridge, Robert L. '38 '63 (WV) C.645 B.S. L.923 LL.B.
Burgin, Rebecca '70 '99 C.205 B.A.A.S. L.1292 J.D.
Cox, Kerri A. '69 '99 C.805 B.A. L.30 J.D.
Dodds, John A. '51 '76 C.390 A.B. L.273 J.D.
Fox, Don W. '56 '82 C.575 B.A. L.896 J.D.
Greskowiak, Denise '69 '95 C.477 A.B. L.128 J.D.
Groner, Laurence M. '51 '81 C.823 B.A. L.273 J.D.
Hass, Daniel P. '50 '80 (IA) C.475 B.A. L.221 J.D.★
Hauslein, Jackson A., Jr. '44 '72 C&L.902 B.A., J.D.
Heady, Douglas J. '51 '76 C.802 B.A. L.893 J.D.
Hoard, E. David '47 '77 (MO) C.246 B.S.E. L.213 J.D.
House, Jacqueline A. '47 '72 (MD) C&L.446 B.A., J.D.
Inazu, John D. '75 '00 C&L.228 B.S.E., J.D.
Janecek, John P. '43 '72 (CA) C.363 B.S. L.426 J.D.
Kean, Barret E. '44 '69 (VA) C&L.893 B.S., J.D.
Kuhn, Fred W. '42 '68 C.602 B.B.A. L.276 J.D.
Leishman, Warren D. '72 '98 C.101 B.A. L.878 J.D.
Loeb, Dorothy P. '35 '72 (NY) C.94 A.B. L.178 J.D.
Loftin, Melinda J. '56 '81 (MI) C.5 B.A. L.213 J.D.
Long, Clarence D., III '43 '72 C.367 B.A. L.446 J.D.
Loslo, Felix '53 '85 C.597 L.469 J.D.
McDade, Joseph M., Jr. '62 '88 C&L.276 B.S.F.S., J.D.
Meek, Philip A. '43 '68 (TX) C&L.802 B.B.A., J.D.
O'Connor, Leta L. '58 '85 C.602 B.A. L.276 J.D.
Passey, Alan K. '51 '80 (UT) C&L.101 B.S., J.D.
Pelletier, Richard A. '45 '74 (PA) C.884 B.S. L.1003 J.D. Assoc. Gen. Coun.
Petkoff, Gregory H. '52 '76 C.276 B.A. L.1049 J.D.
Pettit, John E. '48 '74 (KS) C.378 B.S. L.502 J.D.
Riley, Shaun T. '63 '90 (MA) C.321 B.A. L.45 J.D.★
Rissling, R. Eric '58 '83 (SC) C&L.790 B.A., J.D.★
Shaw, Steven A. '46 '73 C.264 B.A. L.30 J.D.
Sheuerman, Philip '53 '80 C.112 A.B. L.770 J.D.
Stamps, Robert F. '48 '77 C.339 A.B. L.896 J.D.
Trombo, Joseph L. '68 '94 C.886 B.S.B.A. L.208 J.D. Assoc. Gen. Coun.
Wagner, Anthony L. '44 '69 (VA) C.659 B.A. L.178 J.D.★
Walmsley, Robin D. '55 '82 (ME) C.164 B.A. L.1294 J.D.
Willmeth, Roger E. '46 '70 (IL) C.209 L.365 J.D.
Zehner, Michael W. '54 '79 (KS) C.375 B.S. L.900 J.D.

OFFICE OF THE JUDGE ADVOCATE GENERAL

Adams, Frances G., II '55 '79 (WV) C&L.923 B.A., J.D.
Anderson, Gary D. '57 '86 (IA) C.101 B.A. L.221 J.D.
Arnold, Kenneth A. '63 '92 (TX) C.1070 B.S. L.744 J.D.
Bauer, Ralph A. '57 '82 (OH) C&L.608 B.A., J.D.
Baumgartner, Nancy Helen '56 '83 (WV) C.445 B.S. L.923 J.D.
Brocki, John B. '47 '89 (VA) C.645 B.S. L.273 J.D.
Bruce, Gerald Roger '61 '87 (NE) C.542 B.A. L.546 J.D.
Carey, Christopher '62 '88 C.602 B.B.A. L.893 J.D.
Chamblee, John S. '59 '84 (TN) C.838 B.A. L.1015 J.D.
Clements, Paul R. '53 '83 (SC) C.790 B.S. L.976 J.D.★
Coit, Robert '57 '85 (GA) C.838 B.S. L.245 J.D.
Cormier, Paul E. '44 '75 C.723 B.A. L.245 J.D.
Couture, Thomas J. '59 '89 (MA) C.550 B.A. L.1048 J.D.★

DEPARTMENT OF THE AIR FORCE (Continued)

Cox, Douglas B. ... '63 '89 (OH) C.610 B.S.J. L.150 J.D.★
Curtis, Brent G. ... '58 '92 (PA) C.92 B.S. L.200 J.D.
Drew, Rodger A. ... '62 '87 (TX) C.839 B.A. L.326 J.D.★
Erickson, Richard J. ... '43 '70 (MI) L.477 J.D.
Evans, Timothy J. ... '62 '86 C&L.190 B.S.B.A., J.D.★
Farmer, Thomas L. ... '63 '93 (NJ) C.776 B.A. L.724 J.D.
Fiscus, Thomas J. ... '50 '75 (IA) C.1070 B.S. L.608 J.D.★
Forcier, Ronald A. ... '49 '75 (NY) C.94 B.A. L.1009 J.D.
Fried, Eric L. ... '66 '91 (NY) C.688 B.S. L.982 J.D.★
Geraci, Thomas A. ... '45 '69 (OH) C&L.7 B.A., J.D.
Gombis, Albert T. ... '68 '97 C.937 B.A. L.276 J.D.★
Greenfield, Kevin ... '57 '87 (OK) C.623 B.A. L.862 J.D.
Halbert, Gary L. ... '56 '86 (TX) C.1070 B.S. L.846 J.D.★
Hart, Erich O. ... '53 '81 (AZ) C&L.37 B.A., J.D.★
Head, Craig L. ... '48 '73 (IL) C.755 B.A. L.209 J.D.
Henderson, Graeme S. ... '65 '92 (UT) C.1375 B.A. L.878 J.D.
Hughes, Harry M. ... '62 '91 (GA) C.16 B.S. L.280 J.D.
Hunt, Edward E., III ... '56 '84 (IN) C.1070 B.S. L.602 J.D.★
Jacobson, Kyle R. ... '69 '94 (VA) C.839 B.S. L.273 J.D.
Kinney, Zachary Z. ... '54 '83 (WV) C.446 B.A. L.33 J.D.
Leblanc, Andrew ... '73 '98 (ME) C.688 B.S. L.309 J.D.
Lockard, Dennis R. ... '51 '84 (MO) C.1060 B.A. L.464 J.D.★
Love, Jane S. ... '57 '83 (FL) C.259 B.S. L.602 J.D.
Madrid, Michael N. ... '49 '74 (IN) C.249 B.A. L.61 J.D.
Malloy, Timothy J. ... '41 '79 (WI) C.959 B.S. L.966 J.D.
Markiewicz, Thomas S. ... '48 '73 (NY) C.1041 B.A. L.262 J.D.
McCray, David H. ... '62 '93 (CA) C.1042 B.S. L.112 J.D.
McHugh, Paul D. ... '53 '86 (NM) C.645 B.A. L.560 J.D.
Moorman, William A. ... '45 '70 (IL) C&L.339 B.A., J.D.
Murad, Dale ... '— '81 C.228 B.A. L.1065 J.D.★
Murphy, Timothy Ward ... '58 '86 (PA) C&L.229 B.A., J.D.★
O'Boyle, Bryan R. ... '53 '78 (TX) C&L.744 B.B.A., J.D.
Ortiz, Paul J. ... '— '95 (NJ) C.209 B.A. L.93 J.D.
Paknik-Nagem, Brenda A.J. ... '61 '90 (WV) C&L.923 B.A., J.D.
Perlstein, Hildegarde Conte ... '56 '82 C&L.128 B.A., J.D.
Perlstein, Loren S. ... '51 '77 (IL) C.339 B.A. L.209 J.D.
Peterson, Richard A. ... '38 '65 (VA) C&L.30 B.A., J.D.
Powers, John J. ... '47 '78 (NY) C.1505 B.A. L.616 J.D.
Procaccino, Joseph A., Jr. ... '51 '76 C.273 B.A. L.30 J.D.
Regan, Judith M. ... '53 '79 C.216 B.A. L.273 J.D.
Risley, F. Scott ... '59 '90 (VA) C.10 B.A. L.1339 J.D.
Roberts, Keith L. ... '55 '81 (KS) C&L.900 B.A., J.D.
Russell, Floyd, III ... '55 '85 (TX) C.805 B.A. L.602 J.D.★
Schlegel, Thomas E. ... '51 '76 (PA) C&L.229 B.A., J.D.★
Teskey, Mark S. ... '63 '89 (SC) C.160 B.A. L.790 J.D.
Thomas, David L. ... '51 '76 (IA) C.1070 B.S. L.352 J.D.★
Tidmore, Phillip G. ... '— '76 (CA) C.37 B.A. L.810 J.D.
Walters, Barry D. ... '56 '92 C.790 B.A. L.1202 J.D.
Ward, James A. ... '43 '91 (CA) C&L.1049 B.S.E.E., J.D.★
Warring, Paul D. ... '47 '75 C&L.276 B.S.B.A., J.D.
Wendlberger, Joseph C. ... '60 '92 (CA) C.1070 B.S.E.E. L.1097 J.D.
White, Carolyn M. ... '60 '87 C&L.101 B.A., J.D.
Wilder, Harlan G. ... '45 '71 (WA) C.446 B.S. L.911 J.D.★
Wilkov, Scott J. ... '67 '92 (IL) C.29 B.A. L.37 J.D.
Wright, Lauryne ... '61 '92 (CA) C.846 B.J. L.64 J.D.
Young, James A., III ... '46 '75 (PA) C.401 B.A. L.659 J.D.

Furcron, Wyckliffe S. G. ... '51 '77 (NJ) C.825 B.S. L.1194 J.D.★

DEPARTMENT OF THE ARMY

(Vacant), ***General Counsel***
Walter B. Huffman, ***The Judge Advocate General***

OFFICE OF THE GENERAL COUNSEL

Barna, Stephanie A. ... '64 '88 C.901 B.A. L.665 J.D.
Bell, David E. ... '53 '83 C&L.502 B.A., J.D.
Castle, Edwin S. ... '53 '79 (VA) C.945 B.A. L.893 J.D.
Clark, Jonathan D. ... '75 '00 C.884 1997 L.273 J.D.
Davenport, Robert L., Jr. ... '72 '98 (WI) C.1286 B.A. L.966 J.D.
Davis, James Benjamin ... '71 '98 (NC) C.896 B.A. L.976 J.D.
Ecker, Frank Behrens, Jr. ... '46 '72 (WA) C.911 B.S. L.629 J.D.
Hancq, Paul D. ... '57 '83 C.494 B.A. L.793 J.D.★
Hoburg, Paul D. ... '55 '85 (TN) C.659 B.S. L.880 J.D.★
Johnson, Cassandra Tsintolas ... '53 '80 C&L.446 B.A., J.D.
Johnson, Darin E.W. ... '75 '00 (IL) C.976 B.A. L.309 J.D.
Martin, T. Patrick ... '72 '97 (IL) C.602 B.B.A. L.597 J.D.
Morello, Steven J. ... '52 '77 C.276 B.S.F.S. L.215 J.D.
Newhouse, Victoria E. ... '69 '97 (MD) C&L.692 B.A., J.D.
Norsworthy, Levator, Jr. ... '48 '73 C.201 B.S. L.150 J.D.
Reres, Matt ... '42 '67 C&L.190 B.A., J.D.
Rivest, Mark A. ... '59 '84 (MA) C.1021 B.A. L.1048 J.D.
Sprunk, Richard J. ... '60 '85 (MI) C.475 B.A. L.213 J.D.
Stockdale, Earl H., Jr. ... '48 '73 C.25 B.A. L.229 J.D.
Taylor, Thomas W. ... '44 '69 (NC) C.296 B.A. L.575 J.D.

OFFICE OF THE JUDGE ADVOCATE GENERAL

Altenburg, John D., Jr. ... '— '73 (OH) C.912 B.A. L.150 J.D.
Bush, Brian X. ... '49 '74 (UT) C.602 B.B.A. L.878 J.D.
Campanella, Lorianne M. ... '64 '90 (CA) C.1349 B.A. L.61 J.D.
Charvat, John L., Jr. ... '55 '85 (NC) C.870 B.S. L.228 J.D.
Cosgrove, Charles A. ... '46 '72 (PA) C.401 B.A. L.1017 J.D.
Coughlin, Michael J. ... '56 '86 (CT) C.545 B.S. L.546 J.D.
Denny, Michael C. ... '47 '72 C.813 B.A. L.94 J.D.
Eveland, Dean S. ... '48 '78 (MS) C.339 A.B. L.500 J.D.
Fano, Robert M. ... '46 '78 (TX) C.623 B.A. L.744 J.D.
Graham, David Eldridge ... '44 '71 (TX) C.839 B.A. L.846 J.D.★
Huffman, Walter B. ... '44 '77 (TX) C&L.845 B.S., J.D. The Judge Adv. Gen.★
Lassus, Kenneth J. ... '52 '78 (LA) C.418 B.S. L.425 J.D.
Lederer, Calvin M. ... '50 '75 (NJ) C.569 A.B. L.1019 J.D.
Lohmeyer, Charles Edward ... '57 '93 (VA) C.1170 B.S. L.1339 J.D.★
Marchand, Michael J. ... '48 '73 (MN) C.723 B.A. L.494 J.D.
Matthews, Mark D. ... '71 '99 (VA) C.1126 B.A. L.945 J.D.
Mayer, Kirsten M. ... '73 '99 (VA) C.893 B.A. L.692 J.D.
Moreau, Alfred E. ... '51 '76 (NE) C.543 B.S. L.602 J.D.
Novotne, Alfred H. ... '53 '81 (IL) C.145 B.A. L.209 J.D.
Parks, William Hays ... '40 '66 (TX) C&L.69 B.A., J.D.
Passar, Arthur L. ... '49 '75 C.575 B.A. L.1066 J.D.
Patrick, John ... '63 '92 (PA) C.870 B.S. L.893 J.D.
Patterson, Margaret K. ... '43 '70 (PA) C&L.665 B.A., J.D.
Pflieger, Michael C. ... '74 '99 C.367 B.A. L.893 J.D.
Rosen, Richard D. ... '48 '73 (FL) C.608 B.A. L.472 J.D.
Ruppert, Raymond C. ... '46 '76 (OK) C.262 B.S. L.623 J.D.
Slitt, Andrew J. ... '70 '00 (CT) C&L.184 B.A., J.D.
Smawley, George R. ... '66 '91 (PA) C.216 B.A. L.831 J.D.★
Stamets, Eric C. ... '51 '76 (VA) C.276 B.S. L.902 J.D.
Stone, Kathryn ... '57 '82 (FL) C&L.362 B.B.A., J.D.
Thompson, Kevin V. ... '66 '00 (MN) C.1354 M.A. L.300 J.D.
White, Jerusha L. ... '50 '81 (DC) C.134 B.S. L.986 J.D.
White, Ronald W. ... '50 '80 (KY) C&L.383 B.A., J.D.
Willson, Stephanie D. ... '50 '80 C.881 A.B. L.1292 J.D.

ARMY MATERIEL COMMAND

Brognano, Dominick J. ... '42 '70 (NY) C.1093 B.A. L.851 J.D.
Citron, Stanley R. ... '58 '83 (PA) C&L.665 B.A., J.D.
Femino, Dominic A., Jr. ... '47 '72 (MA) C.95 A.B. L.94 J.D.
Harrington, Paul David ... '45 '75 C.197 A.B. L.477 J.D.
Hodge, Craig E. ... '47 '79 (OH) C.531 B.A. L.608 J.D.
Kessler, Jeffrey I. ... '48 '72 (NJ) C.705 B.A. L.178 J.D.
Klatsky, Stephen A. ... '48 '74 (NY) C.1019 B.A. L.982 J.D.
Korte, Edward J. ... '47 '71 (OH) C&L.608 B.S., J.D.
Kranzberg, Joshua A. ... '59 '83 (MO) C&L.734 A.B., J.D.
Lassman, Michael L. ... '63 '88 (MI) C.476 B.S. L.215 J.D.
Medsger, William R. ... '54 '82 (AZ) C.870 B.S. L.36 J.D.
Meza-Dombkowski, Elvira D. ... '52 '81 (MI) C.215 A.B. L.912 J.D.
Mills, Linda B.R. ... '48 '76 (NJ) C&L.705 B.A., J.D.
Rothberg, Louis K. ... '50 '75 C.1044 B.A. L.945 J.D.
Shelton, Sam W., III ... '43 '73 (LA) C.419 B.A. L.420 J.D.
Simon, Lisa R. ... '64 '89 (NY) C.228 A.B. L.178 J.D.
Stolarun, Edward L. ... '41 '70 (VA) C.688 B.S.E.E. L.128 J.D.
Travers, P. Diane ... '63 '88 (VA) C.893 B.A. L.945 J.D.

OFFICE, CHIEF OF ENGINEERS/HEADQUARTERS, U.S. ARMY CORPS OF ENGINEERS

Adams, Michael J. ... '47 '74 (NY) C.321 A.B. L.262 J.D.
Allen, Ronald C. ... '40 '70 (ME) C.431 B.A. L.1294 J.D.
Bayert, William K. ... '51 '77 (ID) C.437 A.B. L.117 J.D.
Beckles, Linda Joyce ... '48 '88 (PA) C.1069 B.A. L.128 J.D.
Bennett, Richard C. ... '51 '80 (OK) C.623 B.A. L.616 J.D.
Bindner, Roseann Rene ... '53 '80 C.790 B.A. L.1209 J.D.
Bond, Susan G. ... '49 '78 (KS) C.734 B.A. L.276 J.D.
Bowen, Elizabeth Karen ... '57 '82 (GA) C.16 B.A. L.245 J.D.
Bryson, Judy Dyke ... '56 '81 (OH) C.418 B.A. L.607 J.D.
Calhoun, Cynthia Miller ... '51 '80 C.183 B.A. L.276 J.D.
Carr, Frank ... '44 '70 (CT) C&L.229 B.A., J.D.
Cohen, David L. ... '31 '60 (PA) C&L.665 B.S., J.D.
Cohen, Martin R. ... '49 '75 (MD) C&L.446 B.A., J.D.
Cooper, Thomas R., Jr. ... '43 '67 (GA) C&L.280 B.A., J.D.
Cribbin, Robert D. ... '59 '84 (OH) C.473 B.S. L.150 J.D.
Edelman, Lester ... '30 '54 (MA) C.93 L.94 J.D.
Fagot, Elizabeth L. ... '52 '77 C.1090 B.S. L.276 J.D.
Ferry, A. Montague, Jr. ... '44 '69 C.324 B.A. L.30 J.D.
Flachbarth, Charles T. P. ... '43 '73 C.311 B.A. L.880 J.D.
Frank, Richard C. ... '54 '83 (MI) C.474 B.S.C.E. L.912 J.D.
Frankel, Barry J. ... '41 '65 (NY) C.107 L.1009 J.D.
Frenzen, Donald W. ... '30 '58 C.72 B.A. L.145 J.D. Adm. J.
Goldman, Howard V. ... '52 '78 (NY) C.1350 B.A. L.569 J.D.
Gruis, Tracy N. ... '62 '88 C&L.945 B.A., J.D.
Hayes, Stephen W. ... '37 '79 (CA) C.502 B.A. L.770 J.D.
Howell, S. Janice ... '47 '74 (MS) C.497 B.S.D. L.500 J.D.
Hylton, Walter H., III ... '41 '65 (VA) C.885 B.A. L.893 J.D.
Jennings, Rupert J., III ... '51 '81 C.431 B.S. L.1294 J.D.
Jockisch, Wesley C. ... '38 '65 C&L.446 A.B., LL.B. Adm. J.
Keiser, Matthew R. ... '62 '94 C.477 A.B. L.128 J.D.
Klements, Newton Leigh ... '47 '72 (NY) C.94 A.B. L.262 J.D.
Krombein, Karlissa B. ... '52 '78 C.890 B.A. L.276 J.D.
Lesser, Monroe L. ... '26 '60 (NY) C.563 B.B.A. L.569 LL.B.
Lynch, Carolyn J. ... '53 '78 C.454 B.A. L.180 J.D.
Mahon, John J. ... '45 '74 (PA) C.728 B.S. L.180 J.D.
Matta, Julia C. ... '71 '97 C&L.276 A.B., J.D.
Meeker, Laura Kuitunen ... '43 '68 C.659 B.S. L.976 LL.B.
Micik, John Andrew ... '49 '85 (VA) C.569 B.A. L.1209 J.D.
Nee, Susan G. ... '56 '80 C.446 B.A. L.276 J.D.
Ng, Lisa M. ... '60 '90 (CA) C.112 A.B. L.945 J.D.
Norman, Laura Ouverson ... '56 '83 C&L.861 B.A., J.D.
Petit, Russell W. ... '45 '75 (NY) C&L.107 B.A., J.D.
Petrowitz, Harold C. ... '21 '50 C.477 B.S. L.276 J.D. Adm. J.
Powers, Kenneth R. ... '44 '69 (OH) C.207 B.A. L.930 J.D.
Pressman, Paul R. ... '48 '72 (MA) C.94 B.A. L.93 J.D.
Schmauder, Craig R. ... '55 '81 (VA) C.415 B.A. L.862 J.D.
Simpson, Noelle J. ... '71 '96 (CT) C.276 B.S. L.1252 J.D.
Steffen, Phillip J. ... '63 '93 C.352 B.A. L.276 J.D.
Taylor, Kendall D. ... '46 '78 C.886 L.1019 J.D.
Waldman, Todd E. ... '68 '94 C.184 B.A. L.273 J.D.
Wood, Lance D. ... '47 '73 C.692 B.A. L.477 J.D.

OFFICE OF THE SECRETARY

Black, Scott C. ... '52 '81 C.1074 B.A. L.61 J.D.
Brockington, Gary J. ... '59 '88 (VA) C.870 B.S. L.893 J.D.
Ehrsam-Holland, Anne E. ... '57 '84 (KS) C.900 B.A. L.880 J.D.
Lancaster, H. Martin ... '43 '67 (NC) C&L.575 A.B., J.D.
Winchester, Robert J. ... '46 '76 C.1113 B.A. L.831 J.D.

OFFICE OF THE ASSISTANT SECRETARY OF THE ARMY
(INSTALLATIONS, LOGISTICS & ENVIRONMENT)

Birney, William T. ... '43 '72 C.1030 B.A. L.904 J.D.

OFFICE OF THE ASSISTANT SECRETARY OF
THE ARMY (MANPOWER & RESERVE AFFAIRS)

Anderson, John C. ... '54 '91 C.477 B.A. L.128 J.D.
McLaurin, John P., III ... '45 '70 (MS) C&L.500 B.A., J.D.
Montgomery, Bronte I. ... '65 '91 (PA) C.1090 B.S. L.1292 J.D.★
Schneider, Karl F. ... '52 '78 C.367 B.A. L.262 J.D.
Serene, Jan W. ... '— '76 (TX) C&L.326 B.A., J.D.★
Spiegel, Jayson L. ... '59 '84 C.276 A.B. L.893 J.D.

U.S. ARMY COURT OF CRIMINAL APPEALS

Brown, Harry D. ... '50 '80 (SC) C.870 B.S. L.790 J.D. Assoc. J.
Cairns, Richard W. ... '46 '72 (TX) C&L.846 B.B.A., J.D. Senior J.
Canner, Demmon F. ... '47 '72 (PA) C.831 B.B.A. L.1017 J.D. Assoc. J.
Carter, Kevin W. ... '52 '78 C.122 B.A. L.45 J.D. Assoc. J.
Chapman, Michael C. ... '50 '75 (TN) C&L.838 B.S., J.D.
Merck, Larry S. ... '47 '72 (SC) C.160 B.A. L.790 J.D. Senior J.
Terwilliger-Stacey, Jodi E. ... '67 '92 (FL) C.475 B.A. L.221 J.D.
Toomey, Allan A. ... '47 '72 C.363 A.B. L.930 J.D. Senior J.

U.S. ARMY LEGAL SERVICES AGENCY

Agar, James R., II ... '64 '90 (OK) C.170 B.A. L.623 J.D.
Baines, Margaret ... '62 '93 (IN) C.602 B.A. L.1119 J.D.
Barfield, Kate S. ... '58 '83 C.178 B.A. L.930 J.D.
Benson, Nolon John, Jr. ... '50 '80 (TN) C.885 B.S. L.838 J.D.
Bobell, Gordon F. ... '36 '76 (CA) C.330 B.A. L.809 J.D.
Borgerding, Karen J. ... '70 '95 (IN) C.210 B.A. L.879 J.D.
Boucher, Leo E., III ... '59 '85 (NY) C.1021 B.A. L.982 J.D.
Broyles, Bryan T. ... '63 '88 (KY) C.531 B.A. L.801 J.D.
Butler, Sheryl A. ... '64 '88 (VA) C.890 B.S. L.692 J.D.
Card, Mary E. ... '71 '96 (CT) C&L.128 B.A., J.D.
Casida, Gary V. ... '45 '75 (CO) C&L.174 B.S., J.D.
Chapman, Linda Ann ... '67 '97 (VA) C.1228 B.S. L.1509 J.D.★
Child, Michael Scott ... '53 '78 (CA) C&L.1049 B.A., J.D.
Clarke, Craig S. ... '46 '78 C.477 B.S.A.E. L.744 J.D.
Coe, Gregory B. ... '— '85 (PA) C.821 B.A. L.1017 J.D.★
Connelly, Timothy M. ... '61 '86 (MN) C.602 B.A. L.494 J.D.★
Crawford, David Tracy ... '66 '91 (PA) C.512 B.A. L.446 J.D.
Cygnarowicz, Paul T. ... '67 '92 (MD) C.423 B.B.A. L.64 J.D.
Diedrichs, Clayton R. ... '61 '87 (CO) C.174 B.A. L.36 J.D.
Elling, Terry L. ... '57 '82 (IL) C&L.339 B.A., J.D.
Erisman, Terri J. ... '72 '98 (NC) C.777 B.A. L.575 J.D.
Felsman, Janine ... '69 '98 (NY) C.1320 B.S. L.1009 J.D.
Fetterman, Joseph Charles ... '64 '89 (NY) C.754 B.S. L.188 J.D.
Fiore, Uldrich L., Jr. ... '51 '79 C.870 B.S. L.705 J.D.
Ganton, Robert A. ... '48 '78 C.276 B.S.F.S. L.30 J.D.
Greco, Carrie M. ... '— '90 (NE) C.174 B.M. L.546 J.D.
Haines, Stephanie L. ... '69 '96 (SC) C.372 B.A. L.607 J.D.
Harvey, Mark W. ... '54 '81 (DC) C.870 B.S. L.273 J.D.
Heslin, Brian S. ... '70 '97 (VA) C.800 B.A. L.1209 J.D.
Kent, John C. ... '58 '83 (VA) C.893 B.A. L.902 J.D.★
King, Francis P. ... '65 '91 (OH) C.901 B.A. L.7 J.D.
Kirchmaier, Charles T. ... '66 '97 (NJ) C.260 B.A. L.831 J.D.
Kittel, Robert N. ... '45 '70 (PA) C.423 B.S. L.884 J.D.
Klein, Alan P. ... '38 '73 (PA) C.659 Ph.D. L.831 J.D.
Ku, Fansu ... '69 '98 (TX) C.454 B.A. L.124 J.D.
Lewenhaupt, Claes H. ... '63 '89 (CA) C.763 B.A. L.1065 J.D.
Lewis, James Arnold ... '64 '91 (OH) C.943 B.A. L.150 J.D.
Lind, Denise R. ... '— '85 (NY) C.1021 B.A. L.982 J.D.
Lind, Scott E. ... '60 '85 (NY) C.158 B.S. L.982 J.D.★
McCommas, Christine Schubert ... '50 '76 C.928 B.A. L.446 J.D.
McCormick, David A. ... '46 '73 C.935 B.A. L.229 J.D.★
McCoy, Toby Dale ... '70 '95 (WV) C&L.902 B.S, J.D.
McFetridge, Robert C ... '52 '81 (CA) C.870 B.S. L.770 J.D.
Mendelson, David Eric ... '69 '94 (FL) C.354 B.S. L.1206 J.D.
Mercader, Braulio ... '66 '96 (PR) C.677 M.P.A. L.1088 J.D.
Mickle, Douglas K. ... '60 '90 C.732 B.S. L.273 J.D.
Mikolashek, Kevin J. ... '— '96 (PA) C.656 B.A. L.645 J.D.
Miller, Joel D. ... '48 '73 C&L.705 B.A., J.D.★
Mitchem, Suzanne ... '67 '93 (FL) C.537 B.A. L.1158 J.D.
Newsome, David, Jr. ... '62 '89 C&L.851 B.A., J.D.★
Nixon, Steven A. ... '50 '75 C&L.502 A.B., J.D.
Nyce, Peter Q., Jr. ... '32 '61 C.902 A.B. L.904 J.D.
O'Keeffe, Richard B., Jr. ... '55 '82 (VA) C.893 B.A. L.945 J.D.★
Osborn, Tara A. ... '62 '87 (SC) C&L.790 B.A., J.D.
Parker, Jennifer A. ... '68 '97 (CA) C.999 B.A. L.1049 J.D.
Reed, Kary B. ... '60 '87 (FL) C.475 B.S. L.1209 J.D.
Roth, Howard W., III ... '61 '86 (VA) C.112 B.A. L.945 J.D.
Salussolia, Paul ... '63 '90 (FL) C.1111 B.A. L.362 J.D.
Sanderson, Stephanie D. ... '72 '97 (AL) C&L.16 B.A., J.D.
Schenk, Lisa M. ... '61 '89 (MA) C.676 B.A. L.602 J.D.
Smith, Gary W. ... '50 '75 (SC) C&L.790 B.S., J.D.★
Spann, Terrance A. ... '62 '87 (WI) C.190 L.436 J.D.
Stockdale, Lee L. ... '52 '89 (FL) C.911 B.A. L.930 J.D.
Tremaglio, Ralph J. ... '63 '93 (MD) C.885 B.A. L.1338 J.D.
Vergona, Mary Catherine ... '65 '97 (VA) C.473 B.S. L.7 J.D.
Watkins, Susana E. ... '63 '90 (TX) C.629 B.S. L.309 J.D.
With, Catherine Marie ... '63 '89 (NY) C.751 B.A.M.A. L.982 J.D.
Witherspoon, Daryl Bernard ... '— '95 (IN) C.1378 B.S. L.879 J.D.

Williamson, Edward ... '54 '79 (PA) C.690 B.A. L.1048 J.D.

DEPARTMENT OF COMMERCE

(Vacant), *General Counsel*

OFFICE OF THE GENERAL COUNSEL

Abney, Wilson R. ... '47 '72 C&L.69 B.A., J.D.
Aldridge, Thomas G. ... '65 '90 C.1243 B.A. L.823 J.D.
Allen, Carol ... '53 '78 C.420 B.A. L.150 J.D.
Andros, Linda Ann ... '49 '80 (MA) C.454 B.A. L.818 J.D.
Aronoff, Arthur I. ... '51 '78 (PA) C.311 B.A. L.309 J.D.
Auber, Robert P. ... '23 '52 C.667 B.S.Ch.E. L.276 J.D.
Austin, Madeleine ... '48 '75 (CO) C.477 B.A. L.208 J.D.
Ballard, Stewart J. ... '53 '85 C.112 B.A. L.861 J.D.
Barbour, Thomas C. ... '46 '73 C.208 B.A. L.228 J.D.
Barnett, Mark A. ... '63 '88 C.216 B.A. L.477 J.D.
Battey, Robert A. ... '54 '96 (MD) C.999 B.M. L.276 J.D.
Behaylo, Michelle K. ... '65 '90 (MI) C.473 B.A. L.880 J.D.
Bevelacqua, Charles A. ... '24 '51 C.665 B.S. L.273 J.D.
Biglow, William A. ... '51 '86 (WI) C.963 B.S. L.966 J.D.
Bird, Otto B. ... '50 '76 C.602 B.A. L.276 J.D.
Bohannon, Mark ... '57 '87 (PA) C.276 B.S.F.S. L.273 J.D.
Borman, Matthew S. ... '55 '89 C.597 B.A. L.569 J.D.
Borofsky, Michael P. ... '60 '88 (PA) C.150 B.F.A. L.831 J.D.
Breed, Pamela M. ... '44 '68 C.518 B.A. L.276 J.D.
Brown, Kelly A. ... '63 '86 (WV) C&L.923 B.A., J.D.
Browne, Berniece A. ... '50 '76 C.431 B.A. L.128 J.D.
Burgess, Jay A. ... '44 '71 (MI) C.103 B.A. L.339 J.D.
Busby, W. Dawn ... '61 '88 (PA) C.860 B.A. L.309 J.D.
Canzano, Diane M. ... '63 '90 C.886 B.A. L.1209 J.D.
Carrara, Steven ... '62 '88 (NY) C.178 B.A. L.30 J.D.
Carson, Cecilia R. ... '65 '91 (TX) C.623 B.A. L.846 J.D.
Chang, Linda S. ... '48 '92 (MD) C.436 B.A. L.273 J.D.
Chang, Lucy M. ... '— '92 C.788 B.A. L.273 J.D.
Clark, Kenneth R. ... '38 '68 C.260 B.A. L.659 LL.B.
Cohen, Daniel ... '64 '89 C.1350 B.A. L.128 J.D.
Connaughton, Anne Q. ... '41 '89 (FL) C.164 B.A. L.362 J.D.
Conner, M. Timothy ... '47 '77 C&L.30 B.A., J.D. Chf., Gen. Litig. Div.
Corrigan, Donald W. ... '43 '70 (MD) C.676 A.B. L.818 LL.B.
Craig, Russell Wells ... '58 '84 (MI) C.477 B.A. L.912 J.D.
Cramer, Lew W. ... '49 '76 (CA) C&L.101 B.A., J.D.
Crotts, Amy K. ... '71 '97 C.576 B.A. L.575 J.D.
Dalmut, Pete M. ... '48 '73 (AR) C&L.45 B.S.B.A., J.D.
Davidson, Frederick S. ... '55 '91 (PA) C.112 B.A. L.276 J.D.
De Blasi, Michelle A. ... '— '98 C.36 B.S. L.911 J.D.
Del Tredici, Gene V. ... '47 '78 C.767 B.A. L.990 J.D.
DeVaughn, Marynell ... '58 '83 C.713 B.A. L.190 J.D.
DiGiacomo, Brian D. ... '57 '83 C.712 B.S. L.823 J.D.
Dolan, Hugh J. ... '28 '53 C&L.724 B.A., J.D. Adm. J.
Ehr, Thomas G. ... '62 '89 C.477 B.A. L.280 J.D.
Eller, Rayna G. ... '52 '84 (IL) C.966 B.A. L.893 J.D.
Ettinger, Stacy J. ... '63 '93 (MD) C.477 B.A. L.30 J.D.
Fields, Gordon B. ... '40 '65 (OR) C.685 B.A. L.629 LL.B.
Fine, Thomas H. ... '66 '92 C.685 B.A. L.188 J.D.
Ford, Harrison S., III ... '59 '84 (MS) C.484 B.A. L.500 J.D.
Fredericks, Barbara S. ... '48 '73 (MD) C.930 B.A. L.94 J.D.
Freije, Philip C. ... '44 '70 (CT) C&L.184 B.A., J.D.
Gallagher, Patrick V., Jr. ... '59 '90 (VA) C.1209 B.A. L.128 J.D.
Gates, Stephen ... '27 '85 (CT) C.882 B.S. L.1040 J.D.
Gillespie, Laura J. ... '67 '91 (VA) C&L.893 B.A., J.D.
Goldenberg, Rina ... '68 '96 (NY) C.347 B.S. L.345 J.D.
Green, Ollie M. ... '60 '85 (IN) C&L.347 B.A., J.D.
Greene, Philip J. ... '61 '86 C.524 B.A. L.425 J.D.
Grier, Jean Heilman ... '47 '73 C.791 B.A. L.494 J.D.
Haflich, Mark R. ... '45 '71 C.688 B.S. L.94 J.D.
Hager, Stephanie Lynn ... '63 '88 C.880 B.A. L.608 J.D.
Hanshaw, Mark E. ... '63 '91 (TN) C&L.838 B.A., J.D.
Heelen, J. Patrick ... '41 '66 C.446 B.A. L.276 J.D.
Heilferty, Robert John ... '63 '88 C&L.128 B.A., J.D.
Hine, Theresa L. ... '62 '90 (PA) C.861 B.A. L.30 J.D.
Hughitt, Elizabeth A. ... '65 '91 C.128 B.A. L.273 J.D.
Hull, Richard E. ... '31 '57 C.197 B.A. L.309 LL.B.
Hunt, Cecil ... '32 '61 C.112 A.B. L.1066 LL.B.
Hurley, Daniel C., Jr. ... '44 '75 C.734 B.S. L.276 J.D.
Isasi, William George ... '71 '99 C.339 B.S. L.276 J.D.
Johnson, Bruce E. ... '51 '77 C.309 A.B. L.228 J.D.
Jones, Roxie J. ... '55 '83 (AL) C.411 B.A. L.30 J.D.
Kalinoski, Carol A. ... '45 '86 C.652 B.A. L.831 J.D.
Kent, Melissa P. ... '57 '84 (AL) C.806 B.A. L.16 J.D.
Kessmeier, Catherine Lavelle ... '69 '95 (NJ) C.522 B.A. L.1338 J.D.
Kleinfeld, Ruth L. ... '40 '65 (MA) C.914 A.B. L.178 LL.B.
Klissas, Nicholas S. ... '59 '90 (NY) C.276 B.S.F.S. L.893 J.D.
Kopatich, Fred L. ... '50 '83 (OR) C.112 B.A. L.1065 J.D.
Kysella, William H., Jr. ... '68 '94 (CA) C.112 B.A. L.1067 J.D.
Labat, Terry Smith ... '52 '77 C&L.280 B.A., J.D.
Langstein, Mark ... '49 '79 (MA) C.1313 B.A. L.93 J.D.
Lawrence, Victor M. ... '67 '93 C.347 B.A. L.692 J.D. Sr. Coun.
Le Blanc, Stacia Davis ... '56 '83 C.475 B.A. L.30 J.D.
Lee, Terry H. ... '— '74 C.94 B.A. L.896 J.D.
Levine, Art ... '34 '63 (NY) C.679 B.S. L.659 J.D.
Levine, Joseph M. ... '48 '72 (NY) C.823 A.B. L.178 J.D.
Levitt, Michael A. ... '48 '73 C&L.309 A.B., J.D.
Lewis, Eleanor Roberts ... '44 '75 C.914 B.A. L.276 J.D.
Liberstein, Kenneth F. ... '58 '89 (PA) C.893 B.A. L.30 J.D.
MacDonald, Roland L., Jr. ... '42 '76 (MD) C.446 B.A. L.64 J.D.
MacKenzie, Joan L. ... '43 '77 (WA) C.1236 B.S. L.1162 J.D.
Madsen, Mark S. ... '64 '95 C.101 B.S. L.596 J.D.
Maggi, David A. ... '54 '79 C.1044 B.A. L.276 J.D.
Magnetti, Thomas O. ... '53 '78 C.276 B.S. L.446 J.D.
Marquez, Awilda R. ... '49 '88 (MD) C.276 B.S.F.S. L.446 J.D.
Martin, Mary Ann ... '42 '67 (MN) C&L.494 B.S., J.D.
Masterson, John T., Jr. ... '51 '77 C.378 B.A. L.976 J.D.
McCartin, Terrence J. ... '55 '81 C.813 A.B. L.276 J.D.
McClelland, Michelle Olivia ... '61 '86 (MD) C&L.64 B.S., J.D.
McClelland, Robert M. ... '33 '60 C&L.276 B.S., J.D.
McCready, Andrew W. ... '56 '85 (WV) C.309 B.A. L.945 J.D.
McDonald, Lauren E. ... '57 '89 (PA) C.802 B.F.A. L.276 J.D.
McInerney, John D. ... '53 '79 C.93 A.B. L.477 J.D.
McKenna, Alice Hannelore ... '58 '84 C.339 B.A. L.30 J.D.
McLellan, Walter J. ... '20 '52 C.103 A.B. L.813 J.D.
Means, Judith F. ... '45 '79 C&L.273 J.D.
Menefee, Mark ... '52 '80 (GA) C.859 B.A. L.280 J.D.

DEPARTMENT OF COMMERCE (Continued)

Min, Timothy James, II ...'71 '99 (MD) C.367 B.A. L.30 J.D.
Mintz, Barbara ...'48 '83 C.831 B.B.A. L.273 J.D.
Moll, Eric W. ...'51 '76 (OH) C.608 B.A. L.117 J.D.
Muller, George ...'34 '62 (OH) C.705 A.B. L.178 J.D.
Mulligan, Robert J. ...'55 '80 (OH) C.473 B.A. L.608 J.D.
Needle, Steven D. ...'47 '72 C.102 B.A. L.188 J.D.
Neuman, Rhonda Cook ...'61 '92 (MD) C.512 B.S. L.446 J.D.
Nielsen, Robert E. ...'41 '82 C.37 B.S. L.879 J.D.
Nottingham, Catherine Casey ...'67 '95 (VA) C.683 A.B. L.861 J.D.
Obayashi, Lisa J. ...'54 '85 C.276 B.A. L.273 J.D.
Odiaga, Ursula M. ...'58 '91 C.860 B.A. L.276 J.D.
Ovca, Jodi E. ...'69 '95 C.914 B.A. L.276 J.D.
Packard, Elise Barry ...'66 '92 (MD) C.103 A.B. L.276 J.D.
Pagan, Maria L. ...'63 '92 (MD) C.860 B.A. L.273 J.D.
Paugh, Jon ...'44 '73 C.216 A.B. L.659 LL.B.
Pender, Erin M. ...'75 '00 C.184 B.A. L.273 J.D. Atty. Advsr.
Pikus, Irwin M. ...'36 '72 C.223 B.S. L.831 J.D.
Potter, Barbara Campbell ...'61 '89 C.477 B.A. L.912 J.D.
Powell, Barbara K. ...'49 '73 (TX) C.228 B.A. L.326 J.D.
Powell, Stephen J. ...'42 '67 (FL) C&L.260 B.A., J.D.
Pratt, Catherine Randall ...'57 '93 (MD) C.118 B.A. L.276 J.D.
Raubitschek, John H. ...'42 '69 C.674 A.B. L.276 J.D.
Recker, David C. ...'71 '97 C.747 B.A. L.1035 J.D.
Reed, Donald J. ...'39 '78 (FL) C.512 B.S. L.329 J.D.
Reese, Rebecca Mei ...'59 '89 C.112 B.A. L.276 J.D.
Reisman, Edward Steven ...'54 '91 (MD) C.696 B.A. L.276 J.D.
Richardson, David W. ...'63 '89 C.478 B.A. L.260 J.D.
Robinson, Judith L. ...'— '98 (MD) C.681 B.A. L.64 J.D.
Rubin, Michael R. ...'50 '76 C&L.276 A.B., J.D.
Ryan, Miles F., III ...'63 '91 (PA) C.309 A.B. L.178 J.D.
Seastrum, Elizabeth C. ...'51 '79 C.118 B.A. L.276 J.D.
Senie, Allyson L. ...'61 '88 C.354 B.A. L.273 J.D.
Sharp, Edward F. ...'49 '83 (MD) C.1169 B.A. L.276 J.D.
Sidney, Arthur Dennis ...'73 '98 (PA) C.881 B.A. L.329 J.D.
Simmons-Benton, Anne F. ...'56 '84 C.276 B.S.F.S. L.1162 J.D.
Sloniewsky, Roman ...'39 '65 C.749 B.S. L.705 LL.B.
Sockowitz, Ira Mitchell ...'61 '90 (NY) C.1349 B.A. L.982 J.D.
Street, Lairold M. ...'52 '82 C.604 A.B. L.1119 J.D.
Styles, Kathleen M. ...'57 '84 C.893 B.A. L.945 J.D.
Taylor, Kathleen J. ...'48 '85 C.1108 B.A. L.273 J.D.
Thoemmes, Boguslawa B. ...'60 '93 (VA) C.800 B.A. L.276 J.D.
Torczon, Andrea G. ...'61 '91 (NJ) C.188 B.A. L.846 J.D.
Trossevin, Marguerite E. ...'49 '85 C&L.884 B.S., J.D.
Truax, Susan K. ...'66 '92 C&L.972 B.S., J.D.
Van Hanswyk, Beth ...'60 '85 (NY) C.1044 B.A. L.982 J.D.
Walz, Jerry A. ...'36 '76 C.851 B.S.E.E. L.425 J.D.
Warren, Arthur A. ...'51 '76 C.397 B.A. L.276 J.D.
Watson, Arthur R. ...'46 '74 (CA) C.309 B.A. L.813 J.D.
Wells, Linda A. ...'57 '83 C.800 B.A. L.659 J.D.
Whitaker, Lorie Beth ...'66 '92 C.861 B.A. L.659 J.D.
White, James K. ...'49 '74 (OK) C.880 B.A. L.623 J.D.
Yue, William C. ...'54 '79 (PA) C.119 B.S. L.659 J.D.
Zia, Hoyt H. ...'53 '81 (CA) C.197 B.A. L.1068 J.D.

ECONOMIC DEVELOPMENT ADMINISTRATION

Abdal-Haqq, Irshad ...'50 '81 C.31 B.A. L.276 J.D.
Bremer, Lisa ...'61 '86 C.831 B.A. L.276 J.D.
Ginsburg, Dayle M. ...'43 '69 C.494 B.A. L.659 LL.B.
Levin, Edward M. ...'34 '58 (IL) C.339 S.B. L.309 LL.B.

NATIONAL OCEANIC AND ATMOSPHERIC ADMINISTRATION

Afzal, Leila J. ...'58 '84 C.103 A.B. L.1292 J.D.
Allison-Browne, Roxie ...'61 '91 C.446 B.G.S. L.803 J.D.
Ben-David, Deborah R. ...'68 '95 (FL) C&L.260 B.A., J.D.
Blum, Branden S. ...'56 '83 C.446 B.A. L.273 J.D.
Briscoe, Nancy ...'61 '89 (NH) C.882 B.S. L.347 J.D.
Burlington, Linda B. ...'47 '82 C.418 B.A. L.208 J.D.
Chi, Samuel S. ...'71 '97 (CT) C.178 A.B. L.107
Cody, Bernard C. ...'53 '82 C.302 B.A. L.276 J.D.
Dacres, Karen D. ...'67 '95 (MD) C.597 B.A. L.273 J.D.
Eckert, Roger B. ...'57 '90 C.893 B.A. L.30 J.D.
Engelke-Ros, Meggan ...'70 '99 (VA) C.367 B.A. L.128 J.D.
Erickson, Kirsten ...'58 '86 C.685 B.A. L.629 J.D.
Feder, Judson J. ...'59 '86 C.668 B.A. L.1066 J.D.
Fenyk, Cynthia S. ...'— '89 C.945 A.B. L.362 J.D.
Fluke, Stephanie W. ...'53 '78 C.205 B.A. L.362 J.D.
Freeman, Martin M. ...'54 '80 (AL) C.10 B.A. L.192 J.D.
Gleaves, Karl D. ...'45 '76 (WI) C.352 B.A. L.966 J.D.
Hannuksela, Jane S. ...'50 '83 (WI) C.860 B.S. L.966 J.D.
Harwood, Deanna R. ...'60 '94 C.1077 B.S. L.809 J.D.
Hayes, Margaret Frailey ...'44 '69 C.378 B.A. L.597 J.D.
Heise, Leah Marie ...'69 '95 C.446 B.A. L.128 J.D.
Hindel, Martin J. ...'65 '91 C&L.608 B.S.M.E., J.D.*
Hogan, Robert J. ...'69 '97 C&L.446 B.A., J.D.
Holt, Mary Gray ...'56 '84 (OR) C.103 A.B. L.629 J.D.
Hytrek, Dan A. ...'— '90 C.628 B.S. L.629 J.D.
Johnson, Linda Sue ...'— '90 (NY) C.475 B.A. L.861 J.D.
Jung, Robin P. ...'63 '90 C.846 B.A. L.472 J.D.
Kraniotis, Patricia ...'44 '69 (WA) C&L.911 B.A., J.D.
Kuruc, Michele ...'57 '85 (WY) C.446 B.A. L.972 J.D.
La Bissonniere, Joel R. ...'57 '84 (MN) C.494 B.A. L.1035 J.D.
Lawrence, Pamela B. ...'— '87 C.569 B.A. L.309 J.D.
Lewers, Catherine R. ...'70 '96 (MO) C.587 B.A. L.174 J.D.
Matera, Marguerite M. ...'50 '79 C.475 B.S. L.588 J.D.
McCall, Mariam E. ...'52 '88 (MT) C.508 B.A. L.1051 J.D.
McIntosh, Dawn Andrews ...'66 '92 C.446 B.S. L.112 J.D.
Messing, Carol ...'65 '90 (PA) C.165 B.A. L.145 J.D.
O'Connor, Craig R. ...'45 '73 (AZ) C.35 B.S. L.36 J.D.
Ortiz, Paul A. ...'65 '93 C.37 B.A. L.569 J.D.
Peaco, James W., Jr. ...'43 '69 C&L.329 B.A., J.D.
Raine, Karen Antrim ...'56 '82 C.381 B.A. L.362 J.D.
Sathre, Constance J. ...'— '87 C.118 B.A. L.1051 J.D.
Schratwieser, Hugh C. ...'53 '86 (VA) C&L.326 B.S., J.D.
Shutler, Sharon K. ...'57 '90 (VA) C.893 B.A. L.1209 J.D.
Tallia, Glenn E. ...'62 '87 C.692 B.S. L.128 J.D.
Varmer, Ole ...'56 '87 C.905 B.S. L.978 J.D.
Williams, Julie A. ...'— '96 (MD) C.197 B.A. L.273 J.D.

OFFICE OF THE INSPECTOR GENERAL

Barlow, Elizabeth T. ...'50 '77 C.788 A.B. L.128 J.D.
Bryan, Jennifer H. ...'70 '95 (GA) C.269 B.A. L.280 J.D.
Croak, Carolyn A. ...'54 '87 (VA) C.473 B.A. L.273 J.D.
Lerner, Allison C. ...'62 '89 C&L.846 B.A., J.D.
Manis, Dean E. ...'54 '80 (NY) C.299 B.A. L.1040 J.D.
Schlee, Teresa M. ...'64 '92 (VA) C.445 B.A. L.273 J.D.

MINORITY BUSINESS DEVELOPMENT AGENCY

Flynn, Dinah I. ...'48 '78 C.66 A.B. L.1162 J.D.
Robinson, Percy E., III ...'54 '80 C.674 A.B. L.228 J.D.

NATIONAL TELECOMMUNICATIONS & INFORMATION ADMINISTRATION

Gattuso, Joseph L. ...'55 '81 C.813 B.A. L.1068 J.D.
Krinsky, Robert Bruce ...'62 '99 C.156 B.A. L.124 J.D.
Lader, Wendy S. ...'64 '93 C.681 B.A. L.659 J.D. Sr. Policy Advisor
Levy, Kelly Klegar ...'62 '89 C.309 A.B. L.812 J.D.
Sloan, Timothy C. ...'53 '79 C.276 B.A. L.228 J.D.
Wasilewski, Cathleen K. ...'— '96 (VA) C.713 B.A. L.30 J.D.
Williams, Tatia Lynne ...'65 '91 C.893 B.A. L.309 J.D.

PATENT AND TRADEMARK OFFICE

Abrahams, David M. ...'69 '96 C.445 B.S. L.904 J.D.
Abrams, Neal E. ...'37 '67 C.790 B.S. L.30 J.D.
Adams, Donald Edward ...'64 '98 (VA) L.1356 J.D.
Aikens, Ronald E. ...'68 '97 (NY) C.197 B.A. L.329 J.D.
Alfieri, Amy L. ...'74 '99 (VA) C.893 B.A. L.1209 J.D.
Alt, Jill C. ...'32 '79 (NY) C&L.107 B.A., J.D.
Anderson, Lawrence E. ...'48 '75 (OH) C.119 B.S. L.930 J.D.
Anderson, Robert M. ...'40 '79 (TX) C.546 B.S. L.107 J.D.
Andrews, Melvyn J. ...'37 '71 (MD) C.423 B.S. L.64 J.D.
Arbes, Carl J. ...'43 '77 C.271 B.S. L.229 J.D.
Arroyo, Teresa M. ...'67 '99 (MD) C.329 B.S.E.E. L.1209 J.D.
Atkinson, Charles E. ...'36 '73 (VA) C.886 B.S.E.E. L.30 J.D.
Awrich, Ellen ...'64 '91 (PA) C.1036 B.A. L.273 J.D.
Baird, Michael W. ...'68 '93 (NY) C.299 A.B. L.262 J.D.
Baldwin, Robert D. ...'38 '65 C.350 B.S. L.221 LL.B.
Ballato, Josie A. ...'58 '89 C.1070 B.S. L.446 J.D.
Barrett, Lee E. ...'49 '77 (MD) C.966 B.S. L.446 J.D.
Barry, Chester T. ...'61 '97 C.453 B.S. L.1356 J.D.
Barry, Lance Leonard ...'65 '95 C.128 B.E.E. L.1209 J.D.
Baxley, Andrew P. ...'60 '92 C.273 B.A. L.128 J.D.
Bayat, Bradley ...'69 '95 (CA) C.112 B.S. L.809 J.D.
Beck, Loretta Christine ...'68 '96 (MD) C.264 B.A. L.273 J.D.
Belenker, Esther ...'55 '86 C.150 B.S. L.276 J.D.
Bello, Zachary R. ...'— '00 (MA) C.999 B.S. L.260 J.D.
Benzmiller, Andrew J. ...'62 '93 (MA) C.93 A.B. L.94 J.D.
Beresford, Lynne Greene ...'42 '78 (PA) C.705 B.A. L.1292 J.D.
Berk, Steven R. ...'70 '96 C.1349 B.A. L.472 J.D.
Bernstein, Hiram H. ...'47 '81 (VA) C.563 B.Ch.E. L.1209 J.D.
Beyer, Brooke A., Jr. ...'65 '91 (MD) C.276 B.S. L.446 J.D.
Biefeld, Diana L. ...'65 '95 (VA) C.608 B.S. L.128 J.D.
Biegel, Ronald L. ...'53 '79 (IL) C.800 Ph.D. L.424 J.D.
Billings, Jessie W. ...'60 '90 (VA) C.183 B.A. L.1209 J.D.
Bishop, Joan Leslie ...'60 '87 (OK) C&L.862 B.A., J.D.
Black, Cheryl Lynn ...'65 '90 C.354 B.S. L.276 J.D.
Blandu, Florentina ...'63 '90 C&L.1158 B.A., J.D.
Blankenship, Howard B. ...'54 '95 (VA) C.16 B.S.E.E. L.273 J.D.
Blohm, Linda E. ...'61 '90 (OK) C.612 B.S. L.862 J.D.
Boagni, Mary E. ...'70 '96 C.1365 B.A. L.245 J.D.
Bodson, Michael E. ...'40 '68 C.30 A.B. L.904 J.D.
Boehler, Anne Marie ...'64 '95 (VA) C.180 B.M.E. L.904 J.D.
Boland, Lois E. ...'55 '85 C.128 B.Ch.E. L.273 J.D.
Bonnet, Odette ...'50 '90 (CA) C.280 M.A. L.861 J.D.
Bora, Roger H. ...'68 '99 (MD) C.745 L.1218 J.D.
Borsuk, Esther Atara ...'62 '87 C.421 B.A. L.945 J.D.
Bottorff, Charles M. ...'59 '87 (OR) C.813 B.A. L.629 J.D.
Boulton, Kelly F. ...'66 '95 (SC) C.1090 B.S. L.790 J.D.
Boyer, George P. ...'50 '81 (MD) C.896 B.A. L.273 J.D.
Bracey, Karen E. ...'62 '94 (VA) C.893 B.A. L.902 J.D.
Bray, Waymond D. ...'40 '68 C.329 B.S.M.E. L.273 LL.B.
Breckenfeld, William G. ...'71 '98 (MD) C.855 B.A. L.884 J.D.
Bresso, Gineen M. ...'73 '99 (MD) C.454 B.S. L.1048 J.D.
Brittingham, Debra S. ...'59 '90 (IL) C.112 B.S. L.801 J.D.
Brown, Barbara T. ...'71 '98 (MD) C.823 B.A. L.1002 J.D.
Brown, Brian D. ...'70 '98 (MD) C.446 B.S. L.930 J.D.
Browne, Dayna Janice ...'66 '98 (NY) C.1248 B.A. L.665 J.D.
Bruce, Mary Frances ...'52 '81 C&L.128 B.A., J.D.
Bruno, James A., Jr. ...'70 '00 (CA) C.1356 B.A. L.284 J.D.
Brust, Jennifer M. ...'62 '89 C.446 B.A. L.831 J.D.
Bryan-Johnson, Hellen M. ...'67 '96 (FL) C.269 B.A. L.1206 J.D.
Bucher, David E. ...'53 '79 C.1124 B.A. L.273 J.D.
Bullock, Darlene D. ...'64 '92 (VA) C.1286 B.S. L.1209 J.D.
Buongiorno, Christopher L. ...'66 '99 (PA) C.1028 B.S. L.645 J.D.
Bush, Karen K. ...'62 '87 (PA) C.602 B.A. L.665 J.D.
Butler, Cheryl A. ...'58 '88 (VA) C.37 B.S. L.1209 J.D.
Calvert, Ian A. ...'39 '62 (TX) C.691 B.A. L.326 LL.B.
Canney, Vincent P. ...'42 '71 C.223 B.S.E.E. L.128 J.D.
Caroff, Marc L. ...'46 '79 (MD) C.186 B.E.Ch.E. L.273 J.D.
Carroll, Doritt ...'64 '90 C&L.276 B.A., J.D.
Carruthers, Alice Sue ...'47 '82 (IL) C.801 B.A. L.352 J.D.
Case, Leigh C. ...'62 '91 C.951 B.A. L.945 J.D.
Cataldo, Peter ...'62 '91 (NY) C.116 B.A. L.982 J.D.
Chapman, Beth A. ...'48 '73 (SD) C&L.793 B.A., J.D.
Chen, Raymond T. ...'68 '94 C.112 B.S.E.E. L.569 J.D.
Chicoski, Jennifer Stiver ...'71 '95 (VA) C&L.276 B.S.B.A., J.D.
Chisolm, Kevon L. ...'69 '98 (NJ) C.222 B.A. L.997 J.D.
Choi, Frank I. ...'67 '95 (IL) C.340 B.A. L.801 J.D.
Chosid, Robin S. ...'63 '90 C.119 B.S. L.215 J.D.

Cissel, Robert F. . . . '48 '74 (MD) C&L.446 B.A., J.D.
Clark, Robert C., Jr. . . . '53 '80 (PA) C.205 B.A. L.469 J.D.
Clarke, Idi Aisha . . . '72 '97 (MD) C.205 B.A. L.923 J.D.
Cofield, Julia Hardy . . . '44 '84 (PA) C&L.574 B.A., J.D.
Coggins, Robert H. . . . '69 '97 C.198 B.S. L.896 J.D.
Cohen, Irwin C. . . . '43 '69 (VA) C.563 B.M.E. L.276 J.D.
Cohen, Lee S. . . . '50 '79 (MD) C.446 B.S. L.64 J.D.
Cohn, Deborah Schaffer . . . '52 '82 (VA) C.30 B.A. L.1209 J.D.
Cole, Jacqueline A. . . . '58 '84 C.346 B.S. L.1187 J.D.
Collins, Alicia P. . . . '69 '96 C.276 B.A. L.446 J.D.
Congo, Cliff . . . '74 '00 C.886 B.A. L.1017 J.D.
Cook, William Bradley . . . '70 '01 (MD) C.1524 B.A. L.128 J.D.
Corbin, Arthur L. . . . '47 '74 (PA) C.446 B.S. L.273 J.D.
Corcoran, Robert J. . . . '38 '67 C.205 B.S.E.E. L.884 J.D.
Cordova, Raul F. . . . '62 '88 C.423 B.A. L.862 J.D.
Corea, Andy . . . '70 '95 C.945 B.A. L.1209 J.D.
Covey, William R. . . . '65 '91 (NY) C&L.262 B.A., J.D. Assoc. Gen. Coun.
Coward, Jeffrey C. . . . '68 '94 (VA) C.328 B.S. L.1509 J.D.
Crane, Sara W. . . . '51 '92 (VA) C.339 B.S. L.276 J.D.
Craven, P. Scott . . . '— '92 (MN) C.602 B.B.A. L.1049 J.D.
Crawford, Murriel E. . . . '53 '80 C.1378 B.S. L.276 J.D.
Critharis, Mary . . . '65 '91 (NY) C.569 B.A. L.1009 J.D.
Crockett, Cynthia E. . . . '63 '95 C.1209 B.S. L.128 J.D.
Cross, Tracy Lanett . . . '72 '98 (GA) C.893 B.A. L.245 J.D.
Crowe, Robert J. . . . '52 '79 C.280 B.A. L.1206 J.D.
Dalier, John D. . . . '64 '90 C&L.420 B.S., J.D.
Dalier, Lauriel F. . . . '68 '98 (MD) C.30 B.A. L.180 J.D.
Dall, Maureen L. . . . '70 '98 (VA) C.886 B.A. L.1209 J.D.
Datri, Alan M. . . . '52 '82 C.732 B.A. L.1209 J.D.
Dawe, William H., III . . . '57 '87 C.884 B.S. L.30 J.D.
Dawson, Robert A. . . . '47 '76 (CT) C.588 B.S. L.904 J.D.
Deane, William J., Jr. . . . '58 '92 (PA) C.928 B.S. L.1338 J.D.
DeFord, Jeffrey S. . . . '61 '90 C.623 BA L.862 J.D.
de Jonge, Kathleen R. . . . '59 '89 (CO) C.054 B.A. L.37 J.D.
Delaney, Zhaleh S. . . . '62 '89 C.893 B.G.S. L.692 J.D.
Del Gizzi, Ronald E. . . . '57 '91 (MA) C.459 B.S. L.818 J.D.
Delmendo, Romulo Hong . . . '62 '96 C.816 B.E. L.128 J.D.
DePumpo, Daniel G . . . '67 '96 C.107 B.S.M.E. L.180 J.D.
Dinallo, Kevin M. . . . '75 '00 (MD) C.529 B.A. L.1338 J.D.
Dixon, Jennifer H. . . . '69 '97 C.688 B.S.E.E. L.30 J.D.
Dixon, Joseph L. . . . '62 '89 (MD) C.446 B.S. L.128 J.D.
Dost, Gerald A. . . . '37 '67 C.237 A.B. L.273 LL.B.
Drost, Albin F. . . . '54 '79 C.321 B.A. L.1017 J.D.
DuBois, Susan Leslie . . . '66 '92 (NY) C.1192 B.A. L.982 J.D.
Dukovcic, Joanna M. . . . '69 '00 (VA) C.665 B.S.E.E. L.1218 J.D.
DuMont, Gregory T. . . . '66 '96 C.107 B.A. L.273 J.D.
Dunn, Drew A. . . . '67 '98 (VA) C.205 B.S. L.1218 J.D.
Dunn, Elizabeth A. . . . '61 '86 (MA) C.94 B.A. L.30 J.D.
Dzenitis, Talis . . . '47 '78 C.446 B.S. L.365 J.D.
Echols, Percy W. . . . '45 '81 (VA) C.893 B.S. L.896 J.D.
Ehard, Andrew S. . . . '69 '97 (VA) C.966 B.A. L.1364 J.D.
Ellis, Joan . . . '50 '92 (MD) C.569 Ph.D. L.273 J.D.
Endieveri, Anne C. . . . '70 '96 C.1021 B.A. L.1364 J.D.
Engel, James Joseph . . . '62 '93 C.477 B.S.Ch.E. L.1209 J.D.
Eulin, Ingrid C. . . . '69 '96 (FL) C.257 B.A. L.472 J.D.
Evanko, Patricia M. . . . '62 '89 C.692 B.S.B.A. L.902 J.D.
Evans, Geoffrey S. . . . '60 '90 (VA) C.800 B.S. L.1209 J.D.
Faint, M. Catherine . . . '— '93 C.296 A.B. L.446 J.D.
Fairbanks, Ronald L. . . . '65 '94 C.571 B.S. L.574 J.D.
Feldman, Dawn J. . . . '68 '93 C.347 B.S. L.546 J.D.
Ferraiuolo, Dominic J. . . . '58 '92 (NY) C.262 B.S. L.724 J.D.
Fetting, Anton W. . . . '50 '87 (MD) C.119 B.S. L.446 J.D.
Fickes, Jeri J. . . . '61 '88 (PA) C.845 B.A. L.378 J.D.
Fingeret, Donald J. . . . '51 '78 (VA) C.665 B.A. L.1209 J.D.
Fink, Gina Marie . . . '69 '95 C.1111 B.A. L.1117 J.D.
Finkel, Sharon E. . . . '63 '93 (VA) C.339 B.S. L.1209 J.D.
Finnegan, Timothy J. . . . '51 '98 (NH) C.550 B.A. L.431 J.D.
First, Vivian Micznik . . . '67 '91 C.994 B.A. L.276 J.D.
Fisher, Hannah Morrison . . . '51 '77 C.477 B.A. L.213 J.D.
Fisher, Richard V. . . . '43 '77 (VA) C.608 B.E. L.64 J.D.
Fleming, Michael R. . . . '55 '86 C.886 M.S.E.E. L.1209 J.D.
Foelak, Morton . . . '31 '72 C.102 B.S. L.273 J.D.
Footland, Lenard A. . . . '43 '69 C.874 B.A. L.831 J.D.
Ford, John K. . . . '55 '94 (VA) C.674 M.S.E. L.273 J.D.
Fosdick, Geoffrey A. . . . '64 '90 C.1044 B.A. L.1019 J.D.
Fowler, Peter N. . . . '51 '84 (CA) C.363 B.A. L.284 J.D.
Frahm, Eric S. . . . '67 '98 (NC) C.886 B.S.E.E. L.30 J.D.
Frankfort, Charles E. . . . '48 '84 (VA) C.446 B.S. L.1209 J.D.
French, Curtis William . . . '67 '97 (TX) C.846 B.A. L.325 J.D.
Friedman, Howard D. . . . '56 '81 (PA) C.446 B.A. L.1338 J.D.
Fries, Kery A. . . . '62 '90 (WV) C.779 B.S. L.923 J.D.
Fromm, Martha L. . . . '69 '95 (MN) C.960 B.B.A. L.300 J.D.
Front, Mitchell . . . '64 '91 C.1111 B.A. L.128 J.D.
Gardiner, J. David . . . '72 '00 (IN) C.347 B.S. L.345 J.D.
Gardner, Dawna Beryl . . . '69 '97 (MD) C.811 B.A. L.884 J.D.
Gardner, Sally . . . '65 '91 (NC) C.576 B.A. L.1345 J.D.
Garner, Christina M . . . '73 '99 (MN) C.665 B.A. L.300 J.D.
Garris, Bradley R. . . . '50 '80 C.223 B.S. L.64 J.D.
Gartner, John M. . . . '68 '96 (NY) C.945 B.A. L.1209 J.D.
Gaskins, Tonja Monique . . . '67 '97 (MD) C.575 B.S. L.1002 J.D.
Gast, Paul F. . . . '45 '70 (IN) C.424 B.S. L.1119 J.D.
Gastelo, Elvia Patricia . . . '71 '99 (NY) C.102 B.A. L.537 J.D.
Gaynor, Barbara A. . . . '62 '88 C.893 B.A. L.945 J.D.
Gearin, Amy L. . . . '58 '98 (MN) C.446 B.A. L.300 J.D.
Gellner, Michael L. . . . '46 '73 (MD) C.446 B.S. L.273 J.D.
Gibson, Robert W., Jr. . . . '50 '85 (VA) C.223 B.S. L.1209 J.D.
Gillis, Deirdre Robertson . . . '71 '98 C.1236 B.A. L.260 J.D.
Gillon, John Joseph, Jr. . . . '49 '80 C&L.425 B.A., J.D.
Glembocki, Erica D.B. . . . '68 '93 (VA) C.893 B.A. L.692 J.D.
Glitz, Susan R. . . . '— '94 (VA) C.311 B.A. L.30 J.D.
Gluck, Richard E. . . . '44 '75 (VA) C.569 B.E. L.128 J.D.
Glynn, Gerald T. . . . '44 '73 (PA) C.884 B.A. L.64 J.D.
Goldberg, Jerome D. . . . '34 '63 (MD) C.446 B.S. L.64 J.D.
Golden, James Brett . . . '71 '97 (VA) C.886 B.S. L.884 J.D.
Goldman, Linda Marie . . . '70 '98 (MA) C.860 B.A. L.30 J.D.
Gonzales, John F. . . . '46 '73 (VA) C.420 B.S. L.273 J.D.
Goodman, Cheryl S. . . . '63 '89 C.339 B.S. L.259 J.D.
Goodman, Wendy B. . . . '71 '97 C.518 B.A. L.569 J.D.
Goodsaid, Ira J. . . . '55 '83 (VA) C.446 B.S. L.1209 J.D.
Gray, Carolyn Chapman . . . '48 '88 C.253 B.A. L.446 J.D.
Greenbaum, Cindy B. . . . '63 '89 C&L.659 B.S., J.D.
Greenlief, Magdalen . . . '56 '85 (VA) C.667 B.S. L.1209 J.D.
Grendzynski, Michael E. . . . '71 '98 (OH) C.385 B.A. L.851 J.D.
Griffith, Venus E. . . . '62 '95 (GA) C.426 B.A. L.800 J.D.
Grimes, Eric B. . . . '63 '98 (VA) C.494 B.S. L.276 J.D.
Grimley, Arthur T. . . . '38 '72 (VA) C.433 B.E.E. L.276 J.D.
Gron, Teddy S. . . . '45 '73 (IL) C.679 B.S. L.424 J.D.
Gross, Anita Pellman . . . '66 '92 (MD) C.453 B.S. L.273 J.D.
Grosz, Alexander . . . '49 '80 (VA) C.563 B.Ch.E. L.30 J.D.
Gunawardhana, Sonali P. . . . '72 '00 (MD) C.823 B.A. L.1218 J.D.
Gushi, Ross N. . . . '66 '95 (HI) C.188 B.S. L.312 J.D.
Hafer, Robert A. . . . '46 '76 C.150 B.S.C.E. L.128 J.D.
Hairston, Kenneth W. . . . '51 '78 (KY) C.1378 B.S.E.E. L.30 J.D.
Hairston, Paula T. . . . '52 '77 C.577 B.A. L.128 J.D.
Hall, Allison Ewing . . . '— '93 (VA) C.893 B.A. L.1209 J.D.
Hall, Michael E. . . . '73 '00 (VA) C.893 B.A. L.945 J.D.
Ham, Seungsook . . . '63 '93 (PA) C.670 B.S.E.E. L.30 J.D.
Hamilton, Michael D. . . . '46 '82 (VA) C.942 B.S. L.378 J.D.
Hanak, Elmer W., III . . . '47 '75 (NY) C.846 B.A. L.309 J.D.
Hanley, John C. . . . '54 '85 (VA) C.893 B.S.E.E. L.1209 J.D.
Hanlon, Adriene Lepiane . . . '63 '91 (PA) C&L.128 B.S.E., J.D.
Hannon, Mary E. . . . '56 '82 C.012 B.A. L.904 J.D.
Hardy, Tarah K. . . . '73 '97 (UT) C.1085 B.A. L.101 J.D.
Harkcom, Gary V. . . . '49 '87 (PA) C.294 B.S. L.30 J.D.
Harrison, Lakeisha R. . . . '— '99 (MI) C.477 B.A. L.329 J.D.
Hastings, Karen M. . . . '59 '88 (VA) C.431 B.S. L.1209 J.D.
Hayash, Susan Carol . . . '70 '97 C.938 B.A. L.1202 J.D.
Hayes, Gail O. . . . '58 '90 (VA) C.453 B.S. L.273 J.D.
Herman, Russ . . . '52 '79 C.966 B.A. L.989 J.D.
Herrell, Robert R. . . . '70 '98 (NY) C.880 B.A. L.861 J.D.
Hershkowitz, Meryl Louise . . . '52 '77 (CT) C.1044 B.A. L.569 J.D.
Hichey, Toni . . . '— '98 C.174 B.S. L.802 J.D.
Hohein, George D. . . . '50 '76 (VA) C&L.893 B.A., J.D.
Hoinkes, H. Dieter . . . '40 '67 C.696 B.S.M.E. L.273 J.D.
Holmes, Angela R. . . . '71 '99 C.852 B.A. L.425 J.D.
Horrall, Patricia A. . . . '64 '90 C.623 B.B.A. L.862 J.D.
Howell, Thomas G. . . . '51 '77 C.999 B.A. L.1209 J.D.
Hunt, Brooks H. . . . '47 '76 (VA) C.679 B.S. L.64 J.D.
Hwang, John C. . . . '69 '96 C&L.446 B.S., J.D.
Isaacson, Virginia T. . . . '— '97 (UT) C&L.1335 B.A., J.D.
Isacson, Linda M. . . . '64 '89 (IL) C.436 B.S. L.597 J.D.
Jackson, Steven W. . . . '70 '00 (NJ) C.390 A.B. L.831 J.D.
Jenkins, Charles L., Jr. . . . '64 '89 (PA) C&L.884 B.S., J.D.
Jenkins, Daniel J. . . . '58 '97 (VA) C.119 M.S. L.128 J.D.
Jennings, Patrick . . . '74 '00 C.1369 B.A. L.645 J.D.
Johnson, Sydney O., Jr. . . . '67 '97 (FL) C.1222 B.S.E.E. L.1206 J.D.
Jones, Josetta I. . . . '70 '97 (TX) C.597 B.S.Che L.325 J.D.
Jones, Richard L. . . . '58 '90 (GA) C.315 B.A. L.245 J.D.
Jones, Yvonne D. . . . '72 '98 C.893 B.A. L.945 J.D.
Judd, Patricia L. . . . '— '98 (CA) C.228 A.B. L.880 J.D.
Kaiser, Theresa K. . . . '64 '90 (FL) C.378 B.S.J.B.A. L.245 J.D.
Kamm, William E. . . . '38 '70 (MD) C.679 B.S. L.446 LL.B.
Kang, Jane C. . . . '71 '00 (MD) C.446 B.A. L.329 J.D.
Keam, Alex S. . . . '70 '96 C.445 B.S. L.446 J.D.
Keating, Dominic J. . . . '67 '96 C.1210 B.S. L.61 J.D.
Keating, Michael P. . . . '65 '89 C&L.128 B.A., J.D.
Keegan, Laura E. . . . '— '97 (VA) C.682 B.A. L.1209 J.D.
Kelly, John M. C. . . . '67 '94 C.228 A.B. L.597 J.D.
Keplinger, Michael S. . . . '40 '72 (MD) C.923 B.S. L.276 J.D.
Khan, Asmat A. . . . '64 '95 C.445 B.A. L.300 J.D.
Kight, John, III . . . '41 '78 (MD) C.1289 B.S. L.64 J.D.
Kim, Sophia Sujin . . . '68 '96 (MD) C&L.446 B.A., J.D.
Kimlin, Edward C. . . . '46 '75 (VA) C.215 B.S.Che. L.128 J.D.
King, Christina Brightmire . . . '63 '88 C.612 B.S. L.862 J.D.
Klass, Jeremy M. . . . '74 '00 (PA) C.645 B.A. L.831 J.D.
Kline, Matthew C. . . . '67 '95 (MD) C.1090 B.A. L.838 J.D.
Knight, Anthony . . . '62 '90 C.223 B.S.M.E. L.1209 J.D.
Knight, Bernard J., Jr. . . . '57 '82 (TX) C.221 B.S.B.A. L.800 J.D.
Koller, Herbert R. . . . '21 '52 C.930 B.S. L.904 J.D.
Kon, Elissa Garber . . . '63 '89 C.705 B.A. L.978 J.D.
Kovalsky, Laura Gorman . . . '69 '97 C.823 B.S. L.128 J.D.
Krass, Errol A. . . . '51 '78 (MD) C.563 B.E. L.273 J.D.
Kratz, Peter F. . . . '50 '83 (MD) C.446 B.S.Ch.E. L.128 J.D.
Krebs, Catherine Kaiser . . . '42 '87 C.276 B.S. L.1209 J.D.
Krehely, Kimberly . . . '56 '80 (PA) C.643 A.B. L.665 J.D.
Krynski, William A. . . . '54 '94 (MD) C.1141 B.S. L.180 J.D.
Kulick, Lizbeth B. . . . '62 '87 (NY) C.319 B.A. L.982 J.D.
Kunin, Stephen G. . . . '48 '75 (VA) C.910 B.S.E.E. L.273 J.D.
Lall, Parshotam S. . . . '39 '74 C.628 Ph.D. L.30 J.D.
LaMarca, William . . . '60 '93 (OH) C.851 B.S.M.E. L.1003 J.D.
Lamone, Thomas S. . . . '43 '79 (CA) C.446 B.S. L.1137 J.D.
Lauterbach, Jodi . . . '— '95 (VA) C.93 B.A. L.744 J.D.
Lawrence, Andrew D. . . . '58 '85 (MA) C.475 B.A. L.1048 J.D.
Le, K. Margaret . . . '61 '86 (LA) C.298 B.A. L.861 J.D.
Le, Khanh . . . '72 '98 (LA) C&L.861 B.A., J.D.
Lecher, Donald J. . . . '68 '96 (VA) C.1229 B.S. L.1339 J.D.
Ledynh, Bot . . . '47 '90 (PA) C.588 M.S. L.818 J.D.
Lee, Betsy P. . . . '67 '96 (MD) C&L.446 B.S., J.D.
Lee, Douglas M. . . . '63 '88 (NY) C.112 B.A. L.1068 J.D.
Lee, Jameson . . . '60 '86 C.453 B.S. L.273 J.D.
Lee, Teresa Coin . . . '55 '86 (NC) C.560 B.A. L.896 J.D.
Leipzig, Marc J. . . . '69 '94 (CO) C&L.893 B.A., J.D.
Leizear, Lisa M. . . . '66 '98 C.446 B.S. L.1364 J.D.
Leonard, John W. . . . '43 '67 C.188 B.A. L.273 J.D.
Lerner, Martin D. . . . '58 '86 C.674 A.B. L.831 J.D.
Levine, Howard B. . . . '63 '88 (MD) C.446 B.A. L.128 J.D.
Levy, Stuart S. . . . '49 '81 (VA) C.563 B.E.E. L.1209 J.D.
Lewis, Michael L. . . . '49 '74 (PA) C.665 B.S. L.229 J.D.

DEPARTMENT OF COMMERCE (Continued)

Lewis, Ralph A. '62 '93 (VA) C.172 B.S. L.128 J.D.
Lieberman, Allan M. '24 '61 C.569 B.A. L.276 J.D.
Lieberman, Paul '37 '71 C.978 B.A. L.128 J.D.
Lisehora, James A. '63 '92 (VA) C.446 B.S. L.1209 J.D.
Long, Janis C. '57 '85 C.1099 B.A. L.861 J.D.
Lorin, Hubert C.L. '55 '95 (VA) C.923 B.Sc.Ch.E. L.30 J.D.
Loughran, Barbara A. '56 '82 C.446 B.A. L.999 J.D.
Lourie, Linda S. '65 '97 (MD) C.681 A.B. L.978 J.D.
Love, John J. '47 '74 (VA) C.215 B.M.E. L.276 J.D.
Lucas, Jay P. '47 '75 (VA) C.659 B.A. L.276 J.D.
Lucas, Jennifer Barton '66 '91 C.575 B.A. L.1209 J.D.
Lueders, April F. '73 '98 (MN) C.1268 B.A. L.1218 J.D.
Luong, Vinh T. '54 '93 (PA) C.420 M.S. L.128 J.D.
Lusignan, Michael R. '37 '66 C.821 B.A. L.607 J.D.
Luthey, Lynn A. '59 '86 (OK) C.623 B.A. L.999 J.D.
Lykos, Angela '65 '91 C.367 B.A. L.228 J.D.
Mack, Mary C. '45 '78 (PA) C.423 B.S. L.64 J.D.
Manalili, Joseph L. '70 '95 C.659 B.A. L.112 J.D.
Mandir, Frederick M. '53 '81 (MD) C.446 B.S. L.425 J.D.
Marcus, James M. '69 '94 C.184 B.A. L.1048 J.D.
Marcus, Stephen '49 '77 (VA) C.688 B.S. L.64 J.D.
Marsh, Sharon R. '56 '82 C.228 A.B. L.245 J.D.
Martin, Eugenia K. '68 '97 (NY) C.893 B.A. L.569 J.D.
Martin, Jennifer McGarry '72 '97 (MD) C.446 PSYC L.1002 J.D.
Martin, John C. '45 '73 C.150 B.S.E.E. L.273 J.D.
Mateja, Joanna '68 '96 C.385 B.A. L.128 J.D.
Matthews, Amos T., Jr. '47 '75 (LA) C.803 B.S. L.329 J.D.
Mayerschoff, Glenn E. '52 '77 (PA) C.308 B.A. L.1017 J.D.
Mayes, Laurie Ann '71 '97 (DC) C.188 B.A. L.260 J.D.
Mays, Paula B. '59 '85 (MD) C.935 B.A. L.607 J.D.
McCamish, Marion E. '41 '68 (KY) C&L.421 B.Ch.E., J.D.
McCauley, Brendan D. '71 '98 (NY) C.714 B.A. L.823 J.D.
McDonald, Thomas D., Jr. '60 '87 C.695 B.A. L.500 J.D.
McGinty, Douglas J. '57 '81 (IL) C.801 B.A. L.339 J.D.
McQuade, John P. '51 '79 C.688 B.S. L.273 J.D.
Medley, Sally '66 '98 (VA) C.383 B.S.E.E. L.1209 J.D.
Meier, Sharon Adinah '67 '94 (CA) C.1356 B.A. L.904 J.D.
Meltzer, Eleanor K. '61 '90 (VA) C.813 A.B. L.276 J.D.
Metz, Andrew Harold '48 '80 (MD) C.446 B.S. L.64 J.D.
Micheli, Angela M. '61 '90 C.705 B.A. L.128 J.D.
Michos, John E. '62 '88 (MD) C.216 B.A. L.273 J.D.
Mickleburgh, Linda B. '61 '87 (VA) C.861 B.A. L.1202 J.D.
Miller, George H., Jr. '33 '69 (VA) C.352 B.S. L.128 J.D.
Milone, Marcie R. Frum '73 '99 (MD) C.105 B.A. L.128 J.D.
Mintel, William A. '47 '90 (PA) C.705 M.S. L.128 J.D.
Mizelle, Dezmona '72 '97 (NC) C&L.574 B.A., J.D.
Moezie, Minna F. '67 '99 (VA) C.999 B.S. L.128 J.D.
Molinoff, Jeffrey Sirota '68 '95 (PA) C.659 B.A. L.94 J.D.
Mooneyham, Janice A. '51 '91 (VA) C.575 B.S. L.1410 J.D.
Moore, William W., 3rd '47 '90 (IA) C.112 B.A. L.221 J.D.
Morris, Theodore '39 '74 (PA) C.831 A.B. L.446 J.D.
Moskowitz, Nelson '47 '76 C.816 M.S. L.128 J.D.
Moskowitz, Sidney I. '51 '78 (VA) C.904 B.A. L.1209 J.D.
Nadelman, Andrea Koyner '65 '91 C.477 B.A. L.273 J.D.
Nagumo, Mark '55 '96 (VA) C.674 A.B. L.1209 J.D.
Nappi, Robert '— '99 (VA) C.160 B.S.E.E. L.30 J.D.
Nase, Jeffrey V. '51 '86 (VA) C.223 B.S. L.1209 J.D.
Neils, Peggy A. '58 '89 C.475 B.S. L.128 J.D.
Nelson, Edward H. '51 '78 C.273 B.A. L.128 J.D.
Nelson, Peter A. '47 '76 (VA) C.588 B.S. L.64 J.D.
Ness, Jennifer Amy '70 '98 C.103 B.A. L.276 J.D.
Nessler, Cynthia L. '54 '95 (VA) C.223 B.S. L.273 J.D.
Niebling, John F., Jr. '42 '76 (VA) C.280 B.S. L.64 J.D.
Niu, Elenore '— '97 C.1375 B.A. L.1068 J.D.
Nuzzolillo, Maria '61 '91 (PA) C.1102 B.S. L.1029 J.D.
Olandria, Warren L. '72 '00 C.629 B.S. L.285 J.D.
Olear, Janice '59 '86 (MD) C.1044 B.S. L.30 J.D.
O'Lear, Michelle R. '71 '97 (FL) C.362 B.A. L.259 J.D.
Omelko, Nancy L. '48 '81 (VA) C.1200 A.B. L.1209 J.D.
Osborne, Stanley I. '68 '93 (VA) C.945 B.A. L.896 J.D.
Oslick, Scott M. '71 '97 (MD) C.446 B.A. L.30 J.D.
Ostrager, Allen M. '46 '78 (PA) C.570 B.S. L.128 J.D.
Oswecki, Jane C. '46 '92 (CT) C.930 B.A. L.1048 J.D.
Otte, Sarah A. '72 '97 (OH) C.347 B.A. L.201 J.D.
Owens, Terry J. '49 '84 (TX) C.421 M.E. L.326 J.D.
Page, Amy C. '70 '95 (VA) C.893 B.A. L.1119 J.D.
Pak, Chung K. '58 '89 C.10 B.S. L.180 J.D.
Pate, William F., III '50 '77 (VA) C.838 B.S. L.904 J.D.
Pearson, Charles A. '51 '77 (OR) C.696 B.S. L.823 J.D.
Pedersen, Chris A.F. '58 '85 (MA) C.276 A.B. L.1048 J.D.
Perkins, Karla '— '95 (MD) C.803 B.S.C.E. L.329 J.D.
Perry, Kimberly Boulware '— '94 (MD) C.446 B.A. L.276 J.D.
Peska, Kevin R. '66 '91 (MD) C.260 B.A. L.273 J.D.
Piccolo, Joseph G. '63 '91 (NY) C.602 B.S. L.569 J.D.
Pignatello, Elizabeth F. '71 '98 C.477 B.A. L.904 J.D.
Powell, Linda A. '54 '98 C.735 B.A. L.623 J.D.
Powell, Steven B. '65 '99 C.896 B.A. L.902 J.D.
Powers, Alexander L. '67 '92 C.477 B.A. L.665 J.D.
Prater, Jill I. '69 '95 C.421 B.A. L.309 J.D.
Preddie, LaVerne T. '60 '90 (VA) C.446 B.A. L.1209 J.D.
Prenty, Mark '61 '94 (PA) C.186 B.S.E. L.273 J.D.
Prescott, Arthur C. '35 '80 (VA) C.818 B.S. L.128 J.D.
Price, Jerry L. '52 '77 (PA) C.1044 B.A. L.1292 J.D.
Price, Wanda Kay Hannon '56 '86 C.329 B.A. L.575 J.D.
Putonen, Derek A. '68 '93 (VA) C.823 B.A. L.904 J.D.
Quinn, Julie C. '63 '89 C.813 B.A. L.1068 J.D.
Quinn, Thomas Jeffrey '54 '80 C&L.861 B.A., J.D.
Rabinowitz, Robert Ira '57 '83 (NJ) C.30 B.A. L.1162 J.D.
Rademacher, Mark A. '70 '98 C.597 B.S.M.E. L.1218 J.D.
Raevis, Robert '57 '84 C.816 B.E. L.1292 J.D.
Rauen, James A. '59 '85 (MD) C.145 B.A. L.945 J.D.
Regan, J. Brendan '72 '98 (MN) C&L.602 B.A., J.D.
Reggy, Auma Ngesa '70 '96 (MD) C.1305 B.A. L.329 J.D.
Reichle, Karin M. '60 '88 (PA) C.228 B.S.E. L.1209 J.D.
Reihner, David C. '46 '74 (PA) C.901 A.B. L.229 J.D.
Reiley, Don C., III '39 '73 (PA) C.264 A.B. L.30 J.D.
Reynolds, Bruce A. '40 '73 (VA) C.184 B.S.E.E. L.276 J.D.
Richards, Leslie L '71 '97 (TX) C.845 B.B.A. L.744 J.D.
Richter, Sheldon J. '44 '73 C.608 B.I.E. L.273 J.D.
Ritchie, Branden Robert '74 '99 (VA) C.945 B.A. L.1209 J.D.
Rizzo, Nicholas S. '30 '59 C.754 B.S. L.276 J.D.
Robinson, Douglas W. '45 '75 (MD) C.612 B.S. L.276 J.D.
Robinson, Elliott S. '69 '95 (PA) C.1373 B.S. L.329 J.D.
Rodriguez, John D. '74 '00 (AL) C.806 B.A. L.192 J.D.
Rodriguez, Joseph C. '— '00 C.846 B.S. L.312 J.D.
Rogers, Gerard F. '— '87 C.454 B.A. L.1202 J.D.
Rolla, Joseph J., Jr. '50 '84 (VA) C.446 B.S. L.30 J.D.
Roskos, Joseph W. '38 '67 (VA) C.816 B.E. L.945 LL.B.
Rossman, Mary J. '50 '79 (CA) C.879 B.A. L.93 J.D.
Roth, Jason I. '74 '99 (MD) C.860 B.A. L.245 J.D.
Ruehl, Charles A. '32 '72 C.610 B.S.E.E. L.128 J.D.
Rupp, Brian A. '70 '98 C.877 B.A. L.770 J.D.
Rupp, Teresa M. '54 '80 (NY) C.116 B.A. L.607 J.D.
Rutland, Barbara A. '62 '91 C.30 B.A. L.180 J.D.
Ryan, Karyn K. '64 '89 C.645 B.S. L.273 J.D.
Salemi, Dominick J. '56 '83 C.602 B.A. L.896 J.D.
Sams, J. David '49 '75 (TN) C.198 B.A. L.880 J.D.
Santamauro, Jon P. '70 '99 (VA) C.454 B.S.E.E. L.273 J.D.
Santomartino, Martha Lewis '64 '89 (MD) C.446 B.A. L.64 J.D.
Sauers, William J. '72 '97 C.1113 B.S. L.884 J.D.
Saunders, Andrea D. '67 '93 C.999 B.S. L.64 J.D.
Sawtelle, Henry G. '71 '97 (NY) C.453 S.B. L.861 J.D.
Schafer, Richard E. '46 '75 (VA) C.475 B.S. L.276 J.D.
Schofer, Joseph L. '28 '57 C.999 B.S. L.273 LL.B.
Schor, Kenneth M. '49 '78 (MD) C.563 B.E.Che. L.64 J.D.
Schwartz, Jordan M. '60 '87 (NY) C.1365 B.A. L.1009 J.D.
Seegars, Gerald C. '61 '91 (MD) C.1044 B.A. L.273 J.D.
Seeherman, Ellen J. '50 '75 (PA) C.1036 A.B. L.569 J.D.
Seidleck, Brian K. '71 '99 (MD) C.446 B.S. L.64 J.D.
Shallant, David E. '47 '72 (NC) C&L.575 A.B., J.D.
Shanahan, Wm. Patrick '58 '90 (VA) C.1209 B.S. L.1048 J.D.
Shanoski, Paul '73 '99 (VA) C.8 B.S. L.1218 J.D.
Sharper, Samuel E., Jr. '55 '86 C.85 B.S. L.329 J.D.
Shaw, Gareth D. '34 '63 (MD) C.999 B.S.E.E. L.64 LL.B.
Shaw, Thomas V. '61 '89 (FL) C.273 B.A. L.472 J.D.
Shay, Frederick B. '22 '60 C.116 B.S. L.276 J.D.
Sheer, Richard M. '43 '72 (MD) C&L.446 B.S., J.D.
Sheffield, Shari L. '69 '96 (VA) C.811 B.A. L.329 J.D.
Shella, Melissa '67 '93 (VA) C.254 B.A. L.893 J.D.
Sherr, Cristina O. '62 '94 C.999 B.A. L.1375 J.D.
Shriver, James Allen, II '72 '98 (VA) C&L.923 B.S.M.E., J.D.
Silverberg, Fred Andrew '53 '81 (VA) C.337 B.S. L.1209 J.D.
Simms, Rany L. '47 '72 (MD) C&L.339 B.A., J.D.
Skoro, Linda '48 '81 (FL) C&L.260 B.A., J.D.
Sloan, Cynthia M. '47 '89 (VA) C.280 B.A. L.1209 J.D.
Slonim, Hope E. '61 '91 (PA) C.183 B.A. L.273 J.D.
Smiga, Howard '64 '90 C.326 B.S. L.201 J.D.
Smith, Anthony '69 '98 (MD) C.112 B.A. L.446 J.D.
Smith, Bridgett Garrett '68 '94 (MD) C.893 B.A. L.446 J.D.
Smith, Esther Belenker '55 '86 C.150 B.S. L.276 J.D.
Smith, Jerry '47 '75 (VA) C.910 B.S. L.273 J.D.
Smith, Jyll A. '59 '89 (VA) C.575 B.A. L.329 J.D.
Smith, Matthew S. '61 '88 (OH) C&L.608 B.S., J.D.
Smith, Michael Lee '61 '86 (TX) C.326 B.A. L.796 J.D.
Smith, Rebecca A. '69 '94 (IL) C.597 B.A. L.209 J.D.
Smith, William F. '50 '77 (VA) C.277 B.Ch.E. L.64 J.D.
Snapp, Tina L. '60 '91 C.893 B.A. L.1209 J.D.
Snyder, Nelson B., III '69 '00 C.1070 B.S. L.945 J.D.
Soroka, David M. '45 '71 C.569 B.A. L.1009 J.D.
Souders, Michael J. '66 '93 (VA) C.945 B.A. L.1509 J.D.
Spar, Robert J. '40 '69 (MD) C.688 B.M.E. L.1002 LL.B.
Sparrow, Mary Ireland '56 '81 C.576 B.A. L.575 J.D.
Spruill, Darryl M. '66 '96 (NJ) C.334 B.S. L.776 J.D.
Staab, Lawrence J. '46 '84 (VA) C.150 B.S. L.1209 J.D.
Stein, Stephen J. '66 '97 (PA) C.30 B.S. L.1338 J.D.
Stern, Ronald J. '42 '70 C.563 B.S. L.537 J.D.
Stevenson, Philip H. '— '97 (VA) L.259 J.D.
Stine, David H. '54 '81 (PA) C.665 B.A. L.588 J.D.
Stokols, Gwen P. '68 '96 (VA) C.705 B.A. L.273 J.D.
Stoll, Robert L. '56 '86 (MD) C.446 B.S. L.128 J.D.
Stoner, Bruce H., Jr. '48 '84 (VA) C.645 B.S. L.30 J.D.
Straser, Richard A. '45 '75 (PA) C.273 B.A. L.896 J.D.
Strecker, Gerard R. '39 '67 (VA) C.223 B.S.E.E. L.273 LL.B.
Striegel, Adam C. '63 '88 C.112 B.A. L.1065 J.D.
Strzyz, Karen M. '70 '96 (NY) C.107 B.S. L.1048 J.D.
Suarez, Maria-Victoria '73 '97 (VA) C.259 B.A. L.30 J.D.
Sussman, Ronald R. '51 '82 (MI) C.475 B.A. L.215 J.D.
Swain, Michele-Lynn J. '65 '92 (PA) C.302 B.S. L.128 J.D.
Sweeney, Megan R. '74 '99 (PA) C.128 B.A. L.1292 J.D.
Sykes, Angela D. '59 '88 (VA) C.861 B.S. L.446 J.D.
Szoke, Michael A. '54 '79 (OH) C.222 B.A. L.607 J.D.
Taylor, Craig D. '47 '82 (PA) C.329 B.A. L.574 J.D.
Therkorn, Ernest G. '51 '77 C.688 B.S. L.273 J.D.
Thomas, Amy E. '62 '97 (NC) C.871 B.S. L.575 J.D.
Thomas, James D. '46 '79 (VA) C.377 B.S. L.128 J.D.
Thompkins, Tricia McDermott '71 '97 (MD) C&L.795 B.A., J.D.
Thompson, Heather D. '67 '99 (VA) C.886 B.A. L.128 J.D.
Tierney, Margery A. '— '83 (VA) C.1044 B.A. L.1356 J.D.
Tierney, Michael P. '66 '91 C&L.911 B.S., J.D.
Timberlake, Edward, Jr. '66 '00 (NC) C.575 B.A. L.896 J.D.
Tingley, John C. '42 '74 (PA) C.445 B.S. L.64 J.D.
Tinyk, Michael D. '68 '98 (CO) C.319 B.A. L.1194 J.D.
Tolin, Gerald P. '45 '73 (VA) C.588 B.S.M.E. L.30 J.D.
Tolpin, Brett '71 '96 (WA) C.352 B.A. L.285 J.D.
Tone, David A. '41 '73 (VA) C.971 B.S. L.30 J.D.
Toupin, James A. '52 '77 C.813 A.B. L.1066 J.D.

Trafton, David L. '39 '70 (MD) C.401 B.S.E.E. L.30 J.D.
Tung, Melanie H. '67 '94 (MD) C.910 B.A. L.273 J.D.
Tyson, Karin '63 '91 (VA) C.459 B.S. L.1209 J.D.
Umansky, Boris '75 '00 (IN) C&L.347 B.A., J.D.
Van Horn, Tawanda '72 '00 C.475 B.A. L.912 J.D.
Vasquez, Edd '64 '98 (TX) C.839 B.S. L.623 J.D.
Vavonese, Daniel P. '69 '95 (MD) C.1372 B.S. L.64 J.D.
Vinson, Brian N. '59 '84 (VA) C.893 B.S. L.1017 J.D.
Vlcek, Tomas V. '64 '90 (NC) C&L.575 B.A., J.D.
Wahlberg, Stacy B. '70 '96 (MD) C.659 B.A. L.273 J.D.
Walberg, Teresa J. '60 '90 (VA) C.688 B.S.E.E. L.1209 J.D.
Walsh, Stephen '47 '98 (VA) C.107 Ph.D. L.1209 J.D.
Walters, Carlisle E. '48 '78 C.156 B.A. L.1202 J.D.
Walton, Kimberly Hubbard '— '89 C.838 B.A. L.180 J.D.
Warren, Charles F. '42 '68 (OH) C.473 A.B. L.607 J.D.
Waters-Perez, Kathryn '69 '96 (PA) C.446 B.A. L.1338 J.D.
Watkins, William P., III '57 '95 (VA) C.223 M.S. L.1356 J.D.
Watson, Robert C. '46 '92 (VA) C.1213 B.S. L.446 J.D.
Wayner, William E. '34 '66 C.1027 B.S. L.30 J.D.
Weber, Brian '65 '91 C.221 B.A. L.352 J.D.
Webster, W. Michael '68 '98 (VA) C.347 B.A. L.1339 J.D.
Weimer, Caroline Fong '65 '96 (MD) C.145 B.A. L.446 J.D.
Weldon, Kevin P. '60 '91 (PA) C.665 B.S.M.E. L.1209 J.D.
Wells, Kelley L. '63 '88 (OK) C.612 B.S. L.623 J.D.
Wells, Kenneth B. '67 '94 (VA) C.867 B.S.E.E. L.273 J.D.
Weltsch, Keith Alan '73 '98 (MD) C.645 B.A. L.273 J.D.
Wendel, Helen R. '36 '73 (VA) C.188 A.B. L.273 J.D.
Westin, Edward P. '53 '79 (NY) C.1029 B.S. L.107 J.D.
Weston, Carl Brandt '58 '86 (CA) C.797 B.A. L.1148 J.D.
Whealan, John M. '63 '91 C.884 B.A. L.309 J.D.
Whitehead, Carl, Jr. '— '00 (MD) C.329 B.S.E.E. L.1002 J.D.
Will, Nora Buchanan '61 '87 (PA) C.754 B.S. L.128 J.D.
Williams, Archie Edward, Jr. '38 '78 (NY) C.569 B.E.E.E. L.262 J.D.
Williams, Irene D. '58 '87 C.37 B.A. L.893 J.D.
Williams, R. Ellsworth '54 '82 (PA) C.302 L.692 J.D.
Willis, Pamela Y. '71 '98 (NJ) C.811 B.A. L.831 J.D.
Wilson, Angela B. '— '91 C.302 B.A. L.945 J.D.
Winter, Elizabeth J. '— '86 C.846 B.A. L.30 J.D.
Winters, Sherman D. '45 '74 C.216 B.Sci. L.273 J.D.
Wise, Robert E. '50 '77 C.846 B.S. L.796 J.D.
Wiseman, Michelle S. Adams '47 '82 (VA) C.347 B.S. L.904 J.D.
Wiseman, Morris '26 '66 C.223 B.S. L.273 J.D.
Witz, Jean C. '59 '94 (PA) L.273 J.D.
Wolff, John H. '— '69 (NY) C.563 B.M.E. L.1009 J.D.
Wolfington, Ronald E. '47 '74 C&L.575 A.B., J.D.
Wong, Albert K. '63 '92 (CA) C.112 B.S.E.E. L.1067 J.D.
Wong, Conrad W. '60 '87 (MD) C.367 B.A. L.276 J.D.
Wood, Caroline E. '71 '96 (MD) C.30 B.A. L.1017 J.D.
Wu, Elaine Tung-Lin '60 '94 C.260 B.S. L.30 J.D.
Yohannan, Kristin L. '67 '94 C.390 B.A. L.273 J.D.
Yontef, David Eric '73 '99 (MD) C.354 B.A. L.1187 J.D.
Young, C. Skye '— '00 (MD) C.999 B.A. L.537 J.D.
Yuen, Henry C. '48 '83 C.672 B.S. L.999 J.D.
Zak, Henry S. '50 '76 (VA) C.1107 A.B. L.180 J.D.
Zalik, Alice T. '40 '81 C.645 B.A. L.273 J.D.
Zarfas, Louis S. '48 '84 (VA) C.453 B.S. L.273 J.D.
Zervas, Albert J. '59 '85 C&L.893 B.S., J.D.
Zirker, Daniel R. '48 '76 (NY) C.602 B.S.Ch.E. L.564 J.D.

Schoeck, Kristen I. '58 '83 (MD) C.446 B.A. L.64 J.D.
Sherman, Paul K. '53 '83 (CA) C.732 B.A. L.215 J.D.
Shuman, John R. '46 '71 C.569 B.S. L.362 J.D.
Skidmore, William V. '29 '59 C.674 A.B. L.976 LL.B.
Stephens, Andrew G. '64 '90 (MO) C.103 B.A. L.502 J.D.
Turner, Roger J. A. '32 '60 (TX) C.228 A.B. L.846 LL.B.
Whitener, Michael L. '54 '84 C.945 B.A. L.893 J.D.

DEPARTMENT OF DEFENSE

(Vacant), *General Counsel*

OFFICE OF THE GENERAL COUNSEL

Allen, James J. '31 '57 C.188 B.A. L.276 J.D.
Aly, Stewart F. '48 '79 C.674 A.B. L.188 J.D.
Aronsson, Patricia '53 '95 C.477 B.A. L.276 J.D.
Bayert, Nicole D. '66 '91 (VA) C.659 B.A. L.945 J.D.
Beard, Jack M. '57 '83 C.276 B.S.F.S. L.477 J.D.
Boyll, Mark S. '52 '82 C.473 B.S. L.345 J.D. Assoc. Dep. Gen. Coun.
Brown, Kathy A. '54 '79 (VA) C.893 B.A. L.945 J.D.
Buchanan, Elizabeth F. '54 '79 (CA) C.767 B.A. L.1065 J.D.
Burger, James A. '43 '68 (NJ) C.749 A.B. L.884 J.D.★
Casciotti, John A. '52 '79 C.645 B.A. L.276 J.D.
Clary, Harold F. '50 '75 (CA) C.112 B.A. L.276 J.D.
Dalton, William H. '40 '65 (NC) C&L.575 B.A., LL.B.
Davidson, Eliana V. '55 '92 (VA) C.260 B.A. L.893 J.D.
Dell'Orto, Daniel J. '49 '80 C.602 B.S. L.724 J.D.
Drake, Gurden E. '43 '68 (NY) C&L.893 B.A., J.D.
Duffy, Thomas J. '— '74 C.602 A.B. L.823 J.D.
Fersht, Eric M. '55 '95 (MD) C.477 A.B. L.276 J.D.
Flanagan, Kevin '49 '76 C.870 B.S. L.623 J.D.
Frothingham, Edward, III '49 '74 C.885 B.A. L.902 J.D.
Gorman, Robert S. '50 '76 C.446 B.S. L.64 J.D.
Grosso, Karen L. '62 '87 (PA) C.901 B.A. L.665 J.D.
Haddad, Richard '38 '66 C&L.309 A.B., LL.B.
Haynes, William J., II '58 '83 C.198 B.A. L.309 J.D.
Hintz, Kimberly '65 '99
Kanamine, Ann M. '53 '79 C.696 B.A. L.1202 J.D.
Koffsky, Paul S. '51 '77 C.309 A.B. L.178 J.D.
McBride, Barbara A. '56 '80 C.893 B.A. L.245 J.D.
Morgan, Tom G. '44 '69 C.188 A.B. L.982 J.D.
Mouyal, Marsha E. '46 '78 C.1365 B.A. L.273 J.D.
Musselman, Donald G. '46 '74 (PA) C.509 B.A. L.208 J.D.
Nathan, Harvey J. '45 '70 C.102 B.A. L.273 J.D.
Neubauer, Ronald G. '31 '60 (WA) C&L.911 B.A., LL.B.
Newman, Melvin D. '51 '79 (AL) C.1091 B.A. L.16 J.D.
Pitkin, Roger F. '43 '68 (NY) C.930 B.A. L.178 J.D.
Reed, Robert E. '48 '72 C.184 B.S. L.818 J.D.
Reyes, William F. '59 '84 C.436 B.A. L.659 J.D.
Russell, Shauna D. '54 '80 C.37 B.A. L.273 J.D.
Ryder, Christopher F.D. '59 '85 (NY) C.95 B.A. L.976 J.D.
Schwartz, Robert S. '50 '77 C.999 B.A. L.245 J.D.
Schwenk, James R. '49 '78 C.871 B.S. L.30 J.D.★
Sharetts-Sullivan, B. Helen '49 '78 (PA) C.651 B.S. L.665 J.D.
Shelley, Henry C., Jr. '55 '81 (MA) C.321 B.A. L.818 J.D.
Smyser, James O. '44 '69 (OR) C.335 B.A. L.950 J.D.
Taylor, Robert S. '50 '75 C&L.309 A.B., J.D.
Van Ness, James G. '49 '74 (IA) C.350 B.S. L.352 J.D.
Wiegmann, J. Bradford '66 '92 C.228 A.B. L.309 J.D.
Yannello, Karen M. '52 '77 C.945 B.A. L.893 J.D.
Yonish, Brian G. '58 '83 C&L.190 B.A., J.D.★

DEFENSE LEGAL SERVICES AGENCY

Standards of Conduct Office

Green, Jeffrey A. '57 '84 C.597 B.A. L.910 J.D.
Mason, Gail D. '48 '87 C.820 B.A. L.276 J.D.
Stoss, Robert F. '47 '77 C.871 B.S. L.276 J.D.

Legislative Reference Service

Brick, Samuel T., Jr. '42 '67 (MD) C.659 B.A. L.446 J.D.

Defense Office of Hearings & Appeals

Benson, Pamela C. '65 '90 (OH) C.608 B.A. L.117 J.D.
Billett, Jeffrey D. '52 '78 C&L.893 B.A., J.D.
Braeman, Kathryn M. '40 '75 C.597 B.A. L.546 J.D.
Cefola, Richard A. '46 '72 (PA) C&L.665 B.A., J.D.
Erck, John R. '43 '68 (IN) C&L.879 B.A., LL.B.
Fields, William S. '54 '79 C.893 B.A. L.945 J.D.
Gales, Robert R. '41 '66 C.611 B.A. L.823 J.D.
Heiny, Claude R., II '53 '78 (IA) C.162 B.A. L.365 J.D.
Hipple, Michael D. '49 '74 (PA) C.276 B.A. L.884 J.D.
Kopocis, Christine M. '55 '80 (VA) C.702 B.S. L.945 J.D.
Leonard, Michael H. '62 '87 (ND) C&L.585 B.A., J.D.
Lokey, Darlene D. '57 '84 (IL) C.112 B.A. L.1049 J.D.
Malone, Matthew E. '57 '93 (VA) C.276 B.S. L.1356 J.D.
Matchinski, Elizabeth M. '56 '84 (OK) C.951 B.A. L.623 J.D.
Metz, John G., Jr. '54 '80 (VA) C.945 A.B. L.128 J.D.
Ra'anan, Michael '58 '83 (MA) C.103 A.B. L.94 J.D.
Ross, Wilford H. '54 '80 (NE) C&L.190 B.S., J.D.
Russell-Hunter, Peregrine D. '64 '90 C.823 B.A. L.597 J.D.
Sax, Barry M. '39 '68 C.112 B.A. L.1066 J.D.
Schachter, Leon J. '42 '67 C.339 B.S. L.597 J.D.
Silber, Jerome H. '35 '59 C&L.966 B.S., LL.B.
Smallin, Jean E. '47 '89 (TX) C.208 B.A. L.326 J.D.
Testan, Joseph S. '57 '81 (CA) C.831 B.A. L.809 J.D.

Defense Contract Audit Agency

Bley, Paul N. '55 '80 (WI) C&L.966 B.B.A., J.D.
Mitchell, Paul C. '41 '67 (WA) C&L.911 B.S., J.D.
Moberley, Kirk B., Jr. '45 '71 (KY) C&L.383 B.A., J.D.

Defense Intelligence Agency

Berry, Robert H., Jr. '43 '76 (CO) C.259 B.A. L.208 J.D.
MacKay, Bruce M. '52 '94 (CA) C.446 B.A. L.101 J.D.
McElligott, Michael J. '49 '76 (ND) C.770 B.A. L.285 J.D.
Meyer, Carl F., Jr. '38 '69 C.150 B.S. L.972 J.D.
Rivera, Nancy '64 '91 (TX) C&L.846 B.S., J.D.
Thornock, John R. '35 '60 (ID) C&L.336 B.A., J.D.

Defense Security Service

Fraude, Jay P. '61 '86 (AZ) C&L.36 B.A., J.D.
Meisner, Roland D. '57 '82 (IN) C.972 B.S. L.879 J.D.
Shaklik, Christine A. '— '93 (CA) C.169 B.A. L.770 J.D.

Defense Logistics Agency

Burton, Robert A. '53 '80 C.945 B.A. L.893 J.D.
Chadick, Mary Susan '47 '72 (TX) C.802 B.A. L.846 J.D.
Drost, Catherine S. '52 '79 (PA) C.651 B.A. L.1017 J.D.
Faris, Jean Marie '62 '88 (MA) C.93 B.A. L.818 J.D.
Ficker, Rodney H. '46 '73 C.103 A.B. L.276 J.D.
Finnegan, Richard N. '40 '69 (TX) C&L.326 B.S., J.D.
Grant, Elizabeth M. '56 '81 C.188 B.A. L.273 J.D.
Haris, Kim N. '65 '91 (MD) C.945 B.A. L.1209 J.D.
Kaufer, Howard M. '57 '82 C.446 B.A. L.273 J.D.
Lussier, Normand V. '44 '72 (CA) C.763 B.A. L.1065 J.D.
Miarecki, Edmund A. '46 '72 C.823 B.A. L.128 J.D.
Pavlak, Michele S. '— '90 (PA) C.145 B.A. L.229 J.D.
Perry, Carolyn J. '54 '79 C.588 B.A. L.273 J.D.
Saviet, Richard D. '50 '75 C.659 B.A. L.904 J.D.

National Imagery and Mapping Agency

Bahr, Barbara J. '56 '82 (IL) C.502 B.S.W. L.339 J.D.
Bailey, Susan Heller '51 '86 (MD) C.188 B.S. L.904 J.D.
Bedlivy, Dawn V. '68 '93 (NJ) C.705 B.A. L.1292 J.D.
Bishop, Howard S., Jr. '47 '75 (IL) C.910 B.S. L.502 J.D.
Cox, Donald F., Jr. '67 '92 (MD) C.446 B.A. L.64 J.D.
Davis, Langston C. '39 '78 C.39 B.A. L.1003 J.D.
Deranger, Andrew H. '53 '81 (MD) C.367 B.A. L.446 J.D.
Ford, Caroline A. '55 '82 (IL) C.93 B.A. L.734 J.D.
Hagberg, Viola Wilgus '52 '78 (OK) C.269 B.A. L.862 J.D.
Hageman, Hilary Lee '68 '95 (NY) C.881 B.A. L.245 J.D.
Hayden, Diane DePriest '54 '85 C.273 B.A. L.1209 J.D.
Hill, David R. '54 '79 (KY) C.421 B.A. L.228 J.D.
Jennings, Laura S. '60 '86 (CA) C.822 B.A. L.464 J.D.
Obloy, Edward J. '48 '73 C.610 B.B.A. L.851 J.D.
Olson, Larry J. '49 '77 (MN) C.491 B.A. L.494 J.D.

DEPARTMENT OF DEFENSE (Continued)

Phifer, Howard Middleton, Jr. ... '54 '82 C.674 A.B. L.30 J.D.
Pittman, Margaret L. ... '50 '92 (MI) C.477 B.A. L.912 J.D.
Rickert, Jack ... '63 '88 (PA) C.831 B.A. L.128 J.D.
Ritter, Barbara R. ... '62 '92 C.446 B.S. L.30 J.D.
Sande, Kermit A. ... '43 '68 C.56 B.A. L.793 J.D.
Slattery, Mary F. ... '50 '74 C&L.900 B.A., J.D.
Sumption, Nancy ... '— '91 (MN) C.747 B.A. L.831 J.D.
Webster, Denise ... '53 '79 (MA) C.645 B.A. L.818 J.D.
Wilbur, Carl E. ... '46 '79 C.311 B.A. L.30 J.D.
Willess, Thomas N. ... '45 '74 C.840 B.B.A. L.744 J.D.

Defense Threat Reduction Agency

Beck, Susana S. ... '53 '80 (TX) C&L.69 B.A., J.D.
Brittigan, Robert L. ... '42 '67 (OH) C&L.608 B.S., J.D.
Burns, John R. ... '57 '86 C.397 B.A. L.276 J.D.
Contento, Denise P. ... '54 '79 (MA) C.1044 B.S. L.1202 J.D.
Durant, James M., III ... '64 '90 (PA) C&L.329 B.A., J.D.★
Heddings, Raymond E. ... '54 '94 C.499 B.A. L.190 J.D.
Rickard, David C. ... '47 '72 (PA) C.390 A.B. L.884 J.D.

Department of Defense Education Activity

Bergosh, Gary L. ... '67 '92 (FL) C.1176 B.A. L.1015 J.D.
Davis, Joseph M. ... '49 '74 C.776 B.A. L.744 J.D.
Garrett, Kemble H. ... '46 '86 C.888 B.A. L.383 J.D.
Schmidt, Ronald W. ... '48 '77 (TX) C.805 B.B.A. L.744 J.D.
Sutemeier, Robert E. ... '47 '72 (MO) C&L.734 B.A., J.D.
Terzian, Robert P. ... '46 '71 C.910 B.A. L.846 J.D.
Wenzel, Wayne R. ... '53 '78 C.573 B.A. L.276 J.D.
Witkin, Maxanne R. ... '56 '88 (VA) C.823 B.A. L.273 J.D.

Defense Security Cooperation Agency

Anderson, Larry D. ... '44 '70 (NE) C&L.546 B.S., J.D.★
Cannon, D. Kay ... '54 '81 (NM) C.494 B.S. L.560 J.D.

National Security Agency

Alexander, Renee Ann ... '61 '94 (PA) C.446 B.A. L.276 J.D.
Anthony, Teisha M. ... '67 '96 (MD) C.445 B.A. L.446 J.D.
Arnold, Susan A. ... '45 '71 C.956 B.A. L.616 J.D.
Badger, Peter R. ... '42 '78 (OH) C.299 A.B. L.117 J.D.
Bloor, Stephen Michael ... '57 '93 (PA) C&L.446 B.S.E.E., J.D.
Cerlenko, Ariane E. ... '66 '91 (MD) C.1044 B.A. L.904 J.D.
Champlain, Laura ... '61 '93 (MD) C.198 B.A. L.446 J.D.
Cook, Darrell F. ... '67 '93 (MD) C&L.446 B.S., J.D.
Deitz, Robert L. ... '46 '76 C.478 B.A. L.309 J.D.
DeRosa, Mary B. ... '59 '85 C.893 B.A. L.273 J.D.
Dufresne, Randi Elizabeth ... '58 '84 (MA) C.128 B.A. L.945 J.D.
Frank, Renee M. ... '— '99 (MD) C.879 B.A. L.446 J.D.
Gibson, Richard D. ... '59 '84 (MS) C.10 B.A. L.500 J.D.
Horrom, Michael H. ... '49 '74 (MD) C.945 A.B. L.64 J.D.
Klugman, Robin ... '55 '92 (PA) C.659 B.A. L.273 J.D.
Kominos, Paul A. ... '65 '93 (PA) C.229 B.A. L.1187 J.D.
Mercurio, Diane M. ... '69 '95 C.397 B.A. L.128 J.D.
Potenza, Vito T. ... '47 '75 C.867 B.A. L.276 J.D. Dep. Gen. Coun.
Powers, W. Kevin ... '46 '81 (MD) C.276 B.S. L.446 J.D.
Prettyman, George B. ... '39 '77 (MD) C.205 B.A. L.446 J.D.
Reynolds, Patrick J. ... '63 '93 C&L.276 A.B., J.D.
Smith, Anna T. ... '47 '85 C.446 B.A. L.276 J.D.
Uchacz, Ronald E. ... '42 '67 (MA) C.860 B.A. L.94 J.D.
White, Patricia Cox ... '57 '82 (MD) C.30 B.A. L.446 J.D.
Williamson, Marcus N. ... '58 '95 (MD) C.446 B.A. L.64 J.D.

TRICARE Management Activity

Altschwager, Howard R. ... '49 '77 (MS) C.966 B.A. L.790 J.D.
Bowman, Roberta K. ... '54 '85 (CO) C&L.174 B.A., J.D.
Callaway, Ellen C. ... '60 '85 (OK) C&L.623 B.A., J.D.
Douglas, James A. ... '60 '88 (CO) C.846 B.A. L.117 J.D.
Gillespie, Laurel C. ... '52 '77 (OH) C.1046 B.A. L.607 J.D.
Hansen, Karl E. ... '49 '76 (IA) C.988 B.A. L.809 J.D.
Hilton, Helen J. ... '52 '78 (NY) C.318 B.A. L.972 J.D.
Jacobs, Mark A. ... '58 '88 (CO) C.170 B.A. L.208 J.D.
Lieb, Kenneth S. ... '52 '77 (CO) C.659 B.A. L.208 J.D.
Mascarenas, Fred L., Jr. ... '53 '87 C.1196 B.S. L.208 J.D.
Saccocci, Donna Lee ... '48 '87 (CO) C.1116 B.A. L.208 J.D.
Seaman, Robert D. ... '44 '69 (CO) C&L.174 B.S., J.D.
Shepherd, Robert L. ... '42 '70 (UT) C&L.878 B.A., J.D.
Totten, Richard G. ... '46 '76 (TX) C.184 B.S. L.802 J.D.★
Voharas, William N. ... '54 '81 C.665 B.A. L.273 J.D.
Wagner, Donald F. ... '40 '75 C.611 B.A. L.273 J.D.
Wesley, Gerald A. ... '45 '77 (MI) C.475 B.A. L.477 J.D.

Ballistic Missle Defense Organization

Ackerman, Mark S. ... '51 '77 (NY) C&L.107 B.A., J.D.
Cifrino, Michael J. ... '50 '75 C.93 B.A. L.446 J.D.
Hightower, Judith L. ... '53 '82 (AL) C.747 B.A. L.481 J.D.
Youmans, Robert A. ... '48 '73 (TX) C.846 B.A. L.744 J.D.★
Zanca, William S. ... '46 '71 (TX) C.172 B.A. L.744 J.D.

Uniformed Services University of the Health Sciences

Baker, John E. ... '49 '79 (ME) C.870 B.S. L.1294 J.D.★
Beall, Bradley S. ... '47 '77 (PA) C.871 B.S. L.64 J.D.
Mannix, Charles R., Jr. ... '50 '76 C&L.229 B.A., J.D.

Defense Prisoner of War/Missing Personnel Office

Gravelle, James F. ... '43 '72 (MI) C.591 B.S. L.469 J.D.★

Washington Headquarters Services

Albanese, John S. ... '51 '77 (NY) C&L.1019 B.B.A., J.D.
Brazis, William E., Jr. ... '56 '90 (MD) C.928 B.A. L.446 J.D.
Brooke, Thomas R. ... '43 '70 C.309 B.A. L.477 J.D.
Clark, James M. ... '54 '89 (FL) C.1083 B.A. L.229 J.D.
Embroski, Paul A. ... '62 '87 C.665 B.A. L.273 J.D.
Goldsmith, Gilah G. ... '50 '76 C.681 B.A. L.273 J.D.
Henderson, William C. ... '66 '94 (VA) C.154 B.A. L.273 J.D.
Hughto, Karen L. ... '— '89 C.280 B.B.A. L.228 J.D.
Perkal, Donald W. ... '35 '62 (CA) C&L.930 B.B.A., J.D.
Repka, Janet N. ... '55 '82 (HI) C.312 B.A. L.276 J.D.
Schall, Jenifer J. ... '62 '87 (OH) C.597 B.A. L.8 J.D.

ARMED SERVICES BOARD OF CONTRACT APPEALS

Coldren, John I. ... '40 '66 C.645 B.S.E.E. L.273 J.D. Adm. J.
Delman, Jack ... '51 '76 C.994 B.A. L.659 J.D. Adm. J.
Dicus, Carroll C., Jr. ... '40 '67 (MD) C&L.64 J.D.
Elmore, Allan F. ... '38 '76 C.1139 B.A. L.262 J.D. Adm. J.
Freeman, Monroe E., Jr. ... '37 '68 C.276 A.B. L.309 LL.B. Adm. J.
Gruggel, John S., Jr. ... '44 '71 C.478 A.B. L.893 J.D. Adm. J.
Hartman, Terrence S. ... '57 '83 C.823 B.S. L.276 J.D.
Harty, Martin J. ... '41 '67 C.424 B.S. L.276 J.D. Adm. J.
Houpe, David V. ... '45 '76 (TN) C&L.836 B.S., J.D.★
James, David W., Jr. ... '37 '67 C.602 A.B. L.145 J.D. Adm. J.
Ketchen, Edward G., Jr. ... '40 '68 C&L.838 B.S., J.D. Adm. J.
Kienlen, Ronald A. ... '39 '64 (IL) C.602 A.B. L.339 J.D. Adm. J.
Lane, John, Jr. ... '40 '64 C.321 A.B. L.262 LL.B. Adm. J.
Lipman, Ronald J. ... '42 '67 C&L.446 J.D. Adm. J.
Moed, Peniel ... '34 '59 (NY) C&L.569 A.B., LL.B. Adm. J.
Page, Reba ... '51 '76 C&L.421 B.A., J.D. Adm. J.
Park-Conroy, Carol N. ... '45 '75 C.966 B.A. L.273 J.D.
Paul, Michael T. ... '46 '78 C.128 B.A. L.893 J.D. Adm. J.
Peacock, Robert T. ... '47 '72 (MD) C&L.446 B.A., J.D. Adm. J.
Reed, Steven L. ... '50 '77 (GA) C&L.280 B.S., J.D. Adm. J.
Rome, Cheryl S. ... '48 '74 C.945 A.B. L.228 J.D. Adm. J.
Schepers, Jean ... '38 '67 C.845 B.S. L.846 LL.B. Adm. J.
Shackleford, Richard ... '46 '76 C.576 B.A. L.329 J.D. Adm. J.
Stempler, Mark N. ... '51 '76 C.893 B.S. L.276 J.D. Adm. J.
Thomas, Eunice W. ... '43 '69 (NY) C.103 B.A. L.976 LL.B. Adm. J.
Ting, Peter D. ... '44 '71 C&L.838 B.S., J.D. Adm. J.
Todd, Lisa Anderson ... '42 '68 C.188 B.A. L.813 LL.B. Adm. J.
Tunks, Elizabeth A. ... '45 '77 C.475 B.A. Adm. J.
Van Broekhoven, Rollin A. ... '40 '68 C.937 B.S. L.69 J.D. Adm. J.
Williams, Paul ... '42 '67 (NH) C.708 B.A. L.94 LL.B. Adm. J., Chmn.
Younger, Alexander ... '43 '70 C.659 A.B. L.273 J.D. Adm. J.

DEFENSE COMMISSARY AGENCY

Alexander, Mark H. ... '58 '86 (KS) C.679 B.A. L.900 J.D.
Baker, Loren L. ... '46 '76 (OK) C&L.623 B.A., J.D.
Bragaw, Rexford T., III ... '48 '73 (OH) C.381 B.B.A. L.150 J.D.
Burr, W. Wilson ... '48 '81 (SC) C&L.790 B.A., J.D.
Clark, Elliot J., Jr. ... '44 '76 (MS) C.497 B.S. L.500 J.D.
England, David M. ... '45 '77 (OR) C.645 B.A. L.629 J.D.
Koren, Philip F. ... '45 '77 (TX) C.363 B.A. L.744 J.D.
Manning, Jay P. ... '44 '70 (SD) C&L.793 B.S.B.A., J.D.
Matheson, Ralph G. ... '46 '72 (MA) C.818 A.B. L.94 J.D.
Rathgeb, Thomas D. ... '52 '76 (PA) C.363 A.B. L.1017 J.D.
Scherer, John P., II ... '67 '92 (NC) C.198 B.A. L.575 J.D.
Seidel, Warren A. ... '62 '87 (OH) C.970 B.A. L.608 J.D.
Sherman, William E. ... '45 '70 (ND) C&L.585 B.A., J.D.

Ady, Howard P. ... '44 '74 (CA) C.1094 B.A. L.1241 J.D.
Alexander, Dwain, II ... '60 '89 (MO) C&L.190 B.S., J.D.
Andersen, Robert M. ... '50 '76 (IA) C&L.352 B.S., J.D.
Armitage, David T. ... '— '78 (GA) C.532 B.A. L.1277 J.D.
Bergquist, Kenneth P. ... '44 '77 (VA) C.813 B.A. L.846 J.D.
Carr, Anthony R. ... '53 '80 (NE) C.546 B.S.B.A. L.190 J.D.
Eatinger, Robert J. ... '57 '82 (CA) C.1110 B.A. L.1049 J.D.
Edwards, D. Rix ... '52 '77 (NC) C&L.575 B.A., J.D.★
Fegley, Gilpin R. ... '51 '76 (PA) C.216 B.A. L.1017 J.D.
Ferrara, Antonio ... '30 '62 (MD) C.446 B.S. L.64 LL.B.
Filice, Marianne ... '47 '78 C&L.128 B.A., J.D.
Fong, Judy A. Lam ... '57 '82 (CA) C.770 B.A. L.1065 J.D.
Franklin, Alfred C. ... '25 '57 C.893 A.B. L.273 LL.B.
Frenette, Richard L. ... '49 '73 (VA) C.347 B.S. L.893 J.D.
Fukumoto, Scott K. ... '60 '85 (OR) C.976 B.A. L.1051 J.D.
Gall, William D. ... '40 '65 (OH) C.597 B.A. L.477 J.D.
Gegan, Jeryl O. ... '44 '80 (MD) C.446 B.A. L.128 J.D.
Gray, Mark Thaddeus ... '59 '89 C.367 B.A. L.446 J.D.
Hansen, Louise E. ... '60 '85 (PA) C.651 B.A. L.30 J.D.
Harrison, Elizabeth ... '36 '71 C.178 B.S. L.276 J.D.
Hejazi, Sharon ... '51 '87 (UT) C&L.878 B.S., J.D.
Herson, Michael ... '65 '90 (PA) C.276 B.A. L.1292 J.D.
Hirsch, John E. ... '47 '76 (KS) C&L.378 B.A., J.D.
Jordan, Mervin L. ... '50 '84 C.8 B.S.M.E. L.1003 J.D.
Kegowicz, Kimberly ... '65 '90 (NY) C.741 B.A. L.201 J.D.
Kelly, Robert W. ... '48 '80 (MA) C.1126 B.A. L.1048 J.D.
Kingsley, William S., II ... '44 '72 (MD) C&L.128 B.E.E., J.D.
Knoche, Karl I. ... '57 '82 (VA) C.1044 B.A. L.945 J.D.
Koepp, Patrick E. ... '60 '85 (WI) C.123 B.A. L.117 J.D.
Lynch, Stephen Thomas ... '54 '83 (MD) C&L.446 B.A., J.D.
Martens, John J. ... '40 '65 C&L.623 B.A., J.D.
Mason, Paul J. ... '48 '75 (OH) C.318 B.A. L.347 J.D.
McClellan, Gerald ... '52 '87 C.94 B.A. L.329 J.D.
McGrath, Brendan ... '— '93 (WI) C&L.436 B.A., J.D.
McLeaish, Laurel Theresa ... '60 '85 (TX) C.846 B.A. L.744 J.D.
Mester, John S. ... '50 '78 (MD) C.321 B.A. L.64 J.D.
Murphy, Kathleen A. ... '62 '87 (VA) C&L.945 B.A., J.D.
Nunn-Gibbs, Barbara L. ... '52 '87 (PA) C.273 B.A. L.329 J.D.
Ralston, John J. ... '58 '83 C.945 A.B. L.128 J.D.
Randolph, William ... '47 '74 C.339 B.S. L.802 J.D.
Reckler, Sherry ... '65 '94 C.273 B.A. L.1202 J.D.
Ritter, Wayne Lyman, Jr. ... '57 '81 (FL) C&L.259 B.A., J.D.★
Rothstein, George J. ... '43 '81 (MD) C.705 B.A. L.446 J.D.
Segal, Cynthia E. ... '56 '85 C.446 B.S. L.128 J.D.
Shaw, Dennis R. ... '— '80 (CA) C.112 A.B. L.1049 J.D.
Shields, William M. ... '50 '77 C.453 S.B. L.178 J.D.
Smith, Michele A. ... '— '90 (PA) C.145 B.A. L.229 J.D.
Spoede, David L. ... '56 '81 (TX) C.946 B.A. L.846 J.D.
Stake, Charles D. ... '43 '73 C&L.273 B.A., J.D.
Summerville, Sarah Falkner ... '50 '84 C.999 B.S. L.481 J.D.

Thomas, Walter, Jr. ... '50 '76 (PA) C&L.329 B.A., J.D.
Travers, Russell E. ... '56 '86 (VA) C.945 B.A. L.273 J.D.
Welber, Kevin A. ... '60 '86 (VA) C.951 B.A. L.945 J.D.
Whealen, John T. ... '29 '55 (KS) C&L.378 A.B., LL.B.
Whitlock, Stephen A. ... '55 '80 (MD) C.10 B.A. L.128 J.D.
Wold, James W. ... '32 '82 (ND) C.477 B.S.E. L.585 J.D.

DEPARTMENT OF EDUCATION

(Vacant), ***General Counsel***

OFFICE OF THE GENERAL COUNSEL

Anthony, Lisa Battalia ... '62 '90 C.183 B.A. L.178 J.D.
Aserkoff, Lisa ... '71 '96 (MA) C.882 B.A. L.910 J.D.
Bardee, Joan Delise ... '52 '77 (VA) C.1102 B.A. L.128 J.D.
Berthiaume, David A. ... '63 '91 (NJ) C.299 B.A. L.276 J.D.
Charboneau, Lynette A. ... '52 '79 (NY) C.590 B.S. L.178 J.D.
Craig, Susan E. ... '49 '76 C.696 B.A. L.976 J.D.
Dailey, Joanna ... '50 '76 C.309 A.B. L.1065 J.D.
Depew, Kenneth C. ... '47 '75 (FL) C.1365 B.A. L.260 J.D.
Deutsch, Nancy Packer ... '54 '84 (VA) C.696 B.A. L.93 J.D.
Dobson, Dana C. ... '71 '98 C.273 B.A. L.329 J.D.
Eichner, Jill Martin ... '59 '84 C.197 B.A. L.477 J.D.
Ellis, Kathryn A. ... '56 '84 C.860 B.A, L.275 J.D. Sr. Coun.
Eshbach, Roseann S. ... '62 '91 (MN) C.886 B.A. L.831 J.D.
Fabia, Robert P. ... '52 '77 C.378 B.A. L.276 J.D.
Finley, Steven Z. ... '56 '85 C.48 B.A. L.30 J.D.
Freid, Stephen H. ... '50 '75 (NJ) C&L.659 B.S., J.D.
Friendly, Deborah ... '63 '90 C.311 B.A. L.30 J.D.
Gault, Pamela L. ... '64 '91 (CA) C.502 A.B. L.1066 J.D.
Gill, Kay Rigling ... '47 '80 C.228 B.A. L.30 J.D.
Goodridge, Marcella ... '— '97 C.659 B.A. L.884 J.D.
Grimes-Miller, Cathy L. ... '63 '88 C&L.893 B.A., J.D.
Hansen, Edwin R., Jr. ... '47 '73 (GA) C.797 B.A. L.280 J.D.
Harris, Lee S. ... '69 '94 C.882 B.A. L.446 J.D.
Harris, Lisa K. Wells ... '61 '86 C.945 B.A. L.659 J.D.
Haubert, William H., II ... '48 '75 (PA) C.30 B.A. L.1049 J.D.
Hess, Jane A. ... '54 '85 (PA) C.648 B.S. L.831 J.D.
Jablonski, Sandra McLean ... '55 '81 (MA) C.103 B.A. L.1202 J.D.
Jenkins, Harold B. ... '46 '71 C.339 B.A. L.309 J.D.
Jenkins, Kimberly Jeneece ... '70 '98 C.893 B.A. L.309 J.D.
Kapfer, Sergio ... '50 '79 C.350 B.S. L.352 J.D.
Koeppel, Dennis P. ... '55 '81 (NY) C&L.107 B.A., J.D.
Kole, Adina Nancy ... '55 '79 (PA) C.1044 B.A. L.831 J.D.
Kraut, Stephen Michael ... '42 '66 (NY) C.563 B.A. L.659 LL.B.
Krim, Daphna ... '— '79 (IL) C.66 B.A. L.178 J.D.
Kristy, John M. ... '46 '75 (MA) C.694 B.A. L.309 J.D.
Lahring, Karl ... '51 '76 (TX) C.893 B.A. L.245 J.D.
Lopez, Francisco ... '62 '92 C.880 B.S. L.276 J.D.
Lustig, Amy W. ... '62 '89 C.347 B.A. L.276 J.D.
Marinucci, Fred J. ... '44 '74 (PA) C.999 B.A. L.831 J.D.
Mason, John R. ... '46 '75 (CA) C.118 B.A. L.94 J.D.
Mayo-Tall, Karen L. ... '63 '91 (PA) C.188 B.S. L.930 J.D.
Mellman, Richard B. ... '49 '76 C.604 B.A. L.569 J.D.
Morelli, Denise ... '61 '86 C.645 B.S. L.904 J.D.
Morhardt, Jeffrey C. ... '46 '89 (VA) C.712 B.A. L.1209 J.D.
Orzechowski, Jennifer S. ... '72 '99 (MD) C.529 B.A. L.128 J.D.
Otero, Jose ... '66 '92 C.472 B.A. L.273 J.D.
Petracca, Ronald B., Jr. ... '56 '81 C.1044 B.A. L.128 J.D.
Pinder, Kamina A. ... '71 '96 C.788 B.A. L.569 J.D.
Riddle, Paul N. ... '51 '77 C.197 B.A. L.228 J.D.
Rosen, Jeffrey B. ... '48 '74 C.264 B.A. L.273 J.D.
Rosenfelt, Philip H. ... '45 '71 (NY) C.659 B.S. L.178 J.D.
Rosenthal, Marci A. R. ... '72 '96 C.188 A.B. L.472 J.D.
Sann, Ronald B. ... '61 '86 C.264 A.B. L.188 J.D.
Santos, Vanessa A. ... '71 '96 (VA) C.676 B.A. L.904 J.D.
Scaniffe, Shelli Dawn ... '65 '91 (FL) C.999 B.A. L.128 J.D.
Shah- Surprenant, Kala ... '— '92 C.569 B.A. L.276 J.D.
Sheridan, Suzanne M. ... '52 '77 C.446 B.A. L.276 J.D.
Siegel, Brian P. ... '58 '83 C.903 B.A. L.659 J.D.
Smith, Mark W. ... '52 '78 C.1019 B.A. L.276 J.D.
Sprague, Marcia C. ... '55 '83 C.197 A.B. L.569 J.D.
Stec, Daria M. ... '52 '77 C.478 B.A. L.128 J.D.
Stevens, Barry W. ... '44 '72 (VA) C.228 B.A. L.276 J.D.
Stewart, Lucinda A. ... '45 '70 (NC) C.915 B.A. L.575 J.D.
Templeman, Lori G. ... '57 '83 C.1109 B.A. L.1049 J.D.
Trepacz, Edmund J., II ... '62 '89 (NY) C.299 B.A. L.567 J.D.
Wanner, Sarah L. ... '55 '82 C.945 B.A. L.910 J.D.
Wathen-Dunn, Peter W. ... '50 '76 C.33 B.A. L.1162 J.D.
Wexler, Robert ... '56 '84 (WI) C.103 A.B. L.966 J.D.
Whitney, Miriam H. ... '48 '78 (OR) C.147 B.A. L.596 J.D.
Winchell, Susan A. ... '56 '88 (NC) C.970 B.A. L.945 J.D.
Winnick, Steven Yale ... '44 '69 (MI) C.976 B.A. L.477 J.D.
Wolff, Russell B. ... '58 '83 C.121 B.A. L.950 J.D.
Woodward, Jennifer L. ... '54 '90 C.911 B.A. L.30 J.D.
Young, Jennifer S. ... '66 '93 C.97 B.A. L.309 J.D.

OFFICE FOR CIVIL RIGHTS

Allen, Beverly Rice ... '66 '91 C.893 B.A. L.575 J.D.
Cantu, Norma V. ... '54 '78 (TX) C.1219 B.S. L.309 J.D.
Choi, Alexander P. ... '68 '95 C.178 B.A. L.597 J.D.
Dorka, Lilian L. Sotolongo ... '62 '88 (PA) C.472 B.A. L.128 J.D.
Foster, Richard L. ... '49 '75 C.475 B.A. L.569 J.D.
Gray, Jan D. ... '61 '88 C&L.329 B.B.A., J.D.
Hakel, Karen E. ... '44 '71 C.494 B.A. L.309 J.D.
Hanrahan, Eileen M. ... '55 '81 (NY) C.724 B.A. L.477 J.D.
Hightower, Anthony ... '61 '86 (GA) C.155 B.A. L.352 J.D.
Hillary, Rosetta ... '51 '77 (IL) C.103 A.B. L.597 J.D.
Hoogstraten, Anne E. Kelleher ... '61 '86 C.918 B.A. L.276 J.D.
Huggins, Nicole A. ... '63 '88 C.216 B.A. L.1017 J.D.
Irvine, Dianne M. ... '48 '78 C.681 A.B. L.976 J.D.
Leeman, David M. ... '45 '70 (WI) C&L.966 B.A., J.D.
Lewis, Cathy H. ... '46 '74 (CO) C.1168 B.A. L.208 J.D.
Lim, Jeanette J. ... '40 '79 (PA) C.477 B.S. L.831 J.D.
Moy, Robert S. ... '50 '84 (MD) C.1350 B.S. L.276 J.D.
Patterson, Lindsay ... '59 '87 (MS) C.797 B.A. L.500 J.D.
Scott-Thomas, Deborah ... '67 '92 (MD) C.276 B.S.B.A. L.446 J.D.
Toliver, Jacques A. ... '57 '84 (PA) C.302 B.S. L.893 J.D.
Tosado, Rebekah ... '64 '90 C&L.93 B.A., J.D.

Bowers, Susan ... '45 '76 C.107 B.A. L.273 J.D.
Kallem, Howard I. ... '51 '78 (VA) C.1044 B.A. L.128 J.D.
Sorensen, Howard D. ... '60 '86 C.754 B.A. L.276 J.D.
Trice, Elisabeth Ann ... '61 '87 (NY) C.880 B.A. L.575 J.D.

DEPARTMENT OF ENERGY

(Vacant), ***General Counsel***

OFFICE OF THE GENERAL COUNSEL

Ahern, Richard F. ... '51 '77 C&L.276 B.S.B.A., J.D.
Asamoah, Harvetta M. ... '61 '89 (PA) C.118 B.A. L.276 J.D.
Barsy, Janet Zoe ... '53 '85 C&L.276 B.S.F.S., J.D.
Beard, Susan F. ... '59 '86 C.668 B.A. L.1068 J.D.
Bradley, Samuel M. ... '44 '70 C.228 B.A. L.893 J.D.
Broker, Anne E. ... '52 '78 C.373 B.A. L.912 J.D.
Bruder, Arthur Perry ... '61 '89 (NY) C.67 A.B. L.659 J.D.
Burgess, W. Gregg ... '61 '89 (AR) C.45 B.S. L.1243 J.D.
Cadieux, Gena E. ... '59 '84 C.645 B.A. L.188 J.D.
Capoferri, Anita ... '61 '88 C.665 B.A. L.575 J.D.
Challandes-Angelini, Sophia ... '— '81 (VA) C.788 B.A. L.1194 J.D.
Clark, Diana D. ... '41 '73 C.788 B.A. L.976 J.D.
Connolly, Vera I. ... '39 '78 (CA) C.112 B.A. L.426 J.D.
Cook, Prentis, Jr. ... '46 '73 C.155 A.B. L.329 J.D.
Cooke, Lot H. ... '52 '84 (VA) C.880 B.A. L.1209 J.D.
Crockett, Don W. ... '38 '66 C.877 B.S. L.309 J.D.
Crook, D. Clifford, III ... '41 '66 C.319 B.A. L.446 J.D.
Davis, L. Dow, IV ... '43 '73 C.623 B.A. L.276 J.D.
Dean, Diana L. ... '49 '77 C.893 A.B. L.1292 J.D.
de Forest, Alicia ... '68 '97 (MD) C.811 B.A. L.477 J.D.
Dennison, William J. ... '51 '76 (KY) C&L.276 A.B., J.D.
DePriest, Thomas B. ... '46 '76 C.228 A.B. L.893 J.D.
Detwiler, R.P. ... '55 '86 C.197 A.B. L.273 J.D.
Dove, Stephen A. ... '50 '77 C.604 B.A. L.477 J.D.
Duarte, Stephen E. ... '— '81 C.676 B.A. L.273 J.D.
Egger, Mary H. ... '52 '77 C.658 B.A. L.201 J.D.
Ferguson, Steven E. ... '45 '73 (IN) C.1229 B.M.E. L.345 J.D.
Fingeret, I. Avrum ... '31 '57 (OH) C.31 A.B. L.607 LL.B.
Forst, Robert L. ... '41 '66 (NY) C.563 B.A. L.178 LL.B.
Foster, Angela Ivy ... '— '87 C.446 B.A. L.790 J.D.
Fullerton, Laura ... '59 '86 (VA) C.893 B.A. L.1209 J.D.
Fygi, Eric J. ... '41 '66 C.885 A.B. L.1065 J.D.
Gervas, Paul A. ... '50 '76 C.445 B.S. L.64 J.D.
Gibson, Joseph L. ... '40 '65 C.69 B.A. L.309 LL.B.
Goldberger, Gustav ... '34 '63 C.041 B.A. L.705 J.D.
Goldenberg, Ralph D. ... '39 '64 (MA) C.309 A.B. L.94 J.D.
Gollomp, Lawrence A. ... '30 '58 C.882 B.A. L.569 LL.B.
Gottlieb, Paul A. ... '47 '73 (IL) C&L.228 B.S.E., J.D.
Graham, Patricia D. ... '52 '83 C.145 B.A. L.276 J.D.
Halpern, Harold L. ... '32 '58 C.659 B.S. L.309 LL.B.
Hanfling, Phyllis A. ... '42 '85 C.994 B.A. L.904 J.D.
Helfrich, Jeanette ... '44 '80 C.378 B.M. L.260 J.D.
Henderson, Robin A. ... '54 '80 (CA) C.1060 B.A. L.169 J.D.
Hoffman, Michael P. ... '44 '76 C.754 B.S. L.904 J.D.
Howe, Lise Courtney M. ... '52 '76 C.228 B.A. L.273 J.D.
Hughes, David R. ... '47 '72 (NJ) C.390 A.B. L.188 J.D.
Jiran, Edward ... '43 '69 C.645 B.A. L.1009 J.D.
Johnson, Linda D. ... '48 '77 C.477 A.B. L.276 J.D.
Johnston, Marc ... '51 '77 (CA) C&L.309 A.B., J.D.
Kasischke, Marc E. ... '57 '86 C.475 B.A. L.30 J.D.
Kelly, Beth Ann ... '64 '89 C.890 B.A. L.273 J.D.
Kemp, Thomas H. ... '44 '69 C.401 B.A. L.930 J.D.
Ketcham, John T. ... '37 '61 C&L.273 B.A., J.D.
Kimbis, Thomas P. ... '71 '97 C.951 B.A. L.893 J.D.
Kirkpatrick, Loy W. ... '31 '57 (KS) C&L.378 B.S., LL.B.
Kumar, Nisha R. ... '62 '87 (IL) C.339 B.S. L.46 J.D.
LeDuc, Edward J. ... '57 '83 C.477 B.S. L.215 J.D.
Lenhard, Joseph A. ... '65 '92 C.911 B.A. L.117 J.D.
Lewis, Paul W. ... '46 '71 C.882 B.A. L.276 J.D.
Liberman Otis, Lee Sarah ... '56 '85 C.976 B.A. L.1191 J.D.
Lucas, John T. ... '64 '91 C.893 B.S. L.1209 J.D.
Madarang, Marilyn M. ... '53 '82 C.856 B.A. L.276 J.D.
Marchick, Robert J. ... '44 '72 (MD) C.223 B.S. L.446 J.D.
Margolis, Eugene ... '35 '61 (NY) C.688 B.M.E. L.276 J.D.
Martin, Kathleen O. ... '53 '80 C.347 B.A. L.276 J.D.
Masters, Janet ... '53 '85 (VA) C.273 B.A. L.1209 J.D.
Masterson, Mary Ann ... '47 '77 C.523 B.A. L.273 J.D.
McRae, James B. ... '50 '77 (MA) C.276 B.S.F.S. L.94 J.D.
Michael, Paul T. ... '46 '71 C&L.190 B.A., J.D.
Miller, Steven Richard ... '53 '78 C&L.569 B.A., J.D.
Monroe, Carl Dean, III ... '60 '86 (AL) C.88 B.A. L.276 J.D.
Moody, Julia Cook ... '67 '99 C.999 B.S. L.276 J.D.
Newton, Robert ... '44 '71 C.410 B.S. L.329 J.D.
Odoulamy, Judy Kosovich ... '49 '80 C.966 B.S. L.273 J.D.
Oliver, Lawrence R. ... '47 '72 (MN) C.699 B.S. L.352 J.D.
Ott, Ellen W. ... '44 '72 C.824 B.A. L.930 J.D.
Phillips, Paul W. ... '41 '69 (MO) C.134 B.A. L.374 J.D.
Pinto, Francine B. ... '50 '75 C.823 B.A. L.93 J.D.
Pulliam, Edward H. ... '43 '68 (NC) C.198 A.B. L.178 LL.B.
Rabben, Robert G. ... '39 '69 C.831 B.A. L.273 J.D.
Renaut, Gilbert T. ... '47 '76 C.722 B.A. L.446 J.D.
Renjilian, James ... '37 '67 C.688 B.M.E. L.273 LL.B.
Ruge, Daniel T. ... '49 '74 C.546 B.S. L.1009 J.D.
Sacco, Thomas W. ... '49 '75 C.1033 B.A. L.1202 J.D.
Schlaifer, Jane P. ... '44 '71 C.681 B.A. L.273 J.D.

DEPARTMENT OF ENERGY (Continued)

Schleck, Peter Michael '69 '95 (MD) C.446 B.A. L.276 J.D. Spec. Advsr. to the Inspec. Gen.
Sherry, Paul J. '46 '73 C&L.93 A.B., J.D.
Skinker, Michael T. '48 '73 C.659 B.A. L.446 J.D.
Skubel, Stephen C. '53 '78 C.321 A.B. L.128 J.D.
Smith, Stephen Page '49 '76 (KY) C.929 B.A. L.228 J.D.
Stephens, William E. '56 '86 (PA) C.1090 B.S. L.574 J.D.
Strauss, Neal J. '47 '73 C.103 A.B. L.145 J.D.
Stubbs, Diane J. '47 '82 C.1222 B.A. L.273 J.D.
Stucky, Jean S. '51 '78 C.914 B.A. L.188 J.D.
Sukol, Judith A. '59 '83 (VA) C.131 B.A. L.945 J.D.
Sulton, Gloria R. '42 '75 C.329 B.A. L.276 J.D.
Sweeny, Janine M. '44 '80 C.542 B.S. L.904 J.D.
Taylor, Jane K. '60 '88 C.788 B.A. L.273 J.D.
Thomson, Margaret A. '48 '87 C.112 B.S. L.276 J.D.
Urie, Matthew C. '55 '82 C&L.101 B.A., J.D.
Waxman, Robert I. '37 '62 C.477 B.B.A. L.597 J.D.
West, Thomas L. '54 '88 (TX) C.760 B.A. L.500 J.D.
White, James K. '40 '65 C.976 B.A. L.178 LL.B.
Williams, JoAnn '48 '73 C.228 B.A. L.575 J.D.

OFFICE OF HEARINGS AND APPEALS

Adeyeye, Valerie Vance '— '93 (MD) C.329 B.B.A. L.276 J.D.
Augustyn, Ann Sweeney '56 '81 C&L.93 B.A., J.D.
Breznay, George B. '41 '69 C&L.309 A.B., LL.B. Dir.
Brown, Fred L. '53 '79 (NY) C.165 B.A. L.273 J.D.
Cronin, Richard A., Jr. '57 '88 C.999 B.S. L.446 J.D.
Fine, Steven L. '60 '88 (MD) C.494 B.A. L.446 J.D.
Freimuth, Janet L. '49 '76 C.659 B.A. L.30 J.D.
Goering, Steven J. '64 '91 (PA) C.378 B.A. L.276 J.D.
Gray, Warren M. '54 '90 (MD) C&L.446 B.A., J.D.
Jenkins-Chapman, Kimberly '66 '92 (PA) C.811 B.A. L.276 J.D.
Klurfeld, Roger J. '51 '76 C.1275 B.A. L.259 J.D.
Lipton, Virginia A. '46 '78 C.994 B.A. L.260 J.D.
Mann, Thomas O. '42 '68 C.910 A.B. L.477 J.D.
Palmer, Robert B. '53 '87 (MA) C.429 B.S. L.477 J.D.
Schwartz, William M. '53 '79 C.309 A.B. L.569 J.D.
VanDoren, E. Barclay '40 '65 C.309 B.A. L.477 J.D. Chief Adm. J.
Woods, Kent S. '53 '79 C&L.477 B.A., J.D.

Becker, Jacqueline M. '67 '93 (IL) C.679 B.A. L.365 J.D.
Crosland, Martha S. '49 '74 (AL) C.822 A.B. L.276 J.D.
Elliott, Russell D. '58 '86 C.556 B.S. L.560 J.D.
Garson, Henry K. '43 '67 C&L.107 B.S., J.D.
Gray, Geoffrey W. '60 '89 C.273 B.A. L.30 J.D.
Hembree, Mary K. '46 '73 C&L.260 B.A., J.D.
Johnson, Harold E. '49 '76 (GA) C&L.469 B.S., J.D.
Klein, Susan E. '46 '75 (OH) C&L.930 B.A., J.D.
Klur, Lawremce R. '43 '85 (PA) C.201 B.A. L.128 J.D.
Lazarus, Linda '51 '76 C.563 B.A. L.904 J.D.
Monlyn, Sylvia McDonald '57 '82 (FL) C&L.259 B.S., J.D.
Palmer, Cynthia M. '66 '93 C&L.309 A.B., J.D.
Parnes, Sanford J. '51 '77 C&L.30 B.A., J.D.
Schneider, Sandra L. '50 '77 C.800 B.A. L.273 J.D.
Shebek, MaryAnn M. '49 '79 C.783 B.A. L.276 J.D.
Sinicropi, Patricia Louise '64 '95 (ME) C.855 B.A. L.1294 J.D.
Slaughter, Leigh '— '88 C.518 B.A. L.276 J.D.
Sohinki, Stephen M. '49 '74 C.665 B.A. L.276 J.D.
Vernet, Jean E. '49 '75 C.475 B.A. L.228 J.D.
Wilchins, Howard M. '45 '69 C.475 B.A. L.145 J.D.

DEPARTMENT OF HEALTH AND HUMAN SERVICES

(Vacant), *General Counsel*

OFFICE OF THE GENERAL COUNSEL

Aibel, Daniel '58 '84 C.881 A.B. L.569 J.D. Health Care Fin. Div.
Altarescu, Louis A. '47 '87 C.30 B.A. L.64 J.D. Civ. Rights
Armstrong, Mary Mitchell '49 '80 C.890 B.A. L.273 J.D. Pub. Health Div.
Azar, Alex M., II '67 '93 C.197 A.B. L.976 J.D.
Bach, Elizabeth H. '64 '92 C.231 B.A. L.659 J.D. Bus. & Admin. Law
Baker, Jonathan A. '59 '91 (VA) C.893 B.A. L.273 J.D. Bus. & Admin. Law
Beckerman, Peter C. '69 '95 C.966 B.A. L.477 J.D.
Bergeron, Richard G. '57 '83 C.431 B.A. L.1294 J.D. Bus. & Admin. Law
Blandford, Marilyn '53 '90 (MD) C.397 B.S. L.446 J.D.
Bobo, Patricia W. '50 '76 C.329 B.A. L.446 J.D. Civ. Rights
Boland, Tara '73 '98 C.188 B.A. L.659 J.D.
Brown, Richard S. '57 '77 C.446 B.A. L.64 J.D.
Brown, Thomas E., Jr. '54 '82 C.446 B.A. L.276 J.D.
Cade, David S. '60 '86 (PA) C.945 B.A. L.446 J.D. Immed. Off.
Caden, Marc L. '68 '96 C.550 B.A. L.692 J.D.
Cain, Kerry Ayers '51 '88 (CO) C.172 B.S. L.174 J.D. Child., Families & Aging Div.
Canfield, Laura E. '62 '87 C.93 B.A. L.823 J.D. Child., Families & Aging Div.
Caplan, Andrew M. '62 '87 C.1036 B.A. L.245 J.D. Ethics Div.
Chen, Shaoyu '— '00 (NE) L.546 J.D. Off. of Chf. Coun.
Chew-Crawford, Debra C. '68 '93 (GA) C.893 B.A. L.30 J.D. Bus. & Admin. Law
Cook, Catherine M. '59 '87 C.821 B.A. L.569 J.D.
Cook, Kay-Ann '59 '87 (VA) C.893 B.A. L.902 J.D.
Craig, Martha C. '66 '95 (TN) C.394 B.S. L.1015 J.D. Bus. & Admin. Law
Dailey, Joan P. '64 '94 C.754 B.S. L.1017 J.D. Health Care Fin. Div.
Damelin, Fara '70 '94 (MD) C.1349 B.A. L.273 J.D. Bus. & Admin. Law
Davis, Jeffrey S. '55 '85 C.839 B.S. L.846 J.D. Bus. & Admin. Law
Davy, Monica H. '69 '95 (PA) C.1356 B.A. L.329 J.D. Bus. & Admin. Law
Drews, Katherine M. '42 '83 (VA) C.945 B.A. L.30 J.D.
Dublin, Robert A. '43 '68 C&L.273 A.B., J.D. Child., Families & Aging Div.
Flynn, Lisa M. '72 '97 (MI) C.477 B.A. L.30 J.D. Bus. & Admin. Law
Foster, Constance L. '67 '92 (NC) C.232 B.A. L.574 J.D. Bus. & Admin. Law
Friedman, Richard M. '49 '75 C.309 A.B. L.276 J.D. Legis. Div.
Frier, Jennifer R. '73 '99 (IL) C.388 B.A. L.910 J.D. Bus. & Admin. Law
Gianturco, Elizabeth Jordan '41 '86 C&L.276 B.S.F.S., J.D. Bus. & Admin. Law
Golland, Jeffrey P. '40 '71 C.910 A.B. L.966 J.D. Health Care Fin. Div.
Gordon, Caryn Beth '69 '95 C.477 B.A. L.94 J.D.
Grabel, Linda J. '50 '76 C.1044 B.A. L.273 J.D. Child., Families & Aging Div.
Hardenbrook, Kristin A. '71 '97 (MD) C.454 B.A. L.884 J.D. Bus. & Law Admin.
Hollis, Debra L. '54 '83 (MD) C&L.446 B.S., J.D. Child., Families & Aging Div.
Hops, Jeffrey S. '62 '91 C.821 B.A. L.569 J.D. Health Care Fin. Div.
Hunsberger, Amy L. '63 '01 C.846 B.B.A. L.1049 J.D.
Jaye, Robert P. '39 '65 C.188 B.A. L.309 LL.B. Health Care Fin. Div.
Johnson, Judith A. '50 '76 (TX) C.846 B.A. L.744 J.D. Civ. Rights
Jones, Jennifer Bragg '71 '96 (MD) C&L.446 B.A., J.D. Asst. Chf. Coun., U.S. FDA
Kagan, Carole F. '54 '82 C.1036 B.A. L.276 J.D. Health Care Fin. Div.
Kanner, Sheree R. '55 '82 C.1350 B.S. L.477 J.D. Health Care Fin. Div.
Keith, Robert E. '48 '74 (IA) C&L.352 B.A., J.D. Child., Families & Aging Div.
Kessler, Carl R. '45 '86 C.94 B.A. L.1209 J.D. Immed. Off.
Ketterer, William G. '41 '66 (PA) C.385 A.B. L.665 LL.B. Sr. Atty., Pub. Health Div.
Kosin, Donald G., Jr. '58 '83 C.597 B.S. L.276 J.D. Health Care Fin. Div.
Kucik, Karen C. '44 '67 C.298 B.A. L.861 J.D. Ethics Div.
Kumar, Mita S. '69 '94 (MD) C.446 B.A. L.273 J.D. Bus. & Admin. Law
Lang, Bradford R. '68 '95
Longe, Janice C. '58 '86 C.475 B.A. L.107 J.D. Child., Families & Aging Div.
Loya, Camille D. '64 '96 C.112 B.A. L.426 J.D. Child., Families & Aging Div.
Lubin, Elaine R. '54 '81 C.188 A.B. L.309 J.D. Health Care Fin. Div.
Lyon, George C. '48 '75 C.588 B.A. L.309 J.D. Civ. Rights
Lyons, Susan M. '64 '91 C.945 B.A. L.145 J.D. Health Care Fin. Div.
Mahler, Christian C '67 '96 C&L.446 B.A., J.D.
Mancuso, Louis J. '46 '73 (MD) C.1122 B.B.A. L.446 J.D. Bus. & Admin. Law
McGraw, Thomas Scott '68 '94 (VA) C.1365 B.A. L.893 J.D. Health Care Fin. Div.
Murphy, James H., Jr. '50 '90 (PA) C.716 B.A. L.276 J.D. Child. Families & Aging Div.
Nelson, Elizabeth Thayer '68 '96 C.118 B.A. L.893 J.D. Legis. Div.
Nesse, Madeline '50 '73 C.178 A.B. L.309 J.D. Child., Families & Aging Div.
Nickerson, Mary H. '69 '99 (NY) C.326 B.A. L.982 J.D. Bus. & Admin. Law
Olesh, Stanley D. '61 '87 C.112 B.A. L.945 J.D. Ethics Div.
Orfield, Sonia Marie '71 '97 (IL) C.145 B.A. L.477 J.D. Health Care Fin. Div.
Page, Leslie C. '72 '97 C.1083 B.S. L.469 J.D. Bus. & Admin. Law
Pailen, Wendy B. '42 '73 C&L.329 B.S., J.D. Civ. Rights
Patrick, Gillian S. '70 '98 (NY)
Patton, Kenneth E. '66 '91 (PA) C.511 B.A. L.276 J.D.
Pennington-Cross, Carla G. '66 '92 C.604 B.M. L.276 J.D. Bus. & Admin. Law
Pierre, Jeffri Thomas '58 '85 C.821 B.A. L.659 J.D.
Richardson, Ami Lynn '69 '98 (CT) C.197 B.A. L.494 J.D. Bus. & Admin. Law
Robbins, Jeffrey P. '44 '70 C.33 B.A. L.477 J.D. Bus. & Admin. Law
Rowthorn, Virginia M. '64 '98 (MD) C.118 B.A. L.446 J.D. Legis. Div.
Russell, Melanie J. '59 '86 (IN) C&L.347 B.A., J.D. Bus. & Admin. Law
Schuler, Laura P. '71 '98 (VA) C.164 B.A. L.893 J.D. Health Care Fin. Div.
Schulkin, Vicki L. '51 '76 C.112 A.B. L.1066 J.D. Health Care Fin. Div.
Shaw, Michael L. '70 '96 C.1044 B.S. L.564 J.D.
Simpson, Christine '71 '97 C.445 B.S. L.64 J.D.
Smith, David R. '50 '75 C&L.1097 A.B., J.D. Health Care Fin. Div.
Sorensen, Heidi A. '— '93 C.165 A.B. L.276 J.D. Sr. Coun.
Stark, Aida O. '62 '88 C&L.677 B.A., J.D. Bus. & Admin. Law
Strojny, Suzanne R. '71 '98 (MD) C.112 B.A. L.904 J.D. Bus. & Admin. Law
Swindell, Edgar M. '55 '80 (NC) C&L.838 B.A., J.D. Ethics Div.
Torres, Meredith '64 '97 (NY) C.354 B.S. L.904 J.D. Bus. & Admin. Law
Tusan, Charlene '51 '78 (PA) C&L.329 B.A., J.D. Civ. Rights
Wallace, Sondra S. '43 '76 C.112 B.A. L.309 J.D. Legis. Div.
Weiser, Amy H. '66 '92 (CA) C.788 B.A. L.273 J.D. Bus. & Admin. Law
White, Timothy M. '42 '67 (MN) C&L.494 B.A., J.D. Bus. & Admin. Law
Woo, Edwin '54 '80 (PA) C.976 B.A. L.659 J.D. Civ. Rights
Woolford, Llewellyn W., Jr. '66 '95 C.273 B.A. L.446 J.D.

OFFICE OF COMMUNITY SERVICES

Harris, Alfred J. '43 '73 C.1115 A.B. L.602 J.D.
Hatwell, Roberta R. '43 '76 C.273 B.A. L.30 J.D.
Heath, James A., Jr. '24 '49 (FL) C.372 A.B. L.362 LL.B.
Horwitz, Carol H. '42 '79 C.499 B.S. L.1162 J.D.
Isralsky, Jeffrey '47 '72 C&L.150 B.A., J.D.
Jordan, Mosina H. '43 '74 (PA) C.569 B.A. L.30 J.D.
Kendall, Leon '45 '78 C&L.329 B.A., J.D.
Lott, Spencer L., II '46 '72 C.966 B.A. L.893 J.D.
Mack, Thomas J. '39 '65 (IL) C.177 B.A. L.145 J.D.
Saul, Richard M. '27 '53 (PA) C.309 A.B. L.659 LL.B.
Valdez, Maria Beatrice '50 '71 C.3 B.A. L.1162 J.D.
Ware, Jeanne D. '26 '65 (WV) C&L.923 B.S., J.D.

FOOD & DRUG ADMINISTRATION

Arcos, Martha '21 '79 (PA) C.055 L.Sc. L.904 J.D.
Arkin, Richard Lance '44 '80 C&L.30 B.A., J.D.
Axelrad, Jane A. '51 '75 C.477 B.A. L.180 J.D.
Benson, Michael T. '41 '77 (NJ) C.446 B.S. L.64 J.D.
Chao, Philip L. '60 '85 C.188 A.B. L.276 J.D.
DeMarco, Carl T. '39 '67 C&L.705 B.S., J.D.
Drezin, Norman A. '42 '74 C.178 B.S. L.64 J.D.
Dutra, Edwin V., Jr. '47 '77 (WA) C.454 B.A. L.285 J.D.
Ensign, John S. '57 '84 (NJ) C.1036 B.A. L.1202 J.D.
Erickson, Margery C. '52 '77 C.964 B.A. L.276 J.D.
Fehnel, Paul O., Jr. '32 '66 C.831 B.S. L.273 J.D.
Forst, Robert '49 '76 (VA) C.477 B.B.A. L.902 J.D.
Hall, Carolyn L. '50 '80 (VA) C.30 B.A. L.1209 J.D.
Howley, Corinne L. '56 '91 (VA) C&L.893 B.A., J.D.
Johnson, Gordon C. '29 '72 (CA) C.339 B.S. L.1026 J.D.
Kimbrough, Carol A. '— '77 C.170 B.A. L.273 J.D.
Klein, Stephen S. '53 '79 C.910 B.A. L.273 J.D.
Kolbye, Albert C., Jr. '35 '67 C.309 A.B. L.446 J.D.
Kuchenberg, Thomas C. '42 '88 C.276 B.S. L.273 J.D.
Lake, L. Robert '41 '67 C.1059 B.A. L.245 J.D.
Lee, Christine Madeleine '67 '91 C.604 A.B. L.309 J.D. Assoc. Chief Coun.
Levitt, Joseph A. '53 '78 (MA) C.188 A.B. L.94 J.D.
Lieberman, Stephen H. '43 '73 (OH) C.667 B.S.M.E. L.1340 J.D.
Mansur, Jean '25 '62 C.378 B.S. L.273 LL.B.
Molinari, Stephen P. '43 '74 C.607 B.S. L.276 J.D.
Norris, John A. '46 '73 (MA) C.696 B.A. L.188 J.D.
O'Shea, Suzanne Matt '53 '78 (IN) C&L.347 B.A., J.D.
Pirt, Nancy E. '52 '79 (PA) C.665 B.A. L.229 J.D.
Price, Richard G. '46 '72 C.749 B.A. L.30 J.D.

Rachanow, Gerald M. '42 '73 (MD) C.446 B.S. L.64 J.D.
Rheinstein, Peter H. '43 '73 C.477 B.A. L.446 J.D.
Steeves, Robert F. '38 '64 C.184 B.S. L.276 J.D.
Tishler, David F. '44 '73 C.690 B. S. L.30 J.D.
Uldriks, Casper Ernest '50 '86 (MA) C.20 B.A. L.818 J.D.
Unger, Steven H. '46 '85 (MD) C.145 B.A. L.705 J.D.
Weeks, Cora E. '35 '66 C.473 A.B. L.273 J.D.
Weinstein, Les '38 '81 C.103 B.A. L.1209 J.D.
Wolfson, I. David '42 '74 (MD) C.446 B.S. L.64 J.D.

PUBLIC HEALTH SERVICE

Carmody, Donald P. '26 '63 C.1044 B.A. L.276 J.D.
Fanning, John P. '36 '65 C.749 A.B. L.976 LL.B.
Hammarlund, John T. '61 '93 C.813 A.B. L.188 J.D.
Hesse, Alice P. '10 '33 L.537 LL.B.
Mardell, Irwin D. '27 '57 (NY) C.415 B.S. L.1009 J.D.
McLeroy, Reuben J. '17 '42 C.273 L.904
Nies, Arthur H. '33 '64 (MD) C&L.276 B.S., J.D.
Oppenheimer, Jack C. '17 '46 C.966 B.A. L.976 LL.B.
Wasserman, Martin P. '42 '77 (MD) C.951 B.A. L.446 J.D.
Waxman, Judith G. '47 '76 C.472 B.Ed. L.30 J.D.

AGENCY FOR HEALTH CARE POLICY & RESEARCH

Hsia, David C. '50 '75 C.311 B.A. L.976 J.D.

Baird, Jane C. '55 '88 C.881 B.A. L.273 J.D.
Barnes, Mark J. '57 '81 C.36 B.S. L.1068 J.D.
Blake, Anne M. '47 '89 C&L.178 B.A., J.D.
Bowers, John S. '39 '80 C.502 B.A. L.273 J.D.
Branning, Earl C. '23 '52 L.362 LL.B. Adm. App. J.
Bueno, Edgar D. '69 '97 (VA) C.145 B.A. L.273 J.D.
Colladay, Coralyn '42 '84 C.999 B.S. L.128 J.D.
Cooper, Erica F. '54 '80 (NY) C.567 B.A. L.724 J.D.
Dawson, Diann '50 '87 (MD) C.1298 B.A. L.128 J.D.
Denkensohn, Sheri N. '67 '93 C.1044 B.S. L.276 J.D.
Drucker, Ellen R. '60 '86 (NY) C.66 B.A. L.1019 J.D.
Fischer, Mary F. '54 '89 (VA) C.107 B.S. L.1209 J.D.
Friedland, Irvin J. '35 '60 (WI) C.966 B.S. L.436 LL.B.
Gershuny, William A. '31 '57 C.229 L.831 LL.B.
Gibbs, Julia D. '50 '75 C.914 B.A. L.309 J.D.
Gitlow, William H. '47 '73 C.156 A.B. L.569 J.D.
Goodman, Susan G. '46 '84 (MO) C.1291 B.A. L.734 J.D.
Grady, Robert J. '50 '75 C.269 B.A. L.790 J.D.
Greenidge-Hoskins, Nicole L. '64 '91 C.103 A.B. L.94 J.D.
Greenlee, Peter A. '41 '73 C.911 B.A. L.329 J.D.
Hadley, Elizabeth Harrison '55 '81 C.976 B.A. L.1066 J.D.
Hays, Louis B. '45 '70 (CA) C.684 B.A. L.1068 J.D.
Hoernig, Glenn A. '54 '89 (VA) C.30 B.S. L.1209 J.D.
Hudson, Helen Clare '48 '77 C.441 B.A. L.477 J.D.
Hyman, Andrew D. '66 '92 (NY) C.178 B.A. L.262 J.D.
Jarett, Linda W. '45 '76 C.446 B.A. L.276 J.D.
Johnson, John M. '48 '75 C.469 B.A. L.280 J.D.
Karpa, Jill L. '71 '98 (MD) C.228 B.A. L.30 J.D.
Kress, Jack M. '— '69 (NY) C&L.178 A.B., J.D.
Leach, Richard A. '59 '85 (CA) C.112 B.A. L.61 J.D.
Lebron, Marion T. '42 '81 (MD) C.289 B.A. L.446 J.D.
Lee, Teresa L. '70 '96 (VA) C.112 B.A. L.273 J.D.
Legler, Paul K. '55 '79 (MN) C.585 B.A. L.494 J.D.
Malamphy, Richard K. '41 '70 C.1062 B.S. L.276 J.D.
Mapes, Paul A. '47 '72 C.1012 B.A. L.569 J.D.
McCloskey, Richard J. '39 '75 (MD) C.705 B.A. L.446 J.D.
McFadden-Elmore, Peggy '53 '78 C.73 B.A. L.790 J.D.
McMaster, Maureen T. '60 '85 (IL) C.424 B.A. L.365 J.D.
McNally, Susan V. '53 '78 C.66 A.B. L.178 J.D.
Miller, Larry A. '52 '78 C.108 B.S. L.273 J.D.
Notar, Susan A. '65 '91 C.966 B.A. L.30 J.D.
Parker, David R. '50 '78 (PA) C.823 B.A. L.477 J.D.
Phillips, Dalton F. '48 '80 (MD) C.569 B.A. L.659 J.D.
Piccione, Joseph J. '52 '88 C.555 B.A. L.128 J.D.
Radinsky, Gregory Scott '72 '97 (MO) C.860 B.A. L.734 J.D.
Robbins, Barbara S. '48 '76 C.787 B.A. L.128 J.D.
Rogers, Suzanne B. '47 '82 C.446 B.A. L.1209 J.D.
Rubenstein, Carl J. '64 '96 (MD) C.273 B.A. L.831 J.D.
Sedivec, Linda A. '46 '78 C.878 B.A. L.575 J.D.
Settle, Norval D. '40 '70 (VA) C.692 B.A. L.30 J.D.
Smith, Merton V., II '46 '84 C.886 Ph.B. L.128 J.D.
Storey, Peter B. '47 '76 (MA) C.976 B.A. L.1048 J.D.
Sussan, Leslie A. '52 '78 C.104 B.A. L.276 J.D.
Tranovich, Andrew F. '43 '69 (PA) C.397 B.A. L.602 J.D.
Vaughn, Jacqueline R. '56 '87 (MD) C.903 B.A. L.64 J.D.
White, David D. '39 '64 C.604 A.B. L.976 LL.B.
Young, Robert W. '52 '81 (MD) C&L.446 B.S., J.D.

DEPARTMENT OF HOUSING AND URBAN DEVELOPMENT

(Vacant), *General Counsel*

OFFICE OF GENERAL COUNSEL

Acevedo, Camille E. '50 '82 (FL) C.846 B.A. L.309 J.D.
Aiosa, Angelo '42 '74 C.331 A.B. L.564 J.D.
Albright, Bruce S. '52 '77 C.529 B.A. L.362 J.D.
Alexander, Donald B. '50 '75 C.821 B.A. L.659 J.D.
Anderson, Boston F., Jr. '31 '56 (MD) L.64 LL.B.
Auerbach, June W. '31 '56 C&L.446 B.A., LL.B.
Bacus, Joseph A. '46 '72 (IL) C.430 B.A. L.339 J.D.
Balis, Steven L. '40 '67 (NY) C.178 A.B. L.309 J.D.
Barksdale, Antoinette '62 '89 (PA) C.347 B.A. L.45 J.D.
Beatley, Patricia G. '52 '76 C.64 B.A. L.1162 J.D.
Belin, Melvin S. '48 '73 C.197 B.A. L.273 J.D.
Bernstein, Carol W. '39 '64 C&L.30 B.A., LL.B.
Bialas, Kathleen M. '57 '82 C.1121 B.A. L.912 J.D.
Block, Frederick E. '65 '93 (NY) C.1349 B.A. L.823 J.D.
Bohling, Gayle E. '63 '89 (VA) C.378 B.A. L.128 J.D.
Bolton, Gregory J. '56 '82 (GA) C.511 B.A. L.329 J.D.
Boyd, Dana G. '54 '81 C.207 B.A. L.276 J.D.
Brain, Deborah D. '59 '85 (MD) C&L.446 B.S., J.D.
Burtschi, Kathleen Furst '63 '88 C.477 B.A. L.208 J.D.
Byrd, Marylea Walker '43 '67 (OK) C.378 B.A. L.862 J.D.
Carey, Harry L. '45 '71 (VA) C.754 B.S. L.128 J.D.
Cassidy, Walter T. '42 '67 (NY) C.724 B.A. L.976 J.D.
Cerny, Stephen A. '54 '89 C.610 B.G.S. L.1003 J.D.
Christopher, Nancy D. '52 '79 (MO) C.741 B.A. L.734 J.D.
Cooper, David R. '40 '65 (VA) C.645 B.A. L.273 J.D.
Coward, Mortimer F. '45 '78 C&L.329 B.B.A., J.D.
Daly, John J. '45 '76 C.363 B.A. L.276 J.D.
Davies, Harry F., Jr. '30 '55 (MD) C.446 B.S. L.276 J.D.
Davies, Katherine '43 '71 C.446 B.A. L.276 J.D.
DeMarco, Anthony J. '42 '67 C.674 A.B. L.93 J.D.
Diaz, Marilyn '56 '97 (CT) C.184 B.A. L.128 J.D.
Dosky, Sharmeen '56 '86 (VA) C&L.1209 B.A., J.D.
Eisenstadt, Mark M. '50 '75 C.966 B.A. L.904 J.D.
Eitches, Edward '49 '75 C.178 B.A. L.309 J.D.
Ellison, Ethel C. '26 '55 (VA) C.999 B.S. L.329 LL.B.
Ferguson, Edward M. '50 '75 (NC) C&L.896 B.B.A., J.D.
Flagg, Patricia Sharin '54 '79 C.696 B.A. L.309 J.D.
Forman, Matthew C. '66 '91 C.446 B.S. L.861 J.D.
Forrester, Althea M. '62 '87 C.145 B.A. L.273 J.D.
Franck, Donald A. '42 '68 C&L.128 B.Ch.E., J.D.
Frank, Elizabeth '59 '88 (OH) C.674 A.B. L.930 J.D.
Gladden, Brenda W. '43 '74 C.129 B.A. L.329 J.D.
Goldblatt, Herbert L. '41 '67 C&L.273 B.A., LL.B.
Goldstein, Steven M. '50 '76 (DE) C.604 A.B. L.930 J.D.
Granik, William R. '37 '62 C&L.309 A.B., LL.B.
Hall, Jeffrey A. '62 '91 C.198 A.B. L.1059 J.D.
Hartenau, Christopher H. '48 '72 (MA) C.103 A.B. L.94 J.D.
Henderson, Bessie C. '51 '88 C.811 B.S. L.128 J.D.
Herold, John W. '46 '74 (PA) C.216 B.A. L.229 J.D.
Hluchyj, Nicholas J. '51 '80 C.128 B.A. L.180 J.D.
Holtz, Rebecca J. '57 '82 (MD) C.518 A.B. L.446 J.D.
Hope, Allen C. '44 '69 (LA) C.1099 B.A. L.420 J.D.
Hopkins, Gains E., Jr. '43 '70 C.999 B.A. L.575 J.D.
Hutchinson, Sam E. '49 '77 (PA) C&L.329 B.S., J.D.
Johnson, A. Victoria '65 '92 (GA) C.788 B.A. L.245 J.D.
Johnson, Sheryl '55 '82 (PA) C.930 B.A. L.329 J.D.
Jordan, Monica '55 '81 C.273 B.A. L.276 J.D.
Kasson, Bruce M. '48 '74 C.994 B.A. L.262 J.D.
Kayagil, Joan Lewis '53 '78 C.473 B.S. L.273 J.D.
Kenison, Robert S. '38 '63 (NH) C.708 B.A. L.309 LL.B.
Kennedy, John P. '42 '67 (VA) C.276 B.S.F.S. L.30 J.D.
Kessner, Audrey Bernstein '59 '83 C.367 B.A. L.276 J.D.
Landau, Vincent R. '30 '54 (MD) C.928 A.B. L.446 LL.B.
Lasner, Richard F. '43 '68 (PA) C.823 B.S. L.665 LL.B.
Laxson, Bradley E. '63 '88 (TN) C.608 B.S. L.880 J.D.
Leon, Barbara A. '64 '90 C.893 B.A. L.276 J.D.
Lester, Elton J. '44 '70 C.54 B.A. L.329 J.D.
Longosz, Vickie Smith '56 '81 (PA) C.651 B.A. L.607 J.D.
MacFarlane, Frances '61 '86 (MA) C.309 A.B. L.276 J.D.
Malech, Robert L. '39 '64 C.188 A.B. L.94 LL.B.
Malmon, Stuart E. '42 '67 C&L.966 B.S., J.D.
Markison, Kenneth A. '47 '72 (MD) C&L.273 B.A., J.D.
Martin, Harwood G. '33 '59 C.918 B.A. L.893
Massman, Kenneth R. '51 '76 (TX) C.659 B.S. L.802 J.D.
McAleer, James P. '30 '66 (MD) C.262 B.S. L.64 LL.B.
McKeever, Benjamin '36 '68 C.309 A.B. L.94 LL.B.
Milner, Michael J. '68 '94 C.705 B.S. L.1292 J.D.
Moran, Michael J. '59 '86 C.436 B.A. L.276 J.D.
Narode, Dana M. '— '86 C.446 B.A. L.273 J.D.
Nash, A. Heaton '37 '64 C&L.976 B.A., LL.B.
Nemec, Gary A. '60 '88 (TX) C.805 B.A. L.796 J.D.
Noonan, Michael D. '41 '66 C.276 B.S.B.A. L.823 J.D.
Opitz, John P. '50 '78 C.546 B.A. L.273 J.D.
Pardo-Kronemann, Jose '52 '92 (PA) C.339 B.S. L.146 J.D.
Park, Betty B. '17 '40 (OR) C&L.629 B.S., J.D.
Patton, Geoffrey L. '45 '73 C.188 A.B. L.273 J.D.
Polatsek, David F. '40 '65 (OH) C.930 A.B. L.309 LL.B.
Polsby, Allen I. '37 '62 C.103 A.B. L.273 J.D.
Pontzer, Peter F. '64 '89 C.216 B.A. L.945 J.D.
Potts, Millicent B. '55 '81 (PA) C.411 B.A. L.329 J.D.
Pratt, Sara K. '49 '75 (AZ) C.1130 B.A. L.37 J.D.
Race, Peter S. '41 '69 (MI) C.813 B.A. L.477 J.D.
Ransick, Myra Lane '39 '83 C&L.45 B.A., J.D.
Ray, Eileen Frances '53 '78 (PA) C.329 B.A. L.128 J.D.
Rennett, Harold J. '54 '78 C.309 A.B. L.477 J.D.
Robinson, Joel D. '35 '60 C.951 B.A. L.178 LL.B.
Robinson, Michael T. '52 '79 (VA) C.966 B.A. L.809 J.D.
Rock, Jeffrey S. '47 '72 (OK) C.623 B.A. L.608 J.D.
Roden, Emmett N., III '43 '73 (MD) C.1036 A.B. L.659 J.D.
Roman, Terri Lynn '65 '97 C.999 B.S. L.472 J.D.
Rothman, Samuel B. '39 '67 (PA) C.659 A.B. L.472 LL.B.
Sacks, Steven J. '44 '69 (NY) C.477 B.A. L.569 J.D.
Salzman, Gerald H. '43 '69 (NY) C.569 B.S. L.1009 J.D.
Santa Anna, Aaron '56 '84 (AZ) C.37 B.A. L.36 J.D.
Schmeltzer, Howard M. '43 '68 C.659 B.A. L.477 J.D.
Shapiro, Barton '56 '83 C.273 B.B.A. L.128 J.D.
Shaw, Stephen I. '57 '86 C.276 B.A. L.930 J.D.
Shorenstein, Ronnie '49 '73 C.823 B.A. L.273 J.D.
Shumway, John B. '59 '85 C.293 B.A. L.352 J.D.
Stephens, Virginia K. '55 '83 (MD) C.788 B.A. L.904 J.D.
Strong, Jonathan '44 '75 C.188 B.A. L.569 J.D.
Swartzbaugh, Jeffrey H. '42 '68 (NY) C.967 B.A. L.477 J.D.
Warren, Walter E. '36 '66 C.260 B.A. L.469 J.D.
Watts, Sally Warner '47 '74 C.347 B.A. L.424 J.D.
Weidenfeller, George L. '47 '75 C.454 B.A. L.818 J.D.
Wiener, Bruce M. '59 '85 C&L.477 A.B., J.D.
Wigglesworth, Leonard '46 '73 C&L.329 B.A., J.D.
Wilson, Carole W. '43 '68 C.881 A.B. L.273 J.D.

DEPARTMENT OF HOUSING AND URBAN DEVELOPMENT (Continued)

Wingard, John P. ....'41 '66 C&L.608 B.S.C., J.D.
Wolf, Mier ....'40 '70 C.659 B.A. L.724 J.D.
Wrin, Evelyn Mittman ....'38 '82 C.530 B.A. L.273 J.D.

WASHINGTON, D. C. OFFICE

Conlan, Russell S. ....'56 '84 (PA) C&L.229 B.A., J.D.
Czauski, Henry S. ....'49 '76 (NJ) C.776 B.A. L.1338 J.D.
Sims, Howard ....'56 '81 (PA) C&L.665 B.A., J.D.

OFFICE OF ADMINISTRATIVE LAW JUDGES

Andretta, Robert A. ....'42 '77 C.871 B.S. L.128 J.D. Admn. Law J.
Cali, Andrea J. ....'54 '79 C.914 A.B. L.930 J.D.
Cregar, William C. ....'44 '69 C.145 A.B. L.339 J.D. Admn. Law J.
Garmeiser, Dori C. ....'61 '86 C.1044 B.A. L.276 J.D.
Heifetz, Alan W. ....'43 '68 C.823 A.B. L.94 J.D. Chief Admn. Law J.
Heinz, Thomas C. ....'41 '72 C.976 B.A. L.629 J.D. Admn. Law J.

BOARD OF CONTRACT APPEALS

Anderson, David T. ....'42 '73 (PA) C.150 B.S. L.273 J.D.
Cooper, Jean S. ....'46 '70 (LA) C.861 B.A. L.245 J.D.
Greszko, Timothy J. ....'49 '75 (MA) C.588 B.S. L.818 J.D.

OFFICE OF THE INSPECTOR GENERAL

Dupuy, John E. ....'65 '98 (VA) C.112 B.A. L.284 J.D.
Hetherton, Judith ....'43 '73 C.702 A.B. L.276 J.D. Coun. to Inspector Gen.
Kemins, Robert A. ....'58 '83 C.1192 B.A. L.1202 J.D.
Kesaris, Philip A. ....'58 '83 (MA) C.299 B.A. L.823 J.D.
Saddler, Bryan P. ....'64 '89 (MD) C.903 B.A. L.64 J.D.

Ambers, Deborah Thalia ....'48 '75 C.216 B.A. L.273 J.D.
Baker, Teresa Lynn ....'69 '96 (VA) C.945 B.A. L.1209 J.D.
Bardack, Paul Roitman ....'53 '80 C.976 B.A. L.904 J.D.
Brown, Luke H. ....'— '93 C.712 B.A. L.273 J.D.
Carroll, Raoul L. ....'50 '76 C.512 B.S. L.724 J.D.
Cashin, Sheryll D. ....'61 '92 (AL) C.880 B.E. L.309 J.D.
Curry, Maynard T. ....'49 '80 C.446 B.S. L.1162 J.D.
Deneau, Irene W. ....'27 '72 (AL) C.028 B.A. L.192 J.D.
Federoff, Carolyn ....'60 '86 C.37 B.A. L.94 J.D.
Gonzales, Ralph E. ....'43 '76 (CO) C.559 B.A. L.208 J.D.
Groberg, Robert P. ....'30 '57 (NY) C.823 B.A. L.178 J.D.
Haines, John M. ....'46 '75 (UT) C.475 B.A. L.813 J.D.
Hampton, Patricia G. ....'39 '85 (PA) C.65 B.A. L.276 J.D.
Harrigan, Robert ....'29 '54 (MA) C.93 L.94
Hedman, Frederick A. ....'37 '74 (MD) C&L.64 B.S., J.D.
Hobson-Phillips, Patricia L. ....'49 '80 (KY) C.999 B.A. L.329 J.D.
Holbert, Kenneth F. ....'24 '51 (TX) C.208 A.B. L.325 LL.B.
Horowitz, Eliot C. ....'49 '75 C.102 B.A. L.1009 J.D.
Hunter, C. Wayne ....'34 '63 C&L.309 A.B., J.D.
Kalish, Robert P. ....'30 '58 C&L.273 A.B., LL.B.
Kaminsky, David R. ....'51 '84 C.94 B.A. L.273 J.D.
Kaplan, Peter ....'43 '77 C.563 B.A. L.569 J.D.
Keeler, Judith A. ....'46 '77 (GA) C.260 B.A. L.245 J.D.
Kuzava, John L. ....'35 '63 C&L.477 A.B., LL.B.
Latimer, George A. ....'35 '63 (MN) C.745 B.A. L.178 LL.B.
Mexic, Scott B. ....'56 '83 C&L.861 B.A., J.D.
Miller, Albert M. ....'31 '58 (VA) C.709 A.B. L.329 LL.B.
Ming, Charles ....'29 '64 (OK) C.623 B.B.A. L.616 J.D.
Morrow, Merle H. ....'41 '66 (LA) C.500 B.A. L.420 J.D.
Mulrain, Lisa V. ....'71 '97 (MA) C&L.818 B.A., J.D.
Norris, George L. ....'13 '54 C.390 A.B. L.537 LL.B.
Papadopoulos, Panagiotis (Peter) ....'43 '78 (PA) C.21 B.S. L.365 J.D.
Pearl, Laurence D. ....'34 '59 C.33 A.B. L.976 LL.B.
Pollack, David J. ....'45 '76 C.966 B.S. L.273 J.D.
Ray, George ....'40 '73 C.217 B.A. L.329 J.D.
Sens, Joseph H. ....'27 '59 C.1019 B.B.A. L.208 J.D.
Sheehan, Kevin J. ....'72 '98 (MD) C.575 B.A. L.329 J.D.
Shields, Cornelius C. ....'33 '57 C&L.436 B.A., LL.B.
Sullivan, Elizabeth M. ....'40 '73 C.423 B.A. L.276 J.D.
Taylor, Jeffrey K. ....'57 '85 (GA) C.838 B.A. L.245 J.D.
Turner, Marvin W. ....'59 '98 (NY) C.329 B.B.A. L.276 J.D.
Villafuerte, Christopher A. ....'68 '94 C.1036 B.A. L.1066 J.D.
Warren, Maureen E. ....'57 '82 (MN) C.713 B.A. L.494 J.D.
Welfeld, Irving H. ....'38 '63 C.102 B.A. L.309 LL.B.
Wilson, Guy S. ....'49 '76 (GA) C.280 A.B. L.51 J.D.

DEPARTMENT OF THE INTERIOR

John Leshy, *Solicitor*

OFFICE OF THE SOLICITOR

Bergstrom, Scott A. ....'68 '94 (KS) C.375 B.S. L.378 J.D.
Blank, Harvey P. ....'54 '79 (OH) C.1036 A.B. L.930 J.D.
Bovard, Thomas A. ....'53 '78 (VA) C.976 B.A. L.893 J.D.
Carlucci, John ....'59 '95 (MD) C.563 B.A. L.893 J.D.
Carr, Michael S. ....'70 '96 (OR) C.174 B.A. L.1051 J.D.
Chalker, Howard W. ....'47 '83 (OK) C.608 B.S. L.862 J.D.
Chang, Wan B. ....'61 '91 C.1036 B.A. L.588 J.D.
Chapman, Miriam R. ....'65 '94 (MD) C.705 B.A. L.329 J.D.
Chester, Beatrice G. ....'25 '48 C.563 L.178 J.D.
Clark, Kristina A. ....'48 '78 C.878 B.A. L.273 J.D.
Coen, Barbara Novak ....'51 '76 C.207 B.A. L.477 J.D.
Cohen, Edward B. ....'49 '75 C.966 B.A. L.276 J.D.
Coleman, W. Jackson ....'53 '78 (MS) C&L.500 B.B.A., J.D.
Conforti, Frank A. ....'49 '76 (CA) C.740 B.A. L.284 J.D.
Crichton, Anne ....'47 '76 C.766 B.A. L.208 J.D.
Daugherty, M. Dennis ....'48 '73 (LA) C&L.420 B.A., J.D.
Dorman, Wendy S. ....'55 '81 (WI) C&L.966 B.A., J.D.
Downes, David R. ....'60 '88 C&L.477 B.A., J.D.
Eisenstein, Eric ....'58 '96 C.446 B.S. L.273 J.D.
Elliott, Timothy S. ....'38 '64 (NY) C.1036 A.B. L.309 J.D.
Fondren, Kimberly L. ....'68 '94 (MD) C.371 B.A. L.16 J.D.
Friedman, Robin A. ....'47 '74 C.959 B.A. L.659 J.D.
Fugate, Barbara B. ....'52 '82 C.914 B.A. L.1066 J.D.
Gayer, David A. ....'51 '77 C.478 A.B. L.309 J.D.
Geigle, Barbara J. ....'53 '88 C.911 B.A. L.273 J.D.
Goldfarb, Joan R. ....'63 '92 (MA) C.918 B.A. L.93 J.D.
Greenwald, Karen ....'74 '99 (MD) C&L.276 A.B., J.D.
Grooms, Thomas Alexander ....'45 '73 C.734 A.B. L.838 J.D.
Hawbecker, Karen ....'64 '90 (PA) C&L.101 B.S., J.D.
Henry, Kathrine L. ....'51 '76 C.280 B.A. L.893 J.D.
Hickey, Michael C. ....'48 '75 C.93 A.B. L.276 J.D.
Inderbitzin, Sarah L. ....'61 '93 (GA) C.446 B.S. L.1059 J.D.
Jackson, Jacqueline ....'50 '92 C.112 B.A. L.329 J.D.
Jasper, John A. ....'54 '83 (KY) C.1161 B.A. L.1162 J.D.
Jesup, Benjamin C. ....'64 '90 C.311 B.A. L.569 J.D.
Kalavritinos, Christina ....'54 '80 C.228 B.A. L.1119 J.D.
Kaswell, Sherry Kinland ....'52 '77 C.446 B.A. L.273 J.D.
Keable, Edward T. ....'61 '87 (NY) C.732 B.A. L.1194 J.D.
Keating, Karen Sprecher ....'54 '78 C.597 B.A. L.273 J.D.
Keep, Scott ....'42 '69 C.154 B.A. L.1049 J.D.
Kelsey, Angela M. ....'54 '89 C.665 B.A. L.546 J.D.
Kilduff, Daniel W. ....'67 '93 (MA) C.860 B.A. L.904 J.D.
Kirton, Paul G. ....'32 '56 (TX) C&L.846 B.A., LL.B.
Koltos, E. Philip ....'37 '64 (NY) C.971 B.S. L.893 LL.B.
Landau, Brenda R. ....'65 '92 (CA) C.112 B.A. L.569 J.D.
Larvie, Veronica I. ....'65 '95 (WY) C&L.972 B.S., J.D.
Leonard, Louis G., III ....'72 '97 (MA) C.276 A.B. L.93 J.D.
Leshy, John D. ....'44 '69 C&L.309 A.B., J.D. Solr.
Lin, Janet H. ....'— '98 (WI) C&L.966 B.A., J.D.
Linscheid, Steven K. ....'55 '86 C.83 B.A. L.378 J.D.
Mason, Milo C. ....'50 '79 C.188 A.B. L.309 J.D.
Mattix, Carla C. ....'67 '95 C.94 B.S. L.276 J.D.
McCarthy, Sabrina A. ....'56 '85 C.145 B.A. L.976 J.D.
Mellinger, Lawrence P. ....'58 '90 (VA) C.797 B.A. L.1209 J.D.
Miller, Scott K. ....'70 '98 (CO) C.880 B.S. L.174 J.D.
Moll, Robert H. ....'46 '71 (PA) C.902 A.B. L.831 J.D.
Moran, David ....'55 '84 (NM) C.560 B.S. L.276 J.D.
More, Robert S. ....'52 '77 (KY) C.93 B.A. L.309 J.D.
Nitta, Kendra ....'66 '96 (CA) C.800 A.B. L.426 J.D.
O'Hara, Kerry Anne ....'60 '87 (WA) C&L.911 B.A., J.D.
O'Malley, Josefa E. ....'— '84 C.909 B.A. L.285 J.D.
Palisoul, Alan A. ....'46 '73 C&L.575 A.B., J.D.
Parks, David B., Sr. ....'38 '72 (VA) C.695 B.A. L.30 J.D.
Pontius, Dale ....'41 '74 (AZ) C.347 A.B. L.37 J.D.
Raynor, Charles P. ....'42 '70 (NY) C.105 A.B. L.188 J.D.
Romanik, Peg A. ....'56 '81 C.475 B.A. L.602 J.D.
Roth, Barry N. ....'49 '74 C.575 A.B. L.276 J.D.
Salotti, Christopher P. ....'64 '95 (NY) C.319 B.A. L.1194 J.D.
Schaumberg, Peter J. ....'50 '75 C.861 B.A. L.273 J.D.
Smathers, John ....'41 '69 (FL) C.674 A.B. L.260 LL.B.
Smyth, Paul B. ....'49 '74 C.855 B.A. L.93 J.D.
Snow, Robert F. ....'62 '95 (NJ) C.1044 B.S. L.1040 J.D.
Sylvester, Cheryl A. ....'47 '73 (WA) C.911 B.A. L.178 J.D.
Taylor, Triscilla P. ....'73 '98 (LA) C.217 B.A. L.803 J.D.
Thompson, Delores Ellen ....'58 '87 C.1161 B.S. L.1340 J.D.
Vinson, Phyllisina L. ....'70 '95 C&L.228 A.B., J.D.
Walline, Megan J. ....'— '97 (OR) C.188 B.S. L.596 J.D.
Walter, Robert E. ....'37 '63 C.724 B.B.A. L.188 J.D.
Watts, David A. ....'37 '62 (MN) C&L.477 B.A., LL.B.
Weiner, James L. ....'60 '87 C.156 B.A. L.30 J.D.
Wheeler, Holly ....'62 '97 (VT) C.502 B.S. L.1194 J.D.
Williams, Pamela S. ....'49 '80 (CA) C.112 B.A. L.1065 J.D.
Wiseman, Maria K. ....'65 '98 (CA) C.112 B.A. L.276 J.D.
Woodcock, Richard J. ....'31 '59 (NY) C.597 B.S. L.178 LL.B.
Woods, Alton ....'51 '76 (PA) C.709 B.A. L.329 J.D.
Young, William Michael ....'54 '77 (AL) C.9 B.B.A. L.192 J.D.
Yudson, Joel M. ....'47 '71 (NY) C.186 B.E. L.659 J.D.

MINERALS MANAGEMENT SERVICE

Anderson, Merrill ....'46 '72 (IA) C.174 B.A. L.352 J.D.
Clark, Platte E. ....'38 '71 C&L.878 B.S., J.D.
Hager, C. Eric ....'44 '73 C.478 A.B. L.273 J.D.
Martinez, Richard R., Jr. ....'46 '89 (PA) C.885 B.A. L.564 J.D.
Roberts, Jane A. ....'50 '77 (VA) C.628 B.A. L.273 J.D.

OFFICE OF HEARINGS & APPEALS

Anthony, Joan Caton ....'39 '80 C.436 A.B. L.128 J.D.
Arness, Franklin ....'33 '58 C&L.506 B.A., J.D. Adm. J.
Ashcraft, Rosalie ....'53 '78 (KY) C&L.383 B.A., J.D.
Burski, James L. ....'47 '73 C.276 B.S.F.S. L.597 J.D. Adm. J.
Byrnes, James L. ....'52 '77 C.229 B.A. L.1338 J.D. Chief Adm. J.
Byrtus, Paul H. ....'49 '81 (WY) C.208 B.A. L.972 J.D.
Clement, Holly Harmuth ....'57 '82 (LA) C.298 B.A. L.861 J.D.
Doyle, Janet R. ....'44 '69 C.201 B.A. L.150 J.D.
Frazier, Gail M. ....'47 '74 C.339 B.A. L.329 J.D. Adm. J.
Grant, C. Randall, Jr. ....'45 '72 C.231 A.B. L.910 J.D. Adm. J.
Greenberg, Sara B. ....'51 '81 C.681 A.B. L.190 J.D.
Harris, Bruce R. ....'45 '72 C.528 B.S. L.945 J.D. Adm. J.
Hughes, David L. ....'47 '75 C.401 B.A. L.276 J.D. Adm. J.
Hunsaker, Hy Dillman ....'55 '82 (UT) C.877 B.S. L.878 J.D.
Irwin, William A. ....'44 '73 C&L.477 A.B., J.D. Adm. J.
Jewett, Richard K., Jr. ....'53 '78 C.659 B.A. L.1202 J.D.
Johnson, Bruce A. ....'49 '74 (PA) C.238 B.A. L.329 J.D.
Kelly, John H. ....'40 '70 C.351 B.A. L.352 J.D. Adm. J.
Kleiler, James R. ....'49 '74 C.276 A.B. L.273 J.D.
Mullen, Robert W. ....'39 '64 C&L.878 B.S., J.D. Adm. J.
Neudorfer, Wolfgang E. ....'43 '71 (KY) C.686 B.S. L.383 J.D.
Parrette, Bernard V. ....'30 '55 C.755 B.A. L.494 J.D. Adm. J.
Price, T. Britt ....'51 '77 C.911 B.A. L.276 J.D.
Rey, F. Cary ....'52 '79 C.477 B.S. L.878 J.D.
Roberts, James F. ....'52 '80 (KY) C.77 B.A. L.383 J.D.
Schwab, Norman K. ....'39 '67 C.446 B.A. L.273 LL.B.

BUREAU OF INDIAN AFFAIRS

Burke, Alan S. ... '48 '74 C.94 B.A. L.276 J.D.
Gary, Arthur E. ... '58 '84 (NY) C.893 B.A. L.945 J.D.
Johnson, David B. ... '59 '87 C.846 B.A. L.188 J.D.
Roff, Jessica ... '71 '98 C.293 B.A. L.904 J.D.
Skibine, George T. ... '52 '77 C.145 B.A. L.494 J.D.
Sneed, Woodrow B. ... '37 '65 C.101 B.S. L.309 J.D.

BUREAU OF LAND MANAGEMENT

Eubanks, Lennie R. ... '38 '74 (OK) C.846 B.B.A. L.862 J.D.
Fry, Thomas ... '44 '69 (TX) C.859 B.S. L.802 J.D.
Hansen, Gordon O. ... '46 '74 (MN) C.747 B.A. L.494 J.D.
Hatfield, Nina R. ... '48 '73 (OH) C.347 A.B. L.1119 J.D.
Hudson, Ted R. ... '47 '74 C.188 A.B. L.446 J.D.
Jorjani, Daniel H. ... '67 '98 C.880 B.A. L.188 J.D.
Nelson, Andrea L. ... '55 '84 C.104 A.B. L.273 J.D.
Niebauer, Peter W. ... '47 '77 (VA) C.966 B.A. L.276 J.D.
Petacchi, Erica L. ... '69 '95 (NY) C.1349 B.A. L.1040 J.D.
Schwartz, Eleanor R. ... '12 '37 (NY) C.331 B.A. L.569 J.D.
Sheehy, Patrick J. ... '49 '74 C.276 B.S. L.744 J.D.

NATIONAL PARK SERVICE

Bradford, Mary R. ... '46 '83 C.446 B.A. L.273 J.D.
Hoogland, Jacob J. ... '52 '78 (UT) C.1085 B.A. L.878 J.D.
Malkin, Karen Anne ... '61 '88 C.367 B.A. L.276 J.D.
Myers, Randolph J. ... '53 '79 (VA) C.893 B.A. L.999 J.D.
Renaud, John W. ... '52 '80 C.951 B.A. L.30 J.D.
Ross, Molly N. ... '50 '76 C.681 A.B. L.145 J.D.
Stone, Renee ... '63 '91 C.699 B.A. L.813 J.D.

OFFICE OF LEGISLATION

Crowell, Barry E. ... '51 '81 C.651 B.A. L.169 J.D.
Lyder, Jane M. ... '50 '75 (NC) C.262 B.A. L.575 J.D.
Simmons, Shayla Freeman ... '57 '83 (TX) C.846 B.B.A. L.802 J.D.
West, Timothy J. ... '48 '74 C.524 B.S. L.64 J.D.

U.S. FISH & WILDLIFE SERVICE

Altemus, Michele J. ... '58 '89 C.800 B.A. L.904 J.D.

Balserak, J. Paul ... '38 '65 C.645 A.B. L.276 LL.B.
Becker, Kathleen C. ... '69 '96 (OR) C.945 B.A. L.1051 J.D.
Gelboin, Tamara R. ... '65 '92 C.66 A.B. L.659 J.D.
Heath, Geoffrey R. ... '52 '78 (UT) C.878 B.A. L.477 J.D. Asst. Solic.
Jodrey, Donald S. ... '62 '96 C.896 B.A. L.904 J.D.
Lobo, Deborah E. ... '70 '94 C.156 B.A. L.273 J.D.
Lurie, Maria Elena ... '67 '95 (NM) C.72 B.A. L.560 J.D.
Simpson, Stephen L. ... '58 '86 C.945 A.B. L.1162 J.D.

DEPARTMENT OF JUSTICE

John D. Ashcroft, *Attorney General*

OFFICE OF THE ATTORNEY GENERAL

Ashcroft, John D. ... '42 '67 (MO) C.976 A.B. L.145 J.D. Atty. Gen.
Ciongoli, Adam G. ... '68 '95 C.659 B.A. L.276 J.D.
Israelite, David M. ... '68 '94 C.947 B.A. L.502 J.D.
Janeway, Kathryn R. ... '56 '98 (IN) C.679 B.A. L.1119 J.D.
Karasiewski, Richard D. ... '51 '89 C.823 B.S. L.1040 J.D.
Nielson, Howard C., Jr. ... '68 '00 C.101 B.A. L.145 J.D.
Page, Allison A. ... '70 '95 C.880 B.A. L.910 J.D.
Prendergast, Richard M. ... '51 '83 (IL) C.589 B.S. L.365 J.D. Asst. Atty. Gen.
Quinlan, Charles A., III ... '49 '88 C.871 B.S. L.602 J.D.
Smith, Sarah Campbell ... '— '99 C.259 B.S. L.362 J.D.

OFFICE OF THE DEPUTY ATTORNEY GENERAL

Collins, Daniel P. ... '63 '89 C.309 A.B. L.813 J.D.
Laufman, David H. ... '58 '88 C.659 B.A. L.276 J.D.
Levey, Stuart A. ... '63 '90 C&L.309 A.B., J.D.
Margolis, David ... '39 '64 (CT) C.103 A.B. L.309 LL.B.
Murray, Patrick B. ... '64 '89 (IL) C.190 B.A. L.209 J.D.
Perry, Philip J. ... '64 '90 C.170 B.A. L.188 J.D.
Sutton, Johnny Keane ... '60 '88 C&L.846 B.A., J.D.
Thompson, Larry D. ... '— '74 C.191 B.A. L.477 J.D.
Wray, Christopher A. ... '66 '93 C&L.976 B.A., J.D.

OFFICE OF THE ASSOCIATE ATTORNEY GENERAL

Friedman, Paul R. ... '44 '72 C.674 B.A. L.976 J.D.
Murphy, Tim ... '29 '54 C.745 B.S. L.276 LL.B.
Onek, Joseph N. ... '42 '68 C.309 A.B. L.976 LL.B.
Sheafor, Catherine M. ... '66 '92 (MD) C.228 A.B. L.910 J.D.
Silverstein, Joan M. ... '65 '93 C.976 B.A. L.276 J.D.
Sutin, L. Anthony ... '59 '85 C.1036 B.A. L.309 J.D.

OFFICE OF ATTORNEY PERSONNEL MANAGEMENT

Barry, Eleanor A. ... '59 '85 C.401 B.S. L.945 J.D.
Cervoni, Rena J. ... '71 '95 (OH) C.529 B.A. L.1003 J.D.
Cinciotta, Linda A. ... '43 '70 C.276 B.S. L.273 J.D.
Gulyassy, Anne M. ... '50 '78 (MI) C.475 B.A. L.912 J.D.
Ho-González, William ... '57 '83 C.178 B.A. L.309 J.D.
Reeves, Catharine E. ... '60 '85 (MD) C.443 B.A. L.64 J.D.
Salans, Marc R. ... '63 '89 C.860 B.A. L.273 J.D.
Smith, Kathleen Conley ... '51 '80 (MD) C.790 B.A. L.273 J.D.
Villa, Aristia K. ... '62 '92 (FL) C.1175 B.A. L.30 J.D.

ANTITRUST DIVISION

Abidin, Elizabeth R. ... '— '97 (MD) C&L.893 B.A., J.D.
Adler, Sanford M. ... '49 '79 (NY) C.688 B.S. L.1019 J.D.
Arnett, John B., Sr. ... '54 '91 (PA) C.475 B.A. L.851 J.D.
Baranko, George S. ... '52 '78 C.602 B.S. L.436 J.D.
Barnett, Belinda A. ... '64 '89 (AL) C&L.16 B.S., J.D.
Bastian, Raphael M. ... '65 '91 (FL) C.276 A.B. L.472 J.D.
Benguerel, Yvette F. ... '61 '86 C.911 B.S. L.823 J.D.
Berlin, William E. ... '63 '88 C.886 B.A. L.893 J.D.
Bickel, David R. ... '44 '72 C.575 A.B. L.326 J.D.
Billiel, Michael D. ... '59 '85 C&L.273 B.A., J.D.
Bitner, Leslie Anne ... '— '98 (TX) C&L.326 B.A., J.D.
Blake-Thomas, David E. ... '70 '98 (MI) C.477 B.A. L.823 J.D.
Block, Ilene Goldman ... '47 '76 C.477 B.A. L.831 J.D. Ethics Offr.
Bloom, Seth E. ... '59 '85 C.696 B.A. L.659 J.D.
Blotner, David A. ... '54 '79 (WI) C&L.966 B.A., J.D. Asst. Chf., Litig. Sect.
Blumenthal, Howard M. ... '52 '76 C.339 B.A. L.309 J.D.
Bobbish, Laury E. ... '62 '88 (MD) C.378 B.S. L.30 J.D. Asst. Chf., Telecom. Task Force
Bodosky, Michael Patrick ... '66 '99 (PA) C.645 B.A. L.229 J.D.
Botti, Mark J. ... '59 '85 C.197 A.B. L.930 J.D.
Bray, A. Jennifer ... '71 '96 (TX) C.839 B.S. L.744 J.D.
Brink, Patricia A. ... '61 '89 (CA) C.605 A.B. L.1067 J.D.
Brodsky, Steven ... '42 '68 C.112 B.A. L.477 J.D.
Brookes, Debra C. ... '71 '99 (NY) C.569 B.A. L.982 J.D.
Brown, Benjamin D. ... '71 '99 C.966 B.A. L.309 J.D.
Brown, Leigh Lani T. ... '53 '91 (AZ) C.735 B.A. L.276 J.D.
Bryce, Rita ... '56 '90 C.880 B.A. L.930 J.D.
Burchuk, Hillary B. ... '57 '82 C.477 A.B. L.904 J.D.
Capone, Joseph A. ... '61 '89 (CA) C.446 B.A. L.61 J.D.
Carter, Erin L. ... '59 '91 (MA) C.454 B.A. L.1202 J.D.
Casey, Maureen T. ... '53 '80 C.262 B.A. L.477 J.D.
Cellini, Dando Belmondo, (P.C.) ... '44 '68 (LA) C&L.861 B.A., J.D.
Chaleff, Michael David ... '66 '96 (CA) C.112 B.A. L.1049 J.D.
Charles, Jillian E. ... '68 '96 C.951 B.A. L.188 J.D.
Chemtob, Stuart M. ... '53 '78 C&L.477 B.A., J.D.
Cheung, Denise ... '70 '95 C.446 B.A. L.309 J.D.
Chick, Patricia G. ... '48 '77 C.66 B.A. L.705 J.D.
Chung, John H. ... '69 '99 (NY) C.597 B.A. L.831 J.D.
Clark, Burney P. ... '48 '73 C.682 A.B. L.276 J.D.
Cohen, Jessica N. ... '63 '89 C.30 B.A. L.276 J.D.
Connor, Deborah L. ... '64 '94 C.473 B.A. L.276 J.D.
Conrath, Craig W. ... '50 '75 (MN) C.429 B.A. L.494 J.D.
Cooney, Theresa ... '64 '89 (PA) C.241 B.S. L.128 J.D.
Cowan, Andrew S. ... '65 '92 (CA) C.976 B.A. L.800 J.D.
Creech, Barry L. ... '60 '87 C.576 B.A. L.575 J.D.
Cummings, Asunción ... '68 '94 C.999 B.A. L.602 J.D.
Davis, Carolyn L. ... '51 '82 (PA) C.645 B.S. L.569 J.D.
DeBusschere, Molly L. ... '47 '81 (WA) C.911 B.A. L.285 J.D.
Dempsey, Justin M. ... '51 '89 C.30 B.A. L.276 J.D.
DeSanto, Sara J. ... '61 '91 (MN) C&L.494 J.D.
Doane, M. Lee ... '44 '86 C.428 B.A. L.902 J.D.
Doidge, J. Richard ... '60 '95 (MA) C.939 B.A. L.188 J.D.
Donaldson, John David ... '67 '95 C.692 B.S. L.705 J.D.
Dorsey-Williams, Juanita ... '59 '94 (TX) C.586 B.B.A. L.325 J.D.
Douglas, Karen Y. ... '58 '96 (MD) C.665 B.S. L.229 J.D.
Dugan, J. Brady ... '65 '90 (VA) C.945 B.A. L.1209 J.D.
Dulmage, Claudia H. ... '47 '79 (OH) C.381 B.A. L.930 J.D.
Duroska, Amelia K. ... '57 '87 C.881 A.B. L.30 J.D.
Eaton, Jade Alice ... '50 '77 C.104 A.B. L.128 J.D.
Edelheit, Susan L. ... '54 '78 C.1044 B.A. L.228 J.D. Asst. Chf., Civil Task Force
Eliasberg, Edward D., Jr. ... '47 '72 C.1111 B.A. L.477 J.D.
Falk, Adam J. ... '72 '99 C.1036 B.A. L.94 J.D.
Faulkner, Robert P. ... '62 '90 (NY) C.30 B.A. L.823 J.D.
Fazio, Catherine E. ... '68 '93 (CA) C.112 B.A. L.813 J.D.
Feiveson, Arthur A. ... '39 '64 (IL) C.475 B.A. L.209 J.D.
Felasco, Michele B. ... '63 '92 (NY) C.999 B.A. L.1048 J.D.
Filippini, John C. ... '43 '73 C.105 A.B. L.823 J.D.
Fishbein, Lauren J. ... '60 '95 C.771 A.B. L.976 J.D.
Fitch, Luin P., Jr. ... '43 '70 (NY) C.367 B.A. L.178 LL.B.
Fonte, John P. ... '48 '78 C.184 B.S.E. L.128 J.D.
Foster, James K. ... '63 '89 (NY) C.1044 B.A. L.1048 J.D.
Foster, Melinda ... '64 '96 C.880 B.A. L.285 J.D.
Frankel, Lawrence M. ... '67 '93 C.188 B.A. L.659 J.D.
Galbreath, Carolyn E. ... '49 '79 C.473 B.S. L.1003 J.D.
Garrison, Nancy C. ... '48 '73 C.103 A.B. L.976 J.D.
Gaul, Kenneth W. ... '59 '85 C.105 B.A. L.477 J.D.
Giliberti, Ben ... '50 '75 C.976 B.A. L.30 J.D.
Goldberg, Peter H. ... '41 '65 C.472 B.B.A. L.309 LL.B.
Goodman, Nancy M. ... '48 '78 C.569 B.A. L.276 J.D. Chf., Computer & Fin. Sect.
Gordon, Stephen C. ... '56 '88 (NC) C.1168 B.A. L.228 J.D.
Gorey, Hays, Jr. ... '44 '69 C&L.878 B.A., J.D.
Gray, Peter A. ... '54 '90 (PA) C.966 B.A. L.831 J.D.
Greaney, John F. ... '50 '77 (MA) C.454 B.A. L.1048 J.D.
Greer, Tracy ... '63 '88 C.103 A.B. L.846 J.D.
Grossman, Benjamin B. ... '39 '64 C.276 A.B. L.309 LL.B.
Grundvig, Mark ... '68 '96 (AZ) C.101 B.S. L.37 J.D.
Grunes, Allen P. ... '57 '83 (OH) C.197 A.B. L.1292 J.D.
Hale, Nina B. ... '55 '82 (CA) C.813 B.A. L.1065 J.D.
Hamilton, Richard T., Jr. ... '62 '87 (PA) C.980 B.A. L.229 J.D.
Hammond, Matthew C. ... '— '97 (IL) C.188 B.A. L.910 J.D.
Hammond, Scott D. ... '63 '88 (NC) C&L.575 J.D.
Hand, Edward T. ... '49 '76 C.880 B.A. L.145 J.D.
Hardee, Norman C. ... '68 '95 C.478 B.A. L.976 J.D.
Harding, Ann Lea ... '41 '80 C.112 B.A. L.276 J.D.
Harmonis, Michael P. ... '46 '73 (PA) C.645 B.A. L.831 J.D.
Harris, Anthony E. ... '53 '76 (IL) C.910 A.B. L.145 J.D.
Harrop, Caldwell ... '55 '83 C.309 B.A. L.588 J.D.
Hart, Kevin B. ... '68 '00 (NY) C.216 B.A. L.982 J.D.
Hegedus, Mark S. ... '63 '91 C.477 B.A. L.569 J.D.
Heiser, Laura ... '57 '82 C.473 A.B. L.823 J.D.
Herman, Deborah Platt ... '63 '89 C.934 B.A. L.893 J.D.
Hesse, Renata B. ... '64 '90 C.914 B.A. L.1066 J.D.
Higgins, Tara Mary ... '66 '93 (FL) C&L.112 B.A., J.D.
Hirrel, Michael J. ... '51 '77 C.93 B.A. L.273 J.D.
Hirsh, Adam D. ... '64 '91 C.976 B.A. L.145 J.D.
Hoffman, Ian D. ... '68 '95 (IA) C.477 B.A. L.352 J.D.
Hollander, Bernard M. ... '16 '49 C.311 B.S. L.309 LL.B.
Hudgins, Willie L., Jr. ... '43 '68 (VA) C&L.329 B.S., J.D. Asst. Chf., Litig. II Sect.
Huffman, Max ... '— '98 (OH) C.188 B.A. L.150 J.D.
Hughes, Angela L. ... '53 '76 C.1377 B.A. L.259 J.D.
Hundley, Joyce B. ... '48 '79 (NY) C.66 B.A. L.178 J.D.

DEPARTMENT OF JUSTICE (Continued)

Irvine, Richard L. '40 '71 (CO) C.174 B.S.E.E. L.208 J.D.
Jacobs, Jon B. '60 '86 C.475 B.A. L.477 J.D.
James, Charles A. '54 '79 C.918 B.A. L.273 J.D.
Jetton, Marion L. '44 '70 C.681 A.B. L.178 J.D.
Jones, Schonette '69 '96 (IL) C.918 L.329 J.D.
Jones, William H., II '72 '97 (TX) C.623 B.A. L.976 J.D.
Jordan, David C. '46 '75 C&L.273 B.A., J.D. Asst. Chf., Health Care Task Force
Kelley, Jacqueline S. '72 '97 C.569 B.S. L.228 J.D.
Knutsen, Karl D. '65 '94 (CO) C.118 B.A. L.494 J.D.
Kooperstein, Donna N. '52 '77 (PA) C.477 B.A. L.1292 J.D. Asst. Chf., Transport., Energy & Agriculture Sect.
Kramer, John R., II '51 '76 (PA) C.216 B.A. L.1017 J.D. Chf., Litig. II Sect.
Kramer, Steven B. '50 '79 (MA) C.188 A.B. L.94 J.D.
Kully, David C. '66 '94 C.197 B.A. L.188 J.D.
Kursh, Gail '53 '79 C.1044 B.A. L.30 J.D.
Larm, Richard P. '45 '72 C&L.309 A.B., J.D.
Lawrence, Sonya Fair '66 '98 C&L.831 B.S.N., J.D.
Leone, Katherine C. '71 '99 (MA) C.188 B.A. L.178 J.D.
Levy, Barton S. '59 '86 (OK) C.623 B.A. L.616 J.D.
Lewis, Cynthia R. '62 '94 (NY) C.273 B.A. L.276 J.D.
Liddle, Thomas H., III '37 '66 (NJ) C.838 B.S.Ch. L.705 J.D.
Limmer, Andrea '42 '75 (NY) C.563 B.A. L.724 J.D.
Lin, Jean '66 '93 (IL) C.112 B.A. L.188 J.D.
Livingston, Michelle I. '— '96 C&L.329 B.A., J.D.
Lubeck, P. Terry '40 '70 (CA) C.878 B.S.M.E. L.813 J.D.
Lynch, John M. '60 '86 C.475 B.A. L.213 J.D.
Marshall, Brent E. '60 '85 (VA) C.92 B.S. L.602 J.D.
Marshall, Frances E. '59 '88 C.118 B.A. L.1066 J.D.
Martin, Richard S. '47 '74 (NY) C.262 A.B. L.145 J.D.
Massa, Salvatore '70 '97 (WI) C.436 B.A. L.966 J.D.
Matelson, Bennett J. '70 '95 C.659 B.A. L.569 J.D.
McGee, Marybeth '54 '81 C.446 B.A. L.273 J.D.
McGeorge, Robert L. '45 '71 C&L.560 B.B.A., J.D.
McMillen, Nancy H. '49 '74 (RI) C.381 A.B. L.309 J.D.
McRae, Lorenzo, II '74 '99 (SC) C.790 B.A. L.329 J.D.
Melillo, Joseph T. '33 '69 C.563 B.S. L.776 J.D.
Meyers, Erika '68 '99 C.880 B.S. L.1209 J.D.
Millen, Robin Ashton '57 '86 (VA) C.477 B.A. L.945 J.D.
Miller, Joseph M. '64 '91 C.1365 B.A. L.1209 J.D.
Moltenbrey, Mary Jean '59 '85 (MA) C&L.93 B.A., J.D. Dir., Civil Non-Merger Enforcement
Morris, Suzanne S. '37 '63 C.103 B.A. L.659 LL.B.
Muoio, Joseph '60 '87 C.918 B.A. L.659 J.D.
Nanni, Anthony V. '42 '68 (NY) C.688 B.E.E. L.262 J.D.
Nash, Janet A. '52 '81 C.477 B.A. L.1162 J.D.
Nicholson, Robert B. '43 '68 C.309 A.B. L.976 LL.B.
Niefer, Mark J. '60 '00 C.896 B.A. L.1209 J.D.
O'Brien, Paul Edward '72 '98 (NY) C&L.276 B.S.F.S., J.D.
O'Donnell, Paul J. '48 '85 (MA) C.436 A.B. L.1066 J.D.
O'Sullivan, Catherine G. '50 '75 C.373 B.A. L.309 J.D.
Parmenter, Frederick H. '52 '78 (VA) C.546 B.A. L.893 J.D.
Pearson, D. Bruce '38 '68 (CT) C.165 A.B. L.309 J.D.
Peel, Donna Alberts '64 '92 (IL) C.475 B.A. L.910 J.D.
Petrizzi, Maribeth '65 '90 C.4 B.B.A. L.93 J.D.
Phelan, Lisa Marie '61 '86 (PA) C.30 B.A. L.904 J.D.
Piccini, Juliette '63 '89 (NY) C.103 A.B. L.976 J.D.
Poole, John W., Jr. '34 '59 C&L.309 A.B., LL.B.
Powers, John J., III '47 '72 C.446 B.A. L.608 J.D.
Purcell, Anne M. '66 '91 (CT) C.1349 B.A. L.107 J.D.
Read, John R. '61 '88 C.101 B.A. L.228 J.D.
Resnikoff, Don A. '40 '66 (NJ) C.705 B.S. L.569 J.D.
Robinson, Constance K. '47 '76 C.588 B.A. L.30 J.D.
Ross, Douglas '48 '73 C.860 A.B. L.273 J.D.
Roy, Deborah A. '51 '95 C.477 B.A. L.1003 J.D.
Sacks, N. Scott '51 '75 C&L.30 B.A., J.D.
Sampson, Karen Elizabeth '58 '85 (PA) C.1222 B.S. L.329 J.D.
Sauntry, John P., Jr. '43 '69 C.276 B.S.F.S. L.273 J.D.
Scanlon, Lisa A. '67 '00 C.436 B.A. L.1065 J.D.
Scheele, Scott A. '65 '90 C.264 B.A. L.884 J.D.
Schlech, Katherine A. '48 '78 (VA) C.822 A.B. L.902 J.D.
Schmoll, Lester J., Jr. '45 '70 (WI) C&L.966 B.S., J.D.
Schwidde, Charles R. '43 '71 C.508 B.A. L.950 J.D.
Seam, Anupama '— '88 (MN) L.1035 J.D.
Segal, Matthew D. '70 '97 (CA) C.178 B.A. L.309 J.D.
Seidman, David '43 '80 C.309 A.B. L.273 J.D.
Sidorov, Jack D. '51 '76 C.367 B.A. L.309 J.D.
Sinkler, Chinita M. '73 '98 (MD) C.512 B.A. L.575 J.D.
Slover, George P. '55 '82 C.880 B.A. L.846 J.D.
Smith, Kimberly A. '69 '98 (OH) C.608 B.S. L.150 J.D.
Smucker, Conrad J. '64 '92 C.231 B.A. L.276 J.D.
Soven, Joshua H. '66 '91 C.659 B.A. L.893 J.D.
Spiegelman, Anne R. '61 '89 (PA) C.914 B.A. L.910 J.D.
Stallings, William H. '70 '94 C&L.575 B.A., J.D.
Steger, Jeffrey I. '62 '94 (PA) C.1036 B.A. L.276 J.D.
Stern, Carla M. '64 '89 (IL) C.436 B.A. L.734 J.D.
Stucke, Maurice E. '65 '95 (NY) C&L.276 A.B., J.D.
Taha, Ahmed E. '67 '96 (CA) C.659 B.A. L.813 J.D.
Tan, Larissa N. '— '99 C.914 B.A. L.112 J.D.
Terres, Nora Todd '58 '86 (MD) C.273 B.A. L.446 J.D.
Thompson, Rosemary Simota '50 '90 (IL) C.424 B.A. L.365 J.D.
Tierney, James J. '54 '86 C.25 B.A. L.678 J.D.
Timberlake, Deana L. '70 '94 (MD) C.94 B.A. L.329 J.D.
Ting, Angela Y. '66 '94 C.645 B.A. L.477 J.D.
Tom, Reginald K. '57 '85 C.881 B.A. L.30 J.D.
Tugander, Steven '64 '90 (NY) C.1044 B.A. L.1019 J.D.
Tween, Douglas M. '62 '90 (NY) C.178 B.A. L.597 J.D.
Urban, Janet R. '48 '74 (MD) C.289 A.B. L.128 J.D.
Vondrak, Frank J. '54 '89 (IL) C.1191 B.A. L.365 J.D.
Wade, James R. '61 '86 C.806 B.A. L.273 J.D.
Wagner, Sarah L. '72 '99 (TX) C.347 L.326 J.D.
Wales, David P., Jr. '69 '96 C.645 B.A. L.823 J.D.
Wang, Weeun '53 '81 (PA) C.205 B.A. L.1338 J.D.
Ward, Margaret A. '73 '98 C.602 B.A. L.309 J.D.
Weis, James L. '54 '88 (GA) C.966 B.A. L.469 J.D.
West, Jeremy K. '65 '94 C.821 B.A. L.813 J.D.
Wiggers, Robert J. '42 '66 (NY) C.1041 B.A. L.569 LL.B.
Wilder, Robert W. '49 '74 C&L.893 B.A., J.D.
Willner, Carl '58 '85 C.732 B.A. L.893 J.D.
Yamanaga, Bruce K. '53 '78 (HI) C.312 B.A. L.911 J.D.
Yingling, Kevin, L '72 '99 C.575 B.A. L.893 J.D.
Young, Frederick Sherwood '61 '89 C.976 B.A. L.276 J.D.
Young, Robert D. '51 '78 C.602 B.A. L.178 J.D.
Yousif, Mona Maria '74 '94 (IL) C&L.477 A.B., J.D.
Zelenko, Daniel L. '71 '98 (NY) C.1365 B.A. L.30 J.D.

CIVIL DIVISION

Alderson, Stanley E., II '51 '80 C.945 A.B. L.893 J.D.
Alexander, Cynthia L. '60 '92 (GA) C&L.880 B.S., J.D.
Alexander, Gerald M. '63 '90 C.178 B.A. L.880 J.D.
Allen, Gary W. '47 '72 (VA) C.608 B.A. L.276 J.D.
Altman, Stephen D. '48 '74 C.228 B.A. L.831 J.D.
Anderson, Daniel R. '54 '79 C.446 B.A. L.64 J.D.
Anderson, David J. '42 '67 C.831 A.B. L.659 LL.B.
Angel, Eric S. '67 '94 C&L.976 B.A., J.D.
Arnold, James E. '62 '89 C.228 A.B. L.976 J.D.
Arnold, Lisa M. '64 '90 C.838 B.A. L.880 J.D.
Ashley, Anjali A. '64 '90 (PA) C.188 B.A. L.309 J.D.
Auerhan, Arnold M. '55 '84 C.446 B.A. L.893 J.D.
Axelrad, Jeffrey F. '42 '67 C.119 B.S. L.597 J.D.
Azar, Henry A., Jr. '61 '88 C.976 B.A. L.569 J.D.
Bain, John Adam '61 '86 (IN) C.679 B.A. L.347 J.D.
Barkoff, Alison Nodvin '74 '00 C.188 B.S. L.1365 J.D.
Baunach, Phyllis Jo '47 '87 C.696 B.A. L.273 J.D.
Bensing, Daniel E. '55 '80 C.188 B.S. L.276 J.D.
Benson, Barry F. '57 '87 (CO) C.1210 B.S. L.831 J.D.
Bentley, Alicia J. '63 '88 (CA) C.8 B.A. L.608 J.D.
Bergmann, William C. '62 '90 (PA) C.674 B.S.E. L.665 J.D.
Bernal, David V. '46 '79 C&L.846 B.A., J.D.
Berns, Philip A. '33 '60 (NY) C.1044 B.S. L.1009 LL.B.
Bernstein, Jeffrey J. '51 '76 (PA) C.645 B.S. L.229 J.D.
Bhambhani, Sanjay M. '62 '89 (NJ) C.910 B.A. L.705 J.D.
Bhattacharyya, Rupa '70 '95 (VA) C.861 B.A. L.309 J.D.
Biddle, Barbara Cozad '49 '77 C.1236 B.A. L.259 J.D.
Bird, C. Coleman '45 '69 C.951 A.B. L.309 J.D.
Blackwell, Craig M. '65 '92 C.103 B.A. L.273 J.D.
Blades, Reginald T., Jr. '57 '80 (LA) C&L.425 J.D.
Blaze, R. Scott '46 '74 C.674 A.B. L.276 J.D.
Bleecker, Kathryn A. '47 '80 C.585 B.A. L.128 J.D.
Bordeaux, JoAnn J. '48 '77 C.907 B.A. L.678 J.D.
Branda, Joyce R. '50 '77 C.860 B.A. L.446 J.D.
Bratt, Jay I. '59 '84 (IL) C.1036 B.A. L.309 J.D.
Brilliant, Shalom '47 '77 C.978 B.A. L.1009 J.D.
Brooker, Renee '65 '91 C.831 B.S. L.276 J.D.
Brown, Jesselyn Alicia '70 '96 C.103 B.A. L.976 J.D.
Brown, Paul Michael '58 '88 (GA) C.1059 B.A. L.280 J.D.
Bruen, James G., Jr. '48 '73 C.103 A.B. L.93 J.D.
Buchan, Frederick, Jr. '39 '65 C.897 B.S.E.E. L.228 LL.B.
Buchholz, David O. '65 '92 (PA) C.821 B.A. L.309 J.D.
Buckingham, Richard T. '50 '81 C.869 B.S. L.472 J.D.
Burdette, Cathy J. '57 '84 C.443 B.A. L.273 J.D.
Burke, Claudia '73 '00 C.311 B.A. L.831 J.D.
Byron, H. Thomas, III '66 '93 C.276 B.A. L.145 J.D.
Caballero, Thomas Edward '71 '97 (FL) C&L.309 A.B., J.D.
Califf, Joan L. '58 '85 (OH) C.676 B.A. L.201 J.D.
Campbell, Stephen Robert '48 '81 C.869 B.S. L.273 J.D.
Candaux, Mary J. '59 '92 (CA) C.763 B.S. L.1049 J.D.
Chambers, Felicia L. '58 '84 C.821 B.A. L.1066 J.D.
Chiang, Chun-I '51 '79 C.966 B.S.E.E. L.276 J.D.
Chiaparas, E. Michael '53 '79 (ME) C.431 B.A. L.1294 J.D.
Chretien, Justin L. '57 '92 C.1070 B.S. L.273 J.D.
Clark, Andrew E. '58 '84 (OK) C.951 B.A. L.276 J.D.
Cohen, David M. '40 '64 C&L.339 A.B., J.D.
Cohen, David T. '62 '87 C.188 B.A. L.569 J.D.
Cohen, Edward R. '39 '64 (NY) C.188 B.S. L.976 J.D.
Cole, William G. '43 '68 C.976 B.A. L.880 J.D.
Collette, Matthew M. '60 '88 C.101 B.A. L.800 J.D.
Collins, Brendan '58 '86 C.94 B.A. L.273 J.D.
Conlin, Colleen L. '52 '78 C.476 B.S. L.1187 J.D.
Connolly, Marie-Therese '57 '84 C.813 B.A. L.588 J.D.
Conry, Colleen A. '62 '90 C.608 B.S. L.93 J.D.
Coppolino, Anthony J. '59 '88 C.321 B.A. L.276 J.D.
Couvillon, Donald A. '41 '70 C.131 A.B. L.128 J.D.
Crocker, Elizabeth '71 '00 C.103 A.B. L.1066 J.D.
Crowley, Ann V. '39 '86 (IN) C.16 B.S. L.347 J.D.
Cunningham, John C. '49 '76 C.569 B.A. L.273 J.D.
Cutini, Drake '48 '79 C.531 B.A. L.383 J.D.
Daiger, Gordon W. '30 '68 C.674 B.A. L.273 LL.B.
D'Alessio, C. Salvatore, Jr. '55 '87 C.1214 B.A. L.1338 J.D.
Dammann, Polly A. '48 '77 C.700 B.A. L.276 J.D.
David, Robert G., Jr. '46 '77 (FL) C&L.472 B.B.A., J.D.
Davidson, Jeanne E. '53 '80 C.112 B.A. L.569 J.D.
Davis, Althea W. '— '93 C.688 B.S.E.E. L.273 J.D.
Davis, John L. '45 '74 C.347 B.S. L.352 J.D.
Davis, Patricia R. '54 '79 C.930 B.A. L.893 J.D.
Davis, Saul '46 '72 (NY) C.563 B.B.A. L.724 J.D.
Dawson, Katherine S. '73 '00 C.976 B.A. L.477 J.D.
Delaney, Maureen A. '67 '92 C.205 B.S. L.904 J.D.
Dinackus, Thomas D. '58 '86 C.216 B.A. L.188 J.D.
Dintzer, Kenneth M. '— '93 (NY) C.1074 B.S. L.477 J.D.
DiPietro, Vito J. '39 '67 C.728 B.S. L.128 LL.B.
Doehl, Robert A. K. '63 '91 (IL) C.399 B.A. L.339 J.D.
Donahue, Mary Jo '57 '88 (NE) C&L.190 B.S.W., J.D.
Donis, Lisa B. '61 '87 (NJ) C.273 B.A. L.128 J.D.
Doroshow, Kenneth L. '63 '91 C.855 B.A. L.188 J.D.
Dover, Marleigh Diane '51 '75 C.66 B.A. L.273 J.D.
Dowdal, Bridgid E. '65 '95 (MN) C.94 B.S. L.494 J.D.

Doyle, Stephen M. ... '63 '88 C.423 B.A. L.225 J.D.
Draycott, Mark Justin ... '60 '89 C&L.276 B.A., J.D.
Drucker, Alison R. ... '48 '85 C.145 B.A. L.276 J.D.
Dufault, Michael S. ... '68 '95 C.867 B.S. L.823 J.D.
Duffy, Jerrob ... '70 '96 C.576 B.A. L.575 J.D.
Durant, Edward Clark ... '— '93 C.264 B.A. L.184 J.D.
Edney, Marsha S. ... '62 '87 C.205 B.A. L.904 J.D.
Egan, Dennis C. ... '39 '69 (WI) C.966 B.S. L.436 J.D.
Einerson, Roger D. ... '— '76 (WI) C&L.966 B.A., J.D.
Eldridge, Lucy E. ... '62 '91 (NY) C.299 A.B. L.262 J.D.
Ellison, Brenda ... '62 '88 C.276 B.A. L.329 J.D.
Epstein, Barbara M. ... '36 '81 (NY) C.665 B.A. L.1009 J.D.
Epstein, David ... '36 '63 C.477 B.A. L.276 LL.B.
Eubanks, Sharon Y. ... '55 '80 C.497 B.A. L.276 J.D.
Evans, Richard M. ... '43 '68 (MN) C.723 B.A. L.494 J.D.
Fadely, Kathlynn G. ... '50 '76 C.280 B.S. L.245 J.D.
Fargo, John ... '50 '77 (NY) C&L.107 B.S., J.D.
Fatouros, Thomas B. ... '72 '99 C.1369 B.A. L.1356 J.D.
Fayngold, Julia ... '69 '97 (NY) C.309 A.B. L.976 J.D.
Federighi, Carol ... '— '91 (TX) C.118 B.A. L.813 J.D.
Felix, Henry R. ... '69 '95 (NJ) C.1376 B.S. L.884 J.D.
Figley, Paul F. ... '49 '74 C.264 B.A. L.802 J.D.
Finnerman, Doris S. ... '50 '87 C.339 B.S. L.276 J.D.
Fischer, Gerard W. ... '57 '82 (MD) C.928 B.A. L.64 J.D.
Fishback, David S. ... '47 '73 C.273 B.A. L.309 J.D.
Floyd, Sheryl L. ... '50 '86 C.216 B.A. L.128 J.D.
Forrest, Bruce G. ... '45 '70 C.659 B.A. L.477 J.D.
Forrest, Herbert E. ... '23 '52 C&L.273 B.A., J.D.
Fortsch, Gregory W. ... '69 '94 C.367 B.A. L.776 J.D.
Fowler, Debra D. ... '59 '89 (VA) C&L.862 B.A., J.D.
Frank, Steve ... '48 '75 (TX) C&L.846 B.A., J.D.
Franken, Jeanne M. ... '53 '84 (CA) C.911 B.A. L.767 J.D.
Freedman, Laurence J. ... '62 '89 C.165 B.A. L.976 J.D.
Frost, Peter F. ... '55 '83 C.112 B.A. L.1065 J.D.
Fuller, Christopher C. ... '51 '84 (UT) C.101 B.S. L.878 J.D.
Fuller, Heather Call ... '68 '94 (NM) C.36 B.A. L.560 J.D.
Gaebler, Helen Anne ... '62 '92 C&L.959 B.A., J.D.
Gale, Alan S. ... '64 '89 C.197 B.A. L.93 J.D.
Gangi, Claudia Barnes ... '63 '91 (NM) C.446 B.S. L.945 J.D.
Gann, Laura L. ... '63 '91 (PA) C.999 B.A. L.945 J.D.
Garland, Seth David ... '70 '95 C.659 B.A. L.1494 J.D.
Garren, Timothy P. ... '54 '81 (SC) C.968 B.A. L.790 J.D.
Garvey, Vincent M. ... '45 '69 C.676 B.A. L.276 J.D.
Gergits, Joseph C. ... '57 '87 (IL) C.424 B.A. L.339 J.D.
Giles, Allison C. ... '61 '92 C.813 B.A. L.276 J.D.
Gillett, Glenn D. ... '51 '76 (VA) C.103 A.B. L.945 J.D.
Gilligan, James J. ... '60 '87 C.367 B.A. L.659 J.D.
Gillingham, Steven ... '52 '80 (NY) C.197 A.B. L.285 J.D.
Ginsburg, Douglas E. ... '60 '85 C.188 B.S. L.904 J.D.
Glass, David M. ... '49 '74 (NY) C.112 A.B. L.1066 J.D.
Gluck, Michelle A. ... '63 '88 (CA) C.112 A.B. L.1066 J.D.
Goldberg, Arthur R. ... '47 '73 C.674 A.B. L.276 J.D.
Goldberg, Helene M. ... '54 '77 (TX) C.280 A.B. L.846 J.D.
Golding, Marshall Tamor ... '25 '53 (NY) C.976 A.B. L.178 L.L.B.
Goldman, Daniel E. ... '69 '95 (MD) C.188 B.A. L.446 J.D.
Gollob-Gomez, Jane ... '64 '89 (NJ) C.276 B.S. L.30 J.D.
Gomez, Jane G. ... '64 '89 C.276 B.S. L.30 J.D.
Gomez, Raphael O. ... '47 '75 C.524 B.A. L.537 J.D.
Gomez, Salomon ... '63 '93 C.999 B.A. L.309 J.D.
Gottesman, David J. ... '56 '82 (IL) C&L.494 B.A., J.D.
Granston, Michael D. ... '66 '92 C.118 B.A. L.976 J.D.
Graves, Lisa R. ... '67 '95 (PA) C.958 B.S. L.188 J.D.
Green, Brenda M. ... '55 '80 C.860 B.A. L.329 J.D.
Green, Phillip J. ... '56 '90 (MO) C.999 B.A. L.734 J.D.
Green, Vanessa I. ... '65 '92 C.1350 B.A. L.904 J.D.
Greenspan, Robert S. ... '37 '63 (NY) C.951 A.B. L.178 LL.B.
Gresser, James A. ... '53 '80 (FL) C&L.602 B.A., J.D.
Griggsby, Lydia K. ... '68 '93 (MD) C.659 B.A. L.276 J.D.
Grimes, James E. ... '— '95 (OH) C.473 B.A. L.608 J.D.
Gripkey, Stephen J. ... '66 '92 (MD) C&L.976 B.A., J.D.
Groner, Arlene Pianko ... '54 '79 C.978 B.A. L.273 J.D.
Gross, Charles R. ... '53 '78 (WI) C&L.966 B.S., J.D.
Gross, Robert J. ... '55 '85 (NY) C.1333 B.S. L.1029 J.D.
Guyton, Marion E. ... '47 '72 C&L.329 B.A., J.D.
Hack, Elizabeth I. ... '63 '89 C.1044 B.A. L.273 J.D.
Hagen, Marie Louise ... '56 '81 C&L.188 A.B., J.D.
Handler, Stephen E. ... '57 '84 (IL) C.960 B.S. L.276 J.D.
Hanower, Patricia L. ... '57 '88 C.1036 B.A. L.145 J.D.
Harris, R. Lynne ... '62 '90 (IL) C.862 B.S. L.910 J.D.
Harvey, G. Michael ... '67 '93 C.228 B.A. L.659 J.D.
Harvey, Ruth A. ... '58 '86 C.112 A.B. L.477 J.D.
Harwell, Lacy R., Jr. ... '60 '87 C.198 B.A. L.818 J.D.
Hausken, Gary L. ... '54 '79 (MT) C.628 B.S. L.508 J.D.
Hausman, Allen W. ... '42 '68 (NY) C.994 B.A. L.569 J.D.
Hawkens, E. Roy ... '53 '83 (VA) C.871 B.S. L.945 J.D.
Henley, Madeline ... '66 '94 C.311 B.A. L.107 J.D.
Henry, Terry M. ... '— '87 (TX) C&L.802 B.S.M.E., J.D.
Hertz, Michael F. ... '49 '74 C.688 B.S. L.597 J.D.
Herwig, Barbara L. ... '44 '71 (CA) C.813 B.A. L.1066 J.D.
Hesch, Joel D. ... '60 '88 C.490 B.S. L.128 J.D.
Hilton, Robert G. ... '46 '71 (WI) C.1070 B.S. L.966 J.D.
Himmelfarb, Edward ... '55 '82 (NY) C.976 B.A. L.309 J.D.
Hirt, Theodore C. ... '50 '75 C.103 B.A. L.144 J.D.
Hockey, Martin F., Jr. ... '63 '89 C.165 A.B. L.1044 J.D.
Hoffman, John J. ... '65 '92 C.165 B.A. L.228 J.D.
Hollis, Robert M. ... '48 '75 C.674 B.S.E. L.276 J.D.
Hosford, Elizabeth M. ... '62 '87 C.699 B.A. L.575 J.D.
Hoyle, John C. ... '42 '67 (NC) C.575 A.B. L.145 J.D.
Hughes, F. Jefferson ... '53 '83 C.870 B.S. L.575 J.D.
Hughes, Todd M. ... '66 '92 (PA) C.309 A.B. L.228 J.D.
Humway, Christina M. ... '60 '87 (WV) C.881 A.B. L.923 J.D.
Hunolt, James A. ... '47 '74 C.784 B.A. L.588 J.D.
Hutchinson, David V. ... '39 '70 (OH) C.871 B.S. L.608 J.D.
Hyman, Lori C. ... '60 '86 C.012 B.A. L.602 J.D.
Igoe, Alison Marie ... '55 '87 (NJ) C.276 B.S. L.564 J.D.
Interrante, John G. ... '62 '91 (PA) C&L.276 A.B., J.D.
Irving, Alfred S., Jr. ... '59 '87 C.896 B.A. L.276 J.D.
Isgro, Francesco ... '53 '83 C.867 B.A. L.1162 J.D.
Issenberg, Adam ... '65 '92 (PA) C.454 B.A. L.665 J.D.
Jackson, Stephanie M. ... '65 '90 (CA) C.800 B.A. L.1097 J.D.
Jackson, Wagner D., Jr. ... '60 '84 C.309 B.A. L.976 J.D.
Jeandheur, Carole A. ... '60 '85 C.604 B.A. L.94 J.D.
Jones, Gordon A. ... '48 '73 (KS) C&L.378 A.B., J.D.
Joseph, Anne M. ... '— '01 (NY) C.951 B.A. L.976 J.D.
Josephs, Mark L. ... '65 '94 C.477 B.A. L.597 J.D.
Jost, Kenneth L. ... '50 '75 (WI) C.959 B.A. L.966 J.D.
Kamenshine, Robert D. ... '40 '64 (NY) C.563 B.A. L.178 J.D.
Kant, Deborah Ruth ... '57 '83 C.103 A.B. L.276 J.D.
Kanter, Ethan Baruch ... '61 '89 (MA) C.659 B.A. L.188 J.D.
Kanter, William ... '39 '66 C.309 A.B. L.178 J.D.
Karaffa, Grace S. ... '61 '90 (NY) C.705 B.A. L.273 J.D.
Kaser, Sylvia T. ... '56 '81 C.851 B.A. L.273 J.D.
Katz, Janet F. ... '53 '80 C.1036 A.B. L.910 J.D.
Keats, Wendy M. ... '49 '74 C.309 B.A. L.659 J.D.
Keener, Donald E. ... '47 '78 C.509 B.A. L.659 J.D.
Kell, Gerald C. ... '46 '73 C.48 B.A. L.575 J.D.
Kelly, Andrea I. ... '67 '93 (TX) C.228 B.A. L.846 J.D.
Kelly, Katherine M. ... '67 '94 C.1031 B.S. L.30 J.D.
Kennedy, Brian G. ... '51 '76 C.475 B.A. L.477 J.D.
Kessler, Amalia Deborah ... '74 '00 (NY) C.309 A.B. L.976 J.D.
Ketyer, Stephen M. ... '56 '85 (NJ) C.867 B.A. L.1325 J.D.
Khandelwal, Sharad S. ... '73 '99 (VA) C.846 B.A. L.477 J.D.
Kijewski, Joseph A. ... '60 '85 C.705 B.A. L.276 J.D.
Kinner, Donald E. ... '57 '84 (VA) C.823 B.A. L.1209 J.D.
Kinner, Russell B. ... '49 '76 C.608 B.A. L.1162 J.D.
Kinsella, James M. ... '48 '78 (NE) C.161 B.A. L.190 J.D.
Kirchner, Domenique ... '52 '77 C.354 B.A. L.145 J.D.
Kirkpatrick, Gregory S. ... '65 '94 (VA) C.347 B.A. L.273 J.D.
Kirschman, Robert E., Jr. ... '59 '84 C.645 B.A. L.273 J.D.
Klein, Alisa B. ... '67 '93 C.674 A.B. L.309 J.D.
Kleinburd, Alan E. ... '50 '75 C.665 B.A. L.273 J.D.
Klontz, David S. ... '49 '76 C.228 B.A. L.273 J.D.
Kofsky, Alina Semo ... '63 '89 C.446 B.A. L.276 J.D.
Kohl, Christine N. ... '48 '73 C.477 B.A. L.665 J.D.
Kohn, J. Christopher ... '48 '73 C.228 B.A. L.273 J.D.
Kopp, Robert E. ... '41 '67 C.604 B.A. L.309 LL.B.
Koppel, John S. ... '56 '82 C.821 B.A. L.569 J.D.
Kosloske, John E. ... '49 '75 C.597 B.A. L.910 J.D.
Kossow, Debra J. ... '49 '75 C.910 A.B. L.472 J.D.
Kovakas, James M. ... '48 '80 (VA) C.446 B.A. L.1209 J.D.
Kroop, Elizabeth F. ... '— '75 C.188 A.B. L.1049 J.D.
Kruse, John C. ... '39 '63 (WY) C.173 L.972 LL.B.
Kurn, Sharon I. ... '60 '86 (AZ) C.1168 B.A. L.37 J.D.
Lacy, Elaine Marzetta ... '59 '85 (MD) C.893 B.A. L.276 J.D.
Laeser, Jason A. ... '73 '98 C&L.472 B.A., J.D.
Lafer, A. David ... '52 '77 C.930 B.S. L.161 J.D.
LaHaie, Henry I. ... '49 '77 (AR) C.999 B.A. L.45 J.D.
Larizza, Raymond M. ... '47 '74 (PA) C.271 B.A. L.229 J.D.
Lau, Lucius Bernard ... '67 '94 C.813 A.B. L.276 J.D.
Lawlor, Jonathan S. ... '64 '91 (NY) C.309 A.B. L.893 J.D.
Leach, Mary McElroy ... '50 '76 (MN) C.713 B.A. L.602 J.D.
Lederman, Thomas C. ... '47 '73 C.309 B.A. L.893 J.D.
Lee, Jeffrica Jenkins ... '57 '82 C.589 B.A. L.329 J.D.
Leidenheimer, Robert E., Jr. ... '62 '88 C.1369 B.A. L.893 J.D.
Leitner, Patricia ... '60 '86 (NY) C.1113 B.A. L.128 J.D.
Lennon, Brian Patrick ... '63 '92 (MI) C.309 B.A. L.602 J.D.
Lennon, Susan H. ... '64 '92 (MI) C.477 B.A. L.602 J.D.
Lepley, Richard G. ... '55 '80 C.339 B.S. L.273 J.D.
Lesperance, Jeannine R. ... '66 '93 (MD) C.276 B.S.F.S. L.893 J.D.
Lester, Harold D., Jr. ... '62 '88 C.269 B.A. L.902 J.D.
Letter, Douglas N. ... '53 '78 C.178 B.A. L.1066 J.D.
Levasseur, Luke P. ... '67 '93 C.1050 B.B.A. L.861 J.D.
Levinson, Lara ... '68 '94 C.477 B.A. L.273 J.D.
Levitt, Peter S. ... '62 '90 C.881 A.B. L.659 J.D.
Lewis, Jacob M. ... '57 '82 C&L.309 B.A., J.D.
Licht, Stuart A. ... '47 '74 (NY) C.560 B.B.A. L.178 J.D.
Lieber, Sheila ... '52 '77 (IL) C.910 A.B. L.276 J.D.
Liebman, Joseph I. ... '45 '70 C.563 B.A. L.724 J.D.
Lindemann, Michael P. ... '52 '80 (VA) C.893 B.A. L.1209 J.D.
Lipstein, Freddi ... '46 '76 C.1036 A.B. L.800 J.D.
Lipton, Joseph Robert ... '68 '94 (IL) C.910 B.A. L.146 J.D.
Lobell, Anne M. ... '62 '94 (MD) C.050 B.A. L.64 J.D.
LoBue, Joseph W. ... '54 '79 C.597 B.A. L.273 J.D.
Long, David W. ... '51 '77 C.112 A.B. L.1065 J.D.
Lord, Sandra Dee ... '50 '80 C.976 B.A. L.276 J.D.
Lo Re, Alan J. ... '63 '90 C.1349 B.A. L.982 J.D.
Love, Lucinda Anne ... '61 '93 (MO) C.804 B.A. L.880 J.D.
Lum, Virginia M. ... '54 '88 C.999 B.M. L.276 J.D.
Macleod, Glenn A. ... '61 '86 (NY) C.732 B.A. L.982 J.D.
Maher, John N. ... '70 '96 (IL) C.98 B.S. L.589 J.D.
Mahon, John J. ... '30 '74 (NY) C.433 B.B.A. L.1019 J.D.
Mahoney, Margaret Jane ... '48 '76 (PA) C.659 B.A. L.1338 J.D.
Maier, Peter R. ... '50 '77 C.976 B.A. L.846 J.D.
Manganiello, Gabrielle ... '66 '92 (MD) C.692 B.A. L.276 J.D.
Marasciullo, Janene M. ... '64 '90 C.264 B.A. L.537 J.D.
Marcus, Stephanie R. ... '66 '91 C.228 A.B. L.976 J.D.
Mark, Carolyn G. ... '53 '78 C.477 B.A. L.273 J.D.
Marlow, Kristal A. ... '69 '95 (NY) C.806 B.A. L.823 J.D.
Mason, Mary H. ... '65 '89 C.65 B.A. L.861 J.D.
McAdams, John M., Jr. ... '52 '81 (VA) C.1150 B.A. L.1209 J.D.
McAuliffe, Robert J. ... '61 '89 C.228 B.S.M.E. L.178 J.D.
McCallum, Robert D., Jr. ... '46 '73 C&L.976 B.A., J.D.
McCarthy, Andrea Wenz ... '58 '84 (CA) C.1044 B.A. L.128 J.D.
McCarthy, Patricia M. ... '62 '89 (MA) C.164 A.B. L.188 J.D.
McConnell, David M. ... '59 '84 (VA) C.893 B.A. L.896 J.D.
McDade, Lawrence G. ... '49 '73 (RI) C&L.93 B.A., J.D.
McKay, Richmond I. ... '47 '72 C.497 B.S. L.500 J.D.
McKinney, Kathryn Marie ... '69 '95 (MD) C.59 B.A. L.988 J.D.

DEPARTMENT OF JUSTICE (Continued)

McLean, Sara '71 '98 (NY) C.674 A.B. L.976 J.D.
Melnick, Mark A. '63 '88 (VA) C.645 B.S. L.893 J.D.
Milanés, Juan E. '65 '91 C.1268 B.A. L.904 J.D.
Miller, Damon C. '47 '75 (PA) C.674 A.B. L.659 J.D.
Miller, Henry T. '61 '86 C.399 B.A. L.420 J.D.
Miller, Katherine A. '69 '96 C.188 B.A. L.976 J.D.
Miller, Peter B. '— '90 C.691 B.A. L.846 J.D.
Miller, Richard A. '52 '77 (SC) C.968 B.A. L.790 J.D.
Millet, Thomas W. '54 '79 C.446 B.A. L.602 J.D.
Milmoe, Michael P. '60 '87 (MD) C.446 B.A. L.64 J.D.
Minch, Lawrence N. '48 '78 C.976 B.A. L.1066 J.D.
Mitsch, Rupert M. '55 '80 C.1044 B.A. L.893 J.D.
Mitzelfeld, James A. '61 '96 (MI) C.475 B.A. L.477 J.D.
Molina, Ernesto Horacio, Jr. '70 '95 (CA) C.1074 B.A. L.770 J.D.
Mollin, Alfred '41 '78 (MD) C.927 B.A. L.446 J.D.
Moltzen, Mary Jo '47 '89 (WA) C.494 B.A. L.285 J.D.
Montague, Richard '63 '89 (CT) C.1044 B.A. L.1019 J.D.
Morgan, Ronald G. '52 '85 C.1070 B.S. L.1017 J.D.
Mullane, Hugh G. '67 '94 (NY) C.1021 B.B.A. L.276 J.D.
Myer, Peter G. '55 '87 C.188 B.S.M.E. L.861 J.D.
Newmark, Andrea '50 '77 C.260 B.A. L.276 J.D.
Niles, Mark C. '66 '92 (MD) C.918 B.A. L.813 J.D.
Nockett, Richard P. '50 '82 C.446 B.A. L.128 J.D.
Norwood, Anthony W. '52 '82 C.273 B.A. L.1338 J.D.
Oberembt, Laurie A. '63 '88 C.602 B.A. L.569 J.D.
O'Connell, Marie V. '61 '88 C.276 B.S.F.S. L.178 J.D.
Olderman, Richard A. '45 '72 C.339 B.A. L.178 J.D.
Olivier, William K. '45 '74 C.694 B.A. L.208 J.D.
Olson, Lisa Ann '58 '84 C.674 A.B. L.893 J.D.
O'Malley, Barbara B. '36 '60 C.914 B.A. L.597 J.D.
Osler, Lois Bonsal '57 '84 C.104 B.A. L.893 J.D.
Packer, Adam '74 '01 (NY) C.276 B.S.F.S. L.178 J.D.
Padda, Darshpaul S. '67 '94 C.145 B.A. L.339 J.D.
Pang, Allie '69 '94 C.112 B.A. L.976 J.D.
Parker, Kristy Lynn '69 '98 (KS) C.579 B.A. L.490 J.D.
Pazar, Charles E. '52 '77 C.94 B.A. L.705 J.D.
Peachey, William C. '58 '85 C.446 B.A. L.45 J.D.
Pelletier, Nina S. '56 '88 (MA) C.460 B.A. L.1194 J.D.
Pennak, Mark W. '50 '75 C.906 B.A. L.911 J.D.
Perry, Margaret J. '49 '78 (MN) C.668 B.A. L.1035 J.D.
Phelps, Alan J. '— '00 (OR) C.546 B.A. L.188 J.D.
Phillips, Dennis L. '52 '82 (NY) C.870 B.S. L.823 J.D.
Phillips, Richard G., Jr. '70 '97 (PA) C.976 B.A. L.276 J.D.
Poirier, James W. '55 '87 C.309 A.B. L.569 J.D.
Pyles, Phyllis '49 '75 C.329 B.A. L.597 J.D.
Quinlivan, Mark T. '65 '92 C.276 B.S. L.659 J.D.
Rabin, Arthur L. '69 '94 (PA) C.1062 B.A. L.124 J.D.
Rabinovitz, Joshua Z. '75 '00 (IL) C.597 B.A. L.145 J.D.
Rabinowitz, Judith Ellen '50 '77 C.705 B.A. L.188 J.D.
Raby, Mark C. '60 '88 C.136 B.S. L.945 J.D.
Radford, Emily Anne '50 '86 (VA) C.1209 B.A. L.945 J.D.
Randolph, Lloyd H. '59 '83 C.383 A.B. L.309 J.D.
Ray, Kathryn D. '61 '86 (VA) C&L.893 B.A., J.D.
Renzi, Linda S. '60 '86 (NY) C.1044 B.A. L.1048 J.D.
Reyna, Nelda C. '66 '93 (TX) C.845 B.A. L.893 J.D.
Richman, Marc P. '46 '73 (PA) C.21 B.S. L.831 J.D.
Riegel, Steven J. '50 '76 (NY) C.966 B.A. L.188 J.D.
Rimerman, Randi-Sue '67 '93 C.188 B.S. L.893 J.D.
Rinaldo, Elizabeth A. '54 '91 (WY) C&L.972 B.S., J.D.
Rivera, Jennifer R. '60 '88 (VA) C.945 B.A. L.893 J.D.
Rivera, Karen A. '71 '99 (MA) L.677 J.D.
Rivera, William Alvarado '69 '95 (CA) C.103 A.B. L.813 J.D.
Robinson, Michael E. '52 '78 C&L.976 B.A., J.D.
Rockafellow, Jack S. '44 '80 (NM) C.1250 B.S. L.560 J.D.
Rogers, Mark W. '54 '79 (MS) C.886 B.A. L.500 J.D.
Rohr, Rebecca A. '73 '99 (CA) C.188 B.A. L.1068 J.D.
Rome, Wendy Leigh '55 '85 C.260 B.S.A. L.30 J.D.
Rosa, Jill Dahlmann '— '94 C&L.477 B.A., J.D.
Rosenfeld, Frank A. '52 '76 (PA) C.229 B.A. L.309 J.D.
Roth, Pamela A. '67 '94 C.659 B.A. L.276 J.D.
Rubin, Amy Michelle '59 '88 (NJ) C.705 B.A. L.569 J.D.
Rudy, Susan K. '57 '83 C.231 B.A. L.273 J.D.
Russell, Elizabeth A. '67 '92 (TX) C.210 B.A. L.1119 J.D.
Russotto, Patricia M. '59 '88 (PA) C.276 B.S.F.S. L.692 J.D.
Ruzich, Richard T. '69 '96 (IL) C.98 B.S.E.E.T. L.801 J.D.
Ryan, William Francis, III '67 '92 (MA) C.860 L.178 J.D.
Sadoff, David '47 '74 C.477 B.A. L.276 J.D.
Sarko, Michele Y.F. '59 '87 C.966 B.A. L.30 J.D.
Sawi, Tarek '58 '83 (NY) C.1044 B.S. L.880 J.D.
Scadron, S. Michael '47 '73 C.611 B.A. L.273 J.D.
Scadron, Terri Jane '62 '89 C.145 B.A. L.273 J.D
Schaitman, Leonard '37 '62 (NY) C&L.178 B.A., LL.B.
Scher, Howard S. '46 '71 C&L.178 A.B., J.D.
Schiffer, Stuart E. '39 '63 C&L.339 B.S., LL.B.
Schneider, Warren A. '36 '62 C&L.128 A.B., J.D.
Schraibman, Sandra M. '47 '73 C&L.790 B.A., J.D.
Schulmeisters, Janis G. '37 '67 (NY) C.1044 B.S. L.1009 LL.B.
Schultz, Cynthia B. '— '90 C.273 B.A. L.30 J.D.
Schumann, John A. '60 '85 (TX) C.839 B.A. L.309 J.D.
Schwarz, Norah Ascoli '— '74 C.94 B.A. L.208 J.D.
Seligman, Phil '64 '90 C.1209 B.A. L.893 J.D.
Shahan, E. Kathleen '48 '75 C.846 B.A. L.796 J.D.
Shaikun, Philip '64 '92 C.228 B.A. L.800 J.D.
Shapiro, Elizabeth J. '60 '88 C.477 B.A. L.276 J.D.
Shealy, Lorri Lee '68 '93 C&L.790 B.A., J.D.
Sher, R. Joseph '42 '75 (MI) C.569 B.S. L.213 J.D.
Sholar, John P. '60 '85 (VA) C.896 B.A. L.276 J.D.
Showalter, John W. '45 '73 C.679 B.A. L.910 J.D.
Siegel, Jay M. '37 '67 C.674 A.B. L.893 J.D.
Sills, Jonathan P. '67 '93 (MD) C.178 A.B. L.893 J.D.
Simkin, Brian M. '64 '92 (GA) C.893 B.S. L.228 J.D.
Simon, Maria '68 '94 C.309 B.A. L.178 J.D.
Simon, Sandra Wien '46 '74 (OH) C.608 B.S. L.1003 J.D.
Simpson, W. Scott '60 '87 (VA) C&L.101 B.A., J.D.
Singer, Michael J. '48 '75 C.367 B.A. L.178 J.D.
Sitcov, Michael '51 '77 C.597 B.A. L.245 J.D.
Slack, Michelle R. '64 '95 (OH) C.381 B.A. L.930 J.D.
Sleater, Susan M. '— '79 (MO) C.734 B.A. L.910 J.D.
Smith, Brian S. '63 '88 (MD) C.886 B.S. L.880 J.D.
Smith, Robin D. '52 '88 (OH) C.999 B.A. L.150 J.D.
Snee, Bryant G. '58 '83 (MO) C.910 B.A. L.734 J.D.
Snyder, Steven B. '59 '88 C&L.893 B.A., J.D.
Solet, Irene M. '50 '75 C.914 B.A. L.976 J.D.
Soni, Sushma '63 '90 (IL) C.597 B.A. L.976 J.D.
Sowles, Marcia K. '50 '75 C.432 B.A. L.879 J.D.
Sperow, Elisabeth Heather '70 '95 (OK) C.112 B.A. L.623 J.D.
Spiro, Daniel A. '60 '84 C.813 B.A. L.309 J.D.
Spooner, Sandra P. '48 '76 C&L.945 B.A., J.D.
Springer, Ann L. '61 '88 C.783 B.A. L.30 J.D.
Steenland, Peter R., Jr. '45 '70 C&L.273 B.A., J.D.
Stein, Elizabeth '48 '75 C.298 B.A. L.597 J.D.
Steinberg, Andrew A. '73 '98 (NJ) C.178 B.A. L.880 J.D.
Steinmeyer, Anthony J. '42 '68 (NY) C.945 B.A. L.309 J.D.
Stemplewicz, John T. '49 '79 (PA) C.728 B.S. L.884 J.D.
Stern, Hillary A. '57 '81 (MA) C.1044 B.A. L.94 J.D.
Stern, Mark '51 '81 C.33 B.A. L.309 J.D.
Stinson, David B. '60 '85 C.446 B.A. L.30 J.D.
Stone, Richard R. '49 '82 C.1176 B.A. L.446 J.D.
Stratvert, Bruce N. '39 '84 (NJ) C.871 B.S. L.178 J.D.
Straus, Lee M. '58 '84 C.311 B.A. L.1068 J.D.
Strichartz, Ina Lee '— '76 C.477 B.A. L.800 J.D.
Subar, Judry L. '56 '81 C.978 B.A. L.276 J.D.
Swingle, Sharon '68 '97 C.659 B.A. L.145 J.D.
Talson, Steven M. '53 '80 (MD) C.112 A.B. L.446 J.D.
Taxay, Michael D. '63 '90 (PA) C&L.228 A.B., J.D.
Terlep, Vincent B., Jr. '46 '73 (WI) C.602 A.B. L.30 J.D.
Terzian, David L. '45 '73 C.367 B.A. L.64 J.D.
Tien, Wendy S. '69 '93 (IL) C.966 B.A. L.494 J.D.
Tiersky, Marcia N. '72 '99 C.896 B.A. L.597 J.D.
Tingle, Michal L. '62 '88 C.112 B.A. L.976 J.D.
Toole, Frances M. '48 '76 C.260 B.A. L.245 J.D.
Touhey, James G., Jr. '56 '82 (MD) C&L.446 B.A., J.D.
Troy, Matthew J. '68 '93 (NY) C.228 A.B. L.880 J.D.
True, Sadhna '64 '91 C.597 B.A. L.477 J.D.
Truscott, Michael Thomas '61 '88 (NY) C.839 B.S. L.1019 J.D.
Tucker, Rina C. '67 '92 C.518 B.A. L.659 J.D.
Tucker, Shelley L. '61 '87 (PA) C.438 B.A. L.878 J.D.
Tyler, John R. '52 '79 C.674 B.A. L.1194 J.D.
Underhill, R. Michael '51 '82 (CA) C.112 B.A. L.767 J.D.
Uygur, Nuriye C. '65 '93 C.401 B.A. L.128 J.D.
Vanderstar, Thankful Townsend '66 '94 C.674 B.A. L.30 J.D.
Vartain, Richard G. '61 '86 C&L.893 B.A., J.D.
Vassanelli, C. Max '39 '66 (PA) C.229 B.A. L.930 J.D.
Vernia, Benjamin J. '61 '93 C.477 A.B. L.880 J.D.
Vu, Quynh '66 '91 (PA) C.216 B.A. L.1017 J.D.
Walser, Mikki Graves '63 '88 (VA) C&L.893 B.A., J.D.
Walthall, Timothy B. '50 '75 C.893 B.A. L.1202 J.D.
Warshawsky, John '56 '82 C&L.502 B.S., J.D.
Wattenbarger, Sherri '68 '93 (TX) C&L.502 B.S., J.D.
Weismann, Anne L. '53 '79 C.103 A.B. L.273 J.D.
Welch, Jonathan P. '61 '87 C.880 B.A. L.273 J.D.
Wells, Carlotta P. '58 '83 (MD) C.659 B.A. L.904 J.D.
Wells, Dodge '45 '72 C.309 A.B. L.145 J.D.
Welsh, Elizabeth A. '63 '91 C.945 B.A. L.128 J.D.
Wendtland, Linda S. '60 '85 C&L.893 B.A., J.D.
Wernery, Linda S. '61 '92 C.150 B.S.N. L.273 J.D.
Whitaker, Tracy J. '44 '69 (VA) C.976 B.A. L.893 LL.B.
White, Franklin E., Jr. '66 '91 (CT) C.893 B.A. L.178 J.D.
Williams, Barbara Silver '58 '83 C.1074 B.A. L.1065 J.D.
Williamson, Donald J. '62 '88 (MA) C.103 B.A. L.94 J.D.
Wilson, James C. '51 '76 (IA) C&L.352 B.B.A., J.D.
Winston, Colette J. '52 '79 C.276 B.S. L.446 J.D.
Wiseman, David B. '61 '95 C.976 B.A. L.93 J.D.
Wong, Burke M. '56 '80 C.276 B.S. L.128 J.D.
Wynn, Constance A. '— '81 (PA) C.347 B.A. L.659 J.D.
Yavelberg, Jamie Ann '68 '93 C&L.228 A.B., J.D.
Zolfaghari, Paul N. '64 '91 C.282 B.A. L.665 J.D.
Zwick, Kenneth L. '45 '76 (PA) C.453 B.S. L.831 J.D.

CIVIL RIGHTS DIVISION

Abraham, Robert K. '60 '85 C.477 B.A. L.912 J.D.
Adelstein, Jay D. '52 '77 C.477 B.G.S. L.383 J.D.
Ahuja, Kiran A. '71 '99 (GA) C.811 B.A. L.280 J.D.
Anderson, James L. '69 '96 C.910 B.A. L.273 J.D.
Andrews, Linda R. '— '83 (WI) C.512 B.A. L.966 J.D.
Angus, James S. '46 '71 C&L.546 B.A., J.D.
Aronowitz, Michelle M. '— '95 C.976 B.A. L.813 J.D.
Axam, Hilary S. '— '95 (PA) C.976 B.A. L.659 J.D.
Baca, A. Baltazar '46 '73 C.174 B.A. L.208 J.D.
Baca, Lawrence R. '50 '77 (VA) C.112 B.A. L.309 J.D.
Bacon, Elizabeth Logsdon '67 '94 C.309 A.B. L.1066 J.D.
Baldwin, Katherine A. '52 '78 C.174 B.A. L.276 J.D.
Barrett, Michael L. '44 '70 C.674 A.B. L.188 J.D.
Barrick, Andrew J. '42 '67 (OH) C.203 B.A. L.851 J.D.
Bass, Alyse Sue '64 '89 C.1036 B.A. L.228 J.D.
Becker, David J. '66 '94 (CA) C.112 B.A. L.1066 J.D.
Bendor, Catherine A. '66 '93 C.188 A.B. L.309 J.D.
Berman, Robert S. '48 '78 (WI) C.72 B.A. L.436 J.D.
Bernstein, Barbara (Bobbi) '68 '95 (VA) C&L.813 B.A., J.D.
Berry, David B. '61 '92 C&L.446 B.A., J.D.
Blackshear, M. Lucia '73 '00 (LA) C.861 B.A. L.425 J.D.
Blizard, Janet L. '47 '80 C.273 B.A. L.128 J.D.
Blumberg, Mark '62 '87 C.339 B.A. L.276 J.D.
Blustein, Benjamin J. '62 '88 C.103 B.A. L.910 J.D.
Bohan, Mary R. '61 '89 C.188 B.A. L.276 J.D.
Bond, Rebecca B. '71 '99 (CA) C.976 B.A. L.309 J.D.

Bowden, Ellen M. ’69 ’94 (TX) C.659 B.A. L.178 J.D.
Bowen, L. Irene ’49 ’76 C.351 B.A. L.273 J.D.
Breen, Philip L. ’52 ’81 C.976 B.A. L.178 J.D.
Brent, Derrick L. ’66 ’96 C.608 B.S. L.597 J.D.
Brewington, Pamela D. ’67 ’92 C&L.575 B.A., J.D.
Brown, Shanetta Y. ’66 ’94 (CA) C.1073 B.S. L.1068 J.D.
Buchko, John P. ’64 ’95 C.645 B.A. L.128 J.D.
Burrell, Meredith L. ’73 ’98 (MD) C.696 B.A. L.30 J.D.
Busansky, Alexander Hendler ’62 ’88 (NY) C.966 B.A. L.276 J.D.
Butler, Steven E. ’63 ’92 C.420 B.A. L.940 J.D.
Calderon, Tovah R. ’72 ’00 C.477 B.A. L.329 J.D.
Campbell, Rhonda Lisa ’69 ’98 C.1494 B.A. L.329 J.D.
Campos, Marta ’60 ’91 (PA) C.66 B.A. L.228 J.D.
Carr, Debra A. ’59 ’86 (TX) C.859 B.A. L.744 J.D.
Carter, Geoffrey L.J. ’— ’96 C.813 A.B. L.145 J.D.
Cass, Jennifer C. ’60 ’89 (PA) C.188 B.A. L.1065 J.D.
Chandler, Thomas E. ’55 ’81 C.477 B.B.A. L.273 J.D.
Cheng, Christopher N. ’68 ’93 (PA) C.659 B.S. L.477 J.D.
Clark, Carolyn ’71 ’96 (MA) C.645 B.A. L.597 J.D.
Clarke, Kristen M. ’— ’00 (NY) C.309 B.A. L.178 J.D.
Cohen, Phyllis M. ’55 ’94 C.446 B.A. L.128 J.D.
Conn, Roy, III ’57 ’84 C.665 B.A. L.329 J.D.
Cooper, Tink D. ’55 ’81 (FL) C.1059 B.A. L.259 J.D.
Davis, Tawana E. ’65 ’91 C.178 B.A. L.309 J.D.
Delaney, Sheila K. ’42 ’74 (VA) C.777 B.A. L.128 J.D.
deLemos, Pedro R. ’50 ’89 C.1280 B.A. L.329 J.D.
Dempsey, Robert N. ’37 ’63 (MN) C.602 B.A. L.796 LL.B.
Dettling, Rosemary ’65 ’92 C.1049 B.A. L.602 J.D.
Deutsch, David ’52 ’78 C.1044 B.A. L.107 J.D.
Dimsey, Dennis J. ’43 ’68 C.659 B.A. L.446 LL.B.
Dorfman, Diane S. ’47 ’71 C.1044 B.A. L.477 J.D.
Dorris, Evanjerl ’47 ’87 (PA) C.1280 B.A. L.325 J.D.
Dougherty, Burtis M., Jr. ’49 ’74 C.976 B.A. L.893 J.D.
Dougherty, Salliann S.M. ’50 ’78 (VA) C.280 B.A. L.1209 J.D.
Dulen, Maureen T. ’60 ’92 (MO) C.734 B.A. L.502 J.D.
Dunne, Sarah A. ’— ’99 (VA) C.813 B.A. L.145 J.D.
Edwards, Lisa W. ’62 ’89 C&L.893 B.A., J.D.
Ehrlich, Anat ’63 ’88 (DC) C.188 B.A. L.94 J.D.
Eichner, James ’68 ’97 C.311 B.A. L.569 J.D.
Einstein, Laura F. ’52 ’80 C.855 B.A. L.30 J.D.
Eisenstein, Miriam R. ’38 ’69 (NY) C.145 A.B. L.569 J.D.
Epstein, Rebecca E. ’69 ’96 C.103 B.A. L.569 J.D.
Eure, Philip K. ’61 ’87 C.813 A.B. L.309 J.D.
Evans, Carol A. ’64 ’95 C.788 A.B. L.309 J.D.
Evans, Kelli M. ’69 ’94 (CA) C.813 B.A. L.112 J.D.
Farano, Richard J. ’64 ’89 C.276 B.S.F.S. L.569 J.D.
Felten-Green, Daphne S. ’65 ’92 C.462 B.A. L.145 J.D.
Fenton, William B. ’39 ’68 C.376 B.A. L.546 J.D.
Ferrante, Teresa A. ’— ’90 C.1097 B.A. L.1066 J.D.
Fitzgerald, Paige M. ’67 ’94 (CA) C.575 B.A. L.893 J.D.
Flynn, David K. ’54 ’79 C.696 B.A. L.976 J.D.
Foran, Sheila M. ’61 ’87 C.339 B.A. L.477 J.D.
Fotopulos, M. Christine ’72 ’97 C.881 B.A. L.861 J.D.
Freedman, Lee J. ’69 ’97 (OH) C.401 B.A. L.608 J.D.
Friedman, Bruce S. ’60 ’85 C.696 B.A. L.273 J.D.
Friel, Gregory B. ’62 ’88 (MD) C.437 B.A. L.309 J.D.
Frohboese, Robinsue ’— ’78 (NE) C.81 B.S. L.546 J.D.
Gadzichowski, John M. ’46 ’71 (WI) C&L.436 B.A., J.D.
Galanter, Seth M. ’68 ’94 (PA) C.178 B.A. L.659 J.D.
Gamondi, Maria Cristina ’68 ’93 C.276 B.A. L.93 J.D.
Ginsburg, Jessica A. ’61 ’87 C.674 A.B. L.893 J.D.
Glassman, Jeremiah ’42 ’72 C.563 B.S. L.128 J.D.
Gordon, Daniel S. ’73 ’00 (NY) C&L.309 A.B., J.D.
Gray, Brent Alan ’64 ’91 C.1237 B.A. L.790 J.D.
Greenbaum, Jon M. ’68 ’93 (CA) C.112 B.A. L.1068 J.D.
Gregory, Claire ’60 ’87 (NH) C.788 A.B. L.893 J.D.
Griffin, Howard R. ’— ’81 C.923 B.A. L.273 J.D.
Gross, Mark L. ’48 ’73 C.705 B.A. L.276 J.D.
Guzman, Javier M. ’66 ’91 (FL) C.420 B.S. L.861 J.D.
Handley, Harvey L., III ’45 ’72 (VA) C&L.902 B.A., J.D.
Harrington, Sarah E. ’72 ’00 (NY) C.976 B.A. L.309 J.D.
Heffernan, Brian F. ’50 ’77 (VA) C.276 A.B. L.128 J.D.
Heilbronner, Susan L. ’66 ’92 C.604 B.A. L.228 J.D.
Hermilla, Nelson D. ’53 ’81 (MO) C.866 B.S. L.502 J.D.
Ho, James C. ’73 ’00 C.813 A.B. L.145 J.D.
Hogan, Gerard V. ’54 ’80 (VA) C.674 A.B. L.30 J.D.
Houk, Diane L. ’59 ’84 (WI) C.970 B.A. L.178 J.D.
Huang, Andrew S. ’70 ’97 (CA) C.1375 A.B. L.1066 J.D.
Hughes, Verlin ’58 ’86 (OK) C.613 B.A. L.560 J.D.
Hume, Gaye L. ’54 ’85 C.845 B.S. L.276 J.D.
Hunter, David H. ’42 ’68 C.674 A.B. L.309 LL.B.
Iyer, Deepa V. ’72 ’97 (IN) C.880 B.A. L.602 J.D.
Jackson, Charla D. ’70 ’96 (MD) C.893 B.A. L.329 J.D.
Jacobs, Gretchen E. ’62 ’88 (CA) C.112 B.A. L.1068 J.D.
Jefferson, Tricia G. ’71 ’98 (MD) C.945 B.A. L.902 J.D.
Jenkins, Sabrina W. ’55 ’80 C.864 B.S. L.329 J.D.
Jerome, Richard B. ’58 ’84 C.103 B.A. L.309 J.D.
Johnson, Alicia D. ’71 ’97 (OH) C.811 B.A. L.329 J.D.
Johnson, Avery L. ’69 ’97 (MD) C.886 B.S. L.665 J.D.
Johnson, Kenneth D. ’62 ’90 C.1109 B.A. L.309 J.D.
Johnson, Michael W. ’71 ’96 C.228 B.A. L.309 J.D.
Jones, Malachi B., Jr. ’70 ’96 C.871 B.S. L.276 J.D.
Kammerman, Barbara ’49 ’78 C.1044 B.A. L.1162 J.D.
Kappelhoff, Mark J. ’61 ’88 (MD) C.723 B.S. L.904 J.D.
Kayyem, Juliette N. ’69 ’96 C&L.309 B.A., J.D.
Keary, Thomas J. ’47 ’73 C.93 B.S. L.273 J.D.
Keefe, Edward S. ’71 ’00 (MA) C.321 B.S. L.659 J.D.
Keith, D. Judith ’47 ’80 C&L.259 B.A., J.D.
Kengle, Robert A. ’56 ’85 (MD) C.25 B.A. L.1162 J.D.
Khoury, Michael K. ’64 ’94 (PA) C.1372 B.A. L.667 J.D.
King, Loretta ’55 ’81 C.228 A.B. L.30 J.D.
Kirkpatrick, Michael T. ’65 ’91 (TX) C.840 B.A. L.30 J.D.
Koffman, Richard A. ’64 ’91 C.918 B.A. L.976 J.D.
Kohrman, Daniel B. ’57 ’85 C.976 B.A. L.178 J.D.
Kowalski, Barry F. ’44 ’73 C.103 A.B. L.128 J.D.
Kuo, Peggy ’64 ’88 C.976 B.A. L.309 J.D.
Kwong, Teresa ’69 ’95 C.668 B.A. L.659 J.D.
Lehtman, Myron S. ’48 ’73 (CA) C.112 B.A. L.1067 J.D.
Lerner, Louise A. ’49 ’74 C.681 B.A. L.93 J.D.
Levy, Allen W. ’— ’86 C.309 B.A. L.893 J.D.
Lewenberg, Sara R. ’70 ’96 (MA) C.188 B.S. L.94 J.D.
Liang, Angela N. ’70 ’99 C.112 B.A. L.446 J.D.
Libman, Robert S. ’63 ’88 C&L.813 B.A., J.D.
Lin, Tana ’— ’91 C.188 B.A. L.569 J.D.
Liu, Andy ’66 ’96 C.401 B.S. L.276 J.D.
Lohier, Raymond J. ’65 ’93 (NY) C.309 A.B. L.569 J.D.
Lowell, Robert P. ’46 ’72 (NY) C.823 B.A. L.107 J.D.
Mabey, Tamara L. ’71 ’98 (MD) C.446 B.A. L.64 J.D.
Mackela, Carol J. ’50 ’89 (MI) C.477 B.A. L.1187 J.D.
Maddox, William G. ’56 ’88 C.309 A.B. L.228 J.D.
Magagna, Joan A. ’47 ’75 C.972 B.A. L.276 J.D.
Mahoney, Cathleen M. ’60 ’85 (IL) C.813 A.B. L.976 J.D.
Maisels, Amanda L. ’70 ’98 C&L.309 A.B., J.D.
Maldonado, Juan ’46 ’76 C.475 B.A. L.477 J.D.
Malek, Alia ’74 ’01 (NY) C.367 B.A. L.276 J.D.
Manickam, Sada ’71 ’97 C.188 B.A. L.107 J.D.
Mansukhani, Sunil H. ’71 ’95 C.339 A.B. L.976 J.D.
Marmolejos, Policarpio ’51 ’81 (MA) C.999 B.A. L.588 J.D.
Marshall, Franz R. ’42 ’74 (PA) C&L.329 B.S., J.D.
Masling, Mark ’55 ’86 (NY) C.174 B.A. L.659 J.D.
Mather, Robert J. ’50 ’77 C.1213 B.S. L.209 J.D.
Maurer, Michael S. ’63 ’88 C.705 B.A. L.273 J.D.
McElderry, Marie Klimesz ’47 ’72 (PA) C.895 B.A. L.665 J.D.
Meacham, Barbara J. ’— ’82 (IN) C.999 B.A. L.608 J.D.
Mendelsohn, Joshua C. ’69 ’95 (CA) C.1077 B.A. L.1068 J.D.
Meyer-Fong, Ming-Yuen ’66 ’94 C.976 B.A. L.112 J.D.
Miller, Pauline A. ’46 ’77 (AZ) C&L.37 B.A., J.D.
Miller, Tamara L. ’60 ’85 C.602 B.A. L.477 J.D.
Milton, Naomi H. ’64 ’91 (PA) C.299 B.A. L.659 J.D.
Mobley, Mary Lou ’65 ’91 (CA) C.605 B.A. L.228 J.D.
Moore, John R. ’51 ’77 C&L.178 B.A., J.D.
Moore, Scott Parrish ’69 ’95 (NE) C.543 B.S. L.190 J.D.
Moossy, Robert J., Jr. ’— ’94 (TX) C.691 B.A. L.326 J.D.
Morales, Eric E. ’68 ’96 (NY) C.846 B.A. L.178 J.D.
Moran, Timothy J. ’64 ’92 (IL) C.802 B.A. L.309 J.D.
Moskowitz, Albert ’49 ’78 (MO) C.563 B.A. L.502 J.D.
Mulroy, Steven J. ’64 ’89 C.188 B.S. L.945 J.D.
Murphy, Donna M. ’64 ’91 (PA) C.30 B.A. L.976 J.D.
Nakata, Ken S. ’64 ’88 C.367 B.A. L.659 J.D.
Nelson, Mellie H. ’45 ’70 C.822 A.B. L.273 J.D.
Nemko, Amy H. ’71 ’97 C.112 B.A. L.976 J.D.
Nicholson, Katherine M. ’64 ’93 (MA) C.64 A.B. L.309 J.D.
O’Beirne, Patricia L. ’63 ’91 C.674 A.B. L.94 J.D.
O’Brian, Valerie R. ’43 ’86 (MD) C.449 B.A. L.128 J.D.
Olesen, Anne K. ’55 ’82 C.1201 B.S. L.569 J.D.
Oliver, Jim U., Jr ’50 ’85 C&L.575 B.S., J.D.
Oliveri, Rigel C. ’72 ’00 (NY) C.893 B.A. L.813 J.D.
Palmer, David J. ’60 ’87 C.178 A.B. L.930 J.D.
Patten, Wendy L. ’65 ’95 C.674 A.B. L.309 J.D.
Peabody, Arthur E., Jr. ’47 ’72 C.588 B.A. L.188 J.D.
Pecht, Anne Marie ’56 ’85 C.576 B.A. L.976 J.D.
Pennington, Kathleen M. ’60 ’85 (NJ) C.705 B.A. L.904 J.D.
Pershing, Stephen B. ’57 ’90 (VA) C.309 B.A. L.893 J.D.
Pincus, Beth ’67 ’93 C.674 A.B. L.309 J.D.
Pinder, Thomas Jones ’76 ’95 C.705 B.A. L.569 J.D.
Pitts, Michael J. ’71 ’99 (NE) C.597 B.S.J. L.276 J.D.
Posner, Mark A. ’52 ’78 (CA) C.1169 A.B. L.1066 J.D.
Preston, Judith C. ’53 ’85 C.103 A.B. L.446 J.D.
Prieto, Margarita M. ’62 ’92 (PA) C.813 A.B. L.309 J.D.
Rao, Sonya A. ’— ’01 (MA) C.860 B.A. L.588 J.D.
Rapp, Kathryn M. ’60 ’92 (OH) C.347 B.A. L.1003 J.D.
Reilly, Susan B. ’52 ’79 C.273 B.A. L.893 J.D.
Resetarits, Jeffrey J. ’69 ’98 (DC) C.276 B.A. L.588 J.D.
Rich, Joseph D. ’42 ’68 C.976 B.A. L.477 J.D.
Riordan, Maureen S. ’59 ’86 (NY) C.776 B.A. L.744 J.D.
Robinson, Sheryl L. ’— ’91 C.329 B.A. L.273 J.D.
Rocah, David R. ’65 ’95 (CA) C.145 B.A. L.569 J.D.
Rosenbaum, Steven H. ’54 ’79 C.1044 B.A. L.477 J.D.
Ross, Alexander C. ’37 ’62 (FL) C&L.472 B.A., LL.B.
Russ, John Albert, IV ’72 ’97 (CA) C.276 B.S. L.813 J.D.
Russell, Kevin K. ’68 ’96 (MD) C.477 A.B. L.976 J.D.
Russo, Joseph C. ’65 ’89 C.276 B.A. L.569 J.D.
Ryan, Kathleen C. ’58 ’91 (PA) C.1077 B.A. L.30 J.D.
Santoro, Christopher A. ’— ’94 C.860 B.A. L.94 J.D.
Schneider, George ’47 ’75 (NY) C.1036 A.B. L.178 J.D.
Schuham, Aaron David ’70 ’96 (IL) C.103 S.B. L.813 J.D.
Searing, Daniel A. ’42 ’70 (MD) C.367 B.A. L.128 J.D.
Seeley, Sharon A. ’55 ’87 (CA) C.165 A.B. L.145 J.D.
Senger, Jeffrey M. ’62 ’88 C&L.309 A.B., J.D.
Seward, Jon M. ’60 ’87 (NJ) C&L.705 B.A., J.D.
Shapiro, Avner M. ’66 ’95 C.1036 B.A. L.94 J.D.
Shoenberg, Dana L. ’68 ’94 C.188 A.B. L.976 J.D.
Silver, Jessica D. ’46 ’72 C&L.273 B.A., J.D.
Simons, Valerie L. ’69 ’98 (CO) C.112 B.A. L.276 J.D.
Singer, Elizabeth A. ’63 ’91 C.976 B.A. L.309 J.D.
Sitton, Janie Allison ’65 ’94 (NC) C&L.575 B.A., J.D.
Sotolongo, Ariel L. ’51 ’78 (CA) C&L.112 B.A., J.D.
Spratt, Jacqueline L. ’59 ’87 (NY) C.703 B.S. L.107 J.D.
Stark, Lisa J. ’53 ’79 C.188 B.S. L.309 J.D.
Stevens, Karen L. ’66 ’94 (IL) C&L.477 B.S., J.D.
Strojny, Andrew M. ’46 ’70 (IL) C.339 B.A. L.597 J.D.
Stumpf, Juliet P. ’66 ’95 C.604 B.A. L.276 J.D.
Stutman, Robin M. ’58 ’82 C.1044 B.A. L.1068 J.D.
Sutherland, Daniel W. ’61 ’85 (KY) C.421 B.S. L.893 J.D.
Tanner, John K. ’49 ’80 C.207 B.A. L.30 J.D.
Taylor, Carl D., Jr. ’67 ’96 C.575 B.A. L.30 J.D.
Taylor, Jane M. ’57 ’83 C&L.879 B.A., J.D.
Thabault, Isabelle M. ’49 ’77 C.1057 B.A. L.1194 J.D.

DEPARTMENT OF JUSTICE (Continued)

Thawley, Barbara E. '55 '81 C&L.128 B.A., J.D.
Thome, Linda F. '50 '78 C.145 B.A. L.273 J.D.
Tingle, Tricia A. '55 '90 (TX) C.805 B.S. L.615 J.D.
Trasvina, John D. '58 '83 (CA) C.309 A.B. L.813 J.D.
Troth, Rebecca K. '55 '84 C.429 B.A. L.477 J.D.
Tunnage, Donald Walker '68 '93 C.511 B.A. L.228 J.D.
Ugelow, Richard S. '44 '68 C.319 B.A. L.30 J.D.
Valdez, Rolando N. '70 '96 C.608 B.A. L.128 J.D.
Vélez, Daniel A. '64 '92 (NY) C.188 B.A. L.150 J.D.
Vieco, Adriana '64 '95 (NY) C.569 B.A. L.1178 J.D.
Waldorf, Lars '63 '90 (CA) C&L.309 B.A., J.D.
Walsh, James D. '72 '01 (NY) C.602 B.A. L.309 J.D.
Ward, Larry G. '— '73 (WI) C.1016 B.A. L.966 J.D.
Weinberg, Barry H. '44 '66 C&L.494 B.A., J.D.
Weinstein, Laurie J. '56 '81 C.651 B.A. L.659 J.D.
Weiss, Daniel H. '65 '90 C.659 B.A. L.446 J.D.
Wertz, Rebecca J. '57 '84 (MA) C.732 B.A. L.823 J.D.
White, Kimberly Heshima '67 '95 C.811 B.A. L.93
Wiener, Ross E. '70 '96 (CA) C.966 B.A. L.273 J.D.
Williams, Barry G. '62 '87 C.893 B.A. L.446 J.D.
Willis, Lauren E. '68 '95 (MD) C.918 B.A. L.813 J.D.
Wiseman, Holly Lee '54 '79 (AL) C.674 A.B. L.94 J.D.
Wodatch, John L., Jr. '44 '69 C.855 B.A. L.276 J.D.
Woodard, Karen D. '68 '93 C.446 B.A. L.228 J.D.
Worthen, William R. '50 '76 C.550 B.A. L.276 J.D.
Yang, Jenny Rae '70 '96 (NJ) C.188 B.A. L.569 J.D.
Yeomans, William R. '50 '76 (CT) C.855 B.A. L.94 J.D.
Younger, LeVern '— '79 C.369 B.S. L.329 J.D.
Zabel, Matthew L. '68 '96 (SD) C.793 B.S. L.597 J.D.
Zebrak, Julie R. '70 '95 C.860 B.A. L.273 J.D.
Zogby, Joseph R. '69 '96 C&L.893 B.A., J.D.
Zubrensky, Michael A. '65 '95 C.309 A.B. L.813 J.D.
Zwibelman, Michael A. '72 '00 (NY) C.813 B.A. L.145 J.D.

COMMUNITY RELATIONS SERVICE

Henderson, George E. '50 '77 (PA) C.469 B.A. L.880 J.D.
Nam, Frances '69 '95 (MD) C.1350 B.S. L.30 J.D.

CRIMINAL DIVISION

Adams, Robert F. '51 '77 C.309 A.B. L.273 J.D.
Albert, Janet E. '65 '92 C.588 B.S. L.30 J.D.
Alexander, Glenn C. '61 '88 (VA) C.885 B.A. L.902 J.D.
Alexandre, Carl '59 '85 C.1139 B.A. L.616 J.D.
Andrews, Paul J. '66 '91 (MA) C&L.93 B.A., J.D.
Arterberry, John D. '43 '74 C.235 B.S. L.880 J.D.
Baker-Wingfield, Catherine S. '62 '93 (VA)
Banks, Miriam Nabors '40 '86 (TN) C&L.836 B.S., J.D.
Bannon, John T., Jr. '39 '76 (PA) C.823 Ph.D. L.602 J.D.
Barr, Jonathan R. '64 '90 C&L.893 B.A., J.D.
Beck, Joseph S. '44 '71 (IA) C.352 B.A. L.221 J.D.
Beste, Eric J. '69 '94 (IL) C.659 B.A. L.597 J.D.
Biehn, Denise E. '66 '95 (MO) C.999 B.S.N. L.734 J.D.
Bikoff, Russell A. '51 '77 C&L.477 B.A., J.D.
Blake, Lystra G. '55 '82 C.569 B.A. L.276 J.D.
Bonner, Mark H. '47 '75 C.276 A.B. L.904 J.D.
Borland, Tressa J. '51 '87 (VA) C.999 B.A. L.1209 J.D.
Bowne, William H., III '53 '86 (NJ) C.896 B.A. L.776 J.D.
Boylan, Scott P. '60 '85 C.264 B.A. L.823 J.D.
Braun, William D. '46 '71 C.165 A.B. L.94 J.D.
Breinholt, Jeffrey A. '63 '88 (CA) C.976 B.A. L.1068 J.D.
Briceno-Hawkins, Rose A. '60 '88 C.1111 B.A. L.904 J.D.
Brown, Edgar N. '28 '57 (TX) C.112 B.A. L.846 LL.B.
Brown, William C. '49 '75 (VA) C.228 B.A. L.862 J.D.
Burke, Betsy E. '56 '83 (TX) C.575 A.B. L.802 J.D.
Burns, Richard E. '64 '90 (NY) C.945 B.A. L.312 J.D.
Burrows, Thomas N. '55 '82 C.381 B.S. L.107 J.D.
Butler, Mary K. '56 '81 C.881 A.B. L.966 J.D.
Bybee, David A. '55 '82 (KY) C.101 B.A. L.383 J.D.
Byrne, James M. '64 '95 C.871 B.S. L.362 J.D.
Carrigan, Araceli G. '49 '81 (GA) C.999 B.S. L.469 J.D.
Carter, Jason E. '67 '93 C.178 B.A. L.569 J.D.
Cassella, Stefan D. '51 '78 (MD) C.188 B.S. L.276 J.D.
Cerese, Georgiann G. '— '88 (IL) C.339 B.S. L.209 J.D.
Chubin, Ellen L. '68 '94 C&L.309 A.B., J.D.
Clabault, William T. '45 '70 (MA) C.860 B.A. L.93 J.D.
Clark, Peter B. '39 '66 C.103 A.B. L.659 J.D.
Coleman, Kathleen N. '47 '72 (PA) C.665 B.A. L.831 J.D.
Connolly, Kevin P. '44 '71 (NY) C.665 B.A. L.930 J.D.
Corcoran, William J. '42 '68 C.754 B.A. L.276 J.D.
Corn, Gavin Alexander '68 '94 (VA) C.216 B.A. L.893 J.D.
Corprew, Barbara A. '49 '74 C.860 B.A. L.659 J.D.
Crawford, Michele L. '59 '85 C.823 B.A. L.472 J.D.
Criscitelli, Sara B. '48 '76 (NY) C.994 B.A. L.1019 J.D.
Dahl, Scott S. '62 '89 C&L.846 B.A., J.D.
Davidson, Hillary A. '67 '93 C.855 B.A. L.976 J.D.
Davitt, Michael E. '54 '85 C.012 B.A. L.276 J.D.
Dempsey, Pamela L. '57 '82 C.228 A.B. L.184 J.D.
Dion, John J. '46 '72 (MA) C.602 B.A. L.273 J.D.
Donsanto, Craig C. '44 '69 (MA) C&L.94 A.B., J.D.
Douglas, Richard J. '56 '91 C.1111 B.A. L.30 J.D.
Downing, Richard W. '— '92 (PA) C.976 B.A. L.813 J.D.
Drew, Joshua W. '67 '99 (MA) C.918 B.A. L.597 J.D.
Drimmer, Jonathan C. '68 '94 C.813 B.A. L.1068 J.D.
DuBose, Michael M. '60 '87 (ME) C.197 A.B. L.309 J.D.
Dunham, Giuliana H. '66 '93 (NY) C.178 B.A. L.569 J.D.
Eckenwiler, Mark '60 '92 (MA) C.309 A.B. L.569 J.D.
Edelman, Ronnie L. '47 '76 C.696 B.A. L.107 J.D.
Ehrenstamm, Faye S. '52 '77 C&L.692 B.A., J.D.
Erickson, Robert J. '49 '74 (ND) C&L.585 B.A., J.D.
Fairfax, Roger Anthony, Jr. '72 '98 C&L.309 A.B., J.D.
Falvo, Vincent J., Jr. '64 '90 (NY) C.188 B.S. L.107 J.D.
Farrington, Jo Ann '52 '77 (IL) C.228 B.A. L.597 J.D.
Felton, Kathleen A. '49 '76 (WI) C.546 B.A. L.966 J.D.
Fischer, Louis M. '47 '72 C.1036 A.B. L.588 J.D.
Fogel, Jeffrey I. '52 '77 C.659 B.S. L.472 J.D.
Folts, David W. '44 '85 C.602 A.B. L.659 J.D.
Frandsen, Peter A. '56 '85 C.446 B.S. L.30 J.D.
Friedman, Judith H. '50 '78 C.575 B.A. L.30 J.D.
Friedman, Richard A. '52 '79 C.976 B.A. L.659 J.D.
Fromstein, Daniel E. '47 '72 C&L.966 J.D.
Gangloff, Joseph E. '52 '77 C.728 A.B. L.659 J.D.
Gannon, Thomas M. '38 '75 C.602 B.A. L.569 J.D.
Gaynus, Deborah M. '61 '86 (PA) C.518 B.A. L.569 J.D.
Geckos, Marietta I. '62 '89 C.322 B.A. L.128 J.D.
Gerardi, Robert H. '62 '93 (VA) C.276 B.S.F.S. L.831 J.D.
Gerbasi, Joseph S. '64 '89 C.93 B.S. L.945 J.D.
Gilpin, Ernestine B. '46 '91 (MD) C.329 B.A. L.30 J.D.
Glavin, Rita M. '71 '97 (NY) C.478 B.A. L.262 J.D.
Glick, Scott J. '— '82 C.446 B.A. L.1019 J.D.
Glover, Eric J. '68 '93 (IL) C.436 B.A. L.228 J.D.
Gold, Robin Kofsky '58 '85 C.367 B.A. L.446 J.D.
Goldberg, Stuart M. '57 '82 C.893 B.A. L.309 J.D.
Goodman, Daniel S. '54 '79 C.309 A.B. L.813 J.D.
Gorman, Tessa M. '— '97 (CA) C.976 B.A. L.1066 J.D.
Grant, Alex J. '— '96 (MA) C.813 B.A. L.188 J.D.
Green, David E. '55 '83 C.604 B.A. L.659 J.D.
Green, Richard D. '58 '85 (PA) C.645 B.S. L.1338 J.D.
Greenberg, Theodore S. '47 '73 C.222 B.A. L.796 J.D.
Greenberg, Todd L. '71 '96 (MD) C.477 B.A. L.309 J.D.
Greenspun, Julian S. '43 '70 C.608 B.S. L.989 J.D.
Groner, Robert '46 '85 C.446 B.A. L.276 J.D.
Grove, Margaret W. '36 '80 C.1278 B.A. L.276 J.D.
Gull, Jason N. '69 '97 (IL) C.951 B.A. L.477 J.D.
Gutierrez, Irene '67 '93 (NY) C.724 B.A. L.1009 J.D.
Hamburg, Mervyn '38 '61 C&L.831 B.S., LL.B.
Hanusik, Thomas A. '64 '91 C.262 A.B. L.228 J.D.
Harbin, Harry S. '51 '82 C.560 B.A. L.276 J.D.
Harris, John E., III '50 '74 C&L.910 B.A., J.D.
Harris, Kenneth J. '57 '82 (CT) C.659 B.A. L.184 J.D.
Hart Nassen, Regina '60 '87 (TX) C.846 B.A. L.276 J.D.
Harwood, Stephen L. '43 '68 (MO) C.228 B.A. L.502 J.D.
Hastings, James R. '37 '66 C.347 B.A. L.972 J.D.
Herrera, Jessica Rae '70 '95 C.976 B.A. L.309 J.D.
Hess, Frederick D. '37 '68 C.178 B.A. L.1009 J.D.
Heyer, Michelle L. '62 '95 (OH) C.94 B.A. L.930 J.D.
Hochberg, Joshua R. '48 '72 (NY) C.178 B.A. L.569 J.D.
Hoppmann, Karin B. '72 '98 (IL) C.976 B.A. L.880 J.D.
Hulser, Raymond N. '— '88 (MA) C.165 B.A. L.659 J.D.
Hunt, Heather H. '61 '89 (VA) C.1369 B.S. L.1209 J.D.
Hyland, John F., Jr. '47 '73 C.309 B.A. L.276 J.D.
Ingersoll, Laura A. '52 '87 (CT) C.914 B.A. L.184 J.D.
Jardini, Nancy J. '64 '88 (FL) C.643 B.A. L.884 J.D.
Joseph, Lester M. '50 '80 (IL) C.477 B.A. L.365 J.D.
Kahn, Lisa Ann '52 '77 C.309 B.A. L.659 J.D.
Katz, James V. '45 '71 (MI) C.932 B.S. L.215 J.D.
Keany, Courtney V. '68 '93 (PA) C.66 B.A. L.273 J.D.
Keegan, Michael J. '58 '84 C.588 B.S. L.124 J.D.
Keeney, John C. '22 '49 C.754 B.S. L.1017 LL.B. Dep. Asst. Atty. Gen.
Kenety, William H., V '48 '75 C.216 B.A. L.309 J.D.
Kerr, Orin S. '71 '97 (NJ) C.674 B.S.E. L.309 J.D.
Killion, Maureen H. '54 '80 C.30 B.A. L.597 J.D.
Kinsey, Gwynn X., Jr. '58 '85 (MD) C.903 B.A. L.446 J.D.
Kockritz, Janis Helen '51 '76 (PA) C.324 B.A. L.128 J.D.
Lamb, Su Zann '47 '85 C.276 B.A. L.128 J.D.
Lantz, William H., Jr. '— '74 (NJ) C.884 B.S.
Lee, Amy Chang '64 '90 (IL) C.103 A.B. L.976 J.D.
Lerner, Jay N. '63 '88 C.339 B.S. L.659 J.D.
Levine, Mia M. '— '93 (MD) C.367 B.A. L.861 J.D.
Levine, Stacey A. '69 '95 C.401 B.A. L.1009 J.D.
Levy, Jennifer E. '55 '79 C.788 A.B. L.128 J.D.
Liebman, Michael C. '64 '90 (NY) C.477 A.B. L.273 J.D.
Liss, Marsha B. '49 '87 C.66 B.A. L.1068 J.D.
Litschewski, Jennafer M. '61 '86 (LA) C.802 B.S.B.A. L.861 J.D.
Loewenberg, Peter B. '46 '73 C.156 A.B. L.569 J.D.
Loomis, Laurel A. '67 '93 (CA) C.112 B.A. L.809 J.D.
Lord, Terry R. '42 '69 (TX) C.802 B.A. L.846 J.D.
Lorenzo-Giguere, Susanna '61 '91 (NY) C.429 B.A. L.1218 J.D.
Lowrie, J. Kenneth '41 '69 (MI) C.477 B.A. L.912 J.D.
Lynch, John T., Jr. '68 '94 (NY) C.696 B.A. L.188 J.D.
Mackay, Donald B. '38 '63 (IL) C.424 B.S. L.365 J.D.
Marcus, Jonathan L. '69 '95 C&L.976 B.A., J.D.
Marine, Frank J. '47 '73 (NY) C.1044 B.A. L.569 J.D.
Marshall, Harry R., Jr. '39 '66 (NY) C.893 B.A. L.659 J.D.
Martin, Jennifer R. '65 '95 C.477 B.S. L.339 J.D.
Martindale, Nancy L. '57 '82 C.446 B.A. L.128 J.D.
Massie, Jerry D. '52 '77 C&L.190 B.A., J.D.
Matz, Harry J. '56 '82 C.156 A.B. L.659 J.D.
Mazurek, Jo '50 '80 C.1111 B.A. L.602 J.D.
McClure, Kathy L. '61 '87 (IL) C.338 B.S. L.339 J.D.
McGarry, Michael S. '66 '95 C.103 A.B. L.178 J.D.
McGorty, Glen G. '73 '98 (NJ) C.674 A.B. L.597 J.D.
McGovern, Clement J., III '60 '85 C.524 B.A. L.128 J.D.
McHenry, Teresa '59 '85 C.691 B.A. L.309 J.D.
McNeil, Ronald M. '47 '76 (NY) C.1044 B.A. L.982 J.D.
Meltzer, Ellen R. '51 '75 C.597 B.A. L.245 J.D.
Menkin, Jeffrey L. '59 '84 C.1036 B.A. L.1292 J.D.
Metcalfe, Joseph C. '65 '92 C.813 B.A. L.309 J.D.
Michelich, John A. '52 '77 (IL) C.340 B.A. L.221 J.D.
Modesti, Claudius B. '64 '92 (NY) C&L.276 B.S.F.S., J.D.
Morrissette, Karen A. '53 '78 C&L.107 B.A., J.D.
Murry, Anthony S. '53 '82 C.674 A.B. L.1162 J.D.
Nesbitt, Joshua W. '58 '89 C.1021 B.A. L.982 J.D.
Newcomb, Nancy Jo '53 '81 C.63 B.S. L.345 J.D.
Newcombe, Catherine L. '66 '94 C.31 B.A. L.012 L.L.B.
Newett, Frank R. '47 '72 C.302 B.A. L.93 J.D.
Norton, Arthur F. '37 '70 (MA) C.598 B.S. L.818 J.D.
O'Donnell, Margaret Anne '57 '85 (VA) C.1030 B.A. L.1209 J.D.

Ohr, Bruce G. '62 '89 (CA) C&L.309 A.B., J.D.
O'Leary, Michael P. '67 '92 C.36 B.S. L.37 J.D.
Oliver, Nancy K. '— '93 C.326 B.A. L.904 J.D.
Orjales, Rodolfo '52 '80 (NY) C.770 B.S. L.823 J.D.
O'Rourke, Marie A. '56 '81 C.659 B.A. L.893 J.D.
Owens, Richard C. '46 '71 (OR) C.285 B.A. L.950 J.D.
Painter, Christopher '58 '85 C.188 A.B. L.813 J.D.
Panagakos, Lynn Elaine '63 '88 C.93 B.A. L.276 J.D.
Park, Robertson T. '57 '83 C.198 A.B. L.1162 J.D.
Park, Susan J. '58 '84 C.518 A.B. L.893 J.D.
Patel, Sejal H. '75 '00 C.859 B.A. L.597 J.D.
Patrick, Jackie B. '49 '77 (OK) C&L.623 B.A., J.D.
Pauley, Roger A. '40 '65 C&L.309 B.A., LL.B.
Pavlock, James R. '58 '83 (NY) C.645 B.S. L.188 J.D.
Payne, Joseph H., III '45 '79 C.976 B.A. L.569 J.D.
Petty, Patricia L. '56 '81 C.604 B.A. L.659 J.D.
Pilger, Richard C. '65 '91 (IL) C.602 B.A. L.347 J.D.
Portney, Vicki '51 '76 C&L.659 B.A., J.D.
Potts, Nancy E. '72 '98 C.674 A.B. L.309 J.D.
Preston, Richard K., II '60 '85 (MD) C.477 B.A. L.446 J.D.
Prior, Jennifer '61 '89 C.674 A.B. L.802 J.D.
Pyne, Rebecca Kettelle '59 '86 (VA) C.938 B.A. L.128 J.D.
Raabe, Wayne C. '53 '85 (ND) C.869 B.S. L.464 J.D.
Radek, Lee J. '43 '71 (IL) C.436 B.A. L.424 J.D.
Raman, Kartik Kalyan '67 '93 (IL) C.145 B.A. L.597 J.D.
Raney, Carla Hope '52 '83 C.446 B.A. L.1209 J.D.
Rao, Sangita K. '69 '96 (IL) C.477 A.B. L.309 J.D.
Raymond, Robert J. '54 '85 (MD) C&L.446 B.A., J.D.
Reardon, Timothy J., III '44 '71 C.575 B.A. L.276 J.D.
Reedy, Patricia J. '59 '87 (OH) C.1118 B.E.S. L.201 J.D.
Reitinger, Philip R. '62 '87 (GA) C.880 B.E. L.976 J.D.
Reynolds, James S. '43 '68 C.231 B.A. L.188 J.D.
Richard, Mark M. '39 '68 C.102 B.A. L.1009 J.D.
Roos, Ronald R. '51 '76 C.446 B.S. L.64 J.D.
Rosenbaum, Eli M '55 '80 C.659 B.S. L.309 J.D.
Ross, Lee Jeffrey, Jr. '50 '75 (GA) C.880 B.A.
Rothstein, Stanley A. '49 '75 C.299 B.A. L.564 J.D.
Rotker, Michael Alan '68 '95 C.477 B.A. L.273 J.D.
Rourke, Mariclaire D. '65 '91 C.741 B.A. L.128 J.D.
Rowan, Patricia B. '49 '88 C.1176 B.S. L.1202 J.D.
Rusch, Jonathan J. '52 '81 C.674 A.B. L.893 J.D.
Salgado, Richard P. '63 '91 (CA) C.560 B.A. L.976 J.D.
Samuel, Linda M. '57 '81 C.645 B.S. L.128 J.D.
Schlesinger, Steven H. '49 '74 (NY) C.563 B.A. L.564 J.D.
Schneider, Gary '54 '78 (FL) C.260 B.A. L.1206 J.D.
Schretter, Judith D. '47 '83 (VA) C.103 B.A. L.1209 J.D.
Schubert, S. Terry '56 '83 C.260 B.S. L.477 J.D.
Schwartz, Jeremy I. '44 '69 (MD) C&L.446 B.A., J.D.
Scott, John W. '59 '85 C&L.276 B.A., J.D.
Seasonwein, Robert G. '46 '75 C.446 B.A. L.823 J.D.
Sellers, William P., IV '45 '71 (VA) C.228 A.B. L.692 J.D.
Sharp, Robert Donald '39 '70 (MI) C.932 B.A. L.912 J.D.
Shave, Betty-Ellen '55 '80 C.860 B.A. L.273 J.D.
Shepherd, Cynthia Marian '67 '92 (VA) C&L.893 B.A., J.D.
Siegal, Susan L. '— '82 C.156 B.A. L.276 J.D.
Silberberg, Wendy J. '54 '91 C.787 B.S. L.128 J.D.
Silverwood, James R. '45 '73 C.339 B.A. L.209 J.D.
Simonson, Andrew Richard '66 '92 C.804 B.S. L.904 J.D.
Simonson, David M. '44 '69 (MD) C&L.446 A.B., J.D.
Simotas, Lisa '67 '93 C.477 B.A. L.569 J.D.
Sinclair, Susan A. '54 '78 C.454 B.A. L.329 J.D.
Smith, Kevin Ryan '58 '85 (MA) C.321 B.A. L.431 J.D.
Smith, Richard C. '61 '88 (FL) C.1010 B.A. L.260 J.D.
Smith, Susan L. '55 '79 (TX) C.59 B.A. L.326 J.D.
Snow, Thomas G. '55 '82 C.945 B.A. L.893 J.D.
Spalding, Jeffery S. '71 '96 C.27 B.A. L.477 J.D.
Spencer, Kara L. '71 '96 (VA) C.160 B.A. L.790 J.D.
Stansell-Gamm, Martha J. '51 '76 (MI) C.210 B.A. L.276 J.D.
Stapleton, William H., Jr. '50 '80 C.893 B.A. L.128 J.D.
Stark, Daniel C. '65 '91 C.1350 B.A. L.1009 J.D.
Stein, Murray R. '31 '63 (MD) C.999 B.S. L.273 LL.B.
Stemler, Patty Merkamp '51 '76 (PA) C.645 B.A. L.665 J.D.
Stevens, Gregory B. '64 '92 C.846 B.A. L.128 J.D.
Stone, Cynthia '58 '94 (NY) C.145 M.A. L.1009 J.D.
Stone, Victor D. L. '47 '72 C.188 B.S. L.309 J.D.
Stutman, Edward A. '45 '71 C&L.831 A.B., J.D.
Surgalla, Michael J., Jr. '58 '83 (NY) C&L.107 J.D.
Sussmann, Michael A. '64 '90 C.705 B.S. L.1009 J.D.
Tafe, Joseph J. '39 '65 (PA) C.390 B.A. L.831
Tamm, Thomas M. '52 '77 C.103 A.B. L.276 J.D.
Taylor, Karen L. '58 '83 (AR) C&L.45 B.S.P.A., J.D.
T'Kach, Stephen J. '56 '88 (MN) C.962 B.S. L.1035 J.D.
Tobin, Yoel '61 '87 (MA) C.178 A.B. L.309 J.D.
Toner, Gerald A. '45 '73 (NY) C.1044 A.B. L.107 J.D.
Torpoco, Edward A. '— '99 C.276 B.S. L.309 J.D.
Urofsky, Philip E. '63 '89 (VA) C&L.893 B.A., J.D.
Vaky, Paul S. '54 '86 (MD) C.446 B.A. L.276 J.D.
Van Lonkhuyzen, John W. '— '85 (MA) C.31 B.A. L.976 J.D.
Varner, Christopher L. '51 '77 C.575 B.A. L.880 J.D.
Vogel, Karen A. '48 '80 C.790 B.S. L.1218 J.D.
Wallace, Ann T. '43 '68 (MA) C.454 B.A. L.818 J.D.
Wallace, Robert E. '59 '85 (MA) C.321 B.A. L.128 J.D.
Walsh, Edward J. '43 '74 (PA) C.728 B.S. L.884 J.D.
Warner, David P. '66 '93 C.608 B.A. L.30 J.D.
Warren, Jimmye S. '45 '78 (CO) C&L.208 B.A., J.D.
Warren, Mary Lee '42 '78 (GA) C.518 A.B. L.93 J.D.
Wasserman, Steven B. '69 '95 C.260 B.A. L.273 J.D.
Watson, Deborah '47 '77 (VA) C&L.945 B.A., J.D.
Weglian, Stephen M., Jr. '41 '67 (MI) C&L.851 B.Ed., J.D.
Weiner, Roger G. '49 '75 (CA) C.107 B.A. L.770 J.D.
Weintraub, Beneva '43 '78 C.605 A.B. L.276 J.D.
Wiedis, Richard N. '63 '88 C.477 B.A. L.276 J.D.
Williams, Marshall R. '40 '72 (VA) C.945 A.B. L.838 J.D.
Wolff, Paula A. '52 '78 C.273 B.A. L.904 J.D.
Wyderko, Joseph C. '56 '81 C.659 B.S. L.188 J.D.
Yost, Mark J. '58 '90 (MD) C.869 B.S. L.276 J.D.
Young, Rex L. '47 '73 (TX) C.623 B.A. L.802 J.D.
Yurek, William '— '97 (VA) C.1070 B.S. L.276 J.D.
Zarate, Juan C. '71 '97 (CA) C&L.309 A.B., J.D.

DRUG ENFORCEMENT ADMINISTRATION

Basnight, Kord H. '62 '89 (VA) C.945 B.A. L.692 J.D.
Bayly, W. Brian '51 '77 C&L.362 B.A., J.D.
Byler, Charles A. '44 '75 (CA) C.112 B.A. L.1049 LL.B.
Clark, John F., IV '62 '88 (LA) C.797 B.A. L.420 J.D.
Clark, M. Wesley '50 '75 C.276 B.S.F.S. L.128 J.D.
Clements, Donald A. '48 '84 (VA) C.122 B.A. L.1209 J.D.
Croft, Julia E. '64 '89 C.569 B.A. L.276 J.D.
Cuilwik, Alysia A. '64 '90 C.788 B.A. L.94 J.D.
Cummings, John M., Jr. '65 '91 (MD) C.30 B.A. L.128 J.D.
D'Orazio, Lawrence A., Jr. '58 '85 (GA) C.999 B.A. L.245 J.D.
Dormont, Daniel '63 '90 (PA) C.659 B.A. L.93 J.D.
Gallagher, Julie C. '60 '85 C.1369 B.S. L.273 J.D.
Gleason, Robert C '62 '87 (VA) C&L.945 B.A., J.D.
Goldman, Bettie E. '58 '87 C.611 B.A. L.128 J.D.
Goldstein, Lynn L. S. '50 '77 C.1140 B.A. L.64 J.D.
Hambuechen, James P. '53 '84 C.174 B.A. L.273 J.D.
Harrison, Ellen '52 '77 (NJ) C.66 B.A. L.705 J.D.
Hieronymus, John O. '— '86 C.912 B.S. L.213 J.D.
Holiman, Susan C. '64 '89 (PA) C.273 B.A. L.128 J.D.
Kaufman, Steven '64 '89 C.273 B.A. L.30 J.D.
King, Terrence J. '62 '88 (MD) C.445 B.S. L.446 J.D.
Medema, Richard A. '56 '81 C.323 B.A. L.912 J.D.
Miles, Victoria Smith '50 '78 C.914 B.A. L.273 J.D.
Mitchell, Gregory J. '58 '83 (VA) C.1329 B.A. L.945 J.D.
Murphy, Elizabeth '59 '87 C.1044 B.S. L.1209 J.D.
Nomady, Mark D. '59 '84 C.801 B.A. L.365 J.D.
Pomares, Carmen R. '63 '88 C.322 B.A. L.128 J.D.
Rashid, Vicki L. '64 '89 (PA) C.665 B.A. L.276 J.D.
Richardson, Robert T. '40 '68 (NY) C&L.724 B.B.A., LL.B.
Ryan, Cynthia R. '54 '79 (DE) C.205 B.A. L.1338 J.D. Chief Coun.
Short, Francis R. '52 '83 (MD) C.871 B.S. L.64 J.D.
Siegel, Steven Nathan '67 '94 (NY) C.645 B.A. L.563 J.D.
Snyder, Eric J. '— '94 (NY) C&L.569 B.S., J.D.
Sola, Stephen A. '63 '89 C.103 A.B. L.1066 J.D.
Spelke, Robert A. '57 '83 C.472 B.B.A. L.1019 J.D.
Vincent, Odessa F. '56 '85 C.1280 B.A. L.329 J.D.
Walker, Jayme S. '61 '89 (IN) C.675 B.A. L.879 J.D.
Walker, Robert W. '58 '89 C.932 B.S. L.329 J.D.
Wilkinson, Carol M. '— '91 (CA) C.741 B.A. L.1049 J.D.
Willingham, Gloria J. '— '75 C.257 B.A. L.276 J.D.

Office of the Administrative Law Judge

Bittner, Mary Ellen '47 '72 C&L.339 B.S., J.D. Chief Adm. Law J.
Randall, Gail A. '49 '84 C.942 B.A. L.910 J.D. Adm. Law J.

FEDERAL BUREAU OF INVESTIGATION

Ainora, Thomas '51 '76 C.276 B.S. L.705 J.D.
Auerswald, Steven C. '51 '76 C.207 B.A. L.692 J.D.
Baker, D. Stephen '54 '86 (VA) C.880 B.A. L.1209 J.D.
Beers, Elizabeth Rae '61 '96 (MD) C.319 B.A. L.446 J.D.
Bessee, Cecilia O. '65 '91 (NY) C.178 B.A. L.1019 J.D.
Blair, Randolph N. '64 '92 C&L.64 B.A., J.D.
Blumenfeld, Laura Ross '48 '73 C.788 B.A. L.659 J.D.
Bobinski, Peter S. '49 '79 (RI) C.676 B.A. L.818 J.D.
Bowman, M. E. '44 '77 (ID) C.950 B.A. L.336 J.D.
Broussard, Edward M. '60 '89 (GA) C&L.280 A.B., J.D.
Brown, Jacqueline FitzGerald '63 '89 C&L.260 B.A., J.D.
Brown, Richard R. '55 '88 C.1113 B.A. L.665 J.D.
Calogero, Valerie P. '62 '88 C.383 B.A. L.276 J.D.
Chabinsky, Steven R. '65 '91 (NY) C&L.228 A.B., J.D.
Cole, Ford R. '47 '76 C&L.602 B.A., J.D.
Cordes, Jack R., Jr. '52 '77 (OH) C&L.930 B.A., J.D.
Coyle, Robert E. '40 '66 C&L.879 B.A., J.D.
Dinoto, Lizanne '59 '99 C.1199 B.A. L.30 J.D.
Donovan, Christopher R. '65 '90 (GA) C.260 B.S. L.362 J.D.
Eller, Amanda L. '70 '97 (NC) C.896 B.A. L.228 J.D.
Falls, Cynthia Ann '59 '85 (AR) C.43 B.A. L.45 J.D.
Feitel, Robert J. '66 '90 C.477 A.B. L.446 J.D.
Franko, Dennis E. '51 '81 (VA) C.754 B.S. L.1209 J.D.
Fudge, Gregory M. '52 '83 (IN) C.344 B.A. L.345 J.D.
Gallagher, Daniel T. '51 '81 (VA) C.886 B.A. L.192 J.D.
Gregor, Bradley S. '59 '85 (IL) C.339 B.S. L.910 J.D.
Grzeskowiak, Colleen B. '56 '89 (NY) C.1044 B.A. L.823 J.D.
Haley, Laura Beth '66 '91 (WV) C&L.923 B.A., J.D.
Hayn, Linda Susan '53 '78 (IL) C.623 B.A. L.893 J.D.
Hazen, Renee L. '61 '93 (PA) C.1356 B.S. L.1187 J.D.
Healy Weigand, Nancy A. '61 '86 (MA) C.454 B.A. L.93 J.D.
Hodes, Scott A. '64 '89 C.347 B.S. L.36 J.D.
Ingber, Laura R. '63 '91 (FL) C&L.472 B.A., J.D.
Ivashkiv, Sophia marta '63 '91 (CA) C.178 B.A. L.94 J.D.
Jacobson, Michael Noam '69 '96 C.1036 B.A. L.93 J.D.
Jensen, David W. '65 '91 (TX) C.880 B.A. L.16 J.D.
Jobe, Stephen J. '61 '90 (VA) C&L.896 B.A., J.D.
Johnson, Octavia R. '66 '93 C.260 B.A. L.325 J.D.
Kaiden, Mindy A. '65 '90 C.188 B.S. L.904 J.D.
Kalisch, Eleni Pryles '61 '87 C.280 A.B.J. L.1059 J.D.
Kelley, Patrick W. '48 '73 (NC) C.475 B.S. L.228 J.D.
Kim, Hyon J. '69 '95 C.976 B.A. L.569 J.D.
Klein, Donald J. '49 '75 (NY) C.610 B.A. L.1019 J.D.
Lammert, Elaine N. '— '94 (NJ) C.821 B.A. L.910 J.D.
Lang, Anthony K. '67 '94 C.145 B.A. L.831 J.D.
Larson, David C. '43 '75 (CA) C.911 B.A. L.770 J.D.
Leons, Natalia R. '63 '89 C.1036 B.A. L.446 J.D.
Levensohn, Betsy J. '69 '96 C.104 B.A. L.1066 J.D.
Leylegian, J. Gregory '65 '90 C.676 B.A. L.904 J.D.
Livingston, John R., Jr. '64 '89 (IN) C&L.347 B.A., J.D.
Lovelace, James G. '50 '79 (OH) C.446 B.A. L.1292 J.D.
Marciano, Charles A. '48 '75 (MA) C&L.93 B.A., J.D.

DEPARTMENT OF JUSTICE (Continued)

Martin, Kristine M.J. '42 '86 (VA) C.1029 B.A. L.128 J.D.
McCullough, I. Charles, III '66 '94 C.383 B.A. L.1017 J.D.
McDonald, Alan R. '47 '74 (IN) C.347 B.A. L.421 J.D.
Miller, William A. '47 '76 (TN) C.910 B.A. L.838 J.D.
Moran, Robert A. '45 '73 C.321 A.B. L.276 J.D.
Motta, Thomas Gregory '59 '84 (ME) C.1200 B.A. L.1294 J.D.
Nigh, Brett '— '92 (VA) C.1 B.A. L.893 B.A.
O'Neill, M. Sean '69 '95 C.602 B.A. L.273 J.D.
O'Neill-Taylor, Kathleen '67 '92 (MA) C.93 B.A. L.818 J.D.
Oswald, Donald E. '58 '88 C.1376 B.S. L.1206 J.D.
Parkinson, Larry R. '54 '83 C.590 B.S. L.309 J.D.
Pavlak, Stanley G., Jr. '61 '86 (OH) C.145 B.A. L.930 J.D.
Pointer, Homer S. '48 '73 (TX) C.47 B.A. L.846 J.D.
Porcelli, Stefania M. '69 '93 (VA) C.228 A.B. L.273 J.D.
Sabol, Sherry E. '65 '93 (MA) C.299 B.A. L.273 J.D.
Sampson, Rita M. '66 '92 (VA) C.945 B.A. L.896 J.D.
Semo, Alina M. '63 '89 C.446 B.A. L.276 J.D.
Stafford, John H. '58 '83 (IL) C.337 B.A. L.801 J.D.
Stonestreet, Kreg S. '61 '87 (KS) C.378 B.S. L.900 J.D.
Szwajkowski, Leslie M. '53 '81 (IL) C.597 B.S. L.910 J.D.
Tate, C. Michelle '58 '84 C.356 B.A. L.500 J.D.
Thomas, Raymond C. '56 '85 C.473 B.A. L.607 J.D.
Tucker, Shelley L. '57 '84 (AL) C&L.16 B.A., J.D.
Vasquez, Mary Hogan '65 '93 C.436 B.A. L.276 J.D.
Wainwright, Duncan J. '54 '79 (IL) C.927 B.A. L.879 J.D.
Waterman, K. Krasnow '57 '90 (AZ) C.659 B.A. L.978 J.D.
Welby, William F. '49 '74 (MA) C.1200 B.A. L.818 J.D.
Williams, Edward L., Jr. '58 '84 (NJ) C.282 B.A. L.776 J.D.
Woods, Michael J. '63 '93 (MA) C.051 B.A. L.309 J.D.
Woods, Stephanie B. '— '96 C.420 B.A. L.861 J.D.
Zall, Terri A. '64 '88 C.446 B.A. L.659 J.D.

FOREIGN CLAIMS SETTLEMENT COMMISSION OF THE UNITED STATES

Barrett, Jaleh F. '44 '86 (VA) C.273 B.A. L.904 J.D.
Bradley, David E. '49 '80 C.198 A.B. L.273 J.D. Chief Coun.
Lacey, John R. '45 '71 C.276 B.S.F.S. L.893 J.D. Chairman
White, Richard Thomas '45 '70 C.511 A.B. L.309 J.D.

EXECUTIVE OFFICE FOR IMMIGRATION REVIEW

Adkins-Blanch, Charles K. '62 '90 C.293 B.A. L.273 J.D.
Agronick, Lois B. '53 '79 (RI) C.103 A.B. L.846 J.D.
Albamonte, Elena Marie '56 '83 (GA) C.446 B.A. L.469 J.D.
Appling, Cathy L. '70 '96 (MD) C.606 B.A. L.30 J.D.
Armstrong, H. Jere '41 '66 C&L.16 B.A., J.D. Judge
Baker, Glen R. '60 '94 (NC) C.1369 B.A. L.1187 J.D.
Barton, Robert L., Jr. '43 '69 C.665 B.A. L.93 J.D.
Bates, Elizabeth Puller '67 '95 C.228 A.B. L.893 J.D.
Bathe, David H. '54 '80 (VA) C.94 B.A. L.588 J.D.
Baumeister, Monica B. '70 '95 (WA) C.367 B.A. L.352 J.D.
Belvedere, Christopher E. '58 '91 C.1044 B.A. L.273 J.D.
Bolyard, David L. '52 '76 C.280 A.B. L.273 J.D.
Bradford, Anne Marie '54 '79 (GA) C.797 B.A. L.228 J.D.
Brady, Laura '— '95 (OH) C.473 B.A. L.608 J.D.
Brooks, Zita H. '49 '77 C.446 B.A. L.1209 J.D.
Brown, Keith O'Brien '61 '87 (SC) C.789 B.A. L.838 J.D.
Buss, Charlyn J. '44 '73 C.293 B.A. L.705 J.D.
Caine, Patrick R. '26 '62 C.500 A.B. L.1048 LL.B.
Campbell, Keith R. '59 '95 (PA) C.436 B.A. L.1338 J.D.
Chapman, Martha '54 '78 (AL) C&L.16 B.A., J.D.
Ching, Pamela K.S. '61 '89 (HI) C.518 A.B. L.30 J.D.
Clark, Molly Kendall '52 '78 C.170 B.A. L.818 J.D.
Crabbs, Karen Yvonne '66 '94 C.763 B.A. L.990 J.D.
Creppy, Michael J. '54 '80 C.254 B.A. L.329 J.D.
de Cardona, Lisa Ann '64 '90 (PA) C.728 B.A. L.1338 J.D.
Donovan, John F. '50 '84 C.999 B.A. L.30 J.D.
Dufresne, Jill H. '53 '78 (VA) C.30 B.A. L.893 J.D.
Dunn, Patricia A. '50 '78 C.1044 B.A. L.602 J.D.
Dunne, Mary Maguire '41 '67 (NY) C.562 B.A. L.724 J.D.
Echavarren, Daniel '49 '80 C.446 B.A. L.276 J.D.
Elliot, Carolyn A. '49 '77 C.494 B.A. L.260 J.D.
Faber, Elise M. '61 '87 (IL) C.597 B.A. L.276 J.D.
Filppu, Lauri Steven '47 '73 (NY) C&L.107 B.A., J.D.
Franco, Danielle '69 '99 (VA) C.128 B.A. L.180 J.D.
Friedrich, Andrea C. '63 '92 (PA) C&L.910 A.B., J.D.
Gipe, Bruce Paul, Jr. '66 '92 C.905 B.S. L.329 J.D.
Greer, Anne J. '58 '92 C.25 B.A. L.1356 J.D.
Grimm, Elizabeth M. '62 '88 (MO) C.910 B.A. L.477 J.D.
Grinberg-Funes, George A. '50 '79 (MA) C.276 B.S.F.S. L.1048 J.D.
Griswold, Stephen S. '56 '86 (MD) C.918 B.A. L.273 J.D.
Grosserode, Kenneth Lee '69 '95 (CA) C.846 B.A. L.767 J.D.
Heilman, Michael J. '46 '77 (WI) C&L.966 B.A., J.D.
Helf, Sheila '62 '89 (MD) C.446 B.A. L.273 J.D.
Hines, Judith K. '46 '80 C.739 B.A. L.910 J.D.
Hoffman, Sharon Corey '55 '81 (VA) C.216 B.A. L.902 J.D.
Holiona, Hope Malia '59 '86 (VA) C.112 B.A. L.273 J.D.
Holmes, David B. '48 '73 C.478 B.A. L.273 J.D.
Hurwitz, Gerald S. '49 '74 C.216 A.B. L.831 J.D.
Huynh Nguyen, Ann '53 '78
Ikezawa, Wendy H. '53 '78 (HI) C.604 A.B. L.276 J.D.
John, Kathy Lanita '54 '80 C.575 B.A. L.128 J.D.
Jones, Philemina McNeill '— '77 (NC) C.369 B.A. L.575 J.D.
Keller, Mary Beth '62 '87 (IA) C.128 B.A. L.893 J.D.
Kelly, Edward F. '60 '87 (VA) C&L.602 B.A.
King, Jean Campbell '66 '95 (CT) C.103 A.B. L.945 J.D.
Kishmir, Anne Greer '58 '92 C.25 B.A. L.1209 J.D.
Kocur, Ana M. '71 '96 (VA) C.645 B.A. L.30 J.D.
Kolbe, Margaret M. '65 '96 (OH) C.150 B.A. L.602 J.D.
Lee, Lori M. '69 '94 (MD) C.228 B.A. L.273 J.D.
Levine, Laurence David '65 '92 C.260 B.A. L.273 J.D.
Liebmann, Beth S. '59 '84 C.1036 B.A. L.472 J.D.
Liebowitz, Ellen '66 '90 (MD) C.205 B.A. L.446 J.D.
Lippman, Daniel '51 '78 (OH) C.30 B.A. L.8 J.D.
Mackey, Deepali Nadkarni '69 '95 (GA) C.469 B.A. L.245 J.D.
Mann, Ana L. '60 '85 (NJ) C.705 B.A. L.273 J.D.
Martin, George R. '57 '84 C&L.945 B.A., J.D.
Mateen, Fatimah A. '68 '95 C.112 B.A. L.30 J.D.
McGoings, Michael C. '43 '74 C.512 B.A. L.128 J.D.
Miller, Neil P. '44 '74 (AZ) C&L.37 B.A., J.D.
Minton, Amy M. '65 '91 (TN) C.837 B.S. L.836 J.D.
Miovski, Lourene Marija '60 '85 (WA) C.911 B.A. L.1358 J.D.
Misra, Neha '69 '94 (PA) C.347 B.S. L.904 J.D.
Monsky, Paul S. '65 '90 C.347 B.A. L.245 J.D.
Morris, James P. '29 '58 (MD) C&L.273 A.B., LL.B.
Morse, Marvin H. '29 '52 (NY) C.165 A.B. L.976 LL.B.
Moscato, Anthony C. '45 '75 C.178 B.A. L.273 J.D.
Neal, David L. '59 '90 C.894 A.B. L.178 J.D.
Nimick, C. Lockhart '61 '90 (NY) C.674 A.B. L.910 J.D.
O'Cadiz, Sergio A. '66 '97 (CA) C.112 B.A. L.1067 J.D.
O'Herron, Margaret M.R. '— '94 (MD) C.104 A.B. L.276 J.D.
Ohlson, Kevin A. '60 '85 C.901 B.A. L.893 J.D.
O'Leary, Brian M. '60 '85 (MA) C.276 B.S.F.S. L.1202 J.D.
Oshinsky, John S. '58 '83 C.446 B.A. L.273 J.D.
Owens, Robert P. '49 '79 C.999 B.S. L.1162 J.D.
Padgett, Gail B. '49 '81 C.1059 B.S. L.276 J.D.
Patel, Rita M. '72 '96 (PA) C.30 B.A. L.1017 J.D.
Payne, Anthony Cardozo '69 '95 (MD) C.893 B.A. L.276 J.D.
Perkins, Jack E. '43 '72 C.768 B.A. L.1065 J.D.
Phelps, George A. '59 '94 (MD) C.446 B.A. L.30 J.D.
Piccotti, Carolyn M. '57 '84 (PA) C.216 B.A. L.1017 J.D.
Premysler, Debra '61 '89 C&L.30 B.A., J.D.
Puffer, Christine E. '65 '90 (MA) C.242 B.A. L.818 J.D.
Pullen, Thomas L. '43 '69 C.927 B.A. L.365 J.D. Judge
Ragland, Thomas K. '66 '94 (MD) C.893 B.A. L.93 J.D.
Rahill, Michael F. '46 '74 (NJ) C.93 B.A. L.564 J.D.
Ramirez, Sergio J. '68 '95 (MD) C.569 B.S. L.30 J.D.
Rappaport, Nolan W. '44 '72 (MD) C&L.879 B.S., J.D.
Riddick, Harry S., Jr. '47 '83 (VA) C.575 A.B. L.692 J.D.
Riemer, Steven R. '49 '74 (OH) C.610 B.B.A. L.608 J.D.
Ries, Lora L. '71 '96 (IL) C&L.879 B.A., J.D.
Riotto, Sharon '52 '78 (NY) C.188 A.B. L.107 J.D.
Rivers, Billy Jack '39 '73 (AL) C.1244 B.A. L.192 J.D.
Rosen, Daisy '62 '88 C&L.472 B.A., J.D.
Rosenberg, Lory D. '46 '77 C.569 B.F.A. L.588 J.D.
Saltsman, Gary D. '51 '79 (OH) C.97 B.S. L.608 J.D.
Scally, Erin L. '56 '81 (OH) C.607 B.A. L.8 J.D.
Schmidt, Paul W. '48 '73 C.399 B.A. L.966 J.D.
Segal, Alice '70 '96 (NJ) C.659 B.A. L.273 J.D.
Smith, Kevin D. '53 '84 (LA) C&L.803 B.A., J.D.
Stogner, W. Wayne '49 '74 (MS) C&L.500 B.A., J.D.
Taylor, Margaret K. '50 '91 (VA) C.101 B.A. L.1209 J.D.
Tousley, Thomas H. '56 '83 (IN) C.30 B.A. L.347 J.D.
Urban, Joan L. '41 '77 C.473 B.A. L.30 J.D.
Vacca, Fred W. '42 '65 C&L.724 B.B.A., J.D.
Venkatraman, Bharathi A. '68 '97 (NJ) L.904 J.D.
Waters, J. Keith '— '86 C.893 B.A. L.1209 J.D.
Waxman, Bruce I. '42 '68 (NY) C.188 B.S. L.178 J.D.
White, Mary B. '54 '84 C.683 B.A. L.421 J.D.

EXECUTIVE OFFICE FOR UNITED STATES ATTORNEYS

Bailie, Michael W. '53 '79 (CT) C.1029 B.A. L.724 J.D.
Benderson, Judith K. '46 '83 C.273 B.A. L.30 J.D.
Bernson, Victor E., Jr. '64 '89 (MA) C.103 B.A. L.94 J.D.
Brewer, C. Madison '42 '68 C.645 B.A. L.273 J.D.
Carey, Tracey Shaffer '57 '84 (VA) C.886 B.S. L.30 J.D.
Coniglio, Peter J. '51 '81 (IA) C.165 A.B. L.221 J.D.
Davis, Teresa '— '92 (MO) L.734 J.D.
DeFalaise, Louis '45 '71 (KY) C.1118 B.A. L.383 J.D.
DeHaan, Richard L. '43 '77 C&L.64 B.S., J.D.
Dettelbach, Steven M. '65 '91 C.197 A.B. L.309 J.D.
Gay, Bonnie Lewis '42 '64 C&L.30 B.A., J.D.
Gess, Nicholas M. '55 '81 (ME) C.95 A.B. L.1294 J.D.
Gontram, Joseph M. '46 '73 C.276 B.S. L.884 J.D.
Howard, Virginia H. '53 '84 (TX) C.846 B.A. L.802 J.D.
Lankler, Tracey Splaine '65 '93 C.446 B.A. L.190 J.D.
Little, Suzanne '54 '84 C.338 B.A. L.1209 J.D.
Moran, Michael P. '60 '85 (CT) C.1350 B.A. L.1019 J.D.
Murguia, Mary H. '60 '86 (KS) C&L.378 B.S.B.A., J.D.
Naimon, David A. '61 '87 C.674 A.B. L.893 J.D.
Newton, F. Page '52 '81 C.311 B.A. L.276 J.D.
Paulose, Rachel K. '73 '97 C.494 B.A. L.976 J.D.
Santelle, James Lewis '58 '83 (WI) C.436 B.A. L.145 J.D.
Solien, Lynne M. '63 '88 (WI) C.489 B.A. L.436 J.D.
Stewart, William Garrett, II '47 '76 C.197 A.B. L.273 J.D.
Wink, Robin S. '62 '92 C.1070 B.S. L.128 J.D.

EXECUTIVE OFFICE FOR UNITED STATES TRUSTEES

Barnhill, Leander D. '58 '89 C.871 B.S. L.259 J.D.
Bridenhagen, Paul W. '57 '85 (PA) C.423 B.A. L.128 J.D.
Ciccone, Anthony J., Jr. '53 '78 C.823 B.A. L.273 J.D.
Daugherty, John L. '63 '88 C&L.893 B.A., J.D.
Davis, Martha L. '51 '80 (VA) C.945 B.A. L.128 J.D. Gen. Coun.
Estryn, Esther I. '— '75 C.951 B.A. L.1202 J.D.
Guzinski, Joseph A. '54 '83 (MD) C.445 B.A. L.893 J.D.
Miller, Jeffrey M. '40 '65 C.102 B.A. L.724 LL.B.
Slates, Sue Ann '— '89 (NM) C&L.560 B.S., J.D.
Sutko, P. Matthew '56 '83 C.434 B.A. L.893 J.D.

IMMIGRATION AND NATURALIZATION SERVICE

Office of the General Counsel

Anderson, Peder A. '44 '69 C&L.585 B.S.B.A., J.D.
Arthur, Andrew R. '66 '92 (MD) C.893 B.A. L.273 J.D.
Baxter, Laura A. '66 '91 (WI) C&L.966 B.A., J.D.
Brown, Robert J. '63 '92 (VA) C.299 A.B. L.273 J.D.
Busby, Scott W. '59 '91 (CA) C.31 B.A. L.1066 J.D.

Busch, Philip B. '62 '90 C.951 B.A. L.893 J.D.
Cameron, Michael Kevin '55 '81 (NC) C.902 B.A. L.896 J.D.
Carpenter, Dea D. '64 '89 (VA) C&L.1209 B.A., J.D.
Cooper, Owen B. '62 '88 (LA) C&L.861 B.A., J.D. Gen. Coun.
Coster, Michael J. '58 '84 (VA) C.945 B.B.A. L.1209 J.D.
Dixon, David M. '32 '59 C&L.880 B.A., LL.B.
Doig, Julia K. '66 '90 (LA) C.518 A.B. L.420 J.D.
Finkelstein, Robert S. '50 '75 (MD) C.282 B.A. L.446 J.D.
Gisser, S. Alexander '57 '87 (CT) C.367 B.A. L.569 J.D.
Gregory, Peter D. '60 '86 (VA) C.436 B.A. L.1209 J.D.
Hamilton, Cristina Navarro '61 '86 (OH) C&L.8 B.A., J.D.
Hernandez, Efren, III '68 '94 (NY) C.843 B.A. L.145 J.D.
Hinds, Ian G. '64 '90 C.31 B.A. L.976 J.D.
Jones, Carolyn D. '60 '87 (MA) C&L.1048 B.S., J.D.
Kendall, Sarah M. '— '96 (TX) C.859 B.A. L.326 J.D.
Kummings, William W. '42 '69 C.623 B.A. L.8 J.D.
Latimer, Kyle D. '59 '86 (UT) C.101 B.A. L.878 J.D.
Lay, Dorothea B. '65 '94 (OR) C.1193 B.A. L.1051 J.D.
Lieberman, Joan S. '50 '76 C&L.446 B.A., J.D.
London, Joanna '— '73 C.681 A.B. L.477 J.D.
Martinez, Janette Marie '71 '96 (FL) C.260 B.A. L.273 J.D.
Mathias, Susan M. '66 '91 C&L.446 B.A., J.D.
McGee, Ramona L. '— '93 (OH) C.93 B.A. L.188 J.D.
Misir, Deborah Nirmala '71 '97 (MA) C.145 B.A. L.494 J.D.
Neifach, Michael '66 '91 C.477 B.A. L.273 J.D.
Parchert, Brett M. '67 '92 (TN) C.340 B.A. L.1015 J.D.
Podolny, Janice B. '49 '75 (MD) C.273 B.A. L.446 J.D.
Raynsford, Craig O. '55 '81 (CA) C.112 B.A. L.276 J.D.
Romig, Jeffrey L. '59 '85 (PA) C.229 B.A. L.665 J.D.
Ryan, J. Kelly '63 '90 (NY) C.861 B.A. L.276 J.D.
Sachs, Martin H. '47 '73 C.705 B.A. L.30 J.D.
Sagerman, Roger F. '66 '94 (CO) C.860 B.A. L.107 J.D.
Sheridan, Michael J. '58 '87 (MN) C.755 B.A. L.1035 J.D.
Slous, Joan '49 '73 C.994 B.A. L.1009 J.D.
Smith, Alice J. '57 '88 C.806 B.A. L.893 J.D.
Steinberg, Andrew J. '64 '91 C.893 B.A. L.1068 J.D.
Strathern, Arthur D. '64 '88 (GA) C.1365 B.A. L.280 J.D.
Tournay, Frederick H. '53 '80 (ID) C.1208 B.S. L.336 J.D.
Whitney, Ronald W. '65 '90 (LA) C&L.420 B.S., J.D.
Wood, Douglas S. '41 '72 (VA) C&L.945 B.A., J.D.

Coven, Phyllis A. '55 '82 (MA) C.94 B.A. L.818 J.D.
Flournoy, David T. '69 '94 C&L.893 B.A., J.D. Coun. to Dep. Commissioner
Hecht, Julie L. '62 '88 C.112 B.A. L.1049 J.D.
Scialabba, Lori L. '— '85 (IL) C.446 B.A. L.836 J.D.
Walton, Kenneth '60 '86 (OH) C.150 B.S. L.930 J.D.

WASHINGTON, D.C. DISTRICT OFFICE

Augustin, Genevieve E. '68 '96 (MD) C.1222 B.S. L.276 J.D.
Dizengoff, Bruce Brian '63 '88 (PA) C.645 B.S. L.831 J.D. Dep. Dist. Coun.
Klauck, Karl D. '49 '74 (PA) C&L.94 A.B., J.D.
Paskey, Stephen '60 '94 (MD) C.475 B.A. L.446 J.D.
Rosas, Eloise '45 '78 C.1125 B.A. L.276 J.D. Dist. Coun.
Todd, Deborah K. '53 '83 C.30 B.A. L.1209 J.D.
Vazquez de Schwartz, Graciela '47 '75 C.677 B.B.A. L.1088 J.D.
Wong, Siu P. '66 '94 (PA) C.273 B.A. L.494 J.D.

ENVIRONMENT AND NATURAL RESOURCES DIVISION

Ahern, Elizabeth M. '63 '88 C.103 A.B. L.893 J.D.
Ahmad, Fataima Z. '68 '95 C.260 B.S. L.904 J.D.
Akers, Susan M. '65 '91 (FL) C.896 B.S. L.228 J.D.
Allen, Leslie '58 '86 C.914 B.A. L.1066 J.D.
Anderson, Esperanza '— '91 (PA) C.183 B.A. L.588 J.D.
Appel, Peter A. '64 '91 C&L.976 B.A., J.D.
Areias, Allison V. '64 '94 C.112 B.A. L.1067 J.D.
Askman, David F. '62 '89 (WY) C&L.972 B.A., J.D.
Ault, Wayne T. '59 '87 C.347 B.A. L.904 J.D.
Baer, Steven R. '49 '74 C.273 B.A. L.276 J.D.
Baker, Michael K. '46 '72 (MA) C.860 B.A. L.93 J.D.
Barr, Lewis M. '53 '78 C.566 B.A. L.273 J.D.
Barry, Patrick '53 '79 (AZ) C&L.629 B.A., J.D.
Barsky, Seth M. '65 '90 (PA) C&L.659 B.A., J.D.
Bartell, Stephen G. '66 '92 (CO) C.472 B.B.A. L.208 J.D.
Basciano, Vincent P. '57 '94 C.446 B.A. L.30 J.D.
Bauer, Scott D. '69 '98 (NC) C.893 B.A. L.575 J.D.
Baylor, Lewis M. '52 '77 (VA) C.893 B.A. L.692 J.D.
Beal, Richard L. '40 '63 (CO) C&L.972 B.A., J.D.
Beckhard, Daniel C. '56 '82 C.309 A.B. L.659 J.D.
Beehler, Alex A. '53 '78 C.674 A.B. L.893 J.D.
Bellas, Leslie Beth '64 '90 C.66 B.A. L.276 J.D.
Bennett, Aaron S. '33 '59 C&L.378 B.A., LL.B.
Bentkover, Frank N. '43 '68 (IL) C.597 B.S.B.A. L.145 J.D.
Berlowe, Andrea L. '64 '93 (MD) C.882 B.S. L.1194 J.D.
Birdsong, Bret C. '64 '94 C.674 A.B. L.1065 J.D.
Birnbaum, Alan '62 '89 (NY) C.188 B.S. L.569 J.D.
Biros, Francis J. '38 '77 (VA) C.1113 B.S. L.30 J.D.
Blackmer, S. Jonathan C. '48 '75 C.575 A.B. L.276 J.D.
Blake, Wendy L. '67 '94 C.893 B.A. L.1209 J.D.
Blanco, Caroline M. '61 '90 C.597 B.A. L.904 J.D.
Blesi, Samuel D. '54 '81 C.150 B.A. L.201 J.D.
Boling, Edward A. '63 '90 (VA) C.890 B.A. L.910 J.D.
Boudreaux, Paul J. '60 '88 C&L.893 B.A., J.D.
Bowman, Warigia M. '68 '94 (TX) C.178 B.A. L.846 J.D.
Brandon, Barry W. '— '88 (WA) C.907 B.A. L.911 J.D.
Brenner, Alan '36 '60 C.228 B.A. L.276 J.D.
Brighton, William D. '52 '79 C.339 A.B. L.477 J.D.
Brock, Matthew T. '52 '82 (ME) C.918 B.A. L.1218 J.D.
Brodney, Robert Michael '— '83 (CA) C.112 B.A. L.809 J.D.
Brook, Robert D. '54 '79 (OR) C.339 B.A. L.1051 J.D.
Brooks, Phillip A. '56 '82 (KY) C&L.383 B.A., J.D.
Brookshire, James E. '51 '76 C.576 B.A. L.790 J.D.
Brown, Mark A. '68 '94 (FL) C.472 A.B. L.260 J.D.
Bryson, John A. '46 '76 C.178 B.A. L.276 J.D.
Buckheit, Bruce C. '48 '75 (NY) C.433 B.S. L.945 J.D.
Burakreis, Dorothy R. '38 '73 C.881 B.A. L.276 J.D.
Burgess, Wells D. '38 '65 (NY) C.309 B.A. L.569 LL.B.
Butler, Virginia Pipes '52 '77 C&L.880 B.A., J.D.
Carman, Sean K. '63 '89 (CO) C.972 B.A. L.188 J.D.
Carroll, Steven E. '41 '73 (CA) C.768 B.A. L.1067 J.D.
Carter, Joan S. '43 '83 (KY) C.10 B.A. L.421 J.D.
Casano, Patricia Kablach '53 '78 C&L.665 B.S., J.D.
Casey, Patrick M. '50 '88 (FL) C.472 B.B.A. L.1194 J.D.
Chassy, Paul L. '40 '73 C.174 B.A. L.477 J.D.
Cherup, Lisa A. '55 '82 (MO) C.893 B.A. L.896 J.D.
Chesslin, Miriam L. '33 '58 C.926 A.B. L.145 J.D.
Christensen, David S. '57 '84 (UT) C.170 B.A. L.285 J.D.
Clear, James J. '42 '68 C&L.276 A.B., J.D.
Cohen, William M. '39 '65 C.475 B.A. L.273 J.D.
Colbourn, Elinor L. '62 '89 C.896 B.A. L.976 J.D.
Collins, N. B. '42 '75 (IL) L.209 J.D.
Connealy, Ross L. '42 '70 (NE) C.945 B.A. L.546 J.D.
Cook, Susan V. '47 '74 (CA) C.37 B.A. L.1049 J.D.
Coppedge, Susan '66 '93 (GA) C.228 B.A. L.813 J.D.
Corcoran, Larry M. '46 '76 C.602 B.S. L.128 J.D.
Corman, Bernice I. '62 '86 (MA) C.861 B.A. L.818 J.D.
Cruden, John C. '46 '75 C.870 B.S. L.770 J.D.
Crum, Matthew Brice '66 '91 (WV) C.886 B.A. L.902 J.D.
Dain, David L. '57 '82 C.362 B.A. L.823 J.D.
Davis, Darlene R. '59 '84 C.1099 B.A. L.861 J.D.
Dertke, Daniel R. '67 '92 (IA) C.228 A.B. L.910 J.D.
Disheroon, Fred R. '31 '56 (TX) C.315 A.B. L.802 J.D.
Dobbins, Jeffrey C. '67 '94 (WV) C.309 A.B. L.228 J.D.
Dodge, Lynn '60 '85 (MI) C.477 B.A. L.215 J.D.
Dodge, Robert I. '62 '88 C.188 B.S. L.178 J.D.
Donahue, Sean H. '66 '94 C.178 B.A. L.145 J.D.
Donnellan, Michael T. '65 '92 (ME) C.164 B.A. L.1194 J.D.
Donohue, Brian G. '53 '78 C.446 B.A. L.276 J.D.
Dooher, Daniel W. '60 '86 (NY) C.602 B.A. L.107 J.D.
Douglas, Nathaniel '47 '73 (PA) C.329 B.M. L.184 J.D.
Doyle, Andrew J. '71 '96 (FL) C.473 B.S. L.362 J.D.
Drew, Cynthia A. '— '92 (IL) C.861 B.A. L.597
Duer, Donna D. '55 '84 C.027 B.A. L.284 J.D.
Durkee, Ellen J. '54 '82 (MI) C.802 B.A. L.477 J.D.
Duval, Natalie M. '67 '92 (NH) C.197 A.B. L.309 J.D.
Dworkin, Karen S. '55 '80 C.1044 B.A. L.904 J.D.
Edgar, Mary F. '50 '81 C.821 B.A. L.276 J.D.
Edmonds, Elizabeth A. '45 '74 C.585 B.A. L.30 J.D.
Egbert, Karen L. '48 '80 C.313 B.A. L.128 J.D.
Ellis, Steven D. '56 '82 (CO) C.170 B.A. L.174 J.D.
Eschen, Andrew M. '53 '79 (VT) C.882 B.A. L.1294 J.D.
Farley, Scott M. '66 '92 (MA) C&L.93 B.A., J.D.
Feingold, Jason W. '68 '94 (IL) C.477 B.A. L.309 J.D.
Ferlo, Albert M., Jr. '54 '79 C.165 A.B. L.472 J.D.
Ferrell, Brian L. '62 '88 (NE) C&L.190 B.A., J.D.
Field, Thornton Withers '48 '79 (CO) C&L.174 B.A., J.D.
Finamore, Barbara A. '54 '80 C.1044 B.A. L.309 J.D.
Findlay, Charles W., III '45 '72 (NY) C.385 A.B. L.930 J.D.
Fingerhood, Karl J. '64 '91 (PA) C.207 B.A. L.692 J.D.
Fish, Gerald S. '30 '61 (MT) C.101 A.B. L.276 LL.B.
Fishel, David L. '58 '91 (PA) L.861 J.D.
Fisher, Gary J. '48 '73 C&L.972 B.A., J.D.
Fisherow, W. Benjamin '46 '74 C.605 B.A. L.1065 J.D.
Fitzgerald, Donna S. '69 '95 (CT) C.184 B.A. L.1194 J.D.
Flanagan, Catherine M. '56 '85 C.659 B.A. L.893 J.D.
Flickinger, Nancy A. '55 '83 C.821 B.A. L.569 J.D.
Flint, Myles E., II '66 '94 (MN) C.1369 B.S. L.1035 J.D.
Flores, Daniel M. '61 '87 C.446 B.A. L.976 J.D.
Flynn, Peter M. '55 '86 C.433 B.E. L.564 J.D.
Fogelson, Matthew A. '70 '97 C.228 A.B. L.569 J.D.
Frankel, Donald G. '56 '82 C.197 B.A. L.569 J.D.
Free, Kalyn Cherie '63 '87 (OK) C.621 B.A. L.623 J.D.
Freeman, James D. '64 '90 C.296 B.S. L.575 J.D.
Friedman, Henry S. '57 '83 (NJ) C.183 B.A. L.94 J.D.
Gallagher, Mark A. '58 '85 C&L.276 B.S.B.A., J.D.
Garbow, Avi Samuel '— '92 (VA) C.477 B.A. L.893 J.D.
Garver, Geoffrey '61 '88 (NY) C.188 B.S. L.477 J.D.
Gelber, Bruce S. '50 '75 C.188 B.A. L.309 J.D.
Gelin, Jacques B. '32 '58 (NY) C.309 A.B. L.178 LL.B.
Gelman, Leonard M. '64 '89 (IL) C.882 B.S. L.146 J.D.
Ghiorzi, Alfred T. '38 '66 (NY) C.433 B.A. L.262 LL.B.
Gilbert, Michelle L. '56 '84 C.112 B.A. L.902 J.D.
Gladstein, Richard M. '54 '82 C.604 B.A. L.1162 J.D.
Gluck, Ronald G. '47 '74 C.107 B.A. L.273 J.D.
Gold, Steve C. '59 '89 (NY) C.309 A.B. L.976 J.D.
Goldfrank, Joan L. '51 '76 C.1365 B.A. L.245 J.D.
Goldman, Greer S. '44 '69 C.188 A.B. L.309 J.D.
Goldsmith, Andrew David '57 '84 (NY) C.188 B.S. L.982 J.D.
Goldstein, Jared A. '68 '95 (MO) C.881 B.A. L.477 J.D.
Goodsell, Glen R. '37 '65 (VA) C.101 B.S. L.30 J.D.
Gordon, Marc E. '62 '90 C.722 B.A. L.446 J.D.
Gormley, Paul '67 '95 C.945 B.A. L.861 J.D.
Gould, Eric S. '45 '75 (OR) C.605 B.A. L.950 J.D.
Greenwald, Robin L. '54 '82 (IL) C&L.339 B.A., J.D.
Grishaw, Letitia J. '54 '80 (WI) C.477 B.A. L.966 J.D.
Haag, Mark R. '55 '84 C.1044 B.A. L.569 J.D.
Haugrud, K. Jack '58 '84 (MN) C.491 B.S. L.813 J.D.
Hazard, Katherine W. '54 '90 (MD) C.999 B.A. L.94 J.D.
Henderson, Susan M. '59 '88 (GA) C.259 B.S. L.260 J.D.
Herm, Stephen R. '51 '91 (MD) C.685 B.A. L.273 J.D.
Himmelhoch, Sarah D. '65 '92 (MD) C.012 B.Sc. L.596 J.D.
Hoang, Anthony P. '64 '89 (FL) C&L.260 B.A., J.D.
Hoilman, Marta '65 '92 C&L.309 A.B., J.D.
Holden, Lisa A. '68 '93 C.575 B.A. L.790 J.D.
Holleman, Paul F. '64 '92 (CO) C.31 B.A. L.174 J.D.
Holm, John O. '50 '75 (ND) C.579 B.A. L.585 J.D.
Homiak, Robert R. '51 '77 C.1044 B.A. L.30 J.D.
Hong, Richard '64 '92 (NJ) C.178 A.B. L.262 J.D.

DEPARTMENT OF JUSTICE (Continued)

Hostetler, Eric G. '67 '93 C.976 B.A. L.813 J.D.
Houston, Drenaye L. '63 '89 (SC) C&L.790 B.A., J.D.
Howard, James C. '55 '83 (MA) C.183 B.A. L.1218 J.D.
Huber, Cynthia S. '55 '79 C.98 B.A. L.608 J.D.
Humm, S. Randall '61 '92 C.347 B.A. L.659 J.D.
Hurley, Ann C. '— '83 C.813 A.B. L.1049 J.D.
Hurley, Joseph E. '51 '76 (PA) C.128 B.A. L.831 J.D.
Hurst, Patricia L. '66 '92 C&L.575 B.A., J.D.
Hutchins, William A. '47 '77 C.311 B.A. L.588 J.D.
Jacobs, Daniel S. '58 '83 (IL) C.478 A.B. L.228 J.D.
Jacobs, Lyn '56 '88 (CA) C.112 B.A. L.1067 J.D.
Jacobsen, Marilyn Perry '50 '77 C.205 B.A. L.276 J.D.
Jacobson, Rachel '58 '84 (IL) C.910 B.A. L.94 J.D.
Jaffe, Gregory A. '62 '88 C.918 B.A. L.309 J.D.
Jakosa, Charles '65 '94 (NM) C.197 A.B. L.494 J.D.
Jimenez, Aimee C. '66 '93 C.260 B.A. L.569 J.D.
Johnson, Herbert G. '36 '69 (NY) C.453 B.S. L.309 J.D.
Johnson, Stephen M. '63 '88 (PA) C&L.884 B.S., J.D.
Jonas, Lori '65 '92 C.951 B.A. L.569 J.D.
Jones, Lisa E. '69 '93 (VA) C.880 B.S. L.893 J.D.
Jordan, Scott J. '60 '88 C.821 B.A. L.93 J.D.
Juliano, Ann C. '67 '94 (CO) C.659 B.A. L.188 J.D.
Kaplan, David J. '59 '87 C.105 B.A. L.1068 J.D.
Kaplan, Julie B. '59 '87 C.659 B.A. L.976 J.D.
Kaplan, Robert A. '65 '91 (MA) C.118 B.A. L.659 J.D.
Katz, Ellen D. '69 '94 C&L.976 B.A., J.D.
Katz, Maureen M. '48 '73 (PA) C.706 B.A. L.588 J.D.
Kautsky, Peter K. '55 '82 C.813 B.A. L.659 J.D.
Kelleher, Gail E. '55 '85 C.705 B.A. L.276 J.D.
Keller, Steven A. '51 '82 (AZ) C.477 B.A. L.36 J.D.
Kellner, Kenneth E. '63 '88 C.188 B.S. L.245 J.D.
Kelso, Harry H. '53 '82 C.1365 B.A. L.796 J.D.
Kilbourne, James C. '51 '77 (MT) C&L.508 B.A., J.D.
Kim, Cecilia Estelle '68 '93 C&L.276 B.A., J.D.
Kim, Todd S. '72 '98 (CA) C&L.309 A.B., J.D.
Klarquist, Robert L. '43 '72 (IL) C&L.339 B.A., J.D.
Klein, Jonathan F. '67 '92 (MA) C.31 B.A. L.309 J.D.
Koester, Kirk W. '55 '84 (OK) C.622 B.A. L.623 J.D.
Kollins, William J. '35 '68 (IL) C&L.424 B.S., J.D.
Korzenik, Jeremy F. '52 '83 (MA) C.976 B.A. L.94 J.D.
Kotila, Mark W. '59 '87 (NY) C.1138 B.B.A. L.1009 J.D.
Kovacs, Kathryn E. '68 '95 C.976 B.A. L.276 J.D.
Ladehoff, Paul H. '63 '94 (NE) C.477 M.S. L.546 J.D.
LaLonde, Martin J. '— '94 (IL) C&L.477 B.B.A., J.D.
Lang, Annette M. '58 '86 C.602 B.A. L.309 J.D.
Lang, Christine '58 '86
Larson, Lary C. '54 '84 C.446 B.A. L.464 J.D.
Lastra, David '64 '91 (PR) C&L.677 B.S., J.D.
Lawrence, Robin E. '60 '91 (PA) C.945 B.B.A. L.878 J.D.
Lazarus, William B. '49 '83 (MA) C.145 B.A. L.659 J.D.
Lazerwitz, David J. '65 '96 (CO) C.170 B.A. L.347 J.D.
Lee, Valerie Ann '53 '84 C.67 B.S. L.976 J.D.
Lefevre, Robert '53 '78 (NY) C.569 B.A. L.1009 J.D.
Lehnert, Leslie E. '— '88 C.297 B.A. L.273 J.D.
Leininger, Roland Lee '57 '93 (CO) C.966 B.S. L.208 J.D.
LePard, Bonnie J. '60 '88 C.918 B.A. L.569 J.D.
Leugers, Mary Jo '55 '85 (VA) C.201 B.S. L.421 J.D.
Levin, Joshua M. '55 '86 (IL) C.604 B.A. L.597 J.D.
Lin, Albert C. '70 '96 C.1365 B.S. L.1066 J.D.
Lindeman, Ralph H. '49 '74 C.207 B.A. L.880 J.D.
Linsin, Gregory F. '49 '79 C.424 B.A. L.1162 J.D.
Lipshultz, Jon M. '62 '87 C.696 B.A. L.477 J.D.
Liu, Sylvia F. '69 '94 C.976 B.A. L.309 J.D.
Lloyd, Rebecca A. '60 '88 C.518 B.A. L.273 J.D.
Loeb, Elizabeth L. '61 '89 C.659 B.A. L.569 J.D.
Lofton, James A. '53 '82 (VA) C.885 B.A. L.692 J.D.
Long, Kenneth G. '61 '86 C.423 B.A. L.216 J.D.
Long, Mariana M. '— '94 (PA) C.197 B.A. L.477 J.D.
Lorenzen, Thomas Allen '60 '85 C.112 B.A. L.309 J.D.
Lyons, Francis X '62 '88 (IL) C.494 B.A. L.424 J.D.
MacAyeal, James R. '57 '83 (IL) C.597 B.A. L.902 J.D.
MacLaughlin, Jerome William '65 '91 C.477 B.A. L.904 J.D.
Mahan, Ellen M. '57 '81 C.1044 B.A. L.273 J.D.
Maher, Robert E., Jr. '58 '87 (NY) C.976 B.A. L.262 J.D.
Mann, Valerie K. '67 '91 C.705 B.A. L.893 J.D.
Mariani, Thomas A., Jr. '57 '85 (NY) C.299 B.A. L.178 J.D.
Marks, Jonathan '59 '85 (FL) C&L.1029 B.A., J.D.
Marshall, John L. '61 '89 (CA) C.604 B.A. L.1067 J.D.
Martella, Roger R., Jr. '70 '97 (MD) C.188 B.S. L.880 J.D.
Martin, John H. '67 '96 C.228 B.A. L.596 J.D.
Martin, Jospeh H. '60 '94 (IL) C.959 B.A. L.597 J.D.
Martin, Michael K. '54 '84 C.976 B.A. L.1066 J.D.
Matzen, Martin W. '44 '75 C.273 B.A. L.537 J.D.
Mayo, A. Kent '67 '95 C.228 B.A. L.910 J.D.
McAliley, Thomas N. '65 '92 (CA) C.309 A.B. L.1066 J.D.
McCabe, Catherine R. '51 '77 (NY) C.66 A.B. L.178 J.D.
McCarthy, Noreen E. '57 '88 (CT) C.829 B.S. L.184 J.D.
McCubbin, Patricia Ross '63 '90 C&L.893 B.A., J.D.
McDermott, Martin F. '55 '82 (IL) C.93 B.A. L.597 J.D.
McDonough, Eileen '56 '85 (MD) C.105 B.A. L.273 J.D.
McIlwain, David L. '48 '78 (NH) C.453 S.B. L.1218 J.D.
McNulty, Michael J. '57 '83 (OH) C.648 B.A. L.831 J.D.
McQuade, Ruth A. '49 '79 (WV) C.437 B.A. L.1162 J.D.
Mears, David K. '63 '91 (TX) C.188 B.S. L.1194 J.D.
Mendelson, Nina A. '64 '91 (WA) C.309 A.B. L.976 J.D.
Mergen, Andrew C. '64 '89 C.966 B.A. L.273 J.D.
Meshorer, Hank '42 '67 (TX) C.156 A.B. L.802 J.D.
Michael, Robin '61 '87 (NC) C&L.575 B.A., J.D.
Milius, Pauline H. '41 '78 C.66 B.A. L.276 J.D.
Milkman, Louise F. '60 '87 C.309 B.A. L.569 J.D.
Miller, Robert H. '57 '86 C.477 B.S. L.94 J.D.
Mohn, Celia '62 '87 (PA) C.228 A.B. L.477 J.D.
Monikowski, Richard A. '57 '94 (NY) C.999 L.560 J.D.
Moreau, Pamela A. '66 '92 (MA) C.893 B.A. L.188 J.D.
Moreno, Ignacia S. '61 '90 C&L.569 B.A., J.D.
Morgulec, James A. '56 '81 C.597 B.S. L.477 J.D.
Morrison, Matthew W. '61 '90 C.401 B.S. L.262 J.D.
Most, John S. '61 '87 (VA) C.893 B.A. L.190 J.D.
Mueller, Jon A. '53 '82 (VA) C.945 B.S. L.692 J.D.
Murtha, Peter J. '53 '78 C.105 B.A. L.273 J.D.
Musel, David F. '61 '93 (IA) C&L.190 B.A., J.D.
Mushal, Raymond W. '44 '73 (PA) C.976 B.A. L.659 J.D.
Nash, Beverly Sherman '47 '74 C.477 A.B. L.273 J.D.
Navaro, Ann D. '66 '91 (PA) C.914 B.A. L.150 J.D.
Nilles, Bruce E. '68 '96 (WI) C&L.966 B.S., J.D.
Nitczynski, Mark A. '63 '91 (CO) C.478 B.A. L.145 J.D.
Oakley, Robert H. '53 '79 C.497 B.A. L.276 J.D.
O'Brien, Eileen F. '50 '74 (MA) C.686 B.A. L.273 J.D.
O'Connell, Angela F. '— '83 C.446 B.S. L.276 J.D.
O'Connell, Charles E., Jr. '41 '70 (MD) C.1244 B.A. L.276 J.D.
Ortiz, Criselda '45 '77 (CA) C.845 B.A. L.1066 J.D.
Osenbaugh, Elizabeth M. '47 '71 (IA) C&L.352 B.A., J.D.
Pacheco, Thomas H. '53 '79 C.103 A.B. L.880 J.D.
Page, Gregory D. '57 '85 C.976 B.A. L.280 J.D.
Pair, Quentin C. '43 '71 C.30 B.S. L.94 J.D.
Parent, Stephanie M. '64 '92 (OR) C.966 B.S. L.1051 J.D.
Pasfield, W. Bruce '59 '84 (FL) C.282 B.A. L.1194 J.D.
Passarelli, Edward J. '51 '76 (VA) C.610 B.A. L.945 J.D.
Patrick, Teresa L. '60 '91 C.235 B.A. L.383 J.D.
Peirce, George A. B. '52 '80 C.870 B.S. L.309 J.D.
Penman, Lynn '60 '85
Pepin, Joan M. '66 '93 (MA) C.197 A.B. L.309 J.D.
Perella, Joseph R. '59 '90 C.454 B.S. L.1194 J.D.
Perry, Christiana P. '65 '91 (FL) C.228 A.B. L.276 J.D.
Persampieri, Nicholas F. '59 '85 (NM) C.31 B.A. L.893 J.D.
Peterson, Elizabeth A. '53 '79 C.722 B.A. L.128 J.D.
Peterson, Gary M. '45 '72 C.350 B.S. L.352 J.D.
Pickering, Cynthia '50 '76
Pirasteh, Gretchen Slosser '59 '87 C.118 B.A. L.494 J.D.
Pisaturo, Catherine C. '63 '89 C.690 B.A. L.904 J.D.
Plaut, Vicki L. '57 '83 C.145 B.A. L.597 J.D.
Puckett, Lawrence W. '54 '81 C.838 B.A. L.861 J.D.
Putnam, Ross E. '45 '73 C.16 B.A. L.146 J.D.
Quast, Sylvia A. '61 '92 (CA) C.494 B.A. L.309 J.D.
Quinn, Thomas Anthony '62 '87 C.31 B.A. L.245 J.D.
Rabinowitz, Judith '58 '89 (AK) C&L.309 A.B., J.D.
Randall, Gary B. '44 '73 (CO) C.911 B.A. L.208 J.D.
Rangarajan, Banumathi '68 '92 (MI) C.912 B.A. L.477 J.D.
Rauch, Samuel D., III '66 '94 (VA) C.893 B.A. L.596 J.D.
Rave, Norman L., Jr. '56 '89 C.309 A.B. L.276 J.D.
Reed, Mary '49 '77 C.1073 B.A. L.425 J.D.
Reed, Michael W. '41 '66 (WA) C.939 B.A. L.911 LL.B.
Reyher, Deborah M. '57 '84 (NY) C.477 B.S. L.976 J.D.
Rigau, Mark A. '— '93 (FL) C.112 B.A. L.1158 J.D.
Rockler, Elliot '50 '84 (ID) C.685 B.A. L.1051 J.D.
Rogers, Barbara A. '56 '85 (MD) C.012 B.A. L.273 J.D.
Rogers, Cherie L. '69 '95 (SC) C&L.790 B.A., J.D.
Rogers, J. Steven '53 '78 (OK) C.613 B.A. L.623 J.D.
Rogers, R. Anthony '40 '69 C.575 B.A. L.893 LL.B.
Romita, Michael N. '65 '91 C.860 B.S. L.477 J.D.
Rosendorf, Donald F. '41 '67 C&L.273 B.A., LL.B.
Rosenthal, Arnold S. '53 '77 (TX) C&L.846 B.A., J.D.
Rosskam, David D. '56 '82 C.674 A.B. L.309 J.D.
Rossmann, Brud '64 '90 (NY) C.477 A.B. L.309 J.D.
Rountree, Tamara N. '61 '94 (NJ) C.674 B.A. L.831 J.D.
Rowe, Michael D. '56 '81 C.893 B.A. L.846 J.D.
Rubin, James W '62 '88 C.309 B.A. L.178 J.D.
Rumsey, Allison B. '62 '93 C.478 B.A. L.276 J.D.
Rusak, Steven E. '67 '92 (DE) C.264 B.A. L.1338 J.D.
Ruvolo, Peter H. '32 '57 C.716 B.A. L.724 LL.B.
Ryan, Anne S. '62 '89 C.976 B.A. L.1066 J.D.
Ryan, Joy '43 '78 (MO) C.502 B.M. L.910 J.D.
Samuels, Stephen L. '52 '78 C.861 B.A. L.813 J.D.
Sands, Jeffrey K. '66 '91 (TX) C.228 B.A. L.846 J.D.
Saxe, Keith E. '55 '89 (AK) C.597 B.A. L.1065 J.D.
Schachter, Scott A. '61 '86 C.94 B.A. L.1029 J.D.
Schaeffer, Paul J. '38 '70 (OR) C&L.629 B.A., J.D.
Schaeffer, Suzanne R. '63 '90 C.945 B.A. L.893 J.D.
Schiffer, Lois J. '45 '69 C.681 A.B. L.309 J.D.
Schmidt, Kathryn '65 '91 (CA) C.112 B.A. L.1065 J.D.
Schneider, Susan L. '52 '78 C.103 B.A. L.276 J.D.
Schoenburg, Stuart B. '38 '63 (CO) C.178 B.S. L.972 J.D.
Schwartz, Jerry M. '54 '79 C.1044 B.A. L.273 J.D.
Schwebs, Monica A. '56 '82 C.674 A.B. L.893 J.D.
Semler, H. Michael '47 '73 C.276 B.S.F.S. L.145 J.D.
Sepulveda-Hambor, Silvia '47 '71 C&L.677 B.A., LL.B.
Shawaker, Edward J. '43 '72 C.477 B.S. L.494 J.D.
Shawley, Dianne '53 '83 C.645 B.A. L.128 J.D.
Sheehan, Charles J. '54 '79 C.93 B.A. L.276 J.D.
Sheehan, John A. '57 '85 C&L.276 B.A., J.D.
Shehabi, Soroush Ricard '65 '94 (CA) C.309 A.B. L.1065 J.D.
Shenkman, Ethan G. '67 '96 C.976 B.A. L.893 J.D.
Shields, Anne H. '40 '77 C.174 B.A. L.128 J.D.
Shilton, David C. '50 '76 C.821 B.A. L.1068 J.D.
Shockey, Charles R. '51 '75 C.197 A.B. L.276 J.D.
Shuey, David F. '56 '81 (LA) C.1365 B.A. L.861 J.D.
Shuff, Sheldon '49 '89 (CA) C.107 B.A. L.426 J.D.
Siff, Scott '64 '91 C&L.309 A.B., J.D.
Silverman, Steven '60 '87 (PA) C.674 A.B. L.813 J.D.
Simon, James F. '56 '83 (CT) C.976 B.A. L.309 J.D.
Sither, John Wright '60 '90 C.118 B.A. L.1066 J.D.
Skelley, Christine Lang '58 '86 (PA) C.645 B.A. L.862 J.D.
Smeltzer, John L. '65 '90 C.311 B.A. L.569 J.D.
Smith, Andrew A. '63 '95 (NM) C.112 B.S. L.560 J.D.
Smith, Deborah M. '52 '78 (AK) C.260 B.S. L.588 J.D.
Smith, Justin '68 '96 C.674 A.B. L.309 J.D.

Smith, Marc A. .... '62 '90 C.446 B.A. L.692 J.D.
Smith, Peter J. .... '40 '71 (PA) C.1113 B.A. L.276 J.D.
Smith, Russell F., III .... '59 '87 C.976 B.A. L.477 J.D.
Smith, Walker Bledsoe, Ms. .... '48 '77 (KY) C.952 B.A. L.421 J.D.
Smout, Cheryl L. .... '58 '86 (VA) C.886 B.S. L.1209 J.D.
Sobeck, Eileen .... '54 '78 C&L.813 B.A., J.D.
Solow, Steven P. .... '58 '86 (NY) C.103 B.A. L.569 J.D.
Spector, Jeffrey A. .... '68 '94 C.367 B.A. L.569 J.D.
Spencer, Nancy J. .... '63 '88 (MD) C.174 B.A. L.813 J.D.
Springer, Caroline T. .... '63 '90 C.674 B.A. L.276 J.D.
Spritzer, Ronald M. .... '54 '82 C.293 B.A. L.659 J.D.
Squires, Susan B. .... '56 '81 (RI) C.103 A.B. L.930 J.D.
Stahr, John T. .... '47 '78 C.31 B.A. L.128 J.D.
Steele, Daniel G. .... '48 '77 C.1182 B.A. L.818 J.D.
Stewart, Howard P. .... '54 '81 (PA) C.655 B.A. L.1017 J.D.
Stolbun, Donna L. .... '54 '81 (TX) C.846 B.B.A. L.326 J.D.
Stone, Randall M. .... '64 '90 C&L.477 B.S., J.D.
Storey, Ruth Ann .... '55 '80 (UT) C&L.878 B.S., J.D.
Strass, Carl .... '39 '64 (NY) C.188 L.823 LL.B.
Street, David E. .... '44 '75 (PA) C.205 B.A. L.831 J.D.
Strouse, Donald E. .... '30 '58 (OH) C.970 B.A. L.608 J.D.
Sukys, Gregory L. .... '48 '84 (VA) C.363 B.A. L.1209 J.D.
Swegle, Thomas W. .... '59 '86 C.602 B.A. L.309 J.D.
Swerdel, Anna .... '48 '78 C.446 B.S. L.904 J.D.
Swift, Joshua E. .... '64 '93 C.951 B.A. L.188 J.D.
Tardiff, Kristine S. .... '66 '93 (NH) C.380 B.A. L.588 J.D.
Tenenbaum, Alan S. .... '56 '82 C.188 B.A. L.309 J.D.
Thode, Anna C. .... '56 '81 C.269 B.A. L.273 J.D.
Thompson, David M. .... '47 '76 (MI) C.347 A.B. L.880 J.D.
Thomsen, Teri R. .... '65 '91 (IA) C&L.352 B.S., J.D.
Thurston, M. Alice .... '57 '85 C.103 B.A. L.178 J.D.
Topol, David H. .... '66 '92 C.188 B.A. L.976 J.D.
Torrent, Karen E. .... '59 '89 C.62 B.A. L.494 J.D.
Udell, Richard A. .... '58 '90 C.95 B.A. L.309 J.D.
Uhlmann, David M. .... '62 '89 C.821 B.A. L.976 J.D.
Upton, James M. .... '43 '68 (NY) C.867 A.B. L.178 J.D.
Vaden, Christopher S. .... '56 '82 C.31 B.A. L.893 J.D.
Van Norman, Mark C. .... '61 '86 (IL) C.1044 B.A. L.309 J.D.
Vollenweider, David O., III .... '53 '81 (FL) C.259 B.S. L.192 J.D.
Walter, Michele L. .... '72 '97 (NE) C&L.190 B.A., J.D.
Ward, Andrea Nervi .... '63 '90 C.674 A.B. L.145 J.D.
Ward, Mary Elizabeth .... '60 '85 (PA) C.645 B.S. L.309 J.D.
Wardzinski, Karen M. .... '55 '80 C.1044 B.A. L.174 J.D.
Washburn, Kevin K. .... '67 '94 (NM) C.623 B.A. L.976 J.D.
Watson, Blake A. .... '56 '82 (TN) C.880 B.A. L.228 J.D.
Watts, John W. .... '64 '95 (CA) C.674 A.B. L.1066 J.D.
Webb, John Thomas .... '47 '78 (PA) C.645 B.A. L.276 J.D.
Weigert, David L. .... '65 '96 (IL) C.821 B.A. L.597 J.D.
Weinischke, William A. .... '50 '80 (MS) C.499 B.S. L.500 J.D.
West, Pamela S. .... '48 '83 (OH) C.475 B.A. L.161 J.D.
Westerfield, William W., III .... '56 '81 (LA) C.575 B.A. L.846 J.D.
White, William A. .... '40 '71 C.478 B.A. L.597 J.D.
Whitney, Claire .... '48 '75 C.475 B.A. L.128 J.D.
Wilkerson-Barron, Yvette .... '65 '91 (MO) C.174 B.A. L.273 J.D.
Willey, Steven J. .... '53 '80 (OH) C.8 B.A. L.608 J.D.
Williams, Eric G. .... '53 '80 (UT) C&L.101 B.A., J.D.
Williams, G. Scott .... '61 '87 (TX) C.846 B.A. L.326 J.D.
Williams, J. Carol .... '46 '82 (VA) C.6 B.A. L.692 J.D.
Williams, Jean E. .... '53 '79 C.289 B.A. L.861 J.D.
Williams, Melaine Aureilia .... '66 '92 (SC) C&L.790 B.A., J.D.
Wilson, Jacqueline Annette .... '65 '94 C.1288 B.A. L.893 J.D.
Wise, Noël .... '— '93 (CA) C.549 B.S. L.1206 J.D.
Wolfteich, Paul G. .... '62 '89 (VA) C.945 A.B. L.880 J.D.
Wright, Douglas R. .... '51 '81 C&L.101 B.A., J.D.
Ying, Evelyn S. .... '60 '89 C.118 B.A. L.273 J.D.
Young, Russell M. .... '49 '81 (VA) C.893 B.A. L.861 J.D.
Yu, Elizabeth .... '50 '78 C.188 B.S. L.273 J.D.
Zander, Caroline M. .... '61 '90 C.597 B.A. L.904 J.D.
Zane, Daria J. .... '58 '86 C.446 B.S. L.273 J.D.
Zellmer, Sandra .... '64 '90 (MN) C.513 B.S. L.793 J.D.
Zevenbergen, Michael J. .... '61 '91 (WA) C.939 B.A. L.309 J.D.
Zizila, Frances .... '71 '95 (CT) C.994 B.A. L.564 J.D.

OFFICE OF THE INSPECTOR GENERAL

Ashbaugh, Robert L. .... '45 '70 C.207 B.A. L.597 J.D.
Fine, Glenn A. .... '56 '85 C&L.309 A.B., J.D.
Francis, Flora A. .... '60 '86 C.604 B.A. L.188 J.D.
Freccero, Francesca .... '60 '87 C.813 A.B. L.1066 J.D.
Gordon, Diana .... '62 '89 C.197 B.A. L.1068 J.D.
Healy, Mary E. .... '67 '94 (MA) C.602 B.A. L.893 J.D.
Kessler, Tamara J. .... '62 '87 (PA) C.914 A.B. L.309 J.D.
Martin, Paul K. .... '59 '91 C.645 B.A. L.276 J.D.
Robinson, Gail A. .... '62 '87 C.705 B.A. L.659 J.D.
Sribnick, Howard L. .... '45 '72 C.105 B.A. L.273 J.D.
Sumner, Patricia A. .... '68 '93 (VA) C&L.893 B.A., J.D.
Weidenbruch, Julie G. .... '60 '86 C.363 B.A. L.276 J.D.
Yanowitch, Paul L. .... '56 '84 C.454 B.A. L.910 J.D.

OFFICE OF JUSTICE PROGRAMS

Alston, Michael L. .... '58 '83 C.329 B.A. L.904 J.D.
Brady, Gregory C. .... '40 '65 C&L.546 B.A., J.D.
Carradini, Rosemary .... '— '98 (MD) C.788 A.B. L.30 J.D.
Cartwright, Heather L. .... '60 '85 C&L.339 B.S., J.D.
Cooper, Scott D. .... '59 '84 (IL) C.605 A.B. L.904 J.D.
Crawford, Cheryl Ann .... '58 '87 (WI) C.961 B.A. L.966 J.D.
Denning, Lowell .... '57 '82 (GA) C.446 B.A. L.280 J.D.
Dodge, Douglas C. .... '40 '65 C.932 B.A. L.912 J.D.
Fallowfield, Linda J .... '64 '95 (MD) C.446 B.S. L.64 J.D.
Feinberg, Donna K. .... '51 '78 C.846 B.A. L.502 J.D.
Fisher, Alan M. .... '69 '95 (MD) C.30 B.A. L.904 J.D.
Gilbert, Karen Lynn .... '68 '94 C.446 B.A. L.64 J.D.
Kaplan, Carol G. .... '39 '62 C.681 B.A. L.178 LL.B.
Kendall, Paul F. .... '55 '85 C.178 B.A. L.180 J.D.
Leary, Mary Lou .... '49 '80 C.823 B.A. L.588 J.D.
Madison, Regina .... '70 '98 C.576 B.A. L.575 J.D.
Mazza, George J. .... '55 '93 C.347 B.A. L.276 J.D.
Merkle, Phillip Kent .... '65 '91 (MD) C.692 B.A. L.128 J.D.
Morrow, Margaret M. .... '— '89 C.67 B.A. L.273 J.D.
Moses, Charles T., III .... '56 '82 (VA) C.885 B.A. L.902 J.D.
O'Brien, Victoria Klekamp .... '56 '82 C.207 L.424 J.D.
Penn, Karen R. .... '69 '96 (MD) C.893 B.A. L.273 J.D.
Pensinger, John .... '49 '76 C.446 B.A. L.64 J.D.
Poston, Catherine Micklitsch .... '64 '89 C.813 B.A. L.276 J.D.
Rizzuto, Christopher A. .... '53 '89 C.276 B.S. L.30 J.D.
Romeo, Jennifer L. .... '65 '93 (IN) C&L.602 B.A., J.D.
Sausjord, Ingrid R. .... '55 '85 (NY) C.112 B.S. L.976 J.D.
Sidley, Janna Beth .... '63 '92 C.112 B.A. L.426 J.D.
Smolover, Deborah S. .... '62 '88 C&L.309 B.A., J.D.
Swartz, Neal James .... '70 '97 (MD) C.602 B.A. L.128 J.D.
Tildon, Rhonda Phoenix .... '70 '94 C.329 B.A. L.30 J.D.
Tompkins, Elena .... '68 '94 (NJ) C.518 B.A. L.1292 J.D.
Trujillo, Olga Rosa .... '61 '88 C.446 B.A. L.273 J.D.
Verveer, Alexandra .... '69 '94 C.597 B.S.J. L.276 J.D.
Wilson, John J. .... '44 '74 (MI) C.477 A.B. L.213 J.D.
Woodard, Kimberly R. .... '72 '97 C.228 A.B. L.273 J.D.

OFFICE OF INTELLIGENCE POLICY AND REVIEW

Barrios, Steven L. .... '58 '83 (NY) C.446 B.A. L.273 J.D.
Connors, John J. .... '47 '77 C.884 A.B. L.228 J.D.
Golrick, Philip D. .... '64 '89 C&L.893 B.A., J.D.
Kennedy, Lionel .... '55 '83 (VA) C.575 B.A. L.893 J.D.
Kornblum, Allan N. .... '38 '61 (NY) C.475 B.S. L.569 LL.B.
Mahler, Richard C. .... '58 '90 (FL) C.1086 B.B.A. L.1206 J.D.
Pastore, Dominic .... '58 '88 C.276 B.S.F.S. L.893 J.D.
Petrow, John E. .... '50 '76 (NY) C.308 B.A. L.1009 J.D.
Pincus, Roger W. .... '62 '87 C.918 B.A. L.659 J.D.
Ryan, David C. .... '49 '82 (MD) C.1115 B.A. L.64 J.D.
Schroeder, Gerald A. .... '46 '72 C.276 A.B. L.345 J.D.
Thren, Christine M. .... '51 '80 C.880 B.A. L.276 J.D.

OFFICE OF LEGAL COUNSEL

Bradshaw, Sheldon Taylor .... '66 '96 C.101 B.A. L.273 J.D.
Cedarbaum, Jonathan G. .... '61 '97 C.309 A.B. L.976 J.D.
Colborn, Paul P. .... '49 '75 C.674 A.B. L.276 J.D.
Delahunty, Robert J. .... '47 '84 (NY) C.178 B.A. L.309 J.D.
Hart, Rosemary .... '53 '80 (CA) C.112 A.B. L.1065 J.D.
Huntington, Clare .... '67 '97 C.604 B.A. L.178 J.D.
Kehne, Jeffrey P. .... '57 '88 (IL) C.311 B.A. L.976 J.D.
Koffsky, Daniel L. .... '53 '78 C.309 A.B. L.976 J.D.
Krass, Caroline D. .... '68 '95 C.813 B.A. L.976 J.D.
Lederman, Martin S. .... '61 '89 C.477 A.B. L.976 J.D.
Lee, Gia B .... '69 '97 (NY) C&L.309 A.B., J.D.
Marcuse, Herman .... '10 '39 (NY) L.178 J.D.
Simon, Leslie A. .... '59 '90 (PA) C&L.976 B.A., J.D.
Singdahlsen, Jeffrey P. .... '65 '91 C.197 A.B. L.893 J.D.
Werner, Robert W. .... '59 '86 (CT) C.31 B.A. L.569 J.D.
Yoo, John .... '— '67 C.309 A.B. L.976 J.D.

OFFICE OF LEGISLATIVE AFFAIRS

Bernhardt, Gena Rae .... '69 '01 (VA) C.902 B.A. L.1209 J.D.
Bryant, Daniel James .... '65 '97 (MD) C&L.30 B.A., J.D. Asst. Atty. Gen.
Burton, M. Faith .... '— '76 C.970 B.A. L.1162 J.D.
Jones, Gregory M. .... '51 '75 C.112 A.B. L.846 J.D.
O'Brien, Patrick M. .... '66 '92 (MN) C.602 B.A. L.494 J.D.
Owen, Peter .... '69 '96 C.893 B.A. L.945 J.D.
Silas, Adrien L. .... '59 '84 (OH) C.608 B.A. L.477 J.D.
Taylor, Velma C. .... '53 '91 (PA) C.597 B.A. L.329 J.D.
Thorsen, Carlyle P. .... '67 '97 (MD) C.754 B.S. L.831 J.D.
Walter, Sheryl L. .... '56 '84 C.293 B.A. L.494 J.D.
Wilson, Karen L. .... '56 '86 (IL) C&L.339 B.A., J.D.

JUSTICE MANAGEMENT DIVISION

Bush, Barbara A. .... '47 '77 C.881 B.A. L.180 J.D.
Caterini, John R. .... '64 '90 C.165 B.A. L.93 J.D.
Dabney, Dolores H. .... '50 '83 (VA) C&L.893 B.A., J.D.
Daniels, Eric S. .... '67 '91 (VA) C&L.893 B.A., J.D.
Donaghy, Linda A. .... '46 '74 (MD) C.122 B.A. L.128 J.D.
Emerson, Catherine V. .... '65 '92 (MD) C&L.128 B.A., J.D.
Ferber, Alan L. .... '48 '73 (MD) C.696 B.A. L.1066 J.D.
Frisch, Stuart .... '46 '72 C.102 B.A. L.309 J.D.
Gallagher, James M. .... '52 '80 C.1030 B.A. L.2 J.D.
Goldsmith, Scott J. .... '51 '81 C.62 B.A. L.273 J.D.
Guerrero, Bernard S. .... '64 '91 C.112 B.A. L.273 J.D.
Haggerty, Kathleen A. .... '50 '76 (NY) C.242 B.A. L.818 J.D.
Harrison, Barbara E. .... '40 '88 (PA) C.823 A.B. L.276 J.D.
Johnston, James W. .... '45 '76 C.352 B.A. L.64 J.D.
Krips, Richard .... '42 '75 C.1044 B.A. L.446 J.D.
Lund, Mary W. .... '44 '81 C.438 B.A. L.273 J.D.
Madan, Rafael A. .... '62 '86 C&L.893 B.A., J.D.
McBurrows, Theodius .... '43 '83 C.382 B.S. L.30 J.D.
Miller, Mark J. .... '51 '76 (NY) C.1350 B.A. L.94 J.D.
Roby, James J. .... '47 '76 C.477 B.A. L.1162 J.D.
Rodgers, Janice M. .... '56 '81 C.188 B.S. L.30 J.D.
Sloan, Vickie Lynn .... '51 '80 (MD) C.446 B.G.S. L.30 J.D.
Sposato, Janis Ann .... '51 '75 C.518 B.A. L.178 J.D.
Tang, Evelyn S. .... '66 '92 C.976 B.A. L.309 J.D.
Theis, Richard P. .... '47 '75 C.112 B.A. L.809 J.D.
Williams, Marcus .... '67 '92 (PA) C.446 B.A. L.273 J.D.
Zanger, Robert M. .... '61 '88 (MN) C.352 B.A. L.597 J.D.

OFFICE OF THE PARDON ATTORNEY

Adams, Roger C. .... '44 '69 (MA) C.95 B.A. L.93 J.D.
Bollwerk, Helen M. .... '51 '78 C.1044 B.A. L.276 J.D.
Hatton, Kathleen G. .... '51 '82 C.966 B.A. L.276 J.D.
Kuzma, Susan M. .... '54 '78 (OH) C&L.608 B.A., J.D.
McGowan, Hope P. .... '55 '83 (CO) C.197 B.A. L.36 J.D.
Morison, Samuel T. .... '63 '91 C.1356 B.S. L.575 J.D.

DEPARTMENT OF JUSTICE (Continued)

U. S. PAROLE COMMISSION

Chickinell, Rockne J. '50 '75 (NE) C&L.190 B.A., J.D.
Gervasoni, Sharon A. '60 '85 C.893 B.A. L.273 J.D.
Posch, Pamela A. '66 '99 (MD) C.446 B.A. L.30 J.D.
Sikkema, P. Dawn '48 '78 (MI) C.114 B.A. L.912 J.D.
Stover, Michael A. '46 '73 C.103 B.A. L.273 J.D. Gen. Coun.
Thiessen, Douglas W. '73 '98 (MD) C.902 B.A. L.896 J.D.

OFFICE OF POLICY DEVELOPMENT

Campbell, Frank A. S. '55 '80 C.390 A.B. L.273 J.D.
Dinh, Viet D. '68 '97 C&L.309 A.B., J.D.
Gormsen, Eric Taylor '63 '90 (VA) C&L.893 B.S., J.D.
Greenberg, Mark D. '63 '85 (CA) C.367 B.A. L.1066 J.D.
Hinchman, Robert '55 '80 (PA) C.665 B.A. L.229 J.D.
Jacobs, Lisalyn R. '65 '91 (PA) C.289 B.A. L.813 J.D.
Jones, Kevin R. '53 '78 C.945 A.B. L.893 J.D.
Karp, David '51 '80 (NY) C&L.178 B.A., J.D.
Keefer, Wendy J. '71 '97 (NC) C.577 B.A. L.1228 J.D.
Klein, Laura F. '68 '95 (OH) C.197 B.A. L.608 J.D.
Mastalli, Grace L. '53 '78 C&L.208 B.A., J.D.
Newstead, Jennifer G. '69 '92 C.309 B.A. L.976 J.D.
Sales, Nathan A. '74 '00 (VA) C.473 A.B. L.228 J.D.
Scheffel, Jocelyn A. '71 '99 (CA) C.178 B.A. L.813 J.D.
Thiemann, Robyn Lynn '73 '98 C.806 B.A. L.569 J.D.
Tisi, Andrea Suzanne '66 '99 (NY) C.054 B.Sc. L.904 J.D.

OFFICE OF INFORMATION AND PRIVACY

Anderson, Cynthia H. '47 '75 C.914 B.A. L.273 J.D.
Bedrick, Benjamin N. '72 '97 (PA) C.319 B.A. L.1017 J.D.
Chason, Kenneth D. '66 '92 (GA) C.1377 B.A. L.192 J.D.
Denk, Laura A. '— '94 (KS) C.945 B.A. L.378 J.D.
Evitt, Brentin Vaughn '67 '98 (TN) L.615 J.D.
Finnegan, Karen M. '59 '92 (PA) C.645 B.S. L.831 J.D.
Hebert, Carol S. '41 '81 (NC) C.569 B.A. L.896 J.D.
Hester, Thomas P., Jr. '63 '97 C.339 M.A. L.146 J.D.
Huff, Richard L. '43 '69 (CA) C.813 B.A. L.1065 J.D.
Kennedy, Rosalind '70 '99 (NY) C.569 B.A. L.537 J.D.
McLeod, Janice Galli '47 '84 C.912 B.S. L.128 J.D.
Menna, Frank P. '72 '98 (VA) C.145 A.B. L.273 J.D.
Metcalfe, Daniel J. '51 '76 C.1350 B.A. L.273 J.D.
Moncada, Kirsten J. '64 '88 C&L.446 B.A., J.D.
Pustay, Melanie '57 '82 C.1209 B.A. L.904 J.D.
Wellman, Tricia S. '70 '96 (VA) C.93 B.A. L.1356 J.D.
Withnell, Elizabeth Ross '50 '83 C.164 B.A. L.276 J.D.
Work, Anne D. '47 '83 C.1060 B.A. L.128 J.D.

OFFICE OF PROFESSIONAL RESPONSIBILITY

Birney, William J. '48 '75 C.378 B.A. L.276 J.D.
Colby, Paul L. '55 '81 C.861 B.A. L.178 J.D.
Duncan, James G. '— '89 C&L.597 B.A., J.D.
Fraase, Mark G. '59 '85 (ND) C.182 B.A. L.585 J.D.
Hoopes, Mary Anne '52 '78 C.991 B.A. L.276 J.D.
Jarrett, Howard Marshall, Jr. '45 '69 C&L.923 B.S., J.D.
Lyon, Robert B., Jr. '48 '77 C&L.790 B.A., J.D.
McCarty, Margaret '62 '87 (IL) C&L.339 B.A., J.D.
Rogers, Richard M. '46 '71 C.262 A.B. L.893 J.D.
Ross, Maurice A. '61 '87 (PA) C.976 B.A. L.309 J.D.
Sargeant, Bernadette '62 '87 C.104 A.B. L.477 J.D.
Talbert, Phillip A. '62 '89 (CA) C.309 A.B. L.1068 J.D.
Wahowiak, Marlene Mary '59 '93 (PA) C.475 B.A. L.273 J.D.
White, Alexander S. '48 '77 C.813 B.A. L.659 J.D.
Will, Candice M. '58 '82 C.560 B.A. L.734 J.D.
Wish, Judith B. '48 '78 C.454 B.A. L.910 J.D.

BUREAU OF PRISONS

Bomson, Scott J. '57 '82 C.1044 B.A. L.30 J.D.
Cantwell, Marianne '64 '91 (VA) C.454 B.A. L.180 J.D.
Cardwell, Bryan Kevin '64 '90 C.893 B.A. L.902 J.D.
Carney, Mary E. '71 '98 C.951 B.A. L.273 J.D.
Chrisler, Tamara E. Lourq '— '93 C&L.339 B.A., J.D.
Crowell, Jane Orci '53 '91 (VA) C&L.273 B.A., J.D.
Daniels-Lewis, Alicia R. '63 '98 C&L.574 B.A., J.D
Day, Katherine A. '57 '84 C.881 A.B. L.982 J.D.
Edson, Elizabeth M. '48 '77 (ME) C.550 B.A. L.1294 J.D.
Erlewine, Christopher '47 '72 C.434 B.A. L.276 J.D.
Fornshill, Renee Brinker '69 '95 C.477 B.G.S. L.215 J.D.
Glassman, Lorna R. '59 '85 (NY) C.659 B.A. L.724 J.D.
Hinkson, Yvonne Elizabeth '54 '85 (NY) C.102 B.A. L.30 J.D.
Holick, Natalie R. W. '73 '98 C.947 B.A. L.1048 J.D.
Hunt, Wanda M. '64 '90 C.235 B.A. L.276 J.D.
Kearns, Thomas William '64 '98 C.665 B.S. L.64 J.D.
Kenney, Kathleen M. '66 '92 C.128 B.A. L.602 J.D.
Kerrigan, Marli J.P. '72 '97 C.893 B.A. L.273 J.D.
Laliberte, Donald '— '83 C.690 B.A. L.1048 J.D.
Layer, Paul W. '62 '90 C.446 B.A. L.1206 J.D.
Lewis, Michael A. '— '95 C&L.276 B.S., J.D.
Marshall, Aaron T. '— '98 C.205 B.A. L.1338 J.D.
Melkin, Matthew W. '64 '89 C.945 B.A. L.659 J.D.
Meyers, Craig F. '54 '80 C.911 B.A. L.678 J.D.
Pybas, Michael j. '57 '81 C.225 B.A. L.623 J.D.
Qureshi, Sarah Nafees '71 '95 C&L.446 B.A., J.D.
Raia, Dominique '63 '88 C.937 B.A. L.884 J.D.
Raskin, Mina '64 '91 C.659 B.A. L.276 J.D.
Ropelewski, James L. '65 '90 (VA) C.1349 B.A. L.945 J.D.
Santucci, Audra E. '69 '00 C&L.436 B.A., J.D.
Sapla, Carolyn Vines '67 '95 C.953 B.A. L.999 J.D.
Schneider, Paul M. '51 '87 C.696 B.A. L.880 J.D.
Tarver, Jerome '— '90 C.103 B.A. L.188 J.D.
Toenges, Jeffrey '64 '91 C.260 B.A. L.300 J.D.
Wills, James C. '— '94 C.511 B.A. L.893 J.D.
Younger, George E. '50 '76 (VA) C.301 B.A. L.692 J.D.
Zoldak, Joyce A. '57 '83 (MA) C.588 B.A. L.1218 J.D.

OFFICE OF THE SOLICITOR GENERAL

Brinkmann, Beth S. '58 '87 (CA) C.112 A.B. L.976 J.D.
Clement, Paul D. '66 '94 C.276 B.S.F.S. L.309 J.D.
Dreeben, Michael R. '54 '82 C.966 B.A. L.228 J.D.
DuMont, Edward C. '61 '86 (CA) C.976 B.A. L.813 J.D.
Feldman, James A. '50 '83 C.659 B.A. L.309 J.D.
Jones, Kent L. '47 '76 C.31 B.A. L.309 J.D.
Kneedler, Edwin S. '46 '75 (OR) C.401 B.S. L.893 J.D.
Lamken, Jeffrey A. '64 '91 C.311 B.A. L.813 J.D.
McDowell, Barbara '52 '86 C.273 B.A. L.976 J.D.
Millett, Patricia A. '63 '88 C.339 B.A. L.309 J.D.
Minear, Jeffrey P. '55 '83 (UT) C.878 B.S.Ch.E. L.477 J.D.
Roberts, Matthew D. '62 '90 C&L.309 A.B., J.D.
Stewart, Malcolm L. '57 '91 C.674 A.B. L.976 J.D.
Wallace, Lawrence G. '31 '60 C.823 A.B. L.178 LL.B.
Wolfson, Paul R. Q. '61 '87 C.309 A.B. L.976 J.D.

OFFICE OF TRIBAL JUSTICE

Araujo, Todd J. '72 '97 C.321 B.A. L.1143 J.D. Dep. Dir.
Gee, Debra E. '69 '95 C.788 B.A. L.36 J.D. Dep. Dir.
Joranko, Timothy W. '61 '86 C.597 B.A. L.309 J.D. Dep. Dir.
Nayback, Kyle T. '70 '96 C.475 B.S. L.560 J.D. Dep. Dir.
Toulou, Tracy S. '— '95 (NM) C.950 B.S. L.560 J.D. Director

OFFICE OF CONSUMER LITIGATION

Arnold, James Elliot '61 '90 C.228 A.B. L.976 J.D.
Ashley, Donald D. '63 '88 C.363 A.B. L.309 J.D.
Autor, Deborah M. '66 '93 C.66 B.A. L.94 J.D.
Furman, Jill P. '66 '92 (MA) C.659 B.A. L.94 J.D.
Gersten, Steven N. '62 '88 C&L.94 B.S.B.A., J.D.
Goldberg, Richard N. '— '98 (MD) C.319 B.A. L.446 J.D.
Harnisch, Allison '73 '99 (MD) C.475 B.A. L.309 J.D.
Hearty, James O. '68 '98 (CO) C.172 B.S. L.174 J.D.
Marks, Linda I. '56 '81 (CA) C.112 B.A. L.426 J.D.
Stearn, Douglas William '64 '92 C.103 B.A. L.188 J.D.
Strawn, Susan L. '— '89 C.674 A.B. L.846 J.D.
Thirolf, Eugene M. '46 '71 (MO) C&L.734 B.A., J.D.

TAX DIVISION

Abate, Mary M. '— '77 (PA) C.228 A.B. L.1292 J.D.
Abbruzzese, Marguerite A. '64 '89 C.1030 B.A. L.273 J.D.
Allen, Gary R. '41 '69 C.597 B.A. L.273 J.D.
Anagnost, Tracy A. '63 '89 (NY) C.165 A.B. L.982 J.D.
Apostolakos, Mary J. '58 '85 C.573 B.S. L.30 J.D.
Bailey, Brian D. '55 '81 (UT) C.101 B.A. L.878 J.D.
Baker, Robert L. '43 '68 C&L.838 B.S., J.D.
Ballweg, Mitchell J. '58 '87 (CO) C.957 B.B.A. L.208 J.D.
Barthel, Carol '46 '86 C.228 B.A. L.276 J.D.
Bassin, Stuart J. '57 '82 C.473 B.Phil. L.188 J.D.
Bender, Joseph E., Jr. '56 '87 C.645 B.S. L.575 J.D.
Berry, Pamela C. '57 '84 C.453 S.B. L.184 J.D.
Bielefeld, Mary Elizabeth '45 '77 C.174 B.A. L.818 J.D.
Bilheimer, John M. '45 '69 (AR) C.45 B.A. L.309 J.D.
Blaskopf, Lawrence '49 '86 (NY) C.696 B.A. L.978 J.D.
Bloch, David P. '63 '89 C.30 B.A. L.1009 J.D.
Blondin, Philip E. '58 '84 (MN) C.311 B.A. L.494 J.D.
Bradley, Janet A. '59 '85 C.128 B.A. L.30 J.D.
Bramson, Nanci S. '67 '93 C&L.659 B.A., J.D.
Branman, Robert J. '62 '88 (CA) C.813 A.B. L.1068 J.D.
Bricken, Charles '47 '79 (OR) C.549 B.S. L.950 J.D.
Brookhart, Charles E. '37 '67 C.350 B.S. L.30 J.D.
Brown, Kevin M. '61 '87 C.299 B.A. L.93 J.D.
Campobasso, Carina J. '59 '90 C&L.309 A.B., J.D.
Cannon, Charles J. '52 '78 C.588 B.S. L.818 J.D.
Carmack, David E. '38 '66 C.692 B.A. L.178 LL.B.
Casper, Lawrence A. '62 '88 C.1036 B.A. L.94 J.D.
Chapman, James W., Jr. '61 '86 (ME) C.550 B.A. L.1294 J.D.
Cihlar, Frank P. '43 '67 C.424 B.S. L.602 LL.B.
Cimino, Ronald A. '43 '68 C&L.665 B.A., J.D.
Cirenza, Bartholomew '60 '90 (NY) C.1040 B.B.A. L.823 J.D.
Clark, Thomas J. '54 '84 (PA) C.724 B.A. L.831 J.D.
Clarke, Russell S. '63 '88 C.207 B.A. L.117 J.D.
Cohen, Jonathan S. '36 '59 C.976 B.A. L.659 LL.B.
Collins, Genevieve J. '57 '88 (NY) C&L.262 B.A., J.D.
Conley, Laura Marie '61 '87 (NY) C.751 B.S. L.982 J.D.
Cronan, Virginia J. '59 '85 (MA) C.454 B.A. L.1202 J.D.
Cronin, Edward F. '54 '82 (MA) C.860 B.A. L.818 J.D.
Csontos, Stephen J. '41 '65 C.1030 B.B.A. L.276 J.D.
Darmstadter, Henry C., III '59 '85 (CA) C.893 B.A. L.800 J.D.
Davis, Evan J. '68 '93 C.165 A.B. L.188 J.D.
Davis, Gregory V. '64 '90 (MN) C.118 B.A. L.494 J.D.
Davis, Michael W. '59 '92 (VA) C.999 B.A. L.276 J.D.
Davis, Nanette L. '62 '90 C.945 B.A. L.276 J.D.
de Leon, Jose F. '57 '85 (FL) C.472 B.A. L.425 J.D.
DelSole, Ellen Page '65 '90 C.1128 B.S. L.575 J.D.
DePriest, Elizabeth D. '— '77 C.611 L.893 J.D.
Determan, Mark S. '65 '95 (CA) C.112 B.A. L.1066 J.D.
DiCicco, John A. '46 '73 (MI) C.475 B.A. L.912 J.D.
DiLeonardo, Thomas S. '64 '91 C.693 B.S. L.1292 J.D.
Donnelly, Deirdre '60 '85 (OH) C.363 B.A. L.930 J.D.
Donohue, Dennis M. '44 '69 (OH) C&L.150 B.A., J.D.
Doolittle, Theodore M. '63 '92 C.309 A.B. L.184 J.D.
Dorosin, Robert N. '39 '64 C.178 A.B. L.477 LL.B.
Dowie, Donald N., Jr. '64 '93 (WA) C.909 B.A. L.1066 J.D.
Doyle, Philip '59 '91 (NJ) C.881 B.A. L.705 J.D.
Dozier, Robert E. '54 '86 C.228 B.A. L.309 J.D.
Dudeck, John A., Jr. '44 '71 C.576 B.S. L.893 J.D.
Duffy, Charles M. '61 '86 (PA) C.1128 B.S. L.665 J.D.
Durney, Ann '43 '67 (OK) C&L.623 B.A., LL.B.
Eliopoulos, George P. '57 '85 C.94 B.A. L.276 J.D.
Ellis, Avery M. '67 '93 (NY) C.446 B.A. L.107 J.D.
Ellisen, Bruce R. '55 '82 (CA) C.112 B.A. L.1065 J.D.
Erickson, Marion E. M. '58 '89 (VA) C.188 B.A. L.1209 J.D.
Estabrook, William S., III '38 '64 (NY) C.604 A.B. L.188 J.D.

Fallon, Claire .... '45 '70 (MA) C.242 A.B. L.93 J.D.
Farber, Richard .... '45 '69 C.105 B.S. L.276 J.D.
Farfante, Darren D. .... '71 '96 (FL) C&L.260 M.A.C.C., J.D.
Farhang, Michael M. .... '71 '95 (CA) C&L.309 A.B., J.D.
Farnham, David .... '52 '82 C.445 B.S. L.446 J.D.
Feldman, Brian J. .... '61 '86 C.645 B.S. L.665 J.D.
Ferrel, J. Brian .... '41 '68 C.276 B.A. L.128 LL.B.
Ferzan, Marc-Philip .... '67 '93 (NJ) C.705 B.A. L.262 J.D.
Fine-Trail, Tamera L. .... '60 '88 (NY) C.502 B.A. L.178 J.D.
Fischbein, Stuart M. .... '40 '65 C.260 B.A. L.273 J.D.
Flynn, Thomas W. .... '56 '81 (IL) C.37 B.S. L.424 J.D.
Fowler, Neal I. .... '62 '87 (MS) C.500 B.B.A. L.228 J.D.
Frahm, Steven I. .... '49 '75 C.446 B.A. L.276 J.D.
Frattarelli, Angelo A. .... '64 '89 (RI) C.1145 B.S. L.1202 J.D.
Fridkin, Jerome H. .... '38 '63 C.659 B.S. L.831 LL.B.
Friedrich, Matthew W. .... '66 '94 (TX) C.893 B.A. L.846 J.D.
Friend, Mark R. .... '49 '78 C.659 B.A. L.30 J.D.
Gavin, Donald J. .... '39 '64 C&L.424 B.S.C., J.D.
Giaimo, Jennifer A. .... '67 '92 (NY) C.94 B.S. L.724 J.D.
Giannullo, Joseph M. .... '62 '88 (MD) C.705 B.S. L.64 J.D.
Gibson, Stuart D. .... '51 '76 (MN) C.597 B.S.J. L.494 J.D.
Gilman, Richard L. .... '63 '89 C.1044 B.S. L.904 J.D.
Grant, Christine A. .... '60 '88 C.705 B.A. L.831 J.D.
Grant, Jian H. .... '68 '97 (PA) C.1288 B.S. L.831 J.D.
Greene, Judybeth .... '62 '87 C.867 B.A. L.273 J.D.
Greene, Kenneth L. .... '52 '77 (MI) C.477 B.A. L.912 J.D.
Groves, Edward E. .... '62 '91 C.36 B.S. L.276 J.D.
Gustafson, David .... '56 '81 C.92 B.A. L.228 J.D.
Hankla, W. Carl .... '58 '85 C.886 B.A. L.902 J.D.
Hardy, Peter Davis .... '68 '94 C&L.477 B.A., J.D.
Heald, Seth G. .... '53 '78 C.311 B.A. L.276 J.D.
Heatley, Berry A. .... '57 '86 (VA) C&L.893 B.S., J.D.
Hechtkopf, Alan .... '44 '69 (VA) C.1083 B.S. L.945 J.D.
Heckman, Tamara S. .... '66 '92 (NY) C&L.107 B.A., J.D.
Higgins, Robert J. .... '50 '76 C.867 B.A. L.128 J.D.
Hinton, John, III .... '55 '81 (PA) C.867 B.A. L.1017 J.D.
Hodgens, John M., Jr. .... '65 '90 (MA) C.93 B.S. L.1202 J.D.
Hogeboom, C. Patrick, III .... '49 '86 (WA) C.556 B.S. L.285 J.D.
Holmes, William D. M. .... '37 '64 (MS) C&L.500 B.P.A., LL.B.
Holton, Melissa Anemojanis .... '67 '94 (VA) C.902 B.S. L.692 J.D.
Horwitz, Murray S. .... '43 '68 (CT) C.976 B.A. L.184 LL.B.
Hough, Shannon L. .... '62 '90 (MD) C.839 B.B.A. L.602 J.D.
Hrebiniak, Gregory S. .... '45 '74 (MD) C.749 A.B. L.64 J.D.
Hurley, Charles P. .... '55 '82 (OH) C.381 B.A. L.930 J.D.
Hutter, Randolph L. .... '58 '89 (MD) C.198 B.A. L.446 J.D.
Ide, Carol Koehler .... '61 '87 C.645 B.A. L.276 J.D.
Ihlo, Jennifer E. .... '55 '83 (TX) C.814 B.A. L.796 J.D.
Jacobs, George J. C., III .... '58 '89 C.103 A.B. L.245 J.D.
Jenkins, Kevin P. .... '63 '92 C.951 B.A. L.309 J.D.
Jennings, Guy P. .... '57 '86 (CA) C.722 B.A. L.464 J.D.
Jonas, Barry .... '65 '89 (CT) C.999 B.A. L.724 J.D.
Kameros, Andrew J. .... '60 '86 C.165 B.A. L.904 J.D.
Karam, Michael E. .... '50 '77 C&L.276 B.S.F.S., J.D.
Karlan, Milan D. .... '38 '63 (OH) C&L.930 B.B.A., LL.B.
Katinsky, David M. .... '61 '86 C.659 B.S. L.893 J.D.
Katon, Glenn M. .... '66 '93 (NY) C.1356 B.A. L.724 J.D.
Kearns, Michael J. .... '50 '75 C.602 B.B.A. L.94 J.D.
Keen, Charles H. .... '52 '90 (GA) C.384 B.A. L.1059 J.D.
Kelcourse, Kevin M. .... '63 '90 C&L.276 B.S.F.S., J.D.
Ketchum, Sara Ann .... '46 '92 (MA) C.881 A.B. L.309 J.D.
Kilgariff, John J. .... '20 '53 (TX) C&L.802 B.B.A., LL.B.
King, Benjamin C., Jr. .... '52 '77 (LA) C.378 B.A. L.861 J.D.
Kloster, Laurie K. .... '58 '83 (MN) C.182 B.A. L.596 J.D.
Kluger, Jerrold L. .... '46 '71 C.705 B.A. L.1009 J.D.
Knutson, Sarah K. .... '61 '90 (WI) C&L.966 B.A., J.D.
Kranz, Stephen P. .... '66 '92 (MN) C.585 B.A. L.221 J.D.
Krysa, Stanley F. .... '29 '56 (TX) C.966 B.S. L.846 LL.B.
Lancaster, Marika .... '48 '75 C.276 B.S. L.602 J.D.
Lawson, Scott R. .... '66 '91 (MA) C.282 B.A. L.569 J.D.
Leedom, Gerald B. .... '47 '75 C.313 A.B. L.477 J.D.
Lena, Manuel P., Jr. .... '52 '89 (TX) C.846 B.S. L.802 J.D.
Lewis, Cynthia M. .... '58 '87 C.385 B.A. L.229 J.D.
Lindquist, John A., III .... '57 '83 C.951 B.A. L.665 J.D.
Lindsay, Robert E. .... '41 '70 C.645 B.A. L.30 J.D.
Lisann, Eric C. .... '60 '86 (MD) C.231 B.A. L.446 J.D.
Lucas, Ruth E. .... '61 '89 (VA) C.575 B.A. L.30 J.D.
Lusty, Kirk C. .... '55 '82 (UT) C&L.878 B.S., J.D.
Lyons, S. Robert .... '59 '91 (WA) C.911 B.A. L.678 J.D.
Lyons, Stephen T. .... '40 '67 (FL) C.228 B.S.E.E. L.260 J.D.
Makl, Glenn A. .... '62 '89 C.1046 B.S. L.1209 J.D.
Maney, John R., Jr. .... '43 '68 C&L.692 B.S., J.D.
Markham, Robert C. .... '44 '68 (MO) C&L.910 A.B., J.D.
Marrella, John A. .... '59 '90 (MA) C.31 B.A. L.309 J.D.
Martineau, Michael J. .... '56 '84 C.951 B.A. L.128 J.D.
May, Caroline F. .... '69 '94 C.421 B.A. L.893 J.D.
McLaughlin, Teresa E. .... '57 '82 (MA) C.681 A.B. L.309 J.D.
Menzer, Susan B. .... '63 '88 C.67 B.A. L.273 J.D.
Metzler, Robert W. .... '49 '82 (VA) C.321 B.A. L.128 J.D.
Meyer, Jeffrey R. .... '63 '91 (MI) L.912 J.D.
Miller, Floyd J., Jr. .... '— '80 (OH) C.161 B.B.A. L.1003 J.D.
Miller, G. Hobart .... '63 '89 (TX) C.839 B.A. L.69 J.D.
Miller, Gayle P. .... '50 '77 (PA) C.659 B.A. L.1292 J.D.
Miller, Gerald C. .... '44 '70 (NY) C.659 A.B. L.94 J.D.
Miller, Karen Davis .... '64 '93 (IL) C.475 B.S. L.597 J.D.
Millstone, Robert D. .... '62 '88 (MO) C&L.910 A.B., J.D.
Mitchell, Richard F. .... '45 '70 (NC) C&L.575 A.B., J.D.
Moody, Herbert L., Jr. .... '33 '61 (SC) C&L.790 B.S., LL.B.
Moriarty, Regina S. .... '61 '87 (VA) C&L.1209 B.S., J.D.
Morrow, William R., Jr. .... '31 '66 C.724 B.A. L.1009 J.D.
Morton, Bruce E. .... '44 '69 (AL) C&L.16 B.A., J.D.
Mullarkey, Daniel P. .... '40 '65 C.436 B.S. L.276 J.D.
Murphy, Lynne M. .... '— '90 (LA) C&L.425 B.B.A., J.D.
Murphy, William T. .... '70 '98 C.1030 B.A. L.184 J.D.
Nicrosi, Michel .... '64 '89 (AL) C&L.16 B.A., J.D.
Nolet, John A. .... '57 '90 (MD) C.454 B.B.A. L.64 J.D.
Notinger, Ramona Stephens .... '57 '84 (TX) C.420 B.S. L.790 J.D.
O'Connor, Michelle B. .... '65 '91 C.184 B.A. L.902 J.D.
Oppenheimer, Joan I. .... '46 '72 (NY) C.881 A.B. L.188 J.D.
O'Reilly, Charles A. .... '62 '92 (CA) C.112 B.A. L.1066 J.D.
Ortega, Beverly Ann .... '62 '89 C.311 B.A. L.1066 J.D.
Ott, Thomas P. .... '59 '88 (MD) C.1044 B.A. L.64 J.D.
Paguni, Rosemary E. .... '51 '76 (CT) C.518 A.B. L.930 J.D.
Pett, Curtis C. .... '53 '88 (IN) C.63 B.S. L.347 J.D.
Pietrofeso, Richard J. .... '65 '90 C&L.37 B.A., J.D.
Pietruszkiewicz, Christopher M. .... '67 '92 C.754 B.S. L.425 J.D.
Pincus, David I. .... '48 '73 (NY) C.102 B.A. L.659 J.D.
Pirkle, John P. .... '58 '89 (CA) C.846 B.B.A. L.61 J.D.
Plepler, Andrew D. .... '60 '86 C.264 B.A. L.472 J.D.
Ponticiello, Stephen .... '59 '85 (PA) C.1044 B.A. L.831 J.D.
Powell, Michael D. .... '49 '79 (FL) C.259 B.A. L.472 J.D.
Pribe, Andrew T. .... '66 '92 (IL) C.112 B.A. L.339 J.D.
Priest, Carol C. .... '63 '88 (LA) C&L.420 B.S., J.D.
Pryor, Walter O. .... '65 '90 C.315 B.A. L.276 J.D.
Putney, Scott W. .... '57 '81 (FL) C.885 B.S. L.862 J.D.
Quarngesser, Susan S. .... '66 '93 C.674 A.B. L.446 J.D.
Riordan, Daniel T. .... '63 '90 C.1369 B.B.A. L.273 J.D.
Riordan, Henry J. .... '60 '86 (MA) C.1155 B.S. L.1202 J.D.
Roetzel, Danny Nile .... '52 '87 (MO) C.1044 B.S. L.734 J.D.
Role, Gerald A. .... '57 '87 C.339 B.A. L.1119 J.D.
Romano, Christopher J. .... '51 '78 (MD) C.445 B.A. L.64 J.D.
Ronk, Alice L. .... '62 '92 (PA) C.674 A.B. L.831 J.D.
Rooney, Jaye E. .... '58 '89 C.882 B.S. L.1294 J.D.
Rosen, Robert A. .... '51 '76 (MD) C.446 B.A. L.64 J.D.
Rosenberg, Kenneth W. .... '51 '87 (PA) C.766 B.A. L.1065 J.D.
Rosenthal, Michael J. .... '63 '89 C.454 B.S. L.904 J.D.
Rossi, Eugene J. .... '56 '82 C.1033 L.30 J.D.
Rothenberg, Gilbert S. .... '51 '75 C.659 B.A. L.30 J.D.
Rovner, Janice .... '63 '88 C.1036 A.B. L.94 J.D.
Rowan, Bridget .... '54 '83 C.563 B.A. L.309 J.D.
Russell, Bruce T. .... '52 '82 (GA) C.575 B.A. L.280 J.D.
Sadler, Alex E. .... '69 '95 C&L.893 B.S., J.D.
Saiz, Beatriz T. .... '70 '95 C.705 B.S. L.1292 J.D.
Salad, Bruce M. .... '54 '79 C.860 B.A. L.273 J.D.
Salem, Michael J. .... '53 '78 (PA) C.654 B.A. L.276 J.D.
Sawyer, Thomas J. .... '62 '87 (IN) C.838 B.S. L.879 J.D.
Schultze, Carol E. .... '62 '87 (MD) C.699 B.A. L.93 J.D.
Seidman, Mildred L. .... '28 '53 (NY) C.102 B.A. L.178 LL.B.
Sergi, Joseph Andrew .... '70 '95 (NJ) C.1040 B.B.A. L.564 J.D.
Seyferth, Mary B. .... '52 '76 C.770 B.S. L.1066 J.D.
Shapiro, Alan M. .... '62 '88 C.1365 B.A. L.245 J.D.
Shapiro, Steven .... '37 '61 (PA) C&L.831 B.S., LL.B.
Sheehan, Anthony T. .... '67 '92 (IL) C.339 B.A. L.477 J.D.
Shellow, Jill R. .... '56 '89 C.367 B.A. L.276 J.D.
Silverman, Steven D. .... '67 '92 C.477 B.A. L.659 J.D.
Singer, Leslie .... '62 '87 (FL) C.861 B.A. L.30 J.D.
Sklarew, Peter .... '51 '79 C.112 B.A. L.1066 J.D.
Smith, Corey J. .... '62 '88 (IL) C.145 B.A. L.818 J.D.
Snoeyenbos, Douglas W. .... '61 '86 C.347 B.S. L.276 J.D.
Snow, Jeffery D. .... '39 '66 C.112 B.A. L.1066 J.D.
Snyder, Edward J. .... '33 '61 C.128 B.A. L.273 LL.B.
Sobotka, Andrew L. .... '63 '89 (TX) C.793 B.S. L.546 J.D.
Speck, Paula K. .... '50 '88 C.309 B.A. L.846 J.D.
Specker, Ellen C. .... '44 '73 C.273 B.A. L.30 J.D.
Spriggs, Jennifer Dover .... '54 '85 C.477 B.A. L.309 J.D.
Springer, James P. .... '42 '74 C.686 B.S. L.276 J.D.
Squires, George L. .... '43 '68 C.867 B.A. L.184 LL.B.
Stehlik, Noreene C. .... '55 '85 C.914 B.A. L.276 J.D.
Stevens, Gregg D. .... '62 '87 (TX) C.473 B.S. L.802 J.D.
Stier, Mark .... '47 '80 C.1169 B.A. L.1066 J.D.
Stoddart, Robert C. .... '51 '84 (PA) C.385 B.A. L.477 J.D.
Taylor-Phillips, LaQuita Joy .... '65 '97 C.421 B.A. L.127 J.D.
Tierney, Carl J. .... '65 '92 (NY) C.881 A.B. L.107 J.D.
Tobin, Donald B. .... '— '96 (MD) C.228 B.A. L.276 J.D.
Tortella, Gregory E. .... '62 '87 (NJ) C.659 B.A. L.117 J.D.
Trissell, Teresa Dondlinger .... '68 '95 C.546 B.A. L.276 J.D.
Ulmer, Joan S. .... '63 '90 C.30 B.A. L.904 J.D.
Vert, Kenneth C. .... '63 '88 (MI) C.475 B.A. L.976 J.D.
Voracek, Thomas G. .... '58 '85 (AZ) C.494 B.A. L.190 J.D.
Vrahoretis, Susan H. .... '62 '88 (NY) C.879 B.A. L.1119 J.D.
Ward, Richard R. .... '63 '90 C.118 B.A. L.494 J.D.
Ward, Steven P. .... '55 '84 C.188 B.A. L.1029 J.D.
Watkins, Robert S. .... '40 '70 C.861 B.A. L.30 J.D.
Webster, Steven M. .... '63 '92 (GA) C&L.362 B.A., J.D.
Wehner, Karen A. .... '51 '84 (PA) C.665 B.A. L.229 J.D.
Weinstein, Elise Caren .... '63 '89 (CT) C.690 B.S. L.1009 J.D.
Welsh, Robert L. .... '47 '72 C.840 B.B.A. L.802 J.D.
Whitledge, William A. .... '45 '70 (IN) C.347 B.S.A. L.1119 J.D.
Williams, Laurence K. .... '59 '87 C.797 B.A. L.893 J.D.
Wollitzer, Rachel I. .... '65 '90 C.659 B.A. L.597 J.D.
Yeaman, Addison Y., Jr. .... '31 '70 (KY) C.976 B.A. L.421 J.D.
Zehnle, Thomas E. .... '61 '87 C.502 A.B. L.945 J.D.

UNITED STATES MARSHALS SERVICE

Auerbach, Gerald M. .... '51 '75 (VA) C.188 B.A. L.276 J.D.
Bordley, William E. .... '56 '85 (VA) C&L.309 B.A., J.D.
Carroll, C. Joseph .... '62 '91 (VA) C.999 B.A. L.893 J.D.
Dickinson, Lisa M. .... '62 '88 C.436 B.A. L.472 J.D.
Elston, Gerald L. .... '54 '80 C&L.276 A.B., J.D.
Gibson, Susan Engelman .... '62 '93 (VA) C.436 B.S. L.128 J.D.
Lazar, Joey B. .... '59 '84 C.874 B.A. L.904 J.D.
Marcovici, Robert X. .... '59 '87 (VA) C.260 B.A. L.30 J.D.
O'Hare, Kevin F. .... '64 '89 C.676 B.A. L.273 J.D.
Roberts, Lucille K. .... '49 '75 (PA) C.205 B.S. L.851 J.D.
Roque, Steven V. .... '67 '92 C.446 B.A. L.30 J.D.
Segars, Ann M. .... '48 '80 (CA) C.893 B.A. L.284 J.D.
Smith, Harvey Y. .... '45 '72 C.893 B.A. L.273 J.D.
Westbrook, Deborah C. .... '51 '76 (KY) C.384 B.A. L.421 J.D. Gen. Coun.

DEPARTMENT OF JUSTICE (Continued)

Addington, Gregory W. ....'56 '82 (CA) C.1144 B.A. L.770 J.D.
Anderson, Linda M. ....'50 '86 (GA) C.813 B.A. L.280 J.D.
Barski, Katherine A. ....'70 '96 C.1206 B.S. L.425 J.D.
Baxter, Felix von ....'50 '75 (MA) C.1350 B.A. L.94 J.D.
Bilchik, Shay ....'53 '77 (FL) C&L.260 B.S.B.A., J.D.
Brigham, Geoffrey R. ....'58 '85 C.347 B.A. L.276 J.D.
Brill, Nathan Lee ....'66 '95 (MD) C.945 B.A. L.30 J.D.
Burke, Michael J. ....'55 '91 C.665 B.A. L.128 J.D.
Cacheris, Lisa ....'57 '86 (VA) C.893 B.A. L.276 J.D.
Cahill, Mary E. ....'43 '88 (NJ) C.1295 A.B. L.180 J.D.
Caldwell, Charles M. ....'54 '79 (IN) C.249 B.S. L.597 J.D.
Caporizzo, Cynthia A. ....'60 '89 C&L.128 B.A., J.D.
Carleton, Brenda Ford ....'51 '87 C.1083 B.A. L.276 J.D.
Clack, Jeanette L. ....'57 '87 C.276 B.S. L.30 J.D.
Clarke, Kerry Jane ....'58 '86 (CA) C.112 A.B. L.1065 J.D.
Clay, Carol A. ....'59 '87 C&L.477 A.B., J.D.
Cohen, Stephen L. ....'71 '97 (FL) C.94 B.A. L.472 J.D.
Coulter, Robert K. ....'55 '81 (LA) C.264 B.A. L.861 J.D.
Crabb, John ....'63 '90 (NY) C.276 B.S.F.S. L.178 J.D.
Crump, Ronald C. ....'51 '80 C.37 B.S. L.602 J.D.
Curt, Suzanne G. ....'54 '78 C.676 B.A. L.818 J.D.
Davis, Alice J.B. ....'46 '79 C.801 B.S. L.597 J.D.
de Ferranti, Margot E. ....'45 '76 C.681 A.B. L.426 J.D.
Delemarre, Michelle T. ....'65 '91 (MA) C.94 B.A. L.1194 J.D.
Deoudes, Katherine Kimi ....'50 '82 C&L.273 B.S., J.D.
de Vallance, Brian ....'58 '92 C.103 A.B. L.36 J.D.
Drew, William K. ....'49 '74 (WA) C&L.911 B.A., J.D.
Fraser, Francis W. ....'47 '73 C&L.190 B.A., J.D.
Gok, Lisa A. ....'53 '79 C.674 A.B. L.178 J.D.
Gregerson, Eva Heffernan ....'56 '81 (MI) C&L.585 B.S.B.A., J.D.
Greiman, Virginia A. ....'46 '80 C.645 B.S. L.818 J.D.
Herbert, Lenese L. ....'63 '89 (PA) C.329 B.S. L.1068 J.D.
Hirata, Irene K. ....'59 '85 (NY) C.188 B.S. L.107 J.D.
Hodges, Barbara I. ....'43 '82 C.610 B.A. L.128 J.D.
Hollenhorst, Thomas M. ....'55 '80 (MN) C&L.494 B.A., J.D.
Horn, Michele Annette ....'63 '89 (VA) C.1099 B.A. L.861 J.D.
Huggard, Stephen G. ....'59 '83 C.893 B.A. L.276 J.D.
Jasinski, James J. ....'49 '77 (NY) C.107 B.A. L.982 J.D.
Johnston, Hugh N., Jr. ....'48 '74 (VA) C.301 B.S. L.945 J.D.
Kane, Michael S. ....'55 '87 C.674 B.A. L.1066 J.D.
Kaplan, Glenn S. ....'65 '91 C.1044 B.S. L.309 J.D.
Karam, Elizabeth Publicover ....'56 '85 (PA) C.446 B.A. L.1162 J.D.
Kirsch, Robert Andrew ....'66 '92 (NY) C.245 B.A. L.262 J.D.
Kukura, Thomas V. ....'57 '83 (PA) C.25 B.A. L.665 J.D.
Levy, Jennifer ....'55 '79 C.788 A.B. L.128 J.D.
Macaluso, Judith N. ....'44 '75 C.446 B.A. L.329 J.D.
Mallin, Letitia J. ....'63 '89 (PA) C.813 B.A. L.178 J.D.
Mapes, Charlotte J. ....'51 '83 (CA) C.547 B.S. L.30 J.D.
McCarrick, John J. ....'47 '72 (CA) C&L.770 B.A., J.D.
Minni, Joseph F. ....'62 '88 (PA) C&L.831 B.B.A., J.D.
Moore, David M. ....'46 '73 C&L.893 B.S., J.D.
Moreland, Jennafer W. ....'61 '86 (LA) C.802 B.S.B.S. L.861 J.D.
Nord, Tim D. ....'62 '88 (OR) C.112 B.A. L.629 J.D.
Olds, Candace A. ....'50 '82 (MD) C.347 B.A. L.446 J.D.
Parshall, Gerald H., Jr. ....'57 '83 C&L.602 B.A., J.D.
Perez, Michael A. ....'46 '82 (MD) C.446 B.S. L.30 J.D.
Rhue, Bond E. ....'39 '68 (MD) C&L.446 B.S., J.D.
Rones, Clifford I. ....'56 '85 (MD) C.696 B.A. L.904 J.D.
Rosen, Eric D. ....'69 '96 (MD) C.659 B.A. L.273 J.D.
Sandhu, Papu ....'68 '96 (MA) C.188 B.A. L.93 J.D.
Schanz, Jeffrey E. ....'52 '92 (VA) C.1262 B.S. L.1209 J.D.
Segall, Eric J. ....'58 '84 C.245 B.A. L.880 J.D.
Sheeham, Mark T. ....'27 '75 C.103 A.B. L.273 J.D.
Sheehan, Eileen Frances ....'61 '86 C&L.575 B.A., J.D.
Smith, John E. ....'63 '94 C.502 B.A. L.178 J.D.
Smith, Walter F. ....'45 '86 (NY) C.645 B.S. L.262 J.D.
Solomon, Edward Robert ....'61 '87 C.881 B.A. L.245 J.D.
Stern, Carl L. ....'37 '66 C.178 A.B. L.1003 J.D.
Stern, Robert H. ....'52 '78 (PA) C&L.831 B.A., J.D.
Stodghill, Charles D. ....'53 '78 C.511 B.A. L.569 J.D.
Strauss, Gerald L. ....'39 '65 (WI) C.966 B.S. L.436 J.D.
Suarez, Michael K. ....'41 '76 (TX) C.1142 B.A. L.309 J.D.
Suarez, Miriam G. ....'62 '88 (FL) C.1278 B.S. L.260 J.D.
Taylor, Jonathan ....'61 '88 (AR) C.315 B.A. L.1243 J.D.
Toledo, Randy ....'62 '89 (FL) C.472 B.A. L.30 J.D.
Torstenson, Karen Fletcher ....'61 '87 (VA) C.893 B.A. L.1209 J.D.
Torwelle, Russell Dean ....'23 '85 C.446 B.A. L.1209 J.D.
Tse, Alex G. ....'65 '91 (CA) C.112 A.B. L.1065 J.D.
Verseman, Scott ....'62 '88 (MO) C&L.734 B.S., J.D.
Vilfer, Donald E. ....'60 '86 (OH) C.97 B.S. L.608 J.D.
Villa, James D. ....'62 '88 C&L.477 B.A., J.D.
Wallace, John K., III ....'46 '71 (MO) C.339 A.B. L.502 J.D.
Webb, Neil E. ....'40 '66 (FL) C.136 A.B. L.362 J.D.
Weckwert, Heidi E. ....'54 '85 (AZ) C.477 B.A. L.37 J.D.
Welch, William M., II ....'63 '89 (IL) C.674 B.A. L.597 J.D.
Welk, Lawrence J. ....'53 '86 (NY) C.116 B.S. L.1040 J.D.
White, Brenda Baldwin ....'61 '86 (PA) C&L.574 B.A., J.D.
White, Clifford J., III ....'56 '83 C&L.273 B.A., J.D.
Wilcove, Michael N. ....'56 '81 C.881 A.B. L.188 J.D.
Zaetta, Christopher R. ....'72 '98 (VA) C.659 B.S. L.665 J.D.
Zatz, Julie ....'48 '86 (IL) C.30 B.A. L.597 J.D.

DEPARTMENT OF LABOR

(Vacant), *Solicitor*

OFFICE OF THE SOLICITOR

Adair, Paul C. ....'65 '92 C.1365 B.A. L.309 J.D.
Aldrich, Robert W. ....'60 '89 C.415 B.A. L.128 J.D.
Alexander, Willie M. ....'51 '77 C.1042 B.S. L.329
Alter, Bruce W. ....'49 '75 C.550 B.A. L.930 J.D.
Apfelbaum, Michael N. ....'54 '78 C.216 B.A. L.273 J.D.
Arnold, L. Carol ....'44 '78 (VA) C.393 B.A. L.273 J.D.
Barber, Christian P. ....'59 '86 (WV) C.654 B.A. L.923 J.D.
Beard, Ellen L. ....'50 '77 C.118 B.A. L.145 J.D.
Beason, Elizabeth Lopes ....'66 '92 C.676 B.A. L.276 J.D.
Bell, Keith E. ....'66 '92 (PA) C&L.574 B.A., J.D.
Benedict, Ria Moore ....'— '97
Bernstecker, Gary E. ....'54 '79 C.347 B.A. L.846 J.D.
Berry, Wayne R. ....'59 '85 (PA) C.754 B.S. L.1029 J.D.
Biersner, Robert J. ....'41 '91 (KY) C.909 B.A. L.1340 J.D.
Blair, James V. ....'58 '86 C.415 B.A. L.276 J.D.
Blair-Kijewski, Cheryl C. ....'54 '86 (PA) C.705 B.A. L.276 J.D.
Bolstein, Arthur ....'37 '62 (NY) C.705 B.A. L.178 LL.B.
Bowen, Frederick ....'53 '78 C.659 B.A. L.273 J.D.
Bray, Karen E. S. ....'42 '69 (MD) C&L.30 B.A., LL.B.
Brenner, Joan ....'25 '87 C.597 B.S. L.273 J.D.
Bryant, Roscoe C., III ....'47 '73 (KY) C.254 B.A. L.574 J.D.
Buckley, Francis P. ....'46 '73 (MA) C.588 B.A. L.818 J.D.
Buff, Gary M. ....'48 '73 C.188 B.A. L.273 J.D.
Calhoun, Sharon D. ....'59 '88 C.314 B.A. L.1243 J.D.
Carter, Donald D., Jr. ....'49 '74 (FL) C&L.260 B.A., J.D.
Chastain, Suzan ....'48 '75 (IA) C&L.221 B.A., J.D.
Chaves, Lillian N. ....'74 '00 (FL) C&L.101 B.A., J.D.
Clair, Edward P. ....'46 '72 C.705 B.A. L.276 J.D.
Cohen, Bruce A. ....'47 '73 C.477 B.A. L.30 J.D.
Cohen, Robert A. ....'41 '68 (OH) C.610 A.B. L.273 J.D.
Coleman, Gail V. ....'46 '72 (MA) C.518 A.B. L.94 J.D.
Coleman, Paula W. ....'49 '78 C.329 B.S. L.665 J.D.
Collver, Geoffrey K ....'72 '99 C&L.629 B.A., J.D.
Costantino, Vincent C. ....'52 '79 (CT) C.1044 B.A. L.1048 J.D.
Cox, Helen H. ....'60 '86 (VA) C&L.945 B.A., J.D.
Craig, James L. ....'60 '85 C.494 B.A. L.273 J.D.
Crawford, James B. ....'49 '80 (VA) C.848 B.A. L.1209 J.D.
Crawford, Sarah C. ....'73 '98 (VA) C&L.945 B.A., J.D.
Cronan, Sheila K. ....'42 '75 (CA) C.668 B.A. L.1066 J.D.
Croydon, Stanley O., Jr. ....'44 '73 C.124 B.S. L.128 J.D.
Curran, Michele W. ....'— '91 (PA) C.446 B.S. L.30 J.D.
Dalzell-Finger, Heidi ....'44 '76 C.914 B.A. L.30 J.D.
Dankowitz, Beverly I. ....'60 '86 C.1044 B.A. L.30 J.D.
Dash, A. Penny ....'50 '75 C.1044 B.A. L.93 J.D.
Davidson, Douglas J. ....'46 '73 (IA) C&L.352 B.A., J.D.
De Deo, Carol A. ....'50 '74 C&L.273 B.A., J.D.
Denney, Michael J. ....'57 '82 (VA) C.299 A.B. L.893 J.D.
Depenbrock, John F., Jr. ....'43 '72 C.893 B.S. L.128 J.D.
Deutsch, Marshall A. ....'39 '64 (CT) C.976 B.A. L.659 LL.B.
Dolan, Peter B. ....'48 '75 (IL) C.20 B.A. L.597 J.D.
Ducharme, D. Alfred ....'67 '95 C.1395 B.A. L.93 J.D.
Durovic, Stevan W. ....'46 '74 C.436 B.A. L.276 J.D.
Durso, Christopher ....'68 '97 C.676 B.A. L.276 J.D.
Dwyer, Adrienne K. ....'64 '90 C.823 B.A. L.904 J.D.
Edmond, Ellen Randi ....'54 '80 C.597 B.A. L.273 J.D.
Elias, Stacey E. ....'60 '85 (NY) C.1036 A.B. L.262 J.D.
Estep, James M. ....'48 '73 C&L.276 A.B., J.D.
Fargas, Laura V. ....'53 '78 (PA) C.112 A.B. L.659 J.D.
Feingold, Jerald S. ....'52 '78 (VA) C.645 B.S. L.831 J.D.
Feldman, Allen H. ....'42 '68 C.659 B.A. L.276 J.D.
Fernandez, Alexander ....'67 '91 (VA) C.1222 B.A. L.276 J.D.
Fitch, Edward H., IV ....'48 '74 C.934 B.A. L.8 J.D.
Flynn, Mark S. ....'52 '78 C.347 B.A. L.477 J.D.
Fort, Linda B. ....'47 '73 C.30 B.A. L.904 J.D.
Frieden, Paul L. ....'53 '78 C&L.273 B.A., J.D.
Fugett, Anne P. ....'50 '79 C.788 B.A. L.273 J.D.
Galgay, Richard T. ....'44 '72 (MA) C.569 A.B. L.818 J.D.
Galvin, Peter D. ....'48 '73 C.976 B.A. L.930 J.D.
Garcia, Gilberto, Jr. ....'— '00 C.846 B.A. L.823 J.D.
Garcia, M. Peter ....'45 '78 C&L.776 B.A., J.D.
Gerdano, Michelle Seyman ....'56 '83 C.665 B.A. L.273 J.D.
Gibbs, Pamela A. ....'62 '92 (VA) C.893 B.A. L.276 J.D.
Gillelan, Joshua T., II ....'46 '73 (MD) C.722 B.A. L.446 J.D.
Gilman, Richard L. ....'53 '78 (VA) C.260 B.S. L.30 J.D.
Given, Whitney R. ....'64 '91 C.914 B.A. L.228 J.D.
Glabman, Scott ....'51 '88 C.674 A.B. L.228 J.D.
Goldberg, Jeff ....'63 '88 (WI) C.112 B.A. L.966 J.D.
Gordon, Charles P. ....'42 '68 (IL) C&L.145 B.A., J.D.
Gottesman, Larry F. ....'53 '81 (FL) C.1111 B.A. L.1209 J.D.
Gottlieb, Ronald J. ....'57 '87 C.994 B.A. L.564 J.D.
Green, Deborah K. ....'51 '79 (WV) C.389 B.A. L.276 J.D.
Greene, James A. ....'47 '78 (NY) C.1041 B.A. L.564 J.D.
Handorf, Karen L. ....'51 '75 (WI) C.962 B.S. L.966 J.D.
Hanley, Sharon E. ....'53 '88 (PA) C.889 B.A. L.945 J.D.
Hauser, Timothy D. ....'59 '85 (MO) C.339 B.A. L.309 J.D.
Heim, Diane A. ....'54 '81 C.651 B.S. L.309 J.D.
Hellman, Kenneth A. ....'48 '73 C&L.273 B.A., J.D.
Helm, Cathryn Celeste ....'52 '86 C.446 B.A. L.425 J.D.
Helm, Edward G. ....'45 '79 C.951 A.B. L.128 J.D.
Henschel, George L. ....'49 '74 (NH) C.188 A.B. L.228 J.D.
Hodge, Charles S. P. ....'46 '71 (MA) C.31 B.A. L.309 J.D.
Hopkins, Elizabeth ....'60 '86 C.37 B.A. L.276 J.D.
Hukill, Craig W. ....'53 '79 (IA) C.350 B.S. L.846 J.D.
Jackson, Charles M. ....'52 '75 C.837 B.A. L.880 J.D.
James, Charles F., II ....'50 '82 C&L.273 B.A., J.D.
James, Rae Ellen ....'49 '75 C.289 B.A. L.273 J.D.
Jones, Stephen R. ....'51 '81 C.264 B.A. L.904 J.D.
Jorgenson, Leif G. ....'44 '69 C.477 B.A. L.421 J.D.
Joyner, Barry H. ....'61 '86 (NM) C&L.560 B.A., J.D.
Justh, Bruce ....'39 '72 (MA) C.665 B.S. L.588 J.D.
Kahl, Barbara E. ....'53 '79 C.477 B.A. L.966 J.D.
Karesh, Lewis J. ....'59 '87 C.576 B.S. L.575 J.D.
Kates, William W. ....'43 '68 C.31 B.A. L.178 J.D.
Klingenberg, Paul J. ....'55 '79 C.973 A.B. L.276 J.D.
Ko, Selene S. ....'71 '97 C&L.309 A.B., J.D.
Koenig, Karen H. ....'59 '85 (MD) C.1350 B.A. L.273 J.D. Sr. Atty.
Kracov, Karen B. ....'61 '86 (MD) C.1044 B.A. L.273 J.D.
Kraft, James M. ....'47 '72 C&L.477 B.A., J.D.
Kramer, Judith E. ....'48 '73 C.339 B.S. L.597 J.D.

Kressley, LuAnn ... '53 '80 (VA) C.665 B.A. L.30 J.D.
Lerner, Mark J. ... '49 '74 (CT) C.918 B.A. L.184 J.D.
Lesser, William ... '56 '85 (NY) C.1044 B.S. L.904 J.D.
Levin, Matthew P. ... '63 '87 C.999 B.A. L.930 J.D.
Levintow, Nicholas J. ... '56 '81 C.164 B.A. L.276 J.D.
Little, Audrey B. ... '55 '80 (NJ) C.674 A.B. L.477 J.D.
Loos, Glenn M. ... '63 '88 (VA) C.381 B.A. L.608 J.D.
Malecki, Mark R. ... '56 '81 (IL) C.959 B.A. L.276 J.D.
Mandel, Steven J. ... '50 '76 C.696 B.A. L.273 J.D.
Mannina, Paul D. ... '55 '91 C.93 B.A. L.30 J.D.
Mascolino, Thomas A. ... '43 '68 C.1323 B.A. L.276 J.D.
McCarthy, Eileen M. ... '57 '84 C.604 A.B. L.273 J.D.
McCracken, J. Matthew ... '60 '90 (VA) C.893 B.A. L.1209 J.D.
McQuade, James E. ... '51 '80 C.846 B.B.A. L.796 J.D.
Mick, Daniel J. ... '47 '73 (MO) C.276 B.A. L.502 J.D.
Millenson, Debra A. ... '47 '70 C.475 B.A. L.477 J.D.
Miller, Karen E. ... '68 '93 C.880 B.A. L.893 J.D.
Miller, Miriam McD. ... '31 '55 (LA) C.298 B.A. L.861 LL.B.
Monarch, Nancy E. ... '61 '86 C.112 B.A. L.145 J.D.
Morin, Mark W. ... '56 '81 (MA) C.893 B.A. L.178 J.D.
Nash, Edith E. ... '39 '65 C.860 B.A. L.569 LL.B.
Nece, Patricia M. ... '58 '84 (NC) C.290 B.S. L.575 J.D.
Newman, Ford F. ... '53 '78 (WV) C.198 A.B. L.923 J.D.
Oshinsky, Samuel J. ... '53 '80 C&L.446 B.A., J.D.
Otte, Jill M. ... '61 '89 (PA) C.1044 B.A. L.276 J.D.
Ozur, Miriam D. ... '63 '88 (MD) C.446 B.A. L.128 J.D.
Pack, Linda Jan S. ... '43 '77 C.59 B.A. L.861 J.D.
Paez, Alan G. ... '66 '91 C.188 B.S. L.276 J.D.
Page, Dorothy L. ... '39 '87 (PA) C.999 B.A. L.1218 J.D.
Paquette, Dennis A. ... '42 '76 C.602 A.B. L.276 J.D.
Parry, Robin Springberg ... '— '94 (VA) C.103 A.B. L.309 J.D.
Peace-Jackson, Marva M. ... '44 '78 C.852 B.A. L.276 J.D.
Pena, David L. ... '48 '79 C.763 B.A. L.1049 J.D.
Perlman, Leslie Canfield ... '53 '79 (NY) C.188 B.S. L.880 J.D.
Perry, Gail A. ... '58 '91 (MD) C.546 B.A. L.276 J.D.
Peters, Brian Earl ... '56 '82 (MD) C&L.597 B.A., J.D.
Pfeffer, Richard M. ... '36 '66 (NY) C.976 B.A. L.309 LL.B.
Plick, Joseph J. ... '59 '87 (VA) C.48 B.A. L.904 J.D.
Powasnik, Jack ... '56 '86 C.705 B.A. L.285 J.D.
Racine, Barbara Eby ... '52 '82 C.705 B.A. L.930 J.D.
Radzely, Howard M. ... '70 '97 C.659 B.S. L.309 J.D.
Raymond, Charles D. ... '45 '72 (PA) C.645 B.A. L.229 J.D.
Reddy, Jayant A. ... '68 '93 (PA) C.350 B.S. L.228 J.D.
Reinhalter, Mark A. ... '56 '82 (MA) C.67 B.A. L.818 J.D.
Reynolds, Lawrence D. ... '54 '90 (VA) C.260 B.A. L.1209 J.D.
Reynolds, Louisa M. ... '— '99 C.267 B.A. L.1067 J.D.
Rieser, Mary J. ... '43 '88 C.1029 B.E.S. L.276 J.D.
Rogoff, Jeffrey Scott ... '68 '93 C.1349 B.A. L.569 J.D.
Rooney, Nancy M. ... '58 '83 (PA) C.884 B.A. L.276 J.D.
Roppolo, Rita ... '50 '77 (MA) C.915 B.A. L.818 J.D.
Rosenthal, Ann ... '49 '77 C.494 B.A. L.94 J.D.
Rutledge, Michael J. ... '57 '82 (FL) C.893 B.A. L.362 J.D.
Sadler, Robert M. ... '53 '91 C.352 B.A. L.128 J.D.
Sandler, Risa D. ... '50 '75 C&L.273 B.A., J.D.
Schloss, Michael A. ... '61 '88 (CA) C&L.978 B.A., J.D.
Schumann, W. Christian ... '47 '72 (MA) C&L.309 B.A., J.D.
Scott, George W., III ... '52 '77 C.228 B.A. L.128 J.D.
Segaar, Ruurd Carel ... '— '72 C.885 H.I. L.1090 J.D.
Seid, Richard A. ... '54 '80 (VA) C.367 B.A. L.902 J.D.
Serrou, Michelle L. ... '71 '98 C.475 B.A. L.30 J.D.
Shaird, Willie B. ... '57 '87 (PA) C.588 B.S. L.329 J.D.
Shalhoub, Donald G. ... '51 '76 C.749 A.B. L.425 J.D.
Shapiro, Robert A. ... '51 '76 C.30 B.A. L.597 J.D.
Sheinfeld, Harry L. ... '49 '75 C.94 A.B. L.569 J.D.
Sherman, Susan J. ... '43 '68 (WI) C&L.966 B.A., J.D.
Shire, Donald S. ... '40 '66 C&L.145 A.B., J.D.
Shortall, John R. ... '49 '76 C.276 A.B. L.724 J.D.
Shteir-Dunn, Vicki J. ... '54 '79 C.367 B.A. L.1292 J.D.
Sieger, Edward D. ... '53 '84 (WI) C.229 B.A. L.966 J.D.
Snashall, Robert C., Jr. ... '48 '73 C.112 B.A. L.597 J.D.
Spiller, Nathaniel I. ... '49 '75 (MA) C&L.309 B.A., J.D.
Stocker, Eva Marie ... '65 '94 (LA) C.1099 B.A. L.425 J.D.
Stomski, Laura J. ... '65 '90 (PA) C.454 B.A. L.464 J.D.
Stone, William J. ... '49 '75 C&L.588 B.S., J.D.
Stovall, Brenda J. ... '51 '80 (PA) C.512 B.A. L.229 J.D.
Strassler, Heidi W. ... '52 '78 (WV) C.446 B.A. L.831 J.D.
Swain, Robert W. ... '48 '77 C.296 B.A. L.1162 J.D.
Taylor, John M. ... '42 '74 (VA) C.276 B.S.F.S. L.911 J.D.
Taylor, William W., III ... '51 '76 (MD) C.575 A.B. L.446 J.D.
Tedesco, William Paul ... '56 '82 (VA) C.1044 B.A. L.273 J.D.
Thurber, Claudia H. ... '44 '83 (WA) C.906 B.A. L.904 J.D.
Toth, Jennifer U. ... '48 '90 C.611 B.A. L.128 J.D.
Tronson, Gregory W. ... '70 '96 C.297 B.A. L.1035 J.D.
Turley, Sheldon G., Jr. ... '58 '83 C.475 B.A. L.276 J.D.
Turow, Stephen D. ... '61 '87 (IL) C.966 B.A. L.339 J.D.
Vassalo, Peter J. ... '71 '96
Waldman, Edward ... '59 '85 C.1044 B.A. L.94 J.D.
Waxman, Jonathan H. ... '42 '67 (CT) C&L.976 B.A., LL.B.
Weglicki, Cynthia Caldwell ... '44 '82 C.104 B.A. L.893 J.D.
Werthmann, Barbara ... '47 '79 C.608 B.A. L.30 J.D.
Wesdock, Sandra M. ... '65 '91 (PA) C.643 B.A. L.128 J.D.
White, Claire B. ... '37 '78 (WV) C.689 Ed.B. L.329 J.D.
White, Douglas N. ... '45 '74 C.105 B.A. L.904 J.D.
Whiting, Ronald G. ... '42 '68 (IA) C&L.352 B.B.A., J.D.
Widom, Barton S. ... '39 '68 C.390 A.B. L.276 J.D.
Wilkinson, Roger W. ... '— '98 C.112 B.A. L.818 J.D.
Williams, Timothy S. ... '60 '87 C.1208 B.A. L.150 J.D.
Wilson, Jordana W. ... '49 '79 (TX) C.1046 B.A. L.846 J.D.
Windle, Suzanne ... '61 '88 C.94 B.A. L.276 J.D.
Woodward, Joseph M. ... '50 '77 (MA) C&L.309 A.B., J.D.
Zeitz, Myron G. ... '46 '78 C.966 B.A. L.64 J.D.
Zinman, Seth D. ... '36 '61 (CT) C.918 B.A. L.309 LL.B.
Zuckerman, Lois R. ... '55 '80 C.1349 B.A. L.178 J.D.
Zuckerman, William ... '32 '56 C&L.575 A.B., J.D.

OFFICE OF SECRETARY

Attwood, Cynthia L. ... '46 '73 C.1154 B.A. L.494 J.D.
Blackburn, Janice K. ... '50 '83 C&L.838 B.A., J.D.
Brooks, Dexter R. ... '69 '96 (MD) C.1378 B.S. L.329 J.D.
Brown, E. Cooper ... '49 '74 C&L.352 B.A., J.D. Adm. Law J.
Brown, Jas. F., Jr. ... '19 '49 C.529 Ph.B. L.659 LL.B. Adm. Appeals J.
Bulger, Craig ... '29 '56 (IL) C.569 B.S. L.477 LL.B.
Dalton, Robert J. ... '60 '91 C.436 B.A. L.1009 J.D.
Dean, Luana M. ... '65 '91 (PA) C.893 B.A. L.446 J.D.
Demopulos, Amelia H. ... '68 '96 (MD) C.103 B.A. L.30 J.D.
Dolder, Nancy S. ... '41 '66 C.112 A.B. L.1065 J.D. Adm. Appeals J.
Drachsler, David A. ... '43 '68 C.569 B.A. L.309 J.D.
Elliott, Gerald R. ... '53 '85 (MD) C.446 B.S. L.127 J.D.
Falzone, Sandra B. ... '61 '88 C.461 B.A. L.180 J.D.
Feigin, Stephen P. ... '41 '66 (CT) C.367 B.A. L.188 LL.B.
Foster, Seena K. ... '64 '89 C.475 B.A. L.273 J.D. Adm. Law J.
Gazda, Deanna L. ... '65 '91 (MD) C&L.446 B.S., J.D.
Gede, Ellen F. ... '60 '86 C.446 B.A. L.796 J.D.
Greenberg, Paul ... '53 '88 C.446 B.S. L.273 J.D. Chair, Adm. Rev. Bd.
Guil, James L. ... '37 '66 C.886 B.S. L.692 J.D. Assoc. Chief Adm. Law J.
Higgins, Cecelia E. ... '50 '79 C.264 A.B. L.174 J.D.
Holmes, John C. ... '34 '64 C.473 B.S. L.128 LL.B. Adm. Law J.
Jones, Carolita V. ... '59 '85 (PA) C.811 B.A. L.831 J.D.
Joyce, Melissa Jo ... '55 '83 (NC) C.1154 B.A. L.838 J.D.
Kallina, Roy Stephen ... '55 '85 C&L.446 B.G.S., J.D.
Kisch, Wendy J. ... '67 '96 (MD) C.1349 B.A. L.30 J.D.
Krizan, Gerald F. ... '53 '79 (MD) C.276 B.A. L.446 J.D.
Lahrman, Lisa L. ... '56 '83 (VA) C.347 B.M.E. L.692 J.D.
Leasure, Linda L. ... '49 '75 (OH) C.967 B.A. L.930 J.D.
Leland, Daniel L. ... '46 '71 C.659 A.B. L.94 J.D. Adm. Law J.
McGranery, Regina ... '45 '71 C.856 B.A. L.893 J.D. Adm. Appeals J.
Miller, Edward Terhune ... '36 '64 C.674 A.B. L.976 LL.B. Adm. Law J.
Morrison, Heidi Regina ... '62 '91 C.999 B.A. L.893 J.D.
Murty, Edward J., Jr. ... '29 '52 C.116 L.107 LL.B. Adm. Law J.
Neal, Mollie W. ... '42 '72 C&L.329 B.A., J.D. Adm. Law J.
Nelson, Malcolm D. ... '54 '80 (PA) C&L.659 B.A., J.D.
Neusner, Frederick D. ... '24 '50 C.855 B.A. L.976 LL.B. Adm. Law J.
Osher, James W. ... '48 '74 (OR) C.855 B.A. L.659 J.D.
Quade, Calvin E., Jr. ... '58 '85 C.273 B.A. L.1187 J.D.
Rosenzweig, Joan Huddy ... '46 '73 C.563 B.A. L.94 J.D. Adm. Law J.
Santacroce, Loretta ... '56 '82 (VA) C.276 A.B. L.945 J.D.
Shepherd, Thomas O., Jr. ... '60 '85 (PA) C&L.665 B.A., J.D.
Sinclair, Mary G. ... '57 '85 (MD) C.446 B.A. L.904 J.D.
Slattery, Daniel J., Jr. ... '40 '70 C.276 A.B. L.128 J.D. Adm. Law J.
Smith, Roy P. ... '33 '65 C.999 B.A. L.262 LL.B. Adm. Appeals J.
Smyth, Todd R. ... '58 '83 C.347 B.A. L.1119 J.D. Adm. Law J.
Stansell-Gamm, Richard T. ... '50 '81 (FL) C.260 B.S.B.A. L.276 LL.M. Adm. Law J.
Sucher, Gabriel ... '56 '85 C.659 B.A. L.276 J.D.
Tureck, Jeffrey ... '45 '69 C.102 B.A. L.705 J.D. Adm. Law J.
Ulan, Janice J. ... '54 '79 C.160 B.A. L.273 J.D.
Vena, John D.A., II ... '59 '85 (CT) C.273 B.A. L.128 J.D.
Vittone, John M. ... '42 '67 C.692 B.A. L.383 J.D. Adm. Law J.
Wieder, Joan ... '39 '64 C.293 B.A. L.880 LL.B.
Witter, Kirsten N. ... '69 '95 (MD) C.950 B.A. L.904 J.D.
Wood, Pamela L. ... '49 '74 C.597 B.A. L.276 J.D. Adm. Law J.

Employees' Compensation Appeals Board

Alsobrook, Mark A. ... '59 '85 (VA) C.945 B.A. L.1209 J.D.
Brandes, Howard P. ... '59 '85 (PA) C.273 B.A. L.30 J.D.
Byrne, Kevin M. ... '53 '78 C.645 B.A. L.276 J.D.
Dunnavant, Barbara Ann ... '47 '89 (MD) C&L.446 B.A., J.D.
Evans-Harrell, Valerie D. ... '55 '81 C.331 B.A. L.273 J.D.
Gerson, David ... '49 '73 (PA) C.874 B.S. L.776 J.D.
Grinvalds, Astra ... '57 '82 (MI) C.932 B.A. L.912 J.D.
Groom, Michael E. ... '55 '80 C&L.190 B.A., J.D.
Keith, Patricia E. ... '64 '90 C.500 B.A. L.880 J.D.
Lucas, Patricia J. ... '42 '91 (PA) C.1111 B.A. L.276 J.D.
Meltzer, Robin Alisa ... '64 '90 (NJ) C.823 A.B., B.S. L.276 J.D.
Mills, Richard E. ... '55 '89 (CT) C.197 B.A. L.879 J.D.
Plegge, Christopher Craig ... '58 '83 C.383 B.A. L.608 J.D.
Rivers, Geo. E. ... '24 '50 (AL) C&L.16 B.S., LL.B.
Scheiner, Leslie H. ... '61 '87 (PA) C.188 B.A. L.128 J.D.
Schwab, Priscilla Anne ... '41 '82 (MD) C.1031 B.A. L.128 J.D.
Sullivan, Dolores Ann ... '40 '78 (MA) C.94 B.S. L.588 J.D.
Sullivan, Nicholle Floyd ... '72 '98 C.347 B.S. L.1119 J.D.
Thoma, Corinth ... '53 '87 C.1376 B.S. L.585 J.D.
Thomas, Willie T.C. ... '42 '74 (PA) C.257 B.S. L.128 J.D.
Trayers, Paul E. ... '48 '79 (MA) C.1107 B.A. L.818 J.D.
Vezzetti, Roxanne ... '64 '89 C.174 B.A. L.904 J.D.
Walsh, Michael J. ... '32 '59 C.670 B.A. L.276 J.D.
Williams, Babette D. ... '60 '86 (MD) C.881 A.B. L.329 J.D.

EMPLOYMENT STANDARDS ADMINISTRATION

Black, Gale Barron ... '50 '76 C&L.30 B.A., J.D.
Brown, Avery L. ... '63 '91 (CT) C.105 B.A. L.893 J.D.
DeMarce, James L. ... '39 '76 (VA) C.962 B.A. L.128 J.D.
Hardin, Robert ... '47 '80 C.999 B.A. L.329 J.D.
Reddig, Jeffrey J. ... '64 '89 (MA) C.459 B.S. L.884 J.D.
Snyder, William M. ... '59 '86 C.273 B.A. L.818 J.D.
Steinberg, Terry N. ... '59 '90 (MA) C.188 B.S. L.94 J.D.
Wilcher, Shirley J. ... '51 '80 (NY) C.518 A.B. L.309 J.D.
Zeigler, Sandra Scott ... '57 '83 C&L.976 B.A., J.D.

EMPLOYMENT & TRAINING ADMINISTRATION

Bright, Melvin J. ... '39 '70 (MO) C.793 B.A. L.986 J.D.
Kontnier, Linda D. ... '42 '78 C.945 A.B. L.30 J.D.
Lowenstein, Frances B. ... '— '65 C&L.190 B.A., J.D.
Muller, Richard G. ... '41 '80 C.276 B.S.F.S. L.64 J.D.
Norris, James H. ... '40 '72 (MD) C&L.446 B.S., LL.B.

OCCUPATIONAL SAFETY & HEALTH ADMINISTRATION

Rogers, Helen Hoban ... '44 '74 C.766 B.A. L.1065 J.D.
Witt, Steven F. ... '45 '73 (NY) C.1019 B.A. L.94 J.D.

DEPARTMENT OF LABOR (Continued)

PENSION AND WELFARE BENEFITS

Arzuaga, Patricia .... '64 '93 (NY) C.976 B.A. L.309 J.D.
Beaver, Clarance E. .... '21 '51 (OH) C.851 B.B.A. L.880 J.D.
Close, Nalini V. .... '71 '96 (MD) C.446 B.A. L.276 J.D.
Feldman, Muriel N. .... '47 '79 C.788 B.A. L.309 J.D.
Fletcher, Linda M. .... '57 '87 C.276 B.A. L.273 J.D.
Gatesman, Valerie A. .... '64 '92 (PA) C.648 B.A. L.229 J.D.
Golding, Debra M. .... '62 '87 (MD) C.659 B.S. L.94 J.D.
Greenstein, Mark A. .... '55 '81 C.659 B.A. L.884 J.D.
Hall, Lyssa Eileen .... '55 '86 (PA) C.329 B.A. L.276 J.D.
Hazlewood, Yanick T. .... '70 '96 (NJ) C.446 B.S. L.64 J.D.
Hobbs, Deborah S. .... '58 '84 C.339 B.A. L.659 J.D.
Hoopes, Terence J. .... '55 '80 C.1275 B.A. L.276 J.D.
Kelly, Carol A. .... '— '94 (MA) L.818 J.D.
Klevan, Morton .... '38 '64 (NY) C.178 B.A. L.309 LL.B.
Kofman, Mila .... '70 '96 C.446 B.A. L.276 J.D.
Lebowitz, Alan D. .... '44 '69 C.454 B.A. L.818 J.D.
Lefkowitz, Gary H. .... '49 '75 C.659 B.A. L.93 J.D.
Levitas, Alan H. .... '47 '74 (MD) C.446 B.S. L.64 J.D.
Lewis, Katherine Dumas .... '53 '79 C.264 B.A. L.930 J.D.
Lindrew, Gerald B. .... '— '74 (WI) C&L.966 B.A., J.D.
Maguire, Daniel J. .... '47 '84 (CA) C.999 B.A. L.61 J.D.
Marchetti, Nancy M. .... '— '89 C.1303 B.A. L.818 J.D.
McColough, Wendy M. .... '52 '81 C.66 B.A. L.178 J.D.
Miller, Virginia J. .... '61 '92 (MA) C.690 B.A. L.818 J.D.
Monhart, Jeffrey A. .... '59 '92 (MT) C.164 B.A. L.508 J.D.
Padams, Allison K. .... '64 '90 (MD) C.938 B.A. L.128 J.D.
Rivera, Norman .... '61 '86 (PR) C&L.677 B.B.A., J.D.
Selinger, Morris L. .... '48 '73 C.4 B.A. L.904 J.D.
Smith, Virginia C. .... '50 '78 (MD) C.289 B.A. L.128 J.D.
Willett, Ronald B. .... '50 '76 (TX) C.846 B.A. L.845 J.D.
Williams, Emmett Filmore, III .... '54 '85 C.301 B.A. L.1017 J.D.

Abdel-Gawad, Jehan A. .... '69 '97 C.112 B.A. L.37 J.D.
Anderson, Sunya .... '47 '74 (TX) C&L.846 B.A., J.D.
Beattie, Patricia A. .... '63 '88 (PA) C.205 B.A. L.659 J.D.
Birek, Stephen J., Jr. .... '47 '75 C&L.229 B.A., J.D.
Blythe, Carol Beth .... '55 '81 C.630 B.A. L.273 J.D.
Boone, Sandra Arcelia .... '— '79 (PA) C.887 B.A. L.329 J.D.
Brookens, Benoit O., II .... '48 '74 (WI) C.966 B.A. L.178 J.D.
Cayode, Carolyn B. .... '— '01 C.860 B.A. L.128 J.D.
Chao, Victor J. .... '32 '60 (NY) C.433 B.B.A. L.569 LL.M.
Ciccone, James .... '56 '84 (NY) C.165 A.B. L.982 J.D.
Colker, Pamela B. .... '64 '92 C&L.107 B.A., J.D.
Corzatt, Jeffrey C. .... '47 '76 C.293 B.A. L.352 J.D.
Crocoll, Kathleen J. .... '61 '87 (NY) C.25 B.S. L.107 J.D.
Day, Heather N. .... '59 '88 (MA) C.454 B.A. L.818 J.D.
Dowdell, Patricia Alicia .... '65 '91 C.273 B.A. L.329 J.D.
Drew, Kathy A. .... '58 '82 C.329 B.A. L.320 J.D.
Edelstein, Janet C. .... '59 '85 (MD) C.390 A.B. L.904 J.D.
Ednie, Regina M. .... '55 '80 (VA) C.443 B.A. L.902 J.D.
Etting, Paula Sutton .... '59 '85 (MD) C.367 B.A. L.446 J.D.
Fields, Lisa M. .... '73 '99 (MA) C.999 B.A. L.94 J.D.
Finnican, Lisa A. .... '65 '92 (MD) C.860 B.A. L.30 J.D.
Forrest, Mary H. .... '62 '87 C&L.862 B.A., J.D.
Forrest, Patrick J. .... '63 '91 C.1115 B.A. L.128 J.D.
Frandsen, Carl F. .... '35 '82 C.197 A.B. L.276 J.D.
Gallo, Coby D. .... '— '87 (CA) C.999 B.A. L.128 J.D.
Glasgow, William A., IV .... '52 '85 C.902 B.A. L.273 J.D.
Goldfarb, David .... '55 '81 C.21 B.S.C. L.30 J.D.
Gresh, Daniel T. .... '63 '88 C.884 B.A. L.273 J.D.
Hardy, Michael R. .... '52 '80 (MD) C&L.446 B.A., J.D.
Heins, Karen J. .... '59 '85 (MD) C.1044 B.A. L.273 J.D.
Henry, Mary E. .... '45 '88 C.446 B.S. L.1048 J.D.
Horowitz, Sylvia Troy .... '35 '59 C.477 B.A. L.273 L.L.B.
Hugler, Edward C. .... '50 '77 C.446 B.A. L.990 J.D.
Johnson, Barbara A. .... '— '89 (NJ) C.1069 B.A. L.107 J.D.
Johnson, Miriam H. .... '48 '78 (MD) C.699 B.A. L.861 J.D.
Jones, Thomas D. .... '36 '71 C.477 B.A. L.912 J.D.
Kelso, Robert B. .... '55 '80 C.477 B.B.A. L.896 J.D.
Kormis, David T. .... '61 '86 (PA) C.1113 B.S. L.229 J.D.
Krishnan, Shuba .... '67 '92 (IL) C.339 B.S. L.347 J.D.
Kultgen, Pamela A. .... '71 '96 (VA) C.221 B.A. L.945 J.D.
Lazar-Meyn, Heidi Ann .... '55 '85 (CA) C.674 A.B. L.1066 J.D.
Lindeman, Alfred .... '40 '65 C.604 B.A. L.569 J.D.
Lockhart, Annabelle T. .... '49 '77 C.1088 B.A. L.329 J.D.
Lubin, Stephen M. .... '39 '76 C.477 B.A. L.446 J.D.
Malis, Michelle C. .... '58 '85 (MD) C.245 B.A. L.64 J.D.
Matthews, Barbara J. .... '46 '83 C.446 B.A. L.846 J.D.
McGregor, Robert L. .... '48 '78 (GA) C.1063 B.B.A. L.969 J.D.
McMullen, James E. .... '52 '78 (IN) C.346 B.A. L.1119 J.D.
Miller, Elissa M. .... '63 '88 C.1044 B.A. L.273 J.D.
Mitten, Raymond E., Jr. .... '60 '85 C.273 B.A. L.1209 J.D.
Miyazawa, James Y. .... '67 '92 (MD) C.823 A.B. L.904 J.D.
Mollick, Helen A. .... '53 '78 C.551 B.A. L.831 J.D. Counsel
Morin, George P. .... '30 '57 C.708 A.B. L.93 LL.B.
Muehlig, Ralph J. .... '30 '75 (NJ) C.197 A.B. L.705 J.D.
Olarinde, Toye A. .... '71 '98 C.1209 B.S. L.329 J.D.
Olszewski, Nancy .... '57 '82 (VA) C.367 B.A. L.276 J.D.
Pleeter, Elizabeth .... '48 '81 (OH) C.107 B.A. L.150 J.D.
Reade, Randall Roger .... '61 '88 (IL) C.107 B.A. L.930 J.D.
Roberts, Carol S. .... '53 '83 C.475 B.A. L.273 J.D.
Robertson, Rhonda F. .... '54 '81 (PA) C.888 B.S. L.273 J.D.
Sarno, Daniel A., Jr. .... '43 '74 (MA) C.860 B.S. L.818 J.D.
Sarpy, John Robert .... '49 '80 (LA) C.902 B.A. L.425 J.D.
Scheingold, Amy J. .... '71 '96 (MD) C.188 B.S. L.273 J.D.
Schumann, Beth E.S. .... '60 '85 C&L.893 B.A., J.D.
Shapiro, Howard L. .... '— '76 C.119 B.A. L.276 J.D. Asso. Counsel
Sims, Yvonne C. M. .... '59 '83 (PA) C.477 B.A. L.665 J.D.
Stepp, Tali R. .... '55 '86 (VA) C.446 B.A. L.64 J.D.
Stokes, E. Francine .... '48 '87 (NJ) C.512 B.S. L.64 J.D.
Szymanski, John Matthew .... '65 '91 (VA) C.288 B.A. L.1339 J.D.
Tate, Kathryn Willcox .... '39 '77 C.274 B.S. L.37 J.D.
Waldbaum, Shari R. .... '65 '90 C.1349 B.A. L.904 J.D.
Washington, Nicole E. .... '63 '88 (NJ) C.811 B.A. L.569 J.D.
White, Arthur C. .... '26 '56 (KY) L.421 J.D.
White, William C. .... '35 '63 C.367 B.A. L.260 J.D.
Wilson, Donnie E. .... '50 '85 C.45 B.A. L.803 J.D.

DEPARTMENT OF THE NAVY

(Vacant), *Judge Advocate General*

OFFICE OF THE JUDGE ADVOCATE GENERAL

Astley, Stephen R. .... '74 '98 (FL) C.259 B.S. L.472 J.D.★
Auclair, Marcella J. .... '62 '87 C.446 B.A. L.30 J.D.
Baggett, Joseph E. .... '49 '77 (FL) C&L.861 B.S., J.D.
Carlos, Tierney Michael .... '59 '87 (NY) C.1044 B.S. L.262 J.D.
Cervi, Gregg A. .... '60 '87 (MI) C.608 B.A. L.1187 J.D.
Garaffa, John V. .... '57 '82 (MN) C.957 B.B.A. L.494 J.D.
Green, Michael G. .... '62 '91 (CA) C.800 B.S.A.E. L.809 J.D.
Haig, Clyde A. .... '65 '92 (PA) C.197 B.A. L.902 J.D.★
Haycock, Steven L. .... '62 '88 (UT) C&L.878 B.A., J.D.
Horgan, Mark M. .... '49 '77 (CA) C.871 B.S. L.990 J.D.
Jenkins, Max B. .... '54 '86 (MA) C.477 B.A. L.93 J.D.
Leonard, Patricia A. .... '57 '83 (MA) C.745 B.A. L.1048 J.D.
Lizzul, Daniel M. .... '57 '82 (FL) C.262 B.A. L.472 J.D.
McAlevy, Mary Grace Manion .... '64 '91 C.201 B.S. L.229 J.D.
McGann, Jeanne .... '47 '80 (CA) C.1116 B.A. L.61 J.D.
McGuire, Carl, III .... '74 '99 (CO) C.172 B.S. L.972 J.D.
Molinengo, Henry R., II .... '56 '82 C&L.127 B.A., J.D.
Myers, David H. .... '50 '78 (IN) C.430 B.A. L.879 J.D.
Nagle, Timothy J. .... '56 '86 (VA) C.871 B.S. L.818 J.D.
Naugle, Kip J. .... '49 '74 (MD) C.436 B.A. L.446 J.D.
Nixon, Nixon S. .... '63 '97 C.864 B.S. L.276 J.D.
Norman, James B. .... '53 '81 (MA) C.308 B.A. L.128 J.D.
Ozmun, Richard R. .... '44 '77 (OK) C.622 B.A. L.623 J.D.
Peterson, Alex G. .... '67 '92 (UT) C.623 B.B.A. L.878 J.D.
Quinn, John P. .... '52 '82 C.228 B.A. L.276 J.D.
Rosen, Mark E. .... '54 '78 (GA) C&L.280 A.B., J.D.★
Storz, William T. .... '55 '82 (NJ) C.1374 B.A. L.705 J.D.
Wagner, David A. .... '57 '83 (PA) C.757 B.A. L.608 J.D.
Walker, Paul A. .... '65 '98 (VA) C.871 B.S. L.945 J.D.
Yacono, Dominick George .... '62 '89 (OH) C.30 B.A. L.608 J.D.★

Board for Correction of Naval Records

Adams, Gary L. .... '44 '70 (NY) C.693 B.S. L.1009 J.D.
Exnicios, James R. .... '49 '74 (CT) C.597 B.A. L.262 J.D.
George, Brian J. .... '52 '80 (NE) C.546 B.A. L.940 J.D.
Goldsmith, Alan E. .... '51 '76 C.385 B.A. L.128 J.D.
Pfeiffer, W. Dean .... '27 '50 (LA) C&L.861 B.S., J.D.
Ruskin, Jonathan S. .... '49 '74 (VA) C&L.188 A.B., J.D.
Zsalman, Robert D. .... '40 '65 (CT) C.93 A.B. L.276 LL.B.

Navy-Marine Corps Appellate Review Activity

Hall, Mary T. .... '56 '78 (GA) C.1301 B.A. L.280 J.D.★
Hammond, Steven P. .... '55 '89 (VA) C.886 B.S. L.902 J.D.
Scudder, Laura L. .... '48 '73 (KY) C.383 B.A. L.421 J.D.
Stallings, Stephen A. .... '53 '83 (TX) C.845 B.B.A. L.93 J.D.
Thompson, Helen B. .... '51 '80 (OH) C.1247 B.A. L.930 J.D.

Navy-Marine Corps Court of Criminal Appeals

DeCicco, William A. .... '49 '75 (CA) C.740 B.A. L.767 J.D. Appl. Judge
Dorman, Charles W. .... '48 '73 (FL) C&L.260 B.A., J.D.★
Rolph, John W. .... '54 '81 (TX) C.843 B.A. L.69 J.D.
Troidl, Robert H. .... '52 '77 (NY) C.229 B.A. L.107 J.D.

Naval Council of Personnel Boards

Wall, Darren S. .... '68 '94 C.1374 B.A. L.1325 J.D.

Office of the Secretary

Houck, James W. .... '58 '85 (MI) C.871 B.S. L.477 J.D.★

Office of Legislative Affairs

Stroble, Kelvin M. .... '64 '89 (SC) C&L.790 B.S., J.D.★
Walsh, Richard F. .... '49 '79 (VA) C.871 B.S. L.893 J.D.★
Waters, Michael A. .... '57 '86 (MI) C.475 B.A. L.1187 J.D.

Naval Legal Service Office

Hsieh, Nathaniel K. .... '65 '91 (IA) C.629 B.A. L.352 J.D.
Hughes, Sally A. .... '— '89 (HI) C&L.312 B.A., J.D.
Little, William C., Jr. .... '49 '82 (PA) C&L.705 B.A., J.D.
McCray, Jeffrey W. .... '65 '89 (OH) C&L.608 B.A., J.D.
Payne, John M. .... '27 '61 (VA) C&L.893 B.A., LL.B.
Peled, Avraham R. .... '66 '92 (MD) C.1213 B.S. L.64 J.D.★
Perdue, William Garrett Roberts .... '66 '98 (PA) C.645 B.S.B.A. L.94 J.D.
Reilly, George F. .... '60 '86 (RI) C.433 B.S. L.724 J.D.
Rosser, Richard L. .... '58 '85 (KY) C.47 B.A. L.383 J.D.
Schminky, John D. .... '54 '81 C.473 B.A. L.280 J.D.
Stallings, Lisa R. .... '58 '83 (SC) C.140 B.A. L.790 J.D.
Veltre, Tracy A. .... '67 '92 (NJ) C.1376 B.S. L.776 J.D.★
Vincent, Robert E., II .... '60 '86 (MD) C&L.446 B.S., J.D.

Headquarters, U. S. Marine Corps

Buckley, Paul J. .... '58 '92 (VA) C.273 B.A. L.30 J.D.
Composto, Joseph .... '49 '75 (NY) C&L.724 B.A., J.D.
Danielson, Edward J. .... '69 '97 (FL) C&L.259 B.S., J.D.★
Euler, John L. .... '44 '69 C.216 B.A. L.276 J.D.
Hess, Theodore G. .... '47 '79 C.188 B.A. L.107 J.D.★
Metcalf, Andrew O. .... '67 '95 (MD) C.881 B.A. L.446 J.D.★
Palmer, Brian .... '60 '86 (CT) C.1044 B.A. L.1048 J.D.
Peters, Danny G. .... '59 '89 (MT) C.1201 B.S. L.508 J.D.★
Posey, Richard B. .... '47 '72 C.205 B.A. L.1292 J.D.
Pugliese, Paul Leonard .... '62 '87

Sennett, Peter H. . . . '63 '88 C.107 B.A. L.823 J.D.★
Tully, Robert S. . . . '54 '80 (MA) C.454 B.A. L.818 J.D.★

Haywood, Herbert H. . . . '40 '73 C.273 A.B. L.276 J.D.
Hurley, Howard E., Jr. . . . '42 '76 (VA) C.454 B.A. L.128 J.D.
Jackson, Samuel E. . . . '64 '92 (PA) C.803 B.S. L.861 J.D.
Kalstein, Allan . . . '51 '77 C.446 B.S. L.128 J.D.
Kopstein, Alexander S. . . . '10 '34 (NY) C&L.262 LL.B.
Manson, William E. . . . '30 '59 (NH) C.550 B.A. L.273 LL.B.
McCabe, Sally J. . . . '46 '79 (CA) C.112 B.A. L.1065 J.D.
Meehan, James P. . . . '51 '81 (PA) C.276 B.A. L.1209 J.D.
Miske, Naomi D. . . . '46 '79 (VA) C.945 B.A. L.30 J.D.
Nash, David M. . . . '56 '81 (PA) C.102 B.A. L.831 J.D.
Prince, Andrew S. . . . '43 '75 (NY) C.871 B.S. L.309 J.D.
Rankin, Daniel F. . . . '28 '71 (MD) C.446 B.A. L.64 LL.B.
Smith, Emory C. . . . '10 '37 (TX) C.586 B.A. L.802 J.D.
Umstattd, Kristen Coles . . . '54 '80 (PA) C&L.976 B.A., J.D.★

Naval Air Test Center, Patuxent River, Md.

Armstrong, Brenda A. . . . '59 '89 (CA) C.836 B.B.A. L.1067 J.D.★

Navy Recruiting Command

Murphy, Eileen M. . . . '66 '91 (MA) C.93 B.A. L.881 J.D.
Ramsay, Kathleen Parker . . . '48 '75 (CA) C.112 A.B. L.61 J.D.★

Adrian, John T. . . . '52 '88 C.326 B.S. L.1015 J.D.
Beers, Robert F. . . . '27 '73 (MD) C&L.665 B.S.E.E., J.D.
Blanchard, John J. . . . '47 '79 C.446 B.S. L.276 J.D.
Brancato, Cynthia C. . . . '47 '90 C.502 B.S. L.276 J.D.
Buechler, Christopher L. . . . '49 '74 (VA) C.674 B.S.E. L.902 J.D.★
Christensen, Linda M. . . . '53 '81 (OK) C&L.878 B.S., J.D.
Clarkson, John B. . . . '65 '91 C.800 B.A. L.809 J.D.
Dobrovits, Paul . . . '66 '91 (IL) C&L.424 B.A., J.D.
Fording, Thomas E. . . . '59 '92 (MA) C.309 B.A. L.818 J.D.
Hanger, Eric W. . . . '62 '90 (MD) C.896 B.A. L.273 J.D.
Jordan, Dawn P. . . . '64 '91 (NC) C.575 B.A. L.1345 J.D.
Kleis, Eric R. . . . '61 '92 (OK) C&L.623 B.A., J.D.
Le, Tai Due . . . '68 '99 (MD) C.1494 B.A. L.615 J.D.
McGavran, Frank J. . . . '40 '69 (OH) C&L.608 B.S., J.D.
McGregor, Michael E. . . . '55 '81 (WA) C&L.285 B.A., J.D.
Morgan, James F., Jr. . . . '44 '78 (VA) C.884 A.B. L.128 J.D.
Munsell, Elsie L. . . . '39 '72 (VA) C.434 A.B. L.945 J.D.
Nixon, Gregory S. . . . '63 '97 (MD) C.864 B.S.M.E. L.276 J.D.
Paddock, Barbara L. . . . '56 '81 (OH) C.608 B.A. L.1003 J.D.
Parker, Steven J. . . . '58 '85 (IL) C.492 B.E.S. L.365 J.D.
Rabinkoff, Penny . . . '53 '81 (NY) C.165 B.A. L.930 J.D.
Stroud, A. Neil . . . '53 '82 (NC) C&L.575 A.B., J.D.
Van Oss, David J. . . . '46 '74 (OH) C.1027 B.S. L.8 J.D.

DEPARTMENT OF STATE

(Vacant), *Legal Adviser*

OFFICE OF THE LEGAL ADVISER

Alphin, Thomas H., Jr. . . . '49 '74 C&L.902 B.A., J.D.
Alvarez, Luisa M. . . . '54 '79 C&L.677 B.A., J.D.
Anderson, James H. . . . '47 '73 (TN) C&L.469 A.B., J.D.
Arbogast, John R. . . . '47 '75 C.674 A.B. L.1066 J.D.
Ballard, Lara Ann . . . '69 '99 (NY) C.276 B.S.F.S. L.178 J.D.
Balton, David . . . '59 '85 (PA) C.309 A.B. L.276 J.D.
Barton, Paula J. . . . '46 '78 C.999 B.A. L.229 J.D.
Benda, Susan R. . . . '57 '89 C.012 B.A. L.276 J.D.
Bettauer, Ronald J. . . . '44 '69 C.951 B.A. L.569 J.D.
Biniaz, Susan . . . '58 '84 C.976 B.A. L.178 J.D.
Bloom, Evan T. . . . '60 '86 C.674 A.B. L.178 J.D.
Borek, Jamison S. . . . '49 '77 C.112 B.A. L.1066 J.D.
Borek, Ted A. . . . '47 '72 (IL) C.276 B.S.F.S. L.178 J.D.
Botet, Violanda . . . '61 '89 C.66 B.A. L.309 J.D.
Brancato, Gilda . . . '49 '78 (NY) C.1044 B.A. L.569 J.D.
Brooks, Jo . . . '49 '75 C.976 B.A. L.1066 J.D.
Brown, Catherine W. . . . '53 '78 C.788 B.A. L.309 J.D.
Buchwald, Todd F. . . . '56 '81 C.188 B.A. L.976 J.D.
Burman, Harold S. . . . '35 '60 (IL) C.966 B.S. L.145 J.D.
Bush, James Daniel . . . '58 '88 (MO) C.1070 B.S. L.880 J.D.
Camponovo, Christopher N. . . . '69 '96 (CA) C.112 B.A. L.1068 J.D.
Caramanica, Janice F. . . . '62 '93 (MD) C.893 B.A. L.30 J.D.
Carlson, Mary Helen . . . '45 '80 C.659 B.A. L.276 J.D.
Chandler, Melinda P. . . . '56 '81 C.347 A.B. L.597 J.D.
Clayman, Paul F. . . . '56 '84 C.1051 B.A. L.904 J.D.
Coffee, Michael S. . . . '71 '96 C.1369 B.S. L.273 J.D.
Cole, Judith K. . . . '43 '87 C.1036 B.A. L.276 J.D.
Collums, Haley D. . . . '47 '80 (VA) C&L.893 B.A., J.D.
Comfort, Mary Wild Ennis . . . '50 '78 C.681 B.A. L.659 J.D.
Crocker, Bathsheba Nell . . . '68 '97 (NY) C.813 B.A. L.309 J.D.
Crook, John R. . . . '47 '72 (IN) C.894 B.A. L.976 J.D.
Cummings, Edward R. . . . '48 '75 (PA) C.367 B.A. L.273 J.D.
Cummins, Sally J. . . . '46 '77 C.378 B.A. L.976 J.D.
Dalton, Robert E. . . . '32 '57 C.321 A.B. L.178 LL.B.
Daumit, Debra M. . . . '70 '95 C.228 B.A. L.575 J.D.
Dickey, Gordon J. . . . '52 '81 (MA) C.174 B.A. L.1202 J.D.
Di Rosa, Paolo . . . '64 '91 C&L.309 B.A., J.D.
Dolan, JoAnn . . . '48 '74 C.276 B.S. L.823 J.D.
Dorosin, Joshua L. . . . '63 '94 C.165 A.B. L.477 J.D.
Gaffney, Francis M. . . . '57 '89 C&L.276 A.B., J.D.
Gallagher, Dennis J. . . . '47 '78 C.602 B.A. L.966 J.D.
Gergen, Jennifer A. . . . '68 '96 (MD) C.276 B.S. L.893 J.D.
Gibbs, Jeffrey J. . . . '48 '81 C.645 B.A. L.128 J.D.
Gleeson, Kevin M. . . . '65 '94 (WA) C.604 B.A. L.494 J.D.
Gorove, Katherine M . . . '59 '86 C.500 B.A. L.178 J.D.
Grosh, Lisa J. . . . '59 '86 (PA) C.655 B.A. L.273 J.D.
Harris, Robert K. . . . '58 '85 (PA) C.188 A.B. L.813 J.D.
Heinemann, Thomas B. . . . '69 '95 C.951 B.A. L.276 J.D.
Hergen, James G. . . . '43 '68 C&L.276 B.S.F.S., J.D.
Herr, Julie Kitzes . . . '46 '74 C.681 A.B. L.813 J.D.
Highsmith, Newell L. . . . '55 '81 C.575 B.A. L.309 J.D.
Hirsch, Theodore M. . . . '64 '93 C.103 A.B. L.309 J.D.
Hollis, Duncan B. . . . '70 '96 C.95 A.B. L.93 J.D.
Holmes, Jessica R. . . . '59 '85 (PA) C.1036 B.A. L.276 J.D.
Hooke, Kathleen H. . . . '61 '87 (NJ) C.354 B.A. L.776 J.D.
Jacobson, Linda . . . '49 '75 C.604 B.A. L.1068 J.D.
Johnson, Clifton M. . . . '64 '90 (MA) C.659 B.A. L.569 J.D.
Johnson, Thomas A. . . . '47 '73 C.95 A.B. L.309 J.D.
Joyce, Anne . . . '63 '90 (NY) C.976 B.A. L.309 J.D.
Kaye, David A. . . . '68 '95 (CA) C.112 B.A. L.1066 J.D.
Khanna, Melanie . . . '70 '98 (NY) C.178 B.A. L.976 J.D.
Kittrie, Orde F. . . . '64 '93 C.976 B.A. L.477 J.D.
Klein, Michele I. . . . '61 '89 (NY) C.165 B.A. L.276 J.D.
Kottmyer, Alice M. . . . '53 '78 (LA) C.1099 B.A. L.425 J.D.★
Kovar, Jeffrey D. . . . '58 '85 (PA) C.951 B.A. L.477 J.D.
Kropf, John W. . . . '61 '88 C.207 B.A. L.665 J.D.
Lahne, Richard K. . . . '48 '81 C.33 B.A. L.893 J.D.
Lamotte, K. Russell . . . '67 '94 (PA) C.188 A.B. L.309 J.D.
Light, Carol J. . . . '45 '75 C&L.30 B.A., J.D.
Loken, Keith . . . '51 '78 C.813 A.B. L.1067 J.D.
Ma'ani, Sovaida . . . '62 '84 C.999 LL.B. L.050 LL.M.
Malin, Mary Catherine . . . '59 '84 C.30 B.A. L.1065 J.D.
Malmborg, Knute E., Jr. . . . '30 '54 (MN) C&L.494 B.S.L., J.D.
Manning, Paul William . . . '51 '77 (MA) C.93 A.B. L.1202 J.D.
Mason, Peter W. . . . '66 '93 (VA) C.597 B.M. L.930 J.D.
Mathias, D. Stephen . . . '55 '80 C.276 B.S.F.S. L.178 J.D.
Mattler, Michael J. . . . '70 '95 C.347 B.A. L.569 J.D.
McCreary, Stephen D. . . . '53 '89 (NY) C.019 B.A. L.025 LL.B.
McLeod, Mary E. . . . '52 '77 C.976 B.A. L.569 J.D.
Menaker, Andrea J. . . . '68 '96 (NY) C.276 B.S. L.911 J.D
Milton, Kathleen M. . . . '58 '86 C.674 B.A. L.309 J.D.
Monahan, William G. P. . . . '64 '94 (VA) C.976 B.A. L.893 J.D.
Moore, Holly Toye . . . '63 '91 (MA) C.311 B.A. L.976 J.D.
Murphy, Kathleen A. . . . '— '93 C.242 B.A. L.128 J.D.
Newman, David S. . . . '62 '87 (MA) C.659 B.S. L.93 J.D.
Nierenberg, Lorie Joan . . . '51 '82 C.788 A.B. L.930 J.D.
O'Brien, James Coad . . . '60 '89 C.429 B.A. L.976 J.D.
Olson, Peter M. . . . '50 '76 C.311 B.A. L.309 J.D.
O'Rourke, Kenneth J. . . . '60 '86 (NY) C.724 B.A. L.1009 J.D.
Osborn, Judith L. . . . '60 '86 C.478 B.A. L.309 J.D.
Page, Kathryn Youel . . . '70 '99 (NY) C.429 B.A. L.477 J.D.
Parker, Lloyd J., Jr. . . . '37 '70 C.896 B.S. L.692 J.D.
Peay, T. Michael . . . '46 '73 C.999 B.A. L.309 J.D.
Pfund, Peter H. . . . '32 '59 C.31 B.A. L.659 J.D.
Pickering, Margaret S. . . . '59 '85 (PA) C.104 A.B. L.309 J.D.
Propp, Kenneth R. . . . '56 '83 C.31 A.B. L.309 J.D.
Purvis, Nigel H. . . . '66 '91 (NY) C.494 B.A. L.309 J.D.
Ramish, Timothy E. . . . '48 '77 (NY) C.976 B.A. L.309 J.D.
Roach, J. Ashley . . . '39 '64 (PA) C&L.659 A.B., J.D.
Rosand, Eric A. . . . '69 '96 (NY) C.311 B.A. L.178 J.D.
Safrin, Sabrina . . . '— '90 (AZ) C.668 B.A. L.1066 J.D.
Salie, David P. . . . '68 '00 C.276 B.S.F.S. L.813 J.D.
Sandage, John Byron . . . '59 '86 C.221 B.A. L.976 J.D.
Sapiro, Miriam . . . '60 '87 (NY) C.951 B.A. L.569 J.D.
Schildge, Heather A. . . . '— '95 (NJ) C.659 B.A. L.309 J.D.
Schnitker, John P. . . . '51 '77 C.31 B.A. L.187 J.D.
Schwab, Carol M. . . . '52 '79 C.881 B.A. L.477 J.D.
Schwartz, Jonathan B. . . . '52 '81 C.821 B.A. L.813 J.D.
Seward, Bernard L., Jr. . . . '56 '84 (VA) C.259 B.S. L.893 J.D.
Shah, Meha . . . '70 '95 C.861 B.A. L.228 J.D.
Sheahan, Cornelia . . . '44 '91 C.732 B.A. L.276 J.D.
Simonoff, Mark A. . . . '62 '88 C.976 B.A. L.309 J.D.
Skipper, Kathryn Nutt . . . '62 '88 (MN) C.713 B.A. L.904 J.D.
Solomon, Steven A. . . . '60 '89 C.178 B.A. L.276 J.D.
Stewart, Cynthia Vuille . . . '69 '98 (NC) C.575 B.A. L.813 J.D.
Stewart, David P. . . . '43 '72 C.674 A.B. L.976 J.D.
Stone, Corin R. . . . '72 '98 C.367 B.A. L.665 J.D.
Sullivan, David Bryan . . . '62 '97 C&L.976 B.A., J.D.
Sulzynsky, Wolodymyr R. . . . '48 '74 C.262 B.S. L.724 J.D.
Surena, Andre M. . . . '46 '72 (NY) C&L.569 B.A., J.D.
Svat, Laura A. . . . '67 '95 C&L.893 B.A., J.D.
Taft, George . . . '40 '70 C.477 B.A. L.276 J.D.
Teel, Elizabeth M. . . . '46 '75 C.914 B.A. L.273 J.D.
Thessin, James H. . . . '48 '74 C.128 A.B. L.309 J.D.
Ugol, Alec I. . . . '64 '89 (PA) C&L.659 B.A., J.D.
Veidenheimer, Paul S. . . . '64 '92 (ME) C.95 A.B. L.228 J.D.
Visek, Richard C. . . . '59 '86 C.813 A.B. L.276 J.D.
Weiner, Allen S. . . . '63 '90 C.309 A.B. L.813 J.D.
Wilcox, Elizabeth R. . . . '68 '99 C.976 B.A. L.309 J.D.
Wilson, Kathleen A. . . . '65 '99 C.945 B.A. L.477 J.D.
Witten, Samuel M. . . . '57 '84 C.446 B.A. L.178 J.D.

OFFICE OF THE SECRETARY

Coran, Paul M. . . . '42 '67 (MA) C.588 B.S.B.A. L.93 J.D.
Gross, Donald G. . . . '52 '80
Holum, John D. . . . '40 '80 C.590 B.S. L.273 J.D. Spec. Advisor
Rosenkrantz, Steven J. . . . '65 '94 C.705 B.A. L.1292 J.D.

BUREAU OF ECONOMIC AND BUSINESS AFFAIRS

Byerly, John R. . . . '53 '79 C.575 B.A. L.976 J.D.
Finston, Matthew A. . . . '— '85 C.821 B.A L.339 J.D.
Finton, Timothy C. . . . '52 '80 C.610 B.A. L.30 J.D.
Perez, Abelardo I. . . . '43 '72 C.326 B.A. L.273 J.D.
Scholz, Wesley S. . . . '50 '77 (WI) C.436 B.A. L.966 J.D.

BUREAU OF LEGISLATIVE AFFAIRS

Trejo, Maria Antonieta . . . '59 '88 C.773 B.A. L.770 J.D.

BUREAU OF INTERNATIONAL ORGANIZATION AFFAIRS

Boyer, Neil A. . . . '38 '64 (NY) C.509 B.S.E. L.569 LL.B.
Zimmerman, Robert A. . . . '61 '87 C.446 B.A. L.64 J.D.

DEPARTMENT OF STATE (Continued)

BUREAU OF OCEANS, INTERNATIONAL ENVIRONMENTAL & SCIENTIFIC AFFAIRS

Blumberg, Robert C. ... '43 '69 (NY) C.477 B.A. L.472 J.D.
Reifsnyder, Daniel A. ... '50 '81 C.855 A.B. L.273 J.D.
Walker, Maureen O. ... '52 '83 C.93 B.A. L.128 J.D.
West, Mary Beth ... '44 '73 C.477 B.A. L.813 J.D.

BUREAU OF CONSULAR AFFAIRS

Aiston, Kevin C. ... '59 '84 (IL) C&L.861 J.D., J.D.
Beirne, Vincent J. ... '50 '79 C.321 B.A. L.184 J.D.
Bellocchi, Luke P. ... '69 '96 C.696 B.A. L.107 J.D.
Betancourt, Edward A. ... '49 '74 C.178 A.B. L.880 J.D.
Bizic, Eli W. ... '39 '64 (TX) C.800 B.A. L.846 LL.B.
Bobotek, Susan Teresa Treadwell ... '59 '85 (VA) C.231 B.A. L.904 J.D.
Cooper, Beth H. ... '64 '91 (PA) C.30 B.S. L.1202 J.D.
Fischel, Stephen K. ... '48 '74 C.937 B.A. L.770 J.D.
Gorsky, Jeffrey ... '52 '78 C&L.273 B.A., J.D.
Kavaler, Howard C. ... '49 '74 C.264 B.A. L.904 J.D.
Meszaros, Michael ... '55 '86 C.980 B.A. L.161 J.D.
Pachon, Consuelo ... '54 '85 (PA) C.276 B.S. L.904 J.D.
Palmer-Royston, Sharon E. ... '43 '75 C.184 B.A. L.904 J.D.

DIRECTOR GENERAL—FOREIGN SERVICE

Brown, Edwin P., Jr. ... '56 '81 (PA) C.207 B.A. L.665 J.D.
Collins, John A. ... '30 '62 (NY) C.724 B.A. L.569 LL.B.
Craig, Sara M. ... '70 '96 (CA) C.966 B.A. L.1066 J.D.
Grundeman, Raymond D. ... '40 '65 (NY) C.747 B.A. L.569 LL.B.
High, George B. ... '31 '59 C.197 A.B. L.178 J.D.
Martin, S. Douglas ... '26 '53 (NY) C.724 A.B. L.178 J.D.
Pernick, Irwin ... '39 '86 (MD) C.563 B.A. L.128 J.D.
Prickett, Russell O. ... '32 '57 (MN) C.300 B.A. L.309 J.D.
Rouse, John H., Jr. ... '33 '61 (MD) C.367 B.A. L.446 J.D.

FOREIGN SERVICE INSTITUTE

Chester, George A., Jr. ... '37 '64 C.813 A.B. L.309 J.D.
Chester, Geraldeen G. ... '44 '69 C.813 A.B. L.309 J.D.
Dinger, Larry M. ... '46 '82 (IA) C.429 B.A. L.309 J.D.
Mathieu, Gail D. T. ... '51 '76 C.33 B.A. L.1292 J.D.
Ordway, John M. ... '50 '75 (CA) C.813 B.A. L.1065 J.D.
Quaglia, Paul L., Jr. ... '49 '80 (IL) C.912 B.A. L.213 J.D.
Simkin, Andrew T. ... '61 '86 C.231 B.A. L.201 J.D.
Washburn, John L. ... '37 '62 C&L.309 A.B., LL.B.

FOREIGN SERVICE OFFICERS (OVERSEAS)

Aldrich, George H. ... '32 '58 (IN) C.210 A.B. L.309 LL.B.
Anderson, Sheila M. ... '54 '79 (MA) C.518 A.B. L.94 J.D.
Angevine, Charles E. ... '34 '60 (CA) C.174 B.A. L.477 J.D.
Baldwin, Malcolm F. ... '40 '66 C.311 B.A. L.145 J.D.
Bright, Ruth E. ... '55 '80 (FL) C.276 B.S. L.362 J.D.
Campbell, Arnold H. ... '50 '75 (IN) C.373 B.A. L.602 J.D.
Campbell, Robert C. ... '47 '73 (OR) C.628 B.A. L.629 J.D.
Cavanaugh, Louis N., Jr. ... '31 '59 C.602 A.B. L.309 J.D.
Cavin, Guyle E. ... '51 '77 (TX) C.691 B.A. L.802 J.D.
Cotter, Michael W. ... '43 '68 (WI) C.276 B.S.F.S. L.477 J.D.
Cummings, Barbara ... '56 '81 C.1036 B.A. L.273 J.D.
Davison, John S. ... '33 '61 C&L.309 A.B., LL.B.
Dayton, John W., III ... '57 '84 (TX) C.31 B.A. L.893 J.D.
Dembski, Sandra A. ... '51 '76 C.821 B.A. L.976 J.D.
Dong, Edward K.H. ... '50 '78 (CA) C.112 A.B. L.1066 J.D.
Doren-Shulkin, Rebecca E. ... '58 '90 (PA) C.276 B.A. L.273 J.D.
Dunn, Bertram F. ... '30 '56 (WV) C&L.923 B.A., J.D.
Dwight, Ronald A. ... '44 '71 (NY) C.103 B.A. L.178 J.D.
Dziatkiewicz, Elizabeth A. ... '48 '83 C.999 B.A. L.30 J.D.
Eighmie, James W., Jr. ... '43 '68 C.976 B.A. L.309 LL.B.
Emmons, Robert D. ... '32 '58 (CA) C.112 B.A. L.1068 LL.B.
Espada-Platet, Luis ... '45 '73 C.677 B.A. L.1088 J.D.
Fagan, Joseph F. ... '29 '57 (PA) C.831 A.B. L.94 LL.B.
Faucher, Robert J. ... '59 '84 C&L.36 B.A., J.D.
Fernandez, John D. ... '42 '77 (VA) C.813 B.A. L.602 J.D.
Fulton, David W. ... '55 '82 (VA) L.945 J.D.
Garcia, Benjamin Andres ... '55 '88 (NJ) C.871 B.S. L.802 J.D.
Gatewood, Jack P. ... '42 '67 (TX) C.45 B.A. L.846 J.D.
Glassman, Jeffrey M. ... '54 '81 (NY) C.178 A.B. L.262 J.D.
Grant, Julie L. ... '— '87 (CA) C.788 B.A. L.800 J.D.
Griffith, William L. ... '51 '90 (NY) C.679 B.A. L.823 J.D.
Grossman, Andrew ... '41 '66 (NY) C.156 B.A. L.178 J.D.
Guerra-Mondragon, Gabriel ... '42 '69 (PR) C.262 B.A. L.677 LL.B.
Hall, Blair Parks, Jr. ... '55 '81 C.446 B.A. L.273 J.D.
Heflin, Donald L. ... '58 '83 (AL) C.88 B.A. L.15 J.D.
Higgins, Richard J. ... '39 '63 C.698 A.B. L.477 LL.B.
Higginson, Charles ... '32 '57 (MA) C&L.309 B.A., LL.B.
Holbrook, Morton J., III ... '42 '72 C.880 B.A. L.145 J.D.
Hughes, Lisa Bobbie Schreiber ... '58 '83 C.705 B.A. L.1292 J.D.
Hume, Cameron R. ... '47 '77 (NY) C.674 A.B. L.30 J.D.
Hyams, Robert S. ... '49 '76 (NY) C.367 B.A. L.569 J.D.
Ito, Pete K. ... '56 '81 C.112 B.A. L.273 J.D.
Jamieson, William J., Jr. ... '49 '79 (GA) C.1059 B.S. L.969 J.D.
Johnson, Donald C. ... '49 '75 C&L.1051 B.A., J.D.
Kahn, Leon E. ... '37 '62 (CO) C&L.174 B.A., LL.B.
Kearns, Kevin L. ... '47 '77 C.262 B.A. L.1009 J.D.
Kelly, George L. ... '31 '58 (GA) C&L.280 A.B., LL.B.
Lea-Brown, Bonnie H. ... '43 '69 C.939 B.A. L.1066 J.D.
Ledogar, Stephen J. ... '29 '59 (NY) C&L.262 B.S., LL.B.
MacDougall, Hugh C. ... '32 '59 (NY) C.309 A.B. L.178 LL.B.
Martinez-Llanes, Hilarión Arnaldo ... '54 '80 C.228 B.A. L.260 J.D.
Morrison, David T. ... '38 '78 C.477 B.A. L.273 J.D.
Murray, Christopher W. ... '53 '80 C.399 B.A. L.188 J.D.
Musch, Donald J. ... '32 '63 C.174 B.A. L.575 J.D.
Nettles, George C. ... '32 '57 (AL) C&L.16 A.B., LL.B.
Otto, Olaf N. ... '48 '73 (GA) C.902 B.A. L.893 J.D.
Phelan, Maureen ... '50 '78 (CO) C.454 B.A. L.1194 J.D.
Rand, S. Richard ... '29 '61 (FL) C&L.472 B.A., LL.B.
Ratigan, John R. ... '39 '64 (MN) C.197 A.B. L.976 LL.B.
Reynders, Thomas R. ... '37 '65 C.674 B.A. L.309 LL.B.
Rosenberg, Richard ... '44 '76 (IL) C.215 B.A. L.309 J.D.
Ruddy, Francis S. ... '37 '67 C.321 A.B. L.425 LL.B.
Rushing, Charles E. ... '29 '54 C.57 A.B. L.228 LL.B.
Samuel, Jeanne J. ... '46 '72 (CA) C.1074 B.S. L.1065 J.D.
Schmitz, Charles A. ... '38 '63 (MO) C&L.976 B.A., LL.B.
Scott, Gail P. ... '52 '77 (VA) C.276 B.S. L.245 J.D.
Sherman, Daryn Z. ... '55 '84 (VA) C.881 A.B. L.1035 J.D.
Sherwood, Nicholas A. ... '47 '75 (MD) C.893 B.A. L.276 J.D.
Shippy, Amelia Ellen ... '44 '77 C.560 B.S. L.273 J.D.
Simon, Anne W. ... '57 '83 C.154 B.A. L.930 J.D.
Sindelar, H. Richard, III ... '49 '83 C&L.276 B.S., J.D.
Smith, Cynthia G. ... '49 '73 C.66 B.A. L.273 J.D.
Snyder, Royce W., Jr. ... '32 '61 C.216 B.A. L.273 J.D.
Suvari, Elizabeth C. ... '45 '75 (RI) C.103 B.A. L.831 J.D.
Sweany, Garett G. ... '35 '61 (WA) C&L.911 B.A., J.D.
Telleen, David R. ... '42 '68 (IL) C.399 B.A. L.477 J.D.
Thompson, Alan R. ... '31 '60 C.813 B.A. L.309 LL.B.
Tousignant, Alan R. ... '55 '81 (MA) C.1107 B.A. L.93 J.D.
van Son, Paul B. ... '49 '80 (FL) C.1236 B.A. L.362 J.D.
Warren, William C. ... '44 '76 C.273 B.A. L.276 J.D.
Weisberg, Robert ... '50 '80 (NY) C.311 B.A. L.575 J.D.
Wilczynski, Alec P. ... '54 '82 (CA) C.696 B.A. L.1049 J.D.
Wilkey, Malcolm R. ... '18 '48 (TX) C&L.309 A.B., J.D.
Williams, Richard H. ... '35 '62 (UT) C&L.878 B.S., J.D.
Williamson, James H. ... '40 '68 C.893 B.M.E. L.30 J.D.
Wilson, Thomas F. ... '27 '56 C.119 B.S. L.477 J.D.
Wohlers, Paul D. ... '52 '83 (WA) C.871 B.S. L.911 J.D.
York, Jo Ann ... '49 '75 (NE) C.768 B.A. L.190 J.D.

U.S. MISSION TO THE UNITED NATIONS

Goldwyn, David L. ... '59 '87 (NY) C.276 A.B. L.569 J.D.
Rosenstock, Robert ... '35 '61 C.188 B.A. L.178 LL.B.

Adler, David B. ... '— '90 (TX) C.354 B.S. L.325 J.D.
Allegra, Theodore ... '53 '81 (CO) C.174 B.A. L.208 J.D.
Allegrone, Charles R. ... '46 '77 C.367 B.A. L.575 J.D.
Alsace, Juan A. ... '57 '83 (MN) C.436 B.A. L.494 J.D.
Archibald, James E. ... '57 '86 (SC) C&L.790 B.A., J.D.
Arvis, Constance C. ... '60 '86 (HI) C.228 A.B. L.1068 J.D.
Bastian, Julie M. ... '54 '81 (IL) C.104 B.A. L.893 J.D.
Bazyluk, Taras A. ... '58 '85 C.309 B.A. L.976 J.D.
Bean, Diane Reimer ... '52 '78 C.813 B.A. L.208 J.D.
Bean, James W. ... '51 '80 C&L.208 B.A., J.D.
Beller, Jeffrey A. ... '57 '85 (CO) C.293 A.B. L.208 J.D.
Bennett, W. Tapley, Jr. ... '17 '50 (GA) C.280 A.B. L.273 LL.B.
Bernstein, David S. ... '63 '89 C.477 B.A. L.309 J.D.
Bialek, Mark ... '55 '82 C.818 B.S. L.1162 J.D.
Blome, Donald A. ... '65 '91 (IL) C&L.477 B.A., J.D.
Boursy, John J., Jr. ... '49 '76 C.971 B.S.E.E. L.273 J.D.
Brajevich, Nikki ... '48 '73 (CA) C.112 B.A. L.1068 J.D.
Brush, Peter N. ... '44 '69 (CT) C.103 A.B. L.184 J.D.
Burgess, David ... '48 '78 C&L.276 B.S.F.S., J.D.
Clark, Bruce W. ... '31 '60 C&L.352 B.A., LL.B.
Clarke, Robert W. ... '42 '90 (VA) C.446 B.A. L.273 J.D.
Degonia, Thomas M., II ... '71 '97 (MD) C.502 B.A. L.904 J.D.
Douglass, William D. ... '59 '89 (NV) C.36 B.S. L.37 J.D.
Driscoll, Richard J. ... '56 '81 C&L.893 B.S., J.D.
Duncan, John D., Jr. ... '50 '76 C.128 B.A. L.180 J.D.
Dunham, Lawrence P. ... '49 '77 C.128 B.A. L.1209 J.D.
Fayen, Molly ... '49 '75 (OH) C.025 B.A. L.1003 J.D.
Fereno, Gary M. ... '35 '76 (VA) C.570 B.S.E.E. L.276 J.D.
Gagné, Clement R., III ... '53 '84 C&L.228 A.B., J.D.
Gainey, Keith E., Jr. ... '56 '81 (PA) C.473 A.B. L.228 J.D.
German, Robert K. ... '27 '52 (TX) C&L.846 B.A., LL.B.
Godwin, Kimberly A. ... '60 '84 C.550 B.A. L.94 J.D.
Grant, Julie ... '64 '87 (CA) C.788 B.A. L.800 J.D.
Grey, Robert T., Jr. ... '36 '72 C.197 B.A. L.477 J.D.
Griffith, Gladis Camilien ... '68 '93 (MA) C&L.93 B.A., J.D.
Hadley, Timothy D. ... '53 '80 C.165 A.B. L.93 J.D.
Hatcher, Stuart M. ... '54 '82 (NJ) C.823 A.B. L.1009 J.D.
Hawthorne, Margaret D. ... '58 '85 C.207 B.A. L.273 J.D.
Hedgbeth, Llewellyn H. ... '52 '88 C.320 B.A. L.902 J.D.
Helling, Lisa L. ... '54 '80 C&L.208 B.A., J.D.
Helman, Gerald B. ... '32 '56 (MI) C&L.477 B.A., LL.B.
Hewitt, Warren E. ... '22 '51 (NY) C.874 B.A. L.178 J.D.
Howard, Howell H., III ... '54 '80 (IL) C.170 B.A. L.1051 J.D.
Huffaker, Thomas K. ... '56 '82 (CA) C.112 B.A. L.1065 J.D.
Hyde, Reginald D. ... '58 '83 (AL) C&L.16 B.S., J.D.
Indahl, Pamela Joan Larson ... '50 '88 (WA) C.1058 B.A. L.1209 J.D.
James, Alan G. ... '20 '48 (NY) C.951 B.A. L.976 J.D.
Johnson, Barbara J. ... '54 '82 (MI) C.475 B.A. L.215 J.D.
Kitchen, R. David ... '58 '83 C.208 B.A. L.276 J.D.
Labowitz, Allan M. ... '23 '56 (VA) C.923 B.S.Ch.E. L.273 J.D.
Leader, Judith K. ... '43 '80 C.881 A.B. L.904 J.D.
Lishman, Joanne M. ... '54 '78 (VA) C.104 A.B. L.904 J.D.
Malkemes, Janet R. ... '55 '80 (PA) C.918 B.A. L.276 J.D.
Mandel, Lawrence C. ... '52 '83 (MA) C.30 B.A. L.588 J.D.
Marshall, Catherine D. ... '51 '78 C.104 A.B. L.273 J.D.
Mayfield, Mark S. ... '56 '80 (TX) C.810 B.A. L.846 J.D.
Melville, James D., Jr. ... '57 '82 (NJ) C.94 B.A. L.705 J.D.
Miller, Dan M. ... '55 '84 (NJ) C.101 B.A. L.178 J.D.
Mills, Richard M., Jr. ... '59 '84 C.276 B.S.F.S. L.846 J.D.
Mueller, Maryann C. ... '61 '87 (PA) C.645 B.A. L.273 J.D.
Murphy, Shaun M. ... '57 '86 C.321 A.B. L.128 J.D.
Nanda, Krishan Kumar Hans ... '59 '85 (VA) C&L.893 B.A., J.D.
Neuling, R. Bruce ... '58 '86 (CA) C.112 B.A. L.629 J.D.
Odom, H. Edward ... '47 '72 (MD) C.901 B.A. L.273 J.D.
O'Herron, Thomas F. ... '39 '66 C.676 A.B. L.128 LL.B.
Oleszycki, Charles R. ... '44 '70 C.475 B.A. L.477 J.D.
Pearson, W. Robert ... '43 '68 (VA) C.880 B.A. L.893 J.D.
Pellington, Joseph O. ... '54 '80 C.210 B.A. L.776 J.D.

Pernick, Matthew H. .... '45 '82 (VA) C.569 B.S. L.30 J.D.
Plofchan, Thomas K., Jr. .... '63 '92 (VA) C.871 B.S. L.893 J.D.
Puhl, Richard J. .... '53 '82 (PA) C&L.229 B.A., J.D.
Rabens, Ronald B. .... '42 '72 (CA) C.209 B.S.C. L.273 J.D.
Reid, Thomas D., Jr. .... '60 '85 (AL) C.245 B.A. L.16 J.D.
Robinson, Susan A. .... '44 '84 (MD) C.774 B.A. L.911 J.D.
Rodriguez, Marian .... '51 '85 C.267 B.S. L.1066 J.D.
Rosenthal, Barry C. .... '58 '84 (MN) C&L.494 B.A., J.D.
Scheffer, David J. .... '53 '79 C.309 A.B. L.051
Schulz, Jeanne .... '46 '72 C.1074 B.S. L.1067 J.D.
Sheehan, Daniel F. .... '56 '81 (MD) C&L.446 B.A., J.D.
Shelton, Grace W. .... '62 '89 (GA) C.105 B.A. L.178 J.D.
Smith, Gene M., (Ms.) .... '50 '76 (KY) C.999 A.B. L.421 J.D.
Stanton, Gregory H. .... '46 '82 (WI) C.604 B.A. L.976 J.D.
Stipkala, Joseph J. .... '29 '61 (OH) C.363 B.S. L.1003 LL.B.
Stone, Richard B. .... '28 '54 C.309 B.A. L.178 LL.B.
Stratford, Richard J.K. .... '48 '75 C.276 B.S.B.A. L.904 J.D.
Sussman, Jerry .... '51 '77 C.1044 B.A. L.273 J.D.
Terrill, Richard W. .... '51 '82 (PA) C.653 B.S. L.564 J.D.
Tesone, Mark F. .... '66 '91 (MD) C.610 B.A. L.30 J.D.
Thurston, Michael E. .... '52 '82 (WA) C&L.911 B.A., J.D.
Tobey, Laurence E. .... '53 '85 C.321 A.B. L.208 J.D.
Topping, Linda M. .... '49 '78 C.970 B.A. L.128 J.D.
Turner, Robert F. .... '44 '82 (VA) C.347 B.A. L.893 J.D.
Vandenberg, Ellie M. .... '50 '81 C.297 B.A. L.300 J.D.
Verville, Elizabeth G. .... '40 '65 C.228 A.B. L.178 LL.B.
Villarosa, Sharon Woods .... '51 '78 (VA) C.575 A.B. L.945 J.D.
Vlcek, Ann Lewis .... '47 '81 C.813 B.A. L.276 J.D.
Wadelton, Joan S. .... '50 '79 (PA) C.788 B.A. L.1292 J.D.
Walton, E. Andrew .... '60 '85 (MA) C.732 B.A. L.1202 J.D.
Walz, Kathleen .... '47 '75 C.245 B.S. L.1065 J.D.
Ward, Kenneth D. .... '57 '90 C&L.276 J.D.
Wilcox, Philip C., Jr. .... '37 '61 (CO) C.951 B.A. L.813 LL.B.
Williams, Stephen B. .... '51 '77 (AR) C.45 B.A. L.802 J.D.
Wooden, Dean B. .... '45 '79 (GA) C.30 B.S. L.1234 J.D.
Wulf, Norman A. .... '40 '65 C.353 B.A. L.352 J.D.
Yager, Brenda Lee .... '49 '81 C.57 B.A. L.209 J.D.
Zeringue, Jeanne-Marie .... '58 '83 (LA) C.220 B.A. L.861 J.D.

DEPARTMENT OF TRANSPORTATION

(Vacant), *General Counsel*

OFFICE OF THE GENERAL COUNSEL

Andrews, Dale C. .... '49 '76 C.273 B.A. L.904 J.D.
Andrews, Julia .... '61 '97 (MD) C.67 B.S. L.904 J.D.
Ashby, Robert C. .... '45 '75 (WI) C.318 B.A. L.966 J.D.
Bates, Michael S. .... '46 '74 (VA) C.198 A.B. L.893 J.D.
Bloch, Peter M. .... '52 '77 (PA) C.696 B.A. L.228 J.D.
Brooks, Joseph A. .... '48 '73 C&L.276 B.S.F.S., J.D.
Carlson, Terence W. .... '62 '88 C.262 B.A. L.128 J.D.
Crouter, Mary M. .... '51 '81 C.550 B.A. L.273 J.D.
Dann, James R. .... '48 '73 C.276 B.S.F.S. L.273 J.D.
DeCell, Jane B. .... '51 '81 C.298 B.A. L.273 J.D.
Diederich, Bernard F. .... '43 '70 C.746 B.A. L.436 J.D.
Eisner, Neil R. .... '43 '67 C.823 A.B. L.178 J.D.
Gabel, Roberta D. .... '52 '76 C.107 B.A. L.30 J.D.
Geier, Paul M. .... '46 '71 C.105 B.A. L.880 J.D.
Goldberg, David J. .... '65 '94 (MA) C.813 B.S. L.93 J.D.
Herlihy, Thomas W. .... '44 '73 C.299 B.A. L.178 J.D.
Holmstrup, Mark A. .... '60 '90 (VA) L.1209 J.D.
Horn, Donald H. .... '45 '70 C.994 B.A. L.309 J.D.
Joost, Robert H. .... '37 '66 C.976 B.A. L.309 J.D.
Kessler, Nancy .... '51 '76 C.518 B.A. L.273 J.D.
Klothe, Robert .... '50 '75 C.994 B.A. L.659 J.D.
Knapp, Rosalind A. .... '45 '73 C&L.813 B.A., J.D.
Langan-Feirson, Mary Kay .... '55 '80 C.37 B.A. L.446 J.D.
Lazarus, Rosalind Avnet .... '— '73 C.788 A.B. L.309 J.D.
Lehman, Dayton, Jr. .... '51 '80 C.908 B.S. L.273 J.D.
Lowry, Nicholas .... '49 '77 C.966 B.A. L.893 J.D.
Mahoney, Thomas F. .... '45 '73 (NY) C.262 B.A. L.273 J.D.
Metoyer, Stephen A. .... '49 '76 C&L.188 A.B., J.D.
Myers, Lawrence R. .... '43 '71 C.31 B.A. L.813 J.D.
Nolan, Michael K. .... '40 '70 (WI) C.884 B.S. L.966 J.D.
Petrie, Joanne .... '55 '81 (NY) C.319 B.A. L.94 J.D.
Plocki, Peter J. .... '57 '83 C.821 B.A. L.273 J.D.
Podberesky, Samuel .... '46 '72 (MD) C&L.446 B.S.A.E., J.D.
Radloff, Gwyneth J. .... '54 '79 C.103 A.B. L.94 J.D.
Ray, Thomas L. .... '44 '70 C.813 A.B. L.145 J.D.
Register, William R. .... '45 '70 (VA) C&L.945 B.S., J.D.
Roh, Audrey .... '75 '00 C.893 B.A. L.128 J.D.
Rosen, Debra J. .... '57 '88 C.454 B.A. L.94 J.D.
Rosenberg, Esta M. .... '54 '79 C.696 B.A. L.276 J.D.
Ross, Robert I. .... '46 '71 C.884 A.B. L.976 J.D.
Rupp, Jeff D. .... '58 '83 (VA) C&L.945 B.A., J.D.
Schwarzkopf, Peter B. .... '31 '56 (NY) C.197 A.B. L.309 J.D.
Smith, Paul S. .... '51 '76 C.276 B.A. L.602 J.D.
Smith, Peter Schuyler .... '— '98 C.165 A.B. L.878 J.D.
Tochen, David K. .... '54 '77 C.1044 B.A. L.273 J.D.
Tourtellot, Christopher T. .... '52 '81 C.976 B.A. L.30 J.D.
Trejo, Laura .... '58 '87 C.788 B.A. L.1066 J.D.
Ulmer, Dorothy J. .... '53 '78 (MS) C.500 B.A. L.325 J.D.
Wagner, William J. .... '45 '71 C.128 B.A. L.966 J.D.
Wildensteiner, Otto M. .... '39 '72 C.556 B.S.M.E. L.184 J.D.
Wolf, Betsy L. .... '51 '78 C.681 B.A. L.569 J.D.

OFFICE OF HEARINGS

Adamson, Eric Andrew .... '70 '97 (VA) C.347 B.S. L.1209 J.D.
Kolko, Burton S. .... '39 '65 C.659 B.S.Econ. L.178 LL.B. Admin. Law J.
Yoder, Ronnie A. .... '37 '61 C&L.893 B.A., J.D. Adm. Law J.

OFFICE OF THE SECRETARY

Clasen, Marc T. .... '35 '63 (NY) C.667 B.C.E. L.564 LL.B.
Keller, Charlene M. .... '71 '97 (PA) C.401 B.A. L.831 J.D.
Kleinberg, David K. .... '38 '65 (NY) C.994 B.A. L.188 LL.B.
Oppler, Edward P. .... '38 '62 (VA) C&L.893 B.A., LL.B.
Peak, John T. .... '45 '71 C&L.276 B.S.B.A., J.D.

BOARD OF CONTRACT APPEALS

Fennessy, Eileen P. .... '48 '74 C.242 B.A. L.818 J.D. Adm. J.
Stern, James L. .... '48 '75 C.1021 B.S. L.564 J.D. Adm. J.
Ware, Thaddeus V. .... '35 '61 C.892 B.A. L.329 J.D. Adm. J.

FEDERAL AVIATION ADMINISTRATION

Office of the Chief Counsel

Armstead, Y. Andrea .... '— '85 C.512 B.S. L.597 J.D.
Baccus, Lisa S. .... '62 '89 (NJ) C.329 B.A. L.705 J.D.
Barry, James A. .... '58 '87 (MD) C.423 B.A. L.64 J.D.
Bennett, Vincent James .... '— '89 C.911 B.A. L.1051 J.D.
Bjornson, Hans I. E. .... '56 '85 C.494 B.A. L.273 J.D.
Bury, Mark W. .... '57 '84 (OH) C&L.608 B.A., J.D.
Byrne, Donald P. .... '43 '69 C.436 A.B. L.383 J.D.
Caron, Susan S. .... '54 '87 (TX) C.347 B.A. L.744 J.D.
Carter, Gregory C. .... '59 '83 C&L.623 B.A., J.D.
Chase, Michael E. .... '49 '75 C.112 A.B. L.1066 J.D.
Conte, Joseph A. .... '60 '86 (MD) C.93 A.B. L.30 J.D.
Cross, Jonathan W. .... '61 '89 C.893 B.A. L.208 J.D.
Cummings-Spickler, Maureen .... '— '82 (PA) C.1261 B.A. L.831 J.D.
Davis, Harold C., Jr. .... '56 '79 (TX) C&L.69 B.A., J.D.
Dilk, Andrew J., Jr. .... '40 '66 (MA) C&L.276 B.A., J.D.
Dillman, James S. .... '46 '70 C.216 B.A. L.229 J.D.
Dominik, Cynthia A. .... '62 '86 C.445 B.S. L.420 J.D.
Donelan, Clare R. .... '51 '78 C.860 B.A. L.30 J.D.
Elmore, Eric M. .... '68 '96 C.329 B.S. L.273 J.D.
Faulkner, LeAnne M. .... '58 '85 (IN) C.210 B.A. L.1119 J.D.
Fuller, Daphne A. .... '56 '81 (NY) C.674 B.A. L.329 J.D.
Hannums, Peter J. .... '44 '80 C.573 B.S. L.128 J.D.
Horowitz, Allan H. .... '47 '74 C.563 B.A. L.1009 J.D.
Jennison, Michael B. .... '45 '79 C&L.378 B.A., J.D.
Jones, Jerome P., Jr. .... '51 '79 (MI) C&L.477 A.B., J.D.
Jordan, Christian F.P. .... '60 '88 (PA) C.446 B.A. L.904 J.D.
Kauffman, Victoria H. .... '67 '93 C.893 B.A. L.1209 J.D.
Kinsey, George P., III .... '63 '88 C.105 B.A. L.273 J.D.
Klang, Jeffrey A. .... '58 '89 C.489 B.A. L.904 J.D.
Leemon, Vicki Sherman .... '55 '80 C.309 A.B. L.30 J.D.
Lewis, Robert B. .... '54 '83 C&L.902 B.A., J.D.
LoBue, Nancy D. .... '54 '79 C.597 B.A. L.30 J.D.
Long, Alison Boothby .... '65 '98 (MD) C.338 B.A. L.128 J.D.
Lynch, Peter J. .... '51 '77 C.454 B.A. L.128 J.D.
Lyons, Holly E. Woodruff .... '65 '91 (CO) C.165 B.A. L.1049 J.D.
Martin, Alan .... '36 '74 C.674 A.B. L.309 J.D.
Martin, Carla J. .... '54 '90 (PA) C.838 B.A. L.904 J.D.
Martinez, Raymond A. .... '— '91 C&L.744 B.A., J.D.
McCarthy, Richard J. .... '59 '89 C.475 B.A. L.851 J.D.
McNall, Patricia A. .... '57 '85 (VA) C.773 B.A. L.273 J.D.
Mellody, Jerome M. .... '53 '81 (PA) C.645 B.S. L.1338 J.D.
Michel, Gary A. .... '47 '72 C.331 A.B. L.30 J.D.
Montgomery, Laura D. .... '61 '87 (MD) C.893 B.A. L.659 J.D.
O'Connor, Cecile .... '— '82 (CT) C.893 B.A. L.262 J.D.
Palladino, Anthony N. .... '52 '80 C.470 B.A. L.1162 J.D.
Pando, Viola M. .... '56 '87 (UT) C&L.878 B.S., J.D.
Peter, Lorelei A. .... '66 '90 (MO) C&L.502 B.BA., J.D.
Petronis, Karen L. .... '58 '84 C.589 B.A. L.30 J.D.
Rabinowitz, Diana R. .... '68 '93 (NJ) C.1044 B.A. L.1019 J.D.
Redos, Joyce L. .... '52 '88 C.653 B.A. L.945 J.D.
San Martin, Frank J. .... '55 '84 C.321 B.A. L.93 J.D.
Skojec, Sheila A. .... '60 '87 C.1349 B.A. L.107 J.D.
Smith, Wilton J. .... '41 '86 (VA) C.871 B.S. L.273 J.D.
Stein, James M. .... '57 '83 (PA) C.976 B.A. L.884 J.D.
Tegtmeier, James W. .... '65 '91 C.427 B.A. L.94 J.D.
Thompson, Mardi Ruth .... '55 '80 C&L.1338 B.S., J.D.
Tomicich, Mark A. .... '60 '90 (PA) C.1235 B.S. L.1218 J.D.
Tonkins, Wayne A., Sr. .... '47 '87 C.828 L.329 J.D.
Uberman, Sara L .... '74 '01 C.855 B.A. L.818 J.D.
Vente, Robert P. .... '62 '87 C.645 B.A. L.229 J.D.
Walsh, John M. .... '34 '72 (MD) C.563 B.E.E. L.273 J.D.
Walsh, Mary Ursula .... '60 '86 C.1030 B.A. L.128 J.D.
Walters, Richard C. .... '46 '71 C&L.659 B.S.E., J.D.
Washington, Anthony L. .... '54 '79 (MA) C.597 B.A. L.93 J.D.
Waters, J. Thomas .... '60 '88 C.575 B.A. L.896 J.D.
Whitlow, James W. .... '51 '77 (NY) C&L.178 B.A., J.D.
Wiegand, David M. .... '52 '81 (FL) C.472 A.B. L.1206 J.D.
Williams, Sheryl L. .... '64 '89 (PA) C.674 A.B. L.276 J.D.
Worden, Dorothy B.A. .... '57 '82 C.4 B.A. L.896 J.D.
Zuckerman, Robert .... '51 '79 (PA) C.831 B.S. L.809 J.D.

Other Offices of F.A.A.

Angle, Richard L. .... '36 '74 C.347 B.S. L.426 J.D.
Bennett, David L. .... '47 '78 (MD) C.105 B.A. L.446 J.D.
Burgess, Quentin L. .... '44 '75 C.1023 B.A. L.329 J.D.
Butcher, Clarence C., Jr. .... '55 '81 C.512 B.A. L.329 J.D.
Coghlan, Malachy T. .... '50 '81 (NV) C.708 B.A. L.61 J.D.
Collins, Marie Adamson .... '62 '88 (IL) C.347 B.A. L.1119 J.D.
Connon, Kathleen A. .... '65 '91 (PA) C.856 A.B. L.128 J.D.
Freeman, Darlene M. .... '51 '77 C.856 B.A. L.276 J.D.
Gilligan, Margaret .... '— '80 (NY) C.706 B.A. L.94 J.D.
Golrick, Richard T. .... '21 '50 (OH) C.363 B.S. L.930 LL.B.
Hart, Christopher A. .... '47 '73 C.674 B.S.E. L.309 J.D.
Hooker, Ann Mead .... '52 '92 C.170 B.A. L.560 J.D.
Jordan, Jon L. .... '36 '67 C.923 A.B. L.893 LL.B.
Kelly, Patrice M. .... '64 '89 C.93 B.A. L.276 J.D.
Maillett, Louise E. .... '53 '78 C.1107 B.A. L.1294 J.D.
Metzbower, S. David, Jr. .... '44 '74 (MD) C&L.64 B.S., J.D.
Molar, Barry L. .... '52 '80 C.475 B.A. L.273 J.D.
Newman, Elizabeth .... '62 '90 (NY) C.540 B.A. L.1187 J.D.
Waters, James T. .... '60 '98 C.575 B.A. L.896 J.D.
Winer, David E. .... '34 '67 C.880 B.E. L.273 LL.B.

DEPARTMENT OF TRANSPORTATION (Continued)

FEDERAL HIGHWAY ADMINISTRATION

Office of the Chief Counsel

Aikens, L. Harold, Jr. ... '42 '75 C.411 A.B. L.276 J.D.
Alsop, Stuart R. ... '40 '68 (CT) C.103 B.A. L.94 LL.B.
Baccus, Wilbert ... '45 '74 C.851 B.A. L.329 J.D.
Black, Robert J. ... '52 '77 (IN) C.894 B.A. L.347 J.D.
Cellini, Sue Anna Moss ... '45 '98 (AZ) C.298 B.A. L.37 J.D.
Cherwek, Virginia I. ... '47 '74 (VA) C.94 B.A. L.273 J.D.
Chess, Florian Frederick ... '57 '85 C.986 B.A. L.1288 J.D.
Cuprill, Raymond W. ... '53 '78 (PR) C&L.1087 B.A., J.D.
Downey, Julie Noelle ... '70 '95 C.260 B.S. L.879 J.D.
Dymond, Kenneth ... '50 '76 C.1349 B.A. L.1009 J.D.
Gainer, Brett J. ... '66 '91 C.1369 B.S. L.273 J.D.
Holian, Thomas P. ... '50 '79 (NY) C.262 B.A. L.564 J.D.
Kussy, Edward V.A. ... '47 '71 (PA) C&L.477 B.A., J.D.
Lemmie, Vanessa Hall ... '60 '88 C.64 B.A. L.446 J.D.
Liff, Diane R. ... '44 '71 C.970 B.A. L.145 J.D.
Macphee, Lisa H. ... '66 '90 (GA) C.245 B.A. L.1059 J.D.
Mobley, Diane K. ... '68 '93 (MD) C.30 B.A. L.446 J.D.
Reidy, Grace E. ... '66 '93 (NY) C.1044 B.A. L.107 J.D.
Rochlis, Steven M. ... '51 '77 (GA) C.645 B.A. L.245 J.D.
Sett, David ... '59 '88 C.112 A.B. L.1097 J.D.
Shaw, Alia C. ... '— '94 C.280 B.A. L.425 J.D.
Thomason, James C., III ... '47 '72 C.280 A.B. L.16 J.D.

FEDERAL RAILROAD ADMINISTRATION

Office of the Chief Counsel

Alpert, Daniel Lee ... '67 '92 (GA) C.293 B.A. L.245 J.D.
Beyer, Christine ... '56 '89 (PA) C.923 B.A. L.273 J.D.
Fashouer, William R., Jr. ... '54 '79 C.347 B.A. L.276 J.D.
Friedman, Nancy L. ... '64 '92 (RI) C.103 A.B. L.930 J.D.
Haley, Michael T. ... '43 '68 (CO) C.174 B.A. L.208 J.D.
Kaplan, Jonathan L. ... '65 '90 C.228 B.A. L.910 J.D.
Kasminoff, David H. ... '60 '85 C.1036 A.B. L.273 J.D.
Kern, John A. ... '51 '76 (PA) C.645 B.A. L.273 J.D.
King, G. Joseph ... '40 '70 C.433 B.A. L.276 J.D.
Lindsey, Seth M. ... '47 '72 (CA) C.800 A.B. L.976 J.D. Chief Coun.
Matsuda, David T. ... '72 '97 (CA) C.1167 B.S. L.1049 J.D.
Nagler, Alan H. ... '66 '92 C.1349 B.A. L.904 J.D.
Phemister, Thomas A. ... '40 '65 (IL) C.118 B.A. L.145 J.D.
Pomponio, Joseph R. ... '49 '76 C.446 B.S. L.30 J.D.
Rosenau, Gareth W. ... '49 '74 C.970 B.A. L.1017 J.D.
Shelton, Kathryn E. ... '72 '96 (VA) C&L.276 B.S.F.S., J.D.
Smith, Daniel C. ... '49 '78 C.215 B.A. L.763 J.D.
Sorrells, Elizaeth Ann ... '61 '95 (TX) C.859 B.A. L.802 J.D.
Stultz, Billie Ann ... '45 '77 C.104 A.B. L.276 J.D.
Sun, Patricia V. ... '56 '81 (PA) C.994 B.A. L.276 J.D.
Tessler, Mark H. ... '48 '75 C.696 B.A. L.569 J.D.
Winkle, John A. ... '70 '96 (MD) C.446 B.S. L.128 J.D.

MARITIME ADMINISTRATION

Agarwal, Julie ... '— '92 C.472 B.B.A. L.260 J.D.
Bloom, Murray A. ... '50 '80 C.184 B.A. L.128 J.D.
Budwick, Philip H. ... '71 '97 (NY) C.1036 B.A. L.861 J.D.
Byrne, Patricia E. ... '46 '70 C.276 B.S.B.A. L.910 J.D.
Feury, Kevin C. ... '41 '67 (NY) C.321 B.S. L.982 J.D.
Gordon, Jay R. ... '50 '75 (MD) C.659 B.A. L.276 J.D.
Gurland, C. Slowikowski ... '61 '87 C.116 B.A. L.823 J.D.
Lorr, Richard M. ... '43 '75 C.563 B.A. L.705 J.D.
Macey, Joe S. ... '36 '67 (TX) C.586 B.A. L.802 J.D.
Main, Larry G. ... '48 '76 (LA) C.259 B.S. L.420 J.D.
Mardula, Francis ... '53 '78 C.831 B.A. L.1017 J.D.
Marquez, John T., Jr ... '67 '92 (MS) C&L.500 B.B.A., J.D.
McMorrow, Michael J. ... '37 '64 (NY) C.116 B.S. L.724 LL.B.
Orenstein, Jean Kirkham ... '— '79 C.378 B.A. L.276 J.D.
Patton, Robert J., Jr. ... '43 '68 C.228 B.A. L.273 J.D.
Richard, Joel Charles ... '49 '89 C.816 B.E. L.276 J.D.
Rodriguez, Janis Parkinson ... '55 '79 C.78 B.A. L.273 J.D.
Rose, Warren M. ... '48 '86 C.502 B.S.B.A. L.893 J.D.
Salisbury, John G. ... '56 '86 C.30 B.A. L.51 J.D.
Sommer, Edmund T., Jr. ... '43 '77 C.1027 B.S. L.273 J.D.
Sutter, Leonard L. ... '30 '59 C.1044 B.S. L.178 J.D.
Vachon, Matthew E. ... '62 '92 (FL) C.1027 B.S. L.472 J.D.
Wiese, John P. ... '47 '77 (VA) C.869 B.S. L.273 J.D.

U. S. COAST GUARD

Office of the Chief Counsel

Abbott, Anita Kay ... '64 '95 (PA) C.869 B.S. L.276 J.D.
Aldana, Benes ... '69 '95 (WA) C.988 B.A. L.911 J.D.
Anderson, Erin W. ... '59 '86 C.835 B.S. L.734 J.D.
Argenti, Laticia ... '61 '91 (VA) C.15 B.A. L.692 J.D.
Augustine, James K. ... '48 '72 C.118 B.A. L.893 J.D.
Barber, Stephen H. ... '42 '69 C.797 B.A. L.469 J.D.
Barton, Michael G. ... '69 '99 (MA) C.823 B.A. L.884 J.D.★
Baum, Joseph H. ... '31 '55 C.145 A.B. L.880 LL.B.
Brophy, J. Stephen ... '44 '69 C&L.879 B.A., J.D.
Chaney, William L. ... '63 '92 (MI) C.455 B.S. L.912 J.D.★
Chenault, Timothy A. ... '52 '77 (VA) C&L.692 B.A., J.D.
Cunningham, Mark A. ... '71 '97 (CO) C.475 B.A. L.245 J.D.
Devine, Michael J. ... '53 '85 (MA) C.869 B.S. L.1048 J.D.
Dixon, C. Warren, III ... '44 '91 (CO) C.1070 B.S. L.208 J.D.
Eder, Elaine A. ... '53 '76 (GA) C.597 B.A. L.245 J.D.
Faleris, Donald W. ... '48 '74 (MI) C.477 B.A. L.912 J.D.
Glomb, Matthew J. ... '60 '94 (PA) C.869 B.S. L.273 J.D.★
Gonzales, Richard V ... '— '90 (WA) C.908 B.A. L.285 J.D.
Hayes, Thomas M., III ... '57 '83 (MO) C.502 B.S. L.734 J.D.
Jackson, Stephen D. ... '46 '73 C.264 A.B. L.1294 J.D.
Mongold, James R. ... '54 '85 (MO) C.869 B.S. L.734 J.D.★
Murray, Patrick J. ... '43 '73 (WA) C.31 B.A. L.976 J.D.
Nicewicz, Walter A. ... '30 '55 (MA) C.1057 B.B.A. L.935 J.D.
Nicholas, Talbot J., II ... '54 '83 C.128 M.A. L.276 LL.M.
Nicholson, James B. ... '56 '99 (NY) C.570 B.S.E. L.776 J.D.
Parks, James G. ... '66 '93 C.546 B.A. L.30 J.D.
Pelcovits, Pamela M. ... '52 '77 C.696 B.A. L.94 J.D.
Pessin, Andrew S. ... '62 '89 C.659 B.A. L.893 J.D.
Reilly, Chris P. ... '— '95 (WA) C.869 B.S.C.E. L.911 J.D.
Russell, Michael D. ... '60 '85 (AL) C.88 B.A. L.16 J.D.
Sullivan, Jacqueline L. ... '49 '83 C.276 B.S. L.128 J.D.
Young, Eric J. ... '58 '83 C.645 B.S. L.229 J.D.★

Other Offices of Coast Guard

Goettle, Daniel J. ... '69 '99 (PA) C.869 B.S. L.273 J.D.
Ingolia, Joseph N. ... '26 '51 C&L.446 B.A., LL.B.
Jordan, George J. ... '49 '77 (MA) C.93 B.A. L.1202 J.D.
Rospars, William ... '67 '97 C.869 B.S. L.178 J.D.

Office of Chief Counsel

Bell, Nancy E. ... '68 '95 C.659 B.A. L.823 J.D.
Bolden, Tyler ... '— '97 C.831 B.B.A. L.276 J.D.
Casey, Dion O. ... '71 '98 C.1273 B.A. L.378 J.D.
Cohen, Steven L. ... '74 '99 C.454 B.A. L.861 J.D.
Coleman, Heidi Lewis ... '57 '82 C.107 B.A. L.273 J.D.
DiMarsico, Andrew J. ... '71 '97 C.423 B.A. L.64 J.D.
Donaldson, K. John ... '56 '84 (MA) C.188 B.A. L.93 J.D.
Feldman, Stanley C. ... '43 '73 C.861 B.A. L.597 J.D.
Fradette, Nicole H. ... '66 '96 (MA) C.518 B.A. L.945 J.D.
Fujita, Deirdre R. ... '57 '83 (CA) C.170 B.A. L.569 J.D.
Glancy, J. Edward ... '54 '80 (PA) C.264 A.B. L.228 J.D.
Goode, Michael T. ... '44 '70 C.902 B.A. L.692 J.D.
Guerci, Lloyd S. ... '47 '73 C.401 B.S.E.E. L.1292 J.D.
Kam, Allan J. ... '48 '72 (NJ) C.222 B.A. L.273 J.D.
Knop, Robert M. ... '67 '99 C.893 B.A. L.30 J.D.
Leahy, Eileen T. ... '49 '77 (MA) C.242 B.A. L.273 J.D.
MacPherson, Rebecca ... '63 '90 (MD) C.425 B.A. L.861 J.D.
Matheke, Otto G., III ... '56 '83 (NH) C.478 B.A. L.94 J.D.
Nakama, Dorothy R. ... '55 '82 C.145 A.B. L.276 J.D.
Rubenstein, Enid ... '45 '69 (NY) C.881 A.B. L.659 J.D.
Sachs, Coleman R. ... '50 '75 (RI) C.103 A.B. L.823 J.D.
Seales, Frank, Jr. ... '49 '75 (PA) C.832 B.S. L.1119 J.D.
Timian, Jennifer T. ... '72 '98 C&L.446 B.A., J.D.
Vaughn, Sharon Y. ... '61 '88 C&L.329 B.A., J.D.
Vinson, Z. T. ... '33 '62 (CA) C.674 A.B. L.893 LL.B.
Wilson, Kenneth V. ... '55 '00 C.999 B.A. L.1202 J.D.
Womack, John G., Jr. ... '42 '67 (NJ) C.309 B.A. L.659 LL.B.
Wood, Stephen P. ... '44 '69 C.951 B.A. L.178 J.D.

DeMeter, Kathleen C. ... '49 '76 C.608 B.A. L.30 J.D.
Parker, Deborah L. ... '43 '94 C.823 A.B. L.276 J.D.

RESEARCH AND SPECIAL PROGRAMS ADMINISTRATION

Betsock, Barbara ... '50 '77 C.262 B.A. L.273 J.D.
Bivins, Renita K. ... '— '97 C.803 B.A. L.425 J.D.
Bonekemper, Edward H., III ... '— '67 C.529 B.A. L.976 J.D.
Christian, Karin V. ... '66 '93 (VA) C.893 B.A. L.128 J.D.
Conkling, Rowena H. ... '36 '78 (MA) C.454 B.S. L.93 J.D.
Furrow, Lucian M. ... '42 '69 (MD) C.892 B.C.E. L.446 J.D.
Glater, David S. ... '44 '68 (NY) C&L.976 B.A., LL.B.
Hilder, Frazer C. ... '43 '68 C.118 B.A. L.477 J.D.
Joost, Elaine Economides ... '48 '77 (MA) C.550 B.A. L.818 J.D.
Kaleta, Judith S. ... '57 '82 (IL) C.209 B.A. L.424 J.D.
Kelly, Katie ... '47 '80 (MA) C.856 B.A. L.588 J.D.
Lopez-Goldberg, Astrid E. ... '66 '95 (MA) C.446 B.S. L.818 J.D.
Machado, Nancy E. ... '60 '85 C.886 B.S. L.273 J.D.
Monniere, Robert A. ... '57 '90 (NE) C.882 B.S. L.546 J.D.
O'Berry, Donna L. ... '63 '95 (MD) C.862 B.A. L.904 J.D.
Pappas, Sherri Lynn ... '55 '87 (WI) C&L.966 B.A., J.D.
Parks, J. Gregory ... '66 '93 (PA) C.546 B.A. L.30 J.D.
Sanchez, Marcel P., Jr. ... '64 '92 C.893 B.A. L.1019 J.D.
Wolanin, Stanley J. ... '49 '79 (PA) C.321 B.A. L.1202 J.D.

ST. LAWRENCE SEAWAY DEVELOPMENT ADMINISTRATION

Office of the Chief Counsel

Owen, Marc C. ... '48 '73 (ME) C.431 B.A. L.1294 J.D. Chief Coun.

SURFACE TRANSPORTATION BOARD

Office of the General Counsel

Cannizzaro, Cecelia ... '50 '79 C.264 A.B. L.174 J.D.
Hanson, Ellen D. ... '50 '75 C.228 A.B. L.575 J.D. Gen. Coun.
Kalick, Theodore K. ... '47 '74 C.477 B.A. L.273 J.D.
Keats, Craig M. ... '47 '73 (PA) C.103 A.B. L.94 J.D.
Kitay, Evelyn G. ... '48 '78 C.643 B.A. L.276 J.D.
Levitt, Marilyn R. ... '46 '98 (MD) C.107 B.A. L.446 J.D.
Oehrle, Christopher ... '64 '92 C.420 B.S. L.260 J.D.

Office of the Board Members

Armstrong, Richard E., III ... '49 '74 C.277 B.S. L.838 J.D.
Clyburn, William, Jr. ... '66 '92 C.277 B.A. L.790 J.D.
Morgan, Linda J. ... '52 '76 C.881 A.B. L.276 J.D. Chmn.

Office of Proceedings

Director's Office

Konschnik, David M. ... '48 '75 C&L.276 B.S., J.D.
Sado, John J. ... '48 '73 C.103 A.B. L.276 J.D.

Section of Administration

Farr, Julia M. ... '63 '87 (VA) C&L.945 B.A., J.D.

Section of Legal Counsel I

Barry, Thomas J. .... '49 '73 (MA) C&L.93 A.B., J.D.
Brown, James L. .... '46 '72 (PA) C.674 A.B. L.477 J.D.
Davis, Eric S. .... '46 '73 C.446 B.S. L.904 J.D.
Fleming, Terrance J. .... '43 '76 (VA) C.1276 B.B.A. L.190 J.D.
Galloway, William D. .... '46 '73 C.347 B.A. L.276 J.D.
Gordon, Beryl .... '51 '77 C.446 B.A. L.329 J.D.
Kronstain, Melissa .... '75 '00 C.645 B.A. L.30 J.D.
Markoff, Paul H. .... '50 '75 C.1044 B.A. L.260 J.D.

Section of Legal Counsel II

Dettmar, Joseph H. .... '44 '70 C.397 B.A. L.273 J.D.
Dixon, Maynard H., Jr. .... '44 '72 C.823 B.A. L.659 J.D.
Lerner, Marc A. .... '47 '74 C&L.273 B.A., J.D.
Levin, Joseph C. .... '40 '64 (MD) C&L.446 A.B., LL.B.
Nellen, David S. .... '46 '73 (MI) C.475 B.A. L.477 J.D.
Nishimoto, Paul K. .... '46 '72 (MD) C.684 B.A. L.1065 J.D.
Schwartz, Kenneth H. .... '47 '72 (MA) C.105 A.B. L.94 J.D.
Strafford, Timothy J. .... '73 '99 (NY) C.705 B.A. L.30 J.D.
Weinstein, Alan R. .... '45 '74 C.563 B.A. L.446 J.D.

Office of the Secretary

Williams, Vernon A. .... '47 '72 C.434 B.A. L.273 J.D.

Office of Economic, Environmental Analysis and Administration

Atkisson, John McE. .... '41 '72 C.112 A.B. L.767 J.D.
Ghosh, Rini .... '— '01 C.197 B.A. L.273 J.D.
Quinlan, Anne K. .... '53 '78 (IA) C.350 B.S. L.221 J.D.
Rutson, Victoria J. .... '58 '85 (PA) C.893 B.A. L.216 J.D.
Stilling, Thomas J. .... '52 '79 (MD) C.446 B.A. L.64 J.D.

Office of Congressional and Public Services

Beiter, Nancy R. .... '46 '74 C.706 B.A. L.273 J.D.
King, Dan G. .... '45 '71 (NC) C&L.575 A.B., J.D.
Saint-Louis, Rudolph A. .... '51 '76 (WI) C.1024 B.A. L.966 J.D.

FEDERAL TRANSIT ADMINISTRATION

Office of the Chief Counsel

Biehl, Scott A. .... '51 '77 (AZ) C.36 B.S. L.1051 J.D.
Durkee, Donald R. .... '45 '81 C.454 B.A. L.128 J.D.
Jackson, Ronald A. .... '64 '90 C.597 B.A. L.569 J.D.
Levy, Trudy B. .... '44 '73 C&L.705 A.B., J.D.
Ludtke, Meghan G. .... '69 '96 (MT) C.966 B.A. L.276 J.D.
Maristch, Rita M. .... '55 '92 C&L.831 B.B.A., J.D.
Martineau, Elizabeth Ada .... '54 '79 C.881 B.A. L.945 J.D.
McBride, Gregory B. .... '45 '74 (MD) C.674 A.B. L.276 J.D.
Portee, Scheryl C. .... '48 '75 C.551 B.A. L.705 J.D.
Sorkin, Linda Watkins .... '42 '65 C.890 B.A. L.945 J.D.
Walker, Bruce .... '59 '96 L.1364 J.D.
Wong, Richard L. .... '— '91 (CA) C.1073 B.A. L.276 J.D.

Barber, Melanie M. .... '58 '87 C.438 B.A. L.902 J.D.
Cook, Christopher A. .... '66 '98 (VA) C.453 B.S. L.260 J.D.
Felder, Richard B. .... '47 '73 C.188 A.B. L.569 J.D.
Jordan, Cedestra L. .... '66 '91 C.999 B.S. L.276 J.D.
Lopez, Arthur A. .... '52 '84 (IL) C.347 B.S. L.1119 J.D.
Mead, Kenneth M. .... '49 '75 C.1102 B.A. L.790 J.D.

TREASURY DEPARTMENT

Neal S. Wolin, *General Counsel*

OFFICE OF THE GENERAL COUNSEL

Baer, Gregory A. .... '62 '88 C.575 A.B. L.309 J.D.
Barber, Francine M. .... '54 '85 C&L.276 B.S., J.D.
Bellew, Sandra C. .... '68 '93 C.309 A.B. L.813 J.D.
Bieger, Peter A. .... '51 '77 C.95 A.B. L.823 J.D.
Booth, Henry H. .... '35 '65 C.585 B.A. L.273 J.D.
Bradley, Billy S. .... '51 '77 C.329 B.A. L.309 J.D.
Carro, Richard S. .... '49 '76 C.228 B.A. L.245 J.D.
Constantine, Eleni M. .... '56 '84 C&L.309 B.A., J.D.
Dorsey, Karen O. .... '50 '87 C.886 B.A. L.30 J.D.
Dougherty, David L. .... '45 '88 C.30 B.A. L.1209 J.D.
Edsall, Alexandra T. Victor .... '67 '95 C&L.309 B.A., J.D.
Gelpern, Anna .... '67 '95 (NY) C.674 B.A. L.309 J.D.
Glaser, Daniel Lawrence .... '68 '94 C.477 B.A. L.178 J.D.
Granat, Rochelle F. .... '58 '84 C.66 B.A. L.273 J.D.
Hingston, Mark K. .... '55 '85 (MA) C.94 A.B. L.818 J.D.
Joy, David D., Jr. .... '54 '81 C.674 A.B. L.893 J.D.
King, Jeffrey C. .... '62 '87 C.823 B.B.A. L.862 J.D.
Lerner, Brad S. .... '58 '83 C.1350 B.A. L.880 J.D.
Levy, Ronald S. .... '43 '68 C.331 B.A. L.904 J.D.
Lurie, Paul D. .... '71 '99 C.1111 B.A. L.259 J.D.
Maguire, Annemarie .... '53 '79 C.823 A.B. L.273 J.D.
Makkreel, Karen Emiko .... '69 '94 C.112 B.A. L.1065 J.D.
McGivern, Thomas M. .... '56 '81 C.350 B.S. L.190 J.D.
McInerney, Roberta K. .... '54 '81 C.393 B.A. L.273 J.D.
Muench, Marilyn L. .... '44 '75 C.939 B.A. L.309 J.D.
Munk, Russell Lewis .... '39 '68 C&L.309 A.B., J.D.
Murphy, John G., Jr. .... '46 '74 C.309 A.B. L.176 J.D.
Murphy, William L. .... '44 '73 C.728 B.S. L.128 J.D.
Nasrah, Melissa M. .... '73 '98 (MD) C.94 B.A. L.30 J.D.
Ratliff, Remi .... '68 '95 (TX) C.914 B.A. L.846 J.D.
Rigrodsky, Marc A. .... '56 '83 C.188 B.S. L.978 J.D.
Salladin, Anne W. .... '57 '89 C.951 B.A. L.893 J.D.
Schmalzbach, Kenneth R. .... '47 '73 C.188 B.S. L.273 J.D.
Schorn, John F. .... '62 '92 (MD) C&L.276 B.A., J.D.
Sim, Randolph B. .... '48 '73 C.145 B.A. L.309 J.D.
Straus, Brandon B. .... '67 '92 C.860 B.A. L.273 J.D.
Wolin, Neal S. .... '61 '89 C&L.976 B.A., J.D. Gen. Coun.
Yetter, John M. .... '64 '89 C.821 B.A. L.976 J.D.

COMMUNITY DEVELOPMENT FINANCIAL INSTITUTIONS

Berg, Jeffrey Christian .... '53 '88 C.128 B.A. L.276 J.D.
Jones, Maurice Antonia .... '64 '94 (VA) C.301 B.A. L.893 J.D.
Laughton, Steven D. .... '61 '86 (MA) C.860 B.A. L.930 J.D.

FINANCIAL CRIMES ENFORCEMENT NETWORK

Angotti, Alma M. .... '57 '82 C.923 B.A. L.893 J.D.
Kroll, Stephen R. .... '46 '73 C&L.309 B.A., J.D. Legal Coun.
Michael, Bess Johnson .... '62 '94 C.197 A.B. L.309 J.D.
Miller, Eileen Hamamura .... '— '73 (CA) C.112 B.S. L.1066 J.D.
Myers, Joseph M. .... '60 '88 (NY) C.976 B.A. L.880 J.D.
Schuetz, Christine L. .... '72 '98 (VA) C.1375 B.A. L.276 J.D.
Zarate, Albert R. .... '67 '94 C.112 B.A. L.1066 J.D.

OFFICE OF THE INSPECTOR GENERAL

Banks, Eric N. .... '50 '83 C.329 B.A. L.1162 J.D.
Doery, Richard .... '57 '85 C.766 B.A. L.273 J.D.
Langwiser, Cynthia A. .... '50 '79 C.19 B.A. L.276 J.D.
Vassar, Lori Y. .... '58 '83 C.893 B.A. L.30 J.D.

OFFICE OF THE COMPTROLLER OF THE CURRENCY

Aldemeyer, Barrett .... '43 '85 C.424 B.A. L.276 J.D.
Alexander, Tena M. .... '60 '88 (IL) C.927 B.S. L.46 J.D.
Allen, June H. .... '55 '80 (GA) C.277 B.S. L.259 J.D.
Amundson, Carolyn M. .... '66 '91 (WI) C&L.966 B.B.A., J.D.
Andrews, Deborah K. .... '55 '85 (MO) C.593 B.S.Ed. L.502 J.D.
Arendal, Rita S. .... '43 '80 C.658 B.S. L.904 J.D.
Arnold, Coreen S. .... '52 '83 C.352 B.B.A. L.128 J.D.
Auerbach, Sue E. .... '49 '76 C.104 A.B. L.30 J.D.
Bailey, Kevin J. .... '59 '86 (PA) C.93 B.S. L.884 J.D.
Barrett, E. Clifford, III .... '44 '69 (VA) C.855 B.A. L.893 LL.B.
Bettauer, Raija H. .... '48 '76 L.999 J.D.
Bhavsar, Saumya R. .... '66 '92 (MI) C.477 B.A. L.215 J.D.
Bialosky, Adam Louis .... '61 '87 C.147 B.A. L.276 J.D.
Blankenheimer, Susan Leslie .... '52 '79 C.823 B.A. L.880 J.D.
Broadman, Ellen .... '50 '76 C.112 B.A. L.588 J.D.
Brown, Stephen B. .... '44 '69 (TX) C.966 B.A. L.802 J.D.
Burch, Alan R. .... '65 '94 (WA) C.911 B.S. L.893 J.D.
Bylsma, Michael S. .... '53 '81 C.273 B.A. L.128 J.D.
Cantor, Eugene H. .... '50 '76 (GA) C.446 B.S. L.245 J.D.
Caouette, Cory Christian .... '72 '96 (MD) C.273 B.A. L.893 J.D.
Chamberlayne, Asa L. .... '62 '88 (MI) C.103 B.A. L.477 J.D.
Clark, Robert M. .... '49 '82 C.546 B.S. L.190 J.D.
Clarke, Martha Vestal .... '54 '81 C.914 A.B. L.309 J.D.
Cleva, Richard H. .... '49 '79 (WA) C.128 B.A. L.911 J.D.
Connelly, Carol M. .... '58 '86 (MA) C.856 B.A. L.93 J.D.
Cooney, Maureen C. .... '57 '86 (NE) C&L.276 A.B., J.D.
Corey, Elizabeth H. .... '45 '81 C.1019 B.B.A. L.326 J.D.
Dehnke, William T. .... '56 '81 C&L.276 B.S., J.D.
Devine, Jeanne N. .... '57 '89 (PA) C.477 A.B. L.846 J.D.
Dierberg, Michael J. .... '70 '99 (TX) C.893 B.A. L.846 J.D.
Douglas, David C. .... '51 '82 (MD) C.264 B.A. L.446 J.D.
Dugas, Michael C. .... '54 '79 C.659 B.A. L.309 J.D.
Gartlir, Kenneth T. .... '50 '76 (GA) C.188 A.B. L.245 J.D.
Gillespie, James F. E., Jr. .... '49 '76 (IN) C.611 B.A. L.1119 J.D.
Glidden, William B. .... '40 '76 (MD) C.95 B.A. L.569 J.D.
Gottfried, Linda A. .... '48 '79 (GA) C.1063 A.B. L.245 J.D.
Grady, Patricia S. .... '62 '87 (VA) C.886 B.S. L.276 J.D.
Greco, Suzette Haynie .... '57 '87 (GA) C.893 B.A. L.280 J.D.
Griffin, L. Robert .... '43 '68 C.1031 B.S. L.309 LL.B.
Hansen, Harold J. .... '46 '73 (SD) C.791 B.S. L.793 J.D.
Hendricks, Myrrel C., Jr. .... '54 '79 C.1110 B.S. L.276 J.D.
Hesse, Margaret C. .... '50 '91 (MT) C.546 B.S. L.508 J.D.
Jackson, John Christopher .... '73 '99 (NC) C&L.575 B.A., J.D.
Jacobsen, Mark P. .... '65 '90 C.937 B.S. L.309 J.D.
Jordan, Douglas Bradford .... '52 '81 C.674 A.B. L.893 J.D.
Kane, David C. .... '48 '73 C.93 B.A. L.276 J.D.
Katz, Deborah .... '56 '87 (NY) C.276 B.S. L.978 J.D.
Key, Steven V. .... '69 '97 (VA) C.228 A.B. L.945 J.D.
Kincaid-Smith, Janet E. .... '62 '89 C.690 B.S. L.893 J.D.
Kirby, Elizabeth J. .... '61 '86 C.838 B.A. L.893 J.D.
Koppel, Rosa M. .... '56 '81 C&L.569 B.A., J.D.
Lamson, Donald N. .... '55 '80 C.309 B.A. L.276 J.D.
Lee, Kevin L. .... '62 '89 (CA) C.259 B.S. L.800 J.D.
Lennon, Kenneth J. .... '61 '94 (MD) C.602 B.A. L.472 J.D.
Liebesman, Peter C. .... '48 '73 C.994 B.A. L.276 J.D.
Linville, Leslie G. .... '49 '77 (MO) C.593 B.S. L.502 J.D.
Manthey, Christopher C. .... '48 '80 (OH) C.318 B.A. L.8 J.D.
Marwell, Emily .... '50 '77 C.681 A.B. L.180 J.D.
Maymir, Javier A. .... '64 '89 (OH) C.973 B.S. L.588 J.D.
McCormally, Brian C. .... '57 '82 (KS) C.376 B.S. L.378 J.D.
McElligot, Ellen M. .... '— '80 (MA) C.93 B.A. L.1202 J.D.
McIntire, Yvonne D. .... '59 '86 C.340 B.A. L.352 J.D.
McSweeney, Karen E. .... '— '93 (FL) C.95 B.A. L.273 J.D.
Mertens, Mitchel G. .... '61 '89 (MN) C&L.494 B.A., J.D.
Meyer, Michele .... '65 '91 (MI) C.477 B.A. L.912 J.D.
Miller, Joel .... '57 '82 C.178 B.A. L.339 J.D.
Miyasato, Sharon .... '52 '77 (CA) C&L.800 B.A., J.D.
Nash, MaryAnn E. .... '62 '87 C.788 A.B. L.818 J.D.
Natter, Raymond .... '50 '75 C.688 B.S. L.276 J.D.
Partridge, Leo F. .... '48 '90 (MD) C.039 B.A. L.64 J.D.
Pasley, Robert S. .... '49 '76 C.299 B.A. L.188 J.D.
Pemberton, Timothy J. .... '57 '91 (TX) C.339 B.S. L.326 J.D.
Petrick, Frederick G., Jr. .... '62 '88 (NC) C.861 B.A. L.575 J.D.
Pogar, Joseph, Jr. .... '43 '70 (VA) C.882 A.B. L.276 J.D.
Principe, Jane A. .... '60 '87 (NJ) C.569 B.S. L.776 J.D.
Rasmussen, Jane .... '39 '84 C.276 B.S. L.273 J.D.
Redwood, Jason D. .... '59 '86 (TX) C.846 B.A. L.998 J.D.
Robbins, Carol Eve .... '48 '85 (PA) C.94 B.A. L.128 J.D.
Robinson, Neil M. .... '57 '89 C.188 A.B. L.276 J.D.
Rushdoony, Jonathan H. .... '57 '83 (NY) C.154 B.A. L.273 J.D.
Rutledge, Virginia S. .... '47 '81 C.788 B.A. L.477 J.D.

TREASURY DEPARTMENT (Continued)

Ryskamp, Randall M. '61 '86 C&L.893 B.A., J.D.
Savoy, Damon J. '63 '89 C.420 B.A. L.190 J.D.
Scall, Lester N. '38 '64 C.102 B.A. L.569 J.D.
Sears, Laurie Page '62 '92 (CT) C.882 B.A. L.184 J.D.
Serino, Robert B. '41 '69 C.860 B.A. L.818 J.D.
Sexton, Gerard J. '52 '89 (MA) C.461 B.S. L.818 J.D.
Sharpe, Ralph E. '47 '74 (WI) C.959 B.A. L.966 J.D.
Sheffield, Joi E. '66 '98 (MD) C.1369 B.A. L.329 J.D.
Shimabukuro, Ronald M. '60 '85 (PA) C.273 B.A. L.904 J.D.
Shuster, Andra J. '66 '92 C.390 A.B. L.276 J.D.
Singh, Manpreet '65 '91 (CA) C.1073 B.S. L.770 J.D.
Sneed, Horace Geoffrey '50 '81 (MI) C.674 A.B. L.477 J.D.
Soboeiro, John Anibal '68 '93 (CT) C&L.309 A.B., J.D.
Solomon, Karen O. '52 '80 C&L.128 B.A., J.D.
Starr, Madonna Kissel '47 '82 C.107 B.A. L.1119 J.D.
Stein, Larry J. '50 '77 C.645 B.S. L.30 J.D.
Stipano, Daniel P. '58 '83 (VA) C.867 B.A. L.945 J.D.
Tenhundfeld, Mark J. '58 '85 C.976 B.A. L.880 J.D.
Thomas, Heidi M. '63 '90 C.550 B.A. L.188 J.D.
Thompson, Eric '42 '67 (VA) C.197 A.B. L.276 J.D.
Tierney, Patrick T. '67 '01 C&L.1529 B.A., J.D.
Van Meter, Stephen G. '61 '86 (MA) C.477 B.A. L.309 J.D.
Vogel, Paul A. '59 '87 (NY) C.755 B.A. L.309 J.D.
Walzer, Lee I. '63 '89 C.477 A.B. L.597 J.D.
Ward, Jay T. '62 '95 (OK) C.1300 B.S. L.623 J.D.
Wheeler, Sarita Suzanne '71 '98 (MA) C.684 B.A. L.472 J.D.
Whittaker, Kristina B. '53 '81 (MD) C.446 B.S. L.64 J.D.
Williams, Julie L. '50 '75 C.1123 B.A. L.1162 J.D.
Worth, Nancy '56 '93 C.156 B.A. L.276 J.D.

BUREAU OF ALCOHOL, TOBACCO AND FIREARMS

Beckman, James A. '67 '93 (FL) C.825 B.A. L.608 J.D.
Chabra, Saleel Roy '67 '94 C.597 B.S. L.276 J.D.
Devoe, Melanie T. '72 '98 (MA) C.012 B.A. L.846 J.D.
Ficaretta, Teresa G. '53 '82 (MD) C.629 B.Mus. L.30 J.D.
Fox, William J. '61 '87 (NE) C&L.190 B.A., J.D.
Hurst, Richard E. '65 '93 C.276 B.S.L.I. L.273 J.D.
Isen, Richard S. '47 '73 (MD) C.446 B.S. L.273 J.D.
Kirkwood, Cheryl L. '60 '88 (KS) C.815 B.A. L.190 J.D.
Ko, Anita H. '73 '97 (MD) C.446 B.A. L.273 J.D.
Kodadek, John R. '48 '86 (VA) C.742 B.A.
Koett, Imelda M. '50 '75 C.263 B.A. L.900 J.D.
Kullman, William F. '58 '94 (PA) C.754 B.A. L.831 J.D.
Lieberman, David C. '65 '90 (MD) C.1365 B.A. L.276 J.D.
Loos, Eleaner R. '52 '81 C.1161 B.S. L.30 J.D.
Manfreda, John J. '45 '71 C.446 B.S.B.A. L.30 J.D.
Milgram, Patricia Weeks '52 '83 (PA) C.654 B.A. L.831 J.D.
Newman, Lynn Green '64 '91 (PA) C.1036 B.A. L.904 J.D.
Orlow, Barry S. '65 '90 C.216 B.A. L.831 J.D.
Rees, John H. '63 '89 (NC) C.797 B.A. L.192 J.D.
Rosen, Michael J. '67 '95 (NY) C.1350 B.A. L.107 J.D.
Roth, Abigail '68 '95 C&L.976 B.A., J.D.
Rubenstein, Stephen R. '50 '76 (NY) C.94 A.B. L.93 J.D.
Ryan, Mary Grace '64 '90 C&L.276 A.B., J.D.
Segal, Jennifer Mann '65 '90 (MD) C.1365 B.A. L.904 J.D.
Slattery, Jeanette N. '60 '85 (VA) C.945 B.A. L.893 J.D.
Smith, G. Elaine '— '84 (PA) C.658 B.A. L.884 J.D.
Tobiassen, Robert M. '52 '78 C.112 A.B. L.1051 J.D.
Torres, Anthony N. '56 '89 (PA) C&L.107 J.D.
Vanneman, Michelle M. '67 '95 (MD) C.188 B.A. L.30 J.D.
Wulf, David M. '69 '93 (GA) C.276 A.B. L.245 J.D.
Zezula, Duane L. '51 '77 C.112 B.A. L.464 J.D.

OFFICE OF DIRECTOR OF PRACTICE

McDonough, Patrick W. '49 '75 (MA) C&L.93 B.S., J.D.
Prater, Earl M., Jr. '45 '75 (VA) C.446 B.A. L.128 J.D.

OFFICE OF FOREIGN ASSETS CONTROL

Office of Chief Counsel

Barkey, Brett D. '61 '86 (CO) C.208 B.A. L.276 J.D.
Hammerle, Barbara C. '46 '75 C.604 A.B. L.309 J.D.
Hoffman, William B. '47 '75 C.951 B.A. L.309 J.D.
Hutner, Susan Klavens '54 '80 C.860 B.A. L.273 J.D.
Mills, David W. '56 '83 C.164 B.A. L.472 J.D.
Monborne, Mark Allen '57 '85 C.264 A.B. L.188 J.D.
Tuchband, Matthew '69 '95 C.1036 B.A. L.276 J.D.

OFFICE OF THRIFT SUPERVISION

Augello, Frances C. '57 '83 (NY) C.4 B.B.A. L.884 J.D.
Bennett, Richard S. '64 '89 C.821 B.A. L.477 J.D.
Bloss, James R. '60 '86 (KS) C.263 B.A. L.378 J.D.
Bonhomme, Evelyne V. '44 '81 (PA) C.918 B.A. L.659 J.D.
Bristol, David J. '48 '75 C.569 B.A. L.273 J.D.
Buck, Carolyn J. '46 '71 C.494 B.A. L.273 J.D.
Cassak, Lance D. '55 '81 (NJ) C.222 B.A. L.94 J.D.
Corcoran, Kevin A. '55 '81 (MN) C.560 B.A. L.494 J.D.
Cureton, Kenneth A. '46 '73 C&L.228 B.A., J.D.
Dakin, Deborah '55 '80 C.475 B.A. L.477 J.D.
Davidson, John J. '62 '88 (VA) C.273 B.A. L.945 J.D.
Davis, Martin Jefferson '42 '69 C.674 A.B. L.188 J.D.
DeCuir, Robert D. '47 '72 C.446 B.S. L.273 J.D.
Dimmick, Steven W. '50 '76 C.732 B.A. L.276 J.D.
Enzel, David H. '55 '79 C&L.665 B.A., J.D.
Fleck, J. Larry '38 '67 (OH) C.608 B.S. L.472 J.D.
Glenn, Paul D. '47 '72 C&L.930 B.A., J.D.
Gong, Kevin A. '59 '84 (CA) C.112 B.A. L.767 J.D.
Griffin, Joseph F. '57 '82 (IL) C&L.145 B.A., J.D.
Guest, M. Lou '50 '86 C.838 B.S. L.273 J.D.
Guido, Kenneth J., Jr. '40 '66 C.1042 B.S. L.800 J.D.
Gutrick, Raynette Rose '71 '97 (MD) C&L.446 B.S., J.D.
Harootunian, John P. '49 '75 (RI) C.94 B.A. L.823 J.D.
Hart, Stephen E. '46 '71 C&L.575 B.A., J.D.
Hawkins-Jones, Vicki L. '51 '77 C.914 B.A. L.93 J.D.
Hendriksen, James A. '54 '81 (PA) C.477 B.A. L.659 J.D.
Herman, Thomas A. '46 '72 C&L.893 B.A., J.D.
Hjerpe, Macrina G. '59 '84 C.321 B.A. L.602 J.D.
Kahn, Aaron B. '44 '70 C.1044 B.S. L.188 J.D.
Lane, Susan '59 '85 (MD) C.1044 B.A. L.273 J.D.
Lassiter, A. Lee, Jr. '46 '75 (GA) C.999 B.B.A. L.705 J.D.
Leary, Timothy D. '63 '88 (VA) C.923 B.A. L.945 J.D.
Leiman, Paul G. '50 '75 C.659 B.A. L.273 J.D.
Lischer, James F., Jr. '48 '74 (IL) C.945 A.B. L.597 J.D.
Lithotomos, Valerie J. '56 '81 (MA) C.94 B.S. L.1202 J.D.
Little, Richard L. '42 '69 (MA) C.696 B.A. L.94 J.D.
Miles, Susan P. '52 '89 (PA) C.446 B.S. L.128 J.D.
Mizuno, Beth N. '55 '80 C.668 B.A. L.276 J.D.
Moore, Elizabeth R. '52 '81 C.400 B.A. L.273 J.D.
Morris, Caroline '43 '74 C.881 B.A. L.273 J.D.
Osterloh, Karen '51 '76 (AZ) C&L.37 B.A., J.D.
Permut, David A. '50 '77 C.94 B.A. L.1202 J.D.
Petrasic, Kevin L. '58 '85 (PA) C.205 B.A. L.128 J.D.
Porreca, James M. '55 '86 (NY) C.1044 B.A. L.564 J.D.
Powers, P. Stacy '56 '81 (IL) C.339 B.S. L.146 J.D.
Rennert, Richard L. '59 '84 C.1349 B.A. L.245 J.D.
Riese, Richard R. '52 '78 C.205 B.A. L.659 J.D.
Rinaldi, Bruce '42 '72 (CA) C.112 B.A. L.1067 J.D.
Roberts, Dirk S. '51 '78 (NY) C.31 B.A. L.569 J.D.
Rosenberg, Steven A. '55 '81 (MA) C.454 B.A. L.930 J.D.
Rosenthal, Dorene Cadoff '63 '89 C.188 B.S. L.245 J.D.
Sazzman, Ellen J. '— '76 C.145 B.A. L.1066 J.D.
Schou, Norman '39 '68 C.813 A.B. L.1065 J.D.
Schwartz, Eugene M. '52 '76 (NJ) C.1044 B.A. L.228 J.D.
Schwartz, Scott E. '61 '86 C.1111 B.A. L.472 J.D.
Scott, Teresa A. '59 '84 (TN) C.838 B.A. L.329 J.D.
Segal, Thomas J. '46 '72 C.475 B.A. L.976 J.D.
Shepard, Catherine A. '48 '83 C.589 B.A. L.128 J.D.
Stearns, Richard C. '48 '73 C.575 B.A. L.893 J.D.
Terango, Ivana '60 '87 (VA) C.273 B.A. L.945 J.D.
Thomas, Randy W. '54 '81 C.443 B.S. L.273 J.D.
Valocchi, Teresa M. '54 '83 (PA) C.37 B.A. L.1338 J.D.
Veis, Bryan T. '51 '81 C.508 B.A. L.276 J.D.

INTERNAL REVENUE SERVICE

Office of Chief Counsel

Abell, Theresa A. '53 '81 (CA) C.284 B.A. L.770 J.D.
Abernathy, David A. '71 '97 (NC) C.575 B.S. L.574 J.D.
Accettura, Paul G. '51 '76 C.273 B.A. L.904 J.D.
Albro, Joyce C. '46 '83 C.889 B.S. L.692 J.D.
Alexander, William D. '56 '82 (NY) C.188 A.B. L.178 J.D.
Allen, Mark A. '52 '80 C&L.893 B.A., J.D.
Allison, Kenneth D. '49 '79 C.228 B.A. L.284 J.D.
Alpern, Ingrid Yollick '47 '83 C.788 B.A. L.904 J.D.
Alsalihi, Linda E. '63 '97 (MA) C.1145 B.S. L.818 J.D.
Alton, Kelly E. '56 '81 (IL) C.94 B.A. L.309 J.D.
Anderson, Grant D. '59 '85 (MN) C.145 B.A. L.494 J.D.
Aqui, Keith A. '45 '77 C&L.329 B.S., J.D.
Aramburu, John '57 '83 C.112 A.B. L.1066 J.D.
Armitage, James Clark '64 '90 C.30 B.A. L.273 J.D.
Armstrong, Willie E., Jr. '49 '82 (VA) C.574 B.S.C. L.893 J.D.
Arndt, Melissa Dawn '73 '98 (WA) C.906 B.A. L.336 J.D.
Arner, Michael R. '35 '61 C&L.608 B.A., J.D.
Athy, Susan '56 '87 C&L.276 B.S., J.D.
Auclair, David B. '59 '84 (NH) C.550 B.A. L.1294 J.D.
Baker, George B. '49 '77 (MA) C.918 B.A. L.94 J.D.
Baker, Susan Thompson '50 '75 (VA) C.915 B.A. L.692 J.D.
Baker, Thomas F. '47 '73 (PA) C.229 B.A. L.665 J.D.
Baldwin, Janis E. '47 '79 C.802 B.A. L.744 J.D.
Baniewicz, Joseph P. '47 '78 C.602 B.S.E.E. L.64 J.D.
Barret, Edward R. '70 '95 (CA) C.103 A.B. L.813 J.D.
Barry, Julie A. '60 '86 C.427 B.A. L.352 J.D.
Barry, William Francis, IV '58 '86 C.1027 B.S. L.861 J.D.
Bass, Christopher Martin '70 '98 (VA) C.575 B.A. L.228 J.D.
Bass, Steven B. '55 '85 (TX) C.94 B.S.B.A. L.616 J.D.
Baughman, Beverly A. '53 '81 C.49 B.A. L.276 J.D.
Baumgarten, J. Peter '51 '80 C.101 B.A. L.285 J.D.
Beker, Harry '47 '75 (NJ) C.994 B.A. L.1292 J.D.
Belzer, Phyllis Magram '50 '75 (MD) C.367 B.A. L.446 J.D.
Bennett, Alice M. '54 '80 (MA) C.588 B.S. L.309 J.D.
Bergkuist, David F. '— '72 (MA) C.860 A.B. L.94 J.D.
Berkovsky, Robert A. '41 '64 (TX) C&L.846 LL.B.
Bernstein, Jamie G. '— '90 C.228 A.B. L.30 J.D.
Bird, Susie Kim '63 '89 (MD) C.383 B.S. L.276 J.D.
Bishop, Alfred C., Jr. '42 '70 C&L.893 B.A., LL.B.
Blaine, George J. '49 '74 C&L.831 B.A., J.D.
Blanchard, William E. '56 '81 (SC) C.140 B.S. L.790 J.D.
Blodgett, William L. '45 '75 C.967 B.A. L.192 J.D.
Bogdonoff, Glenn '52 '80 (CT) C.1192 B.S. L.1029 J.D.
Bogos, Nicholas G. '54 '82 (FL) C.1176 B.A. L.260 J.D.
Boland, Frank K. '47 '76 (TX) C.840 B.A. L.802 J.D.
Bomgardner, Sharon J. '62 '87 C.945 B.A. L.1017 J.D.
Boody, Eric E. '59 '88 C.101 B.S. L.228 J.D.
Bornholdt, Gary W. '67 '95 (NY) L.1019 J.D.
Bowden, George E., III '52 '86 (VA) C.893 B.A. L.1209 J.D.
Brackett, William D. '42 '67 (VA) C.378 B.S. L.945 J.D.
Bracknell, Rebecca Chesno '74 '98 (MD) C&L.446 B.A., J.D.
Bracuti, Guy A. '65 '94 (NJ) C.705 B.A. L.273 J.D.
Bradley, George H. '37 '72 (TN) C.469 A.B. L.838 J.D.
Bray, Patricia C. '— '83 (TX) C.843 B.B.A. L.796 J.D.
Brokaw, James L. '50 '75 (VA) C.893 B.A. L.902 J.D.
Brookens, Marilyn E. '48 '74 (IL) C.293 B.A. L.339 J.D.
Brower, Steve '51 '76 (TX) C.1268 B.A. L.326 J.D.
Brown, K. Scott '64 '98 C.446 B.S. L.64 J.D.
Brown, Roger M. '67 '92 C.105 B.A. L.904 J.D.
Brown, Stuart L. '50 '75 C.976 B.A. L.309 J.D.

Brumley, S. Ray '44 '69 C&L.896 B.A., J.D.
Bryan, Kerry H. '58 '98 (GA) C&L.16 B.A., J.D.
Burnett, Charles B. '55 '82 C&L.101 B.S., J.D.
Burns, Bobby D. '43 '67 (KY) C&L.421 B.A., J.D.
Butler, Deborah A. '50 '74 (MS) C.802 B.A. L.500 J.D.
Butler, Paul T. '69 '94 (MD) C.423 B.B.A. L.446 J.D.
Caden, Stephanie L. '68 '96 C.164 B.A. L.692 J.D.
Cadenas, Ricardo A. '53 '79 (FL) C.184 B.A. L.564 J.D.
Camillo, Lynne '62 '87 (CT) C.1030 B.A. L.823 J.D.
Camp, Bryan T. '60 '87 (VA) C.311 B.A. L.893 J.D.
Campbell, Carol A. '56 '87 (VA) C.893 B.A. L.945 J.D.
Campbell, Geoffrey M. '75 '01 C.861 B.S. L.823 J.D.
Carlisle, Debra L. '51 '81 C.999 B.Mus. L.564 J.D.
Carlisle, Richard L. '51 '79 (MA) C.454 B.A. L.818 J.D.
Carlton, Dale S. '50 '91 (TX) C.802 B.M.E. L.846 J.D.
Carter, Thomas E. '55 '85 (WA) C.906 B.A. L.285 J.D.
Casey, Jean M. '58 '85 (IL) C.436 B.S. L.424 J.D.
Casey, Ken C. '45 '79 C.276 B.A. L.273 J.D.
Casey, Robert M. '54 '86 (NY) C.4 B.A. L.982 J.D.
Cashman, Marie '54 '85 C.454 B.A. L.128 J.D.
Cassano, Daniel A. '57 '83 C.886 B.S. L.945 J.D.
Chandler, John W., Jr. '46 '80 (GA) C.273 B.B.A. L.999 J.D.
Chewning, Richard L. '48 '73 C.182 B.A. L.228 J.D.
Christman, Kenneth P., Jr. '51 '85 (CA) C.674 A.B. L.976 J.D.
Christopher, Charles B. '58 '85 C.299 A.B. L.94 J.D.
Chung, Ginny Y. '71 '97 (GA) C.914 B.A. L.245 J.D.
Chyr, Charlotte '66 '91 (CA) C.112 B.A. L.464 J.D.
Clark, Deborah Y. '52 '79 C.679 B.A. L.94 J.D.
Clark, Graham G. '53 '77 C.1086 B.A. L.896 J.D.
Clark, Joseph W. '47 '77 C&L.329 B.A., J.D.
Clary, Betty J. '45 '81 C&L.383 B.S., J.D.
Cleary, Stephen R. '51 '76 (NJ) C.728 B.A. L.1202 J.D.
Cleverdon, Edwin B. '62 '92 (AL) C.1091 B.A.
Click, David L. '56 '83 C.112 B.A. L.30 J.D.
Coburn, Daniel J. '64 '91 (WI) C.867 B.A. L.966 J.D.
Coe, Sara M. '51 '77 (MD) C.446 B.A. L.273 J.D.
Cohen, Edward S. '41 '67 (VA) C.692 B.A. L.893 LL.B.
Cohen, Judith Cavell '62 '87 C&L.188 A.B., J.D.
Cohen, Kenneth E. '57 '82 (MD) C&L.446 B.S., J.D.
Cohen, Sharon R. '64 '90 (MD) C.205 B.S. L.273 J.D.
Collins, Mary E. '69 '95 (PA) C.754 B.S. L.1202 J.D.
Collins, Raymond L. '44 '73 (IA) C.587 B.S. L.900 J.D.
Collinson, Dale S. '38 '63 (NY) C.976 A.B. L.178 LL.B.
Colson, Faith '56 '94 (NJ) C.198 B.A. L.1292 J.D.
Comeau, John J. '57 '82 C.339 B.S. L.209 J.D.
Conley, Joseph E. '60 '85 (TX) C.917 B.A. L.575 J.D.
Connelly, Kevin B. '55 '80 (VA) C.860 B.A. L.945 J.D.
Cooper, Carl M. '50 '81 (VA) C.945 B.A. L.692 J.D.
Coppersmith, William E. '46 '74 (MD) C&L.446 B.A., J.D.
Corbitt, James W., Jr. '43 '71 (VA) C.893 B.S. L.945 J.D.
Corn, Philip M. '36 '64 C.855 B.S. L.188 J.D.
Coss, Richard E. '46 '73 C&L.608 B.S., J.D.
Coulter, John M., Jr. '43 '68 C.228 A.B. L.276 J.D.
Coumaris, George Tom '49 '75 C.446 B.A. L.280 J.D.
Cox, Richard H. '39 '64 (OH) C.659 B.S.E. L.930 J.D.
Coyne, Michael J. '39 '72 (VA) C.1115 B.S. L.276 J.D.
Crawford, David L., Jr. '42 '67 C.276 B.S.B.A. L.273 LL.B.
Creswell, Lori L. '66 '91 (RI) C.94 B.S. L.818 J.D.
Crisalli, Donna M. '50 '76 (NJ) C&L.569 B.A., J.D.
Crowe, Billie L. '61 '87 (LA) C&L.425 B.B.A., J.D.
Culbertson, Teri A. '55 '80 (IL) C.338 B.S. L.209 J.D.
Culmer, Charles W. '52 '83 (MA) C.494 B.A. L.309 J.D.
Curtin, Mary Anne '47 '82 C.856 A.B. L.128 J.D.
Daly, Richard M. '48 '78 C.976 B.A. L.1066 J.D.
Daly, Vincent '47 '94 (MD) C.262 A.B. L.446 J.D.
Damazo, Herbert Lane '60 '87 (MD) C.234 B.S. L.94 J.D.
Danbury, Michael J. '32 '57 (NY) C.976 A.B. L.188 LL.B.
Dang, Trina L. '69 '96 (NY) C.112 B.A. L.569 J.D.
Danon, Albert E. '47 '74 (PA) C.645 B.A. L.831 J.D.
David, Thomas '57 '82 C.611 B.S. L.64 J.D.
Dean, Mary E. '— '78 C.454 B.A. L.818 J.D.
Delgado, Deborah Harvey '51 '84 (TX) C.691 B.A. L.846 J.D.
De Liee, Charles T. '44 '86 (VA) C.1145 B.B.A. L.128 J.D.
Delmar, Richard K. '52 '77 C.276 A.B. L.569 J.D.
Denick, Robin Williams '55 '80 C.506 B.A. L.1206 J.D.
Desilets, Robert A., Jr. '67 '92 C.896 B.A. L.64 J.D.
Devlin, Peter J. '48 '73 (NY) C&L.724 B.S., J.D.
Dillmann, Delores M. '61 '86 (ND) C.999 B.S. L.585 J.D.
Domike, Joan R. '26 '71 C.518 B.A. L.276 J.D.
Dorfman, Jeffrey '51 '77 (NY) C.608 B.A. L.910 J.D.
Douglas, Winston H. '48 '82 C.688 B.S. L.276 J.D.
Dowling, Patrick J. '47 '72 (IA) C.1182 B.A. L.188 J.D.
Dunn, Judith C. '56 '81 C.754 B.S. L.309 J.D.
Dusenberry, Blaise G. '60 '86 (MD) C.692 B.A. L.64 J.D.
Edwards, Elizabeth '42 '86 (PA) C.821 B.A. L.659 J.D.
Eggeman, James L. '56 '87 (OR) C.886 B.A. L.1209 J.D.
Ehrenberg, Robin J. '57 '88 (MD) C.1044 B.A. L.449 J.D.
Endick, Stuart W. '51 '77 (NY) C.994 B.A. L.569 J.D.
Erickson, Jeffrey A. '65 '91 (PA) C.1111 B.S. L.117 J.D.
Estrada, Arturo '49 '75 (FL) C.843 B.B.A. L.602 J.D.
Evans, Camille B. '62 '87 C.659 B.A. L.309 J.D.
Ewell, Candace B. '68 '00 C.999 L.574
Fahey, Douglas A. '50 '77 C.207 B.A. L.64 J.D.
Fanaroff, Carolyn D. '65 '94 (MD) C.1365 B.A. L.30 J.D.
Farahati, Britta '68 '94 C.93 B.A. L.64 J.D.
Fegan, David C. '44 '70 (MD) C.903 B.A. L.446 J.D.
Feinberg, Paul C. '54 '79 (TX) C&L.846 B.B.A., J.D.
Feldman, Jacob '40 '73 C.994 B.S. L.1009 J.D.
Feldstein, Merrill D. '65 '90 (NJ) C.1044 B.A. L.30 J.D.
Felker, Barbara Allen '55 '82 C.674 A.B. L.309 J.D.
Ferber, Rosamond S. '60 '87 (MD) C.298 B.A. L.446 J.D.
Ferguson, Robin M. '69 '93 (VA) C.378 B.S. L.1209 J.D.
Fernandez, Catherine Livingston '58 '84 (PA) C.821 B.A. L.665 J.D.
Fernandez, Lewis J. '51 '78 (PA) C.999 B.S. L.776 J.D.
Ferrara, Dennis M. '47 '73 C.861 B.A. L.420 J.D.
Fielding, Eliot D. '46 '74 (NY) C.415 B.S. L.1009 J.D.
Finer, Robert M. '52 '77 (GA) C&L.273 B.A., J.D.
Finkelstein, Barry J. '47 '74 (NY) C.1040 B.B.A. L.1009 J.D.
Finkenaur, Bridget E. '71 '96 (MA) C.1349 B.S. L.575 J.D.
Finley, Franklin L. '39 '83 C.759 B.S. L.1209 J.D.
Finley, Michael D. '41 '66 C&L.734 B.S., J.D.
Finlow, Leslie '58 '93 (MD) C.788 A.B. L.904 J.D.
Fischer, John M. '40 '64 (VA) C&L.477 A.B., J.D.
Fish, David L. '61 '86 C.150 B.A. L.608 J.D.
Fitzpatrick, Robert J. '63 '88 (NY) C.107 B.A. L.982 J.D.
Fitzsimmons, Megan R. '73 '99 C.893 B.A. L.276 J.D.
Fleeman, M. Grace '47 '85 C.25 B.S. L.273 J.D.
Fleming, Gerald B. '44 '77 C.623 B.S. L.276 J.D.
Foley, Sean F. '58 '90 C.477 B.S. L.276 J.D.
Foster, Perry T. '40 '65 (TX) C&L.846 B.A., J.D.
France, Renay '41 '79 (PA) C.329 B.S. L.229 J.D.
Francis, Paul A. '42 '74 C&L.93 A.B., J.D.
Frankel, Michael H. '39 '65 C&L.659 B.S.E., LL.B.
Friedman, Peter C. '58 '83 C.659 B.A. L.982 J.D.
Frisch, Jill A. '60 '84 (NY) C.228 A.B. L.800 J.D.
Fuller, Pamela Wilson '63 '88 (PA) C.831 B.A. L.665 J.D.
Fultz, Richard D. '53 '78 (FL) C&L.260 B.S., J.D.
Gabriel, Grant E. '59 '84 (OH) C&L.851 B.B.A., J.D.
Gabrysh, Celia A. '50 '75 C.215 B.A. L.221 J.D.
Galm, Sharon '43 '71 C.119 B.A. L.276 J.D.
Gardner, Lorraine E. '51 '90 C.1086 B.A. L.472 J.D.
Garlett, Philip L. '56 '82 (NY) C.367 B.A. L.569 J.D.
Geber, David M. '41 '65 (MD) C.831 B.S. L.276 J.D.
Gelman, Sheara L. '76 '00 C.446 B.A. L.770 J.D.
Gibbons, James C. '46 '76 C.112 B.A. L.190 J.D.
Gibbs, William D. '50 '76 C.309 B.A. L.893 J.D.
Giblen, Douglas L. '51 '75 C.197 A.B. L.178 J.D.
Gilbert, Craig R. '52 '77 C.473 B.S. L.1003 J.D.
Glyer, Grid Riggle '55 '81 C.385 B.A. L.930 J.D.
Gold, Carol D. '47 '72 C.228 B.A. L.94 J.D.
Goldman, Michael D. '44 '69 C.659 B.A. L.276 J.D.
Goldman, Michael J. '73 '99 (NY) C.696 B.A. L.724 J.D.
Goldman, Richard G. '52 '77 C.339 B.A. L.1292 J.D.
Goldstein, Allen '36 '63 C.563 B.B.A. L.1009 LL.B.
Goldstein, Richard Scott '65 '92 C.945 B.A. L.275 J.D.
Goldwyn, Brant S. '49 '78 C.966 B.A. L.128 J.D.
Gompertz, Michael L., Jr. '49 '75 C.976 B.A. L.94 J.D.
Gootzeit, Ronald M. '56 '82 C&L.339 B.S., J.D.
Gorlick, Warren R. '59 '86 C.1307 B.A. L.188 J.D.
Gray, Carolyn H. '64 '91 C&L.846 B.A., J.D.
Gray, Gary D. '54 '79 C.478 B.A. L.990 J.D.
Gray, Patricia L. '52 '84 (VA) C.276 A.B. L.945 J.D.
Gregg, William J. '58 '87 (CT) C.1044 B.S. L.262 J.D.
Grimm, Danielle M. '— '98 (NJ) C.999 B.A. L.107 J.D.
Grogan, Deborah Marie '63 '88 (CO) C.31 B.A. L.813 J.D.
Gross, Karin Goldsmith '52 '78 C.446 B.A. L.966 J.D.
Gross, Marlene '40 '65 C.659 A.B. L.178 LL.B.
Guiry, James M. '64 '92 (CT) C.188 B.A. L.982 J.D.
Gulas, A. M. '53 '88 (PA) C.665 B.A. L.229 J.D.
Hagen, Holly L. '65 '94 (PA) C.276 B.A. L.128 J.D.
Haglund, David R. '51 '80 C.628 B.S. L.990 J.D.
Hale, Nancy W. '— '83 (NC) C.1318 B.A. L.575 J.D.
Hall, Charles A., III '68 '93 C.446 B.S. L.64 J.D.
Hall, Sharon L. '54 '85 C&L.101 B.S., J.D.
Halley, Joyce J. Green '41 '80 (IA) C&L.221 B.M.E., J.D.
Halpern, Irwin '62 '87 C.1036 B.A. L.893 J.D.
Handleman, Paul F. '56 '83 C.1169 A.B. L.284 J.D.
Handler, Elizabeth A. '62 '87 C.494 B.A. L.910 J.D.
Haney, Phyllis D. '58 '89 (VA) C.893 B.A. L.838 J.D.
Hankin, Steven J. '49 '77 (WI) C&L.966 B.A., J.D.
Hanson, Robert B. '62 '95 (WA) C.205 B.S. L.446 J.D.
Hara, Michael E. '55 '80 (HI) C.312 B.A. L.276 J.D.
Harbourt, Clifford M. '47 '73 (PA) C.884 B.S.Econ. L.229 J.D.
Harrigal, Rebecca L. '— '88 C.665 B.S. L.276 J.D.
Harris, Mark D. '69 '94 (MA) C.696 B.A. L.982 J.D.
Harris, Rebecca D. '60 '87 (TN) C.806 B.A. L.838 J.D.
Harris, Terri L. '61 '90 (CA) C.990 B.S. L.1067 J.D.
Harvey, Bernard P., III '62 '90 (PA) C.446 B.S. L.128 J.D.
Hawkes, Robert T. '60 '86 (FL) C.309 A.B. L.188 J.D.
Heard, William A., III '53 '86 (MD) C.893 B.S. L.30 J.D.
Heinecke, Richard M. '64 '89 (IL) C.1093 B.S. L.801 J.D.
Helke, Joel E. '48 '74 C.958 B.S. L.190 J.D.
Helou, Alexandra K. '72 '99 (NY) C.893 B.A. L.904 J.D.
Herbert, Nancy B. '51 '78 (OH) C.473 B.A. L.150 J.D.
Herring, Thomas G. '56 '80 (CO) C.173 B.A. L.208 J.D.
Hines, J. Thomas '41 '74 C.813 B.A. L.273 J.D.
Hirschhorn, Roy A. '53 '82 (CT) C.30 B.S. L.1029 J.D.
Hodes, Rochelle '63 '89 C.30 B.S. L.904 J.D.
Hoffman, Burton S. '34 '63 (MD) C.64 B.S. L.1002 LL.B.
Hoffman, Marjorie '51 '81 C.118 B.A. L.705 J.D.
Hoffman, Ruth '45 '87 (NY) C.30 B.A. L.1048 J.D.
Hogan, James F. '51 '86 C.712 B.B.A. L.128 J.D.
Holmes, Jerry E. '41 '74 (MD) C.446 B.A. L.30 J.D.
Honigman, Robert G. '67 '92 C.893 B.A. L.94 J.D.
Hooe, Stephen D. '51 '76 C&L.893 B.A., J.D.
Horan, Gerald M. '47 '73 C.610 A.B. L.575 J.D.
Horn, Sharon Y. '59 '83 (PA) C.477 B.A. L.831 J.D.
Horton, Geoffrey C. '42 '73 C.893 B.A. L.30 J.D.
Hossofsky, Katherine A. '46 '71 C.1029 B.A. L.930 J.D.
Howard, Phillip J. '39 '67 (MD) C.446 B.S. L.64 LL.B.
Howe, Miriam A. '48 '78 (MD) C.699 B.A. L.861 J.D.
Howell, Laura '59 '85 C.800 B.A. L.94 J.D.
Howells, Horace White '68 '98 C.94 B.A. L.273 J.D.
Hu, Paula Ping '53 '78 C&L.608 B.A., J.D.
Huffman, John P. '48 '90 (MD) C.446 B.S.E.E. L.276 J.D.
Hughes, Teresa Burridge '51 '85 (VA) C.945 B.A. L.273 J.D.
Hunt, Sylvia Fortney '52 '81 C.893 B.S. L.245 J.D.
Hurwitz, Susan B. '53 '81 C.188 B.S. L.273 J.D.

TREASURY DEPARTMENT (Continued)

Hussey, William D.	'47 '73 C.705 B.A. L.178 J.D.
Hyche, Vicki J.	'63 '87 C&L.469 B.B.A., J.D.
Hyman, Mitchel S.	'58 '82 C.367 B.A. L.273 J.D.
Ingram, Sarah Hall	'57 '83 C.976 B.A. L.276 J.D.
Inhof, Diana April	'72 '97 (PA) C.509 B.S. L.665 J.D.
Inserra, Francis C.	'56 '83 C.319 B.A. L.1019 J.D.
Irving, Andrew M.	'48 '82 (MD) C.311 B.A. L.276 J.D.
Jackel, Monte A.	'51 '78 C.994 B.A. L.1019 J.D.
Jackson, William A.	'56 '83 (VA) C.893 B.A. L.1209 J.D.
Jacobs, Christie J.	'61 '90 C.881 A.B. L.128 J.D.
James, Deirdre A.	'66 '91 (MD) C.446 B.A. L.329 J.D.
Jannotta, Santina M.	'51 '81 (NJ) C.831 B.A. L.705 J.D.
Jennings, Mark S.	'48 '79 (CA) C.1060 B.A. L.464 J.D.
Johnson, George R.	'53 '83 (IL) C.1044 B.A. L.365 J.D.
Jones, Marshall R.	'53 '85 (GA) C.575 B.A. L.178 J.D.
Jordan, Jeff Steven	'63 '89 C.472 B.A. L.117 J.D.
Joseph, Warren M.	'49 '78 (MD) C.165 A.B. L.276 J.D.
Jurovіesky, Henry	'71 '96 (MD) C.102 B.S. L.659 J.D.
Juster, David A.	'53 '79 C.494 B.E.S. L.221 J.D.
Kaizen, Mark S.	'52 '78 (IL) C.705 B.A. L.365 J.D.
Kaminsky, Robert L.	'38 '64 (PA) C&L.659 B.S., LL.B.
Kanuk, Donald W.	'32 '63 (LA) C.861 B.A. L.425 J.D.
Karen, Daniel S.	'72 '98 (GA) C.1292 B.A. L.245 J.D.
Karzon, Elizabeth U.	'55 '85 C.813 B.A. L.569 J.D.
Kassell, Susan J.	'51 '78 C.264 B.A. L.884 J.D.
Kastl, Robert J.	'45 '78 (OH) C.608 B.A. L.117 J.D.
Katz, Beverly Moses	'63 '88 C.260 B.S. L.472 J.D.
Katz, Geraldine Foucault	'41 '78 (WV) C.672 B.S. L.923 J.D.
Keller, Christine L.	'68 '96 (NY) C.24 B.S. L.107 J.D.
Kelley, Christopher Thomas	'70 '94 (IL) C&L.339 B.S., J.D.
Kelley, George P.	'44 '74 C.321 B.A. L.93 J.D.
Kernaghan, Kathleen	'65 '90 (PA) C.728 B.A. L.831 J.D.
Khan, Naseem	'68 '93 (IL) C.424 B.A. L.221 J.D.
Kim, Douglas H.	'72 '99 (WI) C.276 B.S. L.128 J.D.
Kim, Nancy	'61 '89 (NY) C.188 B.A. L.262 J.D.
Kindell, Judith E.	'61 '88 C.36 B.S. L.178 J.D.
Kipnis, Bruce E.	'41 '67 (MD) C.575 B.S. L.30 J.D.
Kirwan, Patrick S.	'57 '82 (MD) C.445 B.S. L.446 J.D.
Kiss, A. Katharine Jacob	'52 '90 C.589 B.S. L.365 J.D.
Kissel, Benedetta A.	'51 '78 (NY) C.1044 B.A. L.602 J.D.
Klotz, Martin F.	'39 '72 (KY) C.63 B.S. L.421 J.D.
Knapp, Nancy Vozar	'58 '83 (IL) C.339 B.S. L.347 J.D.
Kocak, Richard A.	'46 '74 C.276 B.S. L.851 J.D.
Koch, Kimberly L.	'67 '96 (VA) C.1369 B.S. L.1209 J.D.
Kohn, Debra A.	'58 '84 C.228 B.A. L.800 J.D.
Kostak, William Michael	'64 '92 (VA) C.119 B.S. L.893 J.D.
Kosterlitz, David S.	'52 '78 C&L.629 B.A., J.D.
Kramer, John E.	'63 '89 (PA) C.197 A.B. L.107 J.D.
Kroening, Linda Marie	'56 '81 (WI) C.436 B.S. L.966 J.D.
Kugler, Paul F.	'46 '75 (NY) C.262 A.B. L.309 J.D.
Lambert-Dean, Deborah	'57 '86 (VA) C.244 B.A. L.893 J.D.
Landau, Barry S.	'52 '76 C&L.477 B.S., J.D.
Larson, Joni	'— '90 (MT) C&L.508 B.S., J.D.
Larson, Lori R.	'57 '88 (CO) C.273 B.A. L.128 J.D.
Laudeman, Robert A.	'69 '95 (PA) C.679 B.S.A.E. L.347 J.D.
Laufer, Janet A.	'60 '85 C.446 B.A. L.8 J.D.
Law, Roger P.	'48 '73 (CA) C.800 B.A. L.93 J.D.
Lekos, Konstantine	'59 '84 (RI) C.676 B.A. L.94 J.D.
Lesho, Karlene M.	'71 '97 (MD) C.1369 B.A. L.1209 J.D.
Levine, Alan C.	'45 '72 C.103 A.B. L.880 J.D.
Levine, Philip J.	'50 '75 (NY) C.156 B.A. L.107 J.D.
Levy, Charles M.	'39 '64 C.823 B.A. L.569 LL.B.
Lew, Pamela	'66 '95 (MD) C.112 B.A. L.1068 J.D.
Lewis, Harve M.	'— '77 C.30 B.A. L.128 J.D.
Lewis, MaryAnn A.	'47 '88 (NY) C.659 B.A. L.1009 J.D.
Lintz, Judith A.	'65 '92 (PA) C.602 B.A. L.201 J.D.
Liquerman, Melissa C.	'63 '90 L.978 J.D.
Lockwood, Charles D.	'58 '83 (FL) C.1111 B.S. L.260 J.D.
Logan, Ann H.	'48 '77 C.1142 B.A. L.802 J.D.
Lorence, Robert W., Jr.	'57 '85 (FL) C.966 B.S. L.285 J.D.
Lowrance, William B.	'45 '70 (MS) C.206 B.A. L.500 J.D.
Lucas, Patrick W.	'49 '80 (CA) C.763 B.A. L.1049 J.D.
Luong, Quan Kha	'— '97 (VA) C.893 B.A. L.1209 J.D.
Lyons, William T.	'42 '72 (MD) C.1057 B.S. L.276 J.D.
MacEachen, John D.	'50 '79 (OH) C.363 B.S. L.851 J.D.
Madden, Edward B., Jr.	'44 '73 C.208 B.S.B.A. L.846 J.D.
Madden, Erinn M.	'69 '94 (VA) C.893 B.A. L.763 LL.M.
Madigan, Elizabeth R.	'52 '83 (MD) C.112 B.A. L.30 J.D.
Manasevit, Patricia A.	'55 '91 (MD) C.401 B.A. L.904 J.D.
Marcus, Phyllis E.	'48 '75 C.911 B.S.B.A. L.161 J.D.
Margopulos, Theodore N.	'48 '73 (NJ) C.705 B.A. L.776 J.D.
Mark, Valerie A.	'57 '82 (MA) C.518 B.A. L.818 J.D.
Marks, Nancy J.	'— '81 (MA) C.1149 B.A. L.818 J.D.
Marshall, Linda S. F.	'61 '86 C.674 B.S.E. L.477 J.D.
Martin, Margaret Ann	'56 '84 (PA) C&L.945 B.A., J.D.
Martin, Robert A.	'69 '94 (MA) C.93 B.A. L.818 J.D.
Masnik, George L.	'48 '73 (NY) C.102 B.A. L.705 J.D.
Mattson, Cynthia J.	'46 '77 C.475 B.A. L.128 J.D.
McDonnell, David H.	'59 '85 C.273 B.A. L.178 J.D.
McGreevy, Cynthia Ann	'63 '88 (OH) C.608 B.S. L.8 J.D.
McGroarty, Patrick T.	'56 '83 (PA) C.728 B.S. L.831 J.D.
McLeod, Will E.	'44 '76 (MA) C.912 B.A. L.477 J.D.
McManus, Richard F.	'57 '83 (MA) C.321 B.A. L.128 J.D.
McQuillan, John F.	'46 '73 (MA) C.1200 B.A. L.588 J.D.
Meacham, Aimee K.	'71 '00 C.201 B.A. L.30 J.D.
Mellody, Katherine A.	'47 '85 C.452 B.A. L.276 J.D.
Melone, Michael E.	'61 '87 (CA) C.112 B.A. L.1068 J.D.
Mersereau, Lori M.	'63 '89 (CA) C.112 B.S. L.800 J.D.
Michael, Kenneth	'63 '96 C.174 B.A. L.208 J.D.
Michaels, Stanley	'37 '62 (VA) C.188 A.B. L.273 LL.B.
Michur, Adrian L.	'50 '79 (PA) C.645 B.A. L.884 J.D.
Mihelcic, Richard J.	'46 '73 (MD) C.645 B.S. L.276 J.D.
Miller, Robert A.	'43 '71 (WI) C.433 B.B.A. L.966 J.D.
Miller, Stephen M.	'32 '60 (OH) C.665 B.B.A. L.608 LL.B.
Millett, Joan L.	'64 '91 C&L.260 B.S., J.D.
Milnes-Vasquez, Marie C.	'63 '93 C.1109 B.A. L.309 J.D.
Mincey, Glenn E.	'67 '98 C.420 B.A. L.276 LL.M
Miosi, Dianna K.	'52 '79 (OH) C.161 B.B.A. L.1003 J.D.
Misner, Robert B.	'47 '72 (KS) C.221 B.A. L.378 J.D.
Mitchell, Jeffery G.	'68 '93 (TN) C.1064 B.S. L.838 J.D.
Moffitt, Thomas D., III	'54 '80 C.608 B.A. L.930 J.D.
Mombrun, Reginald	'63 '89 (FL) C.94 B.S. L.574 J.D.
Monahan, Charles J.	'36 '59 C.734 B.S. L.276 J.D.
Monica, Christopher T.	'68 '95 (NC) C.659 B.S. L.64 J.D.
Montemurro, Michael J.	'50 '76 C.262 B.A. L.1009 J.D.
Moran, John M.	'53 '79 (NJ) C.884 B.S. L.1292 J.D.
Moriarty, John P.	'57 '82 C.30 B.A. L.276 J.D.
Moriarty, Wahl	'60 '93 (NY) L.574 LL.M.
Morrissey, John	'66 '93 (PA) C.861 B.S.M. L.273 J.D.
Morton, Cynthia D.	'59 '87 (MD) C.893 B.A. L.273 J.D.
Mosley, Susan T.	'56 '87 (VA) C.976 B.A. L.1209 J.D.
Mucha, Donna L.	'67 '92 (MD) C.445 B.A. L.64 J.D.
Muchnikoff, Lee D.	'61 '90 C.1047 B.A. L.904 J.D.
Munroe, David D.	'53 '82 (AZ) C.264 A.B. L.902 J.D.
Musher, Steven A.	'54 '78 C.976 B.A. L.659 J.D.
Nachman, Carol P.	'43 '79 C.280 A.B. L.767 J.D.
Nash, Laura C.	'72 '97 (VA) C.57 B.A. L.221 J.D.
Neal, Linda	'53 '85 (VA) C.886 B.S. L.1209 J.D.
Needle, Martin E.	'64 '89 C.1365 B.A. L.273 J.D.
Nelson, Jeffrey M.	'49 '70 C.276 B.S. L.30 J.D.
Newsome, Helene R.	'63 '90 C.339 B.S. L.597 J.D.
Nixon, Michael A.	'50 '83 (GA) C.1059 B.A. L.280 J.D.
Nolan, Leo F., II	'50 '76 (CA) C.1109 B.A. L.800 J.D.
Novey, Michael S.	'44 '79 C&L.309 A.B., J.D.
Nuding, Jennifer L.	'67 '92 (IL) C&L.339 B.S., J.D.
O'Hara, Brendan Paul	'57 '88 (VA) C.475 B.A. L.896 J.D.
Oldak, Regina L.	'51 '82 C.788 B.A. L.276 J.D.
O'Leary, Colleen A.	'69 '94 (MD) C.705 B.A. L.276 J.D.
Oppenheimer, Mary E.	'42 '77 (CA) C.604 A.B. L.767 J.D.
Osborne, Martin L.	'62 '88 (WI) C.812 B.S. L.966 J.D.
Osborne, Richard L.	'44 '71 C.33 B.A. L.228 J.D.
Oseekey, Cheryl Lynn	'48 '83 (NY) C&L.107 B.S., J.D.
O'Shea, William P.	'53 '78 (MA) C.454 B.A. L.93 J.D.
Ouslander, Andrew	'60 '86 (NJ) C.1019 B.B.A. L.1009 J.D.
Owens, Margaret A.	'53 '79 (PA) C.728 B.A. L.831 J.D.
Palmer, Michele D.	'54 '78 (WI) C.999 B.A. L.329 J.D.
Palmerino, Kim A.	'47 '74 (MD) C.321 B.A. L.128 J.D.
Paris, Dominic A.	'49 '78 (PA) C.223 B.S. L.831 J.D.
Passales, Richard K.	'61 '91 (CT) C.30 B.S.B.A. L.823 J.D.
Patchell, Robert D.	'37 '67 C&L.37 B.A., LL.B.
Patton, Edward L.	'50 '79 C.382 B.S. L.910 J.D.
Paul, Norman A.	'48 '73 C.696 B.A. L.128 J.D.
Paup, Michael L.	'41 '69 (VA) C.178 B.A. L.893 LL.B.
Phillips, Linda Conway	'— '84 (VA) C.423 B.A. L.1209 J.D.
Pickett, D. Lyndell	'56 '83 (KY) C.383 B.B.A. L.421 J.D.
Pinsky, Ronald D.	'46 '75 C.966 B.B.A. L.273 J.D.
Pirfo, Oreste Russ	'51 '79 C.1019 B.A. L.276 J.D.
Pitzer, Robert M.	'48 '73 (MD) C.282 B.A. L.276 J.D.
Platt, Lynnette N. M.	'55 '89 C&L.999 B.A., LL.B.
Pleet, Eric L.	'43 '68 (MD) C.472 B.B.A. L.446 LL.B.
Plucinski, Inga C.	'— '95 C.945 B.A. L.893 J.D.
Pollard, Mark R.	'65 '91 (GA) C.1365 B.A. L.280 J.D.
Press, Cheryl E.	'59 '86 (MD) C.472 B.A. L.978 J.D.
Press, Lyle Bennett	'63 '88 (NJ) C.910 A.B. L.30 J.D.
Preston, Thomas M., Jr.	'49 '75 C&L.597 B.A., J.D.
Purcell, Elizabeth A.	'49 '75 C&L.276 B.S., J.D.
Putzi, Patrick	'34 '60 C.436 B.S. L.966 LL.B.
Quarrie, Karen A. Rennie	'69 '95 (NY) C.1019 B.B.A. L.982 J.D.
Quinn, James A.	'62 '89 (NY) C&L.107 B.A., J.D.
Raineri, Eugene, Jr.	'56 '82 (PA) C.1113 B.A. L.615 J.D.
Ramsey, Charles B.	'44 '74 C.893 B.Ch.E. L.420 J.D.
Rapaport, marnie	'51 '85 (MD) C.882 B.S. L.128 J.D.
Ratchford, Robert M.	'55 '81 (VA) C.888 B.S. L.425 J.D.
Rawlins, Elizabeth Dru	'58 '85 (TN) C.1081 B.S. L.880 J.D.
Reaman, Susan J. Pristo	'48 '74 C.215 B.A. L.365 J.D.
Reed, Kathleen	'53 '91 (NY) C.383 B.S. L.262 J.D.
Reilly, Peter K.	'55 '85 (OK) C.623 B.B.A. L.862 J.D.
Ricca, Bettie N.	'51 '77 C.228 B.A. L.245 J.D.
Richards, John B.	'66 '97 (IL) C.713 B.S. L.209 J.D.
Ricks, Jo Lynn L.	'59 '85 C&L.446 B.A., J.D.
Ricotta, John T.	'58 '84 (NY) C.696 B.A. L.107 J.D.
Roach, Michael J.	'41 '69 C&L.659 A.B., J.D.
Robb, James R.	'58 '90 (CO) C.172 B.S. L.208 J.D.
Robertson, Calder L., Jr.	'48 '74 (TX) C.846 B.A. L.228 J.D.
Romano, Nancy B.	'60 '86 C.401 B.A. L.564 J.D.
Rose, Nancy L.	'56 '80 C.1044 B.S. L.273 J.D.
Rose, Portia N. Toynes	'55 '90 (TX) C.326 B.A. L.325 J.D.
Rosenthal, Joseph M.	'51 '80 (VA) C&L.945 A.B., J.D.
Roth, Kristine A.	'51 '78 C&L.608 B.A., J.D.
Rotunno, Norma C.	'69 '96 (NJ) C.180 B.A. L.1019 J.D.
Roy, James R.	'45 '75 (CT) C.431 B.A. L.184 J.D.
Rutstein, Joel Scott	'61 '86 (IL) C.685 B.A. L.209 J.D.
Ryan, Walter M.	'54 '80 (VA) C.276 B.A. L.30 J.D.
Sabin, Marsha A.	'59 '85 (PA) C.273 B.A. L.61 J.D.
Sabin, William C., Jr.	'52 '79 C.602 B.A. L.446 J.D.
Sams, Lisa G.	'62 '89 C.197 A.B. L.228 J.D.
Samuel, Charles E.	'46 '74 (NC) C&L.574 B.S., J.D.
Samuels, Mayer R.	'75 '00 C&L.112 B.S., J.D.
Sapienza, John T., Jr.	'42 '70 C.659 B.A. L.273 J.D.
Schaffer, Martin L., III	'55 '89 (CA) C.602 B.A. L.945 J.D.
Schattner, Lawrence H.	'50 '76 C.228 A.B. L.446 J.D.
Schell, Rosemary	'— '92 (TX) C.586 B.B.A. L.846 J.D.
Schmit, Michael F.	'47 '74 (NY) C.116 A.B. L.107 J.D.
Schneider, David A.	'60 '86 C.1349 B.S. L.904 J.D.
Schneiderman, Henry S.	'56 '81 (NY) C.910 A.B. L.1292 J.D.
Schroeder, Delilah Seroussi	'63 '95 (MD) C.112 B.A. L.861 J.D.

Schuman, Raymond J. '34 '62 (FL) C.994 B.A. L.472 LL.B.
Schwartz, Carol A. '52 '83 (VA) C.30 B.S. L.1209 J.D.
Schwartz, Edward C. '57 '84 C.112 A.B. L.1065 J.D.
Schwartz, Julie C. '64 '89 C.94 B.A. L.273 J.D.
Schwartzman, Jerome M. '59 '88 (NY) C.999 B.A. L.978 J.D.
Schwimmer, Mark I. '51 '75 C&L.309 A.B., J.D.
Scott, Michelle A. '70 '95 (IA) C.340 B.A. L.221 J.D.
Scully, Martin, Jr. '52 '84 C.588 B.S. L.982 J.D.
Sebastian, Timothy P. '52 '80 (MD) C&L.446 B.S., J.D.
Sekula, Jerome D. '39 '65 (NY) C&L.107 B.A., J.D.
Seller, Allan B. '46 '74 C.895 B.S. L.724 J.D.
Serbes, Filiz A. '63 '88 C.276 B.S.F.S. L.188 J.D.
Shafor, Martha Jane '65 '90 (FL) C.1222 B.S. L.1187 J.D.
Shaheen, Michael E., Jr. '40 '68 (TN) C.976 B.A. L.880 LL.B.
Shapiro, Marc A. '60 '86 (WV) C.473 B.A. L.608 J.D.
Shatz, Eileen M. '62 '88 (NY) C.401 B.A. L.276 J.D.
Shelburne, Anne Pettus '51 '79 C.575 A.B. L.838 J.D.
Shelton, Lori Katrine '70 '98 (MD) C.705 B.A. L.904 J.D.
Shepard, Judith T. '40 '83 (MD) C.339 A.B. L.446 J.D.
Shepardson, Courtney L. '66 '99 (VA) C.999 B.A. L.1209 J.D. Chief Coun.
Shepherd, Neil D. '58 '84 C.112 B.A. L.1065 J.D.
Shiraishi, Jolene J. '— '98 (VA) C.629 B.A. L.273 J.D.
Shuman, Lisa Jane '56 '83 (MD) C.1365 B.A. L.446 J.D.
Silber, David Barry '58 '84 C&L.446 B.A., J.D.
Silva, Cristian P. '72 '98 (NY) C.1099 B.A. L.425 J.D.
Silver, Jonathan D. '55 '81 C.475 B.A. L.94 J.D.
Simonsen, Warren P. '49 '77 (IN) C&L.879 B.A., J.D.
Simpson, Kirsten L. '64 '90 (VA) C.867 B.A. L.904 J.D.
Sissman, Elissa M. '63 '88 C.1044 B.A. L.273 J.D.
Skelton, Jan '66 '92 (IL) C.788 A.B. L.365 J.D.
Smith, Mark S. '58 '85 (MA) C.1288 B.S. L.94 J.D.
Sobczak, Deanne M. '62 '90 (NY) C.188 B.S. L.904 J.D.
Solomon, Louis M. '40 '65 (MD) C&L.446 B.A., J.D.
Spatz, William V. '56 '82 (VA) C&L.893 B.A., J.D.
Speetjens, Amy L. '62 '87 C.676 B.A. L.128
Spielman, Stuart '51 '78 C.1019 B.A. L.966 J.D.
Squires, Donald M. '56 '81 C.1350 B.A. L.976 J.D.
Stabile, Maria Treglia '62 '90 (NY) C.262 B.S. L.1009 J.D.
Stanley, Keith E. '51 '81 C.475 B.S. L.477 J.D.
Starke, Richard C. L. '54 '80 (VA) C.301 B.A. L.893 J.D.
Stevens, Margo L. '55 '79 C.273 B.A. L.537 J.D.
Stewart, Brenda M. '51 '80 C.48 B.A. L.976 J.D.
Storm, Jennifer A. '66 '98 (MD) C.1036 B.A. L.276 J.D.
Strong, Eileen B. '62 '89 (NJ) C.886 B.A. L.1029 J.D.
Strum, Jonathan M. '67 '95 (NY) C.276 B.A. L.1068 J.D.
Subin, Russell P. '63 '89 C.999 B.B.A. L.564 J.D.
Suica, Donald M. '55 '79 (PA) C.1047 A.B. L.851 J.D.
Surabian, Vincent G. '44 '69 (MA) C.164 A.B. L.94 J.D.
Swann, Deborah '56 '86 (NY) C.999 B.F.A. L.978 J.D.
Swim, Michael A. '60 '85 C.893 B.A. L.326 J.D.
Tank, Suzanne K. '54 '80 (MN) C.297 B.A. L.494 J.D.
Tarrant, John F. '55 '80 (NJ) C.705 B.A. L.776 J.D.
Tate, Sarah E. '63 '89 (CT) C.518 A.B. L.188 J.D.
Tawshunsky, Alan N. '54 '85 C.680 B.A. L.276 J.D.
Tellier, Paul E. '53 '78 C.321 A.B. L.880 J.D.
Testoff, Robert Allen '58 '80 (NE) C.446 B.S. L.546 J.D.
Tewel, Eva B. '48 '77 C.588 B.A. L.569 J.D.
Thigpen, Bernita L. '61 '86 (IL) C.679 B.A. L.209 J.D.
Todd, Richard W. '41 '71 C.801 B.A. L.190 J.D.
Tolleris, John A. '52 '79 (NY) C.390 A.B. L.569 J.D.
Tomsic, Alan '56 '81 (CO) C&L.174 B.S., J.D.
Toomey, Stephen J. '58 '83 (MD) C.717 B.S. L.128 J.D.
Toor, Joyce Hendricks '62 '87 (RI) C.103 A.B. L.30 J.D.
Townsend, Brian C. '62 '89 C.443 B.S. L.64 J.D.
Travers, Thomas J. '57 '84 (AL) C.10 B.A. L.861 J.D.
Tretiak, Philip L. '59 '86 (NY) C.1044 B.S. L.1292 J.D.
Trevey, John L., Jr. '— '90 (VA) C.945 B.A. L.902 J.D.
Trice, Ashton P. '59 '85 C.896 B.A. L.945 J.D.
Tucker, Andrea S. '57 '83 (MD) C&L.446 B.A., J.D.
Turley, F. Andrew '55 '84 (MA) C.454 B.A. L.818 J.D.
Tyson, Charles C. '41 '71 (PA) C.757 B.A. L.665 J.D.
Urban, Joseph J. '45 '74 (PA) C.665 B.A. L.276 J.D.
Uze, Barton J. '46 '73 C&L.352 B.S., J.D.
Vanek-Bigelow, Helen '53 '96 (LA) C.797 B.A. L.502 J.D.
van Mullen, Cherish '73 '98 (LA) L.420 J.D.
Veninga, Ann '52 '79 (TX) C.685 B.A. L.846 J.D.
Vinnik, Jeffrey L. '53 '78 (MA) C.976 A.B. L.309 J.D.
Vohs, Cathy A. '57 '89 (NY) C.960 B.S. L.569 J.D.
Vukovich, Joseph M. '38 '67 (OH) C.980 B.S.B.A. L.1003 J.D.
Wade, Roger E. '62 '92 (OH) C.473 B.A. L.8 J.D.
Wahl, Julia L. '57 '84 (PA) C&L.229 B.S., J.D.
Walker, Barbara Burch '55 '88 (IA) C.232 B.S. L.352 J.D.
Walker, John C. '53 '85 C.836 B.A. L.276 J.D.
Walker, Robert A., Jr. '51 '86 C.1123 B.A. L.1194 J.D.
Wall, Judith M. '50 '76 (VA) C.205 B.A. L.945 J.D.
Walton, Deanna '69 '95 (IL) C.679 B.GA. L.347 J.D.
Wassel, Cheryl Rae '59 '85 (MD) C&L.446 B.A., J.D.
Watson, Susan B. '48 '76 (MD) C.19 B.A. L.64 J.D.
Weber, Rose Marie '51 '94 (MD) C.801 B.A. L.64 J.D.
Weberman, Bernard H. '49 '75 C.477 B.S. L.846 J.D.
Weggner, Stephen R. '68 '95 (OR) C.629 B.S. L.950 J.D.
Weinheimer, Russell E. '60 '86 C&L.101 B.A., J.D.
Weinstock, Ronald B. '50 '84 (NY) C.930 B.A. L.262 J.D.
Weissler, Robert C. '54 '82 C.976 B.A. L.1066 J.D.
Welch, Donna Joy '58 '85 (AR) C.112 B.A. L.45 J.D.
Westry, George E. '46 '96 C.1280 B.B.A. L.329 J.D.
Whedbee, Charles M. '38 '64 (NC) C&L.575 A.B., J.D.
Wheeler, Robert G. '45 '75 C.112 B.A. L.128 J.D.
White, David E. '58 '84 (GA) C.301 B.A. L.469 J.D.
Wiener, Howard A. '64 '89 C.94 B.S. L.904 J.D.
Wilder, Michael J. '62 '92 (PA) C.976 B.A. L.477 J.D.
Wiles, Daniel J. '49 '76 (MD) C.928 B.A. L.446 J.D.
Williams, Donald R. '43 '87 (TX) C&L.845 B.B.A., J.D.
Williams, Edward M. '61 '86 (GA) C.880 B.A. L.362 J.D.
Williams, Floyd L., III '46 '72 C.893 B.A. L.45 J.D.
Williams, Melinda Gaugler '70 '95 (VA) C.1369 B.A. L.64 J.D.
Williams, Robert B. '45 '71 (NY) C.228 A.B. L.893 J.D.
Williams, Robert E., Jr. '49 '74 (PA) C.423 B.A. L.64 J.D.
Williams, Rose L. '61 '87 (NE) C.960 B.S. L.546 J.D.
Wilson, Christopher J. '53 '81 (CT) C.1103 B.A. L.1209 J.D.
Wilson, Curtis G. '52 '77 (SD) C.56 B.A. L.793 J.D.
Wojay, Craig R. '52 '79 (MI) C.932 B.B.A. L.1187 J.D.
Wolf, Thomas J. '46 '72 C.910 B.A. L.502 J.D.
Woo, Maxine M. '66 '97 (MD) C.145 B.A. L.30 J.D.
Woo, Walter H. '46 '72 C&L.326 B.A., J.D.
Wood, Richard J. '51 '77 (CA) C.383 B.A. L.608 J.D.
Worden, Neil B. '57 '82 (KY) C.138 B.A. L.421 J.D.
Wright, George F. '43 '74 (PA) C.499 B.S. L.192 J.D.
Yanes, Marta '64 '97 (FL) C.1222 B.A. L.472 J.D.
Yates, Willard W. '51 '79 (PA) C.170 B.A. L.831 J.D.
Young, Donna M. '61 '86 C&L.276 A.B., J.D.
Zech, Felix J. '45 '74 (AZ) C&L.37 B.S., J.D.
Zelnik, Jonathan R. '— '95 (CA) C.164 A.B. L.426 J.D.
Zuba, Kathryn A. '56 '79 C.659 B.A. L.1017 J.D.

Architect, Robert J. '45 '71 C.24 B.A. L.1009 J.D.
Aronson, Robert H. '48 '74 (PA) C&L.831 B.A., J.D.
Bloom, Diane S. '62 '88 (PA) C.104 A.B. L.276 J.D.
Brambilla, Robert C. '52 '78 (VA) C.339 B.A. L.1209 J.D.
Breault, Pamela M. '61 '92 (MD) C.30 B.S.B.A. L.64 J.D.
Brockner, William L. '41 '74 C.1038 B.A. L.30 J.D.
Cantor, Kim A. '58 '82 (AZ) C.173 B.S. L.36 J.D.
Chappell, John Wesley '41 '89 (PA) C.999 B.A. L.329 J.D.
Chasin, Joseph '42 '66 C.569 B.S. L.1009 LL.B.
Crockett, David E., Jr. '47 '74 C.682 B.A. L.273 J.D.
Daume, David O. '48 '73 C.880 B.A. L.861 J.D.
Davis, Karen L. '— '76 C.518 B.A. L.831 J.D.
Devereaux, Anne O'Connell '59 '87 C.945 B.A. L.128 J.D.
Diersen, Kari Lynn '71 '00 C.569 B.F.A. L.276 J.D.
Ehrlich, Amanda A. '— '97 (CA) C.025 B.A. L.831 J.D.
Evans, Daniel S. '51 '79 C.475 B.A. L.276 J.D.
Field, Karen M. '58 '83 (VA) C.893 B.A. L.1209 J.D.
Gamerman, Berel R., (Mr.) '43 '71 C.454 B.A. L.93 J.D.
Gertner, Robert '49 '77 C.575 B.A. L.128 J.D.
Harper, Robert C., Jr. '49 '75 C&L.128 B.A., J.D.
Heben, Lawrence W. '48 '76 (PA) C.229 B.A. L.665 J.D.
Heck, Patrick G. '57 '82 (OH) C.30 B.S. L.851 J.D.
Kawecki, Lynn E. '47 '80 (VA) C.112 B.S. L.426 J.D.
Kuehnle, Roger '55 '84 (MO) C.999 B.S. L.502 J.D.
Liberty, John P. '32 '56 (MA) C.276 B.S. L.94 LL.B.
Linder, Steven J. '51 '77 (NY) C.659 B.A. L.569 J.D.
Logan, Charles E. '46 '73 C.824 B.A. L.273 J.D.
Luft, Edward David '43 '76 C&L.823 A.B., J.D.
Luperini, Joseph A. '29 '54 (MD) C.928 B.A. L.446 LL.B.
Masnik, Robert H. '45 '72 (NY) C.563 B.A. L.1009 J.D.
McWhorter, Terrance '61 '92 C.902 B.S.C. L.150 J.D.
Miller, Joel '42 '68 (WI) C&L.966 B.S., J.D.
Mosakowski, Linda E. '54 '86 (PA) C.1305 B.A. L.1338 J.D.
Nadler, Judith L. '55 '82 (IL) C.1044 B.A. L.910 J.D.
Nix, Jonnie M. '54 '93 (AR) C.314 B.A. L.273 J.D.
O'Donnell, Mark F. '57 '83 (MD) C.893 B.A. L.128 J.D.
Oxman, Bernard '31 '66 C.184 B.A. L.94 LL.B.
Palmer, Oliver S. '42 '84 C.905 B.S. L.446 J.D.
Reich, Albert '59 '86 C.1040 B.B.A. L.982 J.D.
Richardson, James D. '43 '83 (PA) C.259 B.A. L.260 J.D.
Rogers, John W. '60 '90 (NY) C.446 B.A. L.107 J.D.
Rotz, Jay H. '42 '70 C.645 B.S. L.276 J.D.
Rubin, Michael A. '46 '74 C&L.836 B.A., J.D.
Salins, Mary Josephine '56 '82 C.446 B.A. L.128 J.D.
Slayen, Gary '53 '82 (CA) C.112 B.S. L.809 J.D.
Som de Cerff, Johanna L. '56 '92 (MD) C.999 A.B. L.64 LL.M.
Swieca, John J. '43 '72 (NY) C&L.107 B.A., J.D.
Tawares, Lisa A. '68 '96 (MA) C.811 B.A. L.93 J.D.
Taylor, Susan M. '55 '83 (PA) C.423 B.A. L.831 J.D.
Thomas, Geoffrey C. '48 '74 C.103 A.B. L.976 J.D.
Thompson, Leah D. Embry '52 '86 (MD) C.30 B.A. L.273 J.D.
Volkman, Richard W. '46 '75 C.973 B.S. L.30 J.D.
Walsh, Robert M. '52 '78 C.602 B.A. L.128 J.D.
Watkins, Carlton A. '54 '83 (GA) C.999 B.B.A. L.128 J.D.
Welty, David W. '42 '68 (MN) C.429 B.A. L.494 J.D.
Wickersham, Richard J. '43 '70 (CA) C.112 B.S. L.1067 J.D.

Office of the Assistant Commissioner (Employee Plans & Exempt Organization)

Charnoff, Robert J. '44 '73 (MD) C.994 B.A. L.273 J.D.
Cohen, Leonard '29 '71 (GA) L.999 LL.B.
Donoghue, John F. '26 '55 C.128 A.B. L.273 LL.B.
Graham, John F. '49 '75 C.1113 B.A. L.128 J.D.
Griffin, John P. '54 '81 C.445 B.S. L.276 J.D.
Hallsten, Ronald C. '49 '74 (SC) C.324 B.A. L.790 J.D.
Howe, Mary Elizabeth '58 '83 (CA) C.768 B.S. L.770 J.D.
Kochis, William R. '36 '64 (CO) C.172 B.S. L.190 J.D.
Louden, John A. '47 '73 (TX) C.960 B.A. L.326 J.D.
Lynch, Alice Vinson '52 '84 (VA) C.383 B.A. L.1209 J.D.
Mackay, James R. '50 '77 (CA) C.1021 B.B.A. L.1137 J.D.
Michel, Elizabeth B. '56 '83 (VA) C.722 B.A. L.1209 J.D.
Miller, Thomas J. '50 '76 (MN) C.201 B.A. L.494 J.D.
Miller, William W., Jr. '35 '62 (GA) C&L.280 A.B., LL.B.
O'Neill, John F. '34 '62 C&L.128 A.B., LL.B.
Patton, John M. '47 '74 C&L.273 B.A., J.D.
Ruth, Susan D. '51 '76 C.30 B.A. L.669 J.D.
Wolf, Steven '41 '71 C&L.347 A.B., LL.B.
Wright, Richard M. '52 '81 (MD) C.64 B.S. L.128 J.D.

BUREAU OF THE PUBLIC DEBT

Adams, Dean A. '46 '73 (IL) C&L.339 B.S., J.D.
Dunlop, Robin Ellena '68 '98 C.94 B.S. L.262 J.D.
Dyson, Sandra '43 '70 C.347 B.A. L.1119 J.D.

TREASURY DEPARTMENT (Continued)

Eccard, Walter T. '46 '77 C.117 B.A. L.880 J.D.
Gronseth, Edward C. '52 '86 (VA) C.591 B.S. L.990 J.D.
Heye, John J. '22 '49 (SD) C.436 B.N.S. L.793 LL.B.
Hoffman, Brenda Lee '65 '93 (VA) C.966 B.A. L.1148 J.D.
Jackson, Jacqueline L. '50 '75 C.697 B.A. L.904 J.D.
Kalsy, Kavita '— '98 (MA) C&L.30 B.A., J.D.
Kelly, Joseph C. T. '72 '96 (MD) C.197 A.B. L.893 J.D.
Klimas, Susan '50 '81 (WV) C&L.923 B.A., J.D.
Kramer-Wilt, James L. '43 '77 (WV) C&L.923 B.S., J.D.
Martin, Lisa Yoke '55 '80 (WV) C&L.923 B.A., J.D.
Reese, Cynthia E. '50 '77 C.684 B.A. L.30 J.D.
Till, Gregory J. '66 '95 (IA) C.351 B.A. L.352 J.D.

U.S. CUSTOMS SERVICE

Office of the Chief Counsel

Brenner, Lou W., Jr. '65 '90 C&L.602 B.A., J.D.
Chen, Christopher '66 '91 (MD) C.112 A.B. L.597 J.D.
Clarke, Senoria K. '64 '92 C.378 B.A. L.188 J.D.
Cohen, Elana '67 '97 (MD) C.966 B.A. L.446 J.D.
Courey, Marc Bennett '72 '95 (GA) C&L.260 B.A., J.D.
Daly, Ellen '53 '79 C.436 B.A. L.602 J.D.
Daman, Willem A. '71 '95 (FL) C.472 B.A. L.260 J.D.
Dubelier, Kristin L. '66 '92 C.597 B.A. L.30 J.D.
Elam, Nancy L. '48 '74 (MA) C.66 B.A. L.588 J.D.
Hatcher, Drew W. '49 '76 (NY) C.951 B.A. L.893 J.D.
Humphries, Robert H. '59 '89 C&L.896 B.A., J.D.
Lehman, John E. '46 '75 C.31 B.A. L.477 J.D.
Martin, Allan L. '49 '79 (MD) C.446 B.A. L.64 J.D.
McClain, Ellen Y. '56 '82 C.228 B.A. L.1194 J.D.
McGinnies, William P. '61 '86 C.172 B.A. L.862 J.D.
McManus, Richard Karl '62 '87 (FL) C&L.472 B.B.A., J.D.
Rawlings, Dwayne S. '69 '97 C.103 A.B. L.276 J.D.
Rettinger, Arthur I. '48 '73 C&L.273 B.B.A., J.D.
Weddell, Laura J. '62 '87 (MO) C.788 B.A. L.910 J.D.

OFFICE OF REGULATIONS AND RULINGS

Amernick, Marvin M. '42 '66 (MD) C.446 L.64 LL.B.
Atwood, John F. '37 '66 C.309 A.B. L.94 LL.B.
Baiamonte, Josephine M. '65 '92 C.1036 B.A. L.208 J.D.
Baskin, Jeremy '53 '77 C.659 B.A. L.1017 J.D.
Bell, Sandra Gethers '54 '78 (SC) C.329 B.A. L.273 J.D.
Berger, Russell A. '51 '76 (VA) C.1048 B.A. L.692 J.D.
Black, John G. '47 '72 C.207 B.A. L.880 J.D.
Bohannon, Edward A. '50 '75 (AR) C.902 B.A. L.861 J.D.
Bornstein, Benjamin J. '55 '89 C.94 B.A. L.999 J.D.
Bratcher, Steven T. '60 '85 C.705 B.A. L.446 J.D.
Brenner, Monika Rice '66 '91 (VA) C.1369 B.B.A. L.1209 J.D.
Brown, Virginia L. '61 '86 C.352 B.A. L.273 J.D.
Burton, Larry L. '48 '78 C.1209 B.A. L.1162 J.D.
Cascardo, Robert J. '63 '91 (MI) C.912 B.A. L.213 J.D.
Castelli, Laurence E. '62 '90 (PA) C.867 B.A. L.30 J.D.
Castro, Herminio M. '66 '92 (PA) C&L.823 B.A., J.D.
Chapman, Kathleen '63 '88 C.608 B.A. L.117 J.D.
Clark, Craig T. '58 '88 (PA) C.63 B.A. L.347 J.D.
Cohen, Alan C. '50 '79 (MD) C.446 B.A. L.64 J.D.
Cole, Marjorie F. '70 '96 (NJ) C.886 B.A. L.945 J.D.
Conrad, William '53 '87 (MD) C.1044 B.S. L.1003 J.D.
Deutsch, Gregory G. '52 '87 (ND) C.629 B.S. L.585 J.D.
Dinerstein, Robert '59 '87 C.569 B.A. L.107 J.D.
Elkins, John E. '43 '68 (OH) C.381 B.A. L.607 J.D.
Feldman, Leonard P. '66 '92 C.1365 B.A. L.260 J.D.
Foote, Francis W. '45 '71 C.902 B.A. L.273 J.D.
Greene, Karen S. '58 '83 C.608 B.A. L.930 J.D.
Greitzer, Shirley T. '47 '76 C.331 B.A. L.669 J.D.
Grier, Georgina '59 '86 C.174 B.A. L.930 J.D.
Hamill, Gail J. '51 '84 (PA) C.838 B.S. L.276 J.D.
Harmon, Myles B. '53 '78 (MA) C.705 A.B. L.94 J.D.
Hollaway, Rebecca Ann '58 '86 (CO) C.172 B.A. L.744 J.D.
Howard, Joseph E. '53 '83 C.178 B.A. L.597 J.D.
Jennings, Sandra A. '66 '96 C.846 B.A. L.30 J.D.
Johnson, Janet L. '48 '78 (IL) C.597 B.S.J. L.209 J.D.
Karateew, Suzanne '63 '88 (NY) C&L.823 B.S., J.D.
Kennedy, Elena F. '58 '85 (MD) C.446 B.S. L.64 J.D.
King, Norman W. '29 '58 (MA) C&L.818 B.A., LL.B.
Kopitopoulos, Christina '70 '96 (NY) C.1349 B.A. L.790 J.D.
Kramer, Lee H. '29 '52 (MD) L.446 LL.B.
Laderberg, Jerry C. '38 '71 C.886 B.S. L.30 J.D.
Lynch, Peter T. '47 '76 C.276 A.B. L.904 J.D.
McCray, George F. '63 '92 C.94 B.S. L.1009 J.D.
McLoughlin, Mary Elizabeth '67 '92 (MD) C.423 B.A. L.209 J.D.
Minardi, Ann S. '58 '87 C.477 A.B. L.94 J.D.
O'Brien, Gerard J., Jr. '51 '78 C.276 B.A. L.128 J.D.
O'Rourk, Ieva Karklins '61 '86 (NM) C.289 A.B. L.930 J.D.
Plofker, Howard G. '62 '87 (MD) C.1044 B.A. L.904 J.D.
Rastelli, Michele Ann '63 '89 (CA) C.882 B.A. L.575 J.D.
Reese, Cynthia M. '60 '86 C.1111 B.A. L.30 J.D.
Ressin, Charles D. '42 '73 (MD) C.446 A.B. L.64 J.D.
Riley, Matthew '60 '89 (PA) C.31 B.A. L.1218 J.D.
Rimmer, D. R. '53 '80 (CA) C.1077 B.A. L.1095 J.D.
Rodbart, Lorrie R. '52 '78 C.882 B.A. L.276 J.D.
Romero, Richard Thomas '61 '96 (NY) C.178 B.A. L.978 J.D.
Rosoff, William G. '43 '69 C.659 A.B. L.705 J.D.
Ross, Laurie E. '62 '90 C.437 B.A. L.1209 J.D.
Rudich, Keith B. '61 '87 C.1044 B.A. L.30 J.D.
Schlissel, Burton L. '39 '66 (NY) C.102 B.A. L.724 LL.B.
Seal, James A. '44 '74 (MD) C.276 B.A. L.64 J.D.
Shurn, Anthony L. '61 '90 (PA) C.932 B.A. L.30 J.D.
Singer, Harold M. '52 '77 C.4 B.A. L.150 J.D.
Stermasi, Julie '63 '90 (PA) C.94 B.A. L.273 J.D.
Steuart, Charles R. '54 '90 C.054 B.Sc. L.1209 J.D.
Struzzieri, Michele S. '56 '86 (MD) C.950 B.S. L.273 J.D.
Stump, Joanne Roman '60 '86 (TX) C.645 B.A. L.796 J.D.
Suzuki, Shari '69 '94 C.446 B.A. L.1338 J.D.
Terranova, Susan S. '51 '77 (MA) C.93 B.A. L.1202 J.D.
Valentine, John L. '45 '76 C&L.285 B.A., J.D.
Vereb, Glen Edward '57 '84 (MD) C.390 B.A. L.64 J.D.
Ver Steeg, Kristen Kay '61 '89 C.323 A.B. L.221 J.D.
Vilders, Gregory R. '51 '85 C.347 B.A. L.208 J.D.
Walker, Craig A. '46 '72 (MD) C.1047 B.A. L.273 J.D.
Whalen, Jeffrey B. '57 '85 C.228 A.B. L.30 J.D.

UNITED STATES SECRET SERVICE

Cahill, Donna L. '58 '83 C.321 A.B. L.930 J.D.
DeLuca, Mary E. '69 '94 (VA) C.1356 B.A. L.30 J.D.
DiPippa, Kathy O'Brien '60 '85 (VA) C.128 B.A. L.945 J.D.
Dougherty, Thomas E. '54 '83 C.446 B.A. L.260 J.D.
Eckl, Lisa L. '71 '98 C.470 B.A. L.884 J.D.
Fain, Julie A. '65 '91 (OK) C.612 B.A. L.623 J.D.
Foley, Timothy M. '60 '85 (IL) C.424 B.S. L.209 J.D.
Hagen, Andrea D. '60 '85 (CA) C.101 B.A. L.273 J.D.
Kelleher, John J. '45 '73 (VA) C.951 B.A. L.893 J.D.
Murphy, Liza M. '68 '94 C.165 A.B. L.309 J.D.
Personette, Donald B. '55 '82 C&L.575 B.A., J.D.

UNITED STATES MINT

Adler, James L. '62 '91 (WI) C.966 B.A. L.436 J.D.
Ansher, Irwin '56 '82 C.446 B.S. L.425 J.D.
Gentry, Jean A. '55 '80 (SC) C.446 B.A. L.790 J.D.
Gubin, Kenneth B. '44 '68 C.994 B.A. L.446 J.D.
Mattleman, Gwen Hollis '55 '85 (NY) C.788 A.B. L.569 J.D.
Weinman, Greg M. '65 '91 C.150 B.S. L.851 J.D.

BUREAU OF ENGRAVING AND PRINTING

Battle, Michael A. '66 '92 (AR) C.1175 B.A. L.45 J.D.
Kinsey, Carrol H., Jr. '54 '79 C.893 B.A. L.945 J.D.
Mullaney, Diane P. '44 '90 (KY) C.1299 B.S. L.383 J.D.
Portman, Michelle E. '67 '92 (PA) C.861 B.A. L.831 J.D.
Washington, Nichole L. Jenkins '62 '88 (PA) C.846 B.A. L.329 J.D.
Wilson, Suzanne L. '45 '80 C.6 B.A. L.329 J.D.

FEDERAL LAW ENFORCEMENT TRAINING CENTER

Bodolay, Stephen M. '44 '77 C.112 B.A. L.426 J.D.
Brunjes, David H. '51 '80 (KS) C.152 B.A. L.900 J.D.
Nutt, Kimberly '65 '90 (GA) C.1365 B.A. L.469 J.D.
Rowell, Gary L. '50 '80 (MS) C.206 B.S. L.500 J.D.

FINANCIAL MANAGEMENT SERVICE

Curran, Paul M. '53 '78 (PA) C.831 B.A. L.107 J.D.
Diana, Natalie H. '61 '87 C.197 A.B. L.569 J.D.
Falanga, Ingrid D. '46 '85 (MD) C.208 B.A. L.276 J.D.
Ingold, David A. '50 '75 (VA) C.205 B.A. L.790 J.D.
Ipema, Bradley J. '65 '91 (IL) C.114 B.A. L.209 J.D.
James, Janet A. '69 '94 (MA) C.645 B.S. L.93 J.D.
Kent, Ronda L. '59 '83 (CT) C&L.184 B.A., J.D.
Kramer, Beth A. '59 '86 (TX) C.859 B.A. L.845 J.D.
Lewis, Randall M. '62 '92 (TX) C.839 B.B.A. L.846 J.D.
Long, Tricia J. '66 '93 C.597 B.S. L.1065 J.D.
Mazella, Daniel J. '60 '89 (VA) C.1369 B.A. L.896 J.D.
Middlebrook, Stephen T. '63 '93 C.910 B.A. L.273 J.D.
Neubauer, Ellen M. '— '80 (MA) C.164 B.A. L.1202 J.D.
Regan, James J. '58 '92 (PA) C.831 B.A. L.629 J.D.
Seldin, Marc I. '65 '91 (NY) C.222 B.A. L.30 J.D.
Talley, Carolyn D. '59 '88 C.788 B.A. L.276 J.D.

DEPARTMENTAL OFFICES

Arkin, Steven D. '57 '82 C.228 B.A. L.813 J.D.
Askey, Elizabeth P. '65 '90 (PA) C.104 A.B. L.309 J.D.
Belanger, Terri A. '68 '95 (MD) C.367 B.A. L.273 J.D.
Bishop, Toby Frances '44 '93 (VA) C.331 B.A. L.1209 J.D.
Bridges, Donald, Jr. '56 '85 (PA) C.276 B.S.F.S. L.30 J.D.
Brown, Patricia A. '62 '88 (NY) C.276 B.S.F.S. L.1066 J.D.
Brown, Patrick J. '68 '96 (NY) C.893 B.S. L.276 J.D.
Brown, Susan D. '61 '87 (NY) C.569 B.A. L.309 J.D.
Burns, Doreen Emily '54 '95 (MD) C.679 B.S. L.1209 J.D.
Caballero, Michael J. '69 '95 (NY) C.602 B.S. L.276 J.D.
Clark, Larry A. '48 '74 (KS) C&L.378 B.A., J.D.
Connolly, John F. '50 '78 C.276 B.S.F.S. L.30 J.D.
Correa, A. Carlos '51 '78 C.276 B.A. L.560 J.D.
Corwin, Manal S. '64 '93 (MA) C.309 A.B. L.94 J.D.
Ellison, Elton A. '50 '77 (OK) C.612 B.S. L.623 J.D.
Epstein, Louise K. '60 '85 C&L.309 A.B., J.D.
Fisher, P. Ann '44 '80 C.112 B.A. L.276 J.D.
Folsom, George A. '55 '82 C.30 B.A. L.790 J.D.
Gillers, William H. '49 '73 C.569 B.A. L.904 J.D.
Golumbic, Court Edward '64 '91 C.880 B.A. L.893 J.D.
Hanson, Robert P. '60 '89 C.347 B.S. L.477 J.D.
Hoffenberg, Mark R. '67 '92 C&L.309 A.B., J.D.
Kerner, Francine J. '— '74 C.994 B.A. L.569 J.D.
Kilcoyne, John A. '34 '60 C&L.276 A.B., J.D.
Kirsch, Michael S. '62 '88 (CA) C.188 A.B. L.309 J.D.
Knopf, Kevin Paul '60 '85 C&L.352 B.S., J.D.
Lubick, Donald C. '26 '50 C.107 B.A. L.309 J.D.
Ludwig, Eugene A. '46 '73 C.311 B.A. L.976 J.D.
Lund, Allan I. '45 '77 C.860 A.B. L.659 J.D.
Marci, Joan-Ellen '48 '77 (MA) C.273 B.A. L.818 J.D.
McBrien, John R. '44 '69 (MO) C.801 B.A. L.734 J.D.
McHale, Stephen J. '55 '80 C.999 B.A. L.30 J.D.
McKenney, William P. '62 '91 (PA) C.896 B.A. L.904 J.D.
Mikrut, Joseph M. '57 '82 (IL) C.339 B.S. L.209 J.D.
Mundaca, Michael F. '63 '92 (NJ) C.178 B.A. L.1066 J.D.
Newcomb, R. Richard '46 '73 C.385 A.B. L.930 J.D.
O'Connell, Dennis M. '41 '70 C.966 B.S. L.188 J.D.
Parcell, John H. '48 '75 C&L.276 B.S.F.S., J.D.
Pfalzgraf, Amy '66 '93 (IA) C&L.352 B.A., J.D.
Pinter, Steven I. '38 '70 C.1244 B.A. L.276 LL.B.

Roth, John T.	'41 '67 C&L.945 A.B., B.C.L.
Santora, Hugo G.	'41 '69 (MD) C&L.446 B.S., J.D.
Scott, Betsy Sue	'51 '76 C.299 B.A. L.192 J.D.
Sowell, James B.	'64 '90 (FL) C&L.260 B.S.B.A., J.D.
Stark, Theresa A.	'57 '86 (NY) C.881 A.B. L.128 J.D.
Strobel, Richard H.	'43 '79 (MD) C.645 B.A. L.446 J.D.
Talisman, Jonathan	'59 '84 C&L.893 B.S., J.D.
Tick, Alan L.	'51 '77 C&L.823 B.A., J.D.
West, Philip R.	'58 '85 C.1044 B.S. L.564 J.D.
Witzgall, Elizabeth B.	'38 '62 C.289 A.B. L.178 LL.B.

DEPARTMENT OF VETERANS AFFAIRS

(Vacant), *General Counsel*

OFFICE OF THE GENERAL COUNSEL

Adams, James E.	'43 '71 C.262 A.B. L.665 J.D.
Adelman, Martie S.	'56 '81 C.910 B.A. L.273 J.D.
Anderson, Jeanne A.	'56 '85 C.939 B.A. L.904 J.D.
Anderson, Phillipa L.	'51 '76 (SC) C.298 B.A. L.537 J.D.
Arpon, Lavinia E.	'74 '99 (MD) C&L.446 B.A., J.D.
Barrans, David J.	'66 '92 C.800 B.A. L.188 J.D.
Bell, Mary Therese	'49 '74 C.860 B.A. L.1294 J.D.
Bergquist, Stephen A.	'43 '68 (MA) C.674 A.B. L.178 J.D.
Bradshaw, Edward D., Jr.	'49 '74 (VA) C&L.893 B.A., J.D.
Brizzi, Francis J., Jr.	'54 '81 (VA) C.923 B.S. L.1209 J.D.
Broyles, Robert E.	'38 '68 (MD) L.64 J.D.
Butler, Michael P.	'57 '89 C.569 B.A. L.861 J.D.
Campbell, R. Randall	'55 '82 C.610 B.G.S. L.902 J.D.
Cassidy, Edward V., Jr.	'49 '75 (NY) C&L.724 B.S., J.D.
Centanni, Amy E.	'69 '95 (PA) C.94 B.A. L.1252 J.D.
Clegg, Karen W.	'52 '79 C.914 B.A. L.569 J.D.
Cohn, Henry A.	'47 '73 C.932 B.A. L.597 J.D.
Conway, Frederic L., III	'47 '72 (MA) C.454 B.A. L.273 J.D.
Cybulski, Joan W.	'54 '79 C&L.1019 B.A., J.D.
Dangoia, W. James	'44 '81 (VA) C.561 B.S. L.1209 J.D.
Davis, Ralph G.	'51 '79 C.154 B.A. L.770 J.D.
Donawick, Peter M.	'48 '76 (AZ) C&L.36 B.S., J.D.
Flynn, Mary Ann	'60 '85 C.385 B.A. L.896 J.D.
Foley, Dennis M.	'63 '88 (MD) C&L.128 B.A., J.D.
Galla, Karen P.	'60 '88 (PA) C&L.665 B.S., J.D.
Gallin, Dean E.	'46 '75 (MD) C.823 A.B. L.30 J.D.
Garvin, Ron H.	'41 '66 C.170 B.A. L.1017 J.D.
Gessel, Thomas O.	'44 '70 C.243 B.A. L.734 J.D.
Grabelle, Paul M.	'47 '71 (NJ) C.705 B.A. L.273 J.D.
Gurland, Jonathan I.	'62 '88 C.1365 B.A. L.861 J.D.
Halstead, Roland W., Jr.	'47 '74 C.1163 B.A. L.1065 J.D.
Heaphy, Kathleen A.	'61 '86 (NM) C&L.560 B.A., J.D.
Hipolit, Richard J.	'52 '78 (NY) C.696 B.A. L.273 J.D.
Howe, Carl E., Jr.	'46 '71 C.790 A.B. L.145 J.D.
Johnson, Lorraine M.	'51 '78 (MI) C.1044 B.A. L.823 J.D.
Johnston, Sharon M.	'49 '91 C.107 B.A. L.276 J.D.
Joyner, Jane Clare	'59 '87 (MN) C.56 B.A. L.1035 J.D.
Katina, Michele Russell	'54 '83 (FL) C.260 B.S. L.362 J.D.
Kauffman, Philip S.	'52 '77 (PA) C.659 B.A. L.446 J.D.
Klein, John W.	'42 '68 (IA) C&L.352 B.A., J.D.
LaMoure, Patrick J.	'63 '88 (OK) C.903 B.A. L.615 J.D.
Lem, Howard C.	'50 '75 (PA) C.319 B.A. L.94 J.D.
Leonard, Michael A.	'47 '75 (PA) C.112 B.A. L.831 J.D.
Llewellyn, Adam K.	'44 '74 (FL) C.871 B.S. L.472 J.D.
MacKenzie, Kenneth B.	'40 '73 C.871 B.S. L.813 J.D.
Malamud, Leonard J.	'41 '68 C&L.273 A.B., J.D.
McDonough, Mark T.	'51 '81 C.563 B.A. L.1003 J.D.
McKeever, Thomas J., Jr.	'49 '74 (PA) C.728 A.B. L.884 J.D.
McKinney, Timothy J., Jr.	'46 '75 (WA) C.908 B.A. L.285 J.D.
McLaughlin, Thomas A.	'42 '70 (PA) C&L.229 B.A., J.D.
Moriarty, Joan E.	'— '85 (MA) C.518 B.A. L.1048 J.D.
Mullen, Andrew J.	'47 '73 (PA) C.24 B.A. L.94 J.D.
Nazarov, Ari	'71 '97 (CT) C&L.184 B.S., J.D.
O'Connor, Gary E.	'64 '92 (MN) C.429 B.A. L.494 J.D.
Parlow, Dianne N.	'38 '82 C.184 B.S. L.64 J.D.
Pokornicky, Edward J.	'43 '74 C.820 A.B. L.904 J.D.
Prudhomme, Angela M.	'59 '87 (VA) C&L.276 B.A., J.D.
Ptacek, Susan J.	'49 '74 (IL) C.352 B.A. L.597 J.D.
Ragan, Richard Scott	'71 '98 (FL) C.484 B.A. L.362 J.D.
Raun, Eric L.	'54 '81 C.276 B.S.F.S. L.659 J.D.
Richman, Neil S.	'47 '72 (MA) C.550 B.A. L.93 J.D.
Robinson, Richard R.	'47 '77 C.878 B.S. L.284 J.D.
Rogalski, Marilyn Komosa	'65 '90 (IL) C.209 B.A. L.904 J.D.
Sendek, Martin J.	'60 '85 (PA) C.665 B.S. L.1338 J.D.
Shea, Barbara B.	'45 '80 (VA) C.890 B.A. L.1209 J.D.
Sideris, Nicole J.	'62 '87 C.289 B.A. L.893 J.D.
Simmons, Michael R.	'42 '75 (MD) C.446 B.A. L.64 J.D.
Sims, Jacqueline M.	'60 '87 (PA) C&L.329 B.A., J.D.
Smalls, Michael R.	'63 '89 C.329 B.A. L.107 J.D.
Smith, Royce E.	'44 '78 (IA) C.329 B.A. L.352 J.D.
Tapp, Barry M.	'48 '75 C&L.329 B.A., J.D.
Tayman, Barry D.	'43 '71 (MD) C&L.64 LL.B.
Thompson, John H.	'48 '73 (IA) C&L.352 B.A., J.D.
Timinski, Michael J.	'55 '82 C.207 B.S. L.188 J.D.
Trujillo, Patricia	'52 '94 (MD) C.999 B.S.N. L.64 J.D.
Washington, Carolyn F.	'54 '79 (TX) C.355 B.A. L.325 J.D.
Willett, Lisa A.	'69 '93 C.30 B.A. L.930 J.D.
Wuchinich, Susan A.	'48 '88 (PA) C.178 B.A. L.831 J.D.
Zeglin, Donald E.	'47 '74 C.229 B.A. L.665 J.D.

VA REGIONAL COUNSEL OFFICE, WASHINGTON, D.C.

Bolasny, Sheldon I.	'44 '72 C.446 B.S. L.329 J.D.
Hutter, Paul J.	'54 '82 (CA) C.691 B.A. L.770 J.D.
McCallum, Deborah K.	'50 '90 (MD) C.446 B.S. L.64 J.D.
Shaub, Walter M., Jr.	'71 '96 (VA) C.1369 B.A. L.30 J.D.
Thomson, Paul G.	'47 '73 (NY) C.598 B.A. L.569 J.D.

BOARD OF CONTRACT APPEALS

Anders, Dan R.	'33 '58 (MS) C.484 B.S. L.500 J.D.
Krempasky, Richard W.	'48 '73 (MD) C.945 B.A. L.446 J.D.
McMichael, Guy H., III	'39 '67 C.309 A.B. L.477 J.D.
Pullara, Morris, Jr.	'43 '72 C&L.260 B.S.M.E., J.D.
Robinson, James Kenneth	'37 '68 (MD) C&L.446 A.B., J.D.
Sheridan, Patricia J.	'53 '80 C.1303 B.A. L.823 J.D.
Thomas, William E., Jr.	'43 '68 C&L.692 B.S., J.D.

OFFICE OF MANAGEMENT

Arisumi, Steven K.	'— '80 (MD) C&L.446 B.S., J.D.
Eastberg, Kathleen	'56 '94 (MD) C.446 B.A. L.64 J.D.
Krump, Gary J.	'46 '71 C.579 B.A. L.494 J.D.
Mulhern, Peter T.	'47 '78 C&L.128 B.A., J.D.

VETERANS HEALTH ADMINISTRATION

Kelley, Thomas P.	'41 '83 (GA) C.446 B.A. L.1234 J.D.
Maurer, Alan T.	'44 '81 (VA) C.492 B.A. L.273 J.D.

OFFICE OF HUMAN RESOURCES MANAGEMENT

Jacobs, Norman E.	'38 '67 (FL) C&L.823 B.S., LL.B.
Oliver-Simon, Gloria C.	'47 '91 C.446 B.S. L.30 J.D.

BOARD OF VETERANS APPEALS

Aguayo-Pereles, Joaquin	'49 '78 C.1088 B.B.A. L.128 J.D.
Ahlberg, John A.	'66 '91 (PA) C.645 B.A. L.823 J.D.
Allen, Christopher R.	'— '96 (ME) C&L.604 B.A., J.D.
Allen, Keith W.	'66 '92 (NC) C.329 B.S.M.E. L.575 J.D.
Bakke, Lila J.	'63 '96 (WI) C.959 M.A. L.966 J.D.
Berg, William W.	'48 '74 (WI) C&L.966 B.A., J.D.
Betourney, Andrew E.	'67 '95 (MD) C.164 B.A. L.273 J.D.
Blasingame, Jack W.	'26 '70 (MS) C.500 B.A. L.356 LL.B.
Bloomgren, Brynn K.	'63 '91 (CT) C.999 B.F.A. L.1029 J.D.
Bohan, Barry F.	'47 '72 (NY) C.276 A.B. L.966 J.D.
Booher, Alice A.	'41 '66 (IN) C.108 A.B. L.345 J.D.
Bosch, Ronald R.	'44 '73 (NJ) C.776 B.A. L.564 J.D.
Bradican, Michael F.	'64 '95 (AZ) C.754 B.S. L.623 J.D.
Braeuer, Wayne M.	'47 '76 (NJ) C.745 B.A. L.678 J.D.
Brogdon, Siobhan S.	'53 '83 C.33 B.A. L.790 J.D.
Brown, Derek R.	'58 '83 (PA) C.901 B.A. L.161 J.D.
Bruu, Christen Culligan	'67 '93 (NY) C.107 B.A. L.982 J.D.
Catino, Theresa M.	'66 '91 C.264 B.A. L.1017 J.D.
Chamberlain, Richard V.	'40 '72 (MA) C.28 B.S. L.184 J.D.
Chestnutt, Mark D.	'66 '91 (VA) C.945 B.A. L.893 J.D.
Chiappetta, Dennis F., Jr.	'68 '94 C.884 B.A. L.823 J.D.
Christian, Frank L.	'39 '69 (SC) C&L.790 A.B., J.D.
Clarkson, John M., III	'56 '88 (TX) C.575 B.A. L.893 J.D.
Clementi, Vito A.	'54 '82 (LA) C.420 B.A. L.425 J.D.
Cohn, Steven L.	'47 '73 (PA) C.81 B.A. L.665 J.D.
Connolly, Jacqueline O.	'66 '91 (MD) C.884 B.A. L.128 J.D.
Costello, Patrick J.	'57 '86 (IA) C.347 B.A. L.1288 J.D.
Crowley, Christine Runte	'70 '97 (MD) C.963 B.S. L.180 J.D.
Crowley, John J.	'65 '90 C.454 B.A. L.818 J.D.
Dannaher, Thomas J.	'51 '76 (CT) C.1030 A.B. L.809 J.D.
Dean, Dennis P.	'46 '74 C.446 B.A. L.276 J.D.
DoMinh, Bernard T.	'65 '92 (PA) C.1044 B.A. L.982 J.D.
Douglas, Thomas L., Jr.	'60 '92 C.16 B.S. L.192 J.D.
Dunne, Martin F.	'45 '75 C.749 A.B. L.564 J.D.
Dunphy, James J.	'53 '83 (VA) C.870 B.S. L.128 J.D.
Durkin, Shane A.	'54 '79 C.276 B.S.B.A. L.1206 J.D.
Ehrman, Kurt G.	'62 '89 (PA) C.347 B.S. L.665 J.D.
Ethridge, Lisa S.	'63 '94 (CT) C.184 B.A. L.1252 J.D.
Fabian, Nancy W.	'51 '91 (KS) C.63 B.S. L.378 J.D.
Ferner, Raymond F.	'54 '83 (MD) C&L.446 B.A., J.D.
Flatley, Catherine M.	'62 '87 (RI) C.93 A.B. L.128 J.D.
Flowers, Frank J.	'49 '80 (PA) C.974 B.A. L.329 J.D.
Foss, Richard T.	'67 '94 (ME) C.164 B.A. L.1294 J.D.
Gallagher, Bernard P.	'40 '72 (PA) C.397 B.A. L.831 J.D.
Gallagher, Elizabeth	'53 '82 C.228 B.A. L.245 J.D.
Gallagher, Mary	'54 '79 (NC) C.577 B.A. L.228 J.D.
Gervasio, Joseph P., Jr.	'54 '80 (VA) C.262 B.S. L.1209 J.D.
Gick, Gary L.	'44 '79 (OR) C.999 B.A. L.1051 J.D.
Gough, Jerome F.	'47 '72 (VA) C.886 B.A. L.692 J.D.
Graham, Mary Caryn	'67 '93 (VA) C.893 B.A. L.1294 J.D.
Greenstreet, Mark W.	'56 '82 (VA) C.1090 B.A. L.692 J.D.
Guido, George Emil, Jr.	'47 '82 (VA) C.767 B.A. L.692 J.D.
Hackett, William E.	'46 '86 C&L.446 B.A., J.D.
Harner, Heather J.	'67 '93 (PA) C.25 B.A. L.665 J.D.
Harrigan, Terence D.	'43 '72 (TN) C&L.838 B.S., J.D.
Harrison, Kimberly E.	'67 '93 (VA) C.64 B.A. L.896 J.D.
Harryman, William R., Jr.	'47 '89 (VA) C.686 B.S. L.945 J.D.
Havelka, David P.	'65 '94 (CT) C.273 B.A. L.1252 J.D.
Hayden, C. Donald	'40 '72 (NY) C&L.446 B.S., J.D.
Hindin, Mark D.	'55 '81 (VA) C.893 B.A. L.665 J.D.
Hogeboom, Charles E.	'47 '76 (IA) C.513 B.A. L.532 J.D.
Holincheck, Michael A.	'53 '93 (VA) C.872 B.S. L.1356 J.D.
Horrigan, Joseph M.	'47 '77 (MA) C.610 B.A. L.93 J.D.
Howell, Linda A.	'57 '91 C.923 B.S.N. L.30 J.D.
Hutcheson, John T.	'62 '88 (VA) C.945 A.B. L.420 J.D.
Hyman, Bruce E.	'42 '66 (TX) C.472 B.A. L.69 J.D.
Jackson, Adrian D.	'— '90 (LA) C.846 B.S. L.803 J.D.
Janec, Susan J.	'65 '94 C.276 B.A. L.1356 J.D.
Jefferson, William J., III	'59 '86 (OH) C.446 B.S. L.329 J.D.
Jivens-McRae, Grace H.	'55 '87 (PA) C.665 B.A. L.276 J.D.
Johnston, Jesse	'53 '80 (MI) C.476 B.S. L.912 J.D.
Jones, John Z.	'64 '93 (MD) C.893 B.A. L.904 J.D.
Jones, Robert E. P.	'60 '91 (ME) C.015 B.A. L.431 J.D.
Jordan, Vicky Campbell	'50 '74 (PA) C.1077 B.A. L.61 J.D.
Kammel, Carole R.	'68 '95 (MD) C.205 B.A. L.1048 J.D.
Kane, Michelle L.	'68 '96 (ME) C.1248 B.A. L.1294 J.D.
Kannee, Bruce N.	'34 '60 C.464 L.273 LL.B.
Kegerreis, Nancy R.	'31 '86 C.882 B.A. L.845 J.D.
Kelly, Thomas S.	'62 '88 (CT) C.1030 B.A. L.128 J.D.
Kennedy, Susan Lynn	'60 '85 (PA) C.659 B.A. L.276 J.D.

DEPARTMENT OF VETERANS AFFAIRS (Continued)

Kettelle, Nancy S. ....'43 '85 C.293 B.A. L.1209 J.D.
Krenzer, Eileen ....'40 '66 (MA) C.107 B.S. L.94 LL.B.
Kunz, Kirsten J. ....'64 '92 (MD) C.674 A.B. L.904 J.D.
Lambrakopoulos, Panayotis E. ....'65 '91 C&L.276 A.B., J.D.
Larkin, Mary E. ....'59 '92 (MD) C.524 B.A. L.446 J.D.
Lawson, Christopher L. ....'61 '87 (MD) C.443 B.A. L.276 J.D.
Lemoine, Brian W. ....'62 '89 (MA) C.28 B.A. L.1048 J.D.
Loeb, James W. ....'49 '78 C.605 B.A. L.910 J.D.
Lyon, Michael D. ....'53 '78 (PA) C.1047 B.A. L.607 J.D.
Mackenzie, Andrew C. ....'70 '95 (ME) C.178 B.A. L.431 J.D.
Martin, Jeffrey J. ....'50 '77 (OR) C.628 B.S. L.629 J.D.
Martin, Michael D. ....'62 '88 (IN) C.894 A.B. L.1119 J.D.
Maynard, Christopher ....'52 '87 (MS) C.999 B.S. L.356 J.D.
Mazzucchelli, Michael G. ....'63 '91 (VA) C.945 B.A. L.1209 J.D.
McCafferty, Edward J. ....'39 '69 (MD) C.602 B.A. L.446 J.D.
Moehlmann, Holly E. ....'42 '72 (PA) C.228 B.A. L.1017 J.D.
Monroe, Jacqueline E. ....'55 '87 (PA) C.302 B.A. L.945 J.D.
Moore, Joseph R. ....'70 '96 (MD) C.723 B.A. L.494 J.D.
O'Brien, Robert E. ....'47 '76 (MA) C.602 A.B. L.93 J.D.
Parker, Jeffrey D. ....'61 '88 (NC) C.1228 B.A. L.575 J.D.
Peace, Sharon M. ....'— '93 (PA) C.94 B.A. L.107 J.D.
Peevy, Alan S. ....'51 '80 C.232 B.A. L.280 J.D.
Philipp, Robert D. ....'40 '67 (IL) C&L.339 B.A., J.D.
Phillips, Nancy I. ....'46 '79 (MN) C.188 B.A. L.1035 J.D.
Pine, William L. ....'53 '88 C.309 B.L.A. L.273 J.D.
Pluta, Thomas A. ....'50 '75 C.94 B.A. L.93 J.D.
Puchnick, William ....'61 '89 (PA) C&L.665 B.A., J.D.
Ragsdale, Ursula V. ....'55 '83 (VA) C.329 B.A. L.146 J.D.
Reardon, Kathleen P. ....'70 '95 (WI) C.201 B.A. L.436 J.D.
Reddy, William J. ....'48 '81 (PA) C.647 B.A. L.665 J.D.
Regan, Scott D. ....'63 '88 C.1030 B.S. L.945 J.D.
Reiter, Neil S. ....'44 '68 C.102 B.A. L.273 LL.B.
Rice, Warren W., Jr. ....'41 '66 (NY) C.184 B.A. L.564 LL.B.
Roberts, Thomas D. ....'46 '79 C.740 B.S. L.145 J.D.
Robertson, Yvette ....'64 '92 (MD) C.329 B.A. L.107 J.D.
Robin, Nancy R. ....'49 '75 (MD) C.443 B.A. L.446 J.D.
Russell, Craig P. ....'41 '66 (WV) C.81 B.A. L.923 LL.B.
Salas, Keith L. ....'— '95 C.645 B.S. L.1338 J.D.
Samorajczyk, Lisa A. ....'67 '94 (MD) C.30 B.S.B.A. L.575 J.D.
Sampson, William E. ....'60 '92 (VA) C&L.500 B.S., J.D.
Schechter, Dan O. ....'— '94 (FL) C.446 B.A. L.260 J.D.
Schlosser, Caroline G. ....'65 '90 (MO) C.347 B.A. L.502 J.D.
Schueler, Jeffrey J. ....'63 '92 (MN) C.473 B.S. L.1035 J.D.
Schwartz, Howard N. ....'52 '78 (NY) C.331 B.A. L.564 J.D.
Sener, Charles G. ....'61 '90 (OH) C.150 B.S. L.8 J.D.
Senyk, George R. ....'45 '74 (IL) C&L.424 B.A., J.D.
Sessing, Claudia Trueba ....'69 '97 (MD) C.1097 B.S. L.446 J.D.
Sharp, Jane E. ....'38 '73 (VA) C.103 B.A. L.818 J.D.
Shaw, Richard L. ....'47 '73 C.867 B.A. L.273 J.D.
Sherman, Iris S. ....'43 '67 C.1044 B.S. L.30 J.D.
Shufelt, Gordon H. ....'44 '78 C.30 B.A. L.1292 J.D.
Siegel, James R. ....'55 '81 C.659 B.A. L.93 J.D.
Siegel, Michael S. ....'53 '86 (FL) C.367 B.A. L.228 J.D.
Singleton, Deborah W. ....'63 '88 C.329 B.A. L.325 J.D.
Skow, Cynthia A. ....'66 '92 (DE) C.339 B.A. L.1338 J.D.
Smith, Richard E. ....'43 '87 (PA) C.446 B.S. L.273 J.D.
Smith, Sandra L. ....'60 '85 C.1111 B.A. L.259 J.D.
Smith, Terry H. ....'58 '86 (MS) C.497 B.S. L.500 J.D.
Spickler, David C. ....'53 '82 (PA) C&L.831 B.A., J.D.
Standefer, Richard B. ....'42 '66 (OK) C.560 L.623 LL.B.
Sternad, Trudy K. ....'64 '89 (MN) C.118 B.A. L.1035 J.D.
Sullivan, Lawrence M. ....'45 '73 C.1030 B.S. L.128 J.D.
Sullivan, Robert E. ....'48 '75 (MA) C.454 B.A. L.93 J.D.
Swanson, Robert B. ....'61 '91 (OH) C.372 B.S. L.8 J.D.
Swiatek, Mark J. ....'47 '78 (AL) C.16 B.S. L.425 J.D.
Sylvester, Stephen F. ....'50 '86 C.128 B.A. L.273 J.D.
Symanski, Charles W. ....'45 '71 (VA) C.708 B.A. L.128 J.D.
Thompson, Gary W. ....'40 '77 (CA) C.1042 B.A. L.1198 J.D.
Thrasher, Richard C. ....'65 '90 (MN) C.118 B.A. L.1035 J.D.
Tilley, Sabrina Marie ....'58 '83 (PA) C&L.831 B.A., J.D.
Tobias, Constance B. ....'58 '83 C.709 B.A. L.188 J.D.
Tobin, Leo W., III ....'47 '75 (MI) C.477 B.A. L.276 J.D.
Toth, Susan S. ....'67 '93 (NY) C.216 B.A. L.982 J.D.
Vander Meer, Michael Paul ....'49 '88 (KS) C.516 B.A. L.900 J.D.
Weiss, Deirdre B. ....'66 '90 C.1203 B.A. L.446 J.D.
Werdal, Pamela Brown ....'59 '89 C.493 B.S. L.1035 J.D.
Werner, Neil T. ....'— '92 C.1044 B.A. L.564 J.D.
Wetmore, William H., IV ....'27 '74 (MD) C.390 B.A. L.904 J.D.
Wiggins, Carolyn F. ....'54 '86 (AL) C.16 B.A. L.192 J.D.
Williams, Richard ....'50 '83 (LA) C.415 B.S. L.425 J.D.
Witt, Clarence H. ....'41 '66 (TN) C.999 B.S. L.838 J.D. Coun.
Yeager, Thomas A. ....'52 '90 (MD) C.906 B.A. L.276 J.D.
Zapata, Alberto H. ....'64 '93 C.228 B.S. L.472 J.D.

VETERANS BENEFITS ADMINISTRATION

Freiheit, Laurence H. ....'44 '74 (CT) C.829 B.A. L.184 J.D.
Greenberg-Lewis, Erica ....'61 '87 (MD) C.604 A.B. L.446 J.D.
Hricik, James M. ....'49 '77 (PA) C.401 B.A. L.831 J.D.
Ising, Paul D. ....'43 '71 (KY) C.1118 B.A. L.421 J.D.
Sabatiuk, Lynne ....'56 '88 (WA) C.150 B.S. L.336 J.D.
Trowbridge, Paul K. ....'47 '76 (CT) C.94 B.A. L.184 J.D.
White, Robert M. ....'44 '74 (CT) C.855 B.S. L.1048 J.D.

FACILITIES MANAGEMENT

Szwarcman, George L. ....'58 '87 (MD) C&L.446 B.A., J.D.

OFFICE OF THE SECRETARY

Recknor, Ann Kathryn ....'46 '87 C.546 B.A. L.273 J.D.

INSPECTOR GENERAL

Bennett, Michael R. ....'54 '82 C.446 B.A. L.128 J.D.
Regan, Maureen T. ....'51 '82 C.446 B.A. L.128 J.D.
Vallowe, Joseph M. ....'57 '82 C.424 A.B. L.597 J.D.

OFFICE OF EMPLOYMENT DISCRIMINATION COMPLAINTS ADJUDICATION

Delobe, Charles R. ....'47 '75 (RI) C.689 B.A. L.818 J.D. Director
Durden, Chauncey W., III ....'47 '73 (VA) C&L.893 B.A., J.D.
Heywood, Harriett T. ....'47 '72 C.369 B.A. L.329 J.D.
Hume, Johnetta D. ....'— '95 (AL) C.932 M.S.W. L.370 J.D.
Lindsay, John Drew, Jr. ....'50 '84 (NY) C.1030 B.A. Econ. L.705 J.D.
Peters, Marilyn ....'53 '80 C.1044 B.A. L.273 J.D.
Simons, Patricia K. ....'48 '90 (PA) C.415 B.S. L.1209 J.D.
Weber, Donald B. ....'46 '78 (CA) C.112 B.A. L.1049 J.D.
Winkfield, John C. ....'51 '76 C.231 B.A. L.276 J.D.

Brenningmeyer, David Allen ....'64 '93 C.339 B.S. L.431 J.D.
Jones, Thomas D. ....'69 '96 (VA) C.945 B.A. L.1209 J.D.
Orfanoudis, Demetrios ....'67 '93 (MD) C&L.276 B.S., J.D.
Walker, Nancy ....'51 '91 (KS) C.63 B.S. L.378 J.D.

ENVIRONMENTAL PROTECTION AGENCY

(Vacant), *General Counsel*

OFFICE OF THE GENERAL COUNSEL

Immediate Office

Adkins, Jocelyn C. ....'69 '96 C.184 B.A. L.446 JD.
Branning, Amy Huang ....'66 '93 C.188 B.A. L.273 J.D.
Brown, Byron Richard ....'— '99 C.550 B.A. L.352 J.D.
Dubey, Susmita ....'63 '93 C.1060 B.A. L.276 J.D.
Fabricant, Robert Edmund ....'63 '91 C.222 B.A. L.180 J.D.
Gibson, Monica Derbes ....'67 '93 C.438 B.A. L.893 J.D.
Kataoka, Mark M. ....'64 '90 C.309 A.B. L.569 J.D.
Koray, Marilyn J. ....'49 '91 C.205 B.A. L.273 J.D.
Mendez, Lucia C. ....'68 '99 C.744 B.A. L.472 J.D. Reg. Coun.
O'Connor, Jennifer M. ....'66 '97 C.309 A.B. L.276 J.D.
Owens, Jon ....'72 '99 C.606 B.A. L.1000 J.D. Staff Atty.
Pace, Barbara E. ....'57 '84 C.930 B.A. L.976 J.D.
Rodgers, Kerry ....'68 '96 (NY) L.569
Scalise, Laura Jean ....'61 '97 (NY) C.705 B.S. L.776 J.D.
Starrs, Charles G. ....'59 '85 C.1369 B.S. L.273 J.D.
Versace, Paul Rios ....'— '99 (MD) C&L.446 B.A., J.D.
Wernick, Kenneth J. ....'48 '73 C.105 B.A. L.902 J.D.
Wolgast, Anna L. ....'54 '78 (TX) C.845 B.A. L.326 J.D. Princ. Dep. Gen. Coun.

Air and Radiation Law Office

Anderson, M. Lea ....'63 '92 C.839 B.S. L.976 J.D.
Backstrom, Timothy D. ....'51 '79 C.453 B.S. L.976 J.D.
Corrigan, Dara A. ....'65 '91 C.69 B.A. L.893 J.D. Health Care Fin. Div.
Cort, Paul R. ....'67 '96 (CA) C.453 B.S. L.477 J.D.
Eckert, Alan W. ....'43 '68 (VA) C.228 A.B. L.893 J.D. Asso. Gen. Coun.
Embrey, Patricia A. ....'54 '79 C.550 B.A. L.273 J.D.
Foote, Gregory B. ....'53 '85 (MD) C.311 B.A. L.273 J.D.
Gleason, Gerald K. ....'40 '69 (CA) C&L.309 B.A., J.D.
Goo, Michael L. ....'61 '88 C.881 A.B. L.911 J.D.
Hannon, John T. ....'50 '76 C.188 B.A. L.276 J.D.
Horowitz, Michael J. ....'64 '89 C.273 B.A. L.309 J.D.
Ketcham-Colwill, Nancy A. ....'56 '84 (VA) C.604 B.A. L.893 J.D.
Matthews, Keith A. ....'59 '91 (MD) C.355 B.S. L.276 J.D.
McConkey, Diane E. ....'66 '93 C.31 B.A. L.893 J.D.
McLean, Kevin W. ....'57 '81 C&L.893 B.A., J.D.
Ossias, Richard B. ....'55 '80 (CA) C.1044 B.A. L.813 J.D.
Prosper, Michael A. ....'52 '87
Sagoff, Kendra H. ....'49 '75 C.681 A.B. L.309 J.D.
Schneeberg, Sara ....'53 '80 C.156 B.A. L.659 J.D.
Simms, Patrice L. ....'69 '98 (MA) C.588 B.S. L.329 J.D.
Thrift, Michael W. ....'62 '92 (CA) C.112 B.A. L.1068 J.D.
Tierney, Jan M. ....'62 '89 C.623 B.S. L.846 J.D.
Vetter, Richard H. ....'54 '85 (OH) C.347 B.A. L.1119 J.D.
Wilcox, Geoffrey L. ....'61 '87 (VA) C.197 B.A. L.945 J.D.

Alternative Dispute Resolution Law Office

Hill, Tanya Adrienne ....'62 '87 C.1090 B.S. L.329 J.D.
Irmer, Cynthia G. ....'55 '80 C.546 B.A. L.190 J.D.
Lawrence, Tanya Adrienne ....'— '87 C.1090 B.S. L.329 J.D.
Ward, William R., Jr. ....'— '89 C&L.976 B.A., J.D.

Cross-Cutting Issues Law Office

Annear, Craig B. ....'47 '73 C.188 A.B. L.477 J.D.
Chapman, Apple ....'70 '99 (MD) C.35 B.S. L.446 J.D.
Guadagno, Anthony F. ....'58 '84 C.705 B.A. L.30 J.D.
Havard, James J. ....'65 '95
Hawbecker, Hale W. ....'60 '89 (PA) C&L.101 B.A., J.D.
Keohane, Jeffrey R. ....'71 '97 (CA) C.94 B.A. L.813 J.D.
Marshall, Tom ....'60 '87 (PA) C.976 B.A. L.477 J.D.
Nelson, James C. ....'50 '75 C.188 B.A. L.273 J.D. Assoc. Gen. Coun.
Ott, Dana B. ....'52 '77 C&L.846 B.A., J.D.
Siegal, Tod E. ....'67 '92 C.178 A.B. L.477 J.D.

International Environmental Law Office

Freedman, Joseph ....'52 '78 (NY) C.145 A.B. L.477 J.D.
Lallas, Peter L. ....'59 '87 (HI) C.813 B.A. L.309 J.D.
Magraw, Daniel B., Jr. ....'46 '76 C.309 A.B. L.1066 J.D. Assoc. Gen. Coun.
Rowley, Anne ....'62 '91 (UT) C.101 B.A. L.276 J.D.
Singh, Padmini ....'51 '91 C.999 B.S. L.602 J.D.
van Hoogstraten, David J. ....'54 '82 C.659 B.A. L.966 J.D.
Wolfson, Steven ....'59 '85 (CA) C.103 A.B. L.1068 J.D.

Finance and Operations Law Office

Baker, Jonathan S. ....'60 '85 C.197 A.B. L.94 J.D.
Beyer, Anthony G. ....'44 '69 (MN) C&L.494 B.S., J.D.
Binder, Bruce S. ....'62 '87 C.1044 B.A. L.904 J.D.
Carroll, Karen J. ....'55 '91 C.657 B.S. L.276 J.D.
Coleman, Kathleen M. ....'63 '90 (CA) C.886 B.S. L.1049 J.D.

Cooper, Geoffrey K. '54 '85 C.207 B.A. L.930 J.D.
Corcoran, Howard F. '49 '79 C.309 B.A. L.276 J.D.
Cowgill, Carol A. '46 '71 C.228 B.A. L.145 J.D.
Darman, Leslie J. '62 '94 (MA) C.1307 B.A. L.107 J.D.
Darner, Thomas A. '43 '68 (KS) C&L.378 B.S., J.D.
Diamond, Marla E. '51 '79 C.1044 B.S. L.180 J.D. Assoc. Gen. Coun.
Doherty, Thomas J. '53 '82 (OH) C.321 B.A. L.608 J.D.
Drummond, James F., Jr. '52 '87 (MD) C.806 B.A. L.128 J.D.
Ehrlich, Alan M. '40 '91 C.107 B.A. L.273 J.D.
Feldman, Richard D. '51 '76 C.156 B.A. L.1292 J.D.
Friedrich, Robert A. '47 '74 C.112 B.A. L.178 J.D.
Goerke, Ariadne '68 '97 (NJ) C.30 B.A. L.904 J.D.
Guerrero, David P. '57 '83 (LA) C.269 B.A. L.425 J.D.
Heinz, John H. '49 '78 (SC) C.152 B.A. L.790 J.D.
Hess, Stephen B. '54 '87 (VA) C.1369 B.B.A. L.1209 J.D.
Hirsch, Patricia K. '53 '79 (KS) C&L.378 B.A., J.D.
Hogan, Joanne M. '63 '88 (MD) C&L.339 B.A., J.D.
Kavouras, Maria S. '57 '91 (OH) C&L.150 B.S., J.D.
Lee, Susanne M. '45 '77 C.216 B.A. L.273 J.D.
Lloyd, David R. '61 '88 C.273 B.A. L.902 J.D.
Pakula, Kenneth R. '63 '88 C.1044 B.A. L.904 J.D.
Pressman, Stephen G. '49 '75 C.893 B.A. L.910 J.D.
Redden, Kenneth A. '68 '93 C.472 B.A. L.273 J.D.
Rowland, John M. '57 '88 C.604 B.A. L.229 J.D.
Shea, Bridget C. '62 '88 C&L.128 B.A., J.D.
Souzon, Jane C. '47 '78 C.645 B.A. L.893 J.D.
Toohey, Ann C. '74 '98 (MA) C.93 B.A. L.1194 J.D.
Winick, Paul M. '52 '80 C.645 B.S. L.276 J.D.
Zemel, Avital G. '64 '89 C.446 B.A. L.273 J.D.

Pesticides and Toxic Substances Law Office

Aranda, Amber L. '64 '91 (FL) C.362 B.A. L.259 J.D.
Boer, Tom J. '73 '98 (CA) C.605 B.A. L.273 J.D.
Dubois, Roland '53 '85 C.197 A.B. L.893 J.D.
Dyner, Mark A. '63 '89 (UT) C&L.878 B.A., J.D.
Eichenwald, Carl J. '60 '92 (MD) C.563 B.A. L.705 J.D.
Fleuchaus, Jonathan J. '54 '83 (FL) C.311 B.A. L.260 J.D.
Golberg, Aron A. '54 '81 C.976 B.A. L.309 J.D.
Huang, Amy T. '66 '93 (VA) C.188 B.A. L.273 J.D.
Knorr, Michele L. '67 '97 (MD) C.445 B.S. L.64 J.D.
Krolikowski, Suzanne B. '66 '95 (VA) C.453 B.S. L.575 J.D.
Lee, Kevin M. '48 '73 (CA) C.766 A.B. L.1067 J.D.
Medici, Andrea E. '65 '91 (PA) C.569 B.A. L.705 J.D.
Perlis, Robert '54 '79 C.674 B.A. L.569 J.D.
Roberts, Patricia A. '42 '78 C.512 B.S. L.273 J.D. Assoc. Gen. Coun.
Ross, Philip J. '50 '75 C.30 B.A. L.245 J.D.
Sadowsky, Donald A. '54 '84 C.188 B.S. L.904 J.D.
Srinivasan, Gautam '73 '99 (MS) C.198 A.B. L.861 J.D.
Wing, Robert D. '64 '94 C.276 B.S.F.S. L.446 J.D.

Water Law Office

Bangser, Paul M. '55 '83 C.453 B.S. L.93 J.D.
Clark, Karen H. '43 '77 C.629 B.A. L.276 J.D.
Curtin, James H. '50 '81 C.128 B.A. L.276 J.D.
Gravallese, David M. '53 '78 (MA) C.309 A.B. L.188 J.D.
Hill, Randolph L. '62 '87 C.112 B.A. L.1066 J.D.
Le Desma, Michael G. '68 '96 (FL) C.309 B.A. L.178 J.D.
Lee, Michael G. '67 '94 (WI) C.696 B.A. L.966 J.D.
Lepow, Susan G. '49 '75 C.659 B.A. L.276 J.D. Asso. Gen. Coun.
Levine, Mary Ellen '62 '86 C.309 A.B. L.273 J.D.
Neugeboren, Steven M. '61 '86 (CT) C.705 B.A. L.976 J.D.
Schroer, Lee C. '46 '72 (TX) C.546 B.A. L.326 J.D.
Siciliano, Carol Ann '59 '86 C.674 A.B. L.262 J.D.
Sweeney, Stephen J. '— '91 C.475 B.A. L.273 J.D.
Wehling, Caroline H. '60 '85 (IL) C.813 B.S. L.309 J.D.
Wendelowski, Karyn I. '67 '96 C.103 B.A. L.276 J.D.
Winer, Catherine A. '46 '72 C.681 A.B. L.273 J.D.
Witt, Richard T. '45 '73 C.976 B.A. L.893 J.D.

Civil Rights Law Office

Adams, Wendy L. '51 '79 C.800 B.A. L.904 J.D.
Beckman, Maria D. '68 '93 C&L.608 B.A., J.D.
Chang, Patrick S. '69 '94 (MD) C.188 B.A. L.30 J.D.
De Leon, Rafael '59 '84 (PA) C.1036 B.A. L.276 J.D. Assoc. Gen. Coun.
Meinero, Seth Adam '73 '99 (NY) C.188 B.A. L.329 J.D.
Ng, William H. '50 '76 C.309 A.B. L.93 J.D.
Okoye, Winifred N. '63 '91 C&L.999 LL.B., B.L.
O'Lone, Mary M. '64 '90 (MD) C.1369 B.A. L.128 J.D.
Regis-Civetta, Jennifer M. '71 '96 C.880 B.A. L.910 J.D.

Solid Waste and Emergency Response Law Office

Carpien, Alan H. '46 '76 C.103 A.B. L.276 J.D.
Friedman, Lisa K. '47 '73 C.103 A.B. L.309 J.D.
Grant, Brian P. '62 '87 C.597 B.A. L.273 J.D.
Horwitz, Sylvia '52 '79 (VA) C.273 B.A. L.128 J.D.
Igoe, Sheila M. '61 '88 C.882 B.S. L.145 J.D.
Kaneen, Christina '52 '78 (IL) C.378 B.A. L.339 J.D.
Kraus, Karen Kelly '60 '85 (OH) C.473 B.A.B.S. L.1003 J.D.
Messier, Dawn M. '65 '92 (NY) C.705 B.A. L.569 J.D.
Michaud, John R. '58 '84 (ME) C.588 B.S. L.94 J.D.
Nam, Katherine H. '62 '87 C.446 B.A. L.659 J.D.
Openchowski, Charles A. '53 '79 (OR) C.605 B.A. L.1051 J.D.
Rivera, Nina Y. '67 '95 C.103 B.A. L.477 J.D.
Salo, Earl '45 '75 C.112 A.B. L.309 J.D.
Schmandt, Alexander G. '58 '87 (TX) C.691 B.A. L.846 J.D.
Silverman, Steven E. '50 '75 C&L.477 B.Mus., J.D.
Tyner, Lee R. '46 '75 C.722 B.A. L.273 J.D.
Woolf, Malcolm D. '67 '93 C.860 B.A. L.893 J.D.

OFFICE OF ENFORCEMENT AND COMPLIANCE ASSURANCE

Office of the Assistant Administrator

Ambrosino, Helene Cohen '60 '86 (NY) C.4 B.B.A. L.724 J.D.
Gordon, Mark D. '44 '69 C&L.659 B.S., LL.B.
Jonesi, Gary '60 '85 C.339 B.A. L.1019 J.D.
Layne, Kenda '61 '92 C&L.446 B.S., J.D.
Spears, Ray E. '49 '74 (TX) C&L.846 B.A., J.D.
Walker, Michael J. '51 '77 (WI) C.966 B.A. L.851 J.D.

Enforcement Capacity and Outreach Office

Haythe, Winston M. '40 '67 C.804 B.S. L.945 J.D.
Stough, Ellen Cook '49 '74 (TX) C.846 B.A. L.744 J.D.
Wills, Carroll G. '39 '70 (CO) C.792 B.S. L.208 J.D.

Federal Facilities Enforcement Office

Breen, Barry N. '56 '81 C.674 A.B. L.309 J.D.
Dalzell, Sally Mozley '62 '87 (AL) C.945 B.A. L.16 J.D.
Drazan, Daniel '59 '89 (NJ) C.273 B.A. L.978 J.D.
Frank, William H. '48 '73 C.694 A.B. L.273 J.D.
Olin, Joyce A. '44 '86 (IL) C.1077 B.A. L.209 J.D.
Watkins, Susan Cary '45 '81 C.575 M.A. L.945 J.D.

Office of Federal Activities

Cain, C. Marshall '34 '59 (SC) C&L.790 B.S., J.D.

International Enforcement and Compliance Division

Alushin, Michael S. '47 '72 C.604 B.A. L.309 J.D.
Coldiron, Cindy Ann '61 '87 (IN) C.741 B.A. L.879 J.D.
Emory, Richard W., Jr. '41 '67 (MD) C.976 B.A. L.309 LL.B.
Mertz, Gregory J. '63 '92 C.446 B.S. L.273 J.D.
Sperling, Lawrence I. '59 '85 C.893 B.A. L.665 J.D.

National Enforcement Investigations Center

Aschwanden, Charles R. '53 '78 (CO) C.339 A.B. L.208 J.D.
Lattimer, John Mangan '43 '77 (CO) C.259 M.S. L.208 J.D.
Nelson, Eric E. '61 '87 (CO) C.1193 B.A. L.208 J.D.

Office of Regulatory Enforcement

Arnold, Shana '66 '97 (VA) C.1042 B.A. L.36 J.D.
Fisher, Michael R. '67 '94 C.691 B.A. L.976 J.D.
Holloway, Lynn S. '55 '78 C.665 B.A. L.273 J.D.
Kabler, Lauren V. '67 '00 C.682 A.B. L.563 J.D.
Kelley, Rosemarie A. '63 '89 C.945 A.B. L.904 J.D.
O'Keefe, Susan E. '55 '80 C.1044 B.A. L.273 J.D.

Air Enforcement Division

Abdalla, David A. '60 '85 C.839 B.B.A. L.796 J.D.
Adair, Jocelyn L. '52 '85 C.30 B.S. L.329 J.D.
Dresdner, Robert P. '55 '88 (NJ) C.174 B.A. L.705 J.D.
Fergusson, Edgar Bruce '62 '88 (VA) C&L.893 B.A., J.D.
Fitzgerald, Angela E. '46 '86 C.72 B.A. L.1162 J.D.
Garlow, Charles G. '49 '79 (WV) C.309 B.A. L.923 J.D.
Ginley, Marcia S. '52 '78 (CO) C&L.174 B.A., J.D.
Gottfried, David J. '63 '89 C.1369 B.B.A. L.1209 J.D.
Lamason, Fielding E., Jr. '54 '84 (PA) C.674 A.B. L.884 J.D.
Lawrence, George E., Jr. '47 '79 (VA) C.886 B.S. L.692 J.D.
Lubow, Judith Rochelle '46 '74 (NY) C.1044 B.A. L.1009 J.D.
Oif, Leslie A. '61 '88 (IL) C.347 B.S. L.209 J.D.
Pickell, Ervin B. '52 '78 (CO) C.172 B.S. L.208 J.D.
Viggiani, Steven J. '60 '88 C.367 B.A. L.893 J.D.

Multimedia Enforcement Division

DiBona, Caroline A. '62 '88 C&L.893 B.A., J.D.
Harris, Marged G. '46 '80 (VA) C&L.945 B.A., J.D.
Hindin, David A. '58 '86 (CA) C.477 B.S. L.1066 J.D.
Kedzie, Glen Paul '58 '89 (OK) C.961 B.S. L.862 J.D.
Libber, Jonathan D. '53 '79 (MD) C&L.446 B.S., J.D.
Marshall, Melissa Page '50 '81 (VA) C.75 B.A. L.1218 J.D.
Repsher, William C. '— '75 C.262 B.S. L.1292 J.D.
Spiegel, Steven '55 '80 C.1044 B.A. L.273 J.D.

RCRA Enforcement Division

Fogarty, John P. C. '58 '85 C.273 B.A. L.1202 J.D.
Garcia, Susan Jenks '— '91 (MD) C.1044 B.A. L.1194 J.D.
Kline, Deborah A. '57 '87 (WA) C.446 B.S. L.273 J.D.
Olmstead, Joan Wart '57 '86 C.823 B.S. L.910 J.D.
Silberman, Jon D. '57 '82 C.1044 B.A. L.273 J.D.
Smith, Catherine S. '67 '93 (MA) C.478 B.A. L.93 J.D.

Toxics and Pesticides Enforcement Division

Ahearn, Caroline C. '61 '89 (VA) C&L.128 B.A., J.D.
Clark, Kathy M. '53 '86 C.575 B.A. L.790 J.D.
Fournier, Cindy S. '58 '90 C.1154 B.A. L.477 J.D.
Garrison, Scott B. '57 '90 (MD) C.966 B.S. L.446 J.D.
Garvey, Mark '62 '89 C.383 B.S. L.421 J.D.
Handley, F. James '58 '85 C.205 B.Ch.E. L.326 J.D.
Jacobs, Jon D. '56 '83 C.855 B.A. L.978 J.D.
Kresch, Sandra '61 '89 C.475 B.S. L.215 J.D.
Lancaster, Robin P. '58 '85 (PA) C.446 B.S. L.329 J.D.
Rattigan, Ellen '57 '90 C.1115 B.S. L.128 J.D.
Ziegel, Dean B. '61 '89 C.1036 B.A. L.1019 J.D.

Water Enforcement Division

Brin, Marla B. '60 '85 C.475 B.A. L.30 J.D.
Cohen, Nadine Steinberg '64 '88 C.446 B.A. L.94 J.D.
Devlin, Mary Elizabeth '58 '86 C.276 B.A. L.273 J.D.
DiBiagio-Wood, Elyse M. '47 '78 C.262 B.A. L.273 J.D.
Drelich, David '51 '76 C.705 A.B. L.188 J.D.
Kumari Jain, Komal '70 '95 C.1369 B.B.A. L.692 J.D.
Lyon, John W. '39 '65 C.31 B.A. L.976 LL.B.
Morrissey, Alan J. '46 '80 C.688 B.S. L.128 J.D.
Nanda, Sushila R. '61 '87 C.309 B.A. L.945 J.D.
Rice, Cassandra L. '66 '94 C&L.37 B.S./B.A., J.D.
Rose, Cheryl T. '65 '94 C.273 B.A. L.910 J.D.
Sullivan, Susan R. '52 '84 C.34 B.A. L.421 J.D.
Theis, Joseph G. '65 '89 (KY) C.1118 B.A. L.1340 J.D.

Policy and Program Evaluation Division

Batson, David C. '53 '79 (NC) C.232 B.A. L.192 J.D.
Comer, Lisa E. '63 '88 (PA) C.645 B.A. L.831 J.D.

ENVIRONMENTAL PROTECTION AGENCY (Continued)

Harrison, Karen E. '61 '86 C.339 B.A. L.1068 J.D.
Kandell, Ellen F. '54 '83 (PA) C.446 B.S. L.831 J.D.
Kenney, Robert E. '48 '75 C.93 A.B. L.273 J.D.
Lammie, Benjamin J. '— '90 (WA) C.645 B.S. L.1051 J.D.
Patterson, Kenneth W. '56 '82 C&L.896 B.A., J.D.
Rollin, Steven P. '62 '90 (MD) C&L.446 B.S., J.D.

Regional Support Division

Andrews, Mary Sigrid '60 '87 C.732 B.S. L.276 J.D.
Backer, Kathleen '56 '90 C.801 B.A. L.128 J.D.
Botts, Stephen C. '47 '74 (TN) C.893 B.A. L.838 J.D.
Breece, Charles E. '46 '75 C.302 B.S. L.329 J.D.
Bufill, Lourdes M. '57 '86 (PA) C.1209 B.A. L.93 J.D.
Cintron-Silva, Maria I. '47 '79 (PR) C&L.677 B.A., J.D.
Clay, David K. '59 '84 (GA) C&L.469 B.A., J.D.
Cohon, Keith E. '59 '85 (WA) C.679 A.B. L.309 J.D.
Connors, Sandra L. '62 '87 (PA) C.886 B.S. L.273 J.D.
Dixon, Douglas P. '58 '86 (WI) C&L.966 B.S., J.D.
Ergener, Denise '60 '90 (PA) C.1044 B.A. L.904 J.D.
Featherson, Clarence E. '58 '86 C.103 A.B. L.329 J.D.
Gipson, Tracy A. '43 '76 C.658 B.A. L.904 J.D.
Gramelspacher, Meredith M. '71 '98 C.478 B.A. L.904 J.D.
Gutreuter, Julia E. '72 '00 (PA) C.188 B.S. L.861 J.D. Asst. Reg. Coun.
Kenney, Thomas Joseph '59 '86 C.103 A.B. L.893 J.D.
Lane-Wenner, Carolyn M. '58 '89 (WI) C.276 B.S. L.966 J.D.
Linett, Janice Corwin '57 '82 C.103 A.B. L.276 J.D.
Mott, Patricia D. '51 '85 (MD) C.104 B.A. L.273 J.D.
Northridge, Michael Allen '59 '84 C.216 B.A. L.276 J.D.
Roberts, Robert A. '65 '91 (MO) C.675 B.A. L.910 J.D.
St. Peter, Mary '49 '83 (PA) C.645 B.A. L.1338 J.D.
Snyder, Gregory C. '56 '81 C.627 B.S. L.546 J.D.
Steuer, Katherine B. '61 '94 (CA) C.918 B.A. L.309 J.D.
Turner, James L. '49 '80 (TX) C.877 B.S. L.845 J.D. Senior Asst. Reg. Coun.
Wheeler, John H. '45 '73 C&L.260 B.S.A., J.D.
Winder, John S., Jr. '43 '71 C.477 B.A. L.273 J.D.

Office of Compliance

Binder, Jonathan Stuart '65 '92 C.860 B.A. L.1194 J.D.
Colbert, Richard '51 '77 (OR) C.860 B.A. L.276 J.D.
Schaeffer, Eric V. '— '87 (PA) C.880 B.A. L.276 J.D.

Enforcement Planning, Targeting and Data Division

Heiss, Robert G. '46 '72 C.951 B.A. L.309 J.D.
Palmer, Daniel '57 '88 (MD) C.494 B.A. L.30 J.D.
Stiehl, Frederick F. '45 '70 C.705 A.B. L.904 J.D.

Manufacturing, Energy and Transportation Division

Callahan, Joanne M. '55 '84 (PA) C.655 B.A. L.831 J.D.

Chemical, Commercial Services and Municipal Division

Berman, Joanne H. '62 '89 (MD) C.446 B.A. L.64 J.D.
Bromm, Susan E. '55 '79 C.1044 B.S. L.276 J.D.
Cherry, Andrew B. '62 '87 (OR) C.477 B.S. L.1051 J.D.
Gilberg, Elliott J. '52 '78 C.309 B.A. L.1067 J.D.
Guernica, Georgina M. '56 '81 C.367 B.A. L.178 J.D.
Harmon, Kenneth R. '61 '86 (VA) C.228 B.A. L.273 J.D.

Office of Criminal Enforcement

Adler, Mary Kendall '56 '83 C.747 B.A. L.1035 J.D.
Cole, Jonathan S. '55 '80 C.951 B.A. L.94 J.D.
Kime, Roy C. '45 '72 (FL) C.228 B.A. L.665 J.D.
Penders, Michael '60 '86 (NJ) C.188 B.A. L.776 J.D.

Criminal Enforcement Counsel Division

Bellin, Bruce G. '48 '73 (MD) C.445 B.S. L.446 J.D.
Hughes, Kathleen A. '55 '82 (LA) C.836 L.425 J.D.
Kelly, Palmer '43 '72 (TX) C.797 B.A. L.273 J.D.
Ojala, Elizabeth M. '52 '85 (MD) C.446 B.A. L.276 J.D.
Parkinson, Nancy B. '56 '89 (MD) C.347 B.A. L.446 J.D.
Robinson, Milton H. '64 '91 (GA) C.319 B.A. L.245 J.D.
Seaton, Thomas J. '57 '84 (ND) C.184 B.A. L.990 J.D.

Dowton, David C. '72 '97 C.477 B.A. L.61 J.D.
Healey, Michael J. '72 '99 C.690 B.S. L.61 J.D.
Schefski, Kenneth C. '72 '00 C.878 B.A.B.S. L.596 J.D.
Sims, Patricia L. '48 '79 (CO) C.597 B.A. L.208 J.D.

ENVIRONMENTAL APPEALS BOARD

Albores, Richard '66 '93 (CA) C.424 B.S. L.1066 J.D.
Berrios-Colon, Nivea R. '70 '00 C&L.677 B.S., J.D.
Chapman, Jasmine M. '72 '98 (NJ) C.788 B.A. L.329 J.D.
Da Rosa, Carlos D. '63 '95 C.976 B.A. L.588 J.D.
Epp, Timothy R. '64 '90 C.83 B.A. L.309 J.D.
Fidler, Danielle C. '71 '97 C.104 A.B. L.273 J.D.
Fulton, Scott Cole '54 '82 (SC) C.454 B.B.A. L.790 J.D.
Heckler, David R. '59 '88 C.1036 B.A. L.273 J.D.
McCallum, Ronald L. '42 '69 (IN) C.347 B.A. L.1119 J.D. Judge
Miles, Leslie K. '59 '82 C&L.94 B.S., J.D.
Newton, Jonathan V. '67 '96 (NY) C.446 B.A. L.309 J.D.
Reich, Edward E. '44 '68 C.994 B.A. L.276 J.D. Judge
Stein, Kathie A. '52 '79 C.604 B.A. L.276 J.D. Judge
Wegman, Alice P. '40 '65 C.188 B.A. L.309 J.D.
Wenzel, Michelle A. '61 '93 C.477 B.S. L.30 J.D.

OFFICE OF ADMINISTRATIVE LAW JUDGES

Bathersfield, Nizanna '75 '98 (MD) C.273 B.A. L.276 J.D.
Biro, Susan Lori '60 '84 C.1044 B.A. L.904 J.D.
Bullock, Charles E. '46 '71 C.105 A.B. L.273 J.D.
Charneski, Carl C. '51 '76 C.717 B.A. L.724 J.D.
Greene, J. F. '37 '63 C.611 B.A. L.145 J.D.
Gunning, Barbara A. '51 '76 C.529 B.A. L.744 J.D.
Hoya, Thomas W. '31 '58 C.309 A.B. L.477 J.D.
Kaczka, Kelly Ann '75 '00 C&L.128 B.A., J.D.
Knight, M. Lisa '62 '88 (GA) C&L.245 B.S., J.D.
Nissen, Spencer T. '28 '52 C&L.585 LL.B.
Pearlstein, Andrew '51 '77 (NV) C.1036 B.A. L.285 J.D.
Wakefield, Benjamin J. '68 '97 C.1169 B.A. L.596 J.D.

OFFICE OF CONGRESSIONAL AND INTERGOVERNMENTAL RELATIONS

Coronado, Robert P. '56 '87 (ID) C.1074 B.S. L.1067 J.D.
Crews, Bill '52 '78 C&L.352 B.A., J.D.
Deitz, Randolph '57 '83 C.1111 B.A. L.1206 J.D.
Dickerson, Thomas P. '55 '80 (OH) C.610 A.B. L.608 J.D.
Meni, Reynold '49 '77 C.331 B.A. L.128 J.D.
Stevens, Mark E. '51 '76 (WI) C&L.966 B.A., J.D.

PROGRAM OFFICE ATTORNEYS

Alpern, Dwight C. '49 '75 C.367 A.B. L.309 LL.B.
Anderson, Phyllis R. '53 '82 C&L.30 B.A., J.D.
Badalamente, Mark F. '64 '89 (MI) C&L.477 A.B., J.D.
Beale, John C. '48 '79 (WA) C.112 B.A. L.569 J.D.
Beasley, Lynn M. '58 '98 (VA) C.322 B.A. L.180 J.D.
Benson, Robert S. '55 '82 (MD) C.945 B.A. L.904 J.D.
Blunck, Christopher R. '61 '87 C.174 B.A. L.1209 J.D.
Bonanno, Gale Carney '62 '91 (MD) C.276 B.S.L.A. L.446 J.D.
Bunte, Laura Louise '69 '95 C.188 B.S. L.904 J.D.
Canty-Letsome, Rosezella '47 '73 (PA) C.329 B.A. L.229 J.D.
Chanania, Fredric Davis '48 '73 C.188 B.A. L.705 J.D.
Childress, Suzanne M. '68 '95 (MD) C.446 B.A. L.30 J.D.
Cleland-Hamnett, Wendy '54 '79 C.231 B.A. L.273 J.D.
Clovis, Debora L. '53 '85 (MD) C.30 B.A. L.446 J.D.
Cohen, Fran E. '61 '87 C.446 B.A. L.1019 J.D.
Cook, Leila Holmes '61 '88 (MD) C.1021 B.A. L.128 J.D.
Correa, Sylvia I. '52 '80 (NY) C.705 B.A. L.273 J.D.
Cross, John F. '51 '76 C.477 B.A. L.273 J.D.
Dibble, Christine L. '61 '86 (VA) C.976 B.A. L.893 J.D.
Doyle, Robert M. '53 '89 (MD) C.445 B.S. L.1209 J.D.
Dunn, Catherine M. '65 '96 (NC) C.821 B.A. L.228 J.D.
Eby, Louis K. '57 '85 (MD) C.276 B.A. L.446 J.D.
Eng, Myron A. '59 '95 (CA) C.112 B.S. L.284 J.D.
Flint, Karen M. '65 '97 (VA) C.886 B.A. L.1194 J.D.
Ford, Laurie R. Garnand '54 '80 C&L.208 B.A., J.D.
Foster, Barbara '53 '84 (VA) C.886 B.S. L.1209 J.D.
Fugh, Justina C. '61 '88 C.881 A.B. L.273 J.D.
Giamporcaro, David E. '52 '79 C.30 B.A. L.273 J.D.
Graham, Judith E. '52 '79 (CO) C&L.347 A.B., J.D.
Gregg, Charles N., Jr. '26 '53 (MA) C&L.309 A.B., LL.B.
Guernica, Mimi '56 '82 C.367 B.A. L.178 J.D.
Hanley, Mary C. '59 '84 C.754 B.A. L.276 J.D.
Herman, Christopher C. '46 '73 (NY) C&L.976 B.A., J.D.
Hodges, Susan T. '59 '85 C.445 B.S. L.329 J.D.
Horwitz, Paul S. '57 '83 (IL) C.347 B.S. L.1051 J.D.
Hostage, Barbara A. '54 '87 C.1115 B.S. L.276 J.D.
Johnson, William F. '38 '63 (MD) C&L.446 B.Ch.E., LL.B.
Jordan, William L. '49 '76 C.674 A.B. L.276 J.D.
Kaiser, Sven Erik '61 '87 (NY) C&L.823 B.A., J.D.
Keplinger, Helen B. '42 '80 (MD) C.923 B.A. L.128 J.D.
King, Helena Ann '67 '93 (MD) C.473 B.A. L.904 J.D.
Klepp, Robert G. '59 '86 C.273 B.A. L.724 J.D.
Kramer, Kim Michelle '71 '98 (NY) C.454 B.S. L.904 J.D.
LaShier, Richard D. '53 '81 (MD) C.696 B.A. L.273 J.D.
Lee, Robert Wayne '54 '84 (GA) C.140 B.A. L.245 J.D.
Leff, Karin S. '62 '88 C.178 B.A. L.276 J.D.
Lewis, Jennifer Marrero '68 '99 (LA) C.974 B.S. L.861 J.D.
Lindsay, Clare '54 '86 C.788 B.A. L.273 J.D.
Lischinsky, Robert '64 '89 (MA) C.787 B.A. L.904 J.D.
Lowrance, Sylvia K. '52 '82 C.477 A.B. L.128 J.D.
Lynne, Diane S. '58 '86 C.446 B.A. L.862 J.D.
Margolis, Alan D. '60 '85 (PA) C.659 B.A. L.665 J.D.
Marvin, Thomas C. '69 '97 (MI) C.475 B.S. L.912 J.D.
Mazakas, Pamela J. '63 '90 (VA) C.682 B.A. L.1209 J.D.
McLean, Meredith L. '71 '97 (CT) C.478 B.A. L.904 J.D.
Miller, Mamie R. '55 '84 (VA) C.273 B.A. L.904 J.D.
Miller, Wendy Ann '60 '86 (CT) C.477 B.S. L.1019 J.D.
Miller, Wendy J. '57 '83 (MD) C&L.446 B.A., J.D.
Mitchell, Sharon O. '40 '89 C.999 B.S. L.1209 J.D.
Moran, Andrew J. '45 '71 (RI) C.1145 B.S. L.818 J.D.
Morley, Karen D. '40 '79 (CA) C.813 B.A. L.770 J.D.
Nelson, Roger A. '45 '73 (OH) C.701 B.S. L.94 J.D.
Pastorkovich, Anne-Marie C. '65 '90 (PA) C&L.273 B.A., J.D.
Patton, Dorothy E. '38 '77 C.966 B.S. L.178 J.D.
Perlberg, Brian Marc '72 '97 C&L.446 B.A., J.D.
Perry, Kate M. '55 '81 C.918 B.A. L.276 J.D.
Rae, Renelle P. '51 '78 (CO) C.173 B.A. L.208 J.D.
Schaaff, Lesley-Anne '68 '93 C.160 B.A. L.1338 J.D.
Schmidt, Lorie J. '59 '84 C.679 B.S.M.S.E. L.309 J.D.
Schneider, Margaret N. '54 '84 C.66 B.A. L.276 J.D.
Seidenstein, Roy '59 '86 C.112 B.A. L.1051 J.D.
Sherlock, Scott M. '59 '85 (MD) C.264 A.B. L.64 J.D.
Simpson, Julie '55 '83 C.339 B.A. L.276 J.D.
Smith, Mary T. '51 '79 C.1044 B.S. L.273 J.D.
Stelle, William W., Jr. '51 '78 C.94 B.A. L.1294 J.D.
Utting, George '52 '84 C.262 B.S. L.276 J.D.
Weinstock, Lawrence '60 '84 (MD) C.688 B.S. L.273 J.D.
Weisner, Carol C. '52 '77 C.813 B.A. L.1067 J.D.
Weitman, Dov N. '52 '76 (NJ) C.978 B.A. L.309 J.D.
Wyeth, George B. '52 '82 (MN) C.399 B.A. L.976 J.D.
Zeller, Elizabeth A. '41 '85 (MD) C.999 B.S. L.446 J.D.

EQUAL EMPLOYMENT OPPORTUNITY COMMISSION

(Vacant), ***General Counsel***

OFFICE OF THE GENERAL COUNSEL

Arrington, Ronald J. '48 '74 C.1286 B.A. L.329 J.D.
Bernstein, Dori K. '58 '84 C.918 B.A. L.569 J.D.
Blackwood, Vincent '45 '70 (MA) C.433 B.A. L.309 J.D.
Blumner, James '42 '74 C.976 B.A. L.575 J.D.
Bruner, Paula R. '60 '85 (PA) C&L.329 B.A., J.D.
Brusoski, Donna J. '56 '84 (PA) C.347 B.A. L.1119 J.D.
Canary, Janet M. Cook '56 '86 C.25 B.A. L.188 J.D.
Coleman, Gail S. '63 '91 C.103 B.A. L.272 J.D.
Davis, Lorraine C. '53 '80 C.188 B.A. L.329 J.D.
Dougherty, Barbara K. '59 '84 C.1350 B.A. L.276 J.D.
Finney, James N. '38 '66 (PA) C&L.178 B.S., LL.B.
Fredericks, Diane Ellen '62 '88 (PA) C.107 B.A. L.904 J.D.
Gantz, Julie Loraine '68 '97 C.309 A.B. L.893 J.D.
Gilpatrick, Diana J. '54 '82 C.105 B.A. L.276 J.D.
Goldstein, Jennifer S. '64 '90 (CA) C.104 A.B. L.145 J.D.
Gregory, Robert J. '60 '85 C.593 B.S. L.190 J.D.
Johnson, Johnnie L., Jr. '46 '70 C.514 B.A. L.607 J.D.
Kryvoruka, Kenneth J. '51 '77 C.705 A.B. L.8 J.D.
Lage, Christopher '68 '93 (MD) C.575 B.A. L.273 J.D.
Letwin, Gerald D. '48 '71 C.667 B.S. L.145 J.D.
Lisser, Justine S. '52 '78 C.104 A.B. L.276 J.D.
Misicka, Cynthia '58 '88 C.690 B.A. L.1068 J.D.
Oliver, Michele Marie '55 '81 (IL) C&L.329 B.S., J.D.
Powers, Sheryl J. '54 '83 C&L.477 B.A., J.D.
Preston, Carlton L. '40 '73 C.999 B.S. L.329 J.D.
Ramshaw, Paul D. '44 '84 (CA) C.999 B.A. L.1067 J.D.
Reams, Gwendolyn Young '46 '73 C.329 B.A. L.30 J.D.
Rosenblum, Marc J. '36 '89 (PA) C.331 A.B. L.276 J.D.
Scanlan, Jerome N. '43 '71 (OH) C.97 B.A. L.930 J.D.
Sklover, Philip B. '43 '68 C.446 B.S. L.30 J.D.
Sloan, Barbara L. '— '86 C.228 B.A. L.1066 J.D.
Starr, Susan L. P. '57 '86 (MN) C.95 A.B. L.1035 J.D.
Suhre, John F. '44 '69 (IN) C.347 A.B. L.1119 J.D.
Troilo, Nicholas J. '58 '94 (PA) C.223 B.S. L.1338 J.D.
Unitas, Robert D. '54 '80 (MA) C.1030 B.A. L.1202 J.D.
Watson, Jean M. Otey '56 '85 (VA) C.30 B.A. L.273 J.D.
Weeks, Nancy A. '57 '84 C.172 B.S. L.276 J.D.
Wheeler, Carolyn L. '44 '86 (MT) C.502 A.B. L.508 J.D.

OFFICE OF LEGAL COUNSEL

Adams, Colleen Lynn '— '94 C.1044 B.S.W. L.575 J.D.
Anderson, Corbett L. '70 '96 (PA) C.651 B.S. L.329 J.D.
Boymel, Paul E. '47 '76 C.197 A.B. L.966 J.D.
Brenner, Brett A. '68 '97 C&L.378 B.A.B.S., J.D.
Cleary, Joseph N. '43 '77 (MD) C.30 B.A. L.64 J.D.
Cooks, James E. '51 '79 (PA) C&L.329 B.S., J.D.
Courtney, Kathleen H. '54 '81 C.1044 B.A.
Dickinson, Lynn Tunnell '69 '96 C&L.945 B.A., J.D.
Goldstein, Gerald M. '47 '72 C&L.94 B.A., J.D.
Gray, Peter S. '51 '77 C.156 A.B. L.180 J.D.
Guerrant, Teresa '57 '85 C.329 B.A. L.273 J.D.
Gwynn, John C. '55 '81 C.339 B.A. L.329 J.D.
Herskowitz, Elaine N. '58 '83 C.659 B.A. L.276 J.D.
Hozempa, Gary J. '52 '77 C.823 B.A. L.276 J.D.
Inzeo, Nicholas M., II '50 '75 C.276 B.S.F.S. L.273 J.D.
Johnston, Dianna B. '45 '77 C.446 B.A. L.276 J.D.
Liss, David G. '47 '72 (PA) C.602 B.B.A. L.228 J.D.
Mastroianni, Peggy R. '41 '75 C.188 B.A. L.262 J.D.
Mauren, Mary Kay '61 '87 C.475 B.A. L.902 J.D.
Miaskoff, Carol R. '56 '87 C.309 A.B. L.273 J.D.
Murphy, Susan E. '52 '80 C.674 A.B. L.145 J.D.
Oram, Kathleen '58 '85 (MD) C.951 B.A. L.273 J.D.
Ravas, Theodore E., Jr. '43 '69 (MI) C.477 B.A. L.912 J.D.
Rennert, Sharon E. '59 '88 C.112 B.A. L.569 J.D.
Roscio, Richard V. '46 '75 C.93 B.S. L.818 J.D.
Samuels, Jocelyn F. '56 '84 C.478 B.A. L.178 J.D.
Sarpong, Awo A. '67 '91 C.66 B.A. L.569 J.D.
Schlageter, Thomas J. '51 '77 (NY) C.602 B.A. L.659 J.D.
Sober, James M. '47 '77 C.94 B.A. L.588 J.D.
Thompson, Stephanie Garner '47 '77 (NY) C.994 B.A. L.569 J.D.
Thurmond, A. Jacy, Jr. '52 '78 C.165 B.A. L.893 J.D.
Vargyas, Ellen J. '50 '74 C.951 B.A. L.659 J.D.

OFFICE OF THE CHAIRWOMAN

Khare, Laura Noel '69 '96 (SC) C.6 B.A. L.790 J.D.
Lopez, Louis '70 '96 C.378 B.S.J. L.309 J.D.

OFFICE OF THE COMMISSIONERS

Cottle, Lisa Sullivan '63 '88 (FL) C.914 B.A. L.276 J.D.
Eates, Antoinette M. '62 '87 (WV) C&L.923 B.A., J.D.
Levin, Naomi '59 '84 C.156 B.A. L.904 J.D.
Lew, Wallace T. '49 '74 C.911 B.A. L.910 J.D.
Miller, Paul Steven '61 '87 (CA) C.659 B.A. L.309 J.D.
Richard, R. Paul '50 '78 C.103 A.B. L.276 J.D.
Segal, Nancy E. '61 '88 C.604 B.A. L.588 J.D.

OFFICE OF FEDERAL OPERATIONS

Anderson, Clare G. '63 '91 C.569 B.A. L.128 J.D.
Badger, Deborah M. '50 '75 C.914 B.A. L.930 J.D.
Bloomfield, Elaine '45 '71 C.930 B.A. L.273 J.D.
Blumenthal, Ronnie '44 '69 C&L.273 A.B., J.D.
Bryan, Sandra G. '43 '77 C.145 B.A. L.818 J.D.
Caliendo, Madeline '63 '88 (NY) C.1044 B.A. L.30 J.D.
Cook, Susan Louise '59 '84 (PA) C.105 B.A. L.276 J.D.
Culbertson, Andrew '65 '91 (NY) C.696 B.A. L.107 J.D.
Denicoff, Todd Eliot '59 '85 C.445 B.S. L.64 J.D.
Dupont, Robyn Meyer '64 '89 (VA) C.896 B.A. L.273 J.D.
Ellington, A. Tonya '62 '88 (MD) C.329 B.A. L.446 J.D.
Fitzgerald, Marie A. '42 '80 C.273 B.A. L.329 J.D.
Hadden, Carlton Maurice '50 '86 (PA) C.574 B.A. L.128 J.D.
Hannan, Joan E. '38 '78 (VA) C.293 A.B. L.537 J.D.
Harris, William L., Jr. '25 '63 C&L.900 A.B., J.D.
Henry, Varice T. '48 '90 (PA) C.446 B.A. L.276 J.D.
Lee, Carley D. '61 '86 C.454 B.A. L.128 J.D.
Mecherikunnel, Thomas Paul '33 '78 C&L.999 B.S., LL.B.
Menoken, Cassandra M. '49 '74 C&L.329 B.A., J.D.
Miller, Melissa A. '61 '86 (VA) C.21 B.A. L.273 J.D.
Names, Donald J. '56 '86 C.1049 B.A. L.30 J.D.
Newell, Larry W. '52 '78 C&L.329 B.A., J.D.
Plotkin, Marc J. '60 '86 C.705 B.A. L.1292 J.D.
Popiden, Joseph S. '53 '79 C&L.229 B.A., J.D.
Roebuck, Thurman M. '42 '77 (PA) C.999 B.S. L.276
Schandler, Heidi L. '62 '87 C.705 B.A. L.8 J.D.
Vinson, Rosalind R. '62 '88 (MI) C.475 B.A. L.276 J.D.
Walker, Robert L. '43 '77 C.329 B.A. L.705 J.D.
Walker-Jones, Joyce '— '86 (IL) C.399 B.A. L.146 J.D.
Weintraub, Alan '60 '85 C.705 B.A. L.30 J.D.
Zanowic, Steven P. '60 '86 (NJ) C.645 B.A. L.273 J.D.

Office of Field Programs

Cruciani, Linda M. '59 '86 (NC) C.198 B.A. L.575 J.D.
Dougherty, Michael J. '49 '74 (PA) C.1030 A.B. L.734 J.D.
Schmelzer, John D. '48 '74 C.1365 B.A. L.472 J.D.

Washington, D.C. Field Office

Aram, Kathleen '51 '78 C.703 B.A. L.1209 J.D.
Bradley, Diane '62 '90 (PA) C.1042 B.A. L.329 J.D.
Bradley, Matthew E. '61 '89 (VA) C.945 B.A. L.128 J.D.
Brice, Barbara D. '64 '89 C.217 B.A. L.861 J.D.
Brown, Kathryn '64 '92 C.156 B.A. L.273 J.D.
Fellin, John K. '60 '89 (PA) C.560 B.A. L.276 J.D.
Goode, E. Kelly '59 '92 (VA) C.508 B.A. L.273 J.D.
Ichniowski, Stephen P. '60 '86 C&L.128 B.A., J.D.
Shih, Stephen T. '68 '93 C.228 B.S. L.910 J.D.
Teitelman, Samuel '46 '75 C.445 B.S. L.446 J.D.
Venture, Veronica A. '64 '91 (MD) C.183 L.30 J.D.
Walters-Marquez, Jeannette '60 '88 C&L.677 B.A., J.D.
Zeldin, Adria S. '55 '86 C.33 B.A. L.276 J.D.

Barnhart, Robert J. '56 '82 C.509 B.A. L.30 J.D.
Dorsey, William A. '48 '73 (CO) C.174 B.A. L.208 J.D.
Essenfeld, Ann P. '45 '79 (GA) C.999 B.A. L.1000 J.D.
Gonzales, Claire E. '— '84 (TX) C.1105 B.A. L.846 J.D.
Hostetler, Pamela E. '52 '88 (PA) C.970 B.A. L.930 J.D.
Kleinman, Chester J. '48 '83 (MD) C.563 B.S. L.64 J.D.
Kravetz, Joel A. '67 '95 C.945 B.A. L.818 J.D.
Llewellyn, Stephen '49 '75 C.732 B.A. L.276 J.D.
Matthews, Cynthia Clark '41 '75 C.329 B.A. L.273 J.D.
Morse, J. Kenneth L. '47 '75 (MI) C.604 B.A. L.477 J.D.
Pulley, Navarro '66 '98 (MD) C.329 B.A. L.1364 J.D.
Rodwell, Donna N. '59 '85 (TX) C.329 B.B.A. L.326 J.D.
Stephens, Regina Newell '61 '87 (PA) C.575 B.A. L.574 J.D.

EXECUTIVE OFFICE OF THE PRESIDENT

THE WHITE HOUSE OFFICE

Blakeman, Bradley A. '58 '87 C.4 B.A. L.1325 J.D.
Ciccone, Christine '64 '94 C.550 B.A. L.273 J.D.
Flippin, Laura L. '70 '96 C.945 B.A. L.893 J.D.
Jeffcoat, Scott D. '73 '99 (TX) C.839 B.A.B.S. L.326 J.D.
Mehlman, Kenneth B. '66 '91 C.264 B.A. L.309 J.D.
Oldham, Cheryl Ann '68 '93 C.840 B.A. L.744 J.D.
Patel, Neil S. '69 '97 C.855 B.A. L.276 J.D.
Rogers, Edwina Clifton '64 '91 C.16 B.S. L.128 J.D.
Schacht, Diana L. '58 '87 C.976 B.A. L.276 J.D.
Silverberg, Kristen L. '— '96 C.309 B.A. L.846 J.D.
Spagnoli, Deborah Ann '64 '95 C.112 B.A. L.464 J.D.

OFFICE OF ADMINISTRATION

Anderson, Catherine S. '61 '88 (PA) C.651 B.A. L.665 J.D.
Greenstone, Adam F. '63 '91 C.282 B.A. L.273 J.D.

OFFICE OF THE VICE PRESIDENT

Brown, Elizabeth M. '60 '88 C.674 B.A. L.145 J.D.
Samuel, William '56 '85 C.604 B.A. L.273 J.D.

OFFICE OF POLICY DEVELOPMENT

Howard, Heather H. '68 '98 (NY) C.228 B.A. L.569 J.D.
Lee, Malcolm R. '59 '89 C.976 B.A. L.659 J.D.
Punke, Timothy E. '71 '97 C&L.188 B.A., J.D.

NATIONAL SECURITY COUNCIL

Gibson, John D. '63 '87 C.273 B.A. L.893 J.D.

OFFICE OF MANAGEMENT AND BUDGET

Aitken, Steven D. '60 '85 (MA) C&L.309 B.A., J.D.
Alesi, Susan E. '44 '80 (VA) C.522 B.S. L.1209 J.D.
Beynon, Rebecca A. '63 '94 C&L.846 B.S., J.D.
Blum, Mathew C. '63 '88 C.945 B.A. L.273 J.D.
Christopoulos, James P. '66 '91 (MI) C.477 B.A. L.215 J.D.
Daniels, Mitchell E., Jr. '49 '79 C.674 A.B. L.276 J.D.
Dennis, Carol R. '— '84 (VA) C.228 B.A. L.1209 J.D.
Fairhall, Lisa B. '58 '81 (MA) C.1350 B.A. L.94 J.D.
Gerich, Michael D. '50 '78 (MD) C.682 B.A. L.1338 J.D.
Hickey, Michael J. '65 '00 (MD) C.999 L.1194 J.D.
Hill, Jefferson B. '41 '67 C&L.309 B.A., J.D.
Loeb, Richard Charles '56 '82 C.446 B.A. L.930 J.D.
Maris, Karen A. '53 '78 C.446 B.A. L.276 J.D.
Reed, McGavock D. '53 '80 (TN) C.838 B.A. L.836 J.D.

EXECUTIVE OFFICE OF THE PRESIDENT (Continued)

Rettman, Rosalyn J. ... '50 '77 C.604 A.B. L.477 J.D.
Sierra, Leticia ... '62 '89 C.976 B.A. L.101 J.D.
Waxman, Gary ... '52 '77 (PA) C.453 B.S. L.976 J.D.
Weinberg, Jeffrey A. ... '49 '75 C.178 B.A. L.273 J.D.

OFFICE OF THE U.S. TRADE REPRESENTATIVE

Alvarez, Kira M. ... '68 '94 C.681 A.B. L.276 J.D.
Brinza, Daniel E. ... '54 '80 C.477 A.B. L.309 J.D.
Davidson, Peter B. ... '62 '91 (MN) C.118 B.A. L.893 J.D.
Fabry, Steven F. ... '60 '85 C.976 B.A. L.309 J.D.
Field, Catherine R. ... '49 '82 C.37 B.A. L.276 J.D.
Freiberg, Kenneth P. ... '48 '75 C.112 B.A. L.1066 J.D.
Greenidge, Alicia D. ... '60 '92 C.415 B.A. L.93 J.D.
Haverkamp, Jennifer A. ... '57 '89 C.970 B.A. L.976 J.D.
Hirsh, Bruce R. ... '59 '90 C.103 B.S. L.813 J.D.
Hodgson, Mélida N. ... '64 '93 (NY) C.881 B.A. L.569 J.D.
Hunter, William D. ... '49 '77 C.813 A.B. L.273 J.D.
Kho, Stephen ... '69 '98 (MD) C.893 B.A. L.446 J.D.
Martyn, Willis S., III ... '64 '89 C.659 B.A. L.309 J.D.
Mattice, Alice L. ... '44 '77 C&L.309 B.A., J.D.
Millán, Juan A. ... '72 '98 C.674 A.B. L.976 J.D. Asst. Gen. Coun.
Mullaney, L. Daniel ... '57 '85 C.31 B.A. L.276 J.D.
Novelli, Catherine A. ... '57 '82 C.860 B.A. L.477 J.D.
Oliver, David W. ... '60 '87 C&L.012 B.A., LL.B.
Overton, Bruce L. ... '51 '77 C.112 B.A. L.426 J.D.
Peck, Brian ... '— '98 C.1375 B.A. L.1049 J.D.
Ross, David J. ... '67 '93 C.339 B.A. L.228 J.D.
Roth, L. James ... '— '95 C.911 B.A. L.678 J.D.
Schnare, Rhonda K. ... '66 '91 (MO) C.502 B.S.Acct. L.575 J.D.
Shub, Rachel ... '60 '86 C.103 A.B. L.861 J.D.
Winter, Audrey ... '56 '80 C&L.280 B.S., J.D.

COUNCIL ON ENVIRONMENTAL QUALITY

Athas, Ellen M. ... '54 '83 C.165 B.A. L.30 J.D.
Bear, Dinah ... '51 '77 C.502 B.J. L.464 J.D. Gen. Coun.
Connaughton, James L. ... '61 '89 C.976 B.A. L.597 J.D.
Cooney, Philip A. ... '59 '84 C.692 B.A. L.884 J.D.
Greczmiel, Horst G. ... '52 '77 (NJ) C.390 A.B. L.1292 J.D.
Leary, William L. ... '49 '74 (FL) C&L.259 B.A., J.D.

OFFICE OF NATIONAL DRUG CONTROL POLICY

Cichetti, Kevin P. ... '71 '96 (MD) C.1356 B.A. L.904 J.D.
Gottlieb, Michael K. ... '69 '96 C.1369 B.B.A. L.1017 J.D.
Hittle, L. Bradley ... '51 '76 C.911 B.A. L.273 J.D.
Jurith, Edward H. ... '51 '77 C.30 B.A. L.1009 J.D.
Peters, Joseph C. ... '57 '83 (PA) C.1113 B.A. L.1017 J.D.
Petersen, Daniel Robert ... '55 '91 (CO) C.173 B.M. L.1410 J.D.
Priebe, Linda V. ... '59 '90 C.1058 B.A. L.878 J.D.
Shull, David A. ... '46 '72 (FL) C&L.260 B.S.A.D., J.D.

EXPORT-IMPORT BANK OF THE UNITED STATES

John M. Niehuss, *General Counsel*

OFFICE OF THE GENERAL COUNSEL

Adler, Douglas Ochs ... '52 '80 C.273 B.A. L.128 J.D.
Boron, Krystyna ... '— '82 C.999 J.D. L.569 LL.M
Braun, Tracey E. ... '61 '86 C.945 B.A. L.893 J.D.
Cohen, Roger I. ... '62 '87 C.1044 B.A. L.309 J.D.
Connor, John G. ... '55 '85 C.331 B.A. L.145 J.D.
Cook, Kamil Poorman ... '67 '96 (NY) C&L.178 B.A., J.D.
Emery, Louis E. ... '49 '81 C.1266 B.A. L.982 J.D.
Geberth, Lisa G. ... '59 '86 C.183 B.A. L.276 J.D.
Kolstad, Carole Lynn ... '46 '70 C.339 B.S. L.846 J.D.
Lapin, Matthew D. ... '73 '99 (CA) C.112 B.A. L.30 J.D.
Manning, Barbara M. ... '66 '92 C.188 B.S. L.309 J.D.
Morin, Robert A. ... '57 '86 (NY) C.659 B.S. L.178 J.D.
Niehuss, John M. ... '37 '64 (OH) C.31 B.A. L.477 J.D. Gen. Coun.
Ohr, Clara J. ... '71 '99 (NE) C.309 B.A. L.494 J.D.
Philpott, Kathleen R. ... '68 '95 C.165 B.A. L.945 J.D.
Schweitzer, Howard A. ... '— '95 C.477 B.A. L.273 J.D.
Spivey, Michael J. ... '63 '90 (AR) C&L.45 B.A., J.D.
Stangland, Elaine ... '49 '78 C.112 B.A. L.1068 J.D. Dep. Gen. Coun.
Ubamadu, Bert C. ... '62 '91 (CA) C.927 B.A. L.1066 J.D.

FARM CREDIT ADMINISTRATION

Philip J. Shebest, *Acting General Counsel*

OFFICE OF THE GENERAL COUNSEL

Shebest, Philip J. ... '55 '80 (PA) C.649 B.A. L.831 J.D. Acting Gen. Coun.

REGULATORY ENFORCEMENT DIVISION

Cohen, Victor A. ... '46 '72 (PA) C.1044 B.A. L.831 J.D.
Katz, Richard A. ... '56 '81 (MI) C.904 B.A. L.215 J.D.
Orlich, Rebecca S. ... '49 '86 C.6 B.A. L.228 J.D.
Strickland, Joy ... '63 '88 (LA) C&L.420 B.S., J.D.
Van Meter, Gary K. ... '53 '81 (WV) C.250 B.S. L.923 J.D.

LEGAL COUNSEL DIVISION

Buffon, Kathleen V. ... '41 '81 C.518 B.A. L.30 J.D.
Cohn, Jennifer A. ... '67 '93 C.473 B.Phil. L.597 J.D.
Laguarda, Wendy R. ... '55 '86 C.860 B.A. L.273 J.D.
McFarland, Laura D. ... '— '93 C.267 B.S. L.990 J.D.
Morris, James M. ... '52 '78 (NY) C.103 B.A. L.659 J.D.
Rubin, Howard I. ... '62 '90 C.222 B.A. L.30 J.D.
Virga, Jane M. ... '59 '84 (CT) C.184 B.A. L.1048 J.D.

FEDERAL COMMUNICATIONS COMMISSION

(Vacant), *General Counsel*

OFFICE OF THE GENERAL COUNSEL

Aaron, Susan A. ... '62 '87 C.846 B.B.A. L.273 J.D.
Armstrong, Daniel M. ... '41 '66 (TN) C.575 A.B. L.309 J.D.
Barton, Eugenie N. ... '50 '90 C.771 B.A. L.273 J.D.
Bergold, Laurel R. ... '49 '75 C&L.273 B.A., J.D.
Bertman, Marjorie S. ... '48 '80 (VA) C.273 B.A. L.904 J.D.
Bird, James R. ... '47 '79 C.674 A.B. L.145 J.D.
Block, Stewart A. ... '46 '71 C.446 B.A. L.659 J.D.
Boehley, Lisa E. ... '62 '91 C.665 B.A. L.273 J.D.
Bourne, Laurence N. ... '55 '81 C.197 B.A. L.846 J.D.
Brooks, Cornell W. ... '61 '92 (PA) C.355 B.A. L.976 J.D.
Carr, James M. ... '59 '87 C.674 A.B. L.813 J.D.
Christopher, Gregory M. ... '41 '71 (AZ) C&L.36 B.A., J.D.
Conover, Carla ... '— '92 C.878 B.A. L.477 J.D.
Cook, Roberta L. ... '47 '75 C.454 B.A. L.546 J.D.
Dellar, Neil A. ... '58 '84 L.999 LL.B.
Diskin, Sharon R. ... '55 '80 C.1044 B.A. L.273 J.D.
Duignan, Maureen ... '52 '79 C.273 B.A. L.30 J.D.
Ellison, Paula M. ... '56 '81 C.228 A.B. L.329 J.D.
Guttmann, Sheldon M. ... '43 '69 C.494 B.A. L.878 J.D.
Hairston, Pamera D. ... '59 '84 (VA) C&L.945 B.A., J.D.
Halprin, Jane Hinckley ... '61 '86 C.456 B.S. L.818 J.D.
Harrold, Daniel J. ... '47 '72 C.546 B.S.B.A. L.846 J.D.
Horowitz, David E. ... '56 '83 C.145 B.A. L.477 J.D.
Ingle, John E. ... '35 '69 C.880 B.A. L.309 J.D.
Katz, Aliza F. ... '64 '89 C&L.659 B.A., J.D.
Kaufman, Joel ... '60 '85 C.676 B.A. L.228 J.D.
Kelley, Sharon B. ... '54 '80 (PA) C.205 B.A. L.1338 J.D.
Kinney, Linda I. ... '65 '91 C.881 A.B. L.893 J.D.
Krasnow, Michael A. ... '71 '99 (MA) C.216 B.A. L.93 J.D.
Launer, Susan L. ... '56 '82 C.1036 B.A. L.904 J.D.
Mago, Jane E. ... '53 '79 (NY) C&L.567 B.A., J.D.
Marcus, Joel ... '62 '89 C.659 B.S. L.309 J.D.
Martin, S. Lee ... '52 '77 C.188 B.A. L.602 J.D.
Pash, Clifford G., Jr. ... '46 '71 (KY) C.198 A.B. L.383 J.D.
Peraertz, Louis E. ... '63 '89 (MA) C.674 A.B. L.309 J.D.
Rabinovitz, Joel A. ... '62 '88 C&L.309 A.B., J.D.
Riffer, John I. ... '34 '60 (MI) C.228 B.A. L.477 LL.B.
Rifken, Sonja J. ... '64 '89 C.576 B.A. L.575 J.D.
Rogovin, John A. ... '61 '89 C.178 A.B. L.893 J.D.
Sacks, Allan ... '45 '70 (NY) C.563 B.A. L.569 J.D.
Schaffner, Lawrence S. ... '34 '61 C.569 B.S. L.276 J.D.
Schecker, Laurence H. ... '53 '79 (NY) C.659 B.S.B.A. L.94 J.D.
Scheiner, Stanley R. ... '55 '86 C.112 A.B. L.659 J.D.
Schneider, Mark A. ... '58 '84 (IL) C.112 B.A. L.209 J.D.
Senzel, David S. ... '49 '77 C.273 B.S. L.188 J.D.
Silberthau, Paula R. ... '50 '77 C.914 B.A. L.1066 J.D.
Smith, Pamela L. ... '63 '88 C.273 B.A. L.659 J.D.
Sonn, Marilyn D. ... '52 '77 C.477 B.A. L.276 J.D.
Stanley, John P. ... '68 '96 C.309 B.A. L.477 J.D. Asst. Chf. Pol. Div.
Steiman, Susan H. ... '46 '76 C&L.273 B.A., J.D.
Wall, Joanne Foster ... '59 '86 C.321 B.A. L.276 J.D.
Weiner, Debra A. ... '52 '78 C.914 B.A. L.94 J.D.
Welch, Richard K. ... '58 '88 (VA) C.575 B.S. L.902 J.D.

MASS MEDIA BUREAU

Aronowitz, Alan E. ... '54 '79 C.24 B.A. L.1202 J.D.
Baghdadi, Mania K. ... '46 '79 C.102 A.B. L.36 J.D.
Baker, Robert Lawrence ... '46 '72 C.260 B.S. L.276 J.D.
Bash, Eric J. ... '65 '91 (PA) C.228 A.B. L.659 J.D.
Berlin, Mark L. ... '47 '72 C.597 B.A. L.273 J.D.
Bernstein, Joyce L. ... '56 '80 C.610 B.A. L.273 J.D.
Bertelsen, Sharon M. ... '58 '87 C.475 B.A. L.990 J.D.
Bleiweiss, Irene ... '60 '85 C.1044 B.A. L.94 J.D.
Boyce, Roy W. ... '47 '72 C.264 A.B. L.276 J.D.
Brett, Amy L. ... '67 '93 C.446 B.A. L.128 J.D.
Brick, Barrett L. ... '54 '80 (NY) C&L.178 B.A., J.D.
Brown, Amelia Logan ... '60 '93 C.174 B.A. L.180 J.D.
Brown, David ... '69 '96 (NJ) C.188 B.A. L.659 J.D.
Brown, James J. ... '42 '68 C&L.262 B.A., LL.B.
Chessen, Rick Charles ... '61 '86 C.966 B.A. L.309 J.D.
Cooper, Hope G. ... '65 '89 (VA) C&L.893 B.A., J.D.
Dortch, Marlene ... '64 '92 (IL) C.276 A.B. L.608 J.D.
Doyle, Peter H. ... '51 '85 C.696 B.A. L.276 J.D.
Dupont, Deborah A. ... '51 '78 C.373 B.A. L.477 J.D.
Dziedzic, Charles E. ... '46 '71 (FL) C.383 B.A. L.259 J.D.
Fitzgerald, Mary M. ... '46 '72 C.770 B.A. L.1066 J.D.
Gorman, R. Barthen ... '44 '72 C.976 A.B. L.477 J.D.
Gross, Jane C. ... '46 '88 (IL) C.494 B.A. L.976 J.D.
Halprin, Ben ... '50 '86 (OR) C.999 B.A. L.629 J.D.
Hayne, Robert A. ... '44 '69 C.221 B.A. L.352 J.D.
Henry, Shaleim ... '— '96 C&L.329 B.A., J.D.
Holberg, Roger D. ... '49 '74 (MI) C.477 B.A. L.912 J.D.
Kreisman, Barbara A. ... '48 '73 C.446 B.A. L.30 J.D.
Lerner, Bradley E. ... '70 '95 (MI) C.477 B.A. L.912 J.D.
Maher, Shaun A. ... '63 '89 C.454 B.A. L.128 J.D.
Matthews, Ann Kimberly ... '59 '85 C.188 A.B. L.813 J.D.
McCauley, Victoria M. ... '58 '83 (OH) C.363 B.A. L.608 J.D.
McGovern, Jean Ann ... '66 '92 C.893 B.A. L.174 J.D.
McLean, Hae Kyung ... '58 '93 C.385 B.A. L.128 J.D.
Murphy, Mary Beth ... '62 '90 C.276 B.A. L.477 J.D.
Nessinger, Thomas S. ... '60 '85 (CA) C&L.602 B.A., J.D.
Pendarvis, Clay C. ... '42 '70 C&L.329 B.S., J.D.
Pulley, Lewis C. ... '54 '81 C.623 B.A. L.30 J.D.
Ratcliffe, Robert H. ... '45 '74 (MD) C.855 B.A. L.94 J.D.
Rhodes, Andrew J. ... '50 '76 C.112 A.B. L.426 J.D.
Roberts, David N. ... '59 '88 (TX) C.846 B.A. L.326 J.D.
Sabourin, Debra S. ... '51 '90 (PA) C.831 B.A. L.1292 J.D.
Schneider, Alan J. ... '46 '72 C.446 B.A. L.273 J.D.

OFFICE OF ENGINEERING & TECHNOLOGY

Romano, Bruce Alan ... '51 '76 C.1049 B.A. L.1068 J.D.

OFFICE OF THE COMMISSIONERS

Goldstein, Jordan ... '64 '94 C.966 B.A. L.813 J.D.
Scrutchins, Arthur D. ... '52 '80 (PA) C.188 B.S. L.831 J.D.
Shelter, Deen A. ... '64 '93 C.61 L.1068 J.D.

CABLE SERVICES BUREAU

Bartlome, Benigno E., Jr. ... '66 '94 C.112 B.S./B.A. L.128 J.D.
Cox, William P. ... '70 '96 (FL) C.228 A.B. L.464 J.D.
Esbin, Barbara S. ... '53 '82 C.33 B.A. L.228 J.D.
Ferree, Wayne Kenneth ... '60 '92 C.197 B.A. L.276 J.D.
Whitesell, Sarah ... '68 '93 C.198 B.A. L.976 J.D.

COMMON CARRIER BUREAU

Adams, John K. ... '60 '90 (FL) C&L.260 B.A., J.D.
Agee, William P. ... '— '89 C.94 B.A. L.1292 J.D.
Barna, Allen A. ... '49 '74 C.705 B.A. L.945 J.D.
Beers, Thomas J. ... '50 '81 C.494 B.A. L.276 J.D.
Bergmann, Scott K. ... '68 '93 (MD) C.228 B.A. L.800 J.D.
Berresford, John W. ... '50 '76 C&L.910 A.B., J.D.
Blue, Claire ... '— '91 (PA) C&L.990 B.A., J.D.
Burmeister, Theodore H. ... '72 '98 (NY) C.860 B.A. L.347 J.D.
Callahan, Cheryl L. ... '— '86 (MD) C.705 B.S. L.982 J.D.
Carey, Michelle M. ... '69 '93 C&L.276 A.B., J.D.
Chaiton, Shoshanna Kelly Heidi ... '73 '00 C.035 B.A. L.1202 J.D.
Cooke, Gregory M. ... '50 '91 (NY) C.94 B.F.A. L.262 J.D.
Dale, Anthony J. ... '68 '97 (MD) C.216 B.A. L.64 J.D.
Dever, William A., Jr. ... '62 '95 C.831 B.A. L.128 J.D.
Einhorn, Eric N. ... '70 '96 C.188 B.S. L.93 J.D.
Firth, Andrew L. ... '66 '92 C.270 B.A. L.602 J.D.
Fullano, Genaro G. ... '60 '90 C.423 B.A. L.128 J.D.
Garnett, Paul William ... '71 '98 C.867 B.A. L.128 J.D.
Goldschmidt, Aaron R. ... '68 '92 (FL) C.188 B.A. L.259 J.D.
Goyal, Praveen ... '74 '99 C.976 B.A. L.309 J.D.
Grayer, Cara T. ... '75 '01 C.811 B.A. L.30 J.D.
Guice, Gregory W. ... '65 '99 (VA) C.575 B.A. L.1209 J.D.
Harmon, Diane L. Griffin ... '65 '93 C.446 B.S. L.329 J.D.
Hays, John C. K. ... '38 '73 C.363 B.S.S. L.276 J.D.
Hollingsworth, Perlesta A., Jr. ... '70 '00 (CT) C.511 B.S. L.184 J.D.
Jackson, Jane E. ... '50 '76 C.66 B.A. L.880 J.D.
Jacobs, Michael J. ... '68 '94 C.228 A.B. L.800 J.D.
Janckson-Curtis, Ana J. ... '55 '83 C.914 B.A. L.273 J.D.
Jones, Marda ... '— '95 C.918 B.A. L.1009 J.D.
Jones, Marilyn ... '62 '93 (LA) C.1099 B.S. L.770 J.D.
Kehoe, William A., III ... '50 '76 C.197 A.B. L.276 J.D.
King, Katherine Ann ... '— '88 C.494 B.A. L.309 J.D.
Lerner, Richard D. ... '55 '81 C.477 B.A. L.575 J.D.
Libertelli, Christopher D. ... '69 '96 C&L.94 B.A., J.D.
Lien, Rhonda J. ... '— '94 (CA) C.427 B.A. L.1065 J.D.
Lucanik, JoAnn ... '56 '84 C.645 B.S. L.61 J.D.
Magnotti, Susan E. ... '52 '77 (VA) C.881 A.B. L.945 J.D.
Mattey, Carol E. ... '57 '83 C.893 B.A. L.659 J.D.
McDonald, Rodney L. ... '67 '94 (MD) C.188 B.A. L.329 J.D.
McKee, Jennifer K. ... '69 '94 C.823 B.A. L.276 J.D.
Milne, J.L. ... '50 '80 C.208 B.A. L.273 J.D.
Mulitz, Andrew G. ... '51 '85 C.393 B.A. L.128 J.D.
Nadel, Mark S. ... '56 '82 C.31 B.A. L.309 J.D.
Nankin, Helene Schrier ... '63 '88 C.659 B.A. L.904 J.D.
Nolen, Joi Roberson ... '68 '93 (MD) C.302 B.A. L.945 J.D.
Pabo, Claudia ... '51 '75 C.540 B.A. L.904 J.D.
Patterson, Julie Y. ... '69 '95 C.659 B.A. L.945 J.D.
Peterson, Timothy A. ... '54 '80 (GA) C&L.280 B.B.A., J.D.
Preiss, Tamara L. ... '63 '90 C&L.893 B.A., J.D.
Reel, Jonathan R. ... '55 '94 C.273 B.A. L.276 J.D.
Rosenworcel, Jessica ... '71 '98 C.918 B.A. L.569 J.D.
Savir, Mika Z. ... '57 '82 (NC) C&L.575 B.A., J.D.
Scher, William J. ... '65 '91 C.1044 B.A. L.273 J.D.
Schroder, Katherine L. ... '69 '95 C.914 B.A. L.309 J.D.
Schwimmer, Martin L. ... '46 '76 C.112 A.B. L.904 J.D.
Secrest, Jonathan D. ... '67 '00 C.31 B.A. L.597 J.D.
Shetler, Deena M. ... '64 '93 C.112 B.A. L.1068 J.D.
Slotten, Douglas L. ... '46 '76 C.352 B.B.A. L.36 J.D.
Smith, Richard D. ... '65 '90 (CA) C.800 B.S. L.990 J.D.
Smolen, Robin Beth ... '64 '95 C.994 B.A. L.724 J.D.
Stevens, Ann H. ... '51 '75 C.1322 A.B. L.180 J.D.
Stover, Jon R. ... '45 '74 C.918 B.A. L.273 J.D.
Tanner, Robert S. ... '69 '96 C.1074 B.A. L.1065 J.D.
Teicher, Gayle R. ... '55 '80 C.112 A.B. L.426 J.D.
Terry, Renee ... '61 '85 (MA) C.557 B.A. L.329 J.D.
Thaggert, Henry, III ... '65 '94 (PA) C.861 B.A. L.569 J.D.
Thomas, Alan A. ... '59 '88 (PA) C.976 B.A. L.276 J.D.
Tofigh, Katherine S. ... '72 '97 (TX) C.401 B.A. L.802 J.D.
Walters, K. Michele ... '66 '95 C.309 A.B. L.976 J.D.
Ward, David O. ... '53 '88 (NY) C.994 B.A. L.1040 J.D.
Webber, Sharon L. ... '64 '91 C.831 B.S. L.30 J.D.
Williams, Romanda L. ... '— '01 C.945 B.A. L.180 J.D.
Williams, Sanford Scott ... '67 '97 (VA) C.188 B.S. L.893 J.D.
Zinman, Jack S., Jr. ... '69 '94 (PA) C.893 B.S. L.884 J.D.

CONSUMER INFORMATION BUREAU

Blackwell, Geoffrey C. ... '69 '95 (MA) C.197 B.A. L.893 J.D.
Hertz, Roger J. ... '44 '69 (PA) C.659 B.A. L.1017 J.D.
Hlibok, Gregory James ... '67 '95 (NY) C.270 B.A. L.1019 J.D.
Marshall, Scott ... '51 '77 C.696 B.A. L.309 J.D.
Mukhoty, Sumita ... '52 '88 (NM) C.999 B.A. L.560 J.D.
Peltz-Strauss, Karen ... '56 '81 C.94 B.A. L.659 J.D.
Sievert, Janet L. ... '53 '87 (MO) C.1347 B.S. L.734 J.D.
White, George F., III ... '60 '91 C.446 B.A. L.276 J.D.

INTERNATIONAL BUREAU

Albers, Thomas N. ... '45 '70 C&L.588 B.A., J.D.
Ball, James L. ... '48 '73 C.932 B.S. L.30 J.D.
Barrie, Julie A. ... '69 '94 C.696 B.A. L.276 J.D. Sr. Legal Adv.
Bell, William H., Jr. ... '46 '73 (PA) C.228 B.A. L.1017 J.D.
Buchanan, Julia C. ... '65 '91 C.228 A.B. L.188 J.D.
Choi, Lisa C. ... '71 '96 C.945 A.B. L.309 J.D.
Coles, John M. ... '51 '76 (PA) C.188 B.A. L.273 J.D.
Collins, Kathleen ... '48 '87 (VA) C.893 B.A. L.273 J.D.
Connor, Justin A. ... '72 '98 C.231 B.A. L.588 J.D.
Copes, John F. ... '46 '72 (OH) C.967 B.A. L.608 J.D.
Dubroof, Linda B. ... '54 '82 C.454 B.A. L.1049 J.D.
Field, Alexandra M. ... '68 '95 (MD) C.309 A.B. L.276 J.D.
Gerr, Pamela ... '57 '85 C.264 B.A. L.228 J.D.
Gilsenan, Jennifer M. ... '68 '94 (MD) C.205 B.A. L.64 J.D.
Giusti, John V. ... '69 '94 (MA) C.260 B.S. L.94 J.D.
Gomez, Anna M. ... '67 '92 C.645 B.A. L.273 J.D.
Griboff, Howard ... '60 '93 C.659 B.A. L.1068 J.D.
Haller, Linda L. ... '57 '86 C.273 B.A. L.276 J.D.
Holiday, Cecily C. ... '49 '80 (TX) C&L.846 B.A., J.D.
Jarmulnek, Fern J. ... '57 '81 C.102 B.A. L.309 J.D.
Kensinger, Karl A. ... '60 '85 C.145 B.A. L.477 J.D.
Krech, David H. ... '59 '84 C.585 B.A. L.273 J.D.
McElvane, Roxanne ... '59 '84 C.30 B.S. L.329 J.D.
Murphy, Christopher J. ... '64 '90 (CA) C.112 B.A. L.464 J.D.
Nixon, Belinda Elvan ... '68 '94 (MD) C.813 A.B. L.276 J.D.
O'Brien, Kathryn A. ... '63 '93 C.788 B.A. L.588 J.D.
O'Connell, Susan Lee ... '55 '83 C.976 B.A. L.128 J.D.
Reideler, Terrence E. ... '40 '71 C.999 B.A. L.692 J.D.
Somers, Robert Bruce ... '57 '83 C.94 B.A. L.930 J.D.
Spaeth, Steven M. ... '63 '89 (WI) C.476 B.S. L.597 J.D.
Thomas, Cassandra C. ... '54 '81 C.783 B.A. L.93 J.D.
Young, J. Mark ... '59 '92 C.945 A.B. L.276 J.D.

WIRELESS TELECOMMUNICATIONS BUREAU

Abeyta, Dan David ... '54 '80 C.972 B.A. L.823 J.D.
Arsenault, Richard J. ... '61 '91 C.882 B.S. L.273 J.D.
Augustin, Genevieve Elizabeth ... '68 '95 (MD) C.1222 B.S. L.276 J.D.
Benson, Guy N. ... '69 '96 (CA) C.112 B.A. L.128 J.D.
Blakeney, Shellie N. ... '— '97 (MD) C.257 B.S. L.823 J.D.
Borkowski, John Joseph ... '52 '76 (OH) C&L.602 A.B., J.D.
Branscome, John B. ... '64 '92 C.886 B.A. L.902 J.D.
Burnley, Kenneth W. ... '59 '92 C.1042 B.S. L.329 J.D.
Burton, Jennifer A. ... '56 '95 C.846 B.S. L.801 J.D.
Cabral, Rosemary R. ... '— '97 (CT) C.1157 B.A. L.823 J.D.
Cannon, Robert M. ... '64 '92 (VA) C.604 B.A. L.30 J.D.
Carson, Cheryl B. ... '— '97 C.276 A.B. L.309 J.D.
Connelly, Michael E. ... '63 '93 C.112 A.B. L.560 J.D.
Coward, Lloyd W. ... '62 '88 C.446 B.A. L.273 J.D.
Crellin, Rose M. ... '— '94 (PA) L.1209 J.D.
Danner, Sandra K. ... '53 '88 C.945 B.A. L.893 J.D.
D'Ari, Paul ... '54 '90 C.112 B.A. L.446 J.D.
Daronco, Peter J. ... '61 '86 C.30 B.A. L.1040 J.D.
Davenport, Howard C. ... '54 '80 C.94 B.A. L.446 J.D.
Delacourt, Scott D. ... '71 '96 C.276 B.A. L.477 J.D.
Desai, Monica Shah ... '69 '94 C.273 B.B.A. L.276 J.D.
Elder, Alice L. ... '57 '91 C.150 B.A. L.107 J.D.
Evanoff, John A. ... '74 '99 (MD) C.262 B.A. L.30 J.D.
Franklin, Karen D. ... '69 '94 C.329 B.A. L.880 J.D.
Friedman, Suzan ... '52 '78 (PA) C.30 B.A. L.1202 J.D.
Furth, David L. ... '57 '84 C.309 B.A. L.813 J.D.
Gacek, Christopher M. ... '61 '95 C.659 B.S. L.893 J.D.
Guendelsberger, Nese B. ... '63 '95
Ham, Kathleen O'Brien ... '58 '88 C.174 B.S. L.128 J.D.
Harris, Katherine M. ... '56 '81 C.939 B.A. L.309 J.D.
Hayes, Edward L., III ... '57 '97 C.329 B.B.A. L.893 J.D.
Hochstein, Leora ... '65 '92 C.264 B.A. L.659 J.D.
Huber, William W. ... '63 '94 C.674 A.B. L.767 J.D.
Jackler, Leon Jay ... '71 '98 (MD) C&L.861 B.A., J.D.
Johnson, Don ... '62 '90 (FL) C.276 B.A. L.128 J.D.
Johnson, Elias G. ... '61 '87 C.103 B.A. L.276 J.D.
Kim, Won ... '60 '95 (MD) C.999 B.A. L.276 J.D.
Kimmel, Susan Landay ... '48 '96 (MD) C.145 B.A. L.904 J.D.
Kunze, William W. ... '60 '94 C&L.976 B.A., J.D.
Littell, Melinda Skinner ... '65 '91 C.428 B.A. L.276 J.D.
Mackoul, Scott A. ... '71 '96 C.228 B.A. L.260 J.D.
Martin, Regina Marie ... '71 '97 C.411 B.A. L.831 J.D.
McGrath, Erin A. ... '73 '00 (NY) C.645 B.A. L.999 J.D.
Melson, Ramona E. ... '— '85 (PA) C.999 B.A. L.276 J.D.
Michaels, Gary D. ... '55 '80 C.659 B.A. L.273 J.D.
Monteith, Kris Anne ... '55 '88 C.174 B.A. L.273 J.D.
Murray, Paul E. ... '57 '89 C.813 B.A. L.228 J.D.
Mussenden, Roberto Rene ... '65 '94 (NC) C.228 B.S./B.A. L.1209 J.D.
Nakazawa, Zenji ... '— '93 (VA)
Nixon, Wilbert E., Jr. ... '57 '84 C&L.273 B.S.E.E., J.D.
Noone, Paul ... '64 '99 (MD) C.645 B.S. L.1338 J.D.
O'Donnell, Brian C. ... '71 '98 (PA) C.529 B.A. L.1017 J.D.
Ohlson, Barry J. ... '67 '92 C.945 B.A. L.273 J.D.
Phillips, Jane E. ... '44 '77 C.188 B.A. L.94 J.D.
Prime, Jamison S. ... '71 '96 (IN) C.210 B.A. L.1119 J.D.
Ray, Linda C. ... '54 '82 C.788 A.B. L.893 J.D.
Rowan, Michael J. ... '68 '98 C.112 B.A. L.880 J.D.
Rubin, Mark Stuart ... '— '86 (MA) C.860 B.A. L.1202 J.D.
Salhus, Jennifer E. ... '72 '97 (VA) C.93 B.A. L.904 J.D.
Salovaara, Erik Jorma ... '67 '93 C.309 A.B. L.145 J.D.
Schlichting, James D. ... '53 '81 C.976 B.A. L.309 J.D.
Scinto, Blaise A. ... '63 '93 C&L.893 B.A., J.D.
Shields, Christopher M. ... '64 '97 C.754 B.S. L.776 J.D.
Siehl, David H. ... '46 '75 C.188 B.A. L.273 J.D.
Spencer, John M. ... '46 '73 C.475 B.A. L.477 J.D.
Steinberg, Jeffrey S. ... '61 '87 (NY) C&L.976 B.A., J.D.
Stone, Scot ... '64 '89 (CA) C.597 B.A. L.1068 J.D.
Taubenblatt, Joel D. ... '70 '95 C.659 B.A. L.228 J.D.
Terry, D'wana ... '65 '90 C.390 B.A. L.893 J.D.
Thyden, Freda Lippert ... '44 '70 C&L.569 B.A., J.D.
Tomchin, Jennifer B. ... '73 '97 C.309 B.A. L.276 J.D.
Vadas, Gregory R. ... '70 '96 (NJ) C.705 B.A. L.1292 J.D.

FEDERAL COMMUNICATIONS COMMISSION (Continued)

Van Wazer, Lauren Maxim '63 '92 C.659 B.S.E. L.276 J.D.
Weingarten, Steven E. '59 '85 (MD) C.276 B.A. L.659 J.D.
Whaley, John William (Jay) '54 '94 C.1044 B.A. L.285 J.D.
Wiener, Margaret W. '51 '77 C.976 B.A. L.569 J.D.
Wiggins, Stanley P. '48 '76 C&L.477 B.A., J.D.
Wilhelm, Michael J. '38 '76 C.215 Ph.B. L.260 J.D.
Wolfe, Peter G. '40 '65 C&L.178 A.B., J.D.
Woytek, Mary E. '52 '77 C.341 B.A. L.602 J.D.
Wypijewski, Anne Marie '60 '86 C.223 B.S. L.1019 J.D.
Zoslov, Amy J. '58 '83 C.94 B.S. L.930 J.D.

OFFICE OF PLANS AND POLICY

Telecommunications Consumer Division

Carlton, Emmitt H., Jr. '61 '87 C.103 B.A. L.893 J.D.
Goodman, Amy Glatter '60 '85 C&L.446 B.A., J.D.
Heitkamp, Colleen K. '52 '91 (MD) C&L.446 B.S., J.D.
Power, Katherine C. '— '79 (VA) C.806 B.A. L.128 J.D.
Schroeder, Kurt Allan '59 '87 (IA) C.293 B.A. L.352 J.D.
Vermillera, Lynn J. '66 '92 C.66 B.A. L.273 J.D.
Wyatt, Thomas D. '55 '84 C.16 B.A. L.904 J.D.

Market Disputes Resolution Division

Bridgham, Tracy E. '58 '87 C.999 B.S. L.128 J.D.
Cheng, Anita Y. '67 '94 (VA) C.472 B.A. L.276 J.D.
Dygert, Jeffrey H. '63 '90 C&L.893 B.A., J.D.
Karmarkar, Radhika V. '66 '91 C.51 B.A. L.30 J.D.
Lamancusa, Frank G. '63 '88 C.105 B.A. L.930 J.D.
Mette, Roderick A. '36 '62 (IL) C&L.602 B.B.A., LL.B.
Reynolds, Glenn T. '62 '88 C&L.893 B.A., J.D.
Rogers, Wallett Bancroft '43 '73 (IL) C.145 B.A. L.597 J.D.
Royle, Lia B. '56 '87 (NY) C.575 B.A. L.178 J.D.
Scavetta, Joseph F., Jr. '69 '97 C.893 B.A. L.602 J.D.
Seifert, Mark G. '62 '92 C.88 B.A. L.893 J.D.
Strickland, David A. '70 '95 C.893 B.A. L.309 J.D.

Technical & Public Safety Division

Durham, Ricardo M. '54 '80 (PA) C.302 B.A. L.1162 J.D.
Ellington, Jacqueline E. '65 '95 C.999 B.S. L.128 J.D.
Fitz-Gibbon, Thomas D. '— '68 (WI) C&L.966 B.S., J.D.
Hollingsworth, W. Riley '46 '73 (SC) C.790 B.A. L.896 J.D.
Laden, Y. Paulette '48 '78 C.449 B.A. L.276 J.D.
Manuel, Allan Kenneth '66 '91 C.446 B.A. L.472 J.D.

Investigations & Hearings Division

Chakerian, Gerald H. '46 '74 (NM) C.685 B.A. L.560 J.D.
Goldstein, Norman '42 '69 C.145 A.B. L.597 J.D.
Harkrader, Trent Lloyd Bruce '70 '95 (TX) C.228 B.A. L.802 J.D.
Kellett, William K. '62 '88 (PA) C.311 B.A. L.1017 J.D.
Kelley, Charles W. '40 '65 (NY) C&L.262 B.S., J.D.
Remy, Raelynn Tibayan '69 '94 C.205 B.A. L.128 J.D.
Schauble, John J. '60 '85 C.855 B.A. L.273 J.D.
Scheibel, Kenneth M., Jr. '56 '86 (PA) C.446 B.A. L.128 J.D.
Schonman, Gary P. '53 '82 (NY) C.107 B.A. L.1040 J.D.
Shook, James William '51 '77 C.674 A.B. L.276 J.D.
Withers, Catherine M. '63 '88 C.813 B.A. L.1097 J.D.

Berthot, Kathryn S. '64 '90 (MD) C&L.446 B.A., J.D.
Collier, Lloyd D. '66 '92 C.659 B.S. L.976 J.D.
Cyrus-Williams, Donna Marie '65 '96 (FL) C.831 B.S. L.259 J.D.
Davenport, William H. '68 '93 C.597 B.A. L.659 J.D.
DeLaurentis, Anthony J. '58 '84 C.524 B.A. L.128 J.D.
Fowlkes, Lisa M. '65 '90 C.656 B.S. L.665 J.D.
Godschall, Melanie A. '58 '85 C.597 B.A. L.945 J.D.
Griffin, Lisa Burns '65 '90 C.188 B.S. L.309 J.D.
Hardie, Yanic L. '— '96 (NY) C.1093 B.A. L.564 J.D.
Hunt, David L. '58 '87 C.273 B.A. L.276 J.D.
Jackson, Kimberly A. '66 '95 (MD) C.276 B.A. L.329 J.D.
Leavitt, Dana Elizabeth '61 '97
Lee, Sharon D. '— '97 (MD) C.329 B.B.A. L.273 J.D.
Mehta, Tejal '67 '91 (PA) C.691 B.A. L.326 J.D.
Olsen, Christopher N. '64 '89 C.197 A.B. L.893 J.D.
Starr, Alexander P. '59 '85 C.813 B.A. L.309 J.D. Chief
Valinoti, Elizabeth H. '69 '97 C.280 A.B.J. L.128 J.D.

FEDERAL DEPOSIT INSURANCE CORPORATION

William F. Kroener, III, *General Counsel*

SUPERVISION AND LEGISLATION BRANCH

Jones, Douglas H. '47 '73 (MD) C&L.446 B.S., J.D.
Kroener, William F., III '45 '72 C.976 A.B. L.813 J.D. Gen. Coun.

REGULATION AND LEGISLATION SECTION

Anderson, Marilyn E. '58 '85 (MD) C.446 B.S. L.273 J.D.
Basham, James G. '64 '89 (KY) C.27 B.A. L.383 J.D.
Bellotto, Christopher J '51 '81
Borzillo, Michelle M. '56 '85 (OK) C.208 B.A. L.616 J.D.
DiNuzzo, Joseph A. '53 '80 C.569 B.S. L.982 J.D.
Goldstrom, Marc J. '59 '84 (MI) C.475 B.A. L.912 J.D.
Hudson, James D. '57 '82 (TN) C.122 B.A. L.838 J.D.
Jensen, Gail K. '53 '81 C.228 B.A. L.30 J.D.
Jones, William I. '54 '79 (LA) C&L.420 B.A., J.D.
LeCren, Pamela E.F. '51 '78 C.665 B.A. L.831 J.D.
Norcom, Janet V. '60 '86 (PA) C.339 B.A. L.884 J.D.
Phillips, Michael B. '49 '78 (MA) C.454 B.A. L.910 J.D.
Ray, Rodney D. '57 '82 (TN) C.835 B.S. L.838 J.D.
Recchia, Nancy J. Schucker '54 '87 (CT) C.216 B.A. L.831 J.D.
Rollin, Claude A. '61 '86 C.823 B.A. L.1292 J.D.
Sallberg, Leslie S. '59 '85 C.97 B.A. L.990 J.D.

COMPLIANCE AND ENFORCEMENT SECTION

Alper, Nancy L. '51 '79 C.164 B.A. L.30 J.D.
Bogue, Richard A. '48 '75 C.867 B.A. L.228 J.D.
Gardiner, Grovetta N. '60 '88 (PA) C.896 B.A. L.574 J.D.
Gore, Gregory E. '50 '82 C.72 B.A. L.1218 J.D.
Houle, Philip P. '45 '70 (ME) C.1266 B.A. L.1294 J.D.
Winkler, Andrea J. '53 '78 C.318 B.A. L.904 J.D.

Regional Affairs Section

Schulz, Thomas A. '44 '70 (OH) C&L.150 B.S.E.E., J.D.

Receivership Operations and Litigation Section

Bolt, Thomas P. '53 '80 (OK) C.612 B.A. L.623 J.D.
Kaplow, Charlotte M. '44 '80 (IL) C.530 B.A. L.46 J.D.
Lamoreaux, Tina A. '58 '83 C.763 B.A. L.61 J.D.
Lantelme, James T. '53 '80 (MD) C.994 B.A. L.276 J.D.
Liles, John H., Jr. '47 '76 (TX) C.326 B.S. L.796 J.D.
Mitchell, Paul Alan '50 '82 C.276 B.S. L.128 J.D.
Osterman, Richard J., Jr. '55 '80 (MD) C.821 B.A. L.64 J.D.
Peyster, Richard I. '52 '78 C.178 B.A. L.1194 J.D.
Reeves, Tom M. '46 '71 (KS) C&L.378 B.S., J.D.
Ribnick, Catherine A. '46 '75 C.788 B.A. L.273 J.D.
Richards, Daniel R. '53 '79 (MI) C.347 B.A. L.213 J.D.
Spear, Alan L. '57 '83 (TN) C.679 B.A. L.838 J.D.
Stoner, Gordon G. '50 '77 C.37 B.A. L.36 J.D.
Tishuk, Barbara Starke '59 '89 (VA) C.273 B.A. L.30 J.D.
Wall, David N. '56 '80 C.188 B.A. L.477 J.D.

PROFESSIONAL LIABILITY SECTION

Ahrens, Roy '47 '71 (TX) C.805 B.A. L.69 J.D.
Alexis, Agnes '59 '85 (NY) C.659 B.A. L.893 J.D.
Davis, Mary P. '52 '78 (OK) C.623 B.A. L.862 J.D.
DeHenzel, Robert J., Jr. '51 '78 (MN) C.443 B.S. L.300 J.D.
Haygood, Katharine H. '47 '77 C.10 B.A. L.16 J.D.
Powalski, Lynn Marie '62 '88 C.1340 B.A. L.904 J.D.
Robb, Marianne '58 '85 C.856 B.A. L.1040 J.D.
Robinson, Floyd I. '46 '73 C.797 B.A. L.846 J.D.
Satterwhite, Melissa '54 '85 C.1130 B.A. L.280 J.D.
Schwartz, Richard M. '58 '82 C.659 B.A. L.276 J.D.
Sommers, Emily E. '43 '77 C.446 B.A. L.128 J.D.
Thomas, John V. '45 '70 (OH) C.347 B.S. L.976 LL.B.
Topping, Catherine Ray '59 '84 (OH) C.207 B.A. L.117 J.D.
van Berg, Joan S. '53 '82 C.94 B.A. L.978 J.D.
Williams, Jeffrey R. '59 '85 C.886 B.A. L.809 J.D.

APPELLATE LITIGATION SECTION

Boles, Colleen B. '55 '80 (VA) C.30 B.A. L.945 J.D.
DuRoss, Ann S. '43 '68 C.289 B.A. L.128 J.D.
Gunning, Kathleen V. '52 '79 C.788 A.B. L.93 J.D.
McGillicuddy, Robert D. '51 '79 C&L.276 B.A., J.D.
McGuire, Claire L. '52 '77 C.242 B.A. L.93 J.D.
Norcross, Kathryn R. '54 '79 C&L.201 B.A., J.D.
Palau, Manuel A. '53 '78 C.446 B.S. L.128 J.D.
Richmond, Lawrence H. '50 '76 C.1044 B.A. L.276 J.D.
Roach, Jeannette E. '46 '84 C.910 B.A. L.128 J.D.
Sarshik, Barbara '51 '76 C.918 B.A. L.659 J.D.
Taner, Jaclyn C. '48 '74 (NY) C.66 B.A. L.309 J.D.
Watson, James Scott '60 '83 C.1209 B.A. L.273 J.D.
Woodall, Barbara S. '51 '76 C.945 B.A. L.1119 J.D.

TRIAL LITIGATION SECTION

Bank, Susan Kantor '54 '80 C.30 B.A. L.904 J.D.
Biblin, Dina L. '54 '78 C&L.273 B.A., J.D.
Birdwell, Z. Scott '62 '89 (GA) C.1147 B.A. L.280 J.D.
Bunning, Joan J. S. '53 '80 C.914 B.A. L.446 J.D.
Chaly, Ingeborg G. '46 '82 (MD) C.610 B.A. L.1003 J.D.
Clark, Robert G. '42 '69 C.453 B.S. L.273 J.D.
Cope, Charles L., II '42 '70 C&L.477 B.A., J.D.
Davison, Patricia E. '58 '84 C.329 B.A. L.659 J.D.
Downing, John T. '51 '76 C&L.446 B.A., J.D.
Holzman, Thomas L. '50 '77 C.31 B.A. L.659 J.D.
Kloner, Wendy '53 '78 C.1036 B.A. L.1162 J.D.
Miller, Lisa M. '54 '83 C.36 B.A. L.910 J.D.
Owen, Marguerite S. '38 '64 C.881 A.B. L.976 LL.B.
Ross, Daniel F. '43 '68 (MI) C&L.477 A.B., J.D.
Taylor, Gregory '61 '87 (MD) C.945 B.A. L.128 J.D.

CORPORATE AFFAIRS SECTION

Cosgrove, Michael S. '54 '74 (PA) C.1113 B.A. L.665 J.D.
Golden, Gregg H. S. '53 '80 C.293 A.B. L.276 J.D.
Goodman, Larry L. '44 '73 C.150 B.A. L.851 J.D.
Houldsworth, Edwin C. '33 '61 (MI) C.475 B.A. L.912 J.D.
Kurtenbach, Daniel H. '57 '83 C&L.546 B.A., J.D.
Nelson, Pamela C. '48 '91 (PA) C.327 B.S. L.1209 J.D.
Ramirez-Cuebas, Nestor D. '47 '73 (PR) C.677 B.A. L.1087 J.D.
Rego, Linda S. '48 '90 (KY) C&L.383 B.S., J.D.
Rider, Donald G. '47 '88 (MD)
Ross, Rita Wiles '55 '81 (MA) C.860 B.A. L.93 J.D.
Schwartz, Saul Y. '56 '82 C&L.665 B.A., J.D.
Stamp, Linda L. '57 '81 (CO) C.208 B.S. L.174 J.D.
Ward, Kathryn L. '47 '80 (FL) C&L.823 B.S., J.D.

OUTSIDE COUNSEL SECTION

Birch, David A. '44 '73 C.93 B.S. L.776 J.D.
Flake, Kathleen '49 '80 C.101 B.A. L.878 J.D.
Furtney, Gayle L. '54 '86 (TX) C.104 B.A. L.862 J.D.

FINANCIAL CRIMES UNIT

Banks, Jock A. '53 '79 C.30 B.A. L.276 J.D.
Davidovich, John A. '47 '74 (IL) C.121 B.S. L.209 J.D.
Gilbride, Edward F. X. '52 '78 C.116 B.A. L.1009 J.D.

Katron, Barbara A. '59 '83 C.645 B.A. L.665 J.D.
Mahshie, John T. '60 '89 (VA) C.276 B.S. L.823 J.D.

OFFICE OF LEGISLATIVE AFFAIRS

Hooper, Loren T. '43 '75 C.347 B.A. L.1049 J.D.

OFFICE OF THE CHAIRMAN

Hood, Roger A. '32 '60 C&L.575 A.B., J.D.

OFFICE OF THE EXECUTIVE SECRETARY

Feldman, Robert E. '56 '81 (RI) C.103 A.B. L.30 J.D.
Fox, Patti C. '50 '81 C.1130 B.A. L.790 J.D.
Williamson, M. Jane '58 '84 C.309 A.B. L.228 J.D.

OFFICE OF INSPECTOR GENERAL

Bernardo, Andrea Q. '— '87 C.788 A.B. L.818 J.D.

OFFICE OF PERSONNEL MANAGEMENT

Scholl, David B. '53 '79 C.401 B.A. L.128 J.D.

DIVISION OF BANK SUPERVISION

Planning and Program Development

Carley, William P. '31 '66 C.602 B.S. L.276 J.D.
Hrindac, William G. '36 '68 (MD) C.935 B.A. L.659 LL.B.
Ty, Felipe F. '43 '87 (NY) C.397 B.S.C. L.999 LL.B.

Bain, Randolph A. '52 '83 (CA) C.112 B.A. L.1067 J.D.
Barker, James M. '50 '83 (NE) C.350 B.S. L.190 J.D.
Black, Patricia M. '51 '76 C.346 B.S. L.904 J.D.
Breslaw, April Anne '61 '85 (MD) C.472 B.A. L.273 J.D.
Clark, James P. '54 '78 C.546 B.A. L.145 J.D.
Cohen, Alan B. '55 '80 C.216 B.A. L.273 J.D.
Collishaw, William C. '39 '64 C.197 A.B. L.976 LL.B.
Durocher, Joan M. '72 '97 (MI) C.475 B.A. L.446 J.D.
Dyess, William A. '40 '64 (TX) C.921 B.S. L.69 LL.B.
Eisenstein, David G. '47 '72 C.966 B.A. L.309 J.D.
Ely, Donna R. '59 '85 (NJ) C.608 B.M. L.776 J.D.
Falloon, Elizabeth '56 '81 C.446 B.S. L.276 J.D.
Fisher, David '45 '70 C.688 B.Mgt.E. L.184 J.D.
FitzGerald, David M. '47 '73 (MI) C.93 A.B. L.477 J.D.
Gamble, Carl F. '53 '79 (FL) C.150 B.A. L.602 J.D.
Hanas, Stephen M. '54 '83 (IL) C.1024 B.S. L.365 J.D.
Hurrington, R. Kenneth '— '77 (TX) C.846 B.A. L.744 J.D.
Jones, William S. '50 '78 (GA) C.188 B.A. L.280 J.D.
Jupiter, Jay A. '46 '80 C.563 B.B.A. L.128 J.D.
Karjala, John G. '40 '71 C.494 B.A. L.862 J.D.
Kuiper, Gary A. '51 '81 (CO) C.114 A.B. L.276 J.D.
Kusinski, Arthur J. '40 '65 (NY) C.299 A.B. L.178 LL.B.
Lee, Robert '57 '83 (HI) C.628 B.S. L.629 J.D.
Lindenmuth, Philip J. '57 '86 (VA) C.30 B.A. L.1209 J.D.
Manning, Robert A. '51 '78 C.1349 B.A. L.262 J.D.
Marshall, Mira Nan '51 '82 C.454 B.A. L.813 J.D.
McClellan, Martha W. '46 '77 C.1142 B.A. L.273 J.D.
McNamar, Mary Ann '41 '82 (MD) C.20 B.A. L.426 J.D.
Morris, Jo Anne '— '79 C.838 B.A. L.893 J.D.
Mounts, Richard '43 '87 (MD) C.112 B.A. L.904 J.D.
Pinansky, David M. '53 '79 (ME) C.164 B.A. L.1202 J.D.
Rigby, Suzanne '61 '86 (MD) C.877 B.S. L.273 J.D.
Sarisky, Thomas J. '57 '82 (PA) C.264 B.A. L.884 J.D.
Saunders, Pamela H. '56 '89 (OH) C.97 B.S. L.329 J.D.
Shiffrin, David E. '49 '75 C.155 B.A. L.1202 J.D.
Smith, Gregory B. '49 '75 C.1209 B.A. L.128 J.D.
Soffer, Robert J. '59 '86 C.446 B.A. L.904 J.D.
Weight, Wayne V. '49 '83 (NE) C.593 B.S. L.190 J.D.
Ziebert, Peter A. '59 '85 C.276 A.B. L.436 J.D.

FEDERAL ELECTION COMMISSION

(Vacant), *General Counsel*

OFFICE OF THE GENERAL COUNSEL

Allen, Mark R. '63 '89 (MA) C.197 B.A. L.93 J.D.
Bader, Richard B. '47 '75 C.604 A.B. L.800 J.D.
Baker, Gregory R. '62 '90 (PA) C.903 B.A. L.607 J.D.
Baker, Holly '48 '93 (MA) C.966 Ph.D. L.93 J.D.
Bernstein, Jonathan A. '56 '81 C.882 B.A. L.966 J.D.
Blumberg, Peter G. '67 '92 (IL) C.339 B.A. L.209 J.D.
Bonham, Robert W., III '55 '80 C.347 B.S. L.1119 J.D.
Buckley, Anthony T. '61 '87 C.728 B.A. L.884 J.D.
Calvert, Lawrence L., Jr. '64 '93 (MD) C.838 B.S. L.276 J.D.
Clair, Vivien '45 '70 (IL) C.145 B.A. L.597 J.D.
Convery, Vincent J., Jr. '45 '71 C.276 A.B. L.896 J.D.
Deeley, Kevin '73 '00 C.93 B.A. L.309 J.D.
Dillenseger, Dominique '58 '84 C.674 B.A. L.893 J.D.
Dinh, Mai '69 '97 C.659 B.A. L.273 J.D.
Fowle, Cheryl A. '65 '95 C.1248 B.S. L.128 J.D.
Gould, Jack A. '57 '87 C.112 B.A. L.464 J.D
Hart, Kimberly D. '64 '89 C.30 B.A. L.893 J.D.
Heilizer, Ruth I. '55 '89 C.339 B.A. L.145 J.D.
Hershkowitz, Stephen E. '45 '75 C.1019 B.S. L.273 LL.B.
Hildebrand, Leigh Gipson '75 '00 C.934 B.A. L.280 J.D.
Holloway, Lorenzo '64 '89 (PA) C.659 B.A. L.831 J.D.
Kolker, David '58 '85 C.976 B.A. L.309 J.D.
Lerner, Lois G. '50 '78 (MA) C.588 B.S. L.1048 J.D.
Levin, Jonathan M. '53 '80 C.867 B.A. L.273 J.D.
Ligon, Tracey F. '65 '91 (MD) C.302 B.S. L.273 J.D.
Litchfield, N. Bradley '42 '71 C.243 B.A. L.329 J.D.
Marinelli, Michael G. '60 '88 C.178 B.A. L.273 J.D.
McDonnell, Xavier K. '56 '89 (MA) C.455 B.S. L.1202 J.D.
Meeker, Tara D. '70 '95 (TN) C.1081 B.B.A. L.327 J.D.
Monaghan, Erin K. '67 '92 C.893 B.A. L.309 J.D.
Mueller, Gregory J. '72 '98 (VA) C.766 B.A. L.128 J.D.
Odrowski, Dawn M. '58 '90 (WI) C.1151 B.A. L.966 J.D.
Painter, Delanie D. '59 '87 (CA) C.228 A.B. L.1066 J.D.
Pineda, Andre G. '66 '91 C.339 B.S. L.801 J.D.
Pugh, J. Duane, Jr. '66 '91 C.188 B.S. L.659 J.D.
Reimer, Rita Ann '47 '74 (VA) C.205 B.A. L.273 J.D.
Rigsby, Delbert K. '60 '87 (PA) C.511 B.A. L.273 J.D.
Robinson, Kasandra Crystal '71 '00 C.446 B.S. L.329 J.D.
Sands, April J. '70 '94 (MD) C&L.846 B.B.A., J.D.
Sanford, Paul '64 '91 (OH) C.610 B.S. L.851 J.D.
Saulnier, Julie '54 '80 C.928 B.A. L.813 J.D.
Scurry, Michael E. '76 '00 C.1419 B.A. L.585 J.D.
Sealander, Colleen Tove '64 '93 (VA) C.608 B.A. L.273 J.D.
Shackelford, William S. '62 '88 C.478 B.A. L.893 J.D.
Shaine, Abigail A. '54 '78 C.976 B.A. L.94 J.D.
Sharkey, Tracy Lyn '68 '93 (OH) C&L.8 B.A., J.D.
Shonkwiler, Mark D. '63 '88 C.502 B.S.P.A. L.477 J.D.
Smith, Rosemary Claire '55 '84 C.1044 B.A. L.273 J.D. Asst. Gen. Coun.
Summers, Harry Jacobs '64 '90 (CA) C.178 B.A. L.276 J.D.
Toalson, Margaret J. '— '94 C&L.502 A.B., J.D.
Veldhuyzen, Albert R. '63 '90 C.597 B.A. L.1209 J.D.
Vosdingh, Rhonda J. '65 '91 C.352 B.A. L.309 J.D.
Weissenborn, Anne A. '39 '77 C.926 B.A. L.128 J.D.
Wyatt, Jamila Iman '73 '98 C.893 B.A. L.273 J.D.

OFFICES OF THE COMMISSIONERS

Bowman, Jeffrey H. '54 '79 (WI) C.958 B.S. L.273 J.D.
Gillespie, Veronica M. '49 '90 (VA) C.966 B.A. L.1209 J.D.
Johnson, Karen V. '53 '83 (PA) C.665 B.A. L.276 J.D.
McGarry, John W. '25 '56 L.276 J.D. Comr.
Reel, Anton E., III '48 '75 (MS) C&L.500 B.A., J.D.
Thomas, Scott E. '53 '77 C.813 B.A. L.276 J.D. Comr.
Wold, Darryl R. '41 '67 (CA) C.154 B.A. L.813 J.D.

FEDERAL EMERGENCY MANAGEMENT AGENCY

(Vacant), *General Counsel*

OFFICE OF THE GENERAL COUNSEL

Adamcik, Carol Ann '69 '94 C.705 B.S. L.659 J.D.
Bergerbest, Nathan S. '57 '81 C.563 B.A. L.800 J.D.
Brown, Michael D. '54 '81 C.614 B.A. L.616 J.D.
Broyles, Edward A. '50 '80 C.1111 B.A. L.329 J.D.
deBorja, Ramoncito J. '68 '94 C.1042 B.A. L.823 J.D.
Herman, Michael S. '— '90 C.705 B.A. L.1292 J.D.
Hoburg, Leigh M. '55 '81 C&L.770 B.A., J.D.
Montoya, Barbara D. '70 '95 (IA) C.694 A.B. L.221 J.D.
Trissell, David A. '67 '92 (OK) C&L.623 B.A., J.D. Trial Atty.
Watson, Martha J. '32 '73 C.801 B.S. L.128 J.D.
Weinhouse, Amy M. '66 '93 C.103 A.B. L.262 J.D.

General Law Division

Brock, Robert S. '51 '76 (VA) C.896 B.A. L.192 J.D. Assoc. Gen. Coun.
Johnson, Lafayette N. '60 '87 (FL) C.329 B.A. L.276 J.D.
Kleederman, Eva Susan '51 '86 (MD) C.788 B.A. L.273 J.D.
Phillips, Peggy A. '51 '92 (PA) C.273 B.A. L.180 J.D.

Litigation Division

Bees, Margaret M. '43 '85 C.446 B.A. L.64 J.D.
Fried, Jordan S. '58 '90 C.855 B.A. L.273 J.D.
Pilgrim, Lynda K. '60 '88 C&L.45 B.S., J.D.

Program Law Division

Chan, Elaine I. '51 '82 C.674 A.B. L.276 J.D.
Katchka, Elizabeth H. '66 '93 (MD) C.473 B.A. L.276 J.D.
Mazur, Cynthia Stelle '54 '86 C.308 B.A. L.823 J.D.
Miller, H. Crane '35 '60 C.951 A.B. L.893 LL.B.
Neal, Richard L., Jr. '64 '97 (AZ) C.112 B.A. L.1209 J.D.

FEDERAL ENERGY REGULATORY COMMISSION

(Vacant), *General Counsel*

OFFICE OF THE GENERAL COUNSEL

Abendroth, Timm L. '48 '77 C.399 B.A. L.966 J.D.
Albert, Judith '46 '76 C&L.30 B.A., J.D.
Alpert, Hollis J. '54 '78 C.597 B.A. L.575 J.D.
Anas, Demetra E. '60 '86 C.914 B.A. L.904 J.D.
Arneson, Joel K. '54 '80 (SD) C.182 B.A. L.221 J.D.
Arnold, Elizabeth J. '62 '89 (MD) C.280 B.S. L.904 J.D.
Bardee, Michael D. '56 '84 C.623 B.A. L.569 J.D.
Beamon, Charles A. '62 '87 (VA) C.886 B.A. L.893 J.D.
Blakeway, Victor D. '44 '69 (TX) C&L.846 B.A., J.D.
Blome, William O. '51 '76 C.309 A.B. L.659 J.D.
Bose, Kimberly A. '61 '88 C.302 B.S. L.329 J.D.
Brooks, Keith M. '52 '85 (PA) C.645 B.S. L.273 J.D.
Bruno, Kim G. '55 '83 C.1077 B.A. L.770 J.D.
Burgess, Thomas J. '47 '74 (RI) C.676 A.B. L.128 J.D.
Caldwell, Connie '51 '82 C.437 B.A. L.923 J.D.
Christin, Barbara K. '47 '78 (MD) L.276 J.D.
Clark, Anja M. '42 '78 C.606 B.A. L.365 J.D.
Clements, John H. '52 '80 C.477 B.A. L.025 LL.B.
Cockrell, Joel M. '49 '73 C.273 B.A. L.124 J.D.
Coffman, David H. '43 '71 C.802 B.A. L.309 J.D.
Cohen, Gary D. '51 '76 C&L.831 B.A., J.D.
Collins, William J. '49 '83 C.893 B.A. L.245 J.D.
Cotleur, Michael D. '47 '73 C.383 A.B. L.608 J.D.
Court, Susan J. '44 '80 (KY) C.1118 B.A. L.1340 J.D.
Dameron, Sharon L. '55 '84 (VA) C.273 B.S. L.30 J.D.
Denkinger, Marc G. '40 '64 (MI) C&L.477 A.B., LL.B.
Desmond, Cecilia M. '— '87 C.446 B.A. L.904 J.D.
Dickey, David R. '49 '79 (MD) C.640 B.A. L.64 J.D.

FEDERAL ENERGY REGULATORY COMMISSION (Continued)

Dunlap, David W. '54 '79 (VA) C.399 B.A. L.273 J.D.
Elliott, Sandra L. '51 '76 (VA) C.446 B.A. L.945 J.D.
Faerberg, David B. '63 '88 C.446 B.A. L.64 J.D.
Farran, Maria L. '56 '87 C.183 B.A. L.902 J.D.
Fields, Rhodell G. '50 '75 C.302 B.A. L.477 J.D.
First, Jonathan E. '61 '86 C.446 B.S. L.276 J.D.
Fischer, Stuart '61 '86 C.216 B.A. L.273 J.D.
Francese, Albert J. '44 '71 C&L.276 B.S.F.S., J.D.
Froehlich, Jane Elizabeth '55 '82 C.103 A.B. L.245 J.D.
Froehlich, William J. '50 '76 C.1349 B.A. L.1009 J.D.
Gadani, Jignasa '74 '00 C.209 B.A. L.146 J.D.
Gasteiger, Larry D. '64 '89 (PA) C.659 B.A. L.1017 J.D.
Gastilo, J. Carmen '53 '78 C.276 A.B. L.273 J.D.
Gilbert, Linda S. '54 '79 C.604 A.B. L.352 J.D.
Gingold, Edward G. '44 '77 C.861 B.A. L.569 J.D.
Gish, Brian R. '54 '78 C.282 B.A. L.273 J.D.
Goldenberg, Michael '52 '77 C.1044 B.A. L.966 J.D.
Goodson, Andre A. '57 '84 C.329 B.S. L.276 J.D.
Gorton, Ann E. '61 '86 (LA) C.420 B.A. L.861 J.D.
Govan, Cynthia A. '49 '80 C.174 B.A. L.1162 J.D.
Gransee, Marsha L. '52 '78 C.608 B.A. L.1003 J.D.
Greenbaum, Alan '47 '72 C.446 B.A. L.273 J.D.
Greenfield, Lawrence R. '55 '79 C.945 B.A. L.273 J.D.
Hadlock, Lorna J. '56 '83 C.945 B.A. L.692 J.D.
Hathaway, Merrill F., Jr. '45 '73 C&L.309 B.A., J.D.
Hecht, Rachel R. '36 '87 C.188 B.A. L.273 J.D.
Henry, Michael G. '68 '98 C.276 A.B. L.846
Heydt, Donald A. '46 '81 C.604 A.B. L.930 J.D.
Heyman, Amy R. '50 '85 C.608 B.A. L.329 J.D.
Higginbottom, Samuel L., Jr. '48 '74 (GA) C&L.178 B.A., J.D.
Holden, Edwin H., III '47 '73 C.367 B.A. L.904 J.D.
Holmes, Jacqueline S. '— '80 (TX) C&L.846 B.A., J.D.
Hooks, Marcia Connelly '50 '78 C.446 B.S. L.329 J.D.
Howe, Richard, Jr. '47 '72 (WI) C.309 B.A. L.966 J.D.
Huggins, Janet L. Oakley '53 '81 C.597 B.A. L.329 J.D.
Johnson, Carol Cox '58 '88 C.1209 B.S. L.893 J.D.
Kelly, Richard E. '51 '76 C&L.276 B.A., J.D.
Kendall, Jack O. '51 '77 C.923 B.A. L.276 J.D.
Kolotushkina, Olga E. '73 '98 C.1124 B.A. L.150 J.D.
Korthaus-Vos, Ellen J. '66 '91 (IA) C&L.352 B.S., J.D.
Koves, Scott E. '47 '75 C.339 B.A. L.345 J.D.
Kozlowski, Hadas Z. '61 '86 (MA) C.914 B.A. L.94 J.D.
Kroeger, John R. '60 '86 C&L.273 B.A., J.D.
Lake, Julia '48 '86 (VA) C.273 B.A. L.192 J.D.
Lane, Dennis '48 '75 C.321 A.B. L.588 J.D.
Lawson, Quentin A. '47 '80 (MI) C.976 B.A. L.477 J.D.
Lee, Linda L. '48 '73 (KS) C&L.378 B.A., J.D.
Long, Joseph H. '45 '71 C.112 A.B. L.1066 J.D.
Long, Lisa T. '55 '85 C.1280 B.A. L.329 J.D.
Lucas, Jenifer L. '45 '75 (KS) C.862 B.S. L.900 J.D.
Lurensky, Marcia A. '48 '73 (MA) C.938 A.B. L.93 J.D.
Lynch, Joseph C. '40 '66 C.716 B.A. L.262 LL.B.
Lyon, Andrew L. '42 '72 (MD) C.154 B.A. L.1065 J.D.
Macpherson, Janice '54 '78 C.94 B.A. L.276 J.D.
Madden, Kevin P. '52 '80 C.446 B.A. L.1209 J.D.
Mamone, Russell B. '29 '65 C.608 B.M.E. L.930 J.D.
Marlette, Cynthia A. '50 '79 C.1111 B.A. L.30 J.D.
Martin, Dawn Kimberly '60 '85 C.329 B.A. L.30 J.D.
McBride, Suzanne Keppeler '74 '00 C.94 B.A. L.276 J.D.
McLean, Robert D. '59 '85 (ND) C&L.585 B.S.B.A., J.D.
McNamara, Suzanne H. '59 '84 C&L.276 B.A., J.D.
Melvin, Dennis H. '48 '74 C.896 B.B.A. L.776 J.D.
Miller, Thajauna D. '53 '78 C.1036 B.A. L.659 J.D.
Minnis, Frederick G., Jr. '45 '77 C&L.329 B.A., J.D.
Molloy, Elizabeth M. '60 '85 C.216 B.A. L.128 J.D.
Morgan, Ethel L. '34 '84 (NY) C.1057 B.A. L.276 J.D.
Morie, Roger P. '53 '79 C.208 B.A. L.178 J.D.
Myler, John A. '42 '72 C.999 B.A. L.494 J.D.
Notargiacomo, Moira '58 '91 C.446 B.A. L.1218 J.D.
Nygaard, Kristina '47 '74 C.821 B.A. L.930 J.D.
Oberoi, Geeta '71 '96 C.273 B.A. L.692 J.D.
Olson, Ingrid M. '47 '78 C.207 B.A. L.128 J.D.
O'Malley, Joseph B. '47 '73 (MA) C.860 B.A. L.94 J.D.
Pacella, Beth G '— '89 (MA) C.156 B.A. L.94 J.D.
Pease, Robert E. '53 '81 C.216 B.A. L.284 J.D.
Penn-Jenkins, Monique '66 '94 C.893 B.A. L.329 J.D.
Pepper, James A. '58 '83 C.383 B.A. L.608 J.D.
Perry, Lona T. '60 '86 C&L.893 B.A., J.D.
Pulas, Demetrios G., Jr. '49 '75 C.30 B.A. L.276 J.D.
Pursley, Thomas A., III '44 '69 C.165 A.B. L.273 J.D.
Reed, Presley R., Jr. '54 '88 C.94 B.A. L.846 J.D.
Robinson, John M. '44 '70 C.821 B.A. L.659 LL.B.
Roidakis, Peter J. '45 '78 C.276 A.B. L.30 J.D.
Rothenberg, Steven '52 '77 C.659 B.S. L.145 J.D.
Rothman, Steven A. '48 '73 C.910 B.A. L.273 J.D.
Rylander, Elizabeth Evans '73 '99 C.893 B.A. L.945 J.D.
Schall, Ellen K. '47 '75 C.107 B.A. L.537 J.D.
Schratwieser, Diane Beaudry '54 '84 C&L.326 B.A., J.D.
Seigel, Jessica A. '51 '77 C.912 B.A. L.477 J.D.
Shepard, Helen S. '67 '99 C.31 B.A. L.597 J.D.
Sheppeard, Laura K. '53 '79 C.838 B.A. L.273 J.D.
Silverman, Jacob '35 '61 (NY) C.102 B.A. L.178 LL.B.
Soopper, Samuel '48 '76 C.273 B.A. L.128 J.D.
Soto, Andrew K. '62 '87 C.264 B.A. L.884 J.D.
Sultan, Shaheda '44 '85 C.034 B.A. L.128 J.D.
Szopo, Irene E. '46 '87 C.569 B.S. L.276 J.D.
Tao, Leonard Michael '60 '85 C.339 B.S. L.273 J.D.
Thompson, Gilda Ena '52 '80 C.262 B.A. L.569 J.D.
Tishman, David G. '44 '72 C&L.705 B.A., J.D.
Toepfer, Betty Nora '48 '89 (CT) C.563 B.A. L.978 J.D.
Tsang, Lori J. '55 '81 C.347 B.S. L.1119 J.D.
Vallance, Laura Jean '67 '94 (MD) C.30 B.A. L.1209 J.D.
Van Der Jagt, Carolyn '55 '91 (PA) C.586 B.B.A. L.846 J.D.
Vasapoli, Dennis '53 '80 C.276 B.A. L.945 J.D.
Vouras, Maria '— '00 C.893 B.A. L.1209 J.D.
Wagner, Gordon '54 '91 (IL) C.536 B.A. L.339 J.D.
Weiss, Patricia L. '— '83 C.679 B.S. L.273 J.D.
White, Lodie Dianne '64 '00 C.912 B.S. L.904 J.D.
White, Richard A. '49 '82 C.1209 B.A. L.276 J.D.
Whitfield, James, Jr. '42 '72 C&L.325 B.A., J.D.
Withnell, David D. '50 '84 C.164 B.A. L.128 J.D.
Wolf, Stanley '52 '78 C.494 B.A. L.1068 J.D.
Wolfman, Andrea C. '53 '78 C.788 A.B. L.477 J.D.
Wood, Harris S. '37 '68 (TX) C.846 B.A. L.276 J.D.
Wood, Warren C. '51 '78 C&L.902 B.A., J.D.
Wuehrmann, David B. '46 '71 C&L.228 B.A., J.D.
Yanoff, Erica Jay '59 '85 (MD) C&L.446 B.A., J.D.

Office of the Secretary

Boergers, David P. '45 '72 C.573 B.S. L.128 J.D.

OFFICE OF THE ADMINISTRATIVE LAW JUDGES

Birchman, Bruce L. '40 '62 C&L.705 B.A., J.D.
Brenner, Lawrence '46 '74 C.102 B.A. L.107 J.D.
Cintron, Carmen A. '53 '78 C&L.677 B.B.A., J.D.
Cowan, William J. '40 '72 (MA) C&L.588 B.A., J.D. Dep. Chief Admin. Law Judge
Dowd, Judith A. '40 '66 C.1295 B.A. L.276 LL.B.
Grossman, Herbert '34 '61 C.188 B.A. L.178 LL.B.
Harfeld, David I. '35 '59 C.692 B.A. L.477 J.D.
Leventhal, Jacob '16 '42 C.569 B.A. L.1009 J.D.
McCartney, Bobbie J. '54 '79 C.1061 B.A. L.326 J.D.
Nacy, Joseph R. '25 '51 C&L.734 J.D.
Silverstein, Edward M. '42 '71 C.588 A.B. L.94 J.D.
Wagner, Curtis L., Jr. '28 '52 C.834 L.838 LL.B. Chief Admn. Law J.
Zimmet, Raymond M. '36 '61 C.446 B.A. L.893 J.D.

OFFICE OF THE COMMISSIONERS

Benge, Mary E. '56 '88 (OK) C.30 B.A. L.862 J.D.
Ferguson, Walter C. '61 '87 C&L.497 B.B.A., J.D.
Hebert, Curtis L, Jr. '62 '89 C.499 B.S. L.356 J.D.
Hilliard, Andrea Riddle '51 '75 (KY) C&L.383 B.A., J.D.
Massey, William L. '48 '73 C.632 B.A. L.45 J.D.
Miles, Richard L. '47 '73 (MD) C&L.64 B.A., J.D.
Nichols, Nils N. '56 '81 C&L.923 B.A., J.D.
Peters, Philip D. '48 '73 (AR) C.632 B.A. L.45 J.D.
Rokach, Joshua Zev '51 '75 C.563 B.A. L.976 J.D.
Solomon, Robert H. '60 '86 C.659 B.A. L.910 J.D.

OFFICE OF MARKETS, TARIFFS AND RATES

Cannon, Shelton '52 '81 (MD) C.446 B.A. L.339 J.D.
Clarey, Patrick E. '68 '96 (MD) C&L.128 B.A., J.D.
Delude, Sandra J. '54 '80 C.882 B.A. L.180 J.D.
Larcamp, Daniel L. '52 '77 (WV) C&L.923 B.S., J.D.
Norman, Jeffrey B. '46 '73 C.273 B.A. L.1068 J.D.
Pederson, James A. '55 '82 (MD) C.893 B.A. L.64 J.D.
Sparber, Frank A. '46 '76 C.659 B.A. L.1209 J.D.

OFFICE OF ENERGY PROJECTS

McGovern, Peter J. '47 '77 (OK) C&L.862 B.S., J.D.

McIver, Milton E. '55 '86 C.905 B.A. L.329 J.D.

FEDERAL HOUSING FINANCE BOARD

Deborah F. Silberman, *General Counsel*

OFFICE OF GENERAL COUNSEL

Berg, Eric E. '54 '84 (NY) C.1044 B.A. L.107 J.D.
Crowley, Neil R. '54 '79 C.454 B.A. L.818 J.D.
Guy, David A. '44 '73 C.1111 B.A. L.260 J.D.
Kaye, Janice A. '61 '89 C.94 B.S. L.276 J.D.
Like, Sharon B. '57 '83 C.976 B.A. L.276 J.D.
Mantini, John C. '49 '79 (OH) C.201 B.S. L.273 LL.M.
Raudenbush, Eric M. '65 '92 (PA) C.264 L.902 J.D.
Reid, Charlotte A. '53 '82 C.611 B.A. L.128 J.D.
Silberman, Deborah F. '52 '81 C.156 B.A. L.128 J.D. Gen. Coun.

OFFICE OF THE BOARD OF DIRECTORS

Gray, James H., Jr. '58 '84 C.315 B.A. L.880 J.D.

FEDERAL LABOR RELATIONS AUTHORITY

(Vacant), *General Counsel*

OFFICE OF THE GENERAL COUNSEL

Feder, David L. '49 '75 (PA) C.1044 B.A. L.588 J.D.
Svartz, Steven H. '49 '75 C.453 B.S. L.276 J.D.
Zorn, Richard L. '52 '84 (OH) C.319 B.A. L.201 J.D.

OFFICE OF THE CHAIRMAN AND MEMBERS

Armendariz, Othoniel (Tony) '24 '56 C.859 B.S. L.744 J.D. Member
Constantine, Peter John '62 '89 C.970 B.A. L.30 J.D.
Pope, Carol Waller '52 '78 (MA) C.783 B.A. L.588 J.D.

OFFICE OF COLLABORATION AND ALTERNATIVE DISPUTE RESOLUTION

Andary, Robert G. '47 '74 C.276 B.A. L.893 J.D. Inspector Gen.
Feil, Fern Jill '67 '92 C.188 B.S. L.228 J.D.

AUTHORITY MEMBER STAFF

Bachman, Edward F. '39 '74 C.823 B.A. L.273 J.D.
Birch, George W. '46 '73 (OH) C.610 B.B.A. L.608 J.D.

Collins, Dennis B. '46 '82 C.694 B.A. L.904 J.D.
Crawford, Gloria J. '46 '76 C.329 B.A. L.273 J.D.
Eddy, David Sherwood, III '72 '98 (NY) C.696 B.A. L.188 J.D.
Hammer, Arnold A. '42 '67 C.188 B.S. L.276 J.D.
Hutchinson, Peter A. '67 '99 C.446 B.A. L.180 J.D.
Jacob, Nancy S. '51 '93 C.150 B.A. L.446 J.D.
Maldonado, M. E. G. '56 '81 (PR) C&L.677 B.B.A., J.D.
McCluskey, Susan D. '52 '77 C.208 B.A. L.188 J.D.
Naylor, Kathryn A. '64 '98 (IL) C.103 B.A. L.930 J.D.
Nichols, Elvin C. '48 '80 (MA) C.188 B.A. L.93 J.D.
Pass, Sonya Yvette '70 '00 C.1223 B.S. L.245 J.D.
Reinhart, Gail D. '57 '81 C.401 B.A. L.276 J.D.
Ryan, Mary Beth '51 '81 C.338 B.A. L.276 J.D.
Solowiej, Sandra M. '53 '79 C.645 B.A. L.192 J.D.
Spooner, Sarah Whittle '70 '97 (NY) C.461 B.S. L.1009 J.D.
Ullman, Paul H. '70 '96 C.529 B.A. L.329 J.D.
Underwood, William K. '50 '75 (KS) C&L.378 B.A., J.D.
Van Doren, Jon F. '— '97 (MD) C.205 B.A. L.1019 J.D.
Wolcott, Clinton D. '55 '80 C.231 B.A. L.276 J.D.

OFFICE OF THE SOLICITOR

Blandford, James F. '47 '85 (MD) C.903 B.A. L.446 J.D.
Boehm, Ann M. '66 '90 C.575 B.A. L.893 J.D.
Johnson, Pamela P. '52 '79 C.30 B.A. L.329 J.D.
Persina, William E. '46 '73 C.188 B.S. L.273 J.D.
Smith, David M. '49 '74 C&L.16 B.A., J.D.
Tobey, William R. '46 '76 (VA) C.118 B.A. L.273 J.D.

OFFICE OF THE ADMINISTRATIVE LAW JUDGES

Devaney, William B. '20 '49 C&L.608 B.A., J.D. Admn. Law J.
Nash, Eli, Jr. '35 '65 C&L.30 B.A., J.D. Admn. Law J.
Oliver, Garvin L. '37 '64 C.273 B.A. L.30 J.D. Admn. Law J.
Pearson, Richard A. '51 '75 C.893 B.A. L.184 J.D.

WASHINGTON REGIONAL OFFICE

Belasco, Lisa '65 '94 C.823 B.S. L.273 J.D.
Corrado, Jeanne Marie '66 '91 C.884 B.A. L.128 J.D.
Doheny, Michael W. '41 '73 C.781 B.A. L.128 J.D.
Liggett, Barbara S. '52 '78 (TX) C&L.838 B.A., J.D.
Walsh, Sara L. '67 '96 (OH) C.183 B.A. L.596 J.D.

FEDERAL SERVICE IMPASSES PANEL

DiTullio, Donna M. '— '79 C.229 B.A. L.1234 J.D.
Kolansky, Ellen J. '42 '87 (VA) C.273 B.A. L.1209 J.D.
Moffett, Kenneth E., Jr. '58 '89 (NY) C.446 B.A. L.262 J.D.
Perciaccante, Marianne '64 '98 (NY) C.276 A.B. L.188 J.D.

FEDERAL MARITIME COMMISSION

(Vacant), *General Counsel*

OFFICE OF THE GENERAL COUNSEL

Devine, Jennifer C. '70 '96 (NY) C.164 B.A. L.273 J.D.
Dickon-Matney, Rachel E. '72 '97 (MD) C.846 B.A. L.273 J.D.
Dike, Theresa '71 '00 L.30 J.D.
Fenneman, Rebecca A. '67 '96 (MD) C.893 B.A. L.446 J.D.
Hughey, Christopher '71 '97 (NY) C.953 B.A. L.188 J.D.
Larson, Amy Wright '64 '92 C.938 B.A. L.128 J.D.
Miles, David R. '48 '75 C.197 B.A. L.1162 J.D.
Napier, Kim T. '75 '01 C.512 B.A. L.30 J.D.
Neustadt, Carol J. '44 '74 C.24 B.A. L.273 J.D.
Trogdon, Benjamin K. '52 '82 C.575 B.A. L.1194 J.D.

BUREAU OF ENFORCEMENT

Berestov, Julie L. '72 '98 (PA) C.30 B.A. L.831 J.D.
Burns, Heather M. '70 '97 (CA) C.475 B.S. L.273 J.D.
De La Cruz, Zoraya B. '71 '99 C.1375 B.A. L.273 J.D.
Haslup, Charles L., III '41 '70 C.321 B.S. L.446 J.D.
Hill, Vern W. '50 '77 C&L.101 B.A., J.D. Dir.
Keane, Martha S. '64 '89 (PA) C.797 B.A. L.861 J.D.
King, Peter J. '54 '78 C.128 B.A. L.273 J.D.
Kontos, Anargiros N. '74 '00 C.575 B.A. L.273 J.D.

OFFICE OF ADMINISTRATIVE LAW JUDGES

Dolan, Frederick M., Jr. '24 '50 C&L.276 A.B., LL.B.
Kline, Norman D. '30 '59 C.309 A.B. L.94 J.D. Chief
Lang, Paul B. '38 '69 C.871 B.S. L.273 J.D. Admin. Law J.

COMMISSIONERS' OFFICES

Creel, Harold J., Jr. '57 '83 (LA) C.968 B.A. L.790 J.D. Chmn.
Merck, Antony M. '44 '73 (SC) C.893 B.A. L.790 J.D.
Moran, John Austin '54 '81 (VA) C.893 B.A. L.902 J.D.
Najarian, Steven D. '65 '91 C.1036 B.A. L.1294 J.D.
Panebianco, Thomas '51 '77 C.705 A.B. L.659 J.D. Gen. Coun.

OTHER OFFICES OF THE COMMISSION

Carey, James F. '43 '77 (MD) C.446 B.S. L.64 J.D.
Kominoth, Tony P. '42 '74 (MD) C.446 B.S. L.64 J.D.
Murphy, Ronald D. '48 '80 C.886 B.S. L.1209 J.D.
VanBrakle, Bryant L. '45 '71 C&L.329 B.A., J.D.

FEDERAL MEDIATION AND CONCILIATION SERVICE

(Vacant), *Deputy General Counsel*

Hoffman, Eileen B. '47 '86 C.188 B.S. L.276 J.D. Dir. of Spec. Proj.

FEDERAL MINE SAFETY AND HEALTH REVIEW COMMISSION

Norman M. Gleichman, *General Counsel*

OFFICE OF THE COMMISSIONERS

Beatty, Robert H., Jr. '58 '94 C&L.923 B.A., J.D.
Blatnik, Lawrence E. '52 '77 C.477 B.A. L.309 J.D.
Jordan, Mary Lou '49 '77 C.712 B.A. L.1162 J.D.
Riley, James C. '49 '86 (PA) C.09 B.A. L.128 J.D.
Stock, Thomas A. '56 '92 C.945 B.A. L.30 J.D.
Symonds, Elizabeth '52 '80 C.477 B.A. L.1066 J.D.
Verheggen, Theodore F. '58 '85 C&L.893 B.A., J.D. Chmn.

OFFICE OF THE GENERAL COUNSEL

Callear, James Y. '49 '75 C&L.945 B.A., J.D.
Ebner, Elizabeth '60 '85 C.276 B.A. L.945 J.D.
Ghosal, Linda H. '— '98 (MD) C.93 B.A. L.904 J.D.
Gleichman, Norman M. '54 '80 C.112 B.A. L.813 J.D. Gen. Coun.
Moar, Ian Thomas '51 '89 C.999 B.A. L.178 J.D.
Stewart, Sarah L. '61 '87 (VA) C.16 B.S. L.945 J.D.
Sullivan, John T. '— '85 C.754 B.S. L.276 J.D.

OFFICE OF THE ADMINISTRATIVE LAW JUDGES

Barbour, David F. '40 '67 C.477 B.A. L.273 J.D. Chf. Adm. Law J.
Bulluck, Jacqueline R. '52 '80 C.329 B.A. L.446 J.D. Adm. Law J.
Cetti, August F. '19 '48 (CA) C.112 B.S. L.1066 J.D. Adm. Law. J.
Feldman, Jerold '49 '77 C.994 B.A. L.724 Adm. Law J.
Hodgdon, T. Todd '45 '71 C.347 A.B. L.1119 J.D. Adm. Law J.
Manning, Richard W. '49 '74 C.575 A.B. L.446 J.D. Adm Law J.
Melick, Gary '40 '68 C.893 A.B. L.446 LL.B. Adm. Law J.
Schroeder, Irwin '43 '69 C.722 A.B. L.1049 J.D. Adm. Law J.
Weisberger, Avram '39 '63 (NY) C.178 A.B. L.569 LL.B. Adm. Law J.
Zielinski, Michael E. '44 '71 C.679 B.S. L.276 J.D. Adm. Law J.

BOARD OF GOVERNORS OF THE FEDERAL RESERVE SYSTEM

J. Virgil Mattingly, Jr., *General Counsel*

OFFICE OF THE GENERAL COUNSEL

Allison, Heatherun S. '64 '89 (CA) C.112 B.A. L.1068 J.D.
Alvarez, Scott G. '55 '81 C.674 A.B. L.276 J.D.
Anderson, Jean C. '65 '95 (NJ) C.170 B.A. L.276 J.D.
Appelbaum, Karen A. '63 '88 C.659 B.A. L.30 J.D.
Ashton, Richard M. '47 '74 (MD) C&L.128 B.A., J.D.
Baer, Andrew S. '70 '95 C.103 A.B. L.477 J.D.
Bonner, Bryan A. '68 '94 C.893 B.A. L.945 J.D.
Boutilier, Elaine M. '52 '78 (ME) C.174 B.A. L.477 J.D.
Caesar, Camille M. '65 '94 C.309 B.A. L.976 J.D.
Clubb, Christopher W. '58 '88 C.174 B.A. L.893 J.D.
Corsi, Thomas M. '62 '87 C.945 B.A. L.93 J.D.
Crossen, Janet S. '53 '86 C.347 B.M. L.477 J.D.
Elza, Julie B. '74 '01 C.597 B.A. L.93 J.D.
Fallon, Kieran J. '66 '92 C.276 B.S. L.569 J.D.
Fleetwood, Bradford S. '57 '85 (VA) C.1209 B.A. L.128 J.D.
Foster, Alicia Salazar '— '93 C&L.477 B.A., J.D.
Hannah, Paul F. '64 '98 (VA) C.597 B.A. L.273 J.D.
Hochberg, Jory M. '52 '77 C.569 B.A. L.93 J.D.
Holz, Scott J. '59 '84 C.893 B.A. L.273 J.D.
Kee, Joanne D. '72 '96 C.112 B.A. L.339 J.D.
Kuray, John L. '53 '78 (CA) C.436 A.B. L.1049 J.D.
MacDonald, Alison M. '64 '88 (AL) C.1365 B.A. L.976 L.L.M.
Martin, Stephanie '60 '87 (MA) C.914 B.A. L.309 J.D.
Mattingly, James V., Jr. '44 '69 C&L.273 B.B.A., J.D. Gen. Coun.
McEwen, Walter R., Jr. '43 '71 C.31 B.A. L.329 J.D.
Meade, Daniel S. '72 '98 (MA) C.676 B.A. L.127 J.D.
Meyer, Stephen H. '52 '78 C.855 B.A. L.569 J.D.
Milenkovich, Melinda M. '67 '94 (IL) C.30 B.A. L.276 J.D.
Miller, Andrew '66 '96 C.884 B.A. L.128 J.D.
Misback, Ann E. '57 '83 C.674 A.B. L.276 J.D.
Mizusawa, Yvonne F. '61 '88 C&L.893 B.A., J.D.
Nardolilli, Pamela G. '56 '81 C.276 B.S.F.S. L.945 J.D.
O'Day, Kathleen M. '52 '77 (MA) C.1107 B.A. L.93 J.D.
O'Rourke, Michael J., Jr. '53 '80 C.262 B.A. L.477 J.D.
Robinson, Patricia A. '53 '87 C.845 B.S.Ed. L.276 J.D.
Scanlon, Thomas E. '— '98 (GA) C.112 B.A. L.1375 J.D.
Siciliano, Stephen L. '45 '68 C.363 A.B. L.597 J.D.
Stoloff, Jonathan D. '61 '87 (NY) C.103 A.B. L.178 J.D.
Threatt, Adrianne G. '71 '96 (MD) C.228 A.B. L.276 J.D.
Tsai, Gerald Chang-Lih '73 '99 (MA) C.367 B.A. L.94 J.D.
Van Der Weide, Mark E. '70 '96 C.352 B.A. L.976 J.D.
Von-Pervieux, Claudia A. '68 '93 C.1158 B.A. L.29 J.D.
Waldron, Michael W. '63 '94 C.367 B.A. L.477 J.D.
Wheatley, Katherine H. '54 '80 C.681 A.B. L.309 J.D.
Wiederhorn, Andrew Hal '73 '99 (MD) C.860 B.S. L.597 J.D.
Williams, Cary K. '54 '80 C&L.893 B.A., J.D.
Williams, J. Mills '42 '69 (IA) C.631 B.A. L.352 J.D.
Wilson, Maya Y. '74 '01 C.881 A.B. L.329 J.D.

OFFICE OF THE SECRETARY

Frierson, Robert deVere '48 '73 (MD) C&L.893 B.A., J.D.
Johnson, Jennifer J. '47 '75 (PA) C.518 A.B. L.659 J.D.
Shanks, Margaret McCloskey '53 '78 C.209 B.S. L.424 J.D.

OFFICE OF BOARD MEMBERS

Winn, Donald J. '37 '77 C.93 A.B. L.276 J.D.

OFFICE OF INSPECTOR GENERAL

Froehlich, Laurence A. '51 '77 C.976 B.A. L.273 J.D.

DIVISION OF CONSUMER AND COMMUNITY AFFAIRS

Ahrens, Jane E. '51 '79 (ID) C.906 L.336 J.D.
Cook, Robert E. '42 '71 (MA) C.930 B.A. L.93 J.D.
English, Maureen P. '49 '74 C.856 A.B. L.276 J.D.
Gell, Jane Jensen '46 '91 C.930 B.A. L.30 J.D.
Hurt, Adrienne D. '51 '84 (NY) C&L.30 B.A., J.D.
Le, Minh-Duc T. '72 '99 (NY) C.945 B.B.A. L.276 J.D.
Lonergan, Daniel G. '58 '83 C.273 B.A. L.945 J.D.
Loney, Glenn E. '47 '72 (GA) C.475 B.A. L.477 J.D.
Michaels, James A. '55 '80 C.659 B.A. L.273 J.D.

BOARD OF GOVERNORS OF THE FEDERAL RESERVE SYSTEM (Continued)

- Ryan, Kathleen C. '58 '91 (PA) C.1077 B.A. L.904 J.D.
- Smith, Dolores Silva '35 '75 C.846 B.A. L.276 J.D.
- Stein, David A. '64 '91 C.367 B.A. L.273 J.D.
- Taylor, Natalie E. '62 '89 (CA) C.229 B.A. L.329 J.D.
- Tran-Trong, Ky '72 '99 C.228 A.B. L.945 J.D.
- Wood, John C. '45 '74 C.821 B.A. L.569 J.D.

DIVISION OF INFORMATION TECHNOLOGY

- Talley, Gerald W. '38 '74 C.112 B.S. L.273 J.D.

DIVISION OF BANKING SUPERVISION AND REGULATION

- Biern, Herbert A. '47 '73 C.569 B.A. L.1009 J.D.
- Desmond, Angela M. '50 '76 C.1149 B.S. L.30 J.D.
- Hill, Elton D. '53 '80 C.309 A.B. L.276 J.D.
- Monroe, Mary F. '58 '83 C.602 B.A. L.276 J.D.
- Nichols, Nina A. '63 '90 C.976 B.A. L.309 J.D.
- Oakes, Nancy '46 '86 (VA) C.527 B.A. L.1209 J.D.
- Ward, Robert M. '54 '93 (MD) C.446 B.S. L.64 J.D.
- Wolff, Joan Nichols '46 '74 C.112 B.A. L.245 J.D.
- Zawistowski, Leonard A., Jr. '54 '83 (PA) C.1062 B.A. L.1209 J.D.

FEDERAL TRADE COMMISSION

Timothy J. Murris, *General Counsel*

OFFICE OF THE GENERAL COUNSEL

- Arington, Michele '64 '91 C.518 A.B. L.893 J.D.
- Barnouw, Faye Chen '68 '93 C.309 A.B. L.1066 J.D.
- Bergman, Michael D. '62 '91 C.95 B.A. L.569 J.D.
- Cohen, William E. '49 '78 C.813 B.S. L.1066 J.D.
- Coleman, Jill E. '63 '91 (VA) C.475 B.A. L.893 J.D.
- Daly, John F. '52 '79 C.453 S.B. L.477 J.D.
- Dawson, Rachel Miller '50 '75 C&L.309 A.B., J.D.
- DeMille-Wagman, Lawrence '51 '77 C.1038 B.A. L.309 J.D.
- DeSanti, Susan S. '49 '81 C.771 B.A. L.94 J.D.
- Fina, Joan E. '67 '96 (MD) C.1058 B.A.E. L.30 J.D.
- Freedman, Bruce G. '47 '73 C.604 B.A. L.976 J.D.
- Gebhard, Theodore A. '48 '95 C.679 B.S. L.1209 J.D.
- Gold, G. Richard '66 '93 (PA) C.575 B.A. L.276 J.D.
- Golden, William P. '48 '73 C.276 B.S.F.S. L.309 J.D.
- Graubert, John D. '56 '82 C.951 B.A. L.276 J.D.
- Greene, Hillary '68 '99 (NY) C&L.976 B.A., J.D.
- Greenfield, Gary M. '60 '87 C.102 B.S. L.880 J.D.
- Hamill, James C. '47 '72 C.902 B.A. L.623 J.D.
- Hurwitz, James D. '46 '73 C.766 B.A. L.1066 J.D.
- Kane, Maryanne S. '49 '74 C.705 B.A. L.276 J.D.
- Kaye, Ira S. '63 '88 C.205 B.A. L.273 J.D.
- Kerst, Marilyn E. '45 '80 C.966 B.A. L.976 J.D.
- Levine, Gail F. '68 '95 C.846 B.A. L.309 J.D.
- Melman, Leslie Rice '48 '75 C.156 B.A. L.734 J.D.
- Minton, Shira Pavis '68 '96 (OH) C.1349 B.A. L.309 J.D.
- Muris, Timothy J. '49 '74 (CA) C.763 B.A. L.1068 J.D.
- Orlans, Melvin H. '43 '69 (NY) C.1036 B.A. L.178 J.D.
- Patton, Dorothy P. '69 '95 C.188 B.A. L.569 J.D.
- Shonka, David C. '47 '72 C.546 B.A. L.1294 J.D.
- Singer, John A. '58 '85 C.918 B.A. L.446 J.D.
- Stiefel, Alysa M. '73 '99 (MD) C.205 B.A./B.S. L.884 J.D.
- Tang, Alexander C. '58 '85 (MA) C.976 B.A. L.93 J.D.
- Vidas, Sandra M. '44 '79 (MD) C.436 B.A. L.30 J.D.
- Vieux, Steve '74 '00 (NJ) C.188 B.S. L.659 J.D.
- Watts, Marianne R. '58 '89 (VA) C.313 B.A. L.904 J.D.
- White, Christian S. '45 '70 C.951 A.B. L.659 J.D.
- Winerman, Marc L. '51 '77 (NY) C.674 A.B. L.309 J.D.
- Wroblewski, Michael S. '63 '92 C.423 B.B.A./B.S. L.846 J.D.

OFFICE OF ADMINISTRATIVE LAW JUDGES

- Timony, James P. '31 '59 C.610 B.S.C. L.276 LL.B.

OFFICE OF THE CHAIRMAN

- Bowie, Darren A. '67 '92 C.945 B.A. L.659 J.D.
- Greisman, Lois C. '57 '84 C.103 A.B. L.537 J.D.
- Steel, Simon A. '68 '95 (NY) C.050 B.A. L.145 LL.M.

OFFICES OF COMMISSIONERS

- Anthony, Sheila F. '40 '85 C.45 B.A. L.904 J.D. Commissioner
- Armstrong, Katherine L. '57 '82 (OR) C.1168 B.A. L.596 J.D.
- Ballard, Tracy E. '67 '93 C.188 B.A. L.309 J.D.
- Cosgrove, Kellie A. '67 '92 C.1030 B.A. L.575 J.D.
- Demartino, Laura Jean '69 '95 C.216 B.A. L.273 J.D.
- Hughto, Sean D. '64 '89 C.1036 B.A. L.228 J.D.
- Klotz, Thomas J. '59 '93 C.117 B.A. L.276 J.D.
- Kopchik, Lisa B. '56 '81 C.951 B.A. L.94 J.D.
- Koslov, Tara Isa '69 '94 C.103 A.B. L.309 J.D.
- Leary, Thomas Barrett '31 '59 C.674 A.B. L.309 J.D. Commissioner
- Magee, Peder van Wagonen '66 '92 C.966 B.A. L.273 J.D.
- Ohlhausen, Maureen K. '62 '92 (VA) C.893 B.A. L.1209 J.D.
- Pahl, Thomas B. '63 '88 C.755 B.A. L.597 J.D.
- Rozell, Lynda M. '62 '88 C&L.893 B.A., J.D.
- Seesel, John H. '49 '74 C.309 A.B. L.1066 J.D.
- Smollen, Jonathan A. '65 '96 C.276 B.A. L.893 J.D.
- Thompson, Mozelle W. '54 '84 C&L.178 A.B., J.D. Commissioner
- Triggs, Casey R. '59 '86 C.810 B.A. L.846 J.D.
- Vedova, Holly L. '64 '90 (VA) C.231 B.A. L.1209 J.D.

OFFICE OF EXECUTIVE DIRECTOR

- Bailey, Judith '47 '78 C.477 A.B. L.1068 J.D.
- Wiggs, Barbara B. '41 '69 (VA) C.887 B.S. L.329 J.D.

OFFICE OF CONGRESSIONAL RELATIONS

- Davis, Anna Holmquist '59 '86 (VA) C.773 B.A. L.276 J.D. Director
- Kando-Pineda, Carol Ann '61 '90 C.681 A.B. L.818 J.D.
- Simons, Claudia A. '65 '89 C.188 B.A. L.910 J.D.

OFFICE OF ADMINISTRATIVE LAW JUDGES

- Arthaud, Victoria C. '67 '95 (MD) C.855 B.A. L.276 J.D.

OFFICE OF INSPECTOR GENERAL

- Trietsch, Dennis R. '47 '76 C.363 A.B. L.30 J.D.

OFFICE OF THE SECRETARY

- Berman, Benjamin I. '46 '71 C.930 A.B. L.309 J.D.
- Clark, Donald S. '52 '78 C.813 B.A. L.1068 J.D.
- Donohue, Richard C. '45 '73 C&L.128 B.A., J.D.

BUREAU OF CONSUMER PROTECTION

- Abdullah, Raouf M. '51 '83 (MA) C.178 A.B. L.818 J.D.
- Ashe, Gregory A. '66 '95 C&L.893 B.A., J.D.
- Berger, Laura D. '67 '94 (FL) C.861 B.A. L.477 J.D.
- Blickman, Neil J. '50 '75 C.473 B.A. L.744 J.D.
- Blower, Bradley H. '61 '88 C.976 B.A. L.228 J.D.
- Brewer, Joel N. '41 '70 (CA) C.112 B.A. L.1065 J.D.
- Brinckerhoff, Clarke W. '43 '68 (NY) C.951 B.A. L.188 J.D.
- Broder, Betsy '55 '82 (NY) C.170 B.A. L.107 J.D.
- Brof, Julie K. '70 '97 C.188 B.S. L.273 J.D.
- Brown, Allison I. '72 '97 (IL) C.813 B.A. L.309 J.D.
- Chung, Jock K. '55 '87 (NY) C.976 B.A. L.569 J.D.
- Cleland, Richard L. '49 '78 (IA) C&L.352 B.S., J.D.
- Cohen, Stephen L. '49 '83 C.659 B.A. L.831 J.D.
- Cowen, Jonathan M. '66 '92 (PA) C.276 B.S. L.309 J.D.
- Crane, Joanna P. '55 '95 (VA) C.823 B.A. L.1209 J.D.
- Crouse, Jeanne M. '56 '82 C.502 B.J. L.446 J.D.
- Crowley, John A. '31 '61 (NY) C&L.262 B.S., J.D.
- Daynard, Matthew '46 '72 C.611 B.A. L.178 J.D.
- Delaney, Elizabeth A. '62 '92 C.588 B.S. L.1065 J.D.
- Dershowitz, Michael '47 '73 C.563 B.A. L.966 J.D.
- Dolan, James Reilly '65 '91 (MD) C.174 B.A. L.273 J.D.
- Dowdy, Lemuel W. '45 '70 (NC) C&L.329 B.S., J.D.
- Eichorn, L. Mark '66 '92 (VA) C.976 B.A. L.893 J.D.
- Elliott, Ramona D. '65 '88 (MD) C.260 B.S. L.245 J.D.
- Engle, Mary Koelbel '61 '86 C.309 A.B. L.893 J.D.
- Evans, Janet M. '55 '81 C.1044 B.A. L.276 J.D.
- Fair, Lesley Anne '56 '81 C.602 A.B. L.846 J.D.
- Floyd, Angela '72 '99 C.124 B.A. L.276 J.D.
- Forbes, Dean C. '66 '91 (PA) C.103 A.B. L.893 J.D.
- Foster, Helen Goff '70 '96 C.884 B.A. L.276 J.D.
- Francois, Renard C. '71 '00 (NY) C.659 B.A. L.273 J.D.
- Frankel, David P. '55 '80 C.823 A.B. L.472 J.D.
- Frankle, Janice Podoll '51 '80 C.347 B.A. L.472 J.D.
- Frisby, Robert M. '60 '85 C.446 B.A. L.893 J.D.
- Gardner, Delores H. '66 '98 (MD) C.864 B.S.A.E. L.273 J.D.
- Gonzalez, Ricardo A. '74 '99 (MD) C&L.276 B.A., J.D.
- Grant, Elizabeth M. '62 '90 (OR) C&L.1051 B.A., J.D.
- Gray, Jessica D. '58 '90 (MA) C.143 B.S. L.93 J.D.
- Gressin, Seena D. '— '92 C.696 B.A. L.813 J.D.
- Gross, Walter C., III '38 '62 (TN) C&L.880 B.A., LL.B.
- Guerard, Collot '47 '73 C.681 A.B. L.276 J.D.
- Gyamfi, Maame A. '70 '99 C.112 B.A. L.276 J.D.
- Harrington, M. Eileen '52 '82 C.999 B.A. L.1162 J.D.
- Harrington-McBride, Catherine C. '— '94 (VA) L.273 J.D.
- Hart, Melissa D. '73 '98 (MD) C.705 B.A. L.893 J.D.
- Harthun, Annemarie Scanlon '67 '92 C.93 B.A. L.893 J.D.
- Hippsley, Heather A. '56 '84 (OH) C.276 B.S. L.1051 J.D.
- Hodapp, Lawrence M. '48 '74 C.937 B.A. L.339 J.D.
- Hone, Elizabeth A. '65 '93 (NY) C.918 A.B. L.1068 J.D.
- Hoppock, Theodore H. '46 '75 C.401 B.S. L.276 J.D.
- Howard, Myra E. '68 '93 (OR) C.112 B.A. L.629 J.D.
- Hrdy, Alice S. '68 '93 (MD) C.610 A.B. L.276 J.D.
- Huseman, Brian '72 '97 (OK) C.612 B.A. L.615 J.D.
- Isaac, Ronald G. '49 '75 C.578 B.A. L.178 J.D.
- Ivens, Gary L. '61 '88 C&L.309 A.B., J.D.
- Jagielski, Karen '62 '94 (PA) C.67 B.A. L.188 J.D.
- Jennings, Carol J. '44 '76 C&L.569 B.A., J.D.
- Jung, Louise R. '49 '75 C.446 B.A. L.477 J.D.
- Kane, Thomas E. '58 '89 C.893 B.A. L.446 J.D.
- Kapin, Laureen '63 '88 C.454 B.A. L.260 J.D.
- Kaufman, Daniel '67 '95 (NY) C.188 B.A. L.659 J.D.
- Keller, Christopher W. '43 '70 C.367 B.A. L.659 J.D.
- Kelly, Richard F. '46 '72 C&L.724 B.B.A., J.D.
- Kinscheck, Renate '52 '77 C.145 B.A. L.94 J.D.
- Knight, Sydney M. '58 '88 (MD) C.042 B.A. L.329 J.D.
- Kohm, James A. '61 '90 C.477 B.A. L.276 J.D.
- Kolish, Elaine D. '55 '80 (MA) C.454 B.A. L.1048 J.D.
- Koss, Laura Debora '67 '93 (NY) C.188 B.A. L.309 J.D.
- Kresses, Mamie '58 '87 C&L.280 B.A., J.D.
- Leonard, Karen E. '69 '95 C.104 A.B. L.107 J.D.
- Levin, Toby Milgrom '47 '85 (MD) C.273 B.A. L.128 J.D.
- Lisher, Craig R. '74 '99 C&L.30 B.A., J.D.
- Lupovitz, Joni '63 '89 C.012 B.A. L.273 J.D.
- Mandigo, Jennifer '72 '97 C.976 B.A. L.1068 J.D.
- Marcus, Phyllis Hurwitz '68 '93 C.659 B.A. L.477 J.D.
- Matz, Bethany E. '72 '97 C.846 B.A. L.309 J.D.
- Mazzarella, Laura '66 '95 (CA) C.659 B.S. L.893 J.D.
- McCormick, Anne M. '60 '87 (FL) C.321 B.A. L.273 J.D.
- Mithal, Maneesha '70 '95 C&L.276 B.A., J.D.
- Modell, Shira D. '56 '81 C.976 B.A. L.309 J.D.
- Mora, Michael P. '62 '88 (IL) C.424 B.S. L.128 J.D.
- Morris, Lucy E. '61 '86 (WA) C.770 B.A. L.1065 J.D.
- Muoio, Karen Mandel '68 '96 (CA) C.771 B.A. L.1065 J.D.
- Ostheimer, Michael '— '92 (NY) C.659 B.S. L.178 J.D.
- Paoli, Elena I. '64 '92 C.446 B.S. L.273 J.D.
- Parnes, Lydia Bloom '53 '78 C&L.30 B.A., J.D.
- Peeler, Clarence L., III '47 '74 C&L.276 B.A., J.D.

Quaresima, Richard A. ..... '65 '90 (PA) C.262 B.A. L.1292 J.D.
Raymond, Jeanne-Marie S. ..... '72 '97 C.88 B.A. L.902 J.D.
Reynolds, Carole L. ..... '— '77 C.30 B.A. L.588 J.D.
Rich, Jessica ..... '62 '88 C.681 B.A. L.569 J.D.
Richardson, Robin M. ..... '62 '90 C&L.260 B.S., J.D.
Roden, Kathryn M. ..... '72 '98 (NY) C.788 B.A. L.1009 J.D.
Rodriguez, Edwin ..... '— '93 C&L.276 B.A., J.D.
Rosso, Rosemary ..... '51 '81 (NY) C.262 B.A. L.569 J.D.
Rusk, Michelle K. ..... '59 '84 C.309 A.B. L.276 J.D.
Salsburg, Daniel R. ..... '66 '91 C&L.659 B.A., J.D.
Schaefer, Karen A. ..... '71 '96 C.436 B.A. L.424 J.D.
Schwanke, Marianne K. ..... '61 '88 C.165 B.A. L.273 J.D.
Sheer, H. Alain ..... '47 '87 C.529 B.A. L.228 J.D.
Spector, Robin Rosen ..... '68 '94 C&L.273 B.A., J.D.
Spiegel, David R. ..... '46 '71 C&L.178 A.B., J.D.
Spivack, Mona Sedky ..... '66 '93 C.813 A.B. L.276 J.D.
Stevenson, Hugh G. ..... '58 '85 (MD) C&L.309 A.B., J.D.
Sullivan, Laura M. ..... '72 '98 (NY) C.178 B.A. L.945 J.D.
Thomas, Beverly J. ..... '48 '76 C.375 B.S. L.378 J.D.
Toporoff, Steven ..... '57 '85 C.563 B.A. L.446 J.D.
Torok, David M. ..... '60 '86 C&L.273 B.A., J.D.
Twohig, Peggy L. ..... '56 '83 C.608 B.A. L.569 J.D.
Vecchi, Christa Van Anh ..... '61 '86 C.881 B.A. L.893 J.D.
Vecellio, Constance M. ..... '44 '71 C.575 B.A. L.309 J.D.
Viswanathan, Serena ..... '71 '96 C.1375 B.A. L.276 J.D.
Wenger, Eric Andrew ..... '68 '93 C.188 B.S. L.273 J.D.
Wilmore, Sandra M. ..... '45 '72 C.254 B.A. L.976 J.D.
Winston, Joel ..... '51 '76 (MI) C&L.477 B.A., J.D.
Wolfe, Douglas V. ..... '65 '91 C.610 A.B. L.893 J.D.
Zylberglait, Pablo M. ..... '68 '94 C.1077 B.S. L.276 J.D.

BUREAU OF COMPETITION

Abbott, Alden F. ..... '51 '77 C.893 B.A. L.309 J.D.
Abrahamsen, Dana ..... '56 '81 C.347 B.S. L.30 J.D.
Albert, Bradley S. ..... '69 '94 C&L.228 A.B., J.D.
Allen, Sarah O. ..... '62 '91 (VA) C.1090 B.S. L.945 J.D.
Andrinopoulos, Angelike ..... '75 '00 (MD) C.228 B.S. L.910 J.D.
Antalics, Michael E. ..... '51 '78 (PA) C.754 B.A. L.273 J.D.
Apori, Yaa A. ..... '75 '00 (NY) C.518 A.B. L.309 J.D.
Armstrong, Norman Alva, Jr. ..... '— '96 (MD) C.893 B.A. L.329 J.D.
Averitt, Neil W. ..... '46 '74 (MA) C&L.309 B.A., J.D.
Baruch, Roberta S. ..... '49 '75 C.145 A.B. L.309 J.D.
Bayer, Peggy D. ..... '75 '00 C.477 B.A. L.273 J.D.
Bellack, George R. ..... '54 '79 C.1113 B.A. L.276 J.D.
Berg, Karen E. ..... '62 '89 C&L.945 B.A., J.D.
Bernstein, Steven K. ..... '67 '91 (FL) C.472 B.B.A. L.597 J.D.
Bloom, Morris ..... '55 '85 (TN) C.861 B.S. L.836 J.D.
Blumenreich, Linda B. ..... '59 '84 C.446 B.A. L.273 J.D.
Bokat, Karen G. ..... '47 '73 C.788 B.A. L.273 J.D.
Brownman, Joseph S. ..... '40 '66 C.102 B.A. L.569 LL.B.
Bruno, Marian R. ..... '54 '82 C.174 B.F.A. L.1243 J.D.
Campbell, Jay C. ..... '71 '99 (NY) C.112 B.A. L.228 J.D.
Catt, Malcolm L. ..... '61 '91 (ID) C&L.999 B.A., LL.B.
Conn, David F. ..... '56 '85 (MD) C.145 A.B. L.904 J.D.
Costilo, L. Barry ..... '37 '63 C.659 B.S.E. L.309 LL.B.
Cox, Kent Eugene ..... '57 '83 (IA) C&L.352 B.S., J.D.
Dagen, Richard B. ..... '57 '83 C.145 B.A. L.245 J.D.
Dahm, Steven A. ..... '69 '99 (CA) C.312 B.A. L.1494 J.D.
Damtoft, Russell W. ..... '54 '81 C.293 B.A. L.352 J.D.
Davidson, Kenneth M. ..... '41 '67 C.145 B.A. L.659 J.D.
Davis, Rendell A., Jr. ..... '50 '77 (NY) C.821 B.A. L.309 J.D.
Davis, Robert P. ..... '64 '90 C.1044 B.S. L.569 J.D.
Diaz, William ..... '75 '00 (MD) C.260 B.S. L.276 J.D.
Dillon, Sean G. ..... '74 '99 (MD) C.446 B.A. L.30 J.D.
Doying, William A.E. ..... '40 '69 C&L.976 B.A., J.D.
Ducore, Daniel P. ..... '50 '76 C.705 A.B. L.477 J.D.
Dudley, David D. ..... '71 '99 (NY) C.477 B.BA. L.659 J.D.
Eckhaus, Joseph ..... '44 '71 C.705 A.B. L.383 J.D.
Edmondson, Eric D. ..... '63 '93 C.684 B.A. L.273 J.D.
Eisenstat, Philip M. ..... '48 '82 C.831 B.B.A. L.276 J.D.
Elmore, Ernest Eric ..... '64 '91 (NY) C&L.188 A.B., J.D.
Epps, Melea R. ..... '54 '86 (MD) C.228 A.B. L.30 J.D.
Fishkin, James A. ..... '61 '88 (NE) C&L.352 B.A., J.D.
Friedman, Alan J. ..... '53 '78 C.823 B.A. L.273 J.D.
Frumin, Jill M. ..... '53 '79 C.690 B.A. L.910 J.D.
Galvan, Patricia Vizuet ..... '73 '99 (TX) C.326 B.S. L.846 J.D.
Gibbs, Garry R. ..... '55 '81 (NY) C.895 B.S. L.569 J.D.
Green, Geoffrey M. ..... '58 '84 C&L.309 A.B., J.D.
Gruendel, Yolanda R. ..... '70 '95 C.893 B.A. L.276 J.D.
Hegarty, James J. ..... '71 '99 (WI) C.228 A.B. L.145 J.D.
Henning, Renee S. ..... '47 '75 (MA) C.914 B.A. L.893 J.D.
Higgins, Claudia R. ..... '52 '77 C.623 B.A. L.30 J.D.
Hilder, Elizabeth R. ..... '52 '77 C.918 B.A. L.477 J.D.
Holden, James H., Jr. ..... '64 '89 (OK) C.934 B.A. L.623 J.D.
Huber, Susan A. ..... '62 '90 (TX) C.288 B.A. L.1066 J.D.
Inglefield, David L. ..... '58 '91 (VA) C.105 B.A. L.1209 J.D.
Jex, Elizabeth A. ..... '61 '87 C.951 B.A. L.276 J.D.
Johnson, Dennis F. ..... '52 '78 C.30 B.A. L.128 J.D.
Jones, Robert L. ..... '65 '90 (IN) C.94 B.A. L.477 J.D.
Joseph, Anthony L. ..... '35 '61 C.821 B.A. L.659 LL.B.
Kades, Michael B. ..... '68 '95 (WI) C.976 B.A. L.966 J.D.
Kaplan, Jeffrey ..... '53 '82 (SC) C&L.978 B.A., J.D.
Klarfeld, Jonathan S. ..... '70 '97 (NY) C.103 A.B. L.569 J.D.
Koberstein, Nicholas R. ..... '68 '94 C.475 B.A. L.276 J.D.
Krulla, Rhett R. N. ..... '48 '74 C.563 B.A. L.723 J.D.
Lee, Andrew J. ..... '72 '99 (CA) C.367 B.A. L.112 J.D.
Lewers, Joanne C. ..... '70 '96 C.1030 B.A. L.208 J.D.
Libby, Kenneth A. ..... '61 '86 (NY) C.145 B.A. L.107 J.D.
Liebeskind, Richard, Jr. ..... '58 '85 (NY) C.228 B.A. L.178 J.D.
Lipson, Frank ..... '43 '70 C&L.477 A.B., J.D.
Long, Randall Aaron ..... '72 '99 (VA) C.893 B.A. L.273 J.D.
Malester, Ann ..... '52 '77 C.104 B.A. L.273 J.D.
Marks, Randall D. ..... '56 '80 C&L.659 B.S., J.D.
Martin, Kristina C. ..... '69 '00 (CT) C.390 A.B. L.352 J.D.
Marvine, Christopher L. ..... '75 '00 (MO) C.378 B.A. L.846 J.D.
McCartney, P. Abbott ..... '48 '73 C.475 B.A. L.61 J.D.
Mendel, Jacqueline K. ..... '60 '91 (PA) C.105 B.A. L.128 J.D.
Michel, Suzanne T. ..... '62 '95 C.597 B.S. L.1066 J.D.
Mills, Karen A. ..... '59 '85 (IL) C.597 B.A. L.659 J.D.
Moiseyev, Michael R. ..... '63 '90 C.112 B.A. L.1065 J.D.
Mongoven, James ..... '47 '81 C.698 A.B. L.178 J.D.
Moore, Robin L. ..... '— '99 (VA) C.280 B.A. L.1209 J.D.
Moreland, Judith A. ..... '49 '75 C.228 B.A. L.276 J.D.
Moscatelli, Catherine M. ..... '61 '88 C.454 B.A. L.245 J.D.
Nagata, Ernest A. ..... '44 '76 C.112 B.S. L.1066 J.D.
Narrow, David M. ..... '47 '72 (PA) C.705 B.A. L.659 J.D.
Nolan, Arthur J. ..... '48 '77 (TX) C&L.846 B.A., J.D.
Nolan, Paul J. ..... '52 '85 C.94 B.A. L.1338 J.D.
Oliver, Geoffrey D. ..... '57 '85 C.309 B.A. L.188 J.D.
Oppenheim, Martha H. ..... '45 '77 (MD) C.331 A.B. L.831 J.D.
Osnowitz, Steven J. ..... '54 '80 C.1036 B.A. L.588 J.D.
Pak, Chul ..... '62 '90 (NY) C.821 B.A. L.569 J.D.
Parisi, John J. ..... '49 '76 C.373 B.A. L.912 J.D.
Pender, David R. ..... '41 '69 C.659 B.S. L.813 J.D.
Perez, Christina R. ..... '66 '93 (TX) C.859 B.S. L.846 J.D.
Peterson, Mrk D.S. ..... '— '89 (PA) C.747 B.A. L.1035
Pettee, Susan ..... '41 '79 C.681 B.A. L.30 J.D.
Piotrowski, Elizabeth A. ..... '54 '81 C.665 B.S. L.276 J.D.
Prisco, Thadd A. ..... '67 '94 C.602 B.A. L.569 J.D.
Richards, Karin F. ..... '67 '96 (NY) C.319 B.A. L.1356 J.D.
Richman, Peter A. ..... '61 '90 (CA) C.112 B.A. L.1065 J.D.
Riddell, Stephen W. ..... '47 '75 C.105 B.S. L.228 J.D.
Roach, Patrick J. ..... '52 '77 C.602 B.A. L.276 J.D.
Roberti, John ..... '69 '95 (NY) C.103 A.B. L.569 J.D.
Robertie, John A. ..... '24 '54 C&L.276 B.S.S., J.D.
Rohlck, Eric D. ..... '61 '86 C.879 B.A. L.912 J.D.
Rosenthal, Lisa A. ..... '— '85 (FL) C.174 B.A. L.260 J.D.
Royall, M. Sean ..... '64 '91 C.839 B.S. L.145 J.D.
Salemi, Constance M. ..... '48 '76 C.783 B.A. L.93 J.D.
Schenof, Anne R. ..... '45 '73 C.273 B.A. L.309 J.D.
Schneider, Marc W. ..... '56 '87 (FL) C.836 B.A. L.472 J.D.
Schorr, Gary H. ..... '62 '88 C.1044 B.A. L.94 J.D.
Shapiro, Barbara K. ..... '— '77 C.309 M.A. L.94 J.D.
Silber, Seth C. ..... '69 '97 C.1365 B.A. L.273 J.D.
Sockwell, W. Stephen, Jr. ..... '50 '85 C.893 B.A. L.276 J.D.
Southworth, James E. ..... '68 '96 (PA) C.311 B.A. L.477 J.D.
Stephenson, Patricia ..... '56 '81 C.1044 B.A. L.705 J.D.
Strong, Arthur M. ..... '54 '80 (UT) C.431 B.A. L.1294 J.D.
Tabor, April J. ..... '76 '01 (MD) C.178 B.A. L.276 J.D.
Tovsky, Robert ..... '50 '84 (MA) C.659 B.A. L.94 J.D.
Tritell, Randolph W. ..... '53 '77 C.1350 B.A. L.659 J.D.
Vigdor, William R. ..... '59 '90 C.1365 B.A. L.273 J.D.
von Nirschl, David A. ..... '63 '91 (TX) C.339 B.S. L.802 J.D.
Voss, Oscar M. ..... '56 '81 (CA) C.813 A.B. L.976 J.D.
Waldeck, Cecelia M. ..... '— '92 (CA) C.150 B.A. L.1065 J.D.
Walker, Goldie V. ..... '72 '97 (NY) C.302 B.A. L.30 J.D.
Wallace, Kari A. ..... '75 '00 (MN) C.399 B.A. L.494 J.D.
Warden, John B. ..... '45 '74 C.976 B.S. L.846 J.D.
Wilensky, Steven L. ..... '60 '89 C.145 B.A. L.846 J.D.
Wu, Stephen Y. ..... '74 '99 (IL) C.339 B.A./B.S. L.273 J.D.
Zimmerman, Seth B. ..... '52 '78 C.1044 B.A. L.107 J.D.
Zito, Michael A. ..... '71 '96 (MO) C.502 B.A. L.999 J.D.

Balbach, Jeanine K. ..... '69 '98 (MD) C.182 B.A. L.1209 J.D.
Havely, Katherine A. ..... '73 '98 (VA) C&L.846 B.A., J.D.
Steiger, Jonathan Miller ..... '69 '96 C.477 B.A. L.178 J.D.

GENERAL ACCOUNTING OFFICE

Anthony H. Gamboa, *General Counsel*

OFFICE OF THE GENERAL COUNSEL

Ahearn, Marie Penny ..... '52 '84 (MD) C.128 B.A. L.930 J.D.
Armen, Margaret Meis ..... '47 '78 C.521 B.A. L.161 J.D.
Armstrong, Thomas H. ..... '52 '78 (VA) C.945 A.B. L.692 J.D.
Arsenoff, Robert C. ..... '48 '76 (IA) C.446 B.A. L.276 J.D.
Ashen, David Anthony ..... '52 '82 C.112 B.A. L.1065 J.D.
Barker, Jonathan H. ..... '49 '75 C.910 B.A. L.365 J.D.
Belkin, Alan ..... '45 '73 C.831 A.B. L.128 J.D.
Benejam, Aldo A. ..... '57 '89 (PA) C.259 B.S. L.472 J.D.
Berlin, Bertram J. ..... '44 '70 C.831 B.A. L.276 J.D.
Bogart, George ..... '54 '82 C.569 B.A. L.94 J.D.
Botsford, Jessica A. ..... '51 '77 C.604 B.A. L.107 J.D.
Brosnan, John G. ..... '44 '70 (CT) C&L.184 B.A., J.D.
Burkard, Richard P. ..... '63 '88 C.446 B.A. L.128 J.D.
Calhoun, Tania L. ..... '62 '92 (VA) C&L.1209 B.A., J.D.
Cambosos, Richard T. ..... '47 '73 C&L.329 B.A., J.D.
Cohen, Jerold D. ..... '49 '75 (MD) C.401 B.A. L.276 J.D.
Coles, Barbara Carrington ..... '63 '88 (CT) C.1083 B.S. L.945 J.D.
Crystal, Robert G. ..... '47 '71 C.994 B.A. L.273 J.D.
Curcio, Mary G. ..... '56 '83 (NY) C.102 B.A. L.724 J.D.
Davis, Christine F. ..... '64 '90 C&L.477 B.A., J.D.
Desaulniers, Helen T. ..... '64 '89 (VA) C.321 A.B. L.945 J.D.
Diz, Carlos E. ..... '58 '88 C.331 B.A. L.564 J.D.
Dowling, Mark B. ..... '67 '98 (VA) C.893 B.A. L.945 J.D.
Dunn, Herbert I. ..... '46 '71 C&L.446 B.S., J.D.
Easterwood, Oliver H. ..... '40 '70 C.1100 A.B. L.446 J.D.
Emmanuelli-Perez, Edda ..... '63 '88 (MD) C.1088 B.A. L.276 J.D.
Engstrom, David F. ..... '40 '70 (MD) C.799 B.S. L.64 J.D.
Feldman, Doreen S. ..... '53 '78 C.1044 B.A. L.262 J.D.
Finley, Ann H. ..... '43 '68 C&L.734 B.S., J.D.
Forman, Jeffrey S. ..... '45 '77 (MA) C.454 B.A. L.818 J.D.
Formica, John L ..... '59 '87 C.273 B.A. L.107 J.D.
Gamboa, Anthony H. ..... '42 '72 (MD) C.870 B.S. L.446 J.D. Gen. Coun.
Gibson, Lynn H. ..... '56 '81 (VA) C.893 B.A. L.945 J.D.
Gilhooly, Kathleen ..... '52 '85 (MD) C.1044 B.A. L.273 J.D.

GENERAL ACCOUNTING OFFICE (Continued)

Glass, Linda Cannon ... '51 '80 C.302 B.S. L.329 J.D.
Goddard, Victor B. ... '47 '73 C.882 B.A. L.273 J.D.
Goldberg, Alan S. ... '39 '63 C.260 B.A. L.326 J.D.
Golden, Michael R. ... '53 '79 (NY) C.188 B.S. L.1019 J.D.
Gorczycki, Henry J. ... '59 '91 (PA) C.645 B.S. L.665 J.D.
Gordon, Daniel I. ... '51 '86 C.1036 B.A. L.309 J.D.
Hamilton, Geoffrey R. ... '64 '90 (MA) C.734 B.A. L.93 J.D.
Healy, Rosemary B. ... '61 '87 C.385 B.A. L.128 J.D.
Hollenbach, Joan M. ... '46 '71 (GA) C.1365 B.A. L.245 J.D.
Hooper, David K. B. ... '63 '88 C.696 B.A. L.276 J.D.
Iannicelli, Peter A. ... '49 '75 C.705 B.A. L.273 J.D.
Irwin, Susan Wachtel ... '41 '71 C.477 B.A. L.273 J.D.
Isrin, Jeanne White ... '51 '87 C.446 B.A. L.128 J.D.
Jackson, Ernie E. ... '49 '75 C.602 B.A. L.178 J.D.
Jackson, Franklin D. ... '61 '87 (VA) C.893 B.A. L.228 J.D.
Jacobson, Jeffrey A. ... '52 '77 (SC) C.347 B.S. L.790 J.D.
Japikse, Bert ... '41 '70 (OH) C.453 S.B. L.188 J.D.
Johnson, Richard P. ... '62 '91 (IL) C.339 B.A. L.910 J.D.
Jones, Shirley A. ... '64 '90 (PA) C.811 B.A. L.276 J.D.
Jordan, Paul E. ... '54 '79 (GA) C&L.280 A.B.J., J.D.
Kasdan, Alan R. ... '34 '60 C.659 B.A. L.976 LL.B.
Keegan, Karen K. ... '55 '86 C.197 A.B. L.846 J.D.
Kepplinger, Gary L. ... '49 '74 (IL) C.273 B.A. L.209 J.D.
Klazkin, Julian P. ... '53 '83 C.107 B.A. L.128 J.D.
Lager, James M. ... '59 '85 C.475 B.A. L.904 J.D.
Laufe, Hannah R. ... '57 '01 C.289 B.A. L.1209 J.D.
Lebowitz, Linda S. ... '62 '88 C.665 B.A. L.446 J.D.
Levine, Andrea ... '52 '77 C.1044 B.S. L.446 J.D.
Lieberman, Paul ... '44 '77 (MA) C.188 B.S. L.588 J.D.
Maguire, Frank ... '52 '82 C.602 B.A. L.426 J.D.
Martin-Rolsky, Neill W. ... '54 '81 C.347 A.B. L.30 J.D.
May, Stephanie J. ... '58 '83 C.860 B.A. L.276 J.D.
McArthur, C. Douglas ... '47 '74 C.446 B.A. L.273 J.D.
McAuliffe, Susan Kozinn ... '60 '86 (NY) C.1044 B.A. L.107 J.D.
McCaffrey, Philip T. ... '63 '89 (CT) C&L.262 B.A., J.D.
McGrail, John T. ... '— '80 (MA) C.454 B.A. L.93 J.D.
Melody, Christine Saryn ... '55 '79 C&L.276 B.S., J.D.
Melody, John M. ... '54 '79 C.645 B.A. L.273 J.D.
Michal-Smith, Susan ... '53 '78 C.150 B.A. L.245 J.D.
Miller, Behn ... '64 '91 (PA) C.893 B.A. L.1209 J.D.
Morrow, Charles W. ... '55 '81 C.254 B.S. L.329 J.D.
Odiorne, Suzanne ... '44 '75 (PA) C.226 B.S. L.30 J.D.
Peterson, Cheryl M. ... '56 '81 C.518 A.B. L.174 J.D.
Pietrovito, Guy R. ... '54 '81 C.945 B.A. L.117 J.D.
Pogany, Andrew T. ... '49 '74 (NJ) C.776 B.A. L.930 J.D.
Poling, Susan A. ... '48 '82 C.201 B.A. L.273 J.D.
Ratzenberger, Sheila A. ... '55 '79 C.518 B.A. L.276 J.D.
Rebbe, James M. ... '60 '90 (PA) C.339 B.A. L.36 J.D.
Reich, Mary W. ... '61 '87 C.30 B.A. L.904 J.D.
Riback, Katherine Irwin ... '61 '88 (PA) C&L.665 B.A., J.D.
Riback, Scott H. ... '60 '86 (MD) C&L.665 B.A., J.D.
Roney, Charles F. ... '48 '75 (VA) C.556 B.A. L.904 J.D.
Sayre, Jill Poses ... '56 '82 C.228 A.B. L.904 J.D.
Schwimer, Daniel ... '53 '79 (NY) C.188 B.S. L.94 J.D.
Seldin, Richard ... '44 '73 C.569 B.A. L.262 J.D.
Shah, Dayna C. ... '48 '73 C.822 A.B. L.276 J.D.
Shanks, Sylvia L. ... '48 '79 C.838 M.A. L.276 J.D.
Simball, Barbara Joseph ... '54 '80 C.454 B.A. L.1048 J.D.
Sklarew, Christina ... '49 '85 (CA) C.112 B.A. L.1065 J.D.
Spangenberg, James A. ... '46 '73 (MD) C.446 B.A. L.273 J.D.
Speight, Mark C. ... '62 '88 (TX) C.846 B.B.A. L.326 J.D.
Thomas, Roger Jaye ... '49 '76 C.329 B.A. L.276 J.D.
Timmerman, Barbara R. ... '56 '82 (VA) C.1369 B.S. L.893 J.D.
Udell, Sindy Rae ... '60 '86 (NY) C.1044 B.S. L.978 J.D.
Van Schaik, John ... '56 '83 C.608 B.A. L.128 J.D.
Vickers, James W. ... '46 '73 (VA) C.695 B.A. L.30 J.D.
Vodraska, Adam ... '64 '90 C.145 A.B. L.107 J.D.
Volpe, Michael R. ... '49 '74 C.390 A.B. L.276 J.D.
Wannisky, Kathleen E. ... '48 '82 C.522 A.B. L.276 J.D.
Webbink, Amy ... '71 '99 (VA) C.228 A.B. L.945 J.D.
Weldon, Stefanie G. ... '46 '78 C.276 B.S. L.050 LL.B.
Westfall, Jennifer Dunn ... '55 '80 C.518 A.B. L.976 J.D.
White, Ralph O., Jr. ... '56 '86 C.945 B.A. L.128 J.D.
Williams, Paula A. ... '50 '78 C&L.329 B.Sc., J.D.
Winslow, Craig H. ... '53 '87 C.886 B.S. L.128 J.D.
Wolcott, Glenn G. ... '53 '85 C.1209 B.S. L.128 J.D.
Woods, William T. ... '51 '81 (MD) C.454 B.A. L.64 J.D.
Wyrsch, Raymond J. ... '44 '72 (TX) C.776 B.A. L.326 J.D.

OFFICE OF THE COMPTROLLER GENERAL

Walker, David M. ... '65 '92 (NY) C.178 B.A. L.262 J.D. Princ. Asst. Compt. Gen.

OFFICE OF CONGRESSIONAL RELATIONS

Hsing, Helen Hong-hen ... '53 '80 C.446 B.A. L.128 J.D.

PERSONNEL APPEALS BOARD

Don, Beth L. ... '46 '70 C.1349 B.A. L.904 J.D.
Reece, Janice M. ... '49 '75 (KS) C.379 B.A. L.378 J.D.

RESOURCES COMMUNITY AND ECONOMIC DEVELOPMENT DIVISION

Donaghy, James F. ... '42 '75 C.433 B.A. L.128 J.D.
Donahue, Patricia F. ... '37 '65 (IN) C.436 B.A. L.345 J.D.

OFFICE OF OPPORTUNITY AND INCLUSIVENESS

Aponte, Nilda I. ... '44 '77 (PR) C.169 B.A. L.677 J.D.

TAX AND JUSTICE

Burns, R. Rochelle ... '55 '87 C.178 B.A. L.128 J.D.

GENERAL SERVICES ADMINISTRATION

Stephenie Foster, *General Counsel*

OFFICE OF THE GENERAL COUNSEL

Adamson, Marie N. ... '62 '88 (IL) C.347 B.A. L.1119 J.D.
Barclay, George N. ... '51 '78 C.103 B.A. L.94 J.D.
Bazil, Wendy Nevett ... '63 '88 C.893 B.A. L.94 J.D.
Ben, Roland ... '55 '85 C.821 B.A. L.831 J.D.
Biederman, W. James ... '51 '92 C.628 B.A. L.802 J.D.
Binstock, Seth P. ... '59 '86 (MD) C.216 B.A. L.329 J.D.
Bolus, Philip W. ... '60 '87 C.482 B.S. L.150 J.D.
Braswell, Telo ... '50 '74 (PA) C.1298 B.S. L.128 J.D.
Brown, Amy J. ... '62 '89 (CA) C&L.464 B.A., J.D.
Budd, Regina M. ... '43 '83 C.574 B.S. L.180 J.D.
Burton, Jody Berke ... '68 '93 C.1044 B.A. L.904 J.D.
Butterworth, Richard R. ... '61 '86 (VA) C.1369 B.S. L.893 J.D.
Cornell, John E. ... '57 '83 (MI) C.475 B.S. L.1187 J.D.
Crivella, Vincent L. ... '52 '77 C.884 B.S. L.64 J.D.
Domber, Jeffrey H. ... '54 '79 C.867 B.A. L.273 J.D.
Eggers, Harmon R. ... '44 '69 C&L.260 B.S.I.E., J.D.
Erwin, Deborah C. ... '54 '77 (MI) C.477 B.G.S. L.912 J.D.
Ettner, Michael J. ... '53 '77 C&L.659 B.A., J.D.
Foster, Stephenie ... '55 '86 C.112 B.A. L.659 J.D. Gen. Coun.
Fowler, Renn C. ... '41 '67 C.446 A.B. L.273 LL.B.
Frecker, David L. ... '56 '85 (OH) C.1111 B.A. L.1003 J.D.
Glassband, Rick P. ... '— '98 (MD) C.446 B.S. L.1338 J.D.
Grose, Scarlett D. ... '69 '94 (VA) C.240 A.B. L.802 J.D.
Harrington, Laurence ... '48 '83 (NJ) C.410 B.A. L.273 J.D.
Huey, Nora A. ... '65 '90 (CA) C.172 B.A. L.464 J.D.
Lloyd, Glynis ... '67 '92 (IL) C.339 B.A. L.228 J.D.
Loewentritt, Lennard S. ... '47 '72 C.966 B.A. L.30 J.D.
Maus, Helen C. ... '47 '72 (PA) C&L.30 B.A., J.D.
McCann, Joseph L. ... '48 '77 C.999 B.A. L.831 J.D.
McKenna, R. Colette ... '44 '69 C.739 B.A. L.28 J.D.
Miller, John S., III ... '37 '62 (VA) C.299 B.A. L.893 LL.B.
Morris, Samuel J., III ... '52 '79 (SC) C.575 B.S. L.790 J.D.
Pomeranz, Sharon Jane ... '62 '91 (CA) C.763 B.S. L.809 J.D.
Rice, Kevin J. ... '69 '94 (OH) C.602 B.S. L.150 J.D.
Ruttenberg, Victoria A. ... '58 '86 C.976 B.A. L.893 J.D.
Sawyer, John C. ... '43 '81 (PA) C.339 A.B. L.1048 J.D.
Schlattman, Robert W. ... '60 '87 (VA) C&L.945 B.A., J.D.
Schrader, Gerald L. ... '45 '70 C.597 B.A. L.659 J.D.
Segal, Barry D. ... '64 '89 (FL) C.1365 B.A. L.260 J.D.
Smart, Marcia L. ... '61 '88 C&L.329 B.A., J.D.
Smith, Robert C. ... '43 '69 C.188 A.B. L.273 J.D.
Thompson, Thedlus L. ... '53 '91 (CA) C.668 B.A. L.464 J.D.
Tully, Michael D. ... '63 '88 (PA) C.1030 B.A. L.128 J.D.
Wilson, Lesly P. ... '51 '78 (CA) C.1168 B.A. L.309 J.D.
Wootten, Michael J. ... '57 '82 (SC) C.645 B.S. L.790 J.D.

Office of Ethics

Ellison, Eugenia D. ... '58 '83 C.914 B.A. L.180 J.D.

OFFICE OF REGIONAL COUNSEL

Aasmaa, Allan I. ... '57 '82 (CA) C.659 B.S. L.813 J.D.
Allen, Julia C. ... '60 '87 (MD) C.276 B.S.F.S. L.904 J.D.
Batley, Lionel G., Jr. ... '36 '61 (NY) C.1019 B.A. L.262 J.D.
Bonner, Judith A. ... '52 '82 (PA) C.341 B.A. L.831 J.D.
Brincks, Michael T. ... '63 '89 (IA) C&L.352 B.A., J.D.
Crook, Lee W., III ... '52 '80 (OH) C.608 B.A. L.607 J.D.
Dattolo, Alphonse R. ... '46 '80 (GA) C.667 B.S. L.969 J.D.
Davis, Gary F. ... '54 '81 (PA) C.923 A.B. L.229 J.D. Reg. Coun.
del Portillo, Candace ... '50 '75 (CA) C.112 B.A. L.1066 J.D.
Duffy, Mark Alan ... '52 '77 (OK) C.612 B.A. L.616 J.D.
Dunn, Jeffrey H. ... '42 '66 (MD) C&L.446 B.A., J.D.
Feher, Michele M. ... '55 '89 (CA) C&L.284 B.A., J.D.
Foster, Jerry Ann ... '32 '58 (KS) C.378 A.B. L.900 J.D.
Gerwin, Barbara G. ... '— '61 (NY) C.477 B.A. L.569 J.D.
Gherlein, David G. ... '63 '90 (OH) C.608 B.S. L.1003 J.D.
Gleeson, Kurt S. ... '58 '83 C.901 B.A. L.880 J.D.
Goodno, Robin E. ... '51 '83 (CA) C.112 A.B. L.1067 J.D.
Hardegree, Howard L. ... '35 '59 (TX) C&L.69 B.A., J.D.
Hawkins, Thomas Y. ... '62 '87 (CA) C.321 B.A. L.1065 J.D.
Hewins, John M. ... '41 '69 (KS) C&L.900 B.B.A., J.D.
Hoffer, Joan M. ... '— '89 (CT) C.102 B.S. L.1040 J.D.
Holt, Leigh Ann ... '63 '88 C.692 B.A. L.945 J.D.
Hysen, Jeffrey M. ... '58 '84 C.156 B.A. L.724 J.D.
Johnson, Mark S. ... '48 '79 (NY) C.575 B.A. L.94 J.D.
Kendell, Kenneth E. ... '51 '81 (MI) C.693 B.A. L.1187 J.D.
Kruger, Elizabeth L. ... '63 '89 (WA) C.910 A.B. L.911 J.D.
Kuppersmith, Lydia ... '65 '90 (VA) C.705 B.S. L.276 J.D.
Lane, George U., Jr. ... '50 '77 (GA) C.511 B.S. L.309 J.D.
Latterman, Carol Ann ... '52 '77 (NY) C.477 B.A. L.273 J.D.
Malkin, Joel D. ... '59 '84 (IL) C.477 B.A. L.424 J.D.
Maxse, Paul J. ... '47 '73 (OH) C.363 B.A. L.1003 J.D.
McCall, Robert J. ... '56 '83 (PA) C&L.831 B.A., J.D.
McCartney, Kathleen M. ... '49 '73 C.856 A.B. L.276 J.D.
Moen, Richard J. ... '42 '72 (WA) C&L.972 B.A., J.D.
Mulert, Tara Gill ... '59 '83 (IL) C.393 B.A. L.209 J.D.
Myles, Kevin M. ... '48 '78 (CO) C.1201 B.A. L.862 J.D.
Oasin, Manuel B. ... '35 '59 C.98 B.A. L.276 J.D.
O'Connell, Nancy E. ... '45 '86 (MA) C.555 A.B. L.309 J.D.
Paik, Marilyn M. ... '62 '87 (CA) C.112 B.A. L.569 J.D.
Parks, Diana M. ... '66 '91 (GA) C&L.280 B.A., J.D.
Ringhausen, John C. ... '52 '83 (IN) C.347 A.B. L.1119 J.D.
Ross, R. Christina ... '— '84 (NV) C.112 B.A. L.1065 J.D.
Skare, Samuel E. ... '47 '75 (IA) C.352 B.A. L.221 J.D.
Taliaferro, T. Cass ... '51 '76 (TX) C&L.846 B.A., J.D.
Teller, Kathryn G. ... '53 '80 (CA) C.112 B.A. L.284 J.D.
Turchin, Debra J. ... '58 '84 (NY) C.260 B.S. L.472 J.D.
Vine, Adele Ross ... '54 '79 (KS) C&L.900 B.A., J.D.

BOARD OF CONTRACT APPEALS

Borwick, Anthony S. ... '44 '71 C.188 B.A. L.861 J.D. Board J.
Daniels, Stephen M. ... '47 '72 (CA) C&L.976 B.A., J.D. Board J. & Chmn.
DeGraff, Martha H. ... '53 '77 C.502 A.B. L.30 J.D. Board J.
Goodman, Allan H. ... '50 '75 C.276 B.S.F.S. L.851 J.D. Board J.
Hyatt, Catherine B. ... '52 '77 C.289 B.A. L.273 J.D. Board J.
Johnson, James A., Jr. ... '54 '82 C.659 A.B. L.276 J.D.
Neill, Edwin B. ... '37 '74 C.128 Ph.B. L.276 J.D. Board J.
Parker, Robert W. ... '52 '77 C&L.446 B.S., J.D. Board J. & V. Chmn.
Pfunder, Margaret S. ... '50 '77 C.938 A.B. L.30 J.D.
Quigley, Anne M. ... '61 '86 C&L.276 B.S.F.S., J.D.
Williams, Mary Ellen Coster ... '53 '78 C.128 B.A. L.228 J.D. Board J.

OFFICE OF INSPECTOR GENERAL

Alderton, Steven M. ... '— '87 C.960 B.S. L.273 J.D.
Grebasch, Virginia S. ... '— '85 (IA) C.177 B.S. L.190 J.D.
Langello, Chris ... '— '92 (VA) C.1156 B.S. L.273 J.D.
Miller, Eric L. ... '55 '81 C.1036 A.B. L.94 J.D.
Potamianos, Antigone ... '67 '93 (VA) C.945 B.A. L.1209 J.D.
Tighe, Kathleen S. ... '54 '83 C.679 B.A. L.273 J.D.

REGIONAL COUNSEL (NATIONAL CAPITAL REGION)

Kupersmith, Lydia R. ... '65 '90 (VA) C.705 B.A. L.273 J.D.
Vranekovic, James D. ... '44 '78 (OH) C.363 A.B. L.989 J.D.

OFFICE OF GOVERNMENTWIDE POLICY

Drabkin, David A. ... '53 '78 C.901 B.A. L.192 J.D.
Pritzker, David M. ... '41 '75 C.976 B.A. L.188 J.D.
Suda, Donald J. ... '45 '86 C.1113 B.A. L.128 J.D.

Anderson, Kevin S. ... '62 '87 (MD) C.446 B.S. L.64 J.D.
Creed, Gordon S. ... '47 '76 C.30 B.A. L.678 J.D.
Harris, Carolyn A. ... '50 '76 (PA) C.188 B.A. L.276 J.D.
Kim, Rena Y. ... '65 '91 (NE) C&L.546 B.S., J.D.
Ratchford, William R. ... '34 '59 (CT) C.184 B.A. L.276 J.D.
Robinson, Turhan E. ... '45 '94 (FL) C.512 B.A. L.260 J.D.

GOVERNMENT PRINTING OFFICE

Anthony J. Zagami, *General Counsel*

OFFICE OF GENERAL COUNSEL

Fantuz, Jennifer R. ... '73 '98 C.97 B.A. L.665 J.D.
Harris, Joyce B. ... '52 '87 (PA) C.20 B.A. L.276 J.D.
Kelly, Thomas T. ... '59 '89 (PA) C.276 A.B. L.1009 J.D.
Potter, Roy E. ... '40 '64 (KY) C&L.383 B.A., J.D.
Spalding, Drew ... '46 '74 C.95 B.A. L.94 J.D.
Zagami, Anthony J. ... '52 '78 C.446 B.S. L.1209 J.D. Gen. Coun.

DiMario, Michael F. ... '37 '72 C.199 B.A. L.276 J.D. Pub. Printer of U.S.
Fine, Neal H. ... '44 '69 C.107 B.A. L.30 J.D.
Miller, Kerry L. ... '55 '81 C.1356 B.A. L.128 J.D. Adm. Law J., Bd. of Contract Appls.
Storck, Robert M. ... '46 '74 (CA) C.276 B.A. L.767 J.D.

LIBRARY OF CONGRESS

Elizabeth A. Pugh, *General Counsel*

OFFICE OF THE GENERAL COUNSEL

Greenfield, Gary E. ... '53 '88 C.201 B.A. L.329 J.D.
Hughes, Michael H. ... '50 '87 C.276 B.S.F.S. L.128 J.D.
James, Jessie, Jr. ... '46 '75 C.1378 B.S. L.378 J.D.
Jones, Lana Kay ... '44 '77 C.966 B.A. L.128 J.D.
Lincoln, Robert A. ... '38 '69 C.188 B.S. L.276 J.D.
Mack, Frank J. ... '52 '84 C.472 B.S. L.1162 J.D.
McClure, Christa ... '39 '82 L.273 M.C.L.
Pugh, Elizabeth A. ... '49 '78 (OH) C.454 B.A. L.161 J.D. Gen. Coun.
Rader, Daniel S. ... '64 '92 (GA) C.228 A.B. L.245 J.D.
Rubiella, Evelio ... '64 '94 (FL) C.1222 B.A. L.1158 J.D.
Tetreault, Charles L. ... '68 '97 (VT) C.1083 B.A.B.S. L.1194 J.D. Asst. Gen. Coun.
Vartanian, Emily ... '71 '97 C.31 B.A. L.276 J.D. Asst. Gen. Coun.
Williams, Meg ... '60 '98 (VA) C.893 B.A. L.1356 J.D.

CONGRESSIONAL RELATIONS OFFICE

Russell, Pamela J. ... '55 '83 (WI) C.694 B.A. L.966 J.D.

CONGRESSIONAL RESEARCH SERVICE

Ackerman, David M. ... '42 '74 (MD) C.388 B.A. L.276 J.D.
Baldwin, Pamela ... '42 '76 (MD) C.945 B.A. L.446 J.D.
Bazan, Elizabeth B. ... '52 '77 C.945 B.A. L.446 J.D.
Boesman, William C. ... '37 '64 C.901 B.A. L.276 J.D.
Burdette, Robert B. ... '45 '73 (OH) C.178 A.B. L.150 J.D.
Cohen, Henry ... '49 '76 C.994 B.A. L.724 J.D.
Costello, George A. ... '44 '70 (NC) C.367 B.A. L.228 J.D.
Dale, Charles V. ... '46 '71 (MN) C.55 B.A. L.494 J.D.
Doyle, Charles ... '43 '68 C.321 B.S. L.276 J.D.
Duffy, Diane Theresa ... '59 '85 (PA) C.665 B.A. L.229 J.D.
Ehlke, Richard C. ... '46 '72 C&L.966 B.B.A., J.D.
Eig, Larry M. ... '49 '76 C.862 B.A. L.276 J.D.
Elsbree, Hugh L., Jr. ... '44 '70 (NY) C&L.309 A.B., J.D.
Elsea, Jennifer K. ... '63 '00 C.352 B.A. L.30 J.D.
Foley, John R., III ... '44 '80 C.602 B.A. L.128 J.D.
Greely, Kevin B. ... '63 '90 (PA) C.30 B.A. L.128 J.D.
Greenfield, Susan Watkins ... '51 '76 C.654 B.A. L.1017 J.D.
Grimmett, Jeanne J. ... '46 '78 C.562 B.A. L.273 J.D.
Halstead, Terry Jason ... '73 '98 (KS) C&L.378 B.A., J.D.
Jeweler, Robin ... '51 '77 (MD) C.446 B.A. L.273 J.D.
Jones, Kimberly D. ... '70 '96 (MI) C.329 B.A. L.912 J.D.
Jones, Nancy L. ... '50 '75 (VA) C&L.276 A.B., J.D.
Killian, Johnny H. ... '37 '63 (NC) C&L.575 A.B., LL.B.
Lazarus, Ellen M. ... '52 '80 (VA) C.4 B.A. L.64 J.D.
Lee, Margaret Mikyung ... '60 '90 (VA) C.976 B.A. L.945 J.D.
Levis, Marc R. ... '47 '76 C.165 B.A. L.245 J.D.
Lewis, Karen J. ... '46 '75 (NY) C.881 A.B. L.982 J.D.
Luckey, John R. ... '49 '80 (GA) C.712 B.A. L.1234 J.D.
Maizels, Elliott ... '48 '77 C.347 B.A. L.128 J.D.
Maskell, Jack H. ... '47 '72 (MA) C.454 B.B.A. L.30 J.D.
Meltz, Robert ... '44 '75 (PA) C.659 B.A. L.276 J.D.
Morris, Marie B. ... '51 '76 C.945 A.B. L.276 J.D.
Murphy, M. Maureen ... '38 '78 C.562 A.B. L.273 J.D.
Nicola, Thomas J. ... '48 '73 C.813 A.B. L.276 J.D.
Noble, Roger F., Jr. ... '48 '79 C.228 B.S. L.30 J.D.
Overton, Kathryn Reichel ... '46 '76 C.446 B.S. L.276 J.D.
Perl, Raphael ... '46 '72 C&L.276 B.S.F.S., J.D.
Ronhovde, Kent M. ... '46 '75 C.309 B.A. L.276 J.D.
Rosenberg, Morton ... '35 '61 (NY) C.569 B.A. L.309 LL.B.
Rubin, Janice E. ... '41 '74 (FL) C.788 A.B. L.273 J.D.
Seitzinger, Michael V. ... '50 '76 C.228 B.A. L.880 J.D.
Shimabukuro, Jon O. ... '71 '99 (MD) C.881 A.B. L.910 J.D.
Spence, Edward J. ... '54 '79 (OH) C.473 A.B. L.851 J.D.
Stevens, Gina M. ... '59 '91 (NY) C.31 B.A. L.982 J.D.
Swendiman, Kathleen S. ... '49 '75 (MD) C.856 B.A. L.1017 J.D.
Thomas, Kenneth R. ... '58 '83 C.164 B.A. L.273 J.D.
Wallace, Paul S., Jr. ... '41 '70 C&L.574 B.S., J.D.
Warshof, Douglas A. ... '45 '70 (NY) C.94 B.A. L.273 J.D.
Weimer, Douglas R. ... '53 '78 C.665 B.A. L.602 J.D.
Welborn, Angie ... '74 '00 C.326 B.A. L.30 J.D.
Whitaker, L. Paige ... '— '90 (PA) C.446 B.A. L.128 J.D.

COPYRIGHT OFFICE

Berry, Eugene E., Jr. ... '54 '82 C&L.383 B.A., J.D.
Briganti, William R. ... '56 '81 (VA) C.893 B.A. L.945 J.D.
Carson, David O. ... '51 '81 (NY) C.813 B.A. L.309 J.D. Gen. Coun.
Coe, A. Renee ... '54 '91 C.97 B.A. L.893 J.D.
Douglass, Charlotte N. B. ... '40 '74 C.329 B.M.E. L.273 J.D.
Dunlap, John K. ... '44 '71 (KY) C&L.383 B.A., J.D.
Feder, Jesse M. ... '62 '87 (CT) C.976 B.A. L.178 J.D.
Giroux, Virginia M. ... '46 '74 C.689 B.A. L.669 J.D.
Kasunic, Robert J. ... '59 '92 C.178 B.A. L.64 J.D.
Kretsinger, Marilyn J. ... '— '78 (TX) C.59 B.A. L.846 J.D.
Levering, Mary Berghaus ... '40 '77 C.670 B.A. L.276 J.D.
Livanios, Helen ... '64 '94 (FL) C.273 B.A. L.472 J.D.
Martin, John M. ... '62 '88 (MA) C.339 B.A. L.94 J.D.
Peters, Marybeth ... '39 '73 C.689 B.Ed. L.273 J.D.
Petruzzelli, Nanette ... '— '81 (MD) L.128 J.D.
Poor, Marla C. ... '65 '95 (CA) C.623 B.S. L.900 J.D.
Rajapakse, Sayuri ... '70 '97 (NY) C&L.178 B.A., J.D.
Roberts, William J. ... '61 '86 (VA) C.321 A.B. L.893 J.D.
Rosen, Isadore A. ... '48 '73 (MD) C.446 B.A. L.64 J.D.
Sandros, Tanya M. ... '53 '93 (VA) C.145 B.A. L.1209 J.D.
Sinn, Patricia L. ... '54 '89 (OH) C.97 B.A. L.851 J.D.
Tepp, Steven M. ... '69 '94 C.165 B.A. L.904 J.D.

LAW LIBRARY

Atwill, Nicole G. ... '50 '85 L.273 M.C.L.
Craig, Pamela Barnes ... '50 '91 (MI) C.597 B.S. L.339 J.D.
Gee, Robert N. ... '56 '81 C&L.623 B.A., J.D.
Levush, Ruth ... '58 '89 L.999 LL.B.
Mahannah, William J. ... '45 '72 (MD) C.367 B.A. L.446 J.D.
Martin, James William, Jr. ... '55 '83 (AL) C&L.16 A.B., J.D.
Miller, Diana Frazier ... '59 '86 (GA) C.347 A.B. L.1119 J.D.
Palmer, Edith P. ... '40 '74 C&L.057 J.D.
Reitze, Glenn L. ... '42 '76 C.966 B.A. L.273 J.D.
Sarnecka-Crouch, Bozena ... '40 '90 (PA) L.228 J.D.
Shroff, Kersi B. ... '43 '78 (VA) C&L.999 B.A., LL.B.
Strattner, Mark William ... '55 '80 (VA) C&L.945 B.A., J.D.

LABOR RELATIONS

Yee, Harry ... '48 '78 (MA) C.588 B.A. L.93 J.D.

MERIT SYSTEMS PROTECTION BOARD

Mary L. Jennings, *General Counsel*

BOARD MEMBERS

Slavet, Beth S. ... '52 '80 C.1036 B.A. L.910 J.D.

OFFICE OF BOARD MEMBERS

Carnes, Lynore M. ... '45 '88 (VA) C.788 B.A. L.1209 J.D.
Vann, Terry ... '— '68 (NY) C.563 B.A. L.575 J.D.
Wiley, William B. ... '48 '89 (CA) C.420 B.S. L.999 J.D.

OFFICE OF THE GENERAL COUNSEL

Cardoza, William A. ... '47 '74 (PA) C&L.329 B.S., J.D.
Conley, Stephanie M. ... '43 '81 C.276 B.S.N. L.30 J.D.
Flores, Eric D. ... '67 '91 (MD) C.446 B.S. L.273 J.D.
Friedman, Joyce G. ... '52 '78 (NY) C.331 B.A. L.1019 J.D.
Jennings, Mary L. ... '40 '76 (AZ) C.845 B.S. L.36 J.D. Gen. Coun.
Morrow, Calvin M. ... '41 '75 (NC) C.902 B.A. L.575 J.D.
Price, Patricia A. ... '46 '82 (PA) C.1209 B.A. L.446 J.D.
Rearden, Sara B. ... '— '71 C.1378 B.S. L.329 J.D.
Schneider, Martha Barret ... '40 '75 C.806 B.A. L.836 J.D.
Williams, Susan L. ... '41 '78 C.72 B.A. L.273 J.D.

OFFICE OF REGIONAL OPERATIONS

Netherton, Darrell L. ... '43 '78 C.352 B.A. L.30 J.D.

OFFICE OF ADMINISTRATIVE LAW JUDGE

Fisher, Margaret C. ... '44 '83 C.788 A.B. L.276 J.D.

OFFICE OF APPEALS COUNSEL

Alpern, Stephen E. ... '47 '71 C.276 A.B. L.178 J.D.
Anasiewicz, James P. ... '49 '88 C.851 B.A. L.273 J.D.

MERIT SYSTEMS PROTECTION BOARD (Continued)

Angelo, Raymond W., Jr. ... '63 '89 (PA) C.308 B.A. L.30 J.D.
Baker, Margaret ... '46 '88 (VA) C.522 A.B. L.1209 J.D.
Berg, Craig A. ... '67 '96 (PA) C.188 B.A. L.30 J.D.
Bey-Proctor, Charlene D. ... '59 '92 (PA) C.302 B.S. L.329 J.D.
Bledsoe, Monalie E. ... '49 '77 C&L.329 B.A., J.D.
Carroll, Elena T. ... '60 '93 C.659 B.A.S. L.276 J.D.
Clevenger, Catherine M. ... '56 '82 C.937 B.A. L.276 J.D.
Duncan, Patrick Casey ... '52 '77 C.446 B.A. L.64 J.D.
Garrity, Lynn A. ... '63 '88 (CT) C&L.184 B.A., J.D.
Grossman, Adrienne R. ... '61 '86 (NY) C.367 B.A. L.273 J.D.
Hanclich, Charles M. ... '65 '92 (VA) C.951 B.A. L.273 J.D.
Jacobs, Gail Turner ... '61 '89 (PA) C.597 B.S. L.329 J.D.
Kelley, Robert J., Jr. ... '55 '83 (MI) C.477 B.A. L.329 J.D.
Klos, Katharine A. ... '44 '76 C.1115 B.A. L.575 J.D.
Korb, Timothy L. ... '50 '83 (NE) C.263 B.A. L.190 J.D.
Lauren, Barbara ... '47 '89 C.788 B.A. L.276 J.D.
Litoff, Stuart M. ... '52 '79 C.1044 B.A. L.1048 J.D.
Long, Pamela M. ... '65 '94 (VA) C.893 B.A. L.273 J.D.
Maley, Susan Chin ... '55 '86 (MD) C.446 B.A. L.276 J.D.
Martínez, Roberto J. ... '47 '83 (PR) C.1088 B.A. L.677 J.D.
Murphy, John J. ... '47 '73 C.390 B.A. L.276 J.D.
Nelson, Jill L. ... '59 '89 (AZ) C.35 B.S. L.37 J.D.
Read, James M. ... '64 '90 C.299 B.A. L.273 J.D.
Schwartz, Lois Siegel ... '39 '64 C.66 B.A. L.569 J.D.
Schweizer, Linda F. ... '49 '79 C.94 B.A. L.446 J.D.
Sigrist, Heather N. ... '67 '94 C.8 B.A. L.7 J.D.
Thompson, Alexander G. ... '61 '93 C&L.602 B.S., J.D.
Trygar, John Paul ... '— '71 C.652 B.S. L.180 J.D.
Tyson, Rose M. ... '49 '74 C.532 B.A. L.329 J.D.

CLERK OF THE BOARD

McCarthy, Shannon ... '42 '78 C.629 B.S. L.128 J.D.
Shannon, Matthew D. ... '55 '80 C.282 B.A. L.273 J.D.

POLICY AND EVALUATION

Mayor, Bruce ... '39 '64 (CT) C.994 B.A. L.976 LL.B.

WASHINGTON, D.C. REGIONAL OFFICE

Armstrong, Sherry A. ... '61 '90 C.893 B.A. L.30 J.D.
Ben-Ami, Raphael Z. ... '52 '83 (PA) C.1291 B.A. L.665 J.D.
Bogle, Elizabeth Bentley ... '47 '72 (MI) C.475 B.S. L.37 J.D.
Boulden, William L. ... '56 '83 (MD) C.820 B.A. L.446 J.D.
Clancy, Joseph E. ... '49 '75 (MD) C.107 B.A. L.64 J.D.
Clement, Sarah Preston ... '53 '84 C.822 A.B. L.893 J.D.
Hudson, Michelle M. ... '54 '79 C.411 B.A. L.904 J.D.
Jenkins, William C. ... '43 '73 (CA) C.319 B.A. L.1065 J.D.
Manning, Edward F. ... '41 '72 C.560 B.A. L.846 J.D.
Winzer, P. J. ... '47 '72 (CA) C.803 B.A. L.1068 J.D.

NATIONAL AERONAUTICS AND SPACE ADMINISTRATION

Edward A. Frankle, *General Counsel*

OFFICE OF THE GENERAL COUNSEL

Batkin, Mark R. ... '— '97 C.1060 B.S. L.464 J.D.
Borda, Gary G. ... '56 '90 C.886 B.S. L.64 J.D.
Edwards, June ... '48 '76 (NE) C&L.546 B.A., J.D.
Feinberg, Shari R. ... '65 '91 C.1349 B.A. L.904 J.D.
Forbes, David P. ... '44 '69 (VA) C.893 B.A. L.128 J.D.
Frankle, Edward A. ... '46 '74 C.128 B.S.E. L.276 J.D. Gen. Coun.
Gayle, David M. ... '43 '71 C.930 B.S. L.273 J.D.
Giza, Laura M. ... '66 '93 C.446 B.S.A.E. L.273 J.D.
Hall, John F., Jr. ... '64 '89 C.276 B.S.F.S. L.902 J.D.
Hostyk, Aaron ... '50 '79 (OH) C&L.477 B.A., J.D.
Kennedy, Alan J. ... '42 '78 (PA) C.679 B.S.M.E. L.446 J.D.
LaRocca, Francis P., Jr. ... '52 '78 C.262 B.A. L.724 J.D. Coun. to Inspec. Gen.
Lupuloff, Harry ... '58 '83 C.910 B.S.E.E. L.930 J.D.
Lyon, Deborah E. ... '51 '76 C.889 B.S. L.790 J.D.
Miller, Guy M. ... '57 '90 C.446 B.S.E.E. L.64 J.D.
Mirmina, Steven A. ... '67 '93 C.1036 B.A. L.184 J.D.
Palk, Sue Hagarman ... '63 '91 (VA) C.886 B.S. L.1209 J.D.
Roan, Bernard J., III ... '51 '80 (NY) C.869 B.S. L.569 J.D.
Roberts, Margaret A. ... '61 '93 C.856 B.A. L.128 J.D.
Salgado, Vincent A. ... '58 '91 C&L.276 B.S., J.D.
Schlabs, Michael W. ... '51 '76 C.1070 B.S. L.846 J.D.★
Stephens, Robert M. ... '49 '77 (VA) C.529 B.A. L.273 J.D.
Steptoe, E. Jason ... '47 '77 C.659 B.A. L.1162 J.D.
Thomas, Daniel ... '68 '94 C.184 B.A. L.94 J.D.
Thompson-King, Sumara M. ... '59 '85 (PA) C.788 A.B. L.276 J.D.
Werner, Pamela J. ... '59 '85 (MO) C.879 B.A. L.910 J.D.
Wojnarowski, Doris A. ... '56 '81 (PA) C.659 B.A. L.1017 J.D.

GODDARD SPACE FLIGHT CENTER

Bakos, Alexander T. ... '64 '92 C.128 A.B. L.446 J.D.
Kerr, Dorothy C. ... '60 '89 C.881 B.A. L.128 J.D.
Schuman, David S. ... '62 '89 C.311 B.A. L.1294 J.D.
Thompson, Theresa M. ... '63 '88 C.597 B.A. L.30 J.D.
Watson, Lawrence F. ... '49 '76 (NC) C.228 B.A. L.838 J.D.

Andreotta, Donald J. ... '48 '74 (CT) C&L.184 B.S.E., J.D.
Beck, David K. ... '54 '84 C.645 B.S. L.273 J.D.
Brundage, Paul D. ... '50 '76 (GA) C.1044 B.A. L.51 J.D.
Eastwood, Charles R. ... '24 '61 C.893 B.C.E. L.273 J.D.
Kurke, Kathy Ann ... '54 '78 (VA) C.694 A.B. L.273 J.D.
Maguire, Michael A. ... '48 '74 C.597 B.A. L.273 J.D.
Marlaire, Michael L. ... '54 '86 (IL) C&L.801 M.A., J.D.
Schumacher, John D. ... '54 '98 (NY) C.871 B.S. L.178 J.D.
Stehmer, Karl H. ... '51 '76 (OH) C.608 B.A. L.930 J.D.
Whelan, Thomas J., Jr. ... '41 '73 C.446 B.S. L.128 J.D.

NATIONAL ARCHIVES AND RECORDS ADMINISTRATION

Gary M. Stern, *General Counsel*

GENERAL COUNSEL STAFF

Baron, Jason R. ... '56 '80 C.918 B.A. L.94 J.D.
Brooks, Gary L. ... '46 '73 C.197 A.B. L.262 J.D.
Davenport, John E., Sr. ... '55 '96 (MD) C.446 B.A. L.64 J.D.
Krupsky, Amy Eisen ... '51 '78 C.910 B.A. L.1009 J.D.
Landou, Jeffrey A. ... '63 '90 (CT) C.1349 B.A. L.262 J.D.
Leff, Deborah ... '51 '77 C.674 A.B. L.145 J.D.
Rudgers, Sarah B. ... '72 '98 (MD) C.867 B.A. L.904 J.D.
Runkel, Christopher M. ... '59 '85 (MD) C&L.273 B.A., J.D.
Stern, Gary M. ... '60 '88 C.881 A.B. L.976 J.D. Gen. Coun.

OFFICE OF RECORDS SERVICES-WASHINGTON, D.C.

Prechtel-Kluskens, Claire ... '62 '88 C.117 B.A. L.608 J.D.

OFFICE OF THE FEDERAL REGISTER

McDonald, Frances D. ... '49 '82 (VA) C.890 B.A. L.128 J.D.
White, Michael L. ... '56 '82 C.893 B.A. L.945 J.D.

OFFICE OF PRESIDENTIAL LIBRARIES

Peterson, David F. ... '37 '63 C.309 A.B. L.188 LL.B.

OFFICE OF THE INSPECTOR GENERAL

Hepler, Jennifer Cron ... '56 '80 (FL) C&L.260 B.S.; B.A., J.D.

OFFICE OF ADMINISTRATIVE SERVICES

Weir, Forrest V. ... '19 '57 (LA) C.377 B.S. L.425 J.D.

NATIONAL CAPITAL PLANNING COMMISSION

(Vacant), *General Counsel*

Jain, Ash J. ... '69 '95 C.477 B.A. L.276 J.D.

NATIONAL CREDIT UNION ADMINISTRATION

Robert M. Fenner, *General Counsel*

OFFICE OF GENERAL COUNSEL

Albin, Sheila A. ... '49 '79 C.446 B.A. L.273 J.D.
Brewington, Dana L. ... '51 '80 C.446 B.S. L.276 J.D.
Canerday, Jon J. ... '56 '81 (AR) C.1125 B.S. L.45 J.D.
Engel, James J. ... '46 '73 C.717 B.A. L.128 J.D.
Fenner, Robert M. ... '48 '74 (MO) C.378 B.A. L.273 J.D. Gen. Coun.
Ianno, John K. ... '55 '80 C.262 B.A. L.1009 J.D.
Kressman, Frank S. ... '60 '87 C.216 B.A. L.285 J.D.
Loizos, Chrisanthy J. ... '68 '94 (OH) C.608 B.A. L.117 J.D.
McKenna, Michael J. ... '59 '84 C.1044 B.A. L.30 J.D.
McPartlin, Margaret E. ... '59 '87 (NY) C.771 B.A. L.831 J.D.
Meltzer, Allan H. ... '48 '76 C.446 B.A. L.276 J.D.
Metz, Regina M. ... '67 '93 C.276 A.B. L.262 J.D.
Peterson, Paul M. ... '57 '85 (PA) C.1375 B.S.E.E. L.273 J.D.
Poliquin, Gerard S. ... '62 '90 (PA) C.1058 B.A. L.988 J.D.
Roach, Robert D. ... '48 '78 (SC) C.1113 B.A. L.790 J.D.
Rupp, Mary Foote ... '51 '82 C.999 B.A. L.180 J.D.
Sachen-Gute, Kathy M. ... '51 '77 (KS) C&L.900 B.B.A., J.D.
Salva, Dianne M. ... '61 '86 (IL) C.424 B.S. L.365 J.D.
Ulan, Hattie Miriam ... '56 '81 C.659 B.A. L.904 J.D.
Widerman, Steven W. ... '54 '81 C.823 A.B. L.930 J.D.

OFFICE OF INSPECTOR GENERAL

Separ, Sharon ... '58 '88 C.886 B.A. L.945 J.D.

NATIONAL ENDOWMENT FOR THE ARTS

L. Hope O'Keeffe, *Acting General Counsel*

Elias, Karen Lee ... '50 '82 C.454 B.A. L.818 J.D.
O'Keeffe, L. Hope ... '57 '86 C.31 B.A. L.273 J.D. Acting Gen. Coun.

NATIONAL ENDOWMENT FOR THE HUMANITIES

Laura S. Nelson, *Acting General Counsel*

Nelson, Laura S. ... '65 '93 (WI) C.893 B.A. L.957 J.D. Acting Gen. Coun.
Walsh, Lauren M. ... '— '96 C.67 B.A. L.950 J.D. Asst. Gen. Coun.

NATIONAL LABOR RELATIONS BOARD

Leonard R. Page, *General Counsel*

OFFICE OF THE GENERAL COUNSEL

Frankl, Joseph F. ... '53 '80 C.477 B.A. L.588 J.D.
Page, Leonard R. ... '44 '72 (MI) C.477 B.B.A. L.213 J.D. Gen. Coun.

Division of Advice

Bridge, Diane L. ... '62 '86 (PA) C&L.229 B.A., J.D.
Colangelo, David A. ... '52 '77 C.178 B.A. L.276 J.D.
Dodds, Amy Lauren ... '69 '94 (VA) C.886 B.S. L.945 J.D.
Farrell, Ellen A. ... '46 '80 (NY) C.477 B.A. L.569 J.D.
Fener, Alan R. ... '45 '71 C.453 B.S. L.276 J.D.
Fogerty, Michael J. ... '42 '67 (IN) C&L.602 B.A., LL.B.
Friedman, Wilbur H. ... '32 '61 C.477 A.B. L.976 LL.B.
Goodman, Laura ... '56 '82 C.273 B.A. L.128 J.D.
Harris, Ella P. ... '43 '79 C.671 B.A. L.276 J.D.
Hornbeck, John W. ... '44 '69 (NY) C&L.823 A.B., J.D.
Jones, Harry E. ... '55 '88 (OR) C.665 B.A. L.629 J.D.
Karsh, Aaron ... '61 '87 (MA) C.339 B.A. L.93 J.D.
Katz, Judith I. ... '48 '78 C.696 A.B. L.818 J.D.
Kearney, Barry J. ... '42 '71 (MO) C.1033 B.S. L.734 J.D.

Lussier, Richard J. '69 '95 (CT) L.1029 J.D.
Mantz, John A. '48 '87 (MD) C.705 B.A. L.1162 J.D.
Marx, Eric C. '59 '89 (WI) C.999 B.A. L.966 J.D.
McCollum, Carolyn B. '53 '77 C.238 B.A. L.94 J.D.
Merberg, Elinor L. '58 '88 (MA) C.112 B.A. L.588 J.D.
Mirsky, Peter B. '47 '71 (FL) C.893 B.A. L.276 J.D.
Mitz, Lisolette E. '59 '87 C.502 B.S.B.A. L.208 J.D.
Omberg, Robert E. '55 '82 (WA) C.1193 B.A. L.911 J.D.
Rothman, Beryl M. '39 '82 C.94 B.A. L.276 J.D.
Sophir, Jayme L. '58 '85 C.188 B.A. L.659 J.D.
Vazquez, Laura T. '66 '94 (PR) C.309 B.A. L.677 J.D.
Watson, Marjorie H. '43 '78 C.994 B.A. L.273 J.D.
Weiser, Herbert E. '30 '60 (NY) C.608 B.S. L.1009 LL.B.
Young, Jacqueline '48 '85 C.966 B.A. L.1048 J.D.

Division of Enforcement Litigation
Appellate Court Branch

Armstrong, Aileen A. '43 '71 C.856 B.A. L.30 J.D.
Bernstein, William M. '40 '71 (NC) C&L.575 B.S., J.D.
Block, Sharon I. '65 '91 C.178 B.A. L.276 J.D.
Broido, Julie Brock '55 '81 C.104 A.B. L.665 J.D.
Burgoyne, John D. '31 '56 C.128 A.B. L.276 J.D.
Cohen, Richard A. '47 '72 (NY) C.188 B.S. L.273 J.D.
Cornnell, Frederick L., Jr. '51 '78 C.228 B.A. L.831 J.D.
Donnelly, Charles P. '41 '68 (TX) C.797 B.A. L.846 LL.B.
Dreeben, Linda J. '51 '77 C.477 A.B. L.94 J.D.
Englehart, Robert J. '51 '77 C.165 B.A. L.94 J.D.
Ferguson, John H. '40 '69 C.951 B.A. L.145 J.D.
Fleischer, David A. '44 '68 C.976 B.A. L.569 J.D.
Francis, Anna L. '71 '97 C&L.477 B.A., J.D.
Gartner, Rachel I. '68 '94 C&L.813 A.B., J.D.
Goldstein, Dawn L. '70 '95 (MA) C.260 B.A. L.94 J.D.
Griffin, Jill A. '56 '82 C.562 B.A. L.608 J.D.
Griffin, Marion L. '33 '55 (OH) C&L.608 B.A., J.D.
Habenstreit, David S. '61 '90 (MA) C.604 B.A. L.588 J.D.
Havard, Frederick '48 '75 (NE) C.112 B.A. L.976 J.D.
Horowitz, Jeffrey L. '64 '88 C.994 B.A. L.276 J.D.
Hoyte-Hayes, Joan E. '— '91 (NY) C.102 B.A. L.823 J.D.
Jacob, Fred B. '69 '94 C.1036 B.A. L.945 J.D.
Jason, Meredith L. '64 '91 C.94 B.A. L.30 J.D.
Marcus, Julie Freya '63 '98 (MA) C.914 B.A. L.477 J.D.
Messitte, Michael F. '37 '63 (MD) C&L.150 B.B.A., LL.B.
Perlstein, Howard E. '42 '70 C.178 A.B. L.1009 J.D.
Seid, David A. '63 '88 (MD) C.222 B.A. L.128 J.D.
Sher, Linda R. '38 '62 C.145 B.A. L.976 LL.B.
Shrager, Deborah E. '63 '90 C.659 B.A. L.597 J.D.
Winkler, Peter '51 '77 C.31 B.A. L.477 J.D.
Young, Christopher W. '48 '82 C.446 B.A. L.1162 J.D.

Division of Enforcement Litigation
Supreme Court Branch

Arbab, John E. '60 '86 C.309 A.B. L.94 J.D.
Come, Norton J. '19 '42 (IL) C&L.145 A.B., J.D.

Division of Enforcement Litigation
Office of Appeals

Breeskin, Nathan '18 '43 L.904 LL.B.
Brinker, Andrew V. '51 '75 (MO) C&L.502 B.A., J.D.
Dixon, Yvonne Teresa '49 '75 C.231 B.A. L.569 J.D.
Druitt, Beverly F. '47 '75 (MS) C.1044 B.A. L.705 J.D.
Ebert, Tina M. '70 '95 (PA) C.645 B.A. L.273 J.D.
Feldman, Arthur L. '41 '67 C.861 B.A. L.273 LL.B.
Francke, Claude R. '49 '88 (OH) C.473 B.S. L.150 J.D.
Freedman, Stephen '45 '73 C.446 B.A. L.329 J.D.
Hall, Allyson C. '71 '97 (MD) C.103 B.A. L.273 J.D.
Keong, Gail M. '47 '84 C.112 B.A. L.904 J.D.
Levitan, Daniel A. '53 '78 (CA) C.1044 B.A. L.1049 J.D.
McCormick, Linda C. '50 '76 C.881 A.B. L.421 J.D.
Mettler, Annetta Kay '51 '79 C.112 A.B. L.1067 J.D.
Pacheco, Beatrice '56 '81 (PA) C.3 B.A. L.174 J.D.
Pavsner, Susan M. '50 '75 C.477 B.A. L.276 J.D.
Seddelmeyer, David Allan '55 '86 (OR) C.347 B.A. L.596 J.D.
Smith, Angela Todd '65 '92 C.597 B.S. L.910 J.D.
Sykora, Wilfred F. '30 '68 C.627 B.A. L.677 LL.B.
Tate, Farrell D. '52 '78 C.116 B.A. L.329 J.D.
Tendrich, Robert I. '51 '77 C.1044 B.A. L.569 J.D.
Washington, Angela M. '62 '90 C.1083 B.S. L.329 J.D.
Yaden, Linda S. '55 '80 (SC)
Yaffe, Deborah M. P. '50 '77 C.696 B.A. L.273 J.D.
Yanulis, Jane A. '53 '81 C.783 B.A. L.30 J.D.

Division of Enforcement Litigation
Contempt Litigation Branch

Collopy, Daniel F. '57 '83 C.276 B.A. L.174 J.D.
Lerner, Helene D. '63 '89 C.1044 B.A. L.276 J.D.
Mascioli, William G. '56 '85 (NY) C.918 B.A. L.569 J.D.
Misra, Polly '68 '93 (OH) C.893 B.A. L.608 J.D.
Mori, David H. '69 '95 C.1494 B.A. L.93 J.D.
O'Neill, Barbara A. '56 '82 C.216 B.A. L.276 J.D.
Shapiro, Kenneth J. '48 '74 (FL) C&L.260 B.S.B.A., J.D.
Shinners, Gary W. '54 '79 (CA) C.147 B.A. L.464 J.D.
Sullivan, Joan A. '62 '90 C.174 B.S.B.A. L.128 J.D.
Zirkin, Stanley R. '45 '70 C.1044 B.A. L.276 J.D.

Division of Enforcement Litigation
Special Litigation Branch

Burns, Meredith A. '66 '95 C.276 B.S. L.188 J.D.
Dheenan, Usha '70 '96 C.188 B.A. L.477 J.D.
Ketcham, Lori W. '58 '84 (MI) C.228 A.B. L.477 J.D.
Lieber, Margery E. '47 '72 (NY) C.102 B.A. L.569 J.D.
Meiners, Denise F. '65 '90 C.884 B.A. L.30 J.D.
Moskowitz, Eric G. '47 '73 C.477 B.A. L.273 J.D.
O'Connor, Bridget '66 '94 C.518 A.B. L.145 J.D.
Parker, D. Criss '63 '89 (CA) C.112 B.A. L.1066 J.D.
Platt, Nancy E. Kessler '64 '89 C.188 B.S. L.1068 J.D.
Simms, Abby P. '51 '75 C.188 B.S. L.30 J.D.

Division of Administration

Joseph, Gloria J. '48 '74

Division of Operations-Management

Eveleth, Peter Ames '39 '65 C.188 B.S. L.659 J.D.
Holliday-Curtis, Yvette H. '— '83 (PA) C.645 B.A. L.884 J.D.
Kovachich, Jennifer S. '57 '83 (NY) C.477 A.B. L.607 J.D.
Marsh, Helen E. '44 '77 (CA) C.813 B.A. L.426 J.D.
Purcell, Anne '51 '78 (MO) C.502 B.A. L.986 J.D.
Schnabel, Edith J. C. '45 '69 C.228 A.B. L.537 J.D.
Siegel, Richard A. '47 '73 C.339 B.A. L.276 J.D.

BOARD MEMBERS

Fox, Sarah M. '51 '82 C.976 B.A. L.309 J.D.
Hurtgen, Peter J. '41 '66 C&L.276 B.S., J.D.
Truesdale, John C. '21 '72 C.293 A.B. L.276 J.D.

OFFICE OF BOARD MEMBERS

Alden, Anne R. '45 '70 C.473 A.B. L.245 J.D.
Azan-Reyes, Marie E. '62 '88 (FL) C.30 B.A. L.904 J.D.
Beccles, Barbara L. '41 '77 (MA) C.94 B.L.S. L.818 J.D.
Buckley, Douglas P. '48 '74 (PA) C.896 B.B.A. L.575 J.D.
Bunn, James C. '46 '79 C.69 B.A. L.569 J.D.
Carroll, Nora '58 '90 C.910 B.A. L.174 J.D.
Chatterjee, Ella B. '44 '76 (NJ) C.216 B.A. L.831 J.D.
Clark, Thomas H. '48 '83 C.476 B.S. L.1162 J.D.
Constantinople, George R. '44 '86 C.867 B.A. L.893 J.D.
Crump, Karen L. '65 '91 (PA) C.25 B.A. L.128 J.D.
D'Amour, Denise M. '54 '86 (MA) C.273 B.A. L.818 J.D.
Datz, Harold J. '38 '65 (FL) C&L.260 B.A., LL.B.
Davison, Gabrielle Giselle '66 '94 C.646 B.A. L.128 J.D.
Dowling, Maria-Kate '63 '89 (MD) C.446 B.A. L.273 J.D.
Elligers, Sandra S. '49 '74 C.188 B.S. L.93 J.D.
Fox, Marian R. '49 '75 C.881 A.B. L.273 J.D.
Franklin, William S. '45 '82 C.846 B.A. L.976 J.D.
Gilhooley, Paul G. '53 '84 (NJ) C.706 B.A. L.776 J.D.
Gold, Wayne R. '51 '77 C.446 B.A. L.190 J.D.
Graber, Norman L. '57 '81 C.188 B.S. L.276 J.D.
Heilweil, Toby Z. '56 '81 (PA) C.1036 B.A. L.659 J.D.
Hunt, Nancy B. '51 '80 (FL) C.472 B.A. L.260 J.D.
Kachor, Mark A. '50 '75 C.112 B.A. L.930 J.D.
Kane, Robert F. '45 '70 C.712 B.A. L.128 J.D.
Kavanagh, Patrick G. '51 '82 (PA) C.276 B.S. L.128 J.D.
Kehoe, Susan E. '49 '85 (MD) C.856 B.A. L.861 J.D.
Knight, Sherrian Patricia '48 '77 C.999 B.A. L.276 J.D.
Kraus, F. W. Grant '— '86 C.951 B.A. L.569 J.D.
Legum, Radine '58 '85 (VA) C.228 B.S. L.276 J.D.
Lewis, Michael R. '52 '91 C.165 A.B. L.276 J.D.
Martin, David P. '44 '69 C&L.608 B.A., J.D.
Middleton, Edith A. '57 '87 (PA) C.994 B.A. L.982 J.D.
Miller, John R. '49 '76 (MD) C.446 B.A. L.930 J.D.
Miller, Jolynne D. '58 '91 (CT) C.569 B.A. L.563 J.D.
Murphy, James C. '43 '78 C.884 A.B. L.30 J.D.
Murphy, James R. '49 '76 (MD) C.674 A.B. L.30 J.D.
Neighborgall, Linda S. '47 '88 (PA) C.446 B.A. L.273 J.D.
Nemzer, Adam M. '61 '87 (CT) C.367 B.A. L.184 J.D.
Nixon, Kathleen A. '50 '77 C.201 B.S. L.945 J.D.
Novak, David '49 '85 (PA) C.311 B.A. L.276 J.D.
Olbrich, Richard '42 '67 (WI) C&L.966 B.S., J.D.
Perry, Cathleen D. '53 '87 (PA) C.882 B.A. L.276 J.D.
Rappaport, Steven F. '61 '89 (MD) C.446 B.A. L.910 J.D.
Ricca, Alan '51 '76 C.477 A.B. L.215 J.D.
Richards, Robert R., Jr. '42 '68 C.820 A.B. L.208 J.D.
Rosenberg, Rosalind '42 '80 C.477 B.A. L.221 J.D.
Ross, Jonathan R. '50 '76 C.604 A.B. L.276 J.D.
Rossen, Leslie E. '49 '78 C.367 A.B. L.273 J.D.
Schaff, David '53 '90 C.94 A.B. L.588 J.D.
Scheinbart, Jonathan R. '49 '75 C.188 B.S. L.976 J.D.
Schwartz, David B. '61 '89 (IL) C.103 A.B. L.145 J.D.
Seidman, Marc B. '51 '76 (PA) C.339 B.A. L.93 J.D.
Skolnick, Julie F. Rosenbaum '68 '96 C.165 B.A. L.188 J.D.
Socoloff, Jane Ballenger '— '78 (OH) C&L.608 B.S., J.D.
Solomon, Lafe E. '49 '76 C.103 B.A. L.861 J.D.
Stillman, Elinor H. '38 '73 C.378 B.A. L.273 J.D.
Tafe, Elizabeth M. '63 '98 (MA) C.681 B.A. L.588 J.D.
Tansimore, Jeffrey D. '62 '90 C.658 B.A. L.30 J.D.
Thurm, Mary-Ellen '49 '75 C&L.273 B.A., J.D.
Valetich, Stephanie '52 '77 (PA) C&L.665 B.A., J.D.
Voltz, Robert M. '42 '68 C.1031 B.S. L.276 J.D.
Walsh, Dennis P. '54 '85 (NY) C.299 B.A. L.188 J.D.
Waters, Jill E. '— '87 (PA) C.105 B.A. L.273 J.D.
Wedekind, Jeffrey D. '57 '82 C.260 B.A. L.273 J.D.
Wheeler, Jeffrey S. '64 '89 C.790 B.A. L.893 J.D.
Wiener, Rosa D. '34 '88 (PA) C.273 B.A. L.276 J.D.
Williford, Rhonda G. '51 '79 (VA) C.415 B.A. L.945 J.D.
Wolff, Alfred L. '38 '62 (WI) C&L.966 B.S., LL.B.
Wolin, Michele '58 '84 (MN) C.228 A.B. L.477 J.D.
Zuver, Charles O., Jr. '69 '95 C.1494 B.A. L.1117 J.D.

OFFICE OF EXECUTIVE SECRETARY

Heltzer, Lester A. '46 '73 C.930 B.A. L.273 J.D.
Toner, John J. '48 '85 (PA) C.645 B.A. L.1209 J.D.

OFFICE OF SOLICITOR

Breiteneicher, Henry S. '49 '75 C.367 B.A. L.273 J.D.
Higgins, John E., Jr. '39 '64 (MA) C.93 A.B. L.94 LL.B.
Leverone, Susan A. '58 '83 C.973 B.A. L.128 J.D.

DIVISION OF ADMINISTRATIVE LAW JUDGES

Alemán, George '44 '77 (NY) C.415 B.A. L.776 J.D.
Amchan, Arthur J. '46 '73 C.473 B.A. L.309 J.D.
Beddow, Richard H., Jr. '32 '60 C.454 B.S. L.93 LL.B.

NATIONAL LABOR RELATIONS BOARD (Continued)

Bogas, Paul ....'59 '85 (NY) C.1349 B.A. L.976 J.D.
Buschmann, Karl H. ....'37 '63 C&L.30 B.A., J.D.
Evans, David L. ....'41 '66 C.840 B.A. L.846 J.D.
Giannasi, Robert A. ....'39 '65 C.966 B.B.A. L.276 J.D.
Gross, Stephen J. ....'35 '63 C.674 A.B. L.178 LL.B.
Hermele, Jerry M. ....'55 '79 C.24 B.A. L.150 J.D.
Kocol, William G. ....'— '73 (IL) C.339 B.S. L.966 J.D
Ladwig, Marion C. ....'20 '49 C.840 B.S. L.846 LL.B.
Linsky, Martin J. ....'39 '65 C&L.262 B.A., J.D.
Rose, James L. ....'35 '62 C&L.378 B.A., J.D.
Rosenstein, Bruce D. ....'43 '68 C.823 B.S. L.421 J.D.
Schlesinger, Benjamin ....'35 '59 C.299 B.A. L.178 LL.B.
Schwarzbart, Robert M. ....'31 '59 C.569 B.A. L.1009 J.D.
Scully, Richard A. ....'42 '67 C.321 B.S. L.276 LL.B.
Shamwell, Earl E., Jr. ....'— '73 C&L.273 B.A., J.D.
Sherman, Nancy M. ....'25 '49 C&L.145 Ph.B., J.D.
Socoloff, Irwin H. ....'42 '67 C.696 A.B. L.188 J.D.
Wagman, Leonard M. ....'28 '55 C.846 B.A. L.178 LL.B.
West, John H. ....'41 '67 C.94 B.A. L.564 LL.B.
Wilks, Thomas R. ....'34 '61 C&L.215 A.B., LL.B.

WASHINGTON, D. C. RESIDENT OFFICE

Anderson, Angela S. ....'43 '67 (AL) C.812 B.S. L.16 J.D.

NATIONAL MEDIATION BOARD

(Vacant), *General Counsel*

Crable, Stephen E. ....'48 '74 C.473 B.A. L.910 J.D. Chf. of Staf
Duggan, Francis J. ....'38 '67 C&L.724 B.A. Chairman
Etters, Ronald M. ....'48 '76 C.30 B.A. L.904 J.D.
Fisher, Susanna ....'75 '00 C.890 B.A. L.1209 J.D.
Johnson, Mary L. ....'51 '80 (CT) C.66 A.B. L.184 J.D.
Jones, Zachery M. ....'56 '87 C.329 B.A. L.494 J.D.
Livingood, John M. ....'47 '76 C&L.884 A.B., J.D.
Mansfield, Benetta M. ....'52 '78 C.367 B.A. L.588 J.D.
Oppenberg, Gale L. ....'53 '77 C.102 B.A. L.188 J.D.
Rogers, Sean J. ....'47 '78 C&L.276 A.B., J.D.
Watkins, Roland ....'52 '77 (OH) C.390 A.B. L.188 J.D.

NATIONAL SCIENCE FOUNDATION

Lawrence Rudolph, *General Counsel*

OFFICE OF THE GENERAL COUNSEL

Ashley, Christopher L. ....'64 '91 C.821 B.A. L.966 J.D.
Brown, Charles S. C. ....'44 '70 C.309 A.B. L.597 J.D.
Chester, John ....'49 '78 C&L.659 B.S., J.D.
Eisenstadt, Anita R. ....'58 '82 C.477 B.A. L.912 J.D.
Grotke, Lewis E. ....'31 '55 (NY) C.732 A.B. L.982 J.D.
Lasken, Jesse E. ....'41 '67 C&L.477 A.B., J.D.
Miles, Theodore A. ....'38 '64 C.309 B.A. L.329 LL.B.
Paver, Fran L. ....'— '80 C.299 B.A. L.910 J.D.
Powell, Dean M. ....'49 '74 C&L.221 B.A., J.D.
Rudolph, Lawrence ....'51 '76 C.4 B.A. L.276 J.D. Gen. Coun.

OFFICE OF INSPECTOR GENERAL

Allen, Craig ....'— '97 C.1275 B.A. L.902 J.D.
Cusumano, Leanne ....'— '94 C.273 B.A. L.945 J.D.
Stagliano, Kristen ....'70 '99 C.911 B.B.A. L.1059 J.D.
Woodford, Richard F., Jr. ....'61 '97 (FL) C.871 B.S. L.259 J.D.

NATIONAL TRANSPORTATION SAFETY BOARD

Ronald S. Battocchi, *General Counsel*

OFFICE OF THE GENERAL COUNSEL

Bass, David E. ....'46 '71 C.902 B.A. L.893 J.D.
Battocchi, Ronald S. ....'47 '74 C.31 B.A. L.1294 J.D. Gen. Coun.
D'Avella, Denise M. ....'64 '90 (MD) C.93 A.B. L.128 J.D.
Julius, R. Christopher ....'68 '97 (NY)
Silbaugh, Kathleen ....'65 '91 C.390 A.B. L.128 J.D.

OFFICE OF ADMINISTRATIVE LAW JUDGES

Fowler, Wm. E., Jr. ....'21 '55 C.8 B.A. L.7 LL.B.
Geraghty, Patrick G. ....'33 '65 C.216 Sc.B. L.30 J.D.
Heller, Steven M. ....'51 '76 C.102 B.A. L.945 J.D.
Mullins, William R. ....'41 '70 C.639 B.A. L.174 J.D.
Pope, William A., II ....'37 '62 C.273 B.A. L.276 J.D.

MANAGING DIRECTOR'S OFFICE

Campbell, Daniel D. ....'43 '71 C.674 B.A. L.569 J.D. Gen. Coun.

NUCLEAR REGULATORY COMMISSION

Karen D. Cyr, *General Counsel*

OFFICE OF THE GENERAL COUNSEL

Bader, Wendy ....'59 '84 (NY) C.693 B.A. L.276 J.D.
Barber, Katheryn M. ....'75 '00 (OH) C&L.200 B.A., J.D.
Baum, Robin A. ....'57 '83 C.1040 B.S. L.796 J.D.
Berry, Elva Bowden ....'63 '97 (MD) C.475 B.A. L.128 J.D.
Burns, Stephen G. ....'53 '78 C.165 B.A. L.273 J.D.
Cameron, Francis X. ....'45 '72 (PA) C&L.665 B.A., J.D.
Chandler, Lawrence J. ....'46 '70 C.94 B.A. L.273 J.D.
Chidakel, Susan Shirley ....'44 '84 (MD) C.645 B.A. L.30 J.D.
Clark, Lisa B. ....'56 '81 (MD) C&L.446 B.S., J.D.
Coggins, Angela Beth ....'71 '98 (LA) C.140 B.A. L.861 J.D.
Cordes, John F., Jr. ....'49 '74 (NJ) C&L.276 B.S., J.D.
Crockett, Steven F. ....'43 '85 (MD) C.231 A.B. L.976 J.D.
Cyr, Karen D. ....'48 '77 C.350 B.S. L.228 J.D. Gen. Coun.
Dambly, Dennis C. ....'48 '75 C.1111 B.S. L.260 J.D.
Engel, Debra S. ....'56 '81 (SC) C.298 B.A. L.790 J.D.
Euchner, Jennifer M. ....'74 '99 (MD) C.692 B.A. L.273 J.D.
Farrar, Karl L. ....'60 '87 (PA) C.411 L.884
Fehst, Geraldine R. ....'48 '79 (IL) C.339 B.A. L.209 J.D.
Fernandez, Antonio ....'74 '00 (MD) C.200 B.A. L.744 J.D.
Fonner, Susan G. ....'33 '59 (IN) L.178 J.D.
Gauch, Dorothy M. ....'60 '88 C.446 B.A. L.64 J.D.
Goldberg, Jack R. ....'45 '75 C.688 B.S. L.884 J.D.
Gray, Joseph R. ....'46 '76 C.645 B.S. L.1017 J.D.
Grodin, Maryann Lawrence ....'50 '75 (CA) C.1044 B.A. L.61 J.D.
Hassell, Donald F. ....'46 '76 (PA) C.1133 B.S. L.273 J.D.
Hodgdon, Ann Perrine ....'31 '77 C.383 A.B. L.276 J.D.
Hoefling, Richard K. ....'43 '74 C.93 B.S. L.446 J.D.
Holzle, Catherine M. ....'53 '80 C.446 B.A. L.64 J.D.
Hom, Steven R. ....'53 '80 (NY) C.112 A.B. L.569 J.D.
Hull, John T. ....'56 '83 C.575 B.A. L.128 J.D.
Itzkowitz, Marvin L. ....'52 '78 C.978 B.A. L.1019 J.D.
Jensen, E. Neil ....'40 '80 (MD) C.321 B.A. L.446 J.D.
Kim, Grace H. ....'59 '86 (MA) C.914 B.A. L.93 J.D.
Lewis, Stephen H. ....'44 '69 C.309 A.B. L.94 J.D.
Lieberman, James ....'45 '74 (VA) C.690 B.S., M.E. L.273 J.D.
Longo, Giovanna M. ....'45 '72 C&L.477 B.A., J.D.
Marco, Catherine L. ....'67 '92 (MA) C.94 B.A. L.818 J.D.
McAndrew, Sara ....'54 '86 (MA) C.446 B.S. L.818 J.D.
McGurren, Henry J. ....'44 '69 C&L.37 B.A., J.D.
Mizuno, Geary S. ....'55 '80 C.103 A.B. L.276 J.D.
Moore, Janice E. ....'50 '78 C&L.276 B.S.L., J.D.
Mullins, Charles E. ....'48 '82 (KY) C.999 B.S. L.421 J.D.
O'Neill, Martin J. ....'71 '00 C.165 B.A. L.846 J.D.
Rafky, L. Michael ....'65 '90 (MD) C.94 B.A. L.276 J.D.
Rothschild, Irwin B., III ....'50 '75 C.597 B.S. L.1068 J.D.
Rothschild, Marjorie Ulman ....'50 '77 C.966 B.A. L.802 J.D.
St. Amour, Norman D. ....'57 '99 (MD) C.034 B.A. L.273 J.D.
Schwartz, Maria E. ....'50 '91 (PA) C.30 B.A. L.329 J.D.
Siemien, Mary P. ....'59 '86 (GA) C.30 B.A. L.469 J.D.
Slaggie, E. Leo ....'35 '76 (CA) C&L.309 A.B., J.D.
Stein, Michael Hal ....'62 '90 C.696 B.A. L.1009 J.D.
Szabo, John L. ....'43 '68 C.276 B.S.F.S. L.273 J.D.
Treby, Stuart A. ....'41 '66 (NY) C.860 B.A. L.276 LL.B.
Turk, Sherwin E. ....'49 '75 C.597 B.A. L.276 J.D.
Uttal, Susan L. ....'50 '77 (NJ) C.1044 B.S. L.1292 J.D.
Weisman, Robert M. ....'56 '84 (OK) C.494 B.Ch.E. L.623 J.D.
Young, Mitzi A. ....'55 '81 C.188 B.A. L.273 J.D.

ATOMIC SAFETY AND LICENSING BOARD PANEL

Bechhoefer, Charles ....'33 '58 C&L.309 A.B., LL.B. Adm. J.
Bollwerk, G. Paul, III ....'53 '78 C.602 A.B. L.276 J.D.
Dewey, Lee S. ....'37 '65 C&L.880 B.A., LL.B.
Moore, Thomas S. ....'46 '72 C.473 B.A. L.608 J.D.
Young, Ann Marshall ....'45 '79 (TN) C.604 A.B. L.880 J.D.

COMMISSION

Davis, Roger K. ....'46 '73 C.228 B.A. L.276 J.D.
Jones, Bradley W. ....'55 '80 C&L.823 B.A., J.D.
Winsberg, Kathryn L. ....'51 '78 (MA) C.478 A.B. L.94 J.D.

OFFICE OF COMMISSION APPELLATE ADJUDICATION

Carson, M. Cecilia ....'61 '92 (MD) C&L.276 B.A., J.D.
Doane, Margaret M. ....'62 '88 (MD) C.423 B.A. L.446 J.D.
Frye, Roland M., Jr. ....'50 '75 C.674 B.A. L.188 J.D.

OCCUPATIONAL SAFETY AND HEALTH REVIEW COMMISSION

Earl R. Ohman, Jr., *General Counsel*

OFFICE OF THE GENERAL COUNSEL

Bass, Laura K. ....'72 '98 (MD) C.188 B.S. L.659 J.D.
Bookman, Peter A. ....'47 '71 (NJ) C&L.705 B.A., J.D.
Bookman, Shirley B. ....'48 '75 (MD) C.445 B.A. L.276 J.D.
Cerveny, John X. ....'62 '87 C.1365 B.A. L.945 J.D.
Clark, Michael J. ....'69 '94 (MA) C.696 B.A. L.477 J.D.
Griffin, Geraldine ....'55 '98 (MA) C.454 B.A. L.184 J.D.
Loftus, Thomas A. ....'46 '75 C.31 B.A. L.273 J.D.
Lynn, H. Bailey, II ....'45 '71 C.674 A.B. L.902 J.D.
Mancini, Nadine N. ....'66 '91 (PA) C.665 B.A. L.184 J.D.
Moran, Eugene P. ....'47 '76 (VA) C.670 A.B. L.1209 J.D.
Ohman, Earl R., Jr. ....'45 '74 C.871 B.S. L.273 J.D. Gen. Coun.
Scheige, Steven S. ....'50 '75 (MD) C.705 B.A. L.276 J.D.
Strickler, Scott H. ....'46 '71 (WA) C.939 B.A. L.911 J.D.
Tanney, Catherine J. ....'52 '78 C.446 B.A. L.276 J.D.

OFFICE OF THE CHAIRMAN

Huberman, Richard L. ....'53 '79 C&L.309 A.B., J.D.
Jarrell, Ann O. ....'55 '85 (MD) C.454 B.A. L.1162 J.D.
Rogers, Thomasina V. ....'51 '77 (NY) C.597 B.S.J. L.178 J.D. Chmn.

OFFICE OF A COMMISSIONER

Eisenbrey, Ross E. ....'53 '78 C.478 B.A. L.477 J.D.
Glick, Janice L. ....'55 '84 C.112 B.A. L.1065 J.D.

OFFICE OF THE EXECUTIVE SECRETARY

Darling, Ray H., Jr. ....'46 '71 C&L.972 B.S., J.D. Exec. Secy.

ADMINISTRATIVE LAW JUDGES

Barkley, James H. ....'43 '68 C.172 B.S. L.174 J.D.
Bober, Gerald Marvin ....'39 '66 (MD) C.928 A.B. L.446 LL.B.

Goldstein, Sidney J. '14 '36 L.209 J.D.
Kim, Jin H. '72 '99 C.145 B.A. L.945 J.D.
Loye, Benjamin R. '27 '58 C&L.208 A.B., LL.B.
Rooney, Covette '52 '77 (PA) C.165 B.A. L.831 J.D.
Simko, Stephen J., Jr. '46 '72 (GA) C.259 B.S. L.245 J.D.
Sommer, Irving '24 '48 C.563 B.B.A. L.1009 J.D. Chief Judge
Spies, Nancy J. '46 '73 (KS) C.942 B.S. L.378 J.D.
Welsch, Ken S. '44 '72 C.446 B.A. L.469 J.D.
Yetman, Robert A. '41 '70 (MA) C.94 B.S. L.818 J.D.

Faust, Jeanne M. '60 '87 (GA) C.347 B.A. L.1119 J.D.
Goldstein, Samuel E. '50 '77 C.276 B.S.B.A. L.1209 J.D.
Green, Marcella M. '63 '92 C.706 B.A. L.1009 J.D.
Merrifield, Pamela G. '51 '88 (TX) C.612 B.S. L.802 J.D.
Reid, Christian E. '52 '87 (CO) C.1165 B.F.A. L.174 J.D.

OFFICE OF GOVERNMENT ETHICS

Amy L. Comstock, *Director*
Marilyn Glynn, *General Counsel*

OFFICE OF THE DIRECTOR

Comstock, Amy L. '59 '86 C.65 B.A. L.477 J.D. Dir.
Ley, Jane S. '50 '75 (KS) C.375 B.S. L.273 J.D. Dep. Dir.
Mosley, Ferne L. '63 '91 (MD) C.665 B.A. L.446 J.D. Special Asst. to the Dir.

OFFICE OF GENERAL COUNSEL AND LEGAL POLICY

Eirinberg, Julia L. '56 '80 (TX) C.45 B.A. L.846 J.D.
Falcon, R. Andrew '63 '88 (CA) C.228 A.B. L.93 J.D.
Glynn, Marilyn '48 '79 C.242 B.A. L.30 J.D. Gen. Coun.
Gorham, Bryan Gregory '74 '99 (NC) C.893 B.S. L.1128 J.D.
Gressman, William E. '48 '73 C.976 A.B. L.309 J.D.
Kim, Judith A. '65 '91 (MO) C.338 B.S. L.910 J.D.
Kimball, Karen '40 '82 C&L.1209 B.A., J.D.
Newton, Elaine '66 '99 (MD) C.1280 B.A. L.446 J.D.
O'Sullivan, James P. '38 '78 (MD) C.363 A.B. L.276 J.D.
Richman, Kay L. '51 '78 C.112 A.B. L.276 J.D.
Rick, Stuart D. '48 '74 C.264 B.A. L.273 J.D. Dep. Gen. Coun.
Salamone, Vincent J. '62 '87 (MA) C.1107 B.A. L.1048 J.D.
Smith, G. Sid '45 '70 (KS) C&L.378 B.A., J.D.
Smith, Norman B. '42 '67 C.659 B.S. L.273 J.D.
Thomas, Richard M. '58 '88 C.999 B.A. L.823 J.D.

OFFICE OF PERSONNEL MANAGEMENT

(Vacant), *General Counsel*

OFFICE OF THE GENERAL COUNSEL

Watson, Melanie J. '— '95 C.674 B.A. L.575 J.D.

MERIT SYSTEMS DIVISION

Abow, Steven E. '50 '75 C.1044 B.A. L.339 J.D.
Buchanan, Annette M. '56 '92 (PA) C.103 B.A. L.588 J.D.
Hicks, James F., Jr. '45 '73 (VA) C.477 B.A. L.893 J.D.
Jones, Kimya I. '69 '96 (MD) C.446 B.S. L.94 J.D.
Kumar, Becky Christina '65 '95 (CA) C.914 B.A. L.178 J.D.
Limon, Raymond A. '63 '95 C.549 B.A. L.347 J.D.

COMPENSATION DIVISION

Chabot, Jo-Ann '46 '72 C.94 B.A. L.276 J.D.
Gerstenfield, Jill '41 '79 C.446 B.S. L.128 J.D.
Green, James S. '45 '71 C.94 B.S. L.276 J.D. Assoc. Gen. Coun.
Plunkett, Wade M. '56 '81 (AR) C&L.45 B.S.B.A., J.D.
Sanders, Earl A. '45 '70 C&L.276 A.B., J.D.
Scholar, Sandra Kaye '56 '90 C.903 B.A. L.273 J.D.
Whitman, Susan G. '64 '89 C&L.188 B.S., J.D.

OFFICE OF THE INSPECTOR GENERAL

Hutton, E. Jeremy '41 '67 C.165 B.A. L.228 J.D.
Watkins, Timothy C. '57 '83 (IN) C.679 B.A. L.1119 J.D.

PERSONNEL IN NON-LEGAL POSITIONS

Mattox, George F. '26 '51 (MD) C&L.64 LL.B.
McLeod, Fred D. '24 '56 C.369 B.A. L.329 LL.B.
Norris, Joseph A. '23 '49 C&L.276 B.S.S., J.D.
Pettibone, Craig B. '43 '68 (WI) C&L.966 B.B.A., J.D.

Band, Joseph M. '40 '66 C&L.30 B.A., J.D.
Davis, Franklin G. '38 '62 (WV) C.647 B.S. L.923 LL.B.
Diaz, Gregory T. '40 '73 C.260 B.A. L.276 J.D.
Heiss, Sharon K. '48 '87 C.347 A.B. L.128 J.D.
Lancaster, Ronny B. '51 '85 C.128 B.A. L.276 J.D.
Laughnan, Monti S. '49 '75 C.30 B.A. L.1202 J.D.
Mazza, Gary E. '37 '66 (NY) C.569 B.A. L.1009 LL.B.
Newland, Howard T., Jr. '49 '76 (VA) C.886 B.A. L.273 J.D.
Panagakos, John '48 '80 (GA) C.823 B.A. L.1234 J.D.
Reich, David '12 '35 C.563 B.A. L.262 LL.B.
Reidy, Edward J. '27 '57 C.870 B.S. L.276 J.D.
Sanet, John A. '48 '73 C.273 B.A. L.260 J.D.
Siegelman, Harold L. '51 '76 (NJ) C.705 B.A. L.585 J.D.

OFFICE OF SPECIAL COUNSEL

Elaine D. Kaplan, *Special Counsel*

Beard, Heather S. '71 '96 (MI) C&L.339 B.A., J.D.
Bell, Amber A. '71 '98 (CA) C.1073 B.A. L.284 J.D.
Biggs, Tracy L. '62 '96 C.276 B.S. L.1356 J.D.
Boulay, Patrick H. '74 '01 C.103 A.B. L.276 J.D.
Dalheim, Karen L. '— '91 (MA) C.454 B.A. L.823 J.D.
Dribinsky, Leonard M. '50 '75 C.610 B.G.S. L.273 J.D.
Ehlinger, Melissa '76 '01 C.846 B.A. L.273 J.D.
Ellis, Kristin L. '72 '97 (MI) C.851 B.S. L.146 J.D.
Engler, Ronald C. '60 '90 (MI) C.477 B.A. L.588 J.D.
Ertel, Ruth Robinson '43 '83 C.1209 B.A. L.273 J.D.
Galindo-Marrone, Ana '64 '95 (FL) C&L.472 B.A., J.D.
Garnes, Tamara N. '73 '01 C.674 A.B. L.276 J.D.
Gerson, Susan Beth '66 '93 C.454 B.A. L.276 J.D.
Gorman, Karen Ponton '64 '89 C.777 B.A. L.128 J.D.
Gray, Kristin A. '70 '96 (VA) C.423 B.A. L.1209 J.D.
Hannapel, Timothy B. '59 '86 C.103 A.B. L.276 J.D. Dep. Spec. Coun.
Jackson, Kimberly Ann '74 '00 C.502 B.A. L.1065 J.D.
Jaicks, Ronald K. '62 '86 C.886 B.A. L.692 J.D.
Kaplan, Elaine D. '55 '79 C.1044 B.A. L.276 J.D. Spec. Coun.
Lovell, Susan L. '65 '91 (VA) C.1031 B.S. L.128 J.D.
Markovitz, Brian Joseph '72 '00 C.216 B.A. L.276 J.D.
McDonnell, Erin M. '— '72 (NY) C.331 B.A. L.602 J.D.
McMullen, Catherine A. '58 '83 (WV) C&L.923 B.A., J.D.
Mehring, Melissa A. '66 '91 (MD) C.881 B.A. L.861 J.D.
Moazed, Shirine E. '64 '94 (PA) C.446 B.A. L.30 J.D.
Monahan, Mary K. '70 '96 (MD) C.423 B.A. L.1202 J.D.
Patel Martin, Shennie '69 '96 C&L.326 B.A., J.D.
Reukauf, William E. '44 '70 C.299 B.A. L.276 J.D.
Rivera-Fournier, Alberto '70 '98 C.918 B.A. L.273 J.D.
Ruben, Francisco J. '70 '95 C.30 B.A. L.904 J.D.
Sklar, Cary P. '56 '81 C.188 B.S. L.276 J.D. Sr. Advisor
Williamson, Leslie Lubell '63 '88 (CO) C.188 B.S. L.107 J.D.

DALLAS FIELD OFFICE

Cardillo, Anthony T. '53 '86 C.728 B.S. L.1209 J.D.
Elliott, Travis Quintin '70 '96 (VA) C.105 B.A. L.273 J.D.

SAN FRANCISCO FIELD OFFICE

Fong, Bruce D. '53 '80 (CA) C.103 A.B. L.1066 J.D.
Martinez, Jacqueline L. '49 '84 (CA) C.112 B.A. L.284 J.D.

OVERSEAS PRIVATE INVESTMENT CORPORATION

Mark Garfinkel, *General Counsel & Vice President*

Abbey, Michael Hall '63 '89 C.228 B.A. L.893 J.D.
Bayer, Nathan J. '45 '69 C.659 B.A. L.276 J.D.
Chalmers, Jane H. '48 '74 C.681 B.A. L.477 J.D. Assoc. Gen. Coun.
Christaldi, Brian '40 '66 C.31 B.A. L.309 LL.B.
Garfinkel, Mark A. '51 '88 C.1044 B.A. L.326 J.D. Gen. Coun. & V.P.
Hills, Laura H. '61 '88 C&L.813 B.A., J.D.
Jagadesan, Dev '69 '94 (PA) C.128 B.A. L.180 J.D. Asst. Gen. Coun.
Jonkers, Ronald N. '51 '77 (CA) C.813 B.A. L.1065 J.D.
Landy, Eli H. '64 '94 (MD) C.102 B.A. L.276 J.D.
Liu, Merlin '47 '78 (NY) C&L.051 B.A., LL.B. Asst. Gen. Coun.
Mahaffey, Thomas J. '53 '80 (TX) C&L.846 B.A., J.D.
Monheimer, Marc H. '31 '57 (CA) C.112 A.B. L.1066 J.D.
Morgan, Barbara K. '54 '79 C.475 B.A. L.602 J.D. Sr. Comm. Coun.
Naide, Laura A. '66 '92 (VA) C.1042 B.A. L.276 J.D.
Nordgren, Marcia L. '59 '87 (NJ) C.478 B.A. L.705 J.D.
Obegi, Melissa '65 '91 C.276 B.S.F.S. L.112 J.D. Asst. Gen. Coun.
O'Sullivan, Robert C. '46 '75 C.93 A.B. L.309 J.D.
Sarkar, Rumu '60 '83 C.66 B.A. L.1162 J.D. Asst. Gen. Coun.
Valentin, Maria Santos '62 '88 (NY) C.262 B.A. L.976 J.D. Sr. Com. Coun.
West, Karen A. '— '88 C.94 B.S. L.309 J.D. Sr. Com. Coun.

INVESTMENT FUNDS DEPARTMENT

Cowan, Steven J. '60 '86 (NY) C.103 B.A. L.309 J.D.

PANAMA CANAL COMMISSION

John L. Haines, Jr., *General Counsel*

OFFICE OF THE GENERAL COUNSEL

Ballard de Fabrega, Marlene '58 '83 (Panama) L.999 J.D.
Ballenger, R. David '62 '88 C.140 B.A. L.790 J.D.
Cabal, Alvaro A. '52 '81 (Panama) C.999 L.861 LL.M.
Fabrega, Marelisa '71 '97 (NY) C&L.276 B.S.B.A., J.D.
Haines, John L., Jr. '41 '66 (VA) C.152 B.A. L.893 J.D. Gen. Coun.
Heisler, Glenn August '62 '89 (NJ) C.882 B.S. L.1202 J.D.
Joyce, Albert J., III '60 '86 (LA) C.945 B.A. L.425 J.D.
Lopez, Tiany M. '67 '91 (Panama)
Lucas, Theodore G. '55 '82 (WA) C&L.911 B.A., J.D.
Sieleman, Jay '53 '78 (IA) C&L.352 B.A., J.D.
Toth, Aurora G. '43 '81 (WA) C.1081 B.S. L.678 J.D.
Vasquez, Lydia Raquel '50 '80 (Panama) L.999 J.D.
Villalaz, Rene A. '70 '96 (LA) C.128 B.A. L.425 J.D.

PEACE CORPS

Nancy H. Hendry, *General Counsel*

OFFICE OF THE GENERAL COUNSEL

Glasow, Suzanne B. '46 '86 C.763 B.A. L.128 J.D.
Hendry, Nancy H. '49 '75 C.681 B.A. L.813 J.D. Gen. Coun.
Horton, Amy '55 '92 C.362 B.A. L.472 J.D.
Martin, Robert L. '26 '53 (NY) C.165 B.A. L.188 J.D.
Ramsey, Ruth Lauren '63 '93 C.276 B.S.F.S. L.145 J.D.
Schabacker, Emily W. '68 '99 C.012 B.A. L.347 J.D.
Shalhoub, Susan C. '49 '74 C&L.94 A.B., J.D.
Zimmerman, Paul M. '66 '94 C.103 B.A. L.1009 J.D.

PENSION BENEFIT GUARANTY CORPORATION

James J. Keightley, *General Counsel*

OFFICE OF THE GENERAL COUNSEL

Amadeo, Mark A. '67 '96 (WI) C.93 B.A. L.966 J.D.
Armbruster, James J. '52 '83 C.1031 B.A. L.976 J.D.

PENSION BENEFIT GUARANTY CORPORATION (Continued)

Ashner, Harold J. ... '51 '76 C.1044 B.A. L.107 J.D.
Bachman, Brenda A. ... '68 '98 (NY) C.914 B.A. L.276 J.D.
Baird, Rhonda N. ... '65 '97 (MD) C.446 B.Sc. L.280 J.D.
Batsell, Samuel C., III ... '54 '80 (IL) C.424 A.B. L.145 J.D.
Beller, James L., Jr. ... '61 '86 C.821 B.A. L.477 J.D.
Bernsen, Stuart E. ... '50 '83 C.178 B.A. L.1292 J.D.
Beyer, William G. ... '45 '76 C.1356 B.S. L.276 J.D.
Birenbaum, Susan E. ... '52 '79 C.659 B.A. L.1019 J.D.
Bisco, Deborah J. ... '59 '85 (IL) C.659 B.A. L.145 J.D.
Blank, Mark ... '52 '76 C&L.659 B.A., J.D.
Bloom, Marjorie Rosenthal ... '46 '75 C.696 B.A. L.37 J.D.
Boone, Merrill Debs ... '61 '90 (MN) C.429 B.A. L.494 J.D.
Breen, Jean Marie ... '54 '80 (NE) C&L.190 B.A., J.D.
Brickhouse, Gennice D. ... '61 '87 C.329 B.B.A. L.893 J.D.
Burns, Josephine Amato ... '47 '84 C.831 B.S. L.276 J.D.
Campbell, D. Bruce ... '62 '87 (PA) C.645 B.A. L.665 J.D.
Cohen, Jeffrey B. ... '56 '81 C.1349 B.A. L.276 J.D.
Connelly, Paula J. ... '60 '85 C.446 B.A. L.904 J.D.
Cooper, Kenneth J. ... '65 '95 (NY) C.951 B.A. L.494 J.D.
Deneen, Terrence M. ... '51 '78 (IL) C&L.339 B.A., J.D.
Desai, Apurva Drupad ... '68 '94 (MD) C.930 B.A. L.128 J.D.
Eagle, Sara B. ... '62 '88 (MD) C.289 B.A. L.446 J.D.
Endo, Kimiyo Tahira ... '40 '93 C.112 B.A. L.904 J.D.
Finke, Charles L. ... '54 '79 (NE) C&L.546 B.S., J.D.
Forster, Raymond M. ... '51 '76 C.340 B.A. L.339 J.D.
Gabriel, Thomas H. ... '51 '79 (NY) C.107 B.A. L.564 J.D.
Goldowitz, Israel ... '53 '79 C.94 B.A. L.273 J.D.
Gould, Peter H. ... '41 '79 C.103 A.B. L.893 J.D.
Graham, Richard A. ... '45 '70 C.198 A.B. L.893 J.D.
Hecht, Stanley M. ... '50 '75 C.705 B.A. L.273 J.D.
Heermans, Nancy Snyder ... '50 '78 C.577 B.A. L.575 J.D.
Hertz, Philip R. ... '50 '74 (MD) C.477 A.B. L.94 J.D.
Jaffe, Holli Beckerman ... '62 '90 (PA) C.1349 B.A. L.904 J.D.
James, Bruce H. ... '57 '87 (PA) C.273 B.A. L.276 J.D.
Keightley, James J. ... '42 '67 C.884 A.B. L.188 LL.B. Gen. Coun.
Kerns, Mia K. ... '73 '98 (MA) C.569 B.A. L.30 J.D.
Khalsa, Kartar S. ... '55 '93 (VA) C&L.823 B.A., J.D.
Klein, Bernard P. ... '46 '77 C.1036 B.A. L.930 J.D.
Klion, Catherine B. ... '53 '79 C.674 B.A. L.569 J.D.
Lambertsen, Charla Zeller ... '47 '93 (PA) C.608 B.S. L.329 J.D.
Landgraff, Lawrence F. ... '47 '72 C.676 A.B. L.724 J.D.
Landy, Ralph L. ... '57 '84 (PA) C&L.659 B.A., J.D.
Lattimer, Richard M., Jr ... '61 '90 (PA) C.608 B.A. L.831 J.D.
Lazare, Melinda Tell ... '57 '82 (PA) C.643 B.A. L.665 J.D.
McCabe, Donald F. ... '46 '94 (CT) C.051 B.A. L.976 J.D.
McCulloch, Frank H., II ... '46 '75 C.951 B.A. L.128 J.D.
Menke, John A. ... '56 '83 C.309 A.B. L.145 J.D.
Miller, Michael C. ... '52 '77 C.321 A.B. L.145 J.D.
Morris, Karen L. ... '62 '88 C.446 B.S. L.276 J.D.
Murphy, Deborah C. ... '41 '67 C&L.309 A.B., J.D.
Paliga, John R. ... '64 '89 (OH) C.980 B.S. L.608 J.D.
Parks, Lois Bruckner ... '50 '75 C.645 B.A. L.575 J.D.
Phillips, Rosemary Leeds ... '36 '86 (MD) C.188 B.A. L.276 J.D.
Pratt, Sherease R. ... '64 '94 (NY) C.188 B.S. L.861 J.D.
Rayle, Nathaniel ... '58 '87 C&L.273 B.A., J.D.
Reilly, Kathleen C. ... '68 '96 (NY) C.951 B.A. L.347 J.D.
Resnick, Jay A. ... '50 '78 C.918 B.A. L.588 J.D.
Rickett, Tracy ... '59 '89 C.546 B.A. L.276 J.D.
Rogers, Brad Quin ... '63 '90 C.420 B.A. L.178 J.D.
Roth, Peter C.L. ... '60 '90 (MA) C.339 B.A. L.818 J.D.
Rubin, Jill Bishop ... '53 '78 C.210 B.A. L.910 J.D.
Schreiber, Stephen D. ... '49 '75 C.165 B.A. L.982 J.D.
Scott-Clayton, Patricia A. ... '53 '78 (IL) C.597 B.A. L.276 J.D.
Steele, Jared Bentley Seneca ... '71 '98 (ID) C.101 B.A. L.188 J.D.
Teiger, Lawrence T. ... '57 '87 (GA) C.1349 B.A. L.982 J.D.
Vernon, Charles W., III ... '50 '78 C.674 B.A. L.30 J.D.
Weiss, Steven A. ... '51 '76 C.659 B.S. L.884 J.D.
West, Deborah ... '53 '79 C.78 B.A. L.1068 J.D.
Williams, Stephen E. ... '51 '77 C.918 B.A. L.273 J.D.
Wilson, Garth D. ... '51 '80 C.970 B.A. L.145 J.D.
Wong, Andrea M. ... '68 '94 C.881 B.A. L.94 J.D.

OFFICE OF INSPECTOR GENERAL

Stover-Springer, Deborah A. ... '55 '80 C.122 B.A. L.446 J.D.

OTHER LAWYERS IN STAFF OR EXECUTIVE POSITIONS

Beardsley, Donna G. ... '57 '92 C.790 B.A. L.276 J.D.
Bloch, James J. ... '60 '90 (PA) C.910 B.S. L.665 J.D.
Dwyer, Janet ... '64 '95 (VA) C.893 B.A. L.692 J.D.
Forbes, Deborah K. ... '51 '88 C.1209 B.S. L.273 J.D.
Foster, John ... '53 '84 (VA) C.276 B.A. L.1209 J.D.
Guritz, Russlyn Landers ... '48 '75 (WV) C.289 B.A. L.923 J.D.
Sirkin, Stuart A. ... '47 '75 C.273 B.A. L.178 J.D.

POSTAL RATE COMMISSION

Stephen L. Sharfman, *General Counsel*

OFFICE OF THE GENERAL COUNSEL

Corcoran, R. Brian ... '47 '73 C.882 B.S. L.273 J.D.
Gallagher, Patricia A. ... '50 '76 C&L.502 B.J., J.D.
Moench, Malin G. ... '47 '75 (UT) C&L.878 B.A., J.D.
Sharfman, Stephen L. ... '44 '70 C.273 A.B. L.276 J.D. Gen. Coun.
Stephens, Mark T. ... '49 '75 C.602 A.B. L.477 J.D.
Waclawski, James ... '59 '95 (MD) C.971 B.S.E.E. L.128 J.D.

OFFICES OF THE COMMISSIONERS

Metrinko, Peter P. ... '49 '74 C.276 B.S.F.S. L.273 J.D.

OFFICE OF THE CONSUMER ADVOCATE

Costich, Emmett R. ... '46 '71 (VA) C.383 A.B. L.893 LL.B.
Dreifuss, Shelley S. ... '50 '76 (MD) C&L.446 B.A., J.D.
Gerarden, Ted P. ... '48 '73 C&L.276 B.S.F.S., J.D.
Richardson, Kenneth E. ... '43 '69 C.188 B.A. L.94 LL.B.

SECURITIES AND EXCHANGE COMMISSION

Richard H. Walker, *General Counsel*

OFFICE OF THE GENERAL COUNSEL

Albert, Ross A. ... '58 '86 C.309 A.B. L.1066 J.D.
Aronson, Tracey E. ... '61 '88 C.103 A.B. L.276 J.D.
Augustini, Hope Hall ... '68 '94 (ME) C.95 L.1294 J.D.
Avery, John W. ... '48 '75 (CA) C.813 A.B. L.1066 J.D.
Bennett, Timothy Sean ... '69 '99 C.446 B.A. L.30 J.D.
Berman, Michael A. ... '45 '71 C.831 B.S. L.884 J.D.
Bredhoff, Audrey Carter ... '54 '85 C.659 B.A. L.352 J.D.
Bresnan, Peter H. ... '55 '85 (NY) C.385 A.B. L.262 J.D.
Brigagliano, James A. ... '57 '83 (NY) C.31 B.A. L.276 J.D.
Broderick, Catherine A. ... '51 '78 C.119 B.F.A. L.569 J.D.
Brown, George C. ... '53 '82 C.576 B.E.D. L.273 J.D.
Burgess, Karen Buck ... '50 '81 C.604 B.A. L.1162 J.D.
Cagnacci, Paula A. ... '74 '99 C.229 B.A. L.180 J.D.
Callcott, W. Hardy ... '61 '86 C.976 B.A. L.813 J.D.
Capute, Allan A. ... '55 '86 C.367 B.A. L.228 J.D.
Chafer, Anne E. ... '51 '76 C.976 B.A. L.276 J.D.
Citrin, Ilene Fisher ... '54 '82 C&L.477 B.A., J.D.
Cody, Kathleen ... '— '87 C.903 B.A. L.128 J.D.
Connor, Richard E. ... '52 '78 (VA) C.790 B.S. L.893 J.D.
Davis, Charles C., Jr. ... '54 '81 C.674 B.A. L.276 J.D.
Dombalagian, Onnig H. ... '70 '96 C&L.309 B.A., J.D.
Drexler, Kimberley S. ... '71 '97 C.893 B.A. L.976 J.D.
Dunbar, Andrew J. ... '73 '99 C.112 B.S. L.1117 J.D.
Finnell, Jeffrey B. ... '66 '92
Fredrickson, David R. ... '60 '87 (NY) C.1375 A.B. L.276 J.D.
Gilkerson, Christopher P. ... '64 '91 C.608 B.A. L.976 J.D.
Glickman, Andrew Z. ... '63 '92 C&L.893 B.A., J.D.
Goldstein, Miriam J. ... '60 '86 C.976 B.A. L.659 J.D.
Greene, Robert T. ... '58 '85 (GA) C.910 B.A. L.245 J.D.
Gresham, Katharine B ... '45 '82 C.104 A.B. L.276 J.D.
Hannigan, Barbara B. ... '53 '85 C.276 B.A. L.30 J.D.
Hardy, Melinda ... '65 '91 C.101 B.A. L.597 J.D.
Hirsch, Daniel O. ... '54 '83 C.156 B.A. L.309 J.D.
Humes, Richard M. ... '51 '76 (PA) C.103 B.A. L.329 J.D.
Kennedy, Kermit B. ... '59 '86 C.165 A.B. L.228 J.D.
Lal, Arvind K. ... '60 '84 C.205 B.A. L.1338 J.D.
Lee, Sonia Y. ... '72 '99 (MS) C.659 B.A./B.S. L.945 J.D.
Lenox, William ... '55 '80 C.237 B.A. L.659 J.D.
Levine, David M. ... '67 '94 (NY) C.1044 B.A. L.1019 J.D.
Levine, Richard A. ... '56 '81 (NY) C.1044 B.A. L.477 J.D.
Lutz, Hugh P., Jr. ... '63 '94 (MD) C.30 B.A. L.1209 J.D.
Mackert, Kristin S. ... '54 '90 C.107 B.S. L.275 J.D.
Magyar, Laura ... '66 '98 C.597 B.A. L.146 J.D.
Mann, Susan ... '61 '89 C.104 A.B. L.813 J.D.
McCarthy, Joan A. ... '53 '81 C.1097 B.A. L.1068 J.D.
McCormick, Christopher H. ... '59 '86 (NY) C.178 B.A. L.94 J.D.
McDonald, Susan S. ... '47 '77 C&L.273 B.A., J.D.
McNeely, Martha H. ... '46 '79 C.788 B.A. L.1162 J.D.
Meehan, Alexander Duer ... '67 '97 (NY) C.299 A.B. L.950 J.D.
Meltzer, D. Leah ... '49 '80 C.860 B.A. L.276 J.D.
Mitchell, Meridith ... '62 '87 C.604 B.A. L.178 J.D.
Monticciolo, Michael J. ... '71 '98 (NY) C.608 B.A. L.1019 J.D.
Nicholas, John J. ... '61 '86 (PA) C.309 B.A. L.569 J.D.
Olson, Marianne B. ... '70 '96 C.276 B.S.F.S. L.1209 J.D.
Parrino, Mary Jo Grote ... '60 '89 C.128 B.A. L.273 J.D.
Peterson, Robert J. ... '68 '99 C.859 B.A. L.145 J.D.
Preston, Mary M. ... '62 '90 C&L.597 B.S.J., J.D.
Pruitt, Laura S. ... '62 '88 C.309 B.A. L.178 J.D.
Purcell, Anita Tedesco ... '— '88 (MD) C&L.64 B.S., J.D.
Puryear, Jennifer Herndon ... '68 '95 (TN) C.309 A.B. L.575 J.D.
Quinn, Randall W. ... '56 '86 (VA) C.446 B.A. L.893 J.D.
Ragen, Lisa Reid ... '63 '89 (NY) C.645 B.A. L.228 J.D.
Rosen, Kenneth M. ... '70 '94 C.188 B.S.I.L.R. L.976 J.D.
Sanger, Diane ... '53 '79 C.453 S.B. L.94 J.D.
Simpson, Marva D. ... '— '93 (IL) C.238 B.S. L.352 J.D.
Smith, Leslie E. ... '43 '74 C.668 B.A. L.228 J.D.
Stern, William S. ... '32 '56 C&L.309 A.B., J.D.
Stillman, Jacob H. ... '34 '58 (TX) C.846 B.A. L.309 LL.B.
Stirling, Linda Bradley ... '56 '86 (GA) C.259 B.F.A. L.280 J.D.
Straus, Susan K. ... '42 '91 C.910 B.A. L.30 J.D.
Sullivan, Anne H. ... '48 '76 C.597 B.A. L.276 J.D.
Summergrad, Eric ... '53 '78 C.604 B.A. L.569 J.D.
Sumner, Amy A. ... '72 '97 C.174 B.A. L.846 J.D.
Turner, Alton O. ... '73 '99 C.94 B.A. L.904 J.D.
von Eckartsberg, Uta M. ... '— '97 C&L.229 B.A., J.D.
Walker, Richard H. ... '50 '76 C.855 B.A. L.831 J.D. Gen. Coun.
White, Diane Virginia ... '— '87 C.104 A.B. L.228 J.D.
Wyderko, Susan Ferris ... '58 '83 C.914 B.A. L.188 J.D.
Yashar, Susan A. ... '59 '83 C.276 B.A. L.94 J.D.

DIVISION OF CORPORATION FINANCE

Adams, Abby Lynn ... '72 '97 C.205 B.S. L.1338 J.D.
Barone, Anthony G. ... '61 '87 (PA) C.659 B.S. L.904 J.D.
Blye, Cecilia D. ... '54 '79 (KY) C.103 B.A. L.178 J.D.
Britt, John Y. ... '51 '84 C.112 A.B. L.426 J.D.
Budge, James R. ... '58 '85 C&L.101 B.A., J.D.
Calio, Joseph E. ... '67 '93 (PA) C.401 B.S. L.276 LL.M.
Carper, Cheri L. ... '72 '99 (VA) C.665 B.A. L.30 J.D.
Carter, William H. ... '39 '68 C.367 B.E.S. L.446 LL.B.
Chalk, Christina E. ... '66 '92 C.228 B.A. L.30 J.D.
Clampitt, Michael R. ... '54 '92 (MD) C.64 B.S. L.446 J.D.
Coller, Mark D. ... '63 '88 (MD) C.94 B.S. L.276 J.D.
Do, Kim Huong ... '70 '95 (WA) C.1049 B.B.A. L.911 J.D.
Dubberly, Paula ... '61 '89 C.273 B.A. L.30 J.D.
Dudek, Paul M. ... '57 '83 (NY) C.262 B.A. L.569 J.D.
Evans, C. Carnot, III ... '69 '95 (MD) C.860 B.A. L.597 J.D.

Fien-Helfman, L. Jacob . . . '50 '76 C.659 B.S. L.1162 J.D.
Fisher, Peggy A. . . . '— '87 (VA) C&L.1209 B.S., J.D.
Fraser, Mary Brooks . . . '48 '87 (WI) C&L.966 B.A., J.D.
Garnett, Karen J. . . . '64 '90 C.197 B.A. L.846 J.D.
Gottlieb, Jonathan E. . . . '54 '82 (NY) C.103 B.A. L.178 J.D.
Green, Mark W. . . . '60 '85 C.659 B.S. L.309 J.D.
Griffith, Julia E. . . . '57 '88 (NY) C.604 A.B. L.569 J.D.
Harrison, N. Sean . . . '70 '97 C.831 B.B.A. L.276 J.D.
Hurwitz, Michael H. . . . '57 '83 C.659 B.A. L.94 J.D.
Hyatte, Michael . . . '51 '79 (IL) C.145 A.B. L.1119 J.D.
Karu, Anita Elaine . . . '48 '74 C.289 B.A. L.273 J.D.
Kelly, Edward M. . . . '— '89 (PA) C.178 M.B.A. L.560 J.D.
Klein, Anita T. . . . '59 '84 (PA) C.659 B.A. L.665 J.D. Sr. Coun.
Kramer, Stacey B. . . . '69 '94 (MD) C.94 B.S.B.A. L.446 J.D.
Krauskopf, Anne Marie . . . '53 '80 C.103 B.A. L.128 J.D.
Krebs, Kathleen Haller . . . '67 '95 (CO) C.174 B.S. L.221 J.D.
Krug, John L. . . . '46 '71 C&L.893 B.A., J.D.
Kung, Felicia H. . . . '62 '89 (IL) C.502 A.B. L.309 J.D.
Leeb, David . . . '71 '97 (NY) C.112 B.A. L.30 J.D.
Levenberg, Timothy S. . . . '64 '90 C.347 B.A. L.477 J.D.
Link, David J. . . . '60 '92 C.886 B.S. L.1209 J.D.
Livingston, Jessica . . . '66 '92 (LA) C.896 B.A. L.861 J.D.
Maddrey, Nicole M. . . . '64 '92 (MD) C.659 B.A. L.446 J.D.
Mahon, John J. . . . '74 '99 C.692 B.S.B.A. L.276 J.D.
McCarty, Charles Barry . . . '57 '88 (VA) C.886 B.S. L.128 J.D.
Miller, Carolyn A. . . . '62 '96 (NY) C.1111 B.A. L.1009 J.D.
Miller, Patricia A. . . . '61 '90 (NC) C.575 B.A. L.16 J.D.
Miller, Robert Neil . . . '75 '01 C.260 B.S.B.A. L.884 J.D.
Minore, Dominic J. . . . '60 '87 (CA) C.763 B.S. L.221 J.D.
Minton, Jeffrey J. . . . '70 '96 (OH) C.608 B.A. L.309 J.D.
Morley, William E. . . . '42 '69 C.446 B.A. L.273 J.D.
Murphy, Elizabeth M. . . . '60 '85 (VA) C.893 B.S. L.602 J.D.
Oremland, Nancy K. . . . '54 '83 (CA) C.276 B.S. L.893 J.D.
Osheroff, Mauri L. . . . '49 '75 C.681 A.B. L.976 J.D.
Pascale, Joseph K. . . . '64 '91 C.1080 B.B.A. L.838 J.D.
Penn, John C. . . . '72 '97 (MD) C.446 B.A. L.309 J.D.
Plesnarski, Robert T. . . . '65 '91 (PA) C.197 B.A. L.831 J.D.
Reader, Jennifer Screen . . . '54 '83 C.387 L.808 J.D.
Reilly, Susann Reising . . . '39 '79 (OR) C.477 M.A. L.950 J.D.
Romanek, Barak M. . . . '61 '88 C.477 B.B.A. L.446 J.D.
Schiffman, Todd K. . . . '57 '82 (MI) C.475 B.A. L.912 J.D.
Sherman, Carolyn J. . . . '66 '92 C.1036 B.A. L.904 J.D.
Shuman, Mark P. . . . '52 '80 (CO) C&L.174 B.A., J.D. Spec. Coun.
Smith, Barbara C. . . . '61 '86 (CA) C.112 A.B. L.767 J.D.
Smith, Everett, Jr. . . . '55 '90 (ID) C.499 B.S. L.336 J.D.
Staffin, Elliot B. . . . '53 '86 C.273 B.A. L.966 J.D. Spec. Coun.
Summer, Barry N. . . . '57 '82 C.690 B.S. L.276 J.D.
Thorpe, Andrew D. . . . '73 '99 (IL) C.1365 B.A. L.910 J.D.
Toomey, William E. . . . '31 '56 (MA) C.602 A.B. L.976 LL.B.
Walters, Gerald S. . . . '69 '94 (CO) C.502 B.S. L.174 J.D.
Webb, Mark S. . . . '46 '85 (NY) C.691 B.A. L.976 J.D.
Webb, Max A. . . . '46 '85 (NY) C.691 B.A. L.976 J.D.
Weiss, Carol P. Newman . . . '60 '89 (PA) C.223 B.S. L.1209 J.D.
Williams, Timothy L. . . . '— '94 (TX) C.326 M.B.A. L.325 J.D.
Wulff, Richard K. . . . '47 '72 (NY) C.262 A.B. L.724 J.D.
Yarashus, Albert L. . . . '35 '63 (VA) C.717 B.S. L.884 LL.B.

EXECUTIVE STAFF

Capparella, Richard D. . . . '31 '60 C.823 B.A. L.276 LL.B.
Cutler, Stephen M. . . . '61 '85 C&L.976 B.A., J.D.
Forde, Timothy J. . . . '57 '90 C.31 B.A. L.494 J.D.
Hunt, Isaac C., Jr. . . . '— '63 C.254 B.A. L.893 LL.B.
Katz, Jonathan G. . . . '50 '75 C.165 A.B. L.665 J.D.
Kiernan, Peter S. . . . '41 '68 C.976 B.A. L.893 J.D.
Lainoff, Michael A. . . . '62 '88 C.860 B.A. L.569 J.D.
McFarland, Margaret H. . . . '48 '86 C.1209 B.A. L.893 J.D.
Tellini, Mark P. . . . '65 '92 (MA) C.95 A.B. L.93 J.D.
Wallman, Steven M.H. . . . '53 '78 C.453 S.B. L.178 J.D.

OFFICE OF ADMINISTRATIVE LAW JUDGES

Foelak, Carol P. . . . '42 '65 C.821 B.A. L.178 LL.B.
Mahony, Robert G. . . . '39 '66 C.602 A.B. L.145 J.D.
McEwen, Lillian A. . . . '44 '75 C.999 B.S.ED. L.329 J.D.
Murray, Brenda P. . . . '39 '64 C.230 B.A. L.94 J.D. Chief Admin. Law J.

DIVISION OF ENFORCEMENT

Ackerson, Sarah B. . . . '46 '76 C.679 B.A. L.345 J.D.
Anderson, Robert E. . . . '39 '64 C&L.966 B.S., J.D.
Andre, Lionel . . . '62 '87 (PA) C.823 B.S. L.276 J.D.
Anzaldúa, Theresa . . . '62 '90 (OH) C.477 B.A. L.309 J.D.
Armstrong, Kyra C. . . . '67 '92 C&L.309 B.A., J.D.
Baker, William R., III . . . '57 '83 C.602 A.B. L.276 J.D.
Balacek, Gerald T. . . . '65 '93 (CT) C.724 B.A. L.982 J.D.
Bamberger, Joanne Cronrath . . . '58 '88 C.942 B.A. L.378 J.D.
Batterman, Jon S. . . . '65 '92 C.30 B.A. L.1019 J.D.
Beaudreault, Lindi L. . . . '73 '98 (TX) C.446 B.A. L.845 J.D.
Berman, Jacqueline B. . . . '66 '92 C.705 B.A. L.904 J.D.
Besse, Robert C. . . . '52 '81 (MA) C.309 B.A. L.588 J.D.
Bettigole, Bruce M. . . . '56 '81 C.976 B.A. L.178 J.D.
Bourelly, Alex J. . . . '64 '92 C.569 B.A. L.597 J.D.
Braswell, Mark K. . . . '63 '90 (PA) C&L.838 B.A., J.D.
Bruch, Gregory S. . . . '60 '87 C.813 A.B. L.352 J.D.
Bruno, Christopher . . . '56 '84 (NY) C.1044 B.A. L.1029 J.D.
Buck, James Lee, II . . . '62 '88 C.893 B.A. L.276 J.D.
Chion, Antonia . . . '54 '81 C.860 A.B. L.276 J.D.
Chumley, Donald C. . . . '33 '58 (NY) C.659 B.S. L.569 LL.B.
Clarkson, James A. . . . '42 '69 C.674 B.A. L.569 J.D.
Coe, Michael E. . . . '63 '90 C.188 A.B. L.893 J.D.
Coffman, James T. . . . '47 '79 (OH) C.97 B.S. L.117 J.D.
Conte, Christopher R. . . . '61 '88 C.103 A.B. L.128 J.D.
Cottam, M. Catherine . . . '56 '83 (NY) C.659 B.A. L.1066 J.D.
Cox, L. DeLane . . . '63 '87 C.838 B.A. L.260 J.D.
Cranford, Todd L. . . . '63 '89 (NY) C.197 A.B. L.178 J.D.
Currier, G. William . . . '47 '80 C.918 B.A. L.1162 J.D.
Dix, James G. . . . '62 '86 (IL) C.145 B.A. L.893 J.D.
Doherty, Laurie A. . . . '59 '90 (MD) C.950 B.A. L.273 J.D.
Dorsey, Sarah Buchanan . . . '67 '94 C.103 A.B. L.813 J.D.
Dowling, Stacy Ann . . . '70 '97 C.95 A.B. L.776 J.D.
Dupuy, Juliet M. . . . '— '96 (WI) C.967 B.A. L.436 J.D.
Eidt-hyat, Adrienne V. . . . '64 '90 (CT) C.423 B.A. L.1009 J.D.
Faragasso, Gregory G. . . . '63 '89 C.945 B.A. L.1009 J.D.
Fields, Brent J. . . . '63 '93 C.886 B.S. L.280 J.D.
Finston, Nina B. . . . '62 '89 C.914 B.A. L.145 J.D.
Flood, Allen Atlee, Jr. . . . '70 '96 C.893 B.A. L.309 J.D.
Flynn, Rory C. . . . '56 '82 C.1138 B.B.A. L.978 J.D.
Foster, L. Hilton . . . '45 '73 C.31 B.S. L.329 J.D.
Friestad, Scott W. . . . '62 '86 (AZ) C&L.352 B.B.A., J.D.
Frye, David S. . . . '56 '83 C.640 B.A. L.502 J.D.
Fuchs, Michael S. . . . '58 '90 C.569 B.A. L.945 J.D.
Geldzahler, Evan . . . '62 '88 C.846 B.B.A. L.245 J.D.
Gentry, Glenn S. . . . '59 '84 (NC) C&L.575 B.A., J.D.
Gerlach, Paul V. . . . '54 '82 C.1193 B.A. L.902 J.D.
Gilheany, Carolyn-Gail . . . '64 '90 (NJ) C.823 B.A. L.564 J.D.
Gionfriddo, David P. . . . '61 '86 (MA) C&L.93 B.A., J.D.
Gittens, Noel A. . . . '53 '90 (MA) C.999 B.S. L.329 J.D.
Gizzi, Paul G. . . . '62 '92 (NY) C.705 B.A. L.776 J.D.
Goodhand, David B. . . . '62 '91 C.604 B.A. L.569 J.D.
Gordy, Emily P. . . . '58 '85 C.282 B.A. L.30 J.D.
Grant, Shelley Renée . . . '49 '80 C.472 B.A. L.273 J.D.
Gray, Elizabeth Pickar . . . '59 '83 C.197 A.B. L.893 J.D.
Gross, Phil . . . '33 '59 (IA) C.30 M.B.A. L.352 LL.B.
Gulack, Robert . . . '53 '92 (MD) C.1019 B.A. L.976 J.D.
Gumagay, Paul A. . . . '68 '00 C.273 B.B.A. L.552 J.D.
Hall, Kenneth H. . . . '47 '81 C.446 B.A. L.976 J.D.
Hansen, Eric M. . . . '62 '87 (PA) C.477 B.A. L.912 J.D.
Hathaway, William M. . . . '55 '87 C&L.347 B.A., J.D.
Heilizer, Deborah Gail . . . '58 '85 (IL) C.145 B.A. L.597 J.D.
Hunter, John L. . . . '45 '72 (MN) C.602 B.A. L.494 J.D.
Hyat, Adrienne . . . '64 '91 (CT) C.423 B.A. L.1009 J.D.
Ignall, David J. . . . '65 '91 C.188 B.A. L.945 J.D.
Jimenez, Pamela M. . . . '64 '90 C.309 A.B. L.597 J.D.
Josephs, Laura B. . . . '59 '87 C.477 A.B. L.228 J.D.
Joyce, Patrick M. . . . '57 '83 C&L.602 A.B., J.D.
Kaplan, Robert B. . . . '— '92 (MA) C.178 A.B. L.569 J.D.
Kashtan, Paula L. . . . '62 '90 C&L.107 B.A., J.D.
Katz, Barbara J. . . . '42 '86 C.145 B.A. L.1068 J.D.
Keyes, Robert J. . . . '52 '86 C.743 B.A. L.276 J.D.
Kinsey, Walton S., Jr. . . . '50 '88 C&L.259 B.S., J.D.
Klein, Josh . . . '68 '94 (NY) C.477 A.B. L.309 J.D.
Knapton, Donna K. . . . '— '97 C.260 B.S. L.472 J.D.
Korotash, Stephen J. . . . '51 '78 (OK) C.694 B.A. L.276 J.D.
Kreitman, Mark . . . '50 '75 C.976 B.A. L.309 J.D.
Kuehnle, William H. . . . '42 '68 C.976 B.A. L.659 LL.B.
Kurr, Carolyn E. . . . '69 '95 (MD) C.197 B.A. L.893 J.D. Sr. Coun.
Lawrence, Gregory Todd . . . '71 '98 (MD) C.920 B.S. L.1002 J.D.
Lebeaux, Susan L. . . . '51 '77 C.477 B.A. L.94 J.D.
Lee, Jason P. . . . '— '99 (CA) C.112 B.A. L.770 J.D.
Lee, Lani M. . . . '57 '83 C.1090 B.A. L.128 J.D.
Lench, Kenneth R. . . . '62 '87 C.1036 B.A. L.94 J.D.
Levine, Deborah . . . '62 '91 C.188 A.B. L.273 J.D.
Linkins, Tracy R. . . . '70 '96 C.446 B.S. L.329 J.D.
Mann, James G. . . . '43 '72 (VA) C.893 B.S. L.30 J.D.
Markle, John S. . . . '66 '92 C.1044 B.A. L.276 J.D.
McCormick, Kelly A. . . . '71 '98 (MD) C.119 B.S. L.904 J.D.
McCready, Susan E. . . . '62 '92 C.112 B.S. L.1066 J.D.
McKown, Joan E. . . . '57 '83 (IA) C.880 B.A. L.221 J.D.
Mesholam, Deborah R. . . . '56 '81 (NY) C.893 B.A. L.178 J.D.
Meyer, Elizabeth F. . . . '54 '81 C.264 B.A. L.94 J.D.
Miller, Kenneth L. . . . '61 '87 C.188 A.B. L.982 J.D.
Mitchell, Traynham E., Jr. . . . '64 '90 C.976 B.A. L.861 J.D.
Moore, Michael P. . . . '65 '91 (CA) C.705 B.A. L.893 J.D.
Nahrwold, Stacey M. . . . '— '99 C.597 B.A. L.228 J.D.
Nathan, Daniel A. . . . '57 '84 (NY) C.453 B.S. L.569 J.D.
Newkirk, Thomas C. . . . '42 '66 C&L.188 B.A., LL.B.
Ochs, Brian A. . . . '56 '83 C.188 B.A. L.309 J.D.
O'Donnell, Keith A. . . . '48 '75 C.385 B.A. L.128 J.D.
O'Rourke, Kevin P. . . . '52 '78 C.426 B.A. L.846 J.D.
Parrish, Cynthia M. . . . '— '90 (PA) C.831 B.B.A. L.1206 J.D.
Perkins, Carlisle E. . . . '59 '87 C.678 B.A. L.893 J.D.
Peterson, Jill M. . . . '60 '86 C.893 B.S. L.945 J.D.
Podell, Bari S. . . . '59 '85 (MD) C.401 B.A. L.904 J.D.
Porter, Mark W. . . . '59 '86 C.95 A.B. L.178 J.D.
Quigley, Joan E. . . . '64 '92 C.674 A.B. L.945 J.D.
Robertson, Melissa A. . . . '58 '84 C.938 B.A. L.276 J.D.
Roffman, Ian D. . . . '72 '97 C&L.145 B.A., J.D.
Rosenfeld, Richard M. . . . '69 '95 (MD) C.705 B.A. L.188 J.D.
Ross, Ellen B. . . . '56 '82 C.1042 B.A. L.426 J.D.
Ross, Yolanda L. . . . '60 '85 C.846 B.B.A. L.813 J.D.
Rubenstein, Daniel H. . . . '59 '86 C&L.309 A.B., J.D.
Rusch, Alfred E. T. . . . '37 '67 C.705 A.B. L.262 LL.B.
Ryan, Russell G. . . . '60 '86 C.93 A.B. L.724 J.D.
Sauer, Richard C. . . . '51 '82 (CA) C.112 B.A. L.426 J.D.
Scheck, Howard A. . . . '63 '92 C.94 B.S.B.A. L.30 J.D.
Schwartz, Helaine . . . '57 '84 (NY) C.1044 B.A. L.564 J.D.
Shea, Catherine M. . . . '58 '83 C.93 B.A. L.188 J.D.
Silverstein, Thomas D. . . . '53 '78 C.385 B.A. L.276 J.D.
Simpson, Richard E. . . . '57 '83 (NY) C.910 B.A. L.597 J.D.
Smallman, Thomas E. . . . '66 '94 (NJ) C.276 B.S.B.A. L.884 J.D.
Snowdon, Andrew L. . . . '68 '93 C.228 B.A. L.893 J.D.
Sosne, Elinor D. . . . '46 '82 (VA) C.66 B.A. L.945 J.D.
Sporkin, Andrew B. . . . '63 '88 C.264 B.A. L.273 J.D.
Stark, John R. . . . '64 '89 C.867 B.S. L.228 J.D.
Starr, Judith R. . . . '57 '85 C.945 B.A. L.309 J.D.
Stevenson, Michael J. . . . '57 '85 C.475 B.A. L.912 J.D.
Sullivan, William P. . . . '30 '61 (MA) C.602 A.B. L.94 LL.B.
Sulzberg, Ann H. . . . '60 '85 C.145 A.B. L.477 J.D.
Sundick, Gary N. . . . '43 '67 C.667 B.S.E.E. L.477 LL.B.
Thompson, Patricia J. . . . '62 '87 C.674 A.B. L.477 J.D.
Tibbetts, Carl A. . . . '52 '78 C.597 B.A. L.659 J.D.

SECURITIES AND EXCHANGE COMMISSION (Continued)

Veal, Daryl R. '54 '87 (NY) C.103 A.B. L.724 J.D.
Walsh, Geraldine M. '63 '90 C.31 B.A. L.569 J.D.
Wang, Leonard W. '53 '78 (WI) C&L.966 B.A., J.D.
Weimer, Marilyn H. '64 '96 (MD) C.64 B.S. L.273 J.D.
Weiss, Jeffrey P. '63 '88 (MD) C.1036 B.A. L.446 J.D.
Wells, Rose R. '47 '95 C.629 B.S. L.1209 J.D.
Welter, Craig '72 '97 (MD) C.228 B.A. L.945 J.D.
West, Lawrence A. '51 '91 C.309 A.B. L.976 J.D.
Whitcomb, David C., Jr. '62 '89 C.156 B.A. L.284 J.D.
Williams, Cheryl J. '64 '90 C.16 B.A. L.228 J.D.
Wilson, Robert G. '58 '90 (MI) C.20 B.A. L.477 J.D.
Zamore, Sharon '63 '89 C.188 B.S. L.309 J.D.
Zelinsky, Yuri B. '55 '80 (IL) C.367 B.A. L.146 J.D.

DIVISION OF INVESTMENT MANAGEMENT

Alper, Ronald E. '57 '83 C.659 B.S. L.64 J.D.
Bailes, Zandra Y. '60 '88 (MD) C.329 B.A. L.976 J.D.
Baker, Martha Cathey '42 '81 C.846 B.A. L.178 J.D.
Barker, Marilyn D. '61 '89 (CA) C.976 B.A. L.178 J.D.
Boggs, Elaine M. '53 '91 (OH) C.97 B.S. L.930 J.D.
Brandenburg, John P. '44 '69 (OH) C.1024 B.A. L.150 J.D.
Browning, Kimberly A. '61 '89 C.914 B.A. L.276 J.D.
Buescher, Sarah A. '67 '95 (PA) C.597 B.S. L.602 J.D.
Bullard, Mercer E. '61 '91 C.976 B.A. L.893 J.D.
Cayne, Jana M. '62 '87 C.188 B.S. L.94 J.D.
Chiu, Lily R. '54 '82 (WA) C.914 B.A. L.276 J.D.
Chretien-Dar, Barbara C. '56 '88 C.446 B.A. L.623 J.D.
Cimmet, Sidney L. '33 '63 (NY) C.309 A.B. L.569 LL.B.
Cole, Mary A. '42 '75 C&L.184 B.A., J.D.
Curtis, James M. '54 '87 (NY) C.299 B.A. L.569 J.D.
Davis, Emerson S. '51 '78 C.205 B.A. L.161 J.D.
Evans, Donald L. '48 '88 C.383 B.A. L.1137 J.D.
Fisher, Catherine A. '46 '77 C.441 B.A. L.213 J.D.
Frech, Mary Kay Greif '50 '81 C.679 B.A. L.326 J.D.
Friedlander, Wendy Finck '49 '76 C.30 B.A. L.128 J.D.
Fuller, Alison M. '63 '92 C.951 B.A. L.276 J.D.
Ganley, John M. '59 '88 (VA) C.696 B.S.ChE. L.273 J.D.
Geffroy, Mary T. '65 '90 C.610 B.S. L.128 J.D.
Greenlees, Christine Y. '61 '87 (MA) C.860 B.A. L.94 J.D.
Grim, David W. '70 '95 C.228 B.A. L.273 J.D.
Gross, Robin S. '65 '90 C.260 B.A. L.273 J.D.
Grossnickle, Janet M. '68 '97 C.645 B.S. L.93 J.D.
Grzeskiewicz, John C. '48 '76 C.855 B.A. L.184 J.D.
Hallock, Houghton R., Jr. '42 '68 (NY) C.674 A.B. L.309 J.D.
Heussler, Barbara Turney '61 '86 (PA) C.478 B.A. L.608 J.D.
Hong, Peter M. '67 '93 (MD) C.216 B.A. L.904 J.D.
Jacobs, Anna '67 '98 (CA) C.659 B.A. L.1065 J.D.
Jones, C. Hunter '62 '87 C.674 A.B. L.178 J.D.
Kane, Timothy R. '59 '88 (IL) C.602 B.S. L.424 J.D.
Kerwin, Thomas M. J. '55 '81 (CO) C.170 B.A. L.276 J.D.
Knisely, Kathleen L. '70 '96 (PA) C.282 B.A. L.128 J.D.
Krudys, Suzanne '63 '92 (CT) C.69 B.B.A. L.1029 J.D.
LaRoche, David G. '58 '85 C.446 B.A. L.128 J.D.
Mann, Marilyn K. '55 '88 C&L.477 B.A., J.D.
McDonald, Joseph B., Jr. '58 '84 (NY) C.1044 B.A. L.30 J.D.
Mendelson, Barry A. '58 '82 C.881 A.B. L.273 J.D.
Miller, Barry D. '53 '87 C.896 B.S. L.273 J.D.
Nash, Susan '54 '82 C.602 B.A. L.309 J.D.
O'Connell, Keith A. '60 '86 C.692 B.S. L.276 J.D.
Osterman, Elizabeth G. '55 '86 (MD) C.821 B.A. L.64 J.D.
Pai, Deepak T. '66 '93 (PA) C.112 B.A. L.813 J.D.
Pfordte, Richard '55 '80 (AZ) C&L.36 B.S., J.D.
Pickholz, Joyce Merrick '43 '66 C&L.569 B.S., LL.B.
Pisto, Lawrence W. '63 '89 C.67 B.A. L.477 J.D.
Plaze, Robert E. '56 '83 C&L.276 A.B., J.D.
Plesset, Rochelle K. '60 '85 C.659 B.A. L.880 J.D.
Pollack-Matz, Fran M. '61 '86 (MD) C&L.273 B.B.A., J.D.
Pugh, Cynthia Gurnee '66 '91 C.945 A.B. L.659 J.D.
Rappa, Nancy M. '50 '87 C.1142 B.A. L.128 J.D.
Romain, Rene Y. '60 '91 C.118 B.A. L.329 J.D.
Roytblat, Nadya B. '65 '90 C.674 B.A. L.276 J.D.
Rubenstein, Edward J. '55 '84 C.674 B.A. L.178 J.D.
Sanders, Ruth Armfield '55 '88 C.790 B.S. L.128 J.D.
Scheidt, Douglas J. '53 '78 C.597 B.A. L.221 J.D.
Schneider, Linda A. '51 '78 (VA) C.856 B.A. L.276 J.D.
Stam, Heidi '56 '81 C.860 B.A. L.30 J.D.
Thompson, Brian R. '51 '76 C.229 B.A. L.1292 J.D.

DIVISION OF MARKET REGULATION

Andrews, Paul P. '61 '86 C.884 A.B. L.128 J.D.
Baysinger, Brian R. '59 '89 C.494 B.A. L.477 J.D.
Berberi, Victoria '60 '86 (PA) C.112 B.A. L.423 J.D.
Bergmann, Larry E. '49 '75 C.453 S.B. L.93 J.D.
Blaine, Belinda A. '61 '88 C.668 B.A. L.1068 J.D.
Brooks, Herbert F., Jr. '48 '77 C.446 B.S. L.1209 J.D.
Bucci, Lori Rae '64 '90 (MA) C.787 B.A. L.94 J.D.
Carpenter, Jerry W. '59 '85 (IL) C.838 B.A. L.836 J.D.
Chidsey, Marla O. '73 '99 (CA) C.769 B.A. L.1117 J.D.
Childs, Allyson '68 '95 (TX) C.367 B.A. L.846 J.D.
Colby, Robert '55 '81 C.95 B.A. L.309 J.D.
Corkran, M. Blair, Jr. '42 '68 C.674 A.B. L.893 LL.B.
Darroch, Elaine M. '— '94 (VA) C.575 B.A. L.30 J.D.
England, Katherine A. '57 '81 C.446 B.A. L.128 J.D.
Etter, Thomas C., Jr. '38 '76 C.659 B.A. L.1338 J.D.
Ferrara, Barbara N. '46 '76 C.823 B.S. L.1162 J.D.
Flynn, Deborah Lassman '64 '94 (MD) C&L.273 B.B.A., J.D.
Fraticelli, Yvonne '62 '88 (PA) C.25 B.A. L.569 J.D.
Fuller, Gordon K. '53 '81 (VA) C&L.893 B.A., J.D.
Geraghty, Peter R. '65 '90 (PA) C.884 B.S.B.A. L.1338 J.D.
Geyer, Kristen N. '64 '91 C.846 B.J. L.276 J.D.
Gonzalez-Diez, Lourdes '66 '91 C.276 B.S.F.S. L.273 J.D.
Hagen, Lillian S. '63 '90 C.354 B.S. L.276 J.D.
Harvey, Alton Stephen '54 '84 C.276 B.A. L.273 J.D.
Ito, Marie D'Aguanno '55 '86 C.446 B.A. L.904 J.D.
Jenson, Paula R. '54 '89 C.429 B.A. L.362 J.D.
Jessee, Glenn J. '57 '88 C.1209 B.A. L.893 J.D.
Khawly, Marianne H. '69 '94 (PA) C&L.276 A.B., J.D.
Kiggins, Constance B. '65 '91 C.188 A.B. L.477 J.D.
King, Elizabeth K. '66 '91 C.228 A.B. L.659 J.D.
Kroeper, Jon Eric '65 '93 (NJ) C.276 B.A. L.146 J.D.
Lawson, Sharon Dubin '57 '83 (NY) C.30 B.A. L.1019 J.D.
Long, Robert B. '73 '98 (AZ) C.36 B.S. L.128 J.D.
Lopez, Ivette '56 '85 (MD) C.976 B.A. L.569 J.D.
Love, Robert A. '54 '79 (PA) C.1036 A.B. L.831 J.D.
Macchiaroli, Michael A. '39 '65 (PA) C.728 B.S. L.884 J.D.
MacGregor, Elizabeth H. '63 '88 C.323 B.A. L.273 J.D.
McGowan, Thomas K. '60 '87 C.886 B.S. L.893 J.D.
McGuire, Catherine '48 '73 (KS) C.447 B.A. L.378 J.D.
Milone, Michael L. '72 '98 C.105 B.A. L.128 J.D.
Mitnick, Janice S. '64 '91 C.245 B.A. L.273 J.D.
Morris, Matthew S. '69 '94 (PA) C.1036 B.A. L.30 J.D.
Pawelski, Victoria M. '67 '95 C.012 B.Com. L.30 J.D.
Pilpel, Heidi E. '65 '91 C.705 B.A. L.569 J.D.
Pullano, Richard E. '58 '87 C.1044 B.A. L.128 J.D.
Randazzo, Louis A. '64 '90 (OH) C.712 B.B.A. L.851 J.D.
Robb-Blake, Margaret J. '65 '93 C.886 B.A. L.128 J.D.
Russell-Hunter, Janet W. '65 '91 C.914 B.A. L.30 J.D.
Sanow, Nancy J. '48 '81 C.30 B.A. L.276 J.D.
Shillman, David S. '60 '88 C.597 B.A. L.477 J.D.
Sibille, Christine M. '64 '90 C.808 B.A. L.659 J.D.
Slevin, Sheila '61 '87 (TX) C&L.846 B.A., J.D.
Smith, Margaret A. '60 '89 C.197 A.B. L.966 J.D.
Strasser, Richard C. '63 '89 C.339 B.A. L.893 J.D.
Varner, Karl J. '55 '94 (LA) C.155 B.S. L.425 J.D.
Villasana, George V. '67 '93 (FL) C.645 B.S. L.30 J.D.
Walinskas, Michael A. '64 '89 (MD) C.446 B.A. L.276 J.D.
Youhn, Stephen M. '62 '91 (FL) C.1111 B.S. L.362 J.D.

OFFICE OF INTERNATIONAL AFFAIRS

Carpenter, Keith E. '56 '84 C.178 B.A. L.893 J.D.
Corcoran, Andrea M. '— '67 C.813 A.B. L.309 LL.B.
Fillinger, Charles T. '52 '82 (OK) C.1376 B.A. L.615 J.D.
Friedman, Felice B. '57 '84 C.309 A.B. L.276 J.D.
Jacobs, Elizabeth '60 '84 (GA) C.1365 B.A. L.273 J.D.
Kimel, Martin '60 '87 C.659 B.A. L.813 J.D.
Lago, Maria Louise (Marisa) '55 '83 (MA) C.186 B.S. L.309 J.D.
Lavdas, George '58 '84 C&L.477 A.B., J.D.
Nguyen, Suzy Anh '66 '93 (MA) C.914 B.A. L.188 J.D.
Saverson, Ester, Jr. '54 '80 C.339 A.B. L.910 J.D.
Stettner, Barbara Ann '62 '95 C.112 B.A. L.990 J.D.
Strahota, Robert D. '40 '69 C.188 B.A. L.127 J.D.
Swindler, Jo Anne '52 '85 C.930 B.S. L.276 J.D.

OFFICE OF COMPLIANCE INSPECTIONS AND EXAMINATIONS

Alworth, Lance Dwight, Jr. '61 '87 C.309 A.B. L.45 J.D.
Caine, Margaret Moore '61 '89 (SC) C.276 B.S. L.790 J.D.
Chan, James A. Wung-Dart '55 '86 C.94 B.A. L.30 J.D.
Cornelius, Allen R., III '52 '82 C.838 B.S. L.836 J.D.
DeTore, Stephen M. '51 '80 (MA) C.588 B.A. L.818 J.D.
Di Marco, Felicia M. '70 '97 C.299 B.A. L.982 J.D.
Draddy, James J., Jr. '59 '93 (NY) C.188 B.A. L.564 J.D.
Gabilondo, Jose M. '62 '91 (CA) C.309 B.A. L.1066 J.D.
Gadziala, Mary Ann '52 '79 (NY) C.1044 B.A. L.982 J.D.
Garcia, Janis L. '59 '87 (MS) C.36 B.S. L.259 J.D.
Gelinas, Andre A. '74 '01 C.93 B.A. L.818 J.D.
Hannibal, Richard A. '57 '82 C.937 B.A. L.276 J.D.
Hansbrough, Nancy L. '54 '86 C.930 B.S. L.1003 J.D.
Javeri, Vaishali R. '72 '97 (IL) C.597 B.A. L.352 J.D.
Johnson, George G. '57 '86 (CA) C.1109 B.A. L.990 J.D.
Jung, Stephen M. '62 '89 C.103 A.B. L.477 J.D.
Kane, Jill C. '70 '96 (PA) C.823 B.S. L.128 J.D.
Kay, Thomas G. '71 '00 C.705 B.S. L.776 J.D.
Lee, Susan L. '63 '88 (VA) C.1044 B.A. L.273 J.D.
Lever, Kristen T. '66 '98 (FL) C&L.472 B.B.A., J.D.
McCarthy, John A. '64 '91 C.477 A.B./B.S. L.446 J.D.
McGee, Helene K. '64 '89 C.914 B.A. L.273 J.D.
Meehan, A. Duer '67 '97 (NY) C.299 B.A. L.950 J.D.
Minarick, Jean E. '63 '87 C.30 B.A. L.893 J.D.
Moore, Helen J. '59 '91 (CA) L.284 J.D.
Richards, Lori A. '60 '86 (MD) C.589 B.A. L.30 J.D. Dir.
Sheehan, Megan L. '72 '99 C.170 B.A. L.904 J.D.
Swanson, Eric J. '67 '93 (MN) C.494 B.A. L.300 J.D.
Walsh, John H. '52 '85 C.463 B.A. L.276 J.D.
Walters, Susan J. '46 '79 (CT) C&L.184 B.A., J.D.
Wilhelmy, Lisa George '61 '87 (FL) C.260 B.A. L.192 J.D.

OFFICE OF MUNICIPAL SECURITIES

Buford, Charlotte L. '67 '93 (OH) C.1203 B.A. L.930 J.D.
Young, Curtis A. '57 '87 (NJ) C.329 B.A. L.705 J.D.
Zehner, Mark R. '59 '84 (PA) C.197 A.B. L.659 J.D.

OFFICE OF THE CHIEF ACCOUNTANT

Burns, Robert E. '50 '76 (OH) C.980 B.S. L.7 J.D.

OFFICE OF FILINGS AND INFORMATION SERVICES

Stovell, L. Bryce '55 '80 (OH) C.674 B.A. L.145 J.D.

OFFICE OF EQUAL EMPLOYMENT OPPORTUNITY

Berman, Susan L. '44 '91 C.1086 B.A. L.273 J.D.
Burnett, Nancy P. '54 '93 C.838 B.S. L.1162 J.D.
Carr, Rebecca Ann '66 '91 C&L.228 B.A., J.D.
Morales, Robert '37 '62 C&L.677 B.A., J.D.
Smith, Karen MacRae '51 '78 C.860 B.A. L.276 J.D.
Tynes, Victor H., Jr. '50 '84 C&L.329 B.A., J.D.

OFFICE OF FREEDOM OF INFORMATION AND PRIVACY ACT OPERATIONS

Anderson, Leslie Michael '50 '87 (PA) C.999 B.A. L.329 J.D.
Tsai, Elizabeth T. '40 '73 C&L.662 B.S.J., LL.B.

OFFICE OF THE INSPECTOR GENERAL

Jensvold, Jon D. ... '43 '69 C&L.494 B.A., J.D.
Sullivan, Mary Beth ... '59 '86 C.321 B.A. L.893 J.D.

OFFICE OF INVESTOR EDUCATION AND ASSISTANCE

Lapins, Aldis ... '43 '72 C&L.477 A.B., J.D.
Macedo, Augusto D. ... '62 '90 (TX) C.1220 B.S. L.325 J.D.
Niedermeier, Christine M. ... '51 '77 C&L.276 B.A., J.D.

Adler, Mark A. ... '56 '82 (NY) C.860 B.S.E. L.309 J.D.
Albrecht, Patricia Maria ... '66 '91 (TX) C.1096 B.A. L.846 J.D.
Andrews, Kelly J. ... '63 '91 (CT) C.999 B.S. L.30 J.D.
Cohen, Mandy S. ... '60 '91 C.1044 B.A. L.1019 J.D.
Grissom, Valerie S. ... '68 '94 (IL) C.339 B.S. L.276 J.D.
Gross, Kevin M. ... '63 '88 C.813 B.A. L.1068 J.D.
Henderson, Lisa K. ... '58 '85 C.188 B.A. L.30 J.D.
Horn, Kevin J. ... '68 '96 (NY) C.659 B.S.E. L.228 J.D.
Huffman, William H., III ... '69 '94 (AL) C&L.16 B.S., J.D.
Priddle, Steven J. ... '56 '99 (AK) C.999 B.A. L.285 J.D.
Quigley, Elizabeth K. ... '69 '95 C.802 B.B.A. L.228 J.D.
Sutton, Gary W. ... '44 '72 (NY) C.494 A.B. L.309 J.D.
Werner, Eric Raymond ... '70 '96 C.605 A.B. L.910 J.D.
Wiggins, Charles H. ... '67 '95 C.352 B.A. L.477 J.D.

SELECTIVE SERVICE SYSTEM

Henry N. Williams, *General Counsel*

OFFICE OF THE GENERAL COUNSEL

Williams, Henry N. ... '17 '53 C.145 Ph.D. L.880 J.D. Gen. Coun.

SMALL BUSINESS ADMINISTRATION

(Vacant), *General Counsel*

OFFICE OF THE GENERAL COUNSEL

Benderson, Eric S. ... '42 '68 C.823 B.A. L.273 J.D.
Benjamin, Denise M. ... '62 '89 C.012 B.A. L.329 J.D.
Campilongo, Michael ... '46 '73 C.276 B.S. L.902 J.D.
Charette, Deborah S. ... '55 '87 (VA) C.629 B.A. L.128 J.D.
Conrey, Martin E. ... '59 '84 C.1283 B.A. L.900 J.D.
Cooper, Howard S. ... '32 '58 C.705 A.B. L.309 LL.B.
Dodds, Kenneth W. ... '69 '94 C.1369 B.S. L.945 J.D.
Embrey, Arlene M. ... '68 '97 (FL) C.1222 B.A. L.273 J.D.
Fishman, David A. ... '63 '89 C.21 B.A. L.904 J.D.
Forrest, Leslie B. ... '45 '74 C.659 B.A. L.276 J.D.
Fox, Gary ... '51 '77 (NY) C.103 A.B. L.309 J.D.
Gangwere, Robert L. ... '52 '81 (MO) C.502 B.A. L.986 J.D.
Gery, William L. ... '55 '87 (PA) C.831 B.A. L.884 J.D.
Gunn, Deborah Katherine ... '56 '86 C.793 B.A. L.276 J.D.
Harber, Kevin R. ... '68 '98 (VA) C.134 B.S. L.893 J.D.
Harris, Glenn P. ... '60 '88 C.183 B.A. L.273 J.D.
Hazlewood, Beverley E. ... '60 '97 (CA) C.1040 B.B.A. L.1370 J.D.
Hou, Hsin-Pin Ashley ... '71 '98 (MD) C.367 B.A. L.64 J.D.
Kempler, Harry D. ... '34 '59 C&L.569 B.A., LL.B.
Kish, Imelda A. ... '57 '82 C.623 B.A. L.30 J.D.
Klein, John W. ... '58 '84 (NY) C.1044 B.A. L.1019 J.D.
Levine, Nina D. ... '54 '87 (NY) C&L.178 B.A., J.D.
Liebross, Audrey H. ... '54 '81 C.446 B.S. L.273 J.D.
Mann Eyester, Laura J. ... '69 '94 C.446 B.A. L.64 J.D.
McManus Pade, Eugenie Marie ... '68 '97 (NY) C.1044 B.A. L.1218 J.D.
Messinger, Arlene Paula ... '61 '86 (NY) C.1019 B.A. L.29 J.D.
Miranda, Veronica I. ... '71 '96 C.30 B.A. L.904 J.D.
Nunn, Robinson S. ... '44 '73 (AR) C.475 B.A. L.904 J.D.
Rigby, Thomas W. ... '66 '92 (VA) C.893 B.A. L.420 J.D.
Silbermann, John G. ... '65 '96 (MA) C.588 B.S. L.128 J.D.
Simmons, Michael A. ... '62 '88 (NY) C.31 B.A. L.309 J.D.
Spellman, Mark A. ... '59 '89 (MA) C.309 B.A. L.978 J.D.
Stiner, Joel A. ... '56 '86 (TX) C.36 B.S. L.802 J.D.
Sundberg, Susan L. ... '53 '86 C.546 B.S. L.1162 J.D.
Swift, Yolanda V. ... '55 '82 (OH) C.363 B.A. L.569 J.D. Asst. Gen. Coun.
Tigar, Andrea R. ... '54 '88 (NY) C.788 A.B. L.893 J.D.
Todorov, Lynn S. ... '65 '92 (CA) C.691 B.A. L.1049 J.D.
Urban, Tara C. ... '64 '98 (PA) C.1155 B.S. L.831 J.D.
Williams-Gaffney, Diane ... '47 '87 C.1378 B.S. L.329 J.D.
Wolff, Cheri C. ... '60 '85 (MD) C.112 B.A. L.276 J.D.
Wright, Diane K. ... '67 '93 C.93 B.S. L.273 J.D.

OFFICE OF HEARINGS AND APPEALS

Wolter, Michael J. ... '54 '96 C.1164 B.A. L.1017 J.D.

Arkow, Richard S. ... '41 '66 C.273 B.A. L.1009 J.D. Admin. Law J.
Cole, Michael S. ... '38 '72 C.627 B.G.S. L.209 J.D. Adm. J.
Corey, George S. ... '63 '91 (MD) C.986 B.A. L.861 J.D.
DiGiandomenico, Linda M. ... '— '95 (MA) C.687 A.B. L.904 J.D.
Fong, Phyllis K. ... '53 '78 C.668 B.A. L.880 J.D. Inspector General
Gray, David R. ... '49 '75 (GA) C.790 B.S. L.1000 J.D. Coun. to the Inspector Gen.
Haitsuka, Jon M. ... '49 '76 C.312 B.B.A. L.1209 J.D.
Holleman, Christopher ... '51 '77 (MA) C.95 A.B. L.880 J.D.
Leopold, Laurence Scott ... '68 '96 (MD) C.326 B.S. L.862 J.D.
Shalloway, Stuart M. ... '60 '87 C.790 B.S. L.30 J.D.
Singer, Barney ... '61 '86 C.188 B.S. L.930 J.D.
Snook, Sheldon L. ... '57 '84 C.1311 B.A. L.502 J.D.
Steininger, Michael G. ... '60 '90 (MD) C.928 B.A. L.64 J.D.
Usher, Benjamin G. ... '29 '53 C&L.64 J.D. Adm. J.
Whalen, Michele M. ... '52 '88 (PA) C.654 B.A. L.128 J.D.

SOCIAL SECURITY ADMINISTRATION

Alexander, Lois A. ... '— '71 C.477 A.B. L.276 J.D.
Avots, Ivar E. ... '51 '76 (KY) C&L.383 B.A., J.D.
Benice, J. Lee ... '30 '53 C&L.107 LL.B.
Bennett, Thomas E. ... '20 '48 C.612 B.A. L.309 J.D. Adm. Law J.
Berkley, Burton ... '34 '58 (IL) C&L.309 A.B., J.D.
Bice, Debra L. ... '53 '80 (CA) C.848 B.A. L.809 J.D.
Brahm, Hildee J. ... '53 '99 L.139 J.D.
Brooks, J. Andrew ... '27 '55 (WA) C.763 B.A. L.911 LL.B.
Browning, Philip M., Jr. ... '30 '60 C.692 B.S. L.477 J.D.
Cahn, Arthur S. ... '38 '65 (MA) C.309 A.B. L.94 LL.B.
Carpenter, George L. ... '19 '51 (OH) C.339 L.851 J.D.
Carter, Thomasine B. ... '52 '85 (PA) C.999 B.A. L.446 J.D.
Ciaramello, Richard M., Jr. ... '— '99 C.690 B.A. L.1338 J.D. Atty. Advsr.
Cohen, Frederick C. ... '35 '60 (MA) C.156 A.B. L.94 J.D.
Corcoran, John R. ... '30 '57 C&L.276 A.B., J.D.
Crawford, Pamela Denise ... '57 '89 (MD) C&L.446 B.A., J.D.
Davis, William H., Jr. ... '46 '75 (TN) C.806 B.S. L.836 J.D.
DeVance, Curtis ... '38 '74 (MD) C.512 B.S. L.128 J.D.
Dirlam, Charles F. ... '29 '58 C.754 B.S. L.276 J.D.
Doneghy, Joseph E. ... '14 '57 (OH) C&L.851 Ph.B., LL.B.
Dowgiello, Bernard A. ... '32 '57 (MD) C&L.446 LL.B.
Engel, David Wayne ... '56 '81 (VA) C.945 A.B. L.902 J.D.
Feight, James S., Jr. ... '45 '72 C.216 B.A. L.659 J.D. Adm. Law J.
Gardner, Marshall C. ... '18 '55 C&L.273 B.S., J.D.
Gold, Joseph M. ... '30 '87 (NY) C.1027 B.S. L.564 J.D.
Goldfinger, Rea J. ... '54 '81 C.446 B.A. L.273 J.D.
Gordon, Lawrence R. ... '52 '77 C&L.260 B.A., J.D.
Griffin, James H. ... '21 '53 C.862 B.S. L.615 Adm. Law J.
Hardin, Grace A. ... '32 '56 (TX) C&L.846 B.A., LL.B.
Helm, Hugh B. ... '14 '38 (TN) C&L.880
Helsper, William H. ... '45 '73 (KS) C&L.900 B.A., J.D.
Horne, Brockman ... '12 '39 (TX) C&L.846 B.A., LL.B.
Ingles, Richard O. ... '47 '76 C.446 B.S. L.64 J.D.
Jordan, Terral A. ... '15 '41 C&L.273 A.B., J.D.
Joyner, Robert E. ... '21 '47 C&L.838 B.A., J.D.
Kalet, Linda Barbara ... '48 '75 (MD) C.705 B.A. L.64 J.D.
Kopicki, Michael Jesse ... '58 '88 (MD) C.446 B.A. L.64 J.D.
Kreutzer, Edward W. ... '20 '51 (MD) L.64 LL.B.
LeFever, William F. ... '40 '70 (VA) C.874 B.A. L.29 J.D.
Lewandoski, Wanda M. ... '17 '40 (AR) C.1125 L.42 LL.B.
Liljedahl, Gerald V. ... '35 '66 (MO) C.352 B.S.C. L.374 J.D.
Lyons, Donna L. ... '72 '98 (MD) C.445 B.S. L.1002 J.D.
Malick, Gordon R. ... '44 '70 C.963 B.S. L.276 J.D.
Mandel, Harry S. ... '23 '64 C.102 B.A. L.276 J.D.
Masengill, Addison C. ... '53 '90 (MD) C.198 A.B. L.273 J.D.
Mason, Carl R. ... '21 '51 (KS) C&L.900 A.B., LL.B.
May, Joseph M. ... '30 '54 C&L.276 A.B., J.D.
Mayhue, Francis E. ... '35 '61 (OK) C.618 B.A. L.623 LL.B.
Mazumdar, Amitava (Jay) ... '72 '97 C.477 B.A. L.273 J.D. Atty.-Advsr.
McGroarty, Edward P. ... '37 '70 C.524 B.S. L.64 J.D.
McGuire, Joseph E. ... '28 '63 (MO) C&L.734 LL.B.
McLaughlin, James A. ... '30 '56 (CA) C.800 L.426 J.D.
McMenamin, John A. ... '25 '63 C.999 B.A. L.831 LL.B.
Michalski, Jan K. ... '32 '59 (MA) C.156 A.B. L.94 J.D. Adm. Law J.
Milett, Mark E. ... '50 '82 (CA) C.1079 B.A. L.1049 J.D.
Moore, Edward F. ... '45 '70 (MD) C.717 B.A. L.64 J.D.
Moran, William B. ... '50 '75 (MA) C.94 A.B. L.818 J.D.
Mothershead, James O. ... '17 '42 L.904 LL.B.
Nicchitta, Angelo G. ... '26 '55 C.696 B.A. L.564 LL.B.
O'Brien, Walter P. ... '36 '68 C.262 A.B. L.276 J.D.
O'Brien, William J. ... '12 '37 C&L.209 LL.B.
Pace, Timothy C. ... '45 '72 C&L.190 B.A., J.D.
Pietrowicz, Richard R. ... '40 '73 C.1097 B.A. L.800 J.D.
Przybylinski, Donald ... '35 '73 C.347 A.B. L.273 J.D.
Ray, Gerald K. ... '55 '82 (MD) C.645 B.A. L.446 J.D.
Roylance, Wm. G. ... '29 '61 (MD) C.30 B.S. L.446 LL.B.
Ryan, Marguerite L. ... '51 '76 C.128 B.A. L.180 J.D.
Samuels, George H. ... '35 '60 C.516 B.A. L.923 J.D. Adm. Law J.
Sanchez, Alfred C. ... '73 '00 C.424 B.A. L.597 J.D.
Satter, Edwin C., III ... '36 '64 (MA) C.28 B.A. L.1048 LL.B.
Sereboff, Jerome R. ... '39 '66 (MD) C&L.446 B.A., LL.B.
Shraberg, William L. ... '43 '72 (KY) C.696 A.B. L.383 J.D.
Siegel, Harold B. ... '16 '39 (OK) C&L.145 A.B., J.D.
Simon, Harriet A. ... '41 '63 (MD) C&L.446 B.A., LL.B.
Smith, Jackson C. ... '11 '37 (KY) C.383 L.1340
Smith, Robert J. ... '36 '76 (VA) C.802 B.S. L.502 J.D.
Stapleton, James J. ... '30 '53 (MA) C.454 A.B. L.94 J.D.
Stark, Charles A. ... '51 '76 C&L.446 B.S., J.D.
Strayhorn, Eugene H. ... '14 '39 C&L.880 A.B., LL.B.
Sweeney, William J. ... '14 '39 C&L.339 A.B., LL.B.
Taylor, George O., Jr. ... '27 '50 C&L.280 J.D.
Taylor, William C. ... '47 '74 (VA) C.446 B.A. L.276 J.D.
Trachtenberg, Robert L. ... '37 '60 C.1046 B.A. L.569 LL.B.
Underwood, John G. ... '21 '50 (MD) C&L.446 LL.B.
Van Voorhis, John H. ... '32 '58 (GA) C.324 B.A. L.245 LL.B.
Watterson, Margaret ... '40 '76 C.331 B.A. L.273 J.D.
Weixel, Cynthia E. ... '54 '81 C.823 B.A. L.30 J.D.
Whalin, David M. ... '46 '77 C.228 A.B. L.421 J.D.
White, John A. ... '29 '73 (AR) C&L.45 B.S., J.D.
Wieman, F. Joseph ... '28 '56 C&L.446 B.S., LL.B.
Yoffee, William M. ... '32 '65 C.145 B.A. L.446 LL.B.

UNITED STATES INFORMATION AGENCY

Les Jin, *General Counsel*

OFFICE OF THE GENERAL COUNSEL

Colvin, Stanley S. ... '59 '83 (KY) C&L.421 B.S.C., J.D.
Epstein, Carol B. ... '41 '85 C.188 A.B. L.273 J.D.
Higgs-Caldwell, Jacqueline P. ... '56 '83 (PA) C.951 B.A. L.659 J.D.
Jin, Les ... '52 '79 (IL) C.112 B.S. L.629 J.D. Gen. Coun.
Ohlhausen, William G. ... '39 '67 C.734 B.S. L.273 LL.B.
Stuart, R. Wallace ... '41 '72 (OH) C&L.150 B.S., J.D. Dep. Gen. Coun.
Swan, Richard H. ... '44 '70 C.228 A.B. L.846 J.D.
Werksman, Richard S. ... '32 '60 C&L.178 A.B., LL.B.

UNITED STATES INTERNATIONAL TRADE COMMISSION

Lyn M. Schlitt, *General Counsel*

OFFICE OF THE GENERAL COUNSEL

Aranoff, Shara L. '63 '88 C.674 B.A. L.309 J.D.
Bardos, Paul R. '57 '82 C.385 A.B. L.276 J.D.
Bernstein, Marc A. '55 '80 C.228 A.B. L.276 J.D.
Bolick, Thomas N. '63 '96 (NC) C.228 B.S. L.575 J.D.
Casson, Andrea C. '53 '78 C.1365 B.A. L.472 J.D.
DeWinter, Laurent '69 '97 C.260 B.A. L.180 J.D.
Diehl, Michael '61 '91 C.1365 B.A. L.472 J.D.
Driscoll, Karen H. Veninga '58 '83 (TX) C.813 A.B. L.846 J.D.
Gearhart, William W., Jr. '47 '73 (VA) C.216 B.A. L.893 J.D.
Haldenstein, Michael K. '64 '93 C.597 B.A. L.347 J.D.
Hatfield, Kathleen H. '59 '90 C.285 B.A. L.276 J.D.
Henderson, John D. '57 '84 (NY) C.763 B.A. L.1066 J.D.
Hughes, Rhonda M. '55 '81 C.674 A.B. L.893 J.D.
Jackson, Jean H. '51 '83 C.97 B.S. L.245 J.D.
Liberman, Michael '55 '96 C.999 M.S. L.692 J.D.
Lyons, James M. '52 '77 C.1044 B.A. L.276 J.D.
Madaj, Edwin J., Jr. '55 '80 C&L.477 A.B., J.D.
Monaghan, Timothy P. '52 '93 (PA) C&L.831 B.S.E.E., J.D.
Rees, Mark B. '63 '88 (MA) C.67 B.A. L.588 J.D.
Reynolds, Neal J. '60 '86 C.309 A.B. L.276 J.D.
St. Charles, Charles A. '51 '77 C.932 B.B.A. L.426 J.D.
Schlitt, Lyn M. '48 '75 C.352 B.A. L.276 J.D. Gen. Coun.
Smithey, Phyllis N. '51 '78 C.329 B.M. L.276 J.D.
Sultan, Peter L. '56 '83 C.054 B.S. L.94 J.D.
Turner, Robin L. '56 '91 (PA) C&L.273 B.A., J.D.
Verratti, Carol McCue '46 '77 C.103 B.A. L.30 J.D.
Yaworski, Nicholas T. '42 '76 (VA) C.691 B.A. L.273 J.D.

OFFICE OF THE COMMISSIONERS

Brown, June Blanchard '48 '87 C.449 B.A. L.276 J.D.
Johnson, Cynthia P. '60 '89 (VA) C.390 B.S. L.273 J.D.
Reiziss, Jay '63 '89 C.705 B.A. L.904 J.D.

OFFICE OF ADMINISTRATION

McLaughlin, Stephen A. '55 '83 C.945 B.A. L.472 J.D.

OFFICE OF ADMINISTRATIVE LAW JUDGES

Harris, Sidney '31 '58 C.563 B.B.A. L.273 J.D. Adm. Law J.
Luckern, Paul J. '30 '60 C&L.276 B.S., LL.B. Adm. Law J.
Shaw, David P. '61 '86 C.1356 B.A. L.904 J.D.

OFFICE OF UNFAIR IMPORT INVESTIGATIONS

Chubb, T. Spence '54 '80 C.575 B.A. L.893 J.D.
Cockburn, Juan S. '49 '75 (NY) C&L.659 B.A., J.D.
Fusco, Thomas S. '55 '85 (MD) C.37 B.A. L.30 J.D.
Glazer, Steven A. '52 '78 C.453 B.S. L.569 J.D.
Levine, Lynn Iris '53 '77 C.299 B.A. L.188 J.D. Dir.
Whieldon, Jeffrey R. '43 '68 C.165 A.B. L.94 LL.B.

OFFICE OF TARIFF AFFAIRS & TRADE AGREEMENTS

Rosengarden, Eugene A. '40 '65 (MD) C&L.446 B.S., LL.B. Dir.
Shepherdson, Daniel P. '58 '86 (MD) C.880 B.A. L.930 J.D.
Summers, Janis L. '54 '78 (IN) C.347 A.B. L.1119 J.D.

OFFICE OF EXTERNAL RELATIONS

Greer, John J. '50 '77 C.893 B.A. L.276 J.D.

UNITED STATES POSTAL SERVICE

Mary Anne Gibbons, *General Counsel*

LAW DEPARTMENT

Office of the General Counsel

Gibbons, Mary Anne '50 '80 C.530 B.A. L.128 J.D. Gen. Coun.

Corporate Law

Davis, George C. '36 '61 C&L.30 B.A., LL.B.
Green, Catherine A. '67 '94 C.309 B.A. L.178 J.D.
Martin, Elizabeth P. '60 '85 C.228 B.A. L.846 J.D.
O'Connell, Margaret L. '42 '82 (VA) C.966 B.A. L.893 J.D.
Pagano, Catherine V. '53 '84 (MN) C.280 A.B. L.813 J.D.
Poats, Grayson M. '46 '73 (VA) C&L.893 B.A., J.D.
Roma, Mary K. '57 '84 (IL) C.273 B.S. L.209 J.D.
Wackerman, Joseph F. '56 '81 C&L.477 B.A., J.D.

Employment & Labor Law

Butler, George H. '46 '71 C.433 A.B. L.93 J.D.
Champi, Elaine K. '60 '86 C.705 B.A. L.30 J.D.
Drucker, Geoffrey A. '60 '85 C.813 B.A. L.1068 J.D.
Forden, Nancy T. '54 '79 C.555 B.A. L.846 J.D.
Gann, Traci Gabhart '69 '94 (TX) C.69 B.B.A. L.273 J.D.
Goodrich, Joan C. '44 '81 C&L.477 A.B., J.D.
Henry, Peter '71 '97 C.893 B.A. L.477 J.D.
Intrater, Karen A. '43 '81 C.994 B.A. L.904 J.D. Mng. Coun.
Kaufman, Howard J. '46 '72 C.188 B.S. L.273 J.D.
McIntosh, Lynn Saunders '65 '92 C.518 B.A. L.276 J.D.
Poole, Lynn D. '39 '66 C&L.309 A.B., LL.B.
Sindermann, Robert P., Jr. '— '86 C.1036 B.A. L.846 J.D.
Stanton, David A. '51 '86 (PA) C.294 B.A. L.338 J.D.
Taran, Larissa Omelchenko '61 '88 C.994 B.A. L.569 J.D.
Wheeler, Courtney B. '50 '75 (LA) C.885 B.A. L.861 J.D.

Purchasing & Commercial Property Law

Burton, Christopher J. '76 '00 C.575 A.B. L.273 J.D.
Gillespie, Donna S. '55 '80 C.901 B.A. L.477 J.D.
Grady, Janessa L. '61 '87 C.811 B.A. L.846 J.D.
Jones, William J. '43 '68 (MN) C.976 B.A. L.494 J.D.
Klepac, Christopher T. '54 '79 (GA) C.1059 B.A. L.893 J.D.
Mumbach, Michael W. '55 '94 (WV) C.273 B.A. L.902 J.D.
Owczarski, Karen Estilo '63 '89 C.66 B.A. L.569 J.D.
Paine-Powell, Linda S. '54 '86 C.446 B.A. L.1209 J.D.
Robinson, Gerald J. '50 '77 C.178 B.A. L.93 J.D.
Taylor, Christine M. '51 '90 C.767 B.S. L.276 J.D.
Vandamm, Michael J. '46 '74 (VA) C.174 B.A. L.813 J.D.
Zevitas, Alexa '74 '99 (MA) C.855 B.A. L.30 J.D.

Legal Policy & Ratemaking Law

Alverno, Anthony F. '66 '92 (WI) C&L.966 B.A., J.D.
Alvis, William T. '51 '76 (TX) C&L.846 B.A., J.D.
Cooper, Richard T. '54 '81 (CA) C.112 A.B. L.1066 J.D.
DeWeerdt, John L. '44 '70 C&L.911 B.A., J.D.
Duchek, Susan M. '50 '76 C.502 A.B. L.276 J.D.
Eggleston, Fred, Jr. '46 '73 C.228 A.B. L.976 J.D.
Foucheaux, Daniel J., Jr. '47 '76 C.378 B.A. L.846 J.D.
German, R. Andrew '51 '76 C.232 B.A. L.228 J.D.
Hollies, Kenneth N. '55 '82 C.446 B.A. L.893 J.D.
Koetting, Eric P. '56 '80 (MO) C.604 B.A. L.145 J.D.
Mires, Stanley F. '47 '72 C&L.813 B.S., J.D.
Moore, Joseph K. '57 '98 (NC) C.257 B.S. L.575 J.D.
Reiter, Scott L. '54 '79 C.867 B.A. L.276 J.D.
Rubin, David H. '58 '85 (MA) C.309 A.B. L.976 J.D.
Tidwell, Michael T. '56 '80 (TX) C&L.846 B.A., J.D.
Watson, Neva R. '52 '77 C.881 A.B. L.309 J.D.

Civil Practice

Bennett, William P. '45 '74 (NC) C.674 A.B. L.228 J.D.
Durham, Harold E. '54 '88 C.326 B.A. L.846 J.D.
Dym, Lori Joan '55 '80 C.1365 B.A. L.228 J.D.
Hirschauer, Gretchen A. '68 '93 C.363 B.A. L.930 J.D.
Hocking, Wendy A. '59 '89 (WI) C.494 B.A. L.966 J.D.
Karro, David G. '42 '69 (WI) C.604 B.A. L.966 J.D.
Lacy, N. Duane '34 '61 (TN) C&L.837 B.S., LL.B.
McKenzie, Nan K. '58 '83 (IL) C.597 B.A. L.273 J.D.
Reimer, Brian M. '59 '89 (MD) C.602 B.A. L.446 J.D.
Scharf, Eric J. '55 '79 (NJ) C.1349 B.A. L.1292 J.D.
Tyrrell, John P. '48 '73 (CT) C.367 B.A. L.184 J.D.
Zelkowitz, Jeffrey H. '53 '79 C.1036 B.A. L.145 J.D.

OFFICE OF THE DEPUTY GENERAL COUNSEL

Bigelow, Gary W. '53 '84 (NC) C.184 B.A. L.575 J.D.
Gilligan, William R., Jr. '53 '87 (PA) C.658 B.S. L.1338 J.D.
Jensen, Richard C. '52 '77 C.57 A.B. L.309 J.D.
Kappler, Charles F. '51 '78 (PA) C.397 B.A. L.477 J.D. Dep. Gen. Coun.
Koetting, Susan L. '46 '88 (OR) C.447 B.A. L.596 J.D.
Meadows, Benjamin J., III '59 '89 (VA) C.893 B.A. L.273 J.D.

MID-ATLANTIC OFFICE

Benowitz, Mitchell J. '60 '87 C.228 L.575 J.D.
Bisson, Jeannette L. '66 '96 (MD) C.30 B.A. L.446 J.D.
Chakeres, Andrew A. '60 '85 C.229 B.S. L.665 J.D.
Furgeson, Stephen W. '47 '74 C.291 B.A. L.30 J.D.
Griffith-Lesesne, La Donna L. '60 '84 C.860 B.A. L.329 J.D.
Hutcheson, Norma Brown '55 '81 C.105 B.A. L.659 J.D.
Kantorik, Sara K. '74 '99 (PA) C.645 B.S. L.831 J.D.
Loeb, Evelyn M. '65 '90 (CA) C.31 B.A. L.1066 J.D.
Marsh, Jason D '69 '99 (UT) C&L.101 B.S., J.D.
Marshall, Thomas J. '62 '87 C.884 B.A. L.659 J.D.
Neel, William B. '41 '73 C.150 B.S.B.A. L.273 J.D.
Rachel, Kevin B. '54 '79 C.1064 B.A. L.846 J.D.
Vance, Karren M. '61 '89 (MD) C.276 B.S.B.A. L.329 J.D.

JUDICIAL OFFICER

Brochstein, David I. '44 '73 C.188 B.S. L.273 J.D.
Cohen, James A. '37 '62 C&L.352 B.S.C., J.D.
Houston, Bruce R. '42 '66 (NY) C.696 B.A. L.982 J.D.
Mahn, William K. '44 '77 C.763 B.A. L.326 J.D.
Mego, Diane M. '70 '96 (MD) C.311 B.A. L.904 J.D.
Menegat, Norman D. '45 '72 (CA) C.813 A.B. L.1066 J.D.

POSTAL INSPECTION SERVICE

Hyde, Gary D., Jr. '— '97 (FL) C.1111 B.S. L.472 J.D.
McKeown, Terrence P. '— '90 C&L.339 A.B., J.D.
Perez, Maria del Carmen '58 '84 (PR) C&L.677 B.A., J.D.
Wainwright, Ronnie A. '41 '79 C.472 B.A. L.64 J.D. Dep. Asst. Inspector Gen.

Cybulski, David P. '52 '78 C.262 B.S. L.1019 J.D.
Davidson, Wilbur L., Jr. '42 '68 (VA) C.945 B.A. L.893 LL.B.
Harrison, Michael J. '43 '70 (KY) C.960 B.S. L.383 J.D.
Hatcher-Capers, Lola M. '54 '79 C.103 B.A. L.273 J.D.
Manasseh-Chambers, Regina S. '71 '97 C.999 B.A. L.665 J.D.
Michelson, Robert E. '47 '73 C&L.273 B.A., J.D.
Warder-Bayliss, Leslie K. '49 '81 C.112 B.A. L.30 J.D.

UNITED STATES COURTS

ADMINISTRATIVE OFFICE OF THE UNITED STATES COURTS

L. Ralph Mecham, *Director*

Adair, David N., Jr. '45 '72 (MO) C.597 B.A. L.477 J.D.
Anderson, Amanda Lannon '67 '92 C.861 B.A. L.30 J.D.
Asin, Steven G. '50 '76 (NY) C.367 B.A. L.823 J.D.
Augustyn, Noel J. '46 '74 C.197 A.B. L.602 J.D.
Braswell, Mark W. '58 '83 C.575 B.A. L.1228 J.D.
Brown, Elizabeth Allison '62 '90 C.446 L.575 J.D.
Brown, Katharine Mason '65 '92 C.914 B.A. L.930 J.D.

Burchill, William R., Jr. '47 '73 C.659 B.A. L.273 J.D.
Burke, Robert J. '55 '84 C.260 B.A. L.472 J.D.
Channon, Patricia Sugrue '38 '80 C.104 A.B. L.945 J.D.
Chastain, John L. '52 '77 C.145 B.A. L.893 J.D.
Countryman, Joan '44 '80 C.352 B.A. L.276 J.D.
Cunningham, Daniel A. '60 '86 C&L.378 B.S., J.D.
Deyling, Robert P. '60 '87 C.813 B.A. L.569 J.D.
Dolan, Michael W. '42 '69 C.378 B.A. L.273 J.D.
Echard, Roberta M. '52 '89 C.339 B.S. L.276 J.D.
Fitzgerald, John J. '71 '98 C.731 B.A. L.1009 J.D. Reg. Admr.
Gaddy, Susan M. '63 '92 (SC) C.575 A.B. L.356 J.D.
Gallagher, Kevin R. '49 '76 (IL) C.424 B.A. L.276 J.D.
Gardner, Christina '49 '79 (CA) C.675 B.A. L.426 J.D.
Gilbert, Melanie Fess '67 '91 (NJ) C.347 B.A. L.564 J.D.
Goodwin, Catharine M. '45 '80 (FL) C.768 B.A. L.260 J.D.
Graham, Amy R. '59 '86 C.823 B.A. L.982 J.D.
Greenman, Lisa '61 '88 C.976 B.A. L.569 J.D.
Hanchett, Karen M. '57 '82 (MD) C.128 B.A. L.446 J.D.
Hayes, Susan J. '46 '81 C.645 B.S. L.30 J.D.
Hennemuth, Jeffrey A. '56 '81 C.62 B.A. L.608 J.D.
Hnatowski, Thomas C. '50 '77 C.205 B.A. L.30 J.D.
Holmes, Marilyn J. '51 '75 C.228 B.A. L.276 J.D.
Horowitz, Linda '53 '78 C.696 B.A. L.910 J.D.
Howard, John D. '49 '75 C.30 B.A. L.362 J.D.
Huff, George B., Jr. '48 '80 (IN) C.303 B.A. L.589 J.D.
Jackson, Dan S. '60 '86 (ID) C.1032 B.A. L.336 J.D.
Jaffe, Richard A. '62 '87 (PA) C.1044 B.A. L.276 J.D.
Jennis, Wendy '51 '77 C.188 A.B. L.276 J.D.
Kattan, Susan J. '46 '74 C.66 B.A. L.1066 J.D.
Lee, Douglas A. '57 '83 (PA) C.103 B.A. L.659 J.D.
Lee, Duane R. '46 '75 C.197 A.B. L.273 J.D.
Lehman, William J. '43 '72 (CO) C.70 B.S. L.208 J.D.
Lidz, Theodore J. '42 '71 (NY) C.475 B.A. L.912 J.D.
Loesche, Robert K. '51 '77 (PA) C.311 B.A. L.94 J.D.
Long, Clothilde C.J. '42 '71 C.104 A.B. L.893 J.D.
Mahin, Gregory A. '49 '75 C&L.128 B.A., J.D.
Malkin, Gloria J. '53 '83 C.1036 B.A. L.30 J.D.
Mattos, Abel J. '44 '80 C&L.128 B.A., J.D.
McCabe, Peter G. '39 '65 C.178 A.B. L.309 J.D.
Mecham, L. Ralph '28 '59 C.878 B.S. L.273 LL.B. Dir.
Miller, Nancy G. '53 '78 C.112 B.A. L.1066 J.D.
Minor, Laura C. '57 '84 (MD) C&L.273 B.A., J.D.
Miskovsky, Mark S. '61 '91 C.93 B.A. L.273 J.D.
Mitterhoff, Mary Louise '59 '88 C&L.705 B.A., J.D.
Molock, Guy, Jr. '58 '84 C.85 B.A. L.329 J.D.
Mrischin, Sandra L. '42 '89 (TN) C&L.347 M.B.A., J.D.
Peterson, Janice C. '— '89 (PA) C.692 B.A. L.1338 J.D.
Petty, Gary C. '50 '76 (KY) C.150 B.A. L.383 J.D.
Proctor, Judy B. '42 '82 (AR) C.45 B.A. L.1243 J.D.
Rabiej, John '53 '78 C.424 B.A. L.339 J.D.
Reed, Michael E. '64 '90 (NY) C.262 B.A. L.1009 J.D.
Robinson, R. Townsend '50 '75 C.30 B.A. L.309 J.D.
Ross, Donald Dean '55 '82 (NE) C&L.546 B.A., J.D.
Savadow, Mark I. '50 '75 C.30 B.A. L.229 J.D.
Savinski, Sharon Ann '49 '81 (PA) C.205 B.A. L.30 J.D.
Saxe, Bret '58 '88 (NM) C.597 B.S. L.1065 J.D.
Shapiro, Mark D. '62 '88 (NY) C.1044 B.S. L.1009 J.D.
Siegel, Karen K. '47 '72 (FL) C&L.472 A.B., J.D.
Silverman, Meryl A. '53 '77 C.107 B.A. L.1019 J.D.
Six, Charles Edward '51 '87 (MD) C&L.446 B.A., J.D.
Stevens, Dinah '42 '78 C.399 B.A. L.776 J.D.
Tevlowitz, Steven M. '56 '86 (MD) C.446 B.A. L.273 J.D.
Thomas, Sandra S. A. '41 '74 C&L.862 B.A., J.D.
Wannamaker, James Henry, III '48 '82 C.790 B.A. L.446 J.D.
Watkins, Ralph '52 '83 C.381 B.G.S. L.30 J.D.
White, Arthur E. '50 '83 (WA) C.276 B.S.F.S. L.678 J.D.
White, Maurice E. '50 '75 C.329 B.A. L.309 J.D.
Williams, David S. '51 '77 (NC) C&L.896 B.S., J.D.
Williams, Louise Dean '66 '91 (MD) C.914 B.A. L.446 J.D.
Wolff, Richard A. '51 '78 C.31 B.A. L.276 J.D.

FEDERAL JUDICIAL CENTER

Fern M. Smith, *Director*

Arberg, Charles S. '54 '80 (VA) C.893 B.S. L.945 J.D.
Berney, Michael L. Gottlieb '56 '82 C.976 B.A. L.569 J.D.
Cecil, Joe S. '48 '78 (IL) C.623 B.S. L.597 J.D.
Dargan, Richard L. '47 '83 (SC) C.797 B.A. L.790 J.D.
Eaglin, James B. '49 '76 (NY) C.1177 B.A. L.107 J.D.
George, Jody Ellyn '59 '87 C.477 B.A. L.575 J.D.
Gur-Arie, Mira L. '63 '88 C.188 B.A. L.569 J.D.
Hooper, Laural L. '— '91 (PA) C.575 B.S. L.276 J.D.
Leary, Marie '68 '94 C.105 B.A. L.128 J.D.
Loveland, Genevra Kay '40 '77 (CA) C&L.846 B.A., J.D.
Markarian, Kris '62 '91 (IL) C.103 A.B. L.347 J.D.
Neary, Denise M. '57 '85 (PA) C.658 B.A. L.831 J.D.
Niemic, Robert J. '50 '86 C.1113 B.S. L.276 J.D.
Reagan, Robert Timothy '59 '93 (CA) C.309 Ph.D. L.1065 J.D.
Rowland, Robin '53 '86 C.178 B.A. L.188 J.D.
Shapard, John E. '47 '74 (CA) C.668 B.A. L.1068 J.D.
Sherman, Mark A. '64 '89 C.273 B.A. L.472 J.D.
Smith, Fern M. '— '75 (CA) C&L.813 B.A., J.D. Dir.
Sobel, Sylvan A. '55 '83 C.276 B.A. L.966 J.D.
Vamvas, Paul S '50 '96 (MD) C.569 B.A. L.446 J.D.
Wiggins, Elizabeth C. '58 '91 (MD) C.575 B.S. L.446 J.D.
Willging, Thomas E. '40 '66 C&L.128 A.B., J.D.
Withers, Kenneth J. '56 '85 (MA) C.588 B.A. L.597 J.D.
Wood, Jefri '56 '86 (VA) C.821 B.A. L.893 J.D.
Woods, Lauren A. '66 '94 (IL) C.436 B.A. L.365 J.D.

SUPREME COURT OF THE UNITED STATES

William H. Rehnquist, *Chief Justice*

Breyer, Stephen G. '38 '66 C.813 A.B. L.309 LL.B. Assoc. J.
Ginsburg, Ruth B. '33 '59 C.188 B.A. L.178 LL.B. Assoc. J.
Kennedy, Anthony M. '36 '62 C.813 A.B. L.309 LL.B. Assoc. J.
O'Connor, Sandra D. '30 '52 C&L.813 A.B., LL.B. Assoc. J.
Rehnquist, William H. '24 '52 C&L.813 B.A., LL.B. Chief Justice
Scalia, Antonin '36 '62 C.276 A.B. L.309 J.D. Assoc. J.
Souter, David H. '39 '66 C&L.309 A.B., LL.B. Assoc. J.
Stevens, John P. '20 '49 C.145 A.B. L.597 J.D. Assoc. J.
Thomas, Clarence '48 '74 C.321 A.B. L.976 J.D. Assoc. J.

Chhabria, Vince '69 '00 (CA) C.1169 B.A. L.1066 J.D.
Corbelli, Linda C. '56 '83 (NY) C.239 B.A. L.273 J.D. Libr.
Doerhoff, Heidi C. '73 '01 (MO) C.602 B.A. L.502 J.D.
Fallon, Christine Luchok '52 '77 (PA) C.923 B.A. L.128 J.D.
Fitzpatrick, Brian T. '75 '01 (CA) C.602 B.S. L.309 J.D.
Gura, Stephen A. '61 '87 (GA) C.1365 B.A. L.276 J.D. Staff Coun.
Horowitz, Mirah Anne '75 '01 (CA) C&L.228 B.A., J.D.
Leiter, Michael '69 '01 (MA) C.178 A.B. L.309 J.D.
Lorson, Francis J. '43 '71 C&L.128 A.B., J.D.
Petkofsky, Jane E. '53 '78 C.665 B.A. L.273 J.D.
Rider, Sally M. '57 '86 C&L.37 B.A., J.D.
Suter, William K. '37 '62 C.859 B.A. L.861 LL.B. Clerk
Vasil, Christopher W. '48 '75 (OH) C&L.161 B.A., J.D.
Wagner, Frank D. '45 '70 (PA) C.188 A.B. L.1017 J.D. Reporter of Decisions

UNITED STATES COURT OF APPEALS DISTRICT OF COLUMBIA CIRCUIT

Douglas H. Ginsburg, *Chief Judge*

Buckley, James L. '23 '50 C&L.976 B.A., LL.B. Cir. J.
Edwards, Harry T. '40 '65 C.188 B.S. L.477 J.D.
Garland, Merrick B. '52 '79 C&L.309 A.B., J.D. Cir. J.
Ginsburg, Douglas H. '46 '73 C.188 B.S. L.145 J.D. Cheif J.
Henderson, Karen LeCraft '44 '68 C.228 B.A. L.575 J.D. Cir. J.
Randolph, A. Raymond '43 '70 C.223 B.S. L.659 J.D. Cir. J.
Rogers, Judith W. '39 '65 C.681 A.B. L.309 LL.B. Cir. J.
Sentelle, David B. '43 '68 C&L.575 A.B., J.D. Cir. J.
Silberman, Laurence H. '35 '62 C.197 A.B. L.309 LL.B. Cir. J.
Tatel, David S. '42 '66 C.477 B.A. L.145 J.D. Cir. J.
Williams, Stephen F. '36 '62 C.976 B.A. L.309 J.D. Cir. J.

Butler, Mark Allen '55 '90 (MI) C.245 B.A. L.477 J.D.
Dunn, Nancy G. '50 '83 C.966 B.A. L.128 J.D.
Hauser, Tracy C. '67 '92 C.882 B.A. L.30 J.D.
Haven, Gail Reizenstein '55 '81 C.477 B.A. L.831 J.D.
Hohenlohe, Philip A. '67 '95 C.309 A.B. L.273 J.D.
Ihrke, William H. '71 '99 (CA) C.154 B.A. L.273 J.D.
Langer, Mark J. '57 '83 (MD) C.373 B.A. L.228 J.D.
Morris, George E. '50 '83 (MA) C.276 B.A. L.818 J.D.
Nessen, R. Peter '68 '96 (MA) C.881 B.A. L.94 J.D.
O'Brien-Holcomb, Diane J. '64 '89 C.884 B.S. L.1009 J.D.
Padgett, Nancy '32 '77 C.597 B.S. L.276 J.D.
Pearlman, Ellen S. '53 '81 C.188 B.A. L.893 J.D.
Powell, J. Mark '70 '97 (IL) C.118 B.A. L.339 J.D.
Ryan, Melissa McKenney '61 '88 C&L.477 B.S.E., J.D.
Sayenga, Jill C. '54 '79 C.262 B.A. L.276 J.D.
Severy, Karen L. '64 '92 C.446 B.A. L.273 J.D.
Thompson, Rebecca L. '53 '80 C.6 B.A. L.896 J.D.
Tomich, Martha J. '53 '78 C.70 B.A. L.180 J.D.
Viar, Elisabeth Anne '63 '90 (VA) C.945 B.A. L.30 J.D.

UNITED STATES COURT OF APPEALS FOR THE FEDERAL CIRCUIT

Haldane Robert Mayer, *Chief Judge*

Archer, Glenn L., Jr. '29 '54 C.976 B.A. L.273 J.D. Sr. J.
Bryson, William C. '45 '75 C.309 A.B. L.846 J.D. Cir. J.
Clevenger, Raymond C., III '37 '68 C&L.976 B.A., LL.B. Cir. J.
Cowen, Wilson '— '28 Sr. J.
Friedman, Daniel M. '16 '41 C&L.178 A.B., LL.B. Sr. J.
Gajarsa, Arthur J. '41 '68 C.688 B.S.E.E. L.276 J.D. Cir. J.
Linn, Richard '44 '69 C.688 B.E.E. L.276 J.D. Cir.J.
Lourie, Alan D. '35 '70 C.309 A.B. L.831 J.D. Cir. J.
Mayer, H. Robert '41 '71 C.870 B.S. L.945 J.D. Chief J.
Michel, Paul R. '41 '67 C.951 B.A. L.893 LL.B. Cir. J.
Newman, Pauline '27 '58 C.881 B.A. L.569 LL.B. Cir. J.
Plager, S. Jay '31 '58 C.575 A.B. L.260 J.D. Cir. J.
Rader, Randall R. '49 '78 C.101 B.A. L.273 J.D. Cir. J.
Schall, Alvin A. '44 '70 C.674 A.B. L.861 J.D. Cir. J.
Smith, Edward S. '19 '47 C&L.893 B.A., J.D. Sr. J.

Blundall, George W. '43 '92 (CA) C.223 B.S. L.1170 J.D.
Brinckerhoff, Courtenay Cassel '67 '99 (MD) C.893 B.S. L.1209 J.D.
Choi, Rebecca J. '62 '89 C&L.846 B.B.A., J.D.
Cotropia, Christopher '74 '99 (CA) C.597 B.S.E.E. L.846 J.D.
DeMello, Jill E. '67 '99 (CA) C.178 B.A. L.273 J.D.
Dorini, Brian J. '65 '97 C.602 B.S.E.E. L.309 J.D.
Frey, Jeffrey Ira '— '99 (NC) C.188 B.E.E. L.276 J.D.
Green, Richard Gerard '70 '99 (MA) C.188 B.A. L.273 J.D.
Halpern, Melvin L. '44 '72 C.563 B.S. L.273 J.D.
Horbaly, Jan '44 '69 (OH) C&L.930 A.B., J.D.
Kim, Rudolph Y. '69 '98 (CA) C.112 B.S. L.276 J.D.
Knur, Kimberly C. '66 '98 C.870 B.S. L.276 J.D.
Mancuso, Stephen M. '57 '86 C.112 B.A. L.1065 J.D.
McDermott, Patricia M. '53 '82 (PA) C.397 B.A. L.831 J.D.
Pettigrew, Lynne E. '64 '97 C.976 B.S. L.276 J.D.
Pulsinelli, Gary '63 '97 (CA) C.309 A.B. L.1066 J.D.
Robertson, Melissa Lanni '66 '92 C.1021 B.S. L.893 J.D.
Skelton, Byron George '05 '31 (TX) C&L.846 B.A., J.D.
Steere, J. Douglas '63 '89 (MO) C.804 B.A. L.861 J.D.
Stoll, Thomas L. '— '96 (VA) C.446 B.S.E.E. L.180 J.D.
Sullivan, Eugene R., II '71 '00 (NY) C.228 B.A. L.178 LL.M.
Thayer, Eleanor M. '44 '82 C.157 B.A. L.30 J.D.

UNITED STATES COURT OF APPEALS FOR THE FEDERAL CIRCUIT (Continued)

Walker, David B., P.E. ... '— '99 (AK) C.871 B.S. L.813 J.D.
Wennes, Marilyn A. ... '61 '90 C.367 B.A. L.446 J.D.

UNITED STATES DISTRICT COURT FOR THE DISTRICT OF COLUMBIA

Thomas F. Hogan *Chief Judge*

Bryant, William B. ... '11 '48 C&L.329 A.B., LL.B. Sr. J.
Facciola, John M. ... '45 '70 C.321 A.B. L.276 J.D. Mag. J.
Flannery, Thomas A. ... '18 '40 C&L.180 LL.B. Sr. J.
Friedman, Paul L. ... '44 '68 C.188 B.A. L.107 J.D. Judge
Green, Joyce Hens ... '28 '51 C.446 B.A. L.273 J.D. Sr. J.
Harris, Stanley S. ... '27 '53 C&L.893 B.S., LL.B. Sr. J.
Hogan, Thomas F. ... '38 '66 C&L.276 A.B., J.D. Ch. J.
Huvelle, Ellen Segal ... '48 '75 C.914 B.A. L.93 J.D. Judge
Jackson, Thomas P. ... '37 '65 C.197 A.B. L.309 LL.B. Judge
Johnson, Norma Holloway ... '— '62 C.1280 B.S. L.276 J.D.
Kay, Alan ... '34 '59 C&L.273 B.A., J.D. Mag. J.
Kennedy, Henry H., Jr. ... '48 '74 C.674 A.B. L.309 J.D. Judge
Kessler, Gladys ... '38 '63 C.188 B.A. L.309 LL.B. Judge
Kollar-Kotelly, Colleen C. ... '— '68 C&L.128 B.A., J.D. Judge
Lamberth, Royce C. ... '43 '67 C&L.846 B.A., LL.B. Judge
Oberdorfer, Louis F. ... '19 '46 C.197 A.B. L.976 LL.B. Sr. J.
Penn, John Garrett ... '32 '57 C.454 A.B. L.94 LL.B. Sr. J.
Roberts, Richard W ... '53 '79 C.881 A.B. L.178 J.D.
Robertson, James ... '38 '66 C.674 A.B. L.273 LL.B. Judge
Robinson, Deborah A. ... '53 '78 C.512 B.S. L.245 J.D. Mag. J.
Sullivan, Emmet G. ... '47 '73 C&L.329 A.B., J.D. Judge
Teel, S. Martin, Jr. ... '45 '70 C&L.893 B.A., J.D. Bkrptcy. J.
Urbina, Ricardo M. ... '46 '70 C&L.276 B.A., J.D. Judge

UNITED STATES COURT OF FEDERAL CLAIMS

Lawrence M. Baskir, *Chief Judge*

Allegra, Francis M. ... '57 '81 C.999 B.A. L.1003 J.D. Judge
Andewelt, Roger B. ... '46 '71 C.102 B.S. L.273 J.D. Judge
Baskir, Lawrence M. ... '38 '62 C.674 A.B. L.309 LL.B. Chief Judge
Bruggink, Eric G. ... '49 '75 C.10 B.A. L.16 J.D. Judge
Bush, Lynn J. ... '48 '76 C.33 B.A. L.276 J.D. Judge
Damich, Edward J. ... '48 '76 C.65 B.A. L.128 J.D. Judge
Earnest, Margaret M. ... '— '89 C.1356 B.A. L.1209 J.D. Clerk of Court
Firestone, Nancy B., ... '51 '77 C.910 B.A. L.502 J.D. Judge
Futey, Bohdan A. ... '39 '68 C.930 B.A. L.1003 J.D. Judge
Gibson, Reginald W. ... '27 '57 C.892 B.S. L.329 LL.B. Sr. Judge
Harkins, Kenneth R. ... '21 '49 C&L.608 B.A., J.D. Judge
Hewitt, Emily ... '44 '78 C.188 A.B. L.309 J.D. Judge
Hodges, Robert H., Jr. ... '44 '69 C&L.790 B.S., J.D. Judge
Horn, Marian Blank ... '43 '69 C.66 A.B. L.262 J.D. Judge
Lydon, Thomas J. ... '27 '55 C.431 B.A. L.276 J.D. Judge
Margolis, Lawrence S. ... '35 '63 C.223 B.S.M.E. L.273 J.D. Judge
Merow, James F. ... '32 '56 C&L.273 A.B., J.D. Judge
Miller, Christine O'Dell Cook ... '44 '69 C.813 B.A. L.878 J.D. Judge
Robinson, Wilkes C. ... '25 '51 C.16 A.B. L.893 LL.B. Sr. Judge
Smith, Loren A. ... '44 '70 C&L.597 B.A., J.D. Judge
Tidwell, Moody R., III ... '39 '65 C.611 B.A. L.904 J.D. Judge
Turner, James T. ... '38 '65 C.896 B.A. L.893 LL.B. Judge
Weinstein, Diane Gilbert ... '47 '79 C.788 B.A. L.94 J.D. Judge
Wiese, John P. ... '34 '66 C.319 B.A. L.893 LL.B. Judge
Wilson, Sarah L. ... '59 '91 C.951 B.A. L.178 J.D. Judge
Yock, Robert J. ... '38 '62 C.747 B.A. L.377 J.D. Judge

OFFICE OF SPECIAL MASTERS

Abell, Richard B. ... '43 '74 (PA) C&L.273 B.A., J.D. Spec. Master
Edwards, John F. ... '60 '87 C.893 B.A. L.1209 J.D. Spec. Master
French, E. LaVon ... '30 '75 C.1281 B.A. L.221 J.D. Spec. Master
Golkiewicz, Gary J. ... '55 '81 C.116 B.S. L.128 J.D. Chief Spec. Master
Hastings, George L., Jr. ... '53 '78 (MI) C&L.477 B.A., J.D. Spec. Master
Millman, Laura Diane ... '46 '77 C.563 B.A. L.262 J.D. Spec. Master
Wright, Elizabeth E. ... '48 '79 C.298 B.F.A. L.1162 J.D. Spec. Master

UNITED STATES COURT OF APPEALS FOR THE ARMED FORCES

Walter T. Cox, III, *Chief Judge*

Cook, William H. ... '20 '47 C.801 L.910 J.D. Sr. J.
Cox, Walter T., III ... '42 '67 C.160 B.S. L.790 J.D. Chief J.
Crawford, Susan J. ... '47 '77 C.105 B.A. L.1202 J.D. Judge
Darden, William H. ... '23 '48 C&L.280 B.B.A., LL.B. Sr. J.
Effron, Andrew S. ... '48 '76 C&L.309 B.A., J.D. Judge
Gierke, H. F., III ... '43 '66 C&L.585 B.A., J.D. Judge
Sullivan, Eugene R. ... '41 '72 C.870 B.S. L.276 J.D. Judge

Cutts, John A., III ... '42 '66 C&L.790 A.B., J.D.
Dixon, Richard D.S., III ... '40 '65 (NC) C.228 A.B. L.575 LL.B.
Dorsey, Nelson Bernard, Jr. ... '72 '97 (MD) C.228 A.B. L.273 J.D.
Duignan, Kathleen A. ... '67 '91 (CT) C.472 B.A. L.1009 J.D.
Early, William N. ... '31 '56 C&L.273 B.A., J.D.
Foreman, LeRoy F. ... '39 '63 C&L.190 B.A., LL.B. Comr.
Gilligan, Francis A. ... '39 '64 C.24 B.A. L.107 J.D.
Granahan, Thomas F. ... '39 '71 (NY) C.262 A.B. L.1009 J.D. Clerk
Harper, James T. ... '45 '69 (TN) C&L.838 B.S., J.D.
Holt, John B. ... '49 '77 (TN) C.871 B.S. L.880 J.D.
Jameson, M. Alison ... '56 '85 (NE) C.865 B.A. L.546 J.D.
Miele, Robert V. ... '47 '71 C.201 B.A. L.608 J.D.
Mueller, Robert C. ... '46 '71 (IA) C.793 B.A. L.228 J.D.
Presson, Michelle C. ... '70 '98 (VA) C.518 B.A. L.945 J.D.
Richardson, James S., Sr. ... '44 '73 (MD) C.443 B.A. L.446 J.D.
Roup, Rolland S. ... '44 '75 (CA) C.112 A.B. L.1068 J.D.
Smith, Stephen D. ... '48 '74 (CA) C.112 B.A. L.61 J.D.
Sterritt, Christopher J. ... '49 '74 C.321 A.B. L.93 J.D.

UNITED STATES TAX COURT

Thomas B. Wells *Chief Judge*

Beghè, Renato ... '33 '55 C&L.145 A.B., J.D. Judge
Chabot, Herbert L. ... '31 '58 C.563 B.A. L.178 LL.B. Judge
Chiechi, Carolyn P. ... '43 '69 C&L.276 B.S., J.D. Judge
Cohen, Mary Ann ... '43 '67 C.112 B.S. L.800 J.D. Chief Judge
Colvin, John O. ... '46 '71 C.502 A.B. L.276 J.D. Judge
Dawson, Howard A., Jr. ... '22 '49 C.575 B.S. L.273 LL.B. Sr. Judge
Gale, Joseph H. ... '— '80 C.674 A.B. L.893 J.D. Judge
Gerber, Joel ... '40 '65 C.1016 B.A. L.209 J.D. Judge
Halpern, James S. ... '45 '73 C&L.659 B.S., J.D. Judge
Jacobs, Julian I. ... '37 '60 C&L.446 B.A., LL.B. Judge
Laro, David ... '42 '68 (MI) C.477 B.A. L.339 J.D. Judge
Nims, Arthur L., III ... '23 '49 C.951 B.A. L.280 LL.B. Judge
Parr, Carolyn M. ... '38 '77 C.362 B.A. L.276 J.D. Judge
Ruwe, Robert P. ... '41 '70 C.973 B.S.B.A. L.1340 J.D. Judge
Swift, Stephen J. ... '43 '70 C.101 B.A. L.273 J.D. Judge
Thornton, Michael B. ... '54 '82 C.499 B.S. L.228 J.D. Judge
Wells, Thomas B. ... '45 '73 C.473 B.S. L.245 J.D. Ch. J.
Whalen, Laurence J. ... '44 '70 C&L.276 A.B., J.D. Judge

SPECIAL TRIAL JUDGES

Armen, Robert N., Jr. ... '47 '73 (OH) C.229 B.A. L.276 J.D.
Couvillion, D. Irvin ... '34 '59 (LA) C&L.420 B.S., J.D.
Dinan, Daniel J. ... '29 '61 (VA) C.1030 B.S.S. L.276 LL.B.
Goldberg, Stanley J. ... '39 '64 C&L.446 B.S., LL.B.
Pajak, John J. ... '32 '56 C&L.823 B.A., J.D.
Panuthos, Peter J. ... '43 '69 (MA) C.1145 B.S. L.818 J.D.
Powell, Carleton D. ... '39 '67 (VA) C.893 B.A. L.692 LL.B.
Wolfe, Norman H. ... '28 '53 (NY) C.976 B.A. L.178 LL.B.

Auchterlonie, Jennifer D. ... '74 '99 (WA) C.426 B.A. L.285 J.D.
Baltes, Joanna P. ... '73 '99 C.37 B.A. L.1049 J.D.
Blake, Andrea Renae ... '74 '99 (WA) C.941 B.A. L.285 J.D.
Bosworth, Emily Abraham ... '68 '94 C&L.500 B.A., J.D.
Campbell, Tara C. ... '75 '01 C.966 B.A. L.436 J.D.
Casazza, Charles S. ... '32 '59 (NY) C.884 A.B. L.262 LL.B. Clerk
Cords, Danshera ... '72 '98 C.911 B.A. L.1358 J.D.
Fahey, Diane L. ... '53 '83 C.161 B.A. L.989 J.D.
Fee, John T. ... '47 '73 C.216 B.A. L.276 J.D.
Gieseler, Stella Ann ... '46 '82 (OH) C.651 B.S. L.1003 J.D.
Gillis, Harold Timothy ... '73 '98 C.1038 B.A. L.276 LL.M.
Glasser, Lynne ... '50 '75 C.980 B.A. L.8 J.D.
Guy, Daniel A., Jr. ... '61 '87 C.928 B.A. L.64 J.D.
Haney, Nathan ... '72 '99 C.506 B.S. L.508 J.D.
Hirabayashi, Glen T. ... '47 '80 C.870 B.S. L.809 J.D.
Huck, Martin T. ... '65 '90 (MD) C.119 B.S. L.1119 J.D.
Ing, Earl T. W. ... '53 '78 C.312 B.A. L.1065 J.D.
Keahey, Hazel C. ... '54 '80 C.808 B.S. L.425 J.D.
Kelley, R. Matthew ... '73 '99 (KS) C.190 B.A. L.602 J.D.
Lee, Patrick D. ... '71 '99 C.477 B.B.A. L.930 J.D.
Linville, David E. ... '75 '01 C&L.911 B.S., J.D.
Loomis, Mary Alexis ... '62 '91 (MD) C.276 B.A. L.904 J.D.
Orefice, James A. ... '60 '88 (CA) C.1103 B.B.A. L.1049 J.D.
Pomerance, Robert S. ... '47 '77 C.309 A.B. L.93 J.D.
Pretty, William A. ... '— '88 (AZ) C.1042 B.A. L.999 LL.B.
Rifkin, Dave ... '71 '97 C.910 A.B. L.262 J.D.
Rinaldi, Mary Elizabeth ... '72 '98 C.94 B.A. L.472 J.D.
Ro, Juli J. ... '72 '97 (CA) C.112 B.A. L.464 J.D.
Ruggieri, Ellen V. ... '59 '84 (MD) C.276 B.A. L.273 J.D.
Shaw, Stanley S., Jr. ... '44 '74 (OH) C.610 A.B. L.276 J.D.
Trauman, Brian Paul ... '74 '99 (FL) C&L.260 B.S.B.A., J.D.
Wallach, Frederick E. ... '37 '63 (NY) C.951 B.A. L.309 J.D.
Weber, E. Paige ... '54 '78 (WV) C&L.923 B.S., J.D.
Wielobob, Allison E. ... '70 '96 (PA) C.859 B.A. L.831 J.D.
Wilson, Janet L. ... '56 '85 (VA) C.893 B.A. L.245 J.D.

UNITED STATES COURT OF APPEALS FOR VETERANS CLAIMS

Kenneth B. Kramer *Chief Judge*

Farley, John J., III ... '42 '74 C.321 A.B. L.1019 J.D. Judge
Fred, Martha E. ... '50 '82 C.801 B.S. L.190 J.D.
Greene, William P., Jr. ... '43 '68 C.922 B.A. L.329 J.D. Judge
Holdaway, Ronald M. ... '34 '59 C&L.972 B.A., LL.B. Judge
Ivers, Donald L. ... '41 '72 C.560 B.A. L.904 J.D. Judge
Kramer, Kenneth B. ... '42 '66 C.339 A.B. L.309 J.D. Chief Judge
Steinberg, Jonathan R. ... '39 '64 C.188 A.B. L.659 LL.B. Judge

---

Bednar, Richard A. ... '61 '90 (VA) C&L.101 B.A., J.D.
Brandon-Arnold, Cynthia M. ... '60 '85 C.823 B.A. L.273 J.D.
Cuffe, Elizabeth C. K. ... '54 '97 (AZ) C.1349 B.A. L.37 J.D.
Dowd, Jennifer A. ... '69 '95 C&L.128 B.A., J.D.
Herring, Norman Y. ... '46 '76 C.836 B.S. L.1137 J.D. Clerk
Lane, Jack F., Jr. ... '42 '66 (VA) C.797 B.A. L.893 LL.B.
Luthi, Jeffery N. ... '53 '87 C&L.972 B.S., J.D.
Mailander, Rosalind ... '54 '85 (TX) C.308 B.A. L.744 J.D.
Montrose, Sandra P. ... '39 '84 C.719 B.A. L.128 J.D.
Olson, Dayna Kim ... '70 '96 (NY) C&L.569 B.S., J.D.
Talbot, Elizabeth Hessman ... '60 '86 (PA) C.377 B.A. L.276 J.D.
Van Brunt, Roy T., III ... '73 '99 (MD) C.798 B.S. L.64 J.D. Law Clerk

JUDICIAL PANEL ON MULTIDISTRICT LITIGATION

Beck, Michael J. ... '49 '78 (IN) C.276 B.A. L.345 J.D.
Boland, Susan J. ... '55 '81 (TN) C.600 B.A. L.838 J.D.
Cahn, Robert A. ... '46 '72 (MO) C&L.502 B.S.P.A., J.D.
Kalahurka, Terrence M. ... '51 '75 (MO) C.734 A.B. L.309 J.D.
Varano, Michele C. ... '66 '98 (PA) C.884 B.S. L.309 J.D.

PATENT AND TRADEMARK PRACTICE PROFILES SECTION

Legal Professionals Practicing

BEFORE THE

UNITED STATES PATENT AND TRADEMARK OFFICE

CONNECTICUT, DELAWARE
DISTRICT OF COLUMBIA

The listings in this section are, according to information available to the publisher at press time, for those subscribers who are registered to practice Patent Law and for those who practice Trademark Law before the U.S. Patent and Trademark Office and who devote a considerable portion of their time or duties to Patent, Trademark and other related matters. It should be noted that registration is not necessary to practice Trademark Law before the U.S. Patent and Trademark Office.

Firms are not registered with the U.S. Patent and Trademark Office and the listings of such entities are limited to those whose practice includes Patent or Trademark and related matters.

The symbols shown have the same meaning as when used elsewhere in this directory. See page IX for Explanatory Notes and Symbols.

BLOOMFIELD, 18,608, *Hartford Co.*

Bedingfield, Herbert M. .... '72 '99 C.228 B.A. L.184 J.D. [🄰 Cantor C.]
*PRACTICE AREAS: Patent Law; Trademark Law; Copyright Law.
Cantor, Michael, (BV) .... '58 '84 C&L.184 B.S., J.D. [Cantor C.] (⊙Norwalk)
*PRACTICE AREAS: Patent Law; Trademark and Copyright Law; Unfair Competition; Intellectual Property Law.

Cantor Colburn LLP, (BV)
55 Griffin Road South, 06002-1355 ⊙
Telephone: 860-286-2929 Fax: 860-286-0115
Email: iplaw@cantorcolburn.com URL: http://www.cantorcolburn.com
Members of Firm: Michael Cantor; Philmore H. Colburn, II; Keith J. Murphy; Leah M. Reimer; David A. Fox; William J. Cass; Michael J. Rye; Pamela J. Curbelo. Associates: Timothy J. Olson; Herbert M. Bedingfield; Deborah B. Crenshaw (Not admitted in CT); James J. Merrick; Peter R. Hagerty (Not admitted in CT).
Patent, Trademark and Copyright Law, Unfair Competition, Computer and Related Intellectual Property Law including Litigation in all Courts.
Norwalk, Connecticut Office: 101 Merritt 7, 06853. Telephone: 203-849-8266. Fax: 203-849-8292.
See Professional Biographies, BLOOMFIELD, CONNECTICUT

Cass, William J., (BVⓉ) '62 '88 C.971 B.S. L.1048 J.D.
[Cantor C.] (⊙Springfield, MA)
*PRACTICE AREAS: Intellectual Property; Litigation.
Colburn, Philmore H., II, (BV) .... '59 '91 C.588 B.S.E.E. L.1048 J.D. [Cantor C.] ⊙
*PRACTICE AREAS: Patent Law; Trademark and Copyright Law; Unfair Competition; Intellectual Property Law.
Crenshaw, Deborah B. '59 '94 C.326 B.S.E.E. L.845 J.D.
(adm. in TX; not adm. in CT) [🄰 Cantor C.]
*PRACTICE AREAS: Intellectual Property.
Curbelo, Pamela J. .... '66 '91 C.971 B.S. L.1048 J.D. [Cantor C.]
*PRACTICE AREAS: Intellectual Property Law.
Fox, David A. .... '67 '95 C.688 B.S.E.E. L.128 J.D. [Cantor C.]
*PRACTICE AREAS: Patent Law; Trademark Law; Copyright Law; Unfair Competition; Intellectual Property.
Hagerty, Peter R. '61 '94 C.454 B.S.Chem. L.1202 J.D.
(adm. in MA; not adm. in CT) [🄰 Cantor C.]
*PRACTICE AREAS: Intellectual Property; Patents; Trademarks; Copyrights.
Merrick, James J. .... '61 '97 C.999 B.S. L.1048 J.D. [🄰 Cantor C.]
*PRACTICE AREAS: Litigation; Trial Practice; Intellectual Property Litigation; Investigations; Personal Injury.
Murphy, Keith J. .... '65 '94 C.308 B.A. L.724 J.D. [Cantor C.]
*PRACTICE AREAS: Intellectual Property; Patent Law; Trademark; Copyright.
Olson, Timothy J. .... '65 '99 C.1027 B.S. L.306 [🄰 Cantor C.]
*PRACTICE AREAS: Patent Law; Trademark Law; Copyright Law; Intellectual Property Law.
Reimer, Leah M. .... '60 '95 C.69 B.Sc. L.184 J.D. [Cantor C.]
*PRACTICE AREAS: Patent Law; Trademark Law; Copyright Law; Unfair Competition; Intellectual Property.
Rye, Michael J., (BVⓉ) '62 '90 C.494 B.A. L.823 J.D.
[Cantor C.] (⊙Springfield, MA)
*PRACTICE AREAS: Intellectual Property Litigation.

BRIDGEPORT, * 141,686, *Fairfield Co.*

Coleman, Henry D., (AVⓉ) '54 '85 C.1044 B.S. L.966 J.D.
(adm. in WI; not adm. in CT) [Coleman S.S.] ⊙

Coleman Sudol Sapone, P.C., (AVⓉ)
714 Colorado Avenue, 06605-1601 ⊙
Telephone: 203-366-3560 Fax: 203-335-6779
Email: cosud@erols.com URL: http://www.lawyers.com/colemansudolllp
Henry D. Coleman (Not admitted in CT); R. Neil Sudol (Not admitted in CT); William J. Sapone.
Patents, Trademarks, Copyrights, Litigation, Unfair Competition, Trade Secrets, Licensing/Technology Deal Structuring, Business Development, Biotechnology/Pharmaceuticals, Software and Internet Law, Due Diligence for Financial Transactions, Technology Acquisition, Technology Licensing Litigation, Alternative Dispute Resolution including Arbitration and Mediation of Contract/License Disputes.
Mamaroneck, New York Office: 434 Mamaroneck Avenue, 10483. Telephone: 203-366-3560.
See Professional Biographies, BRIDGEPORT, CONNECTICUT

Sapone, William J., (BVⓉ) '54 '84
C.459 B.S. L.1040 J.D. [Coleman S.S.] (⊙New York, NY)
Sudol, R. Neil, (BVⓉ) '51 '84 C.401 B.A.,B.S. L.569 J.D.
(adm. in NY; not adm. in CT) [Coleman S.S.]

FAIRFIELD, 54,849, *Fairfield Co.*

Aker, David '51 '82 C.186 B.S. L.724 J.D.
(adm. in NY; not adm. in CT) [🄰 Perman&G.]
*PRACTICE AREAS: Intellectual Property Matters.
Caulfield, Donald C. .... '42 '68 C.321 B.S. L.93 J.D. [🄲 Perman&G.]
*PRACTICE AREAS: Patent, Trademark, Copyright.
Dowd, Thomas P., (AVⓉ) '33 '63 C&L.262 B.S., LL.B.
(adm. in NY; not adm. in CT) [🄰 Perman&G.]
*PRACTICE AREAS: Patent, Trademark, Copyright.
Gelling, Ralph D. '41 '70 C.971 B.S.E.E. L.724 J.D.
(adm. in NY; not adm. in CT) [🄰 Perman&G.]
*PRACTICE AREAS: Patent, Trademark, Copyright.
Goodwin, John J. '32 '60 C.433 B.S.E.E. L.724 J.D.
(adm. in NY; not adm. in CT) [🄰 Perman&G.]
*PRACTICE AREAS: Patent, Trademark, Copyright.
Green, Clarence A., (AV) .... '38 '66 C.454 B.S.M.E. L.94 J.D. [Perman&G.]
*PRACTICE AREAS: Patent, Trademark, Copyright.
Harrington, Mark F. .... '60 '85 C.885 B.S. L.1040 J.D. [Harrington&S.]
*PRACTICE AREAS: Patent, Trademark, Copyright.

Harrington & Smith, LLP
1809 Black Rock Turnpike, 06432
Telephone: 203-366-4084 Fax: 203-366-4109
Email: patent@hspatent.com
Mark F. Harrington; Harry F. Smith.
Patent, Trademark, Copyright.
See Professional Biographies, FAIRFIELD, CONNECTICUT

Hilburger, Albert W. .... '37 '62 C.477 B.S.M.E. L.276 LL.B. [🄰 Perman&G.]
*PRACTICE AREAS: Patent, Trademark, Copyright.

Perman & Green, LLP, (AV)
425 Post Road, 06430-6232
Telephone: 203-259-1800 Facsimile: 203-255-5170
Email: pgpatent@aol.com URL: http://www.pgpatent.com
Managing Partner: Clarence A. Green. Associates: David M. Warren (Not admitted in CT); Albert W. Hilburger; Thomas L. Tully; Michael J. Tully (Not admitted in CT); John J. Goodwin (Not admitted in CT); Ralph D. Gelling (Not admitted in CT); Thomas P. Dowd (Not admitted in CT); David Aker (Not admitted in CT); Geza C. Ziegler, Jr.; Henry I. Steckler (Not admitted in CT). Of Counsel: Donald C. Caulfield; Paul Weinstein.
Patent, Trademark, Copyright and Related Matters.
See Professional Biographies, FAIRFIELD, CONNECTICUT

Smith, Harry F. .... '49 '86 C.999 B.S.E.E. L.1029 J.D. [Harrington&S.]
*PRACTICE AREAS: Patent, Trademark, Copyright Law.
Steckler, Henry I. '42 '67 C.688 B.S.E.E. L.1009 J.D.
(adm. in NY; not adm. in CT) [🄰 Perman&G.]
*PRACTICE AREAS: Patent, Trademark, Copyright.
Tully, Michael J. '39 '70 C.588 B.S. L.128 J.D.
(adm. in VA; not adm. in CT) [🄰 Perman&G.]
*PRACTICE AREAS: Patent, Trademark, Copyright.
Tully, Thomas L. .... '33 '60 C.93 B.S. L.276 J.D. [🄰 Perman&G.]
Warren, David M. '35 '71 C.453 B.S.E.E. L.818 J.D.
(adm. in MA; not adm. in CT) [🄰 Perman&G.]
*PRACTICE AREAS: Patent, Trademark, Copyright.
Weinstein, Paul .... '40 '70 C.667 B.M.E. L.276 J.D. [🄲 Perman&G.]
Ziegler, Geza C., Jr. .... '61 '94 C.1029 B.S.E.E. L.1252 J.D. [🄰 Perman&G.]
*PRACTICE AREAS: Patent, Trademark, Copyright.

HARTFORD, * 139,739, *Hartford Co.*

Alix, James E., (AV) .... '33 '62 C.321 B.S. L.276 LL.B. [🄲 Alix,Y.&R.]

Alix, Yale & Ristas, LLP, (BV)
(Formerly Chilton, Alix & Van Kirk)
750 Main Street, 06103-2703
Telephone: 860-527-9211 Facsimile: 860-527-5029
Email: ayrllp@pctlaw.com
Members of Firm: Guy D. Yale; L. James Ristas; Richard H. Berneike; Clifford P. Kelly. Associates: James E. Piotrowski; Robert S. Smith. Of Counsel: James E. Alix; Ralph H. Chilton; Roger A. Van Kirk.
Patent, Trademark, Computer, Copyright and Unfair Competition Law and Related Licensing and Litigation.
See Professional Biographies, HARTFORD, CONNECTICUT

Berneike, Richard H. .... '32 '64 C.679 B.S.Ch.E. L.273 LL.B. [Alix,Y.&R.]
Chilton, Ralph H., (AV) .... '30 '61 C.679 B.S.M.E. L.273 J.D. [🄲 Alix,Y.&R.]
Cunningham, Marina F. .... '64 '93 C.178 B.S. L.184 J.D. [McCormick,P.&H.]
*PRACTICE AREAS: Intellectual Property; Patents; Trademarks; Copyrights; E-Commerce.
Dempsey, John J., (AVⓉ) '24 '57 C.871 B.S. L.446 LL.B.
(adm. in MD; not adm. in CT) [🄲 McCormick,P.&H.] ⊙
*PRACTICE AREAS: Patents; Trademarks; Copyrights.
Getz, Richard D. ....'62 '92 C.184 B.S.M.E. L.1048 J.D. [🄰 McCormick,P.&H.]
*PRACTICE AREAS: Intellectual Property Transactions; Licensing; Patents; Trademarks; Copyrights.
Gowanlock, William B. .... '52 '95 C.477 B.S.E. L.128 J.D. [🄰 McCormick,P.&H.]
*PRACTICE AREAS: Intellectual Property; Patent Prosecution; Government Contracts.
Griffith, Wm. Tucker .... '73 '98 C.971 B.S. L.306 J.D. [🄰 McCormick,P.&H.]
*PRACTICE AREAS: Intellectual Property; Litigation; Patents; Trademarks; Copyrights.
Haesche, Frederick J. .... '24 '66 C&L.184 B.S., J.D. [🄲 McCormick,P.&H.] ⊙
*PRACTICE AREAS: Intellectual Property; Patents; Trademarks; Copyrights.
Hilton, John C., (BV) .... '31 '62 C.453 B.S. L.184 J.D. [McCormick,P.&H.]
*PRACTICE AREAS: Trademarks; Patents.
Huber, Donald K., (AV) ....'30 '58 C&L.597 B.S.M.E., J.D. [🄲 McCormick,P.&H.] ⊙
*PRACTICE AREAS: Intellectual Property; Patents; Trademarks; Copyrights.
Kelly, Clifford P., (BV) .... '50 '93 C.871 B.S. L.184 J.D. [Alix,Y.&R.]
Linderman, John C. .... '38 '70 C.453 B.S. L.184 J.D. [McCormick,P.&H.]
*PRACTICE AREAS: Intellectual Property; Patents; Trademarks; Copyrights.
Ma, Shirley S. .... '69 '96 C.1044 B.S. L.201 J.D. [🄰 McCormick,P.&H.]
*PRACTICE AREAS: Intellectual Property.
MacDonald, Donald J. '60 '99 C.1154 B.S. L.1389 J.D.
(adm. in MA; not adm. in CT) [🄰 McCormick,P.&H.]
*PRACTICE AREAS: Intellectual Property Litigation; Patent Prosecution.
Mackas, Daniel G. ....'61 '97 C&L.184 B.S.E., J.D. [🄰 McCormick,P.&H.]
*PRACTICE AREAS: Patents; Trademarks; Copyrights.

McCormick, Paulding & Huber, LLP, (BV)
CityPlace II, 185 Asylum Street, 06103-4102 ⊙
Telephone: 860-549-5290 Fax: 860-527-0464
Email: MPH@IP-Lawyers.com URL: http://www.IP-lawyers.com
Members of Firm: John C. Hilton; John C. Linderman; J. Kevin Grogan (Resident, Springfield, Massachusetts Office); Arthur F. Dionne (Resident, Springfield, Massachusetts Office); Richard R. Michaud; Marina F. Cunningham. Associates: Daniel G. Mackas; Susan C. Oygard (Resident, Springfield, Massachusetts Office); Nicholas J. Tuccillo (Resident, Springfield, Massachusetts Office); Wm. Tucker Griffith; Stephen P. Scuderi (Resident, Springfield, Massachusetts Office); Mary-Jacq Holroyd (Resident, Springfield, Massachusetts Office); Richard D. Getz; William B. Gowanlock; Donald J. MacDonald (Not admitted in CT); Shirley S. Ma. Of Counsel: Theodore R. Paulding; Donald K. Huber; Frederick J. Haesche; John J. Dempsey (Not admitted in CT); Charles E. Sohl.
Patent, Trademark, Copyright, Unfair Competition, Franchise, Computer and Related Intellectual Property Law including Litigation in all Courts.
Springfield, Massachusetts Office: 1350 Main Street, 5th Floor. Telephone: 413-736-5401. Fax: 413-733-4543.
See Professional Biographies, HARTFORD, CONNECTICUT

Michaud, Richard R. ....'63 '96 C.1029 B.S.M.E. L.1252 J.D. [McCormick,P.&H.]
*PRACTICE AREAS: Patents; Trademarks; Copyrights; Intellectual Property; Litigation.
Paulding, Theodore R., (AV) ....'30 '57 C.602 B.S. L.184 J.D. [🄲 McCormick,P.&H.] ⊙
*PRACTICE AREAS: Intellectual Property.
Piotrowski, James E. ....'58 '98 C.184 B.S. L.1252 J.D. [🄰 Alix,Y.&R.]
Ristas, L. James ....'49 '78 C.188 B.S. L.184 J.D. [Alix,Y.&R.]
Smith, Robert S. .... '33 '67 C.454 B.S.M.E. L.569 J.D. [🄰 Alix,Y.&R.]
*PRACTICE AREAS: Patent Law; Trademark Law; Copyright Law; Trade Secrets Law; Computer Law.
Sohl, Charles E. .... '45 '76 C.223 B.S.M.E. L.184 J.D. [🄲 McCormick,P.&H.] ⊙
*PRACTICE AREAS: Intellectual Property Law; Business Law.
Van Kirk, Roger A., (AV) .... '32 '62 C.882 B.S.E.E. L.273 J.D. [🄲 Alix,Y.&R.]
Yale, Guy D. ....'45 '76 C.608 B.S. L.184 J.D. [Alix,Y.&R.]

MILFORD, 48,168, *New Haven Co.*

Stoltz, Melvin I., (AV) '43 '69 C&L.184 B.S.Ch. E., J.D. 🄱🄱
51 Cherry Street, 06460
Telephone: 203-874-8183 Facsimile: 203-878-9607
Email: patlaw@snet.net
Patent, Trademark, Copyright and Unfair Competition. Foreign Patent and Trademark Law and Related Litigation.
See Professional Biographies, MILFORD, CONNECTICUT

MONROE, 14,010, *Fairfield Co.*

Adolphson, K. Bradford .... '56 '83 C.184 B.S. L.273 J.D. [Ware,F.V.S.&A.]
Barber, William J. .... '59 '86 C.1350 B.S. L.1009 J.D. [Ware,F.V.S.&A.]
*PRACTICE AREAS: Patents; Copyrights; Trademarks.
Carvis, Thaddius J. .... '43 '71 C.966 B.S.Ch.E. L.128 J.D. [Ware,F.V.S.&A.]
*PRACTICE AREAS: Patent Law; Trademark Law; Copyright Law; Antitrust Law; Unfair Competition Law.
Frederick, James R., (AV) ....'44 '69 C&L.477 B.S., J.D. [Ware,F.V.S.&A.]
Fressola, Alfred A., (AV) ....'46 '73 C&L.184 B.S.E., J.D. [Ware,F.V.S.&A.]
Hyman, Andrew T. .... '62 '96 C.454 B.S. L.1051 J.D. [Ware,F.V.S.&A.]
*PRACTICE AREAS: Patents; Trademarks; Copyrights; Intellectual Property.
Maguire, Francis J., Jr. .... '47 '83 C.690 B.S.E.E. L.306 J.D. [Ware,F.V.S.&A.]

Oliver, Milton M., (AVⓉ) '51 '75 C.309 B.A. L.284 J.D.
(adm. in MA; not adm. in CT) [Ware,F.V.S.&A.]
*PRACTICE AREAS: International Patent Law; Trademarks; Copyrights; Computer Law; Litigation.
Pasquale, Jack M. .... '43 '81 C.570 B.S.E.E. L.1048 J.D. [Ware,F.V.S.&A.]
*PRACTICE AREAS: Patents; Trademarks; Copyrights; Intellectual Property.
Retter, James A. ....'51 '00 C.228 B.A. L.184 J.D. [Ware,F.V.S.&A.]
Shear, Stephen B. '43 '74 C.861 B.S. L.273 J.D.
(adm. in VA; not adm. in CT) [Ware,F.V.S.&A.]
Ware, Robert H., (AV) ....'27 '51 C.477 B.S.M.E. L.309 LL.B. [Ware,F.V.S.&A.]

Ware, Fressola, Van Der Sluys & Adolphson, LLP, (AV)
Bradford Green, Building Five, 755 Main Street, P.O. Box 224, 06468
Telephone: 203-261-1234 Fax: 203-261-5676
Email: mail@wfva.net
Robert H. Ware; Alfred A. Fressola; K. Bradford Adolphson; Francis J. Maguire, Jr.; William J. Barber; James R. Frederick; Thaddius J. Carvis; Stephen B. Shear (Not admitted in CT); Milton M. Oliver (Not admitted in CT); Jack M. Pasquale; James A. Retter; Andrew T. Hyman.
Patent, Trademark, Copyright, Computer, Antitrust, Unfair Competition, Foreign Patent Law, Litigation and Federal Practice.
See Professional Biographies, MONROE, CONNECTICUT

NEW HAVEN, * 130,474, *New Haven Co.*

Bachman, Robert H. '33 '58 C.184 B.A. L.569 LL.B.
(adm. in NY; not adm. in CT) [Bachman&L.]
*PRACTICE AREAS: Patents; Trademarks; Copyrights; Unfair Competition; Licensing Law.

Bachman & LaPointe, P.C., (AV) BR
900 Chapel Street, Suite 1201, 06510
Telephone: 203-777-6628 Fax: 203-865-0297
Email: iplaw@bachlap.com
Robert H. Bachman (Not admitted in CT); Gregory P. LaPointe; Barry L. Kelmachter; George A. Coury.
Intellectual Property Law including U.S. and International practice in Patent, Trademark, Copyright, International Trade, Unfair Competition, Antitrust and Licensing Law. Trials and Appeals in all Federal Courts and Administrative Agencies.
See Professional Biographies, NEW HAVEN, CONNECTICUT

Coury, George A. .... '63 '90 C.645 B.S. L.1040 J.D. [Bachman&L.]
*PRACTICE AREAS: Patents; Trademarks; Copyrights; Unfair Competition; Licensing Law.
DeLio, Anthony P., (AV) .... '28 '57 C.667 B.S. L.273 J.D. [DeLio&P.]
*PRACTICE AREAS: Patents; Trademarks; Copyrights; Unfair Competition; Intellectual Property Licensing.

DeLio & Peterson, LLC, (AV)
121 Whitney Avenue, 06510-1241
Telephone: 203-787-0595 FAX: 203-787-5818
Email: delpet@delpet.com URL: http://www.lawyers.com/delio
Anthony P. DeLio; Peter W. Peterson;—John J. Tomaszewski (Not admitted in CT).
United States and International Patent, Trademark, Copyright and Unfair Competition Law. Licensing, Franchising and Technology - Litigation.
See Professional Biographies, NEW HAVEN, CONNECTICUT

Kelmachter, Barry L. .... '46 '79 C.823 B.S. L.30 J.D. [Bachman&L.]
*PRACTICE AREAS: Patents; Trademarks; Copyrights; Unfair Competition; Licensing Law.
LaPointe, Gregory P., (AV) .... '46 '78 C.880 B.E. L.30 J.D. [Bachman&L.]
*PRACTICE AREAS: Patents; Trademarks; Copyrights; Unfair Competition; Licensing Law.
Peterson, Peter W., (AV) .... '54 '82 C&L.184 B.S., J.D. [DeLio&P.]
*PRACTICE AREAS: Patents; Trademarks; Copyrights; Unfair Competition; Intellectual Property Licensing.
Tomaszewski, John J. '40 '71 C.569 B.Ch.E. L.724 J.D.
(adm. in NY; not adm. in CT) [A DeLio&P.]
*PRACTICE AREAS: Patents; Trademarks; Copyrights; Intellectual Property Licensing; Unfair Competition.

NORWALK, 78,331, *Fairfield Co.*

Boehm, Christopher C. .... '65 '96 C.690 B.S. L.1252 J.D. [A Cantor C.]
*PRACTICE AREAS: Intellectual Property.
Cantor, Michael, (BV) ....'58 '84 C&L.184 B.S., J.D. [Cantor C.] (⊙Bloomfield)
*PRACTICE AREAS: Patent Law; Trademark and Copyright Law; Unfair Competition; Intellectual Property Law.

Cantor Colburn LLP, (BV)
101 Merritt 7, 06856 ⊙
Telephone: 203-849-8266 Fax: 203-849-8292
Email: iplaw@cantorcolburn.com URL: http://www.cantorcolburn.com
Michael Cantor; Philmore H. Colburn, II; Michael J. Kelly. Associates: Christopher C. Boehm (Resident).
Patent, Trademark and Copyright Law, Unfair Competition, Computer and Related Intellectual Property Law including Litigation in all Courts.
Bloomfield, Connecticut Office: 55 Griffin Road South, 06002. Telephone: 860-286-0115. Fax: 860-286-0115.

(This Listing Continued)

Cantor Colburn LLP (Continued)
See Professional Biographies, NORWALK, CONNECTICUT

Colburn, Philmore H., II, (BV) .... '59 '91 C.588 B.S.E.E. L.1048 J.D. [Cantor C.] ⊙
*PRACTICE AREAS: Patent Law; Trademark and Copyright Law; Unfair Competition; Intellectual Property Law.
Kelly, Michael J. .... '43 '76 C.1046 B.S. L.776 J.D. [Cantor C.]
*PRACTICE AREAS: Intellectual Property Law.

SIMSBURY, 21,161, *Hartford Co.*

Libert, Victor E., (AV) ....'36 '69 C.667 B.Ch.E. L.1009 J.D. [Libert&Assoc.]
*PRACTICE AREAS: Intellectual Property; Patents; Trademarks; Copyrights; Trade Secrets.

Libert & Associates, (AV)
3 Mill Pond Lane Powder Forest Business Park, P.O. Box 538, 06070-0538
Telephone: 860-651-9321 Fax: 860-651-5735
Email: libert.i.p.law@snet.net
Victor E. Libert. Associates: Frederick A. Spaeth.
Patent, Trademark, Copyright, Intellectual Property and Related Matters.
See Professional Biographies, SIMSBURY, CONNECTICUT

Spaeth, Frederick A. ....'59 '86 C.184 B.S. L.1029 J.D. [A Libert&Assoc.]
*PRACTICE AREAS: Patents; Trademarks; Copyrights; Intellectual Property.

SOUTHPORT, —, *Fairfield Co.*

Fattibene, Arthur T. ....'23 '52 C.610 B.S. L.276 J.D. [Fattibene&F.]
*PRACTICE AREAS: Intellectual Property; Patent; Trademark; Copyright.
Fattibene, Paul A. .... '57 '83 C.882 B.S. L.1029 J.D. [Fattibene&F.]
*PRACTICE AREAS: Patent; Trademark; Copyright; Intellectual Property.

Fattibene & Fattibene
2480 Post Road, 06490
Telephone: 203-255-4400 Fax: 203-259-0033
URL: http://www.fattibene.com
Arthur T. Fattibene; Paul A. Fattibene.
Patent, Trademark, Copyright and other Intellectual Property Law.
See Professional Biographies, SOUTHPORT, CONNECTICUT

STAMFORD, 108,056, *Fairfield Co.*

Battersby, Gregory J., (AV) ....'47 '73 C.776 A.B. L.262 J.D. [Grimes&B.]
Coplit, James G. '68 '94 C.188 B.S. L.94 J.D.
(adm. in NY; not adm. in CT) [Grimes&B.]
Greeley, Paul D., (AV) ....'57 '82 C.183 B.A. L.285 J.D. [Ohlandt,G.R.&P.]
Grimes, Charles W., (AV) .... '51 '75 C.645 B.S. L.208 J.D. [Grimes&B.]

Grimes & Battersby L.L.P., (AV)
3 Landmark Square, Suite 405, P.O. Box 1311, 06904-1311
Telephone: 203-324-2828 Telecopy: 203-348-2720
URL: http://www.gandb.com
Charles W. Grimes; Gregory J. Battersby; James G. Coplit (Not admitted in CT).
Patents, Trademarks, Copyrights, Unfair Competition, Trade Secrets, Multimedia, Licensing, Franchising, Litigation and Antitrust.
See Professional Biographies, STAMFORD, CONNECTICUT

Hubbard, Robert R. '37 '65 C.608 B.E.E. L.273 LL.B.
(adm. in DC; not adm. in CT) [C Ohlandt,G.R.&P.]
McAllister, Terrence J. '55 '84 C.1044 B.A. L.1040 J.D.
(adm. in NY; not adm. in CT) [Ohlandt,G.R.&P.]
Ohlandt, John F. '23 '56 C.433 B.E.E. L.724 LL.B.
(adm. in NY; not adm. in CT) [C Ohlandt,G.R.&P.]

Ohlandt, Greeley, Ruggiero & Perle, (AV)
Suite 903 One Landmark Square, 06901
Telephone: 203-327-4500 Facsimile: 203-327-6401
Email: 102001.3251@compuserve.com
Paul D. Greeley; Charles N. J. Ruggiero; Terrence J. McAllister (Not admitted in CT). Associates: John Yankovich (Not admitted in CT). Senior Counsel: John F. Ohlandt (Not admitted in CT). Of Counsel: George W. Rauchfuss, Jr. (Not admitted in CT); Robert R. Hubbard (Not admitted in CT). Practice Limited to Intellectual Property Law and Related Matters.
See Professional Biographies, STAMFORD, CONNECTICUT

Rauchfuss, George W., Jr. '38 '68 C.645 B.S.Ch.E. L.904 J.D.
(adm. in DC; not adm. in CT) [C Ohlandt,G.R.&P.]
Ruggiero, Charles N. J. .... '49 '76 C.563 B.M.E. L.365 J.D. [Ohlandt,G.R.&P.]
Yankovich, John '57 '96 C.667 M.S.E.E. L.1040 J.D.
(adm. in NY; not adm. in CT) [A Ohlandt,G.R.&P.]

WILMINGTON, * 71,529, *New Castle Co.*

Amernick, Burton A., (AVⓉ) '40 '66 C.446 B.S.Ch.E. L.64 J.D.
(adm. in MD; not adm. in DE) [Connolly B.L.&H.]
*PRACTICE AREAS: Biotechnology Patents; Chemical Patents; Medical Patents; Metallurgical Patents; Pharmaceutical Patents.

Barrera, Joseph '62 '99 C.999 B.A. L.560 J.D.
(adm. in NM; not adm. in DE) [🄰 Connolly B.L.&H.] ⊙
*PRACTICE AREAS: Intellectual Property.

Beck, Richard M., (BV) '38 '66 C.688 B.M.E. L.273 J.D.
(adm. in DC; not adm. in DE) [Connolly B.L.&H.]

Bourke, Mary W. .... '59 '85 C.674 B.S.E. L.665 J.D. [Connolly B.L.&H.]

Buchanan Ingersoll, Professional Corporation, (BVⓉ)
1201 North Market Street, Suite 1501, 19801 ⊙
Telephone: 302-428-5500 Fax: 302-428-3996
Antitrust and Trade Regulation, Broadcasting and Cable TV, Commercial Transactions, Computer Law, Construction Industry Law, Corporate Law and Finance, Creditors' Rights and Bankruptcy, Energy, Environmental Law, ERISA and Employee Benefits, Family Law, Financial Institutions, Franchising, Government Relations, Healthcare, Insurance Regulation, Intellectual Property, International Transactions, Labor and Employment, Litigation, Mergers and Acquisitions, Municipal Law, Natural Resources Law, Public Finance, Real Estate, Security Alarm, Tax and Estate Planning, Technology Law, Trade Secret Litigation, Transportation Law, Trust and Estate Administration, Venture Capital.
Pittsburgh, Pennsylvania Office: One Oxford Centre, 301 Grant Street, 20th Floor. Telephone: 412-562-8800. Telecopier: 412-562-1041. URL: http://www.bipc.com.
Philadelphia, Pennsylvania Office: Eleven Penn Center, 14th Floor, 1835 Market Street. Telephone: 215-665-8700.
Bryn Mawr, Pennsylvania Office: 937 East Haverford Road, Suite 201. Telephone: 610-581-7004.
Harrisburg, Pennsylvania Office: One South Market Square, 213 Market Street, 3rd Floor. Telephone: 717-237-4800.
Tampa, Florida Office: SunTrust Financial Centre, 401 East Jackson Street, Suite 2500. Telephone: 813-222-8180.
Aventura, Florida Office: One Turnberry Place, 19495 Biscayne Boulevard, Suite 606. Telephone: 305-933-5600.
Miami, Florida Office: Bank of America Tower, 100 S.E. Second Street, Suite 2100. Telephone: 305-347-4080.
Princeton, New Jersey Office: 700 Alexander Park, Suite 300. Telephone: 609-987-6800.
Buffalo, New York Office: 268 Main Street, Suite 201. Telephone: 716-853-2330.
Washington, D.C. Office: 1776 K Street, N.W., Suite 800. Telephone: 202-452-7900.
Other Washington, D.C. Office: Silverstein and Mullens, 1776 K Street, N.W., Suite 800. Telephone: 202-452-7900.
New York, New York Office: 140 Broadway, 35th Floor. Telephone: 646-458-2340.
McLean, Virginia Office: 8280 Greensboro Drive, Suite 601. Telephone: 703-749-6060.
San Diego, California Office: First National Bank Center, 401 West A Street, Suite 1900. Telephone: 619-578-5000.
London, England Office: Tower 42, The International Financial Centre, Old Broad Street, EC2N 1HQ. Telephone: 44-207-920-3700.
Dublin, Ireland Office: Level 1, 4 Custom House Plaza, IFSC, Dublin 1. Telephone: 011-353-1611-7266. Fax: 3531-836-9305.
See Professional Biographies, WILMINGTON, DELAWARE

Connolly, Arthur G., (AV) .... '05 '32 C.453 B.S. L.309 LL.B. [Connolly B.L.&H.] ‡
Crawford, Paul E., (BV) .... '40 '66 C&L.884 B.M.E., J.D. [Connolly B.L.&H.]
DiGiovanni, Francis .... '65 '93 C.105 B.S.M.E. L.665 J.D. [🄰 Connolly B.L.&H.]
Donnelly, Rex A., IV .... '66 '96 C.886 B.S.M.E. L.1138 J.D. [🄰 Ratner&P.]
*PRACTICE AREAS: Intellectual Property.
Evain, Eric J. .... '60 '98 C.592 B.S. L.644 J.D. [🄰 Connolly B.L.&H.]
Fairchild, John D., (AV) '32 '63 C.30 B.A. L.215 J.D.
(adm. in MI; not adm. in DE) [🄲 Connolly B.L.&H.]
Goldstein, Kevin W. .... '58 '91 C.688 B.S. L.1338 J.D. [Ratner&P.]
*PRACTICE AREAS: Intellectual Property; Intellectual Property Litigation.
Gomez, Brian A. .... '65 '93 C.1119 B.A. L.1338 J.D. [🄰 Huntley&Assoc.]
*PRACTICE AREAS: Intellectual Property; Patent; Trademark; Copyright.
Green, Stanley B., (AVⓉ) '41 '67 C.563 B.E.E. L.273 LL.B.
(adm. in DC; not adm. in DE) [Connolly B.L.&H.]
*PRACTICE AREAS: Patent Litigation; Patent Infringement; Electrical Patents; Electronic Patents; Computer and Software Patents.
Gregory, Theodore C. '26 '68 C.645 B.S. L.8 J.D.
(adm. in OH; not adm. in DE) [🄲 Huntley&Assoc.]
*PRACTICE AREAS: Patent Law; Patent Applications; Litigation; Agreements.
Hansen, Christine M., (BV) .... '64 '92 C.674 A.B. L.659 J.D. [🄰 Connolly B.L.&H.]
Hume, Larry J. '56 '00 C.36 B.S.E.E. L.1209 J.D.
(adm. in VA; not adm. in DE) [🄰 Connolly B.L.&H.]
*PRACTICE AREAS: Patent; Trademark; Litigation Support; Copyright; Trade Secret.
Huntley, Donald W. .... '42 '67 C&L.339 B.S., J.D. [Huntley&Assoc.]
*PRACTICE AREAS: Intellectual Property Law; Patent, Trademark and Copyright Law.

Huntley & Associates
1105 North Market Street, P.O. Box 948, 19899-0948
Telephone: 302-426-0610 Facsimile: 302-426-0612
URL: http://www.monopolize.com
Donald W. Huntley. Associates: Brian A. Gomez. Of Counsel: Theodore C. Gregory (Not admitted in DE).
Intellectual Property; Patent, Trademark and Copyright Law.

(This Listing Continued)

Huntley & Associates (Continued)
See Professional Biographies, WILMINGTON, DELAWARE

Hutz, Rudolf E., (AV) .... '38 '64 C.674 A.B. L.276 J.D. [Connolly B.L.&H.]
Jacobs, Robert, (BV) .... '41 '68 C.563 B.S.Ch.E. L.831 J.D. [Jacobs&C.]
*PRACTICE AREAS: Product Liability; Asbestos Litigation; Medical Malpractice; Business Litigation; Patent Law.

Jacobs & Crumplar, P.A., (BV)
2 East 7th Street, P.O. Box 1271, 19899
Telephone: 1-800-355-1818; 302-656-5445 FAX: 302-656-5875
Email: jcinbox@jacobsandcrumplar.com URL: http://www.jacobsandcrumplar.com
Robert Jacobs.
Personal Injury, Automobile Accidents, Medical Malpractice, Social Security Disability, Products Liability and Toxic Substance, Worker Compensation, Business Litigation, Bankruptcy, Patent and Copyright Law.
See Professional Biographies, WILMINGTON, DELAWARE

Knothe, Charles S., (BV) .... '44 '81 C.971 B.S.M.E. L.1338 J.D. [C.S.Knothe]
*PRACTICE AREAS: Real Estate Law; Collections; Commercial Law; Wills Law; Estates Law.

Knothe, Charles S., P.A., (BV)
#14 The Commons, 3516 Silverside Road, 19810-4932
Telephone: 302-478-8800 Fax: 302-478-8988
Email: cknothe@compuserve.com
Charles S. Knothe.
Real Estate, Collections, Commercial Law, Wills and Estates, Patent, Trademark and Copyright Law.
See Professional Biographies, WILMINGTON, DELAWARE

Krikelis, Costas S. .... '37 '77 C.688 B.S.E.E. L.1338 J.D. [Ratner&P.]
*PRACTICE AREAS: Intellectual Property Law.
Lambert, William E. '41 '69 C.918 B.A. L.309 LL.B.
(adm. in DC; not adm. in DE) [🄲 Connolly B.L.&H.]

Lew, Jeffrey C. '47 '81 C.186 B.S. L.831 J.D.
Silverside Professional Park, 1403 Silverside Road, 19810
Telephone: 302-475-7919 Fax: 302-475-7915
Email: lawoffice@jlew.com
***PRACTICE AREAS: Patents; Patent Applications; Patent Prosecution; Patent Licensing; Trademarks.**
Intellectual Property Law including: Patent, Trademark, Copyright and Related Matters.
See Professional Biographies, WILMINGTON, DELAWARE

Liss, Morris, (AVⓉ) '40 '70 C.563 B.E.E. L.128 J.D.
(adm. in DC; not adm. in DE) [Connolly B.L.&H.]
*PRACTICE AREAS: Computer and Software Patents; Electrical Patents; Electronic Patents; Mechanical Patents; Patent Licensing.
Lovitz, Michael L. '64 '89 C.659 B.A. L.831 J.D.
(adm. in PA; not adm. in DE) [🄰 Connolly B.L.&H.]
*PRACTICE AREAS: Trademarks; Unfair Competition; Copyrights.
McMorrow, Robert G., Jr. '58 '83 C.152 B.A. L.276 J.D.
(adm. in PA; not adm. in DE) [Connolly B.L.&H.]
McShane, William E. '63 '89 C.205 B.S.Ch.E. L.1338 J.D.
(adm. in PA; not adm. in DE) [Connolly B.L.&H.]
Monroe, Bruce M. .... '40 '96 C.894 A.B. L.1338 J.D. [Ratner&P.]
*PRACTICE AREAS: Intellectual Property; Chemical Intellectual Property.
Olsen, James M. .... '67 '98 C.659 B.S.M.E. L.273 J.D. [🄰 Connolly B.L.&H.]
O'Rourke, Gerard M. .... '67 '94 C.367 B.S. L.884 J.D. [🄰 Connolly B.L.&H.]
Pettit, George R., (BVⓉ) '45 '75 C.431 B.S.E.E. L.1009 J.D.
(adm. in IN; not adm. in DE) [Connolly B.L.&H.]
*PRACTICE AREAS: Electrical Intellectual Property; Intellectual Property Infringement; Intellectual Property Licensing; Computer and Software Patents; Electronic Patents.
Pezzner, Ashley I. .... '59 '90 C.790 B.S. L.64 J.D. [Connolly B.L.&H.]
Pezzner, Harold, (BV) .... '36 '62 C.645 B.S. L.273 J.D. [Connolly B.L.&H.]
Prestia, Paul F., (AVⓉ) '37 '67
C.401 B.S.Ch.E. L.276 J.D. [Ratner&P.] (⊙Valley Forge, PA)
*PRACTICE AREAS: Intellectual Property; Litigation; Dispute Resolution; Patents.

Ratner & Prestia, A Professional Corporation, (AVⓉ)
Suite 209, Webster Building, 3411 Silverside Road, P.O. Box 7228, 19803 ⊙
Telephone: 302-479-9470 Fax: 302-479-9480
Email: mail@ratnerprestia.com URL: http://www.ratnerprestia.com
Kevin W. Goldstein; Costas S. Krikelis (Resident Managing Partner); Bruce M. Monroe;—Rex A. Donnelly, IV. Consulting Attorney: Paul F. Prestia.
Domestic and International Intellectual Property Law including Patent, Trademark, Copyright, Unfair Competition, Trade Secret Matters and Related Litigation, Licensing and Antitrust, Biotechnology, Software and Computer Law, Internet Law, Protection and Entertainment Law.
Valley Forge, Pennsylvania Office: Suite 301, One Westlakes (Berwyn), P.O. Box 980. Telephone: 610-407-0700. Facsimile: 610-407-0701.
Allentown, Pennsylvania Office: Suite 265, Commerce Plaza II, 5100 Tilghman Street. Telephone: 610-530-8100. Fax: 610-530-8200.
See Professional Biographies, WILMINGTON, DELAWARE

Rogowski, Patricia Smink .... '62 '88 C.401 B.S.M.E. L.659 J.D. [Connolly B.L.&H.]

WASHINGTON, 606,900

Abrams, David S., (AV) .... '37 '64 C.446 B.S. L.29 J.D. [Roylance,A.B.&G.]
*PRACTICE AREAS: Litigation; Patent Law; Trademark Law.

Adcock, Eric William .... '71 '00 C.446 B.S. L.273 J.D. [[A] Finnegan,H.F.G.&D.]
*PRACTICE AREAS: Intellectual Property Litigation; Chemical Patents; Patent Litigation; Patent Prosecution; Pharmaceutical Patents.

Adduci, Mastriani & Schaumberg, L.L.P., (AV) [BR]
1200 Seventeenth Street, N.W., Fifth Floor, 20036-3006
Telephone: 202-467-6300 Telefax: 202-466-2006
Email: ams@adduci.com URL: http://www.adduci.com
Barbara A. Murphy;—Michael G. McManus (Not admitted in DC); Sarah E. Hamblin (Not admitted in DC). Of Counsel: Robert A. Westerlund; Raymond H. J. Powell, Jr. (Not admitted in DC).
International Trade, Customs, Trade Regulation, Unfair Competition, Patent, Trademark and Copyright, and Government Contract Law.
A list of Representative Clients and References will be furnished upon request.
See Professional Biographies, WASHINGTON, DISTRICT OF COLUMBIA

Adrian, Stephen G. .... '63 '90 C.575 B.S. L.273 J.D. [Armstrong,W.H.M.&N.]

Ahmad, Aisha '— '97 C.446 BSEE L.989 J.D.
(adm. in MD; not adm. in DC) [[A] Roylance,A.B.&G.]
*PRACTICE AREAS: Patent Prosecution.

Aisenberg, Irwin M., (AV) .... '25 '58 C.119 B.S. L.276 J.D. [Jacobson,H.]
*PRACTICE AREAS: Intellectual Property Law; Biotechnology Patents; Chemical Patents.

Aitken, Andrew C. .... '61 '88 C.423 B.S. L.128 J.D. [Venable,A.B.H.&C.]
*PRACTICE AREAS: Patent Litigation; Patent Prosecution; Medical Patents; Mechanical Patents; Intellectual Property Litigation.

Aitken, Richard L., (AV) .... '30 '56 C.188 B.E.E. L.273 J.D. [Venable,A.B.H.&C.]
*PRACTICE AREAS: Intellectual Property; Patents; Trademarks; Computers and Software; Electronic Patents.

Alapati, Nanda K. .... '59 '94 C.436 B.S.E.E. L.276 J.D. [[A] Pennie&E.]
*PRACTICE AREAS: Intellectual Property; Patent.

Albrecht, Ralph P. .... '65 '97 C.886 B.S.E.E. L.1356 J.D. [[C] Venable,A.B.H.&C.]
*PRACTICE AREAS: Intellectual Property; Patents; Trademarks; Copyrights; Computers and Software.

Alcorn, Linda E. .... '69 '94 C.188 B.S. L.94 J.D. [Sterne,K.G.&F.]
*PRACTICE AREAS: Patent Litigation; Business Methods; Medical Devices; Consumer Products; Civil Appeals.

Ali, Zeba T. '74 '00 C.228 B.S. L.575 J.D.
(adm. in NC; not adm. in DC) [[A] Kenyon&K.]
*PRACTICE AREAS: Intellectual Property.

Alprin, Michael Scott '70 '00 C.164 B.A. L.904 J.D.
(adm. in MD; not adm. in DC) [[A] Armstrong,W.H.M.&N.]
*PRACTICE AREAS: Trademark; Patent Litigation; Research.

Altherr, Robert F., Jr. .... '— '80 C.150 B.S.Ch.E. L.117 J.D. [Banner&W.]
*PRACTICE AREAS: Intellectual Property Litigation; Intellectual Property Law; Patents.

Altmiller, John C., (AV) .... '36 '71 C.884 B.E.E. L.188 J.D. [Kenyon&K.]
*PRACTICE AREAS: Intellectual Property.

Amron, Cory M., (AV) .... '53 '77 C.696 B.A. L.309 J.D. [Vorys,S.S.&P.]
*PRACTICE AREAS: Real Estate; Commercial Law; Trademark Law; Copyright Law; Licensing.

Anderson, Chad C. '75 '00 C.576 B.S.E. L.692 J.D.
(adm. in VA; not adm. in DC) [[A] Venable,A.B.H.&C.]
*PRACTICE AREAS: Patent Prosecution; Intellectual Property Litigation.

Angert, Michael I. .... '61 '99 C.645 B.S.E.E. L.64 J.D. [[A] Kenyon&K.]
*PRACTICE AREAS: Intellectual Property.

Antonelli, Terry, Stout & Kraus, LLP
(See Arlington, Virginia)

Anzalone, Steven M., (BV) .... '57 '84 C.674 B.S.E. L.575 J.D. [Finnegan,H.F.G.&D.]
*PRACTICE AREAS: Patent Infringement.

Armstrong, James E., III, (AV) '29 '57
C.475 B.S.Ch.E. L.446 J.D. [Armstrong,W.H.M.&N.]

Armstrong, James Elwood, IV '72 '97
C.367 B.S. L.30 J.D. [[A] Armstrong,W.H.M.&N.] ⊙
*PRACTICE AREAS: Intellectual Property (100%).

Armstrong, Kara M. .... '66 '91 C.518 A.B. L.880 J.D. [Fisher,C.&S.]
*PRACTICE AREAS: Patent; Trademark; Copyright; Unfair Competition and related Litigation.

Armstrong, Westerman, Hattori, McLeland & Naughton, (AV)
1725 K Street, N.W., Suite 1000, 20006 ⊙
Telephone: 202-659-2930 Facsimile: 202-887-0357 (G.P.III); 202-331-7519 (G.P.III) Video: 202-728-6844
Email: information@armstrongpat.com URL: http://www.armstrongpat.com
James E. Armstrong, III; William F. Westerman; Ken-Ichi Hattori; William G. Kratz, Jr. (Resident, Pittsburgh, Pennsylvania); Mel R. Quintos; Donald W. Hanson; Stephen G. Adrian; Scott M. Daniels; William Lee Brooks. Associates: John P. Kong; James Elwood Armstrong, IV; Sadao Kinashi; Nicolas E. Seckel (Not admitted in DC); Thomas E. Brown (Not admitted in DC); Michael Scott Alprin (Not admitted in DC); Joseph L. Felber; Kenneth Harry Salen (Not admitted in DC). Of Counsel: Le-Nhung McLeland; Ronald F. Naughton (Not admitted in DC); Edward F. Welsh (Resident at Pittsburgh, Pennsylvania Office); Michael J. Caridi.
Languages: Japanese, French and Filipino.
Patent, Trademark, Copyright and Unfair Competition Law. Other Matters Involving Technology and Related Litigation in all Courts and Administrative Agencies including The U.S. International Trade Commission. United States and International Patent and Trademark Law.
Pittsburgh, Pennsylvania Office: 429 Fourth Avenue, Suite 707. Telephone: 412-281-2931. Facsimile: 412-281-1821.
See Professional Biographies, WASHINGTON, DISTRICT OF COLUMBIA

Arpin, James B. .... '59 '89 C.659 B.A.S./B.S.E. L.94 J.D. [Baker B.]

Articola, Phillip John .... '— '94 C&L.446 M.S.E.E., J.D. [[A] Foley&L.]
*PRACTICE AREAS: Intellectual Property; Computer Law; Communications Law; Semiconductor Technology.

Babayi, Robert S. .... '59 '92 C.1222 B.S.E.E. L.472 J.D. [[C] Venable,A.B.H.&C.]
*PRACTICE AREAS: Intellectual Property; Patent Prosecution; Technology Licensing.

Bachrach, Max '68 '98 C.178 B.A. L.893 J.D.
(adm. in VA; not adm. in DC) [[A] Pennie&E.]
*PRACTICE AREAS: Patent Prosecution; Patent Litigation; Pharmaceutical Patents.

Badagliacca, Michael John '71 '97 C.188 B.S. L.990 J.D.
(adm. in NY; not adm. in DC) [[A] Staas&H.]
*PRACTICE AREAS: Intellectual Property.

Bailey, Suzin C. '60 '93 C.101 B.S. L.273 J.D.
(adm. in MD; not adm. in DC) [[A] Jacobson,H.]
*PRACTICE AREAS: Patent Prosecution; Litigation; Trademark; Copyright.

Bain, John W. .... '55 '98 C.679 B.S.E.E. L.345 J.D. [[A] Sughrue M.]
*PRACTICE AREAS: Intellectual Property.

Bajefsky, Robert D., (AV) .... '43 '70 C.886 B.S.Ch.E. L.276 J.D. [Finnegan,H.F.G.&D.]
*PRACTICE AREAS: Biotechnology Patents; Chemical Patents; Medical Patents; Patent Litigation; Pharmaceutical Patents.

Baker Botts, L.L.P., (AV) [BR]
A Registered Limited Liability Partnership
The Warner, 1299 Pennsylvania Avenue, N.W., 20004-2400 ⊙
Telephone: 202-639-7700 Fax: 202-639-7832
Email: postmaster@bakerbotts.com URL: http://www.bakerbotts.com
Special Counsel: James B. Arpin; Jay M. Cantor.
Patent, Trademark, Copyright and Unfair Competition Law.
Houston, Texas Office: One Shell Plaza, 910 Louisiana. Telephone: 713-229-1234.
Austin, Texas Office: 1600 San Jacinto Center, 98 San Jacinto Boulevard. Telephone: 512-322-2500.

(This Listing Continued)

Baker Botts, L.L.P. (Continued)
Dallas, Texas Office: 2001 Ross Avenue. Telephone: 214-953-6500.
New York, New York Office: 599 Lexington Avenue. Telephone: 212-705-5000.
London, England Office: 45 Ludgate Hill. Telephone: 0171-778-1400 (Local); 011-44-171-778-1400 (International).
Baku, Azerbaijan Office: 6-10 Vagif Mustafa-zadeh Street, Third Floor, Icheri Sheher, 370004. Telephone: 994-12-97-63-88 (Local); 011-994-12-97-63-88 (International). Fax: 994-12-97-63-91 (Local); 011-994-12-97-63-91 (International).
Associated Firm: Mohammed Bin Saud Al Rasheed, Attorneys and Legal Consultants, Le Cygne Commercial Center, No. 2, Olaya, Main Road, P.O. Box 62982, Riyadh 11595, Saudi Arabia. Telephone: (966-1) 464-3139. Facsimile: (966-1) 464-9264.
See Professional Biographies, WASHINGTON, DISTRICT OF COLUMBIA

Banner, Brian E. .... '— '74 C.37 B.S.B.A. L.365 J.D. [Banner&W.]
*PRACTICE AREAS: Intellectual Property Law; Trademarks; Copyrights; Intellectual Property Licensing.

Banner, Donald W., (AV) .... '— '53 C.679 B.S.E.E. L.215 J.D. [Banner&W.]
*PRACTICE AREAS: Intellectual Property Law; Patents; Intellectual Property Litigation; Intellectual Property Licensing.

Banner, Pamela I., (AV) .... '— '87 C.679 B.S.E.E. L.273 J.D. [Banner&W.]
*PRACTICE AREAS: Intellectual Property Law; Patents; Intellectual Property Litigation; Appellate Practice; Electrical Intellectual Property.

Banner & Witcoff, Ltd., (AV) [BR]
Established In 1920 - Predecessor Parent
1001 G Street, N.W., 20001-4597 ⊙
Telephone: 202-508-9100 Facsimile: 202-508-9299
Email: cooperman@bannerwitcoff.com URL: http://www.bannerwitcoff.com
Robert F. Altherr, Jr.; Brian E. Banner; Donald W. Banner; Pamela I. Banner; Gary D. Fedorochko; William J. Fisher; Christopher R. Glembocki; Brian E. Hanlon; Patricia E. Hong; Dale H. Hoscheit; Thomas H. Jackson; Sarah A. Kagan; Robert S. Katz; Christopher L. McKee; Nina L. Medlock; Frederic M. Meeker; Helen Hill Minsker; Thomas L. Peterson; Joseph M. Potenza; Steven P. Schad; Joseph M. Skerpon; Susan A. Wolffe; Bradley C. Wright. Of Counsel: William W. Beckett; Edward F. McKie, Jr.; William F. Rauchholz; Douglas W. Robinson; Franklin D. Wolffe. Associates: Steve S. Chang; Joseph P. Curtin; Michael David (Not admitted in DC); Catherine A. Ferguson; Lisa M. Hemmendinger; Lin J. Hymel (Not admitted in DC); Richard C. Irving; Anthony W. Kandare (Not admitted in DC); David S. Lee (Not admitted in DC); Darrell Gilbert Mottley (Not admitted in DC); Ajay S. Pathak; Paul M. Rivard; Christopher B. Roth.
Intellectual Property including Procurement of Patents, Trademarks, Copyrights, Trade Secrets, Counseling & Opinions, Unfair Competition, Interferences, Licensing, Antitrust and International Trade Matters. Litigation including Trials and Appeals in Federal and State Courts and International Trade Commission.
Chicago, Illinois Office: Ten South Wacker Drive. Telephone: 312-715-1000. Facsimile: 312-715-1234.
Boston, Massachusetts Office: 28 State Street, 28th Floor. Telephone: 617-227-7111. Fax: 617-227-4399.
Portland, Oregon Office: 601 SW Second Avenue, Suite 1900. Telephone: 503-279-6330. Fax: 503-279-6328.
See Professional Biographies, WASHINGTON, DISTRICT OF COLUMBIA

Banowit, Donald R. .... '73 '98 C.477 B.S.E. L.276 J.D. [[A] Sterne,K.G.&F.]
*PRACTICE AREAS: Intellectual Property.

Barash, Eyal Hanan .... '69 '97 C.347 B.S., B.A. L.597 J.D. [[A] Finnegan,H.F.G.&D.]
*PRACTICE AREAS: Chemical Intellectual Property; Pharmaceutical Intellectual Property.

Barner, Kevin M. '65 '97 C.205 B.E.E. L.64 J.D.
(adm. in MD; not adm. in DC) [[A] Sughrue M.]
*PRACTICE AREAS: Intellectual Property.

Barnes & Thornburg, (AV) [BR]
750 17th Street, N.W. Suite 900, 20006 ⊙
Telephone: 202-289-1313 FAX: 202-289-1330
URL: http://www.btlaw.com
Resident Partners: Perry Palan; Joseph D. Lewis. Of Counsel: Mark M. Newman; Paul E. Fahrenkopf (Not admitted in DC).
Acquisitions and Mergers, Antitrust, Chemical Intellectual Property, Copyrights, Electrical Intellectual Property, Electronic Intellectual Property, Franchise Licensing, Intellectual Property Arbitration, Intellectual Property Infringement, Intellectual Property Litigation, Intellectual Property Portfolio Management, Intellectual Property Licensing, International Intellectual Property, Literary Property, Mechanical Intellectual Property, Medical Intellectual Property, Patents, Patent Litigation, Patent Protection, Pharmaceutical Intellectual Property, Proprietary Rights, Protection of Personality, Software Licensing, Taxation of Intellectual Property, Trademarks, Trademark Litigation, Trademark Registration.
Representative Intellectual Property Clients: Center for Employment Security Education and Research Inc.; Hillenbrand Industries, Inc.; Kistler Instrumente AG; Knorr-Bremse AG; New York Air Brake Company; Paul Reed Smith Guitars; Porter Athletic Equipment Company; Scient Corp.; Society of Government Travel Professionals.
Indianapolis, Indiana Office: 11 South Meridian Street, 46204. Telephone: 317-236-1313. FAX: 317-231-7433.
Fort Wayne, Indiana Office: 600 One Summit Square, 46802. Telephone: 260-423-9440. FAX: 260-424-8316.
South Bend, Indiana Office: 600 1st Source Bank Center, 100 North Michigan, 46601-1632. Telephone: 574-233-1171. FAX: 574-237-1125.
Elkhart, Indiana Office: 121 West Franklin Street, Suite 200, 46516. Telephone: 574-293-0681. FAX: 574-296-2535.
Chicago, Illinois Office: 2600 Chase Plaza, 10 South LaSalle Street, 60603. Telephone: 312-357-1313. FAX: 312-759-5646.
See Professional Biographies, WASHINGTON, DISTRICT OF COLUMBIA

Barney, James R. '68 '00 C.871 B.S. L.976 J.D.
(adm. in VA; not adm. in DC) [[A] Finnegan,H.F.G.&D.]
*PRACTICE AREAS: Patent Litigation; Chemical Intellectual Property; Pharmaceutical Intellectual Property.

Bateman, John W. .... '65 '90 C&L.893 B.A., J.D. [Kenyon&K.]
*PRACTICE AREAS: Intellectual Property.

Beck, George C. .... '— '93 C&L.276 B.S., J.D. [[C] Foley&L.]
*PRACTICE AREAS: Intellectual Property.

Beckers, J. Randall, (AV) .... '52 '80 C.10 B.S.E.E. L.192 J.D. [Staas&H.]
*PRACTICE AREAS: Intellectual Property Law; Patent, Trademark, Copyright and Unfair Competition.

Beckett, William W., (AV) .... '— '56 C.152 B.S. L.273 J.D. [[C] Banner&W.]
*PRACTICE AREAS: Intellectual Property Law; Patents; Trademarks; Intellectual Property Licensing.

Beddard, Cameron W. '67 '01 C.910 B.S.E.E. L.276 J.D.
(adm. in MD; not adm. in DC) [[A] Sughrue M.]
*PRACTICE AREAS: Patent Law.

Behringer, John W., (AV) ..... '38 '68 C.201 B.S.Chem. L.273 J.D. [Fitzpatrick,C.H.&S.]

Bell, Michael J. .... '59 '89 C.602 B.S.M.E. L.276 J.D. [Howrey S.A.&W.]
*PRACTICE AREAS: Intellectual Property.

Belz, John M. .... '48 '80 C.502 B.S.E.E. L.846 J.D. [Leydig,V.&M.]

Bent, Stephen A., (AV) .... '— '81 C.231 B.S. L.273 J.D. [Foley&L.]
*PRACTICE AREAS: Biotechnology; Pharmaceutical; Intellectual Property.

Berdo, Robert H., (AV) .... '30 '60 C.352 B.S. L.273 J.D. [Roylance,A.B.&G.]
*PRACTICE AREAS: Patent Law; Pharmaceutical Patent Law; Chemical Patent Law.

Berkowitz, Jeffrey A. .... '63 '88 C.705 B.A. L.1325 J.D. [Finnegan,H.F.G.&D.]
*PRACTICE AREAS: Patent Prosecution; Computer and Software Patents; Software Copyright.

Berman, Paul J., (AV) .... '51 '75 C&L.309 A.B., J.D. [Covington&B.]

Bernstein, Frank L., (AV) .... '59 '84 C.111 B.S. L.966 J.D. [Sughrue M.] ⊙
*PRACTICE AREAS: Intellectual Property Law; Litigation.

Bernstein, Howard L., (P.C.), (AV) ......'43 '69 C.563 B.E.E. L.1009 J.D. [Sughrue M.]
*PRACTICE AREAS: Intellectual Property Law; Litigation.

Best, George C. '— '97 C&L.145 S.B., J.D.
(adm. in IL; not adm. in DC) [[A] Foley&L.]
*PRACTICE AREAS: Intellectual Property.

Bhatt, Minaksi .... '63 '90 C.914 B.A. L.273 J.D. [⊡ Rothwell,F.E.&M.]
*PRACTICE AREAS: Intellectual Property Litigation.

Bicks, Mark S., (AV) .... '48 '77 C.588 B.S.M.E. L.128 J.D. [Roylance,A.B.&G.]
*PRACTICE AREAS: Litigation; Patent Law; Trademark Law; Copyright Law; Mechanical Patent Law.

Bird, John M. '73 '00 C&L.446 B.S.M.E., J.D.
(adm. in MD; not adm. in DC) [🄰 Sughrue M.]
*PRACTICE AREAS: Patents.

Bjorge, Gerald H., (AV) .... '37 '66 C.597 B.S.Ch.E. L.273 LL.B. [⊡ Keil&W.]
*PRACTICE AREAS: Patents; Trademark Law.

Blank Rome Comisky & McCauley LLP, (AV)
The Farragut Building, 900 17th Street, N.W., Suite 1000, 20006 ⊙
Telephone: 202-530-7400 FAX: 202-463-6915
Email: webmaster@blankrome.com URL: http://www.blankrome.com
Resident Members: Herbert Cohen; Susan B. Flohr; Michael C. Greenbaum; Victor M. Wigman; Charles R. Wolfe, Jr. Senior, Special and Of Counsel: Donald R. Greene; George C. Myers, Jr. (Not admitted in DC); Michael D. White. Resident Associates: David J. Edmondson (Not admitted in DC); Brian C. Jones; Denise Catherine Lane (Not admitted in DC); Peter S. Weissman.
Administrative Law, Administrative Adjudications; Administrative Agency Practice, Administrative Hearings and Appeals, Administrative Litigation, Federal Administrative Law, Professional Licensing, Professional Licensing Regulation, Public Law, Admiralty and Maritime Law, Marine Law, Maritime Contracts, Maritime Finance, Maritime Law, Maritime Liens, Ship Sales and Mortgages, Aged and Aging, Age Discrimination, Elder Care, Elder Law, Agency and Distributorships, Distribution Agreements, International Distribution, Alcoholic Beverages, Liquor Licensing, Alternative Dispute Resolution, Arbitration, International Arbitration, International Dispute Resolution, Mediation, Antitrust and Trade Regulation, Antitrust, Business Combinations, Competition, Covenants Not To Compete, Deceptive Trade Practices, Noncompetition and Non-Solicitation Agreements, Price-Fixing, Restrictive Covenants, Trade Regulation, Unfair Trade, Appellate Practice, Civil Appeals, Art Law, Artists Rights, Museum Law, Asset Protection, International Asset Protection, Aviation and Aerospace, Aircraft Finance and Leasing, Aircraft Sales, Airline Labor Law, Aviation Law, Aviation Defense, Aviation Insurance, Aviation Litigation, Aviation Products Liability, Aviation Regulation, Bankruptcy, Bankruptcy Arbitration, Bankruptcy Chapter 7, Bankruptcy Chapter 11, Bankruptcy Chapter 12, Bankruptcy Chapter 13, Bankruptcy Collections, Bankruptcy Litigation, Bankruptcy Mediation, Bankruptcy Reorganization, Bankruptcy Taxation, Bankruptcy Trustees Rights, Commercial Bankruptcy, Commercial Foreclosure, Commercial Insolvency, Commercial Recovery, Commercial Workouts, Foreclosures, Fraudulent Conveyance, Insolvency, International Bankruptcy, International Insolvency, Liquidations, Out of Court Debt Restructuring, Pre-Bankruptcy Workouts, Receiverships, Repossessions, Workouts, Workouts Taxation, Banks and Banking, ATM Networks, Bank Collections, Bank Directors and Officers Liability, Bank Foreclosures, Bank Mergers and Acquisitions, Banking Antitrust, Banking Law, Banking Litigation, Commercial Banking, Commercial Credit, Commercial Loans, Consumer Banking, Credit Card Law, Credit Finance, Credit Law, Electronic Banking, Fair Lending, Financial Law, Interest and Usury, International Banking Law, International Loans, Lender Law, Lender Liability, Lender Regulation, Lenders Rights, Letters of Credit, Loan Restructuring, Loan Workouts, Loans, Savings and Loan Law, Secured Lending, Truth in Lending, Biotechnology, Biomedical Technology, Biotechnology Licensing, Business Law, Business Arbitration, Business Associations Law, Business Crimes, Business Development, Business Dissolutions, Business Estate Planning, Business Formation, Business Fraud, Business Litigation, Business Mediation, Business Organization, Business Planning, Business Regulation, Business Reorganization, Business Sales, Business Succession Planning, Business Successions, Business Syndication, Business Taxation, Business Torts, Business Transactions, Business Transfers, Business Trusts, Business Valuation, Buying and Selling of Businesses, Capital Formation, Closely Held Business Estate Planning, Closely Held Business Law, Closely Held Business Taxation, Complex Business Litigation, Emerging Business Law, Emerging Growth Companies, Entrepreneurial Business Law, Family Business Law, Family Business Mediation, Family Business Successions, International Business Law, International Joint Ventures, Joint Ventures, Limited Liability Company Law, Privatization, Professional Practices, Small Business Law, Sole Proprietorships, Strategic Alliances, Chancery and Equity, Chancery Practice, Children, Child Custody, Child Support, Civil Practice, Federal Civil Practice, Sex Discrimination, Commercial Collections, Post Judgment Collections, Commercial Law, Commercial Litigation, Complex Commercial Litigation, Secured Transactions, Uniform Commercial Code, Commercial Real Estate, Commercial Real Estate Acquisitions, Commercial Real Estate Development, Commercial Real Estate Finance, Commercial Real Estate Foreclosure, Commercial Real Estate Sales, Commercial Real Estate Syndication, Commercial Real Estate Workouts, Industrial Real Estate Law, Shopping Center Acquisitions, Shopping Center Development, Shopping Center Law, Complex and Multi-District Litigation, Computers and Software, Computer Contracts, Computer Law, Computer Security, Computer Software Law, Computer Technology, Electronic Commerce, Information Technology, Information Technology Contracts, Information Technology Licensing, International Computer Law, Internet Law, Software Copyright, Software Licensing, Software Protection, Year 2000 Computer Conversion, Constitutional Law, First Amendment Law, Construction Law, Construction Finance, Construction Litigation, Construction Workouts, Environmental Construction Law, International Construction Law, Public Construction Law, Consumer Law, Consumer Arbitration, Consumer Class Actions, Consumer Credit, Consumer Credit Compliance, Consumer Finance, Consumer Fraud, Consumer Litigation, Consumer Protection, Consumer Rights, Fair Credit Reporting Act, Contracts, Breach of Contract, Commercial Contracts, Contract Fraud, Contract Litigation, International Commercial Contracts, International Contracts, Copyrights, Copyright Infringement, Copyright Litigation, Copyright Prosecution, Copyright Protection, Copyright Registration, International Copyright Law, Corporate Law, Closely Held Corporations, Corporate Banking Law, Corporate Commercial Law, Corporate Contracts, Corporate Control Contests, Corporate Criminal Law, Corporate Dissolutions, Corporate Ethics, Corporate Fiduciary Law, Corporate Finance, Corporate Formation, Corporate Governance, Corporate Income Tax, Corporate Insurance, Corporate Insurance Defense, Corporate Investigations, Corporate Litigation, Corporate Organization, Corporate Partnerships, Corporate Planning, Corporate Real Estate, Corporate Reorganization, Corporate Successions, Corporate Tax Controversies, Corporate Tax Planning, Corporate Taxation, Corporate Trusts, Corporate Workouts, Family Corporations, Foreign Sales Corporations, Hostile Takeovers, Incorporation, International Corporate Finance, International Corporate Law, International Corporate Taxation, Nonprofit Corporations, Offshore Corporations, Professional Corporations; Proxy Contests, Public Corporations, S Corporations, Securitization, Small Business Corporations, Takeovers, Tender Offers, Transfer Pricing, Criminal Law, Debtor and Creditor, Creditor Bankruptcy, Creditors Rights, Creditors Rights in Bankruptcy, Debtor and Creditor Bankruptcy, Debtor and Creditor Collections, Debtor and Creditor Remedies, Debtor and Creditor Reorganization, Debtor and Creditor Rights, Debtor and Creditor Workouts, Debtor Bankruptcy, International Creditors Rights, Secured Creditors Rights, Unsecured Creditors Rights, Disabilities, Americans with Disabilities Act, Academic Employment, College and University Law, Administrative Lobbying, Executive Lobbying, Legislative Lobbying, Lobbying, Eminent Domain, Employee Benefits, COBRA, Deferred Compensation, Employee Benefit Taxation, Employee Benefit Trusts, Employee Compensation, Employee Stock Ownership Plans, ERISA, Executive Compensation, Executive Compensation Taxation, Flexible Benefit Plans, Multi-Employer Benefits, Multi-Employer Pensions, Non-Qualified Benefits, Pension and Profit Sharing Plans, Pension Plans, Pension Taxation, Profit Sharing, Public Pension Plans, Qualified Retirement Plans, Retirement Benefit Plans, Taft-Hartley Plans, Unemployment Compensation, Music Copyright, Environmental Law, Environmental Compliance, Environmental Liability, Environmental Litigation, Environmental Mediation, International Environmental Law, Equipment Finance and Leasing, Equipment Finance, Equipment Leasing, Vehicle Leasing, Family Law, Divorce, Matrimonial Law, Finance, Asset Based Finance, Financial Institution Reorganization, Financial Institutions Law, Financial Institutions Taxation, Financial Restructuring, International Commercial Finance, International Finance, Franchises and Franchising, Franchise Law, Franchise Licensing, Franchise Litigation, Franchise Taxation, International Franchising, General Practice, Federal Practice, Government, County Government Law, Federal Government Law, Government Affairs, Government Agency Practice, Government Relations, Legislative Practice, Local Government Law, Public Policy, Qui Tam Litigation, State Government Law, State Legislative Practice, Township Law, Government Contracts, Government Construction Contracts, Government Contract Arbitration, Government Contract Fraud, Government Procurement, International Government Contracts, Local Government Contracts, Public Bidding, Public Contract Law, Public Works Contracts, Guardianship and Conservatorship, Health Care, Alternative Health Care Delivery System, Certificates of Need, Health Care Administration, Health Care Contracts, Health Care Corporate Law, Health Care Facility Licensing, Health Care Facility Regulation, Health Care Finance, Health Care Fraud, Health Care Legislation, Health Care Licensing, Health Care Mergers and Acquisitions, Health Care Regulation, Health Care Reimbursement, Health Care Taxation, Health Insurance, Health Insurance Coverage, Health Insurance Defense, Health Insurance Trusts, Health Law, Health Maintenance Organizations, Integrated Health Care Delivery Systems, Long Term Care, Managed Care, Managed Care Contracts, Medical Antitrust, Mental Health Law, Nursing Home Regulation, Pharmacy Law, Physicians Contracts, Hospital Law, Hospital Administration, Medical Staff Contracts, Medical Staff Credentialing, Housing Law, Affordable Housing, Apartment Projects, Housing Finance, Insurance, Commercial Insurance, Insurance Company Taxation, Insurance Litigation,

(This Listing Continued)

Blank Rome Comisky & McCauley LLP (Continued)

Insurance Defense, Intellectual Property, Artistic Property, Chemical Intellectual Property, Electrical Intellectual Property, Intellectual Property Infringement, Intellectual Property Licensing, Intellectual Property Litigation, International Intellectual Property, International Licensing, Mechanical Intellectual Property, Medical Intellectual Property, Pharmaceutical Intellectual Property, Piracy, Proprietary Rights, Taxation of Intellectual Property, International Law, International Trade, Anti-dumping, Countervailing Duties, Customs Law, Export Regulation, Import and Export Law, International Trade Regulation, Latin America Trade, Russia Trade, Investments, Financial Services Law, Financial Services Regulation, Foreign Investment, Foreign Investment in the United States, International Investment, Investment Banking Law, Investment Company Law, Investment Partnerships, Investment Regulation, Labor and Employment, Affirmative Action, Collective Bargaining, Employee Drug Testing, Employer Liability, Employment at Will, Employment Contracts, Employment Discrimination, Employment Litigation, Employment Mediation, Executive Employment Law, Executive Severance Contracts, Fair Labor Standards, Family and Medical Leave Act, Federal Employment Law, Harassment, International Employment Contracts, International Labor Law, Labor Arbitration, Management Labor Law, National Labor Relations Act, Personnel Policies, Public Sector Collective Bargaining, Public Sector Labor Relations, Sexual Harassment, Unfair Labor Practices, Union Contract Negotiations, Union Elections, Union Organization, Wage and Hour Law, WARN Act, Workplace Violence, Wrongful Termination Defense, Leases and Leasing, Commercial Leasing, International Leasing, Landlord and Tenant Law, Lease Finance, Leasing, Leveraged Leasing, Office Leasing, Retail Leasing, Shopping Center Leasing, Legal Ethics and Professional Responsibility, Legal Ethics, Litigation, Civil Litigation, Complex Litigation, Defense Litigation, Federal Civil Litigation, Federal Litigation, International Litigation, Long-Arm Litigation, Trial Practice, U.S. Supreme Court Litigation, Newspaper Contracts, Publishing Contracts, Medical Malpractice, Medicare and Medicaid, Medicaid Planning, Medicare and Medicaid Reimbursement, Medicare Fraud and Abuse, Mergers, Acquisitions and Divestitures, Business Acquisitions, Business Divestitures, International Mergers and Acquisitions, Leveraged Acquisitions, Leveraged Buyouts, Merger Reorganization, Mergers and Acquisitions, Mergers and Acquisitions Finance, Mortgages, Commercial Mortgages, Mortgage Banking Law, Mortgage Bankruptcy, Mortgage Finance, Mortgage Foreclosure, Mortgage Insurance, Mortgage Lien Foreclosure, Mortgage Refinancing, Mortgage Securitization, Mortgage Tax, Mortgage Workouts, Secondary Mortgage Market, Municipal Bonds, Municipal Bonds Taxation, Municipal Contracts, Municipal Corporation Law, Municipal Derivative Products, Municipal Finance, Municipal Labor Law, Municipal Leasing, Municipal Pension Law, Municipal Redevelopment, Municipal Securities, Municipal Taxation, Tax Increment Finance, Natural Resources, Nonprofit and Charitable Organizations, Charitable Limited Partnerships, Charitable Organizations Law, Charitable Trusts and Foundations, Nonprofit Organizations Law, Nonprofit Tax Law, Private Foundations, Tax Exempt Organizations, Occupational Safety and Health, OSHA, Partnership Law, Family Limited Partnerships, Family Partnerships, Limited Liability Partnerships, Limited Partnerships, Partnership Dissolution, Partnership Formation, Partnership Organization, Partnership Syndication, Partnership Taxation, Patents, Biochemical Patents, Biotechnology Patent Prosecution, Biotechnology Patents, Chemical Patent Prosecution, Chemical Patents, Computer and Software Patents, Design Patents, Electrical Patent Prosecution, Electrical Patents, Electronic Patents, International Patents, Mechanical Patent Prosecution, Mechanical Patents, Medical Patents, Metallurgical Patents, Molecular Biology Patents, Patent Applications, Patent Infringement, Patent Interference Practice, Patent Licensing, Patent Litigation, Patent Prosecution, Patent Protection, Pharmaceutical Patents, Personal Injury, Premises Security, Probate, Ancillary Probate, International Probate, Probate Administration, Probate Litigation, Probate Taxation, Products Liability, Drug and Medical Device Defense, Firearms Products Liability, Professional Liability, Public Finance, Bond Finance, Economic Development, Housing and Urban Development, Industrial Development, International Economic Development, International Project Finance, Project Finance, Public Authority Finance, Public Finance Taxation, Public-Private Development, Tax Exempt Bonds, Tax Exempt Finance, Railway Labor Law, Real Estate, Condominium Association Law, Condominium Conversions, Condominium Development, Condominium Law, Conveyancing, Cooperative Association Law, Cooperative Conversions, Cooperative Housing Law, Easements, International Real Estate, Land Acquisitions, Land Sales, Land Trusts, Planned Unit Development Law, Real Estate Acquisitions, Real Estate Arbitration, Real Estate Banking Law, Real Estate Bankruptcy, Real Estate Brokers Licensing, Real Estate Contracts, Real Estate Development, Real Estate Finance, Real Estate Foreclosure, Real Estate Investment, Real Estate Investment Taxation, Real Estate Investment Trusts, Real Estate Joint Ventures, Real Estate Leasing, Real Estate Litigation, Real Estate Mediation, Real Estate Partnerships, Real Estate Restructuring, Real Estate Sales, Real Estate Secured Lending, Real Estate Securities, Real Estate Settlements, Real Estate Syndication, Real Estate Tax Appeals, Real Estate Tax Assessment, Real Estate Taxation, Real Estate Title, Real Estate Transfers, Real Estate Valuation, Real Estate Workouts, Real Property, Real Property Acquisitions, Real Property Development, Real Property Finance, Residential Real Estate, Residential Real Estate Development, Waterfront Development, Regulatory Law, Drug and Medical Device Regulation, Federal Regulatory Law, Regulated Industries, Regulatory Agency Practice, Regulatory Investigations, Religious Nonprofit Corporation Law, RICO, Securities, Bank Securities, Broker-Dealer Arbitration, Broker-Dealer Regulation, Initial Public Offerings, Private Placement, Private Placement Syndication, Public Offerings, SEC Enforcement, Securities Arbitration, Securities Litigation, Securities Offerings, Securities Registration, Securities Regulation, Shareholder Agreements, Shareholder Disputes, Tax Exempt Securities, Sports Contracts, Sports Licensing, Taxation, Employment Tax, Estate and Gift Taxation, Federal Income Tax, Federal Tax Controversies, Federal Taxation, Fiduciary Income Tax, Income Tax, Individual Taxation, International Tax Controversies, International Taxation, Like Kind Exchanges, Local Taxation, Low Income Housing Tax Credits, Property Tax Abatement, Property Tax Appeals, Sales and Use Tax, State Taxation, Tax Appeals, Tax Audits, Tax Collection, Tax Deferred Exchanges, Tax Planning, Tax Shelters, Trusts and Estates Taxation, Electronics, High Technology Contracts, Semiconductor Technology, Technology Contracts, Technology Licensing, Technology Protection, Technology Transfers, Torts, Trade Association Law, Toxic Torts, Trade Secrets, Theft of Trade Secrets, Trademarks, International Trademarks, Trade Dress, Trade Names, Trademark Arbitration, Trademark Infringement, Trademark Licensing, Trademark Litigation, Trademark Prosecution, Trademark Protection, Trademark Registration, Transportation, Common Carrier Law, Mass Transit Law, Public Transportation Law, Transit Labor, Trusts and Estates, Decedents Estates, Estate Administration, Estate Litigation, Estate Planning, Family Trusts, Family Wealth Transfer, Fiduciary Law, Fiduciary Liability, Fiduciary Litigation, Financial Planning, International Estate Planning, International Trusts, Living Trusts, Offshore Trusts, Personal Planning, Retirement Planning, Trust Administration, Trust Law, Trust Litigation, Trust Planning, Wealth Preservation, Unfair Competition, Utility Law, Utility Acquisitions, Utility Contracts, Utility Taxation, White Collar Crime, Embezzlement, White Collar Criminal Defense, White Collar Fraud, Wills, Contested Wills, Inheritance, Living Wills, Successions, Zoning, Planning and Land Use, Building and Public Safety Codes, Cemetery Law, Environmental Land Use, Fire Districts, Improvement Districts, Land Conservation, Land Development, Land Entitlement, Land Use, Land Use Litigation, Land Use Permitting, Land Use Regulation, Rezoning, Special Districts, Subdivisions, Water Districts, Zoning Law, Zoning Variances, Retail Industry Development.
Media, Pennsylvania Office: Rose Tree Corporate Center, 1400 N. Providence Road, Building 1, Suite 301, 19063. Telephone: 610-891-7800. FAX: 610-891-7804.
Philadelphia, Pennsylvania Office: One Logan Square, 19103-6998. Telephone: 215-569-5500. FAX: 215-569-5555.
Cherry Hill, New Jersey Office: Woodland Falls Corporate Park, 210 Lake Drive East, Suite 200, 08002-1164. Telephone: 856-779-3600. FAX: 856-779-7647.
Boca Raton, Florida Office: 1200 North Federal Highway, Suite 417, 33432. Telephone: 561-417-8100. FAX: 561-417-8101.
Allentown, Pennsylvania Office: 1620 Pond Road, Suite 200, 18104-2255. Telephone: 610-706-4300. FAX: 610-706-4343.
Wilmington, Delaware Office: Chase Manhattan Centre, 1201 Market Street, Suite 800, 19801. Telephone: 302-425-6400. FAX: 302-425-6464.
Trenton, New Jersey Office: 200 West State Street, 08608. Telephone: 609-278-2320. FAX: 609-278-2323.
Baltimore, Maryland Office: 250 West Pratt Street, Suite 1100, 21201. Telephone: 410-659-1400. FAX: 410-659-1414.
New York, New York Office: The Chrysler Building, 405 Lexington Avenue, 10174. Telephone: 212-885-5000. FAX: 212-885-5001.
Cincinnati, Ohio Office: PNC Center, 201 East Fifth Street, Suite 1700, 45202. Telephone: 513-362-8700. Fax: 513-362-8787.

See Professional Biographies, WASHINGTON, DISTRICT OF COLUMBIA

Bleeker, Ronald A., (AV) .... '49 '74 C&L.178 B.S., J.D. [Finnegan,H.F.G.&D.]
*PRACTICE AREAS: Intellectual Property Litigation.

Blumenthal, David A., (AV) ..... '— '74 C.945 B.S. L.273 J.D. [Foley&L.] (⊙L.A., CA)
*PRACTICE AREAS: Intellectual Property.

Boalick, Scott R. .... '65 '99 C.659 B.S.E. L.276 J.D. [🄰 Fish&R.]

Bodendorf, Andrew F. '68 '98 C.228 B.S.E.E.
(adm. in VA; not adm. in DC) [Ⓐ Fish&R.]
*PRACTICE AREAS: Intellectual Property.

Boland, Mark, (AV) .... '60 '85 C.321 B.A. L.128 J.D. [Sughrue M.]
*PRACTICE AREAS: Intellectual Property Law; Litigation.

Boland, Thomas R., (AV) .... '36 '66 C.754 B.S. L.276 J.D. [Vorys,S.S.&P.]
*PRACTICE AREAS: Intellectual Properties Law; Licensing Law; Trade Secret Law; Litigation.

Bookoff, Leslie I. .... '68 '93 C.446 B.S. L.659 J.D. [Ⓐ Finnegan,H.F.G.&D.]
*PRACTICE AREAS: Intellectual Property Portfolio Management; Intellectual Property Litigation; Mechanical Intellectual Property; Medical Intellectual Property; Patent Prosecution.

Bosch, Michele C. .... '68 '93 C.893 B.A. L.945 J.D. [Ⓐ Finnegan,H.F.G.&D.]
*PRACTICE AREAS: Pharmaceutical Patents; Chemical Patents; Biochemical Patents; Patent Interference Practice; Patent Prosecution.

Boss, Brandon '73 '98 C.546 B.A. L.861 J.D.
(adm. in LA; not adm. in DC) [Ⓐ Smith,G.&R.]
*PRACTICE AREAS: Patent; Trademarks.

Boughner, Stephen T. '71 '98 C&L.8 B.S.E.E., J.D.
(adm. in OH; not adm. in DC) [Ⓐ Staas&H.]
*PRACTICE AREAS: Intellectual Property; Patents; Trademarks; Copyrights.

Bowditch, Mark I. .... '63 '93 C&L.273 B.S., J.D. [Ⓒ Rothwell,F.E.&M.]

Boyd, Walter Y., Jr., (AV) .... '56 '84 C.240 B.A. L.574 J.D. [Finnegan,H.F.G.&D.]
*PRACTICE AREAS: Patent Prosecution; Patent Licensing.

Boyle, James J. .... '64 '99 C.1172 B.S. L.893 J.D. [Ⓐ Finnegan,H.F.G.&D.]
*PRACTICE AREAS: Patent Prosecution; Patent Protection; Electronics; Fiber Optics; Physics.

Bradley, William E. .... '69 '98 C.1369 B.S. L.1209 J.D. [Ⓐ Fulbright&J.]
*PRACTICE AREAS: Intellectual Property.

Bretscher, Carl P. .... '62 '93 C.339 B.S. L.273 J.D. [Ⓐ Pennie&E.]
*PRACTICE AREAS: Patent Law; Intellectual Property.

Brogan, William J. .... '— '99 C.94 B.S.C.E. L.273 J.D. [Ⓐ Finnegan,H.F.G.&D.]
*PRACTICE AREAS: Computer and Software Patents; Intellectual Property Litigation; Software Protection; Patent Prosecution.

Brooks, William Lee .... '58 '87 C&L.893 B.S.E.E., J.D. [Armstrong,W.H.M.&N.]

Browdy, Roger L., (AV) .... '45 '72 C.477 B.S.E. L.276 J.D. [Browdy&N.]
*PRACTICE AREAS: Pharmaceutical Intellectual Property; Medical Intellectual Property; Chemical Intellectual Property; International Intellectual Property; Intellectual Property Licensing.

Browdy and Neimark, (AV) BB
Suite 300, 624 Ninth Street, N.W., 20001-5303
Telephone: 202-628-5197 Telecopier: 202-737- 3528
Email: pmcinnis@browdyneimark.com URL: http://www.lawyers.com/browdyneimark
Sheridan Neimark; Roger L. Browdy;—Anne M. Kornbau; Norman J. Latker. Of Counsel: Iver P. Cooper; Jay M. Finkelstein.
U.S. and International Intellectual Property including Patent, Trademark, Copyright and Unfair Competition Law.
See Professional Biographies, WASHINGTON, DISTRICT OF COLUMBIA

Brown, Thomas E. '67 '98 C.107 B.S.E.E. L.1356 J.D.
(adm. in VA; not adm. in DC) [Ⓐ Armstrong,W.H.M.&N.]
*PRACTICE AREAS: Patent Prosecution.

Brunsvold, Brian G., (AV) ... '38 '67 C.350 B.S.Ch.E. L.273 J.D. [Finnegan,H.F.G.&D.]
*PRACTICE AREAS: Antitrust and Trade Regulation; Chemical Intellectual Property; Intellectual Property Licensing; Intellectual Property Litigation; Pharmaceutical Intellectual Property.

Buczynski, Joseph J. .... '64 '94 C.1028 B.S.E.E. L.273 J.D. [Roylance,A.B.&G.]
*PRACTICE AREAS: Intellectual Property Law; Electrical Patents; Mechanical Patents; Computer Law.

Bundock, John P., Jr., (AV) ..... '26 '51 C.860 B.S.E.E. L.273 LL.B. [Ⓒ Leydig,V.&M.]

Bundren, William J. .... '56 '83 C.838 B.A. L.902 J.D. [Cahn&S.]
*PRACTICE AREAS: Intellectual Property Law.

Burchfiel, Kenneth J., (AV) .... '51 '78 C.31 A.B. L.188 J.D. [Sughrue M.]
*PRACTICE AREAS: Intellectual Property Law.

Burdett, James R. .... '51 '84 C.871 B.S. L.1338 J.D. [Venable,A.B.H.&C.]
*PRACTICE AREAS: Intellectual Property.

Burgujian, Richard V. .... '49 '85 C.816 B.E. L.705 J.D. [Finnegan,H.F.G.&D.]
*PRACTICE AREAS: Electronic Patents; Patent Infringement; Patent Prosecution.

Burke, Elizabeth Marie '— '00 C.128 B.S. L.180 J.D.
(adm. in VA; not adm. in DC) [Ⓐ Finnegan,H.F.G.&D.]
*PRACTICE AREAS: Patent Prosecution.

Burn, Brian '68 '01 C.387 B.S. L.1356 J.D.
(adm. in VA; not adm. in DC) [Ⓐ Finnegan,H.F.G.&D.]
*PRACTICE AREAS: Chemical Intellectual Property; Pharmaceutical Intellectual Property; Chemical Patent Prosecution; Chemical Patents; Patent Litigation.

Burns, Robert L. ...... '68 '95 C.674 B.S.A. & A.E. L.365 J.D. [Ⓐ Finnegan,H.F.G.&D.]
*PRACTICE AREAS: Mechanical Intellectual Property; Aerospace Law; Technology Law.

Burns, Todd J. .... '— '95 C.107 B.S.Ch.E. L.273 J.D. [Ⓒ Foley&L.]
*PRACTICE AREAS: Intellectual Property; Chemical Patent; Pharmaceutical Patent Law.

Burns, Doane, Swecker & Mathis, L.L.P.
(See Alexandria, Virginia)

Burrous, Beth A. .... '— '93 C.188 B.S. L.276 J.D. [Foley&L.]
*PRACTICE AREAS: Biotechnology; Strategic Business Planning; Patent Validity and Infringement Opinions.

Burwell, L. Scott .... '69 '93 C.31 A.B. L.309 J.D. [Ⓐ Finnegan,H.F.G.&D.]
*PRACTICE AREAS: Intellectual Property Litigation; Pharmaceutical Intellectual Property; Biotechnology Patents; Patent Litigation.

Cahn, Maurice U. .... '55 '82 C.401 B.A. L.128 J.D. [Cahn&S.] ⊙
*PRACTICE AREAS: Intellectual Property Law.

Cahn & Samuels, LLP
2000 P Street, N.W., Suite 200, 20036 ⊙
Telephone: 202-331-8777 Fax: 202-331-3838
URL: http://www.pattmcopy.com
Maurice U. Cahn; Frederick N. Samuels; George A. Metzenthin; William J. Bundren.
Intellectual Property including procurement and protection of Patent, Trademark and Copyright, counseling and preparation of opinions, protection of trade secrets, litigation, International Patent Prosecution and Licensing, Patent Prosecution including Electrical, Mechanical, Medical, Biotechnology, Software, Business Methods, Electronic Commerce and Chemical.
Rockville, Maryland Office: P.O. Box 5565.
See Professional Biographies, WASHINGTON, DISTRICT OF COLUMBIA

Callahan, Celine T. .... '63 '91 C.128 B.Ch.E. L.273 J.D. [Howrey S.A.&W.]
*PRACTICE AREAS: Intellectual Property Law; Patent and Trademark Litigation; Counseling and Procurement.

Callahan, John T. .... '63 '90 C.128 B.Ch.E. L.64 J.D. [Sughrue M.]
*PRACTICE AREAS: Intellectual Property Law.

Calvetti, Frederick F., (AV) .... '45 '78 C.474 B.S. L.64 J.D. [Smith,G.&R.]
*PRACTICE AREAS: Intellectual Property.

Cantor, Alan I., (AV) .... '48 '75 C.186 B.E. L.64 J.D. [Foley&L.]
*PRACTICE AREAS: Intellectual Property.

Cantor, Jay M., (AV) .... '32 '60 C.659 B.S.E.E. L.273 J.D. [Ⓒ Baker B.]

Capuano, Vincent L. .... '64 '99 C.608 B.S. L.7 J.D. [Ⓐ Sterne,K.G.&F.]
*PRACTICE AREAS: Pharmaceutical Patent Procurement; Enforcement; FDA / ANDA.

Caridi, Michael J. .... '72 '97 C&L.128 B.A., J.D. [Ⓒ Armstrong,W.H.M.&N.]
*PRACTICE AREAS: Intellectual Property Litigation; International Trade; Commercial Litigation.

Carrier, Michael K. .... '66 '96 C&L.150 B.S., J.D. [Ⓐ Smith,G.&R.]
*PRACTICE AREAS: Patent Prosecution; Patent Counseling.

Cassidy, Martha .... '58 '97 C.293 B.A. L.893 J.D. [Ⓐ Rothwell,F.E.&M.]

Castellano, Kristina M. .... '71 '96 C.911 B.S. L.1218 J.D. [Ⓐ Kenyon&K.]
*PRACTICE AREAS: Intellectual Property.

Chandler, Sterling W. '— '91 C.131 B.A. L.861 J.D.
(adm. in LA; not adm. in DC) [Ⓐ Lalos&K.]
*PRACTICE AREAS: Intellectual Property.

Chang, Steve S. .... '— '99 C.608 B.S.E.E. L.831 J.D. [Ⓐ Banner&W.]
*PRACTICE AREAS: Intellectual Property Law; Patents; Intellectual Property Litigation; Electrical Intellectual Property; Computer and Software Patents.

Chao, Fei-Fei .... '55 '97 C.999 B.S. L.446 J.D. [Ⓒ Venable,A.B.H.&C.]
*PRACTICE AREAS: Patent Applications; Patent Prosecution; Patent Infringement; Technology Transfers; Technology Licensing.

Chapman, Ernest F., (AV) ...... '35 '72 C.754 B.S. L.831 J.D. [Ⓒ Finnegan,H.F.G.&D.]
*PRACTICE AREAS: Patents; Chemical Patent Prosecution; Chemical Patents.

Chatterjee, Aaron C. .... '— '98 C.999 B.S. L.1209 J.D. [Ⓐ Foley&L.]
*PRACTICE AREAS: Intellectual Property.

Cheek, Warren M., Jr. .... '55 '83 C&L.260 B.S., J.D. [Wenderoth,L.&P.]
*PRACTICE AREAS: Chemical Patents; Biotechnology and Pharmaceutical Patents.

Chen, Jenny W. '73 '99 C.597 B.S.E.S. L.930 J.D.
(adm. in CA; not adm. in DC) [Ⓐ Howrey S.A.&W.]
*PRACTICE AREAS: Intellectual Property; International Trade; Patent Law.

Cheng, Lee .... '66 '96 C.477 B.S. L.823 J.D. [Ⓐ Wenderoth,L.&P.]
*PRACTICE AREAS: Biotechnology Patents; Pharmaceutical Patents; Chemical Patents; Patent Prosecution.

Choi, Alicia M. '66 '99 C.608 B.S.E.E. L.08 J.D.
(adm. in OH; not adm. in DC) [Ⓐ Staas&H.]
*PRACTICE AREAS: Patents.

Chopskie, Gregory A. .... '70 '99 C.276 B.S. L.1209 J.D. [Ⓐ Finnegan,H.F.G.&D.]
*PRACTICE AREAS: Pharmaceutical Patents; Pharmaceutical Intellectual Property; Patent Litigation; Patent Prosecution.

Cimbala, Michele A. .... '50 '91 C.645 B.S. L.273 J.D. [Sterne,K.G.&F.]
*PRACTICE AREAS: Intellectual Property Law; Biotechnology Patents.

Cleary, J. Michael, (AV) .... '43 '69 C.30 B.A. L.273 J.D. [Cleary&K.]
*PRACTICE AREAS: Copyright Law; Trademark Law; Unfair Competition Law; Litigation.

Cleary & Komen, LLP, (AV)
Suite 200, 600 Pennsylvania Avenue, S.E., 20003-4304
Telephone: 202-675-4700 Fax: 202-675-4716
Email: cleary-komen@cleary-komen.com
Members of Firm: J. Michael Cleary; Edwin Komen.
Copyright, Trademark and Unfair Competition Law, Foreign and Domestic. Practice before Federal Courts and Government Departments.
See Professional Biographies, WASHINGTON, DISTRICT OF COLUMBIA

Cohen, Herbert, (AV) .... '33 '69 C.477 B.S.C.E. L.904 J.D. [Blank R.C.&M.]
*PRACTICE AREAS: Trademarks; International Trademarks; Patents; International Patents.

Colaianni, Joseph V., Jr. .... '69 '96 C.446 B.S.E.E. L.273 J.D. [Ⓐ Fish&R.]
*PRACTICE AREAS: Intellectual Property Litigation.

Colbert, Edward T., (AV) .... '47 '73 C&L.446 A.B., J.D. [Kenyon&K.]
*PRACTICE AREAS: Intellectual Property Litigation; Trademark Counseling and Prosecution; Unfair Competition and Related Litigation.

Cole, Carol L. '72 '00 C.446 B.S. L.904 J.D.
(adm. in VA; not adm. in DC) [Ⓐ Finnegan,H.F.G.&D.]
*PRACTICE AREAS: Biotechnology Patent Prosecution; Chemical Patent Prosecution; Patent Infringement; Patent Prosecution.

Converse, Robert E., Jr., (AV) '45 '74 C.597 B.S.E.E. L.229 J.D.
[Finnegan,H.F.G.&D.]
*PRACTICE AREAS: Patent Prosecution; Patent Litigation.

Cooper, Iver P., (AV) .... '53 '78 C.453 B.S. L.94 J.D. [Ⓒ Browdy&N.]
*PRACTICE AREAS: Biotechnology and Biomedical Patents.

Cordell, Ruffin B., (AV) .... '63 '89 C.420 B.S.E.E. L.276 J.D. [Fish&R.]
*PRACTICE AREAS: Litigation; Intellectual Property Law; International Trade Commission Proceedings.

Cornwell, David K.S. .... '58 '83 C&L.560 B.S.M,E., J.D. [Sterne,K.G.&F.]
*PRACTICE AREAS: Litigation; Intellectual Property Law.

Corsello, Kenneth R. .... '65 '92 C.1350 B.S. L.128 J.D. [Ⓐ Kenyon&K.]
*PRACTICE AREAS: Intellectual Property.

Covert, John M. .... '63 '94 C.728 B.S. L.1209 J.D. [Sterne,K.G.&F.]
*PRACTICE AREAS: Patent Law; Chemical Patent; Biotechnology.

Covington & Burling, (AV)
1201 Pennsylvania Avenue, N.W., 20004-2401 ⊙
Telephone: 202-662-6000 Fax: 202-662-6291
Email: postmaster@cov.com URL: http://www.cov.com
Members of Firm: Paul J. Berman; Christopher N. Sipes; Allan J. Topol. Associates: Kurt G. Calia; Jean M. Perron; Grady Lee White.
General Practice, including, but not limited to: Antitrust and Competition, Appellate, Arbitration and Alternative Dispute Resolution, Banking and Financial Services, Bankruptcy and Insolvency, Business Law, Civil Rights, Communications and Media, Copyrights, Corporate, Criminal, Election and Campaign Finance, Emerging Companies, Employee Benefits, Employment, Energy, Environmental, Food, Drug and Cosmetics, Government Contracts, Health Services, Information Services, Insurance, Intellectual Property, International, Information Technology and Internet, Latin America, Legislative, Litigation, Mergers and Acquisitions, Petroleum, Products Liability, Professional Responsibility, Real Estate, Securities, Sports, Taxation, Toxic Torts, Trade Associations, Trade Regulation, Trademarks, Transportation, Trusts and Estates and Year 2000 Computer Conversion.
San Francisco, California Office: 601 California Street, Suite 1900, 94108. Telephone: 415-591-6000.
New York, N.Y. Office: 1330 Avenue of the Americas, 10019-5400. Telephone: 212-841-1000. Telecopier: 212-841-1010.
London, England Office: Leconfield House, Curzon Street, W1Y 8A5. Telephone: 011-44-71-495-5655. Fax: 011-44-71-495-3101.
Brussels, Belgium Office: 44 Avenue des Arts (Bte. 8), 1040. Telephone: 011-32-2-549-5230. Fax: 011-32-2-502-1598.
See Professional Biographies, WASHINGTON, DISTRICT OF COLUMBIA

Cubert, Jack S. '31 '67 C.563 B.E.E. L.831 J.D.
(adm. in NJ; not adm. in DC) [Ⓐ Fitzpatrick,C.H.&S.]

Curry, William E. '58 '97 C&L.446 B.S.E.E., J.D.
(adm. in MD; not adm. in DC) [Ⓐ Kenyon&K.]
*PRACTICE AREAS: Intellectual Property.

Curtin, Joseph P., (BV) .... '— '91 C.576 B.S.E.E. L.446 J.D. [Ⓐ Banner&W.]
*PRACTICE AREAS: Intellectual Property Law; Patents; Electrical Intellectual Property; Computer and Software Patents; Electronic Patents.

Cushing, David J., (AV) .... '52 '77 C.602 B.S.E.E. L.446 J.D. [Sughrue M.]
*PRACTICE AREAS: Intellectual Property Law; Litigation.

Daebeler, Paul F. .... '66 '91 C.401 B.S.E.E. L.1338 J.D. [Ⓒ Venable,A.B.H.&C.]
*PRACTICE AREAS: Intellectual Property.

Daley, Henry J. .... '— '97 C.971 B.S. L.588 J.D. [Ⓐ Pillsbury W.] (⊙Mc Lean, VA)
*PRACTICE AREAS: Intellectual Property; Patent Prosecution; Patent Litigation.

Daley, Kathleen Alice .... '66 '93 C.188 B.S. L.276 J.D. [Ⓐ Finnegan,H.F.G.&D.]
*PRACTICE AREAS: Intellectual Property Licensing; Intellectual Property Litigation; Mechanical Intellectual Property; Biomedical Technology.

Daniels, Scott M., (AV) .... '52 '77 C.118 B.A. L.188 J.D. [Armstrong,W.H.M.&N.]
*PRACTICE AREAS: Intellectual Property Law.

David, Michael '— '00 L.446 J.D.
(adm. in MD; not adm. in DC) [Ⓐ Banner&W.]
*PRACTICE AREAS: Patents; Patent Licensing; Pharmaceutical Intellectual Property; Medical Intellectual Property Law.

Davis, Garrett V. .... '54 '84 C.923 B.S. L.64 J.D. [Roylance,A.B.&G.]
*PRACTICE AREAS: Patent Law; Chemical Patent Law.

Davis, James F., (AV) .... '34 '64 C.339 B.S.Ch.E. L.276 J.D. [Howrey S.A.&W.]
*PRACTICE AREAS: Intellectual Property; Patent Law; Patent, Trademark and Copyright Law.

Davis, Michael R., (AV) .... '42 '70 C.1213 B.S.Chem. L.273 J.D. [Wenderoth,L.&P.]
*PRACTICE AREAS: Chemicals; Pharmaceuticals; Metallurgy; Biochemicals.

Day, Christopher William '69 '00 C.576 B.S. L.180 J.D. (adm. in MD; not adm. in DC) [[A] Finnegan,H.F.G.&D.]
*PRACTICE AREAS: Intellectual Property Infringement; Intellectual Property Litigation; International Intellectual Property; Mechanical Intellectual Property; Computer and Software Patents.

Dechert, (AV) [BR]
1775 Eye Street, N.W., 20006-2401 ⊙
Telephone: 202.261.3300 Telefax: 202.261.3333
URL: http://www.dechert.com
Resident Counsel: Ralph Oman.
Antitrust, Banking, Bankruptcy and Reorganization, Business and Technology, Commercial Litigation, Complex Litigation, Copyrights, Corporate Finance, Competition, Construction, Customs and Excise, Criminal and Civil Fraud, Defamation, Domestic Taxation, Employee Benefits and Executive Compensation, Employment, Environmental, Estate Planning, EU Legislation, Financial Services, First Amendment, Government Affairs, Health Care, Immigration, Insurance, Intellectual Property, Internet and e-Commerce, Information Technology, Insurance, International Business, International Taxation, International Trade, Investment Management, Labor, Latin America, Life Sciences, Mass Torts, Media, Mergers and Acquisitions, Patent Law and Litigation, Privacy, Private Equity, Products Liability, Property Planning, Real Estate and Mortgage Finance, Retail, Securities Litigation and Enforcement, Securitization, State and Local Taxation, Tax-Exempt Organizations, Trademarks, Venture Capital.
Philadelphia, Pennsylvania: 4000 Bell Atlantic Tower, 1717 Arch Street, 19103-2793. Telephone: 215.994.4000.
New York, New York: 30 Rockefeller Plaza, 10112. Telephone: 212.698.3500.
Harrisburg, Pennsylvania: Thirty North Third Street, 17101-1603. Telephone: 717.237.2000.
Princeton, New Jersey: Princeton Pike Corporate Center, P.O. Box 5218, 08543-5218. Telephone: 609.620.3200.
Boston, Massachusetts: Ten Post Office Square South, 12th Floor, 02109-4603. Telephone: 617.728.7100.
Hartford, Connecticut: 90 State House Square, 06103-3702. Telephone: 860.524.3999.
Newport Beach, California: 4675 MacArthur Court, Suite 1400, 92660-8842. Telephone: 949.442.6000.
London, England: 2 Serjeants' Inn, EC4Y 1LT. Telephone: +44 20 7583 5353.
Brussels, Belgium: 65 Avenue Louise 1050. Telephone: +32 2 535 5411.
Paris, France: 55, avenue Kléber, 75116. Telephone: +33 1 53 65 05 00.
Luxembourg: Brucher & Seimetz in association with Dechert, Avocats a la Cour, 10 rue de Vianden B.P. 709, L-2017. Telephone: +352 45 62 62.

See Professional Biographies, WASHINGTON, DISTRICT OF COLUMBIA

DeCosta, Frank A., III .... '63 '96 C.188 B.S. L.276 J.D. [[A] Finnegan,H.F.G.&D.]
*PRACTICE AREAS: Intellectual Property; Computers and Software; Litigation; Patent Licensing; Patent Prosecution.

Degnan, Lauren A. ....'70 '95 C.188 B.S. L.880 J.D. [[A] Fish&R.]

Delaney, Patrick R. ....'63 '00 C.446 B.S. L.128 J.D. [[A] Smith,G.&R.]

DeLuca, Vincent M. ....'60 '87 C.178 B.S.E.E. L.1209 J.D. [Rothwell,F.E.&M.]
*PRACTICE AREAS: Intellectual Property.

de Rosa, Barth X. ....'55 '82 C.273 B.A. L.280 J.D. [Stevens,D.M.&M.]
*PRACTICE AREAS: Intellectual Property; Trademarks; Copyrights; Litigation; Mergers and Acquisitions.

Devlin, Timothy M. .... '70 '97 C.645 B.S. L.477 J.D. [[A] Kenyon&K.]
*PRACTICE AREAS: Intellectual Property.

Dickinson Wright PLLC, (AV)
Suite 800, 1901 L Street, N.W., 20036-3506 ⊙
Telephone: 202-457-0160 Facsimile: 202-659-1559
URL: http://www.dickinson-wright.com
Resident Of Counsel: J. John Shimazaki. Resident Associate: Nicole M. Meyer (Not admitted in DC).
Alternative Dispute Resolution, Antitrust, Appellate Litigation, Banking and Financial Services, Bankruptcy, Business Criminal Defense and Internal Investigations, Commercial and Business Litigation, Construction Law, Corporate, Corporate Finance, Ebusiness, Education and School Law, Employee Benefits, Employment Litigation, Energy and Public Utilities, Environmental, Family and Matrimonial Law, Gaming Law, Immigration, Insurance Industry, Intellectual Property, International, Labor and Employment Relations, Mergers and Acquisitions, Municipal Law and Finance, Private Capital, Product Liability/Personal Injury Litigation, Railroads and Transportation, Real Estate, Regulatory and Administrative Law, Risk Management, Securities, Taxation, Telecommunications, Trade Regulation, Trusts and Estate Planning.
Detroit, Michigan Office: 500 Woodward Avenue, Suite 4000. Telephone: 313-223-3500. Facsimile: 313-223-3598.
Ann Arbor, Michigan Office: 101 North Main Street, Suite 535. Telephone: 734-623-7075. Fax: 734-623-7568.
Bloomfield Hills, Michigan Office: 38525 Woodward Avenue, Suite 2000. Telephone: 248-433-7200. Facsimile: 248-433-7274.
Grand Rapids, Michigan Office: 200 Ottawa Avenue, N.W., Suite 900. Telephone: 616-458-1300. Facsimile: 616-458-6753.
Lansing, Michigan Office: Suite 200, 215 South Washington Square. Telephone: 517-371-1730. Facsimile: 517-487-4700.

See Professional Biographies, WASHINGTON, DISTRICT OF COLUMBIA

Dietze, Paul E. ....'53 '99 C.1178 B.S. L.446 J.D. [[A] Pennie&E.]
*PRACTICE AREAS: Intellectual Property; Patents.

Dorsey, Daniel K. .... '58 '90 C.1048 B.S.E.E. L.1162 J.D. [[A] Jacobson,H.]
*PRACTICE AREAS: Criminal Law; Intellectual Property Law.

Driscoll, Benjamin D. '68 '00 C.659 B.S.E.E. L.1209 J.D. (adm. in VA; not adm. in DC) [[A] Fish&R.]
*PRACTICE AREAS: Patent Prosecution; Patent Litigation.

Dudek, Jean K., (BV) .... '57 '85 C.788 A.B. L.569 J.D. [[A] Fitzpatrick,C.H.&S.]

Dunham, Thomas M. ....'63 '95 C.1349 B.S. L.884 J.D. [Howrey S.A.&W.]
*PRACTICE AREAS: Intellectual Property Law.

Dunner, Donald R., (AV) ..... '31 '58 C.679 B.S.Ch.E. L.276 J.D. [Finnegan,H.F.G.&D.]
*PRACTICE AREAS: Intellectual Property Litigation; Intellectual Property Appeals.

Durkin, Tracy-Gene Graveline, (BV) '61 '89 C.1316 B.S. L.273 J.D. [Sterne,K.G.&F.]
*PRACTICE AREAS: Intellectual Property Law; Mediation; Trademarks; Unfair Competition; Patents.

Edmondson, David J. '62 '92 C.367 B.A. L.477 J.D. (adm. in VA; not adm. in DC) [[A] Blank R.C.&M.]
*PRACTICE AREAS: Intellectual Property; Electrical Intellectual Property; Electrical Patent Prosecution; Computer and Software Patent Protection; International Patents.

Edmondson, James W. .... '57 '88 C.870 B.S. L.276 J.D. [Finnegan,H.F.G.&D.]
*PRACTICE AREAS: Intellectual Property Infringement; Intellectual Property Licensing; Intellectual Property Litigation; Mechanical Intellectual Property; Proprietary Rights.

Eichelburg, Robert J., (AV) ..... '35 '63 C.262 B.S. L.273 J.D. [[C] Finnegan,H.F.G.&D.]
*PRACTICE AREAS: Chemical Patent Prosecution; Coatings Technology; Inorganic Chemistry; Organic Chemistry; Polymers.

Einaudi, Carol P., (AV) .... '37 '85 C.783 B.S. L.273 J.D. [Finnegan,H.F.G.&D.]
*PRACTICE AREAS: Patent Prosecution.

Ellis, William T. ....'— '75 C.339 B.S.E.E. L.128 J.D. [Foley&L.]
*PRACTICE AREAS: Electronics; Patents; Computer Law; E-commerce; Contracts.

Ernst, Barbara G. .... '55 '80 C.928 B.A. L.446 J.D. [Rothwell,F.E.&M.]
*PRACTICE AREAS: Intellectual Property.

Esfahani, Houtan Khalili ....'64 '95 C.178 B.S.E.E. L.1292 J.D. [[A] Finnegan,H.F.G.&D.]
*PRACTICE AREAS: Intellectual Property; Patents.

Esmond, Robert W. .... '53 '89 C.446 B.Sc. L.273 J.D. [Sterne,K.G.&F.]
*PRACTICE AREAS: Intellectual Property Law.

Fahrenkopf, Paul E. '— '79 C.30 B.A. L.472 J.D. (adm. in NJ; not adm. in DC) [[C] Barnes&T.]
*PRACTICE AREAS: Trademark Protection; Trademark Registration; Trade Dress.

Farabow, Ford F., Jr., (AV) '38 '63 C.160 B.S.Ch.E. L.273 J.D. [Finnegan,H.F.G.&D.]
*PRACTICE AREAS: Chemical Intellectual Property; Intellectual Property Arbitration; Intellectual Property Infringement; Intellectual Property Litigation; Pharmaceutical Intellectual Property.

Fasulo, Albert J., II '62 '97 C.054 B.S. L.1002 J.D. (adm. in MD; not adm. in DC) [[A] Sterne,K.G.&F.]
*PRACTICE AREAS: Patent Law.

Featherstone, Donald J. .... '64 '99 C.390 B.S.E.E. L.1356 J.D. [[A] Sterne,K.G.&F.]
*PRACTICE AREAS: Intellectual Property Law.

Fedigan, John T., (AV) '32 '67 C.1031 B.S.Chem. L.128 LL.B. [[C] Wenderoth,L.&P.] ‡
*PRACTICE AREAS: Patents; Chemical Patents; Prosecution; Interference Practice.

Fedorochko, Gary D. ....'— '90 C.688 B.S. L.273 J.D. [Banner&W.]
*PRACTICE AREAS: Intellectual Property Law; Patents; Intellectual Property Licensing; Electrical Intellectual Property; Computer and Software Patents.

Feisthamel, Karen L. .... '65 '90 C.103 Sc.B. L.276 J.D. [[A] Kenyon&K.]
*PRACTICE AREAS: Intellectual Property.

Felber, Joseph L. ....'61 '00 C.893 B.S. L.128 J.D. [[A] Armstrong,W.H.M.&N.]
*PRACTICE AREAS: Patent.

Feldhaus, John J., (AV) '— '80 C.688 B.S. L.1209 J.D. (adm. in VA; not adm. in DC) [Foley&L.]
*PRACTICE AREAS: Electrical and Mechanical Intellectual Property Procurement; Litigation.

Ferguson, Catherine A. ....'— '93 C.550 B.A. L.1338 J.D. [[A] Banner&W.]
*PRACTICE AREAS: Intellectual Property.

Fiala, Thomas C. .... '67 '98 C.688 B.S. L.306 J.D. [[A] Sterne,K.G.&F.]
*PRACTICE AREAS: Patent Law; Intellectual Property Law.

Figg, E. Anthony, (AV) ....'46 '73 C.701 B.S. L.345 J.D. [Rothwell,F.E.&M.]
*PRACTICE AREAS: Intellectual Property.

Filipek, Jeffrey R. ....'70 '00 C.645 B.S.E.E. L.180 J.D. [[A] Wenderoth,L.&P.]
*PRACTICE AREAS: Patents.

Finkelstein, Jay M., (AV) .... '37 '64 C.223 B.S.E.E. L.273 J.D. [[C] Browdy&N.]
*PRACTICE AREAS: Intellectual Property.

Finnegan, Henderson, Farabow, Garrett & Dunner, L.L.P., (AV) [BR]
1300 I Street, N.W., Suite 700, 20005 ⊙
Telephone: 202-408-4000 Facsimile: 202-408-4400
Email: info@finnegan.com URL: http://www.finnegan.com
Members of Firm: Douglas B. Henderson; Ford F. Farabow Jr.; Arthur S. Garrett; Donald R. Dunner; Brian G. Brunsvold; Jerry D. Voight (Resident Partner, Palo Alto, California Office); Laurence R. Hefter; Herbert H. Mintz; C. Larry O'Rourke (Resident Partner, Palo Alto, California Office); Albert J. Santorelli; Michael C. Elmer (Resident Partner, Palo Alto, California Office); Richard H. Smith; Stephen L. Peterson; John M. Romary; Bruce C. Zotter; D. Patrick O'Reilley; Allen M. Sokal; Robert D. Bajefsky; Richard Lee Stroup; David W. Hill; Thomas L. Irving; Charles E. Lipsey; Thomas W. Winland; Basil J. Lewris; Martin I. Fuchs; E. Robert Yoches; Barry W. Graham; Susan Haberman Griffen; Richard B. Racine; Thomas H. Jenkins III; Robert E. Converse Jr.; Clair X. Mullen Jr.; Christopher P. Foley; John C. Paul; Roger D. Taylor (Resident Partner, Atlanta, Georgia Office); David M. Kelly; Kenneth John Meyers; Carol P. Einaudi; Walter Y. Boyd Jr.; Steven M. Anzalone; Jean Burke Fordis (Resident Partner, Palo Alto, California Office); Barbara Clarke McCurdy; James K. Hammond; Richard V. Burgujian; John Michael Jakes; Thomas W. Banks (Resident Partner, Cambridge, Massachusetts Office); Christopher P. Isaac; Bryan C. Diner (Resident Partner, Brussels, Belgium Office); M. Paul Barker (Resident Partner, Palo Alto, California Office); Andrew Chanho Sonu; David S. Forman; Vincent P. Kovalick; Gerson S. Panitch; James W. Edmondson; Michael R. McGurk; Cheri M. Taylor; Joann M. Neth; Linda A. Wadler; Charles E. Van Horn; Jeffrey A. Berkowitz; Michael R. Kelly (Resident Partner, Tokyo, Japan Office); James B. Monroe; Doris Johnson Hines; David Avrum Manspeizer; Lori-Ann Johnson (Resident Associate, Atlanta, Georgia Office); Allen R. Jensen; Ronald A. Bleeker; John A. Rissman (Not admitted in DC; Resident Partner, Cambridge, Massachusetts Office); R. Bruce Bower (Resident Partner, Atlanta, Georgia Office); Yitai Hu; Martin F. Majestic (Resident Partner, Palo Alto, California Office); Therese A. Hendricks (Resident Partner, Cambridge, Massachusetts Office); M. Lawrence Oliverio (Resident Partner, Cambridge, Massachusetts Office). Senior Counsel: Tipton D. Jennings IV; Kenneth E. Payne. Of Counsel: Ernest F. Chapman; William B. Dyer, III (Resident Counsel, Atlanta, Georgia Office); Robert J. Eichelburg; Wayne W. Herrington; Thomas L. Jarvis; William T. McClain; Leslie A. McDonell (Resident Counsel, Boston, Massachusetts Office); Robert F. Rotella; Russell L. Sandidge (Resident Counsel, Atlanta, Georgia Office); Robert F. Ziems. Associates: Eric William Adcock; Adam Avrunin (Resident Associate, Atlanta, Georgia Office); Eyal Hanan Barash; James R. Barney (Not admitted in DC); Kenneth D. Bassinger (Resident Associate, Atlanta, Georgia Office); F. Leslie Bessenger III (Resident Associate, Atlanta, Georgia Office); Leslie I. Bookoff; Michele C. Bosch; James J. Boyle; William J. Brogan; Elizabeth Marie Burke (Not admitted in DC); Brian Burn (Not admitted in DC); Robert L. Burns; L. Scott Burwell; Gregory A. Chopskie; Carol L. Cole (Not admitted in DC); Kathleen Alice Daley; Christopher William Day (Not admitted in DC); Frank A. DeCosta III; Houtan Khalili Esfahani; Michael J. Flibbert; David Penn Frazier; Lawrence Francis Galvin; Stephanie S. Conis Gauthier (Resident Associate, Atlanta, Georgia Office); Jason E. Gorden (Resident Associate, Palo Alto, California Office); C. Gregory Gramenopoulos (Resident Associate, Brussels, Belgium Office); Anthony M. Gutowski; Anthony A. Hartmann; Scott A. Herbst (Resident Associate, Palo Alto, California Office); Timothy M. Hsieh; D. Brian Kacedon (Not admitted in DC); Lara Chapman Kelley; Sang Hui Michael Kim (Resident Associate, Palo Alto, California Office); Christine E. Lehman; Esther H. Lim; Kurt Albert Luther; Keith Douglas MacMillan; Geoffrey Colbourne Mason; Matthew Jerald Mason; Robert A. Matthews, Jr.; Timothy James May (Not admitted in DC); Roland George McAndrews, Jr.; Kevin William McCabe; Rebecca McNeill; Arie M. Michelsohn (Not admitted in DC); Michael A. Morin; Allen J. Moss (Not admitted in DC); Sean Christopher Myers-Payne (Not admitted in DC); William Nakhleh (Not admitted in DC); Charles D. Niebylski (Not admitted in DC); Steven P. O'Connor; Kristen Rae Jakobsen Osenga; Robert A. Pollock; Eric P. Raciti; Richard L. Rainey (Resident Associate, Atlanta, Georgia Office); Aaron M. Raphael; Rafael E. Rosado (Resident Associate, Cambridge, Massachusetts Office); Christopher S. Schultz (Resident Associate, Cambridge, Massachusetts Office); Steven J. Scott (Resident Associate, Brussels, Belgium Office); Parmanand "Anand" K. Sharma; Patricia Ann Shatynski; Michael T. Siekman; Leonard Smith, Jr.; Jemy Soegeng; Jay A. Stelacone; Kara Farnandez Stoll; Pedro F. Suarez (Not admitted in DC); Sanya Sukduang; Jennifer S. Swan (Not admitted in DC); Mark D. Sweet; Jeanne M. Tanner; Susanne C. Tinker (Not admitted in DC); Rachel H. Townsend; Anthony C. Tridico (Not admitted in DC; Resident Associate, Brussels, Belgium Office); Charlena L. Williams (Resident Associate, Atlanta, Georgia Office); James T. Wilson (Not admitted in DC).
Patents, Trademarks, Copyrights, Trade Secrets, Chemical IP, Electrical IP, IP Infringement, IP Licensing, IP Litigation, IP Portfolio Management, IP Procurement, IP Rights, International IP, Mechanical IP, Pharmaceutical IP, Biotechnology IP, Information Technology Licensing.
Reference: Crestar Bank, N.A., Washington, D.C.
Atlanta, Georgia Office: 3200 SunTrust Plaza, 303 Peachtree Street, N.E., 30308. Telephone: 404-653-6400. Facsimile: 404-653-6444.
Cambridge, Massachusetts Office: 55 Cambridge Parkway, 02142. Telephone: 617-444-8508. Facsimile: 617-444-8608.
Palo Alto, California Office: 700 Hansen Way, 94304. Telephone: 650-849-6600. Facsimile: 650-849-6666.
Brussels, Belgium Office: Avenue Louise 326, Box 37, B-1050. Telephone: 011-322-646-0353. Facsimile: 011-322-646-2135.
Tokyo, Japan Office: Toranomon No. 45 Mori Building, Third Floor, 1-5, Toranomon 5-Chome Minato-Ku, 105-0001. Telephone: 011-813-3431-6943. Facsimile: 011-813-3431-6945.

See Professional Biographies, WASHINGTON, DISTRICT OF COLUMBIA

Fish & Richardson P.C., (AV)
601 13th Street N.W., 20005 ⊙
Telephone: 202-783-5070 Fax: 202-783-2331
Email: info@fr.com URL: http://www.fr.com
Ruffin B. Cordell; Alexander J. Hadjis; John F. Hayden; Linda Liu Kordziel; Michael J. McKeon; Ralph A. Mittelberger. Of Counsel: James E. Mrose; Rene D. Tegtmeyer. Associates: Scott R. Boalick; Andrew F. Bodendorf (Not admitted in DC); Joseph V. Colaianni, Jr.; Lauren A. Degnan; Benjamin D. Driscoll (Not admitted in DC); Harold H. Fox; William D. Hare; Joseph Franklin Key; Andrew Kopsidas (Not admitted in DC); Phyllis Kristal (Not admitted in DC); Kevin J. McNeely; Robert V. Racunas (Not admitted in DC); W. Karl Renner (Not admitted in DC); Gary Savitt; Mark Edward Wadrzyk (Not admitted in DC); Gregory A. Walters; R. Whitney Winston.

(This Listing Continued)

Fish & Richardson P.C. (Continued)
Intellectual Property, Complex Litigation, Technology Law: Patents, Trademarks, Copyrights, Trade Secrets, Intellectual Property Litigation, Business Litigation, Technology Regulations, Antitrust Law, Corporate and Securities, White Collar Crime.
Boston, Massachusetts Office: 225 Franklin Street. Telephone: 617-542-5070. Fax: 617-542-8906.
Redwood City, California Office: 500 Aguello Street, Suite 500. Telephone: 650-322-5070. Fax: 650-854-0875.
Minneapolis, Minnesota Office: Fish & Richardson, P.C., P.A., 60 South Sixth Street, 3300 Dain Rauscher Plaza. Telephone: 612-335-5070. Fax: 612-288-9696.
San Diego, California Office: 4350 La Jolla Village Drive, Suite 500. Telephone: 858-678-5070. Fax: 858-678-5099.
New York, N.Y. Office: 45 Rockefeller Plaza, Suite 2800. Telephone: 212-765-5070. Fax: 212-258-2291.
Wilmington, Delaware Office: 919 North Market Street, Suite 1000, P.O. Box 1114. Telephone: 302-652-5070. Fax: 302-652-0607.
Dallas, Texas Office: 5000 Bank One Center, 1717 Main Street. Telephone: 214-747-5070. Fax: 214-747-2091
See Professional Biographies, WASHINGTON, DISTRICT OF COLUMBIA

Fisher, William J. ....'— '86 C.46 B.S.Ch.E. L.776 J.D. [Banner&W.]
*PRACTICE AREAS: Intellectual Property Law; Patents; Intellectual Property Licensing; Chemical Intellectual Property; Pharmaceutical Intellectual Property.

Fisher, Christen & Sabol, (AV)
Suite 1401, 1725 K Street, N.W., 20006
Telephone: 202-659-2000 Fax: 202-659-2015
Email: FCSabol@aol.com URL: http://www.lawyers.com/fisherchristen&sabol
Virgil H. Marsh; Kara M. Armstrong.
Patent, Trademark, Copyright, Unfair Competition and related Litigation. Mechanical Patents, Chemical Patents, Biotechnology Patents.
See Professional Biographies, WASHINGTON, DISTRICT OF COLUMBIA

Fitzpatrick, Cella, Harper & Scinto, (AV) [BR]
1900 K Street, N.W., 20006-1110 ⊙
Telephone: 202-530-1010 Facsimile: 202-530-1055 URL: http://www.fitzpatrickcella.com
Resident Partners: John W. Behringer; Lawrence A. Stahl; William M. Wannisky; Warren E. Olsen; Scott D. Malpede; Thomas J. O'Connell; Steven E. Warner; Mark A. Williamson; Anne M. Maher; Daniel S. Glueck; Brian L. Klock. Counsel: Robert C. Kline. Resident Associates: Christopher Philip Wrist; Gary M. Jacobs; Jack S. Cubert (Not admitted in DC); Jean K. Dudek; Edmund J. Haughey, III; Justin J. Oliver (Not admitted in DC); Simon D. Roberts (Not admitted in DC).
Intellectual Property Practice. Patent, Trademark, Copyright, Trade Secret, Unfair Competition, Computer, Licensing, Antitrust and International Trade Law. Trials and Appeals in Federal and State Courts and Administrative Agencies.
New York, N.Y. Office: 30 Rockefeller Plaza. Telephone: 212-218-2100. Facsimile: 212-218-2200.
Orange County, California Office: 650 Town Center Drive, Suite 1600, Costa Mesa. Telephone: 714-540-8700. Facsimile: 714-540-9823.
See Professional Biographies, WASHINGTON, DISTRICT OF COLUMBIA

Flibbert, Michael J. .... '64 '94 C.276 B.S. L.273 J.D. [[A] Finnegan,H.F.G.&D.]
*PRACTICE AREAS: Chemical Intellectual Property; Chemical Patents; Patent Litigation; Pharmaceutical Patents.

Flohr, Susan B. ....'53 '79 C.1356 B.A. L.904 J.D. [Blank R.C.&M.]
*PRACTICE AREAS: Trademark Law; Copyright Law; Computer Law; Unfair Competition Law; Licensing.

Floyd, Eldora Ellison '66 '99 C.311 B.S. L.276 J.D.
(adm. in MD; not adm. in DC) [[A] Sterne,K.G.&F.]
*PRACTICE AREAS: Patent Law.

Foley, Christopher P., (AV) .... '53 '83 C.871 B.S. L.276 J.D. [Finnegan,H.F.G.&D.]
*PRACTICE AREAS: Trademark Registration; Trademark Litigation; Patent Litigation; Patent Prosecution.

Foley & Lardner, (AV)
Washington Harbour, Suite 500, 3000 K Street, N.W., 20007-5109 ⊙
Telephone: 202-672-5300 Facsimile: 202-672-5399
Email: webmaster@foleylaw.com URL: http://www.foleylardner.com
Partners: Stephen A. Bent; David A. Blumenthal; William T. Ellis; John J. Feldhaus (Not admitted in DC); Patricia D. Granados; John P. Isacson; Michael D. Kaminski; Lyle Kimms; Kenneth E. Krosin; Johnny A. Kumar; Jack L. Lahr; Glenn Law; Peter G. Mack; Brian K. McNamara; Sybil Meloy (Not admitted in DC); Richard C. Peet; George E. Quillin (Not admitted in DC); Colin G. Sandercock; Bernhard D. Saxe (Not admitted in DC); Richard L. Schwaab (Not admitted in DC); Charles F. Schill; Richard L. Schwaab; Arthur Schwartz. Retired Partners: Donald D. Jeffery. Of Counsel: Barbara Ann McDowell (Not admitted in DC). Special Counsel: Jayme A. Huleatt. Associates: Phillip J. Articola; George C. Beck; George C. Best; Paul M. Booth; Todd J. Burns; Beth A. Burrous; Aaron Chatterjee; Matthew R. Cohen; Ronald Coslick; Ronald J. Kamis; Mary Michelle Kile; Stephen B. Maebius (Not admitted in DC); Marvin A. Motsenbocker; Ankur D. Shah (Not admitted in DC); Howard N. Shipley; James M. Silbermann; Marc K. Weinstein.
General Practice. International and Domestic Patent, Trademark, Copyright, Biotechnology and related Intellectual Property Law. Intellectual Property Litigation.
Other Washington, D.C. Office: 888 Sixteenth Street, N.W. Telephone: 202-835-8000. Fax: 202-835-8136.
Los Angeles, California Office: 2029 Century Park East, 35th Floor. Telephone: 310-277-2223. Fax: 310-557-8475.
Sacramento, California Office: 300 Capitol Mall, Suite 1125. Telephone: 916-443-8005. Fax: 916-443-2240.
San Diego, California Office: 402 West Broadway, 23rd Floor. Telephone: 619-234-6655. Fax: 619-234-3510.
San Diego/North County, California Office: 11250 El Camino Real, Suite 200. Telephone: 858-847-6700. Facsimile: 858-792-6773.
San Francisco, California Office: One Maritime Plaza, Sixth Floor. Telephone: 415-434-4484. Fax: 415-434-4507.
Denver, Colorado Office: 1999 Broadway, Suite 2560. Telephone: 303-297-0260. Fax: 303-297-0266.
Jacksonville, Florida Office: The Greenleaf Building, 200 Laura Street. P.O. Box 240. Telephone: 904-359-2000. Facsimile: 904-359-8700.
Orlando, Florida Office: Suite 1800, 111 North Orange Avenue, P.O. Box 2193. Telephone: 407-423-7656. Facsimile: 407-648-1743.
Tallahassee, Florida Office: 106 East College Avenue, Highpoint Center, Suite 900, P.O. Box 1819. Telephone: 850-222-6100. Facsimile: 850-561-6475.
Tampa, Florida Offices: Suite 2700, 100 N. Tampa Street, P.O. Box 3391. Telephones: 813-229-2300; Pinellas County: 813-442-3296. Facsimile: 813-221-4210.
West Palm Beach, Florida Office: 777 South Flagler Drive, Suite 901, West Tower. Telephone: 561-655-5050. Facsimile: 561-655-6925.
Chicago, Illinois Office: One IBM Plaza, 330 N. Wabash Avenue, Suite 3300. Telephone: 312-755-1900. Facsimile: 312-755-1925.
Other Chicago, Illinois Office: Three First National Plaza, 70 West Madison, Suite 4100. Telephone: 312-558-6600. Fax: 312-558-6676.
Annapolis, Maryland Office: Suite 102, 175 Admiral Cochrane Drive. Telephone: 410-266-8077. Facsimile: 410-266-8664.
Detroit, Michigan Office: 150 West Jefferson, Suite 1000. Telephone: 313-963-6200. Fax: 313-963-9308.
Madison, Wisconsin Office: Verex Plaza, 150 East Gilman Street, P.O. Box 1497. Telephone: 608-257-5035. Facsimile: 608-258-4258.
Milwaukee, Wisconsin Office: Firstar Center, 777 East Wisconsin Avenue. Telephone: 414-271-2400. Facsimile: 414-297-4900.
Brussels, Belgium Office: Avenue Louise, 283. Telephone: 32-2-646-2777. Facsimile: 32-2-646-7574.
See Professional Biographies, WASHINGTON, DISTRICT OF COLUMBIA

Forman, David S., (BV) .... '42 '87 C.309 B.A. L.273 J.D. [Finnegan,H.F.G.&D.]
*PRACTICE AREAS: Patent Law.

Foster, John D. .... '43 '70 C.350 B.S.Ch.E. L.276 J.D. [[C] Leydig,V.&M.]

Fox, Harold H. ....'67 '99 C.453 B.S. L.94 J.D. [[A] Fish&R.]
*PRACTICE AREAS: Patent Law.

Frank, Robert J., (AV) .... '24 '60 C.188 B.E.E. L.1009 LL.B. [Venable,A.B.H.&C.]
*PRACTICE AREAS: Patent Law; Trademark Law.

Frazier, David Penn .... '66 '00 C.645 B.S. L.276 J.D. [[A] Finnegan,H.F.G.&D.]
*PRACTICE AREAS: Intellectual Property Portfolio Management; Pharmaceutical Intellectual Property; Biotechnology Patents; Patent Litigation; Pharmaceutical Patents.

Fuchs, Martin L., (AV) .... '52 '78 C.705 B.A. L.273 J.D. [Finnegan,H.F.G.&D.]
*PRACTICE AREAS: Patent Infringement.

Fues, Eric J. ....'62 '95 C.597 B.S. L.424 J.D. [[A] Pennie&E.]
*PRACTICE AREAS: Intellectual Property; Patent Litigation.

Fulbright & Jaworski L.L.P., (AV)
801 Pennsylvania Avenue, N.W., 20004-2604 ⊙
Telephone: 202-662-0200 Fax: 202-662-4643
Email: info@fulbright.com URL: http://www.fulbright.com
Partners: Robert J. Koch (Not admitted in DC); John E. Lynch; Mark E. Ungerman. Counsel: Thomas S. Hahn; Michael J. Strauss. Senior Associates: Mary Anne Schofield (Not admitted in DC). Associates: William E. Bradley; Einar Stole (Not admitted in DC).
General Civil Practice. Trial and Appellate Practice before Federal and State Courts, Departments and Agencies. Administrative and Legislative, Antitrust and Trade Regulations, Banking, Corporate and Securities, Customs, Education and Intercollegiate Sports Law, Energy, Environmental, Health Care, Immigration and Export Law, International, Labor and Employment, Patent, Project Finance, Trademark and Copyright, Taxation, Transportation, White Collar Criminal Law.
Houston, Texas Office: 1301 McKinney, Suite 5100, 77010. Telephone: 713-651-5151. Fax: 713-651-5246.
Austin, Texas Office: 600 Congress Avenue, Suite 2400, 78701. Telephone: 512-474-5201. Fax: 512-536-4598.
San Antonio, Texas Office: 300 Convent Street, Suite 2200, 78205. Telephone: 210-224-5575. Fax: 210-270-7205.
Dallas, Texas Office: 2200 Ross Avenue, Suite 2800, 75201. Telephone: 214-855-8000. Fax: 214-855-8200.
New York, New York Office: 666 Fifth Avenue, 31st Floor. 10103. Telephone: 212-318-3000. Fax: 212-318-3400.
Los Angeles, California Office: 865 South Figueroa Street, 29th Floor, 90017. Telephone: 213-892-9200. Fax: 213-680-4518.
Minneapolis, Minnesota Office: 225 South Sixth Street, Suite 4850, 55402. Telephone: 612-321-2800. Fax: 612-321-9600.
London, England Office: 2 St. James's Place, SW1A 1NP Telephone: 011-4420-7629-1207. Fax: 011-4420-7493-8259.
Hong Kong Office: The Hong Kong Club Building, Nineteenth Floor, 3A Chater Road, Central. Telephone: 011-852-2523-3200. Fax: 011-852-2523-3255.
See Professional Biographies, WASHINGTON, DISTRICT OF COLUMBIA

Galvin, Lawrence Francis .... '55 '98 C.871 B.S. L.276 J.D. [[A] Finnegan,H.F.G.&D.]
*PRACTICE AREAS: Mechanical Intellectual Property; Design Patents; Electrical Patent Prosecution; Mechanical Patents; Patent Prosecution.

Garner, Gene M., II .... '58 '88 C&L.446 B.S.E.E., J.D. [Staas&H.]
*PRACTICE AREAS: Intellectual Property Law; Patents; Trademarks; Copyright Law.

Garrett, Arthur S., (AV) ....'38 '64 C.688 B.S.Ch.E. L.273 LL.B. [Finnegan,H.F.G.&D.]
*PRACTICE AREAS: International Patent Prosecution; International Licensing; Trademark Registration.

Garrett, Patrick E. .... '62 '96 C.1338 B.S.E.E. L.446 J.D. [[A] Sterne,K.G.&F.]
*PRACTICE AREAS: Intellectual Property Law.

Garvey, John C., (AV) ....'53 '79 C.228 B.S.E. L.273 J.D. [Staas&H.]
*PRACTICE AREAS: Intellectual Property Law; Patent, Trademark, Copyright and Unfair Competition.

Gerdine, Clint A. '70 '98 C.813 B.S. L.705 J.D.
(adm. in VA; not adm. in DC) [[A] Kenyon&K.] ‡
*PRACTICE AREAS: Intellectual Property.

Gifford, C. Nichole '74 '99 C.834 B.S. L.836 J.D.
(adm. in TN; not adm. in DC) [[A] Rothwell,F.E.&M.]
*PRACTICE AREAS: Intellectual Property.

Gilsdorf, Christine J. ....'61 '98 C.886 B.S. L.150 J.D. [[A] Staas&H.]
*PRACTICE AREAS: Intellectual Property Law; Patents; Trademarks; Copyrights.

Glembocki, Christopher R. ....'— '95 C.893 B.S.E.E. L.904 J.D. [Banner&W.]
*PRACTICE AREAS: Intellectual Property Law; Patents; Electrical Intellectual Property; Computer and Software Patents; Electronic Patents.

Glueck, Daniel S. .... '66 '93 C&L.309 A.B., J.D. [Fitzpatrick,C.H.&S.]

Goldberg, Joshua L. '— '99 C.910 B.S. L.273 J.D.
(adm. in VA; not adm. in DC) [[A] Nath&Assoc.]

Goldsmith, Barry S. ....'62 '94 C.886 B.S.E.E. L.260 J.D. [[A] Kenyon&K.]
*PRACTICE AREAS: Intellectual Property.

Goldstein, Jorge A., (AV) .... '49 '83 C.688 B.S. L.273 J.D. [Sterne,K.G.&F.]
*PRACTICE AREAS: Agrochemicals; Life Sciences; Technology Transfers; Biotechnology; Intellectual Property.

Goldstein, Melvin '34 '70 C.831 A.B. L.276 J.D.
(adm. in MD; not adm. in DC) [[C] Keil&W.]
*PRACTICE AREAS: Patents.

Gollhofer, Richard A. ....'55 '81 C.701 B.S. L.146 J.D. [Staas&H.]
*PRACTICE AREAS: Intellectual Property Law; Patent, Trademark, Copyright and Unfair Competition.

Gollin, Michael A., (AV) ....'57 '85 C.674 A.B. L.94 J.D. [Venable,A.B.H.&C.]
*PRACTICE AREAS: Intellectual Property; Patent Law; Biotechnology; Trademarks; Environmental Law.

Gonsalves, Gregory J. '60 '97 C.823 Ph.D. L.276 J.D.
(adm. in VA; not adm. in DC) [[A] Pennie&E.]
*PRACTICE AREAS: Intellectual Property.

Goodman, Alfred N., (AV) ......'45 '70 C.696 B.S.M.E. L.276 J.D. [Roylance,A.B.&G.]
*PRACTICE AREAS: Litigation; Patent Law; Trademark Law; Copyright Law; Mechanical Patent Law.

Gorski, Joseph M. '61 '96 C.475 B.S.M.E. L.1209 J.D.
(adm. in VA; not adm. in DC) [[A] Wenderoth,L.&P.]
*PRACTICE AREAS: Mechanical Patent Prosecution; Electrical Patent Prosecution.

Graham, Barry W., (AV) ......'47 '77 C.893 B.S.E.E. L.280 J.D. [Finnegan,H.F.G.&D.]
*PRACTICE AREAS: Electronic Intellectual Property; Intellectual Property Infringement; Intellectual Property Litigation; Computer and Software Patents; Technology Protection.

Grasso, Fred .... '66 '97 C.893 B.S.C.E. L.904 J.D. [[A] Kenyon&K.]
*PRACTICE AREAS: Intellectual Property.

Greenbaum, Michael C. .... '51 '76 C.971 B.S.E.E. L.1292 J.D. [Blank R.C.&M.]
*PRACTICE AREAS: Software Protection; Year 2000 Computer Conversion; Copyright Infringement; Electrical Intellectual Property; Biomedical Technology.

Greene, Donald R., (AV) .... '31 '66 C.472 B.S.E.E. L.273 LL.B. [[C] Blank R.C.&M.]
*PRACTICE AREAS: Electronic Patents; Intellectual Property Licensing; Semiconductor Technology; Technology Licensing; Electronics.

Griffen, Susan Haberman, (AV) ... '56 '82 C.350 B.S. L.352 J.D. [Finnegan,H.F.G.&D.]
*PRACTICE AREAS: Biotechnology Patents.

Grimaldi, Alan M., (AV) ....'44 '72 C.563 B.Ch.E. L.128 J.D. [Howrey S.A.&W.]
*PRACTICE AREAS: Antitrust; Commercial Law; Intellectual Property; Arbitration; Insurance Coverage.

Gruskin, Steven M. .... '66 '91 C.472 B.S.M.E. L.273 J.D. [Sughrue M.]
*PRACTICE AREAS: Intellectual Property Law.

Gubinsky, Louis, (P.C.), (AV) .... '41 '67 C.446 B.S. L.276 LL.B. [Sughrue M.]
*PRACTICE AREAS: Intellectual Property Law; Biotechnology.

Gutowski, Anthony M. ....'67 '94 C.884 B.M.E. L.273 J.D. [[A] Finnegan,H.F.G.&D.]
*PRACTICE AREAS: Mechanical Patents; Electro-Mechanical Patents; Medical Patents; Patent Protection; Patent Prosecution.

Haddaway, Keith G. .... '58 '97 C.1203 B.S. L.273 J.D. [[A] Venable,A.B.H.&C.]
*PRACTICE AREAS: Intellectual Property.

Hadjis, Alexander J. ....'67 '95 C.608 B.S.E.E. L.665 J.D. [Fish&R.]
*PRACTICE AREAS: Intellectual Property Law.

Hahm, W. Douglas '68 '00 C.645 B.S.M.E. L.1356 J.D.
(adm. in VA; not adm. in DC) [[A] Wenderoth,L.&P.]
*PRACTICE AREAS: Patent Prosecution; Mechanical Patents.

Hahn, Thomas S. ....'44 '77 C.645 B.S. L.1209 J.D. [[C] Fulbright&J.]
*PRACTICE AREAS: Intellectual Property; Patents; Trademarks; Copyrights.

Hails, Robert L., Jr. .... '68 '93 C.446 B.S. L.273 J.D. [Ⓐ Kenyon&K.]
*PRACTICE AREAS: Intellectual Property.
Halber, Eric P. .... '63 '90 C.390 B.S.M.E. L.1202 J.D. [Ⓐ Sughrue M.]
*PRACTICE AREAS: Intellectual Property.
Halsey, James D., Jr., (AV) .... '35 '64 C.446 B.S. L.904 J.D. [Staas&H.]
*PRACTICE AREAS: Intellectual Property Law; Patent, Trademark, Copyright and Unfair Competition.
Ham, Yoon S. .... '61 '94 C.999 B.S.E.E. L.264 J.D. [Jacobson,H.]
*PRACTICE AREAS: Intellectual Property Law; Electrical Patents; Mechanical Patents.
Hamblin, Sarah E. '69 '00 C.890 B.S. L.180 J.D.
(adm. in VA; not adm. in DC) [Ⓐ Adduci,M.&S.]
*PRACTICE AREAS: Intellectual Property Litigation.
Hammond, James K., (BV) .... '52 '78 C&L.893 B.S., J.D. [Finnegan,H.F.G.&D.]
*PRACTICE AREAS: Patent Prosecution; Patent Litigation.
Hanlon, Brian E. .... '— '95 C.971 B.S.M.E. L.128 J.D. [Banner&W.]
*PRACTICE AREAS: Intellectual Property Law; Patents; Design Patents; Mechanical Intellectual Property; Medical Intellectual Property.
Hannon, Brian W. .... '57 '87 C.884 B.S.M.E. L.128 J.D. [Sughrue M.]
*PRACTICE AREAS: Intellectual Property Law; Litigation.
Hanson, Donald W., (AV) '46 '74 C.350 B.S.Ch.E. L.273 J.D.
[Armstrong,W.H.M.&N.]
Hare, William D. .... '63 '95 C.160 B.S. L.326 J.D. [Ⓐ Fish&R.]
*PRACTICE AREAS: Intellectual Property Law.

Harness, Dickey & Pierce, P.L.C.
888 Sixteenth Street, N.W., 20006 ⊙
Telephone: 202-835-7480
Email: info@hdp.com URL: http://www.hdp.com
W. R. Duke Taylor.
Patent, Trademark, Copyright, Unfair Competition, Computer Law, Trade Secrets, Trade Regulation. Trial and Appellate Practice in State and Federal Courts.
Representative Clients: The Black and Decker Manufacturing Co.; Daimler-Chrysler Corp.; Emerson Electric Co.; General Motors Corp.; La-Z-Boy Chair Co.; Matsushita Electric; Monroe Auto Equipment Co.; Sun Microsystems; University of Michigan.
Troy, Michigan Office: 5445 Corporate Drive, Suite 400. Telephone: 248-641-1600. Telefacsimile: 248-641-0270.
St. Louis, Missouri Office: 7700 Bonhomme, Suite 400. Telephone: 314-726-7500. Fax: 314-726-7501.
See Professional Biographies, WASHINGTON, DISTRICT OF COLUMBIA

Harper, Blaney .... '60 '92 C.477 B.S. L.276 J.D. [Jones,D.R.&P.]
*PRACTICE AREAS: Intellectual Property; Intellectual Property Litigation.
Harrison, Mark B., (BV) .... '53 '77 C.1044 B.A. L.1292 J.D. [Venable,A.B.H.&C.]
*PRACTICE AREAS: Trademark Law; Copyright Law; Computer Law.
Harroun, John A. '69 '99 C.160 B.S.E.E. L.446 J.D.
(adm. in MD; not adm. in DC) [Ⓐ Sterne,K.G.&F.]
*PRACTICE AREAS: Intellectual Property.
Hartmann, Anthony A. .... '66 '96 C.893 B.S. L.602 J.D. [Ⓐ Finnegan,H.F.G.&D.]
*PRACTICE AREAS: Intellectual Property Litigation; Chemical Intellectual Property.
Hattori, Ken-Ichi, (BV) .... '44 '90 C.999 B.A. L.1209 J.D. [Armstrong,W.H.M.&N.]
Haughey, Edmund J., III .... '72 '98 C.659 B.S.E. L.945 J.D. [Ⓐ Fitzpatrick,C.H.&S.]
Hayden, Christopher G. '57 '97 C.339 B.S. L.326 J.D.
(adm. in TX; not adm. in DC) [Ⓐ Pennie&E.]
*PRACTICE AREAS: Intellectual Property.
Hayden, John F. .... '66 '92 C.150 B.S. L.309 J.D. [Fish&R.]
*PRACTICE AREAS: Intellectual Property; Patents.
Hayes, Jennifer M. .... '68 '94 C&L.329 B.S., J.D. [Ⓐ Sughrue M.]
*PRACTICE AREAS: Patent Law.
Heflin, H. Ray '67 '97 C.277 B.S. L.1218 J.D.
(adm. in VA; not adm. in DC) [Ⓐ Sughrue M.]
Hefter, Laurence R., (AV) .... '35 '64 C.688 B.M.E. L.273 J.D. [Finnegan,H.F.G.&D.]
*PRACTICE AREAS: Trademarks; Trademark Litigation; Unfair Competition; Intellectual Property Litigation; Alternative Dispute Resolution.
Helfrich, George F. '33 '70 C.861 B.S. L.420 J.D.
(adm. in LA; not adm. in DC) [Ⓒ Keil&W.]
*PRACTICE AREAS: Chemical Patents; Litigation; Licensing; Trade Secret and Trademark Law.
Hemmendinger, Lisa M. .... '— '98 C.788 A.B. L.446 J.D. [Ⓐ Banner&W.]
*PRACTICE AREAS: Intellectual Property Law; Patents; Biotechnology; Pharmaceutical Intellectual Property.
Henderson, Douglas B., (AV) .... '35 '62 C.645 B.S. L.273 J.D. [Finnegan,H.F.G.&D.]
*PRACTICE AREAS: Intellectual Property Litigation; Patents; Technology Licensing; Trade Secrets; Trademarks.

Henderson & Sturm LLP, (AV)
1301 Pennsylvania Avenue, N.W. Suite 1020, 20004-1707 ⊙
Telephone: 202-296-3854 Fax: 202-223-9606
URL: http://www.hsllp.com
Members of Firm: William H. Wright; Michael O. Sturm (Not admitted in DC).
Patent, Trademark, Copyright and Unfair Competition Law and Federal Trial Practice Exclusively, Intellectual Property.
Other Offices: Des Moines, Iowa; Davenport, Iowa; Omaha, Nebraska.
See Professional Biographies, WASHINGTON, DISTRICT OF COLUMBIA

Henry, Mark J. .... '67 '92 C.645 B.S.C.E. L.1338 J.D. [Staas&H.]
*PRACTICE AREAS: Intellectual Property Law; Patent, Trademark, Copyright and Unfair Competition.
Herbert, William F. .... '56 '81 C.93 B.A. L.128 J.D. [Staas&H.]
*PRACTICE AREAS: Intellectual Property Law; Patent, Trademark, Copyright and Unfair Competition.
Herrington, Wayne W., (AV) .... '45 '71 C.500 B.A. L.178 J.D. [Ⓒ Finnegan,H.F.G.&D.]
*PRACTICE AREAS: Intellectual Property Litigation; Patent Litigation; Patent Protection; International Intellectual Property.
Herron, David E., II '— '92 C.375 B.S. L.986 J.D.
(adm. in KS; not adm. in DC) [Ⓒ Stevens,D.M.&M.]
*PRACTICE AREAS: Patent Prosecution; Electro-Mechanical Patents; Patent Litigation.
Hill, David W., (AV) .... '46 '77 C.870 B.S. L.273 J.D. [Finnegan,H.F.G.&D.]
*PRACTICE AREAS: Alternative Dispute Resolution; Intellectual Property; Patents; Trademarks; Unfair Competition.
Hilliard, Thomas P. .... '65 '96 C&L.128 B.M.E., J.D. [Ⓐ Pillsbury W.]
*PRACTICE AREAS: Intellectual Property Law; Patent Law.
Hines, Doris Johnson .... '64 '91 C.688 B.S.E.E. L.273 J.D. [Finnegan,H.F.G.&D.]
*PRACTICE AREAS: Patent Litigation; Electrical Patent Prosecution.
Hissong, Drew, Ph.D. .... '67 '99 C.381 B.S. L.930 J.D. [Ⓐ Sughrue M.]
*PRACTICE AREAS: Intellectual Property Law.
Hoel, John E. '42 '74 C.502 B.S. L.276 J.D.
(adm. in VA; not adm. in DC) [Morgan&F.]
Hoffman, Tara Laster '71 '99 C.886 B.S. L.128 J.D.
(adm. in VA; not adm. in DC) [Ⓐ Roylance,A.B.&G.]
*PRACTICE AREAS: Intellectual Property; Intellectual Property Litigation.
Holman, John Clarke, (AV) .... '38 '66 C.966 B.S. L.30 J.D. [Jacobson,H.]
*PRACTICE AREAS: Intellectual Property Law; Chemical Patents; Metallurgical Patents; Mechanical Patents; Trademarks.
Holmes, John E., (AV) .... '53 '78 C.688 B.S.E.E. L.273 J.D. [Roylance,A.B.&G.]
*PRACTICE AREAS: Patent, Trademark and Copyright Law; Technology Licensing; Electrical and Computer Patent Law.
Hong, Patricia E. .... '— '93 C.886 B.S.M.E. L.180 J.D. [Banner&W.]
*PRACTICE AREAS: Intellectual Property Law; Patents; Design Patents; Intellectual Property Litigation.
Horowitz, Karen G. '68 '95 C.674 B.S.E. L.262 J.D.
(adm. in NY; not adm. in DC) [Ⓐ Pennie&E.]
*PRACTICE AREAS: Patent Prosecution; Patent Opinions.

Hoscheit, Dale H., (AV) .... '— '56 C&L.339 B.S., J.D. [Banner&W.]
*PRACTICE AREAS: Intellectual Property Law; Patents; Intellectual Property Licensing; Intellectual Property Litigation; Biotechnology.
Howell, Jeffrey J. '70 '99 C.367 B.S.M.E. L.64 J.D.
(adm. in MD; not adm. in DC) [Ⓐ Roylance,A.B.&G.]
*PRACTICE AREAS: Patent Law; Patent Litigation.

Howrey Simon Arnold & White, LLP, (AV) BB
1299 Pennsylvania Avenue, N.W., 20004-2402 ⊙
Telephone: 202-783-0800 Fax: 202-383-6610
URL: http://www.howrey.com
Members of Firm: Michael J. Bell; Celine T. Callahan; James F. Davis; Thomas M. Dunham; Alan M. Grimaldi; Joseph P. Lavelle; William K. West, Jr.; J. Paul Williamson. Associates: Jenny W. Chen (Not admitted in DC); Donna D. King; Matthew J. Moore.
General and Trial Practice including Antitrust, Commercial Litigation, Corporate and Transactional, Environmental, Government Contracts, Insurance Coverage, Intellectual Property, International Trade, Products Liability, Securities Litigation, Supreme Court and Appellate and White Collar Criminal Defense.
Century City, California Office: 1925 Century Park East, Suite 2100, 90067-2512. Telephone: 310-712-1000. Fax: 310-712-1099.
Los Angeles, California Office: Suite 1400, 550 South Hope Street, 90071-2604. Telephone: 213-892-1800. Fax: 213-892-2300.
Menlo Park, California Office: 301 Ravenswood Avenue, 94025. Telephone: 650-463-8100. Fax: 650-463-8400.
Houston, Texas Office: 750 Bering Drive, 77057-2198. Telephone: 713-787-1400. Fax: 713-787-1440.
Minneapolis, Minnesota Office: 4850 U.S. Bank Place, 601 Second Avenue South, 55402-4320.
Irvine, California Office: 2020 Main Street, Suite 1000. Telephone: 949-721-6900.
Chicago, Illinois Office: 321 North Clark Street, Suite 800, 60610. Telephone: 312-595-1239. Fax: 312-595-2250.
London Office: City Point, One Ropemaker Street, EC2Y 9HS. Telephone: 011 44 207 6283303. Fax: 011 44 207 065 6650.
See Professional Biographies, WASHINGTON, DISTRICT OF COLUMBIA

Hrozenchik, Mark W. .... '62 '97 C.816 B.E.E.E. L.1252 J.D. [Ⓐ Roylance,A.B.&G.]
*PRACTICE AREAS: Electronics; Intellectual Property.
Hsieh, Timothy M. .... '61 '98 C.367 B.E.S. L.893 J.D. [Ⓐ Finnegan,H.F.G.&D.]
*PRACTICE AREAS: Patent Litigation; Patent Prosecution; Fiber Optics; Semiconductor Technology.
Hu, Yitai .... '65 '94 C.378 B.A. L.446 J.D. [Finnegan,H.F.G.&D.]
*PRACTICE AREAS: Intellectual Property Litigation; Intellectual Property Licensing; International Intellectual Property; International Licensing.
Huleatt, Jayme A. .... '— '88 C.658 B.A. L.128 J.D. [Ⓒ Foley&L.]
*PRACTICE AREAS: Patents; Trademarks; Copyrights; Intellectual Property.
Hulina, Amy L. '64 '97 C.645 B.S. L.30 J.D.
(adm. in VA; not adm. in DC) [Ⓐ Kenyon&K.]
*PRACTICE AREAS: Intellectual Property.
Humphries, Nathaniel A., (AV) .... '34 '65 C.790 B.S. L.273 J.D. [Ⓒ Jacobson,H.]
*PRACTICE AREAS: Intellectual Property; Mechanical Patents.
Huppert, Michael S. .... '58 '90 C.506 B.S. L.1209 J.D. [Wenderoth,L.&P.]
*PRACTICE AREAS: Patent Law; Mechanical Patents; Patent Prosecution.
Hurvitz, John A. .... '64 '91 C.311 B.A. L.976 J.D. [Covington&B.]
Hutchins, John R. .... '70 '96 C.477 B.S.E. L.309 J.D. [Ⓐ Kenyon&K.]
*PRACTICE AREAS: Intellectual Property.
Hwa, James '69 '97 C.178 B.S.E.E. L.273 J.D.
(adm. in NY; not adm. in DC) [Ⓐ Morgan&F.]
*PRACTICE AREAS: Intellectual Property.
Hymel, Lin J. '— '01 L.276 J.D.
(adm. in MD; not adm. in DC) [Ⓐ Banner&W.]
*PRACTICE AREAS: Intellectual Property; Patents; Pharmaceutical Intellectual Property; Medical Intellectual Property; Intellectual Property Litigation.
Hyndman, Kelly G. .... '60 '97 C.870 B.S. L.276 J.D. [Ⓐ Sughrue M.]
Hynds, Joseph A. .... '64 '91 C.894 B.A. L.273 J.D. [Rothwell,F.E.&M.]
*PRACTICE AREAS: Intellectual Property.
Ihnen, Jeffrey L., (AV) .... '51 '80 C.898 B.A. L.273 J.D. [Ⓒ Rothwell,F.E.&M.]
*PRACTICE AREAS: Intellectual Property Law.
Inge, John R., (AV) .... '46 '74 C.119 B.S. L.818 J.D. [Sughrue M.]
*PRACTICE AREAS: Intellectual Property Law.
Irving, Richard C. .... '— '93 C.588 B.S. L.273 J.D. [Ⓐ Banner&W.]
*PRACTICE AREAS: Intellectual Property Law; Patents; Computer and Software Patents; Electrical Patents; Patent Prosecution.
Irving, Thomas L., (AV) .... '51 '77 C.878 B.A.Chem. L.228 J.D. [Finnegan,H.F.G.&D.]
*PRACTICE AREAS: Chemical Intellectual Property; Chemical Patent Prosecution; Chemical Patents; Patent Interference Practice.
Isaac, Christopher P., (BV) .... '59 '87 C.665 B.S. L.273 J.D. [Finnegan,H.F.G.&D.]
*PRACTICE AREAS: Patent Prosecution.
Jackman, Peter A. .... '71 '98 C.884 B.S. L.64 J.D. [Ⓐ Sterne,K.G.&F.]
*PRACTICE AREAS: Intellectual Property Law.
Jackson, Thomas H. .... '— '82 C.659 B.S.E.E. L.776 J.D. [Banner&W.]
*PRACTICE AREAS: Intellectual Property Law; Patents; Electrical Intellectual Property; Intellectual Property Litigation; Computer and Software Patents.
Jacob, Matthew M., (AV) .... '39 '70 C.102 B.S.Chem. L.904 J.D. [Wenderoth,L.&P.]
*PRACTICE AREAS: Chemical Patent Prosecution; Patent Interference Practice; Patent Licensing.
Jacobs, Gary M. .... '51 '76 C&L.846 B.A., J.D. [Ⓐ Fitzpatrick,C.H.&S.]
Jacobson, Harvey B., Jr., (AV) .... '36 '62 C.976 B.Ch.E. L.309 LL.B. [Jacobson,H.]
*PRACTICE AREAS: Intellectual Property Litigation; Chemical Patents; Mechanical Patents.

Jacobson, Holman, PLLC, (AV) BB
400 Seventh Street, N.W., 20004
Telephone: 202-638-6666 Cable Address: "Lawpat" Telefax: 202-393-5350; 202-393-5351; 202-393-5352
Email: IP@JHIP.COM URL: http://www.JHIP.COM
Members of Firm: Harvey B. Jacobson, Jr.; John Clarke Holman; Allen S. Melser; Michael R. Slobasky; Jonathan L. Scherer; Irwin M. Aisenberg; William E. Player; Yoon S. Ham. Associates: Linda J. Shapiro; Suzin C. Bailey (Not admitted in DC); Daniel K. Dorsey; Suzannah K. Sundby (Not admitted in DC). Of Counsel: Marvin R. Stern; Nathaniel A. Humphries.
Patent, Trademark, Unfair Competition, Copyright, Computer and Antitrust Law. International Patent and Trademark Practice. Practice before all Federal Courts, U.S. Patent and Trademark Office and other Administrative Agencies.
See Professional Biographies, WASHINGTON, DISTRICT OF COLUMBIA

Jakes, John Michael, (AV) .... '57 '86 C.228 BSEE L.276 J.D. [Finnegan,H.F.G.&D.]
*PRACTICE AREAS: Intellectual Property Litigation; Appellate Practice; Electrical Intellectual Property; Computer and Software Patents; Medical Patents.
Jalali, Laleh .... '67 '94 C.446 B.S.M.E. L.273 J.D. [Ⓐ Kenyon&K.]
*PRACTICE AREAS: Intellectual Property.
Jarvis, Thomas L. .... '56 '86 C&L.575 B.A., J.D. [Ⓒ Finnegan,H.F.G.&D.]
*PRACTICE AREAS: Patent Litigation; Electrical Intellectual Property; Computer and Software Patents; Semiconductor Technology.
Jay, Jeremy M. .... '53 '90 C.184 B.S. L.1209 J.D. [Leydig,V.&M.]
Jeffery, Donald D., (AV) .... '— '61 C.966 B.S. L.273 LL.B. [Foley&L.] ‡
Jenkins, Thomas H., III, (AV) .... '51 '80 C.198 B.S. L.893 J.D. [Finnegan,H.F.G.&D.]
*PRACTICE AREAS: Patent Litigation; Patent Prosecution.
Jennings, Tipton D., IV, (AV) '32 '60 C.472 B.S.E.E. L.273 J.D.
[Ⓒ Finnegan,H.F.G.&D.]
*PRACTICE AREAS: Patent Prosecution; Trademarks; Intellectual Property Licensing; Intellectual Property Litigation; International Intellectual Property.

Jensen, Allen R., (AV) ....'50 '77 C.877 B.S.Chem. L.273 J.D. [Finnegan,H.F.G.&D.]
*PRACTICE AREAS: Chemical Patent Prosecution; Intellectual Property Portfolio Management; Pharmaceutical Patent Prosecution.

Johnson, Lance G. .... '59 '87 C.350 B.S. L.273 J.D. [Roylance,A.B.&G.]
*PRACTICE AREAS: Preparation; Prosecution; Litigation and Licensing of Patents and Trademarks.

Jones, Brian C. ....'56 '94 C.446 B.S.Ch.E. L.273 J.D. [Ⓐ Blank R.C.&M.]
*PRACTICE AREAS: Chemical Intellectual Property; Pharmaceutical Intellectual Property; Mechanical Intellectual Property; International Intellectual Property; Intellectual Property Infringement.

Jones, Day, Reavis & Pogue, (AV)
51 Louisiana Avenue, N.W., 20001-2113 ⊙
Telephone: 202-879-3939 Telecopier: 202-626-1700
Email: counsel@jonesday.com URL: http://www.jonesday.com
Languages: Chinese, Farsi, French, German, Hindi, Greek, Jamaican Patuis, Russian, Spanish, and Tamil.
Associates: Blaney Harper; Brian D. Lefort (Not admitted in DC).
Patent, Trademark and Copyright Law.
In Atlanta, Georgia: 3500 SunTrust Plaza, 303 Peachtree Street, N.E. Telephone: 404-521-3939. Telecopier: 404-581-8330.
In Brussels, Belgium: Avenue Louise 480, Louizalaan 480, 1050 Brussels. Telephone: 32-2-645-14-11. Telecopier: 32-2-645-14-45.
In Chicago, Illinois: 77 West Wacker. Telephone: 312-782-3939. Telecopier: 312-782-8585.
In Cleveland, Ohio: North Point, 901 Lakeside Avenue. Telephone: 216-586-3939. Telecopier: 216-579-0212.
In Columbus, Ohio: 1900 Huntington Center, 41 South High Street. Telephone: 614-469-3939. Telecopier: 614-461-4198.
In Dallas, Texas: 2727 North Harwood Street. Telephone: 214-220-3939. Telecopier: 214-969-5100.
In Frankfurt, Germany: Hochhaus am Park, Grüneburgweg 102, 60323 Frankfurt am Main. Telephone: 49-69-9726-3939. Telecopier: 49-69-9726-3993.
In Hong Kong, China: 31st Floor, Edinburgh Tower, The Landmark, 15 Queen's Road Central. Telephone: 852-2526-6895. Telecopier: 852-2868-5871 or 852-2868-5699.
In Houston, Texas: Chase Tower, 600 Travis Street, Suite 6500. Telephone: 832-239-3939. Telecopier: 832-239-3600.
In Irvine, California: 5 Park Plaza, Suite 1100. Telephone: 949-851-3939. Telecopier: 949-553-7539.
In London, England: Bucklersbury House, 3 Queen Victoria Street. Telephone: 44-20-7236-3939. Telecopier: 44-20-7236-1113.
In Los Angeles, California: 555 West Fifth Street, Suite 4600. Telephone: 213-489-3939. Telecopier: 213-243-2539.
In Madrid, Spain: Velázquez 51. Telephone: 34-91-520-39-39. Telecopier: 34-91-520-39-38.
In New York, New York: 599 Lexington Avenue. Telephone: 212-326-3939. Telecopier: 212-755-7306.
In Palo Alto, California: 1804 Embarcadero Road, Suite 201. Telephone: 650-739-3939. Telecopier: 650-739-3900.
In Paris, France: 120, rue du Faubourg Saint-Honoré. Telephone: 33-1-56-59-39-39. Telecopier: 33-1-56-59-39-38
In Pittsburgh, Pennsylvania: 500 Grant Street, 31st Floor. Telephone: 412-391-3939. Telecopier: 412-394-7959.
In Shanghai, China: 2805 Kerry Centre, 1515 Nanjing Road West. Telephone: 86-21-5298-6568. Telecopier: 86-21-5298-6569.
In Singapore, Singapore: 30 Cecil Street, #29-01 Prudential Tower. Telephone: 65 538 3939. Telecopier: 65 536 3939.
In Sydney, Australia: Governor Phillip Tower, Level 38, 1 Farrer Place. Telephone: 61-2-9210-6921. Telecopier: 61-2-9210-6926.
In Taipei, Taiwan: 8th Floor, 2 Tun Hwa South Road, Section 2. Telephone: (886-2) 2704-6808. Telecopier: (886-2) 2704-6791.
In Tokyo, Japan: Toranomon 45 Mori Building, 3rd Floor, 1-5, Toranomon 5-chome, Minato-ku, Tokyo 105-0001. Telephone: 81-3-3433-3939. Telecopier: 81-3-5401-2725.
See Professional Biographies, WASHINGTON, DISTRICT OF COLUMBIA

Jordan, B. Delano ....'70 '99 C.886 B.S.E.E. L.945 J.D. [Ⓐ Kenyon&K.]
*PRACTICE AREAS: Intellectual Property.

Kacedon, D. Brian '75 '00 C.228 B.S.E. L.569 J.D.
(adm. in MD; not adm. in DC) [Ⓐ Finnegan,H.F.G.&D.]
*PRACTICE AREAS: Mechanical Patents; Patent Licensing; Patent Litigation; Patent Prosecution.

Kagan, Sarah A. .... '— '88 C.1036 B.A. L.273 J.D. [Banner&W.]
*PRACTICE AREAS: Intellectual Property Law; Patents; Biotechnology; Pharmaceutical Intellectual Property.

Kaminski, Jeffri A. .... '68 '97 C.665 B.S.E.E. L.607 J.D. [Ⓐ Venable,A.B.H.&C.]
*PRACTICE AREAS: Intellectual Property; Electrical Patent Prosecution; Technology Licensing.

Kaminski, Michael D., (BV) .... '— '87 C&L.477 B.S.E., J.D. [Foley&L.]
*PRACTICE AREAS: Patent Litigation; Patent Licensing.

Kandare, Anthony W. '— '01 C.101 B.S.M.E. L.912 J.D.
(adm. in VA; not adm. in DC) [Ⓐ Banner&W.]
*PRACTICE AREAS: Intellectual Property.

Karta, Glenn E. ....'57 '82 C.688 B.S. L.146 J.D. [Ⓒ Rothwell,F.E.&M.]
*PRACTICE AREAS: Intellectual Property.

Kasper, Alan J., (AV) ....'43 '68 C.1044 B.S.E.E. L.276 J.D. [Sughrue M.]
*PRACTICE AREAS: Intellectual Property Law; Litigation.

Katz, Robert S. ....'— '92 C.119 B.S. L.273 J.D. [Banner&W.]
*PRACTICE AREAS: Intellectual Property Law; Patents; Design Patents; Mechanical Intellectual Property.

Keil, Herbert B., (AV) .... '27 '53 C.945 B.S. L.146 J.D. [Keil&W.]
*PRACTICE AREAS: Chemical Patent Law; Patent; Trademark Law; Litigation.

Keil & Weinkauf, (AV) BB
1101 Connecticut Avenue, N.W., 20036
Telephone: 202-659-0100 Telecopier: 202-659-0105
Members of Firm: Herbert B. Keil; Russell E. Weinkauf (Not admitted in DC); Jason D. Voight. Special Counsel: Gerald H. Bjorge; Norman G. Torchin; George F. Helfrich (Not admitted in DC); Ronald H. Smith (Not admitted in DC). Associates: David C. Liechty (Not admitted in DC). Of Counsel: Melvin Goldstein (Not admitted in DC). Technical and Foreign Patent Advisor: Barbara A. Schwalge.
Patent, Trademark, Copyright, Unfair Competition, Licensing and Related Antitrust Law. Litigation.
See Professional Biographies, WASHINGTON, DISTRICT OF COLUMBIA

Kelemen, Gabor J. '30 '72 C&L.30 B.A., J.D.
(adm. in VA; not adm. in DC) [Venable,A.B.H.&C.]
*PRACTICE AREAS: Patent Law.

Kelley, Lara Chapman .... '69 '99 C.896 B.S. L.273 J.D. [Ⓐ Finnegan,H.F.G.&D.]
*PRACTICE AREAS: Biotechnology Patent Law; Chemical Patent Law.

Kelly, David M., (AV) .... '57 '83 C.665 B.S. L.229 J.D. [Finnegan,H.F.G.&D.]
*PRACTICE AREAS: Trademark Litigation; Trademark Prosecution; Domain Names; Trade Dress.

Kenehan, Edward F., Jr., (BV) ....'50 '79 C.277 B.S. L.30 J.D. [Sughrue M.]
*PRACTICE AREAS: Intellectual Property.

Kenyon & Kenyon, (AV) BB
1500 K Street, N.W., Suite 700, 20005 ⊙
Telephone: 202-220-4200 Fax: (202) 220-4201, Groups II & III
Resident Partners: John C. Altmiller; Edward T. Colbert; William K. Wells, Jr.; Brian S. Mudge; John W. Bateman; Douglas E. Ringel (Not admitted in DC). Resident Associates: Mark M. Supko; Judith L. Toffenetti; C. Kyle Musgrove; Gary S. Morris; William M. Merone; John McGroarty; Timothy M. Devlin; John R. Hutchins; Robert L. Hails, Jr.; Karen L. Feisthamel; Teresa A. Lavenue (Not admitted in DC); Bradley J. Meier; Kristina M. Castellano; Mark H. Neblett; Fred Grasso; Clint A. Gerdine (Not admitted in DC); Kenneth R. Corsello; Dan Salehi; Michael M. Shen (Not admitted in DC); Barry S. Goldsmith; David J. Zibelli (Not admitted in DC); Ronald E. Prass, Jr.; Jennifer L. King; Sumeet Magoon (Not admitted in DC); Ronald L. Sigworth; Michael I. Angert; Julie E. Stein (Not admitted in DC); Zeba T. Ali (Not admitted in DC); Amy L. Hulina (Not admitted in DC); Michael A. Siem (Not admitted in DC); William E. Curry (Not admitted in DC); B. Delano Jordan; Laleh Jalali; David R. Schaffer (Not admitted in DC); W. David Wallace.
Intellectual Property Practice. Patents, Trademarks, Copyrights, Trade Secrets, Unfair Competition, Computer Law, Licensing and related Trade Regulation, Antitrust and International Trade Matters. Sports Marketing, Entertainment Law, Trials, Appeals and Arbitration.
New York, N.Y. Office: One Broadway, 10004. Telephone: 212-425-7200. Fax: (212) 425-5288.

(This Listing Continued)

Kenyon & Kenyon (Continued)
Munich, Germany Office: Steinsdorfstr. 10, 80538 Munich. Telephone: 49 89 211 134-30. Fax: 49 89 21 134-49.
San Jose, California Office: Riverpark Towers, Suite 600, 333 West San Carlos Street, 95110. Telephone: 408-975-7500. Fax: (408) 975-7501.
See Professional Biographies, WASHINGTON, DISTRICT OF COLUMBIA

Kerr, Don M. '36 '65 C.845 B.S.B.A. L.273 LL.B.
(adm. in DE; not adm. in DC) [Ⓒ Rothwell,F.E.&M.]
*PRACTICE AREAS: Intellectual Property.

Kessler, Edward J., (AV) ....'43 '70 C&L.273 B.S.E.E., J.D. [Sterne,K.G.&F.]
*PRACTICE AREAS: Intellectual Property Law.

Key, Joseph Franklin ....'69 '99 C.884 B.E.E. L.446 J.D. [Ⓐ Fish&R.]
*PRACTICE AREAS: Intellectual Property.

Kile, Mary Michelle ....'— '95 C.228 B.S.E. L.893 J.D. [Ⓒ Foley&L.]
*PRACTICE AREAS: Intellectual Property.

Kim, Judith U. .... '— '95 C&L.446 B.A., J.D. [Ⓐ Sterne,K.G.&F.]
*PRACTICE AREAS: Intellectual Property.

Kimble, Ronald L. '64 '01 C.446 B.S. L.273 J.D.
(adm. in MD; not adm. in DC) [Ⓐ Sughrue M.]
*PRACTICE AREAS: Intellectual Property.

Kimms, Lyle .... '— '90 C.433 B.E.M.E. L.276 J.D. [Foley&L.]
*PRACTICE AREAS: Intellectual Property.

Kinashi, Sadao ....'50 '97 C.999 B.S. L.146 J.D. [Ⓐ Armstrong,W.H.M.&N.]
*PRACTICE AREAS: Intellectual Property (100%).

Kinberg, Robert, (AV) ....'48 '75 C.910 B.S.E.E. L.273 J.D. [Venable,A.B.H.&C.]
*PRACTICE AREAS: Patent Law; Trademark Law.

King, Donna D. .... '68 '99 C&L.880 B.E., J.D. [Ⓐ Howrey S.A.&W.]

King, Jennifer L. .... '72 '99 C.273 B.S. L.276 J.D. [Ⓐ Kenyon&K.]
*PRACTICE AREAS: Intellectual Property.

Kishimoto, Yoshinari '54 '99 C&L.999 B.A., LL.B.
(adm. in NY; not adm. in DC) [Ⓐ Sughrue M.]
*PRACTICE AREAS: Patent Application; Patent Prosecution; Litigation.

Kit, Gordon, (BV) .... '54 '83 C.178 A.B. L.30 J.D. [Sughrue M.]
*PRACTICE AREAS: Intellectual Property Law; Biotechnology.

Kline, Robert C., (AV) .... '27 '55 C.659 B.S. L.273 J.D. [Ⓒ Fitzpatrick,C.H.&S.]

Klock, Brian L. ....'67 '94 C.886 B.S.E.E. L.273 J.D. [Fitzpatrick,C.H.&S.]

Koch, Robert J., (AV) '46 '73 C.215 B.S. L.128 J.D.
(adm. in VA; not adm. in DC) [Fulbright&J.]
*PRACTICE AREAS: Intellectual Property; Technology and Science; Technology Transfers.

Komen, Edwin, (AV) ....'49 '76 C.800 B.A. L.273 J.D. [Cleary&K.]
*PRACTICE AREAS: Copyright Law; Trademark Law; Unfair Competition Law.

Kong, John P. ....'66 '95 C.569 B.S. L.273 J.D. [Ⓐ Armstrong,W.H.M.&N.]
*PRACTICE AREAS: Intellectual Property Law.

Kopsidas, Andrew '70 '99 C.446 B.S.A.E. L.273 J.D.
(adm. in MD; not adm. in DC) [Ⓐ Fish&R.]

Kordziel, Linda Liu ....'68 '93 C&L.228 B.S.E., J.D. [Fish&R.]
*PRACTICE AREAS: Intellectual Property; Patents; Litigation.

Kornbau, Anne M., (AV) .... '44 '70 C.223 B.S.Chem. L.273 J.D. [Ⓐ Browdy&N.]
*PRACTICE AREAS: Intellectual Property Law; Biotechnology Law; Pharmaceuticals; Chemistry Trademark Law.

Kovalick, Vincent P., (BV) ....'61 '88 C.645 B.S.E.E. L.1209 J.D. [Finnegan,H.F.G.&D.]
*PRACTICE AREAS: Patent Litigation; Patent Prosecution; Patent Licensing.

Kramer, Bruce E. ....'63 '89 C.893 B.S.Che. L.8 J.D. [Sughrue M.]
*PRACTICE AREAS: Intellectual Property Law.

Kraus, Heidi L. .... '69 '97 C.645 B.S. L.273 J.D. [Ⓐ Sterne,K.G.&F.]
*PRACTICE AREAS: Intellectual Property Law; Patent Prosecution; Life Sciences; Biomedical Technology; Pharmaceutical Intellectual Property.

Kravetz, Paul I. .... '63 '92 C.352 B.S.E.E. L.209 J.D. [Staas&H.]
*PRACTICE AREAS: Patents; Copyrights; Trademarks.

Krinsky, Richard Paul ....'— '82 C.24 B.S. L.180 J.D. [Ⓒ Barnes&T.]
*PRACTICE AREAS: Patents; Trademarks; Copyrights; Aviation Law; Intellectual Property.

Kristal, Phyllis '— '00 C.453 B.S.M.E. L.818 J.D.
(adm. in MA; not adm. in DC) [Ⓐ Fish&R.] (⊙Boston, MA)
*PRACTICE AREAS: Patent Law.

Krosin, Kenneth E., (AV) ....'— '72 C.674 B.S.E.E. L.273 J.D. [Foley&L.]
*PRACTICE AREAS: Intellectual Property Litigation.

Krugman, Gary D., (AV) ....'48 '73 C.1044 B.S. L.930 J.D. [Sughrue M.]
*PRACTICE AREAS: Trademark Law; Unfair Competition Law; Copyright Law.

Kubovcik, Ronald J., (AV) ....'44 '73 C.665 B.S.Ch.E. L.229 J.D. [Kubovcik&K.]
*PRACTICE AREAS: Chemical Intellectual Property; Pharmaceutical Intellectual Property; Mechanical Intellectual Property; Trademarks; Patent Prosecution.

Kubovcik & Kubovcik, (AV)
The Farragut Building, 900 17th Street, N.W., Suite 710, 20006
Telephone: 202-887-9023 Fax: 202-887-9093
Email: KandK@kubovcik.com URL: http://www.lawyers.com/kubovciklaw
Ronald J. Kubovcik; Keiko Tanaka Kubovcik (Not admitted in the United States).
Intellectual Property Law, Chemical Intellectual Property, Pharmaceutical Intellectual Property, Mechanical Intellectual Property, Patent Interference Practice, Trademarks.
See Professional Biographies, WASHINGTON, DISTRICT OF COLUMBIA

Kumar, Johnny A. ....'— '93 C.846 B.S.E.E. L.1209 J.D. [Foley&L.]
*PRACTICE AREAS: Intellectual Property Law; Electrical and Computer Patent Law.

Kunitz, Norman N., (AV) ...... '35 '61 C.223 B.S.E.E. L.273 J.D. [Venable,A.B.H.&C.]
*PRACTICE AREAS: Patent Law; Trademark Law.

Lahr, Jack L., (AV) ....'— '63 C.851 B.S.M.E. L.273 J.D. [Foley&L.]
*PRACTICE AREAS: Litigation; Intellectual Property Law; Antitrust Law; Administrative Law.

Lalos, Peter N., (AV) .... '34 '61 C.688 B.S.M.E. L.30 LL.B. [Lalos&K.]
*PRACTICE AREAS: Intellectual Property Law; Corporate Law; Litigation; Appellate Practice.

Lalos & Keegan, (AV) BB
1146 Nineteenth Street N.W., Fifth Floor, 20036-3723
Telephone: 202-887-5555 Telecopier: (202) 296-1682
Email: laloskeegan@radix.net URL: http://www.lawyers.com/lalos&keeganlaw
Members of Firm: Peter N. Lalos; Alfred A. Stadnicki (Not admitted in DC). Associates: Sterling W. Chandler (Not admitted in DC).
Intellectual Property Law including Patent, Trademark, Copyright, International Trade and Unfair Competition Law, before Federal Trial and Appeal Courts, International Trade Commission, Federal Agencies and State Trial and Appeal Courts.
See Professional Biographies, WASHINGTON, DISTRICT OF COLUMBIA

Landsman, Sheldon I., (P.C.), (AV) ....'42 '68 C.563 B.E.Ch.E. L.273 J.D. [Sughrue M.]
*PRACTICE AREAS: Intellectual Property Law.

Lane, Denise Catherine '69 '97 C.454 B.S. L.94 J.D.
(adm. in MA; not adm. in DC) [Ⓐ Blank R.C.&M.]
*PRACTICE AREAS: Intellectual Property Litigation; Intellectual Property Licensing; Patent Prosecution.

Langworthy, Elisabeth A. ....'55 '84 C.788 A.B. L.273 J.D. [Sutherland A.&B.]
*PRACTICE AREAS: Trademarks; Copyrights; Intellectual Property Licensing; Intellectual Property Litigation.

Latker, Norman J. ....'31 '56 C&L.339 B.S.C.E., J.D. [Ⓐ Browdy&N.]
*PRACTICE AREAS: Intellectual Property Law; Mechanical; Electro-Mechanical; Chemistry Law; Government Patent Policy.

Lavelle, Joseph P., (AV) ....'57 '82 C.1028 B.S. L.665 J.D. [Howrey S.A.&W.]
*PRACTICE AREAS: Intellectual Property; Antitrust; Complex Litigation.

Lavenue, Teresa A. '66 '98 C.880 B.S. L.910 J.D. (adm. in CA; not adm. in DC) [[A] Kenyon&K.]
*PRACTICE AREAS: Intellectual Property.
Lavine, Irvin A., (AV) .... '25 '50 C.128 B.A. L.273 J.D. [Nath&Assoc.] ‡
Law, Glenn .... '— '92 C.188 B.S.E.E. L.273 J.D. [Foley&L.]
*PRACTICE AREAS: Patent Law and Litigation; Intellectual Property.
Lawrence, Stanton T., III, (AV) '45 '73 C.172 B.S.Chem. L.273 J.D. [Pennie&E.] (⊙New York, NY)
*PRACTICE AREAS: Intellectual Property Litigation.
Lazarus, Richard B. .... '— '74 C.679 B.S.M.E. L.128 J.D. [[C] Barnes&T.]
*PRACTICE AREAS: Patent Prosecution; Patents; Copyrights; Trademarks.
Ledbetter, James E. '50 '77 C&L.260 B.S., J.D. (adm. in GA; not adm. in DC) [Stevens,D.M.&M.]
*PRACTICE AREAS: Patent Law; Electrical Patents; Mechanical Patents; Trademarks; Copyrights.
Lee, David S. '— '92 C.823 B.S.E.E. L.128 J.D. (adm. in MD; not adm. in DC) [[A] Banner&W.]
*PRACTICE AREAS: Intellectual Property.
Lee, Michael Quentin .... '62 '93 C.893 B.S.E.E. L.276 J.D. [Sterne,K.G.&F.]
*PRACTICE AREAS: Intellectual Property Law.
Leff, Elizabeth A. .... '57 '87 C.454 B.S. L.813 J.D. [Rothwell,F.E.&M.]
*PRACTICE AREAS: Intellectual Property; Litigation.
Lefort, Brian D. .... '67 '98 C.454 B.S.M.E. L.818 J.D. [[A] Jones,D.R.&P.]
Lehman, Christine E. .... '70 '94 C.821 B.S. L.569 J.D. [[A] Finnegan,H.F.G.&D.]
*PRACTICE AREAS: Patent Litigation; Intellectual Property Litigation.
Lehnigk, George F., (AV) .... '63 '91 C.228 B.S. L.273 J.D. [Sughrue M.]
*PRACTICE AREAS: Intellectual Property Law.
Lewis, Joseph D., (AV) .... '— '79 C.319 B.A. L.273 J.D. [Barnes&T.]
*PRACTICE AREAS: Intellectual Property; Computer Law; Trademarks; Copyrights; Technology Law.
Lewris, Basil J., (AV) .... '49 '77 C.563 B.S.Ch.E. L.273 J.D. [Finnegan,H.F.G.&D.]
*PRACTICE AREAS: Civil Appeals; Chemical Intellectual Property; Intellectual Property Litigation; Pharmaceutical Intellectual Property; Biotechnology.

Leydig, Voit & Mayer, Ltd., (AV) [BB]
700 Thirteenth Street N.W., Suite 300, 20005-3960 ⊙
Telephone: 202-737-6770 Telecopier: 202-737-6776
Email: mail@leydig.com URL: http://www.leydig.com
John M. Belz (Resident); Jeffrey A. Wyand (Resident); Jeremy M. Jay (Resident);—Xavier Pillai (Not admitted in DC; Resident); Shannon D. Schemel (Not admitted in DC; Resident); Leah C. Oubre (Resident). Of Counsel: John P. Bundock, Jr. (Resident); John D. Foster (Resident).
Patent, Trademark, Copyright, Unfair Competition and Related Antitrust and International Trade Law. Trials and Appeals.
Chicago, Illinois Office: Two Prudential Plaza, Suite 4900. 180 North Stetson Avenue. Telephone: 312-616-5600. Telecopier: 312-616-5700.
Rockford, Illinois Office: 6815 Weaver Road, Suite 300. Telephone: 815-963-7661. Telecopier: 815-963-7664.

See Professional Biographies, WASHINGTON, DISTRICT OF COLUMBIA

Lieberman, Steven .... '59 '85 C.674 A.B. L.178 J.D. [Rothwell,F.E.&M.]
*PRACTICE AREAS: Intellectual Property; Litigation; Constitutional Law.
Liechty, David C. '69 '99 C.101 B.S. L.878 J.D. (adm. in UT; not adm. in DC) [[A] Keil&W.]
*PRACTICE AREAS: Chemical Patents; Biotechnology Patents.
Lim, Esther H. .... '— '95 C.445 B.A. L.446 J.D. [[A] Finnegan,H.F.G.&D.]
*PRACTICE AREAS: Intellectual Property Litigation; Computer and Software Patents; Technology Licensing; International Intellectual Property; Software Protection.
Lindquist, Leigh Ann .... '— '98 C.788 A.B. L.273 J.D. [[A] Sughrue M.]
*PRACTICE AREAS: Intellectual Property.
Liniak, Berenato, Longacre & White, LLC
(See Bethesda, Maryland)
Lipp, Christopher R. '69 '98 C.886 B.S. (adm. in VA; not adm. in DC) [[A] Sughrue M.]
*PRACTICE AREAS: Intellectual Property.
Lipsey, Charles E., (AV) ..... '50 '77 C.277 B.S.Ch.E. L.273 J.D. [Finnegan,H.F.G.&D.]
*PRACTICE AREAS: Intellectual Property Litigation; Patent Infringement.
Livnat, Shmuel (Sandy) .... '48 '92 C.999 B.S. L.273 J.D. [Venable,A.B.H.&C.]
Longanecker, Stacey J. .... '65 '93 C.446 B.S.E.E. L.128 J.D. [Roylance,A.B.&G.]
*PRACTICE AREAS: Patent, Trademark and Copyright Law; Electrical Patent Law; Computer Law.
Ludwig, Steven R. .... '60 '95 C.645 B.S. L.273 J.D. [Sterne,K.G.&F.]
*PRACTICE AREAS: Intellectual Property Law; Interference Law; Litigation; Trade Secrets; Alternative Dispute Resolution.
Luther, Kurt Albert .... '68 '97 C.37 B.S.M.E. L.36 J.D. [[A] Finnegan,H.F.G.&D.]
*PRACTICE AREAS: Patent Prosecution; Patent Litigation; Mechanical Patents; Computer and Software Patents; Electro-Mechanical Patents.
Lutz, Nancy H. .... '59 '95 C.210 B.A. L.365 J.D. [[A] Pennie&E.]
*PRACTICE AREAS: Litigation; Trademark Law; Copyright Law; Unfair Competition Law; Advertising Law.
Lynch, John E., (AV) .... '37 '64 C.262 B.S. L.276 J.D. [Fulbright&J.]
*PRACTICE AREAS: Intellectual Property.
Mack, Peter G., (AV) .... '— '73 C.436 B.M.E. L.273 J.D. [Foley&L.]
*PRACTICE AREAS: Intellectual Property Litigation.
Mack, Susan J., (AV) .... '50 '83 C.174 B.A. L.30 J.D. [Sughrue M.]
*PRACTICE AREAS: Intellectual Property Law; Biotechnology.
MacMillan, Keith Douglas ...... '62 '00 C.205 B.A. L.273 J.D. [[A] Finnegan,H.F.G.&D.]
*PRACTICE AREAS: Chemical Patent Prosecution; Patent Infringement.
Madden, Thomas J., (AV) ...... '41 '68 C.884 B.S.E.E. L.128 J.D. [Venable,A.B.H.&C.]
*PRACTICE AREAS: Government Contract Law; Intellectual Property; Legislative Practice.
Maebius, Stephen B. .... '— '94 C.188 B.A. L.273 J.D. [Foley&L.]
*PRACTICE AREAS: Intellectual Property.
Magoon, Sumeet '71 '99 C.223 B.S.E.E. L.64 J.D. (adm. in VA; not adm. in DC) [[A] Kenyon&K.]
*PRACTICE AREAS: Intellectual Property.
Maher, Anne M. .... '61 '91 C.105 B.A./B.S.E.E. L.276 J.D. [Fitzpatrick,C.H.&S.]
Makuch, Michael A. .... '58 '84 C.976 B.S. L.930 J.D. [Smith,G.&R.]
*PRACTICE AREAS: Intellectual Property Law.
Malpede, Scott D. .... '61 '88 C.645 B.S.M.E. L.273 J.D. [Fitzpatrick,C.H.&S.]
Manbeck, Harry F., Jr. .... '26 '55 C.401 B.S.E.E. L.421 LL.B. [Rothwell,F.E.&M.]
Mandir, William H. .... '60 '87 C.446 B.S.E.E. L.1218 J.D. [Sughrue M.]
*PRACTICE AREAS: Intellectual Property Law; Litigation.
Manspeizer, David Avrum, (BV) '63 '91 C.659 B.A. L.705 J.D. [Finnegan,H.F.G.&D.]
*PRACTICE AREAS: Intellectual Property Litigation; Pharmaceutical Intellectual Property; Federal Litigation; Biotechnology Patent Prosecution; Biotechnology Patents.
Marcus, Michael S., (BV) .... '49 '84 C.563 B.Ch.E. L.1209 J.D. [Morgan&F.]
*PRACTICE AREAS: Intellectual Property; Patents; Reexamination and Petition Practice.
Markow, Scott B. '72 '99 C.188 B.S. L.276 J.D. (adm. in MD; not adm. in DC) [[A] Covington&B.]
*PRACTICE AREAS: Intellectual Property; Litigation; Electronic Commerce; Food and Drug Regulation.
Marsh, Virgil H., (AV) .... '35 '64 C.446 B.S.Ch.E. L.276 J.D. [Fisher,C.&S.]
*PRACTICE AREAS: Patent, Trademark, Copyright; Unfair Competition and related Litigation.
Mason, Geoffrey Colbourne ..... '71 '97 C.309 A.B. L.276 J.D. [[A] Finnegan,H.F.G.&D.]
*PRACTICE AREAS: Pharmaceutical Intellectual Property; Civil Litigation; Biotechnology Patent Prosecution.
Mason, Matthew Jerald .... '70 '00 C.101 B.S.Ch.E. L.846 J.D. [[A] Finnegan,H.F.G.&D.]
*PRACTICE AREAS: Chemical Patents; Pharmaceutical Patents.
Masters, Robert M. .... '63 '90 C.645 B.S.E.E. L.64 J.D. [Sughrue M.]
*PRACTICE AREAS: Intellectual Property Law; Litigation.
Matthews, Robert A., Jr. ..... '63 '92 C.886 B.S.M.E. L.893 J.D. [[A] Finnegan,H.F.G.&D.]
*PRACTICE AREAS: Electro-Mechanical Patents; Patent Infringement; Patent Litigation.
May, Timothy James '68 '98 C.966 B.S.E.E. L.1209 J.D. (adm. in VA; not adm. in DC) [[A] Finnegan,H.F.G.&D.]
*PRACTICE AREAS: Intellectual Property Litigation; Patent Prosecution.
McAndrews, Roland George, Jr. '68 '98 C.884 B.M.E. L.128 J.D. [[A] Finnegan,H.F.G.&D.]
*PRACTICE AREAS: Mechanical Patents.
McCabe, Kevin William .... '70 '99 C.692 B.S. L.273 J.D. [[A] Finnegan,H.F.G.&D.]
*PRACTICE AREAS: Patent Litigation; Biotechnology Patent Prosecution.
McCall, Molly A. .... '63 '98 C&L.665 B.S., J.D. [[A] Sterne,K.G.&F.]
*PRACTICE AREAS: Intellectual Property Law.
McCann, Clifton E., (AV) .... '50 '78 C.697 B.S. L.128 J.D. [Venable,A.B.H.&C.]
*PRACTICE AREAS: Patent Litigation; Patents; Trademarks; Copyrights; New Media Law.
McClain, William T. ...... '26 '58 C.383 B.S.Met.E. L.425 J.D. [[C] Finnegan,H.F.G.&D.]
*PRACTICE AREAS: Chemical Intellectual Property; Intellectual Property Infringement; Intellectual Property Licensing; International Licensing; Mechanical Intellectual Property.
McCurdy, Barbara Clarke .... '60 '86 C.228 B.S.M.E. L.818 J.D. [Finnegan,H.F.G.&D.]
*PRACTICE AREAS: Intellectual Property Infringement; Intellectual Property Litigation; Mechanical Intellectual Property; Medical Intellectual Property; Technology Protection.
McDowell, Barbara Ann '— '87 C.935 B.S. L.273 J.D. (adm. in VA; not adm. in DC) [[C] Foley&L.]
*PRACTICE AREAS: Chemistry; Biotechnology; Patent Prosecution.
McEwen, James G. '70 '96 C.846 B.S. L.273 J.D. (adm. in VA; not adm. in DC) [[A] Staas&H.]
*PRACTICE AREAS: Patent Law; Trademark Law; Trade Secret; Licensing; Intellectual Property Law.
McGee, Peter .... '55 '85 C.188 B.S. L.128 J.D. [[A] Ostrolenk,F.G.&S.]
*PRACTICE AREAS: Patent Law.
McGroarty, John .... '67 '97 C.659 B.S. L.276 J.D. [[A] Kenyon&K.]
*PRACTICE AREAS: Intellectual Property.
McGurk, Michael R., (BV) ... '60 '88 C.205 B.S.Ch.E. L.273 J.D. [Finnegan,H.F.G.&D.]
*PRACTICE AREAS: Intellectual Property Litigation; Patent Interference Practice; Patent Licensing; Patent Prosecution.
McKee, Christopher L. .... '— '88 C.350 B.S. L.273 J.D. [Banner&W.]
*PRACTICE AREAS: Intellectual Property Law; Intellectual Property Litigation; Appellate Practice.
McKenna, Peter A. .... '51 '94 C.570 B.S.E.E. L.776 J.D. [Sughrue M.]
*PRACTICE AREAS: Intellectual Property Law.
McKeon, Michael J. .... '68 '97 C.184 B.S. L.273 J.D. [Fish&R.]
*PRACTICE AREAS: Intellectual Property Litigation.
McKie, Edward F., Jr., (AV) .... '— '52 C.688 B.E.E. L.276 J.D. [[C] Banner&W.]
*PRACTICE AREAS: Intellectual Property Law.
McKiernan, Thomas Edward '62 '95 C.1229 B.S.M.E. L.215 J.D. (adm. in MI; not adm. in DC) [[A] Rothwell,F.E.&M.]
*PRACTICE AREAS: Intellectual Property.
McLeland, Le-Nhung .... '49 '83 C.1209 B.A. L.904 J.D. [[C] Armstrong,W.H.M.&N.]
McManus, Michael G. '69 '94 C.280 B.A. L.45 J.D. (adm. in GA; not adm. in DC) [[A] Adduci,M.&S.]
*PRACTICE AREAS: Customs Law; International Trade Regulation; Patent Litigation.
McMorrow, Robert G., (P.C.), (AV) .... '30 '57 C.999 B.S. L.276 LL.B. [[C] Sughrue M.]
*PRACTICE AREAS: Intellectual Property Law; Trademark Law.
McNamara, Brian J., (AV) '— '86 C.433 B.E.E. L.446 J.D. [Foley&L.] (⊙Annapolis, MD)
*PRACTICE AREAS: Electronics; Intellectual Property.
McNeely, Kevin J. .... '63 '92 C.971 B.S. L.1202 J.D. [[A] Fish&R.]
*PRACTICE AREAS: Patent Prosecution; Telecommunications Law; Regulatory; Internet Law; Intellectual Property.
McNeill, Rebecca .... '70 '97 C.604 B.A. L.276 J.D. [[A] Finnegan,H.F.G.&D.]
*PRACTICE AREAS: Biotechnology Patent Prosecution; International Intellectual Property.
Medlock, Nina L. .... '— '80 C.217 B.S. L.273 J.D. [Banner&W.]
*PRACTICE AREAS: Intellectual Property Law; Patents; Electrical Intellectual Property; Computer and Software Patents.
Meeker, Frederic M. .... '— '92 C.1356 B.S. L.1209 J.D. [Banner&W.]
*PRACTICE AREAS: Intellectual Property Law; Patents; Intellectual Property Litigation; International Trade; Electrical Intellectual Property.
Meier, Bradley J. .... '73 '99 C.902 B.S. L.602 J.D. [[A] Kenyon&K.]
*PRACTICE AREAS: Intellectual Property.
Melser, Allen S., (AV) .... '46 '72 C.659 B.S.E.E. L.276 J.D. [Jacobson,H.]
*PRACTICE AREAS: Intellectual Property; Electrical Patents; Computer and Software Patents; Multimedia Law.
Merone, William M. .... '69 '95 C.800 B.S.B.A. L.893 J.D. [[A] Kenyon&K.]
*PRACTICE AREAS: Intellectual Property.
Metzenthin, George A. .... '69 '95 C&L.930 B.S.E.E., J.D. [Cahn&S.]
*PRACTICE AREAS: Intellectual Property Law.
Mexic, Darryl, (P.C.), (AV) .... '40 '66 C.277 B.E.E. L.276 J.D. [Sughrue M.]
*PRACTICE AREAS: Intellectual Property Law.
Meyer, Jerald L. '— '98 C.477 B.S. L.1218 J.D. (adm. in VA; not adm. in DC) [[A] Nath&Assoc.]
Meyer, Nicole M. '73 '98 C.31 B.A. L.904 J.D. (adm. in VA; not adm. in DC) [[A] Dickinson W.]
*PRACTICE AREAS: Trademark Litigation and Prosecution; Copyright Litigation and Prosecution.
Meyers, Kenneth John, (AV) ...... '40 '71 C.474 B.S. L.276 J.D. [Finnegan,H.F.G.&D.]
*PRACTICE AREAS: Pharmaceutical Patents; Biotechnology Patents.
Michel, Christian C. '70 '99 C.390 B.S.E.E. L.884 J.D. (adm. in PA; not adm. in DC) [[A] Roylance,A.B.&G.]
*PRACTICE AREAS: Electrical Patent Law; Trademark; Computer Law.
Michelsohn, Arie M. '62 '99 C.178 B.A. L.273 (adm. in NY; not adm. in DC) [[A] Finnegan,H.F.G.&D.]
*PRACTICE AREAS: Intellectual Property Litigation; Intellectual Property Portfolio Management; Biotechnology Patents; Chemistry; Life Sciences.
Mickney, Marcus R. '69 '00 C.886 BSAE L.1209 J.D. (adm. in VA; not adm. in DC) [[A] Roylance,A.B.&G.]
*PRACTICE AREAS: Patents; Trademarks; Copyrights.
Miller, John T., (AV) .... '35 '65 C.835 B.A.Chem. L.273 J.D. [[C] Wenderoth,L.&P.]
*PRACTICE AREAS: Patents; Chemical Patents; Pharmaceutical Patents; Interference Practice.
Minsker, Helen Hill, (AV) .... '— '88 C.881 A.B. L.273 J.D. [Banner&W.]
*PRACTICE AREAS: Intellectual Property Law; Trademarks; Copyrights; Intellectual Property Litigation.
Mintz, Herbert H., (AV) .... '46 '72 C.186 B.Ch.E. L.273 J.D. [Finnegan,H.F.G.&D.]
*PRACTICE AREAS: Patent Interference Practice; Patent Litigation.
Mion, John H., (P.C.), (AV) .... '31 '58 C.705 B.S.E.E. L.273 J.D. [Sughrue M.]
*PRACTICE AREAS: Intellectual Property Law.
Mittelberger, Ralph A., (AV) .... '45 '75 C.453 B.S. L.276 J.D. [Fish&R.]
*PRACTICE AREAS: Intellectual Property; Litigation; International Trade Commission.
Monroe, James B. .... '63 '91 C.910 B.S. L.273 J.D. [Finnegan,H.F.G.&D.]
*PRACTICE AREAS: Chemical Intellectual Property; Intellectual Property Litigation; Intellectual Property Portfolio Management; Pharmaceutical Intellectual Property; Patent Litigation.
Montebello, Mary A. .... '60 '85 C&L.383 B.A., J.D. [[A] Smith,G.&R.]
*PRACTICE AREAS: Patents.
Moore, Matthew J. .... '68 '96 C&L.823 B.S., J.D. [[A] Howrey S.A.&W.]
*PRACTICE AREAS: Patent Litigation; Patent Prosecution; Copyright; Trademark; Licensing.

Moran, Michael John '53 '95 C&L.37 B.S., J.D.
(adm. in AZ; not adm. in DC) [A Rothwell,F.E.&M.]
*PRACTICE AREAS: Intellectual Property.

Morgan & Finnegan, L.L.P., (AV) BR
A Registered Liability Partnership
1775 Eye Street, N.W., 4th Floor, 20006 ⊙
Telephone: 202-857-7887 Facsimile: 202-857-7929
URL: http://www.MorganFinnegan.com
Resident Partners: Michael S. Marcus; John E. Hoel (Not admitted in DC). Counsel: Joseph C. Redmond, Jr. Associates: James Hwa (Not admitted in DC); Kenneth P. Waszkiewicz.
Patent and Technology-related law, Trademark, Copyright, Trade Secret and Unfair Competition, Licensing and Related Antitrust, Trade Regulation, Environmental and Food and Drug Law. International Trade Law. Trials and Appeals. Arbitration.
New York, N.Y. Office: 345 Park Avenue, 10154. Telephone: 212-758-4800. Cable Address: "Findurpine". Facsimile: (212) 751-6849. Telex: ITT 421792.
See Professional Biographies, WASHINGTON, DISTRICT OF COLUMBIA

Morin, Michael A. .... '70 '95 C.679 B.S.I.E. L.273 J.D. [A Finnegan,H.F.G.&D.]
*PRACTICE AREAS: Intellectual Property Litigation; Technology Licensing; Civil Appeals.
Morris, Gary S. .... '61 '96 C.688 B.S. L.276 J.D. [A Kenyon&K.]
*PRACTICE AREAS: Intellectual Property.
Moss, Allen J. '64 '97 C.871 B.S. L.36 J.D.
(adm. in AZ; not adm. in DC) [A Finnegan,H.F.G.&D.]
*PRACTICE AREAS: Patent Litigation; Electrical Patent Prosecution; Software Patent Prosecution; Mechanical Patent Prosecution.
Mottley, Darrell Gilbert '— '00 C.886 B.S.E.S.M. L.273 J.D.
(adm. in VA; not adm. in DC) [A Banner&W.]
*PRACTICE AREAS: Intellectual Property; Design Patents; Mechanical Intellectual Property; Computer and Software Patents; Electrical Intellectual Property.
Mrose, James E. .... '64 '89 C.309 S.B.E.E. L.94 J.D. [C Fish&R.]
*PRACTICE AREAS: Intellectual Property; Patents.
Mudge, Brian S. .... '56 '91 C&L.659 B.S., J.D. [Kenyon&K.]
*PRACTICE AREAS: Intellectual Property.
Mullen, Clair X., Jr., (BV) .... '33 '60 C.757 B.S. L.665 LL.B. [Finnegan,H.F.G.&D.]
*PRACTICE AREAS: International Patent Prosecution; Metallurgical Patents; Patent Licensing; Patent Prosecution.
Murphy, Barbara A., (AV) .... '57 '82 C.197 B.A. L.273 J.D. [Adduci,M.&S.]
*PRACTICE AREAS: Antidumping; International Trade Regulation; Unfair Competition; Intellectual Property.
Murphy, Michael T., (BV) .... '58 '83 C.446 B.A. L.64 J.D. [Roylance,A.B.&G.]
*PRACTICE AREAS: Patents; Trademarks; Copyright Law; Litigation; Unfair Competition Law.
Musgrove, C. Kyle .... '70 '96 C.861 B.S. L.1128 J.D. [A Kenyon&K.]
*PRACTICE AREAS: Intellectual Property.
Muskin, Jonathan H. '67 '96 C.861 B.S. L.1000 J.D.
(adm. in NJ; not adm. in DC) [A Staas&H.]
*PRACTICE AREAS: Intellectual Property Law; Patents; Trademarks; Copyright Law.
Myers, George C., Jr., (AV) '38 '73 C.871 B.S. L.93 J.D.
(adm. in MA; not adm. in DC) [C Blank R.C.&M.]
*PRACTICE AREAS: Patent Litigation; Patent Prosecution; Patent Licensing.
Myers-Payne, Sean Christopher '67 '01 C.611 B.A. L.1209 J.D.
(adm. in VA; not adm. in DC) [A Finnegan,H.F.G.&D.]
*PRACTICE AREAS: Patent Prosecution; Biochemical Patents; Pharmaceutical Patents; Biotechnology Patents; Chemical Patents.
Nakamura, Dean H. .... '52 '93 C.312 B.S. L.273 J.D. [Roylance,A.B.&G.]
*PRACTICE AREAS: Intellectual Property Law; Biotechnology.
Nakhleh, William '— '99 C.30 B.S. L.273 J.D.
(adm. in VA; not adm. in DC) [A Finnegan,H.F.G.&D.]
*PRACTICE AREAS: Chemical Intellectual Property; Pharmaceutical Intellectual Property.
Narayanan, Anant S. .... '59 '94 C.999 B.Tech. L.273 J.D. [A Jones,D.R.&P.]
Nath, Gary M., (AV) .... '44 '75 C.693 B.S. L.30 J.D. [Nath&Assoc.] ⊙
*PRACTICE AREAS: Patent and Trademark Prosecution and Litigation; Trade Secrets; Licensing; Acquisitions, Divestitures and Mergers; Joint Ventures.

Nath & Associates, PLLC, (AV) BR
1030 15th Street, N.W. 6th Floor, 20005 ⊙
Telephone: 202-775-8383 or 202-775-9393 Facsimile: 202-775-8396 or 202-882-9409
Email: IP@NATHLAW.COM URL: http://www.NATHLAW.COM
Members of Firm: Gary M. Nath; Harold L. Novick. Associates: Jerald L. Meyer (Not admitted in DC); Joshua L. Goldberg (Not admitted in DC). Retired: Irvin A. Lavine; Donald M. Sandler (Not admitted in DC).
Patent, Trademark, Copyright, Licensing Litigation, International Patents, General Counsel Services.
San Diego, California Office: 110 West C Street, Suite 1300, 92101. Telephone: 619-645-5290. Facsimile: 619-645-5289.
See Professional Biographies, WASHINGTON, DISTRICT OF COLUMBIA

Naughton, Ronald F. '34 '67 C.651 B.S. L.229 J.D.
(adm. in PA; not adm. in DC) [C Armstrong,W.H.M.&N.]
Neal, Chellis E. .... '57 '90 C.446 B.A. L.64 J.D. [A Venable,A.B.H.&C.]
Neblett, Mark H. .... '58 '94 C.339 B.S. L.276 J.D. [A Kenyon&K.]
*PRACTICE AREAS: Intellectual Property.
Neils, Paul F. .... '59 '89 C.475 B.S.M.E. L.128 J.D. [Sughrue M.]
*PRACTICE AREAS: Intellectual Property Law.
Neimark, Sheridan, (AV) .... '35 '62 C.119 B.S. L.273 J.D. [Browdy&N.]
*PRACTICE AREAS: Patent Opinions; Patent Prosecution; Pharmaceuticals and Pesticides; Chemistry; Plastics and Moldings.
Neth, Joann M. .... '59 '89 C.104 A.B. L.893 J.D. [Finnegan,H.F.G.&D.]
*PRACTICE AREAS: Chemical Intellectual Property; Chemical Patents; Patent Infringement; Patent Licensing; Patent Litigation.
Newman, Mark M., (AV) .... '— '62 C.33 B.S. L.904 LL.B. [C Barnes&T.]
*PRACTICE AREAS: Patents; Trademarks; Copyrights.
Niebylski, Charles D. '60 '00 C.602 B.S. L.128 J.D.
(adm. in MD; not adm. in DC) [A Finnegan,H.F.G.&D.]
*PRACTICE AREAS: Chemical Patent Prosecution; Pharmaceutical Intellectual Property; Intellectual Property Portfolio Management.
Novick, Harold L., (AV) .... '42 '73 C.473 B.A. L.273 J.D. [Nath&Assoc.]
*PRACTICE AREAS: Electro-Mechanical Patents; Prosecution; Intellectual Property Licensing; Trademark Prosecution; Copyright Prosecution.

Oblon, Spivak, McClelland, Maier & Neustadt, P.C.
(See Arlington, Virginia)

O'Brien, Patrick D. .... '45 '97 C.885 B.S. L.1209 J.D. [A Sterne,K.G.&F.]
*PRACTICE AREAS: Intellectual Property Law.
O'Connell, Thomas J. .... '48 '86 C.454 B.S. L.904 J.D. [Fitzpatrick,C.H.&S.]
O'Connor, Steven P. .... '60 '96 C.705 B.A. L.893 J.D. [A Finnegan,H.F.G.&D.]
*PRACTICE AREAS: Pharmaceutical Intellectual Property; Biomedical Technology; Microbiology; Biochemical Patents; Biotechnology Patents.
Odedra, Dhiren R. .... '71 '98 C.959 B.S. L.831 J.D. [A Wenderoth,L.&P.]
*PRACTICE AREAS: Patent Law; Electrical Patents; Computer and Software Patents; Patent Prosecution.
Odedra, Kaushal R. .... '69 '95 C.494 B.S. L.436 J.D. [A Wenderoth,L.&P.]
*PRACTICE AREAS: Trademark and Copyright Law.
Olexy, Peter D., (P.C.), (AV) .... '43 '68 C.645 B.S.Ch.E. L.273 J.D. [Sughrue M.]
*PRACTICE AREAS: Intellectual Property Law.
Oliver, Justin J. '72 '97 C.856 B.S. L.904 J.D.
(adm. in VA; not adm. in DC) [A Fitzpatrick,C.H.&S.]
Olsen, Warren E., (AV) .... '46 '75 C.563 B.E. Mech. L.276 J.D. [Fitzpatrick,C.H.&S.]
Oman, Ralph, (AV) .... '40 '73 C.299 A.B. L.276 J.D. [C Dechert]
*PRACTICE AREAS: Intellectual Property.
O'Reilley, D. Patrick, (AV) .... '43 '75 C.871 B.S. L.273 J.D. [Finnegan,H.F.G.&D.]
*PRACTICE AREAS: Intellectual Property Infringement; Intellectual Property Licensing; Intellectual Property Litigation; International Licensing; Mechanical Intellectual Property.
Osenga, Kristen Rae Jakobsen '72 '00 C.352 B.S.E. L.339 J.D.
[A Finnegan,H.F.G.&D.]
Osha, J. Frank, (AV) .... '39 '66 C.453 B.S. L.309 LL.B. [Sughrue M.]
*PRACTICE AREAS: Intellectual Property Law.
Ostroff, Joseph S. .... '72 '97 C.188 B.S. L.273 J.D. [A Sterne,K.G.&F.]
*PRACTICE AREAS: Patents; Chemical Patents; Biotechnology Patents; Patent Interference Practice; Pharmaceutical Patents.

Ostrolenk, Faber, Gerb & Soffen, LLP, (AV)
1725 K Street NW, 20006 ⊙
Telephone: 202-457-7785 Fax: 202-429-8919
Email: email@ostrolenk.com
Stephen A. Soffen. Associates: Peter McGee; Ellen S. Tao. Of Counsel: Leon Zitver.
Patent, Trademark, Copyright and Unfair Competition.
New York, New York Office: 1180 Avenue of the Americas. 10036. Telephone: 212-382-0700. Facsimile: 212-382-0888.
See Professional Biographies, WASHINGTON, DISTRICT OF COLUMBIA

Oubre, Leah C. .... '75 '00 C.420 B.S. L.1509 J.D. [A Leydig,V.&M.]
Palan, Perry, (AV) .... '— '70 C.910 B.S.E.E. L.273 J.D. [Barnes&T.]
*PRACTICE AREAS: Patents; Trademarks; Copyrights; Technology Licensing; Technology Transfers.
Pan, Susan Perng .... '69 '95 C.893 B.S.E.E. L.273 J.D. [Sughrue M.]
*PRACTICE AREAS: Intellectual Property Law.
Panitch, Gerson S. .... '63 '88 C&L.966 B.S.I.E., J.D. [Finnegan,H.F.G.&D.]
*PRACTICE AREAS: Intellectual Property Portfolio Management; Medical Patents; Patent Litigation; Patent Protection.
Pathak, Ajay S. .... '— '93 C.607 B.S. L.161 J.D. [A Banner&W.]
*PRACTICE AREAS: Intellectual Property Law; Patents; Biotechnology; Pharmaceutical Intellectual Property; Chemical Intellectual Property.
Patterson, Kendrick .... '66 '96 C.277 B.S.I.E. L.273 J.D. [A Sterne,K.G.&F.]
*PRACTICE AREAS: Patent; Intellectual Property.
Paul, John C., (AV) .... '54 '79 C.103 A.B. L.930 J.D. [Finnegan,H.F.G.&D.]
*PRACTICE AREAS: Intellectual Property Portfolio Management; Intellectual Property Licensing; Patent Litigation; Patent Prosecution.
Pavelko, Thomas P. .... '49 '80 C.570 B.S.ChE L.1209 J.D. [Stevens,D.M.&M.]
*PRACTICE AREAS: Chemical Patents; Mechanical Patents; Biotechnology Patents.
Payne, Kenneth E., (AV) .... '36 '65 C.378 B.S. L.30 J.D. [C Finnegan,H.F.G.&D.]
*PRACTICE AREAS: Intellectual Property Litigation; Patent Infringement; Technology Transfers; International Intellectual Property; Mechanical Intellectual Property.
Peckarsky, Peter .... '47 '77 C.453 B.S.E.E. L.930 J.D. [C Stevens,D.M.&M.]
*PRACTICE AREAS: Intellectual Property; Complex Litigation; Antitrust; Corporate Law; Fraud.
Pedersen, Nils E. .... '60 '89 C.454 B.S.M.E. L.1209 J.D. [Wenderoth,L.&P.]
*PRACTICE AREAS: Mechanical Patents; Electrical Patents; Prosecution; Licensing.
Peet, Richard C. .... '— '94 C.311 B.S. L.128 J.D. [Foley&L.]
*PRACTICE AREAS: Patents; Trademarks; Licensing; Litigation.
Pellegrini, Carl J. .... '60 '92 C.436 B.S.E.E. L.966 J.D. [A Sughrue M.]
*PRACTICE AREAS: Intellectual Property Prosecution; Intellectual Property Litigation.

Pennie & Edmonds LLP, (AV) BR
1667 K Street, N.W., 20006 ⊙
Telephone: 202-496-4400 Facsimile: 202-496-4444
Email: pennie@info.pennie.com URL: http://www.pennie.com
Partners: Stanton T. Lawrence, III; Paul J. Zegger (Not admitted in DC); Marcia H. Sundeen; Todd A. Wagner (Not admitted in DC). Associates: Nanda K. Alapati; Carl P. Bretscher; Greg P. Roggin; Eric J. Fues; George A. Willinghan, III (Not admitted in DC); Gregory J. Gonsalves (Not admitted in DC); Christopher G. Hayden (Not admitted in DC); Nancy H. Lutz; Max Bachrach (Not admitted in DC); Paul E. Dietze; Serge Sira; Karen G. Horowitz (Not admitted in DC).
Intellectual Property and Technology Litigation including Patent, Trademark, Trade Secrets, Copyright and Unfair Competition Causes, Environmental Law, Communications Law and Related Government Agency Proceedings, Licensing, Arbitration and International Trade Matters. Trials and Appeals in all Federal and State Courts.
New York, New York Office: 1155 Avenue of the Americas. Telephone: 212-790-9090. Facsimile: (212) 869-9741, (212) 869-8864.
Palo Alto, California Office: 3300 Hillview Avenue. Telephone: 650-493-4935. Facsimile: 650-493-5556.
See Professional Biographies, WASHINGTON, DISTRICT OF COLUMBIA

Perron, Jeannie M. .... '57 '85 C.679 B.S. L.273 J.D. [A Covington&B.]
*PRACTICE AREAS: Regulatory Law; Food and Drug Regulation; Regulatory Offences.
Peterson, Stephen L., (AV) .... '44 '74 C.768 B.S. L.117 J.D. [Finnegan,H.F.G.&D.]
*PRACTICE AREAS: Patent Prosecution; Patent Litigation; Trade Secrets.
Peterson, Thomas L. .... '47 '85 C.980 B.S. L.1003 J.D. [Banner&W.]
*PRACTICE AREAS: Intellectual Property Law; Patents; Intellectual Property Licensing; Patent Prosecution; Computer and Software Patents.
Petruzzelli, Julie A. .... '57 '83 C.103 Sc.B. L.893 J.D. [Venable,A.B.H.&C.]
*PRACTICE AREAS: Intellectual Property; Complex Civil Litigation.
Phillips, Lisa N. '64 '01 C.645 B.S. L.1209 J.D.
(adm. in PA; not adm. in DC) [A Rothwell,F.E.&M.]
*PRACTICE AREAS: Patent Prosecution; Patent Litigation.
Pillai, Xavier '52 '94 C.930 Ph.D. L.146 J.D.
(adm. in IL; not adm. in DC) [A Leydig,V.&M.]

Pillsbury Winthrop LLP, (AV) BR
1133 Connecticut Avenue, N.W., 20036 ⊙
Telephone: 202-775-9800 Fax: 202-833-8491
URL: http://www.pillsburywinthrop.com
Senior Attorneys: Henry J. Daley; Thomas P. Hilliard.
General Practice with an emphasis on Administrative, Admiralty and Maritime, Alternative Dispute Resolution, Antitrust and Trade Regulation, Appellate Practice, Art, Aviation and Aerospace, Bankruptcy, Banking, Biotechnology, Business, Civil, Class Actions, Commerce & Technology, Commercial, Communications and Media, Complex and Multi-District Litigation, Construction, Contracts, Corporate, Creditor's Rights, E-Commerce, Emerging Companies, Employee Benefits, Energy, Environmental, Equipment Finance and Leasing, Executive Compensation, Finance, Guardianship and Conservatorship, Health Care and Hospital, International, International Trade, Internet, Labor and Employment, Leases and Leasing, Licensing, Life Sciences, Litigation, Medicare and Medicaid, Mergers, Acquisitions and Divestitures, Natural Resources, Nonprofit and Charitable Organizations, Partnership, Patents, Planning and Land Use, Political, Probate, Products Liability, Project Finance, Real Estate, Regulatory, RICO, Securities, Taxation, Torts, Toxic Torts, Trademark, Trust and Estates, Utility, White Collar Crime, Wills and Zoning Law.
San Francisco, California Office: 50 Fremont Street, 94105-2228. Telephone: 415-983-1000. Fax: 415-983-1200.
New York, New York Office: One Battery Park Plaza, 10004-1490. Telephone: 212-858-1000. Fax: 212-858-1500.
Los Angeles, California Office: 725 South Figueroa Street, Suite 2800, 90017-5406. Telephone: 213-488-7100. Fax: 213-629-1033.
Other Los Angeles, California Office: Century City, 10100 Santa Monica Boulevard, Suite 2300.
Orange County, California Office: 650 Town Center Drive, Seventh Floor, Costa Mesa, California 92626-7122. Telephone: 714-436-6800. Fax: 714-436-2800.
McLean, Virginia Office: 1600 Tysons Boulevard, 22102. Telephone: 703-905-2000. Fax: 703-905-2500.
Palm Beach, Florida Office: 125 Worth Avenue, 33480. Telephone: 561-655-7297. Fax: 561-833-6726.
Sacramento, California Office: 400 Capitol Mall, Suite 1700, 95814-4419. Telephone: 916-329-4700. Fax: 916-441-3583.
San Diego, California Office: 101 West Broadway, Suite 1800, 92101-8219. Telephone: 619-234-5000. Fax: 619-236-1995.

(This Listing Continued)

Pillsbury Winthrop LLP (Continued)

Other San Diego, California Office: 11975 El Camino Real, Suite 200, 92130-5000. Telephone: 619-234-5000. Fax: 858-509-4010.
Silicon Valley, California Office: 2550 Hanover Street, Palo Alto, California 94304-1115. Telephone: 650-233-4500. Fax: 650-233-4545.
Stamford, Connecticut Office: Financial Centre, 695 East Main Street, 06904-6760. Telephone: 203-348-2300. Fax: 203-965-8226.
London, England Office: 54 Lombard Street, EC3V 9DH. Telephone: +44-171-648-9200. Fax: +44-171-283-1656.
Sydney, Australia Office: Level 10, 7 Macquarie Place, NSW2000. Telephone: +612-8214-2200. Fax: 612-8214-2211.
Tokyo, Japan Office: Fuerte Kojimachi Building, 5th Floor, 1-7-25 Kojimachi, Chiyoda-ku, 102-0083. Telephone: +011-81-3-5226-7260. Fax: +011-81-3-5226-7261.
Other Tokyo, Japan Office: 6 Gaikokuho Jimu Bengoshi Jimusho, Fifth Floor, Samon Eleven Building, 3-1, Samon-cho, Shinjuku-ku, 160. Telephone: +813-3354-3531. Fax: +813-3354-3534.
Hong Kong, China Office: 2504-6 Asia Pacific Finance Tower, Citibank Plaza, 3 Garden Road, Central Hong Kong. Telephone: +852-2530-3400. Fax: +852-2530-3355.
Singapore Office: 6 Battery Road #38-01B, 049909. Telephone: +65-227-4700. Fax: +65-227-4711.

See Professional Biographies, WASHINGTON, DISTRICT OF COLUMBIA

Pitcher, David M., (AV) ....'45 '71 C.477 B.S.E. L.823 J.D. [Staas&H.]
*PRACTICE AREAS: Intellectual Property Law; Patent, Trademark, Copyright and Unfair Competition.
Player, William E. ....'51 '82 C.454 B.S. L.93 J.D. [Jacobson,H.]
*PRACTICE AREAS: Intellectual Property Law; Biotechnology Patents; Chemical Patents.
Polk, C. Edward, Jr. '67 '99 C.446 B.S. L.273 J.D.
(adm. in VA; not adm. in DC) [A Covington&B.]
*PRACTICE AREAS: Intellectual Property; Patents.
Pollock, Robert A. .... '62 '99 C.976 B.S. L.273 J.D. [A Finnegan,H.F.G.&D.]
*PRACTICE AREAS: Genetics; Immunology; Biotechnology Patent Prosecution; Biotechnology Patents; Molecular Biology Patents.
Potenza, Joseph M., (AV) ....'— '75 C.999 B.S.E.E. L.276 J.D. [Banner&W.]
*PRACTICE AREAS: Intellectual Property Law; Patents; Copyrights; Intellectual Property Litigation; Intellectual Property Licensing.
Powell, Raymond H. J., Jr. '52 '88 C.152 B.S.E.E. L.273 J.D.
(adm. in VA; not adm. in DC) [C Adduci,M.&S.] (⊙Arlington, VA)
*PRACTICE AREAS: Patent Law.
Prass, Ronald E., Jr. ....'63 '96 C.871 B.S. L.30 J.D. [A Kenyon&K.]
*PRACTICE AREAS: Intellectual Property.
Quillin, George E., (AV) '— '84 C.870 B.S. L.790 J.D.
(adm. in SC; not adm. in DC) [Foley&L.]
*PRACTICE AREAS: Intellectual Property Law.
Quintos, Mel R. ....'56 '86 C.1044 B.E. L.608 J.D. [Armstrong,W.H.M.&N.]
Rabena, John F. ....'65 '94 C.870 B.S.E.E. L.64 J.D. [Sughrue M.]
*PRACTICE AREAS: Intellectual Property Law; Litigation.
Racine, Richard B., (AV) .... '56 '81 C.276 B.S. L.930 J.D. [Finnegan,H.F.G.&D.]
*PRACTICE AREAS: Patent Litigation; Pharmaceutical Patents; Chemical Patents.
Raciti, Eric P. .... '66 '95 C.886 B.S. L.128 J.D. [A Finnegan,H.F.G.&D.]
*PRACTICE AREAS: Intellectual Property Procurement; International Intellectual Property; Electro-Mechanical Patents; Medical Patents; Patent Litigation.
Racunas, Robert V. '71 '96 C.665 B.S. L.273 J.D.
(adm. in VA; not adm. in DC) [A Fish&R.]
Raphael, Aaron M. .... '73 '99 C.477 B.S. L.245 J.D. [A Finnegan,H.F.G.&D.]
*PRACTICE AREAS: Patent Law.
Rauchholz, William F. .... '— '92 C.477 B.S.E. L.1356 J.D. [C Banner&W.]
*PRACTICE AREAS: Intellectual Property; Patents; Chemical Intellectual Property.
Ray, Michael B. .... '64 '90 C.550 B.S.E.E. L.1218 J.D. [Sterne,K.G.&F.]
*PRACTICE AREAS: Intellectual Property Law.
Redmond, Joseph C., Jr. ....'24 '55 C.860 B.E.E. L.273 J.D. [C Morgan&F.]
*PRACTICE AREAS: Patents; Copyright; Trademarks; Intellectual Property Law.
Reister, Andrea G. ....'57 '93 C.911 B.S. L.1209 J.D. [C Covington&B.]
Renner, W. Karl '69 '99 C.446 B.S.E.E. L.273 J.D.
(adm. in VA; not adm. in DC) [A Fish&R.]
Repper, George R. ....'54 '82 C.1044 B.S. L.982 J.D. [Rothwell,F.E.&M.]
Ringel, Douglas E. '66 '93 C.188 B.S. L.477 J.D.
(adm. in NY; not adm. in DC) [Kenyon&K.]
*PRACTICE AREAS: Intellectual Property.
Rivard, Paul M. ....'— '98 C.158 B.S. L.128 J.D. [A Banner&W.]
*PRACTICE AREAS: Intellectual Property Law; Patents; Chemical Intellectual Property; Pharmaceutical Intellectual Property.
Robbins, Thomas D. '70 '00 C.446 B.S.E.E. L.128 J.D.
(adm. in MD; not adm. in DC) [A Wenderoth,L.&P.]
*PRACTICE AREAS: Mechanical Patent Prosecution; Electrical Patent Prosecution.
Roberts, Simon D. '68 '91 C&L.999 B.Sc.
(adm. in NY; not adm. in DC) [A Fitzpatrick,C.H.&S.]
Robins, Eric P. '74 '99 C.893 L.1209 J.D.
(adm. in VA; not adm. in DC) [C Stevens,D.M.&M.]
*PRACTICE AREAS: Patents; Trademarks; Copyright.
Robinson, Douglas W. ....'— '86 C.688 B.S. L.978 J.D. [C Banner&W.]
*PRACTICE AREAS: Patent; Trademark; Copyright and Unfair Competition Law.
Rodgers, Dennis C. ....'62 '89 C.431 B.S. L.273 J.D. [Smith,G.&R.]
*PRACTICE AREAS: Intellectual Property Law; Patent Prosecution; International Patent Prosecution.
Roggin, Greg P. ....'69 '94 C.477 B.A. L.910 J.D. [A Pennie&E.]
*PRACTICE AREAS: Patent Litigation; Intellectual Property Licensing; Intellectual Property Litigation.
Romary, John M., (AV) ....'47 '73 C.401 B.S.E.E. L.276 J.D. [Finnegan,H.F.G.&D.]
*PRACTICE AREAS: Patent Litigation; Patent Prosecution; Patent Licensing.
Rosner, Abraham J. ....'56 '88 C.276 B.S. L.1209 J.D. [Sughrue M.]
*PRACTICE AREAS: Intellectual Property Law.
Rotella, Robert F. .... '41 '68 C.569 B.E.E. L.273 J.D. [C Finnegan,H.F.G.&D.]
*PRACTICE AREAS: Intellectual Property.
Roth, Christopher B. ....'— '99 C.679 B.S. L.494 J.D. [A Banner&W.]
*PRACTICE AREAS: Intellectual Property Law; Intellectual Property Litigation; Chemical Intellectual Property; Patent Prosecution.
Rothwell, G. Franklin, (AV) ..... '28 '56 C.502 B.S.M.E. L.273 J.D. [Rothwell,F.E.&M.]
*PRACTICE AREAS: Intellectual Property.

Rothwell, Figg, Ernst & Manbeck, A Professional Corporation, (AV) BB
Suite 701 East Tower, 555 Thirteenth Street, N.W., 20004 ⊙
Telephone: 202-783-6040 Facsimile: 202-783-6031
Email: info@rothwellfigg.com URL: http://www.rothwellfigg.com
G. Franklin Rothwell; E. Anthony Figg; Barbara G. Ernst; Harry F. Manbeck, Jr.; George R. Repper; Steven Lieberman; Vincent M. DeLuca; Joseph A. Hynds; Robert J. Jondle (Resident, Omaha, Nebraska Office); Elizabeth A. Leff;—Martha Cassidy; Gregg L. Jansen (Not admitted in DC; Resident, Omaha, Nebraska Office); Nancy T. Morris (Not admitted in DC; Resident, Omaha, Nebraska Office); Lisa A. Fahien Uldrich (Not admitted in DC; Resident, Omaha, Nebraska Office); Richard Wydeven; Thomas Edward McKiernan (Not admitted in DC); Jason M. Shapiro (Not admitted in DC); Michael John Moran (Not admitted in DC); Anne M. Sterba; Lisa N. Phillips (Not admitted in DC); Leigh M. Zanowski (Not admitted in DC); C. Nichole Gifford (Not admitted in DC). Of Counsel: Don M. Kerr (Not admitted in DC); Jeffrey L. Ihnen; Glenn E. Karta; Mark I. Bowditch; Minaksi Bhatt; Michael G. Sullivan.
Intellectual Property Law, Practice and Related Litigation, including Patent, Trademark, Copyright, Unfair Competition, Trade Secrets, Licensing and Related Antitrust Law. Defamation Law and other First Amendment Issues.
Omaha, Nebraska Office: 13906 Gold Circle, Suite 204, 68144. Telephone: 402-333-1550. Fax: 402-333-1510.

See Professional Biographies, WASHINGTON, DISTRICT OF COLUMBIA

Roylance, Abrams, Berdo & Goodman, L.L.P., (AV) BB
1300 19th Street, N.W., Suite 600, 20036-1649
Telephone: 202-659-9076 Facsimile: 202-659-9344
Email: RABG@roylance.com URL: http://www.roylance.com
David S. Abrams; Robert H. Berdo; Alfred N. Goodman; Mark S. Bicks; John E. Holmes; Michael T. Murphy; Lance G. Johnson; Dean H. Nakamura; Stacey J. Longanecker; Joseph J. Buczynski; Garrett V. Davis. Associates: Tara Laster Hoffman (Not admitted in DC); Jeffrey J. Howell (Not admitted in DC); Aisha Ahmad (Not admitted in DC); Marcus R. Mickney (Not admitted in DC); Christian C. Michel (Not admitted in DC); Mark W. Hrozenchik.
Patent, Trademark, Copyright and Unfair Competition Law. International Patent and Trademark Practice. Litigation in all Federal Courts.

See Professional Biographies, WASHINGTON, DISTRICT OF COLUMBIA

Ruch, Joseph J., Jr., (BV) '48 '75 C.223 B.S. L.273 J.D.
(adm. in VA; not adm. in DC) [Sughrue M.]
*PRACTICE AREAS: Intellectual Property Law.
Saidman, Perry J., (AV) .... '45 '73 C&L.273 B.S.E.E., J.D. [S.DesignLaw] ⊙
*PRACTICE AREAS: Intellectual Property; Design Patents; Design Law; Trade Dress; Artistic Property.

SAIDMAN DesignLaw Group, (AV)
1201 Connecticut Avenue, Suite 750, 20036 ⊙
Telephone: 202-223-0800 Fax: 202-223-6607
Email: Group@designlaw.com
Perry J. Saidman.
Industrial Designs, Design Protection, Industrial Design Law, Industrial Design Registrations, Design Patents, Design Law, Design Law Expert, Design Law Consulting, Design Patent Prosecution, Design Patent Infringement, Trade Dress, Product Configurations, Trademark Law, Trademark Infringement, Trademark Registration, Unfair Competition Law, Intellectual Property, Patent Protection, Royalty Agreements, Licensing Agreements, Expert Witness, Design Copyrights, Designer Agreements, Hague Agreement, Utility Patents, PCT Applications, Utility Patent Infringement, Copyright Law, Copyright Registration, Mediation.
Representative Clients: Imperial Schrade Corp.; Toyota; Boston Acoustics; The Burdick Group; Design Ideas, Ltd.; Virginia Plastics Co.; Panasonic.
Silver Spring, Maryland Office: 1110 Bonifant Street, Suite 510, 20910. Telephone: 301-585-8601. Fax: 301-585-0138.

See Professional Biographies, WASHINGTON, DISTRICT OF COLUMBIA

Salehi, Dan .... '67 '99 C.1074 B.S. L.1218 J.D. [A Kenyon&K.]
*PRACTICE AREAS: Intellectual Property.
Salen, Kenneth Harry '64 '00 C.446 B.S. L.1209 J.D.
(adm. in VA; not adm. in DC) [A Armstrong,W.H.M.&N.]
*PRACTICE AREAS: Intellectual Property; Patents.
Saliba, Raja N. ....'66 '97 C.999 B.S. L.273 J.D. [A Sughrue M.]
*PRACTICE AREAS: Patent Litigation; Patent Prosecution.
Samuels, Frederick N. ....'63 '90 C.446 B.S.E.G. L.273 J.D. [Cahn&S.] ⊙
*PRACTICE AREAS: Intellectual Property Law.
Sandler, Donald M., (AV) '27 '57 C.367 B.E. L.64 LL.B.
(adm. in MD; not adm. in DC) [Nath&Assoc.] ‡
Santorelli, Albert J., (AV) ....'38 '64 C.688 B.S.E.E. L.276 LL.B. [Finnegan,H.F.G.&D.]
*PRACTICE AREAS: Patent Litigation; Patents; Patent Interference Practice; Patent Infringement.
Sartori, Michael A. .... '— '98 C.602 B.S.E.E. L.276 J.D. [C Venable,A.B.H.&C.]
*PRACTICE AREAS: Intellectual Property.
Savitt, Gary ....'— '99 C.871 B.S.A.E. L.904 J.D. [A Fish&R.]
*PRACTICE AREAS: Intellectual Property.
Saxe, Bernhard D., (AV) .... '— '81 C.367 B.A. L.273 J.D. [Foley&L.]
*PRACTICE AREAS: U.S. and Foreign Chemical, Pharmaceutical; Biotechnological Patent, Licensing and Litigation; Trademarks; Technology Transfers.
Scala, Keith B. '75 '00 C.188 B.S. L.365 J.D.
(adm. in IL; not adm. in DC) [A Sughrue M.]
*PRACTICE AREAS: Patents.
Schad, Steven P. .... '— '87 C.474 B.S.C.E. L.1209 J.D. [Banner&W.]
*PRACTICE AREAS: Intellectual Property Law; Patents; Intellectual Property Licensing; Mechanical Intellectual Property.
Schaffer, David R. '58 '97 C.945 B.A. L.128 J.D.
(adm. in VA; not adm. in DC) [A Kenyon&K.]
*PRACTICE AREAS: Intellectual Property.
Schemel, Shannon D. '73 '00 C.790 B.S. L.273 J.D.
(adm. in VA; not adm. in DC) [A Leydig,V.&M.]
Scherer, Jonathan L. .... '54 '82 C.24 B.S. L.1040 J.D. [Jacobson,H.]
*PRACTICE AREAS: Intellectual Property Law; Electrical Patents; Mechanical Patents.
Schill, Charles F., (AV) ....'— '73 C.1031 B.S. L.117 J.D. [Foley&L.]
*PRACTICE AREAS: International Trade Regulation; Intellectual Property; Litigation; Patents; Trademarks.
Schmidt, Jeffrey A. ....'68 '97 C.107 B.S. L.128 J.D. [A Sughrue M.]
Schneller, Marina V., (AV) .... '43 '72 C.788 A.B. L.30 J.D. [Venable,A.B.H.&C.]
*PRACTICE AREAS: Intellectual Property.
Schofield, Mary Anne '— '98 C.667 B.S. L.262 J.D.
(adm. in NY; not adm. in DC) [A Fulbright&J.]
*PRACTICE AREAS: Intellectual Property; Patent Prosecution.
Schwaab, Richard L., (AV) '— '71
C.966 B.S.Ch.E. L.273 J.D. [Foley&L.] (⊙Milw., WI)
*PRACTICE AREAS: Intellectual Property Law.
Schwartz, Arthur, (AV) ....'— '63 C.350 B.S.I.E. L.273 J.D. [Foley&L.] ‡
*PRACTICE AREAS: Intellectual Property Law.
Sears, Mary Helen, (AV) .... '— '60 C.188 A.B. L.273 J.D. [M.H.Sears]
*PRACTICE AREAS: Intellectual Property; Patents; Trademarks; Copyrights; Trade Secrets.

Sears, M.H., The, Law Firm, Chartered, (AV) BB
910 Seventeenth Street, N.W., Suite 800, 20006
Telephone: 202-463-3892 Facsimile: 202-463-4852 URL: http://www.searshahn.com
Email: mhsears@mhsears.com URL: http://www.lawyers.com/mhsearslaw
Members of Firm: Mary Helen Sears.
Litigation, Counseling and Procurement of Rights in all areas of Intellectual Property, including Patents, Trademarks, Copyrights, Trade Secrets and general Unfair Competition matters.

See Professional Biographies, WASHINGTON, DISTRICT OF COLUMBIA

Seas, Robert J., Jr. (P.C.), (AV) ...... '32 '62 C.119 B.S.E.E. L.273 LL.B. [Sughrue M.]
*PRACTICE AREAS: Intellectual Property Law.
Seckel, Nicolas E. '67 '96 L.999 J.D.
(adm. in NY; not adm. in DC) [A Armstrong,W.H.M.&N.]
*PRACTICE AREAS: Intellectual Property (100%).
Shaffer, Gary L. .... '49 '79 C&L.665 B.S.Che., J.D. [Venable,A.B.H.&C.]
*PRACTICE AREAS: Patent Litigation; Patent Prosecution; Biotechnology; Pharmaceuticals; Medical Devices.
Shah, Ankur D. ....'— '97 C.645 B.S. L.273 J.D. [A Foley&L.]
*PRACTICE AREAS: Intellectual Property.
Shannon, John P., Jr. ....'46 '75 C.215 B.M.E. L.273 J.D. [Venable,A.B.H.&C.]
*PRACTICE AREAS: Intellectual Property; Patents; Mechanical Patents; International Patents; Trademarks.
Shapiro, Jason M. '64 '94 C.367 B.S. L.64 J.D.
(adm. in MD; not adm. in DC) [A Rothwell,F.E.&M.]
*PRACTICE AREAS: Intellectual Property.
Shapiro, Linda J., (AV) .... '52 '77 C.860 B.S. L.273 J.D. [A Jacobson,H.]
*PRACTICE AREAS: Intellectual Property Law; Mechanical Patents; Computer and Software Patents.
Shapiro, Ronald E. .... '53 '78 C.367 B.A. L.446 J.D. [Vorys,S.S.&P.]

Sharma, Parmanand "Anand" K. '71 '98
C.446 B.S.M.E. L.564 J.D. [[A] Finnegan,H.F.G.&D.]
*PRACTICE AREAS: Intellectual Property Litigation; Patent Prosecution; Intellectual Property Portfolio Management.

Shatynski, Patricia Ann ... '62 '99 C.570 B.S.Ch.E. L.1338 J.D. [[A] Finnegan,H.F.G.&D.]
*PRACTICE AREAS: Chemical Patent Prosecution; Pharmaceutical Patent Prosecution; Chemicals; Organic Chemistry; Semiconductor Technology.

Shea, Timothy J., Jr. .... '66 '95 C.902 B.S. L.146 J.D. [[A] Sterne,K.G.&F.]
*PRACTICE AREAS: Intellectual Property; Biotechnology; Patent Prosecution; Licensing.

Sheikerz, Mehdi D. '65 '96 C.886 B.S. L.1218 J.D.
(adm. in FL; not adm. in DC) [[A] Staas&H.]
*PRACTICE AREAS: Intellectual Property; Patents; Licensing; Trademarks; Copyrights.

Shen, Michael M. '73 '98 C.477 B.S.Ch.E. L.276 J.D.
(adm. in NY; not adm. in DC) [[A] Kenyon&K.]
*PRACTICE AREAS: Intellectual Property.

Shimazaki, J. John ....'59 '88 C.1074 B.S. L.101 J.D. [[C] Dickinson W.]
*PRACTICE AREAS: Patent Law; Trademark Law; Licensing.

Shipley, Howard N. ....'— '96 C.886 B.S. L.1209 J.D. [[A] Foley&L.]
*PRACTICE AREAS: Intellectual Property.

Siegel, Neil B., (AV) ....'42 '67 C.339 B.S. L.597 J.D. [Sughrue M.]
*PRACTICE AREAS: Intellectual Property Law; Litigation.

Siekman, Michael T. ....'67 '95 C.67 B.S. L.94 J.D. [[A] Finnegan,H.F.G.&D.]
*PRACTICE AREAS: Pharmaceutical Patent Prosecution; Patent Litigation; Intellectual Property Portfolio Management; Patent Interference Practice.

Siem, Michael A. '73 '01 C.46 B.S. L.477 J.D.
(adm. in NY; not adm. in DC) [[A] Kenyon&K.]
*PRACTICE AREAS: Intellectual Property.

Sigworth, Ronald L. ....'64 '97 C.893 B.S.M.E. L.128 J.D. [[A] Kenyon&K.]
*PRACTICE AREAS: Intellectual Property.

Silbermann, James M. ....'— '96 C.446 B.S.Ch.E. L.128 J.D. [[A] Foley&L.]
*PRACTICE AREAS: Intellectual Property; Patent Law.

Sipes, Christopher N. .... '65 '92 C&L.309 A.B., J.D. [Covington&B.]

Sira, Serge .... '61 '99 C.025 Ph.D. L.446 J.D. [[A] Pennie&E.]
*PRACTICE AREAS: Intellectual Property.

Skerpon, Joseph M. ....'— '82 C.674 B.S.E. L.107 J.D. [Banner&W.]
*PRACTICE AREAS: Intellectual Property Law; Patents; Biotechnology; Pharmaceutical Intellectual Property; Chemical Intellectual Property.

Sloan, Robert V., (P.C.), (AV) '33 '64 C.1031 B.S. L.64 LL.B.
(adm. in MD; not adm. in DC) [Sughrue M.]
*PRACTICE AREAS: Intellectual Property Law.

Slobasky, Michael R., (AV) ....'45 '72 C.912 B.S.E.E. L.273 J.D. [Jacobson,H.]
*PRACTICE AREAS: Intellectual Property Law; Electrical Patents; Mechanical Patents.

Smith, Ellen Resnick ....'70 '97 C.860 B.S. L.1209 J.D. [[A] Sughrue M.]

Smith, Leonard, Jr. .... '61 '95 C.871 B.S. L.276 J.D. [[A] Finnegan,H.F.G.&D.]
*PRACTICE AREAS: Computer and Software Patents; Computer Architecture Patents; Biotechnology Patent Prosecution; Biotechnology Patents; Patent Litigation.

Smith, Richard H., (AV) .... '37 '65 C.401 B.S.I.E. L.273 J.D. [Finnegan,H.F.G.&D.]
*PRACTICE AREAS: Patent Prosecution; Patent Litigation; Patent Licensing; Computer and Software Patents.

Smith, Ronald H. '38 '76 C.966 B.S. L.446 J.D.
(adm. in MD; not adm. in DC) [[C] Keil&W.]
*PRACTICE AREAS: Patents.

Smith, Gambrell & Russell, LLP, (AV)
Suite 800, 1850 M Street, N.W., 20036 ⊙
Telephone: 202-263-4300 Telecopier: 202-263-4329
Partners: Robert G. Weilacher; Frederick F. Calvetti; Michael A. Makuch; Dennis C. Rodgers. Associates: Michael K. Carrier; Brandon Boss (Not admitted in DC); Patrick R. Delaney; Mary A. Montebello.
Patent, Trademark, Copyright, Antitrust, Unfair Competition and Trade Regulation Law. Practice before Federal Courts and Government Departments.
Atlanta, Georgia Office: Suite 3100, Promenade II, 1230 Peachtree Street, N.E. Telephone: 404-815-3500. Fax: 404-815-3509.
Jacksonville, Florida Office: Bank of America Tower, 50 North Laura Street, Suite 2200. Telephone: 904-598-6100. Fax: 904-598-6300.
See Professional Biographies, WASHINGTON, DISTRICT OF COLUMBIA

Snider, Ronald R., (AV) .... '37 '65 C.679 B.S.E.E. L.477 J.D. [Snider&Assoc.]
*PRACTICE AREAS: Litigation; Licensing Law; Intellectual Property Law.

Snider & Associates, (AV)
1054 31st Street, N.W., Suite 400, 20007
Telephone: 202-347-2600 Fax: 202-347-7870
Email: sniderpatent@yahoo.com URL: http://www.lawyers.com/snider&assoclaw
Ronald R. Snider.
Intellectual Property Law, Patents, Trademarks, Copyrights, Government Contracts.
See Professional Biographies, WASHINGTON, DISTRICT OF COLUMBIA

Soegeng, Jemy .... '68 '98 C.1075 B.S. L.629 J.D. [[A] Finnegan,H.F.G.&D.]
*PRACTICE AREAS: Intellectual Property Portfolio Management; Mechanical Patents; Medical Patents; International Patent Prosecution.

Soffen, Stephen A., (AV) ....'56 '83 C.188 B.S.E.E. L.818 J.D. [Ostrolenk,F.G.&S.]
*PRACTICE AREAS: Patent; Trademark; Copyright; Unfair Competition.

Sokal, Allen M., (AV) .... '46 '73 C.659 B.S.Ch.E. L.276 J.D. [Finnegan,H.F.G.&D.]
*PRACTICE AREAS: Intellectual Property Rights; Chemical Patents; Patent Litigation; Patent Prosecution; Pharmaceutical Patents.

Sokohl, Robert E. .... '65 '91 C.823 B.S.C.E. L.904 J.D. [Sterne,K.G.&F.]
*PRACTICE AREAS: Intellectual Property Law.

Son, Anthony H. ....'— '97 C.446 B.S. L.978 J.D. [[A] Foley&L.]
*PRACTICE AREAS: Intellectual Property; Litigation.

Sonu, Andrew Chanho ....'46 '87 C.112 B.S.E.E. L.1338 J.D. [Finnegan,H.F.G.&D.]
*PRACTICE AREAS: Intellectual Property Litigation; Intellectual Property Licensing; Intellectual Property Arbitration; Technology Transfer; Patent Prosecution.

Spencer, George H., (AV) .... '28 '52 C.976 B.E. L.188 J.D. [Venable,A.B.H.&C.]
*PRACTICE AREAS: Intellectual Property Law; Patent Law; Trademark Law; Litigation.

Staas, H. J., (AV) .... '38 '64 C.401 B.S. L.276 LL.B. [Staas&H.]
*PRACTICE AREAS: Intellectual Property Law; Patent, Trademark, Copyright and Unfair Competition.

Staas & Halsey LLP, (AV)
700 Eleventh Street, N.W., Suite 500, 20001
Telephone: 202-434-1500 Facsimile: 202-434-1501
Email: info@s-n-h.com URL: http://www.staasandhalsey.com
Members of Firm: H. J. Staas; James D. Halsey, Jr.; David M. Pitcher; John C. Garvey; J. Randall Beckers; William F. Herbert; Richard A. Gollhofer; Mark J. Henry; Paul I. Kravetz; Gene M. Garner, II; Michael D. Stein. Associates: Jonathan H. Muskin (Not admitted in DC); Stephen T. Boughner (Not admitted in DC); Christine J. Gilsdorf; Mehdi D. Sheikerz (Not admitted in DC); John H. Stowe (Not admitted in DC); James G. McEwen (Not admitted in DC); Michael John Badagliacca (Not admitted in DC); Alicia M. Choi (Not admitted in DC); Heath E. Wells (Not admitted in DC).
Patent, Trademark, Copyright, Unfair Competition and Computer Law. International Patent and Trademark Practice. Practice before Federal Courts and Administrative Agencies.
See Professional Biographies, WASHINGTON, DISTRICT OF COLUMBIA

Stadnicki, Alfred A. '50 '78 C.422 B.S.C.E. L.1048 J.D.
(adm. in MA; not adm. in DC) [Lalos&K.]

Stahl, Lawrence A., (AV) .... '54 '79 C.94 A.B. L.273 J.D. [Fitzpatrick,C.H.&S.]

Steffe, Eric K. .... '64 '94 C.280 B.S. L.1209 J.D. [Sterne,K.G.&F.]
*PRACTICE AREAS: Intellectual Property; Patent Licensing; Patent Infringement; Biochemical Patents; Biotechnology Patents.

Stein, Julie E. '71 '00 C.453 B.S. L.273 J.D.
(adm. in CA; not adm. in DC) [[A] Kenyon&K.]
*PRACTICE AREAS: Intellectual Property.

Stein, Michael D. .... '65 '92 C.30 B.S.E.E. L.659 J.D. [Staas&H.]
*PRACTICE AREAS: Intellectual Property Law; Patent, Trademark and Copyright Law.

Stelacone, Jay A. .... '64 '93 C.645 B.S.A.E. L.546 J.D. [[A] Finnegan,H.F.G.&D.]
*PRACTICE AREAS: Patent Litigation; Patent Infringement; Patent Interference Practice.

Sterba, Anne M. .... '73 '98 C.935 B.A. L.1209 [[A] Rothwell,F.E.&M.]

Stern, Marvin R., (AV) .... '35 '63 C.223 B.S.Ch.E. L.273 J.D. [[C] Jacobson,H.]
*PRACTICE AREAS: Intellectual Property Law; Chemical Patents; Mechanical Patents; Trademarks.

Sterne, Robert Greene, (AV) .... '51 '77 C.860 B.S.E.E. L.446 J.D. [Sterne,K.G.&F.]
*PRACTICE AREAS: Intellectual Property Law.

Sterne, Kessler, Goldstein & Fox P.L.L.C., (AV)
1100 New York Avenue N.W., 20005
Telephone: 202-371-2600 Fax: 202-371-2540
URL: http://www.skgf.com
Members of Firm: Robert Greene Sterne; Edward J. Kessler; Jorge A. Goldstein; David K.S. Cornwell; Robert W. Esmond; Tracy-Gene Graveline Durkin; Michele A. Cimbala; Michael B. Ray; Robert E. Sokohl; Eric K. Steffe; Michael Quentin Lee; Steven R. Ludwig; John M. Covert; Linda E. Alcorn.
Patent, Trademark, Copyright, Unfair Competition, Computer, Electronics, Biotechnology, Chemical, Interference, Alternative Dispute Resolution, Mechanical, Industrial Design, Internet, Related Litigation and Licensing.
See Professional Biographies, WASHINGTON, DISTRICT OF COLUMBIA

Stevens, Davis, Miller & Mosher, L.L.P.
1615 L Street, N.W. Suite 850, 20036
Telephone: 202-408-5100; 202-785-0100 Fax: 202-408-5200; 202-408-5088
Email: sdmm@stevensdavis.com URL: http://www.stevensdavis.com
Members of Firm: James E. Ledbetter (Not admitted in DC); Thomas P. Pavelko; Anthony P. Venturino; Barth X. de Rosa. Of Counsel: Peter Peckarsky; Clifford L. Tager (Not admitted in DC); Eric P. Robins (Not admitted in DC); David E. Herron II (Not admitted in DC).
Domestic and International Practice in the field of Intellectual Property Law, concentrating on: Patents, Trademarks, Copyrights and Trade Secrets. Patent, Trademark, Copyright and Unfair Competition Litigation before Federal and State Courts. Specialized Practice in Patent Interference Proceedings before the Board of Appeals and Patent Interferences and Practice before the Trademark Trial and Appeal Board. Intellectual Property Licensing. Computer and High-Technology Law. Biotechnology Law. Food and Drug Administration Law. Anti-Counterfeiting Enforcement Efforts before the U.S. Customs Service and Federal Courts. Due Diligence Practice emphasizing Intellectual Property in the context of Corporate Acquisitions, Audits, Mergers, Corporate Financing and Initial Public Offerings.
References will be provided upon request.
See Professional Biographies, WASHINGTON, DISTRICT OF COLUMBIA

Stole, Einar '64 '00 C.911 B.S. L.446 J.D.
(adm. in MD; not adm. in DC) [[A] Fulbright&J.]
*PRACTICE AREAS: Intellectual Property; Patents.

Stoll, Kara Farnandez ....'68 '97 C.477 B.S.E.E. L.276 J.D. [[A] Finnegan,H.F.G.&D.]
*PRACTICE AREAS: Intellectual Property Litigation; Electrical Patent Prosecution.

Stowe, John H. '39 '71 C.277 B.E.E. L.347 J.D.
(adm. in IN; not adm. in DC) [[A] Staas&H.]

Strauss, Michael J. .... '54 '87 C.1044 B.A. L.273 J.D. [[C] Fulbright&J.]
*PRACTICE AREAS: Litigation; Antitrust; Intellectual Property; Patent.

Stroup, Richard Lee, (AV) ..... '48 '76 C.607 B.S.ME L.893 J.D. [Finnegan,H.F.G.&D.]
*PRACTICE AREAS: Intellectual Property Litigation; Mechanical Intellectual Property; Civil Litigation; Technology Licensing; Trademarks.

Sturm, Michael O., (AV) '43 '73 C.350 B.S. L.1128 J.D.
(adm. in VA; not adm. in DC) [Henderson&S.] ⊙

Suarez, Pedro F. '64 '00 C.1070 B.S.E.E. L.273 J.D.
(adm. in CA; not adm. in DC) [[A] Finnegan,H.F.G.&D.]
*PRACTICE AREAS: Software Protection; Intellectual Property Infringement; Intellectual Property Litigation; Electrical Patent Prosecution; Electronic Patents.

Subramanian, Chid .... '61 '97 C.8 M.S.Ch.E. L.276 J.D. [[A] Sughrue M.]

Sughrue Mion, PLLC, (AV) [BB]
A Professional Limited Liability Company including Professional Corporations
Suite 800, 2100 Pennsylvania Avenue, N.W., 20037-3213 ⊙
Telephone: 202-293-7060 Facsimile: 202-293-7860
Email: sughrue@sughrue.com URL: http://www.sughrue.com
Members of Firm: John H. Mion (P.C.); Robert J. Seas, Jr. (P.C.); Darryl Mexic (P.C.); Robert V. Sloan (P.C.) (Not admitted in DC); Peter D. Olexy (P.C.); J. Frank Osha; Louis Gubinsky (P.C.); Neil B. Siegel; David J. Cushing; Cynthia Clarke Weber; John R. Inge; Joseph J. Ruch, Jr. (Not admitted in DC); Sheldon I. Landsman (P.C.); Richard C. Turner; Howard L. Bernstein (P.C.); Alan J. Kasper; Kenneth J. Burchfiel; Gordon Kit; Susan J. Mack; Frank L. Bernstein; Mark Boland; William H. Mandir; Gary D. Krugman; Brian W. Hannon; Abraham J. Rosner; Bruce E. Kramer; Paul F. Neils; Brett S. Sylvester; Robert M. Masters; William Mack Webner; George F. Lehnigk; John T. Callahan; Steven M. Gruskin; Peter A. McKenna; Edward F. Kenehan, Jr.; John F. Rabena; Susan Perng Pan. Associates: Lee C. Wright; Stanislav Torgovitsky; Carl J. Pellegrini; Kelly G. Hyndman; Ellen Resnick Smith; Raja N. Saliba; H. Ray Heflin (Not admitted in DC); Chid Subramanian; Jeffrey A. Schmidt; Paul J. Wilson; Eric P. Halber; Christopher R. Lipp (Not admitted in DC); Kevin M. Barner (Not admitted in DC); Leigh Ann Lindquist; John W. Bain; Drew Hissong, Ph.D.; Keith B. Scala (Not admitted in DC); Terrance Jay Wikberg (Not admitted in DC); Mark R. Woodall; Ronald L. Kimble (Not admitted in DC); Cameron W. Beddard (Not admitted in DC); Michael J. Whitehead; Daniel V. Williams; Jennifer M. Hayes; Yoshinari Kishimoto (Not admitted in DC); John M. Bird (Not admitted in DC). Senior Counsel: Robert G. McMorrow (P.C.).
Patent, Trademark, Copyright, Unfair Competition Law. Practice before the Federal Courts and Administrative Agencies. Antitrust, International Trade Regulation, International Patent and Trademark Law.
Tokyo, Japan Office: Toei Nishi Shimbashi Building, Suite 4F, 13-5 Nishi Shimbashi 1-Chome 105. Telephone: (03) 3 503-3760.
Menlo Park, California Office: 1010 El Camino Real, Suite 360. Telephone: 650-325-5800. Facsimile: 650-325-6606.
See Professional Biographies, WASHINGTON, DISTRICT OF COLUMBIA

Sukduang, Sanya ....'73 '99 C.93 B.S. L.30 J.D. [[A] Finnegan,H.F.G.&D.]
*PRACTICE AREAS: Patent Litigation; Patent Interference Practice; Chemical Patent Prosecution; Biotechnology Patent Prosecution.

Sullivan, Michael G. ....'63 '91 C.1119 B.S. L.64 J.D. [[C] Rothwell,F.E.&M.]
*PRACTICE AREAS: Intellectual Property.

Sundby, Suzannah K. '72 '99 C.959 B.S. L.1218 J.D.
(adm. in CA; not adm. in DC) [[A] Jacobson,H.]
*PRACTICE AREAS: Biotechnology Patents; Chemical Patents; Pharmaceutical Patents; Medical Patents; Patent Applications.

Sundeen, Marcia H., (AV) ....'54 '81 C.436 B.S. L.930 J.D. [Pennie&E.]
*PRACTICE AREAS: Intellectual Property; Intellectual Property Litigation; International Trade.

Supko, Mark M. .... '63 '94 C.754 B.S. L.276 J.D. [[A] Kenyon&K.]
*PRACTICE AREAS: Intellectual Property.

Sutherland Asbill & Brennan LLP, (AV)
1275 Pennsylvania Avenue, N.W., 20004-2415 ⊙
Telephone: 202-383-0100 Cable Address: "Sutab Wash" Telex: 89-501 Facsimile: 202-637-3593
Email: info@sablaw.com URL: http://www.sablaw.com
Counsel of the Firm in Washington, D.C.: Elisabeth A. Langworthy.
Patent, Trademark, Copyright, Licensing, Litigation, Trade Secret and Related Intellectual Property Law.

(This Listing Continued)

Sutherland Asbill & Brennan LLP (Continued)
Atlanta, Georgia Office: 999 Peachtree Street, N.E., 30309-3996. Telephone: 404-853-8000.
New York, N.Y. Office: 350 Park Avenue, 25th Floor, 10022. Telephone: 212-655-3883.
Austin, Texas Office: 701 Brazos Street, Suite 1040, 78701-2559. Telephone: 512-478-1665.
Tallahassee, Florida Office: 2282 Killearn Center Boulevard, 32308-3561. Telephone: 850-894-0015.
See Professional Biographies, WASHINGTON, DISTRICT OF COLUMBIA

Swan, Jennifer S. '— '01 C&L.665 B.A., J.D. (adm. in VA; not adm. in DC) [Ⓐ Finnegan,H.F.G.&D.]
*PRACTICE AREAS: Biochemical Technology; Intellectual Property Litigation; Pharmaceutical Intellectual Property.
Sweet, Mark D. .... '66 '99 C.945 B.S. L.180 J.D. [Ⓐ Finnegan,H.F.G.&D.]
*PRACTICE AREAS: Chemical Intellectual Property; Patent Prosecution.
Swenson, George W., Jr. .... '33 '92 C.812 B.S. L.273 J.D. [Vorys,S.S.&P.]
Sylvester, Brett S. .... '62 '87 C.188 B.S. L.365 J.D. [Sughrue M.]
*PRACTICE AREAS: Intellectual Property Law.
Tager, Clifford L., (CV) '— '87 C.161 B.E.E. L.273 J.D. (adm. in PA; not adm. in DC) [Ⓒ Stevens,D.M.&M.]
*PRACTICE AREAS: Intellectual Property (100%); Patents; Trademarks; Copyrights; Trade Secrets.
Tanner, Jeanne M. ....'58 '97 C.453 B.S.M.E. L.1209 J.D. [Ⓐ Finnegan,H.F.G.&D.]
*PRACTICE AREAS: Intellectual Property Litigation; Mechanical Intellectual Property; Mechanical Patents.
Tao, Ellen S. .... '69 '95 C.910 B.S. L.30 J.D. [Ⓐ Ostrolenk,F.G.&S.] ⊙
*PRACTICE AREAS: Patent Prosecution.
Taylor, Cheri M., (AV) .... '48 '86 C.10 B.S. L.1209 J.D. [Finnegan,H.F.G.&D.]
*PRACTICE AREAS: Biotechnology; Pharmaceuticals; Chemical Patents; Cosmetics; International Trade.
Taylor, W. R. Duke ....'58 '84 C&L.8 B.S.M.E., J.D. [Harness,D.&P.] (⊙Troy, MI)
*PRACTICE AREAS: Patent, Trademark and Intellectual Property.
Teel, Keith A. .... '56 '81 C.902 B.S. L.893 J.D. [Covington&B.]
Tegtmeyer, Rene D., (AV) ....'34 '63 C.910 B.S. L.273 J.D. [Ⓒ Fish&R.]
*PRACTICE AREAS: Intellectual Property; Patents; Litigation.
Tiedrich, Lee J. ...... '66 '91 C.228 B.S.E. L.659 J.D. [Covington&B.] (⊙San Fran., CA)
Ting, Henry P. .... '69 '97 C.103 Sc.B. L.188 J.D. [Ⓐ Covington&B.]
Tinker, Susanne C. '70 '01 C.446 B.S.M.E. L.276 J.D. (adm. in VA; not adm. in DC) [Ⓐ Finnegan,H.F.G.&D.]
*PRACTICE AREAS: Mechanical Patents; Medical Patents; Patent Prosecution; Medical Technology.
Toffenetti, Judith L. .... '53 '94 C.66 B.A. L.273 J.D. [Ⓐ Kenyon&K.]
*PRACTICE AREAS: Intellectual Property.
Topol, Allan J., (AV) .... '41 '66 C.119 B.S. L.976 LL.B. [Covington&B.]
Torchin, Norman G. ....'29 '61 C&L.273 B.S., LL.B. [Ⓒ Keil&W.]
*PRACTICE AREAS: Patents; Trademark Law.
Torgovitsky, Stanislav ....'67 '96 C&L.273 B.A., J.D. [Ⓐ Sughrue M.]
*PRACTICE AREAS: Intellectual Property.
Townsend, Rachel H. .... '69 '00 C.860 B.S. L.276 J.D. [Ⓐ Finnegan,H.F.G.&D.]
Troike, Robert L. .... '36 '64 C.1027 B.S. L.1002 LL.B. [Ⓒ Baker B.]
Turner, Richard C. ....'55 '81 C.688 B.S. L.273 J.D. [Sughrue M.]
*PRACTICE AREAS: Patent Law; Intellectual Property Law; Trade Regulation Law; Unfair Competition Law.
Ungerman, Mark E., (AV) .... '59 '88 C.1044 B.S.E.E. L.273 J.D. [Fulbright&J.]
*PRACTICE AREAS: Intellectual Property; Technology and Science Transfers; Patents; Trademarks; Computer and Software Patents.
Van Horn, Charles E. ....'42 '68 C.401 B.S.Ch.E. L.30 J.D. [Finnegan,H.F.G.&D.]
*PRACTICE AREAS: Patents.

Venable, Attorneys At Law, Venable, Baetjer, Howard & Civiletti, LLP, (AV) BB
A Partnership including Professional Corporations
Suite 1000, 1201 New York Avenue, N.W., 20005 ⊙
Telephone: 202-962-4800 Fax: 202-962-8300
URL: http://www.venable.com
Members of Firm: George H. Spencer; Robert J. Frank; Norman N. Kunitz; Thomas J. Madden; Marina V. Schneller; Gabor J. Kelemen (Not admitted in DC); John W. Schneller; Robert Kinberg; Allen Wood; Mark B. Harrison; Ashley J. Wells; Julie A. Petruzzelli; James R. Burdett; Michael A. Gollin. Of Counsel: Gary L. Shaffer (Not admitted in DC). Associates: Fei-Fei Chao; Catherine A. Ferguson; Michael P. Leary (Not admitted in DC); Chellis E. Neal; Michael A. Sartori; Catherine M. Voorhees; George Abe Zachariah.
Baltimore, Maryland Office: Venable, Baetjer and Howard LLP, 1800 Mercantile Bank & Trust Building, 2 Hopkins Plaza. Telephone: 410-244-7400. Fax: 410-244-7742.
McLean, Virginia Office: Venable, Baetjer and Howard LLP, Suite 400, 2010 Corporate Ridge. Telephone: 703-760-1600. Fax: 703-821-8949.
Rockville, Maryland Office: Venable, Baetjer and Howard LLP, Suite 500, One Church Street, P. O. Box 1906. Telephone: 301-217-5600. Fax: 301-217-5617.
Towson, Maryland Office: Venable, Baetjer and Howard LLP, 210 Allegheny Avenue, P. O. Box 5517. Telephone: 410-494-6200. Fax: 410-821-0147.
Revisers of the Maryland Law Digest for this Directory.
See Professional Biographies, WASHINGTON, DISTRICT OF COLUMBIA

Venturino, Anthony P. ....'56 '87 C.433 B.Ch.E. L.273 J.D. [Stevens,D.M.&M.]
*PRACTICE AREAS: Patent Law; Trademark Law; Licensing; Litigation.
Voight, Jason D. .... '68 '96 C.188 B.S. L.846 J.D. [Keil&W.]
*PRACTICE AREAS: Patents; Trademark Law; Litigation.
Voorhees, Catherine M. ...... '60 '88 C.390 B.S.E.E. L.1209 J.D. [Ⓒ Venable,A.B.H.&C.]
*PRACTICE AREAS: Patents; Trademarks; Copyrights.

Vorys, Sater, Seymour and Pease LLP, (AV)
11th Floor, 1828 L Street, N.W., 20036-5109 ⊙
Telephone: 202-467-8800 Telex: 440693 Telecopier: 202-467-8900
URL: http://www.vssp.com
Resident Members: Thomas R. Boland; Ellen A. Efros; W. Mack Webner; Michael A. Grow. Resident Associates: Douglas R. Bush, George W. Swenson, Jr.; Scott D. Balderston.
Patent, Trademark and Copyright Law.
Columbus, Ohio Office: 52 East Gay Street, P.O. Box 1008, 43216-1008. Telephone: 614-464-6400. Telex: 241348. Telecopier: 614-464-6350.
Cleveland, Ohio Office: 2100 One Cleveland Center, 1375 East Ninth Street, 44114-1724. Telephone: 216-479-6100. Telecopier: 216-479-6060.
Cincinnati, Ohio Office: Suite 2100, 221 East Fourth Street, P.O. Box 0236, 45201-0236. Telephone: 513-723-4000. Telecopier: 513-723-4056.
Alexandria, Virginia Office: 277 South Washington Street, Suite 310, 22314. Telephone: 703-837-6999. Facsimile: 703-549-4492.
See Professional Biographies, WASHINGTON, DISTRICT OF COLUMBIA

Wadler, Linda A. .... '63 '88 C.339 B.S. L.477 J.D. [Finnegan,H.F.G.&D.]
*PRACTICE AREAS: Patent Litigation; Patent Prosecution.
Wadrzyk, Mark Edward '68 '98 C.597 B.S.E.E. L.146 J.D. (adm. in IL; not adm. in DC) [Ⓐ Fish&R.]
*PRACTICE AREAS: Patent Law; Intellectual Property; Patent Prosecution; Patent Litigation.
Wagner, Todd A. '66 '91 C.629 B.A. L.982 J.D. (adm. in NY; not adm. in DC) [Pennie&E.]
*PRACTICE AREAS: Intellectual Property; Litigation.
Wallace, W. David .... '68 '96 C.188 B.A. L.930 J.D. [Ⓐ Kenyon&K.]
*PRACTICE AREAS: Intellectual Property.
Walters, Gregory A. ....'67 '96 C.475 B.S.E.E. L.213 J.D. [Ⓐ Fish&R.]
*PRACTICE AREAS: Patents; Trademarks; Intellectual Property; Copyrights; Computer Law.
Wannisky, William M., (AV) .... '48 '75 C.645 B.S. L.276 J.D. [Fitzpatrick,C.H.&S.]
Warner, Steven E. ....'59 '88 C.1213 B.S.M.E. L.273 J.D. [Fitzpatrick,C.H.&S.]
Waszkiewicz, Kenneth P. .... '63 '98 C.446 B.S.C.S. L.64 J.D. [Ⓐ Morgan&F.]
*PRACTICE AREAS: Intellectual Property; Patents.

Watts, Charles R. .... '62 '90 C.205 B.S.M.E. L.1209 J.D. [Wenderoth,L.&P.]
*PRACTICE AREAS: Mechanical Patents; Electrical Patents; Patent Applications; Prosecution; Licensing.
Weaver, Jeffrey S. .... '66 '98 C.339 B.S.E.E. L.446 J.D. [Ⓐ Sterne,K.G.&F.]
*PRACTICE AREAS: Intellectual Property.
Weber, Cynthia Clarke, (AV) .... '51 '76 C.914 B.A. L.128 J.D. [Sughrue M.]
*PRACTICE AREAS: Litigation; Trademark Law; Unfair Competition Law; Copyright Law.
Webner, William Mack, (AV) .... '41 '68 C&L.8 B.S., J.D. [Sughrue M.]
*PRACTICE AREAS: Litigation; Trademark, Copyright and Unfair Competition Law; Trade Secret Law; Licensing.
Wegner, Harold C., (AV) .... '43 '69 C.597 B.A. L.276 J.D. [Foley&L.]
*PRACTICE AREAS: Intellectual Property; Intellectual Property Asset Management.
Weierstall, Eric J. .... '— '99 C&L.823 B.S., J.D. [Ⓐ Venable,A.B.H.&C.]
*PRACTICE AREAS: Patents.
Weilacher, Robert G., (AV) ....'34 '61 C.178 B.S. L.273 LL.B. [Smith,G.&R.]
*PRACTICE AREAS: Intellectual Property Law.
Weinkauf, Russell E. '23 '51 C&L.966 B.S., LL.B. (adm. in WI; not adm. in DC) [Keil&W.]
*PRACTICE AREAS: Patent; Trademark Law.
Weinstein, Marc K. '— '99 C.645 B.S.E.E. L.276 J.D. (adm. in VA; not adm. in DC) [Ⓐ Foley&L.]
*PRACTICE AREAS: Intellectual Property; Software Patents; Computer and Software Patents; Electronic Patents.
Weissman, Peter S. ....'66 '96 C.1350 B.E. L.273 J.D. [Ⓐ Blank R.C.&M.]
*PRACTICE AREAS: Intellectual Property Law; Electrical Patents; Mechanical Patents; Trademarks; Fastener Quality Act.
Wells, Ashley J. ....'43 '80 C&L.770 B.S., J.D. [Venable,A.B.H.&C.]
*PRACTICE AREAS: Intellectual Property Law; Patents.
Wells, Heath E. '69 '98 C.885 B.S.C.E. L.904 J.D. (adm. in VA; not adm. in DC) [Ⓐ Staas&H.]
*PRACTICE AREAS: Intellectual Property; Trademarks; Copyrights; Patents.
Wells, William K., Jr., (AV) .... '43 '74 C.886 B.S. L.893 J.D. [Kenyon&K.]
*PRACTICE AREAS: Intellectual Property.

Wenderoth, Lind & Ponack, L.L.P., (AV) BB
2033 K Street, N.W., Suite 800, 20006-1021
Telephone: 202-721-8200 Fax: 202-721-8250 (G-III) 202-833-3015 (G-IV)
Email: wlp@wenderoth.com URL: http://www.wenderoth.com
Members of Firm: Michael R. Davis; Matthew M. Jacob; Warren M. Cheek, Jr.; Nils E. Pedersen; Charles R. Watts; Michael S. Huppert. Of Counsel: John T. Miller; John T. Fedigan. Associates: Lee Cheng; Kaushal R. Odedra; Dhiren R. Odedra; Joseph M. Gorski (Not admitted in DC); W. Douglas Hahm (Not admitted in DC); Jeffrey R. Filipek; Thomas D. Robbins (Not admitted in DC).
Patent, Trademark, Copyright and Unfair Competition Law. International Patent and Trademark Practice.
See Professional Biographies, WASHINGTON, DISTRICT OF COLUMBIA

West, William K., Jr., (AV) ...... '37 '62 C&L.228 B.S.M.E., LL.B. [Howrey S.A.&W.]
*PRACTICE AREAS: Patent; Trade-dress; Antitrust; Complex Litigation.
Westerlund, Robert A. ...... '56 '80 C&L.861 J.D. [Ⓒ Adduci,M.&S.] (⊙Arlington, VA)
*PRACTICE AREAS: Patent Procurement; Patent Licensing; Litigation.
Westerman, William F., (BV) ...'52 '79 C.675 B.S. L.862 J.D. [Armstrong,W.H.M.&N.]
White, Grady Lee .... '63 '93 C.597 B.S. L.1068 J.D. [Ⓐ Covington&B.]
White, Michael D. ....'52 '82 C.893 B.S. L.838 J.D. [Ⓒ Blank R.C.&M.]
*PRACTICE AREAS: Patent Litigation; Patent Validity and Infringement Opinions; Mechanical Intellectual Property; Electro-Mechanical Patents; Mechanical Patent Prosecution.
Whitehead, Michael J. .... '74 '01 C.608 B.S.E.E L.1218 J.D. [Ⓐ Sughrue M.]
*PRACTICE AREAS: Patent Law.
Wigman, Victor M., (AV) ....'40 '67 C.223 B.S.M.E. L.659 J.D. [Blank R.C.&M.]
*PRACTICE AREAS: Intellectual Property Infringement; International Licensing; Mechanical Patents; Metallurgical Patents; Patent Infringement.
Wikberg, Terrance Jay '70 '00 C.1333 B.S.A.E. L.446 J.D. (adm. in MD; not adm. in DC) [Ⓐ Sughrue M.]
*PRACTICE AREAS: Patents.
Williams, Daniel V. .... '71 '01 C.1213 B.S.M.E. L.1218 J.D. [Ⓐ Sughrue M.]
*PRACTICE AREAS: Intellectual Property.
Williams, Frederick C. '— '74 C.93 B.S. L.477 J.D. [Williams&Assoc.] & [Ⓒ Slater & Z.]

Williams & Associates
1030 Fifteenth Street., N.W. Suite 300, 20005-1501
Telephone: 202-842-0431 Fax: 202-467-4045
Email: fcw@bellatlantic.net URL: http://www.lawyers.com/dc-patentlaw
Frederick C. Williams. Of Counsel: James L. Lewis.
Patent Prosecution, Patent Portfolio and Infringement Analysis, with special emphasis in the areas of Medical and Surgical Devices and Digital Signal Processing; Government Contract Claim Preparation and Prosecution.
See Professional Biographies, WASHINGTON, DISTRICT OF COLUMBIA

Williamson, J. Paul, (AV) .... '48 '73 C.679 B.S.A.E. L.339 J.D. [Howrey S.A.&W.]
*PRACTICE AREAS: Trademarks; International Trademarks; Trademark Litigation; Trademark Prosecution; Trademark Protection.
Williamson, Mark A. ....'62 '90 C.223 B.S.M.E. L.276 J.D. [Fitzpatrick,C.H.&S.]
Willinghan, George A., III '65 '97 C.301 B.S. L.276 J.D. (adm. in VA; not adm. in DC) [Ⓐ Pennie&E.]
*PRACTICE AREAS: Intellectual Property; Patent Prosecution; Patent Litigation.
Wilson, James T. '68 '99 C.645 B.S.E.E. L.904 J.D. (adm. in VA; not adm. in DC) [Ⓐ Finnegan,H.F.G.&D.]
*PRACTICE AREAS: Patent Prosecution; Patent Litigation; Patent Infringement; Intellectual Property Portfolio Management.
Wilson, Paul J. .... '61 '98 C.474 B.S.E.E. L.64 J.D. [Ⓐ Sughrue M.]
*PRACTICE AREAS: Electronics; Computers and Software; Intellectual Property.
Winland, Thomas W., (AV) .... '49 '74 C.608 B.S. L.228 J.D. [Finnegan,H.F.G.&D.]
*PRACTICE AREAS: Intellectual Property Litigation; Intellectual Property Arbitration; Intellectual Property Licensing; Proprietary Rights.
Winston, R. Whitney ....'— '99 C.453 S.B. L.1209 J.D. [Ⓐ Fish&R.]
*PRACTICE AREAS: Intellectual Property; Litigation.
Wiseman, Thomas G. .... '47 '84 C.415 B.S. L.64 J.D. [Venable,A.B.H.&C.]
*PRACTICE AREAS: Patent Prosecution.

Witherspoon, John F., (AV) '33 '65 C.234 B.S. L.276 J.D.
Suite 500, 815 Connecticut Avenue, N.W., 20006-4004
Telephone: 202-835-3700 Facsimile: 202-293-2902
Email: jfw@witherspoonlaw.com
***PRACTICE AREAS: Patent Law.**
Patent, Trademark and Copyright Law.
See Professional Biographies, WASHINGTON, DISTRICT OF COLUMBIA

Wolfe, Charles R., Jr., (AV) '52 '78 C.401 B.S.Ch.E. L.276 J.D. [Blank R.C.&M.] (⊙Phila., PA)
*PRACTICE AREAS: Patent Law; Trademark Law; Unfair Competition Law; Patent Litigation; Copyright Law.
Wolffe, Franklin D., (AV) .... '— '59 C.446 B.S.Ch.E. L.273 J.D. [Ⓒ Banner&W.]
*PRACTICE AREAS: Intellectual Property Law; Patents; Intellectual Property Licensing; Chemical Intellectual Property.
Wolffe, Susan A., (AV) .... '— '90 C.893 B.S.Ch.E. L.1209 J.D. [Banner&W.]
*PRACTICE AREAS: Intellectual Property Law; Patents; Intellectual Property Licensing; Chemical Intellectual Property; Pharmaceutical Intellectual Property.

Wood, Allen .... '45 '75 C.59 B.A. L.30 J.D. [Venable,A.B.H.&C.]
*PRACTICE AREAS: Intellectual Property Law; Patent Law.
Woodall, Mark R. .... '66 '99 C.886 B.S. L.1209 J.D. [🄰 Sughrue M.]
*PRACTICE AREAS: Intellectual Property.
Wright, Bradley C. .... '— '94 C.453 B.S.E.E. L.1209 J.D. [Banner&W.]
*PRACTICE AREAS: Intellectual Property Law; Patents; Appellate Practice; Electrical Intellectual Property; Computer and Software Patents.
Wright, Lee C. .... '61 '96 C.446 B.S. L.1209 J.D. [🄰 Sughrue M.]
*PRACTICE AREAS: Intellectual Property.
Wright, William H., (AV) .... '43 '70 C&L.128 B.S.M.E., J.D. [Henderson&S.]
Wrist, Christopher Philip .... '58 '85 C.174 B.S. L.208 J.D. [🄰 Fitzpatrick,C.H.&S.]
Wyand, Jeffrey A. .... '42 '77 C.401 B.S.E.E. L.446 J.D. [Leydig,V.&M.]
Wydeven, Richard .... '63 '94 C.966 B.S.E.M. L.846 J.D. [🄰 Rothwell,F.E.&M.]
*PRACTICE AREAS: Intellectual Property.
Yee, Edward W. .... '57 '98 C.976 B.A. L.446 J.D. [🄰 Sterne,K.G.&F.]
*PRACTICE AREAS: Patents.
Yoches, E. Robert, (AV) ....'53 '80 C.174 B.S.E.E. L.659 J.D. [Finnegan,H.F.G.&D.]
*PRACTICE AREAS: Information Technology Licensing; Software Copyright; Software Licensing; Software Protection; Intellectual Property Litigation.

Yoo, Anthony S. .... '68 '92 C&L.893 B.A., J.D. [🄰 Covington&B.]
Zanowski, Leigh M. '69 '00 C.699 A.B. L.128 J.D.
(adm. in MD; not adm. in DC) [🄰 Rothwell,F.E.&M.]
*PRACTICE AREAS: Pharmaceutical Patent Litigation; Biotechnology Patent Prosecution.
Zegger, Paul J. '59 '87 C.454 B.S.Ch.E. L.982 J.D.
(adm. in CT; not adm. in DC) [Pennie&E.]
*PRACTICE AREAS: Intellectual Property; Intellectual Property Litigation.
Zibelli, David J. '61 '93 C.94 B.S.E.E. L.1170 J.D.
(adm. in VA; not adm. in DC) [🄰 Kenyon&K.]
*PRACTICE AREAS: Intellectual Property.
Ziems, Robert F., (AV) ....'29 '58 C.474 B.S. L.273 LL.B. [🄲 Finnegan,H.F.G.&D.]
*PRACTICE AREAS: Mechanical Patents; Mechanical Intellectual Property.
Zitver, Leon .... '13 '42 C.563 B.S. L.273 J.D. [🄲 Ostrolenk,F.G.&S.] ⊙
*PRACTICE AREAS: Patent Law.
Zotter, Bruce C., (AV) .... '42 '75 C.454 B.S.M.E. L.273 J.D. [Finnegan,H.F.G.&D.]
*PRACTICE AREAS: Patent Litigation.

PROFESSIONAL BIOGRAPHIES SECTION

CONNECTICUT, DELAWARE
DISTRICT OF COLUMBIA

COHEN & THOMAS

ANSONIA, CONNECTICUT

(See Derby)

General Civil and Criminal Practice. Trials in all Courts. Personal Injury, Negligence and Medical Malpractice Litigation, Real Estate Purchase, Sale, Financing, Zoning and Development, Domestic Law and Divorce, Probate, Wills and Trusts, Banking, Foreclosure and Workouts, Commercial Litigation and Collections, Municipal, Elder Law, Worker's Compensation.

DREW & MERSEREAU, P.C.

Established in 1974

47 WEST MAIN STREET
AVON, CONNECTICUT 06001
Telephone: 860-677-1974
Fax: 860-677-9143
Email: dandmavon@aol.com
URL: http://www.lawyers.com/drew&mersereau

Estate Planning, Business Planning, Estate Settlement, Estate and Gift Taxation and Corporate Law.

JOHN E. DREW, born Rockville Centre, New York, September 2, 1941; admitted to bar, 1967, New York; 1968, Connecticut. *Education:* Colgate University (A.B., 1963); Vanderbilt University (J.D.,1966); New York University (Graduate Tax Program). Phi Delta Phi. Chairman, Avon Zoning Board of Appeals, 1974—. Member, Connecticut Estate and Tax Planning Council, Inc. *Member:* Hartford County, Connecticut and New York State Bar Associations. ***PRACTICE AREAS:*** Estate Planning; Business Planning; Estate Settlement. ***Email:*** JDrewlaw@aol.com

PAUL E. MERSEREAU, born Endicott, New York, January 18, 1939; admitted to bar, 1964, Connecticut. *Education:* Williams College (B.A., 1961); Harvard University (LL.B., 1964). Member: Estate and Business Planning Council of Hartford, 1973—; President, 1983-1984. Connecticut Estate and Tax Planning Council Inc., 1981—. *Member:* Hartford County and Connecticut Bar Associations. Fellow, American College of Trust and Estate Counsel. ***PRACTICE AREAS:*** Estate Planning; Business Planning; Estate Settlement. ***Email:*** PaulMers@aol.com

CHRISTOPHER S. DREW, born New York City, New York, May 19, 1967; admitted to bar, 1995, Massachusetts; 1997, Connecticut. *Education:* Duke University (A.B., 1990); University of Connecticut (J.D., with honors, 1995). *Member:* Hartford County, Connecticut, Massachusetts and American Bar Associations. ***PRACTICE AREAS:*** Estate Planning; Business Planning; Corporate Law; Estate Settlement. ***Email:*** CDrewatty@aol.com

---

ALFRED R. CASELLA, born Springfield, Massachusetts, October 8, 1971; admitted to bar, 1996, Connecticut; 1997, Massachusetts; 1998, U.S. District Court, District of Massachusetts. *Education:* Trinity College (B.S., 1993); University of Connecticut (J.D., 1996); New York University School of Law (LL.M., Taxation, 2001). Phi Beta Kappa; Pi Gamma Mu; Phi Delta Phi. *Member:* Hampshire County and Connecticut Bar Associations. ***PRACTICE AREAS:*** Estate Settlements; Estate Planning; Business Planning. ***Email:*** alfredrcasella@aol.com

DAVID C. GRIMES, born New Haven, Connecticut, November 29, 1974; admitted to bar, 2000, Alabama; 2001, Connecticut. *Education:* Auburn University (B.A., cum laude, 1997); University of Connecticut (J.D., 2000). *Member:* Alabama, Connecticut and American Bar Associations. ***PRACTICE AREAS:*** Estate Planning; Business Planning; Corporate Law. ***Email:*** davidgrimes9@aol.com

---

EDWARD W. GASSER

20 EAST MAIN STREET
P.O. BOX 984
AVON, CONNECTICUT 06001-0984
Telephone: 860-674-8342
Fax: 860-676-8912
Email: egasser@gasserlaw.com

Insurance Law, Insurance Defense, Civil Litigation, Gaming Litigation.

EDWARD W. GASSER, born Litchfield, Connecticut, March 16, 1956; admitted to bar, 1988, Connecticut; 1989, Massachusetts; 1992, Mashantucket Pequot Tribal Court. *Education:* Northwestern Connecticut Community College (A.S., with honors, 1982); Western Connecticut State University (B.S., 1984); Western New England College (J.D., magna cum laude, 1988). *Member:* Hartford County, Connecticut and Mashantucket (President) Bar Associations. ***PRACTICE AREAS:*** Insurance Defense; Professional Liability Law; Real Estate Law; Insurance Law; Gaming Law.

REPRESENTATIVE CLIENTS: Mashantucket Pequot Tribal Nation; Foxwoods Resort & Casino, Zurich Insurance Group; Farmers Insurance; New London County Mutual; ESIS, Inc.; Reliance National; CNA; Crawford & Company; Insurance Company of North America; Houlihan's Restaurant Group; Speedy Muffler.

LITCHFIELD CAVO

40 TOWER LANE, SUITE 200
AVON, CONNECTICUT 06001
Telephone: 860-255-5577
Telefax: 860-255-5566

Chicago, Illinois Office: 303 West Madison Street, 60606. Telephone: 312-781-6677. Fax: 312-781-6630.
Boston, Massachusetts Area Office: 6 Kimball Lane, Suite 100, Lynnfield, Massachusetts, 01940-2682. Telephone: 781-246-0155. Fax: 781-246-0167.
Haddonfield, New Jersey Office: 3 South Haddon Avenue, 08033. Telephone: 856-428-6682. Fax: 856-354-1656.
Milwaukee, Wisconsin Area Office: 4447 North Oakland, Shorewood, Wisconsin, 53211. Telephone: 414-962-7240. Fax: 414-962-7243.

General Civil Practice in State and Federal Courts, Trials and Appeals. Arbitration and Mediation. Business Litigation, Insurance Coverage, Reinsurance, Insurance Litigation, Insurance Defense, Product Liability Defense, Professional Liability Defense, Employment Litigation, Technology Law and Litigation.

FIRM PROFILE: Litchfield Cavo is a litigation firm with a national practice in state and federal trial and appellate courts. From its offices in Chicago, Wisconsin, Connecticut, Massachusetts and New Jersey, Litchfield Cavo represents insurers, their insureds, and other business clients in insurance coverage and defense, product liability, professional liability, tort, employment and commercial litigation. Newly formed in 1998, most of its core partners have practiced together elsewhere for over a decade. The success of our firm is founded upon the values we bring to our practice of law: hard work, responsiveness, litigation focus, creativity, civility, and the desire to build long-term relationships with our clients.

Representative Clients: Ace Re; Aetna, Inc. AIG Technical Services, Inc.; Allstate Life Insurance Company; American Excess Insurance Association; American Home Products Co.; Atlanta International Insurance Co.; AON Risk Services; Argonaut Insurance Co.; Bay View Bank; Bechtel Corporation; Best Buy, Inc.; Cambridge Integrated Services; Chubb Group Insurance; Cincinnati Insurance Company; CNA; Connecticut Life & Casualty Ins. Co.; CP Risk Management, LLC; Du Page Radiologists, S.C.; Essex Insurance Company; Everest National Insurance Co.; Everest Reinsurance Co.; Federated Department Stores; Firemen's Fund Insurance Co.; Gallagher Bassett Services; Gulf Insurance Group; Hermitage Insurance Company; Home Insurance Company; Highlands Insurance Company; Hugo Neu; ICI Americas Inc.; Komori America Corporation; Komori Corporation; Lexington Insurance Company; Lumbermen's Mutual Insurance company; MacSteel International U.S.A. Corp.; Metal Sales Manufacturing Co.; Metro Chicago Security, Inc.; Middlesex Mutual Assurance Co.; Mitsui & Co., Ltd.; Mitsui Marine Fire Insurance Co., Ltd.; Mori Seiki Co., Ltd.; Mori Seki U.S.A., Inc.; Mt. McKinley Insurance Company; Nobel Biocare AB; North American Risk Services; Northland Insurance Group; Risk Enterprise Management, Ltd.; Royal Insurance Company; St. Paul Fire and Marine Insurance Company; Scottsdale Insurance Company; Smithkline Beecham; Societa Industrial Construzioni Meccaniche Electriche, S.P.A.; St. Paul Companies; Stamp Graphic, Inc.; Swiss Reinsurance Company; Travelers Property Casualty Corporation; Unigard Insurance Co.; Utica Mutual Insurance Company; Very Fine Products, Inc.; Yamazen, Inc Wells Fargo Risk Management; Yasuda Fire and Marine Insurance Company, Ltd.; Zurich Insurance Company.

ALAN I. BECKER (Resident, Chicago, Illinois Office).

TRACY C. BEGGS (Resident, Chicago, Illinois Office).

BENJAMIN A. BLUME (Resident, Chicago, Illinois Office).

RICHARD C. CAVO, born Utica, New York, 1957; admitted to bar, 1985, New York; 1989, Connecticut; U.S. District Court, Southern, Eastern and Northern Districts of New York and U.S. District Court, District of Connecticut. *Education:* Niagara University and St. Lawrence University (B.A., 1980); St. John's University School of Law (J.D., 1984). Author: "Survey of New York Practice," St. John's University Law Review, 1983. Co-Author: "Morton International: The Fiction of Regulatory Estoppel," 24 Seton Hall Law Review 847, 1993; "The Polluter's Web: The Pollution Exclusion and the Question of Deception," CPCU Journal, June 1994; "The Sophist's Maze: The Polluter's Revision of the History of the Total Pollution Exclusion," Mealey's Insurance Litigation Reports, September 1994; "A Study of History: The Evolution of Pollution Insurance Regulation," Mealey's Insurance Litigation Reports, July

(This Listing Continued)

LITCHFIELD CAVO, Avon—Continued

1997; "The Path of Least Resistance: Policyholder Export of Expected or Intended Pollution Harms," Mealey's Insurance Litigation Reports, June 1998. Former Employment: Aetna Casualty and Surety Company, 1988-1996. Recipient, Aetna Chairman's Award. Vice Chairman, 1994-1996 and Chairman, 1996-1997, Insurance Environmental Litigation Association. **Email:** cavo@litchfieldcavo.com

ROBERT L. CIOCIOLA (Not admitted in Connecticut; Resident, Lynnfield, Massachusetts Office).

THOMAS M. CRAWFORD (Resident, Chicago, Illinois Office).

MICHAEL W. DONAUBAUER (Resident, Chicago, Illinois Office).

MITCHELL H. FRAZEN (Resident, Chicago, Illinois Office).

MATTHEW J. IVERSON (Resident, Chicago, Illinois Office).

EILEEN P. KAVANAGH (Resident, Lynnfield, Massachusetts Office).

DANIEL G. LITCHFIELD (Resident, Chicago, Illinois Office).

KATHLEEN F. MUNROE, born Manchester, Connecticut, December 5, 1949; admitted to bar, 1988, Connecticut; 1991, U.S. District Court, District of Connecticut. *Education:* Boston College (B.A., 1971); University of Connecticut (J.D., 1987).

HOPE G. NIGHTINGALE (Resident, Chicago, Illinois Office).

MARK W. RATTAN (Also at Chicago, Illinois and Shorewood, Wisconsin Offices).

PATRICK J. SULLIVAN (Resident, Chicago, Illinois Office).

CHARLES E. VERMETTE, JR., born Providence, Rhode Island, October 7, 1964; admitted to bar, 1989, Connecticut; 1990, U.S. District Court, District of Connecticut. *Education:* George Washington University (B.A., 1986); Boston College (J.D., 1989).

ASSOCIATES

JOHN J. CAVO (Resident, Chicago, Illinois Office).

KATHLEEN J. COLLINS (Not admitted in Connecticut; Resident, Chicago, Illinois Office).

GABRIEL DANIEL MARTIN CIOCIOLA (Not admitted in Connecticut; Resident, Lynnfield, Massachusetts Office).

DAVID A. CORBETT

MARC S. EDRICH, born Long Island, New York, December 16, 1964; admitted to bar, 1989, Connecticut; 1990, U.S. District Court, District of Connecticut. *Education:* Cornell University (B.S., 1986); Albany Law School (J.D., cum laude, 1989). Member, Justinian Society. Drafting Committee Member, Connecticut Electronic Communications. *Member:* Hartford, Connecticut and American Bar Associations. ***PRACTICE AREAS:*** Insurance Coverage Defense; Commercial Litigation; Bankruptcy. **Email:** edrich@litchfieldcavo.com

DAWN M. GONZALEZ (Resident, Chicago, Illinois Office).

TIMOTHY S. JAJLIARDO, born Manchester, Connecticut, August 10, 1966; admitted to bar, 1999, Connecticut; 2000, U.S. District Court, District of Connecticut. *Education:* University of Connecticut (B.A., General Studies, 1995; J.D., honors, 1999).

JOHN D. LaBARBERA (Resident, Chicago, Illinois Office).

BRIAN PETER MULARSKI (Resident, Shorewood, Wisconsin Office).

MATTHEW D. WALKER (Resident, Chicago, Illinois Office).

MELICENT B. THOMPSON

STEPHANIE WING TIPTON (Resident, Chicago, Illinois Office).

(For complete biographical data on all personnel, see Professional Biographies at Chicago, Illinois)

PETER D. LURIA

32 EAST MAIN STREET
P.O. BOX 779
AVON, CONNECTICUT 06001
Telephone: 860-674-1411

Civil Litigation, Securities Litigation, Arbitration, Commercial Law, Commercial Litigation, Business Law, Real Estate, Trials in all courts, Arbitration.

PETER D. LURIA, born Boston, September 9, 1953; admitted to bar, 1979, Connecticut, U.S. District Court, District of Connecticut and U.S. Court of Appeals, Second Circuit; 1990, U.S. District Court, Eastern District of New York, U.S. Supreme Court. *Education:* Trinity College (B.A., 1975); California Western School of Law (J.D., 1978). Phi Beta Kappa. ***LANGUAGES:*** French.

(This Listing Continued)

REPORTED CASES: Welch v. Codre Capital 9 23 F. 2nd, 989 (2nd Circuit, 1991).

JUDITH D. MEYER

152 SIMSBURY ROAD
P.O. BOX 451
AVON, CONNECTICUT 06001-0451
Telephone: 860-678-7711
Fax: 860-677-6832
Email: judithdmeyer@nela.org
URL: http://www.lawyers.com/jdmlaw

Mailing Address: P.O. Box 451, Avon, Connecticut 06001-0451

Employment Law, Civil Litigation in all State and Federal Courts and Administrative Agencies, Professional Licensing.

JUDITH D. MEYER, born Brooklyn, New York, July 12, 1949; admitted to bar, 1989, Connecticut; 1990, U.S. District Court, District of Connecticut; 1995, U.S. Court of Appeals, 2nd Circuit; 1998, U.S. Supreme Court. *Education:* Virginia Commonwealth University (B.S., 1972); Queens College of the City University of New York (M.A., 1979); University of Connecticut (J.D., with honors, 1989). *Member:* Hartford County (Chair, Medical-Legal Dinner Committee; Chair, Labor and Employment Committee) and Connecticut (Member, Executive Committee, Labor and Employment Section; Chair, Annual Review Committee, ERISA Sub Committee) Bar Associations; National Employment Lawyers Association; Connecticut Employment Lawyers Association.

MORAN, SHUSTER, CARIGNAN & KNIERIM, LLP

111 SIMSBURY ROAD
AVON, CONNECTICUT 06001
Telephone: 860-678-0450
Fax: 860-676-2507
URL: http://www.lawyers.com/msc&k

Real Estate, Land Use, Probate, Estate Planning, Small Business Representation, Personal Injury, Civil and Criminal Litigation.

CARL H. SHUSTER, born New York, N.Y., May 14, 1936; admitted to bar, 1962, Connecticut. *Education:* Trinity College (B.A., 1958); University of Chicago (J.D., 1961). Pi Gamma Mu. Recipient, National Merit Scholarship. *Member:* Hartford and Connecticut Bar Associations (Member, Real Property Section). ***PRACTICE AREAS:*** Real Property; Estate Planning. **Email:** chshuster@lawyers.com

ROBERT R. MORAN, JR., born Hartford, Connecticut, November 26, 1946; admitted to bar, 1971, Connecticut. *Education:* Syracuse University (B.A., 1968); Suffolk University (J.D., 1971). *Member:* Connecticut Bar Association; Connecticut Mortgage Bankers Association (Closing and Compliance Committee); Litchfield County Board of Realtors (Forms and Bylaws Committees). ***PRACTICE AREAS:*** Real Property; Probate; Estate Planning.

PHILIP J. CARIGNAN, born Hartford, Connecticut, March 28, 1957; admitted to bar, 1982, Connecticut; 1983, Florida. *Education:* Boston College (B.S., cum laude, 1979); Suffolk University (J.D., 1982). Phi Alpha Delta (Vice Justice, Frankfurter Chapter, 1981-1982). *Member:* Connecticut (Member, Planning and Zoning Executive Committee) Bar Association; The Florida Bar. ***PRACTICE AREAS:*** Probate; Estate Planning; Real Property; Land Use.

GLENN E. KNIERIM, JR., born Mt. Clemens, Michigan, September 10, 1953; admitted to bar, 1978, District of Columbia; 1979, Maryland; 1984, Connecticut. *Education:* College of the Holy Cross (A.B., cum laude, 1975); Catholic University of America (J.D., 1978). Phi Beta Kappa. Research Editor, Catholic University Law Review, 1977-1978. *Member:* Hartford County, Connecticut (Member: Committee on Professional Ethics; Criminal Justice Section) and American (Member, Litigation Section) Bar Associations. ***PRACTICE AREAS:*** Litigation.

F. WILLIAM O'CONNOR

20 EAST MAIN STREET
AVON, CONNECTICUT 06001-1224
Telephone: 860-677-2254
Fax: 860-676-8912
Email: fwoc@aol.com
URL: http://www.lawyers.com/oconnorfw

Estate Planning, Tax Law, Real Estate, Corporate Law, Probate.

F. WILLIAM O'CONNOR, born Utica, New York, November 19, 1948; admitted to bar, 1979, Connecticut; 1980, U.S. Tax Court. *Education:* Univer-

(This Listing Continued)

sity of Connecticut (B.A., 1972; J.D., 1978); Trinity College (M.A., 1975). Certified Public Accountant, Connecticut, 1981. Attorney: Coopers & Lybrand, 1978-1983; Emhart, 1984-1989; General DataComm, 1989-1997. *Member:* Connecticut (Member: Estates, Probate and Tax Sections); and American (Member, Federal Tax Committee, 1979—and Real Estate and Probate Committees) Bar Associations; American Institute of Certified Public Accountants (Member, Federal Tax and Personal Financial Planning Committees); Connecticut Society of Certified Public Accountants (Member, Executive Committee: Personal Financial Planning Section). ***PRACTICE AREAS:*** Estate Planning; Tax Law; Real Estate; Corporate Law.

JOHN C. PETERS, P.C.

30 AVON MEADOW LANE
P.O. BOX 797
AVON, CONNECTICUT 06001-0797
Telephone: 860-676-1608
Fax: 860-676-2250
Email: Pete68may@aol.com

General Corporate, Finance, Banking and Securities Law. Litigation, Probate, Elder Law.

JOHN C. PETERS, born Webster, South Dakota, May 16, 1931; admitted to bar, 1959, South Dakota; 1961, New York; 1968, Nebraska; 1974, Connecticut. *Education:* Augustana College (B.A., 1953); University of Michigan (J.D., 1959). Order of the Coif. Associate Editor, Michigan Law Review, 1958-1959. *Member:* Connecticut and Nebraska State Bar Associations; State Bar of South Dakota.

SCIBILIA & McCUIN, P.C.

Established in 1985
WORTHINGTON PROFESSIONAL PARK
1263 WILBUR CROSS HIGHWAY
BERLIN, CONNECTICUT 06037
Telephone: 860-828-8884
Fax: 860-829-0410

Commercial Transactions, Corporate, Business and Securities, Real Estate and Litigation.

FIRM PROFILE: Scibilia & McCuin, P.C. is a specialized corporate and commercial law firm offering a full range of legal services to its clients concentrating on all aspects of corporate finance, commercial lending and workout transactions, including traditional and non-traditional securitization and SBA and government backed loans and grants, banking and securities, including internet integration, emerging company and venture capital, land use and real estate development and financing transactions, general corporate representation and litigation.

Scibilia & McCuin has structured its practice so as to offer a better understanding of its clients' business and legal needs in order to provide prompt and efficient legal services which accommodate those needs and to adapt quickly to the changing nature of today's business and legal environments.

SUZANNE M. SCIBILIA, born Fort Lauderdale, Florida, December 29, 1956; admitted to bar, 1983, New York and Connecticut; 1987, Massachusetts; U.S. District Court, District of Connecticut. *Education:* University of Hartford (B.A., 1978); St. John's University (J.D., 1982). *Member:* Hartford County, Connecticut, New York State and American Bar Associations. ***PRACTICE AREAS:*** Commercial Transactions; Real Estate; General Corporate; Business Law; Securities; Internet Law. ***Email:*** sscibilia@scibilia-mccuin.com

J. SCOTT McCUIN, born Killeen, Texas, October 29, 1965; admitted to bar, 1989, Connecticut and U.S. District Court, District of Connecticut. *Education:* University of Connecticut (B.A., magna cum laude, 1986; J.D., 1989). Phi Beta Kappa; Pi Sigma Alpha. U.S. Senate Aide, U.S. Senator Lowell P. Weiker, Jr., 1986. Law Clerk to the Connecticut State's Attorney Office, 1987. *Member:* Hartford, Connecticut and American Bar Associations; Connecticut Trial Lawyers Association. ***PRACTICE AREAS:*** Real Estate; Land Use; Commercial Transactions; Corporate; Securities Law; Commercial Litigation. ***Email:*** smccuin@scibilia-mccuin.com

LAURA M. MURPHY, born New Britain, Connecticut, June 12, 1966; admitted to bar, 1992, Connecticut; 1993, New York; U.S. District Court, District of Connecticut. *Education:* Trinity College (B.A., 1988); Western New England College School of Law (J.D., 1992). Temporary Assistant Clerk, Foreclosure and Real Property, Superior Court. *Member:* Connecticut and American

(This Listing Continued)

Bar Associations. ***PRACTICE AREAS:*** Real Estate; Commercial Transactions; Corporate Law; Commercial Litigation; Wills; Probate Administration. ***Email:*** lmurphy@scibilia-mccuin.com

JAMES L. CARLSON, born Scottsbluff, Nebraska, June 15, 1956; admitted to bar, 1996, Colorado; 1999, Connecticut. *Education:* University of Nebraska (B.S., Architectural Studies, 1978; Master of Architecture, 1980); Western New England College School of Law (J.D., 1995). Licensed Architect in Colorado since 1986. Member, Construction Panel of the American Arbitration Association. *Member:* Boulder, Colorado and American (Intellectual Property Section) Bar Associations. ***LANGUAGES:*** German. ***PRACTICE AREAS:*** Construction Law; Zoning, Planning and Land Use; Corporate Law; Securities; Real Estate. ***Email:*** jcarlson@scibilia-mccuin.com

OF COUNSEL

JEFFREY P. CUGNO, born New Britain, Connecticut, January 15, 1950; admitted to bar, 1987, Connecticut. *Education:* University of Connecticut (B.S., 1972); University of Hartford (M.A., 1977); University of Bridgeport (J.D., 1986). ***PRACTICE AREAS:*** Real Estate; Land Use; Commercial; Corporate Law.

JOHN K. KNOTT, JR.

BETHANY, CONNECTICUT

(See Cheshire)

General Civil Practice, Municipal and Administrative Law, Land Use Law, Probate and Estate, Real Estate, Selected Civil Trials and Appeals, Education and Special Education.

THE LAW OFFICE OF SCOTT B. CHAMBERLAIN, P.C.

275 GREENWOOD AVENUE
BETHEL, CONNECTICUT 06801
Telephone: 203-798-2877
Fax: 203-798-6359
Email: mx5madness@aol.com
URL: http://www.lawyers.com/chamberlainlaw

Family Law, Divorce, Bankruptcy, Criminal Law, Personal Injury.

SCOTT B. CHAMBERLAIN, born Stamford, Connecticut, May 8, 1954; admitted to bar, 1985, Connecticut; 1986, U.S. District Court, District of Connecticut; 1996, U.S. Supreme Court. *Education:* Louisiana State University and A. and M. College (B.S., 1977; J.D., 1983). *Member:* Danbury and Connecticut Bar Associations; Connecticut Criminal Defense Lawyers Association; Connecticut Trial Lawyers Association; National Association of Consumer Bankruptcy Attorneys; Association of Trial Lawyers of America. ***PRACTICE AREAS:*** Family Law; Divorce; Criminal Law; Personal Injury. ***Email:*** mx5madness@aol.com

GAGER & PETERSON, LLP

Established in 1917
2 STONY HILL ROAD
BETHEL, CONNECTICUT 06801
Telephone: 203-207-5400
Telecopier: 203-207-5407

Waterbury, Connecticut Office: One Exchange Place, P.O. Box 2480. Telephone: 203-597-5100. Telecopier: 203-757-7888.

Litchfield, Connecticut Office: 782 Bantam Road. Telephone: 860-567-0828. Telecopier: 860-567-5844.

Sharon, Connecticut Office: 25 West Main Street, P.O. Box 158. Telephone: 860-364-5531. Telecopier: 860-364-5805.

Southbury, Connecticut Office: 325 Main Street South. Telephone: 203-262-6600. Telecopier: 203-262-6780.

General Practice. Corporate Law, Banks and Banking, Securities, Administrative Law, Litigation, Insurance, Trusts and Estates, Probate, Real Estate, Taxation, Patents, Trademarks, Copyrights, Zoning, Planning and Land Use, Consumer Law, Environmental Law, Computers and Software, Information Technology, Labor and Employment Law, Personal Injury.

RICHARD L. EMERSON, born Orange, New Jersey, September 16, 1946; admitted to bar, 1973, Connecticut. *Education:* Wesleyan University (B.A., 1968); George Washington University (J.D., with honors, 1973). Law Clerk, Appellate Division, U.S. Attorney's Office for the District of Columbia, 1972-1973. Judge of Probate, District of Redding, Connecticut, 1979—. *Member:*

(This Listing Continued)

GAGER & PETERSON, LLP, Bethel—Continued

Connecticut and American Bar Associations. (Also at Waterbury Office). ***PRACTICE AREAS:*** Corporate Law; Banking Law; Trusts and Estates. ***Email:*** emerson@gpbethel.com

THOMAS J. McHALE (See Waterbury listing).

THOMAS M. RICKART, born New Haven, Connecticut, April 7, 1953; admitted to bar, 1981, Connecticut. *Education:* Yale University (B.A., 1975); University of Connecticut (M.A., 1978); Boston College (J.D., cum laude, 1981). Articles and Citations Editor, Boston College Environmental Affairs Law Review, 1980-1981. *Member:* Connecticut and American Bar Associations. ***PRACTICE AREAS:*** Real Estate Law; Environmental Law; Commercial Lending.

KATHY S. BOWER (See Southbury listing).

FRANK J. SCINTO (See Waterbury listing).

ASSOCIATE

PETER A. SCALZO, born Danbury, Connecticut, March 10, 1962; admitted to bar, 1995, Connecticut; 1996, U.S. District Court, District of Connecticut. *Education:* Messiah College (B.S., 1984); Regent University (J.D., 1995). Recipient, American Jurisprudence Award. Zoning Hearing Officer, Brookfield, Connecticut. *Member:* Danbury and Connecticut Bar Associations. ***PRACTICE AREAS:*** Real Estate; Landlord and Tenant Law; Zoning, Planning and Land Use; Wills, Trusts and Estates; Business Law. ***Email:*** scalzo@gpbethel.com

CHRISTIAN LAWRENCE DIPENTIMA (See Southbury listing).

HARVEY J. KULAWITZ, LLC

BETHEL, CONNECTICUT

(See Ridgefield)

All Personal Injury Cases, including Car Accident cases, Aircraft & Boating accidents, Slip & Fall accidents, Dog Bite attacks, and Wrongful Death accidents & claims.

JACKSON, O'KEEFE AND PHELAN

423 MUNGER LANE
BETHLEHEM, CONNECTICUT 06751
Telephone: 203-266-5255
Fax: 203-266-5255

Hartford, Connecticut Office: 36-40 Russ Street. Telephone: 860-278-4040. Fax: 860-527-2500.

General Practice including Civil Trial and Appellate Practice in all Courts, Governmental Law and Relations, Personal Injury, Medical Malpractice, Construction Litigation, Products Liability, Probate and Estate Planning, Residential and Commercial Real Estate, Corporation, Insurance, Banking, Legislative Practice, Mediation and Arbitration.

(For complete biographical data on all personnel, see Professional Biographies at Hartford, Connecticut)

CANTOR COLBURN LLP

55 GRIFFIN ROAD SOUTH
BLOOMFIELD, CONNECTICUT 06002-1355
Telephone: 860-286-2929
Fax: 860-286-0115
Email: iplaw@cantorcolburn.com
URL: http://www.cantorcolburn.com

Norwalk, Connecticut Office: 101 Merritt 7, 06853. Telephone: 203-849-8266. Fax: 203-849-8292.

Patent, Trademark and Copyright Law, Unfair Competition, Computer and Related Intellectual Property Law including Litigation in all Courts.

FIRM PROFILE: In a world of corporate takeovers and merger mania, it's easy for a law firm to try to be everything to everyone. Few succeed. That's why, at Cantor Colburn LLP, intellectual property law is the only type of law we practice. And why we have gained a reputation as a leader in our field.

Our greatest strength is our focus. A focus on managing and protecting the products, processes, systems and inventions of our clients. A focus that extends to all phases of patent, trademark, copyright, unfair competition, computer and trade secret law, and related licensing and litigation. And expertise that includes a wide range of areas such as semiconductors, software, ceramics, polymeric materials, computers, chemical processing, automotive, optical imaging, biotechnology, and oil and gas wells.

MEMBERS OF FIRM

MICHAEL CANTOR, born Hartford, Connecticut, July 10, 1958; admitted to bar, 1984, Connecticut and U.S. District Court, District of Connecticut; 1984, U.S. Court of Appeals for the Federal Circuit; registered to practice before U.S. Patent and Trademark Office. *Education:* University of Connecticut (B.S., with honors, Chemical Engineering/Materials Engineering, 1980; J.D., 1983). Tau Beta Pi. Adjunct Professor in Patent Law, University of Connecticut School of Law, 1993—. *Member:* Connecticut and American Bar Associations; Connecticut Patent Law Association; American Intellectual Property Law Association; International Trademark Association. ***PRACTICE AREAS:*** Patent Law; Trademark and Copyright Law; Unfair Competition; Intellectual Property Law. ***Email:*** mcantor@cantorcolburn.com

PHILMORE H. COLBURN, II, born Springfield, Massachusetts, August 2, 1959; admitted to bar, 1991, Connecticut and U.S. District Court District of Connecticut; 1992, Massachusetts and New York; 1993, U.S. District Court, District of Massachusetts; 1994, U.S. Court for the Federal Circuit 8th Circuit; registered to practice before U.S. Patent and Trademark Office. *Education:* Northeastern University (B.S.E.E., with honors, 1982); University of Massachusetts (M.B.A., 1986); Western New England College School of Law (J.D., 1991). Eta Kappa Nu. Design Engineer, Hamilton Standard division of United Technologies Corporation. *Member:* Hampden County, Connecticut and American Bar Associations; Connecticut Patent Law Association. ***PRACTICE AREAS:*** Patent Law; Trademark and Copyright Law; Unfair Competition; Intellectual Property Law. ***Email:*** pcolburn@cantorcolburn.com

KEITH J. MURPHY, born Manhasset, New York, October 3, 1965; admitted to bar, 1994, New York, Connecticut, U.S. District Court, District of Connecticut, U.S. District Court, Southern and Eastern Districts of New York and U.S Court of Appeals for the Federal Circuit; registered to practice before U.S. Patent and Trademark Office. *Education:* Hartwick College (B.A., Biology, 1987); St. John's University (J.D., 1993). Author, "Win/Win Settlement of Patent Litigation," The Law Works, Vol. 3, No. 4, 1996. *Member:* Connecticut and American Bar Associations; Connecticut Patent Law Association. ***PRACTICE AREAS:*** Intellectual Property; Patent Law; Trademark; Copyright. ***Email:*** kmurphy@cantorcolburn.com

LEAH M. REIMER, born Rapid City, South Dakota, October 31, 1960; admitted to bar, 1995, Connecticut; registered to practice before U.S. Patent and Trademark Office. *Education:* Baylor University (B.Sc., with honors, Chemistry, 1979); Stanford University (Ph.D., Organic Chemistry, 1988); University of Connecticut (J.D., 1995). Research Chemist, EliLilly and DowElanco. *Member:* Connecticut and American Bar Associations; American Chemical Society; American Association for Advancement of Science. ***PRACTICE AREAS:*** Patent Law; Trademark Law; Copyright Law; Unfair Competition; Intellectual Property. ***Email:*** lreimer@cantorcolburn.com

DAVID A. FOX, born Milwaukee, Wisconsin, August 26, 1967; admitted to bar, 1995, Pennsylvania; 1996, Connecticut and U.S. District Court, District of Connecticut; registered to practice before U.S. Trademark and Patent Office. *Education:* Rensselaer Polytechnic Institute (B.S.E.E., 1989); Catholic University (J.D., 1995). Patent Examiner, U.S. Patent and Trademark Office. Formerly with, Ratner & Prestia, Valley Forge, Pennsylvania. *Member:* American Intellectual Property Law Association; Connecticut Patent Law Association. ***PRACTICE AREAS:*** Patent Law; Trademark Law; Copyright Law; Unfair Competition; Intellectual Property. ***Email:*** dfox@cantorcolburn.com

WILLIAM J. CASS, born Springfield, Massachusetts, November 16, 1962; admitted to bar, 1988, Massachusetts; 1990, U.S. District Court, District of Massachusetts; 1998, Connecticut, U.S. District Court, District of Connecticut, U.S. Tax Court and U.S. Court of Appeals for the Federal Circuit; registered to practice before U.S. Patent and Trademark Office. *Education:* Worcester Polytechnic Institute (B.S., with high distinction, Mechanical Engineering, 1985); Western New England College of Law (J.D., cum laude, 1988). Partner, Ryan, Martin, Costello, Leiter, Steiger & Cass, P.S., Springfield, Massachusetts. Commercial Pilot. *Member:* American Bar Association. ***PRACTICE AREAS:*** Intellectual Property; Litigation. ***Email:*** wcass@cantorcolburn.com

MICHAEL J. RYE, born Vermillion, South Dakota, January 14, 1962; admitted to bar, 1990, Massachusetts, U.S. District Court, District of Massachusetts; 1991, New York and U.S. Court of Appeals, First Circuit; 1994, Minnesota; 1999, Connecticut; registered to practice before U.S. Patent and Trademark Office. *Education:* University of Minnesota (B.A., Biology, 1985); Syracuse University (J.D., 1990). Formerly with, Doherty, Wallace, Pillsbury and Murphy, Springfield, Massachusetts. *Member:* Hampden County, Massachusetts and American Bar Associations. ***PRACTICE AREAS:*** Intellectual Property Litigation. ***Email:*** mrye@cantorcolburn.com

PAMELA J. CURBELO, born Fitchburg, Massachusetts, January 19, 1966; admitted to bar, 1991, Massachusetts; 2001, Connecticut; registered to

(This Listing Continued)

practice before U.S. Patent and Trademark Office. *Education:* Worcester Polytechnic Institute (B.S.Chem.Eng., 1988); Western New England College (J.D., cum laude, 1991). Former In-House Intellectual Property Attorney, Corporate Office and United Technologies Research Center, United Technologies Corporation. *Member:* American Bar Association; Connecticut Patent Law Association. ***PRACTICE AREAS:*** Intellectual Property Law. **Email:** pcurbelo@cantorcolburn.com

ASSOCIATES

ANDREW C. RYAN, born Springfield, Massachusetts, October 4, 1968; admitted to bar, 1997, Massachusetts; 1999, Connecticut; registered to practice before the U.S. Patent and Trademark Office. *Education:* Massachusetts College of Pharmacy and Allied Health Services (B.S., Pharmacy, 1992); Western New England College (J.D., 1997). Registered Pharmacist. *Member:* Massachusetts, Connecticut and American Bar Associations; American Pharmaceutical Association. ***PRACTICE AREAS:*** Patent Law; Trademark Law; Intellectual Property Litigation. **Email:** ryan@cantorcolburn.com

WAYNE R. GROHS, born Derby, Connecticut, May 20, 1964; admitted to bar, 1999, Connecticut. *Education:* University of New Haven (B.S., in Chem. Eng., 1993); Quinnipiac College School of Law (J.D., 1998). *Member:* American Intellectual Property Law Association. ***PRACTICE AREAS:*** Patent Law; Trademark Law. **Email:** wgrohs@cantorcolburn.com

TIMOTHY J. OLSON, born Bellevue, Nebraska, December 28, 1965; admitted to bar, 1999, Connecticut; registered to practice before the U.S. Patent and Trademark Office. *Education:* United States Merchant Marine Academy (B.S., Marine Engineering, 1988); Rensselaer Polytechnic Institute (M.S., Mechanical Engineering, 1993); University of Connecticut School of Law (J.D., with honors, 1999); Rensselaer Polytechnic Institute (M.S., Computer Science, 2001). Licensed Professional Engineer, State of Connecticut. Formerly with: Proto-Power Corporation; General Dynamics, Electric Boat Division. *Member:* Intellectual Property Owners Association (Member, Patent Law, E-Commerce/Internet Committee). [Lieut., USNR (1988-1996)]. ***PRACTICE AREAS:*** Patent Law; Trademark Law; Copyright Law; Intellectual Property Law. **Email:** tolson@cantorcolburn.com

HERBERT M. BEDINGFIELD, born Louisville, Kentucky, December 16, 1972; admitted to bar, 1999, Connecticut; registered to practice before the U.S. Patent and Trademark Office. *Education:* Duke University (B.A., 1995); University of Connecticut (J.D., 1999). *Member:* American Bar Association (Member, Sections On: Intellectual Property; Technology; International Law). ***PRACTICE AREAS:*** Patent Law; Trademark Law; Copyright Law. **Email:** budhm@alumni@duke.edu

STEVEN M. COYLE, born Boston, Massachusetts, June 6, 1968; admitted to bar, 1993, Massachusetts, 1994, Connecticut; 1995, U.S. District Court, District of Massachusetts; 1999, U.S. Court of Appeals, First Circuit. *Education:* Trinity College (B.A., 1990); Western New England College (J.D., cum laude, 1993). Law Clerk, Justices of Massachusetts Superior Court, 1993-1994. *Member:* Hampden County, Connecticut, Massachusetts and American Bar Associations. ***PRACTICE AREAS:*** Intellectual Property Litigation. **Email:** scoyle@cantorcolburn.com

CHARLES F. O'BRIEN, born Middletown, Connecticut, May 27, 1970; admitted to bar, 1997, Massachusetts and Connecticut. *Education:* Northeastern University (B.S.M.E., 1993); Western New England College (J.D., 1997). *Member:* Hampden County, Massachusetts, Connecticut and American Bar Associations. ***PRACTICE AREAS:*** Intellectual Property Litigation. **Email:** cobrien@cantorcolburn.com

GEORGE A. PELLETIER, JR., born Springfield, Massachusetts, January 17, 1970; admitted to bar, 1997, Massachusetts; 2001, Connecticut. *Education:* Bard College (B.A., 1992); Western New England College (J.D., 1997). ***PRACTICE AREAS:*** Trademark Law. **Email:** gpelletier@cantorcolburn.com

TROY LAMONTAGNE, born Middletown, Connecticut, December 13, 1962; admitted to bar, 1998, Connecticut. *Education:* Rochester Institute of Technology (B.S.E.E., 1985); Western New England College (J.D., 1998). Member, Institute of Electrical and Electronic Engineers, 1982—. *Member:* Connecticut and American Bar Associations. ***PRACTICE AREAS:*** Intellectual Property. **Email:** tlamontagne@cantorcolburn.com

DEBORAH B. CRENSHAW, born Tripoli, Libya, Africa (Wheelus A.F.B.), January 8, 1959; admitted to bar, 1994, Texas; registered to practice before U.S. Patent and Trademark Office (Not admitted in Connecticut). *Education:* University of Houston (B.S.E.E., 1983); Texas Tech University School of Law (J.D., 1994). Licensed with the Texas Board of Registration for Professional Engineers, 1991—. *Member:* State Bar of Texas; American Intellectual Property Law Association. ***PRACTICE AREAS:*** Intellectual Property. **Email:** dcrenshaw@cantorcolburn.com

LEONARD E. HEYMAN, born Washington, D.C., June 11, 1967; admitted to bar, 2000, Connecticut and New York. *Education:* Old Dominion University (B.S.M.E., 1990); State University of New York at Buffalo (J.D., 1999). ***PRACTICE AREAS:*** Intellectual Property. **Email:** lheyman@cantorcolburn.com

(This Listing Continued)

DANIEL F. DREXLER, born St. Louis, Missouri, October 4, 1972; admitted to bar, 2000, Connecticut. *Education:* Rutgers University (B.S., Environmental Engineering, 1996); Pace University School of Law (J.D., 1999). *Member:* Connecticut (Member, Intellectual Property Section) and American Bar Associations. ***PRACTICE AREAS:*** Patent; Intellectual Property; Trademark. **Email:** ddrexler@cantorcolburn.com

GEORGE J. LYMAN, born Hartford, Connecticut, February 17, 1952; admitted to bar, 2000, Connecticut; registered to practice before the U.S. Patent and Trademark Office. *Education:* University of Hartford (B.S., in Physics, 1989; B.S., 1991, in Engineering, 1991); Tufts University (M.S., in Electro-Optics, 1993); Western New England College (J.D., 1999). Professional Engineer, State of Connecticut, 1995. Member: Institute of Electrical and Electronics Engineers; Optical Society of America, 1999; Society of Photo-Optical Instrumentation Engineers. ***PRACTICE AREAS:*** Patent Prosecution. **Email:** glyman@cantorcolburn.com

JAMES J. MERRICK, born Hartford, Connecticut, June 22, 1961; admitted to bar, 1997, Connecticut; 2000, U.S. District Court, District of Connecticut; registered to practice before U.S. Patent and Trademark Office. *Education:* University of Connecticut, Storrs; Trinity College; Charter Oak College (B.S., with honors, 1991); Western New England College School of Law (J.D., 1997). Judicial Law Clerk to the Appellate Court for the State of Connecticut, 1997-1999. Appointed Special Public Defender, 1997; Certified Legal Intern to State's Attorney's Office G.A. 14, Part A, 1996. ***PRACTICE AREAS:*** Litigation; Trial Practice; Intellectual Property Litigation; Investigations; Personal Injury. **Email:** jmerrick@cantorcolburn.com

SEAN F. SULLIVAN, born Westerly, Rhode Island,; admitted to bar, 1993, Connecticut. *Education:* University of Connecticut (BSEE, 1989); Western New England College (J.D., 1993). ***PRACTICE AREAS:*** Patent.

PAMELA S. CHESTEK, born Cincinnati, Ohio, August 29, 1955; admitted to bar, 2001, Massachusetts, New York and Connecticut. *Education:* Pennsylvania State University (B.F.A., with high distinction, 1977); Western New England College (J.D., summa cum laude, 2000). Member, Western New England Law Review, 1998-1999. *Member:* American Bar Association. ***PRACTICE AREAS:*** Trademarks; Copyrights; Intellectual Property Litigation. **Email:** pchestek@cantorcolburn.com

DANIEL E. BRUSO, born Springfield, Massachusetts, February 20, 1967; admitted to bar, 1996, Massachusetts and U.S. District Court, District of Massachusetts; 1998, U.S. Court of Appeals for the First Circuit and U.S. District Court, District of Connecticut (Not admitted in Connecticut). *Education:* Worcester Polytechnic Institute (B.S., 1989); Western New England College (J.D., 1996). Previously with: Cooley, Shrair, P.C., Springfield, Massachusetts, 1996-2000; Materials Control Specialist for Norton Company, 1989-1990; Production Control Planner with Allegro Microsystems, Inc., 1990-1992. *Member:* Hampden County, Massachusetts (Chair, New Lawyers Section) and American Bar Associations. ***PRACTICE AREAS:*** Commercial Law; Bankruptcy; Creditors Rights; Commercial Litigation; Intellectual Property. **Email:** dbruso@cantorcolburn.com

LISA A. BONGIOVI, born Rantoul, Illinois, October 5, 1966; admitted to bar, 1994, Pennsylvania; 1996, Oregon; 1999, Massachusetts (Not admitted in Connecticut). *Education:* University of Connecticut (B.S., Civil Engineering, 1988); Western New England College School of Law (J.D., summa cum laude, 1994). Author: "Sifting Through the Mixture Problem," 15 W. New Eng. L. Rev. 395, 1993. Foreign Legal Associate, Tozai Sogo Law Office, Tokyo, Japan, 1994-1996. Clerk to Judge Walter I. Edmonds, Jr., Oregon Court of Appeals, 1996-1998. ***PRACTICE AREAS:*** Intellectual Property; Patent. **Email:** lbongiovi@cantorcolburn.com

PETER R. HAGERTY, born Warren, Michigan, September 13, 1961; admitted to bar, 1994, Massachusetts; registered to practice before U.S. Patent and Trademark Office (Not admitted in Connecticut). *Education:* Massachusetts College of Pharmacy (B.S., cum laude, Organic Chemistry, 1987); New England School of Law (J.D., 1994). *Member:* American Bar Association; Cleveland and American Intellectual Property Law Associations. ***PRACTICE AREAS:*** Intellectual Property; Patents; Trademarks; Copyrights. **Email:** phagerty@cantorcolburn.com

MARISA J. DUBUC, born Westfield, Massachusetts, January 22, 1960; admitted to bar, 2001, Massachusetts and Connecticut. *Education:* Westfield State College (B.S., in Computer Science, 1985); Western New England College (J.D., 2000). registered to practice before U.S. Patent and Trademark Office. *Member:* American Bar Association (Section, Intellectual Property). [CTA1, USNR, 1980-1997]. ***LANGUAGES:*** Chinese (Mandarin) and Spanish. ***PRACTICE AREAS:*** Patent Prosecution. **Email:** mdubue@cantorcolburn.com

MICHAEL J. CHANG, born Tarrytown, New York, April 2, 1974; admitted to bar, 2001, Connecticut. *Education:* Vassar College (B.A., Biology, 1996). (Patent Agent).

(This Listing Continued)

CANTOR COLBURN LLP, Bloomfield—Continued

ANNE D. BARRY, born Syracuse, New York, April 11, 1959; admitted to bar, 2001, Connecticut. *Education:* University of Connecticut (B.S., Mathematics and Statistics, 1981); Union College (M.A., Computer Science, 1984); University of Connecticut School of Law (J.D., 2001).

KAREN BEUTEL, born Dayton, Ohio, April 22, 1971; admitted to bar, 2001, Connecticut. *Education:* Loyola University (B.S., 1993; J.D., 2001). ***PRACTICE AREAS:*** Patents. **Email:** kbeutel@cantorcolburn.com

JENNIFER A. D'ERRICO, born Hartford, Connecticut, July 19, 1974; admitted to bar, 2000, New York (Not admitted in Connecticut). *Education:* Syracuse University (B.A., 1996); Benjamin N. Cardozo School of Law (J.D., 1999). *Member:* New York State Bar Association. ***PRACTICE AREAS:*** Intellectual Property.

PATENT AGENTS

PATRICIA S. DeSIMONE, born St. Louis, Missouri, January 12, 1965; admitted to bar, 2001, Connecticut; registered to practice before the U.S. Patent and Trademark Office. *Education:* Fairleigh Dickinson University (B.S., Medical Technology, 1987); Wesleyan University (M.S., Organometallic Chemistry, 2000). Member, American Chemical Society.

J. MICHAEL BUCHANAN, born San Diego, California, October 7, 1959. *Education:* College of William and Mary (B.S., in Chemistry, 1981); University of California at Berkeley (Ph.D., Chemistry, 1985). Formerly with Eastman Kodak Company. (Patent Agent). **Email:** buchanan@cantorcolburn.com

KAREN A. JALBERT, born Putnam, Connecticut, June 10, 1969. *Education:* Rensselaer Polytechnic Institute (B.S., Aeronautical Engineering, 1991). Sigma Gamma Tau Honor Society. Registered Patent Agent, 1995. Patent Examiner, U.S.P.T.O., 1991-1994. *Member:* Rochester Intellectual Property Law Association. (Patent Agent). ***PRACTICE AREAS:*** Patent Prosecution. **Email:** kjalbert@cantorcolburn.com

SUKHEUM KWON, born Seoul, Korea, July 20, 1960; admitted to bar, registered to practice before U.S. Patent and Trademark Office. *Education:* Seoul National University (B.S., 1984; M.S., 1986); Franklin Pierce Law Center (M.I.P., 2000). *Member:* Korean Patent Attorney Association; International Association For the Protection of Industrial Property. **Email:** skwon@cantorcolburn.com

STEVEN M. McHUGH, born Waterbury, Connecticut, October 12, 1962; admitted to bar, registred to practice before U.S. Patent and Trademark Office. *Education:* University of Connecticut (B.S.E.E., 1994); Quinnipiac University School of Law (J.D., 2001). *Member:* American Intellectual Property Law Association.

ROBERTA L. PELLETIER, born Nashua, New Hampshire, January 13, 1970; admitted to bar, registered to practice before U.S. Patent and Trademark Office. *Education:* Rivier College (B.S. in Chemistry, 1992); Boston University (M.A., Chemistry, 1994); University of Connecticut School of Law.

BARRY M.L. STANDIG, born Ridgewood, New Jersey, August 10, 1963. *Education:* Rutgers University (B.S.M.E., 1985); Columbia University (M.B.A., 1989); Nova Southeastern Law Center (J.D., 1994). ***PRACTICE AREAS:*** Patent Prosecution. **Email:** bstandig@cantorcolburn.com

REPRESENTATIVE CLIENTS: General Motors Corp.; General Electric Co.; Rogers Corp.; Raymond Engineering; Baker Hughes, Inc.; The Siemon Co.; American Distilling & Mfg. Co., Inc.; Villeroy & Boch S.a.r.l.; American Optical Corp.; Kaman Corp.; University of Connecticut; JPS Elastomerics Corp.; AEARO Co.; Standard-Knapp, Inc.; Konica Corp.; International Business Machines; Bic Corporation; United States Surgical Corp.; Delphi Technologies Inc.; Jeneric Pentron Inc.; Proton Energy Systems; Sanyo Electric Co., Inc.; Macrovision Corp.

STEPHEN S. CHINITZ & ASSOCIATES

800 COTTAGE GROVE ROAD, SUITE 421
BLOOMFIELD, CONNECTICUT 06002
Telephone: 860-769-6999
Fax: 860-769-6998
Email: ssc@home.com
URL: http://www.lawyers.com/stephenschinitz

Collections, Creditor's Rights, Personal Injury, Insurance, Subrogation, Bankruptcy Court Litigation (Creditors), Legal Malpractice, Domestic Relations and Real Estate, Trials in all Courts.

STEPHEN S. CHINITZ, born Hartford, Connecticut, January 13, 1953; admitted to bar, 1979, Connecticut and U.S. District Court for the District of Connecticut. *Education:* University of Connecticut (B.A., 1975); John Marshall Law School (J.D., 1979). Lecturer: National Association of Savings Banks, 1987—; "Federal Fair Debt Collections Practices Act," National Business Institute, 1988; "Lender Liability in Connecticut," 1991; Lorman Business Center, Inc. 1995, "Small Claims and Garnishment Procedures for Business Professionals". *Member:* Hartford County, Connecticut (Member, Sections on: Litigation; Banking; Commercial Law and Bankruptcy; Lecturer, Uniform Commercial Code, Issues in Secured Transactions, 1982-1984; Lecturer, Selected Issues in Bankruptcy Law, 1985) and American (Member, Sections on: Litigation; Member, Committee on Entertainment and Sports Law, 1980-1987; Family Law Litigation, 1980-1987) Bar Associations; Connecticut Trial Lawyers Association; The Association of Trial Lawyers of America; American Bankruptcy Institute; Commercial Law League of America (Member, Young Lawyers Section; Member, Executive Council, 1986-1988; Recording Secretary, 1988-1989; Treasurer, 1989-1990; Chairman-Elect, 1990-1991; Chairman, 1991-1992; Board of Governors, 1992-1993; Chairman, Membership Committee, State of Connecticut, 1984; Vice-Chairman, National Membership Committee, Lecturer: Proposed Article 2A, Uniform Commercial Code; Lease vs. Secured Loan, 1987; "Connective Consumer Collection Law", Lorman, Inc.; Member, Executive Committee, Future Planning Conference, 1992); Connecticut Creditors' Rights Attorneys Association (Vice President). ***PRACTICE AREAS:*** Commercial Law; Litigation; Bankruptcy Law; Creditor's Rights; Collections; Foreclosures; Personal Injury; Domestic Relations.

ASSOCIATE

ANNA-CRISTINA CABRAL CARUK, born Lisbon, Portugal, January 24, 1966; admitted to bar, 1992, Connecticut, New York and U.S. District Court, District of Connecticut; 1995, U.S. Court of Appeals, Second Circuit. *Education:* Western Connecticut State University (B.A., 1988); University of Connecticut School of Law (J.D., 1991). Pi Gamma Mu; National Honor Society. *Member:* Danbury, New York State, Connecticut and American Bar Associations. Oliver Elsworth Inn of Court (Barrister) 1994-1997. ***LANGUAGES:*** Portuguese and Spanish. ***REPORTED CASES:*** Santiago v. Commissioner of Correction 39 Conn. App. 674 A.2d 304 1995. ***PRACTICE AREAS:*** Collections; Personal Injury; Divorce.

CLAYMAN, MARKOWITZ, TAPPER AND BARAM, L.L.C.

3 REGENCY DR.
BLOOMFIELD, CONNECTICUT 06002-2331
Telephone: 860-242-2221
Telecopier: 860-286-0185
Email: office@ctattys.com
URL: http://www.ctattys.com

Business Law, Commercial, Condominium, Corporate, Criminal Law, Elder Law, Employment Law, Entertainment Law, Estate Planning, Family, Franchise Law, General Practice. Immigration, Municipal Law, Nationality, Negligence, Personal Injury, Planning and Zoning, Probate, Real Estate, Trademarks, Trials in all Courts.

MEMBERS OF FIRM

MARTIN A. CLAYMAN, born Boston, Massachusetts, October 11, 1936; admitted to bar, 1962, Connecticut; 1963, U.S. District Court, District of Connecticut; 1969, U.S. Supreme Court; 1974, U.S. Court of Appeals, Second Circuit. *Education:* Loomis Institute; Yale University (B.A., 1958); University of Connecticut (J.D., 1962). Assistant Prosecutor, 1966-1970. Adjunct Instructor of Law at University of Hartford, 1986-1987. Director, Vernon Bank, 1987-1992. Justice of the Peace, 1989—. *Member:* Connecticut (Chairman, Executive Committee of Franchise Law, 1996-1999) and American (Member, Forum Committee on Franchising, Business Law Section, 1983—) Bar Associations. ***PRACTICE AREAS:*** Franchise Law; Business Law; Commercial Litigation; Commercial Real Estate; Trademark Law. **Email:** mac@ctattys.com

DAVID J. MARKOWITZ, born Hartford, Connecticut, May 19, 1948; admitted to bar, 1974, Connecticut and U.S. District Court, District of Connecticut. *Education:* Clark University (B.A., 1970); University of Connecticut (J.D., 1974). Member, Canton, Connecticut, Inland Wetlands and Watercourses Agency, 1989-1999; Chairman, 1990-1999. Member, Community Associations Institute, 1990—. *Member:* Connecticut (Member: Executive Committee of Real Property Section, 1980-1989; Executive Committee, Sports and Entertainment Section, 1989—; Chairman, Legislative Subcommittee of Real Property Section, 1984-1989) and American Bar Associations. ***PRACTICE AREAS:*** Business Law; Real Estate Law; Planning Law; Zoning Law; Condominium Law; Entertainment Law. **Email:** djm@ctattys.com

PAUL LITMAN, born Springfield, Massachusetts, June 14, 1939; admitted to bar, 1964, Connecticut; 1965, U.S. District Court, District of Connecticut; 1967, U.S. Court of Appeals, Second Circuit. *Education:* American International College (B.S., 1961); Boston University (LL.B., 1964). Author: "The Basics of Connecticut's Mechanics Lien Law," Connecticut Construction Magazine, February-March, 1979. Member, Board of Directors, Jewish Children's Service Organization, 1981-2001. *Member:* Hartford County, Connecticut (Member, Sections on: Family Law; Alternative Dispute Resolution) and American Bar Associations; Connecticut Trial Lawyers Association; Connecticut

(This Listing Continued)

Criminal Defense Lawyers Association. ***PRACTICE AREAS:*** Family Law; Personal Injury; Criminal Law; Arbitration; Mediation; Medical Malpractice; Products Liability. ***Email:*** pl@ctattys.com

JOSEPH M. TAPPER, born New York, N.Y., July 21, 1941; admitted to bar, 1966, Connecticut and U.S. District Court, District of Connecticut; 1976, U.S. Court of Appeals, 2nd Circuit; 1987, U.S. Supreme Court. *Education:* Franklin & Marshall College (A.B., 1963); University of Connecticut (LL.B., 1966). Listed: Woodward/White Inc.'s "The Best Lawyers in America," 2000-2001 Edition; and "International Who's Who of Professionals for 2002". Member, Board of Directors, International Institute of Connecticut, 1985-1996. *Member:* Connecticut Bar Association; American Immigration Lawyers Association (Connecticut Chapter; Treasurer, 1974-1975, Vice President, 1975-1976, 1977-1978, President, 1978-1979 and Chairman, Liaison Committee, 1976-1978; 1979-1980; 2000-2001). ***PRACTICE AREAS:*** Immigration and Nationality Law. ***Email:*** joetap@ctattys.com

FRANCIS J. FARRELLY, born Hartford, Connecticut, April 15, 1941; admitted to bar, 1966, Connecticut and U.S. District Court, District of Connecticut; 1971, U.S. Court of Appeals, 2nd Circuit; 1976, U.S. Supreme Court; 1982, U.S. Tax Court. *Education:* Boston College (B.S., 1963); University of Connecticut (J.D., 1966). Magistrate, Superior Court, G.A. 16, 1982-1985. Chairman, Fair Rent Commission, Town of Wethersfield 1995—. *Member:* Hartford County and Connecticut (Member, Executive Committee of the Elder Law Section; Estate and Probate Sections) Bar Associations. ***PRACTICE AREAS:*** Probate Law; Estate Planning Law; Elder Law; Real Estate Law. ***Email:*** fjf@ctattys.com

JASON Y. GANS, born Boston, Massachusetts, December 3, 1943; admitted to bar, 1968, Massachusetts; 1972, U.S. District Court, District of Massachusetts; 1974, U.S. District Court, District of Connecticut; 1982, Connecticut. *Education:* University of Michigan (B.A., 1965); Boston College (LL.B., 1968). Listed, Woodward/White Inc.'s "The Best Lawyers in America," 2001-2002 Edition. Author: "The Immigration Act of 1990," Connecticut Bar Journal, March, 1991. Chief Legal Officer, Chief Nationality Section and General Attorney, U.S Department of Justice Immigration and Naturalization Service, Hartford, Connecticut, 1973-1985. *Member:* American Immigration Lawyers Association. ***PRACTICE AREAS:*** Immigration and Nationality Practice. ***Email:*** jyg@ctattys.com

DAVID A. BARAM, born 1953; admitted to bar, 1978, Connecticut and U.S. District Court, District of Connecticut. *Education:* University of Connecticut (B.A., 1975); St. Mary's University of San Antonio (J.D., 1978). Mayor, Bloomfield, 1983-1989. Chairman, Capital Region Council of Governments, 1987-1989. President, Bloomfield Chamber of Commerce, 1997-1998. Chairman, Jewish Federation's Community Relation's Council, 1996-1998. Board Member, Jewish Federation of Greater Hartford. President, United Synagogues of Conservative Judaism, Connecticut Valley Region, 1999-2000. Vice President, Schecter Day School, 1996-2001. *Member:* Hartford County, Connecticut (Member, Executive Committee; Labor Law and Family Law Sections) and American (Member, Labor and Employment Law Section) Bar Associations. ***PRACTICE AREAS:*** Family Law; Business Law; Commercial Transactions; Real Estate; Zoning and Municipal Law; Administrative Law; Employment and Discrimination Law. ***Email:*** dab@ctattys.com

KENT D. MAWHINNEY, born Manchester, Connecticut, July 12, 1965; admitted to bar, 1990, Connecticut; 1991, U.S. Tax Court and U.S. Court of Appeals, 2nd Circuit. *Education:* Babson College (B.S., with distinction, 1987); Western New England College (J.D., cum laude, 1990). Phi Alpha Delta. Legal Counsel: Greater Hartford Jaycees, 1999; Greater Hartford Jaycees Foundation, 2000. *Member:* Connecticut Bar Association; American Immigration Lawyers Association; Oliver Ellsworth Inns of Court. ***PRACTICE AREAS:*** Civil Litigation; Immigration Law. ***Email:*** kdm@ctattys.com

---

SUSAN J. CARLSON, born New Britain, Connecticut, September 19, 1956; admitted to bar, 1981, Connecticut and U.S. District Court, District of Connecticut. *Education:* University of Connecticut (B.A., cum laude, 1978; J.D., cum laude, 1981). ***PRACTICE AREAS:*** Business Law; Real Estate; Trademarks. ***Email:*** sjc@ctattys.com

REPRESENTATIVE CLIENTS: Webster Bank; Nickson Industries; World Wrestling Federation Entertaiment; Nestles Research and Development; Rogers Corp.; Connecticut School of Broadcasting; Raveis Affiliates, Inc.
APPROVED ATTORNEYS FOR: Connecticut Attorney's Title Insurance Co.; Chicago Title; Old Republic Title Insurance Co.

NAIR & LEVIN, P.C.

Established in 1975

510 COTTAGE GROVE ROAD

BLOOMFIELD, CONNECTICUT 06002

Telephone: 860-242-7585

Facsimile: 860-242-2980

Commercial Litigation, Collections, General Practice, Bankruptcy, Personal Injury, Creditors' Rights, Real Estate.

(This Listing Continued)

ROBERT M. LEVIN, born Hartford, Connecticut, December 23, 1950; admitted to bar, 1975, Connecticut and U.S. District Court, District of Connecticut; 1991, New York; 1995, Florida; 1996, U.S. District Court, Southern District of Florida. *Education:* Boston University (B.S., 1972); University of Miami (J.D., 1974). *Member:* Connecticut and American Bar Associations; Connecticut Creditors' Rights Attorneys' Association (Founding Director and Past President). (Also of Counsel to Moody, Jones & Montefusco, Plantation, Florida). ***REPORTED CASES:*** Robert M. Elliot, P.C. v. Mark Stuart, 53 Conn. App. 333; 730 A. 2d 1176. ***PRACTICE AREAS:*** Collection Law; Personal Injury; Real Estate; Creditors Rights; Bankruptcy. ***Email:*** rlevin@nairlevin.com

---

LISA K. ANDERSON, born Derby, Connecticut, April 23, 1957; admitted to bar, 1983, Connecticut; 1986, U.S. District Court, District of Connecticut; 1997, Massachusetts; 1998, U.S. District Court, District of Massachusetts. *Education:* Albertus Magnus College (B.A., 1979); Western New England College (J.D., 1983). *Member:* Connecticut Bar Association; Connecticut Creditors' Rights Attorneys' Association. ***PRACTICE AREAS:*** Bankruptcy; Collection Law; Real Estate Law. ***Email:*** landerson@nairlevin.com

DIANA J. KEIR, born Springfield, Massachusetts, June 6, 1963; admitted to bar, 1989, Connecticut; 1991, U.S. District Court, District of Connecticut. *Education:* Wheaton College; University of Connecticut (B.A., 1985); University of Bridgeport School of Law (J.D., 1988). *Member:* Connecticut Bar Association; Connecticut Creditors' Rights Attorneys Association. ***PRACTICE AREAS:*** Collection Law; Commercial Litigation; Creditors Rights; Labor Law. ***Email:*** dkeir@nairlevin.com

MITCHELL J. LEVINE, born Hartford, Connecticut, May 27, 1965; admitted to bar, 1990, Connecticut; 1991, U.S. District Court, District of Connecticut; 1995, Florida; 1996, U.S. District Court, Southern District of Florida; 1998, Massachusetts and U.S. District Court, District of Massachusetts. *Education:* Hofstra University (B.A., 1987); Western New England College (J.D., 1990). *Member:* Connecticut and American Bar Associations; Connecticut Creditors' Rights Attorneys Association. ***PRACTICE AREAS:*** Bankruptcy; Foreclosure; Commercial Litigation; Personal Injury; Creditors' Rights. ***Email:*** mlevine@nairlevin.com

LORI B. MEEKER, born Berlin, Connecticut, December 4, 1964; admitted to bar, 1991, Connecticut; 1992, U.S. District Court, District of Connecticut. *Education:* Wheaton College (B.A., 1986); Western New England College (J.D., 1991). *Member:* Connecticut Creditors' Rights Attorneys Association. ***PRACTICE AREAS:*** Collection Law; Real Estate; Personal Injury; Commercial Law; Probate Administration; Creditors Rights. ***Email:*** lmeeker@nairlevin.com

CATHERINE A. WILOWSKI, born East Orange, New Jersey, August 31, 1956; admitted to bar, 1985, Connecticut and U.S. District Court, District of Connecticut. *Education:* University of Connecticut (B.A., 1978); Northwestern School of Law of Lewis and Clark College (J.D., 1984). Director and President, Friends of Canton Park and Recreation, Inc.; *Member:* Connecticut Creditors' Rights Attorneys Association. ***PRACTICE AREAS:*** Personal Injury; Commercial Litigation; Probate Administration; Real Estate; Collection Law. ***Email:*** cwilowski@nairlevin.com

PETER J. STERLING, born New York, New York, April 2, 1946; admitted to bar, 1974, Connecticut. *Education:* Catholic University (B.S., 1968); University of Delaware (M.S., 1972); George Washington University (J.D., 1974). ***PRACTICE AREAS:*** Creditors' Rights; Personal Injury; Real Estate; Zoning Law; Environmental Law. ***Email:*** psterling@nairlevin.com

MELISSA E. SCHWALBACH, born East Meadow, New York, November 29, 1968; admitted to bar, 1993, Connecticut; 1994, U.S. District Court, District of Connecticut; 1997, Mashantucket Pequot Tribal Court. *Education:* University of Connecticut (B.A., 1990); Western New England College (J.D., 1993). *Member:* Connecticut Creditors' Rights Association (Member, Director, Safe Haven of Greater Waterbury). ***REPORTED CASES:*** Testa v. City of Waterbury, 55 Conn. App. 264, 738 A.2d 740. ***PRACTICE AREAS:*** Commercial Litigation; Civil Litigation; Personal Injury; Creditors' Rights. ***Email:*** mschwalbach@nairlevin.com

REPRESENTATIVE CLIENTS: Hartford Hospital, Inc.; St. Francis Hospital and Medical Center; Ford Motor Credit Co.; General Motors Acceptance Corp.; Chrysler Financial Corp.; Connecticut Natural Gas Co.; World Omni Financial Corp.; American Honda Finance Corp.; Toyota Motor Credit Corp; Superior Bank; American Eagle Federal Credit Union; American Medical Response; United Healthcare.

LAW OFFICES OF MARC N. NEEDELMAN

Established in 1990

SUITE 313
800 COTTAGE GROVE ROAD
BLOOMFIELD, CONNECTICUT 06002-2343
Telephone: 860-242-7174
Telecopier: 860-242-8291

General Practice. Trials in all Courts. Real Estate, Corporate and Commercial, Personal Injury, Criminal, Municipal, Workers Compensation, Zoning, Domestic and Family, Landlord and Tenant.

MARC N. NEEDELMAN, born Hartford, Connecticut, May 13, 1952; admitted to bar, 1977, Connecticut and U. S. District Court, District of Connecticut. *Education:* George Washington University (B.A., 1974); Western New England School of Law (J.D., 1977). Bloomfield Town Attorney, 1991—. Deputy Assistant State's Attorney, 1978-1981. Deputy Mayor, Town of Bloomfield, 1989-1991. Bloomfield Town Councilman, 1985-1991. Chairman, Bloomfield Inland-Wetland and Watercourses Commission, 1978-1985. Member, Bloomfield Planning and Zoning Commission, 1983-1985. Acting Town Manager, Town of Bloomfield, 1998-2000. Member and Former Officer, Bloomfield Fire Department. Trustee, Solomon Schechter Day School, 1992-1995. Director, Federation Homes, 1993-1995, 1998-2000. Lecturer: Heritage Publishing - Landlord/Tenant Law. President, Beth Hillel Synagogue, 1999-2001. *Member:* Hartford County and Connecticut (Member, Litigation, Criminal Justice Sections) Bar Associations; Connecticut Trial Lawyers Association; Connecticut Association of Municipal Attorneys. ***REPORTED CASES:*** Shelby Mutual Insurance Company v. Dennis Della Ghelfa, et. al., 3 Conn. App. 432; Southern New England Telephone Co. v. Board of Tax Review 31 Conn. App. 155. ***PRACTICE AREAS:*** Civil; Real Estate; Corporate; Commercial; Personal Injury; Criminal; Workers' Compensation; Municipal; Zoning; Domestic; Landlord/Tenant.

ASSOCIATE

JOHN M. KELLY, born Hartford, Connecticut, August 5, 1964; admitted to bar, 1991, Connecticut; 1992, U.S. District Court, District of Connecticut. *Education:* Fairfield University (B.A., 1986); Western New England College School of Law (J.D., 1991). Phi Alpha Theta; Phi Alpha Delta. Deputy Mayor, Town of Newington, 1999—; Newington Town Councilman, 1995—. Member, Democratic State Central Committee, 2000—; Secretary, West Meadow Cemetery Expansion Committee (1987-1990), Member, Standing Insurance Committee (1988-1991). Member, Board of Education Space Needs Committee (1994-1995), Town of Newington. Vice President, Newington Chamber of Commerce, 1998—. *Member:* Hartford County and Connecticut Bar Associations. ***PRACTICE AREAS:*** General Litigation; Personal Injury; Real Estate; Municipal; Landlord/Tenant; Commercial Law.

REPRESENTATIVE CLIENTS: Merchants Insurance Group; Acme Auto, Inc.; Bernie's Audio, Video, T.V. & Appliance Co.; First Union Bank; Town of Bloomfield, Connecticut; Wilson (CT.) Fire District; Bloomfield Center Volunteer Fire Company, Inc.; Puritan Furniture Mart; Hartford Distributors, Inc.
APPROVED ATTORNEYS FOR: Connecticut Attorneys Title Insurance Co.; First American Title Insurance Co.
REFERENCES: Acme Auto, Inc.; Town of Bloomfield, CT; Bernie's Audio, Video, T.V. & Appliance Co.; Hartford Distributors, Inc.

CHURCH AND CHURCH

BRANFORD, CONNECTICUT

(See New Haven)

General Civil and Criminal Practice before State and Federal Courts, Municipal Law, Real Estate, Zoning, Land Use, Corporation, Probate, Estate Planning, Elder Law, Commercial, Condominium and Collections, Trials and Appeals.

EDMONDS & BRUNO, P.C.

52 HARRISON AVENUE
P.O. BOX 807
BRANFORD, CONNECTICUT 06405
Telephone: 203-488-1000
Telecopier: 203-488-1200

Estate Planning, Probate, Taxation, Corporation and Real Estate Law, Mediation, Family, Litigation, Workers Compensation, Personal Injury.

CHRISTIAN P. EDMONDS, born Milford, Connecticut, December 24, 1952; admitted to bar, 1978, Connecticut; 1990, Florida. *Education:* Providence College (B.A., cum laude, 1974); University of Connecticut (J.D., 1978). Phi Sigma Tau. Certified Public Accountant, Connecticut, 1981. Instructor, Hurricane Island Outward Bound, 1984—. *Member:* New Haven County, Connecticut (Chairman, Young Lawyers, Estates and Probate Section, 1984-1988; Member, Estates and Probate Executive Committee) and American (Member: Taxation, Real Property and Probate Sections) Bar Associations; The Florida Bar; New Haven Young Lawyers Association (President, 1987-1988); CSCPA; AICPA (Member, Taxation Section). ***PRACTICE AREAS:*** Estate Planning; Probate; Real Estate; Taxation; Corporate Law.

ALICE A. BRUNO, born Waterbury, Connecticut, May 17, 1955; admitted to bar, 1981, Connecticut. *Education:* Tufts University (B.A., 1977); University of Connecticut (M.S.W., 1981; J.D., 1981). *Member:* New Haven County (President, 1993-1994) and Connecticut (Chairperson, Young Lawyers Section, 1987-1988; Assistant Secretary-Treasurer, 1988-1989; Member, Family Law and Elder Law Committees) and American Bar Associations; New Haven Young Lawyers Association (President, 1986-1987); Academy of Family Mediators. ***PRACTICE AREAS:*** Litigation; Mediation; Family Law; Personal Injury; Workers Compensation.

APPROVED ATTORNEYS FOR: Chicago Title Insurance Co.; First American Title Insurance Co.

JOHN F. NAIZBY

10 MIDDLE STREET
BRANFORD, CONNECTICUT 06601
Telephone: 203-315-1000

Personal Injury.

JOHN F. NAIZBY, born Dolgeville, New York, December 29, 1966; admitted to bar, 1993, Florida; 1994, Connecticut; 1996, U.S. Court of Appeals, Second Circuit. *Education:* Hartwick College (B.A., 1989); Quinnipiac College (J.D., 1993). *Member:* Connecticut Bar Association; The Florida Bar; Connecticut Trial Lawyers Association; The Association of Trial Lawyers of America (Member, Litigation Section). ***PRACTICE AREAS:*** Personal Injury.

ADELMAN HIRSCH & NEWMAN, LLP

1000 LAFAYETTE BOULEVARD
BRIDGEPORT, CONNECTICUT 06604
Telephone: 203-331-8888
Fax: 203-333-4650
URL: http://www.ahnlaw.com
Email: ahnlaw@hotmail.com
URL: http://www.lawyers.com/injurylawct

Plaintiff's Personal Injury, Medical Malpractice, Products Liability, Wrongful Death, Automobile Accidents, Truck Accidents and Legal Malpractice.

MEMBERS OF FIRM

ROBERT B. ADELMAN, born Tucson, Arizona, December 24, 1952; admitted to bar, 1978, Connecticut; 1979, U.S. District Court, District of Connecticut; 1981, U.S. Court of Appeals, Second Circuit; 1982, U.S. Supreme Court; Special Master, U.S. District Court, District of Connecticut. *Education:* St. Lawrence University (B.A., 1975); Cornell University (J.D., 1978). Phi Beta Kappa. Co-Author: "Proving Damages," Product Liability Practice Guide, 1988; "The Legal Framework of a Products Liability Case in Connecticut," Connecticut Bar Journal, Vol. 65 No. 5 Oct. 1993; "Contingency Fees Under The Model Rules of Professional Conduct and The Tort Reform Act," CTLA Forum, Vol. 5 No. 1 Jan. 1987; Connecticut Evidence Review," CTLA Forum, Vol. 9 No. 6 Nov. 1991; "Update on Evidence 1992," CTLA Forum, Vol. 10 No. 6 Nov. 1992; "Update on Evidence 1993," CTLA Forum, Vol. 11 No. 6 Nov. 1993; The Trials and Tribulations of 220 (D), CTLA Forum, Vol. 12 No. 1 Jan. 1994; "Update on Evidence 1994," CTLA Forum, Vol. 12 No. 6 Nov. 1994; "BRB Carrier"s Subrogation Rights After the Automobile Insurance Reform Act of 1993," CTLA Forum, Vol. 13 No. 1 Jan. 1995; "Update on Evidence 1995," CTLA Forum, Vol. 13 No. 6 Nov. 1995; "Update on Evidence 1996," CTLA Forum, Vol. 14, No. 6, Nov. 1996; "Update on Evidence 1997," CTLA Forum, Vol. 15, No. 6, Nov. 1997; "Update on Evidence 1998," CTLA Forum, Vol. 16, No. 5, Sept/Dec. 1998. Listed in The Best Lawyers in America. *Member:* Connecticut Trial Lawyers Association (Member, Board of Governors, 1984—; President, 1992-1993); The Association of Trial Lawyers of America; American Board of Trial Advocates (Associate); American College of Trial Lawyers. (Certified as a Civil Trial Advocate by the National Board of Trial Advocacy). ***REPORTED CASES:*** Petriello v. Kalman, 215 Conn. 377 (1990); Bleau v. Ward, 221 Conn. 331 (1992). ***PRACTICE AREAS:*** Personal Injury; Medical Malpractice; Products Liability; Legal Malpractice.

JORAM HIRSCH, born Tel-Aviv, Israel, June 6, 1954; admitted to bar, 1979, Connecticut; 1980, U.S. District Court, District of Connecticut; 1993, U.S. Supreme Court and U.S. Court of Appeals, Second Circuit. *Education:* Wesleyan University (B.A., magna cum laude, 1976); Georgetown University Law School (J.D., 1979). Special Master, U.S. District Court, District of Connecticut. Law Clerk to Hon. John P. Cotter, Chief Justice of the Connecticut

(This Listing Continued)

Supreme Court, 1979-1980. Associate Editor, The Tax Lawyer. "Reimbursements of Collateral Source Benefits Under the 1993 Automobile Insurance Reform Act and Application of ERISA Preemption" CTLA Forum Vol. 11, No. 5, Sept. 1993. *Member:* Connecticut and American Bar Associations; Connecticut Trial Lawyers Association (Member, Board of Governors, 1991—; Chairman, Amicus Committee, 1993—); The Association of Trial Lawyers of America; The Raymond E. Baldwin American Inn of Court. ***REPORTED CASES:*** Gold v. Newman, 211 Conn. 631 (1989); Petriello v. Kalman, 215 Conn. 377 (1990); Hines v. St. Vincent's Medical Center, 232 Conn. 632 (1995); McGlinchey v. Aetna, (amicus) 224 Conn. 133 (1992); Clohessy v. Bachelor, (amicus) 237 Conn. 31 (1996); Mazziotti v. Allstate Insurance Company, (amicus), 240 Conn. 799 (1997). ***PRACTICE AREAS:*** Personal Injury; Medical Malpractice; Products Liability; Legal Malpractice. ***Email:*** jhirsch@ahnlaw.com

RICHARD L. NEWMAN, born Canton, New York, January 16, 1955; admitted to bar, 1979, Wisconsin and U.S. District Court, Western District of Wisconsin; 1982, Connecticut and U.S. District Court, District of Connecticut; 1993, U.S. Supreme Court. *Education:* State University of New York at Albany (B.A., summa cum laude, 1976); University of Wisconsin-Madison (J.D., 1979). Phi Beta Kappa. Law Clerk to Hon. Edmond O. Burke, Justice of the Alaska Supreme Court, 1978. Author: "Physician Liability For Suicide of Noncustodial Patient," Connecticut Medicine, 1998; 62:297-299. "Legal Malpractice and Burden Shifting in Connecticut," 15 CTLA Forum 125, May/June, 1997; "Stamford Hospital vs. Vega: Connecticut Affirms Right to Patient Self-Determination," Connecticut Medicine 1996; 60:481-83. Co-Author: "PTSD in Civil Litigation: Recent Scientific and Legal Developments," 37 Jurimetrics Journal 257-267, 1997; "Tort Remedies in Connecticut," Lexis Law Publishing, 1996; "Proving Damages," Product Liability Practice Guide, 1988. Member, Ethics Committee, Danbury Hospital. *Member:* Connecticut (Member, Medical-Legal Committee) and American Bar Associations; Connecticut Trial Lawyers Association (Member, Board of Governors, 1993—; Public Interest Committee); The Association of Trial Lawyers of America. ***PRACTICE AREAS:*** Personal Injury; Medical Malpractice; Products Liability; Legal Malpractice. ***Email:*** rnewman@ahnlaw.com

NEIL W. SUTTON, born Poughkeepsie, New York, May 29, 1958; admitted to bar, 1984, Connecticut; 1985, U.S. District Court, District of Connecticut; 1993, U.S. Supreme Court; 2000, U.S Court of Appeals, Second Circuit. *Education:* University of Pennsylvania (B.A., cum laude, 1980); Boston College (J.D., cum laude, 1984). Co-Author: "Update on Evidence 1994," CTLA Forum, Vol. 12 No. 6 Nov. 1994; "Update on Evidence 1995," CTLA Forum, Vol. 13 No. 6 Nov. 1995; "Update on Evidence 1996," CTLA Forum, Vol. 14 No. 6 Nov. 1996; "Update on Evidence 1997," CTLA Forum, Vol. 15 No. 6 Nov. 1997; "Update on Evidence 1998," CTLA Forum, Vol. 16 No. 6 Nov. 1998. *Member:* Connecticut Bar Association (House of Delegates; Executive Committee, Litigation Section); Connecticut Trial Lawyers Association; The Association of Trial Lawyers of America. ***REPORTED CASES:*** Bleau v. Ward, 221 Conn. 331 (1992); Curry v. Burns, (amicus) 225 Conn. 782 (1993); Young v. Data Switch Corp., 231 Conn. 95 (1994). ***PRACTICE AREAS:*** Personal Injury; Medical Malpractice; Products Liability; Legal Malpractice; Automobile Accidents and Injuries. ***Email:*** neilwsutton@hotmail.com

MARY ANN CONNORS, born Middletown, Connecticut, August 22, 1962; admitted to bar, 1987, Connecticut; 1988, U.S. District Court, District of Connecticut. *Education:* University of Connecticut (B.A., magna cum laude, with honors, 1984); University of Connecticut School of Law (J.D., 1987). Phi Beta Kappa. Executive Editor, 1985-1986, and Notes and Comments Editor, 1986-1987, University of Connecticut International Law Journal. Associate Editor of the CTLA Forum. Co-Author: "The Legal Framework of a Products Liability Case in Connecticut," Connecticut Bar Journal, Vol. 65 No. 5 Oct., 1993; "The Trials and Tribulations of 220 (D)," CTLA Forum, Vol. 12, No. 1, Jan., 1994; "Supreme and Appellate Court Review 1994," CTLA Forum, Vol. 12, No. 6, November/December 1994; "Supreme and Appellate Court Review 1995," CTLA Forum, Vol. 13, No. 4, July/August 1995; "Supreme and Appellate Court Review 1996," CTLA Forum, Vol. 14, No. 1, January/February 1996; Supreme and Appellate Court Review 1996-1997," CTLA Forum, Vol. 15, No. 4, July/August 1997; "Supreme and Appellate Court Review 1998," CTLA Forum, Vol. 16, No. 4, July/August 1998. Court Appointed Arbitrator, Connecticut Superior Court. *Member:* Connecticut and American Bar Associations; Connecticut Trial Lawyers Association (Member, Board of Governors, 1996—); The Association of Trial Lawyers of America. ***PRACTICE AREAS:*** Personal Injury; Medical Malpractice; Products Liability; Legal Malpractice. ***Email:*** mconnors@ahnlaw.com

MICHAEL F. EWING, born New Brunswick, New Jersey, January 27, 1961; admitted to bar, 1991, Connecticut; 1992, U.S. District Court, District of Connecticut. *Education:* University of Notre Dame (B.A., 1982); Yale University (M.S., 1984; M.Phil, 1985); New York University (J.D., 1991). Staff Editor, Review of Law and Social Change, 1990-1991. Editor-at-Large, Connecticut Bar Journal. Co-Author: "The Trials and Tribulations of 220(D)," CTLA Forum, Vol. 12 No. 1 Jan. 1994. *Member:* Greater Bridgeport, Connecticut and American Bar Associations; Connecticut Trial Lawyers Association; The Association of Trial Lawyers of America. ***REPORTED CASES:*** Stern v. Allied Van Lines, 246 Conn. 170 (1998). ***PRACTICE AREAS:*** Personal Injury; Medical Malpractice; Products Liability; Legal Malpractice. ***Email:*** mewing@ahnlaw.com

(This Listing Continued)

AMENDOLA & AMENDOLA

BRIDGEPORT, CONNECTICUT

(See Fairfield)

Matrimonial Law, Family, Divorce, Child Custody, Domestic Relations and Litigation.

BAI, POLLOCK, BLUEWEISS & MULCAHEY, P.C.

Established in 1973

PARK CITY PLAZA
10 MIDDLE STREET
P.O. BOX 1978
BRIDGEPORT, CONNECTICUT 06604
Telephone: 203-366-7991
Fax: 203-366-4723

Insurance Defense, Civil Trial Practice. Negligence, Professional Liability, Products Liability, Toxic Substances, Real Estate and Commercial Loans.

FIRM PROFILE: The firm was founded in 1973. Bai, Pollock Blueweiss & Mulcahey, P.C. engages in general practice with specialization in all areas of litigation in both state and federal courts throughout Connecticut as well as other jurisdictions. The firm seeks to provide aggressive and effective legal representation on a practical and cost-effective basis.

ARNOLD J. BAI (1931-1992).

PAUL E. POLLOCK, born Freeport, New York, December 11, 1941; admitted to bar, 1970, Connecticut, U.S. District Court, District of Connecticut and U.S. Court of Appeals, Second Circuit. *Education:* University of Notre Dame (B.S., 1963; J.D., 1970). Listed in The Best Lawyers in America. Member, Staff, 1968-1969 and Editorial Board, 1969, Notre Dame Lawyer. Advocate, American Board of Trial Advocates. *Member:* Defense Research Institute. Fellow, American College of Trial Lawyers. ***PRACTICE AREAS:*** Litigation; Professional Liability.

JEFFREY A. BLUEWEISS, born New York, N.Y., May 10, 1956; admitted to bar, 1981, Connecticut; 1982, U.S. District Court, District of Connecticut; 1993, U.S. District Court, Southern and Eastern Districts of New York. *Education:* Washington University, St. Louis (B.S.B.A., summa cum laude, 1978); College of William & Mary (J.D., 1981). Phi Alpha Delta. Recipient, American Jurisprudence Award in Property. Lecturer, Fairfield University, School of Graduate and Continuing Education, 1985-1989. Director, Connecticut Defense Lawyers Association, 1988-1992. Bencher, American Inns of Court, 1988—. *Member:* The Connecticut and American Bar Associations; Defense Research Institute. ***PRACTICE AREAS:*** Civil Litigation; Construction Law; State Liability; Municipal Liability; Business Litigation; Negligence; Professional Liability; Insurance; Products Liability; Domestic Relations; Subrogations.

GARIE J. MULCAHEY, born Stamford, Connecticut, December 7, 1943; admitted to bar, 1981, Connecticut; 1982, New York and U.S. District Court, District of Connecticut. *Education:* University of Connecticut (B.A., summa cum laude, 1978); Pace University (J.D., cum laude, 1981). Listed in The Best Lawyers in America. Case Note and Comment Editor, Pace Law Review, 1980-1981. Recipient, American Jurisprudence Award for Remedies. *Member:* American Board of Trial Advocates (Associate). ***PRACTICE AREAS:*** General Litigation; Professional Liability Law.

RAYMOND J. PLOUFFE, JR., born Bridgeport, Connecticut, October 14, 1959; admitted to bar, 1984, Connecticut; 1985, U.S. District Court, District of Connecticut; 1988, U.S. Court of Appeals, Second Circuit. *Education:* Fairfield University (B.A., magna cum laude, 1981); Villanova University (J.D., 1984). Phi Alpha Theta; Pi Sigma Alpha. Member, Villanova Law Review, 1983-1984. *Member:* Connecticut Bar Association. ***PRACTICE AREAS:*** General Litigation.

MADONNA A. SACCO, born Lynbrook, N.Y., July 18, 1955; admitted to bar, 1985, Connecticut, U.S. District Court, District of Connecticut and U.S. Court of Appeals, Second Circuit. *Education:* Fairfield University (B.A., 1977); University of Bridgeport (J.D., 1984). Bencher, 1995; President, 1997-2000, American Inns of Court. *Member:* Connecticut Bar Association. ***PRACTICE AREAS:*** Professional Liability Litigation.

MICHAEL S. LYNCH, born Bronx, New York, July 4, 1962; admitted to bar, 1987, Connecticut; 1988, U.S. District Court, District of Connecticut. *Edu-*

(This Listing Continued)

BAI, POLLOCK, BLUEWEISS & MULCAHEY, P.C., Bridgeport—Continued

cation: University of Connecticut (B.A., cum laude, 1984; J.D., 1987). *Member:* Connecticut Bar Association. ***PRACTICE AREAS:*** Civil Litigation; Real Estate Law; Professional Liability Law; Probate.

DAVID J. ROBERTSON, born Bridgeport, Connecticut, September 20, 1963; admitted to bar, 1988, Connecticut; 1989, U.S. District Court, District of Connecticut; U.S. Court of Appeals, Second Circuit. *Education:* Fairfield University (B.A., 1985); Georgetown University (J.D., 1988). ***PRACTICE AREAS:*** Civil Litigation; Professional Liability; Products Liability; Municipal Liability.

GAILEEN A. KAUFMAN, born Bridgeport, Connecticut, May 12, 1965; admitted to bar, 1990, Connecticut; 1992, U.S. District Court, District of Connecticut. *Education:* Fairfield University (B.A., 1987); University of Connecticut (J.D., 1990). Barrister, American Inns of Court, 1998—. *Member:* Bridgeport and Connecticut Bar Associations. ***PRACTICE AREAS:*** Professional Liability Law; General Litigation.

HEIDI MARIE CILANO, born Queens, New York, January 15, 1971; admitted to bar, 1996, Connecticut; 1997, New York. *Education:* Catholic University of America (B.A., 1993); Quinnipiac College School of Law (J.D., 1996). Member, Criminal Law Society, 1993-1994. Secretary/Treasurer, Moot Court Honor Society, 1994-1996. Second Best Speaker, Moot Court Competition. Recipient, Distinguished Academic Award, Criminal Procedure. ***PRACTICE AREAS:*** Professional Liability; Civil Litigation; Domestic Relations.

KEITH M. BLUMENSTOCK, born Hackensack, New Jersey, July 23, 1969; admitted to bar, 1999, Connecticut; 2000, New York and U.S. District Court, District of Connecticut. *Education:* Rensselaer Polytechnic Institute (B.S., 1995); Quinnipiac College School of Law (J.D., 1999). Recipient, American Jurisprudence Awards in Legal Skills and Criminal Procedure. *Member:* Connecticut and New York State Bar Associations. ***PRACTICE AREAS:*** Professional Liability; Litigation. ***Email:*** kblumenstock@baipollock.com

MARK S. LESO, born Nutley, New Jersey, November 17, 1969; admitted to bar, 1995, Connecticut; 1996, New York; 2000, U.S. District Court, District of Connecticut. *Education:* Southern Connecticut State University (B.S., cum laude, 1992); Institute on International and Comparative Law, Oxford, England (1993); University of San Diego School of Law (J.D., 1995). Member, National Mock Trial Competition Team, 1993-1995. *Member:* Connecticut Bar Association (Member, Mock Trial Judge, 1998). ***PRACTICE AREAS:*** Professional Liability; Municipal Liability; Directors and Officers Liability; Civil Litigation; Real Estate Law; Commercial Leasing; Residential Leasing; Business Organization; Probate; Subrogation. ***Email:*** mleso@baipollock.com

LINDA D. D'ALBIS, born New Haven, Connecticut, January 11, 1957; admitted to bar, 1984, Connecticut and U.S. District Court, District of Connecticut. *Education:* Williams College (B.A., 1978); Catholic University of America (J.D., 1984). *Member:* New Haven County and Connecticut Bar Associations. ***PRACTICE AREAS:*** Professional Liability; Insurance Defense.

JEFFREY R. OWENS, born Derby, Connecticut, July 22, 1972; admitted to bar, 2000, Connecticut. *Education:* Trinity College (B.A., 1994); Quinnipiac University School of Law (J.D., 2000). *Member:* Sports and Entertainment Law Society. ***PRACTICE AREAS:*** Civil Litigation; Insurance; Real Estate; Probate.

JOSHUA A. YAHWAK, born Morristown, New Jersey, April 17, 1975; admitted to bar, 2000, Connecticut; 2001, New York. *Education:* Franklin and Marshall College (B.A., 1997); Washington and Lee University (J.D., 2000). Phi Alpha Delta, 1997—. *Member:* Connecticut, New York State and American Bar Associations. ***PRACTICE AREAS:*** Insurance Defense; Litigation; Real Estate. ***Email:*** jyahwak@baipollock.com

CATHERINE L. CREAGER, born Philadelphia, Pennsylvania, August 19, 1961; admitted to bar, 2000, Connecticut. *Education:* Western Kentucky University at Bowling Green (B.A., 1982); Carnegie Mellon University, Pittsburgh (M.A., 1989); Quinnipiac College School of Law (J.D., 2000). ***PRACTICE AREAS:*** Civil Litigation; Professional Liability. ***Email:*** ccreager@baipollock.com

MARYANNE EVAN, born Bridgeport, Connecticut, January 6, 1974; admitted to bar, 2000, Connecticut; 2001, New York. *Education:* Eastern Connecticut State University (B.A., 1996); Albany Law School of Union University (J.D., 2000). Albany Law Review. Note and Comment Editor. *Member:* Bridgeport and New York State Bar Associations. ***PRACTICE AREAS:*** Medical Malpractice; Professional Liability. ***Email:*** mevan@baipollock.com

JEFFREY N. GAULL, born Hartford, Connecticut, February 17, 1970; admitted to bar, 2001, Connecticut. *Education:* University of Vermont at Burlington (B.A., 1993); Vermont Law School, South Royalton (J.D., 2000). Debevoise Moot Court. Jessup Moot Court (Best Oralist, 2000). *Member:* Connecticut and American (Member, Section: Environmental, 1998—) Bar Associations. ***PRACTICE AREAS:*** Civil Litigation; Medical Malpractice. ***Email:*** jgaull@baipollock.com

REPRESENTATIVE CLIENTS: Hartford Fire Insurance Co.; Hartford Accident and Indemnity Co.; Connecticut Medical Insurance Company; New London County Mutual Insurance Company; Bridgeport Hospital; Milford Hospital; Griffin Hospital; CNA Insurance Companies; United Services Automobile Association; First State Insurance Co.; Town of Newton; Town of Greenwich; MMI Risk Management Resources, Inc.; Gallagher Bassett Services; Progressive Insurance Company; Zurich Insurance Company; Coregis Group; Medical Inter-Insurance Exchange; Pro-Mutual Group; Fireman's Fund; Media Professional Insurance Co.; SAFECO Insurance Company; Westport Insurance Corporation; Reliant Claims; American Healthcare Indemnity; Farmers Insurance; Danbury Hospital and Services; National Continental Casualty; Travelers Group.

BARR & LaCAVA

BRIDGEPORT, CONNECTICUT

(See Stamford)

General Practice, Franchising and Franchise Law, Litigation in all State and Federal Courts, Real Estate, Probate, Corporate, Estate Planning, Family, Immigration, Petroleum Marketing Practices, Environmental Law, Workers Compensation, Appellate Practice, Personal Injury and Automobile Accidents.

ALFRED R. BELINKIE & ASSOCIATES

Established in 1957

1087 BROAD STREET

BRIDGEPORT, CONNECTICUT 06604-4379

Telephone: 203-368-4201

Fax: 203-368-3075

Email: blink19@aol.com

URL: http://www.lawyers.com/belinkielaw

Family Law, Real Estate, Probate, Personal Injury, Elder Law, Bankruptcy, Divorce, Criminal, Estates, Wills, Workers Compensation.

ALFRED R. BELINKIE, born Bridgeport, Connecticut, February 8, 1924; admitted to bar, 1949, Connecticut; U.S. District Court, District of Connecticut, U.S. Court of Appeals, 2nd Circuit and U.S. Supreme Court. *Education:* Dartmouth College (A.B., 1945); Yale University (LL.B., 1947). Member, Corby Court. Listed in Best Lawyers in America (Family Law). Contributing Author, "The Connecticut Family Law Journal," Butterworth Legal Publishers, 1982—. Lecturer, Family Law, Connecticut Bar Association, 1981—. Director, 1967-1970 and Chairman of the Board, 1971-1972, Bridgeport Legal Services Committee, Inc. General Counsel: University of Bridgeport Student Body, 1972; American Academy of Matrimonial Lawyers, 1990; American Chapter, International Academy of Matrimonial Lawyers, 1990; American College of Family Trial Lawyers, 1995—. Member, Connecticut Statewide Grievance Committee, Branch of The Judiciary. *Member:* Bridgeport (Chairman, Family Law Committee, 1974-1978, 1984-1992; Member, Executive Committee, 1975-1983, 1984-1989) and Greater Bridgeport (President, 1979-1980) Bar Association; American Academy of Matrimonial Lawyers (President, Connecticut Chapter, 1981-1982). ***PRACTICE AREAS:*** Family Law; Divorce; Child Custody; Child Support; Juvenile Law; Paternity; Premarital Agreements; Post Judgment; Domestic Relations.

ASSOCIATES

DONALD J. BOWERS, born Queens, New York, June 17, 1961; admitted to bar, 1989, Connecticut and U.S. District Court, District of Connecticut; 1990, New York; 1994, Florida. *Education:* State University of New York at Binghamton (B.A., 1983); University of Bridgeport (J.D., 1988). Phi Delta Phi. *Member:* Bridgeport and Connecticut Bar Associations; The Florida Bar. ***PRACTICE AREAS:*** Civil Litigation; Commercial Litigation; Collections; Family Law; Foreclosures; Probate; Personal Injury; Bankruptcy; Real Estate; Workers Compensation. ***Email:*** blink19@aol.com

DIANE BELINKIE, born Bridgeport, Connecticut, June 26, 1954; admitted to bar, 1997, Connecticut. *Education:* Clark University (B.A., Psychology, 1975); Yale University (M.P.H., Public Health Services Administration/Long Term Care, 1982); Quinnipiac College (J.D., 1993). Nursing Home Administrator: Oregon, 1977; Connecticut, 1985. Author: "Piecing Together Healthcare Protection, Long-Term Care Options," Vol. 16, No. 1, Summer 1993, American Bar Association Family Advocate; "Health Care for the Elderly: Medicare, Medicaid and Nursing Home Care," Vol. 12, Number 1, Summer 1994, Journal of the American Academy of Matrimonial Lawyers; "Motion Practice in Matrimonial Actions," 1996; "Grandparents Raising Grandchildren: A Legal Guide for Connecticut," 1997. *Member:* Bridgeport, Connecticut and American Bar Associations. ***PRACTICE AREAS:*** Family Law; Elder Law; Criminal Law; Juvenile Law; Childrens Rights; Wills; Estate Planning; Medicare and Medicaid; Drug Crimes; Divorce. ***Email:*** blink19@aol.com

(This Listing Continued)

HOLLY A. HESLIN, born New Rochelle, New York, January 6, 1966; admitted to bar, 1996, New York and Connecticut. *Education:* University of Connecticut (B.A., 1988); Cleveland-Marshall College of Law, Cleveland State University (J.D., cum laude, 1995). Delta Theta Phi. Member, Tribune, 1994-1995. *Member:* Bridgeport (Member, Family Law Committee, 1998—) New York State and Connecticut (Member: Executive Committee, Family Law Section; Executive Committee, Young Lawyers Section, 1998-1999) Bar Associations. ***PRACTICE AREAS:*** Divorce; Real Estate; Wills; Probate; Personal Injury. ***Email:*** blink19@aol.com

ANDREW B. BOWMAN

BRIDGEPORT, CONNECTICUT

(See Westport)

General Civil and Criminal Litigation before all Federal and State Courts. Trials and Appeals. Criminal Defense, Tax Litigation, Employment Law, Construction Litigation, Civil Rights, Environmental Law, Personal Injury, Commercial Litigation and Negligence Law.

BRANDNER & PONZINI

BRIDGEPORT, CONNECTICUT

(See Stamford)

General Civil and Criminal Litigation. Driving While Intoxicated, Personal Injury, Product Liability, Automobile Accidents, Domestic Relations, Commercial, Corporate, Real Estate and Estate Planning.

BRAUNSTEIN & TODISCO, LLC

BRIDGEPORT, CONNECTICUT

(See Fairfield)

Taxation, Business Law, Estate Planning, Elder Law, Trusts, Probate Administration and Probate Proceedings, Commercial Transactions and Real Estate, Criminal and Civil Litigation, Bankruptcy, Trial and Appellate Practice.

BRODY, WILKINSON AND OBER, P.C.

BRIDGEPORT, CONNECTICUT

(See Southport)

General Civil Practice, Corporation, Probate, Estate Planning, Trusts and Estates, Real Estate, Employment, Commercial, Environmental, Creditors Rights, Tax, Pension, Profit Sharing, Entertainment Law, Banking, General Business, Municipal, Freedom of Information Matters, Telecommunications, Public Utilities, Commercial Litigation.

CASPER & DE TOLEDO LLC

BRIDGEPORT, CONNECTICUT

(See Stamford)

Civil Trial and Appellate Practice in all State and Federal Courts. Personal Injury, Medical Malpractice, Product Liability, Workers' Compensation, Employment Discrimination, Employee Rights and Benefits, Civil Rights, Contracts and Family Law.

RICHARD A. CERRATO

SUITE 2A
3180 MAIN STREET
BRIDGEPORT, CONNECTICUT 06606
Telephone: 203-374-4600
Fax: 203-372-0824
URL: http://www.lawyers.com/cerratolaw

General Civil Practice before State and Federal Courts. Family, Personal Injury, Probate, Real Estate, Education, Labor, Bankruptcy and Workers Compensation Law. Trials and Appeals.

RICHARD A. CERRATO, born New York, N.Y., August 4, 1949; admitted to bar, 1983, Connecticut. *Education:* University of Connecticut (B.A., 1971; M.A., 1973); Western New England College (J.D., 1983). *Member:* Connecticut, Bridgeport and American Bar Associations; Connecticut Trial Lawyers Association; American Trial Lawyers Association.

REPRESENTATIVE CLIENTS: Northeastern Pennsylvania Educational Television Association (WVIA); Southwestern Connecticut Agency on Aging, Inc.
REFERENCES: Chase-Connecticut; People's Bank.

LAW OFFICES OF MICHAEL GENE CLEAR

BRIDGEPORT, CONNECTICUT

(See Stamford)

General Civil Trial Practice in State and Federal Courts. Personal Injury, Negligence, Environmental Law and Hazardous Waste Litigation, Insurance Coverage Litigation, Complex Litigation, Commercial Litigation, Alternative Dispute Resolution, Mediation, Municipal Law, Environmental Insurance Defense, Insurance Coverage, Probate Litigation, Wills, Elder Law, Incapacity Planning, Probate Administration.

COHEN AND WOLF, P.C.

Established in 1951
1115 BROAD STREET
BRIDGEPORT, CONNECTICUT 06604
Telephone: 203-368-0211
Facsimile: 203-394-9901
URL: http://www.cohenandwolf.com

Danbury, Connecticut Office: 158 Deer Hill Avenue. Telephone: 203-792-2771. Facsimile: 203-791-8149.
Stamford, Connecticut Office: 112 Prospect Street. Telephone: 203-964-9907. Facsimile: 203-576-8504.
Westport, Connecticut Office: 190 Main Street. Telephone: 203-222-1034.

General Practice. Business Transactions, Commercial Litigation, Employment and Labor, Family and Matrimonial, Land Use, Municipal, Personal Injury, Physicians Practice, Real Estate, Securities, Tax, Trusts and Estates. Litigation in all Courts.

HERBERT L. COHEN (1905-1983).

AUSTIN K. WOLF, born Peoria, Illinois, February 1, 1923; admitted to bar, 1951, Connecticut; 1952, U.S. District Court, District of Connecticut; 1967, U.S. Court of Appeals, Second Circuit. *Education:* Yale University (B.A., 1948); Harvard University (LL.B., cum laude, 1951). Member, Board of Editors, Connecticut Bar Journal, 1979-1984. Member, Board of Directors, Connecticut Bar Foundation, 1979-1981. Attorney Trial Referee, 1983—. Listed in The Best Lawyers In America, 1986-2000. *Member:* Bridgeport, Connecticut (Member: Executive Committee, Section on Planning and Zoning, 1968—; House of Delegates, 1979-1983) and American Bar Associations; American College of Real Estate Lawyers. ***PRACTICE AREAS:*** Land Use; Real Estate. ***Email:*** cw@cohenandwolf.com

RICHARD L. ALBRECHT, born New York, N.Y., July 2, 1938; admitted to bar, 1962, New York; 1964, U.S. District Court, Southern and Eastern Districts of New York; 1968, Connecticut; 1970, U.S. Court of Appeals, Second Circuit. *Education:* Bucknell University (B.S., 1959); Cornell University (J.D., 1962). Phi Delta Phi. Assistant District Attorney, New York County, 1965-1968. *Member:* The Association of the Bar of the City of New York; Connecticut and American Bar Associations. Fellow, American Academy of Matrimonial Lawyers. [Staff Judge Advocate, New York Air National Guard, 1965-1968]. ***PRACTICE AREAS:*** Litigation. ***Email:*** ralbrecht@cohenandwolf.com

JONATHAN S. BOWMAN, born Bridgeport, Connecticut, January 16, 1942; admitted to bar, 1966, Connecticut and U.S. District Court, District of Connecticut; 1967, U.S. Court of Military Appeals; 1970, U.S. Court of Appeals, Second Circuit. *Education:* Indiana University (A.B., 1963); University of Connecticut (J.D., 1966). Phi Eta Sigma. Lecturer on Law, University of Bridgeport, 1971. Member, Fairfield Charter Revision Commission, 1985. *Member:* Bridgeport, Connecticut and American Bar Associations. ***REPORTED CASES:*** Interlude, Inc. v. Skurat, 253 Conn. 531 (2000); Rosenblit v. Williams, 57 Conn. App. 788 (2000); Willow Funding Company, LP v. Grencom Associates et al 246 Conn. 615 (1998); FDIC v. Bombero, 236 Conn. 744 (1996); First Constitution Bank v. Harbor Village Ltd. Partnership, 230 Conn 807 (1994); Uniroyal, Inc., et al v. Board of Tax Review of the Town of Middlebury, 182 Conn. 619 (1981); Michael J. Papa v. Greenwich Green, Inc., et al 177 Conn. 295 (1979). ***PRACTICE AREAS:*** Real Estate; Condominium; Property Tax Appeals; Bankruptcy; Title Insurance. ***Email:*** jbowman@cohenandwolf.com

IRVING J. KERN, born Bridgeport, Connecticut, September 8, 1946; admitted to bar, 1971, Connecticut, U.S. District Court, District of Connecticut and U.S. Court of Appeals, Second Circuit. *Education:* University of Connecticut (B.S., with high honors, 1968); University of Virginia (J.D., 1971). Beta Gamma Sigma; Phi Kappa Phi. Member: Board of Associates, Bridgeport Hospital; Fairfield County Commercial Banking Advisory Board, Fleet Bank. *Member:* Bridgeport, Connecticut and American Bar Associations. ***PRACTICE AREAS:*** Real Estate; Commercial; Corporate; Estate Planning; Health Care; Probate. ***Email:*** ikern@cohenandwolf.com

MARTIN J. ALBERT, born Brooklyn, New York, April 18, 1945; admitted to bar, 1970, New York; 1973, U.S. Tax Court; 1976, Connecticut. *Education:*

(This Listing Continued)

COHEN AND WOLF, P.C., Bridgeport—Continued

University of Pennsylvania (B.S., 1966); Boston University (J.D., 1969); New York University (LL.M., 1972). Certified Public Accountant, New York, 1971. *Member:* Bridgeport (Member and Former Chairman, Tax Section; Chairman, Probate and Estate Planning Section), Connecticut (Member, Executive Committee, Tax Section, 1979—) and American Bar Associations. ***PRACTICE AREAS:*** Taxation; Estate Planning; Probate. ***Email:*** malbert@cohenandwolf.com

STEWART I. EDELSTEIN, born Rochester, New York, October 2, 1948; admitted to bar, 1973, Connecticut; 1974, U.S. District Court, District of Connecticut and U.S. Court of Appeals, Second Circuit; 1978, U.S. Supreme Court; 1981, U.S. District Court, Southern District of New York; 1984, U.S. District Court, Eastern District of New York; 1992—, Special Master, U.S. District Court, District of Connecticut. *Education:* Oberlin College (B.A., magna cum laude, 1970); Cornell University (J.D., 1973). Author: "Bombast v. Cogent," Litigation Magazine, Volume 18, Number 3 (Spring, 1992); "Defense Strategies for a More Level PJR Playing Field," The Connecticut Law Tribune, Volume 20, Number 1 (December 27, 1993); "Update on Evidence: The Attorney/Client Work Product Privilege Thicket," Connecticut Trial Lawyer's Forum, Volume 12, Number 2 (March/April, 1994); "Litigating in Cyberspace: Contracts on the Internet," Trial Magazine (October, 1996); "Preparing Your Client's Testimony," The Connecticut Law Tribune, Volume 24, Number 34 (August 17, 1998); "Escaping Litigation Purgatory: What Every Trial Lawyer Should Know About the Complex Litigation Docket," The Connecticut Law Tribune, Volume 25, Number 32 (August 9, 1999); "CUTPA Punitive Damages and Attorney's Fees: When Are They Recoverable, and How Much Is Enough,?" CTLA Forum, Vol. 18, No. 3 (July/September 2000). Yale Law School, Tutor-in-Law, 1994—. *Member:* Bridgeport, Connecticut and American Bar Associations; Connecticut Trial Lawyers Association; The Association of Trial Lawyers of America. ***PRACTICE AREAS:*** Commercial Litigation; High Technology. ***Email:*** sedelstein@cohenandwolf.com

NEIL R. MARCUS (See Danbury listing for Biography).

G. KENNETH BERNHARD, born White Plains, New York, June 14, 1944; admitted to bar, 1969, New York; 1972, Connecticut; 1973, U.S. Supreme Court; 1975, U.S. District Court, District of Connecticut, U.S. Court of International Trade and U.S. Claims Court; 1975, U.S. Court of Customs and Patent Appeals. *Education:* Yale University (B.A., 1966); New York University (J.D., 1969; LL.M., 1970). Recipient, Clear Fellowship. Assistant Professor of Law, Constitutional Law, United States Military Academy, 1973-1974. Town Attorney, Town of Westport, 1981-1985, 1989-1993; Town Attorney, Town of Wilton, 1991—; Town Attorney, Town of Weston, 2000—. Appointed Trial Referee, Connecticut Superior Court, 1985-1996. Appointed Special Master, Connecticut Superior Court, 1992-1996. Member, Connecticut General Assembly, 1997—. Third Selectman, Town of Westport, 1987-1989. Member, Zoning Board of Appeals, Town of Westport, 1989. *Member:* Westport (President, 1987-1988), Bridgeport and The Connecticut Bar Associations; Connecticut Trial Lawyers Association. [Major, U.S. Army, JAGC, 1970-1993]. ***PRACTICE AREAS:*** Civil Litigation; Municipal; Domestic; Criminal; Zoning Appeals; Real Estate. ***Email:*** kbernhard@cohenandwolf.com

DAVID L. GROGINS (See Danbury listing for Biography).

GRETA E. SOLOMON, born Waterbury, Connecticut, February 10, 1951; admitted to bar, 1976, Connecticut; 1977, U.S. Tax Court; 1978, Florida, New York and U.S. District Court, District of Connecticut. *Education:* Smith College (A.B., 1973); University of Connecticut (J.D., with honors, 1976); New York University (LL.M. in Taxation, 1977). Chairman, Board of Trustees, Y.W.C.A. of Eastern Fairfield County, Inc., 1990-1996. President, Jewish Family Service, 1990-1992. Past Member, Board of Directors, Jewish Center for Community Services. Past Chair, Board of Jewish Community Foundation, Inc., 1995-2001. Member, Board of Directors, 1990-2001; Vice President and Chair, 1990—, Allocations Committee, Greater Bridgeport Area Foundation. Member, Youth Commission, Town of Westport, Connecticut. Chair, Adult Advisory Board, Toquet Hall, Westport, CT. Member, Board of Directors, Jewish Home for the Elderly, 2001—. *Member:* New York State, Connecticut (Member, Executive Committee, Estates and Probate Section, 1989—) and American Bar Associations; The Florida Bar. ***PRACTICE AREAS:*** Taxation; Estate Planning; Trusts and Estates; Elder Law; Retirement Planning. ***Email:*** gsolomon@cohenandwolf.com

ROBIN A. KAHN (See Danbury listing for Biography).

RICHARD G. KENT, born New Haven, Connecticut, January 13, 1951; admitted to bar, 1975, Connecticut, U.S. District Court, District of Connecticut and U.S. Court of Appeals, Second Circuit; 1981, U.S. Supreme Court. *Education:* Rutgers University (B.A., with highest distinction, 1972); Boston College (J.D., 1975). Phi Beta Kappa; Pi Sigma Alpha. Author: Article, "Parental Liability for the Torts of Children," Connecticut Bar Journal, December, 1976. Co-Author: "Fighting For Your Children: A Father's Guide to Custody," Taylor Publishing Company, 1998; "Inside Women's College Basketball, Anatomy of A Season," Taylor Publishing Company, 2000. Lecturer, Bridgeport Bar Association Seminars, 1989-2001. Assistant Town Attorney, Hamden, Connecticut, 1976-1977. *Member:* Bridgeport (Junior Bar President, 1981-1982; Chairman, Family Law Committee, 1994-1998), Connecticut (Member, 1979—, Chairman, 1985, Executive Committee, Young Lawyers Section; Assistant Secretary-Treasurer, 1986; Treasurer, 1989; Member, House of Delegates, 1987, 1988; Member, Board of Governors, 1987, 1988; Member: Executive Committee, Family Law Section, 1987—; Committee on Professional Ethics, 1992—) and American (Editor, Member Net, Young Lawyers Division, 1987) Bar Associations. ***REPORTED CASES:*** Catino v. Bd. of Ed. Town of Hamden, 174 Conn. 414 (1978); Solo v. Solo, 2 Conn. App. 290 (1984); Berg v. Berg, 24 Conn. App. 509 (1991); Albrecht v. Albrecht, 19 Conn. App. 146 (1989); City Savings v. Dessoff, 3 Conn. App. 644 (1988); Miller v. Kirshner, 225 Conn. 185 (1993); Weidenbacher v. Weidenbacher, 234 Conn. 51 (1995); Askinazi v. Askinazi, 34 Conn. App. 328 (1994); Muller v. Muller, 43 Conn. App. 327 (1996); Morgan v. Morgan, Appellate cite; Durkin v. Durkin, 43 Conn. App. 659 (1996). ***PRACTICE AREAS:*** Family; Civil; Criminal Litigation. ***Email:*** rkent@cohenandwolf.com

RICHARD SLAVIN, born Akron, Ohio, March 1, 1947; admitted to bar, 1977, Ohio; 1984, Connecticut. *Education:* Case Western Reserve University (B.A., 1969; M.B.A., 1972); University of Akron (J.D., 1977). Omicron Delta Kappa. Financial Analyst Examiner, 1972-1977, Staff Attorney, 1977-1979 and Attorney Inspector, 1979-1981, Ohio Division of Securities. Director, Connecticut Securities and Business Investments Division, 1981-1983. Participant, Intergovernmental Exchange Act Program, United States Securities and Exchange Commission, 1981. Author, "Securities Regulation in 1990," Connecticut Bar Journal, May, 1990. Member, Connecticut Banking Commissioner's Securities Act Advisory Committee, 1984, 1998—. Secretary, Director and Member, Executive Committee, Chair, Fund Raising Committee, Connecticut Legal Services, Inc., 1993—. Director, Legal Center for Connecticut Non Profit Organizations, Inc., 1992-1996. *Member:* Bridgeport (Chairman, Business Law Committee, 1997-1998), Connecticut (Member, Executive Committee, Business Law Section, 1985—; Chairman, Securities Committee, 1986-1990, 1996—; Chairman, Business Courts Study Committee, 1997-1998; Member: Federal Practice Committee; Pro Bono Committee) and American (Member, Federal Regulation of Securities Committee, State Regulation of Securities Committee, Enforcement, State Liaison, Broker-Dealer, and Small Business Capital Formation Subcommittees; Business Law Section, 1983—; Member, Securities Litigation Committee, Arbitration Subcommittee, Litigation Section) Bar Associations; National Association of Securities Dealers (Member, Board of Arbitrators), National Futures Association (Member, Board of Arbitrators). ***PRACTICE AREAS:*** Securities Regulation; Banking Regulation; Securities, Banking and Corporate Litigation; Arbitrations. ***Email:*** rslavin@cohenandwolf.com

DANIEL S. NAGEL, born New York, N.Y., June 22, 1959; admitted to bar, 1984, Connecticut; 1987, U.S. District Court, District of Connecticut. *Education:* Cornell University (B.S., with distinction, 1981; J.D., 1984). Member, Moot Court Board, 1983-1984. Member, Trumbull Board of Finance, 1991-1995. Member, Board of Directors, Leadership Greater Bridgeport, 1994-1997. Member, Board of Directors, Guenster Rehabilitation Center, Inc., 1994-1999. Secretary/Treasurer, Bridgeport Futures Initiative, 1995-2000. Member, Board of Directors, LMG Programs, Inc., 1999-2001. Member, Board of Directors, Congregation Beth El, 2000-2001. Vice Chairperson, Trumbell Ethics Commission, 2000—. *Member:* Bridgeport (Chairperson, Real Estate Section, 1994-1995), Connecticut (Member, Sections on: Real Property (Executive Committee); Commercial; Conservation and Environmental Quality) and American Bar Associations. ***PRACTICE AREAS:*** Real Estate; Commercial; Environmental. ***Email:*** dnagel@cohenandwolf.com

RICHARD J. DI MARCO, born Pelham Manor, New York, September 30, 1955; admitted to bar, 1984, New York and Connecticut; 1985, U.S. Tax Court. *Education:* State University of New York at Albany (B.A., 1977); Brooklyn Law School (J.D., 1983); New York University (LL.M. in Taxation, 1984). Certified Public Accountant, New York, 1980. *Member:* Bridgeport (Chairman: Tax Committee, 1991-1995; Estate Planning, Probate and Elder Law Committee, 2000-2001; Member, Board of Directors, 1996-1999), Connecticut (Member, Executive Committee, Tax Section, 1990—), New York State and American Bar Associations. ***REPORTED CASES:*** Kimball v. Commissioner of Internal Revenue, 853 F.2d 120 (2d Cir. 1988); Airkaman, Inc. v. Groppo, 221 Conn. 751 (1992). ***PRACTICE AREAS:*** Taxation; Estate Planning; Corporate. ***Email:*** rdimarco@cohenandwolf.com

DAVID B. ZABEL, born Baltimore, Maryland, April 12, 1957; admitted to bar, 1982, New Jersey and U.S. District Court, District of New Jersey; 1986, U.S. Court of Appeals, Third Circuit; 1987, Connecticut and U.S. District Court, District of Connecticut. *Education:* Brown University (A.B., 1979); University of Virginia (J.D., 1982). Member: Executive Committee, Fairfield Chamber of Commerce, 1997-1999; Fairfield Board of Fire Commissioners, 1999—. *Member:* Bridgeport, Connecticut and American Bar Associations; Connecticut Trial Lawyers Association. ***PRACTICE AREAS:*** Employment; Civil Litigation; Bankruptcy. ***Email:*** dzabel@cohenandwolf.com

MARK A. KIRSCH, born New York, N.Y., July 18, 1960; admitted to bar, 1985, Connecticut; 1986, U.S. District Court, District of Connecticut; 1987,

(This Listing Continued)

New York. *Education:* State University of New York at Albany (B.S., magna cum laude, 1982); Boston University (J.D., 1985). Legal Counsel to Board of Directors, 1998—, Member, Board of Directors, 1989-1997 and Treasurer, 1991-1997, Home Builders Association of Fairfield County. Chairman, Board of Directors, 1998-2000 and Member, Board of Directors, 1996—, Leadership Greater Bridgeport. Member, Board of Directors, Jewish Center for Community Services, 1998—. *Member:* Bridgeport, Connecticut, New York State and American Bar Associations. ***PRACTICE AREAS:*** Real Estate. ***Email:*** mkirsch@cohenandwolf.com

DAVID M. LEVINE, born Oceanside, New York, February 17, 1961; admitted to bar, 1986, Connecticut; 1987, U.S. District Court, District of Connecticut; 1988, New York. *Education:* Brandeis University (A.B., magna cum laude, with honors, 1983); Boston University (J.D., 1986). Author: "Counsel's Changing Role in the Health Care Arena," *Connecticut Law Tribune,* Sept. 23, 1996. Lecturer: Limited Liability Companies, Bridgeport Bar Association, 1993 and 2000; Connecticut Business Corporation Act, 1995 and 1996. Member and President, Bridgeport Chamber of Commerce, 2001—. Member, Board of Directors, Connecticut Venture Group, Bridgeport Chapter, 1994-1995. Member, Connecticut Law Revision Committee Special Task Force on Professional Entities, 2001. *Member:* Bridgeport (Chairman, Business Law Committee, 2000-2001), Connecticut (Member, Executive Committee, Business Law Section, 2000—), New York State and American Bar Associations; American Health Lawyers Association; Connecticut Health Lawyers Association. ***PRACTICE AREAS:*** Corporate; Commercial; Health Care; Real Estate. ***Email:*** dlevine@cohenandwolf.com

JOSEPH G. WALSH (See Danbury listing for Biography).

DAVID A. BALL, born Albany, New York, March 1, 1966; admitted to bar, 1991, Connecticut; 1992, U.S. District Court, District of Connecticut. *Education:* Brandeis University (B.A., cum laude, 1988); University of Pennsylvania (J.D., 1991). *Member:* Bridgeport, Connecticut and American Bar Associations; Connecticut Trial Lawyers Association. ***PRACTICE AREAS:*** Commercial Litigation; Securities Litigation; Corporate. ***Email:*** dball@cohenandwolf.com

JOCELYN B. HURWITZ, born Bronx, New York, August 10, 1967; admitted to bar, 1992, Connecticut; 1993, U.S. District Court, District of Connecticut. *Education:* Sarah Lawrence College; Cornell University (B.S., 1989; J.D., 1992). Bench Brief Editor, Moot Court Board, 1991-1992. Member: Connecticut Council for Divorce Mediation; Academy of Family Mediators. *Member:* Bridgeport, Connecticut (Member, Sections on: Family Law; Commercial Litigation) and American (Member, Sections on: Commercial Litigation; Family Law) Bar Associations. ***PRACTICE AREAS:*** Family Law; Commercial Litigation; Divorce Mediation. ***Email:*** jhurwitz@cohenandwolf.com

STUART M. KATZ, born New York, N.Y., September 24, 1967; admitted to bar, 1992, Connecticut; 1993, U.S. District Court, District of Connecticut. *Education:* Johns Hopkins University; Brandeis University (B.A., cum laude, 1989); Boston University (J.D., 1992). Articles Editor, American Journal of Law and Medicine, 1991-1992. Member, Connecticut Regional Board, Anti-Defamation League of B'nai B'rith (ADL). *Member:* Bridgeport, Connecticut and American Bar Associations; Connecticut Employment Lawyers Association; Connecticut Criminal Defense Lawyers Association. ***PRACTICE AREAS:*** Commercial and Criminal Litigation; Employment Law. ***Email:*** skatz@cohenandwolf.com

MONTE E. FRANK (See Danbury listing for Biography).

PATRICIA C. SULLIVAN, born Port Chester, New York, June 17, 1959; admitted to bar, 1989, Connecticut; 1990, New York and U.S. District Court, District of Connecticut; 1991, District of Columbia Court of Appeals; 1992, U.S. Court of Appeals, Second Circuit; 1993, U.S. Supreme Court. *Education:* Fordham University (B.A., 1980; J .D., 1989). Assistant Town Attorney, Westport, 1991-1993. Associate Town Attorney, Wilton, 1992—. Assistant Town Attorney, Weston, 2000—. Assistant Town Attorney, Ridgefield, 2000—. *Member:* Bridgeport, Regional, Westport, Connecticut, New York State and American Bar Associations; District of Columbia Bar. ***Email:*** psullivan@cohenandwolf.com

VINCENT M. MARINO, born West Islip, New York, September 12, 1971; admitted to bar, 1996, Connecticut; 1997, New York and U.S. District Court, District of Connecticut. *Education:* State University of New York at Binghamton (B.A., 1993); Quinnipiac College (J.D., 1996). Co-Author: "Connecticut's PJR After Pinsky," Sidebar, Connecticut Bar Association Litigation Section, Fall, 1996. Member, Milford Chamber of Commerce, 1998. *Member:* Stamford/Norwalk, Bridgeport, Connecticut and American Bar Associations; Connecticut Trial Lawyers Association. ***PRACTICE AREAS:*** Commercial Litigation; Employment Law; Construction Law; Real Estate; Bankruptcy. ***Email:*** vmarino@cohenandwolf.com

ANN B. MULCAHY, born Hartford, Connecticut, October 2, 1973; admitted to bar, 1999, Connecticut; 2000, District of Columbia and U.S. District Court, District of Connecticut. *Education:* Trinity College (B.A., with honors, Political Science, 1996); Cornell University (J.D., 1999). Phi Delta Phi; Pi Gamma Mu. Senior Note Editor, Cornell Journal of Law and Public Policy, 1998-1999. *Member:* Greater Bridgeport, Hartford County, Connecticut and American Bar Associations. ***PRACTICE AREAS:*** Employment Law; Commercial Litigation. ***Email:*** amulcahy@cohenandwolf.com

MARNIE J. RUBIN (See Danbury listing for Biography).

ARI J. HOFFMAN, born Fairfield, Connecticut, June 27, 1974; admitted to bar, 2000, Connecticut; 2001, U.S. District Court, District of Connecticut. *Education:* Brandeis University (B.A., magna cum laude, 1996); Boston College (J.D., 2000). ***PRACTICE AREAS:*** Commercial Litigation. ***Email:*** ahoffman@cohenandwolf.com

BARBARA M. SCHELLENBERG, born New York, N.Y., November 10, 1959; admitted to bar, 1986, Connecticut; 1988, U.S. District Court, District of Connecticut. *Education:* Cornell University (B.S., 1981); University of Pennsylvania (J.D., 1986). ***PRACTICE AREAS:*** Commercial Litigation; Appellate Practice. ***Email:*** bschellenberg@cohenandwolf.com

FREDERIC B. EISMAN, born New York, N.Y., September 24, 1965; admitted to bar, 1992, Connecticut; 1993, New York and U.S. District Court, Southern and Eastern Districts of New York. *Education:* Union College (B.A., 1987); New York University (M.A., 1990); Washington University (J.D., 1992). Recipient, Scribes Award. Executive Articles Editor, Washington University Law Quarterly, 1992. *Member:* Westchester County, New York State, Connecticut and American Bar Associations. ***PRACTICE AREAS:*** Corporate Law; Business Law; Trusts and Estates; Real Estate. ***Email:*** feisman@cohenandwolf.com

OF COUNSEL

MARTIN F. WOLF, born Utica, New York, January 4, 1929; admitted to bar, 1955, Connecticut; 1956, U.S. District Court, District of Connecticut. *Education:* University of Connecticut (A.B., 1952); Harvard University (LL.B., 1955). *Member:* Bridgeport (President, 1982-1983), Connecticut and American Bar Associations. ***PRACTICE AREAS:*** Real Estate; Corporate; Education. ***Email:*** mwolf@cohenandwolf.com

ROBERT J. ASHKINS, born Bridgeport, Connecticut, August 3, 1928; admitted to bar, 1958, Connecticut; 1960, U.S. District Court, District of Connecticut and U.S. Court of Appeals, Second Circuit. *Education:* University of Connecticut and University of Bridgeport (B.A., 1951); Yale University (LL.B., 1958). *Member:* Bridgeport, Connecticut and American Bar Associations. ***PRACTICE AREAS:*** Business; Labor; Health Care. ***Email:*** c&w@cohenandwolf.com

STUART A. EPSTEIN, born Bridgeport, Connecticut, January 31, 1938; admitted to bar, 1962, Connecticut; 1963, California; 1964, U.S. District Court, Southern District of California; 1966, U.S. District Court, District of Connecticut. *Education:* College of William & Mary (B.A., 1959); Yale University (LL.B., 1962). Phi Beta Kappa. *Member:* Connecticut and American Bar Associations; The State Bar of California. ***PRACTICE AREAS:*** Real Estate; Private Syndications of Real Estate Transactions. ***Email:*** c&w@cohenandwolf.com

JACK E. McGREGOR, born Kittanning, Pennsylvania, September 22, 1934; admitted to bar, 1963, Pennsylvania and U.S. District Court, Western District of Pennsylvania; 1971, District of Columbia, U.S. District Court for the District of Columbia and U.S. Supreme Court; 1973, U.S. Court of Appeals for the District of Columbia Circuit; 1996, Connecticut. *Education:* Yale University (B.S., 1956); University of Pittsburgh (LL.B., 1962). Editor-in-Chief, University of Pittsburgh Law Review, 1961-1962. *Member:* Bridgeport, Connecticut and American Bar Associations. ***PRACTICE AREAS:*** Corporate; Finance; Real Estate Development. ***Email:*** cw@cohenandwolf.com

LEGAL SUPPORT PERSONNEL

SHERRY E. SOPIN, born Bridgeport, Connecticut, May 17, 1950. *Education:* University of Vermont; Boston University (B.S., 1972). Member, 1987—, Recording Secretary, 1990-1991, President, 1992-1993 and Bar Liaison, 1997—, Association of Legal Administrators, Nutmeg Chapter. Member, Legal Advisory Board, Legal Assistant Program, Sacred Heart University. *Member:* Bridgeport (Chair, Legal Administrators Committee, 2000—), Regional, Connecticut and American (Associate) Bar Associations; Legal Marketing Association. (Director of Administration). ***PRACTICE AREAS:*** Financial Management; Human Resource Management; Systems Management; Facilities Management; Administration; Marketing. ***Email:*** ssopin@cohenandwolf.com

LOCAL COUNSEL FOR: American Arbitration Association; Anheuser Busch Companies, Inc.; The Chase Manhattan Bank; Coldwell Banker; Commonwealth Land Title Insurance Company; Duracell; Emigrant Savings Bank; Federated Department Stores, Inc.; Fidelity National Title Insurance Company of New York; Illinois Tool Works Inc.; Lawyers Title Insurance Corp.; Marine Midland Bank; Merrill Lynch Credit Corp.; Mobil Oil; The Perrier Group of America; Prudential Insurance Company of America; Stop & Shop Supermarkets Company; Terex Corp.; Toll Brothers, Inc.; United Technologies.

(This Listing Continued)

COHEN AND WOLF, P.C., Bridgeport—Continued

REPRESENTATIVE CLIENTS: Beadsley, Brown & Bassett, Inc.; The Bridgeport and Port Jefferson Steamboat Co.; The Bridgeport Bluefish; City of Meridian Planning Commission; City of Stamford; Electric Indicator Co., Inc.; Enterprise Rent-A-Car; Fleet Bank; Greater Bridgeport Regional Business Council; Heyman Properties; Hudson United Bank; Jewish Home for the Elderly of Fairfield County; Marcus Dairy; New Milford Savings Bank; Norwalk Redevelopment Agency; Omega Engineering, Inc.; Oronogue Village Condominium Association, Inc.; People's Bank; Pepperidge Farm, Inc.; Shepards, Inc.; Tenax Corp.; T. M. Systems, Inc.; Tomlinson, Hawley, Patterson, Inc.; Town of Eaton; Town of Newtown; Town of Westport (land use matters); Town of Wilton; T R Paul, Inc.; University of Bridgeport; Wayside Furniture Shops; William Raveis Real Estate.
REFERENCES: Fleet Bank; Hudson United Bank.

COLEMAN SUDOL SAPONE, P.C.

714 COLORADO AVENUE
BRIDGEPORT, CONNECTICUT 06605-1601
Telephone: 203-366-3560
Fax: 203-335-6779
Email: cosud@erols.com
URL: http://www.lawyers.com/colemansudollp

Mamaroneck, New York Office: 434 Mamaroneck Avenue, 10483. Telephone: 203-366-3560.

Patents, Trademarks, Copyrights, Litigation, Unfair Competition, Trade Secrets, Licensing/Technology Deal Structuring, Business Development, Biotechnology/Pharmaceuticals, Software and Internet Law, Due Diligence for Financial Transactions, Technology Acquisition, Technology Licensing Litigation, Alternative Dispute Resolution including Arbitration and Mediation of Contract/License Disputes.

HENRY D. COLEMAN, admitted to bar, 1985, Wisconsin; 1986, New York; 1987, New Jersey, U.S. District Court, District of New Jersey and U.S. District Court, Southern and Eastern Districts of New York; registered to practice before U.S. Patent and Trademark Office (Not admitted in Connecticut). *Education:* State University of New York at Buffalo (B.S. in Pharmaceutical/Medicinal Chemistry, magna cum laude, 1977; B.A. in Political Science, magna cum laude, 1 977; Ph.D. in Pharmaceutical/Medicinal Chemistry, 1982); University of Wisconsin-Madison (J.D., cum laude, 1985). Thesis: "Studies on the Chemical Synthesis of Oligoribonucleotides Containing 5- Mercaptopyrimidine Bases," 1982. Co-author with John D. Vandenberg: "Protecting Non-U.S. Research in the United States," Biotechnology 6, 791, 1988. *Member:* New York Intellectual Property Law Association; New Jersey Intellectual Property Law Association; American Chemical Society; Association of University Technology Managers.

R. NEIL SUDOL, admitted to bar, 1984, New York; 1988, New Jersey, U.S. District Court, Southern and Eastern Districts of New York and U.S. District Court, District of New Jersey; registered to practice before U.S. Patent and Trademark Office (Not admitted in Connecticut). *Education:* Lehigh University (B.A., Mathematics and Psychology, magna cum laude, 1975; B.S., Engineering Physics, magna cum laude, 1975); New York University (J.D., 1983). *Member:* New York Intellectual Property Law Association; American Intellectual Property Law Association. ***LANGUAGES:*** German.

WILLIAM J. SAPONE, born Waterbury, Connecticut, February 13, 1954; admitted to bar, 1984, Connecticut; 1985, New York; 1991, U.S. Court of Appeals for the Federal Circuit, U.S. District Court, Southern District of New York and U.S. District Court, District of Connecticut; registered to practice before U.S. Patent and Trademark Office. *Education:* University of Lowell (B.S.Ch.E., 1977); Pace University (J.D., 1984). *Member:* Connecticut (Member, Intellectual Property Section), New York State and American (Member: Patent and Trademark Section; Committee on Patent Legislation; Committee on Design Patent Protection) Bar Associations; Connecticut Intellectual Property Law Association (Chairman, Membership Committee; Legislative Committee, 1989-1991); American Intellectual Property Law Association; National Association of Manufacturers (Member, Task Force on Intellectual Property, 1987); New York Intellectual Property Law Association; International Trademark Association; American Chemical Society. (Also Of Counsel, Nims Howes Collison Hansen & Atkins). ***Email:*** wjspatent@aol.com

COLES, O'CONNELL, DOLAN & McDONALD, P.C.

BRIDGEPORT, CONNECTICUT
(See O'Donnell, McDonald and Cregeen, L.L.C.)

COLLINS, HANNAFIN, GARAMELLA, JABER & TUOZZOLO

PROFESSIONAL CORPORATION
BRIDGEPORT, CONNECTICUT
(See Danbury)

General Practice. Real Estate, Estate Planning, Probate, Zoning and Land Use, Tax, Corporation, Commercial, Banking, Family Law, Criminal Law, Negligence, and Civil Trials in all Courts.

GREGORY M. CONTE

4083 MAIN STREET, SUITE 2B-F
BRIDGEPORT, CONNECTICUT 06606
Telephone: 203-371-8137
Fax: 203-371-2304
Email: gmjc123@cs.com
URL: http://www.lawyers.com/gregoryconte

Family Law, Divorce, Child Custody, Real Estate, Zoning Law, Personal Injury.

GREGORY M. CONTE, born Bridgeport, Connecticut, May 8, 1947; admitted to bar, 1980, Connecticut and U.S. District Court, District of Connecticut. *Education:* Sacred Heart University (B.A. 1969); Fairfield University (M.A., 1974); University of Bridgeport (J.D., 1980). Member, Board of Education, Town of Monroe, 1999. City Council, City of Bridgeport, 1974-1978. Attorney Trial Referee, Connecticut State Courts, 1999—. *Member:* Bridgeport and Connecticut Bar Associations; Connecticut Trial Lawyers Association; American Trial Lawyers Association; Connecticut Italian American Bar Association; National Italian American Bar Association. ***REPORTED CASES:*** Jolly Inc. v. ZBA, 237 Conn 184 (1996); Cardoza v. Zoning Commission, 211 Conn 78 (1989); Daughters of St. Paul v. Zoning Board, 17 Conn App 53 (1988); Courchaine v. Shelby Mutual Ins. Co., 2 Conn App 438 (1984). ***PRACTICE AREAS:*** Personal Injury (40%); Real Estate (30%); Family Law (10%); General Practice.

COUSINS, JOHNSON & DESROSIERS, P.C.

BRIDGEPORT, CONNECTICUT
(See Stratford)

Workers' Compensation, Personal Injury, Trials, Real Estate, Probate.

DALY, WEIHING & BOCHANIS

SUITE 710, SECURITY BUILDING
1115 MAIN STREET
BRIDGEPORT, CONNECTICUT 06604
Telephone: 203-333-8500
Fax: 203-334-0305
Email: lawdwb@aol.com

General Trial, Administrative and Appellate Practice including Arbitration, Transportation, Estate Planning, Probate, Corporation, Torts, Workers Compensation, Real Estate, Domestic Relations, Labor and Legislative Law.

MEMBERS OF FIRM

JAMES J. A. DALY (1914-1982).

THOMAS J. WEIHING, born Bridgeport, Connecticut, October 26, 1943; admitted to bar, 1970, Connecticut; 1971, U.S. District Court, District of Connecticut; 1972, U.S. Court of Appeals, Second Circuit. *Education:* New Haven College (B.S., 1965); New England Law School (J.D., 1970). *Member:* Bridgeport and Connecticut Bar Associations; Connecticut Trial Lawyers' Association; The Association of Trial Lawyers of America. ***REPORTED CASES:*** Gray Line Bus Company v. Greater Bridgeport Transit District, 188 Conn 417, 449 A.2d 1036, 35 ALR4th 1252, September 21, 1982. Lee vs. Middlesex Ins. Co. 219 Conn. 644, 594 A.2d 952 (1991). Lee vs. Middlesex Ins. Co. 229 Conn. 842 (1994). ***PRACTICE AREAS:*** Arbitration Law; Transportation Law; Labor Law; Legislative Law; Trials and Appeals. ***Email:*** lawdwb@aol.com

JOHN T. BOCHANIS, born Bridgeport, Connecticut, January 28, 1958; admitted to bar, 1984, Connecticut and U.S. District Court, District of Connecticut; 1985, U.S. Court of Appeals, Second Circuit; 1994, U.S. Supreme Court. *Education:* University of South Carolina (B.A., 1979); Creighton University (J.D., 1984). *Member:* Bridgeport, Connecticut and American Bar Associations; The Association of Trial Lawyers of America. ***LANGUAGES:*** Greek. ***REPORTED CASES:*** Lees vs. Middlesex Ins. Co. 219 Conn. 644, 594 A. 2d 952 (1991). Lees vs. Middlesex Ins. Co. 229 Conn. 842 (1994). ***PRACTICE AREAS:*** Trials and Appeals. ***Email:*** lawdwb@aol.com

(This Listing Continued)

REPRESENTATIVE CLIENTS: Family Garage Inc.; Bridgeport Transit District; Morgan Drive Away, Inc.; Trumbull Housing Authority.

DEPANFILIS & VALLERIE, LLC

BRIDGEPORT, CONNECTICUT

(See Norwalk)

General Civil and Criminal Litigation Practice in all Courts. Negligence, Medical Malpractice, Taxation, Corporation, Estate Planning, Probate, Real Estate, Workers Compensation, Family and Landlord and Tenant Law.

DISERIO MARTIN O'CONNOR & CASTIGLIONI LLP

BRIDGEPORT, CONNECTICUT

(See Stamford)

General Practice. Litigation and Trials in all Courts. Corporate, Commercial Finance, Securities, Taxation, Banking, Foreclosure and Workout, Real Estate Law, Personal Injury and Negligence, Employment Law, Wrongful Termination, Workers Compensation, Insurance Coverage and Defense, Family, Creditors Rights and Bankruptcy, Trusts, Probate, Estate and Tax Planning.

ELSTEIN AND ELSTEIN, P.C.

SUITE 400
1087 BROAD STREET
BRIDGEPORT, CONNECTICUT 06604-4260
Telephone: 203-367-4421
Telecopier: 203-366-8615
Email: belstein@snet.net
URL: http://www.lawyers.com/elsteinandelstein

Trials and Appeals emphasizing Personal Injury and Commercial Law, Real Estate Acquisition, Negotiation and Financing, Domestic Relations, Corporate and Business Planning.

HENRY ELSTEIN, born Bridgeport, Connecticut, April 19, 1934; admitted to bar, 1959, Connecticut; 1985, New York. *Education:* Yale University (B.A., 1956; LL.B., 1959). Lecturer, "Mechanics Liens," Connecticut Bar Association, 1978. Deputy Moderator, Fairfield, Connecticut Representative Town Meeting, 1969-1971. Chairman: Committee on Legislation and Administration, 1965-1967; Committee on Public Works and Planning, 1969-1973, Fairfield, Connecticut Representative Town Meeting. Member, 1979-1984 and Vice-Chairman, 1981-1984, Fairfield, Connecticut Economic Development Commission. Member, Mayor's Task Force on Historic Resources, Bridgeport, Connecticut, 1987-1989. Member, Board of Directors, Child Guidance Center, 1990—. *Member:* Bridgeport (Chairman, Committee on Continuing Legal Education, 1984-1985), Connecticut, New York State and American Bar Associations. ***REPORTED CASES:*** Nash v. the Weed & Duryea Company, 236 Conn. 746 (1996); Kennedy v. Kennedy, 177 Conn. 47 (1979); Berg v. Berg, 24 Conn. App. 509 (1991). ***PRACTICE AREAS:*** Financing; Real Estate; Real Estate Acquisition; Debt Restructuring; Mechanics Liens; Domestic Relations; Corporate; Trials and Appeals. ***Email:*** elstein@snet.net

BRUCE L. ELSTEIN, born New Haven, Connecticut, April 10, 1961; admitted to bar, 1986, Connecticut; 1987, U.S. District Court, District of Connecticut. *Education:* Skidmore College (B.S., 1983); Hofstra University (J.D., 1986). Member and General Counsel, Board of Trustees, Greater Bridgeport Symphony, 1988-1996; Vice President, 1996-1998. Associate Director, Carlson Festivals, 1988-1992. Member, Court Appointed Committee on Foreclosures. *Member:* Bridgeport (Chairman, Unauthorized Practice of Law Committee, 1992-1993), Connecticut (Member, Sections on: Commercial Law and Bankruptcy; Real Estate) and American Bar Associations; The Association of Trial Lawyers of America; Connecticut Trial Lawyers Association. ***REPORTED CASES:*** Sullivan v. Nameaug, 233 Conn. 213 (1995); L&G Associates v. Danbury ZBA 40 Conn. App. 784 (1996); The Cadle Company of Connecticut v. C.F.D. Development Corporation, et al, 44 Conn. App. 409 (1997); Booth v. Flanagan, 19 Conn. App. 413 (1989). ***PRACTICE AREAS:*** Personal Injury; Defamation; Commercial Law and Litigation; Real Estate; Mechanics Lien; Condominium; Trials and Appeals. ***Email:*** belstein@snet.net

REPRESENTATIVE CLIENTS: AutoZone, Inc.; The Bridgeport Lumber Co., Inc.; Scott Swimming Pools, Inc.; WD Capital Holdings, LLC.
REFERENCE: Hudson United Bank; Chase Manhattan.
APPROVED ATTORNEYS FOR: Connecticut Attorneys Title Insurance Company; Lawyers Title Insurance Company; Stewart Title Guaranty Company.

FINN DIXON & HERLING LLP

BRIDGEPORT, CONNECTICUT

(See Stamford)

Corporate Law, Mergers and Acquisitions, Securities Law, Venture Capital Financing, Corporate Finance and Restructuring, Commercial Litigation, Banking and Lending Law, Bankruptcy and Workouts, Employee Benefits and the Federal and State Taxation of Businesses and Business Transactions.

FOGARTY COHEN SELBY & NEMIROFF LLC

BRIDGEPORT, CONNECTICUT

(See Greenwich)

Litigation in all Courts, Real Estate and Land Use, Estate Planning and Probate, Corporate, Matrimonial, Administrative and Environmental, Appellate Practice, Business, Civil Trial, Commercial Litigation, Construction, Family, Labor and Employment, Medical Malpractice, Trust and Product Liability.

LAW OFFICES OF JAMES O. GASTON

239 GOLDEN HILL STREET
BRIDGEPORT, CONNECTICUT 06604
Telephone: 203-334-1656
Fax: 203-333-4532

Personal Injury, Products Liability, Workers Compensation, Medical Malpractice, Commercial Law.

JAMES O. GASTON, born Birmingham, Alabama, February 2, 1959; admitted to bar, 1983, Connecticut; 1991, U.S. Claims Court. *Education:* Lehigh University (B.S., 1980); Duquesne University (J.D., 1983). Assistant Editor, Duquesne University, Legal Periodical, Juris, 1982-1983. Author: "Sex Based Mortality Tables and Manhart, Juris," Vol. XVII No. 3, Spring, 1983. "Direct Action Suits in Uninsured Motorist Cases," Connecticut Lawyer, Vol 3, No. 6, March 1993; "Recall Without Retreat-Assessing the Changes in Personal Injury Automobile Law from the Plaintiff's Perspective," Connecticut Lawyer, Vol. 4, No. 5, February, 1994; "Cutting The Gordian Knot of Apportionment," Connecticut Lawyer, Vol 5 No. 9, June/July, 1995. *Member:* Greater Bridgeport (Member, Civil Trials and Procedure Committee), Connecticut (Member, Board of Governors, 1993—; House of Delegates, 1993—; Executive Committee Litigation Section, 1986—; Chair, Litigation Section, 1996-1999; Client Security Fund, 1993-1997) and American Bar Associations; Connecticut Trial Lawyers Association (Chairman, People's Law School Committee, 1988—; Chairman, Expert Data Bank Committee, 1990-1993; Legislative Committee 1998—; Member, Continuing Legal Education Committee, 1990-1992); The Association of Trial Lawyers of America; Trial Lawyers for Public Justice (State Coordinator, 1990-1994). (Certified as a Civil Trial Advocate by the National Board of Trial Advocacy, 1990—). ***PRACTICE AREAS:*** Personal Injury Law; Products Liability Law; Workers Compensation; Commercial Law.

REPRESENTATIVE CLIENTS: Microboard Processing Inc.; Bridgeport Air Services Inc.; Million-Air Inc.; Milford Seafood Corporation; CME Wire & Cable Inc.

GENUARIO & CONOVER

BRIDGEPORT, CONNECTICUT

(See Norwalk)

General Civil Practice. Trials in all State and Federal Courts. Real Estate, Probate, Employment, Construction, Personal Injury, Foreclosures, Commercial and Zoning Law.

GOLDSTEIN AND PECK, P.C.

Established in 1939
1087 BROAD STREET
P.O. BOX 1538
BRIDGEPORT, CONNECTICUT 06601
Telephone: 203-334-9421
Telefax: 203-334-6949
Email: info@goldsteinandpeck.com
URL: http://www.lawyers.com/goldsteinpeck

General Practice, including Litigation (State and Federal Courts; Trials and Appeals) and Transactional Representation (Banking, Corporate, Real Estate). Arbitration, Domestic Relations, Estate Planning, Insurance, Municipal Law, Personal Injury, Probate, Product Liability, Zoning.

DAVID GOLDSTEIN (1898-1992).

(This Listing Continued)

GOLDSTEIN AND PECK, P.C., Bridgeport—Continued

WILLIAM J. KUPINSE, JR., born New Haven, Connecticut, September 24, 1939; admitted to bar, 1964, Connecticut and U.S. District Court, District of Connecticut; 1967, U.S. Court of Appeals, Second Circuit; 1971, U.S. Tax Court. *Education:* Dartmouth College (A.B., 1961); Cornell University (LL.B., 1964, with distinction). Phi Kappa Phi; Order of the Coif. Member, Board of Editors, Cornell Law Quarterly, 1962-1964. First Selectman, Town of Easton, 1997—. *Member:* Bridgeport, Westport, The Connecticut and American Bar Associations. ***PRACTICE AREAS:*** General Practice; Litigation; Trusts and Estates; Commercial Law; Family Law. ***Email:*** kupinsew@goldsteinandpeck.com

WALTER A. FLYNN, JR., born Bridgeport, Connecticut, August 2, 1943; admitted to bar, 1968, Connecticut; 1971, U.S. Court of Appeals, Second Circuit, U.S. District Court and U.S. Tax Court; 1973, U.S. Supreme Court. *Education:* Boston College (B.S., 1965); Georgetown University (J.D., 1968); New York University (LL.M in Taxation, 1971). Town Attorney, Town of Weston, 1984-1991. *Member:* Bridgeport (President, 1988-1989), Westport, The Connecticut (Member: House of Delegates, 1990-1994; Executive Committee, Estates and Probate Section, 1987—) and American Bar Associations. ***PRACTICE AREAS:*** Wills; Trusts and Estates; Probate; Taxation; Eminent Domain. ***Email:*** info@goldsteinandpeck.com

JOHN G. DZURIK, born Bridgeport, Connecticut, May 2, 1950; admitted to bar, 1975, Connecticut, U.S. District Court, District of Connecticut; 1987, Washington. *Education:* Georgetown University (B.S.F.S., 1972); Georgetown University Law Center (J.D., 1975). Editor, Law and Policy in International Business, 1974-1975. Board of Directors, Georgetown University Alumni Association, 1979-1985. *Member:* Bridgeport (Treasurer, 1993-1994; Secretary, 1994-1995; President, 1996-1997); Connecticut (Member, House of Delegates, 1987-1992), Washington State and American (Member, Executive Committee, Young Lawyers Division, 1981-1983; State Membership Chairman, 1984-1992) Bar Associations. ***PRACTICE AREAS:*** Leases and Leasing; Real Estate Finance; Commercial Real Estate. ***Email:*** dzurikj@goldsteinandpeck.com

DENNIS M. LACCAVOLE, born Bridgeport, Connecticut, February 5, 1953; admitted to bar, 1978, Connecticut; 1979, New York and U.S. District Court, District of Connecticut; 1980, U.S. Court of Appeals, Second Circuit; 1982, U.S. Supreme Court. *Education:* Fairfield University (B.S., 1975); St. John's University (J.D., 1978). *Member:* Bridgeport, Connecticut, New York State and American Bar Associations; Connecticut Defense Lawyers Association (Member, Board of Directors, 1997-2000); Defense Research Institute; Connecticut Trial Lawyers Association. ***PRACTICE AREAS:*** Insurance; Personal Injury; Premises Liability; Products Liability; Professional Liability. ***Email:*** laccavod@goldsteinandpeck.com

ROBERT L. CAVANAUGH, JR., born Waterbury, Connecticut, November 28, 1967; admitted to bar, 1993, Connecticut. *Education:* Northeastern University (B.S., magna cum laude, 1990); Suffolk University (J.D., cum laude, 1993). *Member:* Westport, Bridgeport, Connecticut and American Bar Associations; Connecticut Trial Lawyers Association; Connecticut Defense Lawyers Association. ***PRACTICE AREAS:*** Personal Injury; Insurance Defense; Civil Litigation. ***Email:*** rc@goldsteinandpeck.com

TIZIANA M. SCACCIA, born Frosinone, Italy, October 2, 1964; admitted to bar, 1990, Connecticut; 1991, New York State and U.S. District Court, District of Connecticut; 1995, Massachusetts and U.S. District Court, Southern District of New York; 1998, U.S. Court of Appeals, Second Circuit. *Education:* Fairfield University (B.S., 1987); University of Connecticut School of Law (J.D., 1990). Adjunct Professor, Fairfield University, 1996-1997 & 2000. Treasurer, Mayoral Campaign, City of Bridgeport, 1995. *Member:* Connecticut and American Bar Associations; American Trial Lawyers Association. ***LANGUAGES:*** Italian. ***PRACTICE AREAS:*** Civil and Commercial Litigation; Personal Injury; Family Law; Real Estate; Probate; Debtor and Creditor; Bankruptcy; Securities Litigation; Construction Litigation; Landlord/Tenant Law; Federal Litigation. ***Email:*** scacciat@goldsteinandpeck.com

CHRISTOPHER M. HARRINGTON, born New York, New York, May 3, 1961; admitted to bar, 1995, Connecticut. *Education:* State University of New York (B.A., 1990); Western New England College School of Law (J.D., 1994). Member, Board of Directors, Treasurer Ancient Burying Ground Association, Hartford, 1998—. ***PRACTICE AREAS:*** Insurance Defense; Commercial Litigation; Personal Injury; Environmental Litigation; Family Law. ***Email:*** cmh@goldsteinandpeck.com

OF COUNSEL

PETER B. O'CONNELL, born Bridgeport, Connecticut, September 30, 1944; admitted to bar, 1970, Connecticut; 1975, U.S. District Court, District of Connecticut. *Education:* Georgetown University (B.A., 1966); Fordham University (LL.B., 1970). *Member:* Bridgeport, Connecticut and American Bar Associations. ***PRACTICE AREAS:*** Probate Law; Real Estate Law. ***Email:*** info@goldsteinandpeck.com

(This Listing Continued)

REPRESENTATIVE CLIENTS: The American Fabrics Co.; American Modern Insurance Group; Bankers and Shippers Insurance Co.; Bee Publishing Company, Inc.; Coldwell Banker; Colonial Insurance Agency, Inc.; The Chase Manhattan Bank; Direct Insurance; FDIC; Great American Insurance Company; Integon Insurance Co.; Town of Greenwich-Board of Education; New Jersey Manufacturers Insurance Company; Town of Newtown-Planning and Zoning Commission; Newtown Savings Bank; Ohio Casualty Group; People's Bank; Syntex Rubber Corp.; Valley Container, Inc.; Physicians Health Services, Inc.; Town of Weston; Town of Westport; Worldwide Insurance Group.

GREEN AND GROSS, P.C.

SUITE 401, 1087 BROAD STREET
BRIDGEPORT, CONNECTICUT 06604-4231
Telephone: 203-335-5141
Fax: 203-367-9964
URL: http://www.lawyers.com/green&grosspc

Bankruptcy Law, Commercial and Construction Claims.

BERNARD GREEN, born Bridgeport, Connecticut, February 8, 1926; admitted to bar, 1952, Connecticut. *Education:* Yale University (B.S., 1949); Columbia University (LL.B., 1952). Phi Delta Phi. Member, Connecticut Governor's Council on Mental Retardation, 1963-1971. Member, Bridgeport Hospital Board of Directors, 1986—. Arbitrator, Commercial Disputes (Specialty, litigation and arbitration of commercial disputes and disputes among members of closely-held organizational entities). *Member:* Bridgeport, Connecticut and American Bar Associations. ***Email:*** bg@gglaw.net

ERIC M. GROSS, born New York, N.Y., February 18, 1947; admitted to bar, 1973, Connecticut. *Education:* Middlebury College (B.A., 1969); University of Connecticut (J.D., 1972). Member: U.S. Commission on Civil Rights, 1971-1972; Trumbull Town Council, 1983-1985. *Member:* Bridgeport, Connecticut and American Bar Associations; Connecticut Trial Lawyers Association (Attorney Trial Referee, 1991—). ***Email:*** emg@gglaw.net

SAMUEL T. ROST, born New York, N.Y., April 4, 1943; admitted to bar, 1969, Connecticut. *Education:* Bowdoin College (A.B., 1965); Boston University (J.D., 1968). Instructor, Business Law, Fairfield University, 1979-1984. Member, Drafting Committee, Connecticut Common Interest Ownership Manual, 2nd Edition. *Member:* Bridgeport, Connecticut and American Bar Associations. ***Email:*** srost@gglaw.net

JOEL Z. GREEN, born Bridgeport, Connecticut, October 26, 1957; admitted to bar, 1982, Connecticut. *Education:* Clark University (A.B., 1979); Case Western Reserve University (J.D., 1982). Member: Fairfield Representative Town Meeting, 1997—(Secretary, Committee on Legislation and Administration, 1997—); Fairfield Democratic Town Committee, 1997—. Commodore, Windjammers Sailing Club, 1992. *Member:* Bridgeport, Connecticut and American Bar Associations. ***Email:*** JoelZGreen@gglaw.net

BARBARA F. GREEN, born New Haven, Connecticut, December 24, 1954; admitted to bar, 1986, Connecticut; 1987, Ohio. *Education:* Connecticut College (B.A., with honors, 1976); University of Connecticut School of Social Work (M.S.W., 1978); University of Connecticut (J.D., 1985). Member, Planned Lifetime Assistance Network Legal Advisory Board, 1999—. Member, Board of Directors, 1995— and Vice Chairman, 2001—, Kennedy Center, Inc. *Member:* Bridgeport and Connecticut Bar Associations. ***Email:*** bfg@gglaw.net

JEFFREY W. KEIM, born Hartford, Connecticut, August 19, 1975; admitted to bar, 2000, Connecticut. *Education:* Elon College (B.A., 1997); University of Connecticut (J.D., 2000). *Member:* Bridgeport, Connecticut and American Bar Associations. ***PRACTICE AREAS:*** Civil Litigation; Criminal Defense. ***Email:*** jkeim@gglaw.net

OF COUNSEL

PAUL A. SOBEL, born Bridgeport, Connecticut, November 3, 1954; admitted to bar, 1979, Connecticut; 1980, U.S. District Court, District of Connecticut; registered to practice before U.S. Patent and Trademark Office. *Education:* Rensselaer Polytechnic Institute (B.S., Mechanical Engineering, 1976); Western New England College (J.D., 1979). Co-Author and Lecturer: "Current Issues in Commercial Real Estate Leases - Connecticut, National Business Institute, Inc., 1995; "Connecticut Construction Law: What To Do When," National Business Institute, Inc., 1997. *Member:* Bridgeport and Connecticut Bar Associations. ***PRACTICE AREAS:*** Real Estate; Construction Law. ***Email:*** psobel@gglaw.net

REPRESENTATIVE CLIENTS: Stelco Industries, Inc.; Connecticut Engineering Associates Corp.; Super 8 Motels, Inc.; Hariton Machinery Co., Inc.; Watkins Bros. Machinery Corp.; John Deere Co.; Fairfaxx Corp.; Toyota Motor Credit Corp; Newtown Savings Bank; Gypsum Specialists.
APPROVED COUNSEL FOR: Chicago Title Insurance Co.; First American Title Insurance Co.; People's Bank; Merrill Lynch Mortgage Co.; Newtown Savings Bank.

LAW OFFICES OF
JOHN R. GULASH, JR. & EUGENE J. RICCIO

SUITE 703, 350 FAIRFIELD AVENUE
P.O. BOX 9118
BRIDGEPORT, CONNECTICUT 06601
Telephone: 203-367-7440
Fax: 203-336-8379
Email: gulashandriccio@aol.com

General Civil and Criminal Trial and Appellate Practice before State and Federal Courts. Civil and Criminal Litigation. Personal Injury and Products Liability Law, Professional Grievance and Disciplinary Proceedings.

MEMBERS OF FIRM

JOHN R. GULASH, JR., born Bridgeport, Connecticut, October 27, 1950; admitted to bar, 1976, Connecticut; 1977, Florida; 1981, U.S. District Court, District of Connecticut; 1985, U.S. Court of Appeals, Second Circuit; 1986, U.S. Supreme Court; 1997, U.S. District Court, Eastern District of New York; 1998, U.S. District Court, Southern District of New York. *Education:* Lehigh University (B.A., with honors, 1972); Stetson University (J.D., 1976). Listed, The Best Lawyers in America, 1991—. Lecturer at CLE Seminars on various criminal law topics for University of Bridgeport School of Law, the Connecticut, Bridgeport and New Haven Bar Associations, 1980—. Lecturer, Bridgeport Municipal Police Training Academy and Fairfield County, Detective School, 1989—. Member, Superior Court Criminal Division Task Force, 1993—. *Member:* Bridgeport (Chairman/Co-Chairman 1983-1984, 1989-1995) and Connecticut (Member, Executive Committee, Criminal Justice Section) Bar Associations; The Florida Bar; National Association of Criminal Defense Lawyers; Connecticut Association of Criminal Defense Lawyers (Member, Board of Governors, 1989—; Secretary, 1992-1993; Vice President, 1993-1994; President, 1994-1995). ***LANGUAGES:*** Spanish. ***REPORTED CASES:*** State of Connecticut v. Sivri, 231 Conn. 115 646A.2d169 (1994); State of Connecticut v. Malines, 11 Conn. App. 425 527A.2d1229 (1987); State of Connecticut v. LaTorre, 51 Conn. App. 541 723A.2d1166 (1999); State of Connecticut v. DeBarros, 254 Conn. 931, 761 A.2d 756 (2000); United States v. Pollina, 782 F.2d358 (2d Cir.1986). ***PRACTICE AREAS:*** Criminal Defense Law; Trial Practice; Appellate Practice.

EUGENE J. RICCIO, born New York, N.Y., March 4, 1951; admitted to bar, 1976, Connecticut; 1977, New York; 1982, U.S. District Court, District of Connecticut; 1988, U.S. District Court, Southern and Eastern Districts of New York; 1997, Massachusetts. *Education:* Marquette University (B.A., 1973); New York Law School (J.D., 1976); Fordham University (M.A., 1984). ***PRACTICE AREAS:*** Civil Litigation; Criminal Defense.

ASSOCIATE

C. CHRISTIAN YOUNG, born Binghamton, New York, New York, October 10, 1970; admitted to bar, 1998, Connecticut; 1999, U.S. District Court, District of Connecticut. *Education:* Calvin College (B.A., 1995); Quinnipiac College School of Law (J.D., 1998). *Member:* Connecticut Criminal Defense Lawyers Association. ***PRACTICE AREAS:*** Criminal Defense; Civil Litigation.

HARLOW, ADAMS & FRIEDMAN, P.C.

BRIDGEPORT, CONNECTICUT

(See Milford)

General Civil Practice, General Civil Litigation in State and Federal Courts, Real Estate Conveyancing, Financing and Development, Zoning, Probate, Personal Injury, Commercial Litigation, Construction Law, Bankruptcy, Business Formations, Landlord and Tenant, Title Opinions, Trials and Appeals.

HEAGNEY, LENNON & SLANE LLP

BRIDGEPORT, CONNECTICUT

(See Greenwich)

General Practice, Real Estate, Trusts and Estates, Probate, Corporation and Business Law, Civil and Criminal Litigation, Zoning and Family Law.

HILL RIVKINS & HAYDEN LLP

1115 BROAD STREET
BRIDGEPORT, CONNECTICUT 06601-1821
Telephone: 203-367-5535
Telecopier: 203-367-5536
Email: hillrivkinsct@snet.net

New York, New York Office: c/o Kirlin, Campbell & Keating, 5 Hanover Square, Suite 1400. Telephone: 212-669-0600. Telecopier: 212-669-0698-0699.

(This Listing Continued)

Houston, Texas Office: 712 Main Street, Suite 1515. Telephone: 713-222-1515. Telecopier: 713-222-1359.

Hoboken, New Jersey Office: 96 Hudson Street. Telephone: 201-222-5180. Telecopier: 201-222-5182.

Admiralty, Transportation, Insurance and Reinsurance, International and Commercial Law, including Trial and Appellate Practice and Arbitration.

RESIDENT PARTNER

Richard H. Webber

(For complete biographical data on personnel, see Professional Biographies at New York, New York)

HOLAHAN, GUMPPER & DOWLING

BRIDGEPORT, CONNECTICUT

(See Fairfield)

General Practice. Real Estate, Land Use, Corporation, Estate Planning and Probate Law. Civil Trials in all Courts. Product Liability, Insurance Law, Environmental Law and Arbitration.

HOLLAND KAUFMANN & BARTELS, LLC

BRIDGEPORT, CONNECTICUT

(See Greenwich)

General Practice. Business and Corporate Law, Employment Law, Estate Planning and Probate Law, Family and Matrimonial Law, Litigation, Residential and Commercial Real Estate and Taxation.

IVEY, BARNUM & O'MARA, LLC

BRIDGEPORT, CONNECTICUT

(See Greenwich)

General Practice. E-Commerce, Litigation in all Courts. Corporate, Commercial, Finance, Taxation, Trusts, Probate, Estate Planning, Family Law, Zoning, Environmental, Real Estate, Employment Law and Elder Law.

JACOBS PARTNERS LLC

BRIDGEPORT, CONNECTICUT

(See Norwalk)

Business and Personal Bankruptcy, Workouts, Debtor Creditor's Rights, Commercial Litigation, Contracts and Business Disputes.

THOMAS L. KANASKY, JR.

Established in 1989

180 FAIRFIELD AVENUE
P.O. BOX 9281
BRIDGEPORT, CONNECTICUT 06604-9281
Telephone: 203-366-3156
Fax: 203-331-1802

General Civil Practice. Commercial, Collections, Bankruptcy and Real Estate Law. Litigation.

THOMAS L. KANASKY, JR., born Bridgeport, Connecticut, August 21, 1946; admitted to bar, 1979, Connecticut and U.S. District Court, District of Connecticut; 1983, U.S. Court of Appeals, Second Circuit; 1991, U.S. District Court, Southern District of New York. *Education:* University of Bridgeport (B.S., 1969); Pace University (J.D., 1979). *Member:* Connecticut Bar Association (Member: Executive Committee, Commercial and Bankruptcy Law Section, 1985—; Veterans and Military Affairs, Member, 1987— and Chairman, 1992—); Commercial Law League of America. [Col., USMCR Retired; Active, 1969-1991.]

REFERENCE: First Fidelity.

JONATHAN J. KLEIN

1445 CAPITOL AVENUE
BRIDGEPORT, CONNECTICUT 06604-1619
Telephone: 203-330-1900
Telecopier: 203-330-1526
Email: jjkesq@hotmail.com
URL: http://www.lawyers.com/jjklaw

Commercial, Civil, Tax and Securities Litigation and Appeals in all State and Federal Courts, White Collar Criminal Defense, Corporate Law, Labor and Employment Law, Administrative Law, Military Law.

(This Listing Continued)

JONATHAN J. KLEIN, Bridgeport—Continued

JONATHAN J. KLEIN, born Yonkers, New York, October 11, 1955; admitted to bar, 1981, New York, U.S. District Court, Southern District of Georgia, U.S. Court of Appeals, Fifth and Eleventh Circuits and U.S. Court of Appeals for the Armed Forces; 1984, U.S. Court of Appeals, Second Circuit; 1985, U.S. District Court, Southern and Eastern Districts of New York; 1986, Connecticut, U.S. District Court, District of Connecticut, U.S. Supreme Court and U.S. Army Court of Criminal Appeals; 1993, U.S. Tax Court. *Education:* Yeshiva University (B.A., magna cum laude, 1977); Fordham University (J.D., 1980). Senior Special Counsel, Department of Enforcement, New York Stock Exchange, 1984-1987. Director and Vice President, Hillel Academy, 1987—. Instructor, Military Law, U.S. Army ROTC, University of Connecticut, 1994—. Member, Committee on Military Justice and Military Affairs, Association of the Bar of the City of New York, 1984-1987. *Member:* Greater Bridgeport (Member, Litigation Committee), Connecticut (Veterans and Military Affairs Committee) and American (Member, Litigation Section) Bar Associations; Association of the United States Army. [Lt. Colonel, U.S. Army, JAGC, active duty, 1981-1984; Reserve, 1984—]. ***LANGUAGES:*** Hebrew. ***REPORTED CASES:*** United States v. Jefferson, 22 MJ 315 (C.M.A. 1986) (briefed and argued as amicus curiae on behalf of the Committee on Military Justice and Military Affairs of the Association of the Bar of the City of New York); Bannon v. Schwartz, 215 Conn. 633, 577 A.2d 1025 (1990); Barnett v. Barnett, 26 Conn. App. 355, 600 A.2d 1055 (1992); Green v. Commissioner, 67 T.C.M. 3074, Dec. 49,897 (M), T.C. Memo 1994-264, (U.S. Tax Court, 1994), affirmed, 60 F.3d 142 (2d Cir. 1995); Cody v. Ward, 954 F.Supp. 43, Blue Sky L. Rep. ¶74,151 (D.Conn. 1997); Davenport v. Society of the Cincinnati in the State of Connecticut, 46 Conn. Sup. 411, 754 A.2d 225 (1999); Breiner v. State Dental Commission, 57 Conn. App. 700, 750 A.2d 1111 (2000); Schlicher v. Schwartz, 58 Conn. App. 80, 752 A.2d 517 (2000); Citibank (South Dakota), N.A. v. Gifesman, —Conn.ARP—, —A.2d— (2001).

REPRESENTATIVE CLIENTS: D'Addario Industries; A-P-A Transport Corp.; G.O.D., Inc.; Phoenix Security Corporation; Industrial Wrecking, Inc.; Pulmonary & Internal Medicine Associates, P.C.; Custom Air Systems, Inc.

KOSKOFF, KOSKOFF & BIEDER, P.C.

350 FAIRFIELD AVENUE
BRIDGEPORT, CONNECTICUT 06604
Telephone: 203-336-4421
Fax: 203-368-3244
Email: KKB@KOSKOFF.com
URL: http://www.koskoff.com

Stamford, Connecticut Office: 1172 Bedford Street. Telephone: 203-325-3686.
Danbury, Connecticut Office: 1 Moss Avenue. Telephone: 203-792-7100.

Litigation in all State and Federal Courts. Medical Malpractice, Equal Opportunity, Negligence, Products Liability, Civil Rights, and Class Actions.

FIRM PROFILE: Koskoff, Koskoff & Bieder was founded by a former president of the Association of Trial Lawyers of America, Theodore I. Koskoff. The firm represents clients and their families in personal injury and wrongful death cases arising from medical and professional malpractice, aviation and vehicular accidents, products liability, premises liability, civil rights and other acts of negligence. Several of the firm's partners are listed in "Best Lawyers in America" and are frequent lecturers on trial advocacy. The firm frequently takes a lead position in emerging areas of law.

THEODORE I. KOSKOFF (1913-1989).

RICHARD A. FUCHS (1945-1995).

MICHAEL P. KOSKOFF, born Bridgeport, Connecticut, March 19, 1942; admitted to bar, 1966, Connecticut and U.S. District Court, District of Connecticut; 1973, U.S. Court of Appeals, 2nd Circuit; 1974, U.S. Supreme Court; 1975, U.S. District Court, Southern District of New York. *Education:* Brandeis University and University of Bridgeport (B.A., 1963); University of Connecticut (J.D., 1966). Listed in "Best Lawyers in America." Author: "New Vistas in Employment Discrimination," Connecticut Docket, February 1974; "Trial of a Medical Malpractice Case," (five part series), Connecticut Law Tribune, 1978; "Quiet on the Set; Lights, Cameras, Action," Connecticut Law Tribune, 1981; "Everyone Into the Pool," Connecticut Jury Selection Procedures, Connecticut Bar Journal, 1978. Faculty Member, National College of Advocacy, 1975—, 1991—. Member: Advisory Board, Quinnipiac College, School of Law 1980—. Co-Chair, Special Masters Program, U.S. District Court, District of Connecticut, 1985-1997. Frequent Guest Speaker on Court T.V., featured in *Damages*, highly acclaimed book examining involvement in medical malpractice suit. *Member:* Bridgeport, Danbury, Connecticut and American Bar Associations; Connecticut Trial Lawyers Association (Co-Chair, Continuing Legal Educational Committee, 1990—); The Association of Trial Lawyers of America. Fellow: American College of Trial Lawyers; Advocate, American Board of Trial Advocates (V.P. Connecticut Chapter, 1999—); The Inner Circle of Advocates. ***PRACTICE AREAS:*** Medical Malpractice; Products Liability; Class Actions; Personal Injury; Civil Rights. ***Email:*** mkoskoff@koskoff.com

RICHARD A. BIEDER, born Stamford, Connecticut, September 26, 1940; admitted to bar, 1965, Connecticut and U.S. Court of Military Appeals; 1969, U.S. District Court, District of Connecticut; 1972, U.S. Court of Appeals, 2nd Circuit; 1973, U.S. Supreme Court. *Education:* University of Pennsylvania (B.S., 1962); New York University (LL.B., 1965); National College of Advocacy, 1984. Member, Board of Representatives, Stamford, Connecticut, 1970-1972. State Chairman, National Organization for Legal Problems in Education, 1974. Author: "Primer on Products Liability," Connecticut Law Tribune, 1977; "How to Grab the Jury's Attention in a Medical Case," Trial Diplomacy Journal, 1981-1982; "What It Means to be a Plaintiff's Lawyer," Connecticut Law Tribune, 1988; "The Case for the Plaintiff," Miami Review, 1988. Contributor: The Association of Trial Lawyers of America tape series: "Learn from the Masters," 1982; "Wrongful Death Litigation," 1983. Lecturer: "Proof of Damages," 1983— and "Dramatic Techniques in the Courtroom," 1983—, National College of Advocacy; "Giant Lies Come From Giant Insurance Companies," Australian Labor Lawyers Association, Adelaide, Australia, 1991; "The Training of Advocates in America," International Bar Association, Argentina, September 1988; Netherlands 2000 "History of the Contingency Fee in U.S., South African Association of Personal Injury Lawyers," 2001 - Trial Techniques. Member (President, 1993-1995), National Board of Trial Advocacy, 1988—. *Member:* Connecticut Trial Lawyers Association (Treasurer, 1973-1974; Vice President, 1974-1975; President, 1975-1977); The Association of Trial Lawyers of America (Board Governors, 1979—Amicus Curiae Committee, 1987; Chair, 1988-1989; Ethics Committee, 1987; Co-Chair of ATLA International Lawyer Relations Committee, 1989-1990; Chairman, 1990, and Co-Chair, International Practice Section, 1991; ATLA Product Liability Advisory Committee, 1989-1990; ATLA Political Insight Conference Committee, 1989-1990; ATLA Insurance Bad Faith Litigation Group, 1989-1990; ATLA Constitution Challenge Committee, 1989-1990; ATLA, Chair, Organization and Home Office Committee, 1995-1997; Member, Judicial Independence Committee, 1999—); American Board of Trial Advocates (Advocate); International Society of Barristers; Association of Personal Injury Lawyers, London; Academy of Florida Trial Lawyers; Kentucky Academy of Trial Lawyers; New York State Trial Lawyers Association; Pennsylvania Trial Lawyers Association; Australian Plaintiff Lawyers Association. [Lt., Judge Advocate, U.S. Navy, 1965-1968]. (Certified as a Civil Trial Advocate by the National Board of Trial Advocacy). ***PRACTICE AREAS:*** Aviation Liability; Mass Torts; Commercial Litigation; Personal Injury. ***Email:*** rbieder@koskoff.com

JOEL H. LICHTENSTEIN, born New York City, N.Y., October 20, 1938; admitted to bar, 1964, New York; 1974, Connecticut; U.S. Court of Appeals, Second Circuit; U.S. District Court, Southern District of New York; U.S. Supreme Court; U.S. Court of Claims. *Education:* Boston University (B.A., 1960; LL.B., 1963). Member, Board of Examiners, National Board of Trial Advocacy. Past Chairman, Medical Legal Committee, Connecticut Bar Association. Past Board Member, Connecticut Trial Lawyers Association. *Member:* Bridgeport, Connecticut (Member, Judiciary Committee), New York State and American Bar Associations; Connecticut Trial Lawyers Association; New York State Trial Lawyers Association; Pennsylvania Trial Lawyers Association; The Association of Trial Lawyers of America (Faculty Member, Advanced College of Advocacy, 1979-1980; Chair, Birth Trauma Litigation Group, 1993-1996; Chair, Professional Negligence, 1998-1999). ***PRACTICE AREAS:*** Medical Malpractice; Hospital Liability; Health Maintenance Organizations; Health Care. ***Email:*** jlichtenstein@koskoff.com

JOHN D. JESSEP, born Valparaiso, Indiana, August 14, 1944; admitted to bar, 1972, Indiana; 1973, Connecticut. *Education:* Valparaiso University (B.A., 1969; J.D., 1972). Executive Editor, Valparaiso University Law Review, 1971-1972. Author: "Selective Pacifism, Retroactivity and H.R. 832," 6 Valparaiso University Law Review, 72, 1971. *Member:* Bridgeport, Danbury and Connecticut Bar Associations; The Association of Trial Lawyers of America; Connecticut Trial Lawyers Association. [U.S. Army, 1967-1969]. ***PRACTICE AREAS:*** Personal Injury; Medical Malpractice. ***Email:*** jjessep@koskoff.com

CHRISTOPHER D. BERNARD, born New York, N.Y., November 1, 1954; admitted to bar, 1979, Connecticut; 1980, U.S. District Court, District of Connecticut. *Education:* University of Miami (B.B.A., cum laude, 1975); University of Florida (J.D., with honors, 1979). Listed in Best Lawyers in America. Member, University of Florida Law Review, 1978-1979. Adjunct Faculty Member, Mattatuck Community College, 1984-1986. Attorney Trial Referee and Arbitrator, State of Connecticut Superior Court. Special Master, U.S. District Court, District of Connecticut. *Member:* Bridgeport, Connecticut and American Bar Associations; Connecticut Trial Lawyers Association (Vice President; Member, Executive, Public Relations, and Continuing Legal Education Committee); The Association of Trial Lawyers of America (Sustaining Member); American Board of Trial Advocates (Associate). Fellow: Connecticut Bar Foundation; American College of Trial Lawyers. (Certified as a Civil Trial Advocate by the National Board of Trial Advocacy). ***PRACTICE AREAS:*** Medical Malpractice; Personal Injury. ***Email:*** cbernard@koskoff.com

(This Listing Continued)

CAREY B. REILLY, born Norwalk, Connecticut, August 8, 1957; admitted to bar, 1982, Connecticut; 1983, U.S. District Court, District of Connecticut; 1984, U.S. District Court, Eastern District of New York; 1995, U.S. Court of Appeals, Second Circuit. *Education:* University of Connecticut (B.A., summa cum laude, University scholar, graduation with distinction in political science, 1979; J.D., 1982). Phi Beta Kappa. *Member:* Bridgeport and Connecticut Bar Associations; The Association of Trial Lawyers of America; Connecticut Trial Lawyers Association. ***PRACTICE AREAS:*** Medical Malpractice; Products Liability; Negligence. ***Email:*** creilly@koskoff.com

JAMES D. HORWITZ, born West Orange, New Jersey, June 19, 1957; admitted to bar, 1984, Connecticut; 1985, U.S. District Court, District of Connecticut. *Education:* Colgate University (B.A., 1979); Yeshiva University (J.D., 1984). Lecturer: "Negligent Infliction of Emotional Distress" 1990, 1991, CTLA; "HIV & Hemophilia: A Class Action" 1994; "Negotiation & Pretrials" 1995, Bridgeport Bar "Electromagnetic Fields" 1995, New Haven Bar; "Voir Dire," CTLA, 1995; "Pretrials," Bpt Bar, 1988, 1999; "Opening and Closing Statements," CTLA, 1996; "Brachial Plexus Injury," ATLA, 1998; "Technology in the Courtroom," CTLA, 1998, 1999; "Technology in Medical Malpractice Trials," National College of Advocacy, 1999; Creating Innovative Trial Exhibits," American Trial Lawyers Association, 2000; "Computerized Presentation of Evidence," American Innws of Court, 2000; "dealing With Daubert," National College of Advocacy, 2000. *Member:* Bridgeport (Chair, Civil Trial Section, 1993-1995; Medical/Legal Committee), Connecticut and American Bar Associations; The Association of Trial Lawyers of America; Connecticut Trial Lawyers Association; American Inns of Court. ***PRACTICE AREAS:*** Medical Malpractice. ***Email:*** jhorwitz@koskoff.com

VINCENT M. MUSTO, born Detroit, Michigan, November 27, 1950; admitted to bar, 1986, Connecticut; 1987, New York; 1988, U.S. District Court, District of Connecticut; 1989, U.S. Court of Appeals, Second Circuit; 1991, U.S. Supreme Court. *Education:* University of Michigan (B.S.C.E., Civil Engineering, cum laude, 1972); University of Illinois (MUP, Masters Degree in Urban Planning, 1977); City University of New York Law School at Queens College (J.D., 1986). Tau Beta Pi; Chi Epsilon. Recipient, American Institute of Planners Award, 1977. Lecturer: Premises Liability, Connecticut Trial Lawyers Association, 1995; Lead Paint Litigation, Stamford Norwalk Bar Association, Bridgeport Bar Association, 1995. Special Master, U.S. District Court, District of Connecticut. *Member:* Bridgeport and Connecticut Bar Associations; Connecticut Trial Lawyers Association; The Association of Trial Lawyers of America; Trial Lawyers for Public Justice. Fellow, Connecticut Bar Foundation. ***REPORTED CASES:*** Bridgeport Guardians v. City of Bridgeport, 933 F.2d 1140, cert. denied 502US 924; Paige v. St. Andrews Roman Catholic Church, 247 Conn. 24. ***PRACTICE AREAS:*** Products Liability; Toxic Substances; Motor Vehicle Accidents and Injuries; Premises Liability. ***Email:*** vmusto@koskoff.com

MICHAEL A. STRATTON, born New Haven, Connecticut, July 29, 1965; admitted to bar, 1990, Connecticut; 1991, U.S. District Court, District of Connecticut. *Education:* Colgate University (B.A., 1987); Boston University (J.D., 1990). Author: "Personal Injury," Section of the Connecticut Bar Deskbook, 1999—. President, Board of Directors, Brain Injury Association of Connecticut. President Elect, Connecticut Academy of Certified Trial Lawyers, 2000—. Presentations for the Connecticut Trial Lawyers Association: "The Trial Notebook and Demonstrative Evidence," 1997; "Inadequate Security Cases: Representing the Crime Victim," 1998; "How to Make $$$ on Low Impact Connective Tissue Cases," 1998; "Nuts and Bolts: Handling PI Cases from Beginning to End," 1998; "Learning About the Defendant Biennial Product Liability Seminar, CLA, 2000. Elected to House of Delegates, Connecticut Bar Association Representative for Eastern Fairfield County, 1995—. *Member:* Greater Bridgeport (Chairman, Public Relations, 1990-1994), Connecticut and American Bar Associations; The Association of Trial Lawyers of America; Connecticut Trial Lawyers Association (Member, Board of Governors; Chairman, Statewide Fund Development). (Certified as a Civil Trial Advocacy Specialist by the National Board of Trial Advocacy). ***REPORTED CASES:*** Donner v. Kearse 234 Conn. 660; Steeneck v. University of Bridgeport 235 Conn. 572. ***PRACTICE AREAS:*** Brain Injury; Toxic Torts; Motor Vehicle Accidents and Injuries; Product Liability; Securities; Fraud Litigation; Police Misconduct; Civil Rights. ***Email:*** mstratton@koskoff.com

ROSALIND J. KOSKOFF, born Leeds, England, April 3, 1941; admitted to bar, 1982, Connecticut; 1983, U.S. District Court, District of Connecticut. *Education:* Pembroke College, Brown University (B.A., 1962); Fairfield University (M. Ed., 1973); University of Bridgeport (J.D., magna cum laude, 1982). *Member:* Bridgeport and Connecticut Bar Associations; Connecticut Trial Lawyers Association; The Association of Trial Lawyers of America. ***PRACTICE AREAS:*** Personal Injury; Products Liability; Appellate Practice. ***Email:*** kkb@koskoff.com

---

REGINA M. DELUCA, born Jersey City, New Jersey, November 27, 1957; admitted to bar, 1985, Connecticut; 1986, U.S. District Court, District of Connecticut. *Education:* Rutgers University (B.S.N., summa cum laude, 1979);

(This Listing Continued)

University of Connecticut (J.D., 1985). Registered Nurse, Connecticut, 1981. *Member:* Bridgeport (Member, Medical Legal Committee), Connecticut (Member, Executive Committee, Health Law Section) and American (Member, Medicine and Law Committee) Bar Associations; Connecticut Trial Lawyers Association; Association of Nurse Attorneys; The Association of Trial Lawyers of America (Member, Committee on Courts, 1998—; Birth Trauma Litigation Group); Fellow, Connecticut Bar Foundation. ***PRACTICE AREAS:*** Medical Malpractice. ***Email:*** rdeluca@koskoff.com

GERTRUDE A. KIAUNIS, born Quincy, Massachusetts, April 29, 1953; admitted to bar, 1985, Connecticut; 1986, U.S. District Court, District of Connecticut; 1997, U.S. Supreme Court. *Education:* Boston College (B.S.N., magna cum laude, 1975); University of Connecticut (J.D., 1985). Registered Nurse, Connecticut, 1975. *Member:* Bridgeport, Connecticut and American Bar Associations; Connecticut Trial Lawyers Association; The Association of Trial Lawyers of America; The American Association of Nurse Attorneys (Charter Member, 1982-2000; Secretary and Director, Connecticut Chapter, 1992-1995); American Nurses Association. ***PRACTICE AREAS:*** Medical Malpractice; Products Liability. ***Email:*** tkiaunis@koskoff.com

JOSHUA D. KOSKOFF, born New Haven, Connecticut, August 10, 1966; admitted to bar, 1994, Connecticut; 1995, U.S. District Court, District of Connecticut. *Education:* Syracuse University (B.A., 1988); Suffolk University (J.D., 1994). *Member:* Bridgeport and Connecticut Bar Associations; Connecticut Trial Lawyers Association; The Association of Trial Lawyers of America (Second Circuit). ***REPORTED CASES:*** Danko v. Redway Enterprises Connecticut Supreme Court. ***PRACTICE AREAS:*** Medical Malpractice; Personal Injury. ***Email:*** jkoskoff@koskoff.com

JOEL THOMAS FAXON, born Brattleboro, Vermont, October 1, 1968; admitted to bar, 1994, Vermont; 1995, Connecticut; 1996, U.S. District Court, District of Connecticut; 1997, U.S. Court of Appeals, Second Circuit; 1999, U.S. District Court, District of Vermont. *Education:* Drew University (B.A., 1990); Vermont Law School (J.D., magna cum laude, 1994). *Member:* Bridgeport, Connecticut and Vermont Bar Associations; Connecticut Trial Lawyers Association; Vermont Trial Lawyers Association; The Association of Trial Lawyers of America. ***REPORTED CASES:*** Godno v. Cleatley, 163 Vt. 237, 656 A 2d 991 (1995); Holmberg v. Brent, 161 Vt. 153, 636 A 2d 333 (1993). ***PRACTICE AREAS:*** Securities; Civil Rights; Personal Injury; Products Liability; Aviation Law. ***Email:*** jfaxon@koskoff.com

ANTONIO PONVERT III, born Newport, Rhode Island, July 12, 1962; admitted to bar, 1990, Pennsylvania; 1991, U.S. District Court, Eastern District of Pennsylvania and U.S. District Court, Northern District of California; 1992, California; 1993, U.S. District Court, Eastern District of California and U.S. Court of Appeals, Ninth Circuit; 1997, Connecticut, U.S. District Court, District of Connecticut and U.S. Court of Appeals, Second Circuit; 2000, U.S. Court of Appeals, Sixth Circuit and Eleventh Circuit. *Education:* University of Rhode Island (B.S., 1987); University of Pennsylvania (J.D., 1990). Member, Order of the Coif. Law Clerk to Hon. Edmund V. Ludwig, U.S. District Court, Eastern District of Pennsylvania, 1990-1991. Associate: O'Melveny & Myers, 1991-1992; Law Offices of Amitai Schwartz, 1993-1997; Tyler, Cooper & Alcorn, 1997-1999. ***REPORTED CASES:*** Bitetto v. Harrington, 1997 U.S. App. Lexis 19957 (9th Cir. 1997); Bucholtz v. Belshe, 114 F.3d 923 (9th Cir. 1997); Jackson v. Mcintosh, 90 F.3d 330 (9th Cir. 1996); Dalzin v. Belshe, 993 F.Supp. 732 (N.D.Cal. 1997). ***PRACTICE AREAS:*** Civil Rights; Class Actions; Criminal Appeals. ***Email:*** aponvert@koskoff.com

OF COUNSEL

JAMES WU, born New Haven, Connecticut, July 27, 1949; admitted to bar, 1975, Connecticut and U.S. District Court, District of Connecticut. *Education:* Trinity College (B.A., 1971); University of Connecticut (J.D., 1975). Member, Eminent Domain Advisory Committee, Law Revision Commission, Connecticut Legislature, 1982-1983. Connecticut Attorney Trial Referee, 1986-1992. *Member:* Waterbury, Litchfield, Danbury, Connecticut (Chairman, Family Law Section, 1994-1995; Member: Executive Committee) and American (Member, Sections on Family Law; Litigation; Chairman, Trial Techniques Committee, Family Law Section, 1991-1992) Bar Associations; Connecticut Trial Lawyers Association. ***PRACTICE AREAS:*** Personal Injury; Family Law; Tax Appeals; Condemnations.

ARTHUR C. LASKE, III

BRIDGEPORT, CONNECTICUT

(See Trumbull)

Personal Injury, Contract Disputes, Criminal, Civil Trial Practice, Municipal Liability, Product Liability, Arbitration and Uninsured/Underinsured Motorists.

LEV & BERLIN, P.C.

BRIDGEPORT, CONNECTICUT

(See Norwalk)

Corporation, Securities, Commercial and Investment Banking, Tax, Real Estate, Estate Planning, Intellectual Property and Civil Litigation in all State and Federal Courts.

JACK S. LIPSON

BRIDGEPORT, CONNECTICUT

(See Westport)

Real Estate, Mortgage Finance, Estate Planning.

MAHER & MURTHA, LLC

528 CLINTON AVENUE
P.O. BOX 901
BRIDGEPORT, CONNECTICUT 06601
Telephone: 203-367-2700
Fax: 203-335-0589
Email: maherandmurtha@snet.net

General Insurance Defense Practice including Negligence, Malpractice, Products liability, Errors and Omissions, Worker's Compensation, Municipal Liability, Law Enforcement Liability and Subrogation Law, Trials and Appeals, State and Federal.

JAMES J. MAHER (1931-1998).

THOMAS M. MURTHA, born Hartford, Connecticut, August 20, 1955; admitted to bar, 1981, Connecticut and U.S. District Court, District of Connecticut; 1992, U.S. Court of Appeals, Second Circuit. *Education:* Fairfield University (B.A., 1978); University of Bridgeport (J.D., 1981). Delta Theta Phi. *Member:* Bridgeport, Connecticut and American Bar Associations; Connecticut Defense Lawyers Association; Defense Research Institute. ***PRACTICE AREAS:*** Defense Litigation; Errors and Omissions; Construction Litigation; Municipal Liability. ***Email:*** maherandmurtha@snet.net

GEOFFREY L. SQUITIERO, born Milford, Connecticut, July 4, 1960; admitted to bar, 1985, Pennsylvania; 1988, Connecticut and U.S. District Court, District of Connecticut; 1992, U.S. Court of Appeals, Second Circuit. *Education:* Tulane University of Louisiana (B.S.M., 1982); University of Toledo (J.D., 1985). *Member:* Bridgeport, Connecticut and American Bar Associations; Connecticut Defense Lawyers Association; Defense Research Institute. ***PRACTICE AREAS:*** Litigation; Subrogation; Products Liability; Municipal Liability; Law Enforcement Liability. ***Email:*** maherandmurtha@snet.net

EDWARD V. WALSH, born Queens, New York, October 17, 1955; admitted to bar, 1981, Massachusetts; 1982, New York; 1991, Connecticut and U.S. District Court, District of Connecticut. *Education:* Fairfield University (B.A., 1977); University of Bridgeport (J.D., 1980); Boston University (LL.M., 1981). Trial Attorney, New York City Transit Authority, 1982-1987. *Member:* Connecticut and American Bar Associations; The Association of Trial Lawyers of America. ***PRACTICE AREAS:*** Litigation; Federal Litigation; Subrogation. ***Email:*** maherandmurtha@snet.net

JOHN C. TURNER, JR., born New London, Connecticut, September 18, 1962; admitted to bar, 1999, Connecticut and New York. *Education:* Utica College of Syracuse University (B.A., 1984); Quinnipiac College (J.D., 1998). Recipient, Distinguished Academic Achievement Award, Communications Law, 1998. *Member:* Bridgeport, Connecticut and American Bar Associations. ***PRACTICE AREAS:*** Defense Litigation; Subrogation. ***Email:*** maherandmurth@snet.net

MARK A. PERKINS, born Nashua, New Hampshire, September 21, 1963; admitted to bar, 1998, Connecticut. *Education:* University of New Hampshire (B.S., Political Science, 1986); Quinnipiac School of Law (J.D., 1998). *Member:* Bridgeport, Connecticut and American Bar Associations. ***PRACTICE AREAS:*** Insurance Defense. ***Email:*** maherandmurtha@snet.net

REPRESENTATIVE CLIENTS: Boy Scouts of America, Inc.; CNA Insurance Company; American States Insurance Company; Domino's Pizza, Inc.; Empire Insurance Group; Eveready Insurance Company; Liberty Mutual Insurance Company; Maryland Casualty Company; Peerless Insurance Company; Scott-Wetzel Services, Inc.; The Travelers Insurance Companies; Western World Insurance Company; Zurich Insurance Companies; Amgro Insurance Company; Terminix, International Co., L.P.; Mass. Corp.; Lancer Claims Service, Inc.; Essex Insurance Co.; Main Mutual Fire Insurance Co.; Legion Insurance Co.; Gallagher Bassett Services, Inc.; Frontier Insurance Co.; Ward - THG; Gulf Specialty Claims; Nationwide Mutual Insurance Co.; Harco National Insurance Co.; Providian Property & Casualty Insurance Co.; AON Risk Services; American International Group; AIG Specialty Auto; Zurich Canada; John Deere Transportation Services; Home Indemnity Co.; Risk Enterprise Management Co.; Safeco Ins. Co.; Sentry Ins. Co.; CIRMA; RCA Ins. Co.; Specialty Claims Mgmt.; Georgia Casualty & Surety; Markel Ins. Co.;

(This Listing Continued)

Crawford & Co.; Wilson & Fitzgerald; American Safety Risk Litigation Group; Performance Claims Service; Carolina Casualty Insurance Co.; Paul Davis Restoration, Inc.
REFERENCE: Hudson United Bank.

MAHER AND WILLIAMS

BRIDGEPORT, CONNECTICUT

(See Fairfield)

General and Federal Practice. Workers Compensation, Probate, Insurance, Subrogation, Estate Planning and Administrative Law. Trials.

MICHAEL G. MARONICH

180 FAIRFIELD AVENUE
BRIDGEPORT, CONNECTICUT 06604
Telephone: 203-336-1595
Fax: 203-331-1802
Email: mgmaronich@aol.com

Civil Litigation, Negligence and Personal Injury, Land Title Consulting & Litigation, Probate and Business Law.

MICHAEL G. MARONICH, born Bridgeport, Connecticut, June 21, 1955; admitted to bar, 1980, Connecticut; 1981, Federal District; 1989, U.S. Court of Appeals, Second Circuit. *Education:* Boston College (B.A., 1977); Vermont Law School (J.D., 1980). *Member:* Connecticut Bar Associations; Connecticut Trial Lawyers Association; The Federalist Society for Law and Public Policy Studies.

MARTIN, LUCAS & CHIOFFI, LLP

BRIDGEPORT, CONNECTICUT

(See Stamford)

Business Law, Corporate Finance, Mergers and Acquisitions, Internet Law, Venture Capital, Commercial and Employment Litigation; Securities, Employment, Commercial Litigation, Real Estate, Commercial Leasing, Estate and Tax Planning, Estate Settlement and Trust Administration.

LAW OFFICES OF
ROBERT K. MARZIK, P.C.

BRIDGEPORT, CONNECTICUT

(See Stratford)

General Practice, Civil Litigation, Admiralty, Maritime, Aviation, Probate and Real Estate Law.

McGOVERN & ASSOCIATES

BRIDGEPORT, CONNECTICUT

(See Greenwich)

General Commercial Practice. Corporate (Foreign and Domestic), Mergers and Acquisitions, Securities, Venture Capital, Taxation, Litigation in all Courts. International, Joint Ventures, Admiralty, Sports, Commercial and Residential Real Estate Law. Estates and Trusts.

MEEHAN, MEEHAN & GAVIN

Established in 1975
76 LYON TERRACE
BRIDGEPORT, CONNECTICUT 06604
Telephone: 203-333-1888
Fax: 203-331-0107
Email: thefirm@meehanlaw.com
URL: http://www.meehanlaw.com

Criminal Law, Personal Injury, Medical Malpractice, Dental Malpractice, Legal Malpractice, Wrongful Death, Labor Law, Commercial Litigation, Appellate.

RICHARD T. MEEHAN, SR., born 1923; admitted to bar, 1960, Connecticut, U.S. District Court, District of Connecticut and U.S. Court of Appeals, Second Circuit. *Education:* University of Bridgeport (B.A.); University of Connecticut (LL.B.). Fellow, American College of Trial Lawyers. ***PRACTICE AREAS:*** Criminal Law; Personal Injury; Labor Law. ***Email:*** thefirm@meehanlaw.com

RICHARD T. MEEHAN, JR., born 1949; admitted to bar, 1974, Connecticut, U.S. District Court, District of Connecticut, U.S. Court of Appeals, Second

(This Listing Continued)

Circuit and U.S. Supreme Court. *Education:* University of Notre Dame (B.A., 1970); University of Connecticut (J.D., 1974). Adjunct Professor of Law, Quinnipiac College School of Law. (Certified as a Criminal Trial Specialist by the National Board of Trial Advocacy). ***PRACTICE AREAS:*** Criminal Law; Drug Crimes; Felonies; White Collar Crime; Personal Injury Law; Automobile Accidents and Injuries; Malpractice; Wrongful Death; Labor Law; Commercial; Appellate. ***Email:*** rtmjr@meehanlaw.com

EDWARD J. GAVIN, born Astoria, New York, April 26, 1961; admitted to bar, 1990, Connecticut, New York and U.S. District Court, District of Connecticut. *Education:* State University of New York at Plattsburgh (B.S., 1983); University of Bridgeport (J.D., 1990). *Member:* Bridgeport, Connecticut and American Bar Associations; Connecticut Criminal Defense Lawyers Association; Connecticut Trial Lawyers Association. ***PRACTICE AREAS:*** Criminal Law; Felonies; Drug Crimes; Driving While Intoxicated; Personal Injury; Labor Law; Real Estate. ***Email:*** ejg@meehanlaw.com

ASSOCIATES

MICHAEL T. MEEHAN, born Bridgeport, Connecticut, October 5, 1971; admitted to bar, 1996, Connecticut; 2000, U.S. District Court, District of Connecticut. *Education:* University of Hartford (B.S., 1993); Quinnipiac College (J.D., 1996). ***Email:*** mtm@meehanlaw.com

ROSEMARIE TALIO WEBER, born White Plains, New York, January 1, 1969; admitted to bar, 1999, Connecticut; 2000, New York; U.S. District Court, District of Connecticut. *Education:* University of Pennsylvania (B.A., 1991); Quinnipiac College School of Law (J.D., 1999). ***Email:*** rtw@meehanlaw.com

LAWRENCE J. MERLY

Established in 1964

76 LYON TERRACE

BRIDGEPORT, CONNECTICUT 06604-4022

Telephone: 203-333-1353

Fax: 203-332-7984

Email: lawrencemerly@yahoo.com

General Civil Practice before State Courts. Personal Injury, Medical Malpractice and Workers Compensation Law. Trials and Appeals.

LAWRENCE J. MERLY, born Bridgeport, Connecticut, March 11, 1939; admitted to bar, 1964, Connecticut and U.S. District Court, District of Connecticut; 1968, U.S. Court of Appeals, Second Circuit; 1971, U.S. Supreme Court. *Education:* Fairfield University (B.S.S., 1961); University of Connecticut (J.D., 1964). State Representative from 130th District (Bridgeport), 1969-1970; Chairman: Sub-Committee of Judiciary Committee on Negligence Law and No-Fault Insurance, 1969; Interim Committee on Negligence Law and No-Fault Insurance, 1969-1970; Legal Counsel, Law Committee, 1971; Counsel to Senate Majority, 1972, Legislature of State of Connecticut. Member, 1981-1986 and President, 1981-1983, Bridgeport Civil Service Commission. City Attorney, City of Bridgeport, 1986-1989. *Member:* Bridgeport (Member: Committees on: Continuing Legal Education, 1968-1969; Criminal Law and Procedure, 1971-1972) and Connecticut (Member, Committee on the Administration of Criminal Justice, 1969-1972) Bar Associations; Connecticut Trial Lawyers Association (Member, Board of Governors, 1969-1970); The Association of Trial Lawyers of America. ***REPORTED CASES:*** Pokorny v. Getta's Garage, 219 Conn. 439 (1991); Pokorny v. Getta's Garage, 22 Conn. App. 539 (1990); Marsala v. Bridgeport, 15 Conn. App. 323 (1988); Blue Sky Bar, Inc. v. Stratford, 203 Conn. 14 (1987); Stamford Apartments Co. v. Stamford, 203 Conn. 586 (1987); Blue Sky Bar, Inc. v. Stratford, 4 Conn. App. 261 (1985); Caracansi v. Caracansi, 4 Conn. App. 645 (1985); Grynkewich v. McGinley, 3 Conn. App. 541 (1985); Arseniadis v. Arseniadis, 2 Conn. App. 239 (1984); Norwalk Vault Co. of Bpt., Inc. v. Mt. Grove Cemetery, 180 Conn. 680 (1980); Marsala v. Valve Corporation of America, 157 Conn. 362 (1969); Pascack Valley Bank & Trust Co. v. Ritar Ford Sales, Inc. 6 Conn. Cir. Ct. 646 (1972). Pascack Valley Bank & Trust Co. v. Ritar Ford, Inc. 6 Conn Cir Ct. 489.; Frillici v. Westport, 231 Conn. 418, December, 1994; Eisenbach v. Downey, 45 Conn. App. 165 (1997). ***PRACTICE AREAS:*** Personal Injury Law; Medical Malpractice; Civil Litigation; Trials and Appeals Law.

REFERENCES: Hudson United Bank; First Union Securities.

MURPHY AND KARPIE, LLC

350 FAIRFIELD AVENUE, SUITE 408

BRIDGEPORT, CONNECTICUT 06604

Telephone: 203-333-0177

Fax: 203-333-8475

Email: murphykarpie@aol.com

General Civil Practice before State and Federal Courts. Insurance Defense, Personal Injury, Negligence, Products Liability, Medical Malpractice, Professional Liability, Employment Litigation, Commercial and Civil Rights Law, Appellate Practice, Toxic Torts.

(This Listing Continued)

KEVIN R. MURPHY, born South Bend, Indiana, May 10, 1949; admitted to bar, 1977, Connecticut and U.S. District Court, District of Connecticut; 1979, U.S. Court of Appeals, 2nd Circuit. *Education:* Dartmouth College (A.B., 1971), Rufus Choate Scholar; University of Connecticut (J.D., with honors, 1977). *Member:* Greater Bridgeport and Connecticut Bar Associations; Connecticut Defense Lawyers Association; Defense Research Institute. ***PRACTICE AREAS:*** Personal Injury Law; Litigation; Products Liability Law; Insurance Defense Law; Medical Malpractice.

KAREN L. KARPIE, born Bridgeport, Connecticut, July 5, 1952; admitted to bar, 1977, Connecticut and U.S. District Court, District of Connecticut; 1979, U.S. Court of Appeals, 2nd Circuit. *Education:* University of Connecticut, (B.A., magna cum laude, 1974; J.D., with honors, 1977). Phi Beta Kappa. *Member:* Greater Bridgeport and Connecticut Bar Associations; Connecticut Defense Lawyers Association. ***PRACTICE AREAS:*** Litigation; Insurance Defense Law; Medical Malpractice; Employment; Appellate Practice; Products Liability.

JOHN W. MILLS, born Norwalk, Connecticut, September 23, 1964; admitted to bar, 1990, Connecticut; 1991, New York; U.S. District Court, District of Connecticut; U.S. Court of Appeals, Second Circuit; U.S. Supreme Court. *Education:* University of Connecticut (B.A., cum laude, 1986); Pace University School of Law (J.D., 1990). Phi Alpha Theta; Pi Sigma Alpha. Recipient, American Jurisprudence Book Award for Environmental Law. *Member:* The Association of the Bar of the City of New York; Connecticut and New York State Bar Associations; Connecticut Defense Lawyers Association. ***PRACTICE AREAS:*** Litigation; Insurance Defense; Toxic Torts; Appellate Practice.

MICHAEL CONNELLY, born Long Branch, New Jersey, June 25, 1971; admitted to bar, 1996, Connecticut. *Education:* Catholic University of America (B.A., 1993; J.D., 1996). *Member:* Bridgeport, Connecticut and American Bar Associations. ***PRACTICE AREAS:*** Insurance Defense; Litigation.

MARIA A. CAHILL, born Bridgeport, Connecticut, September 14, 1964; admitted to bar, 2000, Connecticut. *Education:* Charter Oak State College (B.A., with highest honors, 1997); Quinnipiac University (J.D., with honors, 2000). Participant, Moot Court Intramural Competition, 1998; Recipient, Best Oral Advocate, 1998; Deans Award, 2000. ***PRACTICE AREAS:*** Insurance Defense; Litigation.

REPRESENTATIVE CLIENTS: State Farm Insurance Company; Middlesex Mutual Assurance Company; Nationwide; Safeco Insurance Companies of America; Sentry Claims Service; Great American Insurance Companies; Fireman's Fund Insurance Companies; Electric Insurance Company; Canal Insurance Co.; National Chiropractic Mutual Insurance Co.; AIG; Atlanta Casualty Companies; Markel American Insurance Company; Ohio Casualty Group.

O'DONNELL, MCDONALD AND CREGEEN, L.L.C.

BRIDGEPORT, CONNECTICUT

(See Fairfield)

General Practice. Trials in all Courts. Probate, Real Estate, Zoning and Administrative Law, Environmental.

CHARLES D. O'HARA, JR.

2145 NORTH AVENUE

BRIDGEPORT, CONNECTICUT 06604-2412

Telephone: 203-333-3434; 203- 929-8831

Fax: 203-368-1055

Email: coharajr@msn.com

Personal Injury, Real Estate, Wills, Probate, Divorce, Bankruptcy.

CHARLES D. O'HARA, JR., born 1969; admitted to bar, 1994, Connecticut; 1996, U.S. District Court, District of Connecticut. *Education:* Fairfield University (B.A., 1991); Quinnipiac College (J.D., 1994). ***PRACTICE AREAS:*** Personal Injury; Real Estate; Wills; Probate; Divorce; Bankruptcy.

PEARL PROFESSIONAL CORPORATION

BRIDGEPORT, CONNECTICUT

(See Westport)

Business, Corporate and Commercial, Aviation, Tax, Commercial Real Estate.

PEPE & HAZARD LLP

BRIDGEPORT, CONNECTICUT

(See Southport)

Commercial, Construction, Corporations, Taxation, Finance and Real Estate, Commercial and Asset Based Finance, Environmental Health/Safety, Fidelity and Surety, Securities, Labor/Employment and Education, Municipal, Administrative, Health Care, Intellectual Property, Patent, International Trade, Estate Planning, Probate, White Collar Crime, and Bankruptcy. Trials in all Courts.

PIAZZA & PICKEL

BRIDGEPORT, CONNECTICUT

(See Stamford)

Trials and Appeals in State and Federal Courts, Negligence, Medical Malpractice, Divorce and Personal Injury Law, Wrongful Death, Legal Malpractice, Child Custody, Automobile Accidents, Product Liability, Adoption, Family Law.

PULLMAN & COMLEY, L.L.C.

Established in 1919

(Formerly Pullman, Comley, Bradley & Reeves)

850 MAIN STREET
P.O. BOX 7006
BRIDGEPORT, CONNECTICUT 06601-7006
Telephone: 203-330-2000
Telecopier: 203-576-8888
URL: http://www.pullcom.com

Hartford, Connecticut Office: 90 State House Square. Telephone: 860-424-4300. Telecopier: 860-424-4370.
New Haven, Connecticut Office: One Century Tower, 265 Church Street. Telephone: 203-773-3006. Telecopier: 203-776-7075.
Simsbury, Connecticut Office: 720 Hopmeadow Street. Telephone: 860-651-9348. Fax: 860-651-1431.
Southport, Connecticut Office: 200 Pequot Avenue, P.O. Box 510. Telephone: 203-254-5000. Telecopier: 203-254-5070.
Stamford, Connecticut Office: 350 Bedford Street. Telephone: 203-324-5000. Telecopier: 203-363-8659.

General Practice including Administrative, Antitrust, Banking, Bankruptcy and Creditors Rights, Bonds, Business and Commercial, Corporate, Education, Employee Benefits, Environmental, Hospital and Health Care, Labor and Employment, Municipal Finance, Real Estate, Securities, Tax, Trusts and Estates, and Zoning. Energy and Utilities, Litigation in all Courts.

JOHN S. PULLMAN (1871-1943).
ARTHUR M. COMLEY (1883-1969).
J. KENNETH BRADLEY (1903-1969).
WILLIAM REEVES (1906-1967).

MEMBERS OF FIRM

ELIZABETH J. AUSTIN, born New York, N.Y., February 19, 1957; admitted to bar, 1983, Texas, Nebraska and U.S. District Court, Northern District of Texas; 1988, U.S. District Court, Eastern District of Texas; 1989, U.S. District Court, Western District of Texas and District of Connecticut; 1990, Connecticut; 1999, U.S. District Court, Southern District of New York. *Education:* University of Nebraska (B.A., 1979; J.D., 1982). *Member:* Bridgeport (Chairperson, Commercial Law Committee), Connecticut (Chair, Commercial Law and Bankruptcy Section), Nebraska State and American Bar Associations; State Bar of Texas; Commercial Law League of America; American Bankruptcy Institute; International Women's Insolvency and Restructuring Confederation; Women's Bankruptcy Bar Association (Founding Member; Executive Committee Member). (Also at New Haven, Hartford and Stamford Offices). ***PRACTICE AREAS:*** Insolvency Law; Bankruptcy Litigation; Commercial Litigation. ***Email:*** EA@PULLCOM.COM

RAYMOND E. BALDWIN, JR., born New Haven, Connecticut, August 10, 1927; admitted to bar, 1956, Connecticut. *Education:* Kent School; Williams College (B.A., 1950); Yale University (LL.B., 1956). Phi Delta Phi. *Member:* Bridgeport, Connecticut and American Bar Associations; National Association of Bond Lawyers. [USNR, 1945-1946, 1950-1953]. (Also at Southport Office). ***PRACTICE AREAS:*** Public Finance; Bond Finance; Trusts and Estates; Real Estate. ***Email:*** REB@PULLCOM.COM

COLLIN P. BARON, born Neptune, New Jersey, June 27, 1947; admitted to bar, 1973, Virginia; 1974, Connecticut. *Education:* University of Virginia (B.A., 1969); George Washington University (J.D., 1973). *Member:* Bridgeport, Connecticut, Virginia and American Bar Associations; American Health Lawyers Association. ***PRACTICE AREAS:*** Health Care Law; Banking Law; Corporate Law. ***Email:*** CPB@PULLCOM.COM

DEBORAH S. BRECK, born Aurora, Colorado, April 14, 1953; admitted to bar, 1983, Connecticut; 2000, U.S. Tax Court. *Education:* Kingswood-Oxford School; Syracuse University; Southern Connecticut State University (B.A., 1975); University of Connecticut (J.D., with honors, 1982). Associate Editor, Connecticut Law Review, 1981-1982. *Member:* Bridgeport, Connecticut (Member: Estates and Probate Section; Legal Problems of the Elderly Section) and American (Member, Real Property, Probate and Trust Law Section) Bar Associations. (Also at Stamford and Southport Offices). ***PRACTICE AREAS:*** Estates and Trusts; Elder Law; Trust and Probate Litigation. ***Email:*** DSB@PULLCOM.COM

CHARLES K. CAMPBELL, JR., born Evanston, Illinois, May 13, 1949; admitted to bar, 1976, Connecticut. *Education:* Brown University (A.B., 1971); Vanderbilt University (J.D., 1976). Associate Editor, Vanderbilt Law Review, 1975-1976. *Member:* Greenwich, Connecticut (Officer, Executive Committee, Conservation and Environmental Quality Section, 1980-1991) and American Bar Associations. (Resident at Stamford Office). ***PRACTICE AREAS:*** Environmental Law; Land Use Planning; Real Estate Law. ***Email:*** CKC@PULLCOM.COM

FRANK B. CLEARY, born Stamford, Connecticut, April 9, 1947; admitted to bar, 1973, Connecticut. *Education:* Princeton University (B.A., 1970); Fordham University (J.D., 1973). *Member:* Bridgeport, Connecticut and American (Member, Sections on: Tax and Commercial Law) Bar Associations; National Association of Bond Lawyers. ***PRACTICE AREAS:*** Taxation; Public Finance; Commercial Law; State and Local Government Law. ***Email:*** FBC@PULLCOM.COM

SHEILA ANNE DENTON, born Youngstown, Ohio, December 3, 1965; admitted to bar, 1992, Connecticut; 1993, U.S. District Court, District of Connecticut; 1999, U.S. Court of Appeals, Second Circuit, U.S. District Court, Eastern and Southern Districts of New York, and U.S. Supreme Court. *Education:* Sacred Heart University (B.S., 1989); Western New England College School of Law (J.D., 1992). Member, Board of Directors, American Red Cross for Southeastern Fairfield County, 1999—. Member, Board of Directors, Women's Leadership Council, 1996—. Member, Board of Directors, Downtown Cabaret Theatre, 1998—. *Member:* Greater Bridgeport (Member, Sections on: Litigation; Commercial Law), Connecticut (Member, Sections on: Federal Practice; Litigation; Commercial Law; Bankruptcy) and American (Member, Litigation Section) Bar Associations; The Association of Trial Lawyers of America; Connecticut Trial Lawyers Association; Raymond E. Baldwin American Inns of Court. ***PRACTICE AREAS:*** Litigation; Bankruptcy. ***Email:*** SXD@PULLCOM.COM

JAMES G. DOWLING, JR., born Coronado, California, May 31, 1952; admitted to bar, 1978, Connecticut and U.S. District Court, District of Connecticut; 1984, U.S. Supreme Court. *Education:* Tufts University (B.A., 1975); Suffolk University (J.D., 1978). Member, 1976-1978 and Editor, 1977-1978, Suffolk Law Review. Author: "Contingent Interest In Executory Contract Is A Right To Property To Which Federal Tax Lien Can Attach," 11 Suffolk Law Review 1400, 1977; "Impeachment of Witness's General Credibility By Use Of Juvenile Record," 11 Suffolk Law Review 590, 1977. *Member:* Connecticut (Member, Real Estate Law Section) and American (Member: Real Property, Probate and Trust Law Section, Committee on Mortgages and Other Debt Financing, Committee on Foreclosures and Related Remedies; Corporation, Banking and Business Law Section; Forum Committee on the Construction Industry, 1982—) Bar Associations; Association of Commercial Finance Attorneys; The Connecticut Mortgage Bankers Association; First American Title Insurance Corporation (Member, Connecticut Advisory Board). (Also at Hartford Office). ***PRACTICE AREAS:*** Real Estate Law; Commercial Transactions. ***Email:*** JXD@PULLCOM.COM

LAWRENCE J. GOLDEN, born Norwalk, Connecticut, February 9, 1947; admitted to bar, 1973, Connecticut; 1985, U.S. District Court, District of Connecticut. *Education:* University of Virginia (B.A., 1969; J.D., 1973). Phi Beta Kappa. Town Councilman Coventry, Connecticut, 1989-1991. Author: *Equitable Distribution of Property,* Shepard's/McGraw-Hill, 1983. Member, Board of Education, Coventry, Connecticut, 1999—. (Resident at Hartford Office). ***PRACTICE AREAS:*** Energy; Environmental; Public Utility; Land Use; Litigation. ***Email:*** LJG@PULLCOM.COM

IRVE J. GOLDMAN, born Scranton, Pennsylvania, May 31, 1958; admitted to bar, 1985, Pennsylvania and U.S. District Court, Eastern District of Pennsylvania; 1988, Connecticut and U.S. District Court, District of Connecticut; 1990, U.S. District Court, Southern District of New York. *Education:* Temple University (B.B.A., Finance, 1980); Western New England College (J.D., 1984). Member, Law Review, 1983-1984. Author: "What's Left of Lien Stripping in Bankruptcy," Volume 69, Number 6, Conn. B.J. 474 (December 1995); "Significant Bankruptcy Decisions in the Second Circuit," 15 Quinnipiac L. Rev. 497 (Winter 1997); "Some Recent Words to the Wise on Bankruptcy Retainers," 11 Connecticut Lawyer 4 (August/September 2000). Co-

(This Listing Continued)

Author: "Survey of Bankruptcy Cases of Note Decided by the Second Circuit, July 31, 1998 - December 1998" (Summer 2000). *Member:* Bridgeport (Member, Commercial Law Committee) and Connecticut (Executive Committee, Commercial Law and Bankruptcy Section) Bar Associations; American Bankruptcy Institute. (Certified Specialist, Business Bankruptcy Law, American Board of Bankruptcy Certification). ***PRACTICE AREAS:*** Commercial Bankruptcy; Personal Bankruptcy; Bankruptcy Litigation; Commercial Litigation. ***Email:*** IJG@PULLCOM.COM

NANCY A. D. HANCOCK, born Watertown, New York; admitted to bar, 1984, Connecticut. *Education:* Princeton University (A.B., magna cum laude, 1981); Cornell University (J.D., 1984). Bench Brief Editor, Cornell Moot Court Board, 1983-1984. *Member:* Bridgeport, Connecticut and American Bar Associations. ***PRACTICE AREAS:*** Venture Capital; Finance; Corporate Law; Securities Law; International Business Law; Tax Law; Banking Law. ***Email:*** NADH@PULLCOM.COM

DAVID O. JACKSON, born San Juan, Puerto Rico, June 13, 1936; admitted to bar, 1962, Connecticut. *Education:* Swarthmore College (A.B., with honors in social sciences, 1958); Harvard University (LL.B., 1961). Co-Author: "Connecticut Condominium Manual," 1972. Construction Lending, 1974; Workouts, 1976; Shopping Centers, 1979; Sale, Purchase and Financing of Commercial Real Estate, 1987; Dealing with Troubled Properties, 1989. Chairman, CLE Seminar on Condominiums, 1977 and 1980; Residential Real Property Transactions, 1981. Listed, "The Best Lawyers in America," 1983, 1987, 1989-1990, 1991-1992, 1993-1994. *Member:* Bridgeport, Connecticut (Secretary, 1972-1974 and Chairman, 1974-1976, Executive Committee, Real Property Section) and American Bar Associations; American College of Real Estate Lawyers. ***PRACTICE AREAS:*** Real Estate Law. ***Email:*** DOJ@PULLCOM.COM

GEORGE J. KASPER, born Suffern, New York, August 2, 1959; admitted to bar, 1987, New York; 1989, U.S. Tax Court; 1999, Connecticut. *Education:* Walsh University (B.A., cum laude, 1981); Ohio Northern University (J.D., 1985); Villanova University (LL.M. in Taxation). Author, "1996 Pension Legislation: The 'Simplification' of 401(k) Plans," CT Lawyer, February, 1997. *Member:* Bridgeport, New York State and American (Member, Tax Section, Employee Benefits Committee, 1999—) Bar Associations. ***PRACTICE AREAS:*** Employee Benefits; Tax; Corporate. ***Email:*** GJK@PULLCOM.COM

MICHAEL A. KURS, born Manhasset, New York, June 26, 1955; admitted to bar, 1980, Georgia; 1981, U.S. District Court, Northern and Southern Districts of Georgia; Supreme Court of Georgia and Court of Appeals of Georgia; 1982, New York; 1987, U.S. Court of Appeals, Eleventh Circuit; 1988, Connecticut; 1995, Mashantucket Pequot Tribal Court. *Education:* Yale University (B.A., 1977); Antioch School of Law (J.D., 1980). Member: Connecticut State Board of Mental Health, (1990-1995); North Central Connecticut Regional Mental Health Board (1988-1997) and Hartford Mental Health Council. *Member:* Connecticut, New York State and American Bar Associations; American Health Lawyers Association. (Also at Hartford Office). ***PRACTICE AREAS:*** Health Care Law; Litigation and Administrative Law; Education Law; Antitrust Law. ***Email:*** MAK@PULLCOM.COM

NANCY DEFONCE LAPERA, born Bridgeport, Connecticut, August 27, 1952; admitted to bar, 1982, Connecticut and U.S. District Court, District of Connecticut. *Education:* Wells College (B.A., cum laude, distinction in English, 1974); Syracuse University College of Law (J.D., 1980). Survey Editor, Syracuse Law Review, 1979-1980. Listed in The Best Lawyers in America. *Member:* Bridgeport, Connecticut and American Bar Associations. ***PRACTICE AREAS:*** Employee Benefits Law. ***Email:*** NDL@PULLCOM.COM

MICHAEL N. LAVELLE, born Chelsea, Massachusetts, March 10, 1946; admitted to bar, 1975, Connecticut and U.S. District Court, District of Connecticut and U.S. Court of Appeals, Second Circuit; 1980, U.S. Supreme Court; 1981, Massachusetts. *Education:* Harvard University (A.B., 1968); Boston University (J.D., 1975). Author: "Wrongful Discharge in Connecticut: Existing and Potential Causes of Action," 60 Conn. Bar Journal 194 (1986); "Recent Developments in Wrongful Discharge," 65 Conn. Bar Journal 193 (1991). Appointed Special Master, U.S. District Court, District of Connecticut, 1999. *Member:* Bridgeport, Connecticut and American Bar Associations. [1st Lt., USMC, 1968-1972]. ***PRACTICE AREAS:*** Labor Law; Zoning Law; Municipal Law. ***Email:*** MNL@PULLCOM.COM

JOSEPH M. LODATO, born Greenwich, Connecticut, July 12, 1964; admitted to bar, 1989, Connecticut. *Education:* Georgetown University (B.S.B.A., 1986); Georgetown University Law Center (J.D., 1989). Board of Directors, Sound View Community Media, Inc.; Board of Directors and Vice President, Business Legal Services, Inc. *Member:* Bridgeport, Stamford/Norwalk Regional (Co-Chair, Business Law Committee), Connecticut and American Bar Associations. (Resident at Stamford Office). ***PRACTICE AREAS:*** Corporate Law; Partnership Law; Commercial Law; Nonprofit and Charitable Organizations; Securities Law. ***Email:*** JML@PULLCOM.COM

THOMAS F. MAXWELL, JR., born New York, N.Y., January 7, 1941; admitted to bar, 1966, Connecticut; 1967, U.S. District Court, District of Connecticut; 1971, U.S. Court of Appeals, 2nd Circuit; 1975, U.S. Supreme Court.

(This Listing Continued)

Education: University of Notre Dame (B.A., 1962); University of Alabama (J.D., 1965). Assistant U.S. Attorney, District of Connecticut, 1970-1976. Police Commissioner, City of Bridgeport, 1985-1987. Dept. Advocate Police Commission, City of Bridgeport, 1987-1991. Attorney Trial Referee, Superior Court Judicial District of Fairfield, 1998—. Member, Grievance Panel, Stamford/Norwalk Judicial District, 1998—. *Member:* Bridgeport, Connecticut and American (Member, Litigation Section) Bar Associations; Connecticut Trial Lawyers Association; Connecticut Defense Lawyers Association; Defense Research Institute. ***PRACTICE AREAS:*** Civil Litigation; Criminal Litigation; Administrative Law; Arbitration; Personal Injury. ***Email:*** TXM@PULLCOM.COM

EDWARD P. McCREERY III, born Bridgeport, Connecticut, August 31, 1954; admitted to bar, 1979, Connecticut. *Education:* University of Vermont (B.A., 1976); Western New England College (J.D., 1979). Secretary, Connecticut Bar Association, 1998. Vice-Chairman, Greater Valley Chamber of Commerce, 1999—. Member, City of Shelton Conservation Commission. Town Attorney, Brookfield, 2000—. *Member:* Bridgeport (Member: Commercial Law Section; Civil Trial Committee), Connecticut (Member, Executive Committee, Litigation Section; Member, Construction Law Section), Federal and American Bar Associations; The Association of Trial Lawyers of America; Connecticut Trial Lawyers Association. ***PRACTICE AREAS:*** Commercial Litigation; Construction; Insurance Coverage; Product Liability; Admiralty; Creditors Rights; Business Arbitration; Municipal Representation. ***Email:*** EPM@PULLCOM.COM

ANDREW J. McDONALD, born Stamford, Connecticut, March 11, 1966; admitted to bar, 1991, Connecticut; 1992, U.S. District Court, District of Connecticut; 1997, U.S. Court of Appeals, Second Circuit. *Education:* Cornell University (A.B., 1988); University of Connecticut School of Law (J.D., with honors, 1991). Phi Delta Phi. Recipient, George and Lorraine Schatzki Award for Service. Managing Editor, Connecticut Journal of International Law, 1990-1991. Member, Stamford Board of Representatives, 1993-1995. Member, 1995-1999, and Chairman, 1997-1999, Stamford Board of Finance. Member, Board of Directors, Stamford Partnership, 1997—; Member, Board of Directors, Women's Business Development Center, 2000—. Trustee, Certified Employees Retirement Fund, 1997-1999; Director of Legal Affairs and Corporation Counsel, City of Stamford, 1999—. *Member:* Bridgeport, Stamford/Norwalk Regional (Co-Chairman, Municipal Law Section, 2000—), Connecticut and American Bar Associations; Connecticut Trial Lawyers Association. (Resident in Stamford Office). ***PRACTICE AREAS:*** Commercial Litigation; Municipal Law; Property Valuation. ***Email:*** AM@PULLCOM.COM

ROBERT B. MITCHELL, born Bremerton, Washington, March 27, 1953; admitted to bar, 1979, New York and U.S. District Court, Southern District of New York; 1980, Louisiana; 1981, U.S. Court of Appeals, Fifth and Eleventh Circuits; 1987, U.S. District Court, Western District of Louisiana; 1988, Connecticut and U.S. District Court, District of Connecticut; 1989, U.S. Court of Appeals, Second Circuit and U.S. Supreme Court. *Education:* Ohio Wesleyan University (B.A., 1975); Tulane University School of Law (J.D., 1978). Order of the Coif. Member, Board of Student Editors, 1976-1978, and Comments Editor, 1977-1978, Tulane Law Review. Member Monroe, Connecticut Economic Development Commission, 1990-1993; Member Monroe, Connecticut Town Council, 1993-1999. Special Master, United States District Court, District of Connecticut, 1993—. Connecticut State Court Arbitrator and Trial Referee, Connecticut Superior Court, Judicial District of Fairfield at Bridgeport. *Member:* Bridgeport (Member, Sections on: Civil, Labor and Employment, Chair, 1994-1995), Louisiana State, Connecticut (Member: Federal Practice Section; Member, Executive Board, Labor Section, 1997-1999) and American (Member, Sections on Labor and Tort and Insurance Practice) Bar Associations. (Also at Stamford Office). ***PRACTICE AREAS:*** General Civil Litigation; Trial Practice; Labor Law; Employment Law; Civil Rights Law; Insurance Defense. ***Email:*** RXM@PULLCOM.COM

HERBERT H. MOORIN, born Stamford, Connecticut, July 10, 1938; admitted to bar, 1962, Connecticut. *Education:* Trinity College (B.A., 1959); Harvard University (LL.B., 1962). Phi Beta Kappa. Co-Author: "IRS Attorney Audit Program," Connecticut Lawyer, 1995. President, United Cerebral Palsy Association of Fairfield County, Inc., 1977-1980. Chairman, Kennedy Center Inc (for Persons with Disabilities), 1993-1994. Bridgeport Public Education Fund, Inc., Treasurer, 1994-1999, Vice Chairman, 2000-2001. Director, Bridgeport Futures, Inc., 1992-1994. *Member:* Bridgeport, Connecticut and American Bar Associations. ***PRACTICE AREAS:*** Trusts and Estates; Pension and Profit-Sharing Law; Corporate Law. ***Email:*** HHM@PULLCOM.COM

D. ROBERT MORRIS, born Rochester, New York, August 23, 1950; admitted to bar, 1975, Connecticut; 1976, New York; 1977, Florida. *Education:* Cornell University (B.A., cum laude, 1972; J.D., 1975); New York University (LL.M., in Taxation, 1976). Co-Author: "Annual Reporting Requirements for Welfare Benefit Plans and Fringe Benefit Plans," Connecticut CPA Quarterly, September 1990. *Member:* Bridgeport, Connecticut (Member, Executive Committee, Tax Section) and American (Member, Sections on: Taxation; Business

(This Listing Continued)

PULLMAN & COMLEY, L.L.C., Bridgeport—Continued

Law) Bar Associations; The Florida Bar. (Also at Stamford Office). ***PRACTICE AREAS:*** Taxation Law; Corporate Law; Employee Benefits Law; Estate Planning; Computer Law. ***Email:*** DRM@PULLCOM.COM

MARIE V. PHELAN, born Jersey City, NJ, July 14, 1947; admitted to bar, 1989, CT. *Education:* Wesleyan Univ. (B.A., cum laude, 1983); Univ. of Connecticut (J.D. , cum laude, 1989). Phi Beta Kappa; Sigma Xi. Member, Public Finance/Public Law Practice Group. Chairman, State of Connecticut Municipal Finance Advisory Commission; Member, Board of Director's of Hartford Assn. of Women Atty's., 1993-1998; Corporator, Harford Ballet; Member, Local Government Committee, Hartford Chamber of Commerce, 1994-1999. Member, 1984-1987, Vice Chairman, 1985-1987, Killingworth Board of Finance. Advisory Board, Ninth Connecticut Women's Congress, 1991. Member, Wesleyan Univ. Alumni Schools Committee, 1984—. *Member:* Connecticut Bar Association; National Association of Bond Lawyers. (Resident at Hartford Office). ***PRACTICE AREAS:*** Public Finance; Public Law; Commercial Lending. ***Email:*** MVP@PULLCOM.COM

ELLIOTT B. POLLACK, born Brooklyn, New York, January 20, 1943; admitted to bar, 1965, Connecticut; 1966, U.S. District Court, District of Connecticut; 1969, U.S. Court of Appeals, Second Circuit and U.S. Supreme Court. *Education:* Columbia College (A.B., 1962); Columbia University (LL.B., 1965). Law Clerk to Associate Justice Howard W. Alcorn, Supreme Court of Connecticut, 1965-1966. Town Councilman, West Hartford, 1975-1977. Board of Directors, Hartford Dispensary, 1988—. President, Hartford Dispensary, 1991-1996; Board of Directors, Solomon Schechter Day School of Greater Hartford, 1990-1996, 1997-1999. Member, State of Connecticut Medical Examining Board, 1991-1994; Board of Directors, Hartford Stage Company, 1991-1999; Board of Directors, 1993—; Vice President, 1999-2001; President, 2001—; Capital Area Foundation for Equal Justice. Member, Board of Directors and Secretary, Connecticut Health Lawyers Association, 1999—. Adjunct Faculty, University of Connecticut Law School, 1997—. *Member:* Hartford County, Connecticut (Member: Administrative Law Section; Health Law Section) and American (Member, Sections of: Health Law; Antitrust) Bar Associations; American Health Lawyers Association; Healthcare Financial Management Association; Institute for Professionals in Taxation (Legal Committee); International Association of Assessing Officers; American Property Tax Counsel. James W. Cooper Fellow, Connecticut Bar Foundation. (Also at Stamford and Hartford Offices). ***PRACTICE AREAS:*** Health Care; Tax Appeal and Condemnation Law; Commercial Litigation. ***Email:*** EBP@PULLCOM.COM

MICHAEL G. PROCTOR, born Bridgeport, Connecticut, May 29, 1957; admitted to bar, 1983, Connecticut. *Education:* Connecticut College (B.A., cum laude, 1979); Boston College (J.D., magna cum laude, 1983). Managing Editor, Boston College Environmental Affairs Law Review, 1982-1983. Author: "Section 10 of the Rivers and Harbors Act and Western Water Allocations-Are the Western States Up a Creek Without a Permit?" Vol. 10, Boston College Environmental Affairs Law Review, No. 1, 1982. *Member:* Bridgeport, Connecticut and American Bar Associations. ***PRACTICE AREAS:*** Real Estate Law; Commercial Lending Law; Creditors' Rights Law. ***Email:*** MGP@PULLCOM.COM

THOMAS A. ROUSE, born Syracuse, New York, December 2, 1950; admitted to bar, 1975, Connecticut and U.S. District Court, District of Connecticut. *Education:* Trinity College (B.A., 1972); University of Connecticut (J.D., 1975). Phi Beta Kappa. Articles Editor, Connecticut Law Review, 1974-1975. *Member:* Connecticut (Computer Law, Environmental and Antitrust Law Sections) and American Bar Associations. (Also at Hartford Office). ***PRACTICE AREAS:*** Electronic Commerce; Environmental Litigation; Telecommunications Law; Electric Power; Technology Startups. ***Email:*** TAR@PULLCOM.COM

ALAN I. SCHEER, born Yonkers, New York, March 3, 1942; admitted to bar, 1967, Connecticut and U.S. District Court, District of Connecticut; 1970, U.S. Court of Appeals, Second Circuit; 1973, U.S. District Court, Northern District of New York; 1974, U.S. Supreme Court. *Education:* Cornell University and New York University (B.S., 1964); Brooklyn Law School (J.D., 1967). Author: "The Family and Medical Leave Act: A New Dawn in Employee Rights," Connecticut Lawyer, Vol. 2 No. 4, December 1991; "Understanding The State and Federal Leave Acts-Reconciling the Differences," Connecticut Law Tribune, June 20, 1994; "Independent Contractors or Employees? Misclassification May Be Dangerous," Connecticut Lawyer, Vol. 5, No. 3, November, 1994. Member, Board of Directors, Hartford Symphony Orchestra, 1984-1990. Executive Vice President, Hartford Chamber Orchestra, 1980-1984. Trustee, Long Wharf Theatre, New Haven, Connecticut, 1987-2000; Member, Board of Directors of Chamber Music Plus, 1991-1997. Member, Editorial Advisory Board of the Connecticut Lawyer, 1990—. Member, Panel of Commercial Arbitrators, American Arbitration Association, 1976—; Panel of Employment Law Arbitrators, 1992—. *Member:* Hartford County, Connecticut (Member, Board of Governors, 1998-2000. Member, House of Delegates, 1990—; Labor and Employment Law Counsel, 1981—; Member, Executive Committee, 1981— and Chairman, 1994-1995, Labor and Employment Law Section; Executive Committee, Antitrust and Trade Regulation Section, 1991—) and

(This Listing Continued)

American (Labor and Employment Law Section) Bar Associations; Society of Professionals in Dispute Resolution. (At Hartford Office). ***PRACTICE AREAS:*** Labor and Employment Law; Litigation; Health Care; Antitrust. ***Email:*** AIS@PULLCOM.COM

GREGORY F. SERVODIDIO, born Staten Island, New York, May 23, 1961; admitted to bar, 1986, Connecticut; 1987, U.S. District Court, District of Connecticut. *Education:* Georgetown University (A.B., magna cum laude, 1983; J.D., 1986). Phi Beta Kappa; Pi Sigma Alpha. Co-author: Connecticut Chapter of ABA Property Tax Deskbook (5th Ed.). Co-Chair, Municipal Tax Advisory Committee to Superior Court, Tax Session, 1995-1996. Member, Board of Directors, Fellowship Place, 1994—. Member, Marlborough Economic Development Commission, 1999—. *Member:* Hartford County, Connecticut and American Bar Associations; Institute for Professionals in Taxation; International Association of Assessing Officers; Connecticut Association of Assessing Officers; National Council of Property Taxation. (Also at Hartford Office). ***PRACTICE AREAS:*** Property Taxation; Condemnation and Relocation; Land Use; Litigation. ***Email:*** GFS@PULLCOM.COM

RONALD CASE SHARP, born New Haven, Connecticut; admitted to bar, 1964, Connecticut. *Education:* Mount Hermon Academy; Yale University (B.A., 1957); University of Connecticut (LL.B., 1964). Lecturer, Business and Taxation, Connecticut Bar Review, 1970—. Arbitrator, American Arbitration Association, 1975—. *Member:* Bridgeport, The Connecticut and American (Member: Closely Held Corporation Committee, Taxation Section, 1978—; Section of Corporation, Banking and Business Law) Bar Associations. [Lt., U.S. Marine Corps, 1957-1961]. ***PRACTICE AREAS:*** Corporate and Partnership Law; Health Care Law; Commercial Transactions; Banking Law; Tax Law. ***Email:*** RCS@PULLCOM.COM

MARGARET M. SHEAHAN, born Bronx, New York, August 10, 1954; admitted to bar, 1980, New York and Connecticut; 1981, U.S. District Court, District of Connecticut, 1987, U.S. Court of Appeals, Second Circuit. *Education:* Fordham University (B.A., magna cum laude, 1976); New York University (J.D., 1980). *Member:* Bridgeport, Connecticut and American (Member, Section on Labor and Employment Law) Bar Associations. (Also at Stamford Office). ***PRACTICE AREAS:*** Labor Law; Employment Law; Civil Litigation. ***Email:*** MMS@PULLCOM.COM

JAMES T. SHEARIN, born Stauton, Virginia, March 11, 1961; admitted to bar, 1986, Connecticut; 1987, U.S. District Court, District of Connecticut; 1988, U.S. Court of Appeals, Second Circuit; 1995, U.S. Supreme Court; 1997, U.S. Court of Federal Claims. *Education:* University of Connecticut (B.A., summa cum laude, 1983; J.D., with high honors, 1986). Recipient, William F. Starr Outstanding Student Award. Administrative Editor, Connecticut Law Review, 1985-1986. Author: "The Discrimination Statutes and the Supreme Court's Program for Confusion," 17 Conn. L. Rev. 3 (1985). Co-author: "What to do When the Feds Grab for Collateral," ABA Banking Journal, Vol. LXXX16, No. 2; Commentary: "Working for Which Side," The Record, No. 175 (September 10, 1993). Author: "The Expert Witness and Mandatory Disclosure: Comply or Suffer the Consequences," Vol. 14, No. 2, CTLA Forum 136 (March/April, 1996); "Lawyering from the *John*," Vol. 6, No. 7, Connecticut Lawyer 28 (April 1996); "Protecting Your Eventual Judgment for Money Damages," The Banking Law Journal (October, 1998). Co-author: "Zealousness and Honesty in Settlement Discussion," Connecticut Law Tribune Magazine (August 9, 1999); "Medical Malpractice Liability: It's Not Just For Doctors Anymore," Vol. 11, No. 5. Connecticut Lawyer 4 (February 2001). Law Clerk, Hon. Peter C. Dorsey, District of Connecticut, 1986-1988. Member, Raymond E. Baldwin Inn of Courts, 1989—. Appointed Co-Counsel to Federal Grievance Committee (D.Conn.) 1997—. Member and Chairman, Connecticut Legal Services. President, UConn Law School Foundation, Inc. James W. Cooper Fellow, Connecticut Bar Foundation. *Member:* Bridgeport (President), Connecticut (Member: Federal Practice and Intellectual Property Sections, Executive Committees) and American Bar Associations; The Association of Trial Lawyers of America; Connecticut Trial Lawyers Association. (Also at Hartford and Stamford Offices). ***PRACTICE AREAS:*** Litigation; Intellectual Property; Admiralty; Securities. ***Email:*** JTS@PULLCOM.COM

H. WILLIAM SHURE, born New Haven, Connecticut, April 5, 1940; admitted to bar, 1964, Connecticut. *Education:* Dartmouth College (A.B., 1961); University of Virginia (LL.B., 1964). Assistant Minority Counsel to the Senate Select Committee on Presidential Campaign Activities (Watergate Committee, 1973). Consulting Counsel, U.S. Senate Committee on Government Operations, Subcommittee on Federal Spending Practices, Efficiency and Open Government, 1975-1977. President, New Haven Jewish Federation, 1982-1985. National Vice-Chairman, United Jewish Appeal, 1989-1999. (Also at New Haven Office). ***PRACTICE AREAS:*** Commercial Law; Banking Law; Bankruptcy Law; Government Law. ***Email:*** HWS@PULLCOM.COM

CHRISTOPHER J. SMITH, born New Haven, Connecticut, March 30, 1958; admitted to bar, 1983, Connecticut; 1984, U.S. District Court, District of Connecticut. *Education:* Providence College (B.A., cum laude, 1980); University of Connecticut School of Law (J.D., 1983). Phi Sigma Tau; Pi Sigma Alpha. Law Clerk, Hon. Antoinette L. Dupont, Judge, Connecticut Appellate Court, 1983-1984. Member and Secretary, North Branford Economic Development

(This Listing Continued)

Commission, 1982-1984. Member, North Branford Zoning Board of Appeals, 1985. Councilman, North Branford Town Council, 1985-1987. Member, North Branford Town Council Pension Review Committee, 1986-1987; Member and Chairperson, North Branford Conservation and Inland Wetlands and Watercourses Agency, 1988-1999; Member, Connecticut General Assembly's Inland Wetlands and Watercourses Task Force, 1995-1996; Member, State of Connecticut Southwest Corridor Action Council; Member, Connecticut General Assembly's Blue Ribbon Commission on Connecticut's Affordable Housing Land Use Appeals Procedure Act, 1999-2000. Member, State of Connecticut Ethics Commission, 2001—. Special Master for Land Use Appeals, Connecticut Superior Court, 1997—. *Member:* Bridgeport (Chairperson, Land Use and Environmental Committee, 1995-1996), New Haven County, Connecticut (Chairperson, Planning and Zoning Section, 1997-2000, and Member, Executive Committee, Section on Planning and Zoning, 1989—; Sections on Real Estate, Administrative and Conservation and Environmental Quality) and American (Member, Sections on: Natural Resources; Energy and Environmental Law and Urban, State and Local Government Law) Bar Associations. ***PRACTICE AREAS:*** Zoning; Planning; Wetlands; Environmental; Real Estate Litigation. ***Email:*** CJS@PULLCOM.COM

JOHN F. STAFSTROM, JR., born Waterbury, Connecticut, June 14, 1956; admitted to bar, 1981, Connecticut. *Education:* College of the Holy Cross (B.A., 1978); University of Connecticut (J.D., with honors, 1981). Member, 1979-1981, and Note and Comment Editor, 1980-1981, Connecticut Law Review. Author: "Standing Under 42 U.S.C. Sections 1981 and 1982: Direct, Indirect and A New 'Loss of Association ' Standing," Volume 13, Connecticut Law Review, 1981. Bridgeport City Council, 1987-1994. *Member:* Bridgeport, Connecticut and American Bar Associations; National Association of Bond Lawyers. (Also at Hartford Office). ***PRACTICE AREAS:*** Public Finance; Corporate Law; Banking Law; Commercial Law. ***Email:*** JFS@PULLCOM.COM

JAMES B. STEWART, born Rockville Centre, New York, May 30, 1943; admitted to bar, 1968, Connecticut. *Education:* Wesleyan University (B.A., 1965); Vanderbilt University (J.D., 1968). *Member:* Bridgeport, Connecticut (Member, Executive Committee, Estates and Probate Section, 1990—) and American Bar Associations. (Also at Southport Office). ***PRACTICE AREAS:*** Estates and Trusts; Real Estate. ***Email:*** JBS@PULLCOM.COM

GROVE W. STODDARD, born Mt. Kisco, New York, September 26, 1941; admitted to bar, 1966, Connecticut. *Education:* Moravian College & Theological Seminary (B.A., 1963); Dickinson School of Law (J.D., 1966). *Member:* Bridgeport, Connecticut and American (Member, Executive Committee, Consumer Law Section, 1977—) Bar Associations. ***PRACTICE AREAS:*** Banking Law. ***Email:*** GWS@PULLCOM.COM

MARSHALL J. TOUPONSE, born Waterbury, Connecticut, September 18, 1960; admitted to bar, 1985, Connecticut. *Education:* Yale University (B.A., magna cum laude, 1982); University of Connecticut (J.D., with high honors, 1985). Member, 1983-1985, and Executive Editor, 1984-1985, Connecticut Law Review. Law Clerk to Chief Justice Ellen A. Peters, Connecticut Supreme Court, 1985-1986. *Member:* Bridgeport, Connecticut (Member, Sections on: Banking Law; Consumer Law; Intellectual Property Law; Sports and Entertainment Law) and American Bar Associations. ***PRACTICE AREAS:*** E-Commerce Law; Corporate Law; Intellectual Property Law; Banking Law; Health Care; Regulatory Law. ***Email:*** MJT@PULLCOM.COM

JOHN R. WARD, born Farnworth, Lancashire, England, August 4, 1962. admitted, 1984, England and Wales; 1990, Connecticut. *Education:* King's College, London University (LL.B., 1983); University of Connecticut (J.D., magna cum laude, 1990). Assistant Corporation Counsel, 1997 and Deputy Corporation Counsel, 1998-2000, City of New Haven. *Member:* Connecticut Bar Association (Member, Real Property Section). (Resident at New Haven Office). ***PRACTICE AREAS:*** Real Estate Law; Commercial Law; Municipal Law. ***Email:*** JRW@PULLCOM.COM

WILLIAM J. WENZEL, born Detroit, Michigan, August 22, 1951; admitted to bar, 1978, Oklahoma and U.S. District Court, Eastern District of Oklahoma; 1979, U.S. District Court, Northern District of Oklahoma; 1980, U.S. Temporary Emergency Court of Appeals, 1981, U.S. Court of Appeals, Tenth Circuit; 1984, U.S. Supreme Court; 1985, Connecticut and U.S. District Court, District of Connecticut; 1987, U.S. Court of Appeals, Second Circuit. *Education:* Colgate University (B.A., 1974); University of Tulsa (J.D., with honors, 1978). Phi Delta Phi. Staff Member, 1976-1977, and Editor-in-Chief, 1977-1978, Tulsa Law Journal. Author: "Application of Article 2 of the Uniform Commercial Code to Lease Transactions," 12 Tulsa Law Journal 556, 1977. Law Clerk, Hon. Fred Daugherty and H. Dale Cook, U.S. District Court, Eastern District of Oklahoma, 1978-1979. Police Commissioner, Fairfield Police Department, 1989-1999. *Member:* Bridgeport, Greater Bridgeport (Chairperson, Litigation Section, 1997-2000), Connecticut and American Bar Associations. ***PRACTICE AREAS:*** Litigation. ***Email:*** WJW@PULLCOM.COM

JAMES P. WHITE, JR., born Providence, Rhode Island, August 15, 1942; admitted to bar, 1967, Connecticut. *Education:* Fairfield University (B.A., 1964); Fordham University (LL.B., 1967). Gamma Eta Gamma (President, Xi Chapter, 1966-1967). Member, Cardinal Key. Town Counsel, Monroe, Connecticut, 1970-1973; 1975-1995. *Member:* Bridgeport (Member, Executive Committee, 1969-1972, 1991-1994), Connecticut (Member, Executive Committee: Planning and Zoning Section, 1990—; Real Estate Section, 1979—) and American Bar Associations. ***PRACTICE AREAS:*** Real Estate, Environmental and Land Use Law; Municipal Law; Business Enterprises. ***Email:*** JPW@PULLCOM.COM

MARJORIE S. WILDER, born New Haven, Connecticut, August 29, 1943; admitted to bar, 1972, Connecticut; 1975, U.S. District Court, District of Connecticut; 1988, U.S. Supreme Court; 1989, U.S. Court of Appeals, Second Circuit; 1997, U.S. Court of Appeals, Ninth Circuit. *Education:* Smith College (A.B., magna cum laude, 1965); Tufts University (M.A., Economics, 1970); University of Connecticut (J.D., with high honors, 1972). Editor, University of Connecticut Law Review, 1971-1972. Assistant Corporation Counsel, 1983-1985 and Corporation Counsel, 1985-1997, Town of West Hartford. *Member:* Hartford County, Connecticut (Member: Litigation, Planning & Zoning and Real Property Sections) and American (Member: Litigation and State and Local Government Law Taxation) Bar Associations; Institute for Professionals in Taxation; International Association of Assessing Officers; Connecticut Association of Assessing Officers. Fellow, James W. Cooper Connecticut Bar Foundation, 1998—. (Resident at Hartford Office). ***PRACTICE AREAS:*** Administrative Law; Condemnation Law; Real and Personal Property Taxation; Litigation; Planning and Zoning. ***Email:*** MSW@PULLCOM.COM

ASSOCIATES

CHRISTIAN G. BELTZ, born Norwalk, Connecticut, June 6, 1969; admitted to bar, 1995, New York and Connecticut. *Education:* Fordham University (B.S., 1991; J.D., 1994). *Member:* Greater Bridgeport and Connecticut Bar Associations; National Association of Bond Lawyers; Government Finance Officers Association. ***PRACTICE AREAS:*** Municipal Law; Real Estate. ***Email:*** CGB@PULLCOM.COM

CARRIE L. BERNIER, born Massachusetts, April 1, 1970; admitted to bar, 2000, Connecticut. *Education:* Boston College (B.A., cum laude, 1992); University of Massachusetts (Master's Certificate, The Program for Women in Government and Public Policy, 1995); Pace University (J.D., cum laude, 2000). Managing Editor, Pace Law Review; President, Womens Association of Law Students. *Member:* Bridgeport, Connecticut and American Bar Associations. ***PRACTICE AREAS:*** Litigation; Employment Law. ***Email:*** CLB@PULLMAN.COM

KATHERINE E. CAULFIELD, born Arlington, Massachusetts, September 5, 1966; admitted to bar, 1991, Connecticut; 1994, Florida. *Education:* Boston College (B.S., cum laude, 1988); University of Connecticut (J.D., 1991). *Member:* Greater Bridgeport, Connecticut and American (Member, Sections on: Taxation; Probate; Real Estate) Bar Associations; The Florida Bar. (Also at Southport Office). ***PRACTICE AREAS:*** Estate and Gift Planning; Estate and Trust Administration; Elder Law. ***Email:*** KEC@PULLCOM.COM

ADAM J. COHEN, born New York, New York, August 6. 1973; admitted to bar, 1998, Connecticut; 1999, U.S. District Court, District of Connecticut. *Education:* Vassar College (B.A., cum laude, 1995); Cornell University (J.D., 1998). Phi Beta Kappa. Author: "Fire Me Nicely: Negligent Infliction of Emotional Distress Claims in Wrongful Termination Cases," Vol. 10 No. 4 Connecticut Lawyer 4 (January 2000); "Keeping the Promise: Proposed Legislation to Establish Nontransferable Elections Systems in Jurisdictions Covered by Section Four of the Voting Rights Act," Vol. 30 No. 3 St. Mary's Law Journal 655 (Spring 1999); "Disregarding the Quarrel Heard," Vol. 9 No. 4 Connecticut Lawyer 10 (January 1999); "The Open Door: Will the Right to Die Survive *Washington v. Glucksberg* and *Vacco v. Quill* ?" 16 In the Public Interest 79 (1998); "Preparing for 'Dignity ': Will Physician-Assisted Suicide Become Legal in New York?" Vol. 8 No. 1 Elder Law Attorney 13 (Winter 1998). Member, Town of Hamden, Commission on Human Rights and Relations, 2001—. Member, Board of Directors, First Amendment Task Force, 1998—. *Member:* Bridgeport, Connecticut and American Bar Associations. ***PRACTICE AREAS:*** Litigation. ***Email:*** AJC@PULLCOM.COM

RICHARD S. DIPRETA, born Greenwich, Connecticut, November 9, 1968; admitted to bar, 1998, Connecticut. *Education:* Trinity College (B.A., 1991); University of Connecticut (M.B.A., J.D., 1997). *Member:* Greenwich, Connecticut (Co-Chair, Estates and Probate Committee, Young Lawyer Section, 1998-2001; President, Young Lawyers of Lower Fairfield County, 1999-2001) and American (Vice-Chair, Real Property, Probate and Trust, Young Lawyers Division) Bar Associations. (At Southport Office). ***PRACTICE AREAS:*** Estate Administration; Estate Planning; Probate. ***Email:*** RSD@PULLCOM.COM

ERIC J. GEORGE, born New York, N.Y., January 4, 1973; admitted to bar, 2000, Connecticut. *Education:* University of Connecticut (B.A., magna cum laude, English Literature, 1995); University of Connecticut School of Law (J.D., 2000). Phi Beta Kappa. *Member:* Hartford, Connecticut (House of Delegate of the Connecticut Bar Association) and American Bar Associations; The American Hellenic Progressive Association. ***PRACTICE AREAS:*** Corporate Law; Taxation; Limited Liability Company Law; Nonprofit Organizations Law. ***Email:*** EJG@PULLCOM.COM

(This Listing Continued)

PULLMAN & COMLEY, L.L.C., Bridgeport—Continued

MATTHEW M. HAUSMAN, born Bridgeport, Connecticut, April 20, 1959; admitted to bar, 1990, Connecticut and Pennsylvania; 1991, U.S. District Court, District of Connecticut. *Education:* Clark University (B.A., cum laude, 1981); George Washington University (J.D., 1990). Research Clerk, Superior Court, 1990-1991. *Member:* Greater Bridgeport, Connecticut and American Bar Associations; Association of Trial Lawyers of America. ***PRACTICE AREAS:*** Commercial Litigation; Administrative and Zoning Law; Municipal Litigation; Property Valuation and Tax Appeals; ERISA Litigation. ***Email:*** MXH@PULLCOM.COM

MATTHEW P. LUNDY, born Mt. Kisco, New York, 1967; admitted to bar, 1994, Connecticut; 1995, New York; 1999, U.S. District Court, District of Connecticut; 2000, U.S. Court of Appeals, Second Circuit. *Education:* Fordham University (B.A., 1989); Wake Forest University School of Law (J.D., 1994). *Member:* Greater Bridgeport and Connecticut (Federal Practice and Environmental Sections) Bar Associations. ***PRACTICE AREAS:*** Litigation; Construction Law; Intellectual Property.

NORMA R. MANDULAK, born Manchester, Connecticut, July 8, 1970; admitted to bar, 1999, Connecticut. *Education:* Southern Connecticut State University (B.S., 1992); Quinnipiac University School of Law (J.D., 1999). *Member:* Connecticut and American Bar Associations. ***PRACTICE AREAS:*** Corporate. ***Email:*** NRM@PULLCOM.COM

JENNIFER T. McGRATH, born Simsbury, Connecticut, November 12, 1971; admitted to bar, 1998, Connecticut. *Education:* University of Connecticut (B.A., magna cum laude, Phi Beta Kappa, 1993); Trinity College (M.A., 1995); University of Connecticut School of Law (J.D., with honors, 1998). *Member:* Greater Bridgeport, Connecticut and American Bar Associations. (Resident at Southport Office). ***PRACTICE AREAS:*** Estate and Gift Planning; Estate and Trust Administration. ***Email:*** JRT@PULLCOM.COM

JULIE A. MORGAN, born Meriden, Connecticut, February 13, 1969; admitted to bar, 1998, Connecticut; 2001, U.S. District Court, District of Connecticut. *Education:* University of Connecticut (B.A., 1991); Quinnipiac College School of Law (J.D., magna cum laude, 1998). *Member:* Hartford County, Connecticut and American Bar Associations; Association of Trial Lawyers of America. (Resident at Hartford Office). ***PRACTICE AREAS:*** Litigation; Property Taxation; Real Estate and Personal Property Valuation; Land Use. ***Email:*** JAM@PULLCOM.COM

PETER S. OLSON, born Norwalk, Connecticut, 1970; admitted to bar, 1995, Connecticut and Maine; 1996, U.S. District Court, District of Connecticut; 1998, U.S. Court of Appeals, Second Circuit; 1999, U.S. Supreme Court. *Education:* Bates College (B.A., 1992); University of Connecticut (J.D., 1995). *Member:* Danbury, Connecticut (Member, Sections on: Computer Law; Litigation; Science and Technology) and American (Member, Sections on: Computer Law; Litigation; Affordable Housing and Community Development) Bar Associations. ***PRACTICE AREAS:*** Municipal Law; Litigation. ***Email:*** PSO@PULLCOM.COM

MARY BETH K. RAPICE, born Bridgeport, Connecticut, March 24, 1959; admitted to bar, 1985, Connecticut. *Education:* St. Mary's College (B.A., 1981); Quinnipiac School of Law (J.D., 1985). *Member:* Bridgeport and Connecticut Bar Associations. ***PRACTICE AREAS:*** Real Estate Law. ***Email:*** MBR@PULLCOM.COM

BRIAN C. ROCHE, born January 28, 1970; admitted to bar, 1995, Connecticut and U.S. District Court, District of Connecticut. *Education:* Fairfield University (B.A., cum laude, 1992); Northeastern University School of Law (J.D., 1995). Law Clerk, Hon. Alan H. Nevas, District of Connecticut, 1997-1999. *Member:* Connecticut Bar Association (Federal Practice Section). ***PRACTICE AREAS:*** Litigation. ***Email:*** BCR@PULLCOM.COM

PATRICIA SQUIRES, born New York, N.Y., May 16, 1957; admitted to bar, 1994, Connecticut; 1995, U.S. District Court, District of Connecticut. *Education:* University of Bridgeport (B.S.N., summa cum laude, 1986); Quinnipiac College (J.D., cum laude, 1994). Associate Editor, Quinnipiac University Law Review. Registered Nurse, 1986. Law Clerk to Chief Judge Peter C. Dorsey, U.S. District Court, District of Connecticut. *Member:* Connecticut Bar Association (Chairman, Health Law Section); American Health Lawyers Association; Connecticut Health Lawyers Association; American Association of Nurse Attorneys. ***PRACTICE AREAS:*** Health Law; Administrative Law; Corporate Law. ***Email:*** PXS@PULLCOM.COM

LORI L. UNDERBERGER, born New York, N.Y., May 2, 1961; admitted to bar, 1985, Maryland; 1987, Arizona, U.S. District Court, District of Arizona and U.S. Tax Court; 1988, District of Columbia; 1991, Missouri; 1997, Connecticut. *Education:* Brandeis University (B.A., cum laude, 1982); George Washington University (J.D., 1985). *Member:* Bridgeport, Connecticut and American Bar Associations; The Missouri Bar; The District of Columbia Bar. ***PRACTICE AREAS:*** Employee Benefits. ***Email:*** LLU@PULLCOM.COM

AIMEE J. WOOD, born Flushing, New York, October 1972; admitted to bar, 1997, Connecticut; 1998, U.S. District Court, District of Connecticut. *Education:* Washington and Lee University (B.A., 1994); University of Connecticut (J.D., with honors, 1997). Co-author: "Zealousness and Honesty in Settlement Discussion," Connecticut Law Tribune Magazine (August 9, 1999). *Member:* Bridgeport, Connecticut and American Bar Associations. ***PRACTICE AREAS:*** Litigation. ***Email:*** AJW@PULLCOM.COM

(This Listing Continued)

QUATRELLA & RIZIO, LLC

BRIDGEPORT, CONNECTICUT

(See Fairfield)

General Civil Practice, Real Estate, Commercial, Corporate, Probate, Commercial and Residential Landlord and Tenant, Financial, Partnership and Negligence Law.

PATRICIA C. REATH

THE LEGAL CENTER
1087 BROAD STREET, FOURTH FLOOR
BRIDGEPORT, CONNECTICUT 06604
Telephone: 203-331-1206
Fax: 203-331-1337
Email: attyreath@aol.com

Family Law, Domestic Relations, Custody, Children and Mediation.

FIRM PROFILE: Practice limited to the area of family law, representation of children in contested custody cases and mediation of family matters.

PATRICIA C. REATH, born Akron, Ohio, October 5, 1941; admitted to bar, 1987, Connecticut. *Education:* Wittenberg University (B.A., magna cum laude, 1963); The Johns Hopkins University (M.A.T., 1964); University of Bridgeport (J.D., magna cum laude, 1987). *Member:* Bridgeport, Connecticut (Member, Family Section) and American Bar Associations.

GLENN M. REISMAN

BRIDGEPORT, CONNECTICUT

(See Shelton)

Creditors' Rights, Bankruptcy, Risk Management, Workouts.

ROBERTS, ROSE & BATES, P.C.

BRIDGEPORT, CONNECTICUT

(See Stamford)

General Practice, Litigation, Real Estate, Leasing, Banking, Matrimonial, Probate, Estate Planning and Trusts, International Business, Employment Law.

ROME McGUIGAN SABANOSH, P.C.

Established in 1969

1000 LAFAYETTE BOULEVARD
BRIDGEPORT, CONNECTICUT 06604
Telephone: 203-382-8000
Telecopier: 203-382-8005

Hartford, Connecticut Office: One State Street. Telephone: 203-549-1000. Telecopier: 203-724-3921.

Labor and Employment, Education, Administrative Law, Alternative Dispute Resolution, Bankruptcy, Benefits Planning/ERISA, Business Planning, Commercial Finance, Construction, Corporate, Creditor's Rights, Environmental, Estate Planning and Administration, Government Relations, Insurance, Intellectual Property, Investigations, Land Use, Litigation, Municipal, Personal Injury, Product Liability, Real Estate, Tax, Tax and Valuation Appeal, Tribal Gaming, White-Collar Crime.

(For Complete Biographical Data on all Personnel see Professional Biographies at Hartford, Connecticut)

ROSENSTEIN & BARNES

BRIDGEPORT, CONNECTICUT

(See Fairfield)

General Civil and Criminal Practice before State and Federal Courts. Civil Litigation, Employment Litigation, Commercial Litigation and Family Law. Domestic Relations and Child Custody Law, Covenants Not to Compete Litigation, Trials and Appeals.

RUANE ATTORNEYS AT LAW

10 MIDDLE STREET
BRIDGEPORT, CONNECTICUT 06604
Telephone: 203-382-0394
URL: http://www.ctdwi.com;
URL: http://www.connecticutcriminaldefense.com

Criminal Defense, Personal Injury, Appellate, DWI, Drug Crimes, Felonies, White Collar Crime, Automobile Accidents, Medical Malpractice, Wrongful Death.

MEMBERS OF FIRM

JAMES J. RUANE, born Jersey City, New Jersey, June 29, 1949; admitted to bar, 1977, Connecticut; 1978, U.S. District Court, District of Connecticut; 1984, U.S. Court of Appeals, Second Circuit. *Education:* Fairfield University (B.A., 1971); University of Connecticut (J.D., cum laude, 1977). Assistant Public Defender, State of Connecticut, 1977-1983. *Member:* Greater Bridgeport Bar Association (Chairman, Criminal Law Committee, 1989-1990); Connecticut Academy of Certified Trial Lawyers (Secretary, 1989-1990; Treasurer, 1990-1991); National Association of Criminal Defense Lawyers. (Certified as a Criminal Trial Advocate by the National Board of Trial Advocacy, 1985—). ***REPORTED CASES:*** United States vs. Garcia, 926 F.2d 125 (1991); United States vs. Lanese, 890 F.2d 1284 (1989); State vs. Lamme, 216 Conn. 172 (1990); Gaudet v. Safeco Insurance Company, 219 Conn. 391 (1991); Lozada v. Warden 223 Conn. 834 (1992); State v. Hinton, 227, Conn. 301 (1993).

JAMES O. RUANE, born Jersey City, New Jersey, July 24, 1972; admitted to bar, 1998, Connecticut. *Education:* University of Scranton (B.A., 1994); University of Connecticut (J.D., 1998). Recipient: M. Joseph Blumfield Award. Special Deputy Assistant, Public Defender, 1998-2000, Connecticut. *Member:* Connecticut Criminal Defense Lawyers; National Association of Criminal Defense Lawyers. ***PRACTICE AREAS:*** DWI Defense; Criminal Defense; Appellate Practice; Civil Torts; Personal Injury; Medical Malpractice; Wrongful Death.

RUBENSTEIN, GREEN & BASS, LLC

BRIDGEPORT, CONNECTICUT

(See Westport)

General Civil Practice before State and Federal Courts, Real Estate, Corporation, Commercial and Banking, Personal Injury, Medical Malpractice, Estate Planning and Probate, Planning and Zoning Trials and Appeals, Banking Litigation.

SANDAK FRIEDMAN HENNESSEY & GRECO, LLP

BRIDGEPORT, CONNECTICUT

(See Stamford)

Trials and Appeals in all Connecticut and Federal Courts and Administrative Agencies. Personal Injury, Medical Malpractice, Commercial, Environmental Litigation, Real Estate, Zoning and Land Use, Property Tax Appeals.

SCHOONMAKER, GEORGE & COLIN, P.C.

BRIDGEPORT, CONNECTICUT

(See Greenwich)

Matrimonial and Family Law.

SHUMWAY & SPENCER, LLC

BRIDGEPORT, CONNECTICUT

(See Fairfield)

Environmental and Corporate Law.

SILVER, GOLUB & TEITELL LLP

BRIDGEPORT, CONNECTICUT

(See Stamford)

Trial Practice in all State and Federal Courts. Medical Malpractice, Negligence, Commercial Litigation, Family and Criminal Law.

THE SIMKO LAW FIRM, L.L.C.

1087 BROAD STREET, SUITE 201
BRIDGEPORT, CONNECTICUT 06604-4231
Telephone: 203-367-2220
Fax: 203-367-3552
URL: http://www.lawyers.com/simkolaw

Construction Litigation, Mechanics Liens, Workers Compensation, Probate, Personal Injury, Medical Collections, Trials and Appeals.

VINCENT M. SIMKO, born Bridgeport, Connecticut, February 2, 1926; admitted to bar, 1953, Connecticut; 1954, U.S. District Court, District of Connecticut; 1959, U.S. Supreme Court. *Education:* Fordham University (B.S. II, cum laude, 1950); University of Connecticut (LL.B., 1953). State Representative, Connecticut, 1955-1957. Treasurer, City of Bridgeport, 1957-1973. Member, Panel of Arbitrators, American Arbitration Association. *Member:* Bridgeport (President, 1978-1979), Connecticut and American Bar Associations; The Association of Trial Lawyers of America; Connecticut Trial Lawyers Association. ***REPORTED CASES:*** L.F. Pace & Sons, Inc., v. The Travelers Indemnity Co, 514 A.2d 766. ***PRACTICE AREAS:*** Construction Law; Construction Litigation; Litigation; Probate; Real Estate; Investments; Investment Regulation; Estate Litigation. ***Email:*** vms_sr@simkolaw.com

V. MICHAEL SIMKO, JR., born Bridgeport, Connecticut, July 24, 1956; admitted to bar, 1988, Connecticut; 1989, U.S. District Court, District of Connecticut. *Education:* St. Vincent College; Providence College (B.A., 1978); University of Bridgeport (J.D., 1988). *Member:* Greater Bridgeport, Connecticut and American Bar Associations; Connecticut Trial Lawyers Association; National Employment Lawyers Association; Connecticut Employment Lawyers Association; The Association of Trial Lawyers of America. ***PRACTICE AREAS:*** Employment Litigation; Workers Compensation; Construction Litigation; Domestic Relations; Divorce. ***Email:*** veemike@simkolaw.com

LEGAL SUPPORT PERSONNEL

PATRICE M. BROTHERS, (Paralegal). ***Email:*** initials@simkolaw.com

REPRESENTATIVE CLIENTS: Wright Investors Service; Bridgeport Hospital; HRH/Atlas Construction.
REFERENCES: Hudson United Bank.
APPROVED ATTORNEYS FOR: Chicago Title Insurance Company; Connecticut Attorneys Title Insurance Company. Lawyers Title Insurance Company.

SLAVITT, CONNERY & VARDAMIS

BRIDGEPORT, CONNECTICUT

(See Norwalk)

General Practice. Commercial Law, Condemnation, Real Estate, Estate Planning, Probate, Family and Personal Injury Law. Civil and Criminal Trial Practice in all Courts. Agency and Distributorships, Alternative Dispute Resolution, Bankruptcy, Banks and Banking, Business Law, Civil Practice, Debtor and Creditor, Eminent Domain, Inverse Condemnation, Land Annexation, Commercial Real Estate, Construction Law, Contracts, Corporate Law, Equipment Finance and Leasing, Family Law, Finance, Franchises and Franchising, Fire Insurance Subrogation, Uninsured and Underinsured Motorists, Uninsured and Underinsured Motorists Arbitration, Commercial Leasing, Evictions, Landlord and Tenant Law, Lease Finance, Leasing, Office Leasing, Retail Leasing, Shopping Center Leasing, Legal Malpractice, Civil Litigation, Business Acquisitions, Business Divestitures, Mortgages, Negligence, Negligence Defense, Partnership Law, Torts, Civil Liability, Tort Liability, Trusts and Estates, Wills, Workers' Compensation, Zoning, Planning and Land Use.

TELLALIAN & TELLALIAN

Established in 1949
COURT EXCHANGE BUILDING
211 STATE STREET
BRIDGEPORT, CONNECTICUT 06604
Telephone: 203-333-5566
Fax: 203-330-1379

General Practice. Probate, Corporation and Real Estate Law.

MEMBERS OF FIRM

ARAM H. TELLALIAN, JR., born Syracuse, New York, January 16, 1913; admitted to bar, 1936, Connecticut; 1938, U.S. District Court, District of Connecticut. *Education:* Yale University (B.A., 1933; LL.B., 1936). Member, National College of Probate Judges, 1969—. Member, 1959— and Chairman, Nominating Committee, 1978—, Connecticut Probate Assembly. Member, Board of Associates, University of Bridgeport, 1963-1992. Judge of Probate, District of Trumbull, 1959-1979. Chairman: Governors Commission on the Age of Majority, 1971-1972; Fund Committee, University of Bridgeport Law School, 1983-1992. Member, Advisory Committee, University of Bridgeport

(This Listing Continued)

TELLALIAN & TELLALIAN, Bridgeport—Continued

Law School, 1981-1992. *Member:* Bridgeport (Member, Executive Committee, 1963-1970; Vice President, 1966-1967; President, 1967-1968) and The Connecticut (Member, Board of Governors, 1963-1966) Bar Associations. ***PRACTICE AREAS:*** Probate; Wills; Trust.

ROBERT S. TELLALIAN, born New Haven, Connecticut, May 15, 1921; admitted to bar, 1949, Connecticut. *Education:* Yale University (B.A., 1942); University of Connecticut (LL.B., 1949). *Member:* Bridgeport and The Connecticut Bar Associations. ***PRACTICE AREAS:*** Probate; Real Estate; Wills; Trust Law.

ASSOCIATE

WILLIAM T. FRAY, born Bridgeport, Connecticut, September 16, 1963; admitted to bar, 1988, Connecticut. *Education:* Fairfield University (B.A., 1985); Wake Forest University (J.D., 1988). *Member:* Greater Bridgeport and Connecticut Bar Associations. ***PRACTICE AREAS:*** Probate; Real Estate; Wills; Trusts.

REPRESENTATIVE CLIENTS: People's Bank; Chase-Manhattan; Fleet Bank.

TREMONT & SHELDON, P.C.

64 LYON TERRACE
BRIDGEPORT, CONNECTICUT 06604
Telephone: 203-335-5145
Fax: 203-366-8503
Email: lawfirm@tremont-sheldon.com
URL: http://www.tremont-sheldon.com

Civil Litigation in Federal and State Courts. Personal Injury and Commercial Law.

FIRM PROFILE: Tremont & Sheldon, P.C., has traditionally limited its size and specialty in order to give each matter individual care and attention. Since 1961, we have specialized in plaintiff's personal injury litigation in the federal and state courts ranging from simple automotive accidents to complex multi-victim disasters.

Tremont & Sheldon employs an aggressive style in case management which benefits our clients and those of the number of Connecticut law firms which refer cases to us for trial.

The firm has a presence in the judicial community both through its jury trial activity and its involvement with litigation organizations.

REPORTED CASES: Fahey v. Safeco Insurance Company of America, 49 Conn. App. 306 (1998); Mayer v. Biafore, Florek & O'Neill, et al, 245 Conn. 88 (1998); Battistoni v. Weatherking Products, Inc., 41 Conn. App. 555 (1996); Roberts v. Westchester Fire Insurance Co., 40 Conn.App. 294 (1996); McKee v. Erikson, 37 Conn.App. 146 (1995); Tovish v. Gerber Electronics, 229 Conn. 587 (1994); Smith v. Otis Elevator Co., 33 Conn.App. 99 (1993); Tovish v. Gerber Electronics, 32 Conn.App. 595 (1993); Lawrence v. New Hampshire Ins. Co., 29 Conn.App. 484 (1992); Tufaro v. Pepperidge Farm, Inc., 24 Conn.App. 234 (1991); Sanzone v. Board of Police Commissioners, 219 Conn. 179 (1991); Kaminski, Adm., et al, v. Town of Fairfield, et al, 216 Conn. 29 (1990); Vajda v. Tulsa, 214 Conn. 523 (1990); Mendes v. Automobile Ins. Co. of Hartford, 212 Conn. 652 (1989); Shelby Mutual Ins. Co. v. Evans, 20 Conn.App. 1 (1989); Ruhl v. Fairfield, 5 Conn.App. 104 (1985); Meinket v. Levinson, 193 Conn. 110 (1984); A & C Corporation v. Pernaselci, 2 Conn.App. 264 (1984); Royston v. Factor, 1 Conn.App. 576 (1984); Rokus v. Bridgeport, 191 Conn. 62 (1983); Dias v. Adams, 189 Conn. 354 (1983); Tetro v. Stratford, 189 Conn. 601 (1983); Kelepecz v. Kelepecz, 187 Conn. 537 (1982); Vincenzi v. Cerro, 186 Conn. 612 (1982); Davey v. Pepperidge Farm, Inc., 180 Conn. 469 (1980); Greenwich v. Kristoff, 180 Conn. 575 (1980); Robert Lawrence Associates, Inc. v. Del Vecchio, 178 Conn. 1 (1979); Comba v. Ridgefield, 177 Conn. 268 (1979); Robles v. Lavin, 176 Conn. 281 (1978); Bond v. Benning, 175 Conn. 308 (1978); Safeco Ins. Co. v. Vetre, 174 Conn. 329 (1978); Mountainside Assn. v. Mountainside Development, Inc., 172 Conn. 60 (1976); Gibson v. Fullin, 172 Conn. 407 (1977); Board of Police Commissioners v. White, 171 Conn. 553 (1976); State v. Paluga, 171 Conn. 586 (1976); Hayes v. Resource Control, Inc., 170 Conn. 102 (1976); Beik v. Thorsen, 169 Conn. 593 (1975); Fox v. Fox, 168 Conn. 592 (1975); Anderson & McPadden, Inc. v. Tunucci, 167 Conn. 584 (1975); Venezia v. Kennedy, 165 Conn. 183 (1973); In Re Application of Dinan, 157 Conn. 67 (1968); Tartaro v. La Conte, 157 Conn. 583 (1969); Short Beach Cottage Owners Assn. v. Stratford, 154 Conn. 194 (1966).

T. PAUL TREMONT (1933-1999).

ROBERT R. SHELDON, born Bridgeport, Connecticut, February 18, 1949; admitted to bar, 1974, Connecticut. *Education:* College of The Holy Cross (B.A., 1971); University of Connecticut (J.D., 1974). Recipient, American Jurisprudence Award. Lecturer: Continuing Legal Education Program, Connecticut Trial Lawyers Association, 1979—; Continuing Legal Education Program, Connecticut Bar Association, 1980—; Continuing Legal Education Program, Greater Bridgeport Bar Association, 1987—. Member: State of Connecticut Workers Compensation Commission Committee on Uniform Procedures, 1990-1991; State of Connecticut Workers Compensation Legal Advisory Board, 1992—; State of Connecticut Judicial Review Council, 1997-2001. State Trial Referee and Fact-Finder/Arbitrator, State of Connecticut Superior Court, 1990-1997. Special Master, United States District Court, 1994—. *Member:* Greater Bridgeport, Connecticut (Member, Executive Committee, Workers Compensation Section, 1988-1997) and American Bar Associations; Connecticut Trial Lawyers Association (Member, Board of Governors, 1987—; Parliamentarian, 1990-1991; Secretary, 1991-1992; Treasurer, 1992-1993; Vice President, 1993-1994; President-Elect, 1994-1995; President, 1995-1996); The Association of Trial Lawyers of America. Fellow, Connecticut Bar Foundation. ***PRACTICE AREAS:*** Personal Injury; Legal Malpractice; Workers Compensation. ***Email:*** rsheldon@tremont-sheldon.com

(This Listing Continued)

CINDY LORI ROBINSON, born Bridgeport, Connecticut, April 10, 1961; admitted to bar, 1986, Connecticut. *Education:* Wesleyan University (B.A., cum laude, 1983); University of Connecticut (J.D., 1986). Member, Moot Court Board. Barrister, Raymond E. Baldwin American Inn of Court, 1994-1997. Lecturer: Continuing Legal Education Program, Connecticut Trial Lawyers Association, 1992—; Continuing Legal Education Program, Greater Bridgeport Bar Association, 1992—. Member, 1992— and Chairperson, 1995—, Standing Committee on Recommendations for Admission to the Bar of Fairfield County. Special Master, Bridgeport Superior Court, 1998—. *Member:* Greater Bridgeport and Connecticut Bar Associations; Connecticut Trial Lawyers Association (Member: Board of Governors, 1993—; Parliamentarian, 2000-2001; Continuing Legal Education Committee, 1995—; Member, 1994-1998 and Co-Chairperson, 1997-1998, Diversity Committee); The Association of Trial Lawyers of America; American Board of Trial Advocates (Associate). (Certified as a Civil Trial Advocate by the National Board of Trial Advocacy). ***PRACTICE AREAS:*** Medical Malpractice; Personal Injury; Sexual Abuse. ***Email:*** crobinson@tremont-sheldon.com

FRANK A. BAILEY, born New Haven, Connecticut, March 16, 1961; admitted to bar, 1987, Connecticut. *Education:* Cornell University (A.B., 1984); University of Connecticut (J.D., 1987). *Member:* Bridgeport, Connecticut and American Bar Associations; Connecticut Trial Lawyers Association (Member, Amicus Curiae Committee; Instructor, People's Law School); The Association of Trial Lawyers of America. ***PRACTICE AREAS:*** Personal Injury; Commercial Litigation; Workers Compensation; Civil Rights; Appellate Practice. ***Email:*** fbailey@tremont-sheldon.com

JASON E. TREMONT, born Bridgeport, Connecticut, February 16, 1967; admitted to bar, 1992, Connecticut; 1993, U.S. District Court, District of Connecticut. *Education:* Dickinson College (B.A., 1989); University of Baltimore (J.D., cum laude, 1992). Special Master, State of Connecticut Superior Court, 2000—. Lecturer, Continuing Legal Education Program, Connecticut Trial Lawyers Association, 1998—. *Member:* Greater Bridgeport and Connecticut Bar Associations; Connecticut Trial Lawyers Association (Member: Board of Governors, 2000—; Co-Chairman, Young Lawyers Committee and Membership Committee; Public Relations Committee, 1996—); The Association of Trial Lawyers of America (Member, Aquatic Safety Injury Group, 1992-1999). ***PRACTICE AREAS:*** Medical Malpractice; Personal Injury; Products Liability. ***Email:*** jtremont@tremont-sheldon.com

DOUGLAS P. MAHONEY, born New York, New York, August 17, 1967; admitted to bar, 1992, Connecticut; 1993, U.S. District Court, District of Connecticut. *Education:* College of the Holy Cross (A.B., 1989); University of Connecticut (J.D., cum laude, 1992). Alpha Sigma Nu; Phi Alpha Theta. Member, University of Connecticut Moot Court Board. Oralist, National Moot Court Competition. Moot Court Teaching Assistant, 1991-1992, University of Connecticut Law School. Lecturer, CTLA Continuing Legal Education, 2001—. Special Master, Bridgeport Superior Court, 2000—. Chairman, Bridgeport People's Law School, 1996—. *Member:* Greater Bridgeport, Connecticut and American Bar Associations; Connecticut Trial Lawyers Association (Member: Membership Committee, Co-Chair; Public Relations Committee); The Association of Trial Lawyers of America. ***PRACTICE AREAS:*** Personal Injury; Sexual Abuse; Premises Security. ***Email:*** dmahoney@tremont-sheldon.com

---

JENNIFER S. RODRIGUEZ, born New Haven, Connecticut, August 30, 1969; admitted to bar, 2000, Connecticut and New York; 2001, U.S. District Court, District of Connecticut. *Education:* University of Rhode Island (B.A., magna cum laude, 1992); Quinnipiac University School of Law (J.D., cum laude, 1999). Phi Delta Phi. *Member:* Greater Bridgeport, Connecticut Hispanic (Member, Law Student Liasion Committee) and American Bar Associations; Connecticut Trial Lawyers Association; Association of Trial Lawyers of America. ***LANGUAGES:*** Spanish. ***PRACTICE AREAS:*** Personal Injury. ***Email:*** jrodriguez@tremont-sheldon.com

WAKE, SEE, DIMES & BRYNICZKA

BRIDGEPORT, CONNECTICUT

(See Westport)

Business and Corporate Law, Real Estate, Trusts and Probate, Estate Planning, Municipal, Zoning and Land Use Law, Litigation in all Federal and State Courts. Federal, State and Foreign Taxation, Pension and Profit Sharing, and Family Law.

WARE, FRESSOLA, VAN DER SLUYS & ADOLPHSON, LLP

BRIDGEPORT, CONNECTICUT

(See Monroe)

Patent, Trademark, Copyright, Computer, Antitrust, Unfair Competition, Foreign Patent Law, Litigation and Federal Practice.

ELLIOT R. WARREN

BRIDGEPORT, CONNECTICUT

(See Westport)

General Civil and Criminal Litigation before all State and Federal Courts. Trials and Appeals. Criminal Defense, Commercial and Tax Litigation, Personal Injury, Employment and Negligence Law.

WEINSTEIN, WEINER, IGNAL, NAPOLITANO & SHAPIRO, P.C.

Established in 1971

350 FAIRFIELD AVENUE

P.O. BOX 9177

BRIDGEPORT, CONNECTICUT 06601

Telephone: 203-333-1177

Cable Address: "Moot"

Fax: 203-384-9832

URL: http://www.lawyers.com/wwin

General Practice including Personal Injury, Negligence, Commercial, Reorganization, Bankruptcy, Foreclosures, Criminal, Civil Rights, Employee Rights and Benefits, Employment Discrimination, Family, Workers Compensation, Real Estate. Trial and Appellate Practice in all State and Federal Courts and Administrative Agencies.

HOWARD EVAN IGNAL, born New Haven, Connecticut, January 2, 1947; admitted to bar, 1972, Connecticut; 1974, U.S. District Court, District of Connecticut and U.S. Court of Appeals, Second Circuit. *Education:* University of Connecticut (B.A., with distinction, 1968); Cornell University (J.D., 1971). Phi Alpha Theta. *Member:* Bridgeport and Connecticut Bar Associations. ***PRACTICE AREAS:*** Banking; Commercial Law; Workers Compensation.

GERALD T. WEINER, born New York, N.Y., July 8, 1943; admitted to bar, 1968, Connecticut. *Education:* University of Connecticut (B.A., 1965; J.D., 1968). Lecturer in Communications Law, 1974-1979 and Adjunct Professor, 1978-1982, University of Bridgeport. Staff Attorney, CATV Bureau, Federal Communications Commission, 1968-1970. Town Counsel, Borough of Woodmont, 1976—. Chairman: Woodbridge Town Committee, 1980—; Third Congressional District Political Committee, 1990—. Member: Woodbridge Charter Revision Commission, 1986-1990; Connecticut Investment Advisory Council, 1992—; 1993—, Deputy Chairman, 1999—, State Board of Arbitration and Mediation, ; Regional Growth Partnership, New Haven, CT, 1995—; Democratic State Central Committee, 1996—. Member: Board of Directors 1994—, Chairman, 1999—, Griffin Hospital; University of Connecticut President's Athletic Advocacy Committee. *Member:* Connecticut Bar Association (Member: Family Law Section; Executive Committee, Commercial Law Section, 1985—; Committee on Professionalism, 1992—); Commercial Law League of America. ***REPORTED CASES:*** Cosgrove Development Co. v. Cafferty, 179 Conn. 670 (1980); Mihalczo v. Woodmont, 175 Conn. 535 (1978); Mitchell v. King, 169 Conn. 140 (1975); Spencer v. Zoning Board of Appeals, 15 Conn. App. 387 (1988); Costa v. Costa, 11 Conn. App. 74 (1987); American Factors v. Foreign Intrigue, Inc., 6 Conn. App. 656 (1986). ***PRACTICE AREAS:*** Family Law; Divorce; Child Custody; Commercial Law; Bankruptcy; Real Estate; Civil Law; Litigation. ***Email:*** gweiner@aol.com

BURTON M. WEINSTEIN, born Brooklyn, New York, March 15, 1929; admitted to bar, 1959, Connecticut; 1963, U.S. Supreme Court; 1970, U.S. Tax Court; 1977, U.S. Court of Immigration Appeals. *Education:* Syracuse University (A.B., 1950); Yale University (J.D., 1956). Recipient, Distinguished Achievement Award, Connecticut Bar Association, 1986. Associate in Research, Yale Law School, 1956-1957. Lecturer: National Institute of Municipal Law

(This Listing Continued)

Offices, Washington, D.C., May 1986; Mid-West Conference on Domestic Violence, Columbus, Ohio, September 1986, 1988, 1989; "Police Response to Domestic Violence," Seventh Annual National Association of Police Planners Conference, Baltimore, Maryland, September 1987; Kansas City, Kansas, September 1987; Springfield, Illinois, November 1987; Los Angeles, California, May 1988; White Plains, New York, June 1988; Victim Services Agency, Law Enforcement Training Project, Houston, Texas, March 1989. Executive Board Member, Fairfield County Affiliate, 1960—. Member, Connecticut Civil Liberties Union, 1960—. Hearing Examiner, Connecticut State Commission on Human Rights and Opportunities, 1969-1972. Trustee, Connecticut Civil Liberties Foundation, 1978-1986. *Member:* Connecticut (Member, Executive Board Human Rights Section, 1978-1984) and Federal Bar Associations; Commercial Law League of America; The Association of Trial Lawyers of America. [U.S. Army, 1950-1953]. ***REPORTED CASES:*** State v. McNally, 39 Conn. App. 419 (1995); Riley v. Bridgeport, 22 Conn. App. 402 (1990); State v. Marsala, 19 Conn. App. 478 (1989); State v. Marsala, 15 Conn. App. 519 (1988); State v. Warren, 14 Conn. App. 688 (1988); Thurman v. Tornington, 595 F.Supp. 1521 (D.Conn. 1984); American Factors v. Foreign Intrigue, Inc., 6 Conn. App. 656 (1986); Marky v. Santargelo, 195 Conn. 76 (1985); Enquire Printing & Publishing Co. v. O'Reilly, 193 Conn. 370 (1984); United Lid of Conn., Inc. v. Teamsters Local 443, 179 Conn. 211 (1979); Viscelli v. American Fidelity Co., 155 Conn. 622 (1967). ***PRACTICE AREAS:*** Litigation; Criminal Defense; Civil Rights; Labor Law; Medical Malpractice; Employment Law; Driving While Intoxicated.

ROBERTA NAPOLITANO, born Jamaica, New York, September 16, 1958; admitted to bar, 1982, Connecticut; 1985, U.S. District Court, District of Connecticut. *Education:* Bryn Mawr College (A.B., 1979); University of Connecticut (J.D., 1982). Member, Panel of Chapter 7 Trustees for District of Connecticut. *Member:* Bridgeport and Connecticut (Member: Executive Committee, Commercial Law Section; Standards of Title Review Committee, Commercial Bar Section) Bar Associations. ***REPORTED CASES:*** Fichera v. Mine Hill Corporation, 541 A 2d 472, 207 Conn. 204 (1988). ***PRACTICE AREAS:*** Commercial Litigation; Bankruptcy; Foreclosures.

RICHARD J. SHAPIRO, born West Hartford, Connecticut, December 3, 1954; admitted to bar, 1978, Connecticut; 1979, U.S. District Court, District of Connecticut; 1983, U.S. Court of Appeals, Second Circuit. *Education:* Purdue University (B.A., summa cum laude, 1975); Stanford University (J.D., 1978). Phi Beta Kappa. Faculty Member, Fairfield University, School of Graduate and Continuing Education, 1982-1987. *Member:* Bridgeport and Connecticut (Member, Executive Board, Human Rights Section, 1979-1985) Bar Associations. ***REPORTED CASES:*** Sanghavi v. Paul Revere Life Ins. Co., 214 Conn. 303 (1990); Cosgrove Development Co. v. Cafferty, 179 Conn. 670 (1980); United Liq. of Connecticut, Inc. v. Teamsters Local 443, 179 Conn. 211 (1979). ***PRACTICE AREAS:*** Real Estate; Commercial Law.

JUDITH A. MAUZAKA, born New Haven, Connecticut, June 5, 1951; admitted to bar, 1982, Connecticut and U.S. District Court, District of Connecticut; 1988, U.S. Court of Appeals, Second Circuit. *Education:* University of Hartford (B.A., 1976); University of Connecticut (J.D., 1982). *Member:* Connecticut Bar Association; The Association of Trial Lawyers of America; Connecticut Trial Lawyers Association; National Employment Lawyers Association; Connecticut Employment Lawyers Association. ***REPORTED CASES:*** Tracey Thurman v. City of Torrington, 595 F. Supp. 1521 (D. Conn. 1985); Baldwin v. Harmony Builders, 31 Conn. App. 242 (1993). ***PRACTICE AREAS:*** Employment Law; Civil Rights; Personal Injury; Family Law; Divorce; Child Custody; Criminal Defense; Driving While Intoxicated; Felonies; Traffic Violations.

REPRESENTATIVE CLIENTS: Future Industries of America, Inc.; Borough Counsel, Borough of Woodmont; Travelers Insurance Co.; Branford Land Trust; Derby Savings Bank; People's Bank; Bank of Boston Connecticut; Bank of New Haven; ComNet Mortgage Services, Inc.; Essex Savings Bank; Fleet Bank; Lafayette American Bank and Trust Company; McCue Mortgage Co.; The Chase Manhattan Bank; The Prudential Bank.; Merriam Motors; Park City Ford; Key Hundai; Misto, LLC.
APPROVED ATTORNEYS FOR: Lawyers Title Insurance Company; Connecticut Attorneys' Title Insurance Co.; Chicago Title; First Fidelity Title.
REFERENCE: Fleet Bank.

WILLIAMS, COONEY & SHEEHY

BRIDGEPORT, CONNECTICUT

(See Trumbull)

General Civil Practice with emphasis on Civil Litigation including Commercial Litigation, Insurance Defense, Personal Injury, Malpractice and Products Liability, Civil Rights, Zoning and Employment Litigation in State and Federal Courts. Trials and Appeals, OSHA, Environmental, Banking and Municipal.

WILLINGER, WILLINGER & BUCCI, P.C.

855 MAIN STREET
BRIDGEPORT, CONNECTICUT 06604
Telephone: 203-366-3939
Telecopier: 203-337-4588

General Practice. Real Estate, Corporate, Commercial, Foreclosure, Bankruptcy, Secured Financing, Zoning, Labor, Probate, Condemnation, Workers Compensation, Financial, Banking, Personal Injury and Criminal Law. Trials in all Courts.

FIRM PROFILE: The law firm of Willinger, Shepro, Tower & Bucci, P.C., consists of a staff of 12 attorneys. We practice law throughout the state of Connecticut in the areas of foreclosures, loan workouts and bankruptcy collections for institutional clients, commercial and residential real estate development on behalf of institutional and private clients, the negotiation and closing of secured and unsecured transactions, financing, bankruptcy, land use, landlord/tenant matters, leasing and all phases of civil litigation including commercial and personal injury trials in all state and federal courts. A profile of the seven partners and associates follows.

CHARLES J. WILLINGER, JR., born Bridgeport, Connecticut, February 11, 1949; admitted to bar, 1973, Florida and Connecticut; 1975, U.S. District Court, District of Connecticut. *Education:* Fairfield University (A.B., 1970); University of Miami (J.D., 1973). Phi Delta Phi. Author: "Inter-Faces; Coordination of the Criminal Justice System," Commission on Criminal Justice, Standards & Goals (Justice Dept.), 1973. Member: Connecticut Association Board of Educations, 1975-1977; Shelton Board of Education, 1975-1977. Member, Valley Regional Planning Commission, 1977-1978. Member, Panel of Arbitrators, American Arbitration Association. *Member:* Bridgeport, Connecticut and American Bar Associations; The Florida Bar. ***PRACTICE AREAS:*** Land Use; Real Estate; Financing Transactions; Loan Restructures; Corporate Law; Planning and Zoning Commissions; Coastal Area Management Commissions; Inland Wetland Agencies; Department of Transportation; Department of Environmental Protection.

THOMAS W. BUCCI, born Bridgeport, Connecticut, April 17, 1948; admitted to bar, 1973, Connecticut; 1974, U.S. District Court, District of Connecticut; 1978, U.S. Court of Appeals, Second Circuit; 1981, U.S. Supreme Court. *Education:* Sacred Heart University (B.A., 1969); University of Connecticut (J.D., cum laude, 1973). Assistant Corporation Counsel, City of Bridgeport, 1975-1981. Mayor, City of Bridgeport, 1985-1989. Counsel to Greater Bridgeport Food Council, 1992—. *Member:* Bridgeport, Connecticut and American Bar Associations. ***SPECIAL AGENCIES:*** Commission on Human Rights and Opportunities, Connecticut State Board of Labor Relations; Connecticut Board of Mediation and Arbitration. ***REPORTED CASES:*** Lead Counsel in Connecticut v. Teal 457 US 440 (1982). ***PRACTICE AREAS:*** Trial and Appellate Practice; Loan Restructures; Employment Law; Foreclosures; Bankruptcy; Creditor's Rights; Corporate Law. ***Email:*** tbucci@eci.com

ANN MARIE KENT WILLINGER, born Bridgeport, Connecticut, November 20, 1954; admitted to bar, 1981, Connecticut; 1982, U.S. District Court, District of Connecticut; 1985, U.S. Court of Appeals, Second Circuit. *Education:* Wellesley College; Fairfield University (B.A., magna cum laude, 1976); St. John's University; University of Bridgeport (J.D., summa cum laude, 1981). Recipient, Outstanding Legal Scholarship Award, University of Bridgeport. Member, St. John's University Law Review, 1978-1979. *Member:* Bridgeport and Connecticut Bar Associations; American Inn of Courts. ***PRACTICE AREAS:*** Land Use Planning; Civil Litigation; Commercial Litigation. ***Email:*** ririk@aol.com

BRADD S. ROBBINS, born Worcester, Massachusetts, April 24, 1963; admitted to bar, 1988, Connecticut; 1989, Massachusetts and U.S. District Court, District of Connecticut. *Education:* Brandeis University (B.A., 1985); Boston University (J.D., 1988). *Member:* Greater Bridgeport, Connecticut and American Bar Associations. ***PRACTICE AREAS:*** Real Estate Development; Commercial Lending; Workouts; Commercial and Residential Leasing and related Transactions; Corporate Law.

MARK D. ARONS, born Durham, North Carolina, April 26, 1958; admitted to bar, 1983, Connecticut and U.S. District Court, District of Connecticut; 1984, U.S. Court of Appeals, Second Circuit; 1988, U.S. Supreme Court. *Education:* Vanderbilt University (B.A., cum laude, 1980); Case Western Reserve University (J.D., 1983). Recipient, American Jurisprudence Award in Criminal Law. Notes Editor, Case Western Reserve Journal of International Law, 1982-1983. Author: "Life, Liberty and the Preemptory Challenge," Trial Practice, Vol. 10, No. 1, Winter 1995. Special Assistant States Attorney, 1985-1986. Diplomate, National Institute of Trial Advocacy. *Member:* The Association of Trial Lawyers of America; Connecticut Trial Lawyers Association (Member, Public Relations Committee, 1997—). ***PRACTICE AREAS:*** Personal Injury; Medical Malpractice; Governmental Liability; Wrongful Death; Products Liability.

TONI MARIE GELINEAU, born New Haven, Connecticut, June 12, 1955; admitted to bar, 1980, Connecticut and U.S. District Court, District of Connecticut. *Education:* Fairfield University (B.A., 1977); University of Connecticut, School of Law (J.D., 1980). Board Member, Town of Orange, Youth Service Commission, 1974-1977. Commissioner, Town of Island-Wetlands Commission, 1980-1982. Board Member, State of Connecticut, Advisory Board, Office of Protection & Advocacy for Persons with Disabilities, 1980-1985. Committee Member, Town of Orange, School Building Committee, 1985-1989. Board Member, Town of Orange, Townwide Building Committee, 1989-1992. Commissioner, Town of Orange, Human Services Commission, 1990-1992. Board Member, Orange Residential Services group home for persons with developmental disabilities, 1982-1996. ***PRACTICE AREAS:*** Real Estate and Zoning; Probate; Domestic Relations; General Practice.

(This Listing Continued)

HEIDI C. McGEE, born Norwalk, Connecticut, December 13, 1965; admitted to bar, 1992, Connecticut; 1993, U.S. District Court, District of Connecticut. *Education:* Colgate University (B.A., 1987); University of Connecticut (J.D., 1992). *Member:* Bridgeport, Connecticut and American Bar Associations. ***PRACTICE AREAS:*** Mortgage Foreclosure; Municipal Taxation; Commercial Litigation. ***Email:*** hcclark@msn.com

THOMAS W. BUCCI, JR., born Bridgeport, Connecticut, September 30, 1969; admitted to bar, 1995, Connecticut; 1996, U.S. District Court, District of Connecticut. *Education:* University of Connecticut (B.A., 1991); St. Johns University School of Law (J.D., 1994). *Member:* Greater Bridgeport, Connecticut and New York State Bar Associations. ***PRACTICE AREAS:*** Land Use; Civil Litigation; Commercial Litigation; Labor and Employment Law; Municipal Law.

NATHALIE FEOLA-GUERRIERI, born Bridgeport, Connecticut March 2, 1969; admitted to bar, 1996, Connecticut and U.S. District Court, District of Connecticut. *Education:* Fairfield University (B.A., 1991); Quinnipiac College, School of Law (J.D., 1995). *Member:* Greater Bridgeport, Connecticut (Member, Litigation Section; Planning and Zoning Section; Commercial Law and Bankruptcy Section) and American Bar Associations. ***PRACTICE AREAS:*** Land Use Law; Litigation; Bankruptcy Law.

REPRESENTATIVE CLIENTS: People's Bank; Dime Savings Bank of New York, FSB; UST Bank/Connecticut; City of Bridgeport; United Properties; Bridgeport Jai-Alai, Inc.; Kasper Group; YMCA of Greater Bridgeport.
APPROVED CLOSING ATTORNEYS FOR: Chicago Title Insurance Company; Security Title Insurance Company; Lawyers Title Insurance Corp.; First American Title Insurance Co.; Stewart Title Guaranty Company.

BURTON S. YAFFIE

BRIDGEPORT, CONNECTICUT

(See Trumbull)

General Practice. Real Estate, Zoning, Corporation, Probate, Administrative, Commercial, Negligence, Family and Estate Planning Law. Trials in all Courts.

THOMAS M. YUDITSKI

105 BROOKLAWN PLACE
BRIDGEPORT, CONNECTICUT 06604
Telephone: 203-335-5996
Fax: 203-336-5438

Personal Injury, Automobile Accidents, Medical Malpractice, Workers Compensation, Arbitration.

THOMAS M. YUDITSKI, born Bridgeport, Connecticut, September 29, 1946; admitted to bar, 1971, Connecticut; 1975, U.S. District Court, District of Connecticut; 1976, U.S. Court of Appeals, Second Circuit. *Education:* Fairfield University (B.S., 1968); St. John's University (J.D., 1971). Special Master, Superior Court, 1983-1985, 1997-1998, 2000-2001; Special Master, U.S. District Court, District of Connecticut, 1994, 1997, 2000. Author: "What Insurance Companies Don't Want You to Know, 1998." Co-Author: "Personal Injury Litigation Practice in Connecticut 1991"; "Trying the Soft Tissue Injury Case in Connecticut 1992," National Business Institute, Inc. Seminars. Lecturer, Westport Bar Association, April 5, 1995 "How to Aggressively Manage Plaintiffs Personal Injury Cases." Member, Panel of Arbitrators, American Arbitration Association. *Member:* Bridgeport, Connecticut and American Bar Associations; Connecticut Trial Lawyers Association (Member, Board of Governors, 1984-1987); The Association of Trial Lawyers of America. ***PRACTICE AREAS:*** Personal Injury Law; Medical Malpractice; Workers Compensation; Automobile Accidents; Arbitration.

LEGAL SUPPORT PERSONNEL

MARJORIE LEHMAN

ZEISLER & ZEISLER, P.C.

Established in 1965
558 CLINTON AVENUE
P.O. BOX 3186
BRIDGEPORT, CONNECTICUT 06605-0186
Telephone: 203-368-4234
Fax: 203-367-9678
Email: info@zeislaw.com
URL: http://www.zeislaw.com

General Civil Practice. Bankruptcy, Corporate Reorganization, Securities Investor Protection Act Litigation, Real Estate, Probate, Corporation, Family, Personal Injury, Negligence and Commercial Law. Trials.

RICHARD D. ZEISLER, born Bridgeport, Connecticut, June 9, 1937; admitted to bar, 1963, Connecticut. *Education:* University of Pennsylvania (B.A., cum laude, 1959); University of Connecticut (LL.B., 1963). Listed in Best Lawyers in America, Bankruptcy. Author, Bankruptcy Section of Matthew Bender Treatise on Divorce Workbook, 1984-1985. Lecturer: Bridgeport Bar Association Continuing Legal Education Program, 1970—; Connecticut Continuing Legal Education Program, 1980—; Commercial Law and Bankruptcy, BAR/BRI Bar Review Program, 1982-1984; Bankruptcy, Professional Seminars, Inc., 1986—. Adjunct Professor of Bankruptcy, University of Bridgeport School of Law, 1986-1987. Member, Bridgeport City Council, 1965-1973. *Member:* Greater Bridgeport (Member, Committee on Federal Courts, 1974-1976; Chairman, Commercial Section, 1984-1996; President, 1990-2000), Connecticut (Member, Commercial Law and Bankruptcy Section, 1980—) and American (Member, Committee on Commercial Law & Bankruptcy, 1970-1976) Bar Associations. ***PRACTICE AREAS:*** Bankruptcy; Commercial Law. ***Email:*** rdzeisler@zeislaw.com

JAMES G. VERRILLO, born Bridgeport, Connecticut, March 20, 1951; admitted to bar, 1976, Connecticut. *Education:* Georgetown University (A.B., 1973); University of Connecticut (J.D., cum laude, 1976). *Member:* Bridgeport (Member, Commercial Law Committee), Connecticut (Member, Commercial Law Section) and American Bar Associations; American Bankruptcy Institute. ***PRACTICE AREAS:*** Bankruptcy; Commercial Law. ***Email:*** jverrillo@zeislaw.com

JAMES BERMAN, born New Haven, Connecticut, October 18, 1955; admitted to bar, 1981, Connecticut. *Education:* Yale University (B.A., 1977); University of Connecticut (J.D., 1981). Law Clerk to the Hon. Alan H. W. Shiff, U.S. Bankruptcy Judge, District of Connecticut, 1981-1983. Listed in Best Lawyers in America, Bankruptcy Law, 2001-2002. Chairman, 1992-1994, and Vice Chairman, 1990-1992, Commercial and Bankruptcy Section, Connecticut Bar Association. Counsel to Committee for Revision of Local Bankruptcy Rules, 1997. Lecturer, Bankruptcy, Connecticut Bar Association, Professional Seminars, Inc., 1986—. ***PRACTICE AREAS:*** Bankruptcy; Commercial Law. ***Email:*** jberman@zeislaw.com

CRAIG I. LIFLAND, born New York, N.Y., October 27, 1956; admitted to bar, 1983, New York; 1984, Florida; 1990, Connecticut. *Education:* Syracuse University (B.A., 1978); Nova Southeastern University (J.D., 1982). Co-Author, "Personal Bankruptcy Planning," Chapter 247, Ohio Transaction Guide, Matthew Bender, 1984. *Member:* Connecticut (Member: Commercial and Bankruptcy Section; Case Management Committee, U.S. Bankruptcy Court, District of Connecticut, Bridgeport Division, 1993-1995) and American (Member, Corporation, Banking and Business Law Section) Bar Associations; The Florida Bar; American Bankruptcy Institute; Turnaround Management Association. ***PRACTICE AREAS:*** Bankruptcy; Commercial Law. ***Email:*** clifland@zeislaw.com

JED HORWITT, born New York, N.Y., October 9, 1959; admitted to bar, 1988, Connecticut and New York. *Education:* Ithaca College (B.S., cum laude, 1981); Cornell University (J.D., cum laude, 1987). Co-Editor, Stockbroker Liquidation Chapter, *Norton Bankruptcy Law and Practice*, 2nd edition. Lecturer: Connecticut Bar Association; Public Investors Arbitration Bar Association. *Member:* Connecticut Bar Association (Chairman, Commercial Law and Bankruptcy Section, 1998-2000); American Bankruptcy Institute; Association of Commercial Finance Attorneys. ***PRACTICE AREAS:*** Bankruptcy; Creditors Rights; Securities Investor Protection Act; Litigation. ***Email:*** jhorwitt@zeislaw.com

MATTHEW K. BEATMAN, born Hartford, Connecticut, July 2, 1965; admitted to bar, 1990, Connecticut; 1991, U.S. District Court, District of Connecticut; 1996, U.S. District Court, Southern and Eastern Districts of New York. *Education:* University of Connecticut (B.S., Electrical Engineering, magna cum laude, 1987); University of Connecticut School of Law (J.D., with honors, 1990). Tau Beta Pi; Eta Kappa Nu. Contributing Editor, Bankruptcy Bulletin, Connecticut Bar Association, 1998-2000. Law Clerk to the Hon. Alan H. W. Shiff, U.S. Bankruptcy Judge, District of Connecticut, 1991-1992. Lecturer: Connecticut Bar Association; various private and public seminar audiences. Alternate Member, Berlin Planning and Zoning Commission. *Member:* Connecticut (Chair, Consumer Bankruptcy Committee; Member, Executive Committee, Commercial Law and Bankruptcy Section; Co-Chair, Commercial Law and Bankruptcy, Young Lawyers Section) and American Bar Associations; Connecticut Trial Lawyers Association; American Bankruptcy Institute, Turnaround Management Association. ***PRACTICE AREAS:*** Bankruptcy; Commercial Litigation. ***Email:*** mbeatman@zeislaw.com

JEFFREY HELLMAN, born New Haven, Connecticut, October 10, 1961; admitted to bar, 1986, Pennsylvania; 1987, Massachusetts; 1989, Connecticut. *Education:* Duke University (A.B., magna cum laude, 1983); Harvard University (J.D., cum laude, 1986). Lecturer on Changes to the Federal Rules of Civil Procedure, Collection Law in Connecticut. Member: Criminal Justice Action Panel, U.S. District Court; Merit Screening Panel Section of the next U.S. Bankruptcy Judge. Co-Editor, Stockbroker Liquidation Chapter, *Norton Bankruptcy Law and Practiee*, 2nd edition. *Member:* Connecticut (Member: Executive Committee, Federal Practice Section; Commercial Law and Bankruptcy Section) and American Bar Associations. ***PRACTICE AREAS:*** Commercial Litigation; Bankruptcy; Criminal Law. ***Email:*** jhellman@zeislaw.com

COLEEN HURLIE-DUNN, born Mount Vernon, New York; admitted to bar, 1986, Connecticut; 1987, U.S. District Court, District of Connecticut. *Education:* Ithaca College (B.A., summa cum laude, 1982); University of Pennsylvania (J.D.). Phi Kappa Phi. *Member:* Bridgeport, Connecticut (Member, Sections on: Real Property, Commercial Law, Bankruptcy) and American Bar Associations; Commercial Law League of America. ***PRACTICE AREAS:*** Commercial Law; Commercial Leasing; Real Property; Corporate Law; Debtor and Creditor Reorganization. ***Email:*** churlie-dunn@zeislaw.com

DENNIS P. ANDERSON, born New Haven, Connecticut, February 14, 1946; admitted to bar, 1972, Connecticut; U.S. District Court, District of Connecticut; U.S. Court of Appeals, Second Circuit. *Education:* Amherst College (B.A., 1969); University of Connecticut (J.D., 1972). Author: "A Practical Guide To Condominium Law in Connecticut," Connecticut Law Review, Volume 4, Number 4, 1972; "Evaluating the Potential Voidability of Title to Connecticut Real Property Acquired Through a Foreclosure Proceeding," Volume 683, Number 2, Connecticut Bar Journal 95, 1989. Contributing Author: *Connecticut Foreclosures*, Connecticut Law Tribune, 2nd Ed., 1989; *Connecticut Lawyers Deskbook*. Co-Author: *Connecticut Common Interest Ownership Manual*, 1984, Connecticut Bar Association. Lecturer, Connecticut Common Interest Ownership Act and Selected Foreclosure Issues, Connecticut Bar Association Continuing Legal Education Program and Bridgeport Bar Association. Member, Connecticut Standards of Title Committee. Secretary, Milford Zoning Board of Appeals. *Member:* Bridgeport (Chairman, Foreclosure Committee), New Haven, Connecticut (Executive Committee Member, Real Property Section; Member, Commercial Law and Bankruptcy Section) and American Bar Associations. ***PRACTICE AREAS:*** Commercial Real Estate; Commercial Litigation. ***Email:*** danderson@zeislaw.com

---

LAWRENCE S. GROSSMAN, born Brooklyn, New York, May 1, 1960; admitted to bar, 1994, Connecticut. *Education:* Colgate University (A.B., 1982); Fordham University (J.D., 1994). Editor, Fordham Moot Court Board. ***PRACTICE AREAS:*** Commercial Litigation; Bankruptcy Litigation. ***Email:*** lgrossman@zeislaw.com

STEPHEN M. KINDSETH, born Enfield, Connecticut, June 22, 1968; admitted to bar, 1994, Connecticut; 1995, U.S. District Court, District of Connecticut; 1996, U.S. District Court, Southern District of New York. *Education:* Fordham University (B.A., 1990); University of Connecticut (J.D., with honors, 1994). Recipient, William F. Starr Research Fellowship. Contributing Editor, Stockbroker Liquidation Chapter, *Norton Bankruptcy Law and Practice*, 2nd edition. *Member:* Bridgeport and Connecticut (Legislative Liason, 2000—; Member, Commercial Law and Bankruptcy Section; Co-Chair, Bankruptcy and Commercial Law Committee, 1996-1998 and Chair, Bridgeport Local Unit, 1998-1999, Young Lawyers Section) Bar Associations; American Bankruptcy Institute. ***PRACTICE AREAS:*** Bankruptcy; Bankruptcy Litigation; Liquidations; Commercial Litigation. ***Email:*** skindseth@zeislaw.com

JOHNPATRICK O'BRIEN, born Bridgeport, Connecticut, December 15, 1967; admitted to bar, 1995, Connecticut. *Education:* Sacred Heart University (B.S., cum laude, 1989); Southwest Missouri State University (M.P.A., magna cum laude, 1991); Thomas M. Cooley Law School (J.D., 1994). Phi Alpha Delta. *Member:* Connecticut and American Bar Associations; Connecticut Trial Lawyers Association. ***REPORTED CASES:*** Dobozy v. Dobozy, 41 Conn. App. 861 (1996). ***PRACTICE AREAS:*** Personal Injury; Criminal Law; Workers Compensation; Appellate Practice. ***Email:*** jobrien@zeislaw.com

GREGORY B. SCHILLER, born Abington, Pennsylvania, September 4, 1958; admitted to bar, 1999, Connecticut; U.S. District Court, District of Connecticut; U.S. District Court, Southern and Eastern Districts of New York. *Education:* Western Connecticut State University (B.A., 1991); Western New England College (J.D., 1998). *Member:* Connecticut (Member, Commercial Law and Bankruptcy Sections) and American Bar Associations (Member, Busi-

(This Listing Continued)

(This Listing Continued)

ZEISLER & ZEISLER, P.C., Bridgeport—Continued

ness Law Section); American Bankruptcy Institute. ***PRACTICE AREAS:*** Bankruptcy; Commercial Law; Corporate Law; Bankruptcy Litigation. ***Email:*** gschiller@zeislaw.com

NICOLE L. INMAN, born U.S. Air Force Base, Bitburg, Germany, July 16, 1972; admitted to bar, 1999, Illinois; 2001, New York (Not admitted in Connecticut). *Education:* Colorado State University (B.A., 1995); St. John's University School of Law (J.D., 1999). *Member:* American Bar Association. ***PRACTICE AREAS:*** Bankruptcy; Commercial Litigation. ***Email:*** ninman@zeislaw.com

JASON M. VENDITTI, born Bridgeport, Connecticut, March 22, 1973; admitted to bar, 2000, Connecticut. *Education:* University of North Texas (B.A., cum laude, 1996); Quinnipiac University School of Law (J.D., magna cum laude, 2000). Member, Moot Court Honor Society. *Member:* Connecticut and American Bar Associations. ***PRACTICE AREAS:*** Commercial Litigation. ***Email:*** jvenditti@zeislaw.com

OF COUNSEL

ROBERT M. ZEISLER, born Bridgeport, Connecticut, February 25, 1932; admitted to bar, 1957, Connecticut; 1965, U.S. Supreme Court. *Education:* University of Connecticut (B.A., 1953); Boston University (LL.B., 1957). Chairman, Conservation Commission, Town of Fairfield, 1965-1970. *Member:* Bridgeport and Connecticut Bar Associations; Connecticut Trial Lawyers Association; The Association of Trial Lawyers of America. [U.S. Army, 1957, Reserves, 1958-1963]. ***PRACTICE AREAS:*** Civil Practice; Personal Injury; Arbitration.

REPRESENTATIVE CLIENTS: C.R. Klewin, Inc.; Peoples Bank; West End Moving & Storage Co., Inc.; Liquidating Custodian for Handy & Harman Refining Group, Inc.; Patriot National Bank; E&F/Walsh Building Company, LLC; Bridgeport Jai Alai, Inc.; Power Company of America; Worth Construction Co., Inc.

ZELDES, NEEDLE & COOPER

A PROFESSIONAL CORPORATION

Established in 1971

1000 LAFAYETTE BOULEVARD

P.O. BOX 1740

BRIDGEPORT, CONNECTICUT 06601-1740

Telephone: 203-333-9441

Telecopiers: 203-333-1489; 579-2933

Email: znclaw.com

URL: http://www.znclaw.com

Litigation in all Courts. Corporate, Probate, Real Estate, Bankruptcy, Family, Condemnation, Criminal, Administrative and Environmental Law.

FIRM PROFILE: Zeldes, Needle & Cooper, founded in 1971, is a firm of thirty lawyers committed to delivering quality legal services to a wide range of clients in accordance with the highest ethical standards of the profession. We welcome the opportunity to provide effective, tenacious and creative responses to the most challenging and complex situations.

The firm includes component groups focusing on litigation and transactional matters. Our litigation work encompasses the routine and the unusual, including the fields of commercial, corporate, personal injury, securities, aviation, product liability, criminal, construction, lender liability, employment, professional liability and domestic relation law. Our transactional attorneys concentrate on corporate matters, bankruptcy, estate planning and settlement, zoning, real estate, business planning, loan restructuring and workouts, banking and commercial conveyancing.

Our attorneys have exceptionally strong academic credentials; a number have federal and state clerkship experience as well. We have been called upon to represent clients with unique and difficult problems and we take pride in devising innovative solutions to legal problems.

JACOB D. ZELDES, born Galesburg, Illinois, December 10, 1929; admitted to bar, 1957, Connecticut; 1958, U.S. District Court, District of Connecticut; 1959, U.S. Court of Appeals, 2nd Circuit; 1960, U.S. Supreme Court; 1966, U.S. Tax Court; 1993, U.S. Court of Appeals, Federal Circuit. *Education:* University of Wisconsin (B.S., 1951); Yale University (LL.B., 1957). Law Clerk, Hon. Robert P. Anderson, U.S. District Court, District of Connecticut, 1957-1958. Special Counsel, Connecticut House of Representatives, Select Committee to Investigate Impeachment of Probate Judge, 1985. *Member:* Greater Bridgeport, The Connecticut (Chairman, 1973-1974, Member, 1963—, Criminal Justice Committee; Chairman, 1984-1987 and Member, 1984—, Federal Practice Committee; Lawyer to Lawyer Arbitration, 1990—) and American Bar Associations; Connecticut Trial Lawyers Association; The Association of Trial Lawyers of America; Connecticut Bar Foundation; Connecticut Defense Lawyers Association (Lifetime Achievement Award, 1999). Fellow: American College of Trial Lawyers; American Bar Foundation. [With U.S.N.R., 1951-1953]. ***REPORTED CASES:*** Rogers vs Richmond, 365 U.S. 534 (1961); Marchetti vs United States, 390 U.S. 39 (1968); City of Harford vs Chase, 942 F.2d 130 (2d Cir. 1991); Continental Casualty Co. vs Pullman, Comley, Bradley & Reeves, 929 F.2d 103 (2d Cir. 1991);In Re Grievance Committee of U.S. District Court, District of Connecticut, 847 F.2d 57 (2d Cir. 1991); United States vs MacKenzie, 777 F.2d 811 (2d Cir. 1985); United States vs Curcio, 694 F.2d 14 (2d Cir. 1982); United States vs Curcio, 680 F.2d 881 (2d Cir. 1982); New York, New Haven & Hartford Railroad Co. vs Iannotti, 567 F.2d 166 (2d Cir. 1977); Connecticut Bank and Trust Co. vs Coffin, 213 Conn. 573 (1990); Joseph I. Lieberman, Attorney General vs Reliable Refuse Co., Inc. 212 Conn. 661 (1989); In Re Grand Jury Investigation by Judge John M. Alexander, 207 Conn. 98 (1988); Rules Committee of Superior Court of Connecticut vs Freedom of Information Commission, 192 Conn. 234 (1984); Caryl S. Stern vs Harold N. Stern, 165 Conn. 797 (1973); Elizabeth M. Gimbel vs Frederic A. Gimbel, et al, 147 Conn. 561 (1960). ***PRACTICE AREAS:*** Civil and Criminal Litigation. ***Email:*** jzeldes@znclaw.com

CHARLES M. NEEDLE, born Chelsea, Massachusetts, April 28, 1938; admitted to bar, 1963, Connecticut. *Education:* Harvard University (B.A., 1959); Wesleyan University (M.A.T., 1960); Yale University (LL.B., 1963). Member, Representative Town Meeting, Fairfield, 1967-1968. Candidate for State Senator for Twenty-Fifth Senatorial District, 1968. Director, 1968-2001 and President, 1986-1988, Harvard Club of Southern Connecticut. President, Foundation for Discovery Museum, 1999-2001. Regional Director, National Conference of Christians and Jews, 1994-1999. Chairman, Professional Division United Way, 1995. *Member:* Greater Bridgeport (Member, Executive Committee, 1989-1992; Treasurer, 1996-1997; Secretary, 1997-1998; Vice-President, 1999-2000; President, 2000-2001), The Connecticut (Member: House of Delegates, 1981; Member, Commercial Law and Bankruptcy Section, 1985—) and American Bar Associations. Member of Fellows of American Bar Foundation and Connecticut Bar Foundation; Advisory Board of Sacred Heart University Para-Legal Program. ***PRACTICE AREAS:*** Commercial Law and Litigation; Bankruptcy Law; Business Reorganization; Real Estate Law. ***Email:*** cneedle@znclaw.com

ROBERT S. COOPER, born New Haven, Connecticut, October 6, 1938; admitted to bar, 1963, Connecticut and U.S. District Court, District of Connecticut; 1965, U.S. Court of Appeals, 2nd Circuit. *Education:* Dartmouth College (A.B., cum laude, 1960); Yale University (LL.B., 1963). *Member:* Greater Bridgeport, The Connecticut and American Bar Associations. ***PRACTICE AREAS:*** Business Law; Financial Law; Commercial Planning; Transactions; Dispute Resolution. ***Email:*** rcooper@znclaw.com

ALFRED J. JENNINGS, JR., born Bridgeport, Connecticut, May 26, 1939; admitted to bar, 1964, Connecticut and U.S. District Court, District of Connecticut; 1969, U.S. Court of Appeals, 2nd Circuit; 1979, U.S. Supreme Court. *Education:* College of the Holy Cross (B.A., 1961); Yale University (LL.B., 1964). *Member:* Greater Bridgeport (Past Chairman, Business Law Committee), The Connecticut and American Bar Associations; Lawyer Pilot Bar Association; National Health Lawyers Association; Community Association Institute. Fellow, Connecticut Bar Foundation. [U.S.A.F., J.A., 1965-1967]. ***PRACTICE AREAS:*** Transactions; Business Law; Dispute Resolution; Real Estate Law; Health Care Law; Community Association Law. ***Email:*** ajennings@znclaw.com

STUART BEAR, born New Haven, Connecticut, May 6, 1944; admitted to bar, 1968, Connecticut and U.S. District Court, District of Connecticut; 1971, U.S. Court of Appeals, 2nd Circuit; 1972, U.S. Supreme Court. *Education:* Harvard University (A.B., cum laude, 1965; LL.B., cum laude, 1968). *Member:* Greater Bridgeport, The Connecticut (Member, Sections on: Federal Practice; Commercial Law and Bankruptcy; Family Law) and American Bar Associations; The Association of Trial Lawyers of America; Connecticut Trial Lawyers Association. ***REPORTED CASES:*** Young v Chase, 18 Conn.App. 85, 557 A.2d 134 (Conn.App., Apr. 4, 1989); Camp v Chase, 39 Conn. Supp. 264 (Sup. CT. Dec. 7, 1983); F.A.S. Intern., Inc. v. Reilly, 179 Conn. 507, 427 A.2d 392 (Conn., Jan 29, 1980); City of West Haven v. Impact, 174 Conn. 160, 384 A2d 353 (Conn., Jan 3, 1978); Michaud v. Gurney, 168 Conn. 431, 362 A.2d 857 (Conn., May 13, 1975); City of Hartford v. Chase, 942 F.2d 130, 20 Fed.R.Serv.3d 995, 19 Media L. Rep. 1172 (2ndCir.(Conn.), Aug 14, 1991); Christensen v. Kiewit-Murdock Inv. Corp., 815 F.2d 206, 55 U.S.L.W. 2539, 7 Fed.R.Serv.3d 592 (2nd Cir.(Conn.), Mar 26, 1987); Ives v. W.T. Grant Co., 522 F.2d 749 (2nd Cir.(Conn.), Jul 31, 1975); Inre Kokoszka,479 F.2d 990, 74-2 USTC P 9569 (2nd Cir.(Conn.), May 18, 1973); Givens v. W.T. Grant Co., 472 F.2d 1039 (2nd Cir.(Conn.), Dec 8, 1972); Givens v. W.T. Grant Co., 457 F.2d 612 (2nd Cir.(Conn.), Mar. 17, 1972); Campagnuolo v. Harder, 440 F.2d 1225 (2nd Cir.(Conn.), Mar 29, 1971); Connecticut Union of Welfare Emp. v. White, 357 F. Supp. 1378 (D.Conn., Apr 23, 1973); Barber v. White, 351 F.Supp. 1091 (D.Conn., Nov 28, 1972); O'Brien v. Trevethan, 336 F.Supp. 1029 (D.Conn., Jan 3, 1972); Rivera v Dunn, 329 F. Supp. 554 (D.Conn., Jul 29, 1971); Matter of Colonial Realty Co., 134 B.R. 1017, 26 Collier Bkrptcy. Cas.2d 333, 22 Bkrptcy.Ct. Dec. 662, Bkrptcy.L. Rep. P 74, 382 (Bkrptcy. D.Conn., Dec 24, 1991; In

(This Listing Continued)

re Fairfield Lumber & Supply Co., 214 B.R. 441 (Bkrptcy. D.Conn. 1997). ***PRACTICE AREAS:*** Commercial Law and Litigation; Bankruptcy Law; Business Reorganization Law; Matrimonial Law. ***Email:*** sbear@znclaw.com

FRANK J. SILVESTRI, JR., born New York, N.Y., November 15, 1946; admitted to bar, 1974, Connecticut; 1975, U.S. District Court, District of Connecticut and U.S. Court of Appeals, 2nd Circuit. *Education:* Georgetown University (A.B., summa cum laude, 1968); Yale University (J.D., 1974). Phi Beta Kappa. Lecturer: "Litigating Claims Against Failed Banks," Connecticut Trial Lawyers Association, October 26, 1991; "Litigating Against the F.D.I.C.," Bridgeport Bar Association, January 13, 1992; "Preserving Disorder: A Review of Rules and Decisions on Preserving Issues for Federal Appeals," Connecticut Bar Association, May 2, 1997. Law Clerk, Hon. J. Joseph Smith, U.S. Court of Appeals for the Second Circuit, 1974-1975. Member, Civil Justice Advisory Group, United States District Court for the District of Connecticut (1996-2000). *Member:* Greater Bridgeport, The Connecticut (Member, Federal Practice Section Executive Committee and Civil Practice Subcommittee) and American (Member, Sections on: Litigation; Antitrust; Member: Committees on Business Torts Litigation and Commercial and Banking Litigation) Bar Associations; American Health Lawyers Association. Fellow: Connecticut Bar Foundation; American Bar Foundation. [With USNR, 1968-1971]. ***REPORTED CASES:*** First Hartford Realty Corp vs Ellis, 181 Conn. 25 (1980); Pacelli Bros. Transportation, Inc. vs Pacelli, 189 Conn. 401 (1983); New England Dairies, Inc. vs Commissioner of Agriculture, 221 Conn. 422 (1992); Timber Trails Corporation v. Planning and Zoning Commission, 222 Conn. 380 (1992). ***PRACTICE AREAS:*** Commercial Litigation; Arbitration. ***Email:*** fsilvestri@znclaw.com

ROBERT A. HARRIS, born Danville, Virginia, April 27, 1956; admitted to bar, 1982, Connecticut and U.S. District Court, District of Connecticut. *Education:* Haverford College (B.A., 1978); University of Virginia (J.D.,1982). Connecticut Reporter for A.B.A. Business Torts Newsletter. Lecturer: "Providing for ADR in Commercial Contracts," Greater Bridgeport Bar Association, November 15, 2000; Connecticut Bar Foundation John A. Speziale Second Annual Alternate Dispute Resolution Symposium, Court-Annexed ADR, October 29, 1999; "Why Not Mediate Construction Disputes?" National Association of Credit Managers, Connecticut Chapter, October 26, 1999; "Arbitration and Mediation: Things You Should Know," Bridgeport Bar Association, May 27, 1999. Author: "Honeymoons Might Not Last Forever," Connecticut Law Tribune, August 17, 1998; "Litigation Rarely Solution to Business Disputes," Fairfield County Business Journal, December 28, 1998; "Arbitrating Employment Claims Can Avoid a Flood of Lawsuits," Fairfield County Business Journal, January 11, 1999; "Developing a Mediation Culture Among Commercial Litigators," Connecticut Lawyer, May, 2000; "Help Business Clients Mediate, Not Litigate," Fairfield County Business Journal, May 8, 2000; "Mediation: Try It, You'll Like It," Business Matters, May, 2000. Arbitrator, American Arbitration Association. *Member:* Greater Bridgeport, Connecticut and American (Member, Litigation, Business Torts, Dispute Resolution, Business Law, Law Practice Management Sections) Bar Associations; The Association of Trial Lawyers of America; Connecticut Trial Lawyers Association. ***REPORTED CASES:*** Ostrowski v. Avery, 243 Conn. 355 (1997). ***PRACTICE AREAS:*** Commercial Litigation; Arbitration; Mediation. ***Email:*** rharris@znclaw.com

GREGORY J. CAVA, born Colorado Springs, Colorado, January 19, 1958; admitted to bar, 1983, Connecticut; 1984, U.S. District Court, District of Connecticut and U.S. Tax Court; 1985, U.S. Court of Appeals, Second Circuit; 1987, U.S. Supreme Court. *Education:* Boston University (B.A., summa cum laude, 1980; J.D., 1983). Phi Beta Kappa. Commissioner (Alt.), Inland-Wetland Commission, Town of Roxbury, Connecticut, 2000—. Commissioner, Planning and Zoning Commission, Town of Darien, Connecticut, 1989-1993. Commissioner, Environmental Protection Commission, Town of Darien, Connecticut, 1989-1991. *Member:* The Regional (Stamford/Norwalk), Greater Bridgeport (Chairman, Real Property Committee, 1996-1998; Member, Real Property Committee, Land Use Committee), Connecticut (Vice Chair, 2001—; Treasurer, 1999-2001 and Secretary, 1997-1999, Real Property Section; Member: Executive Committee: Real Property Section, 1995—) and American (Member, Real Property Section) Bar Associations; The Association of Trial Lawyers of America. ***PRACTICE AREAS:*** Real Estate Transactions, Financing and Development; Land Use; Condominium Law; Condominium Development; Community Association Law. ***Email:*** gcava@znclaw.com

DAVID P. ATKINS, born Riverside, California, May 9, 1956; admitted to bar, 1982, Virgin Islands; 1983, U.S. Court of Appeals, Third Circuit; 1984, Connecticut and U.S. District Court, District of Connecticut; 1985, U.S. Court of Appeals, Second Circuit; 1986, U.S. Supreme Court; 1990, U.S. Tax Court. *Education:* Columbia University (B.A., summa cum laude, 1978); Yale University (J.D., 1981). Phi Beta Kappa. Co-Author: "Punishment or Compensation: New Constitutional Restrictions on Civil Forfeiture," 11 University of Bridgeport Law Review 371 (1991); "Advancing Client Costs," The Connecticut Law Tribune (May, 17,1997); "Responding to a Disciplinary Complaint," The Connecticut Law Tribune (April 24, 2000). Author: "Safeguarding Funds for Third Parties," The Connecticut Law Tribune (May 20, 1996); "Vicarious Liability: A Risk In Representation Affiliations," The Connecticut Law Tribune (May 4, 1998); "Contacts with An Opposing Party's Employees: When Is A Witness Off Limits?" The Connecticut Law Tribune (April 26, 1999); "Written Fee Agreements In Contingency Cases," Connecticut Lawyer (April, 1997). Law Clerk, Hon. Almeric L. Christian, U.S. District Court, District of the Virgin Islands, 1981-1983. Member, The Connecticut Law Tribune Editorial Board. *Member:* Virgin Islands, Connecticut (Member, Task Force on Attorney Grievance Procedures, 1997-1998; Member, Special Committee on In-House Counsel, 1999-2000) and American (Member, Litigation Section) Bar Associations; American Civil Liberties Union; Association of Professional Responsibility Lawyers (Director, 1996-1998). Fellow, Connecticut Bar Foundation. ***REPORTED CASES:*** Manson v. Stacescu, 823 F. Supp. 76 (D.Conn.) aff'd. 11 F. 3d 1127 (2d Cir. 1993); Federal Paper Board Co. Inc. v Amata, 693 F. Supp. 1376 (D.Conn. 1988); Plasil v. Tableman, 223 Conn. 68 (1992). ***PRACTICE AREAS:*** Criminal and Commercial Litigation; Appeals; Professional Licensing and Discipline; Legal Ethics. ***Email:*** datkins@znclaw.com

MAXIMINO MEDINA, JR., born New York, N.Y., May 20, 1958; admitted to bar, 1984, Connecticut and U.S. District Court, District of Connecticut. *Education:* Harvard University (B.A., 1980); New York University (J.D., 1984). Member, 1988-1991, Board of Directors, and Chairman, 1988-1991, Bridgeport Water Pollution Control Authority, 1988-1991. Member: Bridgeport Board of Education, 1993—. *Member:* Greater Bridgeport (Chairman, Minority Recruitment Committee, 1994-1995; Board of Directors, 1996-1998), Connecticut (Member, Committee to Attract and Promote Minority Participation in the Legal Profession, 1988-1993) and American Bar Associations; Connecticut Trial Lawyers Association; The Association of Trial Lawyers of America; Connecticut Hispanic Bar Association; National Hispanic Bar Association. ***LANGUAGES:*** Spanish. ***PRACTICE AREAS:*** Commercial Litigation; Bankruptcy Law; Personal Injury Litigation. ***Email:*** mmedina@znclaw.com

JONATHAN B. ORLEANS, born Washington, D.C., August 9, 1954; admitted to bar, 1985, New York, Connecticut, U.S. District Court, Southern District of New York and U.S. District Court, District of Connecticut; 1987, U.S. Court of Appeals, Second Circuit; 1999, U.S. Supreme Court. *Education:* Hampshire College (B.A., 1977); Princeton University (M.P.A., 1984); New York University (J.D., cum laude, 1984). Order of the Coif. Associate Editor, New York University Review of Law & Social Change, 1983-1984. Hays Civil Liberties Fellow. Law Clerk, Hon. M. Joseph Blumenfeld, U.S. District Court, District of Connecticut, 1984-1985. *Member:* Greater Bridgeport, Connecticut and American (Member, Litigation and Labor/Employment Sections) Bar Associations. ***REPORTED CASES:*** Stewart B. McKinney Foundation v. Town of Fairfield, 790 F. Supp. 1197 (D. Conn. 1992); Connecticut Air Services Inc. v. Danbury Aviation Commission, 211 Conn 690 (1989). ***PRACTICE AREAS:*** Civil Litigation; Employment Law. ***Email:*** jorleans@znclaw.com

SHELLEY R. SADIN, born Manila, Philippines, March 16, 1957; admitted to bar, 1984, Connecticut and U.S. District Court, District of Connecticut. *Education:* Yale University (B.A., 1979); Georgetown University (J.D., 1984). Member, Criminal Justice Act Standing Committee, 1990-1996. Criminal Justice Act District Representative, 1998—. Member, Federal Grievance Committee, 2000—. *Member:* Connecticut Bar Association (Member, Criminal Justice and Federal Practice Sections); National Association of Criminal Defense Lawyers; Connecticut Criminal Defense Lawyers Association (Member, Board of Governors, 1990—). ***PRACTICE AREAS:*** Criminal Investigations, Trials and Appeals; Civil Litigation and Appeals. ***Email:*** ssadin@znclaw.com

EDWARD R. SCOFIELD, born Bridgeport, Connecticut, October 6, 1961; admitted to bar, 1985, Connecticut; 1986, U.S. District Court, District of Connecticut; 1992, U.S. Court of Appeals, 2nd Circuit; 1994, U.S. Court of Appeals, Federal Circuit; 1996, U.S. District Court, Southern District of New York. *Education:* Yale University (B.A., cum laude, 1982); University of Connecticut (J.D., cum laude, 1985). Associate Editor, Connecticut Law Review, 1984-1985. Law Clerk, Hon. T. Emmet Clarie, U.S. District Judge, District of Connecticut, 1985-1986. Superior Court Attorney Trial Referee, 1996—. *Member:* Greater Bridgeport, Connecticut and American Bar Associations. ***PRACTICE AREAS:*** Civil Litigation; Intellectual Property Litigation. ***Email:*** escofield@znclaw.com

DAVID P. FRIEDMAN, born Montgomery, Alabama, April 23, 1957; admitted to bar, 1984, New York; 1988, Connecticut; 1989, U.S. District Court, District of Connecticut; 1992, U.S. Court of Appeals, Ninth Circuit; 1997, U.S. District Court, Southern District of New York; 1999, U.S. Court of Appeals, Second Circuit. *Education:* Stanford University (B.A., 1979); New York University (J.D., cum laude, 1983). Order of the Coif, 1983. Law Clerk, Hon. Judith S. Kaye, Chief Judge, New York Court of Appeals, 1986-1988. *Member:* Greater Bridgeport, Connecticut and American Bar Associations. ***PRACTICE AREAS:*** Civil Litigation; Commercial Litigation; Legal Malpractice Litigation. ***Email:*** dfriedman@znclaw.com

LESLIE PAIER ACETO, born New Haven, Connecticut, January 11, 1962; admitted to bar, 1988, Connecticut; 1989, U.S. District Court, District of Connecticut. *Education:* Boston College (B.A., cum laude, 1984); University of Connecticut (J.D., cum laude, 1988). *Member:* Greater Bridgeport, New Haven, Connecticut and American Bar Associations. ***PRACTICE AREAS:*** Real Estate; Commercial; Corporate. ***Email:*** laceto@znclaw.com

(This Listing Continued)

ZELDES, NEEDLE & COOPER, A PROFESSIONAL CORPORATION, Bridgeport—Continued

MARTIN L. McCANN, born Bethpage, New York, May 16, 1958; admitted to bar, 1992, Connecticut; 1993, New York, U.S. District Court, District of Connecticut and U.S. Tax Court. *Education:* Fairfield University (B.S., 1980); Quinnipiac College, School of Law (J.D., magna cum laude, 1992). Associate Editor, Law Review, Quinnipiac College. Certified Public Accountant, Connecticut, 1986. Author: Pinsky v. Duncan: Ex Parte Attachment of Real Property in Connecticut and The Antithetical Restrictions of Due Process 11:1 University of Bridgeport Law U. Rev. 201 (1990), Use Tax, Mail Order Sales, and The Constitution: Recent Developments in Connecticut 12:1 University of Bridgeport Law Rev. 137 (1991); Federal Tax Aspects of Bankruptcy for Individuals and Corporations, Kleinrock Publications, TaxExpert Series (1998). *Member:* Greater Bridgeport, Connecticut and American Bar Associations; American Association of Attorney-Certified Public Accountants. ***PRACTICE AREAS:*** Business Law; Commercial Law; Bankruptcy; Taxation. ***Email:*** mmccann@znclaw.com

S. DAVE VATTI, born Philadelphia, Pennsylvania, June 12, 1968; admitted to bar, 1993, Connecticut and U.S. District Court, District of Connecticut. *Education:* Columbia University (B.A., 1989); University of Connecticut (J.D., 1992). Notes and Comments Editor, Connecticut Journal of International Law, 1991-1992. Interscholastic Director, Connecticut Moot Court Board, 1991-1992. First Place, Alva P. Louiselle Moot Court Competition, 1990. Author: "Issue Splitting to Maximize Recovery in Dram Shop Actions," CTLA Forum, Vol. 12, No. 5 (Sept./Oct. 1994). Adjunct Faculty, University of Connecticut School of Law, 1995—. *Member:* Greater Bridgeport and Connecticut Bar Associations; Connecticut Trial Lawyers Association. ***REPORTED CASES:*** Cirillo v. Sardo, 41 Conn. App.664 (1996). ***PRACTICE AREAS:*** Business Litigation; Personal Injury; Civil Rights; Employment Law; Campaign Finance Law. ***Email:*** dvatti@znclaw.com

DOUGLAS J. VARGA, born Bridgeport, Connecticut, August 30, 1963; admitted to bar, 1989, Illinois and U.S. District Court, Northern District of Illinois; 1993, U.S. District Court, Southern District of Illinois and U.S Court of Appeals, Seventh Circuit; 1995, U.S. Supreme Court and U.S. District Court, Northern District of Indiana; 1996, U.S. District Court, Central District of Illinois; 1997, New York and U.S. District Court, Southern and Eastern Districts of New York; 1998, Connecticut and U.S. District Court, District of Connecticut; 2000, U.S. Court of Appeals, Second Circuit. *Education:* Fairfield University (B.A., magna cum laude, 1985); Vanderbilt University (J.D., 1989). Executive Articles Editor, Vanderbilt Journal of Transnational Law, 1988-1989. *Member:* Greater Bridgeport, Connecticut and American Bar Associations. ***PRACTICE AREAS:*** Commercial Litigation; Employment Litigation. ***Email:*** dvarga@znclaw.com

MARIE A. CASPER, born Richmond, California, December 4, 1948; admitted to bar, 1990, Connecticut and U.S. District Court, District of Connecticut. *Education:* University of California at Berkeley (B.A., 1970; M.A., 1972); University of Bridgeport School of Law (1987-1988); Yale Law School (J.D., 1990). Member, Inns of Court, 1996-1999. *Member:* Connecticut Bar Association. ***PRACTICE AREAS:*** Commercial Litigation. ***Email:*** mcasper@znclaw.com

JOSEPH C. HUTCHISON, born Princeton, New Jersey, August 19, 1956; admitted to bar, 1983, New York; 1996, Connecticut. *Education:* Hamilton College (B.A., magna cum laude, 1978); New York University (J.D., 1982). Counsel to the United States Attorney, Senior Litigation Counsel, Assistant U.S. Attorney, Office of the U.S. Attorney, Connecticut, 1988-2000. Assistant Commissioner, Department of Investigation, City of New York, 1986-1988. Office of the Criminal Justice Coordinator, City of New York, 1984-1986. Defense Counsel, Legal Aid Society, New York, 1982-1984. Fulbright Scholar, 1978-1979. ***PRACTICE AREAS:*** Complex Commercial Litigation; White Collar Crime; Health Care Litigation; Environmental Litigation. ***Email:*** jhutchison@znclaw.com

---

MARCY TENCH STOVALL, born Greenville, Mississippi, March 20, 1956; admitted to bar, 1993, Connecticut; 1994, U.S. District Court, District of Connecticut; 1997, U.S. District Court, Southern District of New York; 1999, U.S. Court of Appeals, Second Circuit. *Education:* Stanford University (B.A., 1979); University of Connecticut (J.D., with high honors, 1993). Notes and Comments Editor, University of Connecticut Law Review. Author: "Looking for a Solution: *In Re Valerie D.* and State Intervention in Prenatal Drug Abuse," 25 Conn. L. Rev. 1265 (1993). *Member:* Greater Bridgeport and Connecticut (Member, Committee on Professional Ethics) Bar Associations. ***PRACTICE AREAS:*** Civil Litigation; Professional Licensing; Legal Ethics; Family Law. ***Email:*** mstovall@znclaw.com

SARAH W. POSTON, born Indianapolis, Indiana, May 7, 1965; admitted to bar, 1994, Pennsylvania; 1995, Ohio and New York; 1997, Connecticut. *Education:* Brown University (A.B., 1987); New York University (J.D., 1993). Staff Editor, American Survey of American Law. *Member:* Connecticut Bar Association. ***LANGUAGES:*** French and Spanish. ***PRACTICE AREAS:*** Civil Litigation; Criminal Law. ***Email:*** sposton@znclaw.com

MATTHEW S. HIRSCH, born Bronx, New York, June 16, 1969; admitted to bar, 1995, Connecticut; 1996, New York; 1997, U.S. District Court, District of Connecticut and U.S. District Court, Southern and Eastern Districts of New York; 2000, U.S. Court of Appeals, Second Circuit. *Education:* Lehigh University (B.A., 1991); Albany Law School of Union University (J.D., cum laude, 1995). Co-Author: "Where is the Product and What Do We Do Now (Practical Guide to the Law of Spoliation," Product Liability Law and Strategy, November, 1998. Associate Member, Albany Law School Journal of Science and Technology, 1993-1995. Adjunct Professor, Sacred Heart University. Law Clerk, Hon. E. Eugene Spear, Connecticut Appellate Court, 1995-1996. *Member:* Connecticut, New York State and American Bar Associations. ***REPORTED CASES:*** Moscovitch v. Danbury Hospital, 25 F.Supp. 2d 74 (D.Conn. 1998). ***PRACTICE AREAS:*** Medical Malpractice; Appellate Practice; Professional Liability; Products Liability; Business Litigation; Employment Law. ***Email:*** mhirsch@znclaw.com

ANTHONY R. MINCHELLA, born Phillipsburg, New Jersey, May 27, 1967; admitted to bar, 1997, New Jersey and Connecticut; 1998, U.S. District Court, District of Connecticut. *Education:* St. Bonaventure University (B.A., 1989) Quinnipiac College School of Law (J.D., magna cum laude, 1996). Associate Editor, Quinnipiac Law Review. Recipient: American Jurisprudence Award, Contracts, Legal Skills and Property; Corpus Juris Secundum Award; Contracts and Property; Distinguished Academic Achievement Award; Family Law, Alternative Dispute Resolution and Legal Drafting and Writing; Faculty Awards for Superior Classroom Performance, Excellence in Oral Advocacy, Academic Excellence and Outstanding Legal Scholarship. Author: *Comparative Negligence May Now Be A Defense to Recklessness,* American Law Firm Association's Transportation Update, Spring, 1999. Co-Author: *Connecticut's Law on Comparative Negligence,* American Law Firm Association's Fifty-State Compendium on Comparative Negligence, Summer, 1999. Law Clerk to the Honorable N. Peter Conforti, New Jersey Superior Court, Chancery Division. *Member:* Connecticut (Co-Chair, Federal Practice Section, 1998—; Co-Chair, Ethics and Professional Responsibility Section, 1999—; Member, Executive Board of Young Lawyers Section, 1998—) and American Bar Associations; Connecticut Trial Lawyers Association. ***PRACTICE AREAS:*** Commercial Litigation; Product Liability Litigation; Real Property Litigation; Personal Injury; Family Law. ***Email:*** aminchella@znclaw.com

BARBARA G. HAGER, born Syracuse, New York, April 4, 1957; admitted to bar, 1996, Connecticut; 1997, U.S. District Court, District of Connecticut; 1999, U.S. Court of Appeals, Second Circuit. *Education:* Allegheny College (B.A., magna cum laude, 1979); Princeton Theological Seminary (M.Div., 1982); University of Connecticut School of Law (J.D., 1996). Licensed, Ordained Minister, Presbyterian Church (U.S.A.), 1982—. Judge, Presbyterian Church (U.S.A.) Judicial Commission, 1997—. Director and Officer, Women's Center of Southeastern Connecticut, 1997-1999. *Member:* Connecticut and American Bar Associations. ***PRACTICE AREAS:*** Condominium Law; Business Law; Foreclosures; Municipal Law. ***Email:*** bhager@znclaw.com

KEVIN C. KELLY, born Allentown, Pennsylvania, November 12, 1959; admitted to bar, 1997, Connecticut and New York; 1999, U.S. Tax Court; 2000, U.S. District Court, District of Connecticut. *Education:* Assumption College (B.A., 1982); Fairfield University (M.A., 1985); University of Connecticut (J.D., 1997). Member, Connecticut Insurance Law Journal, 1995-1997. Recipient: Little, Brown & Company Book Award for Excellence: Trusts & Estates; CALI Excellence for the Future Award: Law and Public Health. Author: "Protecting Assets for the Community Spouse when Long-term Care is Needed," Probate & Property, Vol. 13, No. 2 (Mar./Apr. 1999). Member, Connecticut Client Advocacy Board, 1994-1997. Town Attorney, Stratford, Connecticut, 1999—. Commissioner: Stratford Commission on Aging, 1997-1999; Stratford Inland Wetland and Watercourse Commission, 1990-1993; Stratford Community Development Agency, 1989-1993. Board Member: Southwestern Connecticut Agency on Aging, Inc., 2000—; Stratford Visiting Nurses Association, Inc., 1998—. *Member:* Connecticut, New York State and American Bar Associations; National Academy of Elder Law Attorneys. ***SPECIAL AGENCIES:*** Senior Investigator, Connecticut Department of Social Services, 1983-1997. ***PRACTICE AREAS:*** Trusts and Estates; Estate Planning; Probate; Elder Law; Municipal Law. ***Email:*** kkelly@znclaw.com

ROBERT M. FROST, JR., born Manhasset, New York, May 3, 1973; admitted to bar, 1998, Connecticut; 1999, New York and U.S. District Court, District of Connecticut. *Education:* College of the Holy Cross (B.A., 1995); University of Connecticut School of Law (J.D., 1998). Phi Beta Kappa; Pi Sigma Alpha; Phi Delta Phi. Executive Director, Connecticut Moot Court Board. Notes and Comments Editor, Connecticut Law Review. Member, Criminal Justice Act Panel, U.S. District Court, District of Connecticut. *Member:* Greater Bridgeport (Co-Chairman, Young Lawyers Committee, 1999-2001; Member: Litigation Section; Criminal Law Section), Connecticut (Member: Litigation Section; Criminal Justice Section; Young Lawyers Section) and American (Member: Litigation Section; Young Lawyer's Section) Bar Associa-

(This Listing Continued)

tions; American Inns of Court (Raymond E. Baldwin AIC); American Health Lawyers Association. ***PRACTICE AREAS:*** Civil Litigation; State and Federal Criminal Litigation. ***Email:*** rfrost@znclaw.com

ROBERT A. PACELLI, JR., born Bridgeport, Connecticut, July 9, 1972; admitted to bar, 1997, Massachusetts; 1998, Connecticut and U.S. District Court, District of Connecticut. *Education:* Brandeis University (B.A., 1994); Boston University (J.D., 1997). Projects Editor, Probate Law Journal, 1996-1997. Paul J. Liacos Scholar. *Member:* American Bar Association. *Member:* Greater Bridgeport (Member, Sections on: Business Law; Real Property Law), Connecticut (Member, Sections on: Business Law; Real Property Law) and American (Member, Sections on: Business Law; Real Property Law) Bar Associations. ***PRACTICE AREAS:*** Business Law; Commercial Real Estate; Residential Real Estate; Community Association Law. ***Email:*** rpacelli@znclaw.com

OF COUNSEL

JOHN R. BRYK, born Bridgeport, Connecticut, March 29, 1950; admitted to bar, 1974, Connecticut. *Education:* University of Bridgeport (B.A., Pol. Sci., 1971); University of Connecticut (J.D., 1974). *Member:* Bridgeport (Chairman, Professional Conduct Committee, 1986-1989; Secretary, 1991-1993; Vice President, 1994-1996; President-Elect, 1996-1997; President, 1997-1998) and Connecticut (Professional Ethics Committee, 1987-1990) Bar Associations. ***PRACTICE AREAS:*** Business Law; Commercial Litigation; Commercial Real Estate; Residential Real Estate; Municipal Taxation; Probate; Personal Injury; Bankruptcy. ***Email:*** jbryk@znclaw.com

SHERYL J. ROSANDER, born Minneapolis, Minnesota, August 17, 1951; admitted to bar, 1977, Minnesota; 1978, California; 1985, Connecticut. *Education:* Wheaton College (B.A., with honors, 1973); William Mitchell College of Law (J.D., 1977). *Member:* Connecticut Bar Association (Real Property Section); American Bar Association (Real Property Section); Community Associations Institute. ***Email:*** srosander@znclaw.com

REPRESENTATIVE CLIENTS: A Child's Garden, Inc.; Advanced Health Care, P.C.; Advanced Technologies & Services, Inc.; The Albert Schweitzer Institute for the Humanities, Inc.; Alimak Elevator Co.; American Savings Bank; American Society of Travel Agents, Inc.; Atlantic Metals, Inc.; AXA Corporate Solutions; Bayer Corp.; Barry Blau & Partners, Inc.; Bodine Corp.; Bridgeport Jai Alai Associates; Bridgeport Jai Alai LLC; Cable Network Services, LLC; Carpenter Co., Inc.; Carpin Manufacturing, Inc.; Ceebraid Signal Management Group, Ltd.; Cesar Pelli & Associates; Chimaera, Inc.; Christopher Peacock Kitchens, Inc.; C. W. Pond Contractors, Inc.; Collins Prospect, LLC; Complete Newborn Care, P.C.; Connecticut Life and Casualty Insurance, Co.; Consumer Incentive Services, Inc.; Creative Choice Homes, LLC; David T. Chase Enterprises, Inc. (Hartford); DeepGreen, N.Y.; Doncasters, Ltd.; Eldon Capitol, LLC; Far Mill River Condominium Association; The Fieber Group; Financial Security Assurance, Inc.; Finimex, Inc.; Fleet National Bank; Gothia Medical AB; Governor's Ridge Association, Inc.; Great Companies, Inc.; Great West Life & Annuity Insurance Co.; Halox Technologies Corp.; H.B. Nitkin Co.; High Performance Plastics, Inc.; Highland Sanitation, Inc.; Hudson-Baylor, Inc.; Hudson United Bank; Industrial Recycling Services, Inc.; Information Architects, Inc.; ITT Corp.; Jeneric/Pentron, Inc.; Kaufman Fuel Co.; Kelsey-Hayes Co.; Key Bank of New York; Kurt H. Volk, Inc.; Lamar Life Insurance Co.; Ledgebrook Condominium Association, Inc.; Lubrication Management Co., Inc.; Manufacturer's Life Insurance Co.; The Marsilio Group; Mayfairs Wholesale Ptys., Ltd.; Mead School for Human Development, Inc.; Medica Valeggia, S.p.A.; Mercedes-Benz Credit Corp.; Mercury Tool & Mold, Inc.; Merrill Lynch; Metro Taxi, Inc.; MNC Credit Corp.; Moroso Performance Products, Inc.; New Castle Hotels, LLC; New England Consulting Group, Inc.; North American Van Lines; Northbrook Condominium Association, Inc.; Norwalk Medical; Nor-West Association, Inc.; Old Republic National Title Insurance Co.; Opticare Health Systems, Inc.; Outdoor Life Network, LLC; Oxford House, Inc.; Pace Motor Lines, Inc.; Paragon Publishing, Inc.; Pepper Partners Limited Partnership; PCS Health Services, Inc.; Pet Pantry Super Discount Stores, LLC; Pfizer, Inc.; Physicians Choice, LLC; Presence Studios Westport LLC; Progressive Plating Technology, Inc.; Promat, LLC; Radiant Systems, Inc.; RCD - Hudson, LLC; R.C. Dolner Construction, Inc.; Rosenthal & Rosenthal, Inc.; RSI Consulting, Ltd.; The Scott's Co./Earthgrow; Share Logic, P.C.; Shepard's, Inc.; Shoreline Entertainment and Greyhound Park, LLC; Skandinaviska Easkilda Burkem, Corp.; Slim Print International, LLC; Southport Woods Condominium Association, Inc.; SpeedVision Network; S.R. Smith, Inc.; Stamford Apartment Co.; Standard Oil of Connecticut, Inc.; Thomas Faria Corp.; Tomra of North America, Inc.; Town Fair Tire Centers, Inc.; Town of Stratford; Triple S, Inc.; Twombly Nursery, Inc.; Uniroyal Corporation; The Upper Deck Co., LLC; U.S. Trust Co.; Velco Chemicals, Inc.; Visirecord Systems, Inc.; Wallach Surgical Devices, Inc.; West Lyon Farm Condominium Association, Inc.

FUREY, DONOVAN, TRACY & DALY, P.C.

43 BELLEVUE AVENUE
BRISTOL, CONNECTICUT 06011
Telephone: 860-589-4343
Fax: 860-583-8674

General Practice. Probate, Corporation, Real Estate, Land Use, Criminal and Negligence Law. Trials in all Courts. Family Law.

WILLIAM J. TRACY, JR., born Bristol, Connecticut, January 30, 1954; admitted to bar, 1979, Connecticut; 1980, U.S. District Court, District of Connecticut; 1983, U.S. Court of Appeals, Second Circuit; 1986, U.S. Tax Court. *Education:* Middlebury College (A.B., 1975); Lewis and Clark College (J.D., 1978). Member, Lewis and Clark Law Review, 1977-1978. Town Attorney,

(This Listing Continued)

Town of Plymouth, 1988-1994; 1995-1998. *Member:* Bristol and Connecticut Bar Associations. ***PRACTICE AREAS:*** Appellate Law; Civil Litigation; Land Use Law; Estate Planning; Probate.

MICHAEL C. DALY, born Hartford, Connecticut, March 22, 1957; admitted to bar, 1982, Connecticut; 1983, U.S. District Court, District of Connecticut. *Education:* Trinity College (B.A., 1979); Western New England College School of Law (J.D., 1982). *Member:* Bristol, Hartford County, Connecticut (Member: House of Delegates, 1989-2001; Board of Governors, 1993-2001) and American Bar Associations. ***PRACTICE AREAS:*** Criminal Law; Negligence Law; Civil Litigation.

TIMOTHY W. FUREY, born Bristol, Connecticut, May 12, 1959; admitted to bar, 1984, Connecticut and U.S. District Court, District of Connecticut. *Education:* College of the Holy Cross (B.A., 1981); Suffolk University (J.D., cum laude, 1984). ***PRACTICE AREAS:*** Family Law; Land Use Law; Business Law; Elder Law; Bankruptcy.

F. PATRICK O'SULLIVAN, born County Kerry, Ireland, March 10, 1948; admitted to bar, 1974, Connecticut; 1975, Massachusetts and U.S. District Court, District of Connecticut; 1976, U.S. District Court, District of Massachusetts. *Education:* Boston University (B.A., 1971); Suffolk University (J.D., 1974). *Member:* The Association of Trial Lawyers of America; Connecticut Trail Lawyers Association. ***PRACTICE AREAS:*** Personal Injury (Plaintiff and Defendant) Law.

JAMES D. DONOVAN, born Hanover, New Hampshire, December 29, 1955; admitted to bar, 1985, Connecticut. *Education:* Valencia Community College (A.D., 1977); Central Connecticut State University (B.A., 1981); Western New England College (J.D., 1985). Assistant Clerk, Hartford Superior Court, 1982-1985. *Member:* Bristol and Connecticut Bar Associations. ***PRACTICE AREAS:*** Personal Injury; Criminal Law; Family Law.

CHRISTOPHER M. REEVES, born Manchester, Connecticut, December 20, 1956; admitted to bar, 1982, Connecticut; 1985, U.S. District Court, District of Connecticut. *Education:* Trinity College (B.A., 1979); University of Connecticut (J.D., 1982). *Member:* Connecticut Bar Association. ***PRACTICE AREAS:*** Personal Injury; Business Litigation.

ATTORNEYS FOR: Industrial Builders Co.; Barlow Metal Stamping Co.; Tollman Spring, Inc.; Nutrico, Inc.; Quality Coils; Admiral Insurance Co, Baron & Young Co., Inc., Behrens Manufacturing Co., Inc.; Joseph Distel Insurance Brokerage Co.; Signature Security, Inc.; Transportation General, Inc.; World Fulfillment LLC.
APPROVED ATTORNEYS FOR: Connecticut Attorney's Title Insurance Co.; First American Title Insurance Co.
REFERENCE: Webster Bank; Farmington Savings Bank; Valley Bank.

HAMZY & CONLIN

140 FARMINGTON AVENUE
BRISTOL, CONNECTICUT 06010
Telephone: 860-589-6525
Fax: 860-589-7370

Bankruptcy, Real Estate, Small Business Incorporations, Family Law, General Practice.

MEMBER OF THE FIRM

WILLIAM A. HAMZY, born 1966; admitted to bar, 1993, Connecticut. *Education:* University of Connecticut (B.A., 1988); Franklin Pierce Law School (J.D., 1992). Member, Bristol Housing Authority, Plymouth, Connecticut. ***PRACTICE AREAS:*** Bankruptcy; Real Estate; Small Business Corporations.

THOMAS W. CONLIN, born 1960; admitted to bar, 1993, Connecticut and U.S. District Court, District of Connecticut. *Education:* College of St. Rose (B.A., 1983); Western New England College (J.D., 1992). Member, Bristol Board of Finance. Member, Bristol Elks Lodge. Member, Bristol Housing Authority, Plymouth, Connecticut. *Member:* Bristol and Connecticut Bar Associations. ***PRACTICE AREAS:*** Real Estate; Family Law; Bankruptcy; General Practice.

JAMES C. JOHNSON

10 RIVERSIDE AVENUE
P.O. BOX 256
BRISTOL, CONNECTICUT 06011-0256
Telephone: 860-584-0551
Fax: 860-583-4453
Email: jcjohnsonesq@aol.com

Real Estate, Zoning, Wills, Trusts, Probate, Criminal Law, Driving While Intoxicated.

JAMES C. JOHNSON, born Bristol, Connecticut, 1953; admitted to bar, 1978, Connecticut; 1979, New York. *Education:* Villanova University (B.A., 1975); Albany Law School of Union University (J.D., 1978). ***PRACTICE***

(This Listing Continued)

JAMES C. JOHNSON, Bristol—Continued

AREAS: Real Estate; Zoning; Wills; Trusts; Probate; Criminal Law; Driving While Intoxicated.

NEWMAN CREED & ASSOCIATES

99 NORTH STREET, ROUTE 6
P.O. BOX 575
BRISTOL, CONNECTICUT 06010
Telephone: 860-583-5200
Telecopier: 860-582-0012
Email: bnewman@newmancreedlaw.com
URL: http://www.lawyers.com/newmancreed

Deep River, Connecticut Office: One High Street, 06417. Telephone: 860-526-8003.

Civil Litigation, Personal Injury, Employment Law, Product Liability, Commercial Law, Medical Malpractice, Wrongful Death, Aviation Law.

BRUCE E. NEWMAN, born New York, N.Y., October 16, 1964; admitted to bar, 1990, California, New York and Connecticut. *Education:* Colgate University (B.A., 1986); Albany Law School of Union University (J.D., 1989). Member, Jessup International Law Moot Court Competition. Recipient: 2nd Best Brief in the World, 1988; Runner-Up, Baxter Publication Award; L.B.J. Scholarship for Congressional Interns. Note and Comment Editor, Albany Law Review, 1988-1989. *Member:* New York State, Connecticut and American Bar Associations; State Bar of California; Connecticut Trial Lawyers Association. ***PRACTICE AREAS:*** Personal Injury; Labor and Employment Law; Product Liability; Civil Litigation. ***Email:*** bnewman@newmancreedlaw.com

KEVIN E. CREED, born Bridgeport, Connecticut, October 22, 1951; admitted to bar, 1997, Connecticut; 1998, U.S. District Court, District of Connecticut. *Education:* University of New Haven (A.A., 1973); University of Colorado at Colorado Springs (B.A., 1983); De Paul University (J.D., 1996). Member, Connecticut American Legion. *Member:* Connecticut and American Bar Associations; Connecticut Trial Lawyers Association; Connecticut State Police Alumni Association. [Maj., U.S. Army, Ret.; Staff Judge Advocate]. ***PRACTICE AREAS:*** Personal Injury; Product Liability; Employment Law; Aviation Law. ***Email:*** kcreed@newmancreedlaw.com

RUGGIERO, ZIOGAS & ALLAIRE

271 FARMINGTON AVENUE
BRISTOL, CONNECTICUT 06010
Telephone: 860-584-2384
Fax: 860-589-8213
URL: http://www.lawyers.com/rza

General Practice. Probate, Real Estate, Corporate, Negligence, Criminal, Elder Law, Family Law and Litigation.

MEMBERS OF FIRM

JAMES ZIOGAS, JR., born Bristol, Connecticut, August 24, 1952; admitted to bar, 1977, Connecticut. *Education:* Springfield College (B.S., 1974); Western New England College (J.D., 1977). Special Public Defender, State of Connecticut, 1982-1990. *Member:* Bristol (President, 1990-1991), Hartford County, Connecticut and American Bar Associations; The Association of Trial Lawyers of America. ***PRACTICE AREAS:*** Zoning, Planning and Land Use; Real Estate; Family Law; Criminal Law; Personal Injury. ***Email:*** jziogas@rzalawyers.com

STEPHEN O. ALLAIRE, born Bristol, Connecticut, February 25, 1945; admitted to bar, 1975, Connecticut; 1985, U.S. District Court, District of Connecticut and U.S. Court of Appeals, Second Circuit. *Education:* United States Military Academy (B.S., 1969); Georgetown University (J.D., 1975). Clerk to Chief Justice Charles S. House of the Connecticut Supreme Court, 1975-1976. Bristol City Councilman, 1977-1979. Member, Central Connecticut Regional Planning Agency, 1979-1981. Chairman, Bristol Development Authority, 1982-1985. Town Counsel: Towns of Plymouth, Litchfield, Winsted and Barkhamsted, 1989-2000. *Member:* Bristol (President, 1982-1986), Hartford County, Connecticut (Chairman, Human Rights Section, 1981-1982; Elder Law Section Executive Committee, 1998—) and American Bar Associations; Connecticut Association of Municipal Attorneys (Vice President, 1996-1998; President, 1998-2000). [Capt., U.S. Army, 1969-1974]. ***PRACTICE AREAS:*** Trusts and Estates; Elder Law; Probate. ***Email:*** sallaire@rzalawyers.com

REPRESENTATIVE CLIENTS: Dabko, Inc.; Wal-Mart; Home Depot; Town of Barkhamsted; Farmington Savings Bank; Webster Bank; O'Brien Funeral Home.
APPROVED ATTORNEYS FOR: FirstAmerican Title Insurance Co.
REFERENCES: Fleet Bank; Webster Bank; Farmington Savings Bank.

HARVEY J. KULAWITZ, LLC

BROOKFIELD, CONNECTICUT

(See Ridgefield)

All Personal Injury Cases, including Car Accident cases, Aircraft & Boating accidents, Slip & Fall accidents, Dog Bite attacks, and Wrongful Death accidents & claims.

HELEN L. McGONIGLE

Established in 1993

24 MEADOWVIEW
P.O. BOX 540
BROOKFIELD, CONNECTICUT 06804-0540
Telephone: 203-740-0074
Fax: 203-740-1171
Email: attymcg@aol.com
URL: http://www.lawyers.com/hmcgoniglelaw

Litigation, Victims Rights, Real Estate, Land Use, Appellate Law, Insurance Law, Personal Injury Law, Probate, Estate Planning, Wills and Equine Law.

HELEN L. McGONIGLE, born Pittsburgh, Pennsylvania, September 25, 1961; admitted to bar, 1986, Connecticut; 1987, U.S. District Court, District of Connecticut; 1989, U.S. District Court, Southern, Eastern and Northern Districts of New York; 1990, U.S. District Court, Western District of New York and U.S. Court of Appeals, 2nd Circuit; 1994, U.S Supreme Court. *Education:* Fairfield University (B.S., 1983); Loyola University (J.D., 1986). Phi Delta Phi. Author: "U.S. Court of Appeals Adopts Test for Therapeutic Hypnosis," Journal of Hypnotism, September, 1996; "Court Adopts Problematic Legal Test for Therapeutic Hypnosis," Sexual Assault Report, Vol. 1, No. 4, 1998; book review, "Memory, Trauma, Treatment and the Law," Connecticut Trial Lawyers Forum (1999). Member, Advisory Board, Brookfield Craft Center, Inc. *Member:* Danbury, Connecticut (Chair, Victims' Rights Committee, 1998-2002) and American Bar Associations; The Association of Trial Lawyers of America; Connecticut Trial Lawyers Association; International Association of Forensic Hypnosis (IAFH) (Advisory Board Member). ***REPORTED CASES:*** Lauer v. Zoning Commission, 220 Conn. 455 (1991); Pomazi v. Conservation Commission, 220 Conn. 476 (1991); Chmielewski v. Aetna Casualty and Surety Co., 218 Conn. 646 (1991); Sorrento Cheese Co., Inc. v. Silvestri, 23 Conn. App. 820 (1990); Lauer II v. Zoning Commission, 44 Conn. App. 542, 243 Conn. 485 (1997), 246 Conn. 251 (1998); Borawick v. Shay, 842 F.Supp. 1501 (D. Conn. 1994), 68 F.3d 597 (2nd Cir. 1995), 1996 U.S. Lexis 3577 (May 1996). ***PRACTICE AREAS:*** Litigation; Appellate Law; Insurance Law; Probate; Wills; Estate Planning; Personal Injury Law; Real Estate; Equine Law; Victims Rights.

HAMPTON LAW OFFICES, LLC

185 ALBANY TURNPIKE
P.O. BOX 1008
CANTON, CONNECTICUT 06019
Telephone: 860-693-8800
Fax: 860-693-8609
URL: http://www.lawyers.com/hamptonlaw

Civil and Criminal Litigation, Appellate Practice, Personal Injury, Motor Vehicle, Corporate, Business, Commercial, Family, Real Estate, Probate and Estate.

WALTER R. HAMPTON, JR., born Brooklyn, New York, May 7, 1957; admitted to bar, 1984, Connecticut and U.S. District Court, District of Connecticut; 1985, U.S. Court of Appeals, Second Circuit. *Education:* University of Hartford (B.A., summa cum laude, 1979) Cornell University (J.D., cum laude, 1984). Alpha Chi. Member, Cornell International Law Society, 1981-1984. Recipient, International Academy of Trial Lawyers Award. *Member:* Hartford County, Connecticut (Member, Section on Trial Advocacy and Criminal Justice) and American (Member, Section on Trial Advocacy) Bar Associations. ***LANGUAGES:*** Spanish, French and Latin. ***PRACTICE AREAS:*** Civil Litigation; Criminal Litigation; Appellate Practice; Corporate; Business; Commercial.

LAURA A. KLEIN, born Rochester, New York, November 10, 1970; admitted to bar, 1996, Connecticut; 1998, U.S. District Court, District of Connecticut. *Education:* University of Connecticut (B.A., 1992; J.D., 1996). *Member:* Hartford, Connecticut and American Bar Associations. ***PRACTICE AREAS:*** Civil Litigation; Personal Injury; Sexual Abuse; Commercial Litigation; Appellate Practice; Juvenile Law; Real Estate; Family Law; Probate; Estate Litigation.

LISA J. CAPPALLI

673 SOUTH MAIN STREET
CHESHIRE, CONNECTICUT 06410
Telephone: 203-271-3888
Fax: 203-271-3850
Email: lcappalli@abanet.org
URL: http://www.lawyers.com/cappalli

Hartford, Connecticut Office: 43 Woodland Street. 06105-2336. Telephone: 860-251-6792.

Matrimonial Law and Mediation.

FIRM PROFILE: General Background and Philosophy. I practice matrimonial and family law and mediation, meaning matters related to marriage, divorce and custody. I have a full and high quality practice and strive to represent clients in a competent and productive manner as they go through difficult times in their lives. With offices in Hartford and New Haven counties, I represent clients throughout Connecticut.

As an advocate, my primary responsibility is to secure the best result I can for my client. As a mediator, my responsibility is to help and counsel the two spouses toward the best result for the two of them. "Best result" pertains to finances, children and handling cases in such a way that I help ease the emotional and personal turmoil of divorce.

People ask how I can deal with marital and family issues at deep levels day in and day out. I consider my professional life as a positive combination of being a lawyer, working with and helping people, having intellectual and legal stimulation, and making a living.

I prefer clients who want to be constructive rather than destructive and who want to help themselves through the divorce process. My approach is to be firm and fair. I balance being reasonable and conciliatory while, at the same time, strongly advocating for my clients.

I am in a "people practice" and the work I do is demanding. I limit the number of clients I accept, maintain a manageable caseload and demand of myself high quality standards. I consciously take care of myself, believing it best for myself, my family and my clients.

LISA J. CAPPALLI, born Manhasset, New York, April 6, 1958; admitted to bar, 1984, Connecticut. *Education:* Lehigh University (B.A., 1980); Cornell University (J.D., 1984). Phi Beta Kappa. Special Master for Divorce Cases throughout Connecticut, including custody disputes. *Member:* Connecticut Bar Association; MENSA..

DODD, LESSACK, RANANDO & DALTON, L.L.C.

700 WEST JOHNSON AVENUE, SUITE 305
CHESHIRE, CONNECTICUT 06410
Telephone: 203-272-1883
Fax: 203-272-2077
Email: doddlrd@aol.com

Trials in all State and Federal Courts. Personal Injury, Products Liability, Social Security Disability, Workers Compensation and Negligence. Appellate Practice.

FIRM PROFILE: The preeminent firm of Dodd, Lessack, Ranando & Dalton evolved from a sole practice established by Edward Dodd in the 1970's into a highly successful civil trial practice, doing trials and appeals in State and Federal Courts. The firm concentrates on workers compensation and social security disability, but also handles personal injury, products liability and negligence matters. The firm's attorneys are active members of state and national trial lawyer associations.

MEMBERS OF FIRM

EDWARD T. DODD, JR., born Waterbury, Connecticut, November 11, 1944; admitted to bar, 1969, Connecticut; 1971, U.S. Court of Appeals, Second Circuit and U.S. District Court, District of Connecticut; 1972, U.S. Supreme Court. *Education:* University of Maryland (B.S., 1966); American University (J.D., 1969). Lecturer: Workers Compensation Law, National Business Institute, 1990—; Connecticut Bar Association; National Business Institute. Member, Internal Security Division, U.S. Department of Justice, 1968-1969. Special Agent, Federal Bureau of Investigation, 1969-1971. Legal Counsel, Waterbury Police Department, 1971-1972. Justice of the Peace, Waterbury, 1973-1988. Charter Revision Commissioner, 1973-1974. Diplomate, Court Practice Institute, 1975-1982. Member: Board of Aldermen, 1978-1980; Civil Service Commission, 1980-1982, City of Waterbury. *Member:* Waterbury (Vice President, 1978-1979; President, 1979-1980), Connecticut (Chairman, Workers Compensation Section) and American Bar Associations; National District Attorneys Association; The Association of Trial Lawyers of America; Connecticut Trial Lawyers Association. Certified as a Civil Trial Advocate by the National Board of Trial Advocacy. ***REPORTED CASES:*** Stitzer vs. Rinaldi's Restaurant, 557 A.2d 1256, 211 Conn. 116 (1988); Struckman vs. Burns, 534 A.2d 888, 205 Conn. 542 (1987); Paternostro vs. Edward Coon Co., 583 A.2d 1293, 217 Conn. 42 (1991); Roy vs. Centennial Insurance Co., 370 A.2d 1011, 171 Conn. 463 (1976); Trinkley vs. Ellas Grasso Regional Center A.2d, 200 Conn. 739 (1992); Wislocki v. Prospect, 224 Conn. 479 (1993); Cocetto v. Lynn Development, 612 A.2d 212, 223 Conn. 376 (1992); Cappellino v. Town of Cheshire, 608 A.2d 1185, 27 Conn. App. 699 (1992); affirmed, 628 A.2d 595, 226 Conn. 569 (1993); Roswell v. State of Connecticut 615 A 2d 1063, 29 Conn. App. 432 (1992); Wilcox v. Borough of Naugatuck, 548 A.2d 469, 16 Conn. App. 676 (1988); Damelio v. Anaconda, Inc., 542 A.2d 1180, 15 Conn. App. 805 (1988). ***PRACTICE AREAS:*** Personal Injury Law; Workers Compensation Law. ***Email:*** doddlrd@aol.com

ROSS T. LESSACK, born Waterbury, Connecticut, September 9, 1955; admitted to bar, 1980, Connecticut; 1981, Florida; 1983, U.S. District Court, District of Connecticut. *Education:* Northeastern University (B.S., 1977); University of Florida (J.D., 1980). *Member:* The Florida Bar; Connecticut Trial Lawyers Association; Association of Trial Lawyers of America. ***REPORTED CASES:*** Bratz v. Bratz, 4 Conn. App. 504 (1985); Struckman v. Burns, 205 conn. 542 (1987); Paternostro v. Edward Coon Co., 217 Conn. 42 (1990); Ericson v. Perrault Spring, 38 Conn. App. 71 (1995); Gillis v. White Oak Corp., 49 Conn. App. 630 (1998). ***PRACTICE AREAS:*** Personal Injury Law; Appellate Law; Workers Compensation Law. ***Email:*** doddlrd@aol.com

PAUL S. RANANDO, born Waterbury, Connecticut, March 9, 1956; admitted to bar, 1981, Connecticut; 1984, U.S. District Court, District of Connecticut; 1992, U.S. Supreme Court; 2000, U.S. Court of Appeals, Second Circuit. *Education:* University of Connecticut (B.A., 1978; J.D., 1981). Alternate Member, Planning and Zoning Commission, Town of Cheshire. *Member:* Connecticut and American Bar Associations; Connecticut Trial Lawyers Association. ***REPORTED CASES:*** Tartaglino v. State of Connecticut 737 A.2d 993, 55 Conn. App. 190 (1999); In re Teshea D. 519 A.2d 1232, 9 Conn. App. 490 (1985). ***PRACTICE AREAS:*** Personal Injury Law; Products Liability Law; Real Property Law; Workers Compensation Law; Social Security Disability. ***Email:*** doddlrd@aol.com

MARY-MARGARET DALTON BURGDORFF, born Hartford, Connecticut, May 21, 1959; admitted to bar, 1985, Connecticut; 1986, U.S. District Court, District of Connecticut. *Education:* St. Mary's College (B.A., 1981); Gonzaga University (J.D., 1985). Phi Alpha Delta. Instructor, National Academy for Paralegal Studies, Inc., 1992-1996. Member: Waterbury Young Lawyers Association, 1986-1995; Civitan. *Member:* Waterbury and Connecticut Bar Associations; The Association of Trial Lawyers of America; Connecticut Trial Lawyers Association. ***REPORTED CASES:*** Ascuitto v. Farricielli, 244 Conn. 692 (1998). ***PRACTICE AREAS:*** Personal Injury Law; Products Liability Law; Litigation; Workers Compensation Law.

CHARLES F. SENICH, born Waterbury, Connecticut, October 28, 1961; admitted to bar, 1989, Connecticut; 1990, U.S. District Court, District of Connecticut. *Education:* University of Bridgeport (B.S., cum laude, 1984); University of Bridgeport School of Law (J.D., 1988). *Member:* Waterbury and Connecticut Bar Associations; Connecticut Trial Lawyers Association; National Organization of Social Security Claimants' Representatives. ***PRACTICE AREAS:*** Personal Injury Law; Workers Compensation; Social Security Disability; ERISA. ***Email:*** doddlrd@aol.com

---

JONATHAN H. DODD, born Waterbury, Connecticut, July 30, 1974; admitted to bar, 2000, Connecticut. *Education:* Vanderbilt University (B.S., 1996); George Washington University (J.D., 2000). *Member:* Waterbury and Connecticut (Member, Young Lawyers Division) Bar Associations; The Association of Trial Lawyers of America; Waterbury Young Lawyers Association. ***PRACTICE AREAS:*** Personal Injury; Workers Compensation. ***Email:*** doddlrd@aol.com

(This Listing Continued)

HITT, SACHNER & MIELE

Established in 1960

673 SOUTH MAIN STREET
P.O. BOX 724
CHESHIRE, CONNECTICUT 06410
Telephone: 203-272-0371
Fax: 203-272-9854
Email: admin@hittsachnermiele.com
URL: http://www.hittsachnermiele.com

General Practice. Real Estate, Corporate, Business Acquisitions Law, Probate, Estate Planning, Personal Injury, Medical Malpractice, Family, Insurance and Zoning Law. Trials in all Courts.

(This Listing Continued)

HITT, SACHNER & MIELE, Cheshire—Continued

MEMBERS OF FIRM

STEPHEN P. SACHNER, born Waterbury, Connecticut, October 31, 1939; admitted to bar, 1964, Connecticut; 1971, U.S. Supreme Court; 1975, U.S. District Court, District of Connecticut. *Education:* Princeton University (A.B., 1961); New York University (LL.B., 1964). *Member:* Connecticut (Chairman, Junior Bar Section, 1970-1971; Assistant Secretary, 1971-1972) and American Bar Associations. ***PRACTICE AREAS:*** Medical Malpractice; Personal Injury Law; General Defense Law. **Email:** sps@hittsachnermiele.com

JAMES M. MIELE, born Manchester, Connecticut, January 5, 1964; admitted to bar, 1989, Connecticut; 1991, U.S. District Court, District of Connecticut. *Education:* University of Connecticut (B.A.P.S., with high honors, 1986); University of Connecticut School of Law (J.D., with honors, 1989). Phi Beta Kappa; Phi Kappa Phi. *Member:* New Haven County and Connecticut (Member, Conservation and Environmental Quality Section) Bar Associations. ***PRACTICE AREAS:*** General Practice; Business Law; Civil Litigation; Real Estate; Family Law; Trusts and Estates. **Email:** jmm@hittsachnermiele.com

ASSOCIATES

CHRISTINE A. ROBINSON, born Buffalo, New York, March, 4, 1965; admitted to bar, 1997, Connecticut; 1998, U.S. District Court, District of Connecticut; 2000, New York. *Education:* New York University (B.A., 1988); Quinnipiac College (J.D., with honors, 1997). Member, Board of Governors, Midstate Medical Center. *Member:* Meriden, New Haven County and Connecticut Bar Associations. ***PRACTICE AREAS:*** Medical Malpractice Defense; General Practice; Business Law. **Email:** car@hittsachnermiele.com

SCOTT R. PARULSKI, born Bristol, Connecticut, March 13, 1971; admitted to bar, 1999, Connecticut. *Education:* Fairfield University (B.A., Political Science and B.A., Psychology, 1993); Quinnipiac College (J.D., 1999). Member, Executive Board, Moot Court Honor Society, Quinnipiac College School of Law. *Member:* Connecticut and American Bar Associations. ***PRACTICE AREAS:*** General Practice; Civil Litigation; Real Estate; Business Law. **Email:** srp@hittsachnermiele.com

JAY N. HERSHMAN, born Hartford, Connecticut, May 20, 1976; admitted to bar, 2001, Connecticut. *Education:* Bryant College (B.A., 1998); Quinnipiac College (J.D., 2001). Recipient: Bryant College Communication Award. Author: Erickson v. Erickson: Extrinsic Evidence in Probate Cases," Quinnipiac Probate Law Journal, Vol. 12 #182. Lieutenant, Cheshire Fire Department, 2001—. Firefighter, Cheshire Fire Department, 1992-2001. *Member:* Connecticut Bar Association. ***PRACTICE AREAS:*** General Practice; Business Law; Civil Litigation; Real Estate; Trusts and Estates. **Email:** jnh@hittsachnermiele.com

OF COUNSEL

FRED A. HITT, born Hartford, Connecticut, August 14, 1931; admitted to bar, 1958, Connecticut. *Education:* Dartmouth College (A.B., 1953); University of Connecticut (LL.B., 1958). President, 1985; Vice President, 1983-1985, University of Connecticut Law School Alumni Association. President, 1991; Trustee, 1986—, University of Connecticut Law School Foundation. *Member:* New Haven County, Connecticut (Member, Criminal and Real Property Sections) and American Bar Associations; The Association of Trial Lawyers of America. **Email:** fah@hittsachnermiele.com

MAUREEN SULLIVAN DINNAN, born Springfield, Massachusetts, August 16, 1959; admitted to bar, 1984, Connecticut and U.S. District Court, District of Connecticut; 1987, U.S. Court of Appeals, Second Circuit; 1988, U.S. Supreme Court. *Education:* Smith College (A.B., with high honors, 1981); University of Connecticut (J.D., 1984). Oliver Ellsworth Inn of Court, 1985-1987. Editor of the Defense, 1984-1986. *Member:* Connecticut and Federal Bar Associations; Defense Research Institute. ***PRACTICE AREAS:*** Medical Malpractice. **Email:** msd@hittsachnermiele.com

REPRESENTATIVE CLIENTS: Connecticut Medical Insurance Co.; Middlesex Hospital; Harte Nissan, Inc.; Harte Infiniti, Inc.; George Harte Nissan, Inc.; Newburgh Nissan, Inc.; Ravenswood Development Corp.; Ravenswood Realty & Management Corp.; Dalton Enterprises, Inc.; F.F. Hitchcock Co., Inc.
APPROVED ATTORNEYS FOR: Connecticut Attorneys Title Insurance Co.; Chicago Title Insurance Co.; Lawyers Title Insurance Co.
APPROVED CLOSING ATTORNEYS FOR: New Haven Savings Bank; Bank of Boston Connecticut; Lafayette American Bank & Trust Company; Shawmut Bank Connecticut, N.A.; Chase Manhattan Bank of Ct., N.A.; Centerbank; PHH US Mortgage Corporation; Pawling (N.Y.) Savings Bank; Prudential Home Mortgage Corp.; Household Financial Services, Corp.; Fleet Bank, N.A.; Norwest Mortgage Corp.
REFERENCE: Fleet Bank; Webster Bank.

JOHN K. KNOTT, JR.

325 SOUTH MAIN STREET
CHESHIRE, CONNECTICUT 06410
Telephone: 203-271-3031
Fax: 203-272-5388
Email: jknottjr@freewwweb.com

General Civil Practice, Municipal and Administrative Law, Land Use Law, Probate and Estate, Real Estate, Selected Civil Trials and Appeals, Education and Special Education.

JOHN K. KNOTT, JR., born Waterbury, Connecticut, June 8, 1938; admitted to bar, 1964, Connecticut; 1968, U.S. District Court, District of Connecticut; 1971, U.S. Court of Appeals, 2nd Circuit. *Education:* The Citadel (B.A., 1960); Boston University (J.D., 1964). Recipient, American Jurisprudence Book Award in Public Utility Law. Town Attorney: Cheshire, 1971—; Bethany, 1990—. *Member:* New Haven County and Connecticut Bar Associations; National Lawyers Association; Connecticut Association of Municipal Attorneys; International Municipal Lawyers Association. [Capt., U.S. Army, Artillery, 1965-1966]. ***REPORTED CASES:*** Cheshire V. McKenney, 182 Conn. 253, 438 A.2d 88 (1980); Cheshire Taxpayers' Action Committee, Inc. V. Guilford, 193 Conn. 1, 474 A.2d 97 (1984). ***PRACTICE AREAS:*** Municipal Law; Land Use Law; Administrative; Probate Law; Trusts and Estates; Civil Trials and Appeals; Education Law.

ASSOCIATE

PRISCILLA C. MULVANEY, born Hempstead, New York, February 16, 1958; admitted to bar, 1984, New York; 1985, Florida; 1986, Connecticut and U.S. District Court, District of Connecticut. *Education:* State University of New York at Oneonta (B.A., 1980); State University of New York at Buffalo (J.D., 1983). Assistant Town Attorney, Hamden, Connecticut, 1985-1987. *Member:* New Haven County, Connecticut and American Bar Associations; The Florida Bar. ***PRACTICE AREAS:*** Real Estate Law; Municipal and Administrative Law; Civil Trials and Appeals; Education Law; Special Education Law. **Email:** jknottjr@freewwweb.com

REPRESENTATIVE CLIENTS: Town of Cheshire; Town of Bethany; Theis Precision Steel Corp.
REFERENCE: Naugatuck Savings Bank.

MOORE, O'BRIEN, JACQUES & YELENAK

700 WEST JOHNSON AVENUE
SUITE 207
CHESHIRE, CONNECTICUT 06410
Telephone: 203-272-5881
Fax: 203-272-9273

Civil, Trial and Appellate Practice in State and Federal Courts. Negligence, Products Liability, Aviation and Medical Malpractice.

FIRM PROFILE: Moore, O'Brien, Jacques & Yelenak is a five-lawyer firm devoted to protecting victims' rights. The firm specializes in plaintiff's personal injury litigation involving negligence actions, products liability, air crash disasters and medical malpractice. Located in Cheshire, the offices are centrally located to almost all Superior Courts and the State's Supreme Court facilities. The firm handles plaintiff's personal injury claims for individuals throughout the state of Connecticut, as well as many other states across the country.

The firm encourages continuing professional development and all partners and associates participate in continuing legal education seminars and professional associations, with two members currently serving as members of the Board of Governors of the Connecticut Trial Lawyers Association.

MEMBERS OF FIRM

GARRETT M. MOORE, born Waterbury, Connecticut, June 4, 1952; admitted to bar, 1981, Connecticut and U.S. District Court, District of Connecticut. *Education:* University of Connecticut (B.S., summa cum laude, 1978); Georgetown University (J.D., with honors, 1981). *Member:* Waterbury, Connecticut and American (Member, Litigation Section) Bar Associations; Connecticut Trial Lawyers Association (President, 1993; Member, Board of Governors, 1985—); American College of Trial Lawyers; American Board of Trial Advocates; National Board of Trial Advocates; The Association of Trial Lawyers of America. ***PRACTICE AREAS:*** Medical Malpractice Law; Products Liability Law; Personal Injury.

GREGORY E. O'BRIEN, born New Haven, Connecticut, May 5, 1961; admitted to bar, 1987, Connecticut and U.S. District Court, District of Connecticut. *Education:* Providence College (B.A., in History, 1983); University of Bridgeport (J.D., magna cum laude, 1987). Judicial Clerkship, for Hon. T. Clark Hull, Connecticut Supreme Court, 1988-1989. *Member:* New Haven County,

(This Listing Continued)

Connecticut and American Bar Associations; National Board of Trial Advocates; The Association of Trial Lawyers of America; Connecticut Trial Lawyers Association (Member, Board of Governors, 1998—). **PRACTICE AREAS:** Personal Injury; Products Liability.

STEPHEN L. JACQUES, born New York, N.Y., January 13, 1947; admitted to bar, 1983, California; 1990, Connecticut; 1991, Massachusetts; 1992, New York. *Education:* California State University at Northridge (B.A., 1970); Webber Douglas Academy, London, England; Loyola University of Los Angeles (J.D., 1983). Author: "Targeting the Defect Theory in Recreational Vehicle Cases," Advocate, January 1989; "Perspectives on the Windshield Retention Case," Advocate, October 1988; "Prescription for Success in an Oral Contraceptive Case," Advocate, November 1987. *Member:* Los Angeles County, Waterbury, Connecticut and American Bar Associations; State Bar of California; Los Angeles Trial Lawyers Association (Member, Board of Governors, 1989-1990); California Trial Lawyers Association; Connecticut Trial Lawyers Association (Member, Board of Governors, 1999—). **PRACTICE AREAS:** Personal Injury; Medical Malpractice Law.

WILLIAM P. YELENAK, born Southington, Connecticut, July 12, 1953; admitted to bar, 1978, Connecticut and U.S. District Court, District of Connecticut. *Education:* Trinity College (B.A., with honors, 1975); Case Western Reserve University (J.D., 1978). Author: "Technology in Trial Practice," Connecticut Lawyer. Special Master, U.S. District Court, District of Connecticut. *Member:* New Haven, Connecticut and American Bar Associations; Connecticut Trial Lawyers Association; The Association of Trial Lawyers of America. **REPORTED CASES:** In re State Police Litigation, 888 F.Supp. 1235 (1995). **PRACTICE AREAS:** Personal Injury.

NUZZO & ROBERTS, L.L.C.

ONE TOWN CENTER
P.O. BOX 747
CHESHIRE, CONNECTICUT 06410
Telephone: 203-250-2000
Fax: 203-250-3131

Civil Trial Practice in all State and Federal Courts, Insurance Law and Insurance Defense, Coverage and Bad Faith Litigation, Products Liability, Personal Injury, Professional Liability, Directors and Officers Liability, Legal Malpractice, Employment Litigation, School Liability, Appellate Practice and Workers Compensation.

FIRM PROFILE: Nuzzo & Roberts, is a litigation firm serving clients throughout Connecticut consisting of eighteen attorneys and an office staff of thirty personnel.

ANTHONY NUZZO, JR., admitted to bar, 1968, Connecticut and District of Columbia; 1969, U.S. District Court, District of Columbia and U.S. Court of Appeals, District of Columbia; 1971, U.S. District Court of Connecticut. *Education:* University of Connecticut (B.A., 1965; J.D., 1968). Public Defender for District of Columbia, 1968-1970. *Member:* New Haven County (President, 1998-1999); Connecticut Defense Lawyers Association (Director, 1988; President, 1994). **PRACTICE AREAS:** Legal Malpractice; Insurance Defense; Insurance Coverage; Insurance Bad Faith. **Email:** anuzzo@nuzzo-roberts.com

RICHARD A. ROBERTS, admitted to bar, 1984, Connecticut and New York; 1985, U.S. District Court, District of Connecticut. *Education:* State University of New York at Binghamton (B.A., 1979); State University of New York at Buffalo (J.D., 1983). Member, Moot Court Board and National Moot Court Team. District Representative for Connecticut, YLS, 1991-1993). *Member:* Connecticut Defense Lawyers Association; New Haven Young Lawyers (President, 1989-1990). **REPORTED CASES:** Kelley v. Bonney, 221 Conn. 549 (1992); Johnson v. American Employers Ins. Co., 25 Conn. App. 95 (1991); Aetna v. Murphy 206 Conn. 409 (1998). **PRACTICE AREAS:** Insurance Defense; Personal Injury; Employment Litigation; Commercial Litigation; Professional Liability. **Email:** rroberts@nuzzo-roberts.com

FREDERICK L. MUROLO, admitted to bar, 1986, Connecticut; 1987, U.S. District Court, District of Connecticut; 1988, Massachusetts; 1989, U.S. District Court, District of Massachusetts; 1993, U.S. Court of Appeals, Second Circuit. *Education:* Connecticut College (B.A., cum laude, 1979); Pennsylvania State University (M.A., 1983); University of Connecticut (J.D., with honors, 1986). Articles Editor, Connecticut Journal of International Law, 1985-1986. **REPORTED CASES:** Colonial Penn v. Bryant, 45 Conn. App. 558, aff'd 243 Conn. 919 (1998); Smith v. Mitsubishi Motors Credit, 247 Conn. 342 (1998); Ciarelli v. Commercial Union, 234 Conn. 807 (1995); Wynn v. Metropolitan, 30 Conn. App. 803, aff'd 228 Conn. 436 (1994). **PRACTICE AREAS:** Insurance Coverage; Insurance Defense; Uninsured Motorist; Appellate Practice. **Email:** fmurolo@nuzzo-roberts.com

DAVID J. WEIL, admitted to bar, 1988, Connecticut and U.S. District Court, District of Connecticut. *Education:* Franklin & Marshall College (B.A., 1982); George Washington University (J.D., 1988). Moot Court Board. **PRACTICE AREAS:** Workers' Compensation. **Email:** dweil@nuzzo-roberts.com

(This Listing Continued)

KAREN T. GERBER, admitted to bar, 1992, Connecticut; 1993, Florida; 1994, U.S. District Court, District of Connecticut. *Education:* University of Connecticut (B.A., cum laude, 1989); Cornell Law School (J.D., cum laude, 1992). Member, Moot Court Board. **REPORTED CASES:** City of Middletown v. van Mahland, 34 Conn. App. 772 (1994); Doyle v. Metropolitan, 252 Conn. 79 (2000). **PRACTICE AREAS:** Insurance Defense; Appellate Practice. **Email:** kgerber@nuzzo-roberts.com

---

JANE E. STODDARD, admitted to bar, 1994, Connecticut; 1995, U.S. District Court, District of Connecticut. *Education:* Bowdoin College (B.A., 1991); University of Connecticut (J.D., with honors, 1994). Notes and Comments Editor, Connecticut Law Review. Moot Court Board.

MARC J. UBALDI, admitted to bar, 1996, Connecticut; 1998, U.S. District Court, District of Connecticut. *Education:* University of Hartford (B.A., magna cum laude, 1988); University of Connecticut School of Law (J.D., 1996). Moot Court Board.

ROBERT J. CHOMIAK, JR., admitted to bar, 1996, Connecticut and U.S. District Court, District of Connecticut. *Education:* Boston University (B.A., cum laude, 1993); New England School of Law (J.D., 1996). Notes Editor, The Environmental Law Forum, New England School of Law, 1996. **PRACTICE AREAS:** Civil Litigation.

JASON M. LIPSKY, admitted to bar, 1997, Connecticut and U.S. District Court, District of Connecticut. *Education:* Providence College (B.A., magna cum laude, 1994); University of Connecticut School of Law (J.D., with honors, 1997). **REPORTED CASES:** Beasley v. Commissioner of Correction, 47 Conn. App. 253 (1998); Beasley v. Commissioner of Correction, 50 Conn. App. 421 (1998).

NICOLE C. DABEKIS, admitted to bar, 1997, Connecticut; 1998, Massachusetts and U. S. District Court, District of Connecticut. *Education:* Providence College (B.S., 1994); Quinnipiac College School of Law (J.D., cum laude, 1997). Quinnipiac Probate Journal.

MICHELE C. CAMEROTA, admitted to bar, 1998, Connecticut; 1999, U.S. District Court, District of Connecticut. *Education:* Central Connecticut State University (B.A., 1993); University of Connecticut School of Law (J.D., 1998).

OLGA E. ZARGOS, admitted to bar, 1999, Connecticut. *Education:* Fairfield University (B.A., cum laude, 1995); Case Western Reserve University (J.D., 1998). **LANGUAGES:** Greek.

JANE M. CARLOZZI, admitted to bar, 1998, Connecticut and U.S. District Court, District of Connecticut. *Education:* Wesleyan University (B.A., 1978); University of Hartford (M.B.A., 1987); University of Connecticut School of Law (J.D., with high honors, 1998).

JENNIFER J. CAVALIER, admitted to bar, 1999, Connecticut. *Education:* Bryant College (B.S., 1994); Quinnipiac College (J.D., 1999). Quinnipiac Probate Journal.

ROBERT J. JOHNSON, admitted to bar, 1999, Connecticut. *Education:* Central Connecticut State University (B.A., 1996); Quinnipiac College School of Law (J.D., cum laude, 1999). Lead Articles Editor, Law Review.

AMBER BRANCIFORTE, admitted to bar, 1999, Connecticut. *Education:* College of New Rochelle (B.A., summa cum laude, 1994); Quinnipiac College School of Law (J.D., cum laude, 1999). Editor, Quinnipiac Probate Law Journal, 1997.

LISA M. CANNATA, admitted to bar, 1999, Connecticut. *Education:* University of Connecticut (B.A., cum laude, 1996); University of Connecticut School of Law (J.D., 1999).

NADINE PARE, admitted to bar, 2000, Connecticut. *Education:* University of Connecticut (B.A., cum laude, 1996); Quinnipiac College School of Law (J.D., 2000). Lead Articles Editor, Quinnipiac Law Review, 1999-2000.

REPRESENTATIVE CLIENTS: CGU Insurance Co.(f/k/a Commercial Union and General Accident); Utica National Insurance Co.; Chubb Group of Insurance Cos.; Metropolitan Property and Liability Insurance Co.; Great American Insurance Co.; Colonial Penn Insurance Co./GE Financial Service; American Insurance Group; Allstate Insurance Co.; Chubb/Executive Risk; Western Heritage Insurance Co.; Westport Insurance Co.; Lexington Insurance Co.; American Equity Insurance Co.; Fulcrom Insurance Co.; Royal SunAlliance; Travelers Insurance Cos.; Integon Insurance Co.; Keystone Insurance; Crawford & Company; Cumberland Farms, Inc.; Ohio Casualty Group; Managed Comp.; McDonald's Corporation; Gallagher Bassett; Enterprise Rental (Budget Rent-A-Car and Avis Rent-A-Car System, Inc.)

JONATHAN HOYT

10 BLUFF AVENUE
CLINTON, CONNECTICUT 06413-2255
Telephone: 860-669-0182
Fax: 860-669-7893
Email: hoytlaw@aol.com
URL: http://www.lawyers.com/hoytlaw

Real Estate both Residential and Commercial, Probate, Estate Planning, Business and Corporate Law, Commercial Transactions.

JONATHAN HOYT, born Middletown, Connecticut, September 17, 1948; admitted to bar, 1974, Connecticut; 1976, U.S. District Court, District of Connecticut. *Education:* Morningside College (B.A., 1970); Southern Methodist University School of Law (J.D., 1973). Host, "That Legal Show," North American Broadcasting Company Radio Network on WALE 990 AM, Providence, Rhode Island; KFNX 1100 AM, Phoenix, Arizona; Internet at renaissanceradio.com, (2000-2001). Revisor and contributor to the American Bar Association's publication "Guide to Home Ownership" (1995). Revisor and contributor to chapter "Buying and Selling a Home," published in the American Bar Association's Family Legal Guide (1994); Revisor and contributor to chapter 9A "Secondary Financing," published in Matthew Bender's Real Estate Financing series (1993). *Member:* Connecticut and American (Chairman, Purchase and Sale Residential Real Estate Committee, 1990-1994) Bar Associations. ***PRACTICE AREAS:*** Elder Law; Covenants Not To Compete; Restrictive Covenants; Lender Law; Loan Workouts; Business Associations Law; Business Development; Business Dissolutions; Business Formation; Business Organization; Business Planning; Business Start-Ups; Business Transactions; Business Transfers; Buying and Selling of Businesses; Closely Held Business Law; Emerging Business Law; Joint Ventures; Limited Liability Company Law; Small Business Law; Sole Proprietorships; Commercial Transactions; Commercial Transfers; Commercial Conveyancing; Commercial Real Estate Acquisitions; Commercial Real Estate Development; Commercial Real Estate Sales; Commercial Real Estate; Commercial Real Estate Workouts; Computer Software Law; Information Technology Contracts; Construction Contracts; Contractors Liability; Materialmens Liens; Mechanics Liens; Commercial Contracts; Closely Held Corporations; Corporate Organization; Incorporation; Professional Corporations; S Corporations; Small Business Corporations; Advance Directives; Conservatorship; Guardian Ad Litem; Incompetency Proceedings; Senior Citizen Housing; Commercial Landlord and Tenant Law; Landlord and Tenant Law; Office Leasing; Retail Leasing; Shopping Center Leasing; Commercial Mortgages; Mortgage Workouts; Secondary Mortgage Market; Limited Liability Partnerships; Partnership Dissolution; Partnership Formation; Partnership Organization; Ancillary Probate; Probate Administration; Probate Taxation; Boundary Disputes; Common Interest Community Law; Community Association Law; Condominium Conversions; Condominium Development; Condominium Law; Condominium Timeshares; Conveyancing; Easements; Homeowners Association Law; Land Acquisitions; Land Sales; Mobile Home Law; Real Estate Acquisitions; Real Estate Banking Law; Real Estate Brokerage Law; Real Estate Brokers and Agents Liability; Real Estate Contracts; Real Estate Development; Real Estate Exchanges; Real Estate Finance; Real Estate Joint Ventures; Real Estate Leasing; Real Estate Partnerships; Real Estate Sales; Real Estate Settlements; Real Estate Title; Real Estate Title Examination; Real Estate Title Insurance; Real Estate Workouts; Real Property; Real Property Acquisitions; Real Property Development; Real Property Finance; Residential Real Estate; Residential Real Estate Development; Residential Real Estate Finance; Residential Real Estate Sales; Right of Way Easements; Waterfront Development; Estate and Gift Taxation; Federal Estate and Gift Taxation; Federal Taxation; Fiduciary Income Tax; Inheritance Tax; Trusts and Estates Taxation; Trade Names; Trademark Registration; Decedents Estates; Estate Administration; Estate Planning; Estate Planning for the Elderly; Estate Planning for Unmarried Couples; Estate Settlements; Family Trusts; Fiduciary Law; Living Trusts; Trust Administration; Trust Law; Wealth Preservation; Inheritance; Living Wills; Successions; Land Use Regulation; Subdivisions; Zoning Law.

REPRESENTATIVE CLIENTS: Dancing Deer Development, LLC; Greg Faucher-Builder, LLC; Moran Builders, Inc.; Schilling Builders, LLC; Shoreline Stair & Millwork Company; Townsend Excavating Co., Inc.; Town of Westbrook Housing Authority; Windows, Doors & More, Inc.; Madison Flower Shop and Garden Center.
APPROVED ATTORNEY FOR: Chicago Title Insurance Co.; Commonwealth Land Title Insurance Co.; First American Title Insurance Company.

MARIA L. HAMPTON

33 MAPLE AVENUE
COLLINSVILLE, CONNECTICUT 06019
Telephone: 860-693-1100
Fax: 860-693-1100
Email: attymariahampton@snet.net

Real Estate, Collections, Business Law, Employment Law, Litigation.

MARIA L. HAMPTON, born Hanover, New Hampshire, March 9, 1960; admitted to bar, 1986, Connecticut and U.S. District Court, District of Connecticut. *Education:* Smith College (B.A., 1982); Western New England College (J.D., 1986). Attorney, Green & Kleinman, Hartford, Connecticut, 1986-1990. *Member:* Hartford County, Connecticut and American Bar Associations; Hartford Association of Women Attorneys. ***PRACTICE AREAS:*** Real Estate; Collections; Business Law; Employment Law; Litigation.

DONOVAN & MORELLO, LLP

Established in 1987

CROMWELL WEST OFFICE PARK
154 WEST STREET
CROMWELL, CONNECTICUT 06416
Telephone: 860-635-7373
Fax: 860-635-6734
Email: jrd@donmorlaw.com
Email: pam@donmorlaw.com
URL: http://www.donmorlaw.con

Meriden, Connecticut Office: 816 Broad Street. Telephone: 203-635-7373.

General Civil and Criminal Practice before State and Federal Courts. Personal Injury, Product Liability, Workers Compensation Law, Trials, Arbitration, Mediation, Uninsured and Underinsured Motorists, Medical Malpractice.

FIRM PROFILE: Donovan & Morello is a litigation law firm founded in 1987 by John R. Donovan, former chief prosecutor in the Superior Court in Meriden, and Paul A. Morello, Jr., a former partner in a Cheshire law firm that concentrated in insurance defense litigation. The partners have many years of experience in the trial of criminal and civil cases in the Federal and State Courts. Together, they have co-authored "The Handbook of Connecticut Uninsured and Underinsured Motorist Law.".

MEMBERS OF FIRM

JOHN R. DONOVAN, born New Haven, Connecticut, September 12, 1953; admitted to bar, 1979, Connecticut; 1981, U.S. District Court, District of Connecticut. *Education:* University of Virginia (B.A., with distinction, 1975); University of Connecticut (J.D., 1979). Co-Author, "Handbook of Connecticut Uninsured and Underinsured Motorist Law," The Connecticut Law Tribune. Chief Prosecutor, Superior Court, Meriden, Connecticut, 1980-1984. Special Counsel for Wallingford, Connecticut Board of Ethics, 1989. *Member:* Connecticut Criminal Defense Lawyers Association; Connecticut Trial Lawyers Association; The Association of Trial Lawyers of America. ***PRACTICE AREAS:*** Criminal Defense; Driving While Intoxicated; Homicide; Sex Crimes; Drugs and Narcotics. ***Email:*** jrd@donmorlaw.com

PAUL A. MORELLO, JR., born Middletown, Connecticut, January 24, 1954; admitted to bar, 1979, Connecticut; 1981, U.S. District Court, District of Connecticut. *Education:* College of the Holy Cross (B.A., cum laude, 1976); Albany Law School of Union University (J.D., 1979). Special Master, State of Connecticut Superior Court, 1997—; Special Master, United States District Court, 1998—. Co-Author: "Uninsured/Underinsured Motorist Law In Connecticut," Volume 11, Connecticut Law Tribune, Nos. 12, 13, 1985; Author: "The Problem of Multiple Uninsured Motorist Coverages: Who Pays?" 62 Connecticut Bar Journal 358. Cited in Aetna Cas. & Sur. Co. v. CNA Ins. Co. 221 Conn. 779 (1992); Co-Author: "The Misapplication of Workmens' Compensation Exclusively to UM Claims: Ross v. City of New Haven, 7 CTLA Forum No. 6.; Co-Author: "Handbook of Connecticut Uninsured and Underinsured Motorist Law," The Connecticut Law Tribune. *Member:* Connecticut and American (Member: Litigation Section; Torts and Insurance Practice Section) Bar Associations; Connecticut Trial Lawyers Association; The Association of Trial Lawyers of America. ***REPORTED CASES:*** Aetna Ins. Co. v. Colbert, 38 Conn. Sup. 1 (1983); Aetna Cas. and Sur. Co. v. Murphy 206 Conn. 409 (1988). ***PRACTICE AREAS:*** Personal Injury Law; Medical Malpractice; Bicycle Accidents; Head and Spinal Injury; Uninsured and Underinsured Motorists. ***Email:*** pam@donmorlaw.com

REPRESENTATIVE CLIENTS: Metropolitan Property & Liability Insurance Co.; Connecticut Insurance Guarantee Fund; Great American Insurance Co.; Colonial Penn Insurance Company.
REFERENCE: Citizens Bank.

ADELMAN HIRSCH & NEWMAN, LLP

DANBURY, CONNECTICUT

(See Bridgeport)

Plaintiff's Personal Injury, Medical Malpractice, Products Liability, Wrongful Death, Automobile Accidents, Truck Accidents and Legal Malpractice.

(This Listing Continued)

BAKER LAW FIRM, P.C.

Established in 1976

24 DELAY STREET

DANBURY, CONNECTICUT 06810

Telephone: 203-792-8765

Fax: 203-791-1892

Email: Fred@Baker-Law.com

URL: http://www.lawyers.com/bakerlawfirm

New Milford Office: Baker Fields, 4 Mine Hill Road. Telephone: 860-354-9100.

Taxation, Estate Planning, Probate, Business and Corporate, Real Estate.

FIRM PROFILE: Baker Law Firm is dedicated to providing companies, entrepreneurs and high net worth individuals with sophisticated and timely business and legal advice, including estate and financial planning, corporate and real property transactions and related services.

FRED L. BAKER, born Bristol, Connecticut, April 30, 1943; admitted to bar, 1969, Connecticut; 1970, U.S. Tax Court; 1974, U.S. District Court, District of Connecticut. *Education:* University of Connecticut (B.A., 1966; J.D., 1969); New York University (LL.M., Taxation, 1974). Author, Handbook of Connecticut Taxes on Industry 1970, Manufacturers' Association of Connecticut. Trial Attorney, Office of Chief Counsel, Internal Revenue Service, 1970-1974. Town Counsel, Town of Bridgewater, 1977—. President, Western Connecticut Estate and Tax Planning Council, Inc., 1976-1977. Member, 1978-1980 and Vice Chairman, 1978-1979, Town of New Milford Board of Education. Member, Advisory Board, Connecticut National Bank, 1986-1991. Corporator, Union Savings Bank, 1987—. Chairman: DATAHR Rehabilitation Institute, 1990-1994; Hanohoe Children's Clinic, 1991—. Trustee, Waterbury Foundation, 2000—. *Member:* Danbury, Connecticut (Member, Taxation Section) and American (Member, Taxation Section) Bar Associations. ***PRACTICE AREAS:*** Taxation; Estate Planning; Probate; Corporate Law; Business Law; Commercial Law; Finance; Real Estate; Trusts and Estates; Elder Law; Family Business Mediation. ***Email:*** Fred@Baker-Law.com

HILLEL GOLDMAN, born Danbury, Connecticut, May 2, 1959; admitted to bar, 1989, Connecticut; 1990, New York; 1991, U.S. District Court, District of Connecticut. *Education:* Vassar College (A.B., 1981); Cornell Graduate School of Management; Jacob D. Fuchsberg Law Center, Touro College (J.D., 1989). Recipient: 1994 Danbury Jaycees Distinguished Service Award; American Jurisprudence Award, Securities Regulation. Editor-in-Chief, Touro Journal of Transnational Law, 1988-1989. Member: Board of Directors, Hispanic Center of Greater Danbury, Inc., 1995-1999; Board of Directors, The Harambee Center, Inc.; Campaign Cabinet, United way of Northern Fairfield County, 1996. President, Board of Directors, Regional Hospice of Western Connecticut, Inc., 1997—. Member, Board of Directors, Danbury Health Services, Inc., 1998—. Director, State Government Relations, Connecticut Elks, 1998-1999. Chairman, Business Resource Directory Committee, Danbury Community Reinvestment Act Task Force. Mayor, Economic Advisory Panel. *Member:* Danbury, Connecticut (Member: Executive Committee, Business Law Section; Limited Liability Company Subcommittee; Executive Committee, Financial Institutions Section), New York State (Member, Franchise Law Committee) and American (Member, Committees on: Credit Union; Developments in Business Financing) Bar Associations. ***PRACTICE AREAS:*** Business Organizations; Corporate Law; Business Law; Commercial Transactions; Finance; Credit Union Law; Franchise Law; Contracts. ***Email:*** Hillel@Baker-Law.com

REPRESENTATIVE CLIENTS: The Taunton Press, Inc.; Beaver Brook Circuits, Inc.; Teknicircuits, Inc.; Southworths Chrysler; New Milford Savings Bank; Union Savings Bank; Vanguard Products Corp.; Housatonic Valley Insurance; Datahr Rehabilitation Institute; Health Care Solutions, Inc.; Fleet National Bank; Sandlapper Fabrics; Beaver Street Apartments Cooperative, Inc.; Danbury/Torrington Regional Workforce Development Board; Neals Yard (Natural Remedies) Limited; Manitou Systems, Inc.

LAW OFFICES OF DAVID F. BENNETT

72 NORTH STREET, SUITE 103

DANBURY, CONNECTICUT 06810

Telephone: 203-797-9888

Telecopier: 203-743-4672

Email: BULLDOG799@AOL.COM

URL: http://www.lawyers.com/dfblaw

Civil Litigation, Personal Injury, Wrongful Death, Commercial, Real Estate, Trusts and Estates Law. Aviation.

FIRM PROFILE: Our firm has substantial experience in civil litigation, personal injury, and wrongful death, real estate transactions, corporate law, planning and zoning and trusts and estates.

(This Listing Continued)

Prior to opening his office, David F. Bennett practiced for five years with Kelley Drye & Warren, a major New York law firm.

Since 1984, the philosophy of the Law Offices of David F. Bennett has been to represent each client with a high level of professional expertise supported by an experienced staff. Our mission is cost effective representation which is results orientated. We build our practice one client relationship at a time.

DAVID F. BENNETT, born Laconia, New Hampshire, July 17, 1952; admitted to bar, 1977, Connecticut; 1978, Florida; 1979, District of Columbia; 1985, U.S. Supreme Court; 1986, New York. *Education:* Tufts University (B.A., magna cum laude, Political Science, 1974); George Washington University (J.D., 1977). *Member:* Connecticut and American Bar Associations; District of Columbia Bar; The Florida Bar; The Association of Trial Lawyers of America; Connecticut Trial Lawyers Association. ***PRACTICE AREAS:*** Civil Litigation; Personal Injury; Wrongful Death; Commercial; Real Estate; Trusts and Estates Law; Planning and Zoning.

Representative Clients available upon request.
REFERENCE: Fleet Bank, Danbury.

CHIPMAN, MAZZUCCO, LAND & PENNAROLA, LLC

30 MAIN STREET, SUITE 204

DANBURY, CONNECTICUT 06810-3043

Telephone: 203-744-1929

FAX: 203-790-5954

URL: http://www.danburylaw.com

Business Law, Litigation, Real Estate, Trusts and Estates, Taxation, Zoning Law, Computer Law.

DAVID R. CHIPMAN, born Norwalk, Connecticut, October 27, 1933; admitted to bar, 1959, New York; 1962, Connecticut. *Education:* Carleton College (B.A., 1954); Duke University (LL.B., 1957). *Member:* Connecticut (Member, Executive Committee, 1968— and Chairman, 1971-1974, Business Law Section) and American Bar Associations. ***PRACTICE AREAS:*** Business Law; Corporate Law; Taxation; Trusts and Estates; Mergers and Acquisitions.

RICHARD S. LAND, born Milton, Massachusetts, October 1, 1948; admitted to bar, 1975, Connecticut; 1983, New York. *Education:* Dartmouth College (B.A., 1970); Emory University (J.D., 1975). *Member:* Connecticut, New York State and American Bar Associations. ***PRACTICE AREAS:*** Estate Planning; Estate Administration; Elder Law; Taxation; Nonprofit and Charitable Organizations.

WARD J. MAZZUCCO, born Stamford, Connecticut, November 4, 1953; admitted to bar, 1978, Connecticut, U.S. District Court, District of Connecticut, U.S. Tax Court and U.S. Claims Court; 1979, U.S. District Court, Southern District of New York and U.S. Court of Appeals, Second Circuit; 1980, Florida; 1982, U.S. Supreme Court; 1985, New York; 1989, U.S. District Court, Eastern and Northern Districts of New York; 1990, U.S. District Court, Western District of New York. *Education:* Brown University (A.B., 1975); Cornell University (J.D., cum laude, 1978). Member: Danbury Zoning Commission, 1979-1981; Danbury Environmental Impact Commission, 1981-1982. *Member:* Danbury, Connecticut and American Bar Associations; The Florida Bar. ***PRACTICE AREAS:*** Litigation; Business Law; Zoning, Planning and Land Use; Health Law; Construction Law.

FRANCIS G. PENNAROLA, born Danbury, Connecticut, May 30, 1951; admitted to bar, 1976, Connecticut; 1977, U.S. District Court, District of Connecticut; 1987, U.S. Court of Appeals, Second Circuit. *Education:* Wesleyan University (B.A., 1973); University of Connecticut (J.D., with honors, 1976). *Member:* Danbury (President, 1986-1987), Connecticut and American Bar Associations; Association of Trial Lawyers of America; Connecticut Trial Lawyers Association; American Bankruptcy Institute. ***PRACTICE AREAS:*** Litigation; Elder Law; Probate; Computer Law; Workouts.

ELIZABETH LACHTERMAN, born Queens, New York, January 16, 1959; admitted to bar, 1985, Connecticut; 1986, U.S. District Court, District of Connecticut; 1987, District of Columbia. *Education:* Tufts University (B.S., cum laude, 1980); George Washington University (J.D., 1984). *Member:* Danbury and Connecticut Bar Associations. ***PRACTICE AREAS:*** Litigation; Real Estate; Business Law. ***Email:*** esl@danburylaw.com

RYAN J. MORLEY, born Cleveland, Ohio, February 22, 1976; admitted to bar, 2001, Connecticut, U.S. District Court, District of Connecticut. *Education:* Miami University (B.A., 1998); Quinnipiac College (J.D, cum laude, 2001). Editor-In-Chief, Quinnipiac Probate Law Journal, 2000-2001. *Member:* Danbury and Connecticut Bar Associations. ***LANGUAGES:*** Spanish. ***PRACTICE AREAS:*** Litigation; Business Law; Land Use. ***Email:*** rjm@danburylaw.com

COHEN AND WOLF, P.C.

158 DEER HILL AVENUE
DANBURY, CONNECTICUT 06810
Telephone: 203-792-2771
Facsimile: 203-791-8149
Email: c&w@cohenandwolf.com
URL: http://www.cohenandwolf.com

Bridgeport, Connecticut Office: 1115 Broad Street. Telephone: 203-368-0211. Facsimile: 203-394-9901.
Stamford, Connecticut Office: 112 Prospect Street. Telephone: 203-964-9907. Facsimile: 203-576-8504.
Westport, Connecticut Office: 190 Main Street. Telephone: 203-222-1034.

General Practice. Business Transactions, Commercial Litigation, Employment and Labor, Family and Matrimonial, Land Use, Municipal, Personal Injury, Physicians Practice, Real Estate, Securities, Tax, Trusts and Estates. Litigation in all Courts.

NEIL R. MARCUS, born Danbury, Connecticut, July 25, 1947; admitted to bar, 1973, Connecticut; 1974, U.S. District Court, District of Connecticut and U.S. Court of Appeals, Second Circuit. *Education:* University of Pennsylvania (B.A., 1969); New York University (J.D., 1973). Member, Wooster School Board of Trustees, 1984—. Chairman, Danbury Hospital Board of Directors, 1987-1991. Chairman of the Board, Danbury Health Systems. Member, Connecticut Milk Regulations Board, 1993—. Vice Chair, Aldrich Museum. *Member:* Danbury, Connecticut and American Bar Associations. ***PRACTICE AREAS:*** Planning and Zoning; Commercial Real Estate; Corporate. ***Email:*** nmarcus@cohenandwolf.com

DAVID L. GROGINS, born Danbury, Connecticut, June 15, 1945; admitted to bar, 1971, Connecticut and U.S. District Court, District of Connecticut. *Education:* Union College (A.B., 1967); Boston College (J.D., 1971). Town Attorney, Town of Newton, 1990—. Town Attorney, Town of Ridgefield, 2000—. *Member:* Danbury, Connecticut and American Bar Associations. ***PRACTICE AREAS:*** Corporate; Commercial Real Estate; Planning and Zoning; Municipal. ***Email:*** dgrogins@cohenandwolf.com

ROBIN A. KAHN, born New York, N.Y., March 17, 1955; admitted to bar, 1980, Connecticut; 1981, U.S. District Court, District of Connecticut. *Education:* Trinity College (B.A., 1977); University of Connecticut (J.D., 1980). Phi Beta Kappa. *Member:* Danbury, Connecticut and American Bar Associations. ***PRACTICE AREAS:*** Real Estate; Planning and Zoning; Condominium Association Representation. ***Email:*** rkahn@cohenandwolf.com

JOSEPH G. WALSH, born Bayshore, New York, December 5, 1957; admitted to bar, 1984, New York and Massachusetts; 1987, Connecticut, U.S. District Court, District of Connecticut and U.S. District Court, Eastern and Southern Districts of New York. *Education:* Manhattan College (B.S., summa cum laude, 1980); Boston College (J.D., cum laude, 1983). Assistant District Attorney, Suffolk County, New York, 1983-1988. Attorney in Charge, Suffolk County East End Drug Task Force, 1986-1988. Member, Ridgefield Republican Town Committee, 1996-2000. *Member:* Danbury (President, 1997) and Connecticut Bar Associations; Connecticut Trial Lawyers Association; Connecticut Criminal Defense Lawyers Association; The Association of Trial Lawyers of America. ***PRACTICE AREAS:*** Personal Injury; Civil and Criminal Litigation. ***Email:*** jwalsh@cohenandwolf.com

MONTE E. FRANK, born New York, N.Y., August 23, 1968; admitted to bar, 1993, Connecticut; 1994, U.S. District Court, District of Connecticut. *Education:* Cornell University (B.A., magna cum laude, 1990; J.D., 1993). Cornell National Scholar; Quill & Dagger Honor Society. Attorney Trial Referee, Factfinder, Arbitrator (Connecticut Superior Court), 2000—. Adjunct Professor of Government, Housatonic Community College, 1994-1995. Secretary, Ridgefield Democratic Town Committee, 1998-2000. *Member:* Danbury (Secretary, 1998; Treasurer, 2001—), Connecticut and American Bar Associations. ***PRACTICE AREAS:*** Commercial Litigation; Employment. ***Email:*** mfrank@cohenandwolf.com

---

MARNIE J. RUBIN, born Los Angeles, California, January 10, 1971; admitted to bar, 1999, Connecticut; 2000, U.S. District Court, District of Connecticut. *Education:* Vassar College (B.A., 1993); Vanderbilt University (J.D., 1998). Member, Moot Court Board. Associate Justice for Traveling Teams. *Member:* Danbury, Connecticut and American Bar Associations. ***PRACTICE AREAS:*** Commercial Litigation; Family Law; Municipal Law. ***Email:*** mrubin@cohenandwolf.com

(For complete biographical data on all personnel, see Professional Biographies at Bridgeport, Connecticut)

COLLINS, HANNAFIN, GARAMELLA, JABER & TUOZZOLO

PROFESSIONAL CORPORATION
Established in 1963
148 DEER HILL AVENUE
P.O. BOX 440
DANBURY, CONNECTICUT 06810
Telephone: 203-744-2150
Telecopier: 203-791-1126
URL: http://www.chgjtlaw.com

Ridgefield, Connecticut Office: 24 Bailey Avenue, 06877. Telephone: 203-438-7403. Fax: 203-438-7425.

General Practice. Real Estate, Estate Planning, Probate, Zoning and Land Use, Tax, Corporation, Commercial, Banking, Family Law, Criminal Law, Negligence, and Civil Trials in all Courts.

FIRM PROFILE: The law firm is a group of dedicated professionals operating as a team to provide you with full service in all areas of the law. Each of our attorneys practices only in limited areas so that his or her skills and knowledge are maximized for you, the client. At the same time, our firm emphasizes coordination and cooperation between firm members in order to best serve all of your needs.

FRANCIS J. COLLINS, born Danbury, Connecticut, November 20, 1933; admitted to bar, 1962, Connecticut; 1964, U.S. District Court, District of Connecticut; 1975, U.S. Court of Appeals, 2nd Circuit. *Education:* Miami University (B.S., 1955); University of Connecticut (LL.B., 1962). State Representative, 1967-1975; Assistant House Minority Leader, 1969-1971; Minority Leader, 1971-1972; Speaker of The House, 1973-1975, Connecticut General Assembly. Director and Chairman of the Board, Connecticut Attorney's Title Insurance Company, Inc., 1973—. Chairman: Judicial District of Danbury Grievance Committee, 1979-1980; 1983-1985; Judicial District of Litchfield Grievance Panel, 1986-1987. Member, Statewide Grievance Committee, 1980-1983. State Trial Referee, 1984-1987. Member, Judicial Selection Commission, 1986-1992. Member, Panel of Arbitrators, American Arbitration Association. *Member:* Danbury, Connecticut (Member, Executive Committee, Planning and Zoning Section) and American Bar Associations. [With U.S. Army, 1956-1958]. ***PRACTICE AREAS:*** Real Estate Law; Land Use Law; Commercial Law; Administrative Law; Worker's Compensation. ***Email:*** fcollins@chgjtlaw.com

EDWARD J. HANNAFIN, born Providence, Rhode Island, February 3, 1936; admitted to bar, 1965, Connecticut; 1966, U.S. District Court, District of Connecticut. *Education:* Boston College, Brown University (A.B., 1959); University of Connecticut (J.D., 1965). Member, Board of Education, New Fairfield, 1967-1968. Public Defender, Third Circuit Court, Connecticut, 1968-1971. President, Y.M.C.A., 1971-1972. Member, New Fairfield School Building Committee, 1968-1981. Justice of the Peace, 1976-1988. *Member:* Danbury and Connecticut Bar Associations. [1st Lieut, U.S. Marine Corps, 1956-1967, active duty, 1959-1962]. ***PRACTICE AREAS:*** Commercial Law; Corporate Law; Real Estate Law. ***Email:*** ehannafin@chgjtlaw.com

JACK D. GARAMELLA, born Bridgeport, Connecticut, January 30, 1945; admitted to bar, 1969, Connecticut; 1970, U.S. District Court, District of Connecticut; 1974, U.S. Supreme Court; 1986, U.S. Tax Court. *Education:* Dartmouth College (A.B., 1966); Northwestern University (J.D., 1969). Phi Delta Phi. Trustee, Danbury Hospital, 1983-1987. Member, Richter Park Authority, 1985-1993. Special Master, Judicial District of Danbury, 1986-1997. *Member:* Danbury and Connecticut Bar Associations; Connecticut Trial Lawyers Association (Member, Board of Governors, 1976-1980; 1984-1986); The Association of Trial Lawyers of America. [With Connecticut National Guard, 1969-1979]. ***PRACTICE AREAS:*** Civil Litigation; Personal Injury Law; Health Care Law. ***Email:*** jgaramella@chgjtlaw.com

PAUL N. JABER, born Danbury, Connecticut, October 15, 1942; admitted to bar, 1968, Connecticut; 1969, U.S. District Court, District of Connecticut. *Education:* Mount St. Mary's College, Maryland (B.S., 1965); University of Connecticut (LL.B., 1968). Assistant Clerk, Superior Court, Danbury, 1969-1971. Assistant Corporation Counsel, City of Danbury, 1977-1979. Member, Board of Education, City of Danbury, 1972-1977. Chairman, Board of Directors, Nutmeg Federal Savings & Loan Association. *Member:* Danbury, Connecticut (Member, Executive Committee, Real Property Section) and American Bar Associations. [With USAR, 1969-1975]. ***PRACTICE AREAS:*** Real Estate Law; Land Use Law; Commercial Law. ***Email:*** pjaber@chgjtlaw.com

ROBERT M. OPOTZNER, born Bridgeport, Connecticut, November 5, 1953; admitted to bar, 1978, Connecticut; 1979, U.S. District Court, District of Connecticut; 1995, New York. *Education:* Yale University (B.A., magna cum laude, 1975); Duke University (J.D., 1978). Former Member, Shelton, Connecticut, Board of Education. Special Master in Divorce/Custody Cases, Judicial District of Danbury; Member, Board of Education, Ridgefield, Connecticut, 1997—; Former Chairman, Labor Negotiations Committee. *Member:* Bridge-

(This Listing Continued)

port, Danbury, Connecticut and American Bar Associations; Connecticut Trial Lawyers Association. ***PRACTICE AREAS:*** Civil Litigation; Commercial Litigation; Labor Law; Matrimonial Law. ***Email:*** bopotzner@chgjtlaw.com

E. O'MALLEY SMITH, born Ft. Clayton, Panama Canal Zone, September 10, 1948; admitted to bar, 1974, Connecticut and U.S. District Court, District of Connecticut; 1980, U.S. Supreme Court. *Education:* University of Notre Dame (B.A., 1970); Rutgers University (J.D., 1973). Justice of Peace, 1984-1996; Director, Danbury War Memorial Association, Inc.; Kiwanis Club of Danbury, Inc, 1976-1988. *Member:* Danbury (Secretary-Treasurer, 1978) and Connecticut (Member, Sections on Elder Law and Estates and Probate) Bar Associations. [Lt. Cmdr., USAR, 1970-1998]. ***PRACTICE AREAS:*** Residential Real Estate; Commercial Real Estate; Trusts and Estate Planning; Probate; Corporate Law. ***Email:*** eomalleysmith@chgjtlaw.com

THOMAS W. BEECHER, born Waterbury, Connecticut, March 30, 1958; admitted to bar, 1983, Connecticut; 1984, U.S. District Court, District of Connecticut. *Education:* Colgate University (B.A., 1980); Suffolk University Law School (J.D., 1983). Pi Sigma Alpha. Member, Suffolk University Law Review, 1981-1983. Author: "'Topical Survey,' Administrative Law, Criminal Law," 15 Suffolk University Law Review, 1982. Law Clerk to the Hon. T. Clark Hull, Connecticut Appellate Court, 1983-1984. State Trial Referee, 1993—. Litchfield Judicial District Grievance Committee, 1987-1995. *Member:* Danbury and Connecticut Bar Associations; Connecticut Trial Lawyers Association. ***PRACTICE AREAS:*** Civil Litigation; Criminal Litigation; Land Use Law; Appellate Practice. ***Email:*** tbeecher@chgjtlaw.com

EVA M. DeFRANCO, born Danbury, Connecticut, September 6, 1961; admitted to bar, 1986, Connecticut and U.S. District Court, District of Connecticut. *Education:* Southern Connecticut State University (B.S., cum laude, 1983); University of Connecticut (J.D., cum laude, 1986). Adjunct Faculty, Western Connecticut State University, 1990—. Director/Advisory Director: Greater Danbury Commission on Child Care, Rights and Abuse, 1986—; Western Connecticut Chapter, American Red Cross, 1990-1992. Director: Richter Park Authority, 1996—; Mayor's Domestic Violence Prevention Task Force, 1998—; Director, Women's Center of Greater Danbury. *Member:* Danbury (President, 1998-1999) and Connecticut Bar Associations (Member, Sections on: Family Law; Women and The Law); Connecticut Trial Lawyers Association. ***PRACTICE AREAS:*** Civil Litigation; Family Law; Collections; Personal Injury Law. ***Email:*** edefranco@chgjtlaw.com

CHRISTOPHER K. LEONARD, born Red Bank, New Jersey, April 25, 1963; admitted to bar, 1989, Connecticut; 1990, U.S. District Court, District of Connecticut. *Education:* University of Rhode Island (B.S., 1985); New England School of Law (J.D., 1989). Member, 1987-1989 and Executive Case and Note Editor, 1988-1989, New England Journal on Criminal and Civil Confinement. Instructor, Legal Research, Danbury Business Institute, 1990-1994. *Member:* Danbury, Connecticut and American Bar Associations. ***PRACTICE AREAS:*** Civil Litigation; Real Estate Law; Land Use Law; Probate; Bankruptcy Law. ***Email:*** cleonard@chgjtlaw.com

---

LAURA A. GOLDSTEIN, born Manhattan, New York, August 20, 1969; admitted to bar, 1994, Connecticut; 1995, U.S. District Court, District of Connecticut. *Education:* Tufts University (B.A., magna cum laude, 1991); University of Connecticut (J.D., 1994). President, Danbury Regional Commission on Child Care Rights and Abuse, 1998—. Secretary, Board of Directors, Ridgefield Playhouse for Movies and the Performing Arts, Town of Ridgefield Cultural Committee, 1998-1999. *Member:* Danbury and Connecticut (Member, Section on Family Law) Bar Associations; Connecticut Trial Lawyers Association. ***PRACTICE AREAS:*** Civil Litigation. ***Email:*** lgoldstein@chgjtlaw.com

GREGG A. BRAUNEISEN, born Bronx, New York, May 1, 1968; admitted to bar, 1997, Connecticut and New York. *Education:* University of South Carolina (B.S., 1991); University of Richmond (J.D., 1997). Member, Western Connecticut Chapter American Red Cross, 1998—. *Member:* Danbury, Connecticut and New York State Bar Associations. ***PRACTICE AREAS:*** Estate Planning; Real Estate; Corporate Law. ***Email:*** gbrauneisen@chgjtlaw.com

GAIL H. MATTHEWS, born Johnstown, Pennsylvania, May 24, 1958; admitted to bar, 1984, Pennsylvania and U.S. District Court, Western District of Pennsylvania; 2000, Connecticut. *Education:* University of Pittsburgh (B.A., magna cum laude, 1980); Thomas M. Cooley Law School (J.D., 1984). Recipient, Divisional Scholar Award University of Pittsburgh. *Member:* Danbury, Allegheny County and Connecticut Bar Associations. ***PRACTICE AREAS:*** Estate and Trusts. ***Email:*** ghamatymatthews@chgjtlaw.com

OF COUNSEL

JOHN J. TUOZZOLO, born Norwalk, Connecticut, July 20, 1948; admitted to bar, 1973, Connecticut; 1975, U.S. District Court, District of Connecticut. *Education:* University of Dayton (B.A., 1970); College of William and Mary (J.D., 1973); University of Connecticut (M.B.A., 1981); University of Hartford (M.S., Taxation, 1985). Co-Author: "Connecticut Real Property Law," The Atlantic Law Book Company, August, 1984; "Encyclopedia of Estate Planning", Boardroom Classics, 1998. Adjunct Faculty, Western Connecticut State University, 1982—. Corporation Counsel, Town of Bethel, Connecticut, 1982-1984. Member, Panel of Arbitrators, American Arbitration Association. *Member:* Danbury and Connecticut (Member, Executive Committee, Estates and Probate Section) Bar Associations. [Col., JAGC, USAR]. ***PRACTICE AREAS:*** Probate Law; Federal Tax Law; Estate Planning. ***Email:*** jtuozzolo@chgjtlaw.com

(This Listing Continued)

COUNSEL FOR: Nutmeg Federal Savings & Loan Assn.; Ridgefield Board of Realtors, Inc.; List Services Corp.; Direct Marketing Response Co. Pentaal, Ltd.; SEBCO, Inc.; List Marketing, Inc.; Westport Supply Company; Northern Fairfield County Board of Realtors; Fairway & Greene, Ltd.
REPRESENTATIVE CLIENTS: Town of Brookfield, Planning and Zoning; Town of Ridgefield, Planning and Zoning; Bunker Ramo Corp; Columbia Diamond Rings, Inc.; Danbury Printing & Litho, Inc.; Rings End, Inc.; Danbury Yamaha, Inc.; Studer, Inc.; Omaha Beef Co., Inc.; Palazzo D'Oro, Inc.; Comatel, U.S.A.; C.P.S. Communications, Inc.; Regional YMCA; Leahy's Fuels, Inc.; Cotter & Co. Colonial Ford; Colonial Honda; Danbury Autopark; Union Carbide; First Brands Co.; Pilgrim Electric, Inc.; DJM of Norwalk, Inc.; Automated Waste Disposal; Related Properties; Patriot Marketing, Inc.; P.G. Investment Co.; Recycling Technologies, Inc.; Kimchuk, Inc.; Webster Bank.
REFERENCES: Union Trust Co.; Savings Bank of Danbury; Union Savings Bank; Fleet Bank of Connecticut; People's Bank.

CORLETO & ASSOCIATES, P.C.

Established in 1994

107 MILL PLAIN ROAD, SUITE 200
DANBURY, CONNECTICUT 06811
Telephone: 203-790-7540
Fax: 203-790-7536
URL: http://www.corletofirm.com

Insurance Defense, Coverage Dispute and Bad Faith Litigation, Environmental Law, Municipal Liability, Corporate Litigation, Corporate Governance, Intellectual Property, Employment Practices Liability.

ANTHONY B. CORLETO, born Brooklyn, New York, February 22, 1959; admitted to bar, 1989, New York and Connecticut; 1994, U.S. District Court, Southern District of New York and U.S. District Court, District of Connecticut. *Education:* The College of Insurance (B.B.A., 1983); Pace University School of Law (J.D., 1989). *Member:* The Association of Trial Lawyers of America, 1999—. ***REPORTED CASES:*** Inset v. Instruction Set, 937 F. Supp. 161 (USDC, D.Conn., 1996). ***PRACTICE AREAS:*** Insurance Defense; Insurance Bad Faith; Insurance Coverage; Environmental Law; Corporate Litigation; Municipal Liability; Employment Practices Liability Insurance; Intellectual Property; Corporate Governance.

LORI A. EATON, born Danbury, Connecticut, January 7, 1964; admitted to bar, 1997, Connecticut; 1999, New York. *Education:* Western Connecticut State University (B.A., 1992); Quinnipiac College School of Law (J.D., 1997). Moot Court Honor Society, 1995-1996. Recipient, Award for Excellence in Oral Advocacy. ***PRACTICE AREAS:*** Insurance Defense; Municipal Liability; Environmental Law; Employment Practices Liability. ***Email:*** eaton@corletofirm.com

DHARMAN P. NILES, born Jaffna, Sri Lanka, July 22, 1969; admitted to bar, 1995, Maryland; 1998, Connecticut; 2000, New York. *Education:* St. Olaf College (B.A., 1992); American University (J.D., 1995). ***PRACTICE AREAS:*** Corporate Law; Intellectual Property; Contracts; Insurance Defense. ***Email:*** niles@corletofirm.com

HUGH J. DONNELLY, born Manhasset, New York, May 3, 1957; admitted to bar, 1984, New York and New Jersey; 1985, District of Columbia; 1994, Connecticut. *Education:* St. John's University (B.S., 1979); Touro College, Jacob D. Fuchsberg Law Center (J.D., 1983). *Member:* Connecticut and New York State Bar Associations; District of Columbia Bar; New York State Trial Lawyers Association. ***PRACTICE AREAS:*** Litigation.

OF COUNSEL

KENNETH L. ROBINSON, born Brooklyn, New York, February 14, 1953; admitted to bar, 1979, New York; 1988, U.S. Supreme Court; 1987, U.S. Court of Appeals, Second Circuit (Not admitted in Connecticut). *Education:* Antioch College (B.S., 1975); Northeastern University (J.D., 1978). *Member:* Nassau County (Chair, Environmental Law Committee, 1992-1994) and New York State (Member, Environmental Law Committee) Bar Associations. ***PRACTICE AREAS:*** Environmental Law; Insurance; Land Use; Real Estate; Litigation. ***Email:*** robinson@corletofirm.com

---

ANDREW C. COTÉ, P.C.

DANBURY, CONNECTICUT

(See Sharon)

CRAMER & ANDERSON LLP

68 NORTH STREET
DANBURY, CONNECTICUT 06810
Telephone: 203-790-7747
Fax: 203-790-9538
Email: danbury@crameranderson.com
URL: http://www.cramer-anderson.com

Litchfield, Connecticut Office: 46 West Street. P.O. Box 278. Telephone: 860-567-8718. Email: litchfield@cramer-anderson.com
Kent, Connecticut Office: Kent Green, P.O. Box 333. Telephone: 860-927-3568. Email: gnelson@cramer-anderson.com
New Milford, Connecticut Office: 51 Main Street. Telephone: 860-355-2631. Email: newmilford@crameranderson.com
Washington Depot, Connecticut Office: 2 Green Hill Road, P.O. Box, 321. Telephone: 860-868-0527. Email: wfairbairn@cramer-anderson.com

General Practice. Probate, Estate Planning, Municipal, Family and Real Estate. Trials. Planning and Zoning, Corporate, Banking, Securities.

FIRM PROFILE: Cramer & Anderson, founded over one-hundred years ago, is a firm of diversely qualified attorneys that offers a wide range of sophisticated legal services to individual and business clients. In the past decade, Cramer & Anderson has grown to become the largest law firm in Litchfield County, with offices in Kent, Litchfield, New Milford and Washington, as well as an office in Danbury, Fairfield County. Listed in Martindale-Hubbell's Bar Register of Preeminent Lawyers, Cramer & Anderson's principal areas of practice include: general business, corporate and commercial law; estate planning, trusts, probate administration and elder law; litigation in all courts, ranging from commercial litigation to personal injury and family law; planning and zoning, residential and commercial real estate law. Our attorneys regularly appear in Connecticut's Superior and Appellate Courts, as well as in the Federal District Court, Second Circuit Court of Appeals, and bankruptcy courts. The firm has expanded into new areas of the law as its client base has diversified. Cramer & Anderson takes pride in its long tradition of commitment by our attorneys to professional excellence, and to public service with community, charitable and civic organizations. Using the resources of our experienced attorneys, paralegals and staff, together with our advanced technological resources, we are committed to serving our clients personally and professionally.

JOSEPH A. SAFFI, born Danbury, Connecticut, November 9, 1949; admitted to bar, 1977, Connecticut. *Education:* University of Connecticut (B.A., 1973); New England School of Law (J.D., cum laude, 1976). Member, Board of Directors: Connecticut Attorneys Title Insurance Company; Danbury Chamber of Commerce. *Member:* Connecticut (Member, Sections on: Real Estate; Estate) and American Bar Associations. (Resident). ***PRACTICE AREAS:*** Residential Real Estate Law; Commercial Real Estate Law; Estate Planning Law; Corporate Law. ***Email:*** jsaffi@crameranderson.com

DAVID P. BURKE, born Pasadena, California, March 15, 1953; admitted to bar, 1978, Connecticut and U.S. District Court, District of Connecticut; 1979, U.S. Tax Court and U.S. District Court, Southern District of New York; 1980, New York and U.S. Court of Appeals, Second Circuit; 1981, U.S. District Court, Eastern District of Wisconsin; 1982, U.S. Supreme Court; 1983, U.S. Court of Appeals, Eleventh Circuit; 1984, U.S. District Court, Eastern District of New York. *Education:* Miami University (B.A., 1975); George Washington University (J.D., 1978). Phi Kappa Phi; Phi Sigma Alpha. Associate, Breed, Abbott & Morgan, New York, New York, 1981-1982. *Member:* Connecticut (Member, Section on Civil Justice), Federal and American (Member, Sections on: Litigation; Corporation, Banking and Business Law) Bar Associations; The Association of Trial Lawyers of America; Connecticut Trial Lawyers Association. (Resident). ***PRACTICE AREAS:*** Commercial Litigation; Civil Law; Personal Injury Law; Family Law. ***Email:*** dburke@crameranderson.com

COUNSEL FOR: Town of Cornwall; First National Bank of Litchfield; New Milford Hospital, Inc.; Canterbury School; New Mil Bank; South Kent School; Marvelwood School.

(For Complete Personnel and Biographical Data, see Professional Biographies at New Milford, Connecticut).

DRISCOLL, TALARICO, FRIZZELL, OLIVO & DRISCOLL

142 DEER HILL AVENUE
DANBURY, CONNECTICUT 06810-7727
Telephone: 203-792-8333
Facsimile: 203-778-9570
Email: attystfo@snet.net

General Practice in all Courts. Trials, Real Estate, Probate, Corporation and Foreclosure Law, Commercial Litigation.

(This Listing Continued)

JULIUS J. BIELIZNA (1914-1988).
HERBERT B. WANDERER (1902-1979).

ROBERT N. TALARICO, born Danbury, Connecticut, March 14, 1942; admitted to bar, 1965, Connecticut. *Education:* University of Connecticut (B.A., 1964; LL.B., 1965). Assistant Corporation Counsel, City of Danbury, 1967-1977. Judge of Probate, District of Danbury, 1988-1990. Superior Court Attorney Trial Referee, 1985—. *Member:* Danbury, Connecticut and American Bar Associations. ***PRACTICE AREAS:*** Banking Law; Estate Planning; Land Use Law; Landlord and Tenant Law; Probate Law; Real Estate; Real Estate-Commercial Law; Real Estate (Property) Law; Real Estate-Residential Law; Secured Lending; Secured Transaction Law; Zoning and Planning; Zoning and Subdivision Law; Zoning Law.

THOMAS A. FRIZZELL, born Brooklyn, New York, September 24, 1940; admitted to bar, 1968, New York and Connecticut; 1973, U.S. Supreme Court; 1975, U.S. District Court, District of Connecticut. *Education:* St. John's University (B.B.A., 1962; LL.B., 1967). Phi Delta Phi. Associate Editor, St. John's Law Review, 1966-1967. Assistant Corporation Counsel, Zoning, Planning and Environmental Matters, City of Danbury, 1979-1982. Counsel, 1977 and Chairman, 1987, Charter Revision Commission, City of Danbury. Corporator and Trustee, Union Savings Bank. Justice of the Peace, 1977-1981. *Member:* Danbury, Connecticut and American Bar Associations. ***PRACTICE AREAS:*** Real Estate Law; Estates; Wills; Probate; Commercial Law; General Practice.

STEVEN M. OLIVO, born Brooklyn, New York, April 4, 1948; admitted to bar, 1975, Connecticut and U.S. District Court, District of Connecticut. *Education:* Dartmouth College (A.B., magna cum laude, 1970); Boston University (J.D., 1975). Phi Beta Kappa. *Member:* Danbury (Treasurer, 1979-1981) and Connecticut Bar Associations; Connecticut Trial Lawyers Association; The Association of Trial Lawyers of America. ***REPORTED CASES:*** Yankee Gas Services Co. v. DaSilva, 25 Conn. App. 226, 593 A. 2d 158 (1991), 220 Conn. 909, 597 A. 2d 341 (1991); H.G. Bass Associates Inc. v. Ethan Allen Inc., 26 Conn. App. 426, 601 A. 2d 1040 (1992); Connecticut Light & Power Co. v. DaSilva, 231 Conn. 441, 650 A. 2d 551 (1994); Merchants Bank and Trust Co. v. DaSilva, 44 Conn. App. 920, 690 A. 2d 435 (1997); South End Plaza Association, Inc. v. Johnson, 62 Conn.App. 462, 767 A.2d 1267 (2001), 256 Conn. 922, 774 A.2d 138 (2001). ***PRACTICE AREAS:*** Civil Practice; Personal Injury Law; Negligence Law; Landlord and Tenant Law.

THOMAS A. FRIZZELL, JR., born Danbury, Connecticut, July 6, 1969; admitted to bar, 1997, Connecticut; 1998, New York; 1999, U.S. Court of Appeals for the District of Columbia Circuit; 2000, U.S. District Court, Southern and Eastern Districts of New York. *Education:* Florida Institute of Technology, School of Aeronautics; Western Connecticut State University (B.S., summa cum laude, 1993); St. John's University School of Law (J.D., cum laude, 1997). Private Pilot, 1991. Author, "Basic Sources of Information in Air Crash Litigation," ABA Tort and Insurance Practice Section, Litigating The Aviation Case, 1998. Program Committee Member, American Bar Association 1999 Aviation Litigation Seminar. Board of Directors, Friends of the Danbury Library. *Member:* Danbury and Connecticut Bar Associations. ***PRACTICE AREAS:*** Personal Injury Litigation; Wrongful Death Litigation; Products Liability; Aviation Law; International Aviation Law.

RICHARD W. HANNA
GEORGE S. PAPAZOGLOU

FOGARTY COHEN SELBY & NEMIROFF LLC

DANBURY, CONNECTICUT

(See Greenwich)

Litigation in all Courts, Real Estate and Land Use, Estate Planning and Probate, Corporate, Matrimonial, Administrative and Environmental, Appellate Practice, Business, Civil Trial, Commercial Litigation, Construction, Family, Labor and Employment, Medical Malpractice, Trust and Product Liability.

STEPHEN C. GALLAGHER

57 NORTH STREET
SUITE 114
DANBURY, CONNECTICUT 06810
Telephone: 203-792-0525
Fax: 203-792-8182
Email: scgatt@msn.com
URL: http://www.lawyers.com/gallagher&gallagher

General Practice, Real Estate, Municipal, Zoning, Condominium, Probate, Personal Injury, Negligence, Criminal and Family Law, Trials in all Courts.

STEPHEN C. GALLAGHER, born Danbury, Connecticut, July 7, 1942; admitted to bar, 1967, Connecticut; 1980, U.S. District Court, District of Connecticut. *Education:* Fairfield University (B.A., 1964); New York University (J.D., 1967). Town Counsel, Town of Bethel, Connecticut, 1969-1982; 1984-

(This Listing Continued)

1986. *Member:* Danbury (President, 1994) and Connecticut Bar Associations. ***PRACTICE AREAS:*** Municipal Law; Zoning Law; Workers Compensation; Criminal Law; Personal Injury.

APPROVED ATTORNEYS FOR: First American Title Insurance Co.; Stewart Title Guaranty Company.
REFERENCES: Union Savings Bank; Savings Bank of Danbury.

GILL LAW PRACTICE

DANBURY, CONNECTICUT

(See Ridgefield)

Family Law, Real Estate, Business Law, Litigation, Divorce, Child Support, Child Custody.

LIAM DAVIS GLYNN

74 WEST STREET
DANBURY, CONNECTICUT 06810
Telephone: 203-744-5434
Fax: 203-744-1446
Email: liamglynn@gte.net

Real Estate, Personal Injury, Criminal, Commercial Collections.

LIAM DAVIS GLYNN, born New York, N.Y., July 26, 1964; admitted to bar, 1990, Connecticut and New York. *Education:* Ithaca College (B.S., 1986); University of Bridgeport (J.D., 1990).

HALL & SAVARESE, P.C.

DANBURY, CONNECTICUT

(See Newtown)

General Practice. Trials in all State and Federal Courts. Zoning and Land Use, Real Estate, Probate and Estate Planning, Personal Injury, Workers Compensation.

JONES, DAMIA, KAUFMAN, BOROFSKY & DEPAUL, LLC

301 MAIN STREET, 3RD FLOOR
P.O. BOX 157
DANBURY, CONNECTICUT 06813-0157
Telephone: 203-744-1313
Fax: 203-797-8403
Email: info@danburyattorneys.com
URL: http://www.danburyattorneys.com

General Civil and Criminal Practice Including Trials in all Courts, Personal Injury, Workers' Compensation, Family Law/Divorce, Employment and Discrimination Law, Corporate, Wills and Probate, Zoning, Real Estate, Banking and Finance, Foreclosures and Collections.

MEMBERS OF FIRM

A. PETER DAMIA, born Yonkers, New York, July 10, 1933; admitted to bar, 1958, Connecticut. *Education:* University of Connecticut (B.A., 1955); Harvard University (LL.B., 1958). Co-author: "Count-Down to Closing," Count-Down Publications, 1979. Instructor, Western Connecticut State College, Division of Extended Programs and Career Development Course, The Condominium in Connecticut, 1979-1981. *Member:* Danbury Bar Association (Vice President, 1980). ***LANGUAGES:*** Italian. ***PRACTICE AREAS:*** Real Estate Law; Probate Law; Banking Law. ***Email:*** adamia@danburyattorneys.com

SANFORD D. KAUFMAN, born Far Rockaway, New York, August 28, 1933; admitted to bar, 1959, New York; 1962, U.S. Supreme Court; 1973, Connecticut. *Education:* Queens College of the City University of New York (B.A., 1955); University of California at Berkeley; New York Law School (LL.B., 1959). Author: "A Busy Lawyers Guide to the Mechanics Lien Law," Queens County Bar Association Journal, Spring, 1966; "What is a Trade Secret?" Industrial Security, May, 1969. Member, Panel of Arbitrators, American Arbitration Association. Associate Counsel Majority Leader of the New York State Assembly, 1966-1968. Special Hearing Officer to the Department of Justice, 1967. Assistant District Attorney County of Queens, City of New York, 1968-1972. Member, Board of Directors: UST Connecticut, 1988-1992; W. N. deSherbinnin Products, Inc., 1988—. *Member:* Danbury, Queens County, Connecticut, New York State and American Bar Associations; The Association of Trial Lawyers of America; Connecticut Trial Lawyers Association. ***PRACTICE AREAS:*** Corporate Law; Banking Law; Negligence Law; Employment Law. ***Email:*** skaufman@danburyattorneys.com

(This Listing Continued)

MARVIN BOROFSKY, born Bridgeport, Connecticut, April 3, 1948; admitted to bar, 1973, Connecticut; 1978, U.S. Supreme Court. *Education:* The American University (B.A., 1970); Suffolk University (J.D., 1973). Special Master, Family Matters, Judicial District of Danbury and Middletown Regional Family Trial District. *Member:* Danbury (Vice President, 1979; President, 1982; Continuing Legal Education Committee; Family Law Committee) and Connecticut (Member: House of Delegates, 1979-1990; Professional Discipline Committee, 1985-1990; Family Law Section) Bar Associations. ***REPORTED CASES:*** Burritt, Lloyd v. Plate, Edward 9/30/83 40-Conn. Sup 103 481,A2d,425. ***PRACTICE AREAS:*** Family Law; Civil Litigation; Real Estate. ***Email:*** mborofsky@danburyattorneys.com

GUY L. DEPAUL, born Danbury, Connecticut, May 23, 1958; admitted to bar, 1984, Connecticut and U.S. District Court, District of Connecticut. *Education:* Siena College (B.A., 1980); University of Bridgeport (J.D., 1983). Attorney State Trial Referee. *Member:* Danbury and Connecticut Bar Associations; Connecticut Trial Lawyers Association. ***REPORTED CASES:*** Keenan v. Union Camp, 49 CA 280. ***PRACTICE AREAS:*** Workers Compensation; Personal Injury. ***Email:*** gdepaul@danburyattorneys.com

MICHAEL R. KAUFMAN, born Queens, New York, October 28, 1963; admitted to bar, 1988, Connecticut; 1989, New York and U.S. District Court, Southern and Eastern District of New York; 1991, U.S. District Court, District of Connecticut, and U.S. Court of Appeals, Second Circuit; 1996, U.S. Supreme Court. *Education:* Lafayette College (A.B., 1985); New York Law School (J.D., cum laude, 1988). Assistant Corporation Counsel, New York City Law Department, 1988-1991. *Member:* Danbury, Connecticut and New York State Bar Associations; Connecticut Trial Lawyers. ***PRACTICE AREAS:*** Civil Litigation; Personal Injury; Employment Law; Banking Law; Commercial Law. ***Email:*** mkaufman@danburyattorneys.com

OF COUNSEL

WILLIAM R. JONES, born Remsen, New York, January 17, 1920; admitted to bar, 1948, Connecticut. *Education:* St. Lawrence University (B.S., 1943); University of Connecticut (LL.B., 1948). Commissioner, Unemployment Compensation, 1950-1954. Attorney State Trial Referee, 1984—. *Member:* Danbury and Connecticut Bar Associations; Connecticut Trial Lawyers Association. ***PRACTICE AREAS:*** Workers Compensation; Personal Injury.

CHARLES F. STELLJES, born New York, N.Y., November 15, 1928; admitted to bar, 1952, New York; 1956, U.S. District Court, Eastern and Southern Districts of New York; 1969, Connecticut; 1972, U.S. District Court, District of Connecticut. *Education:* New York Law School (LL.B., 1952). *Member:* Queens County, Danbury and Connecticut Bar Associations; Connecticut Trial Lawyers Association. ***REPORTED CASES:*** Success Centers, Inc v. Huntington Learning Centers, Inc. 233 Conn. 761, 613 A.2d 1320. ***PRACTICE AREAS:*** Negligence Litigation; Domestic Litigation; Commercial Litigation.

REPRESENTATIVE CLIENTS: Fairfield Processing Co.; Tesec Corp.; W.N. deSherbinnin Products, Inc.; Danbury Downtown Council; Greentree Toyota Lincoln Mercury.; The Kanthal Corp.; Fleet Bank; Newtown Savings Bank; Union Savings Bank; Summit Bank.
ISSUING AGENTS FOR: Security Title & Guaranty Co.; Chicago Title Insurance Co.; First American Title Insurance Co.
REFERENCES: NMBT; Fleet Bank.

KOSKOFF, KOSKOFF & BIEDER, P.C.

1 MOSS AVENUE
DANBURY, CONNECTICUT 06810
Telephone: 203-792-7100
URL: http://www.koskoff.com

Bridgeport, Connecticut Office: 350 Fairfield Avenue. Telephone: 203-336-4421.
Stamford, Connecticut Office: 1172 Bedford Street. Telephone: 203-325-3686.

Litigation in all State and Federal Courts. Medical Malpractice, Equal Opportunity, Negligence, Products Liability, Civil Rights, Criminal Law and Class Actions.

(For biographical data on all personnel, see Professional Biographies at Bridgeport, Connecticut)

JAMES MARK LAMONTAGNE

68 MAIN STREET
DANBURY, CONNECTICUT 06810
Telephone: 203-778-1422

General Practice.

JAMES MARK LAMONTAGNE, born 1965; admitted to bar, 1992, Connecticut; 1993, New York. *Education:* Western Connecticut State University (B.S., 1988); Pace University (J.D., 1992). ***PRACTICE AREAS:*** Real Estate; Criminal Law; Civil Law.

HELEN L. McGONIGLE

DANBURY, CONNECTICUT

(See Brookfield)

Litigation, Victims Rights, Real Estate, Land Use, Appellate Law, Insurance Law, Personal Injury Law, Probate, Estate Planning, Wills and Equine Law.

LAWRENCE J. MIX

57 NORTH STREET, SUITE 214
DANBURY, CONNECTICUT 06810-5660
Telephone: 203-744-0220

Business Law, Real Estate, Litigation, Labor and Employment, Alternative Dispute Resolution, General Practice.

LAWRENCE J. MIX, born Port Chester, New York, March 7, 1957; admitted to bar, 1981, Massachusetts; 1982, U.S. District Court, District of Massachusetts; 1985, Connecticut, U.S. District Court, District of Connecticut and U.S. Supreme Court. *Education:* Cornell University (B.S., 1978) Boston University (J.D., 1981). Arbitrator, American Arbitration Association. Director and Treasurer, 1987-1988, Hartford Chapter, American Corporate Counsel Association. *Member:* Connecticut (Member, Alternative Dispute Resolution Committee) and American Bar Associations; The Corporate Bar of Westchester-Fairfield. (Also practicing individually at Brookfield, Connecticut). ***PRACTICE AREAS:*** Business Law; Real Estate; Litigation; Labor and Employment; Alternative Dispute Resolution; General Practice.

MOOTS, PELLEGRINI, MANNION, MARTINDALE & DRATCH, P.C.

DANBURY, CONNECTICUT

(See New Milford)

Estate Planning, Probate, Business and Corporate, Real Estate, Domestic Relations, Personal Injury, Workers Compensation, Criminal and Civil Litigation. Planning Zoning and Land Use.

MULVEY & KOROTASH

Established in 1976
THE WEST STREET BUILDING
31 WEST STREET
P.O. BOX 751
DANBURY, CONNECTICUT 06813
Telephone: 203-792-5900
Telecopier: 203-798-2057

General Civil and Criminal Trial Practice. Real Estate, Probate, Corporate, Negligence, Workers Compensation, Commercial and Family Law.

MEMBERS OF FIRM

JAMES RYAN MULVEY, born New Haven, Connecticut, May 25, 1947; admitted to bar, 1972, Connecticut and U.S. District Court, District of Connecticut. *Education:* Dartmouth College (A.B., 1969); Fordham University (J.D., 1972). *Member:* Danbury (Vice President 1999, President 2000), Connecticut and American Bar Associations; The Association of Trial Lawyers of America. ***PRACTICE AREAS:*** Civil and Criminal Litigation; Domestic Relations; Divorce; Real Estate.

MARK W. KOROTASH, born Derby, Connecticut, December 4, 1948; admitted to bar, 1973, Connecticut; 1974, U.S. District Court, District of Connecticut. *Education:* Dartmouth College (A.B., 1970); College of William & Mary (J.D., 1973). Phi Alpha Delta (Vice President, 1971-1972; President, 1972-1973). Member, Newtown Pension Committee, 1979—. Member, Board of Directors, Fairfield County Lawyer Referral Service, 1980-1985. Member, Board of Directors, Danbury Chapter, American Red Cross, 1980-1984. *Member:* Danbury (Member, Committees on: Public Relations, 1978-1979; Unauthorized Practice of Law, 1986-1987), Newtown (Vice-President, 1978-1979; President, 1980-1981), Connecticut (Member: Probate Section; Committee on News Media Legal Resource, 1977-1978) and American Bar Associations; Connecticut Trial Lawyers Association. ***PRACTICE AREAS:*** Real Estate; Probate; Wills; Estate Planning; Civil Litigation.

APPROVED ATTORNEYS FOR: Connecticut Attorneys Title Insurance Co.; First American Title Insurance Co.; Stewart Title Insurance Co.; Fidelity National Title Insurance Co.
REFERENCES: Peoples Bank; Union Savings Bank.

MURPHY AND KARPIE, LLC

DANBURY, CONNECTICUT

(See Bridgeport)

General Civil Practice before State and Federal Courts. Insurance Defense, Personal Injury, Negligence, Products Liability, Medical Malpractice, Professional Liability, Employment Litigation, Commercial and Civil Rights Law, Appellate Practice, Toxic Torts.

PIAZZA & PICKEL

DANBURY, CONNECTICUT

(See Stamford)

Trials and Appeals in State and Federal Courts, Negligence, Medical Malpractice, Divorce and Personal Injury Law, Wrongful Death, Legal Malpractice, Child Custody, Automobile Accidents, Product Liability, Adoption, Family Law.

PINNEY, PAYNE, VAN LENTEN, BURRELL, WOLFE & DILLMAN, P.C.

Established in 1948
LEE FARM CORPORATE PARK
83 WOOSTER HEIGHTS
P.O. BOX 3499
DANBURY, CONNECTICUT 06813-3499
Telephone: 203-743-2721
Fax: 203-792-4759
Email: ppv@ntplx.com

General Practice. Civil and Criminal Litigation in all State and Federal Courts, State and Federal Appeals, Real Estate, Planning, Zoning and Land Use, Estate Planning and Administration, Corporate, Business, Commercial, Banking, Personal Injury, Domestic Relations, Medical Malpractice, Administrative Law, Tax, Native American Law, Corporate Mergers and Acquisitions.

THOMAS W. VAN LENTEN, born Paterson, New Jersey, April 4, 1934; admitted to bar, 1962, Connecticut. *Education:* University of Bridgeport (B.S., 1959); University of Connecticut (LL.B., 1962). Member, Board of Editors, University of Connecticut Law Review, 1961-1962. Member, Moot Court, 1960. Town Counsel for Ridgefield, Connecticut, 1965-1968. Member, Board of Directors, 1974 and Secretary, 1977-1978, The Danbury Hospital. Member, Panel of Arbitrators, American Arbitration Association. *Member:* Danbury, Connecticut and American Bar Associations; Schaghticoke Tribal Nation (Member, General Counsel, 1994—). ***PRACTICE AREAS:*** Commercial Law; Litigation; Banking Law; Construction Law; Probate Law; Native American Law. ***Email:*** tomv@ppvlaw.com

HUGH A. BURRELL, born Port Chester, New York, January 13, 1939; admitted to bar, 1964, Connecticut. *Education:* University of Virginia (B.S. in Com., 1961; LL.B., 1964). Phi Alpha Delta. Member, Business Board, University of Virginia Law Review, 1963-1964. Member, Board of Directors, 1974-1976, Vice President, 1976-1979 and President, 1979-1981, Tax District of Candlewood Isle. Member, New England Land Title Association, 1975—. Member, American Land Title Association, 1985-1989. Secretary, Greater Danbury Chamber of Commerce, 1990-1994. Member, Board of Directors, Greater Danbury Chamber of Commerce, 1988—; Chairman of the Board, 1994-1996. Incorporator - Savings Bank of Danbury, 1994—; Board of Directors, The Ann Olsen Endowment, Inc., 1994—; Board of Directors, Fairfield County Community Foundation, Inc., 1996-1998; Board of Directors, The Ridgewood Country Club, Inc., 1994— (Vice President, 1997; President, 1998-1999). *Member:* Danbury (Vice-President, 1991; President, 1992) and Connecticut (Member, Sections of: Real Estate; Estate and Probate; Panel Member, Legal Fee Arbitration Board, 1981) Bar Associations. ***PRACTICE AREAS:*** Real Estate Law; Estate Law; Probate Law; Banking Law. ***Email:*** hbur@ppvlaw.com

ROBERT J. WOLFE, born New Haven, Connecticut, March 13, 1936; admitted to bar, 1960, Connecticut; 1962, U.S. Court of Appeals, Second Circuit; 1966, U.S. District Court, District of Connecticut. *Education:* University of Vermont (B.S., 1957); University of Virginia (LL.B., 1960). Sigma Nu Phi. Business Manager, Virginia Law Weekly, 1959-1960. Superior Court Attorney Trial Referee, 1984-1986. Superior Court Special Master (Family), 1986. Judiciary Client Security Fund Committee, 1999—. *Member:* Danbury (Secretary-Treasurer, 1966-1968; President, 1980-1981) and Connecticut (Member: House of Delegates, Board of Governors, 1978-1990; Specialization Committee, 1973-1982; Professional Ethics Committee, 1980-1981; Awards Committee, 1981-1982, 1985-1987, 1998; Nominating Committee, 1981, 1987, 1998, 1999, 2000. Admission to the Bar Committee, 1981-1985; Professional Discipline Committee, 1982—, Chairman, 1991-1994; Special Committee on Membership Services, 1983-1985; Chairman, 1985; Committee on the Arbitration of Fee Disputes; Member, 1983—and Chairman, 1999—. Member: Academy of Continu-

(This Listing Continued)

ing Professional Development, 1982—; Judiciary Committee, 1987-1990; Committee on Unauthorized Practice of Law, 1990—; Committee on Constitution and Structures, 1991; Client's Security Fund, 1995-1999) Bar Associations. ***PRACTICE AREAS:*** Commercial Law; Corporations and Other Businesses; Estate Planning; Estate Settlement; Probate Law; Real Estate Law. ***Email:*** wolfe@ppvlaw.com

JOHN M. DILLMAN, born Stratford, Connecticut, May 31, 1939; admitted to bar, 1965, Connecticut. *Education:* Lehigh University (B.S., 1961); University of Connecticut (LL.B., 1965). Editor in Chief, University of Connecticut Law Review, 1964-1965. *Member:* Danbury, Connecticut (Member, Executive Committee, Estates and Probate Section, 1983-1985) and American Bar Associations. ***PRACTICE AREAS:*** Estate Planning and Settlement; Trust Law. ***Email:*** dillman@ppvlaw.com

MARTIN A. RADER, JR., born Danbury, Connecticut, November 30, 1945; admitted to bar, 1970, Connecticut. *Education:* Yale University (B.A., 1967); University of Connecticut (M.B.A., 1979; J.D., with honors, 1970). Assistant States Attorney, Judicial District of Danbury, 1974-1984; Attorney State Trial Referee, 1993—. Board of Directors, The Non-Profit Rental Corporation. Instructor, Paralegal Program Center for Professional Development, University of Connecticut, 1996—. *Member:* Danbury (President, 1991) and Connecticut (Member, Sections on: Estates; Litigation) Bar Associations; Connecticut Trial Lawyers Association; The Association of Trial Lawyers of America. Fellow, Connecticut Bar Foundation, James W. Cooper Fellows. [CAPT (RET.), JAGC, USNR]. ***REPORTED CASES:*** Brown v. Brown 195 Conn 98 (1985); State v. McIntosh 199 Conn 155 (1986); Southbury Land Trust, Inc. v. Ahdricovich, 59 Cohn. App. 785 (2000). ***PRACTICE AREAS:*** Real Estate Law; Personal Injury Litigation; Commercial Litigation; Probate Law. ***Email:*** mrader@ppvlaw.com

WILLIAM S. STEELE, JR., born Yakima, Washington, April 19, 1945; admitted to bar, 1970, Connecticut. *Education:* Yale University (B.A., 1967); New York University (J.D., 1970). *Member:* Danbury and Connecticut (Member, Sections on: Real Property; Planning & Zoning; Environmental Law) Bar Associations. ***PRACTICE AREAS:*** Real Estate Law; Land Use Law. ***Email:*** wss@ppvlaw.com

SHELDON A. ROSENBAUM, born New Haven, Connecticut, September 20, 1948; admitted to bar, 1974, Connecticut; 1975, U.S. District Court, District of Connecticut; 1980, U.S. Supreme Court and U.S. Court of Appeals, Second Circuit. *Education:* Rutgers University (B.A., 1970; J.D., 1973). Author, "Motion Practice Before Trial," Family Law Practice in Connecticut, LPH, 1996. Superior Court Special Master (Family), 1992—. Chairman of the Board of Directors, Regional YMCA of Western Connecticut, Inc., 1989-1991. Member, Town of Bethel Ethics Commission, 1995-2001. *Member:* Danbury and Connecticut (Member, Family Law Section) Bar Associations. ***REPORTED CASES:*** Kioukis v. Kioukis, 185 Conn. 249, 44A. 2d 894 (1981); Cahn v. Cahn, 26 Conn. App. 720 (1992); 225 Conn. 666 (1993); Roberts v. Roberts, 32 Conn. App. 465 (1993). ***PRACTICE AREAS:*** Domestic Relations Law; Personal Injury Law; Real Estate Law. ***Email:*** srosenbaum@ppvlaw.com

JACKIE CHAN, born Canton, China, December 15, 1948; admitted to bar, 1974, Connecticut; 1976, U.S. District Court, District of Connecticut; 1982, U.S. Court of Appeals, Second Circuit and U.S. Supreme Court. *Education:* Colgate University (A.B., 1970); St. John's University (J.D., 1973). State of Connecticut Attorney Fact-Finder, 1984—and Trial Referee, 1984—. Member, Board of Trustees, Danbury Hospital Development Fund, Inc., 1985-1988. Member, Board of Directors, Nutmeg Federal Savings and Loan Association, 1988-2000. *Member:* Danbury (President, 1985-1986) and Connecticut (House of Delegates, 1989-1991; Board of Governors, 1989-1994) Bar Associations; Connecticut Trial Lawyers Association; Connecticut Criminal Defense Lawyers Association. ***LANGUAGES:*** Chinese. ***REPORTED CASES:*** Grenier v. Compratt Construction Co., 189 Conn. 144, 454 A.2d. 1289 (1983); State v. Morrill, 193 Conn. 602, 478 A.2d. 994; Abel v. Zoning Board of Appeals, 172 Conn. 286, 374 A.2d. 227; R. Zemper & Associates v. Scozzafava, 28 Conn. App. 557 (1992). ***PRACTICE AREAS:*** Criminal and Civil Litigation; Personal Injury; Commercial Law. ***Email:*** jackiechan@ppvlaw.com

RICHARD D. ARCONTI, born Danbury, Connecticut, November 16, 1952; admitted to bar, 1977, Connecticut. *Education:* University of Notre Dame (B.A., cum laude, 1974); University of Connecticut (J.D., 1977). Assistant States Attorney, Superior Court, Judicial District of Danbury, Connecticut, 1978-1984. Adjunct Instructor, Western Connecticut State University, 1988-1990. Member, Board of Directors: Western Connecticut State University Foundation; Pope John Paul Health Center. Member, Panel of Arbitrators, American Arbitration Association. *Member:* Danbury (President, 1993) and Connecticut Bar Associations; Connecticut Trial Lawyers Association. (Certified as a Criminal Trial Advocate by the National Board of Trial Advocacy, 1985-1990). ***REPORTED CASES:*** State v. DeBoben, 187 Conn. 469; Sabino v. Ruffalo, 19 Conn. App. 402; Randazzo v. Pitcher, 17 Conn. App. 471; State v. Cimino, 194 Conn. 210; State v. Martin, 2 Conn. App. 605; State v. Ibramov, 137 Conn. 348; State v. Conger, 183 Conn. 386. ***PRACTICE AREAS:*** Civil Litigation; Personal Injury Law; Criminal Law. ***Email:*** arc@ppvlaw.com

(This Listing Continued)

TED D. BACKER, born Islip, New York, July 9, 1952; admitted to bar, 1977, District of Columbia; 1978, Connecticut; 1981, New York. *Education:* George Washington University (B.A., 1974; J.D., 1977). Phi Beta Kappa. Vice President, Family and Children's Aid, Inc., 1995-2000. Member, Still River Alliance, 1997—. *Member:* Danbury and Connecticut Bar Associations; The District of Columbia Bar. ***REPORTED CASES:*** In Re Investigation of Grand Juror into the Bethel Police Department, 188 Conn. 601, 452 A.2d 935; Newtown v Dept. of Public Utility Control, 3 Conn. App 416, 488 A.2d 1286; Rotophone, Inc. v. Danbury Hospital, 13 Conn. App. 230, 535 A.2d 830. ***PRACTICE AREAS:*** Administrative Law; Real Estate Law; Environmental Law. ***Email:*** tbacker@ppvlaw.com

JOSEPH DIMYAN, born Danbury, Connecticut, July 17, 1953; admitted to bar, 1979, Connecticut; 1980, U.S. Court of Military Appeals; U.S. Court of Appeals, Second Circuit; U.S. District Court, District of Connecticut; U.S. District Court, Southern and Eastern Districts of New York. *Education:* Fairfield University (B.A., 1975); Fordham University (J.D., 1979). *Member:* Danbury and Connecticut Bar Associations; Connecticut Trial Lawyers Association; Connecticut Criminal Defense Lawyers Association. ***LANGUAGES:*** Arabic. ***REPORTED CASES:*** L'Ambiance Plaza Plaintiffs Committee; In Re Robert, 199 Conn. 693, 509 A.2d 475; State v. Cimino, 194 Conn. 210, 478 A.2d 1005; State v. Rutan, 194 Conn. 438, 479 A.2d 1209; Dewitt v. John Hancock Met Life Ins., 501 A.2d 768.; United States v. Barton, 76 F.3rd 499; Tanges v. Heidelberg Inc. etal, 92 N.Y. 2d 918 (1999). ***PRACTICE AREAS:*** Personal Injury Law; Criminal and Civil Litigation. ***Email:*** jed@ppvlaw.com

DANIEL E. CASAGRANDE, born New Haven, Connecticut, June 7, 1954; admitted to bar, 1980, New York; 1986, Connecticut. *Education:* Fairfield University (B.A., summa cum laude, 1976); Fordham University (J.D., cum laude, 1979). Recipient, American Jurisprudence Awards in Contracts and Constitutional Law. Commentary Editor, Fordham Law Review, 1978-1979. Author: "The Impact of the Interstate Agreement on Detainers Upon Federal Prisoner Transfer," 46 Fordham Law Review 492, 1977. Law Clerk, Hon. William H. Mulligan, United States Court of Appeals for the Second Circuit, 1979-1981. Associate, Stillman, Friedman & Shaw, New York, N.Y., 1981-1986. President, Connecticut Association of Municipal Attorneys, 1991-1994. *Member:* Danbury, Connecticut and American Bar Associations. ***PRACTICE AREAS:*** Civil Litigation; Commercial Litigation; Municipal Law; Land Use Law. ***Email:*** dcasag@ppvlaw.com

KIM E. NOLAN, born Danbury, Connecticut, July 18, 1949; admitted to bar, 1977, Connecticut; 1986, U.S. District Court, District of Connecticut. *Education:* Norwich University (B.A., English, 1972); Vermont Law School (J.D., 1976). State of Connecticut Attorney Fact-Finder and Trial Referee, 1991—. *Member:* Danbury and Connecticut Bar Associations; Connecticut Trial Lawyers Association; Connecticut Defense Lawyers Association; Association of Trial Lawyers of America. [Capt., U.S. Army Reserve, 1972-1980]. ***PRACTICE AREAS:*** Personal Injury; Civil Litigation; Real Estate Law; Commercial Law; Landlord/Tenant Law. ***Email:*** knolan@ppvlaw.com

WENDY A. GRISPIN, born Bronx, New York, May 26, 1966; admitted to bar, 1993, Connecticut, U.S. District Court, District of Connecticut and Southern District of New York; U.S. Supreme Court. *Education:* Western Connecticut State University (B.B.A., 1990); Pace University (J.D., cum laude, 1993). Managing Editor, Pace International Law Review. *Member:* Danbury (President, 2001), Connecticut (Member, Criminal Justice Section) and American (Member, Criminal Justice Section) Bar Associations; The Association of Trial Lawyers of America; Connecticut Criminal Defense Lawyers Association. ***REPORTED CASES:*** United States v. Barton, 76 F. 3d 499 (2nd Cir. 1996); Russack v. Russack, 58 Conn. App. 517 (2000). ***PRACTICE AREAS:*** Criminal and Civil Litigation; Personal Injury; Domestic Relations Law. ***Email:*** wgrispin@ppvlaw.com

---

JOHN H. VAN LENTEN, born Danbury, Connecticut, November 14, 1962; admitted to bar, 1996, Connecticut and U.S. District Court, District of Connecticut. *Education:* Western Connecticut State University (B.B.A., 1987); Quinnipiac College School of Law (J.D., summa cum laude, 1996). Phi Delta Phi. Member, Burns Inn. Recipient: American Jurisprudence Awards in Evidence; Torts; Federal Income Tax; Legal Skills; Administrative Law; Land Use Planning; Criminal Procedure (Investigative); Advanced Constitutional Law. Law Clerk, Hon. Barry R. Schaller, Connecticut Appellate Court, 1998-1999. *Member:* Danbury, Connecticut and American Bar Associations. ***PRACTICE AREAS:*** Commercial Law; Real Estate; Appellate Practice; Construction Law; Land Use; Native American Law. ***Email:*** jvanlenten@ppvlaw.com

JOSEPH DASILVA, JR., born Danbury, Connecticut, February 5, 1970; admitted to bar, 1999, Connecticut. *Education:* Western Connecticut State University (B.A., 1993; M.A., 1997); Quinnipiac College School of Law (J.D., magna cum laude, 1999). Executive Business Editor, Quinnipiac Health Law Journal, 1998-1999. Recipient, American Jurisprudence Award in Criminal Law, Torts, Evidence, Business Organizations, First Amendment, State Constitutional Law, Lawyers Professional Responsibility, Law of the European Union.

(This Listing Continued)

PINNEY, PAYNE, VAN LENTEN, BURRELL, WOLFE & DILLMAN, P.C., Danbury—Continued

Member: Danbury, Connecticut and American Bar Associations; Associations of Trial Lawyers of America. ***PRACTICE AREAS:*** General Litigation. ***Email:*** jdasilvajr@ppvlaw.com

JEAN YOUNG KIM, born Seoul, Korea, February 22, 1973; admitted to bar, 2001, Connecticut. *Education:* Yale University (B.A., 1995); Hofstra University School of Law (J.D., 2000). *Member:* Danbury and American Bar Associations; National Asian Pacific American Bar Association. ***LANGUAGES:*** Korean, Spanish. ***PRACTICE AREAS:*** Civil Litigation; Commercial Litigation; Land Use; Toxic Torts; Administrative Law; Municipal Law; Real Estate; Commercial Law. ***Email:*** jyk@ppvlaw.com

OF COUNSEL

A. SEARLE PINNEY, born New Milford, Connecticut, September 14, 1920; admitted to bar, 1948, Connecticut. *Education:* Tufts University (B.A., 1942); Harvard University (LL.B., 1948). Town Counsel, Town of Brookfield, 1951-1975. Member, House of Representatives, Connecticut General Assembly, 1955-1961; Minority Leader, House, 1959-1961. Member, Board of Trustees: Wooster School, 1960-1991; Connecticut State University, 1979-1997; Chairman, 1991-1995. Chairman, Grievance Committee, Judicial District of Danbury, 1979-1983. Member, Statewide Grievance Committee, 1979-1980; 1983-89; Chairman, 1985-1989. Chairman, Judicial Council on Legal Ethics, 1990. Chairman, Committee on Professional Discipline, 1990-1991, Member, 1990-1994. Member of Panel, American Arbitration Association. *Member:* Danbury (President, 1969), Connecticut (Recipient, John Eldred Shields Distinguished Professional Services Award, 1991) and American Bar Associations. ***PRACTICE AREAS:*** Estate Planning and Administration.

BOBBY S. PAYNE, born Louisa, Virginia, August 27, 1933; admitted to bar, 1960, Virginia and Connecticut. *Education:* University of North Carolina (B.A., 1955); University of Virginia (LL.B., 1960). Phi Alpha Delta. Member, Board of Directors, Connecticut Golf Foundation, Inc., 1999—. *Member:* Danbury and Connecticut (Member, Real Property Section) Bar Associations. ***PRACTICE AREAS:*** Real Estate Law; Land Use Law. ***Email:*** e:mail@ppvlaw.com

COUNSEL FOR: City of Danbury; Savings Bank of Danbury; Interlab, Inc.; Bethel Consolidated Co.; Berkshire Industrial Corporation; Western Connecticut Sportsplex; Schaghticoke Tribal Nation; Theatre Projects Consultants, Inc.; Hersam-Acorn Press, Inc.; International Fiber Systems, Inc.; International Television Production Group, Inc.; REI Property & Asset Management, Inc.; Subaru of Wilton, Inc.; Georgetown Jeep/Eagle, Inc.; Danbury Mail; Hoya Lens of America; Paul Dinto Electrical Contractors, Inc.; Town of New Fairfield.
LOCAL COUNSEL FOR: First American Title Insurance Co.; Fidelity National Title Insurance, Co.; United Water Connecticut Inc.; Commonwealth Land Title Insurance Co.; Stewart Title Insurance Co.; R.S.A. Corp.; Nutmeg Federal Savings & Loan Association; Chase Manhattan Bank of Connecticut; Summit; Fleet Mortgage Services, Inc.; Exxon, U.S.A.; International Sports & Entertainment Strategies (ISES); Housatonic Area Regional Transit District; United Properties Group Inc.; Druck, Inc.; Union Savings Bank.

SILVER, GOLUB & TEITELL LLP

DANBURY, CONNECTICUT

(See Stamford)

Trial Practice in all State and Federal Courts. Medical Malpractice, Negligence, Commercial Litigation, Family and Criminal Law.

WARE, FRESSOLA, VAN DER SLUYS & ADOLPHSON, LLP

DANBURY, CONNECTICUT

(See Monroe)

Patent, Trademark, Copyright, Computer, Antitrust, Unfair Competition, Foreign Patent Law, Litigation and Federal Practice.

CHRISTOPHER G. WINANS, P.C.

d/b/a Sullivan, Biraglia, Winans and Eberhard

24 SHELTER ROCK ROAD
DANBURY, CONNECTICUT 06810
Telephone: 203-798-1000
Fax: 203-797-0000
Email: CGWinans@aol.com
URL: http://www.lawyers.com/winans

Collections, Commercial Litigation, Civil Litigation and Personal Injury.

(This Listing Continued)

CHRISTOPHER G. WINANS, born Hartford, Connecticut, October 30, 1961; admitted to bar, 1987, Connecticut; 1988, U.S. District Court, District of Connecticut; 1991, U.S. Supreme Court; 1993, U.S. District Court, Southern District of New York and U.S. Court of Appeals, Second Circuit. *Education:* Fairfield University (B.A., 1983); Rutgers University (J.D., 1986). Law Clerk, Superior Court, Connecticut Judicial Department, 1986-1988. Partner, Pinney, Payne, Burrell, Wolfe and Dillman, P.C. 1993-1997. *Member:* Danbury and Connecticut Bar Associations; The Connecticut Trial Lawyers Association. ***REPORTED CASES:*** Chapin v. Freedom of Information Commission, 22 Conn. App. 316 (1990); Mitchell v. Mitchell, 31 Conn. App. 331 (1993); Ridgebury Group v. Mitchell, 31 Conn. App. 938 (1993); Scala v. Datahr Rehabilitation Institute, 38 Conn. App. 906 (1995). ***PRACTICE AREAS:*** Collections; Commercial Law; Construction Litigation; Foreclosures; Landlord and Tenant Law; Civil Litigation; Personal Injury. ***Email:*** CGWinans@aol.com

JACKSON HARRIS BURLINGAME & HUBERT, LLC

Established in 1961

245 MAIN STREET
DANIELSON, CONNECTICUT 06239
Telephone: 860-774-9627
Fax: 860-774-5784
Email: jhbhlaw@snet.net

General Civil Practice. Criminal, Family, Probate, Estate Planning, Corporate, Real Estate, Municipal and Bankruptcy Law. Litigation.

MEMBERS OF FIRM

GEORGE H. JACKSON, III, born Providence, Rhode Island, February 25, 1939; admitted to bar, 1964, Connecticut. *Education:* Dartmouth College (A.B., 1961); University of Pennsylvania (J.D., 1964). Member, 1969-1993 and Chairman, 1977-1993, Board of Finance, Town of Pomfret. Director, Connecticut Attorney Title Insurance Co., 1992—. *Member:* Windham County (President, 1990-1991), Connecticut (Member: Executive Committee, Planning and Zoning Section, 1968-1979; Executive Committee, Real Property Section, 1973—; Standards of Title Committee, 1988—) and American Bar Associations. ***PRACTICE AREAS:*** Real Estate.

JOHN K. HARRIS, JR., born New Bedford, Massachusetts, August 23, 1937; admitted to bar, 1966, Connecticut. *Education:* University of Massachusetts at Amherst (B.S., 1960); University of Connecticut School of Law (LL.B., 1965). Member, 1969-1989, and Chairman, 1973-1988, Brooklyn, Connecticut, Planning and Zoning Commission. Member and Chair, Brooklyn Water Pollution Control Commission, 1988-1994. Hearing Examiner, Connecticut Commission on Human Rights and Opportunities, 1971-1976. Member, 1970-1983 and Chair, 1981-1983, Northeast Connecticut Regional Planning Agency. Member, Northeast Connecticut Council of Governments Planning Commission, 1983-1989. Town Attorney: Thompson, Connecticut, 1972-1983; Eastford, Connecticut, 1978-1985; Sterling, Connecticut, 1980-1998. State of Connecticut Attorney Trial Referee, 1987-1996. *Member:* Windham County (President, 1996) and Connecticut (Clients Security Fund, 1980-1997) Bar Associations. ***PRACTICE AREAS:*** Civil Litigation; Criminal Defense; Bankruptcy; Elder Law. ***Email:*** john.harris@snet.net

STEPHEN J. BURLINGAME, born New Bedford, Massachusetts, March 18, 1943; admitted to bar, 1969, Connecticut. *Education:* Bates College (A.B., 1965); University of Connecticut (J.D., 1969). Selectman, Town of Killingly, 1969-1971. Member, 1975-1987, Vice-Chairman, 1975-1978 and Chairman, 1978-1987, Board of Directors, Day Kimball Hospital. Counsel, Borough of Danielson, Town of Killingly. Chairman, Connecticut Hospital Association, 1991-1992. *Member:* Windham County, Connecticut and American Bar Associations. ***PRACTICE AREAS:*** Probate; Planning; Zoning; Corporate; Municipal; Family. ***Email:*** sjburlingame@snet.net

DAVID M. HUBERT, born Putnam, Connecticut, June 12, 1951; admitted to bar, 1979, Connecticut. *Education:* Georgetown University; University of Connecticut (B.A., magna cum laude, 1973; J.D., 1979). Member, 1973-1975 and Chairman, 1974-1975, Killingly Planning & Zoning Commission. Town Attorney, Town of Pomfret, 1989—. Town Attorney, Town of Brooklyn, 1996-2000. *Member:* Windham County, Connecticut and American Bar Associations; Connecticut Trial Lawyers Association; Association of Trial Lawyers of America; American Council of Life Insurance, Legal Section (Member, Subcommittee on Federal Bankruptcy Legislation, 1982-1985). ***PRACTICE AREAS:*** Real Estate; Personal Injury; Municipal; Landlord/Tenant; Automobile Accidents and Injuries; Dog Bites; Slip and Fall; Wrongful Death.

REPRESENTATIVE CLIENTS: Cargill Bank; The Borough of Danielson, Ct.; Town of Pomfret; S.K. Properties; Town of Killingly; Quinebaug Systems, Inc.
REFERENCES: Fleet Bank (Danielson Branch); Cargill Bank.

LAW OFFICE OF HEATHER M. BROWN, LLC

1051 POST ROAD, SUITE 2
P.O. BOX 37
DARIEN, CONNECTICUT 06820-0537
Telephone: 203-655-1900
Fax: 203-655-2210
Email: darienlaw@snet.net
URL: http://www.lawyers.com/hmbrown

Civil Litigation, Family Law, Divorce, Child Custody, Child Support, Land Use, Real Estate, Real Estate Finance, Probate Administration.

HEATHER M. BROWN, born Danbury, Connecticut, March 29, 1959; admitted to bar, 1984, Connecticut and U.S. District Court, District of Connecticut. *Education:* University of Illinois (B.A., 1979); Pace University (J.D., 1984). Appointed Attorney Trial Referee, Superior Court, 1995—. Magistrate, Superior Court, 2001. *Member:* Connecticut (Member, Sections on: General Practice; Real Property; Family Law) and American (Member, Litigation, Property and Probate Section) Bar Associations; Connecticut Trial Lawyers Association. ***SPECIAL AGENCIES:*** Principal, CT-Title.com. ***REPORTED CASES:*** Masella v. Blue Cross & Blue Shield, 936 F2d 98, 2nd Cir., 1991; Giordano v. Giordano, 9 Conn. App. 641, 1987; Licari v. Blackwelder, 14 Conn. App. 46, 1988; Grady v. Schmitz, 16 Conn. App. 292, 1988; Saradjian v. Saradjian, 25 Conn. App. 411, 1991; D'Addario v. Darien Planning & Zoning, 25 Conn. App. 137, 1991. ***PRACTICE AREAS:*** Real Estate; Probate; Civil Litigation; Family Law. ***Email:*** darienlaw@snet.net

LEGAL SUPPORT PERSONNEL

BARBARA MURRAY. PRACTICE AREAS: Real Estate.

AMELIA AMBROGIO. PRACTICE AREAS: Litigation Support.

KELLY VEGLIANTE. PRACTICE AREAS: Real Estate Compliance.

CURTIS, BRINCKERHOFF & BARRETT, P.C.

DARIEN, CONNECTICUT

(See Stamford)

General Practice, Real Estate, Commercial Real Estate Acquisitions, Municipal Law, Zoning, Planning and Land Use, Banking, Administrative Law, Litigation, Civil Litigation, Commercial Litigation, Tax Appeals, Eminent Domain, Federal Taxation, International Taxation, State Taxation, Estate Planning, Trust and Estate, Probate, Elder Law, Family Law, Domestic Relations, Closely Held Corporations, Business Law, Corporate Law, Commercial Law, Commercial Leasing, Leases and Leasing, Employment Law, Non-Competition and Non-Solicitation Agreements, Commercial Arbitration, Construction Law, Landlord and Tenant Law, Personal Injury and Negligence, Product Liability, Bankruptcy, Civil Trial and Appellate Practice in all State and Federal Courts.

PATRICK J. DAMANTI

777 POST ROAD
P.O. BOX 134
DARIEN, CONNECTICUT 06820-0634
Telephone: 203-655-7104
Fax: 203-655-6417
Email: patdamanti@snet.net

New York, New York Office: 36 West 44th Street, Suite 900, 10036. Telephone:212-764-6206. Fax: 212-997-7686.

Real Estate, Foreclosure, Workouts, Creditors Rights, Bankruptcy, Banking, Probate, Trusts and Estates.

PATRICK J. DAMANTI, born Brooklyn, New York, April 6, 1947; admitted to bar, 1973, New York; 1987, U.S. District Court, Southern and Eastern Districts of New York; 1988, Connecticut; 1990, U.S. District Court, District of Connecticut. *Education:* College of the Holy Cross (A.B., 1968); Villanova University; St. John's University (J.D., 1972). Commissioner, 1994—, Chairman, 1997—; Secretary, 1995-1997, Planning and Zoning Board, and Commissioner, 1991-1994, Zoning Board of Appeals, Town of Darien, CT. *Member:* The Association of the Bar of the City of New York; New York State, Connecticut and American Bar Associations.

ASSOCIATE

CHRISTINA M. COLBERT, born Brooklyn, New York, October 8, 1967; admitted to bar, 1992, Connecticut; 1993, New York and U.S. District Court, Southern and Eastern Districts of New York. *Education:* St. John's University (B.A., cum laude, 1989; J.D., 1992). Member, Moot Court.

FREEHILL HOGAN & MAHAR LLP

Established in 1952
23 OLD KINGS HIGHWAY SOUTH
DARIEN, CONNECTICUT 06820
Telephone: 203-921-1913
Facsimile: 203-358-8377
Email: reception@freehill.com
URL: http://www.freehill.com

Admiralty and Maritime Law, Administrative Law, Charter Parties, Contracts, Marine Pollution and Environmental Law, Ship Finance, Marine Insurance, Personal Injury, General Commercial Litigation, Occupational Disease Defense, Maritime and Environmental Criminal Law, Criminal Law. All aspects of Litigation and Arbitration, including Trials and Appeals in Federal and State Courts.

(For Biographical Data on all Personnel, See Professional Biographies at New York, New York)

GLEASON & HILL, LLC

23 OLD KINGS HIGHWAY SOUTH
P.O. BOX 1636
DARIEN, CONNECTICUT 06820
Telephone: 203-655-9696
Fax: 203-656-2055
Email: attorneys@gleasonlaw.com

Land Use, Commercial and Residential Real Estate, Business, Environmental, Litigation, Family, Personal Injury.

WILDER G. GLEASON, born New York, New York, August 1, 1950; admitted to bar, 1977, Connecticut and U.S. District Court, District of Connecticut. *Education:* Williams College (B.A., 1972); University of Connecticut (J.D., 1977). *Member:* Stamford/Norwalk Regional (Board of Directors, 1993-1997; Member, Sections on: Real Estate; Business; and Co-Chair, Land Use Committee, 1997—), Connecticut (Member, Sections on: Business; Real Estate; Planning and Zoning) and American Bar Associations. ***PRACTICE AREAS:*** Zoning, Planning and Land Use; Real Estate; Leases and Leasing; Environmental. ***Email:*** wilder.gleason@gleasonlaw.com

D.B. HILL, born Norwalk, Connecticut, 1956; admitted to bar, 1987, New York; 1996, Connecticut; U.S. District Court, Southern and Eastern Districts of New York. *Education:* American University (B.S., 1979); University of Bridgeport (J.D., 1986). Assistant District Attorney, Bronx County, New York, 1986-1997. Supervisor, Narcotics Bureau and Narcotics Major Case Unit, 1989-1993. Deputy Chief, Rackets Bureau, 1993-1997. *Member:* Stamford/Norwalk Regional, Connecticut, New York State and American Bar Associations. ***PRACTICE AREAS:*** Administrative Appeals; Zoning, Planning and Land Use; Litigation. ***Email:*** bruce.hill@gleasonlaw.com

---

KATHRYN L. PASTERNAK, born New York, N.Y., July 19, 1951; admitted to bar, 1997, Connecticut; 1998, New York. *Education:* Sweet Briar College (B.A., 1972); University of Virginia (M.A., 1975); Pace University (J.D., 1997). *Member:* New Canaan, Connecticut, New York State and American Bar Associations; Regional Bar Association of Stamford/Norwalk. ***LANGUAGES:*** Spanish. ***PRACTICE AREAS:*** Real Estate; Zoning, Planning and Land Use. ***Email:*** kathryn.pasternak@gleasonlaw.com

OF COUNSEL

JENNIFER N. BOYD, born Meriden, Connecticut, 1952; admitted to bar, 1978, Connecticut. *Education:* Tufts University (B.A., magna cum laude, 1974); University of Connecticut (J.D., cum laude, 1978). *Member:* Connecticut and American Bar Associations. (Also of Counsel to Fogarty Cohen Selby & Nemiroff LLC, Greenwich). ***PRACTICE AREAS:*** Corporate Finance; Corporate Law; Mergers and Acquisitions; Partnership Law; Limited Liability Company Law. ***Email:*** jennifer.boyd@gleasonlaw.com

L. CONRAD AMBRETTE, born New York, New York, January 7, 1947; admitted to bar, 1972, New York; 1973, Connecticut and U.S. District Court, District of Connecticut. *Education:* Middlebury College (B.A., 1968); Cornell University (J.D., 1971). *Member:* Stamford, Connecticut, New York State and American Bar Associations. [1st Lt., U.S. Army, Military Intelligence, 1971-1973]. (Also Member, Millar & Ambrette, Darien, CT). ***PRACTICE AREAS:*** Probate and Estates; Elder Law; Wills; Trusts. ***Email:*** ambrette@optonline.net

HEAGNEY, LENNON & SLANE LLP

DARIEN, CONNECTICUT

(See Greenwich)

General Practice, Real Estate, Trusts and Estates, Probate, Corporation and Business Law, Civil and Criminal Litigation, Zoning and Family Law.

LAW OFFICE OF STEPHEN P. HORNER

Established in 1986

2183 BOSTON POST ROAD

DARIEN, CONNECTICUT 06820

Telephone: 203-655-7905

Facsimile: 203-656-1075

URL: http://www.hornerlaw.com

Email: shorner@sphorner.com

URL: http://www.lawyers.com/hornerlaw

Labor and Employment Practice before State and Federal Courts.

FIRM PROFILE: The Law Office of Stephen P. Horner was founded in 1986. From its beginning, the firm has practiced only employment and labor law. The firm is highly computerized with regard to all aspects of its practice including research, word processing, billing, communication, conflict checking, case management and court calendaring (Westlaw and PRO LAW).

STEPHEN P. HORNER, born New Rochelle, New York, December 24, 1946; admitted to bar, 1974, New York; 1988, Connecticut, U.S. District Court, District of Connecticut and U.S. District Court, Southern and Eastern Districts of New York; 1998, U.S. Court of Appeals, Second Circuit. *Education:* Dickinson College (B.A., 1967); Temple University (M.B.A., 1969; J.D., 1972). Former Labor Counsel to Uniroyal, Inc., 1984-1986. Special Master, U.S. District Court, District of Connecticut, 1999-2001. Member, Town of Darien's RTM (Representative Town Meeting), 1999-2000. *Member:* Norwalk-Stamford Regional (Chairman, Employment Law Section, 1993-1994; 1997-2001) and Connecticut (Member, Labor and Employment Law Section) Bar Associations; The Corporate Bar (Chairman, Employment Law Section, 1989-1990); Connecticut Employment Lawyers Association; National Employment Lawyers Association. [Capt., Military Police, U.S. Army, 1971-1977]. ***PRACTICE AREAS:*** Employment Law; Labor Law.

REPRESENTATIVE CLIENTS: Ventiv Health Communications, Inc.; Edo Corp.; Leggette, Brashears & Graham, Inc.; Drake, Beam & Morin; Chartwell Reinsurance; Uniroyal Holding; G.W. Hoffman, Inc.; Management Resources of America; The Patterson Club; Silvermine Golf Club; The Wilton Bank.

HUMES, BOTZOW, WAGNER & MILLER

DARIEN, CONNECTICUT

(See Davidson, Dawson & Clark LLP)

CHRISTOPHER P. McCLANCY

1051 POST ROAD

SUITE 3

P.O. BOX 1124

DARIEN, CONNECTICUT 06820-1124

Telephone: 203-656-4700

Fax: 203-656-4800

Email: CPMcClancy@msn.com

URL: http://www.lawyers.com/cpmcclancy

General Practice, Trusts and Estates, Civil Litigation, Property Tax Assessments, Business Formation, Commercial Law, Legal Ethics and Professional Responsibility.

CHRISTOPHER P. McCLANCY, born New York, N.Y., July 29, 1961; admitted to bar, 1987, Connecticut, New York, U.S. District Court, District of Connecticut and U.S. District Court, Southern and Eastern Districts of New York; 1988, District of Columbia; 1990, U.S. Court of Appeals for the Federal Circuit and U.S. Court of International Trade. *Education:* Villanova University (B.A., 1983); New York Law School (J.D., cum laude, 1987); The Hague Academy of International Law, The Hague, The Netherlands (1992); Georgetown University Law Center (LL.M., International & Comparative Law, 1995). Co-Author: "Liability and Control, in representing Foreign-Owned Business in Connecticut," Connecticut Bar Association Continuing Legal Education, 1993. Member, 1991-1995 and Chairman, 1993-1995, Town of Darien Board of Tax Review. Member, Selden Society. *Member:* Association of the Bar of the City of New York (Member, Library Committee, 1990-1993; Member, Foreign & Comparative Law Committee, 1996—); Connecticut (Co-Chairman, 1990-1991 and Chairman, 1991-1992, International Law & World Peace Section), New York State and American (Member, Sections on: International Law & Practice; Litigation) Bar Associations; American Society of International Law. ***PRACTICE AREAS:*** General Practice; Probate; Trusts and Estates; Civil Litigation; Business Formation; Corporate Formation; Legal Ethics and Professional Responsibility; Property Tax Appeals; Commercial Law.

MILLAR & AMBRETTE

Established in 1963

23 OLD KING'S HIGHWAY SOUTH

DARIEN, CONNECTICUT 06820-1267

Telephone: 203-655-7931

FAX: 203-656-2055

URL: http://www.lawyers.com/millar&ambrette

Real Estate, Probate and Estate Planning, Elder Law, Corporation, and General Practice.

MEMBERS OF FIRM

SAMUEL D. B. MILLAR, JR., born Montclair, New Jersey, January 16, 1931; admitted to bar, 1957, Connecticut; 1969, U.S. Supreme Court. *Education:* Wesleyan University (B.A., 1953); Rutgers University (LL.B., 1957). Director, Connecticut Attorneys Title Insurance Company. *Member:* Stamford, Connecticut and American Bar Associations. ***PRACTICE AREAS:*** Real Estate; Probate and Estates. ***Email:*** smillar1@optonline.net

L. CONRAD AMBRETTE, born New York, New York, January 7, 1947; admitted to bar, 1972, New York; 1973, Connecticut and U.S. District Court, District of Connecticut. *Education:* Middlebury College (B.A., 1968); Cornell University (J.D., 1971). *Member:* Stamford, Connecticut, New York State and American Bar Associations. [1st Lt., U.S. Army, Military Intelligence, 1971-1973]. (Also Of Counsel, Gleason & Hill, LLC, Darien, CT). ***PRACTICE AREAS:*** Probate and Estates; Elder Law; Real Estate; Wills; Trusts.

ASSOCIATE

PATRICIA MORELAND GROSS, born Hays, Kansas, June 29, 1936; admitted to bar, 1985, Connecticut; 1986, U.S. District Court, District of Connecticut. *Education:* University of Connecticut (B.G.S., with honors, 1979); Pace University (J.D., 1984). *Member:* Stamford Regional, Connecticut and American Bar Associations. ***PRACTICE AREAS:*** General Practice; Real Estate. ***Email:*** pgross1@optonline.net

---

REILLY & REILLY

800 POST ROAD

P.O. BOX 1072

DARIEN, CONNECTICUT 06820-1072

Telephone: 203-655-6785

Fax: 203-655-7462

URL: http://www.reillylaw.com

Email: lawyers@reillylaw.com

URL: http://www.lawyers.com/georgereilly

Family Law, Litigation, Trusts and Estates Planning and Administration, Residential Real Estate.

GEORGE A. REILLY, born Norwalk, Connecticut, September 6, 1954; admitted to bar, 1984, Connecticut; 1985, New York; 1986, U.S. District Court, Southern and Eastern Districts of New York; 1991, U.S. Supreme Court. *Education:* Union College (B.A., 1977); Fordham University (J.D., 1984). Member: Psi Upsilon Fraternity; Kiwanis International; Board of Selectmen, Town of Darien, 1999—; Board of Trustees, King & Low-Heywood Thomas School, 1988-1998 (President, 1990-1997). *Member:* Stamford-Norwalk Regional (Member, Family Law Committee; Co-Chairman, Litigation Committee, 1992-1995), Connecticut (Member, Family Law Section), New York State and American (Member, Family Law Section) Bar Associations. ***PRACTICE AREAS:*** Family Law; Divorce; Post Divorce; Litigation; Residential Real Estate; Trusts and Estates. ***Email:*** george@reillylaw.com

OF COUNSEL

LAWRENCE H. REILLY, born New York, New York, July 27, 1922; admitted to bar, 1950, New York; 1952, Connecticut. *Education:* Fordham University (A.B., 1943); Columbia University (LL.B., 1949). Member, Papal Order of St. Gregory The Great. *Member:* The Association of the Bar of the City of New York; Regional, New York State (Member, Trusts and Estates Law Section), Connecticut (Member, Estates and Probate Section) and American Bar Associations. ***PRACTICE AREAS:*** Elder Law; Trusts and Estates. ***Email:*** larry@reillylaw.com

RUCCI, BURNHAM, CARTA & EDELBERG, LLP

Established in 1978
800 POST ROAD
P.O. BOX 1107
DARIEN, CONNECTICUT 06820
Telephone: 203-655-7695
Facsimile: 203-655-4302
URL: http://www.rbce.com

New Canaan, Connecticut Office: 71 Elm Street, P.O. Box 1680. Telephone: 203-966-6500.

Stamford, Connecticut Office: 6 Landmark Square, Suite 470. Telephone: 203-359-5637.

Commercial and Residential Real Estate, Trusts and Estates, Estate Planning, Civil Trial Practice including Fiduciary Disputes, Employment, Commercial, Construction and Personal Injury Litigation, Corporate, Commercial, Information Technology, Banking, Workouts and Bankruptcy, Business Law, Environmental Law, Pre-Nuptial Agreements, State, Local and Federal Taxation, Zoning, Pensions, ERISA Matters and Charitable Organizations.

FIRM PROFILE: Our firm was founded in 1978 to offer highly skilled and professional legal services to the Fairfield County community.

Today the same philosophy and tradition continue. The firm's practice has grown to serve both individuals and business clients in a responsive, effective manner. Our mission is to act as counselors as well as legal advisors to our clients.

MEMBERS OF FIRM

JOSEPH J. RUCCI, JR., born Norwalk, Connecticut, February 14, 1941; admitted to bar, 1966, Connecticut; 1971, U.S. District Court, District of Connecticut; 1973, U.S. Supreme Court. *Education:* Fairfield University (A.B., 1963); Villanova University School of Law (J.D., 1966). With Federal Bureau of Investigation, 1966-1970. Director, Bank of New Canaan. *Member:* Regional (President, 1991-1992; Member, Executive Committee, 1981-1992), Connecticut (Secretary, 1993-1994) and American Bar Associations. ***PRACTICE AREAS:*** Information Technology; Banking; Business Law; Commercial Law. ***Email:*** jrucci@rbce.com

PAUL H. BURNHAM, born Greenfield, Massachusetts, May 14, 1954; admitted to bar, 1980, Connecticut and U.S. District Court, District of Connecticut; 1986, U.S. Court of Federal Claims; 1987, U.S. Tax Court. *Education:* Yale University (B.A., 1977); University of Connecticut School of Law (J.D., 1980); New York University School of Law (LL.M., in Taxation, 1984). *Member:* Connecticut and American Bar Associations. ***PRACTICE AREAS:*** Estate Planning; Estate Administration; Individual Taxation; Corporate Tax Planning. ***Email:*** pburnham@rbce.com

MARK R. CARTA, born Fairfield, Connecticut, 1950; admitted to bar, 1978, Connecticut; 1998, U.S. Tax Court. *Education:* University of Pennsylvania (B.A., cum laude 1973); University of Connecticut (J.D., 1977). Member, Connecticut Law Review, 1975-1977. Law Clerk to Judge T.F. Gilroy Daly, U.S. District Court, District of Connecticut, 1977-1978. Special Master, U.S. District Court, Stamford/Norwalk Superior Court. *Member:* The Connecticut Bar Association. ***PRACTICE AREAS:*** Commercial Litigation; Employment Discrimination; Fiduciary; Construction Litigation; Civil Appeals; Products Liability Defense; Intellectual Property; Banking Litigation; Business Mediation.

PAUL B. EDELBERG, born Middletown, Connecticut, April 6, 1950; admitted to bar, 1976, Connecticut and U.S. District Court, District of Connecticut; 1982, New York. *Education:* Wesleyan University (B.A., 1972); University of Connecticut Law School (J.D., with honors, 1976). Executive Editor, Connecticut Law Review, 1975-1976. Chairman, Banking Law Section of the Connecticut Bar Association, 1991-1994; Member, Bank Advisory Committee of the Connecticut Law Revision Commission, 1993-1994; Member, Long Island Sound Advisory Committee to The Connecticut Department of Environmental Protection, 1991-1999. Chairman of the Board, Stamford Chamber of Commerce, 2000—. *Member:* The Regional (Member, Board of Directors, 1994-1998), Connecticut and American Bar Associations. (Resident, Stamford Office). ***PRACTICE AREAS:*** Banks and Banking; Corporate Law; Business Law; Mergers, Acquisitions and Divestitures; Finance; Debtor and Creditor; Commercial Law; Real Estate; Nonprofit and Charitable Organizations. ***Email:*** pedelberg@rbce.com

WILLIAM M. CARELLO, born New York, N.Y., November 27, 1962; admitted to bar, 1989, Connecticut; 1990, New York; 1992, U.S. District Court, District of Connecticut. *Education:* University of Connecticut (B.S., magna cum laude, 1985; J.D., with high honors, 1989). Member, Connecticut Moot Court Board, 1988-1989. Notes and Comments Editor, Connecticut Law Review, 1988-1989. President, Darien Lions Club; First Vice President and Director, Darien Chamber of Commerce. *Member:* The Regional (Former Chairman, Business Law Section) and Connecticut Bar Associations. ***PRACTICE AREAS:*** Corporate Law; Business Law; Commercial Law; Mergers and Acquisitions; Real Estate. ***Email:*** wcarello@rbce.com

ROBERT F. MASLAN, JR., born Rockville Centre, New York, December 9, 1951; admitted to bar, 1990, Connecticut; 1991, New York, U.S. District Court, Southern, Northern and Eastern Districts of New York and U.S. District Court, District of Connecticut; U.S. Court of Appeals, Second Circuit. *Education:* Fairfield University (B.S., summa cum laude, 1987); Fordham University (J.D., 1990). Articles & Commentary Editor, Fordham Law Review. Special Master, Superior Court. Former President, Norwalk Seaport Association. *Member:* Stamford/Norwalk Regional and Connecticut (Member, Planning and Zoning Section) Bar Associations. ***PRACTICE AREAS:*** Commercial Litigation; Federal Civil Practice; Real Estate; Zoning, Planning and Land Use. ***Email:*** rmaslan@rbce.com

COLETTE C. SYMON, born Liverpool, England, January 15, 1964; admitted to bar, 1991, Connecticut; 1993, New York. *Education:* Tufts University (B.A., 1985); University of Connecticut School of Law (J.D., with honors, 1991). *Member:* Regional and Connecticut (Co-Chair, Real Property Committee, Young Lawyers Section, 1993-1995 and 1997-1999; Co-Chair, Womens Law Round Table Section 1995-1997; Member: Real Property and Women in the Law Sections) Bar Associations. ***PRACTICE AREAS:*** Residential Real Estate; Zoning; General Business Law. ***Email:*** csymon@rbce.com

ASSOCIATES

DAVID J. RUCCI, born Tupelo, Mississippi, December 9, 1967; admitted to bar, 1997, Connecticut. *Education:* Ohio Wesleyan University (B.A., 1990); Quinnipiac College School of Law (J.D., 1997). *Member:* New Canaan and Connecticut Bar Associations. (Resident, New Canaan Office). ***PRACTICE AREAS:*** Zoning, Planning and Land Use; Residential Real Estate; Commercial Real Estate; Commercial Litigation; Internet Law. ***Email:*** drucci@rbce.com

SANDRA J. AKOURY, born Waterbury, Connecticut, June 16, 1960; admitted to bar, 1998, Connecticut. *Education:* University of Connecticut (B.S., 1982; J.D., 1996). ***PRACTICE AREAS:*** Construction Arbitration; Mechanics Liens; Civil Litigation; Zoning Planning and Land Use; Construction Law; Landlord and Tenant. ***Email:*** sakoury@rbce.com

HAYDEN R. BRAINARD, born Ithaca, New York, August 12, 1973; admitted to bar, 1999, New York; 2000, Connecticut. *Education:* Syracuse University (Economics, 1995); Albany Law School of Union University (J.D., cum laude, 1998). Author: "Survey and Study of Technology Development and Transfer Needs in New York", 9Alb.L.J.Sci. & Tech. 423 (1999). ***LANGUAGES:*** Italian and Spanish. ***PRACTICE AREAS:*** Corporate Law; Internet Law; Business Law; Intellectual Property. ***Email:*** hbrainard@rbce.com

SONIA T. LAROSSA, born Greenwich, Connecticut, September 28, 1974; admitted to bar, 1999, Connecticut; 2000, New York and U.S. District Court, District of Connecticut. *Education:* Bucknell University (B.A., 1996); Villanova University School of Law (J.D., 1999). ***LANGUAGES:*** Italian. ***PRACTICE AREAS:*** Civil Litigation. ***Email:*** slarossa@rbce.com

THERESA ANNE TWIGG, born Springfield, Massachusetts, January 31, 1955; admitted to bar, 1982, Connecticut; 1984, U.S. District Court, District of Connecticut. *Education:* University of Pennsylvania (A.B., 1976; M.A., 1977); University of Connecticut (J.D., 1982). *Member:* Greater Bridgeport and Connecticut Bar Associations. ***PRACTICE AREAS:*** Corporate; Land Use; Employment Law. ***Email:*** ttwigg@rbce.com

CHARLES A. JOHNSON, born Camden, New Jersey, December 15, 1967; admitted to bar, 1994, New Jersey and U.S. District Court, District of New Jersey; 1995, New York; 1996, District of Columbia; 1998, U.S. District Court, Southern and Eastern Districts of New York; 2000, Connecticut and U.S. District Court, District of Connecticut. *Education:* Fairfield University (B.A., cum laude, 1990); Syracuse University (J.D., 1994). Assistant Counsel, U.S. Department of the Navy, Office of the General Counsel, 1995-1998. *Member:* New York State and Connecticut Bar Associations; Connecticut Trial Lawyers Association; U.S. Maritime Law Association. ***PRACTICE AREAS:*** Commercial Litigation; Maritime Admiralty Litigation. ***Email:*** cjohnson@rbce.com

OF COUNSEL

IAN R. CRAWFORD, born Bangkok, Thailand, December 8, 1943; admitted to bar, 1970, New York; 1990, Connecticut. *Education:* Brown University (B.A., 1966); Syracuse University (J.D., 1969); New York University School of Law (LL.M. in Taxation, 1977). Phi Delta Phi. *Member:* New York State Bar Association (Member, Tax Section). (Also practicing individually at New York, N.Y.). ***PRACTICE AREAS:*** Employee Benefits; Deferred Compensation; ERISA; COBRA; Individual Taxation; Corporate Taxation; Estate Planning; Estate Administration. ***Email:*** icrawford@rbce.com

JAMES C. DEMPSEY, born Brooklyn, New York, April 9, 1937; admitted to bar, 1962, New York; 1963, U.S. District Court, Southern and Eastern Districts of New York and U.S. Court of Appeals, Second Circuit; 1971, U.S. Court of Appeals for the Armed Forces; 1972, U.S. Supreme Court; 1987, Connecti-

(This Listing Continued)

RUCCI, BURNHAM, CARTA & EDELBERG, LLP, Darien—Continued

cut; 1988, U.S. District Court, District of Connecticut. *Education:* Fordham University (B.A., 1958; LL.B., 1962). Member, Fordham University Law Review, 1961-1962. *Member:* The Association of the Bar of the City of New York; Stamford Regional and American (Member, Sections on: Business Law; International; Antitrust) Bar Associations; American Corporate Counsel Association (Westchester/Southern Connecticut Chapter). [Lt. Col. Infantry (USAR - Ret.), Continuing Adjunct Faculty Member, U.S. Army Command and General Staff College]. ***PRACTICE AREAS:*** Corporate Law; Securities; Commercial Law; Estate Planning; Estate Administration; Real Estate. ***Email:*** jdempsey@rbce.com

ALBERTO N. MORIS, born Miami, Florida, July 31, 1966; admitted to bar, 1991, Florida; 1995, U.S. District Court, Southern District of Florida (Not admitted in Connecticut). *Education:* University of Miami (B.A., 1987); Emory University (J.D., 1990). ***LANGUAGES:*** Spanish, French and Portuguese. ***PRACTICE AREAS:*** Corporate Law; Commercial Law; Commercial Litigation; Corporate Banking Law; Aviation Law; Corporate Contracts; Internet Law. ***Email:*** amoris@rbce.com

JAMES F. SULLIVAN, born Hartford, Connecticut, June 21, 1950; admitted to bar, 1976, Connecticut; 1977, U.S. District Court, District of Connecticut; 1992, Arizona. *Education:* University of Paris, Paris, France (D.D., 1971); Boston College (A.B., magna cum laude, 1972); St. Louis University (J.D., 1976). Member, St. Louis Law Journal, 1975-1976. *Member:* Stamford Regional, New Canaan, Connecticut (Member, Section on Corporate, Banking and Business Law, Real Property) and American Bar Associations. (Resident, New Canaan Office). ***LANGUAGES:*** French. ***Email:*** jsullivan@rbce.com

REPRESENTATIVE CLIENTS: AmeriCares Foundation, Inc.; Karl Chevrolet Inc.; New England Orthotic and Prosthetic System LLC; Bank of New Canaan; Vanteq Inc.; Pear Tree Point School Inc.; AtNight Media, Inc.; Transonet LLC; Save The Sound, Inc.

PETER M. RYAN

777 POST ROAD
DARIEN, CONNECTICUT 06820
Telephone: 203-655-8921
Fax: 203-656-0019
Email: pryanlex@aol.com

Civil Litigation, Criminal Litigation, Appellate Practice, Administrative Law, Personal Injury.

PETER M. RYAN, born Stamford, Connecticut, June 25, 1937; admitted to bar, 1963, Connecticut; 1965, U.S. District Court, District of Connecticut; 1969, U.S. Supreme Court and U.S. Court of Appeals, Second Circuit; 1975, U.S. District Court, Eastern District of New York. *Education:* La Salette Seminary (A.A., 1957); Seton Hall University (B.S., 1960); University of Pennsylvania (J.D., 1963). Member, Board of Editors, Connecticut Bar Journal, 1972-1974. Special Master, Connecticut Superior Court, 1982—. Trustee, Stamford Bar Association Foundation, 1970-1985. President, 1988-1991 and Chairman of the Board, 1991-1994, Liberation Programs, Inc. *Member:* Stamford (Treasurer, 1965-1968; Vice President, 1968-1972; President, 1972-1973), Connecticut and American Bar Associations; The Association of Trial Lawyers of America; Federal Bar Council. ***REPORTED CASES:*** Fruin v. Colonnade One at Old Greenwich Ltd., 237 Conn. 123, 676 A.2d 369 (1996); Thomason v. Chemical Bank, 234 Conn. 281, 661 A.2d 595 (1995); Hawkins v. Hawkins, 11 Conn. App. 195, 526 A.2d 872; McHale v. W.B.S. Corporation, 187 Conn. 444, 446 A.2d 815 (1982); Abel v. Zoning Boards of Appeals, 172 Conn. 286, 374 A.2d 227 (1977); Nowell v. Nowell, 272 F.Supp. 298 (Conn. 1967); Standard Structural Steel Co. v. Debron Corp., 515 F.Supp. 803, aff'd 657 F.2d 265 (2d Cir., 1981). ***PRACTICE AREAS:*** Civil Litigation; Probate Litigation; Criminal Litigation; Appellate Practice; Administrative Law; Personal Injury.

SCHOONMAKER, GEORGE & COLIN, P.C.

DARIEN, CONNECTICUT

(See Greenwich)

Matrimonial and Family Law.

CAROLYN C. SWIGGART

777 POST ROAD
P.O. BOX 941
DARIEN, CONNECTICUT 06820
Telephone: 203-655-8921
Fax: 203-656-0019
Email: cswiggart@aol.com
URL: http://www.lawyers.com/swiggartfamilylaw

Family Law, Divorce, Child Custody, Domestic Relations.

(This Listing Continued)

CAROLYN C. SWIGGART, born September 19, 1958; admitted to bar, 1983, Massachusetts; 1985, Connecticut. *Education:* Lycée International de St. Germain-en-Laye, France (Baccalauréat International de Genève, bilingue, 1977); Wellesley College (A.B., Wellesley Scholar, 1980); University of Connecticut (J.D., 1983). Member, Moot Court Board, 1981-1983. Member Executive Committee Connecticut Bar Association Young Lawyers Section, 1992-1994. Co-Chairman, 1991-1994 and Member, Board of Editors, 1986-1991, Connecticut Bar Association Basic Practice Manual. Member, Darien Representative Town Meeting, 1990-1994. Member, Executive Committee Connecticut Bar Association Family Law Section, 2001—. *Member:* Stamford Regional (Member, Sections on: Family Law; Probate), Connecticut (Member, Family Law Section) and American Bar Associations. ***LANGUAGES:*** French. ***PRACTICE AREAS:*** Family Law; General Practice.

OF COUNSEL

PIERSON LAW FIRM, Darien, Connecticut.

TIBBETTS KEATING & BUTLER, LLC

43 CORBIN DRIVE
P.O. BOX 5
DARIEN, CONNECTICUT 06820
Telephone: 203-656-1066
Fax: 203-656-2573
http://www.tkblaw.com
URL: http://www.lawyers.com/tibbettskeating&butler

New York City Office: 1155 Avenue of the Americas, 28th Floor, 10036. Telephone: 212-398-9509. Fax: 212-398-9788.

General Practice. Residential Real Estate, Civil Litigation, State and Federal, Bankruptcy Chapter 7, Bankruptcy Litigation, Civil Appeals, Estate Planning, Estate Administration, Family Trusts, Living Trusts, Personal Injury, Commercial Real Estate, Corporate Law, Computer Law, Criminal Law.

ALFRED P. TIBBETTS, born Darien, Connecticut, June, 16, 1956; admitted to bar, 1984, Connecticut. *Education:* Principia College (B.A., 1978); Washington and Lee University (J.D., 1984). Phi Delta Phi. Member, Zoning Board of Appeals, 2000—. President, Darien Chamber of Commerce, 2000—. ***PRACTICE AREAS:*** Real Estate; Trusts and Estates.

MARY P. KEATING, born White Plains, New York, January 1, 1958; admitted to bar, 1986, New York; 1989, Connecticut. *Education:* Manhattanville College (B.A., cum laude, 1979); Yale Law School (J.D., 1985). ***PRACTICE AREAS:*** Computer Law; Contract Law; Real Estate Law; Estate Planning; Corporate Law.

TIMOTHY F. BUTLER, born Port Chester, New York, August 6, 1965; admitted to bar, 1992, Connecticut, New York, U.S. District Court, Eastern and Southern Districts of New York; 1995, U.S. District Court, District of Connecticut; 1997, U.S. Court of Appeals, Eighth Circuit; 2000, U.S. Court of Appeals Second Circuit. *Education:* New York University (B.A., 1987); Fordham University (J.D., 1991). Member: Butler, Fitzgerald & Potter, 1991-1994. *Member:* New York State, Connecticut (Secretary, General Practice Section, 1998-1999) and American Bar Associations; Association of Trial Lawyers of America; National College of Advocacy (Advocate, 2001). ***PRACTICE AREAS:*** Litigation; Corporate; Criminal. ***Email:*** timbutler@aol.com

ASSOCIATES

JOHN R. HALL, II, born Rockville Centre, New York, March 20, 1961; admitted to bar, 1989, Connecticut; 1994, New York and U.S. District Court, Southern District of New York. *Education:* University of Connecticut (B.A., 1984; J.D., cum laude, 1989). Co-Author: "Recent Developments in Excess, Surplus Lines and Reinsurance," 30 Tort and Ins. L.J. 360 (1995). *Member:* Stamford/Norwalk, Connecticut and American Bar Associations. ***PRACTICE AREAS:*** Litigation; Real Estate; Corporate.

JOANNA F. BOWEN, born Dallas, Texas, May 19, 1954; admitted to bar, 1995, Connecticut; 1996, New York. *Education:* University of Oklahoma (B.S., 1975); Pace University (J.D., 1995). Member, Pace Environmental Law Review. Recipient, Environmental Law Certificate, Pace University, 1995. Author: Note, "Atlantic States Legal Foundation, Inc. v. Eastman Kodak Co.: The Second Circuit Affirms the NPDES Permit as a Shield and Tries to Sink the Clean Water Act," 12.1 Pace Environmental Law Review, 1994; "The Connecticut Uniform Prudent Investor Act," The Connecticut Lawyer, Volume 8.3, p. 10, 1997. *Member:* Stanford-Norwalk Regional, Connecticut and New York State Bar Associations; the Regional Bar. ***PRACTICE AREAS:*** Trusts and Estates; General; Real Estate.

OF COUNSEL

CHRISTOPHER P. McCLANCY, born New York, N.Y., July 29, 1961; admitted to bar, 1987, Connecticut, New York, U.S. District Court, District of

(This Listing Continued)

Connecticut and U.S. District Court, Southern and Eastern Districts of New York; 1988, District of Columbia; 1990, U.S. Court of Appeals for the Federal Circuit and U.S. Court of International Trade. *Education:* Villanova University (B.A., 1983); New York Law School (J.D., cum laude, 1987); The Hague Academy of International Law, The Hague, The Netherlands (1992); Georgetown University Law Center (LL.M., International & Comparative Law, 1995). Co-Author: "Liability and Control, in representing Foreign-Owned Business in Connecticut," Connecticut Bar Association Continuing Legal Education, 1993. Member, 1991-1995 and Chairman, 1993-1995, Town of Darien Board of Tax Review. Member, Selden Society. *Member:* Association of the Bar of the City of New York (Member, Library Committee, 1990-1993; Member, Foreign & Comparative Law Committee, 1996—); Connecticut (Co-Chairman, 1990-1991 and Chairman, 1991-1992, International Law & World Peace Section), New York State and American (Member, Sections on: International Law & Practice; Litigation) Bar Associations; American Society of International Law. ***PRACTICE AREAS:*** General Practice; Probate; Trusts and Estates; Civil Litigation; Business Formation; Corporate Formation; Legal Ethics and Professional Responsibility; Property Tax Appeals; Commercial Law.

A list of Representative Clients will be furnished upon request.
REFERENCES: Bank of Darien; People's Bank.

WAKE, SEE, DIMES & BRYNICZKA

DARIEN, CONNECTICUT

(See Westport)

Business and Corporate Law, Real Estate, Trusts and Probate, Estate Planning, Municipal, Zoning and Land Use Law, Litigation in all Federal and State Courts. Federal, State and Foreign Taxation, Pension and Profit Sharing, and Family Law.

WOMER LAW FIRM, LLC

777 POST ROAD
DARIEN, CONNECTICUT 06820
Telephone: 203-656-0753
Fax: 203-656-0019
Email: martinwomer@cs.com
URL: http://www.nnepa.com/WomerLaw

Trusts and Estates, Wills, Non Profit and Charitable Organizations, Conservation Easements, Zoning, Planning and Land Use, Real Estate.

MARTIN C. WOMER, born Indianapolis, Indiana, April 5, 1953; admitted to bar, 1997, Massachusetts; 1998, Maine and New Hampshire; 1999, Connecticut. *Education:* Colby College (A.B., cum laude and distinction in Chemistry, 1975); University of Maine School of Law (J.D., 1997). Articles Editor, Ocean and Coastal Law Journal. Author: "The Ability of Estate Fiduciaries Under State Law to Utilize Congress's 1997-1998 Tax Incentives for Post-Mortem Conversation Easements," presented at Land Conservation Summit 2000, St. Paul, MN, July 29, 2000; "Ballard Shipping Co. v. Beach Shellfish: The End of the Era When Robins Dry Dock Foreclosed State Jurisdiction Over the Recovery of Economic Damages from Oil Spills," 2 Ocean and Coastal Law Journal 435 (1997). Senior Planner, Maine Department of Conservation, Land Use Regulation Commission, 1997-1999. Member, 1980-1987 and Chairman, 1981-1986, Rockport Maine Planning Board. Administrative Director, Coastal Mountains Land Trust, Rockport, Maine, 1991-1994. *Member:* Connecticut (Member, Sections On: Estates & Probate; Planning & Zoning), and American Bar Associations (Member, Real Property, Probate and Trust Section); Regional Bar Association of Stamford, Norwalk, Darien & Wilton; National Network of Estate Planning Attorneys. ***PRACTICE AREAS:*** Trusts and Estates; Probate; Nonprofit and Charitable Organizations; Conservation Easements; Zoning, Planning and Land Use; Real Estate. ***Email:*** martinwomer@cs.com

COHEN & THOMAS

Established in 1936
315 MAIN STREET
P.O. BOX 313
DERBY, CONNECTICUT 06418
Telephone: 203-735-9521
Fax: 203-732-8129
Email: cohen.and.thomas@att.net
URL: http://www.lawyers.com/cohen-and-thomas-attys

Lichtfield, Connecticut Office: 15 Meadow Street, 06759. Telephone: 860-567-3754. Fax: 860-567-3894.

General Civil and Criminal Practice. Trials in all Courts. Personal Injury, Negligence and Medical Malpractice Litigation, Real Estate Purchase, Sale, Financing, Zoning and Development, Domestic Law and Divorce, Probate, Wills and Trusts, Banking, Foreclosure and Workouts, Commercial Litigation and Collections, Municipal, Elder Law, Worker's Compensation.

(This Listing Continued)

FIRM PROFILE: Since 1936, when David B. Cohen began a law practice in Derby, he and his successors have maintained a continuing legal presence in the community. Now known as Cohen & Thomas, the firm offers a wide range of legal services throughout the state of Connecticut, including trials and appeals in all State and Federal Courts.

MEMBERS OF FIRM

DAVID B. COHEN (1913-1991).

JAMES E. COHEN, born New Haven, Connecticut, December 29, 1946; admitted to bar, 1971, Connecticut and U.S. District Court, District of Connecticut; 1975, U.S. Supreme Court. *Education:* University of Pennsylvania (B.A., 1968); University of Connecticut (J.D., 1971). Corporation Counsel, City of Derby, 1973-1980; 1992-1994. Trial Referee, Connecticut Superior Court, 1996—. ***PRACTICE AREAS:*** Real Estate and Mortgage Financing; Probate; Wills and Trusts; Zoning, Planning and Land Use; Municipal Law; Foreclosures. ***Email:*** jecohen@att.net

DOMINICK J. THOMAS, JR., born Derby, Connecticut, September 29, 1946; admitted to bar, 1971, Connecticut and U.S. District Court, District of Connecticut; 1972, U.S. Court of Military Appeals; U.S. Court of Federal Claims. *Education:* College of the Holy Cross (B.A., 1968); University of Virginia (J.D., 1971). Phi Delta Phi. Assistant Professor Department of Law, U.S. Military Academy, 1975-1977. Town Counsel, Oxford, 1985-1986 and 1995-1997. *Member:* Connecticut Trial Lawyers Association; The Association of Trial Lawyers of America. [JAGC, U.S. Army, 1972-1977]. ***PRACTICE AREAS:*** Personal Injury; Medical Malpractice; Criminal Law; Domestic; Appellate Practice; Zoning Law. ***Email:*** djthomas@att.net

ASSOCIATES

IAN A. COLE, born Gainesville, Florida, May 2, 1954; admitted to bar, 1980, Connecticut; 1981, U.S. District Court, District of Connecticut. *Education:* University of Connecticut; University of California at Berkeley (B.A., 1974); Western New England School of Law (J.D., 1980). ***PRACTICE AREAS:*** Commercial Litigation; Bankruptcy; Civil Rights; Appellate Law; Workers Compensation; Elder Law. ***Email:*** iancole@att.net

CHRISTINE L. CURTISS, born New Haven, Connecticut, July 3, 1964; admitted to bar, 1989, Connecticut; 1991, U.S. District Court, District of Connecticut. *Education:* University of New Haven (B.A., magna cum laude, 1986); University of Connecticut School of Law (J.D., with honors, 1989). ***PRACTICE AREAS:*** Civil Rights; Consumer Collections; Commercial Collections; Civil Litigation; Elder Law. ***Email:*** clcurtis@att.net

GAYLE C. CARR, born Buffalo, New York, December 21, 1961; admitted to bar, 1990, Connecticut; 1992, U.S. District Court, District of Connecticut. *Education:* Boston University (B.A., cum laude, 1983); Villanova University (J.D., 1990). (Resident, Litchfield Office). ***PRACTICE AREAS:*** Family Law; Civil Litigation; Personal Injury; Negligence; Medical Malpractice. ***Email:*** gaylecarr@att.net

GREGORY M. THOMAS, born Fort Hood, Texas, October 12, 1972; admitted to bar, 1999, Connecticut. *Education:* Fairfield University (B.A., 1995); Villanova University (J.D., 1998). *Member:* Connecticut Bar Association. ***PRACTICE AREAS:*** Criminal Law; Commercial Collections; Personal Injury; Juvenile Law; Civil Rights. ***Email:*** gmthomas@att.net

REPRESENTATIVE CLIENTS: Birmingham Utilities, Inc.; Bridgeport Hydraulic Co.; F & R Realty; Housatonic Lumber Co.; Wal-Mart Stores, Inc.; Birmingham Group, Inc.; Heyman Properties; United Methodist Homes of Connecticut, Inc.; Town of Oxford; Spectrum Healthcare, LLC; John J. Brennan Construction Co., Inc.

RALPH J. ALEXANDER

330 ROBERTS STREET, SUITE 400
EAST HARTFORD, CONNECTICUT 06108-3694
Telephone: 860-289-5477
Fax: 860-291-9282
Email: bwa@snet.net

General Trial Practice in all Courts, Real Estate, Trusts, Probate, Estate Planning, Business Law, Workers Compensation, Social Security Disability Claims, Municipal, Personal Injury, Family Law, Labor Relations Public Sector, Public Housing, Public Housing Law.

RALPH J. ALEXANDER, born 1946; admitted to bar, 1973, Connecticut; 1974, U.S. District Court, District of Connecticut; 1993, U.S. Supreme Court. *Education:* University of Vermont (B.A., 1970); New England School of Law (J.D., 1973). *Member:* Connecticut and American Bar Associations; Association of Trial Lawyers of America. ***PRACTICE AREAS:*** Administrative Law; Business Law; Commercial Law; Domestic Relations; Estates and Probate; Housing Law (with emphasis on public housing); Litigation; Personal Injury; Real Estate Law.

GILMAN & MARKS

TWO RIVERVIEW SQUARE
99 EAST RIVERVIEW DRIVE
EAST HARTFORD, CONNECTICUT 06108
Telephone: 860-282-0301
Fax: 860-289-3198
Email: gmatty@msn.com

General Practice. Real Estate, Tax and Probate Law, Trials, Corporation, Estate Planning, Zoning and Land Use, Employment Law, Criminal, Banking, Mortgage, Litigation, Mortgage Foreclosures, DUI, Civil Rights, Discrimination, Wrongful Termination, Sexual Harassment, Family and Medical Leave Act, Americans with Disabilities.

FIRM PROFILE: The roots of Gilman & Marks go back to the firm of Hyde & Joslyn in 1875. George H. Gilman. Sr.'s name was added to the firm name in 1893, and Henry Marks and Albert J. Marks, Sr. became part of the firm in 1919. The firm has operated under the name of Gilman & Marks since 1921.

Throughout the years, Gilman & Marks has had a reputation for expertise in all phases of real estate law and particularly, for representation of lending institutions and real estate related activities.

MEMBERS OF FIRM

ROBERT S. CAREY, JR., born Westcliff-On-Sea, Essex, England, June 12, 1949; admitted to bar, 1976, Connecticut. *Education:* University of Connecticut (B.A., 1971; J.D., 1976). Director, Connecticut Attorneys Title Insurance Company, 1987—. *Member:* Hartford County (Vice Chair, Real Property Committee, 1995-1999; Chairman, 1999—), Connecticut and American Bar Associations. ***PRACTICE AREAS:*** Commercial Real Estate; Residential Real Estate; Title Matters; Mortgages.

THOMAS C. AUSTIN, JR., born Hartford, Connecticut, December 11, 1953; admitted to bar, 1980, Connecticut. *Education:* St. Michael's College (B.A., 1975); Quinnipiac College School of Law (J.D., 1980). *Member:* Hartford County, Connecticut and American Bar Associations; Connecticut Trial Lawyers Association; The Association of Trial Lawyers of America; National Association of Criminal Defense Lawyers. ***PRACTICE AREAS:*** Foreclosures Law; Litigation; Commercial Law; Criminal Law; Driving While Intoxicated.

ROBERT W. HEAGNEY, born Stockton, California, May 5, 1953; admitted to bar, 1980, Connecticut. *Education:* Saint Anselm College (B.A., 1975); Quinnipiac College School of Law (J.D., 1980); University of San Diego. State Representative, 1999—. *Member:* Hartford County, Hartford County Federal, Connecticut and American Bar Associations. ***PRACTICE AREAS:*** Employment Law; Estates; Zoning, Planning and Land Use; Civil Litigation; Driving While Intoxicated; Civil Rights; Discrimination; Wrongful Termination; Sexual Harassment; Family and Medical Leave Act; Americans with Disabilities Act.

J. MARK SILHAVY, born Manchester, Connecticut, October 11, 1955; admitted to bar, 1981, Connecticut. *Education:* Hobart College (B.A., 1977); Quinnipiac College School of Law (J.D., 1980); Boston University (LL.M., 1981). Member, University of Bridgeport Law Review, 1979-1980. *Member:* Connecticut and American Bar Associations. ***PRACTICE AREAS:*** Commercial Real Estate; Residential Real Estate; Probate; Estate Planning; Corporate Law.

REPRESENTATIVE CLIENTS: American Savings Bank; Century Federal Savings Bank; Commercial Federal Mortgage Corp.; Fleet Bank; Mechanics Savings Bank; Norwest Mortgage; Peoples Bank; United Carolina Bank; Webster Bank; Mortgage Guaranty Insurance Corporation; Columbia National Inc.
REFERENCES: Fleet Bank, NA.

LEONE, THROWE, TELLER & NAGLE

33 CONNECTICUT BOULEVARD
EAST HARTFORD, CONNECTICUT 06108
Telephone: 860-528-2145
Fax: 860-282-1539
Email: lttn@snet.net
URL: http://www.lawyers.com/lttnlaw

General Trial Practice in all Courts. Real Estate, Trusts, Probate, Estate Planning, Workers Compensation, Municipal, Personal Injury, Family Law and Criminal Law, Divorce, Child Custody, Child Support, Juvenile Law, Business Law, Landlord/Tenant, Drunk Driving Defense.

FIRM PROFILE: LEONE, THROWE, TELLER & NAGLE has served the needs of individuals and businesses in the East Hartford area since its founding by Alvin C. Leone, who for over fifty years prided himself on providing his clients with quality legal services in a timely and cost effective manner. Leone, Throwe, Teller & Nagle has continued a general practice law firm which offers a broad range of legal expertise from personal injury litigation and general litigation to real estate closings and wills. Leone, Throwe, Teller & Nagle maintains an active trial practice with experienced attorneys. At Leone, Throwe, Teller & Nagle, our commitment is to provide our clients quality cost-effective legal service.

ALVIN C. LEONE (1910-1986).

JOHN F. NAGLE (1925-1997).

MEMBERS OF FIRM

WILLIAM A. LEONE, born Hartford, Connecticut, July 19, 1943; admitted to bar, 1969, Connecticut. *Education:* Wesleyan University (B.A., 1966); University of Connecticut (J.D., 1969). Legal Counsel and Director, East Hartford Chamber of Commerce, 1976-1983. State Attorney Trial Referee, 1987—. Special Master, U.S. District Court. Hearing Officer, Town of East Hartford, 1990-1992. *Member:* Hartford County, Connecticut and American Bar Associations; Connecticut Defense Lawyers Association; Connecticut Trial Lawyers Association. ***PRACTICE AREAS:*** Civil and Criminal Litigation; Real Estate; Estate Planning and Probate; Personal Injury; Business Law. ***Email:*** w.leone@snet.net

FRANK A. LEONE, born Hartford, Connecticut, September 29, 1949; admitted to bar, 1975, Connecticut. *Education:* Wesleyan University (B.A., 1971); Suffolk University (J.D., cum laude, 1975). Member, Moot Court Advisory Board and Chairman, First Year Moot Court Program, 1974-1975. *Member:* Hartford County, Connecticut and American Bar Associations; The Association of Trial Lawyers of America; Connecticut Trial Lawyers Association; Connecticut Defense Lawyers Association. ***PRACTICE AREAS:*** Civil and Criminal Litigation; Real Estate; Probate; Estate Planning; Business Law; Personal Injury; Landlord and Tenant Law.

ADAM J. TELLER, born Manchester, Connecticut, January 12, 1963; admitted to bar, 1987, Massachusetts; 1988, U.S. District Court, District of Massachusetts, Connecticut and U.S. District Court, District of Connecticut; 1997, U.S. Court of Appeals, Second Circuit. *Education:* Harvard University (A.B., summa cum laude, 1984); Harvard University (J.D., cum laude, 1987). Presidential Scholar. Tau Beta Pi Prize, 1984. Oliver Ellsworth Inns. of Court, Member, 1991-1993; Treasurer, 1992-1993. Law Clerk, Hon. Peter C. Dorsey, U.S. District Judge, District of Conn., 1987-1989. Dep. Asst. Public Defender, Superior Court, Enfield, CT, 1989-1992. Special Master, U.S. District Court, 1998—. Hearing Officer, Board of Education, Manchester, Connecticut, 1998-1999. Alternate, Town of Bolton Planning & Zoning Commission, 2001—. *Member:* Hartford County, Connecticut and American Bar Associations. ***REPORTED CASES:*** State vs. Diaz, 226 Conn. 514 (1993). ***PRACTICE AREAS:*** Civil and Criminal Litigation; Personal Injury; Drunk Driving Defense; Family Law; Divorce; Child Custody; Child Support; Probate; Civil Rights; Employment Discrimination; Workers' Compensations. ***Email:*** ateller@snet.net

DOUGLAS T. BARALL, born El Paso, Texas, July 9, 1957; admitted to bar, 1988, Connecticut; 1990, U.S. District Court, District of Connecticut. *Education:* University of Hartford (B.A., 1984); Western New England College School of Law (J.D., 1988). Special Master, Superior Court Domestic Relations Cases, 1991—. *Member:* Hartford and Connecticut Bar Associations. ***REPORTED CASES:*** Virginia Riggio vs. Orkin Exterminating Co., 59 Conn. App. 309 (2000). ***PRACTICE AREAS:*** Family Law; Personal Injury; Civil Litigation; Criminal Law; Divorce; Child Custody; Child Support; Juvenile Law.

VALERIE LEONE, born Hartford, Connecticut, July 11, 1975; admitted to bar, 2000, Connecticut and U.S. District Court of Connecticut. *Education:* Lafayette College (B.A., 1997); Suffolk University (J.D., cum laude, 2000). *Member:* Hartford County, Connecticut and American Bar Associations. ***PRACTICE AREAS:*** Civil Litigation; Criminal Litigation; Personal Injury; Real Estate; Estate Planning; Probate; Elder Law; Business Law; Landlord and Tenant Law.

OF COUNSEL

JAMES H. THROWE, born Norwich, Connecticut, May 22, 1930; admitted to bar, 1957, Connecticut. *Education:* University of Connecticut (B.A., 1954; LL.B., 1957). Author: "Joint Tenancy in Connecticut," 31 Connecticut Bar Journal 70, 1957. Law Clerk, U.S. District Court Judge, J. Joseph Smith, 1957-1958. Member: Zoning and Planning Commission, 1960-1962; Town Council, 1963-1965, South Windsor. Mayor, South Windsor, 1965-1967. State Judge Advocate, Connecticut Military Department, 1967-1978. Chairman, South Windsor Sewer Commission, 1971-1978. State Attorney Trial Referee, 1987—. Special Master, Superior Court Domestic Relations Cases, 1986—. *Member:* Hartford County (Chairman, Bench-Bar Committee, 1972-1973), Connecticut (Chairman, Veteran's and Military Affairs Committee, 1989-1990) and American Bar Associations. [Brigadier General, AUS RET]. ***PRACTICE AREAS:*** Civil and Criminal Litigation; Family Law; Divorce; Child Custody.

REPRESENTATIVE CLIENTS: Holland Machine Co.; Unas Grinding Corporation; Munson's Candy Kitchen, Inc., dba Munson's Chocolates; BDK Machine Co., Inc.; Liberty Oil Equipment Co., Inc.; U.S. Trust Company of Connecticut.

(This Listing Continued)

REFERENCES: U.S. Trust Company of Connecticut; Savings Bank of Manchester.

LAW OFFICES
HOWARD LEE SCHIFF, P.C.

510 TOLLAND STREET
P.O. BOX 280245
EAST HARTFORD, CONNECTICUT 06128-0245
Telephone: 860-528-9991, Toll Free: 800-ATTY-HLS
Fax: 860-528-7602
Email: newclaim@hlschiffpc.com
URL: http://www.hlschiffpc.com

Worcester, Massachusetts Office: 340 Main Street, Suite 959. Telephone: 508-753-9991. Fax: 508-753-0260.

Providence, Rhode Island Office: 10 Dorrance Street, Suite 515. Telephone: 401-861-9991. Fax: 401-861-0246.

Augusta, Maine Office: 150 State Street, 04330. Telephone: 207-621-9991. Fax: 207-621-1819.

Concord, New Hampshire Office: 36 Warren Street, Suite 1, P.O. Box 2372, 03302. Telephone: 603-228-4444. Fax: 603-228-6644.

Rutland, Vermont Office: 1 Scale Avenue, Suite 112, 05071. Telephone: 802-775-3988. Fax: 802-773-9990.

Collection Law (Retail and Commercial), Commercial Law, Creditor's Rights, Creditor Bankruptcy, Enforcement of Judgement, Foreclosures, Subrogation in the entire New England region.

FIRM PROFILE: The firm was founded in East Hartford, Connecticut in 1958 by Attorney Howard Lee Schiff and became a professional corporation in 1977. A full-service firm, its practice is primarily devoted to retail and commercial collection law and creditor's rights. The firm practices statewide in Connecticut, Massachusetts, Rhode Island, Maine, Vermont and New Hampshire.

There are twelve attorneys in the firm with 73 personnel in support, including paralegals, collectors and an investigation department. The office is fully computerized, maintains a predictive dialing system and provides for automated account processing and status reporting. National claim referral is available via creditor networks including DozierNet, NARCANET, the National Attorney Network, Recovery1, American Alliance of Creditor Attorneys, Rosenfeld Net and other client-specific protocols.

While the client base includes corporate leaders in banking, insurance, health care, utilities, retail chains, student loan agencies and credit unions, the firm continues to represent many small businesses and individual clients. The office takes pride in its function within the credit community and has endeavored to blend the law with modern technology and traditional professional concerns.

ROY B. BRADRICK, born Putnam, Connecticut, January 4, 1953; admitted to bar, 1984, Connecticut; 1987, U.S. District Court, District of Connecticut. *Education:* University of Connecticut (B.A., 1975); Western New England College (J.D., 1984). Selectman, Union, Connecticut, 1992—. *Member:* Connecticut and American Bar Associations. ***PRACTICE AREAS:*** Collection Law; Commercial Law; Subrogation. ***Email:*** rbradrick@hlschiffpc.com

ROBERT E. JOHNSON, JR., born Bridgeport, Connecticut, February 23, 1959; admitted to bar, 1984, Connecticut; 1985, U.S. District Court, District of Connecticut; 1996, Rhode Island. *Education:* University of Rhode Island (B.A., 1981); University of Bridgeport (J.D., 1984). *Member:* Connecticut (Member, Juvenile Justice Section) and Rhode Island Bar Associations. (Also Member of Providence, Rhode Island Office). ***PRACTICE AREAS:*** Collection Law; Foreclosure; Negligence; Real Estate. ***Email:*** rjohnson@hlschiffpc.com

CHRISTOPHER T. MOYLAN, born Hartford, Connecticut, September 17, 1959; admitted to bar, 1990, Connecticut; 1992, U.S. District Court, District of Connecticut. *Education:* Bates College (B.A., 1981); Western New England College (J.D., 1989). ***PRACTICE AREAS:*** Bankruptcy; Collection Law; Commercial Law; Creditors' Rights; Negligence; Subrogation. ***Email:*** cmoylan@hlschiffpc.com

ADAM J. OLSHAN, born Brooklyn, New York, July 13, 1966; admitted to bar, 1991, Connecticut; 1992, U.S. District Court, District of Connecticut; 1993, New York. *Education:* Yale University (B.A., 1988); Boston College (J.D., 1991). Co-Author, "Successful Judgement Collections in Connecticut." *Member:* National Association of Retail Attorneys (Board Member); Connecticut Creditor's Rights Attorneys Association (Director and Vice President). ***PRACTICE AREAS:*** Collection Law; Commercial Law; Creditors Rights; Health Care Collections; Workers Compensation Law. ***Email:*** aolshan@hlschiffpc.com

---

STEPHEN A. WIENER, born Hartford, Connecticut, April 1, 1947; admitted to bar, 1979, Connecticut; 1981, U.S. District Court, District of Connecticut. *Education:* Brown University (A.B., cum laude, 1969); Bryant College (M.B.A., with honors, 1975); University of Connecticut (J.D., 1979). Delta Mu Delta. *Member:* Connecticut Bar Association; Commercial Law League of America. ***PRACTICE AREAS:*** Bankruptcy; Collection Law; Commercial Law; Creditor's Rights; Mortgage Law. ***Email:*** swiener@hlschiffpc.com

(This Listing Continued)

DAVID F. ERTMAN, born Hartford, Connecticut, December 22, 1942; admitted to bar, 1974, Connecticut and U.S. District Court, District of Connecticut. *Education:* Lycoming College; University of Hartford (B.A., 1969); University of Connecticut (J.D., 1973). Member, Committee on Legal Internship, 1972-1973. Commissioner, Small Claims Hearing Officer, Superior Court at Meriden, Milford, New Haven and West Haven, 1977—. Magistrate, Superior Court, New Haven, 1983—. Arbitrator/Fact Finder, Superior Court, 1983—. State Trial Referee, 1984—. *Member:* Connecticut Bar Association (Member, Committee on Delivery of Legal Services, 1980-1982; Secretary: Section on Human Rights and Responsibilities, 1979-1981; Committee on Juvenile Justice, 1980—). ***PRACTICE AREAS:*** Alternative Dispute Resolution; Civil Litigation; Children's Rights Law; Health Law.

DOUGLAS F. JENNINGS, born New York, New York, March 19, 1952; admitted to bar, 1982, Connecticut and U.S. District Court, District of Connecticut; 1987, Maine. *Education:* Nasson College (B.A., 1977); University of Bridgeport (J.D., 1980). *Member:* Kennebec County, Connecticut and Maine State (Member: Peer Review Committee, 1989—; Lawyer Referral Service Committee, 1989—) Bar Associations; Maine Forest Products Association, 1987—. (Resident Augusta, Maine Office). ***PRACTICE AREAS:*** Litigation; Construction Law; Securities; Collections.

HARRY JOSEPH THEODOSS, born Southbridge, Massachusetts, January 3, 1970; admitted to bar, 1996, Massachusetts; 1997, Connecticut, U.S. District Court, District of Connecticut and U.S. District Court, District of Massachusetts. *Education:* University of Massachusetts (B.A., 1992); Western New England College (J.D., 1995). *Member:* Massachusetts, Connecticut and American Bar Associations.

JOSEPH P. LATINO, born Meadville, Pennsylvania, April 15, 1952; admitted to bar, 1987, Pennsylvania; 1988, Connecticut and U.S. District Court, District of Connecticut. *Education:* University of Massachusetts (B.A., 1975); Quinnipiac College School of Law (J.D., 1987). ***PRACTICE AREAS:*** Collections (80%); Landlord and Tenant Law (15%); Probate (5%). ***Email:*** jlatino@hlschiffpc.com

CARL BRUGNOLI, born Brockton, Massachusetts, January 30, 1974; admitted to bar, 1999, Massachusetts (Not admitted in Connecticut). *Education:* Boston College, Chestnut Hill (B.A., 1996); University of Connecticut Law School (J.D., 1999). (Resident, Worcester, Massachusetts Office). ***PRACTICE AREAS:*** Collections (100%). ***Email:*** cbrugnoli@hlschiffpc.com

JESSICA ELLICOTT, born New Haven, Connecticut, May 15, 1961; admitted to bar, 1995, New York; 1996, Vermont. *Education:* University of California at Santa Barbara (B.A., 1983); Vermont Law School (J.D., 1994). *Member:* Onondaga County and New York State Bar Associations; Vermont Bar Association. (Resident, Rutland, Vermont Office). ***LANGUAGES:*** Dutch. ***PRACTICE AREAS:*** Civil Practice.

KERRY DUNCAN BARNSLEY, admitted to bar, 1987, New Hampshire (Not admitted in Connecticut). ***Email:*** kerrybarnsley@aol.com

OF COUNSEL

HOWARD LEE SCHIFF, born New York, New York, March 20, 1933; admitted to bar, 1958, Connecticut; 1959, U.S. District Court, District of Connecticut. *Education:* Wesleyan University (B.A., 1954); Cornell University (J.D., 1957). Author: "Should A Commercial Attorney Accept Retail Collections— A Critical Analysis," Commercial Law Journal, February 1973. *Member:* Connecticut and American Bar Associations; Commercial Law League of America. ***PRACTICE AREAS:*** Collection Law; Commercial Law; Creditors' Rights; Negligence; Subrogation.

LEGAL SUPPORT PERSONNEL

ELIZABETH G. STEVENSON, born New Britain, Connecticut, 1963. *Education:* Trinity College, Hartford, Connecticut (B.A., 1986). Administrative Manager, Master Collectors, Inc., 1985-1990. (Firm Administrator). ***PRACTICE AREAS:*** Coordinates and Acts as Liaison; Implements and Resolves Client Needs and Concerns. ***Email:*** estevenson@hlschiffpc.com

REPRESENTATIVE CLIENTS: General Electric Capital Corp.; Household Financial Services; Associates National Bank; Discover Card; Capital One; Sears Roebuck & Co.; May Department Stores Co., Inc.; Navy Federal Credit Union; Connecticut Student Loan Foundation; New York Higher Education Assistance Authority; University of Connecticut Health Center-John Dempsey Hospital; Lawrence and Memorial Hospital; Aetna Life & Casualty; United Illuminating; Century Healthcare Collections; Commercial Corporation of America; Connecticut Light & Power; Fleet/Norstar Financial Corp.; Providian National Bankcorp; MBNA.
REFERENCE: Sovereign Bank.

MICHAEL J. WHELTON

111 FOUNDERS PLAZA
SEVENTEENTH FLOOR
EAST HARTFORD, CONNECTICUT 06108
Telephone: 860-289-9358
Fax: 860-289-6210
Email: attorneymwelton@snet.net

General Practice. Trials in all State and Federal Courts. Personal Injury, Criminal, Municipal, Zoning, Family, Divorce, Probate, Wills, and Real Estate Law.

MICHAEL J. WHELTON, born Hartford, Connecticut, December 29, 1947; admitted to bar, 1975, Connecticut; 1977, U.S. District Court, District of Connecticut; 1978, U.S. Court of Appeals, Second Circuit. *Education:* Babson College (B.S., cum laude, 1971); George Washington University School of Law (1972); Suffolk University (J.D., 1974). Special Assistant Corporation Counsel, Town of East Hartford, 1975-1979. Member: Committee on Magistrates, State of Connecticut, 1985—; Bar Examining Committee, State of Connecticut, 1984—; Public Defender Services Commission, 1989-1995; Assistant Counsel, The Metropolitan District, 1977-1988. *Member:* Hartford County and Connecticut Bar Associations; Connecticut Trial Lawyers Association.

REPRESENTATIVE CLIENTS: Charles H. Kaman; Fleagane Enterprises (Wendy's Restaurant); Connecticut National Bank; Hartford National Bank; People's Bank; Women's World, Inc.; D.H.R. Construction Co., Inc.; Hamilton Standard Testing Systems, Inc.; East Hartford Foundation Co., Inc.; East Hartford Visiting Nurses Assn., Inc.; Pizza Time Theatre, Inc.; Podunk Farm, Inc.; D&M Motors, Inc.; Handel Dairy Farms, Inc.; Flintkote, Inc.; Howard Johnsons, Inc.; Stop & Shop, Inc.; Mobil Oil; Sage-Allen, Inc.; Arrow Bus Line; Mitchell Trucking Co.; Riverside Convalescent Home, Inc.

THE LAW OFFICES OF BRIAN J. WOOLF, LLC

Established in 1998
50 FOUNDERS PLAZA
EAST HARTFORD, CONNECTICUT 06108-3209
Telephone: 860-290-8690
Fax: 860-290-8697
Email: woolflaw@rcn.com
URL: http://www.lawyers.com/woolf

Criminal Defense, State and Federal, (including White Collar), Motor Vehicle and DUI's, Civil Litigation including Major Personal Injury and Negligence Matter, Family Law, Divorce, Child Custody, Banking (New Charters Only), Real Estate and Commercial Loan Workouts.

BRIAN J. WOOLF, born Johannesburg, South Africa, September 21, 1947; admitted to bar, 1977, Connecticut and U.S. District Court, District of Connecticut; 1978, Florida; 1996, U.S. District Court, Southern and Eastern Districts of New York; 2000, Massachusetts. *Education:* Hebrew University of Jerusalem, Israel (B.A., 1972); University of Pennsylvania (M.A., 1974); University of Connecticut (J.D., with honors, 1977). Banking Commissioner, with regulatory supervision over Banking, Thrift and Securities Matters, State of Connecticut, 1981-1985. *Member:* Connecticut (Member: Criminal Law and Family Law Sections), and American (Member, Business Law Section) Bar Associations. ***LANGUAGES:*** Hebrew, Afrikaans.

COHEN AND ACAMPORA

8 FRONTAGE ROAD
P.O. BOX 190
EAST HAVEN, CONNECTICUT 06512
Telephone: 203-467-7337
Telecopier: 203-468-7865

New Haven, Connecticut Office: 109 Church Street. Telephone: 203-624-4126.

General Civil and Criminal Practice before State and Federal Courts. Personal Injury, Litigation, Products Liability, Environmental, Real Estate, Zoning, Acquisitions and Development, Probate, Estate Planning, Workers Compensation, Domestic Relations, Foreclosure, Bankruptcy, Insolvency, Maritime Law, Real Estate, Tax Appeals, Business, Commercial and Corporation Law.

MEMBERS OF FIRM

JOHN A. ACAMPORA, born New Haven, Connecticut, March 6, 1944; admitted to bar, 1969, Connecticut; U.S. District Court, District of Connecticut; U.S. Court of Appeals, Second Circuit. *Education:* Quinnipiac College (A.S., 1964; B.S., 1966); Suffolk University (J.D., 1969). Chairman, Moot Court Advisory Board. Associate Professor, Connecticut Practice and Procedure, Quinnipiac College, Hamden, Connecticut, 1975-1978. Town Attorney, East Haven, Connecticut, 1969-1976. Special Public Defender, U.S. District Court, New Haven, Connecticut, 1970-1971. Member, Advisory Board: Quinnipiac College, 1975—; Bank of New Haven, 1984—; Founder's Bank, 1985—. Trustee, St. Michael's Roman Catholic Church, 1983-1991. Member, Municipal Tax Advisory Committee, State of Connecticut Tax Court. *Member:* New Haven County, Connecticut and American Bar Associations; American Trial Lawyers Association. ***LANGUAGES:*** Italian. ***PRACTICE AREAS:*** General Civil and Criminal Litigation; Personal Injury Law; Products Liability Law; Environmental Law; Real Estate Law; Zoning Law; Acquisitions and Development Law; Probate Law; Estate Planning Law; Workers Compensation Law; Domestic Relations Law; Corporate Law.

GARY W. STEGINA, born New Haven, Connecticut, March 30, 1955; admitted to bar, 1980, Connecticut; 1984, U.S. District Court, District of Connecticut. *Education:* University of New Haven (B.S., magna cum laude, 1977); Cleveland State University-Cleveland Marshall College of Law (J.D., 1980). Alpha Chi. Recipient, Lawyers Coop Book Award-Future Interest. *Member:* New Haven County, Connecticut and American Bar Associations. [Capt., Second Company Governor's Foot Guard of Connecticut, 1980—]. ***PRACTICE AREAS:*** Commercial and Residential Real Estate Law; Business and Corporate Law; Mergers and Acquisitions Law; General Practice.

DAVID L. WEISS, born Hartford, Connecticut, April 26, 1963; admitted to bar, 1988, Connecticut. *Education:* University of Chicago (B.A., 1985); Washington University (J.D., 1988). Phi Delta Phi. *Member:* New Haven County (Member, Real Estate Committee), Connecticut and American Bar Associations. ***LANGUAGES:*** French. ***PRACTICE AREAS:*** Real Estate; Civil Litigation; Commercial Litigation; Condemnation; Tax Appeals; Corporate Law; Trusts and Estates.

FRANK S. MARCUCCI, born New Haven, Connecticut, March 27, 1957; admitted to bar, 1982, Connecticut and U.S. District Court, District of Connecticut. *Education:* University of New Haven (B.S., cum laude, 1979); Western New England School of Law (J.D., 1982). Phi Alpha Delta (Arthur Middleton Chapter, Vice Justice, 1979-1982). *Member:* Connecticut Trial Lawyers Association. ***REPORTED CASES:*** MacLellan vs. LER Associates, 27 Conn. App. 913 (1992); Kulisch vs. Aetna Casualty & Surety Co., 36 Conn. App. 938 (1994) Cert. granted, 231 Conn. 938; Pagano vs. Pagano 44 Conn. App. 905 (1997) Cert. denied, 240 Conn. 911 (1997); Solomon vs. Gilmore, 48 Conn, App. (1998); Criscoulo vs. Mauro Motors, Inc., 58 Conn. App. 537 (2000). ***PRACTICE AREAS:*** Civil Trial Litigation; Domestic Relations; Personal Injury Litigation.

OF COUNSEL

EDWARD W. COHEN, born New Haven, Connecticut, October 6, 1912; admitted to bar, 1937, Connecticut. *Education:* Yale University (B.S., cum laude, 1934; LL.B., 1937). Order of the Coif. ***PRACTICE AREAS:*** General Practice.

STEVENS, HARRIS & GUERNSEY, P.C.

EAST LYME, CONNECTICUT

(See Niantic)

General Civil and Criminal Practice before State and Federal Courts. Personal Injury, Wrongful Death, Real Estate, Probate, Corporation, Domestic Relations, Environmental and Workers Compensation Law. Trials and Appeals.

ADAMS & ELIASON

69 HIGH STREET
ENFIELD, CONNECTICUT 06082-3509
Telephone: 860-745-1659

General Practice. Family Law, Children, Civil Litigation, Commercial Law, Real Estate, Wills, Trusts & Estates, Bankruptcy, Municipal Law, Zoning Law.

MEMBERS OF FIRM

DEBORAH W. A. ELIASON, born Hartford, Connecticut, March 28, 1956; admitted to bar, 1983, Connecticut. *Education:* Tufts University (B.A., cum laude, 1978); University of Connecticut (J.D., 1983). *Member:* Connecticut Bar Association; Association of Trial Lawyers of America. ***PRACTICE AREAS:*** Family Law; Children; Civil Litigation; Commercial Law; Real Estate; Wills; Trusts& Estates; Bankruptcy. ***Email:*** deliason@prodigy.net

OF COUNSEL

JOHN D. ADAMS, born Pittsburgh, Pennsylvania, May 9, 1933; admitted to bar, 1959, Connecticut, 1965, U.S. Supreme Court. *Education:* Yale University (B.A., 1954); University of Connecticut (LL.B., 1959). Assistant U.S. Attorney, 1963-1965. Corporation Counsel, Town of Enfield, 1967-1977. Hearing Officer, Commission on Human Rights and Opportunities, 1980—. *Member:*

(This Listing Continued)

Hartford County, Connecticut and Federal Bar Associations; American Judicature Society. ***PRACTICE AREAS:*** Real Property; Municipal Law; Zoning Law; Family and Matrimonial; Commercial Law.

REPRESENTATIVE CLIENTS: Anthony Troiano & Son, Enfield; Brookside Village, Inc.
APPROVED ATTORNEYS FOR: Connecticut Attorney's Title Insurance Co.; Lawyers' Title Insurance Corp.
REFERENCES: Enfield Federal Savings & Loan Assn.; The Savings Institute.

SKOLER, ABBOTT & PRESSER, P.C.

ENFIELD, CONNECTICUT

(See Springfield, Massachusetts)

Representing Management in Labor and Employment Law Including the National Labor Relations Act, Employee Benefit Law, Pension Law, Wage and Hour Law, Immigration Law, Workers Compensation Law, OSHA and Equal Employment Opportunity Law. Trials and Appeals, Including Wrongful Discharge Litigation.

JONATHAN D. CARLISLE

Established in 1985

67 MAIN STREET, CENTER BROOK
P.O. BOX 800
ESSEX, CONNECTICUT 06426
Telephone: 203-629-9600

Greenwich Office: 125 Mason Street, 06830. Telephone: 203-629-9600. Fax: 203-629-9072.

Wills and Estate Planning, Taxation, Trust and Estate Administration, Contested Probate Matters, Residential and Investment Real Estate, Land Use and Zoning Law.

REPRESENTATIVE CLIENTS: McNaught Syndicate, Inc. (Newspaper Features); Pam Marker, Inc. (Consumer Paper Products); Microwave Development, Inc. (Technology); Broadford & Maloney, Inc. (Business Consulting).
APPROVED TITLE ATTORNEYS FOR: Fleet Bank; Peoples Bank; First Constitution Bank; Greenwich Federal Savings and Loan Assn.; Union Trust Co.; Putnam Trust Co.; CityTrust; Commonwealth Land Title Ins. Co.; First American Title Insurance; Center Bank; Chicago Title Ins. Co.
REFERENCE: Putnam Trust Co.

(For complete Biographical Data on all Personnell see Professional Biographies at Greenwich)

GOULD, LARSON, BENNET, WELLS & McDONNELL, P.C.

Established in 1961

ESSEX SAVINGS BANK BUILDING
35 PLAINS ROAD
P.O. BOX 959
ESSEX, CONNECTICUT 06426
Telephone: 860-767-9055
Fax: 860-767-2742
URL: http://www.gould-larson.com
URL: http://www.lawyers.com/glbw&m

General Practice in all Courts. Real Estate, Zoning, Family, Bankruptcy, Banking, Probate, Corporation Law, Estate Planning and Taxation, and Personal Injury Law, Trials, Appeals, Domestic Relations, Municipal Law and Land Use Law, Insurance Defense, Elder Law, Arbitration and Mediation.

FIRM PROFILE: Gould & Larson was established in 1961. The firm is comprised of five lawyers, three paralegals and several support personnel. The firm serves clients throughout Connecticut, concentrating in areas of Real Estate, Probate, Tax, Domestic, Municipal and Civil Litigation. Two former partners have gone on to become Superior Court Judges. All firm members participate in continuing legal education and are active in local community affairs.

JAMES H. GOULD (1911-1985).

JOHN E. LARSON, born Springfield, Massachusetts, December 10, 1924; admitted to bar, 1953, Connecticut. *Education:* Amherst College (B.A., 1949); Harvard University (LL.B., 1952). State Representative, 1957-1959. Public Defender, Middlesex County, 1959-1961. Probate Judge, District of Deep River, 1963-1967. Director, 1974-1988, and Chairman, 1987-1988, Omni Bank of Connecticut. *Member:* Middlesex County and Connecticut Bar Associations. ***PRACTICE AREAS:*** Estate Planning Law; Probate Law; Real Estate Law.

JOHN S. BENNET, born Middletown, Connecticut, August 3, 1951; admitted to bar, 1977, Connecticut. *Education:* American University (B.A., 1973); Franklin Pierce College and Law Center (J.D., 1977). Attorney Trial Referee, 1988—. Federal Editor, Survey of New Hampshire Law, 1976. Town Attorney: Town of East Haddam, 1994—; Town of Clinton, 1994—; Town of Chester, 1991—. *Member:* Middlesex County, Connecticut and American Bar Associations; The Association of Trial Lawyers of America. ***PRACTICE AREAS:*** Civil Law; Commercial Litigation; Banking Law; Municipal Law; Planning and Zoning Law; Corporate Law; Banking Law.

MICHAEL J. WELLS, born Westbrook, Connecticut, December 16, 1956; admitted to bar, 1981, Connecticut. *Education:* Western New England College (B.A., summa cum laude, 1978); Hofstra University (J.D., with distinction, 1981). Member, Hofstra Law Review, 1979-1980. Member, Planning Commission, Westbrook, Connecticut, 1982-1984. Member, Board of Education, Westbrook, Connecticut, 1984-1985. Director: Westbrook Cemetery Association, 1985—; Chester Bank, 1987-1989. Counsel, Zoning Board of Appeals, Westbrook, Connecticut, 1989—. Town Attorney, Town of Westbrook, 1989-1993. *Member:* Middlesex County, Connecticut and American Bar Associations. ***PRACTICE AREAS:*** Real Estate Law; Probate Law; Planning and Zoning Law; Corporation Law; Municipal Law.

KENNETH J. McDONNELL, born Derby, Connecticut, June 7, 1958; admitted to bar, 1983, Connecticut; 1984, U.S. District Court, District of Connecticut; 1985, U.S. Court of Appeals, Third Circuit; 1986, U.S. Court of Appeals, Second Circuit. *Education:* Boston College (B.A., magna cum laude, 1980); University of Connecticut (J.D., 1983). President, Clinton Land Conservation Trust, 1995—. *Member:* Middlesex County and Connecticut Bar Associations; Connecticut Trial Lawyers Association; Association of Trial Lawyers of America; Association of Trial Lawyers of America; Connecticut Academy of Certified Trial Lawyers; National Board of Trial Advocacy. (Board Certified Civil Trial Attorney, National Board of Trial Advocacy). ***PRACTICE AREAS:*** Personal Injury Law; Civil Litigation Law; Domestic Relations; Environmental Law.

HELEN B. BENNET, born Bronxville, New York, July 10, 1953; admitted to bar, 1985, Connecticut. *Education:* Williams College (B.A., cum laude, 1975); Stanford University (M.A., 1979); University of Connecticut School of Law (J.D., with honors, 1985). Probate Judge, District of Saybrook, 1990—. Member, Executive Committee, Connecticut Probate Assembly, 1993-1999. Chairman, Education Committee, Connecticut Probate Assembly, 1993-1999. Member, Tri-Town Juvenile Review Board, 1997—. Member, Chester Board of Education, 1983-1987. *Member:* Middlesex County and Connecticut Bar Associations. ***PRACTICE AREAS:*** Estate Planning Law; Probate Law.

REPRESENTATIVE CLIENTS: Towns of Clinton, East Haddam and Chester; Essex Savings Bank; Town of Ole Lyme, Water Pollution Control Authority; Killingworth Land Conservation Trust; Town of Westbrook, Zoning Board of Appeals; Chicago Title Insurance Co.; Regional School District No. 4.; Homestead Insurance.
APPROVED ATTORNEYS FOR: Commonwealth Land Title Insurance Co.; Chicago Title Insurance Co.; First American Title Insurance Co.

HUDSON AND KILBY

78 MAIN STREET, CENTERBROOK VILLAGE
P.O. BOX 398
ESSEX, CONNECTICUT 06426
Telephone: 860-767-0195
Fax: 860-767-7077
Email: hudson.kilby@snet.net
URL: http://www.lawyers.com/hudsonandkilby

General Practice. Probate, Estate Planning, Real Estate, Zoning and Land Use, Taxation, Business Organizations, and Municipal.

MEMBERS OF FIRM

W. CAMPBELL HUDSON, III, born New York, N.Y., May 7, 1951; admitted to bar, 1976, Connecticut; 1978, U.S. District Court, District of Connecticut. *Education:* Tulane University of Louisiana (B.A., 1973; J.D., 1976). Representative, 1979-1989, Vice Chairman, 1981-1985 and Chairman, 1985-1987, Connecticut River Estuary Regional Planning Agency. Town Counsel, Town of Clinton, 1985-1988. Member: Long Island Sound Study, Citizens Advisory Committee, 1987-2000; Essex Board of Finance, 1997—. Trustee, 1989-1993 and Vice-Chairman, 1990-1992, Connecticut River Watershed Council. Borough Counsel, Borough of Fenwick, 1990—. Member, 1991-1997 and Chairman, 1993-1997, Essex Board of Education. Trustee, 1993—, Vice-President, 1995-2000, and President, 2000—, Connecticut Fund for the Environment. Trustee, 1997— and Vice-Chairman, 2000—, Middlesex County Community Foundation. *Member:* Middlesex County, Connecticut (Member, Sections on: Estates and Probate; Planning and Zoning) and American (Member, Real Property, Probate and Trust Law Section) Bar Associations. ***PRACTICE AREAS:*** Real Property; Estate Planning; Probate; Municipal Law; Land Use Law; Commercial Law.

MARIANNE B. KILBY, born Offenbach a/m, Germany, July 5, 1935; admitted to bar, 1979, Connecticut; 1981, U.S. District Court, District of Connecticut. *Education:* Barnard College (B.A., cum laude, 1957); Johns Hopkins University (M.A., 1959); University of Connecticut (J.D., with honors, 1979). Author, "Contested Name Changes for Minors," The Connecticut Probate Law

(This Listing Continued)

HUDSON AND KILBY, Essex—Continued

Journal, Vol. 1, No. 1, Fall 1985. Member, 1984-1993 and Chairman, 1986-1987, Killingworth Conservation Commission. *Member:* Middlesex County, Connecticut (Member, Sections on: Estates and Probate; Elder Law) and American (Member, Real Property, Probate and Trust Law Section) Bar Associations. ***LANGUAGES:*** German and French. ***PRACTICE AREAS:*** Estate Planning; Probate; Real Property; Taxation; Elder Law; Real Estate.

SUZANNA URBAN, born Norwalk, Connecticut, May 11, 1970; admitted to bar, 1996, Connecticut; 1998, New York. *Education:* Washington University (A.B., 1992); Temple University (J.D., 1996). *Member:* Middlesex County, Connecticut (Member, Elder Law Section) and American Bar Associations. ***LANGUAGES:*** Hungarian and German. ***PRACTICE AREAS:*** Real Property; Land Use; Corporate Law; Probate.

CYNTHIA M. OFFREDI, born New Haven, Connecticut, September 5, 1970; admitted to bar, 1997, Connecticut; 1998, New York. *Education:* Allegheny College (B.A., cum laude, 1993); Pace University School of Law (J.D., certificate in Environmental Law, 1997). Treasurer, Essex Art Association, 2001—. *Middlesex County and Connecticut (Member, Sections on:* Estates and Probate, Planning, and Zoning) Bar Associations. ***PRACTICE AREAS:*** Estate Planning; Probate; Land Use; Real Estate.

REFERENCE: Fleet Bank.

SENNING & RIEDER

16 SAYBROOK ROAD
ESSEX, CONNECTICUT 06426
Telephone: 860-767-2618
Fax: 860-767-2740
Email: jlssealaw@aol.com
URL: http://www.lawyers.com/senningriederlaw

General Practice. Trial and Appellate Practice in all State and Federal Courts, Admiralty, Litigation, Corporate, Estate Planning and Administration, Real Estate and Business Law.

FIRM PROFILE: John L. Senning and Richard E. Rieder have practiced together for over 18 years. Their philosophy is to provide personalized attention to their clients at all junctures while handling their legal matters. They do not run a high volume practice. Mr. Senning and Mr. Rieder have over 40 years of combined experience in Essex while covering southern Connecticut. They mainly concentrate on estate planning and administration, business, real estate and admiralty law.

MEMBERS OF FIRM

JOHN L. SENNING, born New Britain, Connecticut, September 13, 1943; admitted to bar, 1970, Connecticut and Maine; 1976, New York, U.S. District Court, Southern and Eastern Districts of New York, U.S. District Court, District of Connecticut and U.S. Court of Appeals, Second Circuit; 1978, U.S. District Court, District of Rhode Island; 1980, U.S. District Court, District of Maine. *Education:* University of Vermont (B.A., 1966); University of Maine (J.D., 1970); Southern Methodist University; Graduate, 1971, Institute of Aerospace and Aviation Law. Associate, Bigham Englar Jones & Houston, New York, New York, 1972-1976. *Member:* Connecticut (Member: Section on Estates and Probate; Subcommittee on, Private Remedies and Land Donations, Section on Conservation and Environmental Quality, 1979-1989; Executive Committee, Section on International Law and World Peace, 1979-1989) and American (Member, Committee on Admiralty and Maritime Litigation, 1983—) Bar Associations; New York County Lawyers Association; Maritime Law Association of the United States (Member, Committees on: Undersea Exploration and Development, 1975-1989, Marine Ecology, 1975-1992, Marine Fisheries, 1980-1992, and Marine Financing, Subcommittee of Yacht Financing, 1989—). ***PRACTICE AREAS:*** Admiralty; Marine Law; Corporate; Probate/Estate Planning; Administration; Real Estate. ***Email:*** jlssealaw@aol.com

RICHARD E. RIEDER, born Wyandotte, Michigan, March 6, 1937; admitted to bar, 1961, Virginia; 1963, New York and U.S. District Court, Southern District of New York; 1964, U.S. Supreme Court, U.S. Court of Appeals, Second Circuit and U.S. District Court, Eastern District of New York; 1983, Connecticut and U.S. District Court, District of Connecticut. *Education:* University of Michigan (A.B., 1958); University of Virginia (LL.B., 1961); New York University (LL.M., 1969). Associate, Chadbourne, Parke, Whiteside & Wolff, New York, New York, 1967-1972. Associate, 1972 and Partner, 1974-1980, Dunnington, Bartholow & Miller, New York, New York. *Member:* The Association of the Bar of the City of New York; Connecticut (Member: Executive Committee; Corporate Counsel Committee) and American (Member, Committee on Corporate Counsel, Section of Litigation) Bar Associations. [Captain, USNR]. ***PRACTICE AREAS:*** Corporate; Probate/Estate Planning. ***Email:*** riedercom@aol.com

JOHN A. STICHTER

15 NOTT LANE
P.O. BOX 412
ESSEX, CONNECTICUT 06426
Telephone: 860-767-9173
Telecopier: 860-767-8584
Email: jstichter@excelonline.com
URL: http://www.lawyers.com/jastichterlaw

New York, New York Office: 641 Lexington Avenue, 18th Floor. Telephone: 212-751-3488. Telecopier: 212-486-1600.

General Practice, Civil Trials and Appeals in State and Federal Courts. Litigation, Arbitration, Trust, Estate, Probate, Estate Planning, Real Estate and Corporation Law.

JOHN A. STICHTER, born Toledo, Ohio, January 13, 1934; admitted to bar, 1961, New York; 1962, U.S. District Court for the Southern District of New York; 1962, U.S. Court of Appeals, 2nd Circuit; 1970, U.S. Court of Appeals, 3rd Circuit; 1977, U.S. Supreme Court; 1993, Connecticut. *Education:* Northwestern University (B.S., 1955); University of Michigan (LL.B. 1960). Assistant U.S. Attorney, Southern District of New York, Criminal Division, 1964-1967. Associate, Donovan, Leisure, Newton & Irvine, N.Y.C., 1960-1964, 1967-1971. Partner, Dunnington, Bartholow & Miller, N.Y.C., 1971-1980. *Member:* New York State (Member, Sections on: Trial Lawyers; Trust and Estates Law), Connecticut (Member, Sections on: Estates and Probate; Litigation) and American (Member, Sections on: Litigation; General Practice) Bar Associations; Federal Bar Council. ***PRACTICE AREAS:*** Estate Planning; Estate Administration; Real Estate; Corporate Law; Civil Litigation; Appellate Practice.

ALBERT, WARD & JOHNSON, P.C.

FAIRFIELD, CONNECTICUT

(See Greenwich)

General Practice. Real Estate, Zoning, Corporation, Litigation, Probate, Taxation, Construction, Environmental and Family Law.

AMENDOLA & AMENDOLA

A Limited Liability Co.
1248 POST ROAD
P.O. BOX 237
FAIRFIELD, CONNECTICUT 06430-0237
Telephone: 203-319-1143
Fax: 203-319-1196
Email: amrndolalaw@freewweb.com
URL: http://www.lawyers.com/amendola&amendola

Matrimonial Law, Family, Divorce, Child Custody, Domestic Relations and Litigation.

MEMBERS OF FIRM

ELAINE S. AMENDOLA, born New Haven, Connecticut, January 16, 1935; admitted to bar, 1962, Connecticut; 1963, U.S. District Court, District of Connecticut; 1967, U.S. Court of Appeals, Second Circuit and U.S. Supreme Court; 1974, U.S. Tax Court. *Education:* Wellesley College (B.A., 1956); Yale University (LL.B., 1962). Member: Connecticut Task Force on Gender, Justice and the Courts and pro bono legal services. *Member:* Bridgeport (Member, Family Law Committee, 1983—), Connecticut and American (Member: Family Law Section; Executive Committee; Lawyer to Lawyer Arbitration, 1989—) Bar Associations. Fellow: American Academy of Matrimonial Lawyers (Vice President, Connecticut Chapter); The American Bar Foundation. ***PRACTICE AREAS:*** Matrimonial Law. ***Email:*** esamendola@aol.com

BONNIE L. AMENDOLA, born New Haven, Connecticut, December 1, 1966; admitted to bar, 1992, Connecticut and U.S. District Court, District of Connecticut. *Education:* University of Pennsylvania (B.A., 1988); University of Connecticut (J.D., with honors, 1992). Member, Planning and Zoning Commission, Bethany, 1992-1996. *Member:* Greater Bridgeport, New Haven County, Connecticut and American Bar Associations. ***LANGUAGES:*** Italian and French. ***PRACTICE AREAS:*** Litigation; Matrimonial.

BRAUNSTEIN & TODISCO, LLC

Established in 1989

ONE ELIOT PLACE

FAIRFIELD, CONNECTICUT 06430

Telephone: 203-254-1118

Telecopier: 203-254-2453

URL: http://www.btlawfirm.com

New York, New York Office: 820 Second Avenue, 4th Floor, 10017. Telephone: 212-557-6767. Telecopy: 212-557-3760.

Taxation, Business Law, Estate Planning, Elder Law, Trusts, Probate Administration and Probate Proceedings, Commercial Transactions and Real Estate.

SAMUEL L. BRAUNSTEIN, born Chattanooga, Tennessee, November 24, 1941; admitted to bar, 1969, Texas; 1970, U.S. District Court, Western District of Texas, U.S. Tax Court, U.S. Court of International Trade and U.S. Court of Federal Claims; 1972, U.S. Court of Appeals, District of Columbia Circuit and U.S. Supreme Court; 1982, Connecticut; 1984, U.S. District Court, District of Connecticut; 1994, U.S. Court of Appeals, Second Circuit. *Education:* University of Tennessee at Knoxville (B.S.B.A., 1963); St. Mary's University of San Antonio (J.D., 1970); Boston University (LL.M., Taxation, 1975); Century University (M.B.A., 1982). Delta Theta Phi (Member, Bickett Senate, 1967-1969). Recipient, American Jurisprudence Awards. Certified Public Accountant: Texas, 1971; Connecticut, 1976. Author: "Criteria in Selection of a Tax Attorney," CLT Tax Law Supplement, May 10, 1993; "The Cabaret Tax and the Carpenteri Case," CLT Tax Law Supplement, February 13, 1995, p. 21; "Which is Better: To Give or To Receive?" CLT Trusts & Estates and Tax Planning Supplement, February 12, 1996, p. 11; "Timely Tax Issues for Practice and Home," 22 CLT 44, 19 (November 4, 1996); "Special IRS Treatments for Lawyers," 23 CLT 10, 20 (March 3, 1997); "IRA Deathtraps," 23 CLT 16, 20 (April 14, 1997); "Love, Marriage and Taxes," 23 CLT 35, 25 (August 25/September 1, 1997); "How Do You Spell Relief?" 23 CLT 44, 16 (November 3, 1997); "Roth IRA Provides a Valuable Planning Tool," 24 CLT 7, 16 (February 9, 1998); "Attorneys Singled Out for Special IRS Treatment," 24 CLT 13, 16 (March 23, 1998); "Are 'Foreign Trusts' Really Alien to Connecticut Estate Planners?" CLT Magazine, Trusts & Estates Supplement, p. 4 (June 22, 1998). Co-Author: with Carol F. Burger: "Good News in Tax Law," ABA Journal, November 2001; "Tax Outcomes You didn't Expect," ABA Journal, November 2000; "Protecting the Wealth," ABA Journal, November 1999, p. 58; "What To Do When the IRS Calls," ABA Journal, November 1998. Co-Author, with C. Wells Hall, III, "These Taxing Times," ABA Journal, November 1997. Moderator and Panelist: "Estate Planning Workshop for Closely-Held Businesses," ABA Section of Taxation, San Francisco, CA, August 2, 1997; "These Taxing Times," ABA Connection Teleconference, November 19, 1997; "A Business Divorce - The Demise of a Law Firm," ABA Section of Taxation, San Antonio, TX, January 25, 1998; "Passing the Torch," ABA Connection Teleconference, February 18, 1998; "Breaking Up is Hard to Do - A Business Law Primer: Section 355 Divisive Reorganizations," ABA Section of Taxation, Washington, DC, May 16, 1998; "What To Do When the IRS Calls," ABA Connection Teleconference, November 1998; Buying and Selling a Business - A Business Primer - Transactional Analysis of the Mechanics and Issues Involved in Buying or Selling a Business," ABA Section of Taxation, Orlando, Florida, January 16, 1999; "Tax Considerations in Buying and Selling a Business - A Tax Primer," ABA Section of Taxation, Washington, D.C., May 1, 1999; "Fringe Benefits Are Not the Only Hot Issues - Winning at the Appellate Level," ABA Section of Taxation, Washington D.C., May 1, 1999; "To Be Or Not To Be-How Is The Question (Taxable or Non-Taxable)-- A Tax Primer-- A Practical Analysis of Selected (Essential) Tax Issues Involved In Buying, Selling and Restructuring A Business," ABA Section of Taxation, Washington, D.C., May 13, 2000; "Tax Considerations in Buying or Selling a Business," ABA Section of Taxation Teleconference, September 16, 1999; "Tax Considerations in Buying or Selling a Business," ABA Section of Taxation Teleconference, March 21, 2000; "Protecting Wealth," ABA Connection Teleconference, November 18 and 19, 1998; "Tax Outcomes You Didn't Expect," ABA Connection Teleconference, November 15, 2000; "Good News in Tax Law," ABA Conection Teleconference, November 14, 2001. Attorney, Office of the Chief Counsel, Internal Revenue Service, 1970-1972. Chairman: Board of Trustees, The Park City Hospital, 1982-1984; Chairman: Board of Directors, Greater Bridgeport Area Foundation, 1999-2001. Member, Town Council, Trumbull, Connecticut, 1993-1995. *Member:* Greater Bridgeport, Connecticut and American (Chair, 2000-2001, Closely Held Businesses Committee and Chair, 2001—, Professional Services Committee; Member, Nominating Committee, 2000—, Tax Section) Bar Associations; State Bar of Texas; Connecticut Society of Certified Public Accountants; Texas Society of Certified Public Accountants; American Institute of Certified Public Accountants. Fellow: The International Society for Philosophical Enquiry; American College of Tax Counsel. [Capt., U.S. Army, 1964-1968.]. ***REPORTED CASES:*** Green v. Commissioner, 67 R.C.M. 3074, Dec. 49,897 (M), T.C. Memo 1994-264, U.S. Tax Court, 1994. ***PRACTICE AREAS:*** Taxation; Trusts and Estates; Estate Planning; Nonprofit and Charitable Organizations; Business Law. ***Email:*** sam@btlawfirm.com

(This Listing Continued)

AMY E. TODISCO, born Glen Cove, New York, August 13, 1959; admitted to bar, 1984, Connecticut, U.S. District Court, District of Connecticut, U.S. Tax Court and U.S. Court of Federal Claims; 1992, U.S. Supreme Court. *Education:* Skidmore College (B.A., 1981); University of Bridgeport (J.D., 1984; LL.M., Taxation, 1987). Phi Delta Phi (Magistrate, 1983). Member, Periclean Academic Honor Society. Author, "Clients Are Never Too Old to Present Ethical Dilemmas," The Connecticut Law Tribune Magazine - Malpractice, Grievance and Professional Responsibility Supplement, p. 18 (May 4, 1998). Vice President, Stratford Federation of Democratic Women, 1989-1990. Member, Board of Directors, 1992-1996 and President, 1995-1996, Trumbull Chamber of Commerce. Member, Executive Committee, Board of Directors, The Bridgeport Regional Business Council, 1994-1996. Chair, Professional Division and Campaign Captain, United Way of Eastern Fairfield County. Member, Board of Directors: Leadership Greater Bridgeport Alumni Association, 1994-1996; Bridgeport Arts Council. Member, Parish Advisory Council and Religious Education Instructor, St. Catherine of Siena Church, Trumbull, Connecticut. *Member:* Greater Bridgeport (Chairperson: Taxation Section, 1989-1991; Estates and Trusts Section, 1992-1994; Member, Executive Committee, 1989-1992; Treasurer, 1992-1993; Vice President, 1993-1994; President Elect, 1994-1995; President, 1995-1996), Connecticut (Member: Executive Committee, Sections on: Tax, 1989-1994, Elder Law, 2000—; Task Force on Grievance Procedures, 1997-1998; Section on: Estates and Probate) and American (Member, Taxation Section) Bar Associations; Fairfield County Women's Bar Association (Member, Executive Committee, 1989-1991, Treasurer, 1991; Vice-President, 1992-1993); National Academy of Elder Law Attorneys. ***LANGUAGES:*** Italian. ***PRACTICE AREAS:*** Elder Law; Probate; Trusts and Estates; Real Estate. ***Email:*** amy@btlawfirm.com

OF COUNSEL

ROGER L. STAVIS, born New York, New York, November 5, 1958; admitted to bar, 1983, New York and U.S. District Court, Southern and Eastern Districts of New York; 1986, U.S. Supreme Court and U.S. Court of Appeals, Second Circuit; 1988, U.S. Court of Military Appeals, 1991, U.S. Court of Appeals, Fourth Circuit; 1993, U.S. Court of Appeals, Third Circuit; 1998, U.S. District Court, District of Connecticut (Not admitted in Connecticut). *Education:* Queens College of the City University of New York (B.A., magna cum laude, 1979); George Washington University (J.D., with honors, 1982). Trustee Scholar. Recipient, Professional Achievement Award, The George Washington Law Alumni Association, 1995. Contributing Author: Criminal Defense Techniques (Bender 1991); Criminal Trial Advocacy, (Appellate Division, 1992); "Jury Selection in the Robert Chambers Murder Trial: The Successful Use of An Individual Voire Dire," Queens Bar Bulletin, May, 1988. Assistant District Attorney and Supervising Attorney, Bronx District Attorney's Office, 1982-1986. Member, Independent Judicial Screening Panel for the Supreme Court, Democratic County Committee, 1991 and 1997. Guest Commentator, Court T.V. *Member:* Association of the Bar of the City of New York (Member, Committee on Criminal Advocacy, 1996—); American Bar Association; National Association of Criminal Defense Lawyers; New York Council of Defense Lawyers. (Also Member, Stavis & Kornfeld, L.L.P.) (Resident, New York, NY Office). ***REPORTED CASES:*** Associated Press v. Bell, 510 N.E.2d 313 (N.Y. 1987); People v. Robert Chambers, 512 N.Y.S.2d 631 (N.Y. 1987); United States v. El Sayyid Nosair, 854 F.Supp.251 (S.D. N.Y. 1994); United States v. Rahman, 189 F.3d 88 (2d Cir. 1999); United States v. Kirkham, 195 F.3d 126 (2d Cir. 1999); United States v. Pirro, 76 F.Supp. 2d 478 (S.D.N.Y. 1999); United States v. Rodriguez, 968 F.2d 130 (2d Cir. 1992); People v. Maher, 675 N.E. 2d 833 (N.Y. 1996); People v. Class, 494 N.E. 2d 444 (N.Y. 1986). ***PRACTICE AREAS:*** Criminal; Civil Litigation; Appellate Practice. ***Email:*** randlaw@concentric.net

RANDY M. KORNFELD, born New York, New York, November 19, 1954; admitted to bar, 1980, New York, U.S. District Court, Southern and Eastern Districts of New York and U.S. Court of Appeals, Second and Third Districts (Not admitted in Connecticut). *Education:* Brooklyn College of the City University of New York (B.A., 1976); Brooklyn Law School (J.D., 1979). Winner, Moot Court Competition in International Law. *Member:* American Bankruptcy Institute. (Also Member, Stavis & Kornfeld, L.L.P.) (Resident, New York, NY Office). ***REPORTED CASES:*** Webster Soda Fountain Mfg. Corp. v. Chemical Bank, 15 UCC Rep.Serv.2d 999 (N. Y. Sup. 1991); In re Brandt-Airflex Corp., 69 B.R. 701, 59 A.F.T.R.2d 87-1019 (Bankr. E.D.N.Y. 1987) appeal dismissed 73 B.R. 59 (E.D.N.Y. 1987); In re Ms. Interpret, 222 B.R. 409, 40 Collier Bankr.Cas.2d 407, 32 Bankr.Ct.Dec.1091 (Bankr. S.D.N.Y., 1998); In re Patient Educ. Media, Inc., 210 B.R. 237 31 Bankr.Ct.Ccc.49 (Bankr. S.D.N.Y. 1997); In re Lippman, 122 B.R. 2066, 2 Bankr.Ct.Dec.227, Bankr.L.Rep. P73,768 (Bankr. S.D.N.Y. 1990). ***PRACTICE AREAS:*** Bankruptcy; Commercial Litigation. ***Email:*** randlaw@concentric.net

FREDERICK E. SCHMIDT, born 1968; admitted to bar, 1995, New York and Connecticut; 1996, U.S. District Court, Southern and Eastern Districts of New York. *Education:* University of Connecticut (B.S., 1990); Brooklyn Law School (J.D., 1994). *Member:* New York County Lawyers' Association; American Bankruptcy Institute; Brehon Law Society. (Also Member, Stavis & Kornfeld, L.L.P.) (Resident, New York, NY Office). ***REPORTED CASES:*** In re

(This Listing Continued)

BRAUNSTEIN & TODISCO, LLC, Fairfield—Continued

Patient Educ. Media, Inc., 210 B.R. 237, 31 Bankr.Ct.Dec. 49 (Bankr. S.D.N.Y., 1997). ***PRACTICE AREAS:*** Bankruptcy; Criminal; Commercial Litigation; Appellate Practice. ***Email:*** randlaw@concentric.net

REPRESENTATIVE CLIENTS: Daley Construction Company; DeSilva & Phillips, Inc.; Greater Bridgeport Area Foundation, Inc.; Plaza Sweets, Inc.; Timgia, LLC; Weatherhill, Inc.
APPROVED ATTORNEYS FOR: The Boston Company; Chicago Title Insurance Co.; Connecticut Attorneys Title Insurance Co.; Lawyers' Title Insurance Company; Fidelity National Title Insurance Company; North American Mortgage Co.; Washington Mutual Bank, F.A.
REFERENCE: People's Bank.

BRODY, WILKINSON AND OBER, P.C.

FAIRFIELD, CONNECTICUT

(See Southport)

General Civil Practice, Corporation, Probate, Estate Planning, Trusts and Estates, Real Estate, Employment, Commercial, Environmental, Creditors Rights, Tax, Pension, Profit Sharing, Entertainment Law, Banking, General Business, Municipal, Freedom of Information Matters, Telecommunications, Public Utilities, Commercial Litigation.

THE LAW OFFICES OF IRA B. CHARMOY, L.L.C.

Established in 1968

1700 POST ROAD, SUITE D-3
P.O. BOX 745
FAIRFIELD, CONNECTICUT 06430-0745
Telephone: 203-254-9393
Fax: 203-254-9797
Email: charmoy@snet.net
URL: http://www.lawyers.com/charmoy

Consumer and Business Bankruptcy, Commercial and General Civil Litigation, Entity Formation, Wills and Trusts, Probate, and Residential and Commercial Real Estate.

FIRM PROFILE: This firm of two attorneys and four support staff personnel has maintained a presence in Fairfield County for over thirty years. It has earned a reputation for innovative and effective representation in business reorganization, Chapter 11 bankruptcy and commercial litigation. Representation is offered in all Federal and Bankruptcy Courts and State Courts.

IRA B. CHARMOY, born Brooklyn, New York, March 8, 1941; admitted to bar, 1966, Connecticut; 1968, U.S. District Court, District of Connecticut; 1983, U.S. Court of Appeals, Second Circuit. *Education:* University of Connecticut (B.A., 1962; J.D., 1965). Author: "Chapter 13 Bankruptcy and Real Estate," 12 The Connecticut Law Tribune No. 8, February 24, 1986; "Developments in the Second Circuit 1996-1997," Quinnipiac Law Journal, Vol. 17, No. 4, Part II, Winter 1998. Lecturer, Basic Bankruptcy in Connecticut, Connecticut Bar Association Continuing Legal Education Program, 1985—. Adjunct Professor of Law in Bankruptcy, Quinnipiac School of Law, 1991—. *Member:* Bridgeport and Connecticut (Member, Executive Committee, Bankruptcy and Commercial Law Section) Bar Associations; Commercial Law League of America; American Bankruptcy Institute. ***REPORTED CASES:*** In re Bellamy 962 F2d 176 (2nd Cir. 1992); In re Capp Indus., Inc., 257 B.R. 119 (Bankr. D. Conn. 2001). ***PRACTICE AREAS:*** Debtor and Creditor; Bankruptcy; Civil Litigation; Business Litigation; Commercial Litigation; Commercial Real Estate; Residential Real Estate; Business Formation; Probate; Wills; Trusts and Estates. ***Email:*** charmoy@snet.net

SCOTT M. CHARMOY, born Bridgeport, Connecticut, April 14, 1970; admitted to bar, 1995, Connecticut; 1996, Illinois and U.S. District Court, District of Connecticut; 1998, U.S. Court of Appeals, Second and District of Columbia Circuits. *Education:* Duke University (A.B., History, 1992); Washington University (J.D., 1995). *Member:* Greater Bridgeport (Chair, Commercial Law and Bankruptcy Section, 2001-2002), Connecticut (Director, Young Lawyers Section) and American Bar Associations. ***REPORTED CASES:*** Guerrera v. Fleet Credit Card Services, 225 B.R. 32 (Bankr. D. Conn. 1998). ***PRACTICE AREAS:*** Debtor and Creditor; Civil Litigation; Business Litigation; Commercial Litigation; Commercial Real Estate; Residential Real Estate; Probate; Wills; Trusts and Estates; Consumer Bankruptcy; Business Bankruptcy; Business Formation. ***Email:*** charmoy@snet.net

REFERENCE: Webster Bank.

COUSINS, JOHNSON & DESROSIERS, P.C.

FAIRFIELD, CONNECTICUT

(See Stratford)

Workers' Compensation, Personal Injury, Trials, Real Estate, Probate.

FINN DIXON & HERLING LLP

FAIRFIELD, CONNECTICUT

(See Stamford)

Corporate Law, Mergers and Acquisitions, Securities Law, Venture Capital Financing, Corporate Finance and Restructuring, Commercial Litigation, Banking and Lending Law, Bankruptcy and Workouts, Employee Benefits and the Federal and State Taxation of Businesses and Business Transactions.

FITZPATRICK, FRAY & BOLOGNA LLC

1238 POST ROAD
P.O. BOX 278
FAIRFIELD, CONNECTICUT 06430
Telephone: 203-255-3581
Fax: 203-254-7745

General Practice. Wetlands, Zoning and Land Use Litigation and Municipal Board Approvals and Appeals; Personal Injury, Trials in all Courts, Wills and Probate, Real Estate Law.

JOHN T. FITZPATRICK (1925-1989).

WILLIAM J. FITZPATRICK, III, born Bridgeport, Connecticut, August 27, 1949; admitted to bar, 1975, Connecticut. *Education:* University of Notre Dame and Georgetown University (A.B., 1971); University of Connecticut (J.D., cum laude, 1975). Member, Board of Finance, Town of Fairfield, 1981-1997. Counsel, State of Connecticut Joint Committee on the Judiciary, 1982-1983. *Member:* Fairfield, Greater Bridgeport and Connecticut Bar Associations. ***PRACTICE AREAS:*** Zoning and Land Use; Wetland/Conservation Approvals and Appeals; Residential and Commercial Real Estate Closings.

MICHAEL T. BOLOGNA, born Haverhill, Massachusetts, September 26, 1956; admitted to bar, 1981, Connecticut; 1984, U.S. District Court, District of Connecticut. *Education:* College of the Holy Cross (B.A., cum laude, 1978); University of Connecticut (J.D., cum laude, 1981). Member, 1979-1981, and Administrative Editor, 1980-1981, Connecticut Law Review. Attorney Trial Referee, 1989—. Member, 1994 and Chairman, 1997-1998, Town of Fairfield Conservation/Wetlands Commission. Trained AAA Mediator. *Member:* Connecticut Bar Association; Connecticut Trial Lawyers Association. (Also Of Counsel to McNamara & Kenney, Shelton, Connecticut). ***PRACTICE AREAS:*** Personal Injury; Wetlands; Zoning; Real Estate; Wills; Mediation; Arbitration. ***Email:*** MTBologna@worldnet.att.net

OF COUNSEL

JOHN P. FRAY, born New Haven, Connecticut, July 11, 1930; admitted to bar, 1955, Connecticut. *Education:* Fairfield University (B.A., 1952); Yale University (LL.B., 1955).

FOGARTY COHEN SELBY & NEMIROFF LLC

FAIRFIELD, CONNECTICUT

(See Greenwich)

Litigation in all Courts, Real Estate and Land Use, Estate Planning and Probate, Corporate, Matrimonial, Administrative and Environmental, Appellate Practice, Business, Civil Trial, Commercial Litigation, Construction, Family, Labor and Employment, Medical Malpractice, Trust and Product Liability.

GARSON & SLEPIAN

Established in 1977

72 RUANE STREET
FAIRFIELD, CONNECTICUT 06430
Telephone: 203-255-3483
Fax: 203-254-8339
Email: garsnlaw@javanet.com
URL: http://www.lawyers.com/garson&slepian

General Civil Practice. Trusts, Estate Planning, Probate, Estate and Gift Tax, Real Estate, Family, Corporate and Commercial Law.

ANDREW EMERY GARSON, born New York, N.Y., August 15, 1945; admitted to bar, 1972, New York; 1974, U.S. District Court, Eastern District of New York; 1975, Connecticut and U.S. Court of Appeals, 2nd Circuit; 1976,

(This Listing Continued)

U.S. District Court, District of Connecticut; 1977, U.S. Supreme Court; 1983, Florida. *Education:* Oberlin College (B.A., 1967); New York University School of Law (J.D., 1972). Assistant District Attorney, Kings County District Attorney's Office, Brooklyn, New York, 1972-1976. *Member:* Greater Bridgeport, Connecticut, New York State and American Bar Associations; The Florida Bar. ***PRACTICE AREAS:*** Real Estate; Estate Planning; Settlement; Family Law.

DAVID CRAIG SLEPIAN, born Buffalo, New York, 1956; admitted to bar, 1982, Connecticut; 1985, U.S. District Court, District of Connecticut; 1990, U.S. Supreme Court. *Education:* Brown University (A.B., 1978); Boston University (J.D., 1981). Author: "The Fiduciary's Role in The Control of Real Estate," BBA Newsletter, Dec. 1996; "The Slow Death of the Succession Tax," BBA, Aug. 1995; "Focus on the Minority Discount" BBA, March 1994, "A Gift in Time Saves Tax, BBA, April 1992, "The Grantor Retained Interest Trust Gains Favor Under the Revenue Reconciliation Act of 1990," BBA, July/Aug. 1991. President, Brown University Club of Fairfield County, 1994-1996. President, Kiwanis Club of Fairfield, 1989-1990, Board of Trustees, Fairfield Public Library, 1998—. *Member:* Greater Bridgeport (Chair, Tax Committee, 1995-1996) and Connecticut Bar Associations. ***PRACTICE AREAS:*** Tax and Estate Planning; Medicaid Planning; Foreclosure and Litigation.

REFERENCES: Lafayette American Bank; Peoples Bank.

ROBERT W. GREEN

FAIRFIELD, CONNECTICUT

(See Stamford)

Real Estate, Probate and Estate, Elder Law, Zoning, Planning and Land Use, Administrative Law, Financial Law and Legislative Practice.

GROGINS & GROGINS

400 STILLSON ROAD
FAIRFIELD, CONNECTICUT 06430
Telephone: 203-335-2112
URL: http://www.lawyers.com/grogins&grogins

Criminal Defense, DWI, Personal Injury Litigation, Automobile Accidents, Slip and Fall Accidents, Family Law, Divorce and Juvenile Law. Civil Litigation.

AUDEN GROGINS, born Bridgeport, Connecticut; February 5, 1962; admitted to bar, 1989, Connecticut; 1990, U.S. District Court, District of Connecticut; 1991, District of Columbia and U.S. Court of Appeals for the District of Columbia Circuit. *Education:* State University of New York (B.S., 1985); University of Bridgeport (J.D., 1989). City Council Member, City of Bridgeport, 1991—. Special Public Defender, handling Part A and Part B division criminal cases in Danbury, Fairfield, and Litchfield Judicial Districts, 1993—. *Member:* Connecticut and American Bar Associations; Connecticut Criminal Defense Lawyers Association (Member, Board of Governors, 1996—). ***PRACTICE AREAS:*** Criminal Law; Personal Injury Law; Foreclosure Law.

DONALD D. HALL

3366 CONGRESS STREET
FAIRFIELD, CONNECTICUT 06430-2030
Telephone: 203-256-9468
URL: http://www.lawyers.com/hallsavarese

General Practice.

DONALD D. HALL, born Milford, Delaware, November 9, 1951; admitted to bar, 1981, Connecticut. *Education:* University of Delaware (B.S., 1973; M.B.A., 1976); University of Connecticut (J.D., 1981). *Member:* Connecticut Bar Association.

LAW OFFICE OF JOHN H. HARRINGTON, ESQ., LLC

527 TUNXIS HILL ROAD
FAIRFIELD, CONNECTICUT 06432
Telephone: 203-331-1881
Fax: 203-330-9252
Email: JHH@johnharrington.net
URL: http://www.johnharrington.net

International Commercial Arbitration; Real Estate, Land Use, Immigration, Probate.

JOHN H. HARRINGTON, born Bridgeport, Connecticut, July 10, 1966; admitted to bar, 1995, Connecticut; 1997, New York. *Education:* Southern Methodist University (B.A., 1988); Defense Language Institute (Diploma, Russian, 1990); Quinnipiac University School of Law (J.D., 1995). Author: "Public International Law, Arms Control and Disarmament," 35 Int'l Law 579 (2001). *Member:* Connecticut and American (Vice Chair, Committee on Arms Control and National Security) Bar Associations; Greater Bridgeport Bar Association. [U.S. Navy Reserve, 1989-1997]. ***LANGUAGES:*** Russian. ***PRACTICE AREAS:*** International Commercial Arbitration; Real Estate; Land Use; Immigration Law; Probate. ***Email:*** JHH@johnharrington.net

HARRINGTON & SMITH, LLP

1809 BLACK ROCK TURNPIKE
FAIRFIELD, CONNECTICUT 06432
Telephone: 203-366-4084
Fax: 203-366-4109
Email: patent@hspatent.com

Patent, Trademark, Copyright.

MARK F. HARRINGTON, born West Islip, New York, September 9, 1960; admitted to bar, 1985, Connecticut; 1986, New York, U.S. District Court, District of Connecticut and U.S. Court of Appeals for the Federal Circuit; registered to practice before U.S. Patent and Trademark Office. *Education:* Virginia Military Institute (B.S., 1982); Pace University (J.D., 1985). *Member:* Connecticut and New York State Bar Associations; Connecticut Patent Law Association. [1st Lt., U.S. Army, 1982-1990]. ***PRACTICE AREAS:*** Patent, Trademark, Copyright. ***Email:*** mharrington@hspatent.com

HARRY F. SMITH, born Granite City, Illinois, March 19, 1949; admitted to bar, 1986, Connecticut and U.S. District Court, District of Connecticut; U.S. Court of Appeals for the Federal Circuit; registered to practice before U.S. Patent and Trademark Office. *Education:* Bridgeport Engineering Institute (B.S.E.E., 1979); University of Bridgeport (J.D., 1985). [With U.S. Navy, 1967-1973]. ***PRACTICE AREAS:*** Patent, Trademark, Copyright Law. ***Email:*** hsmith@hspatent.com

ASSOCIATE

KEVIN P. CORRELL, born Norwich, New York, April 4, 1956; admitted to bar, 1999, Massachusetts (Not admitted in Connecticut). *Education:* University of Hartford (B.S.E.E., 1989; B.A., Physics, 1989); Rogers Williams Law School (J.D., 1998). *Member:* Massachusetts Bar Association. [U.S. Navy, 1975-1981]. ***PRACTICE AREAS:*** Patent, Trademark, Copyright. ***Email:*** kcorrell@hspatent.com

HEAGNEY, LENNON & SLANE LLP

FAIRFIELD, CONNECTICUT

(See Greenwich)

General Practice, Real Estate, Trusts and Estates, Probate, Corporation and Business Law, Civil and Criminal Litigation, Zoning and Family Law.

HOLAHAN, GUMPPER & DOWLING

Established in 1990

1375 KINGS HIGHWAY EAST
P.O. BOX 320177
FAIRFIELD, CONNECTICUT 06432-0177
Telephone: 203-384-1385
Fax: 203-335-3594
Email: hgd.law@hganddlaw.com

General Practice. Real Estate, Land Use, Corporation, Estate Planning and Probate Law. Civil Trials in all Courts. Product Liability, Insurance Law, Environmental Law and Arbitration.

MEMBERS OF FIRM

EDWARD J. HOLAHAN, JR., born Hempstead, New York, June 5, 1936; admitted to bar, 1967, Connecticut and U.S. District Court, District of Connecticut; 1973, U.S. Court of Appeals, Second Circuit. *Education:* Yale University (B.A., 1958); Georgetown University (J.D., 1966). State Attorney Trial Referee, Fact-Finder/Arbitrator, State of Connecticut Superior Court, 1990—. *Member:* Bridgeport (Member, Civil Trials Section), Connecticut (Member, Civil Justice Section) and American (Member, Tort and Insurance Practice Section) Bar Associations; Connecticut Defense Lawyers Association; Defense Research Institute. [Lt., USNR, 1959-1963]. ***REPORTED CASES:*** Bahr v. Prudential Ins. Co. of America, 5 Conn. Cir. Ct. 620, 260 A.2d 422, Cert. Den. 158 Conn. 634 (1969); Jett v. Dunlap, 179 Conn. 215 (1979); Ochs v. Borrelli, 187 Conn. 253 (1982); Matthews v. FMC Corp., 190 Conn. 700 (1983); Ridingsword v. Liberty Mutual Ins. Co., 224 Conn. 8 (1992). ***PRACTICE AREAS:*** Civil Litigation; Products Liability; Insurance; Uninsured and Underinsured Motorists; Arbitration.

(This Listing Continued)

HOLAHAN, GUMPPER & DOWLING, Fairfield—Continued

KEVIN J. GUMPPER, born Bridgeport, Connecticut, September 17, 1950; admitted to bar, 1975, Connecticut; 1980, U.S. District Court, District of Connecticut. *Education:* Yale University (B.A., 1972); University of Connecticut (J.D., with high honors, 1975). Law Clerk to Justice William P. Barber, Supreme Court of Connecticut, 1975-1976. Member, 1983-1989 and Chairman, 1985-1989, Fairfield Zoning Board of Appeals. Member, 1989-1995 and Vice-Chairman, 1994-1995, Fairfield Conservation Commission. Member, 1995— and Chairman, 1997-1999, Fairfield Town Plan and Zoning Commission. *Member:* Fairfield, Bridgeport and Connecticut (Member, Real Estate Section) Bar Associations. ***REPORTED CASES:*** Forsell v. Conservation Commission, 43 Conn. App. 239 (1996). ***PRACTICE AREAS:*** Real Estate; Land Use; Probate; Estate Planning; Appellate Practice; Environmental Law. ***Email:*** kgumpper@hganddlaw.com

MICHAEL A. DOWLING, born Norwalk, Connecticut, August 29, 1953; admitted to bar, 1979, Connecticut; 1980, U.S. District Court, District of Connecticut; 1989, U.S. Court of Appeals, Second Circuit. *Education:* St. Michael's College (B.A., cum laude, 1975); Western New England College (J.D., 1979). Fire Commissioner, 1989-1999 and Chairman, 1993, 1996, Town of Fairfield. *Member:* Bridgeport (Chairman, Civil Trials Section, 1989), Connecticut (Member, Construction Law Section) and American (Member, Litigation Section) Bar Associations; Connecticut Defense Lawyers Association; Defense Research Institute. Certified as a Civil Trial Advocate by the National Board of Trial Advocacy. ***REPORTED CASES:*** Stewart v. Federated Department Stores, Inc., 234 Conn. 597 (1995). ***PRACTICE AREAS:*** Civil Litigation; Products Liability; Premises Liability; Insurance; Arbitration. ***Email:*** mdowling@hganddlaw.com

ASSOCIATES

JOHN M. ROWAN, born Bethpage, New York, October 29, 1971; admitted to bar, 1996, Connecticut; 1997, New York. *Education:* State University of New York at Binghamton (B.A., 1993); Fordham University (J.D., 1996). *Member:* Greater Bridgeport (Member, Young Lawyers Committee, 1997), Connecticut and American Bar Associations; Connecticut Trial Lawyers Association; Connecticut Defense Lawyers Association. ***PRACTICE AREAS:*** Civil Litigation; Insurance Defense; Premises Liability; Products Liability; Personal Injury; Insurance. ***Email:*** jrowan@hganddlaw.com

WILLIAM P. GUMPPER (Retired).

REPRESENTATIVE CLIENTS: Liberty Mutual Insurance Company; General Star Management Company; Trust Insurance Co.; PHICO Insurance Co.; Bic Corp. APPROVED ATTORNEYS FOR: Connecticut Attorneys' Title Insurance Co.; Lawyers Title Insurance Co.; First American Title Insurance Co.

HOLLAND KAUFMANN & BARTELS, LLC

FAIRFIELD, CONNECTICUT

(See Greenwich)

General Practice. Business and Corporate Law, Employment Law, Estate Planning and Probate Law, Family and Matrimonial Law, Litigation, Residential and Commercial Real Estate and Taxation.

HOPPER & HOPPER

FAIRFIELD, CONNECTICUT

(See Greenwich)

Probate and Estate Planning, Wills, Trusts and Real Estate Law.

JACOBS PARTNERS LLC

FAIRFIELD, CONNECTICUT

(See Norwalk)

Business and Personal Bankruptcy, Workouts, Debtor Creditor's Rights, Commercial Litigation, Contracts and Business Disputes.

JEFFERS & IRELAND

PROFESSIONAL CORPORATION

1248 POST ROAD

FAIRFIELD, CONNECTICUT 06430

Telephone: 203-259-7900

Fax: 203-259-1070

Email: firm@jeffire.com

URL: http://www.jeffire.com

General Corporate and Business. Health Care. Employment. Entertainment. Marketing, Advertising and Sales Promotion. E-Commerce. Copyright and Trademark. Commercial Real Estate.

(This Listing Continued)

KAREN A. JEFFERS, born Baltimore, Maryland, September 2, 1954; admitted to bar, 1979, Connecticut and U.S. District Court, District of Connecticut; 1980, U.S. District Court, Southern and Eastern Districts of New York. *Education:* Trinity College (B.A., 1976); Columbia University (J.D., 1979). Phi Beta Kappa. Harlan Fiske Stone Scholar. *Member:* Connecticut (Member, Labor and Employment Law Section) and American (Member, Intellectual Property Law Section) Bar Associations; National Health Lawyers Association; Promotion Marketing Association of America. ***PRACTICE AREAS:*** Corporate; Business; Advertising and Marketing; Health Care; Employment; Copyright and Trademark; Entertainment. ***Email:*** kjeffers@jeffire.com

PAMELA T. IRELAND, born Bridgeport, Connecticut, November 6, 1953; admitted to bar, 1987, Connecticut. *Education:* Wheelock College (B.S., 1975); University of California, Hastings College of the Law (J.D., 1987). Member, 1985-1986 and Note Editor, 1986-1987, Hastings Law Journal. *Member:* Connecticut (Real Property and Sports Entertainment Law Sections) and American (Business and Labor and Employment Law Sections) Bar Associations. ***PRACTICE AREAS:*** Business; Corporate; Employment; E-Commerce; Marketing; Copyright; Trademark; Commercial Real Estate. ***Email:*** pireland@jeffire.com

---

MARGARET A. BARTIROMO, born Brooklyn, New York, March 16, 1963; admitted to bar, 1992, New York; 1997, Connecticut. *Education:* Hunter College (B.A., 1985); Columbia University Graduate School (M.A., 1988); Columbia University (J.D., 1991). Phi Beta Kappa. Mellon Fellowship in the Humanities. ***Email:*** mbartiromo@jeffire.com

TINA PASSALARIS, born Nassau County, New York, August 13, 1968; admitted to bar, 1995, New York; 1998, U.S. District Court, Southern and Eastern Districts of New York; 2000, U.S. District Court, District of Connecticut; 2001, Connecticut. *Education:* Columbia University (B.A., 1990; J.D., 1993). Phi Beta Kappa. ***Email:*** tpassalaris@jeffire.com

REPRESENTATIVE CLIENTS: St. Vincent's Medical Center; Goodwill Industries; Volume Services America; The Sawtooth Group; Fusion 5 Inc.; Tetley USA Inc.; Guinness Bass Import Company; World Wrestling Federation; Louis Vuitton N.A., Inc.; William Raveis Real Estate, Inc.; North Castle Communications, Inc.; Ketchum, Inc.

JONTOS & LOTTY

1212 POST ROAD

P.O. BOX 218

FAIRFIELD, CONNECTICUT 06430

Telephone: 203-259-7009

Fax: 203-254-7780

Email: lottyesq@aol.com

General Litigation, Insurance Defense, Legal, Medical, Dental and Accountant Malpractice, Uninsured Motorist Arbitration, Claims.

MEMBERS OF FIRM

RICHARD A. JONTOS (1935-1995).

ROBERT W. LOTTY, born Bridgeport, Connecticut, September 3, 1946; admitted to bar, 1974, Wisconsin, Connecticut, U.S. District Court, District of Connecticut and U.S. Court of Appeals, Second Circuit. *Education:* University of Connecticut (B.A., 1968); University of Wisconsin (J.D., 1973). *Member:* Connecticut, Federal and American Bar Associations; State Bar of Wisconsin. (Also of Counsel to Lippman & Ouellette, New Haven, Connecticut). ***PRACTICE AREAS:*** Litigation; Legal Malpractice; Medical Malpractice; Dental Malpractice; Accountants Malpractice; Uninsured and Underinsured Motorists Arbitration; Environmental Litigation.

JANE E. HUGO BURWELL, born Worcester, Massachusetts, March 5, 1958; admitted to bar, 1987, Connecticut; 1990, U.S. District Court. District of Connecticut. *Education:* University of Connecticut (B.A., 1980); University of Bridgeport (J.D., 1986). ***PRACTICE AREAS:*** Insurance Defense; Municipal Law; Trial Practice; Appellate Practice.

REPRESENTATIVE CLIENTS: CNA; Gallagher-Bassett; Adjustco, Inc.; Metropolitan Insurance; National Interstate; Safeco Insurance Co.; USAA.

KELLY AND MOONEY

2452 BLACK ROCK TURNPIKE

FAIRFIELD, CONNECTICUT 06432

Telephone: 203-373-7780

Fax: 203-373-6860

Criminal and Civil Litigation including Personal Injury, Insurance Defense and Uninsured Motorist Arbitration.

RAYMOND J. KELLY, born Biloxi, Mississippi, April 24, 1953; admitted to bar, 1981, Connecticut and U.S. District Court, District of Connecticut.

(This Listing Continued)

Education: Fairfield University (B.A., 1975); Quinnipiac College (J.D., 1981). Assistant Public Defender, Danbury, 1981-1983; Bridgeport, 1983-1985. Hearing Officer, Commission on Victim's Services, 1988-1991. Member, Fairfield County Grievance Panel, Judicial Selection Commission, 1998—. Neutral Arbitrator. *Member:* Stamford, Bridgeport, Connecticut and American Bar Associations; Connecticut Trial Lawyers Association; Connecticut Criminal Defense Lawyers Association. ***PRACTICE AREAS:*** Civil Litigation; Criminal Litigation; Personal Injury; Insurance Defense; Uninsured Motorist Arbitration.

JAMES P. MOONEY, born Bridgeport, Connecticut, September 17, 1956; admitted to bar, 1983, Connecticut; 1984, U.S. District Court, District of Connecticut. *Education:* Boston University (B.S., magna cum laude, 1979); Western New England College (J.D., 1983). Phi Alpha Delta. Chairman: Beacon Falls, Connecticut Planning and Zoning Board, 1993-1994; Board of Finance, 1996-1997. *Member:* Connecticut (Member, Federal Litigation Section) and American Bar Associations. ***PRACTICE AREAS:*** Insurance Defense Work; Uninsured Motorist Arbitration; Plaintiff Personal Injury.

KLEBAN & SAMOR, P.C.

FAIRFIELD, CONNECTICUT

(See Southport)

General Practice. Corporation, Federal, State and Foreign Taxation, Relocation, Residential and Commercial Real Estate, Civil Litigation in Federal and State Courts. Negligence, Estate Planning, Probate, Pension and Profit Sharing, Foreclosure, Banking, Regulatory and Financing, Securities, Zoning, Workers Compensation and Public Utilities Law.

LAX & TRUAX, LLC

THE BRICK WALK
1275 POST ROAD, SUITE 200 C
P.O. BOX 336
FAIRFIELD, CONNECTICUT 06430
Telephone: 203-254-9877
Fax: 203-255-6991
Email: slaxax@aol.com

General Practice.

SANDRA P. LAX, born Brooklyn, New York, December 16, 1951; admitted to bar, 1988, Connecticut; 1989, New Jersey, Colorado, Massachusetts, District of Columbia, U.S. District Court, District of Connecticut and U.S. District Court, District of New Jersey. *Education:* Brooklyn College (B.S., 1971); Queens College (M.L.S., cum laude, 1975); University of Bridgeport (J.D., cum laude, 1988). Phi Delta Phi. Associate Editor, University of Bridgeport Law Review, 1987-1988. Author: "Motion Practice in Matrimonial Actions," 1996; "Grandparents Raising Grandchildren: A Legal Guide for Connecticut", 1997. *Member:* Bridgeport and Connecticut (Member, Sections on: Family Law; Elder Law; Chairperson, Bridgeport Bar Association Committee) Bar Associations; National Association of Elder Law Attorneys; Fellow of American Academy of Matrimonial Lawyers. ***LANGUAGES:*** Spanish. ***PRACTICE AREAS:*** Elder Law; Real Estate; Domestic Relations; Matrimonial Law; Family Law. **Email:** slaxax@aol.com

LOUISE T. TRUAX, born Newton, Massachusetts, May 2, 1962; admitted to bar, 1993, Connecticut. *Education:* University of Vermont (B.A., 1984); Sacred Heart University (A.A., 1986); Pace University (J.D., cum laude, 1993). Member, Board of Editors, Connecticut Family Lawyer, 1994—. Author: "Superior Court Highlights," Connecticut Family Lawyer, Vol. 9, pg. 41, Vol. 10, Pg. 47 Volume 12, Pg 6, Vol. 12 Pg. 13; "Deposition Strategies," Family Advocate, Vol. 19, Pg. 24. Contributor: "Law of the Fifty States," Family Law Quarterly, 1997—. *Member:* Westport, Stamford/Norwalk, Connecticut (Member, Executive Committee, Family Law Section, 1995—) and American (Member, Family Law Section) Bar Associations. ***PRACTICE AREAS:*** Domestic Relations Law; Family Law; Matrimonial Law. **Email:** ltraux5291@aol.com

---

DANIEL J. ROBERTS, born Norwalk, Connecticut, November 22, 1974; admitted to bar, 2000, Connecticut. *Education:* University of Connecticut (B.A., magna cum laude, 1996); Quinnipiac School of Law (J.D., 2000). ***PRACTICE AREAS:*** Domestic Relations; Family Law; Matrimonial Law. **Email:** droberts@aol.com

JAMES H. LEE

140 SHERMAN STREET
FAIRFIELD, CONNECTICUT 06430
Telephone: 203-259-4665

Appellate Practice, Civil Practice, General Practice.

(This Listing Continued)

JAMES H. LEE, born Berkeley, California, August 15, 1947; admitted to bar, 1975, Connecticut; 1976, U.S. District Court, District of Connecticut. *Education:* Amherst College (A.B., 1969); Syracuse University College of Law (J.D., cum laude, 1975). Member, Justinian Society. Member: Board of Editors, 1973-1975, Syracuse Law Review; Board of Editors, Connecticut Bar Journal, 1985-1995. Member, Fairfield Board of Education, 1989-1995, 1997—. *Member:* Greater Bridgeport and Connecticut Bar Associations. [With U.S. Army, 1970-1971]. ***LANGUAGES:*** French.

MAHER AND WILLIAMS

268 POST ROAD
P.O. BOX 550
FAIRFIELD, CONNECTICUT 06430
Telephone: 203-255-7777
Fax: 203-254-6611
URL: http://www.lawyers.com/maher&williams

General and Federal Practice. Workers Compensation, Probate, Insurance, Subrogation, Estate Planning and Administrative Law. Trials.

MEMBERS OF FIRM

KEVIN J. MAHER, born Bridgeport, Connecticut, November 21, 1939; admitted to bar, 1964, Connecticut and U.S. District Court, District of Connecticut. *Education:* Berkshire School; Mount St. Mary's College (B.S., 1961); Wake Forest College (J.D., 1964). Phi Alpha Delta. Lecturer: Bridgeport Bar Association, 1992; Danbury Chamber of Commerce, 1992. *Member:* Bridgeport, Connecticut and American Bar Associations. ***PRACTICE AREAS:*** Workers Compensation.

SCOTT WILSON WILLIAMS, born Fullerton, California, March 11, 1958; admitted to bar, 1984, Connecticut; 1985, U.S. District Court, District of Connecticut. *Education:* Wake Forest University (B.A., cum laude, 1981; J.D., 1984). Member, Advisory Board, Workers' Compensation Commission, 1993—. *Member:* Bridgeport, Connecticut and American Bar Associations. ***PRACTICE AREAS:*** Workers Compensation.

MAUREEN E. DRISCOLL, born Bridgeport, Connecticut, August 23, 1965; admitted to bar, 1990, Connecticut and U.S. District Court, District of Connecticut. *Education:* University of Connecticut (B.A. in Political Science, cum laude, 1987); Western New England College School of Law (J.D., 1990). Phi Alpha Delta. *Member:* Bridgeport, Connecticut and American Bar Associations. ***PRACTICE AREAS:*** Workers Compensation.

JAMES L. SULLIVAN, born Jacksonville, Vermont, September 5, 1964; admitted to bar, 1993, Connecticut. *Education:* Deerfield Academy; Middlebury College (B.A., in History, 1986); Vermont Law School (J.D., cum laude, 1993). ***PRACTICE AREAS:*** Workers' Compensation.

JAMES D. MORAN, JR., born Waterbury, Connecticut, February 16, 1966; admitted to bar, 1992, Connecticut; 1993, New York. *Education:* Cornell University (B.A. in Government, with distinction, 1989); Tulane University School of Law (J.D., cum laude, 1992). *Member:* Connecticut and New York State Bar Associations.

COUNSEL FOR: AlliedSignal, Inc.; Atlantic Mutual Cos.; BIC Corp.; CIRMA; CNA Insurance Cos.; Danbury Hospital; Helmsman Management Services, Inc.; Home Insurance Co.; Kemper Insurance Group; Liberty Mutual Insurance Co.; Maryland Casualty Co.; Public Service Mutual Insurance Co.; Risk Enterprise Management Limited; Royal Insurance Co.; The State Insurance Fund of New York; T.J. Maxx Stores, Inc.; Zurich-American Insurance Group.

DAVID M. McHUGH

1261 POST ROAD
FAIRFIELD, CONNECTICUT 06430
Telephone: 203-319-1970
Facsimile: 203-319-0199
Email: d.mchugh@snet.net
URL: http://www.lawyers.com/mchughlaw

Real Estate, Estate Planning, Probate, Trusts and Estates, Personal Injury, Business Law.

DAVID M. McHUGH, born Holyoke, Massachusetts, July 7, 1939; admitted to bar, 1966, Connecticut; 1967, U.S. District Court, District of Connecticut; 1969, U.S. Court of Appeals, Second Circuit and U.S. Supreme Court; 1985, Massachusetts. *Education:* Deerfield Academy, Deerfield, Massachusetts (1957); Fairfield University (B.S.S., 1962); University of Connecticut School of Law (J.D., 1965).

MEYERS BREINER & NEUFELD, L.L.P.

Established in 1986

55 WALLS DRIVE, SUITE 204

FAIRFIELD, CONNECTICUT 06430

Telephone: 203-255-9410

Fax: 203-254-1388

Email: mbnllp@worldnet.att.net

Family, Corporate, Estate Planning, Real Estate, Negligence and Taxation Law.

MICHAEL A. MEYERS, born New York, N.Y., July 2, 1944; admitted to bar, 1969, Connecticut; 1972, U.S. District Court, District of Connecticut; 1974, U.S. Supreme Court and U.S. Tax Court. *Education:* University of Connecticut (B.A., 1966); Boston University (J.D., 1969; LL.M. in Taxation, 1970). Author: "Application of The Corporate Opportunity Doctrine to the Purchase of A Corporations's Stock by Fiduciaries of the Corporation," 50 Connecticut Bar Journal 111, 1976. Law Clerk to the Honorable John P. Cotter, Chief Justice, Connecticut Supreme Court, 1970-1971. Member, State Bar Examining Committee, 1979-1988. *Member:* Bridgeport, The Connecticut and American Bar Associations. Fellow, American Academy of Matrimonial Lawyers (Secretary, 1985; Vice President, 1985-1987; President Elect, 1988-1989; President, 1989-1990, Connecticut Chapter); International Academy of Matrimonial Lawyers (Charter Member).

ALEXANDER BREINER, born Bridgeport, Connecticut, July 24, 1948; admitted to bar, 1973, Connecticut and U.S. District Court, District of Connecticut; 1974, U.S. Tax Court; 1976, U.S. Supreme Court, U.S. Court of Appeals, 2nd Circuit and U.S. Claims Court; 1976-1982, U.S. Court of Customs and Patent Appeals; 1981, U.S. Court of International Trade; 1985, U.S. Court of Appeals for the Federal Circuit. *Education:* The Johns Hopkins University (B.S., 1970); University of Maryland School of Law (J.D., 1973). *Member:* The Connecticut Bar Association (Member, Sections on: Real Property; Planning and Zoning).

MICHAEL A. NEUFELD, born New York, N.Y., July 1, 1949; admitted to bar, 1977, Connecticut, Florida, U.S. District Court, District of Connecticut, U.S. Tax Court and U.S. Claims Court. *Education:* University of Pennsylvania (B.A., 1970); Columbia University (M.B.A., 1972); University of Miami (J.D., cum laude, 1977). Author: "Arithmetic Formula Helps Determine Qualifications For Section 303 Benefits," 6 Estate Planning 205, 1981; "IRS Unwillingness to Follow Davis on Condemnations Deters Rehabs," 55 Journal of Taxation 50, 1981; "When to Avoid or Cut Back on Use of Unlimited Marital Deduction," 10 Taxation for Lawyers 132, 1981; "Until Death or Divorce Do Us Part: Estate Planning for Clients Who Wish To Insulate Their Assets From Their Spouses," 58 Connecticut Bar Journal 267, 1984; "Estate Planning Ramifications of Public Act 86-397: Section 2056 (b)(5) Revisited," 2 Connecticut Probate Law Journal 197, 1987. Co-Author: "Are Grats Still Great," 70 Connecticut Bar Journal 206, 1996. Certified Public Accountant, Connecticut, 1974. Adjunct Professor of Law, Quinnipiac College School of Law, 1985-1996. Member, Advisory Board, Quinnipiac College School of Law, 1995—. *Member:* Bridgeport, The Connecticut (Member, Executive Committee, 1980—and Editor, Tax Letter, 1982-1993, Taxation Section; Member, Estates and Probate Section; Member and Chairman, Liaison with Accountants Committee, 1985-1987) and American (Member, Sections on: Taxation; Real Property, Probate and Trust Law) Bar Associations; The Florida Bar. Fellow, The American College of Trust and Estate Counsel.

REPRESENTATIVE CLIENTS: Antinozzi Associates, Inc.; Main Street Shopping Center; Star Struck, Inc.; J. Silver; Derosier Moving & Storage Co., Inc.
REFERENCES: People's Bank; Putnam Trust Company; Fleet Bank; Hudson United Bank; 1st Union Bank.

O'DONNELL, McDONALD AND CREGEEN, L.L.C.

Established in 1937

Successor to Coles, O'Connell, Dolan & McDonald, P.C.

2452 BLACK ROCK TURNPIKE, SUITE 2

FAIRFIELD, CONNECTICUT 06432

Telephone: 203-374-9700

Fax: 203-374-9772

General Practice. Trials in all Courts. Probate, Real Estate, Zoning and Administrative Law, Environmental.

FIRM PROFILE: O'Donnell, McDonald and Cregeen, L.L.C. is dedicated to serving the people of Fairfield and surrounding counties. The firm is a general practice with an emphasis in civil litigation.

JAMES E. O'DONNELL, born Toledo, Ohio, July 28, 1952; admitted to bar, 1978, Ohio; 1979, U.S. District Court, Northern District of Ohio; 1980, Connecticut and U.S. District Court, District of Connecticut. *Education:* Columbia University (B.A., 1974); The Ohio State University; Boston College (J.D., cum laude, 1978). Director, 1983— and Secretary Treasurer, 1985—, Board of Directors, Bridgeport Public Library. *Member:* Bridgeport (Member, Civil Trials and Procedures Committee), Connecticut (Member, Civil Justice Section) and American (Member, Litigation Section) Bar Associations; The Association of Trial Lawyers of America; Connecticut Trial Lawyers Association. ***PRACTICE AREAS:*** Civil Trials; Real Estate; Probate; General Practice.

MAURA O'DONNELL, born Bridgeport, Connecticut, April 18, 1953; admitted to bar, 1978, Ohio; 1979, U.S. District Court, Northern District of Ohio; 1980, Connecticut and U.S. District Court, District of Connecticut. *Education:* Newton College (B.A., cum laude, 1975); Boston College (J.D., cum laude, 1978). Recipient, Joseph Oteri Award. *Member:* Bridgeport and Connecticut Bar Associations. ***PRACTICE AREAS:*** General Practice; Probate.

DAVID J. McDONALD, born Waterbury, Connecticut, May 6, 1959; admitted to bar, 1985, Connecticut; 1986, U.S. District Court, District of Connecticut; 1988, U.S. Court of Appeals, Second Circuit. *Education:* College of the Holy Cross (B.A., cum laude, 1981); University of Connecticut (J.D., 1985). Director, 1988-1996 and Secretary, 1989-1996, Board of Directors, Cardinal Shehan Center. *Member:* Bridgeport (Member, Trial and Real Estate Committees), Connecticut and American Bar Associations; Connecticut Trial Lawyers Association. ***PRACTICE AREAS:*** Civil Trials; General Practice; Real Estate; Probate.

SHARON A. CREGEEN, born New York, N.Y., May 18, 1960; admitted to bar, 1985, Connecticut; 1986, U.S. District Court, District of Connecticut. *Education:* Allegheny College (B.A., cum laude, 1982); George Washington University (J.D., 1985); Pace University Law School (LL.M., in Environmental Law, 1993). Pi Gamma Mu. Director and Secretary, Pet Animal Welfare Society of Connecticut, 1989-2000. Director and President, PAWS, Inc., 1999-2001. Member, Easton Conservation Commission, 1993-1999. *Member:* Bridgeport, Connecticut (Member, Section on Trial) and American (Member, Sections on: Litigation; Corporate) Bar Associations; Connecticut Trial Lawyers Association. ***PRACTICE AREAS:*** Trusts and Estates; Probate; General Practice; Litigation; Land Use Law.

LEGAL SUPPORT PERSONNEL

SHARON L. FRASER, born Bridgeport, Connecticut, August 16, 1967. *Education:* Roger Williams College (B.S., Paralegal Studies, 1989). Notary Public. Additional studies: "Residential Real Estate," Connecticut Bar Association, Sept. 1996; "Title Searching," Fairfield University, 1997; "Internet Strategies for the Paralegal in Connecticut," Institute for Paralegal Education; "Basic Estate Administration for the Connecticut Paralegal," Institute for Paralegal Education. (Paralegal). ***PRACTICE AREAS:*** Real Estate; Civil Litigation; Probate; Foreclosures; General Practice.

COUNSEL FOR: Bridgeport Roman Catholic Diocesan Corp.; Allstate Insurance Co.; North American Philips Co.; Philips Medical Systems, North America, Inc.; Travelers Insurance Co.; The U.S. Baird Corp; Chevron U.S.A.; Pet Animal Welfare Society.
REFERENCES: Chancery Office, The Bridgeport Roman Catholic Diocesan Corp.

OWENS, SCHINE & NICOLA, P.C.

53 SHERMAN STREET

FAIRFIELD, CONNECTICUT 06430

Telephone: 203-259-6612

Fax: 203-256-8796

Trumbull, Connecticut Office: 799 Silver Lane, P.O. Box 753.
Telephone:203-375-0600. Fax: 203-375-5003.

General Trial Practice in all Courts. Real Estate, Corporate, Probate, Personal Injury, Criminal, Family, Workers Compensation, University, Labor Law, Commercial and Bankruptcy. Administrative Agency Proceedings and Appeals, Environmental, Construction Law, Arbitration and Land Use.

DANIEL F. CARUSO, born Greenwich, Connecticut, December 12, 1957; admitted to bar, 1983, Connecticut; 1984, U.S. District Court, District of Connecticut. *Education:* University of Connecticut (B.A., 1980); Vermont Law School (J.D., 1983). Member, Connecticut Probate Assembly, 1995—. Member, National College of Probate Judge, Fairfield, 1995—. State Representative, 1989-1994. Treasurer, Town of Fairfield, 1993-1995. *Member:* Fairfield, Connecticut (Member, Section of Probate and Trust Law; Superintendent, Probate of Estates, Adoptions and Parental Rights Matters) and American Bar Associations. ***PRACTICE AREAS:*** Trusts and Estates; Real Estate; Small Business Law; General Practice. **Email:** DFC@OSN-PC.com

OF COUNSEL

J. BRIAN FATSE, born Bridgeport, Connecticut, October 22, 1958; admitted to bar, 1988, Connecticut. *Education:* Franklin & Marshall College (B.A., 1980); Western New England College (J.D., cum laude, 1988). Recipient, American Jurisprudence Book Award in Criminal Law. Member, Western New

(This Listing Continued)

England Law Review. Member, Zoning Board of Appeals, Town of Easton, 1989—. Member, Trumbull Town Attorney, 2000—. **PRACTICE AREAS:** Corporate Law; Bankruptcy; Real Estate. **Email:** JBF@OSN-PC.com

JOHN F. FALLON, born White Plains, New York, January 16, 1950; admitted to bar, 1976, Connecticut and U.S. District Court, District of Connecticut. *Education:* Fairfield University (B.A., 1971); Fordham University (J.D., 1976). Member, Board of Education, Town of Fairfield, 1978-1983. Legal Counsel, Connecticut General Assembly: Judiciary Committee, 1979; Senate Majority, 1980. Chairman, Board of Police Commissioners, Town of Fairfield, 1985-1990. Connecticut State Attorney Trial Referee, 1988—. Member, State of Connecticut Judicial Review Council, 1992 —. Member, Trumbull Town Attorney, 2000—. *Member:* Fairfield, Greater Bridgeport, Connecticut (Member, House of Delegates, 1993—) and American Bar Associations. ***PRACTICE AREAS:*** Litigation; Zoning Law; Administrative Law.

REPRESENTATIVE CLIENTS: Fairfield University; St. Luke's School, New Canaan.
REFERENCES: Citicorp Mortgage; Fleet Bank; Chase Manhattan Bank.

(For complete biographical data on all personnel, see Professional Biographies at Trumbull, Connecticut)

PERMAN & GREEN, LLP

425 POST ROAD
FAIRFIELD, CONNECTICUT 06430-6232
Telephone: 203-259-1800
Facsimile: 203-255-5170
Email: pgpatent@aol.com
URL: http://www.pgpatent.com

Patent, Trademark, Copyright and Related Matters.

MEMBERS OF FIRM

MARTEY R. PERMAN (1939-1993).

MANAGING PARTNER

CLARENCE A. GREEN, born Massachusetts, March 14, 1938; admitted to bar, 1966, Massachusetts; 1967, New York; 1982, U.S. Court of Appeals for the Federal Circuit; 1986, U.S. District Court, District of Connecticut; 1987, Connecticut; registered to practice before U.S. Patent and Trademark Office. *Education:* University of Massachusetts (B.S.M.E., 1962); Boston University (J.D., 1965). Member, 1966-1980 and Vice President, 1978-1980, Rochester Patent Law Association. *Member:* New York State, Connecticut and American Bar Associations; The Corporate Bar; American Intellectual Property Law Association; Connecticut Patent Law Association; Licensing Executives Society. ***PRACTICE AREAS:*** Patent, Trademark, Copyright.

ASSOCIATES

DAVID M. WARREN, born Bronx, New York, August 16, 1935; admitted to bar, 1971, Massachusetts; 1972, U.S. Court of Appeals, First Circuit and U.S. District Court, District of Massachusetts; 1979, U.S. Supreme Court; 1982, New York; registered to practice before the U.S. Patent and Trademark Office (Not admitted in Connecticut). *Education:* Massachusetts Institute of Technology (B.S.E.E., 1957); New York University (M.E.E., 1964); Suffolk University (J.D., 1971). *Member:* New York State and American Bar Associations; New York Patent, Trademark and Copyright Law Association; Institute of Electrical and Electronics Engineers. ***PRACTICE AREAS:*** Patent, Trademark, Copyright.

ALBERT W. HILBURGER, born Buffalo, New York, January 1, 1937; admitted to bar, 1962, Virginia; 1964, District of Columbia and U.S. District Court, District of Columbia; 1972, Connecticut and U.S. District Court, District of Connecticut; 1976, U.S. Supreme Court; registered to practice before U.S. Patent and Trademark Office. *Education:* University of Michigan (B.S.M.E., 1958); Georgetown University (LL.B., 1962). Delta Theta Phi. Licensed Professional Engineer: Rhode Island, 1967; Pennsylvania, 1968. Instructor, Business Law I & II, Paralegal Program, Mitchell College, 1975-1981. Connecticut Small Claims Commissioner, 1981-1983; Water and Sewer Commission: East Lyme, Connecticut, 1980-1983; Arbitrator, American Arbitration Association. *Member:* New London County (Chairman, Educational Committee, 1978-1981) and Connecticut (Member, Section on Patent, Trademark & Copyright Law; Chair, Intellectual Property Section, 1987-1988) Bar Associations; National Lawyers Association; Connecticut Patent Law Association (President, 1992-1993); Virginia State Bar; The District of Columbia Bar. ***PRACTICE AREAS:*** Patent, Trademark, Copyright. **Email:** hilpat@ctol.net

THOMAS L. TULLY, born Boston, Massachusetts, January 23, 1933; admitted to bar, 1960, Connecticut; 1962, U.S. District Court, District of Connecticut; registered to practice before U.S. Patent and Trademark Office. *Education:* Boston College (B.S., 1955); Georgetown University (J.D., 1959). Examiner, U.S. Patent and Trademark Office, 1955-1959. *Member:* Connecticut Bar Association; Connecticut Patent Law Association; American Chemical Society. ***PRACTICE AREAS:*** Patent, Trademark, Copyright.

MICHAEL J. TULLY, born Boston, Massachusetts, May 1, 1939; admitted to bar, 1970, Virginia; 1975, Massachusetts; 1976, U.S. Court of Appeals for the Federal Circuit; 1978, U.S. Supreme Court; registered to practice before U.S. Patent and Trademark Office (Not admitted in Connecticut). *Education:* Northeastern University (B.S., 1964); Catholic University (J.D., 1970). Delta Theta Phi. Examiner for the U.S. Patent and Trademark Office, 1966-1970. *Member:* American Bar Association; American Intellectual Property Law Association; Connecticut Patent Law Association; Patent Office Society. ***LANGUAGES:*** German. ***PRACTICE AREAS:*** Patent, Trademark, Copyright.

JOHN J. GOODWIN, born New York, New York, June 5, 1932; admitted to bar, 1960, New York; 1964, U.S. Supreme Court; 1982 U.S. Court of Customs and Patent Appeals and U.S. Court of Appeals for the Federal Circuit (Not admitted in Connecticut). *Education:* Manhattan College (B.S.E.E., 1954); St. John's University Law School (J.D., 1959). *Member :* American Bar Association. ***PRACTICE AREAS:*** Patent, Trademark, Copyright.

RALPH D. GELLING, born Malverne, New York, April 8, 1941; admitted to bar, 1969, New York; 1970, U.S. Court of Appeals, Second Circuit; 1975, Massachusetts; 1982, U.S. Court of Appcals for the Federal Circuit; registered to practice before U.S. Patent and Trademark Office (Not admitted in Connecticut). *Education:* Worcester Polytechnic Institute (B.S.E.E., 1963); St. John's University (J.D., 1969). *Member:* American Intellectual Property Association; Licensing Executives Society; Boston Patent Law Association. ***PRACTICE AREAS:*** Patent, Trademark, Copyright. **Email:** rdgelling@aol.com

THOMAS P. DOWD, born New York, N.Y., July 29, 1933; admitted to bar, 1963, New York; 1968, U.S. District Court, Southern and Eastern Districts of New York; 1979, U.S. Court of Appeals for the Federal Circuit; 1980, U.S. Supreme Court; registered to practice before U.S. Patent and Trademark Office (Not admitted in Connecticut). *Education:* Manhattan College; Fordham College (B.S., 1958); Fordham University (J.D., 1963). Contributor: "Eckstrom's Licensing in Foreign and Domestic Corporations," Clark-Boardman, 1983. Representative, PTO Commissioner's Ad Hoc Advisory Committee, 1980-1985. Commissioner, 1987— and Vice Chairman, 1990—, City of Yonkers Commission on Human Rights. Panel Member, American Arbitration Association, 1979—. *Member:* New York Intellectual Property Law Association; Licensing Executives Society. ***REPORTED CASES:*** Intra v. Hamar-Laser, 4 U.S.P.Q. 2d 337, 1986-Expert Witness. ***PRACTICE AREAS:*** Patent, Trademark, Copyright.

JANIK MARCOVICI, born Iasi, Romania, April 18, 1963; admitted to bar, 1997, Connecticut; 1998, New York. *Education:* Polytechnic Institute of New York (B.S.A.E., with honors, 1985); Quinnipiac College (J.D., cum laude, 1997). Tau Beta Pi; Phi Delta Phi. *Member:* Connecticut Bar Association. ***PRACTICE AREAS:*** Patent, Trademark, Copyright.

DAVID AKER, born Brooklyn, New York, July 4, 1951; admitted to bar, 1982, New York; 1984, U.S. District Court, Eastern District of New York; 1985, U.S. District Court, Southern District of New York; registered to practice before U.S. Patent and Trademark Office (Not admitted in Connecticut). *Education:* Cooper Union (B.S., 1973); State University of New York at Stony Brook (M.S., 1975); St. John's University School of Law (J.D., 1981). Sigma Pi Sigma. Adjunct Professor of Law, Touro College, Jacob D. Fuchsberg Law Center, Huntington, NY, 1983—. With: IBM Corp., 1990-1996; Gottlieb, Rackman & Reisman, P.C., New York, N.Y., 1987-1990. (Chief Patent Counsel, Analytical Instruments). ***PRACTICE AREAS:*** Intellectual Property Matters.

GEZA C. ZIEGLER, JR., born Greenwich, Connecticut, April 21, 1961; admitted to bar, 1994, Connecticut; 1995, New York; 1996, U.S. District Court, Southern and Eastern Districts of New York; 1998, U.S. District Court, District of Connecticut; registered to practice before U.S. Patent and Trademark Office. *Education:* University of Bridgeport (B.S.E.E., 1984); Sacred Heart University (M.B.A., 1990); Quinnipiac College School of Law (J.D., 1994). *Member:* Connecticut Bar Association; Hungarian-American Engineering Society. ***LANGUAGES:*** Hungarian. ***PRACTICE AREAS:*** Patent, Trademark, Copyright.

HENRY I. STECKLER, admitted to bar, 1967, New York; 1979, New Jersey; U.S. Supreme Court; U.S. District Court, District of New Jersey; U.S. District Court, Southern and Eastern Districts of New York; U.S. Court of Appeals for the Federal Circuit; registered to practice before U.S. Patent and Trademark Office (Not admitted in Connecticut). *Education:* Rensselaer Polytechnic Institute (B..S.E.E., 1962); New York University (M.S.E.E., 1963); Brooklyn Law School (J.D., 1967). Patent Attorney, RCA Labs, 1979-1986. Attorney, Lerner, David, Kromholtz & Metlick, 1979. Patent Attorney, U.S. Philips Corp., 1968-1979. Patent Examiner, U.S. Patent Office, 1967-1968. Associate, Eugene Lovette, Esq., 1964. *Member:* New York and New Jersey State Bar Associations. (Patent Counsel). ***PRACTICE AREAS:*** Patent, Trademark, Copyright. **Email:** pgpatent@aol.com

(This Listing Continued)

PERMAN & GREEN, LLP, Fairfield—Continued

OF COUNSEL

DONALD C. CAULFIELD, born East Stroudsburg, Pennsylvania, February 13, 1942; admitted to bar, 1968, District of Columbia; 1969, New Jersey; 1992, Connecticut; registered to practice before U.S. Patent and Trademark Office. *Education:* College of the Holy Cross (B.S., 1963); Boston College (J.D., 1967). Member, Connecticut Patents and Technology Transfer. *Member:* New Jersey State and American (Member, Patent, Trademark and Copyright Section) Bar Associations; The District of Columbia Bar. ***PRACTICE AREAS:*** Patent, Trademark, Copyright.

PAUL WEINSTEIN, born 1940; admitted to bar, 1970, Connecticut; registered to practice before the U.S. Patent and Trademark Office. *Education:* Polytechnic Institute of New York (B.S., 1961; M.S., Metallurgical Engineering, 1965); Georgetown University (J.D., 1969). Former USPTO Patent Examiner. Former Deputy General Counsel for Intellectual Property, Olin Corporation. *Member:* American Bar Association.

QUATRELLA & RIZIO, LLC

ONE POST ROAD
P.O. BOX 320019
FAIRFIELD, CONNECTICUT 06432
Telephone: 203-335-2222; 203-255-9928
Fax: 203-255-6618

General Civil Practice, Real Estate, Commercial, Corporate, Probate, Commercial and Residential Landlord and Tenant, Financial, Partnership and Negligence Law.

MEMBERS OF FIRM

DAVID L. QUATRELLA, born Bridgeport, Connecticut, May 17, 1955; admitted to bar, 1980, Connecticut and U.S. District Court, District of Connecticut; 1981, Pennsylvania and U.S. District Court, Eastern District of Pennsylvania; 1982, New Jersey and U.S. District Court, District of New Jersey. *Education:* Fairfield University (B.A., cum laude, 1977); Villanova University (J.D., 1980). *Member:* Bridgeport, Connecticut and American Bar Associations. ***PRACTICE AREAS:*** Real Estate Law; Business Organizations Law; Banking Law.

RAYMOND RIZIO, born Copenhagen, Denmark, January 11, 1960; admitted to bar, 1985, Connecticut and U.S. District Court, District of Connecticut; 1986, New York. *Education:* Fairfield University; Franklin & Marshall College (B.A., 1982); University of Bridgeport (J.D., 1984). Member, Moot Court Board. Member: Fairfield Conservation Commission, 1987-1988; Fairfield Zoning Board of Appeals, 1987-1991; Trumbull Economic Development Commission, 1992—. *Member:* Bridgeport, Connecticut and New York State Bar Associations; The Association of Trial Lawyers of America.

ASSOCIATES

JAMES P. BLANCHFIELD, born Springfield, Massachusetts, May 7, 1968; admitted to bar, 1996, Connecticut; 1998, U.S. District Court, District of Connecticut. *Education:* University of Connecticut (B.A., 1994); Quinnipiac College School of Law (J.D., cum laude, 1996). Recipient: Excellence in Oral Advocacy Award; Distinguished Academic Achievement Award, 1996. Member, 1994-1995 and Editorial Board, 1995-1996, Quinnipiac Law Review. *Member:* Connecticut and Regional Bar Associations. ***PRACTICE AREAS:*** Litigation.

PETER V. GELDERMAN, born LaCrosse, Wisconsin, June 2, 1954; admitted to bar, 1979, Illinois; 1980, Connecticut; U.S. Court of Appeals, 2nd Circuit. *Education:* University of Connecticut (B.A., 1976); John Marshall Law School (J.D., 1979). Delta Theta Phi. Assistant Town Attorney, Westport, Connecticut, 1980-1985. Town Attorney, Town of Trumbull, Connecticut, 1989-1990. *Member:* Westport, Illinois State, Connecticut and American Bar Associations.

ROBERT G. GOLGER, born Bridgeport, Connecticut, September 13, 1961; admitted to bar, 1987, Connecticut; 1988, U.S. District Court, District of Connecticut; 1989, U.S. Court of Appeals, Second Circuit. *Education:* Northeastern University (B.A., 1983); Suffolk University (J.D., 1987). Law Clerk, Connecticut Superior Court, 1987-1988. *Member:* Connecticut and American Bar Associations; National Association of Criminal Defense Lawyers (Member, Trumbull Board of Finance, 1994—); Connecticut Trial Lawyers Association. ***PRACTICE AREAS:*** Civil Litigation; Criminal Law; Appellate Practice.

SARAMAE KREITLOW, born Iowa City, Iowa, May 9, 1969; admitted to bar, 1998, Connecticut and U.S. District Court, District of Connecticut. *Education:* Quinnipiac College (B.A., 1992; J.D., 1998). Phi Delta Phi. Recipient: Corpus Juris Secondum Award for Scholastic Excellence; Judge Allan J. Nevas Book Award; Academic Excellence Award. *Member:* Connecticut Bar Association; Connecticut Trial Lawyers Association. ***PRACTICE AREAS:*** Civil Litigation.

(This Listing Continued)

KATHERINE M. MACOL, born Bridgeport, Connecticut, April 2, 1968; admitted to bar, 1993, Connecticut. *Education:* Connecticut College (B.A., 1990); Quinnipiac College School of Law (J.D., 1993). *Member:* Bridgeport and Connecticut Bar Associations.

WILLIAM M. PETROCCIO, born Bridgeport, Connecticut, December 7, 1960; admitted to bar, 1985, Connecticut; 1987, U.S. District Court, District of Connecticut; 1988, New York. *Education:* Southern Connecticut State University (B.S., 1982); University of Bridgeport (J.D., 1985). Associate Editor, University of Bridgeport Law Review, 1983-1985. *Member:* Connecticut (Member, Sections on: Real Property; Probate; Corporations and Business Law; Environmental Law), Greater Bridgeport and American Bar Associations. ***PRACTICE AREAS:*** Business Law; Corporate Law; Real Estate; Commercial Law; Banking Law.

APPROVED ATTORNEYS FOR: Lawyers Title Insurance Co.
REFERENCES: Robert D. Russo M.D. & Associates Radiology, P.C.; PNC Mortgage Corp.; Lawyers Title Insurance Corp.; Peoples Bank; The Home Depot, Inc.; International Developers; United Properties; Anthony Julian Railroad Construction Co., Inc.

ROSENSTEIN & BARNES

1100 KINGS HIGHWAY EAST
P.O. BOX 687
FAIRFIELD, CONNECTICUT 06432-5466
Telephone: 203-367-7922
Fax: 203-367-8110
URL: http://www.rosenbar.com
Email: srosenstein@rosenbar.com
URL: http://www.lawyers.com/rosenbar

General Civil and Criminal Practice before State and Federal Courts. Civil Litigation, Employment Litigation, Commercial Litigation and Family Law. Domestic Relations and Child Custody Law, Covenants Not to Compete Litigation, Trials and Appeals.

MEMBERS OF FIRM

SHEILA K. ROSENSTEIN, born Springfield, Massachusetts, September 18, 1946; admitted to bar, 1981, Connecticut. *Education:* Barnard College (A.B., 1968); Columbia University (J.D., 1971). *Member:* Greater Bridgeport, Connecticut and American Bar Associations. ***REPORTED CASES:*** Newman v. Newman, 235 Conn. 82 (1995), rev'g, 35 Conn. App. 449 (1994). ***PRACTICE AREAS:*** Family Law; Domestic Relations; Child Custody; Civil Litigation; Appeals. ***Email:*** srosenstein@rosenbar.com

WILLIAM B. BARNES, born Newport, Rhode Island, November 29, 1952; admitted to bar, 1979, Connecticut. *Education:* Minneapolis College of Art & Design and Grinnell College (B.A., 1974); University of Connecticut (J.D., 1978). Lead Articles Editor, Connecticut Law Review, 1977-1978. Author: "Competence to Plead and the Mentally Retarded Defendant: United States v. Masthers", Connecticut Law Review, Vol. 9, No. 3, 1977. *Member:* Greater Bridgeport and Connecticut Bar Associations; Connecticut Employment Lawyers Association; National Employment Lawyers Association. ***SPECIAL AGENCIES:*** Connecticut Commission on Human Rights & Opportunities, United States Equal Employment Opportunity Commission. ***REPORTED CASES:*** Bridgeport Guardians, Inc. v. City of Bridgeport, 933 F.2d 1140 (2d Cir. 1991); Burger & Burger, Inc. v. Murren, 202 Conn. 660 (1987); Santora v. Miklus, 199 Conn. 179 (1986). ***PRACTICE AREAS:*** Employment; Litigation; Civil Litigation; Covenants Not To Compete Litigation; Appeals. ***Email:*** wbarnes@rosenbar.com

APPROVED ATTORNEYS FOR: Chicago Title Insurance Co.
REFERENCE: Chase Connecticut.

NANDITA P. RUCHANDANI

161 KINGS HIGHWAY EAST, SUITE 212-214
FAIRFIELD, CONNECTICUT 06432-4837
Telephone: 203-576-9211
Fax: 203-576-9158
Email: attynpr@aol.com
URL: http://www.members.aol.com/attynpr/index/html

Immigration Law, International Business Law, International Corporate Law, Leases and Leasing, Landlord and Tenant Law.

NANDITA P. RUCHANDANI, admitted to bar, 1994, Connecticut; 1995, New York; 1997, District of Columbia. *Education:* Barnard College (B.A., 1990); Columbia University (M.A., 1994); George Washington University (J.D., 1994). ***PRACTICE AREAS:*** Immigration Law; International Business Law; International Corporate Law; Leases and Leasing; Landlord and Tenant Law.

RYAN, MASON & LEWIS, LLP

1300 POST ROAD, SUITE 205
FAIRFIELD, CONNECTICUT 06430
Telephone: 203-255-6560
Fax: 203-255-6570
Email: iplaw@rml-law.com

Locust Valley, New York Office: 90 Forest Avenue. Telephone: 516-759-2772. Fax: 516-759-9512.

Intellectual Property Law, including Patent, Trademark, Copyright, Trade Secret, Unfair Competition, Licensing and Related Matters.

(For Complete Biographical data on all personnel, see Professional Biographies at Locust Valley, New York)

SANDAK FRIEDMAN HENNESSEY & GRECO, LLP

FAIRFIELD, CONNECTICUT

(See Stamford)

Trials and Appeals in all Connecticut and Federal Courts and Administrative Agencies. Personal Injury, Medical Malpractice, Commercial, Environmental Litigation, Real Estate, Zoning and Land Use, Property Tax Appeals.

SHUMWAY & SPENCER, LLC

1 POST ROAD
FAIRFIELD, CONNECTICUT 06430
Telephone: 203-255-7444
Facsimile: 203-255-0365

Environmental and Corporate Law.

FIRM PROFILE: Shumway & Spencer concentrates on all aspects of environmental law, including environmental aspects of business transactions. A primary focus of its environmental practice is the defense of waste site cleanup ("Superfund") claims on behalf of industry, municipalities and individuals. The firm also has a substantial corporate practice.

MEMBERS OF FIRM

SUSAN H. SHUMWAY, born Janesville, Wisconsin, January 12, 1950; admitted to bar, 1975, Illinois and U.S. District Court, Northern District of Illinois; 1976, U.S. Court of Appeals, Seventh Circuit; 1986, Connecticut and U.S. District Court, District of Connecticut. *Education:* University of Wisconsin at Madison (B.A., 1972); Boston University (J.D., 1975). *Member:* Connecticut and American Bar Associations. ***PRACTICE AREAS:*** Environmental Law. ***Email:*** SShumway@Compuserve.com

WILLIAM C. SPENCER, born Philadelphia, Pennsylvania, August 27, 1949; admitted to bar, 1974, New York; 1975, New Jersey; 1990, Connecticut; U.S. District Court, Southern District of New York; U.S. District Court, District of Connecticut. *Education:* Ursinus College (B.A., 1971); St. John's University (J.D., 1974). Editorial Advisor, Regulatory Reporter Connecticut; Member, Connecticut Bureau of Waste Management Advisory Committee. Commissioner, Southbury Inland Wetlands and Water Courses Commission. *Member:* Connecticut (Member, Business and Conservation and Environmental Law Sections) and American (Member, Sections on: Natural Resources, Energy and Environmental Law; Business Law; Law, Science and Technology) Bar Associations; The Corporate Bar Association of Westchester and Fairfield. ***PRACTICE AREAS:*** Environmental Law; Corporate Law; Health Care Law.

REPRESENTATIVE CLIENTS: Uniroyal Chemical Company, Inc.; Sequa Corp.; Clayton, Dubilier & Rice; Naugatuck Savings Bank; Zero Corporation; City Chemical Corp.

SILVER, GOLUB & TEITELL LLP

FAIRFIELD, CONNECTICUT

(See Stamford)

Trial Practice in all State and Federal Courts. Medical Malpractice, Negligence, Commercial Litigation, Family and Criminal Law.

JOSEPH H. SWEENEY

1305 POST ROAD, SUITE 206A
FAIRFIELD, CONNECTICUT 06430-0454
Telephone: 203-256-1299

Taxation, Estate Planning, Trusts, Real Estate, IRS Disputes.

(This Listing Continued)

JOSEPH H. SWEENEY, born Buffalo, New York, November 28, 1936; admitted to bar, 1994, Connecticut. *Education:* Canisius College (B.B.A., 1958); Case Western Reserve University (M.B.A., 1959); Pace University (J.D., 1993). Certified Public Accountant, Connecticut and New York. *Member:* Fairfield, Westport, Connecticut and American Bar Associations; American Institute of Certified Public Accountants. ***PRACTICE AREAS:*** Taxation; Aged and Aging; Trusts and Estates; Real Estate.

WAKE, SEE, DIMES & BRYNICZKA

FAIRFIELD, CONNECTICUT

(See Westport)

Business and Corporate Law, Real Estate, Trusts and Probate, Estate Planning, Municipal, Zoning and Land Use Law, Litigation in all Federal and State Courts. Federal, State and Foreign Taxation, Pension and Profit Sharing, and Family Law.

JAMES RICHARD WITTSTEIN

341 MELVILLE AVENUE
FAIRFIELD, CONNECTICUT 06432
Telephone: 203-334-4552
Fax: 203-330-0369
Email: jrwlaw@cshore.com

Nursing Law, Medical Law, Real Estate.

JAMES RICHARD WITTSTEIN, admitted to bar, 1994, New York; 1995, Connecticut. *Education:* Sacred Heart University (B.S.N., 1986); Pace University (J.D., 1994). ***PRACTICE AREAS:*** Nursing Law; Medical Law; Real Estate.

SUSAN E. BRYANT, P.C.

SIX FOREST PARK DRIVE
P.O. BOX 444
FARMINGTON, CONNECTICUT 06032
Telephone: 860-674-0111
Fax: 860-674-0011
Email: sebry@aol.com

Practice includes Securities, Corporate, Commercial Law.

SUSAN E. BRYANT, born Aiea Heights, Hawaii, January 29, 1948; admitted to bar, 1976, Oklahoma; 1985, Nebraska; 1992, New York; 1995, Connecticut. *Education:* Wellesley College (B.A., cum laude, 1970); University of Oklahoma (J.D., 1975). Order of the Coif. Research Editor, Oklahoma Law Review, 1973-1975. Author: "Comments on Reform of the U.S. Financial and Securities Markets, Toledo Transcript," Spring, 1990; "Oklahoma Securities Act - 1984 Amendments," (with P. David Newsome, Jr.) 55 Okla. B.J. 2659, 1984. Presenter: Numerous presentations nationally on securities and compliance issues; Securities Industry Association, "Securities Activities of Insurance Companies," 1997, Orlando, Florida; Institute for International Research "Variable Product Advertising Issues," 1996, Washington, D.C.; Investment Company Institute "NASD Issues," 1994, Washington, D.C.; Fourth Annual New England Securities Conference "Investment Advisers and Investment Companies," 1994, Boston, Massachusetts; National Regulatory Services, "Broker Dealer Arrangements - Variable Insurance Contracts," 1994, New York, New York. Visiting Assistant Professor of Law, University of Oklahoma School of Law, Norman, Oklahoma, 1988. Adjunct Professor of Law, Oklahoma City University School of Law, 1987-1988; Adjunct Professor of Accounting, Oklahoma City University, Meinders School of Business, Oklahoma City, Oklahoma, 1986-1987. *Member:* Oklahoma, New York State, Connecticut and American (Member, State Regulation of Securities Committee, Business Law Section) Bar Associations; North American Securities Administrators Association (President, 1989-1990; Board of Directors, 1990-1991; Chairman, Task Force on Settlement with Drexel Burnham & Lambert, 1989-1991). ***PRACTICE AREAS:*** Securities; Corporate; Broker-Dealer; Investment Adviser; Business Law.

LOIS L. McGUIRE, born Orlando, Florida, March 20, 1957; admitted to bar, 1983, Connecticut; 1984, U.S. District Court, District of Connecticut. *Education:* University of Central Florida (B.A., cum laude, 1980); University of Connecticut School of Law (J.D., 1983). Formerly: Compliance and Regulatory Counsel, Aetna Life Insurance Company, 1983-1991; General Practice Litigation, 1991-1998. ***PRACTICE AREAS:*** Securities; Corporate Law; Broker-Dealer Arbitration; Investment Management; Business Law.

A list of Representative Clients will be furnished upon request.

FELDMAN & HICKEY, LLC

10 WATERSIDE DRIVE, SUITE 303
FARMINGTON, CONNECTICUT 06032
Telephone: 860-677-0551
Email: michaelfeldman@feldmanhickey.com

FIRM PROFILE: Mr. Feldman is Board Certified in Civil Trial Practice by the National Board of Trial Advocacy. The firm practices in Civil, Insurance, Commercial and Personal Injury Litigation.

MICHAEL FELDMAN, born Queens, New York, December 12, 1954; admitted to bar, 1981, Connecticut and U.S. District Court, District of Connecticut; 1982, New York and U.S. Court of Appeals, Second Circuit. *Education:* State University of New York (B.A., with honors, 1978); Benjamin Cardozo School of Law (J.D., cum laude, 1981). Member, 1979-1980 and Associate Editor, 1980-1981, Cardozo Law Review. Author: "Survey of the Literature: Commercial Speech and Commercial Speakers," Cardozo Law Review, Vol. 2, Issue 3, Spring, 1981. *Member:* Connecticut Bar Association. (Board Certified Civil Trial Specialist by the National Board of Trial Advocacy). **Email:** michaelfeldman@feldmanhickey.com

CHARLES E. NED HICKEY, born New London, Connecticut, September 14, 1953; admitted to bar, 1990, Connecticut; 1991, U.S. District Court, District of Connecticut. *Education:* Merrimack College (B.A., cum laude, 1976); Washington Theological Union (M.A., 1982); University of Connecticut (J.D., with honors, 1990). Notes and Comments Editor, Connecticut Journal of International Law, 1989-1990. Law Clerk to the Honorable Judge John J. Daly, Appellate Court of Connecticut, 1990-1991. Member, 1993—and Chairman, 1998—, Finance Board, Town of Marlborough. *Member:* Connecticut Bar Association. **Email:** nedhicky@feldmanhickey.com

KRISTEN SCHULTZE GREENE, born Dover, New Hampshire, January 9, 1971; admitted to bar, 1996, Connecticut; 1998, U.S. District Court, District of Connecticut. *Education:* University of New Hampshire (B.A., cum laude, 1993); Western New England College School of Law (J.D., cum laude, 1996). Recipient, CALI Excellence for Future Award, 1996. *Member:* Connecticut Bar Association. **Email:** kristengreene@feldmanhickey.com

---

GREEN & LEVINE LLP

231 FARMINGTON AVENUE
FARMINGTON, CONNECTICUT 06032
Telephone: 860-677-7004
Facsimile: 860-677-7005
URL: http://www.lawyers.com/g&llaw

Commercial and Residential Real Estate, Zoning, Development, Finance, Corporate Workouts and Foreclosures, Commercial Leasing, Business Law.

LOUIS F. GREEN, born Hartford, Connecticut, October 25, 1942; admitted to bar, 1968, Connecticut. *Education:* University of Connecticut (B.A., 1964; LL.B., 1968). *Member:* Hartford County, Connecticut (Member, Real Estate, Commercial Law and Bankruptcy Sections), American (Member, Sections on: Real Property, Probate and Trust Law; Committee on Foreclosure and Related Remedies and Committee on Commercial Leasing; Corporation, Banking and Business Law and Foreclosure Procedure) and International (Member, Sections on: Business Law; General Practice) Bar Associations. **PRACTICE AREAS:** Entrepreneurial Business Law; Corporate Law; Commercial Real Estate; Real Estate Development; Real Estate Acquisitions; Real Estate Finance; Loan Workouts; Foreclosures; Commercial Leasing; Probate; Estate Planning. **Email:** lfg101@aol.com

TAMARA KAGAN LEVINE, born Hartford, Connecticut, June 18, 1956; admitted to bar, 1981, Connecticut and U.S. District Court, District of Connecticut. *Education:* Connecticut College (B.A., cum laude, 1978); University of Connecticut (J.D., 1981). *Member:* Hartford County, Connecticut and American (Member, Real Property, Probate and Trust Law Section) Bar Associations. **PRACTICE AREAS:** Commercial Real Estate; Real Estate Development; Real Estate Finance; Commercial Leasing; Affordable Housing; Entrepreneurial Business Law; Real Estate Acquisitions; Zoning Law; Probate; Estate Planning. **Email:** tkl618@aol.com

OF COUNSEL

EUGENE M. KAGAN, born Hartford, Connecticut, July 9, 1930; admitted to bar, 1956, Connecticut. *Education:* University of Connecticut (B.A., 1953; LL.B., 1956). Trustee, University of Connecticut, School of Law Foundation, Inc., 1981-1982. *Member:* Hartford County, Connecticut and American Bar Associations. **PRACTICE AREAS:** Commercial Real Estate; Real Estate Development. **Email:** yichiel@aol.com

LEVY & DRONEY, P.C.

POND VIEW CORPORATE CENTER
74 BATTERSON PARK ROAD
P.O. BOX 887
FARMINGTON, CONNECTICUT 06034-0887
Telephone: 860-676-3000
Telecopier Ext: 860-676-3200
Email: ldlaw.com
URL: http://www.ldlaw.com

Administrative Law, Banking, Business Law, Civil and Criminal Litigation in State and Federal Courts, Condominiums, Construction, Corporate, Environmental Law, Estate Planning, Family Law, Foreclosures, Health Care, Labor and Employment, Mergers and Acquisitions, Municipal, Personal Injury and Insurance Defense Law, Practice Before Federal and State Agencies and Commissions, Probate, Public Finance, Real Estate, Secured and Unsecured Commercial Transactions, Securities, Taxation, Title Insurance Litigation, Zoning.

COLEMAN B. LEVY, born New Haven, Connecticut, May 9, 1939; admitted to bar, 1966, Connecticut and U.S. District Court for Connecticut; 1967, U.S. District Court for Southern District of New York; U.S. Court of Appeals, Second Circuit; 1976, U.S. Supreme Court. *Education:* University of Connecticut (B.A., 1961; M.A., 1962; J.D., 1966). Director, Hartford County Bar Association (Member, Executive Committee for Real Estate Section, 1983-1987). *Member:* Connecticut (Member, Executive Committee For: Corporations and other Business Entities, 1980-1990; Planning and Zoning, 1980-1988) and American Bar Associations. **PRACTICE AREAS:** Real Estate; Corporation; Business; Finance; Mergers and Acquisitions. **Email:** clevy@ldlaw.com

JOHN F. DRONEY, JR., born Hartford, Connecticut, October 8, 1946; admitted to bar, 1973, Connecticut; 1974, U.S. District Court, District of Connecticut and U.S. Court of Appeals, Second Circuit. *Education:* College of the Holy Cross (A.B., 1968); University of Connecticut (J.D., cum laude, 1973). Member, Board of Editors, University of Connecticut Law Review, 1972-1973. Author: "The Specter of State Action in Self Help Repossession," Vol. 5 No. 2 University of Connecticut Law Review, 1972. Recipient, University of Connecticut School of Law Distinguished Alumni Award, 1989. Member, 1974-1977 and Vice Chairman, 1976-1977, Board of Special Assessments, West Hartford. State of Connecticut Public Health Council, 1977-1979. Special States Attorney, Special Assistant Attorney General. Member, Town Council, West Hartford, Connecticut, 1977-1981. *Member:* Hartford, Connecticut and American Bar Associations; The Association of Trial Lawyers of America; Federal Bar Council; Connecticut Trial Lawyers Association; National Association of Criminal Defense Lawyers; James W. Cooper Fellow of The Connecticut Bar Foundation. **PRACTICE AREAS:** Litigation. **Email:** jdroney@ldlaw.com

JOEL MANDELL, born Hartford, Connecticut, July 1, 1939; admitted to bar, 1966, Connecticut; 1967, U.S. District Court, District of Connecticut; 1971, U.S. Supreme Court. *Education:* University of Connecticut (B.A., 1961; J.D., 1966). Marquis' Who's Who in American Law, 1990-2001. Member, Charter Revision Commission, Simsbury (1990-1992). Member, Simsbury Housing Authority, (1992-1993). Selectman, Town of Simsbury, (1993—; Deputy First Selectman, 1999—). Member, State of Connecticut Title Insurance Task Force, 1989-1990. Member of Panel, American Arbitration Association. *Member:* Hartford County, Connecticut (Member: House of Delegates, 1983-1986; Executive Committee, Real Property Section, 1978—, Chairman, 1995-1997) and American Bar Associations; New England Land Title Association (Member, Board of Directors, 1996—). [Capt., U.S. Army, 1961-1963]. **PRACTICE AREAS:** Commercial Real Estate Law; Conveyancing Law; Finance Law; Title Insurance Law. **Email:** jmandell@ldlaw.com

DANE R. KOSTIN, born Hartford, Connecticut, July 16, 1947; admitted to bar, 1972, Connecticut; 1973, U.S. District Court for Connecticut; 1975, U.S. Court of Appeals, Second Circuit; 1976, U.S. Supreme Court. *Education:* Wharton School, University of Pennsylvania (B.S., 1969); Boston University (J.D., 1972). Beta Alpha Psi. Member, Boston University Law Review, 1970-1972. Author: "The Definition of Competition under the Robinson-Patman Act," Vol. 51, Boston University Law Review 54. Member, Advisory Committee to the Banking Commissioner on the Connecticut Uniform Securities Act, 1983-1997. *Member:* Hartford County, Connecticut and American Bar Associations. [Capt., USAR, 1969-1977]. **PRACTICE AREAS:** Securities Law; Business Planning Law; Franchise Law; Corporate Law; Commercial Law; Mergers and Acquisitions. **Email:** dkostin@ldlaw.com

MARVIN H. LAPUK, born Hartford, Connecticut, March 27, 1931; admitted to bar, 1960, Connecticut and U.S. District Court, District of Connecticut. *Education:* University of Connecticut (B.S., 1953; J.D., 1960). Co-author: "Accounting for an Account," 56 Connecticut Bar Journal 469, December, 1982. Member, 1973—, Membership Chairman, 1981-1982 and Member, Board of Directors, 1987-1988, Estate and Business Planning Council of Hartford. *Member:* Hartford (Co-Chairman, Budget Committee, 1974-1999), Connecticut (Member, Sections on: Taxation and Estates; Probate Law) and American (Member, Sections on: Taxation; Real Property, Probate and Trust Law) Bar

(This Listing Continued)

Associations; American Association of Attorney-Certified Public Accountants; Connecticut Society of Certified Public Accountants. [Lt., U.S. Army, 1953-1955]. ***PRACTICE AREAS:*** Estate Planning Law; Business Planning Law; Estate Administration Law. ***Email:*** mlapuk@ldlaw.com

JOHN ROSE, JR., born Falmouth, Massachusetts, September 26, 1940; admitted to bar, 1966, Connecticut; 1967, U.S. District Court, District of Connecticut; 1973, U.S. Supreme Court; 1993, U.S. District Court, Southern District of New York; 1996, U.S. Court of Appeals, Second Circuit. *Education:* Dartmouth College (A.B., 1963); Yale Law School (LL.B., 1966). Assistant Chief Prosecutor, Connecticut Circuit Courts, 1967-1968. Special Master, U.S. District Court, Connecticut, 1984—. Commissioner, Connecticut Human Rights and Opportunities Commission, 1988-1990. Member, Judicial Selection Commission, State of Connecticut, 1994-1996. Chair, Joint Task Force on Equal Access to Justice, 1999—. Member, Editorial Board, Connecticut Law Tribune, 1999—; State Commission of Racial and Ethic Disparity in the Criminal Justice System, 2000—. *Member:* Hartford County (Co-Chair, CLE Committee), Connecticut (Member: Lawyer to Lawyer Dispute Resolution Program; Executive Committee, Construction Law Section; Chair, Federal Judiciary Committee; Member, State Commission on Racial and Ethnic Disparity in the Criminal Justice System) and American Bar Associations; National Bar Association; Connecticut Trial Lawyers Association. ***PRACTICE AREAS:*** Commercial Law; Construction Litigation; Employment Litigation. ***Email:*** jrose@ldlaw.com

DANIEL E. KLEINMAN, born Hartford, Connecticut, November 8, 1944; admitted to bar, 1969, Connecticut; 1970, U.S. District Court, District of Connecticut; 1971, U.S. Court of Appeals, 2nd Circuit; 1973, U.S. Supreme Court. *Education:* Harvard College (A.B., 1966); Boston College (J.D., 1969). Chairman, Governor's Advisory Council. Hartford Regional Center, 1973-1977. Member of Faculty, National Association of Mutual Savings Banks, Consumer Credit Seminar, Advanced Mortgage School, 1975-1977. President, Beth El Temple of West Hartford, 1995-1997. *Member:* Hartford County, Connecticut (Member, Executive Committee, Commercial Law and Bankruptcy Section, 1979-1986; Member, Executive Committee, Planning and Zoning Section, 1990—; Member, Executive Committee Sports and Entertainment Law Section, 1995—) and American (Member, Real Property Section) Bar Associations. [Lt., Connecticut Air National Guard, 1969-1975]. ***PRACTICE AREAS:*** Land Use Law; Real Estate Law; Banking Law; Finance Law; Sports Law. ***Email:*** dkleinman@ldlaw.com

JOMARIE T. ANDREWS, born Providence, Rhode Island, August 6, 1954; admitted to bar, 1979, Connecticut and U.S. District Court, District of Connecticut. *Education:* Colgate University (B.A., 1976); University of Connecticut (J.D., 1979). *Member:* Hartford County, Connecticut (Member, Real Property Section) and American (Member, Real Property Section) Bar Associations; Real Estate Exchange. ***PRACTICE AREAS:*** Commercial Real Estate Law; Real Estate Development Law; Conveyancing Law; Financing Law; Leasing Law. ***Email:*** jandrews@ldlaw.com

JEFFREY J. MIRMAN, born Hartford, Connecticut, July 6, 1953; admitted to bar, 1978, District of Columbia; 1979, Connecticut, U.S. District Court for the District of Columbia and U.S. Court of Appeals for the District of Columbia Circuit; 1980, U.S. District Court, District of Connecticut; 1984, U.S. Court of Appeals, Second Circuit; 1992, U.S. Supreme Court; 2001, U.S. Court of Appeals, Eleventh Circuit. *Education:* Johns Hopkins University (B.A., with honors, 1975); George Washington University (J.D., 1978). Pi Sigma Alpha; Omicron Delta Kappa. *Member:* The District of Columbia Bar; Hartford County, Connecticut (Member, Labor and Employment Section) and American (Member: Labor and Employment Law Section; Antitrust Law Section) Bar Associations. ***REPORTED CASES:*** Abington Limited Partnership v. Heublein, 246 Conn. 815 (1998); Metropolitan Entertainment Co. v. Koplik, 20 F.Supp.2d 354 (D.Conn. 1998); Med-Trans of Connecticut, Inc. v. Department of Pub. Health & Addition Services, 242 Conn. 152 (1997); Levy v. Commission On Human Rights & Opportunities (1996); West Hartford Interfaith Coalition v. Town of West Hartford, 228 Conn. 498 (1994); West Farms v. State Traffic Comm'n, 951 F.2d 469 (2nd Cir. 1991), cert. denied, 112 S.Ct. 1671; Cohen v. Security Title & Guaranty Company, 212 Conn. 436 (1989); Nicotra Wieler Inv. Management, Inc v. Grower, 207 Conn. 441 (1988); Luciani v. The Stop & Shop Companies, 15 Conn. App. 407, cert. denied, 209 Conn. 809 (1988); Hamilton v. Smith, 773 F.2d 461 (2nd Cir. 1985). ***PRACTICE AREAS:*** Litigation. ***Email:*** jmirman@ldlaw.com

ROBIN MESSIER PEARSON, born New York, N.Y., May 26, 1951; admitted to bar, 1980, Connecticut and U.S. District Court, District of Connecticut. *Education:* Trinity College (B.A., with honors, 1973); University of Connecticut (J.D., 1980). Editor, Connecticut Real Estate Law Journal, 1991-1994. *Member:* Hartford County, Connecticut (Member: Executive Committee, Young Lawyers Division, 1981-1987; President, Hartford Young Lawyer Division, 1983-1985; House of Delegates, 1984-1986; Executive Committee, Planning and Zoning Section, 1985—; Section Chairperson, 1991-1994) and American (District Representative to National Executive Council of the Young Lawyers Division, 1985-1987) Bar Associations; Real Estate Exchange (Member, Executive Committee, 1991-1997; President, 1995-1996). ***PRACTICE AREAS:*** Land Use and Environmental Law. ***Email:*** rpearson@ldlaw.com

JOSEPH A. VITALE, born New Haven, Connecticut, June 2, 1956; admitted to bar, 1981, Connecticut; 1983, U.S. District Court, District of Connecticut. *Education:* Boston College (A.B., summa cum laude, 1978); Georgetown University (J.D., 1981). *Member:* Connecticut and American Bar Associations; American Health Lawyers Association; National Association of Bond Lawyers. ***PRACTICE AREAS:*** Health Care Law; Municipal and Public Finance Law. ***Email:*** jvitale@ldlaw.com

RICHARD T. KEPPELMAN, born Buffalo, New York, January 17, 1943; admitted to bar, 1972, New York; 1974, U.S. District Court, Southern District of New York; 1978, Connecticut; 1980, U.S. District Court, District of Connecticut. *Education:* Yale University (B.A., 1968); Columbia University (J.D., 1971). Harlan Fiske Stone Scholar. *Member:* The Association of the Bar of the City of New York; Hartford County, Connecticut (Member: Executive Committee, 1984—; Business Law Section; Commercial Law Section) and American (Member, Sections on Business Law and Tax Law) Bar Associations. ***PRACTICE AREAS:*** Corporate Law; Securities Law; Commercial Finance Law; Mergers and Acquisitions; Health Care Law. ***Email:*** rkeppel@ldlaw.com

WILLIAM C. STOKESBURY, born Derby, Connecticut, April 25, 1959; admitted to bar, 1984, Connecticut; 1985, U.S. District Court, District of Connecticut. *Education:* Yale University (B.A., 1981); Boston University (J.D., 1984). Editor, Connecticut Real Estate Law Journal, 1994-1997. *Member:* Hartford County (Co-Chairman, Real Property/Transactions Committee), Connecticut (Executive Committee, Real Property Section) and American Bar Associations. ***PRACTICE AREAS:*** Real Estate Law; Conveyancing Law; Financing Law; Leasing Law. ***Email:*** wstokesb@ldlaw.com

ROBERT B. LEVINE, born Brooklyn, New York, November 11, 1960; admitted to bar, 1985, Massachusetts; 1986, Connecticut; 1989, U.S. District Court, District of Connecticut. *Education:* Connecticut College (B.A., 1982); Suffolk University (J.D., 1985); Boston University (LL.M., 1986). Recipient: Massachusetts Society of Certified Public Accountants Certificate of Achievement (For Passing CPA Exam at First Sitting). *Member:* Hartford County, Connecticut and American Bar Associations. ***PRACTICE AREAS:*** Estate Planning; Estate Administration; Business Reorganization; Succession Planning. ***Email:*** rlevine@ldlaw.com

DAVID M. SHERIDAN, born Monterey, California, May 16, 1955; admitted to bar, 1985, Connecticut; U.S. District Court, District of Connecticut; U.S. Court of Appeals, Second Circuit. *Education:* U.S. Naval Academy; University of Arizona (B.S., 1981); University of Connecticut (J.D., 1985). Special Master, U.S. District Court for the District of Connecticut. *Member:* Hartford County, Connecticut (Member, Committee on Professional Responsibility and Ethics) and American Bar Associations; The Association of Trial Lawyers of America; Connecticut Trial Lawyers Association; Federal Bar Association; Association of Professional Responsibility Lawyers. ***PRACTICE AREAS:*** Litigation. ***Email:*** dsheridan@ldlaw.com

ROSS G. FINGOLD, born Brooklyn, New York, July 27, 1956; admitted to bar, 1981, Connecticut and U.S. District Court, District of Connecticut. *Education:* University of Pennsylvania (B.A., cum laude, 1978); Syracuse University (J.D., cum laude, 1981). Partner, Schatz & Schatz, Ribicoff & Kotkin, Hartford, Connecticut, 1981-1996. *Member:* Connecticut and American Bar Associations; The Association of Trial Lawyers of America. ***PRACTICE AREAS:*** Commercial and Financial Litigation; Commercial Finance; Asset Based Finance; Real Estate Litigation; Loan Workouts and Restructuring; Commercial and Residential Foreclosures; Lender Liability Defense; Bankruptcy and Insolvency. ***Email:*** rfingold@ldlaw.com

LAWRENCE J. MARKS, born Newark, New Jersey, February 9, 1965; admitted to bar, 1990, Connecticut. *Education:* Trinity College (B.A., with high honors in History, 1987); New York University (J.D., 1990; LL.M. in Taxation, 1991). Phi Beta Kappa. *Member:* Connecticut (Member, Section on Taxation) and American (Member, Tax Law Section) Bar Associations; National Association of Bond Lawyers. ***PRACTICE AREAS:*** Federal and State Taxation; Pension, Profit Sharing and Employee Benefits Law; Municipal and Public Finance Law; Limited Liability Company Law. ***Email:*** lmarks@ldlaw.com

KENNETH J. LEVINE, born New York, New York, January 23, 1965; admitted to bar, 1990, Connecticut and New York; 1991, U.S. District Court, District of Connecticut and Eastern District of New York. *Education:* Union College (B.S., 1987); Emory University (J.D., 1990). *Member:* Hartford County, New York State, Connecticut (Executive Committee, Workers Compensation Section; Editor, Compensation Quarterly Magazine) and American Bar Associations; Connecticut Trial Lawyers Association (Membership and Young Lawyers Committees); Association of Trial Lawyers of America. ***PRACTICE AREAS:*** Civil Litigation; Criminal Litigation; Personal Injury; Workers Compensation; Family Law. ***Email:*** klevine@ldlaw.com

C. ROBERT ZELINGER, born Stockholm, Sweden, December 2, 1955; admitted to bar, 1986, Connecticut and U.S. District Court, District of Connecticut. *Education:* Trinity College (B.A., 1977; M.A., 1985); University of

(This Listing Continued)

LEVY & DRONEY, P.C., Farmington—Continued

Connecticut (J.D., with honors, 1985). *Member:* Connecticut and American Bar Associations. ***PRACTICE AREAS:*** Business Law; Mergers and Acquisitions; Information Technology. ***Email:*** crzeling@ldlaw.com

---

LISA A. ZACCARDELLI, born Hartford, Connecticut, June 8, 1965; admitted to bar, 1990, Connecticut; 1991, U.S. District Court, District of Connecticut. *Education:* Boston College (B.A., magna cum laude, 1987); St. John University (J.D., 1990). Board Member, Moot Court Program. *Member:* Hartford County, Connecticut and American Bar Associations. ***PRACTICE AREAS:*** Litigation. ***Email:*** lzaccard@ldlaw.com

JOSEPH B. SAPPINGTON, born Baltimore, Maryland, June 26, 1972; admitted to bar, 1999, Connecticut and U.S. District Court, District of Connecticut. *Education:* Loyola College (B.A., 1995); Vermont Law School (J.D. and M.S.E.L., 1998). *Member:* Hartford County, Connecticut and American Bar Associations. ***PRACTICE AREAS:*** Environmental Law; Civil Litigation. ***Email:*** jsapping@ldlaw.com

GEORGE A. BAKER, born Putnam, Connecticut, October 7, 1964; admitted to bar, 1989, Connecticut. *Education:* Eastern Connecticut State University (B.S., 1986); Western New England College School of Law (J.D., 1989). Probate Judge Tolland Probate Court, 1995-1998. *Member:* Hartford County and American Bar Associations. ***PRACTICE AREAS:*** Estate Planning; Estate Administration; Business Planning. ***Email:*** gbaker@ldlaw.com

JASON W. COHEN, born Brooklyn, New York, June 9, 1970; admitted to bar, 1995, Connecticut; 1996, U.S. District Court, District of Connecticut. *Education:* Bates College (B.A., cum laude, 1992); Suffolk University (J.D., cum laude, 1995). *Member:* Connecticut (Member, Executive Committees, Sections on Labor and Employment Law; Litigation and Young Lawyers) and American (Member, Labor and Employment Law Section) Bar Associations; American Red Cross Volunteer Services Committee. ***PRACTICE AREAS:*** Civil Litigation; Labor and Employment Law; Municipal Law; Workers' Compensation; Unemployment Compensation. ***Email:*** jcohen@ldlaw.com

COUNSEL

WILLIAM R. BREETZ, born Bridgeport, Connecticut, July 4, 1941; admitted to bar, 1968, Connecticut. *Education:* Dartmouth College (B.A., 1963); University of Virginia (LL.B., 1968). Phi Alpha Delta. Assistant Professor of Law, University of Connecticut, 1970-1972. Member, 1977— and Chairman, 1980-1984, Connecticut Law Revision Commission. Chair, Connecticut Law Revision Study Group on Mortgage Law, 1991. Commissioner, National Conference of Commissioners on Uniform State Laws, 1991—. Reporter, National Conference of Commissioners on Uniform State Laws for Uniform Condominium Act, Uniform Common Interest Ownership Act, 1976-1982. Member, NCCUSL/ABA, Joint Editorial Board on Real Property Acts, 1992—. *Member:* Hartford County, Connecticut and American Bar Associations; American College of Real Estate Lawyers. ***PRACTICE AREAS:*** Real Estate Law; Finance Law; Energy Law. ***Email:*** wbreetz@law.uconn.edu

ROBERT B. COHEN, born Scranton, Pennsylvania, February 13, 1933; admitted to bar, 1957, Connecticut; U.S. District Court, District of Connecticut; 1958, U.S. Court of Appeals, 2nd Circuit; 1974, U.S. Supreme Court 1984, U.S. Tax Court. *Education:* Dickinson College (A.B., 1954); University of Pennsylvania (LL.B., 1957). Contributor and Author, Connecticut Section, Directory of State Environmental Agencies. Contributor, Connecticut Section, Foundational Requirements for Admissibility of Expert Testimony, 1992, DRI. Lecturer, "Environmental Implications of Business Transfers." Member: Who's Who in American Law; Who's Who in Connecticut. Arbitrator, Construction Industry, American Arbitration Association. Former, Chairman and Member, Zoning Board of Appeals, West Hartford, Connecticut. Member, Defense Research Institute. *Member:* Hartford County, Connecticut (Member, Committee on: Conservation and Environmental Quality) and American Bar Associations; Connecticut Trial Lawyers Association; The Association of Trial Lawyers of America. ***REPORTED CASES:*** Yandow vs. City of Bristol, 145 C 703 146 A2D 409; DeLucco vs. Mott's SuperMarkets, Inc. 158 C 615 259 A2D 646; Truck & Trailer Service Company, et al, 169 C 407 363 A2D 86; Emerick vs. Monaco & Sons, 145 C 101 139 A2D 156. ***PRACTICE AREAS:*** Environmental Law; Litigation. ***Email:*** rcohen@ldlaw.com

HOWARD I. GROSS, born Hartford, Connecticut, May 6, 1923; admitted to bar, 1951, Connecticut; 1956, U.S. Supreme Court; 1952, U.S. District Court, District of Connecticut; 1961, U.S. Court of Appeals, Second Circuit. *Education:* University of Connecticut (B.A., 1948; J.D., 1951). Co-Author: "The Individual Trustee's Guide," Tower Publishers, 1999. Corporation Counsel, Town of Marlborough, Connecticut, 1955-1965. President, Estate and Business Planning Council of Hartford, 1975-1976. Attorney State Trial Referee, 1984-1988. Member, Panel of Arbitrators, American Arbitration Association. *Member:* Hartford County, Connecticut (Secretary, 1989-1990; Treasurer, 1988-1989; Member: Board of Governors, 1981-1990; House of Delegates, 1980-1988; Professional Ethics Committee, 1976-1997; Professional Discipline Committee, 1994-1997; Clients Security Fund, 1980-1982) and American (Member, Section on: General Practice) Bar Associations; National Association of Bond Lawyers. [Lt. U.S. Army, 1942-1946]. ***PRACTICE AREAS:*** Business Planning; Estate Planning; Asset Protection. ***Email:*** hgross@ldlaw.com

R. BARTLEY HALLORAN, born Stamford, Connecticut, August 23, 1950; admitted to bar, 1975, Connecticut. *Education:* Georgetown University (B.A., 1972); University of Connecticut (J.D., 1975). Lecturer: No Fault, 1989, Basic Advocacy, 1990-1991, Class Actions, 1992 and Automobile Litigation, 1995, 1996, Connecticut Trial Lawyers Association. Member, 1998 and Chairman, 1999—, Capitol City Economic Development Authority. *Member:* Hartford County, Connecticut (Member, Civil Justice Section) and American Bar Associations; Connecticut Trial Lawyers Association (Member, Board of Governors, 1976; Vice President, 1981; Chairman: Legal Education Basic Advocacy Seminar, 1981; Legislative Committee, 1983-1991; President, 1985-1987); The Association of Trial Lawyers of America (Chairman: State Grants, 1987; Fundraising, 1988; No Fault Committee, 1990-1991; State Relations, 1992-1994; Member, Board of Governors, 1988-1996; Chair, Legal Affairs Committee, 1997); National Association of Criminal Defense Attorneys (Chairman, Criminal Trial Advocacy Seminar, 1981); American Board of Trial Advocates; Judicial Review Commission (Chairman, 1992-1996). ***PRACTICE AREAS:*** Malpractice; Negligence; Class Actions; Commercial Litigation; Securities Litigation; Products Liability; Automobile Accidents and Injuries; Criminal Law. ***Email:*** rhalloran@ldlaw.com

HERBERT G. ISAACSON, born Hartford, Connecticut, August 10, 1936; admitted to bar, 1963, Connecticut; 1978, U.S. District Court, District of Connecticut. *Education:* Dartmouth College (A.B., 1958); London School of Economics, London, England; Harvard Law School (LL.B., 1963). Author: "Notice to Quit," Connecticut Bar Journal, 1969. Co-Author: Connecticut Condominium Manual, 1972; The Connecticut Common Interest Ownership Manual, 1984. *Member:* Litchfield County, Hartford County, Connecticut (Member, Real Property Section) and American Bar Associations. ***PRACTICE AREAS:*** Real Estate Law; Conveyancing Law; Condominium Law; Foreclosure Law. ***Email:*** hisaacson@ldlaw.com

EDGAR A. KING, born McLean, Illinois, November 20, 1923; admitted to bar, 1954, Connecticut. *Education:* Illinois Wesleyan University (Ph.B, 1949); University of Connecticut (J.D., 1954). Judge of Probate (District), 1975-1994. Law Clerk, Town of Farmington, 1975-1999. State Representative, 1969-1976. Chairman, Republican Town Committee, 1969-1973. Town Council, 1961-1966. [U.S. Navy, 1941-1945.]. ***PRACTICE AREAS:*** Estate Planning; Probate Administration.

PETER J. TYRRELL, born Waterbury, Connecticut, August 9, 1944; admitted to bar, 1969, Connecticut; 1971, U.S. District Court, District of Connecticut; 1972, U.S. Court of Appeals, Second Circuit; 1973, U.S. Supreme Court. *Education:* Villanova University (B.S., 1966); Boston College (J.D., 1969). Acting Chairman, Connecticut Office of Protection & Advocacy for the Disabled. Board Member, Huntington's Disease Society of America. *Member:* Connecticut and American Bar Associations. ***PRACTICE AREAS:*** Telecommunications. ***Email:*** ptyrrell@ldlaw.com

LOUIS WANG, born Baton Rouge, Louisiana, April 28, 1950; admitted to bar, 1994, Connecticut. *Education:* Tufts College (B.S., magna cum laude, 1971); Tufts University School of Medicine (M.D., 1975); University of Connecticut (J.D., high honors, 1994). Phi Beta Kappa. Recipient, West Publishing Award, 1991-1992, 1993-1994. Member, Connecticut Law Review, 1991-1994. *Member:* Connecticut and American Bar Associations; American College of Surgeons; American Medical Association; National Health Lawyers Association; College of Legal Medicine. ***Email:*** lwang@ldlaw.com

GEORGE M. HYMAN (1904-1985).

HARRY H. KLEINMAN (1933-1981).

JOHN P. PAVIA, III, born Bridgeport, Connecticut, June 18, 1963; admitted to bar, 1990, New York, Connecticut and U.S. District Court, District of Connecticut. *Education:* Duquesne University (B.A., 1985); American University (J.D., 1988). Adjunct Professor, Quinnipiac College Law School, 1989—. Law Clerk to U.S. District Judge Robert Zampano, 1989-1990. Assistant District Attorney, Brooklyn, New York, 1992-1995. ***PRACTICE AREAS:*** Commercial Litigation; Corporate Transactions; Intellectual Property; Government Relations; Municipal and Public Finance. ***Email:*** jpavia@ldlalw.com

REPRESENTATIVE CLIENTS: Aetna Life Insurance Co.; Chicago Title Insurance Co.; Connecticute Attorneys Title Insurance Company; Fidelity National Title Insurance Co.; First American Title Insurance Co.; Lawyers Title Insurance Corporation; Arrow Line, Inc./Coach USA, Inc.; Canon Greater Hartford Open; Carrier Corporation; Envirotest Systems Corp.; Exxon Mobil Corp.; Rite Aid Corp.; Shell Oil Company; The Trump Organization; Griffin Hospital; Abacus Payroll Systems; Allied Waste Industries, Inc.; ArchivesOne, Inc.; Back Bay Restaurant Group; Beauty Enterprises, Inc.; BJ's Wholesale Club, Inc.; Broilking Corp.; Connecticut Lighting, Inc.; Connecticut Public Broadcasting, Inc.; Dental Associates of Connecticut, P.C.; Devcon Enterprises, Inc.; Dynalock, Inc.; Eastern Investments LLC; Eastland Shoe Mfg. Corp.; Edart Truck Rental Corp.; Electrical Wholesalers, Inc.; Environmental Systems Products, Inc.; The Farmington Company; The Fletcher-

(This Listing Continued)

Terry Company; Georgia Pacific; Gilbane Construction Company; Gold Bond Mattress Co.; ING Northamerica Insurance Corp.; Konover & Associates, Inc.; LesCare Kitchens, Inc.; MarJam Supply Co., Inc.; Miss Porters' School, Inc.; Northeast Utilities System; Oldcastle Precast, Inc.; Omega Engineering, Inc.; Outlet Broadcasting Inc.; Plasma Coatings, Incorporated; Plassein International, Inc.; Quality Coils, Inc.; Rothschild Realty, Inc.; S&S Worldwide, Inc.; Southern New England Telecommunications Corporation (SNET); Staples, Inc.; The Stop & Shop Companies, Inc.; Tilcon, Inc.; Toll Brothers, Inc.; Tomasso Brothers, Inc.; United Technologies Corp.; Wilmorite, Inc.; Amresco Residential Mortgage Co.; BankNorth; Citizens Bank; Connecticut Housing Finance Authority; Liberty Bank; Litchfield Bancorp; National Cooperative Bank; National Iron Bank; People's Bank; Sovereign Bank; Webster Bank; Advest, Inc.; Bear Stearns & Co., Inc.; Dillon, Read & Co., Inc.; Donaldson, Lufkin & Jenrette Securities Co.; Goldman, Sachs & Co.; Herbert J. Sims & Co., Inc.; Lazard Freres & Co.; Merrill Lynch Capital Markets; UBS PaineWebber Inc.; State Street Capital Markets, LLC; Borough of Litchfield; Cities and Towns of Bloomfield, Easton, New Britain, Newington, Norfolk, Waterbury, The Metropolitan District (MDC), Regional School District No. 9, Winchester Housing Authority; State of Connecticut.

MURPHY, LAUDATI & KIEL, P.C.

THE EXCHANGE, SUITE 360
270 FARMINGTON AVENUE
FARMINGTON, CONNECTICUT 06032
Telephone: 860-674-8296
Fax: 860-674-0850
URL: http://www.lawyers.com/mlklaw

Litchfield County Office: Plaza Park North, 249 Winsted Road, Torrington, 06790. Telephone: 860-482-3478. Fax: 860-674-0850.

General Civil and Criminal Practice before State and Federal Courts.

NEIL F. MURPHY, JR., born East Orange, New Jersey, May 19, 1945; admitted to bar, 1970, Connecticut. *Education:* Boston College (A.B., 1967); University of Connecticut (J.D., 1970). Former Corporate Counsel, City of Bristol. Town Attorney, Town of Plymouth. Hearing Examiner, Connecticut Commission of Human Rights and Opportunities, 1976—. *Member:* Bristol (President, 1981-1983), Hartford County and Connecticut Bar Associations; Connecticut Trial Lawyers Association; The Association of Trial Lawyers of America. [Capt., USMCR, active duty, 1970-1974, JAGD.]. ***PRACTICE AREAS:*** Personal Injury Litigation; Criminal Law; Civil Rights; Real Property Litigation.

JOHN L. LAUDATI, born Waterbury, Connecticut, April 6, 1955; admitted to bar, 1981, Connecticut. *Education:* University of Connecticut (B.A. magna cum laude, 1977; J.D., 1981). Associate Editor, The Defense, Journal of The Connecticut Defense Lawyers Association, 1984-1988. Co-Chairperson, Hartford County Practice and Procedure Seminar, 1986-1988. Director, Vice President, Farmington River Watershed Association, 1988—. Member, Executive Committee, Manitook Lake Association, 1988—. *Member:* Bristol, Hartford County and Connecticut (Member, Executive Committee, Young Lawyers Section) Bar Associations; Connecticut Defense Lawyers Association. ***PRACTICE AREAS:*** Commercial Litigation; Criminal Law; Personal Injury; Family Law.

LAWRENCE J. KIEL, born Hartford, Connecticut, October 7, 1957; admitted to bar, 1983, Connecticut. *Education:* University of Connecticut (B.A. cum laude, with distinction, 1979; J.D., M.S.W., 1983). Member: National Association of Social Workers, 1981-1983; National Association of Counsel for Children, 1982-1984; Farmington Watershed Association; West Hartford Credit Union, Inc., Treasurer. *Member:* Hartford County and Connecticut (Member: Real Property, Banking Sections) Bar Associations. ***PRACTICE AREAS:*** Corporate; Real Estate; Commercial Lending; Contracts; Bankruptcy; Collections. ***Email:*** larrykiel@snet.net

---

MARGARET FOGERTY RATTIGAN, born Flushing, New York, February 25, 1960; admitted to bar, 1991, Connecticut; 1992, U.S. District Court, District of Connecticut. *Education:* Fordham University; University of Connecticut (B.A., Psychology, 1981); University of Connecticut School of Law (J.D., with honors, 1991). Recipient: American Jurisprudence Award in Trial Practice; Dean's Fellow. Co-Author, "Banking Law," 1990 and 1991 Cumulative Supplements, Matthew Bender and Company. Author, "Hospitals and Product Liability: Sales or Service," Journal of the Connecticut Defense Lawyers Association, Vol. 5 No. 3, Winter 1989. *Member:* Connecticut and American Bar Associations; Connecticut Trial Lawyers Association. ***Email:*** margaretrattigan@snet.net

LAW OFFICE OF MATTHEW N. PERLSTEIN

10 WATERSIDE DRIVE, SUITE 303
FARMINGTON, CONNECTICUT 06032
Telephone: 860-677-2177
Telecopier: 860-677-1147
Email: mnp@ctcondolaw.com
URL: http://www.ctcondolaw.com

Condominium and Community Association Law.

MATTHEW N. PERLSTEIN, born Hartford, Connecticut, January 16, 1946; admitted to bar, 1973, Connecticut and U.S. District Court, District of Connecticut; 1980, U.S. Supreme Court. *Education:* Bard College (A.B., 1968); Boston University (J.D., 1973). Member, Boston University Law Review, 1972-1973. Author: "When Informal Action by Corporate Directors Will be Permitted to Bind the Corporation," Boston University Law Review, Vol. 53, No. 1. Co-Author, The Connecticut Common Interest Ownership Manual, 1984. Advisor, Connecticut Law Revision Commission on the Connecticut Common Interest Ownership Act, 1982-1983. Author: "How to Terminate A Condominium," *Practical Real Estate Lawyer,* 1990. *Member:* Hartford County, Connecticut (Member, Executive Committee, Real Property Section, 1984—) and American (Co-Chair, Subcommittee on Uniform Laws of Committee on Condominiums, Co-operatives and Homeowners Associations, 1989-1994) Bar Associations; Community Associations Institute (President, Connecticut Chapter, 1990-1991; Chair, National Attorneys Committee, 1993-1994); College of Community Association Lawyers. ***PRACTICE AREAS:*** Condominium Law; Community Association Law.

JULIA DUCHOW THOMPSON, born St. Louis, Missouri, May 11, 1968; admitted to bar, 1996, Connecticut; 1999, U.S. District Court, District of Connecticut. *Education:* Miami University (B.S.Ed., 1990); Northeastern University (J.D., 1996). Editor, Northeastern University Forum, 1995-1996. *Member:* Hartford County and Connecticut Bar Associations; Community Associations Institute. ***PRACTICE AREAS:*** Condominium Law; Community Association Law. ***Email:*** jdt@ctcondolaw.com

HEIDI J. DARASKEVICH, born Glastonbury, Connecticut, September 24, 1964; admitted to bar, 1991, Connecticut; 1992, U.S. District Court, District of Connecticut. *Education:* Trinity College (B.A., 1986); University of Connecticut School of Law (J.D., 1991). *Member:* Connecticut (Young Lawyers Section Chair, 1999-2000; Chair-Elect, 1997-1999; Treasurer) and American Bar Associations. ***PRACTICE AREAS:*** Condominium Association Law; Common Interest Community Law; Commercial Litigation; Civil Litigation; Creditors Rights; Land Use; Land Development. ***Email:*** hjd@ctcondolaw.com

HOWARD M. ROSENFIELD

10 WATERSIDE DRIVE, SUITE 303
FARMINGTON, CONNECTICUT 06032
Telephone: 860-677-4334
Fax: 860-677-1147
Email: howard@stockbrokerproblems.com
Email: howisu4u@aol.com

Securities Arbitration, Arbitration and Mediation, Securities Consumer Arbitration, Shareholders Disputes, Investment Fraud.

HOWARD M. ROSENFIELD, born Waterbury, Connecticut, October 27, 1953; admitted to bar, 1980, Connecticut; 1982, Florida; 1984, U.S. Court of Appeals, 2nd Circuit; 1985, U.S. Court of Appeals, 9th Circuit. *Education:* Evergreen State College (B.A., 1975); California Western School of Law (J.D., 1979). Member, Labor Law Review, California Western School of Law. *Member:* Connecticut Bar Association; The Florida Bar. ***LANGUAGES:*** Spanish. ***PRACTICE AREAS:*** Securities Arbitration; Mediation; Securities Consumer Arbitration; Shareholder Disputes; Investment Fraud.

THE LAW OFFICE OF THOMAS H. WINSLOW, LLC

321 MAIN STREET
FARMINGTON, CONNECTICUT 06032-2976
Telephone: 860-678-4425
Fax: 860-678-4427
Email: thomaswins@aol.com

Insurance, Insurance Defense, Products Liability, Vehicle Rental, Municipal Defense, Health Insurance, ERISA, Litigation, Pharmacists Liability.

(This Listing Continued)

THE LAW OFFICE OF THOMAS H. WINSLOW, LLC, Farmington—Continued

THOMAS H. WINSLOW, born Bristol, Connecticut, November 15, 1955; admitted to bar, 1983, Ohio; 1985, Connecticut; 1986, U.S. District Court, District of Connecticut. *Education:* Ohio Northern University (B.S., Pharmacy, 1978; J.D., 1983). Staff Member, Ohio Northern University Law Review, 1981-1983. Registered Pharmacist: Connecticut, 1979—; Ohio, 1984—. Attorney, Lucas County Common Pleas Court, Toledo, Ohio, 1983-1985. Meriden, Waterbury & New Haven Superior Court fact finder and arbitrator for civil cases under $50,000, 1992-1999. Member, Connecticut Alliance for Safe Prescription Practices, 1999—. *Member:* Connecticut and American Bar Associations; Connecticut Defense Lawyers Association (Board of Director, 1996-1998; Second Vice President, 1998; First Vice President, 1999; President, 2000; Chairman of the Board, 2001); Defense Research Institute (1991—); Connecticut Business & Industry Association (Member, Product Liability Steering Committee, 1995-1999); American Society of Pharmacy and Law. ***REPORTED CASES:*** Demmarais v. Dow Corming Corp., 712 F.Supp. 13 (1989); Winslow v. Lewis-Shepard, 212 Conn. 462 (1989); Crotta v. Home Depot. Inc., 249 Conn. 634 (1999). ***Email:*** Thomaswins@aol.com

REPRESENTATIVE CLIENTS: Avis Rent-A-Car System, Inc.; The Gainsco Companies; Kemper Insurance Companies; Investors Insurance Group; Risk Assessment Strategies; Town of East Hartford.

ALTER AND SHERWOOD, LLC

701 HEBRON AVENUE
P.O. BOX 1420
GLASTONBURY, CONNECTICUT 06033
Telephone: 860-652-4020
Telecopier: 860-652-4022

General Civil Practice before State and Federal Courts. Real Estate, Zoning, Land Use and Administrative Practice, Corporation, Environmental Law and Real Estate Development.

MEMBERS OF FIRM

PETER JAY ALTER, born Waterbury, Connecticut, August 28, 1946; admitted to bar, 1973, Connecticut. *Education:* Harvard University (A.B., 1968); University of Connecticut School of Law (J.D., 1973). *Member:* Hartford County, Connecticut (Member, Executive Committee, Planning and Zoning Section, 1986-1987; 1994-1997) and American Bar Associations. ***PRACTICE AREAS:*** Real Estate Development Law.

DAVID F. SHERWOOD, born Danbury, Connecticut, August 8, 1955; admitted to bar, 1987, Connecticut. *Education:* University of Pennsylvania (B.A., magna cum laude, 1977); Yale University (M.Phil., 1981; Ph.D., with highest honors, 1983); University of Connecticut (J.D., with highest honors, 1987). Sigma Xi. Author: "In Defense of the Golden Arches: The Constitutionality of Municipal Regulation of Commercial Architecture," 60 Conn. Bar J. 271 (1986); "Challenging Inequality in the Connecticut Property Tax," 20 Conn. Law Rev. 479 (1988); "Land Use Appeals Under General Statues § 8-8," Conn. Real Est. L J 13, 6 (1996); "Property Tax," Connecticut Tax Handbook, RIA (1998, 1999); "Property Taxes," Guidebook to Connecticut Taxes, CCH (2000, 2001). Guest Lecturer: "Connecticut State and Local Taxation," Connecticut Bar Association Continuing Legal Education, 1990, 1991: "Regulatory Takings," National Business Institute, 1993. "Zoning Boards of Appeals," National Business Institute, 1994; "Real Estate Transfer Documents," Connecticut Association of Assessing Officers Symposium, 1997; "Connecticut State Taxation," Lorman, 1998; "Property Tax Issues for Manufacturers in Connecticut," National Business Institute, 2001. *Member:* Hartford County, Connecticut and American Bar Associations. ***LANGUAGES:*** Spanish.

RYAN K. McKAIN, born Manchester, Connecticut, January 16, 1974; admitted to bar, 2000, Connecticut; 2001, New York. *Education:* Pennsylvania State University (B.S., 1996); University of Connecticut School of Law (J.D., 2000). Editor-in-Chief: Connecticut Journal of International Law, 1999-2000. Author: "A Critical Evaluation of the Development and Implementation of Forest Preservation Strategies," Connecticut Journal of Intrernational Law, Volume 15, Page 235, 2000. *Member:* Hartford County, Connecticut, American and New York Bar Associations.

AYARS & ASSOCIATES, LLC

131 NEW LONDON TURNPIKE, SUITE 318
GLASTONBURY, CONNECTICUT 06033
Telephone: 860-652-7070
Fax: 860-652-7073
Email: pattylaw50@aol.com

Real Estate, Condominium Law, Cooperative Housing Law, Cooperative Housing Association Law, Real Estate Development, Water Rights, Riparian Rights, Family Law, ADR, Mortgage Financing, Consumer Credit and Finance.

PATRICIA A. AYARS, born Salem, New Jersey, July 21, 1950; admitted to bar, 1983, Connecticut. *Education:* University of Connecticut (B.A., cum laude, 1972; J.D., summa cum laude, 1983). Articles Editor, Connecticut Law Review, 1982-1983. Clerk, Honorable Thomas J. Meskill, Jr., U.S. Court of Appeals, Second Circuit, 1983-1984. Author: "The Flow of Surface Water in Connecticut," Connecticut Law Review 601, 1082. Vice Chair, Subcommittee on Timeshare and Recreational Common Interest Communities, Real Estate Section, American Bar Association, 1989-1990; Chair, Subcommittee on Timeshare and Recreational Common Interest Committee, Real Estate Section, American Bar Association, 1990—. *Member:* Hartford County and Connecticut Bar Associations; Community Association Institute; Hartford Association of Women Attorneys; Arbitrator and Mediator, American Arbitration Association; Hebron Planning and Zoning Commission (Vice-Chair). ***PRACTICE AREAS:*** Condominium Law; Real Estate Law.

BOATMAN, BOSCARINO, GRASSO & TWACHTMAN

Established in 1989
628 HEBRON AVENUE, BUILDING 3
P.O. BOX 650
GLASTONBURY, CONNECTICUT 06033-0650
Telephone: 860-659-5657
Telecopier: 860-657-4549

Commercial, Debtor and Creditor Rights, Bankruptcy, Litigation, Real Estate and Real Estate Development, Estate Planning, Personal Injury, Representation before IRS, Litigation in all Courts.

MEMBERS OF FIRM

PATRICK W. BOATMAN, born Pasadena, California, August 18, 1951; admitted to bar, 1979, Massachusetts; 1980, Connecticut. *Education:* California State Polytechnic University (B.A., 1973); Webster College (M.A., 1975); Boston University (J.D., 1979). Editor and Member, Boston University Law Review, 1977-1979. Law Clerk to Chief Justice William A. Grimes, New Hampshire Supreme Court, 1979-1980. *Member:* Connecticut (Member, Commercial Law and Bankruptcy Section), Massachusetts and American Bar Associations. [Lieut., U.S. Army, 1973-1976; Lieutenant Colonel, Connecticut Army National Guard]. ***PRACTICE AREAS:*** Commercial Law; Bankruptcy; General Litigation; Personal Injury. ***Email:*** pboatman@bbgtattorneys.com

THOMAS C. BOSCARINO, born Hartford, Connecticut, July 12, 1952; admitted to bar, 1977, Connecticut; 1978, U.S. Tax Court; 1982, U.S. District Court, District of Connecticut. *Education:* University of Connecticut (B.A., 1974); Cumberland School of Law (J.D., cum laude, 1977). Phi Alpha Delta (President, 1975-1976). Associate Justice, Cumberland Moot Court Board, 1976-1977. Associate Editor and Member, Cumberland Law Review, 1975-1977. Special Assistant U.S. Attorney, District of Connecticut, 1985-1986. *Member:* Connecticut Bar Association (Member, Commercial Law and Bankruptcy Section). ***PRACTICE AREAS:*** Bankruptcy; Debtor and Creditor Rights; Tax Collection; Commercial Law; Commercial Litigation. ***Email:*** tboscarino@bbgtattorneys.com

JOHN H. GRASSO, born Birmingham, Alabama, August 6, 1956; admitted to bar, 1982, Georgia; 1989, Connecticut and U.S. District Court, District of Connecticut; 1993, Massachusetts and U.S. District Court, District of Massachusetts. *Education:* University of Connecticut (B.A., summa cum laude, 1979); Emory University (J.D., 1982); Cornell University (Certificate in Labor Relations Studies, 1987). Phi Beta Kappa. Visiting Assistant Professor, University of Connecticut School of Business Administration, Storrs, Connecticut. Member, Board of Education, Regional School District No. 8. Special Assistant U.S. Attorney, District of Alaska, 1982-1985. *Member:* Hartford County and Connecticut (Member: Commercial Law, Bankruptcy and Elder Law Sections) Bar Associations; State Bar of Georgia. [Capt., JAGC, U.S. Army, 1982-1988; Lieutenant Colonel, Connecticut Army National Guard]. ***PRACTICE AREAS:*** General Litigation; Debtor and Creditor Rights; Commercial Law; Estate Planning; Personal Injury. ***Email:*** jgrasso@bbgtattorneys.com

WALTER A. TWACHTMAN, JR., born Brooklyn, New York, April 13, 1939; admitted to bar, 1967, Connecticut; 1969, U.S. Court of Appeals, Second

(This Listing Continued)

Circuit. *Education:* University of Connecticut (B.A., 1964; J.D., 1967). Associate Editor, University of Connecticut Law Review, 1966-1967. Member, Board of Editors, Connecticut Bar Journal, 1970-1975. Member, National Moot Court Team, University of Connecticut School of Law, 1966. Author: "De-Facto Segregation-The Northern Problem," 40 Connecticut Bar Journal 493, 1966; "The Connecticut Law of Zoning (Part C)." 41 Connecticut Bar Journal 658, 1967. Contributing Author: "Symposium on 1971 Connecticut Tax and Probate Legislation," Connecticut Bar Journal 129, 236, 1972. Faculty: "The Ethical Use of 'Futility' of Treatment as Rationale for DNR Orders," Fourth International Interdisciplinary Conference Justice in Health Care: Medicine, Ethics, and Economics, 1992; Faculty: "The Future of Surrogate Decision Making in light of Cruzan v. Harmon and In Re: Westchester County Medical Center (O'Connor)," Third National Interdisciplinary Conference Justice in Health Care: Medicine, Ethics, and Economics, 1990. Law Clerk to the Hon. Howard W. Alcorn, Associate Justice of the Connecticut Supreme Court, 1967-1968. *Member:* Hartford County, Connecticut and American (Member, Sections on: Torts and Insurance Practice Law; Litigation; Corporation, Banking and Business Law; Real Property, Probate and Trust Law) Bar Associations; The Association of Trial Lawyers of America; Connecticut Trial Lawyers Association; American Society of Law, Medicine & Ethics. Arbitrator, American Association. [with U.S. Army, 1958-1961]. ***PRACTICE AREAS:*** Zoning, Planning and Land Use; Real Estate; Appellate Practice. ***Email:*** wtwachtman@bbgtattorneys.com

APPROVED ATTORNEY AND AGENT FOR: Lawyers Title Insurance Corp.; Connecticut Attorneys Title Insurance Co.; Chicago Title Insurance Co.

RICHARD G. CONVICER, LLC

41 HEBRON AVENUE
GLASTONBURY, CONNECTICUT 06033
Telephone: 860-657-9040
Fax: 860-657-9039
Email: RConvi3589@aol.com

Civil and Criminal Tax Representation, Business and Tax Planning, IRS Tax Disputes, Estate Planning, Probate.

RICHARD G. CONVICER, born Boston, Massachusetts, November 12, 1948; admitted to bar, 1981, Connecticut, U.S. District Court, District of Connecticut and U.S. Tax Court. *Education:* Boston University (B.A., cum laude, 1971); Boston College (J.D., cum laude, 1981); New York University (LL.M. in Taxation, 1985). Trial Attorney, Office of Chief Counsel, IRS, Hartford, Connecticut, 1981-1985. Adjunct Professor, IRS Practice, University of Hartford Graduate School of Business, 1988-1993. Co-Author: *Connecticut Limited Liability Company Forms and Practice Manual,* Data Trace Publications, Inc., 1995. Author: "New IRS 'Check-the Box' Regulations and Proposed Amendments to Connecticut LLC Act," Connecticut Lawyer, March 1997; "IRS Examinations - Conduct by Agents," Chapter P.12, Benders' Federal Tax Service, Matthew Bender, 1993; "Tax Fraud: Avoiding Pitfalls in Representing Clients before the IRS," Connecticut CPA Quarterly, June 1992. *Member:* Connecticut (Member: Executive Committee, Section on Taxation, 1988—) and American (Member: Section of Taxation, Committee on Court Procedure, 1986—) Bar Associations. Fellow, American College of Trust and Estate Counsel.

LAW OFFICES OF GEORGE J. DUBORG

200 GLASTONBURY BOULEVARD, SUITE 301
GLASTONBURY, CONNECTICUT 06033
Telephone: 860-633-4797
Fax: 860-633-0694

Professional Liability, Products Liability, General Liability and Construction.

STAFF COUNSEL
AMERICAN INTERNATIONAL COMPANIES

MANAGING ATTORNEY

GEORGE J. DuBORG, born Detroit, Michigan, April 18, 1938; admitted to bar, 1971, California, U.S. Court District Court, Southern District of California; 1982, Connecticut and U.S. District Court, District of Connecticut. *Education:* San Jose University (B.A., 1959); University of California, Hastings (J.D., 1971). *Member:* Connecticut Bar Association; Defense Research Institute.

SENIOR TRIAL ATTORNEYS

JULIE A. HARRIS, born Washington, D.C., November 11, 1956; admitted to bar, 1981, Connecticut and U.S. District Court, District of Connecticut. *Education:* University of Hartford (B.A., 1978); University of Connecticut (J.D., 1981). *Member:* Connecticut Bar Association; Connecticut Defense Lawyers' Association.

(This Listing Continued)

THOMAS F. KELSEY, born Bridgeport, Connecticut, July 15, 1943; admitted to bar, 1974, Ohio; 1975, Connecticut and U.S. District Court, District of Connecticut. *Education:* University of Hartford (B.S., 1966); Capital University (J.D., 1974). *Member:* Connecticut and American Bar Associations.

TRIAL ATTORNEYS

DONALD P. GUERRINI, born Hartford, Connecticut, November 29, 1945; admitted to bar, 1981, Connecticut; 1993, U.S. District Court, District of Connecticut. *Education:* University of Connecticut (B.A., 1968; M.B.A., 1974); University of Bridgeport (J.D., 1981). *Member:* Connecticut and American Bar Associations; American Collectors Association.

CARLA OTTAVIANO, born New Haven, Connecticut, November 10, 1952; admitted to bar, 1985, Connecticut; 1986, U.S. District Court, District of Connecticut; 1996, U.S. Court of Appeals, Second Circuit. *Education:* Smith College (A.B., 1974); Franklin Pierce Law Center (J.D., 1985).

BRIAN J. FARRELL, JR., born Wallingford, Connecticut, June 30, 1968; admitted to bar, 1996, Connecticut; 1998, U.S. District Court, District of Connecticut. *Education:* St. Michael's College (B.A., 1990); Quinnipiac College (J.D., 1996). *Member:* American Corporate Counsel Association.

DUHAMEL & SCHOOLCRAFT LLC

131 NEW LONDON TURNPIKE
GLASTONBURY, CONNECTICUT 06033
Telephone: 860-652-0072
Fax: 860-652-8412
Email: duhamel.schoolcraft@snet.net

General Litigation, Insurance Defense, Workers Compensation, Personal Injury and Commercial Litigation.

DIANE D. DUHAMEL, born Nashua, New Hampshire, September 10, 1960; admitted to bar, 1987, New Hampshire; 1988, Connecticut; 1992, U.S. District Court, District of Connecticut; 1998, Massachusetts. *Education:* Saint Michael's College (A.B., 1982); Franklin Pierce Law Center (J.D., 1987). Member, Legal Advisory Committee to Chairman, Workers' Compensation Commission, 1992-1997. Vice-Chair, 1998-2000 and Chair, 2000—, Executive Committee of Workers' Compensation Section. Assistant Attorney General, Office of the Attorney General, Hartford, Connecticut, 1987-1990. Member, Legal Standing & Examining Committee For Workers Compensation Certification, 1999—. *Member:* New Hampshire and Connecticut (Member: Workers' Compensation Section; Executive Committee, 1996—) Bar Associations. ***PRACTICE AREAS:*** Insurance Defense; Workers Compensation; Personal Injury.

DAVID W. SCHOOLCRAFT, born Honolulu, Hawaii, December 29, 1956; admitted to bar, 1985, Connecticut; 1986, U.S. District Court, District of Connecticut. *Education:* University of Connecticut (B.A., 1980); Western New England College (J.D., 1985). Member, Western New England Law Review, 1984-1985. Member, 1997— and Chairman, 1999—, Planning and Zoning Commission, Town of Hebron. Member, Legal Advisory Committee to Chairman, Workers' Compensation Commission, 1999—. *Member:* Connecticut (Chairman, Legislative Committee, 1987-1994 and Executive Board of Workers Compensation Section, 1987—) and American Bar Associations; Connecticut Defense Lawyers Association; Defense Research Institute. ***PRACTICE AREAS:*** Insurance Defense; Workers Compensation; Personal Injury.

REPRESENTATIVE CLIENTS: Liberty Mutual; ACE USA (Formerly Cigna); Safeco; Ward North America; Sedgwick James of Connecticut; Westvaco; Tilcon Connecticut Inc; White Oak Corp.; AIG; United Technologies.

JOHN E. FRANCKLING

41-A NEW LONDON TURNPIKE
GLASTONBURY, CONNECTICUT 06033
Telephone: 860-633-8461
Fax: 860-633-4545

Criminal Law, Family Law, Personal Injury.

JOHN E. FRANCKLING, born Hartford, Connecticut, November 26, 1947; admitted to bar, 1983, Connecticut; 1984, U.S. District Court, District of Connecticut. *Education:* Springfield College (B.S., 1969; M.Ed., 1970); Western New England College (J.D., 1983). Member: Public Building Commission, Town of Glastonbury, 1988-1990; Board of Education, Town of Glastonbury, 1990-1994. *Member:* Hartford County and Connecticut Bar Associations; Connecticut Trial Lawyers Association; The Association of Trial Lawyers of America; Connecticut Criminal Defense Lawyers Association; National Association of Criminal Defense Lawyers.

FRAUENGLASS & EISENBERG

206 NEW LONDON TURNPIKE
GLASTONBURY, CONNECTICUT 06033-0357
Telephone: 860-633-0300
Fax: 860-657-4096
Email: FrauenglassEisenberg@SNET.Net

Visitation, Property Division, Alimony, Child Support, Post-Judgment Modifications, Prenuptial Agreements, Mediation, Practice limited to Divorce and Custody Law.

FIRM PROFILE: Frauenglass and Eisenberg represent our clients as vigorous advocates, while always responsive to their client's concerns and instructions. Dedication to this philosophy continues to be essential to their effective representation of clients.

Our practice is limited to divorce and custody law. We are committed to the resolution of all conflicts that are a part of the divorce process, including post-divorce disputes.

LLOYD FRAUENGLASS, born Hartford, Connecticut, September 27, 1937; admitted to bar, 1966, Connecticut; 1970, U.S. Supreme Court. *Education:* Trinity College (B.S., 1959); Cornell University Graduate School; University of Connecticut Law School (J.D., 1966). Lecturer, Legal and Psychological Perspectives of Divorce, Elmcrest Family Institute, 1979. President, Connecticut Council of Divorce and Family Mediators, 1982-1985. Special Master: Divorce Cases, Superior Court, 1987—; Hartford and New Britain Family Courts. *Member:* Hartford County (Chairman, Family Law Committee, 1981-1984), Connecticut (Member, Executive Committee, Family Law Section, 1975-1985) and American (Member, Family Law Section) Bar Associations. ***PRACTICE AREAS:*** Divorce; Child Custody Law; Family Law; Divorce Mediation.

DEBORAH R. EISENBERG, born Willimantic, Connecticut, July 14, 1954; admitted to bar, 1994, Connecticut; 1995, District of Columbia. *Education:* University of Connecticut (B.A., 1976); George Washington University (M.P.A., 1980; J.D., 1994). Special Master for Divorce Cases, Superior Court, Hartford, Middlesex and Tolland County. *Member:* Hartford County (Member, Family Law Section) and Connecticut (Member, Family Law Section) Bar Associations. ***PRACTICE AREAS:*** Divorce; Child Custody Law; Family Law.

JACONETTA & ASSOCIATES

2934 MAIN STREET
GLASTONBURY, CONNECTICUT 06033
Telephone: 860-657-8805
FAX: 860-657-8617

Taxation, Corporations, Limited Liability Companies, Partnerships, Estate Planning, Probate, Estate Administration, Trusts, Elder Law, Federal and State Tax Controversies.

JOSEPH P. JACONETTA, born Westerly, Rhode Island, April 20, 1961; admitted to bar, 1987, Maryland, District of Columbia and U.S. Tax Court; 1990, Connecticut. *Education:* University of Rhode Island (B.A., with highest distinction, 1983); American University (J.D., 1986); Georgetown University (LL.M. in Taxation, 1990). Phi Beta Kappa. Author: "Purchase Price Allocations to Covenants Not to Compete Under the Internal Revenue Code of 1986," The Tax Lawyer, Fall 1990; "AMT Liability on Buy-Sell Agreements," The Tax Advisor, September 1991; "Reducing Current Gain from Installment Sales of S Corporation Assets," The Journal of S Corporation Taxation, June 1992; "Sale of a Business," Commerce Clearing House, Inc., Federal Tax Service. *Member:* Connecticut, Maryland State and American (Member, Tax Section) Bar Associations; The District of Columbia Bar. ***PRACTICE AREAS:*** Taxation; Trusts and Estates; Business Planning; Elder Law; Probate. ***Email:*** joejac@ntplx.net

---

DAVID P. WIMER, born Lancaster, Pennsylvania, August 13, 1963; admitted to bar, 1995, Connecticut. *Education:* Pennsylvania State University (B.S., 1985); University of Connecticut (J.D., 1995). *Member:* Connecticut and American Bar Associations. ***PRACTICE AREAS:*** Estate Planning; Probate; Real Estate; Elder Law.

ANNE BURNHAM, born Hackensack, New Jersey, January 4, 1966; admitted to bar, 1995, Connecticut. *Education:* University of Connecticut (B.A., 1989; J.D., with honors, 1995). Phi Beta Kappa; Phi Kappa Phi. *Member:* Connecticut and American Bar Associations. ***PRACTICE AREAS:*** Estate Planning; Estate Administration; Real Estate; Probate.

MAYO, GILLIGAN & ZITO, LLP

GLASTONBURY, CONNECTICUT

(See Wethersfield)

Trials in all Courts, Real Estate, Banking and Commercial Finance, Creditors' Rights and Bankruptcy, Employment, Business Law, Zoning, Environmental, Estate Planning, Elder Law, Probate and Personal Injury Law.

MONTSTREAM & MAY, L.L.P.

SALMON BROOK CORPORATE PARK
655 WINDING BROOK DRIVE
P.O. BOX 1087
GLASTONBURY, CONNECTICUT 06033-6087
Telephone: 860-659-1341
Fax: 860-657-8519
Email: email@montmaylaw.com

Workers' Compensation, Civil Litigation, Insurance Defense, Products Liability, Medical Malpractice, Legal Malpractice.

FIRM PROFILE: Montstream and May, L.L.P. is a medium size firm located in Glastonbury, Connecticut. Its primary area of focus is insurance defense, including worker's compensation, civil litigation and all areas of property/casualty and insurance law generally. They handle similar matters for self-insured's. Montstream and May has the greatest number of Board Certified Worker's Compensation Specialists of any firm in the State.

ROBERT G. MONTSTREAM (Retired).

FRANK A. MAY, born 1948; admitted to bar, 1975, Connecticut and U.S. District Court, District of Connecticut; 1981, U.S. Court of Appeals, Second Circuit and U.S. Supreme Court. *Education:* University of Rhode Island (B.S., 1970); University of Connecticut (J.D., with high honors, 1975). *Member:* Hartford County, Connecticut (Member, Executive Board, Workers' Compensation Section) and American (Member, Sections on: Litigation; Torts; Insurance Practice; Products General Liability and Consumer Law Committee; Workers' Compensation and Employee's Liability Law Committee: Property Insurance Law Committee; Excess, Surplus Lines and Reinsurance Special Committee; Environmental Law Section) Bar Associations; Defense Research Institute; Connecticut Defense Lawyers Association; Connecticut Trial Lawyers Association. ***PRACTICE AREAS:*** Civil Litigation; Insurance Defense; Workers Compensation. ***Email:*** fmay@montmaylaw.com

APRIL HASKELL, born New York, N.Y., March 15, 1950; admitted to bar, 1976, California and U.S. District Court, Southern District of California; 1979, Connecticut and U.S. District Court, District of Connecticut; 1996, Supreme Court of Massachusetts. *Education:* University of California at Los Angeles (B.A., 1971); Loyola Marymount University (J.D., 1976). *Member:* Connecticut (Medical Legal Committee) and American (Member, Sections on: Torts; Insurance Practice) Bar Associations; State Bar of California; Defense Research Institute; Board Member, Connecticut Defense Lawyers Association. ***LANGUAGES:*** French. ***PRACTICE AREAS:*** Civil Litigation; Insurance Defense; Medical Malpractice; Products Liability. ***Email:*** ahaskell@montmaylaw.com

DAVID A. KELLY, born Washington, D.C., February 11, 1952; admitted to bar, 1977, Connecticut and U.S. District Court, District of Connecticut. *Education:* American University (B.S., 1974); Suffolk University (J.D., 1977). *Member:* Connecticut Bar Association (Member, Workers Compensation Committee). ***PRACTICE AREAS:*** Insurance Defense; Workers Compensation. ***Email:*** dkelly@montmaylaw.com

MICHAEL J. FINN, born 1961; admitted to bar, 1989, Connecticut and U.S. District Court, District of Connecticut. *Education:* Mount St. Mary's College (B.S., 1983); University of Connecticut (M.S., 1989); Western New England College (J.D., 1989). *Member:* Hartford County, Connecticut and American Bar Associations. ***PRACTICE AREAS:*** Insurance Defense; Workers Compensation. ***Email:*** mfinn@montmaylaw.com

JEAN D. MOLLOY, born Hartford, Connecticut, September 3, 1960; admitted to bar, 1988, Connecticut; 1989, U.S. District Court, District of Connecticut. *Education:* Boston College (B.A., cum laude, 1982); Western New England College (J.D., 1988). *Member:* Hartford County and Connecticut (Member, Workers Compensation Section) Bar Associations. ***PRACTICE AREAS:*** Insurance Defense; Workers Compensation. ***Email:*** jmolloy@montmaylaw.com

DOMINICK C. STATILE, born Jersey City, New Jersey, March 10, 1966; admitted to bar, 1991, Connecticut; 1992, U.S. District Court, District of Connecticut. *Education:* Villanova University (B.A., 1988); University of Connecticut (J.D., 1991). *Member:* Hartford County, Connecticut and American Bar Associations. ***PRACTICE AREAS:*** Workers' Compensation; Insurance Defense. ***Email:*** dstatile@montmaylaw.com

(This Listing Continued)

ASSOCIATES

JOSEPH J. PASSARETTI, JR., born 1968; admitted to bar, 1994, Connecticut, New Jersey and U.S. District Court, District of New Jersey; 1995, U.S. District Court, District of Connecticut. *Education:* Rutgers University (B.A., 1990); Quinnipiac College (J.D., 1993). *Member:* Connecticut Bar Association. ***PRACTICE AREAS:*** Insurance Defense; Workers Compensation. ***Email:*** jpassaretti@montmaylaw.com

MICHAEL M. BUONOPANE, born 1971; admitted to bar, 1996, Connecticut. *Education:* University of Connecticut (B.A., 1993); New England School of Law (J.D., 1996). ***PRACTICE AREAS:*** Workers' Compensation; Civil Litigation; Insurance Defense. ***Email:*** mbuonopane@montmaylaw.com

MARGARET E. McGRAIL, born Hartford, Connecticut, August 22, 1961; admitted to bar, 1986, Connecticut and U.S. District Court, District of Connecticut. *Education:* Fairfield University (B.A., 1983); Western New England College (J.D., 1986). Staff Member, 1984-1985 and Research Editor, 1985-1986, Western New England Law Review. *Member:* Connecticut Bar Association. ***PRACTICE AREAS:*** Workers Compensation Law. ***Email:*** mmcgrail@montmaylaw.com

KAREN A. WRIGHT, born 1972; admitted to bar, 2000, Connecticut. *Education:* Quinnipiac College School of Law (B.A. in Legal Studies; J.D., 2000). ***PRACTICE AREAS:*** Workers Compensation; Personal Injury. ***Email:*** kwright@montmaylaw.com

JOSEPH M. MABE, born 1975; admitted to bar, 2001, Connecticut. *Education:* University of Oregon (B.S., Political Science, Economics, 1997); University of Connecticut School of Law (J.D., 2000). Intramural Director, Moot Court Board, University of Connecticut School of Law. ***Email:*** jmabe@montmaylaw.com

MARIE E. GALLO-HALL, born Brooklyn, N.Y. , April 4, 1962; admitted to bar, 2001, Connecticut. *Education:* University of Connecticut (B.A., 1984; J.D., 2001). ***PRACTICE AREAS:*** Workers Compensation; Personal Injury; Social Security Disability. ***Email:*** mgallo-hall@montmaylaw.com

MELISSA A. MURELLO, born June 25, 1976; admitted to bar, 2001, Connecticut. *Education:* Carnegie Mellon University (B.S., 1998); University of Pittsburgh (J.D., 2001). Interned, Pittsburgh Public Defender's Office.

REPRESENTATIVE CLIENTS: Acadia Insurance; AIG Claims; Safeco; Ames; Amlico; Atlantic Mutual; Berkley; Berkshire Hathaway; Home Insurance Companies; Cambridge Intergrated Services; City of Bridgeport; City of Hartford; Constitution States Services; Crum & Foster; Cunningham Lindsey; Eastern Casualty; EMC Insurance; Friendly's Ice Cream Corp.; GAB Robbins; Gallagher Bassett; Great American Insurance Co.; CT Guaranty Fund; Hartford Insurance; Home Depot; Liberty Mutual; Lowe's; Mastercare of CT, Inc.; McDonald Corp.; One Becon; Peerless Insurance Co.; Reliance Insurance Co.; Royal & Sunalliance; RSKO; Sedgwick James; Sentry Claims; SRS; St. Paul Insurance Co.; TCI; Travelers Insurance; Uniroyal.

POMERANZ, DRAYTON & STABNICK

95 GLASTONBURY BOULEVARD
GLASTONBURY, CONNECTICUT 06033-4412
Telephone: 860-657-8000; 800-246-5541
Fax: 860-657-9838
Email: pdslaw@pdslaw.coom

Workers Compensation Law, Federal Longshore and Harborworkers Act.

DOUGLAS L. DRAYTON, born Hartford, Connecticut, December 30, 1944; admitted to bar, 1969, Connecticut. *Education:* University of Connecticut (B.S., 1966; J.D., 1969). *Member:* Hartford County and Connecticut Bar Associations. ***PRACTICE AREAS:*** Workers Compensation Law. ***Email:*** DougD@pdslaw.com

JAMES L. POMERANZ, born Hartford, Connecticut, February 19, 1946; admitted to bar, 1972, Connecticut. *Education:* Yale University (B.A., 1969); Georgetown University (J.D., 1972). *Member:* Hartford County Bar Association. ***PRACTICE AREAS:*** Workers Compensation Law; Longshore and Harborworkers Compensation Act. ***Email:*** JimP@pdslaw.com

RICHARD T. STABNICK, born Memphis, Tennessee, October 16, 1944; admitted to bar, 1970, Connecticut. *Education:* Wesleyan University (B.A., 1966); University of Connecticut (J.D., 1970). *Member:* Hartford County, Connecticut and American Bar Associations. ***PRACTICE AREAS:*** Workers Compensation Law; Longshore and Harborworkers Compensation Act. ***Email:*** RichardS@pdslaw.com

LUCAS D. STRUNK, born Putnam, Connecticut, September 15, 1956; admitted to bar, 1982, Connecticut. *Education:* College of the Holy Cross (B.A., 1979); University of Connecticut (J.D., 1982). *Member:* Mashantucket, Connecticut and American Bar Associations; Connecticut Trial Lawyers Association. ***PRACTICE AREAS:*** Workers Compensation Law; Longshore and Harborworkers Compensation Act. ***Email:*** LukeS@pdslaw.com

JASON M. DODGE, born Hartford, Connecticut, March 11, 1958; admitted to bar, 1983, Connecticut; 1984, U.S. District Court, District of Connecticut; 1997, U.S. Court of Appeals, 2nd Circuit. *Education:* University of Connecticut (B.A., 1980; J.D., 1983). *Member:* Hartford County and Connecticut Bar Associations; Association of Trial Lawyers of America. ***PRACTICE AREAS:*** Workers Compensation Law; Longshore and Harborworkers Compensation Act. ***Email:*** JasonD@pdslaw.com

(This Listing Continued)

ANNE KELLY ZOVAS, born Hartford, Connecticut, September 29, 1961; admitted to bar, 1986, Connecticut; 1987, U.S. District Court, District of Connecticut; 1993, U.S. Court of Appeals, 2nd Circuit. *Education:* Boston College (B.A., cum laude, 1983); University of Connecticut (J.D., 1986). *Member:* Hartford County, Connecticut and American (Member, Tort and Insurance Practice Section) Bar Associations; Connecticut Trial Lawyers Association. ***PRACTICE AREAS:*** Workers Compensation Law; Civil Litigation; Subrogation. ***Email:*** AnneZ@pdslaw.com

RICHARD L. AIKEN, JR., born Gardner, Massachusetts, May 1, 1956; admitted to bar, 1985, Connecticut; 1986, U.S. District Court, District of Connecticut and Massachusetts. *Education:* University of New Haven (B.S., summa cum laude, 1978); Western New England College (J.D., cum laude, 1985). Alpha Chi. *Member:* Connecticut and American Bar Associations. ***PRACTICE AREAS:*** Workers Compensation Law. ***Email:*** RickA@pdslaw.com

MICHAEL J. McAULIFFE, born Holyoke, Massachusetts, June 29, 1961; admitted to bar, 1986, Connecticut and U.S. District Court, District of Connecticut. *Education:* George Washington University (B.A., 1983); Western New England College (J.D., 1986). *Member:* Connecticut Bar Association (Member, Workers Compensation Section). ***PRACTICE AREAS:*** Workers Compensation Law. ***Email:*** MikeM@pdslaw.com

ASSOCIATE

KRISTEN L. FRAZIER, born Hartford, Connecticut, February 1, 1974; admitted to bar, 1999, Connecticut; 2000, U.S. District Court, District of Connecticut. *Education:* University of Connecticut (B.S., 1996); University of Connecticut School of Law (J.D., 1999). *Member:* Hartford County and Connecticut Bar Associations. ***PRACTICE AREAS:*** Workers Compensation. ***Email:*** KristenF@pdslaw.com

HEATHER KLINEBERG, born New Haven, Connecticut, July 28, 1975; admitted to bar, 2000, Connecticut and New York. *Education:* Syracuse University (B.S., 1997); Quinnipiac College (J.D., 2000). *Member:* Hartford, New Haven and Connecticut Bar Associations. ***PRACTICE AREAS:*** Civil Litigation; Workers Compensation. ***Email:*** HeatherK@pdslaw.com

WILLIAM A. ROBERTO LLC

381 HUBBARD STREET
GLASTONBURY, CONNECTICUT 06033
Telephone: 860-657-3300
Fax: 860-657-2900

Civil Litigation, Criminal Litigation, Personal Injury, Family Law, Probate.

WILLIAM A. ROBERTO, born Hartford, Connecticut, October 13, 1946; admitted to bar, 1971, Ohio and Connecticut; 1973, U.S. District Court, District of Connecticut; 1975, U.S. Supreme Court; 1978-1982, U. S. Court of Customs and Patent Appeals; 1980, U.S. Court of Appeals, Second Circuit, U.S. District Court, Northern District of Ohio and U.S. Court of Appeals for the Federal Circuit. *Education:* University of Connecticut (B.S., 1968); University of Akron (J.D., 1970). Assistant Corporation Counsel, Town of East Hartford, 1975-1983. State Trial Referee, State of Connecticut, 1985-1989. Member, Panel of Arbitrators, American Arbitration Association. *Member:* Hartford County (Co-Chairman, 1988-1993, Bench/Bar Committee; President, 1986-1987), Connecticut (Member: Domestic and Family Law Committee, 1977—; General Practice Executive Committee, 1983-1987; House Of Delegates, 1987-1992; Board of Governors, 1988-1992), Ohio State and American Bar Associations.

KENNETH L. SHLUGER

119 HEBRON AVENUE
GLASTONBURY, CONNECTICUT 06033
Telephone: 860-633-4767
Fax: 860-652-8145
Email: shluger@aol.com
URL: http://www.lawyers.com/shlugerlaw

Hartford, Connecticut Office: 216 Main Street, 06106. Telephone: 860-247-8681.
Hebron, Connecticut Office: 17 Main Street, 06248. Telephone: 860-228-1242.

Civil and Criminal Litigation, Personal Injury, Medical Malpractice, Products Liability, Divorce, Bankruptcy, Driving While Intoxicated; Slip and Fall, Automobile Accidents.

KENNETH L. SHLUGER, born Hartford, Connecticut, January 20, 1955; admitted to bar, 1980, Connecticut and U.S. District Court, District of Con-

(This Listing Continued)

KENNETH L. SHLUGER, Glastonbury—Continued

necticut; 1981, U.S. Court of Appeals, 2nd Circuit. *Education:* University of Connecticut (B.A., in Political Science, with distinction, 1977); University of Connecticut School of Law (J.D., 1980). Research Clerk Intern, Judicial Department, Superior Court, Hartford, State of Connecticut, 1979-1980. Adjunct Professor, Lecturer, Manchester Technical Community College, 1981-1983. Member, 1983-1994 and Secretary and Board of Directors, 1990-1992, University Club, Hartford. Board Member, Andover Hebron Marlborough Youth Services, 1990-1993. Member, 1989-1993 and Secretary, 1991-1993, Marlborough Democratic Town Committee. Counsel and Board of Directors, Greater Harford Marathon Foundation, 1993—. Hearing Officer, Connecticut Commission On Human Rights and Opportunities, 1997—. *Member:* Hartford County (Member, Board of Directors, 1986-1997; Chairman, Long Range Planning Committee; Continuing Legal Education Committee; Annual Outing Committee; Law Day Committee; Road Race Committee; Special Events Committee; Membership Services) and Connecticut (Member, House of Delegates; Formerly Member: Executive Committee; Criminal Justice and Executive Committee Member Services); Connecticut Trial Lawyers Association (Member, Legislative Committee, 1996-1998); The Association of Trial Lawyers of America.

ALBERT, WARD & JOHNSON, P.C.

Established in 1973
125 MASON STREET
P.O. BOX 1668
GREENWICH, CONNECTICUT 06836
Telephone: 203-661-8600
Telecopier: 203-661-8051
URL: http://www.lawyers.com/awj

General Practice. Real Estate, Zoning, Corporation, Litigation, Probate, Taxation, Construction, Environmental and Family Law.

TOM S. WARD, JR., born New York, N.Y., December 25, 1944; admitted to bar, 1969, Connecticut. *Education:* Hamilton College (B.A., 1966); Fordham University (J.D., 1969). Instructor, Real Estate Law, Fairfield University, 1977-1986. *Member:* Greenwich, Connecticut and American (Member, Real Property, Probate and Trust Law Section) Bar Associations. ***PRACTICE AREAS:*** Commercial and Residential Real Estate; Financing. ***Email:*** tward@awjlaw.com

SCOTT R. JOHNSON, born Greenwich, Connecticut, October 25, 1952; admitted to bar, 1980, New York; 1981, U.S. District Court, Southern District of New York; 1983, Connecticut and U.S. District Court, District of Connecticut. *Education:* Cornell University (B.A., magna cum laude, 1975); Vermont Law School (J.D., 1979). Licensed Real Estate Broker, New York, 1982. Associate, Finley, Kumble, Wagner, Heine, Underberg & Casey, 1979-1983. *Member:* Association of the Bar of the City of New York; Greenwich and Connecticut Bar Associations. ***PRACTICE AREAS:*** Real Estate; Environmental; Construction Law. ***Email:*** sjohnson@awjlaw.com

JANE D. HOGEMAN, born Hartford, Connecticut, September 23, 1950; admitted to bar, 1977, New Mexico; 1981, Ohio; 1986, Connecticut. *Education:* Connecticut College For Women; University of Michigan (B.A., 1972; J.D., cum laude, 1976). Counsel, Governor's Organized Crime Prevention Commission, 1977-1980. *Member:* Greenwich and Connecticut Bar Associations. ***PRACTICE AREAS:*** Real Estate and Zoning Law. ***Email:*** jhogeman@awjlaw.com

HOWARD R. WOLFE, born Middletown, Connecticut, January 10, 1960; admitted to bar, 1984, Connecticut; 1985, New York and U.S. District Court, District of Connecticut. *Education:* Northwestern University (B.A., 1981); Boston University (J.D., 1984). Barrister, American Inn of Court-Bridgeport, 1989—. *Member:* Greenwich, Stamford Regional, Connecticut and American Bar Associations; Connecticut Trial Lawyers Association; Association of Trial Lawyers of America. ***PRACTICE AREAS:*** Civil Litigation; Commercial Litigation; Foreclosures; Landlord/Tenant. ***Email:*** hwolfe@awjlaw.com

CHRISTOPHER A. KRISTOFF, born Greenwich, Connecticut, February 27, 1955; admitted to bar, 1985, Connecticut; 1991, U.S. District Court, District of Connecticut. *Education:* Alfred University (B.A., 1977); Thomas M. Cooley Law School (J.D., cum laude, 1985). Note Editor, Law Review, Thomas M. Cooley Law School. *Member:* Greenwich, Connecticut (Member, Probate Law Section, 1992—) and American (Member, Probate Law Section, 1992—) Bar Associations. ***PRACTICE AREAS:*** Probate Administration; Civil Litigation. ***Email:*** ckristoff@awjlaw.com

VICKI K. COMBERIATI, born Bloomsburg, Pennsylvania, August 3, 1954; admitted to bar, 1995, Connecticut and New York. *Education:* California State University at San Bernardino (B.A., 1977); University of Michigan (M.A., 1983); Pace University School of Law (J.D., 1995). *Member:* Connecticut, New York State and American Bar Associations. ***PRACTICE AREAS:*** Real Estate; Corporate. ***Email:*** vcomb@awjlaw.com

(This Listing Continued)

ASSOCIATE

ALBERT T. STRAZZA, born Greenwich, Connecticut, October 6, 1970; admitted to bar, 2001, Connecticut. *Education:* Southern Connecticut State University (B.S., 1995); Pace University (J.D., 2001). [U.S. Marine Corps Reserve]. ***PRACTICE AREAS:*** Real Estate; Business Law; Construction Law; Commercial Real estate. ***Email:*** astrazza@awjlaw.com

OF COUNSEL

DAVID ALBERT, born Naugatuck, Connecticut, June 28, 1928; admitted to bar, 1954, Connecticut; 1978, U.S. Supreme Court. *Education:* Ohio University (A.B., 1951); Yale University (LL.B., 1954). State Trial Referee, 1985—. American Inn of Court-Bridgeport, 1988—. *Member:* Greenwich (President, 1971-1972) and Connecticut Bar Associations; Connecticut Trial Lawyers Association; The Association of Trial Lawyers of America. ***PRACTICE AREAS:*** Zoning; Civil Litigation; Family Law.

C. ROBTON PERELLI-MINETTI, born Petaluma, California, August 12, 1948; admitted to bar, 1983, New York; 1992, Connecticut. *Education:* University of California at Santa Barbara (B.A., history, 1970; M.A., History, 1972); University of California at Los Angeles, (J.D., 1981). Associate Editor, UCLA Law Review, 1980-1981. Author: Causation and Intention in The Entrapment Defense, 28 UCLA Law Review, 859 (1981). Instructor, Quinnipiac College School of Law, Winter, 1995. *Member:* Greenwich, Stamford-Norwalk Regional, New York State (Member, Business Law Section; International Law Section), Connecticut (Member, Business Law Section; Computer Law Section; Bankruptcy Section) and American (Business Law Section; Tax Section; International Section; Law Practice Management Section; Dispute Resolution Section) Bar Associations; Association of the Bar of the City of New York. ***LANGUAGES:*** German. ***PRACTICE AREAS:*** Corporate; Mergers and Acquisitions; Tax. ***Email:*** rpm@awjlaw.com

APPROVED TITLE ATTORNEYS FOR: Fidelity National Title Insurance Co.; Chicago Title Co.; First American Title Insurance Co.; Peoples Bank; The Putnam Trust Company of Greenwich; Lawyers Title Insurance Co.; Sound Beach Financial Corp.; Norwest Mortgage, Inc.; Fleet Bank; Chase Bank of Connecticut; KeyCorp Mortgage Inc.; Pawling Savings Bank; Webster Bank; Alliance Funding; Parallel Commercial Capital.

JOHN LLOYD ANNER, III

Established in 1989
125 MASON STREET
GREENWICH, CONNECTICUT 06830
Telephone: 203-862-9237
New York: 212-645-0779; New York Fax: 212-645-3229
FAX: 203-629-8462

Arbitration, Corporate, Commercial, International, Labor and Benefits Law, Litigation in all Courts, Real Estate, Trusts and Estates.

JOHN LLOYD ANNER, III, born New York, N.Y., May 26, 1937; admitted to bar, 1964, New York; 1965, U.S. District Court, Southern and Eastern Districts of New York and U.S. Court of Appeals, Second Circuit; 1987, Connecticut. *Education:* Fordham University (B.S., 1959; J.D., 1964). Elected Member of Representative Town Meeting, Greenwich, 1982-1997; Member, 1983-1997, and Chairman, 1988-1989, RTM Labor Contracts Committee; Member, 1984 and Chairman, 1990-1998, RTM Finance Committee; Member, RTM Claims Committee, 1986-1992. Contract Arbitrator, Building Services Industry, New York, 1989—. Arbitrator, American Arbitration Association; National Mediation Board; Federal Mediation and Conciliation Service.

BARNETT & ASSOCIATES

ONE LAFAYETTE PLACE, 3RD FLOOR
GREENWICH, CONNECTICUT 06830
Telephone: 203-622-0350
Fax: 203-622-0375
Email: cblegal@aol.com
URL: http://www.lawyers.com/cbarnett

Legal Consulting, Securities, Mergers and Acquisitions, Venture Capital, General Corporate, Business Law, Contracts.

FIRM PROFILE: Charles E. Barnett is the former Vice President and General Counsel of St. Joe Minerals Corporation, Combustion Engineering, Inc. and The Reader's Digest Association, Inc., all publicly owned companies. The firm offers legal consulting services to businesses and leveraged buy-out and venture capital firms and conducts a securities, mergers, acquisitions and general corporate law practice.

CHARLES E. BARNETT, born Charleston, West Virginia, September 25, 1939; admitted to bar, 1965, New York; 1973, Connecticut; 1987, U.S. Supreme

(This Listing Continued)

Court. *Education:* University of Michigan (B.A., 1961; J.D., 1964). Trustee, Practicing Law Institute, 1985—, Member, Committee on Programs and Publications of Board of Trustees. Executive Committee of the Conference Board's Council of Chief Legal Officers, 1992-1994. Legal Advisory Committee to the Board of Directors of the New York Stock Exchange, 1987-1990. Chairman, International and Comparative Law Center of the Southwestern Legal Foundation; Chairman, Annual Symposium for three years. Forum, U.S. Supreme Court and European Court of Justice, 1990-1993. Board of Directors of the Corporate Bar of Westchester-Fairfield Counties, 1989-1993. Vice President and General Counsel, St. Joe Minerals Corporation, New York, N.Y., 1974-1983. Vice-President and General Counsel, Combustion Engineering, Inc., Stamford, Connecticut, 1984-1990. Vice President and General Counsel, The Reader's Digest Association, Inc., Pleasantville, N.Y., 1990-1994. *Member:* The Association of the Bar of the City of New York; New York State, Connecticut and American (Member, Committee on Corporate Law Departments, 1987-1995) Bar Associations; Corporate Bar Association of Westchester-Fairfield. (Also Of Counsel, McGovern & Associates). ***PRACTICE AREAS:*** Legal Consulting; Securities; Mergers and Acquisitions; Venture Capital; Corporate.

BENTLEY, MOSHER, BABSON & LAMBERT, P.C.

Established in 1942

321 RAILROAD AVENUE

P.O. BOX 788

GREENWICH, CONNECTICUT 06836-0788

Telephone: 203-629-2424

Telecopier: 203-629-2545

Email: attysbmbl@aol.com

General Practice. Estates and Trusts, Corporate, Tax, Real Estate, Mortgage and Banking, Consumer Lending. State and Federal Litigation including Domestic Relations.

FIRM PROFILE: Bentley, Mosher, Babson & Lambert, P.C. traces its roots in the Stamford and Greenwich areas back to the 1940's. The firm has a tradition of commitment to professional excellence and to public service with community, charitable, civic and political organizations.

DAVID F. BABSON, born Cambridge, Massachusetts, October 19, 1923; admitted to bar, 1950, Connecticut. *Education:* Harvard University (A.B., 1947); University of Michigan (J.D., 1950). With Office of Solicitor, U.S. Department of Labor, in Boston, Massachusetts and Washington, D.C., 1950-1954. *Member:* Connecticut and American Bar Associations; The Regional Bar. ***PRACTICE AREAS:*** Estates and Trusts; Estate Planning; Personal Taxation. ***Email:*** attysbmbl@aol.com

JOHN F. LAMBERT, born Jersey City, New Jersey, June 19, 1930; admitted to bar, 1956, New York; 1957, Connecticut. *Education:* University of Notre Dame (A.B., 1952); Columbia Law School (LL.B., 1956). Phi Delta Phi. *Member:* Greenwich and Connecticut Bar Associations; The Regional Bar; The Association of Trial Lawyers of America; The Connecticut Trial Lawyers Association. ***PRACTICE AREAS:*** State and Federal Litigation; Domestic Relations. ***Email:*** attysbmbl@aol.com

M. DEAN MONTGOMERY, born Stamford, Connecticut, November 9, 1942; admitted to bar, 1967, Colorado; 1971, Connecticut. *Education:* Middlebury College (B.A., 1964); University of Denver (J.D., 1966). Stamford Police Commissioner, 1977-1981. Stamford Fire Commissioner, 1981-1983. *Member:* Connecticut (Executive Committee, Real Property Section) and American (Member, Real Property, Probate and Trust Law Section, Property Tax Committee) Bar Associations; The Regional Bar (President, 1983-1984). [Captain, U.S. Army, 1968-1970]. ***PRACTICE AREAS:*** Real Estate; Mortgage Banking; Consumer Lending; Property Related Litigation and Appeals. ***Email:*** attysbmbl@aol.com

CHARLES E. MOSHER, born Schenectady, New York, February 9, 1931; admitted to bar, 1959, Connecticut. *Education:* New York University (B.S., 1954); University of Virginia (LL.B., 1959). *Member:* Greenwich (President, 1982-1983), Connecticut and American Bar Associations. [1st Lt. U.S. Marine Corps, 1954-1956]. ***PRACTICE AREAS:*** Estate Planning; Probate; Real Estate; Corporate. ***Email:*** attysbmbl@aol.com

RICHARD J. SLAGLE, born Stamford, Connecticut, October 26, 1948; admitted to bar, 1978, Connecticut. *Education:* University of Connecticut (B.A., 1970); Syracuse University (J.D., 1977). *Member:* Greenwich, Connecticut and American Bar Associations. ***PRACTICE AREAS:*** Estate Planning; Probate; Real Estate. ***Email:*** attysbmbl@aol.com

COUNSEL

PETER BENTLEY, born Jersey City, New Jersey, September 1, 1915; admitted to bar, 1942, New York; 1952, Connecticut. *Education:* Phillips Exeter Academy; Princeton University (A.B., 1938); Yale Law School (J.D., 1941). *Member:* Connecticut and American Bar Associations; The Regional Bar.

(This Listing Continued)

CATHERINE P. WHELAN, born Worcester, Massachusetts, February 19, 1960; admitted to bar, 1985, Connecticut. *Education:* University of Connecticut (B.A., cum laude, 1982); University of Bridgeport (J.D., cum laude, 1985). Pi Sigma Alpha; Phi Delta Phi. Recipient, American Jurisprudence Awards in: Family Law; Insurance Law; Legal Ethics. Member, 1983-1985 and Lead Articles Editor, 1984-1985, University of Bridgeport School of Law Review. Member, Raymond E. Baldwin Chapter, American Inns of Court, Bridgeport. Member, Board of Directors, Nathaniel Witherell Nursing Home, Greenwich, 1989-1993. *Member:* Lower Fairfield County (Member, Young Lawyers Section and President, 1988-1989) and Connecticut (Member, Executive Committee, 1989-1991) Bar Associations; Connecticut Trial Lawyers Association; The Association of Trial Lawyers of America. ***PRACTICE AREAS:*** Litigation; Personal Injury; Divorce. ***Email:*** cpwlaw@aol.com

RETIRED

EDWIN M. JONES, born Bridgeport, Connecticut, May 15, 1916; admitted to bar, 1943, New York; 1947, Connecticut. *Education:* Yale University (B.A., 1937, Phi Beta Kappa); New York University (LL.B., 1942; LL.M. in Taxation, 1951). Executive Director, Pension Benefit Guaranty Corporation, Washington, D.C., 1982-1984. *Member:* The Association of the Bar of the City of New York (Member, Committee on Employee Benefits); Greenwich, Connecticut and New York State (Member, Executive Committee and Committee on Employee Benefits) Bar Associations; The Regional Bar; The Association of Life Insurance Counsel. ***PRACTICE AREAS:*** ERISA Employee Benefits; General Corporate. ***Email:*** attysbmbl@aol.com

REPRESENTATIVE CLIENTS: Carl J. Herzog Foundation, Inc.; Ø-A-O Lssa; E.J. Gaisser, Inc.; Roller Bearing Co.; Tuthill Finance; S.E. Minor & Co.; Scholz Design, Inc.; Wainco Funding, LLC.
APPROVED ATTORNEYS FOR: First American Title Insurance Co.; Connecticut Attorneys Title Insurance Co.; Chicago Title Insurance Co.; Old Republic National Title Insurance Co.; Security Title; Fidelity Title Insurance Co.; Old Republic National Title Insurance Co.
REFERENCE: First Union Bank and Putnam Trust.

BERKOWITZ, MALOWITZ & MULLIN

GREENWICH, CONNECTICUT

(See Stamford)

Personal Injury Litigation, Medical Malpractice, Products Liability Law, Workers' Compensation, and Complex Civil Litigation.

BLEAKLEY PLATT & SCHMIDT LLP

SIXTY-SIX FIELD POINT ROAD

GREENWICH, CONNECTICUT 06830

Telephone: 203-661-5222

Telecopier: 203-661-1197

Email: info@bpslaw.com

URL: http://www.bpslaw.com

White Plains, New York Office: One North Lexington Avenue. Telephone: 914-949-2700. Telecopier: 914-683-6956.

General Civil and Trial Practice. Corporation, Securities, Litigation (including Tax Certiorari), Banking, Probate, Trust, Estate Planning, Life Insurance, Municipal, Zoning, Utility, Real Estate Law, Employment and Environmental Law.

RESIDENT PARTNERS

JOHN J. FERGUSON, born New York, N.Y., October 3, 1939; admitted to bar, 1966, New York; 1979, Connecticut. *Education:* College of the Holy Cross (B.S., 1961); Fordham University (LL.B., 1965). Director, Patriot National Bank, 2001—. Trustee, St. Thomas Acquinas College, 2001—. Chairman of the Board, Catholic Sermons Foundation, 2001—. Trustee, College of New Rochelle, 1995-2001. Trustee, Inner City Foundation Diocese of Bridgeport, 1991-1998. Associate Trustee, College of the Holy Cross, 1975-1981. Trustee, St. Vincent's Hospital, Rye, New York, 1983-1986. Trustee, LaSalle Military Academy, 1990-1993. Member, President's Advisory Board, College of New Rochelle, 1980-1994. Director, Clemons Productions, Inc. Director, Bernard C. Harris Publishing Co. Trustee, Clare Rose Foundation. Trustee, Jane & Ralph Pfeiffer Foundation. *Member:* Greenwich, Westchester County, Connecticut and New York State (Member, Trusts and Estates Law Section) Bar Associations. ***Email:*** jjf@bpslaw.com

JOHN E. MEERBERGEN, born Brooklyn, New York, April 10, 1943; admitted to bar, 1972, Connecticut; 1980, U.S. District Court, Southern and Eastern Districts of New York; 1983, U.S. Court of Appeals, Second Circuit; 1994, U.S. Supreme Court. *Education:* University of Hartford (B.A., 1969); John Marshall Law School (J.D., 1972). Assistant Town Attorney, 1979-1981 and Town Attorney, 1982-1997, Town of Greenwich, Connecticut. *Member:*

(This Listing Continued)

BLEAKLEY PLATT & SCHMIDT LLP, Greenwich—Continued

Greenwich (Member, Sections on Family Law; Probate; Planning and Zoning), Connecticut and American Bar Associations; Connecticut Trial Lawyers Association. ***Email:*** jem@bpslaw.com

STEVEN PAUL DeRICCO, admitted to bar, 1985, New Jersey; 1987, New York, Connecticut and U.S. Tax Court; 1998, U.S. District Court, Southern District of New York. *Education:* St. Francis College (B.S., Accounting, 1981); Fordham University (J.D., 1984); New York University (LL.M., Taxation, 1991). Member, Town Council (RTM) Greenwich, CT, 1998—. Member, Town Claims Committee, Greenwich, CT, 1998—. Member, Board of Directors, American Red Cross, Westchester Affiliate. Chairman, Planned Giving Committee, American Red Cross, Westchester Affiliate. ***PRACTICE AREAS:*** Estate Planning; Trusts and Estates; Surrogates Court Practice; Litigation; Tax Law.

RESIDENT COUNSEL

J. LINCOLN HALLOWELL, born Brooklyn, New York, December 23, 1939; admitted to bar, 1972, New York; 1995, Connecticut. *Education:* Villanova University (B.A., 1960); St. Johns University (J.D., 1971). Trustee, Petroleum Industry Research Foundation, Inc., 1980—. *Member:* New York State Bar Association; Corporate Bar Association of Westchester and Fairfield. ***Email:*** jlh@bpslaw.com

(For Complete Biographical Data on all Personnel, See Professional Biographies at White Plains, New York)

BOEGGEMAN, GEORGE, HODGES & CORDE, P.C.

GREENWICH, CONNECTICUT

(See White Plains)

General Civil Trial Practice. Casualty Insurance, Personal Injury, Negligence, Medical Malpractice, Products Liability, Municipal Law, Commercial Litigation and Employment Law.

CACACE, TUSCH & SANTAGATA

GREENWICH, CONNECTICUT

(See Stamford)

General Civil and Criminal Trial Practice in State and Federal Courts, Administrative Law, Elder Law, Probate, Civil Appeals, Business Law, Creditor and Collections, Commercial Law, Telecommunications Law, Entertainment and the Arts, Contracts, Government, Construction Law, Land Use Litigation, Commercial Litigation, Personal Injury, Domestic Relations, Real Estate, Corporation, Estate Planning, Commercial Leasing, Planning and Zoning, Land Use, Environmental, Eminent Domain and Real Estate Tax Appeals.

J. MICHAEL CANTORE, JR.

GREENWICH, CONNECTICUT

(See Stamford)

Medical Malpractice, Personal Injury, Auto Accident, Product Liability, Civil and Commercial Litigation, Divorce, Family, Child Custody, Real Estate, Wills and Trust, Criminal Defense, DWI, Bankruptcy.

JONATHAN D. CARLISLE

Established in 1985

125 MASON STREET

GREENWICH, CONNECTICUT 06830

Telephone: 203-629-9600

Fax: 203-629-9072

Email: jdcarlisleassoc@aol.com

URL: http://www.lawyers.com/jonathandcarlisle

Essex Office: 67 Main Street Center Brook, P.O. Box 800, 06426.

Wills and Estate Planning, Taxation, Trust and Estate Administration, Contested Probate Matters, Residential and Investment Real Estate, Land Use and Zoning Law.

JONATHAN D. CARLISLE, born Hartford, Connecticut, December 3, 1942; admitted to bar, 1968, Connecticut. *Education:* St. Marks School, Southborough, Massachusetts; Yale University (B.A., 1965); University of Connecticut School of Law (LL.B., 1968). Associate, 1968-1973 and Member, 1974-1985, Badger, Fisher, Cohen & Barnett, Greenwich and Stamford, Connecticut. Member, Attorney/Realtor Panel, Greenwich Board of Realtors, 1985-1986. Director, 1983-1989 and Chairman, 1985-1989, Greenwich Arts Council. Trustee, 1985-1989 and Treasurer, 1988-1989, The Family Center. Trustee, 1986— and Secretary, 1988-1990, The Bruce Museum of the Town of Greenwich. *Member:* Greenwich and Connecticut (Member: Estates and Probate Committee; Real Estate Committee) Bar Associations.

REPRESENTATIVE CLIENTS: McNaught Syndicate, Inc. (Newspaper Features); Pam Marker, Inc. (Consumer Paper Products); Microwave Development, Inc. (Technology); Broadford & Maloney, Inc. (Business Consulting).
APPROVED TITLE ATTORNEYS FOR: Fleet Bank; Peoples Bank; Putnam Trust Co.; First American Title Insurance.
REFERENCE: Putnam Trust Co.

CASPER & de TOLEDO LLC

GREENWICH, CONNECTICUT

(See Stamford)

Civil Trial and Appellate Practice in all State and Federal Courts. Personal Injury, Medical Malpractice, Product Liability, Workers' Compensation, Employment Discrimination, Employee Rights and Benefits, Civil Rights, Contracts and Family Law.

CERUSSI & SPRING

A PROFESSIONAL CORPORATION

66 FIELD POINT ROAD

GREENWICH, CONNECTICUT 06830-6473

Telephone: 203-661-4000

Facsimile: 203-661-1197

White Plains, New York Office: One North Lexington Avenue. Telephone: 914-948-1200. Facsimile: 914-948-1579.

Litigation. Trials and Appeals in all State and Federal Courts. Insurance, Products Liability, Construction, Commercial, Environmental, Toxic Tort and Employment Law.

(For Complete Biographical Data on all Personnel, see Professional Biographies at White Plains, New York)

LAW OFFICES OF MICHAEL GENE CLEAR

GREENWICH, CONNECTICUT

(See Stamford)

General Civil Trial Practice in State and Federal Courts. Personal Injury, Negligence, Environmental Law and Hazardous Waste Litigation, Insurance Coverage Litigation, Complex Litigation, Commercial Litigation, Alternative Dispute Resolution, Mediation, Municipal Law, Environmental Insurance Defense, Insurance Coverage, Probate Litigation, Wills, Elder Law, Incapacity Planning, Probate Administration.

GARY I. COHEN

Established in 1969

781 NORTH STREET

GREENWICH, CONNECTICUT 06831

Telephone: 203-622-8787

Facsimile: 203-622-8798

Email: GICLAW@AOL.COM

URL: http://www.lawyers.com/giclaw

Practice Limited to Family and Matrimonial Law.

GARY I. COHEN, born New Haven, Connecticut, June 19, 1943; admitted to bar, 1968, Connecticut and U.S. District Court, District of Connecticut; U.S. Court of Appeals, 2nd Circuit and U.S. Supreme Court. *Education:* Yale University (B.A., 1965); University of Virginia (LL.B., 1968). Order of the Coif. Member, 1966-1968 and Articles Editor, 1967-1968, Virginia Law Review. Visiting Lecturer, Graduate Department of Psychology, Southern Connecticut State University, 1979-1983. Member, Board of Editors, The Connecticut Family Law Journal, 1982-1989. *Member:* Connecticut Bar Association (Member, Executive Committee: Civil Justice Section, 1978-1983; Criminal Justice Section, 1978-1979; Family Law Section, 1980—); Connecticut Trial Lawyers Association (President, 1981-1982). Fellow: American Academy of Matrimonial Lawyers (Past President, Board of Managers, Connecticut Chapter); International Academy of Matrimonial Lawyers; American College of Family Trial Lawyers (Charter Diplomate). ***PRACTICE AREAS:*** Family Law; Matrimonial Law.

(This Listing Continued)

ASSOCIATE

MARCI E. FINKELSTEIN, born Cleveland, Ohio, June 9, 1972; admitted to bar, 1998, Connecticut. *Education:* University of Florida (B.A., 1995); Touro College Jacob D. Fuchesberg Law Center (J.D., 1998). ***PRACTICE AREAS:*** Family Law; Matrimonial Law. ***Email:*** MARCI@GICLAW.COM

CUMMINGS & LOCKWOOD

TWO GREENWICH PLAZA
P.O. BOX 2505
GREENWICH, CONNECTICUT 06836
Telephone: (203) 869-1200
Telecopier: (203) 869-3120
Email: info@cl-law.com
URL: http://www.cl-law.com

Stamford, Connecticut Office: Four Stamford Plaza, P.O. Box 120, 06904-0120. Telephone: (203) 327-1700. Telecopier: (203) 351-4535.
Hartford, Connecticut Office: CityPlace I, 185 Asylum Street, 36th Floor, 06103-3495. Telephone: (860) 275-6700. Telecopier: (860) 724-3397.
New Haven, Connecticut Office: 700 State Street, P.O. Box 1960. 06509-1960. Telephone: (203) 782-3000. Telecopier: (203) 777-3347.
West Hartford, Connecticut Office: Town Center, 29 South Main Street, Suite 208, 06107. Telephone: (860) 275-6700. Telecopier: (860) 313-0293.
Bonita Springs, Florida Office: 24311 Walden Center, Suite 201, 34134. Telephone: (941) 947-8811. Telecopier: (941) 947-8025.
Naples, Florida Office: 3001 Tamiami Trail North, P.O. Box 413032, 34101-3032. Telephone: (941) 262-8311. Telecopier: (941) 263-0703.

General Practice. National and Regional Litigation Counsel, Corporate Law, Patent and Intellectual Property, Trusts and Estates, Labor and Employment, Mergers and Acquisitions, Partnerships and Joint Ventures, Commercial Lending, Corporate Finance, Creditors' Rights, Bankruptcy and Workouts, Securities Regulation and Litigation, Tax, Arbitration, Insurance, Banking and Financial Services, Leasing, Commercial and Residential Real Estate, Construction, Environmental, Toxic Torts, Health Law, Products Liability Litigation, Probate Litigation, Family Law and International Business.

FIRM PROFILE: Cummings & Lockwood caters both to commercial entities and individual clients, serves as local, regional and national counsel in Corporate, Litigation, and Creditors' Rights matters, and has one of the largest groups of Estate Planning professionals in the country.

Cummings & Lockwood attorneys answer questions and solve problems by having specialists in multiple disciplines practice together from eight offices to address the broad concerns of our diverse clientele. The firm guides corporate transactions and resolves complex business disputes for emerging, middle-market and Fortune 500 businesses, including high tech companies, financial services providers and industrial manufacturers. We are also uniquely positioned to assist affluent families and entrepreneurs in designing wealth preserving estate plans and developing business succession strategies.

PARTNERS

FOSTER BAM, born Bridgeport, Connecticut, January 11, 1927; admitted to bar, 1954, New York; 1968, Connecticut. *Education:* Yale University (B.A., 1950); Columbia University and Yale University (LL.B., 1953). Assistant U.S. Attorney for the Southern District of New York, 1955-1957.

FRANK J. COYLE, born New York, N.Y., August 12, 1919; admitted to bar, 1945, New York; 1947, Connecticut. *Education:* Princeton University (B.A., 1941); Yale University (LL.B., 1943). CEO, The Putnam Trust Company of Greenwich, Greenwich, Conn., 1978-1984. ***PRACTICE AREAS:*** Trusts Law; Estates Law; Real Estate. ***Email:*** fcoyle@cl-law.com

B. CORT DELANY, born Greenwich, Connecticut, August 2, 1955; admitted to bar, 1982, New York, Connecticut, U.S. District Court, Southern and Eastern Districts of New York. *Education:* Dartmouth College (A.B., 1977); Fordham University (J.D., 1981); New York University (LL.M., in Taxation, 1987). Member, Fordham International Law Journal. ***PRACTICE AREAS:*** Real Estate; Will Contests; Taxation; Probate Law; Estate Planning. ***Email:*** cdelan@cl-law.com

PHILIP M. DRAKE, born June 10, 1925; admitted to bar, 1952, New York; 1955, Connecticut. *Education:* Phillips Academy, Andover; Yale University (B.A., 1948); University of Virginia (J.D., 1951). Order of the Coif (Virginia Chapter, 1951). Associated with Sullivan & Cromwell, 1951-1953. Assistant United States Attorney for the Southern District of New York, 1953-1955. Trustee, University of Virginia Law School Foundation. Fellow, American College of Trust and Estate Counsel. ***Email:*** pdrake@cl-law.com

JOHN R. FRENCH, born New York, N.Y., January 2, 1941; admitted to bar, 1966, New York; 1975, U.S. Tax Court; 1977, Florida and Connecticut. *Education:* Harvard University (A.B., cum laude, 1962; LL.B., 1966). Associated with White & Case, 1966-1976. ***PRACTICE AREAS:*** Estate Settlement Law; Trust Administration Law; Taxation Law. ***Email:*** jfrench@cl-law.com

(This Listing Continued)

JESSIE A. GILBERT, born New York, N.Y., 1960; admitted to bar, 1986, New York; 1986, Massachusetts; 1989, Connecticut, California and U.S. Tax Court. *Education:* Hamilton College (A.B., 1982); Case Western Reserve University School of Law (J.D., 1985); New York University (LL.M., Taxation, 1986). Judicial Clerkship, The Honorable Carleton D. Powell, U.S. Tax Court, Washington, D.C., 1986-1987. Co-Author: "Creative Clients Require Creative Planning," Connecticut Law Tribune June 22, 1998, reprinted in Legal Times; "The New Environment in Connecticut for the Investment and Management of Trust and Charitable Assets," 14 Quinnipiac Law Journal, No.3 p.420, 2000. ***PRACTICE AREAS:*** Trusts and Estates; Estate Planning; Estate Administration; Taxation; Family Business Law.

ROBERT T. GILHULY, born Belmont, Massachusetts, May 7, 1930; admitted to bar, 1954, Connecticut. *Education:* College of the Holy Cross (B.A., 1951); Yale University (LL.B., 1954). Order of the Coif. *Member:* Greenwich (President, 1973), Connecticut (Chairman, Tax Section, 1966-1969; Executive Committee, Estates and Probate Section, 1978-1995) and American Bar Associations. Fellow, American College of Trust and Estate Counsel (Chairman, Conn. Chapter 1986-1991; Regent, 1994-1995). ***PRACTICE AREAS:*** Estate Settlement and Trust Administration; Estate Planning; Real Estate Law. ***Email:*** rgilhuly@cl-law.com

ROBERT F. GRELE, born Waterbury, Connecticut, December 29, 1939; admitted to bar, 1964, Connecticut. *Education:* Gettysburg College (A.B., 1961); Cornell University (LL.B., 1964). Order of the Coif. ***PRACTICE AREAS:*** Estate Settlement Law; Trust Administration Law; Real Estate Law. ***Email:*** rgrele@cl-law.com

WILLIAM R. LYNCH, born New York, N.Y., November 17, 1928; admitted to bar, 1959, New York; 1963, Connecticut. *Education:* Phillips Exeter Academy; Yale University (B.A., 1951); Columbia University (LL.B., 1958). Associated with Milbank, Tweed, Hadley & McCloy, 1958-1962. ***PRACTICE AREAS:*** Trusts and Estates Law; Real Estate Law; Business Law. ***Email:*** wlynch@cl-law.com

JONATHAN B. MILLS, born Springfield, Massachusetts, April 28, 1959; admitted to bar, 1985, Connecticut; 1988, U.S. District Court, District of Connecticut; 1991, U.S. Supreme Court. *Education:* Princeton University (A.B., 1981); University of Connecticut (J.D., 1985). ***PRACTICE AREAS:*** Real Estate Law; Leasing; Financing. ***Email:*** jmills@cl-law.com

DOUGLAS H. OLIN, born New Haven, Connecticut, May 3, 1968; admitted to bar, 1994, New York and Connecticut. *Education:* Emory University (B.B.A., 1990); New York University School of Law (J.D., 1993; LL.M. in Taxation, 1995). *Member:* Greenwich and Connecticut Bar Associations. ***PRACTICE AREAS:*** Estate Planning; Tax Planning; Estate Administration; Trust Administration. ***Email:*** dolin@cl-law.com

EDWARD F. RODENBACH, born Phillipsburg, New Jersey, April 16, 1951; admitted to bar, 1976, Connecticut. *Education:* Lafayette College (A.B., summa cum laude, 1973); Cornell University (J.D., cum laude, 1976). Phi Beta Kappa; Phi Alpha Theta. Editor-in-Chief, Cornell International Law Journal, 1975-1976. Author; "Compensation of Fiduciaries and their Counsel in Connecticut," 3 The Connecticut Probate Law Journal 295, 1988. Past President, Estate Planning Council of Fairfield County. ***PRACTICE AREAS:*** Estate Settlement Law; Trust Administration Law; Estate Law; Tax Planning Law; Executive Tax Planning Law. ***Email:*** erodenbach@cl-law.com

RESIDENT ASSOCIATES

April F. Condon ***Rani Newman Mathura***
Eugénie D. Verrillo

(For complete biographical information on personnel, see Professional Biographies at Stamford, CT, Hartford, CT, West Hartford, CT, New Haven, CT, Bonita Springs, FL and Naples, FL)

CURTIS, BRINCKERHOFF & BARRETT, P.C.

GREENWICH, CONNECTICUT

(See Stamford)

General Practice, Real Estate, Commercial Real Estate Acquisitions, Municipal Law, Zoning, Planning and Land Use, Banking, Administrative Law, Litigation, Civil Litigation, Commercial Litigation, Tax Appeals, Eminent Domain, Federal Taxation, International Taxation, State Taxation, Estate Planning, Trust and Estate, Probate, Elder Law, Family Law, Domestic Relations, Closely Held Corporations, Business Law, Corporate Law, Commercial Law, Commercial Leasing, Leases and Leasing, Employment Law, Non-Competition and Non-Solicitation Agreements, Commercial Arbitration, Construction Law, Landlord and Tenant Law, Personal Injury and Negligence, Product Liability, Bankruptcy, Civil Trial and Appellate Practice in all State and Federal Courts.

DAY, BERRY & HOWARD LLP

Established in 1919

ONE EAST PUTNAM AVENUE

GREENWICH, CONNECTICUT 06830

Telephone: 203-862-7800

Fax: 203-862-7801

Email: postmaster@dbh.com

URL: http://www.dbh.com

Hartford, Connecticut Office: CityPlace I. Telephone: 860-275-0100. Telecopier: 860-275-0343.

Stamford, Connecticut Office: One Canterbury Green. Telephone: 203-977-7300. Telecopier: 203-977-7301.

Boston, Massachusetts Office: 260 Franklin Street. Telephone: 617-345-4600. Telecopier: 617-439-4453.

Antitrust, Banking, Bank Lending, Bankruptcy, Bankruptcy Counseling, Benefits and Executive Compensation, Business Succession Planning, Business Transactions and Counseling, Closely Held Businesses, Credit Tenant Lease Financing, Commercial Litigation, Commercial Leasing, Construction, Direct Liability and Casualty Insurance, Disability, Emerging Companies, Energy, Environmental and Land Use, Equipment Finance and Leasing, Employment Law and Litigation, Environmental Law and Litigation, Executive Planning, Family Law, Finance and Investments, First Party Insurance, Franchise and Distributorship Litigation, Government Investigations, Health Care, Insurance Regulation and Proceedings, Insurance Litigation, International Tax, International Transactions, Life Insurance and Annuities, Low Income Housing Tax Credits, Medical and Professional Malpractice, Mergers and Acquisitions, Multi-Property Transactions, Municipal Finance, Negligence Defense, Planning for Entrepreneurs, Private Equity Funds, Product Liability, Real Estate Development, Real Estate Equity Investors, Real Estate Finance, Real Estate Workouts and Restructuring, Regulatory Insurance Proceedings and Litigation, Reinsurance, Securities Law, Securities Litigation, Strategic Joint Ventures, Structured Finance, Tax, Tax Litigation Group, Tax Exempt and Charity Giving, Tax Exempt Organizations, Technology and Intellectual Property Business and Litigation, Torts Litigation, Telecommunications, Trusts and Estates Administration, Trusts and Estates Litigation, Water Companies.

MEMBERS OF FIRM IN GREENWICH

R. SCOTT BEACH, born Newport Beach, CA, 1968; admitted to bar, 1993, Connecticut. *Education:* Emory University (B.A., 1990) Phi Beta Kappa; George Washington University National Law Center (J.D., with honors, 1993). ***PRACTICE AREAS:*** Emerging Companies; Mergers and Acquisitions; Strategic Joint Ventures; Private Equity Funds; Finance and Investments; Telecommunications. ***Email:*** rsbeach@dbh.com

RONALD OSBURN DEDERICK, born Chicago, IL, 1935; admitted to bar, 1963, New York; 1969, Connecticut. *Education:* University of Virginia (B.A., 1957; J.D., 1962). ***PRACTICE AREAS:*** Estate Planning; Tax-Exempt Organizations and Charitable Giving; Trust and Estate Administration; Trust and Estate Litigation. ***Email:*** rodederick@dbh.com

FORREST LEE GRIFFITH III, born Buffalo, NY, 1947; admitted to bar, 1972, Connecticut; 1979, U.S. Supreme Court. *Education:* Williams College (B.A., 1969); Boston University (J.D., cum laude, 1972). Member: Panel of Arbitrators, National Association of Securities Dealers, Inc.; International Bar Association; Connecticut Venture Group. ***PRACTICE AREAS:*** Emerging Companies; Mergers and Acquisitions; Strategic Joint Ventures; Finance and Investments; International Transactions. ***Email:*** flgriffith@dbh.com

AMY K. WILFERT, born New York, NY, 1957; admitted to bar, 1984, New York; 1995, Connecticut. *Education:* Amherst College (B.A., 1979); Fordham University (J.D., 1983). ***PRACTICE AREAS:*** Estate Planning; Entrepreneurs Trust and Estate Administration; Tax-Exempt Organizations. ***Email:*** akwilfert@dbh.com

ASSOCIATES OF THE FIRM IN GREENWICH

Peter Chadwick ***Shawn T. Wooden***

COUNSEL IN GREENWICH

Lesley I. B. Schless (Not admitted in CT)

(For Biographical Data on other firm personnel, see Professional Biographies at Hartford and Stamford, Connecticut and Boston, Massachusetts)

DISERIO MARTIN O'CONNOR & CASTIGLIONI LLP

GREENWICH, CONNECTICUT

(See Stamford)

General Practice. Litigation and Trials in all Courts. Corporate, Commercial Finance, Securities, Taxation, Banking, Foreclosure and Workout, Real Estate Law, Personal Injury and Negligence, Employment Law, Wrongful Termination, Workers Compensation, Insurance Coverage and Defense, Family, Creditors Rights and Bankruptcy, Trusts, Probate, Estate and Tax Planning.

DOUGHERTY, DOUGHERTY & VECCHIOLLA

Established in 1921

28 SOUND VIEW DRIVE

P.O. BOX 4239

GREENWICH, CONNECTICUT 06830

Telephone: 203-869-0290; 869-3085

FAX: 203-869-3159

URL: http://www.lawyers.com/dd&vlaw

General Practice. Estate Planning and Probate Law. Real Estate, Taxation and Corporate Law, Business Law, Trusts and Estates.

JAMES A. DOUGHERTY (1902-1992).

HUGH BRUCE DOUGHERTY (1931-1999).

MEMBERS OF FIRM

JOHN L. VECCHIOLLA, born New London, Connecticut, August 16, 1942; admitted to bar, 1971, Connecticut; 1972, U.S. District Court, District of Connecticut; 1975, U.S. Supreme Court. *Education:* Middlebury College (A.B., with honors in history, 1964); Boston University (J.D., 1967). Phi Alpha Delta. Member, Greenwich Board of Education, 1984-1997. Alternate Member Mediation & Arbitration Board of Connecticut, 1989-1991. *Member:* Greenwich (President, 1992-1993), Connecticut and American Bar Associations. [Capt., U.S. Army, Corps of Army Engineers, 1968-1970]. ***PRACTICE AREAS:*** Probate; Real Estate; General Practice; Taxation; Estate Planning.

JAMES BRUCE DOUGHERTY, born Port Chester, N.Y., June 27, 1958; admitted to bar, 1983, Connecticut. *Education:* Iona College (B.B.A., 1980); University of Connecticut (J.D., 1983). Greenwich Catholic School Board of Education (Member, 1994—; Chairman, 1996—). *Member:* Greenwich (President, 1995-1996), Regional (Vice-Chair Estates and Probate Committee) and Connecticut Bar Associations. ***PRACTICE AREAS:*** Estate Planning; Probate; Real Estate; Land Use; Elder Law; Taxation; General Practice.

REFERENCES: Fleet Bank, N.A.; Putnam Trust Co.

WAYNE D. EFFRON, P.C.

Established in 1979

165 WEST PUTNAM AVENUE

P.O. BOX 499

GREENWICH, CONNECTICUT 06836

Telephone: 203-622-1160

Fax: 203-622-4004

Email: effronlaw@effronlaw.com

URL: http://www.effronlaw.com

Matrimonial Law and Civil Litigation including Personal Injury and Commercial Law at the Trial and Appellate Levels.

WAYNE D. EFFRON, born Derby, Connecticut, August 18, 1950; admitted to bar, 1977, Connecticut and U.S. District Court, District of Connecticut; 1980, U.S. District Court, Southern and Eastern Districts of New York and U.S. Supreme Court; 1983, New York; 1992, U. S. Court of Appeals, Second Circuit. *Education:* University of Connecticut (B.A., summa cum laude, 1972; J.D., cum laude, 1977). Phi Beta Kappa. University Scholar. Listed in Best Lawyers in America, 1997—. Co-Author: "Connecticut Practice Book Annotated," published by West Publishing Company, Second Edition, Vols. 2 and 3, 1979; "Connecticut Practice Book Annotated," Published by West Publishing Company, Third Edition, Vol. 2, 3 and 3A, 1996. Adjunct Professor of Law, Pace University School of Law, 1983-1986. Special Pre-Trial Master, Superior Court, 1983—. *Member:* Greenwich (President, 1993-1994), Stamford/Norwalk Regional, Connecticut (Member, Sections on: Civil Justice; Family Law) and American (Member, Family Law Section) Bar Associations; The Association of Trial Lawyers of America; Connecticut Trial Lawyers Association. Fellow, American Academy of Matrimonial Lawyers (Member, Board of Managers, Connecticut Chapter). ***PRACTICE AREAS:*** Family Law; Civil Litigation; Personal Injury. ***Email:*** wayne@effronlaw.com

ALLEN GARY PALMER, born Bronx, New York, December 8, 1963; admitted to bar, 1988, Connecticut; 1989, New York; 1991, U.S. District Court, District of Connecticut; 1995, U.S. District Court, Eastern District of New York. *Education:* University of Connecticut (B.A., 1985); Inns of the Court School of Law, London, England (Certificate in Comparative Advocacy, 1987); Edinburgh University (Certificate in International Business Transactions, 1987); Benjamin N. Cardozo School of Law, Yeshiva University (J.D., 1988). Paulsen Editor, Moot Court Board, 1987-1988. Brief Writer, Prince Evidence Competition, 1987. Member, Sports Law Society, 1985-1988. Line Editor, Panel Publishers,

(This Listing Continued)

1988-1989. Panel Member, Appointed Counsel, Superior Court for Juvenile Matters, Danbury, Connecticut, 1993-1998. Assistant Corporate Counsel, City of Danbury, 1997-1999. *Member:* Greenwich and Connecticut Bar Associations; Stamford/Norwalk Regional Connecticut Bar Association. ***REPORTED CASES:*** Pangburn v. Klug, 244 A.D. 2d 394 (1997); SFP Tisca v. Robin Hill Farm, Inc., 244 Conn. 721 (1998). ***PRACTICE AREAS:*** Family Law; Civil Litigation; Personal Injury Law. ***Email:*** apalmer@effronlaw.com

OF COUNSEL

JOEL M. KAYE (Also practicing individually, Greenwich).

EPSTEIN FOGARTY COHEN SELBY

GREENWICH, CONNECTICUT

(See Fogarty Cohen Selby & Nemiroff LLC)

FINN DIXON & HERLING LLP

GREENWICH, CONNECTICUT

(See Stamford)

Corporate Law, Mergers and Acquisitions, Securities Law, Venture Capital Financing, Corporate Finance and Restructuring, Commercial Litigation, Banking and Lending Law, Bankruptcy and Workouts, Employee Benefits and the Federal and State Taxation of Businesses and Business Transactions.

FOGARTY COHEN SELBY & NEMIROFF LLC

88 FIELD POINT ROAD
P.O. BOX 2508
GREENWICH, CONNECTICUT 06836-2508
Telephone: 203-661-1000
Telefax: 203-629-7300
URL: http://www.lawyers.com/fcs&n

Litigation in all Courts, Real Estate and Land Use, Estate Planning and Probate, Corporate, Matrimonial, Administrative and Environmental, Appellate Practice, Business, Civil Trial, Commercial Litigation, Construction, Family, Labor and Employment, Medical Malpractice, Trust and Product Liability.

MEMBERS OF FIRM

JAMES R. FOGARTY, born Norwalk, Connecticut, 1943; admitted to bar, 1967, New York; 1968, Connecticut. *Education:* Fordham University (B.A., 1964; LL.B., 1967); New York University (LL.M., 1972). Law Clerk, Hon. Howard W. Alcorn, Chief Justice (Ret.), Connecticut Supreme Court, 1968-1969. Member, Board of Editors, Connecticut Bar Journal, 1976-1982. Special Pre-trial Master, Superior Court, 1979-1985, U.S. District Court, 1991—. Member, Connecticut Statewide Grievance Committee, 1982-1985. *Member:* American Board of Trial Advocates. Fellow, American College of Trial Lawyers. ***PRACTICE AREAS:*** Appellate Practice; Business Torts; Complex Litigation; Personal Injury Law; Malpractice. ***Email:*** jfogarty@fcsn.com

BRUCE F. COHEN, born Everett, Massachusetts, 1935; admitted to bar, 1959, New York; 1965, Connecticut. *Education:* New York University (B.A., 1955); Yale Law School (LL.B., 1958). *Member:* Greenwich, Connecticut, New York State and American Bar Associations; The Association of the Bar of the City of New York. ***PRACTICE AREAS:*** Land Use Law; Real Estate Law; Real Estate Finance Law. ***Email:*** bcohen@fcsn.com

LELAND C. SELBY, born Granite City, Illinois, 1944; admitted to bar, 1969, Connecticut; 1989, New York. *Education:* University of Richmond (B.A., 1966); University of Virginia (LL.B., 1969). Delta Theta Phi. *Member:* Greenwich, Connecticut (Member: Ethics Committee, 1985-1992; Executive Committee, Probate Section, 1985-1990; Chairman, Probate Committee of Young Lawyers Section, 1972-1974) and American Bar Associations. Fellow, American College of Trust and Estate Counsel. ***PRACTICE AREAS:*** Estate Planning and Administration; Trust Law; Estate and Gift Taxation Law; Charitable Organizations. ***Email:*** lselby@fcsn.com

ANDREW P. NEMIROFF, born Brooklyn, New York, September 13, 1951; admitted to bar, 1979, Connecticut and U.S. District Court, District of Connecticut; 1980, U.S. Court of Appeals, Second Circuit. *Education:* Central Connecticut State College (B.S., 1973); University of Utah (M.A., 1975); John Marshall Law School (J.D., with honors, 1979). Member, Order of John Marshall. Editor-In-Chief, John Marshall Law Review, 1978-1979. Law Clerk to Honorable T.F. Gilroy Daly, United States District Court, District of Connecticut, 1979-1981. Author: "The Illinois Abortion Parental Consent Act of 1977: A Far Cry From Permissible Consultation," 12 John Marshall Journal 179, 1979. *Member:* Connecticut and American Bar Associations. ***PRACTICE AREAS:*** Matrimonial Law; Accident and Personal Injury Law; Complex Litigation. ***Email:*** anemiroff@fcsn.com

(This Listing Continued)

STEVEN W. RUSSO, born Plattsburgh, New York, October 19, 1956; admitted to bar, 1981, Connecticut and U.S. District Court, District of Connecticut. *Education:* University of Connecticut (B.S., magna cum laude, 1978); George Washington University (J.D., with honors, 1981). Member, Town of Weston Planning and Zoning Commission, 1995—. Previous Employment: Trager and Trager P.C.; Badger Fisher & Cohen. *Member:* Greenwich, Connecticut and American (Member, Sections on: Real Estate; Corporate Law) Bar Associations. ***PRACTICE AREAS:*** Commercial Real Estate; Banking Law; Real Estate; Real Estate Finance; Land Use; Construction Law. ***Email:*** srusso@fcsn.com

COUNSEL

ROBERT A. EPSTEIN, born New York, N.Y., February 3, 1929; admitted to bar, 1954, Connecticut; 1955, U.S. District Court, District of Connecticut. *Education:* College of William & Mary (B.A., 1951); Yale University (LL.B., 1954). Phi Beta Kappa. Member, Bench and Bar, 1973-1975. Member, Connecticut Statewide Grievance Committee, 1979-1983. Special Pre-trial Master, Superior Court, 1979—. *Member:* Connecticut and American Bar Associations; American Academy of Matrimonial Lawyers; Connecticut Trial Lawyers Association. ***PRACTICE AREAS:*** Matrimonial Law.

EVERETT FISHER, born Greenwich, Connecticut, 1920; admitted to bar, 1948, Connecticut; 1949, New York. *Education:* Yale University (B.A., 1941); Yale Law School (LL.B., 1948). Phi Delta Phi. *Member:* Greenwich (President, 1959-1960), Connecticut and American Bar Associations. Fellow, American College of Trust and Estate Counsel. ***PRACTICE AREAS:*** Probate Law; Estate and Gift Taxation. ***Email:*** evfisher@yahoo.com

JENNIFER N. BOYD, born Meriden, Connecticut, 1952; admitted to bar, 1978, Connecticut. *Education:* Tufts University (B.A., magna cum laude, 1974); University of Connecticut (J.D., cum laude, 1978). *Member:* Connecticut and American Bar Associations. (Also of Counsel to Gleason & Hill, LLC, Darien). ***PRACTICE AREAS:*** Corporate Finance; Corporate Law; Mergers and Acquisitions; Partnership and Limited Liability Companies. ***Email:*** jboyd@fcsn.com

ASSOCIATES

WILLIAM BRADFORD SMITH, JR., born Flushing, New York, 1951; admitted to bar, 1985, Connecticut. *Education:* Pace University (B.S., 1981; J.D., 1985). Previous Employment: Whitman & Ransom; Badger Fisher & Cohen. *Member:* Greenwich and Connecticut Bar Associations. ***PRACTICE AREAS:*** Estate Planning and Administration; Trust Law; Estate and Gift Taxation; Charitable Organizations. ***Email:*** wsmith@fcsn.com

CAROLYN ALEXANDER COLLINS, born Atlanta, Georgia, May 26, 1963; admitted to bar, 1988, Connecticut; 1989, U.S. District Court, District of Connecticut; 1996, U.S. Court of Appeals, Second Circuit. *Education:* Cornell University (B.A., 1985); University of Connecticut School of Law (J.D., cum laude, 1988). Special Pre-Trial Master, Superior Court, 1994—. *Member:* Connecticut and American Bar Associations; Connecticut Trial Lawyers Association; American Trial Lawyers Association; Raymond E. Baldwin American Inn of Court. ***PRACTICE AREAS:*** Appellate Practice; Medical Malpractice; Commercial Litigation; Personal Injury; Business Torts. ***Email:*** ccollins@fcsn.com

LAWRENCE F. REILLY, born Silver Spring, Maryland, October 1, 1963; admitted to bar, 1989, Connecticut; 1990, New York and U.S. District Court, District of Connecticut; 1994, U.S. Court of Appeals, Second Circuit. *Education:* State University of New York at Purchase (B.A., 1986); New York Law School (J.D., cum laude, 1989). Special Pre-Trial Master, Fact Finder and Arbitrator, Superior Court. Listed in Who's Who Among American Law Students. Chief Notes and Comments Editor, New York Journal of Human Rights. Author, "Church and State: A Critical Analysis of the Lemon Test," New York Law School Journal of Human Rights, 1989. Previous Employment: Wofsey, Rosen, Kwaskin & Kuriansky; Williams, Cooney & Sheehy. *Member:* The Greater Bridgeport, Stamford Regional and Connecticut Bar Associations; Connecticut Trial Lawyers Association. ***REPORTED CASES:*** Gore v. People's Savings Bank, 235 Conn. 360, 665 A.2d 1341 (1995). ***PRACTICE AREAS:*** Litigation; Constitutional Law. ***Email:*** lreilly@fcsn.com

ANNE M. PIEDADE, born Des Moines, Iowa, January 21, 1967; admitted to bar, 1996, Connecticut; 1997, New York. *Education:* University of Connecticut (B.A., 1989); University of Connecticut School of Law (J.D., 1996). *Member:* Connecticut, New York State and American Bar Associations. ***PRACTICE AREAS:*** Estate Planning; Estate Administration; Trust Law; Estate and Gift Taxation; Charitable Organizations. ***Email:*** apiedade@fcsn.com

ERIC R. POSMANTIER, born Chicago, Illinois, June 9, 1971; admitted to bar, 1997, Connecticut. *Education:* State University of New York at Albany (B.A., 1993); Rutgers University, Camden (J.D., 1997). Member, Rutgers Law Journal, 1996-1997. ***PRACTICE AREAS:*** Family Law; Civil Litigation. ***Email:*** eposmantier@fcsn.com

GILBRIDE, TUSA, LAST & SPELLANE, LLC

Established in 1983

31 BROOKSIDE DRIVE

P.O. BOX 658

GREENWICH, CONNECTICUT 06836

Telephone: 203-622-9360

Facsimile: 203-622-9392

New York, New York Office: The Graybar Building, 420 Lexington Avenue. Telephone: 212-692-9666. Facsimile: 212-661-6328.

General Practice. Real Estate, Corporation, Securities, Federal and State Courts, Litigation, Franchise Law, Taxation, Admiralty, International, Trademark, Probate, Zoning, Land Use, Family Law and Aviation.

MEMBERS OF FIRM

FRANK J. GILBRIDE, II, born Brooklyn, New York, September 28, 1941; admitted to bar, 1968, New York; 1972, Connecticut; 1976, U.S. Supreme Court. *Education:* Villanova University (B.S., 1963); Fordham University (J.D., 1967). *Member:* Greenwich, Stamford/Norwalk Regional, Connecticut and American (Member, Real Property, Probate and Trust Law Section) Bar Associations; Maritime Law Association of the United States. ***PRACTICE AREAS:*** Trusts and Estates Law; Real Estate Law; Admiralty Law; Family Law. ***Email:*** fjg@gtlslaw.com

CHARLES S. TUSA, born Brooklyn, New York, September 6, 1944; admitted to bar, 1970, New York; 1976, U.S. Supreme Court; 1978, Connecticut. *Education:* Colgate University (B.A., 1966); New York Law School (J.D., 1969). Book Review Editor, New York Law Forum, 1969. Co-Author: Note, "Tort Liability in Light Civilian Aircraft Operation," 13 N.Y.L.F. 545, 1967. Reprinted: 11 Personal Injury Commentator 33, 1968; 18 Law Review Digest 1, 1968. Author: Note, "Churning: A Critical Analysis," 19 N.Y.L.F. 315, 1969. *Member:* Connecticut (Member, Executive Committee, Franchise Law Section) and American (Member, Sections on: Corporation, Banking and Business Law; Franchise Law) Bar Associations. ***PRACTICE AREAS:*** Corporation Law; Commercial Law; Securities Law; Franchise Law. ***Email:*** cst@gtlslaw.com

BENNETT H. LAST, born New York, N.Y., May 23, 1944; admitted to bar, 1969, New York; 1973, U.S. Supreme Court (Not admitted in Connecticut). *Education:* Queens College of the City University of New York (B.A., 1965); Columbia University (LL.B., 1968). Phi Beta Kappa. *Member:* The Association of the Bar of the City of New York (Member, Transportation Law Committee, 1980-1981); American Bar Association (Member, Sections on: Antitrust Law; Litigation). ***PRACTICE AREAS:*** Commercial Litigation. ***Email:*** bhl@gtlsny.com

THOMAS P. SPELLANE, born New York, N.Y., March 17, 1950; admitted to bar, 1976, New York; 1978, U.S. Tax Court; 1985, U.S. Supreme Court; 1993, Connecticut. *Education:* Hamilton College (B.A., 1971); Syracuse University (J.D., 1975); New York University (LL.M. in Taxation, 1982). *Member:* The Association of the Bar of the City of New York; New York State (Member, Taxation Section) and American (Member, Sections on: Taxation; Real Property, Probate and Trust Law) Bar Associations. ***PRACTICE AREAS:*** Taxation Law; Trusts and Estates Law; Real Estate Law. ***Email:*** tps@gtlslaw.com

JOHN P. TESEI, born Greenwich, Connecticut, May 13, 1948; admitted to bar, 1975, Connecticut. *Education:* University of Notre Dame (B.S., 1970); Fordham University (J.D., 1975). *Member:* Greenwich and Connecticut Bar Associations. ***PRACTICE AREAS:*** Environmental Law; Land Use; Commercial Real Estate; Aviation Law. ***Email:*** jpt@gtlslaw.com

ERIC H. SELTZER, born Bay Shore, New York, June 7, 1959; admitted to bar, 1985, New York; 1996, Connecticut. *Education:* Columbia University; University of Colorado (B.A., 1981); Brooklyn Law School (J.D., 1984). Member, Moot Court Honor Society, 1982-1984. Recipient, American Jurisprudence Award in Legal Profession. *Member:* Association of the Bar of the City of New York. ***PRACTICE AREAS:*** Commercial Litigation; Real Estate Law; Public Finance. ***Email:*** ehs@gtlsny.com

DAVID CRYSTAL, II, born New York, N.Y., February 9, 1938; admitted to bar, 1965, New York; 1968, U.S. District Courts, Southern and Eastern Districts of New York and U.S. Court of Appeals, Second Circuit; 1969, U.S. Supreme Court; 1974, Connecticut and U.S. District Court, District of Connecticut. *Education:* St. Lawrence University (B.A., 1961); Edinburgh University, Scotland; Boston University (J.D., 1964). Author: "Anatomy of an Arbitration," Practicing Law Institute, 1996. Assistant Counsel, Joint Legislative Committee, New York State Legislature on Legislative Fiscal Analysis and Review, 1967. Assistant Counsel, Joint Legislative Committee, New York State Legislature on Election Law, 1969-1970. Assistant Counsel, Minority Leader of the New York State Legislature, 1972. Commissioner, Howard-Farrington Commuter Hockey League, 1983-1986. Vice Chairman, Board of Trustees, 1986-1993 and President, 1993-1995, Green Chimneys Children's Services, Inc. Securities/Legal Editor and Columnist, Market Chronical, Weekly Newspaper published since 1839, 1987-1991. Arbitrator: New York Stock Exchange, Inc., 1987—; National

(This Listing Continued)

Association of Securities Dealers, 1988—. *Member:* The Association of the Bar of the City of New York. Securities Industry Association (Member, Compliance and Legal Division). ***PRACTICE AREAS:*** Securities Regulation; Arbitration; Litigation. ***Email:*** dc@gtlsny.com

JAMES P. DONOHUE, JR., born Bronxville, New York, June 28,, 1950; admitted to bar, 1976, New York and U.S. District Court, Southern and Eastern Districts of New York (Not admitted in Connecticut). *Education:* Fordham University (B.A., 1972; M.A., 1973; J.D., 1975). Member, Fordham Urban Law Journal, 1974-1975. Member, International Moot Court Team. Author: Case Note, "Administrative Law— Freedom of Information Act—Renegotiation Procedures Will Not Be Temporarily Stayed While a Controversy Over the Status of Documents Under the Information Act is Settled," III Fordham Urban Law Journal 359, 1975. *Member:* Westchester County, New York State (Member, Litigation Section) and American (Member, Sections on: Litigation; Family Law) Bar Associations. ***PRACTICE AREAS:*** Litigation; Securities Arbitration. ***Email:*** jpd@gtlsny.com

FREDERIC P. RICKLES, born Brooklyn, New York, February 25, 1965; admitted to bar, 1992, New York, Virginia and New Jersey (Not admitted in Connecticut). *Education:* University of Virginia (B.A., 1987); George Washington University (J.D., 1991). *Member:* The Association of the Bar of the City of New York. ***PRACTICE AREAS:*** Commercial Litigation; Real Estate Law; Trusts and Estates Law. ***Email:*** fpr@gtlsny.com

SARAH J. OTIS, born Morristown, New Jersey, 1967; admitted to bar, 1993, Connecticut; 1994, New Jersey. *Education:* Dartmouth College (A.B., 1990); Emory University; Benjamin N. Cardozo School of Law, Yeshiva University (J.D., 1993). ***LANGUAGES:*** French. ***PRACTICE AREAS:*** Trust and Estates. ***Email:*** sjo@gtlslaw.com

---

KENNETH M. GAMMILL JR., born Greenwich, Connecticut, September 29, 1968; admitted to bar, 1995, Connecticut; 1996, New York. *Education:* Hamilton College (A.B., 1990); Vermont Law School (J.D., cum laude, 1995). Best Oralist, 1994; Member, Moot Court Advisory Board, 1994-1995; Semi-Finalist, Debevoise Moot Court Competition and National Moot Court Team. *Member:* Greenwich, Stamford/Norwalk Regional, New York State and Connecticut Bar Associations. ***PRACTICE AREAS:*** Real Estate; Land Use; Environmental Law. ***Email:*** kmg@gtlslaw.com

GLEN J. MOORE, born Darien, Connecticut, July 31, 1972; admitted to bar, 1997, Connecticut. *Education:* Georgetown University (B.A., 1994); Pace University (J.D., 1997). *Member:* Greenwich, Stamford/Norwalk Regional, Connecticut and American Bar Associations. ***PRACTICE AREAS:*** Trusts and Estates; Real Estate. ***Email:*** gjm@gtlslaw.com

THOMAS W. LITTMAN, born New York, N.Y., May 3, 1970; admitted to bar, 1999, New York and Massachusetts (Not admitted in Connecticut). *Education:* Lehigh University (B.A., 1992); Tulane University of Louisiana (J.D., 1998). ***PRACTICE AREAS:*** Civil Litigation; Real Estate. ***Email:*** tl@gtlsny.com

OF COUNSEL

RAYMOND R. FLETCHER, JR., born Schenectady, New York, June 7, 1929; admitted to bar, 1956, New York (Not admitted in Connecticut). *Education:* Rensselaer Polytechnic Institute (B.Ch.E., 1949); Harvard University (LL.B., 1956). *Member:* The Association of the Bar of the City of New York; New York State and American Bar Associations.

ROBERT N. LITTMAN, born Brooklyn, New York, May 4, 1932; admitted to bar, 1961, New York; 1967, U.S. Tax Court (Not admitted in Connecticut). *Education:* Lehigh University (B.S., 1954); Brooklyn Law School (LL.B., 1960); New York University (LL.M., Taxation, 1962). Certified Public Accountant, New York, 1960. [Private, U.S. Army, 1954-1956]. ***PRACTICE AREAS:*** Taxation; Trusts and Estates; Probate. ***Email:*** rlittman@msn.com

---

MYRA L. GRAUBARD

GREENWICH, CONNECTICUT

(See Stamford)

Commercial Law, Commercial Collections, Retail Collections, Enforcement of Judgements, Post Judgment Collections, Civil Litigation, General Civil Practice, Family Law, Divorce, Probate, Wills, Real Estate.

ROBERT W. GREEN

GREENWICH, CONNECTICUT

(See Stamford)

Real Estate, Probate and Estate, Elder Law, Zoning, Planning and Land Use, Administrative Law, Financial Law and Legislative Practice.

GRIMES & BATTERSBY L.L.P.

GREENWICH, CONNECTICUT

(See Stamford)

Patents, Trademarks, Copyrights, Unfair Competition, Trade Secrets, Multimedia, Licensing, Franchising, Litigation and Antitrust.

HEAGNEY, LENNON & SLANE LLP

Established in 1959

248 GREENWICH AVENUE

P.O. BOX 7910

GREENWICH, CONNECTICUT 06836

Telephone: 203-661-8400

Fax: 203-661-7496

Email: slane@prodigy.net

URL: http://www.lawyers.com/hlslaw

General Practice, Real Estate, Trusts and Estates, Probate, Corporation and Business Law, Civil and Criminal Litigation, Zoning and Family Law.

MEMBERS OF FIRM

JOHN G. HEAGNEY (1925-1982).

FRANCIS X. LENNON, JR. (1928-1999).

JOHN F. SLANE, JR., born Jersey City, New Jersey, August 20, 1949; admitted to bar, 1974, Connecticut; 1975, U.S. District Court, District of Connecticut; 1981, New York; 1989, U.S. Tax Court; 1996, U.S. District Court, Southern District of New York; 2000, U.S. Court of Appeals, Second Circuit. *Education:* St. Michael's College (B.A., cum laude, 1971); University of Maine (J.D., 1974). Recipient, American Jurisprudence Awards in Torts and Real Property. Editor, University of Maine Law Review, 1973-1974. Member, Fairfield Board of Education, 1988-1989. Moderator, Fairfield Town Meeting, 1997-1999. *Member:* Connecticut and New York State Bar Associations; The Association of Trial Lawyers of America; Connecticut Trial Lawyers Association. ***PRACTICE AREAS:*** General Practice; Family Law; Real Estate Litigation; Construction Litigation; Civil Litigation; Wills; Trust Law. **Email:** slane@prodigy.net

THOMAS J. HEAGNEY, born New York, N.Y., January 3, 1953; admitted to bar, 1980, Connecticut; 1988, New York. *Education:* Drew University (B.A., 1975); New York Law School (J.D., 1980). Member: Greenwich Representative Town Meeting, 1981-1985; Greenwich Planning and Zoning Commission, 1985-1991. Greenwich Board of Education, 1991-1995. *Member:* Greenwich, Connecticut and American Bar Associations. ***PRACTICE AREAS:*** General Practice; Corporate; Business; Probate Law; Estate Planning; Zoning, Planning and Land Use; Real Estate. **Email:** heagney@prodigy.net

APPROVED TITLE ATTORNEYS FOR: Fleet Bank; Putnam Trust Co.; People's Bank; Fairfield County Savings Bank; New Haven Savings Bank; First American Title Insurance Co.; Pawling Savings Bank; Dime Savings Bank; First Union Bank; Chase; First County Bank; Bank of America; Webster Bank; Wells Fargo Home Mortgage, Inc.; Greenwich Bank And Trust Co.; Summit Bank; Citicorp Mortgage; Astoria Federal Mortgage Corp.; Merrill Lynch Credit Corp.; Washington Mutual Bank, FA; Wilton Bank; Chevy Chase Bank CCB.

KEVIN T. HOFFMAN

Established in 1995

289 GREENWICH AVENUE, SECOND FLOOR

GREENWICH, CONNECTICUT 06830

Telephone: 203-869-8744

Fax: 203-869-8648

Email: KTH9@aol.com

URL: http://www.lawyers.com/kthoffman

Commercial Litigation. Securities Arbitration, Employment and Litigation.

FIRM PROFILE: The Law Offices of Kevin T. Hoffman, established in January, 1995, serve a national client base with specializations in securities arbitrations and related employment matters. The firm also represents clients before regulatory organizations and state regulators.

KEVIN T. HOFFMAN, born Bronxville, New York, August 11, 1956; admitted to bar, 1982, New York and U.S. District Court, Southern and Eastern Districts of New York; 1993, Connecticut and U.S. Supreme Court; 1997, U.S. District Court, District of Connecticut. *Education:* Dartmouth College (A.B., 1978); Fordham University (J.D., 1981). Author: "Campeche Bay Blow-out: A Strict Liability Approach to Damages Resulting from Offshore Drilling Accidents," Vol. 3, Fordham International Law Journal, 1980. Panelist, National Association of Securities Dealers Arbitration Board. Speaker, Securities Industry Association Law and Compliance Seminar, 1997. *Member:* New York State and Connecticut Bar Associations. ***PRACTICE AREAS:*** Securities Arbitration; NASD Arbitration; New York Stock Exchange Arbitration; SEC Enforcement; Securities Litigation; Commercial Litigation; Bankruptcy Matters; Employment Litigation; Executive Severance Contracts.

(This Listing Continued)

HOLLAND KAUFMANN & BARTELS, LLC

289 GREENWICH AVENUE

GREENWICH, CONNECTICUT 06830-6595

Telephone: 203-869-5600

Fax: 203-869-4648

General Practice. Business and Corporate Law, Employment Law, Estate Planning and Probate Law, Family and Matrimonial Law, Litigation, Residential and Commercial Real Estate and Taxation.

ALEXANDER J. HOLLAND, born Brooklyn, New York, October 5, 1931; admitted to bar, 1956, New York; 1959, Connecticut and U.S. Tax Court. *Education:* Hofstra College (B.A., cum laude, 1952); Harvard University (LL.B., 1955). *Member:* The Association of the Bar of the City of New York; Greenwich (President, 1991-1992), Connecticut (Member, Executive Committee, Probate Section, 1977-1992; Co-Chair: Subcommittee on Virtual Representation, 1987-1993; Spousal Rights at Death, 1988-1991 and Creditors Claims Against Estates, 1987) and American Bar Associations. Fellow: American College of Trust and Estate Counsel (Former Member, State Laws Committee; Chair, Subcommittees on Virtual Representation, 1985, and Uniform Laws, 1988); James W. Cooper Fellow, Connecticut Bar Association. ***PRACTICE AREAS:*** Estate Planning Law; Probate Law; Trust Law; Taxation; Family Law. **Email:** aholland@hkbllc.com

CHARLES B. KAUFMANN, III, born Pittsburgh, Pennsylvania, January 13, 1944; admitted to bar, 1969, Connecticut; 1970, New York. *Education:* Yale University (B.A., cum laude, 1966); Columbia University (J.D., 1969). Law Clerk to Justice Charles S. House, Connecticut Supreme Court, 1969-1970. Associate, Simpson Thacher & Bartlett, New York, New York, 1970-1977. *Member:* Greenwich, Stamford-Norwalk Regional, Connecticut (Member, Sections on: Corporations and Other Business Organizations; Banking; Tax) and American Bar Associations; The Corporate Bar Association of Westchester and Fairfield, Inc. ***PRACTICE AREAS:*** Corporate Law; Business Law; Buying and Selling of Businesses; Small Business Law; Real Estate. **Email:** ckaufmann@hkbllc.com

PHILIP H. BARTELS, born Cleveland, Ohio, September 30, 1949; admitted to bar, 1974, Connecticut and U.S. District Court, District of Connecticut; 1975, U.S. District Court, Southern and Eastern Districts of New York; 1976, U.S. District Court, District of Vermont; 1980, New York and U.S. District Court, Northern District of New York. *Education:* Cornell University (B.A., cum laude, 1971); University of Chicago (J.D., 1974). Phi Beta Kappa. Magistrate, Connecticut Superior Court, 1983-1985. Member, 1984-2000, Chairman, 1992-2000, Town of Greenwich Conservation Commission. *Member:* Greenwich, Connecticut, New York State and American Bar Associations. ***PRACTICE AREAS:*** Matrimonial Law; Litigation; Exempt Organizations. **Email:** pbartels@hkbllc.com

HAROLD R. BURKE, born Willimantic, Connecticut, August 13, 1959; admitted to bar, 1988, Connecticut and New York; 1989, U.S. District Court, Southern District of New York and U.S. District Court, District of Connecticut. *Education:* Southern Connecticut State University (B.S., with honors, 1979); University of Connecticut (M.B.A., 1982); Pace University School of Law (J.D., 1987). Recipient: New York State Bar Association, Committee on International Trade and Transactions Writing Award, 1987. *Member:* Greenwich, Connecticut and American Bar Associations; The Association of Trial Lawyers of America; Connecticut Employment Lawyers Association; National Employment Lawyers Association. ***PRACTICE AREAS:*** Litigation; Employment Law; Personal Injury Law; Business Litigation; Matrimonial Law. **Email:** HRBurke@aol.com

JEAN MILLS ARANHA, born Bridgeport, Connecticut, 1955; admitted to bar, 1989, Connecticut; 1990, New York. *Education:* Yale University (B.A., cum laude, 1977); Fordham University School of Law (J.D., cum laude, 1989). Associate, Day, Berry & Howard, Stamford, Connecticut, 1989-1996. *Member:* Stamford-Norwalk Regional, Connecticut (Member: Executive Committee, Elder Law Section; Section on Estate and Probate Section), New York State (Member, Sections on: Trusts and Estates; Elder Law) and American Bar Associations; National Academy of Elder Law Attorneys. ***PRACTICE AREAS:*** Estate Planning; Probate; Administration of Trusts and Estates; Administrative Law. **Email:** jaranha@hkbllc.com

LORI E. ROMANO, born Greenwich, Connecticut, March 10, 1967; admitted to bar, 1992, Connecticut. *Education:* Fairfield University (B.A., magna cum laude, 1989); University of Bridgeport (J.D., magna cum laude, 1992). Phi Delta Phi. Notes and Comments Editor, University of Bridgeport Law Review, 1991-1992. Recipient: American Jurisprudence Award, Estate Planning, 1990; Outstanding Legal Scholarship, 1990 and 1992; American Bar Association Law Award, Section of Urban, State and Local Government, 1992; Recipient, Con-

(This Listing Continued)

HOLLAND KAUFMANN & BARTELS, LLC, Greenwich—Continued

necticut Attorneys Title Insurance Co. Real Property Award, 1992. *Member:* Connecticut and American Bar Associations. ***PRACTICE AREAS:*** Estate Planning Law; Probate Law; Trust Law. ***Email:*** lromano@hkbllc.com

JOHN C. FUSCO, born New Haven, Connecticut, June 26, 1961; admitted to bar, 1993, Rhode Island; 1994, Connecticut; 1997, U.S. District Court, District of Connecticut. *Education:* Providence College (B.A., 1983); University of Bridgeport (J.D., 1992). ***PRACTICE AREAS:*** Litigation; Employment Law; Business Litigation; Real Estate; Small Business Law. ***Email:*** jfusco@hkbllc.com

OF COUNSEL

BETH K. HANSSON, born Pittsburgh, Pennsylvania, June 9, 1961; admitted to bar, 1986, Connecticut. *Education:* University of Richmond (B.A., magna cum laude, 1983); Washington College of Law, American University (J.D., 1986). Phi Beta Kappa. Member, American University Journal of International Law and Policy, 1985-1986. *Member:* Greenwich (Vice President, 1995-1997), Connecticut and American Bar Associations. ***PRACTICE AREAS:*** Corporate Law; Business Law; Small Business Law; Real Estate.

HOPPER & HOPPER

170 MASON STREET

GREENWICH, CONNECTICUT 06830

Telephone: 203-629-1100

Facsimile: 203-629-1104

Email: hopperandhopper@aol.com

URL: http://www.lawyers.com/hopperandhopper

Probate and Estate Planning, Wills, Trusts and Real Estate Law.

MEMBERS OF FIRM

CAMERON F. HOPPER, born Brooklyn, New York, March 9, 1933; admitted to bar, 1959, Connecticut. *Education:* Trinity College (B.A., with honors, 1955); Yale Law School (J.D., 1958). Phi Beta Kappa. Recipient, Citation, Governor of Connecticut and State Legislature for Outstanding Service as Judge of Probate, 1991. Probate Judge, District of Greenwich, 1968-1991. Member, 1991—; Secretary, 1991—, Council on Probate Judicial Conduct. Secretary, Greenwich Board of Health, 1963-1968. Member, Advisory Committee to Probate Court Administrator, 1991-1992. Vice Chairman, Commission on Aging, 1991-1995. Member, 1968-1991; Vice President, 1971, Connecticut Probate Assembly. Secretary and Board Member, The Oaklawn Foundation, 1994—. James W. Cooper Fellow, Connecticut Bar Association. *Member:* Greenwich (President, 1973) and Connecticut (Member, Estates and Probate Section) Bar Associations; National College of Probate Judges. ***PRACTICE AREAS:*** Probate; Estate Planning; Wills; Trusts and Estates; Real Estate.

DAVID W. HOPPER, born Greenwich, Connecticut, March 27, 1965; admitted to bar, 1991, Connecticut, U.S. District Court, District of Connecticut and U.S. District Court, Southern District of New York. *Education:* University of Richmond (B.A., 1987); University of Bridgeport (J.D., 1990). Recipient, American Jurisprudence Award in Environmental Law. Secretary, 1992-1994, Vice Chairman, 1994-1996, and Chairman, 1996-1998, Board of Health, Greenwich, Connecticut. Chairman, Greenwich Republican Town Committee, 1998—. ***PRACTICE AREAS:*** Land Use; Land Development; Real Estate; Probate; Estate Planning; Wills; Trusts and Estates.

VERONICA C. STAPLEFIELD, born Greenwich, Connecticut, March 5, 1956; admitted to bar, 1989, New York and Connecticut. *Education:* Sacred Heart University (B.S., cum laude, 1983); Pace University (J.D., 1988). *Member:* Greenwich, Connecticut and American Bar Associations. ***PRACTICE AREAS:*** Trusts and Estates; Real Estate.

OF COUNSEL

PAMELA D. BOCHINSKI, born Mt. Vernon, New York, October 27, 1941; admitted to bar, 1977, Connecticut; 1990, New York. *Education:* University of Edinburgh, Edinburgh, Scotland; Bucknell University (B.A., 1963); University of Connecticut (J.D., 1977). Justice of the Peace, Weston, Connecticut, 1985—. Member, Panel of Moderators, Weston, Connecticut, 1983-1987. *Member:* Westport, Connecticut (Member: Executive Committee, Estates and Probate Section, 1982—; Board of Editors, Connecticut Bar Journal, 1992—), New York State and American Bar Associations. (Also practicing individually, Westport). ***PRACTICE AREAS:*** Estate Planning Law; Wills Law; Trusts Law; Probate Law; Trust Administration Law; Estate Law; Gift Law; Personal Taxation Law; Civil Practice.

IVEY, BARNUM & O'MARA, LLC

Established in 1950

170 MASON STREET

P.O. BOX 1689

GREENWICH, CONNECTICUT 06830

Telephone: 203-661-6000

Telecopier: 203-661-9462

Email: general@ibolaw.com

URL: http://www.ibolaw.com

General Practice. E-Commerce, Litigation in all Courts. Corporate, Commercial, Finance, Taxation, Trusts, Probate, Estate Planning, Family Law, Zoning, Environmental, Real Estate, Employment Law and Elder Law.

MEMBERS OF FIRM

MICHAEL J. ALLEN, born Corning, New York, February 13, 1960; admitted to bar, 1985, Connecticut and U.S. District Court, District of Connecticut. *Education:* Cornell University (B.S., 1982; J.D., 1985). *Member:* Greenwich and Connecticut Bar Associations. ***PRACTICE AREAS:*** Corporate Law; Commercial Law; Commercial Real Estate. ***Email:*** m-allen@ibolaw.com

ROBERT C. BARNUM, JR., born New York, N.Y., October 27, 1921; admitted to bar, 1948, Connecticut; 1950, U.S. District Court, District of Connecticut; 1954, U.S. Court of Appeals, Second Circuit. *Education:* Dartmouth College (A.B., 1943); Cornell University (LL.B., cum laude, 1948). Prosecutor, 1950-1951. Secretary, Greenwich Board of Health, 1953-1964. Moderator Pro Tem, Representative Town Meeting, 1965-1979. *Member:* Greenwich (President, 1963), Connecticut and American Bar Associations. ***PRACTICE AREAS:*** Trusts and Estates; Tax Planning; Real Estate. ***Email:*** r-barnum@ibolaw.com

EDWARD D. COSDEN, JR., born New York, N.Y., March 28, 1945; admitted to bar, 1971, Connecticut; 1977, U.S. District Court, District of Connecticut and U.S. District Court, Southern and Eastern Districts of New York. *Education:* Westminster College (B.A., 1968); University of Tulsa (J.D., 1970). Phi Delta Phi. Legislation Editor, Tulsa Law Journal, 1970. Author, "The Physician-Patient Privilege in Oklahoma," Tulsa Law Journal, Vol. 7, No. 2, 1971. Member: Darien Conservation Commission and Darien Inland Wetlands Commission, 1980-1986; Darien Planning and Zoning Commission, 1987-1989. Member and Vice Chairman, Darien Environmental Protection Commission, 1986-1989. *Member:* Greenwich, Connecticut and American Bar Associations. ***PRACTICE AREAS:*** Trusts and Estates; Tax Planning. ***Email:*** e-cosden@ibolaw.com

WILMOT L. HARRIS, JR., born Wheeling, West Virginia, February 19, 1941; admitted to bar, 1967, District of Columbia; 1968, Connecticut. *Education:* Washington & Lee University (B.S., 1963); University of Pennsylvania (LL.B., 1966). Member, 1991—, Secretary, 1991-1995 and Chairman, 1995-1999, Greenwich Commission on Aging. *Member:* Greenwich (President, 1989-1990) and Connecticut (Member, House of Delegates, 1988-1990) Bar Associations; District of Columbia Bar. ***PRACTICE AREAS:*** Trusts and Estates; Tax Planning; Real Estate; Corporate Law. ***Email:*** mharris@ibolaw.com

WILLIAM I. HASLUN II, born Hartford, Connecticut, June 21, 1958; admitted to bar, 1987, Connecticut; 1988, U.S. District Court, District of Connecticut; 1989, U.S. District Court, Southern District of New York. *Education:* Phillips Academy; St. Andrews University; Hamilton College (B.A., 1981); University of Connecticut (J.D., 1987). Member, 1992-1999, Treasurer, 1992-1995 and Vice Chairman, 1996-1999, Greenwich Housing Authority. Member, 1994—, Court Operations Chair, 1996—, Citizen's Advisory Council for Housing Matters. Member, Greenwich Housing Partnership, 1991-1993. *Member:* Greenwich (President, 1997-1998), Connecticut (Member, Land Use Section) and American Bar Associations. ***PRACTICE AREAS:*** Civil Litigation; Family Law; Land Use; Zoning Law. ***Email:*** c-haslun@ibolaw.com

JUERG A. HEIM, born Aarau, Switzerland, August 25, 1962; admitted to bar, 1990, New York and Connecticut. *Education:* Connecticut College (B.A., 1984); New York Law School (J.D., 1988). *Member:* Greenwich and Connecticut Bar Associations. ***LANGUAGES:*** German. ***PRACTICE AREAS:*** Corporate Law; Commercial Law; Business Law. ***Email:*** j-heim@ibolaw.com

MICHAEL J. JONES, born Bronx, New York, September 9, 1958; admitted to bar, 1983, Connecticut; 1984, U.S. District Court, District of Connecticut; 1990, U.S. Supreme Court; 1992, New York and U.S. District Court, Southern District of New York. *Education:* Colgate University (B.A., cum laude, 1980); Boston College (J.D., 1983). *Member:* Greenwich, Connecticut, New York State and American Bar Associations; The Association of Trial Lawyers of America; Connecticut Trial Lawyer's Association. ***PRACTICE AREAS:*** General Practice; Residential Real Estate; Commercial Real Estate; Commercial Law; Litigation. ***Email:*** m-jones@ibolaw.com

EDWARD T. KRUMEICH, JR., born Greenwich, Connecticut, June 22, 1950; admitted to bar, 1975, Connecticut; 1977, U.S. District Court, Northern District of Ohio and U.S. Court of Appeals, Sixth Circuit; 1978, New York and

(This Listing Continued)

U.S. District Court, Southern and Eastern Districts of New York; 1984, U.S. District Court, District of Connecticut. *Education:* Hamilton College (A.B., 1972); Case Western Reserve University (J.D., 1975). Order of the Coif. Editor, Law Review, 1974-1975. Law Clerk to the Hon. Anthony J. Celebrezze, Judge, U.S. Court of Appeals, Sixth Circuit. Member and Chairman, Greenwich Board of Social Services, 1990-1995. Member, Board of Estimate and Taxation, Greenwich, 1995—. *Member:* Greenwich, Connecticut, New York State and American (Member, Sections on: Litigation; Family Law; Labor Law) Bar Associations; Association of the Bar of the City of New York (Member: Young Lawyers Committee, 1982-1985; Lectures and Continuing Education Committee, 1985-1988); The Association of Trial Lawyers of America; Connecticut Trial Lawyers Association; National Institute of Trial Advocacy. ***PRACTICE AREAS:*** Litigation; Construction Law; Employment Law; Residential Real Estate. ***Email:*** e-krumeich@ibolaw.com

DONAT C. MARCHAND, born Westmore, Vermont, May 5, 1934; admitted to bar, 1958, Connecticut. *Education:* College of the Holy Cross; University of Connecticut (B.S., 1955); Harvard University (LL.B., 1958); New York University (LL.M., Taxation, 1967). *Member:* Greenwich (President, 1988), Connecticut (Member: House of Delegates, 1984-1998; Board of Governors, 1986-1998; Vice President, 1998-1999; President-Elect, 1999-2000; President, 2000-2001; Immediate Past President, 2001-2002) and American Bar Associations; Fellow, American College of Trust and Estate Counsel; Director, Connecticut Bar Foundation and American Bar Foundation. [Capt., U.S. Air Force, Judge Advocate, 1959-1963]. ***LANGUAGES:*** French. ***PRACTICE AREAS:*** Trusts and Estates; Tax Planning; Real Estate; Taxation; Land Use; Zoning Law; Probate Litigation. ***Email:*** d-marchand@ibolaw.com

MILES F. McDONALD, JR., born Brooklyn, New York, March 10, 1938; admitted to bar, 1964, New York; 1969, Connecticut; U.S. District Court, District of Connecticut; U.S. District Court, Southern and Eastern Districts of New York; U.S. Court of Appeals, Second Circuit. *Education:* Portsmouth Abbey; Columbia University (B.A., 1960; LL.B., 1963). Commissioner, Public Defender Services Commission, 1974-1978. *Member:* Greenwich (President, 1982), Connecticut, New York State and American Bar Associations; The Association of Trial Lawyers of America. Fellow, National Board of Trial Advocacy. Certified as a Civil Trial Advocate by the National Board of Trial Advocacy. ***PRACTICE AREAS:*** Litigation; Probate Litigation. ***Email:*** m-mcdonald@ibolaw.com

EDWIN J. O'MARA, JR., born Holyoke, Massachusetts, June 3, 1920; admitted to bar, 1950, Connecticut. *Education:* Harvard University (A.B., cum laude, 1947; LL.B., 1950). Member, 1952-1962 and Chairman, 1953-1962, Housing Authority of Greenwich. Member, State Bar Examining Committee, 1966-1981. *Member:* Greenwich (President, 1967), Connecticut and American Bar Associations. ***PRACTICE AREAS:*** Real Estate; Trusts and Estates; Tax Planning.

JENNIFER D. PORT, born New York, N.Y., April 26, 1955; admitted to bar, 1984, New York; 1997, Connecticut. *Education:* Union College (B.A., cum laude, 1977); Benjamin N. Cardozo School of Law, Yeshiva University (J.D., 1981). Director, Women's Division, 1984-1990, Director, 1986-1992, Trustee, 1992—, The Jewish Guild for the Blind. Director, J.G.B. Health Care Facilities, Inc., 1987-1989. *Member:* The Association of the Bar of the City of New York; Greenwich, Connecticut, New York State (Member: Committee on Estate and Trust Administration, 1989—; Sections on: Trusts; Estates) and American Bar Associations; Estate Planning Council of Westchester County. ***PRACTICE AREAS:*** Trusts and Estates; Tax Planning; Probate; Estate Litigation; Charitable Trusts and Foundations. ***Email:*** j-port@ibolaw.com

KARLA PANKRATZ RAY, born Sturgeon Bay, Wisconsin, 1966; admitted to bar, 1991, Connecticut, Wisconsin and U.S. District Court, Eastern District of Wisconsin. *Education:* University of Wisconsin-Madison (B.A., 1988); Marquette University (J.D., 1991). Member, 1989-1990 and Managing Editor, 1990-1991, Marquette University Law Review. *Member:* Stamford/Norwalk Regional and Connecticut Bar Associations. ***PRACTICE AREAS:*** Residential Real Estate; Commercial Real Estate; Commercial Finance; Franchise Law. ***Email:*** k-ray@ibolaw.com

GREGORY A. SAUM, born Amsterdam, New York, November 28, 1954; admitted to bar, 1979, Connecticut and U.S. District Court, District of Connecticut. *Education:* Dartmouth College (A.B., magna cum laude, 1976); Boston University (J.D., 1979). *Member:* Greenwich, Connecticut (Member, Estates and Probate Section) and American Bar Associations; Estate Planning Council of Lower Fairfield County. ***PRACTICE AREAS:*** Trusts and Estates; Tax Planning; Probate; Real Estate. ***Email:*** g-saum@ibolaw.com

LORRAINE SLAVIN, born New York, N.Y., September 14, 1953; admitted to bar, 1985, Connecticut; 1986, New York. *Education:* Marymount College (B.A., 1975); Hunter College (M.S., 1976); Manhattanville College (M.P.S., 1981); Fordham University (J.D., cum laude, 1985). Senior Articles Editor, Fordham Law Review, 1984-1985. Law Clerk to Judge William H. Timbers, U.S. Court of Appeals, Second Circuit, 1985-1986. *Member:* Greenwich, Connecticut, New York State and American Bar Associations. ***PRACTICE AREAS:*** Real Estate; Land Use; Zoning Law. ***Email:*** l-slavin@ibolaw.com

(This Listing Continued)

STEVEN B. STEINMETZ, born Mount Vernon, New York, March 19, 1962; admitted to bar, 1985, Connecticut; 1992, New York. *Education:* Yeshiva University (B.A., magna cum laude, 1982); Benjamin N. Cardozo School of Law, Yeshiva University (J.D., 1985). Executive Editor, Cardozo Arts and Entertainment Law Journal, 1984-1985. *Member:* Regional (Chairman, Real Estate Law Section), Connecticut and American Bar Associations. ***PRACTICE AREAS:*** Commercial Real Estate; Commercial Leasing; Franchise Law; Commercial Finance; Secured Lending. ***Email:*** s-steinmetz@ibolaw.com

ASSOCIATES

BETH S. BECKER, born Hartford, Connecticut, April 5, 1962; admitted to bar, 1987, Connecticut; 1988, New York and U.S. District Court, District of Connecticut. *Education:* Connecticut College (B.A., with distinction, 1983); Washington College of Law of the American University (J.D., 1986). *Member:* Connecticut Bar Association. ***PRACTICE AREAS:*** Real Estate; Land Use; Zoning Law. ***Email:*** bbecker@ibolaw.com

JOHN E. CHAFFEE, born Bridgeport, Connecticut, January 20, 1970; admitted to bar, 1997, Connecticut. *Education:* Villanova University (B.S., cum laude, 1991; J.D., 1996). Beta Gamma Sigma; Gamma Phi. *Member:* Connecticut Bar Association. ***PRACTICE AREAS:*** Business Law; Corporate Law; Commercial Law; Real Estate. ***Email:*** j-chaffee@ibolaw.com

MARIANNE HOFFMAN, born Fairfield, Connecticut, September 28, 1968; admitted to bar, 1994, Connecticut; 1995, U.S. District Court, District of Connecticut; 1997, New York; U.S. District Court, Southern and Eastern Districts of New York. *Education:* Wellesley College (A.B., cum laude, 1990); University of Pennsylvania (J.D., 1994). Law Clerk, Hon. William J Lavery, Appellate Court, State of Connecticut. Previous Employment: Kelley Drye & Warren LLP and Federal Emergency Management Agency. ***PRACTICE AREAS:*** Litigation. ***Email:*** m-hoffman@ibolaw.com

JENNIFER B. KALLENBACH, born Los Angeles, California, July 28, 1967; admitted to bar, 1994, Connecticut; 1996, New York. *Education:* Georgetown University (B.A., magna cum laude, 1989); Tulane University (J.D., cum laude, 1994). Phi Beta Kappa. *Member:* Greenwich, Connecticut, New York State and American Bar Associations. ***PRACTICE AREAS:*** Real Estate; Land Use; Zoning Law. ***Email:*** j-kallenbach@ibolaw.com

KURT DAVID KOEHLER, born Mineola, New York, July 12, 1967; admitted to bar, 1994, Connecticut; 1995, New York and U.S. District Court, District of Connecticut. *Education:* University of Colorado at Boulder (B.A., 1989); Quinnipiac College School of Law (J.D., cum laude, 1993); University of Miami School of Law (LL.M., Estate Planning, 2000). Phi Delta Phi. Associate Editor, Quinnipiac Law Review, 1992-1993. Author: "Opposition to Proposed Rule Change: Attorney/Party Certification and Sanctions," Connecticut Trial Lawyers Association "Forum," Vol. 10, No. 4, July/August 1992. Previous Employment, Gallagher & Calistro. *Member:* Greenwich, Regional, Connecticut, New York State and American Bar Associations. ***PRACTICE AREAS:*** Trusts and Estates; Tax Planning; Probate; Estate Litigation. ***Email:*** k-koehler@ibolaw.com

CYNTHIA L. SINGER, born Omaha, Nebraska, April 1, 1961; admitted to bar, 1992, Illinois; 1995, Connecticut. *Education:* University of Nebraska (B.S., 1983); Loyola University (J.D., 1992). *Member:* Greenwich, Regional, Connecticut and American Bar Associations. ***PRACTICE AREAS:*** Estate Planning; Probate. ***Email:*** c-singer@ibolaw.com

OF COUNSEL

DEIRDRE A MARTINI, born Flushing, New York, October 27, 1960; admitted to bar, 1987, Connecticut; 1988, U.S. District Court, District of Connecticut and U.S. Court of Appeals for the Second Circuit. *Education:* New York University (B.A., 1984); Quinnipiac College School of Law (J.D., 1987). Faculty Member, U.S. Department of Justice, Office of the Senior Counsel on Alternate Dispute Resolution, 1996-1999. U.S. Attorneys Office, District of Connecticut, 1988-1999. *Member:* Connecticut (Member, Sections On: Bankruptcy; Commercial Law; Alternate Dispute Resolution; Federal Practice) Bar Association. ***PRACTICE AREAS:*** Bankruptcy; Commercial Law; Federal Litigation; Alternate Dispute Resolution. ***Email:*** d-martini@ibolaw.com

MELISSA TOWNSEND KLAUBERG, born Buffalo, New York, August 7, 1956; admitted to bar, 1981, New York; 1982, Florida; 1988, Connecticut. *Education:* University of Rochester (B.A., 1978); Albany Law School of Union College (J.D., 1981). Member, Albany Law Review, 1979-1981. Author, "Avoiding an Unwanted Invasion of Trusts," Vol. 4, Albany Law Review, 1981. *Member:* Greenwich and Connecticut Bar Associations; The Florida Bar. ***PRACTICE AREAS:*** Real Estate; Land Use; Zoning Law. ***Email:*** m-klauberg@ibolaw.com

PAUL M. O'CONNOR, JR., born Auburn, New York, 1933; admitted to bar, 1961, New York; 1984, Connecticut. *Education:* Cornell University (A.B., 1955); Georgetown University (J.D., 1960). Hearing Officer, Connecticut Commission of Human Rights and Opportunities, 1997—. *Member:* Greenwich, Connecticut, New York State, Stamford Regional and American Bar Associa-

(This Listing Continued)

IVEY, BARNUM & O'MARA, LLC, Greenwich—Continued

tions; Federal Bar Council. ***PRACTICE AREAS:*** General Practice; Real Estate; Civil Litigation; Construction Law; Land Use. ***Email:*** poconnor@ibolaw.com

APPROVED TITLE ATTORNEYS FOR: Fleet Bank, N.A.; First Union Bank of Connecticut; The Putnam Trust Company of Greenwich; People's Bank; First Connecticut Bank; The Boston Company; Citibank, FSB; The Bank of New York; Connecticut Attorneys Title Insurance Co.; Chicago Title Insurance Company; Commonwealth Land Title Insurance Co.; First American Title Insurance Co.

JACQUES & MOGER, P.C.

Established in 1981
530 OLD POST ROAD #3
GREENWICH, CONNECTICUT 06830
Telephone: 203-629-4434
FAX: 203-629-4865
Email: jacmogpc@aol.com
URL: http://www.lawyers.com/jacques&moger

Litigation in all Courts. Wealth Transfer Planning, Probate, Taxation, Real Estate, Family, Banking and Closely Held Corporate Law.

EMILE W. JACQUES, born New Haven, Connecticut, January 22, 1929; admitted to bar, 1958, Connecticut; 1959, Florida. *Education:* Yale University (B.A., 1953; LL.B., 1958). *Member:* Greenwich (President, 1969-1970), Connecticut and American Bar Associations; Connecticut Trial Lawyers Association. ***PRACTICE AREAS:*** Wealth Transfer; Estate Planning; Estate Administration; Estate Settlement; Trust Planning; Trust Administration; Asset Protection; Estate and Gift Taxation; Fiduciary Law; Probate Litigation; Tax Litigation.

DANIEL W. MOGER, JR., born White Plains, New York, July 18, 1941; admitted to bar, 1966, Connecticut. *Education:* Phillips Academy; Yale University (B.A., 1963); University of Pennsylvania (LL.B., 1966). Member, Board of Editors, University of Pennsylvania Law Review, 1964-1966. Law Clerk to Justice Charles S. House, Connecticut Supreme Court, 1966-1967. *Member:* Greenwich, Connecticut, American and Regional Bar Associations; Connecticut Trial Lawyers Association. ***PRACTICE AREAS:*** Real Estate; Civil Litigation; Family Law.

REPRESENTATIVE CLIENTS: Cornerstone Bank; Douglas Elliman-Pickering Associates, Inc.; Harrison Management Co.; Weeks Automobile Corp.; Fuel Tech, Inc.
APPROVED ATTORNEYS FOR: Most Institutions Active in the Local Mortgage Market.

JOEL M. KAYE

165 WEST PUTNAM AVENUE
GREENWICH, CONNECTICUT 06830
Telephone: 203-622-4500
Fax: 203-622-1797
Email: KAYESONGS@AOL.com

General Practice, Real Estate, Probate, Business Law.

JOEL M. KAYE, born Mt. Vernon, New York, December 12, 1953; admitted to bar, 1977, Connecticut and U.S. District Court, District of Connecticut; 1980, U.S. Supreme Court; 1983, New York. *Education:* American University (B.A., 1974); University of Connecticut (J.D., cum laude, 1977). Co-Author: "Connecticut Practice Book Annotated," with Wayne D. Effron, published by West Publishing Company, Second Edition, Vols. 2 and 3, 1979; "Connecticut Practice Book Annotated," with Wayne D. Effron and Johanna L. Kaye, Published by West Publishing Company, Third Edition, Vol 2, 3 and 3A, 1996. *Member:* Greenwich, Connecticut (Member: Real Property Section) and American (Member, Sections on: Real Property, Probate and Trust Law; Law Practice Management) Bar Associations. ***PRACTICE AREAS:*** Real Estate; Commercial Law; Probate.

REPRESENTATIVE CLIENTS: The Chase Manhattan Bank; Fleet Mortgage Corp.; First Republic Bank.
APPROVED TITLE AGENT FOR: Commonwealth Land Title Insurance Co.; First American Title Insurance Co.; Connecticut Attorney's Title Insurance Co.; Fidelity National Title Insurance Co.

KAYE AND HENNESSEY, LLC

71 LEWIS STREET
P.O. BOX 768
GREENWICH, CONNECTICUT 06836
Telephone: 203-625-5300
Fax: 203-625-3161
Email: kayehenlaw.com
URL: http://www.kayehenlaw.com

Real Estate, Probate, Estate Planning.

(This Listing Continued)

JEREMY E. KAYE, born Greenwich, Connecticut, November 2, 1955; admitted to bar, 1980, Connecticut; 1981, New York. *Education:* American University (B.A., 1975); University of Connecticut at Storrs (M.B.A., 1980); University of Connecticut School of Law (J.D., 1980). *Member:* Greenwich (Past President), Stamford/Norwalk (President), Connecticut and American Bar Associations. ***PRACTICE AREAS:*** Real Estate Law; Probate Law. ***Email:*** jek@kayehenlaw.com

JEVERA KAYE HENNESSEY, born Greenwich, Connecticut, November 2, 1960; admitted to bar, 1984, Connecticut; 1985, U.S. District Court, District of Connecticut. *Education:* Georgetown University (B.A., 1981); Boston University, School of Law (J.D., 1984). *Member:* Greenwich (President, 1994-1995), Stamford/Norwalk Regional, Connecticut and American Bar Associations. ***PRACTICE AREAS:*** Estate Planning; Probate Law; Trust Law. ***Email:*** jkh@kayehenlaw.com

DONALD R. KIEFER

OUTDOOR TRADER BUILDING
79 EAST PUTNAM AVENUE
GREENWICH, CONNECTICUT 06830
Telephone: 203-869-5511
Telecopier: 203-869-6855
Email: Ctlawyr@aol.com
URL: http://www.lawyers.com/donladkiefer

General Civil and Taxation, Practice with emphasis in Litigation, Family, Divorce, Domestic Relations, Real Estate, Commercial, Corporate, International, Admiralty; Probate Law & Litigation.

DONALD R. KIEFER, born Paterson, New Jersey, July 8, 1936; admitted to bar, 1962, Connecticut; 1984, New York. *Education:* Colgate University (B.A., 1959); Columbia University (LL.B., 1962). Member, Greenwich Representative Town Meeting, 1984-1998; Greenwich Planning and Zoning Board of Appeals, 1995—, Chairman, 2000. . *Member:* Connecticut Bar Association; Connecticut Trial Lawyers Association; The Association of Trial Lawyers of America; Maritime Law Association of the United States.

REPRESENTATIVE CLIENT: Boat U.S.; Q.S. International, Ltd.; Continental Insurance Co.; Stolt-Nielsen, Inc.
REFERENCES: Putnam Trust Co.

KOSKOFF, KOSKOFF & BIEDER, P.C.

GREENWICH, CONNECTICUT
(See Bridgeport)

Litigation in all State and Federal Courts. Medical Malpractice, Equal Opportunity, Negligence, Products Liability, Civil Rights, and Class Actions.

ROBERT M. LANE

530 OLD POST ROAD NO. 3
GREENWICH, CONNECTICUT 06830
Telephone: 203-869-3700
Telecopier: 203-869-6019
Email: RMLANE530@aol.com

General Practice. Probate, Taxation, Real Estate, Estate Planning.

ROBERT M. LANE, born Kenosha, Wisconsin, May 12, 1928; admitted to bar, 1954, New York; 1958, U.S. Court of Appeals, Second Circuit; 1961, U.S. District Court for the District of Columbia; 1964, Connecticut; 1965, U.S. Supreme Court. *Education:* St. Louis University (B.S., 1950); Columbia University (LL.B., 1953). *Member:* Greenwich, Connecticut, New York State and American Bar Associations. ***PRACTICE AREAS:*** Estate Planning; Real Estate; Taxation; Corporate Law.

LAWRENCE E. LARSON

153 MASON STREET
GREENWICH, CONNECTICUT 06830-6608
Telephone: 203-661-2300
FAX: 203-661-2350

Trusts, Estates, Taxation, Real Estate and Corporate Law, Business Transactions, Elder Law.

LAWRENCE E. LARSON, born February 18, 1932; admitted to bar, 1960, New York; 1963, U.S. District Courts, Eastern and Southern Districts of New York; 1966, Connecticut; 1967, U.S. District Court, District of Connecticut; 1983, Florida; 1989, U.S. Tax Court. *Education:* Colgate University (A.B., 1954); Cornell University (LL.B., 1959); Columbia University (M.B.A., 1965).

(This Listing Continued)

Justice of the Peace, 1995—. *Member:* Greenwich (President, 1981) and Connecticut Bar Associations; The Florida Bar.

LAW OFFICES OF JOHN T. LOFORESE LLC

Established in 1994

25 LEWIS STREET, SUITE 304

GREENWICH, CONNECTICUT 06830

Telephone: 203-625-5594

Fax: 203-625-0154

URL: http://www.lawyers.com/loforese

White Plains, New York Office: 81 Main Street, 10601. Telephone: 914-328-8800.

Civil Litigation, Real Estate, Wills and Probate, Personal Injury, Family Law, Collections.

JOHN T. LOFORESE, born Greenwich, Connecticut, March 28, 1959; admitted to bar, 1984, Connecticut; 1989, U.S. District Court, District of Connecticut; 1991, New York; 1996, U.S. District Court, Southern District of New York. *Education:* Manhattan College (B.A., magna cum laude, 1981); St. John's University (J.D., 1984). Epsilon Sigma Pi; Phi Alpha Theta. *Member:* Greenwich and Connecticut Bar Associations; Connecticut Trial Lawyers Association. ***PRACTICE AREAS:*** Litigation; Real Estate; General Practice.

MAHER AND WILLIAMS

GREENWICH, CONNECTICUT

(See Fairfield)

General and Federal Practice. Workers Compensation, Probate, Insurance, Subrogation, Estate Planning and Administrative Law. Trials.

RICHARD J. MARGENOT

537 STEAMBOAT ROAD

GREENWICH, CONNECTICUT 06830

Telephone: 203-869-7888

Fax: 203-869-0458

URL: http://www.lawyers.com/rjmargenot

Real Estate, Business Law, Wills, Trusts, Probate and Estate Planning Settlement, Conservatorships, Fraud.

RICHARD J. MARGENOT, born Greenwich, Connecticut, November 4, 1957; admitted to bar, 1985, Connecticut and New York. *Education:* Trinity College (B.A., 1980); Pace University (J.D., 1984). Recipient, Jerome T. Orans Memorial Award for Clinical Studies, 1984. *Member:* Connecticut Bar Association.

MARTIN, LUCAS & CHIOFFI, LLP

GREENWICH, CONNECTICUT

(See Stamford)

Business Law, Corporate Finance, Mergers and Acquisitions, Internet Law, Venture Capital, Commercial and Employment Litigation; Securities, Employment, Commercial Litigation, Real Estate, Commercial Leasing, Estate and Tax Planning, Estate Settlement and Trust Administration.

McGOVERN & ASSOCIATES

ONE LAFAYETTE PLACE

GREENWICH, CONNECTICUT 06830

Telephone: 203-622-1101

Telecopier: 203-622-9192

URL: http://www.lawyers.com/mcgovernassociates

Email: kmcgovern@mcgovernlaw.com

URL: http://www.mcgovernlaw.com

New York, N.Y. Office: Trump Tower, 721 5th Avenue, Suite 52-D, 10022. Telephone: 212-697-0955.

General Commercial Practice. Corporate (Foreign and Domestic), Mergers and Acquisitions, Securities, Venture Capital, Taxation, Litigation in all Courts. International, Joint Ventures, Admiralty, Sports, Commercial and Residential Real Estate Law. Estates and Trusts.

FIRM PROFILE: McGovern & Associates is a full-service and highly experienced corporate law firm whose attorneys have an average of 17 years practicing in various specialties. As a result, we provide efficiencies in turnaround time and price that a large firm cannot provide. We also have extensive experience in international law and taxation and have concentrated business in the United Kingdom, Canada, Bermuda, Mexico, Switzerland, China, Taiwan, the Philippines and Hong Kong.

KEVIN M. McGOVERN, born New York, N.Y., July 16, 1948; admitted to bar, 1975, Connecticut; 1980, U.S. District Court, Southern District of New York; 1981, Pennsylvania; 1992, U.S. District Court Eastern District of New York; 1993, New York. *Education:* University of London, England and Cornell University (B.A., 1970); St. John's University (J.D., 1975). Phi Alpha Delta. Former General Counsel, Clabir Corporation (NYSE). Member, Board of Trustees, Brunswick School of Greenwich. Member, Cornell Trustees Board Council. *Member:* Greenwich, Connecticut (Member, Executive Committee, Section on Corporations and Other Business Organizations), Pennsylvania, New York, and American (Member, Sections on: Corporation, Banking and Business Law; Science and Technology) Bar Associations; American Judicature Society (Former Member, Board of Directors and Membership Committee). **Email:** kmcgovern@mcgovernlaw.com

CONSTANCE TILDEN LOESER, born Washington, D.C., November 8, 1945; admitted to bar, 1982, New York (Not admitted in Connecticut). *Education:* Smith College (A.B., 1967); University of Utah (J.D., 1979). Barnard J. Stewart Award. Author: "Effect of the Supreme Court Decision in Tufts on After Tax Rate of Return in Real Estate Investments and Disclosures in Real Estate Offering Materials," 4 The Real Estate Securities Journal 13. U.S. Peace Corps Instructor: Royal Thai Naval Academy, Pak Nam, Thailand and Mahidol University, Bangkok, Thailand, 1970-1972. *Member:* American Bar Association (Member, Sections on: Corporation, Banking and Business Law). ***PRACTICE AREAS:*** Securities Law; Corporate Law; Mergers and Acquisitions Law. **Email:** connie@mcgovernlaw.com

BRIAN T. FOLEY, born Bronxville, New York, April 12, 1959; admitted to bar, 1985, New York, U.S. District Court, Southern and Eastern Districts of New York, Connecticut and U.S. District Court, District of Connecticut; 1986, U.S. Court of Appeals, Second Circuit; 1987, U.S. Court of Appeals, Fifth Circuit; 1988, District of Columbia; 1992, U.S. Court of Appeals, Federal Circuit. *Education:* United States Military Academy; Manhattanville College (B.A., 1981); New York Law School (J.D., cum laude, 1984). Member, New York Law School Law Review, 1982-1984. Formerly, Howery & Simon, Washington, DC, 1987-1994. *Member:* Connecticut, New York State and American Bar Associations; District of Columbia Bar; New York State Trial Lawyers Association; International Trade Commission Trial Lawyers Association. ***PRACTICE AREAS:*** Commercial Litigation; Patent Enforcement Litigation. **Email:** bfoley@mcgovernlaw.com

CHARLES E. BARNETT, born Charleston, West Virginia, September 25, 1939; admitted to bar, 1965, New York; 1973, Connecticut; 1987, U.S. Supreme Court. *Education:* University of Michigan (B.A., 1961; J.D., 1964). Trustee, Practicing Law Institute, 1985—, Member, Committee on Programs and Publications of Board of Trustees. Executive Committee of the Conference Board's Council of Chief Legal Officers, 1992-1994. Legal Advisory Committee to the Board of Directors of the New York Stock Exchange, 1987-1990. Chairman, International and Comparative Law Center of the Southwestern Legal Foundation; Chairman, Annual Symposium for three years. Forum, U.S. Supreme Court and European Court of Justice, 1990-1993. Board of Directors of the Corporate Bar of Westchester-Fairfield Counties, 1989-1993. Vice President and General Counsel, St. Joe Minerals Corporation, New York, N.Y., 1974-1983. Vice-President and General Counsel, Combustion Engineering, Inc., Stamford, Connecticut, 1984-1990. Vice President and General Counsel, The Reader's Digest Association, Inc., Pleasantville, N.Y., 1990-1994. *Member:* The Association of the Bar of the City of New York; New York State, Connecticut and American (Member, Committee on Corporate Law Departments, 1987-1995) Bar Associations; Corporate Bar Association of Westchester-Fairfield. (Also Member, Barnett & Associates). ***PRACTICE AREAS:*** Legal Consulting; Securities; Mergers and Acquisitions; Venture Capital; Corporate. **Email:** cbarnett@mcgovernlaw.com

MARK G. ABERASTURI, born Brooklyn, New York, February 12, 1964; admitted to bar, 1989, New York; 1990, U.S. Tax Court and U.S. District Court, Southern and Northern Districts of New York; 1999, U.S. Court of Appeals, Second Circuit (Not admitted in Connecticut). *Education:* State University of New York at Albany (B.S., 1986); Western New England College School of Law (J.D., 1989); Quinnipiac College School of Law (LL.M., Taxation, 1993). Author: "Exemption Planning," National Business Institute, August, 1994; "Income Tax Aspects of Family Limited Partnerships," National Business Institute, May, 1995. Mid-Hudson Bankruptcy Attorney, 1990. *Member:* Orange County (Member, Tax and Bankruptcy Committees), New York State (Member, Tax, Trust and Estate Section) and American (Member, Sections on: Tax; Real Estate Property; Business Law) Bar Associations. ***PRACTICE AREAS:*** Taxation; Mergers and Acquisitions; Bankruptcy; Trusts and Estates. **Email:** maberasturi@mcgovernlaw.com

EDWARD KANOWITZ, born Brooklyn, New York, August 27, 1951; admitted to bar, 1976, Connecticut; 1979, U.S. District Court, District of Con-

(This Listing Continued)

McGOVERN & ASSOCIATES, Greenwich—Continued

necticut; 1983, U.S. Tax Court. *Education:* Union University (A.B., 1973); New York University (M.B.A., 1976; J.D., 1976). Justice of the Peace, Town of Ridgefield, 1983—. *Member:* Connecticut (Member, Sections on: Estate and Probate; Taxation; Chairman, Corporation, Business and Banking Law Committee, Young Lawyers Section, 1979-1980) and American (Member, Sections on: Taxation; Corporation, Banking and Business Law) Bar Associations. ***PRACTICE AREAS:*** Taxation; Civil Litigation; Corporate Law.

DAVID R. WESTRA, born Wayne, New Jersey, September 3, 1965; admitted to bar, 1999, New York and New Jersey (Not admitted in Connecticut). *Education:* Ramapo College (B.S., 1995); Pace University (J.D., 1998). Member, Pace International Law Review, 1996-1997. *Member:* New York State and American Bar Associations; Westchester Corporate Bar Association. ***PRACTICE AREAS:*** Internet Law; Technology Law; Year 2000 Computer Conversion; Intellectual Property; Corporate Law; Securities. ***Email:*** dwestra@mcgovernlaw.com

OF COUNSEL

LAWRENCE W. CASEY, born Oceanside, New York, November 24, 1949; admitted to bar, 1976, New York; 1978, District of Columbia (Not admitted in Connecticut). *Education:* Alfred University (B.A., 1971); St. John's University (J.D., 1975). Staff Attorney, Securities and Exchange Commission, 1976-1978; Legislative Counsel, Congressman Jack Kemp, 1979; Senior Staff, Senator John Chafee, 1980; Chief of Staff, Congressman George Wortley, 1981-1987; Director of Legislation, Rural Electrification Administration (Presidential Appointment), U.S. Department of Agriculture; Counselor to the Administrator, Food Safety and Inspection Service (Presidential Appointment), 1990-1993. Chief of Staff, Congressman Michael Forbes, 1995—. *Member:* District of Columbia Bar. (Counsel Emeritus). ***PRACTICE AREAS:*** Legislation Regulation; Washington Practice.

JOSEPH P. CONNORS, born New York, N.Y., March 14, 1949; admitted to bar, 1990, New York (Not admitted in Connecticut). *Education:* Johns Hopkins University (B.A., 1971); New York University (J.D., 1974). Corporate Associate, Brown & Wood, 1975-1980; Corporate Associate, LeBoeuf, Lamb, Greene & MacRae, 1980-1984; Corporate and Banking Associate, Winthrop, Stimson, Putnam & Roberts, 1984-1990; Corporate and Banking Partner, Kirlin, Campbell, Meadows & Keating, 1990-1994; Corporate and Banking Partner, Gallet, Dreyer & Berkey, LLP, 1994-1996. *Member:* New York State Bar Association. ***PRACTICE AREAS:*** Banking Law; Securities; Corporate Law.

JAMES J. QUINN, born New York, N.Y., August 13, 1945; admitted to bar, 1975, New Jersey; 1976, New York (Not admitted in Connecticut). *Education:* Fordham University (B.A., 1967); New York University (M.A., 1971; M.B.A., Finance, 1974); St. John's University (J.D., 1975). Certified Public Accountant, New York, 1978. *Member:* The Association of the Bar of the City of New York; New York State (Member, Section on U.S. Activities of Foreign Tax Payers) and American (Member, Section on Taxation) Bar Associations; American Institute of Certified Public Accountants; New York City Institute of Certified Public Accountants. (Resident at New York, N.Y. Office). ***PRACTICE AREAS:*** Taxation; Corporate Law; International Law.

REPRESENTATIVE CLIENTS: Advanced Polymer Systems; Allerx, Inc.; Ambassador Trading Co.; America's Best; Avant Garde Systems, Inc.; Block & Nardizzi, Inc.; Borla Industries; Bowling Corporation of America; Brecker & Merryman, Inc.; Business Acquisition Consultants, Inc.; Capital Sports, Inc.; Coleary Transport Co.; Commonwealth Sprague Capacitor, Inc.; CompuBryte Technology Corp.; The Computer Commission, Inc.; Computer Marketing Corp.; Connecticut Venture Management Group; Cortell USA; Creative Science, Inc.; Cybergnostic; Delta-Omega Technologies; Empery Corp.; Enterprise Associates, Inc.; Environmental Equipment, Inc.; Executors, Inc.; Fairway Intermediaries Ltd.; Falcon Electronics, Inc.; Finevest Services, Inc.; Globe Ticket Co.; Golf Finance Incorporated; The Greenwich Group; Greenwich Money Management, Inc.; Greenwich Partners, Inc.; Greenwich Venture Partners, Inc.; Growth Research Associates, Inc.; Hallmark Packaging Products, Inc.; Helm Resources, Inc.; Hemex, Inc.; Hudson National Golf Club; Imported Cars of Greenwich; Information Center Services, Inc.; Interenergy Corp.; International Interactive Commerce, Ltd.; International Trade Resources, Inc.; JBS Investment Banking, Ltd.; K-L Media; Keystone Filler & Mfg.; Lamalie Amrop Associates, Inc.; F.B. Leopold Company; Lillian August Designs, Inc.; Managed Health Benefits Corp.; Medcraft Corp.; Metedeconk; Milbrook Association; Millenium Management; Morgan Grace; National Fairways, Inc.; National Guardian Corp.; National Semiconductor Corp.; National Video Centers, Inc.; NeoStrata Company, Inc.; Nobel Education Dynamics; Paine-Williams, Inc.; Pegasus International; Petro Canada; Playlands, Inc.; PolyStrata, Inc.; PolyStrata Pharmaceuticals, Inc.; Preferred Links; Premier, Inc.; Premier Sports, Inc.; The Savant Group, Inc.; Security Capital Management, Inc.; Shen Yi Holding; Municipal Government of Shanghai; Slickbar, Inc.; SOBE; Sports Health, Inc.; The Sovran Companies; Sunglass Hut Corp.; Swiss Bank; Thermal Waste Technologies, Inc.; Trakus; TriAsia Ltd.; TriStrata, Inc.; U.S. Automotive; U.S. Sensors, Inc.; Vuarnet U.S.; YWC, Inc.

HILARY B. MILLER

112 PARSONAGE ROAD
GREENWICH, CONNECTICUT 06830-3942
Telephone: 203-861-6262
Facsimile: 203-622-6264
Email: hilary@miller.net
URL: http://www.lawyers.com/hilarymiller

Litigation and Corporate Law. Family Law.

HILARY B. MILLER, born New York, N.Y., February 20, 1951; admitted to bar, 1982, Connecticut; 1983, New York, U.S. District Court, District of Connecticut, U.S. District Court, Southern, Eastern and Northern Districts of New York, U.S. Court of Appeals, First and Second Circuits and U.S. Supreme Court. *Education:* Dartmouth College (A.B., 1973; M.B.A., 1974); Fordham University (J.D., 1982). Phi Beta Kappa. Rufus Choate Scholar. Edward Tuck Scholar. Commercial Pilot, with instrument and multi-engine ratings. Arbitrator, NASD Regulation and American Arbitration Association. Mediator, Special Master, U.S. District Court, Southern District of New York. Arbitrator, New York City Civil Court. Hearing Officer, Connecticut Department of Consumer Protection. Chartered Financial Analyst. *Member:* Connecticut Bar Association; New York County, New York State and American Bar Associations; Lawyer-Pilots Bar Association. ***LANGUAGES:*** French. ***PRACTICE AREAS:*** Litigation; Corporate Law; Intellectual Property; Family Law.

MORE PHILLIPS & DUNCAN, P.C.

95 EAST PUTNAM AVENUE
GREENWICH, CONNECTICUT 06830
Telephone: 203-629-2611
Fax: 203-629-2375
Email: morphildunc@mindspring.com

General Civil Practice, Trials and Appeals in Federal and State Courts, Corporate, Probate.

WILLIAM A. PHILLIPS, born Providence, Rhode Island, December 1925; admitted to bar, 1954, Connecticut; 1956, New York; U.S. District Court, Southern and Eastern Districts of New York and U.S. District Court, District of Connecticut; U.S. Supreme Court; U.S. Court of Appeals, Second and Third Circuits. *Education:* Brown University (A.B., 1950); University of Connecticut (LL.B., 1954). *Member:* Connecticut (Executive Committee, Antitrust Law Section; Federal Practice Section; Litigation Section; Business Law Section) and American (Member, Sections on: Litigation; Business Law) Bar Associations. [USMC, 1943-1946]. ***REPORTED CASES:*** Virginia Corp. v. Galanis, 223 Conn. 436 (set aside of mortgages of white collar felon); In re Nulman's Appeal from Probate, 207 Conn. 806 13 Conn. App. 811 (removal of testamentary executor); Slifkin v. Condec Corp. 13 Conn. App. 538 (employment case); In re Galanis, 71 B.R. 953 (proof of fraud claims in bankruptcy court); American Tel. and Tel. Co. v. Merry, 592 F.2d 118 (no ERISA preemption of state court ordered alimony); Louring v. Kuwait Boulder Shipping Co., 455 F.Supp. 630 (rights of small corporation shareholders and officers); French v. Oberreuter, 157 Conn. 181 Conn. 729 (constructive trust and fiduciary obligations of executor); Mott v. Teagle Foundation, Inc. 156 Conn. 407 (will construction suit); Morgenwick v. Leahy, 384 F.2d 710 (wrongful death claim by reason of gas explosion); Resnik v. Muir, 4 Conn. Cir. Ct. 293 (discovery issue); Fink v. Cox, 154 Conn. 720, 154 Conn. 732, 154 Conn. 733, 154 Conn. 736 (revocation of child adoption); Growth v. Redmond, 24 Conn. Supp. 467 (multiple litigation issue); Redmond v. Matthies, 149 Conn. 423 (corporate and testamentary fiduciary issues); Brown v. Anderson Nichols & Co., 203 Fed. Supp. 489 (pain and suffering not recoverable under Death on the High Seas Act); Matthies v. Seymour Mfg. Co., 271 F.2d 740 (application of Federal Rules to derivative shareholders' suit); Meadows v. Higgins, 49 Conn. App. 286, cert. granted 247 Conn. 910 September 1998 (builder's suit against homeowners); Delacroix v. Lubin Graphics, 993 F.Supp. 74 1997 (French artist's suit against art producer); Andrews v. Gorby, 237 Conn. 12 (testators direction in Will for fiduciary fees); Smith and Smith Bldg. Corp. v. DeLuca, 36 Conn. App. 839 (interpretation of builder's contract). ***PRACTICE AREAS:*** Litigation; Corporate; Probate.

DOUGLAS M. MORE (Retired).

JOHN BRUCE DUNCAN (Retired).

OHLANDT, GREELEY, RUGGIERO & PERLE

GREENWICH, CONNECTICUT

(See Stamford)

Practice Limited to Intellectual Property Law and Related Matters.

RICHARD S. PASTORE, P.C.

125 MASON STREET
GREENWICH, CONNECTICUT 06830
Telephone: 203-661-8988
Fax: 203-661-8051

General and Commercial Practice. Taxation, Estate Planning and Estate Administration, Probate and Real Estate Law.

RICHARD S. PASTORE, born New York, N.Y., September 25, 1932; admitted to bar, 1960, New York; 1966, U.S. Tax Court; 1967, U.S. Supreme Court and Connecticut. *Education:* Amherst College (A.B., 1954); Columbia University (LL.B., 1960). Phi Delta Phi; Kent Court. Associate, Mendes & Mount, New York, N.Y., 1960-1962. Partner, Albert, Pastore & Ward, Greenwich, Ct., 1970-1993. *Member:* Association of the Bar of the City of New York; Greenwich, Connecticut, New York State (Member, Taxation Section) and American (Member, Taxation Section; International and Comparative Law Section) Bar Associations. ***PRACTICE AREAS:*** General and Commercial Practice; Taxation; Estate Planning and Estate Administration.

APPROVED ATTORNEY FOR: First American Title Insurance Co.
REFERENCE: Putnam Trust Co.

PIAZZA & PICKEL

GREENWICH, CONNECTICUT
(See Stamford)

Trials and Appeals in State and Federal Courts, Negligence, Medical Malpractice, Divorce and Personal Injury Law, Wrongful Death, Legal Malpractice, Child Custody, Automobile Accidents, Product Liability, Adoption, Family Law.

ROBERT B. POTASH

Established in 1974
31 BROOKSIDE DRIVE
GREENWICH, CONNECTICUT 06830
Telephone: 203-661-7580
Telecopier: 203-661-7623

General Practice, Real Estate, Probate and Estate Planning.

ROBERT B. POTASH, born Greenwich, Connecticut, April 21, 1948; admitted to bar, 1974, Connecticut and U.S. District Court, District of Connecticut; 1979, U.S. Supreme Court. *Education:* Boston University (B.S., 1970); Suffolk University (J.D., 1974). *Member:* Greenwich, Stamford/Norwalk, Connecticut and American Bar Associations. ***PRACTICE AREAS:*** Real Estate Law; Residential Real Estate; Commercial Real Estate.

APPROVED ATTORNEYS FOR: Peoples Bank; Bank of New York; Bank of America; Webster Bank; Fleet Bank; First American Title Co.; Commonwealth Land Title, Fidelity National Title; PNC Mortgage.

RAMER & RAMER

Established in 1977
21 BENEDICT PLACE
GREENWICH, CONNECTICUT 06830
Telephone: 203-629-1600
Fax: 203-629-1844

General Practice, Family Law, Real Estate, Business Law, Litigation, Zoning, Wills and Estates.

MEMBERS OF FIRM

JEFFREY S. RAMER, born New York, N.Y., June 10, 1944; admitted to bar, 1970, New York; 1971, U.S. District Court, Southern and Eastern Districts of New York and U.S. Court of Appeals, Second Circuit; 1973, U.S. Supreme Court; 1977, Connecticut; 1978, U.S. District Court, District of Connecticut. *Education:* Franklin & Marshall College (A.B., 1966); Fordham University (J.D., 1969). ***PRACTICE AREAS:*** General Practice; Real Estate; Business Law; Zoning; Wills; Estate Administration; Trial Practice; Appellate Practice; Litigation.

NANCY N. RAMER, born Ottawa, Canada, July 25, 1946; admitted to bar, 1974, New York; 1975, Connecticut, U.S. District Court, Southern and Eastern Districts of New York and U.S. Court o f Appeals, Second Circuit; 1978, U.S. District Court, District of Connecticut. *Education:* University of Arizona (B.A., 1968); St. John's University (J.D., 1973). Divorce Mediation Training, 1996. ***PRACTICE AREAS:*** Family Law; Divorce; Child Custody; Visitation Rights; Property Rights; General Practice.

ROBERTS, ROSE & BATES, P.C.

GREENWICH, CONNECTICUT
(See Stamford)

General Practice, Litigation, Real Estate, Leasing, Banking, Matrimonial, Probate, Estate Planning and Trusts, International Business, Employment Law.

ROBINSON & COLE LLP

Established in 1845
80 FIELD POINT ROAD
GREENWICH, CONNECTICUT 06836-1538
Telephone: 203-862-4100
Fax: 203-862-4199
Email: gren.rc.com
URL: http://www.rc.com

Other Offices: Hartford, CT, Stamford, CT, New London, CT, Boston, MA, New York, NY and Manchester, NH.

General Practice including Admiralty, Antitrust and Trade Regulation, Appellate, Banking and Institutional Finance, Bankruptcy and Creditors' Rights, Business Litigation, Business Workouts, Construction, Corporate and Closely Held Business, Criminal Litigation, E-Commerce and Intellectual Property, Employee Benefits and ERISA Litigation, Employment Litigation and Counseling, Environmental, Estate Planning and Probate, Government Relations, Healthcare, Immigration, Insurance, International, Labor Relations and Collective Bargaining, Land Use and Zoning, Personal Injury, Product Liability, Professional Liability, Public Finance, Real Estate Finance, Development and Leasing, Securities, Tax-Exempt Organizations, Tax Planning and Representation, Utilities and Telecommunications.

PARTNERS

KENNETH M. GAMMILL, admitted to bar, 1967, Connecticut. *Education:* Duke University (B.A., 1965); Boston University (LL.B., 1968). Member, Environmental Commission Town of New Canaan, Connecticut, 1980-1990. ***PRACTICE AREAS:*** Trusts and Estates. ***Email:*** kgammill@gren.rc.com

GEORGE L. SMITH, admitted to bar, 1982, New York; 1985, Florida; 1988, Connecticut. *Education:* Trinity College (B.A., 1978); St. John's University (J.D., 1981). Member, Executive Committee, Estates and Probate Section, Connecticut Bar Association, 1993—. (Resident). ***PRACTICE AREAS:*** Trusts and Estates; Wills; Probates. ***Email:*** gsmith@gren.rc.com

OF COUNSEL

Thomas J. McKee (Resident)
Clark Whittemore, Jr.

COUNSEL

ELIZABETH M. GRANT, admitted to bar, 1989, Connecticut; 1990, New York. *Education:* Smith College (A.B., 1975); Fordham University (J.D., 1989). (Resident). ***LANGUAGES:*** French. ***PRACTICE AREAS:*** Trusts and Estates; Wills; Probate. ***Email:*** egrant@gren.rc.com

ASSOCIATE

MEREDITH ANN LEFF, admitted to bar, 1998, New York and New Jersey (Not admitted in Connecticut). *Education:* Cornell University (B.S., 1994); Hofstra Law School (J.D., 1997). Associate Editor, Hofstra Law Review. ***PRACTICE AREAS:*** Real Estate; Trusts and Estates. ***Email:*** mleff@stam.rc.com

Lawyers are members of local, state and national bar associations.

(For biographical data on other personnel, see Professional Biographies at Hartford, New London and Stamford, CT, Boston, MA, New York, NY and Manchester, NH)

PHILIP RUSSELL, P.C.

71 LEWIS STREET
P.O. BOX 1437
GREENWICH, CONNECTICUT 06836
Telephone: 203-661-4200
Fax: 203-661-3666
URL: http://www.lawyers.com/philiprussell

Civil and Criminal Litigation in all State and Federal Courts. Traffic, Automobile Accidents, DWI, DUI, White Collar Crimes.

PHILIP D. RUSSELL, born Brooklyn, New York, October 16, 1958; admitted to bar, 1985, New York; 1986, Connecticut; 1988, U.S. District Court,

(This Listing Continued)

PHILIP RUSSELL, P.C., Greenwich—Continued

District of Connecticut and U.S. District Court Southern and Eastern Districts of New York; 1989, U.S. Supreme Court; 1992, U.S. Court of Appeals, Second Circuit. *Education:* State University at Binghamton (B.A., 1981); Brooklyn Law School (J .D., 1984). Recipient, ABA Silver Key Award, 1984. Assistant District Attorney, Bronx County, 1984-1988; Rackets Bureau, 1986-1988, 1984-1986. Brooklyn Law School Alumni Association, Member, Board of Directors: 1992-1994, Board Member, Westchester County Bar Association, Criminal Justice Section. Moderator, Seminar on Sentencing, Confinement and Supervision, Regional Bar, March 1996. Program Speaker, Cross Examination and Investigative Preparation, Regional Bar, February 9, 1997. Member: National Lawyers Committee; Amicus Curiae Committee, National Organization for Reform of Marijuana Laws. Program Speaker: "Pretrial Investigation in Criminal Defense", NORML Legal Seminar, May 30, 1999, Aspen Colorado; "Connecticut Drunk Driving Law Revisions," Regional Bar, Dec. 1999. *Member:* Greenwich (President, 1996-1997) and Connecticut (Member, Council of Bar Presidents, 1997, Criminal Justice Section) Bar Associations; Connecticut Criminal Defense Lawyers Association (Member, Board of Governors, 1996—); National Association of Criminal Defense Lawyers. (Board Certified Criminal Trial Advocate by the National Board of Trial Advocacy). ***SPECIAL AGENCIES:*** Admitted to practice before the Office of Thrift Supervision. ***REPORTED CASES:*** State v. Ruffin 241 Conn. 502 699 A.2d, 872 (1997); State v. Quinones 21 Conn. App. 506, 574 A.2d 1308 (1990) cert. den., 215 Conn. 816, 576 A.2d. 546 (1990). People v. Alfred Saunders N.Y. Supp (1987). Oliveiras v. Mayer 23 F. 3rd 642, 1994. ***PRACTICE AREAS:*** Civil Litigation; Criminal Litigation.

ROY S. WARD, born Bridgeport, Connecticut, August 15, 1959; admitted to bar, 1992, Connecticut; 1993, U.S. District Court, District of Connecticut and U.S. District Court, Southern District of New York; 1995, Colorado. *Education:* Lake Forest College (B.A., 1981); University of Bridgeport (J.D., magna cum laude, 1991). Law Review, University of Bridgeport. Recipient, Distinguished Academic Achievement. Author: "Michigan Dept. of State Police v. Sitz, The Supreme Court Approves The Use of Drunk Driving Road Blocks" in Bridgeport Law Review, Vol. 12 No., 2. *Member:* Greenwich, Stamford/Norwalk Regional, Connecticut and American Bar Associations. ***REPORTED CASES:*** State v. Decaro, 252 conn.-229, 745 A.2d 800 (2000). ***PRACTICE AREAS:*** Civil Litigation; Criminal Litigation.

JAMES J. PASTORE, born Stamford, Connecticut, December 15, 1972; admitted to bar, 1998, Connecticut; 1999, U.S. District Court, District of Connecticut. *Education:* Marist College (B.S., 1995); Queens College of the City University of New York (J.D., 1998). *Member:* Greenwich, Stamford/Norwalk, Bridgeport, Connecticut and American Bar Associations; Connecticut Trial Lawyers Association; Connecticut Criminal Defense Lawyers Association. ***PRACTICE AREAS:*** Criminal Litigation; Civil Litigation.

CHRISTOPHER W. CALDWELL, born Greenwich, Connecticut, January 2, 1967; admitted to bar, 1992, Connecticut; 1993, New York; 1997, U.S. District Court, District of Connecticut and U.S. District Court, Southern District of New York. *Education:* Pennsylvania State University (B.A., 1989); John Marshall Law School (J.D., 1992). Faculty Research Assistant, The John Marshall Law School. Member: NRA Institute for Legislative Action. *Member:* Greenwich, Stamford/Norwalk Regional and Connecticut Bar Associations. ***REPORTED CASES:*** Thalle Construction Co., Inc. v. Whiting-Turner Contracting Co., Inc., 39 F.3d 412 (2d. Cir. 2000). ***PRACTICE AREAS:*** Commercial Litigation; Criminal Law.

OF COUNSEL

HAROLD H. DEAN, born Passaic, New Jersey, April 12, 1929; admitted to bar, 1957, Connecticut and U.S. District Court, District of Connecticut; 1961, U.S. Supreme Court. *Education:* St. Lawrence University (B.S., 1953); Brooklyn Law School (LL.B., 1957). U.S. Air Force Pilot, 1954. FAA Commercial Pilot, 1958. Prosecutor Circuit Court, 1965-1969. Connecticut Circuit Court Judge, 1969-1974. Connecticut Common Pleas Judge, 1974-1975. Connecticut Superior Court Judge, 1975-1999. Attorney Advisor U.S. Securities and Exchange Commission, 1957-1959. [Lt. Col., U.S. Air Force, Active and Reserve, 1952-1982]. ***PRACTICE AREAS:*** Litigation; Civil Litigation; Arbitration.

ST. JOHN, PARK & SCOTT

Established in 1938

P.O. BOX 697

GREENWICH, CONNECTICUT 06836-0697

Telephone: 203-637-2518

Fax: 203-637-8005

General Practice. Wills and Estate Planning, Probate and Taxation, Trust and Estate Administration, Real Estate, Corporate, Family and Zoning Law. Civil Litigation.

(This Listing Continued)

GEORGE W. SCOTT, JR., born New York, N.Y., November 15, 1941; admitted to bar, 1966, Connecticut; 1968, U.S. District Court, District of Connecticut; 1971, U.S. Court of Appeals, Second Circuit and U.S. Supreme Court; 1985, U.S. Tax Court. *Education:* Dartmouth College (A.B., 1963); Yale University (LL.B., 1966). Special Pre-Trial Master, Superior Court, 1979—. Attorney State Trial Referee, 1985—. *Member:* Greenwich, The Connecticut and American Bar Associations.

ORSON L. ST. JOHN (Retired).

HALFORD W. PARK (1918-1997).

SANDAK FRIEDMAN HENNESSEY & GRECO, LLP

GREENWICH, CONNECTICUT

(See Stamford)

Trials and Appeals in all Connecticut and Federal Courts and Administrative Agencies. Personal Injury, Medical Malpractice, Commercial, Environmental Litigation, Real Estate, Zoning and Land Use, Property Tax Appeals.

SCHOONMAKER, GEORGE & COLIN, P.C.

81 HOLLY HILL LANE

P.O. BOX 5059

GREENWICH, CONNECTICUT 06831-5059

Telephone: 203-862-5000

Fax: 203-862-5099

Email: schoon@sgcfamlaw.com

URL: http://www.sgcfamlaw.com

Matrimonial and Family Law.

FIRM PROFILE: The firm concentrates on complex financial and tax matters in the matrimonial field and on child custody matters, premarital agreements and appeals. This focus allows our attorneys to concentrate all of their talents, skills, and energy on providing high quality representation for our clients.

The very nature of our practice calls for the ability to handle emotionally charged issues. Our attorneys and legal staff have the experience, understanding and discretion necessary to resolve difficult and delicate matters. We are selective with our clientele and therefore can devote the time and attention to each matter that it deserves.

SAMUEL V. SCHOONMAKER, III, born Newburgh, New York, September 1, 1935; admitted to bar, 1961, Connecticut and U.S. District Court, District of Connecticut; 1967, U.S. Court of Appeals, Second Circuit; 1965, U.S. Supreme Court. *Education:* Yale University (B.A., magna cum laude, 1958, J.D., 1961) Phi Beta Kappa. Senior Topical Editor, Connecticut Bar Journal, 1997—. Member, Board of Editors: Fairshare, 1980—; American Journal of Family Law, 1993—. Co-Author, "Connecticut's New Approach to Marriage Dissolution," 47 Connecticut Bar Journal 375, 1974. Author: "Frequently Stated or Unstated Criteria in Equitable Distribution States," Law & Business, Inc., 1980; "Settling Disputes Over Tangible Personal Property," Fairshare, April 1982. Member: Advisory Committee on Reorganization and Unification of Connecticut Courts, 1974-1976; Connecticut Family Support Advisory Committee, 1986—; Advisory Board of National Legal Resource Center for Child Advocacy and Protection, 1988—. Chairman, Connecticut Child Support Commission, 1984-1986. Attorney State Trial Referee, 1989—. Co-Chairperson, Gender Bias in the Workplace Committee, 1991. *Member:* Connecticut (Chairman: Family Law Section, 1971-1974; Bench/Bar Relations Committee, 1976—) and American (Chairman: Bill of Rights of Children Committee; Federal Legislation and the Family Committee; Member of National Council, 1977-1994, Secretary, 1979-1980, Vice Chairman, 1980-1981, Chairman-Elect, 1981-1982 and Chairman, 1982-1983, Family Law Section; Member, House of Delegates, 1984-1994) Bar Associations. Fellow: American Academy of Matrimonial Lawyers (Member, Board of Managers, Connecticut Chapter, 1975—); International Academy of Matrimonial Lawyers; Connecticut Bar Foundation; American Bar Foundation. ***PRACTICE AREAS:*** Matrimonial Law; Family Law. ***Email:*** svs3@sgcfamlaw.com

CYNTHIA COULTER GEORGE, born Connecticut, June 11, 1953; admitted to bar, 1978, Connecticut. *Education:* Cornell University (B.A., 1975); Loyola University (J.D., 1978). Member, Loyola Law Review, 1977-1978. Co-Author, "Connecticut Family Law Citations," Lexis Law Pub., 1994. Chairperson, Connecticut Family Law Section, 1987-1988. *Member:* American Bar Association (Financial Officer, Family Law Section, 1997-1998; 1999-2000). Fel-

(This Listing Continued)

low, American Academy of Matrimonial Lawyers (Counsel, National Chapter, 1996; President, Connecticut Chapter, 1998-1999). ***PRACTICE AREAS:*** Matrimonial Law; Family Law. ***Email:*** CGeorge@sgcfamlaw.com

THOMAS D. COLIN, born Brooklyn, New York, January 2, 1967; admitted to bar, 1992, Connecticut; 1993, New York, Maine, U.S. District Court, District of Connecticut and U.S. District Court, Southern District of New York. *Education:* C.W. Post College of Long Island University (B.S., summa cum laude, 1989); St. John's University (J.D., cum laude, 1992). Member, St. John's Law Review, 1990-1992. Director of Publications, Criminal Law Institute, 1991-1992. Law Clerk to Justice Paul L. Rudman, Supreme Judicial Court of Maine, 1992-1993. Co-Editor, "Connecticut Family Law Citations," Lexis, 1997—. *Member:* Stamford-Norwalk Regional (Co-Chair, Family Law Section), Connecticut (Executive Committee, Family Law Section); and American (Co-Chair, Ethics, Professionalism and Grievance Committee, Family Law Section) Bar Associations. ***PRACTICE AREAS:*** Matrimonial Law; Family Law. ***Email:*** tcolin@sgcfamlaw.com

SAMUEL V. SCHOONMAKER IV, born Stamford, Connecticut, 1967; admitted to bar, 1994, Connecticut. *Education:* Yale University (B.A., magna cum laude, 1990); Cambridge University, Cambridge, England (M.Phil., 1991); Columbia University (J.D., 1994). Law Clerk to Judge William Rush, Stamford Superior Court. Author: "Division and Valuation of Speculative Assets: Reasoned Adjudication or Courthouse Confusion?"; "Consequences and Validity of Family Law Provisions in the Welfare Reform Act," Journal of the American Academy of Matrimonial Lawyers. Managing Editor, The Connecticut Family Lawyer. *Member:* Stamford/Norwalk Regional, Connecticut (Member, Executive Committee, Family Law Section) and American (Financial Officer, 2000-2002; Co-Chair, Congressional Relations Committee, Family Law Section) Bar Associations. ***PRACTICE AREAS:*** Matrimonial Law; Family Law. ***Email:*** svs4@sgcfamlaw.com

JOHN P. EKBERG, III, born St. Louis, Missouri, February 26, 1947; admitted to bar, 1990, Connecticut; 1991, New York. *Education:* College of Wooster (B.A., 1969); Pace University (M.P.A., 1982); Pace University School of Law (J.D., magna cum laude, 1990). Member, Case Note Editor, Pace Law Review, 1989-1990; Moot Court Board, Pace University School of Law, 1988-1989. Author: "Murray v. United States: The Emasculation of the Fourth Amendment Warrant Clause" 10 Pace Law Review 167, 1990; "Limitation on Jurisdiction over Component Parts Manufacturers in Product Liability Actions," Journal of Products Liability 55, 1988. *Member:* Stamford-Norwalk Regional (Board Member), Connecticut (Family Law Section), New York State and American Bar Associations. ***PRACTICE AREAS:*** Matrimonial Law; Family Law. ***Email:*** jekberg@sgcfamlaw.com

JILL HEITLER BLOMBERG, born New York, N.Y., July 18, 1972; admitted to bar, 1997, Connecticut; 1998, New York. *Education:* University of Pennsylvania (B.A., History, 1994); Fordham University (J.D.,1997). *Member:* Stamford-Norwalk Regional, New York State (Member, Family Law Section), Connecticut (Member, Family Law Section) and American (Chair, Family Law Section, Young Lawyers Division; Executive Committee and Co-Chair, Family Law and Child Advocacy Committee, Young Lawyers Section) Bar Associations; New York County Lawyers Association (Member, Family Law Section). ***PRACTICE AREAS:*** Family Law; Matrimonial Law. ***Email:*** jblomberg@sgcfamlaw.com

---

NANCY SEGORE-FRESHMAN

GREENWICH, CONNECTICUT

(See Westport)

Family Law, Divorce Mediation, Collaborative Law, Estate Planning, Estate Administration.

WILLIAM SELSBERG

GREENWICH, CONNECTICUT

(See Stamford)

General Practice including Real Estate, Commercial and Residential, Corporate Law, Common Interest Community Law, Zoning and Subdivision Law, Environmental Law, Commercial and Residential Leases.

LAW OFFICE OF THOMAS M. SHANLEY

Established in 1988

37 ARCH STREET
GREENWICH, CONNECTICUT 06830
Telephone: 203-622-9004
FAX: 203-622-3086
Email: tmshanley@snet.net
URL: http://www.lawyers.com/shanley

Matrimonial, Family, Divorce, Paternity, Custody, Appeals and all areas of Domestic Relations Law.

THOMAS M. SHANLEY, born Bridgeport, Connecticut, 1954; admitted to bar, 1979, Connecticut and U.S. District Court, District of Connecticut; 1986, U.S. Supreme Court. *Education:* Fairfield University (B.A., 1976); New York Law School (J.D., cum laude, 1979). Director and Treasurer, Fairfield University Alumni Association, 1983—. *Member:* Greenwich, Connecticut (Member, Executive Committee of Family Law Committee; Lecturer: 1987-1988, Co-Chairperson of Monthly Seminar Series, Family Law Section "The Anatomy of A Divorce" Trial Series Lectures, 1989; Feb., 1992, Family Law Seminar, "Relocation Issues in Custodial Disputes"; Nov., 1992, Family Law Seminar, "Settlement and The Short Term Marriages and Inherited Property") and American (Member, Family Law Section) Bar Associations; The Association of Trial Lawyers of America. ***PRACTICE AREAS:*** Divorce; Matrimonial Law; Family and Domestic Relations Law.

SHIPMAN & GOODWIN LLP

Established in 1919

43 ARCH STREET
GREENWICH, CONNECTICUT 06830
Telephone: 203-869-6222
Telecopier: 203-869-6565
Email: www@goodwin.com
URL: http://shipman-goodwin.com

Hartford, Connecticut Office: One American Row. Telephone: 203-251-5000.
Lakeville, Connecticut Office: 12 Porter Street, P.O. Box 1809. Telephone: 203-435-2539.
Stamford, Connecticut Office: One Landmark Square. Telephone: 203-324-8100.

General Practice. Banking, Corporation, Tax, Antitrust, Commercial Finance, Securities, Venture Capital, Labor and Employment, Health Care, Environmental, Pension and Employee Benefits, Estate Planning, Estate Settlement, Trust Administration, Real Estate, Municipal Law, Franchise, Dealer and Distributor Litigation. Trials in all Courts.

FIRM PROFILE: Shipman & Goodwin was founded over 80 years ago. Its principal areas of practice include general corporate and securities law, litigation, corporate and commercial finance, tax, bankruptcy and creditors' rights, environmental law, municipal law, administrative law, utility regulation, real estate, construction law, fidelity and surety law, venture capital financing, international trade, antitrust and trade regulation, banking, insurance, labor and employment, trusts and estates, pension, health care law, intellectual property, computer law, tax-exempt organizations, agricultural cooperatives, family law, criminal law, legislation and lobbying. The firm is divided into six departments: Business, Litigation, Labor and Employment, Real Estate, Tax, and Trusts and Estates. In each area of practice, lawyers are assisted by experienced legal assistants. In addition, many lawyers are members of practice groups organized to address specifically the needs of particular clients and/or industries. Among such groups are those serving venture capital investors, high technology and emerging companies, hospitals and health care providers, municipalities and agricultural cooperatives. Within the Trust and Estate Department is a group specializing in Financial Planning and Trust Administration.

OF COUNSEL

GERARD E. JONES, born Cleveland, OH, 1937; admitted to bar, 1966, New York; 1991, Connecticut. *Education:* Yale University (B.A., 1959; LL.B., 1965). *Member:* The Association of the Bar of the City of New York; New York State Bar Association. ***PRACTICE AREAS:*** Corporate Law; Securities Law. ***Email:*** gjones@joodwin.com

Unless otherwise noted, all are members of The Hartford County, Connecticut and American Bar Associations.

REPRESENTATIVE CLIENTS: Aetna Casualty & Surety Co.; Agri-Mark, Inc.; Anthem Blue Cross & Blue Shield of Connecticut.; City of Hartford; Hartford Hospital; Stanadyne, Inc.; United Technologies Corp.; Yankee Energy System, Inc.

SILVER, GOLUB & TEITELL LLP

GREENWICH, CONNECTICUT

(See Stamford)

Trial Practice in all State and Federal Courts. Medical Malpractice, Negligence, Commercial Litigation, Family and Criminal Law.

DAVID M. SINGER

Established in 1982

125 MASON STREET
GREENWICH, CONNECTICUT 06830
Telephone: 203-629-2700
Facsimile: 203-629-8462
Email: d.m.singer@worldnet.att.net
URL: http://www.lawyers.com/dmsinger

General Civil Practice. Business Law, Real Estate, Probate and Estate Planning, Corporate and Mergers and Acquisitions.

DAVID M. SINGER, born Boston, Massachusetts, March 26, 1945; admitted to bar, 1969, Massachusetts; 1977, New York; 1982, Connecticut. *Education:* University of Pennsylvania (B.A., 1966); Boston University (J.D., 1969). Selectman, Town of Greenwich, Connecticut (1993-1997). *Member:* Greenwich and Connecticut Bar Associations. ***PRACTICE AREAS:*** General Civil Practice; Corporation: Mergers and Acquisitions; Real Estate; Wills, Estates and Trusts.

APPROVED ATTORNEY FOR: Fleet Bank of Connecticut; People's Bank; First Union; Putnam Trust Co.; Sound Beach Financial Co.; Connecticut Attorneys Title Insurance Co.; First American Title Insurance Company; Citibank, N.A.; Astoria Federal Savings; The Long Island Savings Bank.

TIERNEY, ZULLO, FLAHERTY & MURPHY, P.C.

GREENWICH, CONNECTICUT

(See Norwalk)

General Practice. Real Estate, Probate, Administrative, Condemnation, Employment, Healthcare, Municipal, Land Use, Planning, Zoning and Family Law. Civil Litigation, State and Federal Courts.

TROW & SANK, P.C.

GREENWICH, CONNECTICUT

(See Stamford)

Trials in all Courts, Personal Injury, Collections, Negligence, Commercial Litigation, Landlord Tenant, Real Estate, Probate, Estate Planning, Tax, Commercial and Corporate Law, Workers Compensation.

TYLER COOPER & ALCORN, LLP

Established in 1847

675 STEAMBOAT ROAD
GREENWICH, CONNECTICUT 06830-7140
Telephone: 203-869-2000
Telecopier: 203-869-2001
URL: http://www.tylercooper.com

Hartford, Connecticut Office: CityPlace. Telephone: 860-725-6200. Telecopier: 860-278-3802.

New Haven, Connecticut Office: 205 Church Street. Telephone: 203-784-8200. Telecopier: 203-789-2133.

Stamford, Connecticut Office: One Landmark Square. Telephone: 203-348-5555. Telecopier: 203-348-3875.

Madison, Connecticut Office: 23 Woodland Road. Telephone: 203-318-3600. Telecopier: 203-318-3609.

Administrative Law, Alternative Dispute Resolution, Antitrust and Trade Regulation, Banking, Bankruptcy and Reorganization, Business Crimes, Business Organizations and Securities Law, Computer Law, Domestic Relations, Environmental Law, Financial Services, Franchising, Health Care, Immigration, Insurance Defense and Insurance Coverage Defense, Intellectual Property, Labor and Employment, Legislative Lawyering, Litigation, Media Law, Medical Malpractice Defense, Pension and Employee Benefits, Public Utilities, Real Estate, Taxation, Trusts and Estates and Workers' Compensation.

SENIOR COUNSEL

HENRY W. PASCARELLA, born New Haven, Connecticut, August 15, 1933; admitted to bar, 1958, Connecticut; 1963, U.S. Supreme Court. *Education:* Wharton School of Finance & Commerce, University of Pennsylvania (B.S., 1955); Yale University (LL.B., 1958). *Member:* Greenwich Bar Association (President, 1972-1973). ***PRACTICE AREAS:*** Trusts and Estates; Real Estate; Environmental and Land Use Regulation; Litigation.

(For all personnel, see Professional Biographies at New Haven)

PETER V. WALL

95 EAST PUTNAM AVENUE
GREENWICH, CONNECTICUT 06830
Telephone: 203-629-2122
Telecopier: 203-629-3822
URL: http://www.lawyers.com/peterwall

New York, NY Office: 305 Madison Avenue, Suite 1146, 10165.

Tax Law. Probate and Estate Planning, Small Business and Real Estate.

PETER V. WALL, born Rome, Georgia, August 3, 1942; admitted to bar, 1968, New York and U.S. District Court, Northern District of New York; 1974, U.S. Tax Court; 1987, Connecticut. *Education:* Dartmouth College (A.B., 1964); Cornell University (M.B.A., 1967; J.D., 1968). Phi Delta Phi. Certified Public Accountant, New York, 1972. Associate, 1973-1979 and Member, 1980-1986, Hale, Grant, Meyerson, O'Brien & McCormick, New York, New York. Trustee, National Hypertension Association, 1986—. *Member:* Greenwich, Connecticut and American (Member, Real Property, Probate and Trust Law Section; Taxation Section) Bar Associations. [Capt., U.S. Army, 1969-1971]. ***PRACTICE AREAS:*** Estate Planning and Probate Law; Real Estate Law; Small Business Law; Taxation Law.

ELLIOT R. WARREN

GREENWICH, CONNECTICUT

(See Westport)

General Civil and Criminal Litigation before all State and Federal Courts. Trials and Appeals. Criminal Defense, Commercial and Tax Litigation, Personal Injury, Employment and Negligence Law.

WHITMAN BREED ABBOTT & MORGAN

100 FIELD POINT ROAD
GREENWICH, CONNECTICUT 06830
Telephone: 203-869-3800
Telecopier: 203-869-1951

Corporate Law, Litigation, Real Estate, Trusts and Estates.

MEMBERS OF FIRM

CHARLES E. COATES, III, born West Point, New York, 1948; admitted to bar, 1974, Connecticut; 1988, New York. *Education:* Harvard University (B.A., magna cum laude, 1970; J.D., 1974). Lecturer on Estate Planning, University of Connecticut School of Law, 1984-1985. *Member:* Greenwich (President, 1987), The Connecticut (Member: Executive Committee, Estates and Probate Section, 1983-1984; House of Delegates, 1985-1988; Board of Governors, 1987-1988) and American Bar Associations. ***PRACTICE AREAS:*** Estate Planning and Administration; Land Use Law; Estate and Gift Taxation Law; Probate Law; Trust Administration. ***Email:*** ccoates@wbamct.com

JAMES A. FULTON, born New York, N.Y., 1952; admitted to bar, 1977, Connecticut and U.S. District Court, District of Connecticut; 1986, U.S. Court of Appeals, Second Circuit. *Education:* University of Connecticut (B.A., summa cum laude, 1974); Cornell University Law School (J.D., 1977). Phi Beta Kappa; Phi Kappa Phi; Pi Sigma Alpha; Phi Delta Phi. Member, Board of Editors, Cornell International Law Journal, 1977. *Member:* The Connecticut Trial Lawyers Association. ***PRACTICE AREAS:*** Litigation; Personal Injury Litigation; Products Liability Litigation; Landlord-Tenant Litigation. ***Email:*** jfulton@wbamct.com

THOMAS F. HARTCH, born Greenwich, Connecticut, 1941; admitted to bar, 1967, Connecticut. *Education:* Yale University (B.A., 1963); New York University (M.P.A., 1968); Columbia University (J.D., 1966). Phi Delta Phi. Author: "The Zoning Board of Appeals: Powers and Practice," 52 Connecticut Bar Journal 380, 1978. *Member:* Greenwich (President, 1984-1985), The Connecticut and American Bar Associations; Christian Legal Society. ***PRACTICE AREAS:*** Real Estate; Trusts and Estates; Land Use.

DALE J. LOIS, born Tarrytown, New York, 1960; admitted to bar, 1990, Connecticut and New York. *Education:* Siena College (B.A., 1983); New York Law School (J.D., 1990). Member and Articles Editor, New York Law School Review, 1989-1990. Law Intern to Hon. J. Costentino, U.S. District Court, Eastern District of New York, 1989. Author: "Racial Integration in Urban Housing: The Method is Legal The Time Has Come," New York Law School Law

(This Listing Continued)

Review, 1991. *Member:* Connecticut and New York State Bar Associations; Regional Bar Association. ***PRACTICE AREAS:*** Commercial Real Estate; Corporate Law; Electronic Commerce. ***Email:*** dlois@wbamct.com

ANTHONY M. MACLEOD, born Manila, Philippines, 1947; admitted to bar, 1972, Connecticut; 1974, U.S. District Court, District of Connecticut; 1975, U.S. Court of Appeals, Second Circuit; 1976, U.S. Supreme Court. *Education:* University of Notre Dame (A.B., magna cum laude, 1969); University of Virginia (J.D., 1972). Member, Editorial Board, Virginia Journal of International Law. Law Clerk to Justices Elmer W. Ryan and Joseph W. Bogdanski, Supreme Court of Connecticut, 1972-1973. Member, Connecticut Supreme Court Law Clerks Association, 1972—. Member, Executive Committee, Young Lawyers Sections, Connecticut Bar Association, 1974-1975. Chair, Public Utility Law Committee, 1995-1998; Executive Committee, 1998. Chair, Regulatory Law Committee, National Association of Water Companies, 1990-1993. Member, Bridgeport Financial Review Board, 1991-1995. Chair, Greenwich Flood and Erosion Control Board, 1988—. *Member:* The Corporate Bar. ***PRACTICE AREAS:*** Corporation Law; Public Utility Law; Real Estate Law. ***Email:*** amacleod@wbamct.com

RICHARD E. MANCUSO, born Bronxville, New York, 1961; admitted to bar, 1988, Connecticut. *Education:* Fordham University; George Washington University (B.A., 1983); Boston College (J.D., cum laude, 1988). *Member:* Connecticut and American Bar Associations. ***PRACTICE AREAS:*** Intellectual Property; Unfair Competition; Corporate Law; Employment Law; Mergers, Acquisitions and Divestitures; Latin America Practice. ***Email:*** rmancuso@wbamct.com

HARRY E. PEDEN, JR., born Norwalk, Connecticut, 1923; admitted to bar, 1948, Connecticut; 1950, Rhode Island. *Education:* Brown University (A.B., 1950); St. John's University (LL.B., 1948); New York University (LL.M., 1960). Chairman, Legislative Committee Representative Town Meeting, Greenwich, CT; Chairman, Town of Greenwich Board of Standards and Appeals. *Member:* Greenwich (President, 1970-1971), The Connecticut and American Bar Associations; Rhode Island State Bar Association. ***PRACTICE AREAS:*** Real Estate; Planning, Zoning and Land Use. ***Email:*** hpedenjr@wbamct.com

HARRY E. PEDEN, III, born Glendale, Arizona, 1945; admitted to bar, 1975, Connecticut; 1984, New York. *Education:* Brown University (B.A., 1968); St. John's University (J.D., cum laude, 1975). *Member:* Connecticut (Member, Executive Committee of the Banking Law Section, 1982—) and American Bar Associations. ***PRACTICE AREAS:*** Corporate Law; Mergers, Acquisitions and Divestitures, Securities. ***Email:*** hpeden@wbamct.com

CHARLES W. PIETERSE, born Springfield, Massachusetts, 1960; admitted to bar, 1986, Connecticut; 1987, Massachusetts and U.S. District Court, District of Connecticut; 1988, New York; 1996, U.S. District Court, Southern and Eastern Districts of New York, U.S. Court of Appeals, Second and Seventh Circuits and U.S. Tax Court. *Education:* University of Massachusetts (B.A., cum laude, 1983); Fordham University (J.D., 1986). Phi Beta Kappa; Phi Kappa Phi; Moot Court Board. Member, Board of Editorial Advisors, Commercial Lending Litigation News and Bank Bailout Litigation News, 1998—. Author: "A Question of Fault—Apportioning Contract Damages," Metropolitan Corp. Counsel, Oct. 1997. Guest Commentary: "Opinions Address Emerging Trend in Standard of Proof of Debt," Bank Bailout Litigation News, November 1998. *Member:* Greenwich, Connecticut and American (Litigation Section) Bar Associations. ***PRACTICE AREAS:*** Civil Litigation; Complex Commercial Litigation; Products Liability; Drug and Medical Device Defense; Creditors Rights; Loan Workouts. ***Email:*** cpieterse@wbamct.com

JAMES C. RILEY, born New York, N.Y., 1960; admitted to bar, 1985, Connecticut; 1986, U.S. District Court, District of Connecticut; 1989, U.S. District Court, Southern District of New York; 1991, U.S. Court of Appeals, Second Circuit. *Education:* Georgetown University (B.A., cum laude, 1982; J.D., 1985). Editor, American Criminal Law Review, 1984-1985. *Member:* Connecticut Bar Association. ***PRACTICE AREAS:*** Commercial Litigation; Employment Litigation. ***Email:*** jriley@wbamct.com

CYD L. SMITH, born Chicago, Illinois, 1958; admitted to bar, 1988, Connecticut and New York. *Education:* Northeastern Illinois University (B.A., summa cum laude, 1980); Pace University (J.D., 1988). Moot Court Competition Award. Member and Articles Editor, Pace University Law Review, 1986-1988. *Member:* Greenwich, Connecticut, New York State and American Bar Associations. (Vice President and Assistant General Counsel, The Ash Forth Company, 1992-2001). ***PRACTICE AREAS:*** Commercial Real Estate; Leasing; Finance; Acquisitions and Divestitures; Residential Real Estate. ***Email:*** csmith@wbamct.com

KEVIN A. WALSH, born Davenport, Iowa, 1950; admitted to bar, 1978, Connecticut; 1979, New York. *Education:* Tulane University of Louisiana (B.A., 1973); St. John's University (J.D., 1978); New York University (LL.M. in Taxation, 1979). *Member:* Connecticut and American Bar Associations. ***PRACTICE AREAS:*** Taxation; Trusts and Estates; Corporate Law; Municipal Finance. ***Email:*** kwalsh@wbamct.com

(This Listing Continued)

ASSOCIATES

A. DUDLEY BELKNAP, born Charleston, West Virginia, 1946; admitted to bar, 1995, Connecticut. *Education:* University of Colorado (B.A., 1969); Pace University School of Law (J.D., 1989). *Member:* Connecticut Bar Association. ***PRACTICE AREAS:*** Estate Administration; Estate Taxation; Estate Planning. ***Email:*** dbelknap@wbamct.com

MARGARET E. CONBOY, born Omaha, Nebraska, 1968; admitted to bar, 1994, Connecticut and New York. *Education:* New York University (B.A., 1990); Pace University (J.D., 1993). *Member:* Greenwich, Stamford/Norwalk Regional and Connecticut (Member, Young Lawyers Section; Real Property Sections) Bar Associations; New York County Lawyers Association. ***PRACTICE AREAS:*** Residential and Commercial Real Estate; Planning and Zoning; Land Use. ***Email:*** mconboy@wbamct.com

ANDREA M. FRALEIGH, born Guelph, Ontario, Canada, 1968; admitted to bar, 1993, Illinois (Not admitted in Connecticut). *Education:* University of Michigan (B.B.A., 1990); Harvard Law School (J.D., cum laude, 1993). Phi Beta Kappa. James B. Angell Scholar. ***PRACTICE AREAS:*** Estate Planning; Estate Administration. ***Email:*** afraleigh@wbamct.com

MACIEJ A. PIATKOWSKI, born Bridgeport, Connecticut, 1971; admitted to bar, 1997, Connecticut. *Education:* Georgetown University (B.A., 1993); University of Connecticut (J.D., 1997). *Member:* American Bar Association. ***LANGUAGES:*** Polish. ***PRACTICE AREAS:*** Litigation; Civil Litigation; Commercial Litigation; Landlord and Tenant Law; Breach of Contract; Foreclosures; Products Liability. ***Email:*** mpiatkowski@wbamct.com

GARY N. MOZER, born 1974; admitted to bar, 1999, CT. *Education:* State University of New York at Binghamton (B.A., cum laude, 1996); University of Connecticut (J.D., with honors, 1999). Commentary Editor, Connecticut Law Review. Author: The Crumbling Wall Between Church and State: Agostini v. Felton, Aid to Parochial Schools and the Establishment Clause in the Twenty-First Century, 31 Conn. L. Rev. 337 (1998); School Vouchers and the Establishment Clause: Introduction, 31 Conn. L. Rev. 803 (1999). *Member:* Stamford Norwalk Regional, Connecticut and American Bar Associations. ***PRACTICE AREAS:*** Corporate Law; Mergers and Acquisitions; Divestitures; Electronic Commerce; Venture Capital.

OF COUNSEL

ROBERT G. KRAUSE, born Manchester, Connecticut, 1931; admitted to bar, 1958, Connecticut. *Education:* University of Connecticut (B.A., 1953); Boston University (LL.B., 1956). ***PRACTICE AREAS:*** Trusts and Estates; Real Estate. ***Email:*** rkrause@wbamct.com

MICHAEL K. MADDEN, born Utica, New York, 1951; admitted to bar, 1978, New York; 1979, District of Columbia; 1986, Maryland (Not admitted in Connecticut). *Education:* Duke University (B.A., magna cum laude, 1973); George Washington University (J.D., with highest honors, 1977). Order of the Coif. Notes Editor, George Washington Law Review, 1976-1977. Law Clerk, Judge Oliver Gasch, U.S. District Court, District of Columbia, 1977-1978. ***PRACTICE AREAS:*** Litigation; Complex Commercial Litigation; Insurance Coverage; Products Liability; Drug and Medical Device Defense; Commercial Arbitration. ***Email:*** mmadden@wbamct.com

DAVID P. TUTTLE, born New York, N.Y., 1960; admitted to bar, 1985, Connecticut; 1987, New York. *Education:* Princeton University (B.A., cum laude, 1982); Duke University (J.D., 1985). *Member:* Connecticut Bar Association (Member, Legislative Committee, Banking Law Section, 1991-1995). ***PRACTICE AREAS:*** Finance; Mergers and Acquisitions; Venture Capital; Securities; Real Estate. ***Email:*** dtuttle@wbamct.com

MICHAEL B. WEIR, born New York, N.Y., 1925; admitted to bar, 1951, New York (Not admitted in Connecticut). *Education:* Yale University (B.A., 1947); University of Pennsylvania (LL.B., 1950). ***PRACTICE AREAS:*** Antitrust; Trade Regulation; Non Profit Organization.

THOMAS J. WILLIAMS

99 INDIAN FIELD ROAD
GREENWICH, CONNECTICUT 06830
Telephone: 203-661-7404
Fax: 203-622-6718
Email: tjwmslaw@aol.com
URL: http://www.lawyers.com/thomasjwilliams

General Practice, Civil, Criminal, Domestic Relations, Family, Divorce.

THOMAS J. WILLIAMS, born Scranton, Pennsylvania, February 19, 1955; admitted to bar, 1982, Connecticut. *Education:* University of West Haven (B.S., 1977); University of Bridgeport (J.D., 1982). ***PRACTICE AREAS:*** General Practice; Civil Practice; Criminal Law.

WILLINGER, WILLINGER & BUCCI, P.C.

GREENWICH, CONNECTICUT

(See Bridgeport)

General Practice. Real Estate, Corporate, Commercial, Foreclosure, Bankruptcy, Secured Financing, Zoning, Labor, Probate, Condemnation, Workers Compensation, Financial, Banking, Personal Injury and Criminal Law. Trials in all Courts.

ZEICHNER ELLMAN & KRAUSE LLP

35 MASON STREET
GREENWICH, CONNECTICUT 06830
Telephone: 203-622-0900
Fax: 203-862-9889
Email: zek@zeklaw.com

New York, N.Y. Office: 575 Lexington Avenue. Telephone: 212-223-0400. Fax: 212-753-0396.

Newark, New Jersey Office: One Gateway Center. Telephone: 973-624-8600. Fax: 973-624-8585.

General Civil Practice. Banking, Corporate, Real Estate, Litigation, Creditor's Rights and Bankruptcy Law.

JOHN T. AVELLINO, born New York, N.Y., February 2, 1947; admitted to bar, 1974, New York and U.S. District Court, Southern and Eastern Districts of New York; 1992, Connecticut and U.S. District Court, District of Connecticut. *Education:* C.W. Post (B.A., 1969); Brooklyn Law School (J.D., 1973). *Member:* New York State Bar Association. [Sgt., U.S. Army National Guard, 1971-1975]. (Also at New York, New York Office). ***Email:*** javellino@zeklaw.com

ASSOCIATE

PIERRE-YVES KOLAKOWSKI, born Bridgeport, Connecticut, September 30, 1967; admitted to bar, 1993, Connecticut; 1994, U.S. District Court, District of Connecticut. *Education:* Fairfield University (B.A., 1989); Quinnipiac College School of Law (J.D., 1993). Recipient, American Jurisprudence Award. *Member:* Greater Bridgeport, Connecticut and American Bar Associations. ***LANGUAGES:*** French. ***Email:*** pkolakowski@zeklaw.com

(For Complete Biographical Data on all Personnel see Professional Biographies at New York, New York)

MOUKAWSHER & WALSH LLC

328 MITCHELL STREET
P.O. BOX 966
GROTON, CONNECTICUT 06340
Telephone: 860-445-1809
Fax: 860-446-8161
URL: http://www.benefitlawyers.com
Email: moukwals@snet.net
URL: http://www.lawyers.com/moukawsher&walshllc

Hartford, Connecticut Office: 21 Oak Street. Telephone: 860-549-8440. Fax: 860-549-8443.

Civil Litigation, ERISA Law, Benefits Law, Estates, Negligence, Personal Injury, Wrongful Death, Medical Malpractice, Products Liability, Commercial Litigation, Employment Law, Trials and Appeals.

JOSEPH E. MOUKAWSHER, born New London, Connecticut, February 5, 1920; admitted to bar, 1949, Connecticut; 1953, U.S. District Court, District of Connecticut; 1980, U.S. Court of Appeals, 2nd Circuit; 1981, U.S. Supreme Court. *Education:* Wesleyan University (B.A., 1942); Harvard University (LL.B., 1948). Phi Beta Kappa. Prosecuting Attorney, Town of Groton, 1955-1960. Borough Attorney, Borough of Groton, 1962-1963. Town Attorney, Town of Groton, 1969-1971; 1977-1983. Coroner, New London County, 1972-1979. Member, Town of Groton Charter Revision Commission, 1991—. *Member:* New London County, The Connecticut and American Bar Associations. ***PRACTICE AREAS:*** Real Estate; Probate; Estate Planning; Civil Litigation. ***Email:*** jemoukawsher@snet.net

MICHAEL J. WALSH, born Nassau, New York, May 31, 1962; admitted to bar, 1987, Connecticut; 1988, New York and U.S. District Court, Southern and Eastern Districts of New York and District of Connecticut; 1993, U.S. Court of Appeals, Second Circuit. *Education:* Stonehill College (B.S., with high honors, 1984); University of Connecticut (J.D., 1987). Member, 1985-1986, and Editor, 1986-1987, Connecticut Law Review. Law Clerk to Hon. Ellen Burns, Chief Judge, U.S. District Court of Connecticut, 1988-1989. Author: "The Disclosure Requirements of 35 U.S.C. 112 and Software-Related Patent Applications: Debugging the System," 18 Conn. L. Rev. 855 (1986). Adjunct Instructor Faculty, University of Connecticut, School of Law, 1994-1999. *Member:* Hartford County, New London County, Connecticut and American Bar Associations; Oliver Ellsworth Inn of Court (Treasurer, 1991-1992); American Trial Lawyers Association; Connecticut Trial Lawyers Association. ***REPORTED CASES:*** Chylinski v. Wal-Mart Stores, 150 F.3d 214 (2d Cir. 1998) (Personal Injury/Premises Liability); Suarez v. Sordo, 43 Conn. App. 756, 685 A.2d 1144, cert. den. 240 Conn. 906, 688 A.2d 334 (1997) (Personal Injury/Premises Liability); Rumbin v. Utica Mutual Insurance, Co., 254 Conn. 290 (2000) (Commercial Contract). ***PRACTICE AREAS:*** Civil Litigation; Personal Injury; Medical Malpractice. ***Email:*** mwalsh7777@aol.com

THOMAS G. MOUKAWSHER, born New London, Connecticut, September 10, 1962; admitted to bar, 1986, Connecticut. *Education:* The Citadel (B.A., magna cum laude, 1983); University of Connecticut (J.D., cum laude, 1986). Phi Kappa Phi. Editor, Conn. L. Rev., 1985-1986. Law Clerk, Office of the Governor, State of Connecticut, 1985-1986. Author: "Mobile Home Parks and Connecticut's Regulatory Scheme," 17 Conn. L. Rev. 811, 1985; "Protecting the Dignity of Privacy Law," 18 Conn. L. Rev. 621, 1986; "Client Perjury Demands Attorney Disclosure," 12 Conn. L. Trib. No. 20, 1986; "Cash Balance Plans: Terminology, Advantages and Disadvantages to Employers and Employees," Connecticut Lawyer, Vol. 10, No. 9, 2000. Member, Town Council, Town of Groton, 1987-1990. Member and Special Counsel, Democratic State Central Committee of Connecticut, 1988-1990. Counsel, Democratic Party, State of Connecticut, 2001—. Member, House of Representatives, State of Connecticut, 40th District, 1991-1993. Special Counsel, President Pro Tempore, Connecticut State Senate, 1993-1995. Counsel, General Assembly, Committee on Commerce, 1993-1995. Member, Democratic State Central Committee of Connecticut, 1997—. Counsel, State of Connecticut Democratic Party, 2001—. Member, Oliver Ellsworth Inn of Court, 1992-1994. *Member:* Connecticut and American Bar Associations. ***REPORTED CASES:*** Mullins v. Pfizer, 23 F.3d 663 (1994) (ERISA); Jackson v. Whipple, 225 Conn. 705 (1993) (unfair trade practices); Kelly v. Bonney, 221 Conn. 549 (1992) (defamation/employment); Adamczyk v. Lever Brothers, 991 F.Supp. 931 (N.D. Ill. 1997) (ERISA); Hudson v. General Dynamics, 186 F.R.D. 271 (D.Conn 1999)(ERISA); Bins v. Exxon, 220 F.3d 1042 (9th Cir. 2000)(en banc)(ERISA). ***PRACTICE AREAS:*** ERISA; Commercial Litigation; Employment Law. ***Email:*** tmoukawsher@snet.net

---

JEFFREY M. SKLARZ, born New Haven, Connecticut, August 15, 1974; admitted to bar, 1999, Connecticut. *Education:* Colby College (B.A., 1996); University of Connecticut (J.D., 1999). Member, Connecticut Journal of International Law, 1996-1999. Author: "Cash Balance Plans: Terminology, Advantages and Disadvantages to Employers and Employees," Connecticut Lawyer, Vol. 10, No. 9, 2000. ***PRACTICE AREAS:*** ERISA; Personal Injury; Employment Law; Civil Litigation; Taxation. ***Email:*** sklarz@aol.com

REFERENCE: Fleet Bank.

O'BRIEN, SHAFNER, STUART, KELLY & MORRIS, P.C.

Established in 1966

475 BRIDGE STREET
P.O. DRAWER 929
GROTON, CONNECTICUT 06340-3723
Telephone: 860-445-2463
Fax: 860-445-4539
Email: osskm@snet.net
URL: http://www.obrienshafner.com

Norwich, Connecticut Office: 138 Main Street. Telephone: 860-889-3855. Fax: 860-886-6352.

Trials in all Courts. Personal Injury, Products Liability, Workers Compensation, Medical Malpractice, Corporations, Estate Planning, Probate, Trust Law, Real Estate, General Practice, Administrative and Admiralty Law.

FIRM PROFILE: Established in 1966, we are a general practice law firm focusing on advocacy, counseling and caring. We can handle almost every type of legal work that a family or business may require. We take great pride in our team approach of lawyers, legal assistants and staff. Each lawyer and legal assistant concentrates their talents in one or more fields. This expertise allows us to provide superior legal services in a number of fields of law as one of southeast Connecticut's most capable and experienced law firms. We emphasize trial work in Personal Injury, Workers Compensation, Probate Appeals and Commercial Litigation. In addition we have expertise in Municipal Law, Estate Planning and Elder Law, Estate and Trust Administration, Business (Corporate) and Real Estate Law.

JOHN C. O'BRIEN, born Hartford, Connecticut, September 9, 1933; admitted to bar, 1962, Connecticut. *Education:* University of Connecticut (B.A., 1956); Georgetown University (J.D., 1962). Staff Attorney, U.S. Senate Juvenile Delinquency Subcommittee, 1962. Secretary, State Occupational Licensing Commission, 1966-1979. President, Board of Governors, Stonington Commu-

(This Listing Continued)

nity Center, Inc., 1968-1970. Chairman, Southeastern Connecticut Regional Planning Agency, 1969-1971. Trustee, Mystic Marine Life Aquarium, 1980-1987. Chairman, Trustee, Westerly Hospital, 1989—. Member, Connecticut Probate Court Advisory Committee, 1981-1987. Trustee, Eastern Connecticut State University Foundation, 1990-1995. *Member:* New London County, Connecticut and American (Member: Economics of the Profession Committee, 1978—; Junior Bar Association Executive Council, 1965-1966; Chairman, Committee on Economics, 1965-1966) Bar Associations. ***PRACTICE AREAS:*** Real Estate Law; Probate Law; Corporations Law.

MATTHEW SHAFNER, born New London, Connecticut, February 23, 1935; admitted to bar, 1959, Connecticut; 1961, U.S. District Court, District of Connecticut; 1963, U.S. Court of Appeals, First and Second Circuits. *Education:* University of Connecticut (B.A., 1958; J.D., 1959). Pi Sigma Alpha. Lecturer, "Triennial World Congress of Pathology, Legal Aspects of Occupational Disease," Mt. Sinai School of Medicine, Connecticut Trial Lawyers Association, 1981. Co-Author: "Maritime Injuries in and Near Connecticut Waters," CTLA Forum, 1987 Chapter; "The Longshore and Harbor Workers' Compensation Act" in Asselin, The Connecticut Workers Compensation Practice Manual, 1988 Supplement. Lecturer, Toxic Torts, March 1985 and Environmental Litigation, New Haven, February 1991, Opening Statements, May 1992, Connecticut Trial Lawyers Association. Member: Hearing Examiner, State Commission on Human Rights and Opportunities, 1967-1971; Asbestos Litigation Group, 1976—. *Member:* New London County Bar Association (President, 1976-1977; Member, Connecticut Council of Bar Presidents, 1975-1977); Connecticut Trial Lawyers Association (Board of Governors; Executive Committee; State Delegate to ATLA, 1984-1999; Co-Chairman, Workers Compensation Section, 1984-1996); New York Academy of Science. ***SPECIAL AGENCIES:*** Disabled Workers Committee of Connecticut. ***REPORTED CASES:*** Original Asbestos Litigation in New England; Champagne v. Raybestos-Manhattan, Inc., 562 A.2d 1100 (1989); McDonough v. CBTG, Inc.; 527 A.2d 664 (1987); Air America v. Director OWCP, 597 F.2d 773 (1st Cir. 1979); Gray V. General Dynamics, 565 F.2d 208 (2nd Cir. 1977); Gencarelle v. General Dynamics, 892 F.2d 173 (2nd Cir. 1989); Peterson v. INA 969 F.2d 1400 (2nd Cir. 1992). ***PRACTICE AREAS:*** Personal Injury Law; Workers Compensation; Admiralty; Asbestos Litigation.

PETER F. STUART, born Savona, New York, June 23, 1939; admitted to bar, 1970, Connecticut; 1974, U.S. Supreme Court, U.S. Tax Court, U.S. Claims Court and U.S. Court of Military Appeals. *Education:* Dartmouth College (A.B., 1961); Dickinson School of Law (J.D., 1969). Member, Dickinson Law Review, 1967-1969. Lecturer: Estate Planning for the Executive, American Life Council, 1972-1973; Instructor of Small Business Seminar, U.S. Small Business Administration, 1978-1979; "Business Law for Small Business Owners," Mohegan Community College, 1988-1992. *Member:* New London County (President, 1981-1982), Connecticut (Member, Executive Committee, Section on Business Law, 1983—) and American (Member, Subcommittee on Closely Held Corporations, 1982—) Bar Associations; National Academy of Elder Law Attorneys, 1990—. [Cmdr., JAGC, USNR, Ret.]. ***PRACTICE AREAS:*** Corporations Law; Business Organizations Law; Elder Law; Estate Planning; Probate Law.

CAROLYN P. KELLY, born Clifton Springs, New York, October 27, 1937; admitted to bar, 1971, Connecticut, U.S. District Court, District of Connecticut, U.S. Court of Appeals, 2nd Circuit and U.S. Supreme Court. *Education:* Syracuse University (B.A., 1959) Phi Kappa Phi; University of Oregon (J.D., 1970). Comments Editor, Oregon Law Review, 1968-1970. Author: "The Case Against Oregon's Dead Man's Statutes," Oregon Law Review, December, 1969. 1989 Connecticut Trial Lawyer's Association Seminar, "Longshore Coverage for Shipbuilding, Harbor Workers and Longshoremen". Selectman, Town of Groton, 1973-1980. Trustee and Vice President, Sea Research Foundation, Inc., 1987—. *Member:* Connecticut (Treasurer, 1985-1988; Vice President, 1988-1989; President, 1990-1991; Member, Board of Governors, 1980-1992) and American (House of Delegates, 1990-1993; Board of Governors, 1996-1999;; State Delegate, 1993-1996) Bar Associations; Connecticut Trial Lawyers Association; The Association of Trial Lawyers of America; Connecticut Bar Foundation (Director, 1985-1989; Vice President, 1985-1988, Fellow). Fellow, American Bar Foundation. ***REPORTED CASES:*** Palumbo v. Director, DW 937 F.2d 70, (2d Cir.); LaFaille v. Benefits Rev. U.S. Dept. of Labor, 884 F.2d 54, (2d Cir.); Pietrunti v. Director, OWCP, 119 F.3d 1035, 31 BRBS84 (CRI)(2nd Cir.). ***PRACTICE AREAS:*** Workers Compensation Law; Civil Litigation; Non-Profit Organizations Law; Employment Law.

GRANVILLE R. MORRIS, born New London, Connecticut, September 9, 1946; admitted to bar, 1974, Connecticut; 1980, U.S. District Court, District of Connecticut; 1981, U.S. Supreme Court. *Education:* Franklin & Marshall College (A.B., 1968); Boston University (J.D., 1974). Phi Alpha Theta; Pi Gamma Mu. Lecturer, Para-Legal Program, Mitchell College, New London, Connecticut, 1977-1980. Instructor, Basic Estate Planning, Connecticut Bar Association Continuing Legal Education Series, 1984-1990. Chairman, Alumni-Admissions Assistants Program, Franklin and Marshall College, 1976-1980. Member, Alumni Board, Franklin and Marshall College, 1990-1993. Member, East Lyme Water and Sewer Commission, Town of East Lyme, 1977-1980. Chairman, East

(This Listing Continued)

Lyme Charter Revision Commission, 1979-1980; Member: East Lyme Board of Finance, 1980-1986; Southeastern Connecticut of Estate and Tax Planning Council, 1979—. Member, Secretary and President, Board of Directors, East Lyme Youth Services Association, 1986-1989. Member, Board of Corporators, Lawrence and Memorial Hospital, 1990—. Member and Secretary, Board of Directors, East Lyme Public Trust Foundation, Inc., 1994—. *Member:* New London County, Connecticut (Member, Real Estate Executive Committee, 1988-1990) and American (Member: Sections on: Real Property Law; Natural Resources Energy and Environmental Law; Reporter for the 1983 Significant Real Estate Legislation Section of Real Property, Probate and Trust Journal) Bar Associations. ***PRACTICE AREAS:*** Estate Planning Law; Probate Administration; Real Estate Law.

FRANK N. EPPINGER, born New Bedford, Pennsylvania, March 24, 1943; admitted to bar, 1973, Connecticut; 1976, U.S. District Court, District of Connecticut; 1989, U.S. Supreme Court; 1993, U.S. Court of Appeals, 2nd Circuit. *Education:* Pennsylvania State University (B.A., 1965); American University (J.D., 1972). Adjunct Lecturer, University of New Haven, 1983-1988. Member, Special Public Defender Panel of the U.S. Magistrate's Court, Naval Submarine Base New London, Groton, Connecticut, 1983-1984. U.S. Naval Military Magistrate, Naval Submarine Base New London, Groton, Connecticut, 1979-1984. President, Board of Trustees, Denison Pequotsepos Nature Center, Inc., 1976-1979. President, North Stonington, Connecticut Historical Society, 1985-1987. President and Member of Board of Trustees of Pequot Audubon Society, Inc., 1983-1989. Counsel, Avalonia Land Conservancy, Inc., 1984—. Counsel, North Stonington Citizens Land Alliance, Inc., 1987—. Town Counsel, Town of North Stonington, 1995—. Counsel and Member of Board of Trustees, Stonington Cemetary Association, 1993—. *Member:* New London County, Connecticut (Member, Executive Committee, Planning and Zoning Section, 1981-1990) and American Bar Associations. [Lt., USN, 1965-1971; Capt., JAGC, USNR Ret.]. ***LANGUAGES:*** Russian. ***SPECIAL AGENCIES:*** Amtrack Customer Advisory Committee, National Passenger Railroad Corp., Washington, D.C. ***REPORTED CASES:*** Ames v. Sears Roebuck and Co., 514 A.2d 352; Ames v. Sears Roebuck and Co., 536 A.2d 563; Christy Hill Builders, Inc. v. Hall, 439 A.2d 1065; Farrington v. Zoning Board of Appeals of Noank Fire District, 413 A.2d 817; General Dynamics Co. v. Groton 440 A.2d 185; Hall v. Planning Commission of Ledyard, 435 A.2d 975; Helbig v. Zoning Board of Appeals for the Noank Fire District, 440 A.2d 940; Helbig v. Zoning Commission of Noank Fire District, 440 A.2d 940; Ilvento v. Frattai, 555 A.2d 985; Spicer v. Noank Fire District Zoning Commission, 562 A.2d 21. ***PRACTICE AREAS:*** Municipal Law; Civil and Probate Litigation; Appellate Litigation; Real Estate Law; Estate Planning Law; Zoning Law.

MARK E. BLOCK, born New York, New York, December 15, 1948; admitted to bar, 1973, Connecticut, U.S. District Court, District of Connecticut and Southern District of New York, U.S. Court of Appeals, Second Circuit and U.S. Supreme Court. *Education:* Ithaca College (B.A., 1970); Brooklyn Law School (J.D., 1973). Advisory Board Member, First American Title Ins. Co. *Member:* New London County (President, 1988-1989), Connecticut (Member: Section on Commercial Law and Bankruptcy, Real Property; Council of Bar Presidents, 1988-1989) and American Bar Associations. (Resident at Norwich Office). ***PRACTICE AREAS:*** Real Estate; Commercial Law; Bankruptcy; Construction Law.

LLOYD L. LANGHAMMER, born Concord, New Hampshire, July 20, 1961; admitted to bar, 1986, Connecticut; 1987, U.S. District Court, District of Connecticut; 1991, U.S. Court of Appeals, Second Circuit. *Education:* Middlebury College (B.A., 1983); University of Connecticut; California Western School of Law (J.D., 1986). Member, Waterford Flood and Erosion Control Board, 1989—. *Member:* New London County, Connecticut and American Bar Associations; The Association of Trial Lawyers of America. (Resident Norwich Office). ***PRACTICE AREAS:*** Commercial Litigation; Bankruptcy.

NATHAN J. SHAFNER, born New London, Connecticut, June 7, 1960; admitted to bar, 1988, Connecticut; 1989, U.S. District Court, District of Connecticut. *Education:* University of Massachusetts (B.A., 1983); Hofstra University (J.D., 1988). Managing Editor of Articles, Hofstra Property Law Journal. *Member:* Connecticut Bar Association (Member, Sections on: Family Law; Labor Law; Workers Compensation); Connecticut Trial Lawyers Association; Connecticut Plaintiff's Employment Law Association; Board of Directors, Connecticut Legal Services, 1992; Connecticut Workers Compensation Advisory Board. ***PRACTICE AREAS:*** Workers Compensation Law; Employment Law; Insurance Disputes.

RICHARD J. PASCAL, born Washington, D.C., June 22, 1959; admitted to bar, 1988, Connecticut; 1989, U.S. District Court, District of Connecticut; 1994, U.S. Supreme Court; 1995, U.S. Tax Court. *Education:* University of Pennsylvania, Wharton School (B.S., magna cum laude, 1981); George Washington University, National Law Center (J.D., 1987). Adjunct Professor, Three Rivers Community Technical College, 1989—. Certified Public Accountant, Maryland, 1982—. Vice President, ECSU Foundation. (Resident Norwich Office). ***PRACTICE AREAS:*** Commercial and General Litigation; Corporate Law; Employment Law; Tax Law.

(This Listing Continued)

O'BRIEN, SHAFNER, STUART, KELLY & MORRIS, P.C., Groton—Continued

ERIC M. JANNEY, born Cleveland, Ohio, April 2, 1966; admitted to bar, 1991, Connecticut; 1995, U.S. District Court, District of Connecticut. *Education:* Georgetown University (B.S. in Foreign Service, cum laude, 1988); University of Connecticut (J.D., with honors, 1991). Phi Alpha Theta; Pi Sigma Alpha. Executive Director, Connecticut Moot Court Board, 1990-1991. Member, 1989-1991, and Moderator, Groton Representative Town Meeting, 1991-1997. Member, Conecticut Republican State Central Committee, 1997—. Board of Directors, American Red Cross, 1992-1995. Faculty Member, The People's Law School, 1994—. Board of Directors, Housing Opportunities for People, Inc., 1997—. Chairman, Georgetown University Alumni Admissions committee. *Member:* New London County, Connecticut and American Bar Associations. ***PRACTICE AREAS:*** Real Estate; Municipal Law; Business Organization. ***Email:*** osskmemj@aol.com

BONDE ERIK JOHNSON, born Springfield, Massachusetts, September 7, 1963; admitted to bar, 1989, Florida; 1996, Connecticut and U.S. District Court, District of Connecticut; 1994, U.S. District Court, Middle District of Florida, U.S. Court of Appeals, 11th Circuit and U.S. Court of Appeals, Federal Circuit. *Education:* Boston University (B.A., 1985); Valparaiso University (J.D., 1989). Executive Managing Editor Law Review, Mock Trial Team, 1988. Legal Writing Teaching Assistant, Valparaiso University School of Law, 1989. *Member:* London County, Connecticut and American Bar Associations; Connecticut Trial Lawyers Association; Association of Trial Lawyers of America. ***PRACTICE AREAS:*** Personal Injury Law; Negligence; Product Liability.

LYNN T. CRAVINHO, born Holyoke, Massachusetts, July 15, 1968; admitted to bar, 1993, Connecticut. *Education:* Providence College (B.S. in Accounting, magna cum laude, 1990); Western New England College School of Law (J.D., cum laude, 1993). Tau Pi Phi, Honor Society. Recipient, American Jurisprudence Award Estate Planning. Certified Public Accountant, Connecticut, January, 1997. Member, Connecticut Society of Certified Public Accountants, 1995—. *Member:* New London County and Connecticut (Tax Section, 1996—; Estates Probate Section, 1997; Elder Law Section, 1998—) Bar Associations; Southeastern Connecticut Estate and Tax Planning Council; National Academy of Elder Law Attorneys. ***PRACTICE AREAS:*** Estate Planning; Probate Administration; Elder Law.

LESTER "L.J." ARNOLD, III, born New London, Connecticut, November 19, 1958; admitted to bar, 1994, Connecticut; 1997, U.S. District Court, District of Connecticut and U.S. Bankruptcy Court. *Education:* Dartmouth College (A.B., 1980); University of Connecticut (J.D., 1994). President, Thames Area Citizens' Advocacy Program, Inc. *Member:* New London County, Connecticut and American Bar Associations (Member, Commercial Law and Bankruptcy Section). (Resident Norwich Office). ***PRACTICE AREAS:*** Commercial Litigation; Foreclosure; Bankruptcy; Construction Law; Real Estate Law.

JAMES HALL, admitted to bar, 1997, Connecticut. *Education:* University of Colorado (B.A., 1992); New York Law School (J.D., 1997). Moot Court. Member, Law Review. *Member:* Connecticut Bar Association; Connecticut Trial Lawyers Association; American Trial Lawyers Association. ***PRACTICE AREAS:*** Personal Injury; Workers Compensation; Unfair Insurance Practices Act; Products Liability.

THOMAS F. COLLIER, born Manchester, Connecticut, September 9, 1961; admitted to bar, 1999, Connecticut. *Education:* University of Connecticut (B.A., 1983); Western New England College, School of Law (J.D., 1998). *Member:* Connecticut (Member, Sections on: Elder Law; Planning and Zoning) and American (Member, Sections on: Business Law; Probate and Trust Law) Bar Associations. ***PRACTICE AREAS:*** Land Use; Elder Law; Estate Planning; Construction Law; Contracts. ***Email:*** osskm@snet.net

APPROVED ATTORNEYS FOR: Chelsea-Groton Savings Bank; Fleet Bank; Citizens Saving Bank; Norwich Savings Bank; The Washington Trust Company; Lawyers Title Insurance Co.

SUISMAN, SHAPIRO, WOOL, BRENNAN, GRAY & GREENBERG, P.C.

GROTON, CONNECTICUT

(See New London)

Administrative Law, Aged and Aging, Appellate Practice, Asset Protection, Business Law, Civil Practice, Civil Rights, Commercial Law, Commercial Real Estate, Constitutional Law, Contracts, Corporate Law, Criminal Law, Debtor and Creditor, Family Law, Finance, Health Care, Indians and Native Populations, Insurance, Intellectual Property, Labor and Employment, Leases and Leasing, Litigation, Medical Malpractice, Municipal Law, Partnership Law, Personal Injury, Probate, Products Liability, Property Law, Real Estate, Regulatory Law, Social Security, Taxation, Torts, Trusts and Estates, Workers Compensation, Zoning, Planning and Land Use.

DELANEY, ZEMETIS, DONAHUE, DURHAM & NOONAN, P.C.

741 BOSTON POST ROAD
GUILFORD, CONNECTICUT 06437
Telephone: 203-458-9168
Fax: 203-458-4424

Wallingford, Connecticut Office: 111 South Main Street, P.O. Box 747, 06492. Telephone: 203-269-1441. Fax: 203-284-9428. Email: dzddn@worldnet.att.net

Practice Primarily Limited to Professional Malpractice, Products Liability, Insurance Defense, Personal Injury, Employment and Commercial Litigation in all Courts.

(For Complete Biographical Data on All Personnel, See Professional Biographies at Wallingford, Connecticut)

JOHN T. DILLON

64 BOSTON STREET
GUILFORD, CONNECTICUT 06437
Telephone: 203-453-9190; 203-453-1234
Fax: 203-453-9889

General Civil Practice, Real Estate, Zoning, Trusts, Estates, Probate and Corporation Law.

JOHN T. DILLON, born New Haven, Conn., March 24, 1937; admitted to bar, 1981, Connecticut and U. S. District Court, District of Connecticut. *Education:* College of the Holy Cross (B.S., 1959); Yale University (M.I.A., 1961); University of Connecticut (J.D., 1981). *Member:* Connecticut Bar Association. ***PRACTICE AREAS:*** Real Estate; Zoning; Trusts; Estates; Probate; Corporation Law.

APPROVED ATTORNEY FOR: Connecticut Title Insurance Co. (Issuing Agent); Lawyers Title Insurance Corp. (Issuing Agent).
REFERENCES: Guilford Savings Bank.

RICHARD M. FRANCHI

206 CHURCH STREET
GUILFORD, CONNECTICUT 06437-2439
Telephone: 203-495-1000
Fax: 203-786-4750
Email: richard.franchi@erols.com
URL: http://www.lawyers.com/rfranchilaw

Products Liability, Personal Injury, Medical Malpractice, Construction Law, Intellectual Property, Copyright Infringement, Copyright Litigation.

RICHARD M. FRANCHI, born Bridgeport, Connecticut, July 4, 1958; admitted to bar, 1989, Connecticut and New York and U.S. District Court, District of Connecticut. *Education:* University of Connecticut (B.S., Mechanical Engineering, 1980); University of Bridgeport (J.D., 1987). Member: Society of Automotive Engineers; American Society of Mechanical Engineers. *Member:* New York State and Connecticut Bar Associations. ***PRACTICE AREAS:*** Products Liability; Personal Injury; Medical Malpractice; Construction Law; Contractor Performance Bonds; Architects and Engineers Liability; OSHA; Aviation Law; Intellectual Property; Copyright Infringement; Copyright Litigation; Patent Litigation; Trademark Litigation.

GAIL S. KOTOWSKI

Established in 1985
397 CHURCH STREET
P.O. BOX 37
GUILFORD, CONNECTICUT 06437-0037
Telephone: 203-453-6030
FAX: 203-458-6981
Email: atty.kotowski@cshore.com
URL: http://www.ct-attorney.com

General Civil and Criminal Practice before State and Federal Courts, Administrative, Corporation, Domestic Relations, Criminal, Personal Injury, Real Estate, Copyright, Trademark, Sports, Trials and Appeals, Social Security, Immigration.

GAIL S. KOTOWSKI, born Brookline, Massachusetts, February 6, 1950; admitted to bar, 1980, Connecticut and U.S. District Court, District of Connecticut. *Education:* Pfeiffer College (A.B., 1972); Western New England College of Law (J.D., 1980). Former State Advocate (Prosecutor), 1986-1990.

(This Listing Continued)

Administrative Law Judge: Commission of Human Rights, 1989-1999; Department of Motor Vehicles, 1990—. Grievance Counsel-Judicial Districts: Danbury, 1987—; Litchfield, 1987—; Waterbury, 1987—. *Member:* New Haven, Connecticut and American Bar Associations. ***LANGUAGES:*** French and German.

LICENSED AGENT FOR: Chicago Title Insurance; New Haven Savings Bank; People's Bank.

JUDITH A. RAVEL

Established in 1993

246 GOOSE LANE
SUITE 201
GUILFORD, CONNECTICUT 06437-2186
Telephone: 203-458-2300
Telecopier: 203-458-8822
Email: J.Ravel@worldnet.att.net
URL: http://www.lawyers.com/ravelaw

Civil Litigation, Family, Municipal, Labor and Employment.

JUDITH A. RAVEL, born San Antonio, Texas, November 27, 1938; admitted to bar, 1984, Connecticut. *Education:* Smith College (A.B., magna cum laude, 1960); University of Connecticut (J.D., with honors, 1984). Phi Beta Kappa. Member, 1982-1983 and Associate Editor, 1983-1984, Connecticut Law Review. Town Counsel: Town of Guilford, 1991-1996; Town of Westbrook, 2000—; Town of Essex. Labor Counsel, Town of Essex, 2000—. *Member:* Connecticut and American Bar Associations; Association of Trial Lawyers of America; Connecticut Employment Law Association; Theodore I Koskoff American Inn of Court (Counselor, 1992-1997). ***PRACTICE AREAS:*** Labor and Employment Law; Civil Litigation; Family; Municipal.

ASSOCIATE

ANNE K. MILLHAM, born Laconia, New Hampshire, April 29, 1967; admitted to bar, 1993, Connecticut; 1994, U.S. District Court, District of Connecticut. *Education:* Bates College (B.A., 1989); University of Connecticut (J.D., 1993). Member, Connecticut Journal of International Law, 1992-1993. *Member:* Connecticut and American Bar Associations; Connecticut Employment Law Association; Theodore I. Koskoff American Inn of Court. ***PRACTICE AREAS:*** Labor and Employment Law; Civil Litigation; Family. **Email:** A.Millham-J.Ravel@worldnet.att.net

OF COUNSEL

MARGOT KENEFICK BURKLE, born Hartford, Connecticut, January 6, 1961; admitted to bar, 1988, Connecticut; 1992, U.S. District Court, District of Connecticut. *Education:* Wheaton College (B.A., cum laude, 1983); University of Bridgeport (J.D., 1988). *Member:* Connecticut Bar Association. ***PRACTICE AREAS:*** Family Law; Civil Litigation; Real Estate.

PAUL K. SULLIVAN, JR.

LIGHTHOUSE SQUARE
705 BOSTON POST ROAD
P.O. DRAWER 327
GUILFORD, CONNECTICUT 06437
Telephone: 203-453-1490
Fax: 203-453-2639
URL: http://www.lawyers.com/sullivan

Estate Planning, Estate Administration, Trusts and Probate Law, Conservatorships.

PAUL K. SULLIVAN, JR., born Landstuhl, West Germany, January 29, 1965; admitted to bar, 1991, Connecticut. *Education:* College of the Holy Cross (B.A., 1987); University of Connecticut (J.D., 1991). *Member:* New Haven County, Connecticut and American Bar Associations; Connecticut Estate and Tax Planning Council. ***PRACTICE AREAS:*** Trust and Estates; Estate Administration; Estate Planning; Probate; Ancillary Probate; Probate Administration; ConservatorshipS.

OF COUNSEL

JEANN R. TERRAZZANO, born New Haven, Connecticut, August 9, 1945; admitted to bar, 1976, Connecticut; 1979, U.S. District Court, District of Connecticut, U.S. Tax Court and U.S. Claims Court. *Education:* Quinnipiac College (B.S., summa cum laude, 1973); University of Connecticut (J.D., 1976); New York University (LL.M. in Taxation, 1980). Certified Public Accountant, Connecticut, 1978. Certified Life Underwriter, Connecticut, 1981. *Member:* Connecticut and American Bar Associations. ***PRACTICE AREAS:*** Trusts and Estates; Estate Administration; Estate Planning; Probate; Ancillary Probate; Probate Administration; Conservatorships.

(This Listing Continued)

REFERENCES: New Haven Savings Bank; Guilford Savings Bank.

PARRETT, PORTO, PARESE & COLWELL, P.C.

Established in 1962

ONE HAMDEN CENTER
2319 WHITNEY AVENUE
HAMDEN, CONNECTICUT 06518
Telephone: 203-281-2700
Fax: 203-281-0700
Email: info@pppclaw.com
URL: http://www.pppclaw.com

North Haven, Connecticut Office: 13 Peck Street, 06473. Telephone: 203-239-1111.

Bankruptcy, Commercial, Construction Litigation, Corporate, Criminal, Elder and Administrative Law, Estate Administration, Estate Planning, Family, Foreclosures, General Civil Practice, Insurance Law, Intellectual Property, Labor and Employment, Medical Malpractice, Municipal, Personal Injury, Products Liability, Real Estate, Taxation, Trials and Appeals in all State and Federal Courts, State Workers Compensation, Zoning.

RICHARD J. PARRETT, born New Haven, Connecticut, February 5, 1932; admitted to bar, 1961, Connecticut; 1962, U.S. District Court, District of Connecticut; 1965, U.S. Supreme Court; 1981, U.S. Court of Appeals, Second Circuit. *Education:* University of Connecticut (B.A., with Honors and Distinction in Government, 1958); Georgetown University (J.D., 1960). Phi Alpha Delta. Selectman, 1967-1973, First Selectman, 1969-1971, Justice of the Peace, 1970-1989, Chairman, North Haven Housing Authority, 1990 - Town of North Haven. Member, Panel of Arbitrators, American Arbitration Association, 1993—. *Member:* New Haven County and Connecticut (Member, Senior Lawyer Section; State Law-Day Chairman, 1966-1967) Bar Associations; The Association of Trial Lawyers of America. [With U.S. Air Force, 1950-1954]. **Email:** rparrett@pppclaw.com

CARL M. PORTO, born Bridgeport, Connecticut, August 31, 1942; admitted to bar, 1967, Connecticut and U.S. District Court, District of Connecticut; 1981, U.S. Court of Appeals, Second Circuit. *Education:* Boston University (B.A., 1964); University of Connecticut (J.D., 1967). Member, Code of Ethics Committee, Town of Hamden, 1968. Civil Service Commissioner, Hamden, 1967-1973. Assistant Town Attorney, 1973-1974, and Town Attorney, 1979-1981, Hamden, Connecticut. Co-Chairman, Federal Masters Program, U.S. District Court, 1989-1997, Attorney State Trial Referee, 1991—. Member, Board of Governors, Quinnipiac Club, 1997-2000. Member, Board of Trustees, 1980-1995 and Vice President, 1990, Hamden Hall Country Day School. Member, Board of Directors and Executive Committee, Bank of New Haven, 1985-1997. Member, Board of Directors: Citizens Bank of Connecticut and Rhode Island, 1997—; Member, Board of Directors, Shubert Performing Arts Center, Inc. Member, Board of New Haven Symphony Orchestra, 1987-1990, St. Raphael's Hospital Foundation, Board of Directors, 1991-1994. Member, Panel of Arbitrators, American Arbitration Association. James W. Cooper Fellow, Connecticut Bar Foundation, Life Fellow. *Member:* New Haven County (Member, Executive Committee, 1981-1987; Secretary 1982-1983; Treasurer, 1983-1984; Vice President, 1984-1985; President, 1985-1986) and Connecticut (Member, Committee on Automobile Reparation, 1977; Committee on Professionalism, 1991-1994; Chair, Committee on the Unauthorized Practice of Law, 1999—; In-House Council Study Committee; Multidisciplinary Practice Committee, 1999—; Multijurisdictional Practice Task Force, 2000—) Bar Associations; Connecticut Trial Lawyers Association. **Email:** cporto@pppclaw.com

JOHN A. PARESE, born Meriden, Connecticut, December 22, 1948; admitted to bar, 1973, Connecticut and U.S. District Court, District of Connecticut. *Education:* Villanova University (B.A., 1970); St. John's University (J.D., 1973). Member, Executive Board, St. John's Moot Court, 1972-1973. Instructor, Real Estate Law, Fairfield University, 1975-1979. Member, North Branford Planning and Zoning Commission, 1978-1981. Co-Town Attorney, Town of North Branford, 1981-1984. Special Master, U.S. District Court, District of Connecticut, 1991—. President, Villanova Club of Greater New Haven, Inc., 1991-1993. *Member:* New Haven County (Member, Executive Committee, 1992—; President, 2000-2001) and Connecticut (Member: House of Delegates, 1984-1990; Board of Governors, 1987-1991; Member, 1991—; Chairman, 1996-1999, Judicial Department Clients' Security Fund Committee, 1999—) Bar Associations. **Email:** jparese@pppclaw.com

WILLIAM S. COLWELL, born New Haven, Connecticut, April 1, 1950; admitted to bar, 1976, Connecticut and U.S. District Court, District of Connecticut. *Education:* Deerfield Academy; Colgate University (A.B., 1973); New

(This Listing Continued)

PARRETT, PORTO, PARESE & COLWELL, P.C., Hamden—Continued

England School of Law (J.D., 1976). Member, Inland Wetland Commission, Town of Cheshire, 1978-1980. Member, 1980-1986 and Chairman, 1982-1985, Planning and Zoning Commission, Town of Cheshire. Special Master, U.S. District Court, District of Connecticut, 1991—. Secretary, Lewis G. Schaeneman, Jr. Foundation, Inc., 1994. President: Quinnipiac Council, Boy Scouts of America, 1993-1995; President, Colgate Club of New Haven, 1986-1997. President, City Missionary Association, Inc., 2000—. *Member:* New Haven County and Connecticut (Member, Sections on: Elder Law; Estate and Probate) Bar Associations; Connecticut Estate and Tax Planning Council. **Email:** wcolwell@pppclaw.com

GREGORY P. KINSELLA, born Pontiac, Michigan, March 6, 1957; admitted to bar, 1982, Connecticut; 1983, U.S. District Court, District of Connecticut. *Education:* Williams College (B.A., cum laude, 1979); University of Miami (J.D., cum laude, 1982). Recipient, American Jurisprudence Award in Criminal Law. Member: Guilford Land Conservation Trust; Guilford Keeping Society; Connecticut Fund for the Environment. Past President and Board of Directors, 1992-2000, Madison Jaycees. *Member:* New Haven County and Connecticut Bar Associations; Connecticut Trial Lawyers Association; Association of Trial Lawyers of America. **Email:** gkinsella@pppclaw.com

MICHAEL DEAN AMATO, born Miami, Florida, June 11, 1955; admitted to bar, 1983, Connecticut; 1984, U.S. District Court, District of Connecticut and U.S. Tax Court. *Education:* University of Connecticut (B.S., 1977; J.D., 1983). Certified Public Accountant, Connecticut, 1979. Member, Pension and Retirement Board, City of Milford, 1983. Vice Chairman, 1984 and Chairman, 1985-1988, Board of Finance, City of Milford. Member, Board of Aldermen, City of Milford, 1989-1993. *Member:* Milford, New Haven County and Connecticut Bar Associations; American Institute of Certified Public Accountants; The Connecticut Society of Certified Public Accountants. **Email:** mamato@pppclaw.com

LOUIS M. FEDERICI, born Philadelphia, Pennsylvania, September 4, 1960; admitted to bar, 1987, Connecticut; 1988, U.S. District Court, District of Connecticut. *Education:* Drexel University (B.S., 1983); Villanova University (J.D., 1987). Recipient, Law Alumni Award, 1986-1987. Legal Research Clerk, Connecticut Superior Court, 1988. Special Master, U.S. District Court, District of Connecticut, 1996—. Alternate Member, Guilford Zoning Board of Appeals. Past President and Board of Directors, New Haven Home Recovery. Past President, Hamden Jaycees. *Member:* New Haven County and Connecticut (Litigation Committee) Bar Associations; Connecticut Trial Lawyers Association. **Email:** lfederici@pppclaw.com

ANTHONY M. SOLOMINE, born New Haven, Connecticut, October 22, 1963; admitted to bar, 1988, Connecticut; U.S. District Court, District of Connecticut. *Education:* Boston College (B.A., cum laude, 1985); Suffolk University (J.D., 1988). Phi Alpha Theta. Commissioner of Civil Service Commission, City of New Haven, 1996—; Commissioner of Affirmative Action Committee, City of New Haven, 1996—. Board of Directors, Farnen House. *Member:* New Haven County and Connecticut (Member, Professional Discipline Committee and Family Law Section) Bar Associations; Young Lawyers Bar Association. **Email:** asolomine@pppclaw.com

CARL M. PORTO II, born New Haven, Connecticut, November, 14, 1967; admitted to bar, 1993, Connecticut; 1994, U.S. District Court, District of Connecticut. *Education:* Boston University (B.A., cum laude 1990); Quinnipiac University School of Law (J.D., 1993). Recipient, American Jurisprudence Award in Trial Practice. Member, Board of Trustees, Hamden Hall Country Day School, 1998—. Member, Connecticut Probate Law Journal. *Member:* New Haven County and Connecticut (Member, Standing Committee on Professionalism) Bar Associations. **Email:** cportoii@pppclaw.com

JOSEPH M. PORTO, born New Haven, Connecticut, August 15, 1970; admitted to bar, 1996, Connecticut; 1997, U.S. District Court, District of Connecticut. *Education:* Trinity College (B.A., 1993); Quinnipiac University School of Law (J.D., 1996). Moot Court Honor Society. *Member:* New Haven County, Connecticut and American Bar Associations; Connecticut Trial Lawyers Association. **Email:** jporto@pppclaw.com

JOHN P. PFANNENBECKER, born New Haven, Connecticut, November 13, 1972; admitted to bar, 1999, Connecticut and U.S. District Court, District of Connecticut. *Education:* University of Rochester (B.A., 1994); Quinnipiac University School of Law and Business (J.D./M.B.A., 1998). Commercial Advocate, Quinnipiac Center for Dispute Resolution. *Member:* Stamford/Norwalk Regional, New Haven County, Connecticut and American Bar Associations; Connecticut Trial Lawyers Association. ***LANGUAGES:*** Italian and Spanish. ***PRACTICE AREAS:*** Corporate Law; Commercial Litigation; Commercial Transactions; Taxation; Internet Law; E-Commerce. **Email:** jpfannenbecker@pppclaw.com

WILLIAM M. RACCIO, born New Haven, Connecticut, December 30, 1956; admitted to bar, 1998, Connecticut. *Education:* Villanova University (B.S.B.A., 1980); Quinnipiac College School of Law (J.D., 1998). Member, Finance Honor Society. Recipient, Outstanding Classroom Performance. License: Property Casualty Life Insurance Health Insurance, State of Connecticut; Series 6 Securities. Member, Chartered Property Casualty Underwriter, Malvern Institute, 1985. Member, Hamden Police Commission, 1999—. Board of Directors, New Haven Jaycees, 1983-1987. Board of Directors, Friendship Gate, 1989-1991. Member, Bank of New Haven Advisory Board, 1985-1992. *Member:* New Haven County, Connecticut and American Bar Associations; American Immigration Lawyers Association. **Email:** wraccio@pppclaw.com

OF COUNSEL

JOHN H. KRICK, born Pittsburgh, Pennsylvania, November 24, 1928; admitted to bar, 1953, Connecticut and U.S. District Court, District of Connecticut; 1966, U.S. Court of Appeals, 2nd Circuit; 1980, U.S. Supreme Court. *Education:* Dartmouth College (B.A., 1950); Columbia University (LL.B., 1953). Representative, Town Meeting, Hamden, Connecticut, 1960-1961. Executive Secretary, 1963 and 1965 and Chairman of Hamden Charter Revision Commission. Member, 1966-1975 and Chairman, 1972-1975, Hamden Board of Education. Consultant to Branford and North Haven Charter Revision Commissions, 1964-1967. *Member:* New Haven County, Connecticut (Member, 1966— and Vice-Chairman, Junior Bar Association, 1968, , Committee on Commercial Law and Bankruptcy) and American Bar Associations; American Judicature Society; Commercial Law League of America (Member, Board of Governors, 1974-1977).

REPRESENTATIVE CLIENTS: A-1 Toyota; Acura of Avon; Acura of Milford; BLCompanies; Burger King; Cable Systems of North Haven, Inc.; Chili's Restaurant; Circuit Wise, Inc.; Citizens Bank of Connecticut; Connecticut Auto Mall; Connecticut Beverage Mart; Connecticut Housing Finance Authority; Connecticut Orthopaedic Specialists, P.C.; Connecticut Stone Supplies; Cumberland Farms, Inc.; Dichello Distributors, Inc.; Doctors' Associates; Executive Auto Group; Fairfield Orthopedic Associates, P.C.; Fleet Pride, Inc.; Gateway Financial Services; Hamden Chrysler Plymouth; Hamden Hall Country Day School, Inc.; Home Town Buffet; J&C Bargas Construction, LLC; J.M. Layton & Company, Inc.; J. Thomas Honda; Juvenile Diabetes Foundation; Landquest, LLC; Lorensen Toyota; MacDonald Companies, Inc.; Mailboxes, Etc.; McDermott Auto Group; McDonald's Restaurants; Merrit Gas Stations; Narang Realty Company, Inc.; New England Flooring Supply Co.; New England Tennis, Inc.; New England Truck Sales and Service, Inc.; New Haven County Sheriff's Association; New Haven Home Recovery; Optima Group, Inc.; Pharmacia-Upjohn Co.; Roche Dinkeloo Architects; Southern New England Telephone Real Estate, Inc.; Town of Hamden; Specialized Packaging Group Inc.; Stop and Shop Supermarkets; Triton Environmental, LLC; Westbrook Honda; Wire and Plastic Machinery, Corp.; Worldtek Travel.
APPROVED ATTORNEYS FOR: American Residential Mortgage Co.; Chicago Title Insurance Co.; Citizens Bank of Connecticut; Commonwealth Title Insurance Co.; Connecticut Attorney's Title Insurance Co.; Connecticut Legal Services Plan; Fleet Bank; GMAC Mortgage Corp; Great Western Mortgage Corp.; Lawyers Title Insurance Corp.; McCue Mortgage Co.; Midwest Legal Services Plan; Milford Bank; New Haven Savings Bank; Peoples Bank; Prudential Legal Services; Sovereign Mortgage Corp.; The Prudential Home Mortgage Co.; United Mortgage; Webster Bank.
REFERENCE: Citizens Bank of Connecticut.

SAXE DOERNBERGER & VITA P.C.

1952 WHITNEY AVENUE
HAMDEN, CONNECTICUT 06517
Telephone: 203-287-8890
Fax: 203-287-8847
URL: http://www.lawyers.com/sevlaw

Complex Commercial Litigation, Insurance Coverage Litigation, Environmental Litigation, Employment, Bankruptcy, Real Estate and Zoning, Construction Litigation.

TRACY ALAN SAXE, born Milford, Connecticut, July 28, 1958; admitted to bar, 1983, Connecticut and U.S. District Court, District of Connecticut; 1996, U.S. District Court, Eastern District of Michigan and U.S. Court of Appeals, Sixth Circuit. *Education:* Syracuse University (B.A., magna cum laude, 1980); Georgetown University (J.D., 1983). Phi Beta Kappa; Pi Kappa Kappa. Adjunct Professor, Insurance Law, Quinnipiac College School of Law, 1997—. Appointed by Department of Justice to Act as Trustee for the United States Bankruptcy Court (1997—). *Member:* Connecticut (Member, Chairman, Basic Practice and Procedures Seminar Committee, 1987-1989) and American Bar Associations; The Association of Trial Lawyers of America; Connecticut Trial Lawyers Association; Corporate Bar (f/k/a Westchester Fairfield County Corporate Counsel Association; Member, Planning Committee for Litigation and Insurance); Orange Little League (Member, Board of Directors, 1996—; Player Agent, 1999—). ***PRACTICE AREAS:*** Complex Commercial Litigation; Insurance Coverage; Employment Law; Bankruptcy; Environmental Litigation. **Email:** tas@sdvlaw.com

JEFFREY J. VITA, born New Haven, Connecticut, March 1, 1965; admitted to bar, 1990, Connecticut and U.S. District Court, District of Connecticut; 1996, U.S. District Court, Eastern District of Michigan and U.S. Court of Appeals, Sixth Circuit. *Education:* University of Connecticut (B.A., cum laude, 1987) Pi Sigma Alpha, Political Science National Honor Society; University of Bridgeport (J.D., 1990). Managing Editor, University of Bridgeport Law Re-

(This Listing Continued)

view. Member, Zoing Board of Appeals, Town of Hamden, Connecticut, 1997—. *Member:* New Haven County and Connecticut Bar Associations; Connecticut Trial Lawyers Association. ***PRACTICE AREAS:*** Complex Commercial Litigation; Insurance Coverage Litigation; Construction Litigation; Bankruptcy; Real Estate. ***Email:*** jjv@sdvlaw.com

EDWIN L. DOERNBERGER, born New York, N.Y., November 6, 1944; admitted to bar, 1976, Hawaii; 1979, Connecticut; 1980, District of Columbia. *Education:* Columbia University (A.B., 1966; M.A., 1969); University of Hawaii (J.D., 1976). *Member:* New Haven County, Connecticut, Hawaii State and American Bar Associations; Connecticut Trial Lawyers Association. ***PRACTICE AREAS:*** Commercial; Bankruptcy; Insurance; Environmental Litigation; Construction; Commercial Litigation. ***Email:*** eld@sdvlaw.com

MARIA A. VANDERLAAN, born Derby, Connecticut, March 9, 1966; admitted to bar, 1992, Connecticut and U.S. District Court, District of Connecticut; U.S. Court of Appeals, Second Circuit. *Education:* Wheaton College (B.A., cum laude, 1988); University of Bridgeport (J.D., 1991). *Member:* New Haven County, Connecticut and American Bar Associations; Connecticut Trial Lawyers Association. ***PRACTICE AREAS:*** Complex Commercial Litigation; Insurance Coverage; Construction Litigation; Bankruptcy; Professional Malpractice Defense. ***Email:*** mav@sdvlaw.com

ASSOCIATES

ALFRED P. BRUNO, born Derby, Connecticut, February 10, 1970; admitted to bar, 1997, Connecticut; 1999, U.S. District Court, District of Connecticut. *Education:* Bates College (B.A., 1992); Quinnipiac College School of Law (J.D., 1997). Member, Moot Court Honor Society, 1996-1997. National Family Law Moot Court Competition Semi-Finalist, 1997. Recipient: Distinguished Academic Achievement Award, Trial Practice; Outstanding Legal Scholarship Award; Service to the Community Award. Volunteer Income Tax Assistance Coordinator, 1995-1997. Bates College President's Advisory Committee, 1989-1992. *Member:* New Haven County, Connecticut and American Bar Associations; Connecticut Defense Lawyers Association; Connecticut Trial Lawyers Association; . ***PRACTICE AREAS:*** Complex Commercial Litigation; Insurance Coverage Litigation; Environmental Litigation; Employment Law; Bankruptcy; Real Estate; Zoning Law; Insurance Defense; Personal Injury. ***Email:*** apb@sdvlaw.com

JENNIFER M. RANCIATO, born New Haven, Connecticut, March 31, 1971; admitted to bar, 2001, Connecticut and U.S. District Court, District of Connecticut. *Education:* Hartwick College (B.A., 1993); Quinnipiac College (J.D., 2000). Member, Moot Court Honor Society, 1998-2000. Recipient, Outstanding Performance in Oral Advocacy Award. *Member:* New Haven County, Connecticut (Member, Young Lawyer's and Labor and Employment Law) Bar Associations. ***PRACTICE AREAS:*** Complex Commercial Litigation; Construction Litigation; Insurance Coverage Litigation; Labor and Employment Law; Civil Rights Law; Bankruptcy Law. ***Email:*** jmr@sdvlaw.com

LAW OFFICES OF ROBERT M. SINGER, L.L.C.

2377 WHITNEY AVENUE
HAMDEN, CONNECTICUT 06518-3225
Telephone: 203-248-8278; Toll Free: 888-218-7772
Fax: 203-407-0602
Email: SingerLawLLC@aol.com
URL: http://www.lawyers.com/rmsinger

General Civil Practice. Business Law, Commercial Litigation, Bankruptcy, Collections, Insurance, Tax Delinquencies, Tax Appeals and Audits, and Tax Planning.

ROBERT M. SINGER, born New Haven, Connecticut, November 20, 1962; admitted to bar, 1988, Connecticut; 1991, U.S. District Court, District of Connecticut and U.S. Tax Court. *Education:* Bryant College (B.S.B.A., Accounting, 1985); Western New England College (J.D., 1988); University of New Haven (Senior Professional Certificate, Taxation of Corporations); Concordia University (New England-Quebec Student Exchange Program, 1983-1984); University of Neuchatal (Summer French Language Program, 1986). Phi Alpha Delta, International Law Fraternity. (Treasurer, Arthur Middleton Chapter, 1987-1988). President, Hamden Jaycees, 1992-1993. Special Master, Connecticut Superior Court, New Britain Judicial District, Tax Session at Hartford. Adjunct Lecturer, Department of Accounting, Southern Connecticut State University, 1998—. Adjunct Assistant Professor, Department of Management, Sacred Heart University, 1991-1993. Author: "Limited Liability Corporations: An Investment Vehicle for Future Income," Financial Freedom Quarterly, Fall 1994, P. 84-88; "Power of Attorney: Planning to Make Life Easy," Caregivers Connection, April 1995; "Law on Delinquent Tax Collection Needs Revision," New Haven Register, August 11, 1996; "Midnight Surprise - Personal Injury Alert," The Tax Advisor, Pages 730-732, December, 1996; "T.R.A. '97: Relief for Some, More Aggravation for Others," The Tax Advisor, pages 767-768, December, 1997; "Reverse Mortgages: Managing Money for Life", Mature Years

(This Listing Continued)

Magazine, Spring, 1998, pages 41-45; "Use of Credit Cards as Sources of Capital for Small Business," Bank Security Report, February 1998, pgs. 7-8; "Those Dwindling Earnings-As Stock Prices Soar," Business Week, Reader's Report, April 20, 1998, Pg. 10; "Grabbing Milk Money: IRS Seizes Tax Refunds During Installment Agreement Status," The Tax Advisor, October 1998, pgs. 674-675; "Greener Pastures Indeed for the Patriots", Business Week, Reader's Report, January 18, 1999, page 10; "Limits on Collection", The Tax Advisor, May 1999, pages 317-318; "Refund Claims: Getting Money Back", The Tax Advisor, May 1999, pages 318-321; "More Becomes Less When Transferee Liability Attaches", Practical Tax Strategies, December 1999, pages 358-364; "Address the Plight of Delinquent Taxpayers," The Hartford Courant, Letters to the Editor, February 15, 2000; "Zero Down and Zero Later - The Problem of Collection: A Comparison of Procedures Under State Collection Law, the Bankruptcy Code, and the Internal Revenue Code," Commercial Law Journal, Volume 105, Number 2, pages 157-216, Summer, 2000; "Stanching the Flow of Bankruptcies," Business Week, Reader's Report, March 19, 2001. Principal, The Alternative Solution Center-Mediation and Arbitration Services for Business and Individuals. *Member:* New Haven County Bar Association; Commercial Law League of America. ***PRACTICE AREAS:*** Bankruptcy; Business Law; Debtor and Creditor; Collections; Insurance; Taxation; Alternative Dispute Resolution. ***Email:*** SingerLawLLC@aol.com

ADVOCATES LAW FIRM, LLC

HARTFORD, CONNECTICUT

(See New Britian)

Criminal Defense, White Collar Criminal Defense, Personal Injury, Medical Malpractice, Legal Malpractice, Legal Ethics and Professional Responsibility, Attorney Discipline. Trials and Appeals in all Courts and Administrative Agencies.

ALDERMAN & ALDERMAN

ONE CORPORATE CENTER
HARTFORD, CONNECTICUT 06103
Telephone: 860-249-0090
Telecopier: 860-249-0117
Email: lawyers@alderman.com
URL: http://www.alderman.com

General Practice, Commercial Law and Bankruptcy, Creditors' Rights, Environmental Law and Land Use, Business and eBusiness, Arbitration, Mediation and Civil Litigation.

MEMBERS OF FIRM

MYLES H. ALDERMAN, JR., born New Haven, Connecticut, August 31, 1959; admitted to bar, 1986, Connecticut. *Education:* Kenyon College (A.B., 1982); Cambridge University; Syracuse University (J.D., cum laude, 1986). Recipient, L.F.E. Goldie Publication Award, 1986. Managing Editor, 1985-1986, Syracuse Journal of International Law and Commerce. Author: "eBusiness 101-A Multipart Series," The Connecticut Lawyer, 2000; "When Is Intellectual Property Not 'Intellectual Property'? Trade-mark, Trade-name, and Trade-dress Law Collides With The Bankruptcy Code, American Lawyer Media Publications, 1999;" "Bankruptcy Law Chapter" of *CBA Basic Practice Manual,* Fall, 1993; "Major Changes Affecting Insolvent Homeowners," *Connecticut Lawyer,* July, 1993; "The FDIC's Power to Stay Proceedings," *Connecticut Lawyer,* February, 1992; "The Securities Acts and International Discovery," 12 Syr. J. Int. L. & Com. 600 (1986). *Member:* Connecticut Bar Association (Member, Executive Committee, Commercial Law and Bankruptcy Section, 1990—; Member, Business Law Section; Chairperson, YLS Section on Bankruptcy and Commercial Law, 1990-1993) and American Bar Association. ***PRACTICE AREAS:*** Commercial Law; Insolvency and Creditors' Rights. ***Email:*** malderman@alderman.com

LINDA WIESENTHAL ALDERMAN, born New York, N.Y., April 29, 1963; admitted to bar, 1987, Connecticut. *Education:* Northwestern University (B.A., 1984); Syracuse University (J.D., 1987). Member, 1985-1987 and Executive Editor, 1986-1987, Syracuse Law Review. Author: Connecticut Chapter, "State Environmental Law Special Report," Government Institutes, 1991; "The Must Carry Rules After Quincy Cable TV, Inc. vs. Federal Communications Commission: The Attempt to Harmonize Mandatory Carriage with Freedom of Speech," 38 Syr. L. Rev. 745, (1987). *Member:* Connecticut Bar Association (Member, Conservation and Environmental Quality Section) and American Bar Association (Member, Section of Natural Resources, Energy and Environmental Law, Environmental Lender Liability and Underground Tank Committees). ***PRACTICE AREAS:*** Land Use and Environmental Law.

OF COUNSEL

FRANCIS J. BROWNE, born New York, N.Y., July 6, 1959; admitted to bar, 1984, Connecticut; 1987, New York. *Education:* University of Notre Dame

(This Listing Continued)

ALDERMAN & ALDERMAN, Hartford—Continued

(B.A., cum laude, 1981); Boston University (J.D., 1984); University of Connecticut (M.B.A., 1990). Staff Editor, Boston University School of Law International Law Journal, 1983-1984. *Member:* Connecticut (Chairperson, YLS Section Corporations, Banking and Business Law, 1987-1990) and American Bar Associations. (Also practicing individually, Stamford). ***PRACTICE AREAS:*** Business Organizations.

REPRESENTATIVE CLIENTS: Agricredit Acceptance Corp.; Chase Manhattan Bank, N.A.; Litton Industries; Metra Health; R.R. Donnelley & Sons Co.; Xerox Business Credit; Henry Butcher Technology Realisation, LTD (England); National Amusements, Inc.; Weyerhaeuser.

RALPH J. ALEXANDER

HARTFORD, CONNECTICUT

(See East Hartford)

General Trial Practice in all Courts, Real Estate, Trusts, Probate, Estate Planning, Business Law, Workers Compensation, Social Security Disability Claims, Municipal, Personal Injury, Family Law, Labor Relations Public Sector, Public Housing, Public Housing Law.

ALFANO & FLYNN, LLC

HARTFORD, CONNECTICUT

(See Suffield)

General Practice. Trials, Negligence, Workers Compensation, Real Estate, Probate, Municipal and Corporation Law, Personal Injury and Domestic Law.

ALIX, YALE & RISTAS, LLP

Established in 1865

(Formerly Chilton, Alix & Van Kirk)

750 MAIN STREET

HARTFORD, CONNECTICUT 06103-2703

Telephone: 860-527-9211

Facsimile: 860-527-5029

Email: ayrllp@pctlaw.com

Patent, Trademark, Computer, Copyright and Unfair Competition Law and Related Licensing and Litigation.

MEMBERS OF FIRM

GUY D. YALE, born San Antonio, Texas, December 4, 1945; admitted to bar, 1976, Connecticut; 1980, U.S. District Court, District of Connecticut; 1982, U.S. Court of Appeals for the Federal Circuit; registered to practice before U.S. Patent and Trademark Office. *Education:* The Ohio State University (B.Sc., magna cum laude, 1967); Yale University; University of Connecticut (J.D., 1976). Sigma Pi Sigma; Phi Beta Kappa. Instructor, Business Law, C.W. Post College, 1977. Probate Judge, District of Bethany, 1979—. *Member:* Connecticut Bar Association (Member, Sections on: Intellectual Property; Trust and Estates; Federal Practice); Connecticut Intellectual Property Law Association; American Intellectual Property Law Association. **Email:** guyyale@pctlaw.com

L. JAMES RISTAS, born Dover, New Jersey, February 2, 1949; admitted to bar, 1978, Connecticut; 1979, U.S. District Court, District of Connecticut; 1982, U.S. Court of Appeals for the Federal Circuit; registered to practice before U.S. Patent and Trademark Office. *Education:* Cornell University (B.S., Eng. Physics, 1971; M.Eng, Nuclear, 1972); University of Connecticut (J.D., 1978). Tau Beta Pi. Author, "Intellectual Property Rights in the Electronics Age," *The Technology Management Handbook,* CRC Press LLC, 1999. Member, Windsor Board of Education, 1982-1987; Windsor Town Council, 1995-2001. Adjunct Faculty, Hartford Graduate Center, 1990-1993. *Member:* Windsor (President, 1985) and Connecticut (Member: Sections on: Commercial Law; Intellectual Property; Chairman, Computer Law Section, 1988-1991) Bar Associations; Connecticut Intellectual Property Law Association. **Email:** jimristas@pctlaw.com

RICHARD H. BERNEIKE, born Lakewood, Ohio, April 5, 1932; admitted to bar, 1964, District of Columbia and Connecticut; 1968, U.S. District Court, District of Connecticut; 1982, U.S. Court of Appeals for the Federal Circuit; registered to practice before U.S. Patent and Trademark Office. *Education:* Purdue University (B.S.Ch., 1958); George Washington University (LL.B., 1963). *Member:* Connecticut Intellectual Property Law Association. [U.S. Army, 1955-1957]

CLIFFORD P. KELLY, born Schenectady, New York, April 10, 1950; admitted to bar, 1993, Connecticut; 1995, U.S. Court of Appeals for the Federal Circuit; 1996, U.S. District Court, District of Connecticut; registered to practice before U.S. Patent and Trademark Office. *Education:* United States Naval Academy (B.S., 1972); University of Connecticut (M.B.A.,1981; J.D., 1993). Member, 1984-1990 and Vice Chairman, 1988-1990, East Granby Planning and Zoning Commission. *Member:* Connecticut (Member, Sections on: Intellectual Property; Computer Law) and American (Member, Section of Intellectual Property) Bar Associations; Connecticut Intellectual Property Law Association. [U.S.N., 1972-1977, Lt.]. **Email:** ckelly@pctlaw.com

ASSOCIATES

JAMES E. PIOTROWSKI, born Bristol, Connecticut, January 7, 1958; admitted to bar, 1998, Connecticut; 2000, U.S. Court of Appeals, Federal Circuit; registered to practice before U.S. Patent and Trademark Office. *Education:* University of Connecticut (B.S., Chemistry, 1980); Quinnipiac College School of Law (J.D., cum laude, 1998). *Member:* Connecticut Bar Association (Member, Intellectual Property Law Section); Connecticut Intellectual Property Law Association. **Email:** jpiotrowski@pctlaw.com

THOMAS J. MENARD, born Manchester, Connecticut, July 11, 1965; admitted to bar, 1998, Connecticut; 2000, U.S. Court of Appeals, Federal Circuit. *Education:* Central Connecticut State University (B.S., Industrial Technology, Electrical Systems, 1991); University of Connecticut (J.D., cum laude, 1998). *Member:* Connecticut (Member, Intellectual Property Section) and American (Intellectual Property Section) Bar Associations; Connecticut Intellectual Property Law Association; American Intellectual Property Law Association. ***PRACTICE AREAS:*** Patents. **Email:** tmenard@pctlaw.com

BENJAMIN Y. AGRESS, born Torrington, Connecticut, March 22, 1972; admitted to bar, 2000, Connecticut. *Education:* Tufts University (B.A., History, 1994); University of Connecticut (J.D., cum laude, 1999). \Recipient, Academic Achievement Award. *Member:* Connecticut (Co-Chair, Intellectual Property and Young Lawyers Sections; Member, Executive Committee, Young Lawyers Section) and American Bar Associations; American Intellectual Property Law Association. ***PRACTICE AREAS:*** Trademarks; Unfair Competition; Copyright Licensing; Noncompetition and Non-Solicitation Agreements. **Email:** bagress@pctlaw.com

ROBERT S. SMITH, admitted to bar, 1967, Connecticut; 1968, District of Columbia; 1982, New York. *Education:* University of Massachusetts (B.S.M.E., 1956); New York University (J.D., 1966). ***PRACTICE AREAS:*** Patent Law; Trademark Law; Copyright Law; Trade Secrets Law; Computer Law.

OF COUNSEL

JAMES E. ALIX, born Worcester, Massachusetts, October 27, 1933; admitted to bar, 1962, Virginia; 1964, Connecticut; 1965, U.S. District Court, District of Connecticut; 1966, U.S. Court of Appeals, Second Circuit; 1982, U.S. Court of Appeals for the Federal Circuit; registered to practice before U.S. Patent and Trademark Office. *Education:* College of the Holy Cross (B.S., Chem., 1955; M.S., Chem., 1956); Cleveland Marshall College of Law; Georgetown University (LL.B., 1962). Graduate Fellow, College of the Holy Cross, 1956. Law Clerk to Chief Judge Eugene Worley, U.S. Court of Customs and Patent Appeals, 1961-1962. President, Connecticut Intellectual Property Law Association, 1974-1975. Member, Panel of Arbitrators, American Arbitration Association. *Member:* Hartford County, Connecticut (Chairman, Patent, Trademark and Copyright Section, 1976-1977; Member, Professional Ethics Committee, Intellectual Property Section) and American Bar Associations; American Intellectual Property Law Association. **Email:** jalix@pctlaw.com

RALPH H. CHILTON, born Dayton, Ohio, August 7, 1930; admitted to bar, 1961, Connecticut; 1965, U.S. District Court, District of Connecticut; 1966, U.S. Court of Appeals, Second Circuit; 1971, U.S. Supreme Court; 1982, U.S. Court of Appeals for the Federal Circuit. *Education:* Purdue University (B.S.M.E., 1952); George Washington University (J.D., 1960). Order of the Coif; Phi Alpha Delta; Tau Beta Pi. *Member:* Connecticut Bar Association; Connecticut Intellectual Property Law Association. [(Comdr., JAGC, U.S. Navy Reserve, Ret.)]

ROGER A. VAN KIRK, born Princeton, New Jersey, August 4, 1932; admitted to bar, 1962, Connecticut and U.S. District Court, District of Connecticut; 1967, U.S. Supreme Court; 1969, U.S. Court of Appeals, Second Circuit; 1982, U.S. Court of Appeals for the Federal Circuit. *Education:* University of Vermont (B.S.E.E., 1957); George Washington University (J.D., 1961). *Member:* Connecticut Intellectual Property Law Association. **Email:** rvankirk@pctlaw.com

APPLETON & APPLETON, LLC

Established in 1958

100 PEARL STREET, SUITE 1210

HARTFORD, CONNECTICUT 06103-4500

Telephone: 860-246-5481

Facsimile: 860-246-5554

URL: http://www.appleton-law.com

Civil Litigation, Litigation, Personal Injury, Medical Malpractice. Commercial Litigation, Employment Litigation, Real Estate, Family, Probate, Appellate Practice.

(This Listing Continued)

MEMBERS OF FIRM

MORTON W. APPLETON, born Hartford, Connecticut, November 13, 1929; admitted to bar, 1955, Connecticut and Massachusetts; 1960, U.S. District Court, District of Connecticut; 1965, U.S. Court of Appeals, Second Circuit. *Education:* University of Connecticut (B.S.); Boston University (J.D.). *Member:* Hartford County and Connecticut Bar Associations. ***PRACTICE AREAS:*** Civil Litigation; Personal Injury; Medical Malpractice; Commercial Litigation; Administrative Law. ***Email:*** mappleton@appleton-law.com

PETER M. APPLETON, born Hartford, Connecticut, October 28, 1962; admitted to bar, 1988, Connecticut; 1989, U.S. District Court, District of Connecticut. *Education:* Trinity College (B.A., 1985); Boston University (J.D., 1988). *Member:* Hartford County and Connecticut Bar Associations; Connecticut Trial Lawyers Association; The Association of Trial Lawyers of America. ***PRACTICE AREAS:*** Civil Litigation; Personal Injury; Medical Malpractice; Product Liability; Employment Litigation; Commercial Litigation. ***Email:*** pappleton@appleton-law.com

ASSOCIATES

LINDA A. KESTEN, born Waterbury, Connecticut; admitted to bar, 1989, Connecticut; 1990, U.S. District Court, District of Connecticut. *Education:* Tufts University (B.A., 1983); University of Connecticut (J.D., 1989). *Member:* Hartford County and Connecticut Bar Associations. ***PRACTICE AREAS:*** Civil Litigation; Personal Injury; Family Law; Real Estate; Probate; Divorce. ***Email:*** lkesten@appleton-law.com

PETER T. EVANS, born Hartford, Connecticut, February 9, 1959; admitted to bar, 1989, Connecticut; 1995, U.S. District Court, District of Connecticut. *Education:* Trinity College (B.A., 1981); University of Connecticut (J.D., with honors, 1989). *Member:* Hartford County and Connecticut Bar Associations. ***PRACTICE AREAS:*** Personal Injury; Insurance Law; Commercial Litigation; Employment Litigation; Appellate Practice. ***Email:*** pevans@appleton-law.com

---

ARNOLD & ASSOCIATES

Established in 1985

80 CEDAR STREET

HARTFORD, CONNECTICUT 06106

Telephone: 860-728-0037

Fax: 860-524-8357

Email: rarnold@ursa.hartnet.org

Civil Litigation, Housing, Landlord Tenant, Public Finance, Securities and Commercial Transactions, Small Business Law and Probate.

FIRM PROFILE: Arnold & Associates is a general practice law firm with special emphasis on housing law. The Firm was established in 1985 and is comprised of skilled and experienced attorneys, paraprofessionals, and support staff dedicated to providing clients with quality, efficient, and effective legal services. The Firm has had extensive experience in civil litigation and handles trial and appellate cases for its clients. The Firm's banking, finance, and general corporate practice includes a broad spectrum of transaction-oriented matters. The Firm consists of three attorneys and one paralegal. Attorney Arnold and Attorney Rodriquez are members in good standing of both the Connecticut and New York Bars. Attorney Arnold is also admitted to practice before the Second Circuit Court of Appeals.

RUDOLPH P. ARNOLD, born New York, N.Y., May 24, 1948; admitted to bar, 1975, Connecticut and U.S. District Court, District of Connecticut; 1979, U.S. Court of Appeals, Second Circuit; 1996, New York. *Education:* Howard University (B.S., 1970); University of Connecticut (J.D., 1975); New York University (LL.M., 1976). Member, Hartford City Council, 1979-1981. Deputy Mayor, City of Hartford, 1981-1983. Director: Hartford Public Library. *Member:* Hartford County, Connecticut and American Bar Associations; National Bar Association; Connecticut Trial Lawyers Association; National Association of Bond Lawyers; Crawford Law Society. ***PRACTICE AREAS:*** Civil Litigation; Landlord and Tenant Law; Housing Law; Public Housing. ***Email:*** rarnold@ursa.hartnet.org

---

RAUL A. RODRIGUEZ, born Buffalo, New York, January 17, 1961; admitted to bar, 1986, Connecticut; 1987, New York and U.S. District Court, District of Connecticut. *Education:* Cornell University (B.A., 1983); State University of New York at Buffalo (J.D., 1986). Author: "One Strike You're Out Evictions In Connecticut" Connecticut Bar Journal, July/August 1997. Chairperson, Latino and Puerto Rican Affairs Commission, State of Connecticut. *Member:* Hartford County and Connecticut Bar Associations; National Hispanic Bar Association; Connecticut Hispanic Bar Association; Connecticut Trial Lawyers Association. ***PRACTICE AREAS:*** Civil Litigation; Landlord and Tenant Law; Foreclosure; Housing Law; Public Housing. ***Email:*** rarnold@ursa.hartnet.org

(This Listing Continued)

LEANNE BAGGETTA, born Meriden, Connecticut, March 23, 1974; admitted to bar, 2000, Connecticut; 2001, U.S. District Court, District of Connecticut. *Education:* Fairfield University (B.A., 1996); Western New England College (J.D., 2000). *Member:* Hartford County, Connecticut and American Bar Associations. ***PRACTICE AREAS:*** Civil Litigation; Landlord and Tenant Law; Foreclosures; Public Housing. ***Email:*** rarnold@ursa.hartnet.org

---

AXINN, VELTROP & HARKRIDER LLP

90 STATE HOUSE SQUARE, 11TH FLOOR

HARTFORD, CONNECTICUT 06103

Telephone: 860-275-8100

Facsimile: 860-275-8101

URL: http://www.avhlaw.com

New York, New York Office: 1370 Avenue of the Americas, 19th Floor. Telephone: 212-728-2200. Facsimile: 212-728-2201.

Washington, DC Office: 1801 K Street, N.W., Suite 411. Telephone: 202-912-4700. Facsimile: 202-912-4701.

Antitrust and Trade Regulation, Intellectual Property, Litigation, and International.

MEMBERS OF FIRM

STEPHEN M. AXINN (Resident, New York, NY Office).

JAMES D. VELTROP, born Jefferson City, Missouri, November 5, 1958; admitted to bar, 1986, Maryland; 1987, District of Columbia; 1996, Connecticut; registered to practice before the U.S. Patent and Trademark Office. *Education:* University of Missouri (A.B., summa cum laude, 1981; M.A., summa cum laude, 1983); Harvard University (J.D., cum laude, 1986). Phi Beta Kappa. Policy Essays Editor, Harvard Journal on Legislation, 1985-1986. Law Clerk to the Hon. Judith W. Rogers, District of Columbia Court of Appeals, 1986-1987. Author: "Understanding Foreign Pre-Merger Filings," 221 N.Y.L.J. 9 (1999); "Invention is the Mother of Litigation," Ct. Law Trib., at 25, Oct. 1997; "Trade Secret Misappropriation: A Federal Crime," Intellectual Property Today, at 6, June 1997; "The New European Union Technology Transfer Block Exemption," Intellectual Property Today, at 29, November 1996; "Tying and Exclusive Purchasing Arrangements under EC Competition Law," 31 Common Market Law Review 549, 1994; "Dévelopments Antitrust Aux Etats-Unis: Analyse Raffinée; Application Aggressive et Internationale," 3 Revue Internationale de Droit Economique 299, 1994; "Common Law and Civil Law Approaches to Investigation and Discovery in the Enforcement of Competition Laws," Due Process and Anticompetitive Practices, ICC Institute of International Business Law and Practice, 1994; "Dual Antitrust Enforcement in the United States: Positive or Negative Lessons for the European Community?" Procedure and Enforcement in E.C. and U.S. Competition Law, P.J. Slot & A. McDonnell eds., 1993. ***PRACTICE AREAS:*** Intellectual Property; Antitrust and Trade Regulation; Litigation. ***Email:*** jdv@avhlaw.com

JOHN D. HARKRIDER (Resident, New York, NY Office).

WILLIAM M. RUBENSTEIN, born Paterson, New Jersey, 1951; admitted to bar, 1981, Connecticut. *Education:* Montclair State College (B.A., 1977); Western New England College (J.D., magna cum laude, 1981). Author: "State Antitrust Enforcement," chapter in *The United States Antitrust Review:* A Global Competition Special Report, 1998; "Antitrust Review of Mergers by State Attorneys General, The New Cops on the Beat," 67 Conn. B.J., 1993; "Connecticut Unfair Trade Practices Act," chapter in *Connecticut Basic Practice Manual*, Connecticut Bar Association, 1989. Adjunct Professor, University of Connecticut School of Business Administration, MBA program, 1990-1997. Trial Attorney, Federal Trade Commission, Bureau of Competition, 1981-1984. Assistant Attorney General, Antitrust Department, State of Connecticut, 1986-1997. ***PRACTICE AREAS:*** Antitrust and Trade Regulation; Litigation. ***Email:*** wmr@avhlaw.com

LAUREN S. ALBERT (Resident, New York, NY Office).

ASSOCIATES

MARK D. ALEXANDER, born Nashville, Tennessee, February 23, 1967; admitted to bar, 1993, New York; 2000, Connecticut. *Education:* Indiana University (B.A., 1989); Cornell University (J.D., cum laude, 1992). Symposium Editor, Cornell Law Review, 1991-1992. Author: "Increased Scrutiny for the Administrative Crime," 77 Cornell Law Review 612 (1992). ***PRACTICE AREAS:*** Litigation; Antitrust and Trade Regulation; Intellectual Property. ***Email:*** mda@avhlaw.com

ERIC D. BEAL, born Lincoln, Nebraska, July 18, 1970; admitted to bar, 2000, Connecticut. *Education:* University of Massachusetts at Amherst (B.A., cum laude, 1993); University of Connecticut School of Law (J.D. with honors, 2000). Judicial Clerk to the Honorable Chief Justice Francis M. McDonald and Justice Peter T. Zarella of the Connecticut Supreme Court, 2000-2001. Author: "Posner and Moral Hazard," 7 Conn. Ins. L.J. 81, 2001; "It's Better To Have Twelve Monkeys Chasing You Than One Gorilla: Humana Inc. v. Forsyth, The

(This Listing Continued)

AXINN, VELTROP & HARKRIDER LLP, Hartford—Continued

McCarran-Ferguson Act, RICO, and Deterrence," 5 Conn. Ins. L.J., 2000. Teaching Assistant: Constitutional Law, University of Connecticut School of Law Academic Support Program, 1999-2000; University of Connecticut School of Law Lawyering Process Program, 1999-2000. Alernate Member, Canton Zoning Board of Appeals, 1999-2001. ***PRACTICE AREAS:*** Antitrust and Trade Regulation; Commercial Litigation.

NICHOLAS EMRYS OWEN GAGLIO (admission pending) (Resident, New York, NY Office).

MICHAEL L. KEELEY (Resident, New York, NY Office).

SIVAN R. KORN (Resident, New York, NY Office).

CHAD A. LANDMON, born Derby, Connecticut, January 13, 1975; admitted to bar, 1999, Connecticut. *Education:* University of Connecticut (B.A., summa cum laude, 1996); University of Connecticut School of Law (J.D., with honors, 1999). Notes and Comment Editor, Connecticut Law Review. Member, Connecticut Moot Court Board. Author: Note, "Creation of a Less Perfect Union: The Implications of General Motors Corp. v. Tracy for Commerce Class Analysis of State Taxation," 30 Conn. L. Rev. 1121, 1998. ***PRACTICE AREAS:*** Commercial Litigation; Antitrust and Trade Regulation. **Email:** cal@avhlaw.com

SONJA A. LARSON (Resident, New York, NY Office).

MARY ELIZABETH LaRUFFA (Resident, New York, NY Office).

CHARLES LOESNER (Resident, New York, NY Office).

ERIC L. PALMQUIST, born Madison, Wisconsin, December 26, 1966; admitted to bar, 2000, New York (Not admitted in Connecticut). *Education:* Bowdoin College (A.B., 1988); Cornell University (J.D., magna cum laude, 1999). Order of the Coif. Member, Cornell University Law Review. *Member:* American Bar Association (Member, Antitrust Section). ***PRACTICE AREAS:*** Antitrust and Trade Regulation; Intellectual Property.

MICHELLE H. SEAGULL, born Fort Knox, Kentucky, October 24, 1975; admitted to bar, 2000, Connecticut. *Education:* Washington University (B.A., 1997); Harvard (J.D., 2000). ***PRACTICE AREAS:*** Antitrust and Trade Regulation; Commercial Litigation. ***Email:*** mhs@avhlaw.com

---

AYARS & ASSOCIATES, LLC

HARTFORD, CONNECTICUT

(See Glastonbury)

Real Estate, Condominium Law, Cooperative Housing Law, Cooperative Housing Association Law, Real Estate Development, Water Rights, Riparian Rights, Family Law, ADR, Mortgage Financing, Consumer Credit and Finance.

BAKER O'SULLIVAN & BLISS PC

HARTFORD, CONNECTICUT

(See Wethersfield)

Litigation, Bankruptcy and Creditors' Rights.

BECK & ELDERGILL, P.C.

97 OAK STREET

HARTFORD, CONNECTICUT 06109

Telephone: 860-646-5606

FAX: 860-646-0054

Email: firm@beckeldergill.com

URL: http://www.beckeldergill.com

General Civil and Criminal Litigation before all State and Federal Trial and Appellate Courts with a concentration on Employment, Civil Rights, Personal Injury, Car Accidents and Divorce.

(For Complete Biographical Data on all Personnel, See Professional Biographies at Manchester, Connecticut)

BERCHEM, MOSES & DEVLIN

A PROFESSIONAL CORPORATION

HARTFORD, CONNECTICUT

(See Milford)

Commercial, Corporate Law, Labor and Employment Law, Litigation, Real Estate, Education, Land Use Planning, Estate Planning, Energy and Utility Law, Environmental, Probate. Partnership Law and Taxation Law. Trials and Appeals in State and Federal Courts.

BERMAN, BOURNS, AARON & DEMBO, LLC

HARTFORD, CONNECTICUT

(See West Hartford)

Family Law, Personal Injury, Litigation, Probate, Estate Planning, Real Estate, Corporate and General Practice.

BERMAN AND SABLE

Established in 1977

100 PEARL STREET

HARTFORD, CONNECTICUT 06103

Telephone: 860-527-9699

Telecopier: 860-527-9077

Email: info@bermansable.com

URL: http://www.bermansable.com

New Haven, Connecticut Office: 195 Church Street. Telephone: 203-495-6200. Fax: 203-495-6220.

Commercial Litigation, Commercial and Corporate Finance Transactions, Real Estate, Corporate Law, Acquisitions, Mergers and Divestitures, Problem Loan Workouts, Loan Restructure and Recoveries, Mortgage and Foreclosure, Creditor's Rights, Defense of Lender Liability Claims, Creditor Bankruptcy Rights, Reorganizations, Tax Appeals, Construction Litigation, Probate and Trials and Appeals in all Courts. FDIC/RTC Approved Counsel.

MEMBERS OF FIRM

MICHAEL P. BERMAN, born Brooklyn, New York, September 13, 1939; admitted to bar, 1969, Connecticut; U.S. District Court, District of Connecticut; U.S. Court of Appeals, Second Circuit. *Education:* Carnegie Institute of Technology (B.S., 1961); University of Cincinnati (M.S., 1964); University of Connecticut (J.D., 1969). Assistant Corporation Counsel, Bloomfield, 1978-1986. Member, Planning Committee for 1989 National Conference of Bankruptcy Judges. *Member:* Connecticut Bar Association (Chairman, 1983-1986, Vice Chairman, 1980-1983, and Member, Executive Committee, 1979-1986, Commercial Law and Bankruptcy Section; Member, Litigation Section); Connecticut Trial Lawyers Association. Lecturer: "Bankruptcy Code, Problems with the Under-secured Creditors," 1983; Selected Issues Concerning Creditors Affected by an Insolvent Debtor," 1985. ***PRACTICE AREAS:*** Commercial Litigation; Litigation on Behalf of Financial Institutions; Defense of Lender Liability Claims; Creditors Rights; Bankruptcy Litigation; Condominium Litigation; Construction Litigation. **Email:** mberman@bermansable.com

JOEL N. SABLE, born New Britain, Connecticut, October 3, 1944; admitted to bar, 1971, Connecticut; U.S. District Court, District of Connecticut; U.S. Court of Appeals, Second Circuit. *Education:* University of Connecticut (B.A., with honors, 1967; J.D., with honors, 1971). *Member:* Hartford County (Treasurer, Young Lawyers Section, 1977-1981), Connecticut (Member: Commercial Law and Bankruptcy Section, Real Property Section; and Lecturer: Bankruptcy Code, 1981: "Automatic Stay, Adequate Protection of Cash Collateral," 1982; Uniform Commercial Code, 1981-1984; "Creditors' Rights and Protection of Security Interests in Bankruptcy," 1987; "Bankruptcy Proceedings," 1988; "Commercially Reasonable Disposition of Collateral Under Article 9-A Case Study," 1989; "Foreclosure and Repossession for Connecticut Lenders - When The Workout Doesn't Work- Repossession of Personal Property," 1990, 1993; "New Legislation Affecting Debtors and Creditors-Connecticut Homestead Exemption," 1993; "Looking for Mr. Green-The Commercial Creditor Perspective," 1996) and American Bar Associations; Commercial Law League of America. ***PRACTICE AREAS:*** Real Estate and Commercial Finance Transactions and Workouts; Corporate Law; Foreclosures; Creditors Rights; Bankruptcy. **Email:** jsable@bermansable.com

STEVEN A. BERMAN, born Brooklyn, New York, October 28, 1947; admitted to bar, 1977, Connecticut. *Education:* Carnegie Mellon University (B.S., 1969); University of New Haven (M.B.A., 1972); University of Connecticut (J.D., with honors, 1977). Lecturer: "Asset Based Lending - How To Lend To The Marginal Borrower," 1987-1989; "What A Clean UCC Search Doesn't Show," 1989-1993; "2001 Revisions to Article 9 and Electronic Transactions," 2000-2001. *Member:* New Haven County, Connecticut (Member, Executive Committee, Commercial Law and Bankruptcy Section, 1984—) and American Bar Associations; Association of Commercial Finance Attorneys (Member, Executive Committee). (Resident Partner, New Haven Office). ***PRACTICE AREAS:*** Commercial Loans; Corporate Acquisitions, Divestitures & Restructures; Construction Loans; Corporate Transactions; Banking Law; Corporate Finance; Real Estate and Leasing Transactions. **Email:** sberman@bermansable.com

JAMES W. OLIVER, born Boston, Massachusetts, October 14, 1959; admitted to bar, 1987, Connecticut; 1988, Massachusetts and U.S. District Court, District of Connecticut. *Education:* Colgate University (B.A., 1982); Boston College (J.D., 1987). Member: Boston College International and Comparative

(This Listing Continued)

Law Review, 1986-1987; Boston College National Mock Trial Team; New England Mock Trial Team. Author: "Local Governments: Are They Immune from CERCLA Liability," Vol. 2 No. 9 Environmental/Hazards The Superfund, RCRA and Toxic Tort Law Advisor 1, September 1990. Lecturer: "Proving and Collecting Judgments by Use of Computer Records," 1998. *Member:* Connecticut Bar Association. ***PRACTICE AREAS:*** Commercial and Complex Litigation; Environmental Law. ***Email:*** joliver@bermansable.com

MARIA K. TOUGAS, born Hartford, Connecticut, August 11, 1963; admitted to bar, 1989, Connecticut and U.S. District Court, District of Connecticut. *Education:* Bowdoin College (A.B., magna cum laude, 1985); Western New England College School of Law (J.D., 1989). Member, Western New England College National Mock Trial Team. Lecturer: "1994 Bankruptcy Reform Act"; "Bankruptcy: A Creditor's Perspective in Connecticut," 2001. *Member:* Connecticut Bar Association (Member: Commercial Law and Bankruptcy Section, Sports and Entertainment Law Section); Connecticut Trial Lawyers Association. ***LANGUAGES:*** Spanish and Greek. ***REPORTED CASES:*** PB Real Estate, Inc. v. DEM II Properties, et al., 50 Conn. App. 74; FDIC v. Carabetta, 55 Conn. App. 384. ***PRACTICE AREAS:*** Bankruptcy; Commercial Litigation; Creditors Rights. ***Email:*** mtougas@bermansable.com

ASSOCIATES

ROBERT J. CAFFREY, born Southington, Connecticut, October 7, 1959; admitted to bar, 1984, Ohio and U.S. District Court, Northern District of Ohio; 1985, U.S. Court of Appeals, Sixth Circuit; 1990, Connecticut and U.S. District Court, District of Connecticut. *Education:* University of Notre Dame (B.A., cum laude, 1981); Case Western Reserve University (J.D., 1984). Associate Member, Case Western Reserve Law Review, 1982-1983. *Member:* Hartford, Connecticut and American Bar Associations. [Army Reserve, Captain (JAG), 1991—]. ***PRACTICE AREAS:*** Commercial Litigation; Construction Litigation; Business Litigation; Products Liability Defense; Insurance; Insurance Coverage; Surety Law. ***Email:*** rcaffrey@bermansable.com

JAMES J. BRAULT, born Bristol, Connecticut, July 4, 1965; admitted to bar, 1991, Connecticut. *Education:* Boston College (B.S., Accounting, 1987); Western New England College School of Law (J.D., 1991); University of Miami School of Law (LL.M., 1995). *Member:* Connecticut and American Bar Associations; National Association of Corporate Real Estate Executives. (Resident, New Haven Office). ***PRACTICE AREAS:*** Commercial Loan Documentation; Real Estate Transactions; Corporate Acquisitions; Contract Law; Corporate Finance; Corporate Mergers and Acquisitions; Divestitures; Restructures. ***Email:*** jbrault@bermansable.com

ALENA C. GFELLER, born Flagstaff, Arizona, June 5, 1969; admitted to bar, 1995, Connecticut; 1996, New York and U.S. District Court, District of Connecticut. *Education:* Arizona State University (B.A., 1991); Widener University (J.D., 1995). *Member:* Connecticut Bar Association (Member, Young Lawyers Section, Commercial Law and Bankruptcy Section). ***LANGUAGES:*** Russian. ***PRACTICE AREAS:*** Commercial Law and Litigation; Bankruptcy; Creditor's Rights; Construction Law; Litigation; Corporate Law and Litigation; Collections; Real Estate; Landlord and Tenant Law. ***Email:*** agfeller@bermansable.com

ANDREW R. SHERRIFF, JR., born Boston, Massachusetts, February 16, 1972; admitted to bar, 1998, Connecticut; 2000, Massachusetts. *Education:* Fordham University (B.A., 1994); Brooklyn Law School (J.D., 1997). Mediator: Academy of Family Mediators (General Member); Society of Professionals In Dispute Resolution; Victim Offender Mediation Association. *Member:* Westport, Connecticut (Dispute Resolution and Real Property Sections) and American Bar Associations. ***PRACTICE AREAS:*** Corporate Law; Real Estate; Commercial Loans; Corporate Finance; Mergers and Acquisitions. ***Email:*** asherrif@bermansable.com

DAVID R. LEVESQUE, born Meriden, Connecticut, July 6, 1972; admitted to bar, 1997, Connecticut; 1998, U.S. District Court, District of Connecticut. *Education:* Middlebury College (A.B., 1994); Western New England College School of Law (J.D., 1997). *Member:* Connecticut Bar Association. ***PRACTICE AREAS:*** Commercial Litigation; Business Litigation. ***Email:*** dlevesque@bermansable.com

SUZANNE LaPLANTE, born Hartford, Connecticut, August 19, 1966; admitted to bar, 1997, New York; 1999, Connecticut. *Education:* University of Aberdeen (M.A., with honors, 1990); Syracuse University College of Law (J.D., 1996). Member, 1994-1996; Lead Articles Editor, 1995-1996, Syracuse Journal of International Law and Commerce. Author: "Facilitating Technology Transfer: Computer Software Development and Cooperative Research and Development Agreements," Syracuse Journal of Legislation and Policy, 1st Issue; Note, "The European Union's General Product Safety Directive: Another Call for U.S. Exporters to Comply with the ISO 9000 Series," Syracuse Journal of International Law & Commerce, 22nd Issue. *Member:* Hartford County and Connecticut Bar Associations; New York County Lawyers' Association. ***PRACTICE AREAS:*** Commercial Litigation. ***Email:*** slaplante@bermansable.com

JACQUELINE FORGIONE, born Southington, Connecticut, May 11, 1964; admitted to bar, 2000, Connecticut. *Education:* Quinnipiac University

(This Listing Continued)

(B.A., cum laude, 1991; J.D., 1998). *Member:* New Haven, Hartford County and Connecticut Bar Associations. ***PRACTICE AREAS:*** Commercial Litigation; Business Litigation; Corporate Transactions. ***Email:*** jforgione@bermansable.com

OF COUNSEL

I. MILTON WIDEM (1923-2000).

BINGHAM DANA LLP

ONE STATE STREET
HARTFORD, CONNECTICUT 06103
Telephone: 860-240-2700
Telefax: 860-240-2800
Email: info@bingham.com
URL: http://www.bingham.com

Boston, Massachusetts Office: 150 Federal Street. Telephone: 617-951-8000. Telecopy: 617-951-8736.

New York, New York Office: 399 Park Avenue. Telephone: 212-318-7700. Fax: 212-752-5378.

Washington, D.C. Office: 1120 20th Street, N.W. Telephone: 202-778-6150. Fax: 202-778-6155.

Los Angeles, California Office: 444 South Flower Street, Suite 4500. Telephone: 213-817-3700. Fax: 213-817-3701.

London, England Office: 39 Victoria Street, SWIH 0EE. Telephone: 011-44-71-799-2646. Telecopy: 011-44-71-799-2654.

Singapore Office: Level 15 Prudential Tower, 30 Cecil Street, 049712. Telephone: 011.65.232.2768. Fax: 011.65.232.2888.

Corporate and Securities Law, Banking and Financial Services, Financial Restructuring, Project/Structured Finance, Technology, Private Equity, Investment Management, Commercial and Criminal Litigation, Corporate Acquisitions, Real Estate, Entrepreneurial Services, Intellectual Property, Tax, Estate Planning, Securities Litigation, Business Regulation and White Collar Defense, Product Liability, Antitrust, Distribution and Franchising, Employment Law, Environmental Law, Sports, Media, Entertainment, International Transactions including International Trade, European, Japanese and Latin American Practices and Alternative Dispute Resolution.

FIRM PROFILE: Bingham Dana LLP is a dynamic and innovative international law firm of more than 500 attorneys that provides a full complement of high-quality legal services, business/governmental consulting, and financial management and investment advisory services. We serve our clients - ranging from small and emerging entrepreneurial businesses to the world's largest corporations and financial institutions - through offices in Boston, New York, London, Washington, Hartford, Los Angeles and Singapore.

PARTNERS

JONATHAN B. ALTER, born 1964; admitted to bar, 1989, Connecticut, New York and U.S. District Court, District of Connecticut and U.S. District Court, Southern, Eastern and Northern Districts of New York; U.S. Court of Appeals, Second Circuit. *Education:* Franklin & Marshall College (B.A., with honors, 1986); Brooklyn Law School (J.D., cum laude, 1989). ***PRACTICE AREAS:*** Commercial Litigation; Financial Law; Loan Workouts; Loan Restructuring; Bankruptcy; Insolvency. ***Email:*** alterjb@bingham.com

FRANK A. APPICELLI, born 1964; admitted to bar, 1989, Connecticut. *Education:* Fairfield University (B.A., 1986); Alma College, Paris, France; Georgetown University (J.D., cum laude, 1989). ***PRACTICE AREAS:*** Commercial Finance; Real Estate; Corporate Law. ***Email:*** appicefa@bingham.com

ROBERT M. BORDEN, born 1955; admitted to bar, 1987, Connecticut. *Education:* State University of New York at Potsdam (B.M., 1977); Teachers College, Columbia University (M.A., 1982); Brooklyn Law School (J.D., 1987). ***PRACTICE AREAS:*** Corporate Trust; Lease and Asset-Based Financing; Trademark Law; Copyright Law; Computer Law. ***Email:*** rmborden@bingham.com

G. ERIC BRUNSTAD, JR., born Holyoke, MA, 1961; admitted to bar, 1986, Connecticut. *Education:* Connecticut College (B.A., magna cum laude, 1983); University of Michigan Law School (J.D., 1986). ***PRACTICE AREAS:*** Appellate; Bankruptcy. ***Email:*** brunstge@bingham.com

ROBERT M. DOMBROFF, born 1947; admitted to bar, 1971, Connecticut; 1999, District of Columbia. *Education:* University of Connecticut (B.A., 1968; J.D., 1971); New York University (LL.M., 1972). ***PRACTICE AREAS:*** Commercial and Financial Litigation; Reinsurance; Loan Workouts and Restructuring; Bankruptcy and Insolvency; Lender Liability Defense. ***Email:*** dombrorm@bingham.com

SCOTT A. FALK, born Buffalo, NY, 1964; admitted to bar, 1989, Connecticut; 1990, U.S. District Court, District of Connecticut; 1992, District of

(This Listing Continued)

BINGHAM DANA LLP, Hartford—Continued

Columbia and New York. *Education:* University of North Carolina, Chapel Hill (B.S., 1985); Duke University (J.D., 1989). ***PRACTICE AREAS:*** Corporate Finance. ***Email:*** safalk@bingham.com

CHESTER L. FISHER III, born New York, NY, 1950; admitted to bar, 1976, New York; 1984, Connecticut. *Education:* Princeton University (A.B., cum laude, 1972); Columbia University (J.D., 1975). ***Email:*** clfisher@bingham.com

EVAN D. FLASCHEN, born Summit, NJ, 1957; admitted to bar, 1982, Connecticut; 1992, U.S. Court of Appeals, First Circuit; 1994, U.S. Court of Appeals, Third Circuit; 1995, U.S. Court of Appeals, Second Circuit. *Education:* Wesleyan University (B.A., 1979); University of Connecticut (J.D., with honors, 1982). ***Email:*** edflaschen@bingham.com

DEBORAH SAMUELS FREEMAN, born Berkeley, CA, 1951; admitted to bar, 1976, District of Columbia; 1977, Connecticut and U.S. District Court, District of Connecticut; 1980, U.S. Court of Appeals, Second Circuit; 1996, U.S. District Court, Southern District of New York. *Education:* Washington University (B.A., 1972); Georgetown University (J.D., 1976). ***Email:*** dsfreeman@bingham.com

F. MARK FUCCI, born 1950; admitted to bar, 1977, Connecticut; 1984, New York. *Education:* Lafayette College (A.B., magna cum laude, 1973); Phi Beta Kappa; University of Connecticut (J.D., 1977). ***PRACTICE AREAS:*** Commercial Finance; Corporate Finance; Loan Workouts and Restructuring; Creditors' Rights; Aviation Law. ***Email:*** fuccifm@bingham.com

JAMES GREENFIELD, born New York, NY, 1947; admitted to bar, 1974, Pennsylvania; 1976, Connecticut; 1981, New York. *Education:* Brown University (A.B., with honors, 1969); Columbia University (M.B.A., 1973; J.D., 1973). ***Email:*** jgreenfield@bingham.com

HAROLD S. HORWICH, born Chicago, IL, 1953; admitted to bar, 1978, Illinois; 1981, Connecticut, U.S. District Court, District of Connecticut and U.S. District Court, District of Massachusetts; 1982, Massachusetts. *Education:* Brown University (A.B., magna cum laude, 1975); Boston University (J.D., 1978). ***Email:*** hshorwich@bingham.com

WILLIAM E. KELLY, born Holyoke, MA, 1947; admitted to bar, 1973, New York; 1974, Connecticut; 1975, U.S. District Court, District of Connecticut. *Education:* Columbia University (B.A., 1969; J.D., 1972). ***Email:*** wekelly@bingham.com

BEN M. KROWICKI, born 1953; admitted to bar, 1981, Connecticut; 1982, New York. *Education:* New York University (B.A., 1974); Vermont Law School (J.D., 1981). ***PRACTICE AREAS:*** Commercial Litigation. ***Email:*** bmkrowicki@bingham.com

GREGORY W. NYE, born Alexandria, VA, 1955; admitted to bar, 1981, Connecticut; 1984, U.S. Court of Appeals, Second Circuit; 1997, U.S. District Court, Southern District of New York. *Education:* University of North Carolina (A.B., 1977); University of Virginia (J.D., 1981). Phi Beta Kappa. ***Email:*** gwnye@bingham.com

THOMAS F. O'CONNOR, born Washington, DC, 1958; admitted to bar, 1990, Missouri; 1991, Illinois; 1994, Connecticut. *Education:* Tulane University (B.A., 1981); University of Missouri at Columbia (J.D., cum laude, 1990). ***Email:*** tfoconnor@bingham.com

MARK OLAND, born 1947; admitted to bar, 1972, Connecticut and U.S. District Court, District of Connecticut. *Education:* University of Vermont (B.A., 1969); Columbia University (J.D., 1972). ***PRACTICE AREAS:*** Commercial Real Estate Law and Finance; Real Estate Loan Workouts; Mortgage Law. ***Email:*** olandm@bingham.com

THOMAS J. O'SHEA, born Springfield, MA, 1962; admitted to bar, 1992, Connecticut. *Education:* University of Hartford (B.S., magna cum laude, 1984); University of Connecticut (M.B.A., 1989); Georgetown University (J.D., cum laude, 1992). Beta Gamma Sigma. *Member:* Hartford County, Connecticut and American Bar Associations. ***PRACTICE AREAS:*** Real Estate; Finance. ***Email:*** tjoshea@bingham.com

DANIEL I. PAPERMASTER, born 1964; admitted to bar, 1989, Connecticut. *Education:* University of Michigan (B.A., with distinction, 1986); University of Texas (J.D., 1989). ***Email:*** papermdi@bingham.com

MICHAEL J. REILLY, born Manchester, CT, 1951; admitted to bar, 1976, Connecticut. *Education:* University of Connecticut (B.A., with honors, 1973; J.D., 1976). ***Email:*** mjreilly@bingham.com

JAMES SCOTT ROLLINS, born 1962; admitted to bar, 1989, Connecticut. *Education:* Princeton University (A.B., cum laude, 1984); University of Virginia (J.D., 1989). ***PRACTICE AREAS:*** Commercial Litigation; Labor and Employment Law; Media Law. ***Email:*** jsrollins@bingham.com

STUART D. ROSEN, born 1956; admitted to bar, 1982, Connecticut and U.S. District Court, District of Connecticut. *Education:* University of Connecticut (B.A., magna cum laude, 1980); Catholic University of America (J.D., 1982). ***PRACTICE AREAS:*** Commercial Litigation; Insurance and Reinsurance Litigation; Business Torts; Real Estate Litigation. ***Email:*** rosensd@bingham.com

JAMES G. SCANTLING, born Pittsburgh, Pennsylvania, April 11, 1949; admitted to bar, 1974, Connecticut. *Education:* Boston University (B.S., 1971); Indiana University (J.D., 1974). ***PRACTICE AREAS:*** Leveraged Leasing; Asset-Based Lending; Project Financing; Mergers and Acquisitions; Lease Finance; Corporate Trusts. ***Email:*** scantljg@bingham.com

BRUCE C. SILVERS, born 1961; admitted to bar, 1986, Connecticut. *Education:* Trinity College (B.A., 1983); Emory University (J.D., 1986). ***PRACTICE AREAS:*** Banking; Finance and Debt Restructuring; Corporate and Securities Law; Public Finance; Project Finance. ***Email:*** silverbc@bingham.com

R. JEFFREY SMITH, born New Haven, CT, 1953; admitted to bar, 1978, Massachusetts and U.S. District Court, District of Massachusetts; 1984, Connecticut. *Education:* Duke University (B.A., cum laude, 1975); Georgetown University (J.D., 1978). ***PRACTICE AREAS:*** Real Estate Finance; Commercial Finance; Workouts. ***Email:*** rjsmith@bingham.com

RESIDENT OF COUNSEL

GARY H. COLLINS, born Islip, New York, December 2, 1965; admitted to bar, 1992, Illinois (Not admitted in Connecticut). *Education:* State University of New York at Buffalo (B.A., 1988); Vanderbilt University (J.D., 1991). ***Email:*** ghcollins@bingham.com

EDWIN GORDON HEBB, JR., born Burlington, VT, 1928; admitted to bar, 1959, Connecticut. *Education:* University of Vermont (B.S., 1956); Georgetown Law School (J.D., 1959). ***Email:*** eghebb@bingham.com

PETER H. LEVINE, born 1949; admitted to bar, 1972, Connecticut and U.S. District Court, District of Connecticut. *Education:* City College of the City University of New York (B.A., 1969); Cornell University (J.D., 1972). ***PRACTICE AREAS:*** Commercial Finance; Corporate and Securities Law; Mergers and Acquisitions. ***Email:*** phlevine@bingham.com

ANN M. SICZEWICZ, born 1955; admitted to bar, 1980, Connecticut and U.S. District Court, District of Connecticut. *Education:* University of Connecticut (B.A., magna cum laude, 1977; J.D., with honors, 1980). ***Email:*** amsiczewicz@bingham.com

RESIDENT ASSOCIATES

NICOLE J. ANKER, born Ann Arbor, MI, 1972; admitted to bar, 1998, Connecticut; 1999, New York and U.S. District Court, District of Connecticut. *Education:* Yale University (B.A., 1994); University of Connecticut (J.D., with high honors, 1998). ***PRACTICE AREAS:*** Litigation. ***Email:*** ankernj@bingham.com

DEBORAH M. BIBBINS, born New Britain, CT, 1965; admitted to bar, 1999, Connecticut; 2000, U.S. District Court, District of Connecticut. *Education:* University of Connecticut (B.S.B.A., cum laude, 1987; J.D., with honors, 1998); University of Massachusetts (M.B.A., 1993). ***PRACTICE AREAS:*** Insurance; Reinsurance; Bankruptcy. ***Email:*** bibbindm@bingham.com

PATTI LYNN BOSS, born Boston, MA, 1967; admitted to bar, 1993, Connecticut; 1994, U.S. District Court, District of Connecticut; 1995, U.S. District Court, Southern District of New York. *Education:* Smith College (B.A. 1989); Boston College Law School (J.D., cum laude, 1993). ***Email:*** plboss@bingham.com

MICHAEL H.M. BROWN, born New York, N.Y., 1967; admitted to bar, 1996, Massachusetts, New Hampshire and U.S. District Court, District of New Hampshire; 1999, Connecticut. *Education:* Oberlin College (B.A., 1990); Northeastern University (J.D., 1995).

ELIZABETH A. CALVERT, born Sydney, New South Wales, Australia, March 19, 1977; admitted to bar, 2001, Connecticut. *Education:* Macquarie University (B.A., 1998); Cornell University (J.D., 2001). ***PRACTICE AREAS:*** Litigation. ***Email:*** eecalvert@bingham.com

LISA M. CIOTTONE, born Bronx, New York, 1970; admitted to bar, 2000, Connecticut. *Education:* Harvard University (A.B., magna cum laude, 1996); Fordham University (J.D., 2000). ***LANGUAGES:*** Spanish. ***PRACTICE AREAS:*** Real Estate. ***Email:*** lmciottone@bingham.com

ALEXIA E. CRUZ, born Manchester, Connecticut, September 5, 1972; admitted to bar, 1997, Connecticut; 1998, New York and U.S. District Court, District of Connecticut. *Education:* Harvard University (A.B., Government, 1994); Pepperdine University School of Law (J.D., 1997). ***PRACTICE AREAS:*** Commercial Litigation. ***Email:*** cruzae@bingham.com

RENÉE M. DAILEY, born New Haven, Connecticut, October 9, 1973; admitted to bar, 1999, Connecticut. *Education:* University of Connecticut (B.A., 1995; B.A., 1996); University of Connecticut School of Law (J.D., 1999). ***PRACTICE AREAS:*** Business; Restructured Finance. ***Email:*** daileyrm@bingham.com

(This Listing Continued)

DAWN E. DUNCAN, born 1963; admitted to bar, 2001, Connecticut. *Education:* Western Carolina University (B.S.Ed., 1985; J.D., 2001). ***PRACTICE AREAS:*** Business. ***Email:*** deduncan@bingham.com

JOHN P. DYRO, SR., born 1965; admitted to bar, 2001, Connecticut. *Education:* Florida International University (B.S., 1989); University of Notre Dame (J.D., 2001). ***Email:*** jpdyro@bingham.com

CELIA EGGERT, born Morristown, New Jersey, May 20, 1961; admitted to bar, 2000, Connecticut. *Education:* University of Connecticut (B.S., 1983); University of Hartford (M.B.A., 1990); Western New England College (J.D., cum laude, 2000). ***PRACTICE AREAS:*** Litigation. ***Email:*** ceggert@bingham.com

WILLIAM F. GOVIER, born Washington, D.C., September 26, 1968; admitted to bar, 1999, Connecticut. *Education:* University of Southern California (B.M., 1993); University of Connecticut School of Law (J.D., with honors, 1999). ***PRACTICE AREAS:*** Restructured Finance; Institutional Finance; Structured Finance. ***Email:*** govierwf@bingham.com

BRENT L. HOFFMAN, born 1971; admitted to bar, 1996, Pennsylvania; 1997, New Jersey; 2000, Connecticut. *Education:* Gettysburg College (B.A., magna cum laude, 1993); Dickinson School of Law of the Pennsylvania State University (J.D., 1996). ***PRACTICE AREAS:*** Commercial Litigation; Securities Litigation; Insurance Litigation; Business Torts; Products Liability. ***Email:*** blhoffman@bingham.com

EDWARD B. KARNS, born 1973; admitted to bar, 2001, Connecticut. *Education:* George Washington University (B.A., 1995); University of Connecticut (J.D., 2001). ***PRACTICE AREAS:*** Business. ***Email:*** ebkarns@bingham.com

SUSAN KIM, born 1972; admitted to bar, 1998, Connecticut and U.S. District Court, District of Connecticut; 1999 U.S. Court of Appeals, First Circuit. *Education:* Tufts University (B.A., 1994); Syracuse University (J.D., cum laude, 1998). ***PRACTICE AREAS:*** Commercial Litigation; Bankruptcy; Appellate Practice. ***Email:*** skim@bingham.com

ALAN H. KOSBERG, born Hartford, Connecticut, June 4, 1964; admitted to bar, 1991, Massachusetts; 1992, Connecticut. *Education:* University of Pennsylvania (B.A., 1986); Boston University (J.D., 1991). ***PRACTICE AREAS:*** Commercial Law; Business Law; Commercial Litigation. ***Email:*** ahkosberg@bingham.com

CHRISTOPHER E. LAWRENCE, born Nyack, New York, November 7, 1972; admitted to bar, 1999, Connecticut. *Education:* Pennsylvania State University (B.A., with honors, 1994); Fordham University (J.D., 1999). ***PRACTICE AREAS:*** Corporate Law; Mergers and Acquisitions; Securities; Venture Capital. ***Email:*** celawrence@bingham.com

MARC R. LEDUC, admitted to bar, 2000, Connecticut and Massachusetts. *Education:* Boston College (B.A., 1996); University of Notre Dame (J.D., 2000). ***PRACTICE AREAS:*** Business Law. ***Email:*** mrleduc@bingham.com

STEWART E. NEWMAN, born 1972; admitted to bar, 1997, Connecticut. *Education:* Yale University (B.A., cum laude, 1994); Boston College (J.D., cum laude, 1997). ***PRACTICE AREAS:*** Litigation. ***Email:*** senewman@bingham.com

CHRISTINE C. PEASLEE, born Poughkeepsie, NY, 1965; admitted to bar, 1998, Connecticut. *Education:* Middlebury College (B.A., magna cum laude, 1989); Western New England College (J.D., cum laude, 1998). ***Email:*** ccpeaslee@bingham.com

RICHARD A. ROCHLIN, born New Haven, Connecticut, July 7, 1975; admitted to bar, 2000, Connecticut; 2001, New York. *Education:* American University (B.A., 1997); University of Connecticut (J.D., 2000). ***PRACTICE AREAS:*** Corporate Law; Structured Finance. ***Email:*** rarochlin@bingham.com

TREVOR T. SANFORD, born Cortland, New York, May 26, 1970; admitted to bar, 1999, Connecticut. *Education:* University of Rochester (B.A., 1992); Washington College of Law, American University (J.D., cum laude, 1999). ***PRACTICE AREAS:*** Finance; Corporate Law. ***Email:*** ttsanford@bingham.com

RUPAL S. SHAH, born Hartford, Connecticut, January 7, 1973; admitted to bar, 1999, Connecticut; 2000, New York. *Education:* College of the Holy Cross (B.A., 1995); Georgetown University (J.D., 1999). ***PRACTICE AREAS:*** Corporate; Bankruptcy. ***Email:*** shahrs@bingham.com

MARGARET J. SHEEHAN, born 1970; admitted to bar, 2001, Connecticut. *Education:* Connecticut College (B.A., 1992); Case Western Reserve University (J.D., 2000). ***PRACTICE AREAS:*** Corporate Finance. ***Email:*** mjsheehan@bingham.com

VI R. SMALLEY, born Hartford, CT, 1968; admitted to bar, 1994, Connecticut; 1995, U.S. District Court, District of Connecticut. *Education:* Smith College (A.B. cum laude with English Honors, 1990); University of Connecticut (J.D. with honors, 1994). ***Email:*** vrsmalley@bingham.com

ANTHONY J. SMITS, born Durban, South Africa, April 8, 1967; admitted to bar, 1994, South Africa; 1997, Massachusetts and U.S. District Court, District

(This Listing Continued)

of Massachusetts; 1998, Connecticut. *Education:* University of Natal (B.Comm, 1987; LL.B., 1989); University of Connecticut (LL.M., 1998). ***PRACTICE AREAS:*** Insolvency; Bankruptcy; Workouts. ***Email:*** smitsaj@bingham.com

CHRISTOPHER S. SNOW, born Middleboro, Massachusetts, April 14, 1971; admitted to bar, 1998, Connecticut; U.S. District Court, District of Connecticut. *Education:* University of Rhode Island (B.S., Education, 1994); Quinnipiac College (J.D., magna cum laude, 1998). ***PRACTICE AREAS:*** Insolvency; Restructured Finance; Corporate Finance; Bankruptcy. ***Email:*** snowcs@bingham.com

MARIALTA Z. SPARAGNA, born Waterbury, Connecticut, September 13, 1960; admitted to bar, 2000, Connecticut. *Education:* Wesleyan University (B.A., 1982); Western New England College (J.D., 1999). ***PRACTICE AREAS:*** Real Estate; Corporate Finance; Insolvency. ***Email:*** sparagmz@bingham.com

SUSANNAH M. STAPLETON, born 1972; admitted to bar, 1998, Connecticut. *Education:* University of Connecticut (B.A., 1994; J.D., 1998). ***PRACTICE AREAS:*** Commercial Real Estate; Finance. ***Email:*** smstapleton@bingham.com

FRANK J. TABOADA, born 1996; admitted to bar, 1996, Ohio; 1999, Connecticut. *Education:* United States Naval Academy (B.S., 1985); Northwestern University (J.D., 1996). ***PRACTICE AREAS:*** Corporate; Mergers and Acquisitions; Finance. ***Email:*** fjtaboada@bingham.com

PATRICK J. TROSTLE, born Carlisle, PA, 1966; admitted to bar, 1992, Connecticut; 1993, New York; 1994, District of Columbia. *Education:* Trinity College (B.A., 1989); Vermont Law School (J.D., 1992). ***PRACTICE AREAS:*** Insolvency. ***Email:*** trostlepj@bingham.com

TANYA TYMCHENKO, born Syracuse, New York; admitted to bar, 2000, Connecticut. *Education:* State University of New York at Binghamton (B.A., 1997); University of Connecticut (J.D., with honors, 2000). ***PRACTICE AREAS:*** Litigation. ***Email:*** ttymchenko@bingham.com

MICHAEL P. UNGARO, born New Britain, Connecticut, January 17, 1965; admitted to bar, 1998, Connecticut; 1999, U.S. District Court, District of Connecticut. *Education:* University of Connecticut (B.A., 1987; J.D., 1998). ***PRACTICE AREAS:*** Litigation; Insurance. ***Email:*** ungarom@bingham.com

OSCAR URIZAR, born Guatemala City, Guatemala, 1958; admitted to bar, 1996, Connecticut; 1998, U.S. District Court, District of Connecticut. *Education:* University of California, Berkeley (B.A., 1982; M.B.A., 1987); University of Connecticut (J.D., 1996). ***Email:*** ourizar@bingham.com

LISA VALENTOVISH, born McKeesport, Pennsylvania, July 4, 1967; admitted to bar, 2000, Connecticut. *Education:* Yale University (B.A., 1989); Quinnipiac College (J.D., 2000). ***PRACTICE AREAS:*** Banking Law; Finance; Corporate Law. ***Email:*** lvalentovish@bingham.com

MARY L. WEIL, admitted to bar, 2001, Connecticut. *Education:* University of Connecticut (J.D., 2001). ***PRACTICE AREAS:*** Business. ***Email:*** mlweil@bingham.com

STEVEN S. WHEELER, born Madison, WI, 1970; admitted to bar, 1998, Connecticut. *Education:* California State University (B.A., 1995); University of Connecticut (J.D., 1998). ***Email:*** sswheeler@bingham.com

SCOTT A. WOOD, born 1970; admitted to bar, 2001, Connecticut. *Education:* Mendoza College of Business (M.B.A., 2001). ***PRACTICE AREAS:*** Business. ***Email:*** sawood@bingham.com

JEFFREY B. ZEMAN, born 1969; admitted to bar, 1995, Connecticut. *Education:* Bowdoin College (A.B., magna cum laude, 1992); Boston College Law School (J.D., cum laude, 1995). ***Email:*** zemanjb@bingham.com

(For Complete Biographical Data on other Personnel, See Professional Biographies at Boston, Massachusetts, London, England, Washington, D.C., Los Angeles, California, New York, New York and Singapore Offices)

BOATMAN, BOSCARINO, GRASSO & TWACHTMAN

HARTFORD, CONNECTICUT

(See Glastonbury)

Commercial, Debtor and Creditor Rights, Bankruptcy, Litigation, Real Estate and Real Estate Development, Estate Planning, Personal Injury, Representation before IRS, Litigation in all Courts.

BONEE LAW OFFICES, LLP

Established in 1883

ONE STATE STREET, SUITE 1510

HARTFORD, CONNECTICUT 06103

Telephone: 860-522-7161

Fax: 860-522-6049

Email: boneelaw@aol.com

URL: http://www.lawyers.com/boneelaw

General Civil, Trial and Appellate Practice in State and Federal Courts, Estate Planning and Probate, Real Estate, Negligence, Wills and Trusts.

FIRM PROFILE: The firm was founded in Hartford in 1883 by Arthur F. Eggleston and John R. Buck. Their successors were John Halsey Buck (1869-1957) and Anson T. McCook (1881-1966), both of Hartford, and Edward H. Kenyon of Wethersfield, retired.

MEMBERS OF FIRM

JOHN L. BONEE, born Hartford, Connecticut, September 26, 1921; admitted to bar, 1950, Connecticut. *Education:* Trinity College (B.S., 1943); Yale University (LL.B., 1947). Member, Court of Common Council, City of Hartford, Connecticut, 1951-1955. Member, Hartford Re-Development Agency, 1955-1965. Clerk, Judiciary Committee, Connecticut General Assembly, 1957. *Member:* Hartford County, Connecticut and American Bar Associations. ***PRACTICE AREAS:*** Elder Law; Estate Planning; Wills; Trust Law; Probate Administration.

JOHN L. BONEE III, born Hartford, Connecticut, December 16, 1947; admitted to bar, 1974, Connecticut and U.S. District Court, District of Connecticut. *Education:* Trinity College (B.A., 1970); Suffolk University (J.D., 1974). Member: Town Council, Town of West Hartford, 1985-1989; Community Planning Advisory Committee, Town of West Hartford, 1984. Board of Education, Town of West Hartford, 1981-1982. Board of Editors, Connecticut Bar Journal, 1978-1985. Corporation Counsel, Town of West Hartford, 1983. *Member:* Hartford County (President, 1995-1996); Connecticut (Member, House of Delegates, 1995—, Family Law and Estates and Probate Sections) and American (Member: House of Delegates, 1996—; Civil Litigation, General Practice and International Law Sections, 1994) Bar Associations. ***PRACTICE AREAS:*** Civil Litigation; Personal Injury; Family Law; Divorce; Estates and Probate; Will Contests; Wrongful Discharge; Appeals.

ERIC H. ROTHAUSER, born Boston, Massachusetts, July 22, 1969; admitted to bar, 1994, Connecticut and Pennsylvania; 1997, U.S. District Court, District of Connecticut. *Education:* University of Connecticut (B.A., 1991); Dickinson School of Law of the Pennsylvania State University (J.D., 1994). *Member:* Hartford County and Connecticut Bar Associations. ***PRACTICE AREAS:*** Civil Litigation; Workers Compensation; Criminal Law; Real Estate; Probate; Wills and Trusts; Personal Injury.

BONNER KIERNAN TREBACH & CROCIATA

Established in 1989

44 CAPITOL AVENUE

SUITE 402

HARTFORD, CONNECTICUT 06106

Telephone: 860-249-9900

FAX: 860-246-3727

URL: http://www.bktc.net

Washington, D.C. Office: 1250 Eye Street, N.W. Telephone: 202-712-7000. Fax: 202-712-7100.

Rockville, Maryland Office: 51 Monroe Street. Telephone: 301-340-9155. Fax: 301-340-1310.

Fairfax, Virginia Office: 10511 Judicial Drive. Telephone: 703-691-0500. Fax: 703-591-5082.

Boston, Massachusetts Office: One Liberty Square. Telephone: 617-426-3900. Fax: 617-426-0380.

New York, New York Office: Empire State Building, Suite 3304. Telephone: 212-268-7535. Fax: 212-268-4965.

Providence, Rhode Island Office: 55 Pine Street. Telephone: 401-273-0100. Fax: 401-273-0101.

General Civil Defense, Appellate and Trial Practice, Civil Mediation and Arbitrations, Product Liability, Malpractice, Property, Casualty, Insurance Law, Construction Litigation, Toxic and Environmental Litigation, Insurance Coverage Disputes, Railroad and Airline Litigation, Employment Law, Commercial Litigation and Counseling, Alternative Dispute Resolutions, Aviation, Computer Law, Technology Law, Consumer Fraud, White Collar Crime.

(This Listing Continued)

OF COUNSEL

Michael J. Smith (Also at Boston, MA and Providence, RI Offices)
Hugh R. Curran (Also at Boston, MA Office)

(For complete biographical data on all personnel, see Professional Biographies at Washington, D.C.)

ANDREW B. BOWMAN

HARTFORD, CONNECTICUT

(See Westport)

General Civil and Criminal Litigation before all Federal and State Courts. Trials and Appeals. Criminal Defense, Tax Litigation, Employment Law, Construction Litigation, Civil Rights, Environmental Law, Personal Injury, Commercial Litigation and Negligence Law.

BRENNER, SALTZMAN & WALLMAN LLP

HARTFORD, CONNECTICUT

(See New Haven)

Corporate, Securities, Federal Income, Estate and Gift Taxation, Real Estate, Estate Planning and Probate, Pension and Profit Sharing, Employee Benefit, Environmental, Health Care Law, Trial Practice and Administrative Law.

BROWN, PAINDIRIS & SCOTT, LLP

Established in 1977

100 PEARL STREET

HARTFORD, CONNECTICUT 06103-4506

Telephone: 860-522-3343

Telecopier: 860-522-2490

URL: http://www.bpslawyers.com

Glastonbury, Connecticut Office: The Old Town Hall, 2252 Main Street, 06033. Telephone: 860-659-0700. Fax: 860-659-8292.

Stamford, Connecticut Office: 6 Landmark Square, Suite 400. Telephone: 203-359-5772.

East Hampton, Connecticut Office: 42 East High Street, 06424. Telephone: 860-267-2044.

Hebron, Connecticut Office: 10 Main Street, 06248. Telephone: 860-228-3506.

General Practice. Administrative, Bankruptcy, Commercial, Communications, Corporate, Criminal, Education, Employment, Estate Planning, Family, Immigration, Insurance, Landlord and Tenant, Municipal, Personal Injury, Probate, Real Estate. Trials and Appeals in all Courts.

MEMBERS OF FIRM

RICHARD R. BROWN, born Boston, Massachusetts, August 13, 1945; admitted to bar, 1971, Connecticut; 1972, U.S. District Court, District of Connecticut, U.S. Court of Appeals, Second Circuit and U.S. Supreme Court. *Education:* University of Massachusetts (B.A., 1968); University of Connecticut (J.D., 1971). Author: Comment, "Declaration Against Penal Interest, Time For Review," 42 Connecticut Bar Journal 276, 1971; "Connecticut's Court System-Criminal," Covering the Courts in Connecticut, Bar-Media Committee of the Hartford County Bar Association, 1982. Assistant Attorney General, 1971-1973. Assistant Prosecutor, State of Connecticut, 1973-1975. *Member:* Hartford County (Chairperson, News Media-Legal Committee, 1980-1981; Chairman, Bar-Media Committee, 1982—) and Connecticut (Chairman, Criminal Law Section, 1982-1985 and Committee on Recommendations for Admission to the Connecticut Bar, 1989—) Bar Associations. Fellow, American College of Trial Lawyers; National Association of Criminal Defense Lawyers; Connecticut Trial Lawyers Association (Member, Board of Directors, 1987—); Inns of Court. ***PRACTICE AREAS:*** Criminal Law; Civil Litigation; Administrative Law. ***Email:*** rbrown@bpslawyers.com

NICHOLAS PAINDIRIS, born Rhodes, Greece, March 25, 1946; admitted to bar, 1973, Connecticut and U.S. District Court, District of Connecticut. *Education:* Yale University (B.A., 1968); University of Connecticut (J.D., 1973). Lecturer, Business Law, Manchester Community College, 1972-1974. Town Attorney, Glastonbury, Connecticut, 1985-1987, 1991-1993. *Member:* Hartford County and Connecticut Bar Associations. (Also at Glastonbury Office). ***LANGUAGES:*** Greek. ***PRACTICE AREAS:*** Corporate Law; Real Estate Law; Commercial Law; Municipal Law; Estate Planning. ***Email:*** npaindiris@bpslawyers.com

RONALD T. SCOTT, born Philadelphia, Pennsylvania, March 31, 1952; admitted to bar, 1978, Connecticut and U.S. District Court, District of Connecticut. *Education:* Alfred University (B.A., 1975); University of Connecticut Law School (J.D., 1978). Special Master, Family Division of Superior Court, 1988—. *Member:* Hartford County, Connecticut (Member, Family Law Section)

(This Listing Continued)

and American Bar Associations; Connecticut Trial Lawyers Association; The Association of Trial Lawyers of America; Collaborative Divorce Lawyers Association. ***PRACTICE AREAS:*** Personal Injury Law; Family Law. ***Email:*** rscott@bpslawyers.com

JOHN D. MAXWELL, born Hartford, Connecticut, September 20, 1952; admitted to bar, 1979, Connecticut; 1980, U.S. District Court, District of Connecticut; 1985, U.S. Court of Appeals, Second Circuit. *Education:* Upsala College (A.B., 1974); William Mitchell College of Law (J.D., 1979). *Member:* Middlesex County and Connecticut Bar Associations; National Association of Criminal Defense Attorneys; Connecticut Trial Lawyers Association. ***PRACTICE AREAS:*** Personal Injury; Workers Compensation; Criminal Defense; Civil Litigation. ***Email:*** jmaxwell@bpslawyers.com

KENNETH T. KELLEY, born Springfield, Massachusetts, October 1, 1939; admitted to bar, 1981, Connecticut; 1982, U.S. District Court, District of Connecticut; 1986, U.S. Tax Court; 1988, Pennsylvania; 1999, New York. *Education:* University of Hartford (B.S., 1976); Western New England College (J.D., 1980). Phi Delta Phi. Co-Author: "Legacy, Plan, Protect & Preserve Your Estate," 1996; "Generations, Planning Your Legacy," 1999, Published by Esperti Peterson Institute. *Member:* Connecticut, Pennsylvania and New York State Bar Associations; National Network of Estate Planning Attorneys. ***LANGUAGES:*** German. ***PRACTICE AREAS:*** Estate Planning; Estate Settlements; Trusts and Estates; Tax Planning; Real Estate. ***Email:*** kkelley@bpslawyers.com

DONALD L. HAMER, born Hartford, Connecticut, August 9, 1950; admitted to bar, 1977, Connecticut; 1978, District of Columbia; 1984, Maryland and U.S. Court of Appeals, District of Columbia Circuit; 1986, U.S. District Court, District of Connecticut. *Education:* Georgetown University (A.B., cum laude, 1972; J.D., 1977). Probate Judge, Glastonbury Probate District, Glastonbury, Connecticut, 1990—; Lecturer, "Conservatorships," Connecticut Bar Association. Member, Executive Committee, 1995— and Chair, Conservator and Guardian Standards Committee, 1992—, Connecticut Probate Assembly. *Member:* Connecticut and American Bar Associations; National College of Probate Judges. (Also at Glastonbury Office). ***PRACTICE AREAS:*** Estate Planning; Probate; Commercial Real Estate; Residential Real Estate; Business Law. ***Email:*** dhamer@bpslawyers.com

KATE W. HAAKONSEN, born Bryn Mawr, Pennsylvania, January 15, 1953; admitted to bar, 1978, Connecticut and U.S. District Court, District of Connecticut; 1979, U.S. Court of Appeals, Second Circuit; 1982, U.S. Supreme Court. *Education:* Ursinus College (B.A., cum laude, 1975); University of Connecticut (J.D., 1978). Lecturer, Family Law, Legal Education Institute, 1990, 1991. Special Master, Family Division of Superior Court, 1988—. Attorney Trial Referee, Superior Court, 1990—. Member, Statewide Grievance Committee, 1994-1996. Member, Board of Directors, Legal Aid Society of Hartford County, 1980-1987. *Member:* Hartford County (Member, Board of Directors, 1985-1986) and Connecticut (Member, Family Law Section, Executive Committee, 1998—) Bar Associations; Academy of Family Mediators (Practitioner Member); Connecticut Council for Divorce Mediation (Member, Board of Directors, 1996—, Secretary, 1998—, Co-President-Elect, 1999-2000, Co-President, 2000-2001). (Also at Glastonbury Office). ***LANGUAGES:*** French. ***PRACTICE AREAS:*** Domestic Relations; Mediation; Civil Litigation; Medical Malpractice; Employment Mediation; Real Estate. ***Email:*** khaakonsen@bpslawyers.com

STEVEN W. VARNEY, born Middletown, Connecticut, May 10, 1959; admitted to bar, 1985, Connecticut; 1986, U.S. District Court, District of Connecticut; 1991, U.S. Court of Appeals, Second Circuit. *Education:* University of Connecticut (B.A., 1981; J.D., 1985). Pi Sigma Alpha. Fact Finder/Arbitrator, Connecticut Superior Court, 1999—. Member, Panel of Arbitrators, American Arbitration Association. *Member:* Hartford County, Connecticut (Member: Executive Committee, Litigation Section; Federal Practice Section) and American Bar Associations. (Also at Glastonbury Office). ***PRACTICE AREAS:*** Litigation; Bankruptcy Law; Criminal Law; Appellate Practice. ***Email:*** svarney@bpslawyers.com

CHRISTOPHER J. McCARTHY, born New Haven, Connecticut, April 14, 1964; admitted to bar, 1989, Connecticut; 1990, U.S. District Court, District of Connecticut; 1991, U.S. Court of Appeals, Second Circuit; 1998, Massachusetts. *Education:* University of Connecticut (B.A., with honors, 1986); New England School of Law (J.D., 1989). Book Review and Casenote Editor, New England Journal on Criminal and Civil Confinement. *Member:* Hartford County and Connecticut Bar Associations. (Also at Glastonbury Office). ***PRACTICE AREAS:*** Criminal Law; Juvenile Law; School Law; Education Law; Civil Litigation; Foreclosure Law; Administrative Law. ***Email:*** cmccarthy@bpslawyers.com

SEAN M. PEOPLES, born Hartford, Connecticut, May 5, 1960; admitted to bar, 1989, Connecticut; 1990, U.S. District Court, District of Connecticut. *Education:* Connecticut College (B.A., 1983); Columbia University (M.A., 1986); Franklin Pierce Law Center (J.D., 1989). Phi Alpha Delta. *Member:* Hartford County (Member, Legal-Medical Committee) and Connecticut (Member: Paralegal Program Advisory Committee and Cooperative Education External Advisory Committee, Manchester Community Technical College; Health Law Committee) Bar Associations. (Also at Glastonbury Office). ***PRACTICE AREAS:*** Civil Litigation; Probate; Residential Real Estate; Immigration Law. ***Email:*** speoples@bpslawyers.com

(This Listing Continued)

DAVID S. RINTOUL, born Westport, Connecticut, July 11, 1961; admitted to bar, 1986, Illinois and U.S. District Court, Northern District of Illinois; 1989, Connecticut; 1991, U.S. District Court, District of Connecticut; 1997, U.S. Court Appeals, Second Circuit. *Education:* The Johns Hopkins University (B.A., 1983); School of International Advanced Studies, Bologna, Italy, (1981-1982); University of Connecticut (J.D., with high honors, 1986). Special Master in Employment law, U.S. District Court, District of Connecticut (1999—). *Member:* Connecticut Bar Association; Connecticut Employment Lawyers Association (Member, Executive Committee, 1996—); National Employment Lawyers Association. (Resident at Glastonbury Office). ***PRACTICE AREAS:*** Employment Litigation; Employee Benefits; ERISA; Wrongful Termination; Age Discrimination; Race Discrimination; Disability Discrimination; Employment Contracts; Covenants Not To Compete; Defamation; Whistleblower Litigation. ***Email:*** drintoul@bpslawyers.com

ASSOCIATES

ROBERT T. RIMMER, born Conway, Arkansas, March 17, 1970; admitted to bar, 1996, Connecticut and U.S. District Court, District of Connecticut. *Education:* Yale University (B.A., 1992); University of Connecticut (J.D., 1996). *Member:* Hartford County, Connecticut and American Bar Associations. ***PRACTICE AREAS:*** Civil Litigation; Criminal Law; Administrative Law; Employment Litigation. ***Email:*** rrimmer@bpslawyers.com

SIMON J. LEBO, born Elizabethville, Pennsylvania, March 12, 1974; admitted to bar, 1999, Connecticut. *Education:* Dickinson College (B.A., magna cum laude, 1996); Dickinson School of Law of the Pennsylvania State University (J.D., cum laude, 1999). Phi Beta Kappa. Woolsack Honor Society. *Member:* Hartford County, Connecticut and American Bar Associations. ***PRACTICE AREAS:*** Estate Planning; Probate Administration; Commercial Law; Real Estate. ***Email:*** slebo@bpslawyers.com

COURTNEY P. STARON, born Hartford, Connecticut, September 12, 1975; admitted to bar, 2000, Connecticut. *Education:* University of Connecticut (B.A., 1997); University of Connecticut School of Law (J.D., 2000). ***PRACTICE AREAS:*** Family Law; Special Education; Litigation. ***Email:*** cstaron@bpslawyers.com

OF COUNSEL

THEODORE J. DiLORENZO, born Hartford, Connecticut, September 22, 1924; admitted to bar, 1953, Connecticut; 1954, U.S. District Court, District of Connecticut. *Education:* Trinity College (B.A., 1950); George Washington University (J.D., 1952). Member, Washington University Law School Law Review, 1951-1952. Chief Counsel, Metropolitan District Commission (MDC), 1973-1976. Councilman, Hartford City Council, 1964-1969; Chairman, Hartford Republican Town Committee, 1967-1970. *Member:* Hartford County, Connecticut and American Bar Associations. ***PRACTICE AREAS:*** Personal Injury; Small Business Law; Business Law; Residential Real Estate; Commercial Real Estate; Estate Administration; Wills.

APPROVED ATTORNEYS FOR: Connecticut Attorneys Title Insurance Co.; First American Title Insurance Co.; Chicago Title Insurance Co.; Lawyer's Title Insurance Co.

BROWN RAYSMAN MILLSTEIN FELDER & STEINER LLP

CITYPLACE II, 185 ASYLUM STREET, 10TH FLOOR
HARTFORD, CONNECTICUT 06103
Telephone: 860-275-6400
Fax: 860-275-6410
URL: http://www.brownraysman.com

New York, New York Office: 900 Third Avenue. Telephone: 212-895-2000. Fax: 212-895-2900.
Los Angeles, California Office: 1880 Century Park East, Suite 711. Telephone: 310-712-8300. Fax: 310-712-8383.
Morristown, New Jersey Office: 55 Madison Avenue, Suite 70. Telephone: 973-285-3222. Fax: 973-285-3262.
Uniondale, New York Office: EAB Plaza, West Tower, 6th Floor, 11556-0615 (Long Island). Telephone: 516-522-2731. Fax: 516-522-2731.
Toronto, Ontario, Canada Office: 2407-40 King Street West, M5H 3 Y2. Telephone: 416-657-4470. Facsimile: 416-657-4475.

General Practice. Computer, Corporate, Securities, Real Estate, Internet, High Technology, Commercial Finance, Employment, Insurance, Patent, Copyright, Trademarks, Bankruptcy, Equipment Leasing and Tax. Trial and Appellate Practice.

(This Listing Continued)

BROWN RAYSMAN MILLSTEIN FELDER & STEINER LLP, Hartford—Continued

MEMBERS OF FIRM

NORMAN H. ROOS, born Ludlow, Massachusetts, February 20, 1948; admitted to bar, 1973, Connecticut. *Education:* Wharton School of Finance and Commerce, University of Pennsylvania (B.S., in Economics, 1969); University of Michigan (J.D., 1972). Phi Alpha Delta. Author: "CMBA Handbook on Connecticut Mortgage Statutes: An Analysis and Compilation of Connecticut Legislation Affecting Residential First Mortgage Lending," published by the Connecticut Mortgage Bankers Association, Inc. (1989, Second Edition, 1991, Third Edition, 1996, Fourth Edition, 1999); "E-Commerce is Here—Can E-Mortgages Be Far Behind?" published by the Real Estate Finance Journal (Summer 2000). Connecticut Law Revision Commission Advisory Committees on Electronic Communications, 1997—, Mortgagor Liability, 1997-1998 and Mortgage Releases, 1993-1994. *Member:* Hartford County, Connecticut (Member, Executive Committee, Consumer Law Section, 1978—, Treasurer, 1983-1985 and Chairman, 1987-1989; Member, Executive Committee, Financial Institutions Law Section, 1991—) and American Bar Associations; Association of Commercial Finance Attorneys; American College of Mortgage Attorneys (Connecticut State Chairman, 1993—); Bank Compliance Association of Connecticut (Board of Governors, 1989-1993; Vice-President and Editor, of Quarterly Newsletter, 1991-1993). ***PRACTICE AREAS:*** Financial Transactions; Electronic Commerce; Banking Law; Financial Services Law; Regulatory Law; Real Estate; Mortgage Banking; Timeshare; Corporate. ***Email:*** nroos@brownraysman.com

BEVERLY W. GAROFALO, born Stamford, Connecticut, February 25, 1963; admitted to bar, 1991, Connecticut; 1992, U.S. District Court, District of Connecticut. *Education:* Colorado College (B.A., 1985); University of Connecticut (J.D., magna cum laude, 1991). Notes and Comments Editor, Connecticut Law Review, 1990-1991. Recipient: Starr Fellow Award for Best Law Review; Jurisprudence Awards in Torts, Property and Income Tax. First Place, Alva P. Loiselle Moot Court Competition. Law Clerk for Chief Justice Ellen A. Peters, Connecticut Supreme Court, 1991-1992. Author: "Treating the Symptom Instead of the Cause: Regulating Student Speech at the University of Connecticut," 23 Conn. L. Rev. 743 (1991); "E-Mail and the Internet: Emerging Issues in Employment Law," Conn. L. Trib. (August 19, 1996); "The Contingent Worker Dilemma: Ninth Circuit Ruling May Prove Costly to Employers," Connecticut Lawyer (May 1997); "Sharing a Middle Ground with Big Brother: How Do You Balance an Employer's Need to Know Against an Employee's Right to Privacy," The Connecticut Law Tribune (May 18, 1998); "Recent Decisions on Harassment Leave Many Questions Unanswered," The Corporate Counsellor (July 1998); "Trade Secrets: Noncompete Agreements," The National Law Journal (January 17, 2000). *Member:* Connecticut (Labor and Employment Law Section, 1992—) and American (Labor and Employment Law Section, 1992—) Bar Associations. ***PRACTICE AREAS:*** Employment Law; Executive Compensation. ***Email:*** bgarofalo@brownraysman.com

ROBERT D. GILBERT, born Plainfield, New Jersey, April 8, 1955; admitted to bar, 1982, Minnesota and U.S. District Court, District of Minnesota; 1983, New Jersey and U.S. District Court, District of New Jersey; 1994, Connecticut; 1997, U.S. District Court, District of Connecticut; 1999, U.S. District Court, Eastern and Southern Districts of New York. *Education:* Princeton University, Woodrow Wilson School of Public and International Affairs (A.B., 1977); Yale University (J.D., 1982). Editor, 1980-1981 and Senior Editor, 1981-1982, Yale Law Journal. Author: Note, "Professional Obligation and the Duty to Rescue: When Must a Psychiatrist Protect His Patient's Intended Victim?" 91 Yale Law Journal 1430, 1982; "Domain-name registrants have new rules to follow," The National Law Journal, January 31, 2000; "Squatters Beware: There are Two New Ways to Get You," New York Law Journal, January 24, 2000; "A New Hook," Cyber Esq., Spring 2000. Treasurer, 1992-1994 and Vice President, 1994-1995, Yale Law School Alumni Association of New Jersey. Health Policy Coordinator, Office of the U.S. Secretary of Health, Education and Welfare, 1977-1978. Special Assistant to the General Counsel, U.S. Department of Health, Education and Welfare, 1979. Special Litigation Counsel, Township of Woodbridge, New Jersey, 1992-1993. Member, Executive Committee, Yale Law School Association, 1997—. Vice Chair, Arbitration and Mediation Committee, Intellectual Property Owners Association. Partner, Edwards & Angell, 1993-1995. Partner, Hellring, Lindeman, Goldstein & Siegal, 1991-1993. *Member:* Connecticut (Member, Litigation Section) and American (Member, Litigation Section) Bar Associations. ***PRACTICE AREAS:*** Complex Civil Litigation; Intellectual Property Litigation; Internet Litigation; Finance Litigation; Franchise Litigation; Employment Litigation. ***Email:*** rgilbert@brownraysman.com

COUNSEL

H. DAVID LEVENTHAL, born Hartford, Connecticut, February 15, 1929; admitted to bar, 1956, Connecticut; U.S. District Court, District of Connecticut; U.S. Court of Appeals, Second Circuit; U.S. Supreme Court. *Education:* Yale University (A.B., 1949); Harvard University (LL.B., 1955). Member, Harvard Legal Aid Bureau, 1952-1955. Co-Author: "The Connecticut Common Interest Ownership Manual," Connecticut Bar Association, 1984. Lecturer in Law, University of Connecticut School of Law, 1971-1980. *Member:* Hartford County, Connecticut (Secretary, Real Property Section, 1970-1972; Chairman, 1972-1974; Member, Executive Committee: Real Property Section, Emeritus and Standards of Title Committee) and American Bar Associations; American College of Real Estate Lawyers. ***PRACTICE AREAS:*** Real Estate; Litigation; Corporate; Information Technology. ***Email:*** dleventhal@brownraysman.com

BRUCE H. LESHINE, born New York, N.Y., November 14, 1960; admitted to bar, 1992, Virginia; 1993, District of Columbia; 1994, New York (Not admitted in Connecticut). *Education:* Rensselaer Polytechnic Institute (B.S.I.E., 1982); College of William & Mary (M.B.A., 1987); Georgetown University (J.D., 1991). ***Email:*** bleshine@brownraysman.com

RICHARD M. BORDEN, born Hartford, Connecticut, August 13, 1965; admitted to bar, 1990, Connecticut; 1991, New York. *Education:* Amherst College (B.A., 1987); New York University School of Law (J.D., 1990). Articles Editor, Annual Survey of American Law, 1989-1990. Member and Director, 1995—, MIT Enterprise Forum of Connecticut . ***PRACTICE AREAS:*** Information Technology; Corporate; Mergers and Acquisitions; Securities. ***Email:*** rborden@brownraysman.com

RESIDENT ASSOCIATES

Samuel L. Molinari	***Nathaniel Selleck***
James R. Kinyon	***Douglas D. Sheehan***
Candace M. Cunningham	***Karen Baldwin Kravetz***
Joseph M. Pastore, III	***Donald R. Ballman***
Diane Duhaime	***Frederik F. Erikson*** (Not admitted in CT)
Mitchell L. Fishberg	***David B. Benoit***
Catherine L. Moreton	

(For complete biographical data on all personnel, see Professional Biographies at New York, New York)

BROWN, RUDNICK, FREED & GESMER

A Partnership of Professional Corporations

CITYPLACE I

185 ASYLUM STREET

HARTFORD, CONNECTICUT 06103-3402

Telephone: 860-509-6500

Fax: 860-509-6501

URL: http://www.brownrudnick.com

Boston, Massachusetts Office: One Financial Center. Telephone: 617-856-8200. Fax: 617-856-8201.

Providence, Rhode Island Office: One Providence Washington Plaza. Telephone: 401-276-2600. Fax: 401-276-2601.

London, England Office: 8 Clifford Street. Telephone: +44-20-7851-6000. Fax: +44-20-7851-6100.

Banking, Bankruptcy, Civil Litigation, Corporate, Employment, Environmental, ERISA, Family, Government Relations, Health Care, High Technology, Insurance Coverage, Intellectual Property, International, Media, Patents, Public and Structured Finance, Real Estate, Secured Lending, Securities, Taxation.

MEMBERS OF FIRM

ROBERT J. ANTHONY, admitted to bar, 1992, Connecticut. *Education:* Boston College (B.A., 1986); Yale University (M.P.H., 1988); University of Connecticut (J.D., 1992). (Resident). ***PRACTICE AREAS:*** Health Care; Business. ***Email:*** ranthony@brfg.com

MARK A. ASMAR, admitted to bar, 1970, Connecticut. *Education:* Indiana University (A.B., 1967); University of Connecticut (J.D., 1970). (Resident). ***PRACTICE AREAS:*** Commercial Real Estate Development; Financing, Leasing and Conveyancing; Loan Workouts; Land Use and Zoning. ***Email:*** masmar@brfg.com

MARK S. BALDWIN, admitted to bar, 1986, Connecticut. *Education:* University of Michigan (A.B., 1983); Boston University (J.D., 1986). (Resident). ***PRACTICE AREAS:*** Complex Commercial, Corporate and Employment Litigation. ***Email:*** mbaldwin@brfg.com

CATHERINE BARR, admitted to bar, 1987, Massachusetts; 2001, Connecticut, Provisional Admission. *Education:* Wellesley College (B.A., 1984); Harvard University (J.D., 1987). (Resident). ***PRACTICE AREAS:*** Commercial and Real Estate Finance; Commercial Lending; Loan Workouts; Bankruptcy. ***Email:*** cbarr@brfg.com

LAWRENCE F. CAFERO, JR., admitted to bar, 1982, Connecticut. *Education:* University of Connecticut (B.A., 1979); Western New England College (J.D., 1982). (Resident). ***PRACTICE AREAS:*** Real Estate; Administrative Law. ***Email:*** lcafero@brfg.com

(This Listing Continued)

DOUGLAS A. COHEN, admitted to bar, 1981, District of Columbia; 1992, Connecticut. *Education:* State University of New York at Buffalo (B.A., 1977); George Washington University (J.D., 1980). (Resident). ***PRACTICE AREAS:*** Environmental; Energy; Administrative Law. ***Email:*** dcohen@brfg.com

SCOTT P. CONSOLI, admitted to bar, 1986, Connecticut; 1987, Massachusetts. *Education:* University of Massachusetts at Amherst (B.A., 1983); Boston College (J.D., 1986). (Resident). ***PRACTICE AREAS:*** Real Estate Development; Commercial Leasing; Commercial Lending; Loan Workouts. ***Email:*** sconsoli@brfg.com

BRIAN C. COURTNEY, admitted to bar, 1987, Connecticut. *Education:* Boston College (B.A., 1984; J.D., 1987). (Resident). ***PRACTICE AREAS:*** Banking Law; Finance; Commercial Lending; Creditors Rights in Bankruptcy. ***Email:*** bcourtney@brfg.com

FRANCA L. DeROSA, admitted to bar, 1990, Connecticut. *Education:* Trinity College (B.A., 1985); American University (J.D., 1990). (Resident). ***PRACTICE AREAS:*** Environmental; Energy; Administrative Law. ***Email:*** fderosa@brfg.com

J. HANSON GUEST, admitted to bar, 1982, New York; 1989, Connecticut. *Education:* University of Chicago (B.A., 1976); Yale University (J.D., 1980); Yale Management School (M.B.A., 1980). (Resident). ***PRACTICE AREAS:*** International Corporate Finance; Corporate Finance; Banking Law; Public Finance; Economic Development; Real Estate. ***Email:*** hguest@brfg.com

HARVEY HOBERMAN, admitted to bar, 1960, Connecticut. *Education:* University of Connecticut (B.A., 1957; LL.B., 1960). (Resident). ***PRACTICE AREAS:*** Commercial Finance; Workouts and Financing; Real Estate Workouts and Financing; Corporate Restructures and Turn-Arounds. ***Email:*** hhoberman@brfg.com

THOMAS D. RITTER, admitted to bar, 1978, Connecticut. *Education:* Amherst College (B.A., 1974); University of Connecticut (J.D., 1977). (Resident). ***PRACTICE AREAS:*** Government Relations (30%); Municipal (20%); Utility (20%); Banking (10%); Environmental (10%); Real Estate (10%). ***Email:*** tritter@brfg.com

HOWARD L. SIEGEL, admitted to bar, 1974, Connecticut. *Education:* Massachusetts Institute of Technology (B.S., 1971); Boston University (J.D., 1974). (Resident). ***PRACTICE AREAS:*** Banking Law; Finance; Commercial Lending; Creditors Rights in Bankruptcy. ***Email:*** hsiegel@brfg.com

PHILIP M. SMALL, admitted to bar, 1978, Connecticut; 1979, District of Columbia. *Education:* University of Pennsylvania (B.A., 1975); George Washington University (M.A., 1979; J.D., 1978). (Resident). ***PRACTICE AREAS:*** Environmental; Energy; Public Utilities; Administrative Law. ***Email:*** psmall@brfg.com

---

Kara L. Brooks (Resident); ***Michael J. Camilleri*** (Resident); ***Sandra K. Davis*** (Resident); ***David E. Golden*** (Resident); ***Michael E. Kozlik*** (Resident); ***Veronica J. Lee*** (Resident); ***Jonathan M. Lewis*** (Resident); ***Thomas J. Regan*** (Resident).

BYRNE & STORM, P.C.

330 MAIN STREET
P.O. BOX 231315
HARTFORD, CONNECTICUT 06123-1315
Telephone: 860-525-3700
Telecopy: 860-525-0287
Email: info@byrnestorm.com
URL: http://www.byrnestorm.com

General Practice, Commercial, Real Estate, Transactions, Foreclosures and Work Outs, Zoning, Corporate, Domestic and Commercial Litigation, Employment Discrimination Defense, Federal and State Court, Trial and Appellate.

JAMES F. BYRNE, born Brooklyn, New York, August 19, 1940; admitted to bar, 1966, New York; 1974, Connecticut. *Education:* Long Island University (B.A., 1962); Fordham University (J.D., 1965). Member, Panel of Arbitrators, American Arbitration Association, U.S. District Court, Southern District of New York, 1975 and District of Connecticut, 1975. *Member:* New York State, Connecticut and American (Member: Real Property, Probate and Trust Law Section International) Bar Associations. ***PRACTICE AREAS:*** Commercial Real Estate; Corporate Law; Commercial Financing; Workouts; Restructuring. ***Email:*** jfb@byrnestorm.com

CHRISTINA M. STORM, born Rockville Centre, New York, October 4, 1952; admitted to bar, 1978, Connecticut; 1979, U.S. District Court, District of Connecticut. *Education:* Manhattanville College (B.A., 1973); New York Law School (J.D., 1977). Listed in Who's Who Among American Law Students. Member: Women In International Security; International Association for Conflict Management. *Member:* Connecticut (Member, Sections on: Pro Bono, Human Rights International Law & World Peace) and American (Member, Sections on: Dispute Resolution; International Law) Bar Associations. ***REPORTED CASES:*** Jazlowiecki v. Cyr, 4 Conn. App. 76, 1985. ***PRACTICE AREAS:*** Conflicts Resolution; Human Rights; International Law. ***Email:*** cms@byrnestorm.com

RODGER C. BOE, born Springfield, Massachusetts, August 12, 1946; admitted to bar, 1977, California and U.S. District Court, Southern District of California; 1982, Connecticut; 1985, U.S. District Court, District of Connecticut. *Education:* Kenyon College (A.B., 1973); Vanderbilt University (J.D. , 1977). *Member:* Hartford County, Connecticut (Member, Litigation Section; Consumer Law Section) and American (Member, Litigation Section) Bar Associations; State Bar of California. ***REPORTED CASES:*** Tolland Enterprises v. Scan-Code, Inc., 684 A.2d 1150, 239 Conn. 326 (1996); Shawmut Bank Connecticut, N.A. v. Connecticut Limousine Service, Inc., 670 A.2d 880, 40 Conn. App. 268 (1996); Morgan v. Brown, 592 A.2d 925, 219 Conn. 204 (1991); Farmers & Mechanics Savings Bank v. Sullivan, 579 A.2d 1054, 216 Conn. 341 (1990); Burleigh v. Norwood Federal Savings & Loan Association, 669 F. Supp. 48 (D. Conn. 1987); Collins v. Dartmouth Plan, Inc., 646 F.Supp. 244 (D. Conn. 1986). ***PRACTICE AREAS:*** Civil Litigation.

ROBERT L. IAMONACO, born Hartford, Connecticut, December 16, 1959; admitted to bar, 1988, Connecticut; 1989, U.S. District Court, District of Connecticut. *Education:* Providence College (B.S., 1981); University of Connecticut (M.B.A., 1985); Western New England College (J.D., cum laude, 1988). Member, Western New England Law Review, 1986-1987. *Member:* Hartford County, Connecticut and American (Member, Sections on: Real Property, Estates and Probate; Business Law; Commercial Law; Bankruptcy) Bar Associations. ***PRACTICE AREAS:*** Commercial Financing; Commercial Real Estate; Residential Real Estate; Corporate Law; Estate Planning. ***Email:*** rli@byrnestorm.com

TENNYSON S. ANTHONY, born Halifax, Nova Scotia, March 31, 1966; admitted to bar, 1995, Connecticut; 1996, U.S. District Court, District of Connecticut. *Education:* University of Hartford (B.A., 1991); Franklin Pierce Law Center (J.D., 1995). *Member:* Connecticut Bar Association (Member, Sections on: Real Estate; Estates and Probate; Planning and Zoning). ***PRACTICE AREAS:*** Residential Real Estate; Commercial Real Estate; Corporate Law; Estate Planning; Probate. ***Email:*** attorneytsa@aol.com

REFERENCES: Fleet Bank; Tolland Bank; Glastonbury Bank & Trust Company; Sovereign Bank.

CAMPBELL CAMPBELL EDWARDS & CONROY

PROFESSIONAL CORPORATION
Established in 1983
TWO RIVERVIEW SQUARE
HARTFORD, CONNECTICUT 06108
Telephone: 860-291-8419
Fax: 860-291-8428
Email: info@campbell-trial-lawyers.com
URL: http://www.campbell-trial-lawyers.com

Portland, Maine Office: 50 Monument Square, 04101. Telephone: 207-780-1190. Fax: 207-780-1194.
Boston, Massachusetts Office: One Constitution Plaza, Third Floor, 02129. Telephone: 617-241-3000. Fax: 617-241-5115.
Concord, New Hampshire Office: 14 South Street, 03301. Telephone: 603-226-4111. Fax: 603-226-4111.
Turnersville, New Jersey Office: Washington Professional Campus II, 901 Route 168, Suite 201, 08012. Telephone: 856-374-8300. Fax: 856-374-8301.
Wayne, Pennsylvania Office: Three Glenhardie Corporate Center, 1265 Drummers Lane, Suite 2000, 19087. Telephone: 610-964-1900. Fax: 610-964-1981.
Providence, Rhode Island Office: 123 Dyer Street, 02903. Telephone: 401-421-5123. Fax: 401-421-5136.

Complex Litigation and Business Counseling, Multi-District Litigation, Class Actions, Products Liability, Business Law, Toxic Torts, Environmental Law, Employment Law and Professional Liability.

JAMES M. CAMPBELL, born Winchester, Massachusetts, October 25, 1958; admitted to bar, 1983, Massachusetts; 1984, Florida, U.S. District Court, District of Massachusetts, U.S. District Court, Middle District of Florida and U.S. Court of Appeals, First and Eleventh Circuits; 1986, New Hampshire, Maine and U.S. District Court, District of New Hampshire; 1991, U.S. District Court, District of Connecticut; 1994, U.S. District Court, District of Maine; 1995, U.S. District Court, District of Vermont (Not admitted in Connecticut). *Education:* Boston College (B.A., magna cum laude, 1980); University of Vir-

(This Listing Continued)

CAMPBELL CAMPBELL EDWARDS & CONROY, PROFESSIONAL CORPORATION, Hartford—Continued

ginia School of Law (J.D., 1983). (Also at Boston, Massachusetts, Concord, New Hampshire, Providence, Rhode Island and Portland, Maine Offices). **Email:** jmcampbell@campbell-trial-lawyers.com

HOLLY M. POLGLASE, born Battle Creek, Michigan, November 2, 1962; admitted to bar, 1988, Massachusetts; 1989, Maine, New Hampshire, U.S. District Court, District of Massachusetts and U.S. Court of Appeals, First Circuit; 1990, U.S. District Court, District of New Hampshire; 1992, U.S. District Court, District of Connecticut; 1996, Connecticut and U.S. District Court, District of Vermont. *Education:* Assumption College (B.A., cum laude, 1985); Suffolk University (J.D., cum laude, 1988). Staff Member, 1986-1987 and Comment Editor, 1987-1988, Suffolk University Law Review. (Also at Boston, Massachusetts, Concord, New Hampshire and Portland, Maine Offices). **Email:** hpolglase@campbell-trial-lawyers.com

(For complete list of Representative Clients, see Representative Clients at Boston, Massachusetts)

(For complete Biographical Data on all Personnel, see Professional Biographies at Boston, Massachusetts)

CANTOR COLBURN LLP

HARTFORD, CONNECTICUT

(See Bloomfield)

Patent, Trademark and Copyright Law, Unfair Competition, Computer and Related Intellectual Property Law including Litigation in all Courts.

AUSTIN CAREY, JR., P.C.

Established in 1993

GOTHIC PARK, SUITE 200
43 WOODLAND STREET
HARTFORD, CONNECTICUT 06105-2340
Telephone: 860-724-0012
Fax: 860-724-1211
Email: acarey@careyfirm.com

Environmental Law, Environmental Insurance Claims, Litigation.

FIRM PROFILE: Our goal is to improve both quality and efficiency in counseling and litigation through enhanced use of technology, project specific collaboration with other specialists, reduced project staffing because of the use of technology, and innovative fee structures that offer alternatives to the traditional hourly rate systems. We subscribe to and, in undertaking any representation, request that our clients agree to, the Guidelines for conduct issued by the Section of Litigation of the American Bar Association.

AUSTIN CAREY, JR., born Hartford, Connecticut, February 6, 1943; admitted to bar, 1968, Connecticut and U.S. District Court, District of Connecticut; 1970, U.S. Court of Military Appeals; 1973, U.S. Claims Court; 1975, U.S. Court of Appeals, Second Circuit and U.S. Supreme Court; 1985, U.S. Tax Court. *Education:* Yale University (B.A., 1965); Ohio State University (J.D., 1968). Adjunct Professor, Environmental Law Clinic, Yale Law School, 1991-1994. Member, Editorial Board, Connecticut Bar Journal, 1976-1986. Member, Environmental Policy Council, Connecticut Business and Industry Association, 1989—. Member, Board of Directors, 1981-1995, and President, 1992-1995, Connecticut Fund for the Environment. Member, Board of Directors, Farmington River Watershed Association, 1987-1994. Member, House of Delegates, Connecticut Bar Association, 1979-1981; 1983-1986. Chairman, West Hartford Human Rights Commission, 1974-1978. Member, West Hartford Conservation Commission, 1981-1983, 1989-1992. Member, Executive Committee, Section on Environmental Law, Connecticut Bar Association. Member, Sections on: Natural Resources and Energy and Environmental Law; Litigation; Economics of Law Practice, Sub-Committee Co-chair, Environmental Litigation Committee, American Bar Association. [Capt., JAGC, U.S. Army, 1969-1973]. ***PRACTICE AREAS:*** Environmental Law; Environmental Insurance Claims; Litigation.

REPRESENTATIVE CLIENTS: Illinois Tool Works Inc.; Southwire Company; Unisys Corporation; Southern New England Telephone Company.
BANK REFERENCES: Fleet Bank, (Hartford, CT.).

STEPHEN S. CHINITZ & ASSOCIATES

HARTFORD, CONNECTICUT

(See Bloomfield)

Collections, Creditor's Rights, Personal Injury, Insurance, Subrogation, Bankruptcy Court Litigation (Creditors), Legal Malpractice, Domestic Relations and Real Estate, Trials in all Courts.

CHORCHES & NOVAK, P.C.

HARTFORD, CONNECTICUT

(See Wethersfield)

Bankruptcy, Asset Protection, Commercial Transactions and Corporate. Civil Litigation in all State and Federal Courts. Representation before Internal Revenue Service.

CLAYMAN, MARKOWITZ, TAPPER AND BARAM, L.L.C.

HARTFORD, CONNECTICUT

(See Bloomfield)

Business Law, Commercial, Condominium, Corporate, Criminal Law, Elder Law, Employment Law, Entertainment Law, Estate Planning, Family, Franchise Law, General Practice. Immigration, Municipal Law, Nationality, Negligence, Personal Injury, Planning and Zoning, Probate, Real Estate, Trademarks, Trials in all Courts.

COHN BIRNBAUM & SHEA P.C.

Established in 1976

100 PEARL STREET
HARTFORD, CONNECTICUT 06103-4500
Telephone: 860-493-2200
Fax: 860-727-0361

Westport, Connecticut Office: 830 Post Road East, 2nd. Floor. Telephone: 203-341-9595. Fax: 203-341-9696.
New York, New York Office: 67 Wall Street, Suite 2411, 10005. Telephone: 212-949-9555. Fax: 212-949-7997.

Banking, Bankruptcy, Business, Commercial, Communications, Condominium, Construction, Contracting, Corporation, Creditors Rights, Employment, Environmental, Finance, Health Care Administrative, Joint Ventures, Land Use, Media, Municipal, Professional Liability Defense, Real Estate, Securities, Shopping Center, Taxation, Technology, Litigation in all State and Federal Courts.

FIRM PROFILE: Our success in building a comprehensive practice in business law is due in part to our demonstrated ability to attract competent legal professionals and back them up with a strong support staff. We have carefully recruited only experienced individuals whose legal expertise is complemented by a strong appreciation of the business environment and a dedication to timely, personalized legal service.

ROBERT E. COHN (Retired).

LESLIE INRIG OLEAR, born Pittsburgh, Pennsylvania, February 27, 1955; admitted to bar, 1981, Connecticut. *Education:* Central Connecticut State College (B.A., summa cum laude, 1977); Western New England College (J.D., cum laude, 1981); Boston University (LL.M., 1984). Corporator, 1995-1997 and Trustee, 1997-1999, Hartford Seminary. Member, The State of Connecticut Risk Management and Insurance Purchasing Board, 1996—. Director, Real Estate Finance Association, Hartford Chapter, 1997—. *Member:* Connecticut and American Bar Associations. ***PRACTICE AREAS:*** Commercial Real Estate Finance; Commercial Real Estate Leasing; Business Law; Communications Law. **Email:** lolear@cb-shea.com

RICHARD J. SHEA, JR., born Bridgeport, Connecticut, March 26, 1957; admitted to bar, 1982, Connecticut; 1983, U.S. Tax Court; 1999, New York. *Education:* Yale University (B.A., 1979); University of Connecticut (M.B.A., 1982; J.D., 1982); Boston University (LL.M., Taxation, 1985). ***PRACTICE AREAS:*** Business Law; Commercial Real Estate; Securities; Technology Law. **Email:** rshea@cb-shea.com

MICHAEL F. MULPETER, born Poughkeepsie, New York, February 21, 1958; admitted to bar, 1984, New York; 1986, Connecticut. *Education:* Union College (B.A., cum laude, 1980); University of Connecticut (J.D., with honors, 1983). Member, 1981-1983 and Lead Articles and Book Reviews Editor, 1982-1983, Connecticut Law Review. ***PRACTICE AREAS:*** Corporate Law; Business Law; Securities; Communications Law. **Email:** mmulpeter@cb-shea.com

(This Listing Continued)

THOMAS W. WITHERINGTON, born Richmond, Virginia, January 12, 1956; admitted to bar, 1982, Connecticut and U.S. District Court, District of Connecticut; 1989, U.S. Court of Appeals, Second Circuit. *Education:* Yale University (B.A., 1978); University of Connecticut School of Law (J.D., with honors, 1982). Co-Author, "Standards of Proof in Employment Law," 57 Connecticut Bar Journal 289, 1983. *Member:* Connecticut and American Bar Associations. ***PRACTICE AREAS:*** Commercial Litigation; Lender Liability; Environmental Litigation. ***Email:*** twitherington@cb-shea.com

SCOTT D. ROSEN, born New York, N.Y., June 8, 1957; admitted to bar, 1986, Connecticut; 1987, U.S. District Court, District of Connecticut. *Education:* Fairfield University (B.A., magna cum laude, 1983); Boston University (J.D., 1986). Member, 1984-1985 and Developments Editor, 1985-1986, Annual Review of Banking Law. Author: "A Construction of Glass-Steagall's Securities Provisions: Clearing the Confusion after Securities Industry Association v. Board of Governors of The Federal Reserve System," 5 Annual Review of Banking Law 307; "Developments in Banking Law: 1985," 5 Annual Review of Banking Law 1. *Member:* Connecticut (Member, Sections on: Commercial Law; Bankruptcy; Banking Law) and American (Member, Sections on: Business Law; Litigation) Bar Associations. ***PRACTICE AREAS:*** Creditors Rights; Bankruptcy Reorganization; Real Estate; Commercial Workouts; Commercial Litigation. ***Email:*** srosen@cb-shea.com

MELVIN A. SIMON, born Montreal, Canada, March 12, 1956; admitted to bar, 1983, Connecticut and U.S. District Court, District of Connecticut. *Education:* Central Connecticut State College (B.A., with honors, 1979); Benjamin N. Cardozo School of Law (J.D., cum laude, 1983). Phi Alpha Theta. Director: Jewish Federation of Greater Hartford; Vice President, Greater Hartford Jewish Community Center. *Member:* Hartford County, Connecticut (Member: Commercial Law and Bankruptcy Section; Lecturer: "Foreclosure and Repossession for Connecticut Lenders-When the Work Out Doesn't Work Out-Repossession of Personal Property," 1999; Connecticut's New Prejudgment Remedy Act, "Prejudgment Remedies-How to Deal With Exemptions and Commercial Waivers," 1994) and American Bar Associations; Association of Trial Lawyers of America; Connecticut Trial Lawyers Association. ***PRACTICE AREAS:*** Commercial Litigation; Bankruptcy; Construction Litigation; Lender Liability Defense; Workouts; Personal Injury; Employment Litigation. ***Email:*** msimon@cb-shea.com

SHARON P. CHURCHILL, born New London, Connecticut, December 31, 1953; admitted to bar, 1992, Connecticut. *Education:* University of Connecticut (B.S., 1976; J.D., with honors, 1992). Member, Moot Court Board. Executive Editor, Conn. Journal of International Law, 1991-1992. *Member:* Connecticut Bar Association. ***PRACTICE AREAS:*** Business Law; Corporate Law; Asset Based Finance; Securities. ***Email:*** schurchill@cb-shea.com

---

MARY E. R. BARTHOLIC, born Hartford, Connecticut, November 13, 1962; admitted to bar, 1993, Connecticut; 1994, Ohio, U.S. District Court, Northern District of Ohio and U.S. District Court, District of Connecticut. *Education:* Elms College (B.A., 1984); University of Pittsburgh (J.D., 1993). Member, Appellate Moot Court Board, 1992-1993. *Member:* Cleveland, Connecticut and Ohio State Bar Associations. ***PRACTICE AREAS:*** Commercial Litigation; Employment Law; Land Use Law. ***Email:*** mbartholic@cb-shea.com

DOUGLAS S. PELHAM, born Hartford, Connecticut, April 27, 1964; admitted to bar, 1998, Connecticut and U.S. District Court, District of Connecticut. *Education:* Lafayette College (B.S., Chemical Engineering, 1986); University of New Haven (M.S., Environmental Engineering, 1993); Quinnipiac College (J.D., magna cum laude, 1998). Professional Engineer, Connecticut, 1992. ***PRACTICE AREAS:*** Commercial Real Estate Finance; Real Estate Leasing; Land Use Law; Environmental Law. ***Email:*** dpelham@cb-shea.com

MATTHEW FEIGENBAUM, born Brooklyn, New York, February 23, 1943; admitted to bar, 1980, New York, Florida and U.S. District Court, Southern District of New York; 1992, California; 1997, Connecticut. *Education:* Brooklyn College of the City University of New York (B.A., 1963); State University of New York at Albany (M.A., 1966); Fordham University (J.D., cum laude, 1979). *Member:* The Florida Bar; State Bar of California. (Resident, Westport Office; Also Of Counsel, New York, NY Office). ***Email:*** mattf@cbsheawestport.com

ROBERT H. FEIGENBAUM, born Middletown, New York, February 6, 1969; admitted to bar, 1996, California; 1998, Connecticut; 1999, New York. *Education:* State University of New York at Albany (B.A., 1991); University of San Diego (J.D., 1995). *Member:* State Bar of California. (Resident, Westport Office). ***Email:*** robf@cbsheawestport.com

MATTHEW C. McGRATH, born Bronx, New York, May 5, 1967; admitted to bar, 1995, Connecticut; 1996, New York, U.S. District Court, District of Connecticut and U.S. District Court, Southern District of New York. *Education:* Manhattan College (B.A., cum laude, 1989); Fordham University School of Law (J.D., 1995). *Member:* Connecticut (Member, Business Law Section), New York State and American (Member, Business Law Section) Bar Associations. ***PRACTICE AREAS:*** Business Law; Corporate Law. ***Email:*** mmcgrath@cb-shea.com

STEPHEN D. OPPENHEIM, born New Haven, Connecticut, September 14, 1967; admitted to bar, 1992, CT; 1993, U.S. District Court, District of CT. *Education:* University of Michigan (B.A., 1989); Washington College of Law of American University (J.D., cum laude, 1992). ***LANGUAGES:*** French, Russian. ***PRACTICE AREAS:*** Commercial Law; Real Estate; Commercial Lending; Creditors Rights. ***Email:*** soppenheim@cb-shea.com

OF COUNSEL

ROBERT J. BIRNBAUM, born New York, N.Y., October 15, 1930; admitted to bar, 1957, New York; 1970, Connecticut. *Education:* Bucknell University (B.A., cum laude, 1952); Harvard University (J.D., 1955). Phi Beta Kappa. Adjunct Professor, University of Connecticut Law School. Member, Law Committee, International Council of Shopping Centers, 1974—. Advisor, Mortgage Reform Committee of the Connecticut Law Review Commission, 1992—. Director, St. Francis Hospital and Medical Center, 1998—. *Member:* Connecticut (Member, Executive Committee, Real Property Section) and American Bar Associations. ***PRACTICE AREAS:*** Commercial Real Estate; Commercial Real Estate Acquisitions; Commercial Real Estate Development; Commercial Real Estate Finance; Leasing; Commercial Real Estate Sales.

REPRESENTATIVE CLIENTS: Amphenol Corporation; American Card Technology, Inc.; Arthur A. Watson & Co., Inc.; The Balf Co.; Collins Enterprises, L.L.C.; E.A. Patten Company; Employers Reinsurance Corporation; Grove Property Trust; Guida-Seibert Dairy Co.; Hamden Plaza; The Hartford Roofing Co., Inc.; Icon International, Inc.; Konover & Associates, Inc.; Lehman Brothers Holdings, Inc.; McDonald's Corporation; New Haven Savings Bank, Inc.; People's Bank; Regency Savings Bank; Sabre Communications, Inc.; St. Francis Hospital & Medical Center; System Pros, Inc.; Tri-City Plaza; Walgreen Co.; Wasley Products, Inc.; Webster Bank; Winstanley Enterprises, L.L.C.
REFERENCE: Webster Bank.

COONEY, SCULLY AND DOWLING

HARTFORD SQUARE NORTH
TEN COLUMBUS BOULEVARD
HARTFORD, CONNECTICUT 06106
Telephone: 860-527-1141
Fax: 860-247-5215

General Practice. Insurance, Corporation, Probate, Construction and Railroad Law. Trials in all Courts.

MEMBERS OF FIRM

JOSEPH P. COONEY (1906-1984).

HENRY COONEY (1951-1991).

RICHARD A. FERRIS (1956-2001).

VINCENT J. DOWLING, born New York City, December 20, 1927; admitted to bar, 1957, Connecticut; 1985, Massachusetts; 1986, Florida. *Education:* Lehigh University (B.S., in Engr. 1949); University of Connecticut (J.D., 1957). *Member:* Hartford County, Connecticut (Chairman, Committee on Specialization, 1974-1981), Federal and American Bar Associations; American Society of Mechanical Engineers. ***PRACTICE AREAS:*** Construction Liability; Litigation; Professional Liability; Mediation.

PATRICK J. FLAHERTY, born Hartford, Connecticut, November 27, 1933; admitted to bar, 1958, Connecticut. *Education:* College of the Holy Cross (A.B., 1955); Yale University (LL.B., 1958). Phi Delta Phi. *Member:* Hartford County, Connecticut and American Bar Associations; National Association of Railroad Trial Counsel (Vice-President, 1995; , National Executive Committee, 1991—). ***PRACTICE AREAS:*** Railroad Liability; Transportation Liability; Food, Drug and Cosmetic Liability; Products Liability; Professional Liability; Domestic Relations.

LOUIS B. BLUMENFELD, born New Britain, Connecticut, October 2, 1945; admitted to bar, 1970, Connecticut. *Education:* University of Vermont (B.A., 1967); Boston College (J.D., 1970). Order of the Coif. Managing Editor, Annual Survey of Massachusetts Law, 1969-1970. Law Clerk to Associate Justice, John R. Thim, Connecticut Supreme Court, 1970-1971. *Member:* Hartford County, Connecticut (Member, 1973-1986 and Chairman, 1979-1982, Committee on the Lawyer and the Community; Member, Environmental Law Section, Federal Practice Section) and American (Natural Resources Law Section) Bar Associations; Connecticut Defense Lawyers Association. ***PRACTICE AREAS:*** Legal Malpractice; Insurance Coverage; Environmental Law; Appellate Practice. ***Email:*** lbb@csd-law.com

JOHN W. SITARZ, born Hartford, Connecticut, May 1, 1947; admitted to bar, 1972, Connecticut. *Education:* Wesleyan University (B.A., 1969); University of Maine (J.D., 1972). *Member:* Hartford County and Connecticut Bar Associations; American Board of Trial Advocates; National Diocesan Attorneys Association; Connecticut Defense Lawyers Association.

(This Listing Continued)

COONEY, SCULLY AND DOWLING, Hartford—Continued

EUGENE A. COONEY, born Hartford, Connecticut, August 14, 1950; admitted to bar, 1977, Connecticut. *Education:* St. Michael's College (B.A., 1972); University of Connecticut (J.D., with honors, 1977). *Member:* Hartford County, Connecticut and American (Member, Sections on: Litigation; Tort and Insurance Practice) Bar Associations; Connecticut Defense Lawyers Association (President, 1996-1997); American Health Lawyers Association; Connecticut Medical Defense Lawyers Association. ***PRACTICE AREAS:*** Medical Malpractice; Insurance Coverage; Administrative Law.

JOHN T. SCULLY, born Hartford, Connecticut, April 1, 1954; admitted to bar, 1980, Connecticut. *Education:* University of Hartford (B.A., cum laude, 1976); University of Connecticut (J.D., 1980). *Member:* Hartford County and Connecticut Bar Associations; Connecticut Trial Lawyers Association; The Association of Trial Lawyers of America. ***PRACTICE AREAS:*** Personal Injury; Criminal Defense; Workers Compensation; Insurance Defense Subrogation.

KAREN JANSEN CASEY, born Brooklyn, New York, October 3, 1955; admitted to bar, 1981, Connecticut. *Education:* University of Vermont (B.A., 1977); University of Connecticut (J.D., 1981). *Member:* Hartford County and Connecticut Bar Associations.

JEFFREY C. PINGPANK, born Stamford, Connecticut, July 6, 1950; admitted to bar, 1975, Connecticut. *Education:* Johns Hopkins University (B.A., 1972); University of Connecticut (J.D., 1975). Author: "Wrongful Discharge, A 'New' Cause of Action," 54 Connecticut Bar Journal 213, 1980. Instructor, Public Sector Labor Relations, Hartford Graduate Center, 1979-1982. *Member:* Connecticut Bar Association (Member, Labor Law Section).

PAUL T. NOWOSADKO, born Norwich, Connecticut, May 7, 1957; admitted to bar, 1983, Connecticut. *Education:* Dartmouth College (B.A., 1979); University of Connecticut (J.D., with honors, 1983). *Member:* Hartford County, Connecticut and American Bar Associations.

HERBERT J. SHEPARDSON, born Westfield, Massachusetts, October 23, 1956; admitted to bar, 1982, Connecticut. *Education:* University of Massachusetts (B.A., 1978); Western New England College (J.D., cum laude, 1981). Pi Sigma Alpha. Member, Western New England Law Review, 1980-1981. Author: "Is Eighth Amendment Proportionately Applicable to Mere Length of Sentence?" 4 Western New England Law Review 335, 1981. Adjunct Professor of Law, Western New England College School of Law, 1984-1988. *Member:* Hartford County, Connecticut (Member, Litigation Section) and American (Member, Litigation Section) Bar Associations; Connecticut Defense Lawyers Association. ***PRACTICE AREAS:*** Medical Malpractice; Civil Litigation.

DAVID A. HAUGHT, born Princeton, New Jersey, March 22, 1960; admitted to bar, 1986, Connecticut. *Education:* Amherst College (B.A., 1982); Suffolk University (J.D., with honors, 1986); University of Connecticut (Visiting, 1986). Staff Member and Associate Editor, Suffolk Transnational Law Journal, 1984-1985. Author: "Constitutional Rights of Excludable Aliens," Suffolk Transnational Law Journal, Vol. 9, 1985; "Foreign Sovereign Immunities Act," Vol. 9, 1986. Contributing Editor, Connecticut Basic Practice Manual. *Member:* Hartford County and Connecticut (Member, Litigation, Construction Law Sections) Bar Associations. ***Email:*** dah@csd-law.com

JAMES T. SCULLY, born Hartford, Connecticut, May 29, 1961; admitted to bar, 1988, Connecticut. *Education:* Salve Regina-The Newport College (B.A., cum laude, 1983); Western New England College (J.D., 1987). *Member:* Hartford County and Connecticut Bar Associations. ***Email:*** js@csd-law.com

WILLIAM J. SCULLY, born Hartford, Connecticut, September 4, 1962; admitted to bar, 1987, Connecticut. *Education:* Connecticut College (B.A., 1984); Western New England College (J.D., 1987). Recipient, Federal Civil Trial Advocacy Book Prize. *Member:* Hartford County and Connecticut Bar Associations.

ROBERT G. CLEMENTE, born Hartford, Connecticut, July 30, 1963; admitted to bar, 1988, Connecticut. *Education:* St. John's University; Boston College (B.A., cum laude, 1985); University of Connecticut (J.D., with honors, 1988). *Member:* Hartford County, Connecticut and American Bar Associations.

OF COUNSEL

JOHN F. SCULLY, born Hartford, Connecticut, October 6, 1925; admitted to bar, 1954, Connecticut. *Education:* Trinity College (A.B., 1950); University of Connecticut (LL.B., 1954). *Member:* Hartford County, Connecticut and American Bar Associations; National Association of Railroad Trial Counsel. Fellow: American College of Trial Lawyers; American Board of Trial Advocates; American Bar Foundation.

ASSOCIATES

LORINDA S. COON, born Monterey, California, October 16, 1957; admitted to bar, 1984, Connecticut; 1985, New York. *Education:* State University of New York at Binghamton (B.S., with honors, 1979); Albany Law School of Union University (J.D., cum laude, 1984). Justinian Society. *Member:* Hartford County, Connecticut and New York State Bar Associations.

REBECCA L. PIDLAK, born Hartford, Connecticut, February 8, 1973; admitted to bar, 1998, Connecticut. *Education:* University of Connecticut (B.S., 1995); Mississippi College School of Law (J.D., with distinction, 1998); Georgetown University Law Center. Phi Alpha Delta.

PAUL A. CROCE, II, born St. Louis, Missouri, April 10, 1970; admitted to bar, 1999, Connecticut. *Education:* Hartwick College (B.A., 1993); University of Connecticut School of Law (J.D., 1999). Executive Editor, Connecticut Insurance Law Journal, 1997-1999. ***Email:*** pac@csd-law.com

JESSICA D. MEERBERGEN, born Greenwich, Connecticut, January 3, 1974; admitted to bar, 1999, Connecticut; 2000, U.S. District Court, District of Connecticut. *Education:* Bates College (B.S., 1996); University of Connecticut (J.D., with honors, 1999). Phi Delta Phi (Officer, 1997-1999). Notes and Comments Editor, Connecticut Insurance Law Journal, 1998-1999. ***Email:*** jdm@csd-law.com

REPRESENTATIVE CLIENTS: Hartford Roman Catholic Archdiocese; St. Francis Hospital; Sisters of Mercy of Connecticut.
TRIAL COUNSEL FOR: The Hartford Insurance Co.; Travelers Aetna Life & Casualty Co.; CNA Insurance Cos.; AMTRAK; CSX Transportation, Inc.; Central Vermont Railway, Inc.; Canadian National Railway Co.; General Reinsurance Co.; Paine, Weber, INAPRO; Safeco Insurance Co.; Catholic Mutual Group I; Imperial Casualty & Indemnity Co.; Gallagher & Bassett; Southern New England Telephone Co.; Mitsui Marine & Fire Insurance Co.; Norfolk Southern Railroad; North American Van Lines; Rapid Adjusting Corp.; St. Paul Fire & Marine; Owens-Corning; The Stanley Works; Sherwin-Williams; Illinois Surplus Lines; Shand Morahan & Co.; American International Underwriters; Connecticut Medical Insurance Co.; Celtic Life Insurance Co.; American Healthcare & Indemnity; Employers Reinsurance Corp.; Pro Mutual Group; The Windsor Group.
REFERENCE: Webster Bank.

COPP & BERALL, LLP

Established in 1955

864 WETHERSFIELD AVENUE

HARTFORD, CONNECTICUT 06114

Telephone: 860-249-5261

Fax: 860-249-4111

Email: frank_berall@coppberall.com

Taxation, Probate, Wills, Trusts and Estate.

FIRM PROFILE: The firm is a specialty boutique, limiting its practice to federal and state taxation, including tax dispute resolution and tax litigation, estate planning and estate administration, probate, trust, estate settlement and post mortem tax planning.

MEMBERS OF FIRM

FRANK S. BERALL, born New York, N.Y., February 10, 1929; admitted to bar, 1955, New York; 1957, U.S. Tax Court, U.S. Court of Appeals, 2nd Circuit and U.S. District Court, Southern District of New York; 1960, Connecticut and U.S. District Court, District of Connecticut; 1961, U.S. Supreme Court; 1969, U.S. Claims Court. *Education:* Yale University (B.S., 1950; J.D., 1955); New York University (LL.M. in Taxation, 1959). Senior Editor, Connecticut Bar Journal, 1970—. Member, Editorial Advisory Boards: Estate Planning, 1973—; The Practical Tax Lawyer, 1988—; The Journal of Taxation of Estates and Trusts, 1988-1992. Listed in Best Lawyers in America for Trusts and Estates, and Tax Law, 1987—. Assistant Instructor in Legal Research, Yale Law School, 1954-1955. Lecturer in Estate Planning Law, University of Connecticut School of Law, 1972-1973. Adjunct Assistant Professor, University of Hartford Graduate Tax Program, 1973-1975. Chair: Tax Section, 1969-1972; Estates and Probate Section, 1984-1986, Connecticut Bar Association. Member, University of Hartford Tax Institute's Advisory Council, 1970-1982; Co-Chair, Notre Dame Estate Planning Institute, 1977—. Co-Chair, Hartford Tax Institute's Advisory Council, 1985-1994. Special Master pre-trying state tax cases in Connecticut Superior Court, 1993—. Co-Chair for Connecticut of I.R.S. Non-Filer Program, 1993-1994. Member and Counsel to Tax Committee of the Governor's Strike Force for Full Employment, 1971-1972. Consultant to Governor's Commission on Tax Reform, 1972-1973. Member: Connecticut State Tax Commissioner's Commission, 1972-1973; Advisory Committee on Tax Law Clarification, 1984-1990. President, Hartford Tax Club, 1975-1976. Senior Tax Counsel, Andros, Floyd and Miller, Hartford, Connecticut. *Member:* Hartford County (Chair, Liaison Committee with Internal Revenue Service, 1972-1974; International Academy of Estate and Trust Law (Executive Counselor, 1978-1982), American College of Trust and Estate Counsel (Regent, 1977-1983; Chair, Estate and Gift Taxation Committee, 1976-1981; Accessions Tax Committee, 1984-1988; State Chair, 1975-1981; Member, Editorial Board, 1975-1987), Connecticut (Chair: Tax Section, 1969-1972; Estate and Probate Section, 1984-1986) and American (Chair, Membership Committee, 1977-1979; Income of Estates and Trusts Committee, 1983-1985; Committee on Economics of Tax Practice, 1987-1989; Continuing Legal Education Committee, Taxation Section, 1992-1994; Chair,

(This Listing Continued)

Committee on Estate Planning and Drafting, Life Insurance, 1979-1985; Task Force on Constitutionality of Tax Law, 1985-1989; Non Tax Issues in Drafting Wills and Revocable Trusts Committee, 1996; Co-Chair, Tax Litigation and Controversy Committee, 1996-1998, Real Property, Probate and Trust Law Section) Bar Associations; American Law Institute (Member, Consultive Groups for restatements of Trusts and Property and Subchapter J Project). [1st Lt., U.S. Army, 1950-1952]. ***REPORTED CASES:*** Commissioner v. Peska, 220 Conn, 77 (1991) (partially released power of appointment not subject to state death tax); Wiegand v. Heffernan, 170 Conn. 567 (1976) (jurisdiction to tax dividends); Naylor v. Brown, 166 Conn. 581 (1974) (special powers of appointment). ***PRACTICE AREAS:*** Probate; Federal and State Taxation; Estate Planning; Trust Administration; Tax Litigation; Tax Planning; Tax Dispute Resolution; Estate Settlement; Post Mortem Tax Planning Law.

OF COUNSEL

BELTON A. COPP, born Chicago Heights, Illinois, May 27, 1920; admitted to bar, 1947, Connecticut. *Education:* Phillips Exeter Academy (cum laude); Yale University (B.A., 1942); Yale Law School (LL.B., 1947). Phi Delta Phi; Corbey Court. Fellow, The American College of Trust and Estate Counsel, 1962-1982. [Lt. Comdr., USNR, 1942-1945, Retired]

MARK H. NEIKRIE, born Hartford, Connecticut, March 8, 1959; admitted to bar, 1984, Connecticut. *Education:* Hobart College (B.S., 1981); Case Western Reserve University (J.D., 1984); Boston University (LL.M. in Taxation, 1986). President, Hartford Tax Club, 1995-1996. *Member:* Connecticut Bar Association (Member, Executive Committee, Tax Section; Chair, Inheritance Tax SubCommittee, 1991-1992; Sales and Use Tax Subcommittee, 1993-1996). ***PRACTICE AREAS:*** Taxation; Probate; Trust; Business; Estate Planning.

REFERENCE: Fleet Bank, N.A.

ANDREW C. COTÉ, P.C.

HARTFORD, CONNECTICUT

(See Sharon)

COWDERY, ECKER & MURPHY, L.L.C.

750 MAIN STREET

HARTFORD, CONNECTICUT 06103-2703

Telephone: 860-278-5555

Facsimile: 860-249-0012

Email: lawyers@cemlaw.com

White Collar Criminal Defense, Commercial Litigation, Personal Injury. Appellate Practice, Professional Discipline.

MEMBERS OF FIRM

JAMES T. COWDERY, born Jacksonville, Florida, December 22, 1953; admitted to bar, 1980, Connecticut; 1982, U.S. District Court, District of Connecticut; 1984, U.S. Court of Appeals, Second Circuit; 1994, U.S. Supreme Court. *Education:* Trinity College (B.A., 1976); University of Connecticut (J.D., magna cum laude, 1980). Phi Beta Kappa. Recipient: William F. Starr Prize Fellowship for Scholarship and Leadership, 1980; Younger Federal Lawyers Award for Outstanding Government Service, 1989. Member, 1978-1979 and Editor-in-Chief, 1979-1980, Connecticut Law Review. Law Clerk to the Hon. Thomas J. Meskill, U.S. Court of Appeals, Second Circuit, 1980-1981. Assistant U.S. Attorney, 1984-1989 and Chief, Criminal Division, 1988-1989, District of Connecticut. Member: Ad Hoc Committee for the Review of the Criminal Justice Act Panel in the District of Connecticut, 1989—; Judicial Review Council, 1992-1996; Committee for Selection of Magistrate for the District of Connecticut, 1996. Chairman, Committee on Criminal Rules and Practice for the District of Connecticut, 1994. *Member:* Hartford County, Connecticut (Member, Sections on: Federal Practice; Criminal Justice and Civil Justice) and American (Member, Sections on: Litigation; Criminal Justice) Bar Associations. ***PRACTICE AREAS:*** White Collar Criminal Defense; Commercial Litigation; Professional Discipline. ***Email:*** jcowdery@cemlaw.com

STEVEN D. ECKER, born Chicago, Illinois, April 19, 1961; admitted to bar, 1988, Connecticut; 1989, U.S. District Court, District of Connecticut; 1990, U.S. Court of Appeals, Second Circuit. *Education:* Yale University (B.A., magna cum laude, 1984); Harvard University (J.D., magna cum laude, 1987). Member, Winning Team, Ames Moot Court Competition, 1987. Recipient, The David H. Neiditz Professional Writing Award for the Best-Written Appellate Brief in Connecticut, 1990, 1992. Editor, Harvard Law Review, 1986-1987. Member, Editorial Board, Connecticut Law Tribune, 1998-2001. Law Clerk to the Hon. Jon O. Newman, Circuit Judge, U.S. Court of Appeals, Second Circuit, 1987-1988. Member, Grievance Committee, U.S. District Court, District of Connecticut, 1995—. *Member:* New Haven County, Hartford County and Connecticut (Chairman, Federal Practice Section, 1998-2000) Bar Associations; Connecticut Trial Lawyers Association (Member, Board of Governors, 1994—); The Association of Trial Lawyers of America. ***PRACTICE AREAS:*** Commercial Litigation; Appellate Practice; Personal Injury; White Collar Criminal Defense. ***Email:*** ecker@cemlaw.com

(This Listing Continued)

THOMAS J. MURPHY, born New York, N.Y., June 27, 1959; admitted to bar, 1986, New York and U.S. District Court, Southern and Eastern Districts of New York; 1988, District of Columbia; 1990, U.S. District Court, District of Columbia; 1991, U.S. District Court, District of Connecticut and U.S. Court of Appeals, Second Circuit; 1995, Connecticut. *Education:* Georgetown University (A.B., magna cum laude, 1981); St. John's University (J.D., magna cum laude, 1985). Phi Beta Kappa. Recipient, Executive Office of United States Attorneys Director's Award for Superior Performance as An Assistant United States Attorney, 1997. Member,1983-1984 and Editor-in-Chief, 1984-1985, St. John's Law Review. Law Clerk to the Hon. George C. Pratt, U.S. Circuit Judge, U.S. Court of Appeals, Second Circuit, 1985-1987. Assistant U.S. Attorney, District of Connecticut, 1990-1997. Instructor, Law, University of Connecticut, Criminal Procedure, 2000-2001 and Moot Court Interterm, 1992-1994. U.S. District Court Magistrate Judge, Merit Review Panel, 2000. *Member:* Hartford County, Connecticut (Member, Federal Judiciary Committee); New York State and American Bar Associations; The District of Columbia Bar. ***PRACTICE AREAS:*** White Collar Criminal Defense; Commercial Litigation; Appellate Practice; Personal Injury. ***Email:*** tmurphy@cemlaw.com

JAMES R. SMART, born Park Ridge, Illinois, April 18, 1967; admitted to bar, 1997, Connecticut. *Education:* Princeton University (A.B., summa cum laude, 1989); University of Washington (M.A., 1994); Harvard Law School (J.D., cum laude, 1997). Phi Beta Kappa. Recipient, School for International Studies Award for Highest Scholarship, University of Washington, 1994. Author, "All the Stars in the Heavens Were in the Right Places: The Passage of the Food Quality Protection Act of 1996," 17 Stanford Environmental Law Journal 273, 1998. Law Clerk: Hon. Robert N. Chatigny, U.S. District Court, District of Connecticut, 1998-1999; Hon. David M. Borden, Connecticut Supreme Court, 1997-1998. *Member:* Oliver Ellsworth Inn of Court. ***PRACTICE AREAS:*** Commercial Litigation; White Collar Defense; Personal Injury; Appellate Practice. ***Email:*** jsmart@cemlaw.com

CRAMER, ALISSI & FONTAINE, P.C.

750 MAIN STREET, 16 FLOOR, SUITE 1600

HARTFORD, CONNECTICUT 06103

Telephone: 860-548-1122

Fax: 860-548-1223

URL: http://www.cafpc.com

URL: http://www.lawyers.com/crameralissi

Civil Litigation, Insurance Defense, Insurance Coverage, Professional Liability, Professional Malpractice, Common Carrier Liability, Personal Injury, Motor Vehicle and Truck Accidents, Liquor Liability, Premises and Product Liability, Trials and Appeals in all courts.

MARK R. CRAMER, born Detroit, Michigan, July 2, 1959; admitted to bar, 1986, Connecticut; 1987, U.S. District Court, District of Connecticut. *Education:* Wesleyan University (B.A., 1982); Western New England College School of Law (J.D., 1986). *Member:* Hartford County, Connecticut and American Bar Associations; Defense Research Institute (DRI). ***PRACTICE AREAS:*** Civil Litigation; Professional Liability; Premises Liability; Insurance; Real Estate Agents and Brokers Errors and Omissions; Liquor Liability. ***Email:*** mccramer@cafpc.com

JAMES A. ALISSI, born Hartford, Connecticut, January 13, 1967; admitted to bar, 1994, Connecticut and U.S. District Court, District of Connecticut. *Education:* Connecticut College (B.A., 1989); District of Columbia School of Law (J.D., 1994). Member, University of District of Columbia Law Review. Member, Moot Court. ***PRACTICE AREAS:*** Civil Litigation; Professional Liability; Premises Liability. ***Email:*** jallissi@cafpc.com

CRAIG A. FONTAINE, born Norwalk, Connecticut, July 27, 1955; admitted to bar, 1983, Kansas; 1984, Connecticut. *Education:* University of New Haven (B.S., 1977); Washburn University of Topeka (J.D., 1982). Associate Editor, ABA Arson Law Reporter, 1990-1992. Vice Chair, ABA Arson Law Project, 1992-1993. *Member:* Topeka, Kansas, Connecticut and American Bar Associations. ***LANGUAGES:*** French. ***Email:*** cfontaine@cafpc.com

MICHAEL J. DUGAN, born Philadelphia, Pennsylvania, June 17, 1963; admitted to bar, 1990, Pennsylvania, New Jersey and U.S. District Court, District of New Jersey; 1997, Connecticut; 1998, U.S. District Court, District of Connecticut. *Education:* Haverford College (B.A., 1985); Temple University (J.D., 1990). Articles Editor, Environmental Law Journal. *Member:* Connecticut and American Bar Associations; Defense Research Institute. ***PRACTICE AREAS:*** Civil Litigation; Personal Injury; Insurance Defense; Products Liability; Professional Malpractice; Toxic Torts; Sick Building Syndrome; Indoor Air Quality. ***Email:*** mdugan@cafpc.com

(This Listing Continued)

CRAMER, ALISSI & FONTAINE, P.C., Hartford—Continued

JAMES M. CELENTANO, born Hartford, Connecticut, October 17, 1969; admitted to bar, 1996, Connecticut; 1997, U.S. District Court, District of Connecticut. *Education:* University of Connecticut (B.A., 1992); University of Connecticut School of Law (J.D., 1996). ***PRACTICE AREAS:*** Insurance Law; Personal Injury; Bad Faith Litigation. ***Email:*** jcelentano@cafpc.com

CHRISTOPHER J. SOCHACKI, born San Antonio, Texas, January 1, 1971; admitted to bar, 1998, Connecticut; 1999, U.S. District Court, District of Connecticut. *Education:* Boston College (B.A., Political Science, 1993); Quinnipiac College (J.D., 1998). Phi Delta Phi. Member, 1996-1997 and Intramural Chairperson, 1997-1998, Moot Court Honor Society. *Member:* Connecticut and American Bar Associations. ***PRACTICE AREAS:*** Insurance Defense; Products Liability; Medical Malpractice; Civil Litigation. ***Email:*** csochacki@cafpc.com

RICHARD A. LORD, JR., born Derby, Connecticut, March 22, 1974; admitted to bar, 2000, Connecticut and U.S. District Court, District of Connecticut. *Education:* University of Connecticut (B.A., 1996); Quinnipiac College (J.D., 2000). Quinnipiac University Law Review, 1998-2000. Mock Trial Society, 1998-2000. *Member:* American Bar Association; Defense Research Institute; Connecticut Defense Lawyers Association. ***PRACTICE AREAS:*** Insurance Defense. ***Email:*** rlord@cafpc.com

STEVEN B. RYAN, born Cleveland, Ohio, June 12, 1974; admitted to bar, 2000, Connecticut; 2001, U.S. District Court, District of Connecticut. *Education:* Catawba College (B.A., 1996); New England School of Law (J.D., 1999). Member and Executive Case and Note Editor, New England Law Review, 1997-1999. Student Representative, Student Bar Association, 1996-1998. Staff Writer, Due Process. Republican Candidate 13th Assembly District Connecticut General Assembly, 2000. Commissioner, Manchester Housing Authority, 2000. *Member:* Hartford County, Connecticut and American Bar Associations; Association of Trial Lawyers of America. ***PRACTICE AREAS:*** Insurance Defense; Civil Rights Defense; Workers Compensation Defense; General Liability Defense. ***Email:*** sryan@cafpc.com

---

CRAMER & ANDERSON LLP

HARTFORD, CONNECTICUT

(See Litchfield)

General Practice. Probate, Estate Planning, Taxation, Municipal, Family, Real Estate, Negligence and Bankruptcy Law. Civil and Criminal Trials. Planning and Zoning, Corporate, Banking, Securities.

CRANMORE, FITZGERALD & MEANEY

49 WETHERSFIELD AVENUE
HARTFORD, CONNECTICUT 06114-1102
Telephone: 860-522-9100
Telecopier: 860-522-3379

Banking, Financial Services, Litigation, Real Estate, Corporate, Bankruptcy, Administrative Law and General Practice.

MEMBERS OF FIRM

J. J. CRANMORE, born Bronxville, New York, February 18, 1955; admitted to bar, 1979, District of Columbia; 1981, U.S. Court of Appeals, Fifth and Eleventh Circuits; 1983, Connecticut; 1991, Massachusetts. *Education:* Bates College (B.A., 1976); Catholic University of America (J.D., 1979); Georgetown University (LL.M., 1983). Catholic University Law Review, 1978-1979. Co-Author: "Banking Law," 1986, 1987, 1988, 1989, 1990, 1991 and 1992 Editions, Matthew Bender and Company; "Considerations Under The Federal Banking and Securities Laws With Respect to Bank Mergers or Takeovers," 36 Oklahoma Law Review 789, 1984. Author: "Court Encounters of The Slowest Kind: The District of Columbia's Implementations of the Amorphous Right to a Speedy Trial," 27 Catholic University Law Review 627, 1978; "Enforcement of Certain Provisions of the Securities Exchange Act of 1934 by the Office of the Comptroller of the Currency," Georgetown University Library, 1983. Attorney-Advisor, Office of the Comptroller of the Currency, Washington, D.C. and New York, N.Y., 1979-1983. Member, Advisory Council to the Banking Commissioner of the State of Connecticut on the Connecticut Securities Act, 1986—. Member, 1983-1984 and Vice Chairman, 1985, Charter Commission and Member, Board of Finance, 1985-1989, Town of Suffield. *Member:* Hartford County, Connecticut (Member, Executive Committee, Banking Law Section, 1986-2000) and American Bar Associations; Connecticut Bankers Association (Associate Member); Connecticut Community Bankers Association (Associate Member); New Hampshire Bankers Association (Associate Member).

(This Listing Continued)

JOHN C. FITZGERALD, JR., born Hartford, Connecticut, July 19, 1955; admitted to bar, 1980, Connecticut and U.S. District Court, District of Connecticut; 1982, U.S. Court of Appeals, Second Circuit; 1991, Massachusetts; 1993, U.S. District Court, District of Massachusetts. *Education:* Hampshire College (B.A., 1977); University of Connecticut (J.D., cum laude, 1980). Recipient, M. Joseph Blumenfeld Award, 1980. Adjunct Faculty: Appellate Advocacy, 1983-1989; Civil Procedure, 1990-1991, University of Connecticut School of Law. Member, Human Resource Committee, Horace Bushnell Memorial Hall, 1994—. Special Master, 1998— and Parajudicial Officer, 1999—, U.S. District Court, District of Connecticut, 1999—. *Member:* Hartford County, Connecticut and American Bar Associations; Connecticut Trial Lawyers Association.

JOSEPH V. MEANEY, JR., born Hartford, Connecticut, April 21, 1955; admitted to bar, 1980, Connecticut and U.S. District Court, District of Connecticut; 1985, District of Columbia; 1989, New York; 1991, Massachusetts; 1993, U.S. District Court, District of Massachusetts; 1995, U.S. Court of Appeals, Second Circuit. *Education:* Cornell University (B.A., 1977); University of Connecticut (J.D., 1980). Special Master, U.S. District Court, District of Connecticut, 1988—. Lecturer: "Lender Liability," Bank Lending Institute, 1988. *Member:* Hartford County, Connecticut and American (Member, Section on Litigation) Bar Associations; Connecticut Trial Lawyers Association; The Association of Trial Lawyers of America.

JOHN P. MCHUGH, born Queens, New York, January 21, 1960; admitted to bar, 1986, Connecticut; 1987, New York and U.S. District Court, District of Connecticut; 1988, New Hampshire. *Education:* State University of New York at Farmingdale (A.S., 1980); College of the Holy Cross (A.B., 1983); St. John's University (J.D., 1986). Contributing Author: Matthew Bender Banking Law Special Alert, March 1988. Co-Author: "Flood Hazard Insurance: Requirements Imposed Upon Bank Lenders When Extending Loans Secured By Real Estate," RELJ, Winter, 1987-1988. Lecturer: "Banking Law Principles and Applications," "Garnishments, Tax Levies, Subpoenas, Financial Privacy and Bankruptcy," American Institute of Banking. *Member:* Hartford County, Connecticut, New Hampshire and American Bar Associations.

PATRICIA D. ANDERSON, born New Haven, Connecticut, March 16, 1965; admitted to bar, 1990, Connecticut. *Education:* Albertus Magnus College (B.A. in Economics, 1987); Western New England College (J.D., cum laude, 1990). Recipient, American Jurisprudence Book Award, Torts. Contributing Author: "Banking Law," Cumulative Supplement, Matthew Bender and Company, 1991. Co-Authored: "Introduction to Federal and Connecticut Bank Regulation," Professional Education Systems, Inc., 1990. *Member:* Connecticut Bar Association (Member, Executive Committee, Financial Institutions Sections); American Society of Corporate Secretaries.

MICHAEL P. MCGOLDRICK, born Hartford, Connecticut, May 10, 1959; admitted to bar, 1991, Connecticut; 1993, U.S. District Court, District of Connecticut. *Education:* University of Notre Dame (B.B.A., 1981); University of Connecticut (J.D., 1991). Corporation Counsel, Town of West Hartford, 1998-1999. Commissioner, Metropolitan District Commission. *Member:* Connecticut and American Bar Associations; Connecticut Trial Lawyers Association.

ASSOCIATE

JENNIFER A. LEVACK, born Hartford, Connecticut, March 18, 1974; admitted to bar, 2000, Connecticut. *Education:* University of Connecticut (B.S., 1996); Western New England College (J.D., 1999). Phi Alpha Delta (Vice Justice, 1997-1998). Member, Western New England Law Review. Legal Counsel, Greater Hartford Junior Chamber of Commerce. *Member:* Connecticut Bar Association. ***LANGUAGES:*** Spanish.

REPRESENTATIVE CLIENTS: People's Bank; First National Bank of Suffield; Salisbury Bancorp, Inc.; Salisbury Bank and Trust Company; First Litchfield Financial Corporation; First National Bank of Litchfield; Citizens National Bancorp, Inc. and Citizens National Bank; Windsor Federal Savings & Loan Association; Liberty Bank; Edgartown National Bank (MA); Rockport National Bank (MA); Randolph National Bank (VT); First Brandon National Bank (VT); BTI Americas, Inc.; Connecticut Fair Plan; Lawrence Brunoli, Inc.; The Cornerstone Companies; The Richardson Mall; Family Meds, Inc.; Precision Dynamics, Inc.; TransAmerica Commercial Finance Corp.; Community Guaranty Savings Bank (NH).

CUMMINGS & LOCKWOOD

CITYPLACE I
185 ASYLUM STREET, 36TH FLOOR
HARTFORD, CONNECTICUT 06103-3495
Telephone: (860) 275-6700
Telecopier: (860) 724-3397
Email: info@cl-law.com
URL: http://www.cl-law.com

Stamford, Connecticut Office: Four Stamford Plaza, P.O. Box 120, 06904-0120. Telephone: (203) 327-1700. Telecopier: (203) 351-4535.

(This Listing Continued)

Greenwich, Connecticut Office: Two Greenwich Plaza, P.O. Box 2505, 06836. Telephone: (203) 869-1200. Telecopier: (203) 869-3120.
New Haven, Connecticut Office: 700 State Street, P.O. Box 1960. 06509-1960. Telephone: (203) 782-3000. Telecopier: (203) 777-3347.
West Hartford, Connecticut Office: Town Center, 29 South Main Street, Suite 208, 06107. Telephone: (860) 275-6700. Telecopier: (860) 313-0293.
Bonita Springs, Florida Office: 24311 Walden Center, Suite 201, 34134. Telephone: (941) 947-8811. Telecopier: (941) 947-8025.
Naples, Florida Office: 3001 Tamiami Trail North, P.O. Box 413032, 34101-3032. Telephone: (941) 262-8311. Telecopier: (941) 263-0703.

General Practice. National and Regional Litigation Counsel, Corporate Law, Patent and Intellectual Property, Trusts and Estates, Labor and Employment Law, Mergers and Acquisitions, Partnerships and Joint Ventures, Commercial Lending, Corporate Finance, Creditors' Rights, Bankruptcy and Workouts, Securities Regulation and Litigation, Tax, Insurance, Banking and Financial Services, Leasing, Commercial and Residential Real Estate, Construction, Environmental, Toxic Torts, Health Law, Products Liability Litigation, Probate Litigation, Family Law and International business.

FIRM PROFILE: Cummings & Lockwood caters both to commercial entities and individual clients, serves as local, regional and national counsel in Corporate, Litigation, and Creditors' Rights matters, and has one of the largest groups of Estate Planning professionals in the country.

Cummings & Lockwood attorneys answer questions and solve problems by having specialists in multiple disciplines practice together from eight offices to address the broad concerns of our diverse clientele. The firm guides corporate transactions and resolves complex business disputes for emerging, middle-market and Fortune 500 businesses, including high tech companies, financial services providers and industrial manufacturers. We are also uniquely positioned to assist affluent families and entrepreneurs in designing wealth preserving estate plans and developing business succession strategies.

PARTNERS

DONALD L. BOROD, born Cleveland, Ohio, June 22, 1947; admitted to bar, 1973, New York; 1983, Connecticut. *Education:* University of Michigan (B.A., 1969); Columbia University (J.D., 1972). Harlan Fiske Stone Scholar. Export Advisory Board, University of Connecticut Small Business Development Center, 1993—. Member, U.S. Department of Commerce Connecticut - Rhode Island District Export Council, 1996—. Advisory Council, University of Connecticut Center for International Business Education and Research (CIBER), 1996—. District Export Council, 1996—. Member: Export Advisory Board, Uconn Small Business Development Center, 1993—; Adjunct Faculty, Rensselaer at Hartford, 1995—; Adjunct Faculty, Uconn School of Business Administration, 1998—. Advisory Counsil, 1996—. *Member:* The Association of the Bar of the City of New York; Connecticut and American Bar Associations. ***PRACTICE AREAS:*** International Business; Distribution and Development Agreements; Joint Ventures; Corporate; Emerging Technologies. ***Email:*** dborod@cl-law.com

PAUL L. BOURDEAU, born Norfolk, Virginia, October 18, 1955; admitted to bar, 1980, Connecticut; 1981, Florida and Massachusetts. *Education:* Yale University (B.A., 1977); Boston University (J.D., cum laude, 1980); New York University (LL.M. in Taxation, 1984). Co-Author: "Connecticut Estates Practice-Trusts," Lawyers Cooperative Publishing Company, 1991. Fellow, American College of Trust and Estate Counsel. Selected for inclusion in The Best Lawyers in America. Past Chair, Estates and Probate Section, Connecticut Bar Association. Chair, Fiduciary Income Tax Committee, Section of Taxation, American Bar Association. ***PRACTICE AREAS:*** Estate Planning; Estate Administration; Charitable Giving. ***Email:*** pbourdeau@cl-law.com

LISA M. BOYLE, born Fall River, Mass., 1964; admitted to bar, 1989, Conn. *Education:* Emmanuel College (B.A., magna cum laude, 1986); Seton Hall Univ. School of Law (J.D., 1989). ***PRACTICE AREAS:*** Health Care; Public Finance; Corporate Finance. ***Email:*** lboyle@cl-law.com

WILLIAM H. BRIGHT, JR., born Camden, New Jersey, August 15, 1962; admitted to bar, 1987, Connecticut, 1988, U.S. District Court, District of Connecticut and Southern and Eastern Districts of New York; 1993, U.S. Court of Appeals, Federal Circuit. *Education:* Dickinson College (B.A., summa cum laude, 1984); University of Chicago (J.D., cum laude, 1987). Member, University of Chicago Law Review. ***PRACTICE AREAS:*** Civil Litigation; Franchise Disputes, Antitrust; Intellectual Property. ***Email:*** wbright@cl-law.com

TIMOTHY S. FISHER, born New Haven, Connecticut, December 12, 1953; admitted to bar, 1978, Connecticut. *Education:* Yale University (B.A., 1975); Columbia University (J.D., 1978). Author: *Connecticut Law of Check Fraud,* Atlantic Law Books, 1991; *Minimizing Risk in Municipal Construction Projects,* CIRMA, 1997. Adjunct Faculty, University of Connecticut School of Law. Faculty, Construction Institute of the University of Hartford Continuing & Professional Education Program. Faculty, "UCC Basic Skills," PLI: Lost, Stolen & Forged Instruments, Wrongful Dishonor, 1986-1990. Presenter, "Will Contests," Annual Connecticut Probate Assembly, 1990. Mediator and Arbitrator, American Arbitration Association, and other private and court-annexed ADR programs. Chair, Construction Advisory Council of American Arbitration Association (Connecticut). *Member:* Connecticut (Past Chair, Alternate Dispute Resolution Section; Executive Committee, Construction Section) and American (Member, Public Contract Law Section; Litigation Law Section; Forum Committee on the Construction Industry) Bar Associations. ***PRACTICE AREAS:*** Construction Disputes; Alternate Dispute Resolution; Check Fraud Law; Probate and Trust Litigation. ***Email:*** tfisher@cl-law.com

MARK D. GIARRATANA, born Montclair, New Jersey, November 2, 1960; admitted to bar, 1987, Connecticut and New York; 1992, U.S. District Court, District of Connecticut and U.S. District Courts, Southern and Eastern Districts of New York; registered to practice before U.S. Patent and Trademark Office. *Education:* Catholic University of America (B.S.M.E., 1982); University of Connecticut (J.D., with honors, 1987). Tau Beta Pi. Staff Member, Connecticut Journal of International Law, 1986-1987. Private Law Practice, 1987—. *Member:* Connecticut and American Bar Associations; American Intellectual Property Law Association; Connecticut Patent Law Association. ***REPORTED CASES:*** Construction Technology, Inc. v. Lockformer ET AL. ***PRACTICE AREAS:*** Patents; Trademarks; Copyrights; Antitrust; Unfair Competition; Computer Law; Intellectual Property. ***Email:*** mgiarratana@cl-law.com

ROBERT B. KATZ, born Hartford, Connecticut, October 16, 1947; admitted to bar, 1983, Connecticut. *Education:* University of Bridgeport (B.S., 1969); Western New England College (J.D., 1982). Special Master: Family Court of Hartford; Family Court of New Britain; Regional Custody Court, Middletown. *Member:* Hartford (Co-Chair, Family Law Committee, 1992-1994) and Connecticut (Member, Executive Committee, Family Law Section, 1996-1997) Bar Associations. ***PRACTICE AREAS:*** Family Law (100%). ***Email:*** rkatz@cl-law.com

WENDI J. KEMP, born Blue Island, Illinois, November 16, 1964; admitted to bar, 1989, Connecticut; 1992, U.S. District Court, District of Connecticut. *Education:* Northwestern University (B.S., with distinction, 1986); University of Connecticut (J.D., with honors, 1989). Recipient, Directors' Award. *Member:* Connecticut (Member, Section on Labor and Employment Law) and American (Member, Section on Labor and Employment Law) Bar Associations. ***PRACTICE AREAS:*** Labor Law; Employment Law; Education Law. ***Email:*** wkemp@cl-law.com

GINA S. LINSTONE (Resident, West Hartford, Connecticut Office).

JAMES I. LOTSTEIN, born Steubenville, Ohio, January 27, 1944; admitted to bar, 1969, Connecticut. *Education:* J.L. Kellogg Graduate School of Management, Northwestern University (B.S., 1965); University of Connecticut (J.D., 1968). Author: "An Introduction to the Connecticut Business Corporation Act," 5 *Connecticut Lawyer* 2 (October 1994); "Ten Things You Can Do Now to Prepare for the New Connecticut Business Corporation Act," 7 Connecticut Lawyer 1 (August/September 1996); "New Indemnification Provisions of the Connecticut Business Corporation Act," 8 Connecticut Lawyer 1 (August/September 1997); "Why Choose Connecticut? Advantages of the Connecticut Business Corporation Act Over the Delaware General Corporation Law," 10 Connecticut Lawyer 7 (April 2000). Co-Author: *Connecticut Business Corporation Act Sourcebook,* published by the Connecticut Bar Association and the Connecticut Law Reporter, 1997. *Member:* Connecticut (Co-Chair, Model Business Corporation Act Task Force, 1993—; Executive Committee, Business Law Section, 1976—, Chairman, 1990-1992) and American (Member, Corporate Laws Committee, 1992—; Chairman, Directors and Officers Task Force, 1994—, Business Law Section) Bar Associations. ***PRACTICE AREAS:*** Corporate Law; Securities Law; Finance; Banking Law. ***Email:*** jlotstein@cl-law.com

JOHN R. MALLIN, born Woonsocket, Rhode Island, July 28, 1950; admitted to bar, 1975, Connecticut and U.S. District Court, District of Connecticut; 1992, U.S. Court of Appeals, Second Circuit. *Education:* Providence College (A.B., summa cum laude, 1972); Harvard Law School (J.D., 1975). Delta Epsilon Sigma. Member, Civil Rights-Civil Liberties Law Review, 1974-1975. Treasurer, Harvard Law School Assn. Ct., 1996—. Member, Executive Committee, Connecticut Rivers Council Boy Scouts of America, 1990—, Counsel President, 1995-1997, Chairman, Corporate Advisory Committee, 1997—. Director, Business for Downtown Hartford, 1995—. ***PRACTICE AREAS:*** Commercial Real Estate; Leasing Law; Finance Law; Construction Law; Land Use Regulations; Corporate Law. ***Email:*** jmallin@cl-law.com

WILLIAM H. NARWOLD, born Miami, Oklahoma, September 11, 1952; admitted to bar, 1979, Connecticut and U.S. District Court, District of Connecticut; 1984, U.S. Court of Appeals, First, Second, Fourth, Fifth, Tenth, Eleventh and Federal Circuits and U.S. Supreme Court; 1985, U.S. District Court, Southern and Eastern Districts of New York. *Education:* Colby College (B.A., 1974); University of Connecticut (J.D., cum laude, 1979). Member, 1977-1978 and Managing Editor, 1978-1979 University of Connecticut Law Review. Law Clerk, Honorable Warren W. Eginton, U.S. District Judge, District of Connecticut, 1979-1981. (Firm Managing Partner) (Also at Stamford, Connecticut Office). ***PRACTICE AREAS:*** Appellate; Products and Professional Liability; Environmental Litigation. ***Email:*** wnarwold@cl-law.com

(This Listing Continued)

CUMMINGS & LOCKWOOD, Hartford—Continued

GREGORY B. NOKES, born Hartford, Connecticut, September 4, 1951; admitted to bar, 1980, Connecticut. *Education:* University of Vermont (B.S., summa cum laude, 1973); University of Connecticut (J.D., with honors, 1980). Member, 1978-1980 and Articles Editor, 1979-1980, Connecticut Law Review. (Also at Stamford, Connecticut Office). ***PRACTICE AREAS:*** Labor Law; Employment Law; Civil Litigation. ***Email:*** gnokes@cl-law.com

KEVIN D. O'LEARY, born Winchester, Massachusetts, December 6, 1963; admitted to bar, 1990, Connecticut and U.S. District Court, District of Connecticut; 1991, Massachusetts. *Education:* Tufts University (B.A., magna cum laude, 1986); University of Connecticut School of Law (J.D., with honors, 1989). *Member:* Connecticut Bar Association (Chair, Young Lawyers' Section, Labor and Employment Law, 1991—). ***PRACTICE AREAS:*** Labor Law; Employment Law; Workers' Compensation. ***Email:*** koleary@cl-law.com

CHARLES D. RAY, admitted to bar, 1989, Connecticut. *Education:* Indiana University of Pennsylvania (1976, B.A.); University of Connecticut (1989, J.D.). ***PRACTICE AREAS:*** Education Law (90%); Criminal Law (10%, 3). ***Email:*** cray@cl-law.com

RICHARD R. RENDEIRO, born New Haven, Connecticut, February 7, 1956; admitted to bar, 1984, Connecticut; 1986, New York; 1990, U.S. District Court, District of Connecticut. *Education:* University of Wisconsin (B.S., 1978); American University (J.D., 1984). ***PRACTICE AREAS:*** Commercial Real Estate; Commercial Finance; Bankruptcy Law. ***Email:*** rrende@cl-law.com

RICHARD VOIGT, born Oskaloosa, Iowa, January 20, 1946; admitted to bar, 1974, Virginia; 1980, Connecticut; 1982, U.S. District Court, District of Connecticut. *Education:* Wesleyan University (B.A., with honors, 1968; Limbach Prize); University of Virginia (J.D., 1974, Michie Legal Writing Award). Listed in Best Lawyers in America, Labor and Employment. *Member:* Connecticut, Federal and American (Member, Sections on: Labor Relations Law; Litigation; Member, Occupational Safety and Health) Bar Associations. ***PRACTICE AREAS:*** Labor Law; Employment Law; Litigation; Occupational Safety and Health Law. ***Email:*** rvoigt@cl-law.com

JANE KIMBALL WARREN, born Bridgeport, Connecticut, June 2, 1961; admitted to bar, 1986, Connecticut. *Education:* Bowdoin College (B.A., cum laude; magna cum laude in history, 1983); University of Connecticut (J.D., 1986). Author: "Lead Paint: Hazardous to Your Health and to the Real Estate Industry," in Probate & Property. Co-Author: "Why Lenders Still Have to Worry About Environmental Liability: An Update," in *Hazardous Waste and Toxic Torts Law and Strategy. Member:* Connecticut (President, Conservation and Environmental Quality Section) and American Bar Associations. ***PRACTICE AREAS:*** Environmental Law. ***Email:*** jwarren@cl-law.com

ERIC WATT WIECHMANN, born Schenectady, New York, June 12, 1948; admitted to bar, 1974, Connecticut; 1982, District of Columbia. *Education:* Hamilton College (B.A., 1970); Cornell University (J.D., 1974). Federal Pretrial Master, U.S. District Court, Connecticut, 1983-1992. State Attorney Trial Referee, 1986-1992. Member, Connecticut Law Revision Commission-Evidence Code Drafting Committee, Connecticut Superior Court-Civil Task Force. *Member:* Hartford, Connecticut (Chairman, Energy Law Committee, 1980-1982; Member, Executive Committee, Antitrust Law Section, 1982-1996; Past Chairman, Court Rules Advisory Committee) and American (Vice Chair, Toxic and Hazardous Substance Committee, TIPS Section) Bar Associations; Federal Bar Council; International Association of Defense Counsel; Defense Research Institute. ***PRACTICE AREAS:*** Civil Litigation; Products Liability; Toxic Tort Litigation; Antitrust Law. ***Email:*** ewiechmann@cl-law.com

HOLLY J. WINGER, born Lancaster, Pennsylvania, December 24, 1956; admitted to bar, 1981, Tennessee; 1983, New York; 1990, Connecticut. *Education:* Duke University (B.A., magna cum laude, with distinction, 1978); Vanderbilt University (J.D., 1981). *Member:* Federal Bar Association; Defense Research Institute. ***PRACTICE AREAS:*** Products Liability Law; Toxic Tort Defense Law; Commercial Litigation. ***Email:*** hwinger@cl-law.com

COUNSEL

LAUREN R. GREENSPOON, born Morristown, NJ, September 25, 1964; admitted to bar, 1989, Connecticut and Pennsylvania; 1990, U.S. District Court, District of Connecticut; 1993, U.S. Court of Appeals, Second Circuit. *Education:* University of Pennsylvania (B.A. cum laude, 1986); University of Pennsylvania Law School (J.D., 1989). ***LANGUAGES:*** French. ***PRACTICE AREAS:*** Securities Litigation; Commercial Litigation; Insurance Coverage; Bad Faith Litigation. ***Email:*** lgreenspoon@cl-law.com

MARGARET M. MURPHY, born Hartford, Connecticut, January 16, 1961; admitted to bar, 1988, Connecticut; 1990, U.S. District Court, District of Connecticut, U.S. Tax Court and U.S. Court of Federal Claims. *Education:* Mount Holyoke College (B.A., Economics, 1983); University of Connecticut (J.D., 1988). *Member:* Connecticut (Member, Estates and Probate Section) and American (Member, Sections on: Tax; Real Property, Probate and Estates) Bar Associations. ***PRACTICE AREAS:*** Estate Planning (60%); Probate (30%); Tax Law (10%). ***Email:*** mmurphy@cl-law.com

SENIOR ATTORNEY

ROBERT B. FAWBER (Resident, West Hartford, Connecticut Office).

RESIDENT ASSOCIATES

Christopher T. Calio
Joel B. Casey
George Chaclas
Karen P. Conway
Patrick J. Day
James F. DeDonato (admission pending)
Mukta Dhumale (admission pending)
Alfred A. DiVincentis, Jr.
Robert J. Gallo
Fiona M. Greaves
Eric E. Grondahl
Kristina M. Hendrickson
Peter W. Hull
David M. Mack
Ingrid L. Moll (admission pending)
W. Joseph Nielsen
Moyahoena N. Ogilvie
Heather J. Rhoades
Robert L. Rispoli
Vanessa D. Roberts
Steven D. Shaffer
Barbara A. Sheehy (admission pending)
Alexandra B. Stevens
Jason C. Welch (admission pending)
Evelyn V. Williams
Allison A. Wood

(For complete biographical information on personnel, see Professional Biographies at Stamford, CT, Greenwich, CT, West Hartford, CT, New Haven, CT, Bonita Springs, FL and Naples, FL)

DANAHER, TEDFORD, LAGNESE & NEAL, P.C.

CAPITOL PLACE
21 OAK STREET
HARTFORD, CONNECTICUT 06106
Telephone: 860-247-3666
Telecopier: 860-547-1321
Email: dtln@dtln.com

Westport Office: 3 Sylvan Road South. Telephone: 203-226-3646.

Litigation in State and Federal Courts, Toxic Tort, Insurance Coverage, Insurance Defense, Product Liability, Personal Injury, Criminal, Corporate, Securities, Commercial, Bankruptcy, Real Estate, Land Use, Environmental, Probate, Estate and Tax Law. Medical, Legal, Accountant, Architect and Engineer Professional Malpractice, Fire and Arson Litigation.

R. CORNELIUS DANAHER, JR., born Washington, D.C., March 15, 1947; admitted to bar, 1973, Connecticut. *Education:* Georgetown University (B.A., 1969; J.D., 1973). Executive Editor, American Criminal Law Review (GULC), 1972-1973. Author: "Duty to Defend," Insurance Coverage and Practice: DRI—Course Book, May, 1985; "Insurance Perspectives in Drug Litigation," Toxic Tort Section of the American Bar Association Convention, Washington, D.C., July, 1985. Member, 1975-1979 and Deputy Mayor, 1977-1979, West Hartford Town Council. Chairman, West Hartford Public Safety Committee, 1975-1979. Member, Board of Directors, West Hartford YMCA, 1982-1985. Chairman, West Hartford Charter Revision Committee, 1982-1983. Member, Board of Governors, 1982-1983 and Member of Senate, 1983—, Georgetown University Alumni Association. *Member:* Hartford County, Connecticut (Member, Executive Committee, Planning and Zoning Section, 1985—), Federal and American (Member, Sections on: Litigation; Insurance, Negligence and Compensation Law; Vice Chairman, Committee on Toxic and Hazardous Substances and Environmental Law, 1985—) Bar Associations; Defense Research Institute; Connecticut Defense Lawyers Association. (Also at Westport Office).

FREDERICK B. TEDFORD, born Manchester, Connecticut, January 22, 1947; admitted to bar, 1972, Connecticut; 1973, U.S. Court of Military Appeals; 1978, U.S. District Court, District of Connecticut. *Education:* University of Connecticut (B.A., 1969); Suffolk University (J.D., 1972). *Member:* Hartford County, Connecticut (Member, Trial Section) and American Bar Associations; Defense Research Institute; Connecticut Defense Lawyers Association; The Association of Trial Lawyers of America (Associate Member); International Association of Arson Investigators; National Fire Protection Association; Connecticut Chapter of International Association of Arson Investigations. [Capt., USAF, 1972-1977]. (Also at Westport Office).

JOYCE A. LAGNESE, born Providence, Rhode Island, May 15, 1955; admitted to bar, 1980, Connecticut; 1981, U.S. District Court for the District of Connecticut. *Education:* State University of New York at Oneonta (B.S., with high honors, 1977); Hofstra University School of Law (J.D., with honors, 1980).

(This Listing Continued)

Member: Hartford County, Connecticut (Member, Sections on: Commercial Law; Civil Justice; Family Law) and American Bar Associations; Defense Research Institute; Connecticut Trial Lawyers Association; The Association of Trial Lawyers of America.

KENNETH R. NEAL, born Philadelphia, Pennsylvania, December 29, 1942; admitted to bar, 1969, Rhode Island; 1971, U.S. District Court, District of Rhode Island; 1974, U.S. Court of Appeals, First Circuit; 1982, District of Columbia and U.S. District Court, District of Columbia; 1986, U.S. District Court, District of Connecticut; 1987, Connecticut. *Education:* Brown University (B.A., 1966); Boston College (J.D., 1969). Member, Commission on Judicial Tenure and Discipline of the State of Rhode Island, 1975-1984. Probate Judge, City of East Providence, 1978-1980. *Member:* Connecticut, Rhode Island and American Bar Associations; The District of Columbia Bar; Defense Research Institute.

FRANK H. SANTORO, born Providence, Rhode Island, July 5, 1942; admitted to bar, 1968, District of Columbia and Maryland; 1976, U.S. District Court, District of Connecticut; 1979, Connecticut. *Education:* Georgetown University (A.B., 1964; J.D., 1967); University of Edinburgh, Scotland; University of London, London, England (LL.M., 1971). Delta Theta Phi. Author: "The National Environmental Policy Act in Connecticut," 62 Connecticut Bar Journal 290 (October 1988); "A Practical Guide to the Federal Tort Claims Act," 63 Connecticut Bar Journal 224 (August 1989); Connecticut Environmental Companies (1993) . Adjunct Lecturer, American University Law School, Washington, D.C., 1973-1974. Assistant U.S. Attorney, Connecticut, 1976-1989. Assistant Public Defender, Montgomery County, Maryland, 1973-1976. Assistant State's Attorney, Montgomery County, Maryland, 1971-1973. Chief, Civil Division, U.S. Attorney's Office, District of Connecticut, 1977-1989. Senior Litigation Counsel, Department of Justice, 1980-1988. Bencher Member, Oliver Ellsworth Inn of Court. Special Counsel, Connecticut State Department of Environmental Protection, 1992-1993. *Member:* Connecticut and American Bar Associations. [Capt., U.S. Army, 1968-1970]

CALUM B. ANDERSON, born Buffalo, New York, July 14, 1951; admitted to bar, 1977, Massachusetts; 1991, Connecticut. *Education:* Gettysburg College (A.B., magna cum laude, 1973); Boston College (J.D., 1976). Phi Beta Kappa. Managing and Business Editor, Boston College Law Review and Annual Survey of Massachusetts Law, 1975-1976. Author: "Analyzing Environmental Insurance Coverage Claims Under Connecticut Law", 66 Connecticut Bar Journal 275 (1992); "Insurance Coverage for Employment Related Litigation: Connecticut Law," 18 W. New England L. Rev. 199 (1996). Trial Advisor, Harvard Law School Trial Advocacy Workshop, 1989-1993. ***Email:*** CANDERSON@DTLN.COM

MATTHEW G. CONWAY, born Buffalo, New York, August 26, 1966; admitted to bar, 1991, Connecticut; 1992, U.S. District Court, District of Connecticut. *Education:* Boston College (B.A., cum laude, 1988); Suffolk University (J.D., cum laude, 1991). Note, "Sports Commissioners or Judges: Who Should Make the Call When the Game is Over?" 24 Suffolk University Law Review 1043, 1990. Lead Articles Editor, 1990-1991, Staff Member, 1989-1990, Suffolk University Law Review. Adjunct Instructor, University of Connecticut School of Law, 1994-1999. *Member:* Hartford County, Connecticut and American Bar Associations; Connecticut Defense Lawyers Association; Connecticut Trial Lawyers Association. ***PRACTICE AREAS:*** Products Liability; Personal Injury. ***Email:*** mconway@DTLN.com

PAUL T. EDWARDS, born Danbury, Connecticut, January 20, 1966; admitted to bar, 1991, Connecticut; 1994, U.S. District Court, District of Connecticut. *Education:* College of William & Mary (B.A., 1988); University of Bridgeport (J.D., cum laude, 1991). Recipient, American Jurisprudence Award for Contracts. Member, University of Bridgeport Law Review, 1989-1991. Law Clerk to Honorable Frederick A. Freedman, Associate Judge, Connecticut Appellate Court, 1991-1992. Adjunct Professor, University of Connecticut School of Law, 1998-2000. *Member:* Hartford County, Connecticut (Member, Young Lawyers Section) and American Bar Associations; Connecticut Medical Defense Lawyers Association. ***PRACTICE AREAS:*** Civil Litigation; Medical Malpractice; Products Liability; Toxic Tort; Professional Liability; Appellate Advocacy. ***Email:*** PEdwards@DTLN.com

ROBERT E. KILEY, born New York, N.Y., December 4, 1962; admitted to bar, 1987, Connecticut; 1988, New York and U.S. District Court, District of Connecticut. *Education:* Connecticut College (B.A., cum laude, 1984); University of Connecticut (J.D., 1987). Law Clerk, Connecticut Superior Court, 1987-1988. *Member:* Hartford County, Connecticut, New York State and Federal Bar Associations; Connecticut Medical Defense Lawyer's Association. ***LANGUAGES:*** Spanish and French. ***PRACTICE AREAS:*** Medical Malpractice Defense; Civil Trial Practice; Insurance Defense. ***Email:*** rkiley@DTLN.com

THOMAS O. ANDERSON, born Brattleboro, Vermont, April 29, 1959; admitted to bar, 1984, Oklahoma; 1985, Massachusetts, U.S. Court of Federal Claims and U.S. Court of Appeals for the Federal Circuit; 1988, Connecticut; 1989, U.S. District Court, District of Connecticut. *Education:* University of Vermont (B.A., 1981); University of Tulsa College of Law (J.D., 1984). Lecturer: "How To Take a Deposition; "How To Try Automobile Case in Connecticut: A Defense Perspective, The Basics of Civil Practice and Advanced Personal Injury: A Defense Perspective (National Business Institute), New Physician's Seminar (CMIC). Author: "The Super Lien and You" (Young, R., Anderson, T. and Grover K.); "Lead litigation: Defendants Beware." Fact Finder and Arbitrator, Superior Court. *Member:* New Britain, Hartford County, Connecticut and Massachusetts Bar Associations. (Certified as a Civil Trial Advocacy Specialist by the National Board of Trial Advocacy). ***PRACTICE AREAS:*** Civil Litigation; Insurance Defense; Medical Malpractice Defense; Professional Liability Defense; Products Liability. ***Email:*** tanderson@dtln.com

(This Listing Continued)

STACEY L. DE ROSA, born New Haven, Connecticut, March 11, 1976; admitted to bar, 2001, Connecticut. *Education:* University of Maryland, College Park (B.A., Government and Politics; Spanish, 1998); Quinnipiac University School of Law (J.D., 2001). Phi Delta Phi. Member, Quinnipiac Law Review, Lead Articles Editor. ***PRACTICE AREAS:*** Litigation. ***Email:*** sderosa@dtln.com

NANCY A. DeROSE, born Stratford, Connecticut, June 10, 1968; admitted to bar, 1993, Connecticut; 1994, U.S. District Court, District of Connecticut. *Education:* Fairfield University (B.A., 1990); Western New England College (J.D., 1993). Phi Sigma Alpha. *Member:* Bridgeport (Member: Criminal Law and Litigation Section) and Connecticut (Member: Litigation Section; Executive Committee; Legislative Liaison) Bar Associations; Connecticut Trial Lawyers Association; Connecticut Criminal Defense Lawyers Association; National Association of Criminal Defense Lawyers. ***REPORTED CASES:*** Luce v. City of West Haven, 238 Conn. 687 (1996); Dubozy v. Dubozy, 41 Conn. App. 861 (1996); State v. Varszegi, 236 Conn. 266 (1996); State v. Swell, 38 Conn. App. 20 (1995). ***PRACTICE AREAS:*** Medical Malpractice; Personal Injury. ***Email:*** nderose@dtln.com

BRIAN P. HENRY, born Magnolia, Arkansas, July 26, 1974; admitted to bar, 1999, Connecticut; 2000, U.S. District Court, District of Connecticut. *Education:* Henderson State University (B.A., 1996); University of Arkansas (J.D., cum laude, 1999). Research Editor, Arkansas Law Review, 1998-1999. Author: "The Moral Watchdogs Ride Again-The Arkansas Supreme Court Condemns An All-American Pastime," 52 Ark. Law Review 453 (1999). *Member:* Connecticut and American Bar Associations. ***PRACTICE AREAS:*** Insurance Defense; Civil Litigation. ***Email:*** bhenry@dtln.com

M. KAREN NOBLE, born Tacloban City, Philippines, July 31, 1968; admitted to bar, 1993, Connecticut; 1994, U.S. District Court, District of Connecticut; 1995, New York. *Education:* Boston College (B.A., 1990; J.D., 1993). Phi Alpha Delta. *Member:* Hartford, Connecticut and American Bar Associations; American Trial Lawyers Association (Member, Medical-Legal Committees, 1994—); Connecticut Defense Lawyers Association; Defense Research Institute. ***LANGUAGES:*** Tagalog, Visayan. ***PRACTICE AREAS:*** Medical Malpractice Defense; Litigation. ***Email:*** KNOBLE@DTLN.COM

ANDREW S. WILDSTEIN, born New Haven, Connecticut, September 11, 1971; admitted to bar, 1996, Connecticut; 1997, New York. *Education:* Connecticut College (B.A., Government, with distinction, 1993); Hofstra University (J.D., 1996). Member, Hofstra Labor Law Journal. Notes and Comments Editor, Hofstra Environmental Law Digest, 1994-1996. *Member:* New York State Bar Association. ***PRACTICE AREAS:*** Medical Malpractice Defense; Civil Litigation. ***Email:*** awildstein@dtln.com

OF COUNSEL

ROBERT C. DANAHER, born Hartford, Connecticut, December 22, 1922; admitted to bar, 1949, Connecticut and District of Columbia. *Education:* Georgetown University (A.B., 1946; J.D., 1948); Duke University. Member, Georgetown University Law Journal, 1948. Author: "The Hartford Letter," 1958-1985. Lecturer in Law, University of Connecticut School of Law, 1951-1971. Member: Board of Governors, 1958-1961; Senate, 1962—, Georgetown University Alumni Association. *Member:* Hartford County (Member, Executive Board, 1964-1965, 1969-1970), Connecticut (Vice Chairman, 1954-1955 and Chairman, 1955-1956, Real Property Section; Chairman, Committee on Legislation, 1961-1971; Member: Joint Committee with State Medical Society, 1957-1959; Administration of Civil Justice Committee, 1969-1971; Bench-Bar Relations Committee, 1972-1976; Secretary, Real Property Committee, 1964-1965; Member, Executive Committee, Civil Justice Section, 1981-1985; Treasurer, 1971-1972), Federal (Hartford County Chapter, Treasurer, 1975-1977) and American (Member, Committee on State Legislation, 1965-1972) Bar Associations; Defense Research Institute; Connecticut Defense Lawyers Association; Connecticut Attorneys Title Insurance Company (Member, 1966—, and Chairman, 1983-1996, Board of Directors).

DAY, BERRY & HOWARD LLP

Established in 1919

CITYPLACE I

HARTFORD, CONNECTICUT 06103-3499

Telephone: 860-275-0100

Telecopier: 860-275-0343

Email: postmaster@dbh.com

URL: http://www.dbh.com

Greenwich, Connecticut Office: One East Putnam Avenue. Telephone: 203-862-7800.

Stamford, Connecticut Office: One Canterbury Green. Telephone: 203-977-7300. Telecopier: 203-977-7301.

Boston, Massachusetts Office: 260 Franklin Street. Telephone: 617-345-4600. Telecopier: 617-345-4745.

Antitrust, Banking, Bank Lending, Bankruptcy, Bankruptcy Counseling, Benefits and Executive Compensation, Business Succession Planning, Business Transactions and Counseling, Closely Held Businesses, Credit Tenant Lease Financing, Commercial Litigation, Commercial Leasing, Construction, Direct Liability and Casualty Insurance, Disability, Emerging Companies, Energy, Environmental and Land Use, Equipment Finance and Leasing, Employment Law and Litigation, Environmental Law and Litigation, Executive Planning, Family Law, Finance and Investments, First Party Insurance, Franchise and Distributorship Litigation, Government Investigations, Health Care, Insurance Regulation and Proceedings, Insurance Litigation, International Tax, International Transactions, Life Insurance and Annuities, Low Income Housing Tax Credits, Medical and Professional Malpractice, Mergers and Acquisitions, Multi-Property Transactions, Municipal Finance, Negligence Defense, Planning for Entrepreneurs, Private Equity Funds, Product Liability, Real Estate Development, Real Estate Equity Investors, Real Estate Finance, Real Estate Workouts and Restructuring, Regulatory Insurance Proceedings and Litigation, Reinsurance, Securities Law, Securities Litigation, Strategic Joint Ventures, Structured Finance, Tax, Tax Litigation Group, Tax Exempt and Charity Giving, Tax Exempt Organizations, Technology and Intellectual Property Business and Litigation, Torts Litigation, Telecommunications, Trusts and Estates Administration, Trusts and Estates Litigation, Water Companies.

MEMBERS OF FIRM IN HARTFORD

J. DANFORD ANTHONY, JR., born Boston, MA, 1935; admitted to bar, 1961, Minnesota; 1964, U.S. Supreme Court, U.S. Tax Court and U.S. Court of Federal Claims; 1965, Connecticut, U.S. Court of Appeals, Second Circuit and U.S. District Court, District of Connecticut. *Education:* Wesleyan University (A.B., 1957); Harvard Law School (LL.B., 1960). ***PRACTICE AREAS:*** Tax; Tax-Exempt Organizations; Municipal Finance. ***Email:*** jdanthony@dbh.com

ELIZABETH C. BARTON, born New Rochelle, NY, July 22, 1952; admitted to bar, 1977, CT. *Education:* Tufts Univ. (B.A., magna cum laude, 1974); Univ. of Connecticut (J.D., 1977). ***PRACTICE AREAS:*** Administrative Law; Environmental; Utility Law; Legislative Representation.

MATTHEW J. BECKER, born Princeton, NJ, 1966; admitted to bar, 1991, Connecticut; 1992, U.S. District Court, District of Connecticut; registered to practice before U.S. Patent and Trademark Office. *Education:* Indiana University (B.S., 1988; J.D., summa cum laude, 1991). ***PRACTICE AREAS:*** Commercial Litigation; Technology & Intellectual Property - Litigation; Technology & Intellectual Property - Business. ***Email:*** mjbecker@dbh.com

PAUL N. BELVAL, born Worcester, MA, 1962; admitted to bar, 1989, Connecticut; 1990, New York. *Education:* University of Massachusetts (B.A., cum laude, 1984); Pace University School of Law (J.D., magna cum laude, 1989). ***PRACTICE AREAS:*** Energy; Telecommunications. ***Email:*** pnbelval@dbh.com

HAROLD M. BLINDERMAN, born Waterford, CT, July 15, 1957; admitted to bar, 1988, CT. *Education:* Clark Univ. (B.A., 1979); Syracuse Univ. (M.P.A., 1987; J.D., 1987). ***PRACTICE AREAS:*** Environmental Law; Administrative Law; Utilities Law.

ROBERT A. BROOKS, born Providence, RI, 1953; admitted to bar, 1981, Connecticut. *Education:* Bates College (B.A., 1975); University of Connecticut (J.D., 1981). ***PRACTICE AREAS:*** Technology & Intellectual Property - Litigation; Commercial Litigation. ***Email:*** rabrooks@dbh.com

MICHAEL A. BUCCI, born Yonkers, NY, 1962; admitted to bar, 1991, California; 1995, Connecticut. *Education:* Syracuse University (B.S., 1984); University of California, Hastings College of the Law (J.D., summa cum laude, 1991). ***PRACTICE AREAS:*** Technology and Intellectual Property - Litigation; Commercial Litigation. ***Email:*** mabucci@dbh.com

VICTORIA WOODIN CHAVEY, born Chattanooga, TN, 1966; admitted to bar, 1992, Connecticut; 1994, U.S. District Court, District of Connecticut. *Education:* Dartmouth College (B.A., cum laude, 1988); Boston University School of Law (J.D., summa cum laude, 1992). ***PRACTICE AREAS:*** Employment Litigation; Employment Law. ***Email:*** vwchavey@dbh.com

(This Listing Continued)

DEAN M. CORDIANO, born Brooklyn, NY, 1952; admitted to bar, 1976, Connecticut and U.S. District Court, District of Connecticut; 1979, U.S. Court of Appeals, Second Circuit. *Education:* State University of New York at Binghamton (B.A., 1973); Duke University (J.D., 1976). ***PRACTICE AREAS:*** Environmental; Land Use. ***Email:*** dmcordiano@dbh.com

DAVID T. DOOT, born Orange, NJ, 1957; admitted to bar, 1985, Connecticut. *Education:* Cornell University (B.S., 1978); T. C. Williams School of Law (J.D., 1985). ***PRACTICE AREAS:*** Energy. ***Email:*** dtdoot@dbh.com

GLENN W. DOWD, born Bridgeport, CT, 1961; admitted to bar, 1989, Connecticut; 1996, U.S. Court of Appeals, Second Circuit. *Education:* Central Connecticut State University (B.S., cum laude, 1984); University of Connecticut (J.D., magna cum laude, 1989). ***PRACTICE AREAS:*** Employment Law; Employment Litigation. ***Email:*** gwdowd@dbh.com

DAVID J. ELLIOTT, born Hartford, CT, 1953; admitted to bar, 1978, Connecticut; 1979, U.S. District Court, District of Connecticut. *Education:* University of Connecticut (B.A., cum laude, 1975); Suffolk University (J.D., cum laude, 1978). ***PRACTICE AREAS:*** Securities Litigation; Commercial Litigation. ***Email:*** djelliott@dbh.com

MICHAEL W. ELSASS, born Heidelberg, Germany, 1952; admitted to bar, 1982, Connecticut. *Education:* Washington University (B.A., 1973); Cornell University (M.A.T., 1975); University of Washington (J.D., cum laude, 1980). ***PRACTICE AREAS:*** Trusts and Estates Administration; Trusts and Estates Litigation; Estate Planning. ***Email:*** mwelsass@dbh.com

STEVEN M. FAST, born New Haven, CT, 1947; admitted to bar, 1971, Connecticut. *Education:* Dartmouth College (B.A., 1968); Columbia University (J.D., 1971). ***PRACTICE AREAS:*** Trusts and Estate Administration; Trust and Estate Litigation; Estate Planning. ***Email:*** smfast@dbh.com

DIANE M. FITZGERALD, born Newport, RI, 1955; admitted to bar, 1982, Maine; 1986, Connecticut. *Education:* Georgetown University (A.B., magna cum laude, 1977); University of Connecticut School of Law (J.D., with high honors, 1982). ***PRACTICE AREAS:*** Benefits and Executive Compensation; Mergers and Acquisitions. ***Email:*** dmfitzgerald@dbh.com

DANIEL L. FITZMAURICE, born Waterbury, CT, 1954; admitted to bar, 1979, Connecticut; 1983, U.S. District Court, District of Connecticut; 1989, U.S. Court of Appeals, Second Circuit; 1990, U.S. Supreme Court; 1994, U.S. Court of Appeals, District of Columbia Circuit; 1995, U.S. Court of Appeals, Third Circuit. *Education:* University of Connecticut (B.S., summa cum laude, 1976); University of Michigan (J.D., cum laude, 1978). ***PRACTICE AREAS:*** Commercial Litigation; Insurance Litigation; Direct Liability and Casualty; Disability Insurance; Life Insurance and Annuities; Franchise and Distributorship Litigation; Reinsurance; Regulatory Insurance Proceedings and Litigation. ***Email:*** dlfitzmaurice@dbh.com

CHARLES W. FORTUNE, born New York, NY, 1957; admitted to bar, 1989, Connecticut; 1990, U.S. District Court, District of Connecticut. *Education:* University of Rochester (B.A., 1979); University of Connecticut School of Law (J.D., 1989). ***PRACTICE AREAS:*** Insurance Litigation; Commercial Litigation; Direct Liability and Casualty; Reinsurance. ***Email:*** cwfortune@dbh.com

GERALD GARFIELD, born Detroit, MI, 1946; admitted to bar, 1971, Connecticut. *Education:* University of Michigan (B.A., 1968; J.D., cum laude, 1971). ***PRACTICE AREAS:*** Energy. ***Email:*** ggarfield@dbh.com

STEVEN M. GREENSPAN, born Hartford, CT, 1960; admitted to bar, 1985, Connecticut and U.S. District Court, District of Connecticut; 1989, U.S. Court of Appeals, First and Second Circuits; 1998, U.S. District Court, Southern District of New York. *Education:* University of Pennsylvania (B.A., 1982); University of Connecticut (J.D., magna cum laude, 1985). ***PRACTICE AREAS:*** Franchise and Distributorship Litigation; Commercial Litigation. ***Email:*** smgreenspan@dbh.com

THOMAS J. GROARK, JR., born Bridgeport, CT, 1937; admitted to bar, 1965, Connecticut. *Education:* College of the Holy Cross (A.B., 1958); University of Connecticut (LL.B., 1965). ***PRACTICE AREAS:*** Securities Litigation; Direct Liability and Casualty; Commercial Litigation; Insurance Litigation; Regulatory Insurance Proceedings and Litigation; Life Insurance and Annuities. ***Email:*** tjgroark@dbh.com

JEFFREY G. GRODY, born Hartford, CT, 1955; admitted to bar, 1980, Connecticut. *Education:* Princeton University (A.B., magna cum laude, 1977); Columbia University (J.D., 1980). ***PRACTICE AREAS:*** Closely Held Businesses; Bankruptcy; Finance and Investments; Emerging Companies; Bankruptcy Counseling. ***Email:*** jggrody@dbh.com

MICHAEL F. HALLORAN, born Waterbury, CT, 1940; admitted to bar, 1965, Connecticut. *Education:* Yale University (B.A., 1962); Yale Law School (LL.B., 1965). ***PRACTICE AREAS:*** Water Companies; Energy. ***Email:*** mfhalloran@dbh.com

J. ROGER HANLON, born Asbury Park, NJ, 1938; admitted to bar, 1964, Connecticut. *Education:* Dartmouth College (B.A., 1960); Cornell University

(This Listing Continued)

(LL.B., 1963). ***PRACTICE AREAS:*** Real Estate Finance; Commercial Leasing; Real Estate Development; Real Estate Workouts and Restructuring. ***Email:*** jrhanlon@dbh.com

MITCHELL R. HARRIS, born White Plains, NY, 1964; admitted to bar, 1990, Connecticut; 1991, U.S. District Court, District of Connecticut. *Education:* Trinity College (B.A., 1987); Georgetown University Law Center (J.D., 1990). ***PRACTICE AREAS:*** Commercial Litigation; Insurance Litigation. ***Email:*** mrharris@dbh.com

RICHARD D. HARRIS, born New York, NY, 1961; admitted to bar, 1990, Connecticut and U.S. District Court, District of Connecticut. *Education:* Wharton School, University of Pennsylvania (B.S.E., magna cum laude, 1983); University of Connecticut School of Law (J.D., with high honors, 1990). ***PRACTICE AREAS:*** Technology and Intellectual Property - Business; Emerging Companies; International Transactions; Strategic Joint Ventures. ***Email:*** rdharris@dbh.com

THOMAS F. HARRISON, born Brooklyn, NY, 1942; admitted to bar, 1967, New York; 1979, Illinois; 1981, Ohio; 1988, District of Columbia; 1989, Connecticut. *Education:* College of the Holy Cross (A.B., 1963); Fordham Law School (J.D., 1966). ***PRACTICE AREAS:*** Environmental and Land Use. ***Email:*** tfharris@dbh.com

TRICIA A. HAUGHT, born Warwick, RI, 1961; admitted to bar, 1989, Connecticut; 1996, Massachusetts. *Education:* Amherst College (A.B., 1983); University of Connecticut (J.D., with high honors, 1988). ***PRACTICE AREAS:*** Environmental and Land Use. ***Email:*** tahaught@dbh.com

PAULA LACEY HERMAN, born Duncan, OK, 1948; admitted to bar, 1978, Connecticut. *Education:* Washburn University (B.A., 1970); State University of New York (M.A., 1975); Yale Law School (J.D., 1978). ***PRACTICE AREAS:*** Mergers and Acquisitions; Emerging Companies; Private Equity Funds; Finance and Investments; Securities Law; International Transactions; Antitrust. ***Email:*** plherman@dbh.com

ROBERT P. KNICKERBOCKER, JR., born Hartford, CT, 1944; admitted to bar, 1969, Connecticut. *Education:* Cornell University (B.A., 1966); University of Connecticut (J.D., 1969). ***PRACTICE AREAS:*** Energy; Telecommunications. ***Email:*** rpknickerbocker@dbh.com

CHARLES H. LENORE, born Jacksonville, FL, 1953; admitted to bar, 1978, Connecticut. *Education:* University of Connecticut (B.A., cum laude, 1975); Syracuse University (J.D., summa cum laude, 1978). ***PRACTICE AREAS:*** Emerging Companies; Technology and Intellectual Property - Business; Closely Held Businesses; Tax. ***Email:*** chlenore@dbh.com

TIMOTHY R. LYMAN, born St. Louis, MO, 1957; admitted to bar, 1987, Connecticut. *Education:* Harvard University (B.A., 1980); New York University (J.D., 1987). ***LANGUAGES:*** Spanish, French, Bosnian, Croatian, Serbian, German, Russian. ***PRACTICE AREAS:*** Finance and Investment; Tax Exempt Organizations; International Transactions. ***Email:*** trlyman@dbh.com

DANIEL S. MATOS, born Hartford, CT, 1950; admitted to bar, 1976, Connecticut. *Education:* University of Connecticut (B.A., 1973); Temple University (J.D., 1976). ***PRACTICE AREAS:*** Real Estate Developments; Real Estate Workouts and Restructuring; Commercial Leasing; Real Estate Finance. ***Email:*** dsmatos@dbh.com

ERNEST J. MATTEI, born New Haven, CT, 1948; admitted to bar, 1975, Connecticut; 1976, U.S. District Court, District of Connecticut and U.S. District Court, Eastern and Southern Districts of New York; U.S. Court of Appeals, Second Circuit. *Education:* Trinity College (B.A., 1970); Georgetown University (J.D., 1975). ***PRACTICE AREAS:*** Insurance Litigation; Commercial Litigation; Family Law; First Party Insurance. ***Email:*** ejmattei@dbh.com

PAUL F. McALENNEY, born Hartford, CT, 1942; admitted to bar, 1967, Connecticut. *Education:* Yale University (B.A., 1964); Yale Law School (LL.B., 1967). ***PRACTICE AREAS:*** Closely Held Businesses; Mergers and Acquisitions; Benefits and Executive Compensation; Banking; Insurance Regulation and Proceedings. ***Email:*** pfmcalenney@dbh.com

JAMES A. McGRAW, born Albany, NY, 1950; admitted to bar, 1975, Connecticut; 1998, Massachusetts. *Education:* Dartmouth College (A.B., 1972); Boston University (J.D., 1975). ***PRACTICE AREAS:*** Real Estate Equity Investors; Real Estate Finance; Real Estate Development; Real Estate Workouts; Real Estate Restructuring. ***Email:*** jamcgraw@dbh.com

KATHLEEN DONDERO MONNES, born Meriden, CT, 1966; admitted to bar, 1992, Connecticut; 1993, U.S. District Court, District of Connecticut. *Education:* Connecticut College (B.A., cum laude, 1988); George Washington University National Law Center (J.D., with high honors, 1992). ***PRACTICE AREAS:*** Insurance Litigation; Commercial Litigation; Direct Liability and Casualty; First Party Insurance; Disability Insurance; Regulatory Insurance Proceedings and Litigation; Life Insurance and Annuities. ***Email:*** kdmonnes@dbh.com

FRANCIS H. MORRISON III, born Springfield, MA, 1947; admitted to bar, 1975, Connecticut; 1999, Massachusetts; U.S. District Court, Southern and Eastern Districts of New York; U.S. Court of Appeals, First and Second Circuits.

(This Listing Continued)

Education: College of the Holy Cross (A.B., 1969); Duke University (J.D., 1975). [Line Officer, U.S. Navy (1969-1972)]. Certified as a Civil Trial Advocate by the National Board of Trial Advocacy. (Chair, Firm Executive Committee, 1996-1999). ***PRACTICE AREAS:*** Commercial Litigation; Trust and Estate Litigation; Disability Insurance; Negligence Defense; Product Liability; Life Insurance and Annuities; Torts Litigation. ***Email:*** fhmorrison@dbh.com

JOHN B. NOLAN, born Providence, RI, 1943; admitted to bar, 1968, Connecticut; 1981, New York. *Education:* Brown University (A.B., 1965); Georgetown University (J.D., 1968). ***PRACTICE AREAS:*** Bankruptcy; Commercial Litigation. ***Email:*** jbnolan@dbh.com

JAMES H. ROTONDO, born Hartford, CT, 1956; admitted to bar, 1981, Connecticut; 1982, U.S. District Court, District of Connecticut; 1989, U.S. Court of Appeals, Second Circuit; 2000, Massachusetts. *Education:* Trinity College (B.A., 1978); Boston University (J.D., 1981). ***PRACTICE AREAS:*** Product Liability; Negligence Defense; Direct Liability and Casualty; Torts Litigation; Insurance Litigation; Commercial Litigation; Disability Insurance. ***Email:*** jhrotondo@dbh.com

EDMUND M. SEE, born Marietta, OH, 1943; admitted to bar, 1971, Connecticut. *Education:* Wesleyan University (B.A., 1965); Harvard Law School (J.D., 1971). ***PRACTICE AREAS:*** Municipal Finance; Finance and Investments; Tax Exempt Organizations. ***Email:*** emsee@dbh.com

JAMES SICILIAN, born Bridgeport, CT, 1956; admitted to bar, 1981, Connecticut; 1982, U.S. District Court, District of Connecticut; 1986, U.S. Court of Appeals, Second Circuit; 1989, U.S. Court of Appeals, First Circuit; 1994, U.S. Tax Court. *Education:* Bucknell University (B.A., cum laude, 1978); University of Connecticut (J.D., 1981). ***PRACTICE AREAS:*** Antitrust; Commercial Litigation; Technology and Intellectual Property - Litigation. ***Email:*** jsicilian@dbh.com

ROBERT G. SIEGEL, born Harrisburg, PA, 1950; admitted to bar, 1976, Connecticut; U.S. Tax Court. *Education:* Wesleyan University (B.A., 1972); Cornell University (M.B.A., 1975; J.D., 1976). ***PRACTICE AREAS:*** Health Care; Tax; Mergers and Acquisitions; Closely Held Businesses. ***Email:*** rgsiegel@dbh.com

FELIX J. SPRINGER, born Salzburg, Austria, 1946; admitted to bar, 1979, Connecticut. *Education:* Amherst College (B.A., 1968); Columbia University (M.A., 1969; M. Phil., 1970); University of Connecticut (LL.B., 1979). ***PRACTICE AREAS:*** Employment Law; Employment Litigation. ***Email:*** fjspringer@dbh.com

JAMES J. TANCREDI, born Hartford, CT, 1954; admitted to bar, 1979, Connecticut, U.S. District Court, District of Connecticut; 1988, U.S. Court of Appeals, Second Circuit and U.S. District Court, Southern District of New York; 1991, U.S. Supreme Court. *Education:* College of the Holy Cross (B.A., magna cum laude, 1976); University of Connecticut (J.D., magna cum laude, 1979). (Certified Specialist, Commercial Bankruptcy, American Bankruptcy Board of Certification) (Chair, Firm Bankruptcy and Creditors Rights Department, 1995-1998). ***PRACTICE AREAS:*** Bankruptcy; Commercial Litigation; Bankruptcy Counseling. ***Email:*** jjtancredi@dbh.com

ALLAN B. TAYLOR, born Cincinnati, OH, 1948; admitted to bar, 1975, Connecticut. *Education:* Harvard University (A.B., 1970); John F. Kennedy School of Government (M.P. P., 1975); Harvard Law School (J.D., magna cum laude, 1975). ***PRACTICE AREAS:*** Commercial Litigation; Insurance Litigation; Direct Liability and Casualty; Life Insurance and Annuities. ***Email:*** abtaylor@dbh.com

ROBERT M. TAYLOR III, born New Haven, CT, 1954; admitted to bar, 1980, Connecticut; 1984, District of Columbia. *Education:* University of Connecticut (B.S., 1977); Western New England College School of Law (J.D., magna cum laude, 1980). ***PRACTICE AREAS:*** Banking; Insurance Regulation and Proceedings; Securities Law. ***Email:*** rmtaylor@dbh.com

LYN GAMMILL WALKER, born New York, NY, 1950; admitted to bar, 1978, Connecticut. *Education:* Wellesley College (B.A., 1972); University of Virginia (J.D., 1978). ***PRACTICE AREAS:*** Planning for Entrepreneurs; Trusts and Estates Administration; Tax Exempt Organizations; Estate Planning. ***Email:*** lgwalker@dbh.com

PHILIP S. WALKER, born New Haven, CT, 1933; admitted to bar, 1960, Connecticut; 1961, U.S. District Court, District of Connecticut; 1966, U.S. Court of Appeals, Second Circuit; 1969, U.S. Supreme Court; 1972, U.S. District Courts, Southern and Eastern Districts of New York; 1990, U.S. District Court, District of Arizona. *Education:* University of Notre Dame (B.A., 1954); Yale Law School (LL.B., 1960). ***PRACTICE AREAS:*** Products Liability; Commercial Litigation; Torts Litigation. ***Email:*** pswalker@dbh.com

RICHARD J. WASSERMAN, born Hartford, CT, 1956; admitted to bar, 1981, Connecticut. *Education:* University of Connecticut (B.A., 1978); Boston University (J.D., 1981). ***PRACTICE AREAS:*** Finance and Investments; Structured Finance; Energy. ***Email:*** rjwasserman@dbh.com

THOMAS R. WILDMAN, born Chicago, IL, 1946; admitted to bar, 1971, Connecticut. *Education:* University of Wisconsin (B.A., 1968; J.D., 1971).

(This Listing Continued)

DAY, BERRY & HOWARD LLP, Hartford—Continued

PRACTICE AREAS: Finance and Investments; Structured Finance; Equipment Finance/Leasing; Private Equity Funds. ***Email:*** trwildman@dbh.com

PAUL D. WILLIAMS, born Brooklyn, NY, 1953; admitted to bar, 1984, Connecticut and U.S. District Court, District of Connecticut; 1985, New York State and U.S. Court of Appeals, Second Circuit. *Education:* City College of New York (B.A., 1976); Brooklyn Law School (J.D., cum laude, 1984). (Certified in Civil Trial Advocacy by the National Board of Trial Advocacy). ***PRACTICE AREAS:*** Torts Litigation; Medical And Professional Malpractice Defense; Franchise And Distributorship Litigation; Commercial Litigation; Product Liability; Negligence Defense. ***Email:*** pdwilliams@dbh.com

MARTIN WOLMAN, born Albany, NY, 1937; admitted to bar, 1964, California; 1965, Connecticut. *Education:* Brown University (A.B., 1958); University of California at Berkeley (LL.B., 1964). ***PRACTICE AREAS:*** Trusts and Estates Administration; Estate Planning; Tax Exempt Organization. ***Email:*** mwolman@dbh.com

ALBERT ZAKARIAN, born Pawtucket, RI, 1940; admitted to bar, 1965, Connecticut. *Education:* Trinity College (B.A., 1962); Columbia University (LL.B., 1965). [Captain, U.S. Air Force (Vietnam), 1965-1968]. ***PRACTICE AREAS:*** Employment Litigation; Employment Law; Commercial Litigation. ***Email:*** azakarian@dbh.com

ASSOCIATES OF FIRM IN HARTFORD

Elizabeth A. Alquist
Christine A. Baily
David M. Bizar
Christopher J. Boccaccio
Mario R. Borelli
Maxwell Branson
Barbara T. Burke
Sam S.F. Caligiuri
Raymond A. Colla, Jr.
C. Simon Davidson
Florence K. S. Davis
Meredith G. Diette
Debra J. Dreibelbis
B. Dane Dudley
William H. Erickson
Alex G. Filotto
Sean M. Fisher
Suzanne Garrow
Patrick M. Gerity
Valicia D. Harmon
Marie C. Kuban
Jonathan M. Levine
Robert J. Lewton
Ronald E. Lyles
Donald J. Marchesseault
Kurosh L. Marjani
Carolyn B. Martino
Kelly G. Miley
Jessica J. Mitchell
Ann Grunbeck Monaghan
Karen A. Moreno
Tracey A. Morgan
Samuel T. D. Neves, Jr.
Leigh A. Newman
Clifford E. Nichols
Vincent P. Pace
Donna Poresky
Samantha A. Pravecek
Deborah S. Russo
Daniel A. Schwartz
James D. Scrimgeour
Sharon M. Seligman
Namita Tripathi Shah
Kathleen A. Shea
Michael P. Shea
Edward S. Shelton
Steven Steinmetz
Erin S. Stephen
Eric L. Sussman
Michelle I. Turner (Not admitted in CT)
Keith S. Varian
Andrew R. Wallace
Darren M. Wallace
Lane T. Watson
Peter Wilson

OF COUNSEL

C. Duane Blinn
Harold C. Buckingham, Jr.
George H. Cain
William H. Cuddy
John C. Glezen
Raymond B. Green
Richard C. MacKenzie
James R. McIntosh
Richard M. Reynolds

COUNSEL

Rosemary G. Ayers
Charlsa D. Broadus (Not admitted in CT)
Douglas E. Fiske
Laurence P. Fleming
David H. Flynn
Douglas W. Gillette
Joseph L. Hammer
Michael P. Hammond, Jr.
Elin Swanson Katz
Edward F. Krzanowski
Barbara B. Lindsay
Priya S. Morganstern
Scott P. Myers
Kevin J. O'Connor
J. James Perkins (Not admitted in CT)

SPECIAL COUNSEL

Judith A. Blank
Stephen B. Middlebrook

(This Listing Continued)

INDEPENDENT CONTRACTOR

Ann K. Anderson
Sarah C. Baskin
Paul Schiff Berman (Not admitted in CT)
Lawrence J. Boudreau

RESIDENT PARTNERS IN BOSTON OFFICE

David B. Broughel
Daniel J. Carragher
Jeffrey A. Clopeck
Nancy M. Cullen
George L. Cushing
Stephen G. Howard
William A. Hunter
J. Charles Mokriski
Francis H. Morrison III
Richard S. Novak
William Shields
H. Lawrence Tafe III
Kenneth E. Werner

PARTNERS IN STAMFORD OFFICE

Jerome Berkman
Martin L. Budd
Michael P. Byrne
Patricia A. Carpenter
Michael G. Considine
Kenneth W. Gage
Andrew P. Gaillard
Thomas D. Goldberg
Gregory A. Hayes
Robert J. Miller
Kenneth W. Ritt
Sabino Rodriguez III
Bonnie J. Roe (Not admitted in CT)
Daniel L. Schwartz
James F. Stapleton
David A. Swerdloff
Stanley A. Twardy, Jr.

PARTNERS IN GREENWICH OFFICE

R. Scott Beach
Ronald Osburn Dederick
Forrest Lee Griffith III
Amy K. Wilfert

RESIDENT COUNSEL IN GREENWICH OFFICE

Lesley I. B. Schless

RESIDENT COUNSEL IN BOSTON OFFICE

Eric K. Runge

RESIDENT OF COUNSEL IN BOSTON OFFICE

Charles Donelan

OF COUNSEL IN STAMFORD OFFICE

Emil H. Frankel

RESIDENT COUNSEL IN STAMFORD OFFICE

Stacey B. Babson-Smith
Patricia M. Canavan
Derek Gilman
Benedicta S. McGrath
Roland A. Paul
Jonathan B. Tropp
Kathleen D. Warner
Paulette Wunsch

STAFF ATTORNEY IN BOSTON OFFICE

Bonny E. Lambert

RESIDENT ASSOCIATSE IN GREENWICH OFFICE

Peter Chadwick
Shawn T. Wooden

RESIDENT ASSOCIATES IN BOSTON OFFICE

John G. Balboni
Kathleen A. Bergin
Viktoria K. Cech-Vinhais
Patricia A. DeJuneas
Tricia F. Deraska
Jonathan I. Handler
Louise A. Handler
Edgar B. Hatrick, IV
Paul J. Keenan, Jr.
Kathleen A. Lind
Shannon A. McAuliffe
John P. McLafferty
Brian T. Moore
Kimberly K. Ryan
Andrea P. Testa

ASSOCIATES IN STAMFORD OFFICE

Tricia S. Begg
Melissa L. Bellavia
Ann Lisa Braun
Rob Roy Buckingham, Jr.
David Y. Choi
Richard P. Colbert
Elizabeth Corwin
Catherine R. Critton (admission pending)
Jamal M. Dawkins
Sarah Moore Fass
Kelly E. P. Flatt
Deborah S. Gordon
Joli Lyn Gross
Lorey Rives Leddy
Natasha M. Lipcan
Margaret A. McComish
Catherine Dugan O'Connor
Thomas J. O'Neill
Brian D. Porch, Jr.
Allen J. Roberts, III
Mark B. Robinson
Jennifer L. Sachs

(This Listing Continued)

ASSOCIATES IN STAMFORD OFFICE (Continued)

Fritz Strohmeyer ***Ray A. Wynter***

LAW OFFICES OF MARTHA A. DEAN

77 BUCKINGHAM STREET
HARTFORD, CONNECTICUT 06106
Telephone: 860-278-6009
Fax: 860-727-4107
Email: mdean@mdeanlaw.com

Environmental Law: Representation of Industrial, Financial, and Commercial Establishments, and Select Citizen Plaintiffs, Litigation in State and Federal Courts.

MARTHA A. DEAN, born Philadelphia, Pennsylvania, March 31, 1959; admitted to bar, 1986, Connecticut; 1995, U.S. District Court, District of Connecticut; 2000 U.S. Court of Appeals, Second Circuit. *Education:* Wellesley College (B.A., 1982); University of Connecticut (J.D., 1986). Member, Connecticut Law Review, 1985-1986. Associate, Robinson & Cole, Hartford, Connecticut, 1990-1994. Member, Steering Committee, Environmental Policies Council, Connecticut Business & Industry Association. *Member:* Connecticut Bar Association (Member, Federal Practice Section and Environmental Section; Past Member, Executive Committee and Co-Chair, Court Watch Committee, Environmental Section); American Trial Lawyers Association; Connecticut Trial Lawyers Association. ***PRACTICE AREAS:*** Environmental.

ASSOCIATE

DAVID R. PURVIS, born New Haven, Connecticut, April 20, 1961; admitted to bar, 1986, Connecticut; 1987, U.S. District Court, District of Connecticut. *Education:* Franklin and Marshall College (B.A., 1983); University of Connecticut (J.D., 1986). Member, 1984-1985 and Notes and Comments Editor, 1985-1986, Connecticut Law Review. Law Clerk to Judge Ellen Bree Burns, U.S. District Court, District of Connecticut, 1986-1988. *Member:* Connecticut Bar Association (Member, Environmental Section); Connecticut Business and Industry Association (Member, Environmental Policies Council). ***PRACTICE AREAS:*** Environmental Law.

MARK H. DEAN, P.C.

241 MAIN STREET
HARTFORD, CONNECTICUT 06106
Telephone: 860-541-6699
Fax: 860-241-7744

Civil Trial Practice. Commercial and Business Litigation, Personal Injury, Employment Law and Administrative Proceedings.

MARK H. DEAN, born Alton, Illinois, November 25, 1958; admitted to bar, 1986, Connecticut; 1987, U.S. District Court, District of Connecticut; 1988, U.S. District Court, Southern District of New York and U.S. Court of Appeals, Second Circuit. *Education:* University of Connecticut (B.A., 1980; J.D., with high honors, 1986). Associate, Reid & Riege, P.C., Hartford, Connecticut, 1986-1991. *Member:* Hartford County, Connecticut (Member, Sections On: Litigation, Commercial Law and Bankruptcy) and American Bar Associations; The Association of Trial Lawyers of America; Connecticut Trial Lawyers Association. [First Lieut., U.S. Army, Infantry, 1980-1983, Awarded the Meritorious Service Medal.]

DECHERT

90 STATE HOUSE SQUARE
HARTFORD, CONNECTICUT 06103-3702
Telephone: 860.524.3999
Fax: 860.524.3930
URL: http://www.dechert.com

Philadelphia, Pennsylvania: 4000 Bell Atlantic Tower, 1717 Arch Street, 19103-2793. Telephone: 215.994.4000.
New York, New York: 30 Rockefeller Plaza, 10112. Telephone: 212.698.3500.
Washington, D.C.: 1775 Eye Street, N.W., 20006-2401. Telephone: 202.261.3300.
Boston, Massachusetts: Ten Post Office Square South, 02109-4603. Telephone: 617.728.7100.
Princeton, New Jersey: Princeton Pike Corporate Center, P.O. Box 5218, 08543-5218. Telephone: 609.620.3200.
Harrisburg, Pennsylvania: Thirty North Third Street, 17101-1603. Telephone: 717.237.2000.
Newport Beach, California: 4675 MacArthur Court, Suite 1400, 92660-8842. Telephone: 949.442.6000.

(This Listing Continued)

London, England: 2 Serjeants' Inn, EC4Y 1LT. Telephone: +44.20.7583.5353.
Brussels, Belgium: 65 Avenue Louise 1050. Telephone: +32.2.535.5411.
Paris, France: 55, avenue Kléber, 75116. Telephone: +33.1.53.65.05.00.
Luxembourg: Brucher & Seimetz in association with Dechert, Avocats a la Cour, 10 rue de Vianden, B.P. 709, L-2017. Telephone: +352.45.62.62.

Antitrust, Banking, Bankruptcy and Reorganization, Business and Technology, Commercial Litigation, Complex Litigation, Copyrights, Corporate Finance, Competition, Construction, Customs and Excise, Criminal and Civil Fraud, Defamation, Domestic Taxation, Employee Benefits and Executive Compensation, Employment, Environmental, Estate Planning, EU Legislation, Financial Services, First Amendment, Government Affairs, Health Care, Immigration, Insurance, Intellectual Property, Internet and e-Commerce, Information Technology, International Business, International Taxation, International Trade, Investment Management, Labor, Latin America, Life Sciences, Mass Torts, Media, Mergers and Acquisitions, Patent Law and Litigation, Privacy, Private Equity, Products Liability, Property Planning, Real Estate and Mortgage Finance, Retail, Securities Litigation and Enforcement, Securitization, State and Local Taxation, Tax-Exempt Organizations, Trademarks, Venture Capital.

PARTNERS

TIMOTHY J. BOYCE, born New Haven, Connecticut, 1954; admitted to bar, 1979, Connecticut. *Education:* Georgetown University (B.S.F.S., 1975); University of Pennsylvania (M.B.A., 1979; J.D., 1979). Phi Beta Kappa; Phi Alpha Theta; Phi Sigma Alpha. Editor, University of Pennsylvania Law Review, 1978-79. Author: "Hotel Revenues in Bankruptcy: An Analysis and Analytic Framework," ABA Real Property, Probate and Trust Journal, Fall, 1993; "The Supreme Court and the Death of Durrett," Real Estate Law Journal, Winter, 1995; "Financing Senior Living Facilities," ABA Probate and Property, March/April, 1996; "Collateralizing Nonassignable Contracts, Licenses and Permits: Half a Loaf Is Better Than No Loaf," The Business Lawyer, 1997; "Recent Developments in Credit Tenant Loans," Real Estate Review, Winter, 1997. Lecturer: "Real Estate Finance Potpourri," American Bar Association annual meeting, 1995; "Credit Tenant Loans," Mortgage Bankers Association annual meeting, February, 1996; Collateralizing Nonassignable Contracts, Permits and Licenses," American Bar Association annual meeting, 1996; "The World's Third Annual Mortgage Financing Program," American Bar Association annual meeting, 1997; "Workout Issues With Commercial Loan Securitizations," American Bar Association annual meeting, 1999; "Defeasance: What It Is and How It Works," National CLE Conference, 2001. *Member:* Connecticut and American (Member, Real Property, Probate and Trust Law Section; Vice Chair, Committee on Foreclosure and Related Remedies, 1996-1999; Vice Chair, Committee on Mortgage Loan Originations, 2001—) Bar Associations; American College of Real Estate Lawyers. ***PRACTICE AREAS:*** Commercial Real Estate; Commercial Leasing; Lease Finance; Real Estate Finance; Leasing. **Email:** timothy.boyce@dechert.com

JOHN J. GILLIES JR., born San Antonio, Texas, 1946; admitted to bar, 1972, New Jersey; 1979, Connecticut. *Education:* Georgetown University (A.B., 1968); Boston College (J.D., 1971). *Member:* Hartford County, Connecticut and American Bar Associations; American College of Investment Counsel; American College of Real Estate Lawyers. ***PRACTICE AREAS:*** Investment Management; Investments; Institutional Investment Law; Investment Partnerships; Debt and Equity Finance; Structured Finance; Real Estate Finance; Real Estate Investment; Real Estate Restructuring. **Email:** john.gillies@dechert.com

ASSOCIATES

IZABELA E. BOLTRYK, born Jaslo, Poland, 1967; admitted to bar, 1999, Connecticut. *Education:* University of Warsaw (M.A., 1994); University of Connecticut (J.D., highest honors, 1999). ***PRACTICE AREAS:*** Real Estate Finance. **Email:** izabela.boltryk@dechert.com

KATHERINE A. BURROUGHS, born Huntington, New York, 1963; admitted to bar, 1988, Connecticut; 1989, Massachusetts and New York. *Education:* Cornell University (B.S., 1985); College of William and Mary (J.D., 1988). Order of the Coif. ***PRACTICE AREAS:*** Real Estate Finance; Securitization; Bankruptcy. **Email:** katherine.burroughs@dechert.com

ROBERT E. GRADY, admitted to bar, 1999, Connecticut. *Education:* University of Massachusetts (B.A., 1993); University of Connecticut (J.D., 1999). ***PRACTICE AREAS:*** Real Estate Finance. **Email:** robert.grady@dechert.com

STEVEN KAPILOFF, born New York, New York, 1961; admitted to bar, 1988, Connecticut. *Education:* Boston University (B.A., cum laude, 1983); University of Southern California (J.D., 1988). ***PRACTICE AREAS:*** Commercial Real Estate. **Email:** steven.kapiloff@dechert.com

ANDREA J. LEVINE, born Hartford, Connecticut, 1966; admitted to bar, 1992, Connecticut. *Education:* Brown University (B.A., 1988); Cornell University (J.D., 1991). ***PRACTICE AREAS:*** Commercial Real Estate Acquisitions; Commercial Real Estate Finance; Commercial Leasing; Office Leasing. **Email:** andrea.levine@dechert.com

(This Listing Continued)

DECHERT, Hartford—Continued

SHARI E. PURRINGTON, (admission pending); admitted to bar, 1991, Connecticut. *Education:* University of Hartford (B.S., magna cum laude, 1987); Western New England College School of Law (J.D., 1991). ***PRACTICE AREAS:*** Commercial Real Estate Finance; Real Estate Finance; Retail Leasing. ***Email:*** shari.purrington@dechert.com

MIRIAM BERLIN SCHNEIDER, born Baltimore, Maryland, 1972; admitted to bar, 1998, New York; 2000, Connecticut. *Education:* University of Pennsylvania (B.A., 1993); New York University (J.D., 1997). ***PRACTICE AREAS:*** Real Estate Finance. ***Email:*** miriam.schneider@dechert.com

NADINE KLINE YOUNG, born Harrisburg, Pennsylvania, 1951; admitted to bar, 1977, Connecticut. *Education:* University of California, Berkeley (B.A., honors, 1973); Cornell Law School (J.D., 1977). ***PRACTICE AREAS:*** Commercial Real Estate Finance; Commercial Leasing; Securitization; Construction Finance; Construction Contracts. ***Email:*** nadine.young@dechert.com

(Partners of the Firm, Counsel, Of Counsel and Associates in Philadelphia and Harrisburg, Pennsylvania; New York, New York; Washington, D.C.; Boston, Massachusetts; Newport Beach, California; Princeton, New Jersey; London, England; Brussels, Belgium; Paris, France and Luxembourg are listed in the Biographical Section respectively.)

DEL NEGRO, FELDMAN & VOLPE, LLC

GOODWIN SQUARE
225 ASYLUM STREET
HARTFORD, CONNECTICUT 06103-1516
Telephone: 860-241-4141
Facsimile: 860-241-4150

Health Care Law, Hospital Law, Managed Care Law.

JOHN T. DEL NEGRO, born Springfield, Massachusetts, 1948; admitted to bar, 1975, Connecticut. *Education:* George Washington University (B.A., 1970); Cornell University (J.D., 1975). ***PRACTICE AREAS:*** Health Care Law; Corporate.

BARRY FELDMAN, born Hartford, Connecticut, 1950; admitted to bar, 1975, Connecticut. *Education:* Princeton University (A.B., 1972); Harvard University (J.D., 1975). ***PRACTICE AREAS:*** Hospital Law; Health Care Law.

MICHELE M. VOLPE, born New Haven, Connecticut, 1966; admitted to bar, 1991, Connecticut. *Education:* Boston College (A.B., 1988); University of Connecticut (J.D., 1991). ***PRACTICE AREAS:*** Health Care Law; Managed Care Law.

REPRESENTATIVE CLIENTS: The Connecticut State Medical Society IPA, Inc.; Fairfield County Physicians Management Corporation; Greenwich Physicians Association, Inc.; Johnson Memorial IPA, Inc.; Norwich Physicians IPA, Inc.; Primary Care Physicians Corporation; PriMed, LLC; Rhode Island Primary Care Physicians Corporation; Saint Francis Hospital and Medical Center; United Hospital Medical Center (Port Chester, New York).

MICHAEL F. DOWLEY

HARTFORD, CONNECTICUT

(See Middletown)

Administrative Law, Alcoholic Beverages, Alternative Dispute Resolution, Banks and Banking, Business Law, Commercial Law, Commercial Real Estate, Computers and Software, Contracts, Copyrights, Corporate Law, Eminent Domain, Environmental Law, Guardianship and Conservatorship, Health Care, Intellectual Property, Leases and Leasing, Litigation, Media Law, Medical Malpractice, Mortgages, Negligence, Nonprofit and Charitable Organizations, Partnership Law, Personal Injury, Premises Liability, Probate, Professional Liability, Real Estate, Resorts and Leisure, Sports Law, Torts, Trademarks, Trusts and Estates, Unfair Competition, Wills, Zoning, Planning and Land Use.

DUHAMEL & SCHOOLCRAFT LLC

HARTFORD, CONNECTICUT

(See Glastonbury)

General Litigation, Insurance Defense, Workers Compensation, Personal Injury and Commercial Litigation.

EDWARDS & ANGELL, LLP

A Partnership including Professional Corporations
90 STATE HOUSE SQUARE
HARTFORD, CONNECTICUT 06103-2715
Telephone: 860-525-5065
Telecopy: 860-527-4198
Email: postmaster@ealaw.com
URL: http://www.ealaw.com

REVISERS OF THE RHODE ISLAND LAW DIGEST FOR THIS DIRECTORY.

Providence, Rhode Island Office: 2800 Financial Plaza. Telephone: 401-274-9200. Cable Address: "Edwangle Providence." Telex: 952001 "E A PVD" Telecopier: 401-276-6611.
Newport, Rhode Island Office: 130 Bellevue Avenue. Telephone: 401-849-7800.
New York, New York Office: 750 Lexington Avenue. Telephone: 212- 308-4411.
West Palm Beach, Florida Office: One North Clematis Street, Suite 400. Telephone: 561-833-7700.
Boston, Massachusetts Office: 101 Federal Street. Telephone: 617-439-4444.
Short Hills, New Jersey Office: 51 John F. Kennedy Parkway. Telephone: 973-376-7700.
Fort Lauderdale, Florida Office: 600 Corporate Drive, Suite 514. Telephone: 954-491-8050.

General Practice.

FIRM PROFILE: Edwards & Angell, LLP, a Massachusetts Limited Liability Partnership, is a full-service law firm with over 200 attorneys. Since our founding in 1894, the Firm has steadily evolved into a major regional law firm with offices in Boston, Massachusetts; Providence and Newport, Rhode Island; New York City; Hartford, Connecticut; Short Hills, New Jersey; and Palm Beach and Fort Lauderdale, Florida.

Edwards & Angell, LLP enjoys long-standing relationships with a broad base of clients ranging from individuals to businesses of every size including small and emerging companies, large publicly and privately held companies, international corporations, financial institutions, all segments of the Insurance industry, venture capital funds, health care providers, municipal bodies, real estate developers, contractors and securities brokers.

Edwards & Angell, LLP has structured its practice to anticipate, respond to and adapt quickly to the economic, regulatory, social and political challenges and opportunities which our clients face daily. Evidence of a strong interdisciplinary approach to client service, the Firm's broad range of practice groups are organized by industry, business or specialized legal services. These practice groups include: Banking, Lending & Commercial Finance, Bankruptcy/Workout, Corporate, Health Care, Insurance, Intellectual Property, International, Labor & Employment, Litigation, Media and Communications, Municipal Finance, Real Estate, Securities, Tax, Technology, Trusts & Estates and Venture Capital.

Edwards & Angell, LLP has earned the reputation of distinguished community leader and spirited citizen. In addition to serving as directors and advisors to numerous community organizations, Edwards & Angell, LLP attorneys have received awards for their steadfast commitment in providing "Pro Bono" services throughout the communities in which they live and work. Further, the Firm has produced several public and private leaders including two current U.S. Senators, as well as Federal and State Judges.

Edwards & Angell, LLP incorporates a team approach Firm-wide maximizing the use of state-of-the-art technology and highly professional paralegal and administrative staff from our various offices to insure timely and efficient service to our clients.

MEMBERS OF FIRM

THEODORE P. AUGUSTINOS, born Syracuse, New York, September 17, 1960; admitted to bar, 1985, Connecticut; 1986, U.S. District Court, District of Connecticut. *Education:* St. Lawrence University (B.A., cum laude, 1982); Boston University School of Law (J.D., 1985). ***PRACTICE AREAS:*** Banking Regulation; General Corporate Law; Mergers and Acquisitions; Insurance Regulation. ***Email:*** taugustinos@ealaw.com

JOHN B. D'AGOSTINO, born Manchester, Connecticut, 1946; admitted to bar, 1972, Connecticut; 1975, U.S. District Court, District of Connecticut. *Education:* University of Connecticut (B.A., cum laude, 1968; J.D., with honors, 1972); Boston University (LL.M., 1974). Member, Connecticut Law Review, 1970-1972. *Member:* Hartford County, Connecticut and American Bar Associations. ***Email:*** jdagostino@ealaw.com

DONALD E. FRECHETTE, born Greenville, Pennsylvania, December 30, 1958; admitted to bar, 1981, Michigan; 1983, Maine and U. S. District Court, District of Maine; 1984, New Hampshire; 1985, Massachusetts; 1988, Connecticut; 1990, U. S. District Court, District of Connecticut; 1991, U. S. District

(This Listing Continued)

Court, District of Massachusetts; 1992, U.S. District Court, District of New Hampshire; 1993, U.S. Court of Appeals, Second Circuit; 1995, U.S. Supreme Court. *Education:* University of New Hampshire (B.A., 1978); New York Law School (J.D., cum laude, 1981); Boston University School of Law (LL.M., 1985). Recipient, Boston University Alumni Academic Achievement Award. Author: "Lending Limits and the Attribution Rules of 12 U.S.C. §84: Congress and the Comptroller Cover the Bases," 2 U. Miami Business Law Rev. 1 (1991); "Expert Opinion Testimony After Porter: Connecticut Adopts the Daubert Standard," 71 Conn. B.J. 346 (Dec. 1997); "The Impact of Late Notice on Excess Insurance Claims — New York Disposes of the Need to Show Prejudice," 5 Journal of Reinsurance 63 (Winter 1997-98); "Retroactive Policy Amendments and the 'Follow the Forms' Doctrine," 5 Journal of Reinsurance 63 (Summer 1998). Member, Redrafting Committee, Connecticut Common Interest Ownership Manual, Second Edition. Adjunct Professor, Moot Court Instructor, University of Connecticut School of Law, 1991-1995. *Member:* Connecticut and New Hampshire Bar Associations. ***PRACTICE AREAS:*** Complex Commercial Litigation; Products Liability; Reinsurance Arbitration; Reinsurance Litigation. ***Email:*** dfrechette@ealaw.com

ALAN J. LEVIN, born Hartford, Connecticut, August 8, 1960; admitted to bar, 1986, Connecticut. *Education:* Clark University (B.A., with honors, 1982); Brooklyn Law School (J.D., 1985). Member, Moot Court Honor Society. ***PRACTICE AREAS:*** Insurance; General Corporate. ***Email:*** alevin@ealaw.com

JOHN H. REID III, born New Britain, Connecticut, March 18, 1944; admitted to bar, 1969, Rhode Island; 1985, Massachusetts; 1992, Connecticut. *Education:* Yale University (B.A., 1966); University of Virginia Law School (LL.B., 1969); Boston University Law School (LL.M. in Taxation, 1974). Member, Advisory Board, Small Business Council of America. *Member:* Rhode Island, Massachusetts, Connecticut and American (Member, Personal Service Organizations Committee, Section on Tax, 1978—) Bar Associations; American Society of Medical Association Counsel. ***PRACTICE AREAS:*** Taxation Law; Employee Benefits Law; Professional Organizations Law; Health Law. ***Email:*** jreid@ealaw.com

MARK B. SEIGER, born Bronx, New York, June 18, 1955; admitted to bar, 1981, Connecticut; 1982, U.S. District Court, District of Connecticut; 1997, Vermont. *Education:* University of Hartford (B.A., summa cum laude, 1978); Case Western Reserve University (J.D., 1981); Georgetown University (LL.M., Commercial Law, 1983). Alpha Chi. Recipient, Blumenthal Memorial Award for Excellence in Economics. Member, Winning Team, Niagara International Moot Court Competition, 1980-1981. Listed in: Who's Who in American Law, 1988—; Who's Who in Emerging Leaders, 1989; Who's Who Worldwide, 1995—. Author: "Effective Risk Management for the Twenty-First Century, Year 2000 and Beyond," *Manufacturers' Risk Prevention,* Summer, 1998. Staff Member, Journal of International Law, 1979. Member, National Young Leadership Cabinet, United Jewish Appeal, 1992-1995. Member, 1990—, Chairman, Young Leadership Council, 1992-1996, Board of Directors, Assistant Secretary and Executive Committee, 1992—, Jewish Federation of Greater Hartford. Member and Trustee, Hebrew Home and Hospital, 1996—. Member, Board of Directors, Connecticut Defense Lawyers Association, 1990-1993. Previous Employment: Halloran & Sage. *Member:* Hartford County, Connecticut and American Bar Associations; Association of Ski Defense Attorneys; Association of Ski Defense Attorneys (Member, Board of Directors, 1995—); Defense Research Institute (Co-Chair, Risk Management Group for Products Liability; Member, Products Liability Steering Committee, 1996—). ***PRACTICE AREAS:*** Products Liability (30%); Risk Management (30%); Complex Civil Litigation (20%); Employment Litigation (10%); Insurance Coverage (10%). ***Email:*** mseiger@ealaw.com

COUNSEL

JANET M. HELMKE-ELMORE, born Rockville Centre, New York, April 19, 1962; admitted to bar, 1988, Connecticut; 1989, New York and U.S. District Court, Southern and Eastern Districts of New York; 1990, District of Columbia; 1992, U.S. District Court, District of Connecticut. *Education:* Syracuse University (B.A., 1984; J.D., magna cum laude, 1988). Member, Order of the Coif, Syracuse University. Associate Editor, Syracuse Law Review, Syracuse University, 1987-1988. Previous Employment: Cadwalader Wickersham & Taft; Halloran & Sage. *Member:* Hartford County, Connecticut, New York State and American Bar Associations; District of Columbia Bar. ***PRACTICE AREAS:*** Commercial Litigation; Products Liability; Personal Injury Defense. ***Email:*** jhelmke@ealaw.com

THOMAS F. X. HODSON, born Mineola, New York, January 2, 1959; admitted to bar, 1988, Connecticut; 1989, New York. *Education:* St. Michael's College (B.A., 1981); Catholic University of America (J.D., 19 87). Associate, Kroll & Tract, New York, N.Y., 1987-1989. Associate, LeBoeuf, Lamb, Green & McRae, New York, N.Y., 1989-1991. Assistant Vice President and Assistant General Counsel, 1995-1997; Vice President and General Counsel, 1997-1999, Orion Capital Companies, Inc., Farmington, Connecticut; Assistant Vice President and Assistant General Counsel, National Reinsurance Corporation, Stamford, Connecticut, 1991-1995. *Member:* Connecticut (Member, Sections on: Corporate Counsel; Business Law), New York State (Member, Sections on: Corporate Counsel; Business Law; Torts, Insurance and Compensation Law) and American (Member, Section on Tort and Insurance Practice) Bar Associations. ***Email:*** thodson@ealaw.com

(This Listing Continued)

ASSOCIATES

DORIS ELLEN DESAUTEL, born Providence, Rhode Island, September 8, 1974; admitted to bar, 1999, Massachusetts; 2000, Connecticut and U.S. District Court, District of Massachusetts; 2001, U.S. District Court, District of Connecticut. *Education:* Colby College (B.A., with distinction, 1996); Suffolk University Law School (J.D., 1999). Phi Alpha Delta. Recipient, Marjorie D. Bither Scholarship, 1999. *Member:* Hartford, Connecticut, Massachusetts and American Bar Associations. ***PRACTICE AREAS:*** Insurance; Reinsurance; Litigation. ***Email:*** ddesautel@ealaw.com

JOHN N. EMMANUEL, born Hartford, Connecticut, November 4, 1969; admitted to bar, 1994, Connecticut; 1995, U.S. District Court, District of Connecticut. *Education:* University of Connecticut (B.S., magna cum laude, 1991); Boston University School of Law (J.D., 1994). Member, Annual Review of Banking Law, 1992-1994. *Member:* Connecticut Bar Association. ***PRACTICE AREAS:*** Insurance; General Corporate; Banking. ***Email:*** jemmanuel@ealaw.com

ANN ELIZABETH FAVALE, born Hartford, Connecticut, October 15, 1975; admitted to bar, 2000, Connecticut. *Education:* University of Connecticut (B.A., 1997; J.D., 2000). *Member:* Connecticut Bar Association. ***PRACTICE AREAS:*** Litigation; Arbitration. ***Email:*** afavale@ealaw.com

MICHAEL T. GRIFFIN, born Norwalk, Connecticut, April 10, 1969; admitted to bar, 1998, Connecticut. *Education:* University of Connecticut (B.A., 1992); University of Connecticut School of Law (J.D., 1998). ***PRACTICE AREAS:*** Insurance; Reinsurance; Corporate Law. ***Email:*** mgriffin@ealaw.com

CATHLEEN TOBIN HEATH, born Rochester, New York, December 28, 1973; admitted to bar, 1999, Connecticut. *Education:* State University of New York at Geneseo (B.A., 1996); University of Notre Dame (J.D., 1999). ***PRACTICE AREAS:*** Insurance Regulation. ***Email:*** cheath@ealaw.com

MATTHEW J. HOBERMAN, born Hartford, Connecticut, May 17, 1971; admitted to bar, 1998, Connecticut and New York. *Education:* Lafayette College (A.B., 1993); University of Miami (J.D., cum laude, 1998). ***PRACTICE AREAS:*** Corporate Law; Business Law; Mergers and Acquisitions; Insurance; Securities. ***Email:*** mhoberman@ealaw.com

TAMARA S. LAPOINTE, born Middletown, Connecticut; admitted to bar, 1999, Massachusetts; 2000, Connecticut. *Education:* Indiana University (B.A., 1995); Suffolk University (J.D., 1998). ***PRACTICE AREAS:*** Corporate Law. ***Email:*** tlapointe@ealaw.com

JEFFREY JOSEPH MEDEIROS, born Elizabeth, New Jersey, February 8, 1966; admitted to bar, 1994, New Jersey; 1995, New York; 1996, Connecticut. *Education:* Western New England College (B.S.B.A., 1989); University of Toledo College of Law (J.D., 1994). Phi Alpha Delta (Vice President, 1992-1994). Member, Moot Court Executive Committee, University of Toledo College of Law. National Champion, Salmon P. Chase Environmental Law Moot Court. Teaching Assistant, Legal Research and Writing/Contracts, University of Toledo, 1993-1994. *Member:* New Jersey State, Connecticut and American Bar Associations; Association of Ski Defense Attorneys. ***PRACTICE AREAS:*** Litigation; Insurance; Reinsurance; Professional Liability Defense; Products Liability; Complex Commercial Litigation. ***Email:*** jmedeiros@ealaw.com

JOSHUA L. MILRAD, born New York, N.Y., March 1, 1968; admitted to bar, 1996, New York and U.S. District Court, Southern and Eastern Districts of New York; 1997, New Jersey and U.S. District Court, District of New Jersey; 1998, Connecticut and U.S. District Court, District of Connecticut. *Education:* Northeastern University (B.S., magna cum laude, 1991); Suffolk University Law School (J.D., cum laude, 1995). Phi Kappa Phi. *Member:* Theodore I. Koskoff American Inn of Court. ***PRACTICE AREAS:*** Civil Litigation. ***Email:*** jmilrad@ealaw.com

REVISERS OF THE RHODE ISLAND LAW DIGEST FOR THIS DIRECTORY.

(For complete biographical data on all personnel, see Professional Biographies at Providence, Rhode Island)

EISENBERG, ANDERSON, MICHALIK & LYNCH LLP

HARTFORD, CONNECTICUT

(See New Britain)

Construction Law, Employment Law, Elder Law, Estate Planning, Taxation Law, Family Law, Federal and State Litigation and Appeals, Municipal, Real Estate, Zoning, Corporate Law, Commercial Law.

JOSEPH S. ELDER

661 WETHERSFIELD AVENUE
HARTFORD, CONNECTICUT 06114-1928
Telephone: 860-296-3247
Fax: 860-296-9131
Email: jselderesq@aol.com
URL: http://www.lawyers.com/jelder

Civil and Criminal Litigation, Felonies, Misdemeanors, Driving While Intoxicated, Personal Injury, Automobile Accidents.

JOSEPH S. ELDER, born New Haven, Connecticut, April 22, 1956; admitted to bar, 1985, Connecticut; U.S. District Court, District of Connecticut. *Education:* University of Connecticut (B.A., 1978; J.D., 1984). Member, Moot Court Board, 1983-1984. Appointed State of Connecticut Board of Pardons, 1994. *Member:* Hartford County Bar Association; Oliver Ellsworth Inns of Court. ***PRACTICE AREAS:*** Civil Litigation; Criminal Law; Felonies; Misdemeanors; Driving While Intoxicated; Personal Injury; Automobile Accidents.

FEINER WOLFSON LLC

100 CONSTITUTION PLAZA, SUITE 600
HARTFORD, CONNECTICUT 06103
Telephone: 860-713-8900
Fax: 860-713-8905

Corporate, Commercial, Franchise, Business Law, Complex Business Litigation, Employment Law and Professional Liability.

ROBERT A. FEINER, born Hartford, Connecticut, January 29, 1958; admitted to bar, 1985, Connecticut. *Education:* University of Connecticut (B.S., magna cum laude, 1979); Cornell University (J.D., cum laude, 1985). Phi Kappa Phi; Beta Alpha Psi; Phi Alpha Delta. Certified Public Accountant, 1981. Previous Employment: Murtha, Cullina Richter and Pinney, 1985-1992. *Member:* Connecticut Bar Association (Executive Committee, Business Law Section). ***PRACTICE AREAS:*** Mergers and Acquisitions; Franchise Law; Corporate Law; Limited Liability Company; Commercial Transactions. ***Email:*** rfeiner@ntplx.net

JOHN M. WOLFSON, born Hartford, Connecticut, April 8, 1958; admitted to bar, 1983, Connecticut; 1984, U.S. District Court, District of Connecticut; 1993, U.S. Supreme Court. *Education:* Drew University (B.A., 1980); University of Connecticut (J.D., 1983). Omicron Delta Epsilon. Associate Director, Moot Court Board. Previous Employment: Rome, Case, Kennelly & Klebanoff, P.C., Bloomfield, Connecticut, Principal, 1991-1994; Edwards & Angel, Hartford, Connecticut, Counsel, 1994-1995. ***PRACTICE AREAS:*** Business and Financial Litigation; Commercial Litigation; Employment Litigation; Tax Controversies; Professional Liability; Lender Liability Law; Franchise Law. ***Email:*** jwolfson@ntplx.net

ANDREA A. HEWITT, born Manchester, Connecticut, October 14, 1955; admitted to bar, 1990, Connecticut and U.S. District Court, District of Connecticut; 1992, U.S. Court of Appeals, 2nd Circuit. *Education:* Post College (B.S., cum laude, 1984); University of Connecticut (J.D., 1990). Previous Employment: Associate, Gersten & Clifford, Hartford, Connecticut, 1990-1995. Counsel, Konica Business Technologies, Inc., 1995-1998. ***PRACTICE AREAS:*** Business Litigation; Commercial Litigation; Employment Litigation. ***Email:*** ahewitt@ntplx.net

FINK & HIGHMARK

HARTFORD, CONNECTICUT

(See West Hartford)

Civil Trial and Appellate Practice in State and Federal Courts. Insurance, Subrogation, Fidelity and Surety, Products Liability, Environmental, Personal Injury, Business, Commercial, Probate, Estate Planning, Corporation, Real Estate, Construction and Workers Compensation.

FINN DIXON & HERLING LLP

HARTFORD, CONNECTICUT

(See Stamford)

Corporate Law, Mergers and Acquisitions, Securities Law, Venture Capital Financing, Corporate Finance and Restructuring, Commercial Litigation, Banking and Lending Law, Bankruptcy and Workouts, Employee Benefits and the Federal and State Taxation of Businesses and Business Transactions.

FITZHUGH & ASSOCIATES

Established in 1984

100 CONSTITUTION PLAZA, SUITE 600
HARTFORD, CONNECTICUT 06106
Telephone: 860-549-6803
Fax: 860-728-0546

Boston, Massachusetts Office: 155 Federal Street, Suite 1700, 02110-1727. Telephone: 617-695-2330. Fax: 617-695-2335.

Cranston, Rhode Island Office: 571 Pontiac Avenue. Telephone: 401-941-3220. Facsimile: 401-941-3055.

General Civil Practice before State and Federal Courts. Insurance Defense, Negligence and Products Liability Defense. Bankruptcy, Environmental and Employment Law.

FIRM PROFILE: A firm of over ten attorneys, Fitzhugh & Associates is a litigation firm that represents only corporate clients. The firm's practice is structured to serve companies that routinely require the services of aggressive outside counsel for defending hazardous waste pollution, personal injury and products' liability claims or handling general corporate litigation, particularly commercial collections involving large dollar amounts.

MICHAEL A. FITZHUGH, born Chicago, Illinois, February 23, 1952; admitted to bar, 1981, Massachusetts; U.S. District Court, District of Massachusetts; U.S. Court of Appeals, First Circuit; U.S. Supreme Court (Not admitted in Connecticut). *Education:* Williams College (B.A., cum laude, 1977); Princeton University; Harvard University (J.D., 1981). *Member:* Boston, American and National Bar Associations; Massachusetts Black Lawyers Association; National Association of Railroad Trial Counsel; Massachusetts Defense Lawyers Association; Defense Research Institute; Federation of Insurance and Corporate Counsel. ***PRACTICE AREAS:*** Products Liability; Employment and Insurance Law. ***Email:*** mfitzhugh@fitzhughlaw.com

REPRESENTATIVE CLIENTS: Allstate Insurance Company; Argonaut Insurance Company; The Boston Housing Authority; Bradlees, Inc.; Chevron U.S.A., Inc.; Federal Deposit Insurance Corporation; Federal Express Corporation; Fleet Bank; The Ford Motor Company; The Ford Motor Credit Company; The Home Insurance Company; IBM, Inc.; Jaguar Cars, Inc.; Liberty Mutual Insurance Company; Maryland Casualty Company; The Massachusetts Bay Transportation Authority ("MBTA"); The Massachusetts Port Authority ("MASSPORT"); The Massachusetts Turnpike Authority; Mobil Oil Corporation; The National Railroad Passenger Corporation ("Amtrak"); Royal Insurance Company; Ryder Truck Rental, Inc.; Sun Refining and Marketing Company ("Sunoco"); The Sentry Insurance Group; Shell Oil Company; TEXACO Inc.; The Travelers Insurance Company; United States Trust Company; Whirlpool Corp.; White Consolidated Industries, Inc.

THOMAS M. FLANAGAN, P.C.

1010 WETHERSFIELD AVENUE
SUITE 202
HARTFORD, CONNECTICUT 06114-3149
Telephone: 860-296-1144
Fax: 860-296-7823
Email: tmfpc@snet.net
URL: http://www.lawyers.com/fpc

Estate Planning, Trust Administration, Estate Administration, Wills and Probate.

THOMAS M. FLANAGAN, born New York, N.Y., September 3, 1949; admitted to bar, 1981, Connecticut; 1982 U.S. District Court, District of Connecticut. *Education:* Cornell University (B.A., 1972; M.A.T., 1975); Syracuse University (J.D., cum laude, 1981). *Member:* Connecticut (Member, Executive Committee, Estates and Probate Section) and American (Member, Real Property, Probate and Trust Law Section) Bar Associations; Estate and Business Planning Council of Hartford; Connecticut Estate and Tax Planning Council (Director, 1998—). ***PRACTICE AREAS:*** Wills; Trusts and Estates; Probate; Estate Planning; Business Planning; Estate Administration Law; Trust Administration Law. ***Email:*** tmfpc@snet.net

KARL FLEISCHMANN, P.C.

CAPITOL PLACE, 21 OAK STREET
SUITE 210
HARTFORD, CONNECTICUT 06106-8002
Telephone: 860-278-5500
Fax: 860-278-5503
Email: kfleischmann@snet.net

Real Estate Investment, Real Estate Finance and Real Estate Litigation.

KARL FLEISCHMANN, born New York, N.Y., January 19, 1937; admitted to bar, 1960, Connecticut; 1961, U.S. District Court, District of Connecticut; 1966, U.S. Court of Appeals, Second Circuit; 1971, U.S. Supreme Court. *Education:* Columbia University (A.B., 1957); Harvard University (LL.B., 1960).

(This Listing Continued)

Phi Beta Kappa. Lecturer, Legal Ethics, School Law and Moot Court, University of Connecticut School of Law, 1968-1973. *Member:* Hartford County and Connecticut (Chairman, Professional Ethics Committee, 1975-1980) Bar Associations. ***Email:*** kfleischmann@snet.net

REPRESENTATIVE CLIENTS: The Wendell Corporation; Atlantic Bank of New York; FinanSkandic Corporation; Peoples Bank; The Meandering Stream Group.

FOGARTY COHEN SELBY & NEMIROFF LLC

HARTFORD, CONNECTICUT

(See Greenwich)

Litigation in all Courts, Real Estate and Land Use, Estate Planning and Probate, Corporate, Matrimonial, Administrative and Environmental, Appellate Practice, Business, Civil Trial, Commercial Litigation, Construction, Family, Labor and Employment, Medical Malpractice, Trust and Product Liability.

CARLO FORZANI

43 WOODLAND STREET, SUITE 500
HARTFORD, CONNECTICUT 06105
Telephone: 860-482-4701
Fax: 860-251-6790
URL: http://www.lawyers.com/forzanilaw

Family Law and Mediation.

CARLO FORZANI, born Stamford, Connecticut, April 20, 1948; admitted to bar, 1976, Connecticut. *Education:* Trinity College (B.A., 1970); University of Connecticut (J.D., with honors, 1976). Author: "Uncontested Matrimonial Actions," Matthew Bender, 1987. Board of Editors, Connecticut Family Lawyer, 1986—. Listed, Best Lawyers in America, 1994—. *Member:* Connecticut (Chair, Family Law Section, 1991-1992) and American (Co-Chair, Law in the Fifty States Committee, Family Law Section, 1985-1994) Bar Associations; American Academy of Matrimonial Lawyers (President-Elect, Connecticut Chapter, 2000-2001). ***REPORTED CASES:*** Burton v. Burton, 189 Conn. 129 (1983).

KARL A. FRANSSON

100 WELLS STREET
HARTFORD, CONNECTICUT 06103
Telephone: 860-728-0259
Facsimile: 860-728-0231
Email: karl.a.fransson@SNET.NET
URL: http://www.lawyers.com/kfransson

Bankruptcy, Collections; Foreclosure, Probate, Wills, Trust and Estates, Elder Law, Commercial, Business Law, Real Estate, General Practice, Living Wills, Powers of Attorney, Health Care, Commercial Bankruptcy, Consumer Bankruptcy, Contested Wills, Guardianship, Conservatorship.

KARL A. FRANSSON, born Hartford, Connecticut, December 1, 1948; admitted to bar, 1975, Connecticut. *Education:* University of Connecticut (B.A., cum laude, 1970; J.D., 1974). Assistant Corporation Counsel, Town of West Hartford, Connecticut, 1977-1979. Member, Ethics Committee, Connecticut Bar Association, 1983-1985. *Member:* Hartford County, Connecticut and American Bar Associations.

FRAUENGLASS & EISENBERG

HARTFORD, CONNECTICUT

(See Glastonbury)

Visitation, Property Division, Alimony, Child Support, Post-Judgment Modifications, Prenuptial Agreements, Mediation, Practice limited to Divorce and Custody Law.

GALE & KOWALYSHYN, LLC

Established in 1968
(Successor to Calvocoressi & Gale)
363 MAIN STREET
HARTFORD, CONNECTICUT 06106
Telephone: 860-522-8296
Fax: 860-522-8298

General Practice. Trials and Appellate Practice in all Courts. Personal Injury, Real Estate, Estate Planning, Family, Administrative, Liquor Licensing and Disciplinary Proceedings, Collections.

(This Listing Continued)

JOHN Q. GALE, born Hartford, Connecticut, June 16, 1951; admitted to bar, 1977, Connecticut. *Education:* University of Pennsylvania (B.S., 1973); University of Connecticut (J.D., 1977). Listed in Marquis Who's Who in American Law, 1996—. *Member:* Hartford County, Connecticut (Chairman Professional Discipline Committee) and American Bar Associations; The Association of Trial Lawyers of America. ***PRACTICE AREAS:*** Personal Injury Law; Estate Planning; Bankruptcy Law; Collections. ***Email:*** jgale@lawlordsofhartford.com

KATHLEEN J. KOWALYSHYN, born Southbridge, Massachusetts, April 8, 1957; admitted to bar, 1990, Connecticut. *Education:* University of Connecticut (B.A., 1980; J.D., 1990); University of Chicago. Member, Ethics Commission, City of Hartford, 1996—. Board of Directors, Connecticut Civil Liberties Union, 2000. *Member:* Hartford County and Connecticut Bar Associations. ***PRACTICE AREAS:*** Family Law; Real Estate; Probate. ***Email:*** kkowalyshyn@lawlordsofhartford.com

JOHN L. CALVOCORESSI (Retired from firm 12/31/99).

REPRESENTATIVE CLIENTS: Zurich Insurance Co.; United Artist Communications and All Lending Institutions; Laboratory Corp. of America; Walmart.
APPROVED ATTORNEY FOR: Connecticut Attorneys Title Insurance Co.

GALLAGHER & CALISTRO

HARTFORD, CONNECTICUT

(See New Haven)

General Civil Litigation and Appellate Practice in all Courts. Personal Injury Litigation, Business Litigation, Commercial Litigation.

GERSTEN & CLIFFORD

Established in 1987
214 MAIN STREET
HARTFORD, CONNECTICUT 06106-1892
Telephone: 860-527-7044
Fax: 860-527-4968

General Practice, Trials in all Courts. Negligence, White Collar Fraud, Securities Litigation, Professional Malpractice, Attorney Malpractice, Family, Real Estate and Probate.

MEMBERS OF FIRM

ELIOT B. GERSTEN, born Hartford, Connecticut, June 2, 1952; admitted to bar, 1979, Connecticut and U.S. District Court, District of Connecticut; 1981, U.S. Court of Appeals, 2nd Circuit; 1984, U.S. Supreme Court. *Education:* George Washington University (B.A., 1975); University of Miami (J.D., 1979). L.E.A.A. Intern, Dade County Public Defenders Office, 1977-1979. *Member:* Hartford County, Connecticut and American Bar Associations; The Association of Trial Lawyers of America. ***PRACTICE AREAS:*** Business Litigation; Securities; White Collar Fraud. ***Email:*** eliotg@gersten-clifford.com

JOHN P. CLIFFORD, JR., born New Haven, Connecticut, October 11, 1954; admitted to bar, 1980, Connecticut and U.S. District Court, District of Connecticut; 1981, Florida. *Education:* Trinity College (B.S., 1976); University of Miami (J.D., cum laude, 1980). *Member:* Hartford County and Connecticut Bar Associations; The Florida Bar; Connecticut Trial Lawyers Association; The Association of Trial Lawyers of America. ***PRACTICE AREAS:*** Personal Injury Litigation; Domestic Relations; Family Law; Workers Compensation Law; Divorce Law; Child Custody Law. ***Email:*** johnc@gersten-clifford.com

ALLAN W. KOERNER, born Putnam, Connecticut, September 4, 1955; admitted to bar, 1982, Connecticut. *Education:* Colby College (B.A., cum laude, 1978); University of Connecticut (J.D., 1982). *Member:* Connecticut Bar Association. ***PRACTICE AREAS:*** Real Estate Law; Corporate Law; Estate Planning Law; Probate Law; Wills; Trust Law. ***Email:*** allank@gersten-clifford.com

ASSOCIATES

WENDY J. DAVIES, born Hartford, Connecticut, March 2, 1965; admitted to bar, 1990, Connecticut; 1991, U.S. District Court, District of Connecticut. *Education:* University of Hartford (B.A., 1987); Western New England College (J.D., 1990). *Member:* Hartford County and Connecticut Bar Associations; Connecticut Trial Lawyers Association; Hartford Association of Women Attorneys; The Association of Trial Lawyers of America. ***PRACTICE AREAS:*** Personal Injury Law; Domestic Law; Criminal Law; Civil Litigation; Divorce Law; Driving While Intoxicated (DWI). ***Email:*** wendyd@gersten-clifford.com

JOHN JOSEPH ROBACYNSKI, born Bridgeport, Connecticut, August 17, 1955; admitted to bar, 1981, Connecticut; 1982, U.S. District Court, District of Connecticut; 1995, U.S. Court of Appeals, 2nd Circuit. *Education:* Fairfield University (A.B., 1977); Ohio Northern University (J.D., 1981); Quinnipiac

(This Listing Continued)

GERSTEN & CLIFFORD, Hartford—Continued

School of Law (LL.M., 1992). ***PRACTICE AREAS:*** Corporate Law; Business Litigation; Mergers and Acquisitions; Environmental Law. ***Email:*** robacjo@ci.bridgeport.ct.us

OF COUNSEL

CHARLES D. GERSTEN, born Simsbury, Connecticut, May 28, 1922; admitted to bar, 1949, Connecticut. *Education:* George Washington University (B.A., 1943); Harvard University (LL.B., 1949). *Member:* Hartford County, Connecticut and American Bar Associations.

GERSTEN & GERSTEN

Established in 1946

234 PEARL STREET

HARTFORD, CONNECTICUT 06103

Telephone: 860-522-0173

URL: http://gerstenandgersten.com

Email: legal@gerstenandgersten.com

URL: http://www.lawyers.com/gersten&gersten

Trial Practice in State and Federal Courts, including plaintiffs in all types of Personal Injury, Malpractice, Workers Compensation, Probate, Real Estate, Matrimonial and Domestic Relations. Bankruptcy, Small Business, Professional Misconduct, Employee Discrimination, and Wrongful Termination.

FIRM PROFILE: Founded in 1946, representing plaintiffs in all types of Personal Injury, Malpractice, Workers' Compensation; also Probate, Real Estate, all phases of Matrimonial and Domestic Relations, Bankruptcy, Small Business, Professional Misconduct; Employment Discrimination and Wrongful Termination.

MEMBERS OF FIRM

MAURICE R. GERSTEN, born East Granby, Connecticut; admitted to bar, 1941, District of Columbia; 1946, Connecticut. *Education:* George Washington University (A.B., 1937; LL.B., 1941). Examiner, Interstate Commerce Commission, Washington, D.C., 1941-1942. Representative, Connecticut Legislature, 1956-1960. Member, Commission to Revise Connecticut Corporation Law, 1960. *Member:* Hartford County, Connecticut and American Bar Associations; The District of Columbia Bar.

AARON L. GERSTEN, born Tariffville, Connecticut, April 21, 1926; admitted to bar, 1954, Connecticut; 1958, U.S. Supreme Court. *Education:* University of Connecticut (B.S. Pharm., 1948); George Washington University (B.A., 1951); University of Connecticut (LL.B., 1954). *Member:* Hartford County, Connecticut and American Bar Associations.

ASSOCIATES

PHILIP K. MEISTER, born Wauseon, Ohio, March 12, 1955; admitted to bar, 1979, Connecticut. *Education:* Trinity College (B.A., 1976); University of Connecticut (J.D., 1979). *Member:* Hartford County, Connecticut and American Bar Associations.

THOMAS D. JACOBS, born Hartford, Connecticut, May 22, 1953; admitted to bar, 1978, Wisconsin; 1987, Connecticut. *Education:* University of Connecticut (B.A., 1975); Marquette University (J.D., 1978). *Member:* Connecticut Bar Association.

KAREN S. GERSTEN, born Hartford, Connecticut, January 11, 1965; admitted to bar, 1990, Connecticut. *Education:* Clark University (B.A., 1987); Suffolk University (J.D., 1990). *Member:* Hartford County, Connecticut and American Bar Associations. ***PRACTICE AREAS:*** Family Law.

GILMAN & MARKS

HARTFORD, CONNECTICUT

(See East Hartford)

General Practice. Real Estate, Tax and Probate Law, Trials, Corporation, Estate Planning, Zoning and Land Use, Employment Law, Criminal, Banking, Mortgage, Litigation, Mortgage Foreclosures, DUI, Civil Rights, Discrimination, Wrongful Termination, Sexual Harassment, Family and Medical Leave Act, Americans with Disabilities.

GOODMAN, ROSENTHAL & McKENNA, P.C.

HARTFORD, CONNECTICUT

(See West Hartford)

Corporation, Real Estate, Pension, Employment, Antitrust, Litigation, Estate Planning.

GORDON, MUIR AND FOLEY, LLP

HARTFORD SQUARE NORTH

TEN COLUMBUS BOULEVARD

HARTFORD, CONNECTICUT 06106-5123

Telephone: 860-525-5361

Telecopier: 860-525-4849

Email: admin@gmflaw.com

URL: http://www.gmflaw.com

General Practice. Trials in all Courts. Insurance, Construction, Fidelity, Surety, Product Liability, Toxic Substances, Personal Injury, Professional Malpractice, Commercial, Real Estate, Probate, Corporation and Administrative Law.

MEMBERS OF FIRM

WILLIAM S. GORDON, JR. (1946-1956).

GEORGE MUIR (1939-1976).

EDWARD J. FOLEY (1955-1983).

JOHN J. REID, born Manchester, Connecticut, June 9, 1943; admitted to bar, 1968, Connecticut; 1969, U.S. District Court of Connecticut; 1986, U.S. Court of Appeals, Second Circuit. *Education:* Clark University (A.B., 1965); Boston College (J.D., 1968). Member, 1966-1968; Editor, 1967-1968, Boston College Industrial and Commercial Law Review. Law Clerk to Justice Charles S. House, Supreme Court of Connecticut, 1968-1969. Lecturer: "Building Contracts Seminar - or - What Happens When the Roof Collapses?" Connecticut Bar Association, 1979; Conference on "Construction Disputes: How to Prevent Them; How to Resolve Them," American Arbitration Association, 1983; Seminar on "Connecticut Construction Law: What to Do When . . .," National Business Institute, Inc., 1986, 1987; Conference on "Arbitrating and Moderating Construction Conflicts," American Arbitration Association, 1989; "Seminar on Construction Law or: What Happens When the Roof Collapses!," Connecticut Bar Association, 1990; "Pitfalls in the Takeover and Recovery Process - Protecting the Rights of the Surety," New England Bond Claim Association, 1991; "Construction Contracts: A Practical Law Seminar," Connecticut Associated Builders and Contractors, Inc., 1991; "Construction Litigation in the Nineties--and Beyond," Connecticut Bar Association, 1992; "Joint Venturing--Opportunities and Pitfalls," Construction Institute, 1993; "Latest Developments in Construction Law," Connecticut Bar Association, 1994; "Doing It Right! Project Delivery Systems," Construction Institute, 1995; "New Developments in Construction Law", Connecticut Bar Association, 1995; "What! Another Change Order?," Construction Institute, 1995; "Latest Developments in Construction Law," Connecticut Bar Association, 1996; "Program Manager, What is it? Is it right for you?," Construction Institute, 1999. Author: "Mechanics Liens - How to Get Cash When No One in the Construction Industry is Paying," Connecticut Bar Association, 1991; "How to Prove and Price Contractor's Claims for Delays, Disruptions and Accelerations--Attorney's Perspective," Connecticut Bar Association, 1992. Co-Author: "The Legal Liabilities of the Construction Manager--Neither Fish nor Fowl--But With the Liability of Both," Connecticut Bar Association, 1994; "Recent Developments in Construction Law-Construction Contract Clauses", Connecticut Bar Association, 1995; "Design-Build Contracts-The Benefits and the Pitfalls," Connecticut Bar Association, 1996. Master, Panel of Special Masters, U.S. District Court of Connecticut, 1988—. Member, Executive Committee and Chair, Construction Institute, 1993—; Panel of Arbitrators and Mediators, American Arbitration Association. *Member:* Hartford County, Connecticut (Member, Sections on: Construction, Executive Committee, Chair, 1994—; Civil Justice) and American (Member: Litigation Section, Committee on Construction Litigation, 1979—; Forum on the Construction Industry, 1976—; Tort and Insurance Practice Section; Fidelity and Surety Law Committee, 1979—; Public Contract Law Section, Vice Chair - Connecticut, 1993—) Bar Associations. ***PRACTICE AREAS:*** Construction Law; Fidelity and Surety Law; Alternate Dispute Resolution; Civil Litigation; Commercial Litigation. ***Email:*** jreid@gmflaw.com

JOHN H. GOODRICH, JR., born Hartford, Connecticut, August 2, 1943; admitted to bar, 1968, Virginia; 1971, Connecticut and U.S. District Court of Connecticut. *Education:* University of Massachusetts (B.A., 1965); College of William & Mary (J.D., 1968). *Member:* Hartford County, Connecticut, Virginia State and American (Member, Practice Management Section; Real Property, Probate and Trust Section) Bar Associations; National Academy of Elder Law Attorneys. [Captain, U.S. Army, 1968-1970]. ***PRACTICE AREAS:*** Real Estate; Probate; Elder Law; Estate Planning. ***Email:*** jgoodrich@gmflaw.com

R. BRADLEY WOLFE, born New York, N.Y., August 10, 1948; admitted to bar, 1974, Connecticut, U.S. District Court of Connecticut and U.S. Court of Appeals, Second Circuit. *Education:* Haverford College (B.A., 1970); University of Connecticut (J.D., 1973). Member, Panel of Special Masters, U.S. District Court of Connecticut, 1989—. Member, Panel of Arbitrators, American Arbitration Association. *Member:* Hartford County, Connecticut and American (Member: Forum Committee for the Construction Industry, 1983—; Tort and

(This Listing Continued)

Insurance Practice Section; Fidelity and Surety Committee, 1982—; Section of Business Law) Bar Associations. ***PRACTICE AREAS:*** Construction Law; Surety Law; Commercial Litigation. ***Email:*** rbwolfe@gmflaw.com

JON STEPHEN BERK, born New York, N.Y., April 1, 1950; admitted to bar, 1975, Connecticut; 1976, U.S. District Court of Connecticut; 1977, U.S. Court of Appeals, Second Circuit; 1980, U.S. Supreme Court. *Education:* Wesleyan University (B.A., 1972); Boston University (J.D., 1975). Co-Author, "Connecticut Law of Uninsured and Underinsured Motorist Coverage," Atlantic Law Book Company, 1999. *Member:* Hartford County and Connecticut Bar Associations; Connecticut Defense Lawyers Association; Defense Research Institute. ***PRACTICE AREAS:*** Automobile Liability; Commercial Liability; Insurance Coverage; Product Liability; Municipal Liability; Agents and Brokers Errors and Omissions; Employment Litigation. ***Email:*** jberk@gmflaw.com

WILLIAM J. GALLITTO, born Middletown, Connecticut, May 22, 1950; admitted to bar, 1976, Connecticut; 1979, U.S. District Court of Connecticut. *Education:* Wesleyan University (B.A., 1972); Boston College (J.D., 1976). Special Master, New Britain Superior Court, 1984-1986. New Britain Superior Court Attorney-Trial Referee, 1985-1987. Hartford Superior Court Attorney-Trial Referee, 1985-1987. *Member:* Hartford County and Connecticut (Vice Chairman, Medical-Legal Committee, 1983—) Bar Associations; The Association of Trial Lawyers of America (Member: Mediation Dispute Committee; Coalition and Victims Committee); Connecticut Trial Lawyers Association. ***PRACTICE AREAS:*** Personal Injury Law; Medical Malpractice; Product Liability. ***Email:*** wgallitto@gmflaw.com

GERALD R. SWIRSKY, born New Haven, Connecticut, February 16, 1941; admitted to bar, 1966, Connecticut. *Education:* Yale University (B.A., 1962); University of Connecticut (LL.B., 1966). Lecturer: "Legal Implications of Patient's Records," University of Connecticut Dental School, 1986—. Adjunct Member of Faculty, University of Connecticut Dental School, 1986—. *Member:* Hartford County, Connecticut and American (Member: Tort and Insurance Practice Law Section; Tort and Insurance Practice Section) Bar Associations. ***PRACTICE AREAS:*** Civil Litigation; Insurance Law; Legal Malpractice Defense; Medical Malpractice Defense; Dental Malpractice Defense; Commercial Litigation. ***Email:*** gswirsky@gmflaw.com

ROBERT J. O'BRIEN, born Camden, New Jersey, September 29, 1954; admitted to bar, 1979, Connecticut; 1980, U.S. District Court, District of Connecticut; 1986, U.S. Court of Appeals, Second Circuit; 1988, U.S. Court of Federal Claims. *Education:* Amherst College (B.A., 1976); Case Western Reserve University (J.D., 1979). Lecturer: National Association of Women in Construction program on Connecticut Construction Law, Fidelity and Surety Law, March, 1986. Co-Author and Lecturer: National Business Institute, Inc.'s program on "Construction Law: What Do You Do When. . . .?" 1987. Lecturer: Construction Law Section, Connecticut Bar Association, 1993, 1994, 1996, 1999. Lecturer: Hartford County Bar Association Program on "Arbitration," 1996. Director, Connecticut Association of Builders and Contractors. Member: Construction Institute Education Committee; Program Committee; Town of Avon Planning and Zoning Committee. *Member:* Hartford County, Connecticut (Member, Executive Committee, Section on: Construction Law) and American Bar Associations. ***Email:*** ro'brien@gmflaw.com

PHILIP J. O'CONNOR, born Hartford, Connecticut, May 24, 1949; admitted to bar, 1976, Connecticut; 1979, U.S. District Court of Connecticut; 1986, U.S. Court of Appeals, Second Circuit. *Education:* Johns Hopkins University (B.A., 1971); University of Connecticut (J.D., with honors, 1976). *Member:* Connecticut Bar Association (Member, Civil Litigation Section); Connecticut Defense Lawyers Association (President, 1993-1994); Defense Research Institute (Member, Drug and Medical Device, Insurance Law, Product Liability, Toxic Torts and Environmental Law Committees). ***PRACTICE AREAS:*** Litigation; Products Liability; Insurance Coverage; Toxic Torts; Negligence Defense. ***Email:*** po'connor@gmflaw.com

KENNETH G. WILLIAMS, born Willimantic, Connecticut, July 28, 1956; admitted to bar, 1982, Connecticut and U.S. District Court, District of Connecticut. *Education:* University of Connecticut (B.A., magna cum laude, honors scholar in Economics, 1978; J.D., with honors, 1982). Fellow, Connecticut Bar Foundation. Lecturer: "Lead Litigation Strategies," Connecticut Bar Association, 1996. *Member:* Connecticut and American Bar Associations; Connecticut Defense Lawyers Association; Defense Research Institute. ***PRACTICE AREAS:*** Tort Liability; Products Liability; Toxic Torts; Environmental Law; Employment Law; Insurance Law. ***Email:*** kwilliams@gmflaw.com

MARY ANNE ALICIA CHARRON, born Haverhill, Massachusetts, September 16, 1961; admitted to bar, 1986, Massachusetts; 1987, Connecticut; 1988, U.S. District Court, District of Connecticut. *Education:* College of the Holy Cross (A.B., 1983); Catholic University of America (J.D., 1986). Senior Staff Member, Catholic University Law Review, 1985-1986. Legal Research Clerk to Judges of the Superior Court of Connecticut, 1986-1987. *Member:* Connecticut (Member, Sections On: Construction Law; Elder Law) and American Bar Associations; Connecticut Volunteer Lawyers for the Arts; National Association of Women in Construction (Hartford County Chapter, 1991—); National Organization of Social Security Claimants Representatives. ***PRACTICE AREAS:*** Construction; Surety/Fidelity; Social Security Disability; Probate. ***Email:*** mcharron@gmflaw.com

ANDREẆ JAMES HERN, born Boston, Massachusetts, December 2, 1962; admitted to bar, 1989, Connecticut; 1990, Massachusetts, U.S. District Court, District of Connecticut. *Education:* Trinity College (B.A., 1986); University of Connecticut (J.D., 1989). Member, Editorial Board of Compensation Quarterly. *Member:* Connecticut Bar Association (Member, Executive Committee, Workers Compensation Section). ***PRACTICE AREAS:*** Insurance Defense; Workers Compensation; Bad Faith Insurance Claims. ***Email:*** ahern@gmflaw.com

RENEÉ W. DWYER, born Hartford, Connecticut, November, 3, 1966; admitted to bar, 1991, Connecticut. *Education:* Providence College (B.S., cum laude, 1988); Catholic University of America (J.D., 1991). Recipient: American Jurisprudence Awards in Family Law and Professional Responsibility; Trial Practice Award. Author: Lead Paint Liability: For The Defense, Sidebar, the Connecticut Bar Association Litigation Quarterly, Spring, 1995, Vol. 3 Number 3; Strict Liability Ruling Overturned, Sidebar, The Connecticut Bar Association Litigation Quarterly, Spring 1996, Volume 4, Number 2; Lead Paint Litigation, The Connecticut Bar Association Litigation Quarterly, Summer 1997, Volume 5, Number 3. *Member:* Hartford County, Connecticut and American Bar Associations. ***PRACTICE AREAS:*** Insurance Defense; Civil Litigation; Retail Liability; Premises Liability. ***Email:*** rdwyer@gmflaw.com

PATTY G. SWAN, born Watertown, Connecticut, July 20, 1969; admitted to bar, 1994, Connecticut; 1995, U.S. District Court, District of Connecticut. *Education:* University of Connecticut (B.A., cum laude, 1991); Western New England College (J.D., cum laude, 1994). Recipient: United States Law Week Award; American Jurisprudence Award in Products Liability; Semi-Finalist, National Environmental Moot Court Competition. *Member:* Hartford County and Connecticut Bar Associations. ***PRACTICE AREAS:*** Insurance Defense; Litigation; Civil Litigation; Insurance Coverage Litigation; Employment Law; Premises Liability; Appellate Advocacy. ***Email:*** pswan@gmflaw.com

ERIK E. ROBERTS, born Charlottesville, Virginia, December 6, 1964; admitted to bar, 1995, Connecticut. *Education:* Wake Forest University (B.A., cum laude, 1987); University of Connecticut School of Law (J.D., 1995). *Member:* Connecticut Bar Association. ***PRACTICE AREAS:*** Insurance Defense; Civil Litigation; Workers Compensation. ***Email:*** eroberts@gmflaw.com

ASSOCIATES

DOREEN WEST AMATA, born New London, Connecticut, January 2, 1967; admitted to bar, 1992, Connecticut, U.S. District Court, District of Connecticut; Mashantucket Pequot Tribal Court and the Mohegan Pequot Tribal Court. *Education:* Providence College (B.S., cum laude, 1989); Western New England College (J.D., Honors, Legal Writing, 1992). *Member:* Connecticut and American Bar Associations; Connecticut Defense Lawyers Association. ***PRACTICE AREAS:*** Insurance Defense; Premises Liability; Medical Malpractice Defense; Legal Malpractice Defense. ***Email:*** dwest@gmflaw.com

DURWIN P. JONES, born New Haven, Connecticut, April 13, 1968; admitted to bar, 1993, Connecticut; U.S. District Court, District of Connecticut. *Education:* Rutgers College (B.A., 1990); Temple University (J.D., 1993). *Member:* Connecticut Bar Association (Member, Construction Law, Commercial Law and Bankruptcy). ***PRACTICE AREAS:*** Commercial Litigation; Construction Litigation; Federal Practice; Creditor's Rights; Lender Liability Defense; Bankruptcy; Foreclosures; Condominium Law; Real Estate Transactions; Corporate Law. ***Email:*** djones@gmflaw.com

MELISSA B. GEETTER, born Hartford, Connecticut, April 14, 1972; admitted to bar, 1997, Connecticut; 1998, U.S. District Court, District of Connecticut. *Education:* State University of New York at Albany (B.S., 1994); University of Connecticut School of Law (J.D., 1997). Member, University of Connecticut Law Review, 1996-1997. *Member:* Hartford County and Connecticut (Member: Labor and Employment Section; Young Lawyers Section) Bar Associations. ***PRACTICE AREAS:*** Employment Litigation; Labor Law; Insurance Defense; Product Liability; Civil Litigation. ***Email:*** mgeetter@gmflaw.com

CHRISTINE L. CHIPMAN, born Brooklyn, New York, March 6, 1958; admitted to bar, 1987, Connecticut. *Education:* Carleton College (B.A., 1980); University of Connecticut School of Law (J.D., 1987). *Member:* Connecticut Bar Association. ***PRACTICE AREAS:*** Corporate Law; Limited Liability Company Law; Real Estate; Commercial Finance. ***Email:*** cchipman@gmflaw.com

WILLIAM P. MASTROGIOVANNI, JR., born Sumter, South Carolina, January 25, 1968; admitted to bar, 1993, Connecticut; 1999, U.S. District Court, District of Connecticut. *Education:* Fairfield University (B.A., cum laude, 1990); University of Connecticut School of Law (J.D., 1993). ***PRACTICE AREAS:*** Litigation. ***Email:*** wmastrogiovanni@gmflaw.com

(This Listing Continued)

(This Listing Continued)

GORDON, MUIR AND FOLEY, LLP, Hartford—Continued

OF COUNSEL

PETER C. SCHWARTZ, born New York, N.Y., May 31, 1938; admitted to bar, 1965, New York; 1967, Connecticut, U.S. District Court of Connecticut and U.S. Court of Appeals, Second Circuit; 1969, U.S. Supreme Court. *Education:* Dartmouth College (A.B., 1960); University of Pennsylvania (LL.B., 1963). "The Internet: How To Protect Yourself from the Perils of Cyberspace," *Defense Counsel Journal,* 2001. Lecturer: "Legal Malpractice Risk Seminars," Connecticut, 1997. *Member:* Hartford County, Connecticut and American (Tort and Insurance Practice Section - TIPS) Bar Associations; International Association of Defense Counsel (Chairman, Legal Malpractice Committee); Connecticut Defense Lawyers Association; Defense Research Institute. ***PRACTICE AREAS:*** Products Liability; Legal Malpractice; Accountants Malpractice. ***Email:*** pschwartz@gmflaw.com

REPRESENTATIVE CLIENTS: AIG; Alamo Rent-A-Car, Inc.; Amenta/Emma Architects, P.C.; American Express IDS; The Atlanta Casualty Insurance Co.; Blue Ridge Insurance Co.; Cannondale Corporation; Century Workers' Compensation; C.H. Nichusm; Chubb; CIGNA; CIRMA; CNA Insurance Companies; Coca-Cola Enterprises; Combustion Engineering Co.; Cranford and Company; CVCS; CVS; D-Tox, Inc.; The Dow Chemcial Co.; Dow Corning Corporation; Emerson Electric Co.; Federal Insurance Co.; First State Insurance Co.; FIP Construction, Inc.; Fireman's Fund Insurance Cos.; Fleet Bank; Florist Mutual; Frito Lay, Inc.; Gallagher Bassetts Services; Gilbane Building Co.; Goodwill Industries of the Springfield/Hartford Area, Inc.; Gulf Insurance Co.; Hanover Insurance Co.; Hertz Corp.; INAPRO; The Infinity Insurance Co.; Lancer Claims, Inc.; Liberty Mutual Insurance Co.; Markel Insurance Co.; May Department Stores Co.; Middlesex Mutual Insurance Co.; Montagno Construction Co., Inc.; National Car Rental Systems, Inc.; National Union; Nationwide Insurance Co.; Nautilus Insurance Co.; Paul S. Yoney, Inc.; Peerless Insurance Co.; Penske Trucking Co. LLP; People's Bank; PneumoAbex Corporation; Professional Medical Insurance Co.; Progressive Casualty Co.; Providence Washington Group; Reliant Insurance Co.; Reliance National Insurance Co.; Rite Aid, Inc.; Riverfront Recapture, Inc.; Safeco Insurance; Security Insurance of Hartford; Shelby Insurance Group; Shepard Steel Co., Inc.; Shoprite Supermarkets; Sterling Risk Services; Titan Mechanical Contractors, Inc.; Transamerica Insurance Co.; Travelers Insurance Co.; Unistress Corp.; United Rentals, Inc.; United National Insurance Co.; University of Connecticut; Utica Mutual Insurance Co.; Wallgreen's Pharmacy; Western Surety; Westport Insurance Co.; W.E. O'Neil Construction Co.; Worcester Mutual Insurance Co.; Zurich American.

JONATHAN GOULD

214 MAIN STREET
HARTFORD, CONNECTICUT 06106-1817
Telephone: 860-278-9115
Fax: 860-278-9124
Email: jgould@nela.org

All aspects of Labor and Employment Law, Employee Benefits, Workplace and Other Injuries.

JONATHAN GOULD, born New Haven, Connecticut, August 18, 1951; admitted to bar, 1976, Connecticut and U.S. District Court, District of Connecticut; 1980, U.S. Court of Appeals, Second Circuit; 1996. U.S. Supreme Court. *Education:* Trinity College (A.B., 1973); University of Connecticut (J.D., 1976). Author: "A Reply to Wiggins and Reicher," 65 Conn. Bar Journal 167, 1991; Worker's Compensation Section 31-290a Claims," Connecticut Workers' Compensation Quarterly, Fall 1993. "Wrongful Discharge Section, Employee and Union Member Guide to Labor Law," 1998. *Member:* Connecticut Bar Association; Connecticut Trial Lawyers Association; National Employment Lawyers Association. ***PRACTICE AREAS:*** Labor Law; Workers Compensation Law.

GOULD, KILLIAN & WYNNE

Established in 1954
280 TRUMBULL STREET, 25TH FLOOR
HARTFORD, CONNECTICUT 06103-3595
Telephone: 860-278-1270
Telecopier: 860-244-9290

General Practice. Real Estate, Probate, Corporation, Estate Planning, Family, Education, Personal Injury, Divorce and Child Custody, Trials and Appeals in all Courts.

MEMBERS OF FIRM

SAMUEL GOULD (1905-1994).

ROBERT K. KILLIAN, born Hartford, Connecticut, September 15, 1919; admitted to bar, 1948, Connecticut. *Education:* Union College (B.A., 1942); University of Connecticut (LL.B., 1948). Assistant Corporation Counsel, Hartford, 1951-1954. Attorney General, 1968-1974 and Lieutenant Governor, 1975-1979, State of Connecticut. *Member:* Hartford County, Connecticut and American Bar Associations; The Association of Trial Lawyers of America.

(This Listing Continued)

FRANCIS J. WYNNE, born Hartford, Connecticut, December 17, 1923; admitted to bar, 1960, Connecticut. *Education:* University of Connecticut (B.S., 1950; LL.B., 1960). Member: Charter Revision Commission, 1965; Zoning Board of Appeals, Wethersfield, Connecticut, 1961-1966. *Member:* Hartford County and Connecticut Bar Associations. ***PRACTICE AREAS:*** Personal Injury; Insurance Defense; Medical Malpractice.

MARTIN A. GOULD, born Hartford, Connecticut, July 4, 1940; admitted to bar, 1965, Connecticut. *Education:* Boston University (B.A., 1962; LL.B., cum laude, 1965); Harvard University (LL.M., 1966). Editor, Boston University Law Review, 1963-1965. Author, "Termination of Trusts," Boston University Law Review, Vol. XLIII, page 562; "The Rejection and Funding of Teacher Contracts in Connecticut," Connecticut Law Review, Vol. 9, page 608. *Member:* Hartford County, Connecticut and American Bar Associations. ***REPORTED CASES:*** Sample List: Bleiler v. Cristwood Construction Company, Inc., et al, 72 F.3d 13 (2d Cir. 1995), 19 Employee Benefit Cases, 2356 and Pension Plan Guide, p. 23915; Torosyan v. Boehringer Ingelheim Pharmaceuticals, Inc., 234 Conn. 1, 662 A.2d 89, (1995); Monroe v. Crandall, 3 Conn. App. 214, 486 A.2d 657 (1985); Tucker v. Norfolk Bd. of Education, 177 Conn. 572, 418 A.2d 933 (1979); Board of Education v. Frey, 174 Conn. 578, 392 A.2d 466 (1978); McTigue v. New London Education Assn., 164 Conn. 348, 321 A.2d 462 (1973). ***PRACTICE AREAS:*** Estate Planning; Probate; Commercial Real Estate; Residential Real Estate; Civil Litigation; Corporate Law; Family Law. ***Email:*** mgould@gkwlaw.com

MARK W. BARONAS, born Greenfield, Massachusetts , July 15, 1954; admitted to bar, 1981, Connecticut. *Education:* Amherst College (B.A., cum laude, 1977); University of Connecticut (J.D., 1981). Law Clerk, Superior Court of Connecticut, 1981-1982. *Member:* Hartford County and Connecticut Bar Associations. ***PRACTICE AREAS:*** Personal Injury; Insurance Defense; Medical Malpractice; Employment Law. ***Email:*** mbaronas@gkwlaw.com

NANCY E. GOULD, born Boston, Massachusetts, June 21, 1966; admitted to bar, 1991, Connecticut. *Education:* Union College (B.S., cum laude, 1988); Boston University (J.D., 1991). Psi Chi. Staff Member, 1989-1990 and Note and Comment Editor, 1990-1991, Annual Review of Banking Law. Author, "The Trend Toward a Cashless Society-The Point of Sale Electronic Fund Transfer," Annual Review of Banking Law, Volume 10. *Member:* Hartford County and Connecticut Bar Associations. ***PRACTICE AREAS:*** Employment Law; Real Estate; Family Law; Civil Litigation; Divorce; Commercial Law. ***Email:*** ngould@gkwlaw.com

ROBERT O. WYNNE, born Hartford, Connecticut, November 26, 1959; admitted to bar, 1991, Connecticut. *Education:* University of Connecticut (B.S., 1982); New England School of Law (J.D., 1991). *Member:* Hartford County and Connecticut Bar Associations. ***PRACTICE AREAS:*** Personal Injury; Insurance Defense; Civil Litigation; Divorce. ***Email:*** rwynne@gkwlaw.com

REPRESENTATIVE CLIENTS: Connecticut Education Assn.; American International Pacific Insurance Co.; Travelers Insurance Co.; The St. Paul Insurance Co.; Keystone Insurance Co.; Cunningham Supply, Inc.; Huntergreen Dental Laboratories; On-Line Technologies Inc.; Advanced Fuel Research, Inc.; Carpenters, Operating Engineers and Teamsters Fringe Benefits Funds.
REFERENCE: Hudson United Bank.

GREEN AND GROSS, P.C.

HARTFORD, CONNECTICUT

(See Bridgeport)

Bankruptcy Law, Commercial and Construction Claims.

GREEN & LEVINE LLP

HARTFORD, CONNECTICUT

(See Farmington)

Commercial and Residential Real Estate, Zoning, Development, Finance, Corporate Workouts and Foreclosures, Commercial Leasing, Business Law.

HAESE, LLC

100 PEARL STREET, 14TH FLOOR
HARTFORD, CONNECTICUT 06103
Telephone: 860-249-7194
Facsimile: 860-249-7195
URL: http://www.haese.com

Boston, Massachusetts Office: 70 Franklin Street, 9th Floor. Telephone: 617-428-0266. Facsimile: 617-428-0276. URL: http://www.haese.com.

Construction and Design Law, Insurance, Fidelity and Surety, Environmental Law, Government Contract Law, Commercial, OSHA Laws and Regulations, Real Property and Finance, Banking and Trial and Appellate Practice in all State and Federal Courts.

(This Listing Continued)

GLENN H. HAESE, born El Campo, Texas, April 7, 1957; admitted to bar, 1983, Colorado and U.S. District Court, District of Colorado; 1996, U.S. Court of Appeals, Fifth Circuit; 1998, U.S. Court of Appeals, Fourth Circuit (Not admitted in Connecticut). *Education:* University of Arizona (B.S.C.E., 1980); University of Colorado; University of Denver (J.D., 1983). McGill Scholar. Co-Author: Chapter, "Changes in Scope," Proving and Pricing Construction Claims, Wiley, 1990; Chapter, "Types of Claims," Proving and Pricing Construction Claims, Wiley, 2001. Lecturer: Competitive Bidding Issues, Concerns, and Resultant Litigation, Southwestern Regional Conference, American Society of Civil Engineers, May, 1979; Construction Litigation and Lender-Borrower Relations, University of Hartford, Construction Institute, April 1991; Proving and Pricing Construction Claims, University of Hartford, Construction Institute, September, 1991; Construction Litigation and Real Estate Projects involving Litigation, Northeast Real Estate Exchange Conference, October, 1991; Efficient and Effective Discovery and Document Control in Construction and Engineering Litigation, Connecticut Bar Association, April, 1992; The New Procurement Law - Construction Management Process Implementation and Claims, University of Hartford, Construction Institute, October, 1992; Resolving Construction Claims in Mediation and Arbitration - Evaluating the Claim, Albany, New York, Hartford, Connecticut and Manchester, New Hampshire. Former Director, Coopers & Lybrand. *Member:* Denver County, Boulder County, Colorado (Member, Alternative Dispute Resolution Committee), Connecticut (Associate Member, Construction Law Section), Massachusetts (Associate Member, Alternative Dispute Resolution Committee), New York State (Associate Member) and American (Co-Vice Chairman, Public Contract Law Section, Committee on International Procurement, Construction Law Section, Science and Technology Section) Bar Associations; American Arbitration Association; American Society of Civil Engineers; Associated General Contractors of America; Connecticut Construction Industries Association; Construction Industries of Massachusetts. ***LANGUAGES:*** French. ***PRACTICE AREAS:*** Construction Law; Engineering Law; Environmental Law; Government Contract Law; Hazardous Waste; Real Estate Law; International Business Law; International Arbitration Law; Alternative Dispute Resolution; Civil Litigation. ***Email:*** ghaese@haese.com

(For Complete Biographical Data on all Personnel, see Professional Biographies at Boston, Massachusetts)

LAW OFFICES OF
R. BARTLEY HALLORAN

HARTFORD, CONNECTICUT

(See Levy and Droney, P.C. in Farmington)

HALLORAN & SAGE LLP

Established in 1935

ONE GOODWIN SQUARE

225 ASYLUM STREET

HARTFORD, CONNECTICUT 06103

Telephone: 860-522-6103

Fax: 860-548-0006

URL: http://www.halloran-sage.com

Middletown, Connecticut Office: 300 Plaza Middlesex, 06457. Telephone: 860-346-8641. Fax: 860-344-1641.

Westport, Connecticut Office: 315 Post Road West, 06880-4739. Telephone: 203-227-2855. Fax: 203-227-6992.

Washington, D.C. Office: 1627 I Street, N.W., Suite 610, 20006. Telephone: 202-496-9270. Fax: 202-496-9279.

Administrative Law, Administrative Hearings and Appeals, Alternative Dispute Resolution, Appellate Practice, Aviation Products Liability, Bad Faith Litigation, Banking Law, Bankruptcy, Breach of Contract, Business Disputes, Business Law, Business Litigation, Business Planning, Casualty Insurance Litigation, Civil Appeals, Civil Litigation, Civil Rights Litigation, Class Action, Commercial Litigation, Complex Civil Litigation, Construction and Design Law, Construction Litigation, Corporate Contracts, Corporate Law, Criminal Litigation, Drug and Medical Device Litigation, Employment Law, Energy and Health Law, Environmental Law, Excess Insurance, Family Business Succession, Fidelity and Surety Law, Finance, Education Law, Employment Law, Environmental, Environmental Insurance Coverage, ERISA, ERISA Litigation, Estate Administration, Estate and Gift Taxation, Estates Law, Excess Insurance, General Corporate Law, General Liability, Government Contracts, Government Finance, Government Relations, Health and Life Insurance Litigation, Insurance Bad Faith Litigation, Insurance Coverage, Institutional Liability Law, Insurance Litigation, Insurance Regulation, Intellectual Property Litigation, International Law, Judicial Review, Labor and Employment, Land Use Planning Law, Lead Paint Litigation, Legislative Practice, Liquor Liability, Lobbying, Marine Insurance Defense, Medical Malpractice, Mergers and Acquisitions and Divestitures, Municipal Law, Municipal Liability, Probate Law, Products Liability Litigation, Professional Liability Litigation, Professional Regulation, Premises Liability, Property Insurance, Psychological Injury Claims, Public Utilities Law, Public Utility Regulation, Real Estate Transactions, Reinsurance Law, Risk Management Consulting, Secured Lending, Securities Law, Subrogation, Taxation Law, Telecommunications Law, Torts, Trade Association, Trucking Transportation Litigation, Trust Law, Unfair Trade, Uninsured and Underinsured Motorists, University Law, Workers Compensation Law, Zoning, Planning and Land Use.

FIRM PROFILE: Halloran & Sage is a large, progressive firm with one of the largest litigation practices in Connecticut. Founded in 1935, the firm also has earned a nationwide reputation because of its litigation work for companies located throughout the United States.

In addition to litigation, Halloran & Sage has expertise in all areas of corporate and commercial law, including national and international capabilities provided by membership in specialized associations such as the American Law Firm Association, the Defense Research Institute, the Federation of Insurance and Corporate Counsel and the International Association of Defense Counsel.

MEMBERS OF FIRM

JOSEPH G. LYNCH, born Newark, New Jersey, August 12, 1924; admitted to bar, 1951, Connecticut; U.S. District Court, District of Connecticut; U.S. District Court, Southern and Eastern District of NY; U.S. Court of Appeals, Second Circuit; U.S. Supreme Court. *Education:* Wesleyan University (A.B., cum laude, 1947); Harvard University (LL.B., 1951). Listed in Best Lawyers in America, 1993—. Administrative Assistant to U.S. Senator Raymond E. Baldwin, 1947-1948. Probate Judge for Portland District, 1963-1983. Town Counsel for Portland, 1963—. General Counsel, Wesleyan University, 1967—. Member, Board of Directors: Rockfall Foundation; New England Air Museum, 1990—; Fidelco Guide Dog Foundation, 1997—. Member, Connecticut State Insurance Purchasing and Risk Management Board. *Member:* Hartford County, Middlesex County, Connecticut (Chairman, Judiciary Committee, 1989-1991) and American Bar Associations; American Judicature Society; Defense Research Institute; Connecticut Defense Trial Lawyers Association; Federation of Insurance and Corporate Counsel; National Association of College and University Attorneys. Fellow: American College of Trial Lawyers. Life Fellow, American Bar Foundation (State Chairman, 1998—). ***PRACTICE AREAS:*** Civil Litigation; Insurance Litigation; Educational Law. ***Email:*** lynchj@halloran-sage.com

JOSEPH T. SWEENEY, born New Haven, Connecticut, September 7, 1937; admitted to bar, 1962, Connecticut. *Education:* College of the Holy Cross (A.B., 1959); Georgetown University (J.D., 1962). Phi Delta Phi. Member, Board of Editors, Georgetown Law Journal, 1961-1962. Law Clerk, Chief Justice Raymond E. Baldwin, Connecticut Supreme Court, 1962-1963. Member, Manchester Town Board of Directors, 1977-1979. *Member:* Hartford County, Connecticut and American Bar Associations; International Association of Defense Counsel (Secretary, Committee on Professional Errors and Omissions, 1990-1991); Connecticut Defense Lawyers Association; Defense Research and Trial Lawyers Association; National Board of Trial Advocacy (Diplomat, 1983-1993); American Board of Trial Advocates. ***REPORTED CASES:*** Nutt v. Norwich Roman Catholic Diocese, 921 F. Supp. 66 (D.Conn., 1995); Silverberg v. Great Southwest Fire Ins. Co., 214 Conn. 632, 573 A.2d 724 (1990); Krawczyk v. Stingle, 208 Conn. 239, 543 A.2d 733 (1988); Mullen v. Horton, 46 Conn.App. 759, 700A.2d 1377 (1997); Dimeo v. Burns, Brooks & McNeil, 6 Conn. App. 241, 504 A.2d 557, cert. denied, 199 Conn. 805, 508 A.2d 31 (1986). ***PRACTICE AREAS:*** Professional Liability Litigation; Clergy Malpractice; Clergy Sexual Misconduct; Insurance Litigation. ***Email:*** sweeney@halloran-sage.com

GEORGE ROYSTER, born Hartford, Connecticut, August 28, 1941; admitted to bar, 1966, Connecticut and U.S. District Court, District of Connecticut; 1968, U.S. Court of Appeals, Second Circuit; 1973, U.S. Supreme Court. *Education:* Lafayette College (A.B., 1963); Washington University (J.D., 1966). Phi Delta Phi. Listed in: Who's Who in American Law and International Law. Author: "Joint and Several Liability and Collateral Sources Under the 1987 Tort Reform Act," Vol. 62, Connecticut Bar Journal, No. 5, 1988; "The Products Liability Statute of Limitation in Connecticut," Volume 9, Connecticut Law Tribune No. 31, 1983; "Jurisdiction under Section 33-411 (b) (Long arm) and forum non-conveniens," CBA seminar on Products Liability, Jan. 1983; "Punitive Damages in Connecticut under the Products Liability Act," CBA seminar on advanced Products Liability, May, 1983; "Challenging the Validity of Neuropsychological Scientific Principles," Neuropsychology for Lawyers Seminar, PES, October, 1988. Author and Speaker at: CBA seminars on Products Liability Tactics and Strategy on subject of long-arm jurisdiction, 1983; CT's Tort Reform Act on subject of joint and several liability, 1986; CT's Tort Reform Act II on the subject of joint and several liability and collateral sources, 1987; Opening Statements and Closing Arguments in Personal Injury Cases, 1989; National Business Associations seminar of Recision of Insurance Contracts in AIDS Cases, 1995. Editor and Contributing Author of 50-State Compendium on Third Party Indemnity in Products Liability Actions, 1995. Member: Connecticut Judicial Selection Commission, 1996—; Glastonbury Town Council, 1975-

(This Listing Continued)

HALLORAN & SAGE LLP, Hartford—Continued

1977; Glastonbury Board of Education, 1969-1975. Counsel to President Ford Committee in Connecticut, 1975-1976. Member, Panel of Arbitrators, American Arbitration Association. *Member:* Connecticut Bar Association (Chairman, Sub-Committee on Trial Specialization, 1975-1976; Chairman, 1984-1987 and Vice Chairman, 1982-1984, Executive Committee on Civil Justice); American Board of Trial Advocates (President, Connecticut Chapter, 1984-1988); National Board of Trial Advocacy; Connecticut Academy of Certified Trial Lawyers (Vice Chairman, 1998—); Connecticut Trial Lawyers Association; Association of Ski Defense Attorneys. Fellow, American Board of Trial Advocates Foundation. (Certified Civil Trial Advocate by the National Board of Trial Advocacy, 1982). ***PRACTICE AREAS:*** Commercial Litigation; Products Liability; Torts. ***Email:*** royster@halloran-sage.com

ARTHUR P. McGOWAN, JR., born Hartford, Connecticut, September 14, 1936; admitted to bar, 1968, Connecticut. *Education:* Worcester Polytechnic Institute (B.S., 1958); Catholic University of America (J.D., 1968). *Member:* Hartford County, Connecticut (Member, Probate and Trust and Corporate Sections) and American (Member, Probate and Real Property, Tax and Business Sections) Bar Associations. ***PRACTICE AREAS:*** Estate Planning; Trust Law; Estates Law; Estate Administration; General Corporate Law; Family Business Succession; Taxation Law; Estate and Gift Taxation. ***Email:*** mcgowan@halloran-sage.com

JOHN W. LEMEGA, born Hartford, Connecticut, September 20, 1943; admitted to bar, 1968, Connecticut; 2001, Massachusetts. *Education:* Trinity College (B.A., cum laude, 1965); Boston College (LL.B., 1968). Phi Beta Kappa. Managing Editor, Annual Survey of Massachusetts Law, 1967-1968. Author: "Fleet Stacking and *Gode,* or: Is There Life After Footnote 9," Vol. 2, The Defense No. 2, June, 1985; "Dram Shop Payments as An Offset to Underinsured Motorist Coverage," Vol. 11, The Connecticut Law Tribune No. 38, September 23, 1985; "Seeking Judicial Review of Arbitration Awards," Vol. 3, The Defense No. 2, June, 1986; "Uninsured Motorist Arbitration— The Scope of 'Limited ' Review," Vol. 5, The Defense, No. 1, October 1988. Lecturer and Co-Author: "Connecticut Structured Settlements," PESI, 1988; "Connecticut Update on Uninsured and Underinsured Motorist Coverage," PESI, 1990, 1991, 1992, 1993, 1994, 1995; "Connecticut Insurance Bad Faith Litigation," PESI, 1990; "Insurance and Tort Law Update," PESI, 1991; Uninsured and Underinsured Motorist Seminar, CTLA, 1995, 1996; "Declaratory Judgements Practical Considerations," American Law Firm Assoc. Health Insurance seminar, 1995. Law Clerk, Justice Elmer W. Ryan of the Connecticut Supreme Court, 1968-1969. Member, 1989-1993, Vice-Chairman, 1990-1991, Chairman, 1991-1993, West Hartford Board of Education, President, Noah Webster House and West Hartford Historical Society, 1998-2000. *Member:* Hartford County, Connecticut and American Bar Associations; Defense Research Institute; Connecticut Defense Lawyers Association (Member, Board of Directors, 1986-1989). ***REPORTED CASES:*** USF&G v. Hutchinson, 710 A.2d 1343; Potter v. Chicago Pneumatic Tool Co., 694 A. 2d 1319; Hansen v. Ohio Casualty Co., 687 A. 2d 1262; O'Brien v. USF&G Co., 669 A. 2d 1221; Horn v. Maryland Casualty Co., 661 A. 2d 1032; Williams v. State Farm Mutual Auto Ins. Co., 641 A. 2d 783; Ceci v. National Indemnity Co., 622 A. 2d 545; Lees v. Middlesex Ins. Co., 581 A. 2d 287; Oldread v. National Union Fire Ins. Co., 500 A. 2d 956; DeDominicus v. American National Fire Ins. Co., 483 A. 2d 616; Farm and City Ins. Co. v. Stevens, 574 A. 2d 1300; Verdon v. Transamerica Ins. Co., 446 A. 2d 3; Burritt Mut. Sav. Bank v. Transamerica Ins. Co., 428 A. 2d 333. ***PRACTICE AREAS:*** Insurance Coverage; Insurance Bad Faith Defense; Insurance Litigation; Fire Insurance Defense; Property Insurance; Civil Appeals. ***Email:*** lemega@halloran-sage.com

VINCENT M. MARINO, born Middletown, Connecticut, April 7, 1944; admitted to bar, 1971, Connecticut. *Education:* University of Bridgeport (B.S., cum laude, 1968); University of Connecticut (J.D., 1971). President, Student Bar Association, 1970-1971. Attorney State Trial Referee, 1988—. *Member:* Middlesex County (President, 1998-1999), Connecticut and American Bar Associations. (Resident, Middletown Office). ***PRACTICE AREAS:*** Residential Real Estate; Commercial Real Estate; Land Use Planning Law; Estate Planning and Administration. ***Email:*** marino@halloran-sage.com

RICHARD C. TYNAN, born Waterbury, Connecticut, August 22, 1947; admitted to bar, 1972, Connecticut. *Education:* Niagara University (B.A., magna cum laude, 1969); Cornell University (J.D., 1972). Author: "Evaluation of Damages in Civil Rights Litigation," Federation of Insurance Counsel Quarterly, Vol. 25, No. 2, 1975. *Member:* Hartford County, Connecticut (Member: Civil Justice, Executive Committee, 1988-1990; Medical Legal Committee, 1989-1990) and American (Member: Economics of Law Practice Section; Civil Litigation Section) Bar Associations. Fellow: American College of Trial Lawyers; Federation of Defense and Corporate Counsel; Defense Research and Trial Lawyers Association; Connecticut Medical Defense Lawyers Association; Connecticut Trial Lawyers Association; American Board of Trial Advocates. Special Master: United States District Court; Superior Court, Hartford/New Britain Judicial District. ***REPORTED CASES:*** Calandro v. Allstate Insurance Co., 63 Conn.App. 202, 2001; McGloin v. Town of Southington 546 A.2d 906, 15 Conn. App. 668, Conn., 1988; State Farm Life and Acc. Assur. Co. v. Jackson 448 A.2d 832, 188 Conn. 152, Conn., 1982; Mausch v. Hartford, 184 Conn. 467, 440 A2d 157, 1981; Burritt Mut. Sav. Bank of New Britain v. Transamerica Ins. Co. 428 A.2d 333, 180 Conn. 71, 1980; Hoadley v. University of Hartford, 176 Conn. 669, 410 A.2d 472, 1979; Mausch v. Hartford, 184 Conn. 467, 440 A.2d 157, 1981. ***PRACTICE AREAS:*** Medical Malpractice; Professional Liability; Civil Litigation; Alternative Dispute Resolution. ***Email:*** tynan@halloran-sage.com

WILLIAM P. BORCHERT, born Hartford, Connecticut, June 24, 1950; admitted to bar, 1974, Connecticut. *Education:* Trinity College (B.A., 1971); Duke University (J.D., 1974). Co-Author: "Considerations in Buying or Selling a Business in Connecticut," National Business Institute, 1987, 1989, 1991, 1994; "Basic Corporate Law in Connecticut," 1992. *Member:* Hartford County, Connecticut and American Bar Associations. ***PRACTICE AREAS:*** Business Law; Corporate Law; Mergers, Acquisitions and Divestitures. ***Email:*** borchert@halloran-sage.com

THOMAS J. HAGARTY, JR., born Hartford, Connecticut, May 19, 1952; admitted to bar, 1977, Connecticut. *Education:* College of the Holy Cross (B.A., 1974); University of Connecticut (J.D., cum laude, 1977). *Member:* Hartford County and Connecticut Bar Associations; International Association of Defense Counsel (Member, State Membership Committee); Defense Research Institute. ***REPORTED CASES:*** Kelly v. Bonney 221 CONN 549, 565 (1992); Alfano v. Insurance Center of Torrington 203 Conn. 607 (1987). ***PRACTICE AREAS:*** Professional Liability; Insurance Defense; Workers Compensation Law. ***Email:*** hagarty@halloran-sage.com

PAUL V. KNOPF, born New York, NY, May 24, 1947; admitted to bar, 1977, Connecticut. *Education:* Amherst College (B.A., 1969); Vanderbilt University (J.D., 1977). *Member:* Hartford County, Connecticut (Member, House of Delegates, 1995-1998) and American Bar Associations; Connecticut Mortgage Bankers Association (Director, 1990-1991). ***PRACTICE AREAS:*** Banking Law; Real Estate Law; Secured Lending; Government Finance. ***Email:*** knopf@halloran-sage.com

BRIAN J. DONNELL, born Glen Cove, New York, October 27, 1955; admitted to bar, 1980, Connecticut; 1981, U.S. District Court, District of Connecticut; 1991, U.S. Supreme Court; 1994, U.S. Court of Appeals, Second Circuit. *Education:* Trinity College (B.A., 1977); Boston College (J.D., cum laude, 1980). Pi Gamma Mu. List in Who's Who in American Law. Editor-in-Chief, Uniform Commercial Code Reporter-Digest, 1979-1980. Member, Connecticut Lawyer Advisory Committee, 1993—. Member, Panel of Arbitrators, American Arbitration Association. *Member:* Hartford County, Connecticut (Member: Antitrust, Construction Law, Commercial Law and Bankruptcy Sections; Construction Law Executive Committee, 1990—) and American Bar Associations; University of Hartford Construction Institute. ***REPORTED CASES:*** Lawrence Brunoli, Inc. v. Branford, 247 Conn. 407 (1999); Connecticut Business & Industry Association, Inc. et al v. Commission on Hospitals & Health Care, 214 Conn. 726, 1990 (CBIA I) and 218 Conn. 335, 1991 (CBIA II); Della Construction Co., Inc. v. The Lane Construction Corp., 42 Conn. Sup. 202, 1991; Sebago, Inc., et al. v. Beazer East, Inc., et al., 1998 18 F.Supp.2d (D.Mass.1998); Mather, et al v. Birken Mfgr. Co. 1998 Conn. Super., LEXIS 3669; Wayne Constr. Corp. v. Reg. School Dist. No. 9, 2000 Conn. Super., LEXIS 1285. ***PRACTICE AREAS:*** Construction Litigation; Construction and Design Law; Corporate Contracts; Business Litigation; Class Actions; Unfair Trade. ***Email:*** donnell@halloran-sage.com

JAMES J. SZEREJKO, born Hartford, Connecticut, October 3, 1948; admitted to bar, 1974, Connecticut, U.S. District Court, District of Connecticut and U.S. Court of Appeals, Second Circuit; U.S. Supreme Court. *Education:* University of Connecticut (B.A., 1970); University of Hartford (M.P.A., 1973); Suffolk University (J.D., 1974). Member, Connecticut General Assembly, Legislative Commissioners' Office, 1977 Legislative Session. Deputy Counsel, Senate Majority, Connecticut General Assembly, 1978 and 1979 Legislative Sessions. Member, Connecticut Medical Examining Board, 1979-1983. Assistant Corporation Counsel, City of Hartford, 1980-1985. Counsel, Hartford Redevelopment Agency, 1980-1984. Member, 1979-1989, and Vice-Chairman, 1982-1989, Connecticut State Board of Education. Deputy Counsel to Chair of Credentials Committee, Democratic National Convention, 1980. Chairman, Connecticut Criminal Justice Commission, 1989-1991. Member, City of Hartford Charter Revision Commission, 1992. *Member:* Hartford County (Treasurer, 1994; Secretary, 1995; President-Elect, 1996; President, 1997; Past President, 1998), Connecticut (Legislative Chairman, 1987) and American Bar Associations; Connecticut Academy of Certified Trial Lawyers. (Board Certified Civil Trial Specialist by the National Board of Trial Advocacy). ***REPORTED CASES:*** Ricketts v. City of Hartford, 74 F.3d 1397 (2d Cir. 1996, cert. denied, 1175.ct.65, 1996); Warren v. Dwyer, 906 F.2d 70 (2d Cir. 1990, cert. denied, 498 U.S. 967, 1990); Brady v. Colchester, 863 F.2d 205 (2d Cir. 1988); Cabinet Realty, Inc. v. Planning and Zoning Commission of Town of Mansfield, 552 A. 2d 1218 (1989). ***PRACTICE AREAS:*** Insurance Litigation; Municipal Law; Civil Rights Litigation; Trade Associations. ***Email:*** szerejko@halloran-sage.com

(This Listing Continued)

WILLIAM J. McGRATH, JR., born Meriden, Connecticut, January 15, 1958; admitted to bar, 1983, Connecticut and U.S. District Court, District of Connecticut. *Education:* LeMoyne College (B.A., magna cum laude, 1980); Cornell University (J.D., cum laude, 1983). *Member:* Hartford County and Connecticut Bar Associations; Defense Research Institute; Connecticut Defense Lawyers Association. ***PRACTICE AREAS:*** Civil Litigation; Personal Injury Law; Insurance Litigation. ***Email:*** mcgrath@halloran-sage.com

DENNIS C. CAVANAUGH, born New Bedford, Massachusetts, December 25, 1956; admitted to bar, 1981, Connecticut; 1998, Massachusetts and U.S. District Court, District of Connecticut and District of Massachusetts. *Education:* University of Connecticut (B.A., with distinction, 1978); University of Miami (J.D., 1981). State of Connecticut Justice of the Peace. *Member:* Hartford County, Connecticut (Member, Section on Federal Practice; Member, Executive Committee, Construction Law Section), Massachusetts and American (Member: Fidelity and Surety Law Committee, Tort and Insurance Practice Section and Construction Industry Forum) Bar Associations; Defense Research and Trial Lawyers Association (Member, Construction Law and Surety Law Committees); American Arbitration Association. ***REPORTED CASES:*** Balfour Beatty Constr. Inc. v. National Surety Corporation, et al., 986 F.Supp. 82 (D. Conn. 1997); Bass Plating Co. v. Town of Windsor, 639 F. Supp. 873 (D. Conn. 1986); Steeltech Building Products Inc. v. Edward Sutt Associates, Inc., 18 Conn. App. 469 (1989); PDS Engineering and Construction Inc. v. Double RS a/k/a et. al., 5 Conn. L. Rptr. No. 12, 306 (Jan. 6, 1992), Modified, 6 Conn. L. Rptr. No. 7, 181 (April 20, 1992). ***PRACTICE AREAS:*** Construction Law; Fidelity and Surety Law; Business Litigation. ***Email:*** cavanaugh@halloran-sage.com

CHRISTOPHER J. LYNCH, born Painesville, Ohio, May 27, 1958; admitted to bar, 1984, Connecticut and U.S. District Court, District of Connecticut; 1986, District of Columbia. *Education:* Wesleyan University (B.A., 1981) Phi Beta Kappa; University of Connecticut (J.D., with honors, 1984). *Member:* Connecticut (Member, Section on Litigation) and American (Member, Sections on: Litigation; Torts and Insurance Practice; Committees on: Products; General Liability and Consumer Law; Self Insurers and Risk Managers; Trial Techniques) Bar Associations; Defense Research Institute (Member, Sections on: Drug and Medical Devices and Products Liability); Connecticut Defense Lawyers Association; American Law Firm Association (Member, Steering Committee of Products Liability Practice Group). ***PRACTICE AREAS:*** Products Liability Litigation; Drug and Medical Device Litigation; Complex Civil Litigation. ***Email:*** lynchc@halloran-sage.com

PAUL D. MEADE, born Waltham, Massachusetts, June 22, 1959; admitted to bar, 1985, Connecticut; 1986, U.S. District Court, District of Connecticut. *Education:* Colby College (B.A., 1981); Duke University (J.D., 1985). *Member:* Hartford County and Connecticut Bar Associations; Connecticut Defense Lawyers Association. ***REPORTED CASES:*** Port Clinton Associates et al v. Board of Selectmen of Clinton, 217 Conn. 588, 587 A. 2nd 126, cert. denied —U.S. —112 S.Ct. 64 (1991). ***PRACTICE AREAS:*** Insurance Defense; Insurance Litigation; Products Liability; Marine Insurance Defense; Insurance Coverage; Environmental Insurance Coverage. ***Email:*** meade@halloran-sage.com

JOSEPH G. FORTNER, JR., born New York, NY, April 19, 1956; admitted to bar, 1983, New York; 1984, U.S. District Court, Southern and Eastern Districts of New York; 1990, Connecticut and U.S. District Court, District of Connecticut. *Education:* Duke University (A.B., 1978); Vanderbilt University (J.D., 1982). Phi Delta Phi. Recipient, American Jurisprudence Award in Conflict of Laws. Member, Board of Trustees, Noah Webster House. *Member:* Connecticut, New York State and Federal Bar Associations; Defense Research Institute (Member, Business Litigation and Products Liability Sections); Federalist Society. ***REPORTED CASES:*** In re Robert A. Bonito, et al., 1997 U.S. App. LEXIS 27068 (9th Cir. 1997); University Savings Assn. v. Bank of New Haven, 765 F.Supp. 35 (D. Conn. 1991); USA Network v. Jones Intercable, Inc., 704 F.Supp. 488 (S.D.N.Y. 1989). ***PRACTICE AREAS:*** Civil Litigation; Complex Litigation; Federal Litigation; Commercial Litigation; Torts; Intellectual Property Litigation; Electronic Commerce. ***Email:*** fortner@halloran-sage.com

STEPHEN P. FOGERTY, born New York, NY, July 18, 1961; admitted to bar, 1986, Connecticut and New York. *Education:* The Catholic University of America (B.A., Honors Philosophy, 1983); Fordham University (J.D., 1986). *Member:* American Board of Trial Advocates (1998—); Defense Research Institute. (Board Certified Civil Trial Specialist by the National Board of Trial Advocacy) (Westport Office). ***PRACTICE AREAS:*** Complex Litigation; Commercial Litigation; Employment Litigation; Governmental Liability; Professional Liability. ***Email:*** fogerty@halloran-sage.com

PETER G. BOUCHER, born Hartford, Connecticut, February 16, 1945; admitted to bar, 1972, Connecticut; 1973, U.S. District Court, District of Connecticut. *Education:* University of Connecticut (B.S., 1967; M.B.A., 1969; J.D., 1972). Assistant Corporation Counsel, City of Hartford, 1972-1976. Counsel to Insurance Commissioner, State of Connecticut, 1976-1979. Commissioner, Department of Public Utility Control, 1987-1991. Council Member, Connecticut Siting Council, 1987-1991. First Vice President, 1990-1991, Chairman, Executive Committee, 1990-1991, Chairman, Subcommittee on Gas Integrated Resource Planning, 1989-1991, National Association of Regulatory Utility Commissioners (NARUC). Member, Board of Directors, National Regulatory Research Institute, 1989-1991. Co-Chairman, Power Planning Committee, New England Governors Conference, Inc., 1990. President, New England Conference of Public Utility Commissioners, 1988-1989. *Member:* Hartford County, Connecticut (Public Utility Section - Executive Committee) and American Bar Associations. ***PRACTICE AREAS:*** Administrative Hearings and Appeals; Administrative Litigation; Judicial Review; Professional Regulation; Telecommunications Law; Government Relations; Legislative Practice; Lobbying; Public Utilities; Public Utility Regulation; Utility Law. ***Email:*** boucher@halloran-sage.com

STEVEN H. MALITZ, born Hartford, Connecticut, September 19, 1961; admitted to bar, 1986, Connecticut, New York; U.S. District Court, District of Connecticut; U.S. District Court, District of Vermont; U.S. District Court, Southern, Eastern and Western Districts of New York. *Education:* Clark University (B.A., with honors in Government and International Relations, 1983); Albany Law School of Union University (J.D., 1986); Graduate, Mayflower Transit Transportation Training Institute. *Member:* Hartford County, Connecticut, New York State and American (Member, Tort and Insurance Practice Litigation, Products Liability and Aviation Practice Sections) Bar Associations; American Law Firm Association (ALFA) (Transportation and Products Liability Groups); Trucking Industry Defense Association (TIDA); American Trucking Association; Defense Research Institute. ***PRACTICE AREAS:*** Insurance Defense Litigation; Trucking Transportation Litigation; Products Liability Litigation; Aviation Products Liability. ***Email:*** malitz@halloran-sage.com

JOHN B. FARLEY, born Willimantic, Connecticut, August 2, 1958; admitted to bar, 1987, Connecticut; 1988, U.S. District Court, District of Connecticut; 1989, U.S. District Court, Southern and Eastern Districts of New York; 1991, U.S. Supreme Court; 1994, U.S. Court of Appeals, Second Circuit; 1999, U.S. Court of Appeals, First Circuit. *Education:* Georgetown University (A.B., 1980); University of Connecticut (M.A., 1983; J.D., with honors, 1987). *Member:* Hartford County (Co-Chairman, Civil Litigation Committee), Connecticut (Member, House of Delegates, 1998-2001) and American Bar Associations; Defense Research Institute. ***REPORTED CASES:*** Branhaven Plaza, LLC v. Inland Wetlands Commission of the Town of Branford, 251 Conn. 269, 740 A.2d 847 (1999); Paige v. St. Andrews Roman Catholic Church Corp., 250 Conn.14, 734 A.2d 85 (1999); Phillip v. Fairfield University, 118 F.3d.131 (2d Cir.1997); Kelley v. Bonney, 221 Conn. 549, 606 A.2d 693 (1992); Hanover Ins. Co. v. Fireman's Fund Ins. Co. 217 Conn. 340, 586, A.2d 567 (1991); A.G. Foods, Inc. v. Pepperidge Farm, Inc. 216 Conn. 200, 579 A. 2d 69 (1990). ***PRACTICE AREAS:*** Appellate Practice; Commercial Litigation; Insurance Litigation; Insurance Regulation; Legal Malpractice. ***Email:*** farley@halloran-sage.com

DAVID B. LOSEE, born Milwaukee, Wisconsin, July 7, 1945; admitted to bar, 1971, Connecticut, U.S. District Court, District of Connecticut and U.S. Court of Appeals, Second Circuit; 1973, U.S. Supreme Court. *Education:* Wesleyan University (B.A., 1968); University of Connecticut (J.D., 1971). Instructor, University of Hartford, Barney School of Business Administration, M.B.A. Program, "Environmental Law and Administration," 1974. *Member:* Hartford County, Litchfield County, Connecticut (Member, Conservation and Environmental Quality Section) and American Bar Associations. ***PRACTICE AREAS:*** Environmental; Zoning, Planning and Land Use; Real Estate Law; Real Estate Development. ***Email:*** losee@halloran-sage.com

MARK T. ALTERMATT, born New Milford, Connecticut, April 8, 1960; admitted to bar, 1988, Connecticut; 1991, U.S. District Court, District of Connecticut. *Education:* Washington and Lee University (B.A., 1982); Syracuse University (J.D., 1988). Recipient, American Jurisprudence Award in Insurance Law. Member, 1986-1988 and Managing Editor, 1987-1988, Syracuse Law Review. *Member:* Connecticut (Member, Executive Committee, Litigation Section) and American Bar Associations. [USMC, 1982-1985]. ***PRACTICE AREAS:*** Civil Litigation. ***Email:*** altermatt@halloran-sage.com

HENRY M. BECK, JR., born New York, NY, March 17, 1951; admitted to bar, 1977, Massachusetts; 1978, Connecticut. *Education:* Duke University (B.S., summa cum laude, 1973); Harvard Law School (J.D., cum laude, 1976). Phi Beta Kappa. Author: "Connecticut Business Law 1994: A Tour of a New Edifice, The Connecticut Business Corporation Act, and a Brief Survey of the Business Law Landscape," 69 CBJ 445 (1995); "Connecticut Corporation Law In the Direction of the Year 2000," 64 CBJ SI-69 (1990). Faculty, ABA National Institute on Closely Held Businesses, 1997. Member: Board of Trustees, Executive Committee, Corporate Secretary, Science Center of Connecticut, 1995—; Board of Directors, Executive Committee, Business Council Chairman, Greater Hartford Chamber of Commerce, 1991-1993; Board of Directors, 1985-1988, and Executive Committee, 1986-1988, Duke University, General Alumni Association; CBA Business Law Section Executive Committee, 1979-1982 and 1984—; ABA Business Law Section Small Business Committee, 1992—; Association of Commercial Finance Attorneys, 1989—; UCC Article 6 Advisory Committee to the Connecticut Law Revision Commission, 1990-1991. Chairman, Hebron Water Pollution Control Authority, 1980-1982. *Member:* Connecticut and American Bar Associations. ***PRACTICE AREAS:*** Business Planning; Closely Held Business Law; Business Reorganization; Securities Law;

(This Listing Continued)

HALLORAN & SAGE LLP, Hartford—Continued

Private Placement; Public Offerings; Shareholder Disputes; Corporate Law; Closely Held Corporations; Commercial Law; Nonprofit Corporations; Internet Law; E-Commerce; Taxation; Financial Transactions. ***Email:*** beck@halloran-sage.com

SUSAN O'DONNELL, born Danbury, Connecticut, June 13, 1964; admitted to bar, 1989, Connecticut; 1990, U.S. District Court, District of Connecticut. *Education:* Sacred Heart University (B.S., cum laude, 1986); Suffolk University (J.D., 1989). *Member:* Connecticut and American Bar Associations; National Association of College and University Attorneys; Connecticut Defense Lawyers Association. ***PRACTICE AREAS:*** Civil Litigation; Civil Practice; University Law; Personal Injury; Insurance Defense. ***Email:*** odonnell@halloran-sage.com

BRUCE H. RAYMOND, born Holden, Massachusetts, November 12, 1964; admitted to bar, 1989, Connecticut, Massachusetts and U.S. District Court, District of Connecticut. *Education:* University of Connecticut (B.A., Political Science, 1986); New England School of Law (J.D., cum laude, 1989). Phi Alpha Delta. Recipient, American Jurisprudence Award, Local Government Law. Best Advocate, North-Eastern Region, American Bar Association National Appellate Advocacy Competition, 1989. Case and Note Editor, New England Journal on Criminal and Civil Confinement, 1988-1989. *Member:* Connecticut Bar Association (Member: Litigation Section; Federal Practice Section); Defense Research Institute (Member, Board of Directors; Connecticut State Representative, 1996-1999; Member, Products Liability Committee; Chair, Specialized Litigation Group for Agricultural, Construction, Mining and Industrial Equipment); Connecticut Defense Lawyers Association. (First Vice President and Member, Board of Directors). ***PRACTICE AREAS:*** Litigation; Products Liability Law; Toxic Tort; Business Disputes; Risk Management. ***Email:*** raymond@halloran-sage.com

KEVIN M. ROCHE, born Bethpage, New York, July 20, 1961; admitted to bar, 1987, Massachusetts; 1988, Connecticut and U.S. District Court, District of Massacusetts; 1993, U.S. District Court, District of Connecticut. *Education:* Siena College (B.A., English, 1983); Western New England College School of Law (J.D., 1987). *Member:* Massachusetts and Connecticut Bar Associations; Connecticut Defense Lawyers Association; Defense Research Institute. ***PRACTICE AREAS:*** Breach of Contract; General Liability; Insurance Contracts; Insurance Coverage; Insurance Litigation; Property Insurance; Subrogation; Defense Litigation. ***Email:*** roche@halloran-sage.com

DAVID G. HILL, born New London, Connecticut, May 16, 1962; admitted to bar, 1988, Connecticut; 1992, U.S. District Court, District of Connecticut. *Education:* Trinity College (B.A., Political Science, 1984); University of Connecticut (J.D., 1988). Connecticut Lawyer Pro Bono Honor Roll. *Member:* Hartford County, Connecticut (Member: Sections on Labor and Employment; Workers' Compensation; Municipal Law and Government Law) and American (Member, Sections on: Civil Litigation; Labor and Employment; Tort and Personal Injury) Bar Associations; Oliver Ellsworth Inn of Court; Connecticut Trial Lawyers Association. ***PRACTICE AREAS:*** Litigation; Professional Liability; Personal Injury Law; Product Liability Law; Construction Law; Insurance Defense Law. ***Email:*** hill@halloran-sage.com

DANIEL P. SCAPELLATI, born Hartford, Connecticut, August 18, 1957; admitted to bar, 1982, Connecticut; 1989, U.S. District Court, District of Connecticut; 1994, U.S. District Court, Southern District of New York; 1997, U.S. Court of Appeals, Second Circuit. *Education:* Villanova University (B.S., 1979); University of Bridgeport (J.D., 1982). *Member:* Connecticut Bar Association; Connecticut Defense Lawyers Association; Defense Research Institute. ***REPORTED CASES:*** Hanson v. Ohio Casualty Ins. Co., 239 Conn. 537, 687 A. 2d 1262 (1996); O'Brien v. United States Fidelity & Guaranty Co., 235 Conn. 837, 669 A. 2d 1221 (1996); Hertz Corp. v. Federal Ins. Co., 245 Conn. 374, 713 A.2d 820 (1998); Amica Mut. Ins. Co. v. Franklin, 147 F.3d 238 (2d Cir. Conn. 1998). ***PRACTICE AREAS:*** Civil Appeals; Civil Litigation; Arson and Insurance Fraud; First Party Insurance Defense; Insurance Bad Faith Defense; Insurance Coverage Defense; Property Insurance Defense. ***Email:*** scapella@halloran-sage.com

JAMES M. SCONZO, born Staten Island, New York, August 13, 1963; admitted to bar, 1989, Connecticut; 1990, U.S. District Court, District of Connecticut; 1992, U.S. Court of Appeals, Second Circuit; 1997, U.S. District Court, Southern, Eastern, Northern and Western Districts of New York. *Education:* University of Connecticut (B.A., 1986), Phi Alpha Theta; Syracuse University (J.D., 1989). Member, Board of Editors, Connecticut Bar Journal. Editor, Connecticut Employment Law Letter. Publications: "Big Brother is Watching," (Electronic Monitoring), Connecticut Employment Law Letter, July 2001; "Have the Conflicts Over Arbitration Finally Been Resolved?", Connecticut Employment Law Letter, June 2001; "EEOC Cries Foul On Denial Of Prescription Contraceptive Coverage," Connecticut Employment Law Letter, Jan. 2001; "Winning The Battle, But Losing The War," (Employer Retaliation), Connecticut Employment Law Letter, Jan. 2001; "Control Your Worker's Behavior," Connecticut Employment Law Letter, Nov. 2000; "Don't Disclose What You Agreed Not To," Connecticut Employment Law Letter, Nov. 2000; "Congress

(This Listing Continued)

Clarifies Stock Option Impact on Overtime Calculations," Connecticut Employment Law Letter, October 2000; "Inevitable Disclosure Can Bar Unfair Competition," Connecticut Law Tribune, Nov. 20, 2000; "Do Hours Make Them Ours? Potential Problems From Using 'Contingency' Workers," The Connecticut Law Tribune, Nov. 1, 1999; "Employer Monitoring in the Workplace: Right of Risk? What to do About Personnel Problems in Your State," Business and Legal Reports, Summer 1999; "Settlement of Employment Practices Liability Claims," Occam's Razor, Jan.-March 1998; "Violence In the Workplace: 50 State Compendium of Significant Case and Statutory Laws," American Law Firm Association, 1997; "Compendium of Significant Employment-Related Case Law and Statutes," American Law Firm Association, First-Fourth Editions, 1996-2000; "U.S. District Court Compilation of "Chambers' Practices", Connecticut Bar Association, October 2000. Special Master, U.S. District Court, District of Connecticut. *Member:* Hartford County, Connecticut (Member: Labor and Employment Section, Legislative and Human Rights Subcommittees; Litigation Section; Federal Practice Section, Local Rules Advisory Committee) and American Bar Associations; Defense Research Institute (Member: Alternative Dispute Resolution; Labor and Employment and Professional Liability Committees); Connecticut Defense Lawyers Association. ***REPORTED CASES:*** Violissi v. City of Middletown, 990 F. Supp. 93 (D.Conn. 1998); Hill v. Pinkerton Security and Investigation Services, Inc., 977 F. Supp. 148 (D. Conn. 1997); Gibbons v. NER Holdings, Inc., 983 F. Supp. 310 (D. Conn. 1997); Nutt v. Norwich Roman Catholic Diocese, 921 F.Supp. 66 (D. Conn. 1995); Fulco v. Norwich Roman Catholic Diocesan Corp., 27 Conn. App. 800, 609 A.2d 1034 (1992), app., dismissed, 226 Conn. 404, 627 A.2d 931 (1993). ***PRACTICE AREAS:*** Labor and Employment; Litigation; Professional Liability; Torts; Alternative Dispute Resolution; Civil Rights. ***Email:*** sconzo@halloran-sage.com

ROBERT B. COX, born Providence, Rhode Island, June 1, 1954; admitted to bar, 1980, Connecticut, U.S. District Court, District of Connecticut and U.S. Court of Appeals, Second Circuit. *Education:* Boston University (B.A., magna cum laude, 1976); University of Connecticut (J.D., 1980; M.B.A., 1980). *Member:* Hartford, Connecticut and American Bar Associations. ***PRACTICE AREAS:*** Finance; Bankruptcy; Corporate Law; Real Estate; Energy; Health Law. ***Email:*** cox@halloran-sage.com

THOMAS P. O'DEA, JR., born Montclair, New Jersey, March 31, 1966; admitted to bar, 1991, Connecticut; 1992, U.S. District Court, District of Connecticut; 1994, U.S. Court of Appeals, Second Circuit. *Education:* Providence College (1988); University of Fribourg, Switzerland; Catholic University of America; Columbus School of Law (J.D., 1991). Appointed by: Governor John Rowland as a Public Member of the Police Officer Standards and Training Council, 1995; Victim Compensation Commissioner, 1997. Appointed by the Board of Selectmen for Town of New Canaan to Personnel Advisory Board, January 1999. *Member:* Connecticut and American Bar Associations. (Resident, Westport Office). ***PRACTICE AREAS:*** Civil Litigation; Torts; Civil Rights; Government Tort Liability; Labor and Employment Law. ***Email:*** odea@halloran-sage.com

GREGORY R. FAULKNER, born New Haven, Connecticut, July 22, 1966; admitted to bar, 1991, Connecticut; 1992, U.S. District Court, District of Connecticut. *Education:* Providence College (B.S., cum laude, 1988); Columbus School of Law (J.D., 1991). Member, Connecticut Building Congress Board of Directors and Industry Practices and Steering Committees. *Member:* Connecticut (Member, Construction Law Section) and American (Member: Tort and Insurance Practice Section, Fidelity and Surety Law Committee; Forum on Construction Industry; Young Professionals Subcommittee to the Fidelity and Surety Law Committee) Bar Associations. ***REPORTED CASES:*** Balfour Beatty Constr. Inc. v. Colonial Ornamental Iron Works, et al., 968 F. Supp. 82 (D.Conn. 1997); First Nat'l Bank of Stanford v. Hemingway Ctr. L.P., et al., 846 F. Supp. 186 (D.Conn. 1994); Forge Square Associates Limited Partnership v. Construction Services of Bristol, Inc., 33 Conn. App. 669 (1994); cert. denied, 229 Conn. 913 (1994). ***PRACTICE AREAS:*** Construction Litigation; Surety and Fidelity; Creditor's Rights; Bankruptcy. ***Email:*** faulkner@halloran-sage.com

DAN E. LaBELLE, born Hartford, Connecticut, May 7, 1955; admitted to bar, 1981, New York; 1987, Connecticut. *Education:* Colgate University (A.B., 1977); Albany Law School of Union University (J.D., 1980). (Resident, Westport Office). ***PRACTICE AREAS:*** Civil Litigation; Environmental Law; Criminal Law. ***Email:*** labelle@halloran-sage.com

DUNCAN J. FORSYTH, born New Haven, Connecticut, November 19, 1951; admitted to bar, 1977, Connecticut; 1981, U.S. District Court, District of Connecticut; 1995, U.S. Court of Appeals, Second Circuit; 1999, U.S. Supreme Court. *Education:* Washington & Jefferson College (B.A., 1974); Wake Forest University (J.D., 1977). Author: "Dilemma of the Duty to Defend," The Defense, Journal of the Connecticut Defense Lawyers Association, September 1986. Co-Author: with Ellen L Sostman, "Mechanics' Lien Waivers in Connecticut: The Myths and the Realities," 63 Connecticut Bar Journal, No. 4, August 1989; with Matthew W. Den Ouden, "Municipal Immunity: A Potential Shield From Liability," The Defense, Journal of Connecticut Defense Lawyers Association, Fall 1990. Lecturer: Greater Hartford Community College, 1981-

(This Listing Continued)

1983; Hartford Police Academy, 1985. Member of Faculty, National College of District Attorneys, 1980. Assistant State's Attorney, 1977-1981. Chairman, Rocky Hill Economic Development Commission, 1982-1989. Member, Charter Revision Commission, Town of Rocky Hill, 1984-1985. Vice President, 1985-1986 and President, 1986-1988, Washington & Jefferson College Alumni Association. President, Farmington Youth Baseball League, 2000. *Member:* Connecticut and American Bar Associations; Defense Research Institute; Connecticut Defense Lawyers Association. ***REPORTED CASES:*** Faria v. First National Supermarkets, Inc. (36 Conn. App. 945); Koepke v. Zoning Board of Appeals (230 Conn. 452); Stannard Beach Association, Inc. v. Zoning Board of Appeals (34 Conn. App. 917); Koepke v. Zoning Board of Appeals (30 Conn. App. 395); Koepke v. Zoning Board of Appeals (223 Conn. 171); Koepke v. Zoning Board of Appeals (25 Conn. App. 611); BCBS Goshen Realty, Inc. v. Planning & Zoning Commission (22 Conn. App. 407). ***PRACTICE AREAS:*** Civil Litigation; Commercial Litigation; Land Use; Administrative; Environmental; Labor and Employment. ***Email:*** forsyth@halloran-sage.com

ANN M. CATINO, born Hartford, Connecticut, October 14, 1960; admitted to bar, 1987, Connecticut; 1988, U.S. District Court, District of Connecticut. *Education:* St. Anselm College (A.B., 1982); Maxwell School of Citizenship and Public Affairs, Syracuse University (M.P.A., 1983); University of Kentucky College of Law (J.D., 1987). Executive Editor, Journal of Mineral Law and Policy. Member, The Real Estate Exchange. *Member:* Connecticut (Member, Conservation and Environmental Quality Section, 1987—) and American (Member, Natural Resources, Energy and Environmental Law, 1987—) Bar Associations; American Law Firm Association (Member, Environmental Law Section); Defense Research Institute (Member, Toxic Torts & Environmental Law Section); Society of Women Environmental Professionals. ***PRACTICE AREAS:*** Environmental Law; Environmental Litigation; Land Use; Administrative Law. ***Email:*** catino@halloran-sage.com

JAMES P. MAHER, born Waterbury, Connecticut, April 20, 1961; admitted to bar, 1987, Connecticut and U.S. District Court, District of Connecticut. *Education:* Fairfield University (A.B., 1983); University of Connecticut (J.D., 1987). *Member:* Hartford and Connecticut (Chairperson, Real Property and Land Use Committee, Young Lawyers Section, 1991-1992) Bar Associations; Real Estate Finance Association. ***PRACTICE AREAS:*** Real Estate; Financial Transactions; Internet and E-Business Law; Business Organization; Creditors Rights. ***Email:*** maher@halloran-sage.com

CARL R. FICKS, JR., born Stamford, Connecticut, October 25, 1963; admitted to bar, 1988, Connecticut; 1989, U.S. District Court, District of Connecticut; 1990, District of Columbia; 1991, U.S. Court of Appeals, Second Circuit; 1992, U.S. District Court, Eastern District of New York. *Education:* Providence College (B.A., 1985); Catholic University (J.D., 1988). Recipient, American Jurisprudence Award in Federal Practice and Procedure. *Member:* Hartford County, Connecticut (Co-Chair, Young Lawyers' Section, Labor and Employment Law, 1992-1995) and American Bar Associations. ***REPORTED CASES:*** Town Close Associates v. Planning and Zoning Commission of Town of New Canaan, 42 Conn. App. 94, 679 A.2d 378 (1991); A. Aiudi & Sons v. Town of Plainville, 862 F.Supp. 737 (D.Conn. 1994); Tomasso Brothers, Inc. v. October Twenty Four, Inc., 230 Conn. 641, 646 A.2d 133 (1994); Forbes v. Ballaro, 31 Conn. App. 235, 624 A.2d 389 (1993); Moffitt v. Town of Brookfield, 759 F.Supp 94 (D.Conn. 1991); LoSacco v. City of Middletown, 745 F.Supp. 812 (D.Conn. 1990). ***PRACTICE AREAS:*** Construction Litigation; Litigation; Civil Rights; Insurance Defense; General Practice. ***Email:*** ficks@halloran-sage.com

ROBERT M. BARRACK, born Metz, France, November 26, 1957; admitted to bar, 1990, Connecticut and U.S. District Court, District of Connecticut. *Education:* Vassar College (B.A., 1979); Rutgers University School of Law (J.D., with honors, 1990). Member, Rutgers Law Journal, 1989-1990. Recipient: American Bar Association Land Use Law Award; American Jurisprudence Award in Property. *Publications:* "Connecticut Construction Law: Can this job be saved?" Lorman Education Services Dec. 17, 1998, Aug. 19, 1999, Feb. 24, 2000, Feb. 1, 2001; "Construction Case Law Summary and Legislative Review," CBA Construction Law Section 1995, 1996, 1997; "Mechanic's Lien in Connecticut, A Practical Guide," Lorman Education Services May 16, 1997. *Member:* Connecticut Bar Association (Member, Construction and Litigation Sections). [U.S. Army, 1980-1983]. ***REPORTED CASES:*** Spicer v. Spicer, 33 Conn. App. 152, 634 A.2d 902 (1993); Lawrence Brunoli, Inc. v. Town of Branford, 247 Conn. 407, 722 A.2d 271 (1999); Middletown Commer. Assocs. L.P. v. City of Middletown, 53 Conn. App. 432, 730 A.2d 1201 (1999); Remington Invs. v. National Props., Inc., 49 Conn. App. 789, 716 A.2d 141 (1998); Sebago, Inc. v. Beazer East, Inc., 18 F.Supp.2d 70 (D.Mass. 1998). ***PRACTICE AREAS:*** Commercial Litigation; Construction Litigation; Breach of Contract; Business Torts; Creditors Rights. ***Email:*** barrack@halloran-sage.com

JOHN W. DIETZ, born Rochester, New York, March 15, 1968; admitted to bar, 1993, Connecticut; 1994, New York and U.S. District Court, District of Connecticut; 1996, U.S. District Court, Southern, Northern and Western District of New York and U.S. Court of Appeals, Second Circuit; 1997, U.S. District Court, Eastern District of New York; 1998, Mohegan Tribe Gaming Disputes Court; 1999, Mashantucket Pequot Tribal Court. *Education:* St. Lawrence University (B.A., 1990); Albany Law School of Union University (J.D., 1993). Omicron Delta Kappa. *Member:* Transportation Lawyers Association; American Law Firm Association (ALFA); Transportation Practice Group; Defense Research Institute. (Resident, Westport Office). ***PRACTICE AREAS:*** Products Liability; Transportation Litigation; Trucking Law; Indian Law. ***Email:*** dietz@halloran-sage.com

BRIAN P. LEAMING, born Philadelphia, Pennsylvania, April 25, 1965; admitted to bar, 1991, Maryland; 1992, Florida; 1993, Connecticut; 1996, U.S. District Court, District of Connecticut. *Education:* Providence College (B.A., 1987); Catholic University of America (J.D., 1991). *Member:* Maryland State Bar Association; The Florida Bar. ***REPORTED CASES:*** Sanchez v. City of Hartford, 10 F.Supp.2d 162 (D.Conn.1999); City of Bristol v. Dickau Bus Co., 63 Conn. App. 770 (2001); Mack v. Lavalley, 55 Conn. App.150 (1999). ***PRACTICE AREAS:*** Municipal Law; Governmental Liability; Constitutional Law; Professional Liability; Premises Liability; Homeowners Liability. ***Email:*** leaming@halloran-sage.com

JAMES C. STEARNS, born Minneapolis, Minnesota, February 11, 1950; admitted to bar, 1977, District of Columbia (Not admitted in Connecticut). *Education:* Dartmouth College (A.B., cum laude, 1972); University of Manchester (M.A., 1974); Georgetown University (J.D., 1976). Member, National Moot Court Team. Editor, Law and Policy in International Business, 1975-1976. Author: "Renewal of the Export Administration Act of 1979: An Overview," Middle East Executive Reports, April, 1983. Counsel, Georgetown University, Health Policy Center, 1976-1977. Special Assistant to the Commissioner, Public Buildings Service, GSA, 1977-1978. Chief Counsel, GSA Board of Contract Appeals, 1978-1980. Deputy Assistant Secretary, Department of Education, 1980-1981. Legislative Counsel, Department of Commerce, 1981-1984. Acting Chief Counsel, Minority Business Development Agency, 1984. Member, Chamber of Commerce Council on Small Business, 1984-1987. Trustee, The Holderness School, 1985-1994. President, United Cerebral Palsy Association, Inc., 1993-1995; Vice Chairman, United Cerebral Palsy Association, Inc., 1995-1997. *Member:* The District of Columbia Bar. (Also at Washington, D.C.). ***PRACTICE AREAS:*** Administrative; Government Contracts; International Trade. ***Email:*** stearns@halloran-sage.com

THERESA W. HAJOST, admitted to bar, 1985, Maryland; 1988, District of Columbia (Not admitted in Connecticut). *Education:* University of Dallas (B.A., cum laude, 1977); University of Toledo (M.A., 1981); George Washington University (J.D., cum laude, 1984). (Also at Washington, D.C.). ***PRACTICE AREAS:*** Litigation; Arbitration; Insurance; Reinsurance; Commercial Litigation. ***Email:*** hajost@halloran-sage.com

ASSOCIATES

Richard P. Roberts	***Alan P. Curto***
John S. Rosania	***Kevin J. Greene***
Mark T. Livesay	***Mark R. Giuliani***
Thomas P. Lambert (Resident, Westport Office)	***Brian C. Clifford***
	N. Kane Bennett
Robert A. Rhodes (Resident, Westport Office)	***Kristin T. Alix***
	Lori D. DiBella
Laura A. Zaino	***John C. Huggins***
Reed A. Slatas	***Patrick M. Birney***
Thomas J. Finn	***Stephanie J. Sweeney***
Janice D. Lai	***Gregory K. Holness***
Melissa Rotenberg Arcaro	***Stephen H. Broer***
Ralph W. Johnson, III	***Peter E. Strniste, Jr.***
Martin A. Onorato	***Erik J. Ness***
Jeffrey F. Gostyla	***Andrew D. Moore***
Elizabeth A. Fitzsimmons	***Salvatore N. Fornaciari***
Pasquale Amodeo	***Amy Sargeant Lang***
Brett M. Szczesny (Resident, Westport Office)	***Annmarie P. Briones***
	Kristie E. Mackin

OF COUNSEL

IRWIN J. MITTLEMAN, born Newark, New Jersey, January 11, 1953; admitted to bar, 1985, New Jersey (Not admitted in Connecticut). *Education:* George Washington University (M.B.A., 1978); New York Law School (J.D., 1985). ***PRACTICE AREAS:*** Taxation (State) Law (100%, 10).

ROBERT C. ENGSTROM, born Worcester, Massachusetts, September 28, 1941; admitted to bar, 1966, Massachusetts; 1971, Connecticut. *Education:* University of Pennsylvania (B.A., 1963; M.B.A., 1970); Boston College (J.D., 1966). *Member:* Hartford County Bar Association. ***PRACTICE AREAS:*** ERISA; Tax Law; Trusts and Estates Law; Corporate Law. ***Email:*** engstrom@halloran-sage.com

ALAN S. RUBENSTEIN, born Far Rockaway, New York, November 5, 1957; admitted to bar, 1991, Connecticut; 1992, New York and U.S. District Court, District of Connecticut. *Education:* University of Rochester (B.A., with honors, 1979); San Francisco State University (M.S., with honors, 1983); Yale

(This Listing Continued)

HALLORAN & SAGE LLP, Hartford—Continued

University; Brooklyn Law School (J.D., 1991). *Member:* Greenwich, Stamford/Norwalk Regional, Connecticut and New York State Bar Associations; Association of Family and Conciliation Courts; Academy of Family Mediators; Connecticut Trial Lawyers Association. (Resident, Westport Office). ***PRACTICE AREAS:*** Family Law; Matrimonial Law; Children; Mediation and Collaboration Law. ***Email:*** rubensteina@halloran-sage.com

MARY L. BARROW, born August 8, 1958; admitted to bar, 1984, New York and U.S. District Court, Southern District of New York; 1986, Florida; 1987, Connecticut. *Education:* Brown University (B.A., 1980); University of Pennsylvania (J.D., 1983). *Member:* Hartford County, Middlesex County and Connecticut Bar Associations. ***PRACTICE AREAS:*** Estate Planning; Family Wealth Transfer; Trust Planning. ***Email:*** barrow@halloran-sage.com

GINA L. SCHAECHER, admitted to bar, 1994, Nebraska and U.S. District Court, District of Nebraska; 2000, U.S. Court of Appeals, Sixth Circuit; 2001, District of Columbia and U.S. Court of Federal Claims (Not admitted in Connecticut). *Education:* University of Nebraska at Omaha (B.S.B.A., magna cum laude, 1990); University of Nebraska at Lincoln (J.D., with distinction, 1993). (Also at Washington, D.C.). ***REPORTED CASES:*** Willers v. Willers, 255 Neb. 769, 587 N.W.2d 390 (1998). ***PRACTICE AREAS:*** Commercial Litigation; Construction Law; Government Contracts. ***Email:*** schaecher@halloran-sage.com

LISA M. KOWTKO, born Waterbury, Connecticut, March 15, 1958; admitted to bar, 1987, Connecticut; 1990, U.S. District Court, District of Connecticut. *Education:* Western Connecticut State University (B.S., in Nursing, 1980); University of Bridgeport School of Law (J.D., cum laude, 1987). Phi Kappa Phi. Associate Editor, Bridgeport Law Review. *Member:* Connecticut and American Bar Associations; Connecticut Society for Healthcare Risk Management; Connecticut Defense Lawyers Association. (Resident, Westport Office). ***PRACTICE AREAS:*** Medical Malpractice; Health Care; Liability. ***Email:*** kowtko@halloran-sage.com

REPRESENTATIVE CLIENTS: Advest Bank; Allied Van Lines; Beech Aircraft; Carolina Casualty; Catholic Mutual Relief Society; CGU Insurance; CNA; Colonia Insurance; The Coca-Cola Co., Inc.; Connecticut Medical Ins. Co.; Consolidated Freightways, aka CNF Transporation, Inc.; Coregis Group, Inc.; Cumis Ins. Society, Inc.; Executive Risk Management Associates; Factory Mut. Ins. Co.; Farmers & Mechanics Savings Bank; Federal Express Corp.; Fidelity & Deposit Co. of Maryland; Fieldcrest Mills, Inc.; Fireman's Fund Inc. Co.; Fleet Bank,, N.A.; Frontier Ins. Co.; The Gainsco Companies; GEICO; Great West Casualty Co.; Guardian Life Insurance Co.; Gulf Insurance Co.; Hallmark Cards, Inc.; The Har-Conn Chrome Co.; The Hartford Insurance Co.; HCM Claim Management; Health Facilities Ins. Co.; Hertz Corp.; Holyoke Mutual Ins. Co.; Honda North America, Inc.; Jeter, Cook & Jepson - Architects, P.C.; Landstar Systems; Marriott Corporation; McDonald's Corp.; National Chriopractic Mutual Ins. (NCMIC); Nationwide Insurance; MEDMARC; Ohio Casualty Group; Olympic Underwriters Management; Orion Capital Cos.; Overnite Transporation Co.; People's Bank; Professional Risk Management Services, Inc.; Ramco Technologies, Inc.; Ranger Ins. Co.; Reliance National Ins. Co.; Risk Enterprise Management, Inc.; Royal Insurance Group; Sanborn Mortgage Farm; State Street Bank & Trust Co.; TIG Ins. Co.; Topolis and Harding, Inc.; Transamerica Inc. Co.; The Burton Corp.; The St. Paul; The Travelers; Tri Star Risk Mgt.; Underwriters Adj. Co.; Universal Underwriters Ins. Co.; Vermont Mutual Ins. Co.; Warner Lambert; Wesleyan University; Western Heritage Ins. Co.; Western Surety Co.; Western World Ins. Co.; W.R. Peterson Oil Co., Inc.; Zurich-American.

HASSETT & GEORGE, P.C.

555 FRANKLIN AVENUE
HARTFORD, CONNECTICUT 06114
Telephone: 860-296-2111
Fax: 860-296-8494
Email: info@hgesq.com
URL: http://www.hgesq.com

Civil Litigation, Commercial Law, Real Estate, Commercial Real Estate, Internet Law, PACA Litigation, Family Law, Criminal Law, Appellate Practice.

FIRM PROFILE: Hassett & George, P.C., is a general practice law firm committed to the service of its clients in a timely and cost-effective manner. While the firm has handled matters for Fortune 500 companies, commercial institutions and governmental agencies, each client is treated and dealt with in a personable, professional and accessible manner. At Hassett & George, P.C., each client's matter is of the utmost concern and importance.

RAYMOND M. HASSETT, born Springfield, Massachusetts, December 28, 1962; admitted to bar, 1987, Connecticut and U.S. District Court, District of Connecticut; 1989, U.S. Court of Appeals, Second Circuit; 1998, U.S. Supreme Court. *Education:* Catholic University of America (B.A., 1984); Quinnipiac College School of Law (J.D., 1987). Adjunct Professor, University of Connecticut. Former Special Assistant U.S. Attorney. Member, Glastonbury Republican Town Committee. President, South Hartford Initiative, elected member alumni Board of Governors, Catholic University of America. *Member:* Hartford County and Connecticut Bar Associations. ***PRACTICE AREAS:*** Criminal Law; Driving While Intoxicated; Divorce; Separation Agreements; Labor and Employment. ***Email:*** rhassett@hgesq.com

LOUIS N. GEORGE, born Southbridge, Massachusetts, November 24, 1961; admitted to bar, 1987, Connecticut and U.S. District Court, District of Connecticut; 1995, Mashantucket Pequot Tribal Court; 1997, U.S. Court of Appeals, Second Circuit and Mohegan Tribe Gaming Disputes Court; 1998, Massachusetts and U.S. Supreme Court. *Education:* Union College (B.A., 1984); Quinnipiac College School of Law (J.D., 1987). Phi Delta Phi. Recipient, American Jurisprudence Award in Criminal Procedure. Member, Simsbury Republican Town Committee. Member: Zoning Board of Appeals and Economic Development Commission, Town of Simsbury. *Member:* Hartford County, Connecticut and American Bar Associations; Connecticut Trial Lawyers Association; The Association of Trial Lawyers of America; Connecticut Defense Lawyers Association. ***LANGUAGES:*** Albanian and Greek. ***REPORTED CASES:*** Dodd v. Middlesex Mutual Assurance Co., 242 Conn. 375, 698 A.2d 819, (1997); Pagano v. Ippoliti et al., 245 Conn. 640, 716 A.2d 848 (1998); McClellan v. Cablevision, 149 F.3d 161 (1998). ***PRACTICE AREAS:*** Civil Litigation; Commercial Litigation; Personal Injury; Worker's Compensation; Internet Law; Appellate Practice. ***Email:*** lgeorge@hgesq.com

---

JOHN S. RUBRICH, born Chicago, Illinois, September 22, 1966; admitted to bar, 1992, Connecticut and U.S. District Court, District of Connecticut; 1998, U.S. Supreme Court. *Education:* University of Notre Dame (B.A., 1988); Quinnipiac School of Law (J.D., 1991). Member, University of Bridgeport Law Review. *Member:* Hartford County and Connecticut Bar Associations; Connecticut Trial Lawyers Association; Association of Trial Lawyers of America. ***REPORTED CASES:*** Dodd v. Middlesex Mutual Assurance Co., 242 Conn. 375, 698 A.2d 819 (1997); Pagano v. Ippoliti, et al, 245 Conn. 640, 716 A.2d 848 (1998). ***PRACTICE AREAS:*** Civil Litigation; Trial Practice; Computer Law; Corporate Law; Estate Planning; Real Estate; Business Law. ***Email:*** jrubrich@hgesq.com

MICHELLE KILLION, born Abington, Pennsylvania, May 7, 1973; (admission pending). *Education:* University of Connecticut (B.S., 1995); Quinnipiac College (J.D., cum laude, 2001). ***Email:*** mkillion@hgesq.com

REPRESENTATIVE CLIENTS: Atlantic Mutual Insurance; Benevolent and Protective Order of Elks, Lodge #771; C.G.A. Electric, Inc.; Chemical Bank; Connecticut Mortgage, LLC; East Hartford Government Workers Federal Credit Union; Electric Works of Westport, Inc.; Empire Insurance Company; Enfield Ford; EZ Publishing; Fleet Bank; Guaranty Federal Financial Corporation; Gulf Western Insurance Company; Hartford Steel Erectors, Inc.; Kimberly-Clark Integrated Corp.; Miller Builders, Inc.; Mortgage Capital Group, LLC; National City Mortgage, Inc.; NetMarketing, LLC; Network Adjusters, Inc.; Northland Insurance Company; O'Connor Electric, Inc.; People's Bank; Response Insurance Company; SAFECO (American States Insurance Company); Sail Sports International, Ltd.; San Juan Center, Inc.; SICO International Technologies, Inc.; Startech Environmental Corp.; State of Connecticut, Office of Attorney General; State of Connecticut, Second Injury Fund; Stejo Construction Co., Inc.; Sullivan & LeShane, Inc.; Town of Southhington; Town of Winchester; Traf-O-Data, Inc.; Trash Away, Inc.; Webgard, LLC; Webster Theater; Zurich Insurance.

HAWKINS, DELAFIELD & WOOD

CITY PLACE
185 ASYLUM STREET
HARTFORD, CONNECTICUT 06103
Telephone: 860-275-6260
Fax: 860-527-5786

New York, N.Y. Office: 67 Wall Street. Telephone: 212-820-9300. Fax: 212-514-8425.

Newark, New Jersey Office: One Gateway Center. Telephone: 973-642-8584. Fax: 973-642-6773.

Los Angeles, California Office: 633 West Fifth Street, Suite 3550. Telephone: 213-236-9050. Fax: 213-236-9060.

Washington, D.C. Office: 601 13th Street., N.W., Suite 800 South. Telephone: 202-682-1480. Fax: 202-682-1497.

San Francisco, California Office: One Embarcadero, Suite 1040. Telephone: 415-486-4200. Fax: 415-397-1513.

General Practice. Probate, Tax, Domestic and International Corporate and Banking, Federal Securities, Real Estate and Litigation. Law of State, Municipal and Public Authority Financing.

MEMBERS OF FIRM

MICHELA DALIANA, born Florence, Italy, January 26, 1962; admitted to bar, 1987, New York. *Education:* Georgetown University School of Foreign Service (B.S.F.S., 1983); New York Law School (J.D., cum laude, 1986); New York University School of Law (LL.M., in Taxation, 1987). *Member:* New York State and American Bar Associations; National Association of Bond Lawyers. (Resident, New York Office). ***Email:*** mdaliana@hdw.com

(This Listing Continued)

C. STEVEN DONOVAN, born New York, N.Y., October 24, 1951; admitted to bar, 1976, New Jersey; 1977, New York. *Education:* University of Notre Dame (B.A., cum laude, 1973); Fordham University (J.D., 1976). Member, Fordham Urban Law Journal, 1974-1976. *Member:* National Association of Bond Lawyers; National Health Lawyers Association. (Resident, New York Office). ***Email:*** csdonovan@hdw.com

RONALD C. GROSSER, born New York, N.Y., September 7, 1949; admitted to bar, 1983, New York. *Education:* Queens College of the City University of New York (B.A., 1971); Adelphi University (M.S., 1974); Boston University (J.D., 1981). Articles Editor, American Journal of Law and Medicine, 1980-1981. *Member:* New York State Bar Association. (Resident, New York Office). ***Email:*** rcgrosser@hdw.com

KENNETH B. ROBERTS, born New York, N.Y., March 21, 1954; admitted to bar, 1982, New York. *Education:* Duke University (B.A., cum laude, 1976); University of Michigan (J.D., 1980). Member, Michigan Yearbook of International Legal Studies, 1979-1980. *Member:* The Association of the Bar of the City of New York (Member: Committee on State Legislation, 1984-1986, 1998-2000; Municipal Affairs Committee, 1988-1991; Task Force on the New York State Constitutional Convention, 1996-1997). (Resident, New York Office). ***Email:*** kbroberts@hdw.com

RICHARD L. SIGAL, born Hartford, Connecticut, January 27, 1939; admitted to bar, 1964, New York. *Education:* Yale University (B.A., 1960); University of Chicago (J.D., 1963). *Member:* The Association of the Bar of the City of New York; New York State (Member, Executive Committee, 1971-1981 and Chairman, 1979-1981, Municipal Law Section) and American Bar Associations. (Resident, New York Office). ***Email:*** rlsigal@hdw.com

JEAN E. WINN, born Bridgeport, Connecticut, February 9, 1955; admitted to bar, 1989, Connecticut. *Education:* Alderson Broaddus (B.S., summa cum laude, 1985); University of Bridgeport School of Law (J.D., magna cum laude, 1989). Member, Law Review, 1987-1989. *Member:* Connecticut Bar Association; National Association of Bond Lawyers. (Resident). ***Email:*** jewinn@hdw.com

KAM WONG, born New York, N.Y.; admitted to bar, 1981, New York. *Education:* Rensselaer Polytechnic Institute (B.S.E.E.; M.S.E.E.); Baylor University (M.B.A.; J.D.). Tau Beta Pi; Eta Kappa Nu. (Resident, New York Office). ***Email:*** tkwong@hdw.com

HEFFERNAN & FARR, L.L.P.

Established in 1973

650 FARMINGTON AVENUE

HARTFORD, CONNECTICUT 06105

Telephone: 860-233-6336

Fax: 860-523-0419

Email: heffernan-farr@lawyers.com

General Practice. Probate, Real Estate, Construction Arbitration, Corporation, Workers Compensation, Personal Injury Law, Development, Family, Elder Law, Commercial Collections. Trials in all Courts.

MEMBERS OF FIRM

JOHN CONNERY HEFFERNAN, born New York, N.Y., June 26, 1944; admitted to bar, 1973, Connecticut; 1974, U.S. District Court, District of Connecticut; 1981, U.S. Court of Appeals for the Second Circuit and U.S. Court of Federal Claims; 1981-1982, U.S. Court of Customs and Patent Appeals; 1982, U.S . Court of Appeals for the Federal Circuit and U.S. Tax Court; 1996, Mashantucket Pequot Tribal Court. *Education:* Fairfield University (B.A., 1966); Catholic University of America (J.D., 1973). Editor, Catholic University Law Review, 1972-1973. Author: "Whither The Indigent Civil Litigant: Boddie v. Connecticut," 22 Catholic University Law Rev. 473, 1973; "Finding Fault with No-Fault Divorce: The Proposed Connecticut Divorce Statute," 47 Connecticut Bar Journal 99, 1973; "Professional Malpractice Insurance: Let the Attorney Beware," 48 Connecticut Bar Journal 347, 1974; "Initiative Ordinances and Home Rule," 25 Municipal Attorney 12, 1984; "Title Agents Liability Endorsement: The Right Hand Giveth And The Left Hand Taketh Away," 6 Perspectives Issue 4 at 3, 1986. Assistant Corporation Counsel, Town of West Hartford, 1981-1984. Member, Panel of Construction Arbitrators, American Arbitration Association. *Member:* Hartford County, Connecticut and American Bar Associations. ***PRACTICE AREAS:*** Probate; Real Estate; Family Law; Divorce; Child Support; Child Custody; Estate Planning.

ROBERT FARR, born Hartford, Connecticut, December 28, 1943; admitted to bar, 1969, Connecticut; 1973, U.S. Supreme Court; 1978, U.S. Tax Court and U.S. Court of Appeals, Second Circuit; 1978, U.S. Court of Federal Claims; 1978-1982, U.S. Court of Customs and Patent Appeals; 1982, U.S. Court of Appeals for the Federal Circuit. *Education:* University of Connecticut (B.S.E.E., 1966; J.D., 1969). Assistant Corporation Counsel, Town of West Hartford, 1970-1972. Member, West Hartford Town Council, 1976-1977. Member, Connecticut State Legislature, 19th District, 1981—. *Member:* Hartford County, Connecticut and American Bar Associations; Institute of Electrical and Electronic Engineers. ***PRACTICE AREAS:*** Real Estate; Corporate Law; Family Law; Divorce.

REPRESENTATIVE CLIENTS: Northeast Group, Inc.; Hartford Services, Inc.; Chase Manhattan Mortgage Corp.; Hannibal Holdings, L.L.C.

HORTON, SHIELDS & CORMIER, P.C.

Established in 1976

90 GILLETT STREET

HARTFORD, CONNECTICUT 06105

Telephone: 860-522-8338

Fax: 860-728-0401

Email: hsclaw@hsclaw.com

Trial and Appellate Practice in all State and Federal Courts. Personal Injury, Insurance Defense, Insurance Coverage, Commercial, Business Organization, Professional Grievance, Workers Compensation, Products Liability and Real Estate Law.

FIRM PROFILE: Horton, Shields & Cormier, P.C. was established in 1976. The members of the firm are experienced appellate and trial lawyers, who annually author the Connecticut Practice Book Annotated, Superior Court Rules and the Connecticut Rules of Appellate Procedure Annotated.

The firm provides a broad range of legal services to its clients, both corporate and individual.

WESLEY W. HORTON, born Hartford, Connecticut, April 16, 1942; admitted to bar, 1970, Connecticut and U.S. District Court, District of Connecticut; 1971, U.S. Court of Appeals, Second Circuit; 1975, U.S. Supreme Court. *Education:* Harvard University (A.B., 1964); University of Connecticut (J.D., 1970). Co-Author: "Supreme Court Rules Annotated," West Publishing Company, annually, 1977—; "Superior Court Civil Rules Annotated," West Publishing Company, annually, 1979—; "Connecticut Appellate Review," Connecticut Bar Journal, annually, 1985—; "Rules of Appellate Procedure Annotated," West Publishing Company, annually, 1993—. Author: "Connecticut Constitution: A Handbook," Greenwood Press, 1993; "Annotated Debates of the 1818 Constitutional Convention," Special Edition, Connecticut Bar Journal, January, 1991. Law Clerk to Chief Justice Charles S. House, Connecticut Supreme Court, 1970-1971. Recipient, Medal of Excellence, University of Connecticut Law School Alumni Association, 1989. Lecturer and Adjunct Professor, University of Connecticut Law School, 1970—. Member, Board of Editors, Connecticut Law Tribune, 1986—. *Member:* Hartford County, Connecticut (Member, 1978—, and Chair., 1997—, Committee on Professional Ethics) and American Bar Associations; Connecticut Trial Lawyers Association; American Academy of Appellate Lawyers. ***PRACTICE AREAS:*** State and Federal Appellate Litigation; Constitutional Law; Insurance Law; Professional Grievance. ***Email:*** hsclaw@hsclaw.com

ROBERT M. SHIELDS, JR., born New York, N. Y., December 14, 1951; admitted to bar, 1978, Connecticut; 1983, U.S. District Court, District of Connecticut; U.S. Court of Appeals, Second Circuit. *Education:* College of the Holy Cross (B.A., 1973); University of Connecticut (J.D., 1978). Co-Author: "Superior Court Civil Rules Annotated," West Publishing Co., annually, 1989—. Assistant City Attorney, Milford, 1978-1982. Special Master, 1995— and Mediator/Arbitrator, 1999—, Connecticut Superior Court. Lecturer, National Business Institute. *Member:* Hartford County, Connecticut and American Bar Associations; Connecticut Defense Lawyers Association. ***PRACTICE AREAS:*** Civil Litigation; Appellate Litigation; Insurance Law; Corporate Law; Real Estate. ***Email:*** rshields@hsclaw.com

KIMBERLY A. KNOX, born Hartford, Connecticut, September 1, 1960; admitted to bar, 1986, Connecticut; 1987, U.S. District Court, District of Connecticut; 1991, U.S. Court of Appeals, Second Circuit. *Education:* Connecticut College (B.A., 1982); University of Connecticut (J.D., 1986). Co-Author: "Superior Court Civil Rules Annotated," West Publishing Co., annually, 1989—; "State Variations of Commercial Law —Connecticut," Oceana Publications, 1988; With Wesley W. Horton, "Code to Rules: From Black and White to Grey," 61 Connecticut Bar Journal 146, 1987. *Member:* Hartford County, Connecticut (Member, Committee on Professional Ethics; Former Chair, Litigation Section; Member, Task Force on Judicial Independence) and American Bar Associations. ***PRACTICE AREAS:*** Professional Grievance; Civil Litigation; Insurance Defense; Insurance Coverage; Personal Injury; Product Liability. ***Email:*** kknox@hsclaw.com

KAREN L. DOWD, born Surrey, England, August 7, 1967; admitted to bar, 1991, Connecticut; 1992, U.S. District Court, District of Connecticut; 1997, U.S. Court of Appeals, Second Circuit. *Education:* University of Virginia (B.A., 1988); University of Connecticut (J.D., 1991). Co-Author: "Superior Court Rules Annotated," West Publishing Co., annually, 1994—. Moot Court Instructor, University of Connecticut School of Law, 1995—. *Member:* Hartford County and Connecticut (Member: Executive Committee, Litigation Section)

(This Listing Continued)

HORTON, SHIELDS & CORMIER, P.C., Hartford—Continued

Bar Associations; Connecticut Trial Lawyers Association; Connecticut Defense Lawyers Association; Defense Research Institute. ***PRACTICE AREAS:*** Civil Litigation; Appellate Practice; Insurance Defense; Personal Injury; Product Liability. ***Email:*** kdowd@hsclaw.com

MICHAEL S. TAYLOR, born Manchester, Connecticut, August 15, 1968; admitted to bar, 1994, Connecticut; 1995, U.S. District Court, District of Connecticut; 1997, U.S. Court of Appeals, Second Circuit. *Education:* University of Connecticut (B.A., cum laude, 1991; J.D., 1994). Author: "Recent Developments in Connecticut Product Liability Law," Conn. B. Journal, Vol. 73, No. 1, 1999. Co-Author: "Superior Court Rules Annotated," West Publishing Co., annually, 2000—. Board of Trustees, University of Connecticut, 1992-1993. *Member:* Hartford County and Connecticut Bar Associations; Defense Research Institute. Oliver Ellsworth, Inns of Court. ***PRACTICE AREAS:*** State and Federal Appellate Litigation; Insurance Law; Insurance Defense; Civil Litigation; Product Liability. ***Email:*** mtaylor@hsclaw.com

KENNETH J. BARTSCHI, born Walton, New York, May 25, 1965; admitted to bar, 1996, Connecticut; 1997, New York and U.S. District Court, District of Connecticut; 2000, U.S. Court of Appeals, Second Circuit. *Education:* State University of New York at Potsdam (B.M., 1987); Arizona State University (M.M., 1989); University of Connecticut (J.D., 1996). Managing Editor, Connecticut Journal of International Law. Author: "Legislative Responses to HIV/AIDS in Africa," 11 Connecticut Journal of International Law 169 (1995). Co-Author: "Superior Court Rules Annotated," West Publishing Co., annually, 2000— "Connecticut Appellate Review," Connecticut Bar Journal, Annually, 2000—. *Member:* Hartford County and Connecticut (Member: Estates and Probate Section; Executive committee of Human Rights and Responsibilities Section) Bar Associations. ***PRACTICE AREAS:*** Civil Litigation; Appellate Practice; Civil Rights; Constitutional Law; Wills. ***Email:*** kbartschi@hsclaw.com

---

DANIEL JONAH KRISCH, born Hartford, Connecticut, November 16, 1973; admitted to bar, 1999, Connecticut; 2000, New York and U.S. District Court, District of Connecticut. *Education:* Columbia University (B.A., 1995); University of Connecticut (J.D., 1999). Author: "Vogt v. Germany: The European Court of Human Rights Expands the Scope of Arhues 10 and 11 of the European Convention on Human Rights to Include the Political Activities of Civil Servants," 14 Connecticut Journal of International Law 237 (1999). *Member:* Connecticut and New York State Bar Associations. ***PRACTICE AREAS:*** Appellate Litigation; Civil Litigation; Criminal Law. ***Email:*** dkrisch@hsclaw.com

OF COUNSEL

SUSAN M. CORMIER, born New Bedford, Massachusetts, November 8, 1954; admitted to bar, 1982, Connecticut and U.S. District Court, District of Connecticut; 1985, U.S. Court of Appeals, Second Circuit; 1987, U.S. Supreme Court. *Education:* Providence College (B.A., 1976); University of Connecticut (J.D., 1982). Co-Author: With Wesley W. Horton, "Rules of Appellate Procedure Annotated," West Publishing Co., Annually, 1993—; "Superior Court Civil Rules Annotated," West Publishing Co., annually, 1989—; "Connecticut Appellate Review," Connecticut Bar Journal, annually, 1994-2000. Law Clerk, Connecticut Superior Court, Appellate Session, 1982-1983. *Member:* Hartford County and Connecticut Bar Associations. ***PRACTICE AREAS:*** Civil Litigation; Appellate Practice; Insurance Litigation. ***Email:*** hsclaw@hsclaw.com

REPRESENTATIVE CLIENTS: AIG Aviation; Chrysler Corp.; Clark Equipment Co.; Colonial Insurance; First Financial Insurance Co.; Gallagher Bassett Services, Inc.; General Dynamics Corp.; Heritage Insurance; INA; Jensen's, Inc.; Konover Development Corp.; Liberty Mutual Insurance Co.; Lloyds of London; Nationwide Insurance Co.; Northland Insurance Co.; Phillips International Holding Corp.; Ranger Insurance Co.; Reliance Insurance Co.; St. Paul Insurance Co.;Tishman Realty & Construction Co.; Town of Burlington; Unigard Security Insurance Co.; United Capitol Insurance Co.; Westwood Restaurant Group; Woodbridge Lake Sewer District.

APPROVED ATTORNEYS FOR: Fidelity National Title Insurance Company of New York; Lawyers Title Insurance Corp.

HOWARD, KOHN, SPRAGUE & FITZGERALD

Practice established by Enoch Perkins in 1786.

237 BUCKINGHAM STREET

P.O. BOX 261798

HARTFORD, CONNECTICUT 06126-1798

Telephone: 860-525-3101

Telecopier: 860-247-4201

Email: atty@hksflaw.com

URL: http://www.hksflaw.com

Manchester, Connecticut Office: 99 East Center Street, 06040. Telephone: 203-646-8075.

(This Listing Continued)

Glastonbury, Connecticut Office: 41B New London Turnpike, 06033. Telephone: 203-633-3373.

General Practice. Corporation, Probate, Insurance, Aviation, Medical-Legal Law, Real Estate, Environmental Law, Family Law, Admiralty, Medical Malpractice, Longshoremen's, Harborworker's Compensation Act and Worker's Compensation Law. Trials in all Courts.

FIRM PROFILE: Howard, Kohn, Sprague & FitzGerald, one of the oldest law firms in the country, was founded in 1786 and has been in continuous practice since that time. The firm provides a diverse range of legal services and represents clients statewide.

The firm participates in the prosecution and defense of lawsuits in both the state and federal courts, in pretrial, trial and appellate stages. Resources include in-house library and computer services as well as specialized paralegal staff.

MEMBERS OF FIRM

JOHN R. FITZGERALD, born Danbury, Connecticut, June 26, 1927; admitted to bar, 1953, Connecticut. *Education:* University of Connecticut (B.A., 1951); University of Connecticut Law School (J.D., high honors, 1953). Co-Author: "Connecticut Law of Torts," 3rd Edition, 1991; "Connecticut Trial Practice," 1987. Adjunct Professor of Law, Connecticut University Law School, 1953-1991. Prosecuting Attorney, Manchester Town Court, 1955-1959. *Member:* Hartford County (President, 1979-1980), Manchester (President, 1972-1973), Connecticut and American Bar Associations; American Judicature Society; Defense Research Institute, Inc.; The Association of Trial Lawyers of America. ***PRACTICE AREAS:*** Trial Practice. ***Email:*** jrf@hksflaw.com

JOHN STEPHEN PAPA, born New Haven, Connecticut, October 1, 1942; admitted to bar, 1967, Connecticut and District of Columbia. *Education:* Fordham University (A.B., 1964; J.D., 1967); University of Hartford (M.S. in Taxation, 1976). Special Master, Superior, Court-Hartford County and U.S. District Court, District of Connecticut. *Member:* Manchester, Hartford County, Connecticut and American Bar Associations. [Judge Advocate and Military Judge, United States Marine Corps, 1967-1970]. ***PRACTICE AREAS:*** Litigation; Real Estate Development. ***Email:*** jsp@hksflaw.com

JAMES M. MOHER, born New Haven, Connecticut, March 18, 1947; admitted to bar, 1972, Connecticut; U.S. District Court, District of Connecticut, 1975. *Education:* Providence College (B.A., magna cum laude, 1969); University of Connecticut (J.D., 1972). *Member:* Hartford County and Connecticut Bar Associations; Connecticut Defense Lawyers Association. ***PRACTICE AREAS:*** Civil Litigation.

ROBERT P. VOLPE, born Hartford, Connecticut, December 19, 1934; admitted to bar, 1959, Connecticut. *Education:* Harvard University (B.A., cum laude, 1956); University of Michigan (J.D., 1959). Member, Board of Editors, University of Michigan Law Review, 1958. Assistant Corporation Counsel, Town of West Hartford, Connecticut, 1976-1979. Corporation Counsel, 1979-1981. *Member:* Hartford County and The Connecticut Bar Associations; Connecticut Defense Lawyers Association. ***PRACTICE AREAS:*** Civil Litigation; Estate Planning and Settlement. ***Email:*** rpv@hksflaw.com

CONSTANCE L. EPSTEIN, born Rockford, Illinois, July 3, 1943; admitted to bar, 1979, Connecticut and U.S. District Court, District of Connecticut; 1983, U.S. Court of Appeals, Second Circuit; 1988, U.S. Supreme Court. *Education:* Illinois State University (B.A., 1965); University of Connecticut (J.D., with high honors, 1979). Contributing Author, The Defense. *Member:* Manchester, Hartford County and Connecticut Bar Associations; Connecticut Trial Lawyers Association; Connecticut Defense Lawyers Association (President). ***PRACTICE AREAS:*** Civil Litigation; Arbitration; Appeals. ***Email:*** cle@hksflaw.com

THOMAS P. CELLA, born New Rochelle, New York, December 4, 1957; admitted to bar, 1983, Connecticut; 1984, U. S. District Court, District of Connecticut. *Education:* University of Connecticut (B.A., 1979); Western New England College (J.D., 1983). Law Clerk, Superior Court, State of Connecticut, 1983-1984. Assistant Town Attorney, Town of Manchester, 1986-1989, 1991—. Member, Economic Development Commission, Town of Manchester, 1986. Special Master, United States District Court, District of Connecticut, 1988—. *Member:* Manchester, Hartford County, Connecticut and American Bar Associations; Connecticut Defense Lawyers Association; Connecticut Trial Lawyers Association; Defense Research Institute, Inc. (Board Certified Civil Trial Lawyer, National Board of Trial Advocacy). ***PRACTICE AREAS:*** Civil Litigation. ***Email:*** tpc@hksflaw.com

JACK G. STEIGELFEST, born Milwaukee, Wisconsin, July 20, 1960; admitted to bar, 1984, Connecticut; 1985, U.S. District Court, District of Connecticut; 1987, U.S. Court of Appeals, Second Circuit. *Education:* Lehigh University (B.S., 1981); University of Connecticut (J.D., high honors, 1984). Executive Editor, Connecticut Law Review, 1983-1984. Judicial Law Clerk for Justice Shea, Connecticut Supreme Court, 1984-1985. Senior Editor, Connecticut Bar Journal, 1995— *Member:* Connecticut and American Bar Associations;

(This Listing Continued)

Connecticut Defense Lawyers Association (Second Vice President, 2001-2002); Defense Research Institute. ***PRACTICE AREAS:*** Civil Litigation; Appeals; Insurance Coverage. ***Email:*** jgs@hksflaw.com

JAMES F. SULLIVAN, born New Britain, Connecticut, September 18, 1963; admitted to bar, 1992, Connecticut; 1993, U.S. District Court, District of Connecticut. *Education:* Boston College (B.A., summa cum laude, 1986); University of Connecticut (M.A., 1989; J.D., with honors, 1992). Phi Beta Kappa. Recipient: American Jurisprudence Award for Property; Thomas Gallivan, Jr. Memorial Prize. Editor-in-Chief, The Connecticut Law Review. Law Clerk to Judge Robert Callahan, Connecticut Supreme Court. Member, Editorial Board, Connecticut Bar Journal, 1993—. Author: "Successor Corporate Liability in Product Liability Actions in Connecticut," 73 Conn. Bar J. 297 (1999); "The Scope of Procedural Rule-making in Connecticut," 65 Conn Bar J. 411 (1991); "Initial Automatic Disclosure Regime of Federal Rule 26," Conn. Lawyer (May, 1994); "Insurer's Duty to Preserve the Fire Scene in Subrogation Cases," (co-author, ABA Monogram 1996). President, The University of Connecticut Law School Alumni Association, 2000. Lecturer: "Motion Practice in Connecticut," topic - "Trial Motions" (Lorman, 1999—); Automobile College of Law, topic - "Biomechanical Experts" (CTLA, 2001). Chairman, Ethics Commission, City of New Britain, 1996-1999; Chairman, CTLA People's Law School (Newington, New Britain and Berlin). *Member:* Connecticut and American (Co-Chair, Litigation Trial Practice Subcommittee on Experts, 2000—) Bar Associations; Connecticut Trial Lawyers Association. ***PRACTICE AREAS:*** Products Liability; Personal Injury; Premises Liability; Professional Malpractice; Construction; Municipal; Employment; Trade Regulation; Commercial Litigation. ***Email:*** jfs@hksflaw.com

ASSOCIATES

TODD W. WHITFORD, born Lowell, Massachusetts, October 6, 1970; admitted to bar, 1995, Connecticut; 1996, U.S. District Court, District of Connecticut; 1996, Massachusetts and U.S. District Court, District of Massachusetts. *Education:* Albright College (B.A., 1992); University of Connecticut (J.D., 1995). Member, Connecticut Moot Court Board, 1992-1995. Associate Editor, Connecticut Insurance Law Journal, 1995. *Member:* Tolland County, Greater Enfield, Connecticut and Massachusetts Bar Associations; Connecticut Defense Lawyers Association. ***PRACTICE AREAS:*** Civil Litigation; Personal Injury; Insurance Defense; Land Use; Domestic Relations; Criminal Law; Estate Planning; Real Estate. ***Email:*** tww@hksflaw.com

STEVEN J. BARBER, born Middletown, Connecticut, October 5, 1972; admitted to bar, 1997, Connecticut; 1998, Massachusetts, U.S. District Court, District of Connecticut and U.S. District Court, District of Massachusetts. *Education:* Stonehill College (B.A., 1994); Western New England College School of Law (J.D., 1997). Distinction in Oral Advocacy, Moot Court. Participant, Phillip C. Jessup International Moot Court Team, 1995-1996. Associate Editor, The Defense, 2000— *Member:* Hartford County, Middlesex County, Connecticut, Massachusetts and American Bar Associations; Connecticut Defense Lawyers Association. ***PRACTICE AREAS:*** Insurance Defense; Personal Injury; Civil Litigation; Domestic Relations; Criminal Law; Workers Compensation; Bankruptcy; Estate Planning; Mediation; Arbitration. ***Email:*** sjb@hksflaw.com

KEVIN LADIEU, admitted to bar, 1996, Connecticut. *Education:* University of Connecticut (B.A., 1991); Quinnipiac College School of Law (J.D., 1996). *Member:* Connecticut Bar Association; Connecticut Trial Lawyers Association. ***PRACTICE AREAS:*** Litigation; Personal Injury; Medical Malpractice; Criminal Law; Products Liability. ***Email:*** kxl@hksflaw.com

JOSEPH E. MASCARO, born Hartford, Connecticut, June 5, 1967; admitted to bar, 1992, Connecticut. *Education:* Fordham University (B.A., Political Science, 1989); University of Connecticut School of Law (J.D., 1992). *Member, Connecticut Defense Lawyers Association.* ***PRACTICE AREAS:*** Civil Litigation; Insurance Defense; Immigration and Naturalization; Criminal Law. ***Email:*** jem@hksflaw.com

REPRESENTATIVE CLIENTS: Allied Van Lines; Allstate Insurance Company; Amica Mutual Insurance Co.; The Commerce Insurance Company; Connecticut Guaranty Fund; Employers of Wausau; Farm Family Mutual Insurance Co.; Fleet Bank, N.A.; Great American Insurance Company; Hartford Accident & Indemnity Co.; Home Insurance Co.; Landfill Management Company, Inc.; Liberty Mutual Insurance Co.; London Market Insurers; Middlesex Mutual Insurance Co.; Mobil Oil Company; National Grange Mutual Liability Co.; Otis Elevator Company; Patron's Mutual Insurance Co.; Peerless Insurance Company; Peter Rock Associates Limited Partnership; Purity Supreme, Inc.; Reliance Insurance Co.; Ridge Road Real Estate Limited Partnership; Royal Globe Insurance Co.; Security Insurance Co.; Sentry Insurance Co.; Supermarkets General, Inc.; Town of Manchester; Travelers Ins. Fund; United Technologies Corp.; Montgomery Elevator Co.
APPROVED ATTORNEYS FOR: Connecticut Attorneys Title Insurance Co.
REFERENCE: Fleet Bank.

HOWD & LUDORF

65 WETHERSFIELD AVENUE
HARTFORD, CONNECTICUT 06114
Telephone: 860-249-1361
Fax: 860-249-7665
URL: http://www.hl-law.com

Products Liability Litigation, Insurance Defense Litigation, Commercial Litigation, Toxic Tort, Municipal Litigation, Medical Malpractice, General Trial and Appellate Practice.

MEMBERS OF FIRM

JOHN R. LILLIENDAHL, III, born Philadelphia, Pennsylvania, July 22, 1945; admitted to bar, 1970, Connecticut and U.S. District Court, District of Connecticut; 1990, Florida; 1992, U.S. District Court, Middle District of Florida. *Education:* Middlebury College (B.A., 1967); University of Connecticut (LL.B., 1970). *Member:* Hartford County and Connecticut Bar Associations; The Florida Bar. ***PRACTICE AREAS:*** Product Liability Litigation; Insurance Defense Litigation; General Trial and Appellate Practice; Toxic Tort; Commercial Litigation.

JOHN J. BOGDANSKI, born Meriden, Connecticut, December 12, 1953; admitted to bar, 1979, Connecticut; 1980, Massachusetts and U.S. District Court, District of Connecticut; 1981, U.S. District Court, District of Massachusetts; 1985, U.S. Court of Appeals, 2nd Circuit. *Education:* Tufts University (B.A., 1976); Western New England College (J.D., cum laude, 1979). Editor, Western New England Law Review, 1978-1979. Law Clerk, Appellate Session of Superior Court, 1979-1980. *Member:* Hartford County, Connecticut and American Bar Associations; Connecticut Defense Lawyers Association. ***PRACTICE AREAS:*** Product Liability Litigation; Insurance Defense Litigation; Toxic Tort.

PHILIP T. NEWBURY, JR., born Westerly, Rhode Island, October 21, 1955; admitted to bar, 1981, Rhode Island and Massachusetts; 1982, Connecticut and U.S. District Court, District of Connecticut; 1985, U.S. Court of Appeals, 2nd Circuit; 1986, U.S. Supreme Court; 1994, U.S. District Court, District of Massachusetts. *Education:* University of Connecticut (B.S., 1977); Suffolk University (J.D., cum laude, 1981). Phi Delta Phi. Editor, Suffolk Transnational Law Journal, 1980-1981. Law Clerk, Appellate Session of Superior Court, 1982-1983. Author: "International Law: The Canadian Arctic Waters Pollution Prevention Act and its Effect," Suffolk Transnational Law Journal 139, 1980. *Member:* Hartford County, Connecticut and American Bar Associations. ***PRACTICE AREAS:*** Products Liability Litigation; Insurance Defense Litigation; Toxic Tort; Municipal Litigation; General Trial and Appellate Practice.

THOMAS R. GERARDE, born Hartford, Connecticut, September 4, 1956; admitted to bar, 1981, Connecticut and U.S. District Court, District of Connecticut; 1987, U.S. Supreme Court. *Education:* Fairfield University (B.S., 1978); Suffolk University (J.D., cum laude, 1981). Staff Member, 1979-1980 and Comment Editor, 1980-1981, Suffolk University Law Review. Author: "Application of the Final Judgement Rule: Attorney Disqualification Order Issued During Grand Jury Proceeding Not Immediately Appealable," 14 Suffolk U. L. Rev. 311, 1980. Law Clerk, Connecticut Superior Court, 1981-1982. *Member:* American Bar Association (Member, Tort and Insurance Practice, Litigation, State and Local Government Law Sections). ***PRACTICE AREAS:*** Municipal Litigation; Product Liability Litigation; Insurance Defense Litigation; Employment Litigation; Appellate Practice.

MARK J. CLAFLIN, born Topeka, Kansas, March 15, 1959; admitted to bar, 1984, Connecticut; 1985, U.S. District Court, District of Connecticut. *Education:* Providence College (B.S., 1981); University of Connecticut (J.D., 1984). *Member:* Hartford County and Connecticut Bar Associations; The Association of Trial Lawyers of America; Connecticut Trial Lawyers Association. ***PRACTICE AREAS:*** Products Liability Litigation; Insurance Defense Litigation; General Trial and Appellate Practice.

CHRISTOPHER M. VOSSLER, born Bridgeport, Connecticut, May 27, 1960; admitted to bar, 1985, Connecticut, U.S. District Court, District of Connecticut and U.S. Court of Appeals, Second Circuit; 1992, New York. *Education:* Boston College (B.A., cum laude, 1982); University of Bridgeport School of Law (J.D., 1985). *Member:* Connecticut, New York State and American Bar Associations; Defense Research Institute; Connecticut Defense Lawyers Association (Board of Directors). ***PRACTICE AREAS:*** Products Liability Litigation; Commercial; Premises Liability Litigation; Environmental Insurance Claims; General Trial and Appellate Practice.

WILLIAM F. CORRIGAN, born Hartford, Connecticut, October 23, 1959; admitted to bar, 1987, Connecticut; 1988, U.S. District Court, District of Connecticut. *Education:* Fairfield University (B.A., 1981); Western New England College (J.D., 1987). Litigation Instructor, Legal Assistance Program, Morse School of Business, 1990-1992. *Member:* Hartford County and Connecticut Bar Associations. ***PRACTICE AREAS:*** Products Liability Litigation; Insurance Defense; Commercial Litigation; Municipal Litigation.

(This Listing Continued)

HOWD & LUDORF, Hartford—Continued

DAVID S. MONASTERSKY, born Boston, Massachusetts, March 28, 1968; admitted to bar, 1993, Connecticut; 1994, U.S. District Court, District of Connecticut. *Education:* Tufts University (B.A., cum laude, 1990); Boston College (J.D., cum laude, 1993). ***PRACTICE AREAS:*** Insurance Defense; Municipal Litigation; Products Liability; Toxic Tort; General Trial and Appellate Practice.

MICHAEL J. ROSE, born Providence, Rhode Island, January 14, 1966; admitted to bar, 1994, Connecticut; 1995, U.S. District Court, District of Connecticut. *Education:* University of New Hampshire (B.A., cum laude, 1989); Franklin Pierce Law Center (J.D., 1994). Mortar Board Honor Society. Pi Gamma Mu. Co-Author: "ADR in Patent Dispute Resolution," vol 32 Idea No 4, 1992. Legislative Assistant, Representative Richard Swett, U.S. House of Representatives, 1991-1994. ***PRACTICE AREAS:*** Civil Rights; Employment Law; Municipal; Insurance Defense.

COLETTE S. GRIFFIN, born Bronxville, New York, June 2, 1958; admitted to bar, 1987, Connecticut; 1990, U.S. Court of Appeals, Sixth Circuit. *Education:* University of California (B.A., 1983); Quinnipiac College School of Law (J.D., 1987). Phi Delta Phi Honor Society (Treasurer, 1986-1987). Member, Probate Law Journal. *Member:* Connecticut Bar Association (Member Worker's Compensation Section). ***PRACTICE AREAS:*** Insurance Defense; Workers Compensation.

MELINDA A. POWELL, born Ft. Lauderdale, Florida, February 10, 1971; admitted to bar, 1996, Connecticut and U.S. District Court, District of Connecticut. *Education:* Florida Atlantic University (B.P.A., Valedictorian, 1991); Vermont Law School (J.D., 1995). Jonathan B. Chase Scholar. *Member:* Connecticut (Co-Chair, Practice Development Committee, 1998-2000) and American (Delegate, Young Lawyers Division, 1997-1999; Associate Editor, The Affiliate, Young Lawyers Division, 1998-2000; Vice-Chair, Women in the Profession, Young Lawyers Division, 1998-1999) Bar Associations; Connecticut Trial Lawyers Association. ***PRACTICE AREAS:*** Insurance Defense Law; Personal Injury Law; Litigation; Trial Practice; Products Liability.

KEITH E. MARQUIS, born Hartford, Connecticut, August 24, 1965; admitted to bar, 1997, Connecticut; 1998, U.S. District Court, District of Connecticut. *Education:* Southern Connecticut State University (B.S., 1990); Quinnipiac College (J.D., 1996). Member, Police Association of Connecticut, 1994-1997. *Member:* New Haven County and Hartford County Bar Associations; Connecticut Defense Lawyers Association. [U.S. Army, 1983-1986 and Connecticut Army National Guard, 1986-1991]. ***PRACTICE AREAS:*** Insurance Defense; Workers Compensation.

PAUL ERICKSON, born Milford, Connecticut, April 5, 1965; admitted to bar, 1994, Massachusetts; 1996, Illinois; 1997, Connecticut. *Education:* Western New England College (B.A., 1988); University of Florida (J.D., 1994). ***PRACTICE AREAS:*** Insurance Defense Litigation; Municipal Liability; Medical Malpractice; Products Liability.

DANIEL C. DeMERCHANT, born Middletown, Connecticut, October 4, 1970; admitted to bar, 1997, Connecticut and U.S. District Court, District of Connecticut; 1998, Florida. *Education:* Stetson University (B.B.A., 1992); Quinnipiac College School of Law (J.D., 1997). Associate Editor, Quinnipiac Probate Law Journal, 1996-1997. *Member:* Middlesex County Bar Association. ***PRACTICE AREAS:*** Products Liability; Insurance Defense; Municipal; General Trial and Appellate Practice.

BRUCE J. GELSTON, born Montreal, Quebec, Canada, December 30, 1969; admitted to bar, 1997, Connecticut; 1998, U.S. District Court, District of Connecticut. *Education:* Western Washington University (B.A., 1993); Quinnipiac College School of Law (J.D., 1997). Member, National Probate Law Journal, 1995-1997. ***PRACTICE AREAS:*** Insurance Defense; Products Liability; Municipal Law.

LISA K. TITUS, born New Haven, Connecticut, August 18, 1971; admitted to bar, 1996, Connecticut. *Education:* Bucknell University (B.A., 1993); University of Connecticut School of Law (J.D., 1996). *Member:* New Haven County and Connecticut Bar Associations. ***PRACTICE AREAS:*** Insurance Defense; Municipal Litigation.

ALEXANDRIA L. BUFFORD, born Nashville, Tennessee, January 24, 1973; admitted to bar, 1999, Connecticut; 2000, New York. *Education:* University of Michigan (B.A., 1995); University of Connecticut (J.D., 1999). Phi Alpha Delta. *Member:* New York Bar Association. ***PRACTICE AREAS:*** Municipal Litigation; Insurance Defense Litigation; Employment Law.

BEATRICE D. SUKHDEO, born New York, New York, April 4, 1974; admitted to bar, 1999, Connecticut. *Education:* St John's University (B.S., 1996); University of Connecticut (J.D., 1999). ***PRACTICE AREAS:*** Insurance Defense Litigation; Municipal Litigation.

JAY THOMAS DON FRANCISCO, born Putnam, Connecticut, January 1, 1973; admitted to bar, 1999, Connecticut. *Education:* Connecticut College (B.A., 1995); Vermont Law School (J.D., 1999). National Political Honor Society, Connecticut College. *Member:* Windham County Bar Association. ***PRACTICE AREAS:*** Insurance Defense; Litigation; Municipal Law.

JOHN J. RADSHAW, born Bridgeport, Connecticut, October 7, 1971; admitted to bar, 1998, Connecticut; 1999, New York and U.S. District Court, District of Connecticut; 2000, U.S. District Court, Souther and Eastern Districts of New York. *Education:* Mary Washington College (B.A., 1993); Quinnipiac College, School of Law (J.D., cum laude, 1998). Editor-in-chief, Quinnipiac Probate Law Journal, 1997-1998. Member, Quinnipiac Probate Law Journal, 1996-1997. *Member:* Connecticut, New York State and American Bar Associations. ***PRACTICE AREAS:*** Municipal Law; Insurance Defense Litigation; Civil Litigation. ***Email:*** jradshaw@hl-law.com

DEANN K. SEYMOUR, born Abington, Pennsylvania, September 15, 1964; admitted to bar, 2001, Connecticut. *Education:* Hartford College for Women (B.S., 1998); Western New England College School of Law (J.D., 2001). ***PRACTICE AREAS:*** Workers Compensation; Insurance Defense; Municipal Law.

RETIRED

EDWARD S. LUDORF, born Simsbury, Connecticut, August 17, 1928; admitted to bar, 1958, Connecticut. *Education:* Trinity College (B.A., 1951); Boston University (LL.B., 1957). *Member:* Hartford County and Connecticut Bar Associations.

REPRESENTATIVE CLIENTS: Black & Decker; CIGNA; Coleman Co.; Columbia Manufacturing; Harsco Corp.; Honda North America Inc.; Hyster Co.; Hyundai; Ladder Management Service Inc.; MHT Products, Inc.; MTD Products Inc.; Mitsubishi; Pennzoil Co.; Pfizer, Inc.; Renault; Toyota Motor Sales, USA, Inc.; United Technologies Corp.; American Empire Surplus Lines Ins. Co.; Reliance Insurance Co.; Travelers Insurance Co.; Pittway Industries; BRK Brands, Inc.; Norton Company; Liberty Mutual Insurance; Werner Co.; Allstate Ins. Co.; British Petroleum Co.; Burger King Corp.; Better Brands, Inc.; Heublein, Inc.; Sharplan Lasers, Inc.; Ford New Holland; Texaco, Inc.; Mobil Corp; Gulf Oil Corp.; Atlantic Mutual Ins. Co.; General Motors Corp.; Huffy Corp.; Trek Bicycle Corp.; OneSource Facilities Services, Inc.; Baxter International Inc.; Safeco/American States Insurance Co.; Daimler Chrysler; TIG Insurance Co.; K&K Insurance Co.; HSBC Bank USA; Gulf Insurance Co.; Great American Insurance Co.; Connecticut Interlocal Risk Management Agency; Nationwide Insurance Co.; Reliant Insurance Co.; Glatfelter Insurance Co.; Lennox Industries; ACE, USA; CNA Insurance Co.; Polaris Industries, Inc.

HUNT LEIBERT CHESTER & JACOBSON, P.C.

94 HUNGERFORD STREET
HARTFORD, CONNECTICUT 06106-4626
Telephone: 860-808-0606
Fax: 860-549-0163; 524-5602; 522-4815
URL: http://www.hlcj.com

Foreclosure, Bankruptcy, Real Estate, Personal Injury, Criminal.

KIMBALL HAINES HUNT, born Dobbs Ferry, New York, September 20, 1948; admitted to bar, 1974, Connecticut; 1975, U.S. District Court, District of Connecticut; 1988, U.S. Court of Appeals, Second Circuit. *Education:* University of New Hampshire (B.A., 1971); North Carolina Central University (J.D., 1974). ***PRACTICE AREAS:*** Personal Injury; Criminal; Litigation; Commercial; Driving While Intoxicated. ***Email:*** khunt@hlcj.com

RICHARD M. LEIBERT, born Hartford, Connecticut, May 3, 1951; admitted to bar, 1979, Connecticut and U.S. District Court, District of Connecticut; 1987, U.S. Court of Appeals, Second Circuit. *Education:* Long Island University (B.A.); University of Connecticut (J.D., 1979). Pi Gamma Mu. Who's Who in American Universities and Colleges. Recipient: American Jurisprudence Award, 1978; Connecticut Bar Association Pro Bono Award, 1993. Member, U.S. Foreclosure Network, 1994. Past Chairman of the Board, Connecticut Consumer Counseling Service. *Member:* Hartford County and Connecticut (Member, Commercial and Bankruptcy Committee, 1979—) Bar Associations; American Bankruptcy Institute. ***REPORTED CASES:*** Savings Bank of Rockville v. Valente; Bristol Savings Bank v. Cellino; Barrett Builders v. Miller; Glastonbury Bank & Trust Co. v. Corbett Construction; BayBank Connecticut, N.A. v. Thumlert; In re Silver. ***PRACTICE AREAS:*** Foreclosure; Bankruptcy; Commercial Litigation; Real Estate. ***Email:*** rleibert@hlcj.com

SAMUEL D. CHESTER, born New Britain, Connecticut, January 11, 1949; admitted to bar, 1974, Connecticut; 1979, U.S. District Court, District of Connecticut. *Education:* University of Wisconsin (B.A., 1971); California Western School of Law (J.D., 1974). *Member:* Hartford County, Connecticut and American Bar Associations. ***PRACTICE AREAS:*** Foreclosure; Commercial Litigation; Collection. ***Email:*** schester@hlcj.com

RICHARD C. JACOBSON, born Brookline, Massachusetts, April 27, 1952; admitted to bar, 1977, Connecticut and U.S. District Court, District of Connecticut; 1982, U.S. Supreme Court; 1984, U.S. Claims Court. *Education:* University of Connecticut (B.A., cum laude, 1974; J.D., cum laude, 1977).

(This Listing Continued)

Co-Author: "Negative Declaration: The Practical Problems," Chicago Title Insurance Company, *Perspectives,* Spring, 1986. Lecturer, Real Estate Law, University of Hartford. *Member:* Hartford County (Member, Commercial Law and Bankruptcy Section), Connecticut and American Bar Associations. ***PRACTICE AREAS:*** Real Estate Law; Corporate Law; Commercial Litigation; Foreclosure. ***Email:*** rjacobson@hlcj.com

---

GERALD BEAUDOIN, born Casablanca, Morocco, June 16, 1960; admitted to bar, 1990, Connecticut. *Education:* Florida State University (B.S., 1986); Florida State University, College of Law (J.D., 1989). *Member:* Windham County, Connecticut and American Bar Associations; Connecticut Trial Lawyer's Association.

THOMAS J. FARRELL, born Providence, Rhode Island, August 27, 1954; admitted to bar, 1985, Connecticut; 1986, U.S. District Court, District of Connecticut; 1987, Rhode Island and U.S. District Court, District of Rhode Island; 1996, U.S. District Court, Western District of Michigan and U.S. Court of Appeals, 6th Circuit. *Education:* University of Rhode Island (B.A., with high distinction, 1981); University of Connecticut (J.D., 1985). Phi Beta Kappa. Recipient, Herman W. Churchill Award for Excellence in History, 1981. Member: National Moot Court Competition Team, 1983; Moot Court Board, 1983-1985. *Member:* Connecticut (Member: Commercial Law, Bankruptcy and Administrative Law Sections) and Rhode Island Bar Associations; Connecticut Trial Lawyers Association.

GEOFFREY KENT MILNE, born Hartford, Connecticut, June 6, 1965; admitted to bar, 1990, Connecticut; 1993, U.S. District Court, District of Connecticut; 1997, U.S. District Court, Southern and Eastern Districts of New York. *Education:* Marist College (B.A., cum laude, 1987); Villanova University (J.D., 1990). Moot Court Regional Finalists. Temporary Assistant Clerk, New Britain Superior Court, 1991-1993. Member, Young Lawyers Executive Committee, 1993—; Co-Chair Corporations and Transactional Law Committee. *Member:* New Britain, Regional (Co-Chair, Young Lawyers Committee; Vice Chair Bench Bar Committee, 1997—) and Connecticut (Member, Pro Bono Committee, 1991-1992) Bar Associations; Connecticut Trial Lawyers Association. ***PRACTICE AREAS:*** Commercial Litigation; Personal Injury Litigation.

KATHRYN R. SYLVESTER, born Camden, New Jersey, January 20, 1968; admitted to bar, 1996, Connecticut and U.S. District Court of Connecticut. *Education:* Rosemont College (B.A., 1990); Vermont Law School (M.S.L., 1991; J.D., 1994). Phi Delta Phi. *Member:* New Haven County and American Bar Associations. ***PRACTICE AREAS:*** Real Estate; General Practice; Environmental Law.

SEAN E. SWEENEY, born Hartford, Connecticut, August 8, 1958; admitted to bar, 1983, Connecticut. *Education:* Stonehill College (B.A., 1980); Western New England College (J.D., 1983). *Member:* Connecticut Bar Association.

REPRESENTATIVE CLIENTS: American Bank of Connecticut; Aurora National Bank; BayBank Connecticut; BancOklahoma; BISYS Mortgage Service; Berkeley Federal Bank & Trust Company; Bristol Savings Bank; Centerbank Mortgage Company; Chemical Residential Mortgage Corporation; Contimortgage Corporation; Citicorp Mortgage, Inc.; City of Hartford; City of New Haven; Commercial Financial Services; Countrywide Funding Corporation; Crown Bank; Empire of America Realty Credit Corporation; FANNIE MAE; Farmers and Mechanics Bank; First National Bank of New England; First Union Mortgage Corp.; Fleet Bank, N.A.; Ford Consumer Co.; FGB Realty Advisors, Inc.; FSB Mortgage Corp.; FTB Mortgage Companies; GE Capital Mortgage Services; GF Mortgage Corporation; Glastonbury Bank and Trust Company; GMAC; Grossmont Bank; Green Tree Financial Corp.; Household Finance Corporation; Leader Federal; Lee Servicing; LSI Financial Group; Market Street Mortgage Company; Mellon Mortgage Company; Merrill Lynch Credit Corporation; Mundaca Investment Corporation; National Mortgage Corporation; NationsBanc Mortgage Corp.; New England Savings Bank; Norwest Mortgage, Inc.; Parmann Mortgage Association; PNC Mortgage Corporation; PaineWebber Mortgage; Savings Bank of Rockville; Standard Mortgage Corp.; TeleBank; Tolland Bank; U.S. Bancorp Mortgage Co.; Walsh Securities; Webster Bank.

HENRY B. HURVITZ

HARTFORD, CONNECTICUT

(See West Hartford)

Real Estate, Family Law, Personal Injury, Wills, Probate.

JACKSON LEWIS SCHNITZLER & KRUPMAN

55 FARMINGTON AVENUE
HARTFORD, CONNECTICUT 06105
Telephone: 860-522-0404
Facsimile: 860-247-1330
Email: hartford@jacksonlewis.com
URL: http://www.jacksonlewis.com

Other offices located in: Atlanta, Georgia; Boston, Massachusetts; Chicago, Illinois; Dallas, Texas; Greenville, South Carolina; Long Island, New York; Los Angeles, California; Miami, Florida; Minneapolis, Minnesota; Morristown, New Jersey; New York, New York; Orlando, Florida; Pittsburgh, Pennsylvania; Sacramento, California; San Francisco, California; Seattle, Washington; Stamford, Connecticut; Washington, D.C.; White Plains, New York.

Labor Relations, Employment Discrimination, Wrongful Discharge and Other Employment-Related Litigation, Employee Benefits and Pension Law, Wage and Hour, OSHA, Immigration Law, Public Sector and State Labor Relations Law, On Behalf of Management.

MEMBERS OF FIRM

WILLIAM J. ANTHONY, born Troy, New York, March 8, 1963; admitted to bar, 1989, California; 1992, New Jersey; 2000, Connecticut. *Education:* Hamilton College (B.A., 1985); Boston University (J.D., 1989). Co-Author: "What To Do When Workers Can't Work," New Jersey Law Journal, April 11, 1994.

THOMAS R. GIBBONS, born 1951; admitted to bar, 1980, PA; 1990, NJ; 1996, CT & U.S. Dist. Ct., D. of Conn. *Education:* Franklin and Marshall College (B.A., 1973); Univ. of Baltimore (J.D., 1980). National Labor Relations Board, 1980-1995; Supervisory Attorney, 1989-1995.

SUSAN K. KRELL, born 1941; admitted to bar, 1975, Connecticut; 1976, U.S. Court of Appeals, 2nd Circuit; 1981, U.S. Supreme Court; 1994, U.S. District Court, Southern District of New York; 1997, U.S. District Court, Northern and Western Districts of New York. *Education:* Queens College (B.A., 1963); University of Connecticut (J.D., 1975). Author: *Employer's Guide to Affirmative Action Compliance,* C.B.I.A. (1991). Contributing Author: *Employment at Will: A 1984 State-By-State Survey,* Nat. Empl. Law Inst., 1986 and 1989 Volumes; *Employment Discrimination Law,* BNA Books, 1985, 1989, 1996 and 1999 updates. Member, Legal Staff, Conn. Comm. on Human Rights and Opp., 1975-1977. Included in "Best Lawyers in America" in Emp. and Labor Law, 1991—. Chair, Liaison Comm. of the Conn. Bar Assoc. to Conn. Comm. on Human Rights and Opp., 1982-1985, 1989-1997. Chair, Emp. Disc. Comm., 1998-2000. Chair, Labor and Emp. Law Section, Conn. Bar Assoc., 1988-1989.

MARGARET J. STRANGE, born 1963; admitted to bar, 1990, CT and U.S. District Court, District of CT. *Education:* Curry College (B.A., magna cum laude, 1985); Suffolk Univ. Law School (J.D., cum laude, 1990). Frequent author and speaker on Employment Law. Adjunct Professor, Employment Law, St. Joseph's College.

OF COUNSEL

ALLAN S. FRIEDLAND, born Philadelphia, PA, March 25, 1955; admitted to bar, 1982, Pennsylvania; 1985, New Jersey; 1992, Connecticut. *Education:* University of Pennsylvania (B.S., 1977); Widener University (J.D., 1982). ***Email:*** friedlaa@jacksonlewis.com

EDWARD M. RICHTERS, born Dover, New Jersey, February 28, 1952; admitted to bar, 1981, Michigan; 1982, U.S. District Court, Eastern District of Michigan; 1983, U.S. Court of Appeals, Sixth Circuit; 1984, Connecticut; U.S. District Court, District of Connecticut; 1987, U.S. Court of Appeals, Second Circuit. *Education:* University of Connecticut (B.A., 1978); Catholic University of America (J.D., 1981). Associate: Dykema, Gossett, Spencer, Goodnow & Trigg, 1981-1983; Day, Berry & Howard, 1983-1988. Senior Counsel, Northeast Utilities, 1989-1994; Vice President Human Resources and Ethics Officer, Northeast Utilities, 1994-1997. *Member:* Connecticut Bar Association. ***PRACTICE AREAS:*** Labor and Employment; Arbitration; Mediation.

ASSOCIATES

TASOS C. PAINDIRIS, born 1970; admitted to bar, 1995, CT; 1996, U.S. District Court, District of CT. *Education:* Wesleyan University (B.A., 1992); Univ. of Conn. (J.D., 1995). *Member:* Hartford County (Labor and Employment Law Section) and Connecticut Bar Associations.

MICHAEL G. PETRIE, born 1971; admitted to bar, 2000, CT. *Education:* Univ. of Connecticut (B.A., 1994; J.D., 2000). *Member:* American Bar Association (Member, Labor & Employment Law Section). ***PRACTICE AREAS:*** Employment Law. ***Email:*** petriem@jacksonlewis.com

JAMES F. SHEA, born 1970; admitted to bar, 1996, MA, CT and U.S. Dist. Ct., Dist. of CT. *Education:* College of the Holy Cross (B.A., 1992); Univ. of Notre Dame (J.D., 1995). Book Review Editor, Journal of College and University Law, 1994-1995.

JENNIFER TINDALL, born 1971; admitted to bar, 1997, FL; 2001, CT. *Education:* Mount Holyoke College (B.A., cum laude, 1993); Florida State Univ. (J.D., magna cum laude, 1997). Order of the Coif. Member, Florida State University Moot Court Team. Member, Florida State University Law Review, 1997. Classes and Seminars Taught: *Sexual Harassment in the Workplace,* November 1998 and March 1999. *Member:* Hillsborough County Bar Association; The Florida Bar; Hillsborough County Association of Women Lawyers

(This Listing Continued)

JACKSON LEWIS SCHNITZLER & KRUPMAN, Hartford—Continued

(HAWL). ***LANGUAGES:*** Russian. ***PRACTICE AREAS:*** Employment Law. ***Email:*** jtindall@jacksonlewis.com

JACKSON, O'KEEFE AND PHELAN

36-40 RUSS STREET
HARTFORD, CONNECTICUT 06106-1571
Telephone: 860-278-4040
Fax: 860-527-2500
URL: http://www.joplaw.com

Bethlehem, Connecticut Office: 423 Munger Lane. Telephone/Fax: 203-266-5255.

General Practice including Civil Trial and Appellate Practice in all Courts, Governmental Law and Relations, Personal Injury, Medical Malpractice, Construction Litigation, Products Liability, Probate and Estate Planning, Residential and Commercial Real Estate, Corporation, Insurance, Banking, Legislative Practice, Mediation and Arbitration.

MEMBERS OF FIRM

JAY W. JACKSON, born Albany, New York, January 31, 1930; admitted to bar, 1958, Connecticut; 1960, U.S. District Court, District of Connecticut. *Education:* Washington and Lee University (B.A., 1953; J.D., 1958). Legal Counsel to: Governor William A. O'Neill, 1980-1988, and Governor Ella Grasso, 1976-1980. Connecticut Commissioner of Insurance, 1975-1976. Connecticut State Senator, 1967-1973. Chairman: Public Utilities Committee, 1967-1969; General Law Committee, 1969-1971; Judiciary Committee, 1971-1973, and Regulations Review Committee, 1971-1973. West Hartford Town Councilman, 1963-1967. *Member:* Hartford County and Connecticut Bar Associations. ***PRACTICE AREAS:*** Governmental Law; Government Relations; Legislative Practice; Administrative Law; Estate Planning; Banking Law; Probate. ***Email:*** jwjackson@joplaw.com

ANDREW J. O'KEEFE, born Middletown, Connecticut, October 23, 1931; admitted to bar, 1956, Connecticut; 1960, U.S. District Court, District of Connecticut; 1961, U.S. Court of Appeals, Second Circuit; 1972, U.S. Supreme Court. *Education:* College of the Holy Cross (B.S., 1953); University of Connecticut (J.D., with honors, 1956). Member, Board of Student Editors, Connecticut Bar Journal, 1954-1956. Member of Faculty: Lecturer in Law, 1957-1983 and Adjunct Professor of Law, 1984—; Subjects: Contracts, Criminal Law, Torts, Advanced Torts, University of Connecticut, School of Law. Member, Zoning Board of Appeals, Town of Wethersfield, 1959. Assistant Prosecutor, 1959 and Prosecutor, 1960-1961. Wethersfield Town Court. Member, Charter Revision Commission, Wethersfield, 1963-1964; 1969. Town Attorney, Town of Wethersfield, 1966-1967. Commissioner, Freedom of Information Commission, 1995—. *Member:* Hartford County, Connecticut (Member, Committee on Professionalism, 1992-1996), Federal and American Bar Associations. ***PRACTICE AREAS:*** Medical Malpractice; Insurance Defense; Civil Practice; Appellate Practice; Civil Trial Practice; Estate Planning; Probate; Wills; Trust Law. ***Email:*** ajokeefe@joplaw.com

DENISE MARTINO PHELAN, born Waterbury, Connecticut, July 6, 1954; admitted to bar, 1980, Connecticut and U.S. District Court, District of Connecticut; 1985, U.S. Court of Appeals, Second Circuit; 1988, U.S. Supreme Court. *Education:* Boston College (B.A., summa cum laude, 1976); University of Connecticut (J.D., 1980). Phi Beta Kappa. Member, Connecticut Bar Examining Committee, 1992—. *Member:* Hartford County, Connecticut and Federal Bar Associations. ***PRACTICE AREAS:*** Civil Trial Practice; Medical Malpractice Law; Insurance Defense Law. ***Email:*** dmphelan@joplaw.com

MICHAEL E. RILEY, born Providence, Rhode Island, March 7, 1950; admitted to bar, 1979, Connecticut; 1980, U.S. District Court, District of Connecticut; 1991, U.S. Supreme Court. *Education:* University of Connecticut (B.A., 1972); Western New England School of Law (J.D., 1978). Chairman, Zoning Board of Appeals, Town of Ellington. Special Counsel, Town of Ellington. *Member:* Hartford, Tolland County (President, 1993-1994), Connecticut and American Bar Associations; Connecticut Trial Lawyers Association; Connecticut Defense Lawyers Association; The Association of Trial Lawyers of America; Defense Research Institute. (Certified as a Civil Trial Specialist by the National Board of Trial Advocacy). ***PRACTICE AREAS:*** Civil Trial Practice; Insurance Defense Law; Personal Injury Law. ***Email:*** meriley@joplaw.com

MATTHEW J. O'KEEFE, born Wethersfield, Connecticut, May 31, 1957; admitted to bar, 1982, Connecticut and U.S. District Court, District of Connecticut; 1987, U.S. Court of Appeals, Second Circuit; 1988, U.S. Supreme Court. *Education:* College of the Holy Cross (B.A.,1979); Suffolk University (J.D., 1982). Chairman, Conservation Commission, City of New Britain, 1986—. Special Assistant Corporation Counsel, City of New Britain, 1986-1987. Member, Central Connecticut Regional Planning Agency. Special Masters Hartford Superior Court and Family Matters. *Member:* Hartford County, Connecticut (Member, Hartford County Chapter) and Federal (Member, Hartford County Chapter; Member at large, 1984-1985; Secretary, 1985; Vice President, 1986; President Elect, 1987; President, 1988-1989) Bar Associations. ***PRACTICE AREAS:*** Estate Planning and Administration; Real Estate; Family Law; Divorce; Child Custody; Spousal Support. ***Email:*** mjokeefe@joplaw.com

(This Listing Continued)

PETER K. O'KEEFE, born Hartford, Connecticut, April 9, 1960; admitted to bar, 1985, Connecticut and U.S. District Court, District of Connecticut; 1987, U.S. Court of Appeals, Second Circuit; 1989, U.S. Supreme Court. *Education:* College of the Holy Cross (B.A., 1982); Suffolk University (J.D., with honors, 1985). Member, Conservation Commission, Town of Wethersfield, 1995—. Commissioner, Wethersfield Housing Authority, 1998—. *Member:* Hartford County, Connecticut, and Federal Bar Associations; Connecticut Defense Lawyers Association; Defense Research Institute. ***PRACTICE AREAS:*** Civil Trial Practice; Insurance Defense; Personal Injury Law; Medical Malpractice Law. ***Email:*** pkokeefe@joplaw.com

PHILIP R. DUNN, JR., born Hartford, Connecticut, May 17, 1963; admitted to bar, 1988, Connecticut; 1989, U.S. District Court, District of Connecticut. *Education:* Fairfield University (B.A., 1985); University of Connecticut (J.D., 1988). *Member:* Hartford County, Connecticut, Federal and American Bar Associations. ***PRACTICE AREAS:*** Civil Trial Practice; Insurance Defense Law; Personal Injury Law. ***Email:*** prdunn@joplaw.com

KATHRYN M. CUNNINGHAM, born Kansas City, Missouri, November 12, 1963; admitted to bar, 1995, Connecticut; 1996, U.S. District Court, District of Connecticut. *Education:* Brigham Young University (B.A., 1986); Trinity College (M.A., 1991); University of Connecticut (J.D., 1995). Recipient, American Jurisprudence Award for Excellence in Administrative Law. ***PRACTICE AREAS:*** Civil Trial Practice; Insurance Defense Law; Appellate Practice. ***Email:*** kmcunningham@joplaw.com

JOSEPH M. BUSHER, JR., born New Haven, Connecticut, October 2, 1970; admitted to bar, 1996, Connecticut; 1997, U.S. District Court, District of Connecticut. *Education:* College of the Holy Cross (A.B., cum laude, 1993); University of Connecticut (J.D., with honors, 1996). *Member:* Connecticut and American Bar Associations. ***PRACTICE AREAS:*** Civil Trial Practice; Insurance Defense; Appellate Practice.

JAMES M. JOSEPH, born New York, N.Y., February 11, 1975; admitted to bar, 2000, Connecticut. *Education:* College of the Holy Cross (B.A., 1997); Suffolk University (J.D., with honors, 2000). *Member:* Hartford County and Connecticut Bar Associations. ***PRACTICE AREAS:*** Estate Planning; Estate Administration; Real Estate; Family Law; Divorce; Child Custody; Child Support. ***Email:*** jmjoseph@joplaw.com

REPRESENTATIVE CLIENTS: Travelers Property Casualty Co.; Kell-Strom Tool Co., Inc.; Liberty Mutual Insurance Co.; MacDonald's Trailer Sales, Inc.; Allstate Insurance Co.; Connecticut Medical Ins. Co.; JME Graphics, Inc.; Old Colony Beach Club Association; ITT Hartford; Harleysville Insurance Co.; Highlands Insurance Group; Hanover Insurance Co.; Firemans' Fun Risk Management Services; State of Connecticut.
APPROVED ATTORNEYS FOR: Fleet Bank; Connecticut Attorneys Title Insurance Co.; New Haven Savings Bank; Travelers Mortgage Services, Inc.; The First National Bank of Litchfield; Litchfield Bancorp; Norwest Bank; Bank America Mtge; Citizens Mortgage Co.; Eagle Federal Savings Bank; Fleet Real Estate Funding Corp.

JACOBS PARTNERS LLC

HARTFORD, CONNECTICUT

(See Norwalk)

Business and Personal Bankruptcy, Workouts, Debtor Creditor's Rights, Commercial Litigation, Contracts and Business Disputes.

JACOBS, WALKER, RICE & BASCHE, P.C.

HARTFORD, CONNECTICUT

(See Manchester)

General Practice. Banking, Probate and Estate Planning, Commercial Transactions, Secured Transactions, Commercial and Residential Real Estate, Zoning, Corporation and Taxation Law, Civil and Commercial Litigation, Creditors Rights.

JANUSZEWSKI, MCQUILLAN AND DENIGRIS

HARTFORD, CONNECTICUT

(See New Britain)

General Practice, Civil and Criminal Litigation, Real Estate, Family Law, Administrative Agency Proceedings, Workers Compensation, Personal Injury, Products Liability, Professional Malpractice, Probate, Representation to Professional Responsibilities, Trials in State and Federal Courts.

KAINEN, ESCALERA & McHALE, P.C.

21 OAK STREET
HARTFORD, CONNECTICUT 06106
Telephone: 860-493-0870
Facsimile: 860-493-0871
Email: kemlaw@kemlaw.com
URL: http://www.lawyers.com/kemlaw

Management Representation in Employment and Labor Law and Related Litigation.

BURTON KAINEN, born Huntington, New York, December 8, 1942; admitted to bar, 1971, Connecticut and U.S. District Court of Connecticut; 1975, U.S. Court of Appeals, Second Circuit; 1980, District of Columbia; 1998, Mashantucket Pequot Tribal Court. *Education:* St. Lawrence University (B.A., 1964); Columbia University (M.B.A., 1966); University of Connecticut (J.D., with honors, 1971). Author: "Political Forces in Public Sector Collective Bargaining," Catholic University Law Review, 1972; "Standards of Proof in Employment Law," Connecticut Bar Journal, 1983. Contributing Author: "Handbook for Connecticut Elected Officials," University of Connecticut, 1985; "Labor Arbitration," BNA, 1990; Employment Litigation Deskbook, ABA, 1998; "Using Surreptitious Tape-Recordings and E-Mail Intrusions......," Labor Law Journal, 1997. Fellow, College of Labor and Employment Lawyers. *Member:* Connecticut (Member, Sections on: Labor and Employment Law; Litigation) and American (Member, Labor and Employment Law Section; Co-Chairman, Committee on Labor Arbitration and Law of Collective Bargaining Agreements, 1982-1985; Co-Chair, Committee on Membership and Finance, 1986-1992; Member, Litigation Section) Bar Associations; The District of Columbia Bar. ***PRACTICE AREAS:*** Employment Law; Litigation; Labor Law. ***Email:*** bkainen@kemlaw.com

MIGUEL A. ESCALERA, JR., born Bronx, New York, April 13, 1955; admitted to bar, 1981, District of Columbia; 1988, U.S. Supreme Court; 1989, U.S. Court of Appeals for the Federal Circuit and U.S. Court of Appeals, Ninth Circuit; 1990, U.S. Court of Appeals, Sixth, Tenth and Second Circuits; 1991, Connecticut. *Education:* Georgetown University (B.S.F.S., 1977); American University (J.D., 1980); Army Judge Advocate General's School, Charlottesville, Virginia (LL.M., 1988). Co-Author, "Nonreferral Unions and Equal Employment Opportunity," Report U.S. Commission on Civil Rights, March, 1982. *Member:* American Bar Association (Member, Sections on Labor and Employment Law; Litigation). [Major, U.S. Army Judge Advocate General's Corps, 1981-1990]. ***LANGUAGES:*** Spanish. ***PRACTICE AREAS:*** Employment Law; Litigation; Labor Law. ***Email:*** mescalera@kemlaw.com

PATRICK J. McHALE, born Lansing, MI., 1964, October 16, 1964; admitted to bar, 1991, Connecticut; 1992, U.S. District Court, District of Connecticut; 1996, U.S. Court of Appeals, Second Circuit. *Education:* Fairfield University (B.A., cum laude, 1986); Western New England College School of Law (J.D., magna cum laude, 1991). *Member:* Connecticut (Member, Labor Law Section) and American (Member, Labor and Employment Law Section) Bar Associations; Connecticut Public Employer Labor Relations Association. ***PRACTICE AREAS:*** Employment Law; Labor Law. ***Email:*** pmchale@kemlaw.com

DIANA GARFIELD, born New York, N.Y., March 16, 1944; admitted to bar, 1975, Massachusetts; 1977, U.S. District Court of Connecticut and U.S. Court of Appeals, Second Circuit; 1979, Connecticut; 1980, U.S. District Court of Massachusetts. *Education:* University of Rochester (A.B., 1965); University of California at Berkeley (M.S.W., 1968); University of Connecticut (J.D., summa cum laude, 1975). Author: "The Right to Rebut; Conclusive Presumptions in Civil Cases," 6 Connecticut Law Review 725, 1974. Law Clerk, Circuit Judge Thomas J. Meskill, U.S. Court of Appeals for the Second Circuit, 1975-1976. Assistant U.S. Attorney for the District of Connecticut, 1976-1978. Special Master, Civil Cases, U.S. District Court, Hartford, 1991—. *Member:* Connecticut and American Bar Associations. ***PRACTICE AREAS:*** Employment Law; Litigation; Labor Law. ***Email:*** dgarfield@kemlaw.com

SHELDON D. MYERS, born New Haven, Connecticut, January 26, 1967; admitted to bar, 1993, Connecticut; 1994, U.S. District Court, District of Connecticut; 1998, Mashantucket Pequot Tribal Court. *Education:* Brandeis University (B.A., summa cum laude, 1988); Yale University (M.A., 1990); University of Connecticut (J.D., 1993). Phi Beta Kappa. Author: "Turning Off the Power on Employees: Using Surreptitious Tape Recordings and E-Mail Intrusions by Employees in Pursuit of Employer Rights," Vol. XXVII, Stetson Law Review, No. 1 at 91 (Summer, 1997). *Member:* Hartford County, Connecticut and American (Member, Sections on: Labor and Employment Law) Bar Associations. ***PRACTICE AREAS:*** Employment Law; Litigation; Labor Law. ***Email:*** smyers@kemlaw.com

JENNIFER LIAN DIXON, born Traverse City, Michigan, June 9, 1964; admitted to bar, 1994, Connecticut; 1996, U.S. District Court of Connecticut. *Education:* University of Michigan (A.B., 1986); New England School of Law (J.D., cum laude, 1993). Editor, New England Journal on Criminal and Civil Confinement. Author: "The Right of The Mentally Ill To Refuse Antipsychotic Drugs During Trial," 19:2 New England Journal on Criminal and Civil Confinement 373, 1993. *Member:* Connecticut and American Bar Associations; National Asian Pacific American Bar Association. ***PRACTICE AREAS:*** Employment Law; Litigation; Labor Law. ***Email:*** jdixon@kemlaw.com

JOSEPH W. McQUADE, born New Haven, CT., 1967, February 12, 1967; admitted to bar, 1992, Connecticut, U.S. District Court, District of Connecticut, U.S. District Court, Southern District of New York and U.S. Court of Appeals, Second Circuit. *Education:* Yale University (B.A., 1989); University of Connecticut School of Law (J.D., 1992). Notes and Comments Editor, Connecticut Law Review. Co-Author: "A Recent Ruling Enhances Private Health Care Payers' Recovery Efforts," Mealey's Litigation Report Insurance Fraud," Vol. 4 Issue 18, Nov. 1997. Law Clerk to the Honorable Joan Glazer Margolis, U.S. Magistrate Judge, 1992-1994. *Member:* Connecticut, Hartford and American Bar Associations. ***PRACTICE AREAS:*** Litigation; Employment Law; Civil Rights Litigation; Labor Law. ***Email:*** jmcquade@kemlaw.com

KATZ AND SELIGMAN

130 WASHINGTON STREET
HARTFORD, CONNECTICUT 06106
Telephone: 860-547-1857
Fax: 860-241-9127
Email: katzandseligman@aol.com

Insurance Defense and Coverage Issues, Professional Licensure Representation (Lawyers and Doctors), Legal Estate; Lawyers Discipline; Plaintiffs Medical Malpractice, Personal Injury, Criminal Defense: State and Federal Courts, Municipal Law.

LESTER KATZ, born 1924; admitted to bar, 1950, Connecticut. *Education:* Harvard University (B.A. 1945; J.D., cum laude, 1950). ***PRACTICE AREAS:*** Civil Litigation; Insurance Defense.

STEVEN L. SELIGMAN, born 1952; admitted to bar, 1979, Connecticut and U.S. District Court, District of Connecticut. *Education:* Yale University (B.A., 1975); University of Connecticut School of Law (J.D., 1979). Lecturer, Trial Practice, University of Connecticut School of Law, 1990—. *Member:* Connecticut Trial Lawyers Association; Connecticut Defense Lawyers Association. ***PRACTICE AREAS:*** Civil Litigation; Professional Licensing Regulation; Legal Ethics and Professional Responsibility; Criminal Litigation; Insurance Defense; Personal Injury; Medical Malpractice; Insurance Coverage; Legal Malpractice. ***Email:*** slskk@aol.com

JAMES A. ARMENTANO, born 1949; admitted to bar, 1975, Connecticut. *Education:* Trinity College (B.A., 1971); Boston University (J.D., 1975). *Member:* Hartford County and Connecticut Bar Associations; Association of Trial Lawyers of America. ***PRACTICE AREAS:*** Civil Litigation; Insurance Defense.

DONALD R. HOLTMAN, born 1936; admitted to bar, 1958, Connecticut; 1961, U.S. Supreme Court; 1967, U.S. District Court, District of Connecticut; 1980, U.S. Court of Appeals, Third Circuit. *Education:* Valparaiso University (B.A., 1956; LL.B., 1958); New York University (LL.M., 1963). Author, "Squire Marsden in Connecticut: Non-assertive Conduct As Hearsay," 40 Connecticut Bar Journal 27, March, 1966. Member: East Granby Planning and Zoning Commission, 1970-1974; East Granby Board of Selectmen, 1974-1976; East Granby Board of Finance, 1977-1985. Hearing Examiner, Connecticut Commission on Human Rights and Opportunities, 1975—. Corporate Counsel Towns of: Hebvron, East Granby and Granby. Town Counsel, Town of Litchfield, 1978—. *Member:* Hartford County, Connecticut and American (Member, Section on Litigation) Bar Associations; Connecticut Trial Lawyers Association. [Capt., JAGC, U.S. Army, 1959-1965]. ***LANGUAGES:*** German. ***PRACTICE AREAS:*** Civil Litigation; Insurance Defense. ***Email:*** ariaserena@aol.com

PAUL A. KEILY

HARTFORD, CONNECTICUT

(See West Hartford)

Civil Litigation. Commercial Real Estate, Residential Real Estate, Landlord and Tenant Law, Bankruptcy, Probate and Family Law, Divorce, Child Custody, Child Support, Adoptions.

KENNY, BRIMMER, MELLEY & MAHONEY

Established in 1955
5 GRAND STREET
HARTFORD, CONNECTICUT 06106
Telephone: 860-527-4226
FAX: 860-527-0214
URL: http://www.lawyers.com/kbmmlaw

General Practice. Personal Injury, Litigation, Products Liability, Medical Malpractice, Insurance, Corporation, and Administrative Law. Trials in all Courts.

(This Listing Continued)

KENNY, BRIMMER, MELLEY & MAHONEY, Hartford—Continued

JOSEPH P. KENNY (1920-1993).

MEMBERS OF FIRM

WILLIAM J. MELLEY, III, born Hartford, Connecticut, June 20, 1953; admitted to bar, 1979, Connecticut and U.S. District Court, District of Connecticut; 1993, U.S. Court of Appeals, Second Circuit; 2000, U.S. Supreme Court. *Education:* College of the Holy Cross (B.A., 1975); Western New England College (J.D., 1979). *Member:* Hartford County, Connecticut and American Bar Associations; Federal District Bar of Connecticut; Connecticut Trial Lawyers Association; The Association of Trial Lawyers of America; Connecticut Defense Lawyer's Association; Certified in Civil Trial by the National Board of Trial Advocacy. ***PRACTICE AREAS:*** Personal Injury; Medical Malpractice; Insurance Defense; Products Liability. ***Email:*** wmelley@kbmm.com

RICHARD C. MAHONEY, born Hartford, Connecticut, May 19, 1953; admitted to bar, 1979, Connecticut; 1993, Mashantucket Pequot Tribal Court. *Education:* Williams College (B.A., with honors, 1975); University of Connecticut (J.D., 1979). Temporary Assistant Clerk, Superior Court for Hartford County, 1978-1979. *Member:* Hartford County, Connecticut and American Bar Associations; Federal District Bar of Connecticut; Connecticut Trial Lawyers Association; The Association of Trial Lawyers of America; Connecticut Defense Lawyers Association. ***PRACTICE AREAS:*** Personal Injury; Real Estate; Insurance Defense. ***Email:*** rmahoney@kbmm.com

ANITA M. VARUNES, born Hartford, Connecticut, March 7, 1963; admitted to bar, 1989, Connecticut. *Education:* Mount Holyoke College (B.A., 1985); Western New England College, School of Law (J.D.,1989). *Member:* Hartford County, Connecticut and American Bar Associations; Connecticut Defense Lawyers Association; Connecticut Trial Lawyers Association. ***PRACTICE AREAS:*** Personal Injury; Workers' Compensation; Employment Law. ***Email:*** avarunes@kbmm.com

DENNIS F. McCARTHY, born Hartford, Connecticut, October 23, 1963; admitted to bar, 1989, Connecticut. *Education:* Hartwick College (B.A., magna cum laude, 1986); Washington College of Law, American University (J.D., 1989). *Member:* Hartford County, Connecticut and American Bar Associations; Connecticut Defense Lawyers Association; Connecticut Trial Lawyers Association. ***PRACTICE AREAS:*** Insurance Defense; Personal Injury; Civil Litigation. ***Email:*** dmccarthy@kbmm.com

ASSOCIATES

SHANNON K. McCARTHY, born New London, Connecticut, April 5, 1972; admitted to bar, 1998, Connecticut; 1999, New York. *Education:* Providence College (B.A., cum laude, 1994); Western New England College (J.D., 1998). *Member:* Hartford County, Connecticut and American Bar Associations. ***PRACTICE AREAS:*** Insurance Defense; Personal Injury; Real Estate; Litigation. ***Email:*** smccarthy@kbmm.com

NICHOLAS C. VARUNES, born Hartford, Connecticut, February 17, 1965; admitted to bar, 1997, Connecticut. *Education:* University of Rochester (B.A., 1988); Western New England College (J.D., 1996). *Member:* Hartford County and American Bar Associations. ***LANGUAGES:*** Greek. ***PRACTICE AREAS:*** Insurance Defense; Personal Injury; Real Estate. ***Email:*** nvarunes@kbmm.com

TERRANCE M. BRENNAN, born Pittsburgh, Pennsylvania, January 9, 1974. *Education:* University of Connecticut (B.A., 1996); Western New England (J.D., 1999). *Member:* Hartford County, Connecticut and American Bar Associations; Connecticut Trial Lawyers Association. ***PRACTICE AREAS:*** Insurance Defense; Personal Injury; Real Estate. ***Email:*** tbrennan@kbmm.com

OF COUNSEL

LESLIE R. BRIMMER, born Hartford, Connecticut, August 20, 1929; admitted to bar, 1957, Connecticut; 1961, U.S. Supreme Court and U.S. Court of Appeals, 2nd Circuit. *Education:* Fairfield University (B.S., 1951); Boston College (LL.B., 1956). Member, Panel of Arbitrators, American Arbitration Association. *Member:* Hartford County, Connecticut and American Bar Associations; Federal District Bar of Connecticut; Connecticut Defense Lawyers Association; Connecticut Trial Lawyers Association; American Board of Trial Advocates (Advocate). Fellow: James W. Cooper Fellows Program, Connecticut Bar Foundation; American College of Trial Lawyers. ***PRACTICE AREAS:*** Alternative Dispute Resolution; Insurance Defense; Personal Injury.

REPRESENTATIVE CLIENTS: Allstate Insurance Co.; American Arbitration Association; American States Insurance; Andover Insurance Company; Berkshire Mutual Fire Insurance Company; Bettom Medical Management, Inc.; California Union Insurance Company; Central Connecticut Celtic Cultural Committee, Inc.; Connecticut Fair Plan; Connecticut Surgery Center, Inc.; Connecticut Transit Authority; Dispute Resolution, Inc.; Dorchester Mutual Fire Insurance Company; Fireman's Fund Insurance Company; Health Care and Retirement Corporation of America, Inc.; Insurance Company of North America; Litigation Alternatives; Middlesex Mutual Assurance Company; National Surety Assurance Company; New England Mutual Association; New London County Mutual Insurance Company; Norfolk & Dedham Insurance Company; Nusil Silicone Technology f/k/a McGhan Nusil Corporation; Pacific Employers Insurance Company; Peerless Insurance Company; Providence Mutual Fire Insurance Company; Prudential Insurance Company; Roncalli Health Care Management; Shawmut Bank; SNETCO; Travelers Insurance Company; Underwriters Adjusting Company; Vermont Mutual; Worcester Insurance Company.

(This Listing Continued)

KILLIAN, DONOHUE & JAFF, LLC

363 MAIN STREET
HARTFORD, CONNECTICUT 06106-1885
Telephone: 860-560-1977
Telecopier: 860-249-6638

Simsbury, Connecticut Office: 141 West Street. Telephone: 860-658-0436. Telecopier: 860-249-6638.

General Practice. Litigation, Administrative, Banking, Municipal, Public Utility, Insurance, Real Estate and Regulatory, Government Relations and Health Care.

ROBERT K. KILLIAN, JR., born Hartford, Connecticut, January 29, 1947; admitted to bar, 1972, Connecticut; 1973, U.S. District Court, District of Connecticut and U.S. Court of Appeals, Second Circuit; 1974, District of Columbia Court of Appeals; 1976, U.S. Court of Appeals for the District of Columbia Circuit and U.S. Supreme Court. *Education:* Union College and University (B.A., 1969); Georgetown University (J.D., 1972). Probate Judge, State of Connecticut, District of Hartford, 1984—. Chief Judge, Connecticut Probate Assembly, 1997-2000. Recipient, Connecticut Probate Assembly's Outstanding Probate Judge, 1990. Member, Connecticut Investment Advisory Council, 1995-2001. Regent, University of Hartford, 1993—. Member, Chief Justice, Committee on Attorney Ethics, 1990—. *Member:* Hartford County, Connecticut and American (Member, Real Estate and Probate Section; Entertainment and Sports Committee); Bar Associations; Connecticut Trial Lawyers Association; The Association of Trial Lawyers of America; National College of Probate Judges; American Arbitration Association. ***PRACTICE AREAS:*** Government Relations; Municipal; Land Use; Administrative Law; Arbitration; Corporate and Utility.

THOMAS J. DONOHUE, JR., born Hartford, Connecticut, June 18, 1951; admitted to bar, 1976, Connecticut and U.S. District Court, District of Connecticut. *Education:* College of the Holy Cross (B.A., 1973); University of Connecticut (J.D., 1976). Counsel: Democratic House Majority Leader, 1976-1977; Lieutenant Governor, 1977-1979. Member, Simsbury Planning Commission, 1982-1984. Selectman, Town of Simsbury, 1984-1986. ***PRACTICE AREAS:*** Real Estate; Zoning and Planning; Banking; Corporate and Utility; Governmental Relations; Administrative Law. ***Email:*** tj@kdjlaw.com

JENNIFER C. JAFF, born New York, N.Y., June 12, 1957; admitted to bar, 1985, New York; 1991, Connecticut; 1992, U.S. District Court, District of Connecticut; 1994, U.S. Court of Appeals, Second Circuit; 1996, U.S. Supreme Court; 2000, District of Columbia. *Education:* Queens College of the City University of New York (B.A., 1981); Georgetown University (J.D., cum laude, 1984). Phi Beta Kappa. Member, Georgetown Law Journal. Law Clerk to Judge Danny J. Boggs, U.S. Court of Appeals, Sixth Circuit. Member, Sprenger & Lang, PLLC, 2000. Assistant Attorney General, State of Connecticut, 1993-1999. Adjunct Professor, Administrative Law, Legal Research and Writing and Women and Law, University of Connecticut, 1990-1991. Visiting Assistant Professor, Administrative Law, Legal Research and Writing and Women and Law, University of Miami School of Law, 1986-1989. Author: "Goliath as Victim: Can the State Bring a Civil Action Under RICO?" 3 Quinnipiac College School of Law Health Law Journal 5, 2000; "Wedding Bell Blues: The Position of Unmarried People in American Law," 30 Arizona Law Review 207, 1988; "Frame-Shifting: An Empowering Methodology for Teaching and Learning Legal Reasoning," 36 Journal of Legal Education 249, 1986. *Member:* Connecticut Bar Association; The District of Columbia Bar. ***PRACTICE AREAS:*** Health Care; Health Care Fraud; Civil RICO; Civil Rights; Complex Litigation. ***Email:*** jennifer@kdjlaw.com

REPRESENTATIVE CLIENTS: Aetna Life & Casualty; Connecticut Natural Gas; The Energy Network; Fleet Bank, N.A.; State of Connecticut; Village Water Company; Connecticut State Dental Assoc.; Space Fitters, Inc.; Shepard Steel; CTG Resources; Boston Market Strategies; TIAA-CREF; Energy East.
REFERENCE: Fleet Bank, N.A.

KLEINMAN & ASSOCIATES, P.C.

2 CONGRESS STREET
HARTFORD, CONNECTICUT 06114-1024
Telephone: 860-525-2930
Email: stewart.kleinman@snet.net
URL: http://www.lawyers.com/kleinmanlaw

New London, Connecticut Office: 22 Masonic Street. Telephone: 860-437-2342. Facsimile: 860-437-2346.

(This Listing Continued)

Business Law, Commercial Real Estate, Leases and Leasing, Mortgages, Loan Workouts, Corporate Finance, Contracts, Corporation, Commercial, Collections, Banking, Bankruptcy, Probate, Estate Planning, Real Estate, Construction Contracts, Family Law, Mortgage Foreclosures, Landlord and Tenant, Zoning, Personal Injury, Consumer Law, Partnership Law, Property Law.

STEWART F. KLEINMAN, born New York, N.Y., July 14, 1940; admitted to bar, 1966, New York; 1971, Connecticut; 1979, Florida. *Education:* New York University, School of Commerce Accounts and Finance (B.S., 1963); Brooklyn Law School (LL.B., 1966). Instructor for Professional Education Systems, Inc., giving seminars in Real Property Law, 1985-1992 . Instructor, University of Connecticut CLE, 1986-1990. Member, 1977-1979 and Vice Chairman, 1979-1980, Board of Special Assessments, Town of West Hartford. Alternate Member, West Hartford Zoning Board of Appeals, 1980-1984. Member, Panel of Arbitrators and Mediators, American Arbitration Association. *Member:* Hartford County (Member: Real Property Committee, 1976-1994; Unauthorized Practice of Law Committee, 1976-1981), Connecticut (Member, Ethics Committee, 1976-1983), New York State and American (Member: Environmental Law Committee, Real Property, Probate and Trust Law Section, 1975—; Title Insurance Committee, 1982—) Bar Associations; The Florida Bar. ***PRACTICE AREAS:*** Commercial Real Estate Development and Finance Law; Loan Workouts Law; Corporate Law; Commercial Leasing Law; Contracts; Construction Contracts; Mortgage Foreclosures; Zoning; Arbitration; Mediation.

(For complete biographical data on all personnel, see Professional Biographies at New London, Connecticut)

ARMAND A. KORZENIK

436 FARMINGTON AVENUE
HARTFORD, CONNECTICUT 06105
Telephone: 860-236-1665
Fax: 860-231-7035
Email: armkor@ntplx.net

General Practice, including Personal Injury, Workers Compensation, Real Estate, Wills and Probate, Divorce, Motor Vehicle, Municipal and Administrative Law, Collection, Civil and Criminal Litigation.

ARMAND A. KORZENIK, born Hartford, Connecticut, October 31, 1927; admitted to bar, 1951, Connecticut; 1952, U.S. District Court of Connecticut; 1959, U.S. Supreme Court and U.S. Court of Military Appeals; 1969, U.S. Court of Appeals, Second Circuit. *Education:* Harvard University (A.B., magna cum laude, 1951); Harvard Law School (J.D., 1951); Yale School of Law (LL.M., 1952). Phi Beta Kappa. Member, City of Hartford: Board of Education, 1953-1959; Zoning Board of Appeals, 1960-1966. Justice of Peace, 1960-1973, 1988—; Assistant Corporation Counsel, 1966-1972; Counsel to Redevelopment Agency, 1966-1968; Counsel to Board of Education, 1968-1972. Member, Panel of Arbitrators, American Arbitration Association. Instructor, Business Law, Hartford Institute of Accounting, 1973-1974. Mayor's Representative, Library Board, 1990-1991. Member, Hartford Democratic Town Committee, 1985-1991. *Member:* Hartford County (Editor, The Bar-Fly, 1975-1978; Chairman: Publications Committee, 1975-1978; Family Relations Committee, 1975-1978; Public Relations Committee, 1975-1978) and Connecticut (Board of Editors, Connecticut Bar Journal, 1971-1979; Member, Executive Committee, General Practice Section, 1983—; Chairman, 1997; Treasurer, 1984-1991; Vice Chairman, 1994—. Chairman, Sub-Committee on Practice and Procedure, 1983-1984; Committee on Criminal Law, 1960-1961; Delegate, House of Delegates, 1975-1978, 1988-1991) Bar Associations; Connecticut Criminal Defense Lawyers Association. [Col., Staff Judge Advocate, 1953-1982 and Brigadier General, 1982—, Connecticut Air National Guard]

KOSKOFF, KOSKOFF & BIEDER, P.C.

HARTFORD, CONNECTICUT

(See Bridgeport)

Litigation in all State and Federal Courts. Medical Malpractice, Equal Opportunity, Negligence, Products Liability, Civil Rights, and Class Actions.

KOSLOFF & HARDING

HARTFORD, CONNECTICUT

(See West Hartford)

Environmental Law.

KRASOW, GARLICK & HADLEY, LLC

ONE STATE STREET
HARTFORD, CONNECTICUT 06103
Telephone: 860-549-7100
Facsimile: 860-728-1651
Email: mail@krasowgarlick.com
URL: http://www.krasowgarlick.com

General Practice including Real Estate, Commercial Litigation, Finance, Common Interest Communities, Banking, Corporate, Real Estate Development, Land Use, Shopping Centers, Insurance Defense, Family, Creditor's Rights.

HERBERT A. KRASOW, born Waterbury, Connecticut, August 25, 1938; admitted to bar, 1964, Pennsylvania; 1965, Connecticut. *Education:* University of Connecticut (B.A., 1960); Temple University (LL.B., 1963). Tau Epsilon Rho. Associate Editor, Temple Law Review, 1962-1963. Author: "Criminal Procedure: Deposition and Change of Venue," 36 Temple Law Quarterly, 1963. Co-Author: "The Connecticut Common Interest Ownership Manual," Connecticut Bar Association, 1984. Advisor, Connecticut Law Revision Commission on The Connecticut Common Interest Ownership Act, 1982-1983. Advisor, Connecticut Law Revision Commission on the Uniform Land Security Interest Act, 1991-1992 and 1995. Advisor, Connecticut Law Revision Commission on Open-End Mortgages as Security for the Guaranty of an Open-End Loan, 1995. Advisor, Connecticut Law Revision Commission on Mortgagor Liability, 1997-1998. Advisor, Connecticut Law Revision Commission on the Connecticut Validating Acts, 1998; Advisor, Connecticut Law Revision Commission on Revised Article 9 of The Uniform Commercial Code, 2000-2001. Member, Panel of Arbitrators, American Arbitration Association. *Member:* Hartford County, Connecticut (Member, Executive Committee, Real Property Section, 1980—) and American Bar Associations; American College of Real Estate Lawyers; Real Estate Finance Association. ***Email:*** hkrasow@krasowgarlick.com

GERALD L. GARLICK, born Elmira, New York, August 21, 1954; admitted to bar, 1979, Connecticut; U.S. District Court, District of Connecticut; U.S. Court of Appeals, Second Circuit. *Education:* State University of New York at Albany (B.A., magna cum laude, 1976); Georgetown University (J.D., 1979). Phi Delta Phi. Editor, Law and Policy in International Business, 1978-1979. Co-Author, "Administrative Survey —International Trade Commission," Law and Policy in International Business, Vol. II, No. 1, 1979. *Member:* Hartford County, Connecticut (Member, Executive Committee, Commercial Law and Bankruptcy Section, 1982-1997; Litigation Section, 1997—; Real Property Section, 2000—) and American Bar Associations. ***Email:*** ggarlick@krasowgarlick.com

LINDA CLIFFORD HADLEY, born Bangor, Maine, June 25, 1959; admitted to bar, 1984, Connecticut. *Education:* Colby College (B.A., magna cum laude, 1981); Boston College (J.D., 1984). Phi Beta Kappa. Case Editor, 1984 and Staff Writer, 1983, Uniform Commercial Code Reporter Digest. Instructor, Greater Hartford Association of Realtors. Founding Member and Member, Board of Advisors, Connecticut Women's Hall of Fame. Member, Middlesex Business Council, 1997-2000. *Member:* Hartford County, Connecticut (Member, Executive Committee, Consumer Law Section, 1986-1988; Commercial Law and Bankruptcy Section) and American Bar Associations. ***Email:*** lhadley@krasowgarlick.com

ASSOCIATE

KENNETH M. ROZICH, born Poughkeepsie, New York, April 13, 1973; admitted to bar, 1998, Connecticut. *Education:* Niagara University (B.A., 1995); Western New England College School of Law (J.D., 1998). Junior Staff Member, Western New England Law Review, 1996-1997. Member, Board of Directors, Connecticut Consortium for Law and Citizenship Education, Inc. *Member:* Hartford County, Connecticut and American Bar Associations; Connecticut Defense Lawyers Association. ***Email:*** krozich@krasowgarlick.com

KENNETH A. GOSS, born Bridgeport, Connecticut, October 7, 1974; admitted to bar, 2000, Connecticut; 2001, New York and U.S. District Court, District of Connecticut. *Education:* Fairleigh Dickinson University (B.A., 1996); Quinnipiac University School of Business (M.B.A., 2000); Quinnipiac University School of Law (J.D., 2000). Recipient, Outstanding Academic Achievement Award, Corporate Finance, 1999. *Member:* New Haven County, Hartford County, Connecticut, New York State and American Bar Associations; The Association of the Bar of the City of New York. ***PRACTICE AREAS:*** Commercial Real Estate; Banking Law; Finance; Corporate Law; Bankruptcy. ***Email:*** kgoss@krasowgarlick.com

KREVOLIN, ROTH & CONNORS LLC

HARTFORD, CONNECTICUT

(See West Hartford)

General Civil Litigation, Personal Injury, Medical Malpractice, Products Liability, Workers Compensation, Commercial Litigation, Matrimonial and Insurance.

KROLL, McNAMARA & EVANS, LLP

HARTFORD, CONNECTICUT

(See West Hartford)

General Practice, Commercial Real Estate, Commercial Litigation, Real Estate Development, Property Management, Real Estate Leasing, Real Estate Acquisitions and Dispositions, Real Estate Construction and Asset Management, Hotels, Real Estate Finance, Zoning, Planning and Land Use, Civil Litigation, Trial Practice, Appeals, Foreclosures, Creditors Rights, Bankruptcy, Contracts, Commercial Collections, Real Estate Litigation, Lender Liability, Landlord and Tenant Law, Trusts and Estates, Probate.

LeBOEUF, LAMB, GREENE & MacRAE L.L.P.

A Limited Liability Partnership including Professional Corporations

Formerly LeBoeuf, Lamb, Leiby & MacRae

GOODWIN SQUARE
225 ASYLUM STREET, 13TH FLOOR
HARTFORD, CONNECTICUT 06103
Telephone: 860-293-3500
Facsimile: 860-293-3555
URL: http://www.llgm.com

Eastern United States:
New York, N.Y. Office: 125 West 55th Street. Telephone: 212-424-8000. Facsimile: 212-424-8500. Telex: 423416 or 1561363.
Washington, D.C. Office: 1875 Connecticut Avenue, N.W. Telephone: 202-986-8000. Facsimile: 202-986-8102. Telex: 440274.
Albany, New York Office: One Commerce Plaza, 99 Washington Avenue, Suite 2020. Telephone: 518-626-9000. Facsimile: 518-626-9010.
Boston, Massachusetts Office: 260 Franklin Street. Telephone: 617-439-9500. Facsimile: 617-439-0341; 439-0342.
Harrisburg, Pennsylvania Office: 200 North Third Street, Suite 300, P.O. Box 12105. Telephone: 717-232-8199. Facsimile: 717-232-8720.
Newark, New Jersey Office: The Legal Center, One Riverfront Plaza. Telephone: 973-643-8000. Facsimile: 973-643-6111.
Pittsburgh, Pennsylvania Office: One Gateway Center, Fort Duquesne Boulevard, Suite 1600. Telephone: 412-594-2300. Facsimile: 412-594-5237.
Western United States:
Denver, Colorado Office: 633 17th Street, Suite 2000. Telephone: 303-291-2600. Facsimile: 303-297-0422.
Los Angeles, California Office: 725 South Figueroa Street, Suite 3100. Telephone: 213-955-7300. Facsimile: 213-955-7399. Telex: 678982.
Salt Lake City, Utah Office: 1000 Kearns Building, 136 South Main Street. Telephone: 801-320-6700. Facsimile: 801-359-8256.
San Francisco, California Office: One Embarcadero Center, Suite 400. Telephone: 415-951-1100. Facsimile: 415-951-1180; 951-1181. Telex: 470167.
Southern United States:
Houston, Texas Office: 1000 Louisiana Avenue. Telephone: 713-287-2000. Facsimile: 713-287-2100.
Jacksonville, Florida Office: 50 North Laura Street, Suite 2800. Telephone: 904-354-8000. Facsimile: 904-353-1673.
European Offices:
Brussels, Belgium Office: Kunstlaan/Avenue des Arts, 19H, B-1000 Brussels, Belgium. Telephone: 011-32-2-227-0900. Facsimile: 011-32-2-227-0909.
London, England Office: LeBoeuf, Lamb, Greene & MacRae (A London Based Multinational Partnership); One Minster Court, Mincing Lane, 6th Floor, London EC3R 7AA England. Telephone: 011-44-20-7-459-5000. Facsimile: 011-44-20-7-459-5099.
Moscow, Russian Federation Office: Nikitsky Pereulok, 5 (formerly Ulitsa Belinskogo) 103473 Moscow, Russian Federation. Telephone: 011-7-095-737-5000. Facsimile: 011-7-095-737-5050.
Paris, France Office: 130, rue du Faubourg Saint-Honoreé75008 Paris, France. Telephone: 011-33-1-53-93-77-00. Facsimile: 011-33-1-42-56-08-06.
Asian Offices:
Almaty, Kazakhstan Office: Prospect Seyfullin, 531, 5th Floor, 480083, Almaty, Republic of Kazakhstan. Telephone: 011-7-3272-50-7575. Facsimile: 011-7-3272-50-7576.
Bishkek, Kyrgyz Office: Ulitsa Panfilova, 205 Bishkek, Kyrgyz Republic. Telephone: 011-996-3312-22-2994. Facsimile: 011-996-3312-66-2233.
Tashkent, Uzbekistan Office: Ulitsa Turab Tula, 1 700003 Tashkent Republic of Uzbekistan. Telephone: 011-7-3712-40-6050. Facsimile: 011-7-3712-40-6052.
African Office:
Johannesburg, South Africa Office: 11 Alice Lane, 2nd Floor, West Wing, Standard Bank Building, Sandton 2196 Johannesburg, South Africa. Telephone: 27-011-784-0233. Fax: 27-011-784-2855.

(This Listing Continued)

General Practice including Administrative, Corporate, Securities, Venture Capital Financing, Banking, Environmental, Insurance, Litigation, Municipal Bonds, Copyrights, Trademarks and Patents.

PARTNERS

ANDREW N. DAVIS, born 1959; admitted to bar, 1990, Connecticut; 1991, U.S. District Court, District of Connecticut; 1998, Massachusetts. *Education:* Trinity College (B.S., 1981); University of Massachusetts at Amherst (M.S., 1983; Ph.D., 1987); George Washington University (J.D., 1990). Albert L. Delisle Botany Fellowship, 1982. ***PRACTICE AREAS:*** Environmental Law; Land Use Law; Health and Safety Law. ***Email:*** adavis@llgm.com

THOMAS G. ROHBACK, born 1951; admitted to bar, 1979, New York; 1993, Pennsylvania; 1998, Connecticut. *Education:* Union College (B.A., summa cum laude, 1973), Phi Beta Kappa; Columbia University (M.A., 1974; J.D., 1978). Harlan Fiske Stone Scholar. Writing and Research Editor, Columbia Journal of Transnational Law. ***PRACTICE AREAS:*** Litigation. ***Email:*** trohback@llgm.com

JAMES A. THOMPSON, JR., born 1945; admitted to bar, 1974, Massachusetts; 1983, District of Columbia; 1989, Connecticut. *Education:* University of Pennsylvania (B.A., 1967); George Washington University (J.D., 1973). ***PRACTICE AREAS:*** Environmental; Health and Safety Law. ***Email:*** jthompso@llgm.com

CHARLES R. WELSH, born 1960; admitted to bar, 1988, Connecticut. *Education:* Trinity College (B.A., 1982); University of Connecticut (J.D., with honors, 1988). ***PRACTICE AREAS:*** Insurance; Business Law; Mergers and Acquisitions; Venture Capital. ***Email:*** cwelsh@llgm.com

DIANE WOODFIELD WHITNEY, born 1945; admitted to bar, 1985, Connecticut; 1986, U.S. District Court, District of Connecticut; 1992, U.S. Supreme Court; 1994, U.S. District Court, District of Vermont; 1997, Mashantucket Pequot Tribal Court (Connecticut). *Education:* William Smith College (B.A., 1967); Colgate University (M.A.T., 1968); University of Connecticut (J.D., with honors, 1985). Instructor, University of Connecticut School of Law, 1992-1997. ***PRACTICE AREAS:*** Environmental; Land Use; Civil Litigation; Appeals; Juvenile. ***Email:*** dwwhitne@llgm.com

RONALD W. ZDROJESKI, born 1960; admitted to bar, 1983, New York; 1986, Connecticut. *Education:* George Washington University (B.A., 1980); The National Law Center at George Washington University (J.D., 1983). Assistant District Attorney, Office of the District Attorney, Kings County, Brooklyn, New York, 1983-1985. ***PRACTICE AREAS:*** Environmental; Litigation. ***Email:*** rzdrojes@llgm.com

OF COUNSEL

ROBERT P. WAX, born 1948; admitted to bar, 1974, Connecticut and U.S. District Court, District of Connecticut; 1977, U.S. Court of Appeals, District of Columbia Circuit and U.S. Court of Appeals, First Circuit. *Education:* Tufts University (B.A., magna cum laude, 1971); University of Virginia (J.D., 1974). Phi Beta Kappa. ***PRACTICE AREAS:*** Utility; Energy. ***Email:*** rpwax@llgm.com

SPECIAL COUNSEL

DENNIS O. BROWN, born 1954; admitted to bar, 1989, Connecticut; 1995, Michigan. *Education:* Michigan State University (B.A., 1976); University of Connecticut (J.D., with high honors, 1989). ***PRACTICE AREAS:*** Commercial Litigation; Employment Law; Business Law. ***Email:*** dbrown@llgm.com

DENNIS F. KERRIGAN, JR., born 1965; admitted to bar, 1991, Connecticut. *Education:* College of the Holy Cross (B.A., 1988); College of William & Mary (J.D., 1991). Phi Delta Phi. Executive Editor, William and Mary Journal of Bill of Rights Law and Public Policy, 1990-1991. Associate Editor, Tort and Insurance Law Journal (TIPS), 1996—. Member, Editorial Board, Young Lawyer Magazine (YLD), 1997—. Special Master, Hartford Superior Court. ***PRACTICE AREAS:*** Litigation. ***Email:*** dennis.kerrigan@llgm.com

CATHERINE K. LIN, born 1954; admitted to bar, 1991, Connecticut. *Education:* Wellesley College (B.A., 1976); Columbia University (M.A., 1986); Yale Law School (J.D., 1990). ***LANGUAGES:*** Chinese. ***PRACTICE AREAS:*** Environmental Law; International Environmental Law. ***Email:*** cklin@llgm.com

(Biographical data on all Members of the Firm, Counsel, Of Counsel and Special Counsel in New York, New York, Washington, D.C., Los Angeles, California, San Francisco, California, Newark, New Jersey, Boston, Massachusetts, Hartford, Connecticut, Salt Lake City, Utah, Jacksonville, Florida, Houston, Texas, Albany, New York, Harrisburg, Pennsylvania, Denver, Colorado, Pittsburgh, Pennsylvania, London, England, Brussels, Belgium, Almaty, Kazakhstan, Moscow, Russian Federation and Paris, France are listed in the respective Biographical Sections)

LEETE & KOSTO, LLP

Established in 1981
21 OAK STREET
SUITE 309
HARTFORD, CONNECTICUT 06106-8002
Telephone: 860-249-8100
Fax: 860-727-9184
Email: lk@visacounsel.com
URL: http://www.visacounsel.com

Limited to Immigration and Naturalization Law, including Visas, Employment Visas, Business Immigration and Citizenship.

MEMBERS OF FIRM

ELIZABETH B. LEETE, born Frankfort, Kentucky, July 31, 1933; admitted to bar, 1976, Connecticut and U.S. District Court, District of Connecticut. *Education:* Wellesley College (B.A., 1954); University of Connecticut (J.D., with highest honors, 1976). Recipient: West Hornbook Awards, 1974, 1975, 1976; Starr Fellowship Award for Outstanding Scholastic Achievement, 1976; American Jurisprudence Awards in Civil Procedure, Corporate Taxation, Property, Torts, Secured Transactions, Trial Practice and Uniform Commercial Code. Administrative Editor, Connecticut Law Review, 1975-1976. Law Clerk, Connecticut Supreme Court, 1976-1977. Author: "Changes in Taxation Relative to Aliens," 11 C.L.T., No. 28, 1985; "Legalization: Remedy or Wrong?" 13 C.L.T. No. 1, 1987. Instructor, Immigration Law, CLE, Connecticut Bar Association and University of Connecticut, 1989—. *Member:* Connecticut Bar Association; American Immigration Lawyers Association. ***LANGUAGES:*** French. ***PRACTICE AREAS:*** Immigration and Naturalization; Visas; Business Immigration. ***Email:*** eleete@visacounsel.com

GALE S. KOSTO, born Springfield, Massachusetts, July 19, 1937; admitted to bar, 1979, Connecticut and U.S. District Court, District of Connecticut. *Education:* Smith College (B.A., 1962); Yale Graduate School (M.A., 1962); University of Connecticut (J.D., 1979). *Member:* Connecticut Bar Association; American Immigration Lawyers Association. ***PRACTICE AREAS:*** Immigration and Naturalization; Visas; Business Immigration. ***Email:*** gkosto@visacounsel.com

ANDREW L. WIZNER, born Detroit, Mich., 1962; admitted to bar, 1989, Connecticut. *Education:* Georgetown Univ. (B.S., Sigma Delta Phi, 1984); Universidad de Barcelona, Barcelona, Spain; Vanderbilt Univ. (J.D., 1989). *Member:* Connecticut Bar Association; American Immigration Lawyers Association. ***LANGUAGES:*** Spanish. ***PRACTICE AREAS:*** Immigration Law; Visas; Employment Visas. ***Email:*** awizner@visacounsel.com

ERIC FLEISCHMANN, born Hartford, Connecticut, November 1, 1961; admitted to bar, 1987, Massachusetts; 1988, Connecticut. *Education:* Yale University (B.A., cum laude, 1983); University of Virginia (J.D., 1987). Recipient, First prize, Burkan Memorial Competition. Author: "The Impact of Digital Technology on Copyright Law," 8 Computer/Law Journal, 1-22, 1987, 70 Journal of the Patent and Trademark Office Society 5-26, 1988, 23 New England Law Review 45-65, 1988. *Member:* Connecticut Bar Association; American Immigration Lawyers Association. ***PRACTICE AREAS:*** Immigration Law; Business Immigration. ***Email:*** ericf@visacounsel.com

REPRESENTATIVE CLIENTS: United Technologies Corp.; Kaman Corp.; ESPN, Inc.; Zygo Corp.; MTU Aero Engine Design Inc.; Bombardier Aerospace; Lydall, Inc.

THE LAW OFFICES OF MATTHEW J. LEFEVRE, ESQ., P.C.

241 ASYLUM STREET, 3RD FLOOR
HARTFORD, CONNECTICUT 06103
Telephone: 860-522-6288
Fax: 860-522-7585
Email: mjlesqpc@snet.net
URL: http://www.lawyers.com/lefevrelaw

Torrington, Connecticut Office: 94 Church Street, 06790. Telephone: 860-626-8590. Fax: 860-489-4316.

Tax Law, Estate Planning and Administration, Trust, Elder Law, Business Planning, Corporate, Partnership, Limited Liability Company, Commercial Law and Financing.

MATTHEW J. LEFEVRE, born New Haven, Connecticut, September 27, 1962; admitted to bar, 1987, Connecticut; 1988, U.S. District Court, District of Connecticut and U.S. Tax Court. *Education:* Clark University (B.A., magna cum laude, 1984); University of Connecticut (J.D., with high honors, 1987). Phi Beta Kappa. Associate, Andros, Floyd and Miller, P.C., 1988-1992; Partner, 1992-1996. *Member:* Connecticut (Member: Taxation Section; Estates and Probate Section; Executive Committee, Elder Law Section) and American (Member, Real Property, Probate and Trust Law Section) Bar Associations; National

(This Listing Continued)

Association of Elder Law Attorneys. ***PRACTICE AREAS:*** Estate Planning Law; Elder Law; Estate Administration Law; Trust Administration Law; Tax Law; Corporate Law; Partnership Law; Limited Liability Company Law; Business Planning; Commercial Financing.

OF COUNSEL

REGINA WEXLER LEFEVRE, born Putnam, Connecticut, June 3, 1962; admitted to bar, 1987, Connecticut. *Education:* Trinity College (B.A., 1984); University of Connecticut (J.D., 1987). *Member:* Litchfield County and Connecticut Bar Associations; Litchfield County Association of Women Attorneys.

LEONE, THROWE, TELLER & NAGLE

HARTFORD, CONNECTICUT

(See East Hartford)

General Trial Practice in all Courts. Real Estate, Trusts, Probate, Estate Planning, Workers Compensation, Social Security Disability Claims, Municipal, Personal Injury, Family Law and Criminal Law, Divorce, Child Custody, Adoptions.

MARY ALICE LEONHARDT

102 OAK STREET
HARTFORD, CONNECTICUT 06106
Telephone: 860-727-8874
Fax: 860-525-2194
Email: maleonhardt@email.msn.com
URL: http://www.lawyers.com/bsn-jd

Health Care, Administrative Law, Corporate Law, Employment Law, Personal Injury, Medical Malpractice.

MARY ALICE LEONHARDT, born Waterbury, Connecticut, June 25, 1956; admitted to bar, 1985, Connecticut; 1988, U.S. District Court, District of Connecticut; 1991, U.S. Supreme Court. *Education:* Georgetown University (B.S.N., cum laude, 1978); Suffolk University (J.D., 1984). Sigma Theta Tau. Registered Nurse: Massachusetts, 1978-1984. Formerly with Pullmen & Conley, 1994-1997; Brown, Rulnick Freed & Gesmer, 1997-1999. *Member:* Connecticut (Member, Executive Committee and Vice President, Administrative Law Section; Member, Executive Committee, Antitrust Section; Member, Executive Committee and Legislative Liaison, Secretary, Health Law Section) and American Bar Associations; Connecticut Trial Lawyers Association; The Association of Trial Lawyers of America; The American Association of Nurse Attorneys (The Connecticut Chapter); The American Society of Law, Medicine and Ethics; The Connecticut SIDS Center, Inc. (President, 1995-1997 and Trustee, 1991-1994); National and Connecticut Health Lawyers Associations; St. Raphael Foundation (Member, Board of Trustees, 1991); Connecticut Women in Healthcare and Management.

LEVIN, FORD & PAULEKAS, LLP

Established in 1979
ONE STATE STREET
HARTFORD, CONNECTICUT 06103
Telephone: 860-527-0400
Telecopier: 860-249-7500
Email: info@lfpllp.com
URL: http://www.lfpllp.com

Commercial Finance, Real Estate Finance, Investment and Development, Business and Corporate Finance, Creditors Rights and Bankruptcy, Environmental and Land Use, International Business Practice, and Litigation in all State and Federal Courts.

MEMBERS OF FIRM

PAUL W. FORD, born Hingham, Massachusetts, May 14, 1950; admitted to bar, 1978, Massachusetts; 1979, Connecticut; 1991, U.S. District Court, District of Connecticut; 1993, U.S. District Court, District of Massachusetts. *Education:* Boston University (B.A., magna cum laude, 1972; Phi Beta Kappa); University of Pennsylvania (M.A., 1975); University of Maine School of Law (J.D., 1978). Member: University of Maine Law Review, 1976-1978. *Member:* Connecticut, Massachusetts, American and International Bar Associations. ***PRACTICE AREAS:*** Commercial Real Estate; Real Estate; Finance; Leases and Leasing; Securities; Contracts; Mergers, Acquisitions and Divestitures; Business Law. ***Email:*** pford@lfpllp.com

WALTER E. PAULEKAS, born Sharon, Pennsylvania, August 28, 1956; admitted to bar, 1986, Connecticut; U.S. District Court, District of Connecticut, U.S. Court of Appeals, Second Circuit, U.S. Supreme Court. *Education:* U.S. Military Academy (B.S., 1978); Western New England College School of Law (J.D., 1986). Phi Alpha Delta. WNEC Law Review. Past President, West Point

(This Listing Continued)

LEVIN, FORD & PAULEKAS, LLP, Hartford—Continued

Society of Connecticut. *Member:* Connecticut and American Bar Associations; Commercial Law League of America. ***PRACTICE AREAS:*** Commercial Litigation; Bankruptcy; Corporate and Business Law; Creditors Rights; Environmental. ***Email:*** wpaulekas@lfpllp.com

WILLIAM J. EGAN, born Chicago, Illinois, August 27, 1965; admitted to bar, 1990, Connecticut; 1991, U.S. District Court, District of Connecticut; 1997, Massachusetts; 2000, U.S. District Court, District of Massachusetts. *Education:* Harvard University (A.B., 1987); University of Connecticut (J.D., 1990). Recipient, American Jurisprudence Award for Trial Practice, 1990. Associate Editor, Connecticut Journal of International Law, 1989-1990. *Member:* Connecticut (Commercial Law and Bankruptcy Section) and American Bar Associations. ***PRACTICE AREAS:*** Commercial Litigation; Bankruptcy; Creditors Rights and Collections; E-Commerce; Commercial Leasing; Lease Litigation; Landlord and Tenant Law; Contract Negotiations; Business Representation. ***Email:*** wegan@lfpllp.com

DAVID A. HILL, JR., born Long Branch, New Jersey, April 4,1966; admitted to bar, 1992, Connecticut; 1993, Massachusetts; U.S. District Court, District of Connecticut; 1994, New York; U.S. District Court, District of Massachusetts; 1996, U.S. District Court, Southern District of New York; 2000, U.S. Court of Appeals, First Circuit. *Education:* Wesleyan University (B.A., 1988); University of Connecticut (J.D., with honors, 1992). Managing Editor, Connecticut Law Review, 1991-1992, Member, 1990-1991. ***PRACTICE AREAS:*** Commercial Litigation; Civil Litigation; Commercial Foreclosure; Commercial Workouts; Creditor Bankruptcy; Commercial Collections; Landlord and Tenant Law; Private Placement Syndication. ***Email:*** dhill@lfpllp.com

LAWRENCE A. DVORIN, born West Hartford, Connecticut, August 31, 1961; admitted to bar, 1989, Connecticut; 1990, U.S. District Court, District of Connecticut. *Education:* University of Rochester; University of Miami (B.M., 1984); Suffolk University (J.D., cum laude, 1989). Staff Member, 1987-1988 and Comment Editor, 1988-1989, Suffolk University Law Review. Author: "Criminal Defendants' Right to a Speedy Trial," Suffolk University L. Rev., Vol. 22, No. 2, 1988; "An Examination of Attorney Disbarment," Suffolk University L. Rev., Vol. 22, No. 2, 1988; "Prosecutors' Right to Qualified Immunity," Suffolk University L. Rev., Vol. 22, No. 4, 1988. *Member:* Connecticut Bar Association (Member, Commercial Law, Bankruptcy and Corporate Law Sections); American Federation of Musicians (Member, Local 400). ***PRACTICE AREAS:*** Commercial Litigation; Commercial Workouts; Commercial Finance; Corporate Transactions. ***Email:*** ldvorin@lfpllp.com

ASSOCIATES

MATTHEW H. YOUMANS, born Hartford, Connecticut, July 7, 1965; admitted to bar, 1991, Connecticut; 1992, U.S. Court of Appeals, 5th Circuit; 1995, U.S. District Court, District of Connecticut. *Education:* Tufts University (B.A., cum laude, 1987); University of Connecticut School of Law (J.D., with honors, 1991). Member, 1989-1991; Executive Editor, 1990-1991, Connecticut Journal International Law. *Member:* Connecticut and American Bar Associations; Connecticut Trial Lawyers Associations. ***PRACTICE AREAS:*** Labor and Employment Litigation; Commercial Litigation; Corporate Transactions. ***Email:*** myoumans@lfpllp.com

ELEANOR N. BORTOLAN, born Clovis, New Mexico, May 3, 1965; admitted to bar, 1990, Connecticut. *Education:* Boston University (B.A., 1987); Catholic University (J.D., 1990). *Member:* Connecticut Bar Association. ***PRACTICE AREAS:*** Commercial Real Estate; Finance. ***Email:*** ebortolan@lfpllp.com

OF COUNSEL

MICHAEL R. LEVIN, born Philadelphia, Pennsylvania, July 30, 1939; admitted to bar, 1969, California and Connecticut. *Education:* Tufts College (A.B., 1961); University of Michigan (J.D., 1967). *Member:* Hartford County, Connecticut and American Bar Associations; State Bar of California; American College of Real Estate Lawyers; Anglo-American Real Property Institute; The Urban Land Institute. ***PRACTICE AREAS:*** Real Estate; Corporate Finance; Business Law; Securities. ***Email:*** mlevin@lfpllp.com

PETER MENTING, born New York, New York, September 19, 1944; admitted to bar, 1973, District of Columbia, U.S. District Court, District of Columbia, U.S. Court of Appeals for the District of Columbia and U.S. District Court, District of Connecticut (Not admitted in Connecticut). *Education:* Hamburg University; George Washington University (B.A., 1967; J.D., 1972); University College London (LL.M., 1974); University Dundee. International Who's Who, 1988. Author: "The Last Crusade," Sunstone Press, 1993. *Member:* District of Columbia Bar; International Bar Association. [U.S. Army, 1968-1969]. ***LANGUAGES:*** German; Italian; French. ***PRACTICE AREAS:*** International & European Community Law; Immigration & Trade. ***Email:*** pmenting@hotmail.com

(This Listing Continued)

LEGAL SUPPORT PERSONNEL

PETER R. BORTOLAN, born New Haven, Connecticut, November 26, 1937. *Education:* Providence College (B.S., 1960); University of Connecticut (M.B.A., 1963). Member, Association of Legal Administrators (Nutmeg Chapter). [1st. Lt., USAF, 1962-1965]. ***Email:*** pbortolan@lfpllp.com

VICTORIA DePERGOLA, born Camden, New Jersey, August 14, 1971. *Education:* University of Delaware (B.A., 1994); Manchester Community College (A.S., 1999). ***PRACTICE AREAS:*** Commercial Litigation; Bankruptcy. ***Email:*** vdepergola@lfpllp.com

REPRESENTATIVE CLIENTS: Aid Association for Lutherans; All American Life Insurance Co.; American Bank of Connecticut; AMRESCO; Atlantic National Trust LLC; Berwind Property Group; Bank of America; Cambridge Realty Partners, LLC; Capital Crossing Bank; Cargill Financial Services Corp.; Citizens Bank; The Davis Companies; Deburring Laboratories, Inc.; Ensign Bickford Realty Corporation; Farm Bureau Insurance Co.; Federal Deposit Insurance Co.; Flanagan Industries; Fleet National Bank; The Fowler & Hunting Company; Glastonbury Bank & Trust Company; H.L. Diehl Co., Inc.; City of Hartford; Health Information Systems, Inc.; Inrange Technologies Corp.; Lawyers Title Insurance Co.; Lexington Partners; Lutheran Brotherhood; The Manufacturers Life Insurance Co.; Metropolitan Life Insurance Company; National Cooperative Bank; Putnam Investments; Shaw's Supermarkets; Security National Bank Limited Partners; Webster Bank; WPI Financial Services; People's Bank; Unity Bank.

LEVY & DRONEY, P.C.

HARTFORD, CONNECTICUT

(See Farmington)

Administrative Law, Banking, Business Law, Civil and Criminal Litigation in State and Federal Courts, Condominiums, Construction, Corporate, Environmental Law, Estate Planning, Family Law, Foreclosures, Health Care, Labor and Employment, Mergers and Acquisitions, Municipal, Personal Injury and Insurance Defense Law, Practice Before Federal and State Agencies and Commissions, Probate, Public Finance, Real Estate, Secured and Unsecured Commercial Transactions, Securities, Taxation, Title Insurance Litigation, Zoning.

LEWIS, LEWIS & FERRARO, L.L.C.

HARTFORD, CONNECTICUT

(See West Hartford)

Family Law, Divorce, Personal Injury, Automobile Accidents, Real Estate, Medical Malpractice, Bankruptcy, Wills, Probate, Estate Planning, Trusts and Estates.

LIBERT & ASSOCIATES

HARTFORD, CONNECTICUT

(See Simsbury)

Patent, Trademark, Copyright, Intellectual Property and Related Matters.

LOUDEN LEGAL GROUP LLC

638 PROSPECT AVENUE
HARTFORD, CONNECTICUT 06105
Telephone: 860-231-7150
Fax: 860-231-7425
Email: info@loudenlegalgroup.com
URL: http://www.loudenlegalgroup.com

Divorce, Divorce Mediation, Matrimonial Law, Premarital Agreements.

FIRM PROFILE: Recognized for excellence through a blend of traditional divorce practice and pioneering in mediation, we believe that constructive resolutions are best for our clients and their families, whether through negotiation or litigation. We have extensive experience in complex cases and are on the cutting edge in effective and caring service to clients, approach to cases and technology.

WM. BRUCE LOUDEN, born Fairfield, Iowa, May 14, 1938; admitted to bar, 1963, Florida; 1970, Connecticut. *Education:* University of Florida (B.A., 1961; J.D., 1963). Phi Beta Kappa. Editor-in-Chief, University of Florida Law Review. Author: "Managing to Maximize Productivity and Fulfillment," ABA Family Advocate, 1994. Listed, Best Lawyers in America, 1983—. *Member:* Connecticut (Chair, Professional Discipline Committee, 1979-1983) and American (Standing Committee on Professional Discipline, 1973-1979) Bar Associations; American Academy of Matrimonial Lawyers (President, Connecticut Chapter, 1991-1992). ***REPORTED CASES:*** Hunter, 177 Conn. 327 (1979); Blake, 211 Conn. 485 (1988); Kronholm, 16 Conn. App. 124 (1988). ***Email:*** blouden@loudenlegalgroup.com

SHANNON O. LOUDEN, born Gainesville, Florida, March 31, 1963; admitted to bar, 1993, Connecticut. *Education:* Swarthmore College (B.A., 1985); University of Pennsylvania (J.D., 1993). *Member:* Connecticut Bar Association

(This Listing Continued)

(Member, Executive Committee, Family Law Section, 1996—); Connecticut Council for Divorce Mediation (Member, Board of Directors, 2000—). ***LANGUAGES:*** Spanish. ***Email:*** slouden@loudenlegalgroup.com

SUSAN BUSBY, born Montreal, Canada, November 15, 1961; admitted to bar, 1993, Connecticut. *Education:* McGill University (B.A., 1988); University of Connecticut (J.D., 1993). Executive Editor, Connecticut Law Review, 1992-1993. ***Email:*** sbusby@loudenlegalgroup.com

ROBERT F. LUDGIN

33 LINDEN PLACE
P.O. BOX 261775
HARTFORD, CONNECTICUT 06126-1775
Telephone: 860-549-3920
Fax: 860-524-8238

Civil and Criminal Litigation, Motor Vehicle, D.W.I., Personal Injury, Commercial, Collections, Estates, Family Law, Real Estate, Landlord and Tenant.

ROBERT F. LUDGIN, born Boston, Massachusetts, April 15, 1940; admitted to bar, 1966, Connecticut; 1967, U.S. District Court, District of Connecticut; 1968, U.S. Court of Appeals, 2nd Circuit and U.S. Supreme Court. *Education:* Princeton University (A.B., cum laude, 1962; Woodrow Wilson School of Public and International Affairs); The University of Michigan Law School (LL.B., 1966). Budget Examiner, U.S. Bureau of Budget, 1966-1967. Government Appeals Agent, Hartford Local Board No. 1 of the Selective Service System, 1967-1969. Councilman, Hartford City Council, 1977-1981. Deputy Mayor, City of Hartford, 1979-1981. *Member:* Hartford County, Connecticut and American Bar Associations; The Association of Trial Lawyers of America.

LYNCH, TRAUB, KEEFE AND ERRANTE

A PROFESSIONAL CORPORATION

HARTFORD, CONNECTICUT

(See New Haven)

General Practice. Corporation, Employment Law, Computer Law, Transportation, OSHA, Tax, Probate, Real Estate, Social Security, Criminal, Negligence, Medical Malpractice and Products Liability Law. Trials and Appeals in all Civil, Administrative and Criminal Courts, Federal and State. Family Law, Workers Compensation, Bankruptcy Law.

MACDERMID, REYNOLDS & GLISSMAN, P.C.

Established in 1992
86 FARMINGTON AVENUE
HARTFORD, CONNECTICUT 06105
Telephone: 860-278-1900
Telecopier: 860-547-1191
URL: http://www.lawyers.com/mrglaw

Civil Litigation; Commercial and Residential Real Estate Litigation; Real Estate, Conveyancing, Leasing, Workout and Finance; Environmental and Land Use Law; Real Estate Brokerage; Communications; Construction Law; Surety; Probate and Estate Law; Employment Law, Alternative Dispute Resolution and Family Law.

PAUL W. ORTH, born Baltimore, Maryland, 1930; admitted to bar, 1954, Massachusetts; 1957, Connecticut. *Education:* Dartmouth College (A.B., magna cum laude, 1951); Harvard Law School (J.D., 1954). Phi Beta Kappa. Instructor, University of Connecticut School of Law, 1960-1980. *Member:* Hartford County (President, 1983-1984) and Connecticut Bar Associations. Fellow, American Bar Foundation. ***LANGUAGES:*** German. ***PRACTICE AREAS:*** Civil Litigation; Employment Litigation; Alternative Dispute Resolution. ***Email:*** porth@mrglaw.com

BRUCE G. MACDERMID, born Hartford, Connecticut, May 12, 1947; admitted to bar, 1975, Connecticut. *Education:* Bowdoin College (A.B., 1969); Boston University (J.D., 1975). *Member:* Hartford County, Connecticut and American Bar Associations. [Lt., USNR, 1969-1972]. ***PRACTICE AREAS:*** Civil Litigation; Real Estate Litigation; Personal Injury; Family Law; Corporate Litigation; Probate Litigation; Commercial Real Estate; Brokerage Litigation; Landlord Tenant Disputes. ***Email:*** bmacdermid@mrglaw.com

PETER R. REYNOLDS, born Mineola, New York, September 4, 1956; admitted to bar, 1984, Connecticut; 1985, U.S. District Court, District of Connecticut; 1997, U.S. Court of Appeals, Second Circuit. *Education:* Harvard University (A.B., 1979); University of Connecticut, School of Law (J.D., with honors, 1984). *Member:* Hartford County, Connecticut and American Bar Associations; Connecticut Trial Lawyers Association. ***PRACTICE AREAS:*** Litigation; Fidelity and Surety; Construction Law; Commercial Law; Insurance. ***Email:*** preynolds@mrglaw.com

(This Listing Continued)

DAVID R. GLISSMAN, born Santa Cruz, California, 1957; admitted to bar, 1984, Connecticut and Massachusetts. *Education:* San Diego State University (B.S., Real Estate, 1979); McGeorge School of Law, University of the Pacific (J.D., 1983); Boston University (LL.M., Taxation, 1984). *Member:* Connecticut (Member, Executive Committee, Real Property Section) and American (Member, Real Property, Probate and Trust Law Section) Bar Associations. ***PRACTICE AREAS:*** Real Property; Conveyancing; Leasing; Workouts; Finance; Land Use; Environmental; Real Estate Brokerage. ***Email:*** dglissman@mrglaw.com

JEANNE S. ROBERTS, born Hartford, Connecticut, November 23, 1965; admitted to bar, 1990, Connecticut; 1991, U.S. District Court, District of Connecticut; 1994, Florida. *Education:* University of Michigan (B.A., 1987); Suffolk University (J.D., 1990). Adjunct Faculty Member, University of Connecticut, School of Law. *Member:* Hartford County and Connecticut (Member, Real Property Sections) Bar Associations. ***PRACTICE AREAS:*** Real Property; Conveyancing; Leasing; Finance; Land Use; Environmental; Real Estate Brokerage. ***Email:*** jroberts@mrglaw.com

MICHAEL S. STIEBEL, born Brooklyn, New York, March 22, 1949; admitted to bar, 1975, Connecticut. *Education:* Virginia Commonwealth University (B.A., 1971); St. Mary's University School of Law (J.D., 1975). *Member:* Connecticut Bar Association (Member, Executive Committee, Real Property Section). ***PRACTICE AREAS:*** Real Property; Conveyancing; Leasing; Workouts; Communications; Finance. ***Email:*** mstiebel@mrglaw.com

MADSEN, PRESTLEY & PARENTEAU, LLC

44 CAPITOL AVENUE SUITE 201
HARTFORD, CONNECTICUT 06106
Telephone: 860-246-2466
Facsimile: 860-246-1794
Email: mppjustice.com
URL: http://www.lawyers.com/mppllc

New London Office: 111 Huntington Street, P.O. Box 1631. Telephone: 860-442-2466. Facsimile: 860-447-9206.

Employment, Benefits Law and Related Litigation. Employment Contracts; Age, Race, Sex and Disability Discrimination; Civil Rights, Section 1983. Wage and Hour Law, Class Actions and Qui Tam Actions, Negotiations, Mediations, Arbitrations, Trials.

FIRM PROFILE: Experienced counselors, litigators and trial attorneys with practice devoted to the representation of individuals in all areas of employment and benefits law and litigation.

WILLIAM G. MADSEN, born Danbury, Connecticut, 1959; admitted to bar, 1990, Maine; 1992, Connecticut. *Education:* University of Massachusetts (B.A., 1985); Yale University (M.A.R., 1987); Vermont Law School (J.D., 1990). Managing Editor, Law Review, 1990. Law Clerk to Hon. Conrad K. Cyr, U.S. Court of Appeals for the First Circuit, 1990-1991. ***PRACTICE AREAS:*** Labor and Employment Law; Civil Rights Law; Age Discrimination Law; Sexual Harassment Law; Employment Disability Law; Employment Contracts Law; Wage and Hour Law. ***Email:*** wmadsen@mppjustice.com

PETER B. PRESTLEY, born 1945; admitted to bar, 1972, Connecticut. *Education:* Wesleyan University (B.A., 1969); University of Connecticut (J.D., 1972). Editor-in-Chief University of Connecticut Law Review. Deputy General Counsel of the Travelers (complex litigation and employment and benefits law) (1975-1994). Simpson Thacher & Bartlett, N.Y, NY (complex coverage litigation) (1994-1997). Chair American Bar Association (Tort and Insurance Practice Section 1992-1993; Chair, Joint Committee on Employee Benefits, 1990). *Member:* National Employment Lawyers Association; Connecticut Employment Lawyers Association. ***LANGUAGES:*** French. ***PRACTICE AREAS:*** Employment Law; Benefits Law; Class Actions; Age Discrimination; False Claims Act; Qui Tam Litigation; Benefits Litigation; Executive Compensation; Mediation; Arbitration. ***Email:*** pprestley@mppjustice.com

JACQUES J. PARENTEAU, born Woonsocket, Rhode Island, June 1, 1957; admitted to bar, 1982, Rhode Island; 1984, Connecticut. *Education:* University of Massachusetts (B.A., magna cum laude, 1979); Washington College of Law of American University (J.D., 1982). Past Member of the Board of Directors and Vice Chairman, Connecticut Legal Services Corporation. Vice Chairman and Member of the Board of Directors of the Connecticut Community Credit Union, Inc.; Arbitrator, Connecticut Automobile Dispute Settlement Program. *Member:* New London County and Rhode Island Bar Associations; Connecticut Trial Lawyers Association; The Association of Trial Lawyers of America. ***PRACTICE AREAS:*** Employment Law; Academic Employment; Commercial Litigation; Personal Injury; Products Liability. ***Email:*** jparenteau@mppjustice.com

ASSOCIATE

CRAIG THOMS DICKINSON, born Bridgeport, Connecticut, September 23, 1963; admitted to bar, 1994, Connecticut, New York and U.S. District Court,

(This Listing Continued)

MADSEN, PRESTLEY & PARENTEAU, LLC, Hartford—Continued

Southern District of New York; 1995, U.S. District Court, Northern District of New York; 1996, U.S. Court of Appeals, Second Circuit; 1997, U.S. District Court, District of Connecticut. *Education:* Fairfield University (B.A., 1985; M.A., 1988); Pace University (J.D., 1993). Member, Pace University Law Review. *Member:* Connecticut and American Bar Associations; New England Lawyers Association. ***REPORTED CASES:*** Leather v. Eyck, 180 F.3d 420 (1999); O'Connor v. Davis, 126 F.3d 112 (1997); Kracunas v. Iona, 119 F.3d 80 (1997); Todaro v. Norat, 112 F.3d 598 (1997); Marshall v. Sullivan, 105 F.3d 47 (1996); Mascetta v. Miranda, 957 F.Supp. 1346 (S.D.N.Y. 1997). ***PRACTICE AREAS:*** Labor and Employment; Civil Rights. ***Email:*** cdickinson@mppjustice.com

MAYO, GILLIGAN & ZITO, LLP

HARTFORD, CONNECTICUT

(See Wethersfield)

Trials in all Courts, Real Estate, Banking and Commercial Finance, Creditors' Rights and Bankruptcy, Employment, Business Law, Zoning, Environmental, Estate Planning, Elder Law, Probate and Personal Injury Law.

McCARTER & ENGLISH, LLP

Established in 1844

ONE FINANCIAL PLAZA
755 MAIN STREET
HARTFORD, CONNECTICUT 06103
Telephone: 860-493-3900
URL: http://www.mccarter.com

Newark, New Jersey Office: Four Gateway Center, 100 Mulberry Street. P.O. Box 652. Telephone: 973-622-4444. Telecopier: 973-624-7070.
Cherry Hill, New Jersey Office: 1820 Chapel Avenue West, Suite 380. Telephone: 609-662-8444. Telecopier: 609-662-6203.
New York, New York Office: 300 Park Avenue, 18th Floor. Telephone: 212-466-9018. Telecopier: 212-432-6568.
Wilmington, Delaware Office: Mellon Bank Center, 919 Market Street. Telephone: 302-654-8010. Telecopier: 302-654-0795.
Philadelphia, Pennsylvania Office: One Commerce Square, 2005 Market Street, Suite 3600. Telephone: 215-557-7700. Telecopier: 215-557-6544.
Baltimore, Maryland Office: 201 North Charles Street. Telephone: 410-385-1088.

Administrative Law, Alternative Dispute Resolution, Antitrust and Trade Regulation, Appellate Practice, Aviation and Aerospace, Bankruptcy, Banks and Banking, Business Law, Civil Practice, Class Actions, Commercial Law, Commercial Real Estate, Communications and Media, Complex and Multi-District Litigation, Computers and Software, Contracts, Copyrights, Corporate Law, Debtor and Creditor, Education Law, Eminent Domain, Employee Benefits, Environmental Law, Equipment Finance and Leasing, Finance, General Practice, Health Care, Insurance, Insurance Coverage, Intellectual Property, International Law, Investments, Labor and Employment, Leases and Leasing, Litigation, Mergers, Acquisitions and Divestitures, Natural Resources, Nonprofit and Charitable Organizations, Patents, Probate, Products Liability, Professional Liability, Public Finance, Real Estate, Taxation, Torts, Toxic Torts, Trade Secrets, Trademarks, Transportation, Trusts and Estates, Unfair Competition, White Collar Crime, Wills, Zoning, Planning and Land Use.

MEMBER OF FIRM

CATHERINE ANN MOHAN, born 1958; admitted to bar, 1985, Connecticut. *Education:* Wheaton College (B.A., magna cum laude, 1980); Georgetown University (J.D., 1985). Phi Beta Kappa. *Member:* Hartford County, Connecticut and American Bar Associations. ***PRACTICE AREAS:*** Litigation; Mass Torts. ***Email:*** cmohan@mccarter.com

ASSOCIATES

JOHN J. ROBINSON, born 1965; admitted to bar, 1994, Connecticut; 1995, U.S. District Court, District of Arizona and U.S. District Court, District of Connecticut. *Education:* Catholic University of America (B.S., 1990; J.D., cum laude, 1994). *Member:* Connecticut Bar Association; Defense Research Institute. ***PRACTICE AREAS:*** Products Liability; Nursing Home Litigation; Tort Litigation. ***Email:*** robinson@mccarter.com

CHRISTINE S. SYNODI, admitted to bar, 1996, Connecticut and U.S. District Court, District of Connecticut. *Education:* Connecticut College (B.A., with honors, 1988); University of Connecticut School of Law (J.D., 1996). Clerk to the Honorable Stuart Schimelman, Hartford Superior Court, Criminal Division, 1995-1996. *Member:* Connecticut and American Bar Associations. ***PRACTICE AREAS:*** Products Liability; Toxic Torts; Civil Litigation. ***Email:*** csynodi@mccarter.com

DONALD J. McCARTHY, JR.

107 OAK STREET
HARTFORD, CONNECTICUT 06106
Telephone: 860-560-0468
Fax: 860-560-0763

General Civil Litigation, Personal Injury, Product Liability, Medical Malpractice, Criminal Trials and Family Law.

DONALD J. McCARTHY, JR., born Hartford, Connecticut, February 3, 1950; admitted to bar, 1980, Connecticut. *Education:* University of Connecticut (B.A., 1973); University of Bridgeport (J.D., 1980). Recipient, American Jurisprudence Award for the study of Remedies. *Member:* Hartford County, Connecticut (Member, House of Delegates, 1982-1996) and American (Member, Sections on: Litigation; Torts and Insurance Practice Law) Bar Associations; Connecticut Trial Lawyers Association; The Association of Trial Lawyers of America. (Also Member, McCarthy, Schuman & Coombes).

McCORMICK, PAULDING & HUBER, LLP

CITYPLACE II
185 ASYLUM STREET
HARTFORD, CONNECTICUT 06103-4102
Telephone: 860-549-5290
Fax: 860-527-0464
Email: MPH@IP-Lawyers.com
URL: http://www.IP-lawyers.com

Springfield, Massachusetts Office: 1350 Main Street, 5th Floor. Telephone: 413-736-5401. Fax: 413-733-4543.

Patent, Trademark, Copyright, Unfair Competition, Franchise, Computer and Related Intellectual Property Law including Litigation in all Courts.

FIRM PROFILE: McCormick, Paulding & Huber, established in Hartford over 50 years ago as a full-service intellectual property firm, and Chapin, Neal & Dempsey, in Springfield for over 80 years, merged in 1995. The firm continues to practice exclusively in this specialized area of the law today. The firm has offices conveniently located in Hartford, Connecticut and Springfield, Massachusetts, midway between New York and Boston for easy access by air, rail and interstate highway, and provides comprehensive service to a host of domestic and international clients. The present partners, associate attorneys, paralegals and support staff number over 40. All partners and associate attorneys are members of the bar of one or more states, are registered to practice before the United States Patent and Trademark Office, and collectively hold degrees in a wide range of engineering and scientific disciplines. Whether your company is an entrepreneurial start-up or multinational conglomerate, the firm offers a full range of services in intellectual property matters throughout the United States and around the world. Working relationships with highly qualified law firms in every major U.S. city and in more than fifty foreign commercial centers allow us to provide you with intellectual property services unconstrained by regional or national boundaries.

MEMBERS OF FIRM

JOHN C. HILTON, born Boston, Massachusetts, May 20, 1931; admitted to bar, 1962, Connecticut; registered to practice before U.S. Patent and Trademark Office. *Education:* Massachusetts Institute of Technology (B.S.A.E., 1953); University of Connecticut (J.D., 1962). Author, "Developments in Design Patent Law," Joint Seminar of New York, Pennsylvania, New Jersey and Connecticut Patent Law Association, 1988. *Member:* Hartford County, Connecticut and American (Member, Sections on: Patent, Copyright and Trademark; Litigation) Bar Associations; American Intellectual Property Law Association; Connecticut Patent Law Association. ***REPORTED CASES:*** Fisher Stove Inc., vs. All Nighter Stove Works Inc., District Court of New Hampshire, 1979 (205USPQ1009) Affirmed 626 F2d 193 (1st Cir. 1980); Atlanta Motoring v. Saratoga Technologies, (N.D. Ga.), reversed on appeal, 33 F.3d 1362, 31 U.S.P.Q.2d 1929 (Fed. Cir. 1994). ***PRACTICE AREAS:*** Trademarks; Patents. ***Email:*** Hilton@IP-Lawyers.com

JOHN C. LINDERMAN, born Norristown, Pennsylvania, January 16, 1938; admitted to bar, 1970, Connecticut; 1996, Massachusetts; registered to practice before U.S. Patent and Trademark Office. *Education:* Massachusetts Institute of Technology (B.S., 1959); University of Connecticut (J.D., 1970). Pi Tau Sigma. Author: "How To Fashion A Protective Order In Patent Litigation," The Licensing Journal Vol. 11, No. 5; "The Ascending Role of Secondary Considerations," Third Annual Joint Seminar Program of Patent Law Associations, 1987. Past Chairman, The MIT Enterprise Forum of Connecticut, 1993-

(This Listing Continued)

1996. *Member:* Hartford County, Connecticut (Chairman, Patent, Trademark and Copyright Section, 1980-1981) and American Bar Associations; American Intellectual Property Law Association; Connecticut Patent Law Association (President, 1977-1978). ***PRACTICE AREAS:*** Intellectual Property; Patents; Trademarks; Copyrights. ***Email:*** Lind@IP-Lawyers.com

J. KEVIN GROGAN (Resident, Springfield, Massachusetts Office).

ARTHUR F. DIONNE (Resident, Springfield, Massachusetts Office).

RICHARD R. MICHAUD, born Bridgeport, Connecticut, November 3, 1963; admitted to bar, 1996, Connecticut. *Education:* University of Bridgeport (B.S.M.E., 1986; M.S.M.E., 1992); Quinnipiac College (J.D., 1995). Tau Beta Pi. *Member:* Hartford County Bar Association; Connecticut Patent Law Association. ***PRACTICE AREAS:*** Patents; Trademarks; Copyrights; Intellectual Property; Litigation.

MARINA F. CUNNINGHAM, born U.S.S.R., May 19, 1964; admitted to bar, 1993, Connecticut; registered to practice before the U.S. Patent and Trademark Office. *Education:* Columbia University (B.S.M.E., 1986); Massachusetts Institute of Technology (M.S., 1988); University of Connecticut (J.D., 1993). Tau Beta Pi. Member, MIT Enterprise Forum. Member, Board of Directors; Co-Chair, Technology and Intellectual Property Committee. *Member:* Hartford County Bar Association; Connecticut Patent Law Association. ***LANGUAGES:*** Russian and Ukrainian. ***PRACTICE AREAS:*** Intellectual Property; Patents; Trademarks; Copyrights; E-Commerce; Litigation. ***Email:*** cunningham@ip-lawyers.com

ASSOCIATES

DANIEL G. MACKAS, born Hartford, Connecticut, November 19, 1961; admitted to bar, 1997, Connecticut; registered to practice before U.S. Patent and Trademark Office. *Education:* University of Connecticut (B.S., Electrical Engineering, cum laude, 1985; J.D., 1997). Tau Beta Pi; Eta Kappa Nu. *Member:* Connecticut and American Bar Associations; Connecticut Intellectual Property Law Association. ***PRACTICE AREAS:*** Patents; Trademarks; Copyrights. ***Email:*** Mackas@IP-Lawyers.com

SUSAN C. OYGARD (Resident, Springfield, Massachusetts Office).

NICHOLAS J. TUCCILLO (Resident, Springfield, Massachusetts Office).

WM. TUCKER GRIFFITH, born Worcester, Massachusetts, April 19, 1973; admitted to bar, 1998, Connecticut; 1999, U.S. District Court, District of Connecticut; registered to practice before U.S. Patent and Trademark Office. *Education:* Worcester Polytechnic Institute (B.S., with distinction, 1995); University of Connecticut, School of Law (J.D., with honors, 1998). Tau Beta Pi; Pi Tau Sigma. Managing Editor, Connecticut Law Review, 1996-1998. Author: "Beyond the Perfect Score: Protecting Routine-Oriented Athletic Performance with Copyright Law," Winter 1998, Connecticut Law Review. *Member:* Hartford County, Connecticut and American Bar Associations; American Intellectual Property Law Association. ***PRACTICE AREAS:*** Intellectual Property; Litigation; Patents; Trademarks; Copyrights. ***Email:*** Tucker@IP-Lawyers.com

STEPHEN P. SCUDERI (Resident, Springfield, Massachusetts Office).

MARY-JACQ HOLROYD (Resident, Springfield, Massachusetts Office).

RICHARD D. GETZ, born Hartford, Connecticut, August 12, 1962; admitted to bar, 1992, Connecticut; registered to practice before U.S. Patent and Trademark Office. *Education:* University of Connecticut (B.S.M.E., 1987); Western New England College of Law (J.D., 1992). Pi Tau Sigma. *Member:* Connecticut and American Bar Associations (Member, Intellectual Property Section); Connecticut Patent Law Association. ***PRACTICE AREAS:*** Intellectual Property Transactions; Licensing; Patents; Trademarks; Copyrights; U.S. Government Contracting. ***Email:*** getz@ip-lawyers.com

WILLIAM B. GOWANLOCK, born Detroit, Michigan, July 15, 1952; admitted to bar, 1995, Connecticut; 1997, District of Columbia; registered to practice before the U.S. Patent and Trademark Office. *Education:* University of Michigan (B.S.E., 1974); Catholic University (J.D., cum laude, 1994). ***PRACTICE AREAS:*** Intellectual Property; Patent Prosecution; Government Contracts. ***Email:*** gowanlock@ip-lawyers.com

DONALD J. MACDONALD, born Huron City, Michigan, October 24, 1960; admitted to bar, 1999, Massachusetts; 2000, U.S. District Court, District of Massachusetts; registered to practice before the U.S. Patent and Trademark Office (Not admitted in Connecticut). *Education:* Oakland University (B.S., Comp. Eng., 1986); Massachusetts School of Law (J.D., 1999). *Member:* Boston, Massachusetts and American Bar Associations; American Intellectual Property Law Association. (Also Member, Lambert & Associates, PLLC). ***PRACTICE AREAS:*** Intellectual Property Litigation; Patent Prosecution. ***Email:*** macdonald@lp-lawyers.com

SHIRLEY S. MA, born Hong Kong, January 5, 1969; admitted to bar, 1996, Ohio; 1998, District of Columbia; 1999, Connecticut; U.S. District Court, District of Columbia; 2000, U.S. District Court, District of Connecticut and U.S. Court of Appeals, Federal Circuit; registered to practice before U.S. Patent and Trademark Office. *Education:* State University of New York at Albany (B.S., Chemistry, 1990); University of Dayton (J.D., 1996). *Member:* New Haven County and American Bar Associations; American Intellectual Property Law Association. ***LANGUAGES:*** Cantonese. ***PRACTICE AREAS:*** Intellectual Property. ***Email:*** ma@ip-lawyers.com

OF COUNSEL

THEODORE R. PAULDING, born Great Barrington, Massachusetts, June 19, 1930; admitted to bar, 1957, Connecticut; registered to practice before U.S. Patent and Trademark Office. *Education:* University of Notre Dame (B.S.M.E., 1952); University of Connecticut (J.D., 1957). Member and Chairman, Wethersfield Planning and Zoning Commission, 1964—. Director, Eli Whitney Fund Connecticut Innovations, Inc., 1984—. *Member:* Hartford County, Connecticut (Chairman, Patent and Trademark Section, 1963-1964) and American Bar Associations; American Intellectual Property Law Association; Connecticut Patent Law Association. ***PRACTICE AREAS:*** Intellectual Property. ***Email:*** Paulding@IP-Lawyers.com

DONALD K. HUBER, born Salford, Pennsylvania, July 7, 1930; admitted to bar, 1958, District of Columbia; 1960, Connecticut; registered to practice before U.S. Patent and Trademark Office. *Education:* Northwestern University (B.S.M.E., 1953; J.D., 1956); University of Hartford (B.S.E.E., 1965). Phi Delta Phi; Pi Tau Sigma. *Member:* Hartford County, Connecticut and American Bar Associations; The District of Columbia Bar; American Intellectual Property Law Association; Connecticut Patent Law Association; International Association for the Protection of Industrial Property. ***LANGUAGES:*** German and English Technical Translations. ***PRACTICE AREAS:*** Intellectual Property; Patents; Trademarks; Copyrights. ***Email:*** Huber@IP-Lawyers.com

FREDERICK J. HAESCHE, born New Haven, Connecticut, December 8, 1924; admitted to bar, 1966, Connecticut; registered to practice before U.S. Patent and Trademark Office. *Education:* College of the City of New York; University of Connecticut (B.S., 1950; J.D., 1966). *Member:* Hartford County, Connecticut and American Bar Associations; American Intellectual Property Law Association; Connecticut Patent Law Association. ***PRACTICE AREAS:*** Intellectual Property; Patents; Trademarks; Copyrights. ***Email:*** Haesche@IP-Lawyers.com

JOHN J. DEMPSEY, born New York, N.Y., August 18, 1924; admitted to bar, 1957, Maryland; 1959, Massachusetts; 1967, U.S. Supreme Court; registered to practice before U.S. Patent and Trademark Office (Not admitted in Connecticut). *Education:* Manhattan College; United States Naval Academy (B.S., 1946); University of Maryland (LL.B., 1957). Examiner, U.S. Patent Office, 1957-1958. *Member:* Hampden County, Massachusetts and American Bar Associations; American Intellectual Property Law Association. ***PRACTICE AREAS:*** Patents; Trademarks; Copyrights.

CHARLES E. SOHL, born Philadelphia, Pennsylvania, November 6, 1945; admitted to bar, 1976, Connecticut; registered to practice before the U.S. Patent and Trademark Office. *Education:* Drexel University (B.S., 1968); University of Kentucky (M.S., 1970); University of Connecticut (J.D., 1976). Member, Board of Education , 1984-1990. Treasurer, Secretary, Vice President, Connecticut Patent Law Association, 1995—. ***PRACTICE AREAS:*** Intellectual Property Law; Business Law. ***Email:*** sohl@ip-lawyers.com

REFERENCE: Fleet Bank.

MCGOVERN & ASSOCIATES

HARTFORD, CONNECTICUT

(See Greenwich)

General Commercial Practice. Corporate (Foreign and Domestic), Mergers and Acquisitions, Securities, Venture Capital, Taxation, Litigation in all Courts. International, Joint Ventures, Admiralty, Sports, Commercial and Residential Real Estate Law. Estates and Trusts.

F. TIMOTHY MCNAMARA, P.C.

102 OAK STREET

HARTFORD, CONNECTICUT 06106

Telephone: 860-249-8458

Fax: 860-249-8850

Email: ftimothymcnamara@aol.com

URL: http://www.lawyers.com/timothy_mcnamara

Insurance, Corporate and Administrative Law. Criminal Law, Appellate Practice, Eminent Domain, Aviation. Practice restricted to Litigation.

F. TIMOTHY MCNAMARA, born Hartford, Connecticut, February 19, 1926; admitted to bar, 1955, Connecticut. *Education:* University of Connecticut (B.A., 1953; M.A., 1956; J.D., with honors, 1955). Law Clerk to Chief Judge J. Joseph Smith, U.S. District Court, 1955-1956. Corporation Counsel, East Hartford, Connecticut, 1966-1967; 1973-1979. *Member:* Hartford County, Connecticut and American Bar Associations; American Board of Trial Advocates.

(This Listing Continued)

F. TIMOTHY McNAMARA, P.C., Hartford—Continued

Fellow, American College of Trial Lawyers. ***LANGUAGES:*** Spanish. ***Email:*** ftimothymcnamara@aol.com

RAMONA MERCADO-ESPINOZA

250 MAIN STREET
HARTFORD, CONNECTICUT 06106-1867
Telephone: 860-560-8188
Fax: 860-560-8189

Civil and Criminal Litigation, Personal Injury, Family Law and Real Estate.

RAMONA MERCADO-ESPINOZA, born Puerto Rico, August 6, 1957; admitted to bar, 1986, Connecticut; 1990, U.S. District Court, District of Connecticut; 1991, U.S. Court of Federal Claims. *Education:* Central Connecticut State University (B.A., cum laude, 1983); University of Connecticut (J.D., 1986). Prior Deputy Assistant Public Defender, 1987-1990. *Member:* Hartford and Connecticut Bar Associations; Hispanic Bar Association; Connecticut Trial Lawyers Association. ***LANGUAGES:*** Spanish.

METZGER & ASSOCIATES

25 CAPITOL AVENUE
HARTFORD, CONNECTICUT 06106-1867
Telephone: 860-549-5026
Fax: 860-549-5224
Email: dmetzger@snet.net

Labor and Employment.

DAVID L. METZGER, born Hartford, Connecticut, 1948; admitted to bar, 1985, Connecticut; U.S. Court of Appeals, Second Circuit and U.S. Supreme Court. *Education:* University of Connecticut (B.A., 1970; J.D., 1984). Connecticut Commission on Human Rights and Opportunities (CHRO), 1974-1986. CHRO Chief of Compliance, 1985-1986. Member: Task Force on CHRO Hearing Process; Americans With Disabilities Act Drafting Committee to the Connecticut Law Revision Commission (1995-1996); Advisory Committee on Human Rights and Opportunities Complaint Process to Connecticut Law Revision Commission (1996-1997). Participant in Legislative Program Review and Investigations Committee Study of CHRO (1999). Member, Connecticut Business Industry Association (CBIA) Labor and Employment Council. Former Partner, Siegal O' Conner Schiff & Zangari, 1986-1994; Jackson, Lewis, Schnitzler & Krupman, 1994-1997. *Member:* Hartford County (Co-Chair, Labor & Employment Committee), Connecticut (Member, Labor and Employment Law Section Executive Committee; Co-Chair, Employment Discrimination Law Subcommittee) and American Bar Associations. ***Email:*** dmetzger@snet.net

JUDITH D. MEYER

HARTFORD, CONNECTICUT

(See Avon)

Employment Law, Civil Litigation in all State and Federal Courts and Administrative Agencies, Professional Licensing.

MICHELSON, KANE, ROYSTER & BARGER, P.C.

93 OAK STREET
HARTFORD, CONNECTICUT 06106
Telephone: 860-522-1243
Fax: 860-548-0194
Email: mkrb@snet.net

Construction Law, Civil Litigation, Surety Law, Labor & Employment Law, Public Utilities, Commercial Law, Personal Injury and Workers Compensation.

FIRM PROFILE: The firm was founded in 1963 with a principal emphasis on construction law. While the firm continues to concentrate in all areas of construction law, representing contractors, architects, engineers, municipalities, private owners and surety companies, the scope of its practice now reaches into nearly all phases of civil law. The firm is very active in arbitration, litigation, and appellate work throughout the Northeast. The firm's offices are located on Oak Street, adjacent to the Superior Court, the Appellate Court, the Supreme Court, and the State Capitol.

RICHARD L. BARGER, born Hartford, Connecticut, April 20, 1944; admitted to bar, 1969, Connecticut; 1971, U.S. District Court, District of Connecticut; 1973, U.S. Court of Appeals for the District of Columbia Circuit; 1986, U.S. Court of Appeals, Second Circuit; 1998, U.S. Claims Court. *Education:* University of Connecticut (B.S., 1966); Suffolk University Law School; University of Connecticut (J.D., 1969). Member, Suffolk University Law Review, 1968. Guest Lecturer, University of Connecticut School of Law, 1990-1992. Author: "Public Construction Contracting in Connecticut," Lorman, 1998. Assistant Attorney General, representing the Connecticut Public Utilities Commission, 1970-1975. Corporation Counsel, Town of Bolton. WPCA Counsel for the Southeastern Regional Resource Recovery Authority and the Towns of Ledyard and Stonington. *Member:* Hartford County and Connecticut Bar Associations; The Association of Trial Lawyers of America. ***PRACTICE AREAS:*** Public Utilities; Administrative Law; Municipal Law; Construction Law; Civil Litigation; Real Estate. ***Email:*** bargerrl@snet.net

STEVEN B. KAPLAN, born New York, N.Y., March 31, 1953; admitted to bar, 1982, Connecticut and U.S. District Court, District of Connecticut; 1983, U.S. Court of Appeals, Second Circuit. *Education:* Columbia University (B.A., 1974); University of Massachusetts (M.A., 1978); University of Connecticut (J.D., 1982). Editor-in-Chief, Connecticut Law Review, 1981-1982. Author: "Payment for Construction Claims in Connecticut," Lorman, 1990, 1998, 1999, 2000, 2001; "Public Construction Contracting in Connecticut," Lorman, 1998, 1999, 2000, 2001; "Bid Disputes," CBA Construction Law Seminar, May 1996; "Union Project Labor Agreements," CBA Annual Meeting Construction Law Section, June 1996; "Performance Bond Claims: The Surety's Defenses-An Update," ABA Surety/TIPS Mid-winter Conference, 1991; Co-Author: "Connecticut Mechanics' Liens and Payment Bonds," PESI, 1987; "Connecticut Construction Claims and Collections," PESI 1988, 1991; "Termination for Cause From the Surety's Perspective," CBA Construction Law Seminar, March 25, 1994; Co-Editor, 1995-2001, Connecticut Bar Association Construction Case Law Summary, Legislative Review. Adjunct Professor of Law, Public Construction Contracts, University of Connecticut School of Law. Member, Panel of Arbitrators, American Arbitration Association. *Member:* Hartford County, Connecticut (Member, Executive Committee, Construction Law Section) and American (Member: Forum Committee on the Construction Industry; Fidelity & Surety Law Committee; Tort & Insurance Practice Section) Bar Associations; Connecticut Trial Lawyers Association. ***PRACTICE AREAS:*** Civil Litigation; Construction Law; Fidelity and Surety. ***Email:*** sbkaplan@snet.net

MARK E. BLAKEMAN, born Chicago, Illinois, March 10, 1951; admitted to bar, 1984, Connecticut; 1985, U.S. District Court, District of Connecticut; 1993, Massachusetts. *Education:* Dartmouth College (A.B., cum laude, 1973); Western New England College (J.D., cum laude, 1984). Recipient, American Jurisprudence Awards in Remedies and Family Law. *Member:* Hartford County and Connecticut Bar Associations; Connecticut Trial Lawyers Association; The Association of Trial Lawyers of America. ***PRACTICE AREAS:*** Civil Litigation; Construction Law; Workers Compensation Law. ***Email:*** mblakeman@snet.net

JOSEPH B. MATHIEU, born Hartford, Connecticut, December 29, 1968; admitted to bar, 1994, Connecticut. *Education:* Providence College (B.A., summa cum laude, 1991); University of Connecticut School of Law (J.D., with high honors, 1994). Contributing Author and Co-Editor, "Payment for Construction Claims in Connecticut," (Lorman, 1998, 1999, 2000, 2001). *Member:* Hartford County and Connecticut (Member, Construction Law Section) Bar Associations. ***PRACTICE AREAS:*** Civil Litigation; Surety Law; Bankruptcy; Construction Law. ***Email:*** jbmathieu@snet.net

CHRISTOPHER W. HUCK, born Hartford, Connecticut, February 18, 1968; admitted to bar, 1994, Massachusetts; 1995, Connecticut and U.S. District Court, District of Connecticut; 1996, U.S. District Court, District of Massachusetts. *Education:* Bates College (B.A., 1990); University of Connecticut (J.D., 1994). Law Clerk to the Honorable Thomas P. Smith, U.S. Magistrate Judge, District of Connecticut, 1995. Contributing Author and Co-Editor: "Public Construction Contracting in Connecticut," (Lorman, 1998, 2000, 2001). *Member:* Hartford County, Connecticut and Massachusetts Bar Associations. ***PRACTICE AREAS:*** Construction Law; Surety Law; Estate Planning; Employment Law; Commercial Litigation. ***Email:*** cwhuck@snet.net

PAUL S. TAGATAC, born Bridgeport, Connecticut, August 30, 1965; admitted to bar, 1990, Connecticut; 1991, U.S. District Court, District of Connecticut. *Education:* University of Connecticut (B.A., magna cum laude, 1987; J.D., 1990). Phi Beta Kappa. ***PRACTICE AREAS:*** Labor and Employment. ***Email:*** ptagatac@snet.net

ASSOCIATES

JUSTINE R. TOBIS, born Bridgeport, Connecticut, June 28, 1951; admitted to bar, 1992, Connecticut; 1993, U.S. District Court, District of Connecticut. *Education:* Central Connecticut State University (B.F.A., 1974); University of Connecticut (M.A., 1975); Western New England College, School of Law (J.D., cum laude, 1992). Recipient, American Jurisprudence Award for Constitutional Law. *Member:* Hartford County and Connecticut Bar Associations. ***PRACTICE AREAS:*** Corporate Law; Real Estate; Workers' Compensation; Personal Injury. ***Email:*** jtobis@snet.net

(This Listing Continued)

BETH MERCIER, born New Haven, Connecticut, May 24, 1969; admitted to bar, 1995, Connecticut; 1996, U.S. District Court, District of Connecticut. *Education:* University of Connecticut (B.A., summa cum laude, 1991; J.D., 1995). Phi Kappa Phi. Contributor, CBA Annual Construction Case Law Summary, 1999-2000. *Member:* Hartford County Bar Association; Connecticut Trial Lawyers Association. ***PRACTICE AREAS:*** Civil Litigation; Construction Law; Personal Injury; Workers' Compensation. ***Email:*** bmercier@snet.net

OF COUNSEL

JAMES N. ROYSTER, born Hartford, Connecticut, September 16, 1944; admitted to bar, 1971, Connecticut. *Education:* Hanover College (B.A., 1968); University of Connecticut (J.D., 1971).

THOMAS H. CONNELL, born Greenwich, Connecticut, October 2, 1934; admitted to bar, 1966, Connecticut and U.S. District Court, District of Connecticut; 1967, U.S. Court of Appeals, Second Circuit; 1971, U.S. Supreme Court. *Education:* Wesleyan University (B.A., 1956); University of Connecticut (J.D., 1966). Recipient, American Jurisprudence Award in Administrative Law and Uniform Commercial Code Law. Contributing Legal Editor, Plastics Engineering, the Official Publication of the Society of Plastics Engineers, 1983. Author: "Impact Cost Claims," Construction, January/February, 1985; "Technical Advertising Claims," Construction, March/April, 1985; "Public Construction Bidding," The Connecticut Law Tribune, April, 1985; "Can This Project be Saved?" (Lorman, 1999). Member, Panel of Arbitrators, American Arbitration Association. *Member:* Hartford County and Connecticut (Member: Executive Committee, Construction Law Section; Labor Section) Bar Associations. ***PRACTICE AREAS:*** Civil Litigation; Construction Law; Corporate Law; Labor Law.

CHESTER J. BUKOWSKI, JR., born Bristol, Connecticut, April 16, 1952; admitted to bar, 1977, Connecticut; 1978, U.S. District Court of Connecticut; 1979, U.S. Court of Appeals, Second Circuit; 1990, California; 1991, U.S. Claims Court. *Education:* Trinity College (B.A., with honors, 1974); Columbia University (J.D., 1977). Phi Beta Kappa. Affiliate Member, AIA Connecticut, 1995—. Member, Panel of Arbitrators, American Arbitration Association. *Member:* Connecticut (Member, Sections on: Construction Law; Alternative Dispute Resolution) and American (Member: Section of Litigation; Forum Committee on the Construction Industry, 1983—) Bar Associations. ***PRACTICE AREAS:*** Construction Law; Design Professional Liability; Appellate Practice. ***Email:*** cbukowski@snet.net

REPRESENTATIVE CLIENTS: B-G Mechanical Contractors, Inc.; CFL, Incorporated; Claywell Electric Co.; CNA Insurance Co.; Connecticut Heating and Cooling Contractors Association; Connecticut Independent Electrical Contractors Association; Connecticut Surety Co.; Costello Industries, Inc.; Ducci Electrical Contractors, Inc.; East P.B.E., Inc.; Electrical Contractors, Inc.; Greiner Engineering Sciences, Inc.; The Hartford; J.H. Lynch & Sons, Inc.; Kiewit Eastern Co.; Kovacs Construction Corp.; National Grange Mutual Insurance Co., Inc.; New England Mechanical Services; Old Newgate Ridge Water Co., Inc.; Peerless Insurance Co.; Polychem Corp.; Regenesis, Inc.; Southeastern Regional Resource Recovery Authority; St. Paul Surety; Topstone Hydraulic Co.; *Municipalities:* Bolton, Cheshire, Ledyard, New Britain, Stonington, Sprague, Oxford, Windham.

MINITER AND ASSOCIATES

Established in 1990

147 CHARTER OAK AVENUE
HARTFORD, CONNECTICUT 06106
Telephone: 860-560-2590
Telefax: 860-560-3238
Email: miniter@attglobal.net

Corporate, Commercial, Bankruptcy, General Litigation, Commercial and Construction Litigation, Environmental, Real Estate and Zoning Law. Commercial, Employment, Estate Planning and Administrative Law, International Sales, Immigration, Family Law, ERISA, Health Care.

FIRM PROFILE: Miniter and Associates is a firm of four attorneys founded by Francis A. Miniter in 1990, concentrating in commercial trade, contract employment, environmental issues and immigration.

FRANCIS A. MINITER, born Hartford, Connecticut, September 15, 1948; admitted to bar, 1978, New York; 1979, Connecticut and U.S. District Court, Eastern and Southern Districts of New York; 1980, U.S. District Court, District of Connecticut; 1992, U.S. Tax Court; 1997, U.S. Court of Appeals, Second Circuit; 1998, U.S. Court of Appeals, First Circuit. *Education:* Trinity College (B.A., 1970; M.A., 1970); University of Toronto, Toronto, Ontario, Canada (LL.B., 1976); Columbia University (LL.M., 1978). Articled Clerk to Borden & Elliot, Toronto, Ontario, 1976-1977. Law Clerk to the Honorable Lawrence Bilder, Judge, Superior Court, Law Division, New Jersey, 1978-1979. Author: "Misleading Advertising: The Standard of Deception," 1 Canadian Business Law Journal 435, 1976; "What Was Said: A Summary of the Proceedings of the 1976 Annual Conference on Commercial and Consumer Law," 2 Canadian Business Law Journal 364, 1978; "Buyer's Right of Rejection: A Quarter Century Under the Uniform Commercial Code and Recent International Developments," 13 Georgia Law Review 805, 1979; "Is Foreclosure Your Best and Only Option?" NBI Connecticut Foreclosure and Repossessions, 1997; "Dealing with Reform," NBI Commercial Lending in Connecticut, 1999. *Member:* Hartford County, Connecticut (Member: Commercial Law and Bankruptcy Section; Executive Committee, 1991-1992) and American (Member: Section Committee on UCC, Electronic Funds Transfer; Sections on: General Practice; Business Law) Bar Associations. ***PRACTICE AREAS:*** Corporate Transactions; Commercial Transactions; International Sales; Bankruptcy; Real Estate; Zoning Law; Commercial Litigation; Construction Litigation; Civil Rights Litigation.

ASSOCIATES

DANIEL C. SPINETI, born Hartford, Connecticut, June 30, 1964; admitted to bar, 1992, Connecticut; 1993, U.S. District Court, District of Connecticut. *Education:* University of Connecticut (B.A., 1986); Western New England College School of Law (J.D., 1990). Phi Alpha Delta. Instructor, National Academy of Paralegal Studies, 1995. *Member:* Hartford County Bar Association; National Italian American Bar Association. ***PRACTICE AREAS:*** Real Estate; Litigation; Family Law; Corporate Law; Criminal Law. ***Email:*** dspineti@aol.com

CHRISTINE E. CORRIVEAU, born New Haven, Connecticut, February 20, 1967; admitted to bar, 1999, Connecticut; 2000, U.S. District Court, District of Connecticut. *Education:* Syracuse University (B.S., 1989); University of Connecticut School of Law (J.D., with honors, 1999). Recipient: Corpus Jurissecundum Award for Scholastic Excellence in Contracts, 1996; CALI Excellence for the Future Award in Contracts, 1999; CALI Excellence for the Future Award - Federal Taxation, 1999; CALI Excellence for the Future Award - Taxation for Non-Profit Organization; CALI Excellence for the Future Award - Liability Insurance. Member, Connecticut Law Review, 1997-1999. ***PRACTICE AREAS:*** Civil Rights; Employment Law; Insurance Law. ***Email:*** cec1803@prodigy.net

MICHAEL T. LANDINO, born New Haven, Connecticut, April 2, 1958; admitted to bar, 1983, Connecticut; 1988, U.S. District Court, District of Connecticut; 1993, U.S. Court of Appeals, Second Circuit and U.S. Supreme Court. *Education:* University of Connecticut (B.A., 1980); Western New England College (J.D., 1983). Member, Barrister's Society, 1982-1983. *Member:* New Haven County, Hartford County and Connecticut (Member, Litigation Section) Bar Associations. ***PRACTICE AREAS:*** Construction Litigation; Corporate Law; Land Use; Technology Law; Employment Law.

GEORGE C. SPRINGER, JR., born Bristol, Connecticut, September 19, 1963; admitted to bar, 1988, Connecticut; 1989, U.S. District Court, District of Connecticut; 1990, U.S. District Court, Southern and Eastern Districts of New York; 1993, U.S. Court of Appeals, Second Circuit and U.S. Supreme Court. *Education:* University of Connecticut (B.A., 1985; J.D., 1988). Member, Connecticut Moot Court Board, 1986-1987. Regional Participant, Philip C. Jessup International Moot Court Competition, 1987. Recipient: Bureau of National Affairs Award for Senior Scholastic Achievement; New Britain NAACP 1995 Shaw Community Service Award; Outstanding Young Lion of the Year Award. Associate Editor, Connecticut Journal of International Law, 1987-1988. Law Clerk, The Honorable Herbert J. Hutton, District Judge for the Eastern District of Pennsylvania, 1990-1991. Publications: Connecticut Legal Developments in International Legal Affairs, 3 Conn. J. Intl. L. 262 (1987); Connecticut Developments, 3 Conn. J. Intl. L. 529 (1988). Principal, George C. Springer, Jr., LLC (1994-2000). President, Walicki-A.W.-Stanley Little League, Inc. (2000—). Member, Board of Directors, New Britain-Berlin YMCA (1996—). Member, Little League International Advisory Board (2000—). Member, Board of Directors, Shelter for the Homeless, Inc. (1993-1994). Executive Secretary, U.S. Civil Rights Commission, Connecticut Advisory Committee (1997-1999). Member, CCARC, Inc. Member, Board of Directors, Connecticut Civil Liberties Union (1993-1995). Chairman, Due Process Committee (1994-1995). Hearings Officer, Connecticut Department of Consumer Protection (1993-1998). President, NAACP, New Britain Chapter (1995-1996). Second Vice President, NAACP, New Britain Chapter (1994-1995). Chair Legal Research Committee, New Britain Chapter, NAACP (1993-1995). Member, New Britain Lion's Club (1994-1995). American Inn of Court (1988-1994). ***PRACTICE AREAS:*** Civil Rights; Employment; Wrongful Termination; Domestic Relations; Workers Compensation; Real Estate; Commercial Litigation; Criminal Law; Labor Law.

(This Listing Continued)

MONTSTREAM & MAY, L.L.P.

HARTFORD, CONNECTICUT

(See Glastonbury)

Workers' Compensation, Civil Litigation, Insurance Defense, Products Liability, Medical Malpractice, Legal Malpractice.

MORRISON, MAHONEY & MILLER, LLP

ONE CONSTITUTION PLAZA, 10TH FLOOR
HARTFORD, CONNECTICUT 06103
Telephone: 860-616-4441
Facsimile: 860-244-3800
Email: info@mail.mm-m.com
URL: http://www.mm-m.com

Boston, Massachusetts Office: 250 Summer Street, 02210. Telephone: 617-439-7500. Facsimile: 617-439-7590.
Fall River, Massachusetts Office: 10 North Main Street, 02722. Telephone: 508-677-3100. Facsimile: 508-672-3840.
London, England Office: 60 Lombard Street, EC3V 9EA. Telephone: 011-44-0207-464-8499. Facsimile: 011-44-0207-509-7238.
New York, N.Y. Office: 100 Maiden Lane, 22nd Floor, 10038-4892. Telephone: 212-825-1212. Facsimile: 212-825-1313.
Providence, Rhode Island Office: One Providence Washington Plaza, 02903. Telephone: 401-331-4660. Facsimile: 401-351-4420.
Springfield, Massachusetts Office: Tower Square, 1500 Main Street, Suite 2400, 01115. Telephone: 413-737-4373. Facsimile: 413-739-3125.
Worcester, Massachusetts Office: One Chestnut Place, 10 Chestnut Street, Suite 470, 01608. Telephone: 508-757-7777. Facsimile: 508-752-6224.

The firm represents its clients in a broad range of Civil matters, including: Property and Liability Insurance Coverage Claims and Issues, Appellate Reinsurance, Environmental and Pollution Defense and Coverage, Arson, and other Insurance Fraud, Professional Liability including Medical, Legal, Accounting, Directors and Officers, Architects and Engineers, Insurance Agents and Brokers, Fidelity and Surety Bond Claims, Insurance Regulatory and Governmental Affairs, Subrogation, Regulatory, General and Corporate Representation of Insurers, Agents and Brokers, Life, Accident, Health, including Sports, Employee Benefits and ERISA, Health Law, Employment Law, Products Liability including Pharmaceutical and Medical Devices, General Liability, Construction Law, Emerging Businesses Consulting, Commercial/Business Litigation Energy, Premises Liability, Retail Premises Liability, Lead Paint, Transportation, Marine and Inland Marine, Workers Compensation for Insurers and Self-Insureds, and General Litigation in State and Federal Courts in numerous jurisdictions throughout the country.

LAW FIRM ALLIANCES/ASSOCIATIONS: **ALFA INTERNATIONAL - AMERICAN LAW FIRM ASSOCIATION**

(For complete biographical data on all personnel, see Professional Biographies at Boston, Massachusetts)

MOUKAWSHER & WALSH LLC

21 OAK STREET
HARTFORD, CONNECTICUT 06106
Telephone: 860-549-8440
Fax: 860-549-8443
URL: http://www.lawyers.com/moukawsher&walshllc

Groton, Connecticut Office: 328 Mitchell Street, P.O. Box 966. Telephone: 860-445-1809. Fax: 860-446-8161. Internet E-Mail: moukwals@snet.net

Civil Litigation, ERISA Law, Benefits Law, Estates, Negligence, Personal Injury, Wrongful Death, Medical Malpractice, Products Liability, Commercial Litigation, Employment Law, Trials and Appeals.

JOSEPH E. MOUKAWSHER, born New London, Connecticut, February 5, 1920; admitted to bar, 1949, Connecticut; 1953, U.S. District Court, District of Connecticut; 1980, U.S. Court of Appeals, 2nd Circuit; 1981, U.S. Supreme Court. *Education:* Wesleyan University (B.A., 1942); Harvard University (LL.B., 1948). Phi Beta Kappa. Prosecuting Attorney, Town of Groton, 1955-1960. Borough Attorney, Borough of Groton, 1962-1963. Town Attorney, Town of Groton, 1969-1971; 1977-1983. Coroner, New London County, 1972-1979. Member, Town of Groton Charter Revision Commission, 1991—. *Member:* New London County, The Connecticut and American Bar Associations. **PRACTICE AREAS:** Real Estate; Probate; Estate Planning; Civil Litigation. **Email:** jemoukawsher@snet.net

MICHAEL J. WALSH, born Nassau, New York, May 31, 1962; admitted to bar, 1987, Connecticut; 1988, New York and U.S. District Court, Southern and Eastern Districts of New York and District of Connecticut; 1993, U.S. Court of Appeals, Second Circuit. *Education:* Stonehill College (B.S., with high honors, 1984); University of Connecticut (J.D., 1987). Member, 1985-1986, and Editor, 1986-1987, Connecticut Law Review. Law Clerk to Hon. Ellen Burns, Chief Judge, U.S. District Court of Connecticut, 1988-1989. Author: "The Disclosure Requirements of 35 U.S.C. 112 and Software-Related Patent Applications: Debugging the System," 18 Conn. L. Rev. 855 (1986). Adjunct Instructor Faculty, University of Connecticut, School of Law, 1994-1999. *Member:* Hartford County, New London County, Connecticut and American Bar Associations; Oliver Ellsworth Inn of Court (Treasurer, 1991-1992); American Trial Lawyers Association; Connecticut Trial Lawyers Association. **REPORTED CASES:** Chylinski v. Wal-Mart Stores, 150 F.3d 214 (2d Cir. 1998) (Personal Injury/Premises Liability); Suarez v. Sordo, 43 Conn. App. 756, 685 A.2d 1144, cert. den. 240 Conn. 906, 688 A.2d 334 (1997) (Personal Injury/Premises Liability); Rumbin v. Utica Mutual Insurance, Co., 254 Conn. 290 (2000) (Commercial Contract). **PRACTICE AREAS:** Civil Litigation; Personal Injury; Medical Malpractice. **Email:** mwalsh7777@aol.com

(This Listing Continued)

THOMAS G. MOUKAWSHER, born New London, Connecticut, September 10, 1962; admitted to bar, 1986, Connecticut. *Education:* The Citadel (B.A., magna cum laude, 1983); University of Connecticut (J.D., cum laude, 1986). Phi Kappa Phi. Editor, Conn. L. Rev., 1985-1986. Law Clerk, Office of the Governor, State of Connecticut, 1985-1986. Author: "Mobile Home Parks and Connecticut's Regulatory Scheme," 17 Conn. L. Rev. 811, 1985; "Protecting the Dignity of Privacy Law," 18 Conn. L. Rev. 621, 1986; "Client Perjury Demands Attorney Disclosure," 12 Conn. L. Trib. No. 20, 1986; "Cash Balance Plans: Terminology, Advantages and Disadvantages to Employers and Employees," Connecticut Lawyer, Vol. 10, No. 9, 2000. Member, Town Council, Town of Groton, 1987-1990. Member and Special Counsel, Democratic State Central Committee of Connecticut, 1988-1990. Member, House of Representatives, State of Connecticut, 40th District, 1991-1993. Special Counsel, President Pro Tempore, Connecticut State Senate, 1993-1995. Counsel, General Assembly, Committee on Commerce, 1993-1995. Member, Democratic State Central Committee of Connecticut, 1997—. Counsel, State of Connecticut Democratic Party, 2001—. Member, Oliver Ellsworth Inn of Court, 1992-1994. *Member:* Connecticut Bar Association. **REPORTED CASES:** Mullins v. Pfizer, 23 F.3d 663 (1994) (ERISA); Jackson v. Whipple, 225 Conn. 705 (1993) (unfair trade practices); Kelly v. Bonney, 221 Conn. 549 (1992) (defamation/employment); Adamczyk v. Lever Brothers, 991 F.Supp. 931 (N.D. Ill. 1997) (ERISA); Hudson v. General Dynamics, 186 F.R.D. 271 (D.Conn 1999)(ERISA); Bins v. Exxon, 220 F.3d 1042 (9th Cir. 2000)(en banc)(ERISA). **PRACTICE AREAS:** ERISA; Commercial Litigation; Employment Law. **Email:** tmoukawsher@snet.net

---

JEFFREY M. SKLARZ, born New Haven, Connecticut, August 15, 1974; admitted to bar, 1999, Connecticut. *Education:* Colby College (B.A., 1996); University of Connecticut (J.D., 1999). Member, Connecticut Journal of International Law, 1996-1999. Author: "Cash Balance Plans: Terminology, Advantages and Disadvantages to Employers and Employees," Connecticut Lawyer, Vol. 10, No. 9, 2000. **PRACTICE AREAS:** ERISA; Personal Injury; Employment Law; Civil Litigation; Taxation. **Email:** sklarz@aol.com

REFERENCE: Fleet Bank.

THE LAW OFFICE OF JOHN F. MURPHY

1324 ASYLUM AVENUE
HARTFORD, CONNECTICUT 06105-6011
Telephone: 860-233-9946
Fax: 860-523-5065
Email: jmurphy@Internet-95.com
URL: http://www.lawyers.com/connecticutaccidentlawyer

Personal Injury, Medical Malpractice, Federal False Claims, Products Liability.

FIRM PROFILE: After thirty years in one of Hartford's largest law firms, Mr. Murphy opened his own office in 1996.

JOHN F. MURPHY, born Hempstead, New York, May 11, 1936; admitted to bar, 1967, Connecticut and U.S. District Court, District of Connecticut. *Education:* Dartmouth College (B.A., 1958); Boston College (J.D., 1967). Author: "Errors in the Charge," Litigation, The Journal of the Section of Litigation of the American Bar Association, Vol. 14, No. 3, Spring 1988; "Powers of the Trial Judge Regarding Conduct of the Trial," Edited Revision, Chapter 13, *The Federal Evidence Practice Guide,* 1990. *Member:* Connecticut, Federal (President, 1984) and American Bar Associations; Connecticut Defense Lawyers Association (Founding and First President, 1977-1978); Defense Research Institute (Chairman, 1984-1990); Association of Trial Lawyers of America; Connecticut Trial Lawyers of America. [Capt., U.S. Marine Corps, 1958-1961]. **LANGUAGES:** French and Spanish. **PRACTICE AREAS:** Personal Injury; Medical Malpractice; False Claims Act; Products Liability; Government.

MURPHY, LAUDATI & KIEL, P.C.

HARTFORD, CONNECTICUT

(See Farmington)

General Civil and Criminal Practice before State and Federal Courts.

MURTHA CULLINA LLP

Established in 1937

CITYPLACE I
185 ASYLUM STREET
HARTFORD, CONNECTICUT 06103-3469
Telephone: 860-240-6000
Facsimile: 860-240-6150
Email: firm@murthalaw.com
URL: http://www.murthalaw.com

New Haven, Connecticut Office: Whitney Grove Square, 2 Whitney Avenue, P.O. Box 704-A, 06503-0704. Telephone: 203-772-7700. Facsimile: 203-772-7723.
Boston, Massachusetts Office: Murtha Cullina Roche Carens & DeGiacomo. 99 High Street. Telephone: 617-457-4000. Facsimile: 617-482-3868.
Woburn, Massachusetts Office: 600 Unicorn Park Drive. Telephone; 781-933-5505. Facsimile: 781-933-1530.

General Practice. Administrative, Antitrust, Banking, Bankruptcy, Cable Television, Commercial, Communications, Construction, Copyright, Corporation, Criminal, Employee Benefits, Energy, Environmental, Estate Planning and Administration, Exempt Organizations, Government Contracts, Health Care, Hospital, Insurance Litigation for Policyholders, Labor, Limited Liability Company Law, Litigation, Mergers and Acquisitions, Municipal Law and Finance, Patents, Probate, Product Liability, Public Utility, Real Estate, Securities, Taxation and Trademark.

MEMBERS OF FIRM

MARCEL J. BERNIER, born Miami, Fl., 1958; admitted to bar, 1982, Conn.; 1983, U.S. Dist. Court, Dist. of Conn. and U.S. Tax Court. *Education:* Florida State Univ. (B.A., magna cum laude, 1979); Univ. of Conn. (J.D., 1982); Boston Univ. (LL.M. in Taxation, 1985). *Member:* Conn. (Member, Exec. Comm., Taxation Sect.; Member, Corporation Sect.) and Amer. (Member, Sections on: Taxation; Business Law) Bar Associations. ***PRACTICE AREAS:*** Business Law; Limited Liability Company Law; Mergers and Acquisitions Law; Business Successions; Tax Law; Estate Planning. ***Email:*** mbernier@murthalaw.com

FRANCIS J. BRADY, born Springfield, Mass., 1945; admitted to bar, 1974, Dist. of Columbia and Conn. *Education:* Worcester Polytechnic Institute (B.S., 1967); George Washington Univ. (J.D., 1973); Harvard Univ. (LL.M., 1974). Mayor, Town of Windsor, 1994-1997. Chair, Civil Justice Advisory Group., 1996-2000; Co-Chair, Local Rules Advisory Comm., Dist of Conn. *Member:* Hartford County (Pres., 2000-2001;) and Conn. (Federal Prac. Exec. Comm.) Bar Assocs. ***PRACTICE AREAS:*** Insurance Litigation For Policyholders; Securities Litigation; Environmental Litigation. ***Email:*** fbrady@murthalaw.com

THOMAS M. CLOHERTY, born Boston, Mass., 1940; admitted to bar, 1973, Penn; 1975, Conn. *Education:* Boston College (A.B., 1963); Duquesne Univ. (J.D., 1973). *Member:* Conn. (Former Chair: Labor and Employment Law Section; Liaison Comm. to Comm. on Human Rights and Opportunities; Labor and Employment Law Program Comm.; NLRB Liaison Comm.) and American (Subcomm. on Alternative Dispute Resolution and Development of Law under NLRA) Bar Assoc. ***PRACTICE AREAS:*** Labor Law; Employment Law. ***Email:*** tcloherty@murthalaw.com

BURTON B. COHEN, born New Haven, Conn., 1951; admitted to bar, 1984, Conn.; 1991, U.S. Court of Appeals, 2nd. Circuit. *Education:* Trinity College (B.A., 1973); Western New England College (J.D., summa cum laude, 1984). Law Clerk to The Hon. Arthur H. Healey, Supreme Court of Conn., 1984-1985. Member: Exec. Comm., Public Utility Law Section, Conn. Bar Assoc. ***PRACTICE AREAS:*** Communications Law and Litigation; Cable Television Law; Administrative Law; State Tax. ***Email:*** bcohen@murthalaw.com

GEORGE A. DAGON, JR., born Hartford, Conn., 1954; admitted to bar, 1979, Conn.; 1982, U.S. Court of Appeals, 2nd Circuit; 2000, U.S. Supreme Court. *Education:* Yale Univ. (B.A., cum laude, 1976); Univ. of Virginia (J.D., 1979). Special Master, U.S. Dist. Court. Member, Exec. Comm., Litigation Section of Conn. Bar Assoc. *Member:* Fed. and Amer. (Litigation and TIPS Sections, Product Liability Comm., Insurance Coverage Comm.) Bar Assns.; National Association of Railroad Trial Counsel; Defense Research Institute. ***PRACTICE AREAS:*** Product Liability; Tort Litigation; Probate Litigation; Trust Litigation; Insurance Litigation for Policyholders. ***Email:*** gdagon@murthalaw.com

THOMAS M. DANIELLS, born Newtown, Conn., 1954; admitted to bar, 1982, Conn. *Education:* Dartmouth College (A.B., cum laude, 1976); Suffolk Univ. (J.D., 1982). Law Clerk to The Hon. Anthony J. Armentano and The Hon. Anthony E. Grillo, Supreme Court of Conn., 1982-1983. ***PRACTICE AREAS:*** Real Estate; Corporate; Financing. ***Email:*** tdaniells@murthalaw.com

JOSEPH P. FASI, born Hartford, Conn., 1954; admitted to bar, 1979, Conn. *Education:* Univ. of Conn. (B.A., cum laude, 1976; J.D., 1979). Treas., Conn. Assoc. of Municipal Attys. *Member:* Nat'l Assoc. of Bond Lawyers. ***PRACTICE AREAS:*** Public and Corporate Finance; Securities; Municipal. ***Email:*** jfasi@murthalaw.com

FRANK GIORDANELLA, born Bridgeport, Conn., 1959; admitted to bar, 1985, N.Y.; 1986, Conn. *Education:* Georgetown Univ. (B.S.F.S., 1981); Harvard Univ. (J.D., 1984). *Member:* Nat'l Assn of Bond Lawyers; Conn. Govt. Finance Officers Assoc. (Assoc. Member). ***PRACTICE AREAS:*** Finance Law; Municipal Bond Law; Resource Recovery Law. ***Email:*** fgiordanella@murthalaw.com

ROBERT V. GIUNTA, JR., born Hartford, Conn., 1949; admitted to bar, 1977, Conn. *Education:* American Univ. (B.A., 1971); Trinity College (M.A., 1977); Univ. of Conn. (J.D., 1977). Co-author: "Workouts for Distressed Continuing Care Retirement Communities," The Practical; Real Estate Lawyer, Vol. 14, No. 4, July 1998. *Member:* Nat'l Assoc. of Bond Lawyers. ***PRACTICE AREAS:*** Bond Finance Law; Real Estate and Housing Law. ***Email:*** rgiunta@murthalaw.com

IRWIN J. HAUSMAN, born Bridgeport, Conn., 1943; admitted to bar, 1968, Conn. *Education:* Univ. of Conn. (B.A., 1965; J.D., 1968). Co-Author, "Workouts for Distressed Continuing Care Retirement Communities," The Practical Real Estate Lawyer, Vol. 14, No. 4, July 1998. Member: Board of Director, Hartford County Bar Assn. Past Chair, Hartford County Bar Assn. Real Estate Comm. ***PRACTICE AREAS:*** Real Estate Law; Commercial Lending Law; Commercial Litigation. ***Email:*** ihausman@murthalaw.com

H. KENNEDY HUDNER, born Boston, Mass., 1950; admitted to bar, 1978, Conn. *Education:* Northeastern Univ. (B.A., 1973); Yale Univ. (J.D., 1978). Author: "Physician Negotiations with Managed Care Plans: An Antitrust Primer," The Medical Staff Counselor, Vol. 7, No. 3, Summer 1993. ***PRACTICE AREAS:*** Business Litigation; Health Care Litigation; Antitrust; Intellectual Property; Computer Law; Commercial (Sales) Law. ***Email:*** khudner@murthalaw.com

DWIGHT A. JOHNSON, born Huntington, W.V., 1945; admitted to bar, 1975, Conn. and Dist. of Columbia. *Education:* Princeton Univ. (B.A., 1968); Yale Univ. (J.D., 1974). Member: Exec. Comm., Public Utility Law Section, Conn. Bar Assoc., 1981—; Town Attorney, Town of Avon, Conn., 1997—. ***PRACTICE AREAS:*** Communications Law; Public Utilities Law; Energy Law; Corporate Law; Municipal Law. ***Email:*** djohnson@murthalaw.com

ROBERT E. KAELIN, born Oceanside, N.Y., 1965; admitted to bar, 1992, Conn.; 1993, U.S. Dist. Ct., Dist. of Conn.; 1997, U.S. Court of Appeals, 2nd Cir.; 1999, Vermont. *Education:* Miami Univ. (B.A., 1988); Duke Univ. School of Law (J.D., 1992). ***PRACTICE AREAS:*** Bankruptcy; Creditors Rights; Commercial Litigation. ***Email:*** rkaelin@murthalaw.com

WILLIAM J. KEENAN, JR., born Hartford, Conn., 1951; admitted to bar, 1976, Conn. *Education:* Amherst College (B.A., magna cum laude, 1973); Univ. of Virginia (J.D., 1976). ***PRACTICE AREAS:*** Employee Benefits Law. ***Email:*** wkeenan@murthalaw.com

MARK F. KORBER, born Buffalo, N.Y., 1947; admitted to bar, 1978, Conn. *Education:* Univ. of Maryland (B.A., 1970); Catholic Univ. of America (M.A., 1974); Univ. of Conn. (J.D., 1978). ***PRACTICE AREAS:*** Corporate Law; Health Care Law; Estate Planning Law; Estate and Trust Administration Law; Resources Recovery Law. ***Email:*** mkorber@murthalaw.com

TIMOTHY L. LARGAY, born Boston, Mass., 1943; admitted to bar, 1969, Conn. *Education:* Georgetown Univ. (A.B., 1965; J.D., 1969). Director, Lex Mundi, 1996-1999. ***PRACTICE AREAS:*** Securities Law; Corporate Law; Mergers and Acquisitions Law. ***Email:*** tlargay@murthalaw.com

KENNETH L. LEVINE, born New York, N.Y., 1953; admitted to bar, 1978, New York; 1981, District of Columbia; 1983, Ohio; 1986, Rhode Island; 1988, Mass.; 1998, Conn. *Education:* Hobart College (B.A., cum laude, 1974); Case Western Reserve Univ. Law School (J.D., 1977); New York Univ. Law School (LL.M., in Taxation, 1983). Phi Beta Kappa. Author: "The Tax Status of Vertically Integrated Health Care Delivery Systems," Journal of Health and Hospital Law, September 1993. Member: Amer. Bar Assoc., Tax Section; Conn. Bar Assoc. ***PRACTICE AREAS:*** Tax Law; Tax Planning; Exempt Organizations Tax; Partnership Taxation. ***Email:*** klevine@murthalaw.com

RICHARD A. MARONE, born New York, N.Y., 1956; admitted to bar, 1981, Conn. and U.S. Dist. Ct. District of Conn.; 1989, U.S. Tax Ct.; 1990, U.S. Ct. of Federal Claims. *Education:* Fairfield Univ. (B.A., magna cum laude, 1978); College of William and Mary (J.D., 1981); Boston Univ. (LL.M., in Taxation, 1990). Phi Alpha Delta; Order of Barristers. Fellow: Am. College of Trust & Estate Counsel. Member, Exec. Comm., Estates and Probate Section, Tax Section and Business Law Section, Conn. Bar Assoc.; Member, Real Property, Probate and Trust Law Section, Law Practice Mgt. Section, Amer. Bar Assoc. ***PRACTICE AREAS:*** Trusts and Estates; Probate; Taxation; Business Law; Corporate Law; Partnership Law; Limited Liability Company Law; Exempt Organizations; Federal Tax Controversies. ***Email:*** rmarone@murthalaw.com

PAUL R. McCARY, born New London, Conn., 1952; admitted to bar, 1979, Conn. *Education:* Univ. of Conn. (B.A., 1974); Western New England

(This Listing Continued)

MURTHA CULLINA LLP, Hartford—Continued

College (J.D., magna cum laude, 1979). Author: "Cogeneration in Connecticut," 59 Conn. Bar Journal 365, Oct., 1985. Law Clerk to The Hon. Leo Parskey, Conn. Supreme Court, 1980-1981. ***PRACTICE AREAS:*** Public Utilities Law; Energy Law. ***Email:*** pmccary@murthalaw.com

HUGH P. McGEE, JR., born Boston, Mass., 1943; admitted to bar, 1972, Conn. *Education:* Dartmouth College (A.B., with distinction, 1965); Univ. of Conn. (J.D., with high honors, 1972); Trinity College (M.A., Economics, 1984). Member, Exec. Comm., Business Law Section, Conn. Bar Assoc. [LT.jg. U.S. Navy, 1966-1969]. ***PRACTICE AREAS:*** Corporate Law; Non-Stock Corporations; Commercial Law. ***Email:*** hmcgee@murthalaw.com

MARTHA E. MENG (See New Haven listing for Biography).

NATALE A. MESSINA, born New York, N.Y., 1952; admitted to bar, 1981, Conn. and U.S. Dist. Ct., Dist. of Conn.; 1984, U.S. Tax Ct. *Education:* Univ. of Conn. (B.S., cum laude, 1974; J.D., 1981); Boston Univ. (LL.M., Taxation, 1987). Certified Public Accountant, Connecticut, 1976. Past-Adjunct Professor of Taxation: University of Hartford; Quinnipiac College. Member, Tax Sec. Conn. Bar Assn.; Member, Tax Sec. Amer. Bar Assn. *Member:* Connecticut Society of Certified Public Accountants (Federal Tax Committee); American Institute of Certified Public Accountants (Member, Tax Section); American Association of Attorney/CPA's; Estate & Business Planning Council of Hartford; Conn. Estate and Tax Planning Council. ***PRACTICE AREAS:*** Business Law; Corporate Law; Federal Tax Controversies; Limited Liability Company Law; Partnership Law; Probate; Taxation; Trusts and Estates. ***Email:*** nmessina@murthalaw.com

HUGH F. MURRAY, III, born Arlington, Mass., 1965; admitted to bar, 1990, Mass.; 1991 Me. and Conn. *Education:* Harvard Univ. (A.B., cum laude, 1987); Boston College Law School (J.D., magna cum laude, 1990). Law Clerk to Hon. Joseph R. Nolan, Mass. Supreme Judicial Court, 1990-1991; Law Clerk to Hon. Thomas J. Meskill, U.S. Court of Appeals, 2nd Circuit, 1991-1992. Member: Am. Bar Assoc., Equal Employment Opportunities Subcomm. ***PRACTICE AREAS:*** Labor Law; Employment Litigation. ***Email:*** hmurray@murthalaw.com

EVERETT E. NEWTON, born Hartford, Conn., 1948; admitted to bar, 1986, Conn. *Education:* Univ. of Hartford (B.S., cum laude, 1976); Univ. of Conn. (M.B.A., 1980; J.D., with high honors, 1986). Law Clerk to Hon. Thomas J. Meskill, U.S. Court of Appeals, 2nd Circuit, 1986-1987. ***PRACTICE AREAS:*** Litigation; Appeals. ***Email:*** enewton@murthalaw.com

LISSA J. PARIS, born Paterson, N.J., 1950; admitted to bar, 1978, N.Y.; 1979, Conn. *Education:* Univ. of Chicago (B.A., 1972); Yale Univ. (J.D., 1977). Phi Beta Kappa. Member, Am. Bar Assoc., Employee Benefits Subcomm., Labor and Employment Section. ***PRACTICE AREAS:*** Employment and ERISA Litigation. ***Email:*** lparis@murthalaw.com

WILLARD F. PINNEY, JR., born Springfield, Mass., 1943; admitted to bar, 1968, Conn. *Education:* Yale Univ. (B.A., 1965); Univ. of Mich. (J.D., cum laude, 1968). Member, 1976—, and Chair., 1988-1999, Securities Advisory Council of the Conn. Dept. of Banking; Member, Exec. Comm. and Chair., 1994-1996, Business Law Section, Conn. Bar Assoc. ***PRACTICE AREAS:*** Corporate Law; Securities Law. ***Email:*** wpinney@murthalaw.com

DAVID PLATT, born Lewiston, Me., 1961; admitted to bar, 1987, Conn.; 2000, Mass. *Education:* Univ. of Vermont (B.S., 1983); S.U.N.Y. at Buffalo (J.D., 1987). Member, Environmental Law and Planning and Zoning Law Sections, Conn. Bar Assoc.; Environment, Energy and Resources and Litigation Sections, Am. Bar Assoc. ***PRACTICE AREAS:*** Environmental Law; Litigation; Land Use Law; Land Conservation Law. ***Email:*** dplatt@murthalaw.com

R. WILLIAM REINSMITH, born Pipestone, Mn, 1936; admitted to bar, 1961, Conn.; 1962, U.S. Court of Military Appeals; registered to practice before U.S. Patent and Trademark Office. *Education:* South Dakota School of Mines and Technology (B.S.M.E., 1958); Yale Univ. (LL.B., 1961). *Member:* American Intellectual Property Law Association. ***PRACTICE AREAS:*** Intellectual Property; Copyrights; Patent and Trademark; Foreign Patents and Trademarks. ***Email:*** wreinsmith@murthalaw.com

STEPHEN E. RONAI (See New Haven listing for Biography).

FRANK J. SACCOMANDI, III, born Philadelphia, Pa., 1955; admitted to bar, 1980, Penn.; 1984, Conn. *Education:* Temple Univ. (B.A., summa cum laude, 1977); Univ. of Penn. (J.D., magna cum laude, 1980). ***PRACTICE AREAS:*** Commercial; Real Estate Law; Commercial Finance Law. ***Email:*** fsaccomandi@murthalaw.com

BARBARA A. SARRANTONIO, born Hartford, Conn., 1947; admitted to bar, 1985, Conn. *Education:* Univ. of Hartford (A.S., 1967; B.A., magna cum laude, 1982); Univ. of Conn. (J.D., with high honors, 1985). Member: Exec. Comm., Real Property Section (Secretary, 1993-1995; Treasurer, 1995-1997; Vice Chair, 1997-1999, Chair, 1999-2001); Commercial Law Section, Conn. Bar Assoc. Member, Comm. on Foreclosure and Related Remedies, Am. Bar Assoc. ***PRACTICE AREAS:*** Commercial Real Estate Law; Commercial Finance Law. ***Email:*** bsarrantonio@murthalaw.com

GREGORY A. SHARP, born Jersey City, N.J., 1944; admitted to bar, 1978, Conn.; 1982, U.S. Court of Appeals, 2nd Circuit; 1996; U.S. Supreme Court. *Education:* Dartmouth College (B.A., 1967); Yale Univ. (M.F.S., 1969); Univ. of Conn. (J.D., 1978). Author: "1995 Legislation Opens New Era of Environmental Regulation," Conn. Lawyer, Aug./Sept. 1995; "DEP Adopts Comprehensive Clean-up Regulations," Conn. Lawyer, Mar. 1996; "The 1996 Amendments to the Inland Wetlands and Watercourses Act: A Municipal Perspective," The Habitat, Jan. 1997. Adjunct Lecturer in Environmental Law, Univ. of Conn. School of Law. Member, 1985-1994, Chair., 1985-1991, Conn. Council on Environmental Quality. Dept. of Env. Protection, Long Island Sound Fund Advisory Comm., 1993—. Member, Administrative Law, Planning and Zoning (Exec. Comm., 1997—), Conservation and Environmental Law (Exec. Comm., 1981—; Chair., 1987-1990) Sections, Conn. Bar Assoc. Member, Litigation, Environment, Energy and Natural Resources Law (Vice Chair, Water Quality and Wetlands Comm., 2000—) Sections, Am. Bar Assoc. ***PRACTICE AREAS:*** Environmental Law; Site Remediation; Environmental Enforcement; Water Resource and Wetlands Regulation. ***Email:*** gsharp@murthalaw.com

JAMES H. SHULMAN, born Hartford, Conn., 1946; admitted to bar, 1971, Conn.; 1972, Dist. of Columbia. *Education:* George Washington Univ. (B.A., 1968; J.D., with honors, 1971). Exec. Vice President and Gen. Counsel, Ahold Real Estate Company, 1993-1996. Member: Int'l Council of Shopping Centers (ICSC), 1993—; Real Property, Planning and Zoning Law, Conn. Bar Assn. ***PRACTICE AREAS:*** Commercial Real Estate Law; Zoning and Land Planning. ***Email:*** jshulman@murthalaw.com

ALFRED E. SMITH, JR. (See New Haven listing for Biography).

RICHARD S. SMITH, JR., born Hartford, Conn., 1959; admitted to bar, 1984, Conn. *Education:* Duke Univ. (A.B., 1981); Washington Univ.; Duke Univ. (J.D., with honors, 1984). Member, Exec. Comm., Business Law Section (Asst. Secy., 1994-1997; Secy, 1997-1998, Vice Chair, 1998—), Conn. Bar Assoc., 1994—; Chair, Task Force on Conn. Business Trusts, 1994—. ***PRACTICE AREAS:*** Corporate Law; Securities Law; Mergers and Acquisitions; Divestitures. ***Email:*** rsmith@murthalaw.com

SARA R. STADLER (See New Haven listing for Biography).

ELIZABETH J. STEWART (See New Haven listing for Biography).

MARK R. SUSSMAN, born Brooklyn, N.Y., 1952; admitted to bar, 1977, Penn.; 1980, Dist. of Columbia; 1981, Conn. *Education:* Tufts Univ. (B.S., summa cum laude, 1974); Univ. of Penn. (J.D., cum laude, 1977). Author: "Air Pollution Control," Chapter in Kosloff & Batchelor, Conn. Environmental Practice, 1996. Atty, U.S. Dept. of Justice, Land and Natural Resources Div., 1977-1981. Member, Chair., 1984-1987, Exec. Comm, 1982—, Environmental Law Section, Conn. Bar Assoc.; Conn. Business & Industry Assoc. (Chair, Air Task Force, 2001—). ***PRACTICE AREAS:*** Environmental Law. ***Email:*** msussman@murthalaw.com

LOUIS B. TODISCO (See New Haven listing for Biography).

BARRY J. WATERS (See New Haven listing for Biography).

ROBERT A. WHITE, born Philadelphia, Pa., 1948; admitted to bar, 1976, N.Y.; 1979, Conn. *Education:* Tufts Univ. (B.A., 1970); Univ. of Chicago; New York Univ. (J.D., 1975). Woodrow Wilson Fellow. Member, Exec. Comm., Commercial Law and Bankruptcy Section, Conn. Bar Assoc.; Chair, Environmental and Mass Torts Subcomm., Business Bankruptcy Comm., Am. Bar Assoc.; Member, Alternative Dispute Resolution, Conn. Bar Assoc. *Member:* Am. Bankruptcy Institute. (Certified Specialist, Business Bankruptcy Law, American Bankruptcy Board of Certification). ***PRACTICE AREAS:*** Bankruptcy; Creditors' Rights and Commercial Litigation; Alternative Dispute Resolution. ***Email:*** rwhite@murthalaw.com

JOHN C. YAVIS, JR., born New Haven, Conn., 1936; admitted to bar, 1961, Conn. *Education:* Univ. of Conn. (B.A., 1957); Yale Univ. (LL.B., 1961). Fellow, Am. College of Trial Lawyers. Member, Exec. Comm., Construction Law Section, Conn. Bar Assoc., 1989—. ***PRACTICE AREAS:*** Litigation; Government Contracts Law; Construction Law. ***Email:*** jyavis@murthalaw.com

MICHAEL A. ZIZKA, born Willimantic, Conn., 1954; admitted to bar, 1982, Conn. *Education:* Rensselaer Polytechnic Institute (B.S., in Geology, cum laude, 1975); Univ. of Conn. (M.S., in Geology, 1978; J.D., with honors, 1982). Adjunct Faculty: Univ. of Conn. Dept. of Natural Resources Management and Engineering. Author: "What's Legally Required?: A Guide to the Legal Rules for Making Local Land-Use Decisions," Conn. Dept. of Environmental Protection (6th ed. 1997). Co-Author: "State and Local Government Land Use Liability," West Group (1997). ***PRACTICE AREAS:*** Environmental; Land Use Law; Municipal Law; Litigation. ***Email:*** mzizka@murthalaw.com

COUNSEL

RUSSELL L. BRENNEMAN, born Springfield, Ill., 1928; admitted to bar, 1953, Dist. of Columbia; 1956, Conn. *Education:* The Ohio State Univ. (B.A.,

(This Listing Continued)

1950); Harvard Univ. (LL.B., 1953). Lecturer in Law, Univ. of Conn. School of Law, 1979-1989. Pres., Conn. Resources Recovery Authority, 1976-1980. Special Counsel, Commissioner of Environmental Protection, Conn., 1972-1973. Member, 1974-1994 and Chair., 1975-1976, Conn. Energy Advisory Board. Chair., Conn. Greenways Comm., 1992-1995. Co-Reporter, Uniform Conservation Easements Act, Nat'l Conference of Commissioners on Uniform State Laws, 1976-1981. Chair., Comm. on Historic Preservation and Easements, Section on Real Property, Probate and Trusts, Am. Bar Assoc., 1982-1985. Member, Internatl. Council of Environmental Law, 1977—. ***PRACTICE AREAS:*** Environmental Law. ***Email:*** rbrenneman@murthalaw.com

WILLIAM M. CULLINA, born Hartford, Conn., 1921; admitted to bar, 1948, Conn. *Education:* Catholic Univ. of America (A.B., 1942); Yale Univ. (LL.B., 1948). Phi Beta Kappa. Member: Labor and Employment Law Section, Am. Bar Assoc. ***PRACTICE AREAS:*** Labor and Employment Law; Health Care Law. ***Email:*** wcullina@murthalaw.com

MICHAEL J. DONNELLY, born Bridgeport, Conn., 1963; admitted to bar, 1990, Conn. *Education:* Washington Univ.; College of the Holy Cross (B.A., 1985); Univ. of Conn. (J.D., cum laude, 1990). ***PRACTICE AREAS:*** Litigation; Environmental Litigation. ***Email:*** mdonnell@murthalaw.com

CHARLES E. DRUMMEY, born Hartford, Conn., 1933; admitted to bar, 1974, Conn. *Education:* Yale Univ. (B.A., 1954); Univ. of Conn. (J.D., 1974). ***PRACTICE AREAS:*** Estate Planning Law; Estate and Trust Administration Law. ***Email:*** cdrummey@murthalaw.com

JULIE FAIRCHILD GREY, born New Haven, Conn., 1962; admitted to bar, 1988, Conn. *Education:* Wheaton College (B.A., cum laude, 1984); Suffolk Univ. Law School (J.D., 1988). Editor, Transnational Law Journal. ***PRACTICE AREAS:*** Commercial Real Estate; Transactional. ***Email:*** jgrey@murthalaw.com

BRANDON J. HICKEY, born New Britain, Conn., 1930; admitted to bar, 1957, Conn. *Education:* Yale Univ. (B.A., 1952; LL.B., 1957); Certificate, Sorbonne, 1951. ***Email:*** bhickey@murthalaw.com

MICHAEL T. KOGUT, born Ludlow, Mass, 1955; admitted to bar, 1981, Mass.; 1984, U.S. Dist. Court, Dist. of Mass. (Not admitted in Connecticut). *Education:* Springfield College (B.A., summa cum laude, 1976); Western New England School of Law (J.D., 1980). Phi Delta Phi. Charter Member, Archibald Cox Inn, 1979. Adjunct Faculty, Western New England College School of Business, 1986-1989; Western New England College School of Law, 1989-1992. Assistant District Attorney, Worcester County, Mass, 1981-1983. Assistant Attorney General, Commonwealth of Mass, 1983-1986. Director, Mass. Medicaid Fraud Control Unit, 1991-1996. Corp. Counsel, City of Springfield, Mass., 1996. Assistant Attorney General, Mass for Elder Protection, 1997-1999. *Member:* Hampden County and Mass. (Member, Health Law Section) Bar Assocs.; The Assoc. of Trial Lawyers of Amer; Ameri. Health Lawyers Assoc. ***PRACTICE AREAS:*** Health Care Regulation; Health Care Litigation; Long Term Care Facilities; Health Care Fraud; Abuse Counseling. ***Email:*** mkogut@murthalaw.com

JAMES B. LYON, born New York, N.Y., 1930; admitted to bar, 1955, Conn. *Education:* Amherst College (B.A., 1952); Yale Univ. (LL.B., Phi Beta Kappa, 1955). Lecturer 1994 and 1995: Conferences on Tax Planning for the Charitable Sector, N.Y. Univ. on Federal Taxation. Member: Comm. on Exempt Organizations, Section on Taxation, 1982—; Chair., Subcomm. on Museums and Other Cultural Organizations, Am. Bar Assoc. Editorial Board Conn. Law Trib.; Am. Law Institute. Fellow: Am. College of Tax Counsel; Am. Bar Foundation. ***PRACTICE AREAS:*** Tax Exempt Organizations Law; Corporate Income Tax Law; State and Local Tax Law. ***Email:*** jlyon@murthalaw.com

JOHN S. MURTHA, born Hartford, Conn., 1913; admitted to bar, 1938, Conn. *Education:* Yale Univ. (B.A., 1935; LL.B., 1938). Fellow, Am. College of Trial Lawyers. ***Email:*** jmurtha@murthalaw.com

DONALD P. RICHTER, born New Britain, Conn., 1924; admitted to bar, 1951, N.Y.; 1953, Conn. *Education:* Bates College (A.B., 1947); Yale Univ. (LL.B., 1950). Phi Beta Kappa. Member, Exec. Comm., Section on Taxation, Conn. Bar Assoc., 1977—. Member, Section on Taxation, Am. Bar Assoc. Fellow, Am. College of Trust and Estate Counsel. ***PRACTICE AREAS:*** Corporate Law; Estate Planning Law; Taxation Law. ***Email:*** drichter@murthalaw.com

MICHAEL SUDARSKY, born Hartford, Conn., 1924; admitted to bar, 1950, N.Y.; 1951, Conn. *Education:* Yale Univ. (B.A., 1947); Columbia Univ. (LL.B., 1950). ***PRACTICE AREAS:*** Corporate Law; Mergers and Acquisitions Law; Estate and Trust Administration Law. ***Email:*** msudarsky@murthalaw.com

ROBERT W. SULLIVAN, born Hartford, Conn., 1944; admitted to bar, 1969, Conn.; 1985, U.S. District Court, District of Conn. *Education:* Yale Univ. (B.A., 1966); Univ. of Connecticut School of Law (J.D., 1969). ***PRACTICE AREAS:*** Real Estate; Land Use; Construction; Financing. ***Email:*** rsullivan@murthalaw.com

PHILIP J. TELLERINE, born Elmont, New York, 1956; admitted to bar, 1982, CA; 1983, U.S. Dist. Ct., Central Dist. of CA and U.S. Tax Court; 2001 Conn. *Education:* State Univ. of NY at Stony Brook (B.A., 1978); Southwestern Univ. School of Law (J.D., 1982); Georgetown Univ. (LL.M., in Taxation, 1983). *Member:* Los Angeles County and American (Member, Taxation Section) Bar Associations; The State Bar of California. ***PRACTICE AREAS:*** Trusts and Estates; Closely Held Business Law; Federal Taxation. ***Email:*** ptellerine@murthalaw.com

ASSOCIATES

DIANE C. BELLANTONI, born Yonkers, N.Y., 1960; admitted to bar, 1995, Conn. *Education:* Stockton State College (B.S., with high honors, 1982); State Univ. of N.Y. at Stony Brook (M. S., 1987); Univ. of Conn. (J.D., with honors, 1995). ***Email:*** dbellatoni@murthalaw.com

MARVIN P. BELLIS, born New Haven, Conn., 1962; admitted to bar, 1998, Conn. and U.S. Dist. Ct., Dist. of Conn. *Education:* Southern Conn. State Univ. (B.S., 1989); Univ. of Conn. School of Law (J.D., 1998). Member: Environmental Law Section, Planning & Zoning Section, Litigation Section and Young Lawyer's Section, Conn. Bar Assoc., 1998—; Natural Resources, Energy and Environmental Law Section and International Environmental Law Section, Am. Bar Assoc., 1998—. ***LANGUAGES:*** German. ***Email:*** mbellis@murthalaw.com

MATTHEW J. BUDZIK, born New London, Conn., 1965; admitted to bar, 1998, Conn. and U.S. Dist. Ct., Dist. of Conn. *Education:* Am. Univ. (B.A., 1987); Georgetown Univ. (J.D., 1998). ***Email:*** mbudzik@murthalaw.com

SHARON L. CODEANNE, born New Haven, Conn., 1967; admitted to bar, 1994, Conn.; 1995, N.Y. *Education:* Trinity College (B.A., 1989); Pace Univ. (J.D., 1994). Notes and Comments Editor, Pace Environmental Law Review. ***Email:*** scodeanne@murthalaw.com

JENNIFER MORGAN DelMONICO (See New Haven listing for Biography).

JEAN C. FUNG, born San Jose, Ca., 1969; admitted to bar, 1995, Ca.; 1998, Conn. *Education:* Stanford Univ. (A.B./B.S., 1992); Boalt Hall School of Law, Univ. of Ca., Berkeley (J.D., 1995). Recipient, Ellis J. Harmon Environmental Law Writing Competition Award, Boalt Hall School of Law, Univ. of Ca., Berkeley. 1994-1995. Articles Editor, High Technology Law Journal, 1993-1994. Author: "KFC Western Inc. v. Meghrig: The Merits and Implications of Awarding Restitution to Citizen Plaintiffs Under RCRA §6972 (a)(1)(B)," Ecol. Law Quarterly, Vol. 22, No. 4, 1995. *Member:* State Bar of Ca. (Member, Environmental Section, 1995—). ***LANGUAGES:*** Chinese. ***Email:*** jfung@murthalaw.com

SUSAN L. GAETANO, born New York, N.Y., April 22, 1970; admitted to bar, 2000, Conn. *Education:* Rensselaer Polytechnic Institute (B.S., magna cum laude, 1992); Univ. of Conn. (J.D., high honors, 2000). ***Email:*** sgaetano@murthalaw.com

MICHAEL C. HARRINGTON, born Springfield, Mass., 1969; admitted to bar, 1995, Conn.; 1997, U.S. Dist. Ct., Dist. of Conn.; 2000, U.S. Ct. of Appeals, 2nd Cir. *Education:* McGill Univ. (B.Comm., great distinction, 1991); Syracuse Univ. (J.D., summa cum laude, 1995). Member: Justinian Honorary Law Society, 1994; Order of Barristers, 1995; Order of the Coif, 1995. Law Clerk to The Hon. Robert I. Berdon, Conn. Supreme Court. ***Email:*** mharrington@murthalaw.com

ALICE M. S. HOOTSMANS, born Boston, Mass., 1963; admitted to bar, 1989, Mass.; 1997, Conn. *Education:* Harvard University (B.A., cum laude, 1986; J.D., 1989). Co-Author: "Tax, Fraud and Other Concerns in Joint Ventures," 24 Conn. Law Trib. 38, 1998. ***Email:*** ahootsmans@murthalaw.com

NICOLE A. F. INGLE, born Mattoon, Ill., 1972; admitted to bar, 1998, Conn. *Education:* Univ. of Va. (B.A., with distinction, 1995; J.D., 1998). Co-Author: "Workouts for Distressed Continuing Care Retirement Communities," The Practical Real Estate Lawyer, V.14, No.4, July 1998. Member, Real Estate Section, Conn. Bar Assoc., 1998-1999. ***Email:*** ningle@murthalaw.com

JENNIFER D. JANELLE, born New Haven, Conn., 1972; admitted to bar, 1997, Conn.; 1998, Mass. *Education:* Boston Univ. (B.A., cum laude, 1994; J.D., 1997). Golden Key National Honor Society; G. Joseph Tauro Scholar. *Member:* Conn. Bar Assoc. (Public Utility Law Sect.). ***Email:*** jjanelle@murthalaw.com

RACHEL SNOW KINDSETH (See New Haven listing for Biography).

ANDREW W. LORD, born Manchester, Conn., 1961; admitted to bar, 1996, Conn. *Education:* Univ. of Maine (B.S., 1982); Univ. of Conn. (J.D., 1996). Recipient: Gerald F. Stevens Memorial Award for Excellence in Environmental Law. ***Email:*** alord@murthalaw.com

MICHAEL E. McDONOUGH, born Tacoma, Wash., 1963; admitted to bar, 1997, Conn. *Education:* Univ. of Conn. (B.A., 1986; M.A., 1989; J.D., with high honors, 1997). *Member:* Nat'l Assoc. of Bond Lawyers; Conn. Govt. Finance Officers Assoc. ***Email:*** mmcdonough@murthalaw.com

(This Listing Continued)

MURTHA CULLINA LLP, Hartford—Continued

LAURIE K. MOLINARI, born Hartford, Conn., 1964; admitted to bar, 1994, Conn. *Education:* Mount Holyoke College (B.A., cum laude, 1986); Univ. of Conn. School of Law (J.D., 1994). ***Email:*** lmolinari@murthalaw.com

KARI L. OLSON, born Hartford, Conn., 1963; admitted to bar, 1998, Conn. *Education:* Univ. of Conn. (B.S., cum laude, 1985); Univ. of Conn. School of Law (J.D., with high honors, 1998). Phi Delta Phi (Vice Magister, 1996-1997). ***Email:*** kolson@murthalaw.com

AARON SARRA, born New Britain, Connecticut, May 5, 1971; admitted to bar, 2001, Connecticut. *Education:* Liberty University (B.S., cum laude, 1994); University of Dayton (J.D., 1999). *Member:* Connecticut Bar Association. ***Email:*** asarra@murthalaw.com

ROBERT L. SCANLON, born New York, N.Y., 1967; admitted to bar, 1999, Conn. *Education:* Univ. of Conn. (B.A., 1990); Univ. of Conn. School of Law (J.D., with honors, 1999). *Member:* Conn. Bar Assoc. (Business Law Sect.). ***Email:*** rscanlon@murthalaw.com

EDWARD B. WHITTEMORE, born New York, N.Y., 1968; admitted to bar, 1995, Conn.; 1996, N.Y. and D.C. *Education:* Dartmouth College (B.A., 1990); George Washington Univ. (J.D., cum laude, 1995). *Member:* Conn. and Amer. Bar Assocs. (Business Law Sects.). ***Email:*** ewhittemore@murthalaw.com

SETH M. WILSON, born 1971; admitted to bar, 1998, Mass.; 1999, Conn.; 2000, U.S. Dist. Court, Dist of Mass.; registered to practice before USPTO. *Education:* College of William & Mary (B.S., Chemistry, 1994); Western New England College (J.D., magna cum laude, 1998). Staff, Senior Articles Editor, Western New England Law Review. Law Clerk to the Hon. Frank H. Freedman, Sr. Judge U.S. Dist. Court, Dist. of Mass. ***LANGUAGES:*** French. ***Email:*** swilson@murthalaw.com

All members, counsel and associates are members of Connecticut and American Bar Associations.

REPRESENTATIVE CLIENTS: Ahold Real Estate Co.; Anold U.S.A., Inc.; AT&T Broadband; Town of Avon; Central Connecticut Health Alliance, Inc.; Charter Communications, Inc.; Connecticut Association of Health Care Facilities, Inc.; Connecticut Business and Industry Assn.; Connecticut Resources Recovery Authority; Cox Communications; Danaher Corporation; E.I. du Pont de Nemours and Co.; ESPN, Inc.; Enron Corp.; Fleet Bank; H.N.S. Management Company, Inc. (Connecticut Transit); John Deere; Kaman Corp.; Lydall, Inc.; MBIA-Municipal Investors Service Corporation; Mercedes-Benz Credit Corp.; The Milford Hospital, Inc.; New Haven Register; O & G Industries, Inc.; Saint Francis Hospital and Medical Center; The Sharon Hospital, Inc.; South Central Connecticut Regional Water Authority; Spirol International Corp.; Stop & Shop Cos., Inc.; SunBridge Healthcare Corporation; Tilcon, Inc.; Trinity College; Tweed New Haven Airport Authority; U.S. Generating Co.; United Parcel Service of America, Inc.; United Technologies Corp.; United Way of the Capitol Area, Inc.; Westinghouse Electric Corp.; Winn Development Co.; Yale University.

NAIR & LEVIN, P.C.

HARTFORD, CONNECTICUT

(See Bloomfield)

Commercial Litigation, Collections, General Practice, Bankruptcy, Personal Injury, Creditors' Rights, Real Estate.

LAW OFFICES OF MARC N. NEEDELMAN

HARTFORD, CONNECTICUT

(See Bloomfield)

General Practice. Trials in all Courts. Real Estate, Corporate and Commercial, Personal Injury, Criminal, Municipal, Workers Compensation, Zoning, Domestic and Family, Landlord and Tenant.

LAW OFFICES OF ELIOT J. NERENBERG

HARTFORD, CONNECTICUT

(See West Hartford)

Family Law, Divorce, Child Custody, Divorce Mediation.

NIXON PEABODY LLP

CITY PLACE
185 ASYLUM STREET
HARTFORD, CONNECTICUT 06103
Telephone: 860-275-6820
FAX: 860-275-6821
Email: nixonpeabody@nixonpeabody.com
URL: http://www.nixonpeabody.com

Rochester, New York Office: Clinton Square. Telephone: 716-263-1000. Fax: 716-263-1600.
New York, N.Y. Office: 437 Madison Avenue. Telephone: 212-940-3000. Fax: 212-940-3111.
Washington, D.C. Office: 401 9th Street, N.W., Suite 900. Telephone: 202-585-8000. Fax: 202-585-8080.
Garden City, New York Office: 990 Stewart Avenue. Telephone: 516-832-7500. Fax: 516-832-7555.
Buffalo, New York Office: 1600 Main Place Tower. Telephone: 716-853-8100. Fax: 716-853-8109.
Boston, Massachusetts Office: 101 Federal Street. Telephone: 617-345-1000. Fax: 617-345-1300.
Manchester, New Hampshire Office: 889 Elm Street. Telephone: 603-628-4000. Fax: 603-628-4040.
Providence, Rhode Island Office: One Citizens Plaza. Telephone: 401-454-1000. Fax: 401-454-1030.
McLean, Virginia Office: 8180 Greensboro Drive, Suite 800. Telephone: 703-790-9110. Telecopier: 703-883-0370.
Costa Mesa, California Office: 600 Anton Boulevard, Suite 1600, 92626. Telephone: 714-241-0101. Fax: 714-241-0105.
San Francisco, California Office: Two Embarcadero Center, Suite 2700, 94111-3996. Telephone: 415-984-8200. Fax: 415-984-8300.

General Practice with an emphasis on Public Finance.

FIRM PROFILE: Nixon Peabody LLP is a general practice law firm that offers services in complex multijurisdictional and International matters involving antitrust, corporate and business law, bank regulatory law, bankruptcy, commercial lending, commercial litigation, employee benefits and labor and employment law, environmental law, estate planning and administration, franchising, healthcare law, housing and community development and syndication, loan enforcement, project finance, public finance, public utilities and energy law, real estate, securities law, tax law, and technology and intellectual property.

PARTNER

ALPHONSO E. TINDALL, JR., born Pittsburgh, Pennsylvania, 1955; admitted to bar, 1985, Connecticut; 1987, New York. *Education:* St. Olaf College (B.A., 1976); University of Connecticut (J.D., 1981). Member, Advisory Board, The Ronald H. Brown Foundation, 1997—. *Member:* The Association of the Bar of The City of New York; New York State, Connecticut, National and American Bar Associations; The National Association of Securities Professionals (Chairman, 1993—). (Also at New York, New York Office). ***Email:*** atindall@nixonpeabody.com

(For biographical data on other personnel, see Professional Biographies at Rochester, New York, New York, New York, Washington, D.C., Albany, New York, Garden City, New York, Buffalo, New York, Boston, Massachusetts, Manchester, New Hampshire, Providence, Rhode Island and McLean, Virginia)

NOBLE, YOUNG & O'CONNOR, P.C.

Established in 1994
1 CONGRESS STREET
HARTFORD, CONNECTICUT 06114-1067
Telephone: 860-525-9975
Fax: 860-525-9985
URL: http://www.nyolaw.com

Practice concentrating in the defense and trial of motor vehicle, premises liability, product liability, medical device and malpractice actions.

FIRM PROFILE: Noble, Young & O'Connor, P.C. specializes in the defense and trial of motor vehicle, premises liability, wrongful detention, product liability, municipal, law enforcement, environmental, pharmaceutical, medical device and malpractice actions. We recognize and are committed to providing the most cost effective, highest quality legal services to our clients.

Today's economic realities dictate that every defense activity be considered in relation to the value of a case and its necessity for the adequate preparation of a file. We accomplish this by maintaining a close dialogue with the file manager and developing a comprehensive defense strategy prior to undertaking any activity.

(This Listing Continued)

Our success in representing insureds, insurers, companies, organizations and municipalities in all stages of adversarial proceedings and the firm's trial experience permit us to offer the highest level of competence in any area of civil litigation.

Noble, Young & O'Connor, P.C. believes that fully serving our insurance clients means more than merely representing their insureds. We offer numerous seminars on a variety of subjects important to the insurance claims area and continually monitor the changing legislative and regulatory arenas in order to keep our clients informed. These seminars are offered to you at no expense. We would be pleased to discuss with you any topics of interest.

CESAR A. NOBLE, born Havana, Cuba, March 21, 1958; admitted to bar, 1983, Connecticut; 1984, U.S. District Court, District of Connecticut. *Education:* Wesleyan University (B.A., with honors, 1980); University of Connecticut (J.D., 1983). Author: "Offers of Judgment, C.G.S. Sec. 52-192," The Defense, Journal of The Connecticut Defense Lawyers Association, Vol. 6, No. 2; "The Continued Vitality of Joint & Several Liability," The Defense, Journal of The Connecticut Defense Lawyers Association, Vol. 8, No. 1; "ADR," The Defense, Journal of the Connecticut Defense Lawyers Association, Vol. 7, No. 3. *Member:* Hartford County and Connecticut Bar Associations; The Association of Trial Lawyers of America; Connecticut Defense Lawyers Association; Defense Research Institute. ***LANGUAGES:*** Spanish. ***PRACTICE AREAS:*** Insurance Defense; Products Liability; Medical Malpractice. ***Email:*** noble@nyolaw.com

ROBERT E. YOUNG, born Danbury, Connecticut, February 21, 1958; admitted to bar, 1984, Connecticut; 1985, U.S. District Court, District of Connecticut. *Education:* University of Connecticut; Western Connecticut State University (B.A., 1981); Western New England College School of Law (J.D., 1984). Phi Alpha Delta. Member, Defense Counsel Trial Academy, 1989. *Member:* Hartford County (Member, Insurance Section) and Connecticut (Member: Litigation Section; Professional Discipline Committee; Connecticut Lawyer Advisory Committee) Bar Associations; Connecticut Defense Lawyers Association; Defense Research Institute. ***PRACTICE AREAS:*** Insurance Defense; Products Liability; Medical Malpractice; Municipal Law; Law Enforcement; Insurance Coverage; Premises Liability; Wrongful Termination; Personal Injury. ***Email:*** young@nyolaw.com

DENNIS P. O'CONNOR, II, born Washington, D.C., January 31, 1955; admitted to bar, 1984, Connecticut; 1986, Maryland; 1987, U.S. District Court, District of Connecticut; 1990, U.S. District Court, District of New York. *Education:* Georgetown University (B.A., 1979; J.D., 1984). Phi Delta Phi. *Member:* Hartford County, Connecticut and American (Member, Sections on: Litigation; Insurance) Bar Associations. ***PRACTICE AREAS:*** Insurance Defense; Products Liability. ***Email:*** oconnor@nyolaw.com

---

JOHN H. HANKS, born Albany, New York, March 23, 1959; admitted to bar, 1987, Connecticut; 1988, U.S. District Court, District of Connecticut. *Education:* Princeton University (A.B., 1982); University of Connecticut (J.D., 1987). Member, Connecticut Bar Examining Committee. *Member:* Middlesex County, Connecticut and American Bar Associations. ***PRACTICE AREAS:*** Insurance Defense. ***Email:*** hanks@nyolaw.com

PETER J. BROWN, born New York, New York, January 30, 1960; admitted to bar, 1990, Connecticut and U.S. District Court, District of Connecticut. *Education:* Fairfield University (B.A., 1982); Western New England College (J.D., 1989). *Member:* Hartford County and Connecticut Bar Associations. ***PRACTICE AREAS:*** Insurance Defense; Personal Injury; Products Liability. ***Email:*** brown@nyolaw.com

AMELIA NORD, born Akron, Ohio, February 7, 1970; admitted to bar, 1997, Connecticut. *Education:* California State University at Long Beach (B.A., 1994); De Paul University (J.D., 1997). Phi Alpha Delta. *Member:* Connecticut and American Bar Associations. ***PRACTICE AREAS:*** Insurance Defense. ***Email:*** nord@nyolaw.com

ELIZABETH A. MORESHEAD, born Norwich, Connecticut, September 10, 1965; admitted to bar, 1993, Connecticut; 1994, Rhode Island and U.S. District Court, District of Connecticut. *Education:* Connecticut College (B.A., 1987); Quinnipiac College (J.D., 1993). Adjunct Faculty, Civil Litigation, University of Hartford, 1999—. *Member:* Hartford County, Connecticut (Member: House of Delegates, 1994-1997; Board of Governors, 1995-1997) and Rhode Island Bar Associations; Connecticut Trial Lawyers Association; Defense Research Institute. ***PRACTICE AREAS:*** Insurance Defense; Personal Injury; Products Liability. ***Email:*** moreshead@nyolaw.com

STEPHANIE P. TIBBETTS, born Worcester, Massachusetts, April 10, 1970; admitted to bar, 1997, Connecticut. *Education:* Catholic University (B.A., 1992); Pepperdine University (J.D., 1995). *Member:* American Bar Association. ***PRACTICE AREAS:*** Insurance Defense. ***Email:*** tibbetts@nyolaw.com

REPRESENTATIVE CLIENTS: Agency Rent-A-Car; Allstate Insurance Company; Altra Auto Rental; American International Group; Avis Rent-A-Car; Cal-Ark Industries, Inc.; Camrac, Inc.; City of Milford; Dollar Rent-A-Car; Elrac, Inc.; Enterprise Rent-A-Car Systems, Inc.; Gulf Insurance Co.; The Infinity Group; INS Insurance Company; McDonalds Corp.; National Auto Credit, Inc.; Nationwide Insurance Company; New London County Insurance Companies; Nobel Insurance Company; Progressive Insurance Companies; Quincy Mutual Insurance Company; Reliant Insurance Company; Replacement Rent-A-Car, Inc.; Safeco Insurance Companies; Schneider National Trucking Company; Snappy Rent-A-Car; Travelers Insurance Co.; United Financial Adjusting Co.

(This Listing Continued)

M. HATCHER NORRIS

254 PROSPECT AVENUE
HARTFORD, CONNECTICUT 06106-2041
Telephone: 860-236-6951
Fax: 860-236-5263
Email: rnorris@bnglaw.com

General Civil, Criminal, Trials and Appellate Practice in all State and Federal Courts. Personal Injury Law.

M. HATCHER NORRIS, born Paterson, New Jersey, October 22, 1949; admitted to bar, 1974, Connecticut and U.S. District Court, District of Connecticut; 1975, U.S. Court of Appeals, Second Circuit; 1978, U.S. District Court, District of Rhode Island; 1982, U.S. Supreme Court. *Education:* Rutgers University (B.A., 1971); University of Connecticut (J.D., 1974). Assistant U.S. Attorney, District of Connecticut, 1975-1978. Attorney Trial Referee, Superior Court, State of Connecticut, 1982—. Special Master, U.S. District Court, District of Connecticut, 1997—. *Member:* Hartford County and Connecticut (Chairman, Executive Committee and Criminal Law Section, 1998-2000) Bar Associations; Connecticut Trial Lawyers Association; The Association of Trial Lawyers of America; National Association of Criminal Defense Lawyers; Connecticut Criminal Defense Lawyers Association (President, 1993-1994); Connecticut Academy of Certified Trial Lawyers (Pres. 1994-1995). Certified as a Criminal and Civil Trial Advocate by the National Board of Trial Advocacy (Also Member of Butler, Norris & Gold).

O'BRIEN, SHAFNER, STUART, KELLY & MORRIS, P.C.

HARTFORD, CONNECTICUT

(See Groton)

Trials in all Courts. Personal Injury, Products Liability, Workers Compensation, Medical Malpractice, Corporations, Estate Planning, Probate, Trust Law, Real Estate, General Practice, Administrative and Admiralty Law.

O'BRIEN, TANSKI & YOUNG

CITYPLACE II
HARTFORD, CONNECTICUT 06103
Telephone: 860-525-2700
Telefax: 860-247-7861

Civil Trial and Appellate Practice, Healthcare Law and Professional Medical Liability. Negligence, Products Liability, Workers Compensation, Admiralty, Maritime. Trials in all Courts.

FIRM PROFILE: O'Brien, Tanski & Young was established in order to provide its clients with a unique smaller firm approach while providing high-quality legal representation reflecting the experience of larger firms. The firm has a broad-based civil litigation practice but is perhaps known the most for its risk management consulting, administrative and regulatory law, professional liability defense and hospital healthcare law. O'Brien, Tanski & Young extends statewide and in Western Massachusetts and is listed in the Bar Register of Preeminent Lawyers.

MEMBERS OF FIRM

JAMES M. TANSKI, born Bristol, Connecticut, February 11, 1946; admitted to bar, 1976, Connecticut, U.S. District Court, District of Connecticut and U.S. Court of Appeals, 2nd Circuit. *Education:* United States Military Academy (B.S., 1968); University of Connecticut (J.D., 1976). *Member:* Hartford County (Co-Chair, Legal-Medical Committee, 1999-2000) and Connecticut (Member, Committee on Professional Ethics, 1982-1983) Bar Associations; Defense Research and Trial Lawyers Association; Connecticut Defense Attorneys Association. [Capt., U.S. Army, 1968-1973]. ***PRACTICE AREAS:*** Medical Malpractice Defense; Health Care Law; Product Liability Defense; Civil Trial Practice; Insurance Defense Law; Personal Injury Law.

ROLAND F. YOUNG, III, born Norway, Maine, April 8, 1954; admitted to bar, 1979, Connecticut, U.S. Tax Court, U.S. District Court, District of Connecticut and U.S. Court of Appeals, Second Circuit. *Education:* Cornell University (B.A., 1976); University of Connecticut (J.D., 1979). Lecturer: Hartford Graduate Center "Hospital Risk Management - Hospital Administrative Law," New England Healthcare Assembly Faculty (1992-1997), Healthcare Financial Managers Assn., Connecticut Chapter, Contributing Editor "CT Scanner." Au-

(This Listing Continued)

O'BRIEN, TANSKI & YOUNG, Hartford—Continued

thor: "Legal Concepts: 'Loss of Chance' and Increase Risk of Future Harm,'" Viewpoint, Vol. 5, No. 3, October, 1992 (Young, R. and Silva, R.); "Hospitals and Product Liability," Viewpoint Vol. 5, No. 4, December, 1992 (Young R. and Grover, K.); "An Argument for Ex-Parte Communications with Treating Physicians," The Defense, Vol. 6, No. 2, December, 1989; "Confidentiality and Aids-Related Testing Under Connecticut Law," (Young, R. and Kasprak, J.), The Defense, Vol. 7, Nos. 1 and 2, Summer, Fall, 1990; "Confidentiality of Medical Records", - Seminar Booklet, 1989, 1992; "Limiting Damages in Civil Litigation," - Seminar Booklet, 1990; "Medical Malpractice in Connecticut," - Seminar Booklet, 1992, 2000; "Healthlaw Update: What's New in 1993," - Seminar Booklet, 1993; "Healthlaw Update: What's New in 1994," - Seminar Booklet, 1994; "Fair Debt Collection Practices Act," CT Scanner, Vol IV, No. 4, November, 1994 (Young, R. and Cox, J.); "The 'Super Lien'," The Connecticut Law Tribune, September, 1994 (Young, R., Anderson T., and Grover, K.); "The 'Super Lien' and You," CT Scanner Volume IV, No. 3, 1993/1994 February/March 1994 (Young, R., Anderson, T. and Grover, K.); "The Evolving Role of Placental Pathology in the Defense of Medical Negligence Claims," Viewpoint Vol. 6, No. 4, December 1993 (Young, R. and Goodusky, A.); "Litem Intendo - Litem Intendes (I sue, You sue)," The Connecticut Law Tribune, October, 1993; "Caveat Hospital: The Risks of Contracting with HMO's," Viewpoint Vol. 6, No. 1, February 1993 (Young, R. and Burgh, J.); "Time Will Tell on Tort Reform III," The Connecticut Law Tribune, September 18, 1995 (Young, R. and Schnog, C.); "A Legislative Update on the Status of Medical Malpractice Reform: A Lay Person's Version," CT Scanner, Sept./Oct. 1995 (Young, R and Nazarov, A.); "Emtala - Emergency Medical Treatment and Active Labor Act," CT Scanner, Vol. V, No. 4, May/June 1995 (Young, R. and Cox, J.); "Illegality Defense for Contracts," CT Scanner, Vol. V, No. 3, February/March 1995 (Young, R and Cox, J.); "IPA's: The Basics," CT Scanner, Vol. VI, No. 3, March 1996 (Young, R. and Feliciano, T.). Editor: Connecticut Society for Health Care Risk Management Policy Manual. Honors: Who's Who in Rising Young Americans, 1991; Who's Who in American Law, 1994; Who's Who in America, 1994-1995; Who's Who in Industry and Business, 1994-1995. *Member:* Hartford County Bar Association (Medico-Legal Liaison Committee); The American Society of Law and Medicine (1982-1998); American Academy of Hospital Attorneys (Chairman: Publications and Programs Subcommittee: Teaching Hospitals, 1991-1996); National Association of Health Law Attorneys (1996—); Connecticut Hospital Association; Defense Research Institute, Inc. (1984-1992); American College of Healthcare Executives (1993-1998); H.F.M.A. Connecticut Chapter (1994—). ***PRACTICE AREAS:*** Health Care Law; Civil Litigation; Medical Malpractice Defense; Insurance Defense; Personal Injury. ***Email:*** rf_young@otylaw.com

ROBERT D. SILVA, born Waterbury, Connecticut, December 6, 1964; admitted to bar, 1990, Connecticut; 1991, New York, Massachusetts and U.S. District Court, District of Connecticut. *Education:* University of Connecticut (B.S., in Accounting, 1986); University of Bridgeport (J.D., 1990). Phi Delta Phi. Recipient, American Jurisprudence Award in Trial Practice. *Member:* Hartford County and Connecticut Bar Associations. ***PRACTICE AREAS:*** Civil Litigation; Medical Malpractice Defense; Products Liability Defense.

HILARY FISHER NELSON, born New Milford, Connecticut, May 5, 1955; admitted to bar, 1986, Connecticut; U.S. District Court, District of Connecticut. *Education:* College of the Holy Cross (B.S., cum laude, 1977); Connecticut College (M.A., 1979); University of Connecticut (J.D., 1986). Author: "Medical Legal Update", The Unicorn Perinatal Newsletter, 15 Summer, 1998. Assistant Clinical Professor, Department of Community Medicine and Health Care, University of Connecticut School of Medicine, 1986—; Clinical Instructor Department of Psychiatry, University of Connecticut School of Medicine, 1986-1992. "Legal Aspects of Peer Review and Sentinel Events," Connecticut Primary Care Association, September 13, 2000; Legal Issues in Parental Nursing Woman & Infant's Health Nursing Symposium, University of Connecticut Health Center, May 10, 1999. Lecturer: "Legal Ramifications Shoulder Dystocia A Team Approach," Connecticut Perinatal Association, Inc., University of Connecticut School of Medicine, March 27, 1996; "Childbirth-Refusing Treatment," Medicolegal Link Rounds, Department of Obstetrics & Gynecology, University of Connecticut School of Medicine, May 1996; "Brain Damaged Infant," Medicolegal Link Rounds Department of Obstetrics and Gynecology, University of Connecticut School of Medicine, March 6, 1995 & April 3, 1991; "Legal and Ethical Issues in Childbirth," LEA Lecture/Discussion, University of Connecticut School of Medicine, January 18, 1995 & February 4, 1994. Presentation, "Legal and Ethical Aspects of Artificial Insemination in the United States., Institute de Recherche Juridiques Comparatives Conference November 13, 1985, Paris, France. Appellate Supreme Court Briefs: Scofield, G.R. and Nelson, H.F., Concern for Dying Amicus Curiae Brief for McDonnell v. Beverly Enterprises, (CV 13477, CV 13478 and CV 13479) State of Connecticut Supreme Court filed September 29, 1988. *Member:* Connecticut Bar Association; Connecticut Trial Lawyers Association; Connecticut Women in Healthcare Management (Member, Membership Committee, 1994—); Connecticut

(This Listing Continued)

Society for Healthcare Risk Management; Connecticut Defense Lawyers Association. ***PRACTICE AREAS:*** Medical Malpractice Defense; Product Liability; Health Law.

DONNA R. ZITO, born Hartford, Connecticut; admitted to bar, 1980, Connecticut and U.S. District Court, District of Connecticut. *Education:* Trinity College (B.A., 1974); University of Connecticut (J.D., cum laude, 1980). Recipient, American Jurisprudence Award, Constitutional Law. Law Clerk, Connecticut Superior Court and Appellate Session, 1980-1982. *Member:* Connecticut and American Bar Associations; The Association of Trial Lawyers of America; Defense Research Institute; Connecticut Defense Lawyers Association. ***PRACTICE AREAS:*** Medical Malpractice Defense; Civil Trial Practice.

ALBERT G. DANKER, JR., born Plainfield, New Jersey, April 13, 1955; admitted to bar, 1992, Connecticut; U.S. District Court, District of Connecticut. *Education:* Wesleyan University (B.A., 1977); Yale School of Medicine Physician Associate Program (Cert., 1981); University of Connecticut (J.D., 1992). Certified Physician Assistant, 1981-1994. *Member:* Hartford County Bar Association. ***PRACTICE AREAS:*** Litigation; Medical Malpractice Defense; Workers Compensation.

RICHARD A. O'CONNOR, born Bronx, New York, June 28, 1960; admitted to bar, 1985, Connecticut, U.S. District Court, District of Connecticut and U.S. Court of Appeals, Second Circuit. *Education:* Fairfield University (B.S., cum laude, 1982); Catholic University of America (J.D., 1985). Law Clerk, Connecticut Superior Court, 1985-1986. *Member:* Connecticut Bar Association (Member, Medical-Legal Committee); Connecticut Defense Lawyers Association; National Health Lawyers Association; Defense Research Institute; Raymond E. Baldwin American Inn of Court. ***PRACTICE AREAS:*** Medical Malpractice Defense; Civil Trial Practice.

COUNSEL

STEPHEN V. MANNING, born Melrose, Massachusetts, June 16, 1956; admitted to bar, 1982, Massachusetts; 1986, U.S. District Court, District of Massachusetts; 1987, U.S. Court of Appeals, First Circuit; 1990, U.S. District Court, District of Connecticut; 1991, U.S. Court of Appeals, Second Circuit; 2000, Connecticut. *Education:* The College of the Holy Cross (B.A., 1978); Suffolk University (J.D., cum laude, 1982). Staff Member, Suffolk University Law Review, 1981-1982. Recipient: American Jurisprudence Award, Contracts; American Jurisprudence Award, Trusts. Law Clerk to the Hon. T.F. Gilroy Daly, Chief U.S. District Judge, District of Connecticut, 1982-1984. Assistant U.S. Attorney, District of Connecticut, Criminal Division, 1989-1999. Appellate Supervisor, U.S. Attorney's Office, 1996-1999. Author: *Insurance Law - Intra-policy Stacking of Uninsured Motorist Coverage* - Taft v. Cerwonka, 433 A.2d 215 (R.I. 1981), 16 Suffolk U.L. Rev. 435 (1982); *Timing of Loss in Secured Loan Cases*, Federal Sentencing Reporter, Vol. 10, No. 3 (Nov./Dec. 1997) (with B. Jongbloed). *Member:* Hartford County and Connecticut Bar Associations. ***REPORTED CASES:*** United States v. Santopietro, 166 F.3d 88 (2d Cir. 1999); United States v. Ortiz, 143 F.3d 728 (2d Cir. 1998); United States v. Paul, 156 F.3d 403 (2d Cir. 1998); United States v. Larson, 112 F.3d 600 (2d Cir. 1997); United States v. Garcia, 56 F.3d 418 (2d Cir. 1995); United States v. Amato, 46 F.3d 1255 (2d Cir. 1995); United States v. Villeda, 764 F. Supp. 736 (D. Conn. 1991). ***PRACTICE AREAS:*** Civil Litigation; Appellate Practice; White Collar Criminal Defense. ***Email:*** sv_manning@otylaw.com

MELINDA S. MONSON, born Chicago, Illinois, September 29, 1959; admitted to bar, 1990, Connecticut; 1991, U.S. District Court, District of Connecticut. *Education:* Northern Illinois University (B.S.N., 1982; M.S.N., 1985); University of Bridgeport (J.D., 1990). Sigma Theta Tau. Associate Editor, University of Bridgeport Law Review, 1989-1990. Editorial Board, Journal of Nursing Law. Registered Nurse: Illinois, 1981-1985; Connecticut, 1985—. Author: "Physicians as Professional Peer Reviewers," The University of Bridgeport Law Review, 1990. Adjunct Professor, Western Connecticut State University. *Member:* Connecticut Bar Association; The Association of Trial Lawyers of America; The American Association of Nurse Attorneys; Connecticut Defense Lawyers Association; Connecticut Health Lawyers Association. ***PRACTICE AREAS:*** Medical Malpractice Defense; Civil Trial Practice; Health Law. ***Email:*** msm@otylaw.com

ASSOCIATE

AMY F. GOODUSKY, born New York, N.Y.; admitted to bar, 1996, Connecticut; 1997, U.S. District Court, District of Connecticut. *Education:* Hampshire College (B.A., 1978); University of Connecticut (J.D., 1996). *Member:* Hartford County and Connecticut Bar Associations; Lawyers Concerned for Lawyers. ***PRACTICE AREAS:*** Litigation; Medical Malpractice Defense; Workers Compensation.

OF COUNSEL

DONALD W. O'BRIEN, born New Britain, Connecticut, April 27, 1925; admitted to bar, 1951, District of Columbia and Connecticut; 1962, U.S. District Court, District of Connecticut, U.S. Court of Appeals, 2nd Circuit, U.S. Supreme Court and U.S. Court of Military Appeals. *Education:* Catholic Univer-

(This Listing Continued)

sity of America (B.A., cum laude, 1948); Georgetown University (J.D., 1951). Phi Delta Phi. Staff Member, Georgetown Law Journal, 1949-1951. Author: "Loss of Use of a Motor Vehicle As An Item of Damage," 38 Georgetown Law Journal 635, 1950. *Member:* Hartford County, Connecticut (Chairman, Veterans and Servicemen Affairs Committee, 1976-1979; Medical-Legal Committee, 1981—) and American Bar Associations; Defense Research Institute; Connecticut Defense Attorneys Association; Maritime Law Association of the United States; The Association of Trial Lawyers of America; Connecticut Trial Lawyers Association. [Lt. Col., USAF, 1943-1945; 1951-1969]. ***PRACTICE AREAS:*** Admiralty; Health Care Law; Civil Litigation.

REPRESENTATIVE CLIENTS: Hartford Hospital; St. Francis Hospital; Midstate Medical Center; University of Connecticut Health Center; Greenwich Hospital Assn.; New Britain General Hosp.; Bradley Memorial Medical Center; Gaylord Hospital; New Milford Hospital; Sharon Hospital; PHICO; M.I.I.X.; A.I.G.; St. Paul's; C.N.A.; C.M.I.C.; Nobel Insurance Co.; Bristol Hospital; State of Connecticut; National Amusements; Apple Healthcare.
APPROVED ATTORNEYS FOR: Chicago Title Insurance Co.; Lawyers Title Insurance Co.; St. Paul Insurance Cos.; Pro Select.

O'CONNELL, FLAHERTY & ATTMORE, L.L.C.

280 TRUMBULL STREET
HARTFORD, CONNECTICUT 06103-3598
Telephone: 860-548-1300
Facsimile: 860-548-0023;
Telecopier: 860-548-0023
Email: mac@ofalaw.com

Springfield, Massachusetts Office: 1350 Main Street. Telephone: 413-747-1773. Telecopier: 413-746-1529.
Moosup, Connecticut Office: 22 Main Street, 06354. Telephone: 860-564-4064. Telecopier: 860-564-1536.
Danbury, Connecticut Office: 50 Newtown Road, 06810. Telephone: 203-748-6632. Telecopier: 203-743-8823.
West Hartford, Connecticut Office: 993 Farmington Avenue, 06107. Telephone: 860-570-1004.
Old Saybrook, Connecticut Office: 163 Saybrook Road, 06457. Telephone: 860-388-6173. Telecopier: 860-388-6865.

Trials, State and Federal Courts. Family, Probate, Estate Planning, Taxation, Corporation, Real Estate, Insurance, Commercial, Criminal, Environmental, Labor, Zoning, Hazardous and Toxic Substances, Wetlands and Land Use, Health and Administrative Law, Indian Law.

FIRM PROFILE: The law firm of O'Connell, Flaherty & Attmore is a general practice firm serving clientele throughout Southern New England states. In its four offices, the firm has a balance of litigation, commercial and personal practitioners offering a broad spectrum of legal services. These include continuing commercial representation, acquisitions and sales of businesses, real estate development including zoning and syndications, insolvency and commercial workouts, lending and related areas. In the area of personal representation, we have an active practice encompassing residential real estate, estate planning, probate and domestic relations. The firm also has an extensive practice in civil and criminal litigation matters, insurance and environmental law.

MEMBERS OF FIRM

MICHAEL D. O'CONNELL, born Hartford, Connecticut, July 14, 1945; admitted to bar, 1972, Connecticut. *Education:* University of Notre Dame (B.A., 1967); University of Connecticut (J.D., 1972). Member: West Hartford Parks and Recreation Advisory Board, 1975-1976; West Hartford Bicentennial Commission, 1975-1976; West Hartford Charter Revision Commission, 1977; West Hartford Human Rights Commission, Special Projects Committee, 1977-1978. Recipient, David H. Neiditz Award for Best Appellate Brief in State of Connecticut, 1997. Editor, Trial Technical Newsletter, DRI Products Liability Section. *Member:* Hartford County, Connecticut (Member: Real Property Section; Administration of Civil Justice Section) and American (Member, Sections on: Litigation; Tort and Insurance Practice; Member, Committee on Trial Techniques, 1976—; Products, General Liability and Consumer Law Committee, 1982—) Bar Associations; Connecticut Defense Lawyers Association (Treasurer, 1982-1983; Vice President, 1983-1985; President, 1985-1986); Defense Research Institute (Member, Committee on Products Liability, 1984—). ***PRACTICE AREAS:*** Employment Law; Product Liability; Commercial Law; Commercial Litigation; Civil Litigation; Indian and Gaming Law. ***Email:*** moconnell@ofalaw.com

JAMES T. FLAHERTY, born Lockport, New York, November 16, 1946; admitted to bar, 1977, Connecticut. *Education:* Tufts University (B.A., 1968); State University of New York at Buffalo (J.D., 1977). Justice of the Peace. *Member:* Hartford County, Connecticut and American Bar Associations; Connecticut Trial Lawyers Association; Defense Research Institute; Connecticut Defense Lawyers Association; The Association of Trial Lawyers of America (Associate Member). [Lieut., U.S. Navy, 1968-1974]. ***PRACTICE AREAS:*** Civil Litigation; Domestic Relations. ***Email:*** jflaherty@ofalaw.com

(This Listing Continued)

GARY G. ATTMORE, born Stillwater, Oklahoma, June 9, 1946; admitted to bar, 1974, Connecticut. *Education:* Northeastern University (B.S., 1970); Suffolk University (J.D., 1974); George Washington University (LL.M. in Taxation, 1976). Delta Theta Phi. Member, Tax Club of Hartford. *Member:* Hartford County, Connecticut (Executive Committee, Tax Section, 1986—) and American (Member, Sections on: Taxation; Real Property, Probate and Trust Law) Bar Associations. ***PRACTICE AREAS:*** Taxation; Estate Planning; Closely-held Business Planning. ***Email:*** gattmore@ofalaw.com

STEPHEN H. SOLOMSON, born Hartford, Connecticut, December 6, 1948; admitted to bar, 1974, Connecticut and U.S. District Court for the District of Connecticut. *Education:* Providence College (B.A., 1970); University of Connecticut (J.D., 1974). Recipient, American Jurisprudence Award in Conflict of Laws. Assistant State's Attorney, 1976-1981. Member, Advisory Committee to Banking Commissioner on Connecticut Uniform Securities Act, 1985—. *Member:* Hartford County and Connecticut Bar Associations; Defense Research Institute; Connecticut Defense Lawyers Association. [Capt., U.S. Army Reserve, 1970-1977]. ***PRACTICE AREAS:*** Insurance Litigation; Commercial Litigation; Securities Law; Criminal Defense. ***Email:*** ssolomson@ofalaw.com

ROBERT A. DeFRINO, born Hartford, Connecticut, July 22, 1949; admitted to bar, 1978, Massachusetts; 1979, U.S. Court of Appeals, First Circuit and U.S. District Court, District of Massachusetts; 1982, Connecticut and U.S. District Court, District of Connecticut. *Education:* Boston College (B.A., 1971); University of Denver (M.S., 1972); New England School of Law (J.D., magna cum laude, 1978). Recipient, American Jurisprudence Book Award. Member and Research Editor, New England Law Review, 1976-1978. Author: Comment, "Aldinger v. Howard: Pendent Party Jurisdiction in Federal Question Cases," 13 New England Law Review 170, 1977. Instructor of Legal Methods, New England School of Law, Boston, Massachusetts, 1980-1981. *Member:* Connecticut (Member, Sections on: Commercial Law and Bankruptcy; Corporations), Massachusetts and American Bar Associations; Association of Commercial Finance Attorneys; World Affairs Council. ***PRACTICE AREAS:*** Business Law; Commercial Law; Bankruptcy Law; Real Estate Law. ***Email:*** rdefrino@ofalaw.com

LAWRENCE H. ADLER, born Hartford, Connecticut, June 16, 1960; admitted to bar, 1985, Connecticut and U.S. District Court, District of Connecticut. *Education:* University of Connecticut (B.S., magna cum laude, 1982); Western New England College (J.D., cum laude, 1985). Phi Alpha Delta, Phi Kappa Phi, Beta Gamma Sigma. Member, Mortar Board-Historian, Chairman of Finance and Projects Committees, 1981-1982. *Member:* Hartford County and Connecticut Bar Associations; Association of Trial Lawyers of America; Connecticut Trial Lawyers Association. ***PRACTICE AREAS:*** Civil Litigation; Insurance Defense; Product Liability Law. ***Email:*** ladler@ofalaw.com

PAUL J. APARO, born New Britain, Connecticut, November 13, 1949; admitted to bar, 1976, Connecticut; 1977, U.S. District Court, District of Connecticut. *Education:* Fairfield University (B.S., 1971); University of Connecticut (J.D., with honors, 1976). *Member:* Connecticut Bar Association (Member, Estate and Probate Committee, Young Lawyers Section, 1977). ***PRACTICE AREAS:*** Real Estate; Probate; Zoning; Corporations; Business Law. ***Email:*** paparo@ofalaw.com

HAROLD F. KEITH, born Newark Valley, New York, February 20, 1922; admitted to bar, 1948, Massachusetts; 1949, Connecticut. *Education:* Northeastern University (LL.B, cum laude, 1948); Providence College. Best Lawyers in America Real Estate, 1987—. Mayor, West Hartford, 1955-1959. Chairman, Capitol Region Planning Agency, 1959-1962. Member, 1956— and Chairman, 1963-1986, Greater Hartford Flood Commission. Member, Board of Parole, 1965-1968. Public Utilities Commissioner, 1968-1971. *Member:* Hartford County (Chairman, Real Estate Committee, 1963-1968), Connecticut and American Bar Associations. ***PRACTICE AREAS:*** Real Estate; Probate; Zoning; Corporations; Business Law. ***Email:*** hkeith@ofalaw.com

ALAN J. SOBOL, born Newark, New Jersey, December 18, 1948; admitted to bar, 1974, Ohio; 1978, District of Columbia and Maryland; 1987, Connecticut. *Education:* University of Maryland (B.A., 1971); University of Akron (J.D., 1974). Phi Alpha Delta. U.S. Attorney General's Honor Law Graduate, 1974. Member, 1972-1973, and Case and Comments Editor, 1973-1974, Akron Law Review. Trial Attorney, Criminal Division, 1974-1979; Special Assistant U.S. Attorney, 1979-1981; Prosecutor, General Litigation Section, U.S. Department of Justice, 1980-1982. Associate General Counsel, National Railroad Passenger Corporation (Amtrak), 1982-1986. Member, Board of Education, Town of Cheshire Board of Directors, Chairman and President, The Cheshire Education Foundation, Inc., 1999—; Executive Secretary and Director, 1995-1999. Member, Board of Directors, The Apple Valley Bank and Trust Company, an organization, 2000—. *Member:* Connecticut (Member, Sections On: Construction Law and Federal Practice; Member, Executive Committee) and American (Member, Criminal Law Section; Forum on the Construction Industry) Bar Associations. ***PRACTICE AREAS:*** Litigation; Construction Law; Criminal Law. ***Email:*** asobol@ofalaw.com

(This Listing Continued)

O'CONNELL, FLAHERTY & ATTMORE, L.L.C., Hartford—Continued

STEPHEN J. SINATRO, born Hartford, Connecticut, March 18, 1964; admitted to bar, 1989, Connecticut; 1990, U.S. District Court, District of Connecticut. *Education:* University of Connecticut (B.A., 1986); Western New England College School of Law (J.D., 1989). Law Clerk to the Honorable F. Owen Eagan, U.S. Judge. *Member:* Connecticut Bar Association. ***PRACTICE AREAS:*** Commercial Litigation; Domestic Law. ***Email:*** ssinatro@ofalaw.com

JOHN ADAM CVEJANOVICH, born Baton Rouge, Louisiana, May 28, 1953; admitted to bar, 1977, Louisiana and U.S. District Court, Eastern District of Louisiana; 1987, Massachusetts; 1995, Connecticut. *Education:* Tulane University of Louisiana (B.A., 1974); Louisiana State University (J.D., 1977). Member, Moot Court; National Moot Court. *Member:* Massachusetts and Connecticut Bar Associations; Massachusetts Association of Defense Counsel. (Resident, Springfield, Massachusetts Office). ***PRACTICE AREAS:*** Personal Injury Litigation; Insurance Defense. ***Email:*** jcvejanovich@ofalawmass.com

MATTHEW W. DEN OUDEN, born Grand Rapids, Michigan, May 25, 1965; admitted to bar, 1992, Connecticut; 1993, U.S. District Court, District of Connecticut. *Education:* University of Hartford (B.A., 1987); University of Connecticut (J.D., 1992). Recipient, David H. Neiditz Award for Best Appellate Brief in State of Connecticut, 1997. *Member:* Connecticut (Member, Computer Law Executive Committee) and American (Member, Tort and Insurance Practice Section) Bar Associations; Defense Research Institute (Member, Product Liability and Litigation Technology Sections); Oliver Ellsworth Inn of Court (Barrister). ***PRACTICE AREAS:*** Indian Law; Products Liability Defense; Computer Law; Risk Management; Insurance Defense. ***Email:*** MWD@OFALaw.com

DENNIS R. LAVETTE, born New Britain, Connecticut, September 30, 1954; admitted to bar, 1981, Connecticut and U.S. District Court, District of Connecticut. *Education:* Vanderbilt University (B.A., 1976); DePaul University (J.D., 1980). Phi Alpha Delta. *Member:* Hartford County (Member, Real Property Committee; Closing Committee) and Connecticut (Member, Sections on: Real Property, Probate and Trust Law; Member) Bar Associations; Connecticut Mortgage Bankers Association (Member, Closing Committee). ***PRACTICE AREAS:*** Residential Real Estate Law; Probate Law; Family Law. ***Email:*** dlavette@ofalaw.com

CLAUDIA M. SKLAR, born Baltimore, Maryland, September 25, 1952; admitted to bar, 1977, Connecticut and U.S. District Court, District of Connecticut. *Education:* Adelphi University (B.A., summa cum laude, 1974); University of Connecticut (J.D., with honors, 1977). Recipient, Hartford County Bar Association Scholarship. Member: Board of Trustees, Adelphi University, 1974-1977; Bloomfield Youth Adult Council, 1978-1980. *Member:* Hartford County and Connecticut (Member, Executive Committee, Commercial Law and Bankruptcy Section, 1985-1996) Bar Associations; Hartford Association of Women Attorneys (Member, Board of Directors, 1988-1991, Vice President, 1989-1992); Connecticut Trial Lawyers Association. ***PRACTICE AREAS:*** Civil Litigation; Commercial Litigation; Real Estate; Bankruptcy; Foreclosure Law; Corporate Law. ***Email:*** csklar@ofalaw.com

JULIA B. MORRIS, born Norwalk, Connecticut, November 15, 1969; admitted to bar, 1994, Connecticut and U.S. District Court, District of Connecticut. *Education:* Lehigh University (B.A., Phi Beta Kappa, 1991); Boston College (J.D., cum laude, 1994). Recipient, David H. Neiditz Award for Best Appellate Brief in State of Connecticut, 1997. *Member:* Connecticut Bar Association (Member, Appellate Division). ***PRACTICE AREAS:*** Business Law; Construction Law; Commercial Litigation; Commercial Transactions; Appellate Practice. ***Email:*** jmorris@ofalaw.com

---

ANNE R. HOYT, born Putnam, Connecticut, May 31, 1955; admitted to bar, 1980, Connecticut and U.S. District Court, District of Connecticut. *Education:* Connecticut College (B.A., with distinction, 1977); University of Connecticut (J.D., 1980). Recipient, American Jurisprudence Award, Administrative Law. Co-Author: "Civil Commitment of Juveniles," bound for honors display University of Connecticut, 1980. Member, Statewide Grievance Committee, 1995—. Attorney Trial Referee, 1990—. Special Master, 1992-1996, Trustee, 1996—; Member, Board of Directors, 1988-1991; Vice President, 1991, Norwich Quinebaug Unit of the American Cancer Society. President, Plainfield Chamber of Commerce, 1992-1993 and Member, Board of Directors, 1992-1998; Trustee, 1998—. *Member:* Windham County and Connecticut Bar Associations. ***REPORTED CASES:*** Douglas Gaynor v. Union Trust Company, 216 Conn. 458, 1990; Fleet Bank of Connecticut v.. Allan J. Breed, et al, 29 Conn. App 924, 1992, cert. den. 225 Conn. 903, 1993; In the matter of Flynn Funeral Home, Inc., Debtor, U.S. Bankruptcy, District of Conn. No. 2-81-01105, 8 C.L.T. No. 12, p. 12 Column 2, 12/10/81. ***PRACTICE AREAS:*** Residential Real Estate Law; Domestic Relations Law; Commercial Law; Civil Litigation; Workers Compensation. ***Email:*** annehoyt@snet.net

(This Listing Continued)

CHARLES I. MILLER, born Newington, Connecticut, October 19, 1964; admitted to bar, 1990, Connecticut; 1991, U.S. District Court, District of Connecticut. *Education:* University of Connecticut (B.A., 1987; J.D., 1990). Member, Connecticut Bar Association, 1990-1998. *Member:* Hartford Bar Association (Member, Sections on: Commercial Law; Litigation). ***PRACTICE AREAS:*** Commercial Law; Commercial Litigation; Foreclosures; Collections. ***Email:*** cmiller@ofalaw.com

LAURA WALTMAN, born Hartford, Connecticut, April 5, 1973; admitted to bar, 1998, Connecticut; 1999, U.S. District Court, District of Connecticut. *Education:* University of Connecticut (B.A., summa cum laude, 1995; J.D., 1998). Phi Beta Kappa. Connecticut Moot Court Board, 1996-1998. Symposium Editor, Connecticut Insurance Law Journal, 1997-1998. *Member:* Connecticut Bar Association. ***PRACTICE AREAS:*** Civil Litigation; Commercial Litigation. ***Email:*** lwaltman@ofalaw.com

DIANE C. MOKRISKI, born Framingham, Massachusetts, December 9, 1970; admitted to bar, 1998, Connecticut; 2000, U.S. District Court, District of Connecticut. *Education:* Colgate University (B.A., magna cum laude, 1993); University of Connecticut School of Law (J.D., 1998). Phi Beta Kappa. Executive Editor, Connecticut Law Review. *Member:* Connecticut and American Bar Associations. ***PRACTICE AREAS:*** Labor and Employment; Products Liability; Insurance Defense; Civil Litigation; Indian Law. ***Email:*** dmokriski@ofalaw.com

MARY ANN SANTACROCE, born New Haven, Connecticut, February 27, 1961; admitted to bar, 1986, Connecticut and U.S. District Court, District of Connecticut. *Education:* Boston College (B.A., summa cum laude, Phi Beta Kappa, 1983); University of Connecticut (J.D., cum laude, 1986). Adjunct Professor, Law of Business Enterprises, Manchester Community Technical College. Former Adjunct Professor, Law of Business Enterprises, Quinnipiac College, 1990. *Member:* Hartford County, Connecticut (Member, Sections on: Real Estate; Corporate, Banking and Business) and American (Member, Business Law Section) Bar Associations. ***PRACTICE AREAS:*** Business; Corporate; Commercial; Real Estate; Commercial Transaction; Bankruptcy. ***Email:*** msantacroce@gmflaw.com

GERARD S. COLLINS, born Winchester, Massachusetts, September 18, 1967; admitted to bar, 1997, Massachusetts and Connecticut; 1998, U.S. District Court, District of Massachusetts; 2001, U.S. District Court, District of Connecticut. *Education:* Boston College (B.A., cum laude, 1989); Western New England College School of Law (J.D., 1996). Member, National Slavic Honor Society. Member: Jessup International Law Moot Court Team. *Member:* Hampden County, Massachusetts, and Connecticut Bar Associations. ***PRACTICE AREAS:*** Insurance Defense; Civil Litigation; Commercial Collections; Real Estate; Federal Criminal Law; Pharmacy Law. ***Email:*** gcollins@ofalaw.com

JEFFREY R. MARTIN, born London, England, July 7, 1953; admitted to bar, 1979, Connecticut and U.S. District Court, District of Connecticut; 1981, Massachusetts; 1982, U.S. District Court, District of Massachusetts. *Education:* Trinity College (B.A., 1975); University of Connecticut (J.D., with honors, 1979). *Member:* Connecticut and American (Member, Section on Litigation) Bar Associations; The Association of Trial Lawyers of America; Connecticut Trial Lawyers Association. ***PRACTICE AREAS:*** Litigation; Personal Injury. ***Email:*** jmartin@ofalaw.com

JOSEPH Z. GERSTEN, admitted to bar, 1998, Connecticut and U.S. District Court, District of Connecticut. *Education:* George Washington University (M.F.S., 1994); Quinnipiac College School of Law (J.D., 1994). Vice Magister, Phi Delta Phi, 1997-1998. Fellow, American College Forensic Examiners. Commissioner, Town of Hamden Inland Wetlands Commission, 2000-2001. ***Email:*** jgersten@ofalaw.com

NICHOLAS J. GORRA, II, born New London, Connecticut, November 8, 1963; admitted to bar, 1992, Connecticut and U.S. District Court, District of Connecticut. *Education:* Clark University (B.A., 1985); New England School of Law (J.D., 1990). *Member:* Connecticut Bar Association (Commercial and Real Estate Sections). ***REPORTED CASES:*** Steiger v. J&S Builders; Slack v. Slack; Fitzgerald v. Legnos. ***PRACTICE AREAS:*** Commercial Transactions; Commercial Litigation; Real Estate; Estate Planning; Civil Litigation. ***Email:*** n.j.gorra@att.net

SANDI BETH GIROLAMO, born Fort Knox, Kentucky, February 28, 1971; admitted to bar, 2001, Connecticut. *Education:* University of Connecticut (B.A., 1993); Quinnipiac University (J.D., summa cum laude, 2001). Recipient, American Jurisprudence Award in Workers Compensation. *Member:* Connecticut and American Bar Associations. ***PRACTICE AREAS:*** Ciovil Litigation; Family Law.

CHRISTOPHER J. ALBANESE, born Danbury, Connecticut; admitted to bar, 2001, Connecticut. *Education:* State University of New York at Albany (B.A.); University of Connecticut (J.D., 2001). *Member:* Connecticut Bar Association (Indian Law Committee). ***PRACTICE AREAS:*** Litigation; Real Property; Bankruptcy; Indian Law.

OHLANDT, GREELEY, RUGGIERO & PERLE

HARTFORD, CONNECTICUT

(See Stamford)

Practice Limited to Intellectual Property Law and Related Matters.

O'NEIL & ASSOCIATES, P.C.

38 HUNGERFORD STREET, SUITE 300
HARTFORD, CONNECTICUT 06106
Telephone: 860-522-5188
Fax: 860-247-3468

Civil Litigation, Personal Injury, DUI, DWI, Slip and Fall, Dog Bites, Automobile Accidents, Product Liability, Family, Real Estate.

FIRM PROFILE: Ms. O'Neil has been practicing family law and personal injury, since, 1985.

PATRICIA A. O'NEIL, born Waterbury, Connecticut, May 18, 1960; admitted to bar, 1985, Connecticut and U.S. District Court, District of Connecticut. *Education:* Catholic University (B.A., 1982; J.D., 1985). *Member:* Connecticut and American Bar Associations; Connecticut Trial Lawyers Association; Association of Trial Lawyers of America. **PRACTICE AREAS:** Personal Injury Law; Real Estate Law; Domestic Relations Law; DUI; DWI; Slip and Fall; Dog Bites; Automobile Accidents and Injuries.

J. LAWRENCE PRICE, born Oklahoma City, Oklahoma, January 6, 1951; admitted to bar, 1986, Connecticut and U.S. District Court, District of Connecticut. *Education:* Purdue University (B.A., 1973); Catholic University of America (J.D., 1985). Town Council, West Hartford, Connecticut, 1986-1995; Deputy Mayor, 1989-1991; West Hartford Democrat Town Chairperson, 1998—; Connecticut Science Center Trustee, 1992-1997. *Member:* Hartford County and Connecticut (Member, Sections on Litigation and Labor and Employment) Bar Associations; Connecticut Trial Lawyers Association; Connecticut Defense Lawyers Association. **PRACTICE AREAS:** Litigation; Commercial Litigation; Employment Litigation.

APPROVED ATTORNEYS FOR: Connecticut Attorney Title.

LAW OFFICE OF ANTHONY J. PALERMINO, LLC

Established in 1980

945 WETHERSFIELD AVENUE
HARTFORD, CONNECTICUT 06114
Telephone: 860-296-0035
FAX: 860-296-9468
Email: a.palermino.atty@snet.net
URL: http://www.lawyers.com/apalermino

Labor and Employment Law, Labor Relations (Private and Public Sector), Civil Rights, Administrative Law, Workers Compensation, Personal Injury, Real Estate, Business Law, Probate Law, Legislative Practice, Community Action Law, Litigation in all Courts.

ANTHONY J. PALERMINO, born Hartford, Connecticut, August 20, 1950; admitted to bar, 1975, Connecticut; 1976, U.S. District Court, District of Connecticut; 1977, U.S. Court of Appeals, First Circuit; 1978, U.S. Court of Appeals, Second Circuit; 1980, U.S. Supreme Court. *Education:* College of the Holy Cross (A.B., magna cum laude, 1972); University of Connecticut (J.D., with honors, 1975). Alpha Sigma Nu. Recipient, Governor's Appointment to the Connecticut Convention Authority, 1996-1998. Commissioner, Commission on Hospitals and Health Care of the State of Connecticut, 1980-1981. Legal Assistance Director, South End Community Services, Inc., 1981-1985. State Representative, Connecticut General Assembly, 1983-1985, 1985-1987, 1987-1989, 1989-1991. Member: Education Committee, 1983-1985, 1985-1987; Finance, Revenue and Bonding Committee, 1983-1985, 1985-1987, 1987-1989, 1989-1991; Transportation Committee, 1985-1987, 1987-1989; Insurance Committee, 1987-1989, 1989-1991; Program and Review Investigations Committee, 1987-1988; Banks Committee, 1989-1991. Special Counsel to Speaker of House of Representatives, 1990. *Member:* Hartford County, Connecticut (Member, Labor Section) and American (Member, Labor and Employment Law Section) Bar Associations. **REPORTED CASES:** Metropolitan District Commission v. AFSCME, Council #4, AFL-CIO, 237 Conn. 114 (1996); North Haven Association of Educational Support Staff v. North Haven Board of Education, 209 Conn. 280 (1988). **Email:** a.palermino.atty@snet.net

(This Listing Continued)

GARY R. ATKINSON, born Middletown, Connecticut, May 31, 1953; admitted to bar, 1985, Connecticut; 1990, U.S. District Court, District of Connecticut. *Education:* Boston University (B.A., cum laude, 1975); University of Connecticut (J.D., 1985). *Member:* Middlesex County, Connecticut (Member, Labor Section) and American (Member, Labor and Employment Law Section) Bar Associations. **Email:** gratkinson@snet.net

REPRESENTATIVE CLIENTS: Metropolitan District Commission; Community Renewal Team, Inc.; Town of Ellington; People's Bank; Fleet Bank; Webster Bank; Healthtrax International, Inc.; Connecticut Association For Community Action; Meadows Real Estate Management and Developement Corporation; Connecticut Non-Profit Energy, Inc.

PEPE & HAZARD LLP

Established in 1983

GOODWIN SQUARE
HARTFORD, CONNECTICUT 06103-4302
Telephone: 860-522-5175
FAX: 860-522-2796
URL: http://www.pepehazard.com

Southport, Connecticut Office: 30 Jelliff Lane, 06490-1436. Telephone: 203-319-4000. Fax: 203-259-0251.
Boston, Massachusetts Office: 150 Federal Street, 02110-1745. Telephone: 617-695-9090. Fax: 617-695-9255.

Commercial, Construction, Corporations, Taxation, Finance and Real Estate, Commercial and Asset-Based Finance, Environmental/Health/Safety, Fidelity and Surety, Securities, Labor/Employment and Education, Municipal, Administrative, Health Care, Intellectual Property, Patent, International Trade, Estate Planning, Probate, White Collar Crime, and Bankruptcy. Trials in all Courts.

FIRM PROFILE: At Pepe & Hazard LLP, we believe that today's profound social and economic changes affect what a law firm must contribute to its clients' services. There are new problems and new opportunities. There must, then, be new solutions - addressed with traditional skills, tempered by cold, hard experience - leavened with a contemporary perspective. Established in 1983, Pepe & Hazard brings this perspective to the intricate and evolving needs of business. That we have remained relevant to our clients through more than a decade and a half of economic change is testimony to the innovative and progressive practice of law that we embrace.

MEMBERS OF FIRM

KATHLEEN F. BORNHORST, born Fort Wayne, Indiana, May 10, 1941; admitted to bar, 1984, Ohio; 1985, Connecticut; 2000, Massachusetts. *Education:* University of Dayton (A.B., cum laude, 1962); University of Toledo (J.D., cum laude, 1984); Boston University (LL.M. in Taxation, 1990). Order of the Coif; Order of the Barristers. Member: Albert R. Mugel National Moot Court Tax Team, 1982-1983; Moot Court Board, 1983-1984. Instructor of Law, University of Toledo, 1984-1985. *Member:* Connecticut (Member, Estates and Probate Section), Ohio State and American (Member, Real Property, Probate and Trust Law Section) Bar Associations. **PRACTICE AREAS:** Business Estate Planning; Charitable Trusts and Foundations; Probate; Estate and Gift Taxation; Trusts and Estates. **Email:** kbornhorst@pepehazard.com

TIMOTHY T. COREY, born Hartford, Connecticut, May 7, 1957; admitted to bar, 1984, Connecticut; 1986, U.S. District Court, District of Connecticut; 1991, U.S. Court of Appeals, Second and Federal Circuits and U.S. Claims Court; 2000, Massachusetts. *Education:* St. Thomas University, Fredericton, New Brunswick, Canada (B.A., with honors, 1979); Salzburg University, Salzburg, Austria (Certificate in International Law, 1981); University of New Brunswick, Fredericton, New Brunswick, Canada (LL.B., 1982); McGeorge School of Law, University of the Pacific (LL.M., International Business, 1983). Member, Jessup International Moot Court Team, 1981. Recipient, Charles A. Dana Fund Scholarship. Book Review Editor, University of New Brunswick Law Journal, 1981-1982. Second Vice President, Connecticut Preservation Society. Board of Trustees, Antiquarian & Landmarks Society. *Member:* Connecticut (Member, Construction Law Executive Committee) and American (Member: Tort and Insurance Practice Section; Fidelity and Surety Law Committee; Forum Committee on the Construction Industry) Bar Associations; Connecticut Construction Industry Association (Member: Mechanics' Lien Task Force); Connecticut Associated Builder's and Contractors. **PRACTICE AREAS:** Construction and Surety; Litigation. **Email:** tcorey@pepehazard.com

PETER L. COSTAS, born Binghamton, New York, March 7, 1931; admitted to bar, 1954, New York; 1960, Connecticut. *Education:* Syracuse University (B.S. in Chem., 1951; J.D., 1954). Phi Delta Phi. Recipient, Connecticut Bar Association John Eldred Shields Memorial Award, 1987. Author: "Discovery and the Issue of Commercial Success in Patent Infringement Action," Federal Rules Decisions, December, 1962; "Patents, Trademarks and Copyrights, The

(This Listing Continued)

PEPE & HAZARD LLP, Hartford—Continued

Legal Monopolies, Part I— Patents," Connecticut Bar Journal, December, 1962; "Part II— Trademarks and Related Law of Unfair Competition," Connecticut Bar Journal, September, 1963; "Part III— Copyrights Protection for Literary and Artistic Creativity," Connecticut Bar Journal, February, 1978; "Today's Challenge to the Bar," Connecticut Bar Journal, September, 1965; "The 1970's: Will We Respond to the Need to Modernize Connecticut's Judicial System?," Connecticut Bar Journal, December, 1970; Audio Course, "Introduction to Patents," American Chemical Society, 1974. Short Course, "Patents, Trademarks and Copyrights—Recognition and Protection of Creativity," 1975, American Chemical Society; "How Shall We Judge the Judges?" Connecticut Bar Journal, March, 1975; "Evaluating the Connecticut Judiciary: A Significant Step Forward," Connecticut Bar Journal, December, 1976; "The CBA Judgeship Poll: A Critical Reappraisal," Connecticut Bar Journal, February, 1979; "Unfair Competition and Unfair Trade Practices-Transplants to the Unfair Trade Practices Act," Connecticut Bar Journal, October, 1980; "Trade Secrets Law—Principles, Pitfalls and Pronouncements," Connecticut Bar Journal, December, 1997. President, Connecticut Patent Law Association, 1966. Vice Chairman, 1967-1971 and Member, 1978-1984, Drug Advisory Council, State of Connecticut. Board of Editors, 1964—, Editor-in-Chief, 1976-1979 and Managing Editor, 1983-1996. Connecticut Bar Journal. Contributor, Connecticut Chapter, "State Trademark and Unfair Competition Law," 1989—. *Member:* Hartford County, Connecticut (President, 1997; President-Elect, 1996-1997; Vice President, 1995-1996; Chairman: Federal Civil Trial Advocacy Program Committee, 1976-1984; Chairman: Federal Practice Section, 1987-1990), New York State and American Bar Associations; American Intellectual Property Law Association; International Trademark Association; American Chemical Society. ***PRACTICE AREAS:*** Antitrust and Trade Regulation; Intellectual Property; International Trade; Civil Litigation. ***Email:*** pcostas@pepehazard.com

JEANINE M. DUMONT, born Los Angeles, California, October 27, 1958; admitted to bar, 1984, California; 1985, Connecticut; 1988, U.S. Court of Appeals, Second Circuit; 1993, U.S. Supreme Court; 1999, Massachusetts. *Education:* University of California, Los Angeles (B.A., 1981); Loyola Law School, Los Angeles (J.D., cum laude, 1984). St. Thomas More Law Honor Society, 1982-1984. Recipient: American Jurisprudence Award in Insurance Law, Advanced Insurance Law, Secured Transactions and Evidence; West Publishing Award for Writing. Author: "Pleadings and Pretrial Practice: a Deskbook for Connecticut Litigators," Connecticut Law Tribune, 1994, 1995, 1996, 1997 and 1998; "What Every Professional Should Know Before Buying Claims-Made Liability Insurance," 35 Federation of Insurance Counsel Quarterly 363, Summer, 1985. Law Clerk, Connecticut Superior Court, 1985. *Member:* Hartford County, Connecticut and American Bar Associations; State Bar of California. ***PRACTICE AREAS:*** Commercial Litigation; Debtor and Creditor; Collections; Civil Fraud; Litigation; Utility. ***Email:*** jdumont@pepehazard.com

MARK I. FISHMAN, born New York, N.Y., September 25, 1945; admitted to bar, 1970, Massachusetts; 1971, U.S. District Court, District of Massachusetts; 1972, New York, U.S. District Court, Southern and Eastern Districts of New York; 1974, U.S. Supreme Court; 1979, U.S. District Court, District of Connecticut; 1980, Connecticut. *Education:* Harvard University (A.B., magna cum laude, 1967; J.D., 1970). Law Clerk, Supreme Judicial Court of Massachusetts, 1970-1971. Member, Connecticut Law Revision Commission Advisory Committee on Article 6 of the Uniform Commercial Code. Director, New Haven Jewish Federation, 1996—. *Member:* Bridgeport (Chairman, Commercial Law Committee, 1997-1998) and Connecticut (Member, Executive Committee, Commercial Law and Bankruptcy Section, 1986-1996, 1999—) Bar Associations; Commercial Law League of America; Association of Commercial Finance Attorneys. (Certified Specialist, Business Bankruptcy Law, American Board of Certification). ***REPORTED CASES:*** In re Cuisinarts, Inc., 115 B.R. 744 (Bkrptcy. D. Conn. 1990). ***PRACTICE AREAS:*** Bankruptcy Law; Commercial Litigation. ***Email:*** mfishman@pepehazard.com

MICHAEL E. FOLEY, born Honolulu, Hawaii, January 7, 1961; admitted to bar, 1987, Connecticut; 1988, U.S. District Court, District of Connecticut. *Education:* University of Massachusetts (B.A., cum laude, 1983); Western New England College (J.D., 1987). Editor, Connecticut Employment Law Letter. Lecturer and Author: Seminars and Periodicals sponsored by The Connecticut Conference of Municipalities, National Public Employer Labor Relations Association and Connecticut Association of Boards of Education, National Business Institute, Connecticut Business and Industry Association. *Member:* Hartford County, Connecticut and American Bar Associations; Connecticut School Attorneys Council (Member, Secretary, 1992-1993; Vice President, 1993-1994; President, 1994-1995); Connecticut Public Employer Labor Relations Association (Executive Board Member, 1996-2000); National School Attorneys Council; National Organization on Legal Problems of Education; National Public Employers Labor Relations Association; National Multiple Sclerosis Association (Board of Director, Connecticut Chapter). (Also at Boston, Massachusetts Office). ***PRACTICE AREAS:*** Management Labor Law; Unfair Labor Practice; Collective Bargaining; Municipal Labor Law; School Board Defense. ***Email:*** mfoley@pepehazard.com

(This Listing Continued)

JAMES C. GRAHAM, born Far Rockaway, N.Y., September 2, 1955; admitted to bar, 1980, District of Columbia; 1981, Virginia; 1982, U.S. Court of Appeals, District of Columbia Circuit, U.S. District Court, District of Columbia; 1984, Connecticut and U.S. District Court, District of Connecticut. *Education:* Yale University (B.A., cum laude, 1977); University of Virginia (J.D., 1980). Author: "Lien Stripping Causes Confusion for Lenders in Chapter 13 Bankruptcy Cases," The Commercial Record, January, 1992; "Lien Stripping Revisited," The Commercial Record, April, 1993; "Bankruptcy Puts a New Spin on Environmental Claims," Connecticut Environmental Compliance Update, July, 1993; "Bankruptcy," Chapter, Connecticut Lawyers' Deskbook: A Reference Manual (Connecticut Bar Association, 1998). *Member:* Connecticut (Executive Committee, Commercial Law and Bankruptcy Section; Member, Litigation and Federal Practice Sections) and American (Member, Sections on: Business Law; Federal Practice; Litigation) Bar Associations; American Bankruptcy Institute. ***PRACTICE AREAS:*** Bankruptcy; Litigation; Commercial Law; Legal Ethics and Professional Responsibility; Debtor and Creditor. ***Email:*** jgraham@pepehazard.com

JAMES G. GREEN, JR., born Buffalo, New York, March 3, 1955; admitted to bar, 1980, Connecticut. *Education:* Boston College (B.A., magna cum laude, 1977); University of Virginia (J.D., 1980). Moderator: "From Claim To Judgment In Less Than Eternity," Hartford County Bar Association, February, 1985. Speaker: "Lender Liability, RICO and CUTPA," Connecticut Bar Association, June, 1986; "Amicable Demand and Judgments," National Business Institute Seminar, August, 1988; "Computer Generated Evidence," Connecticut Bar Association, October, 1990; "Effective and Efficient Discovery in Complex Litigation," Connecticut Trial Lawyers Association, January, 1993; "Liability of Accountants and Lawyers to Third Parties," Lorman Education Services, June, 1993; "Current Topics Regarding Professional Liability of Accountants," Connecticut Society of C.P.A's November, 1993; "Federal Rules Changes Affecting Discovery," Lorman Education Services, January, 1994. Co-Author: "Liability of Accountants to Third Parties," Connecticut Trial Lawyers Association Forum, March/April, 1994. Instructor: Connecticut Trial Advocacy Institute, Connecticut Bar Association/National Institute for Trial Advocacy, March, 1994, 1995. *Member:* Hartford County (President, 1996-1997; Member, Board of Directors, 1990-1994), Connecticut (Member: Litigation Section) and American (Member, Litigation Section) Bar Associations. ***PRACTICE AREAS:*** Business Litigation; Contract Litigation; Accountants' Liability; Corporate Litigation; Civil Appeals. ***Email:*** jgreen@pepehazard.com

URSULA L. HAERTER, born Southampton, New York, July 4, 1962; admitted to bar, 1993, Connecticut. *Education:* New York State School of Industrial and Labor Relations at Cornell University (B.S., 1987); University of Connecticut (J.D., 1992). Editor: Connecticut Employment Law Letter. *Member:* Hartford County, Connecticut (Executive Committee, Labor and Employment Law Section) and American (Committee on the Development of the Law Under the National Labor Relations Act) Bar Associations. ***PRACTICE AREAS:*** Labor and Employment; Employment Defense; Management Labor Law. ***Email:*** uhaerter@pepehazard.com

DAN A. HAYNES, born Honolulu, Hawaii, August 11, 1950; admitted to bar, 1977, Virginia; 1980, District of Columbia; 1994, Connecticut, U.S. Supreme Court, U.S. Court of Federal Claims, U.S. District Court, Eastern District of Virginia, U.S. District Court, District of Columbia, U.S. Court of Appeals, Fourth Circuit and U.S. Court of Appeals, District of Columbia Circuit. *Education:* American University (B.S., 1974); Georgetown University (J.D., 1977). *Member:* District of Columbia Bar; Virginia State Bar (Member, Construction Law Section); Connecticut (Member, Construction Law Section) and American (Member: Public Contract Law; Corporation, Banking and Business Law; International Law and Practice Sections; Forum on the Construction Industry) Bar Associations; International Bar Association (Member: Section on Business Law, Committee on International Construction Contracts). ***LANGUAGES:*** French. ***PRACTICE AREAS:*** Construction and Design Law; Construction Contracts; International Construction Law; Public Construction Law; Government Procurement. ***Email:*** dhaynes@pepehazard.com

STEPHEN B. HAZARD, born Dayton, Ohio, April 28, 1945; admitted to bar, 1973, Connecticut. *Education:* Brown University (B.A., 1967); University of Washington (J.D., 1973); Boston University (LL.M. in Taxation, 1976). Member, Board of Editors, Washington Law Review, 1972-1973. *Member:* Connecticut (Member, Corporations and Tax Sections) and American (Member, Sections on: Business Law; Health; Taxation; Antitrust; Law Practice Management) Bar Associations; American Health Lawyers Association; Connecticut Technology Council. [Lt. (j.g.), USNR, 1967-1970]. (Also at Boston, Massachusetts Office). ***PRACTICE AREAS:*** Corporate Law; Mergers, Acquisitions and Divestitures; Venture Capital; Technology Transfer; Emerging Growth Companies. ***Email:*** shazard@pepehazard.com

ROBERT L. KEEPNEWS, born New York, New York, March 8, 1947; admitted to bar, 1975, New York; 1976, Connecticut. *Education:* Georgetown University (B.S., 1968); Fordham University (J.D., 1974). Member, Fordham Urban Law Journal, 1973-1974. Law Clerk to Hon. Frank J. Battisti, Chief Judge, U.S. District Court, Northern District of Ohio, 1974-1976. Author: "The Fairness Doctrine: Time for the Graveyard?" 2 Ford. Urb. L.J. 563 (1974).

(This Listing Continued)

Special Master, United States District Court. Attorney Trial Referee, State of Connecticut. *Member:* Connecticut and American (Member, Sections on Litigation and Labor and Employment Law) Bar Associations. [Capt., U.S. Marine Corps, 1968-1971]. ***PRACTICE AREAS:*** Commercial Litigation; Employment Litigation; Alternative Dispute Resolution. ***Email:*** rkeepnews@pepehazard.com

THOMAS G. LIBRIZZI, born San Juan, Puerto Rico, September 6, 1959; admitted to bar, 1984, Connecticut; 1985, U.S. District Court, District of Connecticut; 1991, U.S. Court of Appeals, Second Circuit; 1994, U.S. Court of Federal Claims. *Education:* Gettysburg College (B.A., 1981); The John Marshall Law School (J.D., with distinction, 1984). Author: The Design/Build Process: A Guide to Licensing and Procurement Requirement in the 50 States (Connecticut), 1997; Prompt Pay Laws in the 50 States (Connecticut Chapter); Lien and Bond Claims In the 50 States (Connecticut); Reference Guide to Licensing and Registration Requirements in the 50 States (Connecticut); "Pay When/If Paid," CFMA Building Profits, May/June, 1996; Co-Author: "Bid Protests: Substance and Procedure on Publicly Funded Construction Projects," The Construction Lawyer, January, 1987. Member, Panel of Arbitrators, American Arbitration Association. *Member:* Hartford County, Connecticut (Member, Construction Law Section) and American (Member: Public Contract Section; Forum on the Construction Industry; Steering Committee for the Construction Management and Design Build Division of ABA Forum on the Construction Industry) Bar Associations. ***PRACTICE AREAS:*** Alternative Dispute Resolution; Construction Law; Contracts; Government Contracts; Insurance. ***Email:*** tlibrizzi@pepehazard.com

THOMAS B. MITCHELL, born Springfield, Massachusetts, May 4, 1956; admitted to bar, 1981, Massachusetts; 1982, U.S. District Court, District of Massachusetts; 1985, Connecticut. *Education:* Amherst College (B.A., 1978); Vanderbilt University (J.D., 1981). Associate Editor, Vanderbilt Law Review, 1979-1981. *Member:* Connecticut (Member, Real Property Section) and American (Member, Section on Real Property, Probate and Trust Law) Bar Associations; Real Estate Finance Association (Hartford, CT. Section). (Also at Boston, Massachusetts Office). ***PRACTICE AREAS:*** Banks and Banking; Commercial Real Estate; Capital Markets; Leases and Leasing; Mortgages; Real Estate. ***Email:*** tmitchell@pepehazard.com

ANTHONY J. NATALE, born Providence, Rhode Island, October 20, 1964; admitted to bar, 1990, Connecticut; 1991, U.S. District Court, District of Connecticut; 1994, U.S. Court of Appeals, Second Circuit; 1996, U.S. Court of Appeals, Fourth Circuit; 1999, U.S. Court of Appeals, First Circuit; 2000, Massachusetts. *Education:* Providence College (B.A., cum laude, Political Science, 1987); Suffolk University (J.D., cum laude, 1990). Pi Sigma Alpha. Semi-Finalist, Irving Kaufman National Securities Law Moot Court Competition. Co-Author: "The Summary Enforceability of Agreements to Settle Lawsuits: A Deal is a Deal!" CTLA Forum, July/August, 1995; "Connecticut State Variations of Commercial Law," Digest of Commercial Laws of The World, 1994, 1997; "The New Unity of Interest Rule In Voir Dire, and Its Applicability to Pending Cases," CTLA Forum, September/October, 1993. Member, Board of Trustees, Manchester Public Library, 1996-1998. *Member:* Hartford County (Board of Directors, 1998—), Connecticut and American Bar Associations; Connecticut Defense Lawyers Association; Defense Research Institute. ***PRACTICE AREAS:*** Civil Litigation. ***Email:*** anatale@pepehazard.com

SUSAN M. ORR, born Hartford, Connecticut, July 24, 1956; admitted to bar, 1980, Connecticut; 1993, U.S. District Court, District of Connecticut; 2000, Massachusetts. *Education:* Colgate University (B.A., magna cum laude, 1977); Boston University (J.D., 1980). Phi Beta Kappa. Recipient, Achievement Award for Excellence in Real Estate Transactions. Author: "Co-Lending For Real Estate," American Bar Association, 1995; "Lenders Beware: Non-Disclosure of Material Facts in Foreclosed Real Estate Sales," The Commercial Record, January 17, 1997; "Commercial Mortgages: A New Business Loan Collateral," The Commercial Record, February 28, 1997; "Title Searching: The Next Generation," The Connecticut Law Tribune, June 30, 1997; "The CMBS Phenomenon: Mortgage Rateability Issues," Pepe & Hazard LLP Real Estate Law Letter, November, 1997; "Office Leasing: The Millennium Issues," The Commercial Record, April 9, 1998; "The Good, the Bad and the Ugly: A Lender Liability Update," American Bar Association, 1998; "Commercial Real Estate Purchase and Sale Transactions," Connecticut Lawyer's Deskbook, Connecticut Bar Association, 1998; "Smart Grown: Designing Communities for the New Mellenium," The Connecticut Law Tribune, September 13, 1999. *Member:* Connecticut (Member: Executive Committee, Young Lawyers Section, 1981-1982; Section on Real Property, Probate and Trust Law) and American (Member, Real Property and Probate Section; Committees on Mortgage Loan Structure and Origination and Loan Practices and Lender Liability) Bar Associations; Real Estate Finance Association; National Network of Commercial Real Estate Women. ***PRACTICE AREAS:*** Commercial Real Estate Finance; Real Estate Leasing; Real Estate Transfers; Real Estate Workouts. ***Email:*** sorr@pepehazard.com

LOUIS R. PEPE, born Derby, Connecticut, March 7, 1943; admitted to bar, 1970, Connecticut. *Education:* Rensselaer Polytechnic Institute (B.Mgt.E, 1964; M.S., 1967); Cornell University (J.D., with distinction, 1970). Phi Kappa Phi.

(This Listing Continued)

Author: "Connecticut Lien and Bond Law," Wiley Law Publications, 1993, 1994, 1995, 1996, 1997, 1998 and 1999; "Changes in Scope Claims," Wiley Law Publications, 1990. Adjunct Associate Professor, Hartford Graduate Center, 1972-1987. American Arbitration Association Connecticut Advisory Council, 1983—. Member: American Arbitration Association Large Complex Case Panel; Member, American Arbitration Association Construction ADR Task Force, 1994-1995; Cornell Law School Advisory Council, 1990—; University of Hartford Construction Institute, Board of Governors, 1995-1996, Executive Committee, 1996-2000; Capital Area Foundation for Equal Justice, Board of Directors, 1993—, President, 1999—. Listed in "Who's Who in America," Who's Who in American Law," and "Best Lawyers in America." *Member:* Hartford County, Connecticut (Chairman, Construction Law Section, 1989-1992; Chairman, Task Force on Grievance Procedures, 1996-1997; Chairman, Task Force on Professionalism (Civility), 1998-1999; Chairman, Standing Committee on Professionalism, 1999—) and American (Member: Public Contract Law Section and Litigation Section; Articles Editor, Committee on Litigation); Bar Associations. Fellow: American College of Trial Lawyers; American Bar Foundation; Connecticut Bar Foundation (James W. Cooper Fellow). Associate, American Board of Trial Advocates. [1st Lieut., U.S. Army, 1964-1966]. ***PRACTICE AREAS:*** Construction Law; Commercial Litigation; Alternative Dispute Resolution; Appellate Practice; Complex Litigation. ***Email:*** lpepe@pepehazard.com

THOMAS J. RECHEN, born Kingston, New York, August 14, 1963; admitted to bar, 1988, Connecticut; 1989, U.S. District Court, District of Connecticut; 1993, U.S. Court of Appeals, Second Circuit and U.S. Supreme Court; 1998, U.S. Court of Appeals for the Federal Circuit. *Education:* State University of New York at Buffalo (B.A., cum laude, 1985); Boston University (J.D., 1988). Author: "Are the Crown Jewels Protected? Steps Your Business Can Take to Guard Trade Secrets," Connecticut Employment Law Letter, May, 1993. Co-Author: "State Variations of Commercial Law For Connecticut," Digest of Commercial Laws of The World, 1994; "The Arbitrator's Obligation to Apply Established Law After Garrity v. McCaskey: A New Era or Just More of the Same?" CTLA Forum, September/October, 1994; "Commercial Litigation: Selection and Presentation of Expert Witnesses: How to Avoid the Pitfalls and Hazards," Connecticut Trial Lawyers Association, December, 1994; "Litigation Issues in Commercial Real Estate Transactions," Connecticut Bar Association, January 1998, and June 1999. Vice Chairman, Board of Managers, Greater Hartford YMCA; Leadership Seminar, Inc. *Member:* Hartford County, Connecticut (Member, Litigation, Federal Practice), Federal and American (Tort and Insurance Practice Section) Bar Associations; Connecticut Defense Lawyers Association; Defense Research Institute. ***PRACTICE AREAS:*** Business Litigation; Business Tort; Complex Litigation; Premises Liability Defense; Professional Liability. ***Email:*** trechen@pepehazard.com

DAVID E. ROSENGREN, born New York, N.Y., July 30, 1951; admitted to bar, 1981, Connecticut. *Education:* Randolph-Macon Woman's College (B.A., cum laude, 1978); University of Virginia (J.D., 1981). Phi Beta Kappa. Author: "The Contractor's Right to Recover Delay Damages Even Though He Has Completed a Job on Time or Ahead of Schedule," Construction Law Adviser, June, 1986. Co-Author: "Bid Protests: Substance and Procedure on Publicly Funded Construction Projects," The Construction Lawyer, January, 1987; "Local Governments: Are They Immune from CERCLA Liability?" Environmental Hazards, September, 1990. Lecturer: "Construction Law: What Happens When The Roof Collapses!" Connecticut Bar Association, 1990; "Construction Litigation in the Nineties and Beyond," Connecticut Bar Association, 1992; "Latest Development in Construction Law," Connecticut Bar Association, 1994; "Drafting Contracts," Connecticut Bar Association, 1994—. Chairman of Publications, University of Hartford Construction Institute, 1989-1991. Member, National Panel of Arbitrators, American Arbitration Association. *Member:* Hartford County, Connecticut (Member, Executive Committee, Secretary, 1990-1992; Vice Chairman, 1992-1994; Chairman, 1994-1997, Construction Law Section) and American (Member: Litigation Section; Forum Committee on the Construction Industry) Bar Associations. ***PRACTICE AREAS:*** Construction Litigation; Complex Commercial Litigation; Environmental Litigation. ***Email:*** drosengren@pepehazard.com

REED D. RUBINSTEIN, born East Lansing, Michigan, July 5, 1960; admitted to bar, 1985, Virginia; 1986, District of Columbia; 1987, Michigan; 1992, Connecticut. *Education:* The University of Michigan (A.B., high honors and distinction in Political Science, 1982; M.A., 1985; J.D., 1985). Recipient, Scribes Award. Author: "The First Step: The Asset Conservation, Lender, and Deposit Insurance Protection Act of 1996," 22 Conn. Law Trib. p. 20 (Oct. 21, 1996); "Financing Vehicles for Brownfield Development," Pennsylvania's Environment, p. 10 (Feb. 1996); "Shortening the 10-Foot Pole: Changes in CRA Should Stimulate Brownfield Lending," 21 Conn. Law Trib. 25 (May 15, 1995); "Rethinking Environmental Justice," Conn. Law Trib. (Supp. Dec. 1994; "Innocent Owner Liability For Environmental Contamination Under Connecticut Law," 67 Conn. Bar J. 398 (1993); "Clean Up Superfund Or Write Off Urban Redevelopment," 19 Conn. L. Trib. 20 (May 3, 1993); "Coaxing the Phoenix: Environmental Remediation Industrial Redevelopment and Municipal Control," 10 Conn. Real Est. L.J. 69 (1993); "Walking The Line: Integrating The Requirements of OSHA's Bloodborne Pathogen Regulation and the Mandates of

(This Listing Continued)

PEPE & HAZARD LLP, Hartford—Continued

the ADA," 66 Conn. Bar J. 451 (1992); "Using David's Slingshot: Handling the Plaintiff's Cost Recovery Suit," 6 Toxics L. Rep. (BNA) 1283 (1992); "A Survey of Recent Environmental Law Developments," 38 Wayne L. Rev. 977 (1992); "A Practical Guide to the National Environmental Policy Act," *Michigan ICLE Environmental Deskbook* (1992); "Environmental Law and Foreign Investment in the United States and in the EEC: A Practitioner's Guide," 69 Mich. B. J. 642 (1990); "A New Export Policy: The Foreign Sales Corporation and State Unitary Taxation of Foreign Source Income," 6 Mich. Y.B. Intl. Legal Stud. 61 (1986). Adjunct Professor of Environmental Law: Western New England College School of Law, Springfield, Mass.; Thomas Cooley Law School, Lansing, Mich., 1991. *Member:* Connecticut and American (Member, Sections of: International; Litigation) Bar Associations; State Bar of Michigan; District of Columbia Bar; Virginia State Bar. ***PRACTICE AREAS:*** Environmental Liability; Real Estate Finance; Land Use and Zoning. ***Email:*** rrubinstein@pepehazard.com

WALTER W. SIMMERS, born Philadelphia, Pennsylvania, March 4, 1948; admitted to bar, 1979, Connecticut. *Education:* University of Pennsylvania (B.S.M.E., 1970); University of Virginia (J.D., 1979). Order of the Coif. Member, Institutional Review Board, The University of Connecticut Health Center, 1998—. *Member:* Connecticut and American (Member: Sections on Business Law and Science and Technology) Bar Associations. [Lt., USN, 1970-1976]. ***PRACTICE AREAS:*** Corporate; Corporate Finance; Securities. ***Email:*** wsimmers@pepehazard.com

ALFRED A. TURCO, born Orange, New Jersey, January 28, 1945; admitted to bar, 1969, Connecticut; 1973, U.S. District Court, District of Connecticut. *Education:* Fordham University (b.A., 1966); University of Connecticut (J.D., 1969). Author: Chapter 17, *The Hardbook of Stable Value Investments,* Frank J. Fabozzi Publisher, 1998. Councillor, West Hartford Town Council, 1993-2000. *Member:* Stable Value Investment Association (Secretary, 1993-2000). ***PRACTICE AREAS:*** ERISA; Insurance. ***Email:*** aturco@pepehazard.com

ANNE NOBLE WALKER, born Salem, Massachusetts, March 24, 1963; admitted to bar, 1992, Connecticut; 1993, U.S. District Court, District of Connecticut. *Education:* Cornell University (B.S., 1985); State University of New York at Buffalo (J.D., cum laude, 1992). Contributor: Connecticut Employment Law Letter. President, Children's Law Centers. *Member:* Hartford, Connecticut (Executive Committee and Labor and Employment Section) and American Bar Associations. ***PRACTICE AREAS:*** Disabilities; Employee Benefits; Labor and Employment. ***Email:*** awalker@pepehazard.com

RICHARD F. WAREING, born New Bedford, Massachusetts, March 2, 1968; admitted to bar, 1993, Massachusetts; 1994, Connecticut and U.S. District Court, District of Massachusetts; 1996, U.S. Court of Appeals for the Federal Circuit; 1997, U.S. District Court, District of Connecticut and U.S. Court of Appeals, Second Circuit; 1999, U.S. District Court, Southern and Eastern Districts of New York. *Education:* College of the Holy Cross (A.B., magna cum laude, 1990); Harvard Law School (J.D., cum laude, 1993). *Member:* Hartford County and American Bar Associations. ***PRACTICE AREAS:*** Civil Appeals; Construction Litigation; Civil Litigation. ***Email:*** rwareing@pepehazard.com

EDWARD C. WHITE, born Providence, Rhode Island, October 30, 1958; admitted to bar, 1990, California; 1995, Massachusetts; 1996, Rhode Island; 1997, Connecticut. *Education:* University of Rhode Island (B.S., 1980); University of the Pacific-McGeorge School of Law (J.D., with great distinction, 1990); Georgetown University Law Center (LL.M., Securities Regulation, 1995). Order of the Coif. *Member:* Connecticut (Member, Business Law Section), Rhode Island and American Bar Associations. ***PRACTICE AREAS:*** Securities Regulation; Mergers and Acquisitions; Emerging Growth Companies. ***Email:*** ewhite@pepehazard.com

ADAM F. ZWEIFLER, born New York, N.Y., March 15, 1960; admitted to bar, 1986, California; 1992, Connecticut. *Education:* State University of New York Binghamton (B.A., 1983); Boalt Hall School of Law, University of California (J.D., 1986). Articles Editor, Ecology Law Quarterly, 1985-1986. *Member:* Connecticut and American (Member, Real Property and Probate Section; Business Law Section) Bar Associations; State Bar of California. ***PRACTICE AREAS:*** Real Estate; Real Estate Finance; Estate Planning; Probate. ***Email:*** azweifler@pepehazard.com

OF COUNSEL

DAVID A. DELMAN, born Indianapolis, Indiana, January 21, 1962; admitted to bar, 1987, Indiana; 1988, California (Not admitted in Connecticut). *Education:* American University, School of International Service (B.A., summa cum laude, 1984); Georgetown University (J.D., magna cum laude, 1987). Order of the Coif. ***PRACTICE AREAS:*** Construction Litigation; Insurance; Environmental Law; Commercial Law. ***Email:*** ddelman@pepehazard.com

ROBERT C. HUNT, JR., born New York, N.Y., July 1, 1925; admitted to bar, 1954, Connecticut. *Education:* Dartmouth College (B.A., 1948); University of Connecticut (LL.B., 1953). Town Attorney, Town of Avon, 1965-1997. Member, Panel of Arbitrators, American Arbitration Association. *Member:* Hartford County, Connecticut (Member, Real Property Section; Committee on Law Office Economics, Chairman, 1967-1969) and American (Member, Sections on: Public Contract Law; Tort and Insurance Practice; Law Practice Management) Bar Associations. [U.S. Army, 1943-1945]. ***PRACTICE AREAS:*** Fidelity and Surety; Municipal Law. ***Email:*** rhunt@pepehazard.com

GLENN J. MACGRADY, born Staten Island, New York; admitted to bar, 1975, Florida; 1977, New York; 1981, California; 1993, Connecticut. *Education:* Columbia College (A.B., 1970); Florida State University College of Law (J.D., with high honors, 1974); Harvard Law School (LL.M., 1975); New York University School of Law (LL.M. in Taxation, 1998). Phi Alpha Delta. Note and Comment Editor, Florida State University Law Review. Recipient, American Jurisprudence Book Awards: Property, Labor Law and Advanced Criminal Procedure. Visiting Professor of Law, Florida State University College of Law, 1988-1989. Counsel, IBM Corporation, 1975-1992. American Arbitration Association (Certified as Computer Law Mediator, 1991). Publications: "Paying Estate Expenses from Estate Income: A Practice and Policy Analysis of the Supreme Court's Hubert Decision and the Proposed Hubert Regulations," 78 Boston U. L.Rev. 1393 (1998); "1997 Connecticut Probate Law," 72 Conn. Bar J. 245 (1998); "What Part of the Estate Should Pay the Estate Expenses?" 72 Fla. Bar J. 10 (1998); "Protection of Computer Software—An Update and Practical Synthesis," 20 Houston L.Rev. 1033 (1984); "The Navigability Concept in the Civil and Common Law: Historical Development, Current Importance, and Some Doctrines that Don't Hold Water," 3 Fla. State U.L.Rev. 511 (1984); "Florida's Submerged Sovereignty Lands: What Are They, Who Owns Them, and Where is the Boundary?" 1 Fla. State U. L.Rev. 596 (1973); Comment, "Worley v. State," 1 Fla. State U. L.Rev. (1973). *Member:* Connecticut, New York State and American (Member, Sections On: Tax Law; Real Property and Probate Law; Business Law; Patent, Trademark and Copyright Law; Science and Technology Law; Legal Education) Bar Associations; State Bar of California; The Florida Bar; Computer Law Association. ***PRACTICE AREAS:*** Tax Law; Employee Benefits; Corporate Law; Estate Planning; Computer Law. ***Email:*** gmacgrady@pepehazard.com

SUSAN E. NEUBERG, born Brooklyn, New York, June 7, 1958; admitted to bar, 1984, New York and U.S. Court of Appeals, Tenth Circuit; 1993, Connecticut. *Education:* State University of New York at Binghamton (B.A., with honors, 1979); Stanford University (A.M., 1980); Benjamin N. Cardozo School of Law (J.D., 1983). Adjunct Lecturer, Insurance Finance Law, University of Connecticut School of Law, 1999. Adjunct Assistant Professor, Real Estate Finance, Real Estate Institute, New York University. *Member:* Association of the Bar of the City of New York (Member: Real Property Law Committee, 1992-1995; Mortgage Loan Opinions Subcommittee, 1992-1995; Mortgage Transfer Gains Tax Subcommittee, 1992-1995; ULSIA Subcommittee, 1992-1995), Connecticut, New York State (Member, Real Estate Financing and Lien Committee, 1990—) and American Bar Associations. ***LANGUAGES:*** Spanish, Portuguese. ***PRACTICE AREAS:*** Real Estate Finance; Real Estate Development; Leasing; Asset Management and Recovery; Workouts; Restructuring. ***Email:*** sneuberg@pepehazard.com

ASSOCIATES

NICOLE M. BAUMMER, born Hartford, Connecticut, January 9, 1974; admitted to bar, 2000, Connecticut; 2001, New York and Massachusetts. *Education:* University of Connecticut (B.A., 1995); University of Connecticut School of Law (J.D., 2000). Recipient, Cali Award, Trial Practice, Fall 1999. Moot Court Teaching Assistant, 1998. Managing Editor, Connecticut Insurance Law Journal, 1999-2000. *Member:* Hartford County, Connecticut (Member, Sections on: Labor and Employment; Litigation), Massachusetts, New York State and American (Member, Sections on: Litigation; Labor and Employment) Bar Associations. ***Email:*** nbaummer@pepehazard.com

FRANK N. CASSETTA, born Waterbury, Connecticut, July 31, 1963; admitted to bar, 1997, Connecticut; 1998, New York. *Education:* University of Connecticut (B.F.A., 1986); Brooklyn Law School (J.D., 1997). *Member:* Connecticut Bar Association; New York County Lawyers Association. ***Email:*** fcassetta@pepehazard.com

ISAIAH D. COOPER, born Middletown, New York, June 9, 1955; admitted to bar, 1991, Connecticut; 1992, New York and U.S. Tax Court. *Education:* State University of New York at Buffalo (B.F.A., summa cum laude, 1978); Youngstown State University (M.M., 1981); New York University (J.D., 1991). Member: International Trombone Association, 1979-1988; American Federation of Musicians, 1978-1988; Orchestra New England Board of Directors, 1994-1995, Vice-President, 1995-1996 and President, 1996; Connecticut Venture Group, 2000—. *Member:* New York State, Connecticut and American Bar Associations. ***LANGUAGES:*** German and Hebrew. ***Email:*** icooper@pepehazard.com

CHRISTOPHER B. CRAMER, born Long Island, New York, May 11, 1972; admitted to bar, 2000, Connecticut. *Education:* St. Michaels's College (B.A., 1994); Texas A&M University (Special Education Certificate, 1995); Sam Houston State University (Special Education Certificate, 1997); Quinnipiac College (J.D., 2000). *Member:* Hartford County, Connecticut and American Bar Associations. ***Email:*** ccramer@pepehazard.com

(This Listing Continued)

JAMES J. FLAHERTY, JR., born Rockville Centre, New York, January 31, 1960; admitted to bar, 1995, Connecticut; 1998, U.S. Tax Court, U.S. District Court, District of Connecticut and U.S. Court of Federal Claims; 1999, U.S. Supreme Court. *Education:* Fairfield University (B.S. Finance, cum laude, 1991); University of Connecticut School of Law (J.D., 1995). Associate Editor, Connecticut Journal of International Law, 1993-1995. Member, Board of Directors, Morris Foundation, 1995—. Lecturer, Naugatuck Valley Community College, 1999—. *Member:* Connecticut (Member: Probate and Trust Section; Elder Law Section; Tax Section) and American (Member: Real Property, Probate and Trust Section; Tax Section) Bar Associations; National Academy of Elder Law Attorneys; Connecticut Estate and Tax Planning Council. (Southport Office). **Email:** jflaherty@pepehazard.com

MICHAEL A. FUSCO, born New Haven, Connecticut, May 15, 1972; admitted to bar, 1997, Connecticut; 1999, New York; 2000, U.S. District Court, District of Connecticut. *Education:* Boston College (B.A., 1994); Quinnipiac College School of Law (J.D., 1997). Symposium Editor, Quinnipiac Law Review. *Member:* Hartford County and Connecticut Bar Associations. **Email:** mfusco@pepehazard.com

JENNIFER W. HADDAD, born Arlington, Massachusetts, May 5, 1972; admitted to bar, 1997, Connecticut. *Education:* Fairfield University (B.S., 1994); University of Connecticut (J.D., 1997). *Member:* Connecticut Bar Association. **Email:** jhaddad@pepehazard.com

VINCENT J. INGRAM, born Pinehurst, North Carolina, October 27, 1972; admitted to bar, 2001, Connecticut. *Education:* Howard University (B.A., 1996; J.D., 2000). *Member:* American Bar Association. **Email:** vingram@pepehazard.com

JENNIFER HAMILTON LEWIS, born Hot Springs, Arkansas, April 25, 1972; admitted to bar, 1997, Connecticut. *Education:* University of Arizona (B.A., magna cum laude, 1993); University of Connecticut (J.D., 1997). *Member:* Hartford County, Connecticut and American Bar Associations. **Email:** jhamiltonlewis@pepehazard.com

JAMES T. MURPHY, born Torrington, Connecticut, August 10, 1966; admitted to bar, 2000, Connecticut. *Education:* Tulane University of Louisiana (B.Arch., 1989); Western New England College (J.D., 2000). Member, Editorial Board, Western New England Law Review, 1999-2000. Member, American Institute of Architects Association, 2000. **Email:** jmurphy@pepehazard.com

JENNIFER A. OSOWIECKI, born Hartford, Connecticut, November 9, 1962; admitted to bar, 1994, Connecticut; 1995, U.S. District Court, District of Connecticut, U.S. Court of Appeals, Second Circuit. *Education:* University of Connecticut (B.S., 1985; J.D., with honors, 1994). Winner, William Hastie Memorial Moot Court Competition. Licensed Pharmacist, Connecticut, 1985. Member, Board of Directors, TAINO Housing and Development Corp., Inc. *Member:* Connecticut and American (Litigation Section) Bar Associations; Connecticut Pharmacists Association; American Inns of Court. **Email:** josowiecki@pepehazard.com

DOUGLAS M. POULIN, born Waterbury, Connecticut, April 3, 1965; admitted to bar, 1991, Connecticut; 1999, Washington. *Education:* Miami University (B.A., 1987); Boalt Hall School of Law, University of California at Berkeley (J.D., 1991). *Member:* Connecticut and Washington State Bar Associations. **Email:** dpoulin@pepehazard.com

A. RACHEL ROTHMAN, born Syracuse, New York, July 14, 1975; admitted to bar, 2000, Connecticut. *Education:* University of Pennsylvania (B.A., 1997); Cornell Law School (J.D., 2000). **Email:** rrothman@pepehazard.com

SHELLIE D. ROSAN, born New York, N.Y., June 26, 1963; admitted to bar, 1996, Connecticut; 1997, New York. *Education:* University of Pennsylvania (B.A., 1986; M.S., 1987); New York University (Diploma, Real Estate Investment Analysis, 1989); Benjamin N. Cardozo School of Law (J.D., 1996). **Email:** srosan@pepehazard.com

GARY F. SHELDON, born Ogdensburg, New York, June 30, 1965; admitted to bar, 1994, Connecticut; 1995, New York and U.S. District Court, District of Connecticut; 1996, U.S. Court of Appeals, Second Circuit. *Education:* Clarkson University (B.S.M.E., 1987); University of Connecticut (J.D., 1994). Member, Forum on the Construction Industry, 1995—. *Member:* Hartford County, Connecticut, New York and American Bar Associations. **Email:** gsheldon@pepehazard.com

WENDY KENNEDY VENOIT, born Meriden, Connecticut, June 2, 1971; admitted to bar, 1997, Connecticut, New Jersey, New York and U.S. District Court, District of New Jersey; 1998, U.S. District Court, Southern, Eastern and Northern Districts of New York and U.S. Court of Appeals, Third Circuit; 1999, U.s. District Court, District of Connecticut. *Education:* College of the Holy Cross (B.A., 1993); Pace University (J.D., magna cum laude, valedictorian, 1996). Research and Writing Editor, Pace Law Review. Author: "The Constitutionality of Punitive Damages and Recent Legislation," Journal of Products and Toxics Liability, vol. 15:3 (1995); Comment, "The Taxation of Punitive Damages: Recent Interpretation of the Section 104(a)(2) Exclusion," Pace Law Review, vol. 16:1 (1995). **Email:** wkennedy@pepehazard.com

(This Listing Continued)

KENNETH S. WEINSTOCK, born Newark, New Jersey, August 23, 1968; admitted to bar, 1993, Massachusetts, New Jersey and U.S. District Court, District of New Jersey; 1994, U.S. District Court, District of Massachusetts; 1996, Connecticut. *Education:* Boston University (B.A., magna cum laude, 1990; J.D., 1993). Edward F. Hennessey Scholar, 1993. *Member:* Massachusetts (Member, Sections on: Labor and Employment; Young Lawyers Division) Connecticut (Member, Young Lawyers Division: Labor and Employment Law Section) and American (Member, Labor and Employment Law Section) Bar Associations; Connecticut Industrial Relations Research Association; Connecticut Public Employer Labor Relations Association; National Public Employer Labor Relations Association. **Email:** kweinstock@pepehazard.com

BRIAN L. WOLINETZ, born Brooklyn, New York, November 27, 1972; admitted to bar, 1998, Florida; 2001, Connecticut. *Education:* University of Florida (B.A., with honors, 1994; J.D., with honors, 1997). Member, Jessup International Moot Court Team. *Member:* Palm Beach County and American Bar Associations; The Florida Bar. ***LANGUAGES:*** Russian. **Email:** bwolinetz@pepehazard.com

DAVID ANDRE WOODARD, born Houston, Texas, November 13, 1974; admitted to bar, 2000, Connecticut. *Education:* Texas Southern University (B.S., 1997); Howard University School of Law (J.D., 2000). Member, Howard Law Journal, 1998-2000. *Member:* Connecticut Bar Association. **Email:** dwoodard@pepehazard.com

RESIDENT PARTNERS IN BOSTON OFFICE

Thomas H. Brantley
Bret A. Cohen
Michael C. Gilleran
Sean W. Gilligan
Timothy Mark Hughes
David M. McGlone
David S. Mortensen

PARTNERS IN SOUTHPORT OFFICE

Suzanne E. Baldasare
Joseph W. Martini (Not admitted in CT)
Harold James Pickerstein

OF COUNSEL IN BOSTON OFFICE

Jane L. King
Richard S. Rosenstein
Sari Ann Strasburg

RESIDENT ASSOCIATES IN BOSTON OFFICE

Katharine P. Costello (Not admitted in CT)
Brendan J. Faulkner
Paul O. Mulroney
Neal F. Splaine

ASSOCIATES IN SOUTHPORT OFFICE

Stephan B. Grozinger
Kristin B. Mayhew

COUNSEL IN SOUTHPORT

JENNIFER L. COX, born New Haven, CT, May 11, 1968; admitted to bar, 1993, CT; 1994, U.S. District Court, District of CT. *Education:* Univ. of Connecticut (B.A., 1990; J.D., 1993). Member: CT Moot Court Board, 1991-1993; National Moot Court Competition. *Member:* American Bar Assn. (Health Law Section); American Health Lawyers Assn; CT Health Lawyers Assn. **Email:** jcox@pepehazard.com

(For biographical data on other firm personnel, see Professional Biographies at Southport, Connecticut and Boston, Massachusetts)

PHELON, FITZGERALD & WOOD, P.C.

HARTFORD, CONNECTICUT

(See Manchester)

General Civil and Criminal Litigation before all State and Federal Courts. Commercial Litigation, Corporation, Workers' Compensation, Zoning, Wills and Probate, Personal Injury, Medical Malpractice.

PIAZZA & PICKEL

HARTFORD, CONNECTICUT

(See Stamford)

Trials and Appeals in State and Federal Courts, Negligence, Medical Malpractice, Divorce and Personal Injury Law, Wrongful Death, Legal Malpractice, Child Custody, Automobile Accidents, Product Liability, Adoption, Family Law.

POLINSKY, SANTOS, SIEGEL & POLINSKY, LLC

890 WEST BOULEVARD
HARTFORD, CONNECTICUT 06105-4139
Telephone: 860-232-9959
Fax: 860-236-8337
Email: eapolinsky@mindspring.com
URL: http://www.lawyers.com/psplaw

Civil Litigation, Personal Injury, Workers Compensation, Negligence, Criminal Law, Real Estate, Wills, Divorce, Employment Law.

JEFFREY POLINSKY, born Norwich, Connecticut, March 15, 1956; admitted to bar, 1982, Connecticut and U.S. District Court, District of Connecticut. *Education:* Boston University (B.A., cum laude, 1978); Franklin Pierce Law Center (J.D.,1982). *Member:* Connecticut Bar Associations; Connecticut Trial Lawyers Association; The Association of Trial Lawyers of America; Connecticut Head Injury Association. **PRACTICE AREAS:** Civil Litigation; Personal Injury; Workers Compensation; Head Injury; Insurance.

ERIC A. POLINSKY, born Winchester, Connecticut, August 24, 1966; admitted to bar, 1991, Connecticut; 1993, U.S. District Court, District of Connecticut. *Education:* Brandeis University (B.A., cum laude, 1988); New England School of Law (J.D., 1991). *Member:* Connecticut Bar Association; Connecticut Trial Lawyers Association; The Association of Trial Lawyers of America. **PRACTICE AREAS:** Personal Injury; Estate Planning; Wills; Trust Law; Real Estate.

CARLOS M. SANTOS, born Cantanhede, Portugal, January 7, 1964; admitted to bar, 1989, Connecticut; 1990, U.S. District Court, District of Connecticut. *Education:* Trinity College (B.A., 1986); University of Connecticut (J.D., 1989). *Member:* Hartford County and Connecticut Bar Associations; Connecticut Trial Lawyers Association; The Association of Trial Lawyers of America. **LANGUAGES:** Portuguese, Spanish. **PRACTICE AREAS:** Civil Litigation; Criminal Litigation; Personal Injury; Workers Compensation; Administrative Law.

DAVID H. SIEGEL, born West Hartford, Connecticut, August 7, 1959; admitted to bar, 1987, Massachusetts and U.S. District Court, District of Massachusetts; 1988, New York, U.S. District Court, Southern and Eastern Districts of New York and U.S. Court of Appeals, Second Circuit; 1991, District of Columbia and Connecticut; 1994, U.S. District Court, District of Connecticut. *Education:* Northeastern University (B.S., cum laude, 1982); Pepperdine University (J.D., 1986). Certified Flight Instructor Certificate, 1982. Commercial Pilot Certificate, Multi and Single Engine Land Ratings and Instrument Ratings, 1983. *Member:* The Association of the Bar of the City of New York; New York State and American (Member, Aviation and Space Law Committee) Bar Associations; The District of Columbia Bar; The Association of Trial Lawyers of America (Member, Aviation Law Section); New York State Trial Lawyers Association; Lawyer-Pilots Bar Association. **PRACTICE AREAS:** Aviation Accidents; International Aviation; Personal Injury; Wrongful Death; Catastrophic Injury; Products Liability.

POLIVY & TASCHNER, LLC

Established in 1993
SIX CENTRAL ROW
HARTFORD, CONNECTICUT 06103
Telephone: 860-560-1180
Telecopier: 860-560-1354
Email: RPolivy@AOL.COM

Mailing Address: P.O. Box 230294, Hartford, Connecticut 06123-0294

Corporate, Financial Transactions, Real Estate Transactions, State and Federal Court Commercial Litigation, Workouts, Bankruptcy and Collections.

MEMBERS OF FIRM

RICHARD B. POLIVY, born New York, N.Y., November 6, 1946; admitted to bar, 1971, Connecticut; 1972, U.S. District Court, District of Connecticut and U.S. Court of Appeals, Second Circuit; 1977, U.S. Supreme Court. *Education:* Case Western Reserve University (B.A., 1968); Boston College (J.D., 1971). Adjunct Professor, University of Bridgeport School of Law, 1980-1988. Author: "Connecticut Construction Lending and the Law;" "Use of Arbitration Clauses in Commercial Loan Documents." President, The Association of Commercial Finance Attorneys, Inc. 1985-1987. Member: American College of Investment Counsel; American College of Finance Lawyers. *Member:* Connecticut (Commercial Law and Bankruptcy Section, Executive Committee, 1971—; Corporate Counsel Section, President, 1982-1984; Executive Committee, 1974-1992) American (Section on: Business Law and Communications Law) and Lawyers Pilots Bar Associations. **PRACTICE AREAS:** Bankruptcy; Secured, Asset-Based and Unsecured Commercial Loan Documentation; Real Estate; Creditor's Rights; Workouts; Business Finance Law. **Email:** RPolivy@AOL.COM

CRAIG S. TASCHNER, born Hartford, Connecticut, June 4, 1962; admitted to bar, 1987, Connecticut; 1988, U.S. District Court, District of Connecticut. *Education:* Daniel Webster College (B.S., cum laude, 1984); New York Law School (J.D., cum laude, 1987). Member, New York Law School Law Review, 1986-1987. Author: "Recovery of Interest and Attorney's Fees," The Contractor's Handbook of Law and Business, 1990. *Member:* Hartford County, Connecticut and American Bar Associations; Connecticut Trial Lawyers Association. **PRACTICE AREAS:** Commercial Law; Commercial Litigation; Creditors Rights; Bankruptcy; Workouts; Lender Liability Defense; Construction Litigation. **Email:** ctaschner@aol.com

ASSOCIATE

DALE M. CLAYTON, born South Windsor, Connecticut, January 25, 1961; admitted to bar, 1994, Connecticut and U.S. District Court, District of Connecticut. *Education:* American International College (B.S., 1983); McGeorge School of Law (J.D., 1993). Governing Board, Community Legal Services, 1992-1993. *Member:* Connecticut Bar Association (Member, Sections On: Commercial Law and Bankruptcy). **PRACTICE AREAS:** Commercial Litigation; Bankruptcy; Real Estate; Secured and Unsecured Lending. **Email:** dclayton@aol.com

PULLMAN & COMLEY, L.L.C.

Established in 1919
(Formerly Pullman, Comley, Bradley & Reeves)
90 STATE HOUSE SQUARE
HARTFORD, CONNECTICUT 06103-3702
Telephone: 860-424-4300
Telecopier: 860-424-4370
URL: http.//www.pullcom.com

Bridgeport, Connecticut Office: 850 Main Street. Telephone: 203-330-2000. Telecopier: 203-576-8888.
New Haven, Connecticut Office: One Century Tower, 265 Church Street. Telephone: 203-773-3006. Telecopier: 203-776-7075.
Simsbury, Connecticut Office: 720 Hopmeadow Street. Telephone: 860-651-9348. Fax: 860-651-1431.
Southport, Connecticut Office: 200 Pequot Avenue, P.O. Box 510. Telephone: 203-254-5000. Telecopier: 203-254-5070.
Stamford, Connecticut Office: 350 Bedford Street. Telephone: 203-324-5000. Telecopier: 203-363-8659.

General Practice including Administrative, Antitrust, Banking, Bankruptcy and Creditors Rights, Bonds, Business and Commercial, Corporate, Education, Employee Benefits, Environmental, Hospital and Health Care, Labor and Employment, Municipal Finance, Real Estate, Securities, Tax, Trusts and Estates, and Zoning. Energy and Utilities, Litigation in all Courts.

JOHN S. PULLMAN (1871-1943).
ARTHUR M. COMLEY (1883-1969).
J. KENNETH BRADLEY (1903-1969).
WILLIAM REEVES (1906-1967).

MEMBERS OF THE FIRM

ELIZABETH J. AUSTIN, born New York, N.Y., February 19, 1957; admitted to bar, 1983, Texas, Nebraska and U.S. District Court, Northern District of Texas; 1988, U.S. District Court, Eastern District of Texas; 1989, U.S. District Court, Western District of Texas and District of Connecticut; 1990, Connecticut; 1999, U.S. District Court, Southern District of New York. *Education:* University of Nebraska (B.A., 1979; J.D., 1982). *Member:* Bridgeport (Chairperson, Commercial Law Committee), Connecticut (Chair, Commercial Law and Bankruptcy Section), Nebraska State and American Bar Associations; State Bar of Texas; Commercial Law League of America; American Bankruptcy Institute; International Women's Insolvency and Restructuring Confederation; Women's Bankruptcy Bar Association (Founding Member; Executive Committee Member). (Also at New Haven, Bridgeport and Stamford Offices). **PRACTICE AREAS:** Insolvency Law; Bankruptcy Litigation; Commercial Litigation. **Email:** EA@PULLCOM.COM

MORRIS W. BANKS, born Hartford, Connecticut, May 3, 1939; admitted to bar, 1964, Connecticut. *Education:* Dartmouth College (A.B., 1961); Columbia University (LL.B., 1964); New York University (LL.M. in taxation, 1965). Adjunct Faculty Member, University of Connecticut School of Law, Lecturing in "Business Planning" 1980—. Alternate Member, Zoning Board of Appeals, Town of Bloomfield, 1969. Member, Bloomfield Town Council, 1969-1973. Panel Member, ALI-ABA New England Federal Securities Law Institute and author of "Current Developments in Real Estate Limited Partnership Financ-

(This Listing Continued)

ings," October, 1986; Panel Member, ALI-ABA Third New England Federal Securities Law Institute and author of "Issuance of Legal Opinions in Connection with Private Placements," September, 1990. Panel Member, Connecticut Bar Association and author of "Divisive Reorganizations"; Panel Member, Connecticut Bar Association and author of "Coping with the New Connecticut Tax Act, Subchapter S Corporations and Partnerships," June, 1993; Panel Member, The President's Forum of Hartford and author of "Financial Structuring Strategies, Venture Capital and Initial Public Offerings as Sources of Funding Growth," March, 1994; Panel Member, Forum on Venture Capital, Southeastern Connecticut Business Association and author of "Forms of Venture Capital and Structure of Venture Capital Pools"; Panel Member, Connecticut Business and Industry Association and author of "Taxable and Tax Free Mergers and Acquisitions," January, 1993; Panel Member, Connecticut Bar Association and author of "Dissolving the Corporate Business Marriage, Tax Aspects of Division of Corporate Assets," April, 1982; Panel Member, Hartford County Bar Association and author of "Tax Aspects of Corporate Distribution and Liquidations," February, 1989; Panel Member, Hartford County Bar Association and author of "Tax Considerations in the Purchase and Sale of Business Interests," May, 1995; Panel Member and author of "How to Steer Clear of Tax Surprises in the Purchase and Sale of Business Interests," November, 1995; Panel Member, seminar sponsored by the Hartford County Bar Association, February, 1986 and author of "Tax Aspects of Real Estate Transactions"; Panel Member and author of "Tax Considerations in the Purchase and Sale of a Small Business," presented to Hartford County Bar Association; Panel Member and author of "Tax Considerations in the Purchase and Sale of Business Interests," presented to the University of Connecticut Income Tax School, November 1998 and November 2000. *Member:* Hartford County (Member, Committee on Liaison with Internal Revenue Service, 1970-1985, Chairman, 1976-1985) and Connecticut (Member, Executive Committee, Tax Section, 1979—; Chairman, 1996-1999; Lecturer in Taxation, Continuing Legal Education, 1971—; Member, Committee on Corporations and Other Business Organizations, 1970-1976) Bar Associations. ***PRACTICE AREAS:*** Corporate Law; Corporate Securities; Taxation; Mergers and Acquisitions; Succession Planning for Closely-Held Business. ***Email:*** MWB@PULLCOM.COM

JAMES G. DOWLING, JR., born Coronado, California, May 31, 1952; admitted to bar, 1978, Connecticut and U.S. District Court, District of Connecticut; 1984, U.S. Supreme Court. *Education:* Tufts University (B.A., 1975); Suffolk University (J.D., 1978). Member, 1976-1978 and Editor, 1977-1978, Suffolk Law Review. Author: "Contingent Interest In Executory Contract Is A Right To Property To Which Federal Tax Lien Can Attach," 11 Suffolk Law Review 1400, 1977; "Impeachment of Witness's General Credibility By Use Of Juvenile Record," 11 Suffolk Law Review 590, 1977. *Member:* Connecticut (Member, Real Estate Law Section) and American (Member: Real Property, Probate and Trust Law Section, Committee on Mortgages and Other Debt Financing, Committee on Foreclosures and Related Remedies; Corporation, Banking and Business Law Section; Forum Committee on the Construction Industry, 1982—) Bar Associations; Association of Commercial Finance Attorneys; The Connecticut Mortgage Bankers Association; First American Title Insurance Corporation (Member, Connecticut Advisory Board). (Also at Bridgeport Office). ***PRACTICE AREAS:*** Real Estate Law; Commercial Transactions. ***Email:*** JXD@PULLCOM.COM

ANDREW C. GLASSMAN, born Hartford, Connecticut, May 26, 1960; admitted to bar, 1985, Connecticut; 1986, U.S. District Court, District of Connecticut. *Education:* Cornell University (B.S., 1982); University of Connecticut School of Law (J.D., 1985). Member, 1983-1985, and Editor, 1984-1985, University of Connecticut Law Review. Frequent lecturer: business acquisition topics; issues involving management of employees, human resource functions. Author: "A Future for Cogeneration: FERC v. American Electric Power Service Corporation," 16 Connecticut Law Review, 1984; "A Summary of the Americans With Disabilities Act," and "Substance Abuse in The Workplace and Employee Assistance Programs". Adjunct Faculty Member: Labor and Personnel Relations, Hartford Graduate Center, 1989-1990; Employee Relations, Teikyo Post University, 1993-1994. Member: Simsbury Rotary; Simsbury Democratic Town Committee, 1988—; Simsbury Main Street Partnership, 1999—. Simsbury Charter Revision Commission, 1990-1991. *Member:* Connecticut and American Bar Associations. (Also at Simsbury Office). ***PRACTICE AREAS:*** Corporate Law; Mergers and Acquisitions; Employment Law; Commercial Transactions. ***Email:*** AXG@PULLCOM.COM

LAWRENCE J. GOLDEN, born Norwalk, Connecticut, February 9, 1947; admitted to bar, 1973, Connecticut; 1985, U.S. District Court, District of Connecticut. *Education:* University of Virginia (B.A., 1969; J.D., 1973). Phi Beta Kappa. Town Councilman Coventry, Connecticut, 1989-1991. Author: *Equitable Distribution of Property,* Shepard's/McGraw-Hill, 1983. Member, Board of Education, Coventry, Connecticut, 1999—. ***PRACTICE AREAS:*** Energy; Environmental; Public Utility; Land Use; Litigation. ***Email:*** LJG@PULLCOM.COM

BARRY D. GREENE, born New Haven, Connecticut, October 22, 1934; admitted to bar, 1959, Connecticut; 1961, U.S. District Court, District of Connecticut. *Education:* Brown University (A.B., cum laude, 1956); University of

(This Listing Continued)

Connecticut (LL.B., 1959). Associate Editor, Board of Student Editors, Connecticut Bar Journal, 1958-1959. Member, 1967-1971 and Chairman, 1969-1971, Bloomfield Board of Education. Hartford Jewish Community Center (Honorary Life Officer). Member, Panel of Arbitrators, American Arbitration Association. *Member:* Hartford County and Connecticut Bar Associations. ***PRACTICE AREAS:*** Real Estate; Corporate Law; Business Law. ***Email:*** BDG@PULLCOM.COM

JOSHUA A. HAWKS-LADDS, born Rochester, New York, February 5, 1965; admitted to bar, 1991, Connecticut; 1992, U.S. District Court, District of Connecticut; 1994, U.S. Court of Appeals, Second Circuit. *Education:* University of Connecticut (B.A., 1987); Western New England College (J.D., cum laude, 1991). Author: Connecticut Bar Journal Official Annual Survey: "Labor Relations and Employment Law: Developments in Connecticut," 74 Conn. Bar Journal 3 (2000); "State Court Adds Twist to Intracorporate Communications," 396 Fair Employment Practices Guidelines at 5 (Nov. 25, 1995). Member: Town of Bolton Planning and Zoning Commission, 1998—; Bolton Board of Finance, 1997; Town of Bolton Economic Development Commission, 1995-1997. Director, March of Dimes, 1998—. Member, 1994—, Chair, 2000—, Bolton Democratic Town Committee. *Member:* Hartford County (Chair, Labor and Employment Committee, 1994-1996) and Connecticut (Labor and Employment Law Section, 1992—) Bar Associations; Connecticut Trial Lawyers Association; Association of Trial Lawyers of America. ***PRACTICE AREAS:*** Civil Litigation; Labor and Employment Law; Municipal Law; Workers' Compensation. ***Email:*** JAH@PULLCOM.COM

JOHN J. KINDL, born Hartford, Connecticut, December 13, 1951; admitted to bar, 1977, Connecticut; 1979, U.S. District Court, District of Connecticut. *Education:* Trinity College (B.A., 1974); University of Connecticut (J.D., 1977). Clerk to Chief Justice John P. Cotter, Connecticut Supreme Court, 1977-1979. *Member:* Hartford County and Connecticut (Member, Real Estate Law Section) Bar Associations. ***PRACTICE AREAS:*** Real Estate Law. ***Email:*** JJK@PULLCOM.COM

MICHAEL A. KURS, born Manhasset, New York, June 26, 1955; admitted to bar, 1980, Georgia; 1981, U.S. District Court, Northern and Southern Districts of Georgia; Supreme Court of Georgia and Court of Appeals of Georgia; 1982, New York; 1987, U.S. Court of Appeals, Eleventh Circuit; 1988, Connecticut; 1995, Mashantucket Pequot Tribal Court. *Education:* Yale University (B.A., 1977); Antioch School of Law (J.D., 1980). Member: Connecticut State Board of Mental Health, (1990-1995); North Central Connecticut Regional Mental Health Board (1988-1997) and Hartford Mental Health Council. Board of Directors, Yale Club and Scholarship Foundation of Hartford, 1999—. *Member:* Connecticut and American Bar Associations; American Health Lawyers Association. (Also at Bridgeport Office). ***PRACTICE AREAS:*** Health Care Law; Litigation and Administrative Law; Employment Law; Education Law; Antitrust Law. ***Email:*** MAK@PULLCOM.COM

LISA A. MAGLIOCHETTI, born New Haven, Connecticut, October 12, 1961; admitted to bar, 1987, Connecticut and U.S. District Court, District of Connecticut; 1989, Massachusetts. *Education:* Quinnipiac College (B.S., magna cum laude, 1983); Boston College (J.D., cum laude, 1987). *Member:* Hartford (Family Law Section), New Haven County, Connecticut (Member, Sections on: Family Law and Civil Justice), Massachusetts and American (Member, Section on Tort and Insurance Practice) Bar Associations; The Association of Trial Lawyers of America; Connecticut Trial Lawyers Association. ***PRACTICE AREAS:*** Litigation; Family Law. ***Email:*** LAM@PULLCOM.COM

ALAN S. PARKER, born Far Rockaway, New York, January 29, 1955; admitted to bar, 1980, New York and Connecticut. *Education:* State University of New York at Binghamton (B.A., 1976); University of Toledo (J.D., cum laude, 1979); New York University (LL.M. in Taxation, 1988). Articles Editor, University of Toledo Law Review, 1979. *Member:* Connecticut (Member, Sections on Taxation and Estates and Probate), New York State and American Bar Associations. (Also at Simsbury Office). ***PRACTICE AREAS:*** Probate and Estate Planning; Tax Law. ***Email:*** ASP@PULLCOM.COM

MARIE V. PHELAN, born Jersey City, NJ, July 14, 1947; admitted to bar, 1989, CT. *Education:* Wesleyan Univ. (B.A., cum laude, 1983); Univ. of Connecticut (J.D. , cum laude, 1989). Phi Beta Kappa; Sigma Xi. Member, Public Finance/Public Law Practice Group. Chairman, State of Connecticut Municipal Finance Advisory Commission; Member, Board of Director's of Hartford Assn. of Women Atty's., 1993-1998; Corporator, Harford Ballet; Member, Local Government Committee, Hartford Chamber of Commerce, 1994-1999. Member, 1984-1987, Vice Chairman, 1985-1987, Killingworth Board of Finance. Advisory Board, Ninth Connecticut Women's Congress, 1991. Member, Wesleyan Univ. Alumni Schools Committee, 1984—. *Member:* Connecticut Bar Association; National Association of Bond Lawyers. ***PRACTICE AREAS:*** Public Finance; Public Law; Commercial Lending. ***Email:*** MVP@PULLCOM.COM

ELLIOTT B. POLLACK, born Brooklyn, New York, January 20, 1943; admitted to bar, 1965, Connecticut; 1966, U.S. District Court, District of Connecticut; 1969, U.S. Court of Appeals, Second Circuit and U.S. Supreme Court. *Education:* Columbia College (A.B., 1962); Columbia University (LL.B., 1965). Law Clerk to Associate Justice Howard W. Alcorn, Supreme Court of

(This Listing Continued)

PULLMAN & COMLEY, L.L.C., Hartford—Continued

Connecticut, 1965-1966. Town Councilman, West Hartford, 1975-1977. Board of Directors, Hartford Dispensary, 1988—. President, Hartford Dispensary, 1991-1996; Board of Directors, Solomon Schechter Day School of Greater Hartford, 1990-1996, 1997-1999. Member, State of Connecticut Medical Examining Board, 1991-1994; Board of Directors, Hartford Stage Company, 1991-1999; Board of Directors, 1993—; Vice President, 1999-2001; President, 2001—; Capitol Area Foundation for Equal Justice. Member, Board of Directors and Secretary, Connecticut Health Lawyers Association, 1999—. *Member:* Hartford County, Connecticut (Member: Administrative Law Section; Health Law Section) and American (Member, Sections of: Health Law; Antitrust) Bar Associations; American Health Lawyers Association; Healthcare Financial Management Association; Institute for Professionals in Taxation (Legal Committee); International Association of Assessing Officers; American Property Tax Counsel. James W. Cooper Fellow, Connecticut Bar Foundation. (Also at Bridgeport and Stamford Offices). ***PRACTICE AREAS:*** Health Care; Tax Appeal and Condemnation Law; Commercial Litigation. ***Email:*** EBP@PULLCOM.COM

LEWIS RABINOVITZ, born Hartford, Connecticut, November 14, 1935; admitted to bar, 1960, Connecticut. *Education:* Yale University (B.A., 1957); Harvard University (LL.B., 1960). Phi Beta Kappa. Member, Connecticut Bar Examining Committee, 1978-1996. Director, Greater Hartford Jewish Federation, 1967—. President, 1980-1982, Chairman of the Board, 1982-1984 and Life Director, Greater Hartford Jewish Community Center. *Member:* Hartford County, Connecticut and American Bar Associations. ***PRACTICE AREAS:*** Corporate Law; Tax Law; Family Law; Litigation. ***Email:*** LR@PULLCOM.COM

RICHARD C. ROBINSON, born Hartford, Connecticut, August 26, 1945; admitted to bar, 1971, Connecticut. *Education:* University of Pennsylvania (B.A., 1967); University of Connecticut School of Law (J.D., with honors, 1971). Member, Board of Editors, Connecticut Law Review, 1969-1971. Recipient: West Hornbook Award; American Jurisprudence Award in Jurisprudence, Labor Law, Corporations. Author: "Coordinated Bargaining —G.E. and Beyond," 2 Connecticut Law Review 375. Law Clerk to Justice Elmer W. Ryan, Connecticut Supreme Court, 1971-1972. Lecturer, Seminar on Alternative Dispute Resolution, Hartford County Bar Association, 1982. Moderator, Seminar on Jury Persuasion, Hartford County Bar Association, 1989. Member: Bloomfield Board of Education, 1975-1981; Bloomfield Town Council, 1981-1983. Vice President, Greater Hartford Jewish Community Center, 1984-1988; President, 1988-1991. Director, Federation Homes, 1983-1990. Director, Hartford Jewish Federation, 1989-2000. Trustee, Hebrew Home and Hospital, 1995—. *Member:* Hartford County (Chairperson, Continuing Legal Education Committee, 1988-1990), Connecticut (Member, Executive Committee, Civil Justice Section, 1980-1982) and American (Member, Sections on: Labor Law; Litigation; Torts and Insurance Practice; Member, Forum Committee on the Construction Industry) Bar Associations. ***PRACTICE AREAS:*** Litigation; Employment Law. ***Email:*** RCR@PULLCOM.COM

THOMAS A. ROUSE, born Syracuse, New York, December 2, 1950; admitted to bar, 1975, Connecticut and U.S. District Court, District of Connecticut. *Education:* Trinity College (B.A., 1972); University of Connecticut (J.D., 1975). Phi Beta Kappa. Articles Editor, Connecticut Law Review, 1974-1975. *Member:* Connecticut (Computer Law, Environmental and Antitrust Law Sections) and American Bar Associations. (Also at Bridgeport Office). ***PRACTICE AREAS:*** Electronic Commerce; Environmental Litigation; Telecommunications Law; Electric Power; Technology Startups. ***Email:*** TAR@PULLCOM.COM

ALAN I. SCHEER, born Yonkers, New York, March 3, 1942; admitted to bar, 1967, Connecticut and U.S. District Court, District of Connecticut; 1970, U.S. Court of Appeals, Second Circuit; 1973, U.S. District Court, Northern District of New York; 1974, U.S. Supreme Court. *Education:* Cornell University and New York University (B.S., 1964); Brooklyn Law School (J.D., 1967). Author: "The Family and Medical Leave Act: A New Dawn in Employee Rights," Connecticut Lawyer, Vol. 2 No. 4, December 1991; "Understanding The State and Federal Leave Acts-Reconciling the Differences," Connecticut Law Tribune, June 20, 1994; "Independent Contractors or Employees? Misclassification May Be Dangerous," Connecticut Lawyer, Vol. 5, No. 3, November, 1994. Member, Board of Directors, Hartford Symphony Orchestra, 1984-1990. Executive Vice President, Hartford Chamber Orchestra, 1980-1984. Trustee, Long Wharf Theatre, New Haven, Connecticut, 1987-2000; Member, Board of Directors of Chamber Music Plus, 1991-1997. Member, Editorial Advisory Board of the Connecticut Lawyer, 1990—. Member, Panel of Commercial Arbitrators, American Arbitration Association, 1976—; Panel of Employment Law Arbitrators, 1992—. *Member:* Hartford County, Connecticut (Member, Board of Governors, 1998-2000. Member, House of Delegates, 1990—; Labor and Employment Law Counsel, 1981—; Member, Executive Committee, 1981— and Chairman, 1994-1995, Labor and Employment Law Section; Executive Committee, Antitrust and Trade Regulation Section, 1991—) and American (Labor and Employment Law Section) Bar Associations; Society of Professionals in Dispute Resolution. ***PRACTICE AREAS:*** Labor and Employment Law; Litigation; Health Care; Antitrust. ***Email:*** AIS@PULLCOM.COM

(This Listing Continued)

GREGORY F. SERVODIDIO, born Staten Island, New York, May 23, 1961; admitted to bar, 1986, Connecticut; 1987, U.S. District Court, District of Connecticut. *Education:* Georgetown University (A.B., magna cum laude, 1983; J.D., 1986). Phi Beta Kappa; Pi Sigma Alpha. Co-author: Connecticut Chapter of ABA Property Tax Deskbook (5th Ed.). Co-Chair, Municipal Tax Advisory Committee to Superior Court, Tax Session, 1995-1996. Member, Board of Directors, Fellowship Place, 1994—. Member, Marlborough Economic Development Commission, 1999—. *Member:* Hartford County, Connecticut and American Bar Associations; Institute for Professionals in Taxation; International Association of Assessing Officers; Connecticut Association of Assessing Officers; National Council of Property Taxation. (Also at Bridgeport Office). ***PRACTICE AREAS:*** Property Taxation; Condemnation and Relocation; Land Use; Litigation. ***Email:*** GFS@PULLCOM.COM

JAMES T. SHEARIN, born Stauton, Virginia, March 11, 1961; admitted to bar, 1986, Connecticut; 1987, U.S. District Court, District of Connecticut; 1988, U.S. Court of Appeals, Second Circuit; 1995, U.S. Supreme Court; 1997, U.S. Court of Federal Claims. *Education:* University of Connecticut (B.A., summa cum laude, 1983; J.D., with high honors, 1986). Recipient, William F. Starr Outstanding Student Award. Administrative Editor, Connecticut Law Review, 1985-1986. Author: "The Discrimination Statutes and the Supreme Court's Program for Confusion," 17 Conn. L. Rev. 3 (1985). Co-author: "What to do When the Feds Grab for Collateral," ABA Banking Journal, Vol. LXXX16, No. 2; Commentary: "Working for Which Side," The Record, No. 175 (September 10, 1993). Author: "The Expert Witness and Mandatory Disclosure: Comply or Suffer the Consequences," Vol. 14, No. 2, CTLA Forum 136 (March/April, 1996); "Lawyering from the *John*," Vol. 6, No. 7, Connecticut Lawyer 28 (April 1996); "Protecting Your Eventual Judgment for Money Damages," The Banking Law Journal (October, 1998). Co-author: "Zealousness and Honesty in Settlement Discussion," Connecticut Law Tribune Magazine (August 9, 1999); "Medical Malpractice Liability: It's Not Just For Doctors Anymore," Vol. 11, No. 5. Connecticut Lawyer 4 (February 2001). Law Clerk, Hon. Peter C. Dorsey, District of Connecticut, 1986-1988. Member, Raymond E. Baldwin Inn of Courts, 1989—. Appointed Co-Counsel to Federal Grievance Committee (D.Conn.) 1997—. Member and Chairman, Connecticut Legal Services. President, UConn Law School Foundation, Inc. James W. Cooper Fellow, Connecticut Bar Foundation. *Member:* Bridgeport (President), Connecticut (Member: Federal Practice and Intellectual Property Sections, Executive Committees) and American Bar Associations; The Association of Trial Lawyers of America; Connecticut Trial Lawyers Association. (Also at Bridgeport and Stamford Offices). ***PRACTICE AREAS:*** Litigation; Intellectual Property; Admiralty; Securities. ***Email:*** JTS@PULLCOM.COM

JOHN F. STAFSTROM, JR., born Waterbury, Connecticut, June 14, 1956; admitted to bar, 1981, Connecticut. *Education:* College of the Holy Cross (B.A., 1978); University of Connecticut (J.D., with honors, 1981). Member, 1979-1981, and Note and Comment Editor, 1980-1981, Connecticut Law Review. Author: "Standing Under 42 U.S.C. Sections 1981 and 1982: Direct, Indirect and A New 'Loss of Association' Standing," Volume 13, Connecticut Law Review, 1981. Bridgeport City Council, 1987-1994. *Member:* Bridgeport, Connecticut and American Bar Associations; National Association of Bond Lawyers. (Also at Bridgeport Office). ***PRACTICE AREAS:*** Public Finance; Corporate Law; Banking Law; Commercial Law. ***Email:*** JFS@PULLCOM.COM

BARRIE K. WETSTONE, born Hartford, Connecticut, May 8, 1938; admitted to bar, 1963, Connecticut. *Education:* Harvard University (B.A., 1960); Columbia University (LL.B., 1963); New York University (LL.M. in Taxation, 1964). Co-Author: "Estate Planning by Lifetime Charitable Giving under the 1976 Tax Reform Act," CLU Journal, January 1978. Lecturer, Forty-first New York University Annual Institute on Federal Taxation, 1982. Member, Adjunct Faculty, Federal Estate and Gift Taxation, University of Connecticut School of Law, 1980-1982. President, Simsbury Light Opera Company, 1980-1982, 1992-1993. *Member:* Hartford County (Member, Internal Revenue Service Bar Liaison Committee, 1967-1969) and Connecticut (Chairman, Bar Association Liaison with Accountants Committee, 1969-1972); Member, Tax Section, Executive Committee, 1990-1991 and 1997—) Bar Associations. ***PRACTICE AREAS:*** Tax Law; Pension and Profit Sharing Law; Estate Planning Law. ***Email:*** BKW@PULLCOM.COM

MARJORIE S. WILDER, born New Haven, Connecticut, August 29, 1943; admitted to bar, 1972, Connecticut; 1975, U.S. District Court, District of Connecticut; 1988, U.S. Supreme Court; 1989, U.S. Court of Appeals, Second Circuit; 1997, U.S. Court of Appeals, Ninth Circuit. *Education:* Smith College (A.B., magna cum laude, 1965); Tufts University (M.A., Economics, 1970); University of Connecticut (J.D., with high honors, 1972). Editor, University of Connecticut Law Review, 1971-1972. Assistant Corporation Counsel, 1983-1985 and Corporation Counsel, 1985-1997, Town of West Hartford. *Member:* Hartford County, Connecticut (Member: Litigation, Planning & Zoning and Real Property Sections) and American (Member: Litigation and State and Local Government Law Taxation) Bar Associations; Institute for Professionals in Taxation; International Association of Assessing Officers; Connecticut Associa-

(This Listing Continued)

tion of Assessing Officers. Fellow, James W. Cooper Connecticut Bar Foundation, 1998—. ***PRACTICE AREAS:*** Administrative Law; Condemnation Law; Real and Personal Property Taxation; Litigation; Zoning, Planning and Land Use. ***Email:*** MSW@PULLCOM.COM

ASSOCIATE

ROD W. FARRELL, born Stamford, Connecticut, July 25, 1958; admitted to bar, 1985, Connecticut and U.S. District Court, District of Connecticut. *Education:* Yale University (B.A., cum laude, 1980); University of Connecticut (J.D., 1985). Author: "Preserving Grand Jury Secrecy: United States v. Baggot," 16 Conn. Law Review 371. *Member:* Connecticut Bar Association. ***PRACTICE AREAS:*** Bankruptcy; Litigation; Business Financing. ***Email:*** RWF@PULLCOM.COM

JULIE A. MORGAN, born Meriden, Connecticut, February 13, 1969; admitted to bar, 1998, Connecticut; 2001, U.S. District Court, District of Connecticut. *Education:* University of Connecticut (B.A., 1991); Quinnipiac College School of Law (J.D., magna cum laude, 1998). *Member:* Hartford County, Connecticut and American Bar Associations; Association of Trial Lawyers of America. ***PRACTICE AREAS:*** Litigation; Property Taxation; Real Estate and Personal Property Valuation; Land Use. ***Email:*** JAM@PULLCOM.COM

JONATHAN M. SHAPIRO, born Middletown, Connecticut, March 25, 1976; admitted to bar, 2001, Connecticut. *Education:* Boston College (B.A., 1998); University of Connecticut School of Law (J.D., 2001). ***PRACTICE AREAS:*** Health Care; Litigation. ***Email:*** JMS@PULLCOM.COM

GWEN P. WEISBERG, born Mount Vernon, New York, July 29, 1958; admitted to bar, 1986, Massachusetts; 1989, U.S. District Court, District of Massachusetts; 1991, Connecticut and U.S. District Court, District of Connecticut. *Education:* University of Massachusetts (B.S., cum laude, 1980); Temple University School of Law (J.D., 1986). Eta Sigma Delta. Member, Moot Court Honor Society (Treasurer, 1985-1986). Member, Board of Directors, 1993-2001, Member, Executive Committee, 1995-2001, Officer, 1999-2001, University of Massachusetts Amherst Alumni Association. *Member:* Connecticut, Massachusetts and American Bar Associations. ***PRACTICE AREAS:*** Litigation; Civil Litigation; Commercial Law; Construction Law; Real Estate Law. ***Email:*** GPW@PULLCOM.COM

(For Complete Biographical Data on all Personnel, See Bridgeport, Connecticut Professional Biographies).

REGNIER, TAYLOR, CURRAN & EDDY

CITYPLACE
HARTFORD, CONNECTICUT 06103-4402
Telephone: 860-249-9121
FAX: 860-527-4343
Email: RTCE@SNET.NET

General Practice. Trials in all Courts. Probate, Insurance, Corporations and Real Estate Law. Family and Municipal Law, Professional Malpractice, Municipal Litigation, Professional Malpractice, Municipal Litigation.

MEMBERS OF FIRM

J. RONALD REGNIER (1906-1987).

ROBERT F. TAYLOR (1930-1994).

EDMUND T. CURRAN, born Bridgeport, Connecticut, July 11, 1937; admitted to bar, 1962, Connecticut, 1970, U.S. District Court, District of Connecticut; 1971, U.S. Court of Appeals, Second Circuit and U.S. Supreme Court. *Education:* Yale University (B.A., 1959; LL.B., 1962). Editor, Bar-Fly (Hartford County Bar Association periodical), 1966-1973. Member: Bloomfield Town Planning and Zoning Commission, 1971-1977; Bloomfield Inland Wetlands Commission, 1973-1977; Bloomfield Town Council, 1977-1981. Bloomfield, Deputy Mayor, 1980-1981. Member, Section of Insurance, Negligence and Compensation Law, American Bar Association. *Member:* Association of Defense Trial Attorneys (Member, Executive Council, 1982-1985; Treasurer, 1986—); Connecticut Defense Lawyers Association (Member, Board of Directors, 1982); Defense Research Institute. ***PRACTICE AREAS:*** General Practice; Trial Practice; Insurance; Toxic Torts; Products Liability; Personal Injury; Professional Malpractice; Premises Liability; Municipal Litigation; Aviation Litigation; Real Estate; Probate; Family Law. ***Email:*** ecurran@rtcelaw.com

RALPH G. EDDY, born Southbridge, Massachusetts, June 4, 1947; admitted to bar, 1972, Connecticut; 1974, U.S. District Court, District of Connecticut; 1979, U.S. Court of Appeals, Second Circuit. *Education:* Bowdoin College (A.B., 1969); University of Connecticut (J.D., 1972). Phi Beta Kappa. James Bowdoin Scholar. Lecturer: Advanced Skills Institute of Insurance Practices, Aetna, Hartford, Connecticut, March, 1990. *Member:* American Bar Association (Member, Tort and Insurance Practice Section); Connecticut Defense Lawyers Association; Association of Defense Trial Attorneys; Defense Research Institute. Fellow, Connecticut Bar Foundation. ***PRACTICE AREAS:*** General

(This Listing Continued)

Practice; Trial Practice; Insurance; Toxic Torts; Products Liability; Personal Injury; Professional Malpractice; Premises Liability; Municipal Litigation; Aviation Litigation. ***Email:*** reddy@rtcelaw.com

JACK D. MILLER, born Paris, France, November 12, 1952; admitted to bar, 1979, Connecticut and U.S. District Court, District of Connecticut. *Education:* Case Western Reserve University (B.A., 1974); Cleveland Marshall College of Law (J.D., 1978). *Member:* Hartford County (Chairman, Bench-Bar Committee, 1988-1989) and American (Member, Sections on: Tort and Insurance Law; Family Law) Bar Associations; Connecticut Trial Lawyers Association; Connecticut Defense Lawyers Association; The Association of Trial Lawyers of America; Association of Defense Trial Attorneys. ***PRACTICE AREAS:*** General Practice; Trial Practice; Insurance; Toxic Torts; Products Liability; Personal Injury; Professional Malpractice; Premises Liability; Municipal Litigation; Aviation Litigation. ***Email:*** jmiller@rtcelaw.com

LAWRENCE L. CONNELLI, born Hartford, Connecticut, July 3, 1958; admitted to bar, 1983, Connecticut; 1984, U.S. District Court, District of Connecticut. *Education:* University of Connecticut (B.A., with distinction, magna cum laude, 1980; J.D., 1983). Author: "TMJ Syndrome: Fact or Fiction," Journal of the Connecticut Defense Lawyers Association, Dec., 1986. *Member:* Connecticut Defense Lawyers Association (Associate Editor, The Defense, 1984—); National Institute of Trial Advocacy (Diplomate). ***PRACTICE AREAS:*** General Practice; Trial Practice; Insurance; Toxic Torts; Products Liability; Personal Injury; Professional Malpractice; Premises Liability; Municipal Litigation; Aviation Litigation; Real Estate; Probate; Family Law. ***Email:*** lconnelli@rtcelaw.com

ASSOCIATES

JAY F. HUNTINGTON, born Hartford, Connecticut, August 4, 1955; admitted to bar, 1981, California; 1984, U.S. District Court, Central District of California; 1987, Connecticut; 1988, U.S. District Court, District of Connecticut. *Education:* Northeastern University (B.S., with honors, 1978); Santa Clara University (J.D., 1981). Lecturer: "Depositions: Strategies, Tactics, and Mechanics," PESI, 1995; "Taking Effective Depositions", Lorman Education Services, 1997. Member, Deputy District Attorneys Association, Ventura County, California, 1981-1984. *Member:* New Haven County, 1988-1992, Hartford County (Litigation Section, 1992—) and Middlesex County Bar Associations; Ventura County Criminal Defense Bar Association (Secretary/Treasurer, 1985; Vice-President, 1986); California Attorneys for Criminal Justice; Connecticut Defense Lawyers Association. ***PRACTICE AREAS:*** General Practice; Trial Practice; Insurance; Toxic Torts; Products Liability; Personal Injury; Professional Malpractice; Premises Liability; Municipal Litigation; Aviation Litigation; Real Estate; Probate; Family Law. ***Email:*** jhuntington@rtcelaw.com

FREDERICK M. O'BRIEN, born Palmyra, New York, October 7, 1946; admitted to bar, 1990, Connecticut; 1991, U.S. District Court, District of Connecticut. *Education:* Valley College; University of California at Berkeley (A.B., summa cum laude, 1975); University of Connecticut (J.D., 1990). Phi Beta Kappa. *Member:* New Haven County Bar Associations. Connecticut Defense Lawyers Association; Connecticut Trial Lawyers Association. ***PRACTICE AREAS:*** General Practice; Trial Practice; Insurance; Toxic Torts; Products Liability; Personal Injury; Professional Malpractice; Premises Liability; Municipal Litigation; Aviation Litigation; Criminal Law. ***Email:*** fobrien@rtcelaw.com

KEITH S. McCABE, born Washington, D.C., July 31, 1966; admitted to bar, 1991, Connecticut. *Education:* Trinity College (B.A., 1988); University of Bridgeport (J.D., cum laude, 1991). *Member:* Connecticut Defense Lawyers Association. ***PRACTICE AREAS:*** General Practice; Trial Practice; Insurance; Toxic Torts; Products Liability; Personal Injury; Professional Malpractice; Premises Liability; Municipal Litigation; Aviation Litigation; Real Estate; Probate; Family Law. ***Email:*** kmccabe@rtcelaw.com

DOUGLAS E. GILMORE, born Boston, Massachusetts, March 10, 1966; admitted to bar, 1991, Connecticut. *Education:* Skidmore College (B.A., 1988); New England School of Law (J.D., 1991). ***PRACTICE AREAS:*** General Practice; Trial Practice; Insurance; Toxic Torts; Products Liability; Personal Injury; Professional Malpractice; Premises Liability; Municipal Litigation; Aviation Litigation; Real Estate; Probate; Family Law. ***Email:*** dgilmore@rtcelaw.com

PETER J. CASEY, born Heilbronn, Germany, February 13, 1964; admitted to bar, 1990, Connecticut; 1991, U.S. District Court, District of Connecticut. *Education:* Boston University (B.S., 1986); University of Bridgeport (J.D., cum laude, 1989). ***PRACTICE AREAS:*** General Practice; Trial Practice; Insurance; Toxic Torts; Products Liability; Personal Injury; Professional Malpractice; Premises Liability; Municipal Litigation; Aviation Litigation; Real Estate; Probate; Family Law. ***Email:*** pcasey@rtcelaw.com

ANDREW W. BRAY, born Hartford, Connecticut, October 18, 1959; admitted to bar, 1991, Connecticut; 1992, U.S. District Court, District of Connecticut. *Education:* University of Connecticut (B.A., magna cum laude, 1988; J.D., 1991). *Member:* Litchfield County Bar Association; Connecticut Trial Lawyers Association; Association of Trial Lawyers of America. ***PRACTICE AREAS:*** General Practice; Trial Practice; Insurance; Toxic Torts; Products

(This Listing Continued)

REGNIER, TAYLOR, CURRAN & EDDY, Hartford—Continued

Liability; Personal Injury; Professional Malpractice; Premises Liability; Municipal Litigation; Aviation Litigation; Real Estate; Probate; Family Law. ***Email:*** abray@rtcelaw.com

SANDRA R. BAKER, born Hartford, Connecticut, November 10, 1969; admitted to bar, 1994, Connecticut; 1995, U.S. District Court, District of Connecticut. *Education:* Wesleyan University (B.A., 1991); University of Connecticut (J.D., with honors, 1994). ***PRACTICE AREAS:*** General Practice; Trial Practice; Insurance; Toxic Torts; Products Liability; Personal Injury; Professional Malpractice; Premises Liability; Municipal Litigation; Aviation Litigation; Real Estate; Probate; Family Law.

MICHAEL P. HENDRICKSON, born New Britain, Connecticut, September 20, 1961; admitted to bar, 1988, Illinois; 1994, U.S. Federal Court, Northern District; 1998, Connecticut. *Education:* State University of N.Y. (B.A., 1983); John Marshall Law School (J.D., 1988). ***PRACTICE AREAS:*** General Practice; Trial Practice; Insurance; Toxic Torts; Products Liability; Personal Injury; Professional Malpractice; Premises Liability; Municipal Litigation; Aviation Litigation; Real Estate; Probate; Family Law. ***Email:*** mhendrickson@rtcelaw.com

M. PAULA SILVA, born Azores, Portugal, April 12, 1972; admitted to bar, 2000, Connecticut. *Education:* University of Hartford (B.S., 1994); Western New England College (J.D., 2000). ***PRACTICE AREAS:*** General Practice; Trial Practice; Insurance; Toxic Torts; Products Liability; Personal Injury; Professional Malpractice; Premises Liability; Municipal Law; Real Estate; Probate; Family Law. ***Email:*** mpsilva@rtcelaw.com

All Members and Associates of the Firm are Members of Hartford County, Connecticut and American Bar Associations.

REPRESENTATIVE CLIENTS: Aetna Life and Casualty; Ambassador Insurance Co.; American Centennial Insurance Co.; American Empire Surplus Lines Insurance Co.; American Mutual Insurance Co.; American Universal Insurance Co.; Atlantic Mutual Insurance Co.; Berkshire Mutual Insurance Co.; Colonial Penn; The Concord Group; Criterion Insurance Co.; DeRand Real Estate Investment Trust; Dailey's Express; Eli Lilly and Co.; First Financial Insurance Co.; Frito Law; General Accident Group; Government Employees Insurance Co.; Great Atlantic & Pacific Tea Co.; Great Southwest Insurance Co.; Hartford Accident & Indemnity Co.; Hartford Fire Insurance Co.; INA Life Insurance Co.; Industrial Indemnity Insurance Co.; Integrity Insurance Co.; Kemper Insurance Co.; Life Insurance Company of North America; Lumber Insurance Co.; Lumbermens Mutual; May Co.; Mayflower Group Inc.; The Moore Group; National Union Fire Insurance Company of Pittsburgh; New York Bankers & Shippers; Norfolk & Dedham; Pioneer Co-Operative Fire; Penn-America Insurance Co.; P.M.A. Group; Roadway Express; Ryder Truck Rental; The Scott-Fetzer Co.; Scottish & York; Shop-Rite Markets; United Services Automobile Assn.; U.S. Aviation Underwriters; Universal Underwriters; Utica Mutual Insurance Co.; Vermont Mutual Insurance Company.

REID AND RIEGE, P.C.

Established in 1950

ONE STATE STREET
HARTFORD, CONNECTICUT 06103
Telephone: 860-278-1150
FAX: 860-240-1002
URL: http://www.reidriege.com

West Hartford, Connecticut Office: 65 LaSalle Road. Telephone: 860-232-6565. FAX: 860-232-6066.
Lakeville, Connecticut Office: 322 Main Street. Telephone: 860-435-9894. FAX: 860-240-1002.
Woodbury, Connecticut Office: 47 Sherman Hill Road. Telephone: 203-267-6680. FAX: 860-240-1002.

Alternative Dispute Resolution. Antitrust & Trade Regulation. Bankruptcy. Business Law. Commercial Law. Commercial Real Estate/Finance. Corporate Law. Employee Benefits/Pension Plans. Employee Benefits/Taft-Hartley Plans. Environmental Law. Health Care. Labor and Employment. Litigation. Mergers and Acquisitions. Nonprofit and Charitable Organizations. Occupational Safety & Health. Probate. Real Estate. Securities. Taxation. Trade and Professional Associations. Trusts & Estates. Zoning, Planning and Land Use.

FIRM PROFILE: Reid and Riege, P.C. was founded in 1950 by John Reid and John H. Riege. The philosophy of the firm is to provide quality, imaginative legal services to privately held and publicly held businesses and financial institutions, and to individuals throughout the State of Connecticut. The firm is comprised of the following practice groups: Corporate and Securities; Commercial; Environmental; Litigation; Real Estate; Tax; Health Care; Employee Benefits and Pension; Estate Planning and Estate Settlement; Bankruptcy and Insolvency; Taft-Hartley (multi-employer) Pension and Benefits Law; and Employment Law.

The firm encourages its attorneys to participate actively in a wide variety of civic and professional organizations and activities. Some of the organizations in which the firm's attorneys have actively served include the Connecticut Business and

(This Listing Continued)

Industry Association, Association of Commercial Finance Attorneys, Council on Foundations, Hartford Downtown Corporation, Connecticut Bar Foundation, and National Conference of Commissioners on Uniform State Laws.

ANDREW J. HOWAT, born Hartford, Connecticut, November 15, 1946; admitted to bar, 1971, Connecticut. *Education:* University of Connecticut (B.A., cum laude, 1968); Cornell University (J.D., with distinction, 1971). Order of the Coif; Phi Kappa Phi; Pi Sigma Alpha. *Member:* Connecticut and American Bar Associations. ***PRACTICE AREAS:*** Commercial Law; Corporate Law; Labor and Employment; Mergers and Acquisitions; Securities; Taxation. ***Email:*** ahowat@reidandriege.com

TRAVERS T. AUBURN, born Winsted, Connecticut, April 10, 1946; admitted to bar, 1972, Connecticut. *Education:* Williams College (B.A., 1968); University of Connecticut (J.D., 1972). *Member:* Litchfield County, Connecticut and American Bar Associations. ***PRACTICE AREAS:*** Probate; Real Estate; Trusts and Estates. ***Email:*** tauburn@reidandriege.com

MAURICE T. FITZMAURICE, born Waterbury, Connecticut, August 15, 1944; admitted to bar, 1971, Connecticut. *Education:* University of Connecticut (B.S., 1967); University of Notre Dame (J.D., 1971). Articles Editor, Notre Dame Law Review, 1970-1971. Law Clerk to Judge Myron H. Bright, U.S. Court of Appeals for the Eighth Circuit, 1971-1972. Author: Note, 44 Notre Dame Law Review 252 (1968). Lecturer: Evidence, Trial Practice, Appellate Practice, Prejudgment Remedies, Injunction Practice, Comparative Negligence and OSHA, Connecticut Bar Association; Pensions, Connecticut State Judges, ERISA, Taft Hartley Trustees. Member, Editorial Board, Connecticut Bar Journal, 1973-1976. Chairperson, Connecticut State Ethics Commission, 1996-1997; Special Master, U.S. District Court, District of Connecticut, 1989—. ***PRACTICE AREAS:*** Litigation. ***Email:*** fitz@reidandriege.com

BRUCE M. LUTSK, born New York, New York, May 2, 1942; admitted to bar, 1974, Connecticut. *Education:* Bowdoin College (B.A., 1964); Harvard University (M.A.T., 1965); Duke University (Ph.D., 1970); University of Connecticut (J.D., 1974). Phi Beta Kappa. Speaker: National Health Lawyers Association; Continuing Care Retirement Communities. *Member:* Connecticut and American Bar Associations; National Health Lawyers Association. ***PRACTICE AREAS:*** Commercial Law; Commercial Real Estate and Financing; Health Care; Real Estate; Zoning, Planning and Land Use. ***Email:*** blutsk@reidandriege.com

TUCK MILLER, JR., born Cleveland, Ohio, June 22, 1947; admitted to bar, 1972, New Jersey; 1974, Connecticut. *Education:* Dartmouth College (A.B., 1969); Georgetown University (J.D., 1972). Law Clerk to the Honorable George H. Barlow, United States District Court, New Jersey, 1972-1974. *Member:* Connecticut and American Bar Associations; National Health Lawyers Association; Connecticut Health Lawyers Association. ***PRACTICE AREAS:*** Health Care. ***Email:*** tmiller@reidandriege.com

MICHAEL L. COYLE, born Mechanicsburg, Pennsylvania, October 2, 1944; admitted to bar, 1972, New York; 1975, Connecticut. *Education:* Syracuse University (B.S., 1966; J.D., 1971); Georgetown University (LL.M., in Taxation, 1975). Member, Justinian Society. Member and Articles Editor, Syracuse Law Review, 1970-1971. Attorney-Advisor, Interpretative Division, IRS Office of Chief Counsel, 1971-1973. Law Clerk to Judge Darrell D. Wiles, U.S. Tax Court, 1973-1975. Listed in Best Lawyers in America, 1988-2002. Lecturer: Connecticut Limited Liability Companies and Limited Liability Partnerships, 1995-1996; Connecticut Sales & Use Tax, 1986-1994 and Connecticut Corporate Business Tax, 1989-1994, National Business Institute Seminars; Connecticut Sales & Use Tax - General and Contractors, Connecticut Business and Industry Association Seminars, 1989-2000. Speaker, "Planned Giving Programs," Not-for-Profit Organizations Conference, Connecticut Society of CPAs, 1998. *Member:* Connecticut (Member, Tax Section Executive Committee, 1991-2001) and American (Chairman, Sales and Financial Transactions Committee, Section of Taxation, 1983-1985) Bar Associations. [With U.S. Army, 1966-1968]. ***PRACTICE AREAS:*** Taxation. ***Email:*** mcoyle@reidandriege.com

SUZANNE S. BOCCHINI, born Chicago, Illinois, February 24, 1947; admitted to bar, 1973, Missouri; 1974, Connecticut. *Education:* The Catholic University of America (B.A., 1969); St. Louis University (J.D., cum laude, 1973). *Member:* Connecticut and American Bar Associations; Connecticut Estate and Tax Planning Council (President, 1996-1997); Hartford Estate and Business Planning Council. Fellow, American College of Trust and Estate Counsel. ***PRACTICE AREAS:*** Probate; Trusts and Estates. ***Email:*** sbocchini@reidandriege.com

JOHN J. JACOBSON, born Washington, D.C., August 10, 1951; admitted to bar, 1976, Connecticut. *Education:* Bowdoin College (A.B., summa cum laude, 1973); Georgetown University (J.D., 1976). Phi Beta Kappa. Co-Author: with William R. Judy, "Courts Back IRS Denials on Plans," National Law Journal 15 (August 18, 1980). *Member:* Connecticut and American Bar Associations. ***PRACTICE AREAS:*** Employee Benefits; Pension Plans; Executive Compensation. ***Email:*** jjacobson@reidandriege.com

JOHN E. D'AMICO, born Waterbury, Connecticut, March 14, 1952; admitted to bar, 1976, Connecticut. *Education:* Tufts University (B.S., cum laude,

(This Listing Continued)

1973); University of Connecticut (J.D., with honors, 1976); New York University (LL.M. in Taxation, 1977). Speaker, "Bankruptcy Tax and Compliance Issues," Connecticut Society of CPA's. Member, American Bar Association Section of Taxation Section 108 Real Estate and Partnership Task Force. Speaker, "The Revised Uniform Partnership Act in Connecticut". Adjunct Professor, University of Hartford, Barney School, Real Estate Taxation. *Member:* Connecticut (Member, Tax Section) and American (Member, Partnership and International Law Committee) Bar Associations. ***PRACTICE AREAS:*** Bankruptcy; Business Law; Commercial Law; Commercial Real Estate and Finance; Corporate Law; Real Estate; Securities; Taxation. ***Email:*** jdamico@reidandriege.com

LAWRENCE H. LISSITZYN, born New York, New York, September 1, 1944; admitted to bar, 1974, New York; 1979, Connecticut. *Education:* Columbia University (B.A., 1966); Vanderbilt University (J.D., 1973). Associate, Davis Polk & Wardwell, N.Y., N.Y., 1974-1979. *Member:* Connecticut and American Bar Associations. [Capt., USMC, 1966-1970]. ***PRACTICE AREAS:*** Litigation. ***Email:*** llissitzyn@reidandriege.com

FREDERICK J. MULLEN, JR., born Providence, Rhode Island, December 30, 1951; admitted to bar, 1977, Connecticut. *Education:* Yale University (B.A., 1974); University of Virginia (J.D., 1977). Articles Editor, Virginia Journal of International Law, 1976-1977. *Member:* Connecticut (Chair, Executive Committee, Probate Section) and American Bar Associations; Hartford Estate and Business Planning Council; Connecticut Estate and Tax Planning Council. Fellow, American College of Trust and Estate Counsel. ***PRACTICE AREAS:*** Probate; Trusts and Estates. ***Email:*** fmullen@reidandriege.com

EDMUND A. MIKOLOWSKY, born Manchester, Connecticut, April 5, 1952; admitted to bar, 1979, Connecticut. *Education:* College of the Holy Cross (B.A., summa cum laude, 1974); Yale University (J.D., 1979). *Member:* Connecticut (Member, Executive Committee, Corporations and Other Business Organizations, 1984-1986) and American Bar Associations. ***PRACTICE AREAS:*** Business Law; Corporate Law; Labor and Employment; Mergers and Acquisitions. ***Email:*** emikolowsky@reidandriege.com

ROBERT U. SATTIN, born Hartford, Connecticut, October 28, 1948; admitted to bar, 1974, Connecticut. *Education:* University of Rochester (A.B., 1970); University of Connecticut (J.D., 1974). Member, Hartford County Bar Association, Continuing Legal Education Committee, 1981-1990. Member, Merit Screening Committee for District of Connecticut Bankruptcy Judgeship, 1998. Member, Advisor Board, Taglaw International Network, 1999—. *Member:* Connecticut (Member, Commercial Law and Bankruptcy Section; Chairman, 1988-1990; Member: Alternative Dispute Resolution Section, 1995—; Banking Law Section, 1976-1994, Task Force on Plain Language Legislation, 1979) and American Bar Associations; Association of Commercial Finance Attorneys (Vice-President, 1991-1997); American Bankruptcy Institute; Turnaround Management Association (Director, Connecticut Chapter, 1993-1999. Advisory Member, Committee to State Law Revision Commission on Revised UCC Article 9, 1999-2000). ***PRACTICE AREAS:*** Alternative Dispute Resolution; Bankruptcy; Business Law; Commercial; Commercial Real Estate and Finance; Litigation. ***Email:*** rsattin@reidandriege.com

JOHN M. HORAK, born Chicopee, Massachusetts, August 29, 1954; admitted to bar, 1980, Connecticut. *Education:* Dartmouth College (B.A., magna cum laude, 1976); University of Notre Dame (J.D., 1980). Co-Author: "Interstate Sales and Small Business - The Potential For Unforeseen Tax Liabilities," Connecticut CPA Quarterly, June, 1992; "Quill and Wrigley - Their Effect on Potential Tax Liabilities in Other States," Connecticut CPA Quarterly, Sept., 1992. Author: "Taking Trusteeship Seriously," Philanthropy Magazine, July 2000. "Recent Connecticut Sales and Use Tax Development," Connecticut CPA Quarterly, September, 1987. Member, West Hartford Board of Tax Review, 1988-1989. Member, West Hartford Ethics Commission, 1998-2000. Chairman, Reid and Riege, Non Profit Organization Practice Group. *Member:* Hartford County, Connecticut and American Bar Associations. ***PRACTICE AREAS:*** Corporate Law; Nonprofit and Charitable Organizations; Taxation; Trade and Professional Associations. ***Email:*** jhorak@reidandriege.com

EDWARD F. SPINELLA, born Hartford, Connecticut, May 28, 1952; admitted to bar, 1978, Connecticut. *Education:* College of the Holy Cross (B.A., 1974); University of Connecticut (J.D., with honors, 1978). Law Clerk, Connecticut Superior Court, 1978-1979. Lecturer: Evidence, Criminal Law, Construction Law; Health Care Fraud, Hartford County Bar Association, 1991. Deputy Assistant State's Attorney, Hartford Judicial District, 1979-1980. Assistant State's Attorney, Hartford Judicial District, 1980-1983. *Member:* Hartford County and Connecticut Bar Associations. ***PRACTICE AREAS:*** Criminal Law; Civil Litigation; Health Care. ***Email:*** espinella@reidandriege.com

CRAIG L. SYLVESTER, born Wichita, Kansas, September 12, 1951; admitted to bar, 1981, Connecticut. *Education:* American University (A.B., cum laude, 1973); University of Connecticut (J.D., with high honors, 1981). Managing Editor, Connecticut Law Review, 1980-1981. Lecturer, "Understanding Stock Purchase Agreements," Connecticut Society of Certified Public Accountants, 1991. Member: Board of Directors, Riverfront Recapture, Inc., 1999—, Board of Commissioners, West Hartford Housing Authority, 1986-1998, Vice

(This Listing Continued)

Chairman, 1990-1995 and Chairman, 1995-1998. Member: Advisory Board, University of Connecticut Family Business Program, 1994—; Small Business Advisory Council, Connecticut Business and Industry Association, 1991-1997; Advisory Board, Hartford Enterprise Zone, 1986-1988; Entrepreneur Institute of Greater Hartford, 1987-1989. *Member:* Connecticut (Member, Sections on: Corporations and Other Business Organizations; Antitrust) and American (Member, Section of Corporation, Banking and Business Law) Bar Associations. ***PRACTICE AREAS:*** Business Law; Corporate Law; Mergers and Acquisitions; Securities. ***Email:*** csylvester@reidandriege.com

ROBERT M. MULÉ, born New York, N.Y., April 15, 1955; admitted to bar, 1981, Connecticut. *Education:* Harvard University (A.B., cum laude, 1977); Boston University (J.D., 1981). Speaker: "New Directions in Business Planning: Update on LLC's and LLP's," seminar sponsored by the Connecticut Bar Association, November 18, 1998; Speaker: "Creditors Rights and Remedies at the End of the '90s," sponsored by the Connecticut Bar Association, October 16, 1998; Speaker: "New Opportunities for LLC's and LLP's," seminar sponsored by the Connecticut Bar Association, August 29, 1996; "Updates in Business Law," Annual Survey of Connecticut Law sponsored by the University of Connecticut Law School Alumni Association, Inc., February 28, 1997 and January 29, 1994. Chair, "Limited Liability Companies and Limited Liability Partnerships," seminar sponsored by the Connecticut Bar Association, June 2, 1995; Speaker: "Limited Liability Companies: The Entity of Choice in Connecticut," seminars sponsored by National Business Institute 1994, 1995 and 1996; "Corporate Counsel: Advising Your Client," seminar sponsored by Lorman Education Services, July 15, 1994; Moderator, "The New Connecticut Limited Liability Company Act," seminar sponsored by the Connecticut Bar Association, October 26, 1993. Author: "Greenmail Legislation — A Report of the Section on Corporations and Other Business Organizations of the Connecticut Bar Association," prepared for the Judiciary Committee of the Connecticut General Assembly, January 30, 1990. Moderator, "Closing Our Doors Forever-Benefits and Issues of an Orderly Business Shutdown," Seminar sponsored by the Connecticut Bar Association, October 13, 1989. Speaker: "Nonbankruptcy Issues in a Business Winddown/Shutdown," seminar sponsored by the Association of Commercial Finance Attorneys, February 25, 1991. Chairman, Connecticut Limited Liability Company Act Subcommittee of the Connecticut Bar Association's Business Law Section, 1992-1996. Member, Connecticut Venture Group, 1992—. Member, Entrepreneurship Institute of Greater Hartford, 1990-1992, 1995-1999. *Member:* Hartford County, Connecticut (Secretary, Executive Committee, Section on Corporations and Other Business Organizations, 1987-1990) and American Bar Associations. ***SPECIAL AGENCIES:*** Member, Bank of Boston Connecticut's Hartford Advisory Board, 1994-1996. Simsbury Town Moderator, 1998—; Alternate, Simsbury Zoning Board of Appeals, 1995-1999. Chairman, Simsbury Charter Revision Commission, 1991-1992; Member, Simsbury Planning Commission, 1992-1993. Member, Simsbury Affordable Housing Partnership, 1990-1994. ***TRANSACTIONS:*** Initial Public Offering for Helpmate Robotics Inc.; Organization of Trust Company of Connecticut. ***PRACTICE AREAS:*** Bankruptcy; Business Law; Commercial Law; Commercial Real Estate and Finance; Corporate Law; Mergers and Acquisitions; Real Estate; Securities. ***Email:*** lawtalk@reidandriege.com

EILEEN M. MARKS, born Hartford, Connecticut, November 18, 1950; admitted to bar, 1979, Connecticut. *Education:* Manhattanville College (A.B., 1972); University of Connecticut (J.D., 1979). *Member:* Connecticut and American Bar Associations. ***PRACTICE AREAS:*** Employee Benefits; Pension and Health Plans; Taft-Hartley Plans. ***Email:*** emarks@reidandriege.com

EARL F. McMAHON, born Providence, Rhode Island, May 31, 1960; admitted to bar, 1985, Connecticut. *Education:* Dartmouth College (B.A., magna cum laude, 1982); Georgetown University (J.D., cum laude, 1985). Phi Beta Kappa. *Member:* Connecticut and American Bar Associations. ***PRACTICE AREAS:*** Commercial Real Estate and Finance; Health Care; Real Estate. ***Email:*** emcmahon@reidandriege.com

JON P. NEWTON, born Milford, Connecticut, January 24, 1962; admitted to bar, 1988, Connecticut. *Education:* Brown University (A.B., magna cum laude, 1984); University of Connecticut School of Law (J.D., 1988). Articles and Book Reviews Editor, Connecticut Law Review. Author: "Suggestions for the New Collective Bargaining Agreement in Professional Basketball," 19 Conn. L. Rev. 1001 (1987). Contributing Author: "The Connecticut Uniform Commercial Code," 64 Conn. B. J. SI-173 (1990). *Member:* Connecticut (Member, Executive Committee, Commercial Law and Bankruptcy Section) and American (Member, Business Law Section) Bar Associations. ***PRACTICE AREAS:*** Bankruptcy; Commercial Law; Commercial Real Estate and Finance; Litigation. ***Email:*** jnewton@reidandriege.com

MARK X. RYAN, born Buffalo, New York, February 14, 1963; admitted to bar, 1988, Connecticut. *Education:* Georgetown University (A.B., magna cum laude, 1985); University of Notre Dame (J.D., cum laude, 1988). *Member:* Connecticut (Member, Antitrust and Corporations Sections) and American (Member, Antitrust and Business Law Sections) Bar Associations. ***PRACTICE AREAS:*** Antitrust; Trade Regulation; Business Law; Corporate Law; Mergers and Acquisitions; Securities. ***Email:*** mryan@reidandriege.com

(This Listing Continued)

REID AND RIEGE, P.C., Hartford—Continued

JOHN D. NEWMAN, born Washington, D.C., May 18, 1959; admitted to bar, 1984, Connecticut. *Education:* Duke University (A.B., summa cum laude, 1981; J.D., 1984). Phi Beta Kappa. William Neal Reynolds Scholar of the Law. Listed in Best Lawyers in America, 1997, 1999-2000. *Member:* Connecticut and American Bar Associations; National Health Lawyers Association; Connecticut Health Lawyers Association. ***PRACTICE AREAS:*** Corporate Law; Health Law; Administrative Law. ***Email:*** jnewman@reidandriege.com

JOSEPH K. FORTIER, born Willimantic, Connecticut, July 17, 1958; admitted to bar, 1984, Connecticut. *Education:* University of Connecticut (B.A. B.S., magna cum laude, 1981); Cornell University (J.D., 1984). Phi Kappa Phi; Phi Beta Kappa. Member, Board of Editors, Cornell International Law Journal, 1983-1984. *Member:* Connecticut and American Bar Associations. ***PRACTICE AREAS:*** Commercial Real Estate; Commercial Leasing. ***Email:*** jfortier@reidandriege.com

THOMAS M. ARMSTRONG, born Albany, New York, April 23, 1946; admitted to bar, 1973, Connecticut. *Education:* Westminster College (B.A., 1968); University of Connecticut School of Law (J.D., cum laude, 1973). Co-author: "Settlement at Bluff Road: An Innovative Administrative Order," Toxic Law Reporter (1988). Author: "Alternative Dispute Resolution: Use in Private and Public Sector to Resolve Environmental Disputes," Environmental Hazards (1988). Co-author: "Environmental Disputes May be Handled Better Without Lawsuits," Compliance and Litigation Strategy (1993). Author: "Expedited Redevelopment Under Connecticut's Revised Transfer Act and Licensed Environmental Professional Programs," Environmental Law & Practice (1995). Member: Steering Committee, Environmental Policy Council of Connecticut Business and Industry Association, 1993-1995; Federal ADR Panel for Environmental Disputes. Chairman, American Heart Association, Connecticut Affiliate, 1993-1995. *Member:* Hartford County, Connecticut (Chairman, Environmental Law Section, 1995-1996) and American (Co-Chairman, Toxic and Environmental Litigation Subsection, Natural Resources, Energy and the Environment Section, 1988-1990) Bar Associations; Greater Hartford Chamber of Commerce. ***PRACTICE AREAS:*** Environmental Law; Occupational Safety and Health; Land Use. ***Email:*** tarmstrong@reidandriege.com

ERIC A. HENZY, born San Diego, California, February 23, 1962; admitted to bar, 1989, New York; 1996, Connecticut. *Education:* University of Connecticut (B.A., magna cum laude, 1984; J.D., 1988). Law Clerk to the Honorable Alan H.W. Shiff, U.S. Bankruptcy Court, District of Connecticut, 1988-1990. *Member:* Connecticut (Secretary and Treasurer, 1998-1999, and Member, Executive Committee, Commercial Law and Bankruptcy Section) and American (Member, Business Law Section) Bar Associations; American Bankruptcy Institute. ***PRACTICE AREAS:*** Bankruptcy; Commercial Law; Litigation. ***Email:*** ehenzy@reidandriege.com

ALAN BIRMINGHAM, born Hartford, Connecticut, June 3, 1943; admitted to bar, 1969, Connecticut and U.S. District Court, District of Connecticut. *Education:* Tufts University (B.A., 1966); Georgetown University (J.D., 1969). *Member:* Connecticut (Member, Executive Committee, Estates and Probate Section, 1984—; Chairman, Legal Problems of the Elderly Committee, 1985-1988 and Member, Executive Committee, Elder Law Section, 1991—); American Bar Associations; Connecticut Estate and Tax Planning Council, Inc. (Director, 1985-1993; President, 1992-1993). Fellow, American College of Trust and Estate Counsel. ***PRACTICE AREAS:*** Probate; Real Estate; Trusts and Estates. ***Email:*** abirmingham@reidandriege.com

JOHN V. GALIETTE, born Waterbury, Connecticut, July 6, 1954; admitted to bar, 1979, Connecticut; 1980, U.S. District Court, District of Connecticut. *Education:* Harvard University (B.A., magna cum laude, 1976); Boston College (J.D., magna cum laude, 1979). Executive Editor, Environmental Affairs Law Review, 1978-1979. Co-author: "Planning For Retirement Benefit Distributions," Elder Law Portfolio Series, Little Brown and Company (1999). Program Chairman, Hartford Chapter, Web-Worldwide Employee Benefits Network. *Member:* Connecticut and American Bar Associations. ***PRACTICE AREAS:*** Employee Benefits; Pension Plans; Executive Compensation; Securities. ***Email:*** jgaliette@reidandriege.com

DOMINIC FULCO, III, born Hartford, Connecticut, December 4, 1959; admitted to bar, 1984, Connecticut; U.S. District Court, District of Connecticut; 1996, U.S. Court of Appeals, Second Circuit. *Education:* University of Hartford (B.A., magna cum laude, 1981); Temple University (J.D., 1984). Alpha Chi. Staff Member, 1982-1983 and Business Editor, 1983-1984, Temple Law Quarterly. Author, Note: "Constitutional Law - 1981 Pennsylvania Reapportionment Plan Meets the Requirements of the United States Constitution and the Pennsylvania Constitution - In Re Reapportionment Plan for the Pennsylvania General Assembly," 56 Temp. L.Q. 787, 1983; "Taxation - Franchise Tax Option Given Only to Domestic Corporations Held Unconstitutional - Gilbert Associates v. Commonwealth of Pennsylvania," 56 Temp. L.Q. 867, 1983. *Member:* Hartford County, Connecticut and American Bar Associations. ***REPORTED CASES:*** PPG Industries, Inc. v. Webster Auto Parts, Inc. 128 F.3d 103 (2d.Cir. 1997); Fulco v. Norwich Roman Catholic Diocesan Corp., 27 Conn. App. 800,

(This Listing Continued)

609 A.2d 1034 (1992), app., dismissed, 226 Conn. 404, 627 A.2d 931 (1993); John Baker, Jr. v. Sun Refining and Marketing Company, 14 Conn. App. 804 (1988); Yost v. Seaboard Surety Company, 182 B.R. 375 (Bankr. D.Conn. 1995); In re: Dazic Controls Corp., 178 B.R. 328 (Bkrptcy.D.Conn. 1995). ***PRACTICE AREAS:*** Alternative Dispute Resolution; Bankruptcy; Litigation. ***Email:*** dfulco@reidandriege.com

DOUGLAS K. KNIGHT, born Rochester, New York, November 29, 1966; admitted to bar, 1992, Connecticut. *Education:* University of Massachusetts (B.B.A., cum laude, 1989); Syracuse University (J.D., magna cum laude, 1992). Order of the Coif. Justinian Honorary Law Society. Associate Editor, Syracuse Law Review. *Member:* Connecticut and American Bar Associations; International Foundation of Employee Benefit Plans. ***PRACTICE AREAS:*** Employee Benefits; Pension Plans; Taft-Hartley Plans. ***Email:*** dknight@reidandriege.com

JOHN R. IVIMEY, born Teaneck, New Jersey, April 12, 1963; admitted to bar, 1991, Connecticut. *Education:* Colgate University (B.A., 1985); University of Connecticut (J.D., with high honors, 1991). *Member:* Connecticut and American Bar Associations. ***PRACTICE AREAS:*** Probate; Trusts and Estates. ***Email:*** jivimey@reidandriege.com

LOUIS J. DONOFRIO, born Rahway, New Jersey, July 4, 1967; admitted to bar, 1992, Connecticut. *Education:* George Washington University (B.A., 1989); Catholic University of America (J.D., 1992). Member, Catholic University Journal of Contemporary Health Law and Policy, 1991-1992. *Member:* Connecticut and American Bar Associations. ***PRACTICE AREAS:*** Commercial Real Estate and Finance; Real Estate; Leasing. ***Email:*** ldonofrio@reidandriege.com

SENIOR ATTORNEYS

KAREN L. BRAND, born Clearwater, Florida, August 18, 1961; admitted to bar, 1986, Connecticut. *Education:* University of Florida (B.A., 1983); Duke University (J.D., 1986). Phi Beta Kappa. *Member:* Connecticut (Member, Sections on: Corporations and Other Business Organizations; Labor and Employment Law) and American (Member, Sections on: Corporations and Other Business Organizations; Labor and Employment Law) Bar Associations. ***PRACTICE AREAS:*** Business Law; Corporate Law; Labor and Employment; Mergers and Acquisitions. ***Email:*** kbrand@reidandriege.com

ROBERT C. REICHERT, born Great Falls, Montana, June 30, 1952; admitted to bar, 1982, Montana; 1990, Connecticut. *Education:* University of Montana (B.A., 1976); Indiana University (M.A., 1980); University of Montana (J.D., with honors, 1982). Recipient, Kilbourne Award for Legal Writing, 1979-1981. Member, Editorial Board, Montana Law Review, 1980-1982. Law Clerk for Chief U.S. District Court Judge James F. Battin for District of Montana, 1982-1984. *Member:* Connecticut and American Bar Associations. ***PRACTICE AREAS:*** Alternative Dispute Resolution; Bankruptcy; Litigation. ***Email:*** rreichert@reidandriege.com

LEAH COHEN CHATINOVER, born Englewood, New Jersey, September 14, 1957; admitted to bar, 1984, Connecticut. *Education:* Barnard College (B.A., summa cum laude, 1979); Yale University (J.D., 1984). Phi Beta Kappa. *Member:* Hartford County, Connecticut and American Bar Associations. ***LANGUAGES:*** Hebrew. ***PRACTICE AREAS:*** Business Law; Corporate Law; Nonprofit Organizations Law; Intellectual Property. ***Email:*** lchatinover@reidandriege.com

---

MICHAEL T. WADE, born San Diego, California, December 10, 1965; admitted to bar, 1992, Connecticut and U.S. District Court, District of Connecticut. *Education:* Yale University (B.A., 1987); University of Connecticut (J.D., 1992). ***PRACTICE AREAS:*** Litigation. ***Email:*** mwade@reidandriege.com

AMES B. SHEA, born Winnetka, Illinois, September 12, 1968; admitted to bar, 1993, Pennsylvania; 1995, Connecticut. *Education:* Denison University (B.A., 1990); Washington & Lee University (J.D., 1993). *Member:* Connecticut Bar Association. ***PRACTICE AREAS:*** Corporate Law; Mergers and Acquisitions; Nonprofit and Charitable Organizations. ***Email:*** ashea@reidandriege.com

THOMAS R. KASPER, born Hartford, Connecticut, April 21, 1964; admitted to bar, 1995, Connecticut. *Education:* University of Connecticut (B.A., cum laude, 1986); Western New England College School of Law (J.D., cum laude, 1995). *Member:* Connecticut and American Bar Associations. ***PRACTICE AREAS:*** Commercial Real Estate and Finance; Real Estate. ***Email:*** tkasper@reidandriege.com

BARBARA A. TAYLOR, born Hartford, Connecticut, June 3, 1972; admitted to bar, 1999, Connecticut. *Education:* Lehigh University (B.S., 1995); University of Connecticut (J.D., with honors, 1999). Phi Delta Phi. *Member:* Connecticut (Estates and Probate Section) and American Bar Associations. ***PRACTICE AREAS:*** Probate; Trusts and Estates. ***Email:*** btaylor@reidandriege.com

(This Listing Continued)

RONALD JOHN KONIUTA, born Meriden, Connecticut, December 17, 1955; admitted to bar, 1995, Connecticut, U.S. District Court, District of Connecticut and U.S. Tax Court. *Education:* University of Connecticut (B.A., 1979; M.B.A., with honors, 1987); Western New England College (J.D., 1994). *Member:* Connecticut and American Bar Associations. ***PRACTICE AREAS:*** Employee Benefits; Pension Plans; Executive Compensation; Taxation; Trusts and Estates. ***Email:*** rkoniuta@reidandriege.com

JOSEPH A. CIPPARONE, born Indianapolis, Indiana, April 29, 1957; admitted to bar, 1983, Connecticut; 1985, U.S. District Court, District of Connecticut. *Education:* University of Michigan (B.A., with high distinction, 1978; M.P.P., 1982; J.D., 1983). Associate Editor, University of Michigan Journal of Law Reform, 1981-1982. CFP Licensee, Certified Financial Planners Board of Standards, Inc., 2000. Author: "Advance Notice of Plant Closings: Toward National Legislation," University of Michigan Journal of Law Reform, Winter, 1981; "The Home Improvement Act Defense," Connecticut Bar Journal, December 1989; "The Roth IRA Exemption From Execution," Connecticut Lawyer, November, 1999. Member, Representative Town Meeting, Town of Waterford, Connecticut, 1985-1991. *Member:* Connecticut (Member: Estate Planning and Probate Section) Bar Association; Financial Planners Association. ***PRACTICE AREAS:*** Trusts and Estates; Probate; Business Law. ***Email:*** jcipparone@reidandriege.com

INDREK H. BUTTNER, born Washington, D.C., May 4, 1951; admitted to bar, 1981, Connecticut; 1983, Florida. *Education:* University of Connecticut (B.A., 1976); Syracuse University (J.D., 1981). Member, Syracuse University Law Review, 1980. *Member:* Connecticut and American Bar Associations; The Florida Bar. ***PRACTICE AREAS:*** Real Estate; Real Estate Finance; Real Estate Acquisitions; Real Estate Sales; Commercial Leasing. ***Email:*** ibuttner@reidandriege.com

JENNIFER R. LUCARELLI, born Derby, Connecticut, January 14, 1973; admitted to bar, 1999, Connecticut; 2000, New York. *Education:* Yale University (B.A., 1995); University of Notre Dame (J.D., 1999). ***LANGUAGES:*** Spanish. ***PRACTICE AREAS:*** Litigation. ***Email:*** jlucarelli@reidandriege.com

DOREEN J. FARINA, born Hartford, Connecticut, April 20, 1950; admitted to bar, 1998, Connecticut. *Education:* University of Connecticut (B.A., 1972); Western New England College (J.D., 1997). ***PRACTICE AREAS:*** Employee Benefits. ***Email:*** dfarina@reidandriege.com

EVAN S. GOLDSTEIN, born Hartford, Connecticut, February, 17, 1973; admitted to bar, 2000, Connecticut. *Education:* University of Vermont (B.A., 1995); Benjamin N. Cardozo School of Law, Yeshiva University (J.D., 2000). *Member:* Connecticut Bar Association. ***PRACTICE AREAS:*** Bankruptcy. ***Email:*** egoldstein@reidandriege.com

RISCASSI AND DAVIS, P.C.

Established in 1955

131 OAK STREET

P.O. BOX 261557

HARTFORD, CONNECTICUT 06126-1557

Telephone: 860-522-1196

Fax: 860-246-5847

URL: http://www.riscassi-davis.com

Civil, Trial and Appellate Practice in State and Federal Courts. Negligence, Products Liability, Aviation and Medical Malpractice.

FIRM PROFILE: RisCassi and Davis, P.C. is a law firm of eleven attorneys which has represented plaintiffs in personal injury litigation since 1955.

Five members of the firm are certified as Civil Trial Advocates by the National Board of Trial Advocacy. Four attorneys, William Davis, James Barolini, Michael Jainchill and John Houlihan are listed in "The Best Lawyers in America," 2001-2002, Woodward/White, Inc., Aiken, SC., in the area of civil and personal injury litigation. Mr. Davis, Mr. Bartolini, John Houlihan, Michael Jainchill and Eugene Swain are all members of the American Board of Trial Advocates. Mr. Jainchill is the co-author of a treatise on Connecticut uninsured motorist law. The late founder of RisCassi and Davis, P.C., Leon RisCassi, served as senate majority and minority leader and was a founder of the Connecticut Trial Lawyers Association.

The members of the firm work with a wide range of cases, including motor vehicle collisions, medical, legal and other professional malpractice, industrial accidents, airplane crashes and product liability cases. RisCassi and Davis, P.C. will also handle cases for plaintiffs other than for personal injury, such as claims arising from business loss or the destruction of property. Located in Hartford, the firm brings personal injury claims throughout Connecticut. Where appropriate, RisCassi and Davis, P.C. will represent plaintiffs from across the country who have claims in Connecticut. RisCassi and Davis, P.C., has teamed with other attorneys where representation of the interests of the client may require attorneys in different states.

(This Listing Continued)

RisCassi and Davis, P.C., strongly supports the involvement of its attorneys in professional and civic activities, particularly in the area of legal education. Members of the firm are extremely active in state and national trial lawyer associations, with five of the eleven attorneys previously having served as presidents of the Connecticut Trial Lawyers Association. Six are presently on its Board of Governors. Many of the attorneys regularly lecture to state and national legal associations on issues relating to personal injury litigation and trial practice. Many have also served on the faculty of the University of Connecticut School of Law where the firm is helping to fund the building of a new courtroom facility for mock trial practice.

LEON RISCASSI (1908-1986).

WILLIAM R. DAVIS, born Waterbury, Connecticut, September 15, 1930; admitted to bar, 1955, Connecticut; 1958, U.S. District Court, District of Connecticut; 1960, U.S. Supreme Court. *Education:* Providence College (B.A., summa cum laude, 1952); University of Connecticut (LL.B., 1955). Member: Board of Student Editors, Connecticut State Bar Journal, 1955; Board of Editors, Connecticut NACCA Journal, 1955-1956. Co-Author, "Uniform Laws in Connecticut," Connecticut Bar Journal, June 1954. Author, "Wrongful Death in Connecticut," NACCA Journal, December 1955. Instructor, Trial Practice, University of Connecticut School of Law, 1971—. Member, Governor's Criminal Justice Commission, 1985—. *Member:* Hartford County (Member, Bench-Bar Relations Committee, 1962; Co-Chairman, Medico-Legal Committee, 1962-1965; Treasurer, 1969-1971; Secretary, 1971-1972; Vice President, 1972-1973; President, 1973-1974), Connecticut (Member: Committee on Medical-Legal Problems and Interprofessional Codes, 1962—; Civil Justice Section; Judiciary Committee, 1979-1982; Chairman, Statewide Grievance Committee, 1982-1985) and American Bar Associations; American Judicature Society; The Association of Trial Lawyers of America (Member, Board of Governors, 1968-1969, 1969-1970, 1970-1971); Roscoe Pound Foundation (Treasurer, 1981-1983); Connecticut Trial Lawyers Association (Treasurer for Connecticut, 1959-1960; Second Vice President, 1960-1961; President, 1962-1963); American Board of Trial Advocates (Diplomat). Fellow: American College of Trial Lawyers; American Bar Foundation; International Society of Barristers. ***PRACTICE AREAS:*** Medical Malpractice; Products Liability; Negligence.

JAMES D. BARTOLINI, born New Haven, Connecticut, April 13, 1946; admitted to bar, 1975, Connecticut and U.S. District Court, District of Connecticut. *Education:* Trinity College (B.A., 1968); Hartford Seminary (M.A., 1970; M.Div., 1972); University of Connecticut (J.D., with honors, 1975). Associate Editor, University of Connecticut Law Review, 1974-1975. Author: "Preparing the Expert Witness for Trial," Connecticut Law Tribune, Vol. 8, No. 22, May 31, 1982; "Trial by Analogy," CTLA Forum, Vol. 6, No. 1, Jan./Feb., 1988. Co-Author: "A Functional Approach to Habeas Corpus Jurisdiction," University of Connecticut Law Review, Spring 1974; "Bystander Recovery for Emotional Distress," Connecticut Bar Journal, Vol. 64, No. 4, August 1990. Instructor, Trial Practice, University of Connecticut School of Law, 1986-1999. Editor in Chief, Connecticut Bar Journal, 1999-2000. *Member:* Hartford County (Co-Chairman, Medical/Legal Committee, 1982-1986) and Connecticut Bar Associations; Connecticut Trial Lawyers Association (Vice-President, 1987-1988; President Elect, 1988-1989; President, 1989-1990); The Association of Trial Lawyers of America; Roscoe Pound Foundation; American Board of Trial Advocates; Connecticut Academy of Certified Trial Lawyers (President, 1988-1989). Fellow, American College of Trial Lawyers. Certified as a Civil Trial Advocate by the National Board of Trial Advocacy. ***PRACTICE AREAS:*** Medical Malpractice; Negligence; Products Liability.

ANDREW S. GROHER, born New York, N.Y., March 10, 1952; admitted to bar, 1978, Connecticut and U.S. District Court, District of Connecticut; 1988, U.S. Court of Appeals, Second Circuit. *Education:* University of Virginia (B.A., 1974); University of Connecticut (J.D., with honors, 1978). Instructor, Trial Practice, University of Connecticut School of Law, 1989—. Special Master: U.S. District Court, 1988—; Hartford Superior Court, 1992—. Member, Board of Directors, Connecticut Traumatic Brain Injury Association, 1993-1998. Member, Connecticut Appleseed Foundation (Member, Board of Directors, 1998—). *Member:* Hartford County Bar Association; Connecticut Trial Lawyers Association (Member, Board of Governors, 1986—; Vice President, 1996-1997; President-Elect, 1997-1998; President, 1998-1999); The Association of Trial Lawyers of America. ***PRACTICE AREAS:*** Medical Malpractice; Negligence; Products Liability. ***Email:*** agroher@riscassidavis.com

MICHAEL C. JAINCHILL, born Hartford, Connecticut, April 7, 1953; admitted to bar, 1978, Connecticut and U.S. District Court, District of Connecticut. *Education:* University of Connecticut (B.A., cum laude, 1975; J.D., with honors, 1978). Pi Sigma Alpha. Selected for inclusion, Best Lawyers in America, 2001. Contributing Author and Researcher, "A Digest of Supreme Court Decisions Affecting Education," 1978. Author: "The Law of Video Tape Evidence," CTLA Forum, Vol. 5, No. 2, April 1987; "Connecticut Law of Uninsured and Underinsured Motorist Coverage: A Guide," Atlantic Law Book Co., 1993, 2nd Edition, 1999. Associate Editor, Connecticut Trial Lawyers Association Forum, 1986—. Special Master: U.S. District Court, 1988—; Hart-

(This Listing Continued)

RISCASSI AND DAVIS, P.C., Hartford—Continued

ford Superior Court, 1992-1995. Commissioner, Occupational Safety and Health Commission, 1991—. Member, American Board of Trial Advocates, 1998—. *Member:* Hartford County, Connecticut (Member, House of Delegates, 1986-1992) and American Bar Associations; Connecticut Trial Lawyers Association (Member, Board of Governors, 1990—); The Association of Trial Lawyers of America. (Board Certified, Civil Trial Advocate Specialist by the National Board of Trial Advocacy). ***PRACTICE AREAS:*** Products Liability; Negligence; Medical Malpractice; Uninsured and Underinsured Motorists.

JOHN J. HOULIHAN, JR., born Hartford, Connecticut, September 19, 1955; admitted to bar, 1980, Connecticut and U.S. District Court, District of Connecticut. *Education:* Providence College (B.A., cum laude, 1977); St. John's University (J.D., 1980). Selected for inclusion, Best Lawyers in America, 2001. Instructor: Moot Court, University of Connecticut School of Law, 1990-1992; Trial Practice, University of Connecticut School of Law, 1999—. *Member:* Hartford County, Connecticut and American Bar Associations; Connecticut Trial Lawyers Association (Member, Board of Governors, 1993—); The Association of Trial Lawyers of America; American Board of Trial Advocates; Connecticut Academy of Certified Trial Lawyers. Certified as a Civil Trial Advocate by the National Board of Trial Advocacy. ***PRACTICE AREAS:*** Negligence; Products Liability; Medical Malpractice.

DAVID W. COONEY, born Jersey City, New Jersey, November 30, 1953; admitted to bar, 1978, Connecticut and U.S. District Court, District of Connecticut; 1993, U.S. Claims Court. *Education:* Rutgers University (B.A., with honors, 1975); University of Connecticut (J.D., 1978); Wesleyan University (M.A., 1998). Phi Beta Kappa. Fact Finder/Arbitrator, Superior Court for the State of Connecticut, 1986—. Special Master: Hartford, New Britain, Waterbury and Middlesex Superior Courts, 1992—; United States District Court, 1996—. *Member:* Hartford County (Medical-Legal Committee, 1984-1988; Chairman, Continuing Legal Education Committee, 1994-2000; Co-Chair, Bench-Bar Committee, 2000—), Connecticut (Member, Executive Committee, Litigation Section, 1984-1993; Professional Discipline Committee, 1997—) and American (Member, Sections on: Litigation; Tort and Insurance Practice Law) Bar Associations; The Association of Trial Lawyers of America; Connecticut Trial Lawyers Association (Member, Connecticut Legal Education Committee, 1992—). Certified as a Civil Trial Advocate by the National Board of Trial Advocacy. ***PRACTICE AREAS:*** Insurance Litigation; Professional Liability; Medical Malpractice; Negligence.

EUGENE K. SWAIN, born Philadelphia, Pennsylvania, December 4, 1947; admitted to bar, 1977, Georgia; 1978, Alabama and U.S. District Court, Middle District of Georgia; 1983, Connecticut and U.S. District Court, District of Connecticut; 1987, Rhode Island and U.S. District Court, District of Rhode Island. *Education:* University of Maryland (B.A., 1975); University of Georgia (J.D., 1977). *Member:* New London County (Board of Directors, 1990—; President, 1995-1996) and Rhode Island Bar Association; State Bar of Georgia; Alabama State Bar; Connecticut Trial Lawyers Association (Member, Board of Directors, 1990—; President, 1999-2000); The Association of Trial Lawyers of America; National Board of Trial Advocacy (Diplomate); American Board of Trial Advocates (Advocate); The Connecticut Academy of Certified Trial Lawyers. ***PRACTICE AREAS:*** Personal Injury; Products Liability; Professional Malpractice.

KATHRYN CALIBEY, born Pawtucket, Rhode Island, July 30, 1953; admitted to bar, 1982, Connecticut and U.S. District Court, District of Connecticut; 1988, U.S. Court of Appeals, Second Circuit. *Education:* University of Connecticut (B.A., 1975); Western New England College (J.D., cum laude, 1982). Recipient: United States Law Week Award; Henry Downey Award; Benjamin Novak Writing Award. Note and Comment Editor, Western New England Law Review, 1981-1982. Senior Editor, Civil Litigation, Board of Editors, Connecticut Bar Journal, 1992—; Associate Editor, CTLA Forum-Supreme and Appellate Court Review, 1996—. Author: "Are Policy Arbitration Clauses Enforceable," CTLA Forum, Vol. 7, No. 1 (1989); "Connecticut Appellate Law Overview-1988," CTLA Forum (1989); "Connecticut Appellate Law Overview-1989," CTLA Forum (1990); Connecticut's Parent-Child Immunity Doctrine, 65 C.B.J. 210, June 1991; "Childs v. Bainer: A Misstep in the Application of Connecticut Damage Law," CTLA Forum, Nov./Dec. 1995. Co-Author: "Civil Liability of Gun Manufacturers for Criminal Use of Handguns," 12 Trial Diplomacy J. (1989); "Bystander Recovery for Emotional Distress," 64 C.B.J. 275, August 1990; "Developments in Tort Law - Annual Survey," C.B.J., 1997—. Instructor, Moot Court, University of Connecticut School of Law, 1992-1995. Special Master, Hartford Superior Court, 1992—. Appointed to the Joint Committee for Judicial Branch Civil Jury Instruction Project, 1993—; Oral History of Connecticut Women in the Legal Profession Project, 1999—. *Member:* Hartford County (Member, Board of Directors, 1997—), Connecticut (Member, Appellate Practice Section) and American Bar Associations; Connecticut Trial Lawyers Association (Member, Amicus Curiae Committee); The Association of Trial Lawyers of America; Hartford County Bar Foundation (Founding Member and Officer, Board of Directors, 1999—); Oliver Ellsworth Inns of Court (Bencher, 1998—). ***PRACTICE AREAS:*** Negligence; Medical Malpractice; Appellate Practice.

(This Listing Continued)

DOUGLAS W. HAMMOND, born New London, Connecticut, April 5, 1960; admitted to bar, 1988, Connecticut; 1989, U.S. District Court, District of Connecticut. *Education:* Yale University (B.A., cum laude, 1982); University of Connecticut (J.D., with highest honors, 1988). Author: "The Conscience of the State," Connecticut Bar Journal, Vol. 72, No. 6 (1998); Author or Co-Author, Annual Tort Law Survey, Connecticut Bar Journal, 1994-1999. Member, Connecticut Law Review. *Member:* Hartford County and Connecticut Bar Associations; Connecticut Trial Lawyers Association; The Association of Trial Lawyers of America. ***PRACTICE AREAS:*** Personal Injury; Products Liability; Negligence.

EVERETT HOWARD MADIN, JR., born Winsted, Connecticut, February 7, 1951; admitted to bar, 1992, Connecticut; 1993, U.S. District Court, District of Connecticut. *Education:* Syracuse University (B.F.A., magna cum laude, 1975); University of Connecticut (J.D., with honors, 1992). Member, Roscoe Pound Foundation. Law Clerk to Judge Edward Y. O'Connell, Connecticut Appellate Court, 1992-1993. Co-Author: "1994 Connecticut Tort Review," Connecticut Bar Journal, Vol. 69, No. 1, February 1995. *Member:* Hartford County, Litchfield County and Connecticut (Member, Young Lawyers Division, Litigation Committee) Bar Associations; Connecticut Trial Lawyers Association; The Association of Trial Lawyers of America. ***PRACTICE AREAS:*** Personal Injury; Products Liability; Medical Malpractice.

PAUL M. IANNACCONE, born Waterbury, Connecticut, November 10, 1961; admitted to bar, 1994, Connecticut. *Education:* University of Connecticut (B.A., 1985); Western New England College (J.D., with honors, 1994). Member, Western New England College Law Review, 1993-1994. Senior Probation Officer, State of Connecticut Judicial Department, 1985-1992. *Member:* Connecticut Bar Association; Connecticut Trial Lawyers Association; Oliver Ellsworth Inns of Court (Barrister); The Association of Trial Lawyers of America. ***PRACTICE AREAS:*** Personal Injury; Products Liability; Medical Malpractice; Civil Litigation.

ROBINSON & COLE LLP

Established in 1845

280 TRUMBULL STREET

HARTFORD, CONNECTICUT 06103-3597

Telephone: 860-275-8200

Fax: 860-275-8299

Email: rc.com

URL: http://www.rc.com

Stamford, Connecticut Office: Financial Centre, P.O. Box 10305, 695 East Main Street. Telephone: 203-462-7500. Fax: 203-462-7599.

Greenwich, Connecticut Office: 80 Field Point Road. Telephone: 203-862-4100. Fax: 203-862-4199.

New London, Connecticut Office: 75 Eugene O'Neill Drive. Telephone: 860-437-5000. Fax: 860-437-5099.

Boston, Massachusetts Office: One Boston Place. Telephone: 617-557-5900. Fax: 617-557-5999.

New York, N.Y. Office: 4th Floor, 780 Third Avenue. Telephone: 212-451-2900. Fax: 212-451-2999.

Manchester, New Hampshire Office: Robinson & Cole & Craig, 84 Bay Street. Telephone: 603-641-2500. Fax: 603-669-1310.

General Practice including Admiralty, Antitrust and Trade Regulation, Appellate, Banking and Institutional Finance, Bankruptcy and Creditors' Rights, Business Litigation, Business Workouts, Construction, Corporate and Closely Held Business, Criminal Litigation, E-Commerce and Intellectual Property, Employee Benefits and ERISA Litigation, Employment Litigation and Counseling, Environmental, Estate Planning and Probate, Government Relations, Healthcare, Immigration, Insurance, International, Labor Relations and Collective Bargaining, Land Use and Zoning, Personal Injury, Product Liability, Professional Liability, Public Finance, Real Estate Finance, Development and Leasing, Securities, Tax-Exempt Organizations, Tax Planning and Representation, Utilities and Telecommunications.

LAW FIRM ALLIANCES/ASSOCIATIONS: ***UNITED STATES LAW FIRM GROUP***

STATE CAPITAL LAW FIRM GROUP

PARTNERS

BRADFORD S. BABBITT, admitted to bar, 1993, Connecticut; 1994, Massachusetts and U.S. District Court, Districts of Connecticut and Massachusetts; 1995, U.S. Court of Appeals, Second Circuit; 1997, U.S. Supreme Court. *Education:* Trinity College (B.A., 1987); Boston College (J.D., magna cum laude, 1993). Order of the Coif. Note Editor, Boston College Law Review. Law Clerk

(This Listing Continued)

to Judge William J. Lavery, Connecticut Appellate Court, 1993-1994. Adjunct Instructor, University of Connecticut School of Law, 1997-2000. ***PRACTICE AREAS:*** Business Litigation. ***Email:*** bbabbitt@rc.com

KENNETH C. BALDWIN, admitted to bar, 1994, Connecticut. *Education:* State University of New York at Geneseo (B.A., 1982); State University of New York at Stony Brook (M.A., 1984); Western New England College (J.D., 1994). *Member:* American Planning Association (Planning and Law Division); Federal Communication Bar Association. ***REPORTED CASES:*** Cellco Partnership v. Town of Farmington, 5 F. Supp. 2d 178 (D. Conn. 1998). ***PRACTICE AREAS:*** Energy; Zoning, Planning and Land Use; Real Estate. ***Email:*** kbaldwin@rc.com

BRUCE B. BARTH, admitted to bar, 1981, District of Columbia; 1982, U.S. Tax Court, U.S. Court of Appeals, Federal Circuit and U.S. District Court, District of Columbia; 1983, Colorado and U.S. District Court, District of Colorado; 1985, Connecticut; 1992, U.S. District Court, District of Connecticut. *Education:* University of Connecticut (B.S., honors scholar, magna cum laude, 1978); George Washington University (J.D., with honors, 1981); Georgetown University (M.L.T., 1983). ***PRACTICE AREAS:*** Employee Benefits; Labor and Employment; Taxation. ***Email:*** bbarth@rc.com

GURDON H. BUCK, admitted to bar, 1965, Connecticut. *Education:* Lehigh University (B.A., 1958); University of Pennsylvania (J.D., 1965). Title Insurance Agent, Connecticut, 1970—. Licensed Real Estate Broker, Connecticut, 1969-2000. *Member:* American Institute of Certified Planners. ***PRACTICE AREAS:*** Real Estate; Zoning, Planning and Land Use; Common Interest Communities; Condominiums; Urban Villages; Mixed Use Land Development. ***Email:*** gbuck@rc.com

LAWRENCE P. COASSIN, admitted to bar, 1983, Connecticut; 1996, New York. *Education:* Babson College (B.S., with distinction, 1980); University of Miami (J.D., cum laude, 1983). Phi Alpha Delta. Associate Editor, The University of Miami International Law Journal, 1982-1983. ***PRACTICE AREAS:*** Mergers and Acquisitions; Corporate Law; Business Law; Finance. ***Email:*** lcoassin@rc.com

THOMAS P. CODY, admitted to bar, 1991, Connecticut; 1992, U.S. District Court, District of Connecticut. *Education:* Bucknell University (B.A., 1980); University of Colorado at Denver (M.P.C.D., 1984); College of William and Mary (J.D., 1991). Member, Board of Editors, William and Mary Law Review, 1990-1991. ***PRACTICE AREAS:*** Zoning, Planning and Land Use; Environmental Law. ***Email:*** tcody@rc.com

FRANK F. COULOM, JR., admitted to bar, 1982, Connecticut, New York and Pennsylvania; U.S. District Court, District of Connecticut; U.S. Court of Appeals, Second Circuit; U.S. District Court, Eastern District of Pennsylvania. *Education:* St. Anselm College (B.A., summa cum laude, 1976); St. John's University (J.D., 1981). Editor-in-Chief, St. John's Law Review, 1980-1981. Clerk, Honorable Alfred L. Luongo, Chief Judge, U.S. District Court, Eastern District of Pennsylvania, 1981-1983. *Member:* Connecticut Bar Foundation. ***PRACTICE AREAS:*** Litigation; Reinsurance; Insurance. ***Email:*** fcoulom@rc.com

ERIC D. DANIELS, admitted to bar, 1986, Connecticut; 1987, U.S. District Court, Districts of Connecticut and Hawaii; 1988, U.S. Court of Appeals, Ninth Circuit; 1991, U.S. Supreme Court and U.S. Court of Appeals, Second Circuit. *Education:* Brown University (B.A., 1983); Boston College Law School (J.D., magna cum laude, 1986). Order of the Coif. Managing Editor, Boston College Law Review, 1985-1986. Attorney Trial Referee, Hartford Superior Court, 1993—. Member, Products Liability Committee, American Bar Association. ***PRACTICE AREAS:*** Litigation; Products Liability. ***Email:*** edaniels@rc.com

S. FRANK D'ERCOLE, admitted to bar, 1968, Connecticut. *Education:* Colby College (A.B., 1961); University of Perugia, Italy; Cornell University (J.D., 1968). Chairman: Committee on General Obligation Bonds, 1982-1986, Legislative Action Committee, 1992-1993 and Co-Chair, Committee on Bankruptcy, 1997-1998, National Association of Bond Lawyers. Governor's Appointment to Commission on Local Government of the State of Connecticut, 1981. ***PRACTICE AREAS:*** Finance; Securities; Government. ***Email:*** sdercole@rc.com

ALICE E. DeTORA, admitted to bar, 1984, Connecticut; U.S. District Court, District of Connecticut. *Education:* Michigan State University (B.A., high honors, 1975); Vermont Law School (J.D., magna cum laude, 1984). Managing Editor, Vermont Law Review. Law Clerk, Connecticut Supreme Court, 1984-1985. *Member:* American Immigration Lawyers Association. ***PRACTICE AREAS:*** Labor and Employment; Immigration. ***Email:*** adetora@rc.com

MICHAEL R. ENRIGHT, admitted to bar, 1981, Illinois and U.S. District Court, Northern District of Illinois; 1992, Connecticut and U.S. District Court, District of Connecticut and Northern District of Illinois. *Education:* University of Illinois (B.A., 1978); Loyola University (J.D., cum laude, 1981). ***PRACTICE AREAS:*** Creditors' Rights; Bankruptcy; Workouts. ***Email:*** menright@rc.com

STEPHEN E. GOLDMAN, admitted to bar, 1980, Connecticut; 1984, Massachusetts. *Education:* Wesleyan University (B.A., magna cum laude, 1976);

(This Listing Continued)

New York University School of Law (J.D., 1980). Phi Beta Kappa. Recipient, University of Connecticut Award for Best Appellate Brief, 1992. Regional Editor, Defense Research Institute, Coverage Newsletter. Adjunct Professor of Law, University of Connecticut School of Law, 1998-1999. Chair, 1997-1998, Property Insurance Law Committee of Tort and Insurance Practice Section, American Bar Association. President of Board of Directors, Greater Hartford Legal Assistance, 1997—. *Member:* Federation of Insurance and Corporate Counsel (Chair, Property Insurance Section); International Association of Defense Counsel; Defense Research Institute; Loss Executives Association; National Association of Property Insurance Lawyers, Connecticut Defense Lawyers Association. ***PRACTICE AREAS:*** Litigation; Insurance. ***Email:*** sgoldman@rc.com

J. C. DAVID HADDEN, admitted to bar, 1980, New York and U.S. Tax Court; 1981, U.S. District Court, Southern and Eastern Districts of New York; 1983, Connecticut. *Education:* Harvard University (A.B., cum laude, 1974); University of Virginia (J.D., 1979). Member: Estate and Business Planning Council of Hartford, Inc.; Exempt Organizations Subcommittee, Section on Taxation, American Bar Association. Fellow, American College of Trust and Estate Counsel. Cooper Fellow, Connecticut Bar Association. ***PRACTICE AREAS:*** Trusts and Estates; Wills; Probate; Tax Exempt Organizations. ***Email:*** dhadden@rc.com

EDWARD F. HENNESSEY, admitted to bar, 1962, Connecticut. *Education:* Dartmouth College (A.B., 1956); Boston College (J.D., 1961). Member, Boston College Law Review. Law Clerk to the Hon. M. Joseph Blumenfeld, U.S. District Court, District of Connecticut. Fellow, American College of Trial Lawyers. Cooper Fellow, Connecticut Bar Association. Board Certified in Civil Trial Advocacy, National Board of Trial Advocacy. ***PRACTICE AREAS:*** Litigation. ***Email:*** ehennessy@rc.com

EDWARD S. HILL, admitted to bar, 1972, Connecticut; 1973, U.S. District Court, District of Connecticut; 1985, U.S. Claims Court. *Education:* Trinity College (B.A., 1969); University of Connecticut (J.D., with honors, 1972). ***PRACTICE AREAS:*** Real Estate; Finance; Bankruptcy; Litigation; Zoning, Planning and Land Use. ***Email:*** ehill@rc.com

BRIEN P. HORAN, admitted to bar, 1979, Massachusetts; 1986, Connecticut. *Education:* Amherst College (B.A., 1975); Institut d'Études Politiques de Paris (C.E.P., 1977); University of Connecticut (J.D., 1979). *Member:* Defense Research Institute; American Intellectual Property Law Association; International Bar Association. ***PRACTICE AREAS:*** Products Liability; Litigation. ***Email:*** bhoran@rc.com

CHRISTOPHER J. HUG, admitted to bar, 1989, Connecticut; U.S. District Court, District of Connecticut. *Education:* Brown University (A.B., 1981); Western New England College (J.D., cum laude, 1989). ***PRACTICE AREAS:*** Litigation; Bankruptcy; Construction Law. ***Email:*** chug@rc.com

STEVEN R. HUMPHREY, admitted to bar, 1966, Massachusetts; 1967, Connecticut; U.S. Court of Appeals, Second Circuit; U.S. District Court, Districts of Connecticut and Massachusetts; U.S. Supreme Court. *Education:* Wesleyan University (B.A., 1963); Vanderbilt University (J.D., 1966). Phi Alpha Delta. ***PRACTICE AREAS:*** Litigation; Administrative Law; Energy; Telecommunications. ***Email:*** shumphrey@rc.com

JACK S. KENNEDY, admitted to bar, 1972, Connecticut. *Education:* Harvard University (B.A., magna cum laude, 1967); University of Virginia (J.D., 1972). Order of the Coif. Member, Editorial Board, Virginia Law Review, 1970-1972. Chairman, Business Law Section, Connecticut Bar Association, 1998-2000. ***PRACTICE AREAS:*** Mergers and Acquisitions; Corporate Law; Business Law; Closely-Held Business Planning. ***Email:*** jkennedy@rc.com

JUDITH M. KEPPELMAN, admitted to bar, 1979, Connecticut. *Education:* Vassar College (A.B., 1971); Fordham University School of Law (J.D., 1978). Member, Executive Committee, Estates and Probate Section, Connecticut Bar Association, 1986—. Fellow: American College of Trust and Estate Counsel (ACTEC); Past President, Estate and Business Planning Council of Hartford. ***PRACTICE AREAS:*** Trusts and Estates; Wills; Probate. ***Email:*** jkeppelman@rc.com

DAVID A. KULLE, admitted to bar, 1985, Connecticut; U.S. District Court, District of Connecticut; U.S. Court of Appeals, Second Circuit; U.S. Supreme Court. *Education:* Hamilton College (B.A., 1975), Phi Beta Kappa; Yale University (M.M., 1978); University of Connecticut (J.D., with honors, 1985). Editor in Chief, Connecticut Law Review, 1984-1985. ***PRACTICE AREAS:*** Labor and Employment; Litigation. ***Email:*** dkulle@rc.com

ERIC LUKINGBEAL, admitted to bar, 1974, Connecticut and U.S. District Court, District of Connecticut; U.S. Court of Appeals, 2nd Circuit. *Education:* Williams College (B.A., 1971); University of Virginia (J.D., 1974). Member, Planning and Zoning Commission, Town of Granby, 1987-2000. Member, Inland Wetlands and Watercourses Commission, Town of Granby. Special Master, U.S. District Court. ***REPORTED CASES:*** Andrews vs. MetroNorth Commuter Railroad, 882 F.2d 705, 2d Cir, 1989; Bernbach v. Timex Corp., 989 F.

(This Listing Continued)

ROBINSON & COLE LLP, Hartford—Continued

Supp 403 (D. Conn. 1997); B.F. Goodrich v. Betkosky, 99 F.3d 503 (2nd Cir. 1996). ***PRACTICE AREAS:*** Environmental Law; Zoning, Planning and Land Use; Litigation; Toxic Torts. ***Email:*** elukingbea@rc.com

JOHN B. LYNCH, JR., admitted to bar, 1984, Connecticut. *Education:* College of the Holy Cross (B.A., cum laude, 1981); University of Virginia (J.D., 1984). Phi Beta Kappa. ***PRACTICE AREAS:*** Mergers and Acquisitions; Finance; Corporate Law; Banking Law. ***Email:*** jlynch@rc.com

DIANA MACPHERSON, admitted to bar, 1978, Connecticut; 1980, U.S. District Court, District of Connecticut. *Education:* Scripps College (B.A., 1965); University of Connecticut School of Law (J.D., 1977). Author, "Ethical and Other Issues for Counsel in Multi State Real Estate Transactions," American College of Real Estate Lawyers, October 1999. *Member:* American College of Real Estate Lawyers; National Network of Commercial Real Estate Women. ***PRACTICE AREAS:*** Real Estate; Finance; Leasing; Construction Law. ***Email:*** dmacpherso@rc.com

MICHAEL F. MAGLIO, admitted to bar, 1982, Connecticut and U.S. District Court, District of Connecticut. *Education:* University of Connecticut (B.A., cum laude, 1979); Suffolk University (J.D., cum laude, 1982). Editor and Staff Writer, Suffolk University Law Review. Member, Export Advisory Board, University of Connecticut Small Business Development Center. Lecturer, Commercial Finance, Asset-Based Lending and Trade Finance. Law Clerk, Superior Court of Connecticut, 1982-1983. ***PRACTICE AREAS:*** Debtor and Creditor; Commercial Law. ***Email:*** mmaglio@rc.com

LINDA J. MCDOWELL, admitted to bar, 1986, Connecticut. *Education:* Dickinson College (B.A., cum laude, 1972); College of William & Mary, Marshall-Wythe School of Law (J.D., 1986). Order of the Coif. Member, Executive Committee, Estates and Probate Section, Connecticut Bar Association. *Member:* Greater Hartford Probate Forum; Central Connecticut Business and Estate Planning Council; The Estate and Business Planning Council of Hartford, Inc. ***PRACTICE AREAS:*** Trusts and Estates; Wills; Probates. ***Email:*** lmcdowell@rc.com

ROBERT S. MELVIN, admitted to bar, 1991, Connecticut; 1992, U.S. District Court, District of Connecticut. *Education:* University of Connecticut (B.S., Chemical Engineering, magna cum laude, 1986; J.D., with high honors, 1991). Tau Beta Pi; Omega Chi Epsilon. Co-Author: Connecticut Chapter, "Brownfields Law and Practice," Matthew Bender, 1997, revised 2001. Member, Waste Management Section, Environmental Policies Council of Connecticut Business and Industry Association, 1991—. ***PRACTICE AREAS:*** Environmental Law; Litigation. ***Email:*** rmelvin@rc.com

DWIGHT H. MERRIAM, admitted to bar, 1978, Connecticut; 1980, Massachusetts; 1981, U.S. District Court, District of Connecticut; 1984, U.S. District Court, District of Hawaii; 1990, U.S. Supreme Court. *Education:* University of Massachusetts (B.A., cum laude, 1968); University of North Carolina (Master of Regional Planning, 1973); Yale University (J.D., 1978). Phi Kappa Phi. Author: "The Palazzolo Decision: Time for Damage Control," *Municipal Lawyer* July-August 2001; "Will Federal Brownfields Legislation Prove a Cruel Hoax," *The Retail Law Strategist* August 2001. Director, American Planning Association, 1988-1990. President, American Institute of Certified Planners, 1988-1990. Fellow, American College of Real Estate Lawyers. [Commissioned Officer, 1968-1975, Capt., 1975-1990, U.S. Navy]. ***PRACTICE AREAS:*** Zoning, Planning and Land Use; Environmental Law; Real Estate; Retail Development. ***Email:*** dmerriam@rc.com

DAVID M. PANICO, admitted to bar, 1989, Connecticut, U.S. District Court, District of Connecticut and U.S. Tax Court. *Education:* Fairfield University (B.S., 1983); University of Connecticut (J.D., with honors, 1989). Author: "Survey of the Final Arbitrage Regulations," The Urban Lawyer, Fall 1993. *Member:* Connecticut Society of Certified Public Accountants; American Institute of Certified Public Accountants; National Association of Bond Lawyers. ***PRACTICE AREAS:*** Indians and Native Populations. ***Email:*** dpanico@rc.com

EARL W. PHILLIPS, JR., admitted to bar, 1980, Connecticut; 1981, Maine. *Education:* Wesleyan University (B.A., cum laude 1977); University of Pittsburgh and Catholic University of America (J.D., 1980). Co-Author, Brownfields Law and Practice for Matthew Bender, 1997, revised 2001. Member: Chair, Waste Management Section, Environmental Policies Council of Connecticut Business & Industry Association, 1987—; Connecticut's Council of Environmental Quality (Senate Appointment); Governor's Environment 2000 Committee. Advisory Committee(s) to the Connecticut Department of Environmental Protection (Hazardous Waste, Water, Spills, Ash). ***PRACTICE AREAS:*** Environmental Law. ***Email:*** ephillips@rc.com

EMANUEL N. PSARAKIS, admitted to bar, 1959, Connecticut. *Education:* University of Connecticut (A.B., 1954); Boston University (LL.B., 1959); Columbia University (LL.M., in Labor Law, 1960). Editor, Boston University Law Review, 1958-1959. ***PRACTICE AREAS:*** Civil Rights; Labor and Employment; Discrimination Law; Litigation. ***Email:*** epsarakis@rc.com

(This Listing Continued)

CRAIG A. RAABE, admitted to bar, 1988, Connecticut; U.S. Supreme Court; U.S. Court of Appeals, Second and District of Columbia Circuits; U.S. District Court, District of Connecticut. *Education:* Valparaiso University (B.A., with honors, 1985); Western New England College School of Law (J.D., cum laude, 1988). Editor in Chief, Western New England Law Review. Law Clerk to Hon. Arthur H. Healey, Connecticut Supreme Court, 1988-1989. Chair, Robinson & Cole Trial and Appellate Advocacy Section. *Member:* Criminal Justice Act Panel, District of Connecticut; National Association of Criminal Defense Lawyers; Connecticut Criminal Defense Lawyers Association. ***PRACTICE AREAS:*** Criminal Law. ***Email:*** craabe@rc.com

JAMES P. RAY, admitted to bar, 1992, Connecticut; 1993, Massachusetts and U.S. District Court, District of Connecticut; 1994, New York. *Education:* University of Connecticut (B.S., cum laude, 1984; M.B.A., 1992; J.D., with honors, 1992). Former Co-Chairman, Young Lawyers Section, Environmental Committee, Connecticut Bar Association. ***PRACTICE AREAS:*** Environmental Law; Litigation. ***Email:*** jray@rc.com

DAVID THOMAS RYAN, admitted to bar, 1966, Connecticut. *Education:* University of Maryland (B.S., 1961); Georgetown University (LL.B., 1965). Associate Editor, Georgetown Law Journal, 1964-1965. Law Clerk for Justice Charles S. House, Connecticut Supreme Court, 1965-1966. *Member:* American Board of Trial Advocates (Advocate). Fellow, American College of Trial Lawyers. ***PRACTICE AREAS:*** Personal Injury; Medical Malpractice; Litigation; Trusts and Estates. ***Email:*** dryan@rc.com

EDWARD J. SAMORAJCZYK, JR., admitted to bar, 1980, Connecticut. *Education:* Harvard University (A.B., with honors, 1977); University of Connecticut School of Law (J.D., with honors, 1980). Articles Editor, Connecticut Law Review. Law Clerk to Hon. Arthur H. Healey, Connecticut Supreme Court, 1980-1981. ***PRACTICE AREAS:*** Corporate Law; Securities; Finance; Insurance. ***Email:*** esamorajcz@rc.com

GLENN A. SANTORO, admitted to bar, 1989, Connecticut; U.S. District Court, District of Connecticut. *Education:* Boston College (B.S. 1983); University of Connecticut (J.D., with honors, 1989). Certified Public Accountant, Connecticut. *Member:* Connecticut Society of Certified Public Accountants; American Institute of Certified Public Accountants; National Association of Bond Lawyers. ***PRACTICE AREAS:*** Mergers and Acquisitions; Corporate; Municipal Law; Government; Finance. ***Email:*** gsantoro@rc.com

EDWARD P. SCHERER, admitted to bar, 1971, Connecticut. *Education:* Colby College (B.A., 1967); Boston College and Loyola University (J.D., 1971). Vice Chair, Committee on Commercial Leasing, American Bar Association, 1987-1992. *Member:* International Council of Shopping Centers; Real Estate Finance Association. ***PRACTICE AREAS:*** Real Estate; Real Estate Leasing; Government. ***Email:*** escherer@rc.com

WILLIAM T. SELLAY, admitted to bar, 1971, Connecticut. *Education:* Michigan State University (B.S., with honors, 1968); University of Michigan (J.D., 1971). Co-Editor, *eCounsel, The Executives Guide to Electronic Commerce*. (Also at New York, N.Y. Office). ***PRACTICE AREAS:*** Business Law; Mergers and Acquisitions; Antitrust and Trade Regulation; Intellectual Property; Technology and Science; International Law. ***Email:*** wsellay@rc.com

BRIAN R. SMITH, admitted to bar, 1985, Connecticut; 1986, U.S. District Court, District of Connecticut; 1989, U.S. Supreme Court; 1995, U.S. Court of Appeals, Second Circuit. *Education:* Colgate University (B.A., cum laude, with honors, 1977); Cornell University (J.D., 1985). Vice President, Sister Cities International, 2000. Trustee, The Hartt School. Member, Executive Committee, Planning and Zoning Section, Connecticut Bar Association. Member, Cornell University Real Estate Council. ***LANGUAGES:*** Japanese. ***PRACTICE AREAS:*** Zoning, Planning and Land Use; Real Estate; Litigation. ***Email:*** bsmith@rc.com

ROBERT H. SMITH, JR., admitted to bar, 1969, Connecticut. *Education:* Harvard University (B.A., 1965); Boston University (LL.B., 1968). Director, Museum Trustee Association, 1989-1994. Trustee, Watkinson Library (Trinity College), 1986—. Member, Board of Managers, Lewis Walpole Library (Yale University), 1995—. *Member:* Connecticut Estate and Tax Planning Council; New England Museum Association; American Museum Association; Central Connecticut Business and Estate Planning Council; Planned Giving Group of Connecticut. Fellow, American College of Trust and Estate Counsel. ***PRACTICE AREAS:*** Wills; Probate; Trusts and Estates; Taxation. ***Email:*** rhsmith@rc.com

W. RICHARD SMITH, JR., admitted to bar, 1983, Connecticut; U.S. District Court, District of Connecticut. *Education:* Southern Connecticut State University (B.S., Biology, 1976; M.S., Biology, 1980); Syracuse University (J.D., 1983). Notes and Comments Editor, Syracuse University Journal of International Law and Commerce, 1982-1983. ***REPORTED CASES:*** Enthone, Inc. v. Commissioner of Revenue Services, 211 Conn. 655, 1989. ***PRACTICE AREAS:*** Environmental Law; Aquaculture and Coastal Development Projects. ***Email:*** wrsmith@rc.com

ALAN R. SPIER, admitted to bar, 1964, Connecticut. *Education:* Harvard University (A.B., 1960; J.D., 1964). Director, Connecticut Legal Services, Inc.,

(This Listing Continued)

1994—. Director, World Affairs Council of Hartford, 1997. Member, Committee on Minority Participation in the Legal Profession, Connecticut Bar Association. ***PRACTICE AREAS:*** Corporate Law; Securities; Banking Law; Business Law. ***Email:*** aspier@rc.com

DANIEL F. SULLIVAN, admitted to bar, 1987, Connecticut; 1988, U.S. District Court, District of Connecticut; 1992, Court of Appeals, Second Circuit; 1993, U.S. Tax Court. *Education:* George Washington University (B.A., with distinction, 1983; J.D., with high honors, 1987). Phi Beta Kappa; Order of the Coif. Adjunct Faculty, University of Connecticut Law School, Insurance Law Center. Vice Chair, Property Insurance Law Committee, American Bar Association, 1999—. ***PRACTICE AREAS:*** Insurance; Litigation. ***Email:*** dsullivan@rc.com

JOHN O. TANNENBAUM, admitted to bar, 1972, New York; 1972, U.S. Tax Court; 1980, Connecticut and U.S. District Court, District of Connecticut; 1981, U.S. Court of Appeals, Second Circuit. *Education:* Pennsylvania State University (B.A., 1968); Brooklyn Law School (J.D., 1971); Boston University (LL.M. in Taxation, 1975). Member, Brooklyn Law Review. Adjunct Instructor, University of Hartford Graduate Tax Program, 1981-2001. Member: Executive Committee, Tax Section, Connecticut Bar Association. ***PRACTICE AREAS:*** Taxation. ***Email:*** jtannenbau@rc.com

RICHARD W. TOMEO, admitted to bar, 1966, Connecticut. *Education:* University of Connecticut (B.A., 1963; J.D., 1966); George Washington University (LL.M. in Taxation, 1970). Senior Editor for Taxation, Connecticut Bar Journal, 1976—. Editor, Journal of Multistate Taxation, 1990—. Chairman, Section on Taxation, Connecticut Bar Association, 1989-1991. Chairman, Corporation Business Tax Subcommittee, 1991—. ***REPORTED CASES:*** Steelcase, Inc. v. Commissioner, 238 Conn. 571 (1996); Foodways National, Inc. v. Commissioner, 232 Conn. 325 (1995). ***PRACTICE AREAS:*** Taxation. ***Email:*** rtomeo@rc.com

THEODORE J. TUCCI, admitted to bar, 1982, Connecticut; 1986, U.S. Court of Appeals, Second Circuit; 1996, U.S. Supreme Court. *Education:* Williams College (B.A., cum laude, 1979); Case Western Reserve University (J.D., 1982). Editor, Case Western Reserve Law Review, 1981-1982. *Member:* Connecticut and American Bar Associations (Member, Life and Health Insurance Committee); Defense Research Institute (Member, Life, Health and Disability Subcommittee); Connecticut Defense Lawyers Association; American Health Lawyers Association. ***PRACTICE AREAS:*** Litigation; Health; Insurance. ***Email:*** ttucci@rc.com

JAMES A. WADE, admitted to bar, 1962, Connecticut. *Education:* Yale University (B.A., 1959); University of Virginia (LL.B., 1962). *Member:* American College of Trial Lawyers. ***PRACTICE AREAS:*** Litigation; Criminal Law. ***Email:*** alarussa@rc.com

OF COUNSEL

Raymond S. Andrews, Jr.	***Reginald Endicott Francklyn***
R. Regner Arvidson	***George C. Hastings***
Lucian E. Baldwin	***John W. Hincks***
Charles J. Cole	***Bruce W. Manternach***
William K. Cole	***Barclay Robinson, Jr.***
John M. Donahue	***Clark Whittemore, Jr.***

COUNSEL

STEPHEN W. ARONSON, admitted to bar, 1987, Connecticut and U.S. District Court, District of Connecticut; 1992, U.S. Supreme Court; 1994, U.S. Court of Appeals, 2nd Circuit. *Education:* Tufts University (B.A., cum laude, 1984); University of Connecticut (J.D., 1987). Assistant Vice President and Assistant General Counsel, Orion Capital Corporation, 1998-2001. ***PRACTICE AREAS:*** Litigation; Labor and Employment. ***Email:*** saronson@rc.com

EILEEN P. BALDWIN, admitted to bar, 1986, Connecticut. *Education:* University of Michigan (B.B.A., 1983); Boston University School of Law (J.D., cum laude, 1986). Paul J. Liacos Scholar, 1985; Edward F. Hennessey Scholar, 1986. Recipient, American Jurisprudence Award for Achievement in the Study of Commercial Law; Student Award in Taxation in Recognition of Achievement in Tax Subjects. ***PRACTICE AREAS:*** Finance; Banking Law. ***Email:*** ebaldwin@rc.com

FELICIA DeDOMINICIS, admitted to bar, 1990, Connecticut. *Education:* Brown University (A.B., 1983); University of Connecticut (J.D., with honors, 1990). ***LANGUAGES:*** Italian. ***PRACTICE AREAS:*** Health Care; Business Law; Mergers and Acquisitions. ***Email:*** fdedominic@rc.com

DINA SCHWARZ FISHER, admitted to bar, 1994, Connecticut. *Education:* Brown University (A.B., cum laude, 1975); University of Connecticut (J.D., with honors, 1994). Associate Editor, Connecticut Law Review. *Member:* American Trial Lawyers Association. ***PRACTICE AREAS:*** Products Liability; Litigation; Intellectual Property. ***Email:*** dfisher@rc.com

MIMI M. LINES, admitted to bar, 1980, Connecticut and U.S. District Court, District of Connecticut. *Education:* Yale University (B.A., magna cum laude, 1977); University of Connecticut (J.D., 1980). ***PRACTICE AREAS:*** Real Estate. ***Email:*** mlines@rc.com

(This Listing Continued)

LINDA L. MORKAN, admitted to bar, 1987, Connecticut; U.S. District Court, District of Connecticut; 1992, U.S. Court of Appeals, 2nd Circuit and U.S. Supreme Court. *Education:* Western Connecticut State College (B.S., cum laude, 1981); University of Connecticut School of Law (J.D., with honors, 1987). Chair, Appellate Practice Committee, Connecticut Bar Association. Technical Editor, Connecticut Bar Journal. ***REPORTED CASES:*** Community Action v. American Alliance, 254 Conn. 387 (2000); Wichers v. Hatch, 252 Conn. 174 (2000); HESCO v. Allen-Bradley Co., 250 Conn. 334 (1999); Yellow Page Consultants v. Omni Home health, 59 Conn. App. 194 (2000); SKW Real Estate v. Mitsubishi Motor Sales, 56 Conn. App. 1 (1999). ***PRACTICE AREAS:*** Appellate Practice; Indians and Native Populations; Litigation. ***Email:*** lmorkan@rc.com

RAFAEL A. SANTIAGO, admitted to bar, 1983, Connecticut; 1984, U.S. District Court, District of Connecticut. *Education:* Tufts University (B.S.E.E., 1973); University of Connecticut (M.B.A., 1983; J.D., 1983). *Member:* International Bar Association; Inter-American Bar Association; Connecticut Hispanic Bar Association (Vice President, 1993-1995; Director, 1993—); Hispanic National Bar Association; Association of Commercial Finance Attorneys. ***LANGUAGES:*** Spanish. ***PRACTICE AREAS:*** Business Law; International Law. ***Email:*** rsantiago@rc.com

JOHN R. SHAUGHNESSY, JR., admitted to bar, 1968, Massachusetts; 1975, U.S. Court of Military Appeals; 1990, Connecticut. *Education:* College of the Holy Cross (A.B., 1965); Boston College (J.D., 1968); Georgetown University (LL.M., (Tax), 1989). Author: Connecticut Chapter, *American Bar Association Sales & Use Tax Desk Book*, 1990—; "Annual Survey of Connecticut Tax Developments," Connecticut Bar Journal, 1990—. *Member:* Boston and Connecticut (Vice Chair, Tax Section, 1999—) Bar Associations. ***REPORTED CASES:*** Muro Pharmaceutical, Inc. v. Crystal; Steelcase Inc. v. Crystal; Anderson Consulting v. Gavin (amicus). ***PRACTICE AREAS:*** Taxation. ***Email:*** jshaughnes@rc.com

KEVIN C. SULLIVAN, admitted to bar, 1993, Connecticut and New York. *Education:* State University of New York at Albany (B.S., magna cum laude, 1987); Hofstra Law School (J.D., with distinction, 1993). ***Email:*** ksullivan@rc.com

RHONDA J. TOBIN, admitted to bar, 1990, Connecticut; 1991, U.S. District Court, District of Connecticut. *Education:* Duke University (B.A., cum laude, 1984; J.D., with honors, 1990). Vice Chair, Professionals, Officers and Directors Liability Committee, American Bar Association. *Member:* Defense Research Institute. ***PRACTICE AREAS:*** Professional Liability; Insurance; Litigation. ***Email:*** rtobin@rc.com

RICHARD F. VITARELLI, admitted to bar, 1994, Connecticut; 1995, Massachusetts, U.S. District Court, District of Connecticut and U.S. District Court, District of Massachusetts. *Education:* Boston College (B.A., magna cum laude, 1991); Suffolk University Law School (J.D., cum laude, 1994). ***LANGUAGES:*** Spanish. ***Email:*** rvitarelli@rc.com

AMY SPAN WERGELES, admitted to bar, 1987, Virginia; 1988, District of Columbia; U.S. Court of Appeals, District of Columbia Circuit; U.S. Court of Appeals, Fourth Circuit; U.S. District Court, Eastern District of Virginia; 1999, Connecticut. *Education:* Rutgers University, Douglass College (B.A., magna cum laude, 1983); University of Virginia (J.D., 1987). Phi Beta Kappa; Pi Sigma Alpha. Author: "What's Your IP Worth? You Should Know," 1998; "The 'DOT Com' Wars: The Collision of Trademarks on the Internet," 1998. *Member:* International Trademark Association. ***PRACTICE AREAS:*** Intellectual Property; Technology and Science. ***Email:*** awergeles@rc.com

ASSOCIATES

MARIA T. ACKLEY, admitted to bar, 1996, Connecticut; 1997, U.S. District Court, District of Connecticut, Mashantucket Pequot Tribal Court and Mohegan Gaming Disputes Court. *Education:* Randolph-Macon College (B.A., English, 1991); Western New England College (J.D., cum laude, 1996). ***Email:*** mackley@rc.com

MARTIN T. BOOHER, admitted to bar, 1998, Connecticut; 1999, New York. *Education:* Bucknell University (B.A., cum laude, 1995); Pace University School of Law (J.D., cum laude, Certificate in Environmental Law, 1998). ***Email:*** mbooher@rc.com

DEIRDRE A. DEVANEY, admitted to bar, 1998, Connecticut; 1999, New York. *Education:* New York University (B.A., cum laude, 1990); University of Connecticut (J.D., with honors, 1998). ***LANGUAGES:*** Icelandic and French. ***Email:*** ddevaney@rc.com

GERALD P. DWYER JR., admitted to bar, 1995, Massachusetts; 1998, Connecticut; 2000, New York. *Education:* Colgate University (A.B., 1990); Gonzaga University School of Law (J.D., magna cum laude, 1995); Georgetown University Law Center (LL.M., with distinction, 1996). ***Email:*** gdwyer@rc.com

RICHARD M. FIL, admitted to bar, 1994, Pennsylvania and Connecticut; 1997, U.S. District Court, District of Connecticut. *Education:* Rensselaer Polytechnic Institute (B.S., 1986); University of Connecticut (J.D., 1994). *Member:*

(This Listing Continued)

ROBINSON & COLE LLP, Hartford—Continued

Connecticut, Pennsylvania and American Bar Associations. ***PRACTICE AREAS:*** Environmental Law; Zoning, Planning and Land Use. ***Email:*** rfil@rc.com

BRIAN C. S. FREEMAN, admitted to bar, 1991, Connecticut and Virginia. *Education:* Georgetown University (B.A., summa cum laude, 1985) Phi Beta Kappa; University of Virginia (J.D., 1989). Member, Virginia Law Review, 1989. Law Clerk to the Hon. Albert J. Engel, Jr., U.S. Court of Appeals, Sixth Circuit, 1989-1990. ***PRACTICE AREAS:*** Environmental; Zoning, Planning and Land Use. ***Email:*** bfreeman@rc.com

ANDREW S. GOLDEN, admitted to bar, 1996, Connecticut; 1997, Massachusetts. *Education:* University of Connecticut (B.A., 1990); University of Massachusetts (M.Ed., 1993); Western New England College School of Law (J.D., cum laude, 1996). Member, Board of Editors, Western New England College Law Review, 1995-1996. ***PRACTICE AREAS:*** Labor and Employment; Litigation. ***Email:*** agolden@rc.com

EDWARD J. HEATH, admitted to bar, 1999, Connecticut and U.S. District Court, District of Connecticut. *Education:* Florida Atlantic University (B.A., 1996); University of Notre Dame (J.D., 1999). ***Email:*** eheath@rc.com

HELEN M. KEMP, admitted to bar, 1994, Connecticut; 1995, U.S. District Court, District of Connecticut and Mashantucket Pequot Tribal Court. *Education:* Amherst College (B.A., magna cum laude, 1975); University of Connecticut (M.A., 1977); Boston University (J.D., cum laude, 1994). ***Email:*** hkemp@rc.com

JEFFREY C. KESTENBAND, admitted to bar, 1997, Connecticut; 1998, U.S. District Court, District of Connecticut and U.S. Court of Appeals, Second Circuit. *Education:* Wesleyan University (B.A., 1993); University of Connecticut (J.D., with honors, 1997). ***Email:*** jkestenban@rc.com

JASON KUSELIAS, admitted to bar, 1998, Connecticut. *Education:* Trinity College (B.A., 1994); Boston University, J.D., 1998). ***Email:*** jkuselias@rc.com

KEVIN E. MAJEWSKI, admitted to bar, 1994, Connecticut; 1999, U.S. District Court, District of Connecticut. *Education:* Wesleyan University (B.A., 1989); University of Connecticut (J.D., 1994). ***Email:*** kmajewski@rc.com

MARION B. MANZO, admitted to bar, 1999, Connecticut. *Education:* Fairfield University (B.A., cum laude, 1996); University of Connecticut (J.D., with high honors, 1999). ***Email:*** mmanzo@rc.com

MELISSA M. MARTIN, admitted to bar, 2000, Connecticut. *Education:* Boston College (B.A., with honors,1993); University of Connecticut (J.D., with honors, 2000). ***Email:*** mmartin@rc.com

GREGORY W. McCRACKEN, admitted to bar, 1993, California; 2000, Illinois; 2001, Connecticut. *Education:* University of Chicago; University of California at Davis (B.A., 1985); McGeorge School of Law, University of the Pacific (J.D., with distinction, 1993); University of Illinois (M.U.P., 2000). ***LANGUAGES:*** Spanish. ***Email:*** gmccracken@rc.com

JOEY LEE MIRANDA, admitted to bar, 1998, Connecticut; 1999, U.S. District Court, District of Connecticut; 2000, District of Columbia. *Education:* Hofstra University (B.B.A., 1991); Quinnipiac College School of Law (J.D., magna cum laude, 1998); University of Connecticut (M.B.A., 2000). ***Email:*** jmiranda@rc.com

JOSHUA S. MIRER, admitted to bar, 2000, Connecticut. *Education:* Lehman College of the City University of New York (B.A., 1992); Western New England College (J.D., 2000); Springfield College (M.Ed., 1995). ***Email:*** jmirer@rc.com

MEGAN R. NAUGHTON, admitted to bar, 1998, Connecticut. *Education:* Syracuse University (B.A., B.S., magna cum laude, 1994); University of Connecticut (J.D., with honors, 1998). ***Email:*** mnaughton@rc.com

ERIN K. O'BRIEN, admitted to bar, 1997, Connecticut; 1998, U.S. District Court, District of Connecticut. *Education:* College of the Holy Cross (B.A., in cursu honoris, cum laude, 1994); Columbia University School of Law (J.D., 1997). ***Email:*** eobrien@rc.com

KAREN A. PERRY, admitted to bar, 1994, Connecticut; 1995, U.S. District Court, District of Connecticut; 1996, Maine. *Education:* Union College (B.A., 1991); University of Connecticut (J.D., 1994). ***LANGUAGES:*** French. ***Email:*** kperry@rc.com

KEVIN S. RASCH, admitted to bar, 1998, Connecticut. *Education:* Albertus Magnus College (B.A., 1992); Trinity College (M.P.P.S., 1995); College of William and Mary (J.D., 1998). ***Email:*** krasch@rc.com

CATHRYN A. REYNOLDS, admitted to bar, 1999, Connecticut. *Education:* Colby College (B.A., cum laude, 1994); University of Connecticut (J.D., 1999). ***Email:*** cczernicki@rc.com

GLENN G. RYBACKI, admitted to bar, 1998, Connecticut; 1999, New York. *Education:* Providence College (B.S., 1984); Quinnipiac College (J.D., 1998). ***Email:*** grybacki@rc.com

(This Listing Continued)

JACQUELINE PENNINO SCHEIB, admitted to bar, 1996, Connecticut; 1997, New York. *Education:* Franklin and Marshall College (B.A., 1991); University of Connecticut (J.D., with honors, 1996). ***Email:*** jpennino@rc.com

JOHN A. SCHUSTER, admitted to bar, 2000, Connecticut. *Education:* Union College (B.A., 1993); Northeastern University (J.D., 2000). ***Email:*** jschuster@rc.com

JEANMARIE B. SHEA, admitted to bar, 1985, Connecticut. *Education:* Yale University (B.A., 1980); University of Connecticut (J.D., with honors, 1985). Executive Editor, Connecticut Law Review, 1983-1984. Member, Greater Hartford Probate Forum. ***PRACTICE AREAS:*** Trusts and Estates; Corporate Law. ***Email:*** jshea@rc.com

CAROL A. SHUBINSKI, admitted to bar, 1995, Virginia; 1996, District of Columbia; 1999, Connecticut. *Education:* Duke University (A.B., 1992); Washington University (J.D., 1995). ***Email:*** cshubinski@rc.com

ROBERT J. SITKOWSKI, admitted to bar, 1995, Pennsylvania; 1997, Connecticut, U.S. District Court, Middle District of Pennsylvania and U.S. District Court, District of Connecticut. *Education:* University of Illinois at Chicago (B.Arch., 1985); University of Pittsburgh (J.D., 1994; M.U.R.P., 1994). ***Email:*** rsitkowski@rc.com

JEFFREY M. THOMEN, admitted to bar, 1998, New Jersey and U.S. District Court, District of New Jersey; 1999, New York; 2000, Connecticut and U.S. District Court, District of Connecticut. *Education:* Fairfield University (B.A., cum laude, 1995); Seton Hall University (J.D., 1998). ***Email:*** jthomen@rc.com

DAWN N. ZAMMITTI, admitted to bar, 1989, Connecticut and U.S. District Court, District of Connecticut. *Education:* University of North Dakota (B.S., 1983); University of Connecticut (J.D., magna cum laude, 1989). ***PRACTICE AREAS:*** Labor and Employment; Trusts and Estates. ***Email:*** dzammitti@rc.com

JENNIFER CROTEAU ZETTERGREN, admitted to bar, 1998, Connecticut. *Education:* University of Connecticut (B.A., 1995); Quinnipiac College of Law (J.D., 1998). ***Email:*** jzettergren@rc.com

Lawyers are members of local, state and national bar associations.

(For biographical data on other personnel, see Professional Biographies at Stamford, Greenwich and New London, CT, Boston, MA, New York, NY and Manchester, NH)

ROGIN, NASSAU, CAPLAN, LASSMAN & HIRTLE, LLC

Established in 1948

CITYPLACE I, 22ND FLOOR
185 ASYLUM STREET
HARTFORD, CONNECTICUT 06103-3460
Telephone: 860-278-7480
Fax: 860-278-2179

General Practice, including Administrative, Antitrust and Trade Regulation, Banking, Bankruptcy, Civil Rights, Commercial, Commercial Leasing Law, Condominium and Other Common Interest Communities; Construction Law, Corporate, Corporate Reorganization, Eminent Domain, Employment, Environmental, Estate Planning and Administration, Family, Franchise Regulation, Health Care, Internet Law, Legislative Practice, Pension and Profit Sharing, Personal Injury, Land Use, Probate, Real Estate, Securities, Surety, Tax Law and Workers Compensation Law. Trials and Appeals in all Courts.

MEMBERS OF FIRM

EDWARD S. ROGIN (1908-2000).

LOUIS E. NASSAU (1908-1999).

ROBERT L. HIRTLE, born Milton, Massachusetts, October 5, 1937; admitted to bar, 1962, Virginia; 1963, Connecticut; 1969, U.S. Supreme Court. *Education:* Fairfield University (B.S., 1959); University of Virginia (J.D., 1962). Awarded LL.D.-Hon. by the National College of Chiropractic, 1990. Assistant Attorney General, State of Connecticut, 1965-1971. President, National Association of Chiropractic Attorneys, 1984-1985. *Member:* Hartford County, Connecticut (Member: Municipal Law and Governmental Services Committee, 1972-1976; Executive Committee, Administrative Law Section) and American Bar Associations; Connecticut Trial Lawyers Association; The Association of Trial Lawyers of America. [Judge Advocate, U.S. Navy, 1962-1965]. ***PRACTICE AREAS:*** Litigation; Appellate Practice; Administrative Law; Health Care. ***Email:*** rhirtle@roginlaw.com

STEVEN D. BARTELSTONE, born Bridgeport, Connecticut, November 23, 1947; admitted to bar, 1972, Connecticut. *Education:* University of Connecticut (B.A., cum laude, 1969; J.D., with high honors, 1972). Assistant to the Speaker of the House of Representatives, 1970-1971. Attorney for the Demo-

(This Listing Continued)

cratic Majority in the House of Representatives, Connecticut General Assembly, 1972-1973. Member, Advisory Committee to the Banking Commissioner on the Uniform Securities Act, 1982-1985. Vice-President, Law, 1985-1986, Vice President, General Counsel and Secretary, 1986, and Senior Vice President, General Counsel and Secretary, Coleco Industries, Inc., 1986-1989. *Member:* Hartford County, Connecticut (Member, Sections on: Commercial Law and Bankruptcy; Corporations and Other Business Organizations; Real Estate Law) and American Bar Associations. ***PRACTICE AREAS:*** Commercial Law; Corporate Law; Real Estate. ***Email:*** sbartelstone@roginlaw.com

DAVID M. CALL, born Hartford, Connecticut, March 21, 1943; admitted to bar, 1968, New York; 1974, Connecticut. *Education:* University of Connecticut (B.A., with highest honors, 1965); Columbia University (LL.B., cum laude, 1968). Phi Beta Kappa. Author: "Attorneys' Malpractice Insurance —Does Your Policy Cover Rule 10b-5 Liability?" 30 The Business Lawyer 1095, 1975. Confidential Law Assistant, Supreme Court of New York, Appellate Division, Third Department, 1968-1969. *Member:* Hartford County, Connecticut (Member, Committee on Professional Ethics) and American Bar Associations. ***PRACTICE AREAS:*** Business Law; Securities Regulation; Taxation; Estate Planning. ***Email:*** dcall@roginlaw.com

PAUL B. ZOLAN, born Bridgeport, Connecticut, June 25, 1951; admitted to bar, 1977, Connecticut. *Education:* Trinity College (B.A., 1973); University of Connecticut (J.D., with honors, 1977). Member, 1975-1976 and Associate Editor, 1976-1977, Connecticut Law Review. Author: Note, "Stock Exchange Investigations," 8 Connecticut Law Review 725, 1976. Panel of Neutrals, Commercial Panel, American Arbitration Association, 1992—. Panel of Mediators, State of Connecticut Department of Education, 1997—. Commissioner and Chairman, West Hartford Housing Authority, 1985-1995. Member, West Hartford Charter Revision Commission, 1995-1996. Member, West Hartford Housing Partnership Committee, 1989-1991. *Member:* Hartford County (Member: Board of Directors, 1997—; Committee on Continuing Legal Education, 1983—), Connecticut (Member: Real Property Section; Consumer Law Section, Lawyers Committee on Affordable Housing and Homelessness) and American (Member, Sections on: Antitrust Law; Construction Law) Bar Associations; Connecticut Trial Lawyers Association. ***PRACTICE AREAS:*** Commercial Law; Corporate Law; Commercial Litigation; Real Estate. ***Email:*** pzolan@roginlaw.com

DAVID J. HEINLEIN, born New London, Connecticut, August 25, 1951; admitted to bar, 1976, Connecticut; 1977, Pennsylvania. *Education:* Trinity College (B.A., 1973); University of San Diego (J.D., cum laude, 1976). Recipient, American Jurisprudence Award, Constitutional Law, 1974-1975. *Member:* Hartford County and Connecticut Bar Associations; Connecticut Trial Lawyers Association; The Association of Trial Lawyers of America. ***PRACTICE AREAS:*** Personal Injury; Workers Compensation; Bankruptcy Litigation; Commercial Litigation. ***Email:*** dheinlein@roginlaw.com

LEWIS K. WISE, born Hartford, Connecticut, March 6, 1947; admitted to bar, 1974, Connecticut; 1980, District of Columbia. *Education:* Columbia University (B.A., 1969); University of Connecticut (J.D., magna cum laude, 1973). Member, University of Connecticut Law Review, 1971-1973. Law Clerk, Chief Judge Frederick J.R. Heebe, U.S. District Court, Eastern District, Louisiana, 1973-1975. Trial Attorney, 1976-1979 and Assistant Director, 1979-1985, Civil Division, U.S. Department of Justice. *Member:* Hartford County, Connecticut (Member, Executive Committee, Planning and Zoning Section) and American Bar Associations; The District of Columbia Bar; Connecticut Health Lawyers' Association. ***PRACTICE AREAS:*** Litigation; Administrative Law; Land Use; Employment Law. ***Email:*** lwise@roginlaw.com

MARK A. ROSENBLUM, born Sharon, Pennsylvania, October 23, 1953; admitted to bar, 1979, Georgia and Pennsylvania; 1987, Connecticut; 1996, U.S. Supreme Court. *Education:* Harvard University (A.B., cum laude, 1975); Emory University (J.D., 1979). Panel of Neutrals, Commercial Panel, American Arbitration Association, 1996—. *Member:* Hartford County, Connecticut and American Bar Associations; State Bar of Georgia; The Association of Trial Lawyers of America. ***PRACTICE AREAS:*** Commercial Litigation; Construction Litigation. ***Email:*** mrosenblum@roginlaw.com

BARRY S. FEIGENBAUM, born Hartford, Connecticut, October 1, 1957; admitted to bar, 1981, Connecticut. *Education:* George Washington University (B.B.A., with distinction, 1978); University of Connecticut (J.D., with honors, 1981). Associate General Counsel, Coleco Industries, Inc., 1986-1989. Zoning Alternate, West Hartford Town Council, 1985-1992. *Member:* Hartford County, Connecticut (Member, Corporate Counsel Section; Executive Committee, Commercial Law and Bankruptcy Section) and American Bar Associations; American Bankruptcy Institute; Commercial Law League of America (Member, Sections on: Bankruptcy and Insolvency). ***PRACTICE AREAS:*** Bankruptcy; Corporate Law; Commercial Law. ***Email:*** bfeigenbaum@roginlaw.com

PETER S. SOROKIN, born Richmond, Virginia, November 28, 1951; admitted to bar, 1976, Connecticut. *Education:* University of Rochester (B.A., 1973); Boston University School of Law (J.D., 1976). *Member:* Connecticut and American Bar Associations. ***PRACTICE AREAS:*** Real Estate; Commercial Leasing. ***Email:*** psorokin@roginlaw.com

(This Listing Continued)

IRIS JUNE BROWN, born New Haven, Connecticut, July 24, 1948; admitted to bar, 1977, Connecticut and U.S Claims Court; 1979, District of Columbia and U.S. Tax Court; 1980, U.S. District Court, District of Connecticut; 1981, U.S. Supreme Court; 1982, U.S. Court of Appeals for the Federal Circuit. *Education:* University of Colorado (B.A., 1973); University of Connecticut (J.D., with high honors, 1977). Author: "Striking May Be a Surprisingly Taxing Experience: Federal Income Tax Consequences of Illegal Public Employee Strikes," 9 Conn. L. Rev. 711 (1977); "Planning Can Reduce Out-of-Bankruptcy Workout Tax Cost," 55 Tax'n Accts. 275 (Nov. 1995); 24 Tax'n Lawyers 218 (Jan./Feb., 1996); "Representing Bankrupt Companies With Underfunded Single-Employer Defined Benefit Plans," 5 Journal of Taxation of Employee Benefits 162 (Nov./Dec. 1997). Adjunct Professor, University of Connecticut Law School, 1981-1983. Trial Attorney, Tax Division, U.S. Department of Justice, Washington, D.C., 1977-1979. Counsel, Aetna Life and Casualty Company, 1979-1984. Arbitrator, Commercial Panel, American Arbitration Association, 1997—. Panelist, Federal Tax Expert Panel, internal revenue Service Arbitration Program, 2000—. Member, Tax Club of Hartford. *Member:* Hartford County, Connecticut (Member, Executive Committee, Tax Section; Chair, Liaison with Accountants Subcommittee; Member and Chair, 1995-1997, Liaison with Accountants Committee) and American (Member, Committee on Individual Investments and Workouts, Tax Section) Bar Associations. ***PRACTICE AREAS:*** Tax Law; Business Law. ***Email:*** ibrown@roginlaw.com

BENJAMIN ENGEL, born Princeton, New Jersey, December 8, 1954; admitted to bar, 1987, Connecticut. *Education:* Princeton University (A.B., cum laude, 1977); Stanford University (A.M., 1979); University of Connecticut School of Law (J.D., with honors, 1987). Member, 1984-1985, 1986-1987, and Executive Editor, 1985-1986, Connecticut Law Review. Author: "Sticks and Stones in Connecticut Criminal Courts: State v. Couture," 18 Conn. L. Rev. 407, 1986. *Member:* Hartford County, Connecticut (Member, Sections of: Corporations and Other Business Organizations; Commercial Law and Bankruptcy) and American (Member, Section of Business Law) Bar Associations. ***PRACTICE AREAS:*** Corporate Law; Commercial Law. ***Email:*** bengel@roginlaw.com

THOMAS M. DIVINE, born Minneapolis, Minnesota, July 28, 1947; admitted to bar, 1978, Connecticut; 1980, U.S. Tax Court; 1984, Massachusetts. *Education:* Columbia College (B.A., magna cum laude, 1969; M.A., Ph.D., 1973); Yale University (J.D., 1977). Phi Beta Kappa. Law Clerk to Judge J. Joseph Smith, U.S. Court of Appeals, Second Circuit, 1977-1978. Author: "Women in the Academy: Sex Discrimination in University Faculty Hiring and Promotion," 5 Journal of Law and Education 429, 1976. *Member:* Connecticut Bar Association (Member, Tax and Executive Committee, Estates and Probate Sections, 1985-1987). ***PRACTICE AREAS:*** Taxation; Trusts and Estates. ***Email:*** tdivine@roginlaw.com

LAWRENCE G. ROSENTHAL, born New York, N.Y., May 19, 1956; admitted to bar, 1982, Texas and U.S. Court of Appeals, Fifth and Eleventh Circuits; 1985, District of Columbia and Maryland; 1986, U.S. Court of Appeals, Third Circuit; 1989, U.S. Court of Appeals for the Federal Circuit and U.S. District Court, District of Connecticut; 1991, Connecticut; 1996, Mashantucket Pequot Tribal Court. *Education:* University of Texas (B.A., with honors, 1978); University of Houston (J.D., 1981). Articles Editor, Houston Journal International Law, 1980-1981. Author: "Equipment Costs in Construction Contract Disputes," 17:2 Public Contract Law Journal, June 1988, reprinted in 6:2 The International Construction Law Review, April 1989. *Member:* The District of Columbia Bar; State Bar of Texas; American (Member, Public Contract Law Section; Tort and Insurance Law Section) Bar Association. ***PRACTICE AREAS:*** Construction Law; Surety and Fidelity Law; Insurance Defense Law; Maritime Law; Litigation. ***Email:*** lrosenthal@roginlaw.com

ASSOCIATES

MARK J. LASSMAN, born Hartford, Connecticut, April 28, 1954; admitted to bar, 1982, Connecticut. *Education:* University of Connecticut (B.A., 1977); Western New England College (J.D., 1981). Special Deputy Assistant State's Attorney, 1984-1985. *Member:* Hartford County and Connecticut Bar Associations. ***PRACTICE AREAS:*** Criminal Law; Construction Litigation. ***Email:*** mlassman@roginlaw.com

BRENDAN T. FLYNN, born Hartford, Connecticut, February 22, 1964; admitted to bar, 1989, Connecticut; 1990, U.S. District Court, District of Connecticut; 1996, U.S. Court of Appeals, Second Circuit and U.S. Supreme Court. *Education:* Swarthmore College (B.A., 1986); University of Connecticut (J.D., with honors, 1989). Associate Editor, Connecticut Journal of International Law, 1988-1989. Author: "Connecticut Developments in International Law," Connecticut Journal of International Law, Volume 4, Issue 1, Volume 4, Issue 3. Law Clerk to Judge Edward Y. O'Connell, Connecticut Appellate Court, 1989-1990. Member, Wethersfield Planning and Zoning Commission, 1994-1995. Member, Wethersfield Town Council, 1995—. Deputy Mayor, 1999—. *Member:* Connecticut (Member, Sections on: Litigation; Conservation and Environmental Quality) and American (Member, Litigation Section) Bar Associations; Connecticut Trial Lawyers Association. ***PRACTICE AREAS:*** Appellate Practice; Administrative Law; Litigation; Commercial Litigation. ***Email:*** bflynn@roginlaw.com

(This Listing Continued)

ROGIN, NASSAU, CAPLAN, LASSMAN & HIRTLE, LLC, Hartford—Continued

LISA M. ANDERSON, born Bridgeport, Connecticut, February 16, 1968; admitted to bar, 1993, Massachusetts; 1994, Connecticut; 1996, U.S. District Court, District of Connecticut. *Education:* Bentley College (B.S., magna cum laude, 1990); Western New England College, School of Law (J.D., cum laude, 1993). Member, Western New England Law Review, 1991-1992. Law Clerk, Connecticut Superior Court, 1993-1994. *Member:* Connecticut Bar Association; Connecticut Trial Lawyers Association. ***PRACTICE AREAS:*** Construction Law; Surety Law; Commercial Litigation; Litigation. ***Email:*** landerson@roginlaw.com

ELIZABETH J. ROBBIN, born Hartford, Connecticut, November 15, 1969; admitted to bar, 1994, Connecticut; 1995, U.S. District Court, District of Connecticut. *Education:* Dartmouth College (B.A., 1991); University of Connecticut (J.D., with honors, 1994). *Member:* Hartford County, Connecticut and American Bar Associations; Connecticut Trial Lawyers Association (President and Member, Board of Directors); Hartford Association of Women Attorneys (Member, Board of Directors). ***PRACTICE AREAS:*** Civil Litigation; Commercial Litigation. ***Email:*** erobbin@roginlaw.com

JONATHAN M. STARBLE, born Bristol, Connecticut, September 10, 1970; admitted to bar, 1995, Connecticut. *Education:* University of Connecticut (B.A., magna cum laude, 1992; J.D., with honors, 1995). Editor-in-Chief, Connecticut Insurance Law Journal. Executive Director, Moot Court Board. *Member:* Connecticut Bar Association. ***PRACTICE AREAS:*** Commercial Litigation; Construction Litigation. ***Email:*** jstarble@roginlaw.com

MONIQUE R. POLIDORO, born Hartford, Connecticut, July 14, 1970; admitted to bar, 1997, Connecticut; 1998, U.S. District Court, District of Connecticut; 1999, U.S. Tax Court. *Education:* University of Connecticut (B.A., magna cum laude, 1994); University of Connecticut School of Law (J.D., with honors, 1997). *Member:* Hartford County, Connecticut and American Bar Associations; Connecticut Trial Lawyers Association; American Trial Lawyers Association. ***PRACTICE AREAS:*** Trusts and Estates; Taxation; Corporate Law; Securities Regulation. ***Email:*** mpolidoro@roginlaw.com

STEPHEN M. HRYNIEWICZ, born Springfield, Massachusetts, June 8, 1973; admitted to bar, 1999, Connecticut; 2000, U.S. District Court, District of Connecticut. *Education:* University of Notre Dame (B.A., cum laude, 1995); University of Connecticut (J.D., with honors, 1999). ***PRACTICE AREAS:*** Bankruptcy Litigation; Civil Litigation; Commercial Litigation. ***Email:*** shryniewicz@roginlaw.com

RANDY P. KABAKOFF, born New Haven, Connecticut, October 23, 1973; admitted to bar, 1999, Connecticut ; 2000, U.S. District Court, District of Connecticut. *Education:* University of Connecticut (B.S., magna cum laude, 1995; J.D., 1999). *Member:* Hartford, Connecticut and American Bar Associations. ***PRACTICE AREAS:*** Real Estate; Corporate Law. ***Email:*** rkabakoff@roginlaw.com

OF COUNSEL

JEROME E. CAPLAN, born New Haven, Connecticut, October 25, 1927; admitted to bar, 1951, Connecticut; 1961, U.S. Supreme Court. *Education:* University of Pennsylvania (B.S., 1948); University of Pennsylvania and Yale University (LL.B., 1951). Law Clerk to U.S. District Judge J. Joseph Smith, 1951-1952. *Member:* Hartford County and Connecticut Bar Associations. ***PRACTICE AREAS:*** Bankruptcy Litigation; Corporate Law; Partnership Law; Commercial Law. ***Email:*** jcaplan@roginlaw.com

EDWIN A. LASSMAN, born Hartford, Connecticut, October 13, 1928; admitted to bar, 1953, Connecticut. *Education:* University of Connecticut (B.A., 1950); Cornell University (LL.B., with distinction, 1953). Phi Alpha Delta; Order of the Coif. Member, Board of Editors, Cornell Law Review, 1952-1953. Corporation Counsel, South Windsor, 1957-1963. State Representative, 1967-1969. *Member:* Hartford County, Connecticut and American Bar Associations. ***PRACTICE AREAS:*** Construction Litigation; Health Care Litigation; Long Term Care; Commercial Real Estate; Corporate Law. ***Email:*** elassman@roginlaw.com

REPRESENTATIVE CLIENTS: American Tower Corporation; Atlantic Pipe Corp.; Baldwin & Lyons, Inc; Bally Total Fitness Corp.; Cigna Corp.; Connecticut Chiropractic Assn.; Connecticut Podiatric Medical Assn.; Connecticut Society of Oral and Maxillofacial Surgeons, Inc.; Dynamic Gunver Technologies, Inc.; Exel Logistics, Inc.; Familymeds, Inc.; George Weiss Associates, Inc.; Industrial Risk Insurers; John Hancock Mutual Life Insurance Co.; Konover Investments Corporation; Lend Lease Real Estate Investments, Inc.; Lexington Healthcare Group; Louis Dreyfus Property Group; The Metro Realty Group, Ltd.; National Chiropractic Mutual Insurance Co.; National Eastern Corp.; OUM & Associates; Phoenix Home Life Insurance Co.; Podiatry Insurance Company of America; Professional Relief Nurses, Inc.; Proprietary Health Care Facilities; Shell Oil Company; Starwood/Ceruzzi, LLC; Sonitrol Communications Corp.; Sonitrol Security Systems of Hartford, Inc.; Videojet International, Inc.; Weiss Asset Management L.P.; White Oak Corp.

THE ROMANELLI LAW OFFICES

255 MAIN STREET, SUITE 303
HARTFORD, CONNECTICUT 06106
Telephone: 860-560-0611
Facsimile: 860-724-6002
Email: iromanelli@yahoo.com
URL: http://www.lawyers.com/romanellilaw

Real Estate, Foreclosures, Collections, contracts, Business Law, Immigration, Wills and Probate, U.S. Law for International Clients, Probate Litigation.

IRENE PYSARIW ROMANELLI, born Cesky Brod, Czechoslovakia, April 21; admitted to bar, 1988, Connecticut; 1991, U.S. District Court, District of Connecticut. *Education:* University of Rhode Island (B.A., 1971); Western New England School of Law (J.D., 1988). Jessup International Moot Court Team, (1987). Positions: 1983, Secretary, Judiciary Committee, Connecticut Legislature; 1984, Republican Clerk, House of Representatives, Special Legislative Committee, Connecticut State Capitol; 1985, Committee Clerk, Finance Review and Bonding Committee, Connecticut State Capitol; Fall, 1987, Judicial Intern to The Honorable Judge Norris O'Neil, Hartford Superior Court, 1988, Country Researcher, ARTICLE 19, the international human rights organization dealing with freedom of expression, London, England; 1990, United States Representative to the United Nations, ARTICLE 19; 1990, Managing Editor, Diplomatic World Observer, New York. Functional Foundations, 2001. Publisher and Edior-in-Chief, DWO. Chairman, PSARGUS Foundation, Inc., 2001. *Member:* Hartford County and Connecticut Bar Associations; Ukrainian American Bar Association; Connecticut Trial Lawyers Association. ***LANGUAGES:*** Ukrainian, Czech, Russian, Polish and French.

ROME McGUIGAN SABANOSH, P.C.

Established in 1969

ONE STATE STREET
HARTFORD, CONNECTICUT 06103
Telephone: 860-549-1000
Telecopier: 860-724-3921
URL: http://www.rms-law.com

Bridgeport, Connecticut Office: 1000 Lafayette Boulevard. Telephone: 203-382-8000. Telecopier: 203-382-8005.

Litigation, Investigations, Intellectual Property, Tax and Valuation Appeal, Tribal Gaming, Administrative Law, Alternative Dispute Resolution, Bankruptcy, Benefits Planning/ERISA, Business Planning, Commercial Finance, Construction, Corporate, Creditor's Rights, Criminal Defense, Education, Environmental, Estate Planning and Administration, Government Relations, Insurance, Labor and Employment, Land Use, Matrimonial Law, Municipal, Personal Injury, Product Liability, Real Estate, Tax, White-Collar Crime.

LAW FIRM ALLIANCES/ASSOCIATIONS: **THE NETWORK OF TRIAL LAW FIRMS, INC.**

INTERNATIONAL SOCIETY OF PRIMERUS LAW FIRMS

LEWIS B. ROME, born Hartford, Connecticut, September 12, 1933; admitted to bar, 1957, Connecticut. *Education:* University of Connecticut (B.A., 1954; LL.B., 1957). Recipient: Eagleton Institute Outstanding Legislator Award, 1972; Charter Oak Leadership Medal, Greater Hartford Chamber of Commerce, 1975; Connecticut Magazine, Outstanding Legislator, 1975; Council of Small Towns, Outstanding Legislator, 1975; Connecticut Magazine, Outstanding Senator, 1976; University of Connecticut Outstanding Alumnus, 1979; Outstanding Alumnus Award, University of Connecticut School of Law, 1981. Republican Candidate for Lieutenant Governor of Connecticut, 1978. Republican Candidate for Governor of Connecticut, 1982. Member, Town Council of Bloomfield, 1961-1969. Mayor, Town of Bloomfield, 1965-1969. Chairman: Greater Hartford Transit District, 1965-1966; Capitol Regional Council of Elected Officials, 1967-1969. Connecticut State Senator, 1970-1979; Senate Majority Leader, 1973-1975; Senate Minority Leader, 1975-1979. Advisor, Office of Economic Opportunities, 1973-1974. Chairman, Greater Hartford Visitors and Convention Bureau, 1980-1981. Director, Coordinating Council For Foundations, Inc., 1973-1990. Member: Executive Committee of National Conference of State Legislatures, 1975-1979; Board of Directors of Mount Sinai Hospital, 1975-1991. Trustee and Executive Committee, Connecticut Public Television, 1975-1982. Trustee and Executive Committee, Connecticut Public Television, 1975-1982. Trustee, 1975-1982 and President, 1980, University of Connecticut Law School Foundation, Inc. Corporator: Winsted Memorial Hospital, 1975-1980; St. Francis Hospital, 1976-1982; Hartford Hospital, 1975—. Member, Department of Higher Education Task Force, 1984-1986. Member, University of Connecticut Task Force on Athletics, 1986-1989. Member, Executive Committee, Board of Directors of Riverfront Recapture, Inc., 1985—. Member, Board of Directors of Blue Ridge Health Services, Inc., 1987-1990. Member, 1988-1997 and Chairman, 1992-1997, Connecticut Advisory Commission on Intergovernmental Relations. Member, American Judicature Society,

(This Listing Continued)

1990—. President, The Toga Club, 1993-1995. Member, Chairman of Connecticut Convention Center Authority, 1990-1997. Member, 1991-1997 and Chairman, 1992-1997, Board of Trustees, University of Connecticut. Chairman, Board of Directors, University of Connecticut Hospital Finance Corporation, 1992-1997. Member, Professional Advisory Board of Connecticut United for Research Excellence, Inc., 1994-2000. Member, Executive Board of Hartford Downtown Council, 1994—. *Member:* Hartford County and Connecticut Bar Associations. **Email:** lrome@rms-law.com

AUSTIN J. McGUIGAN, born Melrose, Massachusetts, September 20, 1943; admitted to bar, 1972, Connecticut; 1974, U.S. District Court, District of Connecticut; 1981, U.S. Supreme Court; 2001, Massachusetts. *Education:* Merrimack College (B.A., 1965); Boston University (J.D., cum laude, 1972). Law Clerk to Justice John P. Cotter, Connecticut Supreme Court, 1972-1973. Author: Law Enforcement Officer's Handbook on Gambling, 1975; Manual on Court Authorized Wire Interception, 1975. "The Grand Jury A Necessary Investigative Tool," Conn. Bar Journal, Vol. 54, No. 1, Feb., 1980; Co-Author: "Report re Adoption of Casino Gambling Legislation," Connecticut Legislative Casino Gambling Task Force, Dec., 1992; "How to Use the Economic Espionage Act to Protect Your Corporate Assets," The Corporate Counselor, Vol. 15, Nos. 2 and 3, 2000. Adjunct Professor, University of New Haven, 1975-1981. Assistant Prosecuting Attorney, State of Connecticut, 1973-1975. Chief Prosecutor, Statewide Organized Crime Task Force, 1975-1978. Liaison, Executive Working Group, U.S. Department of Justice. Chief State's Attorney, State of Connecticut, 1978-1985. Member: National District Attorneys Association (Vice President, 1980-1985; Lecturer on Organized Crime and Corruption); Board of Directors, National Board of Trial Advocacy, 1979-1988. Member: Board of Directors, American Prosecutors Research Institute, 1996; International Prosecutors Association, 1998—. *Member:* Connecticut (Member: Executive Committee, Criminal Justice Section and Intellectual Property Section; Connecticut State Bar Examining Committee, 1990-1993) and American (Member, Criminal Justice and Intellectual Property Sections) Bar Associations; The Association of Trial Lawyers of America; Connecticut Trial Lawyers Association; National Association of Criminal Defense Lawyers; Connecticut Criminal Defense Lawyers Association. [With U.S. Army Intelligence]. ***LANGUAGES:*** German. ***PRACTICE AREAS:*** Theft of Trade Secrets; Corporate Investigations; Government Investigations; Commercial Litigation; White Collar Criminal Defense; Product Liability. **Email:** amcguigan@rms-law.com

JOHN A. SABANOSH, born Bridgeport, Connecticut, December 10, 1938; admitted to bar, 1963, Connecticut; U.S. District Court, District of Connecticut; U.S. Court of Appeals, Second Circuit; U.S. Supreme Court. *Education:* University of Virginia (B.A., 1960; LL.B., 1963). Phi Alpha Delta. Practices before National Labor Relations Board in several of its Regional Offices, including Connecticut, New York City, Boston, Minneapolis, Philadelphia and San Francisco and before the Board in Washington, D.C., Connecticut State Board of Labor Relations, Connecticut State Board of Mediation and Arbitration in grievance and interest arbitrations under State Teacher Negotiation Act and Municipal Employee Relations Act, American Arbitration Association under its Voluntary Rules for Labor Arbitration, industry panels and other private and public agencies in grievance arbitrations. Collective bargaining spokesman for public school boards, municipalities and public utilities and for private sector clients in manufacturing, construction, health care, printing, institutions of higher education, service and other industries. Lectures and seminars on a variety of labor-and employment-related topics for corporate, professional and public sector audiences, including annual lectures on teacher bargaining issues to doctoral candidates at Teachers College, Columbia University. Courses in personnel administration and the law at Sacred Heart University, Fairfield, Connecticut, and in advanced collective bargaining at the University of Bridgeport Graduate Program in Governmental Affairs and Management, Bridgeport, Connecticut. *Member:* Bridgeport, The Connecticut and American (Member, Labor and Employment Law Sections) Bar Associations. (See Bridgeport for full Biographical information). ***PRACTICE AREAS:*** Management Labor and Employment Law; Education Law; Public Education; Private Education. ***Email:*** jsabanosh@rms-law.com

RICHARD F. BANBURY, born Hartford, Connecticut, August 20, 1938; admitted to bar, 1964, Connecticut; 1965, U.S. District Court, District of Connecticut, 1970, U.S. Court of Appeals, Second Circuit; 1972, U.S. Supreme Court. *Education:* Yale University (B.A., Economics, 1960; J.D., 1963). Author: "Noncultural Determinants of Criminal Behavior," 50 Connecticut Bar Journal 315, 1976. Law Clerk, Justice John Cotter Supreme Court of Connecticut, 1965-1967. Assistant State's Attorney, Hartford County, 1970-1975. Chief Assistant State's Attorney, 1975-1978. Guggenheim Visiting Fellow, Yale Law School, 1976-1977. Vice-President, 1977-1979; President, 1980-1981; Connecticut Halfway House, Inc. Member: Connecticut Bar Examining Committee, 1980—; Executive Committee, 1982—. Attorney and Executive Director for Council on Probate Judicial Conduct, 1989—. Member, Panel of Arbitrators, American Arbitration Association, Litigation Alternatives and Dispute Resolution, Inc. *Member:* Connecticut Bar Association; Connecticut Trial Lawyers Association. ***PRACTICE AREAS:*** Litigation; Professional Liability; Alternative Dispute Resolution. ***Email:*** rbanbury@rms-law.com

(This Listing Continued)

MORRIS R. BOREA, born Hartford, Connecticut, April 25, 1957; admitted to bar, 1982, Connecticut; 1985, U.S. District Court, District of Connecticut; 1993, U.S. Court of Appeals, Second Circuit. *Education:* Trinity College (B.S., 1979); University of Connecticut (J.D., 1982). Author: "Municipal Liability, The Public Duty Doctrine Revisited," CTLA Forum, Vol. 10, No. 1, February, 1992. Program Chair, Product Liability Litigation, CTLA CLE Seminar, 2001. Program Chair, Suing the Federal, State and Local Government, Connecticut Trial Lawyers Association Continuing Legal Education Seminar, 1999. Chairman, 1997— and Secretary, 1996-1997, Wethersfield Zoning Board of Appeals. Chairman, Connecticut Trial Lawyers Association People's Law School, Wethersfield, Connecticut, 1993-1997. *Member:* Connecticut Trial Lawyers Association (Member: Continuing Legal Education Committee, 1996—; Membership Committee, 1997—); The Association of Trial Lawyers of America. ***LANGUAGES:*** Italian. ***PRACTICE AREAS:*** Civil Litigation; Complex Commercial Litigation; Personal Injury; Medical Malpractice; Products Liability; Trade Secret Litigation. ***Email:*** mborea@rms-law.com

JOHN W. BRADLEY, JR., born Middletown, Connecticut, June 17, 1948; admitted to bar, 1976, Connecticut; 1977, U.S. District Court, District of Connecticut. *Education:* College of the Holy Cross (B.A., 1970); University of Puget Sound-Seattle University (J.D., 1976). Town Attorney: Town of Cromwell, 1997—; Town of Wethersfield, 2001—; Special Counsel, Town of Malborough. *Member:* Hartford County and Connecticut (Sections on: Litigation and Administrative Law, Executive Committee) Bar Associations; Connecticut Trial Lawyers Association; Defense Research Institute; Connecticut Defense Lawyers Association; Connecticut Association of Municipal Attorneys; Union Internationale des Avocats. ***LANGUAGES:*** French. ***PRACTICE AREAS:*** Litigation; Administrative Law. ***Email:*** jbradley@rms-law.com

ROBERT J. T. BRITT, born Hartford, Connecticut, January 12, 1959; admitted to bar, 1984, Connecticut; 1988, U.S. District Court, District of Connecticut. *Education:* Fairfield University (B.A., 1981); New England School of Law (J.D., 1984). Assistant State's Attorney, 1985-1988. Author: "A DUI Arrest from Start to Finish," Connecticut Trooper, Vol. 3, No. 1 (1996). Lecturer: Operating Under the Influence Defense (Hartford County Bar Association), November 1993; March 1996-November, 1999; Strategies in Defending DUI Cases (Connecticut Bar Association), October 1996; Defense of a DWI Case (Connecticut Public Defenders), 1998. *Member:* Hartford County (Chair, Criminal Justice Committee, 1996—) and Connecticut (Secretary, Executive Committee, Criminal Justice Section) Bar Associations; National Association of Criminal Defense Lawyers; Connecticut Criminal Defense Lawyers Association; National College for DUI Defense (Founding Member). ***PRACTICE AREAS:*** DUI Defense; Criminal Litigation. ***Email:*** rbritt@rms-law.com

JOSEPH B. BURNS, born New Haven, Connecticut, March 6, 1960; admitted to bar, 1985, Connecticut; 1986, U.S. District Court, District of Connecticut; 1992, U.S. Court of Appeals, Second Circuit; 1994, U.S. Supreme Court; 1997, Mohegan Gaming Disputes Court and Mashantucket Pequot Tribal Court; 2000, U.S. Court of Appeals, First Circuit. *Education:* Boston University (B.A., 1982); Western New England College (J.D., 1985). Phi Delta Phi. Special Master, New Britain Superior Court, 1996—. Fact Finder/Arbitrator, Connecticut Superior Court, 1998—; Attorney Trial Referee, Connecticut Superior Court, 1999—. *Member:* New Britain, Hartford County, Connecticut (Member, Indian Law Committee; Member, Sections on: Litigation, Federal Practice and Intellectual Property) and American (Member, Sections on: Litigation and Torts and Insurance Practice) Bar Associations; Connecticut Trial Lawyers Association. ***PRACTICE AREAS:*** Litigation. ***Email:*** jburns@rms-law.com

JOSEPH J. CASSIDY, born Caracas, Venezuela, January 11, 1958; admitted to bar, 1984, Connecticut; 1985, New York and U.S. District Court, Southern and Eastern Districts of New York; 1990, U.S. District Court, District of Connecticut, U.S. Court of Appeals, Second Circuit, U.S. Supreme Court and U.S. Tax Court; 2001, Massachusetts and U.S. District Court, District of Massachusetts. *Education:* University of Connecticut (B.A., magna cum laude, 1980); Oxford University, England; Hofstra University (J.D., 1984). Hofstra Law Review, Member, 1982-1983 and Managing Editor, 1983-1984. Moderator and Lecturer, Annual Symposium on Connecticut Property Tax, 1997—. Lecturer, University of Connecticut Annual School for Tax Assessors. Member, Board of Governors, Arthritis Foundation, 1992—. *Member:* Hartford County and Connecticut (Sections on: Litigation, Intellectual Property and Commercial Law and Bankruptcy) Bar Associations; Connecticut Association of Assessing Officers. ***PRACTICE AREAS:*** Commercial and Tax Litigation; Intellectual Property Litigation; General Civil Litigation; Appellate Practice. ***Email:*** jcassidy@rms-law.com

GLENN E. COE, born Canal Zone, Panama, August 18, 1944; admitted to bar, 1974, Connecticut; 1993, Massachusetts; 1995, New York; U.S. District Court, District of Connecticut; U.S. District Court, District of Massachusetts; U.S. Court of Appeals, Second Circuit; U.S. Supreme Court. *Education:* Andrews University (B.A., 1966; M.A., summa cum laude, 1967); University of Connecticut (J.D., 1973). Editor: Connecticut Trial Judges Benchbook, 1974; Connecticut Sentencing Benchbook, 1974; Court of Common Pleas Benchbook, 1974. Co-author: with Francis Cady (University of Connecticut Law School Dean), "Judicial Education: Coals to Newcastle?" University of Con-

(This Listing Continued)

ROME McGUIGAN SABANOSH, P.C., Hartford—Continued

necticut Law Review, Spring, 1974. Chief Trial Attorney, Office of the Chief State's Attorney, Connecticut, 1978-1983. *Member:* Hartford County (President, 2001), Connecticut (Member, Criminal Justice Executive Committee, 1984; Intellectual Property Executive Committee, 1993; Delegate, 2000—) and American Bar Associations. ***PRACTICE AREAS:*** Commercial Litigation; Intellectual Property Litigation; Corporate Investigations and Litigation; Government Investigations; White Collar Crime; Wrongful Death and Personal Injury; Bad Faith Litigation; Accountants Liability; Professional Liability. ***Email:*** gcoe@rms-law.com

RICHARD P. HEALEY, born Salem, Massachusetts, December 12, 1951; admitted to bar, 1977, Massachusetts, Connecticut and U.S. District Court, District of Massachusetts; 1978, U.S. District Court, District of Connecticut; 1991, U.S. Supreme Court. *Education:* Boston College (A.B., cum laude, 1973); Boston College Law School (J.D., 1976). Recipient, Alumni Award for Outstanding Contribution to the Development of the Law School. Chairman, American Diabetes Association, Connecticut Affiliate, 1993-1995. Connecticut Judicial Performance Evaluation Advisory Panel, 1995-1999; Connecticut Prison and Jail Overcrowding Commission, 1999—. *Member:* Massachusetts, Connecticut (Member, Executive Committee, Real Property Section, 1979-1988) and American Bar Associations. ***PRACTICE AREAS:*** Commercial Real Estate Finance and Development; Litigation; Employment Law. ***Email:*** rhealey@rms-law.com

ANDREW L. HOULDING, born Cardiff, Wales, U.K., May 30, 1945; admitted to bar, 1992, Connecticut; 1993, U.S. District Court, District of Connecticut; U.S. Court of Appeals, Second Circuit; Mohegan Gaming Disputes Court. *Education:* Boston University (B.A., 1966); University of Connecticut (J.D., with honors, 1992). *Member:* Bridgeport and Connecticut (Co-Chairman, Indian Law Section; Member, Labor and Employment Section) Bar Associations. ***LANGUAGES:*** French. ***PRACTICE AREAS:*** Labor and Employment; Litigation; Indian Law. ***Email:*** ahoulding@rms-law.com

WILLIAM W. KALIFF, born Providence, Rhode Island, January 27, 1963; admitted to bar, 1988, Connecticut; 1989, U.S. District Court, District of Connecticut. *Education:* Boston College (B.A., summa cum laude, 1985); Boston College Law School (J.D., cum laude, 1988). Phi Beta Kappa; Phi Alpha Theta. *Member:* Connecticut (Member, Sections on: Litigation; Intellectual Property; Commercial Law and Bankruptcy) and American (Member, Section on Intellectual Property Law) Bar Associations. ***PRACTICE AREAS:*** Civil and Commercial Litigation; Intellectual Property Litigation. ***Email:*** wkaliff@rms-law.com

RICHARD J. KENNY, born Newark, New Jersey, March 27, 1950; admitted to bar, 1975, Connecticut; 1976, U.S. District Court, District of Connecticut; 1984, U.S. Court of Appeals, Second Circuit; 1998, Massachusetts. *Education:* College of the Holy Cross (B.A., summa cum laude, 1972); University of Connecticut (J.D., with honors, 1975). *Member:* Hartford County, Connecticut and American Bar Associations; Defense Research Institute; Connecticut Defense Lawyers Association (President, 1997-1998); Connecticut Trial Lawyers Association; International Association of Defense Lawyers. ***PRACTICE AREAS:*** Civil Litigation; Commercial Litigation; Products Liability; Medical Malpractice. ***Email:*** rkenny@rms-law.com

ANTHONY B. LUDOVICO, born New Haven, Connecticut, April 19, 1943; admitted to bar, 1968, Connecticut and U.S. District Court, District of Connecticut. *Education:* Brown University (B.A., 1965); University of Connecticut School of Law (J.D., 1968). *Member:* Connecticut Bar Association (Member, Estates & Probate Executive Committee, 1998-2001; Member, Elder Law Section). ***PRACTICE AREAS:*** Trusts and Estates. ***Email:*** aludovico@rms-law.com

JEFFREY L. MENT, born Bridgeport, Connecticut, February 10, 1967; admitted to bar, 1992, Connecticut, U.S. District Court, District of Connecticut and U.S. Tax Court. *Education:* University of Connecticut (B.S., cum laude, 1989); University of Miami (J.D., 1992). Author: "Recent Case Law on Police Liability," Connecticut Trooper, Vol. 2, No. 2, Fall, 1995; "Fourth Amendment-Friend or Foe," Connecticut Trooper, Vol. 4, No. 1, Spring/Summer, 1997. *Member:* Connecticut (Member, Litigation Section) and American (Member, Sections on Litigation and Air Space Law) Bar Associations; Connecticut Trial Lawyers Association; Defense Research Institute (Professional Liability Steering Committee). ***PRACTICE AREAS:*** Civil Liability; Commercial Litigation; Products Liability; Professional Liability. ***Email:*** jment@rms-law.com

PUTNAM H. PERRY, born Hartford, Connecticut, January 29, 1959; admitted to bar, 1993, Connecticut; 1994, U.S. District Court, District of Connecticut. *Education:* Boston University (B.A., 1983); University of Cambridge, England (LL.M., 1986); University of Virginia (J.D., 1993). ***PRACTICE AREAS:*** Litigation. ***Email:*** pperry@rms-law.com

DEBRA C. RUEL, born Hartford, Connecticut, December 14, 1953; admitted to bar, 1984, Connecticut; 1985, U.S. District Court, District of Connecticut. *Education:* College of New Rochelle (B.A., 1975); University of Connecticut (J.D., 1984). Recipient, American Jurisprudence Book Award in Conflict of Laws. Adjunct Faculty, Lawyering Process, University of Connecticut School of Law, 1994-1998. Member, Board of Directors, Children's Law Center of Connecticut, Inc. *Member:* Hartford County (Co-Chair, Family Law Section, 1999-2000, 2000-2001), Connecticut and American (Member, Family Law Section) Bar Associations; Collaborative Divorce Lawyers' Association. ***PRACTICE AREAS:*** Matrimonial Law. ***Email:*** druel@rms-law.com

HELGA MAYER WOODS, born Philadelphia, Pennsylvania, February 15, 1957; admitted to bar, 1983, Connecticut; U.S. District Court, District of Connecticut. *Education:* University of Pennsylvania (B.A., 1979); Ludwig-Maximilians University, Munich, Germany; University of Connecticut School of Law (1982-1983); Villanova Law School (J.D., 1983). Delta Phi Alpha. Member, Board of Trustees, The Greater Hartford Easter Seal Rehabilitation Center, Inc., 1993-1996. Member: Board of Directors, Connecticut Attorneys Title Insurance Company; Board of Directors, Vested Technologies, Inc. *Member:* Hartford County, Connecticut (Co-Chair, Indian Law Section, 2000—) and American Bar Associations. ***PRACTICE AREAS:*** Commercial Finance; Commercial Real Estate Finance; Commercial Real Estate Development. ***Email:*** hwoods@rms-law.com

---

JONATHAN J. BLAKE, born Hartford, Connecticut, July 10, 1961; admitted to bar, 2000, Connecticut. *Education:* University of Connecticut (B.A., 1983); Boston University (M.A., Creative Writing, 1991); Suffolk University Law School (J.D., cum laude, 2000). Staff Member, 1997-1998 and Note Editor, 1998-1999, Suffolk Transnational Law Review. Recipient, American Jurisprudence Award, Labor Law. ***PRACTICE AREAS:*** Labor and Employment; Indian Law; Litigation. ***Email:*** jblake@rms-law.com

JULIE D. BLAKE, born Manchester, Connecticut, February 10, 1975; admitted to bar, 1999, Connecticut. *Education:* University of Virginia (B.A., 1996); Suffolk University Law School (J.D., 1999). McLaughlin Competition Winner - Oral Advocacy. *Member:* Connecticut Bar Association. ***PRACTICE AREAS:*** Litigation; Internet Law; E-Commerce; Appellate Practice. ***Email:*** julieblake@rms-law.com

ZISCA BURKLEY, born Brooklyn, New York, October 1, 1974; admitted to bar, 2000, Connecticut and U.S. District Court, District of Connecticut. *Education:* State University of New York at Buffalo (B.A., 1996); Hofstra University (J.D., 2000). *Member:* Hartford County, Connecticut and New York State Bar Associations. ***Email:*** zburkley@rms-law.com

ALEXANDER J. CHOTKOWSKI, born Cambridge, Massachusetts, August 7, 1970; admitted to bar, 1996, Connecticut and U.S. District Court, District of Connecticut; U.S. Court of Appeals for the Armed Forces; U.S. Supreme Court. *Education:* Washington & Jefferson College (B.A., 1993); Franklin Pierce Law Center (J.D., 1996). Marine Judge Advocate, Special Assistant U.S. Attorney, 1997-2000. *Member:* Hartford County Bar Association; Connecticut Trial Lawyers Association; Connecticut Defense Lawyers Association. [USMC, Active Duty, 1996-2000; Captain, USMC Reserves, 2000—]. ***PRACTICE AREAS:*** Commercial Litigation; Insurance Defense; Products Liability Defense. ***Email:*** achotkowski@rms-law.com

BERNARD F. GAFFNEY, born New Britain, Connecticut, October 30, 1966; admitted to bar, 1993, Connecticut and U.S. District Court, District of Connecticut; 1994, Massachusetts and U.S. District Court, District of Massachusetts. *Education:* St. Anselm College (B.A., 1989); Suffolk University School of Law (J.D., 1993). Editor-in-Chief, Adelphia Law Journal. Co-Counsel, Asian Americans of Connecticut, Inc., 1993-1994. Commissioner, Board of Finance, City of New Britain, 1993-1995. *Member:* New Britain and Hartford County Bar Associations; Connecticut Defense Lawyers Association. ***PRACTICE AREAS:*** Civil and Commercial Litigation; Products Liability Defense. ***Email:*** bgaffney@rms-law.com

THOMAS J. LENGYEL, born Waterbury, Connecticut, April 30, 1973; admitted to bar, 1999, Connecticut; 2000, U.S. District Court, District of Connecticut. *Education:* University of Pittsburgh (B.A., 1995); Quinnipiac College (J.D., 1999). Vice-President, Phi Delta Phi, 1998-1999. ***PRACTICE AREAS:*** Commercial Litigation; Civil Litigation; Securities Regulation; Ad Valorem Tax; Business Consultation; Construction Litigation. ***Email:*** tlengyel@rms-law.com

JAYME E. STAMPER, born Rocky Hill, Connecticut, August 1, 1965; admitted to bar, 2000, Connecticut. *Education:* University of Hartford, Hartford College for Women (B.A., 1995); University of Connecticut (J.D., 2000). ***PRACTICE AREAS:*** Civil Litigation; Family Law; Municipal Law. ***Email:*** jstamper@rms-law.com

JACQUELINE A. WILSON, born Hartford, Connecticut, August 28, 1951; admitted to bar, 1986, Connecticut; 1991, U.S. District Court, District of Connecticut. *Education:* St. Anselm College (B.S., Registered Nursing, 1973); Western New England College School of Law (J.D., 1986). Registered Nurse, 1973. ***REPORTED CASES:*** Favrow v. Vargus, 222 Conn 699 (1992); Papa v. Papa, 55 Conn App 47 (1999). ***PRACTICE AREAS:*** Family Law; Juvenile Law; Civil Litigation. ***Email:*** jwilson@rms-law.com

(This Listing Continued)

COUNSEL

HORACE G. FLINN, JR., born McPherson, Kansas, July 2, 1938; admitted to bar, 1987, Connecticut. *Education:* University of North Texas (B.S., with honors, 1959); Harvard University (E.D.M., 1960); University of Hartford (M.B.A., 1981); University of Connecticut (J.D., with honors, 1987). [Capt., U.S. Air Force, 1961-1966]. ***LANGUAGES:*** German. ***PRACTICE AREAS:*** Estate Planning.

GEORGE P. GENERAS, JR, born Erie, Pennsylvania, December 24, 1943; admitted to bar, 1992, Connecticut; 1996, U.S. District Court, District of Connecticut; 1999, U.S. Supreme Court. *Education:* University of Scranton (B.S., 1966; M.B.A., 1968); University of Connecticut (J.D., 1991). Certified Public Accountant, New York, 1973 and Connecticut, 1979. *Member:* Connecticut and American Bar Associations; American Association of Attorney-Certified Public Accountants; American Institute of Certified Public Accountants; Connecticut Society of Certified Public Accountants. [Sgt. U.S. Army, 1969-1971.]. ***PRACTICE AREAS:*** General. ***Email:*** ggeneras@rms-law.com

JOHN F. STROTHER, born Marion, Ohio, June 22, 1942; admitted to bar, 1970, New York; 1972, U.S. Tax Court; 1975, Connecticut; 1979, U.S. District Court, District of Connecticut. *Education:* Phillips Exeter Academy and Princeton University (A.B., cum laude, 1964); Yale University (LL.B., 1967). Legal Advisor, Ministry of Justice, Republic of Somalia, 1968-1969. Treasurer, Yale Law School Alumni Association of Fairfield County, 1978-1986. Director, Connecticut Retirement Consultants Association, 1993-1995. *Member:* Bridgeport (Chairman, Tax Section, 1996-1997), Connecticut (Treasurer, Executive Committee, Tax Section, 1979-1982; Secretary-Treasurer, 1982-1985) and American Bar Associations. ***PRACTICE AREAS:*** Employee Benefits Law; ERISA; General Practice. ***Email:*** jstrother@rms-law.com

---

RUBEN, JOHNSON & MORGAN, P.C.

CITYPLACE II
185 ASYLUM STREET
HARTFORD, CONNECTICUT 06103
Telephone: 860-275-6888
Telecopier: 860-275-6884

Real Estate, Corporate, Bankruptcy, Litigation.

MARSHALL S. RUBEN, born Alexandria, Virginia, May 28, 1960; admitted to bar, 1985, California; 1987, District of Columbia; 1990, Connecticut. *Education:* Yale University (B.A., 1982); Columbia University (J.D., 1985); New York University (LL.M., Taxation, 1996). *Member:* Connecticut Bar Association; State Bar of California; The District of Columbia Bar. ***PRACTICE AREAS:*** Real Estate; Real Estate Finance; Corporate; Taxation. ***Email:*** mruben@rjmlawct.com

DEREK M. JOHNSON, born Bethlehem, Pennsylvania, September 21, 1957; admitted to bar, 1985, Texas; 1992, Connecticut. *Education:* University of Washington (B.A., cum laude, 1979; M.A., 1981); Emory University (J.D., 1985). Editor-in-Chief, 1984-1985, Bankruptcy Developments Journal. Adjunct Professor, University of Connecticut. *Member:* Connecticut and American Bar Associations; State Bar of Texas. ***PRACTICE AREAS:*** Bankruptcy; Corporate Litigation. ***Email:*** djohnson@rjmlawct.com

LISA KELLY MORGAN, born Darby, Pennsylvania, September 25, 1962; admitted to bar, 1987, Connecticut and U.S. District Court, District of Connecticut;1992, U.S. District Court, Southern and Eastern Districts of New York. *Education:* Villanova University (B.A., cum laude, 1984); University of Connecticut (J.D., with honors, 1987). Commissioner, National Conference of Commissioners on Uniform State Laws, 1999—. Member, NCCUSL Drafting Committee on Non-Judicial Foreclosure Act, 2000— Member, NCCUSL Study Committee on Certificate of Title Laws, 1999—. *Member:* Hartford County, Connecticut and American Bar Associations. ***PRACTICE AREAS:*** Litigation; Real Estate. ***Email:*** lmorgan@rjmlawct.com

OF COUNSEL

MAURA HUGHES HORAN, born Hartford, Connecticut, August 17, 1962; admitted to bar, 1988, Connecticut. *Education:* University of California, San Diego (B.A., cum laude, 1984); University of Connecticut (J.D., 1988). ***PRACTICE AREAS:*** Litigation; Real Estate. ***Email:*** mhoran@rjmlawct.com

---

RUBENSTEIN, GREEN & BASS, LLC

HARTFORD, CONNECTICUT

(See Westport)

General Civil Practice before State and Federal Courts, Real Estate, Corporation, Commercial and Banking, Personal Injury, Medical Malpractice, Estate Planning and Probate, Planning and Zoning Trials and Appeals, Banking Litigation.

BARBARA J. RUHE

HARTFORD, CONNECTICUT

(See Wethersfield)

Adoption, Matrimonial, Juvenile and Custody Law.

SABATINI AND ASSOCIATES, LLC

HARTFORD, CONNECTICUT

(See Newington)

General Civil Practice. Trials in all State and Federal Courts. Litigation, Probate, Corporate, Personal Injury, Commercial, Zoning.

SABIA & HARTLEY, LLC

190 TRUMBULL STREET
SUITE 202
HARTFORD, CONNECTICUT 06103-2205
Telephone: 860-541-2077
Facsimile: 860-713-8944
URL: http://www.sabiahart.com

Commercial Law and Transactions, Employment Law, Civil Litigation, Commercial Litigation, Tort Litigation, Corporate Transactions, Real Estate and Banking.

RANDALL J. SABIA, born Manchester, Connecticut, April 6, 1957; admitted to bar, 1985, Connecticut and U.S. District Court, District of Connecticut. *Education:* Middlebury College (A.B., 1979); University of Connecticut (J.D., with honors, 1985). *Member:* Connecticut Bar Association; Commercial Finance League of America; Commercial Law League; Association of Commercial Finance Attorneys; Connecticut Community Banker's Association. ***PRACTICE AREAS:*** Commercial Transactions; Uniform Commercial Code; Commercial Foreclosures; Commercial Collections; Bankruptcy; Corporate Law. ***Email:*** rsabia@sabiahart.com

JILL HARTLEY, born Hartford, Connecticut, April 17, 1964; admitted to bar, 1989, Texas and U.S. District Court, Northern District of Texas; 1992, Connecticut and U.S. District Court, District of Connecticut; 1994, U.S. Court of Appeals, Second Circuit; 1995, Massachusetts; 2000, U.S. Supreme Court. *Education:* University of Texas (B.A., with honors, 1984); University of Houston (J.D., with honors, 1989). Order of the Coif. *Member:* Connecticut Bar Association (Labor Law Section). ***PRACTICE AREAS:*** Employment Law; Commercial Litigation; Tort Litigation. ***Email:*** jhartley@sabiahart.com

EDWARD C. TAIMAN, JR., born North Tarrytown, New York, November 1, 1956; admitted to bar, 1986, Connecticut and U.S. District Court, District of Connecticut. *Education:* University of Connecticut (B.S., 1978); Pepperdine University (J.D., 1985). Law Clerk, Hon. Louise DeCarl Malugen, U.S. Bankruptcy Court, Southern District of California, 1985-1986. President, Student Bar Association, Pepperdine University, 1984-1985. *Member:* Tolland County, Connecticut and American Bar Associations. ***PRACTICE AREAS:*** Bankruptcy Law; State and Federal Litigation. ***Email:*** etaiman@sabiahart.com

---

EILEEN C. MOSKEY, born Bristol, Connecticut, May 24, 1964; admitted to bar, 1995, Connecticut. *Education:* University of Connecticut (B.A., cum laude, 1986); Western New England College School of Law (J.D., 1994). Pi Sigma Alpha. *Member:* Connecticut and American Bar Associations. ***PRACTICE AREAS:*** Commercial Transactions; Real Estate; Uniform Commercial Code; Commercial Foreclosures; Commercial Collections; Corporate Law; Landlord and Tenant Law. ***Email:*** emoskey@sabiahart.com

MICHAEL G. ALBANO, born New York, New York, August 16, 1953; admitted to bar, 1996, New York, New Jersey and U.S. District Court, District of New Jersey; 2000, Connecticut and U.S. District Court, District of Connecticut. *Education:* State University of New York at Oneonta (B.S., 1975); Tufts University (M.A., 1981); Yale School of Drama (M.F.A., 1982); Brooklyn Law School (J.D., cum laude, 1995). Executive Editor, Brooklyn Journal of International Law. Author: Note, "Agency as a Means of Obtaining Jurisdiction in New York Over Foreign Corporations: A Failed Theory," Brooklyn Journal of International Law 1, Vol. XX, No. 1. ***PRACTICE AREAS:*** Commercial Litigation; Torts. ***Email:*** malbano@sabiahart.com

EDWARD M. ROSENTHAL, born Albany, New York, June 17, 1968; admitted to bar, 1992, Florida; 1993, Connecticut and U.S. District Court, District of Connecticut. *Education:* Boston University (B.S.B.A., 1989); University of Miami (J.D., 1992). Member and Notes and Comments Editor, University of Miami Business Law Journal. *Member:* Connecticut Bar Associations; Connecticut Trial Lawyers Association; The Association of Trial Lawyers of America. ***PRACTICE AREAS:*** Commercial Litigation; Civil Litigation; Personal Injury. ***Email:*** erosenthal@sabiahart.com

(This Listing Continued)

SABIA & HARTLEY, LLC, Hartford—Continued

RYAN P. BARRY, born Manchester, Connecticut, June 28, 1972; admitted to bar, 2000, Connecticut and U.S. District Court, District of Connecticut. *Education:* University of Connecticut (B.A., cum laude, 1994); University of Connecticut School of Law (J.D., 1999). Phi Delta Phi. Member, Connecticut Law Review, 1998-1999. Author: "Erisa's Purpose: The Conveyance of Information From Trustee to Beneficiary," 31 Conn. L. Rev. 735, 1999. Director, Greater Hartford Transit District, 1999—. Member: Town of Manchester Ethics Commission; Manchester Democratic Town Committee, 1994—. *Member:* Manchester and Connecticut (Member, Litigation Section) Bar Associations. ***PRACTICE AREAS:*** Commercial Litigation. ***Email:*** rpbarry@sabiahart.com

SANDAK FRIEDMAN HENNESSEY & GRECO, LLP

HARTFORD, CONNECTICUT

(See Stamford)

Trials and Appeals in all Connecticut and Federal Courts and Administrative Agencies. Personal Injury, Medical Malpractice, Commercial, Environmental Litigation, Real Estate, Zoning and Land Use, Property Tax Appeals.

SANDLER, GOLDSTEIN & MARA, P.C.

ONE HARTFORD SQUARE WEST
SUITE 302
HARTFORD, CONNECTICUT 06106
Telephone: 860-241-7700
Fax: 860-241-7701

General Commercial Practice including Litigation, Corporations, Administrative, Real Estate, Public Utilities, Communications, Zoning, Energy, Environmental, Labor Relations, Municipal and Public Agency, Public Finance and Entertainment Law, Personal Injury.

JAMES P. SANDLER, born New York, N.Y., April 12, 1936; admitted to bar, 1962, Connecticut, U.S. District Court, District of Connecticut and U.S. Court of Appeals, Second Circuit. *Education:* Princeton University (A.B., 1957); Harvard University (J.D., 1962). Connecticut Law Revision Commission, 1993-1997; Connecticut Commission on the Arts, Secretary/Treasurer, 1992-1995. Co-Chairman, Governor's Commission on Quality and Integrated Education, 1989-1991. Chairman, Development Commission, City of Hartford, 1972-1987. Secretary and Director, Hartford Economic Development Corp., 1973-1998 . Member, 1975— and Chairman, 1976-1993, Connecticut Energy Advisory Board. Chairman, Junior Bar Section, 1967-1968 and Member, Board of Governors, 1968-1970, Connecticut Bar Association. Member, Connecticut Legislative Task Force for Restructuring the Electric Industry, 1995-1997. Member, Bloomfield Economic Development Commission, 1995—. ***PRACTICE AREAS:*** Municipal; Public Agency; Public Employment; Energy; Corporate Law; Business Law; Entertainment Law; Elder Health Care. ***Email:*** jpsandler@snet.net

RICHARD H. GOLDSTEIN, born Hartford, Connecticut, December 5, 1949; admitted to bar, 1976, Connecticut and U.S. District Court, District of Connecticut. *Education:* Bates College (B.S., 1971); American University, Washington College of Law (J.D., 1975). Member, American University Law Review, 1974-1975. Corporation Counsel, City of Hartford, 1982-1988. Member, State Commission on Compensation of Elected State Officials and Judges, 1991-1999. Member, National Association of Bond Lawyers, 1999—. ***PRACTICE AREAS:*** Municipal and Public Agency. ***Email:*** rhgesq@worldnet.att.net

DANIEL N. MARA, born Winooski, Vermont, October 21, 1960; admitted to bar, 1985, Connecticut and U.S. District Court, District of Connecticut. *Education:* Hamilton College (A.B., 1982); University of Connecticut (J.D., 1985). Delegate to the Connecticut Bar Association, 1998—. *Member:* Hartford County, Connecticut and American (Litigation Section) Bar Associations; Connecticut Trial Lawyers Association. ***REPORTED CASES:*** Connecticut Light and Power Co. v. South Eastern Connecticut Regional Resources Recovery Authority. 822 F.Supp. 888, 143 P.U.R. 4th 292; CTB Realty Ventures XXII, Inc. v. Markoski, 33 Conn. App. 388; Bristol Savings Bank v. Cellino, 34 Conn. App. 914. ***PRACTICE AREAS:*** Trial Practice; Commercial Law; Litigation; Employment Litigation; Real Estate; Foreclosures; Collections; Personal Injury. ***Email:*** dmara@snet.net

All Lawyers in the Firm are Members of the Connecticut and American Bar Associations.

REPRESENTATIVE CLIENTS: Abrahms Agencies; Alliance Limousine; Aplicare, Inc.; Town of Bloomfield; The ctnow.com Meadows Music Centre; Clinton Harborside Marina, Inc.; Community Housing and New Commercial Enterprises; Eastern Connecticut State University Foundation; Harbor Petroleum of New England; Hartford Economic Development Corp.; Hartford Housing Authority; Hartford Distributors, Inc.; The Hebrew Home and Hospital; iProjects, LLC; Manafort Brothers; Managed Construction Resources, LLC; The Michael Bolton Charities; OTOhealth, Inc.
LEGAL COUNSEL TO: The Metropolitan District Commission.
REFERENCE: Webster Bank.

SANTOS & SEELEY, P.C.

51 RUSS STREET
HARTFORD, CONNECTICUT 06106
Telephone: 860-249-6548
Fax: 860-724-5533

Trial and Appellate Practice in State and Federal Courts, Criminal Law, White Collar Crime, Employment, Personal Injury, Commercial Litigation, Civil Rights.

HUBERT J. SANTOS, born Springfield, Massachusetts, September 12, 1944; admitted to bar, 1969, Connecticut; 1970, U.S. District Court, District of Connecticut; 1971, U.S. Court of Appeals, Second Circuit; 1972, U.S. Supreme Court; 1979, U.S. Claims Court; 1982, U.S. Tax Court. *Education:* University of Hartford (B.A., magna cum laude, 1966); University of Connecticut (J.D., cum laude, 1969). Recipient: Regents Honor Award; Handley Award; Corporation Award; Barristers Ball Award; 1993 Distinguished Graduate Award, University of Connecticut, School of Law Alumni Association; 1995 Vincent Brown Coffin Award, University of Hartford. Lead Articles Editor, Connecticut Law Review, 1968-1969. Adjunct Faculty, Trial Practice, University of Connecticut, 1976-1986. Assistant Federal Public Defender, District of Connecticut, 1972-1974. Corporation Counsel, City of Hartford, 1978-1979. Member: Standing Discovery Committee, 1984— and Grievance Committee, 1984-1987, Oliver Ellsworth Inn of Court, 1987—, U.S. District Court, District of Connecticut. Commissioner, Judicial Selection Commission for the State of Connecticut, 1987-1994. *Member:* Hartford County, Connecticut (Member: Criminal Law Committee, 1977-1978; Continuing Legal Education Committee, 1983-1984; State Judicial Screening Committee, 1983-1986) and American Bar Associations; Connecticut Trial Lawyers Association; The Association of Trial Lawyers of America. Fellow: American College of Trial Lawyers; American Board of Trial Advocates. ***PRACTICE AREAS:*** Criminal Defense; Commercial Law; Business Litigation; Personal Injury; Appellate Practice; White Collar Crime.

HOPE C. SEELEY, born Bridgeport, Connecticut, February 25, 1964; admitted to bar, 1989, Connecticut; 1990, U.S. District Court, District of Connecticut; 1994, U.S. Court of Appeals, Second Circuit; 1998, U.S. Supreme Court. *Education:* University of Connecticut (B.A., magna cum laude, 1986; J.D., with honors, 1989). Phi Beta Kappa; Phi Kappa Phi; Pi Sigma Alpha. Member: Mortar Board; Moot Court Board. Finalist, 1987 Alva P. Loiselle Moot Court Competition. Recipient: Alvin B. Dozeman Writing Award, 1985, 1986; Augusta Gerberich Scholarship, 1986; Joseph Blumenfeld Award, 1989; Maxwell Heiman Memorial Award, 1998. Instructor, University of Connecticut School of Law: Appellate Moot Court Inter-Term, 1989—; Legal Methods, 1990-1993; Lawyer Processing, 1995—. *Member:* Hartford County and Connecticut (Member, Executive Committee, Criminal Justice Section) Bar Associations; Connecticut Trial Lawyers Association; Connecticut Criminal Defense Lawyers Association (Member, Executive Board, 1997—); National Criminal Defense Lawyers Association; Oliver Ellsworth Inn of Court (Barrister, 1992-1995). ***PRACTICE AREAS:*** Criminal Defense; White Collar Crime; Civil Litigation; Appellate Litigation. ***Email:*** seeley@home.com

---

PATRICK S. BRISTOL, born East Greenwich, Rhode Island, December 6, 1971; admitted to bar, 1996, Connecticut; 1997, U.S. District Court, District of Connecticut. *Education:* University of New Hampshire (B.A., 1993); University of Connecticut (J.D., 1996). *Member:* Hartford County and Connecticut Bar Associations. ***PRACTICE AREAS:*** Criminal Defense; Civil Litigation; White Collar Crime.

SCHATZ & NOBEL, P.C.

330 MAIN STREET
HARTFORD, CONNECTICUT 06106
Telephone: 860-493-6292
Telecopier: 860-493-6290
Email: SN06106@aol.com
URL: http://www.snlaw.net

General Business Litigation in all Federal and State Courts. Securities Litigation, including class and derivative actions and licensing proceedings. Antitrust Litigation, Employment Litigation, Professional Liability Litigation.

ANDREW M. SCHATZ, born Hartford, Connecticut, April 6, 1951; admitted to bar, 1976, Illinois; 1980, Connecticut; U.S. District Court, District of Connecticut and Northern and Southern Districts of Illinois; U.S. Court of Appeals, Second and Seventh Circuits. *Education:* Cornell University (B.A., with honors, 1972); Harvard University (J.D., with honors, 1976). Phi Beta

(This Listing Continued)

Kappa. Member, 1973-1976 and Articles Editor, 1975-1976, Harvard Civil Rights-Civil Liberties Law Review. Member, Securities Advisory Council to the Connecticut Department of Banking. Formerly with: Sachnoff Weaver & Rubenstein, Chicago, Illinois, 1976-1987; Schatz & Schatz, Ribicoff & Kotkin, Hartford, Connecticut, 1987-1995. *Member:* Connecticut and American Bar Associations. ***PRACTICE AREAS:*** Securities Litigation; Business Litigation; Professional Liability; Antitrust. ***Email:*** andy@snlaw.net

JEFFREY S. NOBEL, born Brooklyn, New York, October 14, 1964; admitted to bar, 1989, Connecticut and U.S. District Court, District of Connecticut. *Education:* University of Connecticut (B.A., cum laude, 1986); Albany Law School (J.D., 1989). Associate Editor, Albany Law Review, 1987-1989. Formerly with Schatz & Schatz, Ribicoff & Kotkin, Hartford, Connecticut, 1989-1995. ***PRACTICE AREAS:*** Securities Litigation; Commercial Litigation; Professional Liability; Business Litigation; Employment Litigation. ***Email:*** jeff@snlaw.net

ROBERT ANDREWS IZARD, JR., admitted to bar, 1983, North Carolina; 1987, Connecticut; U.S. District Court, District of Connecticut and Middle and Western Districts of North Carolina; U.S. Court of Appeals, Second and Fourth Circuits; U.S. Supreme Court. *Education:* Yale University (B.A., 1978); Emory University (J.D., with honors, 1983). Order of the Coif. Former Chair, Commercial and Business Litigation Committee, American Bar Association (Member, Litigation Section). Distinguished Neutral, CPR Institute for Dispute Resolution. Notes and Comments Editor, Emory Law Journal. Author: "Lawyers and Lawsuits: A Guide to Litigation". ***PRACTICE AREAS:*** Complex Commercial Litigation; Securities Litigation. ***Email:*** rizard@snlaw.net

---

PATRICK A. KLINGMAN, born Poughkeepsie, New York, 1965; admitted to bar, 1991, New York; 1992, District of Columbia; 1994, U.S. District Court, Southern District of New York and U.S. District Court, District of Columbia; 1995, U.S. District Court, Western District of New York; 1997, U.S. District Court, District of Connecticut; 1998, Connecticut. *Education:* Villanova University (B.A.,1987); Maxwell School of Citizenship and Public Affairs (M.A., international relations, 1990); Syracuse University (J.D., cum laude, 1990). Lead Articles Editor, Syracuse Journal of International Law and Commerce, 1989-1990. *Member:* Hartford County, Connecticut and New York State Bar Associations; The District of Columbia Bar. ***PRACTICE AREAS:*** Securities Litigation; Commercial Litigation. ***Email:*** patrick@snlaw.net

WAYNE T. BOULTON, born Alhambra, California, December 2, 1970; admitted to bar, 1997, Connecticut; U.S. District Court, District of Connecticut. *Education:* Colgate University (B.A., cum laude, 1993); University of Connecticut School of Law (J.D., with honors, 1997). *Member:* Connecticut and American Bar Associations. ***PRACTICE AREAS:*** Securities Litigation; Commercial Litigation. ***Email:*** wayne@snlaw.net

LAW OFFICES
HOWARD LEE SCHIFF, P.C.

HARTFORD, CONNECTICUT

(See East Hartford)

Collection Law (Retail and Commercial), Commercial Law, Creditor's Rights, Creditor Bankruptcy, Enforcement of Judgement, Foreclosures, Subrogation in the entire New England region.

SCIBILIA & McCUIN, P.C.

HARTFORD, CONNECTICUT

(See Berlin)

Commercial Transactions, Corporate, Business and Securities, Real Estate and Litigation.

DAVID M. S. SHAIKEN, P.C.

Established in 1991

330 MAIN STREET

HARTFORD, CONNECTICUT 06106

Telephone: 860-244-0720
Facsimile: 860-244-0725
Email: david.shaiken@snet.net
URL: http://www.shaiken.com

Bankruptcy, Insolvency, Creditor's Rights, Commercial Law, Commercial Litigation, Commercial Finance, Commercial Arbitration and Mediation, Family Law, Alternative Dispute Resolution.

(This Listing Continued)

DAVID M. S. SHAIKEN, born New York, NY, August 24, 1960; admitted to bar, 1987, Connecticut; 1988, U.S. District Court, District of Connecticut. *Education:* Swarthmore College (B.A., 1982); University of Connecticut (J.D with honors, 1987). Law Clerk to the Honorable Robert L. Krechevsky, U.S. Bankruptcy Judge, 1987-1989. Co-Author: Chapters 3 and 8, *Automatic Stay Litigation in Bankruptcy,* Wiley Law Publications, John Wiley & Sons, 1995. Lecturer: "Chapter 11 Bankruptcy: What the Business Lawyer Needs to Know When Someone (Other Than Their Client) Files a Chapter 11 Case," Connecticut Bar Association, 1999; Local Rules Committee, U.S. Bankruptcy Court, District of Connecticut; "Collision At the Intersection of Divorce and Bankruptcy: Is A Divorce Court's Division of Assets an Avoidable Transfer?" Connecticut Bar Association, 2001. *Member:* Hartford County, Connecticut (Member, Executive Committee and Chairman, 1996-1998, Commercial Law and Bankruptcy Section; Member, Family Law Section) and American (Member, Business and Family Law Sections) Bar Associations; American Bankruptcy Institute; The National Association of Consumer Bankruptcy Attorneys; Turnaround Management Association; Family Firm Institute.

RALPH D. SHERMAN

HARTFORD, CONNECTICUT

(See West Hartford)

Criminal and Civil Litigation. Civil Rights, Second Amendment Law, Firearms, Pistol Permits, Pardons, Landlord Tenant, Collections and Real Estate.

SHIPMAN & GOODWIN LLP

Established in 1919

ONE AMERICAN ROW

HARTFORD, CONNECTICUT 06103-2819

Telephone: 860-251-5000
Telecopier: 860-251-5099
Email: www@goodwin.com
URL: http://shipman-goodwin.com

Greenwich, Connecticut Office: 43 Arch Street. Telephone: 203-869-6222.
Lakeville, Connecticut Office: 12 Porter Street, P.O. Box 1809. Telephone: 203-435-2539.
Stamford, Connecticut Office: One Landmark Square. Telephone: 203-324-8100.

General Practice. Banking, Corporation, Tax, Antitrust, Commercial Finance, Securities, Venture Capital, Labor and Employment, Health Care, Environmental, Pension and Employee Benefits, Estate Planning, Estate Settlement, Trust Administration, Real Estate, Municipal Law, Franchise, Dealer and Distributor Litigation. Trials in all Courts.

FIRM PROFILE: Shipman & Goodwin was founded over 80 years ago. Its principal areas of practice include general corporate and securities law, litigation, corporate and commercial finance, tax, bankruptcy and creditors' rights, environmental law, municipal law, administrative law, utility regulation, real estate, construction law, fidelity and surety law, venture capital financing, international trade, antitrust and trade regulation, banking, insurance, labor and employment, trusts and estates, pension, health care law, intellectual property, computer law, tax-exempt organizations, agricultural cooperatives, family law, criminal law, legislation and lobbying. The firm is divided into six departments: Business, Litigation, Labor and Employment, Real Estate, Tax, and Trusts and Estates. In each area of practice, lawyers are assisted by experienced legal assistants. In addition, many lawyers are members of practice groups organized to address specifically the needs of particular clients and/or industries. Among such groups are those serving venture capital investors, high technology and emerging companies, hospitals and health care providers, municipalities and agricultural cooperatives. Within the Trust and Estate Department is a group specializing in Financial Planning and Trust Administration.

MEMBERS OF FIRM

STUYVESANT K. BEARNS, born Washington, DC, 1937; admitted to bar, 1965, Virginia; 1966, New York; 1975, Connecticut. *Education:* Yale University (B.A., magna cum laude, 1959); University of Virginia (LL.B., 1965). Order of the Coif. Member, Editorial Board, University of Virginia Law Review, 1962-1965. *Member:* Litchfield County and Connecticut (Chairman, 1986-1988, Executive Committee, Estates and Probate Section, 1978-2000) Bar Associations. Fellow, The American College of Trust and Estate Counsel (Member, 1977—; Connecticut Chairman, 1991-1996). (Lakeville Office). ***PRACTICE AREAS:*** Estate Planning and Settlement; Probate Matters; Trust Administration; Land Preservation Law. ***Email:*** sbearns@goodwin.com

PETER W. BENNER, born Newark, NJ, 1950; admitted to bar, 1976, Connecticut. *Education:* Princeton University (A.B., magna cum laude, 1972); Georgetown University (J.D., 1975). Executive Board, Georgetown Law Jour-

(This Listing Continued)

SHIPMAN & GOODWIN LLP, Hartford—Continued

nal, 1973-1975. Law Clerk to U.S. District Court Judge Thomas A. Flannery, 1975-1976. ***PRACTICE AREAS:*** Commercial Litigation; Bankruptcy Litigation; Health Care Litigation. ***Email:*** pbenner@goodwin.com

JAMES W. BERGENN, born Brooklyn, NY, 1954; admitted to bar, 1979, Connecticut. *Education:* The Catholic University of America (B.A., summa cum laude, 1976); Columbia University (J.D., 1979). Phi Beta Kappa. Law Clerk to U.S. District Court Chief Judge T. Emmet Clarie, 1979-1980. Lecturer, Trial Practice, University of Connecticut Law School, 1986—. Assistant Federal Public Defender, U.S. District Court, District of Connecticut, 1981-1983. Instructor, Connecticut Trial Advocacy Institute, 1994—. Appointed Special Prosecutor by Chief State's Attorney, 1994-1995. *Member:* National Association of Criminal Defense Lawyers; Connecticut Criminal Defense Lawyers Association; Connecticut Trial Lawyers Association. ***PRACTICE AREAS:*** Trial Practice; White Collar Litigation; Criminal Litigation; Antitrust Litigation; Health Care Litigation. ***Email:*** jbergenn@goodwin.com

JAMES T. BETTS, born Springfield, MA, 1943; admitted to bar, 1968, Connecticut. *Education:* Yale University (B.A., summa cum laude, 1965; LL.B., 1968). Phi Beta Kappa; Order of the Coif. Member, Board of Editors, Yale Law Journal, 1966-1968. Law Clerk to Judge Robert P. Anderson, U.S. Court of Appeals, Second Circuit, 1968-1969. *Member:* The American College of Trust and Estate Counsel. ***PRACTICE AREAS:*** Estate Planning and Settlement Law; Probate Matters; Financial Planning and Trust Administration Law. ***Email:*** jbetts@goodwin.com

DONNA L. BROOKS, born Richmond, VA, 1960; admitted to bar, 1985, Connecticut. *Education:* College of William and Mary (B.A., 1982); University of Virginia (J.D., 1985). Phi Beta Kappa. ***PRACTICE AREAS:*** Venture Capital; Emerging Growth Companies; Business Law; Commercial Finance; Mergers and Acquisitions; Securities Law. ***Email:*** dbrooks@goodwin.com

DANIEL P. BROWN, JR., born Evanston, IL, 1943; admitted to bar, 1968, Connecticut; 1984, Massachusetts. *Education:* Williams College (B.A., cum laude, 1965); Yale University (LL.B., 1968). Phi Beta Kappa. Selectman, 1969-1974. Member, Planning and Zoning Commission, Town of Granby, 1974—. ***PRACTICE AREAS:*** Corporate Law; Business Law; Corporate Finance; Corporate Trust Law. ***Email:*** pbrown@goodwin.com

COLEMAN H. CASEY, born Bryn Mawr, PA, 1947; admitted to bar, 1973, Connecticut; 1984, Massachusetts. *Education:* Amherst College (B.A., magna cum laude, 1969); Yale University (J.D., 1973). Phi Beta Kappa. Member, Board of Editors, Yale Law Journal, 1972-1973. Author: Note, "A First Amendment Right of Access to the Courts for Indigents," 82 Yale Law Journal 1055, 1973. *Member:* American College of Real Estate Lawyers; National Association of Bond Lawyers. ***PRACTICE AREAS:*** Real Estate Law; Public Finance; Commercial Finance; Independent Schools Law. ***Email:*** ccasey@goodwin.com

ROBERT J. CATHCART, born Cleveland, OH, 1935; admitted to bar, 1962, Ohio; 1964, Connecticut. *Education:* Harvard University (B.A., 1958); Western Reserve University (LL.B., 1961). Town Attorney, Town of Wethersfield, 1979-1981. *Member:* The Association of Trial Lawyers of America; Connecticut Trial Lawyers Association. ***PRACTICE AREAS:*** Civil Litigation; Insurance Coverage and Defense; ERISA Litigation; Personal Injury Law. ***Email:*** rcathcart@goodwin.com

CHRISTINE L. CHINNI, born Detroit, MI, 1962; admitted to bar, 1991, Massachusetts; 1992, Connecticut. *Education:* University of Michigan (B.A., with high honors, 1984); University of California (M.A., 1985); Western New England College School of Law (J.D., summa cum laude, 1991). Editor-in-Chief, Western New England Law Review. Law Clerk to Supreme Judicial Court of Massachusetts Judge John M. Greaney, 1991-1992. President, Connecticut School Attorneys' Council. *Member:* Hartford County, Connecticut and American Bar Associations. ***PRACTICE AREAS:*** Management Labor Law; Public School Law; School Board Defense; School Equal Protection. ***Email:*** cchinni@goodwin.com

BRUCE A. CHUDWICK, born Hartford, CT, 1957; admitted to bar, 1988, Connecticut. *Education:* Bryant College (B.S., summa cum laude, 1979); University of Hartford (M.S., 1988); University of Connecticut (J.D., 1988). Certified Public Accountant, Connecticut, 1982. Member, Town Council, Farmington, Connecticut, 1995—. *Member:* Connecticut and American Bar Associations; National Association of Bond Lawyers; American Institute of Certified Public Accountants; Connecticut Society of Certified Public Accountants (Former Chair, State Taxation Committee). ***PRACTICE AREAS:*** Municipal Law; Public Finance. ***Email:*** bchudwick@goodwin.com

BRIAN CLEMOW, born Hartford, CT, 1944; admitted to bar, 1969, Connecticut. *Education:* Harvard University (B.A., cum laude, 1966); University of Pennsylvania (LL.B., cum laude, 1969). Adjunct Professor, Labor Law, University of Connecticut Law School, 1975-1985. Editor: "Employer's Guide to Labor and Employment Laws and Regulations," published by Connecticut Business and Industry Association, 1988-1995. *Member:* Connecticut (Chairman, Labor and Employment Section, 1979-1981) and American Bar Associations; Connecticut School Attorneys Council (President, 1979-1980). ***PRACTICE AREAS:*** Labor Relations; Employment Law; Education Law. ***Email:*** bclemow@goodwin.com

(This Listing Continued)

RICHARD I. COHEN, born Brooklyn, NY, 1958; admitted to bar, 1984, Connecticut. *Education:* Wesleyan University (B.A., 1981); Cornell Law School (J.D., 1984). Member, Northeast Key District Pension Liaison Group, Internal Revenue Service. *Member:* Connecticut Bar Association (Member, Executive Committee, Section on Taxation);. ***PRACTICE AREAS:*** ERISA; Pension and Profit Sharing Plans; Employee Benefits. ***Email:*** rcohen@goodwin.com

GLENN M. CUNNINGHAM, born Denville, NJ, 1966; admitted to bar, 1991, Connecticut; 1992, U.S. District Court, District of Connecticut; 1996, U.S. Court of Appeals, First Circuit. *Education:* Villanova University (B.A., 1988); Villanova University School of Law (J.D., 1991). Pi Sigma Alpha. Order of Omega. Adjunct Professor, Trial Advocacy, University of Connecticut School of Law, 1999—. *Member:* Hartford County (Past Member, Bench-Bar Committee), Connecticut (Member: Federal Practice Section, Local Rules Committee; Intellectual Property Section), Federal (President, Hartford County Chapter) and American Bar Associations; Connecticut Trial Lawyers Association. ***PRACTICE AREAS:*** Intellectual Property Litigation; Business Litigation; Business Torts Litigation. ***Email:*** gcunningham@goodwin.com

LESLIE L. DAVENPORT, born Hartford, CT, 1956; admitted to bar, 1987, Connecticut; 1988, U.S. District Court, District of Connecticut. *Education:* Fairfield University (B.A., cum laude, 1978); Rensselaer Polytechnic Institute (M.S., Business, 1986); University of Connecticut School of Law (J.D., magna cum laude, 1987). Law Clerk, Honorable Ellen Bree Burns, U.S. District Court, District of Connecticut, 1987-1989. Executive Editor, Connecticut Law Review, 1986-1987. ***PRACTICE AREAS:*** Corporate Finance; Securities Regulation. ***Email:*** ldavenport@goodwin.com

BRENDA A. ECKERT, born Hartford, CT, 1945; admitted to bar, 1973, Connecticut. *Education:* Sarah Lawrence College (B.A., 1967); University of Connecticut (J.D., magna cum laude, 1973). Member, Board of Editors, Connecticut Law Review, 1971-1973. Law Clerk to U.S. District Court Judge Jon O. Newman, 1973-1974. Member, Grievance Committee, U.S. District Court, 1986-1987. *Member:* American Immigration Lawyers Association. Fellow, American Bar Foundation. Fellow, The Connecticut Bar Foundation. ***PRACTICE AREAS:*** Civil Litigation; Employment Litigation; Immigration Law. ***Email:*** beckert@goodwin.com

JOAN W. FELDMAN, born New York, NY, 1956; admitted to bar, 1986, Connecticut. *Education:* State University of New York, Downstate Medical Center, College of Nursing (B.S.N., magna cum laude, 1977); University of Connecticut School of Law (J.D., with honors, 1986). *Member:* American Health Lawyers Association. ***PRACTICE AREAS:*** Business Law; Health Care Law. ***Email:*** jfeldman@goodwin.com

VAUGHAN FINN, born Tokyo, Japan, 1951; admitted to bar, 1977, District of Columbia; 1994, Connecticut and U.S. District Court, District of Connecticut. *Education:* Radcliffe College (B.A., magna cum laude, 1973); Harvard Law School (J.D., 1977). Phi Beta Kappa. Law Clerk, Judge Morris E. Lasker, U.S. District Court, Southern District of New York, 1977-1979. Associate, Wald, Harkrader & Ross, Washington, D.C., 1979-1985. Trial Attorney and Senior Trial Counsel, Civil Division, U.S. Department of Justice, 1985-1992. ***PRACTICE AREAS:*** Employment Law; Litigation. ***Email:*** vfinn@goodwin.com

THOMAS P. FLYNN, born Mount Kisco, NY, 1964; admitted to bar, 1989, Connecticut. *Education:* University of Connecticut (B.A., summa cum laude, 1986; J.D., summa cum laude, 1989). Phi Beta Kappa. Member: Licensing Executives Society; Connecticut Venture Group; Board of Directors, MIT Entrepreneur Forum of Connecticut. *Member:* National Association of Stock Plan Professionals. ***PRACTICE AREAS:*** Corporate Law; Business Law; Corporate Finance Law; Corporate Trust Law; Emerging Growth and High Tech Companies; Venture Capital Law; Mergers and Acquisitions; Technology; Corporate Finance. ***Email:*** tflynn@goodwin.com

SUSAN C. FREEDMAN, born Colchester, CT, 1949; admitted to bar, 1989, Connecticut; 1991, District of Columbia. *Education:* University of Connecticut (B.A., with honors, 1971; M.A., with honors, 1975); National Law Center George Washington University (J.D., with high honors, 1989). Order of the Coif. Law Clerk to Judge John H. Pratt, U.S. District Court, District of Columbia, 1989-1990. *Member:* Connecticut and American Bar Associations; Connecticut Trial Lawyers Association; Connecticut School Board Attorneys Council. ***PRACTICE AREAS:*** College and University Law; Independent School Law; School Board Defense; Special Education Litigation. ***Email:*** sfreedman@goodwin.com

DEBORAH SMITH FRISONE, born Hartford, CT, 1951; admitted to bar, 1987, Connecticut. *Education:* University of Connecticut (B.A., cum laude, 1974); University of Florida (M.A., 1976); University of Connecticut (J.D., magna cum laude, 1987). ***LANGUAGES:*** Italian. ***PRACTICE AREAS:*** Business Law; Computer and Technology Law; Electronic Commerce; Commercial Finance; Corporate Trust Law; Securities Law; Bankruptcy Law. ***Email:*** dfrisone@goodwin.com

(This Listing Continued)

STEPHEN K. GELLMAN, born Washington, DC, 1963; admitted to bar, 1989, Connecticut. *Education:* Trinity College (B.A., honors, 1985); University of Pennsylvania (J.D., 1989). Member, Executive Committee Connecticut Bar Association, Estates and Probate Section. ***PRACTICE AREAS:*** Estate Planning; Probate Matters; Trusts Administration. ***Email:*** sgellman@goodwin.com

IRA H. GOLDMAN, born New York, NY, 1947; admitted to bar, 1972, Connecticut. *Education:* Cornell University (B.A., 1968); Yale University (J.D., 1972). Adjunct Professor, Employee Benefits Law, University of Connecticut Law School, 1987—. ***PRACTICE AREAS:*** Bankruptcy and Reorganization Law; Pension, Compensation and Employee Benefit Planning Law. ***Email:*** igoldman@goodwin.com

GARY S. HAMMERSMITH, born Manhasset, NY, 1960; admitted to bar, 1986, New York and U.S. District Court, Southern and Eastern Districts of New York; 1988, District of Columbia (inactive); 1989, U.S. District Court, District of Connecticut; 1990, Connecticut. *Education:* College of William & Mary (A.B., 1981); University of Virginia (J.D., 1985). Pi Sigma Alpha (National Political Science Fraternity). *Member:* New York State and American Bar Associations; The District of Columbia Bar. Fellow, American College of Investment Counsel, 1994. ***PRACTICE AREAS:*** Business Law; Venture and Intellectual Property; Mergers and Acquisitions; Corporate Transactions; Commercial Law. ***Email:*** ghammersmith@goodwin.com

JOHN T. HARRIS, born Detroit, MI, 1942; admitted to bar, 1967, Wisconsin; 1974, California; 1979, Connecticut; 1984, Pennsylvania. *Education:* Princeton University (B.S.E., 1964); University of Wisconsin (J.D., 1967). Author: "Application of the Abstention Doctrine to Inverse Condemnation Actions in Federal Court," 4 Pepperdine University Law Review 1, 1975. Chairman, Town of Simsbury Zoning Commission, 1981-1987. Adjunct Professor of Law, Fidelity and Surety Law, University of Connecticut School of Law, Insurance Law center, 1998—. Member, University of Hartford Board of Regents, 2000—. Member, Board of Trustees, Hartt School of Music, 1996—. *Member:* Connecticut Bar Association (Member, Standing Committee on Dispute Resolution in the Courts, 2000—). ***PRACTICE AREAS:*** Civil Litigation; Insurance Coverage and Defense Law; Fidelity and Surety Law; Construction Law. ***Email:*** jharris@goodwin.com

BARRY C. HAWKINS, born Portland, ME, 1943; admitted to bar, 1968, Connecticut. *Education:* Bowdoin College (A.B., with honors, 1965); University of Virginia (J.D., 1968). Member: Connecticut Uniform Laws Commissioners, 1999— NCCUSL Drafting Committee for Revised Uniform Arbitration Act; Governor, 1994-1997 and Member, American College of Real Estate Lawyers. Director, 1994-1999 and Member, Stamford Regional Bar Association; Chairman, Real Property Section, 1993-1995 and Member, Executive Committee, 1978—, Connecticut Bar Association. Director, Connecticut Chapter, Community Associations Institute, 1998— Member, Gallivan Foundation Advisory Board, 1992— Trustee, Housatonic Community College Foundation, 1996—. Author: "Can Rent Receivers Be Liable Under Environmental Laws?", The Practical Real Estate Lawyers, Vol. 12, No. 2, March, 1996; "The 1995 Amendments to the Connecticut Transfer Act", Connecticut Real Estate law Journal, Vol. 13 no. 3 (1995); "Alternative Dispute Resolution in Real Estate Litigation," American Bar Association, ACREL Papers; (1994). *Member:* Connecticut and American (Real Property, Probate and Trust Law Section) Bar Associations. (Stamford Office). ***PRACTICE AREAS:*** Real Estate; Land Use Regulation; Community Association Law; Environmental Law; Business Litigation; Commercial Litigation. ***Email:*** bhawkins@goodwin.com

TIMOTHY S. HOLLISTER, born Brooklyn, NY, 1957; admitted to bar, 1982, Connecticut. *Education:* Wesleyan University (B.A., cum laude, 1978); Occidental College (M.A. in Urban Studies, 1980); Boston University (J.D., 1982). Co-Author: "*State and Local Land Use Liability,*" West, 1998. Coro Foundation Fellow in Public Affairs, St. Louis, Missouri, 1978-1979. Chair, Environmental Law Section, Connecticut Bar Association, 1996-1997. Regional Vice President, National Institute of Municipal Law Officers, 1999—. Member, Governor's Blue Ribbon Commission to Study Affordable Housing, 1999-2000. ***PRACTICE AREAS:*** Land Use Law; Environmental Law and Litigation. ***Email:*** thollister@goodwin.com

CHARLES L. HOWARD, born Alamogordo, NM, 1950; admitted to bar, 1975, Missouri; 1977, Connecticut. *Education:* Princeton University (A.B., cum laude, 1972); University of Virginia (J.D., 1975). Assistant Attorney General of Missouri, 1975-1976. Commissioner, Connecticut Commission on Compensation of State Elected Officials and Judges, 1983-1991. Commissioner, Connecticut Judicial Selection Commission, 1992-1995. Commissioner, Connecticut Criminal Justice Commission, 1995—. Member, Board of Trustees, Connecticut Policy and Economic Council, Inc. Member, Board of Directors, Connecticut World Trade Association, 1984-1990; Public Act Section 7-52 Task Force on Study of Civil Victims Trust Fund. *Member:* Connecticut Association of Municipal Attorneys (Board of Directors, 1986-1993); National Health Lawyers' Association; Defense Research Institute. ***PRACTICE AREAS:*** Civil Litigation; Intellectual Property Litigation; ERISA Litigation; Municipal Litigation; Representation of Corporate Ombudsman; Appellate Practice. ***Email:*** choward@goodwin.com

(This Listing Continued)

SHEILA A. HUDDLESTON, born El Dorado, AR, 1953; admitted to bar, 1990, Connecticut; 1994, U.S. Court of Appeals, First and Second Circuits; 2000, U.S. Supreme Court; U.S. Court of Appeals for Frederal Circuit. *Education:* Yale University (B.A., summa cum laude, 1977; M.A., 1984; J.D., 1990). Recipient: 1994 David H. Neiditz Professional Writing Award for Best Appellate Brief in Connecticut. Adjunct Instructor, Appellate Advocacy, University of Connecticut School of Law. Law Clerk to Chief Justice Ellen A. Peters, Connecticut Supreme Court, 1990-1991. *Member:* Hartford County and Connecticut Bar Associations; American Health Lawyers Association; Defense Research Institute. ***PRACTICE AREAS:*** Civil Appeals; Complex Litigation; Antitrust; Medical Antitrust; Criminal Appeals. ***Email:*** shuddleston@goodwin.com

JOHN E. KREITLER, born East Orange, NJ, 1946; admitted to bar, 1974, Wisconsin; 1975, Connecticut. *Education:* Wesleyan University (B.A., 1968); University of Wisconsin (J.D., cum laude, 1974). Order of the Coif. Member, Board of Editors, Wisconsin Law Review, 1972-1973. Law Clerk to Justice Conner T. Hansen, Wisconsin Supreme Court, 1974-1975. Secretary, Connecticut Venture Group's Hartford Chapter. Member: Connecticut Technology Council. Member: Hartford Advisory Board, The Entrepreneurship Institute; Rising Star Advisory Board. Past Member, Computer Law Section, Connecticut Bar Association. *Member:* Computer Law Association. ***PRACTICE AREAS:*** Corporate Law; Computer Law; Mergers and Acquisitions Law; Health Insurance Law; Venture Capital Finance Law; Commerce Law. ***Email:*** jkreitler@goodwin.com

KATHERINE J. LAMBERT, born Montreal, QU, 1950; admitted to bar, 1981, Connecticut; 1982, U.S. District Court, District of Connecticut; 1983, U.S. Court of Appeals, Second Circuit. *Education:* Kirkland College (B.A., 1973); Suffolk University (J.D., cum laude, 1981). Member, 1979-1981 and Note Editor, 1980-1981, Suffolk University Law Review. Adjunct Faculty Member, University of Connecticut School of Law, 1982-1984. Law Clerk, Hon. Anthony J. Armentano, Connecticut Supreme Court, 1981-1982. Deputy Assistant States Attorney (Appellate), 1982-1983. President, 1993-1994, Executive Committee, 1989-1995, and Member, 1987—, The Real Estate Exchange. Member, National Council, The National Network of Commercial Real Estate Women, 1990-1992. Advisor, Mortgage and Foreclosure Law Study Committee of the Connecticut Law Revision Commission, 1991-1992. Member, Connecticut Executive Committee, Real Estate Finance Association, 1993-1997. *Member:* Connecticut Bar Association (Member, Real Property Section, 1989—); Real Estate Finance Association (1993—); International Council of Shopping Centers; Downtown Hartford YMCA (Vice Chair, Board of Managers, 1997-1998); Hartford Stage Company (Board of Directors). ***PRACTICE AREAS:*** Real Estate; Finance; Leases and Leasing; Zoning, Planning and Land Use. ***Email:*** klambert@goodwin.com

JOHN H. LAWRENCE, JR., born Orange, NJ, 1946; admitted to bar, 1975, Connecticut; 1981, Pennsylvania. *Education:* Washington & Lee University (B.S., 1968); University of Virginia (J.D., 1975). *Member:* American Health Lawyers Association; Healthcare Financial Management Association; Connecticut Health Lawyers Association. ***PRACTICE AREAS:*** Health Care Law; Corporate Law; Business Law; Insurance Law; Federal and State Taxation Law. ***Email:*** jlawrence@goodwin.com

ALAN E. LIEBERMAN, born New York, NY, 1956; admitted to bar, 1982, Connecticut. *Education:* Yale University (B.A., cum laude, 1978); University of Michigan (J.D., magna cum laude, 1982). Order of the Coif. Member, Executive Committee, Taxation Section, Connecticut Bar Association. *Member:* Internal Revenue Service Key District Exempt Organization Liaison Group; Connecticut General Assembly Task Force on the Taxation of Financial Institutions (Chair); Hartford Tax Club (President, 1996-1997); National Association of Bond Lawyers; Department of Revenue Services (Member, Commissioner's Committee on the Taxation of Partnerships and Limited Liability Companies); Connecticut Business and Industry Association (Member, Standing Tax Committee). ***PRACTICE AREAS:*** Federal and State Taxation; Business Law. ***Email:*** alieberman@goodwin.com

ALEX LLOYD, born Atlantic, IA, 1942; admitted to bar, 1967, Connecticut. *Education:* Colby College (B.A., 1964); Yale University (LL.B., 1967). Co-Author: "The Service Business: Partnership or Corporation," 43 Connecticut Bar Journal 259, 1969; "Immunity for Peer Review Participants in Hospitals," A.A.H.A., 1989. *Member:* American Health Lawyers Association; Connecticut Health Lawyers Association. Fellow: American Bar Foundation; Connecticut Bar Foundation. ***PRACTICE AREAS:*** Health Care Law; Corporate Law; Business Law; Federal Taxation; State Taxation; Securities Law. ***Email:*** alloyd@goodwin.com

JULIE A. MANNING, born Manchester, CT, 1961; admitted to bar, 1988, Connecticut, U.S. District Court, District of Connecticut, U.S. District Court, Southern and Eastern Districts of New York and U.S. Court of Appeals, Second Circuit. *Education:* Fairfield University (B.A., 1983); Suffolk University (J.D., 1988). *Member:* Connecticut, Federal and American Bar Associations; American Bankruptcy Institute. ***PRACTICE AREAS:*** Bankruptcy Litigation; Bankruptcy Reorganization; Commercial Law; Creditors Rights; Foreclosures. ***Email:*** jmanning@goodwin.com

(This Listing Continued)

SHIPMAN & GOODWIN LLP, Hartford—Continued

RICHARD A. MILLS, JR., born Middletown, NY, 1960; admitted to bar, 1986, Connecticut. *Education:* University of Virginia (B.A., 1982; J.D., 1986). Law Clerk to Judge Joseph J. Longobardi, U.S. District Court, District of Delaware, 1986-1987. *Member:* Connecticut School Attorneys Council. ***PRACTICE AREAS:*** Public and Private Sector Labor Relations and Employment Law; Education Law. ***Email:*** rmills@goodwin.com

THOMAS B. MOONEY, born Oak Park, IL, 1951; admitted to bar, 1976, Connecticut. *Education:* Yale University (B.A., magna cum laude, 1973); Harvard University (J.D., cum laude, 1976). Phi Beta Kappa. Articles Editor, Harvard International Law Journal, 1975-1976. Co-Author: "Impasse Resolution in Local Government Relations: The Connecticut Approach," 9 Connecticut Law Review 579, 1977; "Wrongful Discharge; A 'New' Cause of Action," 54 Connecticut Bar Journal 213, 1980; "Solomon Revisited: Separating Educational and Other Than Educational Needs in Special Education Residential Placements," 14 Connecticut Law Review 531, 1982. Author: "Student Searches," School Law in Review, 1991; "Related Services and Extracurricular Activities under IDEA and Section 504," School Law in Review, 1994; "A Practical Guide to Connecticut School Law," (2nd ed. 2000); "See You in Court: The Annuals of the Nutmeg Board of Education," CABE Journal, 1980—. Adjunct Professor, Law and Public Education, University of Connecticut Law School, 1985—. Professor in Residence, Neag. School of Education, University of Connecticut, 2001—. ***LANGUAGES:*** German. ***PRACTICE AREAS:*** Education Law; Public Sector Labor Relations; Labor and Employment Law. ***Email:*** tmooney@goodwin.com

SCOTT L. MURPHY, born Hartford, CT, 1947; admitted to bar, 1973, Connecticut; 1984, Massachusetts. *Education:* Williams College (B.A., 1969); Columbia University (J.D., 1973). Harlan Fiske Stone Scholar. Member, Connecticut Law Revision Commission. *Member:* National Association of Bond Lawyers. ***PRACTICE AREAS:*** Corporate Law; Securities Law; Public Finance; Corporate Finance and Corporate Trust Law. ***Email:*** smurphy@goodwin.com

SARANNE P. MURRAY, born Manchester, CT, 1947; admitted to bar, 1983, Connecticut. *Education:* Emmanuel College (B.A., 1969); University of Connecticut (J.D., summa cum laude, 1983). Associate Editor, Connecticut Law Review, 1981-1983. Author: "Partial Closing of a Business Is Not Mandatory Subject of Bargaining Under the NLRA: First National Maintenance Corp. v. NLRB," 14 Connecticut Law Review 435, 1982. *Member:* Connecticut Public Employer Labor Relations Association (Counsel and Member, Executive Board, 1986—); National Public Employer Labor Relations Association (Co-Counsel, 1997—). ***PRACTICE AREAS:*** Public and Private Sector Labor Relations and Employment Law. ***Email:*** smurray@goodwin.com

RICHARD D. NICHOLSON, born Hartford, CT, 1948; admitted to bar, 1973, Connecticut. *Education:* College of the Holy Cross (A.B., 1970); University of Connecticut (J.D., 1973). Author: "Preemption of State Sales & Use Taxes on Goods Purchased Over the Internet," State Tax Notes, January 18, 2000. Adjunct Professor, State and Local Taxation, Western New England College Law School, 2000-2001. First Assistant Commissioner and General Counsel, Connecticut Department of Revenue Services. *Member:* Connecticut (Member, Executive Committee, Tax Section) and American (Member, Tax Section) Bar Associations. ***PRACTICE AREAS:*** State Taxation (100%); Local Taxation; Taxation; State Legislative Practice. ***Email:*** rnicholson@goodwin.com

MARK K. OSTROWSKI, born Manchester, CT, 1963; admitted to bar, 1988, Connecticut. *Education:* University of Connecticut (B.A., cum laude, 1985; J.D., with honors, 1988). Lecturer, Trial Practice, University of Connecticut School of Law. *Member:* Defense Research Institute; Connecticut Trial Lawyers Association. ***PRACTICE AREAS:*** Civil Litigation; Insurance; Health Care; Business; Torts; Products Liability Litigation. ***Email:*** mostrowski@goodwin.com

HOWARD L. PIERCE, born Lakewood, NJ, 1948; admitted to bar, 1991, Connecticut; 1992, U.S. District Court, District of Connecticut; 1998, U.S. District Court, Southern District of New York and U.S. Supreme Court. *Education:* University of Buffalo (B.S., 1971); Quinnipiac College (J.D., 1990). Author: "American Health Lawyers Association, Fraud and Abuse: Compliance and Enforcement Seminar," November 2, 2000, Washington, D.C.; Co-Author: "A Recent Ruling Enhances Private Healthcare Payers' Recovery Efforts," Mealey's Litigation Report Insurance Fraud, Vol. 4 Issue 18, Nov. 1997; "Forfeiture Under State and Federal Statutes," Continuing Education Division and Law Review CLE, 1990; Author: "Fraud and Abuse in Private Insurance Programs," seminar outline, ABA Section of Litigation, Semi-annual Meeting, Scottsdale, Arizona, November 5, 1992. General Counsel, New England Anti-Fraud Association. Lecturer: Trial Practice, University of Connecticut School of Law. *Member:* Connecticut, Federal and American Bar Associations; American and Connecticut Trial Lawyers (Former Co-Chair, Fraud and Abuse Subcommittee, ABA Health Law Litigation Section, 1992-1994) Association; National Health

(This Listing Continued)

Lawyers Association. ***PRACTICE AREAS:*** Health Care Fraud and Abuse Litigation; Insurance Fraud; Criminal Fraud; Civil Rights Litigation. ***Email:*** hpierce@goodwin.com

WILLIAM G. ROCK, born Brooklyn, NY, 1959; admitted to bar, 1984, Connecticut. *Education:* Villanova University (B.A., summa cum laude, 1981); University of Virginia (J.D., 1984). Phi Kappa Phi. Adjunct Faculty Member, University of Hartford Barney School of Business. *Member:* National Association of Bond Lawyers. ***PRACTICE AREAS:*** Real Estate Law; Commercial Finance Law; Corporate Trust Law. ***Email:*** wrock@goodwin.com

PAUL D. SANSON, born Dayton, OH, 1949; admitted to bar, 1977, Connecticut; 1978, District of Columbia. *Education:* Princeton University (A.B., 1974); Georgetown University Law Center (J.D., 1977). Law Fellow. Managing Editor, The Tax Lawyer, Georgetown University Law Center, 1976-1977. Law Clerk to U.S. District Court Judge Charles R. Richey, 1977-1978. Trial Attorney, (Honors Program) Antitrust Division, U.S. Department of Justice, 1978-1981. Member, Executive Committee and Past Chair, Franchise Law Section and Member, Executive Committee, Federal Practice Section, Connecticut Bar Association. Member, Forum on Franchising, American Bar Association. ***PRACTICE AREAS:*** Business Litigation; Franchise Litigation; Distribution Litigation; Antitrust Litigation; Environmental Litigation; Petroleum Marketing Law; Franchises and Franchising. ***Email:*** psanson@goodwin.com

LOUIS B. SCHATZ, born Hartford, CT, 1954; admitted to bar, 1981, New York; 1988, Connecticut and U.S. Tax Court. *Education:* Cornell University (B.A., 1976); Cornell Law School (J.D., 1979); New York University (LL.M., in Taxation, 1980). Speaker: "Impact of Connecticut Transfer Taxes on Workouts Involving Distressed Real Estate," Hartford Tax Institute, 1991 and 1993; "Limited Liability Companies: The Entity of Choice in Connecticut," National Business Institute, 1994, 1995 and 1996; "Like-Kind Exchanges," National Business Institute, 1994; "Update on Limited Liability Companies," Stamford Regional Bar Association, 1993, 1994; "Connecticut Tax Developments," National Conference of CPA Tax Practitioners, 1995—; "Limited Liability Companies and Limited Liability Partnerships," Connecticut Bar Association, 1995, 1996, 1997; "Connecticut Sales and Use Taxes on the Construction Industry," Conn. Bus. and Industry Assoc., Oct. 1995; "Federal Income Tax Developments: U. Conn Tax School, Oct. 1995, Oct. 1999; " Overview of LLCS," University of Connecticut Tax School, Oct. 2000; "Connecticut Tax Developments," Foundation for Accounting Education, January 1996, January 2000; "Connecticut Sales and Use Tax Update," Conn. Bus. and Industry Assoc., May 1997; "Limited Liability Companies," Connecticut Society CPA's annual Real Estate Conference, Oct. 1999. Co-Author: "Connecticut Limited Liability Company Act: Forms and Practice Manual," Data Trace Legal Publishers, 1995 (2000, supplement); "Recent IRS Revenue Procedure Provides Welcome Flexibility in Using LLC's," Connecticut Lawyer, April 28, 1995. Author: "Choosing Between an LLC and LLP," Connecticut Lawyer, November 1996. Author: Chapter 8, Real Estate Conveyance Tax, "1999 Connecticut Tax Handbook," Research Institute of America. *Member:* Connecticut (Member, Executive Committee, Tax Section, 1988—; Chairman, Subcommittee on Connecticut Conveyance Taxes, 1992—; Member, Subcommittee on Connecticut Limited Liability Companies, 1992—), New York State (Member, Section on Taxation) and American (Member, Section on Taxation) Bar Associations. ***PRACTICE AREAS:*** Tax Law; Limited Liability Company Law; State Taxation; Partnership Taxation; Partnership Law. ***Email:*** lschatz@goodwin.com

JAMES C. SCHULWOLF, born Forest Hills, NY, 1956; admitted to bar, 1980, Massachusetts; 1993, Connecticut. *Education:* Amherst College (B.A., cum laude, 1977); New York University (J.D., 1980). Author: "Controlling Your Destiny: Key Issues in Subordination and Intercreditor Agreements," The Secured Lender, November/December, 1995. Lecturer, Executive Enterprises Conference on Loan Documentation and Asset Based Lending. Fellow and Regional Coordinator, Joint Task Force Re: Adoption of Revised Article 9, American College of Commercial Finance Lawyers. *Member:* American Bar Association (Co-Chair, Subcommittee on Intellectual Property Financing; Committee on Commercial Financial Services; Member: Committee on Commercial Financial Services; Committee on Uniform Commercial Code); Association of Commercial Finance Attorneys. ***PRACTICE AREAS:*** Asset Based Lending; Commercial Lending; Mergers and Acquisitions; Electronic Commerce; Equipment Leasing; Mezzanine Finance; Equity Financing; Venture Capital; Loan Syndications and Participations. ***Email:*** jschulwolf@goodwin.com

THEODORE M. SPACE, born Binghamton, NY, 1938; admitted to bar, 1966, Connecticut. *Education:* Harvard University (A.B., cum laude, 1960); Yale University (LL.B., 1966). Member, 1973-1985 and Chairperson, 1975-1985, Board of Education, Town of Bloomfield. *Member:* Connecticut Bar Association (Member, Administrative Law Section, Executive Committee, 1980—); American Law Institute (Member, Members Consultative Group, Restatement of the Law, The Law Governing Lawyers); American Health Lawyers Association; Connecticut Health Lawyers Association. ***PRACTICE AREAS:*** Administrative Law; Complex Litigation; Health Care Law; Real Estate Law; Copyright Law. ***Email:*** tspace@goodwin.com

GARY S. STARR, born Bridgeport, CT, 1950; admitted to bar, 1975, Connecticut; 1976, U.S. District Court of Connecticut; 1985, U.S. Court of Appeals,

(This Listing Continued)

Second Circuit. *Education:* Union College (B.A., cum laude, 1972); University of Connecticut (J.D., with honors, 1975); New York University (LL.M., Labor Law, with honors, 1978). Member, 1973-1974 and Editor, 1974-1975, Connecticut Law Review. Member, Sections on: Labor and Employment Law and Federal Bar, Connecticut Bar Association. Member, Sections on: Labor and Employment Law and Litigation, American Bar Association. ***PRACTICE AREAS:*** Employment Law; Litigation; Labor Law. ***Email:*** gstarr@goodwin.com

JANET S. STULTING, born Richmond, VA, 1948; admitted to bar, 1980, Connecticut and U.S. District Court, District of Connecticut. *Education:* Converse College, Sorbonne University, Paris, France and University of Connecticut (B.A., summa cum laude, 1971) Phi Beta Kappa; University of Connecticut (J.D., cum laude, 1980). Member, 1978 and Notes and Comments Editor, 1979-1980, Connecticut Law Review. *Member:* Connecticut and American Bar Associations; American Academy of Adoption Attorneys. ***PRACTICE AREAS:*** Trusts and Estates; Adoption; Assisted Reproduction Technology. ***Email:*** jstulting@goodwin.com

THOMAS F. TRESSELT, born Evansville, IN, 1943; admitted to bar, 1968, California; 1976, Connecticut; 1984, Massachusetts. *Education:* Yale University (B.A., cum laude, 1965); University of Michigan (J.D., cum laude, 1968). Associate Editor, University of Michigan Law Review, 1967-1968. Assistant Dean, Yale Law School, 1974-1977. ***PRACTICE AREAS:*** Antitrust and Trade Regulation Law; Corporate Law; Business Law; Corporate Trust Law. ***Email:*** ttresselt@goodwin.com

NATALIE W. WELSH, born Tripoli, Libya, 1964; admitted to bar, 1994, Connecticut. *Education:* University of Virginia (B.A., with high distinction, 1986); University of Pennsylvania (M.G.A., 1988); University of Connecticut School of Law (J.D., with high honors, 1994). ***PRACTICE AREAS:*** Employee Benefits; Pension and Profit Sharing Plans; Public Pension Plans. ***Email:*** nwelsh@goodwin.com

JOHN E. WERTAM, born Troy, NY, 1957; admitted to bar, 1986, Connecticut. *Education:* University of Maine at Orono (B.S., with high honors and high distinction, 1980); Vermont Law School (M.S.L., Environmental Law, 1981); University of Connecticut School of Law (J.D., 1986). Author: Book, *Connecticut Environmental Law Handbook,* Government Institutes, Inc., First Edition, July, 1988, Second Edition, March, 1990, Third Edition, October, 1992, Fourth Edition, December, 1995, Fifth Edition, spring, 2000. Member, Environmental Law Section, Connecticut Bar Association. *Member:* Connecticut Business and Industry Association (Member, Environmental Policies Council); Connecticut Environmental Forum (Chair, Board of Directors); Board of Editorial Advisors, Regulatory Reporter Connecticut; Environmental Law Institute (Associate). ***PRACTICE AREAS:*** Environmental Law; Land Use Law. ***Email:*** jwertam@goodwin.com

MARCUS D. WILKINSON, born London, England, 1962; admitted to bar, 1988, California; 1991, New York; 1998, Connecticut. *Education:* Haverford College (B.A., 1984); Columbia Law School (J.D., 1988); European Institute of Business Administration, Fontainebleau, France (M.B.A., 1993). Harlan Fiske Stone Scholar; Kitchener European Scholar. Articles Editor, Columbia Journal of Transnational Law, 1987-1988. Author: Note, "Judicial Review of Foreign Arbitral Awards on Antitrust Matters After *Mitsubishi Motors,*" 26 Columbia Journal of Transnational Law 407, 1988. Co-Author: with Ford Holbrook, Clare O'Brien and Henry Winters, "The Emergence of Cross-Border Stock-for-Stock Transactions," International Financial Law Review 1996 Mergers & Acquisitions Yearbook; with Bruce A. Mann, "The Role of Counsel in Venture Capital Transactions If Disputes Arise," The Business Lawyer, May 1991; with Harry Rubin, "What is 'Substantially All' of a Corporation's Assets for Purposes of an Indenture Governed by New York or Delaware Law?" Insights: The Corporate and Securities Law Advisor, July 1991. ***LANGUAGES:*** French. ***PRACTICE AREAS:*** Mergers and Acquisitions; Corporate Law; Securities; Finance; Venture Capital. ***Email:*** mwilkinson@goodwin.com

JOSEPH P. WILLIAMS, born Philadelphia, PA, 1968; admitted to bar, 1994, Connecticut; 1995, Pennsylvania and U.S. District Court, District of Connecticut; 1996, U.S. Court of Appeals, Second Circuit. *Education:* The American University (B.A., magna cum laude, 1991); Georgetown University Law Center (J.D., cum laude, 1994). Senior Notes Editor, Georgetown Journal of Legal Ethics. Author: "Client Perjury and The Duty of Candor," 6 Geo. J. Legal Ethics 1005 (1993); "Lower Pay for Women's Coaches: Refuting Some Common Justifications," 21 J. College and Univ. Law 643 (1995); Co-Author: *Connecticut Environmental Law Handbook* (4th Ed. 1995). *Member:* Hartford County, Connecticut and American Bar Associations. ***PRACTICE AREAS:*** Environmental Law; Land Use Law. ***Email:*** jwilliams@goodwin.com

ROBERT L. WYLD, born Oak Ridge, TN, 1951; admitted to bar, 1976, Connecticut. *Education:* University of Vermont (B.A., summa cum laude, 1973); Georgetown University (J.D., 1976). Phi Beta Kappa. Notes Editor, American Criminal Law Review, 1975-1976. Law Clerk to U.S. District Court Judge Frank J. Murray, 1976-1977. Author: "Summary Contempt May Properly Be Applied to the Orderly Refusal of Witnesses to Testify at Trial After Grant of Immunity —U.S. v. Wilson," 13 American Criminal Law Review 27, 1975;

(This Listing Continued)

"Whether Servicing and Safety Checks of Industrial Machinery Constitute Control Under Connecticut's Product Liability Statute of Repose," 2 Products Liability Commentary and Cases 5, 1987. Special Master, U.S. District Court, District of Connecticut, 1987—; Special Master, Superior Court for the Judicial District of Hartford-New Britain, 1992—. The Hartford County Bar Association, President, 1991-1992. ***PRACTICE AREAS:*** Civil Litigation; Business Litigation; Securities Litigation; Intra-Corporate Disputes; Health Care Litigation; Trusts and Estates Litigation; Health, Life, Disability & ERISA Litigation. ***Email:*** rwyld@goodwin.com

LINDA L. YODER, born St. Mary's, PA, 1957; admitted to bar, 1981, District of Columbia, 1983, New Jersey; 1987, Connecticut. *Education:* Grove City College (B.A., magna cum laude, 1978); Georgetown University (J.D., magna cum laude, 1981). Editor, Georgetown Law Review, 1980-1981. Member, Executive Committee, Labor and Employment Law Section, Connecticut Bar Association. ***PRACTICE AREAS:*** Civil Litigation; ERISA Litigation; Employment and Education Law. ***Email:*** lyoder@goodwin.com

COUNSEL

MAUREEN J. ANDERSON, admitted to bar, 1992, Connecticut. *Education:* University of Connecticut (B.A., summa cum laude, 1988); University of Connecticut School of Law (J.D., with honors, 1992). Phi Beta Kappa. Notes and Comments Editor, University of Connecticut Law Review. Law Clerk to Justice Flemming L. Norcott, Connecticut Supreme Court, 1992-1993. *Member:* Connecticut and American Bar Associations; American Health Lawyers Association; Connecticut Health Lawyers Association. ***LANGUAGES:*** French. ***PRACTICE AREAS:*** Health Law; Corporate Law; Insurance Law. ***Email:*** manderson@goodwin.com

MARY JO BLAIN ANDREWS, born Providence, RI, 1955; admitted to bar, 1989, Connecticut. *Education:* Trinity College, Washington, D.C. (A.B., magna cum laude, 1977); Harvard Law School (J.D., 1989). Law Clerk, Judge Ernest C. Torres, U.S. District Court, District of Rhode Island, 1989-1990. ***PRACTICE AREAS:*** Real Estate; Zoning, Planning and Land Use; Municipal Corporation Law. ***Email:*** mandrews@goodwin.com

THOMAS A. KLEE, born Buffalo, NY, 1944; admitted to bar, 1969, New York; 1979, Connecticut and U.S. Supreme Court. *Education:* Cornell University (B.S., 1966; J.D., 1969). *Member:* Hartford County, Connecticut (Member, Executive Committee, Business Law Section, 1988—) and American Bar Associations; American Society of Corporate Secretaries. [Capt., U.S. Army, 1969-1972]. ***PRACTICE AREAS:*** Securities; Corporate Law; Corporate Finance. ***Email:*** tklee@goodwin.com

JENNIFER BROWN MAILLY, born Malden, MA, 1960; admitted to bar, 1987, New York; 1992, Connecticut. *Education:* Brown University (A.B., magna cum laude, 1982); Ohio State University (J.D., summa cum laude, 1986). Order of the Coif. Managing Editor, Ohio State University Law Journal, 1985-1986. ***PRACTICE AREAS:*** Labor and Employment. ***Email:*** jmailly@goodwin.com

ARNOLD K. SHIMELMAN, born Hartford, CT, 1945; admitted to bar, 1971, Connecticut; 1975, U.S. District Court, District of Connecticut; 1979, U.S. Court of Appeals, Second Circuit. *Education:* University of Vermont (B.S., 1967); Suffolk University (J.D., 1971). Assistant Attorney General, Connecticut, 1972-1997. *Member:* Hartford County, Connecticut and American Bar Associations. ***PRACTICE AREAS:*** Real Estate Law; Transportation Law; Land Use Law. ***Email:*** ashimelman@goodwin.com

GERALD P. STERGIO, born Brooklyn, NY, 1953; admitted to bar, 1993, Connecticut. *Education:* University of Connecticut (B.A., magna cum laude, 1975); University of New Haven (M.A., 1983); University of Connecticut School of Law (J.D., 1992). *Member:* Hartford, Connecticut and American Bar Associations. ***Email:*** gstergio@goodwin.com

ASSOCIATES

JENNIFER L. ADAMY, born New York, NY, 1965; admitted to bar, 1995, New York; 2000, Connecticut and U.S. District Court, District of Connecticut. *Education:* State University of New York at Binghamton (B.A., 1987); Hofstra University (J.D., 1994). Staff Member, 1992-1993 and Managing Editor of Articles, 1993-1994, Hofstra Property Law Journal. Adjunct Professor, The Writing Program, New York Law School, 1998-2000. *Member:* Hartford County, Connecticut and American Bar Associations; American Bankruptcy Institute; Hartford Association of Women Attorneys. ***REPORTED CASES:*** Chase Manhattan Bank, N.A. v. Travelers Group, 702 N.Y.S. 2d 60 (1st Dep't 2000); Essex v. Newman, 220 A.D. 2d 639, 632 N.Y.S. 2d 636 (2d Dep't 1995). ***PRACTICE AREAS:*** Commercial Litigation; Bankruptcy Law. ***Email:*** jadamy@goodwin.com

LAURA L. ANASTASIO, born Sharon, CT, 1965; (admission pending). *Education:* Emory University (B.A., 1987); University of Connecticut, School of Law (J.D., with honors, 2001). Phi Alpha Delta. ***LANGUAGES:*** Spanish.

(This Listing Continued)

SHIPMAN & GOODWIN LLP, Hartford—Continued

MONICA A. BENNETT, born Milton, FL, 1977; (admission pending). *Education:* Tuskegee University (B.S., Psychology, 1998); Howard University (J.D., 2001). ***Email:*** mbennett@goodwin.com

CATHERINE M. BRENNAN, born Greenwich, CT, 1968; admitted to bar, 1994, New York, Connecticut and U.S. District Court, Southern and Eastern Districts of New York; 1995, New Jersey and U.S. District Court, District of New Jersey. *Education:* College of the Holy Cross (A.B., 1990); Pace University (J.D., cum laude, 1993); New York University (LL.M., Taxation, 1996). Casenote and Comment Editor, Pace Law Review, 1992-1993. *Member:* Greenwich and Regional Bar Associations. (Stamford Office). ***PRACTICE AREAS:*** Estate Planning; Trust Administration; Estate Settlements. ***Email:*** cbrennan@goodwin.com

JAMES J. CARROLL, born Hartford, CT, 1972; admitted to bar, 1998, Connecticut; 1999, New York. *Education:* University of Connecticut (B.A., cum laude, 1994; J.D., 1998). *Member:* Hartford County, Connecticut (Member, Tax Section), New York State (Member, Tax Section) and American (Member, Tax Section) Bar Associations; National Association of Bond Lawyers. ***PRACTICE AREAS:*** Federal Taxation; State and Local Tax; Tax Exempt Organizations; Partnership Taxation. ***Email:*** jcarroll@goodwin.com

RAYMOND J. CASELLA, born Springfield, MA, 1966; admitted to bar, 1999, Massachusetts; 2000, Connecticut. *Education:* Bentley College (B.S., Accountancy, 1988); Western New England College School of Law (J.D., cum laude, 1999); New York University (LL.M., 2000). Certified Public Accountant, 1991. *Member:* Hartford County, Connecticut and American Bar Associations. ***PRACTICE AREAS:*** Tax. ***Email:*** rcasella@goodwin.com

ANNE E. K. DACEY, born Atlanta, GA, 1969; admitted to bar, 1995, Pennsylvania; 1997, Connecticut and U.S. District Court, District of Connecticut. *Education:* Wittenberg University (B.A., summa cum laude, 1991); Northeastern University (J.D., 1995). Law Clerk to the Hon. Peter C. Dorsey, Chief Judge, U.S. District Court, District of Connecticut, 1995-1997. ***PRACTICE AREAS:*** Health Care Law; Corporate. ***Email:*** adacey@goodwin.com

CATHERINE M. ESPOSITO, born Newhaven, CT, 1975; admitted to bar, 2001, Connecticut. *Education:* University of Connecticut (B.S., 1997); Quinnipiac College (J.D., magna cum laude, 2001). Editor-In-Chief , Quinnipiac Law Review, 2000-2001. *Member:* Connecticut Bar Association (Member: Young Lawyers Section; Executive Committee). ***Email:*** cesposito@goodwin.com

PATRICK FAHEY, born Worcester, MA, 1968; admitted to bar, 1993, Connecticut; 1994, U.S. District Court, District of Connecticut; 2000, U.S. Court of Appeals, Federal Circuit. *Education:* College of the Holy Cross (A.B., 1990); University of Connecticut (J.D., with honors, 1993). Managing Editor, Connecticut Law Review. Law Clerk to: the Hon. Ellsworth A. Van Graafeiland, U.S. Court of Appeals for the Second Circuit, 1996-1997; the Hon. Dominic J. Squatrito, U.S. District Judge, District of Connecticut, 1994-1996; the Hon. Thomas P. Smith, U.S. Magistrate Judge, District of Connecticut, 1993-1994. Author: "Payne v. Tennessee: An Eye for an Eye and then Some," 25 Conn. L. Rev. 205, 1992. Co-Author: "Some Points on Litigating Title II and Title XVI Disability Claims," 14 Quinnipiac L. Rev. 243, 1994. ***Email:*** pfahey@goodwin.com

JULIE C. FAY, born Northampton, MA, 1969; admitted to bar, 2001, Massachusetts (Not admitted in Connecticut). *Education:* Williams College (B.A., cum, laude, 1991); Middlebury College (M.A., 1995); University of Connecticut School of Law at Hartford (J.D., with honors, 2001). Author; "Gebser v. Vista, Independent School District, Is it Really the Final Word in School Liability for Teacher-N-Student Sexual Harassment", 31 Conn. L.Rev., 1985 & 1999. *Member:* American Bar Association. ***LANGUAGES:*** Spanish. ***PRACTICE AREAS:*** Education; Labor and Employment. ***Email:*** jfay@goodwin.com

DANIELLE P. FERRUCCI, born Waterbury, CT, 1973; admitted to bar, 1999, Connecticut. *Education:* University of Connecticut (B.A., cum laude, 1995; M.P.A., J.D., with honors, 1999). Law Clerk to Justice Joette Katz and Richard N. Palmer, CT Supreme Court, 1999-2000. ***PRACTICE AREAS:*** Trusts and Estates. ***Email:*** dferrucci@goodwin.com

TAMMI TUVE FLOWERS, born Sacramento, CA, 1971; admitted to bar, 1996, Massachusetts; 1997, New York (Not admitted in Connecticut). *Education:* Boston College (B.A., History; Economics, 1993; J.D., 1996). Phi Beta Kappa. Member, Business Law Section, American Bar Association. *Member:* The Association of the Bar of the City of New York; New York State Bar Association.

ROSS H. GARBER, born New London, CT, 1967; admitted to bar, 1992, Connecticut; 1993, District of Columbia; 1997, U.S. District Court, District of Connecticut. *Education:* University of Connecticut (B.A., with honors, 1989; J.D., with honors, 1992). William F. Starr Research Fellow. Member, Moot Court Board. Research and Book Reviews Editor, Connecticut Journal of International Law. Adjunct Instructor of Law, University of Connecticut School of Law, 1998. . Law Clerk to the Hon. Robert N. Chatigny, U.S. District Judge for the District of Connecticut, 1994-1996. *Member:* Connecticut (Member, Section on: Litigation) and American (Member, Section on: Litigation) Bar Associations; Oliver Ellsworth Inn of Court. ***PRACTICE AREAS:*** Civil Fraud; Criminal Fraud; Criminal Defense; Health Care Fraud. ***Email:*** rgarber@goodwin.com

LISA DENISE GLADKE, born New Britain, CT, 1973; admitted to bar, 1998, Connecticut. *Education:* Connecticut College (B.A., magna cum laude, 1995); Boston College (J.D., 1998). Member, Connecticut Government Finance Association. *Member:* National Association of Bond Lawyers. ***PRACTICE AREAS:*** Public Finance; Real Estate. ***Email:*** lgladke@goodwin.com

GREGG P. GOUMAS, born Derby, CT, 1970; admitted to bar, 1997, Connecticut; 1998, U.S. District Court, District of Connecticut; 2000, Massachusetts and U.S. District Court, District of Massachusetts. *Education:* Williams College (B.A., 1992); Western New England College (J.D., cum laude, 1997). *Member:* Connecticut (Member, Sections on: Young Lawyers; Labor and Employment) and American Bar Associations. ***PRACTICE AREAS:*** Employment Litigation. ***Email:*** ggoumas@goodwin.com

BRYON W. HARMON, born Middletown, CT, 1967; admitted to bar, 1996, Connecticut; 1997, New York and U.S. District Court, District of Connecticut; 1999, U.S. District Court, District of New York. *Education:* University of Connecticut (B.A., 1992); Western New England College (J.D., 1996). *Member:* Connecticut (Member, Estates and Probate Section) New York State (Member, Trusts and Estates Section) and American (Member, Real Property, Probate and Trust Section) Bar Associations. ***PRACTICE AREAS:*** Trusts and Estates. ***Email:*** bharmon@goodwin.com

JILL CUTLER HODGMAN, born Englewood, NJ, 1973; admitted to bar, 1999, Connecticut. *Education:* Cornell University (B.A., 1995); University of Connecticut School of Law (J.D., with honors, 1999). Member, 1997-1998 and Associate Editor, 1998-1999, Connecticut Insurance Law Journal. ***PRACTICE AREAS:*** Education Law; School Law; Labor and Employment. ***Email:*** jhodgman@goodwin.com

JEFFREY W. HUSSEY, born Evanston, IL, 1963; admitted to bar, 1998, Massachusetts, Connecticut and U.S. District Court, District of Massachusetts; 1999, U.S. District Court, District of Connecticut; 2000, U.S. District Court, Southern and Eastern Districts of New York. *Education:* University of Maine (B.S., Business Administration, 1987); Western New England College School of Law (J.D., cum laude, 1997). Note Editor, 1996-1997 and Staff Member, 1995-1996, Western New England Law Review. Member, Philip C. Jessup International Law Moot Court Team, 1995. Law Clerk to the Honorable Barry R. Schaller, Connecticut Appellate Court, 1997-1998. *Member:* Hartford County, Connecticut and American Bar Associations. ***PRACTICE AREAS:*** Corporate; Mergers and Acquisitions; Venture Capital; Finance Law; Corporate Trust. ***Email:*** jhussey@goodwin.com

CATHERINE FRANKLIN INTRAVIA, born Texas City, TX; admitted to bar, 1999, Connecticut. *Education:* University of Connecticut (B.S., in Business Administration & Marketing, 1977); Western New England College School of Law (J.D., magna cum laude, 1999). Member, Western New England College Law Review, 1997-1998. Recipient, Abraham Smith Award for Outstanding Performance in Probate Law. Intern to the Honorable Alfred V. Covello, U.S. District Court, District of Connecticut, 1997. Connecticut Licensed Realtor, 1987—. *Member:* Connecticut (Member, Sections on: Intellectual Property; Computer Law) and American (Member, Sections on: Intellectual Property; Real Property) Bar Associations. ***PRACTICE AREAS:*** Real Estate; Intellectual Property; Computer Law; E-Business; Corporate Law; Mergers and Acquisitions. ***Email:*** cintravia@goodwin.com

LORI B. IZZO, born Newark, NJ, 1958; (admission pending). *Education:* Bucknell University (B.S.B.A., 1981); Fairfield University (M.S., Finance, 1992); University of Connecticut School of Law (J.D., with high honors, 2001). Author; "Doe v. Mutual of Ohaha Insurance Co.: The ADA Does Not Regulate the Content of Insurance Policies, But What Have Cameras, Braille Books or Wheelchairs Got To Do With It?", Connecticut Insurance Law Journal, vol. 7:1. Certified Public Accountant, 1981-2001. *Hartford and American Bar Associations.* ***PRACTICE AREAS:*** Employee Benefits.

GABRIEL J. JIRAN, born Niskayuna, NY, 1971; admitted to bar, 1996, Ohio; 1999, Colorado and U.S. District Court, Southern District of Colorado; 2000, U.S. Court of Appeals, Sixth Circuit (Not admitted in Connecticut). *Education:* Miami University (B.S., 1993); University of Cincinnati (J.D., 1996). *Member:* Ohio State Bar Association. ***PRACTICE AREAS:*** Labor and Employment.

AMY R. KIRSCHBAUM, born Norwich, CT, 1971; admitted to bar, 1997, Connecticut; 1998, U.S. District Court, District of Connecticut. *Education:* Georgetown University (B.A., magna cum laude, 1993); University of Connecticut (J.D., with honors, 1997). Judicial Clerkship, State of Connecticut Appellate Court, the Honorable Edward O'Connell, 1997-1998. *Member:* Connecticut and American Bar Associations. ***PRACTICE AREAS:*** Pension Plans; Employee Benefits. ***Email:*** akirschbaum@goodwin.com

(This Listing Continued)

SHARON SLOAN KOZIOL, born Manchester, CT, 1969; admitted to bar, 1996, Connecticut; 1997, New York. *Education:* University of Connecticut (B.S., magna cum laude, 1991); Albany Law School of Union University (J.D., 1996). Alpha Lamda Delta. *Member:* Hartford County, New York State and American Bar Associations; Hartford Association of Women Attorneys. ***PRACTICE AREAS:*** Commercial Litigation; Collections and Foreclosures; Healthcare Fraud. ***Email:*** ssloan@goodwin.com

KATHLEEN M. LaMANNA, born Smithtown, NY, 1970; admitted to bar, 1995, Connecticut; 1996, U.S. District Court, District of Connecticut; 2000, U.S. District Court, Southern and Eastern Districts of New York. *Education:* Boston College (B.A., cum laude, 1992); University of Connecticut (J.D., 1995). Charter Member and Associate Editor, University of Connecticut Insurance Law Review, 1994-1995. *Member:* Hartford and Connecticut Bar Associations; Hartford Association of Women Attorneys. ***PRACTICE AREAS:*** Litigation; Commercial Litigation; Creditors Rights; Bankruptcy; Workouts. ***Email:*** klamanna@goodwin.com

CHRISTOPHER R. LaSARACINA, born Norwich, CT, 1974; admitted to bar, 1999, Connecticut; 2001, U.S. District Court, District of Connecticut. *Education:* University of Connecticut (B.S., Accounting, 1996); Quinnipiac College (J.D., 1999). Member, Quinnipiac Probate Law Journal, 1997-1999. *Member:* Tolland County Bar Association. ***PRACTICE AREAS:*** Litigation; Labor Law.

ANNE H. LITTLEFIELD, born Hartford, CT, 1967; admitted to bar, 1995, Connecticut and U.S. District Court, District of Connecticut; 1997, Rhode Island. *Education:* Boston College (A.B., magna cum laude, 1989); Harvard University (M.T.S., 1992); University of Virginia School of Law (J.D., 1995). ***PRACTICE AREAS:*** Labor and Employment Law; Education Law. ***Email:*** alittlefield@goodwin.com

COURTNEY B. MASIULIS, born Waterbury, CT, 1976; (admission pending). *Education:* Connecticut College (B.A., 1998); University of Michigan at Ann Arbor (J.D., 2001). ***LANGUAGES:*** French. ***PRACTICE AREAS:*** Litigation. ***Email:*** cmasiulis@goodwin.com

ALEXANDRA M. McHUGH, born Boston, MA, 1965; admitted to bar, 2000, Connecticut. *Education:* Harvard University (B.A., cum laude, 1987); University of Connecticut (J.D., with honors, 2000). Recipient, John Harvard Scholarship. Associate Editor, Connecticut Law Review. ***PRACTICE AREAS:*** Commercial Litigation. ***Email:*** amchugh@goodwin.com

LISA BANATOSKI MEHTA, born Bristol, CT, 1973; admitted to bar, 1998, Connecticut; 1999, U.S. District Court, District of Connecticut. *Education:* George Washington University (B.A., cum laude, 1995); University of Pennsylvania (J.D., 1998). Member, Connecticut Public Employer Labor Relations Association. *Member:* Hartford County, Connecticut (Member, Sections on: Labor and Employment; Litigation) and American (Member: Labor and Employment Law Section; Government and Public Sector - Lawyer's Division) Bar Associations; Hartford Association of Women Attorneys; Industrial Relations Research Association; Connecticut Labor & Employment Women. ***PRACTICE AREAS:*** Public Sector Labor Relations Law; Labor and Employment Law; Privacy and Publicity Law; Employment Law. ***Email:*** lbanatoski@goodwin.com

CRAIG S. MEUSER, born Milford, CT, 1964; admitted to bar, 1997, Connecticut; 1999, U.S. District Court, District of Connecticut. *Education:* Dartmouth College (B.A., cum laude, 1986); University of Bridgeport (M.Ed., 1987); Quinnipiac College School of Law (J.D., summa cum laude, 1997). Executive Editor, Quinnipiac Health Law Journal, 1995-1997. Law Clerk to Hon. Justice Robert I. Berden, Connecticut Supreme Court, 1997-1998. *Member:* Connecticut and American Bar Associations; National School Board Association Council of School Attorneys; Connecticut School Attorneys' Council. ***PRACTICE AREAS:*** Education; Labor; Employment. ***Email:*** cmeuser@goodwin.com

DEREK L. MOGCK, born Edina, MN, 1971; (admission pending). *Education:* Gordon College (B.A., cum laude, 1993); University of Massachusetts at Boston (M.S.P.A., 1998); University of Connecticut College of Law (J.D., with honors, 2001). Articles Editor, Connecticut Law Review. Recipient: Best Oralist Award, 1999 Alva P. Loiselle Moot Court Competition; CALI Excellence Awards in Appellate Advocacy and Trial Practice. Intern to the Honorable Alfred V. Covello, U.S. District Court, District of Connecticut, 1999. Author: "Are We There Yet?: Refining the Test for Expert Testimony through Daubert, Kumho Tire and Proposed Federal Rule of Evidence 702,33 Conn. L. Rev. 303 (2000); "Connecticut Federalists in President Jefferson's (Republican) Court: United States v. Hudson and Goodwin and the national controversy regarding federal criminal common law jurisdiction", Connecticut History (forthcoming). ***Email:*** dmogck@goodwin.com

MAYA N. PERRY, born Dover, NH, 1975; admitted to bar, 2000, Connecticut. *Education:* Connecticut College (B.A., cum laude, 1997); Georgetown University (J.D., cum laude, 2000). ***Email:*** mperry@goodwin.com

JASON M. PRICE, born Columbus, OH, 1971; admitted to bar, 1996, Connecticut; 1999, U.S. District Court, District of Connecticut; 2000, New York. *Education:* Miami University (B.A., 1993); Western New England College (J.D., cum laude, 1996). Articles Editor, Western New England Law Review. Author: "Sex, Lies and Rape Shield Statutes," Western New England Law Review, Vol. 18 No. 2. Completed National Institute of Trial Advocacy, 2000. *Member:* Connecticut and American Bar Associations; Defense Research Institute. ***PRACTICE AREAS:*** Litigation; Insurance; Torts; Products Liability; ERISA.

GIAN-MATTHEW RANELLI, born Hartford, CT, 1965; admitted to bar, 1994, Connecticut; 1997, New York. *Education:* DePauw University (B.A., 1988); Vermont Law School (J.D., 1994; MLS, summa cum laude, 1997). Philip Jessup International Moot Court. *Member:* Connecticut and American Bar Associations. ***PRACTICE AREAS:*** Environmental Law; Land Use Law. ***Email:*** mranelli@goodwin.com

JERI E. REUTENAUER, born New Haven, CT, 1970; admitted to bar, 2000, Connecticut; 2001, New York. *Education:* Quinnipiac University (B.A., cum laude, 1992; J.D., cum laude, 2000); Sarah Lawrence College (M.S., 1994). Managing Editor, Quinnipiac Law Review, 1999-2000. Author: "Medical Malpractice Liability in the Era of Genetic Susceptibility Testing," 19 Quinnipiac Law Review, 539 (2000). *Member:* American Bar Association (Member, Health Law Section, 1997—); American Society of Law, Medicine and Ethics. ***Email:*** jreutenauer@goodwin.com

JOSE M ROJAS, born Madrid, Spain, 1972; admitted to bar, 1997, Wisconsin; 1999, Connecticut. *Education:* Bentley College (B.S., 1994); Quinnipiac College (J.D., 1997). Recipient: American Jurisprudence Award in Criminal Law and Legal Writing. Lead Article's Editor, Connecticut Probate Law Journal. Special Assistant United States Attorney, 1998-2000. *Member:* Connecticut Bar Association. [U.S. Army, JAGC, 1997-2000]. ***LANGUAGES:*** Spanish. ***PRACTICE AREAS:*** Litigation; Criminal Law. ***Email:*** jrojas@goodwin.com

MORGAN P. RUECKERT, born Rochester, NY, 1970; admitted to bar, 1998, Connecticut and U.S. District Court, District of Connecticut; 1999, New York. *Education:* University of Connecticut (B.A., 1994; J.D., 1998). Phi Beta Kappa. New England Scholar; Golden Key National Honor Society. Recipient: The Honorable Joseph M. Blumenfeld Prize; The Ralph Colucci Award. [Sergeant, U.S. Marine Corps, 1989-1996]. ***PRACTICE AREAS:*** Litigation. ***Email:*** mrueckert@goodwin.com

ROBERT C. SCOTT, born Kingston, Jamaica, 1968; admitted to bar, 1998, Connecticut. *Education:* Drew University (B.A., 1989); University of Connecticut (J.D., 1998). *Member:* American Bar Association; National Association of Bond Lawyers. ***PRACTICE AREAS:*** Business Law; Public Finance; Banking Law; Corporate; Government Relations. ***Email:*** rscott@goodwin.com

STEPHEN M. SEDOR, born Rancocas, NJ, 1969; admitted to bar, 1995, Connecticut; 1996, New York; 1997, U.S. District Court, Northern District of New York; 2000, U.S. District Court, District of Connecticut. *Education:* Clarkson University (B.S., 1991); Quinnipiac College (J.D., 1995). Recipient: Distinguished Academic Achievement Award; American Jurisprudence Award, Labor Law. Business Managing Editor, Connecticut Probate Law Journal. ***PRACTICE AREAS:*** Employment Litigation; Litigation. ***Email:*** ssedor@goodwin.com

AMY E. SOUCHUNS, born Meriden, CT, 1974; admitted to bar, 1999, Connecticut; U.S. District Court, District of Connecticut. *Education:* College of the Holy Cross (B.A., 1996); Catholic University of America (J.D., cum laude, 1999). Delta Theta Phi. Note and Comment Editor, Catholic University Law Review, 1998-1999. Author: "Old Paint, New Laws: Achieving Effective Compliance with the Lead-Based Paint Hazard Reduction Act," 47 Catholic U. L. Rev. 1412, 1998; Volume 47, No. 4, Catholic University Law Review. Intern to the Honorable Alan H. Nevas, U.S. District Court, District of Connecticut, 1997. ***PRACTICE AREAS:*** Land Use; Environmental Law. ***Email:*** asouchuns@goodwin.com

KAREN THERESE STAIB, born Hartford, CT, 1972; admitted to bar, 1998, Connecticut. *Education:* Dartmouth College (B.A., with honors, 1994); University of Connecticut School of Law (J.D., with honors, 1998). Editor-in-Chief, Connecticut Insurance Law Journal, 1997-1998. Law Clerk to the Honorable Flemming L. Norcott, Jr., Connecticut Supreme Court, 1998-1999. Secretary, Board of Directors, University of Connecticut School of Law Alumni Association, 1998-1999. *Member:* Hartford County, Connecticut and American Bar Associations. ***PRACTICE AREAS:*** Intellectual Property. ***Email:*** kstaib@goodwin.com

KARA LAWSON VAN AUSDALL, born Hartford, CT, 1973; admitted to bar, 2000, Connecticut. *Education:* Providence College (B.A., summa cum laude, 1995); Boston College (J.D., 2000). Executive Editor, 1999-2000 and Member, 1998-1999, Boston College Third World Law Journal. ***PRACTICE AREAS:*** Litigation. ***Email:*** kvanausdall@goodwin.com

JENNIFER C. VICKERY, born Chicago, IL, 1964; admitted to bar, 2000, Connecticut. *Education:* Hampshire College (B.A., 1989); University of Massachusetts (M.A., 1994); Western New England College School of Law (J.D.,

(This Listing Continued)

(This Listing Continued)

SHIPMAN & GOODWIN LLP, Hartford—Continued

1999). Member, Independent Computer Consultant Association, 2000—. ***PRACTICE AREAS:*** Intellectual Property; Business Law. ***Email:*** jvickery@goodwin.com

MARIANNE MONTI WALLACE, born Waterbury, CT, 1972; admitted to bar, 1997, Connecticut. *Education:* Fairfield University (B.A., 1994); University of Connecticut at Hartford (J.D., 1997). ***LANGUAGES:*** Italian. ***PRACTICE AREAS:*** General Litigation; Commercial Litigation; Insurance Defense; Bankruptcy. ***Email:*** mwallace@goodwin.com

HENRY J. ZACCARDI, born Hartford, CT, 1956; admitted to bar, 1989, Connecticut. *Education:* Tufts University (B.A., 1979); Suffolk University Law School (J.D., cum laude, 1989). Recipient, American Jurisprudence Award in Advanced Tort Law. Member, Suffolk University Law Review, 1988-1989. ***PRACTICE AREAS:*** Labor and Employment. ***Email:*** hzaccardi@goodwin.com

OF COUNSEL

GEORGE C. JEPSEN, born Hattiesburg, MS, 1954; admitted to bar, 1982, Connecticut. *Education:* Dartmouth College (B.A., summa cum laude, 1976); Kennedy School of Government, Harvard University (M.P.P., 1982); Harvard Law School (J.D., cum laude, 1982). Phi Beta Kappa. Teaching Fellow, Constitutional Law, Harvard College, 1981. State Representative, Connecticut General Assembly, 1987-1991. State Senator, Connecticut General Assembly, 1991—; Co-Chairman, Judiciary Committee, 1993. (Stamford Office). ***LANGUAGES:*** French, Spanish and Chinese. ***PRACTICE AREAS:*** General Practice; Tax Law; Estate Planning. ***Email:*** gjepsen@goodwin.com

CHARLES B. MILLIKEN, born New Haven, CT, 1931; admitted to bar, 1957, Connecticut. *Education:* Yale University (B.A., 1952); Harvard University (J.D., 1957). Fellow: American College of Trust and Estate Counsel; American College of Tax Counsel. ***Email:*** cmilliken@goodwin.com

ROBERT L. ROSENSWEIG, born New Britain, CT, 1928; admitted to bar, 1952, Connecticut; 1953, New York. *Education:* Yale University (B.A., 1949); Fordham University (LL.B., cum laude, 1952). ***Email:*** rrosensweig@goodwin.com

Unless otherwise noted, all are members of The Hartford County, Connecticut and American Bar Associations.

REPRESENTATIVE CLIENTS: ATMI, Inc.; Aetna U.S. Healthcare Inc.; Agri-Mark, Inc.; American Home Assurance Co.; Anthem Blue Cross & Blue Shield of Connecticut, Connecticut Region Red Cross Blood Services; The American School for the Deaf; CIGNA; City of Hartford; Coltec Industries, Inc.; Connecticut Association of Independent Schools, Inc.; Connecticut Bankers Association; Connecticut Development Authority; Connecticut Health and Educational Facilities Authority; Connecticut Health System, Inc.; Connecticut Innovations, Inc.; Connecticut Institute for the Blind; Danbury Board of Education; Ensign-Bickford Industries, Inc.; Exxon; Federal Land Bank; Fleet National Bank; Gartner Group, Inc.; Green Mountain Partners, L.P.; The Hartford Club; Hartford Hospital; LEGO Systems, Inc.; The Merrow Machine Co.; Occupational Health & Rehabilitation, Inc.; Ogden Projects, Inc.; People's Bank; Shell Oil Co.; Stamford Board of Education; Stanadyne, Inc.; State Street Bank & Trust Co.; TransAct Technologies Incorporated; United Technologies Corp.; Yankee Energy System, Inc.

SIEGEL, O'CONNOR, SCHIFF & ZANGARI, P.C.

150 TRUMBULL STREET
HARTFORD, CONNECTICUT 06103
Telephone: 860-727-8900
Telecopier: 860-527-5131
Email: first initial last name @soszlaw.com
URL: http://www.soszlaw.com

New Haven, Connecticut Office: 171 Orange Street, P.O. Drawer 906. Telephone: 203-789-0001. Telecopier: 203-782-2766.

Labor Relations and Employment Law representing management in the private and public sectors, including related Litigation in Federal and State Courts, Tax Law, Education Law, Municipal Law, Commercial Law, Corporate Law, Estate Planning and Estate Administration Matters.

FIRM PROFILE: Siegel, O'Connor, Schiff & Zangari, P.C. is a Connecticut based law firm whose practice is exclusively dedicated to the representation of management in labor and employment matters and specialized business and tax representation.

CHRISTINE A. BARKER (Resident, New Haven, Connecticut Office).

JOHN W. BECK, born Providence, Rhode Island, May 16, 1954; admitted to bar, 1979, Connecticut. *Education:* Dartmouth College (B.A., cum laude, 1976); University of Connecticut (J.D., 1979); New York University (LL.M., 1980). Recipient, Bobbs-Merrill Award for Outstanding Achievement. *Member:* Connecticut and American Bar Associations. (Resident). ***PRACTICE AREAS:*** Real Estate Law; Business Law; Taxation Law; Low Income Tax Credits; Affordable Housing. ***Email:*** jbeck@soszlaw.com

GREGORY J. BEZZ, born New Britain, Connecticut, October 14, 1955; admitted to bar, 1980, Connecticut. *Education:* Rensselaer Polytechnic Institute (B.S., cum laude, 1977); University of Connecticut School of Law (J.D., 1980). *Member:* Connecticut and American Bar Associations. (Resident). ***PRACTICE AREAS:*** Business Law; Tax Law; Commercial Law. ***Email:*** gbezz@soszlaw.com

ROBERT F. COHN (Resident, New Haven, Connecticut Office).

HUGH W. CUTHBERTSON (Resident, New Haven, Connecticut Office).

FREDERICK L. DORSEY (Resident, New Haven, Connecticut Office).

GLENN A. DUHL, born New York, New York, April 2, 1961; admitted to bar, 1986, Louisiana, U.S. District Court, Eastern, Middle and Western Districts of Louisiana, U.S. Court of Appeals, Fifth Circuit; 1987, Connecticut and U.S. District Court, District of Connecticut; 1993, New York and U.S. District Court, Eastern and Southern Districts of New York; 1998, U.S. Court of Appeals, Second Circuit and U.S. Supreme Court. *Education:* Wesleyan University (B.A., 1983); Tulane University of Louisiana (J.D., 1986). *Top Ten Things Every Lawyer Should Know About Employment Law,* ABA Mtg., 7/00, 8/01, *FLSA Legislation Committee,* "2001 Report of the Subcommittee on Developments Under the ADEA," (2/01); Nat'l Business Institute, "Basic Wage and Hour Law in CT.," (1998, 1999); ALI-ABA, *The Practical Litigator,* Vol. 10, No. 6, Nov. 1999, "Conducting Sexual Harassment Investigations;" Council on Education in Management, *Personnel Law Update, 1999,* "How to Avoid the Devastation of Increasing Class Action Lawsuits and Disparate Impact Claims," (1999); CT Restaurant Ass'n., "Currect Issues in Wage & Hour Law," (3/00)); *Connecticut Labor and Employment Law,* "The Employment Agreement," 1995, rev. 2001. *Member:* Louisiana State, Connecticut (Former-Chair, Young Lawyers Section) and American (Member, Young Lawyers Division; Former Liaison to Labor and Employment Law Section) Bar Associations. (Resident). ***PRACTICE AREAS:*** Labor Law; Employment Law; Litigation; NASD Arbitration. ***Email:*** gduhl@soszlaw.com

NICHOLAS J. GRELLO, JR., born Bronx, New York, March 18, 1963; admitted to bar, 1989, Connecticut; 1990, New York, U.S. District Court, District of Connecticut and U.S. Court of Appeals, Second Circuit. *Education:* Boston University (B.A., cum laude, 1986; J.D., 1989). Co-Editor: "Connecticut Labor & Employment Law," 1995. Co-Author: "Connecticut Bar Association's Seventeenth Annual Survey: Connecticut Labor and Employment Law in 1995--Federal Labor Decisions," 1996. *Member:* Hartford County, Connecticut (Member, Labor and Employment Section), New York State and American (Member, Labor and Employment Section) Bar Associations; Connecticut School Attorneys Council (President, 2000-2001). (Resident). ***LANGUAGES:*** Spanish. ***PRACTICE AREAS:*** Labor Relations; Privacy Law; Public Sector Labor Relations; Employment Law; Education Law; Municipal Law; Litigation. ***Email:*** ngrello@soszlaw.com

PETER D. HERSHMAN (Resident, New Haven, Connecticut Office).

PETER A. JANUS, born Monza, Italy, February 25, 1946; admitted to bar, 1970, Connecticut; 1976, District of Columbia; 1977, U.S. District Court of Connecticut, U.S. Supreme Court and U.S. Court of Appeals, First Circuit; 1978, U.S. Court of Appeals, Second Circuit. *Education:* Cornell University (A.B., 1967); The Wharton School (M.B.A., 1974); Boston University (J.D., 1970). Co-Author: "NLRB Regulation of Election Conduct," 1974; "NLRB Remedies for Unfair Labor Practices," 1976. Contributing Editor and Assistant Editor, 1976-1996, and Associate Editor, 1997—, "The Developing Labor Law," Bureau of National Affairs. Co-Editor, "Connecticut Labor and Employment Law," 1995 and 1997 and 1998 Cumulative Supplements. Fellow, College of Labor and Employment Lawyers. Vice-Chairman, Greater Hartford YMCA Board of Managers, 1989-1992. Advisory Board, The Connecticut Law Tribune. President, Cornell University Alumni Federation, 1993-1995; Cornell University Council, 1990—. Member, The American Employment Law Council, 1996. *Member:* Connecticut (Member: Executive Committee, Labor and Employment Law Section; Education Law Committee) and American (Member: Labor and Employment Law Section; Committee on the Development of the Law Under the National Labor Relations Act, 1976—; Litigation Section) Bar Associations; District of Columbia Bar. (Resident). ***PRACTICE AREAS:*** Labor Law; Employment Law; Litigation; Education Law. ***Email:*** pjanus@soszlaw.com

GEORGE J. KELLY, JR. (Resident, New Haven, Connecticut Office).

RICHARD D. O'CONNOR, born Worcester, Massachusetts, October 22, 1937; admitted to bar, 1964, Connecticut and U.S. District Court, District of Connecticut; 1969, U.S. Court of Appeals, Second Circuit; 1971, District of Columbia; 1973, U.S. Supreme Court; 1974, U.S. Court of Appeals, District of Columbia Circuit; 1985, Massachusetts and U.S. District Court, District of Massachusetts; 1997, U.S. District Court, Southern and Eastern Districts of New York. *Education:* College of the Holy Cross (B.S., 1959); Georgetown University (LL.B., 1964). Phi Delta Phi. Co-Author: "An Analysis of the 'No Strike Clause' In Contemporary Collective Bargaining Agreements," 7 Western

(This Listing Continued)

New England Law Review 147, 1984. Law Clerk to Honorable T. Emmet Clarie, U.S. District Judge, District of Connecticut, 1964-1965. Member, Connecticut School Attorneys' Council, 1975—. Member, Magistrate Selection Committee, U.S. District Court, District of Connecticut, 1983-1990. Member, Governor's Panel for the Resolution of Educational Disputes, 1985-1997. *Member:* Hartford County, Connecticut (Member, 1969—and Chairman, 1977-1978, Labor and Employment Law Section; Member, Executive Committee, 1985-1989), Massachusetts (Member, Labor and Employment Law Section, 1985—) and American (Member: Labor and Employment Law Section, 1969—; Committee on International Labor Law, 1985—; Management Co-Chairman, 1991-1995; Section on Dispute Resolution, 1998—) Bar Associations; The Association of Trial Lawyers of America; American Association of Hospital Attorneys; Federal Bar Council; International Society for Labor Law and Social Security. [Lt., U.S. Navy, active duty, 1959-1961]. (Resident). ***PRACTICE AREAS:*** Labor Law; Litigation; Employment Law; Education Law. ***Email:*** roconnor@soszlaw.com

EDWARD F. O'DONNELL, JR., born Waterbury, Connecticut, May 13, 1950; admitted to bar, 1977, Connecticut; 1978, South Carolina; 1979, U.S. District Court, District of South Carolina; 1980, U.S. District Court, District of Connecticut, U.S. Court of Appeals, First Circuit and U.S. Court of Appeals, Second Circuit. *Education:* St. Anselm's College (B.A., 1972); University of Connecticut (J.D., 1977). *Member:* Connecticut and American (Member: Labor and Employment Law Section; Committee on Practice and Procedure under the National Labor Relations Act) Bar Associations; South Carolina Bar. (Resident). ***PRACTICE AREAS:*** Labor Law; Employment Law; Litigation. ***Email:*** eodonnell@soszlaw.com

ROBERT J. PERCY, born Port Chester, New York, June 19, 1945; admitted to bar, 1973, Connecticut; 1974, U.S Tax Court; 1986, U.S. District Court, District of Connecticut. *Education:* Rensselaer Polytechnic Institute (B.M.E., 1967); University of Connecticut (J.D., 1973). Tau Beta Pi. Adjunct Professor of Law, University of Hartford, 1996—. *Member:* Connecticut (Member, Executive Tax Committee, 1992—) and American Bar Associations. (Resident). ***PRACTICE AREAS:*** Taxation Law; Employee Benefit Law; Business Law; Criminal Tax Defense. ***Email:*** rpercy@soszlaw.com

DONALD W. STRICKLAND, born Springfield, Massachusetts, February 8, 1945; admitted to bar, 1973, Connecticut and U.S. District Court of Connecticut; 1978, U.S. Court of Appeals, Second Circuit; 1980, District of Columbia. *Education:* Marietta College (B.A., 1966); University of Connecticut (J.D., 1969). Elected Office: Town Moderator, Russell, Massachusetts, 1967-1969. Special Agent, FBI, U.S. Department of Justice, 1969-1973. President, 1977-1978 and Member, Executive Committee, 1977-1983, Connecticut School Attorneys Council. Adjunct Professor of Law, Sacred Heart University, Graduate School, 1994-1999. Contributing Editor, Conn. Labor and Employment Law, Law Trib. Pub., 1995. Director, Thorndike Pond Conservation Association, Jaffrey Center, N.H., 1995—; President, 2000—. Director, Glastonbury A Better Chance (ABC) House Foundation, 2001—. *Member:* Connecticut (Chairman, Labor and Employment Law Section, 1982; Member, Executive Committee, 1980-1988; Editor, "Annual Survey of Connecticut Labor Law Developments," 1979-1980) and American Bar Associations. (Resident). ***PRACTICE AREAS:*** Labor Law; Employment Law; Education Law; Municipal Law. ***Email:*** dstrickland@soszlaw.com

MARIO J. ZANGARI (Resident, New Haven, Connecticut Office).

OF COUNSEL

ROBERT W. BLYTHE (Resident, New Haven, Connecticut Office).

JAY S. SIEGEL, born New York, New York, August 14, 1929; admitted to bar, 1955, New York; 1956, Connecticut; 1958, U.S. District Court of Connecticut; 1959, U.S. Court of Appeals, Second Circuit and U.S. Supreme Court; 1967, U.S. Court of Appeals, First Circuit; 1971, District of Columbia and U.S. Court of Appeals, District of Columbia Circuit. *Education:* New York University (A.B., 1950; J.D., 1954). Fulbright Scholar, Japan Today Program, 1993-1994. Visiting Scholar, Harvard Law School, 1995-1996. Co-Editor: "The Developing Labor Law-The Board, The Courts and The National Labor Relations Act," Bureau of National Affairs, 1971. Columnist: Employment Law, National Law Journal, 1978-1982. Author: "Deferral to Arbitration Awards in Title VII Actions," Labor Law Journal, July, 1974; "Employers Evidentiary Burden in Suits under Title VII," Federal Bar Journal, September, 1981; "Changing Public Policy: Private Arbitration to Resolve Statutory Employment Disputes," The Labor Lawyer, Summer, 1997. Lecturer: Public Policy and Alternative Dispute Resolution (ADR), John F. Kennedy School of Government, Harvard University, 1992—. *Member:* The Connecticut (Chairman, Labor Law Section, 1961-1963) and American (Chairman, Labor and Employment Law Section, 1977-1978; Delegate, House of Delegates, 1980-1981) Bar Associations. (Resident). ***Email:*** jsieg14@aol.com

---

JODY PAGANO BENBOW (Resident, New Haven, Connecticut Office).

(This Listing Continued)

SHAWN P. COYNE, born Portland, Maine, October 20, 1970; admitted to bar, 1998, Massachusetts; 1999, Connecticut and U.S. District Court, District of Massachusetts. *Education:* University of New Hampshire (B.A., cum laude, 1993); Western New England College (J.D., 1998). *Member:* Hartford County, Connecticut and American Bar Associations. (Resident). ***PRACTICE AREAS:*** Labor Law; Employment Law; Municipal; Education; Immigration; Litigation. ***Email:*** scoyne@soszlaw.com

ANA ISABEL DEMOURA, born Montalegre, Portugal, October 15, 1970; admitted to bar, 1998, Connecticut; 1999, U.S. District Court, District of Connecticut. *Education:* Fairfield University (B.A., 1992); Western New England College (J.D., cum laude, 1998). Member, Western New England Law Review, 1996-1998. Law Clerk to Hon. Sidney Landau, Connecticut Appellate Court, 1998-1999. *Member:* Hartford County (Member, Education Committee, 2000), Connecticut and American Bar Associations; Oliver Ellsworth Inn of Court (Pupil, 1999-2000). (Resident). ***LANGUAGES:*** Spanish and Portuguese. ***PRACTICE AREAS:*** Employment Law; Litigation; Labor Law; Education Law. ***Email:*** ademoura@soszlaw.com

KEVIN J. DIADAMO (Resident, New Haven, Connecticut Office).

PAUL H. GAMACHE, born Quincy, Massachusetts, July 4, 1970; admitted to bar, 1995, Connecticut; 1996, U.S. District Court, District of Connecticut. *Education:* Tufts University (B.S., cum laude, 1992); University of Connecticut (J.D., honors, 1995). *Member:* Hartford County, Connecticut and American Bar Associations. (Resident). ***PRACTICE AREAS:*** Employment Litigation; Civil Rights Litigation; Commercial Litigation. ***Email:*** pgamache@soszlaw.com

DANIEL P. MURPHY (Resident, New Haven, Connecticut Office).

JOHN J. O'CONNELL, born Hartford, Connecticut, December 29, 1970; admitted to bar, 1998, Connecticut. *Education:* Fairfield University (B.A., 1993); Connecticut School of Law (J.D., 1997). Legal Aid, 1998—. *Member:* New Haven County, Connecticut and American Bar Association; Connecticut Trial Lawyers Association. ***PRACTICE AREAS:*** Employment; Labor; Litigation; Education; Business. ***Email:*** joconnell@soszlaw.com

REPRESENTATIVE CLIENTS: Accessory Controls & Equipment Corp.; Allan S. Goodman, Inc.; Anthem-Blue Cross/Blue Shield of Connecticut; Bristol Hospital; Brockway-Smith Company; C.I.A.C.; State of Ct. Judicial Dept.; Connecticut Lodging & Attraction Association; Connecticut Restaurant Association; Connecticut Tool & Manufacturing Association; Dana Corporation; Data-Mail, Inc.; Fordham Distributors; Franklin Distributors, Inc.; Hartford Distributors, Inc.; Hospital of St. Raphael; Kimberly-Clark Corp.; Kollmorgen Corp.; Madison Square Garden; Mechanics Uniform Services, Inc.; New Britain General Hospital; New London Board of Education; Rogers Corp.; Rogo Distributors; Unisource; Seviroli Foods, Inc.; Stanadyne Automotive Corp.; SuperValu; Wallingford Board of Ed.; Wild Oats Markets, Inc.; Woodstock Academy.

(For Biographical Data on Personnel at New Haven, see New Haven, Connecticut Professional Biographies).

LAW OFFICES OF ALAN B. SILVER, LLC

HARTFORD, CONNECTICUT

(See Wethersfield)

Bankruptcy, Business Law, Commercial Law, Real Estate, Personal Injury.

SILVER, GOLUB & TEITELL LLP

HARTFORD, CONNECTICUT

(See Stamford)

Trial Practice in all State and Federal Courts. Medical Malpractice, Negligence, Commercial Litigation, Family and Criminal Law.

SILVESTER & DALY

72 RUSS STREET

HARTFORD, CONNECTICUT 06106

Telephone: 860-278-2650
Fax: 860-727-9243

General Insurance Defense, Fire, Arson and Fraud Matters, Automobile Liability, Medical and Legal Malpractice Defense, Workers' Compensation, Construction Litigation, Labor Law and Relations, Personal Injury, Residential and Commercial Real Estate, Civil and Criminal Trials in all Courts.

EDWARD J. DALY, JR., born Hartford, Connecticut, January 11, 1929; admitted to bar, 1957, Connecticut. *Education:* Cornell University (B.A., 1950); University of Connecticut (LL.B., 1957). Assistant States Attorney, Hartford County, 1965-1969. Claims Commissioner, State of Connecticut, 1987-1991. Counsel to Oliver Ellsworth, Inn of Court. *Member:* Hartford County, Connecticut and American Bar Associations; American Board of Trial Advocates; National Association of Criminal Defense Lawyers.

(This Listing Continued)

SILVESTER & DALY, Hartford—Continued

ROBERT F. KAPPES, born 1968; admitted to bar, 1993, Connecticut; 1994, U.S. District Court, District of Connecticut; 1997, California. *Education:* St. Anselm College (B.A., 1990); New England School of Law (J.D., 1993). *Member:* Hartford County, Connecticut and American Bar Associations; State Bar of California. ***Email:*** Kappes@erols.com

OF COUNSEL

FRANK J. SZILAGYI, born Hartford, Connecticut, October 2, 1959; admitted to bar, 1990, Connecticut; 1991, U.S. District Court, District of Connecticut; 1993, U.S. Court of Appeals, Second Circuit. *Education:* University of Connecticut (B.S., 1981); Western New England College (J.D., 1990). Contributing Author: "Banking Law," 1989 and 1990, Cumulative Supplements, Matthew Bender and Company. President, Hungarian Club of Hartford, 1992-1996. *Member:* Hartford County, Connecticut and American Bar Associations; The Association of Trial Lawyers of America; Connecticut Trial Lawyers Association; Oliver Ellsworth Inn of Court. ***LANGUAGES:*** Hungarian. ***REPORTED CASES:*** Gaynor Elec. Co., Inc. v. Hollander, 618 A.2d 532 (Conn.App. 1993); Cruz v. Meachum, 159 F.R.D. 366 (D.Conn. 1994). Labbe v. Hartford Pension Comm., 682 A2d 490 (Conn.1996). ***Email:*** fjsesq@aol.com

REPRESENTATIVE CLIENTS: AON Services Group; Connecticut Medical Insurance Company; EMCOR Group, Inc.; Hartford Municipal Employees Association, Inc.; Hartford Police Union; PHICO Insurance Company; Reliance Insurance; R.W. Granger & Sons, Inc.; Semac Electrical Company, Inc.; SMS Financial II, LLC; The Hartford Steam Boiler and Inspection Company; The May Department Stores Company (including Filene's and Lord & Taylor); OKEE Industries, Inc.; Omar Coffee Company, Inc..

SKELLEY ROTTNER P.C.

Established in 1962

P.O. BOX 340890

HARTFORD, CONNECTICUT 06134-0890

Telephone: 860-561-7077

Telecopier: 860-561-7088

Email: postmaster@skelleyrottner.com

URL: http://www.skelleyrottner.com

Trials in all Courts. Casualty Insurance, Fire and Property Insurance, Insurance Fraud, Bad Faith and Unfair Insurance Practice Claims, Insurance Coverage, Plaintiff's Personal Injury Litigation, Professional Liability, Environmental Law, Liquor Liability, Products Liability and Toxic Tort Litigation, Subrogation and Recovery, Commercial Litigation.

JOSEPH F. SKELLEY, JR. (1927-1995).

JOEL J. ROTTNER, born Hartford, Connecticut, December 21, 1944; admitted to bar, 1973, Connecticut. *Education:* Wesleyan University (B.A., 1967); University of Connecticut (J.D., with honors, 1973). State Attorney Trial Referee. *Member:* Hartford County (Member, Executive Committee, Litigation Section), Connecticut and American (Member, Sections of: Tort and Insurance Practice; Litigation) Bar Associations; Connecticut Defense Lawyers Association; American Board of Trial Advocates; Defense Research Institute; International Association of Defense Counsel. ***PRACTICE AREAS:*** Products Liability and Toxic Torts; Property Insurance; Arson and Insurance Fraud; Insurance Coverage. ***Email:*** jrottner@skelleyrottner.com

SUSAN L. MILLER, born Brooklyn, New York, December 27, 1948; admitted to bar, 1983, Connecticut; 1984, U.S. District Court, District of Connecticut. *Education:* University of Connecticut (B.S., 1970); Southern Connecticut State College (M.S., 1973); Western New England College (J.D., cum laude, 1983). *Member:* Hartford County, Connecticut and American Bar Associations; Defense Research Institute; Connecticut Defense Lawyers Association (Board of Directors). ***PRACTICE AREAS:*** Insurance Defense Law; Products Liability Law; Plaintiff Personal Injury; Underinsured/Uninsured Motorist; Toxic Torts. ***Email:*** smiller@skelleyrottner.com

JAMES G. GEANURACOS, born Bridgeport, Connecticut, October 25, 1954; admitted to bar, 1983, Connecticut; 1984, U.S. District Court, District of Connecticut; 1986, U.S. Court of Appeals, Second Circuit; 1987, U.S. Supreme Court. *Education:* Columbia College (B.A., 1976); University of Connecticut (J.D., 1983). *Member:* Hartford County and Connecticut Bar Associations. ***PRACTICE AREAS:*** Personal Injury Law; Insurance Defense; Products Liability Law; Professional Liability; Workers Compensation Law. ***Email:*** jgeanuracos@skelleyrottner.com

RANDALL M. HAYES, born Washington, D.C., June 1, 1956; admitted to bar, 1983, Connecticut. *Education:* Hobart College (B.A., with honors in history, 1978); Western New England College (J.D., 1983). Member: Oliver Ellsworth Inn of Court, 1987-1992; Board of Managers, West Hartford YMCA, 1985-1992, Chairman of Board, 1990-1992. Board of Trustees, Metropolitan YMCA of Greater Hartford, 1992—. *Member:* Hartford County, Connecticut (Member, Committees on: Professional Ethics, 1985-1989; Alternative Methodist of Dispute Resolution, 1991-1993; and Computer Law, 1998-2000) and American (Member, Section of Law Practice Management) Bar Associations; Connecticut Defense Lawyers Association; Defense Research Institute. ***PRACTICE AREAS:*** Insurance Defense; Professional Liability; Municipal Liability. ***Email:*** rhayes@skelleyrottner.com

KIRBY G. HUGET, born Ann Arbor, Michigan, June 1, 1960; admitted to bar, 1985, Connecticut. *Education:* The Citadel (B.A., 1982); Western New England College (J.D., 1985). Staff Member, 1983-1984 and Articles Editor, 1984-1985, Western New England Law Review. Author: "Conflict of Laws —Tort Choice of Law Principles Applied to a Breach of Warranty Claim in Cohen v. McDonnell Douglas Corp., 389 Mass. 327, 450 N.E. 2d 581 (1983)," 7 W. New Eng. L. Rev. 95 (1985). Associate Editor, 1989-1995 and Editor-in-Chief, 1996-2000, The Defense, The Journal of the Connecticut Defense Lawyers Association. *Member:* Hartford County, Connecticut and American Bar Associations; Connecticut Defense Lawyers Association (Member, Board of Directors); Defense Research Institute. ***PRACTICE AREAS:*** Insurance Defense; Insurance Fraud; Liquor Liability Law; Products Liability Law; Wrongful Death Law. ***Email:*** khuget@skelleyrottner.com

MATTHEW DALLAS GORDON, born San Juan, Puerto Rico, March 22, 1956; admitted to bar, 1987, Connecticut; U.S. District Court, Southern District of New York; U.S. Supreme Court. *Education:* Bard College (B.A., 1980); University of Connecticut School of Law (J.D., 1987). Member, 1984-1987, and Managing Editor, 1996-1997, Connecticut Law Review. *Member:* Hartford County (Board of Directors, 1996—) Connecticut (Chairman, Commercial Law and Bankruptcy Law Section; Member, Young Lawyers Division, 1992-1993; Delegate, House of Delegates, 1992—) and American Bar Associations. ***PRACTICE AREAS:*** Insurance Defense Law; Commercial Litigation; Professional Liability; Municipal Liability. ***Email:*** mgordon@skelleyrottner.com

CARL F. YEICH, born Dayton, Ohio, March 27, 1956; admitted to bar, 1982, Connecticut and U.S. District Court, District of Connecticut; 1986, Pennsylvania; 1989, New York. *Education:* Johns Hopkins University (B.A., 1978); Cornell University (J.D., 1981). *Member:* Hartford County, Connecticut and American Bar Associations; Connecticut Defense Lawyers Association. ***PRACTICE AREAS:*** Property Insurance Law; Subrogation; Insurance Recovery; Casualty Defense; Arson and Insurance Fraud. ***Email:*** cyeich@skelleyrottner.com

LAURA ONDRUSH, born Manhattan, New York, November 26, 1956; admitted to bar, 1989, Connecticut. *Education:* Gettysburg College (B.S., 1978); Western New England College (J.D., 1988). *Member:* Hartford, Connecticut and American Bar Associations. ***PRACTICE AREAS:*** Insurance Defense Litigation; Personal Injury; Products Liability. ***Email:*** londrush@skelleyrottner.com

OF COUNSEL

SUSAN E. MALLIET, born Hartford, Connecticut, September 24, 1954; admitted to bar, 1979, Connecticut. *Education:* Vassar College (A.B., cum laude, 1976; Phi Beta Kappa); University of Connecticut (J.D., 1979). *Member:* Hartford County, The Connecticut and American Bar Associations; Connecticut Trial Lawyers Association. ***PRACTICE AREAS:*** Insurance Defense Litigation; Personal Injury; Professional Liability. ***Email:*** smalliet@skelleyrottner.com

REPRESENTATIVE CLIENTS: Allstate Insurance Co.; Amica Ins. Co.; Avis Rent A Car; Citicorp Life Insurance Company; CGU Insurance Co.; CNA Insurance Cos.; Colonial Farm Ins. Co.; Coregis Group; Crawford and Company; Hanover Insurance Co.; Interstate Insurance Co.; Liberty Mutual; The May Department Stores Company; Metropolitan Property and Casualty Insurance Co.; Middlesex Mutual Insurance Co.; Northland Insurance Co.; Peerless Insurance Co.; Preferred Mutual Insurance Co.; Stop and Shop Companies, Inc.; Travelers Property Casualty Co.; Underwriters at Lloyds; Vermont Mutual Insurance Co.; Worcester Insurance Co.; Zurich American Insurance Co.
REFERENCES: Fleet Bank and Liberty Bank.

SOEDER & ASSOCIATES, L.L.C.

241 ASYLUM STREET

SUITE 700

HARTFORD, CONNECTICUT 06103

Telephone: 860-246-1600

Fax: 860-246-1700

Email: lsoeder@soeder-associates.com

URL: http://www.soeder-associates.com

Municipal Finance, Business Development, Federal Tax Law.

LISA P. SOEDER, born Beacon, New York, 1958; admitted to bar, 1984, New York; 1986, Connecticut. *Education:* State University of New York at Oneonta (B.A., magna cum laude, 1980); University of Notre Dame (J.D., 1983); New York University (LL.M. in Taxation, 1988). Editor-in-Chief: Federal

(This Listing Continued)

Taxation of Municipal Bonds. Former Partner: Hawkins, Delfield & Wood, 1990-1996; Nixon, Peabody, LLP, 1996-2000. *Member:* Hartford County, New York State (Member, Taxation Section), Connecticut (Member, Taxation Section) and American (Member, Tax-Exempt Financing Section) Bar Associations; National Association of Bond Lawyers (Former Director; Former Steering Committee Member); American College of Bond Lawyers. ***PRACTICE AREAS:*** Municipal Finance; Tax; Business Development. ***Email:*** lsoeder@soeder-associates.com

OF COUNSEL

CHARLES D. KATZ, born New York, N.Y., March 13, 1959; admitted to bar, 1985, New York (Not admitted in Connecticut). *Education:* Union College (B.A., 1981); Fordham University (J.D., 1984). Member, International Law Journal. Recipient, American Jurisprudence Award in Decedents' Estates. Author: "Manhattan on Film: Walking Tours of Hollywood's Fabled Front Lot," Limelight Editions, January 2000; Note: "Recognizing the Need for International Exclusion of Pleasure Craft From Limitation of Liability Statutes," 6 Fordham International Law Journal 421, 1983. Former Associate: Hawkins, Delafield & Wood, 1986-1994; LeBoeuf, Lamb, Greene & Macrae LLP, 1994-1998. *Member:* American Bar Association; New York County Lawyers Association; National Association of Bond Lawyers. ***PRACTICE AREAS:*** Municipal Finance; Tax; Business Development. ***Email:*** cdkatz@soeder-associates.com

---

PAUL H. D. STOUGHTON

241 MAIN STREET
5TH FLOOR
HARTFORD, CONNECTICUT 06106
Telephone: 860-525-5529
Fax: 860-241-7744

Trials and Appeals. General Business Litigation, Negligence and Personal Injury, Probate Litigation, Labor and Employment Law.

PAUL H. D. STOUGHTON, born Hartford, Connecticut, December 20, 1959; admitted to bar, 1986, Connecticut; 1987, U.S. District Court, District of Connecticut; 1988, U.S. District Court, Southern District of New York and U.S. Court of Appeals, Second Circuit. *Education:* St. Lawrence University (B.A., cum laude, 1982); Hastings College of Law, University of California (J.D., 1986). Lecturer: Avoiding OSHA Citations and Liability. *Member:* Hartford County, Connecticut and American Bar Associations; The Association of Trial Lawyers of America; Connecticut Trial Lawyers Association. ***LANGUAGES:*** French. ***REPORTED CASES:*** Naftzger v. Naftzger & Kuhe, Inc. 602 A-2d 606 (1992).

SUMMA & RYAN, P.C.

HARTFORD, CONNECTICUT

(See Waterbury)

Management, Labor and Employment Law, Labor Relation, Equal Employment Opportunity.

TINLEY, NASTRI, RENEHAN & DOST, LLP

HARTFORD, CONNECTICUT

(See Waterbury)

Trial Practice in State and Federal Courts. Commercial Litigation, Bankruptcy, Employment Law, Personal Injury, Workers Compensation, Collections, Elder Law, Estate Planning, Probate.

TOBIN, CARBERRY, O'MALLEY, RILEY & SELINGER, P.C.

Established in 1963

3RD FLOOR, 330 MAIN STREET
HARTFORD, CONNECTICUT 06106
Telephone: 860-541-6438
Fax: 860-541-6484
Email: govrelations@tcors.com

New London, Connecticut Office: 43 Broad Street, P.O. Box 58, 06320. Telephone: 860-447-0335. Fax: 860-442-3469.

Government Relations, General Civil and Criminal Practice, Trials and Appeals in all Courts, Administrative Law, Banking and Commercial Law, Commercial Real Estate, Contract Law, Employment Law, Public Finance, Health Care Law, Land Use Law, Personal Injury, Product Liability, Estate Planning and Probate, Real Estate Law, Sports Law, Federal, State and Local Tax Law.

(This Listing Continued)

ROBERT D. TOBIN, born Boston, Massachusetts, September 15, 1942; admitted to bar, 1968, Connecticut; 1969, U.S. District Court, District of Connecticut and U.S. Court of Appeals, Second Circuit. *Education:* Boston College (B.A., cum laude, 1964; J.D., 1968). Author: "Teacher Negotiations Into the Seventies," 12 William & Mary Law Quarterly 711, 1971; "Section 9-103 and the Interstate Movement of Goods," Boston College Industrial and Commercial Law Review, Vol. IX, p. 72, 1968. Staff, Boston College Industrial and Commercial Law Review, 1967-1968. Lecturer, Preparation for Trial: From Opening the File Through Starting the Case," Connecticut Bar Association Seminar on Estate Practice, 1983. Member, Connecticut General Assembly, 37th District, 1975-1976. State of Connecticut Trial Referee, 1985—. *Member:* New London County (Member, Board of Directors, 1984-1985), The Connecticut and American Bar Associations; Connecticut Trial Lawyers Association; The Association of Trial Lawyers of America. ***REPORTED CASES:*** Simond v. Board of Education, 473 F.2d 988 (2d Cir. 1973); Sanderson v. Banigai, 690 F.2d 337 (2d Cir. 1982); Tinnerello and Sons, Inc. v. Town of Stonington, 141 F.3d 46 (2d Cir. 1998); In re: Election for Second Congressional Districts, 231 Conn. 602 (1994); Washington Trust Co. v. Smith, 42 Conn. App. 300 (1666), rev'd 241 Conn. 734 (1997). ***PRACTICE AREAS:*** Commercial Law; Litigation; Real Estate; Zoning; Administrative Law. ***Email:*** rdtobin@tcors.com

GLENN T. CARBERRY, born Norwich, Connecticut, January 29, 1955; admitted to bar, 1979, District of Columbia; 1982, Connecticut. *Education:* Gettysburg College (B.A., summa cum laude, 1976); University of Pennsylvania (J.D., 1979). Phi Beta Kappa. Comment Editor, University of Pennsylvania Law Review, 1978-1979. Recipient: Citizen of the Year, Eastern Connecticut Chamber of Commerce, 1995; Distinguished Service Award, Chamber of Commerce of Southeastern Connecticut, 1996. Author: "Laetrile: Statutory and Constitutional Limitations on the Regulation of Ineffective Drugs," 127 University of Pennsylvania Law Review 233, 1978; "Ex Parte Communications in Off-the-Record Administrative Proceedings: A Proposed Limitation on Judicial Innovation," 1980 Duke Law Journal, 130. Co-Author: "Government Contract Bidders Should be Permitted to Extend Short Bid Acceptance Periods," Public Contract Law Journal, Volume 13, No. 2, February, 1983; "Waiver of the Government's Right to Terminate for Default in Defense Contracts," Public Contract Law Journal, Vol. 17, No. 2, June 1988. Associate, Hogan & Hartson, Washington, D.C., 1979-1982. Candidate, United States House of Representatives, 1988 and 1992. *Member:* New London County, Connecticut and American Bar Associations. ***SPECIAL AGENCIES:*** Connecticut Development Authority; Connecticut Department of Public Utility Control. ***PRACTICE AREAS:*** Banking Law; Corporate Law; Land Use; Administrative Law; Telecommunications Law. ***Email:*** gtcarberry@tcors.com

JOSEPH J. SELINGER, JR., born Rockville Center, New York, March 10, 1952; admitted to bar, 1978, Connecticut. *Education:* Amherst College (B.A., 1974); University of Connecticut (J.D., 1978). Member, National Moot Court Team, 1978. Author: "The Use of Real Estate Rehabilitation Credits by Limited Partnership," The Journal of Real Estate Taxation, Winter, 1983; "TEFRA: High Bracket Tax Payers in the Wake of the AMT," Connecticut Law Tribune, October, 1982. Co-Author: "How to Negotiate PCTV Agreements," Private Cable, March/April 1984; "Napoletano vs. Cigna: An Evolving Standard of MCO Legal Compliance?" Connecticut Medicine, The Journal of the Connecticut State Medical Society, 1996. Lecturer: "Evaluating Client Suitability for a Real Estate Limited Partnership Investment," Connecticut Bar Association Annual Tax Planning Institute, 1985; "Tax Treatment of Vacation Homes," National Institute of Real Estate Taxation, Washington, D.C., 1989; "Annual Survey of Connecticut Law: Current Developments in Business and Banking," Section on Corporations and Other Business Organizations, Connecticut Bar Association, 1991; "Risks and Benefits of Medicaid Managed Care to Long Term Care Providers," Health Care Financial Management Association, 1995; "Legal Issues Update Medicaid Managed Care," Health Care Financial Management Association and Connecticut Health Lawyers Association, 1996; "Choice of Business Entity in Connecticut: How to do it Right," National Business Institute, 1998. State of Connecticut Small Claims Court Commissioner, 1989-1995. Member, State of Connecticut Law Review Commission, 1997. *Member:* Connecticut and American Bar Associations; American Bankruptcy Institute; National Association of Health Care Lawyers; National Association of Bond Lawyers. ***PRACTICE AREAS:*** Corporate Finance; Securities Law; Health Care Law; Public Finance. ***Email:*** jjselinger@tcors.com

LEGAL SUPPORT PERSONNEL

ALAN J. DECKMAN. *Education:* Assumption College (B.S., 1993); Suffolk University (M.P.A., 1995). *Member:* American Society of Public Administrators; American College of Healthcare Executives. ***Email:*** ajdeckman@tcors.com

JAMES P. LEAHY, born Milford, Connecticut, April 27, 1962. *Education:* Brandeis University (B.A., 1985). *Areas of Responsibility:* Government Relations.

(For complete biographical data on all personnel, See Professional Biograhies at New London, Connecticut)

TYLER COOPER & ALCORN, LLP

Established in 1847

CITYPLACE

HARTFORD, CONNECTICUT 06103-3488

Telephone: 860-725-6200

Telecopier: 860-278-3802

URL: http://www.tylercooper.com

New Haven, Connecticut Office: 205 Church Street. Telephone: 203-784-8200. Telecopier: 203-789-2133.

Stamford, Connecticut Office: One Landmark Square. Telephone: 203-348-5555. Telecopier: 203-348-3875.

Greenwich, Connecticut Office: 675 Steamboat Road. Telephone: 203-869-2000. Telecopier: 203-869-2001.

Madison, Connecticut Office: 23 Woodland Road. Telephone: 203-318-3600. Telecopier: 203-218-3609.

Administrative Law, Alternative Dispute Resolution, Antitrust and Trade Regulation, Banking, Bankruptcy and Reorganization, Business Crimes, Business Organizations and Securities Law, Computer Law, Domestic Relations, Environmental Law, Financial Services, Franchising, Health Care, Immigration, Insurance Defense and Insurance Coverage Defense, Intellectual Property, Labor and Employment, Legislative Lawyering, Litigation, Media Law, Medical Malpractice Defense, Pension and Employee Benefits, Public Utilities, Real Estate, Taxation, Trusts and Estates and Workers' Compensation.

MEMBERS OF FIRM

RALPH GREGORY ELLIOT, born Hartford, Connecticut, October 20, 1936; admitted to bar, 1961, Connecticut. *Education:* Yale University (B.A., 1958; LL.B., 1961). Phi Beta Kappa. Law Clerk to Justice William J. Shea, Connecticut Supreme Court, 1961-1962. Adjunct Professor of Law, University of Connecticut School of Law, 1973—. Member, State Criminal Justice Commission, 1991-1995. Town Counsel, Town of Salisbury, 1981—. Chairman, Connecticut Legal Specialization Screening Committee, 1981—. Chairman, U.S. District Court Panel of Special Masters, 1983-1988. Connecticut Superior Court Trial Referee, 1984-1995. Co-Chairman, United States Constitution Bicentennial Commission of Connecticut, 1986-1991. Chairman, Board of Editors, Connecticut Law Tribune, 1986-1987. President, 1988-1990, and Chairman, Executive Committee, 1990-1992, Yale Law School Association. Chairman, Health Insurance Law Committee, Tort and Insurance Practice Section, 1985-1986, Member, Standing Committee on Ethics and Professional Responsibility, 1989-1995, Standing Committee on Amicus Curiae Briefs, 1996-1998 and Standing Committee on Professional Discipline, 1998—, American Bar Association. President, Connecticut Bar Association, 1985-1986. *Member:* American Law Institute. Fellow, American Bar Foundation. ***PRACTICE AREAS:*** Litigation; Constitutional Law; Media Law; Municipal; Legal Ethics.

LEWIS SEGAL, born New York, N.Y., April 26, 1935; admitted to bar, 1960, Connecticut. *Education:* Columbia University (A.B., 1956); Yale University (LL.B., 1959). Chief Executive Officer, Century Brass Products, Inc., 1981-1987. ***PRACTICE AREAS:*** Business Law; Corporate Finance; Commercial Finance; Mergers and Acquisitions. ***Email:*** segal@tylercooper.com

WILLIAM H. CHAMPLIN III, born Hartford, Connecticut, December 25, 1946; admitted to bar, 1972, Connecticut. *Education:* Georgetown University (B.S.F.S., 1968); University of Connecticut (M.B.A., 1975; J.D., 1972). Law Clerk to Justice Alva P. Loiselle, Connecticut Supreme Court, 1972-1973. ***PRACTICE AREAS:*** Litigation, Alternative Dispute Resolution. ***Email:*** champlin@tylercooper.com

ROBERT J. METZLER II, born Allentown, Pennsylvania, February 5, 1948; admitted to bar, 1974, New York; 1976, Connecticut. *Education:* Princeton University (A.B., 1970); University of Connecticut (J.D., 1973); New York University. Law Clerk to Judge Thomas J. Meskill, U.S. Court of Appeals, Second Circuit, 1975-1976. Chairman, Public Utility Law Section, Connecticut Bar Association, 1981-1984. Fellow, American College of Investment Counsel. ***PRACTICE AREAS:*** Corporate, Public Utilities, Business Finance. ***Email:*** metzler@tylercooper.com

WILLIAM W. BOUTON III, born Glen Cove, New York, March 14, 1953; admitted to bar, 1980, Connecticut. *Education:* Ohio Wesleyan University (B.A., 1976); University of Connecticut (J.D., 1980). Pi Sigma Alpha. ***PRACTICE AREAS:*** Banking, Corporate, Securities. ***Email:*** bouton@tylercooper.com

THOMAS C. CLARK, born Randolph, Vermont, September 3, 1942; admitted to bar, 1969, Connecticut; 1970, U.S. District Court, District of Connecticut. *Education:* Dartmouth College (B.A., 1964); Cornell University (J.D., 1969). Chancellor, Moot Court Board, 1968-1969. State Representative, 1975-1977. House Counsel, Connecticut General Assembly, 1977-1979; 1981-1983. Clerk, Connecticut House of Representatives, 1979-1981. Chairman: Connecticut Committee on Alternate Methods of Sentencing 1977-1978; Board of Protection and Advocacy for Handicapped. *Member:* Hartford County, Connecticut

(This Listing Continued)

and American Bar Associations. ***PRACTICE AREAS:*** Insurance Coverage Litigation; Civil Litigation; Bad Faith; E-Commerce; Franchise Law. ***Email:*** clarkt@tylercooper.com

MARK V. CONNOLLY, born Danbury, Connecticut, January 3, 1957; admitted to bar, 1982, Connecticut; 1983, New York. *Education:* University of Connecticut (B.A., 1979; J.D., 1982). Phi Beta Kappa. Member, 1980-1981, and Administrative Editor, 1981-1982, Connecticut Law Review. ***PRACTICE AREAS:*** Litigation. ***Email:*** connolly@tylercooper.com

WILLIAM S. FISH, JR., born Manhasset, New York, May 20, 1958; admitted to bar, 1983, Connecticut. *Education:* State University of New York at Buffalo (B.A., 1980); University of Virginia (J.D., 1983). Phi Beta Kappa. Adjunct Professor of Law, University of Connecticut School of Law. Member, Executive Committee, Commercial Law and Bankruptcy Section, Connecticut Bar Association. *Member:* American Bankruptcy Institute. ***PRACTICE AREAS:*** Bankruptcy and Creditors' Rights; Commercial Litigation. ***Email:*** fish@tylercooper.com

KEVIN McCANN, born Roslyn Park, New York, March 8, 1954; admitted to bar, 1983, Connecticut. *Education:* Furman University (B.A., 1976); College of William & Mary (J.D., 1983); Boston University (LL.M., Taxation, 1994). Member, Board of Editors, William & Mary Law Review, 1982-1983. Director, Connecticut Breast Cancer Coalition. ***PRACTICE AREAS:*** Estate Planning; Trusts and Estates; Elder Law; Retirement Planning. ***Email:*** mccann@tylercooper.com

DAVID J. WIESE, born New Britain, Connecticut, January 13, 1958; admitted to bar, 1984, Connecticut. *Education:* Boston College (B.S., 1980); Syracuse University (M.B.A., 1983; J.D., 1983). Member, 1981-1982, and Notes and Comments Editor, 1982-1983, Syracuse Journal of International Law and Commerce. Director, Bank Compliance Association of Connecticut, 1989-1993. Chairman, Consumer Law Section, Connecticut Bar Association, 1991-1994. Instructor, Connecticut School of Finance and Management. ***PRACTICE AREAS:*** Banking; Regulatory Compliance; Corporate. ***Email:*** wiese@tylercooper.com

FILLIS W. STOBER, born Hartford, Connecticut, October 20, 1949; admitted to bar, 1979, Connecticut. *Education:* University of Connecticut (B.A., 1971; J.D., 1979). Phi Beta Kappa. Member, Executive Committee, Banking Law Section, Connecticut Bar Association, 1985—. Secretary, Consumer Law Section, Connecticut Bar Association, 1994—. ***PRACTICE AREAS:*** Bank Regulation; E-Commerce; ATM Networks; Bank Collections; Bank Fraud; Check Fraud; Credit Union Law; Electronic Banking; Escrow Agent Liability; Truth in Lending. ***Email:*** stober@tylercooper.com

THOMAS S. MARRION, born New London, Connecticut, December 17, 1960; admitted to bar, 1985, Connecticut. *Education:* College of the Holy Cross (A.B., 1982); University of Connecticut (J.D., 1985). Member, 1983-1984, and Associate Editor, 1984-1985, Connecticut Law Review. Law Clerk to Chief Judge Robert L. Krechevsky, U.S. Bankruptcy Court, District of Connecticut, 1985-1987. Instructor, Creditors' Rights and Bankruptcy, University of Connecticut School of Law, 1992—. Member: Bolton Zoning Commission, 1989-1991, 1992-1993; Bolton Charter Revision Commission, 1988, 1992-1993. Member, Executive Committee, Commercial Law and Bankruptcy Section, Connecticut Bar Association, 1994—. ***PRACTICE AREAS:*** Corporate Law; Commercial Finance; Creditors Rights in Bankruptcy; Municipal Law; Health Care; Real Estate. ***Email:*** marrion@tylercooper.com

KEVIN G. FERRIGNO, born Hartford, Connecticut, June 15, 1962; admitted to bar, 1989, Connecticut. *Education:* Union College (B.S., Chemistry, 1984); Western New England College School of Law; University of Connecticut (J.D., 1989). Member, 1993-1999 and Chairman, 1999—, Connecticut Historical Commission. Chairman, St. James Board of Education, 1999—. ***PRACTICE AREAS:*** Corporate Law; Real Estate; Environmental Law; Commercial Law; Mergers and Acquisitions. ***Email:*** ferrigno@tylercooper.com

WILLIAM F. CUMMINGS, born Buffalo, New York, May 23, 1963; admitted to bar, 1988, Pennsylvania; 1990, New York; 1992, Connecticut. *Education:* Fordham University; State University of New York at Buffalo (B.S., 1985; M.B.A., 1988; J.D., 1988). ***PRACTICE AREAS:*** Corporate; Banking; Securities; Investments. ***Email:*** cummings@tylercooper.com

GLORY MARTYN LENA, born Bryn Mawr, Pennsylvania, May 29, 1966; admitted to bar, 1991, Connecticut. *Education:* Dartmouth College (B.A., 1988); Boston University (J.D., 1991). Member, 1989-1990, and Editor, 1990-1991, Boston University Law Review. ***PRACTICE AREAS:*** Civil Litigation; Products Liability; Medical Malpractice Defense; Appellate Practice. ***Email:*** lena@tylercooper.com

OF COUNSEL

WILLIAM S. ROGERS, born Hartford, Connecticut, July 1, 1932; admitted to bar, 1960, Connecticut. *Education:* Boston University School of Management (B.S., 1954); University of Connecticut (J.D., 1960). Member, Board of Editors, University of Connecticut Law Review, 1959-1960. Town Counsel, Town of Glastonbury, 1976—. Member, Securities Advisory Council, Connecti-

(This Listing Continued)

cut Department of Banking, 1993—. Securities Arbitrator, NYSE, NASD and AAA. Faculty Member, Broker-Dealer Institute, PLI, 1991. Panel Member, Securities Forum 1991 and 1994, Connecticut Department of Banking. Special Master, U.S. District Court, 1986-1988. Chairman, Municipal Law and Governmental Services Committee, 1983-1986, Judiciary Committee, 1985-1991, Connecticut Bar Association. [Pilot, U.S. Air Force, 1954-1957]. ***PRACTICE AREAS:*** Securities Law, Litigation and Regulation; Municipal Law and Litigation; Administrative Law and Litigation; Appellate Practice.

ROGER E. KOONTZ, born Quincy, Illinois, May 21, 1940; admitted to bar, 1965, Connecticut. *Education:* University of Illinois (B.S., 1962); Yale University (J.D., 1965). ***PRACTICE AREAS:*** Public Utility; Administrative Law; Energy Law. ***Email:*** koontz@tylercooper.com

COUNSEL

KURT W. JOHNSON, born New Britain, Connecticut, July 8, 1941; admitted to bar, 1972, Connecticut. *Education:* University of Connecticut (B.A., 1964; J.D., 1972). Vice President and Group Counsel, Asea Brown Boveri Inc., 1972-1991. *Member:* Connecticut Power and Energy Society. [Lieut., U.S. Army, 1964-1966]. ***PRACTICE AREAS:*** Independent Power Production and Cogeneration; Corporate; Environmental Law; International Law; Real Estate Law. ***Email:*** johnson@tylercooper.com

BARRY M. WINNICK, born New Haven, Connecticut, June 30, 1962; admitted to bar, 1987, Connecticut. *Education:* Tufts University (B.A., 1984); Syracuse University College of Law (J.D., 1987). ***PRACTICE AREAS:*** Commercial Litigation; Collections; Foreclosures; Municipal Law. ***Email:*** winnick@tylercooper.com

RESIDENT ASSOCIATES

JAMES R. BYRNE, born New York, N.Y., February 28, 1969; admitted to bar, 1994, Connecticut; 1995, U.S. District Court, District of Connecticut and Massachusetts. *Education:* Boston University (B.A., magna cum laude, 1990); University of Connecticut (J.D., 1994). *Member:* Connecticut Bar Association. ***PRACTICE AREAS:*** Commercial Litigation. ***Email:*** byrne@tylercooper.com

CHRISTOPHER MARKHAM HADDAD, born Washington, D.C. April 10, 1969; admitted to bar, 1995, Connecticut. *Education:* University of Virginia (B.A., 1991); University of Connecticut (J.D., 1995). *Member:* American Health Lawyers Association. ***Email:*** haddad@tylercooper.com

MICHAEL T. McCORMACK, born Westchester, Pennsylvania, May 12, 1967; admitted to bar, 1993, Connecticut. *Education:* Providence College (B.S., 1989); Catholic University of America (J.D., 1992). Editor, The Journal of Contemporary Health Law and Policy, 1991-1992. Family Law, 1992. Law Clerk to the Honorable Fred B. Ugast, Chief Judge of the Superior Court of the District of Columbia, 1992-1993. ***Email:*** mmccormack@tylercooper.com

CAROL L. LOOMIS, born Drexel Hill, Pennsylvania, December 30, 1954; admitted to bar, 1997, Connecticut. *Education:* Mount Holyoke College (B.A., 1977); University of Connecticut Law School (J.D., 1997). Member, 1995-1996 and Executive Editor, 1996-1997, Connecticut Law Review. Law Clerk to Associate Justice, Honorable Richard N. Palmer, Connecticut Supreme Court, 1997-1998. ***Email:*** loomis@tylercooper.com

ELIZABETH M. SMITH, born Buffalo, New York, November 25, 1960; admitted to bar, 1998, Connecticut. *Education:* Mississippi State University (B.S., 1982); The University of Connecticut (M.B.A., 1998); The University of Connecticut School of Law (J.D., 1998). ***Email:*** smithe@tylercooper.com

SUSAN E. TAYLOR, born Portland, Maine, January 17, 1971; admitted to bar, 1999, Connecticut. *Education:* University of Maine (B.S., 1993); Quinnipiac School of Law (J.D., 1999). ***Email:*** taylor@tylercooper.com

ELIZABETH K. ANDREWS, born Buffalo, New York, May 19, 1973; admitted to bar, 1999, Connecticut. *Education:* State University of New York at Buffalo (B.S., 1995); Case Western Reserve University School of Law (J.D., 1999). ***Email:*** eandrews@tylercooper.com

PAUL GUGGINA, born Cambridge, Massachusetts, October 4, 1965; admitted to bar, 2001, Connecticut. *Education:* Southern Illinois University (B.S., 1989); Boston College School of Law (J.D., 2001). ***Email:*** pguggina@tylercooper.com

All Partners and Associates are Members of the Connecticut and American Bar Associations

REPRESENTATIVE CLIENTS: Fleet National Bank; The Hartford Courant Co.; Hospital of St. Raphael; Science Park Development Corp.; The Stanley Works; Town of Salisbury; Town of Woodstock; Yale-New Haven Hospital, Inc.; Gaylord Hospital; Connecticut American Water Co.; The Southern Connecticut Gas Co.; Connecticut Energy Corporation; Birmingham Utilities; Southern New England Telephone Co.; American Society of Composers, Authors and Publishers (ASCAP); Asea Brown Boveri Inc.; Honeywell, Inc.; Kraft General Foods, Inc.; Prudential Securities, Inc.; Sears, Roebuck & Co.; The Travelers Companies; Town of Guilford; Connecticut Bankers Association; Horton Medical Center; New Britain Transportation Corp.; Westfield Corporation, Inc.; Philip Morris Incorporated; Mechanics Savings Bank; Webster Bank; Norwalk Savings Society; Farmington Savings Bank; Union Savings Bank; First Union National Bank; Prudential Insurance Company.

(For all personnel, see Professional Biographies at New Haven)

UPDIKE, KELLY & SPELLACY, P.C.

Established in 1967

ONE STATE STREET
P.O. BOX 231277
HARTFORD, CONNECTICUT 06123-1277
Telephone: 860-548-2600
Cable Address: "Ukslaw."
Fax: 860-548-2680
Email: Info@uks.com
URL: http://www.uks.com

New Haven, Connecticut Office: 265 Church Street, 10th Floor. Telephone: 860-786-8300. Fax: 203-772-2037.

Stamford, Connecticut Office: 6 Landmark Square, Fourth Floor. Telephone: 203-359-5749. Fax: 203-359-5858.

Administrative Law, Appellate Law, Brownfields Redevelopment, Business Law, Commercial Lending and Banking, Commercial Litigation, Complex Litigation, Creditors' Rights and Bankruptcy, Criminal, Design/Construction Law, Electronic Commerce Law, Employment Based Immigration Law, Environmental Law, Franchise Law, Human Service Law, Insurance Coverage Defense, Insurance Defense Law, Labor and Employment Law, Legislative Representation, Personal Law, Probate Law, Product Liability Law, Professional Defense Law, Public Finance/Public Law, Real Estate Law, Taxation, Trusts and Estates and Utilities Law.

LAW FIRM ALLIANCES/ASSOCIATIONS: **COMMERCIAL LAW AFFILIATES (CLA)**

STUART N. UPDIKE (1904-1983).

PETER G. KELLY, born Hartford, CT, June 30, 1937; admitted to bar, 1962, CT; 1963, NY; 1981, DC. *Education:* Georgetown Univ. (B.S., magna cum laude, 1959); Yale Law School (J.D., 1962). Phi Beta Kappa; Alpha Sigma Nu; Phi Delta Phi. Member, Board of Editors, Yale Law Journal, 1960-1962. Author: "Reconsideration of Subrogative Rights of Miller Act Payment Bond Surety," 71 Yale Law Journal 1274, 1962. Chairman, Charter Revision Commission, City of Hartford, 1967. Member: Board of Governors, 1970-1973; Senate, 1973—, Georgetown Univ. Alumni Assn., Washington, D.C. Member, Board of Directors, 1970-1983 and Vice Chairman, 1975-1983, Greater Hartford Process, Inc. Trustee, 1972-1984, Exec. Comm., 1977-1980, CT Public Television. Member, Board of Directors, 1973-1980 and Chairman, 1974-1977, The Greater Hartford Convention and Visitors Bureau. Co-Chairman, 1983-1995 and Director, 1983—, Nat'l. Conf. of Christians and Jews (Western New England). Member, Board of Regents, Georgetown Univ. 1973-1980; Emeritus, 1981—. Member, Board of Directors, 1975-1982, Secy. and Member, Exec. Comm., 1975-1980, Greater Hartford Arts Council. Member, Board of Directors: Greater Hartford Leadership Program, 1983-1992; St. Francis Hosp. Assn., Inc., 1978-1983. Trustee, 1979-1988 and Member, Nat'l. Board of Governors, 1988-1997, Inst. of Living. Director 1979-1983 and Treas., 1981-1983, Amer. Political Found. Member and Treas., Exec. Board, The Democracy Program, 1983-1984. Director, 1984-1999; and Treas. 1987-1991, Nat'l. Democratic Inst. for Int'l. Affairs. Public Member, Pennsylvania Avenue Development Corp., 1981-1986. Director and Chairman, The Center for Democracy (Washington, D.C.), 1985-1997. Member, Board of Directors, Holy Apostles College and Seminary, 1985—. Director: St. Francis Hospital and Medical Center, 1992—; Director, St. Francis *Care* Inc., 1997—. Member, Board of Trustees, The CNA Corporation (Center for Naval Analysis), 1992—. Member, Exec. Comm., Yale Law School Assn., 1994-1997. Member, Board of Directors, The Nat'l. Symphony Orchestra, 1994-1996. Director, International Foundation for Electoral Systems, 1995—. Member, 1976-1992, Nat'l. Treas., 1979-1981 and Nat'l. Finance Chairman, 1981-1985, Democratic Nat'l. Comm. Finance Co-Chairman, Democratic Congressional Campaign Committee, 1989-1991. Chairman, Metro Hartford Chamber of Commerce, 1999-2001. Director, U.S. Chamber of Commerce, 1999—. Member, Advisory Board, Connecticut Inner City Business Strategy Initiative, 1999—. Member, Board of Directors, Gore 2000, 1999-2000. President and Director, Saint Francis Hospital Foundation, 1999—. Member, Board of Regents, University of Hartford, 1999—. Director, Capitol Region Growth Council, 1999—. Member, International Advisory Board, Geneva Centre for Democratic Control of Armed Forces, 2000—. Recipient: 1990 John Carroll Award, Georgetown Univ.; Yale Law School Assn. Distinguished Service Award, 1983; The National Conference Human Rights Award, 1991. *Member:* NY State Bar Assn.; Bar Assn. of the District of Columbia. ***PRACTICE AREAS:*** Business Law; Design/Construction; Legislative Representation; Professional Defense. ***Email:*** pgkone@aol.com

BOURKE G. SPELLACY, born Hartford, CT, May 23, 1937; admitted to bar, 1961, CT. *Education:* Princeton Univ. (A.B., cum laude, 1958); Yale Law School (J.D., 1961). Asst. Corp. Counsel, City of Hartford, 1964-1965. Asst.

(This Listing Continued)

UPDIKE, KELLY & SPELLACY, P.C., Hartford—Continued

Counsel, 1966-1973 and General Counsel, 1977—, The Metropolitan District, Hartford County. Member, Commission on Creation of Judicial Districts, State of CT, 1965. Member, Board of Directors: Symphony Society of Greater Hartford, 1968-1974; The Hartford Ballet, Inc., 1978-1982, Honorary Trustee, 1983—. Member, Board of Directors, 1978-1993, Vice Chairman, 1981 and Chairman, 1987, CT Law Revision Commission. Member, Board of Directors and Secy., Greater Hartford Arts Council, 1981-1993. *Member:* Amer. Judicature Soc. ***PRACTICE AREAS:*** Administrative Law; Appellate Law; Business Law; Commercial Litigation; Legislative Representation; Personal Law; Professional Defense; Taxation. ***Email:*** bspellacy@uks.com

THOMAS J. SHORTELL (1942-1997).

THOMAS W. DEMILLE, born Boston, MA, October 9, 1938; admitted to bar, 1969, CT. *Education:* Northeastern Univ. (B.S., magna cum laude, 1961); Univ. of Connecticut (J.D., cum laude, 1969). Editor, CT Law Review, 1968-1969. Member, Board of Editors, The CT Bar Journal, 1977-1982. Member, Board of Directors, 1976-1981 and Chairman, 1977-1980, Hartford Chamber Orchestra. Member, Glastonbury Fine Arts Commission, 1977-1978. Member, Board of Directors, 1978; V.P., 1978-1981, CT Advocates for the Arts. Elector, Wadsworth Atheneum 1978-1986. Trustee and V.P., Wethersfield Preservation Trust, 1980—. Director and V.P., 1983 and Pres., 1984-1987, Wethersfield Historical Society. Member, 1977-1978 and V.P., 1983, Greater Hartford Leadership Program. Member, Wethersfield Affordable Housing Task Force, 1985-1986. CT State Chairman, Govt. Affairs Committee of the Intl. Council of Shopping Centers, 1985-1994. Member, Wethersfield Economic Develop. Commission, 1987-1991. Town Attorney, Town of Wethersfield, 1989-1994. Chairman, State Issues Committee, Intl. Council of Shopping Centers, 1994—. Member, Internet Task Force, 1999—. ***PRACTICE AREAS:*** Real Estate. ***Email:*** tdemille@uks.com

PAUL L. McCORMICK, born Hartford, CT, August 21, 1940; admitted to bar, 1965, CT; 1977, U.S. Tax Court. *Education:* Brown Univ. (A.B., 1962); Harvard Univ. (J.D., 1965). Adjunct Professor of Law, Univ. of Bridgeport, 1985-1986. Member, Board of Directors, Family Service Society, 1979-1980. Member, Board of Directors, Visiting Nurse and Home Care, Inc., 1980-1985. Trustee, CT Opera Assn., Inc., 1983-1992. Member, Executive Committee, Board of Directors, Mark Twain Memorial, 1991-1998. Member, Charter Revision Commission, Town of Bloomfield, 1980-1981. Member, Fair Rent Commission, Town of Bloomfield, 1980-1983. Alternate Member, 1982-1985, Member, 1985-1987 and Chairman, 1988-1991, Zoning Board of Appeals, Town of Bloomfield. Vice Chairman, 1983-1985, and Chairman, 1985-1987, Inland Wetlands Commission, Town of Bloomfield. Chairman, Town of Bloomfield Housing Authority, 1997—. ***PRACTICE AREAS:*** Business Law; Taxation; Trusts and Estates; Probate. ***Email:*** pmccormick@uks.com

JAMES H. LLOYD, III, born Philadelphia, PA, October 20, 1943; admitted to bar, 1973, CT. *Education:* Princeton Univ. (A.B., cum laude, 1965); Univ. of Pennsylvania (M.B.A., 1967); Univ. of Connecticut (J.D., magna cum laude, 1973). Editor-in-Chief, CT Law Review, 1972-1973. Author: "Airport Noise: An Inadequate Judicial Response," 4 CT Law Review 634, 1972; "Local vs. State and Regional Zoning: The Tragedy of the Commons Revisited," 47 CT Bar Journal 249, 1973. Member, Glastonbury Charter Revision Commission, 1978-1979, 1988-1989. Commissioner, 1979-1981, Vice Chairman, 1983-1985, and Chairman, 1985-1987, Glastonbury Plan and Zoning Commission. Member, Greater Hartford Leadership Program, 1979-1980. Advisory Council, Univ. of Connecticut Health Center, 1986-1992. Board of Directors, CT World Trade Assn., 1989-1990. Board of Directors, Commercial Law Affiliates, 1990-1992. Member, Advisory Council, New England Legal Found., 1991-1997. *Member:* Amer. Planning Assn. ***PRACTICE AREAS:*** Public Finance; Public Law; Commercial Law; Utilities Law. ***Email:*** jlloyd@uks.com

JOHN C. KING, born Bridgeport, CT. November 14, 1946; admitted to bar, 1973, CT. *Education:* Georgetown Univ. (B.S.F.S., 1968; J.D., 1973). Law Clerk to Honorable John P. Cotter, Justice, Chief Court Admin., CT Supreme Court, 1973-1974. Member, 1979—, Member, Exec. Board, 1986—, Comptroller, 1988-1990, Pres., 1990-1998, New Britain Municipal Economic Develop. Agency. Chairman, Civil Service Commission, 1979-1984. Member, 1980— and Chairman, 1982—, Charter Revision Commission, City of New Britain. Member, Greater Hartford Leadership Program, 1983-1984. Member, Board of Ed., 1984— and Pres., 1986—, St. Joseph School. Member of the Board, 1984— and Chairman, Hartford Branch, 1985-1987, Amer. Red Cross. Member, Article 2A Subcommittee Law Revision Committee, 1987-1988. Member of the Board, 1988-1990, Vice Chairman, 1990, Mooreland Hill School, Board of Trustees and Chairman, 1994—. Chairman, Blue Ribbon Commission, Multiple Family Housing and Fire Prevention, City of New Britain, 1991. Member, New Britain Vision 2000 Committee, 1992. Chairman, Site Selection Committee, Christmas in April, New Britain, 1992. Corporator, Hospital for Special Care, 1992. Corporator, New Britain General Hosp., 1993—. Member, Executive Board, New Britain Chamber of Commerce, 1995—. Corporator, Hospital for Special Care, 1994—. Member, Board of Trustees, Community Mental Health Affiliates, Inc., 1995—. Corporator, CW Group, Inc., 1995—. Member,

(This Listing Continued)

Board of Directors, Greater New Britain Teen Pregnancy Prevention, Inc., 1996—, Vice-Chairman, 1997—. Member, Board of Governors, Fairfield College Preparatory School, 1998—. Chairman, New Britain Democratic Town Committee, 1984-1989. Member, Democratic State Central Committee, 1992—. Member, Board of Directors, CT Bar Assn., 2000. *Member:* Nat'l Assn of Railroad Trial Counsel. ***PRACTICE AREAS:*** Labor and Employment; Litigation; Legislative Representation; Utilities Law. ***Email:*** jking@uks.com

JAMES M. CONNOR, born Hartford, CT, February 3, 1956; admitted to bar, 1980, CT. *Education:* Harvard Univ. (A.B., magna cum laude in Economics, 1977); Georgetown Univ. Law Center (J.D., cum laude, 1980). Member, Leadership Greater Hartford, 1989. Director, World Affairs Council of Connecticut, Inc., 1992—, Nominating Comm., 1993, Executive Comm., 1998—. Director, Hill Housing, Inc., 1992-1996, V.P., 1994-1995; Pres., 1995-1996. Member, CT Advisory Council, Food for All, Inc., 1992-1998, Vice-Chair, 1993-1996. Secy, Harvard-Radcliffe Club of Northern CT, 1992-1994, V.P., 1994-1996; Pres., 1996-1998. Exec. Comm., Real Property Section, CT Bar Assn., 1994—. Member, International Business Council, Metro Harford Chamber of Commerce, 1997—. Member, Advisory Board, Intl. Business Center, Teikyo Post Univ., 1994-1997. ***PRACTICE AREAS:*** Business Law; Commercial Lending; Real Estate. ***Email:*** jconnor@uks.com

R. DIAL PARROTT, born Greenville, MS, December 14, 1943; admitted to bar, 1980, MA; 1984, CT. *Education:* Princeton Univ. (A.B., cum laude, 1966); Univ. of Virginia (M.A., 1976; J.D., 1980). Author: "Resource Recovery: Guideline for Public Officials," *Cities and Villages,* April, 1990. Co-Author: with Henry K. Brown, "How to Choose a Solid Waste System," *The Management of World Wastes,* July, 1990. Author: "A Load of Garbage," *Hartford Business Journal,* October 1993. Chairman, CT Law Firm Group on Minority Hiring and Retention, 1997—. Secy, Municipal Law and Gov't Services Committee, CT Bar Assn, 1989-1990. *Member:* Nat'l Assn. of Bond Lawyers; CT Conf. of Municipalities; Hartford Society of Municipal Analysts; CT Gov't Finance Officers Assn; Municipal Waste Management Assn. ***PRACTICE AREAS:*** Public Finance; Public Law; Solid Waste. ***Email:*** dparrott@uks.com

DAVID E. STURGESS, born New Haven, CT, March 21, 1956; admitted to bar, 1981, CT. *Education:* Univ. of Connecticut (B.S., magna cum laude, 1978); Duke Univ. (J.D., 1981). Beta Gamma Sigma; Phi Kappa Phi. Herman Crown Scholarship Winner. Co-Author: "Wraparound Lease Financing of Personal Property," 41 The Business Lawyer No. 3, May, 1986; "Flood Hazard Insurance: Requirements Imposed on Banks Extending Loans Secured by Real Property," 16 Real Estate Law Journal No 3, Winter, 1988. Contributing Author, Estate Planning and Admin. Service (Warren, Gorham & Lamont, 1989). Member, Board of Directors, 1989-1992, Chairman, Develop. Committee, 1990-1992, The APT Found. Member, Leadership Greater Hartford, 1990. Member, Board of Directors, 1990-1993 and Member, Finance Committee, 1992-1993, United Cerebral Palsy Assn. of Greater Hartford. Member, Board of Directors, 1991—, Chairman, 1995-1998, Vice Chairman, 1994, Member, Exec. Comm., 1994—, Member, Finance Committee, 1992-1994 and Chairman, Organization and Governance Committee, 1993-1994, Community Health Charities of Connecticut. Member, Board of Directors and Disaster Chairman, Amer. Red Cross, Hartford Chapter, 1984-1988. Member, 1986—, Membership Committee, 1988, Board of Directors, 1994-1995, CT Venture Group. Member, CT Technology Council, 1997—. Member Wethersfield Administrative Organization, Private Citizens Committee, 1992. Member, Hartford County Recycling Advisory Committee, 1992-1993. Member, Wethersfield Republican Town Committee, 1987-1990. Member, International Council of Shopping Centers, 1996—. Board of Directors, United Way of the Capitol Area, 1997—. Member, Special Services District Committee, Metro Hartford Chamber of Commerce, 1999—. ***PRACTICE AREAS:*** Business Law; Commercial Lending; Human Service; Real Estate Leasing; Finance. ***Email:*** dsturgess@uks.com

MARK J. ZIMMERMANN, born Passaic, NJ, July 5, 1956; admitted to bar, 1981, CT. *Education:* Georgetown Univ. (B.S.B.A., 1978); Boston Univ.; Tulane Univ. (J.D., cum laude, 1981). Member, CT Business and Industry Assn. (Member, Environmental Policies Council, 1988—; Member, Steering Committee, 1994-1997). Member, CT Environmental Forum, 1986—. Member, Executive Comm., Environmental Law Section, CT Bar Assn, 1998—. Board of Editors, Envir. Compliance and Litigation Strategy, 1990—. Member, Amer. Arbitration Assn., Envir. Advisory Counsel, 1992—. Member, Leadership Greater Hartford, 1993. Participant, CT Envir. Roundtable, Superfund Roundtable, 1993. Member, State of CT Superfund Legislative Task Force, 1993. Board of Managers, Glastonbury Branch, YMCA, 1995—. ***PRACTICE AREAS:*** Environmental; Administrative Law. ***Email:*** mzimmermann@uks.com

CHARLES J. NICOL, born Biddeford, ME, August 9, 1956; admitted to bar, 1983, CT. *Education:* Univ. of Rhode Island (B.S., with high distinction, 1978); Cornell Univ.; Yale Univ. (J.D., 1983). Member, Exec. Comm., Envir. Law Section, CT Bar Assn., 1987—; Secy., 1993-1994; Chairman, 1994-1995; Exec. Comm. Admin. Law Section, 1996—, CT Bar Assn. Chairman, 1995-1997, Envir. Law Comm., Hartford County Bar Assn.; Board of Editorial Advisors, "Regulatory Reporter: Connecticut". Member, Commercial Law Affiliates, Envir. Law Committee, 1991—. Member, CT Business and Industry As-

(This Listing Continued)

sociation, Environmental Policies Council, 1994—. Member and Secy., Zoning Board of Appeals, Town of Simsbury, 1989-1993; Recycling Committee, Town of Simsbury, 1992-1996. Member, Culture, Parks and Recreation Committee, Town of Simsbury, 1993—. Member, Planning Commission, Town of Simsbury, 1993-1996. Board of Directors, Connecticut Groundwater Assn., 1995—. Member, Simsbury Democratic Town Committee. ***PRACTICE AREAS:*** Administrative Law; Environmental Litigation; Utilities Law. ***Email:*** cnicol@uks.com

RICHARD S. ORDER, born Worcester, MA, August 14, 1956; admitted to bar, 1982, NY; 1988, CT; 1982, U.S. District Court, Southern and Eastern Districts of NY; 1988, U.S. District Court, District of CT; 1990, U.S. Court of Appeals, Second Circuit; 1996, U.S. District Court, Eastern District of MI; 1999, U.S. Supreme Court. *Education:* Wesleyan Univ. (B.A., summa cum laude, 1978); Columbia Univ. (J.D. , 1981). Phi Beta Kappa. Managing Editor, Columbia Human Rights Law Review, 1980-1981. Author, "Are Aliens Still a Suspect Class After NORWICK?," 11 Columbia Human Rights L. Rev. 227 (1979-1980). Member, Electronic Filing Comm., U.S. District Court, District of CT, 1997—. Co-Chairman, Alternative Dispute Resolution Subcommittee, ABA Litigation Section, Committee on Corporate Counsel, 1999—. Member, Federal Practice (Chairman, 1995-1998, Secy, 1992-1993, Treas., 1993-1995, and Member, Exec. Comm. 1992—), Corp. Counsel (Secy/Treas., 1994-1995) and Franchise Law (Exec. Comm., 1994-1997) Sections, CT Bar Assn. Affiliate Member, American Franchisee Assn., 2000—. ***PRACTICE AREAS:*** Commercial Litigation; Franchise Law; Human Service. ***Email:*** rorder@uks.com

HUGH I. MANKE, born West Hartford, CT, December 9, 1942; admitted to bar, 1976, CT. *Education:* Princeton Univ. (A.B., 1964); State Univ. of New York (J.D., 1975). Senior Editor, Buffalo Law Review, 1974-1975. Author: "Exhaustion of Local Remedies in the Subcommission on Prevention of Discrimination and Protection of Minorities," 24 Buffalo Law Review 643, 1975. Law Clerk, Hon. Arthur Healey, CT Superior Court, 1975-1976. Assoc. Counsel, CT Conf. of Municipalities, 1976-1979. Special Counsel, CT Dept. of Trans. 1979-1981. Member, Exec. Comm. Young Lawyers Section, CT Bar Assn., 1976-1978. Member, Board of Directors, CT Assn. of Municipal Attorneys, 1982—. Member, Board of Directors, Greater New Haven Chamber of Commerce, 1997—. Chairman, Board of Directors, International Voluntary Services, 1993—. Member, Board of Directors, Junior Achievement, 1996—. ***LANGUAGES:*** Vietnamese and German. ***PRACTICE AREAS:*** Administrative Law; Business Law; Public Finance/Public Law; Real Estate. ***Email:*** hmanke@uks.com

KATHERINE C. CALLAHAN, born Hartford, CT, January 21, 1959; admitted to bar, 1984, CT. *Education:* Boston College (B.A., magna cum laude, 1981); Univ. of Connecticut (J.D., with high honors, 1984). Member, 1982-1983 and Lead Articles Editor, 1983-1984, CT Law Review. Author: Note, "The Bottom Line Concept in Title VII Litigation; Connecticut v. Teal and the Relevance of End Results," 15 CT Law Review, Summer, 1983. ***LANGUAGES:*** French. ***PRACTICE AREAS:*** Professional Defense; Appellate Law; Commercial Litigation. ***Email:*** kccallahan@uks.com

SUSAN A. HAYS, born Waltham, MA, September 9, 1959; admitted to bar, 1984, CT; 1985, MA; 1992, RI. *Education:* Bowdoin College (A.B., magna cum laude, 1981); Boston College (J.D., magna cum laude, 1984). Order of the Coif. Member, Real Estate Exchange, 1990—, Prof. Develop. Committee Chair, 1993-1994, Vice President, 1997-1998, President, 1998-1999, Past President and NNCREW Delegate, 1999-2000; Blue Ribbon Committee, 2000-2001. Member, Junior League of Hartford, 1989—, Admin. Council Director, 1993-1994, V.P., 1994-1995, Show House Board, 1995-1996. Intl. Council of Shopping Centers CT Govt. Affairs Co-Chairman, 1994-1999, State Director, 1999—. Member: First Night Hartford Planning Committee, 1991-1994; Leadership Greater Hartford, 1995; Board Member, Twin Oaks Condo Assoc., 1993—; Vice President, 1993-1994; Treasurer, 1994—. Member, BASIC, 1984—, Chairman, Greater Hartford Area, 1996—, Chairman, CT, 1999—. ***PRACTICE AREAS:*** Business Law; Real Estate. ***Email:*** shays@uks.com

ROBERT J. MARTINO, born Hartford, CT, April 18, 1960; admitted to bar, 1985, CT. *Education:* Johns Hopkins Univ. (B.A., 1982); Univ. of Connecticut (J.D., 1985). Board of Directors, Vice Chairman, Real Estate Finance Assn, Hartford Chapter, 1995-1998; National Lawyers Council of Democratic National Committee, 1992—; 1988-1992; Avon Old Farms Alumni Assn., 1986—; Wethersfield Town Council, 1990-1995; Glastonbury Democratic Town Committee, 1995—; Wethersfield Democratic Town Committee, 1990-1995; Board of Directors, Wethersfield Chapter of UNICO Nat'l, 1990—; Board of Directors, Nat'l Conf. of Christians and Jews, Western New England, 1993—; Leadership Greater Hartford, 1994-1995; Board of Directors, Hartford Police Athletic League, Inc., 1994—. The Greater Hartford Convention and Visitors Bureau, Executive Committee, 1998—, Vice-Chairman, 1998-2000, Chairman, 2000—. ***PRACTICE AREAS:*** Commercial Lending; Banking Law; Real Estate; Real Estate Finance. ***Email:*** rmartino@uks.com

JOHN F. WOLTER, born Stamford, CT, October 15, 1961; admitted to bar, 1986, CT; 1988, NH. *Education:* Saint Anselm College (B.A., summa cum laude, 1983); Georgetown Univ. (J.D., cum laude, 1986). Member, 1986— and Chairman, 1990-1996, East Haddam Democratic Town Committee. Member, East Haddam Planning and Zoning Commission, 1988-1995. Chairman, East

(This Listing Continued)

Haddam Charter Commission, 1988-1990. Member, East Haddam Charter Study Committee, 1987-1988. Member: Board of Trustees, Brian House, Inc., 1992— and Adult Vocational Program, Inc., 1999—. Delegate, White House Conference on Small Business, 1995. *Member:* American Health Lawyers Assn.; Association of Commercial Finance Attorneys. ***PRACTICE AREAS:*** Business Law; Commercial Lending; Human Service; Franchise Law; Utilities Law. ***Email:*** jwolter@uks.com

FRANK G. USSEGLIO, born Boston, MA, September 15, 1961; admitted to bar, 1986, ME, MA and U.S. Court of Military Appeals; 1991, CT. *Education:* College of the Holy Cross (B.A., 1983); Albany Law School of Union Univ. (J.D., 1986). Certified Trial Advocacy Instructor, National Institute of Trial Advocacy, 1987. Chair, Hartford County Young Lawyers Section, Connecticut Bar Association, 1993-1994. Executive Committee, Veteran's and Military Affairs Section, Connecticut Bar Association, 1993—. Author: "How to Limit Opposing Counsel's Access to Former Employees," Leader's Product Liability Law & Strategy, Vol. XV, No. 6, December 1996. Chairman, Marlborough Republican Town Committee, 1996-1999; Marlborough Zoning Board of Appeals, 1997—; Chairman, 1998—. Adjunct Instructor, Naval Justice School, Newport, R.I., 1997-2000. Adjunct Faculty Member, Defense Research Institute of International Legal Studies, Newport, R.I., 2000—. Member, Leadership Greater Hartford, 1996. Member, Eastern Association of Intercollegiate Football Officials, 1999—. Member, Connecticut Association of Interscholastic Officials, 1995—. Member, National Ice Hockey Officials, 1998—. Member, National Federation of Interscholastic Officials, 1995—. Member, U.S.A. Hockey, 1995—. Member, American Society of Mechanical Engineers. Recipient: Senior Judge Advocate Naval Reserve Commendation Award, 1996-1998; Navy Outstanding Volunteer Service Award, 1999. [U.S. Navy, 1984-1991; CDR, U.S. Naval Reserve]. ***PRACTICE AREAS:*** Product Liability; Design/Construction; Insurance Defense; Professional Defense; Personal Law. ***Email:*** fusseglio@uks.com

DAVID J. MONZ, born Scotch Plains, NJ, October 18, 1958; admitted to bar, 1989, CT. *Education:* Franklin and Marshall College (B.S., 1980); Virginia Polytechnic Inst. and State Univ. (M.S., 1983); Univ. of Connecticut School of Law (J.D., high honors, 1989). Articles and Book Reviews Editor, CT Law Review. Clerk, Honorable Thomas J. Meskill, U.S. Court of Appeals, Second Circuit, 1989-1990. Member, Criminal Justice Act Panel. Member, North Haven Republican Town Comm., 1996—. Member, North Haven Inland Wetlands Commission, 1997—. Environmental Coordinator, Town of North Haven, 1994—. Member, National Assn., of College and University Attorneys, 1997—; Co-Chair, Environmental Law Section, 2000—. ***PRACTICE AREAS:*** Environmental Law; Administrative Law; Criminal Law. ***Email:*** dmonz@uks.com

THOMAS A. GUGLIOTTI, born Waterbury, CT, July 22, 1949; admitted to bar, 1975, CT and U.S. District Court, District of CT; 1995, U.S. District Court, Southern and Eastern Districts of NY. *Education:* Fairfield Univ. (A.B., 1971); Suffolk Univ. (J.D., cum laude, 1975). Lecturer on bankruptcy and related issues, National Business Institute, CT Bar Assn. and The Corporate Bar. Member: District of CT Local Bankruptcy Rules Committee, 1985-1993; District of Connecticut Bankruptcy Venue Redistricting Committee, 1998; Member: Past Treasurer, Vice Chairman and Member, Executive Committee, Commercial Law and Bankruptcy Section, CT Bar Assn; Chairman, Connecticut Bar Association Standards of Title and Bankruptcy Subcommittee; Member, Executive Committee, Commercial Law and Bankruptcy Section of the Hartford County Bar Assn.; Panel of Bankruptcy Mediators, Hartford County Bar Assn.; Avon, CT Board of Finance. Former Chairman, Avon Democratic Town Committee. *Member:* American Bankruptcy Institute. (Certified in Commercial Bankruptcy Law by the American Board of Certification). ***PRACTICE AREAS:*** Bankruptcy, Loan Workouts, Creditors' Rights; Commercial Foreclosures and Related Litigation; Real Estate and Title Litigation. ***Email:*** tgugliotti@uks.com

EDWARD J. PONTACOLONI, born Hartford, CT, November 12, 1950; admitted to bar, 1979, CT; 1981, U.S. District Court, District of CT; 1983, U.S. Court of Appeals, Second Circuit. *Education:* Marquette Univ. (B.A., 1972); Western New England College (J.D., 1979). ***SPECIAL AGENCIES:*** Assoc. Member, National Assn. of Government Guaranteed Lenders. Member, National Assn. of Development Companies. ***PRACTICE AREAS:*** Commercial Lending; Secured Transactions; Commercial Litigation; Creditors Rights; Banking. ***Email:*** epontacoloni@uks.com

KERRY R. CALLAHAN, born Norwalk, CT, March 30, 1961; admitted to bar, 1989, CT; 1990, U.S. District Court, District of CT. *Education:* Middlebury College (B.A., cum laude, 1983); Univ. of Connecticut (J.D., with high honors, 1989). Notes and Comments Editor, CT Law Review. Recipient, American Jurisprudence Awards: Conflicts of Law; Trial Practice; Corp. Finance. Author: "Protecting Child Sexual Abuse Victims in Connecticut," Univ. of Connecticut Law Review, Volume 21-2, Winter, 1989. Adult Probation Officer, State of CT, 1983-1986. Factfinder/Arbitrator, Superior Court, CT. ***LANGUAGES:*** Spanish. ***PRACTICE AREAS:*** Civil Litigation; Professional Malpractice and Insurance Defense; Personal Injury Law; Insurance Coverage; Construction Litigation; Commercial Litigation. ***Email:*** krcallahan@uks.com

(This Listing Continued)

UPDIKE, KELLY & SPELLACY, P.C., Hartford—Continued

DONALD W. DOEG, born New York, N.Y., April 15, 1960; admitted to bar, 1991, CT; 1992, U.S. District Court, District of CT. *Education:* Duke Univ. (B.S.C.E., 1982); Univ. of Southern Mississippi (M.B.A., 1984); Univ. of Connecticut (J.D., 1991). Prof. Engineer, States of CT and MS. Member: Nat'l Soc. of Prof. Engineers; Amer. Soc. of Civil Engineers. Chairperson, Business Practices of CT Engineers in Private Practice; Avon Old Farms Alumni Assn. Allied Individual Member, American Institute of Architects. Member, Exec. Comm. of Construction Law Section of CT Bar Assn. Member, Construction Specifications Institute. [Captain, USAF, 1982-1986]. ***PRACTICE AREAS:*** Construction and Design Litigation; Professional Defense; Insurance Defense; Civil Litigation. ***Email:*** ddoeg@uks.com

MARIA S. SPALDING, born Poughkeepsie, NY, August 9, 1955; admitted to bar, 1987, CT; 1992, U.S. District Court, District of CT. *Education:* Russell Sage College (B.S.N., 1977); Univ. of Bridgeport (J.D., 1987). Registered Nurse: NY, 1975; CT, 1977. Member: CT Hospital Assn. of Risk Managers; CT Medical Defense Society. ***PRACTICE AREAS:*** Product Liability; Professional Defense. ***Email:*** mspalding@uks.com

KEVIN N. REYNOLDS, born New Haven, CT, September 18, 1962; admitted to bar, 1991, CT; 1992, U.S. District Court, District of CT. *Education:* Kenyon College (A.B., 1985); Univ. of Virginia (J.D., 1991). Legislative Staff Asst. to U.S. Senator Christopher J. Dodd, 1985-1988. Member, CT Democratic Leadership Coalition, 1994—. Chief Legal Counsel, Democratic State Central Committee, 2001—. Member, West Hartford Democratic Town Committee, 1998—. Member, Leadership Greater Hartford, 1999. ***PRACTICE AREAS:*** Administrative Law; Legislative Representation; Litigation. ***Email:*** kreynolds@uks.com

ROBERT M. DeCRESCENZO, born Hartford, CT, September 8, 1957; admitted to bar, 1988, CT. *Education:* Univ. of Connecticut (B.A., 1981; M.P.A., with distinction, 1985; J.D., with honors, 1988). Recipient, American Jurisprudence Awards in Contracts and Professional Responsibility. Recipient: Distinguished Community Service Award, Anti-Defamation League; Distinguished Service Award, Capitol Region Council of Governments. Mayor, East Hartford, 1993-1997. Vice-Chairman, Transportation Committee, Capitol Region Council of Governments, 1993-1997. Member, Board of Trustees, Science Center of Connecticut, Inc., 1993—. Member, Board of Trustees, Main Street Plus, Inc., 1994—. Vice-Chair, Riverfront Recapture, Inc., 1995—. Elector, Wadsworth Athenaeum, 1996-1999. Chairman, Old State House, 1998—. Member, Board of Directors, Metro Hartford Chamber of Commerce, 1998—. Member, Board of Directors, First Federal Savings and Loan Association of East Hartford, 1998—. President, East Hartford Interfaith Ministries, 1998—. Fellow, American Leadership Forum, 1994—. Paul Harris Fellow, Rotary International. ***PRACTICE AREAS:*** Municipal; Litigation; Public Policy; Land Use; Land Development; Legislative Representation. ***Email:*** rdecrescenzo@uks.com

BERNARD E. JACQUES, born New York, N.Y., 1946; admitted to bar, 1986, NY; 1993, CT; U.S. Court of Appeals, Second Circuit; U.S. Supreme Court. *Education:* Marist College (B.A., 1969); New York Univ. (M.A., 1974); St. John's Univ. (J.D., 1986). Moot Court Board; Winner, Tinnelly Competition and Bosch Award for Oral Advocacy. Recipient, Amer. Jurisprudence Award in Advanced Labor Law. Member: West Hartford Town Council, 1996; CT Business and Industry Assn. Employment Law Council. ***PRACTICE AREAS:*** Employment Litigation; Labor and Employment Law. ***Email:*** bjacques@uks.com

CHRISTOPHER L. BRIGHAM, born Danbury, CT, October 19, 1962; admitted to bar, 1992, CT; 1993, U.S. District Court, District of CT. *Education:* Middlebury College (B.A., 1986); Vermont Law School (J.D., cum laude, 1992). Chair, CT Court Visitation Program-GA6. Member, Leadership Greater New Haven. ***PRACTICE AREAS:*** Labor and Employment; Professional Defense. ***Email:*** cbrigham@uks.com

DONALD R. SEIFEL, JR., born New Britain, Connecticut, October 16, 1957; admitted to bar, 1983, CT and U.S. District Court, District of CT; 1984, U.S. Tax Court. *Education:* Univ. of Michigan (A.B., 1980); Boston University (J.D., 1983); New York University (LL.M., Taxation, 1984). Member, Connecticut Estate and Tax Planning Council. ***PRACTICE AREAS:*** Business Law; Trusts and Estates; Probate; Taxation. ***Email:*** drseifel@uks.com

ROBERT R. SIMPSON, born New Rochelle, NY, October 2, 1968; admitted to bar, 1993, CT; 1995, U.S. District Court, District of CT and U.S Court of Appeals, Second Circuit. *Education:* Boston Univ. (B.A., 1989); Case Western Reserve Univ. (M.B.A., 1993; J.D., 1993). Recipient: Amer. Jurisprudence Award for Trial Advocacy; Best Advocate, ABA Region VI Trial Competition, 1993; Best Brief and National Finalist, Frederick Douglas Moot Court Competition, 1992; George Crawford Law Assn. 1996 Tomorrow Award. Member, Board of Directors, George Crawford Law Assn., 1996—. Barrister, American Inns of Court; Board of Directors, Capitol Foundation for Equal Justice, 1998—. Member, Board of Directors, Riverfront Recapture, Inc. Member, Board of Directors, Hartford County Bar Foundation, 2000—. Member, Litigation Exec. Committee, CBA, 2000—; Loan Committee, Urban League of Greater Hartford. ***PRACTICE AREAS:*** Complex Litigation; Professional Liability Defense; Employment Litigation. ***Email:*** rsimpson@uks.com

AMY E. ALISSI, born Cleveland, Ohio, February 28, 1967; admitted to bar, 1992, CT; 1993, U.S. District Court, District of CT. *Education:* Trinity College (B.A., 1989); Catholic Univ. (J.D., 1992). Member, Catholic University Journal of Contemporary Health Law and Policy. Member, National Assn. of Government Guaranteed Lenders. ***PRACTICE AREAS:*** Commercial Finance; Real Estate. ***Email:*** aalissi@uks.com

R. ALISHA VERDONE, born Queens, NY, September 17, 1962; admitted to bar, 1990, CT; 1991; U.S. District Court, District of CT; 1995, NY. *Education:* Univ. of Connecticut (B.A., 1984); Univ. of Bridgeport (J.D., 1990). Connecticut Probate Law Journal, Developments Editor, 1989-1990. Member: Real Estate Finance Association; Real Estate Exchange. ***LANGUAGES:*** French. ***PRACTICE AREAS:*** Business Law; Commercial Lending; Real Estate; Creditor's Rights. ***Email:*** raverdone@uks.com

ROLAN J. YOUNG, born New Haven, CT, November 15, 1960; admitted to bar, 1993, CT. *Education:* Dartmouth College (A.B., 1982); American Univ., Washington College of Law (J.D., 1985). Recipient: Minority Business Person of the Year Award, Business New Haven, 1999; 20 Noteworthy Women, New Haven Business Times, 1999. First Vice-President, Greater New Haven NAACP, 1998—; President, 2000—. Member, Board of Directors, Visiting Nurses Association of Southeastern Connecticut, 1998-2000. Member, Board of Directors, Greater New Haven Community Loan Fund, 1998-2000. Board of Directors, State of CT NAACP, 1999—. Member, George Crawford Law Assn. Member, CT Housing Coalition, 1999—. Tutor, Yale University Law School Housing and Community Development Clinic. General Counsel, New Haven Housing Authority, 2000—. Member, Board of Trustees, St. Raphael's Foundation, 2000—; Member, Board of Directors, NHSB Community Development Corporation, 2000—. ***LANGUAGES:*** Chinese. ***PRACTICE AREAS:*** Business Law; Commercial Lending; Public Finance/Public Law; Real Estate; Affordable Housing; Community Development. ***Email:*** ryoung@uks.com

OF COUNSEL

ERNEST N. ABATE, born New Haven, CT, August 10, 1943; admitted to bar, 1969, CT; 1972, U.S. District Court, District of CT; 1990, U.S. Supreme Court. *Education:* Villanova Univ. (B.S., 1965); Univ. of Notre Dame (J.D., 1968). Member, City Committee, Stamford, CT, 1973-1978. Member, House of Representatives, CT Legislature, 1975-1983. Designated "Best Legislator" in Polls conducted by CT Magazine, 1982. Chairman, House Judiciary Committee, 1977-1978. Speaker of the House, 1979-1983. Chairman, Legislative Management Committee. Connecticut Gubernatorial Candidate, 1982. Delegate for Senator Edward M. Kennedy 1980 National Convention. Chairman: CT Bar Association Law Day Committee, 1975-1976; Legislative Liaison Committee, 1976. Member, CT Law Revision Commission, 1983-1985. Counsel to Stamford Board of Realtors, 1989-1994. Member, Special Civilian Conference with Secretary of U.S. Department of Defense, 1984. Member, Board of Trustees, Ferguson Library, 1989-1993; 1995-2001; Chairman, 1993, 2000; President, State of CT Regional Action Council, 1992-1993. Member, Board of Directors: Senior Services of Stamford, Inc., 1991—; Kids In Crisis, Inc., 1999—. Member, Board of Trustees, CT Public Television and Radio, 1978-1983. Member, Mayor's Ethics Panel, City of Stamford, 1993. Past Member, Board of Trustees: Federal Health Systems Agency; Child Guidance Center. [Capt., USMC, 1969-1972]. (Also Member, Abate and Abate, Stamford, Connecticut). ***PRACTICE AREAS:*** Business; Trusts and Estates; Wills; Real Estate; Zoning. ***Email:*** ernestabate@msn.com

DOUGLAS M. COSTLE, born Long Beach, CA, July 27, 1939; admitted to bar, 1965, DC; 1968, CA (Not admitted in Connecticut). *Education:* Harvard Univ. (B.A., 1961); Univ. of Chicago (J.D., 1964). Author: "Environmental Regulation and Regulatory Reform," Washington Law Review, June, 1981. Adjunct Professor, John F. Kennedy School of Gov't, 1981. Visiting Scholar, Harvard School of Public Health, 1981. Fellow, Woodrow Wilson Natl. Center for Scholars, 1971. Dean, VT Law School, June 1, 1987-1991. Chairman of the Board and Distinguished Senior Fellow, Institute for Sustainable Communities, Montpelier, VT. Directorships: Co-Chairman of the Board of Trustees of a Family of Mutual Funds Managed by John Hancock Company, Boston, MA, 1992—; Niagara Mohawk Power Corp., Syracuse, NY, 1991—; Mitretek Systems, Inc., McLean, VA., 1995—; Concept Five Technologies Corp., McLean, VA, 1996—; Living Technologies, Inc., Burlington, VT, 1996—; Co-Chair: Envir. Management Advisory Board, U.S. Department of Energy, 1993—; National Audubon Society, New York, NY, 1993—; Health Effects Institute, Cambridge, MA, 1993—. Deputy Commissioner, 1972 and Commissioner, 1973-1975, Dept. of Envir. Prot. Agency, State of CT. Asst. Director, U.S. Congressional Budget Office, 1975-1976. Admin., U.S. Envir. Protection Agency, 1977-1981. President's Rep., NATO, Committee on Challenges to Modern Society, 1977-1981. Co-Chairman, U.S. - USSR Joint Committee on the Envir., 1977-1981. Chairman, U.S. Regulatory Council, 1979-1981. Chairman, Exec. Comm., Envir. Testing & Certification Corp., Edison, NJ, 1981-1986.

(This Listing Continued)

COUNSEL

MICHAEL P. BOTELHO, born New Bedford, MA, March 14, 1966; admitted to bar, 1991, CT; 1992, U.S. District Court, District of CT. *Education:* Bowdoin College (A.B., magna cum laude, 1988); Georgetown Univ. (J.D., cum laude, 1991). James Bowdoin Scholar. General Counsel to CT State Treasurer, 1997-1999. Pres., Bowdoin College Club of Connecticut. Member: Securities Law and Disclosure Committee, National Association of Bond Lawyers; CT Government Finance Officers Association; Administrative Law Section Executive Committee (CT Bar Assn.). First Vice-Chairman, Glastonbury Republican Town Committee. ***PRACTICE AREAS:*** Public Finance/Public Law; Administrative Law; Commercial Lending; Real Estate. ***Email:*** mbotelho@uks.com

KAREN KEEFE CLARK, born Hartford, CT, June 1, 1965; admitted to bar, 1990, CT; 1991, U.S. District Court, District of CT; 1992, MA and RI; 1996, U.S. District Court, District of MA; 1999, U.S. Court of Appeals, Second Circuit. *Education:* Holy Cross College (A.B., 1987); Univ. of Connecticut (J.D., 1990). Managing Editor, 1989-1990, CT Journal of Int'l Law. Chair, CBA's Hartford County Young Lawyers, 1994-1995. ***PRACTICE AREAS:*** Appellate; Product Liability; Professional Defense; Commercial Litigation. ***Email:*** kclark@uks.com

---

JOHN J. ALISSI, born Hartford, CT, October 5, 1970; admitted to bar, 1998, CT. *Education:* Williams College (B.A., 1993); Univ. of Connecticut School of Law (J.D., 1998). Member, 1996-1997 and Associate Editor, 1997-1998, CT Journal of Int'l Law. Listed in Who's Who of American Law Students, 1996 and 1998. Author: "Revolutionizing The Telephone Industry: The World Trade Organization Agreement on Basic Telecommunications and the Federal Communications Order," CT Journal of Int'l Law, Vol. 13-2, Spring 1999. Recipient: Excellence for the Future Award, Problems in Criminal Law. ***PRACTICE AREAS:*** Business Law; Commercial Lending; Real Estate. ***Email:*** jalissi@uks.com

EDWARD C. ANDREWS, II, born Marquette, MI, September 11, 1973; admitted to bar, 1999, CT. *Education:* Hobart and William Smith Colleges (B.A., 1995); Case Western Reserve Univ. School of Law (J.D., 1999). ***PRACTICE AREAS:*** Litigation. ***Email:*** eandrews@uks.com

LAURA FLYNN BALDINI, born Hartford, CT, August 17, 1970; admitted to bar, 1997, CT and NY; 1998, U.S. District Court, District of CT. *Education:* Yale Univ. (B.A., 1992); Seton Hall Univ. (J.D., 1996). Member, Seton Hall U. Journal of Sports Law. ***LANGUAGES:*** Spanish. ***PRACTICE AREAS:*** Insurance Defense Litigation; Personal Injury; Commercial Litigation. ***Email:*** lbaldini@uks.com

IRENE E. BASSOCK, born Hartford, CT, November 15, 1968; admitted to bar, 1995, CT; 1996, MA and U.S. District Court, District of CT; 1997, U.S. District Court, District of MA; 1998, U.S. Court of Appeals, First Circuit. *Education:* Gettysburg College (B.A., magna cum laude, 1990); Boston Univ. (J.D., cum laude, 1995). Phi Beta Kappa. Member, Wagner Labor Law National Moot Court. Edward F. Hennessey Scholar. ***PRACTICE AREAS:*** Commercial Litigation; Employment Based Immigration Law; Labor and Employment Law. ***Email:*** ibassock@uks.com

DANA RENE BAUGHNS, born New Haven, CT, November 30, 1968; admitted to bar, 1998, CT; U.S. District Court, District of CT. *Education:* Howard Univ. (B.A., 1992); Univ. of Connecticut (J.D., 1998). Member, Board of Directors, George Crawford Law Association., 1999—. Co-Chair, Hartford County Bar Scholarship Committee, 1999—. ***PRACTICE AREAS:*** Employment Litigation; ERISA Litigation; Collective Bargaining. ***Email:*** dpetaway@uks.com

MICHEL BAYONNE, born Port au Prince, Haiti, July 13, 1976; admitted to bar, 2001, CT. *Education:* Fairfield University (B.A., 1998); Univ. of Connecticut School of Law (J.D., 2001). ***PRACTICE AREAS:*** Business Law. ***Email:*** mbayonne@uks.com

COURTNEY R. BLAIR, born New Britain, CT, January 12, 1976; admitted to bar, 2001, CT. *Education:* Connecticut College (B.A., 1998); Quinnipiac College School of Law (J.D., 2001). ***PRACTICE AREAS:*** Government Relations; Legislative Representation. ***Email:*** cblair@uks.com

MICHAEL J. BRANDI, born New Haven, CT, March 2, 1971; admitted to bar, 1996, CT; 1997, U.S. District Court, District of CT. *Education:* College of the Holy Cross (B.A., 1993); Univ. of Connecticut (J.D., 1996). Member, 1994-1995 and Editor in Chief, 1995-1996, CT Insurance Law Journal. Author: "The Paradox of Technological Progress in Health Insurance Contracts: Experimental Treatment Clauses and Breast Cancer," CT Insurance Law Journal, Vol. 2, No. 1, Spring, 1996. Member, Board of Fire Commissioners, Town of Hamden, 1997-1999. Member, Democratic Town Committee, Town of Hamden, 1997-1999. Member, Board of Directors, Fellowship Place, 2000—. ***PRACTICE AREAS:*** Business Law; Real Estate; Commercial Lending; Municipal Law. ***Email:*** mbrandi@uks.com

(This Listing Continued)

HEATHER WILSON BUCKNAM, born New Haven, CT, October 9, 1969; admitted to bar, 1996, CT; 1997, U.S. District Court, District of CT. *Education:* Bucknell Univ. (B.A., 1991); Univ. of CT (J.D., 1996). Member, 1994-1995 and Notes and Comments Editor, 1995-1996, CT Insurance Law Journal. Author: "John Hancock Mutual Life Insurance Company v. Harris Trust & Savings Bank: The Applications of ERISA's Guaranteed Benefit Policy Exception to General Account Insurance Contracts," CT Insurance Law Journal, Vol. 2, No. 1, Spring 1996. ***PRACTICE AREAS:*** Business Law; Commercial Lending; Real Estate. ***Email:*** hbucknam@uks.com

CARRIE J. CAMPION, born West Islip, NY, 1974; admitted to bar, 2000, CT. *Education:* State Univ. of New York at Binghamton (B.A., cum laude, 1996); Boston College Law School (J.D., cum laude, 2000). ***PRACTICE AREAS:*** Labor and Employment; Municipal Law. ***Email:*** ccampion@uks.com

DANIEL R. CANAVAN, born Hartford, CT, March 7, 1975; admitted to bar, 2000, CT. *Education:* Eastern Connecticut State Univ. (B.S., 1997); Quinnipiac College School of Law (J.D., cum laude, 2000). Lead Articles Editor, Quinnipiac Law Review. Law Clerk to the Hon. Joseph H. Pellegrino, CT Appellate Court, 2000-2001. ***PRACTICE AREAS:*** Insurance Defense; Appellate; Litigation. ***Email:*** dcanavan@uks.com

TODD E. CUSANO, born New Haven, CT, November 28, 1972; admitted to bar, 2000, CT. *Education:* Univ. of Connecticut (B.A., summa cum laude, 1997); Univ. of Connecticut School of Law (J.D., 2000). Phi Beta Kappa. Member, Golden Key National Honor Society. Editor-in-Chief, CT Insurance Law Journal. Vice Magister, Phi Delta Phi, 19990-2000. Treasurer, CT Italian-American Bar Assn., 2001—. Member, UNICO National; Rocky Hill Republican Town Committee. ***PRACTICE AREAS:*** Commercial Litigation; Insurance Defense; Professional Defense. ***Email:*** tcusano@uks.com

RICHARD M. DIGHELLO, JR., born Meriden, CT, July 14, 1969; admitted to bar, 1996, CT; 1997, U.S. District Court, District of CT. *Education:* Quinnipiac College (B.A., 1993); Boston Univ. School of Law (J.D., 1996). Phi Alpha Delta. ***PRACTICE AREAS:*** Professional Defense; Construction and Design Litigation; Insurance Litigation. ***Email:*** rdighello@uks.com

ANTONIO E. DOS SANTOS, born Springfield, MA, February 6, 1975; admitted to bar, 2000, CT; 2001, U.S. District Court, District of CT. *Education:* Boston College (B.A., 1997); Univ. of Connecticut School of Law (J.D., 2000). Associate Editor, CT Journal of Int'l Law. ***PRACTICE AREAS:*** Business Law. ***Email:*** adossantos@uks.com

THOMAS W. EDGINGTON, born Kansas City, KS, February 10, 1975; admitted to bar, 2000, CT; 2001, Federal District of CT. *Education:* St. Bonaventure Univ. (B.A., cum laude, 1997); Albany Law School of Union Univ. (J.D., cum laude, 2000). Member, Moot Court Advisory Board. Chairperson, Morse Competitions, 1999-2000. Finalist, New York,/New England Region, ABA National Negotiation Competition. ***PRACTICE AREAS:*** Commercial Litigation. ***Email:*** tedgington@uks.com

BARBARA A. FREDERICK, born Brooklyn, NY, December 9, 1949; admitted to bar, 1997, CT. *Education:* Marymount College (B.A., with honors, 1971); Boston College (M.A., 1973); Univ. of Connecticut (J.D., 1997). Recipient: Cali Excellence for the Future Awards in Statutory Interpretation and Administrative Law; West Publishing Corporation Award for Outstanding Scholastic Achievement; Little, Brown & Company Award in Evidence. Adjunct Professor, Univ. of CT School of Law Moot Court, 2000. Law Clerk and Exec. Asst. to Chief Justice Robert Callahan, CT Supreme Court, 1997-1999. ***PRACTICE AREAS:*** Appellate Law; Litigation. ***Email:*** bfrederick@uks.com

PAUL N. GILMORE, born Ft. Lauderdale, FL, January 25, 1963; admitted to bar, 1988, CT; 1989, U.S. District Court, District of CT; 1990, U.S. District Court, Eastern and Southern Districts of NY; 1994, U.S. Court of Appeals, Second Circuit. *Education:* Florida State Univ. (B.S. in Finance, magna cum laude, 1984); Univ. of North Carolina at Chapel Hill (J.D., 1988). Phi Kappa Phi; Beta Gamma Sigma. Recipient, American Jurisprudence Award for Achievement in the Study of Torts. Member, Simsbury Zoning Board of Appeals, 1993-1998; Member, Simsbury Water Pollution Control Authority, 1999—. ***PRACTICE AREAS:*** Commercial Litigation; Appellate Law; Creditors' Rights; Bankruptcy; Loan Workouts. ***Email:*** pgilmore@uks.com

DREW S. GRAHAM, born Hartford, Connecticut, August 12, 1967; admitted to bar, 1995, CT; 1996, U.S. District, District of CT. *Education:* Tufts Univ. (B.A., with honors, 1989); Univ. of Connecticut (J.D., 1995). Member, World Affairs Council, 2000. ***LANGUAGES:*** Spanish. ***REPORTED CASES:*** Eidshahen v. Pizza Hut, 973 F.Supp. 113 (D.Con. 1997). ***PRACTICE AREAS:*** Insurance Defense; Personal Injury; Municipal Law. ***Email:*** dgraham@uks.com

SUZANNE E. GRAVES, born Needham, MA, February 24, 1976; admitted to bar, 2001, CT. *Education:* Franklin & Marshall College (B.A., cum laude, 1998); Univ. of Connecticut School of Law (J.D., 2001). Articles Editor, CT Law Review. Author: "Checkpoints and the Fourth Amendment: Saving Grace or Constitutional Martyr," 32 Conn. L.Rev. 1487, 2000. ***PRACTICE AREAS:*** Commercial Litigation; Personal Law. ***Email:*** sgraves@uks.com

(This Listing Continued)

UPDIKE, KELLY & SPELLACY, P.C., Hartford—Continued

JENNIFER L. GROVES, born Bridgeport, CT, May 15, 1973; admitted to bar, 1998, CT; U.S. District Court, District of CT. *Education:* Yale Univ. (B.A., distinction in Psychology, 1995); Boston College (J.D., 1998). Psi Chi. Member, Uniform Commercial Code Reporter Digest, 1996-1998 and Administrative Editor, 1997-1998. ***PRACTICE AREAS:*** Professional Liability Defense; Insurance Defense; Human Services. ***Email:*** jgroves@uks.com

ROBERT HICKS, born Waterbury, CT, April 2, 1974; admitted to bar, 2001, CT. *Education:* Connecticut College (B.A., 1996); Univ. of Connecticut School of Law (J.D., 2001). Notes and Comments Editor, CT Law Review, 2000-2001. ***PRACTICE AREAS:*** Business Law. ***Email:*** rhicks@uks.com

KATHLEEN A. HUDZIKIEWICZ, born Springfield, MA, April 30, 1974; admitted to bar, 2000, CT. *Education:* Westfield State College (B.A., 1996); Western New England College School of Law (J.D., 2000); New York Univ. School of Law (LL.M., 2001). Member, 1998-1999 and Note Editor, 1999-2000, Western New England Law Review, 1999-2000. ***PRACTICE AREAS:*** Tax Law; Trusts and Estates. ***Email:*** khudzikiewicz@uks.com

DEBORAH L. HUTTON, born Middletown, CT, June 10, 1971; admitted to bar, 2000, CT. *Education:* Univ. of Connecticut (B.A., 1993); Univ. of Connecticut School of Law (J.D., 2000). ***PRACTICE AREAS:*** Government Relations; Legislative Representation. ***Email:*** dhutton@uks.com

JOHN B. KENNELLY, born Hartford, CT, June 12, 1969; admitted to bar, 1996, CT and U.S. District Court, District of CT. *Education:* Wesleyan Univ. (B.A., 1991); Univ. of Connecticut (J.D., 1996). Author: CT Chapter, "Workers Compensation: A State by State Analysis," 3rd Edition, 1997. Member, Vision Hartford, 1999—. ***PRACTICE AREAS:*** Construction and Design Law; Real Estate Law. ***Email:*** jkennelly@uks.com

SHEA S. KINNEY, born Hartford, CT, March 12, 1974; admitted to bar, 1999, CT. *Education:* Mount Holyoke College (B.A., cum laude, 1996); Univ. of Connecticut (J.D., with honors, 1999). Recipient: Bristol Bar Association Scholarship, 1997-1999. ***PRACTICE AREAS:*** Personal Injury Law; Product Liability; Insurance Defense Law. ***Email:*** skinney@uks.com

SCOTT N. KOSCHWITZ, born Milford, CT, June 2, 1967; admitted to bar, 1995, CT; 2000, NY. *Education:* Univ. of Connecticut (B.A., 1989); Pace Univ. School of Law (J.D., Environmental Law Certificate, 1995). Notes and Comments Editor, Pace Environmental Law Review, 1994-1995. ***PRACTICE AREAS:*** Environmental Law; Commercial Litigation. ***Email:*** skoschwitz@uks.com

KATE F. KOTSAFTIS, born Waterbury, CT, July 30, 1976; admitted to bar, 2001, CT. *Education:* Univ. of Connecticut (B.A., magna cum laude, 1998); Univ. of Connecticut School of Law (J.D., 2001). Recipient, CALI Excellence for the Future Award for Legal Writing. ***PRACTICE AREAS:*** Commercial Litigation. ***Email:*** kkotsaftis@uks.com

GREGG J. LALLIER, born Hartford, CT, August 14, 1972; admitted to bar, 1998, CT. *Education:* Boston College (B.S., magna cum laude, 1994); Emory Univ. School of Law (J.D., 1998). ***PRACTICE AREAS:*** Business Law; Intellectual Property; Electronic Commerce Law. ***Email:*** glallier@uks.com

BRAD N. MONDSCHEIN, born Plainview, NY, March 12, 1968; admitted to bar, 1993, CT; 1994, U.S. District Court, District of CT; 1995, U.S. Court of Appeals, Second Circuit. *Education:* Union College (B.A., 1990); Western New England College School of Law (J.D., cum laude, 1993). Member, Western New England Law Review, 1991-1992. Law Clerk to Judge Maxwell Helman, CT Appellate Court, 1993-1994. ***PRACTICE AREAS:*** Utility Law; Franchise Law; Litigation. ***Email:*** bmondschein@uks.com

ROBERT ANDREW MORGAN, born St. Louis, MO, April 16, 1973; admitted to bar, 1999, CT; 2001, U.S. District Court, District of CT. *Education:* Santa Clara Univ. (B.S., 1995); New England School of Law (J.D., 1999). Recipient: New England Scholar Award, 1997, 1998; CALI Award in Administration Law and Business Organization. Staff Editor, Environmental Law Forum, 1996-1998. Co-author, "Cleaning Up, Redeveloping and Reusing Contaminated Properties," 33 New England Law Review 667, Spring 1999. ***PRACTICE AREAS:*** Commercial Litigation. ***Email:*** rmorgan@uks.com

TIMOTHY L. O'KEEFE, born Lowell, MA, August 31, 1967; admitted to bar, 1992, MA; 1993, CT; 1995, U.S. District Court, District of CT; 2000, U.S. District Court, District of MA. *Education:* College of The Holy Cross (B.A., 1989); Western New England College School of Law (J.D., 1992). *Member:* CT Bar Association (Co-Chair, Young Lawyers Litigation Section Executive Committee, 2000); The Association of Trial Lawyers of America. ***PRACTICE AREAS:*** Personal Injury; Product Liability; Worker's Compensation; Domestic Relations. ***Email:*** tokeefe@uks.com

SCOTT S. ORENSTEIN, born Pittsburgh, PA, July 25, 1967; admitted to bar, 2001, CT. *Education:* Univ. of Massachusetts, Amherst (B.S.C.E., 1990); Quinnipiac College School of Law (J.D., 2001). Prof. Engineer, State of CT. ***PRACTICE AREAS:*** Construction and Design Litigation; Professional Defense. ***Email:*** sorenstein@uks.com

(This Listing Continued)

CRAIG LYLE PERRA, born Cranston, RI, June 6, 1971; admitted to bar, 1997, CT; 1998, U.S. District Court, District of CT and U.S. Court of Appeals, Second Circuit; 2001, U.S. Supreme Court. *Education:* Univ. of Connecticut (B.A., 1993; J.D., with honors, 1997). Research Editor, CT Insurance Law Journal, 1996-1997. ***PRACTICE AREAS:*** Commercial Litigation; Creditors Rights; Bankruptcy. ***Email:*** cperra@uks.com

VANESSA L. RAMIREZ, born Ponce, Puerto Rico, October 23, 1973; admitted to bar, 2001, CT. *Education:* Univ. of Pennsylvania (B.A., 1995); Univ. of Connecticut (M.P.H., magna cum laude, 1997); Univ. of Pennsylvania Law School (J.D., 2001). Senior Editor, Univ. of Pennsylvania Journal of International and Economic Law. ***PRACTICE AREAS:*** Business Law. ***Email:*** vramirez@uks.com

RUSSELL F.A. RIVIERE, born Castries, St. Lucia, October 23, 1974; admitted to bar, 2000, CA; 2001, CT. *Education:* Univ. of Florida (B.A., 1996); Georgetown Univ. Law Center (J.D., 1999). ***PRACTICE AREAS:*** Labor and Employment; Litigation. ***Email:*** rriviere@uks.com

JOSEPH A. ROSENTHAL, born West Islip, NY, July 17, 1969; admitted to bar, 1996, CT. *Education:* State Univ. of NY at Binghamton (B.A., with honors, 1990; M.A., 1993); Boston College Law School (J.D., magna cum laude, 1996). ***PRACTICE AREAS:*** Environmental; Administrative Law; Utilities Law. ***Email:*** jrosenthal@uks.com

R. SCOTT SLIFKA, born Chicago, IL, March 5, 1974; admitted to bar, 1999, CT. *Education:* George Washington Univ. (B.A., 1996; J.D., 1999). Member, Executive Board, Moot Court Board. ***PRACTICE AREAS:*** Design/Construction; Professional Defense Law. ***Email:*** sslifka@uks.com

JOHN G. STRETTON, born New Haven, CT, January 12, 1973; admitted to bar, 1998, CT and U.S. District Court, District of CT. *Education:* Boston College (B.A., cum laude, 1995); Boston Univ. (J.D., cum laude, 1998). ***PRACTICE AREAS:*** Civil Litigation; Professional Liability Defense; Employment Litigation; Personal Injury Defense; Insurance Coverage Defense; Municipal Liability Defense; Commercial Litigation. ***Email:*** jstretton@uks.com

JAMES N. TALLBERG, born Phoenix, AZ, May 13, 1965; admitted to bar, 1996, CT, U.S. District Court, District of CT and U.S. Court of Appeals, Second Circuit. *Education:* Southern CT State Univ. (B.S., 1987); Univ. of Connecticut (J.D., with honors, 1996). Assoc. Editor, CT Insurance Law Journal, 1995-1996. Member, Rocky Hill Republican Town Comm., 1997—. Member, Cora J. Belden Library Advisory Board, 1997—. Member, Rocky Hill Economic Development Commission, 2000—. *Member:* CT Bar Association (Co-Chair, Young Lawyers Section Civil Rights Committee, 2001—); Defense Research Institute. ***PRACTICE AREAS:*** Civil Litigation; Municipal Liability Defense; Professional Liability Defense; Insurance Coverage Defense. ***Email:*** jtallberg@uks.com

AMY L. VAN DYKE, born Manhasset, NY, September 5, 1972; admitted to bar, 1999, NJ and U.S. District Court, District of NJ; 2000, PA; 2001, CT. *Education:* Muhlenberg College (B.A., cum laude, 1994); Widener Univ. School of Law (J.D., 1999). ***PRACTICE AREAS:*** Commercial Litigation; Professional Defense; Products Liability. ***Email:*** avandyke@uks.com

CORINNA M. WARHURST, born Providence, RI, April 22, 1974; admitted to bar, 2000, CT and NY; 2001, U.S. District Court, District of CT. *Education:* Bucknell Univ. (B.A., 1997); Case Western Reserve Univ. School of Law (J.D., 2000). Associate Editor and Executive Notes Editor, Journal of Int'l Law. ***PRACTICE AREAS:*** Construction and Design Law; Professional Defense. ***Email:*** cwarhurst@uks.com

An Independent Member of Commercial Law Affiliates, an affiliation of business, commercial litigation and commercial real estate law firms serving clients in more than 145 cities worldwide.
All Personnel are members of the Hartford or New Haven County, Connecticut and American Bar Associations.

REPRESENTATIVE CLIENTS: AT&T Wireless; CNA Insurance; City of Bridgeport; City of Hartford; Connecticut Innovations, Inc.; Coregis Group; ; Design Professionals Insurance Company; First American Title Insurance Company; First International Bank; FleetBoston Financial; Hartford Insurance Group; Ingersoll-Rand Company; The Metropolitan District; Microsoft Corporation; New England Development Co.; Northeast Utilities; Saint Francis *Care*, Inc.; Schindler Elevator; State Farm Insurance; State of Connecticut (including the Office of the State Treasurer and the Department of Economic and Community Development); Target Corporation; Travelers Property Casualty Corporation; Yale University.

WALLER, SMITH & PALMER, P.C.

HARTFORD, CONNECTICUT

(See New London)

General Practice. Corporation, Commercial, Estate Planning, Probate, Real Estate, Personal Injury, Municipal, Banking and Trials in all Courts.

CHRISTINE M. WHITEHEAD

241 MAIN STREET
HARTFORD, CONNECTICUT 06106
Telephone: 860-241-7797
Fax: 860-241-7744

Matrimonial, Custody, Mediation.

CHRISTINE M. WHITEHEAD, born Patterson, New Jersey, September 5, 1950; admitted to bar, 1975, Connecticut and U.S. District Court, District of Connecticut. *Education:* Smith College (B.A., magna cum laude, 1972); University of Connecticut (J.D., 1975). Phi Beta Kappa. *Member:* Hartford County and Connecticut Bar Associations; American Academy of Matrimonial Lawyers. ***PRACTICE AREAS:*** Family Law (80%, 50); Personal Injury Law (20%, 3).

WIGGIN & DANA LLP

ONE CITYPLACE
HARTFORD, CONNECTICUT 06103-3402
Telephone: 860-297-3700
Telefax: 860-525-9380
URL: http://www.wiggin.com

New Haven, Connecticut Office: One Century Tower, P.O. Box 1832. Telephone: 203-498-4400. Telefax: 203-782-2889.
Stamford, Connecticut Office: 400 Atlantic Street, P.O. Box 110325. Telephone: 203-363-7600. Telefax: 203-363-7676.
Berwyn, Pennsylvania Office: 1055 Westlake Drive. Telephone: 610-727-4153. Telefax: 610-727-4085.
Cherry Hill, New Jersey Office: 402 Park Boulevard North, 08802. Telephone: 856-662-3331. Telefax: 856-662-1783.

Antitrust and Trade Regulation, Appellate, Automotive Industry Law, Banking and Financial Services, Bankruptcy Law, Biotechnology Law, Civil Litigation, Closely Held Business, Cogeneration, Construction Law, Employee Benefits and ERISA Law, Environmental Law, Estate Planning and Settlement Law, Franchise Law, Governmental Affairs, Health Care, Hospital Law, Institutional Finance, Insurance Coverage Litigation, Intellectual Property, Internal Corporate Investigations and White Collar Criminal Defense Law, International Transactions, Labor Law, Litigation, Long Term Care Facilities and Financing, Mental Health Law, Mergers and Acquisitions, National and Regional Litigation Counsel, Partnerships and Joint Ventures, Patent Prosecution and Litigation, Professional Malpractice Litigation, Public Finance, Public Utilities, Real Estate Leasing, Development and Finance, Secured Transactions, Securities Regulation, State and Federal Tax Law, Tax Exempt Organizations, Technology Licensing, Telecommunications, Trademarks and Copyright, Trust and Estates Administration, Venture Capital and Zoning.

MEMBERS OF FIRM

VALERIE A. SEILING, born Staten Island, New York, 1957; admitted to bar, 1982, New York; 1984, Connecticut. *Education:* Cornell University (B.S., with honors, 1978; J.D., 1981). Editor, Cornell Law Review, 1979-1981. (Resident). ***PRACTICE AREAS:*** Corporate Finance; Secured Transactions; Mergers and Acquisitions; Commercial Mortgages; Real Estate Finance. ***Email:*** vseiling@wiggin.com

PATRICK J. MONAHAN, II, born New Haven, Connecticut, 1958; admitted to bar, 1983, Connecticut. *Education:* Stonehill College (B.A., 1980); Boston College (J.D., cum laude, 1983). Editor, Boston College International and Comparative Law Review, 1982-1983. (Resident). ***PRACTICE AREAS:*** Litigation. ***Email:*** pmonahan@wiggin.com

ROBERT M. LANGER, born Norwalk, Connecticut, 1948; admitted to bar, 1973, Connecticut. *Education:* Franklin & Marshall College (A.B., 1970); University of Connecticut School of Law (J.D., 1973). Co-Author: "The Connecticut Unfair Trade Practices Act," 54 Conn. B.J. 388 (1980); "Antitrust Review of Mergers by State Attorneys General, The New Cops on the Beat," 67 Conn. B.J. 1 (1993); *The Connecticut Unfair Trade Practices Act 2v (1994). Author:* "A Practitioner's Guide to State Antitrust Health Care Issues," Antitrust (ABA) Fall, 1995; "Should the Antitrust Division, the FTC and State Attorneys General Formally Allocate the Market for Antitrust Enforcement?" Antitrust Report (Matthew Bender) October 1998; "60 Minutes with Robert M. Langer, Assistant Attorney General and Chair, NAAG Multistate Antitrust Task Force," 60 Antitrust L.J. 197 (1991); 61 Antitrust L.J. 211 (1992). Assistant Attorney General, State of Connecticut, 1973-1994, Department Head - Antitrust and Consumer Protection. Chair: National Association of Attorney Generals, Multistate Antitrust Task Force, 1990-1992; Eastern States Antitrust Committee, 1988-1990; State Antitrust Enforcement Committee, Section of Antitrust Law, American Bar Association, 1992-1995. Co-Chair, Federal and State Legislative Policy Task Force, 1996-1997; Legislation Committee, 1997-1998. Chair, Consumer Protection Committee. Council Member, Section of Antitrust Law, ABA, 1990-1992. Member, Board of Editors, Matthew Bender Antitrust Report, 1992—. Member, Bureau of National Affairs Antitrust and Trade Regulation Report Advisory Board, 1994—. Adjunct Professor, University of Connecticut School of Business Administration, MBA Program, 1979—. Chair, Antitrust Section, Connecticut Bar Association, 1979-1980. Chair, Antitrust & Trade Regulation Committee, 1998—. WESFACCA Chair, James W. Cooper Fellows Program: Connecticut Bar Foundation, 2000; Fellow, American Bar Foundation, 2000. (Resident). ***PRACTICE AREAS:*** Antitrust and Trade Regulation; Administrative Law; Consumer Law; Medical Antitrust. ***Email:*** rlanger@wiggin.com

STEPHEN B. HARRIS, born New York, N.Y., 1961; admitted to bar, 1987, New York and U.S. District Court, Eastern and Southern Districts of New York; 1988, Minnesota; 1993, U.S. District Court, District of Connecticut; 1996, Connecticut; 1998, U.S. District Court, Western District of New York. *Education:* Brandeis University (B.A., magna cum laude, 1983); Hofstra University (J.D., 1986). Articles Editor, 1985-1986 and Staff Member, 1984-1985, Hofstra Law Review. *Member:* American Bar Association (Member, Employment and Labor Relations Litigation Committee, Litigation Section); Connecticut Business and Industry Association (Member, Labor and Employment Law Council). (Resident). ***PRACTICE AREAS:*** Employment Litigation; Wrongful Termination Defense; Employcr Rights; Sexual Harassment; Wage and Hour Law. ***Email:*** sharris@wiggin.com

DANIEL J. KLAU, born Hartford, Connecticut, 1961; admitted to bar, 1991, Connecticut and Massachusetts. *Education:* University of California, San Diego (B.A., with distinction in Political Science, 1984, cum laude, outstanding senior distinguished student); Boston University School of Law (J.D., summa cum laude, 1990). Recipient, Melville Bigelow Award (for student showing most promise as scholar and teacher of law). Note Editor, Boston University School of Law - Law Review, 1988-1990. Author: "What Price Certainty," Corbin, Williston and the Restatements of Contracts to B.V.C. Rev. 511 (1990). Law Clerk, Chief Justice Ellen A. Peters, Connecticut Supreme Court, 1990-1991. (Resident). ***Email:*** dklau@wiggin.com

PETER M. WENDZEL, born Kalamazoo, Michigan, 1967; admitted to bar, 1992, Connecticut. *Education:* George Washington University (B.A., magna cum laude, 1989) Phi Beta Kappa; University of Virginia School of Law (J.D., 1992). (Resident). ***Email:*** pwendzel@wiggin.com

RESIDENT COUNSEL

SHARYN B. ZUCH, born New Hyde Park, New York, 1956; admitted to bar, 1981, Florida; 1999, Connecticut; U.S. District Court, Middle District of Florida; U.S. Court of Appeals, Eleventh Circuit. *Education:* Cornell University (B.S., with distinction, 1977); University of Chicago (J.D., 1981). Phi Kappa Phi; Omicron Nu. Author: "Battling in Bankruptcy Court," Federal Bar News & Journal, June/July 1991; "Bankruptcy Mediation," Hillsborough County Bar Bulletin, May 1990; "Selected Problems in Discovery," Chapter, Business Litigation in Florida, 1989; "Trade Secrets and High-Tech Industries," 59 Florida Bar Journal 37, 1985; "Discovery of Facts Known and Opinions Held By Experts," 58 Florida Bar Journal 225, 1984; "A Critical Analysis of Recent Federal Appellate Decisions on Predatory Pricing," 55 Antitrust Law Journal 401, 1982. Editor, "The Quarterly Report," Florida Bar Business Law Section, 1987-1990. Contributor, ARTSNEWS, on law and the arts, 1987-1988. Bankruptcy Mediator, Middle District of Florida. *Member:* The Florida Bar (Member, Business Law Executive Council, Chair, Business Litigation Committee); American Bar Association (Member: Litigation and Business Law Sections); American Bankruptcy Institute; Tampa Bay Bankruptcy Bar Association (Secretary). Master, American Inns of Court (Secretary, Ferguson White Chapter). ***PRACTICE AREAS:*** Antitrust; Bankruptcy. ***Email:*** szuch@wiggin.com

MARCIA KENNY KEEGAN, born Poughkeepsie, New York, 1958; admitted to bar, 1989, Connecticut. *Education:* Union College, Schenectady, New York (B.A., cum laude, 1980); Cornell Law School (J.D., cum laude, 1989). Senior Editor, Cornell International Law Journal. ***PRACTICE AREAS:*** Employment Law. ***Email:*** mkeegan@wiggin.com

RESIDENT ASSOCIATES

CATHERINE P. BAATZ, born Holyoke, Massachusetts; admitted to bar, 1996, Connecticut. *Education:* Mount Holyoke College (A.B., magna cum laude, 1981) Phi Beta Kappa; Harvard Law School (J.D., 1996). Member, 1993-1996 and Managing Editor, 1994-1995, Woman's Law Journal. ***Email:*** cbaatz@wiggin.com

LORI R. CLARK, born Middletown, Connecticut, 1964; admitted to bar, 1998, Connecticut. *Education:* University of Connecticut (B.A., Economics and Political Science, 1993); Western New England College (J.D., cum laude, 1997). Member, Western New England Law Review, 1995-1997. Law Clerk: The Honorable Alfred V. Covello, Chief Judge, U.S. District Court, 1998-1999. ***Email:*** lclark@wiggin.com

MICHELLE WILCOX DEBARGE, born New Britain, Connecticut, 1965; admitted to bar, 1993, Connecticut. *Education:* Williams College (B.A., 1987); University of Connecticut School of Law (J.D., magna cum laude, 1993). Mem-

(This Listing Continued)

WIGGIN & DANA LLP, Hartford—Continued

ber, 1991-1992 and Editor-in-Chief, 1992-1993, University of Connecticut Law Review. Author: "The Performance of Invasive Procedures by HIV-Infected Doctors: The Duty to Disclose under the Informed Consent Doctrine," 25 Conn. Law Review 991 (1993). ***Email:*** mdebarge@wiggin.com

MICHAEL J. DEVINE, born Milford, Connecticut, 1968; admitted to bar, 1995, Nebraska and U.S. District Court, District of Nebraska; 1997, Illinois; 2000, Connecticut. *Education:* University of Connecticut (B.A., 1990); Creighton University School of Law (J.D., cum laude, 1995). Associate Editor, Creighton Law Review. Law Clerk to the Honorable Edward E. Hannon, Nebraska Court of Appeals, 1995-1997. ***Email:*** mdevine@wiggin.com

RICHARD H. LUGLI, born Bristol, Connecticut, 1964; admitted to bar, 1990, Connecticut; 1991, Maine. *Education:* Amherst College (A.B., 1986); University of Connecticut School of Law (J.D., with honors, 1990). ***Email:*** rlugli@wiggin.com

STEVEN P. MALECH, born Silver Spring, Maryland, 1966; admitted to bar, 1995, Connecticut; 1996, U.S. District Court, District of Connecticut and U.S. Court of Appeals, Federal Circuit. *Education:* University of Texas at Austin (B.A., with special honors in Psychology, 1988); University of Connecticut (J.D., with honors, 1995). (Resident). ***Email:*** smalech@wiggin.com

GAYLE CAROL WINTJEN, born Brooklyn, New York, 1964; admitted to bar, 1990, Massachusetts and U.S. District Court, District of Massachusetts; 1991, New York and U.S. District Court, Southern and Eastern Districts of New York; 1996, New Jersey and U.S. District Court, District of New Jersey; 2001, Connecticut; U.S. Court of Appeals, 1st and 4th Circuits. *Education:* University of Massachusetts (B.B.A., 1986); New England School of Law (J.D., 1990); New York University (LL.M., 1995). Case and Note Editor, New England Law Review, 1989-1990. Author: "Make Room for Daddy: A Putative Father's Rights to His Children," 24:3 NEL. Rev. (1990); Update, "-Constitutional Law-Obscenity and the First Amendment," 25:4 NEL. Rev. (1991). ***Email:*** gwintjen@wiggin.com

(For complete biographical data on all personnel, see Professional Biographies at New Haven, Connecticut)

THOMAS P. WILLCUTTS & ASSOCIATES

CAPITOL PLACE
21 OAK STREET SUITE 602
HARTFORD, CONNECTICUT 06106-8002
Telephone: 860-524-6800
Fax: 860-524-7766
Email: tpw@ntplx.net
URL: http://www.lawyers.com/willcuttslaw

Securities Litigation and Arbitration, Commercial Litigation, Legal Malpractice, Professional Malpractice, Products Liability, Personal Injury and General Civil Litigation in Federal and State Courts.

THOMAS P. WILLCUTTS, born Oakland, California, February 1, 1959; admitted to bar, 1984, Connecticut and U.S. District Court, District of Connecticut. *Education:* Rice University (B.A., 1981); Washington University (J.D., 1984). Staff Member, 1982-1983 and Associate Editor, 1983-1984, Washington University Law Quarterly. Law Clerk to Honorable James Reinhard, Missouri Court of Appeals, St. Louis, Missouri, 1983. Author: "Actions for Products Liability," Connecticut Actions & Remedies-Tort Law (Butterworth, 1993). *Member:* Hartford County and Connecticut Bar Associations; The Association of Trial Lawyers of America; Connecticut Trial Lawyers Association. ***REPORTED CASES:*** Levine et al. v. Advest, Inc., 244 Conn. 732, 128 Ed. Law Rep. 1085 (1998). ***PRACTICE AREAS:*** Securities Litigation; Securities Arbitration; Commercial Litigation; Legal Malpractice; Professional Malpractice; Products Liability; Personal Injury; Civil Litigation.

ASSOCIATES

JOHN JAY PAVANO, born New Britain, Connecticut, December 4, 1964; admitted to bar, 1994, Connecticut; 1995, U.S. District Court, District of Connecticut. *Education:* University of Connecticut (B.A., 1987); Quinnipiac College (J.D., 1994). Recipient: American Jurisprudence in Legal Writing; Zeldes, Needle & Cooper Award for Excellence in Legal Writing; Wofsey, Rosen, Kweskin & Kuriansky Award for Appellate Brief Writing; Superior Classroom Performance Award. General Counsel to the Connecticut State Police Academy Alumni Association. *Member:* Connecticut Bar Association. ***REPORTED CASES:*** Levine et al. v. Advest, Inc., 244 Conn. 732, 128 Ed. Law Rep. 1085 (1998); United States v. Mendez, _F. 3d _ (2d Cir., 1998). ***PRACTICE AREAS:*** Securities Litigation; Securities Arbitration; Commercial Litigation; Legal Malpractice; Professional Malpractice; Products Liability; Personal Injury; Civil Litigation.

(This Listing Continued)

DOUGLAS A. CHO, born Baltimore, Maryland, January 21, 1962; admitted to bar, 1991, Connecticut; 1992, U.S. District Court, District of Connecticut; 1994, Massachusetts; 1996, U.S. Court of Appeals, Second Circuit. *Education:* Wesleyan University (B.A., 1984); University of Connecticut (J.D., with honors, 1991). *Member:* Connecticut and American Bar Associations. ***PRACTICE AREAS:*** Securities Litigation; Securities Arbitration; Commercial Litigation; Legal Malpractice; Professional Malpractice; Products Liability; Personal Injury; Civil Litigation.

OF COUNSEL

MARVIN S. BLOOM, born Hartford, Connecticut, October 9, 1929; admitted to bar, 1954, Connecticut and Massachusetts. *Education:* Washington University (A.B., 1951); Boston University (J.D., 1954). Phi Eta Sigma. Chairman, Board of Revision and Special Assessments, West Hartford, 1970-1974. Member, Panel of Arbitrators, American Arbitration Association. *Member:* Hartford County, Connecticut and American Bar Associations; American Judicature Society; Connecticut Trial Lawyers Association; Association of Trial Lawyers of America. [Lt., Staff Judge Advocate, USAF, 1954-1956]

WILLINGER, WILLINGER & BUCCI, P.C.

HARTFORD, CONNECTICUT

(See Bridgeport)

General Practice. Real Estate, Corporate, Commercial, Foreclosure, Bankruptcy, Secured Financing, Zoning, Labor, Probate, Condemnation, Workers Compensation, Financial, Banking, Personal Injury and Criminal Law. Trials in all Courts.

HENRY C. WINIARSKI, JR.

941 WETHERSFIELD AVENUE
HARTFORD, CONNECTICUT 06114-3137
Telephone: 860-296-2127
Fax: 860-296-2131
Email: hcwjr53@msn.com

General Practice, Real Estate, Probate and Conservatorship Law, Wills, Trusts, Zoning, Title Insurance, Civil Litigation and Commercial Law.

HENRY C. WINIARSKI, JR., born Hartford, Connecticut, August 18, 1953; admitted to bar, 1978, Connecticut; 1979, U.S. District Court, District of Connecticut. *Education:* Central Connecticut State College (B.A., 1975); University of Connecticut (J.D., 1978). Recipient, Hartford County Bar Association Scholarship, 1977. Member: Connecticut Capitol Center Commission, 1979-1982; Connecticut Board of Accountancy, 1982-1984. *Member:* Hartford County, Connecticut and American Bar Associations.

WOLF, HOROWITZ, ETLINGER & CASE, L.L.C.

241 MAIN STREET
HARTFORD, CONNECTICUT 06106-1817
Telephone: 860-724-6667
Facsimile: 860-293-1979

Litigation in all Courts. Insurance Defense, Fidelity, Surety, Construction Law, Professional Malpractice, Insurance Coverage, Toxic Torts, Products Liability, Commercial Litigation and Subrogation.

PENROSE WOLF, born Rockwood, Pennsylvania, October 17, 1925; admitted to bar, 1967, Connecticut. *Education:* Pennsylvania State University (B.S., 1948); University of Connecticut (J.D., 1967). Author: "Munsey Trust and The Federal Tax Lien," The Forum, Vol. VI, #4, 1971; "Deviations in Relet Contract Complete Discharge of the Surety," The Forum,. Vol. X, #1, 1974; "New Limitations and Penalties on Surety's Exercise of its Traditional Rights," The Forum, Vol. XVII, #2, 1981. Architect-Engineer Liability under comm. law, 1986. Corporate Counsel, Hartford Insurance Group, 1980-1984. Chairman, Claims Advisory Committee, Surety Association of America, 1981-1982. Editor, Fidelity and Surety Law Committee Publication, American Bar Association, 1986-1992. Member, National Panel of Arbitrators (Commercial), American Arbitration Association. *Member:* Connecticut and American (Member, 1968— and Vice Chairman, 1975—, Fidelity and Surety Law Committee, Tort and Insurance Practice Section; Member, The Forum Committee on the Construction Industry, 1976—; Chairman, Government Committee, 1983-1984) Bar Associations. ***PRACTICE AREAS:*** Fidelity; Surety; Construction; Subdivisions. ***Email:*** pwolf@wolfhorowitz.com

MATTHEW M. HOROWITZ, born New York City, N.Y., April 23, 1952; admitted to bar, 1976, District of Columbia; 1977, U.S. Court of Appeals, Fifth Circuit; 1978, Texas and U.S. District Court, Southern District of Texas; 1984, Massachusetts; 1985, U.S. District Court, District of Massachusetts; 1988, Con-

(This Listing Continued)

necticut and U.S. District Court, District of Connecticut. *Education:* Tufts University (B.A., summa cum laude, 1973); New York University (J.D., 1976). Order of the Coif. Contributing Author: "The Law of Payment Bonds", American Bar Association, Fidelity and Surety Law Committee; "The Law of Miscellaneous Bonds", American Bar Association, Fidelity & Surety Law Committee; "Miscellaneous Bond Monograph," American Bar Association Tort and Insurance Practice Section. Lecturer: University of Houston Law Center, Spring, 1981; Lecturer and Clinical Instructor, University of Connecticut School of Law, 1981-1984. Assistant Professor, Western New England College of Law, 1984-1987. *Member:* Connecticut and American (Vice Chair, Fidelity and Surety Law Committee) Bar Associations; The District of Columbia Bar; State Bar of Texas. ***PRACTICE AREAS:*** Fidelity and Surety; Construction. ***Email:*** mhorowitz@wolfhorowitz.com

DEBORAH ETLINGER, born New York, N.Y., March 13, 1957; admitted to bar, 1987, Pennsylvania; 1988, Connecticut; 1993, Massachusetts. *Education:* University of Massachusetts (B.A., 1979); Western New England Law School (J.D., cum laude, 1987). Recipient, American Jurisprudence Book Award — Business Organizations, Contracts, Professional Responsibility. Contributing Author "Law and Practice of Insurance Coverage Litigation", West Group & ABA Tort and Insurance Practice Section, 2000. *Member:* Connecticut (Member, Sections on: Environmental; Litigation; Executive Committee; Gender Equity Committee) and American (Member, Sections on: Tort and Insurance Practice; Litigation and Environmental) Bar Associations; Defense Research Institute. ***PRACTICE AREAS:*** Civil Litigation; Insurance Defense; Employment Defense; Health Insurance; ERISA; Defense; Products Liability; Professional Malpractice; Toxic Tort. ***Email:*** detlinger@wolfhorowitz.com

GARY M. CASE, born Milford, Connecticut, July 29, 1966; admitted to bar, 1991, Connecticut; 1992, U.S. District Court, District of Connecticut; 1992, U.S. Court of Appeals, Second Circuit. *Education:* Fairfield University (B.S., cum laude, 1988); University of Connecticut (J.D., with high honors, 1991). Adjunct Instructor, University of Connecticut School of Law, Moot Court Program, 1994—. Contributing Author: "Law and Practice of Insurance Coverage Litigation," West Group & ABA Tort and Insurance Practice Section 2000. "The Law of Payment Bonds", American Bar Association, Tort and Insurance Practice Section, 1998. *Member:* Connecticut Bar Association. ***PRACTICE AREAS:*** Civil Litigation; Insurance Defense; Fidelity and Surety; Toxic Torts. ***Email:*** gcase@wolfhorowitz.com

JAN MARIA LOCALIO, born Hartford, Connecticut, April 27, 1967; admitted to bar, 2001, Connecticut. *Education:* Williams College (B.A., 1989); University of Connecticut (J.D., 2001); University of Michigan (M.M.A., 1996). Fiedlity and Surety Editor, 2000-2001, Connecticut Law Journal. ***PRACTICE AREAS:*** Insurance Defense; Toxic Torts; Fidelity and Surety; Construction Law. ***Email:*** jlocalio@wolfhorowitz.com

LEGAL SUPPORT PERSONNEL

CATHY BLAISDELL JOHNSON. *Education:* The American University (B.A., 1983). Former Deputy Clerk, U.S. District Court, District of Connecticut. (Paralegal). ***PRACTICE AREAS:*** Fidelity Investigation/Litigation; Surety Investigation/Litigation; General Insurance Defense; Construction Loss/Litigation; Creditors Rights/Bankruptcy. ***Email:*** cblaisdell@wolfhorowitz.com

REPRESENTATIVE CLIENTS: Allstate Reinsurance Company; American Home Assurance Company; American Insurance Company; American International Adjustment Company, Inc.; American International Group, Inc.; American Modern Home Insurance Company; Amwest Surety Insurance Company; Chubb Group of Insurance Cos.; Connecticut General Life Insurance Co.; Cumis Insurance Society, Inc.; CUNA Mutual Group; Fireman's Fund Insurance Company; First Indemnity of America; Frontier Insurance Company; Great American Insurance Company; Greenwich Insurance Co.; International Fidelity Insurance Company; Kember Insurance Co.; Lexington Insurance Company; National Union Fire Insurance Co. of Pittsburg, P.A.; New Hampshire Insurance Company; Ohio Casualty Insurance Company; Philadelphia Insurance Co.; Republic Western Insurance Company; Fire and Marine Insurance Company; Sentry Select Insurance Co.; The Mountbatten Insurance Co.; Travelers Property and Casualty; U.S. United Pacific Insurance Company; Western Surety Company; General Star Management Co.; Arkwright Insurance Co.; Liberty Mutual Insurance Co.; Cigna; National Grange Mutual Ins. Co.; Liberty Bond Services Inc.; Reliance National.

THE LAW OFFICES OF BRIAN J. WOOLF, LLC

HARTFORD, CONNECTICUT

(See East Hartford)

Criminal Defense, State and Federal, (including White Collar), Motor Vehicle and DUI's, Civil Litigation including Major Personal Injury and Negligence Matter, Family Law, Divorce, Child Custody, Banking (New Charters Only), Real Estate and Commercial Loan Workouts.

YULES & YULES, LLC

P.O. BOX 230278
HARTFORD, CONNECTICUT 06123-0278
Telephone: 860-724-5815

New Haven, Connecticut Office: 195 Church Street, Seventeenth Floor. 06510. Telephone: 203-789-1000. Fax: 203-789-6320.
Stamford, Connecticut Office: P.O. Box 522. 06904-0522. Telephone: 203-327-9200.
New York, N.Y. Office: Grand Central Station, P.O. Box 4419. 10163-4419. Telephone: 203-327-9200.

Trial Practice, Automobile, Mobile Carrier, Bad Faith, Corporate Business Torts, Drug and Medical Device Litigation, Fraud, Insurance, Products Liability, Professional Malpractice, Transportation, Workers' Compensation Law, Securities Arbitration and Financial Institutions Litigation.

REPRESENTATIVE CLIENTS: Allstate Insurance Co.; The Atlantic Cos.; Nationwide Insurance Co.; Transamerica Insurance Group; Zurich-American Insurance Cos.; Chubb Group of Insurance Cos.; Dow Corning Corp.; Chrysler Corp.; Air Products & Chemicals, Inc.; Kellogg Co.; Orion Group; American Medical Systems, Inc.; United Farm Bureau Mut. Ins. Co.; National Freight Trucklines, Inc.; Pfizer Inc.; Brethren Mut. Ins. Co.

(For complete biographical data on all personnel, see Professional Biographies at New Haven, Connecticut)

PEASE & SHORTZ, P.C.

52 CHAMBERLAIN HIGHWAY
KENSINGTON, CONNECTICUT 06037
Telephone: 860-828-4879
Fax: 860-828-9432
Email: pease-shortz@erols.com

Taxation and Estate Planning, Probate, Estate and Trust Administration, Business Planning, Business Mediation.

ALLEN H. PEASE, born New Britain, Connecticut, June 15, 1925; admitted to bar, 1954, New York; 1955, Connecticut; 1991, Massachusetts. *Education:* University of Chicago (A.B., 1948); University of Virginia (LL.B., 1953). Phi Alpha Delta. Member, Board of Editors, University of Virginia Law Review, 1952-1953. *Member:* New Britain, Hartford County, Connecticut, New York State, Massachusetts and American Bar Associations. ***PRACTICE AREAS:*** Taxation (20%); Estate Planning (20%); Estate Administration; Trust Administration; Corporate Law. ***Email:*** pease-shortz@erols.com

FREDERICK M. SHORTZ, born Wilkes-Barre, Pennsylvania, June 30, 1955; admitted to bar, 1985, Connecticut. *Education:* Tufts University (B.A., cum laude, 1981); Hastings College of Law, University of California (J.D., 1985). *Member:* Connecticut (Member, Estates and Probate Section, Tax Section) and American (Member, Section of Taxation; Section of Real Property, Probate and Trust Law) Bar Associations. ***PRACTICE AREAS:*** Taxation (10%); Estate Planning (40%); Estate Administration; Trust Administration; Closely Held Corporations (10%). ***Email:*** pease-shortz@erols.com

CRAMER & ANDERSON LLP

KENT GREEN
P.O. BOX 333
KENT, CONNECTICUT 06757
Telephone: 860-927-3568
Fax: 860-927-4194
Email: gnelson@cramer-anderson.com
URL: http://www.cramer-anderson.com

Danbury, Connecticut Office: 68 North Street. Telephone: 203-790-7747. Email: danbury@crameranderson.com
Litchfield, Connecticut Office: 46 West Street. P.O. Box 278. Telephone: 860-567-8718. Email: litchfield@cramer-anderson.com
New Milford, Connecticut Office: 51 Main Street. Telephone: 860-355-2631. Email: newmilford@crameranderson.com
Washington Depot, Connecticut Office: 2 Green Hill Road, P.O. Box 321. Telephone: 860-868-0527. Email: wfairbairn@cramer-anderson.com

General Practice. Probate, Estate Planning, Municipal, Family and Real Estate Law. Trials. Planning and Zoning, Corporate, Banking, Securities.

RESIDENT PARTNER

GRANT J. NELSON, born Clinton, Iowa, November 29, 1935; admitted to bar, 1964, Connecticut. *Education:* Drake University (B.A., 1961); Yale University (LL.B., 1964). Counsel, Town of Kent, 1976-1989. *Member:* Litchfield County (President, 1992-1994) and Connecticut (Member, Executive Commit-

(This Listing Continued)

CRAMER & ANDERSON LLP, Kent—Continued

tee, Real Estate Section, 1986—) Bar Associations. (Resident). ***PRACTICE AREAS:*** Estate Planning Law; Probate Administration Law; Real Estate Law. ***Email:*** gnelson@cramer-anderson.com

COUNSEL FOR: Town of Cornwall; First National Bank of Litchfield; New Milford Hospital, Inc.; Canterbury School; New Mil Bank; South Kent School; Marvelwood School.

(For Complete Personnel and Biographical Data, see Professional Biographies at New Milford, Connecticut).

SIENKIEWICZ & McKENNA, P.C.

25 NORTH MAIN STREET, SUITE 13A
KENT, CONNECTICUT 06757
Telephone: 860-927-4640
Fax: 860-927-1909
URL: http://www.lawyers.com/smlaw

New Milford, Connecticut Office: 9 South Main Street, P.O. Box 786. Telephone: 860-354-1583. Fax: 860-355-4439.

Civil Practice. Personal Injury, Medical Malpractice, Product Liability, Real Estate, Commercial Law, Administrative Law, Family Law, Mediation, Trusts and Estates, Zoning, Planning and Land Use, Contracts, Appellate Practice.

COUNSEL FOR: Town of Kent; New Milford Water Pollution Control Authority; Brookfield Water Pollution Control Authority; Ernest P. Riva & Son, Inc.; Stor-It-All, Inc.; Northeast Communications, Inc.
LOCAL AGENT FOR: Connecticut Attorney's Title Insurance Company; Commonwealth Land Title Ins. Co.
REFERENCES: Town of New Milford; Town of Kent.

(For complete Biographical Data on all Personnel, See Professional Biographies at New Milford, Connecticut)

JONATHAN HOYT

KILLINGWORTH, CONNECTICUT

(See Clinton)

Real Estate both Residential and Commercial, Probate, Estate Planning, Business and Corporate Law, Commercial Transactions.

REID AND RIEGE, P.C.

322 MAIN STREET
LAKEVILLE, CONNECTICUT 06039
Telephone: 860-435-9894
FAX: 860-240-1002
URL: http://www.reidriege.com

Hartford, Connecticut Office: One State Street. Telephone: 860-278-1150. FAX: 860-240-1002.
West Hartford, Connecticut Office: 65 LaSalle Road. Telephone: 860-232-6565. FAX: 860-232-6066.
Woodbury, Connecticut Office: 47 Sherman Hill Road. Telephone: 203-267-6680. FAX: 860-240-1002.

Alternative Dispute Resolution. Antitrust & Trade Regulation. Bankruptcy. Business Law. Commercial Law. Commercial Real Estate/Finance. Corporate Law. Employee Benefits/Pension Plans. Employee Benefits/Taft-Hartley Plans. Environmental Law. Health Care. Labor and Employment. Litigation. Mergers and Acquisitions. Nonprofit and Charitable Organizations. Occupational Safety & Health. Probate. Real Estate. Securities. Taxation. Trade and Professional Associations. Trusts & Estates. Zoning, Planning and Land Use.

TRAVERS T. AUBURN, born Winsted, Connecticut, April 10, 1946; admitted to bar, 1972, Connecticut. *Education:* Williams College (B.A., 1968); University of Connecticut (J.D., 1972). *Member:* Litchfield County, Connecticut and American Bar Associations. ***PRACTICE AREAS:*** Probate; Real Estate; Trusts and Estates. ***Email:*** tauburn@reidandriege.com

SHIPMAN & GOODWIN LLP

12 PORTER STREET
P.O. BOX 1809
LAKEVILLE, CONNECTICUT 06039
Telephone: 860-435-2539
Telecopier: 860-435-0011
Email: www@goodwin.com
URL: http://shipman-goodwin.com

Greenwich, Connecticut Office: 43 Arch Street. Telephone: 203-869-6222.
Hartford, Connecticut Office: One American Row. Telephone: 203-251-5000.
Stamford, Connecticut Office: One Landmark Square. Telephone: 203-324-8100.

General Practice. Banking, Corporation, Tax, Antitrust, Trade Regulation, Finance and Securities, Venture Capital, Labor and Employment, Health Care, Environmental, Professional Liability, Pension and Profit Sharing, Estate Planning, Probate, Trust Administration and Financial Management, Real Estate, Municipal Law. Trials in all Courts.

PARTNER

STUYVESANT K. BEARNS, born Washington, DC, 1937; admitted to bar, 1965, Virginia; 1966, New York; 1975, Connecticut. *Education:* Yale University (B.A., magna cum laude, 1959); University of Virginia (LL.B., 1965). Order of the Coif. Member, Editorial Board, University of Virginia Law Review, 1962-1965. *Member:* Litchfield County, Connecticut (Chairman, 1986-1988, Executive Committee, Estates and Probate Section, 1978-2000) and American Bar Associations. Fellow, American College of Trust and Estate Counsel (Member, 1977—; Connecticut Chairman, 1991-1996). ***PRACTICE AREAS:*** Estate Planning and Settlement Law; Probate Matters; Trust Administration Law; Land Preservation Law. ***Email:*** sbearns@goodwin.com

REPRESENTATIVE CLIENTS: Salisbury Bank & Trust Dept.

(For complete biographical data on all personnel, see Professional Biographies at Hartford, Connecticut)

COHEN & THOMAS

Established in 1936
15 MEADOW STREET
LITCHFIELD, CONNECTICUT 06759
Telephone: 860-567-3754
Fax: 860-567-3894
Email: cohen.and.thomas@att.net
URL: http://www.lawyers.com/cohen-and-thomas-attys

Derby, Connecticut Office: 315 Main Street, P.O. Box 313, 06418. Telephone: 203-735-9521. Fax: 203-732-8129.

General Civil and Criminal Practice. Trials in all Courts. Personal Injury, Negligence and Medical Malpractice Litigation, Real Estate Purchase, Sale, Financing, Zoning and Development, Domestic Law and Divorce, Probate, Wills and Trusts, Banking, Foreclosure and Workouts, Commercial Litigation and Collections, Municipal, Elder Law, Worker's Compensation.

(For Complete biographical data on all personnel, See Professional Biographies at Derby, Connecticut)

CRAMER & ANDERSON LLP

46 WEST STREET
P.O. BOX 278
LITCHFIELD, CONNECTICUT 06759-0278
Telephone: 860-567-8718
Fax: 860-567-4531
Email: litchfield@cramer-anderson.com
URL: http://www.cramer-anderson.com

Danbury, Connecticut Office: 68 North Street. Telephone: 203-790-7747. Email: danbury@crameranderson.com
Kent, Connecticut Office: Kent Green, P.O. Box 333. Telephone: 860-927-3568. Email: gnelson@cramer-anderson.com
New Milford, Connecticut Office: 51 Main Street. Telephone: 860-355-2631. Email: newmilford@crameranderson.com
Washington Depot, Connecticut Office: 2 Green Hill Road, P.O. Box 321. Telephone: 860-868-0527.Email: wfairbairn@cramer-anderson.com

General Practice. Probate, Estate Planning, Taxation, Municipal, Family, Real Estate, Negligence and Bankruptcy Law. Civil and Criminal Trials. Planning and Zoning, Corporate, Banking, Securities.

FIRM PROFILE: Cramer & Anderson, founded over one-hundred years ago, is a firm of diversely qualified attorneys that offers a wide range of sophisticated legal services to individual and business clients. In the past decade, Cramer & Anderson has grown to become the largest law firm in Litchfield County, with offices in Kent, Litchfield, New Milford and Washington, as well as an office in Danbury, Fairfield County. Listed in Martindale-Hubbell's Bar Register of Preeminent Lawyers, Cramer & Anderson's principal areas of practice include: general business, corporate and commercial law; estate planning, trusts, probate administration and elder law; litigation in all courts, ranging from commercial litigation to personal injury and family law; planning and zoning, residential and commercial real estate law. Our attorneys regularly appear in Connecticut's Superior and Appellate Courts, as well as in the Federal District Court, Second Circuit Court of Appeals, and bankruptcy courts. The firm has expanded into new areas of the law as its client base has diversified. Cramer & Anderson takes pride in its long tradition of

(This Listing Continued)

commitment by our attorneys to professional excellence, and to public service with community, charitable and civic organizations. Using the resources of our experienced attorneys, paralegals and staff, together with our advanced technological resources, we are committed to serving our clients personally and professionally.

MEMBERS OF FIRM

DAVID CRAMER (1902-1981).

CLAYTON L. BLICK, born Waterbury, Connecticut, August 7, 1917; admitted to bar, 1941, Connecticut. *Education:* New York University (A.B., 1938); New York University School of Law (J.D., 1941). *Member:* Litchfield County, Connecticut and American Bar Associations. (Resident). ***PRACTICE AREAS:*** Real Estate Law; Probate Administration Law; Estate Planning Law. ***Email:*** cblick@cramer-anderson.com

PERLEY H. GRIMES, JR., born Portland, Maine, June 7, 1944; admitted to bar, 1969, Connecticut; 1971, U.S. District Court, District of Connecticut. *Education:* Dartmouth College (B.A., 1966); Georgetown University (J.D., 1969). Phi Delta Phi. Town Counsel: Litchfield, 1970-1974; Cornwall, 1978—. *Member:* Litchfield County, Connecticut and American Bar Associations; Connecticut Trial Lawyers Association. (Resident). ***PRACTICE AREAS:*** Estate Planning; Probate Administration; Real Estate; Zoning, Planning and Land Use. ***Email:*** pgrimes@cramer-anderson.com

ROBERT L. FISHER, JR., born New York, N.Y., August 3, 1946; admitted to bar, 1976, Connecticut; 1977, U.S. District Court, District of Connecticut; 1984, U.S. Supreme Court. *Education:* Princeton University (A.B., 1972); University of Connecticut (J.D., 1976). Director, Connecticut Attorneys Title Insurance Co. *Member:* Litchfield County and Connecticut Bar Associations; The Association of Trial Lawyers of America; The Connecticut Trial Lawyers Association. [1st Lt., U.S. Army, 1966-1969]. (Resident). ***PRACTICE AREAS:*** Real Estate Law; Planning and Zoning Law; Civil Litigation; Elder Law. ***Email:*** rfisher@cramer-anderson.com

WILLIAM C. FRANKLIN, born New Milford, Connecticut, June 30, 1953; admitted to bar, 1978, Connecticut and U.S. District Court, District of Connecticut. *Education:* Bates College (B.A., 1975); Rutgers University (J.D., 1978). State Attorney Trial Referee, 1994—; State Fact Finder, 1994—. *Member:* Litchfield County and Connecticut Bar Associations; The Association of Trial Lawyers of America; Connecticut Trial Lawyers Association. (Resident). ***PRACTICE AREAS:*** Commercial Litigation; General Civil Litigation; Personal Injury Litigation; Civil Appeals. ***Email:*** wfranklin@cramer-anderson.com

BARRY S. MOLLER, born Simsbury, Connecticut, February 27, 1956; admitted to bar, 1987, Connecticut and U.S. District Court, District of Connecticut. *Education:* Nasson College (B.A., 1978); Drake University (M.A., 1984); University of Bridgeport (J.D., 1986). *Member:* Litchfield County and Connecticut (Member, Executive Committee, Litigation and Workers Compensation Sections, 1997—) Bar Associations. (Resident). ***PRACTICE AREAS:*** Personal Injury; Workers Compensation Law. ***Email:*** bmoller@cramer-anderson.com

JAMES D. HIRSCHFIELD, born Westbury, New York, July 13, 1957; admitted to bar, 1985, Connecticut and U.S. District Court, District of Connecticut; 1986, New Hampshire; 1996, U.S. Supreme Court. *Education:* Central Connecticut State College (B.A., 1980); University of Bridgeport (J.D., 1985). Phi Delta Phi. Recipient, American Jurisprudence Award for Property. *Member:* Litchfield County and Connecticut Bar Associations. (Resident). ***PRACTICE AREAS:*** Family Law; Divorce; Custody and Visitation; Support; Paternity; Criminal Defense; Civil Litigation; Trials and Appeals. ***Email:*** jhirschfield@cramer-anderson.com

GRANT J. NELSON (for complete biographical date, See Professional Biographies at Kent, CT).

REGINALD WILLIAM H. FAIRBAIRN (for complete biographical data, See Professional Biographies at Washington Depot, CT).

RANDALL J. BREECKNER (for complete biographical data, See Professional Biographies at New Milford, CT).

ARTHUR C. WEINSHANK (for complete biographical data, See Professional Biographies at New Milford, CT).

DAVID P. BURKE (for complete biographical data, See Professional Biographies at Danbury, CT).

JOSEPH A. SAFFI (for complete biographical data, See Professional Biographies at Danbury, CT).

D. RANDALL DiBELLA (for complete biographical data, See Professional Biographies at New Milford, CT).

MITCHELL J. MELNICK (for complete biographical data, See Professional Biographies at New Milford, CT).

JOHN D. TOWER (for complete biographical data, See Professional Biographies at New Milford, CT).

(This Listing Continued)

LISA L. BUZAID (for complete biographical data, See Professional Biographies at New Milford, CT).

ASSOCIATES

DENISE M. CLOUTIER, born Gardner, Massachusetts, September 2, 1961; admitted to bar, 1991, Connecticut; U.S. District Court, District of Connecticut. *Education:* Dartmouth College (B.A., 1983); Columbia University (J.D., 1991). Law Clerk to Magistrate Judge Donna Martinez, U.S. District Court, District of Connecticut, 1996-1998. (Resident). ***LANGUAGES:*** French. ***PRACTICE AREAS:*** Civil Litigation; Family Law. ***Email:*** dcloutier@cramer-anderson.com

ROSEMARY B. JONES (for complete biographical data, See Professional Biographies at New Milford, CT).

OF COUNSEL

ROBERT M. FITZGERALD, born Torrington, Connecticut, October 14, 1926; admitted to bar, 1950, Connecticut; 1951, Colorado; 1952, U.S. District Court, Connecticut; 1959, U.S. Court of Appeals, 2nd Circuit. *Education:* Yale University (B.A., 1948); New York University (LL.B., 1950). Phi Delta Phi. Assistant United States Attorney, District of Connecticut, 1953-1955. ***Email:*** rfitzgerald@cramer-anderson.com

STEPHEN N. HUME (for complete biographical data, See Professional Biographies at New Milford, CT).

HENRY B. ANDERSON (for complete biographical data, See Professional Biographies at New Milford, CT).

PAUL B. ALTERMATT (for complete biographical data, See Professional Biographies at New Milford, CT).

COUNSEL FOR: Town of Cornwall; First National Bank of Litchfield; New Milford Hospital, Inc.; Canterbury School; New Mil Bank; South Kent School; Marvelwood School.

(For Complete Personnel and Biographical Data, see Professional Biographies at New Milford, Connecticut).

GAGER & PETERSON, LLP

Established in 1917

782 BANTAM ROAD

LITCHFIELD, CONNECTICUT 06759

Telephone: 860-567-0828
Telecopier: 860-567-5844

Mailing Address: 782 Bantam Road, P.O. Box 815, Bantam, CT 06750-0815

Waterbury, Connecticut Office: One Exchange Place, P.O. Box 2480. Telephone: 203-597-5100. Telecopier: 203-757-7888.

Bethel, Connecticut Office: 2 Stony Hill Road. Telephone: 203-207-5400. Telecopier: 203-207-5407.

Sharon, Connecticut Office: 25 West Main Street, P.O. Box 158. Telephone: 860-364-5531. Telecopier: 860-364-5805.

Southbury, Connecticut Office: 325 Main Street South. Telephone: 203-262-6600. Telecopier: 203-262-6780.

General Practice. Corporate Law, Banks and Banking, Securities, Administrative Law, Litigation in all Courts, Insurance, Trusts and Estates, Probate, Health Care, Real Estate, Commercial Real Estate, Commercial Law, Taxation, Patents, Trademarks, Copyrights, Consumer Law, Computers and Software, Family Law, Environmental Law, Employment Law.

MARY M. ACKERLY, born Stamford, Connecticut, August 21, 1947; admitted to bar, 1977, Connecticut. *Education:* Barnard College (B.A., magna cum laude, 1970); Yale University (J.D., 1977). Phi Beta Kappa. Judge of Probate, District of Norfolk, Connecticut, 1987-1995. Member: Probate Advisory Committee, Connecticut Law Revision Commission, 1988—; Council on Probate Judicial Conduct, 1989-1994. *Member:* Litchfield County, The Connecticut (Member, Executive Committee, Estates and Probate Section, 1984—) and American Bar Associations. Fellow, American College of Trust and Estate Counsel. (Resident). ***PRACTICE AREAS:*** Estate Planning; Probate; Estate and Trust Administration; Elder Law; Real Estate. ***Email:*** mackerly@gplitchfield.com

J. MICHAEL SCONYERS, born Yazoo City, Mississippi, November 23, 1946; admitted to bar, 1976, Virginia; 1979, District of Columbia; 1981, Connecticut. *Education:* Georgia State University (A.B., summa cum laude, 1973); George Washington University (J.D., 1976). *Member:* The District of Columbia Bar; Virginia State Bar; Litchfield County, Connecticut and American Bar Associations. [LT. Col., USMCR, Ret.]. (Also at Sharon Office). ***PRACTICE AREAS:*** Civil Litigation; Real Property Law; Family Law; Planning and Zoning Law.

DONNA D. VINCENTI, born New Britain, Connecticut, February 7, 1956; admitted to bar, 1983, Maine; 1984, Connecticut. *Education:* Colby College

(This Listing Continued)

GAGER & PETERSON, LLP, Litchfield—Continued

(B.A., cum laude, 1978); University of Maine School of Law (J.D., 1983). Member: Connecticut Estate and Tax Planning Council; Greater Hartford Probate Forum. *Member:* Litchfield County, Connecticut (Member, Estates and Probate Section; Elder Law and Tax Sections) and American (Member, Real Property, Probate and Trust Law Section) Bar Associations. ***PRACTICE AREAS:*** Estate Administration; Trust Administration; Probate; Estate Planning; Elder Law; Business Succession Planning. **Email:** dvincenti@gplitchfield.com

JO E. FRIDAY (See Sharon listing).

LAW OFFICES OF PETER C. HERBST

LITCHFIELD, CONNECTICUT

(See Torrington)

Land Use Law, Land Development Law, Zoning Law, Wetlands Law, Real Estate Transactions.

WILLIAM H. CLENDENEN, JR.

A PROFESSIONAL CORPORATION

MADISON, CONNECTICUT

(See New Haven)

General Civil and Appellate Practice. Banking, Civil Rights, Employment, Construction, Consumer, Commercial Litigation, Estates and Probate, Real Estate, Personal Injury. General Litigation in all Courts.

MARSHAL D. GIBSON

PROFESSIONAL CORPORATION

MADISON, CONNECTICUT

(See New Haven)

Federal Income Taxation, Estate Planning, Corporate, Pension, Probate Law and Tax Litigation.

SNOW, ATTICKS & HOLLO, LLC

69 WALL STREET
P.O. BOX 247
MADISON, CONNECTICUT 06443
Telephone: 203-245-4800
Facsimile: 203-245-4495
Toll Free: 888-9-THE-LAW
Email: sahattys@aol.com
URL: http://www.lawyers.com/sahattys

General Practice including Real Estate, Financing, Banking, Business Law, Probate, Wills, Tax, Trusts and Estates, Personal Injury and Civil and Criminal Litigation, Family Law, Trials in all State and Federal Courts.

DONALD F. SNOW, JR., born July 5, 1947; admitted to bar, 1972, Connecticut. *Education:* Norwich University Vermont College (B.A., 1969); William and Mary College (J.D., 1972). Member, Board of Finance, Town of Madison, Connecticut. *Member:* Connecticut and American Bar Associations. ***PRACTICE AREAS:*** Real Estate; Corporate; Banking; Financing.

JOHN K. ATTICKS, III, born Hartford, Connecticut, June 15, 1938; admitted to bar, 1972, Connecticut and U.S. District Court, District of Connecticut. *Education:* University of Connecticut (B.A., 1964; J.D., 1972). Member, Panel of Arbitrators, American Arbitration Association. Treasurer, Democratic Town Committee, Town of Madison, Connecticut. *Member:* Hartford County and Connecticut Bar Associations. ***PRACTICE AREAS:*** Real Estate; Foreclosures; Workouts; Commercial Litigation; Probate; Contracts; Business Organization; Condominium Law.

LESLIE S. HOLLO, born New York, N.Y., September 14, 1963; admitted to bar, 1988, New York and U.S. District Court, Southern and Eastern Districts of New York; 1992, Connecticut and U.S. District Court, District of Connecticut; 1994, U.S. Claims Court. *Education:* Columbia University (B.A., summa cum laude, 1986; J.D., 1987). Phi Beta Kappa. Research and Writing Editor, Columbia Human Rights Law Review, 1986-1987. Pro-Bono Attorney, The Law Works for People. Volunteer Lecturer, School Volunteers for New Haven, Inc. Member, Board of Directors, SARAH Tuxis Residential Services. *Member:* New Haven County, Connecticut (Member, Committee on Solo and Small Firm Practice) and American (Member, Tort and Insurance Practice Section) Bar Associations; Association of the Bar of the City of New York. ***PRACTICE AREAS:*** Litigation; Negligence; Personal Injury Law; Criminal Defense; Family Law.

BARLOW, MURPHY & LAVIGNE, LLP

Established in 1984

172 EAST CENTER STREET
MANCHESTER, CONNECTICUT 06040-5252
Telephone: 860-646-4081
Fax: 860-645-1608
Email: info@barlow-murphy.com
URL: http://www.lawyers.com/barlowmurphy

General Civil Practice before State and Federal Courts. Personal Injury, Real Estate, Estate Planning, Elder Law and Probate Administration, Trials and Appeals, Probate, Elder Law, Business Law, Foreclosure, Bankruptcy.

MEMBERS OF FIRM

MALCOLM F. BARLOW, born Manchester, Connecticut, July 20, 1943; admitted to bar, 1978, Connecticut. *Education:* University of Connecticut (B.A., 1965; J.D., 1977). *Member:* Manchester, Hartford County, Connecticut and American Bar Associations. ***PRACTICE AREAS:*** Real Estate; Probate; Elder Law. **Email:** mfbarlow@barlow-murphy.com

BRIAN J. MURPHY, born Manchester, Connecticut, August 11, 1958; admitted to bar, 1996, Connecticut; 1999, U.S. District Court, District of Connecticut. *Education:* Eastern Connecticut State University (B.S., magna cum laude, 1989); University of Connecticut (J.D., 1995). *Member:* Manchester, Hartford County, Connecticut and American Bar Associations. ***PRACTICE AREAS:*** Real Estate; General Practice; Construction Law. **Email:** bjmurphy@barlow-murphy.com

GARY D. LAVIGNE, born Dallas, Texas, May 4, 1953; admitted to bar, 1980, Connecticut and U.S. District Court, District of Connecticut. *Education:* University of Connecticut (B.A., 1974); Western New England School of Law (J.D., 1978). Member: Willimantic Chamber of Commerce; Business Network International; Tri-County Board of Realtos (Board Attorney). ***PRACTICE AREAS:*** Residential Real Estate; Commercial Real Estate; Corporate Law; Business Law; Foreclosures; Bankruptcy; Estate Planning; Securities. **Email:** gdlavigne@barlow-murphy.com

REPRESENTATIVE CLIENTS: Housing Authority of the Town of Manchester; The Donwell Co.
REFERENCES: Connecticut Attorney's Title Insurance Co.; Savings Bank of Manchester.

BECK & ELDERGILL, P.C.

447 CENTER STREET
MANCHESTER, CONNECTICUT 06040
Telephone: 860-646-5606
FAX: 860-646-0054
Email: firm@beckeldergill.com
URL: http://www.beckeldergill.com

Hartford, Connecticut Office: 97 Oak Street. 06109. Telephone: 860-522-5606.

General Civil and Criminal Litigation before all State and Federal Trial and Appellate Courts with a concentration on Employment, Civil Rights, Personal Injury, Car Accidents and Divorce.

BRUCE S. BECK, born Brooklyn, New York, September 3, 1946; admitted to bar, 1973, Connecticut and U.S. District Court, District of Connecticut; 1974, U.S. Court of Appeals, Second Circuit; 1977, U.S. Supreme Court. *Education:* University of Maryland (B.S., 1969); Catholic University of America (J.D., 1973). State of Connecticut Attorney Trial Referee. Special Master, Superior Court. *Member:* Manchester Bar Association (President); Connecticut Trial Lawyers Association (Member, Board of Governors, 1992-1996). ***REPORTED CASES:*** Silver v. Jacobs, 43 Conn. App. 184 (1996); Karen v. Parciak Karen, 40 Conn. App. 697 (1996); Battersby v. Battersby, 218 Conn. 467 (1991); Mulholland v. Mulholland, 26 Conn. App. 585 (1992); Watson v. Watson, 20 Conn. App. 551 (1990); Banks v. Vito, 19 Conn. App. 256 (1989); SHVC, Inc. v. Roy, 188 Conn. 503 (1982); Hryniewicz v. Wilson, 51 Conn. App. 440 (1998); Lewin v. U.S. Sergical Corp., 21 Conn. App. 629 (1990); Double I Limited Partnership v. Town of Glasonbury, 14 Conn. App. 77 (1998); In re West Service Corp., 225 B.R. 537 (Bankr.D.Conn., 1998); In re Hryniewicz, 222 B.R. 14 (Bankr.D.Conn. 1998); Matter of Fiore, 27 B.R. 48 (Bankr.D.Conn. 1998); Matter of Gorin, 18 B.R. 151 (Bankr.D.Conn. 1982); Matter of Win-Sum Sports, Inc., 14 B.R. 389 (Bankr.D.Conn. 1981); Matter of Begley, 12 B.R. 839 (Bankr.D.Conn. 1981); Matter of Majewski, 7 B.R. 904 (Bankr.D.Conn. 1981); Matter of Grimaldi, 3 B.R. 533 (Bankr.D.Conn. 1980); Thompson v. Orcutt 257 Conn. 301 (2001); Pospisil v. Pospisil 59 Conn. App. 446 (2000). ***PRACTICE AREAS:*** Commercial Litigation; Domestic Relations; Bankruptcy.

(This Listing Continued)

KATHLEEN ELDERGILL, born Mount Kisco, N.Y., January 16, 1953; admitted to bar, 1981, Connecticut and U.S. District Court, District of Connecticut; 1983, U.S. Court of Appeals, Second Circuit; 1988, U.S. Supreme Court. *Education:* University of Connecticut (B.A., highest honors , Phi Beta Kappa, 1975; J.D., with high honors, 1981). Small Claims Commissioner State of Connecticut. Special Master, United States District Court for the District of Connecticut. *Member:* Manchester Bar Association; Association of Trial Lawyers of America; Connecticut Trial Lawyers Association; Connecticut Employment Lawyers Association; National Employment Lawyers Association. Fellow: American College of Trial Lawyers; Connecticut Bar Foundation, James W. Cooper Fellows Program. (Certified in Civil Trial Advocacy by the National Board of Trial Advocacy). ***REPORTED CASES:*** Meyers v. Cornwell Quality Tools, Inc., 41 Conn. App. 19 (1996); Starr v. Commissioner of Environment Protection, 236 Conn. 722 (1996); Sadloski v. Manchester, 235 Conn. 637 (1995); Schnabel v. Tyler, 230 Conn. 735 (1994); Tyler v. Schnabel, 34 Conn. App. 216 (1994); Sadloski v. Manchester, 228 Conn. 79 (1993); Schnabel v. Tyler, 32 Conn. App. 704 (1993); State v. Ball, 226 Conn. 265 (1993); Starr v. Commissioner of Environmental Protection, 226 Conn. 358 (1993); Lester v. Resort Camplands International, Inc. 27 Conn. App. 59 (1992); Killingly v. Connecticut Siting Council, 220 Conn. 516 (1991); Double 1 Ltd. Partnership v. Plan & Zoning Comm. 218 Conn. 65 (1991); Preston v. Department of Environmental Protection, 218 Conn. 821 (1991); Concerned Citizens of Sterling v. Ct. Siting CNCl., 215 Conn. 474 (1990); Preston v. Connecticut Siting Council, 21 Conn. App. 85 (1990); Lewin v. United States Surgical Corporation, 21 Conn. App. 629 (1990); Preston v. Connecticut Siting Council, 20 Conn. App. 474 (1990); Zinker v. Doty, 907 F.2d 357 (2d Cir. 1990) and 637 F. Supp. 138 (D. Conn. 1986); Connecticut Light & Power Co. v. Dept., Pub. UTIL., 210 Conn. 349 (1989); Dorman v. Satti, 862 F.2d 432 (2d Cir. 1988) and 678 F. Supp. 375 (D. Conn. 1988); Brady v. Town of Colchester, 863 F.2d 205 (2d Cir. 1988); Frost v. Chromalloy Aero. Tech. Corp., 697 F. Supp. 82 (D. Conn. 1988); Sadlowski v. Manchester, 206 Conn. 579 (1988); United States v. Rosario, 820 F. 2d 584 (2d Cir. 1987); Concerned Citizens of Sterling v. Town of Sterling, 204 Conn. 551 (1987); Mumford Cove Assn., Inc. v. Town of Groton 786 F. 2d 530 (2d Cir. 1986); State v. Ostroski, 201 Conn. 534 (1986); State v. Shifflett, 199, Conn. 718 (1986); Coollick v. Windham, 7 Conn. App. 142 (1986); State v. Stanley, 197 Conn. 309 (1985); State v. Pelletier, 196 Conn. 32 (1985); Acheson v. White, 195 Conn. 211 (1985); State v. McCulley 5 Conn. App. 612 (1985); Southland Corp. v. Vernon, 1 Conn. App. 439 (1984); Williams v. CHRO on Human Rights & CHRO 257 Conn. 258 (2001). ***PRACTICE AREAS:*** Employment; Civil Rights; Civil Litigation; Consumer Law; Environmental Law.

KENNETH I. FRIEDMAN, born Sayre, Pennsylvania; December 17, 1962; admitted to bar, 1988, Connecticut and U.S. District Court, District of Connecticut; 2000, U.S. Court of Appeals, Second Circuit. *Education:* Cornell University (A.B., with distinction, 1985); Vanderbilt University (J.D., 1988). Phi Delta Phi. Associate Editor, Vanderbilt University Law Review, 1987-1988. Factfinder/Arbitrator, State of Connecticut Superior Court. *Member:* Manchester, Connecticut and American Bar Associations; Connecticut Trial Lawyers Association; Connecticut Employment Lawyers Association; National Employment Lawyers Association. ***REPORTED CASES:*** Pintavalle v. Valkanos, 216 Conn. 412 (1990); Lacasse v. Burns, 214 Conn. 464 (1990); Blake v. H-2A & H-2B Voluntary Employees Beneficiary Association, 952 F.Supp. 927 (D.Conn. 1997); Reynolds v. Frank, 786 F. Supp. 168 (D.Conn 1992); Gandelman v. Aetna Ambulance Service, Inc., 48 F. Supp. 2d 169 (D. Conn. May 10, 1999); Zoldak v. Tacala, Inc., 2000 WL 1576419 (D. Conn. 2000). ***PRACTICE AREAS:*** Employment; Personal Injury; Civil Litigation; Civil Rights.

MARC P. MERCIER, born Hartford, Connecticut, July 4, 1965; admitted to bar, 1991, Connecticut and U.S. District Court, District of Connecticut. *Education:* University of Connecticut (B.A., 1987; J.D., with honors, 1991). *Member:* Manchester and Hartford County Bar Associations; Connecticut Employment Lawyers Association. ***REPORTED CASES:*** Gerber & Hurley, Inc. v. CCC Corp., 36 Conn.App. 539 (1995); Albuquerque v. Albuquerque, 42 Conn.App. 284 (1996); Silver v. Jacobs, 43 Conn.App. 184 (1996). ***PRACTICE AREAS:*** Civil Litigation; Employment; Civil Rights; School and Education Law.

FATIMA T. LOBO, born Chaves, Portugal, August 7, 1966; admitted to bar, 1991, Connecticut and U.S. District Court, District of Connecticut. *Education:* University of Connecticut (B.A. magna cum laude, 1988; J.D., with honors, 1991). Small Claims Commissioner, State of Connecticut. *Member:* Manchester, Connecticut and American Bar Associations; Connecticut Trial Lawyers Association. ***REPORTED CASES:*** Woronecki v. Trappe, 228 Conn. 574 (1994); Wilson v. Planning and Zoning Com'n of the Town of East Granby, 729 A.2d 791, 53 Conn. App. 182 (Conn. App. 1999), cert. granted; Wilson v. Planning and Zoning Com'n of the Town of East Granby, 733 A.2d 850, 249 Conn. 927 (Conn. 1999). ***PRACTICE AREAS:*** Domestic Relations; Probate; Real Estate; Bankruptcy and Credit Problems.

DAVID R. KRITZMAN, born Waterbury, Connecticut, April 8, 1958; admitted to bar, 1984, Connecticut; 1985, U.S. District Court, District of Connecticut. *Education:* University of Connecticut (B.A., magna cum laude, 1980; J.D., 1984). *Member:* Connecticut Bar Association; Connecticut Trial Lawyers Association; Association of Trial Lawyers of America; Connecticut Criminal Defense Lawyers Association. ***REPORTED CASES:*** Michaud v. Wawruck, 209 Conn. 407 (1998). ***PRACTICE AREAS:*** Criminal; Personal Injury; Family Litigation.

MATTHEW R. POTTER, born Windham, Connecticut, March 25, 1969; admitted to bar, 1994, Connecticut; 1995, U.S. District Court, District of Connecticut. *Education:* George Washington University (B.A., with honors, 1991); Western New England School of Law (J.D., 1994). *Member:* Manchester, Connecticut and American Bar Associations. ***PRACTICE AREAS:*** Personal Injury; Domestic Relations; Criminal Litigation; Bankruptcy and Credit Problems.

DEREK V. OATIS, born Meriden, Connecticut, September 2, 1966; admitted to bar, 1998, Connecticut. *Education:* Southern Connecticut State University (B.A., 1991); University of Connecticut School of Law (J.D., 1998). *Member:* Manchester Bar Association. ***REPORTED CASES:*** Hyllen-Davey v. Plan and Zoning Com'n of Town of Glastonbury, 57 Conn. App. 589, (2000), cert denied 253 Conn. 926, (2000); Animal Rights Front v. Rocque, 63 Conn. App. 207, (2001). ***PRACTICE AREAS:*** Employment; Environmental Law; Criminal Litigation; Zoning Law.

MARIA C. MONICK, born Greenwich, Connecticut, April 30, 1965; admitted to bar, 1996, Connecticut; 1997, U.S. District Court, District of Connecticut. *Education:* Bryant College (B.S., 1987); Western New England College (J.D., 1996). ***PRACTICE AREAS:*** Criminal Law; Foreclosures; Probate; Real Estate; Bankruptcy.

ELAINE N. CAMPOSEO

445 CENTER STREET
P.O. BOX 741
MANCHESTER, CONNECTICUT 06045-0741
Telephone: 860-643-8330
Telefax: 860-646-0054
Email: ENCamposeo@aol.com

Probate, Wills and Estate Planning, Real Estate, Parental Rights, Landlord & Tenant Law, Mortgages.

ELAINE N. CAMPOSEO, born Hartford, Connecticut, May 24, 1947; admitted to bar, 1989, Connecticut. *Education:* Hartford College for Women (A.A., 1969); Eastern Connecticut State University (B.S., magna cum laude, 1983); Western New England College (J.D., 1988). Judge of Probate; Executive Committee, Chairperson, Financial Advisory Committee and Planning Committee, District of Andover (Andover, Bolton and Columbia), 1991—. *Member:* Manchester, Connecticut and American Bar Associations; National College Probate Judges.

JACOBS, WALKER, RICE & BASCHE, P.C.

146 MAIN STREET
P.O. BOX 480
MANCHESTER, CONNECTICUT 06045-0480
Telephone: 860-646-0121
Fax: 860-645-6229
Email: jwrblaw@hotmail.com

General Practice. Banking, Probate and Estate Planning, Commercial Transactions, Secured Transactions, Commercial and Residential Real Estate, Zoning, Corporation and Taxation Law, Civil and Commercial Litigation, Creditors Rights.

RONALD JACOBS, born Hartford, Connecticut, January 27, 1927; admitted to bar, 1952, Connecticut; 1967, U.S. Tax Court. *Education:* Trinity College (B.A., 1948); University of Connecticut (LL.B., with honors, 1952); Boston University (LL.M. in Taxation, 1966). *Member:* Manchester and Connecticut Bar Associations. ***PRACTICE AREAS:*** Corporation; Taxation; Probate; Estate Planning and Administration; Commercial Transactions. **Email:** jacobs1946@hotmail.com

LEONARD JACOBS, born Hartford, Connecticut, June 24, 1943; admitted to bar, 1968, Connecticut. *Education:* University of Connecticut (B.S., 1965; LL.B., 1968); Boston University (LL.M. in Taxation, 1974). Phi Kappa Phi; Beta Gamma Sigma. *Member:* Manchester and Connecticut Bar Associations. ***PRACTICE AREAS:*** Zoning; Commercial Real Estate; Commercial Transactions; Secured Transactions; Banking. **Email:** lenjacobs@hotmail.com

JEAN T. WALKER, born Torrington, Connecticut, September 1, 1943; admitted to bar, 1985, Connecticut. *Education:* Connecticut College (B.A., summa cum laude, 1965); Harvard University (M.A.T., 1967); University of Connecticut (J.D., with honors, 1985). Phi Beta Kappa. Woodrow Wilson Fel-

(This Listing Continued)

JACOBS, WALKER, RICE & BASCHE, P.C., Manchester—Continued

lowship, 1965-1966. *Member:* Manchester, Connecticut and American Bar Associations. ***PRACTICE AREAS:*** Commercial and Residential Real Estate. ***Email:*** jatwalker@hotmail.com

MICHAEL J. RICE, born Hartford, Connecticut, August 27, 1961; admitted to bar, 1986, Connecticut. *Education:* University of Connecticut (B.S., 1983); Vermont Law School (J.D., 1986); Boston University (LL.M., in Taxation, 1991). *Member:* Manchester and Connecticut Bar Associations. ***PRACTICE AREAS:*** Corporation; Taxation; Probate; Estate Planning and Administration; Commercial Transactions; Secured Transactions; Residential Real Estate. ***Email:*** mjarice@hotmail.com

STEVEN M. BASCHE, born Boston, Massachusetts, May 30, 1961; admitted to bar, 1986, Connecticut and U.S. District Court of Connecticut. *Education:* University of Connecticut (B.A., magna cum laude, 1983; J.D., with honors, 1986). Phi Beta Kappa. Member, Moot Court Board, 1983-1986. *Member:* Manchester, Hartford County, and Connecticut (Member, Commercial Law and Bankruptcy Sections) Bar Associations. ***PRACTICE AREAS:*** Civil Litigation; Commercial Litigation; Construction Litigation; Intellectual Property Litigation; Commercial Real Estate; Residential Real Estate; Creditors Rights. ***Email:*** sbasche@hotmail.com

---

DAVID M. BARRY, JR., born Manchester, Connecticut, December 3, 1963; admitted to bar, 1992, Connecticut. *Education:* Trinity College (B.A., 1985); University of Connecticut (J.D., 1992). Connecticut Law Review; Associate Editor, 1991-1992, Member, 1990-1992. *Member:* Manchester and Connecticut Bar Associations. ***PRACTICE AREAS:*** Zoning; Commercial Transactions; Secured Transactions; Commercial Real Estate; Residential Real Estate. ***Email:*** dmbarrylaw@hotmail.com

CATHERINE J. KULAK, born New York, New York, October 9, 1971; admitted to bar, 2000, Connecticut. *Education:* Douglass College at Rutgers University (B.A., 1993); University of Connecticut (J.D., 2000). *Member:* Manchester and Connecticut Bar Associations. ***PRACTICE AREAS:*** Residential Real Estate; Civil Litigation; Commercial Litigation. ***Email:*** cjkulak@hotmail.com

---

PHELON, FITZGERALD & WOOD, P.C.

Established in 1956

773 MAIN STREET

MANCHESTER, CONNECTICUT 06040

Telephone: 860-643-1136

Fax: 860-643-5773

Email: PFW_LAWFIRM@COMPUSERV.COM

General Civil and Criminal Litigation before all State and Federal Courts. Commercial Litigation, Corporation, Workers' Compensation, Zoning, Wills and Probate, Personal Injury, Medical Malpractice.

FIRM PROFILE: Phelon, FitzGerald & Wood, P.C. was established in 1956 by Herbert A. Phelon, Jr. and the late Philip Bayer. The firm now serves central and eastern Connecticut and offers a wide range of legal services. The firm encourages continuing professional development and all partners and associates participate in continuing legal education seminars, professional association activities and civic affairs.

HERBERT A. PHELON, JR. (1925-2000).

THOMAS P. FITZGERALD, born Manhasset, New York, February 20, 1944; admitted to bar, 1969, Connecticut; 1975, U.S. Supreme Court; 1978, U.S. District Court, District of Connecticut. *Education:* St. Bonaventure University (B.B.A., 1966); Syracuse University (J.D., 1969). Contributing Author: "Litigating Head Trauma Cases," Professional Education Systems, Inc., 1989. Guest Lecturer, Professional Education System, Incorporated (CLE Program), 1988. Special Master, and Member, Grievance Committee, U.S. District Court, District of Connecticut. Member, Board of Directors, Connecticut Traumatic Brain Injury Association. *Member:* Manchester and Connecticut Bar Associations; Connecticut Trial Lawyers Association; The Association of Trial Lawyers of America. ***PRACTICE AREAS:*** Personal Injury; Commercial Litigation; Civil Litigation.

HOWARD M. WOOD, III, born Lawrence, Massachusetts, December 31, 1940; admitted to bar, 1965, Texas; 1971, Connecticut; 1976, U.S. District Court, District of Connecticut. *Education:* University of Hartford (B.S., magna cum laude, 1970); Baylor University (LL.B., 1965); Denver Seminary (M.A., with honors, 1981). *Member:* Connecticut Bar Association; Christian Legal Society. ***PRACTICE AREAS:*** Civil Litigation; Construction Law; Church and Non-Profit Law; Commercial Law.

(This Listing Continued)

MICHAEL M. DARBY, born Manchester, Connecticut, June 13, 1957; admitted to bar, 1982, Connecticut. *Education:* University of Hartford (B.A., summa cum laude, 1978); Duke University (J.D., with honors, 1982). Adjunct Faculty Member, Business Law, University of Hartford, 1985-1988. Town Attorney, Town of Manchester, 1992—. Director: Manchester Chamber of Commerce, 1989-1997; United Way of Manchester, 1986—. *Member:* Manchester, Hartford County and Connecticut Bar Associations. ***PRACTICE AREAS:*** Real Estate; Probate Administration; Estate Planning; Elder Law; Zoning; Small Business Matters.

THOMAS S. FIORENTINO, born Hartford, Connecticut, May 6, 1957; admitted to bar, 1982, Connecticut. *Education:* Fairfield University (B.A., 1979); St. John's University (J.D., 1982). *Member:* Manchester, Hartford County and American Bar Associations. ***PRACTICE AREAS:*** Family and Juvenile Law; Real Estate; Personal Injury; Probate and Estate Planning; Criminal.

JAMES H. HOWARD, born Manchester, Connecticut, April 30, 1963; admitted to bar, 1988, Connecticut; 1990, U.S. District Court, District of Connecticut; 1997, U.S. Court of Appeals, Second Circuit. *Education:* Hobart College (B.A., 1985); University of Connecticut (J.D., 1988). *Member:* Manchester and Connecticut Bar Associations. ***PRACTICE AREAS:*** Civil Litigation; Real Estate.

JAMES J. SULLIVAN, born Hartford, Connecticut, April 7, 1948; admitted to bar, 1973, Connecticut; U.S. District Court, District of Connecticut. *Education:* Providence College (B.A., 1970); University of Fribourg, Fribourg, Switzerland; Suffolk University (J.D., 1973). Phi Alpha Delta. *Member:* Manchester, Hartford County and Connecticut Bar Associations; Connecticut Trial Lawyers Association. ***PRACTICE AREAS:*** Family Law; Real Estate; Probate; Criminal Law; Zoning Law. ***Email:*** pfw_lawfirm@compuserv.com

---

NANCY JEANNE JOHNSON, born Plainfield, New Jersey, August 3, 1957; admitted to bar, 1983, Connecticut; 1985, U.S. District Court, District of Connecticut. *Education:* Georgian Court College (B.A., cum laude, 1979); Western New England College (J.D., cum laude, 1983). Recipient, American Jurisprudence Awards in Administrative Law and in Constitutional Law. Instructor, Introductory Law Courses and CPA Review Course, University of Hartford, 1986-1987. *Member:* Hartford County and Connecticut Bar Associations. ***LANGUAGES:*** French. ***PRACTICE AREAS:*** Probate Administration; Estate Planning; Elder Law.

PETER J. PETRONE, born Manchester, Connecticut, March 1, 1954; admitted to bar, 1982, Connecticut. *Education:* University of Hartford (B.A., magna cum laude, 1978); St. Mary's University of San Antonio (J.D., 1981). *Member:* Connecticut and American Bar Associations. ***PRACTICE AREAS:*** Real Estate; General Practice. ***Email:*** pfw_lawfirm@compuserve.com

REPRESENTATIVE CLIENTS: CFM Construction, Inc.; Christian Radio Fellowship; Dean Machine Products, Inc.; Empire Industries; Encore Productions, Inc.; First Federal Savings & Loan Association; GMAC Mortgage Corp.; Highland Park Market; Liberty Bank; MAP Good Products, Inc.; Northwest Mortgage Co.; PNC Mortgage Corp. of America; The Salvation Army of Connecticut; Town of Manchester; Town of East Windsor; Town of South Windsor; Quarry Ridge Golf Club; Webster Bank.
REFERENCE: First Federal Savings & Loan Association.

BROWN & WELSH, P.C.

Established in 1928

MERIDEN EXECUTIVE PARK

530 PRESTON AVENUE, 2ND FLOOR

P.O. BOX 183

MERIDEN, CONNECTICUT 06450-0183

Telephone: 203-235-1651

Telecopier: 203-235-9600

http://www.brownwelsh.com

URL: http://www.brown&welsh@brownwelsh.com

Domestic and International Business Law and related Litigation, including Contracts, Uniform Commercial Code, Bankruptcy, Arbitration, Corporate Law, Computer Law, Real Property and Probate.

THOMAS J. WELSH, born Milford, Connecticut, July 26, 1953; admitted to bar, 1980, Connecticut and U.S. District Court, District of Connecticut; 1984, U.S. Court of Appeals, Second Circuit; 1988, New York. *Education:* University of Connecticut (B.S., magna cum laude, 1975); Massachusetts Institute of Technology; University of Connecticut (J.D., 1980). Phi Beta Kappa; Phi Kappa Phi; Sigma Pi Sigma. ***REPORTED CASES:*** Shelton v. Commissioner, 193 Conn. 506 (1984). ***PRACTICE AREAS:*** Commercial Law; Uniform Commercial Code; Real Property; Bankruptcy. ***Email:*** tjwelsh@brownwelsh.com

HOUSTON PUTNAM LOWRY, born New York, N.Y., April 1, 1955; admitted to bar, 1980, Connecticut; 1985, District of Columbia; 1989, New York. *Education:* Pitzer College (B.A., 1976); University of Connecticut

(This Listing Continued)

(M.B.A., 1980); Gonzaga University (J.D., cum laude, 1980); University of Cambridge (LL.B., with honors, in International Law, 1981, Redesignated LL.M., 1998); Hague Academy of International Law, The Hague, The Netherlands, 1981 and 1982. Adjunct Faculty Member, University of Connecticut Law School, International Commercial Law and International Commercial Arbitration, 1990—. Law Clerk, U.S. District Court Judge, William M. Acker, Jr., 1982-1983. Visiting Scholar, Yale Law School, 1981-1982. ***REPORTED CASES:*** Figeora v. C&S Ball Bearing, 237 Conn 1 (1996); Bergeron v. Mackler, 225 Conn. 391 (1993); Bell Food Services, Inc. v. Sherbacow, 217 Conn. 476 (1991); Citizens of Bank of Clearwater v. Hunt, 927 F.2d 707 (2d Cir. 1991); 294 Farmington Realty Company v. CFM of Connecticut, Inc., 23 Conn. App. 499, (1990). ***PRACTICE AREAS:*** Business Law; Civil Litigation; Arbitration; International; Appellate Practice; Computer Law. ***Email:*** hplowry@brownwelsh.com

OF COUNSEL

DAVID BROWN, born Waterbury, Connecticut, June 21, 1930; admitted to bar, 1962, Connecticut; 1975, U.S. Court of Appeals, Second Circuit; 1963, U.S. District Court, District of Connecticut. *Education:* University of Connecticut (B.S., 1952; J.D., 1962). ***REPORTED CASES:*** Dick Warner Cargo Handling Corp. v. Aetna Business Credit, Inc. 700 F 2d 858 (CA2, 1983); In Re Brookside Drug Store, Inc. 3 BR 120 (BCD Conn. 1980). ***PRACTICE AREAS:*** Commercial Law; Uniform Commercial Code; Bankruptcy; Probate.

DONOVAN & MORELLO, LLP

Established in 1987
816 BROAD STREET
MERIDEN, CONNECTICUT 06450
Telephone: 860-635-7373
URL: http://www.donmorlaw.com

Cromwell, Connecticut Office: Cromwell West Office Park, 154 West Street. Telephone: 860-635-7373. Fax: 860-635-6734.

General Civil and Criminal Practice before State and Federal Courts. Personal Injury, Product Liability, Workers Compensation Law, Trials, Arbitration, Mediation, Uninsured and Underinsured Motorists, Medical Malpractice.

FIRM PROFILE: Donovan & Morello is a litigation law firm founded in 1987 by John R. Donovan, former chief prosecutor in the Superior Court in Meriden, and Paul A. Morello, Jr., a former partner in a Cheshire law firm that concentrated in insurance defense litigation. The partners have many years of experience in the trial of criminal and civil cases in the Federal and State Courts. Together, they have co-authored "The Handbook of Connecticut Uninsured and Underinsured Motorist Law.".

MEMBERS OF FIRM

JOHN R. DONOVAN, born New Haven, Connecticut, September 12, 1953; admitted to bar, 1979, Connecticut; 1981, U.S. District Court, District of Connecticut. *Education:* University of Virginia (B.A., with distinction, 1975); University of Connecticut (J.D., 1979). Co-Author, "Handbook of Connecticut Uninsured and Underinsured Motorist Law," The Connecticut Law Tribune. Chief Prosecutor, Superior Court, Meriden, Connecticut, 1980-1984. Special Counsel for Wallingford, Connecticut Board of Ethics, 1989. *Member:* Connecticut Criminal Defense Lawyers Association; Connecticut Trial Lawyers Association; The Association of Trial Lawyers of America. ***PRACTICE AREAS:*** Criminal Defense; Driving While Intoxicated; Homicide; Sex Crimes; Drugs and Narcotics. ***Email:*** JRD@Donmorlaw.com

PAUL A. MORELLO, JR., born Middletown, Connecticut, January 24, 1954; admitted to bar, 1979, Connecticut; 1981, U.S. District Court, District of Connecticut. *Education:* College of the Holy Cross (B.A., cum laude, 1976); Albany Law School of Union University (J.D., 1979). Special Master, State of Connecticut Superior Court, 1997—; Special Master, United States District Court, 1998—. Co-Author: "Uninsured/Underinsured Motorist Law In Connecticut," Volume 11, Connecticut Law Tribune, Nos. 12, 13, 1985; Author: "The Problem of Multiple Uninsured Motorist Coverages: Who Pays?" 62 Connecticut Bar Journal 358. Cited in Aetna Cas. & Sur. Co. v. CNA Ins. Co. 221 Conn. 779 (1992); Co-Author: "The Misapplication of Workmens' Compensation Exclusively to UM Claims: Ross v. City of New Haven, 7 CTLA Forum No. 6.; Co-Author: "Handbook of Connecticut Uninsured and Underinsured Motorist Law," The Connecticut Law Tribune. *Member:* Connecticut and American (Member: Litigation Section; Torts and Insurance Practice Section) Bar Associations; Connecticut Trial Lawyers Association; The Association of Trial Lawyers of America. ***REPORTED CASES:*** Aetna Ins. Co. v. Colbert, 38 Conn. Sup. 1 (1983); Aetna Cas. and Sur. Co. v. Murphy 206 Conn. 409 (1988). ***PRACTICE AREAS:*** Personal Injury Law; Medical Malpractice; Bicycle Accidents; Head and Spinal Injury; Uninsured and Underinsured Motorists. ***Email:*** PAM@Donmorlaw.com

(For Complete Biographical Data on all Personnel, see Professional Biographies at Cromwell, Connecticut)

SANDRA K. GERBER

636 BROAD STREET
P.O. BOX 2420
MERIDEN, CONNECTICUT 06450
Telephone: 203-238-1010
Fax: 203-630-1930
URL: http://www.lawyers.com/sgerber,atty

Family, Real Estate, Negligence, Civil Litigation, Workers Compensation, Products Liability, Medical Liability and Professional Malpractice Law.

SANDRA K. GERBER, born Dayton, Ohio, July 10, 1948; admitted to bar, 1983, Connecticut; 1984, U.S. District Court, District of Connecticut. *Education:* University of Bridgeport (B.S., magna cum laude, 1973; J.D., 1983). *Member:* Meriden-Wallingford-Southington and Connecticut Bar Associations. ***PRACTICE AREAS:*** Family Law; Personal Injury; Workers Compensation; General Practice; Civil Litigation; Divorce; Child Custody; Paternity; Child Support.

JACOBS & JACOBS, P.C.

71 CATLIN STREET
P.O. BOX 193
MERIDEN, CONNECTICUT 06450-0193
Telephone: 203-235-5787
Fax: 203-235-0447
Email: jacobs.jacobs@snet.net
URL: http://www.lawyers.com/jacobs&jacobs

Litigation, Civil Trial, Real Estate, Construction, Personal Injury, Workers Compensation, Criminal Defense, Domestic Relations, Real Estate and Social Security Disability Law.

FIRM PROFILE: Jacobs & Jacobs, P.C. is dedicated to providing professional , experienced representation in many areas of the law. The firm is also active in numerous charitable organizations throughout Connecticut. We strive to achieve the most favorable results possible for our clients.

STEPHEN D. JACOBS, born Meriden, Connecticut, December 13, 1946; admitted to bar, 1972, Connecticut; 1980, U.S. District Court, District of Connecticut. *Education:* Georgetown University (A.B., 1969); University of Miami (J.D., 1972). Alderman, Town of Meriden, 1974-1976. Chairman: Meriden Human Rights Commission, 1973-1974; Meriden Community Action Agency, 1977-1979. Justice of the Peace, Connecticut, 1995—. Member, Board of Tax Review, Town of Warren. Former Town Councilman, City of Meriden. Former Member, Zoning Board, Town of Cheshire. Former Chairman, American Red Cross. Member, Caldwell Legal Services. *Member:* Meriden-Wallingford-Southington, Connecticut and American Bar Associations; Connecticut Trial Lawyers Association; The Association of Trial Lawyers of America. ***LANGUAGES:*** Spanish. ***PRACTICE AREAS:*** Personal Injury Law; Criminal Law; Domestic Relations Law; Workers Compensation Law; Real Estate Law. ***Email:*** stephenjacobs@lawyer.com

BARRY JACOBS, born Meriden, Connecticut, March 12, 1952; admitted to bar, 1981, Connecticut; 1982, U.S. District Court, District of Connecticut. *Education:* Alfred University; University of Miami (B.A., 1975); University of Bridgeport (J.D., 1980). Former Local Chairman, March of Dimes. Former Board Member, The Catholic Family, Meriden, CT. Former President, Bradley Park Neighborhood. Member, Caldwell Legal Services. *Member:* Meriden-Wallingford-Southington, Connecticut and American Bar Associations; The Association of Trial Lawyers of America. ***LANGUAGES:*** Spanish. ***PRACTICE AREAS:*** Personal Injury; Real Estate Law; Domestic Relations Law; Criminal Law; Probate.

(Member, Caldwell Legal Services)
REFERENCE: Center Bank.

LAW OFFICES OF NORMAN B. TEAGUE

204 EAST MAIN STREET
P.O. BOX 2404
MERIDEN, CONNECTICUT 06450
Telephone: 203-238-4242
Fax: 203-630-1133
Email: nbt425@hotmail.com
URL: http://www.lawyers.com/teague

Criminal Trial Practice in all State Courts including DWI/DUI/OUI Law, Department of Motor Vehicles License Suspension Hearing Practice in all Connecticut locations including Administrative Per Se Law, Commercial Driver's License Law, Work Permit Law, Medical Unit Law and Traffic Law, Criminal Appeals, Family Law, Automobile Accident and Personal Injury Law.

(This Listing Continued)

LAW OFFICES OF NORMAN B. TEAGUE, Meriden—Continued

NORMAN B. TEAGUE, born Camden, New Jersey, November 1, 1946; admitted to bar, 1982, Connecticut and U.S. District Court, District of Connecticut. *Education:* University of Bridgeport (B.S., 1970; J.D., 1981). Program Chair and Speaker: "Driving Under the Influence Cases," May 14, 1990, Connecticut Bar Association; "Representing Your Client at the DMV and in State Court Proceedings," 1991, Connecticut Bar Association. Program Chair, "DWI-Per Se-Work Permits," April 29, 1994, Connecticut Bar Association. Speaker: "Handling Driving Under the Influence Cases," December 10, 1988, Connecticut Trial Lawyers Association; "Per Se and DWI Defense," Nov. 30, 1990, May 3, 1991, June 7, 1991, Connecticut Criminal Defense Lawyers Association; "Driving Under the Influence," April 7, 1995, Middlesex County Bar Association; "Strategies in Defending DUI Cases," October 11, 1996, Lorman Education Services, Inc. Trial Consultant, Connecticut Criminal Defense Lawyers Association, Tactics and Strategy Clinic, 1991, 1992. Author: "Practicing Before the Administrative 'Per Se' Unit of Department of Motor Vehicles," Connecticut Criminal Defense Lawyers Association Quarterly Newsletter, Vol. II, No. 2, March/April 1991. *Member:* Meriden-Wallingford-Southington (Member, Nomination Committee Chair, 1993—; Soiré Committee Chair, 1990—) and Connecticut (Member, Criminal Justice Section; Member, 1986, Executive Committee Member, 1988—; Secretary, 1991-1994, Chair, 1994-1997) Bar Associations; Connecticut Criminal Defense Lawyers Association (Charter Member, Board of Governors, 1990—, Secretary, 1990-1992, Vice President, 1992-1994, President, 1994-1996; Committee on DWI and Per Se, 1990—); National Association of Criminal Defense Lawyers; National College for DUI Defense (Founding Member). ***PRACTICE AREAS:*** Criminal Law; DWI/DUI/OUI; Drivers License Suspension Law; Family Law; Automobile Accident; Personal Injury.

WEIGAND, MAHON AND ADELMAN ATTORNEYS AT LAW, P.C.

Established in 1974

636 BROAD STREET
P.O. BOX 2420
MERIDEN, CONNECTICUT 06450
Telephone: 203-238-1010
Fax: 203-630-1930
URL: http://www.lawyers.com/wma
Email: info@wmalawyer.com
URL: http://www.wmalawyer.com

General Civil Practice before State and Federal Courts. Personal Injury, Products Liability, Medical Malpractice, Tort, Workers Compensation, Labor, Real Estate, Estate Planning, Probate, Commercial, Domestic Relations Law, and Social Security Law.

JOSEPH F. WEIGAND, JR., born Meriden, Connecticut, August 9, 1936; admitted to bar, 1966, Connecticut; 1969, U.S. Court of Appeals, Second Circuit; 1973, U.S. District Court, District of Connecticut. *Education:* University of Connecticut (B.S., 1958; LL.B., 1965). State Representative, 1974-1976. Clerk, House of Representatives, 1976-1978. Member, Board of Trustees, Meriden YMCA, 1985—. Member, Board of Directors, 1985-1990 and President, 1988-1990, University of Connecticut Alumni Association. *Member:* Meriden-Wallingford-Southington and Connecticut (Member, Executive Committee, Elder Law Section, 1995—) Bar Associations. ***PRACTICE AREAS:*** Commercial Real Estate; Residential Real Estate; Probate; Estate Planning; Commercial Law; Elder Law. ***Email:*** weigand@wmalawyer.com

BRIAN T. MAHON, born Meriden, Connecticut, February 18, 1948; admitted to bar, 1973, Connecticut; 1974, U.S. District Court, District of Connecticut. *Education:* College of the Holy Cross (A.B., 1970); Vanderbilt University (J.D., 1973). Associate Brief Editor, Moot Court Board. Member, Editorial Board, "Barrister" Magazine, 1983. Contributor, ABA Journal, 1984. Legal Advisory Committee to the State of Connecticut, Worker's Compensation Commission Chairman. *Member:* Meriden-Wallingford-Southington (President, 1981-1982), New England (President, 1997-1998), Connecticut (President, 1995-1996; Chairman, Young Lawyers Section, 1981-1982; Chairman, Continuing Legal Education Committee, 1990-1993; Chairman, Pro Bono Committee, 1993-1994; Member, Workers Compensation Committee, 1989—; Member, Solo and Small Firm Task Force, 1992-1993) and American (House of Delegates, 1993—; Member, Standing Committee on Solo and Small Firms, 1997—; Chairman, Standing Committee on Lawyer Title Guaranty Funds, 1990-1993; Chairman, Juvenile Justice Committee, Young Lawyers Section, 1981-1987) Bar Associations; Connecticut Trial Lawyers Association (Member, Education Committee of Workers' Compensation Committee, 1992—). Fellow, Connecticut Bar Foundation. ***PRACTICE AREAS:*** Plaintiff's Negligence; Workers' Compensation; Labor Law; Civil Trials. ***Email:*** mahon@wmalawyer.com

(This Listing Continued)

GERARD I. ADELMAN, born Brooklyn, New York, June 15, 1946; admitted to bar, 1982, Connecticut and U.S. District Court, District of Connecticut. *Education:* Ohio State University (B.A., 1970); Southern Connecticut State University (M.A., 1977); University of Connecticut (J.D., with honors, 1982). Phi Beta Kappa. Recipient, American Jurisprudence Book Award. Vice-President, Meriden Board of Education, 1991-1999. Advisor, Women's & Family Center. Member, Board of Governors, Veterans Memorial Medical Center. President, Rotary Club of Meriden, 1990-1991. Special Master: Regional Family Docket; Judicial District at Meriden; Judicial District of Middlesex. *Member:* Meriden-Wallingford-Southington (President, 1990-1991), Connecticut (Member, Family Law Section) and American (Member, Family Law Section) Bar Associations. ***REPORTED CASES:*** Rau v. Rau, 37 Conn.App.209 (1995). ***PRACTICE AREAS:*** Divorce Mediation; Family; Social Security; Landlord and Tenant Law; General Practice. ***Email:*** adelman@wmalawyer.com

---

MICHAEL D. QUINN, born Meriden, Connecticut, April 13, 1968; admitted to bar, 1997, Connecticut. *Education:* American International College (B.S., 1990); Thomas M. Cooley Law School (J.D., 1996). Recipient, Book Award, Advanced Trial Workshop. Commissioner/Vice Chairman: Meriden Housing Authority Board, 1997—; Mills Study Committee, 1998-2000. Treasurer, Meriden Democratic Committee, 1997—. Member, Board of Directors, Meridan YMCA. President, Board of Directors, Meridan Wallingford Chrysalis, Inc. *Member:* Meridan- Wallingford- Southington (Vice-President), Connecticut and American Bar Associations. ***PRACTICE AREAS:*** Personal Injury; Workers' Compensation; Criminal Law. ***Email:*** quinn@wmalawyer.com

OF COUNSEL

JOHN F. STANTON, born New Britain, Connecticut, August 28, 1947; admitted to bar, 1975, Connecticut; 1976, U.S. District Court, District of Connecticut. *Education:* College of the Holy Cross (B.A., 1969); University of Connecticut (J.D. with honors, 1975). Omicron Delta Epsilon. *Member:* Meriden-Wallingford Southington (President, 1986-1987), Connecticut and American (Vice-President) Bar Associations. ***PRACTICE AREAS:*** Commercial Law; Real Property Law; Probate Law. ***Email:*** wma@snet.net

GENERAL COUNSEL FOR: Meriden-Wallingford Physicians Center, P.C.
REFERENCES: Fleet Real Estate Funding Corp.; Hudson United Bank; Castle Bank; Fresh Impressions, LLC.

RICHARD G. ADAMS & ASSOCIATES, LLC

Established in 1978

JACOB FREDERICK HUBER HOUSE
163 COLLEGE STREET
MIDDLETOWN, CONNECTICUT 06457
Telephone: 860-347-4696
Fax: 860-347-0295
Email: richardgadams@snet.net
URL: http://www.lawyers.com/richardgadams

General Trial, Appellate and Administrative Practice before all Courts. Litigation. Environmental Law, Health and Safety, Health Care, Real Estate, Land Use, Corporate, Commercial, Taxation, Estate Planning, and Legislative Lobbying and Mediation.

MEMBERS OF FIRM

RICHARD G. ADAMS, born West Reading, Pennsylvania, March 21, 1941; admitted to bar, 1967, Connecticut; U.S. District Court, District of Connecticut. *Education:* Princeton University (A.B., cum laude, 1963); Yale University (M.A., 1967; LL.B., 1967). Board of Editors, Yale Law Journal, 1964-1965. Member, 1970-1972 and Chairman, 1971-1972, Middlefield Planning and Zoning Commission. Member: State Legislative Task Force on DEP Permit Streamlining, 1992-1993; Academy of Continuing Professional Development, Connecticut Bar Association. *Member:* Middlesex County, Connecticut (Member, Executive Committees: Administrative Law Section, 1980—; Conservation & Environmental Quality Section, 1983-1989) and American Bar Associations. ***SPECIAL AGENCIES:*** U.S. E.P.A.; Army Corps of Engineers; CT D.E.P.; DOT. ***TRANSACTIONS:*** Comprehensive permitting for Bristol & Lisbon, CT resource recovery facilities and for other CT incinerators and landfills, industrial parks and a golf course. ***PRACTICE AREAS:*** Environmental Law; Land Use Regulation; Legislative Lobbying.

PAUL D. BUHL

THE CALEB FULLER HOUSE
49 MAIN STREET
MIDDLETOWN, CONNECTICUT 06457
Telephone: 860-347-0879
Fax: 860-344-8876

Civil Trials and Appeals in all Courts. General Commercial Practice, Business Organizations Law, Real Estate, Securities, Zoning, Land Use, Construction, Environment, Banking, Employment, Estate Planning and Probate Law.

PAUL D. BUHL, born Minneapolis, Minnesota, May 17, 1960; admitted to bar, 1985, Illinois and U.S. District Court, Northern District of Illinois; 1987, Connecticut; 1989, U.S. District Court, District of Connecticut. *Education:* St. Mary's College (B.A., magna cum laude, 1982); University of Notre Dame (J.D., 1985). Phi Alpha Theta; Pi Gamma Mu; Delta Epsilon Sigma; Alpha Mu Gamma. Managing Editor, Journal of Legislation, 1984-1985. Author: "Protecting Business Entities Under the Federal Anti-Tampering Act," Vol. XI, Journal of Legislation, 1984. Chairman, Legislation Committee, Connecticut Community Associations Institute, 1989-1991, Construction Institute, 1993-1994. Member, East Haddam Planning & Zoning Commission, 1993-1996. Probate Judge, District of East Haddam, 1994—. Member, Endowment Committee, Connecticut Rivers Council, B.S.A., 1996—. *Member:* Connecticut Bar Association. ***REPORTED CASES:*** Tucker v. Pace Investment Associates, 32 Conn. App. 384; Pelletier v. Goodnoff. 45 Conn. Supp. 563, affirmed 52 Conn. App. 360.

MICHAEL F. DOWLEY

Established in 1982
116 WASHINGTON STREET
P.O. BOX 1235
MIDDLETOWN, CONNECTICUT 06457
Telephone: 860-347-9987
Fax: 860-347-3597
URL: http://www.dowleyandassociates.com

Administrative Law, Alcoholic Beverages, Alternative Dispute Resolution, Banks and Banking, Business Law, Commercial Law, Commercial Real Estate, Computers and Software, Contracts, Copyrights, Corporate Law, Eminent Domain, Environmental Law, Guardianship and Conservatorship, Health Care, Intellectual Property, Leases and Leasing, Litigation, Media Law, Medical Malpractice, Mortgages, Negligence, Nonprofit and Charitable Organizations, Partnership Law, Personal Injury, Premises Liability, Probate, Professional Liability, Real Estate, Resorts and Leisure, Sports Law, Torts, Trademarks, Trusts and Estates, Unfair Competition, Wills, Zoning, Planning and Land Use.

FIRM PROFILE: Since its inception, the law firm of Michael F. Dowley has been dedicated to serving the people of Connecticut. Based in Middletown, the firm extends service to the counties of New Haven, Hartford and New London. The firm specializes in the areas of Civil Litigation and Real Estate Law. The firm is committed to providing quality, cost-effective representation reflecting the highest diligence and integrity.

MICHAEL F. DOWLEY, born Hartford, Connecticut, September 25, 1943; admitted to bar, 1968, Connecticut; 1969, U.S. Court of Appeals, Second Circuit; 1971, U.S. Tax Court; 1972, U.S. District Court, District of Connecticut; 1979, U.S. Supreme Court. *Education:* Providence College (A.B., magna cum laude, 1965); Villanova University (J.D., 1968). Member, Panel of Arbitrators, American Arbitration Association. *Member:* Hartford County, Middlesex County (Chairman: Practice and Procedure Committee, 1976-1986; Medical Legal Committee, 1976-1988; Member, Board of Directors; Vice President, 1993-1994, President Elect, 1994-1995, President, 1995-1996), Connecticut (Member: Executive Committee, Civil Justice Section, 1979—; Professional Ethics Committee, 1980-1985) and American Bar Associations; Connecticut Trial Lawyers Association; The Association of Trial Lawyers of America; Middlesex Preservation Trust (Director, 1987-1993). (Certified as a Civil Trial Specialist by the National Board of Trial Advocacy). ***REPORTED CASES:*** Larson v. Fazzino, 216 Conn. 431 (1990); Bishop v. Bordonaro, 20 Conn. App. 58 (1989); Atlantic Richfield Co. v. Canaan Oil Co., 202 Conn. 234 (1987); Cook v. Nye, 9 Conn. App. 221 (1981); Gionfrido v. Wharf Realty, Inc., 193 Conn. 28 (1984); Waterbury Petroleum Products, Inc. v. Canaan Oil and Fuel Company, Inc., 193 Conn. 208 (1984); Szypula v. Szypula, 2 Conn. App. 650 (1984); Kowal v. Hofher, 181 Conn. 358 (1980); First Federal Savings v. Charter Appraisal, 724 A.2d 497 (1999). ***TRANSACTIONS:*** Comprehensive Permitting of Development on Long Island Sound, DEP Coastal Area Management, Excavation Approvals; Complete State and Local Permitting of Regional Wal-Mart Center. ***PRACTICE AREAS:*** Civil Litigation; Environmental Law; Real Estate Development; Regulatory Law.

(This Listing Continued)

ASSOCIATES

JENNIFER A. BERNAZANI, born November 30, 1975; admitted to bar, 2000, Connecticut. *Education:* College of the Holy Cross (B.A., 1997); University of Connecticut (J.D., 2000). Phi Alpha Theta. Author, "The Eagle, the Turtle, the Shrimp and the WTO: Implications for the Future of Environmental Trade Measures," 15 Conn. J. Int'l L. 207 (2000).

LEGAL SUPPORT PERSONNEL

JEAN M. ANDERSON, born Fort Monmouth, New Jersey, August 8, 1954. *Education:* Middlesex Community College (A.S., 1974); Hartford College for Women (Legal Asst. Cert., 1989). *Member:* Central Connecticut Association of Legal Assistants. (Legal Assistant/Office Manager). ***PRACTICE AREAS:*** Real Estate; General Office Management; Bookkeeping.

BRENDA D. PICCIOLO, born New Brunswick, Canada, June 30, 1954. *Education:* Manchester Community College (Associate in Paralegal Studies, 1996). ***LANGUAGES:*** French. ***PRACTICE AREAS:*** Probate; Estate Planning; Real Estate.

REPRESENTATIVE CLIENTS: Insurance: Chicago Title Insurance Co.; Connecticut Attorneys Title Insurance Co.; Lawyers Title Insurance Co.; Real Estate: D'Amato Construction; C.W. Builders & Developers, Inc.; David G. Sierpinski, Builder, Inc.; The Flatley Co.; Coughlin & Coughlin, Inc.; The Zalia Group; W.S. Development; Ruby Tuesday; Walmart. Banking: Liberty Bank; People's Bank; Ulster Savings Bank; Webster Bank. Business: Auto Body Specialties, Inc.; B & B Equipment, Inc.; Cameron Plumbing and Heating; Casserino's Moving and Storage Co.; Coleman Bros. Shows, Inc.; Landmark Development Group, LLC; Perficient Computers; Next Century Solutions; Covenant Village; Lutheran Elderly Housing; West Hartford Interfaith Coalition; Financial Services Associates; Industry for Middletown, Inc.; Life Innovators Corporation; Middlesex Industrial Development Corporation; Middlesex Industrial Development Council, Ltd.; Naek Construction; New England Gasket; NatureMost, Inc.; Old Mill Wayside Furniture; R. O. Nelson Plumbing, Inc.; Tara Hotels; Tricon International, Ltd. Health: Mayfield Congregate Housing; 3 Oaks Medical Associates; Anesthesiologists of Middletown, P.C.; Family Practice of Middletown, P.C.; Higganum Family Medical Group; Middlesex Gastroenterology Associates.
REFERENCES: Liberty Bank; First Union.

DZIALO, PICKETT & ALLEN, P.C.

Established in 1964
200 COURT STREET
P.O. BOX 661
MIDDLETOWN, CONNECTICUT 06457
Telephone: 860-638-5400
Fax: 860-638-5410
Email: welcome@dpapc.com
URL: http://www.lawyers.com/dpapc

Old Saybrook, Connecticut Office: 15 Elm Street, P.O. Box 779. Telephone: 203-395-6340. Fax: 203-388-9399. Email: welcome@dpapc.com.

General Practice. Litigation in all Courts, Residential Real Estate, Commercial Real Estate, Zoning and Land Use, Corporate, Estate Planning, Elder Law, Probate Law, Personal Injury Litigation, Municipal Law.

FIRM PROFILE: Progressive and dynamic full service law firm. Outgrowth of politically active law firm. The firm prides itself on the quality of its work, its personnel, and the attention given to clients' needs. The firm encourages the professional dvelopment of its principals, associates, and paralegals through continuing legal education, seminars, professional association membership, and participation in civic affairs. Each of the lawyers and paralegals in the firm has developed and maintains a specific area of legal concentration. The firm maintains two fully staffed offices, one in Middletown, which serves northern Middlesex County, and the New Haven and Hartford areas, and one in Old Saybrook, which serves the southern portion of Middlesex County and the shoreline area, including New London, Waterford, Old Lyme and Madison.

DAVID M. ROYSTON, born Hartford, Connecticut, March 20, 1939; admitted to bar, 1964, Connecticut. *Education:* Fairfield University (B.S., cum laude, 1961); Georgetown University (J.D., 1964). President and Director. Member, Middlesex Shoreline Board of Realtors. Member and Former Chairman, Old Saybrook Democratic Town Committee and Old Saybrook Charter Revision Commission. Town Counsel, Essex, Connecticut, 1973—. Represents Old Lyme Zoning Commission and Zoning Board of Appeals, Chester Planning and Zoning Commission and Deep River Zoning Board of Appeals. Attorney Trial Referee, State of Connecticut. *Member:* Middlesex County (Past President), Connecticut and American Bar Associations. ***PRACTICE AREAS:*** Real Estate; Municipal Law; Land Use Regulation.

PHILIP F. KARPEL, born New Haven, Connecticut, July 3, 1942; admitted to bar, 1967, Connecticut; 1969, U.S. Court of Appeals, Second Circuit; 1973, U.S. District Court, District of Connecticut. *Education:* College of the Holy Cross (B.S., 1964); University of Connecticut (LL.B., 1967). Vice President and Director. Associate Editor, University of Connecticut Law Review,

(This Listing Continued)

DZIALO, PICKETT & ALLEN, P.C., Middletown—Continued

1965-1967. Law Clerk to The Honorable Elmer O. Ryan, Connecticut Supreme Court, 1967-1968. Member, Connecticut Developers' Council and Middletown Democratic Town Committee. Corporator, Middlesex Hospital. Director, MARC: Community Resources, Ltd. *Member:* Middlesex County (Past President), Connecticut (Member: Executive Committee on Real Property, Planning and Zoning, and Health Care Law Sections) and American (Member, Planning and Zoning, Real Property, Probate and Economic Sections) Bar Associations. ***PRACTICE AREAS:*** Commercial Real Estate; Residential Real Estate; Corporate Law; Land Use Regulation; Environmental Law; Health Care Law.

ROBERT P. DUTCHER, born Philadelphia, Pennsylvania, January 22, 1950; admitted to bar, 1975, Connecticut and U.S. District Court, District of Connecticut. *Education:* Wesleyan University (B.A., cum laude, 1971); Georgetown University Law Center (J.D., 1975). Vice President and Director. Associate Editor, Georgetown Law Journal, 1973-1975. *Member:* Middlesex County, Connecticut and American (Member, Litigation Section) Bar Associations; Connecticut Trial Lawyers Association; The Association of Trial Lawyers of America. ***PRACTICE AREAS:*** Litigation; Plaintiffs Personal Injury.

GREGORY M. HARRIS, born Mount Vernon, New York, July 23, 1951; admitted to bar, 1976, Connecticut; 1978, U.S. District Court, District of Connecticut. *Education:* Yale University (B.S., 1972); University of Connecticut (J.D., 1976). Secretary. Phi Alpha Delta. Member, Middletown Charter Revision Commission, 1982. Trustee, St. Agnes Home, Inc., West Hartford, Connecticut. Member, Middletown Board of Education, 1989-1993. Member, Middletown Republican Town Committee and Middletown Exchange Club. Attorney Trial Referee, Connecticut. *Member:* Middlesex County and Connecticut Bar Associations. ***PRACTICE AREAS:*** Real Estate Litigation; Consumer Litigation; Commercial Litigation; Foreclosures; Property Rights; Debtor Collection.

D. JEANNE MESSICK, born Middletown, Connecticut, October 22, 1953; admitted to bar, 1981, Connecticut. *Education:* Connecticut College (B.S., magna cum laude, 1975); Universidad Nacional, Autonoma de Mexico; University of Connecticut (J.D., 1981). Assistant Secretary. Phi Beta Kappa. Past President, Mercy High School Alumnae Association. Past President and Director, Central Connecticut Business and Estate Planning Council, Inc.; Trustee, Barinerd Memorial Library. Member, Haddam Zoning Board of Appeals. Counsel, Mercy High School, Town of Essex Water Pollution Control Authority and Sanitary Waste Commission. *Member:* Middlesex County and Connecticut (Member, Probate, Estates and Elder Law Sections) Bar Associations. ***LANGUAGES:*** Spanish. ***PRACTICE AREAS:*** Estate Planning; Probate Law; Elder Law; Planned Residential Communities; Condominium Law; Taxation Law.

JOHN N. MONTALBANO, born Brooklyn, New York, March 1, 1954; admitted to bar, 1980, Connecticut; 1981, Massachusetts, U.S. District Court, District of Connecticut, U.S. District Court, District of Massachusetts and U.S. Court of Appeals, Second Circuit. *Education:* Boston College (B.S., magna cum laude, 1976; J.D., 1980). Treasurer. Lecturer in Law, Boston College, 1979-1980; Post College, 1980-1981. Contributing Book Reviewer, Trial Magazine and The Connecticut Law Tribune, 1985. Past Director, Affirmation Counseling Center, Inc. Member, The Guild of Catholic Lawyers, Diocese of Norwich and Connecticut and Massachusetts Camps Farthest Out. *Member:* Middlesex County and Connecticut Bar Associations; Connecticut Trial Lawyers Association; Connecticut Defense Lawyers Association; The Association of Trial Lawyers of America; Christian Legal Society. ***PRACTICE AREAS:*** Litigation; Plaintiffs Personal Injury.

SEAN E. DONLAN, born Mount Kisko, New York, February 4, 1965; admitted to bar, 1997, Massachusetts; 1998, Connecticut. *Education:* Babson College (B.S., cum laude, 1992); Suffolk University Law School (J.D., 1997). Member: Suffolk University Law School Trial Team, 1996-1997; The Association of Trial Lawyers of America National Trial Competition, 1997. *Member:* Middlesex County and Connecticut Bar Associations; Connecticut Trial Lawyers Association. ***PRACTICE AREAS:*** Real Estate; Litigation; Personal Injury.

SCOTT A. CARTA, born Middletown, Connecticut, July 2, 1973; admitted to bar, 1999, Connecticut. *Education:* University of Connecticut (B.A., 1996); University of Connecticut School of Law (J.D., 1999). *Member:* Middlesex County and Connecticut Bar Associations; Connecticut Trial Lawyers Association. ***PRACTICE AREAS:*** Litigation; Personal Injury.

REPRESENTATIVE CLIENTS: *Associations:* Industry for Middletown, Inc. *Banking:* Liberty Bank; Connecticut National Bank; The Farmers and Mechanics Bank. *Business:* Kabel Luggage Shops, Inc; Kogel/Giant Network; Kogel Lumber Company. *Communications:* The Middletown Press Publishing Co.; Howard A. McAuliffe, Inc. (communications systems). *Insurance:* Connecticut Attorneys Title Insurance Co.; Liberty Mutual. *Municipal:* Town of Essex; Essex Sewer Authority; Old Lyme Zoning Board. *Real Estate:* Hill Development Corp.; Real Estate Service of Connecticut, Inc.

GOULD, LARSON, BENNET, WELLS & McDONNELL, P.C.

MIDDLETOWN, CONNECTICUT

(See Essex)

General Practice in all Courts. Real Estate, Zoning, Family, Bankruptcy, Banking, Probate, Corporation Law, Estate Planning and Taxation, and Personal Injury Law, Trials, Appeals, Domestic Relations, Municipal Law and Land Use Law, Insurance Defense, Elder Law, Arbitration and Mediation.

HOWARD, McMILLAN & D'AQUILA

Established in 1976

386 MAIN STREET
MIDDLETOWN, CONNECTICUT 06457
Telephone: 860-346-1377
Fax: 860-346-5121
Email: hmd@snet.net

General Trial, Appellate and Administrative Practice before all Courts. Municipal, Real Estate, Environmental, Zoning, Corporate, Commercial, Tax, Probate and Estate Planning Law.

WILLIAM HOWARD, born Norwalk, Connecticut, November 16, 1938; admitted to bar, 1967, Connecticut; 1972, U.S. Tax Court; 1973, U.S. District Court, District of Connecticut; 1979, U.S. Court of Appeals, Second Circuit. *Education:* University of Connecticut (B.A., 1964); Harvard University (J.D., 1967); Georgetown University (LL.M. in Taxation, 1971). Phi Beta Kappa; Phi Kappa Phi. Law Clerk to U.S. Tax Court Judge Samuel B. Sterrett, 1970-1972. *Member:* Middlesex County (President, 1991-1992; Member, Standing Committee on Recommendations for Admission to the Bar of Middlesex County) and Connecticut Bar Associations; Connecticut Association of Municipal Attorneys (Member, Executive Board). ***PRACTICE AREAS:*** Real Estate Law; Business Law; Litigation; Taxation Law; Municipal Law.

JANE S. McMILLAN, born New York, N.Y., November 28, 1937; admitted to bar, 1975, Connecticut; 1976, U.S. District Court, District of Connecticut and U.S. Court of Appeals, Second Circuit; 1981, U.S. Tax Court. *Education:* University of Pennsylvania (B.A., cum laude, 1969); State University of New York at Buffalo (J.D., 1974); Wesleyan University (MALS, 1999). *Member:* Middlesex County and Connecticut (Member, Elder Law Section; Executive Committee, Estate and Probate Section) Bar Associations. ***PRACTICE AREAS:*** Estate Planning Law; Business Law; Taxation Law.

JEAN M. D'AQUILA, born New Britain, Connecticut, June 4, 1959; admitted to bar, 1984, Connecticut; 1987, U.S. District Court, District of Connecticut. *Education:* University of Connecticut (B.A., with honors, magna cum laude, 1981; J.D., 1984). *Member:* Middlesex County and Connecticut (Member, Planning and Zoning Section) Bar Associations; Connecticut Association of Municipal Attorneys. ***PRACTICE AREAS:*** Municipal Law; Government; Real Estate; Zoning Law; Land Use.

REPRESENTATIVE CLIENTS: Town of Killingworth; Town of East Hampton; The New St. Luke's Housing Corp.; O'Rourke's Diner; Bailey's Express, Inc.; American Red Cross; The Smith and Bishel Co.; A.R. Mazzotta; Middlesex County Chamber of Commerce; Historic Resources Consultants, Inc.; Fleet Bank; Liberty Bank; People's Bank; Mohawk Manufacturing Co.; Community Health Center, Inc.; Northern Middlesex Habitat for Humanity, Inc.
APPROVED ATTORNEYS FOR: Connecticut Attorneys Title Insurance Co.; Stewart Title Guaranty Co.
REFERENCES: Fleet Bank; Webster Bank.

JOZUS, MILARDO & THOMASSON

THE WILLIAM SOUTHMAYD HOUSE
73 MAIN STREET
MIDDLETOWN, CONNECTICUT 06457
Telephone: 860-347-4686
Telecopier: 860-347-2283
Email: jmtlaw@snet.net
URL: http://www.lawyers.com/jmtlaw

Trial and Appellate Practice in all Courts. Corporate and Commercial Law, Domestic Relations, Estate Planning and Probate, Municipal Law, Personal Injury and Products Liability Law, Residential and Commercial Real Estate, Land Use, Zoning and Development.

FIRM PROFILE: Jozus, Milardo & Thomasson was founded in Middletown, Connecticut in 1973 by Ivar A. Jozus and Joseph E. Milardo, Jr. The firm handles a broad array of practice areas throughout central Connecticut. The firm believes in providing its clients with personalized attention and quality legal services.

MEMBERS OF FIRM

IVAR A. JOZUS, born Riga, Latvia, July 18, 1938; admitted to bar, 1970, Connecticut; 1971, U.S. District Court, District of Connecticut. *Education:*

(This Listing Continued)

Dartmouth College (A.B., 1961); University of Connecticut (J.D., 1970). Instructor in Business Law, Central Connecticut State University, 1984-1986. Member, Portland Planning and Zoning Commission, 1978-1984. *Member:* Middlesex County (President, 1997-1998), Connecticut (Chairman, Law Office Economics Committee, 1982-1993. Military and Veterans Affairs Committee, 1980-1988) and American Bar Associations. [Captain, JAGC, U.S. Naval Reserve, 1964-1996.]. ***LANGUAGES:*** Latvian. ***PRACTICE AREAS:*** Corporate Law; Real Estate Law; Estate Planning Law; Probate Law. ***Email:*** jmtlaw@snet.net

JOSEPH E. MILARDO, JR., born Middletown, Connecticut, October 5, 1948; admitted to bar, 1974, Connecticut; 1975, U.S. District Court, District of Connecticut; 1979, U.S. Supreme Court. *Education:* Fordham University (B.A., 1970); Suffolk University (J.D., 1974). Corporation Counsel, City of Middletown, 1975; 1991-1993. City Councilman, 1979-1980, 1993-1997 and Probate Judge, 1980-1987, Middletown, Connecticut. Member, Connecticut Probate Assembly, 1982—. *Member:* Middlesex County (Secretary, 1977-1980; Director, 1981), Connecticut and American Bar Associations; Connecticut Trial Lawyers Association. [Major, U.S. Army Reserves, Retired]. ***PRACTICE AREAS:*** Civil Law; Criminal Litigation; Probate Law; Workers Compensation Law; Family Law. ***Email:*** jmtlaw@snet.net

DEAN A. THOMASSON, born Chicago, Illinois, March 27, 1948; admitted to bar, 1981, Connecticut; 1983, U.S. District Court, District of Connecticut. *Education:* Illinois Institute of Technology (B.S.C.E., 1970; M.S.C.E., 1972); Western New England College (J.D., 1981). Tau Beta Pi; Chi Epsilon. Licensed Professional Engineer, Connecticut, 1978. Member, Board of Finance, Town of Durham, 1985-1991. *Member:* Middlesex County, Connecticut and American Bar Associations. ***PRACTICE AREAS:*** Planning and Zoning Law; Land Use Law; Real Estate Development Law. ***Email:*** jmtlaw@snet.net

ASSOCIATE

LINDA J. CANNATA, born Middletown, Connecticut, October 4, 1961; admitted to bar, 1989, Connecticut. *Education:* Bath University, Bath, England; Connecticut College (B.A., with honors and distinction in Government and History, cum laude, 1983); Dickinson School of Law (J.D., 1989). Phi Beta Kappa; Pi Sigma Alpha. Recipient, American Jurisprudence Award in Legal Research. *Member:* Hartford County, Connecticut (Member, Construction Law Section) and American Bar Associations; Connecticut Trial Lawyers Association. ***PRACTICE AREAS:*** Civil Litigation; Personal Injury. ***Email:*** jmtlaw@snet.net

REPRESENTATIVE CLIENTS: Ameritage Corp., Inc.; Apple Tree Childrens Center; Jackson Corrugated Container Corp.; Reliance Automotive, Inc.; Bysiewicz Corporation; Perma-Treat Corporation; Federal Home Loan Mortgage Corporation; Federal National Mortgage Association; Fleet Bank; Yellow Freight System, Inc.; Jem Wire Products, Inc.; Children's Home of Cromwell, Inc.; Seaworthy Systems, Inc.; Hays Haven Marina, Inc.
APPROVED ATTORNEYS FOR: Chicago Title Insurance Co.; Connecticut Attorneys Title Insurance Co.; First American Title Insurance Co.; Fleet Bank; New Haven Savings Bank; People's Bank; Liberty Bank; Commonwealth Land Title Insurance Co.
REFERENCES: Fleet Bank, N.A.; Liberty Bank.

MAYO, GILLIGAN & ZITO, LLP

MIDDLETOWN, CONNECTICUT

(See Wethersfield)

Trials in all Courts, Real Estate, Banking and Commercial Finance, Creditors' Rights and Bankruptcy, Employment, Business Law, Zoning, Environmental, Estate Planning, Elder Law, Probate and Personal Injury Law.

RICHARD W. TOMC & ASSOCIATES, P.C.

CALEB FULLER HOUSE
49 MAIN STREET
MIDDLETOWN, CONNECTICUT 06457
Telephone: 860-347-4415
Fax: 860-347-1930
Email: RiTom@aol.com

Business Organizations, Commercial Loan Transactions, Trusts and Estates.

RICHARD W. TOMC, born Cleveland, Ohio, April 5, 1945; admitted to bar, 1971, New York and U.S. District Court, Southern District of New York; 1973, Connecticut and U.S. District Court, District of Connecticut. *Education:* John Carroll University (A.B., magna cum laude, 1967); Harvard University (J.D., 1970); Wesleyan University (M.A.L.S., 1982).

REFERENCES: Liberty Bank.

BERCHEM, MOSES & DEVLIN

A PROFESSIONAL CORPORATION
Established in 1933
75 BROAD STREET
MILFORD, CONNECTICUT 06460-3363
Telephone: 203-783-1200
Facsimile: 203-878-2235; 203-877-8422
URL: http://www.bmd-law.com

Commercial, Corporate Law, Labor and Employment Law, Litigation, Real Estate, Education, Land Use Planning, Estate Planning, Energy and Utility Law, Environmental, Probate. Partnership Law and Taxation Law. Trials and Appeals in State and Federal Courts.

FIRM PROFILE: From its roots in the general law practice established by William Gitlitz in 1933, Berchem, Moses & Devlin has grown to a sophisticated multispecialty practice. Our growth has been strategic to ensure that each client receives the most comprehensive legal representation, in a personalized environment, which allows our attorneys to fully understand and evaluate our clients' needs and objectives.

All our highly credentialed lawyers concentrate in one or more practice sections, thereby enabling each to develop the specialized knowledge necessary to serve the needs of our clients. These practice sections, discussed in further detail on the pages that follow, include Business Services, Education, Labor and Employment, Litigation and Real Estate Services. The interconnection of these practice groups also enables us to provide a variety of multidisciplinary services to our public sector clients in our Municipal Services Section.

In addition, recognizing that a commitment to our communities is a vital element of our profession, our attorneys are actively involved in a wide range of nonbusiness activities. These activities include participation in local, civic and charitable organizations, serving on the boards of educational and medical institutions, maintaining political leadership roles and holding positions on various local administrative boards and agencies.

ROBERT L. BERCHEM, born Milford, Connecticut, August 17, 1941; admitted to bar, 1965, Connecticut; 1966, U.S. District Court, District of Connecticut; 1969, U.S. Supreme Court; 1977, U.S. Court of Appeals, Second Circuit. *Education:* Fairfield University (A.B., cum laude, 1962); Villanova University (J.D., 1965); University of Michigan (LL.M., Labor Relations, 1967). Alpha Sigma Nu. Order of the Coif. Recent Developments Editor, Villanova Law Review, 1964-1965. Law Clerk, Hon. William H. Timbers, Chief Judge, U.S. District Court, District of Connecticut, 1965-1966. Author: "Recent Development," 9 Villanova Law Review 155, 1963; Comment, 9 Villanova Law Review 306, 1964. Assistant Prosecutor, Fifth Circuit Court, 1967-1974. Member, Finance Committee, Bridgeport Hospital, 1995—. Trustee, Fairfield University, 1991-1996. *Member:* New Haven County, Connecticut (Member, Commercial Law Section) and American Bar Associations. William W. Cook Fellow, University of Michigan Law School, 1966-1967. ***PRACTICE AREAS:*** Commercial Law; Real Estate; Land Use Planning; Energy Law; Utility Law. ***Email:*** rberchem@bmd-law.com

MARSHA BELMAN MOSES, born Pittsburgh, Pennsylvania, October 25, 1948; admitted to bar, 1976, Connecticut; 1977, U.S. District Court, District of Connecticut and U.S. Court of Appeals, Second Circuit. *Education:* Miami University (B.A., 1970); Wayne State University (J.D., summa cum laude, 1975). Pi Sigma Alpha. Member, 1973-1974; Note and Comment Editor, Scribes, 1974-1975. Member, Connecticut Regional Board, Anti-Defamation League, August 1995. President, Connecticut School Board Attorneys Council, 2000. *Member:* New Haven County, Connecticut (Member, Education Law Section) and American Bar Associations; The Association of Trial Lawyers of America. ***PRACTICE AREAS:*** Education Law; Labor and Employment. ***Email:*** mmoses@bmd-law.com

MICHAEL P. DEVLIN, born Milford, Connecticut, June 12, 1950; admitted to bar, 1976, New York; 1988, Connecticut; U.S. District Court, District of Connecticut; U.S. District Court, Northern, Eastern and Southern Districts of New York. *Education:* Boston College (B.A., magna cum laude, 1972); Columbia University (J.D., 1975). Phi Beta Kappa. *Member:* Connecticut (Member, Labor and Employment Law Section) and American (Member, Labor and Employment Law Section) Bar Associations. ***PRACTICE AREAS:*** Labor and Employment. ***Email:*** mdevlin@bmd-law.comcom

STEPHEN W. STUDER, born Cambridge, Massachusetts, January 23, 1950; admitted to bar, 1977, Massachusetts; 1978, Connecticut and U.S. District Court, District of Connecticut; 1980, U.S. District Court, District of Massachusetts. *Education:* Stonehill College (B.A., magna cum laude, 1972); Suffolk University (J.D., cum laude, 1977). Member, Suffolk University Law Review, 1975-1977. Author: Case Comments, 10 Suffolk University Law Review 938, 1976; 11 Suffolk University Law Review 171, 1976. Chairman, Civil Service

(This Listing Continued)

BERCHEM, MOSES & DEVLIN, A PROFESSIONAL CORPORATION, Milford—Continued

Commission, Milford, Connecticut, 1989-1997. Former Judge of Probate, District of Milford. *Member:* New Haven County, Connecticut (Member, Committees on: Planning and Zoning, 1985—; Environmental Law, 1992—; Family Law Section) and American Bar Associations. ***PRACTICE AREAS:*** Land Use; Environmental Law; Estate Planning; Family Law; Trusts. ***Email:*** sstuder@bmd-law.com

RICHARD J. BUTURLA, born Milford, Connecticut, June 29, 1957; admitted to bar, 1982, Connecticut, U.S. District Court, District of Connecticut and U.S. Court of Appeals, Second Circuit. *Education:* Southern Connecticut State College (B.S., magna cum laude, 1979); Villanova University (J.D., 1982). Associate Editor, Villanova Law Review, 1981-1982. Author: Note, "In re Bollinger Corp., A Financing Statement, Promissory Note and Letters Constituting The Course of Dealing are Sufficient to Serve as A Valid Security Agreement," 26 Villanova Law Review 931, 1981; Comment, "The Handicapped Child's Right to A Free Appropriate Education: Defining The Limits of Responsibility," 27 Villanova Law Review 567, 1982; "Limitations on Discovery, Civil Discovery Practice Law Connecticut," 1995. Director, Southern Connecticut State College Alumni Association, 1983-1985. Councilman at Large, Chairman of Town Council, Stratford, Connecticut, 1987-1989. Town Attorney, Stratford, Connecticut, 1995—. Corporation Counsel, Derby, Connecticut, 1997—.. *Member:* Connecticut and American Bar Associations; Connecticut Trial Lawyers Association; The Association of Trial Lawyers of America. ***REPORTED CASES:*** Armac Industries, Ltd. v. Citytrust, 203 Conn. 394, 525 A.2d 77 (1987); B.A. Ballou and Company, Inc. v. Citytrust, 218 Conn. 749, 591 A.2d 126 (1991); Bombero, Jr., Etal v. Planning and Zoning Commission of the Town of Monroe, Etal, 17 Conn. App. 150, 550 A.2d 1098 (1988); Citytrust v. Page, Etal, 28 Conn. App. 907, 610 A.2d 197 (1992); D.J. Quarry Products, Inc. v. Planning and Zoning Commission of the Town of Beacon Falls, 217 Conn. 447, 585 A.2d 1227 (1991); Dean v. Filipowich, Etal, 20 Conn. App. 825, 570 A.2d 243 (1990); Dennin, Etal v. The Connecticut Interscholastic Athletic Conference, Inc., 94 F.3d 96 (1996); Dennin, Etal v. The Connecticut Interscholastic Athletic Conference, Inc., 913 F.Supp. 663 (1996); Federal Deposit Insurance Corporation v. Sextant Development Corporation, Etal, 142 F.R.D. 55 (1992); Federal Deposit Insurance Corporation v. SUNA Associates, Inc., 80 F.3d 681 (1996); J.F. Barrett and Sons, Inc. v. Rosenshein, 23 Conn. App. 817, 582 A.2d 919 (1990); Hedberg v. Pantepec International, Inc., 35 Conn. App. 19, 645 A.2d 543 (1994); Huff v. West Haven Board of Education, Etal, 1998 WL 286167 (D.Conn.) (1998); Kornatowski v. Wallingford Police Department, Etal, 1993 WL 299032 (D.Conn.) (1993); Meyers v. Arcudi, Etal, 947 F.Supp. 581 (1996); Meyers v. Arcudi, Etal, 915 F.Supp. 522 (1996); Mrs. B. on her behalf and as a mother and guardian of M.M. v. Milford Board of Education, Etal, 103 F.3d 1114 (1997); Smart SMR of New York Inc. d/b/a v. The Zoning Commission of the Town of Stratford, 9 F.Supp. 2d 143, (1998); Smart SMR of New York, Inc. d/b/a v. The Zoning Commission of the Town of Stratford, 995 F.Supp. 52 (1998); Smith v. Planning and Zoning Board of the City of Milford, Etal, 3 Conn.App. 550, 490 A.2d 539 (1985); Smith v. Planning and Zoning Board of the City of Milford, Etal, 203 Conn. 317, 524 A.2d 1128 (1987); Town of Monroe, Etal v. Renz, Etal, 46 Conn. App. 5, 698 A.2d 328 (1997); Town of Stratford v. International Association of Firefighters, AFL-CIO, Local 998, 48 Conn. App. 849, 713 A.2d 269 (1998); Howley v. Stratford, 87 F.Supp.2d 97 (1999); Omnipoint Communications, Inc. v. Planning & Zoning Commission of the Town of Wallingford, 91 F.Supp.2d. 497 (2000); Howley v. Stratford, 217 F.3d. 141 (2000); Lillibasle v. Sergi, 117 F.Supp.2d 182 (2000). ***PRACTICE AREAS:*** Litigation; Insurance Defense. ***Email:*** rbuturla@bmd-law.com

FLOYD J. DUGAS, born New Orleans, Louisiana, September 2, 1959; admitted to bar, 1986, Connecticut; 1987, U.S. District Court, District of Connecticut; 1993, U.S. Court of Appeals, Second Circuit and U.S. Court of Appeals, District of Columbia Circuit. *Education:* University of Connecticut (B.S., 1981); Temple University (J.D., 1986). Member, Moot Court Board. *Member:* Connecticut (Corporate, Commercial, Labor and Employment Law Section; Executive Committee, 1989-1990; Vice President, Secretary Young Lawyers Division, 1991-1993) and American (Member, Corporate, Commercial and Labor and Employment Law Section) Bar Associations; School Board Attorneys Council. ***PRACTICE AREAS:*** Labor and Employment; Corporate Law; Education. ***Email:*** fdugas@bmd-law.com

KENNETH R. PLUMB, born Holyoke, Massachusetts, February 5, 1957; admitted to bar, 1984, Connecticut; 1985, U.S. District Court, District of Connecticut; 1986, U.S. Claims Court; 1993, U.S. Court of Appeals, Second Circuit. *Education:* Union College (B.A., 1980); Western New England College (J.D., 1984). Member, 1982-1983 and Executive Editor, 1983-1984, Western New England Law Review. Author: "Draft Committees: A Loophole in the Federal Election Laws," 6 Western New England Law Review 555, 1983; Annual Connecticut Bar Journal Labor and Employment Law Surveys, 1985-1996; Connecticut Bar Journal, Senior Topical Editor, Labor and Employment Law, 1991-1997. Connecticut Lawyers Deskbook, Labor and Employment Law Chapter, 1998-1999. Contributing Author: Covenants Not To Compete, Employee Duty of Loyalty & Trade Secrets. *Member:* Hartford County, Connecticut (Member, Executive Committee, Labor and Employment and Workers' Compensation Law Sections, 1986—) and American (Member: Labor and Employment Law Section; Executive Council Member, 1991-1993) Bar Associations; American Employment Law Council, (Charter Member, 1993). ***PRACTICE AREAS:*** Employer-Employee Relations; Employment Discrimination; Labor (Management); Workers Compensation. ***Email:*** kplumb@bmd-law.com

LAWRENCE B. PELLEGRINO, born Bridgeport, Connecticut, November 5, 1966; admitted to bar, 1991, Connecticut; 1992, U.S. District Court, District of Connecticut. *Education:* Connecticut College (B.A., summa cum laude, 1988); University of Virginia (J.D., 1991). Phi Beta Kappa. Order of the Coif. Editor, Virginia Environmental Law Journal, 1989-1991. Member, Government Finance Officer Association of Connecticut. *Member:* Greater Bridgeport, New Haven County and Connecticut Bar Associations; National Association of Bond Lawyers. ***REPORTED CASES:*** In re Smart, 214 B.R. 63 (Bankruptcy. D. Conn. 1997). ***PRACTICE AREAS:*** Public Finance; Commercial Law; Real Estate; Bankruptcy. ***Email:*** lpellegr@bmd-law.com

---

BRIAN A. LEMA, born Westerly, Rhode Island, August 21, 1965; admitted to bar, 1990, Connecticut; 1991, U.S. District Court, District of Connecticut. *Education:* University of Bristol, Bristol, England UK; Georgetown University (B.A., cum laude, 1987; J.D., 1990). *Member:* New Haven County, Connecticut and American (Member, Sections on: Business Law; Litigation) Bar Associations. ***PRACTICE AREAS:*** Litigation; Land Use; Commercial Law. ***Email:*** blema@bmd-law.com

WARREN L. HOLCOMB, born Durham, North Carolina, April 12, 1950; admitted to bar, 1977, California; 1993, Connecticut; 1994, U.S. District Court, District of Connecticut. *Education:* Butler University; University of Connecticut at Storrs (B.A., 1972); Southwestern University School of Law (J.D., 1977). *Member:* State Bar of California; Connecticut and American (Member, Labor and Employment Law Section) Bar Associations. ***PRACTICE AREAS:*** Labor and Employment; Entertainment Law. ***Email:*** wholcomb@bmd-law.com

MICHELLE C. LAUBIN, born Mahopac, New York, August 1, 1971; admitted to bar, 1996, Connecticut; 1997, New York and U.S. District Court, District of Connecticut. *Education:* Wells College (B.A., summa cum laude, 1993); Northeastern University (J.D., 1996). Phi Beta Kappa. *Member:* Connecticut and American Bar Associations. ***PRACTICE AREAS:*** Education Law. ***Email:*** mlaubin@bmd-law.com

JONATHAN DAVID BERCHEM, born Milford, Connecticut, September 6, 1969; admitted to bar, 1995, Connecticut and Pennsylvania; 1999, U.S. Supreme Court. *Education:* Fairfield University (B.A., 1992); Syracuse University (J.D., 1995). *Member:* Milford, Connecticut and American Bar Associations. ***PRACTICE AREAS:*** Litigation; Insurance Defense; Labor and Employment. ***Email:*** jberchem@bmd-law.com

DEAN R. SINGEWALD, born New Haven, Connecticut, December 23, 1964; admitted to bar, 1990, Connecticut; 1996, U.S. District Court, District of Connecticut. *Education:* Brown University (B.A., 1987); New England School of Law (J.D., cum laude, 1990). *Member:* Connecticut Bar Association (Member, Sections On: Labor and Employment; Litigation; Young Lawyers; Education Law Committee; Officer, Executive Committee; Director, Executive Committee); Connecticut School Attorneys Council. ***PRACTICE AREAS:*** Labor and Employment; Education. ***Email:*** drs@bmd-law.com

MICHAEL V. VOCALINA, born New London, Connecticut, November 2, 1964; admitted to bar, 1993, Connecticut. *Education:* Eastern Connecticut University (B.S., 1986); Thomas M. Cooley Law School (J.D., cum laude, 1992). Author: Criminals Profit Through Chapter 13: Pennsylvania Dept. of Public Welfare, 110 S. Adjunct Professor, Three Rivers Community College, 1992-1995. *Member:* Connecticut Bar Association; Connecticut Trial Lawyers Association. ***PRACTICE AREAS:*** Workers Compensation; Personal Injury; General Litigation.

BRYAN L. LeCLERC, born Waterbury, Connecticut, April 6, 1962; admitted to bar, 1987, Connecticut and U.S. District Court, District of Connecticut; 1988, New York; 1993, U.S. District Court, Southern District of New York; 1996, U.S. Supreme Court. *Education:* Fairfield University (B.A., 1984); University of Connecticut (J.D., with honors, 1987). Pi Sigma Alpha. Elected Member, Representative Town Meeting, Town of Fairfield, 1991—. Member, Board of Directors, Fairfield University Alumni Association, 1993—. Author: Three chapters in Estate Planning and Administration Service, Warren, Gorham & Lamont, 1989. *Member:* Westport and Connecticut (Young Lawyers Section, Career Development Committee Chair, 1990-1993) Bar Associations; Connecticut Trial Lawyers Association; The Association of Trial Lawyers of America. ***REPORTED CASES:*** Maloney v. Conrey, 208 Conn. 392, 1988; Rogo Zruski v. American Food Services Equipment Corp. 211 Conn. 431, 1989; Mack Financial Corporation v. Crossley 209 Conn. 163, 1988. ***PRACTICE AREAS:*** Litigation; Probate.

(This Listing Continued)

BRIAN W. SMITH, born New York, N.Y., May 2, 1957; admitted to bar, 1981, Connecticut; 1982, U.S. District Court, District of Connecticut. *Education:* University of Buffalo (B.A., magna cum laude, 1978); Duke University (J.D, 1981). Phi Alpha Delta. *Member:* New Haven County and Connecticut Bar Associations; Connecticut Defense Lawyers Association. ***PRACTICE AREAS:*** Litigation; Insurance.

CAROLYN MAZANEC DUGAS, born Jersey City, New Jersey, May 5, 1962; admitted to bar, 1987, Connecticut. *Education:* Temple University (B.A., 1984; J.D., 1987). Member, Temple Mock Trial Team. Formerly with Donnarumma, Derby & Tramuta. ***PRACTICE AREAS:*** Education Law.

OF COUNSEL

THOMAS GALVIN COTTER, born Bridgeport, Connecticut, May 5, 1956; admitted to bar, 1984, Connecticut and U.S. District Court, District of Connecticut. *Education:* Nichols College (B.S., 1978); University of Bridgeport (J.D., 1982). Member: I.A.I.A.B.C.; Chairman and Commissioner Town of Stratford Zoning Commission, 1990-1995. State of Connecticut Workers' Compensation Commissioner appointed by Governor John G. Rowland, 1996-1997; State of Connecticut Attorney Trial Referee, State of Connecticut Factfinder/Arbitrator appointed by Chief Justice Robert Callahan and Chief Administrative Judge Arron Ment. Member, Board of Directors, YMCA. *Member:* Bridgeport (Former Co-Chairman of Rules and Procedures Committee), Millford/Ansonia, Connecticut and American Bar Associations; Connecticut Trial Lawyers Association. ***PRACTICE AREAS:*** Workers Compensation; Bad Faith Litigation; Professional Liability; General Litigation; Personal Injury Litigation; Environmental Claims; Toxic Tort Litigation; Uninsured and Underinsured Motorist Arbitration; Construction Litigation; Products Liability; Subrogation.

MARK J. ROSEN, born Mount Vernon, New York, September 22, 1946; admitted to bar, 1975, Connecticut; 1977, New York and Rhode Island; 1979, U.S. Court of Appeals, First and Second Circuits and U.S. Court of Customs and Patent Appeals. *Education:* University of Michigan (B.A., 1968); University of Connecticut (J.D., 1973). Author: "Connecticut Unfair Trade Practices Act," 1985, "Connecticut Foreclosures," 1985, 1987, 1989, "Enforcing Secured Claims in Connecticut," 1985 and "Connecticut Collection Law," 1985, published by Professional Education Systems, Inc.; "Problem Loans in Connecticut," National Business Institute, 1988. Alternate, West Hartford Zoning Board of Appeals, 1979. Superior Court Trial Referee, 1988—. Formerly with Zeisler & Zeisler P.C. *Member:* Hartford County, Rhode Island, Connecticut and American Bar Associations; The Association of Trial Lawyers of America. ***PRACTICE AREAS:*** Domestic Law; Childrens Rights; Foreclosures; Collections. ***Email:*** mrosen@bmd-law.com

REPRESENTATIVE CLIENTS: *Corporate:* Alinabal; American Airlines; Amgraph Packaging, Inc.; ANCO Engineering; Ann Taylor; ASSA Abloy; Allas Copco-North America; Arrow Lock; Atlas Fence Company; AVA/RAV Communities; Black & Decker/BAHCO Tools; Bigelow Tea; CASCO Products; Car Temps USA; Bridgeport Health Care Center, Inc.; C. Cowles & Company; Circuit-Wise, Inc.; Colonial Toyota; Commonwealth Land Title Insurance Co.; Cook-Willow Convalescent Home; Crabtree Cadillac/Oldsmobile; Datco Bus Co.; Diocesse of Bridgeport; Domino Sugar Corporation; Esstar, Inc.; Essex Industries; Extended Stay America; Federal Express; Federal Home Loan Mortgage Corp.; First Group America; Fleet Bank; Fletcher Thompson Architects; Friendly's Ice Cream Corporation; Gateway Bank; Golden Heights Health Center; Goodwin College; Great Atlantic Pacific Tea Company; Hammerson Property Corp.; Heyman Properties; Hillman Properties; Hilton Corp.; Hoffman Materials; Jefferson Smurfit; McDonald Corp.; Marriott Corporation; Mercy Housing and Shelter Corp.; Milford Jai Alai; Milwaukee Electric Tool Corporation; National Car Rental; National Casualty Company; National Westminister Bank; Northeast Restaurant Company; People's Bank; Peter Pan Bus Lines; PETCO Animal Supplies, Inc.; Power Development Corporation; Price-Costco; RPS/Fedex Ground; R.C. Bigelow, Inc.; R.J. Guerrera, Inc.; Refined Sugars; Ryder Systems; Samsung Electronics America, Inc.; Samsung Electronics Co., LTD.; Stevens of Milford; Sandvik Milford, Inc.; Sargent Manufacturing; Scottsdale Insurance Company; Service Merchandise; Standadyne Automotive Group; Stop & Shop Supermarkets, Inc.; Thomas Industries; Thornton Oil Company; Tishman Sepayer Properties, Inc.; TOMRA North America; Trefz Corporation; Unillever; U.S. Repeating Arms/Browing Firearms; U.S. Trust Co.; Vantage Group; Vespell USA; Village Manor Health Care, Inc.; Waldbaums; Warunco; Warner Bros., Inc.; Westport Lexus; Westfield Properties; William Pritt Realty; Yale Security.
BOARDS OF EDUCATION: Easton/Redding; Fairfield; Milford; Monroe; New Britain; New Haven; Norwalk; Orange; Straford; Sterling; Trumbell; West Haven; Weston; Woodbridge.
MUNICIPALITIES: City of Bridgeport; City of Derby; Town of Madison; Town of Newtown; Town of Orange; City of Shelton; Town of Stratford; Town of Trumbell; City of Waterbury; Town of Wethersfield; City of West Haven; Housing Authority for the City of Meriden; Housing Authority for the City of New Haven; Housing Authority for the City of West Haven; New Haven Parking Authority.
INSURANCE COMPANIES: Aceptance; AIG; Allstate; CGU; CNA; Commercial Union; Connecticut Guaranty Fund; Chubb Executive Risk; Crawford and Company; Housing Authority Risk Rentention Group; Farmers Insurance Co.; Gallagher Bassett Services; Housing Authority Risk Retention; Interstate Insurance; ITT Hartford; Liberty Mutual; Lexington; Mac Risk Management; National Union; Pennsylvania Lumbermans Mutual; Providence/Washington; R.E.M.; Scottsdale Insurance Co.; 21st Century Ins. Co.
THIRD PARTY ADMINISTRATORS: Crawford & Co.; Cunningham Lindsey Morton; GAB Robins; Gallagher Bassett; Sedgewich James; Gates McDonald; Mac Risk Management; Stirling & Stirling; Toko-Marine; RSKCO.

ANDREW J. BROUGHEL

243 BROAD STREET
P.O. BOX 45
MILFORD, CONNECTICUT 06460
Telephone: 203-874-6166
Fax: 203-878-1681

General Civil Practice. Real Estate, Probate, Family.

ANDREW J. BROUGHEL, born Bridgeport, Connecticut, September 8, 1938; admitted to bar, 1964, Connecticut; 1967, U.S. Supreme Court; 1969, U.S. Court of Appeals, 2nd Circuit. *Education:* Fairfield University (B.S.S., 1960); Georgetown University (J.D., 1963). Delta Theta Phi. Counsel, Milford Housing Authority, 1972-1976. Executive Secretary, Milford Charter Revision Commission, 1972-1973. Adjudicator, Department of Motor Vehicles, State of Connecticut, 1973-1975. Member, 1973-1976 and Chairman, 1975-1976, Milford Pension and Retirement Board. Trial Attorney, City of Milford, 1977-1982. Fact Finder, Judicial District of Ansonia-Milford, 1983-1989. Trial Referee, 1990-1996; Member, Panel of Arbitrators, American Arbitration Association, 1994. *Member:* Connecticut Bar Association. ***PRACTICE AREAS:*** Real Estate; Zoning; Probate; Family Law; Trials in all Courts.

HARLOW, ADAMS & FRIEDMAN, P.C.

300 BIC DRIVE
MILFORD, CONNECTICUT 06460
Telephone: 203-878-0661
Fax: 203-878-9568
Email: attorney@quidproquo.com
URL: http://www.harlowadamsfriedman.com

General Civil Practice, General Civil Litigation in State and Federal Courts, Real Estate Conveyancing, Financing and Development, Zoning, Probate, Personal Injury, Commercial Litigation, Construction Law, Bankruptcy, Business Formations, Landlord and Tenant, Title Opinions, Trials and Appeals.

FIRM PROFILE: We are a regional law firm which is dedicated to finding practical, workable solutions to your family and business needs. These needs might range from a simple home closing to a financial restructuring of your assets and liabilities to a complex Chapter 11 business bankruptcy to obtaining a just settlement for a personal injury lawsuit. Solutions are always designed to minimize our client's tax burden. Whatever need presents itself, our primary concern is to provide the best representation possible for our clients.

WILLIAM D. HARLOW (1921-1988).

GEORGE W. ADAMS, III, born Lancaster, Pennsylvania, February 17, 1949; admitted to bar, 1975, Connecticut; 1977, U.S. District Court, District of Connecticut; 1979, U.S. Supreme Court. *Education:* Yale University (B.A., 1971); Boston University (J.D., 1975). *Member:* Milford, Bridgeport (Chair, Lawyers Concerned for Lawyers), Connecticut and American (Member, Sections on: General Practice; Real Property, Probate and Trust) Bar Associations. ***PRACTICE AREAS:*** Real Estate; Zoning Law; Probate. ***Email:*** gwa@quidproquo.com

DANA ERIC FRIEDMAN, born Mineola, New York, December 11, 1946; admitted to bar, 1971, Virginia; 1972, District of Columbia and U.S. Court of Federal Claims; 1977, U.S. Tax Court; 1978, Connecticut; 1990, U.S. District Court, District of Connecticut. *Education:* University of Michigan (B.A., 1968); George Washington University (J.D., 1971; LL.M., 1975). Order of the Coif. Member, George Washington Law Review, 1970-1971. Attorney, Office of Chief Counsel, Internal Revenue Service, 1971-1977. *Member:* Milford, Connecticut and American (Member, Sections on: Taxation; Real Property, Probate and Trust Law) Bar Associations; The District of Columbia Bar; Virginia State Bar. ***PRACTICE AREAS:*** Real Estate Acquisitions; Real Estate Development; Real Estate Finance; Probate; Estate Settlements; Corporate Law. ***Email:*** def@quidproquo.com

THEODORE H. SHUMAKER, born Bridgeport, Connecticut, October 9, 1955; admitted to bar, 1981, Connecticut; 1983, U.S. District Court, District of Connecticut. *Education:* University of Connecticut (B.S., 1978); University of Miami (J.D., 1981); George Washington University (LL.M., Labor, 1982). *Member:* Milford, Bridgeport, Connecticut and American (Member, Sections on: Business Law; Real Property, Probate and Trust Law) Bar Associations. ***PRACTICE AREAS:*** Real Estate; Zoning Law; Probate; Estate Planning. ***Email:*** ths@quidproquo.com

STEPHEN P. WRIGHT, born Newport, Rhode Island, October 22, 1954; admitted to bar, S1981, Texas; 1986, U.S. District Court, Southern District of Texas and U.S. Court of Appeals, Fifth Circuit; 1987, Connecticut and U.S. District Court, District of Connecticut. *Education:* Florida State University (B.S., 1976); Western New England College (J.D., 1980). Town Councilman, Town of Trumbull, 1995—. Town of Trumbull, Chairman, Affordable Housing

(This Listing Continued)

HARLOW, ADAMS & FRIEDMAN, P.C., Milford—Continued

Committee, 1997-1998 and Chairman, Land Acquisition and Preservation Committee, 1998—. Monitor and Lecturer: "Recent Developments Debtor/Creditor Relationships," 1999, 2000; "Collection of Judgments in Connecticut - Ethical Considerations," 1998. Monitor/Lecturer/Author: "Recent Developments in Debtor/Creditor Relationships and Asset Protection," College of the State Bar of Texas. Co-Author: "Current Issues in Debtor/Creditor Relations," State Bar of Texas Tenth Annual General Practice Institute, 1987. Lecturer: "Considerations in Workouts," State Bar of Texas Dealing with Insolvency Institute, 1986; "Collection of Judgement," State Bar of Texas Practice Skill Course, 1986; "Current Issues in Debtor/Creditor Relations," State Bar of Texas Tenth General Practice Institute, 1987. Author/Lecturer: "Exemptions in Bankruptcy," New Haven County Bar Association Continuing Legal Education, Bankruptcy Seminar, 1995. Co-Author and Lecturer: "Bankruptcy and Reorganization: The Lawyer/Paralegal Team in Practice," Commercial Law League of American Satellite Broadcast, 1991. Author and Lecturer: "Recent Developments Under Article 2," of U.C.C. - Commercial Law League of America, Eastern Section Convention, 1989; "Automatic Stay and Section 105 Litigation," Connecticut Trial Lawyers Association, Bankruptcy Seminar, 1993; "Environmental Issues in Bankruptcy," National Business Institute, 1992. *Member:* New Haven and Houston Bar Associations; State Bar of Texas (Member, Litigation Section); The Association of Trial Lawyers of America; Connecticut Trial Lawyers Association (Board Sustaining Member). (Board Certified Civil Law Specialist, Tax Board of Legal Specialization, 1986-1991). ***PRACTICE AREAS:*** Civil Litigation; Debtor and Creditor Rights; Debtor and Creditor Bankruptcy. ***Email:*** spw@quidproquo.com

JAMES M. NUGENT, born Cranford, New Jersey, December 3, 1955; admitted to bar, 1980, Connecticut; 1981, U.S. District Court, Southern and Eastern Districts of New York. *Education:* University of Connecticut (B.A., 1977); University of Bridgeport (J.D., 1980). *Member:* Bridgeport and Connecticut Bar Associations; American Bankruptcy Institute; Commercial Law League. ***REPORTED CASES:*** Conn. National Bank v. N.E.O. II, Inc., 22 Conn. App 468; Conn. National Bank v. Great Neck Development Corp., 215 Conn. 143. ***PRACTICE AREAS:*** Bankruptcy; Commercial Litigation; Real Estate; Civil Litigation; Commercial Law. ***Email:*** jmn@quidproquo.com

MICHAEL P. A. WILLIAMS, born Bridgeport, Connecticut, September 1, 1945; admitted to bar, 1974, Connecticut and U.S. District Court, District of Connecticut; 1979, U.S. Court of Appeals, Second Circuit. *Education:* Boston University (A.B., 1968); Cumberland School of Law of Samford University (J.D., 1974). Phi Alpha Delta; Order of Barristers. Member, National Moot Court Team, 1972. Chief Justice, Cumberland Moot Court Board, 1973-1974. *Member:* Bridgeport, Connecticut and American Bar Associations. ***PRACTICE AREAS:*** Real Estate; Freedom of Information. ***Email:*** mpaw@quidproquo.com

ERIC R. GAYNOR, born Philadelphia, Pennsylvania, June 10, 1962; admitted to bar, 1987, Connecticut; 1988, U.S. District Court, District of Connecticut. *Education:* Emory University (B.A., 1984); University of Connecticut (J.D., 1987). Phi Sigma Alpha, National Political Science Honor Society, 1983. Author and Lecturer: "Residential and Commercial Evictions in Connecticut," National Business Institute Seminar, 1998 and 2000. *Member:* Orange (Member and Chairman, Board of Ethics, 1998—) and Connecticut (Member, Membership Services Committee) Bar Associations. ***REPORTED CASES:*** Peter-Michael, Inc. vs. Sea Shell Associates, 244 Conn. 269 (1998); Branhaven Associates vs. Vitrom, 40 Conn. App. 513 (1996); State vs. Fox, 22 Conn. App. 449 (1990); Fischel vs. Verkerke Reproductions USA, Inc., 21 Conn. App. 339 (1990); Red Hill Coalition vs. Town Plan & Zoning Comm., 212 Conn. 727 (1989); Red Hill Coalition vs. Conservation Commission, 212 Conn. 710 (1989); Double I Limited Partnership vs. Town of Glastonbury, 208 Conn. 802 (1988). ***PRACTICE AREAS:*** Commercial Litigation; Collections; Bankruptcy; Landlord and Tenant Law; Personal Injury. ***Email:*** erg@quidproquo.com

JOSEPH A. KUBIC, born Bridgeport, Connecticut, April 18, 1961; admitted to bar, 1992, Connecticut; 1993, U.S. District Court, District of Connecticut. *Education:* University of Connecticut (B.A., 1983; M.A., Economics, 1985); University of Bridgeport (J.D., 1991). Member, Town Council, Town of Stratford, 1991-1995. President, Connecticut Rugby Foundation, Inc. Director, Connecticut Parents Advocacy Counsel, Inc., 1999—. *Member:* Milford, Bridgeport and Connecticut Bar Associations. ***LANGUAGES:*** English and French. ***PRACTICE AREAS:*** Construction Law; Real Estate; Personal Injury. ***Email:*** jak@quidproquo.com

JAMES R. WINKEL, born Cleveland, Ohio, December 4, 1963; admitted to bar, 1996, Connecticut; 1997, U.S. District Court, District of Connecticut. *Education:* Bryant College (B.A., 1985); University of Connecticut School of Law (J.D., high honors, 1996). *Member:* Connecticut Bar Association. ***PRACTICE AREAS:*** Commercial Law; Civil Litigation; Personal Injury. ***Email:*** jrw@quidproquo.com

(This Listing Continued)

APPROVED ATTORNEYS FOR: Fidelity National Title Insurance Co.; Lawyers Title Insurance Corp.; First American Title Insurance Co.; Stewart Title Guaranty Co.
REFERENCES: The Milford Bank; Citizens Bank; First Union New Haven; Countrywide Home Loan Corporation.

JACOBI, KAPPEL & CASE, P.C.

300 BIC DRIVE
MILFORD, CONNECTICUT 06460
Telephone: 203-874-7110
Fax: 203-874-6469
Email: info@jkc-law.com

Environmental, Real Estate, Planning and Zoning, Motor Vehicle Accidents, Personal Injury, Estate Planning and Administration, Business Law. Litigation in all Courts.

PAUL JACOBI, born Bronx, N.Y., September 17, 1950; admitted to bar, 1976, New York and U.S. District Court, Southern and Eastern Districts of New York; 1988, Connecticut and U.S. District Court, District of Connecticut. *Education:* Hofstra University (B.A., magna cum laude, 1972; J.D., 1975); Sacred Heart University (M.B.A., 1984). Author: "The Environmental Liability of Trustees," Connecticut Lawyer, September, 1992; "How the New Transfer Act Will Affect You," Connecticut's Environment, August, 1995. Chairman, Milford Inland Wetlands Agency, 1988-1989. Member, Milford Board of Aldermen, 1989-1993. Member: State of Connecticut Cleanup Standards Advisory Committee; State of Connecticut Transfer Act Advisory Committee. Chairman, Environmental Committee, Corporate Bar Association, 1992; Real Estate Finance Association. *Member:* New Haven County (Chairman, Environmental Committee), Connecticut (Member, Conservation and Environmental Quality Section) and American (Member, Natural Resources Committee) Bar Associations. ***PRACTICE AREAS:*** Environmental Law. ***Email:*** pjacobi@jkc-law.com

ROBERT KAPPEL, born Brooklyn, N.Y., November 21, 1950; admitted to bar, 1977, New York; 1981, U.S. District Court, Eastern and Southern Districts of New York; 1991, Connecticut; 1992, U.S. District Court, District of Connecticut; 2000, U.S. Court of Appeals, Second Circuit. *Education:* Queens College of the City University of New York (B.A., cum laude, 1972); Hofstra University (J.D., 1975). Arbitrator, Civil Court of the City of New York, 1988-1990. Board of Trustees, Adelphi University Paralegal Institute, 1988-1990. President, 1994-1996, Greater Milford Business Association. Member, Board of Directors, Milford Progress, Inc., 1999. President, 2000 and Member, Board of Directors, 2001—, Milford Chamber of Commerce Trust. President, 1999, and Member, Board of Directors, Milford Chamber of Commerce, 1995-2000. Member, Board of Directors: City of Milford Council on Aging, 1994-1998. President, 2001 and Member, Board of Directors, Combined Parishes Action Committee, Inc., 1993—; Literacy Center of Milford, Inc., 1997-1998. *Member:* Connecticut (Member: Litigation Section; Environmental Section) and New York State (Member, Insurance Committee) Bar Associations; Connecticut Trial Lawyers Association. ***PRACTICE AREAS:*** Environmental Law; Civil Litigation; Commercial Transactions; Personal Injury Litigation. ***Email:*** rkappel@jkc-law.com

MAX S. CASE, born Hartford, Connecticut, March 9, 1947; admitted to bar, 1974, Pennsylvania; 1974, U.S. District Court, Eastern District of Pennsylvania; 1975, Connecticut and U.S. District Court, District of Connecticut. *Education:* University of Pennsylvania (B.A., 1969); Temple University (J.D., 1974). Trial Counsel, City of Milford, 1992-1995. Legislative Commissioner, Connecticut State Legislature, 1993—. Connecticut State Senator, 1991-1993. Member, Board of Aldermen, Milford, Connecticut, 1981-1985. Corporator, Milford Hospital, Inc., 1983—. Chairman, Milford Superior Courthouse Building Committee, 1987-1989. Member, Advisory Committee, Municipal Tax Appeals, 1995-1996. Member, Board of Directors, Tower One/Tower East, 1997—. Attorney Trial Referee, 1997—. *Member:* Milford (Secretary, 1989—) and Connecticut (Member, Planning and Zoning Executive Committee) Bar Associations. ***REPORTED CASES:*** State of Connecticut v. Cain, 223 Conn. 731 (1992). ***PRACTICE AREAS:*** Real Estate; Land Use; Tax Appeals; Civil Litigation. ***Email:*** mcase@jkc-law.com

LOUIS J. BONSANGUE, born Milford, Connecticut, October 18, 1968; admitted to bar, 1993, Connecticut; 1995, New York and U.S. District Court, District of Connecticut; 2000, U.S Court of Appeals, Second Circuit. *Education:* Fordham University (B.S., cum laude, Business Administration and Finance, 1990); Hofstra University (J.D., 1993). Member, Hofstra Property Law Journal. President, Devon Rotary Club, 2000. *Member:* Connecticut Bar Association (Member, Law-Related Education Committee, 1994—); Connecticut Trial Lawyers Association. ***PRACTICE AREAS:*** Civil Litigation; Personal Injury Litigation; Environmental Law. ***Email:*** lbonsangue@jkc-law.com

---

DAVID SPERANZINI, born New Haven, Connecticut, August 20, 1965; admitted to bar, 1997, Connecticut. *Education:* University of Connecticut (B.S.,

(This Listing Continued)

magna cum laude, 1988; M.S., 1990; J.D., 1997). Tau Beta Pi; Omega Chi Epsilon. *Member:* Connecticut and American Bar Associations. ***PRACTICE AREAS:*** Environmental Law. ***Email:*** dsperanzini@jkc-law.com

REPRESENTATIVE CLIENTS: Satin American Corporation; Loctite Corp.; Perkin Elmer; Hudson United Bank; Voltarc Technologies, Inc.; A.B. Dick Corp.; United Aluminum Corp.; The Broadstone Group; Town of Branford, Connecticut; Milford Bank; Lake Phipps Special Taxing District; Hines Interests Limited Partnership; Fusco Corp.; Norwalk Savings Society; Emsar Corp.; Winkle Bus Co.
REFERENCES: The Milford Bank; Stewart Title Insurance Co.

KARP & LANGERMAN, P.C.

MILFORD PLACE CORPORATE CENTER
185 PLAINS ROAD
MILFORD, CONNECTICUT 06460
Telephone: 203-876-0606
Westport: 203-866-5892
Fax: 203-876-0768

Corporation, Probate, Estate Planning, Taxation, Pension and Profit Sharing, Commercial, Real Estate.

JOEL C. KARP, born Stamford, Connecticut, April 9, 1940; admitted to bar, 1964, Connecticut and U.S. District Court, District of Connecticut; 1972, U.S. Tax Court; 1980, U.S. Supreme Court. *Education:* Brown University (B.A., 1961); University of Connecticut (J.D., with honors, 1964). Director, 1973-1985 and 1990—, New Haven Jewish Federation. Director, 1996—and President, 1998—, Jewish Community Center of Greater New Haven. Campaign Chairman, 1977-1978, Vice President, 1980-1985, and Chairman, 1981—, Committee on Study of the Elderly. Director, Camp Laurelwood, Inc., 1970-1985. President, 1975-1976; Director, 1978-1979, New Haven Jewish Home for the Aged. Director and Vice President, Ezra Academy, 1985-1995 . Director, Greater New Haven Chapter of Juvenile Diabetes Foundation, 1985—. *Member:* Milford, New Haven, Connecticut and American (Member, Corporation, Banking and Business Law Section) Bar Associations. ***PRACTICE AREAS:*** Tax; Business; Estate Planning; Probate.

LAWRENCE LANGERMAN, born New Haven, Connecticut, September 19, 1951; admitted to bar, 1976, Connecticut and U.S. District Court, District of Connecticut; 1977, U.S. Tax Court; 1980, U.S. Supreme Court. *Education:* University of Vermont (B.A., 1973); Catholic University of America (J.D., 1976); New York University (LL.M. in Taxation, 1980). Member, 1985—, and Board of Directors, 1986-1989 and 1991, Connecticut Consultants Retirement Association. Board of Directors, 1995—and Vice President, 1998—, United Way of Milford. *Member:* Milford, New Haven, Connecticut (Member: Executive Committee Tax Section, 1979-1989; Commercial Law Section) and American (Member, Sections on: Tax; Corporation, Banking and Business Law) Bar Associations. ***PRACTICE AREAS:*** Corporate; Tax; Estate Planning; Business; Pension and Profit Sharing; Real Estate.

REFERENCE: Fleet Bank.

KERIN & CANTY, P.C.

120 BROAD STREET
MILFORD, CONNECTICUT 06460
Telephone: 203-876-9831
Fax: 203-876-0100
Email: blackfin34@aol.com
URL: http://www.lawyers.com/kcjlaw

Personal Injury, Workers' Compensation.

BRENDAN T. CANTY, born Worcester, Massachusetts, September 22, 1958; admitted to bar, 1987, Connecticut. *Education:* Northeastern University (B.S., in Criminal Justice, 1981); University of Bridgeport (J.D., 1987). Phi Delta Phi. *Member:* Norwalk/Wilton and Connecticut Bar Associations; International Association of Arson Investigators.

MICHAEL R. KERIN, born New Haven, Connecticut, July 3, 1958; admitted to bar, 1988, Connecticut; 1989, U.S. District Court, District of Connecticut. *Education:* Vassar College (B.A., 1980); American University (M.F.A., 1984); Middlebury College; University of Bridgeport (J.D., summa cum laude, 1987). Phi Delta Phi. Recipient: American Jurisprudence Award in Products Liability; Tort Law Award. *Member:* Connecticut and American Bar Associations; Connecticut Trial Lawyers Association. ***PRACTICE AREAS:*** Personal Injury; Workers' Compensation.

LYNCH, TREMBICKI, MARTELON AND BOYNTON

Established in 1947
63 CHERRY STREET
P.O. BOX 453
MILFORD, CONNECTICUT 06460
Telephone: 203-878-4669
Fax: 203-876-0644
URL: http://www.lawyers.com/llmtblaw

Westport, Connecticut Office: 225 Main Street, Suite 103. Telephone: 203-227-6808. Fax: 203-226-6215.

General Practice. Probate, Real Estate, Zoning, Negligence, Workers' Compensation and Labor Relations, Domestic Relations and Municipal Law. Trials in all Courts.

FIRM PROFILE: Founded in 1947 by Richard H. Lynch, the firm Lynch, Trembicki, Martelon and Boynton offers a wide range of practice areas to both individual and corporate clients in New Haven and Fairfield Counties. The firm's four attorneys have a combined experience of over seventy-five years of practice. Practice areas include civil and criminal litigation in state and federal courts including appeals, complex personal injury, wrongful death and product liability claims. The firm also has an extensive real estate, land use and zoning practice including all aspects of commercial and residential real estate transactions and financing.

MEMBERS OF FIRM

RICHARD H. LYNCH (1912-1991).

THOMAS B. LYNCH, born New Haven, Connecticut, February 14, 1955; admitted to bar, 1980, Connecticut and U.S. District Court, District of Connecticut. *Education:* Boston College (B.A., magna cum laude, 1977); University of Connecticut (J.D., 1980). Phi Alpha Delta. Deputy Assistant States Attorney, New Haven, 1982-1985. Chairman, Charter Revision Commission, City of Milford, 1982-1983. Member, Board of Finance, City of Milford, 1986-1989. Member, Board of Directors, Milford Chapter, American Red Cross, 1989-1995. Member, Board of Trustees, The Milford Bank, 1990—. Member, Board of Directors, Milford Mental Health Center 1997—. *Member:* Milford (Treasurer, 1983—), New Haven County, Connecticut (Member, Estate, Probate and Real Estate Sections) and American Bar Associations; Connecticut Trial Lawyers Association. ***PRACTICE AREAS:*** Commercial Real Estate; Residential Real Estate; Residential Development; Zoning, Planning and Land Use; Estate Planning; Estate Administration; Family Law; Divorce; Criminal Litigation; Education Law.

GEORGE F. MARTELON, JR., born Boston, Massachusetts, October 4, 1949; admitted to bar, 1974, Connecticut and U.S. District Court, District of Connecticut. *Education:* Boston College (B.A., cum laude, 1971), Order of Cross & Crown; Washington & Lee University (J.D., 1974). Assistant City Attorney, 1974-1978 and City Attorney, 1981-1987, City of Milford, Connecticut. Member: Connecticut Public Employer Labor Relations Association, 1984—; Panel of Arbitrators, American Arbitration Association. *Member:* Milford and Connecticut Bar Associations. ***PRACTICE AREAS:*** Probate Law; Real Estate; Labor and Employment; Civil Litigation; Family Law; Education Law; Estate Administration; Estate Planning for the Elderly; Elder Law; Homeowners Association Law; Real Estate; Conveyancing; Public Sector Employment Law; Union Contract Negotiations; Municipal Law; Special Education Law.

ALEXANDER J. TREMBICKI, born Bridgeport, Connecticut, June 10, 1955; admitted to bar, 1980, Connecticut and U.S. District Court, District of Connecticut. *Education:* University of Connecticut (B.A., cum laude, 1977; J.D., 1980). Chairman, Milford Board of Finance, 1983-1984. Member: Fairfield Representative Town Meeting, 1997—; Connecticut Judicial Department - Attorney Trial Referee/Fact Finder, 1999—; Million Dollar Advocates Forum, 1999—. *Member:* Westport, Bridgeport and Connecticut Bar Associations; Connecticut Trial Lawyers Association; The Association of Trial Lawyers of America. (Resident, Westport Office). ***PRACTICE AREAS:*** Civil Litigation; Personal Injury; Commercial Litigation; Employment Law; Family Law; Product Liability; Aviation Accidents; Wrongful Death; Medical Malpractice; Uninsured and Underinsured Motorist; Covenants Not To Compete; Collections; Corporate Litigation; Theft of Trade Secrets; Contract Litigation; Construction Litigation; Creditors Rights; Restrictive Covenant; Deceptive Trade Practices; Business Litigation; Federal Civil Practice; Alternative Dispute Resolution.

MICHAEL S. BOYNTON, born New Haven, Connecticut, July 26, 1960; admitted to bar, 1986, Connecticut and U.S. District Court, District of Connecticut. *Education:* Stonehill College (B.A., 1983); University of Bridgeport (J.D., 1986). Assistant Public Defender, State of Connecticut, 1986-1992. *Member:* Milford, Valley, New Haven County, Connecticut (Member, Criminal Law Section) and American Bar Associations; Connecticut Trial Lawyers Association. ***PRACTICE AREAS:*** Civil Litigation; Personal Injury; Criminal De-

(This Listing Continued)

LYNCH, TREMBICKI, MARTELON AND BOYNTON, Milford—Continued

fense; Drug Crimes; Driving While Intoxicated; Family Law; Divorce; Workers Compensation; Motor Vehicle Accidents and Injuries; Accidents; Felonies; Misdemeanors; Dram Shop Liability.

STEVENS, CARROLL & CARVETH

Established in 1969

26 CHERRY STREET
P.O. BOX 432
MILFORD, CONNECTICUT 06460
Telephone: 203-877-5471
Fax: 203-877-3970
Email: email@stevenscarrollcarveth.com

Real Estate, Zoning, Condominium, Family, Civil Litigation, Criminal Litigation, Corporate Law, Business Law, Appeals in all Courts, Workers Compensation, Estate Planning, Wills, Probate.

FIRM PROFILE: Since 1969, the highly rated firm of Stevens, Carroll & Carveth has offered clients in Milford and coastal Connecticut a full-service practice, including Civil Litigation, Criminal Litigation, and appeals, in State and Federal Courts. In addition, the firm concentrates on matters concerning Real Estate; Planning and Zoning; Estate Planning, Wills, Trusts and Probate; Workers Compensation Law; Corporate Law and Business Law. Attorneys with the firm are active members of state and national lawyers associations and participants in local governance.

MEMBERS OF FIRM

GERALD F. STEVENS (1938-1990).

LEO P. CARROLL, born Bridgeport, Connecticut, July 5, 1944; admitted to bar, 1969, Connecticut and U.S. District Court, District of Connecticut; 1970, U.S. Court of Appeals, 2nd Circuit. *Education:* Villanova University (A.B., 1966); Boston College (J.D., 1969). Trial Counsel, City of Milford, 1973-1977. Director, Connecticut Attorneys Title Insurance Co., Inc., 1991—. Trustee, The Milford Bank, 1993—. *Member:* Milford, Connecticut and American Bar Associations. ***PRACTICE AREAS:*** Planning and Zoning Law; Commercial and Residential Real Estate Law; Estates and Trusts. ***Email:*** lcarroll@stevenscarrollcarveth.com

CHRISTOPHER B. CARVETH, born Montreal, Quebec, June 9, 1950; admitted to bar, 1975, Connecticut; 1976, U.S. District Court, District of Connecticut, U.S. Court of Appeals, 2nd Circuit and U.S. Tax Court. *Education:* University of Bridgeport (B.A., 1972); Catholic University of America (J.D., 1975); University of Notre Dame, London, England. Adjunct Associate Professor, University of Bridgeport, 1984-1985. Small Claims Commissioner, Connecticut Superior Court, 1984-1987. *Member:* Milford and Connecticut Bar Associations; The Association of Trial Lawyers of America; Connecticut Trial Lawyers Association (Director, 1989-2001). ***PRACTICE AREAS:*** Civil Litigation-Plaintiff Law; Criminal Defense Law; Workers Compensation Law. ***Email:*** cbcarveth@stevenscarrollcarveth.com

ASSOCIATE

KRISTIN DORNEY FOLEY, born Boston, Massachusetts, January 13, 1962; admitted to bar, 1986, Massachusetts and U.S. District Court, District of Massachusetts; 1987, Connecticut; 1988, U.S. District Court, District of Connecticut. *Education:* Middlebury College (B.A., cum laude, 1983); Boston College Law School (J.D., 1986). Member, 1996-2001, Board of Editors, Connecticut Bar Journal; Workers' Compensation Quarterly, Editor and Chief, 1996-1999. *Member:* New Haven County, Milford, Bridgeport and Connecticut Bar Associations. ***PRACTICE AREAS:*** Workers' Compensation Law; General Practice; Real Estate Law; Estates and Trusts. ***Email:*** kdfoley@stevenscarrollcarveth.com

KEVIN J. CURSEADEN, born Montebello, California, March 27, 1969; admitted to bar, 1997, Connecticut. *Education:* Boston College (B.A., 1991); Quinnipiac University School of Law (J.D., 1997). Formerly with Bai Pollock & Cuyne, PC. [Captain, Army Reserve, 1991—]. ***REPORTED CASES:*** Kolomiets v. Syncor International Corp., et al. 51 Conn App 523 (1999). ***PRACTICE AREAS:*** Litigation; Real Estate. ***Email:*** kcurseaden@stevenscarrollcarveth.com

REPRESENTATIVE CLIENTS: The Milford Bank; Circuit City Stores; Chelsea GCA Realty, Inc.; Southern New England Telephone Real Estate; Shaw's Supermarket; Water's Construction Co., Inc.; Wal-Mart Stores, Inc.; Heritage Village Commercial Center.
APPROVED ATTORNEYS FOR: Catic Connecticut Title Insurance Co.; Chicago Title Insurance Co.

MELVIN I. STOLTZ

51 CHERRY STREET
MILFORD, CONNECTICUT 06460
Telephone: 203-874-8183
Facsimile: 203-878-9607
Email: patlaw@snet.net

Patent, Trademark, Copyright and Unfair Competition. Foreign Patent and Trademark Law and Related Litigation.

MELVIN I. STOLTZ, born Hartford, Connecticut, 1943; admitted to bar, 1969, Connecticut; 1970, U.S. District Court, District of Connecticut; 1975, U.S. Court of Appeals, Second Circuit; registered to practice before U.S. Patent and Trademark Office. *Education:* University of Connecticut (B.S., Chem. Eng., 1965); University of Connecticut School of Law (J.D., 1969). Tau Beta Pi. *Member:* Milford, The Connecticut (Chairman, Patent, Trademark and Copyright Section, 1977-1978) and American Bar Associations; American Intellectual Property Law Association; American Institute of Chemical Engineers; Connecticut Patent Law Association (Member, Federal Practice Committee, 1984—).

WARE, FRESSOLA, VAN DER SLUYS & ADOLPHSON, LLP

Established in 1921

BRADFORD GREEN, BUILDING FIVE
755 MAIN STREET
P.O. BOX 224
MONROE, CONNECTICUT 06468
Telephone: 203-261-1234
Fax: 203-261-5676
Email: mail@wfva.net

Patent, Trademark, Copyright, Computer, Antitrust, Unfair Competition, Foreign Patent Law, Litigation and Federal Practice.

ROBERT H. WARE, born Kansas City, Missouri, 1927; admitted to bar, 1951, Massachusetts; 1952, New York; 1958, Connecticut; 1959, U.S. Court of Appeals, Second Circuit; 1989, U.S. Court of Appeals for the Federal Circuit; registered to practice before U.S. Patent and Trademark Office. *Education:* University of Michigan (B.S.M.E., 1947); Harvard University (M.S.M.E., 1948); Harvard Law School (LL.B., 1951). Tau Beta Pi. Member, Panel of Arbitrators, American Arbitration Association. *Member:* Bridgeport, Danbury, Connecticut (Member, House of Delegates, 1976-1979; Chairman, Antitrust Section, 1977-1979) and American Bar Associations; Connecticut Intellectual Property Law Association (President, 1969-1970); Institute of Electrical and Electronics Engineers. ***Email:*** rhw@wfva.net

ALFRED A. FRESSOLA, born Bridgeport, Connecticut, 1946; admitted to bar, 1973, Connecticut; 1975, U.S. District Court for the District of Connecticut and U.S. Court of Appeals, Second Circuit; 1993, U.S. Court of Appeals for the Federal Circuit; registered to practice before U.S. Patent and Trademark Office. *Education:* University of Connecticut (B.S.E.E., with honors, 1968; M.S.E.E., 1970); University of Connecticut School of Law (J.D., with honors, 1973). Tau Beta Pi; Eta Kappa Nu. Member, Computer Science and Engineering Advisory Board, University of Connecticut. *Member:* Bridgeport, Connecticut (Chairman, Intellectual Property Law Section, 1986-1987) and American Bar Associations; Connecticut Intellectual Property Law Association; Institute of Electrical and Electronics Engineers. ***Email:*** aaf@wfva.net

PETER C. VAN DER SLUYS (1939-1991).

K. BRADFORD ADOLPHSON, born Bridgeport, Connecticut, 1956; admitted to bar, 1983, Connecticut; 1984, U.S. District Court, District of Connecticut; 1986, U.S. Court of Appeals for the Federal Circuit; 1987, District of Columbia; registered to practice before U.S. Patent and Trademark Office. *Education:* University of Connecticut (B.S.M.E., 1978); George Washington University (J.D., 1983). Pi Tau Sigma. Patent Examiner, U.S. Patent and Trademark Office, 1978-1983. *Member:* Bridgeport, Connecticut and American Bar Associations; American Intellectual Property Law Association; Connecticut Intellectual Property Law Association (President, 1997-1998); Federal Circuit Bar Association. ***Email:*** kba@wfva.net

FRANCIS J. MAGUIRE, JR., born Providence, Rhode Island, 1947; admitted to bar, 1983, Connecticut; 1993, U.S. Court of Appeals for the Federal Circuit; 1994, U.S. District Court, District of Connecticut; registered to practice before U.S. Patent and Trademark Office. *Education:* University of Rhode Island (B.S.E.E., with honors, 1974); University of Connecticut School of Law (J.D., 1983). Senior Engineer: General Dynamics, Electric Boat Division, 1974-1980; ABB Combustion Engineering, 1980-1982. Patent Attorney, United Technologies Corporation, 1982-1991. *Member:* Connecticut and American Bar As-

(This Listing Continued)

sociations; American Intellectual Property Law Association; Connecticut Intellectual Property Law Association; International Association for the Protection of Industrial Property. **Email:** fjm@wfva.net

WILLIAM J. BARBER, born Jamaica, New York, 1959; admitted to bar, 1986, New York; 1993, U.S. Court of Appeals for the Federal Circuit; 1995, Connecticut; registered to practice before U.S. Patent and Trademark Office. *Education:* State University of New York at Stony Brook (B.S., Computer Science/Engineering, 1981); Brooklyn Law School (J.D., 1984). *Member:* Connecticut Intellectual Property Law Association. ***PRACTICE AREAS:*** Patents; Copyrights; Trademarks. **Email:** wjb@wfva.net

JAMES R. FREDERICK, born Findlay, Ohio, September 9, 1944; admitted to bar, 1969, Connecticut; 1970, U.S. District Court for the District of Connecticut; 1974-1982, U.S. Court of Customs and Patent Appeals; 1983, U.S. Court of Appeals for the Federal Circuit; registered to practice before U.S. Patent and Trademark Office. *Education:* University of Michigan (B.S., Physics, 1966); University of Michigan Law School (J.D., 1969). Phi Delta Phi. *Member:* Connecticut (Chairman, Patent, Trademark and Copyright Section, 1982-1983) and American Bar Associations; The Connecticut Intellectual Property Law Association (President, 1993-1994). **Email:** jrf@wfva.net

THADDIUS J. CARVIS, born Waukegan, Illinois, 1943; admitted to bar, 1971, Virginia; 1972, Connecticut; 1979, U.S. District Court, District of Connecticut; 1984, U.S. Court of Appeals for the Federal Circuit; registered to practice before U.S. Patent and Trademark Office. *Education:* University of Wisconsin-Madison (B.S.Ch.E., 1965); Catholic University of America (J.D., 1970). *Member:* Connecticut Bar Association (Member, Executive Committee, Patent Law Section, 1977-1984; Vice Chairman, 1980-1981; Chairman, 1981-1982); Virginia State Bar; Connecticut Intellectual Property Law Association (President, 1990-1991). ***PRACTICE AREAS:*** Patent Law; Trademark Law; Copyright Law; Antitrust Law; Unfair Competition Law. **Email:** tjcarvis@email.com

STEPHEN B. SHEAR, born Washington, D.C., December 8, 1943; admitted to bar, 1974, Virginia; 1977, New York and U.S. District Court, Southern and Eastern Districts of New York; 1980, U.S. Supreme Court; registered to practice before U.S. Patent and Trademark Office (Not admitted in Connecticut). *Education:* Tulane University of Louisiana (B.S., Chemistry, 1966); New Mexico State University (M.S., Chemistry, 1969); The George Washington University (J.D., with honors, 1974). Order of the Coif. Clerk to Hon. Caleb M. Wright, U.S. District Court, District of Delaware, 1974-1976. Patent Examiner, U.S. Paten and Trademark Office, 1969-1974. *Member:* The Association of the Bar of The City of New York; American Bar Association; New York Intellectual Property Law Association; American Chemical Society. (Chief Patent Counsel). **Email:** SBS@wfva.net

MILTON M. OLIVER, born Columbia, South Carolina, 1951; admitted to bar, 1975, California and Massachusetts; 1978, Florida; 1979, U.S. Supreme Court and U.S. Court of Customs and Patent Appeals; 1983, District of Columbia; 1984, New York; registered to practice before U.S. Patent and Trademark Office (Not admitted in Connecticut). *Education:* Harvard University (B.A., 1972); Hastings College of Law, University of California and Golden Gate University (J.D., 1975). *Member:* Boston Bar Association; American Intellectual Property Law Association; Boston and New York Patent Law Associations; Computer Law Association; German-American Law Association; Institute of Electrical & Electronics Engineers. ***LANGUAGES:*** German, French and Russian. ***PRACTICE AREAS:*** International Patent Law; Trademarks; Copyrights; Computer Law; Litigation. **Email:** milton_oliver@post.harvard.edu

JACK M. PASQUALE, born Torrington, Connecticut, 1943; admitted to bar, 1981, Connecticut; registered to practice before U.S. Patent and Trademark Office. *Education:* Ward Technical Institute; Newark College of Engineering (B.S.E.E., 1971); Western New England College (J.D., 1981). Tau Beta Pi. Cheshire Inland Wetlands and Watercourses Commission, Member, 1976— and Chairman, 1978—. Crescent Beach Niantic Zoning Board of Appeals, Member, 1994— and Chairman, 1996—. Legal Counsel, United States Junior Chamber International Senate. *Member:* Bridgeport, Connecticut (Member, Sections on: Patent and Trademark; Computer Law) and American Bar Associations; Connecticut Intellectual Property Law Association; Institute of Electrical and Electronic Engineers. ***PRACTICE AREAS:*** Patents; Trademarks; Copyrights; Intellectual Property. **Email:** jackpasquale@compuserve.com

JAMES A. RETTER, born Cleveland, Ohio, 1951; admitted to bar, 2000, Connecticut; registered to practice before the U.S. Patent and Trademark Office. *Education:* Duke University (B.A., Physics and B.A., Mathematics, 1973); University of Connecticut (Ph.D., Physics, 1979; J.D., with honors, 2000). Phi Kappa Phi. Pi Mu Epsilon. Sigma Pi Sigma. Formerly: Teledyne, 1983-1985; Sort, Inc., 1985-1988; Computer Sciences Corp., 1989-1991; Consulting Engineer, 1991-1995. [U.S. Air Force, 1979-1983]. **Email:** jar@wfva.net

ANDREW T. HYMAN, born Boston, Massachusetts, 1962; admitted to bar, 1996, Connecticut; 1998, District of Columbia; 1999, U.S. Court of Appeals, Fourth Circuit; 2000, U.S. Supreme Court; registered to practice before the U.S. Patent and Trademark Office. *Education:* University of Massachusetts at Amherst (B.S., Physics, cum laude, 1987); Lewis and Clark's Northwestern School of Law (J.D., 1994). ***PRACTICE AREAS:*** Patents; Trademarks; Copyrights; Intellectual Property. **Email:** mrandrewhyman@aol.com

PATENT AGENT

KENNETH Q. LAO, born Qui Nhon, Vietnam, 1943. *Education:* National Cheng Kung University (B.S., 1966); State University of New York at Stony Brook (Ph.D., Physics, 1975); Stanford University (Postdoctoral Fellow, Department of Chemistry, 1975-1977). Registered to practice before the U.S. Patent and Trademark Office. Formerly: General Electric Company, 1977-1979; Nimslo Technology, 1979-1983; Lockheed Aeronautical Systems Company, 1983-1987; Nova Technology, 1987-1998. ***LANGUAGES:*** Chinese and Vietnamese. **Email:** kql@wfva.net

---

WEEKS LAW FIRM

337 MONROE TURNPIKE
MONROE, CONNECTICUT 06468
Telephone: 203-261-6052
Telecopier: 203-452-7563
Email: weekslaw@aol.com
URL: http://www.lawyers.com/weekslawfirm

Civil Litigation, Real Estate.

ROBERT W. WEEKS, JR., born 1945; admitted to bar, 1970, Connecticut. *Education:* Rutgers University (B.A.); University of Connecticut (J.D.). ***PRACTICE AREAS:*** Civil Litigation; Real Estate.

ADVOCATES LAW FIRM, LLC

11 FRANKLIN SQUARE
NEW BRITAIN, CONNECTICUT 06051
Telephone: 860-348-1900
Facsimile: 860-348-1942
URL: http://www.advocateslawfirm.com

Criminal Defense, White Collar Criminal Defense, Personal Injury, Medical Malpractice, Legal Malpractice, Legal Ethics and Professional Responsibility, Attorney Discipline. Trials and Appeals in all Courts and Administrative Agencies.

RON MURPHY, born Wantagh, New York, May 16, 1958; admitted to bar, 1983, Connecticut and U.S. District Court, District of Connecticut; 1985, Massachusetts and U.S. District Court, District of Massachusetts. *Education:* Springfield College (B.S., summa cum laude, 1980); University of Connecticut (J.D., 1983). National Criminal Defense College, July 1991. Trial Lawyers College, August 1995. Judicial Law Clerk, Superior Court of Connecticut, 1983-1984. Author: "Medical Malpractice Claims; Connecticut Action and Remedies-Tort Law," (Butterworth, 1993); "Ethical Considerations in Criminal Defense," National Business Institute, 1996; "Taking the Criminal Case to Trial," National Business Institute, 1996; "Grievance Defense: Should You Respond on the Merits at the Local Panel?" Connecticut Law Tribune, 1998. Lecturer: "DWI Dealing with the New Laws and Regulations," Hartford, 1993; "Brave New World - The Many Changes in State and Federal Criminal Law," Hartford, 1995; "Strategies in Defending DUI Cases," Hartford, 1996; "Criminal Defense Litigation in Connecticut," New Haven, 1996; "Protect Yourself Against Claims by Prospective Clients," Connecticut Law Tribune, 2000. Adjunct Faculty, Legal Ethics, University of Connecticut School of Law, 2000—. Faculty Trial Lawyers College, 2001—. Certified Emergency Medical Technician, 1999—. *Member:* Hartford County (Chairman, Criminal Law, 1990-1993), Connecticut (Member, Professional Discipline Committee; Task Force on Grievance Procedures; Member, Committee on Professional Ethics), Massachusetts and American Bar Associations; Connecticut Trial Lawyers Association; The Association of Trial Lawyers of America; Massachusetts Academy of Trial Attorneys; National Association of Criminal Defense Lawyers; Connecticut Criminal Defense Lawyers Association (President, 2000-2001); Massachusetts Association of Criminal Defense Lawyers. (Certified as a Civil Trial Advocacy Specialist by the National Board of Trial Advocacy). ***REPORTED CASES:*** State v. Miller, 29 Conn. App. 207 (1992), affd, 227 Conn. 363 (1993); State v. Figueroa, 22 Conn. App. 73, cert den, 215 Conn. 814 (1990). ***PRACTICE AREAS:*** Criminal Defense; White Collar Criminal Defense; Personal Injury; Medical Malpractice; Legal Malpractice; Legal Ethics and Professional Responsibility; Attorney Discipline.

FRANCIS D. PAOLA, JR., born 1949; admitted to bar, 1980, Connecticut. *Education:* Villanova University (A.B.); Quinnipiac College (J.D.).

MICHAEL G. RIGG, born Pointe-Claire, Quebec, Canada, December 4, 1970; admitted to bar, 1996, Connecticut and U.S. District Court, District of Connecticut, 1988. *Education:* Elizabethtown College (B.A., 1992); Quinnipiac

(This Listing Continued)

ADVOCATES LAW FIRM, LLC, New Britain—Continued

College (J.D., 1996). Member, Moot Court Honor Society. *Member:* Hartford County and Connecticut Bar Associations; Connecticut Criminal Defense Lawyers Association; Connecticut Trial Lawyers Association. ***PRACTICE AREAS:*** Criminal Defense; Personal Injury.

JANIS K. MALEC, born Hartford, Connecticut, May 28, 1958; admitted to bar, 1996, Connecticut; 1997, U.S. District Court, District of Connecticut. *Education:* University of Connecticut (B.S., 1981); St. Joseph College (M.A., 1990); Western New England College (J.D., 1996). Registered Nurse, Connecticut, 1981—. *Member:* Hartford County and Connecticut Bar Associations; Association of Trial Lawyers of America; Connecticut Criminal Defense Lawyers Association; Connecticut Trial Lawyers Association. ***PRACTICE AREAS:*** Medical Malpractice; Personal Injury; Criminal Defense.

REFERENCE: Webster Bank.

EISENBERG, ANDERSON, MICHALIK & LYNCH LLP

Established in 1987

136 WEST MAIN STREET
P.O. BOX 2950
NEW BRITAIN, CONNECTICUT 06050-2950
Telephone: 860-229-4855; 225-8403
Fax: 860-223-4026
URL: http://www.eaml.com

Construction Law, Employment Law, Elder Law, Estate Planning, Taxation Law, Family Law, Federal and State Litigation and Appeals, Municipal, Real Estate, Zoning, Corporate Law, Commercial Law.

FIRM PROFILE: Eisenberg, Anderson, Michalik & Lynch was founded in 1987 with the merger of two established firms dating back to 1961. The firm has a comprehensive and diverse practice with emphasis in several areas of specialization including Federal and State Litigation and Appeals, Personal Injury and Products Liability, Medical Malpractice, Workers Compensation, Banking, Corporate and Commercial Law, Bankruptcy and Creditors Rights, Foreclosures, Real Estate including Complex Commercial and Residential, Labor Relations, Equal Employment and Civil Rights Litigation, Municipal Law, Environmental Law, Trust and Estates Planning, Elder Law, Federal and State Taxation, Family Law and Related Areas, Zoning, Public Health, Social Security Disability.

HAROLD J. EISENBERG (1906-1995).

MEMBERS OF FIRM

STEPHEN J. ANDERSON, born New Britain, Connecticut, September 6, 1936; admitted to bar, 1961, Connecticut; 1963, U.S. District Court, District of Connecticut; 1969, U.S. Court of Appeals, Second Circuit; 1979, U.S. Supreme Court. *Education:* University of Connecticut (B.A., 1958; J.D., 1961). Corporation Counsel, Town of Berlin, 1985-1987, 1994-1997. Connecticut State Trial Referee, 1986—. *Member:* New Britain and Connecticut Bar Associations. ***PRACTICE AREAS:*** Commercial Law; Real Estate Law; Planning and Zoning Law. ***Email:*** steveanderson@eaml.com

ROBERT A. MICHALIK, born Bristol, Connecticut, September 21, 1941; admitted to bar, 1966, Connecticut, U.S. District Court, District of Connecticut, U.S. Court of Appeals, Second Circuit and U.S. Tax Court. *Education:* University of Connecticut (B.A., 1963; J.D., 1966). Lecturer, Principles of Law and Advanced Law, Central Connecticut State University, 1975-1981, 1985-1986. Member, 1969-1973 and Chairman, 1971-1973, Plainville Town Council. Town Attorney, Town of Plainville, 1979—. Member, Board of Directors, 1984-1986 and General Counsel, 1977—, CenConn Credit Union. General Counsel: Regional Recycling Operating Committee, 1989—; United Business and Industry Federal Credit Union, 1989—; and other financial institutions; Regional Resource Recovery Facility Operating Committee, 1986—. Member, Tunxis Community College Regional Advisory Board and Foundation, 1993—. *Member:* New Britain, Hartford County, Connecticut and American Bar Associations. ***PRACTICE AREAS:*** Municipal Law; Banking Law; Family Law. ***Email:*** bobmichalik@eaml.com

EDWARD T. LYNCH, JR., born Hartford, Connecticut, June 17, 1945; admitted to bar, 1970, Connecticut and U.S. District Court, District of Connecticut; 1971, U.S. Court of Appeals, Second Circuit; 1972, U.S. Tax Court and U.S. Claims Court; 1973, District of Columbia and U.S. Supreme Court; 1977, U.S. District Court, Southern District of New York, U.S. District Court, District of Rhode Island and U.S. Court of Military Appeals; 1981, U.S. District Court, District of Massachusetts, U.S. Court of Appeals, First Circuit; 1982, U.S. Court of Appeals for the Federal Circuit. *Education:* Georgetown University (A.B., 1967); University of Connecticut (M.B.A., 1976; J.D., 1970). Associate Professor, Finance Department, Central Connecticut State University, 1971-1997. Corporation Counsel, City of New Britain, 1984-1989. General Counsel, Connecticut Police Chief's Association, 1978—. General Counsel, International Association of Campus Law Enforcement Administrators, 1982—. [Lieutenant Colonel, Judge Advocate Troop Command, Connecticut National Guard, 1972-1993]. ***PRACTICE AREAS:*** Corporate Litigation; Business Litigation; Labor and Employment Litigation; Construction Litigation; Arbitration. ***Email:*** edlynch@eaml.com

CHARLES W. BAUER, born Hartford, Connecticut, November 26, 1943; admitted to bar, 1971, Connecticut; 1975, U.S. District Court, District of Connecticut and U.S. Court of Appeals, Second Circuit; 1985, U.S. Supreme Court. *Education:* Hamilton College (A.B., 1965); University of Connecticut School of Law (J.D., 1968). Judge of Probate, Burlington, 1979—. Corporation Counsel, Town of Burlington, 1983—. President, Board of Directors, New Britain Foundation for Public Giving, 1994-1997. *Member:* New Britain and Connecticut Bar Associations; National Academy of Elder Law Attorneys, Inc. ***PRACTICE AREAS:*** Municipal Law; Elder Law; Estate Planning; Construction Law; Land Use. ***Email:*** charlesbauer@eaml.com

DENNIS G. CICCARILLO, born New Britain, Connecticut, November 11, 1953; admitted to bar, 1979, Connecticut; 1980, U.S. District Court, District of Connecticut; 1984, U.S. Court of Appeals, First and Second Circuits. *Education:* Brown University (A.B., 1975); University of Connecticut (J.D., 1978). Instructor: Principles of Law, Advanced Law and Legal Environment of Business, Central Connecticut State University, 1979—. Superior Court Attorney Trial Referee, Fact Finder and Arbitrator, 1987—. Hearing Officer: Connecticut Commission on Human Rights & Opportunities, 1992-1997. Board of Directors, Connecticut Legal Services, Inc. (Past President). *Member:* New Britain Bar Association; Connecticut Trial Lawyers Association; National Organization of Social Security Claimants' Representatives. ***PRACTICE AREAS:*** Labor and Employment Law; Social Security; Disability. ***Email:*** dennisciccarillo@eaml.com

PAMELA REARDON REYNOLDS, born Danbury, Connecticut, July 14, 1952; admitted to bar, 1985, Connecticut; 1987, U.S. District Court, District of Connecticut. *Education:* Southern Connecticut State University (B.S., 1974; M.S., 1979); University of Connecticut (J.D., 1985). Member, Connecticut Law Review, 1982-1985. Author: "The Significance of Congressional Intent and Statutory Purpose in Defining Profits Realized in Section 16 (b) Litigation: CBI Industries v. Horton," Connecticut Law Review, Vol. 16, Winter, 1984, No. 2. President, Board of Directors, New Britain Chamber of Commerce. *Member:* Connecticut Bar Association. ***PRACTICE AREAS:*** Corporate Law; Commercial Law; Trust and Estate Planning; Mergers and Acquisitions Law; Franchise Law. ***Email:*** pamreynolds@eaml.com

JoANN CENTRILLA-SILVIA, born Bronx, New York, September 29, 1960; admitted to bar, 1989, Connecticut; 1990, New York and U.S. District Court, Southern and Eastern Districts of New York; 1991, U.S. District Court, District of Connecticut. *Education:* Fordham University (B.A., 1982); University of Bridgeport School of Law (J.D., 1988). Fact Finder, Superior Court, 1990—. Board Member, Connecticut Creditors Rights Attorneys Assoc. *Member:* New Britain and New York State Bar Associations. ***PRACTICE AREAS:*** Commercial Collections; Consumer Collections; Bankruptcy Law. ***Email:*** joannsilvia@eaml.com

KENNETH R. SLATER, JR., born Stafford Springs, Connecticut, July 27, 1966; admitted to bar, 1991, Connecticut; 1992, U.S. District Court, District of Connecticut; 1994, U.S. Court of Appeals, Second Circuit. *Education:* University of Rochester (B.A., cum laude, highest distinction in economics, 1988); University of Connecticut (J.D., cum laude, 1991). Omicron Delta Epsilon. *Member:* New Britain and Connecticut (Member, Planning and Zoning, Environmental Quality and Legal Technology Sections; Former Chair, Environmental Law Committee, Young Lawyers Section, 1993-1997) Bar Associations. ***PRACTICE AREAS:*** Environmental Law; Land Use Law; Litigation; Arbitration. ***Email:*** kenslater@eaml.com

PETER N. UPTON, born New York, New York, November 7, 1944; admitted to bar, 1973, Rhode Island; 1974, U.S. Court of Military Appeals; 1976, Connecticut and U.S. District Court, District of Connecticut. *Education:* Princeton University (B.A., Philosophy, 1966); Boston University Law School (J.D., 1973). Editor, Boston University Law Review, 1972-1973. Chief Defense Counsel, Judge Advocate General Corps Officer, Naval Legal Service Office, Norfolk, VA. *Member:* Connecticut Bar Association. [LCDR, USNR, 1966-1976]. ***PRACTICE AREAS:*** Litigation. ***Email:*** peterupton@eaml.com

GREGORY J. SPUCHES, born Syracuse, New York, July 31, 1960; admitted to bar, 1988, Connecticut, New York, U.S. Tax Court and U.S. District Court, District of Connecticut; 1991 U.S. District Court, Northern District of New York. *Education:* Bryant & Stratton Business Institute (A.O.S., Accounting, 1979); State University of New York College of Technology at Utica/Rome (B.P.S., Accounting/Business Administration, 1982); University of Bridgeport College of Law (J.D., 1985); Syracuse University Graduate School of Management. Phi Alpha Delta. *Member:* Connecticut (Member: Tax, Elder Law and Estates and Probate Sections), New York State (Member: Tax, Elder Law and

(This Listing Continued)

Estates and Probate Sections) and American (Member: Taxation, Real Property, Probate and Trust Sections) Bar Associations; National Academy of Elder Law Attorneys, Inc. ***PRACTICE AREAS:*** Taxation; Estate Planning; Probate; Estate Administration; Elder Law; Taxpayer Representation. ***Email:*** gregoryspuches@eaml.com

LAURIE G. DeNIGRIS, born New Haven, Connecticut, February 1, 1959; admitted to bar, 1984, Connecticut; 1985, U.S. District Court, District of Connecticut. *Education:* Skidmore College (B.A., 1981); Ohio Northern University (J.D., 1984). Delta Theta Phi. Recipient, American Jurisprudence Award in Contracts. Managing Editor, Ohio Northern University Law Review, 1983-1984. Special Master for Matrimonial Matters in Hartford, New Britain and Litchfield. *Member:* Hartford County, Connecticut and American (Member, Family Law Section; Former Co-Chair, Family Law and Child Advocacy Committee) Bar Associations; Collaborative Divorce Lawyers Association. ***PRACTICE AREAS:*** Family Law; Childrens Rights; Social Security; Litigation. ***Email:*** lauriedenigris@eaml.com

ASSOCIATES

DAVID G. JORDAN, born Danbury, Connecticut, July 16, 1974; admitted to bar, 1999, Connecticut; 2000, U.S. District Court, District of Connecticut. *Education:* Fairfield University (B.A., 1996); University of Connecticut (J.D., 1999). *Member:* New Britain and Connecticut Bar Associations. ***PRACTICE AREAS:*** Litigation. ***Email:*** davidjordan@eaml.com

BRUCE A. ZAWODNIAK, born Newton, Massachusetts, March 22, 1961; admitted to bar, 1988, Connecticut; 1989, U.S. District Court, District of Connecticut; 1990, District of Columbia. *Education:* Trinity College (B.A., 1983); University of Connecticut (J.D., 1988). Member: Community Associations Institute; Rocky Hill Zoning Board of Appeals. Justice of the Peace. *Member:* New Britain and Connecticut (Member, Real Property Section) Bar Associations. ***PRACTICE AREAS:*** Real Estate Law; Real Estate Foreclosures; Condominium Law; Landlord/Tenant Law; Commercial Law; Consumer Collections. ***Email:*** brucezawodniak@eaml.com

REPRESENTATIVE CLIENTS: Acme Monaco, Inc.; Amco Precision Tool; Amodio Moving & Storage, Inc.; Apple Health Care; ARNA Machine; Branford Steam Railroad Co.; Bristol Resource Recovery Facility Operating Committee; First Bristol Federal Credit Union; Central Connecticut Chiropractic, P.C.; CIGNA; Connecticut Employees Union "Independent"; Connecticut Police Chief's Association; Connecticut Postal Federal Credit Union; Connecticut State Employees Credit Union; Covenant Home/Pilgrim Manor; Dutch Point Credit Union, Inc.; Cenconn Credit Union, Inc.; First City Bank; Fleet Bank, N.A.; United Business & Industry Employees Federal Credit Union; Nutmeg State Federal Union; Hartford Federal Credit Union; YWCA; New Britian Board of Education; International Association of Campus Law Enforcement Administrators; ITT Sealectro; Macristy Industries, Inc.; Magson Uniform Corp.; Manafort Brothers, Inc.; Meriden Municipal Federal Credit Union; New Britain Chamber of Commerce; New Britain Municipal Employees Credit Union; Newington VA Federal Credit Union; Pinstripe Marketing; Prime Healthcare, P.C.; Southern New England Ice & Oil; Spring Brook Service, Incorporated; Swift Textile Metalizing, LLC; Tenergy, LLC; Textron, Inc.; TILCON Connecticut Inc.; TILCON Inc.; TILCON Minerals, Inc.; Tomasso Brothers, Inc.; Town of Burlington; Town of Plainville; Town of Stafford; Town of Wallingford; Tunxis Obstetrics and Gynecologists, P.C.; Tunxis Recycling Operating Committee; Webster Bank; Shein, Cohen & Palmer, L.L.C.

JANUSZEWSKI, McQUILLAN AND DeNIGRIS

Established in 1952

165 WEST MAIN STREET
P.O. BOX 150
NEW BRITAIN, CONNECTICUT 06050-0150
Telephone: 860-225-7667
Fax: 860-826-1814
Email: JMDNBCT@WORLDNET.ATT.NET

General Practice, Civil and Criminal Litigation, Real Estate, Family Law, Administrative Agency Proceedings, Workers Compensation, Personal Injury, Products Liability, Professional Malpractice, Probate, Representation to Professional Responsibilities, Trials in State and Federal Courts.

FIRM PROFILE: Founded by the late Judge Roman Lexton in 1952, the firm of Januszewski, McQuillan & DeNigris has provided high quality legal services to individuals and businesses for more than 40 years. The continuing commitment of the firm members to their clients, and through volunteer service to their community and profession, has led to a statewide practice marked by stability, integrity, and quality service.

MEMBERS OF FIRM

EDWARD JANUSZEWSKI (1921-1999).

PAUL J. McQUILLAN, born Bristol, Connecticut, September 19, 1928; admitted to bar, 1957, Connecticut. *Education:* Georgetown University (B.S. in F.S., 1952; J.D., 1956). Corporation Counsel, City of New Britain, 1960-1962. Chairman, State Board of Pardons, 1977-1984. Member and Chairman, Criminal Injuries Compensation Board, 1982-1984. Chairman, Connecticut Judicial Selection Commission, 1986-1992. Fellow, American College of Trial Lawyers, 1987. *Member:* New Britain (President, 1974-1975), Hartford County (Member, Executive Committee, 1970—), Connecticut and American Bar Associations; Connecticut Trial Lawyers Association (Member, Board of Governors, 1970—; President, 1987-1988); The Association of Trial Lawyers of America (Member, Board of Governors, 1979-1992); American Board of Trial Advocates (Advocate); American Board of Criminal Lawyers; Association of Professional Responsibility Lawyers. ***PRACTICE AREAS:*** Personal Injury Law; Criminal Law; Malpractice; Professional Ethics.

NICHOLAS E. DeNIGRIS, born New Britain, Connecticut, May 9, 1935; admitted to bar, 1960, Connecticut. *Education:* Clark University (B.A., 1957); Boston University and University of Connecticut (J.D., 1960). Member, 1964-1968; 1971-1975 and President, 1973-1975, New Britain Board of Education. Assistant Prosecutor, 15th Circuit Court of Connecticut, 1965-1967. President, The Boy's and Girl's Club, Corporator, YMCA. Special Assistant Corporation Counsel of New Britain. *Member:* New Britain (President, 1980), Hartford County and Connecticut Bar Associations. ***PRACTICE AREAS:*** Real Estate Law; Domestic Relations Law; Criminal Law; Personal Injury; Corporate Law; Probate Law; Estates.

JOHN C. MATULIS, JR., born New Britain, Connecticut, May 21, 1950; admitted to bar, 1976, Connecticut and U.S. District Court, District of Connecticut; 1986, U.S. Court of Appeals, Second Circuit; 1998, U.S. Supreme Court. *Education:* Trinity College (A.B., 1972); University of Connecticut (J.D., 1975). Author: Chapter, "Motions to Preclude Experts," *Civil Discovery Practice in Connecticut,* Law Practice Handbooks, Inc. (1995). Director: Connecticut Legal Services, Inc., 1976-1983; YMCA of Berlin-New Britain, 1986-1992. Director, 1976-1989, and President, 1987-1988, Sheldon Child Guidance Clinic. Director: Community Mental Health Affiliates, Inc., 1992-1998; Reid Treatment Center, Inc. 1998—. *Member:* New Britain (President, 1991-1992), Hartford County (Co-Chair, Bench-Bar Committee, 1993-1995, Chair, Civil Litigation Committee, 1996—), Connecticut and American Bar Associations; Connecticut Trial Lawyers Association. ***PRACTICE AREAS:*** Civil Litigation; Professional Malpractice; Domestic Relations Law.

STEVEN D. ANDERSON, born Malden, Massachusetts, April 28, 1954; admitted to bar, 1984, Connecticut, 1985, U.S. District Court, District of Connecticut. *Education:* United States Military Academy (B.S., 1976); University of Connecticut (J.D., 1984). President, Board of Directors, New Britain-Berlin YMCA, 1987—. Member, Ethics Commission, Town of Berlin, 1998—. President, New Britain Chapter, American Heart Association, 1988-1990. President, New Britain Lions Club, 1993—. *Member:* New Britain, Hartford County, Connecticut (Member, House of Delegates, 1989—; Board of Governors, 1989-1993) and American Bar Associations; Connecticut Trial Lawyers Association. [Capt. U.S. Army 1972-1981; Lieut. Col. USAR/Conn. Nat. Guard 1981—]. ***PRACTICE AREAS:*** Personal Injury Law; Criminal Law; Family Law; Workers Compensation Law; Probate Law.

MARTIN McQUILLAN, born New Britain, Connecticut, May 16, 1962; admitted to bar, 1990, Connecticut; 1991, U.S. District Court, District of Connecticut. *Education:* Georgetown University (B.A., 1986); Western New England College (J.D., 1990). Member, Board of Directors, Connecticut Legal Services, Inc., 1991; Chair, People's Law School, New Britain, 1993. President, New Britain Bar Association, 1998. *Member:* New Britain, Hartford County and Connecticut Bar Associations; Connecticut Trial Lawyers Association. ***PRACTICE AREAS:*** Personal Injury Law; Workers Compensation Law; Criminal Law.

REPRESENTATIVE CLIENTS: Tilcon, Inc.; Webster Bank; Peoples' Bank; First City Bank; Reno Machine Company, Inc.; Dattco Bus Company; J. Dorio Builders & Realty, Inc.; Coppermine Estates, Inc.; B & R Machine Company, Inc.; Acmat, Inc.

ALBERT, WARD & JOHNSON, P.C.

NEW CANAAN, CONNECTICUT

(See Greenwich)

General Practice. Real Estate, Zoning, Corporation, Litigation, Probate, Taxation, Construction, Environmental and Family Law.

CURTIS, BRINCKERHOFF & BARRETT, P.C.

NEW CANAAN, CONNECTICUT

(See Stamford)

General Practice, Real Estate, Commercial Real Estate Acquisitions, Municipal Law, Zoning, Planning and Land Use, Banking, Administrative Law, Litigation, Civil Litigation, Commercial Litigation, Tax Appeals, Eminent Domain, Federal Taxation, International Taxation, State Taxation, Estate Planning, Trust and Estate, Probate, Elder Law, Family Law, Domestic Relations, Closely Held Corporations, Business Law, Corporate Law, Commercial Law, Commercial Leasing, Leases and Leasing, Employment Law, Non-Competition and Non-Solicitation Agreements, Commercial Arbitration, Construction Law, Landlord and Tenant Law, Personal

(This Listing Continued)

CURTIS, BRINCKERHOFF & BARRETT, P.C., New Canaan—Continued

Injury and Negligence, Product Liability, Bankruptcy, Civil Trial and Appellate Practice in all State and Federal Courts.

DAVIDSON, DAWSON & CLARK LLP

Established in 1949

36 GROVE STREET

NEW CANAAN, CONNECTICUT 06840

Telephone: 203-966-8759

Telecopier: 203-966-7894

New York, New York Office: 330 Madison Avenue. Telephone: 212-557-7700. Telecopier: 212-286-8513.

General Civil Practice. Trust and Estate Planning and Administration, Probate, Taxation, Corporate, Real Estate and Non-Profit Organizations.

MEMBERS OF FIRM

BERKELEY D. JOHNSON, JR., born Yonkers, New York, April 22, 1931; admitted to bar, 1960, Connecticut; 1961, New York; 1981, Florida. *Education:* Harvard University (A.B., 1953); University of Connecticut (LL.B., 1960). *Member:* The Association of the Bar of the City of New York; New Canaan, New York State, Connecticut and American Bar Associations; The Florida Bar. (Resident Partner). ***PRACTICE AREAS:*** Estate Planning; Wills and Trusts; Probate; Zoning Law. ***Email:*** bdjohnson@davidsondawson.com

ALAN P. DONALDSON, born New York, N.Y., October 29, 1947; admitted to bar, 1973, Connecticut. *Education:* Princeton University (A.B., cum laude, 1970); Northwestern University (J.D., cum laude, 1973); New York University (LL.M. in Taxation, 1981). Member, Northwestern University Law Review, 1972-1973. Trustee, New Canaan Nature Center, 1986-1992; Trustee, 1994—and President, 2000—, New Canaan Community Foundation. Trustee, 1995—and Vice President, 1996—, New Canaan Library. *Member:* New Canaan, Connecticut and American Bar Associations. (Resident Partner). ***PRACTICE AREAS:*** Estate Planning; Wills and Trusts; Probate; Federal Income, Estate and Gift Taxation. ***Email:*** apdonaldson@davidsondawson.com

OF COUNSEL

WILLIAM M. THROOP, JR., born Mt. Vernon, New York, September 19, 1924; admitted to bar, 1951, New York; 1958, Connecticut. *Education:* Princeton University (A.B., 1945); Yale University (LL.B., 1950). Phi Delta Phi. *Member:* The Association of the Bar of the City of New York (Member: Trusts, Estates and Surrogates Courts Committee, 1968-1971; Committee on Professional and Judicial Ethics, 1976-1979); New Canaan, New York State, Connecticut and American Bar Associations. ***PRACTICE AREAS:*** Estate Planning; Wills and Trusts; Probate; Not-for-Profit Organizations. ***Email:*** wmthroop@davidsondawson.com

ASSOCIATES

MARTIN P. DANIELS, born New York, N.Y., May 2, 1963; admitted to bar, 1990, Connecticut; 1991, New York and Massachusetts; U.S. District Court, Southern and Eastern Districts of New York; U.S. District Court, District of Connecticut; 1992, U.S. Court of Appeals, Second Circuit. *Education:* Skidmore College (B.A., 1985); London School of Economics and Political Science (M.Sc., 1986); Syracuse University (J.D., 1990). Order of the Barrister, 1989-1990. Phillip C. Jessup International Law Moot Court Competition, 1988-1990. Member, 1988-1990, Finance Director, 1989-1990, Syracuse University College of Law Moot Court Board. Recipient, International Legal Studies Award, 1989-1990. Member, Syracuse Journal of International Law and Commerce, 1988. Member, Estate Planning Council of Lower Fairfield County. *Member:* The Association of the Bar of the City of New York; New York (Member, Trusts and Estates and Real Property Sections), New Canaan and Connecticut (Member, Estates and Probate, Real Estate and Planning and Zoning Sections) Bar Associations. (Resident). ***PRACTICE AREAS:*** Estate Planning; Wills and Trusts; Probate; Real Estate and Zoning. ***Email:*** mpdaniels@davidsondawson.com

THOMAS M. SHEEHAN, born Heidelburg, Germany, March 14, 1971; admitted to bar, 1997, Connecticut. *Education:* Providence College (B.A., English, 1993); Roger Williams University School of Law (J.D., 1997); Boston University (LL.M. in Taxation, 1998). Recipient, CALI Excellence in Legal Drafting. Listed in Who's Who 1997 Law School Graduates. *Member:* Connecticut (Chair, Taxation Committee, Young Lawyers Section) and American Bar Associations. (Resident). ***PRACTICE AREAS:*** Trusts and Estates; Estate Planning; Estate Administration; Tax Law. ***Email:*** tmsheehan@davidsondawson.com

(For complete biographical data on all personnel, see Professional Biographies at New York, N.Y.)

SPERRY A. DE CEW

22 EAST AVENUE

P.O. BOX 1056

NEW CANAAN, CONNECTICUT 06840

Telephone: 203-966-6019

Facsimile: 203-972-3780

Email: dqlaw@snet.net

General Civil and Criminal Practice. Trials and Appeals in State and Federal Courts. Domestic Relations, Personal Injury, Commercial Litigation, Business, Real Estate and Probate Law.

SPERRY A. DE CEW, born Bronxville, New York, September 9, 1946; admitted to bar, 1975, Connecticut and U.S. District Court, District of Connecticut; 1980, U.S. District Court, Southern and Eastern Districts of New York; 1981, New York, U.S. Court of Appeals, Second Circuit and U.S. Supreme Court. *Education:* Cornell University (B.A., 1972); University of Connecticut (J.D., 1975). Phi Alpha Delta. Member, New Canaan Town Council, 1977-1989. Member, Board of Selectman, 1997-1999. *Member:* Connecticut and American Bar Associations; Connecticut Trial Lawyers Association; The Association of Trial Lawyers of America. [With U.S. Army, 1967-1970]. ***REPORTED CASES:*** Connecticut Institute for the Blind, Inc. v. Connecticut Commission of Human Rights and Opportunities, 176 Conn. 88, 405 A.2d 618 (1978) (Amicus); Allen v. Nissley, 184 Conn. 539, 440 A.2d 231 (1981) (Real Estate Contract); Campisano v. Nardi, 212 Conn. 282, 562 A.2d 1 (1989) (Construction Contract; Corporation); Roach v. Roach, 20 Conn. App 500, 568 A.2d 1037 (1990) (Domestic-Divorce); Kane v. Parry, 24 Conn. App. 307, 588 A.2d 227 (1991) (Domestic-Divorce); Oppenheimer v. State, 25 Conn. App. 802 (1991) (Tort-Auto); Kane v. Parry, 27 Conn. 923, 608 A.2d 108 (1992) (Domestic-Divorce); Kane v. Parry, 226 Conn. 817 (1993) (Domestic-Divorce); Bishops v. Hastings, 33 Conn. App. 933 (1994) (Real Estate Contract). ***PRACTICE AREAS:*** Civil Litigation; Personal Injury; Real Estate; Family Law.

REFERENCES: Chase Manhattan Bank; Summit Bank; Connecticut Attorney's Title Insurance Co.; Lawyers Title Insurance Co.

FINN DIXON & HERLING LLP

NEW CANAAN, CONNECTICUT

(See Stamford)

Corporate Law, Mergers and Acquisitions, Securities Law, Venture Capital Financing, Corporate Finance and Restructuring, Commercial Litigation, Banking and Lending Law, Bankruptcy and Workouts, Employee Benefits and the Federal and State Taxation of Businesses and Business Transactions.

FRANCO & ASSOCIATES

125 ELM STREET

NEW CANAAN, CONNECTICUT 06840

Telephone: 203-972-7339

Fax: 203-972-7321

Email: mfranco@francolaw.com

URL: http://www.lawyers.com/francolaw

Real Estate, Real Estate Development, Zoning, Planning and Land Use, Corporate Law, Commercial Law, Partnership Law, Securities Law, Trusts and Estates.

MEMBER OF FIRM

MICHAEL J. FRANCO, born Stamford, Connecticut, November 19, 1959; admitted to bar, 1985, Vermont; 1986, Massachusetts; 1987, New Hampshire and Connecticut. *Education:* Merrimack College (B.A., 1981); Vermont Law School (J.D., 1985). President, Student Bar Association, 1983-1985. *Member:* Connecticut (Member, Planning and Zoning Section), Massachusetts and New Hampshire Bar Associations; Rotary International. ***PRACTICE AREAS:*** Real Estate; Real Estate Development; Zoning, Planning and Land Use; Corporate Law; Commercial Law; Partnership Law; Estate Planning. ***Email:*** mfranco@francolaw.com

ASSOCIATE

MORRIS L. BAROCAS, born Stamford, Connecticut, May 25, 1968; admitted to bar, 1996, Connecticut. *Education:* George Washington University (B.B.A., 1990); Quinnipiac College (J.D., 1995). *Member:* American Bar Association. ***TRANSACTIONS:*** Nynex-Bell Atlantic Merger, 1996-1997. ***PRACTICE AREAS:*** Residential Real Estate; Commercial Real Estate; Banking Law; Corporate Law; Trusts and Estates. ***Email:*** mbarocas@francolaw.com

GOGICK, BYRNE & O'NEILL, LLP

280 ELM STREET
NEW CANAAN, CONNECTICUT 06840-5313
Telephone: 203-327-7561
Fax: 203-966-1431

New York, New York Office: 26 Broadway. Telephone: 212-422-9424. Facsimile: 212-422-9429.
West Orange, New Jersey Office: 80 Main Street. Telephone: 973-778-7074. Facsimile: 973-731-9319.

Professional Liability, Construction, Environmental, Surety and General Litigation, Mediation, Arbitration and Employment Discrimination.

(For Complete Biographical Data on all Personnel, see Professional Biographies at New York, NY)

HENRY L. GOLDSTEIN

Established in 1980
46 MAIN STREET
NEW CANAAN, CONNECTICUT 06840-4523
Telephone: 203-356-9511
Fax: 203-357-1445
URL: http://www.lawyers.com/henrygoldstein

Estate Planning, Probate, Real Estate and Corporate Law.

HENRY L. GOLDSTEIN, born New York, N.Y., August 12, 1941; admitted to bar, 1966, New York; 1973, Connecticut. *Education:* Cornell University (A.B., 1963); University of Pennsylvania (J.D., 1966). *Member:* Stamford, Connecticut, New York State and American Bar Associations; American Judicature Society.

REFERENCE: First Union Bank.

HAWTHORNE, ACKERLY & DORRANCE, LLC

Established in 1926
25 SOUTH AVENUE
P.O. BOX 937
NEW CANAAN, CONNECTICUT 06840
Telephone: 203-966-9583
Fax: 203-966-1296

General Practice. Probate, Estate Planning, Business Planning, Real Estate, Taxation, Family, Litigation, Employment and Elder Law.

JEREMIAH S. MILLER, born New York, N.Y., July 4, 1945; admitted to bar, 1973, Connecticut; 1976, U.S. District Court, District of Connecticut. *Education:* Kenyon College (B.A., 1967); Washington & Lee University (J.D., 1972). *Member:* New Canaan (President, 1979-1980), The Connecticut and American Bar Associations. ***PRACTICE AREAS:*** Estate Settlements; Trust Administration; Conservatorships; Elder Law; Real Estate; Estate Planning; Family Law Mediation.

MICHELLE R. HUBBARD, born New York, N.Y., May 19, 1947; admitted to bar, 1985, Connecticut. *Education:* Manhattanville College (B.A., 1972); New York Law School (J.D., cum laude, 1984). Member, New York Law School Journal of International and Comparative Law, 1983-1984. *Member:* New Canaan, Stamford/Norwalk Regional, Connecticut and American Bar Associations. ***PRACTICE AREAS:*** Estate Planning; Probate; Trust Administration; Real Estate.

LAWRENCE S. MANNIX, born Norwalk, Connecticut, January 18, 1962; admitted to bar, 1987, Massachusetts; 1988, District of Columbia and U.S. Tax Court; 1994, Connecticut. *Education:* College of the Holy Cross (B.A., 1984); Catholic University of America (J.D., 1987); Boston University (LL.M., 1995). Litigation Attorney, Internal Revenue Service, National Office, 1988-1992. *Member:* Connecticut (Member, Estates and Probate Section) and American (Member, Taxation Section) Bar Associations. ***PRACTICE AREAS:*** Taxation; Estate Planning and Administration; Business Planning and Administration.

GEORGE W. BAKER, born New York, N.Y., April 25, 1948; admitted to bar, 1973, Connecticut; 1975, U.S. District Court, District of Connecticut; 1976, U.S. Supreme Court and U.S. Court of Appeals, Second Circuit. *Education:* Columbia University (B.A., 1969; J.D., 1973). Member, New Canaan Town Council, 1989—. Connecticut Superior Court Attorney Trial Referee, 2000—. *Member:* New Canaan, Connecticut and American Bar Associations; Connecticut Trial Lawyers Association. ***PRACTICE AREAS:*** General Litigation; Employment Law.

(This Listing Continued)

MICHAEL NEDDER, born Boston, Massachusetts, April 4, 1973; admitted to bar, 1999, Connecticut. *Education:* Fairfield University (B.S., 1996); Fordham University (J.D., 1999). *Member:* New Canaan and The Connecticut Bar Associations. ***PRACTICE AREAS:*** Estate Planning; Business Planning; Real Estate; Taxation. ***Email:*** mnedder@hadlaw.com

OF COUNSEL

DANA C. ACKERLY, born New York, N.Y., June 9, 1920; admitted to bar, 1948, Connecticut; 1972, U.S. District Court, District of Connecticut. *Education:* Williams College (A.B., 1941); Yale University (LL.B., 1948). *Member:* New Canaan (President, 1967-1969) and The Connecticut Bar Associations. ***PRACTICE AREAS:*** Estate and Trust Administration; Taxation.

MARVIN I. GRUSS, born Bridgeport, Connecticut, January 14, 1924; admitted to bar, 1962, Connecticut. *Education:* Brown University; Massachusetts Institute of Technology; Clark University (A.B., summa cum laude, 1944); Yale University (LL.B., 1962). Order of the Coif. *Member:* New Canaan (President, 1975-1976), Stamford-Norwalk Regional and The Connecticut Bar Associations; Estate Planning Council of Lower Fairfield County (President, 1987-1988). ***PRACTICE AREAS:*** Trust Administration; Estate Administration; Real Estate; Taxation; Closely Held Corporations. ***Email:*** migruss@hadlaw.com

LOUIS S. PRYOR, born Washington, D.C., March 6, 1934; admitted to bar, 1960, Connecticut; 1961, U.S. Court of Military Appeals; 1963, U.S. District Court, District of Connecticut; 1964, New York; 1970, U.S. Tax Court. *Education:* United States Naval Academy (B.A., magna cum laude, 1957); Yale University (LL.B.,. 1960). *Member:* Connecticut and American Bar Associations. [With JAGC, USAF, 1960-1963]. ***PRACTICE AREAS:*** Taxation; Estate Planning; Trust Administration.

REFERENCES: First Union Bank; Fleet Bank; U.S. Trust Co. of Connecticut; Summit Bank; Putnam Trust.

JACOBS PARTNERS LLC

NEW CANAAN, CONNECTICUT

(See Norwalk)

Business and Personal Bankruptcy, Workouts, Debtor Creditor's Rights, Commercial Litigation, Contracts and Business Disputes.

KOSKOFF, KOSKOFF & BIEDER, P.C.

NEW CANAAN, CONNECTICUT

(See Bridgeport)

Litigation in all State and Federal Courts. Medical Malpractice, Equal Opportunity, Negligence, Products Liability, Civil Rights, and Class Actions.

MELLICK & SEXTON, P.C.

Established in 1976
70 PINE STREET
NEW CANAAN, CONNECTICUT 06840
Telephone: 203-972-0200
Fax: 203-972-0708
Email: emellick@aol.com

Real Estate and Zoning Law.

EDWARD G. MELLICK, born Evanston, Illinois, July 9, 1945; admitted to bar, 1970, Connecticut; 1975, U.S. Supreme Court; 1979, Florida. *Education:* Dartmouth College (B.A., 1967); American University (J.D., 1970). Associate Editor-in-Chief, American University Law Review, 1969-1970. Director, New Canaan Community Foundation, 1988-1994. *Member:* New Canaan, Stamford and Connecticut Bar Associations; The Florida Bar. ***Email:*** emellick@aol.com

OF COUNSEL

MARLENE E. MACAUDA, born Bridgeport, Connecticut, July 3, 1955; admitted to bar, 1981, Connecticut and U.S. District Court, District of Connecticut. *Education:* Providence College (B.A., 1977); Quinnipiac College School of Law (J.D., 1980). *Member:* Westport and Connecticut Bar Associations. ***SPECIAL AGENCIES:*** President, Long Lots PTA, Westport Connecticut, 1997-1999. ***PRACTICE AREAS:*** Real Estate; Zoning. ***Email:*** marlenmail@aol.com

O'ROURKE & ASSOCIATES, LLC

Established in 1987

27 PINE STREET

NEW CANAAN, CONNECTICUT 06840

Telephone: 203-966-6664

Fax: 203-966-5710

Email: obrendan@aol.com

Commercial and Securities Litigation, Corporate and Real Estate Law, Entertainment Law.

BRENDAN J. O'ROURKE, born Bronxville, New York, August 4, 1958; admitted to bar, 1985, Connecticut and U.S. District Court, District of Connecticut. *Education:* University of Virginia (B.A., Economics, with distinction, 1980; M.A., International Law and Political Science, 1985; J.D., 1985). Executive Editor, University of Virginia Journal of Law and Politics, 1984-1985. Associate, Day, Berry and Howard, 1985-1987. Hearing Officer, Connecticut Commission on Human Rights and Opportunities, 1989-2000. *Member:* New Canaan (President 1994-1995), Connecticut and American (Member, Sections on: Business Law; Individual Rights) Bar Associations. ***PRACTICE AREAS:*** Commercial Litigation; Commercial Arbitration; Corporate Law; Real Estate.

JEFFREY M. McCORMICK, born February 16, 1972; admitted to bar, 1998, Connecticut; 2000, U.S. District Court, District of Connecticut. *Education:* Loyola College (B.A., 1995); Widener University School of Law (J.D., 1998). Widener Law Review, 1996-1998. *Member:* Connecticut and American (Member, Sections on: Commercial Law; Litigation; Sports and Entertainment Law) Bar Associations. ***PRACTICE AREAS:*** Commercial Litigation; Corporation Law; Sports Law; Entertainment Law.

CHARLINE V. DALE, born Bowling Green, Kentucky, August 4, 1925; admitted to bar, 1949, Kentucky and Ohio; 1951, District of Columbia; 1956, Michigan and U.S. Tax Court; 1960, New York; 1986, Texas; 1996, Connecticut. *Education:* University of Cincinnati (B.A., 1946; LL.B., 1949). Special Consultant, Tax Management, Inc., Bureau of National Affairs, 1990—. *Member:* Dallas (Member, Sections on: Solo & Small Firm Officer, 1992-1994; Tax Section; Probate Section) and American (Member, Tax Section, Domestic Relations Tax Committee Officer, 1993—; Estates and Trusts Section) Bar Associations; State Bar of Texas (Member, Tax Section). Fellow, Texas Bar Foundation. ***PRACTICE AREAS:*** Taxation; Trusts and Estates; Probate.

PIAZZA & PICKEL

NEW CANAAN, CONNECTICUT

(See Stamford)

Trials and Appeals in State and Federal Courts, Negligence, Medical Malpractice, Divorce and Personal Injury Law, Wrongful Death, Legal Malpractice, Child Custody, Automobile Accidents, Product Liability, Adoption, Family Law.

RUCCI, BURNHAM, CARTA & EDELBERG, LLP

Established in 1978

71 ELM STREET

P.O. BOX 1680

NEW CANAAN, CONNECTICUT 06840

Telephone: 203-966-6500

URL: http://www.rbce.com

Darien, Connecticut Office: 800 Post Road, P.O. Box 1107. Telephone: 203-655-7695.

Stamford, Connecticut Office: 6 Landmark Square, Suite 470. Telephone: 203-359-5637.

Commercial and Residential Real Estate, Trusts and Estates, Estate Planning, Civil Trial Practice including Fiduciary Disputes, Employment, Commercial, Construction and Personal Injury Litigation, Corporate, Commercial, Information Technology, Banking, Workouts and Bankruptcy, Business Law, Environmental Law, Pre-Nuptial Agreements, State, Local and Federal Taxation, Zoning, Pensions, ERISA Matters and Charitable Organizations.

(For biographical data on all personnel, see Professional Biographies at Darien, Connecticut)

SANDAK FRIEDMAN HENNESSEY & GRECO, LLP

NEW CANAAN, CONNECTICUT

(See Stamford)

Trials and Appeals in all Connecticut and Federal Courts and Administrative Agencies. Personal Injury, Medical Malpractice, Commercial, Environmental Litigation, Real Estate, Zoning and Land Use, Property Tax Appeals.

SCHOONMAKER, GEORGE & COLIN, P.C.

NEW CANAAN, CONNECTICUT

(See Greenwich)

Matrimonial and Family Law.

SILVER, GOLUB & TEITELL LLP

NEW CANAAN, CONNECTICUT

(See Stamford)

Trial Practice in all State and Federal Courts. Medical Malpractice, Negligence, Commercial Litigation, Family and Criminal Law.

LAW OFFICES OF RICHARD C. STEWART

237 ELM STREET

NEW CANAAN, CONNECTICUT 06840

Telephone: 203-966-5949

Facsimile: 203-972-0784

Email: rcstewart@aol.com

General Civil and Criminal Practice. Trials and Appeals in all State and Federal Courts. Domestic Relations, Personal Injury, Commercial Litigation, Business, Real Estate and Probate Law.

RICHARD C. STEWART, born Norwalk, Connecticut, July 15, 1943; admitted to bar, 1972, Connecticut; 1973, U.S. District Court, District of Connecticut; 1981, New York; 1983, U.S. Court of Appeals, Second Circuit and U.S. Supreme Court; 1984, U.S. District Court, Southern and Eastern Districts of New York; 1985, U.S. District Court, Northern and Western Districts of New York. *Education:* Beloit College (B.A., 1965); University of Connecticut (J.D., 1972). Appointed: Fact Finder/Arbitrator, by Judicial Branch, State of Connecticut, February 4, 2000-June 30, 2001; Attorney Trial Referee, by Chief Justice of the Connecticut Supreme Court, February 4, 2000-June 30, 2001. Member, Town Council, 1977-1989 and Chairman, Municipal Services Committee, 1977-1989, Town of New Canaan. *Member:* New Canaan and Connecticut Bar Associations; Connecticut Trial Lawyers Association; The Regional Bar Association of Stamford, Norwalk, Darien and Wilton. [1st Lt., U.S.A.R., 1966-1969]. ***REPORTED CASES:*** Cromwell v. Cromwell, 31 Conn.App. 937, 626 A.2d 1344 (1993) (DIVORCE); Griffin v. Planning and Zoning Commission, 30 Conn.App. 643,621 A.2d 1359 (1993) (MANDAMUS); Bank of Montreal v. Gallo, 3 Conn.App. 268,487 A.2d 1101 (1985) (COMMERCIAL GUARANTY); Dei Cas v. Mayfield, 3 Conn.App. 106, 485 A.2d 584 (1985) (WILL CONSTRUCTION); Carpenter v. Planning and Zoning Commission, 176 Conn. 581,409 A.2d 1029 (1979) (ZONING); Jones v. Ricker, 172 Conn. 572,375 A.2d 1034 (1977) (MANDAMUS).

AL P. TREBING & ASSOCIATES, P.C.

106 MAIN STREET

NEW CANAAN, CONNECTICUT 06840

Telephone: 203-972-5856

Fax: 203-972-6307

Email: alptrebing@aol.com

URL: http://www.lawyers.com/alptreb

Ridgefield, Connecticut Office: 54 Danbury Road, Suite 266. Telephone: 203-798-8851. Fax: 203-730-0061.

Corporations, Partnerships and Limited Liability Companies, Small Businesses, Taxation, Contracts and Commercial Transactions, Estate and Trust Planning, Probate.

FIRM PROFILE: The firm limits its practice to business, tax and estate planning matters and advises a wide range of small to mid-size businesses, business owners and individuals on such things as business formation, tax planning, contract ne-

(This Listing Continued)

gotiation and drafting, tax proceedings, business purchase and sale, commercial loan transactions, estate planning and estate administration. We are committed to providing expert legal advice with a personal touch.

•

AL P. TREBING, born Mineola, New York, November 9, 1951; admitted to bar, 1980, New York; 1981, Connecticut. *Education:* Rider College (B.S., summa cum laude, 1974); Pace University (J.D., cum laude, 1979); New York University (LL.M., in Taxation, 1985). Andrew J. Rider Scholar. Recipient, Leonard A. Olson Alumni Award. Editor, Pace Law Review, 1978-1979. Author: "The Contemporaneous Ownership Rule in New York," Issue 1, Vol. 1, Pace Law Review, 1980. Certified Public Accountant, New York, 1977. *Member:* New Canaan, Stamford Regional and Connecticut Bar Associations. (Also Of Counsel to Kay Parker Jex, LLC).

WAKE, SEE, DIMES & BRYNICZKA

NEW CANAAN, CONNECTICUT

(See Westport)

Business and Corporate Law, Real Estate, Trusts and Probate, Estate Planning, Municipal, Zoning and Land Use Law, Litigation in all Federal and State Courts. Federal, State and Foreign Taxation, Pension and Profit Sharing, and Family Law.

ROGERS LAW FIRM LLC

7 CHURCH STREET NORTH
P.O. BOX 1020
NEW HARTFORD, CONNECTICUT 06057
Telephone: 860-379-9600
Facsimile: 860-379-8560
URL: http://www.lawyers.com/kwlaw
Email: attorneyrogers@aol.com
URL: http://www.rogerslawfirm.com

Commercial, Real Estate, Estate Planning, Corporate, Business Law.

NORMAN E. ROGERS, JR., born Winsted, Connecticut, February 10, 1951; admitted to bar, 1979, Connecticut; 1980, U.S. District Court, District of Connecticut. *Education:* Hartwick College (B.A., 1972); Western New England College School of Law (J.D., cum laude, 1979); Boston University School of Law (LL.M., 1997). Member: New Hartford Board of Finance, 1982-1984; New Hartford Board of Selectmen, 1984-1988; Field Staff, U.S. Senator Lowell P. Weicker, Jr., 1982-1987; Executive Secretary, Probate Assembly, 1993—. Probate Judge, District of New Hartford, 1990—. Chair, Farmington River Wild and Scenic Study Committee, 1989-1995. *Member:* Litchfield County, Connecticut and American Bar Associations. [U.S. Navy, 1972-1975]. ***PRACTICE AREAS:*** Commercial Law; Real Estate; Estate Planning.

BACHMAN & LAPOINTE, P.C.

Established in 1978

900 CHAPEL STREET, SUITE 1201
NEW HAVEN, CONNECTICUT 06510
Telephone: 203-777-6628
Fax: 203-865-0297
Email: iplaw@bachlap.com

Intellectual Property Law including U.S. and International practice in Patent, Trademark, Copyright, International Trade, Unfair Competition, Antitrust and Licensing Law. Trials and Appeals in all Federal Courts and Administrative Agencies.

ROBERT H. BACHMAN, born Hartford, Connecticut, February 5, 1933; admitted to bar, 1958, New York; 1959, U.S. District Court, Western District of New York; 1961, U.S. District Court, District of Connecticut (Not admitted in Connecticut). *Education:* University of Connecticut (B.S., 1954); New York University (J.D., 1957). ***PRACTICE AREAS:*** Patents; Trademarks; Copyrights; Unfair Competition; Licensing Law; Litigation. ***Email:*** bachmanr@bachlap.com

GREGORY P. LAPOINTE, born Manhattan, New York, September 29, 1946; admitted to bar, 1978, Connecticut. *Education:* Vanderbilt University (B.E., 1971); American University (J.D., 1976). Patent Examiner, United States Patent and Trademark Office, 1972-1977. ***PRACTICE AREAS:*** Patents; Trademarks; Copyrights; Unfair Competition; Licensing Law; Litigation. ***Email:*** lapointeg@bachlap.com

BARRY L. KELMACHTER, born Brooklyn, New York, March 25, 1946; admitted to bar, 1979, Virginia; 1988, Connecticut; registered to practice before U.S. Patent and Trademark Office. *Education:* Syracuse University (B.S., 1968; M.S., 1971); American University (J.D., 1979). ***PRACTICE AREAS:*** Patents; Trademarks; Copyrights; Unfair Competition; Licensing Law; Litigation. ***Email:*** kelmachterb@bachlap.com

(This Listing Continued)

GEORGE A. COURY, born Danbury, Connecticut, August 2, 1963; admitted to bar, 1990, Connecticut; 1991, New York; registered to practice before U.S. Patent and Trademark Office. *Education:* Pennsylvania State University (B.S., 1985); Pace University School of Law (J.D., cum laude, 1990). ***PRACTICE AREAS:*** Patents; Trademarks; Copyrights; Unfair Competition; Licensing Law; Litigation. ***Email:*** couryg@bachlap.com

BARR & LACAVA

NEW HAVEN, CONNECTICUT

(See Stamford)

General Practice, Franchising and Franchise Law, Litigation in all State and Federal Courts, Real Estate, Probate, Corporate, Estate Planning, Family, Immigration, Petroleum Marketing Practices, Environmental Law, Workers Compensation, Appellate Practice, Personal Injury and Automobile Accidents.

BARTHOLOMEW & PRICE

104 LINDEN STREET
NEW HAVEN, CONNECTICUT 06511
Telephone: 203-777-4505
Fax: 203-777-5330
Email: bartholomew@bartholomewandprice
URL: http://www.lawyers.com/bartholomew&price

Medical Malpractice, Personal Injury, Employment Litigation.

SUSAN H. BARTHOLOMEW, born Latrobe, Pennsylvania, July 28, 1944; admitted to bar, 1978, Connecticut; 1979, U.S. District Court, District of Connecticut; 1992, U.S. Court of Appeals, Second Circuit. *Education:* The Ohio State University (B.A., 1966); Capital University (J.D., cum laude, 1978). Member, Order of the Curia. Co-author: "Social Experimentation and the Changing World of Work," The Planning of Change, 3rd edition, 1976. Member, Board of Directors, 1980-1985; Chairperson, 1982-1984 and President, 1983-1985, Connecticut Women's Education and Legal Fund. *Member:* Connecticut and American (Member, Labor Law Section) Bar Associations; The Association of Trial Lawyers of America; Connecticut Trial Lawyers Association; National Employment Lawyers Association. ***REPORTED CASES:*** Lyte v. Sara Lee Corp., 950 F.2d 101 (2d Cir. 1991) (employment); Quinnipiac Council, Boy Scouts of America, Inc. v. Commission on Human Rights and Opportunities, 204 Conn. 287, 528 A.2d 352 (1987) (civil rights); Rauccio v. Frank, 750 F.Supp. 566 (D.Conn. 1990) (employment). ***PRACTICE AREAS:*** Personal Injury Litigation; Medical Malpractice Litigation; Business Litigation; Employment Litigation. ***Email:*** bartholomew@bartholomewandprice.com

CHARLES B. PRICE, JR., born Detroit, Michigan, February 21, 1958; admitted to bar, 1983, Connecticut and U.S. District Court, District of Connecticut; 1991, U.S. Court of Appeals, Second Circuit. *Education:* Northeastern University (B.S., with highest honors, 1980); Temple University (J.D., 1983). Member, Moot Court Board. Member, Temple Law Review, 1982. *Member:* Connecticut and American Bar Associations; Connecticut Trial Lawyers Association (Member, Continuing Legal Education Committee); The Association of Trial Lawyers of America. ***PRACTICE AREAS:*** Personal Injury Litigation; Medical Malpractice Litigation; Employment Litigation; Insurance Litigation. ***Email:*** price@bartholomewandprice.com

BARTLETT LAW OFFICES, P.C.

Established in 1989

742 CHAPEL STREET
NEW HAVEN, CONNECTICUT 06510
Telephone: 203-772-4844
Fax: 203-772-2773
Email: bartlettlaw@yahoo.com
URL: http://www.lawyers.com/bartlettpc

Plaintiff Personal Injury, Wrongful Death, Plaintiff Medical Malpractice, Personal Bankruptcy, Probate, Criminal.

KENNETH G. BARTLETT, born New York, N.Y., February 13, 1954; admitted to bar, 1981, Connecticut and U.S. District Court, District of Connecticut; 1982, U.S. Court of Appeals, Second Circuit; 1983, New Jersey; 1990, U.S. Claims Court. *Education:* University of Vermont (B.A., 1977); Quinnipiac College (J.D., 1981). Contributing Editor, Toxic Substances Journal, 1982—. Author: "Recent Sediment Dating through Cinders," Green Mountain Geology, Vol. 22, No. 1 (paper given at Vermont Geological Society Annual Meeting, April 13, 1975; "The Battle to Control Hazardous Wastes, 6 Conn. Law Tribune No. 12, p. 3, March 24, 1980; "The Constitutional Framework of RCRA," Toxic Substances Journal, Vol. 3. No. 1, Summer, 1981; "The Legal Development of a Viable Remedy for Toxic Pollution Victims," Toxic Substances Journal, Vol. 4, No. 4, p. 277, Spring, 1983; "Office Hazards: A Legal Survey," Toxic Sub-

(This Listing Continued)

BARTLETT LAW OFFICES, P.C., New Haven—Continued

stances Journal, Vol. 5. No. 3, p. 199, Winter, 1983-1984; "Notice Defects in Connecticut Zoning Actions," University of Bridgeport Law Review Vol. 6, No. 2, Spring, 1985; "Office Illnesses," Trial Magazine Vol. 22, No. 5, May, 1986; "Screening and Developing the Medical Malpractice Case," (four-part article) Conn. Law Tribune, Vol. 12, No. 18, May 5, 1986, Vol. 19, May 12, 1986, No. 23, June 23, 1986 and Vol. 24, June 30, 1986; "Preparing the Medical Negligence Case," Trial Magazine Vol. 23, No. 8, August, 1987. Co-Author: "Controlling Parameters of Phosphate Absorption on Two Reference Clays," (paper given at NSF Symposium on Trace Metal at University of New Hampshire, August 25-26, 1976); "Motion for Review," 5 Conn. Law Tribune, No. 51, P. 2, December 17, 1979; "Toxic Torts," Faculty, ATLA's National College of Advocacy, Yale Law School, New Haven Connecticut, June 10-12, 1984; "Connecticut Unfair Trade Practices and Connecticut Unfair Insurance Practices Act: Expanding Legal Horizons," Conn. Bar Journal Vol. 58, No. 4., p. 302, August, 1984; *Hazardous Waste Management:* The Law of Toxics and Toxic Substances, CRC Press, Inc., September, 1986. Lecturer: "The Legal Development of a Viable Remedy for Toxic Pollutant victims," Belli Society Seminar, ATLA annual convention, Washington, D.C., July 16, 1983) Paper published in ATLA convention proceedings, 1983 and Barrister, Vol. 10, No. 4, pp. 41-46, Fall, 1983; "How Do We Handle Victim Compensation?" Northeast Conference on Hazardous Waste, Boston, Mass., November 29, 1983; "Occupational Disease: Law and Medicine - Selected Legal Issues," Connecticut Bar Association Seminar, January 14, 1984; "Private Remedies for Toxic Tort/Hazardous Waste Victims," New England Environmental Conference, Tufts University, Medford, Massachusetts, March 27, 1984; "Legal Claims From Illnesses in the Office Workplace: A Legal and Medical Primer," Belli Society Seminar, ATLA Annual Convention, San Francisco, California, July 11, 1987, published in the Belli Society Journal, October, 1987; American Paralegal Institute, New Haven, CT, September, 1981, June, 1982. Panelist: Greater Bridgeport Hazardous Waste Management Conference, Bridgeport, Connecticut, March 20, 1980; "Roundtable Discussion of Hazardous Waste Issues," New England Environmental Conference, Tufts University, Medford, Massachusetts, March 29, 1980. Speaker: "Superfund," New England Environmental Conference, Tufts University, Medford, Massachusetts, March 28, 1981; "Continuing Trends in Toxic Tort Litigation," Northeast Conference on Hazardous Waste, Ocean City, New Jersey, November 11, 1982; "Critical Care Nursing: A Survey of Contemporary Legal Issues," Veterans Administration Hospital, West Haven, Connecticut to Connecticut Chapter of Critical Care Nurses, February 22, 1983; "Screening and Developing the UBCLE, Bridgeport, Connecticut, March 24, 1984; Planning Co-Chairman, Connecticut Bar Association, "Medical Malpractice; Screening the Medical Negligence Case," November 15, 1985, October 28, 1989; trial demonstration, Annual ILCA Conference, Toronto, Canada, July 8, 1989; trial demonstration, International Conference Lactation Consultants, Toronto, Canada, July 30, 1989; Personal Injury Practice in Connecticut, Hartford, New Haven, February 8 and 9, 1990; Trying the Automobile Injury Case in Connecticut, October 9, 1991. Lecturer, Use of an Expert Physician to Prove a Crucial Medical Fact: A Case Study Connecticut Trial Lawyers Association, March 17, 1994. *Member:* American Bar Association; The Association of Trial Lawyers of America; Connecticut Academy of Certified Trial Lawyers. (Certified as a Civil Trial Advocate by the National Board of Trial Advocacy). ***PRACTICE AREAS:*** Personal Injury Law; Medical Malpractice Law; Workers Compensation; Bankruptcy.

CHARLES A. EGGERT, JR., born Stamford, Connecticut, February 17, 1948; admitted to bar, 1981, Illinois and U.S. District Court, Northern District of Illinois; 1985, Connecticut and U.S. District Court, District of Connecticut. *Education:* University of Connecticut (B.A., 1976); John Marshall Law School (J.D., 1981). Phi Beta Kappa. *Member:* Illinois State, Connecticut and American Bar Associations. ***PRACTICE AREAS:*** Bankruptcy; Family Law; Social Security Disability; Probate; Real Estate.

REFERENCE: Fleet Bank.

BERCHEM, MOSES & DEVLIN

A PROFESSIONAL CORPORATION

NEW HAVEN, CONNECTICUT

(See Milford)

Commercial, Corporate Law, Labor and Employment Law, Litigation, Real Estate, Education, Land Use Planning, Estate Planning, Energy and Utility Law, Environmental, Probate. Partnership Law and Taxation Law. Trials and Appeals in State and Federal Courts.

BERDON, YOUNG & MARGOLIS, P.C.

132 TEMPLE STREET
NEW HAVEN, CONNECTICUT 06510
Telephone: 203-772-3740
Fax: 203-492-4444
Email: yberdon@snet.net
URL: http://www.lawyers.com/berdonyoung&margolis

Automobile Accidents, Bankruptcy, Business Law, Child Custody, Child Support, Construction Law, Consumer Law, Contracts, Criminal Law, Debtor and Creditor, Discrimination, Divorce, Driving While Intoxicated, Eminent Domain, Employment Law, Estate Planning, Family Law, General Practice, Landlord and Tenant, Legal Malpractice, Personal Injury, Products Liability, Real Estate, Sexual Harassment, Social Security, Traffic Violations, Trust and Estates, Wills and Probate, Worker's Compensation, Zoning and Land Use.

PASQUALE YOUNG, born New Haven, Connecticut, August 19, 1936; admitted to bar, 1963, Connecticut and U.S. District Court, District of Connecticut; 1969, U.S. Court of Appeals, 2nd Circuit and U.S. Supreme Court. *Education:* United States Merchant Marine Academy (B.S., 1959); Yale University (LL.B., 1963). Prosecutor: Connecticut Circuit Court, 1965-1967; North Branford Town Council, 1971-1980. Mayor, North Branford, 1983-1984. Chairman, State of Connecticut Grievance Panel, Ansonia-Milford Judicial District, 1986—. Trial Referee, State of Connecticut, 1991—. *Member:* New Haven County, Connecticut and American Bar Associations. ***PRACTICE AREAS:*** Real Estate; Zoning and Land Use; Litigation; Family Law; Criminal Law. ***Email:*** pasqualeyoung@snet.net

STUART A. MARGOLIS, born New Haven, Connecticut, September 23, 1953; admitted to bar, 1978, Connecticut and U.S. District Court, District of Connecticut. *Education:* Carleton College; Brandeis University (B.A., cum laude, 1975); University of Connecticut (J.D., cum laude, 1978). Recipient, American Jurisprudence Award in Contracts. Associate Editor, Connecticut Law Review, 1978. Author: Note, "Protection From Discovery of Researchers' Information," 9 Connecticut Law Review 326, 1977; Article, "Sanctions Against Accountants For Violations of The Securities Laws: A Reappraisal," 4 Delaware Journal Corporate Law 399, 1979. *Member:* New Haven County and Connecticut Bar Associations. ***PRACTICE AREAS:*** Corporate Law; Administrative Law; Commercial Law; Bankruptcy; Personal Injury. ***Email:*** yberdon@snet.net

PETER A BERDON, born New Haven, Connecticut, February 22, 1966; admitted to bar, 1991, Connecticut and U.S. District Court, District of Connecticut. *Education:* Duke University (B.A., 1988); University of Connecticut J.D., with honors, 1991). Recipient: American Jurisprudence Award in Evidence; The Little, Brown & Company Award in Evidence. *Member:* New Haven County, Connecticut and American Bar Associations; The Association of Trial Lawyers of America. ***PRACTICE AREAS:*** Business Law; Alcoholic Beverage Law; Government Relations; Litigation; Trusts and Estates. ***Email:*** pberdon@snet.net

---

PAUL E. BARRETT, JR. (1955-1995).

DAVID D. BERDON (1925-1998).

REPRESENTATIVE CLIENTS: Steak Loft of Mystic, Inc.; Brodach Builders, Inc.; Jeremy Homes, Inc.; Great Atlantic & Pacific Tea Co.; Lakepoint Condominiums; North Farms East Condominium; Wine & Spirits Wholesalers of Connecticut; Chamard Vineyards, Inc. ; The Coastal New England Wine Group, Inc.; Nutmeg Housing Development Corp.; Price Costco; Keyboard Acceptance Corp.; Baldwin Pianos, Inc.; Habitat for Humanity of Greater New Haven, Inc.; Lipper International, Inc.; Town of Branford; Branford Housing Authority.

BERGMAN, HOROWITZ & REYNOLDS, P.C.

Established in 1962

157 CHURCH STREET, 19TH FLOOR
P.O. BOX 426
NEW HAVEN, CONNECTICUT 06502-0426
Telephone: 203-789-1320
Fax: 203-785-8127
Email: bhr@taxlawyers.com
URL: http://www.taxlawyers.com

New York, N.Y. Office: 499 Park Avenue, 26th Floor. Telephone: 212-688-4150 Fax: 212-688-4236.

Practice restricted to Federal, State and Foreign Taxation. Estate Planning, Probate, Corporation, Financing, Employee Benefits, Pension and Profit Sharing Law. Real Estate, Commercial.

FIRM PROFILE: Established in 1962 as a tax-oriented firm, Bergman, Horowitz & Reynolds, P.C. has maintained its financial focus while expanding its practice to include corporate and commercial law.

(This Listing Continued)

We practice extensively in areas of tax, business (corporate and partnership), estate planning, acquisitions, employee benefits and trusts and estates. Our clients include closely held businesses of all sizes, entrepreneurs, celebrities and wealthy families, domestic and international. Our clients use our planning expertise to provide for themselves and future generations.

Our clients value our comprehensive approach. They rely on us to minimize taxes while helping them achieve their goals.

Based in New Haven, Connecticut, we maintain a satellite office at 499 Park Avenue, Manhattan. Our firm consists of 33 attorneys and paralegal assistants.

STANLEY N. BERGMAN, born New London, Connecticut, May 30, 1933; admitted to bar, 1959, Connecticut; 1970, U.S. Tax Court. *Education:* Dartmouth College (A.B., cum laude, 1955; M.B.A., 1956); University of Michigan (J.D., 1959). Co-author: "Plan Selection—Pension and Profit Sharing Plans," Tax Management Portfolio No. 350. Certified Public Accountant, Connecticut, 1962. *Member:* Connecticut (Member, Section of Taxation) and American (Member, Section of Taxation) Bar Associations. ***PRACTICE AREAS:*** Business; ERISA; Estate Planning; Taxation (Local, Personal Property, State, Federal or International Law). ***Email:*** bergman@taxlawyers.com

DAVID L. REYNOLDS, born Tulsa, Oklahoma, July 17, 1941; admitted to bar, 1966, Oklahoma; 1970, Connecticut. *Education:* Yale University (B.A., 1963; LL.B., 1966). Phi Alpha Delta. Co-author: "Plan Selection—Pension and Profit Sharing Plans," Tax Management Portfolio No. 350. Trustee, St. Raphael Healthcare System. Corporator, The Milford Bank. Secretary, the Quinnipiac Club. *Member:* Connecticut, Oklahoma and American (Member, Section of Taxation) Bar Associations. [1st Lt., U.S. Army, 1966-1969]. ***PRACTICE AREAS:*** Business; ERISA; Estate Planning and Administration; Taxation (Local Personal Property, State, Federal or International Law); Corporate Law; Partnerships. ***Email:*** reynolds@taxlawyers.com

MELVIN DITMAN, born Munich, Germany, November 12, 1946; admitted to bar, 1971, Connecticut and U.S. District Court, District of Connecticut; 1973, U.S. Court of Appeals, Second Circuit. *Education:* University of Connecticut (B.A., 1968); Cornell University (J.D., 1971). Member, Inland and Wetland Commissions, Town of Woodbridge, 1980-1982. Member, Panel of Arbitrators, American Arbitration Association. *Member:* New Haven County (President, Young Lawyers Section, 1977), Connecticut (Member, Executive Board, Commercial Law and Bankruptcy Section, 1977—) and American Bar Associations; Commercial Law League of America. ***PRACTICE AREAS:*** Bankruptcy; Business; Commercial; Litigation; Real Estate; Finance and Real Estate Property Law. ***Email:*** ditman@taxlawyers.com

WILLIAM C. G. SWIFT, JR., born White Plains, New York, October 29, 1948; admitted to bar, 1973, Connecticut; 1977, U.S. Tax Court; 1979, U.S. District Court, District of Connecticut; 1990, U.S. Claims Court. *Education:* Wharton School, University of Pennsylvania (B.S., 1970); University of Connecticut (J.D., 1973). Certified Public Accountant, Connecticut, 1975. Member, Board of Trustees, Connecticut Trust for Historic Preservation. *Member:* Connecticut and American (Member, Taxation Section) Bar Associations; Connecticut Society of Certified Public Accountants. ***PRACTICE AREAS:*** Business; Estate Planning; Taxation (Local, Personal Property, State, Federal or International Law). ***Email:*** swift@taxlawyers.com

PAUL L. BEHLING, born Washington, D.C., 1948; admitted to bar, 1973, Connecticut; 1980, District of Columbia. *Education:* University of Hartford (B.S., cum laude, 1970); University of Connecticut (J.D., with high honors, 1973); New York University (LL.M. in Taxation, 1974). Author: "Taxation of 401(k) and Other Salary Reduction Plans," Warren, Gorham & Lamont (1994). Adjunct Professor, Deferred Compensation, Advanced Corporate Taxation, Quinnipiac College School of Law, 1982—. Chair, Tax Section, Connecticut Bar Association, 1982-1985. *Member:* The District of Columbia Bar; American Bar Association (Section of Taxation; Member, Committee on Defense and Prosecution Tax Crimes, Criminal Justice Section, 1979-1990, Member, Corporate Tax Committee, 1977-1990; Member, Employee Benefits Committee, 1990—). ***PRACTICE AREAS:*** Business; Employee Benefits; Taxation. ***Email:*** behling@taxlawyers.com

RICHARD J. KLEIN, born New York, N.Y., November 20, 1946; admitted to bar, 1977, New York; 1978, Connecticut and U.S. Tax Court; 1986, Florida. *Education:* Massachusetts Institute of Technology (S.B., 1968); Fordham University School of Law (J.D., cum laude, 1976); New York University (LL.M. in Taxation, 1978). *Member:* Connecticut (Member, Section of Taxation) New York State and American (Member, Sections of: Taxation; Real Property, Probate and Trust Law) Bar Associations; The Florida Bar. ***PRACTICE AREAS:*** Business; Estate Planning; Estate Administration; Taxation (Local, State, Federal Law). ***Email:*** klein@taxlawyers.com

JAMES RUSSELL BROCKWAY, born Baltimore, Maryland, March 5, 1952; admitted to bar, 1976, Maryland; 1979, Connecticut, U.S. Tax Court and Court of Federal Claims. *Education:* Dartmouth College (A.B., summa cum laude, 1973); Duke University (J.D., 1976). Phi Beta Kappa. *Member:* Connecticut (Member, Sections of: Taxation; Corporations), American (Member,

(This Listing Continued)

Sections of: Taxation; Real Property, Probate and Trust Law) and International Bar Associations; Society of Trust and Estate Practitioners. ***PRACTICE AREAS:*** Business; Estate Planning; State Taxation; Federal Taxation; International Taxation. ***Email:*** brockway@taxlawyers.com

BRUCE I. JUDELSON, born Lynn, Massachusetts, June 13, 1952; admitted to bar, 1977, Massachusetts; 1980, U.S. District Court, District of Massachusetts and Court of Federal Claims; 1981, Connecticut; 1984, U.S. Tax Court; 1995, New York. *Education:* Massachusetts Institute of Technology (B.S., 1974); Harvard University (J.D., magna cum laude, 1977). Tau Beta Pi. *Member:* Massachusetts (Member, Section of Taxation), Connecticut (Member, Section of Taxation) and American (Member, Section of Taxation) Bar Associations. ***PRACTICE AREAS:*** Business; Estate Planning; Taxation (Local, Personal Property, State, Federal or International Law). ***Email:*** judelson@taxlawyers.com

DAVID A. RINGOLD, born Pittsburgh, Pennsylvania, October 25, 1956; admitted to bar, 1980, District of Columbia; 1981, U.S. Tax Court; 1982, Connecticut; 1995, New York. *Education:* Georgetown University (B.A., magna cum laude, 1977); Yale Law School (J.D., 1980). *Member:* Connecticut, New York State and American Bar Associations; The District of Columbia Bar. ***PRACTICE AREAS:*** Business; ERISA; Estate Planning; Taxation (Local, Personal Property, State, Federal or International Law). ***Email:*** ringold@taxlawyers.com

DAVID L. DUBROW, born New York, N.Y., January 1, 1957; admitted to bar, 1983, New York; 1984, Connecticut; 1990, New Hampshire. *Education:* Vassar College (A.B., with honors in Economics, 1978); New York University (J.D., 1982). Omicron Delta Epsilon. New Hampshire Reporter for State Tax Notes. *Member:* New Hampshire, Connecticut, New York State and American (Member, Section of Taxation and Real Estate Committee) Bar Associations. ***PRACTICE AREAS:*** Tax Law; Business Planning; Personal Planning; Non-Profit Organizations; Partnership Planning; Corporate Planning; International Taxation; State Taxation; Estate Planning. ***Email:*** dubrow@taxlawyers.com

PAUL M. ROY, born Fitchburg, Massachusetts, April 29, 1958; admitted to bar, 1983, Connecticut; 1985, U.S. Tax Court; 1986, Massachusetts; 1991, Court of Federal Claims. *Education:* Wharton School, University of Pennsylvania (B.S.; B.A., cum laude, 1980); Georgetown University (J.D., 1983). *Member:* Connecticut, Massachusetts and American Bar Associations. ***PRACTICE AREAS:*** Business; Estate Planning; Taxation (Local, Personal Property, State, Federal or International Law); Nonprofit and Charitable Organizations. ***Email:*** roy@taxlawyers.com

JEREMY A. MELLITZ, born Bridgeport, Connecticut, May 28, 1955; admitted to bar, 1981, Connecticut; 1982, District of Columbia; 1984, U.S. District Court, District of Connecticut; 1992, U.S. Court of Appeals, Second Circuit. *Education:* Boston University (B.A., magna cum laude, 1977); Emory University (J.D., 1980). Recipient, American Jurisprudence Award in Torts. *Member:* New Haven, Connecticut and American Bar Associations; The District of Columbia Bar; Connecticut Trial Lawyers Association. ***PRACTICE AREAS:*** Business; Commercial Litigation; Labor and Employment; Real Estate Finance; Real Estate Property Law. ***Email:*** mellitz@taxlawyers.com

LOUIS R. PISCATELLI, born Boston, Massachusetts, June 8, 1960; admitted to bar, 1989, Connecticut. *Education:* Colby College (B.A., 1982); Cornell University (M.B.A., 1986); University of Connecticut (J.D., with high honors, 1989). *Member:* American Bar Association. ***PRACTICE AREAS:*** Business; ERISA; Estate Planning; Taxation (Local, Personal Property, State, Federal or International Law). ***Email:*** piscatelli@taxlawyers.com

EDWARD A. RENN, born Bridgeport, Connecticut, June 20, 1958; admitted to bar, 1988, Connecticut. *Education:* Syracuse University (A.B., 1984); University of Connecticut (J.D., high honors, 1988). Member, Connecticut Law Review, 1986-1988. *Member:* Connecticut and American Bar Associations. ***PRACTICE AREAS:*** Employee Benefits; Business Planning; Estate Planning; Taxation (Federal, State and International). ***Email:*** renn@taxlawyers.com

ELIZABETH A. WHALEN, born New York, N.Y., October 13, 1957; admitted to bar, 1990, New York; 1993, U.S. Tax Court; 1998, Connecticut. *Education:* Brooklyn College of the City University of New York (B.S., summa cum laude, 1984; M.A., 1986); Columbia University School of Law (J.D., 1989) Harlan Fiske Stone Scholar; New York University School of Law (LL.M., 1995). *Member:* New York State (Member, Tax Section), Connecticut and American Bar Associations (Member Tax Section). ***PRACTICE AREAS:*** Partnership Law; Real Estate; International Taxation; Financial Investments. ***Email:*** whalen@taxlawyers.com

OF COUNSEL

KENNETH N. MUSEN, born Lawrence, Massachusetts, April 2, 1950; admitted to bar, 1975, Connecticut and U.S. Tax Court; 1997, New York. *Education:* Massachusetts Institute of Technology (S.B., 1972); Harvard University (J.D., cum laude, 1975). Phi Beta Kappa. *Member:* American Bar Association (Taxation Section). ***PRACTICE AREAS:*** Business; Estate Planning; Taxation; State and Federal Tax; International Tax Law. ***Email:*** musen@taxlawyers.com

(This Listing Continued)

BERGMAN, HOROWITZ & REYNOLDS, P.C., New Haven—Continued

PATRICIA A. CAMPANA, born New York, New York, March 11, 1959; admitted to bar, 1985, Illinois and U.S. District Court, Northern District of Illinois; 1992, Connecticut. *Education:* University of Chicago (B.A., 1981); Chicago-Kent College of Law, Illinois Institute of Technology (J.D., 1985). Emeritus Scholar, University of Chicago. Instructor, Real Estate Law, Morse School of Business, 1997-1998. *Member:* Connecticut, Illinois State and American Bar Associations; American College of Investment Counsel. ***LANGUAGES:*** French, Spanish and Italian. ***PRACTICE AREAS:*** Corporate Law; Commercial Law; Real Estate; Investments; Securities.

RAQUEL S. COLBY, born Summit, New Jersey, April 13, 1966; admitted to bar, 1991, New Jersey; 1992, New York and U.S. District Court, Southern and Eastern Districts of New York and District of New Jersey; 1994, New Hampshire and U.S. Court, District of New Hampshire (Not admitted in Connecticut). *Education:* University of Rhode Island (B.S., with high honors, 1988); Seton Hall University (J.D., cum laude, 1991); New York University (LL.M. in taxation, 1994). Associate Editor, Seton Hall Law Review, 1990-1991. Note, Hoffman v. Connecticut Department of Income Maintenance, 21 Seton Hall 88, 1990. *Member:* New Jersey State, New Hampshire, New York State and American Bar Associations. ***LANGUAGES:*** Spanish. ***PRACTICE AREAS:*** Tax Law; Business Planning for Individuals; Partnerships and Corporations; State Taxation; Estate Planning. ***Email:*** colby@taxlawyers.com

RICHARD A. FAVA, born Bronx, New York, October 14, 1974; admitted to bar, 2000, New York (Not admitted in Connecticut). *Education:* University of Pennsylvania (B.S., 1995); American University (J.D., 1999). ***LANGUAGES:*** Italian. ***Email:*** fava@taxlawyers.com

BRYAN P. GALAT, born New Haven, Connecticut, December 16, 1976; admitted to bar, 2001, Connecticut. *Education:* Dartmouth College (B.A., 1998); University of Connecticut (J.D., 2001).

JACLYN S. KIM, born Seoul, Korea, April 29, 1973; admitted to bar, 2001, Connecticut. *Education:* Cornell University (B.S., 1996); Fordham University (J.D., 2001).

MITCHELL R. KOPS, born Bethpage, New York, June 27, 1968; admitted to bar, 1995, New York; 1996, Oregon; 2001, Connecticut. *Education:* University of Virginia (B.A., 1990); Fordham University (J.D., 1994); New York University (LL.M., Taxation, 1995). *Member:* Oregon State Bar; New York State Bar Association. ***PRACTICE AREAS:*** Estate Planning; Federal Taxation; State Taxation; Local Taxation. ***Email:*** kops@taxlawyers.com

JAY F. KRAUSE, born Philadelphia, Pennsylvania, March 30, 1966; admitted to bar, 1991, California; 1994, District of Columbia; 1995, Connecticut. *Education:* Georgetown University (B.S.B.A., 1988); London School of Economics, London, England; University of Pennsylvania (J.D., 1991); New York University (LL.M., 1994). Co-Author: "Connecticut Tax Handbook," RIA Group, 1998 and "Counseling California Corporations, Update," Continuing Education of the Bar, 1993. *Member:* Connecticut and American (Member, Sections on: Taxation, Real Property, Probate and Trusts) Bar Associations; State Bar of California; District of Columbia Bar. ***PRACTICE AREAS:*** Business; Estate Planning; Personal Taxation; Corporate Taxation; Partnership Taxation; International Taxation. ***Email:*** krause@taxlawyers.com

STEPHEN LISS, born Bayside, New York, September 30, 1975; admitted to bar, 2001, Connecticut and New York. *Education:* Vassar College (B.A., 1997); Georgetown University (J.D., cum laude, 2000); New York University (LL.M., Tax, 2001). Recipient, Nelson T. Hartson Award for Excellence in Tax Law. ***PRACTICE AREAS:*** Estate Planning; Trusts and Estates; Partnership Taxation.

HUNTER N. NORTON, born Bridgeport, Connecticut, September 20, 1967; admitted to bar, 1993, Pennsylvania and New Jersey; 1999, Connecticut. *Education:* University of Connecticut (B.S., magna cum laude, 1989); Temple University (J.D., 1992); Georgetown (LL.M., Taxation, 1993). Managing Editor, Temple Political and Civil Rights Law Review, 1992. Certified Public Accountant, Connecticut, 1998. *Member:* American Bar Association. ***PRACTICE AREAS:*** Federal Taxation; International Taxation; State and Local Taxation; Estate Planning; Business Law. ***Email:*** norton@taxlawyers.com

JEFFREY H. ROBERTS, born Rutland, Vermont, March 4, 1973; admitted to bar, 2001, Connecticut. *Education:* University of Vermont (B.A., 1997); Georgetown University Law Center (J.D., 2000). Executive Editor, The Tax Lawyers, Georgetown University, 1999-2000. Member, The Federalist Society, 1997-2000. Author, Cite as: Note, Allocation of Costs of Common Improvement to Bases of Benefited Properties Disallowed Under Section 1016 (a)(1) *Norwest v. Commissioner,* 52 Tax Law 925 (Winter) 1998. ***PRACTICE AREAS:*** Taxation; Estate Planning. ***Email:*** roberts@taxlawyers.com

JAY H. RUBINSTEIN, born Springfield, Massachusetts, July 31, 1960; admitted to bar, 1989, Massachusetts; 1990, New York; 1997, Connecticut. *Education:* Syracuse University (B.S., Accounting, 1982); University of Hartford (M.S., Taxation, 1986); Northeastern University Law School (J.D., 1989). Co-Author: "Deductibility of Private Securities Partnership Expenses after Mayer," Tax Notes, March 13, 1995. *Member:* Connecticut, New York State and American (Member, Sections on: Taxation; Real Property; Probate; Trusts) Bar Associations. ***PRACTICE AREAS:*** Federal Taxation; International Taxation; State and Local Taxation; Estate Planning; Business Law. ***Email:*** rubinstein@taxlawyers.com

JASON S. RUDNICK, born New York City, New York, June 9, 1975; admitted to bar, 2000, Connecticut. *Education:* Johns Hopkins University (B.A., 1997); University of Connecticut School of Law (J.D., 2000). Member, Connecticut Journal of International Law, 1998-2000. ***PRACTICE AREAS:*** Tax; Litigation; Commercial. ***Email:*** rudnick@taxlawyers.com

VON E. SANBORN, born Manchester, New Hampshire, January 19, 1968; admitted to bar, 1997, New York; 1999, New Hampshire and U.S. Tax Court; 2001, Connecticut. *Education:* Boston University (B.A., 1991); Albany Law School of Union College (J.D., 1995); Villanova University (LL.M., in Taxation, 1996). *Member:* New York State (Member, Tax Section) New Hampshire and American (Member, Tax Section) Bar Associations; International Fiscal Association. ***LANGUAGES:*** English. ***PRACTICE AREAS:*** International Tax Planning; Corporate Tax Planning; Multi-State Tax Planning; Tax Litigation; Business. ***Email:*** sanborn@taxlawyers.com

DEBORAH K. SNYDER, born Bronx, New York, August 31, 1967; admitted to bar, 1992, Connecticut; 1993, New York and U.S. District Court, District of Connecticut; 1997, U.S. Court of Appeals, Second Circuit. *Education:* Johns Hopkins University (B.A., M.A., 1989, Phi Beta Kappa); Harvard University (J.D., cum laude, 1992). Executive Editor, Harvard Civil Rights-Civil Liberties Law Review. Law Clerk, Honorable Peter C. Dorsey, Chief Judge, U.S. District Court, District of Connecticut, 1992-1994. *Member:* Connecticut and American Bar Associations. ***PRACTICE AREAS:*** Taxation; Estate Planning. ***Email:*** snyder@taxlawyers.com

KAREN E. YATES, born New Haven, Connecticut, November 14, 1971; admitted to bar, 1996, Connecticut. *Education:* American University (B.A., 1993); Cornell Law School (J.D., 1996). *Member:* Connecticut and American (Member, Real Property, Probate, Trust and Taxation Sections) Bar Associations. ***PRACTICE AREAS:*** Estate Planning; Estate Administration; Tax. ***Email:*** yates@taxlawyers.com

LEGAL SUPPORT PERSONNEL

SUSAN H. RYAN, born New Haven, Connecticut, January 20, 1952. *Education:* Albertus Magnus College (A.A., 1985). Alpha Sigma Lambda. (Legal Administrator). ***PRACTICE AREAS:*** General Staff Support Functions including: Personnel,; Marketing; Equipment; Facilities/Space Utilization; Purchasing; Systems and Records. ***Email:*** ryan@taxlawyers.com

---

BERMAN AND SABLE

Established in 1977

195 CHURCH STREET
NEW HAVEN, CONNECTICUT 06510
Telephone: 203-495-6200
FAX: 203-495-6220
Email: info@bermansable.com

Hartford, Connecticut Office: 100 Pearl Street. Telephone: 203-527-9699. Telecopier: 203-527-9077.

Commercial Litigation, Commercial and Corporate Finance Transactions, Real Estate, Corporate Law, Acquisitions, Mergers and Divestitures, Problem Loan Workouts, Loan Restructure and Recoveries, Mortgage and Foreclosure, Creditor's Rights, Defense of Lender Liability Claims, Creditor Bankruptcy Rights, Reorganizations, Tax Appeals, Construction Litigation, Probate and Trials and Appeals in all Courts. FDIC/RTC Approved Counsel.

(For Complete Biographical Data on All Personnel, see Professional Biographies at Hartford, Connecticut)

BERSHTEIN, LIPPMAN, BACHMAN & McKEON, P.C.

59 ELM STREET
NEW HAVEN, CONNECTICUT 06510-2047
Telephone: 203-777-5800
Fax: 203-777-5806
Email: blbm@reallawyers.com
URL: http://www.lawyers.com/blbm

Westport, Connecticut Office: 735 Post Road East. Telephone: 203-222-7048. Fax: 203-777-5806.

(This Listing Continued)

General Practice including Real Estate, Federal and State Court Litigation, Public and Private Finance, Banking, Leasing, Business, Municipal Tax Law, Health Care, Creditors and Debtors Rights including Workouts, Collections and Foreclosures, Landlord and Tenant, Estate Planning, Probate and Personal Injury.

RAYMOND C. BERSHTEIN, born New Haven, Connecticut, June 3, 1958; admitted to bar, 1983, District of Columbia; 1985, Connecticut. *Education:* Emory University (B.A., 1980); George Washington University (J.D., 1983). *Member:* Connecticut and American (Member, Municipal Law and Governmental Services Committee) Bar Associations. ***PRACTICE AREAS:*** Real Estate; Municipal Tax Liens; Finance; Business Law. ***Email:*** rcb@reallawyers.com

NEIL A. LIPPMAN, born Woodmere, New York, May 6, 1965; admitted to bar, 1990, Connecticut; 1991, Florida and U.S. District Court, District of Connecticut. *Education:* Washington University (A.B., 1987); University of Miami (J.D., magna cum laude, 1990). Order of the Coif. Member, University of Miami Law Review. Board Member, 1992-1996, Treasurer, 1997-1999 and Chairman, 1999-2001, New Haven Jewish Home for the Aged. *Member:* New Haven, Connecticut and American Bar Associations. ***PRACTICE AREAS:*** Commercial Litigation; Foreclosures; Collections; Creditors Rights. ***Email:*** nal@reallawyers.com

STACI H. BACHMAN, born Cincinnati, Ohio, July 24, 1966; admitted to bar, 1991, Connecticut; 1998, Massachusetts. *Education:* Wellesley College (B.A., cum laude, with honors, 1988); The George Washington University (J.D., 1991). *Member:* Connecticut and American Bar Associations. ***PRACTICE AREAS:*** Real Estate; Leasing; Finance; Business Law. ***Email:*** shb@reallawyers.com

CHRISTOPHER M. McKEON, born Stoughton, Massachusetts, October 18, 1966; admitted to bar, 1991, Connecticut; 1992, U.S. District Court, District of Connecticut; 1998, Pennsylvania. *Education:* Fairfield University (B.A., 1988); Quinnipiac College School of Law (J.D., magna cum laude, 1991). Author: "Rape Trauma Syndrome: A Proposal for Liberal Admissibility in Connecticut," 11 University of Bridgeport Law Review 623, 1992. *Member:* New Haven, Connecticut (Chairman, Young Lawyers Division, Bridgeport Local Unit, 1993-1994) and American Bar Associations. ***PRACTICE AREAS:*** Commercial Litigation; Landlord and Tenant; Foreclosures; Collections; Real Estate; Zoning Law; Business Law. ***Email:*** cmm@reallawyers.com

---

MICHAEL J. AJELLO, born New Haven, Connecticut, January 13, 1967; admitted to bar, 1996, Connecticut and Mohegan Tribe Gaming Disputes Court; U.S. District Court, District of Connecticut. *Education:* Northeastern University (B.S., 1989); Thomas M. Cooley Law School (J.D., 1995). Recipient, Book Award in Trial Workshop. Commissioner, Planning and Zoning Commission, Town of Hamden, 1998. *Member:* New Haven County Bar Association (Member, Executive Committee, 1999—); New Haven Young Lawyers Association (President, Executive Committee, 1996-2000; Chairman, Planning Section, 1999-2001); Connecticut Trial Lawyers Association. ***PRACTICE AREAS:*** Commercial Litigation; Civil Litigation; Real Estate; Landlord and Tenant; Foreclosures; Collections. ***Email:*** mja@reallawyers.com

OF COUNSEL

LESLIE A. ZACKIN, born New York, New York, August 28, 1964; admitted to bar, 1990, Connecticut. *Education:* Tufts University (B.A., magna cum laude, 1986); Fordham University School of Law (J.D., 1990). Recipient: Keith C. Miller Memorial Award, 1990. Member, Board of Directors, Jewish Federation of Greater New Haven. Member, Tax and Legal Committee, Jewish Foundation of Greater New Haven, 1997—. Member, Connecticut Estate and Tax Planning Council, 1998—. *Member:* New Haven, Greater Bridgeport, Connecticut (Member, Sections on: Estates and Probate and Elder Law; Co-Chair, Young Lawyers Section, Estates and Probate Committee, 1994-1995) and American (Member, Real Property, Probate and Trust Law Section) Bar Associations. ***LANGUAGES:*** French. ***PRACTICE AREAS:*** Estate Planning; Probate; Business Law. ***Email:*** laz@reallawyers.com

THOMAS P. McKEON, born New Haven, Connecticut, September 2, 1938; admitted to bar, 1963, Connecticut; 1968, U.S. District Court, District of Connecticut. *Education:* Providence College (A.B., 1960); Boston University (J.D., 1963). Chairman, North Haven Board of Ethics, 1998—. Elected Member, North Haven Board of Education, 1974-1978. Construction Industry and Commercial Transactions Arbitrator, American Arbitration Association. *Member:* New Haven County, Connecticut and American Bar Associations. [Lt., U.S. Navy Reserve Law Specialists, 1963-1967]. ***PRACTICE AREAS:*** Real Estate Transactions; Probate; Estate Planning; Planning and Zoning.

THE BOHONNON LAW FIRM, LLC

205 CHURCH STREET
NEW HAVEN, CONNECTICUT 06510
Telephone: 203-787-2151
Fax: 203-773-1427
Email: bohonnon.com
URL: http://www.lawyers.com/bohonnonlaw

General Practice. Admiralty, Corporation, Insurance, Probate, Estate Planning, Real Estate, Zoning, Family, Administrative and Taxation Law. Trials, Aviation, Bankruptcy and Environmental.

FIRM PROFILE: R. William Bohonnon has been a practicing attorney in New Haven, Connecticut since 1947. He succeeds the firm of his father-in-law, Kenneth Wynne, Chief Justice of the Supreme Court of Connecticut in 1959-1961. The firm is comprised of Wynne Bohonnon and David Bohonnon, the sons of R. William Bohonnon. The firm is actively engaged in professional association activities, continuing legal education seminars and civic affairs. The firm serves the entire state with two offices offering a wide range of legal services.

MEMBERS OF FIRM

K. WYNNE BOHONNON, born New Haven, Connecticut, October 11, 1952; admitted to bar, 1982, Connecticut and U.S. District Court, District of Connecticut; 1987, U.S. Court of International Trade; 1988, U.S. Supreme Court. *Education:* Wesleyan University (B.A., 1975); Connecticut College (M.A., 1977); Quinnipiac College Law School (J.D., 1980). *Member:* Westport, Connecticut and American Bar Associations; Connecticut Trial Lawyer's Association (Member, Computer and Technology Committee, 1998—); Maritime Law Association. ***SPECIAL AGENCIES:*** President, Saugatuck Child Care Services, Westport, Connecticut, 1993-1994. ***PRACTICE AREAS:*** Admiralty and Maritime Law; Family Law; Personal Injury; Civil Litigation; Computer Law; Contract; Construction Law; Probate. ***Email:*** wynne@bohonnon.com

DAVID M. BOHONNON, born New Haven, Connecticut, October 10, 1956; admitted to bar, 1982, Connecticut and U.S. District Court, District of Connecticut. *Education:* Connecticut College (B.A., 1978); Quinnipiac College School of Law (J.D., 1982). *Member:* New Haven County, Connecticut (Member, Taxation Section) and American Bar Associations; Connecticut Trial Lawyer's Association; Maritime Law Association (Member, Subcommittee on Yacht Financing); National Business Aircraft Association. ***PRACTICE AREAS:*** Admiralty and Maritime Law; Aviation Law; State and Federal Taxation; Corporate Law; Venture Capital; Real Estate; Zoning; Contract. ***Email:*** david@bohonnon.com

OF COUNSEL

R. WILLIAM BOHONNON, born Northfield, Vermont, January 13, 1921; admitted to bar, 1944, New York; 1946, Connecticut and U.S. District Court for District of Connecticut. *Education:* Wesleyan University (1943); Brooklyn Law School (LL.B. cum laude, 1943). *Member:* Connecticut and American Bar Associations; Connecticut Trial Lawyer's Association. ***PRACTICE AREAS:*** Admiralty and Maritime Law; State and Federal Taxation; Probate; Trust Administration; Contract; Family Law; Civil Litigation; Real Estate; Personal Injury; Construction Law. ***Email:*** bill@bohonnon.com

DEAN W. BAKER, born New Haven, Connecticut, May 7, 1956; admitted to bar, 1983, Connecticut; U.S. District Court, District of Connecticut. *Education:* Duke University (B.A., magna cum laude, 1978; J.D., 1983). *Member:* Connecticut (Executive Member, Chairman, 1994-1996; Member, Commercial Law and Bankruptcy Section) and American Bar Associations; Association of Commercial Finance Attorneys. ***PRACTICE AREAS:*** Bankruptcy; Commercial Transactions; Commercial Litigation; Contract Law. ***Email:*** dean@bohonnon.com

---

BRENNER, SALTZMAN & WALLMAN LLP

A Limited Liability Partnership including Professional Corporations
Established in 1963
271 WHITNEY AVENUE
P.O. BOX 1746
NEW HAVEN, CONNECTICUT 06507-1746
Telephone: 203-772-2600
Facsimile: 203-562-2098
Email: postmaster@bswlaw.com

Corporate, Securities, Federal Income, Estate and Gift Taxation, Real Estate, Estate Planning and Probate, Pension and Profit Sharing, Employee Benefit, Environmental, Health Care Law, Trial Practice and Administrative Law.

NEWTON D. BRENNER, (P.C.), born Meriden, Connecticut, December 30, 1934; admitted to bar, 1958, Connecticut; 1959, New York and U.S. Tax

(This Listing Continued)

BRENNER, SALTZMAN & WALLMAN LLP, New Haven—Continued

Court; 1978, Florida. *Education:* Wharton School, University of Pennsylvania (B.S., 1955); Yale University (LL.B., 1958). Order of the Coif. Editor, Yale Law Journal, 1957-1958. Lecturer, Regulation of Financial Reporting, Yale School of Organization and Management, 1978-1979, 1979-1980. *Member:* New Haven County, Connecticut and American Bar Associations; The Florida Bar. ***PRACTICE AREAS:*** Taxation; Acquisitions and Mergers; Corporate Reorganization; Estate Planning. ***Email:*** nbrenner@bswlaw.com

STEPHEN L. SALTZMAN, (P.C.), born Providence, Rhode Island, April 6, 1937; admitted to bar, 1963, Connecticut; 1966, U.S. Tax Court and U.S. Court of Claims. *Education:* Wharton School; University of Pennsylvania (B.S., 1958); Boston University (LL.B., cum laude, 1961); New York University (LL.M., in Taxation, 1963). Member, Board of Editors, Boston University Law Review, 1960-1961. Editor, Intramural Law Review, 1961-1962. Research Associate, New York University School of Law, 1961-1962. *Member:* New Haven County, Connecticut (Secretary, 1970-1973 and Chairman, 1973-1976, Taxation Section) and American Bar Associations.

MARC A. WALLMAN, (P.C.), born Queens, New York, December 31, 1942; admitted to bar, 1966, Connecticut; 1978, Florida. *Education:* Queens College (B.A., 1963); Yale University (LL.B., 1966). Phi Beta Kappa. *Member:* New Haven County, Connecticut and American (Member, Section on Business Law) Bar Associations; The Florida Bar. ***PRACTICE AREAS:*** Corporate; Real Estate; Commercial Law; Health Care Law. ***Email:*** mwallman@bswlaw.com

DAVID R. SCHAEFER, (P.C.), born Hartford, Connecticut, June 12, 1948; admitted to bar, 1973, Massachusetts; 1980, Connecticut, U.S. Tax Court, U.S. District Court, District of Massachusetts, U.S. District Court, District of Connecticut, U.S. Court of Appeals, First and Second Circuits and U.S. Supreme Court. *Education:* University of Wisconsin (B.A., 1971); New York University (J.D., cum laude, 1973). Order of the Coif; Phi Kappa Phi. Root Tilden Scholar. *Member:* New Haven County (Past President), Connecticut and American Bar Associations; Federal Bar Council. ***PRACTICE AREAS:*** Federal Litigation; Commercial Litigation including Employment; Environmental; Real Estate; Banking; Contracts and Securities. ***Email:*** dschaefer@bswlaw.com

STUART JAY MANDEL, (P.C.), born Bronx, New York, January 25, 1949; admitted to bar, 1974, New York; 1982, Connecticut. *Education:* Harpur College (B.A., summa cum laude, 1970); Harvard University (J.D., 1973). *Member:* The Association of the Bar of the City of New York; New Haven County, Connecticut, New York State and American (Member, Sections on: Corporation, Business Law) Bar Associations. ***PRACTICE AREAS:*** Business; Corporate; Securities. ***Email:*** smandel@bswlaw.com

DONALD W. ANDERSON, (P.C.), born Chicago, Illinois, September 16, 1944; admitted to bar, 1973, New York; 1982, Connecticut. *Education:* Villanova University (B.A., cum laude, 1966); Columbia University (J.D., 1972). Harlan Fiske Stone Scholar. *Member:* New Haven County, Connecticut (Member, Sections on Trusts and Estates) and New York State (Member, Sections on: Trusts and Estates) Bar Associations. ***PRACTICE AREAS:*** Trusts and Estates. ***Email:*** danderson@bswlaw.com

SAMUEL M. HURWITZ, born New Haven, Connecticut, November 8, 1953; admitted to bar, 1983, Connecticut; 1984, U.S. Tax Court and 1996, U.S. District Court, District of Connecticut. *Education:* Columbia University (B.A., magna cum laude, 1976); Stanford University (J.D., 1983). Phi Beta Kappa. Order of the Coif. *Member:* New Haven County, Connecticut (Member, Tax Section) and American (Member, Taxation Section; Business Law Section) Bar Associations. ***PRACTICE AREAS:*** Taxation; Estate Planning; Business. ***Email:*** shurwitz@bswlaw.com

WAYNE A. MARTINO, (P.C.), born Danbury, Connecticut, April 18, 1959; admitted to bar, 1984, Connecticut. *Education:* American University (B.A., cum laude, 1981); University of Connecticut (J.D., with honors, 1984). ***PRACTICE AREAS:*** Internet Law; Business Start-Ups; Corporate; Securities. ***Email:*** wmartino@bswlaw.com

JOHN R. BASHAW, born Hartford, Connecticut, December 4, 1960; admitted to bar, 1987, Connecticut. *Education:* University of Vermont (B.S., 1982); University of Maine at Orono; Vermont Law School (J.D., magna cum laude, 1987). Member, Vermont Law Review, 1985-1987. *Member:* Connecticut (Member, Conservation and Environmental Quality Section, 1987— and American (Member, Section on Natural Resources, Energy and Environmental Law) Bar Associations. ***PRACTICE AREAS:*** Environmental Regulation; Environmental Litigation. ***Email:*** jbashaw@bswlaw.com

MITCHELL S. JAFFE, (P.C.), born Brooklyn, New York, September 26, 1955; admitted to bar, 1979, Connecticut. *Education:* Harpur College, State University of New York at Binghamton (B.A., 1976); New York University (J.D., 1979). Phi Beta Kappa; Phi Sigma Alpha. President, Student Bar Association. Member, Moot Court Board. Member, Board of Directors, 1983-1990 and

(This Listing Continued)

President, 1988-1990, Connecticut Chapter, Community Associations Institute. Member, Connecticut Chapter, Real Estate Finance Association. *Member:* Connecticut (Member: Executive Committee, Real Property Section) and American Bar Associations. ***PRACTICE AREAS:*** Commercial Real Estate; Commercial Leasing; Real Estate Finance; Condominium Law; Loan Workouts. ***Email:*** mjaffe@bswlaw.com

ALICE J. MICK, (P.C.), born Norfolk, Virginia, November 7, 1944; admitted to bar, 1989, Connecticut; 1990, New York and U.S. District Court, District of Connecticut. *Education:* Stanford University (B.A., 1966); Yale University (M.A.T., 1968; J.D., 1989). Member: New Haven Federation of Teachers, 1969-1984; New England Board of Higher Education, 1982-1983. President, Connecticut Association of Alternative Schools and Programs, 1982-1984. *Member:* New Haven, Connecticut and American Bar Associations; American Health Lawyers Association. ***LANGUAGES:*** French. ***PRACTICE AREAS:*** Corporate Law; Health Law; Employment Law. ***Email:*** amick@bswlaw.com

KENNETH ROSENTHAL, born Tallahassee, Florida, September 25, 1944; admitted to bar, 1978, Connecticut; 1979, U.S. District Court, District of Connecticut and U.S. Tax Court. *Education:* Yale University (B.A., cum laude, 1967); University of Connecticut (J.D., with high honors, 1978). Author: "Prosecutor Misconduct, Convictions and Double Jeopardy," 71 Temple Law Rev. 887, (1998); "Connecticut's New Preliminary Hearing," 5 Bridgeport L. Rev. 1 (1983); "New Appellate Court System," 9 Conn. L. Trib. No 37. p. 1 (Sept. 12, 1983). *Member:* Connecticut Bar Association (Member, Committee on Liaison with Accountants). ***PRACTICE AREAS:*** Federal Litigation; Commercial Litigation; Business Disputes; Real Estate; Construction; Environmental; Health Care Reimbursement; Bankruptcy; Creditors Rights; Tax Litigation; Professional Liability; Probate Litigation; Personal Injury; Criminal Defense; White Collar Crime. ***Email:*** krosenthal@bswlaw.com

CAROLYN W. KONE, born New Haven, Connecticut, March 16, 1950; admitted to bar, 1975, Connecticut; 1977, U.S. District Court, District of Connecticut; 1980, New York and U.S. Court of Appeals, Second and Third Circuits. *Education:* Barnard College (B.A., magna cum laude, 1972); Boston University (J.D., 1975). Instructor, University of Bridgeport School of Law, 1980-1984. City of New Haven Assistant and Deputy Corporation Counsel, 1984-1990. Attorney Trial Referee for the Connecticut State Judicial Department, Commission on Human Rights and Opportunities Hearing Examiner, 1982-1997. Member, Legal Committee, Connecticut Fund for the Environment. Former Member, Board of Directors, Congregation Beth El Keser Israel. Vice-President and Former Member, Board of Directors, New Haven Preservation Trust. Member, Legal Advisory Committee, Connecticut Fund for the Environment. *Member:* New Haven County and Connecticut Bar Associations; Theodore Koskoff Inns of Court (Bencher). Fellow, Connecticut Bar Foundation. ***PRACTICE AREAS:*** Federal Litigation; Commercial Litigation; Municipal Law; Foreclosures; Real Estate Contracts; Probate Litigation; Employment Law; Civil Rights Litigation; Administrative Law. ***Email:*** ckone@bswlaw.com

BRIAN P. DANIELS, born Meriden, Connecticut, April 25, 1966; admitted to bar, 1992, Connecticut; 1993, U.S. District Court, District of Connecticut; 1998, U.S. Court of Appeals, Second Circuit; 1999, U.S. Tax Court. *Education:* California Institute of Technology (B.S., cum laude, 1988); Harvard Law School (J.D., cum laude, 1992). *Member:* New Haven County, Connecticut (Member, Litigation Section) and American Bar Associations. ***PRACTICE AREAS:*** Federal Litigation; Commercial Litigation; Environmental; Contracts; Insurance Coverage; Trade Secrets; Unfair Trade; Arbitration. ***Email:*** bpdaniels@bswlaw.com

GEORGE BRENCHER IV, born Hartford, Connecticut, July 28, 1966; admitted to bar, 1992, Connecticut and U.S. District Court, District of Connecticut; 1996, New York. *Education:* University of Pennsylvania (B.A., 1988; J.D. magna cum laude, 1992). Order of the Coif, 1992—. Law Clerk to the Hon. José A. Cabranes, Chief Judge, District of Connecticut, 1992-1993. Author: "Formalism, Positivism and Natural Law in Ernest Weinrib's Tort Theory," 42 U. Toronto L.J. 318, 1992. ***LANGUAGES:*** French. ***PRACTICE AREAS:*** Internet Law; Business Start-Ups; Corporate; Securities. ***Email:*** gbrencher@bswlaw.com

---

JENNIFER DOWD DEAKIN, born Torrington, Connecticut, February 9, 1968; admitted to bar, 1993, Massachusetts; 1994, Connecticut. *Education:* Boston College (B.A., summa cum laude, 1990; J.D., cum laude, 1993). Phi Beta Kappa; Order of the Coif. Executive Editor, Boston College Law Review. Author: "A Selective View of History: *Feist Publications, Inc. v. Rural Telephone Services, Inc.*," B.C.L.Review, December, 1992. Law Clerk to Justice Joette Katz, Connecticut Supreme Court, 1993-1994. ***PRACTICE AREAS:*** Corporate Law; Commercial Law. ***Email:*** jdeakin@bswlaw.com

MICHELLE GOGLIA, born New Haven, Connecticut, October 22, 1975; admitted to bar, 2000, Connecticut; 2001, District of Columbia. *Education:* Colgate University (B.A., 1997); University of Connecticut School of Law (J.D., 2000). ***PRACTICE AREAS:*** Commercial Litigation; Corporate Law; Environmental. ***Email:*** mgoglia@bswlaw.com

(This Listing Continued)

ROWENA A. MOFFETT, born Montreal, Canada, March 24, 1967; admitted to bar, 1998, Connecticut; 1999, U.S. District Court, District of Connecticut; 2001, U.S. Court of Appeals, Third District. *Education:* University of North Carolina at Chapel Hill (B.A., with distinction, 1989); University of Connecticut School of Law (J.D., with high honors, 1997). Phi Beta Kappa. Associate Editor, University of Connecticut Law Review. Member, University of Connecticut Moot Court. President, William F. Starr Insurance Law Moot Court Competition. Law Clerk to: the Honorable Thomas P. Smith, United States Magistrate Judge, District of Connecticut, 1997-1998; the Honorable Dominic J. Squatrito, United States District Judge, District of Connecticut, 1998-2000. Member, Board of Directors, University of Connecticut School of Law Alumni Association, 2000—. *Member:* New Haven County, Connecticut and American Bar Associations; Federal Bar Council. ***LANGUAGES:*** Spanish. ***PRACTICE AREAS:*** Federal Litigation; Commercial Litigation; Employment Litigation; Civil Rights Litigation; Administrative Law. ***Email:*** rmoffett@bswlaw.com

SARAAB A. SALEH, born New Haven, Connecticut, July 1, 1971; admitted to bar, 1996, Connecticut. *Education:* St. Lawrence University (B.S., magna cum laude, 1993) Phi Beta Kappa; Washington & Lee University (J.D., 1996). Zoning Board of Appeals Member: Town of Woodbridge, 1999-2001. ***PRACTICE AREAS:*** Internet Law; Corporate Law; Securities. ***Email:*** ssaleh@bswlaw.com

OF COUNSEL

SHARON KOWAL FREILICH, born Rochester, New York, November 7, 1956; admitted to bar, 1980, District of Columbia; 1981, Georgia; U.S. District Court, Southern District of Georgia; U.S. District Court, District of Connecticut; U.S. Court of Appeals, Eleventh Circuit; 1986, Connecticut. *Education:* George Washington University (B.A., 1977; J.D., 1980). Instructor, Law and Medicine, Augusta College, 1981-1982. Adjunct Professor, University of Hartford, Deferred Compensation, 1993-1995. Director: Greater Hartford Jewish Federation, 1996—; Commission on Jewish Education of Greater Hartford, 1995-2000; Anti-Defamation League, 1991-1997; Connecticut State Chairperson for A World of Difference Campaign, 1992-1995. Director, Bess and Paul Sigel Hebrew Academy of Greater Hartford, 1997—. Member, West Hartford School Board Ad Hoc Committee on the Recognition of religious holidays in the public schools, 1989. *Member:* Hartford County and Connecticut (Member, Section on Corporation, Banking and Business Law) Bar Associations; The District of Columbia Bar; State Bar of Georgia. (Also of Counsel to Brenner Satlzman & Wallman LLP). ***PRACTICE AREAS:*** Intellectual Property; Corporate Law; Securities Law; Pension Law; Employee Benefits Law. ***Email:*** sfreilich@bswlaw

STEPHEN M. PINCUS, born Brooklyn, New York, June 10, 1967; admitted to bar, 1993, Maryland (inactive); 1994, Connecticut and U.S. District Court, District of Connecticut; 1995, U.S. Court of Appeals, Second Circuit. *Education:* University of Michigan, Ann Arbor (A.B., with honors, 1989); University of Maryland School of Law (J.D., with honors, 1993). Clinical Teaching Fellow, Yale Law School, 1993-1995. Law Clerk to the Honorable Janet Bond Arterton, U.S. District Judge, District of Connecticut, 1995-1996. President, Congregation Beth El Keser Israel, 2001—. *Member:* Connecticut Bar Associations; New Haven Inn of Court. ***PRACTICE AREAS:*** Federal Litigation; Commercial Litigation; Employment Litigation; Civil Rights; Employment Law. ***Email:*** spincus@bswlaw.com

---

BUCKLEY & WYNNE

Established in 1986

685 STATE STREET

NEW HAVEN, CONNECTICUT 06511

Telephone: 203-776-2278

Fax: 203-495-6020

Email: buckley.and.wynne@snet.net

Hartford, Connecticut Office: 10 Columbus Boulevard. Telephone: 203-560-2278.

General Civil and Criminal Practice before State and Federal Courts. Personal Injury, Medical and Legal Malpractice, Product Liability, Probate, Workers Compensation Law. Trials and Appeals.

MEMBERS OF FIRM

JOHN F. WYNNE, born New Haven, Connecticut, September 18, 1920; admitted to bar, 1951, Connecticut. *Education:* Dartmouth College (B.A., 1943); St. John's University (J.D., 1951). Member, Board of Education, Town of Woodbridge, 1955-1963. Member, Board of Fire Commissioners, Town of Woodbridge, 1970-1987. *Member:* New Haven County and Connecticut Bar Associations. ***PRACTICE AREAS:*** Probate Law.

JOHN F. BUCKLEY, JR., born Boston, Massachusetts, October 5, 1959; admitted to bar, 1984, Connecticut; 1985, U.S. District Court, District of Connecticut. *Education:* Middlebury College (B.S., cum laude, 1981); University of Connecticut (J.D., with honors, 1984). Member, Panel of Arbitrators, American Arbitration Association. *Member:* Hartford County, Connecticut and American Bar Associations; Connecticut Trial Lawyers Association; The Association of Trial Lawyers of America. ***PRACTICE AREAS:*** Personal Injury Litigation; Product Liability; Medical Malpractice; Legal Malpractice.

(This Listing Continued)

JOHN F. WYNNE, JR., born New Haven, Connecticut, March 30, 1958; admitted to bar, 1984, Connecticut; 1985, U.S. District Court, District of Connecticut. *Education:* University of Connecticut (B.A., magna cum laude, 1980; J.D./M.B.A., with highest honors, 1984). Instructor, Finance and Real Estate Law, University of New Haven, 1982—. Member, Panel of Arbitrators, American Arbitration Association. *Member:* New Haven County, Connecticut and American Bar Associations; The Association of Trial Lawyers of America; Connecticut Trial Lawyers Association. ***REPORTED CASES:*** Nicolletta v. Nationwide Insurance Co., 211 Conn. 640, 560 A 2nd 964 1989 (Uninsured Motorist). ***PRACTICE AREAS:*** Personal Injury Litigation; Product Liability; Medical Malpractice; Legal Malpractice.

REFERENCE: First Union National Bank.

CARMODY & TORRANCE LLP

195 CHURCH STREET

P.O. BOX 1950

NEW HAVEN, CONNECTICUT 06509-1950

Telephone: 203-777-5501

Facsimile: 203-784-3199

Email: contactus@carmodylaw.com

URL: http://www.carmodylaw.com

Waterbury, Connecticut Office: 50 Leavenworth Street. P.O. Box 1110, 06721-1110. Telephone: 203-573-1200. Facsimile: 203-575-2600.

Southbury, Connecticut Office: 900 Main Street South. P.O. Box 410, 06488-0410. Telephone: 203-264-7882. Facsimile: 203-264-7847.

General Practice including Administrative, Alternative Dispute Resolution, Antitrust and Trade Regulation, Arbitration, Banking, Bankruptcy, Bond Finance, Closely Held Business, Commercial Real Estate, Commercial Litigation, Complex Litigation, Construction, Contracts, Corporate, Creditors' Rights, Employment Benefits, Employer Defense, Energy, Environmental, ERISA, Estate Planning, Family Business Successions, Finance, Freedom of Information, Government (State and Municipal Contracts), Health Care, Insurance, Intellectual Property, Patents and Trademarks, Labor and Employment, Land Use, Management Counseling, Medical Malpractice Defense, Municipal, Nonprofit Organizations, Pension, Privatization, Probate, Products Liability, Professional Liability Defense, Profit Sharing, Public-Private Finance, Public Utility, Securities, Tax, Toxic Torts, Zoning Law. General Civil, Criminal and Appellate Practice in all Courts.

FIRM PROFILE: 61 Attorneys Firmwide.

PARTNERS

ANTHONY M. FITZGERALD, born Waterbury, Connecticut, May 16, 1944; admitted to bar, 1969, Connecticut; 1972, District Court, District of Connecticut; 1975, U.S. Supreme Court; 1978, U.S. Court of Appeals, Second Circuit; 1994, U.S. District Court, Southern District of New York. *Education:* Yale University (A.B., cum laude, 1966); Columbia University (J.D., cum laude, 1969). Stone Scholar. Listed in "The Best Lawyers in America," 1995—. *Member:* Connecticut Bar Association (Member, Board of Governors, 1984-1987); American Board of Trial Advocates. Fellow, American College of Trial Lawyers. ***PRACTICE AREAS:*** Civil Litigation; Business Torts; Public Utilities. ***Email:*** afitzgerald@carmodylaw.com

BURTON Z. ALTER, born New York, New York, July 11, 1940; admitted to bar, 1967, New York; 1991, Connecticut; U.S. District Court, Southern District of New York. *Education:* Princeton University (A.B., cum laude, 1962); Columbia University (J.D., 1965). Phi Delta Phi. Contributing Editor: *New York Corporate Handbook,* New York State Bar Association, 1983. Consultant: *New York Practice Guide,* Matthew Bender, 1987. Member, Securities Advisory Council, Office of the Banking Commissioner, State of Connecticut, 1995—. *Member:* The Association of the Bar of the City of New York; American Law Institute. ***PRACTICE AREAS:*** Corporate Law; Mergers and Acquisitions; International Mergers and Acquisitions. ***Email:*** balter@carmodylaw.com

CHARLES F. CORCORAN, III, born Westfield, Massachusetts, July 26, 1945; admitted to bar, 1971, Connecticut; U.S. District Court, District of Connecticut; 1973, U.S. Court of Appeals, Second Circuit; 1989, U.S. Supreme Court. *Education:* Yale University (A.B., magna cum laude, 1967; J.D., 1971); Gonville & Caius College, Cambridge University, England. Phi Beta Kappa. Member, Connecticut Commission to Study Alternate Methods of Sentencing, 1977-1978. Member, Board of Governors, 1987-1992 and Legal Counsel, 1988-1990, University of Hartford Construction Institute. Adjunct Professor, Trial Methods, Western New England College School of Law, 1990-1994; Author: "Reinsurance Litigation: A Primer," 16 Western New England Law Review 41,

(This Listing Continued)

CARMODY & TORRANCE LLP, New Haven—Continued

1994, and Volume 7, National Insurance Law Review, No. 2. Member, Panel of Arbitrators, American Arbitration Association. *Member:* Connecticut Trial Lawyers Association. ***LANGUAGES:*** French, Italian, Spanish and Czech. ***PRACTICE AREAS:*** Trials and Appeals; Environmental Law; Professional Malpractice Law; Labor and Employment; Commercial and Contract Law; Insurance, Reinsurance and Surety Bond Law; Construction Litigation. ***Email:*** ccorcoran@carmodylaw.com

THOMAS R. CANDRICK, JR., born Lewisburg, Pennsylvania, November 14, 1947; admitted to bar, 1975, Connecticut; 1978, U.S. District Court, District of Connecticut. *Education:* Cornell University (A.B., 1969); University of Pennsylvania (M.B.A., 1975; J.D., 1975). Beta Sigma Gamma. *Member:* Connecticut Bar Association (Member, Executive Committee, Business Law Section, 1987—); American Arbitration Association. ***PRACTICE AREAS:*** Corporate Law; Commercial Law; Bankruptcy; Banking. ***Email:*** tcandrick@carmodylaw.com

SUSAN SEIDLER CHAMBERS, born New York, New York, February 9, 1955; admitted to bar, 1980, Connecticut, U.S. District Court, District of Connecticut and U.S. Court of Appeals, Second Circuit. *Education:* Cornell University (B.A., 1977); University of Edinburgh, Edinburgh, Scotland; University of Connecticut (J.D., cum laude, 1980). *Member:* Connecticut Bar Association (Chair, Federal Practice Section, 2000—); The Association of Trial Lawyers of America. ***PRACTICE AREAS:*** Construction; Contract Litigation; Insurance Litigation; Employer Defense. ***Email:*** schambers@carmodylaw.com

ANN HARRIS RUBIN, born Hartford, Connecticut, April 4, 1957; admitted to bar, 1983, Connecticut and U.S. District Court, District of Connecticut; 2001, U.S. Court of Appeals, Second Circuit. *Education:* Wellesley College; Cornell University (B.A., 1979); University of Connecticut School of Law (J.D., 1983). Special Master, U.S. District Court, District of Connecticut, 1992—. Arbitrator-Fact Finder, Connecticut Superior Court, 1992—. *Member:* Theodore I. Koskoff American Inn of Court. ***PRACTICE AREAS:*** Civil Litigation; Business Litigation; Insurance Law; Banking; Creditors Rights Law; Arbitration; Mediation. ***Email:*** arubin@carmodylaw.com

THOMAS J. SANSONE, born Danbury, Connecticut, December 31, 1960; admitted to bar, 1985, Connecticut; 1986, U.S. District Court, District of Connecticut; U.S. Tax Court; 1993, U.S. District Court, Southern and Eastern Districts of New York. *Education:* Boston University (B.A., magna cum laude, 1982; J.D., 1985). Member, Mortar Board. Instructor, American Institute of Banking (Waterbury Chapter), 1987-1991. *Member:* Connecticut Bar Association (Chairman, Commercial Litigation Committee, 1994-1996 and Member, Executive Committee, 1994—, Commercial Law and Bankruptcy Section); Waterbury Young Lawyers Association (President, 1991-1992); Connecticut Young Lawyers Association (Member, Executive Committee, 1991-1992). ***PRACTICE AREAS:*** Civil Litigation; Creditors Rights Law; Bankruptcy. ***Email:*** tsansone@carmodylaw.com

ANN HEDGES ZUCKER, born Columbus, Ohio, May 23, 1959; admitted to bar, 1985, Connecticut; 1986, U.S. District Court, District of Connecticut and New York. *Education:* Yale University (B.A., 1981); Fordham University (J.D., 1985). *Member:* American Health Lawyers Association; National Association of Bond Lawyers. ***PRACTICE AREAS:*** Banking; Public Finance; Health Care; Corporate Law; Commercial Real Estate. ***Email:*** azucker@carmodylaw.com

CHRISTOPHER ROONEY, born Argentia, Newfoundland, Canada, November 1, 1955; admitted to bar, 1984, Pennsylvania and U.S. District Court, Eastern District of Pennsylvania; 1988, Connecticut; 1989, U.S. District Court, District of Connecticut. *Education:* University of Virginia (B.A., 1977); University of Connecticut School of Law (J.D., 1984). Assistant District Attorney, Philadelphia, 1984-1989. *Member:* Connecticut Defense Lawyers Association. ***PRACTICE AREAS:*** Commercial Litigation; Land Use; Environmental Law; Criminal Law; Antitrust; Civil Rights; Health Care. ***Email:*** crooney@carmodylaw.com

HOWARD K. LEVINE, born New York, New York, September 30, 1964; admitted to bar, 1990, Connecticut; 1991, New York; 1992, U.S. District Court, District of Connecticut; 1993, U.S. Tax Court; 1994, U.S. Court of Appeals, Second Circuit; 1998, U.S. District Court, Southern and Eastern Districts of New York. *Education:* University of Connecticut (B.S., magna cum laude, 1986); University of Bridgeport (J.D., magna cum laude, 1990). ***PRACTICE AREAS:*** Civil Litigation; Labor and Employment. ***Email:*** hlevine@carmodylaw.com

ASSOCIATES

DAVID S. HARDY, born New Haven, Connecticut, 1973; admitted to bar, 1999, Connecticut. *Education:* Colgate University (A.B., 1996); University of Connecticut (J.D., 1999). ***PRACTICE AREAS:*** Civil Litigation. ***Email:*** dhardy@carmodylaw.com

(This Listing Continued)

ANNE D. PETERSON, born Nashville, Tennessee, June 27, 1969; admitted to bar, 1998, Connecticut. *Education:* Bates College (B.A., 1991); University of Connecticut School of Law (J.D., 1998). ***PRACTICE AREAS:*** Civil Litigation; Commercial Real Estate; Construction Law. ***Email:*** apeterson@carmodylaw.com

WILLIAM G. LEWIS, born Bronx, New York, September 18, 1964; admitted to bar, 1998, Connecticut. *Education:* Ithaca College (B.A., 1986); University of Connecticut (J.D., 1998). ***PRACTICE AREAS:*** Corporate Law; Commercial Law; Intellectual Property. ***Email:*** wlewis@carmodylaw.com

LUCY M. ROMEO, born Greenwich, Connecticut, September 5, 1973; admitted to bar, 1998, Connecticut; 1999, New York. *Education:* Yale University (B.A., cum laude, 1995); University of Connecticut (J.D., 1998). Member, Connecticut Law Review, University of Connecticut School of Law, 1997-1998. ***PRACTICE AREAS:*** Civil Litigation; Products Liability Defense; Insurance Defense. ***Email:*** lromeo@carmodylaw.com

REPRESENTATIVE CLIENTS: Algonquin Gas Transmission Co.; Anthem Blue Cross & Blue Shield of Connecticut, Inc.; Capital City Economic Development Authority; City of Waterbury; Clear Channel Communications Connecticut Development Authority; Connecticut Health and Educational Facilities Authority; Connecticut Housing Finance Authority; Connecticut Housing Finance Authority; ConnectiCare, Inc.; Connecticut Innovations, Inc.; Connecticut Lottery Corporation; Crompton Corporation; Fleet Boston Financial Co.; Hospital for Special Care; Iroquois Gas Transmission System; MacDermid, Inc.; Mercator Software, Inc.; Middlebury Water Pollution Authority; New Haven Savings Bank; New Opportunities for Waterbury, Inc.; Northeast Utilities; People's Bank; State of Connecticut; Teleflex Incorporated; Timex Corporation; Town of New Hartford; Town of Prospect; Town of Watertown; Town of Woodbury; Transwitch, Inc.; USCO Logistics; Verizon Wireless; Waterbury Companies; Waterbury Foundation; Waterbury Hospital; Waterbury Republican-American; Waterbury Spirit Professional Baseball Club; Webster Bank.
TRIAL COUNSEL FOR: Aetna Life and Casualty; Attorney's Liability Assurance Society, Inc.; Professional Risk Management Services, Inc.; Reliance National Insurance Co.; St. Paul Fire & Marine Insurance.

(For complete biographical data on all personnel, see Professional Biographies at Waterbury, Connecticut)

CARTER & CIVITELLO

NEW HAVEN, CONNECTICUT

(See Woodbridge)

Workers Compensation, Social Security, Disability Law, Personal Injury.

LAW OFFICES OF
PAUL V. CARTY

Established in 1997
506 WHALLEY AVENUE
P.O. BOX 3192
NEW HAVEN, CONNECTICUT 06515-0292
Telephone: 203-387-5400
Fax: 203-387-5402
Email: pvcartyesq@aol.com
URL: http://www.lawyers.com/pvcartyesq

Criminal Defense, Personal Injury, Civil Litigation, Workers Compensation, Family Law, Landlord and Tenant Law, Driving While Intoxicated, Civil Litigation.

PAUL V. CARTY, born Uchitomari, Okinawa, August 2, 1954; admitted to bar, 1985, Connecticut; 1992, U.S. District Court, District of Connecticut; 1995, Mashantucket Pequot Tribal Court. *Education:* The Choate School; Wesleyan University (B.A., 1977); University of Connecticut (J.D., 1985). Chairman, West Haven Board of Ethics, 1988-1990. *Member:* West Haven, New Haven County, Connecticut and American Bar Associations; Connecticut Criminal Defense Lawyers Association; George Crawford Law Association; Connecticut Trial Lawyers Association. ***PRACTICE AREAS:*** Criminal Defense; Personal Injury; Workers Compensation; Family Law; Landlord and Tenant Law; Driving While Intoxicated; Civil Litigation.

CHURCH AND CHURCH

35 ELM STREET
P.O. BOX 78
NEW HAVEN, CONNECTICUT 06501-0078
Telephone: 203-562-0300
Fax: 203-624-5134
Email: nwchurch@gateway.net
URL: http://www.lawyers.com/churchandchurch

General Civil and Criminal Practice before State and Federal Courts, Municipal Law, Real Estate, Zoning, Land Use, Corporation, Probate, Estate Planning, Elder Law, Commercial, Condominium and Collections, Trials and Appeals.

(This Listing Continued)

MEMBERS OF FIRM

NORBERT W. CHURCH, JR., born New York, N.Y., August 13, 1952; admitted to bar, 1979, Massachusetts, Connecticut and U.S. District Court, District of Massachusetts; 1980, U.S. District Court, District of Connecticut. *Education:* Bucknell University (B.S.B.A., 1974); New England School of Law (J.D., 1978). Delta Mu Delta; Omicron Delta Kappa. Member, 1982-1988; President, 1987-1988, Board of Directors, Branford Visiting Nurses Association. Member, Board of Directors, Quinnipiac Club, 1986-1988; 1995-1999, President, 1999-2000. Secretary, Committee on Recommendations for Admission to the Connecticut Bar for New Haven County, 1983-1992. Assistant Town Attorney, Town of Branford, 1984-1987. Town Attorney, Town of Branford, 1987-1996. *Member:* New Haven County (Board of Directors, 1998—; Co-Chair, Continuing Legal Education Committee) and Connecticut (Member, Executive Committee, Planning and Zoning Section) Bar Associations; Connecticut Association of Municipal Attorneys. ***REPORTED CASES:*** Castellon v. Board of Zoning Appeals, 221 Conn. 374 (Zoning) (1992); TLC Development, Inc. v. Planning and Zoning Commission, 215 Conn. 527 (Zoning) (1990). ***PRACTICE AREAS:*** Municipal Law; Planning and Zoning Law; Real Estate; Condominium Law; Probate; Estate Planning; Litigation; Collections; Land Use.

MARGARET KEZER CHURCH, born Boston, Massachusetts, December 20, 1953; admitted to bar, 1980, Massachusetts; 1981, Connecticut. *Education:* Wheaton College (B.A., cum laude, 1975); New England School of Law (J.D., 1978). *Member:* New Haven County and Connecticut Bar Associations. ***PRACTICE AREAS:*** Probate Law; Estate Planning Law; Real Estate Law; Elder Law.

DAVID T. TOTMAN, born Pittsburgh, Pennsylvania, December 14, 1938; admitted to bar, 1966, District of Columbia; 1967, Connecticut, Florida and U.S. District Court, District of Connecticut; 1970, U.S. Tax Court; 1994, Mashantucket Pequot Tribal Court. *Education:* Yale University (B.A., magna cum laude, 1961; LL.B., 1965); University of Stockholm, Sweden (M.A., 1962); College of Advocacy, Hastings College of Law, University of California. Adjunct Professor, Business Law, Albertus Magnus College, New Haven, Connecticut, 1974—. Lecturer, History, Quinnipiac College, Hamden, Connecticut, 1966—. *Member:* New Haven County, The Connecticut and American (Member, Family Law Section) Bar Associations; The Florida Bar. ***LANGUAGES:*** Swedish. ***PRACTICE AREAS:*** Corporations; Family Law; Estate Planning; Probate; Real Estate.

REPRESENTATIVE CLIENTS: Town of Branford; Town of North Branford; Flexo Converters; Fleet Bank; Village Commons Condominiums; Quonnipaug Hills Condominiums, Bay View Place Condominiums; Town of North Branford; Lakeview Condominiums; Harbor Crest Condominiums; The Oaks Condominiums; Harbor Village Condominiums; Forest Edge Recreation Association.
APPROVED ATTORNEY FOR: Chicago Title Insurance Co.; Lawyers Title Insurance Co.; Connecticut Attorneys Title Insurance Co.; New Haven Savings Bank; People's Bank; Webster Bank; Fleet Mortgage; First Union Bank; PHH Mortgage; Guilford Savings Bank; Sikorsky Federal Credit Union; GMAC Mortgage Corp.; Chase Mortgage Co.
REFERENCES: Fleet Bank.

CICCHETTI & TANSLEY

NEW HAVEN, CONNECTICUT

(See Waterbury)

General Civil and Criminal Practice before State and Federal Courts; Trial and Appeals, Real Estate, Residential and Commercial, Real Estate Development, Planning and Zoning, Corporate/Business Law, Municipal Law, Commercial Litigation, Personal Injury, Domestic Relations, Workers Compensation Law, Criminal Law, Probate.

CIULLA & DONOFRIO, LLP

NEW HAVEN, CONNECTICUT

(See North Haven)

Civil Litigation in all State and Federal Courts, Commercial Litigation, Business Law, Municipal and Governmental Law, Construction and Surety Law, Product Liability, Personal Injury, Employment Law, Insurance Litigation, Tax and Zoning Appeals, Antitrust, Securities, Tax and Corporate Law.

WILLIAM H. CLENDENEN, JR.

A PROFESSIONAL CORPORATION

400 ORANGE STREET
P.O. BOX 301
NEW HAVEN, CONNECTICUT 06502-0301
Telephone: 203-787-1183
Fax: 203-787-2847

General Civil and Appellate Practice. Banking, Civil Rights, Employment, Construction, Consumer, Commercial Litigation, Estates and Probate, Real Estate, Personal Injury. General Litigation in all Courts.

(This Listing Continued)

FIRM PROFILE: William H. Clendenen, Jr. represents small businesses, corporations and individuals throughout the state of Connecticut. He has a legal support staff to assist with matters. Mr. Clendenen maintains a general practice and he is listed in the Bar Register of Preeminent Lawyers.

WILLIAM H. CLENDENEN, JR., born New London, Connecticut, December 2, 1942; admitted to bar, 1967, Connecticut; 1968, U.S. District Court, District of Connecticut and U.S. Court of Appeals, Second Circuit; 1971, U.S. Supreme Court; 1976, U.S. Claims Court; 1977, U.S. District Court, Southern District of New York and U.S. District Court, District of Rhode Island. *Education:* Providence College (B.A., 1964); Catholic University of America (J.D., 1967). Reginald Heber Smith Community Lawyer Fellowship, University of Pennsylvania, 1967. Author: "Connecticut Consumer Law - The Transition From Caveat Emptor," 64 Conn. B. J. S I 290 1990. Supervising Attorney, Yale Law School, 1981. Alternate Public Member, Connecticut State Board of Mediation and Arbitration, 1976-1978. Co-Chairman, U.S. District Court, District of Connecticut, Special Masters Committee, 1986-1989. Attorney State Trial Referee, 1991—; Fact-finder/Arbitrator, 1991—. Member, Connecticut Law Library Advisory Committee, 1993—. *Member:* New Haven County (Member, Executive Committee, 1984—; Secretary, 1986-1987; Treasurer, 1987-1988; Vice President, 1988-1989; President, 1989-1990; Chairman: Continuing Legal Education Committee, 1984-1986; Lawyer Referral Committee, 1986-1989), Connecticut (Chairman: Consumer Law Section, 1974-1978; Lawyer Referral Committee, 1987-1989; Member, Federal Practice Section, 1974—) and American Bar Associations; The Association of Trial Lawyers of America; Connecticut Trial Lawyers Association. Life Fellow, Connecticut Bar Foundation (Member, Board of Directors, 1991—; Treasurer, 1992—). Fellow, American College of Trial Lawyers. ***PRACTICE AREAS:*** Litigation; Personal Injury Law; Estates; Probate Law; Civil Rights Law; Commercial Law; Real Estate.

JAMES E. CLIFFORD, born New Haven, Connecticut, September 19, 1959; admitted to bar, 1985, Connecticut; 1987, U.S. District Court, District of Connecticut. *Education:* Georgetown University (B.A., 1981); University of Kent, Canterbury, England; Columbus School of Law, Catholic University of America (J.D., 1985). Legal Advisor, Milford Independent Disabled Persons, Milford, Connecticut, 1985-1990. *Member:* New Haven County (Member, Lawyer Referral Committee, 1991-1996) and Connecticut Bar Associations. ***PRACTICE AREAS:*** Litigation; Personal Injury Law; Real Estate Law; Commercial Law.

NANCY L. WALKER, born Pasadena, California, October 6, 1953; admitted to bar, 1983, Connecticut, U.S. District Court, District of Connecticut. *Education:* University of California (B.A., with honors, 1976); Hastings College of Law, University of California (J.D., magna cum laude, 1983). Thurston Society; Order of the Coif. Member, Hasting Law Journal, 1981-1983. Recipient, American Jurisprudence Awards in: Corporations, 1982; Secured Transactions, Legal Professional Responsibility, 1983. Author: Note, "Committee to Defend Reproductive Right v. Myers: The Constitutionality of Conditions on Public Benefits in California," 33 Hastings Law Journal 1475, 1982. Law Clerk, Hon. Arthur H. Latimer, U.S. Magistrate, New Haven, Connecticut, 1983-1985. Professor, Legal Research and Writing, University of Bridgeport, School of Law, 1987-1988. *Member:* New Haven (Chair, Recycling Committee Chair, 1990-1991) Bar Association. ***LANGUAGES:*** French. ***PRACTICE AREAS:*** Litigation; Appellate Practice; Commercial Law.

THOMAS C. PELLEGRINO, born New Haven, Connecticut, September 5, 1968; admitted to bar, 1993, Connecticut; 1995, U.S. District Court, District of Connecticut. *Education:* Fairfield University (B.A. in Politics, 1990); Syracuse University (J.D., 1993). Recipient, New York State Bar Association Legal Ethics Award for "Attorney Paternalism and the Child Client: Does 'Father' Always Know Best?" 1992. *Member:* New Haven County and Connecticut Bar Associations; Inns of Court (Associate, 1995-1996). ***PRACTICE AREAS:*** Litigation; Commercial Law; Real Estate; Family Law.

KEVIN C. SHEA, born Bridgeport, Connecticut, April 14, 1966; admitted to bar, 1993, Connecticut and U.S. District Court, District of Connecticut; 2000, U.S. Court of Appeals, Second Circuit. *Education:* University of Connecticut (B.S., 1988); University of Connecticut School of Law (J.D., magna cum laude, 1993). Member, University of Denver Law Review, 1993. Recipient, American Jurisprudence Award, Torts, 1991. Law Clerk Intern, Honorable Alfred D. Covello, U.S. District Court, District of Connecticut, 1993. Member, Westbrook Zoning Commission, 1999—. *Member:* New Haven County, Connecticut and American Bar Associations. ***PRACTICE AREAS:*** Civil Litigation; Medical Malpractice; Professional Liability; Products Liability; Labor and Employment; Education Law; Commercial Litigation. **Email:** kcs@clenlaw.com

COAN, LEWENDON, GULLIVER & MILTENBERGER, LLC

Established in 1981

495 ORANGE STREET

NEW HAVEN, CONNECTICUT 06511

Telephone: 203-624-4756

Fax: 203-865-3673

URL: http://www.lawyers.com/clrglawoffices

General Civil Practice. Bankruptcy, Commercial, Banking, Personal Injury, Real Estate, Corporation, Probate, and Estate Planning Law, Elder Law, Trials and Appeals before all Courts.

MEMBERS OF FIRM

RICHARD M. COAN, born Brooklyn, New York, September 17, 1948; admitted to bar, 1974, Connecticut; 1981, U.S. District Court, District of Connecticut; 1982, U.S. Court of Appeals, Second Circuit. *Education:* University of Rochester (A.B., magna cum laude, 1969); Yale University (J.D., 1974). Member, Panel of Bankruptcy Trustees, District of Connecticut, 1986—. *Member:* New Haven County, Connecticut (Member, Sections on: Commercial and Bankruptcy Law) and American (Member, Sections on: Corporation, Banking and Business Law) Bar Associations; National Association of Bankruptcy Trustees. **PRACTICE AREAS:** Real Estate Law; Bankruptcy Law; Commercial Law. **Email:** richcoan@aol.com

WHITNEY M. LEWENDON, born White Plains, New York, November 30, 1948; admitted to bar, 1973, Connecticut; 1974, U.S. District Court, District of Connecticut; 1976, U.S. Supreme Court; 1983, U.S. Court of Appeals, Second Circuit. *Education:* Columbia University (B.A., 1970); Northeastern University (J.D., 1973). Lecturer, Bridgeport University Law School, 1977. Visiting Professor, Law and Older Persons, Quinnipiac College, Hamden, Connecticut, 1987. *Member:* New Haven County and Connecticut (Member, Sections on: Elder Law; Estates and Probate) Bar Associations; National Academy of Elder Law Attorneys (Regional Coordinator). **PRACTICE AREAS:** Elder Law; Probate Law; Estate Planning Law. **Email:** wmlewendon@aol.com

CARL T. GULLIVER, born Indianapolis, Indiana, March 6, 1951; admitted to bar, 1980, District of Columbia; 1981, U.S. District Court, District of Columbia; 1982, Maryland and New York; 1983, U.S. District Court, District of Maryland; 1984, U.S. Court of Appeals, Fourth Circuit; 1985, Connecticut; 1986, U.S. District Court, District of Connecticut. *Education:* Ohio Wesleyan University (B.A., 1973); George Washington University (J.D., 1980). *Member:* New Haven and Connecticut (Member, Commercial Law and Bankruptcy Section) Bar Associations; The District of Columbia Bar (Member, Bankruptcy Committee, 1982-1986); American Bankruptcy Institute. (Board Certified, Business Bankruptcy Law, American Board of Certification). **PRACTICE AREAS:** Bankruptcy Law; Creditors Rights Law; Commercial Law.

TIMOTHY D. MILTENBERGER, born Buffalo, N.Y., October 22, 1964; admitted to bar, 1990, Connecticut; 1992, U.S. District Court, District of Connecticut; 1998, U.S. Court of Appeals, Second Circuit; 1999, U.S. Court of Appeals, Ninth Circuit. *Education:* Washington University (A.B., 1986); Boston University (J.D., cum laude, 1990). *Member:* Connecticut Bar Association (Member, Sections on Commercial Law and Bankruptcy; Federal Practice); Association of Trial Lawyers of America. **PRACTICE AREAS:** Bankruptcy Law; Commercial Litigation; Creditors Rights. **Email:** tmilten@aol.com

OF COUNSEL

E. HUNTINGTON DEMING, born New Haven, Connecticut, July 22, 1950; admitted to bar, 1977, District of Columbia; 1979, U.S. District Court, District of Columbia; 1987, Connecticut; U.S. District Court, District of Connecticut. *Education:* Stanford University (B.A., 1972); American University (J.D., 1977). Clerk to the Hon. Bruce S. Mencher, Superior Court, District of Columbia, 1978-1980. Assistant Corporation Counsel, District of Columbia, 1980-1986. *Member:* New Haven County, Connecticut and American Bar Associations. **PRACTICE AREAS:** Civil Law; Commercial Litigation.

REPRESENTATIVE CLIENTS: Guida-Seibert Dairy Co.; Tilden Financial Corp.; J.H. Daly Co.; Hartford Bindery, Inc.; Circle Business Credit, Inc.; Professional Leasing Services; Fair Haven Community Health Center.
APPROVED ATTORNEYS FOR: Lawyer's Title Insurance Corp.; Title USA Insurance Corp.; First American Title Insurance Corp.; Chicago Title Insurance Co.; New Haven Savings Bank; Fleet Bank; People's Bank.
REFERENCE: Fleet Bank.

COHEN AND ACAMPORA

109 CHURCH STREET

NEW HAVEN, CONNECTICUT 06510

Telephone: 203-624-4126

East Haven, Connecticut Office: 8 Frontage Road, P.O. Box 190. Telephone: 203-467-7337. Telecopier: 203-468-7865.

(This Listing Continued)

General Civil and Criminal Practice before State and Federal Courts. Personal Injury, Litigation, Products Liability, Environmental, Real Estate, Zoning, Acquisitions and Development, Probate, Estate Planning, Workers Compensation, Domestic Relations, Foreclosure, Bankruptcy, Insolvency, Maritime Law, Real Estate, Tax Appeals, Business, Commercial and Corporation Law.

(For Complete Biographical Data on all Personnel, see Professional Biographies at East Haven)

COHEN & THOMAS

NEW HAVEN, CONNECTICUT

(See Derby)

General Civil and Criminal Practice. Trials in all Courts. Personal Injury, Negligence and Medical Malpractice Litigation, Real Estate Purchase, Sale, Financing, Zoning and Development, Domestic Law and Divorce, Probate, Wills and Trusts, Banking, Foreclosure and Workouts, Commercial Litigation and Collections, Municipal, Elder Law, Worker's Compensation.

LAW OFFICES OF JOHN W. COLLERAN, P.C.

19 WHITNEY AVENUE

NEW HAVEN, CONNECTICUT 06510

Telephone: 203-865-2899

Fax: 203-777-4587

Email: colleran@iconn.net

URL: http://www.lawyers.com/jwcolleranatty

General Practice in all Courts. Corporation, Negligence, Probate, Environmental, Zoning, Real Estate and Administrative Law, Personal Injury. Trials.

JOHN W. COLLERAN, born New Haven, Connecticut, July 13, 1930; admitted to bar, 1955, Connecticut; 1958, U.S. District Court of Connecticut; 1965, U.S. Court of Appeals, Second Circuit and U.S. Supreme Court. *Education:* Yale University (B.A., 1952; LL.B., 1955). Phi Alpha Delta. Member, Yale Law Journal, 1955. Member, Board of Directors, The Bank of New Haven, 1986-1991. Member, Board of Directors, BNH Bancshares, Inc., 1988-1991. Member, Board of Directors, 1982-1994 and Treasurer, 1989-1994, New Haven Symphony Orchestra. Member of Panel, American Arbitration Association. *Member:* New Haven County, The Connecticut and American Bar Associations; Connecticut Trial Lawyers Association. **PRACTICE AREAS:** Real Estate Law; Administrative Law; Hazardous Waste Law; Personal Injury Law.

APPROVED ATTORNEYS FOR: Stewart Title Insurance Corporation; Fidelity National Title Insurance Company.
REFERENCES: New Haven Savings Bank. Representative Clients: Ulbrich Stainless Steels & Special Metals, Inc.; Ulbrich Realty, Inc.; Southern New England Federal Credit Union; Flight Support, Inc.; Metro Taxi, Inc.; Transportation General, Inc.

COUSINS, JOHNSON & DESROSIERS, P.C.

NEW HAVEN, CONNECTICUT

(See Stratford)

Workers' Compensation, Personal Injury, Trials, Real Estate, Probate.

CUMMINGS & LOCKWOOD

700 STATE STREET

P.O. BOX 1960

NEW HAVEN, CONNECTICUT 06509-1960

Telephone: (203) 782-3000

Telecopier: (203) 777-3347

Email: info@cl-law.com

URL: http://www.cl-law.com

Stamford, Connecticut Office: Four Stamford Plaza, P.O. Box 120, 06904-0120. Telephone: (203) 327-1700. Telecopier: (203) 351-4535.

Greenwich, Connecticut Office: Two Greenwich Plaza, P.O. Box 2505, 06836. Telephone: (203) 869-1200. Telecopier: (203) 869-3120.

Hartford, Connecticut Office: CityPlace I, 185 Asylum Street, 36th Floor, 06103-3495. Telephone: (860) 275-6700. Telecopier: (860) 724-3397.

West Hartford, Connecticut Office: Town Center, 29 South Main Street, Suite 208, 06107. Telephone: (860) 275-6700. Telecopier: (860) 313-0293.

Bonita Springs, Florida Office: 24311 Walden Center, Suite 201, 34134. Telephone: (941) 947-8811. Telecopier: (941) 947-8025.

Naples, Florida Office: 3001 Tamiami Trail North, P.O. Box 413032, 34101-3032. Telephone: (941) 262-8311. Telecopier: (941) 263-0703.

(This Listing Continued)

General Practice. National and Regional Litigation Counsel, Corporate Law, Patent and Intellectual Property, Trusts and Estates, Labor and Employment, Mergers and Acquisitions, Partnerships and Joint Ventures, Commercial Lending, Corporate Finance, Creditors' Rights, Bankruptcy and Workouts, Securities Regulation and Litigation, Tax, Insurance, Banking and Financial Services, Leasing, Commercial and Residential Real Estate, Construction, Environmental, Toxic Torts, Health Law, Products Liability Litigation, Probate Litigation, Family Law and International Business.

FIRM PROFILE: Cummings & Lockwood caters both to commercial entities and individual clients, serves as local, regional and national counsel in Corporate, Litigation, Intellectual Property and Creditors' Rights matters, and has one of the largest groups of Estate Planning professionals in the country.

Cummings & Lockwood attorneys answer questions and solve problems by having specialists in multiple disciplines practice together from eight offices to address the broad concerns of our diverse clientele. The firm guides corporate transactions and resolves complex business disputes for emerging, middle-market and Fortune 500 businesses, including high tech companies, financial services providers and industrial manufacturers. We are also uniquely positioned to assist affluent families and entrepreneurs in designing wealth preserving estate plans and developing business succession strategies.

MEMBERS OF FIRM

MICHAEL N. DELGASS, born Berkeley, California, May 16, 1969; admitted to bar, 1995, Illinois; 1999, Florida and Connecticut; 2000, New York. *Education:* Indiana University (B.S., Geology, 1992; B.S., Biology, 1992; B.A., Chemistry, 1992); University of Chicago (J.D., 1995). Phi Beta Kappa. Author: *Pecuniary Dynastic Offshore Trusts: New Offshore Opportunities for U.S. Citizens,* 138 Trusts & Estates 12 (July 1999); *Financial Reporting for the Family Office, Reducing Fiduciary Exposure,* 135 Trust & Estates 12 (April 1999). Contributing Editor (1998 Update), *Illinois Estate Planning, Will Drafting and Estate Administration Forms,* Michie, 2d ed. (1996). Adjunct Professor, Northwestern University School of Law, Chicago, Illinois, 1999. Instructor: American Bankers Association, National Trust School, 1998; American Bankers Association, National Graduate Trust School, 1998. *Member:* Chicago (Probate Practice Committee: Member, Executive Committee, 1998-1999; Vice-Chairman, 1998-1999; Secretary, 1997-1998), Connecticut (Estates and Probate Section, Member, Executive Committee; Business Law Section) and American (Member, Sections on: Taxation and Real Property; Probate and Trust Law) Bar Associations; Family Firm Institute. ***PRACTICE AREAS:*** Trusts and Estates. ***Email:*** mdelgass@cl-law.com

CHARLES J. FILARDI, JR., born New Haven, Connecticut, April 8, 1956; admitted to bar, 1991, Connecticut; 1992, U.S. District Court, District of Connecticut. *Education:* Lafayette College (A.B., 1978); University of Bridgeport School of Law (J.D., magna cum laude, 1991). Recipient, American Jurisprudence Award, Commercial Law. *Member:* New Haven County, Connecticut and American Bar Associations; The Association of Trial Lawyers of America; Connecticut Trial Lawyers Association. [with U.S. Navy, 1980-1985; CDR, U.S. Naval Reserve, 1985—]. (Also in Stamford, Connecticut Office). ***PRACTICE AREAS:*** Bankruptcy; Debtor and Creditor; Commercial Litigation; Creditors Rights.

JAMIE JOHNSON FITZGERALD, born New York, New York, November 16, 1947; admitted to bar, 1972, Illinois; 1980, New York; 1988, Connecticut. *Education:* Middlebury College (A.B., English Literature, 1969); University of Chicago (J.D., 1972). Phi Beta Kappa. Contributor, "Trademark Law Practice Forms," Clark Boardman Company, Ltd., 1988-1991. Member, Editorial Board, The Trademark Reporter, 1990-1991. *Member:* Connecticut Patent Law Association; American Intellectual Property Law Association; United States Trademark Association (Associate Member). ***PRACTICE AREAS:*** Trademarks; Copyrights; Intellectual Property. ***Email:*** jfitzgerald@cl-law.com

KEITH BRADOC GALLANT, born New Haven, Connecticut, February 28, 1952; admitted to bar, 1978, Connecticut; 1981, U.S. District Court, District of Connecticut; 1985, U.S. Court of Appeals, Second Circuit. *Education:* Pembroke College, University of Cambridge (B.A., with honours, 1975; M.A., 1979); University of Connecticut (J.D., cum laude, 1978); University of London (LL.M., 1979). *Member:* National Academy of Elder Law Attorneys. Fellow, American College of Trust and Estate Counsel. ***PRACTICE AREAS:*** Estate Planning and Administration; Probate Litigation; Elder Law; Disabilities Law; Fiduciary Litigation; Disabilities; Special Education. ***Email:*** kgallant@cl-law.com

DAVID W. KESNER, born Pensacola, Florida, November 22, 1955; admitted to bar, 1992, Maine; 1993, Massachusetts; 1998, Connecticut. *Education:* New York Institute of Technology (B.S., summa cum laude, 1989); New York Law School (J.D., magna cum laude, 1992). Law Review. ***PRACTICE AREAS:*** Trusts and Estates; Estate Planning. ***Email:*** dkesn@cl-law.com

DAVID A. REIF, born Pittsburgh, Pennsylvania, April 24, 1946; admitted to bar, 1971, Connecticut; 1977, U.S. Supreme Court. *Education:* Lafayette College (A.B., magna cum laude, 1968); Harvard University (J.D., 1971). Phi Beta Kappa. Law Clerk, Hon. William H. Timbers, U.S. Court of Appeals, 1971-1972. Special Master, U.S. District Court, 1993—. Author: "Product Liability and CUTPA," *Sidebar,* Vol. 1, No. 3 (1993); "The Use of Patents in Plaintiff's Product Liability Litigation," *Sidebar,* Vol. 1, No. 4 (1993); "Product Liability: Of Toys and Cars and Purple Chicks," *Sidebar,* Vol. 2, No. 3 (1994); "While You Were at the Beach: A Product Law Update," SIDEBAR, Vol. 5, No. 2 (1997); "Inadvertent Disclosure," For the Defense, December 2000. Lecturer: Connecticut Franchise Law, PEI, 1989; Franchise Termination and Litigation, Connecticut Bar Association, 1991; Products Liability Law, Connecticut Bar Association, 1993, 1995, 1997, 1999. Instructor, Connecticut Institute of Trial Advocacy, 1996-1998. *Member:* New Haven County, Connecticut (Chair, Franchise Law Committee, 1993-1995; Vice Chair, Litigation Section, 1999-2001) and American Bar Associations; Connecticut Trial Lawyers Association; Defense Research Institute; American Board of Trial Advocates. (Board Certified Civil Trial Advocate by the National Board of Trial Advocacy). ***PRACTICE AREAS:*** Civil Trials; Personal Injury Trials; Products and Professional Liability Litigation; Franchise Law; Bankruptcy; Debtor and Creditor. ***Email:*** dreif@cl-law.com

MARK G. SKLARZ, born Irvington, New Jersey, November 18, 1945; admitted to bar, 1970, Connecticut and U.S. District Court, District of Connecticut; 1975, U.S. Supreme Court. *Education:* Franklin & Marshall College (B.A., 1967); University of Connecticut (J.D., with honors, 1970); New York University (LL.M. in Taxation, 1974). Member: Board of Editors, Connecticut Law Review; Connecticut Bar Journal, 1977. *Member:* Connecticut (Employee Benefits Section; Executive Committee of the Business Organization Section) and American Bar Associations. ***PRACTICE AREAS:*** Taxation; Business and Corporate; Trust and Estates; Licensing. ***Email:*** msklarz@cl-law.com

CHARLES M. TATELBAUM (See Biography at Naples, Florida Office).

COUNSEL

KEITH N. COSTA, born Newtown, Massachusetts, September 6, 1958; admitted to bar, 1985, New York; 1994, Connecticut. *Education:* University of Connecticut (B.A., 1980); Washington College of Law of American University (J.D., 1983). ***PRACTICE AREAS:*** Corporate Law; Creditors Rights; Bankruptcy; Debtor and Creditor. ***Email:*** kcosta@cl-law.com

ASSOCIATES

Holley L. Claiborn ***Thomas J. Dufour***
Joshua W. Cohen ***Sean P. Merrill***
Timothy W. Crowley ***Graceann A. Pisano***

(For complete biographical information on personnel, see Professional Biographies at Greenwich, CT, Hartford, CT, West Hartford, CT, Stamford, CT, Bonita Springs, FL and Naples, FL)

DELANEY, ZEMETIS, DONAHUE, DURHAM & NOONAN, P.C.

NEW HAVEN, CONNECTICUT

(See Wallingford)

Practice Primarily Limited to Professional Malpractice, Products Liability, Insurance Defense, Personal Injury, Employment and Commercial Litigation in all Courts.

DELIO & PETERSON, LLC

121 WHITNEY AVENUE
NEW HAVEN, CONNECTICUT 06510-1241
Telephone: 203-787-0595
FAX: 203-787-5818
Email: delpet@delpet.com
URL: http://www.lawyers.com/delio

United States and International Patent, Trademark, Copyright and Unfair Competition Law. Licensing, Franchising and Technology - Litigation.

ANTHONY P. DELIO, born Brooklyn, New York, 1928; admitted to bar, 1957, District of Columbia; 1958, Connecticut; 1959, U.S. District Court, District of Connecticut; 1965, U.S. Supreme Court; 1982, U.S. Court of Appeals, Federal Circuit; 1984, U.S. Court of Appeals, Second Circuit; registered to practice before U.S. Patent and Trademark Office. *Education:* Polytechnic Institute of Brooklyn (B.S., Physics, 1953); George Washington University (J.D., cum laude, 1957). Member, George Washington University Law Review, 1956-1957. Patent Advisor, Office of Naval Research, 1956-1957. *Member:* New Haven County, Connecticut and American Bar Associations; The District of Columbia Bar; Connecticut Patent Law Association; American Intellectual Property Law Association; International Patent Law Association. ***LAN-***

(This Listing Continued)

DELIO & PETERSON, LLC, New Haven—Continued

GUAGES: Italian and German. ***PRACTICE AREAS:*** Patents; Trademarks; Copyrights; Unfair Competition; Intellectual Property Licensing; Franchise Law; Technology Law.

PETER W. PETERSON, born Connecticut, August 7, 1954; admitted to bar, 1982, Connecticut; 1986, U.S. District Court, District of Connecticut and U.S. Court of Appeals for the Federal Circuit; registered to practice before U.S. Patent and Trademark Office. *Education:* University of Connecticut (B.S., Mech. Engr. and Material Science, 1976; M.S., Metallurgy, 1979; J.D., 1982). Member, Town of Southbury Zoning Board of Appeals, 1991—. *Member:* New Haven County and Connecticut Bar Associations. ***PRACTICE AREAS:*** Patents; Trademarks; Copyrights; Unfair Competition; Intellectual Property Licensing; Franchise Law; Technology Law; Litigation; Patent Applications; Patent Interference Practice; Trademark Litigation.

JOHN J. TOMASZEWSKI, born Brooklyn, New York, January 12, 1940; admitted to bar, 1971, New York; 1973, U.S. District Court, Eastern and Southern Districts of New York and U.S. Court of Appeals, Federal Circuit; registered to practice before U.S. Patent and Trademark Office (Not admitted in Connecticut). *Education:* New York University (B.Ch.E., 1963); Fairleigh Dickinson University (M.B.A., 1966); St. John's University (J.D., 1970). Phi Delta Phi. Recipient, American Jurisprudence Award in Federal Jurisdiction. *Member:* American Intellectual Property Law Association. ***PRACTICE AREAS:*** Patents; Trademarks; Copyrights; Intellectual Property Licensing; Unfair Competition; Franchise Law; Technology Law.

ROBERT CURCIO, born New Haven, Connecticut, May 15, 1958; admitted to bar, 1997, Connecticut; 1999, District of Columbia; U.S. District Court, District of Connecticut and District of Columbia and U.S. Court of Appeals, Federal Circuit; registered to practice before U.S. Patent and Trademark Office. *Education:* University of Vermont (B.A., Physics, 1980); University of Connecticut (M.S., Physics, 1984); Seattle University School of Law (J.D., 1997). *Member:* Connecticut and American (Member, Sections on: Intellectual Property; Federal Practice) Bar Associations; Federal Circuit Bar Association (Member, Amicus Committee); Connecticut Intellectual Property Lawyers Association. ***PRACTICE AREAS:*** Intellectual Property Litigation; Patents; Trademarks; Copyrights; Unfair Competition; Intellectual Property Licensing; Patent Interference Practice; Technology Law.

KELLY REYNOLDS NOWAK, born New Haven, Connecticut, January 18, 1968; admitted to bar, 2000, Connecticut; registered to practice before the U.S. Patent and Trademark Office. *Education:* Southern Connecticut State University (B.S., Chemistry, 1991); University of New Haven (M.S., Environmental Science, 1995); Quinnipiac College School of Law (J.D., 1998). *Member:* New Haven County and Connecticut Bar Associations. ***PRACTICE AREAS:*** Patents; Trademarks; Copyrights; Intellectual Property; Litigation. ***Email:*** delpet@delpet.com

MICHAEL A. PETROCELLI, born New York, June 28, 1960; admitted to bar, 1999, Coneticut. *Education:* New York Institute of Technology (B.S.M.E., 1985); New York Law school (J.D., 1990). ***PRACTICE AREAS:*** Patents; Trademarks; Copyrights; Intellectual Property Litigation.

DEL SOLE & DEL SOLE, L.L.P.

27 ELM STREET

NEW HAVEN, CONNECTICUT 06510

Telephone: 203-785-8500

Fax: 203-777-4485

Email: delsole@delsoledelsole.com

URL: http://www.lawyers.com/delsoledelsole

Mailing Address: 46 South Whittlesey Avenue, Wallingford, Connecticut 06492

Wallingford, Connecticut Office: 46 South Whittlesey Avenue, 06492. Telephone: 203-284-8000. Fax: 203-284-9800.

Trials and Appeals in all Courts. General, Tort and Malpractice, Litigation, Probate, Workers Compensation, Corporate, Real Estate Law and Insurance Law.

FIRM PROFILE: Del Sole & Del Sole is a mid-sized firm specializing in civil litigation of all types, with a significant concentration in the defense of personal injury claims. The firm provides representation to insurers, manufacturers, health care and other municipalities, professionals, national trucking companies and other corporations in diverse areas including products liability, medical and other professional negligence, vehicular mishaps, actions for declaratory relief, insurance coverage litigation and general liability issues.

The firm also practices in the areas of commercial and residential real estate, corporate law, workers's compensation and probate. It handles matters before all state and federal tribunals within the state of Connecticut, at both the trial and appellate levels, and has substantial expertise in mediation and arbitration. The firm is listed in the Bar Register of Preeminent Lawyers.

MEMBERS OF FIRM

STEPHEN P. DEL SOLE, born Brooklyn, New York, March 27, 1952; admitted to bar, 1977, Connecticut; 1979, U.S. District Court, District of Connecticut. *Education:* Boston College (B.A., 1974); Brooklyn Law School (J.D., 1977). *Member:* New Haven County and Connecticut Bar Associations; The Connecticut Defense Lawyers Association; Defense Research Institute. ***PRACTICE AREAS:*** Litigation; Insurance Law. ***Email:*** sdelsole@delsoledelsole.com

MICHAEL P. DEL SOLE, born Brooklyn, New York, August 13, 1953; admitted to bar, 1979, Connecticut; 1980, U.S. District Court of Connecticut; 1993, U.S. Court of Appeals, Second Circuit. *Education:* Boston College (A.B., summa cum laude, 1975); University of Connecticut (J.D., with honors, 1979). Recipient, American Jurisprudence Award in Civil Procedure. Law Clerk to the Judges of the Appellate Session of the Connecticut Superior Court, 1979-1980. *Member:* New Haven County and Connecticut Bar Associations; The Connecticut Defense Lawyers Association. ***REPORTED CASES:*** Gaetano Marino v. Edward J. Peters, 39 Conn. App. 907; Aetna Life and Casualty Co. v. Braccidiferro, 232 Conn. 901; Remington v. Aetna Casualty and Surety Co., 35 Conn. App. 581; Aetna Life and Casualty Co. v. Braccidiferro, 34 Conn. App. 833; Mulrooney v. Wambolt, 215 Conn. 211; Connell v. Colwell, 214 Conn. 242; Olstza v. Fenton, 19 Conn. App. 802; Vessichio v. Hollenbeck, 18 Conn. App. 515; Maloney v. Conroy, 208 Conn. 392; General Motors Acceptance Corp. v. Pumphrey, 13 Conn. App. 223; Zichichi v. Middlesex Memorial Hospital, 204 Conn. 399; Wesson v. City of Milford, 5 Conn. App. 369; Conti v. Rose Hill Poultry Co., Inc., 3 Conn. App. 246; Sturdivant v. Yale-New Haven Hospital, 2 Conn. App. 103; Pavlinko v. Yale-New Haven Hospital, 192 Conn. 138; American Laundry Machinery, Inc. v. Hartford National Bank, 190 Conn. 212; Exel Logistics v. Maryland Casualty Co., 40 Conn. App. 415. ***PRACTICE AREAS:*** Litigation; Insurance Law; Appellate Practice. ***Email:*** mdelsole@delsoledelsole.com

DENISE DEL SOLE-KENNEDY, born Meriden, Connecticut, July 18, 1957; admitted to bar, 1990, Connecticut and U.S. District Court, District of Connecticut. *Education:* Quinnipiac College (A.S., 1977; B.A., 1980); University of Bridgeport (J.D., 1988). *Member:* New Haven County and Connecticut Bar Associations; Connecticut Defense Lawyers Association. ***PRACTICE AREAS:*** Litigation; Real Estate Law.

ASSOCIATES

ELLEN M. COSTELLO, born Waterbury, Connecticut, July 31, 1947; admitted to bar, 1988, Connecticut; U.S. District Court, District of Connecticut. *Education:* St. Joseph's College (B.S., Health Care Administration, 1984); Suffolk University (J.D., 1988). Registered Nurse: Connecticut and Massachusetts, 1968; District of Columbia and Bridgeport, Connecticut, 1971; Pennsylvania, 1976. *Member:* Connecticut and American Bar Associations; American Association of Nurse Attorneys (Director and Treasurer, Connecticut Chapter); Connecticut Defense Lawyers Association. ***PRACTICE AREAS:*** Medical and Dental Malpractice; General Litigation.

RENE GERARD MARTINEAU, born Lowell, Massachusetts, September 4, 1961; admitted to bar, 1987, Connecticut; 1988, Massachusetts and U.S. District Court, District of Massachusetts; 1992, U.S. Supreme Court. *Education:* University of Lowell (B.S., cum laude, 1984); Western New England College of Law (J.D., cum laude, 1987). *Member:* New Haven County and Connecticut Bar Associations; Connecticut Defense Lawyers Association. ***PRACTICE AREAS:*** Civil Litigation. ***Email:*** rmartineau@delsoledelsole.com

EDWARD F. PIAZZA, born New Haven, Connecticut, July 16, 1941; admitted to bar, 1966, Connecticut; 1967, U.S. District Court, District of Connecticut. *Education:* Fordham University (B.S., 1963); Boston College (J.D., 1966). Member, New Haven Board of Aldermen, 1971-1976. Democratic Majority Leader of Board of Aldermen, 1973-1976. Deputy Corporation Counsel, 1980-1984. *Member:* New Haven County and Connecticut Bar Associations; The Connecticut Defense Lawyers Association. ***PRACTICE AREAS:*** Trials; Workers Compensation; Probate; Real Estate.

ALFRED P. BRUNO, born Derby, Connecticut, February 10, 1970; admitted to bar, 1997, Connecticut. *Education:* Bates College (B.A. History, 1992); Quinnipiac College School of Law (J.D., 1997). Member, Moot Court Honor Society, 1996-1997. National Family Law Moot Court Competition Semi-Finalist, 1997. Recipient: Distinguished Academic Achievement Award, Trial Practice; Outstanding Legal Scholarship Award. Bates College President's Advisory Committee, 1989-1992. *Member:* New Haven County and Connecticut

(This Listing Continued)

Bar Associations; Connecticut Defense Lawyers Association. ***PRACTICE AREAS:*** Insurance Defense Litigation; Personal Injury Law. ***Email:*** alfredb@delsoledelsole.com

OF COUNSEL

DOMINIC P. DEL SOLE, born Brooklyn, New York, January 25, 1926; admitted to bar, 1962, Connecticut; 1963, U.S. District Court, District of Connecticut. *Education:* University of Notre Dame (B.S., 1948); University of Connecticut (LL.B., 1962). President, New Haven County Insurance Claim Managers Council, 1958. Chairman, New Haven County Inter Company Arbitration Committee, 1961. Member, National Panel of Arbitrators, American Arbitration Association. *Member:* New Haven County and Connecticut Bar Associations; Defense Research and Trial Lawyers Association; The Connecticut Defense Lawyers Association; American Judicature Society. ***PRACTICE AREAS:*** Litigation; Insurance Law.

REPRESENTATIVE CLIENTS: Alexis, Inc.; Cigna Insurance Co.; American International Adjustment Co.; Automobile Club of Southern California; Chicago Insurance Co.; Chubb & Son; CNA Insurance Co.; Gerling-Konzern (Germany); Hanover Insurance Group; Occidental Fire & Casualty; The Orion Group; Process Technology Inc.; Puritan Insurance Co.; Recovery Services International; Reliance Insurance Co.; St. Paul Fire & Marine Insurance Co.; Security Insurance Co.; Zurich Insurance Co.; Podiatry Insurance Company of America; Harleysville Insurance Co.; State of Connecticut (Department of Transportation); Caterpillar, Inc.; Connecticut Limousine Service; Constitution State Service Co.; First National Supermarket, Inc.; Home Insurance Co.; Honeywell, Inc.; Textron, Inc.; The America Group; Great Atlantic & Pacific Tea Company; Crawford & Co.; Progressive Insurance Co.; National Continental Ins. Co.; Nissan Motor Insurance Co.; Travelers; First Trenton Indemnity Co.; Hubbell, Inc.; Motorists Insurance Co.; MIC/PDP; Countrywide Insurance Cos.; Transtar, Inc.; Kemper Insurance Co.; Integon; J.B. Hunt Transport, Inc.; APA Truck Leasing; Proline Carriers, Inc.; Utah Home Fire Insurance Co.; Fidelity and Deposit Company of Maryland; Safeco; Yasuda; ARAMARK; Associates Financial Services, Inc.; CHC Physicians; American Healthcare Indemnity Co.; CMIC; City of New Haven; CNA Health Pro; CNA Commercial Insurance; CNA Pro; Clarendon Insur. Co.; Allstate Insurance Co.; Naughton Insurance Co.; Coca Cola Bottling Co. of NY; Danbury Insurance Co.; Brown & Brown, Inc.; MAC Risk Management, Inc.; Stop & Shop; Encompass; Affinity Insurance Co.; Safeco Excess & Select; Cambridge Claims Service; RSK Co.; York Claims Service; Kendall Life Insurance Company; Gulf Risk Services; Utah Home Fire Insurance Co.; State Auto Insurance Co.; Liberty Insurance Services; Connecticut Specialty; Windsor Group; Temtex Industries, Inc.; Houston General Claims; Executive Auto Group; Smeal Manufacturing Company; Chesterfield Services, Inc.; SeaCo Insurance Co.; Tristar Risk Management; Lindsey Morden Claims Management, Inc.; Cunningham Lindsey U.S., Inc.; Edwards Food Services.

DISESA & DISESA

Established in 1984

385 ORANGE STREET

NEW HAVEN, CONNECTICUT 06511

Telephone: 203-781-0870

Telefax: 203-781-0861

Email: v.disesa@snet.net

General Practice. Real Estate, Trusts and Estates, Small Business.

JOSEPH D. DISESA (1944-1983).

VICTORIA M. DISESA, born New Haven, Connecticut, August 24, 1952; admitted to bar, 1979, Connecticut and U.S. District Court for District of Connecticut. *Education:* University of Pennsylvania (B.A., 1974); Georgetown University (J.D., 1978). Author: "Professional Responsibility: Issues for Solo Practitioners and Small Firms," Connecticut-Lawyer, Vol 5, No. 6, March, 1995. *Member:* New Haven County (President-Elect, 1999-2000; Member: Real Estate Committee, 1990—; Chair, Pro Bono Committee, 1992-1996; Executive Committee, 1992—), Connecticut (Member, Solo and Small Firm Practice, 1995—) and American Bar Associations. ***PRACTICE AREAS:*** Real Estate; Trusts and Estates; Small Business. ***Email:*** v.disesa@snet.net

APPROVED ATTORNEY FOR: Chicago Title Insurance Co.; Connecticut Attorneys Title Insurance Co. (CATIC).
REFERENCE: Fleet Bank.

GERALD P. DWYER

Established in 1964

377 ORANGE STREET

P.O. BOX 1975

NEW HAVEN, CONNECTICUT 06511

Telephone: 203-865-2392

Fax: 203-785-1749

General Practice, Negligence, Personal Injury, Municipal, Insurance and Arbitration Law. Trials in all Courts.

GERALD P. DWYER, born New Haven, Connecticut, February 16, 1936; admitted to bar, 1964, Connecticut; 1985, Massachusetts. *Education:* University of Connecticut (B.A., 1958; J.D., 1963). Town Counsel, Bethany, Connecticut,

(This Listing Continued)

1969-1990. Town Counsel, City of West Haven, 1989-1991. Member, Panel of Arbitrators, American Arbitration Association. *Member:* New Haven County, Connecticut and Massachusetts Bar Associations. ***PRACTICE AREAS:*** Negligence Law; Municipal Law; Insurance Law; Arbitration Law.

REPRESENTATIVE CLIENTS: Travelers Insurance Co.; Greyhound Lines; Greater New York Mutual Insurance Co.; Shell Oil Co.; Connecticut Insurance Guaranty Fund.

EARLY, LUDWICK & SWEENEY, L.L.C.

ONE CENTURY TOWER, 11TH FLOOR

265 CHURCH STREET

P.O. BOX 1866

NEW HAVEN, CONNECTICUT 06508-1866

Telephone: 203-777-7799

Fax: 203-785-1671

Email: INFO@ELSLAW.COM

URL: http://www.lawyers.com/elslaw

Plaintiffs' Toxic Tort Litigation, Products Liability, Personal Injury and Industrial Accidents, Workers' Compensation, Lead Paint Litigation, Asbestos Disease Litigation, Fen-Phen Litigation, FELA and Railroad Litigation, Criminal Law, Wrongful Termination, Malpractice, and Trials and Appeals.

JAMES F. EARLY, born Derby, Connecticut, April 23, 1946; admitted to bar, 1971, New Hampshire and U.S. District Court, District of New Hampshire; 1973, U.S. Court of Appeals, 1st Circuit; 1975, Connecticut and U.S. District Court, District of Connecticut; 1977, U.S. Court of Appeals, 2nd Circuit; 1987, Rhode Island. *Education:* Harvard College (A.B., 1968); Boston University (J.D., 1971). *Member:* New Haven County, Connecticut, New Hampshire and American Bar Associations; The Association of Trial Lawyers of America; Connecticut Trial Lawyers Association (Member, Asbestos Litigation Group). (Also Member, Early & Strauss, New York, New York). ***PRACTICE AREAS:*** Toxic Torts; Asbestos Disease; Lead Paint and Personal Injury Litigation; Trials. ***Email:*** jfe@elslaw.com

LINDALEA P. LUDWICK, born Duluth, Minnesota, July 17, 1945; admitted to bar, 1983, Connecticut and U.S. District Court, District of Connecticut. *Education:* University of Wisconsin (B.S., with honors, 1967); University of Connecticut (J.D., 1983). *Member:* Connecticut and American Bar Associations; Connecticut Trial Lawyers Association (Member, Workers Compensation Committee). (Also Member, Early & Strauss, New York, New York). ***PRACTICE AREAS:*** Trials; Workers Compensation Law; Asbestos Disease; Toxic Torts. ***Email:*** lpl@elslaw.com

ROBERT J. SWEENEY, born Danbury, Connecticut, February 10, 1952; admitted to bar, 1977, Connecticut; 1978, U.S. District Court, District of Connecticut; 1998, Rhode Island. *Education:* Providence College (B.A., magna cum laude, 1974); University of Connecticut (J.D., with honors, 1977). Lecturer, Juvenile Law and Criminal Justice, Department of Sociology, Southern Connecticut State University, 1977-1982; 1986—. Public Defender, State of Connecticut, 1979-1986. Member, Inland Wetlands Commission, Town of North Haven, 1986—. ***PRACTICE AREAS:*** Trials; Personal Injury Litigation; Civil Litigation; Criminal Litigation. ***Email:*** bsweeney@elslaw.com

BRIAN C. FOURNIER, born New Haven, Connecticut, November 22, 1969; admitted to bar, 1995, Connecticut; 1996, Massachusetts and U.S. District Court, District of Connecticut; 1998, Rhode Island. *Education:* Boston College (B.A., 1992); Catholic University of America (J.D., 1995). *Member:* New Haven County, Connecticut and Massachusetts Bar Associations; Connecticut Trial Lawyers Association. ***PRACTICE AREAS:*** Toxic Torts; Lead Poisoning; Civil Litigation; Criminal Defense; Personal Injury. ***Email:*** brianf@elslaw.com

CHRISTOPHER MEISENKOTHEN, born New Haven, Connecticut, May 20, 1974; admitted to bar, 1999, Connecticut and U.S. District Court, District of Connecticut; 2000, New York, Maine and U.S. District Court, Northern District of Texas. *Education:* University of Connecticut (B.A., with distinction, 1996; J.D., 1999). Phi Alpha Theta; Phi Delta Phi. Member, 1997-1999 and Articles Editor, 1998-1999, Connecticut Journal of International Law. Author: "Chemical Castration: Breaking the Cycle of Paraphiliac Recidivism," Social Justice, Vol. 26, 1999; "Sub Seabed Disposal of Nuclear Waste: An International Policy Perspective," 14 Conn. J. Intl. L. 631, 1999. *Member:* Connecticut, New York State and American Bar Associations; The Association of Trial Lawyers of America; Connecticut Trial Lawyers Association; New York State Trial Lawyers Association. ***PRACTICE AREAS:*** Products Liability; Personal Injury; Toxic Torts; Workers' Compensation. ***Email:*** cmeisenkothen@elslaw.com

ETHAN EARLY, born Dover, New Hampshire, March 29, 1972; admitted to bar, 1999, Connecticut; 2000, New York. *Education:* Princeton University (B.A., Philosophy, 1995); University of Connecticut (J.D., 1999). Member, 1997-1998, and Associate Editor, 1998-1999, Connecticut Journal of Interna-

(This Listing Continued)

EARLY, LUDWICK & SWEENEY, L.L.C., New Haven—Continued

tional Law. Author, "Flatow v. Islamic Republic of Iran and the Foreign Immunities Act: Is a Piece of Mind Enough?" Volume 14, Number 1. (Also Associate, Early & Strauss, New York, New York). ***Email:*** eearly@elslaw.com

MICHAEL J. LUZZI, born New Haven, Connecticut, December 22, 1962; admitted to bar, 1991, Connecticut; 1993, U.S. District Court, District of Connecticut. *Education:* Yale University (B.A., 1985); University of Dayton (J.D., 1991). Delta Kappa Epsilon. *Member:* New Haven County, Connecticut and American Bar Associations. ***PRACTICE AREAS:*** Tort Defense; Asbestos Defense. ***Email:*** mluzzi@elslaw.com

ENGELMAN & WELCH-RUBIN, L.L.P.

(Formerly Schwartz & Knight; Schwartz & Engelman)

278 ORANGE STREET
NEW HAVEN, CONNECTICUT 06510
Telephone: 203-787-4249
Fax: 203-785-8378

General Practice. Probate, Estate Planning, Corporate, Litigation, Family, Personal Injury and Appellate Practice.

MEMBERS OF FIRM

ROBERT J. ENGELMAN, born New York, N.Y., October 16, 1932; admitted to bar, 1959, Connecticut; 1960, U.S. District Court, District of Connecticut. *Education:* Yale University (B.A., 1954; LL.B., 1959). Phi Beta Kappa; Order of the Coif. Article and Book Review Editor, Yale Law Journal, 1958-1959. Law Clerk to Judge Robert P. Anderson, U.S. District Court, 1959-1960. Law Tutor, 1961-1963 and Visiting Lecturer in Law, 1966-1967, Yale Law School. *Member:* The Connecticut and American Bar Associations. ***PRACTICE AREAS:*** Probate Law; Estate Planning Law; Corporate Law; Family Law; Litigation.

LORI A. WELCH-RUBIN, born Waterbury, Connecticut, July 11, 1959; admitted to bar, 1991, Connecticut and U.S. District Court, District of Connecticut. *Education:* Harvard University (B.A., 1981); Columbia University (M.A., 1983); Yale University (J.D., 1991). Presidential Fellow, 1981-1984. Lecturer, Yale Medical School, 1989-1998. Law Clerk to Chief Justice Ellen Ash Peters, Connecticut Supreme Court, 1989-1990. *Member:* New Haven County and Connecticut Bar Associations; Connecticut Trial Lawyers Association. ***REPORTED CASES:*** Representative Cheshire Mortgage Services v. Montes, 223 Conn. 80 (1992); Ireland v. Ireland, 246 Conn. 413 (1998). ***PRACTICE AREAS:*** Litigation; Family Law; Appellate Practice; Divorce.

DAVID WELCH-RUBIN, born New Haven, Connecticut, November 27, 1954; admitted to bar, 1984, Connecticut; 1986, U.S. District Court, District of Connecticut. *Education:* Yale University (B.A., 1977); Columbia University (J.D., 1984). Phi Beta Kappa. *Member:* New Haven County and Connecticut Bar Associations. ***PRACTICE AREAS:*** Litigation; Family Law; Personal Injury; Divorce.

MAX H. SCHWARTZ (Retired).

J. STEPHEN KNIGHT (1912-1961).

REFERENCES: Sovereign Bank, Connecticut; Citizens Bank Connecticut.

ESTY & BUCKMIR, LLC

714 STATE STREET
NEW HAVEN, CONNECTICUT 06511
Telephone: 203-495-9999
Fax: 203-495-9662
Email: estyandbuckmir@aol.com

General Insurance Defense. Motor Vehicle, Premises Liability, Product Liability, Professional, Medical and Legal Malpractice, Construction Litigation, Commercial Litigation, Worker's Compensation and Miscellaneous Personal Injury Litigation.

MILES N. ESTY, born Bayshore, Long Island, New York, June 13, 1962; admitted to bar, 1989, Connecticut; 1990, New York and U.S. District Court, Southern and Eastern Districts of New York; 1991, U.S. District Court, District of Connecticut; 1992, U.S. Court of Appeals, Second Circuit. *Education:* Trinity College (B.A., 1985); New York Law School (J.D., 1989). *Member:* The Association of the Bar of the City of New York; New Haven, Connecticut and American Bar Associations; Connecticut Defense Lawyers Association. ***PRACTICE AREAS:*** Insurance Defense; Civil Practice.

ELIZABETH M. BUCKMIR, born Bridgeport, Connecticut, April 19, 1963; admitted to bar, 1988, Connecticut; 1989, U.S. District Court, District of Connecticut. *Education:* University of Connecticut (B.A., 1985); University of

(This Listing Continued)

Connecticut School of Law (J.D., 1988). *Member:* Bridgeport, Connecticut and American Bar Associations; Connecticut Defense Lawyers Association. ***PRACTICE AREAS:*** Insurance Defense; Civil Practice.

ASSOCIATE

MARLA L. SELIGSON, born New Haven, Connecticut, August 22, 1972; admitted to bar, 1998, Connecticut. *Education:* Southern Connecticut State University (B.S., cum laude, 1994); Syracuse University (J.D., cum laude, 1998). *Member:* Connecticut Bar Association; Defense Lawyers Association. ***PRACTICE AREAS:*** Insurance Defense; Civil Practice.

JONATHAN A. BEATTY, born New Haven, Connecticut, December 8, 1972; admitted to bar, 1999, Connecticut; 2000, U.S. District Court, District of Connecticut. *Education:* Boston College (B.A., 1996); University of Connecticut School of Law (J.D., 1999). *Member:* Connecticut and American Bar Associations. ***PRACTICE AREAS:*** Insurance Defense; Civil Practice.

REPRESENTATIVE CLIENTS: Nationwide Mutual Insurance Co.; Kemper National Insurance Cos.; Providence Washington Insurance Co.; Public Service Mutual Insurance Co.; Penn National Insurance Co.; National Indemnity Co.; Metropolitan Property & Casualty; Risk Services Inc.; Carl Warren & Co.; Airborne Freight; Costco Companies, Inc.; United Technologies, Sikorsky Aircraft Division; Lumber Insurance Co.; Housing Authority Insurance Co.

EVANS, FELDMAN & BOYER, L.L.C.

Established in 1937
261 BRADLEY STREET
P.O. BOX 1694
NEW HAVEN, CONNECTICUT 06507-1694
Telephone: 203-772-4900
Telecopier: 203-782-1356
Email: Judgment@Iconn.net

General Practice. Transactions and Litigation involving Commercial, Banking, Equipment Leasing, Corporation, Taxation, Estate Planning, Probate, Environmental, Real Estate, Condemnation, Negligence and Personal Injury and Employment Law. Trials in State and Federal Courts. Appeals, Administrative, Bankruptcy.

FIRM PROFILE: Evans, Feldman & Boyer serves the legal and credit departments of numerous financial institutions, commercial finance companies, banks and leasing companies by providing cost-effective representation throughout the state.

PHOEBE BENNET BOYER (Retired).

JACK H. EVANS, born New Haven, Connecticut, February 6, 1915; admitted to bar, 1937, Connecticut; 1948, U.S. District Court of Connecticut; 1963, U.S. Supreme Court. *Education:* University of Connecticut; Boston University (J.D., 1937). Recipient, John Eldred Shields' Distinguished Professional Services Award, 1992. Consultant, Veterans Administration Medical Research Service, 1973-1994. Member, Connecticut Advisory Panel—Judicial Performance and Evaluation, 1983-1992. Member: Advisory Board Quinnipiac College School of Law and Legal Studies Department, 1992—. *Member:* New Haven County (President, 1972-1973; Member, Committee on Admissions to the Bar, 1978—), The Connecticut (Chairman, Clients' Security Fund, Committee, 1969-1972; Vice President, 1980; President, 1982; Vice Chairman, Senior Lawyers Section, 1993-1994) and American (Member, Sections on: Real Property, Probate and Trust Law; Insurance, Negligence and Compensation Law; Corporation, Banking and Business Law; Chairman, Clients Security Fund Committee, 1976-1979; Member: Senior Lawyers Section, 1991—; House of Delegates, 1981-1984) Bar Associations. Fellow, American Bar Foundation. ***PRACTICE AREAS:*** Real Property Law; Probate Law; Trust Law; Corporation Law; Insurance Law; Personal Injury Law.

RICHARD C. FELDMAN, born New Haven, Connecticut, May 23, 1943; admitted to bar, 1968, Connecticut; 1969, U.S. Court of Appeals, 2nd Circuit; 1970, U.S. District Court, District of Connecticut; 1975, U.S. Supreme Court. *Education:* Rutgers University (B.A., 1965); University of Connecticut (J.D., 1968). Member, Legal Committee, Eastern Association of Equipment Lessors, 1983—. Co-Author: "Collecting a Judgement in Connecticut," National Business Institute, 1991 and 1994. Contributing Author: "Warranties," Equipment Leasing, Matthew Bender, 1995. Member, Panel of Commercial Arbitrators, American Arbitration Association. *Member:* New Haven County, Connecticut (Member: Commercial Law and Bankruptcy Section; Executive Committee, 1987—; Chairman, UCC Committee) and American (Member: Section on Real Property, Probate and Trust Law; Section on Business Law) Bar Associations; Commercial Law League of America. ***PRACTICE AREAS:*** Commercial Litigation; Banking Law; Leasing Law; Commercial Finance Law; Real Property. ***Email:*** judgment@iconn.net

KEITH R. AINSWORTH, born Trenton, New Jersey, March 17, 1965; admitted to bar, 1990, Connecticut; 1991, U.S. District Court, District of Connecticut; 1995, U.S. Court of Appeals, 2nd Circuit. *Education:* Tufts University (B.S., 1987); University of Miami (J.D., 1990). Editor-in-Chief, Environmental Law Bulletin, 1989-1990. Co-Author: "The 1994 Amendment to the Marine

(This Listing Continued)

Mammal Protection Act," Natural Resources & Environment, Spring, 1995. Board of Finance, Town of Haddam, 1992-1997; First Selectman, Town of Haddam, 1997-1999; Selectman, 1999—. *Member:* New Haven, Connecticut (Member, Section on, Environmental Law, 1991—; Executive Committee, 1994—); Young Lawyer's Environmental Law Committee, 1994—; Connecticut Trial Lawyers Association. ***LANGUAGES:*** French. ***PRACTICE AREAS:*** Environmental Law; Civil Litigation; Commercial Litigation. ***Email:*** judgment@iconn.net

JAMES P. BROCHIN, born New Haven, Connecticut, 1953; admitted to bar, 1987, Connecticut and U.S. District Court, District of Connecticut; 1990, U.S. Court of Appeals, Second Circuit. *Education:* Brown University (A.B., History, 1976); University of Connecticut (J.D., with honors, 1987). Co-Editor-in-Chief, Connecticut Bar Association Bankruptcy Bulletin, 1993-1995. Author: "Judgment Enforcement in Connecticut," National Business Institute. Commissioner, New Haven Development Commission. *Member:* New Haven County, Connecticut (Member, Commercial Law and Bankruptcy and Federal Practice Sections) and American (Member, Business Law Section) Bar Associations. ***PRACTICE AREAS:*** Commercial Law; Litigation; Bankruptcy. ***Email:*** jblaw@snet.net

REPRESENTATIVE CLIENTS: Advanta Leasing Corp.; AT&T Capital Corp.; Dyck & O'Neill; The Bank of New York; CIT Group; Chase Manhattan Bank; Conscco Finance Vendor Services Corp.; Hudson United Bank; Mortgage Guaranty Insurance Corp; Nations Bank; Finova Capital Corp.; De Lage Landen Financial Services; National Union Fire Insurance.
APPROVED ATTORNEYS FOR: Lawyers Title Insurance Corp.; Chicago Title Guaranty Co.

FARREN AND KING

Established in 1967

94 PROSPECT STREET
P.O. BOX 1989
NEW HAVEN, CONNECTICUT 06521-1989
Telephone: 203-562-9813
Fax: 203-562-3248
Email: administrator@farrenkinglaw.com
URL: http://www.lawyers.com/farrenandking

General Practice including Personal Injury, Workers Compensation, Domestic Relations, Real Estate, Criminal, Probate, Corporations, Labor Relations and Zoning. Trials and Appeals in State and Federal Courts. Municipal, State and Federal Administrative Practice.

MEMBERS OF FIRM

PAUL E. FARREN (1915-1992).

JACKSON T. KING, born New Haven, Connecticut, October 10, 1929; admitted to bar, 1960, Connecticut; 1961, U.S. District Court, District of Connecticut; 1967, U.S. Court of Appeals, Second Circuit. *Education:* Suffield Preparatory; Colgate University (A.B., 1952); Columbia University (LL.B., 1958). Phi Delta Phi; Kent Court. *Member:* New Haven County and The Connecticut Bar Associations; Connecticut Trial Lawyers Association. [Lieut., U.S. Marine Corps, active duty, 1953-1955]. ***PRACTICE AREAS:*** Personal Injury Law; Domestic Relations; Probate Law; Workers' Compensation; Criminal Law; Real Estate.

PAUL E. FARREN, JR., born Philadelphia, Pennsylvania, January 8, 1945; admitted to bar, 1969, Connecticut; 1975, U.S. District Court, District of Connecticut. *Education:* The Loomis School; Yale University (B.A., 1966); Northwestern University and University of Connecticut (J.D., 1969). Phi Delta Phi. Associate Court Advocate, Juvenile Court for the State of Connecticut, Second District at New Haven, 1975-1977. *Member:* New Haven County and American Bar Associations; The Connecticut Bar Association; Connecticut Trial Lawyers Association; American Trial Lawyers Association. ***PRACTICE AREAS:*** Personal Injury; Workers' Compensation; Domestic Relations; Real Estate; Trusts and Estates; Criminal. ***Email:*** pfarren@farrenkinglaw.com

SUSAN KING SHAW, born New Haven, Connecticut, June 24, 1959; admitted to bar, 1985, Connecticut; 1986, U.S. District Court, District of Connecticut; 1996, U.S. Court of Appeals, Second Circuit. *Education:* Colgate University (B.A., with honors, 1981); University of Connecticut (J.D., 1985). Note and Comment Editor, Connecticut Law Review, 1984-1985. Member, Connecticut Moot Court Board, 1984-1985. Winner, Alva P. Loiselle Upper Class Moot Court Competition, 1985. Author: Note, "Disparate Impact and Meaningful Access Under Section 504 of the Rehabilitation Act of 1973: Jennings v. Alexander," 16 Conn. L. Rev. 3, 1984. *Member:* New Haven County and The Connecticut Bar Associations; Connecticut Trial Lawyers Association. ***REPORTED CASES:*** Beers v. Bayliner Marine Corp., 236 Conn. 769 (1996); East Haven v. Afscme, 212 Conn. 368 (1989); Battista v. United Illuminating Company, 10 Conn. App. 486, 523 A.2d 1356 (1987). ***PRACTICE AREAS:*** Trials; Personal Injury Law; Workers' Compensation; Domestic Relations; Employment Law. ***Email:*** skshaw@farrenkinglaw.com

(This Listing Continued)

REPRESENTATIVE CLIENTS: Continental Transport Systems, Inc.; National Education Association Legal Services Program; St-Al-Mac Corporation of Connecticut; Universal Trucking Corp.; CDW Trucking, Inc.

JOHN A. FERRANTI

45 COURT STREET
NEW HAVEN, CONNECTICUT 06511
Telephone: 203-562-1354
Fax: 203-498-2692
URL: http://www.lawyers.com/jaferrantilaw

Real Estate, Personal Injury, Landlord and Tenant Law, Collections, Criminal Law.

JOHN A. FERRANTI, born New Haven, Connecticut, September 29, 1963; admitted to bar, 1989, Connecticut; 1990, U.S. District Court, District of Connecticut. *Education:* Villanova University (B.A., 1986); University of Bridgeport School of Law (J.D., 1989). Recipient, American Jurisprudence Trial Practice Award. *Member:* New Haven County, Connecticut and American Bar Associations; Connecticut Trial Lawyers Association. ***PRACTICE AREAS:*** Real Estate Law; Personal Injury Law; Landlord and Tenant Law; Collections; Criminal Law.

FINN DIXON & HERLING LLP

NEW HAVEN, CONNECTICUT

(See Stamford)

Corporate Law, Mergers and Acquisitions, Securities Law, Venture Capital Financing, Corporate Finance and Restructuring, Commercial Litigation, Banking and Lending Law, Bankruptcy and Workouts, Employee Benefits and the Federal and State Taxation of Businesses and Business Transactions.

RICHARD M. FRANCHI

NEW HAVEN, CONNECTICUT

(See Guilford)

Products Liability, Personal Injury, Medical Malpractice, Construction Law, Intellectual Property, Copyright Infringement, Copyright Litigation.

GALLAGHER & CALISTRO

1377 BOULEVARD
P.O. BOX 1925
NEW HAVEN, CONNECTICUT 06509
Telephone: 203-624-4165
Fax: 203-865-5598
URL: http://www.gallagher-calistro.com
Email: lawoffices@gallagher-calistro.com
URL: http://www.lawyers.com/gallagher-calistro

General Civil Litigation and Appellate Practice in all Courts. Personal Injury Litigation, Business Litigation, Commercial Litigation.

FIRM PROFILE: Since the firm's establishment by William F. Gallagher, the firm has maintained a practice focusing on personal injury and appellate matters. The firm primarily represents individuals throughout the state of Connecticut, and is listed in the Bar Register of Preeminent Lawyers.

For a list of Second Circuit, Connecticut Supreme Court and Connecticut Appellate Court reported decisions, and a full list of publications, see our website at www-.gallagher-calistro.com.

WILLIAM F. GALLAGHER, born New Haven, Connecticut, June 28, 1937; admitted to bar, 1963, Connecticut; 1964, U.S. District Court, District of Connecticut; 1966, U.S. Court of Appeals, Second Circuit; 1969, U.S. Supreme Court. *Education:* Fairfield University (B.S.S., 1959); University of Connecticut (LL.B., 1963). Recognized in The Best Lawyers in America for Appellate Litigation and Personal Injury Litigation. Author: "Connecticut Post Trial Motions," Connecticut Law Tribune Co., 1980. Co-Author: Connecticut Laws and Their Impact on Business Entities: Connecticut Product Liability Act, 64 Conn. B.J. Special Issue-364 (1990). Lecturer: Connecticut Bar Association Trial Advocacy Program, 1976-1990; Advanced Civil Procedure, 1993—; Connecticut Trial Lawyers Association, College of Evidence, 1987-1997; Supreme and Appellate Court Review, 1987—; Tort Reform, 1988-1990; Advocacy Seminars, 1983—. Assistant Corporation Counsel, West Haven, Connecticut, 1969-1972. Special Assistant State's Attorney, New Haven County, 1974-1982. Connecticut State Trial Referee, 1984—. Member: Board of Editors, Connecticut Law Tribune, 1986—; ; Legal Internship Committee, 1983—; Civil Rules Task Force, 1993—; Appellate Rules Advisory Committee, 1996—; Commission to Study the Attorney Grievance Process, 2000-2001. Editor, Connecticut Trial Lawyers

(This Listing Continued)

GALLAGHER & CALISTRO, New Haven—Continued

Association "Forum", 1993—. Advocate, American Board of Trial Advocates. *Member:* New Haven County (President, 1993-1994), Connecticut (President, 1999-2000) and American (Member, Family Law Section, Tort and Insurance Practice Section, Litigation Section) Bar Associations; Connecticut Trial Lawyers Association (President, 1990-1991; Member, Board of Governors, 1983—); American Judicature Society; The Association of Trial Lawyers of America; Trial Lawyers for Public Justice; Association of Professional Responsibility Lawyers; National Panel of Arbitrators; American Arbitration Association; American Academy of Appellate Lawyers. Fellow: American College of Trial Lawyers; American Bar Foundation; Roscoe Pound Foundation; American Academy of Appellate Lawyers. Charter Fellow, Connecticut Bar Foundation. (Certified as a Civil Trial Advocate, National Board of Trial Advocacy). ***PRACTICE AREAS:*** Civil Litigation; Trials; Appeals; Personal Injury Litigation. ***Email:*** wfg@gallagher-calistro.com

ROGER B. CALISTRO, born New Haven, Connecticut, May 21, 1954; admitted to bar, 1979, Connecticut; 1980, U.S. District Court, District of Connecticut. *Education:* Cornell University (B.A., with honors, 1976); Duke University (J.D., 1979). Special Public Defender, West Haven, Connecticut, 1979-1983. Assistant Corporation Counsel, New Haven, Connecticut, 1984-1988. Special Master, U.S. District Court, 1990, 1994. Lecturer: Connecticut Trial Lawyers Association, College of Evidence, 1992; Quinnipiac College School of Law, 1993, 1995; Trial Advocacy, Practising Law Institute, 1994. *Member:* New Haven County, Connecticut and American (Litigation, 1979—) Bar Associations; Connecticut Trial Lawyers Association; The Association of Trial Lawyers of America; State of Connecticut Civil Jury Instruction Committee Task Force. (Certified as a Civil Trial Advocate, National Board of Trial Advocacy). ***PRACTICE AREAS:*** Trials; Appeals. ***Email:*** rcalistro@gallagher-calistro.com

BARBARA L. COX, born Frankfurt a.m., Germany, February 16, 1951; admitted to bar, 1982, Connecticut; 1983, U.S. District Court, District of Connecticut; 1988, U.S. Court of Appeals, Second Circuit. *Education:* Wesleyan University; Pennsylvania State University (B.A., with highest distinction, 1974; Sigma Tau Delta); University of Connecticut (J.D., 1982). Recipient: Connecticut Law Tribune Award for Excellence in Writing; University of Connecticut Law School Library Award for Written Work of Excellence. Law Clerk to Honorable Ralph K. Winter, U.S. Circuit Judge, U.S. Court of Appeals for the Second Circuit, 1982-1983. *Member:* New Haven County, Connecticut and American Bar Associations; Connecticut Trial Lawyers Association; The Association of Trial Lawyers of America. ***PRACTICE AREAS:*** Trials; Appeals. ***Email:*** bcox@gallagher-calistro.com

THOMAS J. AIRONE, born New Haven, Connecticut, July 6, 1966; admitted to bar, 1996, Connecticut and U.S. District Court, District of Connecticut. *Education:* Bates College (B.A., 1988); Quinnipiac College School of Law (J.D., cum laude, 1996). Associate Editor, Quinnipiac Law Review, 1994-1995. Author: "Hedonic Damages and the Admissibility of Expert Testimony in Connecticut after *Daubert v. Merrell Dow Pharmaceuticals, Inc.*," 15 Quinnipiac Law Review 235, 1996. *Member:* New Haven County (Member, Court Relations Committee), Connecticut and American (Member, Litigation Section) Bar Associations; Connecticut Trial Lawyers Association (Member, Executive Committee, Young Lawyers Section); Association of Trial Lawyers of America. ***PRACTICE AREAS:*** Trials; Appeals. ***Email:*** tairone@gallagher-calistro.com

HUGH D. HUGHES, born Rochester, New York, April 20, 1970; admitted to bar, 1997, Connecticut; 1998, New York; 1999, Massachusetts. *Education:* Princeton University (A.B., Philosophy, 1992); University of Connecticut (J.D., cum laude, 1997). Member, Connecticut Law Review. Recipient, Cornelius Wickersham Prize in Constitutional Law. Law Clerk to Justice Francis M. McDonald, Jr., Connecticut Supreme Court, 1997-1998. *Member:* New Haven County, Connecticut and American Bar Associations; Christian Legal Society. ***PRACTICE AREAS:*** Appeals. ***Email:*** hhughes@gallagher-calistro.com

GARCIA & MILAS

A PROFESSIONAL CORPORATION

44 TRUMBULL STREET

NEW HAVEN, CONNECTICUT 06510-1001

Telephone: 203-773-3824

Facsimile: 203-782-2312

URL: http://www.lawyers.com/garciamilaslaw

Construction Litigation, Real Estate, Arbitration, Mediation, Commercial Litigation, Franchise Litigation.

RAYMOND A. GARCIA, born New Haven, Connecticut, February 9, 1950; admitted to bar, 1979, Connecticut and U.S. District Court, District of Connecticut; 1982, U.S. Court of Appeals, Second Circuit; 1985, U.S. Claims Court. *Education:* Southern Connecticut State College (B.A., 1971); John Marshall Law School (J.D., 1979). The Gavel Society. Executive Candidacy Editor and Associate Articles Editor, John Marshall Law Journal. *Member:* Connecticut (Member, Executive Committee, Construction Law Section) and American (Member: Litigation Section; Construction Disputes and Forum Committee) Bar Associations. ***PRACTICE AREAS:*** Construction Litigation; Franchise Litigation. ***Email:*** rgarcia@garciamilas.com

JANE I. MILAS, born Meriden, Connecticut, August 18, 1954; admitted to bar, 1986, Connecticut; 1987, U.S. District Court, District of Connecticut. *Education:* Bryn Mawr College (A.B., cum laude, 1976); Northwestern University (M.A., 1978; M.A., 1981); University of Connecticut School of Law (J.D., 1986). Member, Connecticut Law Review. *Member:* New Haven County (Chair, New Haven Women Attorneys Committee), Connecticut (Secretary, Executive Committee, Construction Law Section) and American (Member, Forum Committee on the Construction Industry) Bar Associations. ***PRACTICE AREAS:*** Construction Litigation; Contracts; Commercial Litigation; Real Estate. ***Email:*** jmilas@garciamilas.com

WILLIAM S. WILSON, II, born Middletown, Connecticut, April 17, 1966; admitted to bar, 1996, Connecticut; 1997, U.S. District Court, District of Connecticut. *Education:* University of New Hampshire (B.S.C.E., 1988); Western New England School of Law (J.D., 1996). *Member:* Connecticut Bar Association (Member, Executive Committee, Construction Section). ***PRACTICE AREAS:*** Construction Law; Contracts; Commercial Law. ***Email:*** wwilson@garciamilas.com

DOUGLAS A. FREY, born Norwalk, Connecticut; admitted to bar, 1995, Connecticut. *Education:* Worcester Polytech Institute (B.S.C.E., 1982); University of Connecticut (J.D., 1995). Phi Delta Phi. *Member:* New Haven County Bar Association. ***PRACTICE AREAS:*** Construction Litigation; Arbitration. ***Email:*** dfrey@garciamilas.com

WARREN F. SASSO, JR., born Derby, Connecticut, October 7, 1970; admitted to bar, 1997, Connecticut and U.S. District Court, District of Connecticut. *Education:* Fordham University (B.A., 1992); University of Connecticut School of Law (J.D., 1997). Recipient, Corpus Juris Secundum Award, in Civil Procedure. Member, Connecticut Client Advocacy Board. *Member:* Connecticut and American Bar Associations; Connecticut Trial Lawyers Association; The Association of Trial Lawyers of America. ***PRACTICE AREAS:*** Civil Litigation; Commercial Litigation. ***Email:*** wsasso@garciamilas.com

LORI A. PETRUZZELLI, born Bronx, New York, September 18, 1970; admitted to bar, 1995, Connecticut and U.S. District Court, District of Connecticut. *Education:* Fairfield University (B.A., summa cum laude, 1992); College of William and Mary (J.D., 1995). Member, Moot Court Bar. Administrative Justice, Moot Court Board. Best Brief, Rendigs National Products Liability Moot Court Competition. Associate Editor, William and Mary Journal of Women and the Law. Author: "Copyright Problems in Post-Modern Art," 5 DePaul J. Art. and Enter. Law 115. *Member:* New Haven and Connecticut Bar Associations. ***PRACTICE AREAS:*** Construction Litigation; Franchise Litigation. ***Email:*** lpetruzzelli@garciamilas.com

FREDERICK E. HEDBERG, born Meriden, Connecticut, September 20, 1966; admitted to bar, 1998, Connecticut. *Education:* University of Connecticut (B.S.E., 1988); Rensselaer Polytechnic Institute (M.S.E., 1991); Quinnipiac College (J.D., 1998). Outstanding Academic Achievement in Computer Law. Licensed Professional Engineer, 1993. Member, American Society of Civil Engineers, 1989-1995. *Member:* Connecticut Bar Association (Member, Construction Law Section). ***PRACTICE AREAS:*** Construction Law; Commercial Litigation. ***Email:*** fhedberg@garciamilas.com

STEVEN R. KOLODZIEJ, born Hartford, Connecticut, October 26, 1964; admitted to bar, 2000, Connecticut. *Education:* University of Connecticut at Storrs (B.A., 1986); Quinnipiac College School of Law (J.D., 2000). Note and Casenote Editor, Quinnipiac Law Review Association, 1999-2000. Author, "Prejudgment Interest on Antitrust Treble Damages in Connecticut after Westport Taxi Service v. Westport Transit District," 19 Quinnipiac L. Rev. 209, 2000. *Member:* New Haven County and Connecticut Bar Associations. ***PRACTICE AREAS:*** Construction Law. ***Email:*** skolodziej@garciamilas.com

(This Listing Continued)

GARRISON LEVIN-EPSTEIN CHIMES & RICHARDSON, P.C.

405 ORANGE STREET

NEW HAVEN, CONNECTICUT 06511

Telephone: 203-777-4425

Fax: 203-776-3965

URL: http://www.garrisonlaw.com

General Civil and Criminal Practice before State and Federal Courts. Labor, Employee Rights and Benefits, Personal Injury, Product Liability, Professional Negligence, Civil Rights, Professional Licensure and Discipline, Workers Compensation Law. Trials and Appeals.

(This Listing Continued)

JOSEPH D. GARRISON, born Merced, California, November 21, 1943; admitted to bar, 1968, Connecticut; 1970, U.S. District Court, District of Connecticut; 1974, U.S. Supreme Court; 1977, U.S. Court of Appeals, Second Circuit. *Education:* Wesleyan University (B.A., 1965); Cornell University (J.D., 1968). Lecturer: Connecticut Bar Association and Connecticut Trial Lawyers Association Continuing Legal Education Programs, 1981—; American Bar Association Legal Education Program, 1989—; National Employment Lawyers Association, 1990—. Listed in Best Lawyers in America, 1987—. Member, Task Force on the Due Process Protocol. *Member:* American Bar Association (Member, ADR Committee, Labor and Employment Section); College of Labor and Employment Lawyers (Board of Governors); National Employment Lawyers Association (Member, Executive Board, 1988—; Vice President, 1991-1992; President, 1993-1995); Connecticut Trial Lawyers Association (Board of Governors). ***PRACTICE AREAS:*** Employment Law; Personal Injury Law. ***Email:*** jgarrison@garrisonlaw.com

ETHAN A. LEVIN-EPSTEIN, born New York, New York, May 2, 1947; admitted to bar, 1972, New York and Massachusetts; 1974, U.S. Court of Appeals, Second Circuit and U.S. District Court, Southern and Eastern Districts of New York; 1975, U.S. Supreme Court; 1987, U.S. District Court, District of Connecticut; 1988, Connecticut. *Education:* Syracuse University (B.A., 1968; J.D., 1971). Adjunct Professor: Brooklyn Law School, 1980-1986; University of Bridgeport Law School, 1986-1988. First Assistant U.S. Attorney, District of Connecticut, 1986-1988. Assistant U.S. Attorney, Eastern District of New York, 1973-1979, 1983-1988. Assistant District Attorney, New York County District Attorney's Office, 1980-1983. Legal Advisor, New York City Police Department, 1972-1973. Best Lawyers In America, 2000. *Member:* Connecticut Bar Association; Federal Bar Council (Trustee, 1997—); National Association of Criminal Defense Lawyers; Connecticut Criminal Defense Lawyers Association; National Employment Lawyers Association. ***PRACTICE AREAS:*** Litigation; Criminal Law; Civil Law. ***Email:*** elevin-epstein@garrisonlaw.com

LEWIS H. CHIMES, born New Haven, Connecticut, February 11, 1960; admitted to bar, 1985, Connecticut; 1986, New York; 1989, Massachusetts; 1990, U.S. District Court, District of Connecticut; U.S. Court of Appeals, Second Circuit. *Education:* Tufts University (B.A., summa cum laude, 1982); Columbia University (J.D., 1985). Harlan Fiske Stone Scholar. Assistant District Attorney, New York County District Attorney's Office, 1985-1990. Co-Author, Connecticut Bar Association Federal Employment Law Update, 1996-1997. *Member:* Connecticut Bar Association; Connecticut Trial Lawyer's Association; Connecticut Employment Lawyers Association; Connecticut Criminal Defense Lawyers Association; National Employment Lawyer's Association. ***PRACTICE AREAS:*** Criminal and Civil Litigation; Employment Law; Personal Injury. ***Email:*** lchimes@garrisonlaw.com

ROBERT A. RICHARDSON, born Bethany, Connecticut, July 15, 1966; admitted to bar, 1991, Connecticut; 1992, U.S. District Court, District of Connecticut; 1995, U.S. Court of Appeals, Second Circuit; 1996, U.S. Supreme Court. *Education:* Pennsylvania State University (B.A., 1988); Ohio State University (J.D., 1991). Managing Editor, Ohio State Law Journal, 1990-1991. Recipient: American Jurisprudence Award; Judge Joseph Harter Award. Externship, The Honorable Herbert R. Brown, Supreme Court of Ohio, 1991. Author: "The Use of After Acquired Evidence in Employment Discrimination Cases," 9(1) St. John's Journal of Legal Commentary, Fall, 1993. Member, Executive Board, Connecticut Civil Liberties Union, 1996-1999. *Member:* Connecticut Bar Association (Member: Labor & Employment Division Executive Board, 1996—; Federal Grievance Committee, 1996—); National Employment Lawyers Association. ***PRACTICE AREAS:*** Employment Law; Criminal Defense. ***Email:*** rrichardson@garrisonlaw.com

JEFFREY S. BAGNELL, born Brighton, Massachusetts, May 20, 1966; admitted to bar, 1992, Massachusetts; 1993, Connecticut; 1998, U.S. District Court, District of Connecticut and Eastern and Southern Districts of New York. *Education:* College of the Holy Cross (B.A., 1988); Boston College (J.D., 1992). *Member:* Connecticut Bar Association; National Employment Lawyers Association; Connecticut Employment Lawyers Association. ***LANGUAGES:*** Spanish. ***PRACTICE AREAS:*** Civil Litigation; Employment Law. ***Email:*** jbagnell@garrisonlaw.com

---

STEPHEN J. FITZGERALD, born Danbury, Connecticut, May 13, 1963; admitted to bar, 1989, New York and Connecticut; 1998, U.S. District Court, Southern District of New York. *Education:* Boston College (B.A., 1985); Fordham University (J.D., 1988). New York County District Attorney's Office, 1988-1998. ***PRACTICE AREAS:*** Litigation.

MORRIS J. "MICKEY" BUSCA, born New London, Connecticut, December 20, 1947; admitted to bar, 1998, Massachusetts and Connecticut; 1999, U.S. District Court, District of Connecticut. *Education:* University of Connecticut (B.A., 1969); University of Massachusetts (M.S. in Labor Relations, 1980); Massachusetts School of Law (J.D., 1997). *Member:* Connecticut and Massachusetts Bar Associations; Connecticut and National Employment Lawyers Associations; Connecticut Trial Lawyers Association. [With U.S. Army, 1969-1971]. ***PRACTICE AREAS:*** Labor; Employment; Workers Compensation; Civil Litigation.

REFERENCE: Bank of New Haven.

THOMAS M. GEISLER, JR.

205 CHURCH STREET, SUITE 508
NEW HAVEN, CONNECTICUT 06510
Telephone: 203-787-0077
Fax: 203-773-1427
Email: T1827@aol.com
URL: http://www.lawyers.com/tmgeisler

General Civil Practice and Litigation in State and Federal Courts, Corporate, Commercial and Business Law, Appellate Practice and Arbitrations.

THOMAS M. GEISLER, JR., born Orange, New Jersey, January 16, 1943; admitted to bar, 1968, New Jersey and U.S. District Court, District of New Jersey; 1972, U.S. Supreme Court; 1974, New York and U.S. District Court, Southern and Eastern Districts of New York; 1975, U.S. Court of Appeals, Second Circuit; 1994, Connecticut; 1995, U.S. District Court, District of Connecticut. *Education:* Harvard University (B.A., cum laude, 1965; J.D., 1968). Recipient, "Litigation Star," Litigation Section, American Bar Association, 1997. President, Harvard Law Record, 1968. Author: "Proof of Violation of Federal Rule of Civil Procedure 11 and of Sanctions Thereunder," 47 am Jur Proof of Facts 3d 241 (1998); "Proof of Employer Liability for Sexual Harassment Claims Under Title VII of the Civil Rights Act of 1964," 52 Am Jur Proof of Facts 3d 1 (1999); "Proof of Matters by Judicial Notices," 60 Am Jur Proof of Facts 3d 175 (2001). Member, Board of Directors, Friends of the Harvard Law Record, 1997—. *Member:* Association of the Bar of the City of New York; Connecticut and American (Member, Litigation Section; Co-Chair, Publication Subcommittee, 1986— and Vice Chair, Trial Practice Committee; Editor, Trial Practice Newsletter) Bar Associations. [Lt., JAG Corps, U.S. Naval Reserve, 1969-1972]. ***REPORTED CASES:*** Middendorf v. Henry, 47 L.Ed.2d 556(1976); Ganton Technologies v. NIGPP, 76 F.3d 462 (2d Cir. 1996); Daw v. Westport, 63 Conn. App. 176 (Conn. App. 2001); Babcock & Wilcox Co. v. Allied-General Nuclear Services, 555 N.Y.S.2d 313 (1st Dept. 1990); Evanston Insurance Co. v. GAB Business Systems, 521 N.Y.S.2d 692 (1st Dept. 1987).

COLIN M. GERSHON

1 CENTURY TOWER, 5TH FLOOR
265 CHURCH STREET
NEW HAVEN, CONNECTICUT 06510
Telephone: 203-782-7798
Fax: 203-776-7075

Employee Benefits Law, Estates and Trusts.

COLIN M. GERSHON, born Keighley, Yorkshire, England, 1946; admitted to bar, 1971, Nebraska; 1975, U.S. Tax Court; 1976, Connecticut, U.S. District Court, District of Connecticut and U.S. Claims Court. *Education:* Colgate University (A.B., Honors in History, 1967); Washington & Lee University (J.D., 1970); New York University (LL.M. in Taxation, 1976). Author: Comment, "Ancillary and Pendent Jurisdiction in Federal Courts," Washington & Lee Law Review, Spring, 1970. *Member:* Connecticut (Member, Sections on: Estates and Probate; Legal Problems of the Elderly) and American (Member, Real Property, Probate and Trust Law Section) Bar Associations. [Lt., JAGC, U.S. Naval Reserve, 1971-1976]. (Also at New Haven Office). ***PRACTICE AREAS:*** Employee Benefits Law; Estates and Trusts.

MARSHAL D. GIBSON

PROFESSIONAL CORPORATION
Established in 1975
2 WHITNEY AVENUE
NEW HAVEN, CONNECTICUT 06510
Telephone: 203-562-8080
Fax: 203-624-3388
Email: mgibtax@aol.com
URL: http://www.lawyers.com/mgibson-tax-atty

Federal Income Taxation, Estate Planning, Corporate, Pension, Probate Law and Tax Litigation.

MARSHAL D. GIBSON, born Montreal, Quebec, December 14, 1944; admitted to bar, 1970, Connecticut, New York and U.S. Tax Court; 1971, U.S. District Court, District of Connecticut; 1972, U.S. Circuit Court of Appeals, Second Circuit and U.S. Claims Court; 1975, Florida. *Education:* Clark University (A.B., 1966); Brooklyn Law School (J.D., 1969); New York University

(This Listing Continued)

MARSHAL D. GIBSON, PROFESSIONAL CORPORATION, New Haven—Continued

School of Law (LL.M. in Taxation, 1970). Member, Connecticut Estate and Tax Planning Council, Board of Directors, 1981-1984. Chairman, Zoning Board of Appeals, Woodbridge, Connecticut, 1983-1995, 1997—. Connecticut Pension Consultants, Member, 1981-1990 and Director, 1985-1988. Town Moderator, Town of Woodbridge, 1994-1998. *Member:* Connecticut (Member: Section on Taxation; Executive Committee Young Lawyers Section, 1976-1980; Young Lawyers Tax Section; Chairman, 1976-1980), New York State and American (Member: Section on Taxation; Committee on Civil and Criminal Tax Penalties, Subcommittee on Criminal Penalties, 1975-1983) Bar Associations; The Florida Bar (Member, Section on Taxation). (Board Certified Taxation Lawyer, Florida Bar Board of Legal Specialization and Education). ***PRACTICE AREAS:*** Estate Planning; Pension; Federal Income Taxation; Corporate; Probate. ***Email:*** mgibtax@aol.com

REFERENCES: New Haven Savings Bank; US Trust Co. of CT.

GILLIS & GILLIS, P.C.

Established in 1978

TWO WHITNEY AVENUE, SUITE 502
NEW HAVEN, CONNECTICUT 06510
Telephone: 203-562-5104
Telefax: 203-495-6476
Email: gillislawct@snet.net
URL: http://www.lawyers.com/gillis&gillis

General Practice including Litigation, Personal Injury including Automobile, Fall Down and Work Related Injuries, Business, Family, Real Estate, Probate, Trust and Wills, Estate and Tax Planning, Criminal, Employment, Social Security Disability and Transportation Law. Trials in all State Courts, Federal Courts and Administrative Agencies.

FIRM PROFILE: Gillis & Gillis, P.C. has over 60 years combined experience practicing law in the New Haven area. The firm's objective is to alleviate their clients of all responsibilities so that they may have time to recover from any injuries they have received. The firm strives to obtain the maximum dollars and benefits possible through whatever course is necessary--negotiation or trial. Gillis & Gillis, P.C. offers their clients personalized service and a "no recovery, no fee" policy.

HOWARD T. GILLIS, born Derby, Connecticut, February 22, 1935; admitted to bar, 1960, Connecticut; 1961, Interstate Commerce Commission. *Education:* Choate Rosemary Hall; International Exchange Student, Stoneyhurst College, England; Yale University (B.A., 1957); Columbia University Law School and University of Connecticut School of Law (J.D., 1960). Phi Delta Phi. Member, National Moot Court Team, 1959. Commissioner, Superior Court, County of New Haven, Connecticut, 1960. Member of Panel, American Arbitration Association. *Member:* New Haven County, Connecticut and American (Member, Sections on: Family Law; Corporation and Business Law; Real Property, Probate and Trust Law) Bar Associations; The Association of Trial Lawyers of America; Connecticut Trial Lawyers Association. ***PRACTICE AREAS:*** Personal Injury; Worker's Compensation; Family Law; Business Law; Probate. ***Email:*** gillislawct@snet.net

JOSEPH L. GILLIS, born New Haven, Connecticut, August 9, 1963; admitted to bar, 1991, Connecticut and U.S. District Court, Southern District of Connecticut. *Education:* Choate Rosemary Hall; University of Colorado at Boulder (B.S., 1986); Vermont Law School (J.D., 1990). Commissioner, Superior Court, County of New Haven, Connecticut, 1991. *Member:* New Haven County, Connecticut and American (Member, Sections on: Litigation; Tort and Insurance Practice; Criminal; Family Law) Bar Associations; The Association of Trial Lawyers of America; Connecticut Trial Lawyers Association. ***PRACTICE AREAS:*** Personal Injury; Workers Compensation; Family Law; Criminal Law; Business Law; Probate; Social Security Disability. ***Email:*** gillislawct@snet.net

EDWARD M. GILLIS, born New Haven, Connecticut, May 10, 1965; admitted to bar, 1992, Connecticut. *Education:* Stratton Mountain School; University of Colorado, at Boulder (B.A., 1988); Vermont Law School (J.D., 1992). Commissioner, Superior Court, County of New Haven, Connecticut, 1992. *Member:* New Haven County, Connecticut and American (Member, Sections on: Litigation; Tort and Insurance Practice; Criminal; Family Law) Bar Associations; The Association of Trial Lawyers of America; Connecticut Trial Lawyers Association. ***PRACTICE AREAS:*** Personal Injury; Worker's Compensation; Family Law; Criminal Law; Business Law; Probate. ***Email:*** gillislawct@snet.net

LISA M. KOLB, born Pawtucket, Rhode Island, April 8, 1972; admitted to bar, 1999, Connecticut. *Education:* Rhode Island College (B.A., cum laude, 1994); Roger Williams University School of Law (J.D., cum laude, 1998). Delta Theta Phi. Member, 1996-1997 and Survey Editor, 1997-1998, Roger Williams University Law Review. Member, American Inns of Court, 1997—. Commissioner Superior Court, County of New Haven, Connecticut, 1999. *Member:* New Haven County, Connecticut and American Bar Associations. ***PRACTICE AREAS:*** Personal Injury; Workers' Compensation; Real Estate; Wills; Trust and Estates; Probate. ***Email:*** gillislawct@snet.net

(This Listing Continued)

ENZO A. PELLEGRINO, born New Haven, Connecticut, January 17, 1970; admitted to bar, 1997, Connecticut. *Education:* Southern Connecticut State University (B.S., 1992); Quinnipiac College School of Law (J.D., 1997). Phi Delta Phi. Recipient, Dean's Scholarship Award, 1994-1997; Academic Achievement Award, 1997. Associate Editor, Probate Law Journal, 1995-1997. *Member:* New Haven and Connecticut Bar Associations; Connecticut Trial Lawyers Association. ***LANGUAGES:*** Italian. ***PRACTICE AREAS:*** Personal Injury; Workers Compensation; Criminal Law; Divorce. ***Email:*** gillislawct@snet.net

APPROVED ATTORNEY FOR: Commonwealth Land Title Insurance, Co.; Stewart Title Guaranty Company; Lawyers Title Insurance.
REFERENCES: New Haven Savings Bank; Hudson United Bank.

EARLE GIOVANNIELLO

59 ELM STREET
SUITE 215
NEW HAVEN, CONNECTICUT 06510
Telephone: 203-777-4003
Fax: 203-777-3993
Email: egiovanniello@erols.com
URL: http://www.lawyers.com/giovanniellolaw

Commercial Litigation, Criminal, Appellate Practice, Foreclosures, Class Actions, Civil Rights and Bankruptcy.

EARLE GIOVANNIELLO, born Queens, New York, June 22, 1959; admitted to bar, 1985, New York, U.S. District Court, Eastern and Southern Districts of New York, U.S. District Court, District of Connecticut, U.S. Court of Appeals, Second and Fourth Circuits and U.S. Supreme Court; 1993, Connecticut. *Education:* Harvard University (B.A., cum laude, 1981); University of Michigan (J.D., 1984). Editor, International Law Review, 1983-1984. Trial Attorney, United States Department of Justice, 1985-1986. Assistant District Attorney, Kings County, New York, 1986-1989. Adjunct Lecturer, University of New Haven, 1999. *Member:* Connecticut Bar Association. ***PRACTICE AREAS:*** Foreclosures; Bankruptcy; Civil Litigation; Commercial Litigation; Appellate Practice; Civil Rights; Class Actions.

LAW OFFICES OF JERRY GRUENBAUM

205 CHURCH STREET, THIRD FLOOR
NEW HAVEN, CONNECTICUT 06510
Telephone: 203-498-6080
Fax: 203-498-6022
Email: jerry@seclawyer.org
URL: http://www.lawyers.com/gruenbaum

Corporate Law, Securities, Business Law, Business Tax, Mergers and Acquisitions, Trusts and Estates, International Law.

JERRY GRUENBAUM, born Israel, June 15, 1955; admitted to bar, 1979, Massachusetts; 1980, Florida; 1984, Connecticut; 1996, California. *Education:* Brooklyn College of the City University of New York (B.S., 1976); Northeastern University (M.S., 1982); Western New England College (J.D., 1979); University of Miami (LL.M., 1983). Phi Alpha Delta. Member, American Institute of Certified Public Accountants. Former Tax Attorney: Peat Marwick Mitchell & Company; Arthur Anderson & Company. Former Compliance Director, CIGNA Securities. ***PRACTICE AREAS:*** Securities Law; Corporate Law; Taxation; Franchise Law; Trust and Estate Law.

HARLOW, ADAMS & FRIEDMAN, P.C.

NEW HAVEN, CONNECTICUT

(See Milford)

General Civil Practice, General Civil Litigation in State and Federal Courts, Real Estate Conveyancing, Financing and Development, Zoning, Probate, Personal Injury, Commercial Litigation, Construction Law, Bankruptcy, Business Formations, Landlord and Tenant, Title Opinions, Trials and Appeals.

HOGAN & RINI, P.C.

234 CHURCH STREET, SUITE 803
NEW HAVEN, CONNECTICUT 06510-1804
Telephone: 203-787-4191
Telecopier: 203-777-4032
URL: http://www.lawyers.com/hogan&rini

Business Formation, Commercial Banking, Civil Rights Section 1983, Public Construction Law, International Commercial Contracts, Executive Compensation, Medical Staff Contracts, Real Estate Development, Probate Administration, Land Use Regulation, Limited Liability Corporations, Contested Trusts and Estates, Municipal Redevelopment, Mergers and Acquisitions, Civil Litigation, Commercial Real Estate Finance, Economic Development, Taxation, Banking Regulation, Business Development, Commercial Real Estate Development, Shopping Center Development, Corporate Law, Corporate Finance, Corporate Governance, Nonprofit Organizations Law, Nonprofit Corporations, Employee Benefits, Employer Rights, Estate Planning, Local Government Civil Rights, Municipal Law, Municipal Civil Rights, Municipal Redevelopment, Appellate Practice, Civil Appeals.

FIRM PROFILE: Hogan & Rini, P.C. and its predecessors have counseled individuals, foreign and domestic businesses and municipal economic development agencies for over two decades. The firm has assisted businesses from formation through public offerings, from regulatory compliance through governmental financing from sales of products through the enforcement of sales agreements and from shareholder and executive agreements through corporation successions. The firm's economic public development work includes advice to municipalities, their commissions, agencies and authorities on all aspects of development, including constitutional as well as statutory challenges to the plans, projects and activities.

REPORTED CASES: Arsen Lazaros, et al v. City of West Haven, et al 45 Conn. App. 571 (1997); George Thomas, et al. v. City of West Haven, et al., 249 Conn. 385 (1999).

JOHN W. HOGAN, JR., born New Haven, Connecticut, February 22, 1939; admitted to bar, 1964, Connecticut; 1965, U.S. District Court, District of Connecticut; 1969, U.S. Tax Court. *Education:* College of the Holy Cross (A.B., 1961); University of Connecticut (LL.B., 1964). Recipient: John Eldred Shields Memorial Distinguished Professional Service Award, Connecticut Bar Association, 1995; Connecticut Courts of Probate 1989 Citizen of the Year Award. Member, Connecticut Board of Healing Arts, 1967-1973. Vice Chairman, Connecticut Commission on Obscenity and Pornography, 1969-1971. Chairman, Governors Prayer Breakfast, 1973. Director, 1984-1989 and Chairman, 1989-1994, New Haven Development Commission. Director, New Haven Regional Leadership Council (1989-1996); Secretary/General Counsel, The Foundation of the Greater New Haven Chamber of Commerce, Inc. (1988—); Trustee, Saint Raphael Healthcare System, Inc. and Hospital of Saint Raphael, (1988-1996); Secretary/Director, Shubert Performing Arts Center, Inc. (1987-1994); Chairman, New Haven Urban Retail Center Advisory Committee, 1991-1993. *Member:* New Haven County, Connecticut (Banking Law, Business Law and Commercial Sections; Member, 1976— and Chairman, 1985-1991, Clients' Security Fund Committee; House of Delegates, 1978-1983; Executive Committee, Banking Law Section, 1981—; Chairman, Awards Committee, 1996—) and American Bar Associations. ***PRACTICE AREAS:*** Commercial Banking; Mergers and Acquisitions; Corporate Planning; Commercial Real Estate; Commercial Contracts; Shopping Center Development; Office Leasing; Estate Planning; Trusts and Estates; Wills; Probate; Nonprofit Corporations; Nonprofit Organizations.

JOSEPH L. RINI, born Cleveland, Ohio, May 14, 1949; admitted to bar, 1975, New York and U.S. Court of Appeals, Second Circuit; 1976, Connecticut and U.S. District Court, Southern and Eastern Districts of New York; 1977, U.S. District Court, District of Connecticut. *Education:* Boston University (A.B., cum laude, 1970); New York University (J.D., 1974). Special Assistant, 1977-1979 and Deputy, 1979-1981, Corporation Counsel, City of New Haven. Associate Counsel, 1977-1980 and General Counsel, 1980-1981, New Haven Redevelopment Agency. Trustee, Saint Brendan's Church, 1994—; Trustee St. Brendan Board of Education, 1988-1995. Director, Visiting Nurse Association of South Central Connecticut, Inc., 1993-1996. Director, VNA Health Services, Inc., 1996—. Vice President, New Haven County Bar Foundation, Inc., 1999—. Court Appointed Trustee, Practice Book 2-64 - Protect interest of clients of disbarred attorney. SBA Designated 504 Closing Attorney. *Member:* New Haven County (Executive Committee, 1984—), Connecticut (Litigation; Construction Law; Federal Practice and Planning and Zoning; Municipal Law and Governmental Relations Committee) and American (Litigation, Affordable Housing, Construction Industry, Law Practice Management, Government and Public Sector and State and Local Government) Bar Associations. [Capt., USAR, 1970-1978]. ***PRACTICE AREAS:*** Civil Litigation; Land Use Regulation; Local Government Law; Public Construction Law; Municipal Contracts; Economic Development; Municipal Redevelopment; Local Government Civil Rights; Municipal Civil Rights; Long-Arm Litigation; Civil Rights Section 1983.

(This Listing Continued)

SPECIAL COUNSEL TO: Krause Bia gosah, gmbH; Emil Kemper, gmbH; City of West Haven; New Haven Community Investment Corporation; Tallmadge Brothers, Inc.; Chase Manhattan Bank; South Central Regional Council of Governments; The David T. Lungrock Foundation; Foundation of Greater New Haven Chamber of Commerce, Inc.
GENERAL COUNSEL TO: Chapel Square of New Haven, Inc.; City of New Haven Parking Authority; Kemper Bakery Systems, Inc.; Krause America, Inc.; Precision Aerospace, Inc.; Juvenile Forensic Services, LLP; Starr Financial Group, LLC; Guilford Veterinary Hospital, LLP.
APPROVED ATTORNEYS FOR: Chicago Title Insurance Co.; Commonwealth Title Co.; Lawyers Title Insurance Co.; First American Title Insurance Co.; Fidelity National Title Insurance Co.
REFERENCES: Hudson United Bank; Chase Manhattan Bank.

HUDSON COOK, LLP

Established in 1997
BUILDING ONE, UNIT 7, 3RD FLOOR
85 WILLOW STREET
NEW HAVEN, CONNECTICUT 06511
Telephone: 203-776-1911
Fax: 203-776-1922
Email: contact@hudco.com
URL: http://www.hudco.com

Linthicum, Maryland Office: 971 Corporate Boulevard, Suite 301, 21909-2232. Telephone: 410-684-3200. Fax: 410-684-2001.
Gardena, California Office: 1515 West 190th Street, Suite 410, 90248. Telephone: 310-851-5522. Fax: 310-851-5526.
Charlottesville, Virginia Office: 301 E. Market Street, 22902. Telephone: 804-220-9310. Fax: 804-220-9311.
Clifton Park, New York Office: 632 Plank Road, Suite 201, 12065. Telephone: 518-383-9440. Fax: 518-383-9401.

Consumer Financial Services.

FIRM PROFILE: Hudson Cook, LLP is one of the nation's most highly regarded law firms practicing exclusively in the area of consumer financial services. Led by Thomas B. Hudson and Robert A. Cook, both Fellows of the American College of Consumer Financial Services Lawyers, Hudson Cook offers a full range of legal services to local, national and international clients.

Hudson Cook, LLP helps clients establish and maintain consumer financial service programs. The firm focuses on a wide array of issues that arise in connection with such programs, including documentation, consumer disclosures, and state licensing.

ELIZABETH C. YEN, born Chicago, Illinois, February 22, 1957; admitted to bar, 1980, Connecticut and U.S. District Court, District of Connecticut. *Education:* Yale University (B.A., cum laude, 1976); University of Michigan (J.D., cum laude, 1980). Author: "Single-Sex Schools and Sex Discrimination," 55 Connecticut Bar Journal 387, 1981. Board of Editors and Contributor, Banking Law Journal. Instructor: Continuing Legal Education Program, Connecticut Bar Association, 1984, 1986, 1987, 1990. Director and Vice President, Bank Compliance Association of Connecticut, 1992-1997. Director, Connecticut Mortgage Bankers Association, 1999-2000. *Member:* Connecticut (Member and Chair, 1984-1987, Executive Committee, Consumer Law Section; Member, Executive Committee, Banking Law Section; Member and Chair, Committee on Publications, 1993-1997; Association Treasurer, 1999-2000) and American (Chair, Truth in Lending Subcommittee, Committee on Consumer Financial Services) Bar Associations. ***LANGUAGES:*** French, German and Chinese. ***PRACTICE AREAS:*** Banking Law; Consumer Law; Financial Services Law. ***Email:*** ecyen@hudco.com

REPRESENTATIVE CLIENTS: Reynolds & Reynolds; The Chase Manhattan Bank, N.A.; Wells Fargo Bank; Bank of America; World Omni Financial Corp.; Mercedes Benz Credit Corporation; Auto One Acceptance Corp.; Banc One Corporation; Merrill Lynch Credit Corporation; Honda North America, Inc.; Toyota Motor Credit Corporation; Nissan Motor Acceptance Corporation; Transamerica Financial Services; MBNA America Bank; Long Beach Acceptance Corporation; Chase Auto Finance; Goldman, Sachs & Company; Smith Barney, Inc.; First Union; AutoNation USA Corporation; American Automobile Leasing Association; American Financial Services Association; National Automotive Finance Association; Harland Financial Services; Bank of America; PeopleFirst Finance; DealerTrack.com Inc; Stoneage.com; CityFinancial, Inc..

JACOBI, KAPPEL & CASE, P.C.

NEW HAVEN, CONNECTICUT

(See Milford)

Environmental, Real Estate, Planning and Zoning, Motor Vehicle Accidents, Personal Injury, Estate Planning and Administration, Business Law. Litigation in all Courts.

JACOBS, GRUDBERG, BELT & DOW, P.C.

Established in 1947

350 ORANGE STREET

P.O. BOX 606

NEW HAVEN, CONNECTICUT 06503

Telephone: 203-772-3100

Fax: 203-772-1691

URL: http://www.lawyers.com/jgb&d

Email: jacobslaw@jacobslaw.com

URL: http://www.jacobslaw.com

General Trial and Appellate Practice in all Courts. Personal Injury, Medical Malpractice, Product Liability, Insurance, Criminal, Constitutional, Civil Rights, Unfair Competition, Antitrust, Securities, Business Torts, Employment, Environmental, Real Estate, Construction and Family Law Litigation.

FIRM PROFILE: In 1947, Howard A. Jacobs joined the law practice of his father, Israel J. Jacobs, who began his law practice in New Haven in 1918. The present firm, Jacobs, Grudberg, Belt & Dow, P.C., has grown to 13 lawyers, with offices occupying all four floors of two joined and restored red brick townhouses, within walking distance of both the state and federal courts. The firm concentrates almost entirely on litigation. It represents plaintiffs in all types of personal injury claims, including those occurring through medical malpractice and product liability. It represents people in the defense of all types of criminal charges. It also represents people in family law litigation, in employment discrimination and wrongful discharge matters, and in other civil disputes. The firm also represents businesses in a broad range of civil and criminal disputes, including antitrust and business torts, stockholder and partnership litigation, securities litigation, breach of contract, employment, franchise and environmental litigation as well as civil and criminal RICO matters. The firm's practice is statewide in both state and federal courts.

Howard A. Jacobs (Personal Injury Litigation for Plaintiffs, Family Law), Ira B. Grudberg (Personal Injury for Plaintiffs, Criminal Defense, Business Litigation) and William F. Dow, III (Criminal Defense) are listed in The Best Lawyers in America. The law firm is listed in the Bar Register of Preeminent Lawyers.

ISRAEL J. JACOBS (1918-1963).

HOWARD A. JACOBS, born New Haven, Connecticut, November 28, 1924; admitted to bar, 1947, Connecticut; 1948, U.S. District Court, District of Connecticut; 1953, U.S. District Court, Eastern and Southern Districts of New York; 1961, U.S. Court of Appeals, Second Circuit; 1971, U.S. Supreme Court; 1981, U.S. Court of Appeals, Ninth Circuit. *Education:* University of Michigan (B.A., 1945; J.D. with distinction, 1947). Senior Editor, Michigan Law Review, 1946-1947. President, Plaintiffs' Trial Lawyers Association of Connecticut, 1961-1962. *Member:* New Haven County, The Connecticut and American Bar Associations; Connecticut Trial Lawyers Association; The Association of Trial Lawyers of America. Fellow: Connecticut Bar Foundation (Charter Fellow). ***REPORTED CASES:*** State of Connecticut v. Aillon, 164 Conn. 661, 295 A.2d 666 (1972) (criminal); Aillon v. State of Connecticut, 173 Conn. 334, 377 A.2d 1087 (1977) (criminal); United States ex rel. Annunziato v. Manson, 425 F.Supp. 1272 (D. Conn.), aff'd, 566 F.2d 410 (2d Cir. 1977) (criminal); Siligato v. Welch, 607 F.Supp. 743 (D.Conn. 1985) (insurance); Reinke v. Greenwich Hospital Association, 175 Conn. 24, 392 A.2d 966 (1978) (medical malpractice); Biller v. Lopes, 655 F.Supp. 292 (D.Conn. 1987) (criminal); Voloshin v. Voloshin, 12 Conn. App. 626, 533 A.2d 573 (1987) (domestic relations); Erickson v. Erickson, 246 Conn. 359, 716 A.2d 92 (1998) (wills); Issler v. Issler, 250 Conn. 226, 737 A.2d 383 (1999) (divorce). ***PRACTICE AREAS:*** Personal Injury Litigation; Domestic Relations Litigation. ***Email:*** hjacobs@jacobslaw.com

IRA B. GRUDBERG, born New York, N.Y., August 6, 1933; admitted to bar, 1960, Connecticut and U.S. District Court, District of Connecticut; 1963, U.S. Court of Appeals, Second Circuit; 1964, U.S. Supreme Court; 1978, U.S. Court of Appeals, Ninth Circuit. *Education:* Yale University (B.A., magna cum laude, 1957; LL.B., cum laude, 1960). Phi Beta Kappa; Order of the Coif. Instructor in Law, Yale University School of Law, 1961-1963. Visiting Lecturer, Yale University School of Law, 1976. Law Clerk to the Honorable J. Joseph Smith, U.S. Circuit Judge, U.S. Court of Appeals, Second Circuit, 1960-1961. *Member:* New Haven County, Connecticut and American Bar Associations; Connecticut Trial Lawyers Association (Treasurer, 1967-1968; Vice President, 1968-1969; President, 1969-1970); The Association of Trial Lawyers of America; National Association of Criminal Defense Lawyers; Connecticut Criminal Defense Lawyers Association. Fellow: American Board of Criminal Lawyers; American College of Trial Lawyers; Connecticut Bar Foundation (Charter Fellow). Certified as Criminal Trial Advocate by the National Board of Trial Advocacy. ***REPORTED CASES:*** United States v. Autuori, 49 F.Supp.2d 321 (D.Conn. 1998), aff'd in part, rev'd in part, 212 F.3d 105 (2d Cir. 2000) (criminal); Bohan v. Last, 236 Conn. 670, 674 A.2d 839 (1996) (personal injury); D'Addio v. Connecticut Insurance Guaranty Association, 30 Conn. App. 729, 622 A.2d 609, cert. denied, 226 Conn. 903, 625 A.2d 1375 (1993)

(This Listing Continued)

(personal injury); State of Connecticut v. Outlaw, 216 Conn. 492, 582 A.2d 751 (1990) (criminal); Rothstein v. United States, 735 F.2d 704 (2d Cir. 1984) (tax); Pfeiffer v. Silver, 712 F.2d 799 (2d Cir. 1983) (personal injury); SCM Corp. v. Xerox Corp., 463 F.Supp. 983 (D.Conn. 1978), remanded, 599 F.2d 32 (2d Cir. 1979), on remand, 474 F.Supp. 589 (D.Conn. 1979), aff'd, 645 F.2d 1195 (2d Cir. 1981), cert. denied, 455 U.S. 1016 (1982) (antitrust); State of Connecticut v. Onofrio, 179 Conn. 23, 425 A.2d 560 (1979) (criminal); Long v. Abbott Mortgage Corp., 459 F.Supp. 108 (D.Conn. 1978) (securities); United States v. Cappabianca, 398 F.2d 356 (2d Cir. 1968) (criminal); State v. Licari, 153 Conn. 127, 214 A.2d 900 (1965) (criminal); United States v. Cianchetti, 315 F.2d 584 (2d Cir. 1963) (criminal). ***PRACTICE AREAS:*** Criminal Defense; Personal Injury Litigation; Business Litigation; Appellate Practice. ***Email:*** igrudberg@jacobslaw.com

DAVID L. BELT, born Wheeling, West Virginia, January 13, 1944; admitted to bar, 1970, Connecticut and U.S. District Court, District of Connecticut; 1971, U.S. Court of Appeals, Second Circuit; 1974, U.S. Supreme Court; 1975, U.S. District Court, Southern and Eastern Districts of New York; 1981, U.S. District Court, District of Rhode Island. *Education:* Yale University (B.A., magna cum laude, 1965; LL.B., 1970). Phi Beta Kappa; Omicron Delta Epsilon. Co-Author: *The Connecticut Unfair Trade Practices Act,* (1994, Supp. 1996). Author: "The Connecticut Anti-Trust Act: A Guide to Interpretation," Vol. 54, No. 5, Connecticut Bar Journal, October, 1980; "Private Actions Under the Connecticut Unfair Trade Practices Act," Vol. 64, Special Issue, Connecticut Bar Journal, May, 1990; "Unfair Trade Practices," in Connecticut Lawyers' Deskbook (CBA, 1998, 2d ed. 2000). Lecturer: "Commercial Litigation," CTLA, November, 1978, 1982; "The Connecticut Anti-Trust Act: A Guide to Interpretation," CBA, November, 1980; "Recognizing and Analyzing the Antitrust Problem," CBA, 1982; "Recognizing and Analyzing the Antitrust Problem in Distribution," November, 1985; "Creative Uses of CUTPA by Business Plaintiffs" and "Defending CUTPA Actions," CBA, December, 1988; "Federal Appellate Overview," CBA, March, 1989; "Private Actions Under the Connecticut Unfair Trade Practices Act," CBA, May, 1990; "Initial Considerations in Case Evaluation," National Business Institute, Inc., October, 1990; "Current Issues Concerning the Connecticut Unfair Trade Practices Act," CBA, June, 1992; "The Connecticut Unfair Trade Practices Act: Developments - 1993," CBA, June, 1993; "Procedural Attacks on a CUTPA Complaint," "Discovery in a CUTPA Action," "Limiting Remedies in a CUTPA," and "Jury Trial of CUTPA Claims," CBA, June, 1994; "Private Actions and Remedies Under CUTPA," CBA, May, 1995; "Common Law Fraud and Misrepresentation in Connecticut," CBA, June, 1997; "Private Actions, Remedies and Jury Instructions Under CUTPA," CBA, May, 1998; "How to Try the CUTPA Case," CBA, May 2000. *Member:* New Haven County, Connecticut (Member, 1976—, and Chairperson, 1980-1983, Executive Committee, Antitrust Section; Member, Federal Practice Section, 1985—) and American (Member, Sections on: Litigation; Antitrust Law) Bar Associations; Federal Bar Council; Connecticut Trial Lawyers Association; The Association of Trial Lawyers of America; National Association of Criminal Defense Lawyers; National Health Lawyers Association; Theodore I. Koskoff American Inn of Court (Secretary, 1991-1992). Fellow: Connecticut Bar Foundation (Life Fellow). [Capt., Military Intelligence, USAR, 1965-1974]. ***REPORTED CASES:*** SCM Corp. v. Xerox Corp., 463 F.Supp. 983 (D. Conn. 1978), remanded, 599 F.2d 32 (2d Cir., 1979), on remand, 474 F.Supp. 589 (D. Conn., 1979), aff'd, 645 F.2d 1195 (2d Cir., 1981), cert. denied, 455 U.S. 1016 (1982) (antitrust); Pfeiffer v. Silver, 712 F.2d 699 (2d Cir. 1983) (personal injury); Madrigal Audio Laboratories, Inc. v. Cello, Ltd., 799 F.2d 814 (2d Cir. 1986) (trademark); Heller v. Champion International Corporation, 891 F.2d 432 (2d Cir. 1989) (employment); Automated Salvage Transport, Inc. v. Wheelabrator Environmental Systems, Inc., 155 F.3d 59 (2d Cir. 1998) (antitrust, environmental); Venterina v. Cummings & Lockwood, 117 F.Supp.2d 114 (D.Conn. 1999) (employment); Federal Paper Board Company, v. Amata 693 F. Supp. 1376 (D. Conn., 1988) (antitrust, civil RICO); Plessey Precision Metals, Inc. v. Metal Center, Inc., 31 B.R. 458 (Bankr. D.Conn. 1983) (bankruptcy); Plastic and Metal Fabricators, Inc. v. Roy, 163 Conn. 257, 303 A.2d 725 (1972) (trade secret); Feen v. Benefit Plan Administrators, Inc., 1999 WL 33972 (Conn. Super Ct. Jan. 13, 1999), 2000 WL 1398898 (Conn. Super. Ct. Sept. 7, 2000 (contract, unfair trade practices); Sabanosh v. Durant, 1997 WL 804871 (Conn. Super. Ct. Dec. 17, 1997) (intracorporate dispute); Alexander & Alexander of Connecticut, Inc. v. Cronin, 1996 WL 409227 (Conn. Super. Ct. June 27, 1996) (noncompete); Conning Corp. v. Davenport Group, 1992 WL98135 (Conn. Super. Ct. April 30, 1992), 1992 WL 329298 (Conn. Super. Ct. Nov 2, 1992) (unfair trade practices, tortious interference with contract, breach of fiduciary duty); Whitfield v. Cooper, 30 Conn. Supp 47, 298 A2d 50 (Super Ct. 1972) (product liability). . ***PRACTICE AREAS:*** Business Litigation; Antitrust; Business Torts Litigation; Employment Litigation; Appellate Practice. ***Email:*** dbelt@jacobslaw.com

WILLIAM F. DOW, III, born New Haven, Connecticut, December 7, 1941; admitted to bar, 1968, Florida; 1969, Connecticut, District of Columbia and U.S. District Court, District of Columbia and Middle District of Florida; 1970, U.S. Court of Appeals, District of Columbia; 1974, U.S. District Court, District of Connecticut; 1975, U.S. Court of Appeals, Second Circuit; 1977, U.S. Court of Appeals, Third Circuit; 1981, U.S. Supreme Court; 1995, U.S.

(This Listing Continued)

District Court, District of Vermont. *Education:* Yale University (B.A., 1963); University of Pennsylvania (LL.B., 1968). Lecturer, Yale Law School, 1975—. Trial Attorney, 1970-1973 and Chief of Juvenile Division, 1973-1974, Public Defender Service of the District of Columbia. Assistant U.S. Attorney for the District of Connecticut, 1974-1976. Chair, Public Defender Services Commission, 1992-1994. Member: Superior Court Criminal Division Task Force, 1993—; Judicial Selection Committee, 1993-1998; Second Circuit Committee on Admissions and Grievances, 1983-1993; Chair, Merit Review Panel Regarding Reappointment of Federal Public Defender for the District of Connecticut, 2000; Connecticut Law Revision Commission, Evidence Code Drafting Committee, 1995-1998; Task Force on Post-Verdict Interviews of Juries , 1996. *Member:* New Haven County (Member, Executive Committee, 1999—; Member, Committee for Development of Opportunities for Minority Lawyers, 1990—; Member, Continuing Legal Education Committee, 1994—), Connecticut (Member, Executive Committee Secretary 1989-1991 and Chair 1992-1994; Section for Administration of Criminal Justice, 1991; Co-Chairman, Trial Advocacy Seminar Program Committee, 1979—; Secretary, Special Committee on Certification of Specialists, 1981, Court Rules Advisory Committee, 1991—; Committee on Liaison with State Courts, 1991-1994; Federal Practice Section, 1988—(Executive Committee, 1995—; Chair, Criminal Practice Subcommittee; Awards Committee) and American Bar Associations; The District of Columbia Bar (Member, Committee for Revision of Criminal Jury Instructions for D.C., 1972); Connecticut Trial Lawyers Association; The Association of Trial Lawyers of America; National Association of Criminal Defense Lawyers; Connecticut Criminal Defense Lawyers Association (President, 1990-1992); Federal Bar Council. Fellow: American College of Trial Lawyers; American Board of Criminal Lawyers; Connecticut Bar Foundation (Charter Fellow). ***LANGUAGES:*** Spanish. ***REPORTED CASES:*** Clisham v. Board of Police Commissioners, 223 Conn. 354, 613 A.2d 254 (1992) (employment); State of Connecticut v. Morrissey, 216 Conn. 185, 577 A.2d 1060 (1990) (criminal); United States v. Dennis, 843 F.2d 652 (2d Cir. 1988) (criminal); Tsokalas v. Purtill, 756 F.Supp. 89 (D.Conn. 1991) (first amendment); Rauccio v. Frank 750 F.Supp. 566 (D.Conn. 1990) (employment); State of Connecticut v. Milum, 197 Conn. 602, 500 A.2d 555 (1985) (criminal); Williams v. Warden, Federal Correctional Institution, Danbury, Connecticut, 470 F.Supp. 1123 (D.Conn. 1979) (civil rights). ***PRACTICE AREAS:*** Criminal Defense; Personal Injury. **Email:** wdow@jacobslaw.com

JONATHAN KATZ, born Syracuse, New York, August 18, 1953; admitted to bar, 1979, Connecticut and U.S. District Court, District of Connecticut; 1981, U.S. Court of Appeals, Second Circuit; 1981, U.S. Tax Court; 1990, U.S. Supreme Court. *Education:* University of Connecticut (B.A., magna cum laude, 1975); Northeastern University (J.D., 1979). Phi Beta Kappa. Attorney State Trial Referee, 1991—. *Member:* New Haven County (Member, Environmental Law Committee), Connecticut (Member, Environmental Law Section) and American (Member, Environmental Law Section) Bar Associations; The Association of Trial Lawyers of America; Connecticut Trial Lawyers Association. ***REPORTED CASES:*** Coregis Ins. Co. v. Goldstein, 32 F.Supp. 2d 508 (D.Conn. 1998) (insurance); Shirvani v. Capital Investing Corporation, Inc. 112 F.R.D. 389 (D.Conn. 1986) (securities); Samperi v. West Haven Inland Wetlands Agency, 226 Conn. 579, 628 A.2d 1286 (1993) (environmental); Samperi v. Planning & Zoning Commission, 40 Conn. App. 840, 674 A.2d 432 (1996) (environmental); Van Dyck Printing Company v. Johnson Graphics, Ltd., 15 Conn. App. 119, 543 A.2d 1349 (1988) (contract). ***PRACTICE AREAS:*** Personal Injury Litigation; Environmental Litigation. **Email:** jkatz@jacobslaw.com

WILLIAM M. BLOSS, born Milwaukee, Wisconsin, November 1, 1957; admitted to bar, 1984, Connecticut; 1985, New York and U.S. District Court, District of Connecticut; 1986, U.S. Court of Appeals, Fifth Circuit; 1988, U.S. Court of Appeals, Second Circuit; 1995, U.S. District Court, Southern and Eastern Districts of New York; 1996, U.S. Court of Appeals, First Circuit and U.S. Tax Court. *Education:* Wake Forest University (B.A., cum laude, 1979); American University (J.D., summa cum laude, 1984). Omicron Delta Kappa. Articles Editor, American University Law Review, 1983-1984. Author: Note, "Gross Receipts Taxes: Toward Parity in State Energy Industry Taxation," 32 American University Law Review 873, 1983. Law Clerk to the Honorable Robert C. Zampano, U.S. District Judge, District of Connecticut, 1984-1985; Honorable Carolyn Dineen King, U.S. Circuit Judge, U.S. Court of Appeals, Fifth Circuit, 1985-1986. Defender Services Advisory Group, Administrative Office of the U.S. Courts, 1995-1996. Member, Board of Education, Town of Guilford, 1999—. *Member:* New Haven County, Connecticut (Chairman, Criminal Justice Committee, Young Lawyers Section, 1987-1991) and American (Member, Criminal Justice Section, U.S. Sentencing Guidelines Committee, 1991—) Bar Associations; Connecticut Trial Lawyers Association; The Association of Trial Lawyers of America; National Association of Criminal Defense Lawyers; Connecticut Criminal Defense Lawyers Association; Theodore I. Koskoff American Inn of Court. Fellow: Connecticut Bar Foundation. ***REPORTED CASES:*** Cowras v. Hard Copy, 56 F.Supp. 2d 207 (D.Conn. 1999) (first amendment); United States v. Autuori, 49 F.Supp.2d 321 (D.Conn. 1998), aff'd in part, rev'd in part, 212 F.3d 105 (2d Cir. 2000) (criminal); Bernet v. Bernet, 56 Conn. App. 661, 745 A.2d 827 (2000) (corporate dissolution);

(This Listing Continued)

Schaeffer v. Vera Wang Bridal House, Ltd., 64 F.Supp.2d 286 (S.D.N.Y. 1999) (personal injury); Automated Salvage Transport, Inc. v. Wheelabrator Environmental Systems, Inc., 155 F.3d 59 (2d Cir. 1998) (antitrust, environmental); Tsokalas v. Purtill, 756 F.Supp. 1737 (D.Conn. 1991) (First Amendment); United States v. Sicignano, 78 F.3d 69 (2d Cir. 1996) (criminal); Ranciato v. CIR, 52 F.3d 23 (2d Cir. 1995) (tax); Roesch v. Otarola, 980 F.2d 850 (2d Cir. 1992) (civil rights); Kamasinski v. Rubin, 764 F.Supp. 741 (D.Conn. 1991), aff'd 962 F.2d 3 (2d Cir. 1992) (civil rights); State of Connecticut v. Russell, 218 Conn. 273, 588 A.2d 1376 (1991) (criminal); United States v. Palacio, 735 F.Supp. 484 (D.Conn. 1990) (criminal); State of Connecticut v. Sierra, 213 Conn. 422, 568 A.2d 448 (1990) (criminal). ***PRACTICE AREAS:*** Criminal Defense; Civil Rights Litigation; Business Litigation; Appellate Practice. **Email:** bbloss@jacobslaw.com

DAVID T. GRUDBERG, born Hartford, Connecticut, December 11, 1960; admitted to bar, 1986, Connecticut and U.S. District Court, District of Connecticut; 1987, New York and U.S. District Court, Southern and Eastern Districts of New York; 1989, U.S. Court of Appeals, Second Circuit. *Education:* Yale University (B.A., cum laude, 1982); University of North Carolina at Chapel Hill (J.D., with high honors, 1985). Order of the Coif. Note and Comment Editor, North Carolina Law Review, 1984-1985. Author: Note, "Illinois v. Gates: A New Test for Informers' Tips," 62 North Carolina Law Review 1024; "The Safe Roads Act: The Constitutionality of the Roadblock and Chemical Test Affidavit Sections," 62 North Carolina Law Review 1230. Law Clerk to the Honorable Ralph K. Winter, U.S. Circuit Judge, U.S. Court of Appeals, Second Circuit, 1985-1986. *Member:* National Association of Criminal Defense Lawyers; Connecticut Criminal Defense Lawyers Association; New Haven County, Connecticut and American Bar Associations; Connecticut Trial Lawyers Association; Association of Trial Lawyers of America. ***REPORTED CASES:*** United States v. Autuori, 49 F. Supp. 2d 321 (D.Conn. 1998), aff'd in part, rev'd in part, 212 F.3d 105 (2d Cir. 2000) (criminal); Skakel v. Benedict, 54 Conn. App. 663, 738 A.2d 170 (1999) (privacy rights); Elm City Cheese Company, Inc. v. Federico, 251 Conn. 59 (1999) (trade secrets); United States v. Doyle, 130 F.3d 523 (2d Cir. 1997) (criminal); Conway v. Town of Wilton, 238 Conn. 653, 680 A.2d 242 (1996) (personal injury); United States v. Whiteley, 54 F.3d 85 (2d Cir. 1995) (sentencing guidelines); Lash v. Aetna Casualty & Surety, 236 Conn. 318, 673 A.2d 84 (1996) (personal injury); DeLuca v. Lord, 858 F. Supp. 1330 (S.D.N.Y. 1994), aff'd, 77 F.3d 578 (2d Cir.), cert. denied, 117 S. Ct. 83 (1996) (habeas corpus); United States v. Melendez, 41 F.3d 797 (2d Cir. 1994) (criminal); United States v. Duncan, 42 F.3d 97 (2d Cir. 1994) (criminal); United States v. Bonds, 933 F.2d 152 (2d Cir. 1991) (criminal); United States v. Nerlinger, 862 F.2d 967 (2d Cir. 1988) (criminal). ***PRACTICE AREAS:*** Criminal Defense; Personal Injury Litigation; Business Litigation; Appellate Practice. **Email:** dgrudberg@jacobslaw.com

STEVEN J. DEFRANK, born Passaic, New Jersey, July 1, 1958; admitted to bar, 1988, Connecticut; 1990, U.S. District Court, District of Connecticut; 1991, U.S. Court of Appeals, Second Circuit. *Education:* Ramapo College (B.A., 1982); University of Bridgeport (J.D., 1988). Phi Delta Phi (Treasurer, 1988). Lead Articles Editor, University of Bridgeport Law Review. *Member:* Connecticut Bar Association; The Association of Trial Lawyers of America; Connecticut Trial Lawyers Association. ***REPORTED CASES:*** Giles v. City of New Haven, 228 Conn. 441, 636 A.2d 1335 (1994) (personal injury); Bourquin v. Melsungen, 40 Conn. App. 302, 670 A.2d 1322 (1996) (wrongful death). ***PRACTICE AREAS:*** Personal Injury Litigation; Product Liability Litigation. **Email:** sdefrank@jacobslaw.com

BERNARD C. CHRISTIANSON, born Bridgeport, Connecticut, September 2, 1944; admitted to bar, 1987, Connecticut. *Education:* Fairfield University (B.A., 1966); University of Rhode Island (M.A., 1972); Southern Connecticut State College (M.S., 1975); University of Connecticut (J.D., 1987). Arbitration Panel Member, State Department of Education, 1987-1992. Member, Mediation Panel, State Department of Education, 1980-1994. *Member:* New Haven County, Connecticut (Member, Family Law Section) and American Bar Associations; Connecticut Trial Lawyers Association; The Association of Trial Lawyers of America. ***PRACTICE AREAS:*** Matrimonial and Family Law. **Email:** bchristianson@jacobslaw.com

---

JOSEPH J. PACKTOR, born Hamden, Connecticut, September 30, 1963; admitted to bar, 1991, Connecticut; 1992, U.S. District Court, District of Connecticut; 2000, U.S. District Court, Southern and Eastern Districts of New York. *Education:* University of Central Florida (B.A., cum laude, 1988); Duke University Law School (J.D., with honors, 1991). Recipient, American Jurisprudence Award in Contracts and Trial Practice. *Member:* Connecticut Bar Association; Connecticut Trial Lawyers Association; Theodore I. Koskoff American Inn of Court. ***REPORTED CASES:*** Fullerton v. Department of Revenue Services, Gaming Policy Board, 245 Conn. 601, 714 A.2d 1203 (1998) (gaming); Lukos v. Bettencourt, 23 F.Supp. 2d 175 (D.Conn, 1998) (civil rights); Custard v. Ins. Adjusters, Inc. v. Nardi, 2000 WL 562318 (Conn. Super. Ct. April 20, 2000) (non-compete, interference with contract, trade secrets, unfair trade prac-

(This Listing Continued)

JACOBS, GRUDBERG, BELT & DOW, P.C., New Haven—Continued

tices). ***PRACTICE AREAS:*** Personal Injury Litigation; Business Litigation; Employment Litigation; Medical Malpractice; Products Liability Litigation. ***Email:*** jpacktor@jacobslaw.com

ROSEMARIE PAINE, born New Haven, Connecticut, September 16, 1966; admitted to bar, 1992, Connecticut; 1993, New York; 1995, U.S. District Court, District of Connecticut; 1996, U.S. Court of Appeals, Second Circuit; 1999, U.S. District Court, Southern and Eastern Districts of New York. *Education:* Southern Connecticut State College (B.S., 1989); University of Connecticut (J.D., 1992). Board Member, West Haven Land Trust, 1997-1998. *Member:* New Haven County (Executive Board Member, 1997-1998) and Connecticut Bar Associations; Connecticut Trial Lawyers Association. ***PRACTICE AREAS:*** Personal Injury Litigation; Criminal Defense; Civil Rights Litigation. ***Email:*** rpaine@jacobslaw.com

ALINOR C. STERLING, born San Francisco, California, May 16, 1967; admitted to bar, 1996, Connecticut; 1997, New York and U.S. District Court, District of Connecticut; 1999, U.S. Court of Appeals, Second Circuit. *Education:* Princeton University (B.A., 1989); University of California at Los Angeles (J.D., 1995). Order of the Coif. Member, UCLA Law Review; Articles Editor, UCLA Women's Law Journal. Law Clerk to the Honorable Lourdes G. Baird, U.S. District Judge, Central District of California, 1995-1996. *Member:* New Haven County and American Bar Associations. ***LANGUAGES:*** French; Russian. ***REPORTED CASES:*** Erickson v. Erickson, 246 Conn. 359, 716 A.2d 92 (1998) (wills); State of Connecticut v. Nunes, 61 Conn. App. 668, —A.2d— (2001) (criminal); Coregis Ins. Co. v. Goldstein, 32 F.Supp. 2d 508 (D.Conn. 1998) (insurance). . ***PRACTICE AREAS:*** Litigation. ***Email:*** asterling@jacobslaw.com

TRISHA MORRIS PORTO, born New Bedford, Massachusetts, February 10, 1969; admitted to bar, 1995, Connecticut; 1997, U.S. District Court, District of Connecticut. *Education:* Northeastern University (B.A., summa cum laude, 1992; J.D., 1995). Teaching Assistant, Legal Practice Program, Northeastern University School of Law, 1995. Law Clerk to the Honorable Janet Bond Arterton, U.S. District Judge, District of Connecticut, 1996-1998. *Member:* New Haven County, Connecticut and American Bar Associations. ***PRACTICE AREAS:*** Business Litigation; Personal Injury Litigation.

REPRESENTATIVE CLIENTS: *Business Torts and Unfair Trade Practices:* The Council for Tobacco Research - U.S.A., Inc.; Ragozzino Foods, Inc.; Sharp Electronics, Inc.; CBS, Inc.; Macmillan, Inc.; Simon & Schuster, Inc.; WVIT, Inc.; Norwest Corp.; Matsushita Corporation of America. *Contract Litigation:* Van Dyck Press, Ltd.; Star Distributors, Inc. Williams Energy Services. *Employment Litigation:* Paramount Communications, Inc.; E.&J. Gallo Winery; United Aluminum Corporation; Champion International Corp.; Valassis Communications, Inc.; Collagen Corporation. *Environmental Litigation:* Heyman Properties; Simkins Industries, Inc. *Insurance Litigation:* Mohawk Mountain Ski Area, Inc. *Real Estate and Construction Litigation:* ED-MOR Electric Co.; The Stop & Shop Companies, Inc.

JACOBS & JACOBS

Established in 1982

GRANITE SQUARE
700 STATE STREET, 3RD FLOOR
NEW HAVEN, CONNECTICUT 06511
Telephone: 203-777-2300
Fax: 203-787-5628
Email: info@jacobs-jacobs.com
URL: http://www.jacobs-jacobs.com

Practice Limited to Personal Injury, Medical Malpractice and Products Liability Law.

FIRM PROFILE: Jacobs & Jacobs concentrates almost exclusively on representing plaintiffs in medical malpractice, personal injury and product liability cases. Recent jury verdicts include: $9,000,000.00 (medical malpractice, birth trauma), $5,350,000.00 (FELA, electrical injury), $8,000,000.00 (medical malpractice, birth trauma), $1,500,000.00 (premises liability, closed head injury). Recent settlements include: $5,200,000.00 (emergency room malpractice), $6,000,000.00 (emergency room malpractice), $4,500,000.00 (medical malpractice, birth trauma), $3,000,000.00 (medical malpractice, family practice), $1,750,000.00 (medical malpractice, radiology).

MEMBERS OF FIRM

ISRAEL J. JACOBS (1918-1963).

STANLEY A. JACOBS, born New Haven, Connecticut, April 23, 1926; admitted to bar, 1950, Connecticut; 1951, U.S. District Court, District of Connecticut; 1953, U.S. District Court, Eastern and Southern Districts of New York; 1958, U.S. Court of Appeals, Second Circuit. *Education:* Yale University and U.S. Naval Academy (B.S., 1947); Yale University (LL.B., 1950). Lecturer, "Continuing Legal Education Program," Connecticut Bar Association, 1974-1988. Attorney Trial Referee, Superior Court Alternative Dispute Resolution Program, 1987—. *Member:* New Haven County (Treasurer, 1968-1973), Connecticut and American Bar Associations; Connecticut Trial Lawyers Association (Lecturer, 1986—); The Association of Trial Lawyers of America. ***LANGUAGES:*** Italian, Spanish, and French. ***REPORTED CASES:*** Mather v. Griffin Hospital 540 A.2d 666, 210 Conn. 125, 1988 (Medical Malpractice). ***PRACTICE AREAS:*** Personal Injury Law; Medical Malpractice; Products Liability Law; Civil Law. ***Email:*** sjacobs@jacobs-jacobs.com

BRUCE D. JACOBS, born New Haven, Connecticut, October 11, 1951; admitted to bar, 1977, Connecticut and U.S. District Court, District of Connecticut. *Education:* Washington University (B.A., 1974; J.D., 1977). *Member:* New Haven County and Connecticut Bar Associations; The Association of Trial Lawyers of America; Connecticut Trial Lawyers Association. ***SPECIAL AGENCIES:*** President, JCC of Greater New Haven. ***PRACTICE AREAS:*** Personal Injury Law; Medical Malpractice; Products Liability Law; Civil Trial Practice. ***Email:*** bjacobs@jacobs-jacobs.com

IRENE PROSKY JACOBS, born New York, N.Y., October 5, 1951; admitted to bar, 1986, Connecticut; 1989, U.S. District Court, District of Connecticut. *Education:* State University of New York at Buffalo (B.A., magna cum laude, 1973); Wesleyan University (M.A., 1980); Yale University School of Law; University of Connecticut (J.D., 1986). Phi Beta Kappa. Alpha Lambda Delta. *Member:* Connecticut and American Bar Associations; The Association of Trial Lawyers of America. ***LANGUAGES:*** French. ***PRACTICE AREAS:*** Personal Injury Law; Medical Malpractice; Products Liability Law; Civil Trial Practice. ***Email:*** ijacobs@jacobs-jacobs.com

CHARLES R. DOUTHAT, born Santa Monica, California, April 12, 1950; admitted to bar, 1982, Connecticut and U.S. District Court, District of Connecticut. *Education:* Stanford University (B.A., with distinction in history, 1972); Hastings College of Law, University of California (J.D., 1977). Special Master, Superior Court, 1990-1994; Attorney Trial Referee, Subcourt, 1997. *Member:* New Haven County and Connecticut (Member, Family Law Section) Bar Associations; Connecticut Trial Lawyers Association; The Association of Trial Lawyers of America. ***LANGUAGES:*** Spanish. ***REPORTED CASES:*** Worrell v. Sachs 41 Conn. Supp. 179, 363 A2d 1387 (1989) (Product Liability). ***PRACTICE AREAS:*** Personal Injury Law; Products Liability Law; Medical Malpractice; Civil Trial Practice. ***Email:*** cdouthat@jacobs-jacobs.com

KEVIN RYDER, born New Haven, Connecticut, January 28, 1949; admitted to bar, 1993, Connecticut; 1994, U.S. District Court, District of Connecticut. *Education:* University of New Haven (B.S., 1989); University of Connecticut (J.D., 1993). *Member:* New Haven and Connecticut Bar Associations. ***PRACTICE AREAS:*** Personal Injury; Medical Malpractice; Products Liability. ***Email:*** kryder@jacobs-jacobs.com

REFERENCE: BankBoston.

JACOBS, JACOBS & SHANNON, P.C.

Established in 1997

265 ORANGE STREET
NEW HAVEN, CONNECTICUT 06510
Telephone: 203-562-6111
Fax: 203-624-8752
Email: jjslaw@msn.com

General Trial Practice in all Courts. Tort, Personal Injury, Malpractice, Products Liability, Federal Employers Liability Act, Employment Discrimination, Criminal, Workers Compensation, Family, Eminent Domain, Appellate Practice.

FIRM PROFILE: A tradition of three generations of trial lawyers dedicated to giving competent, caring and aggressive representation.

ISRAEL J. JACOBS (1918-1963).

RICHARD L. JACOBS, born New Haven, Connecticut, May 5, 1930; admitted to bar, 1957, Connecticut; 1958, U.S. District Court, District of Connecticut and U.S. Court of Appeals, Second Circuit; 1973, U.S. Supreme Court. *Education:* Yale University (B.A., 1952; LL.B., 1957). Phi Beta Kappa; Phi Alpha Delta; Book and Gavel. President, New Haven Legal Assistance Association, Inc., 1969-1971. Member, Board of Directors, Friends of Legal Services, 1983—. *Member:* New Haven County (Member, Medical-Legal Committee, 1983—; Chairman, 1991-1995); Connecticut (Member, Executive Committee on Criminal Justice, 1963—) and American Bar Associations; Connecticut Trial Lawyers Association; The Association of Trial Lawyers of America; Connecticut Criminal Lawyers Association. ***PRACTICE AREAS:*** Personal Injury; Medical Malpractice; Products Liability; Workers Compensation; Federal Employers Liability Act; Employment Discrimination; Criminal; Family. ***Email:*** jjslaw@msn.com

STEVEN D. JACOBS, born New Haven, Connecticut, September 27, 1958; admitted to bar, 1985, Connecticut; 1986, U.S. District Court, District of Con-

(This Listing Continued)

necticut; 1994, Illinois; 1995, U.S Court of Appeals, Second Circuit. *Education:* Trinity College (B.A., 1980); University of Pittsburgh (J.D., 1985). *Member:* New Haven County, Connecticut, Illinois State and American Bar Associations; Connecticut Trial Lawyers Association; The Association of Trial Lawyers of America; Connecticut Criminal Defense Lawyers Association. ***PRACTICE AREAS:*** Personal Injury; Medical Malpractice; Product Liability; Federal Employers Liability Act; Criminal; Family; Workers Compensation; Appellate Practice; Employment Discrimination. ***Email:*** jjslaw@msn.com

JOHN M. SHANNON, born Jacksonville, Florida, January 24, 1962; admitted to bar, 1988, Connecticut; 1991, U.S. District Court, District of Connecticut; 1997, U.S. Court of Appeals, Second Circuit. *Education:* Florida Junior College (A.A., 1983); Florida State University (B.S., in Criminology, 1985); University of Florida (J.D., 1988). Golden Key. *Member:* New Haven County and Connecticut Bar Associations; Connecticut Trial Lawyers Association; Connecticut Criminal Defense Lawyers Association; The Association of Trial Lawyers of America. ***PRACTICE AREAS:*** Personal Injury; Medical Malpractice; Products Liability; Employment Discrimination; Workers Compensation; Family Law; Real Estate. ***Email:*** jjslaw@msn.com

REFERENCE: New Haven Savings Bank

JACOBS PARTNERS LLC

NEW HAVEN, CONNECTICUT

(See Norwalk)

Business and Personal Bankruptcy, Workouts, Debtor Creditor's Rights, Commercial Litigation, Contracts and Business Disputes.

JANUSZEWSKI, McQUILLAN AND DeNIGRIS

NEW HAVEN, CONNECTICUT

(See New Britain)

General Practice, Civil and Criminal Litigation, Real Estate, Family Law, Administrative Agency Proceedings, Workers Compensation, Personal Injury, Products Liability, Professional Malpractice, Probate, Representation to Professional Responsibilities, Trials in State and Federal Courts.

KAHN AND STARK, LLC

110 WHITNEY AVENUE
NEW HAVEN, CONNECTICUT 06510
Telephone: 203-777-0506
Facsimile: 203-777-9971
URL: http://www.mediator.com/divorceresources
URL: http://www.lawyers.com/kahnandstark

Family Law.

GERALD H. KAHN, born Buffalo, New York, August 11, 1944; admitted to bar, 1970, New York, Missouri and U.S. District Court, Western District of Missouri; 1971, Connecticut and U.S. District Court, District of Connecticut. *Education:* Yale University (B.A., 1966); University of Michigan (J.D., cum laude, 1969). Lecturer: Connecticut Bar Associations; Continuing Legal Education Program; National Business Institute; Law Education Institute. *Member:* New Haven County, (Member Family Law Section Executive Committee); Connecticut (Member, Family Law Section, Executive Committee; Chair, 1997-1998) and American (Member, Family Law Section) Bar Associations; Connecticut Trial Lawyers Association; The Association of Trial Lawyers of America. ***LANGUAGES:*** Spanish. ***PRACTICE AREAS:*** Family Law; Divorce; Custody; Alimony; Child Support. ***Email:*** ghkahn@snet.net

BARBARA KAHN STARK, born Baltimore, Maryland, March 19, 1950; admitted to bar, 1976, Colorado; 1992, Connecticut. *Education:* University of Maryland (B.A., 1972); University of Denver (J.D., 1976). President, Connecticut Council for Divorce Mediation. Member, Academy of Family Mediators. *Member:* The Colorado (Chair, Family Law Section, 1995), Connecticut (Member, Executive Council, Family Law Section) and American (Council Member, Family Law Section, 1999) Bar Associations. Fellow, American Academy of Matrimonial Lawyers. ***PRACTICE AREAS:*** Divorce Mediation; Divorce Collaboration; Divorce Financial Planning. ***Email:*** barbara.k.stark@snet.net

---

SHERI L. BERMAN, born Westerly, Rhode Island; admitted to bar, 1998, Connecticut. *Education:* Quinnipiac College (B.A., 1993; J.D., 1998). *Member:* New Haven and Connecticut (Family Law Section) Bar Associations. ***PRACTICE AREAS:*** Family Law. ***Email:*** sberman@snet.net

KENNEDY, JOHNSON, D'ELIA & GILLOOLY L.L.C.

LONG WHARF MARITIME CENTER
545 LONG WHARF DRIVE
NEW HAVEN, CONNECTICUT 06511
Telephone: 203-865-8430
Fax: 203-865-5345
URL: http://www.kennedyjohnson.com
URL: http://www.lawyers.com/kjdglaw

General Civil Practice. Personal Injury, Medical Malpractice, Professional Malpractice, Products Liability, Workers Compensation, Family Law, Real Estate and Probate Law. Trials before all State and Federal Courts.

MEMBERS OF FIRM

DAVID H. JOHNSON, born Lafayette, Indiana, April 17, 1950; admitted to bar, 1976, Illinois and U.S. District Court, Northern District of Illinois; 1979, Connecticut; 1981, U.S. District Court for the District of Connecticut and U.S. Court of Appeals, Second Circuit. *Education:* United States Naval Academy and University of Illinois (B.S., 1972); Chicago-Kent College of Law (J.D., with honors 1976). Legal Counsel, Illinois Department of Corrections, 1976-1978. *Member:* New Haven County (Lecturer: Continuing Education Program, 1987—) and Connecticut (Lecturer, Continuing Legal Education Program, 1987—) Bar Associations; Connecticut Trial Lawyers Association (Lecturer, Continuing Legal Education Program, 1987—); Association of Trial Lawyers of America. ***PRACTICE AREAS:*** Personal Injury Law; Medical Malpractice Law; Products Liability Law.

JOHN J. KENNEDY, JR., born New Haven, Connecticut, November 20, 1953; admitted to bar, 1978, Connecticut and U.S. District Court for District of Connecticut. *Education:* Yale University (B.A., 1975); University of Connecticut (J.D., with honors, 1978). Lecturer, Connecticut Continuing Legal Education Seminar, 1986—. *Member:* New Haven County (Treasurer, 1990-1991; President, 1991-1992), The Connecticut (Lecturer, Continuing Legal Education Program, 1987—) and American Bar Associations; Connecticut Trial Lawyers Association (Lecturer, Continuing Legal Education Program, 1987—; Member, Board of Governors, 1990—); The Association of Trial Lawyers of America; American Board of Trial Advocates. ***PRACTICE AREAS:*** Personal Injury Law; Medical Malpractice Law; Products Liability Law.

JOHN J. D'ELIA, born Hartford, Connecticut, September 24, 1961; admitted to bar, 1986, Connecticut. *Education:* Trinity College, Hartford (B.A., 1983); University of Connecticut (J.D., 1986). Member, Moot Court Board, 1985-1986. Awarded, Fifth Best Oralist and Writer of Best Brief, Philip C. Jessup International Law Moot Court Competition, 1986. *Member:* New Haven County and Connecticut Bar Associations; Connecticut Trial Lawyers Association. ***PRACTICE AREAS:*** Personal Injury Law; Workers Compensation.

DENNIS W. GILLOOLY, born New Haven, Connecticut, February 23, 1960; admitted to bar, 1986, Connecticut; 1987, U.S. District Court, District of Connecticut. *Education:* Trinity College (B.A., 1982); University of Connecticut (J.D., 1986). Arbitrator/Mediator for American Arbitration Association. Fact Finder/Arbitrator for State of Connecticut Superior Court. *Member:* New Haven County, Connecticut and American Bar Associations; Association; Connecticut Trial Lawyers Association. ***PRACTICE AREAS:*** Personal Injury Law; Products Liability Law; Workers Compensation; Professional Malpractice; Insurance Disputes.

ROBERT L. SCHWAB, born New Haven, Connecticut, December 20, 1959; admitted to bar, 1990, Connecticut; 1998, U.S. Supreme Court and U.S. District Court, District of Connecticut. *Education:* Amherst College (B.A., 1982); University of Bridgeport (J.D., 1990). *Member:* New Haven County and Connecticut Bar Associations; Connecticut Trial Lawyers Association. ***PRACTICE AREAS:*** Personal Injury; Workers' Compensation; Products Liability; Criminal Law.

ASSOCIATES

STEPHANIE Z. ROBERGE, born Teaneck, New Jersey, January 9, 1965; admitted to bar, 1990, Connecticut; 1991, New York and U.S. District Court, District of Connecticut. *Education:* University of Rhode Island (B.S., Pharmacy, 1987); Quinnipiac College (J.D., 1990). President, Moot Court Society. Member, Connecticut Pharmaceutical Association. Member, Representative Town Meeting, Town of Fairfield, 1993-1997. *Member:* Connecticut and American Bar Associations. ***SPECIAL AGENCIES:*** Connecticut Dept. of Public Health. ***PRACTICE AREAS:*** Medical Malpractice; Personal Injury; Commercial Litigation; Products Liability.

CHRISTOPHER D. DE PALMA, born New Haven, Connecticut, December 26, 1974; admitted to bar, 1999, Connecticut; 2000, U.S. District Court, District of Connecticut. *Education:* Fairfield University (B.A., 1996); Quinnipiac College (J.D., 1999). Recipient: Northeastern Regional Winner, ATLA,

(This Listing Continued)

KENNEDY, JOHNSON, D'ELIA & GILLOOLY L.L.C., New Haven—Continued

National Student Trial Advocacy Competition, 1999. Vice President, Mock Trial Honor Society, 1998-1999. *Member:* Connecticut Trial Lawyers Association. ***PRACTICE AREAS:*** Personal Injury; Workers Compensation.

REPRESENTATIVE CLIENTS: Yellow Freight Systems, Inc.; Bituminous Insurance Co.
APPROVED ATTORNEYS FOR: Security Title Insurance Co. (Issuing Agent); Chicago Title Insurance Co.
REFERENCE: Citizens Bank Connecticut.

KOSKOFF, KOSKOFF & BIEDER, P.C.

NEW HAVEN, CONNECTICUT

(See Bridgeport)

Litigation in all State and Federal Courts. Medical Malpractice, Equal Opportunity, Negligence, Products Liability, Civil Rights, and Class Actions.

KREVOLIN & DONATO, P.C.

59 ELM STREET
P.O. BOX 612
NEW HAVEN, CONNECTICUT 06503
Telephone: 203-624-3191
Fax: 203-624-4187
Email: krevolin.donato.pc@snet.net
URL: http://www.lawyers.com/krevolinanddonatoattys

General Civil Practice. Probate, Estate Planning, Elder Law, Asset Protection, Pension and Profit Sharing, Corporation, Real Estate, Gift Estate, Taxation, Personal Injury, Family and Workers Compensation Law. Trials.

SHERMAN H. KREVOLIN, born New Haven, Connecticut, September 5, 1929; admitted to bar, 1954, Connecticut; 1958, U.S. District Court, District of Connecticut. *Education:* Yale University (B.A., 1951; LL.B., 1954). Deputy Town Meeting Moderator, Town of Orange, 1967-1969. *Member:* New Haven, Connecticut and American Bar Associations; Connecticut Estate and Tax Planning Council (Secretary, 1972-1973). ***PRACTICE AREAS:*** Probate; Estate Planning; Profit Sharing; Corporation; Elder Law; Tax Law.

CHARLES J. DONATO, born Moultrie, Georgia, June 24, 1945; admitted to bar, 1972, Connecticut. *Education:* Fairfield University (B.A., 1967); University of Connecticut (J.D., 1972). Lecturer, Adjunct Professor of Law, University of New Haven, 1985. *Member:* New Haven, Connecticut and American Bar Associations; Connecticut Estate and Tax Planning Council (President, 1980-1981). [SSG, U.S. Army, 1969-1971]. ***PRACTICE AREAS:*** Real Estate; Probate; Corporation; Tax Law.

JOHN E. LEE

205 CHURCH STREET, SUITE 406
NEW HAVEN, CONNECTICUT 06510-1805
Telephone: 203-865-6499
Fax: 203-865-0236
Email: johnelee@iconn.net
URL: http://www.lawyers.com/jeleeatty

General Civil Practice before State and Federal Courts. Real Estate, Business Law, Personal Injury, Family Law, Corporate Law, Construction Law, Trusts and Estates, Commercial Real Estate, Contracts, Leases and Leasing, Litigation, Mortgage, Probate, Products Liability, Torts, Wills, Zoning, Planning and Land Use, Trials and Appeals.

JOHN E. LEE, born New Haven, Connecticut, July 30, 1944; admitted to bar, 1969, Connecticut; 1972, U.S. District Court, District of Connecticut; 1973, U.S. Court of Appeals, Second Circuit; 1975, U.S. Supreme Court. *Education:* Georgetown University (A.B., 1966); University of Connecticut (J.D., 1969). *Member:* New Haven County (Chairman, Young Lawyers Section, 1975-1976), Connecticut (Chairman: Young Lawyers Section, 1979-1980; Law Day USA Committee, 1980-1981; Member: Long Range Planning Committee, 1979-1985; Board of Governors, 1980-1981; Judiciary Committee, 1981-1987; Committee on Scope and Correlation, 1983-1984; Arbitration of Fee Disputes Committee, 1983-1986; Assistant Secretary-Treasurer, 1980-1981) and American Bar Associations. ***REPORTED CASES:*** Morello v. J.H. Hogan, Inc., 1 Conn. App. 150; Miller v. Miller, 16 Conn. App. 412. ***PRACTICE AREAS:*** Real Estate; Business Law; Personal Injury; Family Law; Corporate Law; Construction Law; Trusts and Estates; Commercial Real Estate; Contracts; Leases and Leasing; Litigation; Mortgages; Probate; Products Liability; Torts; Wills; Zoning, Planning and Land Use.

(This Listing Continued)

APPROVED ATTORNEY FOR: Chicago Title Insurance Co.; Commonwealth Land Title Insurance Co.; First American Title Insurance Co.
REFERENCES: First Union Bank.

LEVY, LEFF & TOOLE

129 CHURCH STREET
NEW HAVEN, CONNECTICUT 06510-2026
Telephone: 203-777-6887
Fax: 203-776-9448

Business Litigation, Appellate Practice and Personal Injury.

LEONARD L. LEVY, born New Haven, Connecticut, June 3, 1922; admitted to bar, 1948, Connecticut. *Education:* Yale University (B.A, 1944; J.D., 1948). ***LANGUAGES:*** Spanish. ***PRACTICE AREAS:*** Personal Injury; Negligence; Divorce; Real Estate.

DAVID A. LEFF, born New Haven, Connecticut, July 12, 1963; admitted to bar, 1988, Connecticut; 1989, New York; 1990, U.S. District Court, District of Connecticut and U.S. Court of Appeals, Second Circuit; 1993, U.S. Supreme Court. *Education:* University of Connecticut (B.A., magna cum laude, 1985); Duke University (J.D., with honors, 1988). Editor, Law & Contemporary Problems, 1987-1988. *Member:* The Association of the Bar of the City of New York; Connecticut Bar Association; Connecticut Trial Lawyers Association; Association of Trial Lawyers of America. ***REPORTED CASES:*** Bohan v. Last, 236 Conn. 670, 674 A.2d 839 (1996) (personal injury); Gemmell v. Lee, 42 Conn. App. 682, 680 A.2d 346 (1996) (real estate). ***PRACTICE AREAS:*** Personal Injury; Business Litigation; Appellate Practice.

ELIZABETH TOOLE, born New Haven, Connecticut, April 16, 1967; admitted to bar, 1994, Massachusetts; 1995, Connecticut. *Education:* Haverford College (B.A., 1989); New England School of Law (J.D., 1994).

LICARI & WALSH LLC

105 COURT STREET
NEW HAVEN, CONNECTICUT 06511
Telephone: 203-752-1450
Fax: 203-752-1401

General Practice, including Civil Litigation, Labor and Employment Law, Workers' Compensation, Real Estate.

CHRISTOPHER M. LICARI, born Philadelphia, Pennsylvania, March 1, 1967; admitted to bar, 1992, Connecticut and U.S. District Court, District of Connecticut; 1994, U.S. Court of Appeals, Second Circuit. *Education:* Tufts University (B.A., cum laude, 1989); University of Bridgeport (J.D., cum laude, 1992). Recipient, American Jurisprudence Book Award. Member, 1990-1992 and Lead Article Editor, 1991-1992, University of Bridgeport Law Review. Author, "State v. Boyd: Probable Cause Beyond a Reasonable Doubt?" University of Bridgeport Law Review, Vol. 12, no. 4, pp. 1035-55 (1992). *Member:* New Haven County (Member, Executive Committee, 1996—), Connecticut and American Bar Associations; Connecticut Trial Lawyers Association; The Association of Trial Lawyers of America; New Haven Inn of Court (Treasurer, 2001—); New Haven County Young Lawyers Association (Member, Executive Committee, 1993-1997; President, 1996-1997). ***PRACTICE AREAS:*** Civil Litigation; Personal Injury; Real Estate. ***Email:*** clicari@licari-walsh.com

JOHN M. WALSH, JR., born New Haven, Connecticut, May 10, 1964; admitted to bar, 1990, Connecticut; 1991, U.S. District Court, District of Connecticut. *Education:* Boston College (B.A., 1986); Catholic University of America Columbus School of Law (J.D., 1990). Member, Moot Court Association, 1987-1990. Participant, U.S. Attorney General Advocacy Program, 1988. Author, "Taking Land Without Compensation, At Last, A New Direction!" 68 Realtor 50 (1989). Adjunct Professor, Tort Law, Branford Hall School of Business. Member and Contract Advisor, National Football League Players Association. *Member:* New Haven County, Connecticut (Member: Labor and Employment Law Section) Bar Associations. ***PRACTICE AREAS:*** Labor and Employment; Workers' Compensation; Civil Litigation. ***Email:*** jwalsh@licari-walsh.com

---

EMMET P. HIBSON, JR., born New Haven, Connecticut, July 26, 1964; admitted to bar, 2000, Connecticut; 2001, U.S. District Court, District of Connecticut. *Education:* Old Dominion University (B.S.B.A., 1989); Sacred Heart University (M.B.A., 1995); Quinnipiac College (J.D., 2000). *Member:* New Haven County and Connecticut Bar Associations; Connecticut Trial Lawyers Association; New Haven County Young Lawyers Association; New Haven Inn of Court. [U.S. Navy, 1982-1986]. ***PRACTICE AREAS:*** Labor and Employment; Civil Litigation; Workers' Compensation. ***Email:*** ehibson@licari-walsh.com

LYNCH, TRAUB, KEEFE AND ERRANTE

A PROFESSIONAL CORPORATION

Established in 1955

52 TRUMBULL STREET
P.O. BOX 1612
NEW HAVEN, CONNECTICUT 06506-1612
Telephone: 203-787-0275
Fax: 203-782-0278
URL: http://www.lawyers.com/ltke
Email: lawyers@ltke.com
URL: http://www.ltke.com

General Practice. Corporation, Employment Law, Computer Law, Transportation, OSHA, Tax, Probate, Real Estate, Social Security, Criminal, Negligence, Medical Malpractice and Products Liability Law. Trials and Appeals in all Civil, Administrative and Criminal Courts, Federal and State. Family Law, Workers Compensation, Bankruptcy Law.

FIRM PROFILE: Lynch, Traub, Keefe and Errante, P.C. is a law firm of attorneys engaged in the general practice of law, with an emphasis on litigation of all types and in all courts and other general areas mentioned above. The firm is located in New Haven, a short distance from the Superior Court and the United States District Court, and has attorneys representing the firm's clients in all courts throughout the state of Connecticut as well as a national level. The firm has been engaged in the practice of law in New Haven since 1955.

The members of the firm work with a wide range of cases in matters of litigation, including criminal law, vehicle collisions, professional malpractice of all types, product liability cases, airplane crashes, industrial accidents, and commercial litigation of all types, workers compensation and domestic relations.

In addition to the above, the firm has active and continuous engagement on behalf of industrial and municipal clients in the area of labor relations, transportation law, negotiation of labor and transportation and other arbitrated disputes, commercial practice and an active real estate practice, both residential and commercial.

Several members of the firm are board certified as civil &/or trial advocates of the National Board of Trial Advocacy. Two partners of the firm, Stephen I. Traub and Hugh F. Keefe, are listed in The Best Lawyers in America in the area of personal injury and criminal litigation. Attorney Stephen Traub and Attorney Hugh Keefe are also fellows of the American College of Trial Lawyers. Attorney Traub and Attorney Errante and Attorney Swift are also members of the American Board of Trial Advocates.

Attorney Hugh F. Keefe is a part-time instructor at Yale Law School and Attorney Steven J. Errante is a part-time instructor at Quinnipiac College School of Law. (Formerly Known as University of Bridgeport School of Law).

HUGH F. KEEFE, born Boston, Massachusetts, January 10, 1943; admitted to bar, 1967, Connecticut; 1968, U.S. District Court, District of Connecticut; 1969, U.S. Court of Appeals, Second Circuit; 1971, U.S. Supreme Court; 1982, U.S. Tax Court. *Education:* Quinnipiac College (B.S., Accounting, 1964); University of Connecticut (J.D., 1967). Phi Theta Kappa. George J. Sherman Scholar, University of Connecticut Law School, 1966-1967. Recipient: Distinguished Alumni Award, University of Connecticut School of Law, 1985; Distinguished Alumnus Award, Quinnipiac College, 1991. Member, Board of Editors, Connecticut Law Tribune, 1986—. Author: "Advocacy and The Criminal Trial Judge," *Trial Magazine,* July 1977; "Dragging the Bar Before Federal Grand Juries," Connecticut Law Tribune, June 1987; "Makeup of Jury is Critical When Defense Is Self-Defense," *Hartford Courant* OP-ED, June 23, 1987; "In Defense of the Peremptory Jury Challenge," Connecticut Trial Lawyers Association *Forum,* July 1987; "Courts not Always Faithful to Spirit of the Constitution," *New Haven Register, 1987. Instructor, Trial Practice, Yale Law School, 1979—. Member:* Town Counsel, Town of East Haven, 1971-1975; Advisory Board, Legal Studies Program, Quinnipiac College, 1974-1981; Connecticut Commission to Study Criminal Pre-Trial Programs, 1978-1980; Quinnipiac College Board of Trustees, 1994—. Trial Counsel, Town of East Haven, 1975—. Member, Board of Directors, 1968-1976 and President, 1975-1976, University of Connecticut Law School Alumni Association. Member: Connecticut Public Defender Commission, 1982-1990; Connecticut Judicial Selection Commission, 1986-1993, 2001—; Advisory Group on Civil Justice Expense and Delay Reduction in Federal Courts, 1991. Special Master, U.S. District Court, 1982—. Attorney Trial Referee, Connecticut Superior Court, 1983—. Bencher, New Haven American Inns of Court, 1989-1994. Member, 1995-2000 and Chairman, 1997-2000, Connecticut Judicial Review Council. Member, Panel of Arbitrators, American Arbitration Association. *Member:* New Haven County (President, Young Lawyers Section, 1970-1971), Connecticut (Member, 1970— and Chairman, 1979-1982, Executive Committee on the Administration of Criminal Justice; Chairman: Special Committee on the Penal System, 1973-1974; Criminal Justice Section, 1979—; Chairman, Officer Nominating Committee, 1997 and 2000; Member, 1973-1977 and Chairman, Sub-Committee of Bench-Bar Relations on Criminal Law, 1977, Committee on Bench-Bar Relations; Member: Special Committee on Unifications of the Courts, 1976-1977; Committee on Trial Advocacy Seminars, 1976-1985; Special Committee on Judicial Evaluation Questionnaire, 1977-1978; Special Committee on Administration of Civil and Criminal Justice, 1977; Federal Practice Committee, 1981—; Judiciary Committee, 1982-1986; Academy of Continuing Professional Development, 1982—), Federal and American (Member, Criminal Justice Section) Bar Associations; Connecticut Trial Lawyers Association; Connecticut Association of Municipal Attorneys; The Association of Trial Lawyers of America; Federal Bar Council. Fellow: American College of Trial Lawyers; American Bar Foundation; American Board of Criminal Lawyers. Certified as a Civil and Criminal Trial Advocate by the National Board of Trial Advocacy. [USAR, National Guard, 1967-1973]. ***PRACTICE AREAS:*** Civil Litigation; Criminal Litigation; Matrimonial Law. ***Email:*** hkeefe@ltke.com

(This Listing Continued)

STEVEN J. ERRANTE, born Queens, New York, April 20, 1953; admitted to bar, 1979, Connecticut and U.S. District Court, District of Connecticut; 1980, New York; 1981, U.S. Court of Appeals, Second Circuit; 1983, U.S. Supreme Court. *Education:* Hofstra University (B.A., magna cum laude, 1975); State University of New York at Buffalo (J.D., 1978). Phi Beta Kappa. Member: Moot Court Board, 1976-1978; National Moot Court Competition, 1977. Member, Board of Editors and Editor at Large, 1986—, Connecticut Bar Journal. Law Clerk, Connecticut Supreme Court, 1978-1979. Lecturer: Pretrial Discovery and Inspection, 1986 and Tort Liability Arising from Security Negligence, University of Bridgeport Law Center Continuing Education, 1986; Pre Trial Preparation, 1987, Nuts and Bolts of Trial Advocacy, 1989-1990, 1991, Trying the Personal Injury Case: Demonstration, 1992, "Is There a Doctor in the Case?" Medical Malpractice, 1994 and Screening, Preparing and Winning the Medical Malpractice Case, 1994, Connecticut Trial Lawyers Association; Tort Reform I, 1988, Tort Reform II, 1989, The Grievance Procedure, 1989, Recent Developments in Medical Malpractice, 1990, Connecticut Uninsured and Underinsured Motors Coverage, 1994-1995, 1997, 1998, 1999, 2001, Effect of New Code of Evidence in the Courtroom, Connecticut Bar Association, 2000, Client Security Fund, 1996— and Winning Auto Collision Cases, 1997, Connecticut Bar Association; Medical Malpractice in Connecticut, 1988, Trial Advocacy in Connecticut, 1989-1990, Determining and Proving Damages, 1990, Trying the Automobile Injury Case, 1991-1992, Medical Malpractice in Connecticut, 1994, Trying the Soft Tissue Injury Case in Connecticut, 1995, Trying the Soft Tissue Case, 1996, 1998 and Trying the Wrongful Death Case, 1997, NBI; Connecticut Bar Association Trial Advocacy Institute, NITA, 1994-2000; "Taking Your First Deposition," NBI, 2001. Personal Injury Settlements in Connecticut, NBI, 1999; Medical Malpractice in Connecticut, NBI, 2000; Taking Your First Deposition, NBI, 2001. Adjunct Professor: Legal Studies, University of New Haven, 1981-1991; University of Bridgeport School of Law, 1986—; Quinnipiac School of Law, FKA. Chairperson, Connecticut Lawyers Advisory Committee, 1990—. Trial Referee Attorney, Superior Court, 1992—. Co-Chair, Trial Practice Workshop-Cross Examination, CTLA, 1993-2000. Member, National Panel of Arbitrators, American Arbitration Association. *Member:* New Haven County (Member: Nominating Committee, 1987; Bench Bar Committee, 1987—; Executive Committee 1992—; Committee on Recommendations for Admission to the Bar, 1996—), Connecticut (Member: Medical-Legal Committee, 1981-1982; Products Liability Committee, 1982-1984; Executive Committee Civil Justice Section, 1985—; Publications Committee, 1993—; New Haven Delegate, House of Delegates, 1986—) and American Bar Associations; American Board of Trial Advocates; Connecticut Trial Lawyers Association (Member: Continuing Legal Education Committee, 1986—; Board of Governors, 1991—; New York Trial Lawyers Association; The Association of Trial Lawyers of America; National Organization of Social Security Claimants Representatives. ***PRACTICE AREAS:*** Medical Malpractice; Negligence; Products Liability; Commercial Litigation; Sports Law; Entertainment Law. ***Email:*** serrante@ltke.com

JOHN J. KEEFE, JR., born Somerville, Massachusetts, May 20, 1947; admitted to bar, 1980, Connecticut and U.S. District Court, District of Connecticut; 1981, U.S. Court of Appeals, Second Circuit; 1983, U.S. Supreme Court. *Education:* University of New Haven (B.S., 1970; M.B.A., 1972); University of San Diego (1979); University of Connect icut (J.D., 1980). Adjunct Professor, Criminal Justice, Quinnipiac College, 1983—. Lecturer, "Defending Drunk Drivers," New Haven County Bar Association, 1987, 1990. Member: American Allocation for Paralegal Education; Advisory Board, Legal Studies Program, Quinnipiac College, 1994-1999. Special Master, mediating family cases in Middletown, Milford and New Haven Superior Courts. Member, Middletown Superior Court pro bono program, Family Law Cases, 1998—. *Member:* New Haven County (Member, Executive Committee, 1984-1992), Connecticut (Member, Family Law Section), West Haven and American Bar Associations; National Association of Criminal Defense Lawyers (Criminal Coordinator, 1986-1989); Connecticut Trial Lawyers Association; Connecticut Criminal Defense Lawyers Association. Certified as a Criminal Trial Advocate

(This Listing Continued)

LYNCH, TRAUB, KEEFE AND ERRANTE, A PROFESSIONAL CORPORATION, New Haven—Continued

by the National Board of Trial Advocacy. [USAR, 1965-1971]. ***PRACTICE AREAS:*** Criminal Law; Domestic Relations; Workers Compensation. ***Email:*** jkeefe@ltke.com

DONN A. SWIFT, born Waterbury, Connecticut, August 18, 1956; admitted to bar, 1981, Connecticut; 1982, U.S. District Court, District of Connecticut; 1991, U.S. Court of Appeals, 2nd Circuit and U.S. Supreme Court. *Education:* Assumption College (B.A., 1978); University of San Francisco (J.D., magna cum laude, 1981). Member, McAuliffe Law Honor Society. Recipient, American Jurisprudence Awards: Criminal Procedure; Insurance. Law Clerk, Connecticut Superior Court Research Department, 1981-1982. Lecturer: Pretrial Discovery, Bridgeport Law School, 1986; Tort Reform I, Connecticut Bar Association, 1989; Pretrial Preparation, New Haven Bar Association, 1990; Bad Faith, National Business Institute, 1990; Evidence in Trial Practice in Connecticut, National Business Institute, 1991; Premises Liability, National Business Institute, 1992, 1994; Bad Faith, National Business Institute, 1993; Trying the Automobile Injury Case in Connecticut, National Business Institute, 1995; Premises Liability, National Business Institute, 1997; Insurance Law in Connecticut, National Business Institute, 1998; A Practical Guide to Federal Court Ruler and Procedures in Connecticut, National Business Institute, 1999; Trying The Soft Tissue Injury Case, National Business Institute, 1999; A Guide to Federal Court Practice, NBI, 1999; Adjusting the Auto Claims, NBI, 2000. Damages in Civil Trial Practice, NBI, 2000. How to Litigate Your First Case, NBI, 2001. U.S. District Court Special Master, 1990—. Attorney State Trial Referee, October 1991—. Fact Finder, Arbitrator Superior Court, October 1991—. *Member:* New Haven (Chairman, Mentor Program, 1996-1998; Member, CLE Committee, 1995-1997, Connecticut (Member, Civil Justice Section; Pro Bono Volunteer, Law Works for People, 1991-1997) and American (Member, Tort and Insurance Practice Section) Bar Associations; Connecticut Defense Lawyers Association; American Board of Trial Advocates; Defense Research Institute; Connecticut Academy of Certified Trial Lawyers. Certified as a Civil Trial Advocate by the National Board of Trial Advocacy. ***PRACTICE AREAS:*** Products Liability; Negligence; Personal Injury. ***Email:*** dswift@ltke.com

CHARLES E. TIERNAN, III, born New Haven, Connecticut, August 15, 1958; admitted to bar, 1983, Connecticut and U.S. District Court, District of Connecticut; 1984, U.S. Tax Court; 1987, U.S. Court of Appeals, Second Circuit; 1991, U.S. Supreme Court. *Education:* Trinity College (B.A., 1980); Drake University (J.D., 1982). Member, Board of Editors, Drake Law Review, 1981-1982. Law Clerk, Connecticut Superior Court, 1983. Author: Note, "Standing Barriers to Citizen and Taxpayers Suits in the Federal Court," 32 Drake Law Review 2, 1983; "Safety and Security In The Workers' Compensation Forum," Compensation Quarterly, Volume 5, Number 3, Summer 1995. Lecturer: "Defending Drunk Drivers," New Haven County Bar Association, 1987; "What's New In Worker's Compensation Law?" New Haven County Bar Association, 1991; Workers' Compensation Update 1993, Council on Education in Management, 1993; Examining the Workers' Compensation Process, Connecticut Labor and Employment Law, National Business Institute, 1993; Workers' Compensation Update 1994, Council on Education in Management, 1994; Workers' Compensation Update, 1995, Council on Education in Management, 1995; "Defending Drinking Drivers," New Haven County Bar Association, 1999-2001; Advanced Workers Compensation in Connecticut, Lorman Education Services, 1999; Adjunct Professor, Introduction to Law, 1989-1996 and Family Law, 1997—, Quinnipiac College. *Member:* New Haven County, Connecticut (Member: Executive Committee; Workers Compensation Section) and American Bar Associations; Connecticut Criminal Defense Lawyers. ***PRACTICE AREAS:*** Criminal Law; Workers Compensation; Matrimonial Law. ***Email:*** ctiernan@ltke.com

ROBERT W. LYNCH, born Washington, D.C., October 17, 1949; admitted to bar, 1983, Connecticut; 1985, U.S. District Court, District of Connecticut. *Education:* Brown University (B.S., 1971); University of Baltimore (J.D., magna cum laude, 1983). Member, Heuisler Honor Society. Professional Engineer: 1978, District of Columbia; 1980, Maryland; 1983, Connecticut. Lecturer: "Advanced Principles of Title Insurance in Connecticut," National Business Institute, 1999; "Mastering Real Estate Titles and Title Insurance in Connecticut," National Business Institute, 2000. *Member:* New Haven County, Connecticut and American Bar Associations; American Bankruptcy Institute (Member, U.S. Bankruptcy Court, District of Connecticut, pro bono panel, 1984-2001). ***PRACTICE AREAS:*** Real Estate; Business Law; Consumer Law; Probate; Estate Planning; Bankruptcy; Commercial Litigation. ***Email:*** rwlynch@ltke.com

RICHARD W. LYNCH, born New Haven, Connecticut, October 17, 1960; admitted to bar, 1987, Connecticut; 1988, U.S. District Court, District of Connecticut; 1992, U.S. Court of Appeals, Second Circuit and U.S. Supreme Court. *Education:* Florida Institute of Technology (A.S., 1980; B.S., cum laude, 1983, Alpha Epsilon); University of Bridgeport (J.D., 1987). Author: "Connecticut's Workers' Compensation Act - New and Improved?" Connecticut Lawyer Magazine, Vol. 4, No. 1, September 1993. Coach, Quinnipiac College School of Law's Trial Team, National Association of Criminal Defense Lawyer's Trial Competition, Chicago, Illinois, Fall 1993. *Member:* New Haven County and Connecticut (Member: Criminal Justice Committee, Young Lawyers Section, 1990-1992; Workers Compensation Section) Bar Associations; Connecticut Mortgage Bankers Association (Member, Young Mortgage Bankers Committee, 1987-1990); National Association of Criminal Defense Lawyers; Connecticut Criminal Defense Lawyers Association (Member, Board of Governors); Connecticut Trial Lawyers Association. ***PRACTICE AREAS:*** Domestic Relations; Workers Compensation; Criminal Law; Forfeiture Defense; Administrative Law. ***Email:*** rlynch@ltke.com

TIMOTHY P. POTHIN, born Tacoma, Washington, December 11, 1958; admitted to bar, 1985, Connecticut; 1986, New York; 1988, U.S. District Court, District of Connecticut; 1994, U.S. Court of Appeals, Second Circuit. *Education:* University of Florida (B.A., 1980); Quinnipiac College School of Law (J.D., 1985). Phi Delta Phi. Member and Associate Editor, University of Bridgeport Law Review, 1983-1985. Lecturer, "Defending Clients Charged in Federal Drug Conspiracy Cases," Connecticut Bar Association 1994. Guest Lecturer, Quinnipiac College School of Law, 1994, 1999. Faculty Member, CBA Trial Advocacy Institute, 2001. Assistant District Attorney, Nassau County, New York, 1985-1986. Deputy Assistant States Attorney, New Haven County, 1986-1988. Court Appointed Arbitrator, Attorney Trial Referee and Special Master, 1998-2001, Connecticut Superior Court. . *Member:* Connecticut Bar Association (Member, Executive Committee, Criminal Justice Section, 1999); National Association of Criminal Defense Lawyers; Connecticut Criminal Defense Lawyers Association; Connecticut Trial Lawyers Association. ***PRACTICE AREAS:*** Negligence; Products Liability; Professional Malpractice; Criminal Defense; Business Litigation. ***Email:*** tpothin@ltke.com

ERIC P. SMITH, born Newport News, Virginia, January 24, 1971; admitted to bar, 1995, Connecticut; 1996, U.S. District Court, District of Connecticut, U.S. District Court, Northern District of New York and U.S. Court of Appeals, Second Circuit. *Education:* University of New Haven (B.S., cum laude, 1992); Quinnipiac College (J.D., cum laude, 1995). Member, 1993-1995 and Legal Writing Assistant Editor, 1994-1995, Moot Court Honor Society. Recipient, Distinguished Academic Achievement Award, Labor Law, 1994. Adjunct Professor, Gateway Community-Technical College, 1999-2000. Lecturer, "Analyzing Medical Records for the Connecticut Paralegal," June 2000.; "Advanced Issues in Connecticut Medical Malpractice," November, 2000. *Member:* New Haven, Connecticut (Member, Section on: Federal Practice) and American Bar Associations; Connecticut Trial Lawyers Association. ***PRACTICE AREAS:*** Medical Malpractice; Personal Injury; Civil Litigation; Appellate Practice. ***Email:*** esmith@ltke.com

---

LEE KENNEDY TIERNAN, born New Haven, Connecticut, June 18, 1961; admitted to bar, 1991, Massachusetts; 1992, U.S. District Court, District of Massachusetts; 1993, U.S. Court of Appeals, 1st Circuit; 1995, U.S. District Court, District of Connecticut; 1996, Connecticut. *Education:* Clark University (B.A., 1983); Suffolk University (J.D., 1989). Semi-Finalist, Justice Thomas C. Clark Moot Court Competition, 1988. Associate Editor, Journal of Affordable Housing and Community Development Law, 1995. Lecturer, "Evictions and Landlord/Tenant Law in Connecticut," 2000-2001. Lecturer: Landlord and Tenant Law, 2001; New Connecticut (3) Small Business Forum. Member, Consumer Advisory Panel, Boston Edison, 1994-1995. General Counsel, New Haven Housing Authority, 1997-2000. *Member:* Boston, New Haven, Connecticut (Delegate, House of Delegates, 1997—), Massachusetts and American Bar Associations; The Association of Trial Lawyers of America. ***PRACTICE AREAS:*** Negligence; Personal Injury; Social Security; Landlord and Tenant Law; Labor and Employment. ***Email:*** ltiernan@ltke.com

NICOLE M. FOURNIER, born Providence, Rhode Island, March 6, 1971; admitted to bar, 1997, Connecticut; 1998, U.S. District Court, District of Connecticut; 2001, U.S. Court of Appeals, Second Circuit. *Education:* Rhode Island College (B.A., 1994); Quinnipiac College (J.D., magna cum laude, 1997). Honor Scholar, 1994-1997. Recipient: Distinguished Academic Achievement Awards, Legal Skills, 1995 and Business Organizations, 1996; Outstanding Legal Scholarship Award, 1997; Academic Excellence, 1997. Member, 1995-1997 and Case Note Editor, 1996-1997, Quinnipiac College School of Law Review. *Member:* New Haven County (Member: Steering Committee, Women and the Law Section; Young Lawyers), Connecticut (Member: Executive Committee, Women and the Law Section; Federal Practice Section) and American Bar Associations. ***PRACTICE AREAS:*** Civil Litigation; Appellate Practice; Criminal Defense. ***Email:*** nfournier@ltke.com

LOUIS MARK RUBANO, born USS Kennedy, Florida, October 14, 1970; admitted to bar, 1998, Connecticut; 1999, U.S. District Court, District of Connecticut. *Education:* Boston College (B.A., cum laude, 1992); Suffolk University School of Law (J.D., cum laude, 1998). Semifinalist, Walter H. McLaughlin Competition, 1997. Vice President, S.U.R.F. (Student Urban Reform Foundation), 1997-1998. *Member:* New Haven County, Connecticut (Member, Executive Committee, Litigation and Civil Justice Section) and American Bar Asso-

(This Listing Continued)

ciations; Connecticut Trial Lawyers Association; New Haven County Young Lawyers Association; Connecticut Trial Lawyers Association (Member, Executive Committee, Young Lawyers Section). ***PRACTICE AREAS:*** Personal Injury; Civil Litigation; Products Liability; Negligence. ***Email:*** lrubano@ltke.com

SONIA M. JONES, born Hartford, Connecticut, January 8, 1974; admitted to bar, 2000, Connecticut; 2001, U.S. District Court, District of Columbia. *Education:* University of Connecticut (B.A., 1996); Roger Williams University School of Law (J.D., 2000). *Member:* Hartford (Member, Criminal Law, 2000) and Connecticut (Member, Sections on: Criminal Law and Womens Law, 2001) Bar Associations. ***PRACTICE AREAS:*** Civil Litigation; Criminal Defense. ***Email:*** sjones@ltke.com

OF COUNSEL

STEPHEN I. TRAUB, born McKeesport, Pennsylvania, April 1, 1930; admitted to bar, 1960, Connecticut; 1961, U.S. District Court, District of Connecticut; 1967, U.S. Supreme Court; 1969, U.S. Court of Appeals, Second Circuit. *Education:* Cornell University; University of Connecticut (B.A., 1957); University of Virginia (LL.B., J.D., 1960). Phi Alpha Delta. Co-Author, with Ann Taffel, "Economic Loss in Death and Disability Cases in Connecticut," Connecticut Bar Association Continuing Legal Education Book, December 13, 1976. Author: "Pre-Trial Investigation and Discovery, a Must," Connecticut Law Tribune, August 22, 1977; "Preparation, Pleadings and Trial of a Medical Malpractice Case in Connecticut," Connecticut Law Tribune, November 6, 1978. Chairman and Lecturer, Connecticut Bar Association Continuing Legal Education Seminar, "Using the Economist" and "Medical Malpractice in Connecticut," 1978. Lecturer: Connecticut Bar Association Seminar on Connecticut Civil Trial Advocacy, 1977-1990; "Medical Malpractice in Connecticut," 1978, 1985, 1986; "Structured Insurance Settlements," Connecticut Bar Association, 1980; "Third Party Claims," Connecticut Trial Lawyers Association, 1980; "Structured Settlements," The Association of Trial Lawyers of America, April 1981. Instructor, Trial Practice and Procedure, Quinnipiac College, 1978-1979. Member, 1964-1966 and Vice Chairman, 1966, Board of Finance, City of Milford. Assistant City Attorney and Trial Counsel, City of Milford, 1966-1973. Member, Executive Board, Quinnipiac School of Law. *Member:* New Haven County (Chairman, Lawyer Referral Service, 1970-1978; Vice-President, 1974-1975; President, 1975-1976), Connecticut (Vice President, 1984-1985; Member: Civil Justice Executive Committee, 1976-1982; Nominating Committee, 1977, 1983; Client's Security Fund Committee, 1978-1981; Hull Commission on Legal Ethics, 1988-1990; Member, 1965-1966 and 1976-1982 and Chairman, 1981, Committee on the Judiciary; Vice Chairman, Statewide Grievance Committee, 1978-1982; Chairman, Committee on Liaison with State Court, 1987-1994) and American (Member, Litigation Section); Bar Associations; The Association of Trial Lawyers of America; Lawyer-Pilot Bar Association; Connecticut Trial Lawyers Association (Member, Board of Directors, 1980-1991; Vice-President, 1982; President, 1984-1985); American Board of Trial Advocates (Civil Trial Advocate; President, 1988-1990; Board of Directors, 1988—); Connecticut Academy of Certified Trial Lawyers. Fellow: American College of Trial Lawyers (Member, State Committee, 1995-2000); American Bar Foundation; Connecticut Bar Foundation. Certified as a Civil Trial Advocate by the National Board of Trial Advocacy, 1981. [Captain, U.S. Army Reserve, active duty, 1951-1955]. ***PRACTICE AREAS:*** Professional Malpractice; Negligence; Commercial Litigation; Airplane Crash Litigation. ***Email:*** straub@ltke.com

WILLIAM C. LYNCH (Retired).

LOCAL COUNSEL: American Trucking Assns., Washington, D.C.; Transport Insurance Co., Dallas, Texas; Roadway Express, Inc., Akron, Ohio; Consolidated Freightways; Johnny Barton, Inc.; Vallerie's Transportation Service, Inc.; ARA Services, Philadelphia, Pennsylvania; Manhattan Life Insurance Co.; National Food Processors Assn.; U-Haul Corp.; The Dow Chemical Co.; Cincinnati Milacron; Alexsis, Inc.; Connecticut Transit; The Stanley Works; Central Insurance Co.; Emery Worldwide; Stanley-Bostitch, Inc.; United States Surgical Corp.; United Coastal Insurance Co.; Republic Claims Service Co.; Stanley Magic Door Inc.; Southern Connecticut Gas Co.; Housing Authority Risk Retention Group, Inc.; Gallagher Bassett Services, Inc.; United Illuminating Co.; Republic Insurance Co.; Nations' Care Inc.; Connecticut Life and Casualty Insurance Company.
GENERAL COUNSEL: Seaboard, Inc.; Cleary Millwork, Inc.
LABOR COUNSEL: J.B. Nafito Corp; Madison Medical LLC.
APPROVED ATTORNEYS FOR: Chicago Title Insurance Co.

McCORMICK, PAULDING & HUBER, LLP

NEW HAVEN, CONNECTICUT

(See Hartford)

Patent, Trademark, Copyright, Unfair Competition, Franchise, Computer and Related Intellectual Property Law including Litigation in all Courts.

STEVEN G. MEDNICK

195 CHURCH STREET
P.O. BOX 1747
NEW HAVEN, CONNECTICUT 06507
Telephone: 203-784-3116
Fax: 203-784-3119
URL: http://www.mednicklaw.com
Email: smednick@snet.net
URL: http://www.lawyers.com/smednick

Government Relations and Legislative Practice, Labor and Employment, Technology Contracts, State, County and Local Government Law, Contracts and Procurement, and Zoning, Planning and Land Use.

STEVEN G. MEDNICK, born Waterbury, Connecticut, February 22, 1952; admitted to bar, 1979, Connecticut and U.S. District Court, District of Connecticut; 1981, U.S. Court of Appeals, Second Circuit; 1996, U.S. Supreme Court. *Education:* Fairfield University (B.A., 1974); University of Connecticut (J.D., 1978). Corporation Counsel, 1994-1996 and Member, Board of Aldermen, 1982-1991, City of New Haven. Associate Fellow: Ezra Stiles College, Yale University; Government Finance Officers of Connecticut. ***PRACTICE AREAS:*** Government Relations; Legislative Practice; Labor and Employment; Technology Contracts; State Government Law; County Government Law; Local Government Law; Contracts; Zoning, Planning and Land Use.

MILANO & WANAT, LLC

205 CHURCH STREET, THIRD FLOOR
NEW HAVEN, CONNECTICUT 06510
Telephone: 203-315-7000; 203-498-6061
Fax: 203-315-7007

Branford, Connecticut Office: 471 East Main Street, 06405. Telephone: 203-315-7000. Fax: 203-315-7007.

Trial Counsel for Commercial Insurance, Construction, Employment, Products Liability, Trade Secrets, Medical Malpractice Defense and Professional Malpractice Defense.

CHRISTOPHER F. WANAT, born Boston, Massachusetts, June 5, 1962; admitted to bar, 1987, Connecticut. *Education:* Connecticut College (B.S., with honors and distinction, 1984); Dickinson School of Law (J.D., 1987). Member, Dickinson Law Review, 1985-1987. Adjunct Professor, Business Law, University of New Haven. Member, National Board of Trial Advocacy, 1998. Serves as Special Master in State and Federal Courts. (Board Certified Civil Trial Advocacy Specialist by the National Board of Trial Advocacy). ***PRACTICE AREAS:*** Commercial Litigation; Construction Litigation; Employment Litigation; Insurance Defense; Trade Secrets; Appellate Practice; Products Liability; Medical Malpractice Defense.

MARK A. MILANO, born New Haven, Connecticut, February 20, 1960; admitted to bar, 1985, Connecticut. *Education:* Boston College (B.A., summa cum laude, 1982); University of Connecticut (J.D., with honors, 1985). Phi Beta Kappa; Phi Alpha Theta. President, University of Connecticut School of Law Alumni Association, 1996-1997. Law Clerk to Justice Angelo G. Santaniello, Connecticut Supreme Court, 1985-1986. President, New Haven Young Lawyers Association, 1990-1991. Graduate, National College of Trial Advocacy, 1991. (Board Certified Civil Trial Advocacy Specialist by the National Board of Trial Advocacy). ***PRACTICE AREAS:*** Insurance Defense; Premises Liability; Product Liability; Appellate Practice; Environmental Law; Medical Malpractice Defense; Commercial Litigation.

SEAN C. CONNORS, born Hillsdale, New Jersey, January 28, 1966; admitted to bar, 1992, Connecticut; 1993, U.S. District Court, District of Connecticut. *Education:* Providence College (B.A., 1988); University of Bridgeport (J.D., 1992). University of Bridgeport School of Law Moot Court Society Executive Board Member, 1991-1992. ***PRACTICE AREAS:*** Products Liability; Insurance Defense Litigation; Municipal Litigation; General Trial and Appellate Practice. ***Email:*** Connors4m@aol.com

STEPHEN G. MURPHY, JR., born New Bedford, Massachusetts, August 12, 1953; admitted to bar, 1987, Connecticut and U.S. District Court, District of Connecticut. *Education:* Williams College (B.A., 1975); University of Connecticut (J.D., with high honors, 1987). Member, 1985-1986, and Articles Editor, 1986-1987, Connecticut Law Review. Law Clerk to Justice Arthur H. Healey, Connecticut Supreme Court, 1987-1988. ***PRACTICE AREAS:*** Insurance Defense; Commercial Litigation; Products Liability; ERISA; Appellate Practice.

ASSOCIATES

ADAM F. ACQUARULO, born New Haven, Connecticut, May 23, 1965; admitted to bar, 1992, Connecticut; 1995, U.S. District Court, District of Con-

(This Listing Continued)

MILANO & WANAT, LLC, New Haven—Continued

necticut. *Education:* University of Connecticut (B.S., 1987); University of Maryland (J.D., 1992). ***PRACTICE AREAS:*** Commercial Litigation; Insurance Defense.

GARY C. KAISEN, born New Haven, Connecticut, September 18, 1966; admitted to bar, 1995, Connecticut. *Education:* Trinity College (B.A., 1991); Boston College (J.D., 1995). ***PRACTICE AREAS:*** Litigation; Commercial Litigation; General Practice.

JEFFREY W. KENNEDY, born Tarrytown, New York, November 1, 1967; admitted to bar, 1994, Hawaii and U.S. District Court, District of Hawaii; 1995, Connecticut and U.S. District Court, District of Connecticut; 1996, U.S. Tax Court. *Education:* University of Connecticut (B.A., cum laude, 1990); Western New England School of Law (J.D., 1994). Pi Sigma Alpha. Golden Key National Scholar. *Member:* New Haven County, Connecticut and American Bar Associations; Inns of Court. ***PRACTICE AREAS:*** Insurance Defense; Workers Compensation; Products Liability; Appellate Practice.

LAWRENCE D. PAELET, born Peekskill, New York, August 28, 1965; admitted to bar, 1992, Connecticut; 1996, U.S. District Court, District of Connecticut. *Education:* Southern Connecticut State University (B.A., magna cum laude, 1987); University of Connecticut (J.D., M.B.A., 1992). Member, Tau Pi Sigma Honor Society. Author: "A Legal Guide for Connecticut Entrepreneurs," State of Connecticut Small Business Development Center, 1992. Volunteer, Volunteer Income Tax Assistance, 1991—. *Member:* New Haven and Connecticut Bar Associations; Connecticut Trial Lawyers Association. ***PRACTICE AREAS:*** Insurance Defense; Workers Compensation.

KENNETH J. MASTRONI, born Hamden, Connecticut, April 15, 1964; admitted to bar, 1989, Connecticut. *Education:* Fairfield University (B.A., 1985); Western New England College (J.D., 1989). ***PRACTICE AREAS:*** Municipal and Governmental Litigation; Commercial Insurance Defense; Employment Litigation; Federal Practice; Civil Rights Defense; Americans with Disabilities Act.

JACK S. TAYLOR, born Guatemala City, Guatemala, May 4, 1971; admitted to bar, 1997, Connecticut. *Education:* Connecticut College (B.A., 1993); University of Iowa College of Law (J.D., 1996). ***PRACTICE AREAS:*** Insurance Defense; Commercial Litigation.

INDEG M. RAIMUNDO, born Dhahran, Saudi Arabia, December 3, 1973; admitted to bar, 1999, Connecticut. *Education:* Muhlenberg College (B.A., 1995); Quinnipiac College (J.D., 1998). ***PRACTICE AREAS:*** Commercial Litigation; Insurance Defense.

ANTHONY J. SARACO, born Bridgeport, Connecticut, January 29, 1972; admitted to bar, 1999, Connecticut and U.S. District Court, District of Connecticut. *Education:* University of Connecticut (B.S., 1994); Quinnipiac College (J.D., 1999). ***PRACTICE AREAS:*** Commercial Litigation; Insurance Defense. **Email:** ajsrc@aol.com

NAUREEN R. WEISSMAN, born Karachi, Pakistan, August 12, 1970; admitted to bar, 1995, Texas; 2000, Connecticut. *Education:* University of Texas at Austin (B.A., 1991; J.D., 1995). ***PRACTICE AREAS:*** Insurance Defense; Commercial Litigation; Administrative Law.

KAREN L. ZIELINSKI, born New Haven, Connecticut, April 14, 1974; admitted to bar, 2000, Connecticut and U.S. District Court, District of Connecticut. *Education:* University of Connecticut (B.A., 1996); University of Connecticut School of Law (J.D., 1999). ***PRACTICE AREAS:*** Insurance Defense; Commercial Litigation. **Email:** karziel@justice.com

JOSEPH G. RINALDI, born Toronto, Ontario, Canada, October 15, 1972; admitted to bar, 2000, Connecticut. *Education:* University of Toronto (B.S., honors, Human Toxicology, 1996); Quinnipiac University School of Law (J.D., 2000). ***PRACTICE AREAS:*** Insurance Defense; Commercial Litigation.

Members of the Firm are Members of New Haven, West Haven, Connecticut and American Bar Associations; Connecticut Trial Lawyers Association; Connecticut Defense Lawyers Association; The Association of Trial Lawyers of America; American Inns of Court.

MINTZ, LEVIN, COHN, FERRIS, GLOVSKY AND POPEO, P.C.

157 CHURCH STREET
NEW HAVEN, CONNECTICUT 06510
Telephone: 203-777-8200
Fax: 203-777-7111
Internet: Each Attorney's Internet Address takes the following form: first initial, last name @mintz.com (e.g., rmintz@mintz.com)
URL: http://www.mintz.com

Boston, Massachusetts Office: One Financial Center. Telephone: 617-542-6000. Fax: 617-542-2241.

New York, N.Y. Office: Chrysler Center, 666 Third Avenue. Telephone: 212-935-3000. Fax: 212-983-3115.

Washington, D.C. Office: 701 Pennsylvania Avenue, N.W. Telephone: 202-434-7300. Fax: 202-434-7400.

Reston, Virginia Office: One Fountain Square, 11911 Freedom Drive. Telephone: 703-464-4800. Fax: 703-464-4895.

Administrative Law, Business Law, Commercial Finance, Commercial Litigation, Commercial Real Estate Finance, Corporate, Emerging Growth Companies, Employment Law, Employment Litigation, Executive Severance Contracts, High Technology, Medicare Fraud and Abuse, Nonprofit Organizations Law, Personnel Policies, Public Finance, Public Law, Public Offerings, Tax, Venture Capital.

FRANK J. MARCO, born March 2, 1947; admitted to bar, 1973, NY; 1980, CT. *Education:* St. Lawrence University (B.S., 1969); Fordham Law School (J.D., cum laude, 1972). Associate Editor, Fordham Law Review, 1971-1972. Member, Advisory Committee, Banking Commissioner on the Connecticut Uniform Securities Act, 1984-1999. Executive Committee, Connecticut Technology Council. Chairman, 1994-1998 and Member, Executive Committee, MIT Enterprise Forum of Connecticut. President, 1997-1998, Chairman, 1998-1999 and Board of Directors, Hartford and Stamford Chapters, Connecticut Venture Group. ***PRACTICE AREAS:*** Venture Capital; Emerging Growth Companies; Mergers and Acquisitions; Public Offerings; High Technology. **Email:** fjmarco@mintz.com

PAUL A. HUGHES, born November 10, 1963; admitted to bar, 1993, CT. *Education:* University of Connecticut (B.A., 1989; J.D., with honors, 1993). Articles Editor, Connecticut Law Review, 1992-1993. Law Clerk to Justice Fleming L. Norcott, Jr., Connectucit Supreme Court, 1993-1994. ***PRACTICE AREAS:*** Venture Capital; Emerging Growth Companies; Mergers and Acquisitions; Public Offerings; Joint Ventures; Strategic Alliances; High Technology; Health Care. **Email:** phughes@mintz.com

All of the firm's attorneys are members of the American Bar Association.

(For complete biographical data on Boston, MA, Reston VA , Washington, D.C. and New York, NY attorneys, see Professional Biographies at Boston, MA, Reston, VA, Washington, D.C. and New York, NY).

(This Listing Continued)

MULVEY, OLIVER & GOULD

83 TRUMBULL STREET
NEW HAVEN, CONNECTICUT 06511
Telephone: 203-624-5111
Telecopier: 203-789-8371
Email: mog@moglaw.com
URL: http://www.lawyers.com/moglaw

Insurance, Workers Compensation and Negligence Law. General Trial and Appellate Practice in all Courts. Real Estate, Corporation and Probate Practice.

MEMBERS OF FIRM

KENNETH J. MULVEY, JR., born New Haven, Connecticut, November 19, 1950; admitted to bar, 1975, Connecticut and U.S. District Court, District of Connecticut. *Education:* Boston College (B.S., cum laude, 1972); Fordham University (J.D., 1975). Author, Note, "Constitutional Law-Sixth Amendment-Systematic Exclusion of Women From Jury Service," Taylor v. Louisiana, 95 S. Ct. 692, Fordham Urban Law Journal, Vol. III, No. 3 at 733. *Member:* New Haven County and The Connecticut Bar Associations; Connecticut Trial Lawyers Association (Board of Directors, 1998—) ; Defense Research Institute; Connecticut Defense Lawyers Association. ***PRACTICE AREAS:*** Insurance Law; Commercial Litigation; Civil Litigation. **Email:** kmulvey@moglaw.com

ROBERT G. OLIVER, born San Diego, California, June 5, 1940; admitted to bar, 1965, Connecticut and U.S. District Court, District of Connecticut; 1971, U.S. Court of Appeals, Second Circuit; 1974, U.S. Supreme Court and U.S. Court of Military Appeals. *Education:* Yale University (B.A., magna cum laude, 1962); Yale Law School (LL.B., 1965). Member, Board of Aldermen, New Haven, Connecticut, 1965-1967. Member, House of Representatives, Connecticut General Assembly, 1967-1973 (Member, Committees on: Judiciary and Appropriations, 1967-1973; Insurance, 1967-1970; Vice-Chairman, Committee on Public Health and Safety, 1971-1973). Counsel, Temporary Nuclear Power Evaluation Council, 1976-1977. Member, 1997— and Chair, 2000—, Federal Grievance Committee for the District of Connecticut. *Member:* New Haven County (President, 1979-1980) and Connecticut (Member, House of Delegates, 1975-1978; Member: Federal Practice Committee and Federal Judiciary Committee, 1993-1995) Bar Associations; Connecticut Defense Lawyers Association; Retired Navy and Marine Corps Judge Advocates Association; Naval Reserve Association; Retired Officers Association; U.S. Naval Institute. [Capt., JAGC, USNR, Ret.]. ***PRACTICE AREAS:*** Trials; Federal Practice; Civil Litigation; Appeals. **Email:** oliver@moglaw.com

CAROLYN P. GOULD, born Seattle, Washington, August 25, 1937; admitted to bar, 1971, Connecticut; 1972, U.S. District Court, District of Connecticut; 1994, U.S. Court of Appeals, Second Circuit. *Education:* Wellesley

(This Listing Continued)

College (A.B., 1959); University of Connecticut (J.D., with honors, 1971). Member, Board of Editors, Connecticut Law Review, 1969-1971. Author, "Significant Developments in Probate Law," 55 Conn. B. J. 119, 1981; "Probate Law," 56 Conn. B.J. 152, 1982; "Connecticut Probate Law 1982," 57 Conn. B.J. 14, 1983; "Connecticut Probate Law 1983," with Sara R. Stadler, 58 Conn. B.J. 22, 1984; "Connecticut Probate Law 1984," with Sara R. Stadler, 59 Conn. B.J., 1985. Advisor, State of Connecticut Law Revision Commission Probate Revision Committee, 1985—. Fact-Finder and Arbitrator, Connecticut Superior Court. *Member:* New Haven County, The Connecticut (Member, Board of Editors, 1973—, and Editor-in-Chief, 1985-1988, Connecticut Bar Journal; Member, Executive Committee, Estates and Probate Section, 1984—; Member, Executive Committee, Elder Law Section, 1990—) and American Bar Associations; Connecticut Defense Lawyers Association. Fellow, The American College of Trust and Estate Counsel (Member: Editorial Board; State Laws Committee; State Chair, 2000—). ***PRACTICE AREAS:*** Insurance Law; Estate Administration; Estate Planning. ***Email:*** cgould@moglaw.com

BARBARA N. BELLIS, born Toms River, New Jersey, July 12, 1961; admitted to bar, 1986, Connecticut; 1987, U.S. District Court, District of Connecticut. *Education:* Boston College (B.A., 1983); Catholic University of America (J.D., 1986). Recipient, American Jurisprudence Award in Bankruptcy, 1985. *Member:* New Haven County (Member: Bench-Bar Committee, 1996—; Medical-Legal Committee, 1996—) and Connecticut Bar Associations; Connecticut Trial Lawyers Association; Connecticut Defense Lawyers Association. ***PRACTICE AREAS:*** Trials; Negligence; Civil Litigation; Commercial Litigation; Criminal Litigation.

DAVID J. CROTTA, JR., born New Haven, Connecticut, August 25, 1960; admitted to bar, 1988, Connecticut; 1989, U.S. District Court, District of Connecticut; 1992, U.S. Court of Appeals, Second Circuit; 1998, U.S. Supreme Court. *Education:* Fairfield University (A.B., cum laude, 1982); University of Connecticut (J.D., 1988). Phi Alpha Theta. Recipient: American Jurisprudence Award in Torts; Milton Horwitz Memorial Award in Torts. *Member:* New Haven County (Member, Committee on Professional Responsibility, 1993—) and Connecticut Bar Associations; Connecticut Defense Lawyers Association. ***PRACTICE AREAS:*** Trials; Negligence and Commercial Litigation; Civil Litigation; Appeals; Probate Appeals. ***Email:*** crotta@moglaw.com

ASSOCIATES

JAMES M. HYLAND, born Brooklyn, New York, January 11, 1962; admitted to bar, 1990, Connecticut; 1991, New York, U.S. District Court, Eastern District of New York and U.S. District Court, District of Connecticut. *Education:* Boston College (A.B., 1984); Brooklyn Law School (J.D., 1990). *Member:* New Haven County and Connecticut Bar Associations; Connecticut Defense Lawyers Association; Defense Research Institute. ***PRACTICE AREAS:*** Trials; Civil Litigation. ***Email:*** hyland@moglaw.com

BRIAN J. RIEGER, born Bridgeport, Connecticut, May 13, 1972; admitted to bar, 1999, Connecticut. *Education:* Ohio State University (B.A., magna cum laude, 1995); University of Connecticut (J.D., 1999). Phi Beta Kappa. *Member:* Connecticut Bar Association; Connecticut Defense Lawyers Association. ***PRACTICE AREAS:*** Trial Practice; Negligence; Civil Litigation. ***Email:*** rieger@moglaw.com

REPRESENTATIVE CLIENTS: Allstate Insurance Co.; Amica Mutual Insurance Co.; Blackmoor Group; Central Insurance Co.; Carolina Casualty; Fireman's Fund Insurance Cos.; Fraternal Insurance Co.; Frontier Insurance Co.; General Motors Corp.; John Hancock Insurance Co.; Interstate National Insurance Co.; Monarch Life Insurance Co.; National Indemnity Co.; Orion Specialty; Parkway Insurance Company; Paul Revere Life Insurance Co.; Pennsylvania Millers Mutual Insurance Company; Pioneer Cooperative Insurance Co.; Prudential Property & Casualty Insurance Co.; Reliance Insurance Co.; Royal and Sunalliance; Sentry Insurance Transportation Division; Underwriters at Lloyds, London; Utica Mutual Insurance Co.; Vermont Mutual Insurance Company; Western World Insurance Group.

MURTHA CULLINA LLP

A Limited Liability Partnership

Established in 1937

WHITNEY GROVE SQUARE, 2 WHITNEY AVENUE
P.O. BOX 704-A
NEW HAVEN, CONNECTICUT 06503-0704

Telephone: 203-772-7700
Facsimile: 203-772-7723
Email: mcrp@mcrp.com
URL: http://www.murthalaw.com

Hartford, Connecticut Office: CityPlace I, 185 Asylum Street, 06103-3469. Telephone: 860-240-6000. Facsimile: 860-240-6150.

Boston, Massachusetts Office: Murtha Cullina Roche Carens & DeGiacomo. 99 High Street. Telephone: 617-457-4000. Facsimile: 617-482-3868.

Woburn, Massachusetts Office: 600 Unicorn Park Drive. Telephone; 781-933-5505. Facsimile: 781-933-1530.

(This Listing Continued)

General Practice. Administrative, Antitrust, Banking, Bankruptcy, Cable Television, Commercial, Communications, Construction, Copyright, Corporation, Employee Benefits, Energy, Environmental, Estate Planning and Administration, Exempt Organizations, Government Contracts, Health Care, Hospital, Insurance Litigation for Policyholders, Intellectual Property, Labor, Litigation, Mergers and Acquisitions, Probate, Product Liability, Public Utility, Real Estate, Securities, Taxation and Trademark.

RESIDENT MEMBERS OF FIRM

BURTON B. COHEN (See Hartford listing for Biography).

MARTHA E. MENG, born Burlington, Vt., 1943; admitted to bar, 1985, Conn. *Education:* Smith College (B.A., magna cum laude, 1968); Yale Univ. (M.Phil., 1972); Univ. of Conn. (J.D. with highest honors, 1985). Author: "Legal Issues," *HDR Affordable Seniors Housing Handbook*, ed. E. Howard, et al. (West, 1999); "Assisted Living Overview," *The Long Term Care Handbook*, ed. K. Goldsmith, et al. (Amer. Health Lawyers Assoc., 2000). ***PRACTICE AREAS:*** Health Care Law; Long Term Care; Retirement Housing and Assisted Living. ***Email:*** mmeng@murthalaw.com

STEPHEN E. RONAI, born Szikso, Hungary, 1936; admitted to bar, 1960, Conn.; 1965, U.S. Supreme Court. *Education:* Columbia Univ. (A.B., 1957); Yale Univ. (LL.B., 1960). Listed in Best Lawyer's in America (Health Care) 1990-2000 Editions. Law Clerk, Hon. David N. Edelstein, U.S. Dist. Judge, Southern Dist. of NY, 1962-1964. Author: "Adapting to the Stark II Antireferral Ban: A Practical Analysis of the Prohibition and Exceptions," 59 Conn. Medicine 157 (1995); "Managed Care Credentialing: Limited Access and Limited Rights," 21 Conn. Law Trib. 37 (1996); Physician Deselection," 22 Conn. Law Trib. 38 (1996). Co-Author: "Tax, Fraud and Other Concerns in Joint Ventures," 24 Conn. Law Trib. 38 (1998). Trustee, 1978-1983, and Chair., 1981-1982; Conn. Hospital Assoc. Member: Health Law Section, Am. Bar Assoc; Amer. Health Lawyer's Assn .; Member: Am. Academy of Health Care Attys.; Conn. Health Lawyers Assoc. (President, 1987-1988); Amer. Health Lawyers Assoc. (Director, 1989-1995). ***PRACTICE AREAS:*** Health Care Law; Health Care Networks; Physician Practice Regulation; Administrative Law. ***Email:*** sronai@murthalaw.com

ALFRED E. SMITH, JR., born New Haven, Conn., 1956; admitted to bar, 1986, Conn. *Education:* Georgetown Univ. (B.A., 1978); Univ. of Conn. (J.D., with honors, 1986). Author: "Laws Herald a New Wave in Medical Waste Regulation," Conn. Law Tribune, Apr., 1989. Co-Author: "Superfund: New Responsibilities, New Opportunities," Conn. Law Tribune, Nov., 1987. The Best Lawyers in America, 1997-1998, 1999-2000 Ed. Member, Conservation and Environmental Quality Section (Member, Exec. Comm., 1993—; Chair, Legislation Subcomm., 1990-1998; Secy., 1998-1999; Vice-Chair, 1999-2000; Chair, 2000-2001), Member, Environmental Law Comm. (Secy., 1990-1992, Vice-Chair., 1992-1993, Chair., 1993—, Recycling Comm. (Chair, 1990-1993) New Haven County Bar Assoc. ***PRACTICE AREAS:*** Environmental Law; Health Care Law. ***Email:*** asmith@murthalaw.com

SARA R. STADLER, born Lincoln, Neb., 1943; admitted to bar, 1979, Conn. *Education:* Univ. of Neb. (B.A., 1965); Southern Conn. State College (M.S . in Urban Studies, 1976); Univ. of Conn. Law School (J.D., 1979). Chair, Estates and Probate Section, Conn. Bar Assoc., 1994-1996. Member: Exec. Comm., Estates and Probate Section, Conn. Bar Assoc. *Member:* Conn. Estate and Tax Planning Council. Fellow: Conn. Bar Foundation; Fellow: Am. College of Trust and Estate Counsel. ***PRACTICE AREAS:*** Estate Planning Law; Estate and Trust Administration Law; Tax Exempt Corporations Law. ***Email:*** sstadler@murthalaw.com

ELIZABETH J. STEWART, born New Haven, Conn., 1961; admitted to bar, 1986, Conn. *Education:* Univ. of Virginia (B.A., 1983; J.D., 1986). Member, Exec. Comm. of Litigation Section, Conn. Bar Assoc. Member, Fed. Practice Section, Conn. Bar Assoc.; Fed. Bar Council; Securities Litigation Comm., Amer. Bar Assoc. ***PRACTICE AREAS:*** Corporate and Securities Litigation; Antitrust Litigation; Insurance Coverage Litigation. ***Email:*** estewart@murthalaw.com

LOUIS B. TODISCO, born Bridgeport, Conn., 1949; admitted to bar, 1977, Conn. *Education:* Univ. of Conn. (B.A., 1970); Univ. of New Haven (M.S.C.J., 1975); Univ. of Miami (J.D., cum laude, 1977). Chair, Administrative Law Section, Conn. Bar Assoc., 1995-1998. Member: Nat'l Health Lawyers Assoc.; Conn. Health Lawyers Assoc. (President, 1995). ***PRACTICE AREAS:*** Health Care Law; Labor and Employment Law. ***Email:*** ltodisco@murthalaw.com

BARRY J. WATERS, born Syracuse, N.Y., 1952; admitted to bar, 1981, Conn.; 2000, Mass. *Education:* Georgetown Univ. (A.B., 1974); Univ. of Maryland (M.A., 1977); George Washington Univ. (J.D., 1981). Member, Individual Rights and Responsibilities Comm., Labor and Employment Section, Am. Bar Assoc.; Exec. Comm., Labor and Employment Law Section, Conn. Bar Assoc. ***PRACTICE AREAS:*** Employment; Litigation; Noncompetition; Trade Secrets. ***Email:*** bwaters@murthalaw.com

(This Listing Continued)

MURTHA CULLINA LLP, New Haven—Continued

COUNSEL

NAN MEAD BIRDWHISTELL, born Louisville, Ky., 1954; admitted to bar, 1979, Conn. *Education:* Emory Univ. (B.A., 1976); Harvard Univ. (J.D., 1979); Yale School of Management (M.P.P.M., 1986). First Selectwoman (Mayor) Woodbridge, Conn., 1991-1997. Member, Mediation Panel, Connecticut State Board of Education. ***PRACTICE AREAS:*** Municipal Law; Health Care Law. ***Email:*** nbirdwhistell@murthalaw.com

MARILYN B. FAGELSON, born Bay Shore, N.Y., 1956; admitted to bar, 1984, New York; 1992, Conn. *Education:* Wesleyan University (B.A., 1978); Hofstra University (J.D., 1983). Law Clerk to The Hon. David F. Jordan, U.S. Magistrate Judge, E.D.N.Y., 1983-1984. Law Clerk to The Hon. Donna F. Martinez, U.S. Magistrate Judge, D. Conn., 1995-1997. ***PRACTICE AREAS:*** Commercial Litigation; Insurance Coverage; Appellate Practice. ***Email:*** mfagelson@murthalaw.com

JOHN M. MONAHAN, born New York, N.Y., 1954; admitted to bar, 1984, Conn.; 1985, ME. and N.Y. *Education:* Columbia College, Columbia Univ. (B.A., 1977); St. John's Univ. School of Law (J.D., 1984). Adjunct Professor, Indiana University School of Law, 1996-1997. *Member:* New Haven County Bar Assoc.; Conn. Estate and Tax Planning Council. ***PRACTICE AREAS:*** Trusts and Estates. ***Email:*** jmonahan@murthalaw.com

LAURA K. NORDEN, born Bethesda, Md., 1965; admitted to bar, 1990, Va.; 1991, Dist. of Col. and Md.; 1994, Tx.; 1996, Conn.; 2001, Mass. *Education:* Univ. of Mich. (B.A., 1987); Univ. of Richmond (J.D., 1990). Member, Women in Cable and Telecommunications, Commission on Women in the Bar. ***PRACTICE AREAS:*** Communications Law; Utility Law; Commercial Litigation. ***Email:*** lnorden@murthalaw.com

ROBERT N. SCHMALZ, born Boston, Mass., 1932; admitted to bar, 1959, Conn. *Education:* Princeton Univ. (A.B., 1954); Harvard Law School (LL.B., 1959). Member, State Bar Examining Comm., 1970-1982. Member, Board of Aldermen, City of New Haven, 1994-2001. ***PRACTICE AREAS:*** Estate Planning Law; Estate and Trust Administration Law. ***Email:*** rschmalz@murthalaw.com

RESIDENT ASSOCIATES

JENNIFER MORGAN DELMONICO, born Urbana, Ill., July 19, 1973; admitted to bar, 1997, Georgia; 1998, U. S. Dist. Court, Northern Dist. of Georgia; 2000, Connecticut and U.S. Dist. Court, Northern Dist. of Il. *Education:* Northwestern Univ. (B.Mus., 1994); Univ. of Virginia (J.D., 1997). Articles Editor, Virginia Journal of Social Policy and the Law, 1996-1997. ***Email:*** jdelmonico@murthalaw.com

RACHEL SNOW KINDSETH, born Natick, Mass., 1971; admitted to bar, 1996, Conn. *Education:* Bates College (B.A., 1993); Univ. of Conn. (J.D., with honors, 1996). Member, Moot Court Board. Member, Connecticut Journal of International Law. ***Email:*** rkindseth@murthalaw.com

HEATHER LYNN OVERHOLSER, born Long Beach, Calif., 1969; admitted to bar, 1995, Mass. and U.S. District Court, District of Mass.; 1999, Conn. *Education:* Univ. of Calif. at Berkeley (B.A., 1991); Boston Univ. (J.D., 1994). *Member:* Mass. Bar Assoc.; Amer. Health Lawyers Assoc.; Conn. Health Lawyers Assoc. ***Email:*** hoverholser@murthalaw.com

All members, counsel and associates are members of Connecticut and American Bar Associations.

(For Biographical Data on other Personnel and a complete list of Representative Clients, see Professional Biographies at Hartford, Connecticut)

NEUBERT, PEPE & MONTEITH, P.C.

195 CHURCH STREET
13TH FLOOR
NEW HAVEN, CONNECTICUT 06510
Telephone: 203-821-2000
Facsimile: 203-821-2009
Email: thm@npmlaw.com
URL: http://www.lawyers.com/npmpclaw

Southport, Connecticut Office: 30 Jelliff Lane, 06490. Telephone: 203-254-9332. Facsimile: 203-254-9239.

General Civil and Appellate Practice before State and Federal Courts, Commercial and Banking Litigation, Product Liability, Hospital Liability, Medical Malpractice, Lawyer Malpractice, Design Professional Malpractice, Employment Discrimination and Wrongful Discharge, Health Care Law, Managed Care, Physicians Contract, Physicians Licensing, Bankruptcy, Creditors's Rights, Real Estate, Corporations, Business, Banking, Environmental Law, Trials and Appeals.

(This Listing Continued)

MICHAEL D. NEUBERT, born Rochester, New York, June 28, 1952; admitted to bar, 1978, Connecticut; 1984, U.S. District Court, District of Connecticut; 1987, California and Massachusetts. *Education:* University of Notre Dame (B.A., cum laude, 1974); University of Connecticut (J.D., 1978). *Member:* New Haven County, Massachusetts, Connecticut (Member: Civil Litigation Committee; Medical Legal Committee) and American (Member, Tort and Insurance Practice Sections; Litigation Section) Bar Associations; The Association of Trial Lawyers of America; Defense Research Institute; Connecticut Trial Lawyers Association; Connecticut Defense Lawyers Association. ***PRACTICE AREAS:*** Hospital Liability; Commercial Litigation; Professional Malpractice Defense; Products Liability Defense; Health Care Law. ***Email:*** mdn@npmlaw.com

GREGORY J. PEPE, born Derby, Connecticut, July 28, 1955; admitted to bar, 1982, Connecticut; 1986, U.S. District Court, District of Connecticut. *Education:* Hamilton College (B.A., 1977); University of Bridgeport (J.D., 1982). *Member:* New Haven County, Connecticut and American Bar Associations. ***PRACTICE AREAS:*** Health Care; Real Estate; Banking-Workout; Lender Representation. ***Email:*** gjp@npmlaw.com

DEBORAH MONTEITH NEUBERT, born Hartford, Connecticut, July 26, 1955; admitted to bar, 1980, Connecticut and U.S. District Court, District of Connecticut; 1993, U.S. District Court, Southern and Eastern Districts of New York. *Education:* Williams College (B.A., cum laude, 1977); University of Connecticut School of Law (J.D., 1980). *Member:* New Haven County, Connecticut (Member, Sections on: Construction Law; Labor and Employment) and American (Member: Forum or the Construction Industry; Labor and Employment Law Section) Bar Associations. ***PRACTICE AREAS:*** Design Professional Liability; Construction; Employment Law; Commercial Litigation. ***Email:*** dmn@npmlaw.com

DOUGLAS S. SKALKA, born New York, N.Y., September 28, 1960; admitted to bar, 1985, Connecticut and U.S. District Court, District of Connecticut; 1986, New York; 1990, U.S. District Court, Eastern and Southern Districts of New York. *Education:* Cornell University (A.B., 1982); Boston University (J.D., 1985). Editor-in-Chief, Probate Law Journal, 1984-1985. *Member:* Stamford/Norwalk Regional (Co-Chairman, Bankruptcy Committee), Connecticut (Executive Committee, Commercial Law and Bankruptcy Section) and American (Member, Business Law Section) Bar Associations; American Bankruptcy Institute; Turnaround Management Association (President, Connecticut Chapter, 1999-2000). ***PRACTICE AREAS:*** Bankruptcy; Commercial Litigation; Corporate Finance; Real Estate. ***Email:*** dss@npmlaw.com

JUDY K. WEINSTEIN, born Malden, Massachusetts, July 10, 1955; admitted to bar, 1980, Connecticut; 1986, Massachusetts. *Education:* Wellesley College (B.A., 1977) University of Connecticut (J.D., 1980). Phi Beta Kappa. Recipient, Wellesley College Scholar. *Member:* Connecticut (Member, Sections on: Commercial Law and Bankruptcy; Real Property), Massachusetts and American Bar Associations; National and Connecticut Health Lawyers Associations. ***PRACTICE AREAS:*** Health Law; Commercial Finance; Commercial Real Estate; Banking Law; Workouts. ***Email:*** jkw@npmlaw.com

PETER T. FAY, born Rockville Centre, New York, May 17, 1965; admitted to bar, 1990, Connecticut; 1991, U.S. District Court, District of Connecticut. *Education:* Fairfield University (B.A., 1987); College of William & Mary, Marshall-Wythe School of Law (J.D., 1990). *Member:* New Haven County, Connecticut and American Bar Associations; Connecticut Defense Lawyers Association; Connecticut Trial Lawyers Association; The Association of Trial Lawyers of America; Defense Research Institute. ***PRACTICE AREAS:*** Commercial Litigation; Professional Malpractice Defense; Products Liability; Personal Injury. ***Email:*** ptf@npmlaw.com

ERIC I. B. BELLER, born New York, N.Y., July 17, 1950; admitted to bar, 1979, Pennsylvania; 1987, Connecticut. *Education:* Harvard College (A.B., cum laude, 1971); Yale Law School (J.D., 1978). Law Clerk, Honorable Norma L. Shapiro, U.S. District Court, Eastern District of Pennsylvania, 1979-1980. Staff Attorney, Environmental Cancer Prevention Center, Public Interest Law Center of Philadelphia, 1978-1979. Assistant District Attorney, Philadelphia, Pennsylvania, 1980-1984. Author: "Regulatory Compliance Meets Managed Care: New Challenges for the Physicians," Connecticut Law Tribune (December 25, 2000); "Legal Issues in the Development and Management of Geriatric Psychiatry Practice," Geriatric Psychiatry Practice Management Handbook, American Association of Geriatric Psychiatry ," 1997; "Health Care Reform Brought Increased Profits, Not Coverage," Connecticut Law Tribune (Sept. 18, 1995), reprinted in Connecticut Medicine (Nov. 1995). Member, Board of Advisors, Center on Health Care Law and Policy, Quinnipiac College School of Law, 1997—. *Member:* New Haven County (Chairman, Environmental Law Committee, 1990-1993; Member, Medical Legal Committee, 1994-1999), Connecticut (Chairman, 1993-1994, Vice Chairman, 1992-1993, Secretary, 1990-1992; Member, Executive Committee, 1988—, Conservation and Environmental Quality Section, 1988—; Member, Health Law Section) and American (Member, Health Law and Natural Resources Law Sections) Bar Associations; American Health Lawyers Association; Connecticut Health Lawyers Association; Bridgeport Hospital (Member, Ethics Committee, 1990-1993); Harvard Club of Southern Connecticut (Member, Board of Directors, 1997—); Joseph

(This Listing Continued)

Slifka Center for Jewish Life at Yale, Inc.. (Secretary, 1989-1990; Secretary-Treasurer, 1990-1991; Chair, Legal Committee, 1994-2001; Member, Executive Committee, 1989-2001; Member, Board of Trustees, 1989—); Member, Legal Advisory Committee, Connecticut Fund for the Environment, 1994—. ***PRACTICE AREAS:*** Health Law; Managed Care; Physicians Contracts; Physicians Licensing; Environmental Law; Business Law. ***Email:*** eibb@npmlaw.com

NANCY L. BOHAN KINSELLA, born Bronx, New York, December 31, 1965; admitted to bar, 1991, Connecticut and New York; 1992, U.S. District Court, Southern District of New York; 1993, U.S. District Court, District of Connecticut and Eastern District of New York. *Education:* St. Thomas Aquinas College (B.S., magna cum laude, 1987); Fordham University School of Law (J.D., 1991). *Member:* New York State and American (Member, Business Law Section) Bar Associations. ***PRACTICE AREAS:*** Corporate Law; Commercial Litigation; Bankruptcy. ***Email:*** nbk@npmlaw.com

ERIC J. STOCKMAN, born Stamford, Connecticut, 1967; admitted to bar, 1994, Connecticut and U.S. District Court, District of Connecticut; 1998, U.S. District Court, Southern District of New York and U.S. Court of Appeals, Second Circuit. *Education:* University of Connecticut (B.A., magna cum laude, 1989); University of Connecticut School of Law (J.D., with honors, 1994). Phi Beta Kappa. Recipient, American Jurisprudence Award, Trial Practice. Commentary Editor, University of Connecticut Law Review, 1993-1994. Author: "Constitutional Gerrymandering," Summer 1993 Vol. 25 pg. 1227-1264. Member, Connecticut Society of Health Care Risk Management. *Member:* New Haven County and Connecticut Bar Associations. ***PRACTICE AREAS:*** Professional Liability; Toxic Torts; Products Liability; Personal Injury. ***Email:*** ejs@npmlaw.com

---

SIMON I. ALLENTUCH, born New York, N.Y., April 20, 1968; admitted to bar, 1994, New York and U.S. District Court, Eastern, Northern and Southern Districts of New York; 1999, Connecticut and U.S. District Court, District of Connecticut. *Education:* University of Chicago (B.A., European History with honors, 1990); New York University (J.D., 1993). *Member:* New Haven County and Connecticut Bar Associations. ***PRACTICE AREAS:*** Civil Litigation; Federal Civil Litigation; Employment Litigation; Employment Law; Physicians Licensing. ***Email:*** sia@npmlaw.com

SONJA GOLDSTEIN, born Leipzig, Germany, December 20, 1926; admitted to bar, 1952, District of Columbia; 1962, Connecticut; 1976, U.S. Supreme Court. *Education:* London School of Economics, London University (B.Sc. Econ., 1947); Yale University (LL.B., 1952). Order of the Coif. Co-Author: with A. J. Solnit, "Divorce and Your Child—Practical Suggestions for Parents," Yale University Press, 1984; with J. Goldstein, A. Freud and A.J. Solnit, "In the Best Interests of the Child," The Free Press, 1986; with J. Goldstein, A.J. Solnit and A. Freud, "The Best Interests of the Child: The Least Detrimental Alternative," The Free Press, 1996. Lecturer, "Children & the Law," Child Study Center, Yale University, 1978—. Visiting Lecturer, Yale Law School, 1995-1996. Board Member: Woodbridge Town Planning and Zoning Commission, 1972-1983; Friends of Legal Services, South Central Connecticut, 1981—; Ethics Committee of Bridgeport Hospital, 1994-1996. *Member:* New Haven County and Connecticut Bar Associations. ***PRACTICE AREAS:*** Health Law; Managed Care; Physicians Contracts. ***Email:*** slg@npmlaw.com

CAMERON C. STAPLES, born Salem, Massachusetts, March 25, 1958; admitted to bar, 1989, Connecticut. *Education:* Wesleyan University (B.A., 1980); University of Pennsylvania (M.G.A., 1984); University of Connecticut (J.D., 1989). Samuel A. Fels Scholar. Frank Ryder Scholarship for Public Service. *Member:* New Haven County and American Bar Associations. ***PRACTICE AREAS:*** Health Care; Corporate Law.

JAMES A. LENES, born White Plains, New York, September 21, 1964; admitted to bar, 1991, Connecticut; 1992, New York and U.S. District Court, District of Connecticut; 1993, U.S. Court of Appeals, Second Circuit. *Education:* Lehigh University (B.S., 1986); University of Connecticut School of Law (J.D., with honors, 1991). Associate Editor, Connecticut Law Review, University of Connecticut School of Law. *Member:* Stamford and Connecticut Bar Associations; Connecticut Trial Lawyers Association. ***PRACTICE AREAS:*** Civil Litigation; Commercial Law; Bankruptcy; Immigration Law. ***Email:*** jal@npmlaw.com

KEVIN M. GODBOUT, born North Kingstown, Rhode Island, February 18, 1968; admitted to bar, 1994, Connecticut; 1995, New York and U.S. District Court, District of Connecticut. *Education:* Colgate University (B.A., 1990); Quinnipiac University School of Law (J.D., cum laude, 1994). Phi Delta Phi (Burns Honors Inn). Recipient, American Jurisprudence Award, Trial Practice. Notes & Comments Editor, Quinnipiac Law Review, 1993-1994. *Member:* New Haven County and Connecticut Bar Associations. ***PRACTICE AREAS:*** Commercial Litigation; Construction Litigation; Premises Liability; Products Liability. ***Email:*** kmg@npmlaw.com

KERRY E. KNOBELSDORFF, born Boston, Massachusetts, August 14, 1965; admitted to bar, 1993, Connecticut; 1996, U.S. District Court, District of Connecticut. *Education:* Trinity College (B.A., with honors, 1986); University of Connecticut School of Law (J.D., with honors, 1993). Phi Beta Kappa. Dean's Fellow. Articles Editor, Connecticut Journal of International Law. Author: " INS v. Canas-Segovia: Keeping Politics In and Refugees Out," 8 Conn. J Int'l. L. 653, (1993). *Member:* Connecticut Bar Association. ***PRACTICE AREAS:*** Insurance Defense; Commercial Litigation. ***Email:*** kek@npmlaw.com

TINA CLARK BEAMON, born New Haven, Connecticut, 1972; admitted to bar, 1997, Virginia; 1998, Connecticut. *Education:* University of Connecticut (B.A., Psychology, magna cum laude, 1994); Washington & Lee University (J.D., 1997). Phi Beta Kappa; Delta Sigma Theta; Phi Alpha Delta. Burkes Scholar. Managing Editor, Race and Ethnic Ancestry Law Journal, 1996. Member, ATLA Mock Trial Team, 1997; Finalist, Washington & Lee Mock Trial, 1997. Recipient, Randall Bezanson Award. Member, Thirty-First Judicial Circuit, Prince William County, VA, 1997-1998. *Member:* American Health Lawyers Association; Connecticut Health Lawyers Association. ***PRACTICE AREAS:*** Health Law; Medical Malpractice; Civil Litigation; Charitable Organizations Law. ***Email:*** tcb@npmlaw.com

ROMEY K. HORNKOHL, born Bristol, Connecticut, September 5, 1973; admitted to bar, 1999, Connecticut; 2001, U.S. District Court, District of Connecticut. *Education:* Quinnipiac College (B.A., 1995); University of Connecticut (J.D., 1999). Dean's Fellow. Recipient: Cali Excellence Award for Trusts and Estates and Aspen Business Law. *Member:* New Haven County, Hartford County, Connecticut and American Bar Associations. ***PRACTICE AREAS:*** Health Care Law; Commercial Litigation; Bankruptcy. ***Email:*** rkh@npmlaw.com

---

NUZZO & ROBERTS, L.L.C.

NEW HAVEN, CONNECTICUT

(See Cheshire)

Civil Trial Practice in all State and Federal Courts, Insurance Law and Insurance Defense, Coverage and Bad Faith Litigation, Products Liability, Personal Injury, Professional Liability, Directors and Officers Liability, Legal Malpractice, Employment Litigation, School Liability, Appellate Practice and Workers Compensation.

PEPE & HAZARD LLP

NEW HAVEN, CONNECTICUT

(See Hartford)

Commercial, Construction, Corporations, Taxation, Finance and Real Estate, Commercial and Asset-Based Finance, Environmental/Health/Safety, Fidelity and Surety, Securities, Labor/Employment and Education, Municipal, Administrative, Health Care, Intellectual Property, Patent, International Trade, Estate Planning, Probate, White Collar Crime, and Bankruptcy. Trials in all Courts.

LAW OFFICE OF
W. MARTYN PHILPOT, JR. L.L.C.

Established in 1994

409 ORANGE STREET
NEW HAVEN, CONNECTICUT 06511
Telephone: 203-624-4666
Fax: 203-624-5050
Email: philpot.law@snet.net
URL: http://www.lawyers.com/wmphilpot

General Trial Practice before State and Federal Courts, Civil Litigation, Employment, Civil Rights, Personal Injury and Medical Malpractice Law, Trials and Appeals, Workers' Compensation, Criminal Defense, Family Law, Education Law, Landlord/Tenant Law, Product Liability, Probate and Administrative Law.

W. MARTYN PHILPOT, JR., born Hartford, Connecticut, August 31, 1956; admitted to bar, 1982, Connecticut and U.S. District Court, District of Connecticut; 1987, U.S. District Court, District of Maryland; 1992, U.S. Court of Appeals, Second Circuit; 1993, U.S. District Court, Southern and Eastern Districts of New York; 2000, U.S. Supreme Court. *Education:* Cornell University (B.S., 1978); Georgetown University (J.D., 1981). Member, Executive Committee, Section on Human Rights and Responsibilities, Connecticut Bar Association, 1984-1985. President, George W. Crawford Law Association, 1984-1986. Member, Board of Directors, Urban League of Greater Hartford, Inc., 1982-1985. General Counsel for NAACP State Conference, 2000—. Minority Delegate for Connecticut Trial Lawyers Association, 2000—. Program Chairperson and Executive Committee Member, New Haven Colony Historical Society, 2000—. Member, Executive Committee, Greater New Haven NAACP, 1994-2000. Recipient, Christian, Community and Professional Services Achievement Award, Christ Chapel New Testament Church, 1999; NAACP Distinguished Service Award, 1997. Assistant Corporation Counsel, City of New Haven, 1985-1994. *Member:* New Haven County, Connecticut, National

(This Listing Continued)

LAW OFFICE OF W. MARTYN PHILPOT, JR. L.L.C., New Haven—Continued

and American Bar Associations; The Association of Trial Lawyers of America; Connecticut Trial Lawyers Association. ***REPORTED CASES:*** Joseph Genovese v. Gallo Wine Merchants, Inc., 226 Conn. 475 (1993); Gant v. Wallingford Board of Education, et al, No. 1765 U.S. Court of Appeals for the Second Circuit (1995); Trevor Thomas v. John Roach, et al, No. 98-7623 U.S. Court of Appeals, for the Second Circuit (1999). ***PRACTICE AREAS:*** Litigation; Employment; Civil Rights; Personal Injury; Medical Malpractice; Workers' Compensation; Criminal Defense; Family Law; Education Law; Landlord/Tenant Law.

LAURA LEE A. DORFLINGER, born Middletown, Connecticut, February 7, 1969; admitted to bar, 1996, Connecticut and U.S. District Court, District of Connecticut; 1998, U.S. Court of Appeals, Second Circuit; 2000, U.S. Supreme Court. *Education:* Southern Connecticut State University (B.S., Business Economics, 1991); Quinnipiac College School of Law (J.D., 1995). Delta Phi Epsilon. Recipient: Southern Connecticut State University Scholarship Award for Study Abroad; Lydia Lundbord Award for Writing Proficiency. Former Member: Substance Abuse Action Council (Drafted and Enacted, Public Act 95-314, Section 2), Middlesex County, 1992; Mayoral Economic Development Committee, 1991. *Member:* New Haven County, Connecticut and American Bar Associations; Association of Trial Lawyers of America; National Association for the Advancement of Colored People. ***REPORTED CASES:*** Gant Ex Rel. Gant v. Wallingford Bd of Educ., 195 F.3d 134 (2nd Cir. 1999); Kellman v. Yale-New Haven Hosp., 64 F. Supp 2nd 35 (D. Conn. 1999); Stubbs v. City of New Haven, _ F. Supp. _, New Haven District Court, Civil No. 3:96CV01363 (JBA) (D. Conn. 1998); Zamfino v. Pace Motor Lines, 1997 WL 306660 (Conn. Super). ***PRACTICE AREAS:*** Litigation; Employment Discrimination; Torts; Family Law; Bankruptcy; Contracts.

MARC L. GLENN, born Stamford, Connecticut, June 15, 1970; admitted to bar, 1999, Connecticut; 2000, U.S. District Court, District of Connecticut. *Education:* Temple University (B.A., 1993); Quinnipiac College School of Law (J.D., 1998). Recipient: Outstanding Academic Achievement Award; Service to Law School Award. *Member:* Connecticut Bar Association; National Association for the Advancement of Colored People (Member, Greater New Haven Chapter). ***Email:*** philpot.law@snet.net

---

PULLMAN & COMLEY, L.L.C.

Established in 1919

(Formerly Pullman, Comley, Bradley & Reeves)

ONE CENTURY TOWER
265 CHURCH STREET
NEW HAVEN, CONNECTICUT 06510-7000
Telephone: 203-773-3006
Telecopier: 203-776-7075
URL: http//www.pullcom.com

Bridgeport, Connecticut Office: 850 Main Street, P.O. Box 7006, Telephone: 203-330-2000. Telecopier: 203-576-8888.
Hartford, Connecticut Office: 90 State House Square. Telephone: 860-424-4300. Telecopier: 860-424-4370.
Simsbury, Connecticut Office: 720 Hopmeadow Street. Telephone: 860-651-9348. Fax: 860-651-1431.
Southport, Connecticut Office: 200 Pequot Avenue, P.O. Box 510. Telephone: 203-254-5000. Telecopier: 203-254-5070.
Stamford, Connecticut Office: 350 Bedford Street. Telephone: 203-324-5000. Telecopier: 203-363-8659.

General Practice including Administrative, Antitrust, Banking, Bankruptcy and Creditors Rights, Bonds, Business and Commercial, Corporate, Education, Employee Benefits, Environmental, Hospital and Health Care, Labor and Employment, Municipal Finance, Real Estate, Securities, Tax, Trusts and Estates, and Zoning. Energy and Utilities, Litigation in all Courts.

JOHN S. PULLMAN (1871-1943).
ARTHUR M. COMLEY (1883-1969).
J. KENNETH BRADLEY (1903-1969).
WILLIAM REEVES (1906-1967).

MEMBERS OF FIRM

ELIZABETH J. AUSTIN, born New York, N.Y., February 19, 1957; admitted to bar, 1983, Texas, Nebraska and U.S. District Court, Northern District of Texas; 1988, U.S. District Court, Eastern District of Texas; 1989, U.S. District Court, Western District of Texas and District of Connecticut; 1990, Connecticut.

(This Listing Continued)

Education: University of Nebraska (B.A., 1979; J.D., 1982). *Member:* Bridgeport (Chairperson, Commercial Law Committee), Connecticut (Vice Chairman, Commercial Law and Bankruptcy Section), Nebraska State and American Bar Associations; State Bar of Texas; Commercial Law League of America; American Bankruptcy Institute; International Women's Insolvency and Restructuring Confederation; Women's Bankruptcy Bar Association (Founding Member; Executive Committee Member). (Also at Bridgeport, Hartford and Stamford Offices). ***PRACTICE AREAS:*** Insolvency Law; Bankruptcy Litigation; Commercial Litigation. ***Email:*** EA@PULLCOM.COM

H. WILLIAM SHURE, born New Haven, Connecticut, April 5, 1940; admitted to bar, 1964, Connecticut. *Education:* Dartmouth College (A.B., 1961); University of Virginia (LL.B., 1964). Assistant Minority Counsel to the Senate Select Committee on Presidential Campaign Activities (Watergate Committee, 1973). Consulting Counsel, U.S. Senate Committee on Government Operations, Subcommittee on Federal Spending Practices, Efficiency and Open Government, 1975-1977. President, New Haven Jewish Federation, 1982-1985. National Vice-Chairman, United Jewish Appeal, 1989-1999. (Also at Bridgeport Office). ***PRACTICE AREAS:*** Commercial Law; Banking Law; Bankruptcy Law; Government Law. ***Email:*** HWS@PULLCOM.COM

JOHN R. WARD, born Farnworth, Lancashire, England, August 4, 1962; admitted to bar, 1990, Connecticut. admitted, 1984, England and Wales; 1990, Connecticut. *Education:* King's College, London University (LL.B., 1983); University of Connecticut (J.D., magna cum laude, 1990). Assistant Corporation Counsel, 1997 and Deputy Corporation Counsel, 1998-2000, City of New Haven. *Member:* Connecticut Bar Association (Member, Real Property Section). ***PRACTICE AREAS:*** Real Estate Law; Commercial Law; Municipal Law. ***Email:*** JRW@PULLCOM.COM

(For Complete Biographical Data on all Personnel, See Bridgeport, Connecticut Professional Biographies)

JUDITH A. RAVEL

NEW HAVEN, CONNECTICUT

(See Branford)

Civil Litigation, Family, Municipal, Labor and Employment.

ROSEN & DOLAN, P.C.

Established in 1972

400 ORANGE STREET
NEW HAVEN, CONNECTICUT 06511
Telephone: 203-787-3513
Fax: 203-789-1605
Email: david.rosen@rosendolan.com
URL: http://www.lawyers.com/rosen&dolan

Trial and Appellate Practice before State and Federal Courts. Plaintiffs' Personal Injury, Civil Rights, Employment Discrimination, Class Actions, Divorce, Family and Criminal Defense Law.

FIRM PROFILE: Rosen & Dolan is committed to providing the highest quality legal services in its specialty areas, with the informality and accessibility of a small firm. The firm has argued and won many reported cases in the Connecticut Supreme Court, Second Circuit Court of Appeals and the United States Supreme Court.

DAVID N. ROSEN, born New York, New York, May 20, 1944; admitted to bar, 1969, Connecticut; 1970, U.S. District Court, District of Connecticut; 1972, U.S. Court of Appeals, 2nd Circuit; 1974, U.S. Supreme Court; 1976, California. *Education:* Harvard University (B.A., magna cum laude, 1965); Yale University (LL.B., 1969). Member, Board of Editors, Yale Law Journal, 1969. Listed in *Best Lawyers in America.* Lecturer, Yale University, 1969-1970; 1981—. Author: "Testifying in Court: A Trial Lawyer's Perspective," in Lewis *Child and Adolescent Psychiatry,* William and Wilkins, 1996; "Rhetoric and Result in the Bobby Seale Trial," *Law's Stories,* Yale Press, 1996. *Member:* New Haven County and Connecticut Bar Associations; The Association of Trial Lawyers of America. ***LANGUAGES:*** French. ***PRACTICE AREAS:*** Appellate Practice; Employment; Personal Injury; Civil Rights. ***Email:*** david.rosen@rosendolan.com

EDWARD J. DOLAN, born Concord, Massachusetts, December 18, 1944; admitted to bar, 1969, Connecticut and U.S. District Court, District of Connecticut; 1974, U.S. Supreme Court. *Education:* Boston College (A.B., cum laude, 1966); University of Connecticut (J.D., 1969). Lecturer, Criminal Law and Family Law, University of New Haven, West Haven, Connecticut, 1972-1976. *Member:* New Haven County and Connecticut Bar Associations. ***PRACTICE AREAS:*** Family Law; Divorce Law; Child Custody Law; Criminal Defense.

REFERENCE: Peoples Bank.

MARY ANNE ROYLE

27 ELM STREET
NEW HAVEN, CONNECTICUT 06510
Telephone: 203-624-7752
Fax: 203-785-0778
Email: mroylelaw@msn.com

General Practice.

MARY ANNE ROYLE, born Vancouver, Washington, August 24, 1952; admitted to bar, 1990, Wisconsin; 1994, Connecticut. *Education:* Willamette University (B.A., 1974); Emory University (M.L.N., 1978); University of Wisconsin (J.D., 1990). Member, National Organization of Veteran's Advocates, 1998—. *Member:* New Haven, Connecticut and Federal Bar Associations; State Bar of Wisconsin; Connecticut Trial Lawyers Association. ***REPORTED CASES:*** Robinson v. Commissioner, 26 Conn. L. Retr. 573, 2000; Daniels v. Warden, 1999 WL 259658. ***PRACTICE AREAS:*** Veterans Appeals; Appellate Practice; Administrative Law; General Practice.

RUBIN & ELDRICH, P.C.

59 ELM STREET
P.O. BOX 1422
NEW HAVEN, CONNECTICUT 06506-1422
Telephone: 203-821-3023
Fax: 203-821-3026
URL: http://www.lawyers.com/rubin&eldridge

Practice Limited to All Areas of Family and Matrimonial Law including Divorce, Custody, Property Distribution and Support Issues.

KENNETH B. RUBIN, born Brooklyn, New York, November 3, 1948; admitted to bar, 1977, Connecticut; 1978, U.S. District Court, District of Connecticut. *Education:* George Washington University; Brooklyn College (B.A., 1971); University of Baltimore (J.D., 1976). Special Master: Superior Court Family Division; Regional Family Trial Docket. *Member:* New Haven County, Connecticut (Member: Family Law Section; Family Law Executive Committee; Committee on Gender Equity in the Profession) and American (Member, Family Law Section) Bar Associations. Fellow, American Academy of Matrimonial Lawyers. ***PRACTICE AREAS:*** Family Law; Matrimonial Law; Child Custody; Marital Property Distribution.

SARAH D. ELDRICH, born New Haven, Connecticut, January 8, 1951; admitted to bar, 1983, Connecticut; 1984, U.S. District Court, District of Connecticut. *Education:* Quinnipiac College (B.A., with honors, 1974; J.D., 1982). Member, Board of Editors, Connecticut Family Lawyer. Assistant Professor of Legal Studies, 1982-1985 and Lecturer in Legal Studies, 1988-1995, Quinnipiac College. Special Master: Superior Court Family Division; Regional Family Trial Docket. *Member:* New Haven County, Connecticut (Past Chair, Family Law Section; Member: Family Law Executive Committee; State Court Liaison Committee) and American (Member, Family Law Section) Bar Associations. Fellow, American Academy of Matrimonial Lawyers. ***PRACTICE AREAS:*** Family Law; Matrimonial Law; Divorce; Child Custody; Alimony.

PAUL A. SCHOLDER ATTORNEY AT LAW, P.C.

Established in 1958
2 WHITNEY AVENUE
P.O. BOX 1722
NEW HAVEN, CONNECTICUT 06507
Telephone: 203-777-7218
Fax: 203-772-2672
Email: PaulA.Scholder,P.C.102261.2673@CompuServe.com
URL: http://www.lawyers.com/paulascholderlaw

General Civil Practice before State and Federal Courts. Civil Litigation, Personal Injury, Products Liability, Workers Compensation Insurance, Family and Probate Law, Environmental Law. Trials and Appeals.

FIRM PROFILE: Paul A. Scholder, Attorney at Law, P.C., is a small law firm, founded in 1958, located in downtown New Haven providing litigation and counselling services in all trial and appellate courts, State and Federal, having jurisdiction over the state of Connecticut.

While providing a broad spectrum of legal services, the firm has always specialized in providing the highest level of representation for insurance carriers, their insureds, municipalities and several multi-national corporations. We are most commonly involved with insurance coverage, products liability, personal injury, municipal liability, civil rights, bad faith, uninsured and underinsured motorist, premises liability and worker's compensation claims and litigation.

(This Listing Continued)

The firm prides itself on its ability to utilize its courtroom, counseling and communication skills to create and implement safe, effective and innovative solutions to the real problems facing our clients. Since our firm has the skill, experience and resources found in large firms, without the burdens of an extensive corporate structure, we have the flexibility to respond to the needs of our clients on a case-by-case basis, providing optimal service at reasonable rates.

PAUL A. SCHOLDER, born New York, N.Y., October 19, 1933; admitted to bar, 1958, Connecticut; 1959, U.S. District Court, District of Connecticut; 1962, U.S. Court of Appeals, Second Circuit; 1963, U.S. Supreme Court. *Education:* Tufts University (B.S., 1955); New York University (LL.B., 1958). *Member:* New Haven County, Connecticut (Member, Executive Committee, Litigation Section, 1987—) and American (Member: Torts & Insurance Practice Law Section; Products Liability Committee) Bar Associations; The Defense Research Institute, Inc. ***PRACTICE AREAS:*** Insurance Law; Product Liability Law; Negligence Law; Civil Litigation. ***Email:*** PaulA.Scholder,P.C.102261.2673@CompuServe.com

REPRESENTATIVE CLIENTS: Berkshire Mutual Insurance Co.; CGU Insurance Cos.; American Hallmark Insurance Co.; Lloyds of London; The Proctor & Gamble Co.; Wells Fargo Alarm Services, Inc.; White Consolidated Industries, Inc.; Chart House, Inc.; National Car Rental Co.; Exxon Corp.; National Food Processors Association; American Bankers Insurance Cos.
REFERENCES: Peoples Bank; Hudson United Bank.

SEELEY & BERGLASS

Established in 1992
121 WHITNEY AVENUE
NEW HAVEN, CONNECTICUT 06510
Telephone: 203-562-5888
Fax: 203-562-9365
Email: wps3695@aol.com

Commercial Litigation, Insurance Claims Litigation, Personal Injury, and Appeals in all Courts, Arbitration and Employment Law, General Practice of Corporate and Commercial Law.

FIRM PROFILE: Southport Office: 3695 Post Road, P.O. Box 858. Telephone: 203-256-3250. Fax: 203-256-3252.

W. PARKER SEELEY, JR., born Bridgeport, Connecticut, January 7, 1937; admitted to bar, 1964, Connecticut and U.S. District Court, District of Connecticut; 1965, U.S. Court of Appeals, Second Circuit; 1966, U.S. Supreme Court. *Education:* Yale University (B.A., 1959); University of Virginia (LL.B., 1964). Law Clerk to Judge Walter E. Hoffman, Chief Judge, U.S. District Court, Eastern District of Virginia, 1963. Private Sector Participant, 1996 SEC Government-Business Forum on Small Business Capital Formation. Bond Counsel, City of Bridgeport, 1982-1985. Member, Advisory Council, Corporation Division Office of the Secretary of State of Connecticut, 1992—. Chairman, Bridgeport Branch of the Southern Connecticut Coast YMCA. *Member:* Bridgeport, Connecticut (Member, Sections on: Corporations; Taxation; Commercial Law) and American (Member, Sections on: Taxation; Corporations; Probate and Trust Law) Bar Associations. (Resident, Southport Office). ***PRACTICE AREAS:*** Corporate Law; Corporate Governance; Corporate Reorganization; Securities; Business Planning; Commercial Transactions; Financial Planning; Estate Planning.

STEVEN BERGLASS, born Jamaica, New York, October 16, 1953; admitted to bar, 1978, Connecticut; 1979, U.S. District Court, District of Connecticut; 1980, U.S. District Court, Southern and Eastern Districts of New York. *Education:* Yale University (B.A., summa cum laude, 1975, Phi Beta Kappa; J.D., 1978). Thomas Swann Barrister's Union. Yale Moot Court of Appeals. Lifetime Member, AHRC. *Member:* Connecticut Bar Association; The Corporate Bar; The Association of Trial Lawyers of America. ***PRACTICE AREAS:*** Insurance Coverage; Commercial Litigation.

ROSWITHA MILLER, born Tampa, Florida, December 3, 1964; admitted to bar, 1995, Connecticut; 1996, U.S. District Court, District of Connecticut; 1997, New York. *Education:* University of Arizona (B.A., 1990); Quinnipiac College (J.D., cum laude, 1995). Associate Editor, Quinnipiac Law Review, 1994-1995. Member, International Law Society. ***LANGUAGES:*** German. ***PRACTICE AREAS:*** Litigation.

SLOAN W. FARRELL, born Easton, Pennsylvania, November 7, 1965; admitted to bar, 1999, Connecticut; 2000, U.S. District Court, District of Connecticut. *Education:* Washington and Lee University (B.A., 1988); Quinnipiac College School of Law (J.D., 1999). Recipient, Distinguished Academic Achievement Award, Mock Trial Association. Member: Disabled American Veterans; Habitat for Humanity. *Member:* Connecticut and American Bar Associations. [First Lt., Infantry, U.S. Army, 1988-1992]. ***LANGUAGES:*** German. ***PRACTICE AREAS:*** Commercial Litigation; Insurance Coverage; Employment Law.

(This Listing Continued)

SEELEY & BERGLASS, New Haven—Continued

JOHN W. SULLIVAN, born Teaneck, New Jersey, September 18, 1970; admitted to bar, 1999, California; 2001, Connecticut. *Education:* Arizona University (B.S., 1994); Quinnipiac University School of Law (J.D., 1998). Recipient, Distinguished Academic Achievement Award. ***PRACTICE AREAS:*** Commercial Litigation.

REPRESENTATIVE CLIENTS: Advance Machinery Co., Inc.; ANC Management Co.; Bridgeport Machines, Inc.; City of Bridgeport; Cabot Paints; Consolidated Development Corporation; Cooperative Retirement Services of America, Inc.; Coram Healthcare, Inc.; Diaxotics, Inc.; Electronic Date Systems Corporation; Fairfield County Sprinkler Co., Inc.; First National Bank of New England; Gale Research, Inc.; General Electric Credit; Gerosa, Inc.; Heyman Properties; Homestead of Connecticut, LLC; Kaba, Inc.; Kirchhoff Construction Co.; Lionheart Group, Inc.; Marcon, Inc.; Middlebury Venture Partners, Inc.; NEON, Inc.; North American Philips Corp.; Phoenix Engineering Services, Inc.; Plaza Hall Assoc.; Richards and Ellis Group; Samsung International; St. James Press, Inc.; Shoreline Motors Corporation; Spectrum Mortgage Bankers, Inc.; Spencers Restaurants, Inc.; Target Capital Group, LLC; Valmont Industries, Inc.; Wall Data, Inc.; Windsor Companies; Xenex, LLC; Yale University.

SIEGEL, O'CONNOR, SCHIFF & ZANGARI, P.C.

171 ORANGE STREET
P.O. DRAWER 906
NEW HAVEN, CONNECTICUT 06510
Telephone: 203-789-0001
Telecopier: 203-782-2766
Email: first initial last name @soszlaw.com
URL: http://www.soszlaw.com

Hartford, Connecticut Office: 150 Trumbull Street. Telephone: 860-727-8900. Telecopier: 860-527-5131.

Labor Relations and Employment Law representing management in the private and public sectors, including related Litigation in Federal and State Courts, Tax Law, Education Law, Municipal Law, Commercial Law, Corporate Law, Estate Planning and Estate Administration Matters.

FIRM PROFILE: Siegel, O'Connor, Schiff & Zangari, P.C. is a Connecticut based law firm whose practice is exclusively dedicated to the representation of management in labor and employment matters and specialized business and tax representation.

CHRISTINE A. BARKER, born Rye, New York, November 21, 1959; admitted to bar, 1987, New York, New Jersey and U.S. District Court, District of New Jersey; 1989, Connecticut. *Education:* Southern Connecticut State University (B.S., 1983); Detroit College of Law, Michigan State University (J.D., cum laude, 1987); New York University (LL.M., 1990). Recipient, American Jurisprudence Award in Debtor/Creditor Law. Staff Member, 1985-1986, and Managing Editor, 1986-1987, Detroit College of Law Review, Michigan State University. *Member:* Connecticut and American Bar Associations. (Resident). ***PRACTICE AREAS:*** Business Law; Computer Law; Taxation Law. ***Email:*** cbarker@soszlaw.com

JOHN W. BECK (Resident, Hartford, Connecticut Office).

GREGORY J. BEZZ (Resident, Hartford, Connecticut Office).

ROBERT F. COHN, born Queens, New York, October 31, 1954; admitted to bar, 1979, New York; 1981, Connecticut. *Education:* State University of New York at Binghamton (B.S., 1976); Washington University (J.D., 1979); New York University (LL.M. in Taxation, 1981). Associate Editor, Washington University Urban Law Annual, 1979. Vice-President, Cornerstone, Inc., 1989—. Member, Tax Committee, The Jewish Foundation, New Haven, Connecticut. *Member:* Connecticut Bar Association (Member, Estates and Probate Law Section). (Resident). ***PRACTICE AREAS:*** Estate Planning Law; Trust Law; Elder Law; Taxation Law; Corporate Law. ***Email:*** rcohn@soszlaw.com

HUGH W. CUTHBERTSON, born Greenwich, Connecticut, November 9, 1946; admitted to bar, 1973, Massachusetts; 1975, U.S. Court of Appeals for the District of Columbia Circuit and Fifth Circuit; 1976, U.S. Court of Appeals, Second Circuit and U.S. District Court, District of Connecticut; 1981, Connecticut, U.S. Court of Appeals, Fifth and Eleventh Circuits and U.S. District Court, District of Massachusetts; 1998, U.S. Supreme Court. *Education:* Case Western Reserve University (B.A., 1969); Boston College (J.D., 1973). Member, National Moot Court Team, Winner, Region I Best Brief and Oral Argument Awards. Trial Attorney, Office of General Counsel, Interstate Commerce Commission, Washington, D.C., 1973-1976. Assistant U.S. Attorney, District of Connecticut, 1976-1981. Member, Panel of Special Masters for New Haven Seat of U.S. District Court, District of Connecticut, 1983—. *Member:* New Haven County, Connecticut, Federal and American Bar Associations; Connecticut Trial Lawyers Association; Connecticut Defense Lawyers Association. (Resident). ***PRACTICE AREAS:*** Labor Law; Employment Law; Litigation. ***Email:*** hcuthbertson@soszlaw.com

(This Listing Continued)

FREDERICK L. DORSEY, born Kenova, West Virginia, April 19, 1953; admitted to bar, 1984, Connecticut; 1985, U.S. District Court, District of Connecticut. *Education:* United States Coast Guard Academy; Marshall University (B.A., cum laude, 1976); University of New Haven (M.B.A., 1978); Western New England College (J.D., 1984). Co-Author: "An Analysis of the 'No-Strike Clause' In Contemporary Collective Bargaining Agreements," 7 Western New England Law Review 147, 1984. *Member:* New Haven County, Connecticut (Member, State Board of Labor Relations Liaison Subcommittee and Education Law Committee) and American Bar Associations; Connecticut School Attorneys Council; National School Board Association Council of School Attorneys. (Resident). ***PRACTICE AREAS:*** Labor Law; Employment Law; Litigation; Education Law; Special Education of Disabled Children Law. ***Email:*** fdorsey@soszlaw.com

GLENN A. DUHL (Resident, Hartford, Connecticut Office).

NICHOLAS J. GRELLO, JR. (Resident, Hartford, Connecticut Office).

PETER D. HERSHMAN, born New Haven, Connecticut, February 18, 1947; admitted to bar, 1972, Connecticut; 1973, U.S. District Court, District of Connecticut; 1975, U.S. Court of Appeals, Second Circuit; 1982, U.S. Tax Court. *Education:* University of Pittsburgh (B.A., 1968); University of Connecticut (J.D., 1972); New York University (LL.M. in Taxation, 1973). Member, Board of Editors, 1970-1972 and Lead Articles Editor, 1971-1972, University of Connecticut Law Review. Recipient, American Jurisprudence Award in International Business Transactions. Lecturer, Federal Estate and Gift Tax and Qualified Retirement Programs, Quinnipiac College, 1982-1984. Member, State Advisory Committee to Study the Recodification of the Connecticut Banking Laws and Related Statutes, 1976-1978. Fire Commissioner, 1987+ and Chairman, 1991-1996, Town of Woodbridge, Connecticut. *Member:* New Haven County, Connecticut and American Bar Associations. (Resident). ***PRACTICE AREAS:*** Corporate Law; Estate Planning Law; Employee Benefit Plans Law. ***Email:*** phershman@soszlaw.com

PETER A. JANUS (Resident, Hartford, Connecticut Office).

GEORGE J. KELLY, JR., born Washington, D.C., January 22, 1947; admitted to bar, 1974, Connecticut and U.S. District Court, District of Connecticut; 1975 Massachusetts and U.S. District Court, District of Massachusetts. *Education:* University of Notre Dame (A.B., 1968); Harvard Law School (J.D., 1974). Law Clerk, Honorable T. Emmet Claire, U.S. District Judge, District of Connecticut, 1974-1975. Assistant U.S. Attorney, District of Connecticut, 1977-1982. Adjunct Mediation Clinic, University of Connecticut School of Law, 1994-1995. Instructor, Lawyering Process, University of Connecticut School of Law, 1996. *Member:* Hartford County, Connecticut and American Bar Associations. ***PRACTICE AREAS:*** Commercial Litigation; Labor and Employment Litigation. ***Email:*** gkelly@soszlaw.com

RICHARD D. O'CONNOR (Resident, Hartford, Connecticut Office).

EDWARD F. O'DONNELL, JR. (Resident, Hartford, Connecticut Office).

ROBERT J. PERCY (Resident, Hartford, Connecticut Office).

DONALD W. STRICKLAND (Resident, Hartford, Connecticut Office).

MARIO J. ZANGARI, born Providence, Rhode Island, September 13, 1940; admitted to bar, 1970, Connecticut and U.S. Tax Court. *Education:* Bryant College (B.S., magna cum laude, 1966); Suffolk University (J.D., 1969); New York University (LL.M. in Taxation, 1970). Note Editor, Suffolk University Law Review, 1968-1969. Author: "Planning Retirement From A CPA Practice," Practicing CPA, March, 1983. Co-Author: "Dower As A Marital Deduction; What Current Factors Influence A Court's Decision," Journal of Taxation, May, 1971. Member, New Haven Technology Investment Fund, Inc., 1991—. *Member:* Connecticut (Member, Tax Law, Business Law Sections, Professional Ethics Committee) and American (Member, Sections on: Taxation Law; Business Law) Bar Associations. Charter Fellow, Connecticut Bar Foundation (Member, James W. Cooper Fellows Program). (Resident). ***PRACTICE AREAS:*** Business Law; Taxation Law; Estate Planning Law. ***Email:*** mzangari@soszlaw.com

OF COUNSEL

ROBERT W. BLYTHE, born Derby, Connecticut, March 28, 1955; admitted to bar, 1980, Connecticut and U.S. District Court, District of Connecticut. *Education:* University of Connecticut (B.A., B.S., magna cum laude, with distinction, 1977); Temple University (J.D., cum laude, 1980). Pi Sigma Alpha; Phi Alpha Delta. Member, 1978-1979 and Executive Editor, 1979-1980, Temple Law Quarterly. Author: Notes, "52 Temple Law Quarterly 854 and 350," 1979. Chairman, Inland Wetlands Agency, Woodbridge, Connecticut, 1993—. *Member:* Connecticut and American Bar Associations. (Resident). ***PRACTICE AREAS:*** Real Estate Law; Commercial Law. ***Email:*** rblythe@soszlaw.com

JAY S. SIEGEL (Resident, Hartford, Connecticut Office).

JODY PAGANO BENBOW, born New Haven, Connecticut, January 17, 1970; admitted to bar, 1996, Connecticut; 1998, U.S. District Court, District of

(This Listing Continued)

Connecticut. *Education:* University of Connecticut (B.A., cum laude, 1992); Western New England College School of Law (J.D., cum laude, 1996). *Member:* Connecticut and American Bar Associations; Connecticut School Attorney Council; National School Board Association Council of School Attorneys. (Resident). ***PRACTICE AREAS:*** Labor Law; Employment Law; Education Law; Special Education Law. ***Email:*** jbenbow@soszlaw.com

SHAWN P. COYNE (Resident, Hartford, Connecticut Office).

ANA ISABEL DeMOURA (Resident, Hartford, Connecticut, Office).

KEVIN J. DIADAMO, born New Haven, Connecticut, October 15, 1973; admitted to bar, 1998, Connecticut; 1999, District of Columbia. *Education:* College of the Holy Cross (B.A., 1995); Quinnipiac College (J.D., 1998). Recipient, Distinguished Academic Achievement Award, 1997, 1998. Associate Editor, Quinnipiac Probate Law Journal, 1997-1998. Quinnipiac Probate Law Journal, "In Re Estate of Cooper: Washington's Revised Prudent Investor Rule," Vol. 12, No. 2, 1997. *Member:* New Haven County and Connecticut Bar Associations; District of Columbia Bar (Member, Estates, Trusts and Probate Law Section, 2001). (Resident). ***PRACTICE AREAS:*** Estate Planning; Corporate; Tax. ***Email:*** kdiadamo@soszlaw.com

PAUL H. GAMACHE (Resident, Hartford, Connecticut Office).

DANIEL P. MURPHY, born New York, N.Y., June 4, 1968; admitted to bar, 1994, New Jersey; 1995, New York, U.S. District Court, District of New Jersey and U.S. Court of Appeals, Third Circuit; 1998, Connecticut and U.S. District Court, District of Connecticut. *Education:* Lafayette College (A.B., 1990); Seton Hall University (J.D., 1994). Municipal Prosecutor, Borough of Roselle Park, NJ, 1995. (Resident). ***PRACTICE AREAS:*** Employment Law; Labor Law; Education Law; Immigration Law. ***Email:*** dmurphy@soszlaw.com

JOHN J. O'CONNELL (Resident, Hartford, Connecticut Office).

REPRESENTATIVE CLIENTS: Accessory Controls & Equipment Corp.; Allan S. Goodman, Inc.; Anthem-Blue Cross/Blue Shield of Connecticut; Bristol Hospital; Brockway-Smith Company; C.I.A.C.; State of Ct. Judicial Dept.; Connecticut Lodging & Attraction Association; Connecticut Restaurant Association; Connecticut Tool & Manufacturing Association; Dana Corporation; Data-Mail, Inc.; Fordham Distributors; Franklin Distributors, Inc.; Hartford Distributors, Inc.; Hospital of St. Raphael; Kimberly-Clark Corp.; Kollmorgen Corp.; Madison Square Garden; Mechanics Uniform Services, Inc.; New Britain General Hospital; New London Board of Education; Rogers Corp.; Rogo Distributors; Unisource; Seviroli Foods, Inc.; Stanadyne Automotive Corp.; SuperValu; Wallingford Board of Ed.; Wild Oats Markets, Inc.; Woodstock Academy.

(For Biographical Data on Personnel at Hartford, see Hartford, Connecticut Professional Biographies).

SILVER, GOLUB & TEITELL LLP

NEW HAVEN, CONNECTICUT

(See Stamford)

Trial Practice in all State and Federal Courts. Medical Malpractice, Negligence, Commercial Litigation, Family and Criminal Law.

SILVERSTEIN & OSACH, P.C.

Established in 1973

SUITE 903, 234 CHURCH STREET
P.O. BOX 1727
NEW HAVEN, CONNECTICUT 06507
Telephone: 203-865-0121
Fax: 203-865-0255
Email: taxlawyer@worldnet.att.net

General Tax Practice. Federal and State Tax Litigation. Estate Planning, Probate, Corporation, Pension and Profit Sharing Law.

NATHAN M. SILVERSTEIN, born Hartford, Connecticut, February 1, 1924; admitted to bar, 1950, Connecticut; 1951, U.S. Tax Court; 1965, U.S. Claims Court. *Education:* St. Olaf College; University of Connecticut; Boston University (LL.B., 1950); New York University (LL.M. in Taxation, 1951). Trial Attorney, Office of Chief Counsel, Internal Revenue Service, 1951-1956. *Member:* New Haven County, The Connecticut (Member, Executive Committee, Taxation Section, 1981—) and American (Member, Civil and Criminal Tax Penalties Committee, 1971—, Section on Taxation) Bar Associations. ***PRACTICE AREAS:*** Tax Law; Litigation; Estate Planning Law. ***Email:*** nsilverstein@so-law.com

RONALD C. OSACH, born New York, N.Y., February 3, 1948; admitted to bar, 1975, New York; 1977, Connecticut and U.S. Claims Court; 1981, U.S. Tax Court. *Education:* Bucknell University (B.A., 1970); New England Law School (J.D., cum laude, 1974); New York University (LL.M. in Taxation, 1975). Author: "New Election Extends Estate Tax Payment Up To 15 Years," Estate Planning, January, 1977; "Economic Recovery Act Changes, Enhance The Benefits of Electing Special Use Valuation," Estate Planning, March, 1982. Chairman, Tax Section, Connecticut Bar Association. Chairman, Committee on Arts and the Law, 1979-1984. *Member:* New Haven County, The Connecticut (Member, Executive Committee of Tax Section, Young Lawyers Section, 1979-1982) and American (Member, Taxation Section) Bar Associations. ***PRACTICE AREAS:*** Tax Law; Tax Litigation; Estate Planning; Corporate Pension. ***Email:*** rosach@so-law.com

(This Listing Continued)

KURT F. ZIMMERMANN, born Milwaukee, Wisconsin, May 23, 1947; admitted to bar, 1977, Massachusetts; 1982, U.S. Court of Appeals, Second Circuit; 1986, Connecticut and U.S. District Court, District of Connecticut. *Education:* University of Connecticut (B.A., 1971); New England School of Law (J.D., 1976); Georgetown University (LL.M. in Taxation, 1977). Recipient, American Jurisprudence Book Awards in Evidence and Equity. Student Articles Editor, New England Law Review, 1975-1976. Trial Attorney, Tax Division, U.S. Department of Justice, Washington, D.C., 1977-1982. Assistant U.S. Attorney, District of Connecticut, 1982-1986. Adjunct Professor, University of Bridgeport School of Law, Graduate Tax Program, Tax Practice and Procedure/Criminal Tax, 1988—. *Member:* Westport and Connecticut (Member, Tax Section) Bar Associations. ***PRACTICE AREAS:*** Tax Law; Litigation. ***Email:*** kzimmermann@so-law.com

---

LEONARD K. ATKINSON, JR., born Bridgeport, Connecticut, February 13, 1966; admitted to bar, 1991, Connecticut. *Education:* University of Connecticut (B.A., 1988); University of Bridgeport (J.D., cum laude, 1991). Notes and Comments Editor, University of Bridgeport Law Review. Recipient, American Jurisprudence Award-Evidence; Merit Scholarship. Author: Note, "The Origins of Wiretapping in Connecticut," University of Bridgeport Law Review, Volume 12, Issue 1. Commissioner of the Superior Court, 1991—. *Member:* New Haven County and Connecticut Bar Associations. ***PRACTICE AREAS:*** Tax; Estate Planning; Pensions. ***Email:*** latkinson@so-law.com

TAX COUNSEL: Birken Manufacturing Co.; The Edart Truck Rental Corp.; General Plasma, Inc.

LAW OFFICES OF ROBERT M. SINGER, L.L.C.

NEW HAVEN, CONNECTICUT

(See Hamden)

General Civil Practice. Business Law, Commercial Litigation, Bankruptcy, Collections, Insurance, Tax Delinquencies, Tax Appeals and Audits, and Tax Planning.

BENSON A. SNAIDER, P.C.

Established in 1972

389 ORANGE STREET
NEW HAVEN, CONNECTICUT 06511
Telephone: 203-777-6426
Fax: 203-782-0366
Email: bslaw@snet.net
URL: http://www.lawyers.com/bslaw

Condemnation, Zoning, Real Estate Development, Land Use.

BENSON A. SNAIDER, born New Haven, Connecticut, October 2, 1937; admitted to bar, 1962, Connecticut; 1966, Florida, U.S. Court of Appeals, Second Circuit, U.S. Court of Military Appeals and U.S. Supreme Court; 1967, U.S. District Court, District of Connecticut; 1985, U.S. Court of Appeals, Eighth Circuit; 1984, U.S. Tax Court. *Education:* University of Vermont (B.A., 1959); University of Virginia (LL.B., 1962). Sigma Nu Phi. Author: "Recognition of Fixture Loss in Condemnation Proceedings," Connecticut Bar Journal, June, 1973; "Condemnation Procedures: The Need for Uniformity," Connecticut Bar Journal, September, 1975. Assistant Attorney General, State of Connecticut, 1966-1967; 1969-1970. Secretary, Shubert Performing Arts Center, Inc., 1983-1987. Trial Attorney Referee, 1991—. *Member:* New Haven County (Member, Executive Committee, 1977—; Chairman, Lawyers Brokers Committee, 1979-1989; Lawyers Referral Committee, 1983-1987; Secretary, 1985-1986), Connecticut (Member: House of Delegates, 1977-1978; Real Property Section; Executive Committee, 1984-1988) and American (Member: Committee on Condemnation Law, Local Government Law Section, 1973—; Litigation Section, 1978—) Bar Associations; The Florida Bar; Connecticut Trial Lawyers Association; The Association of Trial Lawyers of America. [Capt., JAGC, U.S. Army, 1963-1966]. ***REPORTED CASES:*** Corbin Development Company, Inc. v. Commissioner of Transportation, 176 Conn. 63 (1978); Caserta v. Zoning Board of Appeals, 226 Conn. 80 (1993); Giovacchino v. Licsak, 34 Conn. App. 906 (1994); Newman v. Schiff, 778 F.2d 460 (8th Cir. 1985). ***PRACTICE AREAS:*** Condemnation; Eminent Domain; Zoning Law; Divorce.

REPRESENTATIVE CLIENTS: Bank of New Haven; Walbro Automotive Co.; Priority Care Inc.; Nationwide Insurance Co.

(This Listing Continued)

BENSON A. SNAIDER, P.C., New Haven—Continued

APPROVED ATTORNEY FOR: First American Title Insurance Co.; Connecticut Attorneys Title Insurance Co.
REFERENCES: The Bank of New Haven.

SNOW, ATTICKS & HOLLO, LLC

NEW HAVEN, CONNECTICUT

(See Madison)

General Practice including Real Estate, Financing, Banking, Business Law, Probate, Wills, Tax, Trusts and Estates, Personal Injury and Civil and Criminal Litigation, Family Law, Trials in all State and Federal Courts.

STEVENS, CARROLL & CARVETH

NEW HAVEN, CONNECTICUT

(See Milford)

Real Estate, Zoning, Condominium, Family, Civil Litigation, Criminal Litigation, Corporate Law, Business Law, Appeals in all Courts, Workers Compensation, Estate Planning, Wills, Probate.

J. MICHAEL SULZBACH

385 ORANGE STREET

NEW HAVEN, CONNECTICUT 06511

Telephone: 203-781-0880

Fax: 203-781-0861

Trials and Appeals in State and Federal Courts. Insurance, Real Estate, Products Liability and Probate Law.

J. MICHAEL SULZBACH, born Long Beach, California, July 5, 1947; admitted to bar, 1972, Connecticut; 1975, U.S. Supreme Court; 1990, U.S. Tax Court. *Education:* University of Pennsylvania (B.A., with honors in History, 1969; J.D., 1972). Associate Editor, 1970-1971 and Editor, 1971-1972, University of Pennsylvania Law Review. Attorney Trial Referee, State of Connecticut, 1992—. *Member:* New Haven County (President, 1986-1987; Chairman, Real Estate Committee, 1988—; Member, Executive Committee, 1978—; Chairman, Lawyer Referral Committee, 1979-1982, President, 1986-1987), Connecticut (Member, House of Delegates, 1988—) and American Bar Associations. [LTC, USAR, Ret.]. ***REPORTED CASES:*** New England Savings Bank v. Bedford Realty Corp., 238 Conn. 745. ***PRACTICE AREAS:*** Trials and Appeals in State and Federal Courts; Insurance; Real Estate; Products Liability; Probate Law; Health Care.

COUNSEL FOR: Hill Central Community Cooperative, Inc.; Madison Beach Club, Inc.; Tuxis Lumber Co., Inc.; Berkshire Petroleum, Inc.; Marathon Ink Co.; SMS Textile Mills, Inc.; Spantex, Inc.
LOCAL COUNSEL FOR: American Telephone & Telegraph Co.; Chrysler Motors Corp.; Data General Corp.; Cushman & Wakefield Inc.; Merrill Lynch; Public Service Mutual Insurance Co.; Smith & Wesson.

SUMMA & RYAN, P.C.

NEW HAVEN, CONNECTICUT

(See Waterbury)

Management, Labor and Employment Law, Labor Relation, Equal Employment Opportunity.

SUSMAN, DUFFY & SEGALOFF, P.C.

Established in 1977

55 WHITNEY AVENUE

NEW HAVEN, CONNECTICUT 06510-1300

Telephone: 203-624-9830

Fax: 203-562-8430

URL: http://www.lawyers.com/susmanduffy

Mailing Address: P.O. Box 1684, New Haven, Connecticut 06507-1684

Administrative, Appellate, Banking, Bankruptcy, Business, Civil Trial, Commercial, Commercial Litigation, Corporate, Construction, Creditors Rights, Criminal Trial, Employment Law, Eminent Domain, Environmental, Family, Franchise, Governmental Relations Law, Healthcare, Housing, Insurance Defense, Land Use, Legal Malpractice Defense, Medical Malpractice Defense, Municipal Bond Public Authority Financing, Non Profit and Tax Exempt Organizations Municipal, Personal Injury, Product Liability, Probate, Professional Liability Defense, Real Estate, Trial Practice in all State and Federal Courts, Trusts and Estates, Wills and Probate, Urban Development, Zoning.

(This Listing Continued)

ALLEN H. DUFFY (1931-1986).

MICHAEL SUSMAN, born New Haven, Connecticut, March 20, 1931; admitted to bar, 1955, Connecticut. *Education:* University of Connecticut (B.A., 1952; LL.B., 1955). Member, Board of Editors, University of Connecticut Law Review, 1954-1955. *Member:* New Haven County, Connecticut and American Bar Associations. ***PRACTICE AREAS:*** Real Estate Development Law; Real Estate Leasing; Municipal Law; Commercial Law. ***Email:*** msusman@susmanduffy.com

JAMES H. SEGALOFF, born New Haven, Connecticut, September 1, 1943; admitted to bar, 1969, Connecticut. *Education:* Syracuse University (A.B., 1965); University of Connecticut (LL.B., 1968). *Member:* New Haven County and Connecticut Bar Associations. ***PRACTICE AREAS:*** Commercial Law; Real Estate Law; Corporate Law. ***Email:*** jsegaloff@susmanduffy.com

JOSEPH E. FAUGHNAN, born New Haven, Connecticut, August 25, 1950; admitted to bar, 1976, Connecticut. *Education:* Fordham University (B.A., 1972); University of Connecticut (J.D., with honors, 1976). Member and Chairman, North Branford Planning and Zoning Commission, 1987—. Waterbury Judicial District Grievance Panel. *Member:* New Haven County and Connecticut (Member, Academy of Continuing Professional Development, 1984-1985) Bar Associations; Connecticut Trial Lawyers Association. ***PRACTICE AREAS:*** Civil Litigation; Commercial Law; Construction Law. ***Email:*** jfaughnan@susmanduffy.com

SUSAN W. WOLFSON, born Brooklyn, New York, May 2, 1938; admitted to bar, 1976, Connecticut. *Education:* Barnard College (B.A., 1959); University of Connecticut (J.D., with honors, 1976). Certified Mediator, Academy of Family Mediators, Connecticut Council For Divorce Mediation. President, Statewide Legal Services, 1996-1998. Chief Victims Compensation Commissioner, State of Connecticut, 1993-1997. Member, Board of Directors, New Haven Legal Assistance Association, 1982-1992. Director, Connecticut Legal Services Corporation, 1989-1991. President, Board of Directors, Statewide Legal Services, 1996. Member, Board of Directors, 1996-2000. Member, Judicial Council on Legal Ethics, 1990-1992. Director, Sta-Fed ADR, Inc., 1993-1994. Editorial Board, Connecticut Law Tribune, 1998—. *Member:* New Haven County (President, 1983-1984), Connecticut (President, 1991-1992; Member, Executive Committee, Family Law Section, 1982—; Chair, Family Law Section Clinic, 1987-1991; Member: Board of Governors, 1983-1987; Task Force on Court Delay, 1984. Chair, Judiciary Committee, 1992-1994; Chair, Ad Hoc Committee on Arbitration of Disputes between Lawyers, 1989; Chair, Pro Bono Committee, 1989-1990; Chair, Gender Equity Committee, 1993-1999) and American (Member, House of Delegates, 1989-1993; Family Law Section, 1980—; Chair, Alimony and Spousal Support Committee, 1995—, Member Council, 1999—; Standing Committee on Competence in the Profession, 1995-1998; Standing Committee on Professionalism, 1999—) Bar Associations; Connecticut Trial Lawyers Association. Fellow: Connecticut Bar Foundation (Member, Board of Directors, 1992—); American Bar Foundation. ***PRACTICE AREAS:*** Family Law; Civil Litigation. ***Email:*** swolfson@susmanduffy.com

LAURA M. SKLAVER, born Waterbury, Connecticut, April 23, 1950; admitted to bar, 1981, Connecticut. *Education:* Wellesley College (B.A., 1972); Case Western Reserve University (M.S.L.S., 1975); University of Connecticut (J.D., with honors, 1981). *Member:* New Haven County, Connecticut (Member: Executive Committee, Business Law Section, 1994—; Secretary, 1996-1997; Treasurer, 1997-1998; Elder Law; Estates and Tax Sections) and American Bar Associations. ***PRACTICE AREAS:*** Business Law; Closely Held Corporations; Limited Liability Company; Partnership Law; Real Estate Financing Law; Estate Planning Law; Healthcare Law; Franchise Law. ***Email:*** lsklaver@susmanduffy.com

ANDREW R. LUBIN, born Hackensack, New Jersey, December 15, 1954; admitted to bar, 1979, Illinois; 1982, Connecticut. *Education:* Clark University (B.A., 1976); John Marshall Law School (J.D., with distinction, 1979). Member, Order of John Marshall. Judicial Law Clerk, Connecticut Superior Court, 1982-1983. Advisor, Connecticut Law Revision Commission Re: Revised Article 9 of the UCC, 2000; Connecticut Law Revision Commission, Re: Electric Communications, 1999. *Member:* New Haven County (Member, Real Property Committee), Connecticut (Member: House of Delegates, 1990-1996; Board of Governors, 1992-1995; Real Property Section, Executive Committee, 1989—, Chairman, 1997-1999; Financial Institutions Section; Commercial Finance Committee, Chairman, 1999—; Commercial Law and Bankruptcy Section; Member: UCC Committee; Revision Committee for "The Connecticut Common Interest Ownership Manual"; Committee on Legal Opinions) and American (Member: Real Property, Probate and Trust Law Section; Leasing Subcommittee) Bar Associations; American College of Real Estate Lawyers. Fellow: Connecticut Bar Foundation. ***PRACTICE AREAS:*** Real Estate Law; Real Estate Finance; Commercial and Finance Law; Leasing Law; Common Interest Community (Condominium) Law; Business Law. ***Email:*** alubin@susmanduffy.com

JAMES J. PERITO, born Wolfeboro, New Hampshire, July 23, 1956; admitted to bar, 1983, Connecticut; 1984, Florida; U.S. Supreme Court; Mashantucket Pequot Tribal Court. *Education:* Lafayette College (B.S. Biology,

(This Listing Continued)

1978); University of Connecticut (J.D., 1983). Joseph Bogdanski Moot Court Award. Judicial Law Clerk, Connecticut Superior Court, 1983-1985. Past Member: Branford Inland Wetlands Commission and Conservation Commission. Member, Branford Land Trust. *Member:* New Haven County and Connecticut (Member: Sections on Conservation and Environmental Quality, Planning & Zoning, Consumer Law; Committee on Professional Ethics) Bar Associations. ***PRACTICE AREAS:*** Zoning Law; Environmental Law; Commercial Law; Real Estate Law; Civil Litigation. ***Email:*** jperito@susmanduffy.com

MATTHEW C. SUSMAN, born New Haven, Connecticut, November 26, 1957; admitted to bar, 1984, Connecticut; 1985, New York; 1986, Vermont. *Education:* Cornell University; Columbia University (A.B., 1979); Fordham University (J.D., 1984). Member: Fordham Urban Law Journal, 1982-1984; Town of Hamden Board of Ethics, 1992-1996; Economic Development Commission, 1996—; Board of Directors, South Central Connecticut Regional Growth Partnership, 1996—. *Member:* New Haven County, Connecticut (Member: Executive Committee, Commercial Law and Bankruptcy Sections) and American (Member, Business Law Section) Bar Associations. ***PRACTICE AREAS:*** Commercial Law; Corporate Law; Real Estate Law; Municipal Finance. ***Email:*** mcsusman@susmanduffy.com

THOMAS E. KATON, born Hartford, Connecticut, August 25, 1959; admitted to bar, 1986, Connecticut and U.S. District Court, District of Connecticut; 1997, U.S. Court of Appeals, Second Circuit. *Education:* University of Pennsylvania (B.A., 1981); University of Bridgeport (J.D., 1986). Associate Editor, University of Bridgeport Law Review, 1985-1986. Author: Note, "Connecticut Mandatory Cable Access Statute: Ripe for Review," 7 Univ. of Bridgeport Law Review 329, 1986. Member, Theodore I. Koskoff American Inns of Court. *Member:* New Haven County, Connecticut and American Bar Associations; Connecticut Trial Lawyers Association; Defense Research Institute (Member, Steering Committee, Professional Liability Section; State Liaison to Business Litigation Committee); Professional Liability Underwriters Society; Connecticut Defense Lawyers Association; Association of Trial Lawyers of America. ***REPORTED CASES:*** Hotz Corporation v. Carabetta, 226 Conn. 812, (1993). ***PRACTICE AREAS:*** Civil Litigation; Insurance Defense; Employment Law; Criminal Law. ***Email:*** tkaton@susmanduffy.com

---

JENNIFER L. SCHANCUPP, born Danbury, Connecticut, December 29, 1961; admitted to bar, 1992, Connecticut; 1993, U.S. District Court, District of Connecticut. *Education:* Kenyon College (A.B., magna cum laude, 1983); University of Connecticut (J.D., 1992). Phi Beta Kappa. *Member:* Connecticut and American Bar Associations. ***PRACTICE AREAS:*** Civil Litigation; Commercial Litigation; Creditors Rights; Employment Law; Bankruptcy; Insurance Defense. ***Email:*** jschancupp@susmanduffy.com

PETER G. KRUZYNSKI, born Mineola, New York, September 14, 1966; admitted to bar, 1993, Connecticut. *Education:* Georgetown University (B.S., 1988); Syracuse University (J.D., 1993). Associate Editor, Syracuse Law Review, 1991-1993. *Member:* New Haven County and Connecticut Bar Associations. ***REPORTED CASES:*** Okemo Mountain, Inc. v. Sikorski (In Re Sikorski 239 B.R. 661 (D. Conn 1999). ***PRACTICE AREAS:*** Litigation; Banks and Banking; Collections; Commercial Law; Bankruptcy. ***Email:*** pkruzynski@susmanduffy.com

MICHAEL C. CONROY, born Hartford, Connecticut; admitted to bar, 1995, Vermont; 1996, U.S. District Court, District of Vermont; 2001, Connecticut and U.S. District Court, District of Connecticut. *Education:* Dartmouth College (A.B., 1989); Vermont Law School (J.D., 1995). *Member:* New Haven County and Vermont Bar Associations; Vermont Trial Lawyers Association. ***LANGUAGES:*** Spanish. ***PRACTICE AREAS:*** Civil Litigation; Insurance Defense; Insurance Coverage; Professional Malpractice Defense. ***Email:*** mconroy@susmanduffy.com

BAIER S. STEPHANIE, born New London, Connecticut, June 26, 1971; admitted to bar, 2001, Connecticut. *Education:* Eastern Connecticut State University (B.S., 1993); University of Connecticut (J.D., 2001). ***PRACTICE AREAS:*** Commercial Law; Business Law; Family Law. ***Email:*** sbaier@susmanduffy.com

OF COUNSEL

DIANA C. BALLARD, born Mahopac, New York, October 9, 1945; admitted to bar, 1986, Connecticut. *Education:* Bellevue School of Nursing (R.N., with honors, 1968); University of New Haven (M.B.A., 1978); Pace University (J.D., 1986). Member, Connecticut Health Lawyers, 1988—; American Association of Nurse Attorneys, 1990—. Certified Healthcare Executive, American College of Healthcare Executives, 1985-1997. Registered Nurse, Connecticut and New York, 1968. *Member:* Connecticut (Member, Elderly Law Section, 1992—) and American (Member, Sections on: Administrative, Medicine and Law Committee) Bar Associations; American Health Lawyers Association. ***PRACTICE AREAS:*** Healthcare Law; Mediation.

(This Listing Continued)

DAVID P. HAMBLETON, born Nashua, New Hampshire, 1939; admitted to bar, 1964, Connecticut. *Education:* Dartmouth College (A.B., cum laude, 1960); Columbia University (LL.B., 1963); New York University (LL.M. in Taxation, 1973). Editor, Columbia Law Review, 1962-1963. Clerk, Judge M. Joseph Blumenfeld, U.S. District Court, Connecticut, 1963-1964. *Member:* Connecticut Bar Association. ***PRACTICE AREAS:*** Corporation Law; Business Law.

REPRESENTATIVE CLIENTS: Architects & Engineers Insurance Company; Bank of New York; Carabetta Enterprises, Inc.; Chicago Title Insurance Co.; Citizens Bank; Deitsch Plastic Co.; First City Servicing, Inc.; First State Insurance Company; First Union National Bank; Fleet Bank, N.A.; Gulf Insurance Company; Harbor Health Services, Inc.; Hartford Insurance Company of Illinois; Hudson United Bank; Kmart Corporation; M & M Investments; New Haven Savings Bank; The New Haven Rowing Club; New Haven Water Pollution Control Authority; Peoples Bank; The Related Companies; SKM, Inc. d/b/a Toad's Place; Southern New England Telephone Co., Inc.; Southland Corporation; Town of Woodbridge; Twin City Fire Insurance Company; Webster Bank; West Haven Water Pollution Control Commission; Yale Ambulatory Services Corporation; Yale New Haven Hospital.

TINLEY, NASTRI, RENEHAN & DOST, LLP

NEW HAVEN, CONNECTICUT

(See Waterbury)

Trial Practice in State and Federal Courts. Commercial Litigation, Bankruptcy, Employment Law, Personal Injury, Workers Compensation, Collections, Elder Law, Estate Planning, Probate.

TYLER COOPER & ALCORN, LLP

Established in 1847

205 CHURCH STREET
P.O. BOX 1936
NEW HAVEN, CONNECTICUT 06509-1910
Telephone: 203-784-8200
Telecopier: 203-789-2133
URL: http://www.tylercooper.com

Hartford, Connecticut Office: CityPlace. Telephone: 860-725-6200. Telecopier: 860-278-3802.

Stamford, Connecticut Office: One Landmark Square. Telephone: 203-348-5555. Telecopier: 203-348-3875.

Greenwich, Connecticut Office: 675 Steamboat Road. Telephone: 203-869-2000. Telecopier: 203-869-2001.

Madison, Connecticut Office: 23 Woodland Road. Telephone: 203-318-3600. Telecopier: 203-318-3609.

Administrative Law, Alternative Dispute Resolution, Antitrust and Trade Regulation, Banking, Bankruptcy and Reorganization, Business Crimes, Business Organizations and Securities Law, Computer Law, Domestic Relations, Environmental Law, Financial Services, Franchising, Health Care, Immigration, Insurance Defense and Insurance Coverage Defense, Intellectual Property, Labor and Employment, Legislative Lawyering, Litigation, Media Law, Medical Malpractice Defense, Pension and Employee Benefits, Public Utilities, Real Estate, Taxation, Trusts and Estates and Workers' Compensation.

MEMBERS OF FIRM

RALPH GREGORY ELLIOT, born Hartford, Connecticut, October 20, 1936; admitted to bar, 1961, Connecticut. *Education:* Yale University (B.A., 1958; LL.B., 1961). Phi Beta Kappa. Law Clerk to Justice William J. Shea, Connecticut Supreme Court, 1961-1962. Adjunct Professor of Law, University of Connecticut School of Law, 1973—. Member, State Criminal Justice Commission, 1991-1995. Town Counsel, Town of Salisbury, 1981—. Chairman, Connecticut Legal Specialization Screening Committee, 1981—. Chairman, U.S. District Court Panel of Special Masters, 1983-1988. Connecticut Superior Court Trial Referee, 1984-1995. Co-Chairman, United States Constitution Bicentennial Commission of Connecticut, 1986-1991. Chairman, Board of Editors, Connecticut Law Tribune, 1986-1987. President, 1988-1990, and Chairman, Executive Committee, 1990-1992, Yale Law School Association. Chairman, Health Insurance Law Committee, Tort and Insurance Practice Section, 1985-1986, Member, Standing Committee on Ethics and Professional Responsibility, 1989-1995, Standing Committee on Amicus Curiae Briefs, 1996-1998 and Standing Committee on Professional Discipline, 1998—, American Bar Association. President, Connecticut Bar Association, 1985-1986. *Member:* American Law Institute. Fellow, American Bar Foundation. (Resident at Hartford Office). ***PRACTICE AREAS:*** Litigation; Constitutional Law; Media Law; Municipal; Legal Ethics.

MICHAEL J. DORNEY, born Ansonia, Connecticut, November 21, 1938; admitted to bar, 1963, Connecticut. *Education:* Boston College (B.A., 1960; LL.B., 1963). National President, American Law Student Association, 1962-1963. Town Counsel, Town of Orange, 1969-1995. Member, 1970-1985, and Chairman, 1973-1976, Executive Committee, Labor and Employment Law Sec-

(This Listing Continued)

TYLER COOPER & ALCORN, LLP, New Haven—Continued

tion; Member, 1985—, Federal Practice Committee, Connecticut Bar Association. *Member:* Defense Research Institute. Certified as a Civil Trial Advocate by the National Board of Trial Advocacy. ***PRACTICE AREAS:*** Litigation, Labor and Employment Law, Municipal.

BRUCE LEWELLYN, born Hutchinson, Kansas, December 15, 1938; admitted to bar, 1967, California and Connecticut. *Education:* University of Kansas (B.S., 1960); Stanford University (LL.B., 1966). Phi Beta Kappa. Member, Board of Editors, Stanford Law Review, 1965-1966. ***PRACTICE AREAS:*** Pension and Employee Benefits; Real Estate; Banking. ***Email:*** lewellyn2@tylercooper.com

JOSEPH C. LEE, born New Haven, Connecticut, December 8, 1939; admitted to bar, 1967, Connecticut. *Education:* Georgetown University (A.B., 1961); University of Connecticut (J.D., 1967); Wesleyan University (M.A.L.S., 1999). Member, Board of Editors, Connecticut Law Review, 1965-1967. Author: "Administrative Law in Connecticut," 64 Connecticut Bar Journal SI-259 (1990). Chairman, Administrative Law Section, Connecticut Bar Association, 1989-1992. (Managing Partner of the Firm). ***PRACTICE AREAS:*** Energy; Public Utility Law; Secured Transactions; Cogeneration; Real Estate; Administrative Law. ***Email:*** lee@tylercooper.com

LEWIS SEGAL, born New York, N.Y., April 26, 1935; admitted to bar, 1960, Connecticut. *Education:* Columbia University (A.B., 1956); Yale University (LL.B., 1959). Chief Executive Officer, Century Brass Products, Inc., 1981-1987. (Resident at Hartford Office). ***PRACTICE AREAS:*** Business Law; Corporate Finance; Commercial Finance; Mergers and Acquisitions. ***Email:*** segal@tylercooper.com

IRVING S. SCHLOSS, born New York, N.Y., February 3, 1945; admitted to bar, 1972, Connecticut. *Education:* Harvard University (A.B., 1966); Yale University (LL.B., 1970). Phi Beta Kappa. Projects Editor, Yale Law Journal, 1969-1970. Law Clerk to Judge Spottswood W. Robinson, U.S. Court of Appeals, District of Columbia Circuit, 1970-1971. Chairman, Corporations and Other Business Organizations Section, 1988-1990 and Member, Executive Committee, Estates and Probate Section, Connecticut Bar Association. Member, Tax Management Advisory Board—Estates, Gifts and Trusts. *Member:* American College of Trusts and Estates Counsel; Connecticut Estate and Tax Planning, Inc. ***PRACTICE AREAS:*** Estate and Gift Taxation; Federal Tax Controversies; Trusts and Estates Taxation; Tax Litigation; Retirement Planning; Estate Planning. ***Email:*** ischlos@attglobal.net

JON T. HIRSCHOFF, born Minneapolis, Minnesota, September 23, 1941; admitted to bar, 1967, Connecticut. *Education:* Stanford University (A.B., 1963); Yale University (LL.B., 1967). Law Clerk to Judge J. Joseph Smith, U.S. Court of Appeals, Second Circuit, 1967-1968. Assistant Professor, 1972-1975, Associate Professor, 1975-1977, Indiana University School of Law. Adjunct Professor, Quinnipiac College School of Law, 1996—. Member, Section on Business, Law committee on Negotiated Acquisitions, American Bar Association, 1995—. ***PRACTICE AREAS:*** Corporate, Mergers and Acquisitions, Securities. ***Email:*** hirschoff@tylercooper.com

WILLIAM H. CHAMPLIN III, born Hartford, Connecticut, December 25, 1946; admitted to bar, 1972, Connecticut. *Education:* Georgetown University (B.S.F.S., 1968); University of Connecticut (M.B.A., 1975; J.D., 1972). Law Clerk to Justice Alva P. Loiselle, Connecticut Supreme Court, 1972-1973. (Resident at Hartford Office). ***PRACTICE AREAS:*** Litigation, Alternative Dispute Resolution. ***Email:*** champlin@tylercooper.com

TIMOTHY W. BINGHAM, born Washington, D.C., February 9, 1945; admitted to bar, 1971, Connecticut; 1972, District of Columbia. *Education:* Yale University (B.A., 1967; J.D., 1971). Phi Beta Kappa. Assistant to Dean, Yale Law School, 1970-1971. Law Clerk to Judge Gerhard A. Gesell, U.S. District Court, District of Columbia, 1971-1972. Chairman, Practising Law Institute Program on Repurchase Agreements and New Deposit Instruments, 1982. Chairman, New Haven Subcommittee, Computer Law Committee, 1984-1986, Vice Chairman, Consumer Law Section, 1986-1987, Connecticut Bar Association. ***PRACTICE AREAS:*** Banking, Consumer Credit, Computer Law. ***Email:*** bingham@tylercooper.com

DAVID W. SCHNEIDER, born Chillicothe, Ohio, September 7, 1942; admitted to bar, 1971, Connecticut. *Education:* Gettysburg College (B.A., 1964); Yale University (B.D., 1967; J.D., 1971). Phi Beta Kappa; Phi Alpha Theta. Member, Board of Editors, Yale Law Journal, 1969-1971. Law Clerk to Judge Robert P. Anderson, U.S. Court of Appeals, Second Circuit, 1971-1973. Chairman, Committee on Liaison with the State Courts, Connecticut Bar Association, 1985-1987. ***PRACTICE AREAS:*** Probate Litigation; Commercial Litigation. ***Email:*** schneider@tylercooper.com

ROBERT W. ALLEN, born Bridgeport, Connecticut, September 13, 1948; admitted to bar, 1973, Connecticut. *Education:* Wesleyan University (B.A., 1970); University of Connecticut (J.D., 1973). Law Clerk to Justice Herbert S. MacDonald, Connecticut Supreme Court, 1973-1974. ***PRACTICE AREAS:*** Litigation; Environmental Law; Consumer Credit; Insurance. ***Email:*** allen@tylercooper.com

RICHARD W. BOWERMAN, born New Haven, Connecticut, February 5, 1946; admitted to bar, 1975, Connecticut. *Education:* Gettysburg College (B.A., 1968); University of Connecticut (J.D., 1975). President, Connecticut Defense Lawyers Association, 1987-1988. Connecticut State Chairman, Defense Research Institute, 1990—. Certified as a Civil Trial Advocate by the National Board of Trial Advocacy. ***PRACTICE AREAS:*** Personal Injury; Employment Law; Entertainment Law; Commercial Litigation. ***Email:*** eagleye@iconn.net

GEORGE E. O'BRIEN, JR., born Holyoke, Massachusetts, January 31, 1947; admitted to bar, 1975, Connecticut. *Education:* Princeton University (A.B., 1969); University of Connecticut (J.D., 1975). Editor-in-Chief, Connecticut Law Review, 1974-1975. Law Clerk to Chief Judge T. Emmet Clarie, U.S. District Court, District of Connecticut, 1975-1976. ***PRACTICE AREAS:*** Litigation; Labor and Employment; Management Labor Law; Collective Bargaining; Labor Arbitration. ***Email:*** obrien@tylercooper.com

ROBERT J. METZLER II, born Allentown, Pennsylvania, February 5, 1948; admitted to bar, 1974, New York; 1976, Connecticut. *Education:* Princeton University (A.B., 1970); University of Connecticut (J.D., 1973); New York University. Law Clerk to Judge Thomas J. Meskill, U.S. Court of Appeals, Second Circuit, 1975-1976. Chairman, Public Utility Law Section, Connecticut Bar Association, 1981-1984. Fellow, American College of Investment Counsel. (Resident at Hartford Office). ***PRACTICE AREAS:*** Corporate, Public Utilities, Business Finance. ***Email:*** metzler@tylercooper.com

RONALD J. COHEN, born New York, N.Y., October 7, 1950; admitted to bar, 1975, Connecticut. *Education:* Trinity College (B.A., 1972); New York University (J.D., 1975). Order of the Coif. Member, 1973-1974, and Note and Comment Editor, 1974-1975, New York University Law Review. Law Clerk to Judge Jon O. Newman, U.S. District Court, District of Connecticut, 1975-1976. ***PRACTICE AREAS:*** Commercial Litigation; Commercial Landlord and Tenant Law; Antitrust and Trade Regulation; Health Care. ***Email:*** cohen@tylercooper.com

MARGARET P. MASON, born Radford, Virginia, March 6, 1944; admitted to bar, 1978, Connecticut. *Education:* Randolph-Macon Woman's College; Goucher College (B.A., 1975); Yale University (J.D., 1978). Phi Beta Kappa. Danforth Fellow. Member, Board of Editors, Yale Law Journal, 1977-1978. Chair, Statewide Grievance Committee, Director and Vice Chair, New Haven Legal Assistance Association, Inc., 1988—. Member, Executive Committee, Federal Practice Section, Connecticut Bar Association, 1985—. Director and Past President, New Haven County Bar Association, 1994-1995. President, New Haven County Bar Foundation, 1994-1997. Arthur Groman Trial Advocacy Fellow, Yale Law School, 1997. ***PRACTICE AREAS:*** Civil Litigation; Employment Law; Medical Malpractice Defense. ***Email:*** mason@tylercooper.com

WILLIAM W. BOUTON III, born Glen Cove, New York, March 14, 1953; admitted to bar, 1980, Connecticut. *Education:* Ohio Wesleyan University (B.A., 1976); University of Connecticut (J.D., 1980). Pi Sigma Alpha. (Resident at Hartford Office). ***PRACTICE AREAS:*** Banking, Corporate, Securities. ***Email:*** bouton@tylercooper.com

THOMAS C. CLARK, born Randolph, Vermont, September 3, 1942; admitted to bar, 1969, Connecticut; 1970, U.S. District Court, District of Connecticut. *Education:* Dartmouth College (B.A., 1964); Cornell University (J.D., 1969). Chancellor, Moot Court Board, 1968-1969. State Representative, 1975-1977. House Counsel, Connecticut General Assembly, 1977-1979; 1981-1983. Clerk, Connecticut House of Representatives, 1979-1981. Chairman: Connecticut Committee on Alternate Methods of Sentencing 1977-1978; Board of Protection and Advocacy for Handicapped. *Member:* Hartford County, Connecticut and American Bar Associations. (Resident at Hartford Office). ***PRACTICE AREAS:*** Insurance Coverage Litigation; Civil Litigation; Bad Faith; E-Commerce; Franchise Law. ***Email:*** clarkt@tylercooper.com

MARK V. CONNOLLY, born Danbury, Connecticut, January 3, 1957; admitted to bar, 1982, Connecticut; 1983, New York. *Education:* University of Connecticut (B.A., 1979; J.D., 1982). Phi Beta Kappa. Member, 1980-1981, and Administrative Editor, 1981-1982, Connecticut Law Review. (Resident at Hartford Office). ***PRACTICE AREAS:*** Litigation. ***Email:*** connolly@tylercooper.com

WILLIAM S. FISH, JR., born Manhasset, New York, May 20, 1958; admitted to bar, 1983, Connecticut. *Education:* State University of New York at Buffalo (B.A., 1980); University of Virginia (J.D., 1983). Phi Beta Kappa. Adjunct Professor of Law, University of Connecticut School of Law. Member, Executive Committee, Commercial Law and Bankruptcy Section, Connecticut Bar Association. *Member:* American Bankruptcy Institute. (Resident at Hartford Office). ***PRACTICE AREAS:*** Bankruptcy and Creditors' Rights; Commercial Litigation. ***Email:*** fish@tylercooper.com

KEVIN McCANN, born Roslyn Park, New York, March 8, 1954; admitted to bar, 1983, Connecticut. *Education:* Furman University (B.A., 1976); College of William & Mary (J.D., 1983); Boston University (LL.M., Taxation, 1994).

(This Listing Continued)

Member, Board of Editors, William & Mary Law Review, 1982-1983. Director, Connecticut Breast Cancer Coalition. (Resident at Hartford Office). ***PRACTICE AREAS:*** Estate Planning; Trusts and Estates; Elder Law; Retirement Planning. ***Email:*** mccann@tylercooper.com

DAVID J. WIESE, born New Britain, Connecticut, January 13, 1958; admitted to bar, 1984, Connecticut. *Education:* Boston College (B.S., 1980); Syracuse University (M.B.A., 1983; J.D., 1983). Member, 1981-1982, and Notes and Comments Editor, 1982-1983, Syracuse Journal of International Law and Commerce. Director, Bank Compliance Association of Connecticut, 1989-1993. Chairman, Consumer Law Section, Connecticut Bar Association, 1991-1994. Instructor, Connecticut School of Finance and Management. (Resident at Hartford Office). ***PRACTICE AREAS:*** Banking; Regulatory Compliance; Corporate. ***Email:*** wiese@tylercooper.com

EMMETT E. BROWN III, born Olean, New York, August 29, 1947; admitted to bar, 1978, New York; 1985, Connecticut. *Education:* Wharton School, University of Pennsylvania (B.S., 1972); Cornell University (M.B.A., 1976; J.D., 1977). [Capt., U.S. Army Special Forces, 1967-1971]. (Resident at Stamford Office). ***PRACTICE AREAS:*** Corporate Law; Intellectual Property; Emerging Growth Companies; Licensing Law; Franchise Law. ***Email:*** browne@tylercooper.com

JON P. LECKERLING, born Brooklyn, New York, August 17, 1948; admitted to bar, 1978, Connecticut. *Education:* United States Military Academy (B.S., 1970); Washington & Lee University (J.D., 1978). Omicron Delta Kappa. Managing Editor, Washington & Lee Law Review, 1977-1978. General Counsel: Armtek Corporation, 1986-1988; Echlin Inc., 1990-1999. Member, Section on Business, Committee on Negotiated Transactions, American Bar Association. [Capt., U.S. Army, 1970-1975]. (Resident at Madison Office). ***PRACTICE AREAS:*** Corporate; Mergers and Acquisitions; Real Estate; Estate Planning; Retirement Planning.

BEN A. SOLNIT, born New Haven, Connecticut, February 7, 1957; admitted to bar, 1984, Connecticut. *Education:* Wesleyan University (B.A., 1979); Yale University (J.D., 1984). Phi Beta Kappa. Law Clerk to Chief Justice Ellen A. Peters, Connecticut Supreme Court, 1984-1985. ***PRACTICE AREAS:*** Commercial Litigation; Appellate Practice. ***Email:*** solnit@tylercooper.com

JACQUELINE DeANDRUS BUCAR, born New Haven, Connecticut, September 9, 1944; admitted to bar, 1986, Connecticut. *Education:* University of Connecticut (B.S., 1966); Wesleyan University (M.A.L.S., 1973); University of Connecticut (J.D., 1986). Phi Beta Kappa; Pi Delta Phi. *Member:* American Immigration Lawyers Association; French-American Chamber of Commerce. ***LANGUAGES:*** French. ***PRACTICE AREAS:*** Labor and Employment; Immigration; Commercial Litigation. ***Email:*** bucar@tylercooper.com

FILLIS W. STOBER, born Hartford, Connecticut, October 20, 1949; admitted to bar, 1979, Connecticut. *Education:* University of Connecticut (B.A., 1971; J.D., 1979). Phi Beta Kappa. Member, Executive Committee, Banking Law Section, Connecticut Bar Association, 1985—. Secretary, Consumer Law Section, Connecticut Bar Association, 1994—. (Resident at Hartford Office). ***PRACTICE AREAS:*** Bank Regulation; E-Commerce; ATM Networks; Bank Collections; Bank Fraud; Check Fraud; Credit Union Law; Electronic Banking; Escrow Agent Liability; Truth in Lending. ***Email:*** stober@tylercooper.com

THOMAS S. MARRION, born New London, Connecticut, December 17, 1960; admitted to bar, 1985, Connecticut. *Education:* College of the Holy Cross (A.B., 1982); University of Connecticut (J.D., 1985). Member, 1983-1984, and Associate Editor, 1984-1985, Connecticut Law Review. Law Clerk to Chief Judge Robert L. Krechevsky, U.S. Bankruptcy Court, District of Connecticut, 1985-1987. Instructor, Creditors' Rights and Bankruptcy, University of Connecticut School of Law, 1992—. Member: Bolton Zoning Commission, 1989-1991, 1992-1993; Bolton Charter Revision Commission, 1988, 1992-1993. Member, Executive Committee, Commercial Law and Bankruptcy Section, Connecticut Bar Association, 1994—. (Resident at Hartford Office). ***PRACTICE AREAS:*** Corporate Law; Commercial Finance; Creditors Rights in Bankruptcy; Municipal Law; Health Care; Real Estate. ***Email:*** marrion@tylercooper.com

CHRISTOPHER P. McCORMACK, born Pittsburgh, Pennsylvania, January 16, 1957; admitted to bar, 1987, Connecticut. *Education:* Yale University (B.A., 1978); Eastman School of Music, University of Rochester (M.A. 1981); Fordham University (J.D., 1987). Pi Kappa Lambda. Writing and Research Editor, Fordham Law Review, 1986-1987. Law Clerk to Judge Thomas J. Meskill, U.S. Court of Appeals, Second Circuit, 1987-1988. ***PRACTICE AREAS:*** Commercial Litigation; Environmental Law; Environmental Insurance Coverage Law. ***Email:*** mccormac@tylercooper.com

CHRISTOPHER L. ULRICH, born Chicago, Illinois, June 27, 1953; admitted to bar, 1979, New York; 1990, Connecticut. *Education:* Georgetown University (A.B., 1975); Boston College (J.D., 1978). Senior Trial Attorney, District Attorney's Office, Kings County, New York, 1978-1986. Special Attorney, Organized Crime Strike Force, Eastern District of New York, U.S. Department of Justice, 1986-1989. (Resident at Stamford Office). ***Email:*** ulrich@tylercooper.com

(This Listing Continued)

KEVIN G. FERRIGNO, born Hartford, Connecticut, June 15, 1962; admitted to bar, 1989, Connecticut. *Education:* Union College (B.S., Chemistry, 1984); Western New England College School of Law; University of Connecticut (J.D., 1989). Member, 1993-1999 and Chairman, 1999—, Connecticut Historical Commission. Chairman, St. James Board of Education, 1999—. (Resident at Hartford Office). ***PRACTICE AREAS:*** Corporate Law; Real Estate; Environmental Law; Commercial Law; Mergers and Acquisitions. ***Email:*** ferrigno@tylercooper.com

LORI B. ALEXANDER, born Keene, New Hampshire, February 3, 1956; admitted to bar, 1990, Connecticut. *Education:* Dartmouth College (B.A., 1978); New York University (M.A., 1985); University of Connecticut (J.D., 1990). Member, 1988-1990, and Articles Editor, 1989-1990, Connecticut Law Review. ***PRACTICE AREAS:*** Employment Law; Personal Injury Defense; Immigration Law. ***Email:*** alexande@tylercooper.com

GREG R. BARRINGER, born Riverton, Wyoming, February 2, 1957; admitted to bar, 1988, Connecticut; 1991, Vermont. *Education:* University of Montana (B.A., 1980); Yale University; Columbia University (J.D., 1988). ***PRACTICE AREAS:*** Estate Planning; Probate; Elder Law; Real Estate. ***Email:*** barringe@tylercooper.com

WILLIAM F. CUMMINGS, born Buffalo, New York, May 23, 1963; admitted to bar, 1988, Pennsylvania; 1990, New York; 1992, Connecticut. *Education:* Fordham University; State University of New York at Buffalo (B.S., 1985; M.B.A., 1988; J.D., 1988). (Resident at Hartford Office). ***PRACTICE AREAS:*** Corporate; Banking; Securities; Investments. ***Email:*** cummings@tylercooper.com

PATRICIA E. REILLY, born Hartford, Connecticut, November 12, 1960; admitted to bar, 1991, Connecticut. *Education:* Wesleyan University (B.A., 1983); Boalt Hall School of Law, University of California, Berkeley (J.D., 1990). Articles Editor, Berkeley Women's Law Journal, 1989-1990. ***PRACTICE AREAS:*** Civil Litigation; Employment Law; Employment Discrimination; Sexual Harassment. ***Email:*** reilly@tylercooper.com

NOBLE F. ALLEN, born Banjul, The Gambia, November 13, 1959; admitted to bar, 1991, Connecticut. *Education:* Military College of Vermont; Norwich University (B.A., 1982); The American University (M.A., 1985; J.D., 1991). Chair, American Immigration Lawyers Association, 1999—. *Member:* Connecticut Defense Lawyers Association. ***PRACTICE AREAS:*** Litigation; Commercial Landlord and Tenant Law; Landlord and Tenant Law; Immigration Law. ***Email:*** allen@tylercooper.com

GLORY MARTYN LENA, born Bryn Mawr, Pennsylvania, May 29, 1966; admitted to bar, 1991, Connecticut. *Education:* Dartmouth College (B.A., 1988); Boston University (J.D., 1991). Member, 1989-1990, and Editor, 1990-1991, Boston University Law Review. (Resident at Hartford Office). ***PRACTICE AREAS:*** Civil Litigation; Products Liability; Medical Malpractice Defense; Appellate Practice. ***Email:*** lena@tylercooper.com

ROBERT B. FLYNN, born Baltimore, Maryland, May 5, 1963; admitted to bar, 1991, New Jersey; 1992, New York; 1995, Connecticut. *Education:* University of Notre Dame (B.A., 1985); Georgetown University Law Center (J.D., 1991). ***Email:*** flynn@tylercooper.com

NICLAS A. FERLAND, born Hartford, Connecticut, August 27, 1967; admitted to bar, 1992, Connecticut. *Education:* Kenyon College (B.A., with high honors, 1989); University of Connecticut (J.D., with honors, 1992). Law Clerk to the Hon. Alan H. W. Shiff, U.S. Bankruptcy Judge for the District of Connecticut, 1992-1993. ***PRACTICE AREAS:*** Bankruptcy; Commercial Finance. ***Email:*** ferland@tylercooper.com

OF COUNSEL

RICHARD G. BELL, born New York, N.Y., March 6, 1932; admitted to bar, 1960, Connecticut. *Education:* Yale University (B.A., 1954); Harvard University (LL.B., 1960). Author: "Acid Rain," 57 Conn. Bar Journal 261 (1983); "The Cross of Gold," 71 Conn. Bar Journal 261 (1997). President, New Haven County Bar Association, 1977-1978. Fellow: American Bar Foundation; Connecticut Bar Foundation. [U.S. Navy, 1954-1957]. ***PRACTICE AREAS:*** Banking, Corporate, Cable Television.

MILTON P. DeVANE, born New Haven, Connecticut, June 20, 1929; admitted to bar, 1958, Connecticut. *Education:* Yale University (B.A., 1950; LL.B., 1958); King's College, Cambridge, England. Phi Beta Kappa. Order of the Coif. Articles Editor, Yale Law Journal, 1957-1958. Law Clerk to Judge Carroll C. Hincks, U.S. Court of Appeals, Second Circuit, 1958-1959. Fellow: American Bar Foundation; Connecticut Bar Foundation. ***PRACTICE AREAS:*** Estate Planning, Probate and Trust Administration, Corporate.

WILLIAM S. ROGERS, born Hartford, Connecticut, July 1, 1932; admitted to bar, 1960, Connecticut. *Education:* Boston University School of Management (B.S., 1954); University of Connecticut (J.D., 1960). Member, Board of Editors, University of Connecticut Law Review, 1959-1960. Town Counsel, Town of Glastonbury, 1976—. Member, Securities Advisory Council, Connecticut Department of Banking, 1993—. Securities Arbitrator, NYSE, NASD and AAA. Faculty Member, Broker-Dealer Institute, PLI, 1991. Panel Member,

(This Listing Continued)

TYLER COOPER & ALCORN, LLP, New Haven—Continued

Securities Forum 1991 and 1994, Connecticut Department of Banking. Special Master, U.S. District Court, 1986-1988. Chairman, Municipal Law and Governmental Services Committee, 1983-1986, Judiciary Committee, 1985-1991, Connecticut Bar Association. [Pilot, U.S. Air Force, 1954-1957]. (Resident at Hartford Office). ***PRACTICE AREAS:*** Securities Law, Litigation and Regulation; Municipal Law and Litigation; Administrative Law and Litigation; Appellate Practice.

JAMES R. GREENFIELD, born Philadelphia, Pennsylvania, March 31, 1926; admitted to bar, 1950, Connecticut; 1951, U.S. District Court, District of Connecticut; 1959, U.S. Supreme Court; 1966, U.S. Court of Appeals, 2nd Circuit. *Education:* Bates College (B.S., 1947); Yale University (LL.B., 1950). Member, Board of Editors, Connecticut Bar Journal, 1962-1978. Instructor in Law, University of Connecticut Law School, 1968-1969; 1972-1973; 1975-1976. Member, Board of Directors, 1978-1984 and Secretary, 1982-1984, National Judicial College. Chairman, Committee of Professional Ethics, 1963-1968; Member, 1960-1963; 1969-1971; 2nd Vice President, 1971-1972; Vice President, 1972-1973 and President, 1973-1974, Board of Governors; Chairman, Judiciary Committee, 1974-1977; Member, Committees on: Minorities, 1988—; Gender Bias, 1991—, Connecticut Bar Association. Member: Board of Governors, 1978-1981; House of Delegates, 1972-1983; Chairman, Standing Committee National Conference Groups, 1981-1982; Member, 1982-1987 and Chairman, 1985, Committee on Scope and Correlation; Member, Commission on Status of Women, 1987-1991 American Bar Association. *Member:* New Haven County Bar Association (Treasurer, 1963-1968; Vice President, 1968-1969; President, 1969-1970; Recipient, Life Time Achievement Award); American Judicature Society (Member, Board of Directors, 1983-1985); Connecticut Bar Foundation (President, 1975-1977); American Law Institute. Fellow: American Bar Foundation; American Academy of Matrimonial Lawyers; (President, Connecticut Chapter, 1993-1994); International Academy of Matrimonial Lawyers. ***PRACTICE AREAS:*** Trial Law; Family Law; Matrimonial Law; Divorce. ***Email:*** greenfield@tylercooper.com

WILLIAM R. MURPHY, born New Haven, Connecticut, October 6, 1927; admitted to bar, 1953, Connecticut. *Education:* Yale University (B.A., 1950; LL.B., 1953). Executive Editor, Yale Law Journal, 1952-1953. *Member:* International Association of Defense Counsel. Fellow: American College of Trial Lawyers; American Bar Foundation. ***PRACTICE AREAS:*** Litigation, Antitrust and Trade Regulation.

ROGER E. KOONTZ, born Quincy, Illinois, May 21, 1940; admitted to bar, 1965, Connecticut. *Education:* University of Illinois (B.S., 1962); Yale University (J.D., 1965). (Resident at Hartford Office). ***PRACTICE AREAS:*** Public Utility; Administrative Law; Energy Law. ***Email:*** koontz@tylercooper.com

RICHARD K. SNYDER, born Richmond, Virginia, August 31, 1935; admitted to bar, 1964, Connecticut. *Education:* University of Michigan (A.B., 1957; J.D., 1963). ***LANGUAGES:*** German. ***PRACTICE AREAS:*** Estate Planning; Estate Administration; Estate Litigation; Real Estate. ***Email:*** snyder@tylercooper.com

SAMUEL W. BOWLBY, born Davenport, Iowa, April 11, 1938; admitted to bar, 1966, Connecticut. *Education:* Dartmouth College (A.B., 1960); Yale University (LL.B., 1966). Phi Alpha Delta. [First Lieut., U.S. Marine Corps, 1960-1963]. ***PRACTICE AREAS:*** Corporate Law; Public Utility Law; Securities. ***Email:*** sbowlby@tylercooper.com

SENIOR COUNSEL

HENRY W. PASCARELLA, born New Haven, Connecticut, August 15, 1933; admitted to bar, 1958, Connecticut; 1963, U.S. Supreme Court. *Education:* Wharton School of Finance & Commerce, University of Pennsylvania (B.S., 1955); Yale University (LL.B., 1958). *Member:* Greenwich Bar Association (President, 1972-1973). (Resident at Greenwich Office). ***PRACTICE AREAS:*** Trusts and Estates; Real Estate; Environmental and Land Use Regulation; Litigation.

COUNSEL

KURT W. JOHNSON, born New Britain, Connecticut, July 8, 1941; admitted to bar, 1972, Connecticut. *Education:* University of Connecticut (B.A., 1964; J.D., 1972). Vice President and Group Counsel, Asea Brown Boveri Inc., 1972-1991. *Member:* Connecticut Power and Energy Society. [Lieut., U.S. Army, 1964-1966]. (Resident at Hartford Office). ***PRACTICE AREAS:*** Independent Power Production and Cogeneration; Corporate; Environmental Law; International Law; Real Estate Law. ***Email:*** johnson@tylercooper.com

NAN BUDDE CHEQUER, born New York, N.Y., August 19, 1938; admitted to bar, 1986, Connecticut. *Education:* Vassar College (A.B., 1960); Yale University (J.D., 1986). (Resident at Stamford Office). ***PRACTICE AREAS:*** Real Estate; Trusts and Estates; Corporate. ***Email:*** chequer@tylercooper.com

(This Listing Continued)

KATHLEEN A. MAHER, born St. Louis, Missouri, June 17, 1956; admitted to bar, 1984, New York; 1991, Connecticut. *Education:* University of Missouri (B.A., 1978); Washington University (J.D., 1983). Order of the Coif. Articles Editor, Washington University Law Quarterly, 1982-1983. ***PRACTICE AREAS:*** Corporate; Finance; Securities; Business Law; Mergers and Acquisitions.

CHARLES R. ANDRES, born Wellesley, Massachusetts, November 2, 1955; admitted to bar, 1984, Connecticut. *Education:* Middlebury College (B.A., 1977); Yale University (M.A.R., 1981); University of Connecticut (J.D., 1984). Notes and Comments Editor, Connecticut Law Review, 1983-1984. Law Clerk to Judge Daniel Spallone, Connecticut Appellate Court, 1986-1987. ***PRACTICE AREAS:*** Land Use; Litigation. ***Email:*** andres@tylercooper.com

BARRY M. WINNICK, born New Haven, Connecticut, June 30, 1962; admitted to bar, 1987, Connecticut. *Education:* Tufts University (B.A., 1984); Syracuse University College of Law (J.D., 1987). (Resident at Hartford Office). ***PRACTICE AREAS:*** Commercial Litigation; Collections; Foreclosures; Municipal Law. ***Email:*** winnick@tylercooper.com

DEBORAH D. CANNAVINO, born Aurora, Illinois, May 29, 1965; admitted to bar, 1990, Connecticut. *Education:* Northwestern University (B.A., 1987); University of California, Hastings College of Law (J.D., 1990). (Resident at Stamford Office). ***PRACTICE AREAS:*** Employment Law; Civil Litigation. ***Email:*** cannavino@tylercooper.com

REGINA DUCHIN KRAUS, born Liberty, New York, January 11, 1947; admitted to bar, 1991, Connecticut. *Education:* George Washington University (B.A., 1969); University of Connecticut (J.D., 1991). ***LANGUAGES:*** Italian. ***PRACTICE AREAS:*** Commercial Litigation; General Civil Litigation; Professional Liability Defense. ***Email:*** kraus@tylercooper.com

SHAWN L. O'SULLIVAN, born Providence, Rhode Island, June 28, 1953; admitted to bar, 1980, Connecticut. *Education:* Providence College (A.B., 1975); Western New England College School of Law (J.D., 1980). ***PRACTICE AREAS:*** Estate Planning; Probate Administration; Trust Administration; Taxation. ***Email:*** osulliva@tylercooper.com

ASSOCIATES

RENEE M. REED, born New Haven, Connecticut, January 1, 1967; admitted to bar, 1992, Connecticut. *Education:* Fairfield University (B.A., 1989); Case Western Reserve School of Law (J.D., 1992). ***PRACTICE AREAS:*** Insurance Defense; Medical Malpractice Defense; Plaintiffs Personal Injury; Workers Compensation. ***Email:*** reed@tylercooper.com

LISA N. DAVIS, born Philadelphia, Pennsylvania, May 14, 1960; admitted to bar, 1990, Connecticut; 1994, U.S. District Court, District of Connecticut. *Education:* Yale University (B.A. in History, magna cum laude, 1982; J.D., 1990). Law Clerk to Justice David M. Shea, Connecticut Supreme Court, 1990-1991. Director, The Legal Center for Connecticut Non-Profit Organizations, Inc., 1994. *Member:* Connecticut (Member: Estates and Probate Section; Tax Section; Legislation Committee, Elder Law Section, 1993-1995) and American (Member, Exempt Organization Committee, Tax Section, 1993-1995) Bar Associations; Connecticut Health Lawyers Association; National Health Lawyers Association. ***LANGUAGES:*** French. ***PRACTICE AREAS:*** Estate Planning; Administration; Probate Law; Disabilities Law; Nonprofit Organizations. ***Email:*** davis@tylercooper.com

JAMES R. BRYNE, born New York, N.Y., February 28, 1969; admitted to bar, 1994, Connecticut; 1995, U.S. District Court, District of Connecticut and U.S. District Court, District of Massachusetts. *Education:* Boston University (B.A., magna cum laude, 1990); University of Connecticut (J.D., 1994). *Member:* Connecticut Bar Association. ***PRACTICE AREAS:*** Commercial Litigation. ***Email:*** bryne@tylercooper.com

S. PETER SACHNER, born New Haven, Connecticut, June 26, 1965; admitted to bar, 1992, Connecticut; 1993, U.S. District Court, District of Connecticut. *Education:* Princeton University (A.B., with distinction, 1987); University of Connecticut School of Law (J.D., 1992). Articles and Book Reviews Editor, Connecticut Law Review, 1991-1992. ***LANGUAGES:*** Spanish. ***PRACTICE AREAS:*** Litigation; Medical Malpractice Defense Law; Personal Injury Law. ***Email:*** sachner@tylercooper.com

ROBERT C. HINTON, born Manhasset, New York, February 20, 1962; admitted to bar, 1995, Connecticut; 1997, New York. *Education:* United States Military Academy (B.S., 1984); University of Connecticut Law School (J.D., 1995). Associate Editor, Connecticut Insurance Law Journal, 1994-1995. Law Clerk to Chief Judge Antoinette L. Dupont, Connecticut Appellate Court, 1995-1996. [Capt., U.S. Army, Armor Branch, 1984-1992]. ***Email:*** hinton@tylercooper.com

MICHAEL C. D'AGOSTINO, born Hanover, New Hampshire, March 4, 1971; admitted to bar, 1996, Connecticut. *Education:* University of Virginia (B.A., 1993; J.D., 1996). ***Email:*** dagostin@tylercooper.com

PAUL L. BADER, born Bronxville, New York; admitted to bar, 1994, Georgia; 1998, Connecticut. *Education:* Duke University (B.A., 1988); Mercer

(This Listing Continued)

University (J.D., 1994). Brainard Currie Honor Society. Moot Court Board. Mercer Law Review. ***PRACTICE AREAS:*** Labor and Employment. ***Email:*** bader@tylercooper.com

CHRISTOPHER MARKHAM HADDAD, born Washington, D.C. April 10, 1969; admitted to bar, 1995, Connecticut. *Education:* University of Virginia (B.A., 1991); University of Connecticut (J.D., 1995). *Member:* American Health Lawyers Association. (Resident at Hartford Office). ***Email:*** haddad@tylercooper.com

MICHAEL T. McCORMACK, born Westchester, Pennsylvania, May 12, 1967; admitted to bar, 1993, Connecticut. *Education:* Providence College (B.S., 1989); Catholic University of America (J.D., 1992). Editor, The Journal of Contemporary Health Law and Policy, 1991-1992. Family Law, 1992. Law Clerk to the Honorable Fred B. Ugast, Chief Judge of the Superior Court of the District of Columbia, 1992-1993. (Resident at Hartford Office). ***Email:*** mmccormack@tylercooper.com

TIMOTHY P. JENSEN, born Woburn, Massachusetts, December 14, 1967; admitted to bar, 1997, Connecticut. *Education:* Trinity College (B.A., 1990); Quinnipiac College School of Law (J.D., 1997). Notes and Case Notes Editor, Quinnipiac Law Review, 1996-1997. ***Email:*** jensen@tylercooper.com

GERALD T. GIAIMO, born New Haven, Connecticut, May 11, 1969; admitted to bar, 1994, Connecticut. *Education:* College of the Holy Cross (B.A., 1991); University of Strasbourg, France, 1989; University of Connecticut (J.D., 1994). Chair, Young Lawyers Section, Connecticut Bar Association, 2000-2001; Young Lawyers' Division Liaison to Antitrust, RICO and Labor Law Committee of American Bar Association Labor and Employment Law Section, 2000-2001. ***LANGUAGES:*** French. ***PRACTICE AREAS:*** Bodily Injury Litigation; Criminal Defense; Employment Law. ***Email:*** giaimo@tylercooper.com

CAROL L. LOOMIS, born Drexel Hill, Pennsylvania, December 30, 1954; admitted to bar, 1997, Connecticut. *Education:* Mount Holyoke College (B.A., 1977); University of Connecticut Law School (J.D., 1997). Member, 1995-1996 and Executive Editor, 1996-1997, Connecticut Law Review. Law Clerk to Associate Justice, Honorable Richard N. Palmer, Connecticut Supreme Court, 1997-1998. (Resident at Hartford Office). ***Email:*** loomis@tylercooper.com

ELIZABETH M. SMITH, born Buffalo, New York, November 25, 1960; admitted to bar, 1998, Connecticut. *Education:* Mississippi State University (B.S., 1982); The University of Connecticut (M.B.A., 1998); The University of Connecticut School of Law (J.D., 1998). (Resident at Hartford Office). ***Email:*** smithe@tylercooper.com

STUART WEICHSEL, born New York, N.Y., June 3, 1965; admitted to bar, 1994, New York (Not admitted in Connecticut). *Education:* Tufts University (B.A., 1986); Georgetown University (J.D., cum laude, 1993). ***Email:*** sweichsel@tylercooper.com

MALGORZATA J. BOCHENEK, born Wroclaw, Poland, May 4, 1972; admitted to bar, 1999, Connecticut. *Education:* Music Conservatory, Wroclaw, Poland (B.A., 1993); University of Connecticut Law School (J.D., 1999). ***Email:*** bochenek@tylercooper.com

SUSAN TAYLOR, born Portland, Maine, January 17, 1971; admitted to bar, 1999, Connecticut. *Education:* University of Maine (B.S., 1993); Quinnipiac School of Law (J.D., 1999). (Resident at Hartford Office). ***Email:*** taylor@tylercooper.com

MATTHEW A. SOKOL, born Poughkeepsie, New York, December 31, 1972; admitted to bar, 1999, Connecticut. *Education:* State University of New York College at Geneseo (B.A., 1995); Pace University School of Law (J.D., 1999). ***Email:*** sokol@tylercooper.com

ELIZABETH K. ANDREWS, born Buffalo, New York, May 19, 1973; admitted to bar, 1999, Connecticut. *Education:* State University of New York at Buffalo (B.S., 1995); Case Western Reserve University School of Law (J.D., 1999). (Resident at Hartford Office). ***Email:*** eandrews@tylercooper.com

ELLEN JEAN BEARDSLEY, admitted to bar, 1999, Connecticut. *Education:* Case Western Reserve University (B.A., 1989); Quinnipiac College (J.D., 1999). ***Email:*** ebeardsley@tylercooper.com

CHRISTOPHER A. KELLAND, born New Britain, Connecticut, December 9, 1971; admitted to bar, 1999, Connecticut. *Education:* University of Connecticut (B.A., 1995); University of Connecticut School of Law (J.D., 1999). ***Email:*** ckelland@tylercooper.com

W. JOE WILSON, born Taylor, Texas, February 19, 1947; admitted to bar, 1999, Connecticut. *Education:* Southern Methodist University (B.A., 1968); University of Connecticut School of Law (J.D., 1999). ***Email:*** jwilson@tylercooper.com

KELLY P. LUTZ, born Milford, Connecticut, September 20, 1974; admitted to bar, 2000, Connecticut. *Education:* George Washington University (B.A., 1996); University of Connecticut School of Law (J.D., 2000). ***Email:*** klutz@tylercooper.com

(This Listing Continued)

TRICIA WHITE, born New Milford, Connecticut, April 27, 1969; admitted to bar, 2001, Connecticut. *Education:* Western Connecticut State University (B.S., 1992); Quinnipiac College School of Law (J.D., 2001). ***Email:*** twhite@tylercooper.com

COURTNEY LANE, born New Haven, Connecticut, April 27, 1967; admitted to bar, 2001, Connecticut. *Education:* Skidmore College (B.A., 1989); Sage Graduate School (M.S. Ed., 1993); University of Connecticut School of Law (J.D., 2001). ***Email:*** clane@tylercooper.com

SARAH LOMBARD, born New Haven, Connecticut, May 12, 1975; admitted to bar, 2001, Connecticut. *Education:* College of the Holy Cross (B.A., 1997); Harvard University Graduate School of Education (Ed.M., 1998); Suffolk University Law School (J.D., 2001). ***Email:*** slombard@tylercooper.com

PAUL GUGGINA, born Cambridge, Massachusetts, October 4, 1965; admitted to bar, 2001, Connecticut. *Education:* Southern Illinois University (B.S., 1989); Boston College School of Law (J.D., 2001). (Resident at Hartford Office). ***Email:*** pguggina@tylercooper.com

All Partners and Associates are Members of the Connecticut and American Bar Associations

REPRESENTATIVE CLIENTS: Fleet National Bank; The Hartford Courant Co.; Hospital of St. Raphael; Science Park Development Corp.; The Stanley Works; Town of Salisbury; Town of Woodstock; Yale-New Haven Hospital, Inc.; Gaylord Hospital; Connecticut American Water Co.; The Southern Connecticut Gas Co.; Connecticut Energy Corporation; Birmingham Utilities; Southern New England Telephone Co.; American Society of Composers, Authors and Publishers (ASCAP); Asea Brown Boveri Inc.; Honeywell, Inc.; Kraft General Foods, Inc.; Prudential Securities, Inc.; Sears, Roebuck & Co.; The Travelers Companies; Town of Guilford; Connecticut Bankers Association; Horton Medical Center; New Britain Transportation Corp.; Westfield Corporation, Inc.; Philip Morris Incorporated; Mechanics Savings Bank; Webster Bank; Norwalk Savings Society; Farmington Savings Bank; Union Savings Bank; First Union National Bank; Prudential Insurance Company.

UPDIKE, KELLY & SPELLACY, P.C.

Established in 1967

265 CHURCH STREET, TENTH FLOOR

NEW HAVEN, CONNECTICUT 06510-7002

Telephone: 203-786-8300

Fax: 203-772-2037

Email: Info@uks.com

URL: http://www.uks.com

Hartford, Connecticut Office: One State Street, P.O. Box: 231277. Telephone: 860-548-2600. Cable Address: "Ukslaw." Fax: 860-548-2680.

Stamford, Connecticut Office: 6 Landmark Square, Fourth Floor. Telephone: 203-359-5749. Fax: 203-359-5858.

Administrative Law, Appellate Law, Business Law, Commercial Lending and Banking, Commercial Litigation, Creditors' Rights, Design/Construction Law, Employment Law, Environmental Law, Franchise Law, Human Service Law, Legislative Representation, Personal Law, Product Liability Law, Professional Defense Law, Public Finance/Public Law, Real Estate Law, Taxation, Financial and Estate Planning and Pensions, and Probate Law, Venture Capital.

HUGH I. MANKE, born West Hartford, CT, December 9, 1942; admitted to bar, 1976, CT. *Education:* Princeton Univ. (A.B., 1964); State Univ. of New York (J.D., 1975). Senior Editor, Buffalo Law Review, 1974-1975. Author: "Exhaustion of Local Remedies in the Subcommission on Prevention of Discrimination and Protection of Minorities," 24 Buffalo Law Review 643, 1975. Law Clerk, Hon. Arthur Healey, CT Superior Court, 1975-1976. Assoc. Counsel, CT Conf. of Municipalities, 1976-1979. Special Counsel, CT Dept. of Trans. 1979-1981. Member, Exec. Comm. Young Lawyers Section, CT Bar Assn., 1976-1978. Member, Board of Directors, CT Assn. of Municipal Attorneys, 1982—. Member, Board of Directors, Greater New Haven Chamber of Commerce, 1997—. Chairman, Board of Directors, International Voluntary Services, 1993—. Member, Board of Directors, Junior Achievement, 1996—. ***LANGUAGES:*** Vietnamese and German. ***PRACTICE AREAS:*** Administrative Law; Business Law; Public Finance/Public Law; Real Estate. ***Email:*** hmanke@uks.com

JOHN F. WOLTER, born Stamford, CT, October 15, 1961; admitted to bar, 1986, CT; 1988, NH. *Education:* Saint Anselm College (B.A., summa cum laude, 1983); Georgetown Univ. (J.D., cum laude, 1986). Member, 1986— and Chairman, 1990-1996, East Haddam Democratic Town Committee. Member, East Haddam Planning and Zoning Commission, 1988-1995; Chairman, East Haddam Charter Commission, 1988-1990. Member, East Haddam Charter Study Committee, 1987-1988. Member, Board of Trustees, Brian House, Inc. and Adult Vocational Program, Inc., 1992—. Delegate, White House Conference on Small Business, 1995. *Member:* American Health Lawyers Assn.; Association of Commercial Finance Attorneys. ***PRACTICE AREAS:*** Business Law; Commercial Lending; Human Service; Franchise Law; Utilities Law. ***Email:*** jwolter@uks.com

(This Listing Continued)

UPDIKE, KELLY & SPELLACY, P.C., New Haven—Continued

DAVID J. MONZ, born Scotch Plains, NJ, October 18, 1958; admitted to bar, 1989, CT. *Education:* Franklin and Marshall College (B.S., 1980); Virginia Polytechnic Inst. and State Univ. (M.S., 1983); Univ. of Connecticut School of Law (J.D., high honors, 1989). Articles and Book Reviews Editor, CT Law Review. Clerk, Honorable Thomas J. Meskill, U.S. Court of Appeals, Second Circuit, 1989-1990. Member, Criminal Justice Act Panel. Member, North Haven Republican Town Committee, 1996—. Member, North Haven Inland Wetlands Commission, 1997—. Environmental Coordinator, Town of North Haven, 1994—. Member, National Assn. of College and University Attorneys, 1997—; Co-Chair, Environmental Law Section, 2000—. ***PRACTICE AREAS:*** Environmental Law; Administrative Law; Criminal Law. ***Email:*** dmonz@uks.com

MARIA S. SPALDING, born Poughkeepsie, NY, August 9, 1955; admitted to bar, 1987, CT; 1992, U.S. District Court, District of CT. *Education:* Russell Sage College (B.S.N., 1977); Univ. of Bridgeport (J.D., 1987). Registered Nurse: NY, 1975; CT, 1977. Member, CT Hospital Assn. of Risk Managers. Member, CT Medical Defense Society. ***PRACTICE AREAS:*** Product Liability; Professional Defense. ***Email:*** mspalding@uks.com

CHRISTOPHER L. BRIGHAM, born Danbury, CT, October 19, 1962; admitted to bar, 1992, CT; 1993, U.S. District Court, District of CT. *Education:* Middlebury College (B.A., 1986); Vermont Law School (J.D., cum laude, 1992). Chair, CT Court Visitation Program-GA6. Member, Leadership Greater New Haven. ***PRACTICE AREAS:*** Labor and Employment; Professional Defense. ***Email:*** cbrigham@uks.com

ROLAN J. YOUNG, born New Haven, CT, November 15, 1960; admitted to bar, 1993, CT. *Education:* Dartmouth College (A.B., 1982); American Univ., Washington College of Law (J.D., 1985). Recipient: Minority Business Person of the Year Award, Business New Haven, 1999; 20 Noteworthy Women, New Haven Business Times, 1999. First Vice-President, Greater New Haven NAACP, 1998—; President, 2000—. Member, Board of Directors, Visiting Nurses Association of Southeastern Connecticut, 1998-2000. Member, Board of Directors, Greater New Haven Community Loan Fund, 1998-2000. Board of Directors, State of CT NAACP, 1999—. Member, George Crawford Law Assn. Member, CT Housing Coalition, 1999—. Tutor, Yale University Law School Housing and Community Development Clinic. General Counsel, New Haven Housing Authority, 2000—. Member, Board of Trustees, St. Raphael's Foundation, 2000—; Member, Board of Directors, NHSB Community Development Corporation, 2000—. ***LANGUAGES:*** Chinese. ***PRACTICE AREAS:*** Business Law; Commercial Lending; Public Finance/Public Law; Real Estate; Affordable Housing; Community Development. ***Email:*** ryoung@uks.com

---

MICHEL BAYONNE, born Port au Prince, Haiti, July 13, 1976; admitted to bar, 2001, CT. *Education:* Fairfield University (B.A., 1998); Univ. of Connecticut School of Law (J.D., 2001). ***PRACTICE AREAS:*** Business Law. ***Email:*** mbayonne@uks.com

JENNIFER L. GROVES, born Bridgeport, CT, May 15, 1973; admitted to bar, 1998, CT, U.S. District Court, District of CT. *Education:* Yale Univ. (B.A., distinction in Psychology, 1995); Boston College (J.D., 1998). Psi Chi. Member, Uniform Commercial Code Reporter Digest, 1996-1998 and Administrative Editor, 1997-1998. ***PRACTICE AREAS:*** Professional Liability Defense; Insurance Defense; Human Services. ***Email:*** jgroves@uks.com

GREGG J. LALLIER, born Hartford, Connecticut, August 14, 1972; admitted to bar, 1998, Connecticut. *Education:* Boston College (B.S., magna cum laude, 1994); Emory Univ. School of Law (J.D., 1998). ***PRACTICE AREAS:*** Business Law; Intellectual Property; Electronic Commerce Law. ***Email:*** glallier@uks.com

JOSEPH A. ROSENTHAL, born West Islip, NY, July 17, 1969; admitted to bar, 1996, CT. *Education:* State Univ. of NY at Binghamton (B.A., with honors, 1990; M.A., 1993); Boston College Law School (J.D., magna cum laude, 1996). Member, St. Joseph's Church Action for Justice. ***PRACTICE AREAS:*** Environmental; Administrative Law; Utilities Law. ***Email:*** jrosenthal@uks.com

JOHN G. STRETTON, born New Haven, CT, January 12, 1973; admitted to bar, 1998, CT and U.S. District Court, District of CT. *Education:* Boston College (B.A., cum laude, 1995); Boston Univ. (J.D., cum laude, 1998). (Also at Hartford, CT Office). ***PRACTICE AREAS:*** Civil Litigation; Professional Liability Defense; Employment Litigation; Personal Injury Defense; Insurance Coverage Defense; Municipal Liability Defense; Commercial Litigation. ***Email:*** jstretton@uks.com

(For Complete Biographical Data on all Personnel, see Professional Biographies at Hartford, Connecticut)

VOTRE & ASSOCIATES, P.C.

105 COURT STREET, SUITE 405
NEW HAVEN, CONNECTICUT 06511-6957
Telephone: 203-498-0065
Fax: 203-821-3595
Email: kvotre@aol.com
URL: http://www.lawyers.com/votre&associates

Commercial Litigation, Taxation, Tax Litigation, International Business Litigation, Health Care Regulation, Health Care Finance, Intellectual Property, Personal Injury, Corporate Law.

KENNETH A. VOTRE, born Bridgeport, Connecticut, September 14, 1960; admitted to bar, 1984, Connecticut, New York and U.S. District Court, District of Connecticut; 1985, U.S. Tax Court; 1993, U.S. Court of Appeals, Federal Circuit and Second Circuit; U.S. Court of International Trade; U.S. Supreme Court. *Education:* University of Bridgeport (B.E.S., 1981; J.D., magna cum laude, 1983; LL.M., in Taxation, 1990); Georgetown University Law Center (LL.M., International and Comparative Law, 1992). Phi Alpha Delta. Author: "Trade in Services: Proposals For the Liberalization of International Trade in Insurance," Volume 13-3, Bridgeport Law Review, 1993. Article, "Opportunities Under GATT & NAFTA," American Lawyer Management Service, Vol. 1, pg 3.67 (1995). Adjunct Professor, Quinnipiac College School of Law, 1993—. ***PRACTICE AREAS:*** Commercial Litigation; Taxation; Tax Litigation; International Business Litigation; Health Care Regulation; Health Care Finance; Intellectual Property. ***Email:*** kvotre@aol.com

---

JOHN-HENRY M. STEELE, born Middlebury, Vermont, October 29, 1962; admitted to bar, 1991, Connecticut; 1992, U.S. District Court, District of Connecticut. *Education:* Trinity College (B.A., 1985); Western New England College School of Law (J.D., 1991). Best brief, Appellant Canner, Pace University's Third Annual National Environmental Moot Court. *Member:* Connecticut Bar Association; Connecticut Trial Lawyers Association. ***PRACTICE AREAS:*** Commercial Litigation; Toxic Torts; Lead Poisoning; Litigation; Personal Injury; Trial Practice.

TARA JUSTINE GALBO, born Danbury, Connecticut, October 2, 1974; admitted to bar, 2000, Connecticut and U.S. District Court, District of Connecticut. *Education:* St. Anselm College (B.A., 1996); Quinnipiac College, School of Law (J.D., 1999). Phi Alpha Phi (Clerk and Historian). Member, Italian Justinian Law Society, 1997. Editor, Health Law Journal, 1998-1999. Law Clerk, Office of Public Defender, Bridgeport, Connecticut, 1999. *Member:* New Haven, Danbury and Connecticut Bar Associations. ***PRACTICE AREAS:*** Commercial Law; Personal Injury; Tax Law; International Business Law; Corporate Law. ***Email:*** taragalbo@aol.com

OF COUNSEL

NEIL K. RUTTER, born Bracebridge, Ontario, Canada, April 12, 1947; admitted to bar, 1980, Ontario; 1994, New York and Connecticut. *Education:* Queen's University, Kingston, Canada (B.A., Hon., 1970); University of Windsor (LL.B., 1978); New York University (LL.M., 1994). Author: "Legal Guide to Countertrade," The Countertrade Lexicon, published by the American Countertrade Association, 1994. Lecturer, "Countertrade and Offset Contracts," American Graduate School of International Management (Thunderbird), 1992—. Member, American Countertrade Association, 1986—. Director, U.S. Business Counsel for Southeastern Europe, 1986—. Formerly: Secretary and General Counsel, Combustion Engineering Canada Inc., 1982-1986; Vice President, ABB Project and Trade Finance (USA) Inc., 1986-1992. [Capt., Canadian Forces, 1965-1975; Major, Canadian Reserves, 1976-1982]. ***PRACTICE AREAS:*** International Commercial Arbitration; International Commercial Law; International Commercial Contracts; Corporate Law; Immigration and Naturalization.

WEINSTEIN, WEINER, IGNAL, NAPOLITANO & SHAPIRO, P.C.

NEW HAVEN, CONNECTICUT

(See Bridgeport)

General Practice including Personal Injury, Negligence, Commercial, Reorganization, Bankruptcy, Foreclosures, Criminal, Civil Rights, Employee Rights and Benefits, Employment Discrimination, Family, Workers Compensation, Real Estate. Trial and Appellate Practice in all State and Federal Courts and Administrative Agencies.

JEAN L. WELTY

385 ORANGE STREET
P.O. BOX 1662
NEW HAVEN, CONNECTICUT 06507
Telephone: 203-781-0877
Fax: 203-781-0899
URL: http://www.lawyers.com/jlwelty

Matrimonial and Family Law, Child Custody, Child Support, Paternity.

JEAN L. WELTY, born Boulder, Colorado, November 21, 1949; admitted to bar, 1975, Connecticut and U.S. District Court, District of Connecticut; 1977, U.S. Court of Appeals, Second Circuit. *Education:* Cornell College (B.A., cum laude, 1971); Yale University (J.D., 1975). Phi Beta Kappa. Tutor in Clinical Studies, Yale Law School, 1979-1993. *Member:* New Haven County (President, Young Lawyers, 1979-1980; Executive Committee, 1979-1982; Law Day Chairman, 1980; Chairman, Family Law Committee, 1993-1996), Connecticut (Assistant Secretary-Treasurer, 1983-1984; Chairman: Young Lawyers Section, 1982-1983; Family Law Section; Judicial Appointments Recommendation Committee, 1978-1980; Member, Judiciary Committee, 1985-1986) and American (Member, Section of Family Law, 1979—) Bar Associations; Connecticut Trial Lawyers Association (Member, Board of Governors, 1978-1986); The Association of Trial Lawyers of America. Fellow, American Academy of Matrimonial Lawyers (President, 1992-1993, Connecticut Chapter). ***PRACTICE AREAS:*** Matrimonial and Family Law.

REFERENCE: People's Bank.

WIGGIN & DANA LLP

Established in 1934

ONE CENTURY TOWER
P.O. BOX 1832
NEW HAVEN, CONNECTICUT 06508-1832
Telephone: 203-498-4400
Telefax: 203-782-2889
URL: http://www.wiggin.com

Hartford, Connecticut Office: One CityPlace. Telephone: 860-297-3700. Telefax: 860-525-9380.

Stamford, Connecticut Office: 400 Atlantic Street, P.O. Box 110325. Telephone: 203-363-7600. Telefax: 203-363-7676.

Berwyn, Pennsylvania Office: 1055 Westlake Drive. Telephone: 610-727-4153. Telefax: 610-727-4085.

Cherry Hill, New Jersey Office: 402 Park Boulevard North, 08802. Telephone: 856-662-3331. Telefax: 856-662-1783.

Antitrust and Trade Regulation, Appellate, Automotive Industry Law, Banking and Financial Services, Bankruptcy Law, Biotechnology Law, Civil Litigation, Closely Held Business, Cogeneration, Construction Law, Employee Benefits and ERISA Law, Environmental Law, Estate Planning and Settlement Law, Franchise Law, Governmental Affairs, Health Care, Hospital Law, Institutional Finance, Insurance Coverage Litigation, Intellectual Property, Internal Corporate Investigations and White Collar Criminal Defense Law, International Transactions, Labor Law, Litigation, Long Term Care Facilities and Financing, Mental Health Law, Mergers and Acquisitions, National and Regional Litigation Counsel, Partnerships and Joint Ventures, Patent Prosecution and Litigation, Professional Malpractice Litigation, Public Finance, Public Utilities, Real Estate Leasing, Development and Finance, Secured Transactions, Securities Regulation, State and Federal Tax Law, Tax Exempt Organizations, Technology Licensing, Telecommunications, Trademarks and Copyright, Trust and Estates Administration, Venture Capital and Zoning.

MEMBERS OF FIRM

FREDERICK H. WIGGIN (1882-1963).

J. DWIGHT DANA (1889-1951).

JOHN Q. TILSON, born New Haven, Connecticut, 1911; admitted to bar, 1936, Connecticut. *Education:* Yale University (B.A., 1933; LL.B., 1936). Phi Beta Kappa; Order of the Coif. Lecturer in Hospital Law, Yale University Medical School, 1958—. Representative, State Legislature, 1953-55. President, Connecticut Bar Association, 1961-1962. ***PRACTICE AREAS:*** Health Care Law; Hospital Law; Tax Exempt Organizations Law; Estate Planning; Estate Settlements.

JOHN W. BARNETT, born Cleveland, Ohio, 1927; admitted to bar, 1953, Connecticut. *Education:* Oberlin College (A.B., 1950); Harvard University (LL.B., cum laude, 1953). Phi Beta Kappa; Delta Sigma Rho. Member, Connecticut Bar Examining Committee, 1973—. Fellow, American College of Trust and Estate Counsel. ***PRACTICE AREAS:*** Estate Planning; Trusts and Estates; Estate Litigation; Property Tax Appeals. ***Email:*** jbarnett@wiggin.com

WILLIAM C. BASKIN, JR., born Pittsburgh, Pennsylvania, 1931; admitted to bar, 1958, Connecticut. *Education:* Yale University (B.A., 1953; LL.B., 1958). Phi Beta Kappa. Managing Editor, Yale Law Journal, 1957-1958. Visiting Lecturer in Corporate and Securities Law, Yale Law School, 1993-2001. Chair, Public Utility Law Section, Connecticut Bar Association, 1984-1986. ***PRACTICE AREAS:*** Corporation Law; Public Utility Law; Securities Law. ***Email:*** wbaskin@wiggin.com

ROBERT F. CAVANAGH, born Framingham, Massachusetts, 1936; admitted to bar, 1959, Connecticut. *Education:* Yale University (B.A., 1956; LL.B., 1959). Order of the Coif. ***PRACTICE AREAS:*** Corporation Law; College Law; Health Care Law; Hospital Law. ***Email:*** rcavanagh@wiggin.com

CHARLES C. KINGSLEY, born New York, N.Y., 1937; admitted to bar, 1962, Connecticut. *Education:* Yale University (A.B., 1959); Harvard University (J.D., cum laude, 1962). President, Connecticut Bar Foundation, 1980-1984. Fellow, American College of Trust and Estate Counsel. Fellow, American Bar Foundation. Member, American Law Institute. ***PRACTICE AREAS:*** Estate Planning; Trust and Estates; Tax Exempt Organizations; Taxation; Closely Held Business Law. ***Email:*** ckingsley@wiggin.com

WILLIAM J. DOYLE, born Boston, Massachusetts, 1936; admitted to bar, 1962, New York; 1963, Connecticut. *Education:* Fairfield University (B.B.A., cum laude, 1958); St. John's University (LL.B., magna cum laude, 1961). Thomas More Scholar, 1958-1961. Managing Editor, St. John's Law Review, 1960-1961. Lecturer in Trial Practice, University of Connecticut Law School, 1975-1977. Instructor in Trial Practice, Yale Law School, 1988—. Chair, Federal Practice Committee, Connecticut Bar Association, 1979-1981. Chair, Lawyer-to-Lawyer Dispute Resolution Committee, Connecticut Bar Association, 1989-1990. Fellow: American College of Trial Lawyers (State Chair, 1987-1988); American Bar Foundation; Connecticut Bar Foundation. ***PRACTICE AREAS:*** Business Litigation; Complex Litigation; Civil Litigation; Commercial Litigation; Health Care Litigation. ***Email:*** wdoyle@wiggin.com

NOEL E. HANF, born Ossining, New York, 1940; admitted to bar, 1965, New York; 1969, Connecticut. *Education:* Yale University (A.B., 1962); Harvard University (LL.B., 1965). *Member:* The Association of the Bar of the City of New York (Member, Committee on Nuclear Technology and the Law, 1990-1993); Connecticut Bar Association (Member, Executive Committee, Public Utility Law Section). ***PRACTICE AREAS:*** Public Utility Law; Tax Exempt Organizations Law. ***Email:*** nhanf@wiggin.com

SHAUN S. SULLIVAN, born Albany, New York, 1940; admitted to bar, 1967, New York; 1970, Connecticut. *Education:* Fairfield University (A.B., cum laude, 1962); Fordham University (LL.B., 1966). Co-Author: "The Military Aircraft Manufacturer - Caught Between Country and the Courts," 3 Defense Research Monograph (October 1979); "Damages for Securities Fraud under United States Law," 1995 International Bar Association Series. Special Master, U.S. District Court, Remington Products, Inc. v. North American Philips Corp., N.V. Philips and Schick, Inc., 107 F.R.D. 642 (D.Conn. 1985). *Member:* International Bar Association (International Litigation Committee, Co-Chair, United States, 1988-1994; Vice Chair, 1995-1999; Chair, 2000—). Fellow: American Bar Foundation; Connecticut Bar Foundation James W. Cooper Fellows Program; American College of Trial Lawyers (State Committee, 1989-1995; Chair, 1997-1999; Committee on Alternatives for Dispute Resolution, 1991—, Chair, 1993-2000). ***PRACTICE AREAS:*** Litigation. ***Email:*** ssullivan@wiggin.com

JEREMY G. ZIMMERMANN, born New Haven, Connecticut, 1941; admitted to bar, 1966, Connecticut. *Education:* Brown University (A.B., 1963); Georgetown University (LL.B., 1966). Editor, Georgetown Law Journal, 1966-1967. Clerk, Judge Luther Youngdahl, U.S. District Court, District of Columbia, 1966-1967. Sustaining Member, Product Liability Advisory Council. ***PRACTICE AREAS:*** Litigation; Insurance Defense Law; Product Liability Defense Law; Professional Liability Defense Law. ***Email:*** jzimmermann@wiggin.com

J. MICHAEL EISNER, born Cleveland, Ohio; admitted to bar, 1971, Connecticut. *Education:* Western Reserve University (A.B., summa cum laude); University of Illinois (M.A.); University of Wisconsin (Ph.D.); Yale University (J.D.). Phi Beta Kappa. Editor, Yale Law Journal. Author: *William Morris Leigerson: A Biography*, University of Wisconsin Press. Co-Author: *Hospital Contracts Manual*, Aspen Publishers; *Physician Organizations and Medical Staff*, Aspen Publishers. ***PRACTICE AREAS:*** Health Care Law; Hospital Law; Medical Staff Law; Election Law; Campaign Law; Political Law. ***Email:*** meisner@wiggin.com

NORMAN FINEBERG, born Portland, Maine, 1941; admitted to bar, 1971, Massachusetts; 1972, Connecticut. *Education:* Worcester Polytechnic Institute (B.S., cum laude, 1963); Yale University (M.Eng., 1964); Boston University (J.D., cum laude, 1971). Editor, Boston University Law Review, 1970-1971. Clerk, Judge Louis Shapiro, Connecticut Supreme Court, 1971-1972. ***PRACTICE AREAS:*** Real Property Law; Real Estate Development; Real Estate Leasing; Condominium Law; Land Use Law. ***Email:*** nfineberg@wiggin.com

WILLIAM H. PROUT, JR., born New Haven, Connecticut, 1945; admitted to bar, 1973, Connecticut. *Education:* Yale University (B.A., 1967); Boston University (J.D., cum laude, 1973). Member, Executive Committee, New Haven County Bar Association. Member, Committee on Professional Ethics, Construction Law Section, Connecticut Bar Association. Member, Forum on the Con-

(This Listing Continued)

WIGGIN & DANA LLP, New Haven—Continued

struction Industry, Construction Litigation Committee, Section of Litigation Committee on Ethics and Professionalism, American Bar Association. ***PRACTICE AREAS:*** Litigation; Construction Law; Professional Responsibility. ***Email:*** wprout@wiggin.com

LINDA L. RANDELL, born Chicago, Illinois, 1950; admitted to bar, 1974, New York and Illinois; 1976, Connecticut. *Education:* University of Michigan (A.B., magna cum laude, 1970); Yale University (J.D., 1973). Phi Beta Kappa. Editor, Yale Law Journal, 1972-1973. Chair, Antitrust Section, Connecticut Bar Association, 1988-1991. Vice Chair, Antitrust Committee, ABA Section of Public Utility, Communications and Transportation Law, 1997. Member, Statewide Grievance Committee, 1991-1994. ***PRACTICE AREAS:*** Public Utility Law; Regulatory Law; Antitrust Law. ***Email:*** lrandell@wiggin.com

D. TERENCE JONES, born New Brunswick, New Jersey, 1946; admitted to bar, 1974, New York; 1978, Connecticut. *Education:* University of Rochester (B.A., cum laude, 1969); Yale Law School (J.D., 1973). ***PRACTICE AREAS:*** Corporation Law; Mergers and Acquisitions Law; Securities Law. ***Email:*** tjones@wiggin.com

MARK R. KRAVITZ, born Philadelphia, Pennsylvania, 1950; admitted to bar, 1975, Connecticut. *Education:* Wesleyan University (B.A., magna cum laude, 1972); Georgetown University (J.D., 1975). Phi Beta Kappa. Managing Editor, Georgetown Law Review, 1974-1975. Clerk: Judge James Hunter, III, U.S. Court of Appeals, Third Circuit, 1975-1976; Justice William H. Rehnquist, U.S. Supreme Court, 1978-1979. Adjunct Professor of Law, University of Connecticut Law School, 1995—. *Member:* American Law Institute; American Academy of Appellate Lawyers. ***PRACTICE AREAS:*** Appellate Practice; Civil Appeals; Media Law; First Amendment; Libel and Slander; Privacy Law; Newspaper Law. ***Email:*** mkravitz@wiggin.com

MELINDA A. AGSTEN, born Charleston, West Virginia, 1950; admitted to bar, 1975, Connecticut. *Education:* Duke University (A.B., magna cum laude, 1972); Vanderbilt University (J.D., 1975). Associate Editor, Vanderbilt Law Review, 1974-1975. ***PRACTICE AREAS:*** Health Care Law; Hospital Law; Tax Exempt Organizations Law; Nonprofit Corporations; Charitable Organizations Law. ***Email:*** magsten@wiggin.com

EDWARD WOOD DUNHAM, born New Haven, Connecticut, 1953; admitted to bar, 1978, Connecticut; 1980, U.S. District Court, District of Connecticut; 1991, U.S. Court of Federal Claims; 1992, U.S. Court of Appeals, First Circuit; 1992, U.S. Court of Appeals, Seventh Circuit; 1994, U.S. Court of Appeals, Second Circuit; 1996, U.S. Supreme Court; 1997, U.S. Court of Appeals, Fifth Circuit. *Education:* Trinity College (B.A., 1975); New York University (J.D., 1978). Phi Beta Kappa. Note and Comment Editor, New York University Law Review. Clerk, Judge Robert A. Ainsworth, Jr., U.S. Court of Appeals, Fifth Circuit, 1978-1979. Fellow, American College of Trial Lawyers. Editor-in-Chief, ABA Franchise Law Journal. ***PRACTICE AREAS:*** Franchise Litigation; Litigation; Complex Litigation; Corporate Litigation; Franchises and Franchising; Franchise Arbitration; Medical Malpractice Litigation. ***Email:*** edunham@wiggin.com

NORMAN J. FLEMING, born Lawrence, Massachusetts, 1953; admitted to bar, 1979, Massachusetts; 1982, Connecticut. *Education:* Harvard University (A.B., 1975; M.B.A., 1979; J.D., 1979). ***PRACTICE AREAS:*** Corporation Law; Mergers and Acquisitions Law; Securities Law; Debt and Equity Finance; Bond Finance. ***Email:*** nfleming@wiggin.com

PETER J. LEFEBER, born Winchester, Connecticut, 1955; admitted to bar, 1980, Connecticut. *Education:* St. Michael's College (A.B., summa cum laude, 1977); University of Connecticut (J.D., with honors, 1980). Delta Epsilon Sigma. Administrative Editor, Connecticut Law Review, 1979-1980. ***PRACTICE AREAS:*** Labor Law; Employment Law. ***Email:*** plefeber@wiggin.com

JOHN G. ZANDY, born Evergreen Park, Illinois, October 22, 1948; admitted to bar, 1975, New York; 1988, Connecticut. *Education:* Miami University (B.A., 1970); Valparaiso University School of Law (J.D., 1974); New York University Graduate School of Law (LL.M. in Labor Law, 1975). Attorney, Solicitor's Office of the U.S. Department of Labor, Region 2, 1975; Attorney, National Labor Relations Board, Region 29, 1975-1977. ***PRACTICE AREAS:*** Labor Law; Employment Law. ***Email:*** jzandy@wiggin.com

SHERRY L. DOMINICK, born Boise, Idaho, 1956; admitted to bar, 1981, Connecticut. *Education:* Yale University (B.A., summa cum laude, 1978); New York University (J.D., 1981). Phi Beta Kappa. ***PRACTICE AREAS:*** Employee Benefits Law; Executive Compensation Law. ***Email:*** sdominick@wiggin.com

ALAN G. SCHWARTZ, born Bethlehem, Pennsylvania, 1956; admitted to bar, 1981, Connecticut. *Education:* University of Pennsylvania (B.A., cum laude, 1978); New York University (J.D., 1981). ***PRACTICE AREAS:*** Civil Litigation; Utility Law; Environmental Litigation; Construction Law; Real Estate Litigation. ***Email:*** aschwartz@wiggin.com

VALERIE A. SEILING, born Staten Island, New York, 1957; admitted to bar, 1982, New York; 1984, Connecticut. *Education:* Cornell University (B.S., with honors, 1978; J.D., 1981). Editor, Cornell Law Review, 1979-1981. (Resident, Hartford Office). ***PRACTICE AREAS:*** Corporate Finance; Secured Transactions; Mergers and Acquisitions; Commercial Mortgages; Real Estate Finance. ***Email:*** vseiling@wiggin.com

BENNETT J. BERNBLUM, born Hartford, Connecticut, 1947; admitted to bar, 1982, Connecticut. *Education:* Yale University (B.A., cum laude, 1969); New York University (J.D., 1982). ***PRACTICE AREAS:*** Business Law; Corporate Law; Corporate Health Care Law; Mergers and Acquisitions Law; State Taxation Law. ***Email:*** bbernblum@wiggin.com

SUSAN J. BRYSON, born Portland, Oregon, 1948; admitted to bar, 1977, Connecticut. *Education:* Stanford University (B.A., 1970); University of Connecticut Law School (J.D., with high honors, 1977). Member, University of Connecticut Law Review, 1975-1977. Clerk, Hon. Alva P. Loiselle, Connecticut Supreme Court, 1977-1978. Tutor, Clinical Studies, Jerome N. Frank Legal Services Organization, Yale Law School, 1992-1996. Member, Board of Directors, Connecticut Bar Foundation, 1998. Member, Executive Committee, Real Property Section, Connecticut Bar Association, 1998. ***PRACTICE AREAS:*** Commercial Real Estate; Development; Downtown Development; Corporate Real Estate; Zoning, Planning and Land Use; Real Estate Finance. ***Email:*** sbryson@wiggin.com

JEANETTE CARPENTER SCHREIBER, born Orlando, Florida, 1955; admitted to bar, 1982, Connecticut. *Education:* Emory University (B.A., with high honors, 1976); Florida State University (M.S.W., 1978); Harvard University (J.D., cum laude, 1982). Phi Beta Kappa. Author: "Medicaid Financial Planning After the Medicare Catastrophic Coverage Act," 63 Conn. Bar Journal 211 (1989); "AIDS Related Testing and Confidentiality: Connecticut's New Legislation," 53 Connecticut Medicine 515 (1989); Chapter, "Decision-Making in Treatment Issues," in *The Long Term Care Handbook,* National Health Lawyers Assoc. (1991). ***PRACTICE AREAS:*** Health Care; Managed Care; Mental Health; Hospital Law; Medical Staff. ***Email:*** jschreiber@wiggin.comM

PATRICK J. MONAHAN, II, born New Haven, Connecticut, 1958; admitted to bar, 1983, Connecticut. *Education:* Stonehill College (B.A., 1980); Boston College (J.D., cum laude, 1983). Editor, Boston College International and Comparative Law Review, 1982-1983. (Resident, Hartford Office). ***PRACTICE AREAS:*** Litigation. ***Email:*** pmonahan@wiggin.com

PETER H. GRUEN, born New York, N.Y., 1954; admitted to bar, 1979, Massachusetts; 1981, Connecticut. *Education:* University of Connecticut (B.A., 1976); Boston University (J.D., 1979). ***PRACTICE AREAS:*** International and Federal Taxation Law; Low Income Housing Tax Credits; Connecticut Taxation Law. ***Email:*** pgruen@wiggin.com

MARY R. NORRIS, born Cincinnati, Ohio, 1955; admitted to bar, 1984, Georgia; 1985, Connecticut. *Education:* University of Cincinnati (B.S., summa cum laude, 1977); Emory University; Georgetown University (J.D., 1984). Phi Beta Kappa. Chair, Intellectual Property Law Section, Connecticut Bar Association, 1992-1994. Member, Licensing Executives Society. ***PRACTICE AREAS:*** Information Technology Contracts; Publishing Contracts; New Media Law; Intellectual Property Licensing; Copyright Protection. ***Email:*** mnorris@wiggin.com

MAUREEN WEAVER, born Bryn Mawr, Pennsylvania, 1955; admitted to bar, 1986, Connecticut. *Education:* Duke University (A.B., magna cum laude, 1977); University of California School of Law, Los Angeles (J.D., 1986). ***PRACTICE AREAS:*** Health Law; Long Term Care; Health Care Compliance; Hospital Law; Administrative Law. ***Email:*** mweaver@wiggin.com

ROBERT M. LANGER, born Norwalk, Connecticut, 1948; admitted to bar, 1973, Connecticut. *Education:* Franklin & Marshall College (A.B., 1970); University of Connecticut School of Law (J.D., 1973). Co-Author: "The Connecticut Unfair Trade Practices Act," 54 Conn. B.J. 388 (1980); "Antitrust Review of Mergers by State Attorneys General, The New Cops on the Beat," 67 Conn. B.J. 1 (1993); *The Connecticut Unfair Trade Practices Act 2v (1994). Author:* "A Practitioner's Guide to State Antitrust Health Care Issues," Antitrust (ABA) Fall, 1995; "Should the Antitrust Division, the FTC and State Attorneys General Formally Allocate the Market for Antitrust Enforcement?" Antitrust Report (Matthew Bender) October 1998; "60 Minutes with Robert M. Langer, Assistant Attorney General and Chair, NAAG Multistate Antitrust Task Force," 60 Antitrust L.J. 197 (1991); 61 Antitrust L.J. 211 (1992). Assistant Attorney General, State of Connecticut, 1973-1994, Department Head - Antitrust and Consumer Protection. Chair: National Association of Attorney Generals, Multistate Antitrust Task Force, 1990-1992; Eastern States Antitrust Committee, 1988-1990; State Antitrust Enforcement Committee, Section of Antitrust Law, American Bar Association, 1992-1995. Co-Chair, Federal and State Legislative Policy Task Force, 1996-1997; Legislation Committee, 1997-1998. Chair, Consumer Protection Committee. Council Member, Section of Antitrust Law, ABA, 1990-1992. Member, Board of Editors, Matthew Bender Antitrust Report, 1992—. Member, Bureau of National Affairs Antitrust and Trade Regulation Report Advisory Board, 1994—. Adjunct Professor, University of Connecticut School of Business Administration, MBA Program, 1979—. Chair, Antitrust Section, Connecticut Bar Association, 1979-1980. Chair, Antitrust & Trade Regulation Committee, WESFACCA, 1998—. Chair, James W. Cooper Fellows Program: Connecticut Bar Foundation, 2000; Fellow, American Bar Foundation,

(This Listing Continued)

2000. (Resident, Hartford Office). ***PRACTICE AREAS:*** Antitrust and Trade Regulation; Administrative Law; Consumer Law; Medical Antitrust. ***Email:*** rlanger@wiggin.com

JAMES F. FARRINGTON, JR., born Waterbury, Connecticut, 1952; admitted to bar, 1984, Connecticut; 1985, New York. *Education:* University of Notre Dame (B.Ch.E., 1974); Quinnipiac University School of Law (J.D., magna cum laude, 1984). Associate Editor, University of Bridgeport Law Review, 1981-1984. Author: "Product and Process Patent Confusion under Antitrust Analysis," 4 Bridgeport L. Rev. 109 (1982); "Piercing the Connecticut Corporate Veil," 5 Bridgeport L. Rev. 109 (1983). Partner, Mannheimer Swartling Advokatbyrå, 1991-1995. Associate and Partner, Reid & Priest, 1985-1991. (Resident, Stamford Office). ***PRACTICE AREAS:*** International Corporate; Pharmaceutical Strategic Alliances; Technology Transfer. ***Email:*** jfarrington@wiggin.com

KAREN L. CLUTE, born Ithaca, New York, 1956; admitted to bar, 1986, Connecticut. *Education:* State University of New York at Binghamton (B.A., 1977; M.Mus., 1981); New York University (J.D., 1986). ***PRACTICE AREAS:*** Employee Benefits; Executive Compensation; Estate Planning; Tax Exempt Organizations; Trusts and Estates. ***Email:*** kclute@wiggin.com

LEONARD LEADER, born New York, N.Y., 1950; admitted to bar, 1974, New York; 1975, U.S. Court of Appeals, Second Circuit and U.S. District Court, Southern District of New York; 1983, Connecticut. *Education:* City College of the City University of New York (B.A., cum laude, 1970); Fordham Law School (J.D., cum laude, 1973); New York University Graduate School of Law (LL.M. in Taxation, 1982). Phi Beta Kappa. Member, Fordham Urban Law Journal, 1972-1973. Author: "Excluded Gifts Are Not Necessarily GST-Exempt," Probate & Property, November/December 1991; "Review of Recent Developments in Estate & Gift Taxation," The Tax Lawyer, 1975-1981. Estate Planning Instructor, Westport School of Continuing Education, 1983. Associate, Parker Chapin Flattau & Klimpl., LLP, New York, NY, 1973-1981. Member, Kleban & Samor, P.C., Southport, CT, 1981-1996. *Member:* Greater Bridgeport (Member, Probate Section), Connecticut (Member, Estates and Probate Section), New York State (Member, Trusts and Estates Section) and American (Member, Sections on: Taxation, Estate and Gift Taxes Committee, Chairman, Task Force on Charitable Easements, 1982; Real Property, Probate and Trust Law, Committee on Estate Planning and Estate Administration for Business Owners) Bar Associations. (Resident, Stamford Office). ***PRACTICE AREAS:*** Estate Planning; Trusts and Estates; Closely Held Business Law; Taxation. ***Email:*** lleader@wiggin.com

JEFFREY R. BABBIN, born Queens, New York, 1960; admitted to bar, 1984, District of Columbia; 1993, Connecticut. *Education:* University of Pennsylvania (B.S. Econ., magna cum laude, 1981); Stanford University (J.D., 1984). ***PRACTICE AREAS:*** Appellate Practice; Civil Appeals; Administrative; U.S. Supreme Court Litigation; Personal Injury. ***Email:*** jbabbin@wiggin.com

IAN E. BJORKMAN, born Stamford, Connecticut, 1958; admitted to bar, 1987, Connecticut; 1988, New York and U.S. District Court, Eastern and Southern Districts of New York. *Education:* New York University (B.A., 1980); Brooklyn Law School (J.D., cum laude, 1987). Staff Member/Notes Editor, Brooklyn Law Review, 1986-1987. Clerk, Hon. Stanley Marcus, United States District Court for the Southern District of Florida, 1987-1988. ***PRACTICE AREAS:*** Litigation. ***Email:*** ibjorkman@wiggin.com

DALE L. CARLSON, born Buffalo, New York, 1946; admitted to bar, 1976, New York and U.S. District Court, Eastern and Southern Districts of New York; 1978, District of Columbia and U.S. Supreme Court; 1982, U.S. Court of Appeals for the Federal Circuit; 1988, Connecticut; registered to practice before U.S. Patent and Trademark Office. *Education:* State University of New York at Buffalo (B.S., Chemical Engineering, 1968; M.B.A., 1969); Syracuse University College of Law (J.D., 1975); New York University School of Law (LL.M. in Trade Regulation, 1979). Associate Editor, Syracuse Journal of International Law & Commerce, 1974-1975. Author: "International Protection of Computer Programs," 3 Syracuse Journal of International Law & Commerce 205 (1975); "The Best Mode Disclosure Requirement in Patent Practice," 60 Journal of the Patent Office Society 171 (1978); 13 New England Law Review 246 (Fall 1977); See Manual of Patent Examining Procedure, § 2004.3; "New Patent Court: A Good Idea," National Law Journal (December 1979); "Effect of Uruguay Round Agreement Amendments Upon Patent Term Extension," Twelfth Annual Joint Seminar Sponsored by the CT, NY, NJ and Philadelphia Intellectual Property Law Associations (Presented at the Grand Hyatt Hotel, NYC, April 17, 1996); "Presto Change-O: Can There Be Liability for Pre-Issuance Activity Leading to Post-Issuance Infringement? Pending Legislation Provides A Retrospective Perspective," Thirteenth Annual Joint Seminar Sponsored by the CT, NY, NJ and Philadelphia Intellectual Property Law Associations (Presented at the Grand Hyatt Hotel, NYC, April 9, 1997); "Changes in Patent Office Rules Relating to Inventorship and Continuation Practice," Fourteenth Annual Joint Seminar Sponsored by the CT, NY, NJ and Philadelphia Intellectual Property Law Associations (Presented at the Grand Hyatt Hotel, NYC, April 28, 1998; "Litigating Reexamined Patents (or Rebaking the Cake)", Fifteenth Annual Joint Seminar by the CT, NY, NJ and Philadelphia Intellectual Property Associations (Presented at the Union League of Philadelphia, April 20,

(This Listing Continued)

1999). Co-Author: "Recent Developments In Correcting Inventorship: Stark, Ewen and the New Final Rule Changes," 4 Intellectual Property Law Today 11 (November 1997); "Who Owns What's in Your Patent?", 5 Intellectual Property Today 8 (June 1998); "It's Broke and You Can't Fix It: 'Uncorrectability' as an Affirmative Defense Against Patent Infringement," 5 Intellectual Property Today 18 (Dec. 1998); "The Division of Rights Among Joint Inventors: Public Policy Concerns After Ethicon v. US Surgical," 39 IDEA 251 (1999); " 'Uncorrectability' as an Affirmative Defense Against Patent Infringement: Managing the Burden of Proof," The Federal Circuit Bar Journal, v.8,n.3,pp.23-38 (1999); "Reexamination: A Viable Alternative to Patent Litigation?" Yale Symposium on Law and Technology, Vol. 3 (Fall 2000); "Exploring the Patents/Antitrust Interface: CSU v. Xerox," Intellectual Property Today, Pg. 7-9 (August 2001). Member, Editorial Advisory Board, "Obtaining Patents," James Publishing, 1997. Adjunct Professor of Intellectual Property, Quinnipiac University School of Law, Hamden, Connecticut, 1999—. Member, Board of Directors, Gateway Community College Foundation, New Haven, Connecticut, 2000—. *Member:* Federal Circuit Bar Association; New York Intellectual Property Law Association (Member: Committee on Consonance and Harmonization in the Profession, 1997-1998; Committee on Professional Ethics and Grievances, 1995-1997; Chair, Committee on License to Practice Requirements, 1992-1994; Chair, Continuing Legal Education Committee, 1985-1988; Board of Directors' Nominating Committee, 1985-1986 and 1991-1992; Member, Board of Directors, 1988-1991; Chair, License to Practice Requirements Committee, 1999-2000); Regional Bar of Stamford, Norwalk, Wilton and Darien (Co-Chair, Intellectual Property Law Committee, 1999-2000); American Intellectual Property Law Association; Connecticut Patent Law Association; International Intellectual Property Association; Licensing Executives Society. ***PRACTICE AREAS:*** Intellectual Property; Chemical Patents; Technology and Science; Trade Secrets; Patent Licensing. ***Email:*** dcarlson@wiggin.com

WILLIAM A. SIMONS, born Kalamazoo, Michigan, 1946; admitted to bar, 1973, Virginia; 1975, California; 1999, Connecticut; registered to practice before U.S. Patent and Trademark Office. *Education:* Michigan State University (B.S., Chem. Eng., 1968); Georgetown Law Center (J.D., 1972); University of New Haven (M.B.A., 1987). *Member:* Connecticut and Federal Circuit Bar Associations; State Bar of California; Virginia State Bar; American Intellectual Property Law Association; Connecticut Intellectual Property Law Association; International Association of Industrial Property Attorneys. ***PRACTICE AREAS:*** Chemical Patents; Intellectual Property Infringement; Intellectual Property; Portfolio Management; International Intellectual Property; Design Patents. ***Email:*** wsimons@wiggin.com

DAVID B. FEIN, born New York, N.Y., 1960; admitted to bar, 1987, New York, Connecticut and U.S. District Court, Southern and Eastern Districts of New York; 1990, U.S. Court of Appeals, Second Circuit; 2000, U.S. Supreme Court. *Education:* Dartmouth College (A.B., cum laude, 1982); New York University School of Law (J.D., cum laude, 1985). Order of the Coif. Senior Board Member, New York University Law Review. Clerkship, Judge Frank M. Coffin, U.S. Court of Appeals for the First Circuit, 1986. Former White House Associate Counsel to the President, 1995-1996. U.S. Attorney's Office, Southern District of New York, 1989-1995: Deputy Chief of the Criminal Division; Counsel to the U.S. Attorney. Visiting Professor of Law, Yale Law School, 1999—. *Member:* Federal Bar Council (Trustee, 1999—); American Bar Association (Criminal Litigation Committee). (Resident, Stamford Office). ***PRACTICE AREAS:*** White Collar Defense; Internal and External Investigations; Corporate Compliance; Appellate; First Amendment. ***Email:*** dfein@wiggin.com

WILLIAM A. PERRONE, born New York, N.Y., 1952; admitted to bar, 1979, Connecticut; 1981, U.S. District Court, District of Connecticut. *Education:* Brooklyn College of the City University of New York (B.A., cum laude, 1974); Western New England College School of Law (J.D., cum laude, 1979). (Resident, Stamford Office). ***PRACTICE AREAS:*** Corporate; Emerging Growth Companies; Information Technology; Mergers and Acquisitions; Securities. ***Email:*** wperrone@wiggin.com

MERTON G. GOLLAHER, born New London, Connecticut, 1962; admitted to bar, 1991, Connecticut. *Education:* Amherst College (B.A., 1984); University of Connecticut (J.D., with high honors, 1991). Member, Connecticut Law Review, 1988-1991. ***PRACTICE AREAS:*** Corporate Law; Health Care; Biotechnology; Business Law; Mergers, Acquisitions and Divestitures. ***Email:*** mgollaher@wiggin.com

STEPHEN B. HARRIS, born New York, N.Y., 1961; admitted to bar, 1987, New York and U.S. District Court, Eastern and Southern Districts of New York; 1988, Minnesota; 1993, U.S. District Court, District of Connecticut; 1996, Connecticut; 1998, U.S. District Court, Western District of New York. *Education:* Brandeis University (B.A., magna cum laude, 1983); Hofstra University (J.D., 1986). Articles Editor, 1985-1986 and Staff Member, 1984-1985, Hofstra Law Review. *Member:* American Bar Association (Member, Employment and Labor Relations Litigation Committee, Litigation Section); Connecticut Business and Industry Association (Member, Labor and Employment Law Council).

(This Listing Continued)

WIGGIN & DANA LLP, New Haven—Continued

(Resident, Hartford Office). ***PRACTICE AREAS:*** Employment Litigation; Wrongful Termination Defense; Employer Rights; Sexual Harassment; Wage and Hour Law. ***Email:*** sharris@wiggin.com

PHYLLIS M. PARI, born New Haven, Connecticut, 1965; admitted to bar, 1990, Connecticut. *Education:* Boston University (B.S., summa cum laude, 1987); Boston University (J.D., magna cum laude, 1990). Note Editor, Boston University Law Review 1989-1990. ***PRACTICE AREAS:*** Litigation. ***Email:*** ppari@wiggin.com

GREGORY S. ROSENBLATT, born Brooklyn, New York, 1955; admitted to bar, 1984, New York; 1997, Connecticut. *Education:* Cornell University (B.S., 1977); New York Law School (J.D., 1983). Member: The Metallurgical Society of AIME; American Electroplaters and Surface Finishers Society. *Member:* Connecticut and American Bar Associations; Connecticut Intellectual Property Law Association. ***PRACTICE AREAS:*** Metallurgical Patents; Patent Prosecution; Patent Litigation; International Patents; Mechanical Patents. ***Email:*** grosenblatt@wiggin.com

FRANCIS J. DUFFIN, born Greenwich, Connecticut, 1962; admitted to bar, 1988, Connecticut and Virginia; 1990, New York. *Education:* Central Connecticut State University (B.A., 1984); University of Bridgeport School of Law (J.D., 1987). *Member:* Connecticut (Member, Intellectual Property Law Section) and Virginia Bar Associations; International Trademark Association; European Communities Trademark Association (ECTA); Institute of Trademark Agents (ITMA). ***PRACTICE AREAS:*** Trademarks; Copyrights; Intellectual Property; Unfair Competition; Computers and Software. ***Email:*** fduffin@wiggin.com

KEVIN M. KENNEDY, born Stratford, Connecticut, 1966; admitted to bar, 1991, Connecticut. *Education:* Connecticut College (B.A., summa cum laude, 1988); University of Connecticut (J.D., with honors, 1991). ***PRACTICE AREAS:*** Litigation; Arbitration; Franchise Litigation; Franchise Arbitration; Business Litigation. ***Email:*** kkennedy@wiggin.com

MICHAEL GRUNDEI, born New York, N.Y., 1964; admitted to bar, 1990, New York; 1996, Connecticut. *Education:* University of Pennsylvania (B.A., magna cum laude, 1986); Duke University School of Law (J.D., 1989). (Resident, Stamford Office). ***LANGUAGES:*** German. ***PRACTICE AREAS:*** Corporate Finance; Securities; Venture Capital; Public Offerings; Mergers and Acquisitions. ***Email:*** mgrundei@wiggin.com

PATRICIA KAVEE MELICK, born New York, N.Y., 1962; admitted to bar, 1988, New York; 1997, Connecticut. *Education:* Lehigh University (B.A., summa cum laude, 1984); University of Chicago Law School (J.D., 1987). Phi Beta Kappa. (Resident, Stamford Office). ***PRACTICE AREAS:*** Mergers, Acquisitions and Divestitures; Biotechnology Licensing; Commercial Transactions; Contracts; Corporate Law. ***Email:*** pmelick@wiggin.com

WILLIAM J. SPERANZA, born Poughkeepsie, New York, 1949; admitted to bar, 1976, New York; 1977, U.S. District Court, Southern and Eastern Districts of New York and U.S. Court of Appeals, Fifth Circuit; 1984, U.S. Court of Appeals for the Federal Circuit; 1985, Connecticut; 1986, U.S. District Court, District of Connecticut; 1989, U.S. Court of Appeals, Third Circuit; 1993, U.S. Supreme Court; 1997, U.S. Court of Appeals, Sixth Circuit; registered to practice before U.S. Patent and Trademark Office. *Education:* University of Notre Dame (B.S.Ch.E., cum laude, 1971); Fordham University (J.D., cum laude, 1975). Member, Fordham Law Review, 1973-1975. Author: "Re-examination - The Patent Challenger's View," 15 A.I.P.L.A. Q.J. 85, 1987. *Member:* American Bar Association; Connecticut Patent Law Association. (Resident, Stamford Office). ***PRACTICE AREAS:*** Patent Law; Intellectual Property; Litigation. ***Email:*** wsperanza@wiggin.com

LISA PAGE HESLIN, born New Haven, Connecticut, 1966; admitted to bar, 1991, Connecticut; 1994, New York. *Education:* Yale University (B.A., 1988); Georgetown University (J.D., 1991). Managing Editor, Journal of Law and Technology, 1990-1991. ***LANGUAGES:*** French. ***Email:*** pheslin@wiggin.com

MARK E. HARANZO, born Wheeling, West Virginia, September 8, 1959; admitted to bar, 1986, West Virginia, Massachusetts and U.S. District Court, Southern District of West Virginia; 1987, Florida and New York; 1989, New Jersey and U.S. District Court, District of New Jersey; 1990, Connecticut. *Education:* Wittenberg University; University of South Florida (B.A., 1981); Stetson University (J.D., 1985). Attorney, Internal Revenue Service, 1986-1988. Co-Author: "Harris Estates Practice Guide, 4th Edition," 1994 Annual Supplements; "Harris 5th Edition New York Estates," West Group, 1996 Edition, 1997-2000 Annual Supplements. Member, Archdiocese of New York, Planned Giving Committee (Co-Chair, Education Committee). *Member:* The Association of the Bar of the City of New York (Member, Estate and Gift Taxation Committee, 1993-1995); New York State (Member, Trusts and Estates Law Section), Massachusetts (Member, Probate Law Section), Connecticut (Member, Estates and Probate Section), Stamford Norwalk Regional and American (Member, Sections on: International Law and Practice; Real Property, Probate and Trust Law) Bar Associations; The West Virginia State Bar; The Florida Bar (Member: Real Property, Probate and Trust Law Section; Tax Section, Federal Estate and Gift Taxation Committee); New York County Lawyers Association (Member, Section on Estates, Trusts and Surrogate's Court Practice; Co-Chair, Committee on Surrogate's Court Practice and Trust and Estate Administration, 1992-1994). Fellow, The American College of Trust and Estate Counsel. (Resident, Stamford Office). ***PRACTICE AREAS:*** Trusts Law; Estates Law; Estate Planning Law; Estate Litigation; Taxation of Trusts and Estates; Not-For-Profit Institutions Law. ***Email:*** mharanzo@wiggin.com

LAWRENCE PEIKES, admitted to bar, 1987, California; 1990, Connecticut; 1996, New York. *Education:* University of Maryland (B.A., 1984); The National Law Center, George Washington University (J.D., with honors, 1987). *Member:* American Bar Association (Member, Section of Labor and Employment Law, 1993—). (Resident, Stamford Office). ***PRACTICE AREAS:*** Labor and Employment Law; Alternative Dispute Resolution; Employee Benefits; Trade Secrets. ***Email:*** LPeikes@wiggin.com

JAMES H. BICKS, born 1962; admitted to bar, 1989, New York; 1999, Connecticut. *Education:* Pomona College (B.A., cum laude, 1984); New York University (J.D., 1988). Editor, Moot Court Board. (Resident, Stamford Office). ***Email:*** jbicks@wiggin.com

DANIEL J. KLAU, born Hartford, Connecticut, 1961; admitted to bar, 1991, Connecticut and Massachusetts. *Education:* University of California, San Diego (B.A., with distinction in Political Science, 1984, cum laude, outstanding senior distinguished student); Boston University School of Law (J.D., summa cum laude, 1990). Recipient, Melville Bigelow Award (for student showing most promise as scholar and teacher of law). Note Editor, Boston University School of Law - Law Review, 1988-1990. Author: "What Price Certainty," Corbin, Williston and the Restatements of Contracts to B.V.C. Rev. 511 (1990). Law Clerk, Chief Justice Ellen A. Peters, Connecticut Supreme Court, 1990-1991. (Resident, Hartford Office). ***Email:*** dklau@wiggin.com

PETER M. WENDZEL, born Kalamazoo, Michigan, 1967; admitted to bar, 1992, Connecticut. *Education:* George Washington University (B.A., magna cum laude, 1989) Phi Beta Kappa; University of Virginia School of Law (J.D., 1992). (Resident, Hartford Office). ***Email:*** pwendzel@wiggin.com

JOSEPH SCHUMACHER, born New York, N.Y., July 31, 1954; admitted to bar, 1986, Pennsylvania, U.S. District Court, Eastern District of Pennsylvania and U.S. Court of Appeals, Third and Ninth Circuits; U.S. District Court, Eastern District of Michigan. *Education:* St. Francis College (B.A., 1976); Delaware Law School of Widener University (J.D., magna cum laude, 1985). External Managing Editor, Delaware Journal of Corporate Law, 1984-1985. Listed in An International Who's Who of Franchise Lawyers (Second Edition) - Law Business Research Limited, London, England. Co-Author: "Recovering Lost Future Royalities in a Franchise Termination Case," Franchise Law Journal, Winter 2001; "Managing Environmental Risks In a Franchising," Franchise Law Journal, January/February, 1990. Speaker: "Franchisee Association and Advisory Councils,"; "Troubled Franchisees," International Franchise Association Legal Roundtables, Philadelphia, Pennsylvania, 2001; "Effective Relationships with Franchisee Associations-Legal and Practical Aspects," International Franchise Association 34th Annual Legal Symposium, Washington, DC, 2001; "Settling Franchise Disputes: The Settlement Process and Agreement," American Bar Association Forum on Franchising, Annual Forum, New Orleans, Louisiana, 2000; "Judicial Remedies - the Ultimate Issue," American Bar Association Forum on Franchising, Annual Forum, Colorado Springs, Colorado, 1997; "Alternative Dispute Resolution in Franchising," American Association of Franchisees and Dealers Annual Convention, Chicago, Illinois, 1997; "Franchise Law Issues," Philadelphia Bar Association, Philadelphia, Pennsylvania, 1996; "Development Issues in Franchising," International Franchise Association Annual Convention Puerto Rico, 1995; "Master Franchising in Brazil," Second Seminar on Franchising in Northeast Brazil, Salvador, Bahia, Brazil, 1992; "The Socio-Economic Impact on Franchising on a Developing Economy," First Seminar on Franchising in Northeast Brazil, 1991. Guest Lecturer - Temple University School of Law, 1991; 1992; "Career Opportunities in Franchising," Temple School of Business Management - The Entrepreneurial Institute, 1991. Corporate Counsel, Maaco Enterprises, Inc., 1986-1987. *Member:* American Bar Association (Member: Litigation Section; Forum Committee on Franchising). (Resident, Berwyn, Pennsylvania Office and Cherry Hill, New Jersey). ***PRACTICE AREAS:*** Franchise Litigation; Franchise Distribution; Commercial Litigation; Commercial Transactions; Alternative Dispute Resolution. ***Email:*** jschumacher@wiggin.com

SENIOR COUNSEL

WILLIAM E. CRAIG, born Springfield, Massachusetts, 1942; admitted to bar, 1967, Connecticut. *Education:* Dartmouth College (B.A., cum laude, 1964); Yale University (LL.B., 1967). Phi Beta Kappa. ***PRACTICE AREAS:*** Real Property Law; Mortgage Law; Municipal Law. ***Email:*** wcraig@wiggin.com

S. ROBERT JELLEY, born Newark, New Jersey, 1930; admitted to bar, 1961, Connecticut. *Education:* Dartmouth College (A.B., 1952; M.S., 1953); Harvard University (LL.B., 1961). Phi Beta Kappa. ***PRACTICE AREAS:*** Litigation; Environmental Law. ***Email:*** rjelley@wiggin.com

(This Listing Continued)

ROBERT M. McANERNEY, born Greenwich, Connecticut, 1924; admitted to bar, 1954, Connecticut; 1959, U.S. District Court, District of Connecticut; 1969, U.S. Supreme Court. *Education:* Williams College (B.A., 1947); University of Virginia (J.D., 1953). Associated with Sullivan & Cromwell, New York, N.Y., 1953. Partner, Durey & Pierson, Stamford, Connecticut, 1954-1963. Founder and Senior Partner, McAnerney & Miller, Darien, Connecticut, 1963-1995. Major Contributing Author: "Proposal for Revision of Connecticut Statutes Relative to Divorce," 44 Connecticut Bar Journal 411 (1970). Co-Author: "Connecticut's New Approach to Marriage Dissolution," 47 Connecticut Bar Journal 375 (1973). Director and Member, Executive Committee, Connecticut Attorneys Title Insurance Company, 1970-1994. *Member:* Connecticut (Member, Board of Governors, 1964-1967; Chairman, Family Law Committee, 1967-1971; Vice Chairman, Family Law Section, 1971-1973; Chairman, Law Office Economics Committee, 1973-1975; Chairman, Special Committee on Legislative Liaison, 1977-1978; Vice-Chairman, Commission on the Legal Profession, 1978-1980; Vice-President, 1978-1979, President-Elect, 1979-1980 and President, 1980-1981) and American (Member, House of Delegates, 1978-1982) Bar Associations; New England Bar Association (Director, 1980-1984); Connecticut Bar Foundation (Director, 1978-1979). Life Fellow, American Bar Foundation. (Resident, Stamford Office). ***PRACTICE AREAS:*** Estate Planning; Trusts and Estates; Family Law; Real Estate.

CHARLES N. SCHENCK, III, born Englewood, New Jersey, 1923; admitted to bar, 1948, New York; 1954, Connecticut. *Education:* Yale University (B.A., 1943); Columbia University (LL.B., 1948). Fellow, American Bar Foundation. ***PRACTICE AREAS:*** Estate Planning; Trusts and Estates; Business Venture Law; Taxation; Closely Held Business.

COUNSEL

PENNY QUINN SEAMAN, born Mount Vernon, New York, 1951; admitted to bar, 1980, Pennsylvania; 1981, District of Columbia; 1983, Virginia; 1984, Connecticut. *Education:* College of William and Mary (B.A., 1972); Delaware Law School (J.D., magna cum laude, 1980). ***PRACTICE AREAS:*** Litigation. ***Email:*** pseaman@wiggin.com

SHARYN B. ZUCH, born New Hyde Park, New York, 1956; admitted to bar, 1981, Florida; 1999, Connecticut; U.S. District Court, Middle District of Florida and U.S. Court of Appeals, Eleventh Circuit. *Education:* Cornell University (B.S., with distinction, 1977); University of Chicago (J.D., 1981). Phi Kappa Phi; Omicron Nu. Author: "Battling in Bankruptcy Court," Federal Bar News & Journal, June/July 1991; "Bankruptcy Mediation," Hillsborough County Bar Bulletin, May 1990; "Selected Problems in Discovery," Chapter, Business Litigation in Florida, 1989; "Trade Secrets and High-Tech Industries," 59 Florida Bar Journal 37, 1985; "Discovery of Facts Known and Opinions Held By Experts," 58 Florida Bar Journal 225, 1984; "A Critical Analysis of Recent Federal Appellate Decisions on Predatory Pricing," 55 Antitrust Law Journal 401, 1982. Editor, "The Quarterly Report," Florida Bar Business Law Section, 1987-1990. Contributor, ARTSNEWS, on law and the arts, 1987-1988. Bankruptcy Mediator, Middle District of Florida. *Member:* The Florida Bar (Member, Business Law Executive Council, Chair, Business Litigation Committee); American Bar Association (Member: Litigation and Business Law Sections); American Bankruptcy Institute; Tampa Bay Bankruptcy Bar Association (Secretary). Master, American Inns of Court (Secretary, Ferguson White Chapter). (Resident, Hartford Office). ***PRACTICE AREAS:*** Antitrust; Bankruptcy. ***Email:*** szuch@wiggin.com

MARCIA KENNY KEEGAN, born Poughkeepsie, New York, 1958; admitted to bar, 1989, Connecticut. *Education:* Union College, Schenectady, New York (B.A., cum laude, 1980); Cornell Law School (J.D., cum laude, 1989). Senior Editor, Cornell International Law Journal. (Resident, Hartford Office). ***PRACTICE AREAS:*** Employment Law. ***Email:*** mkeegan@wiggin.com

CYNTHIA BRODHEAD, born Lockport, New York, September 25, 1946; admitted to bar, 1982, Connecticut and U.S. District Court, District of Connecticut. *Education:* Syracuse University (B.A., magna cum laude, 1968); Yale University (M.A., 1970); University of Connecticut School of Law (J.D., with honors, 1982). Phi Beta Kappa. Member, Connecticut Law Review. ***PRACTICE AREAS:*** Utility Law; Regulated Industries. ***Email:*** cbrodhead@wiggin.com

MARTIN H. DODD, born Hartford, Connecticut, 1953; admitted to bar, 1983, Connecticut and U.S. District Court, District of Connecticut; 1988, New York. *Education:* Trinity College (B.S., 1975); University of Connecticut (J.D., cum laude, 1983). Lecturer, Environmental Insurance Coverage, ABA/PLI, 1992. Formerly associated with: General Electric Co., Fairfield, Connecticut and Schenectady, New York, 1983-1993. General Counsel, TRC Companies, Inc., Windsor, Connecticut, 1993-1997 and 1999—. *Member:* Corporate Bar (Member, Environmental Section). ***PRACTICE AREAS:*** Environmental; Corporate Law. ***Email:*** mdodd@wiggin.com

CHRISTINE OWENS MORGAN, born Cambridge, Massachusetts, 1965; admitted to bar, 1990, Connecticut. *Education:* Connecticut College (B.A., 1987); University of Connecticut (J.D., 1990). ***PRACTICE AREAS:*** Commercial Real Estate Finance; Commercial Real Estate Development; Commercial Real Estate Acquisitions; Real Estate Finance; Real Estate Secured Lending. ***Email:*** cmorgan@wiggin.com

TODD E. GARABEDIAN, born Los Angeles, California, 1962; admitted to bar, 1994, Massachusetts; 1999, Connecticut; registered to practice before U.S. Patent and Trademark Office. *Education:* University of California, Los Angeles (B.S., 1985); Washington State University (M.S., BioChemistry, 1988; Ph.D., BioChemistry, 1991); New England School of Law (J.D., 1994). ***PRACTICE AREAS:*** Intellectual Property; Biochemical Technology; Pharmaceutical Intellectual Property; Biotechnology Licensing; Trademarks. ***Email:*** tgarabedian@wiggin.com

GATES GARRITY-ROKOUS, born 1963; admitted to bar, 1993, Massachusetts; 1994, Connecticut; 1995, U.S. District Court, District of Connecticut. *Education:* Trinity College (B.A., with highest honors, 1986); Yale University (J.D., 1992). Editor-in-Chief, Yale Journal of International Law, 1991-1992. Member, Yale Law Journal. Law Clerk to: Hon. T.F. Gilroy Daly, U.S. District Court, District of Connecticut; Hon. Thomas J. Meskill, U.S. Court of Appeals, Second Circuit. Former Assistant United States Attorney and Criminal Health Care Fraud Coordinator, U.S. Attorney's Office, Connecticut. *Member:* Connecticut and American Bar Associations. ***PRACTICE AREAS:*** Litigation; White Collar Criminal Defense; Corporate Law; Criminal Law; Civil Litigation; Federal Regulatory Law; Regulatory Law; Health Care. ***Email:*** ggarrity_rokous@wiggin.com

ASSOCIATES

WILLIAM JOHN ALBINGER, born New Haven, Connecticut, 1967; admitted to bar, 1997, Connecticut. *Education:* University of New Haven (B.S., Marketing, summa cum laude, 1990); Quinnipiac University (J.D., magna cum laude, 1997). Recipient: West Publishing Company Award for Outstanding Scholastic Achievement; Corpus Juris Secundum Award for Scholastic Excellence. Notes and Casenotes Editor, Quinnipiac Law Review, 1996-1997. Law Clerk to Honorable Paul M. Foti, Connecticut Appellate Court, 1997-1998. ***Email:*** walbinger@wiggin.com

ERIKA L. AMARANTE, born New Haven, Connecticut, 1973; admitted to bar, 1998, Connecticut. *Education:* Cornell University (B.A., with distinction, 1995); New York University (J.D., cum laude, 1998). Member, 1997 and Editor in Chief, 1998, New York University Environmental Law Journal. Law Clerk, Hon. Francis McDonald and Hon. Richard Palmer, U.S. Supreme Court, Connecticut, 1998-1999. Executive Assistant, Hon. Francis McDonald, 1999-2000. Author: "Water Resources: Agriculture, the Environment and Society," Bioscience V. 47n.2, February, 1999; "The International Obligation to Conduct an Environmental Impact Assessment: The ICJ Case Concerning the Gabcikovo-Nagymaros Project," 7 NYU Envtl. L.J. 30, 1999. ***Email:*** eamarante@wiggin.com

JEFFREY RUSSELL AMBROZIAK, born Okinawa, Japan, 1966; admitted to bar, 1998, Connecticut. *Education:* Princeton University (B.S.E., 1989); College of William & Mary (J.D., 1998). ***Email:*** jambroziak@wiggin.com

BETHANY L. APPLEBY, born Monterey, California, 1967; admitted to bar, 1997, Connecticut. *Education:* Yale University (B.A., magna cum laude, 1989); University of Connecticut School of Law (J.D., highest honors, 1997). Notes and Comments Editor, Connecticut Law Review. Semi-finalist, Duberstein Bankruptcy Moot Court Competition, 1997. Moot Court Teaching Assistant. Certified Financial Planner, College for Financial Planning, 1994. ***Email:*** bappleby@wiggin.com

CATHERINE P. BAATZ, born Holyoke, Massachusetts; admitted to bar, 1996, Connecticut. *Education:* Mount Holyoke College (A.B., magna cum laude, 1981) Phi Beta Kappa; Harvard Law School (J.D., 1996). Member, 1993-1996 and Managing Editor, 1994-1995, Woman's Law Journal. (Resident, Hartford Office). ***Email:*** cbaatz@wiggin.com

JESSICA A. BALLOU, born Cincinnati, Ohio, 1975; admitted to bar, 2000, Connecticut; 2001, New York. *Education:* Roanoke College (B.A., 1997); Quinnipiac University (J.D., cum laude, 2000). Member, Quinnipiac Law Review. Author: "Above the Law?: Prosecutorial Tactics After United States v. Singleton, 19 Quinnipiac L. Rev. 173, 2000. ***Email:*** jballou@wiggin.coms

KENNETH F. BAUM, admitted to bar, 2001, Connecticut. *Education:* University of California at Berkeley (B.A., with highest distinction, 1994); Yale Law School (J.D., 2001); Yale School of Medicine (M.D., 2001) Junior Phi Beta Kappa. Editor, Yale Journal of Health Policy, Law & Ethics. Author: "Golden Eggs: Toward the Rational Regulation of Oocyte Donation," Bringham Young University Law Review, March, 2001. Founder and Director, Yale Health Law Society. ***Email:*** kbaum@wiggin.com

PATRICIA R. BEAUREGARD, born Stamford, Connecticut, 1960; admitted to bar, 1998, Connecticut; 1999, New York; 2001, U.S. District Court, District of Connecticut. *Education:* Fairfield University (B.A., English, Writing and Literature, magna cum laude, 1991); Quinnipiac University (J.D., magna cum laude, 1998). Alpha Sigma Lambda; Phi Delta Phi. Member, Quinnipiac Law Review Association, 1996-1998. Editor, Research and Symposium, 1997-

(This Listing Continued)

(This Listing Continued)

WIGGIN & DANA LLP, New Haven—Continued

1998. Co-Author, with Jessie A. Gilbert, "The New Environment in Connecticut for the Investment and Management of Trust and Charitable Assets," The Quinnipiac Probate Law Journal, March 2000. Lecturer, Estate Planning and Fiduciary Law. Instructor, Westport Continuing Education Program. ***Email:*** pbeauregard@wiggin.com

EILEEN REYNOLDS BECKER, born Bridgeport, Connecticut, 1967; admitted to bar, 1992, Pennsylvania and New Jersey; 1994, Connecticut. *Education:* Syracuse University (A.B., 1989); Rutgers University School of Law, Camden (J.D., magna cum laude, 1992). Managing Editor, Rutgers Law Journal, 1991-1992. ***Email:*** ebecker@wiggin.com

PENELOPE I. BELLAMY, born Palatka, Florida, 1947; admitted to bar, 1984, Connecticut. *Education:* Swarthmore College (B.A., 1969); University of Connecticut (J.D., with high honors, 1984). ***Email:*** pbellamy@wiggin.com

ELIZABETH ANNE BLOOMFIELD, born Greenville, Pennsylvania, 1971; admitted to bar, 2000, New York; 2001, Connecticut. *Education:* Vassar College (A.B., 1993); New York University. Member, Order of Barristers. Casebook Editor, Moot Court Board, 1998. (Resident, Stamford Office). ***Email:*** ebloomfield@wiggin.com

VICTOR ALLEN BOLDEN, born New York, N.Y., 1965; admitted to bar, 1990, New York; 2000, Connecticut. *Education:* Columbia University; Harvard University. Member, Harvard Blackletter Journal. Author: "Where Does New York City Go From Here: Chaos or Community?" 23 Fordham Urban Law Journal, 1031, 1996; "Judge Not That Ye Be Not Judged: A Dramatic Call for a More Enlightened Approach to Judicial Decision-Making in Race Discrimination Cases," 7 Harvard Blackletter Journal 33, 1990; "Salvaging Black Males," in Racial Reflections: Dialogues in the Direction of Liberation, 37 U.C.L.A. L. Rev. 1037, 1084, 1990, edited by Derrick Bell, Tracy Higgins and Sung-Hee Suh. Adjunct Professor, New York Law School. ***Email:*** vbolden@wiggin.com

KEVIN S. BUDGE, born Waterbury, Connecticut, 1971; admitted to bar, 1996, Connecticut. *Education:* University of Connecticut (B.A., magna cum laude, 1993); Western New England College School of Law (J.D., 1996). ***Email:*** kbudge@wiggin.com

DYLAN S. CALSYN, born Chicago, Illinois, 1971; admitted to bar, 2000, Connecticut. *Education:* Northwestern University (B.A., with highest honors, 1993; M.A., 1993); Yale University (J.D.). Edit Team, Yale Law and Policy Review, 1997. Law Clerk, Hon. William J. Sullivan, U.S. Supreme Court, Connecticut, 1999-2000. Author: "Block Grants, Entitlements and Federalism: A Conceptual Map of Contested Terrain," Jerry L. Mashaw and Dylan S. Calsyn, 14 Yale Law and Policy Review, 297, 1996. ***Email:*** dcalsyn@wiggin.com

JULIE MIN CHAYET, born Bay Shore, New York, 1969; admitted to bar, 1999, Connecticut and New York. *Education:* Haverford College (B.A., 1991); Columbia University (M.P.A., 1995); Fordham University (J.D., 1998). Associate Editor, 1996-1997 and Staff Member, Environmental Law Journal. (Resident, Stamford Office). ***LANGUAGES:*** Korean and Spanish. ***Email:*** jminchayet@wiggin.com

LORI R. CLARK, born Middletown, Connecticut, 1964; admitted to bar, 1998, Connecticut. *Education:* University of Connecticut (B.A., Economics and Political Science, 1993); Western New England College (J.D., cum laude, 1997). Member, Western New England Law Review, 1995-1997. Law Clerk: The Honorable Alfred V. Covello, Chief Judge, U.S. District Court, 1998-1999. (Resident, Hartford Office). ***Email:*** lclark@wiggin.com

MONIKA DOROTA CORNELL, born Warsaw, Poland, 1964; admitted to bar, 2000, Connecticut. *Education:* University of Michigan (A.B., with highest distinction, 1995); Institut D'Etudes Politiques De Paris (Cert. with honors, 1999); Boston University (J.D., 2000). Phi Beta Kappa. Note Editor, Public Interest Law Journal. ***LANGUAGES:*** French, Polish and Russian. ***Email:*** mcornell@wiggin.com

DAVID COTTA, born 1972; admitted to bar, 1999, New York (Not admitted in Connecticut). *Education:* Trinity College (B.A., 1994); Cornell University (J.D., 1997). ***Email:*** dcotta@wiggin.com

JAMES O. CRAVEN, born New York, N.Y., 1968; admitted to bar, 1994, Connecticut; 1995, New York and U.S. Court of the Armed Forces; 1997, U.S. District Court, District of Connecticut. *Education:* Dickinson College (B.A., Economics and Political Science, 1990); Case Western Reserve University (J.D., cum laude, 1994). ***Email:*** jcraven@wiggin.com

JEFFREY JOHN DANILE, born New York, N.Y., 1975; admitted to bar, 2000, Connecticut. *Education:* New York University (B.A., Political Science, cum laude, 1996); St. John's University (J.D., 2000). Executive Publications Editor, St. John's Law Review. Author: "Recent Developments in NY Law," 73 St. John's L. Rev. 613, 1999. (Resident, Stamford Office). ***Email:*** jdanile@wiggin.com

(This Listing Continued)

KEVIN PAUL DEAN, born Englewood, New Jersey, 1966; admitted to bar, 1998, Connecticut. *Education:* Fairfield University (B.S., 1988); University of Connecticut School of Law (J.D., 1998). Associate Editor, University of Connecticut Law Review, 1998. ***Email:*** kdean@wiggin.com

MICHELLE WILCOX DeBARGE, born New Britain, Connecticut, 1965; admitted to bar, 1993, Connecticut. *Education:* Williams College (B.A., 1987); University of Connecticut School of Law (J.D., magna cum laude, 1993). Member, 1991-1992 and Editor-in-Chief, 1992-1993, University of Connecticut Law Review. Author: "The Performance of Invasive Procedures by HIV-Infected Doctors: The Duty to Disclose under the Informed Consent Doctrine," 25 Conn. Law Review 991 (1993). (Resident, Hartford Office). ***Email:*** mdebarge@wiggin.com

W. BRUCE DelMONICO, born New Haven, Connecticut, 1969; admitted to bar, 1997, Connecticut; 1998, U.S. District Court, District of Connecticut; 1999, Georgia and U.S. District Court, Northern District of Georgia. *Education:* Brown University (B.A., in Honors English, 1991); University of Texas at Austin (M.A., in English, 1994, Phi Kappa Phi); University of Virginia (J.D., 1997). Dillard Fellow, 1995-1996. Essays Editor, Virginia Journal of Social Policy & The Law, 1996-1997. (Resident, Stamford Office). ***Email:*** bdelmonico@wiggin.com

JODY L. DeSTEFANIS, born Bronx, New York, 1970; admitted to bar, 1999, Connecticut; registered to practice before U.S. Patent and Trademark Office. *Education:* University of Connecticut (B.S.E., 1992); Quinnipiac University (M.B.A., 1998; J.D., 1998). (Resident, Stamford Office). ***Email:*** jdestefanis@wiggin.com

MICHAEL J. DEVINE, born Milford, Connecticut, 1968; admitted to bar, 1995, Nebraska and U.S. District Court, District of Nebraska; 1997, Illinois; 2000, Connecticut. *Education:* University of Connecticut (B.A., 1990); Creighton University School of Law (J.D., cum laude, 1995). Associate Editor, Creighton Law Review. Law Clerk to the Honorable Edward E. Hannon, Nebraska Court of Appeals, 1995-1997. (Resident, Hartford Office). ***Email:*** mdevine@wiggin.com

TIMOTHY A. DIEMAND, born Waterbury, Connecticut, 1967; admitted to bar, 1992, Maryland; 1993, District of Columbia; 1997, Connecticut and U.S. District Court, District of Connecticut. *Education:* Clark University (B.A., cum laude, 1989); George Washington University National Law Center (J.D., with honors, 1992). Staff Member, Journal of International Law and Economics, 1990-1992. ***Email:*** tdiemand@wiggin.com

ANITA C. DiGIOIA, born New Haven, Connecticut, 1971; admitted to bar, 1997, Louisiana; 1998, Connecticut; 1999, New York. *Education:* Siena College (B.A., magna cum laude, 1994); Tulane University (J.D., magna cum laude, 1997). Order of the Coif. Member, 1995-1997, Notes and Comments Editor, 1996-1997, Tulane Law Review. Law Clerk, Judge Steven R. Plotkin, U.S. Court of Appeals, Fourth Circuit, Louisiana, 1997-1999. ***Email:*** adigioia@wiggin.com

ADAM PAUL DOHERTY, born Hartford, Connecticut, 1974; admitted to bar, 2001, Connecticut. *Education:* Yale University (B.A., 1996); University of Hartford (M.S., 1997); William & Mary School of Law (2001). Administrative Justice and Member, William and Mary Moot Court Board. Member, William and Mary Environmental Law and Policy Review. ***Email:*** adoherty@wiggin.com

MEGHAN E. DOHERTY, born New Haven, Connecticut, 1974; admitted to bar, 2001, Connecticut. *Education:* University of Connecticut (B.A., 1996); Quinnipiac College (J.D., magna cum laude, 2001). ***Email:*** mdoherty@wiggin.com

CHRISTOPHER D. FASANO, born Waterbury, Connecticut, 1975; admitted to bar, 2000, Connecticut. *Education:* Villanova University (B.A., cum laude, 1997); Syracuse University (J.D., cum laude, 2000). Member, Syracuse Journal of Law and Technology, 1998-2000. ***Email:*** cfasano@wiggin.com

CECILE MONIQUE FRASER, born Kingston, Jamaica, West Indies, 1965; admitted to bar, 2000, Connecticut. *Education:* Fordham University (B.A., Political Science, 1987); The Graduate Faculty, New School for Social Research (M.A., Political Science, 1997); Rutgers University School of Law (J.D., 2000). ***Email:*** cfraser@wiggin.com

JESSE M. FURMAN, born New York, N.Y., June 7, 1972; admitted to bar, 1999, New York; 2000, U.S. District Court, Southern District of New York (Not admitted in Connecticut). *Education:* Harvard University (A.B., summa cum laude, 1994); Oxford University, England (1995); Yale University (J.D., 1998). Phi Beta Kappa. Henry Fellow. Executive Editor, Yale Law Journal, 1997-1998; Articles Editor, Yale Law and Policy Review, 1996-1997. Law Clerk to: Judge Michael B. Mukasey, U.S. District Court, Southern District of New York, 1998-1999; Judge José A. Cabranes, U.S. Court of Appeals, Second Circuit, 1999-2000. Prospective Clerk to Justice David H. Souter, U.S. Supreme Court, 2002-2003. Author: Note, "Political Illiberalism: The Paradox of Disenfranchisement and the Ambivalences of Rawlsian Justice," 106 Yale Law Journal 1157, 1997. *Member:* New York State and American Bar Associations; Federal Bar Council. (Resident, Stamford Office). ***Email:*** jfurman@wiggin.com

(This Listing Continued)

ELIZABETH MARY GARRETT, born Framingham, Massachusetts, 1968; admitted to bar, 1999, Connecticut. *Education:* Southern Connecticut State College (B.S., Computer Science, cum laude, 1999); University of Connecticut (J.D., with honors, 1999). Member, University of Connecticut Law Review, 1998-1999. *Member:* American Bar Association (Member, Sections on: Taxation; Labor and Employment). ***Email:*** egarrett@wiggin.com

MICHELE B. GERROIR, born Cleveland, Ohio, July 21, 1970; admitted to bar, 1996, Ohio and U.S. District Court, Southern District of Ohio; 2001, Connecticut. *Education:* Syracuse University (B.A., magna cum laude, 1992); Case Western Reserve University (J.D., 1996); University of Houston Law Center (LL.M. in Health Law, 1999). Member, National Moot Court Team. Associate Editor, 1994-1995 and Topic Development Manager, 1995-1996, Health Matrix Journal of Law Medicine. *Member:* Ohio State Bar Association (Member, Health Law Section); American Health Lawyers Association; Society of Ohio Healthcare Attorneys. ***Email:*** mgerroir@wiggin.com

SARA A. GOLDBERG, born Miami, Florida, 1970; admitted to bar, 1996, New York (Not admitted in Connecticut). *Education:* Princeton University (A.B., History, magna cum laude, 1992); New York University (J.D., cum laude, 1995). Developments Editor, New York University Environmental Law Journal, 1994-1995. Law Clerk to the Honorable Michael H. Dolinger, U.S. Magistrate Judge, U.S. District Court, Southern District of New York, 1995-1996. Author, "Lender Liability Under CERCLA: Shaping a New Legal Rule," N.Y.U. Environmental Law Journal, reprinted in Banking Law Anthology. (Resident, Stamford Office). ***LANGUAGES:*** Hebrew. ***Email:*** sgoldberg@wiggin.com

NICOLE H. GOLLAHER, born New York, N.Y., 1969; admitted to bar, 1996, Connecticut. *Education:* Brown University (A.B., 1991); University of Connecticut School of Law (J.D., with honors, 1996). Associate Editor, Connecticut Journal of International Law, 1994-1996. ***LANGUAGES:*** German, French, Spanish. ***Email:*** ngollaher@wiggin.com

NAOMI B. GRAUBARD, born New York, N.Y., 1971; admitted to bar, 1996, Connecticut; 1997, New York; U.S. District Court, District of Connecticut. *Education:* Washington University (B.A., 1993); Boston University (J.D., cum laude, 1996). Editor-in-Chief, Boston University Probate Law Journal, 1995-1996. (Resident, Stamford Office). ***Email:*** ngraubard@wiggin.com

DAVID C. GRIGSBY, born Elmhurst, Illinois, 1967; admitted to bar, 1996, Connecticut. *Education:* Yale University (B.A., Philosophy, 1989); University of Michigan (J.D., 1996). Author: The Island Press Bibliography of Environmental Literature, Yale School of Forestry and Environmental Studies Staff. ***Email:*** dgrigsby@wiggin.com

ALEXANDER J. GRODSKI, born Rahway, New Jersey, 1970; admitted to bar, 2000, Connecticut. *Education:* Seton Hall University (B.A., 1993); University of Connecticut (J.D., with honors, 2000). ***Email:*** agrodski@wiggin.com

JONATHAN W. HARAY, born New York, N.Y., 1969; admitted to bar, 1995, New York; 1999, Connecticut. *Education:* State University of New York at Albany (B.A., 1991); Syracuse University (J.D., cum laude, 1994). ***Email:*** jharay@wiggin.com

MARK W. HEAPHY, born Nutley, New Jersey, 1969; admitted to bar, 1996, Connecticut. *Education:* College of William & Mary (B.A., 1990) Phi Beta Kappa; Yale University (M.A., 1993); University of Virginia (J.D., 1996). Adjunct Professor, Quinnipiac University School of Law, 2000—. ***LANGUAGES:*** German. ***Email:*** mheaphy@wiggin.com

KENNETH DECATUR HEATH, born Augsburg, Germany, 1970; admitted to bar, 1999, Connecticut. *Education:* University of Virginia (B.A., with high distinction, 1992); Princeton University (M.P.A., 1994); Yale University (J.D., 1999). Phi Beta Kappa. Recipient, Distinguished Student Award. Editor-in-Chief, Journal of Public and International Affairs. Managing Editor, The Yale Law Journal, 1998-1999. Author: "The Symmetries of Citizenship: Welfare, Expatriate Taxation and Stakeholding," 13 Geo. Immigr. L. J. 533, Summer, 1999; "Could We Have Armed the Kosovo Liberation Army? The New Norms Governing Intervention in Civil War," 4 University of California at Los Angeles Journal of International Law and Foreign Affairs, Winter, 2000. Presidential Management Intern, Office of the Secretary of Defense, 1994-1996. ***Email:*** kheath@wiggin.com

BART DUNCAN JEFFRESS, born Middletown, Ohio, September 26, 1971; admitted to bar, 1999, Oregon; 2001, Connecticut. *Education:* Johns Hopkins University (B.A., with general and departmental honors, 1993); Harvard University (M.A., 1996); Yale University (J.D., 1999). ***Email:*** bjeffress@wiggin.com

STUART C. JOHNSON, born Cleveland, Ohio, 1963; admitted to bar, 1995, Massachusetts and Connecticut; 1999, U.S. District Court, District of Connecticut. *Education:* Colby College (B.A., 1985); Northeastern University (J.D., 1994). ***Email:*** sjohnson@wiggin.com

RUSSELL G. KAUFF, born New York, N.Y., July 4, 1969; admitted to bar, 1997, Connecticut. *Education:* Trinity College (B.A. with faculty honors in Economics, 1991); University of Connecticut (J.D., 1997). Director, Intramural

(This Listing Continued)

Competition, Connecticut Moot Court Board, 1996-1997. Symposium Editor, Connecticut Law Review, 1996-1997. (Resident, Stamford Office). ***LANGUAGES:*** French. ***Email:*** rkauff@wiggin.com

WILLIAM JAMES KELLEHER, III, born Flushing, New York, 1970; admitted to bar, 1996, New York and U.S. District Court, Southern and Eastern Districts of New York; 2001, Connecticut. *Education:* Fairfield University (B.A., 1992); St. John's University (J.D., 1995). Executive Publications Editor, 1994-1995, Staff Member, 1993-1994, American Bankruptcy Institute Law Review. Staff Member, New York International Law Review, 1993-1994. Author: Note, "Jury Trials in Bankruptcy Court," 2 Am. Bankr. Inst. L. Rev. 477, 1994; Recent Decision, "United World Trade v. Mangyshlakneft Oil Production Assn.," 7 N.Y. Int'l L. Rev. 75, 1994. Law Clerk to Hon. Dorothy Eisenberg, U.S. Bankruptcy Court, Eastern District of New York, 1995-1996. (Resident, Stamford Office). ***Email:*** wkelleher@wiggin.com

STACIE A. KELLY, born New Haven, Connecticut, 1975; admitted to bar, 2000, Connecticut. *Education:* University of Miami (B.A., 1997); Harvard University (J.D., 2000). ***Email:*** skelly@wiggin.com

MICHAEL K. KINNEY, born New Haven, Connecticut, 1963; admitted to bar, 1996, Connecticut; registered to practice before U.S. Patent and Trademark Office. *Education:* University of Connecticut (B.S., Computer Science and Engineering, 1985); Quinnipiac College (J.D., cum laude, 1995). Engineer, Sikorsky Aircraft Corp., 1986-1997. ***Email:*** mkinney@wiggin.com

ROBERT E. KOOSA, born Waterbury, Connecticut, February 13, 1976; admitted to bar, 2001, Connecticut. *Education:* Merrimack College (B.A., cum laude, 1995); Quinnipiac College (J.D., summa cum laude, 2001). Finalist, 1-L Mock Trial Competition. Note and Casenote Editor, Quinnipiac Law Review. Member, Trial Lawyers of America, Student Trial Advocacy Competition. ***Email:*** rkoosa@wiggin.com

SIGRID E. KUN, born Boston, Massachusetts, 1966; admitted to bar, 1998, Connecticut. *Education:* Ithaca College (B.S., magna cum laude, 1988); Centre International D'Etudes Francais, Universite Lumiere Lyon II, Lyon, France (Premier Degre, June 1989); Ludwig Maximillian University, Munich, Germany (Geschaftsstelle Deutsches Sprachdiplom, August 1990); Quinnipiac University (J.D., 1998). Lead Articles Editor, Law Review. Recipient, Distinguished Academic Achievement Awards. Author: "Racehorse and Intellectual Property Rights: Racing Towards Recognition," 17 Quinnipiac Law Review No. 2, Summer 1997. ***LANGUAGES:*** German and French. ***Email:*** skun@wiggin.com

STEPHEN JARED LABLE, admitted to bar, 1999, Connecticut; 2000, District of Columbia. *Education:* Brandeis University (B.A., cum laude, 1994); Yale University (M.A., Ethics, 1996); Benjamin N. Cardozo School of Law, Yeshiva University (J.D., 1999). Law Clerk to the Hon. Alan H. Nevas, Senior U.S. District Court Judge, Bridgeport, Connecticut, 2000-2001.

MONIKA NIVA MARIE LAHIRI, born Hartford, Connecticut, 1971; admitted to bar, 1995, Connecticut; 1996, New York and U.S. District Court, District of Connecticut; 1997, U.S., District Court, Southern District of New York. *Education:* Providence College (B.A., summa cum laude, 1992); Yale University (J.D., 1995). Member: Yale Journal of International Law, 1993-1995; Yale Journal of Law & Humanities, 1994-1995. ***LANGUAGES:*** German. ***Email:*** mlahiri@wiggin.com

DAVID A. LEVENSTEIN, born Brooklyn, New York, August 24, 1963; admitted to bar, 2001, Connecticut. *Education:* Haverford College (B.A., 1985); University of Washington (M.A., 1988); Western New England College (J.D., magna cum laude, 2001). Holmes Scholar. ***LANGUAGES:*** German. ***Email:*** dlevenstein@wiggin.com

RICHARD H. LUGLI, born Bristol, Connecticut, 1964; admitted to bar, 1990, Connecticut; 1991, Maine. *Education:* Amherst College (A.B., 1986); University of Connecticut School of Law (J.D., with honors, 1990). (Resident, Hartford Office). ***Email:*** rlugli@wiggin.com

STEVEN P. MALECH, born Silver Spring, Maryland, 1966; admitted to bar, 1995, Connecticut; 1996, U.S. District Court, District of Connecticut and U.S. Court of Appeals, Federal Circuit. *Education:* University of Texas at Austin (B.A., with special honors in Psychology, 1988); University of Connecticut (J.D., with honors, 1995). (Resident, Hartford Office). ***Email:*** smalech@wiggin.com

BRUCE L. McDERMOTT, born Cleveland, Ohio, 1964; admitted to bar, 1989, Connecticut; 1993, New Jersey and New York. *Education:* Lafayette College (B.A., 1986); Case Western Reserve University (J.D., 1989); Pace University School of Law (LL.M., Environmental Law, 1992). Managing Editor, Case Western Reserve Law Review. Author: "Outer Space: The Latest Polluted Frontier," 36 Air Force Law Review; "Fundamentalists' Efforts to Intervene in Curricular Decisions," 34 Case Western Reserve Law Review 911 (1989). ***Email:*** bmcdermott@wiggin.com

ERIK L. MENGWALL, born Västerås, Sweden, 1974; admitted to bar, 2001, Connecticut. *Education:* Yale University (B.A., 1997); George Washington University Law School (J.D., 2001). Managing Editor, *Note Bene*, George Washington University. ***LANGUAGES:*** Swedish. ***Email:*** emengwall@wiggin.com

(This Listing Continued)

WIGGIN & DANA LLP, New Haven—Continued

JAMES J. MENNA, admitted to bar, 1999, Connecticut. *Education:* State University of New York at Binghamton; New England School of Law (J.D., magna cum laude, 1999). Symposium Editor, New England Law Review, 1998-1999. ***Email:*** jmenna@wiggin.com

PAMELA P. MILLMAN, born Kearny, New Jersey, 1957; admitted to bar, 1984, Connecticut; U.S. District Court, District of Connecticut. *Education:* Duke University (A.B., magna cum laude, 1980); Emory University School of Law (J.D., 1984). Member, Moot Court. ***Email:*** pmillman@wiggin.com

CLEMENT J. NAPLES, admitted to bar, 2000, Connecticut. *Education:* Southern Connecticut State College (B.S., 1994); Quinnipiac University School of Law (J.D., 2000). Phi Delta Phi. Member, Quinnipiac Law Review. (Resident, Stamford Office). ***Email:*** cnaples@wiggin.com

MAUREEN O'CONNOR, born Manchester, New Hampshire, 1975; admitted to bar, 2000, Connecticut. *Education:* Notre Dame University (B.A., cum laude, 1997); University of Connecticut (J.D., 2000). Member, Moot Court Board. Assistant Managing Editor, Connecticut Insurance Law Journal, 1998-2000. ***Email:*** moconnor@wiggin.com

THERESA M. PARIETTI, born Long Island, New York, 1968; admitted to bar, 1998, Connecticut. *Education:* Rutgers University (B.A., Communications; M.S., Industrial Relations and Human Resources); University of Connecticut Law School (J.D., with honors, 1998). Member, 1996-1997, Articles Editor, 1997, Connecticut Law Review. Clerkship, Justice Borden, Connecticut Supreme Court, 1998-1999. Author: "Adding to the Confusion Surrounding Employment Discrimination Actions in the Second Circuit: Chetkova v. Connecticut General Life Insurance Company," 27 Conn. Law Review 1827 (1997). ***Email:*** tparietti@wiggin.com

BONNIE LYNNE PATTEN, born Buffalo, New York, 1966; admitted to bar, 1992, Connecticut. *Education:* University of Pennsylvania (B.A., 1989); Boston University (J.D., cum laude, 1992). ***Email:*** bpatten@wiggin.com

CHRISTOPHER R. PERRY, born New Haven, Connecticut, 1974; admitted to bar, 2001, Connecticut. *Education:* American University, Washington, D.C. (B.A., cum laude, 1996); University of Connecticut (J.D., 2001). Recipient, Alumni Foundation Award for Excellence in Legal Scholarship, 2001. Editor in Chief, Connecticut Law Review. Author: "Trademarks as Commodities: The 'Famous' Roadblock to Applying Trademark Dilution Law in Cyberspace," Connecticut Law Review, 2000. ***Email:*** cperry@wiggin.com

CHRISTINA KAM PETERSON, born New York, N.Y., November 28, 1970; admitted to bar, 1996, New York and New Jersey; 1997, Pennsylvania and U.S. District Court, Eastern District of Pennsylvania; 1999, U.S. District Court, District of New Jersey. *Education:* University of Michigan (B.A., 1992); Hofstra University School of Law (J.D., 1995). Staff Editor, Hofstra Labor Law Journal. *Member:* American Bar Association (Member, Business Law Section, Forum Committee on Franchising). (Resident, Berwyn, Pennsylvania Office and Cherry Hill, New Jersey). ***Email:*** cpeterson@wiggin.com

JOAN ALLEN ROWE, born Pittsfield, Massachusetts, 1961; admitted to bar, 1988, Connecticut. *Education:* University of Vermont (B.A., 1983); Boston University School of Law (J.D., 1987). ***Email:*** jrowe@wiggin.com

MARGARET A. RUTHERFORD, born White Plains, New York, 1965; admitted to bar, 2001, Connecticut. *Education:* Wesleyan University (B.A., 1997); Georgetown University (J.D., 2000). Associate Editor, Georgetown International Environmental Law Review. Law Clerk, Hon. Chief Judge William J. Lavery, Appellate Court of Connecticut. ***Email:*** mrutherfurd@wiggin.com

JOSEPH A. SANFILIPPO, born Manhasset, New York, 1966; admitted to bar, 1993, Massachusetts; 1994, New York and Tennessee; 1999, District of Columbia; 2000, Connecticut and U.S. Tax Court. *Education:* Providence College (B.A., 1988); New York Law School (J.D., magna cum laude, 1992); New York University (LL.M., Taxation, 1996). Member, 1990-1991 and Articles Editor, 1991-1992, New York Law School Law Review. Law Clerk: Honorable Howard M. Kirshbaum, Associate Justice, Colorado Supreme Court, 1992-1993; Honorable H. Ted Milburn, U.S. Circuit Judge, U.S. Court of Appeals, Sixth Circuit, 1993-1994. ***Email:*** jsanfilippo@wiggin.com

G. ADAM SCHWEIKERT, III, admitted to bar, 1999, Connecticut. *Education:* University of Notre Dame (B.A., magna cum laude, 1991); University of Connecticut School of Law (J.D., with highest honors, 1999). Phi Beta Kappa. Law Clerk to: Judge Robert N. Chatigny, U.S. District Court, District of Connecticut, 1999-2000; Judge Wade Brorby, U.S. Court of Appeals, Tenth Circuit, 2000-2001.

GEORGE AUSTIN SELMONT, born Clinton, Connecticut, 1967; admitted to bar, 1999, Connecticut; 2000, U.S. District Court, District of Connecticut. *Education:* Bard College (B.A. Filmmaking); Harvard University (A.L.M., Government); Northeastern University (J.D., 1999). Recipient, William J. Lockwood prize for Campus Leadership. Semifinalist, Evans Constitutional Law Moot Court Competition, University of Wisconsin, 1999. Co-Author: "The Uniform Computer Information Transaction Act —The Future and New of Computer Information," Conn. Law Trib., July 2000. Appointed by Senate President Pro Tempore to the Commission for Educational Technology. ***Email:*** gselmont@wiggin.com

(This Listing Continued)

WILLIAM B. SLATE, born New York, N.Y., 1966; admitted to bar, 1992, California; 2000, Connecticut; registered to practice before U.S. Patent and Trademark Office. *Education:* California Institute of Technology (B.S., Engineering and Applied Science, with honors, 1988); University of California, Los Angeles (J.D., 1992). Tau Beta Pi. ***Email:*** wslate@wiggin.com

LAUREN A. SULLIVAN, born Hartford, Connecticut, 1962; admitted to bar, 1995, Pennsylvania; 2000, Connecticut. *Education:* Widener University (B.S., 1990; J.D., 1994). ***Email:*** lasullivan@wiggin.com

CHRISTINE P. TEIXEIRA, born Melrose, Massachusetts, 1975; admitted to bar, 2000, Connecticut. *Education:* Villanova University (B.S., 1997); University of Connecticut (J.D., 2000). Board Member, Moot Court. ***LANGUAGES:*** Portuguese and French. ***Email:*** cteixeira@wiggin.com

KIMBERLY S. TOOMEY, born Philadelphia, Pennsylvania, June 11, 1969; admitted to bar, 1995, Pennsylvania and New Jersey; U.S. District Court, District of New Jersey; 1996, U.S. District Court, Eastern District of Pennsylvania; 2000, U.S. Court of Appeals, Third Circuit. *Education:* LaSalle University (B.A., cum laude, 1991); Villanova University (J.D., 1994). Student Works Editor, Villanova Environmental Law Journal. Co-Author: "Recovering Lost Future Royalties in a Franchise Termination Case," Franchise Law Journal, Winter 2001. Speaker, "Discovery Dilemmas and Opportunities: Ethical, Practical and Legal Issues in the Discovery Process," American Bar Association Forum on Franchising, 2001, Annual Forum, San Francisco, California. *Member:* American Bar Association (Member, Business Law Section, Forum Committee on Franchising). (Resident, Berwyn, Pennsylvania Office and Cherry Hill, New Jersey). ***Email:*** ktoomey@wiggin.com

JANIE L. TREANOR, born San Antonio, Texas, 1973; admitted to bar, 1998, Texas; 2001, Connecticut. *Education:* University of Texas (B.A., 1994); Southern Methodist University (J.D., 1998). Member, Moot Court Board, 1996-1977. Moot Court Board, Director of Education, 1997-1998. Moot Court Board Best Brief Nominee, 1996. Editor of the SMU Law Review, 1998. Author: Comment, "Privatization v. Corporatization of the Federal Aviation Administration: Revamping Air Traffic Control," Journal of Air Law and Commerce, Vol. 63, Feb-March, 1998. (Resident, Stamford Office). ***Email:*** jtreanor@wiggin.com

JOSEPH R. TRISTINE, born Bridgeport, Connecticut, 1971; admitted to bar, 1997, Connecticut. *Education:* Harvard University (A.B., magna cum laude, 1993); University of California School of Law (J.D., 1997). ***Email:*** jtristine@wiggin.com

SUZANNE E. WACHSSTOCK, born Long Beach, New York, 1969; admitted to bar, 1994, Connecticut; 1995, New York; 1996, U.S. District Court, Southern and Eastern Districts of New York and U.S. Court of Federal Claims. *Education:* Harvard University (A.B., magna cum laude, 1990; (J.D., cum laude, 1994). Phi Beta Kappa. (Resident, Stamford Office). ***LANGUAGES:*** Hebrew. ***Email:*** swachsstock@wiggin.com

JENNIFER NEYAN WILLCOX, born Berkeley, California, January 30, 1969; admitted to bar, 1998, Connecticut and New York. *Education:* Yale University (B.A., 1991); Northeastern University (J.D., 1998). Member, Craven Moot Court Competition. Law Clerk to the Hon. Janet Bond Arterton, U.S. District Court, District of Connecticut. ***Email:*** fwilcox@wiggin.com

AMY GHORY WINNICK, born Cincinnati, Ohio, 1957; admitted to bar, 1983, District of Columbia; 1986, Connecticut. *Education:* Cornell University (B.A., Psychology, 1979); Georgetown University (J.D., 1982). ***Email:*** awinnick@wiggin.com

GAYLE CAROL WINTJEN, born Brooklyn, New York, 1964; admitted to bar, 1990, Massachusetts and U.S. District Court, District of Massachusetts; 1991, New York and U.S. District Court, Southern and Eastern Districts of New York; 1996, New Jersey and U.S. District Court, District of New Jersey; 2001, Connecticut; U.S. Court of Appeals, 1st and 4th Circuits. *Education:* University of Massachusetts (B.B.A., 1986); New England School of Law (J.D., 1990); New York University (LL.M., 1995). Case and Note Editor, New England Law Review, 1989-1990. Author: "Make Room for Daddy: A Putative Father's Rights to His Children," 24:3 NEL. Rev. (1990); Update, "-Constitutional Law-Obscenity and the First Amendment," 25:4 NEL. Rev. (1991). (Resident, Hartford Office). ***Email:*** gwintjen@wiggin.com

WILLIAMS AND PATTIS, LLC

Established in 1971

51 ELM STREET

NEW HAVEN, CONNECTICUT 06510

Telephone: 203-562-9931

Fax: 203-776-9494

Email: jrw@johnrwilliams.com

Criminal and Civil Trial Practice before all State and Federal Courts. Civil Rights Law. Appellate Practice.

(This Listing Continued)

JOHN R. WILLIAMS, born Fargo, North Dakota, August 11, 1941; admitted to bar, 1968, Connecticut and U.S. District Court, District of Connecticut; 1971, U.S. Court of Appeals, 2nd Circuit; 1973, U.S. Supreme Court. *Education:* Harvard University (A.B., cum laude, 1963); Georgetown University (J.D., 1967). Associate Editor, Georgetown Law Journal, 1967. Editor, *PLI Unreasonable Force Litigation Handbook,* 1992-1994, 1998-2000. Legislative Assistant to U.S. Senator M. R. Young, 1963-1967. Author, "The Constitutionality of Basic Protection," 1 Conn. Law Review 44, June 1968. Contributor: PLI Section 1983 Civil Rights Litigation Manual, 1985—; *1988 Civil Rights Litigation and Attorney Fees Annual Handbook,* Clark Boardman Co.; *Convicting the Innocent,* Connery Ed., 1996. Tutor in Clinical Studies, Yale Law School, 1980-1994. *Member:* New Haven County, Connecticut (Member, Federal Practice Section, 1987—) and American Bar Associations; Connecticut Trial Lawyers Association; Connecticut Criminal Defense Lawyers Association; The Association of Trial Lawyers of America (Past Chair, Civil Rights Section); National Association of Criminal Defense Lawyers (Life Member); National Lawyers Guild. ***PRACTICE AREAS:*** Criminal Law; Civil Practice; Civil Rights; Appellate Practice.

NORMAN A. PATTIS, born Chicago, Illinois, September 21, 1955; admitted to bar, 1993, Connecticut. *Education:* Purdue University (B.A., 1977); University of Connecticut (J.D., with honors, 1993). ***PRACTICE AREAS:*** Criminal Law; Civil Practice; Civil Rights; Appellate Practice. ***Email:*** NormPattis@aol.com

---

KATRENA ENGSTROM, born Brooklyn, New York, January 7, 1947; admitted to bar, 1975, New York; 1978, District of Columbia; 1980, Connecticut. *Education:* Vassar College (B.A., 1968); Boston University (J.D., 1973). *Member:* New Haven County Bar Association; The District of Columbia Bar; National Health Lawyers Association. ***PRACTICE AREAS:*** Criminal Law; Civil Practice; Civil Rights; Appellate Practice.

WILLIAM S. PALMIERI, born New Haven, Connecticut, October 1, 1963; admitted to bar, 1994, Connecticut and U.S. District Court, District of Connecticut. *Education:* Albertus Magnus College (B.A. summa cum laude, 1990); Vermont Law School (J.D., 1993). Alpha Sigma Lambda. Notes Editor, Vermont Law School, 1992-1993. *Member:* American Bar Association. ***PRACTICE AREAS:*** Criminal Law; Civil Practice; Civil Rights; Appellate Practice.

ANGELICA N. PAPASTAVROS-CORBO, born Bridgeport, Connecticut, February 21, 1969; admitted to bar, 1996, Connecticut and U.S. District Court, District of Connecticut. *Education:* University of Bridgeport (B.A., 1991); Quinnipiac College (J.D., 1995). ***LANGUAGES:*** Greek. ***PRACTICE AREAS:*** Criminal Law; Civil Practice; Civil Rights; Appellate Practice.

DAWNE WESTBROOK, born Dayton, Ohio, January 22, 1970; admitted to bar, 1999, Connecticut. *Education:* Fisk University (B.A., 1992); Vanderbilt University (J.D., 1995). CLEO Fellow, National Nelson Mandela Scholar. ***PRACTICE AREAS:*** Employment Discrimination; Police Misconduct; Civil Rights; Criminal Law. ***Email:*** dawne_westbrook@yahoo.com

ROBERT BERKE, born Queens, New York, June 21, 1966; admitted to bar, 1992, Connecticut; 1993, New York; 2001, U.S. District Court, District of Connecticut. *Education:* State University of New York at Albany (B.A., 1988); Quinnipiac College (J.D., 1992). Member, Town Plan and Zoning Commission, Woodbridge, CT, 1998—. ***PRACTICE AREAS:*** Criminal Law; Civil Rights; Employment Discrimination.

REFERENCES: Webster Bank; Citizens Bank.

WINNICK, RUBEN, CHAMBERS, EVANS AND HOFFNUNG, LLC

Established in 1927

110 WHITNEY AVENUE
NEW HAVEN, CONNECTICUT 06510-1238
Telephone: 203-772-4400
Fax: 203-772-2763

Corporate, Commercial, Real Estate, Litigation, Personal Injury, Family, Probate, Taxation, Estate Planning and Estate Administration, Commercial Lending, Creditors' Rights, Business Bankruptcy.

FIRM PROFILE: The firm was founded in 1927 by Alexander Winnick, a Yale Law School graduate and early prominent member of the Connecticut Bar, specializing in personal injury, medical malpractice and representation of family-owned businesses.

The firm's breadth allows it to assist clients in all aspects of their professional and personal lives, ranging from commercial and real estate work to wills and trusts, divorce, and personal injury. It has expertise in workers compensation, property tax appeals, probate administration, commercial bankruptcy, and business lending. The firm maintains an active trial practice, representing individuals in accident and product liability actions. It offers strategic planning for closely held and family businesses, including retirement and business succession services. It serves commercial clients in seeking court ordered remedies, and defending against litigation. It handles criminal law matters (including driving violations), gift and estate tax planning, contracts, leasing and zoning matters. A team can be assembled from within the firm to provide for this range of needs.

ALEXANDER WINNICK (1903-1989).

GILBERT H. WINNICK (1928-1999).

EDWARD B. WINNICK, born New Haven, Connecticut; admitted to bar, 1959, Connecticut; 1960, U.S. District Court, District of Connecticut; 1966, U.S. Court of Appeals, Second Circuit. *Education:* Dartmouth College (B.A., 1954); Yale University (LL.B., 1959). [Lt., USNR]. ***PRACTICE AREAS:*** Commercial Law; Litigation; Property Tax Appeals; Business Litigation.

DIANE DASKAL RUBEN, born Chicago, Illinois; admitted to bar, 1973, Connecticut; U.S. District Court, District of Connecticut. *Education:* Wellesley College and University of Chicago (B.A., summa cum laude, 1967); Harvard University (M.A.T., 1968); George Washington University (J.D., with honors, 1973). Phi Beta Kappa. ***PRACTICE AREAS:*** Commercial; Real Estate; Medical Corporations; Professional Corporations; Litigation; Estate Planning; Estate Administration; Business Litigation; Personal Injury.

WICK R. CHAMBERS, born New Haven, Connecticut; admitted to bar, 1979, Connecticut; 1980, U.S. District Court, District of Connecticut. *Education:* Yale University (B.A., 1971); Vermont Law School (J.D., cum laude, 1978). *Member:* New Haven County, Connecticut (Vice Chair Committee on Professional Ethics; Member, Business Law, Commercial Law and Bankruptcy, and Estates and Probate Sections) and American (Member, Business Law Section; Center for Professional Responsibility) Bar Associations; Computer Law Association and Information Technology Association of American. ***PRACTICE AREAS:*** Legal Ethics; Software Licensing; Computer Law; Technology Law; Estate Planning; Business Law; General Practice.

JOSHUA A. WINNICK, born New Haven, Connecticut; admitted to bar, 1986, Connecticut. *Education:* Harvard University (A.B., cum laude, 1978); American University (J.D., 1986). Town Attorney, Hamden, Connecticut, 1997-1999. ***PRACTICE AREAS:*** Civil Litigation; Real Estate; Commercial Litigation; Personal Injury; Domestic Relations.

ROBERT S. EVANS, born New Haven, Connecticut; admitted to bar, 1960, Connecticut; 1963, California; 1965, U.S. Supreme Court; 1992, Vermont. *Education:* Cornell University (B.A., 1958; J.D., 1960). Phi Alpha Delta. *Member:* New Haven County, Connecticut (Member, Executive Committee, 1980— and Chairman, 1988-1991, Banking Law Section; Vice Chairman, Commercial Law and Bankruptcy Section, 1978-1979), Vermont and American (Member, Business Law Section, Sub-Committee on Loan Workouts and Bankruptcy, 1990—) Bar Associations. [Captain, Judge Advocate, U.S.A.F., 1961-1964]. (Also Of Counsel to McCarty Law Offices, Brattleboro, Vermont). ***PRACTICE AREAS:*** Creditors Rights; Business Bankruptcy; Business Reorganization; Workouts; Business Litigation.

DANIEL N. HOFFNUNG, born New York, N.Y.; admitted to bar, 1987, Connecticut; 1988, U.S. District Court, District of Connecticut and U.S. Tax Court; 1995, U.S. District Court, Southern District of New York. *Education:* Quinnipiac College (B.A., with honors, 1974); University of Connecticut (J.D., with honors, 1987). Recipient, Callaghan & Company Book Award for Property. Contributor: *Warren Gorham & Lamont Estate Planning and Administration Service* (R. Whitman ed. 1989). *Member:* New Haven County, Connecticut (Member, Business Law and Real Property Sections) and American (Member, Business Law and Probate and Real Property Sections) Bar Associations. ***PRACTICE AREAS:*** Commercial Law; Finance; Real Property; Business Organization; Licensing; Estate Planning; Probate. ***Email:*** hoffnung@iconn.net

---

YOLEN AND PERZIN, LLC

Established in 1982

5 TRUMBULL STREET
P.O. BOX 1990
NEW HAVEN, CONNECTICUT 06521
Telephone: 203-562-5100
Fax: 203-562-5211
URL: http://www.lawyers.com/yolen&perzin

General and Trial Practice in State and Federal Courts. Negligence, Malpractice, Commercial Litigation, Family and Special Education Law, Real Estate, Zoning. Trials in all Civil, Administrative and Criminal Courts.

TIMOTHY B. YOLEN, born New Haven, Connecticut, September 25, 1949; admitted to bar, 1980, Connecticut and U.S. District Court, District of Connecticut. *Education:* Hobart College (B.A., 1972); Western New England College (J.D., magna cum laude, 1980). *Member:* New Haven County and Connecticut Bar Associations; Connecticut Trial Lawyers Association; The As-

(This Listing Continued)

YOLEN AND PERZIN, LLC, New Haven—Continued

sociation of Trial Lawyers of America. ***PRACTICE AREAS:*** Business Law; Commercial Litigation; Commercial Real Estate; Residential Real Estate; Zoning, Planning and Land Use.

MICHAEL PERZIN, born Philadelphia, Pennsylvania, July 26, 1955; admitted to bar, 1981, Connecticut and U.S. District Court, District of Connecticut; 1986, U.S. Supreme Court; 1987, U.S. District Court, Eastern and Southern Districts of New York. *Education:* Swarthmore College; Rutgers University (B.A., 1978); Yale University (J.D., 1981). Appointed Small Claims Commissioner, Housing Matters, 1984-1986. *Member:* New Haven County, Stamford, Connecticut (Member, Sections on: Family Law; Consumer Law) and American (Member, Litigation Section) Bar Associations; The Association of Trial Lawyers of America; Connecticut Trial Lawyers Association. ***PRACTICE AREAS:*** Family Law; Negligence; Medical Malpractice; Education Law.

REFERENCES: Union Trust Company; First Fidelity Bancorporation; Federal Deposit Insurance Corp; Centerbank.

YULES & YULES, LLC

195 CHURCH STREET, SEVENTEENTH FLOOR
NEW HAVEN, CONNECTICUT 06510
Telephone: 203-789-1000
Fax: 203-789-6320
Email: yuleslaw@yuleslaw.com
URL: http://www.lawyers.com/yules&yules

Hartford, Connecticut Office: P.O. Box 230278, 06123-0278. Telephone: 860-724-5815.
Stamford, Connecticut Office: P.O. Box 522. 06904-0522. Telephone: 203-327-9200.
New York, N.Y. Office: Grand Central Station, P.O. Box 4419. 10163-4419. Telephone: 203-327-9200.

Trial Practice, Automobile, Mobile Carrier, Bad Faith, Corporate Business Torts, Drug and Medical Device Litigation, Fraud, Insurance, Products Liability, Professional Malpractice, Transportation, Workers' Compensation Law, Securities Arbitration and Financial Institutions Litigation.

FIRM PROFILE: Since 1938, Yules & Yules has represented insurers and self-insureds in New York and Connecticut in complex litigation. We are trial lawyers with experience in products liability, professional malpractice, insurance law, corporate business torts, wrongful death claims, workers' compensation, and motor carrier, rail and transportation law. We have experience with first and third-party coverages and bad faith. Our representation of financial institutions includes securities arbitration. We service Connecticut and New York, particularly the New York City metropolitan area and Long Island.

HERMAN YULES (1910-1999).

ROBERT B. YULES, born Hartford, Connecticut, April 18, 1952; admitted to bar, 1978, Connecticut, U.S. District Court, District of Connecticut, U.S. Court of Appeals, Second Circuit, U.S. Tax Court and U.S. Claims Court. *Education:* Ohio Wesleyan University (B.A., cum laude, 1974); University of Toledo (J.D., 1977). Author: Connecticut Trial Practice, West Group, 2001; "An Analysis of Connecticut's New Product Liability Law," 56 Conn. Bar Journal 269, 1982; Chapter 7, "Types of Defects," Products Liability Practice Guide, Matthew Bender, 1988; "Human-Factors Experts in Products Liability Litigation," 9 J of Products Liability 107, 1986; "Asserting Legal Defenses in an Products Liability Case," 8 J of Products Liability No. 189, 1985; "Connecticut Insurance Law Review—, Bond Press, 1981—; "Insurance Bad Faith Litigation," 67 Conn. Bar J.380, 1993. Lecturer: "Insurance Bad Faith Litigation," 67 Conn. Bar J. 380, 1993; Products Liability, Seminar Sponsored by Defense Research Institute, Inc., Atlanta, 1984 and San Diego, 1985; American Bar Association's National Insititute on Medical Malpractice, Charleston, 1991. Southern Methodist University 6th Annual Product Liability Symposium, Houston, Texas, 1985. City Attorney, City of New Britain, Conn., 1978-1979; DRI Insurance Claims Supervision Seminar, Hartford, CT, 1989. *Member:* Connecticut, New York State and American Bar Associations; International Association of Defense Counsel; Defense Research Institute; Trucking Industry Defense Association. ***PRACTICE AREAS:*** Drugs and Medical Devices; Insurance; Products Liability; Professional Malpractice; Transportation; Securities.

ASSOCIATE

RICHARD W. MATHER, born Hartford, Connecticut, October 22, 1958; admitted to bar, 1990, Connecticut and U.S. District Court, District of Connecticut. *Education:* University of Connecticut (B.A., 1981; J.D., with honors, 1990); Trinity College (M.A., 1986). *Member:* Connecticut and American Bar Associations. ***PRACTICE AREAS:*** Insurance; Products Liability; Workers Compensation; Medical Negligence.

(This Listing Continued)

REPRESENTATIVE CLIENTS: Allstate Insurance Co.; The Atlantic Cos.; Nationwide Insurance Co.; Transamerica Insurance Group; Zurich-American Insurance Cos.; Chubb Group of Insurance Cos.; Dow Corning Corp.; Chrysler Corp.; Air Products & Chemicals, Inc.; Kellogg Co.; Orion Group; American Medical Systems, Inc.; United Farm Bureau Mut. Ins. Co.; National Freight Trucklines, Inc.; Pfizer Inc.; Brethren Mut. Ins. Co.

ZELDES, NEEDLE & COOPER

A PROFESSIONAL CORPORATION
NEW HAVEN, CONNECTICUT

(See Bridgeport)

Litigation in all Courts. Corporate, Probate, Real Estate, Bankruptcy, Family, Condemnation, Criminal, Administrative and Environmental Law.

MAYO, GILLIGAN & ZITO, LLP

NEWINGTON, CONNECTICUT

(See Wethersfield)

Trials in all Courts, Real Estate, Banking and Commercial Finance, Creditors' Rights and Bankruptcy, Employment, Business Law, Zoning, Environmental, Estate Planning, Elder Law, Probate and Personal Injury Law.

SABATINI AND ASSOCIATES, LLC

ONE MARKET SQUARE
NEWINGTON, CONNECTICUT 06111
Telephone: 860-667-0839
Fax: 860-667-0867
Email: LAWNEW@aol.com

General Civil Practice. Trials in all State and Federal Courts. Litigation, Probate, Corporate, Personal Injury, Commercial, Zoning.

FIRM PROFILE: Sabatini and Associates was established in 1974. The firm primarily engages in general civil litigation in state and federal courts as well as appellate. There is special emphasis on land use litigation, especially obtaining permits before local planning and zoning agencies and wetlands commissions. The firm has represented developers in many towns throughout Hartford and Litchfield counties and is active statewide. The firm also has experience in employment cases, ERISA matters, pension and insurance related litigation and major injury litigation. The firm has a history of involvement with Bar related activities, with Mr. Sabatini having served as President of the Hartford County Bar Association. The firm is centrally located and its staff of paralegals and personnel are experienced and knowledgeable.

VINCENT F. SABATINI, born Providence, Rhode Island, April 16, 1942; admitted to bar, 1969, Connecticut; 1972, U.S. District Court, District of Connecticut; 1975, U.S. Court of Appeals, Second Circuit; 1983, U.S. Supreme Court. *Education:* University of Rhode Island (B.S., 1965); Suffolk University (J.D., 1969). Member, Wethersfield Town Council, 1973-1979. Deputy Mayor, Town of Wethersfield, 1978-1979. Corporation Counsel, Town of Wethersfield, 1981-1990. Attorney State Trial Arbitrator, 1985—. Special Master, Superior Court. *Member:* Hartford County (President, 1993-1994), Connecticut and American Bar Associations; The Association of Trial Lawyers of America; Connecticut Trial Lawyers Association. ***PRACTICE AREAS:*** Land Use; Civil Litigation. ***Email:*** LAWNEW@aol.com

ASSOCIATE

JAMES V. SABATINI, born Hartford, Connecticut, September 29, 1971; admitted to bar, 1998, Connecticut; 1999, U.S. District Court, District of Connecticut. *Education:* Hamilton College (B.A., 1994); Case Western Reserve University (J.D., 1998). *Member:* Hartford County and Connecticut Bar Associations; Connecticut Trial Lawyers Association; The Association of Trial Lawyers of America. ***PRACTICE AREAS:*** Civil Litigation.

REPRESENTATIVE CLIENTS: Pizza Hut of America, Inc.; Midas Muffler; Piper Brook Associates; Farmers and Mechanics Bank; Keeney Manufacturing; Crest Mazda; Town of Wethersfield; RD Management; Webster Bank; Eastco Development.
REFERENCE: Webster Bank.

ANDREWS, YOUNG & GERAGHTY, P.C.

Established in 1988

216 BROAD STREET
P.O. BOX 751
NEW LONDON, CONNECTICUT 06320-0751
Telephone: 860-444-2101
Fax: 860-440-2615
URL: http://www.lawyers.com/andrewscosgrove&young
URL: http://www.newlondonlegal.com

General Civil Practice. Real Estate, Estate Planning, Probate, Elder Law, Corporations, Business Law, Commercial and Financial Transactions, Creditors' Rights, Bankruptcy, Collections, Personal Injury, Trials and Appeals, Municipal Law, Foreclosure, Land Use and Development, Zoning.

LOIS G. ANDREWS, born Madera, California, September 6, 1947; admitted to bar, 1973, California; 1976, Connecticut. *Education:* University of California at Davis (B.A., cum laude, 1969; M.A., 1970); University of California at Los Angeles (J.D., 1973). Pi Sigma Alpha. Recipient: National Science Foundation Fellowship, 1969-1970; Ann Rosenthal Stein Scholarship, 1971-1972. Director, 1988-1995, Treasurer, 1989-1992, Vice-President, 1992-1993 and President, 1993-1994, Estate and Tax Planning Council of Eastern Connecticut. Contributing Author: Connecticut Elder Law, A Desktop Manual, CBA, 1995. *Member:* New London County, Connecticut (Member, Sections on: Estates and Probate; Real Property; Member, Executive Committee, Elder Law and Estates and Probates Sections) and American (Member, Sections on: Real Property, Probate and Trust Law) Bar Associations; State Bar of California; National Academy of Elder Law Attorneys. ***PRACTICE AREAS:*** Estate Planning; Probate; Elder Law; Real Estate; Business Law; Municipal Law. ***Email:*** andrews@newlondonlegal.com

JAMES L. YOUNG, JR., born Derby, Connecticut, December 11, 1951; admitted to bar, 1981, Oregon; 1987, Connecticut. *Education:* Southern Connecticut State College (B.A., 1975); Northwestern School of Law of Lewis and Clark College (J.D., 1981). Assistant General Counsel, 1981-1983 and Trust Officer, 1983-1985, The Oregon Bank. Assistant General Counsel, First Interstate Bank of Oregon, 1985-1987. Member, Town of Groton Economic Development Commission. Past Chairman Board of Directors, Chamber of Commerce of Southeastern Connecticut. Director, United Cerebral Palsy Association of Southeastern Connecticut. *Member:* New London County and Connecticut (Member, Sections on: Commercial Law, Business, Bankruptcy, Real Estate, Elder Law, Estates and Probate) Bar Associations; Commercial Law League. ***PRACTICE AREAS:*** Debtor and Creditor; Commercial Law; Business Law; Zoning; Real Estate; Estate Planning, Wills and Trusts. ***Email:*** young@newlondonlegal.com

PAUL M. GERAGHTY, born Babylon, New York, January 25, 1957; admitted to bar, 1984, Connecticut; 1985, New York. *Education:* Northeastern University; University of Maine (B.A., cum laude, 1980); University of Bridgeport (J.D., 1984). Phi Delta Phi. President, Jessup International Law Society, 1983-1984. Jessup International Moot Court Competition, 1983. Assistant District Attorney, Nassau County District Attorney's Office, 1985-1986. Chairman, Haddam Planning and Zoning Commission. *Member:* New London County, Connecticut (Member, Sections on: Commercial Law and Bankruptcy; Real Estate) and American Bar Associations. ***REPORTED CASES:*** New England Savings Bank v. Maureen Clark, 54 Conn. App. 121 (1999); Clinton v. Rogers Lake West Association 40 Conn. App. 454 (1996); Steiger v. J.S. Builders, 39 Conn. App. 32 (1995); Williams v. Breyer, 21 Conn. App. 380 (1990); Vespoli v. Pagliarulo, 212 Conn. 1 (1989). ***PRACTICE AREAS:*** Commercial Transactions; Commercial Litigation; Business Law; Municipal Law. ***Email:*** geraghty@newlondonlegal.com

ASSOCIATE

BARBARA ARNOLD, born Easton, Maryland, November 27, 1971; admitted to bar, 1998, Maryland; 2000, Connecticut. *Education:* St. Johns College (B.A., 1993); University of Maryland School of Law (J.D., 1998). Author, "The New Leviathan: Can The Immigration Act of 1996 Really Transfer Power Over Public Benefits to State Governments", 21 Md. J. Int'l L. & Trade 225 (1998). Assistant District Counsel, Immigration and Naturalization Service, New York (1998-2000). *Member:* New London County, Connecticut and Maryland State Bar Associations. ***PRACTICE AREAS:*** Litigation; Commercial Law; Municipal Law; Real Property; Personal Injury. ***Email:*** arnold@newlondonlegal.com

RYAN M. SUERTH, born Savannah, Georgia, December 6, 1974; admitted to bar, 2000, Connecticut. *Education:* Pepperdine University (B.A., Sociology, 1997); Southwestern University School of Law (J.D., 2000). Staff Member, Southwestern University Law Journal. *Member:* New London and Connecticut Bar Associations. ***PRACTICE AREAS:*** Commercial Law; Business Law; Debtor and Creditor; Estate Planning. ***Email:*** suerth@newlondonlegal.com

REPRESENTATIVE CLIENTS: Connecticut Attorneys Title Insurance, Co.; Black Bear Golf Resort, Inc.; Montville Water Pollution Control Authority; National Loan Investors, L.P.; Citizens Bank; Phoenix Soil, LLC; Rogovin Moving & Storage Co.; Dovenmuehle Mortgage, Inc.; Opsail Ct 2000; Sail New London.

(This Listing Continued)

REFERENCES: Chamber of Commerce of Southeastern Connecticut; The Dime Savings Bank of Norwich.

BEEBE AND O'NEIL

NEW LONDON, CONNECTICUT

(See Norwich)

General Civil and Criminal Practice before State and Federal Courts. Corporation, Personal Injury, Medical Malpractice, Family Law, Commercial, Workers Compensation, Real Estate, Zoning, Wills, Probate, Bankruptcy, Collections and Taxation Law. Trials and Appeals. Banking, Lender Liability, FDIC, Governmental Bank Acquisitions.

BROWN JACOBSON P.C.

NEW LONDON, CONNECTICUT

(See Norwich)

General Practice in all Courts. Trials, Probate, Insurance, Real Estate, Corporate, Commercial and Administrative Law.

CONWAY & LONDREGAN, P.C.

Established in 1962

38 HUNTINGTON STREET
NEW LONDON, CONNECTICUT 06320-6170
Telephone: 860-447-3171
Fax: 860-444-6103
Email: conway.londregan@snet.net
URL: http://www.lawyers.com/clpc

Mystic, Connecticut Office: Masons Island Road, P.O. Box 396, 06355-0396. Telephone: 203-536-4991.

General Practice in all Courts. Municipal Law, Administrative, Real Estate, Commercial Loans, Personal Injury, Probate, Zoning and Real Estate Law, Corporation, Estate Planning, Civil and Commercial Litigation.

KEVIN W. CONWAY, born Norwich, Connecticut, October 17, 1932; admitted to bar, 1957, Connecticut; 1959, U.S. District Court, District of Connecticut. *Education:* College of the Holy Cross (B.A., with honors, 1954); University of Connecticut (LL.B., 1957). Co-Author: "Recent Developments in Connecticut Zoning Law," Connecticut Bar Journal Vol. XXXI No. 3, September 1957; Case Notes, 30 Connecticut Bar Journal, 1967. Editor, University of Connecticut Law Review, 1955-1957. Vice Chairman, Groton Charter Revision Committee, 1959-1960. Member, Executive Council, Connecticut Junior Bar Association, 1960. Special Public Defender, Superior Court, New London County, 1966-1971. *Member:* New London County (Secretary, 1964-1967; President, 1979-1980) and Connecticut Bar Associations (Member, Board of Governors, 1968-1971, 1985-1987; Treasurer, 1972-1975; Member, House of Delegates, 1982-1987; Chairman, Committee on Unauthorized Practice of Law, 1975-1977; Chairman, Connecticut Bar Association Task Force on Delivery of Legal Services, 1980-1981; Chairman, CBA Special Joint Committee on Real Estate Paralegals, 1984-1985; President, Southeastern Connecticut Estate and Tax Planning Counsel, 1985; Member, New London County Grievance Committee, 1985—; Chairman, Middlesex County Grievance Committee, July 1986-July 1992). ***PRACTICE AREAS:*** Estate Planning; Probate; Real Estate; Business Law; Municipal Law. ***Email:*** kconway.c-l@snet.net

FRANCIS T. LONDREGAN, born Norwich, Connecticut, January 17, 1935; admitted to bar, 1960, Connecticut; 1961, U.S. District Court, District of Connecticut. *Education:* College of the Holy Cross (B.S., 1957); University of Connecticut (LL.B., 1960). Member, Executive Council, Connecticut Junior Bar Association, 1962. City Councilman, 1964-1970. Mayor, City of New London, 1965-1966. Town Counsel, Town of Montville, 1973-1979. Counsel: Montville Water and Sewer Commissioner, 1975; Waterford Water Pollution Control Authority, 1980. Member and Legal Representative, Lawrence & Memorial Hospital Legal-Medical Ethics Committee, 1989; Diocese of Norwich Committee on Medical Ethics, 1990—; Associate Director of Law, City of New London for Land Use Matters and Charter Revision. General Counsel: Southeast Area Transit District; Garde Arts Center, Inc. *Member:* New London County and Connecticut Bar Associations; Connecticut Association of Municipal Attorneys (Director, 1974; Vice President, 1975; President, 1978-1979). ***PRACTICE AREAS:*** Commercial Law; Corporate Law; Banking; Secured Transactions; Real Estate; Land Use; Estate Planning; Probate. ***Email:*** flondregan.c-l@snet.net

THOMAS J. LONDREGAN, born New London, Connecticut, February 14, 1944; admitted to bar, 1969, Connecticut; 1979, U.S. District Court, District of Connecticut. *Education:* Fairfield University (A.B., 1966); University of Connecticut (J.D., 1969). Member: Advisory and Planning Council, Seaside Regional Center, State of Connecticut, 1979-1988; Board of Directors, South-

(This Listing Continued)

CONWAY & LONDREGAN, P.C., New London—Continued

eastern Connecticut Estate and Tax Planning Council, 1980-1982; Board of Trustees, The Public Library of New London, 1980-1991. Counsel, New London Charter Revision Commission, 1981. President, Eastern Connecticut Transportation Consortium, 1992-1996. Co-Counsel, New London Redevelopment Agency, 1983. Director of Law, City of New London, 1992—. Town Counsel, Town of Stonington, 1992—. Judge, Mashantucket Pequot Tribal Court, Mashantucket, Connecticut, 1992—. *Member:* New London and Connecticut Bar Associations; Connecticut Trial Lawyers Association. ***REPORTED CASES:*** Edward P. Vallerie, et al v. Town of Stonington, 253 Conn 371 (2000); Malcolm Robertson v. Town of Stonington, 253 Conn. 255 (2000); Kroll v. Sebastian, 58 Conn. App. 262 (2000); New London v. Zoning Board of Appeals, 29 Conn. App. 402 (1992); Caltabiano v. Phillips, 23 Conn. App. 258 (1991); Phillips v. Palakewitz, 17 Conn. App. 476 (1989); Caltabiano v. Salem Planning & Zoning, 211 Conn. 662 (1989); Filosi v. Hawkins, 1 Conn. App. 634 (1984); Powers v. Powers, 186 Conn. 8 (1982); Fromer v. Reynolds Metals Development Company; Gardiner v. Conservation Commission, 222 Conn. 98 (1992); Fromer v. Lombardi, et al, 33 Conn. App. 910 (1993); Honan v. Greene et al, 37 Conn. App. 137 (1995); Carpenteri-Waddington, Inc. v. Commissioner of Revenue Services, 234 Conn. 355 (1994); H H Holding Co. v. Board of Tax Review, 37 Conn. App. 917 (1995); M. DeMatteo Construction Co. v. City of New London, 236 Conn. 710 (1996); Harrall-Michalowski v. Shippee, 40 Conn. App. 613 (1996); Branch v. Occhionero, 239 Conn. 199 (1996); New Milford Block v. Grondahl, 51 Conn. App. 454 (1999). ***PRACTICE AREAS:*** Municipal Law; Estate Planning; Probate; Business Law and Zoning; Commercial Litigation; Appellate Practice. ***Email:*** tlondregan.c-l@snet.net

MICHAEL W. SHEEHAN, born New London, Connecticut, October 10, 1960; admitted to bar, 1989, Connecticut. *Education:* College of the Holy Cross (B.A., 1982); Rensselaer Polytechnic Institute (M.B.A., 1986); University of Connecticut (J.D., 1989). Instructor, Law and Banking Principles, Real Estate Loan Documentation, American Institute of Banking, 1991—. *Member:* New London County and Connecticut Bar Associations; Southeastern Connecticut Board of Realtors; The Children's Museum of Southeastern Connecticut (Board of Trustees, 1997—); New London Rotary Club (1995—). ***PRACTICE AREAS:*** Banking Law; Commercial Law; Real Estate Law; Probate Law; Estate Planning. ***Email:*** msheehan.c-l@snet.net

RALPH J. MONACO, born Bronx, New York, June 17, 1967; admitted to bar, 1993, Connecticut, New Jersey and U.S. District Court, District of New Jersey; 1994, U.S. District Court, District of Connecticut; U.S. Court of Appeals, Second Circuit. *Education:* Fordham University (B.A., cum laude, 1989); New York Law School; Quinnipiac College School of Law (J.D., with honors, 1993). Recipient: American Jurisprudence Awards in Trial Practice, Advanced Trial Practice and Products Liability; Award for Excellence in Oral Advocacy. *Member:* New London County and Connecticut (Member, House of Delegates, 1999—; Young Lawyers' Section, Secretary, 1998-1999; Treasurer, 1999-2000; Chair-Elect, 2000-2001; Director, 1998-2000) Bar Associations; Connecticut Trial Lawyers Association; New London County Young Lawyers Association (President, 1995-1998). ***REPORTED CASES:*** Honan v. Greene, et al, 37 Conn. App. 137 (1995); Branch v. Occhionero, 239 Conn. 199 (1996); McIntosh v. McIntosh, 47 Conn. App. 907 (1997); New Milford Block v. Grondahl, 51 Conn. App. 454 (1999); Kroll v. Sebastian, 58 Conn. App. 262 (2000). ***PRACTICE AREAS:*** Civil Litigation; Commercial Litigation; Product Liability; Personal Injury; Municipal Litigation; Appellate Practice. ***Email:*** rmonaco.c-l@snet.net

SUSAN B. POCHAL, born Winchester, Connecticut, January 2, 1960; admitted to bar, 1985, Massachusetts; 1986, Connecticut. *Education:* Western Connecticut State University (B.S., cum laude, 1982); Western New England College School of Law (J.D., 1985). Instructor: Real Estate Law and Contract Law for Landry, Lyons and Whyte, Better Homes and Gardens Real Estate School, 1987-1988. President, Three Rivers College Foundation, 1994-1996, 1998-1999. *Member:* Massachusetts, Connecticut and American Bar Associations; Estate and Tax Planning Council of Eastern Connecticut. ***PRACTICE AREAS:*** Probate Law; Estate Planning; Trusts and Estates Taxation. ***Email:*** spochal.c-l@snet.net

BRIAN K. ESTEP, born Brookville, Pennsylvania, January 2, 1960; admitted to bar, 1986, New York; 1987, U.S. District Court, Western District of New York; 1988, U.S. District Court, Northern District of New York; 1993, Pennsylvania; 1994, U.S. District Court, Eastern District of Pennsylvania; 1996, Connecticut; 1997, U.S. District Court, District of Connecticut. *Education:* Allegheny College (B.A., magna cum laude, 1982); Dickinson School of Law (J.D., 1985). Phi Beta Kappa; Pi Gamma Mu. ALJ New York State Dept. of Labor Unemployment Appeals Board, 1992-1993. *Member:* Monroe County, Albany County, New London County, Schenectady County, New York State and American Bar Associations. ***REPORTED CASES:*** People v. Cowie 134 AD2d 844 (Fourth Dept 1987); New Milford Block v. Grondahl, 51 Conn. App. 454 (1999). ***PRACTICE AREAS:*** Litigation; Worker Compensation; Municipal. ***Email:*** bestep.c-l@snet.net

JEFFREY T. LONDREGAN, born New London, Connecticut, January 1, 1971; admitted to bar, 1998, Connecticut. *Education:* Fairfield University (B.A., 1993); Quinnipiac College (J.D., 1998). *Member:* Connecticut Bar Association; Connecticut Trial Lawyers Association; Connecticut Young Lawyers Society. ***Email:*** jlondregan.c-l@snet.net

REPRESENTATIVE CLIENTS: The L. C. Doane Company; City of New London; M. J. Sullivan Automotive Corner; Garde Arts Center; Southeast Area Transit District; F & F Distributors, Inc.; Hedden Insurance Agency; New London Country Club, Inc.; Town of Stonington; Town of Bozrah; Brustolon Buick-Pontiac, Inc.; Wilcox Marine Supply Co.; Chelsea Groton Savings Bank; Charter Oak Federal Credit Union; Citizen's Savings Bank; People's Bank; Liberty Bank; Masons Island Co.; Groton Long Point Assn.; Designers Group; Mystic Fire District; Old Mystic Fire District; Noank Fire District; Fairview Nursing Home; Cumis Insurance Society, Inc.; Southern New England Chapter; American Institute of Banking; St. Matthew's Church Corp.; Connecticut Interlocal Risk Management Agency; Indian Town Assoc. of Old Saybrook.
LOCAL COUNSEL FOR: Outdoor Systems, Inc.; Bess Eaton Donut & Flour Co.; Reynolds Metals Development Company; Southern New England AIB, Inc.

(This Listing Continued)

DUPONT AND RADLAUER, L.L.P.

CAPTAIN'S WALK
165 STATE STREET, SUITE 502
P.O. BOX 710
NEW LONDON, CONNECTICUT 06320-0710
Telephone: 860-447-0090
Fax: 860-437-7442
Email: radlaw@snet.net
URL: http://www.lawyers.com/dupontandradlauer

Litigation, Probate, Business Organization.

MEMBERS OF FIRM

RALPH P. DUPONT, born Fall River, Massachusetts, May 21, 1929; admitted to bar, 1956, Connecticut; 1961, U.S. District Court, District of Connecticut; 1967, U.S. Supreme Court and U.S. Court of Appeals, Second Circuit; 1980, U.S. Tax Court; 1985, U.S. District Court, Southern District of New York. *Education:* Brown University (A.B., cum laude, with highest honors, American Civilization, 1951); Harvard University (J.D., cum laude, 1956). Member, Board of Editors, Harvard Law Review, 1955-1956. Author: "Dupont on Connecticut Civil Practice," 1998; *Litigation,* Attorney's Desk Library, 1994; Lecturer, Law, University of Connecticut Law School, 1980-1985. Adjunct Professor of Law, Quinnipiac College School of Law, 1994-1995. Visiting Professor of Law: Western New England College School of Law, 1992-1994; Bridgeport School of Law, Quinnipiac College, 1991-1992; Northeastern University School of Law, 1977-1978. Member, Executive Board, Quinnipiac University School of Law, 1994—. *Member:* Connecticut (Lecturer, Continuing Legal Education Program, 1972—) and American Bar Associations; National Board of Trial Advocacy (Diplomate); International Academy of Trust and Estate Law. Fellow, American College of Trust and Estate Counsel. [Lt. (jg), U.S.N.R., 1951-1953]. ***REPORTED CASES:*** Stanford v. Kuwait Airways Corp., et al, 89 F.3d 117 (2d Cir. 1996); Frito-Lay, Inc. v. Killingly Planning and Zoning Commission, 206 Conn. 554, 538 A.2d 1039 (1998); Sanderson v. Banigan, 690 F.2d 337 (2nd. Cir. 1982); Swenson v. Dittner, 183 Conn. 289, 439 A.2d 334 (1981); Red Top, Inc. v. Ledyard, 181 Conn. 343; 435 A.2d 364 (1980); Schenck v. Sears, Roebuck, et al, 176 Conn. 245; 405 A.2d 665 (1979); McKay v. McKay, 174 Conn. 1, 381 A.2d 527 (1977). ***PRACTICE AREAS:*** Litigation; Probate; Business Organization. ***Email:*** radlaw@snet.net

BARBARA J. RADLAUER, born New York, New York, April 23, 1961; admitted to bar, 1995, Connecticut; 1996, U.S. District Court, District of Connecticut and U.S. District Court, Southern and Eastern Districts of New York; 1999, U.S. Supreme Court; 2000, U.S. District Court, District of Columbia. *Education:* State University of New York (B.S.N., 1985); Mercy College (M.S.N., with distinction, 1991); Quinnipiac University (J.D., 1994). Sigma Theta Tau; Registered Nurse, New York, 1985—. Assistant Professor, 1995-1996; Adjunct Associate Professor, Quinnipiac University, 1994—. *Member:* The Association of the Bar of the City of New York; New York State, Connecticut and American Bar Associations; American Association of Nurse Attorneys (President, 1999—; Connecticut Chapter, 1997-1999;Member, Board of Directors, 2000—). ***REPORTED CASES:*** Simmons v. Simmons, 244 Conn. 158, 708 A.2d 949 (1997); Simmons v. Simmons, 1998 Conn. Super. LEXIS 1324; Stanford & Hegna v. KAC, 89.F.3d 117; 1996 U.S. App. Lexis 17811; Mathews v. Nolan, 26 Conn. App. 920, 599 A.2d 747 (1991). ***PRACTICE AREAS:*** Civil Litigation; Personal Injury. ***Email:*** radlaw@snet.net

FAULKNER & BOYCE, P.C.

Established in 1986

216 BROAD STREET
P.O. BOX 391
NEW LONDON, CONNECTICUT 06320
Telephone: 860-442-9900
Fax: 860-443-6428
Email: law@faulknerandboyce.com
URL: http://www.faulknerandboyce.com

FIRM PROFILE: Since the firm's inception, Faulkner & Boyce, P.C. has achieved and maintained Martindale-Hubbell's highest rating for legal ability and ethical conduct. With over 90 years of legal experience, the firm focuses only on Civil Litigation. The firm extends its service throughout Connecticut as well as parts of Rhode Island.

DALE PATRICK FAULKNER, born New Haven, Connecticut, September 23, 1938; admitted to bar, 1963, Connecticut. *Education:* Providence College (A.B., magna cum laude, 1960); University of Connecticut (LL.B., 1963). Editor-in-Chief, University of Connecticut Law Review, 1962-1963. Editor, Forum, 1985-1993. Law Clerk to the Honorable T. Emmet Clarie, U.S. District Court Judge, District of Connecticut, 1963-1964. Co-Author: *Connecticut Trial Evidence Notebook,* Lexis Law Publishing. Lecturer in Law, 1975-1985 and Adjunct Professor of Law, 1986-1997, University of Connecticut School of Law. *Member:* Connecticut Bar Association (Member, State Judicial Selection Commission, 1994-1997); Connecticut Trial Lawyers Association (Member, Board of Governors, 1982-1993) ; National Board of Trial Advocacy (Diplomate). Fellow, American College of Trial Lawyers. ***PRACTICE AREAS:*** Personal Injury; Premises Liability; Wrongful Death; Professional Liability.

THOMAS W. BOYCE, JR., born New Haven, Connecticut, March 12, 1951; admitted to bar, 1976, Connecticut; 1977, New York; 1978, U.S. District Court, Eastern District of New York; 1980, U.S. District Court, District of Connecticut. *Education:* Universite de Fribourg, Fribourg, Switzerland; Providence College (B.A., 1973); Brooklyn Law School (J.D., 1976). With Kings County District Attorneys Office, Brooklyn, New York, 1976-1979. *Member:* Connecticut Bar Association; Connecticut Defense Lawyers Association; National Board of Trial Advocacy (Diplomate); American Board of Trial Advocates (Advocate). Fellow, American College of Trial Lawyers. ***PRACTICE AREAS:*** Personal Injury; Medical Malpractice Defense; Products Liability Defense; Insurance Litigation.

HUMBERT J. POLITO, JR., born Cleveland, Ohio, February 19, 1956; admitted to bar, 1986, Connecticut; 1987, Rhode Island; 1988, U.S. District Court, District of Connecticut and U.S. District Court, District of Rhode Island; 1993, U.S. Court of Appeals, Second Circuit. *Education:* College of the Holy Cross (B.A., magna cum laude, 1978); University of Connecticut (J.D., with honors, 1986). Phi Beta Kappa. Law Clerk to the Honorable Donald F. Shea, Associate Justice, Supreme Court of Rhode Island, 1986-1987. Lecturer in Law, University of Connecticut School of Law, 1998—. Member, Board of Directors, Brain Injury Association of Connecticut, 1992-1998. *Member:* Connecticut Bar Association; Connecticut Trial Lawyers Association (Member, Board of Governors, 1993—); National Board of Trial Advocacy (Advocate); American Board of Trial Advocates (Advocate)Rhode Island Trial Lawyers Association. ***PRACTICE AREAS:*** Personal Injury; Product Liability; Medical Malpractice; Premises Liability; Wrongful Death.

SHELLEY L. GRAVES, born New London, Connecticut, December 15, 1968; admitted to bar, 1994, Connecticut and U.S. District Court, District of Connecticut. *Education:* University of Connecticut (B.A., 1990; J.D., 1994). Co-Author: *Connecticut Trial Evidence Notebook* (Lexis Law Publishing, 1994). *Member:* Connecticut Bar Association; Connecticut Trial Lawyers Association; The Association of Trial Lawyers of America. ***PRACTICE AREAS:*** Personal Injury; Premises Liability.

JOHN PATRICK CASEY, born Springfield, Massachusetts, March 7, 1968; admitted to bar, 1997, Connecticut; 2000, U.S. District Court, District of Connecticut; 2001, Rhode Island. *Education:* University of Connecticut (B.A., 1991); American University (J.D., summa cum laude, 1997). *Member:* Connecticut Bar Association; Connecticut Trial Lawyers Association. [With U.S. Navy Judge Advocate General's Corps. (1997-2000).]. ***PRACTICE AREAS:*** Personal Injury; Premises Liability.

REFERENCE: Fleet National Bank of Connecticut.
REPRESENTATIVE CLIENTS: AIU/AIAC/AIG Insurance Co.; Chicago Pneumatic Tool Co.; Citizens Bank; Club Med; Connecticut Medical Insurance Co.; Smurfit-Stone Container; The Day Publishing Co.; Mack Trucks, Inc.; Travelers Insurance Co.

HORVITZ & CAISSE

NEW LONDON, CONNECTICUT

(See Norwich)

Practice Limited to Matrimonial Law.

KLEINMAN & ASSOCIATES, P.C.

22 MASONIC STREET
NEW LONDON, CONNECTICUT 06320-6404
Telephone: 860-437-2342
Facsimile: 860-437-2346
Email: stewart.kleinman@snet.net
URL: http://www.lawyers.com/kleinmanlaw

Hartford, Connecticut Office: 2 Congress Street. Telephone: 860-525-2930.

Business Law, Commercial Real Estate, Leases and Leasing, Mortgages, Loan Workouts, Corporate Finance, Contracts, Corporation, Commercial, Collections, Banking, Bankruptcy, Probate, Estate Planning, Real Estate, Construction Contracts, Family Law, Mortgage Foreclosures, Landlord and Tenant, Zoning, Personal Injury, Consumer Law, Partnership Law, Property Law.

STEWART F. KLEINMAN, born New York, N.Y., July 14, 1940; admitted to bar, 1966, New York; 1971, Connecticut; 1979, Florida. *Education:* New York University, School of Commerce Accounts and Finance (B.S., 1963); Brooklyn Law School (LL.B., 1966). Instructor for Professional Education Systems, Inc., giving seminars in Real Property Law, 1985-1992. Instructor, University of Connecticut CLE, 1986-1990. Member, 1977-1979 and Vice Chairman, 1979-1980, Board of Special Assessments, Town of West Hartford. Alternate Member, West Hartford Zoning Board of Appeals, 1980-1984. Member, Panel of Arbitrators and Mediators, American Arbitration Association. *Member:* Hartford County (Member: Real Property Committee, 1976-1994; Unauthorized Practice of Law Committee, 1976-1981), Connecticut (Member, Ethics Committee, 1976-1983), New York State and American (Member: Environmental Law Committee, Real Property, Probate and Trust Law Section, 1975—; Title Insurance Committee, 1982—) Bar Associations; The Florida Bar. ***PRACTICE AREAS:*** Commercial Real Estate Development and Finance Law; Loan Workouts Law; Corporate Law; Commercial Leasing Law; Contracts; Construction Contracts; Mortgage Foreclosures; Zoning; Arbitration; Mediation.

MEREDITH E. RUSSELL, born Cambridge, Massachusetts, November 10, 1949; admitted to bar, 1989, Connecticut; 1990, U.S. District Court, District of Connecticut. *Education:* Boston University (B.A., 1972); University of Bridgeport School of Law (J.D., 1989). Member: Groton Board of Education, 1992-1996; Groton City Council, 1999—. *Member:* New London County and Connecticut (Member, Commercial Law, Bankruptcy Section) Bar Associations. ***PRACTICE AREAS:*** Foreclosures; Bankruptcy; Evictions; Real Estate; Family Law.

MADSEN, PRESTLEY & PARENTEAU, LLC

111 HUNTINGTON STREET
P.O. BOX 1631
NEW LONDON, CONNECTICUT 06320
Telephone: 860-442-2466
Facsimile: 860-447-9206

Hartford Office: 44 Capitol Avenue, Suite 201. Telephone: 860-246-2466. Facsimile: 860-246-1794.

Employment, Benefits Law and Related Litigation. Employment Contracts; Age, Race, Sex and Disability Discrimination; Civil Rights, Section 1983. Wage and Hour Law, Class Actions and Qui Tam Actions, Negotiations, Mediations, Arbitrations, Trials.

WILLIAM G. MADSEN, born Danbury, Connecticut, 1959; admitted to bar, 1990, Maine; 1992, Connecticut. *Education:* University of Massachusetts (B.A., 1985); Yale University (M.A.R., 1987); Vermont Law School (J.D., 1990). Managing Editor, Law Review, 1990. Law Clerk to Hon. Conrad K. Cyr, U.S. Court of Appeals for the First Circuit, 1990-1991. ***PRACTICE AREAS:*** Labor and Employment Law; Civil Rights Law; Age Discrimination Law; Sexual Harassment Law; Employment Disability Law; Employment Contracts Law; Wage and Hour Law. ***Email:*** pprestley@mppjustice.com

PETER B. PRESTLEY, born 1945; admitted to bar, 1972, Connecticut. *Education:* Wesleyan University (B.A.); University of Connecticut (J.D., 1972). ***LANGUAGES:*** French. ***PRACTICE AREAS:*** Labor and Employment Law. ***Email:*** wmadsen@mppjustice.com

JACQUES J. PARENTEAU, born Woonsocket, Rhode Island, June 1, 1957; admitted to bar, 1982, Rhode Island; 1984, Connecticut. *Education:* University of Massachusetts (B.A., magna cum laude, 1979); Washington College of Law of American University (J.D., 1982). Past Member of the Board of

(This Listing Continued)

MADSEN, PRESTLEY & PARENTEAU, LLC, New London—Continued

Directors and Vice Chairman, Connecticut Legal Services Corporation. Vice Chairman and Member of the Board of Directors of the Connecticut Community Credit Union, Inc.; Arbitrator, Connecticut Automobile Dispute Settlement Program. *Member:* New London County and Rhode Island Bar Associations; Connecticut Trial Lawyers Association; The Association of Trial Lawyers of America. ***PRACTICE AREAS:*** Employment Law; Academic Employment; Commercial Litigation; Personal Injury; Products Liability. ***Email:*** jparenteau@mppjustice.com

MARIANI & RECK, LLC

83 BROAD STREET
NEW LONDON, CONNECTICUT 06320-1630
Telephone: 860-443-5023
Fax: 860-443-8897
Email: info@marianireck.com

General Civil and Criminal Practice before State and Federal Courts. Personal Injury, Product Liability, Medical Malpractice, Domestic Relations, Child Custody, Labor and Employment, Municipal, Real Estate, Landlord and Tenant Law, Probate and Corporate Law. Trials and Appeals. Mediation.

LINDA L. MARIANI, born Philadelphia, Pennsylvania, May 12, 1952; admitted to bar, 1977, Massachusetts; 1978, Connecticut; 1979, District of Columbia; 1982, U.S. District Court, District of Connecticut and U.S. Supreme Court; 1997, Mohegan Gaming Disputes Court. *Education:* Cornell University (B.A., 1974); Suffolk University (J.D., 1977). Recipient, State of Connecticut Judicial Department Certificate of Commendations, 1987, April and August, 1999. Listed, Best Lawyers in America, Woodward White Inc., 2001. Deputy Assistant States Attorney, 1980-1986. Member, Marine Commerce and Development Committee, City of New London, 1978-1990. Fact Finder, Special Master and Trial Referee for State of Connecticut Judicial Department. Arbitrator-Court Annexed Arbitration Program, 1997—. Member, Middlesex Judicial District Grievance Panel, 1992-1998. *Member:* New London County (President, Family Law Section, 1987; Co-Chair, Women in the Law Section, 1991—), Connecticut (Member: Executive Committee, Family Law Section, 1988 and 2001) and American Bar Associations; Connecticut Trial Lawyers Association; The Association of Trial Lawyers of America; National District Attorney's Association; Connecticut Council of Divorce and Family Mediators (Training, 1983); Academy of Family Mediators (Practitioner Member); American Arbitration Association. ***LANGUAGES:*** Spanish, French and Italian. ***PRACTICE AREAS:*** Matrimonial Law; Personal Injury; Family Mediation; Mediation. ***Email:*** lmariani@marianireck.com

STEPHEN E. RECK, born Brooklyn, New York, September 4, 1965; admitted to bar, 1990, Connecticut; 1991, U.S. District Court, District of Connecticut; 1998, U.S. Supreme Court and U.S. Tax Court; 2001, Mashantucket Tribal Court. *Education:* University of Connecticut (B.A., cum laude, 1987); Western New England College School of Law (J.D., cum laude, 1990). Political Science Honor Society, University of Connecticut. Member, Western New England Law Review, 1989-1990. Special Master, Superior Court Family Division, 1999—. *Member:* New London County (Member, Board of Directors 2001—) and Connecticut Bar Associations; Connecticut Trial Lawyers Association; Connecticut Criminal Defense Lawyers Association. ***REPORTED CASES:*** Citicorp Mortgage v. Burgos, 227 Conn. 116 (1993); Miner v. Miner, 48 Conn. App. 409 (1998); Panganiban v. Panganiban, 251 Conn. 920 (1999); Panganiban v. Panganiban, 54 Conn. App. 634 (1999); Taylor v. Taylor, 57 Conn. App. 528 (2000); Way v. Way, 60 Conn.App. 189 (2000). ***PRACTICE AREAS:*** Family Law; Personal Injury; Criminal Law; Real Estate; Probate; Trusts and Estates; Bankruptcy. ***Email:*** sreck@marianireck.com

---

MICHAEL J. CARTIER, born Exeter, New Hampshire, March 5, 1959; admitted to bar, 1985, New Hampshire; 1987, Connecticut; 1989, U.S. District Court, District of Connecticut. *Education:* St. Anselm College (A.B., cum laude, 1982); Ohio Northern University; Franklin Pierce Law Center (J.D., 1985). Recipient: History Book Award; Contracts Book Award, Ohio Northern University, 1983. Instructor: Business Law, Three River Community College, 1991-1996; Paralegal Studies, University of Connecticut, 1994-1996. *Member:* New Hampshire Bar Association; Connecticut Bar Association; Connecticut Defense Attorneys Association. [LT., U.S. Navy, Judge Advocate General's Corp., 1985-1989; LCDR USNR-R, 1989-1998]. ***PRACTICE AREAS:*** Personal Injury; Criminal Law; Negligence Law; Employment Discrimination; Military Law.

KEVIN B. F. EMERSON, born Camden, New Jersey, 1970; admitted to bar, 1995, Connecticut. *Education:* Eastern College (B.A., 1992); Georgetown University Law Center (J.D., 1995). Special Master, Judicial District of New London (!999—). *Member:* New London and Connecticut (Family Law Section) Bar Associations. ***PRACTICE AREAS:*** Divorce; Family Law. ***Email:*** kemerson@marianireck.com

RACHEL M. PROULX, born Derby, Connecticut, December 13, 1971; admitted to bar, 1999, Connecticut. *Education:* State University of New York at Stony Brook (B.A., 1993); University of Bridgeport (M.S., 1996); Quinnipiac College (J.D., 1999). Phi Delta Phi; Phi Alpha Delta. *Member:* Connecticut Bar Association. ***PRACTICE AREAS:*** Family Law; Probate.

McGARRY, PRINCE, McGARRY, P.C.

Established in 1923

58 HUNTINGTON STREET
NEW LONDON, CONNECTICUT 06320
Telephone: 860-443-1818
Fax: 860-443-1810
Email: tfmcal@aol.com
URL: http://www.lawyers.com/mcgarryprincemcgarry,law

General Practice. Probate, Estate Planning, Real Estate, Corporation, Municipal, Banking and Commercial Law, Zoning and Condominium Law. Trials in all Courts.

S. VICTOR PRINCE (1892-1991).

JOHN J. McGARRY (1900-1973).

THOMAS F. McGARRY, born New London, Connecticut, November 7, 1939; admitted to bar, 1964, Connecticut. *Education:* Providence College (A.B., 1961); University of Connecticut (LL.B., 1964). Director, McCurdy-Salisbury Foundation, 1976—. Counsel, Regional School District #18, Old Lyme and Lyme, 1975—. *Member:* New London County, The Connecticut and American Bar Associations.

REPRESENTATIVE CLIENTS: Fleet Bank; Regional School District #18, Old Lyme and Lyme; Abco. Welding & Industrial Supplies, Inc.
APPROVED ATTORNEY FOR: Chicago Title Insurance Co.; First American Title Insurance Co.; Commonwealth Land Title Insurance Co.
REFERENCES: Fleet Bank.

McGUIRE & McGUIRE

Established in 1901

68 FEDERAL STREET
P.O. BOX 270
NEW LONDON, CONNECTICUT 06320
Telephone: 860-443-4357
Fax: 860-440-3817
Email: mcguire@ctol.net
URL: http://www.lawyers.com/mcguire&mcguire

General Civil Practice. Corporate, Probate, Estate Planning, Real Estate, Business, Land Use.

FRANCIS F. McGUIRE (1910-1982).

FRANK L. McGUIRE (1940-1990).

JAMES C. McGUIRE, born New London, Connecticut, 1947; admitted to bar, 1973, Connecticut; 1976, U.S. District Court, District of Connecticut. *Education:* Yale University (B.A., 1969); University of Pennsylvania (J.D., 1973). Chairman, 1984-1997, Treasurer, 1997-1999, Director, 1981—, Board of Directors, Lawrence and Memorial Hospital, New London. Secretary and Treasurer, 1975-1994, President, 1994-1997, Secretary, 1997—, Board of Directors, Williams School, New London. *Member:* New London County, Connecticut and American Bar Associations; National Association of College and University Attorneys. ***Email:*** jcm@ctol.net

REPRESENTATIVE CLIENTS: Connecticut College; Day Publishing Co.; Lawrence and Memorial Hospital; Whaling City Dredge & Dock Corp.; Fleet Bank.
APPROVED ATTORNEYS FOR: Chicago Title Insurance Co.; Connecticut Attorneys Title Insurance Co.; First American Title Insurance Co.
REFERENCE: Fleet Bank.

LUCIA M. MERCURIO, LLC

470 BANK STREET, SECOND FLOOR
NEW LONDON, CONNECTICUT 06320
Telephone: 860-447-9942
Fax: 860-447-8157
Email: lmm@lmercuriolaw.com
URL: http://www.lawyers.com/mercurio

Automobile Accidents, Wrongful Death, Personal Injury, Employment Law, Discrimination, Premises Liability.

(This Listing Continued)

LUCIA M. MERCURIO, born East Orange, New Jersey, March 21, 1962; admitted to bar, 1989, Connecticut; 1990, U.S. District Court, District of Connecticut; 1992, Rhode Island; 1993, U.S. District Court, District of Rhode Island. *Education:* Fairfield University (B.A., magna cum laude, 1984); University of Connecticut School of Law (J.D., with honors, 1989). Recipient: American Jurisprudence Award; University of Connecticut Hornbook Award. Note Editor, University of Connecticut Law Review, 1988-1989. Appointments: Trial Referee, Arbitrator and Special Master, New London Judicial District, 1996—. Lecturer: "Employment Law for Trial Lawyers," Connecticut Trial Lawyers Association, 1999; "Swing the Federal, State & Local Government," Connecticut Trial Lawyers Assoc., 1999. Instructor, Peoples Law School, 1996-2000. *Member:* New London County, Rhode Island, Connecticut and American Bar Associations; Connecticut Trial Lawyers Association (Member, Board of Governors); The Association of Trial Lawyers of America. ***LANGUAGES:*** Spanish. ***PRACTICE AREAS:*** Automobile Accidents and Injuries; Wrongful Death; Personal Injury; Employment Law; Discrimination; Premises Liability.

O'BRIEN, SHAFNER, STUART, KELLY & MORRIS, P.C.

NEW LONDON, CONNECTICUT

(See Groton)

Trials in all Courts. Personal Injury, Products Liability, Workers Compensation, Medical Malpractice, Corporations, Estate Planning, Probate, Trust Law, Real Estate, General Practice, Administrative and Admiralty Law.

PECK & TUNESKI, P.C.

10 PEARL STREET
P.O. BOX 37
NEW LONDON, CONNECTICUT 06320
Telephone: 860-447-3370
Telefax: 860-447-3150
http://www.peck-tuneski.com
URL: http://www.lawyers.com/peck&tuneski

Old Saybrook Office: 6 Business Park Road 06475. Telephone: 860-395-1811. Fax: 860-395-1812.. Url: http://www.peck-tuneski.com.

Lender Representation in Loan Workouts and Bankruptcy, Commercial Collections, Real Estate and Foreclosure, both residential and commercial, Land Use and Zoning, Probate, Estate and Tax Planning, Business and Corporate Law, Employment and Labor Law, Family Law, Personal Injury, Wrongful Death, Leasing, Zoning and Litigation in all Courts.

ROBERT D. PECK (1935-2000).

PATRICIA H. MODZELEWSKI, born New Britain, Connecticut, August 15, 1958; admitted to bar, 1984, Connecticut; 1985, U.S. District Court, District of Connecticut. *Education:* University of Connecticut (B.A., 1980); University of Bridgeport (J.D., 1983). Phi Delta Phi. Member, Board of Directors, Shoreline Visiting Nurses Association, 1985—. Member, Board of Directors, Lawrence and Memorial Hospital Auxiliary, 1991—. City Representative, Southeastern Connecticut Regional Planning Agency, 1985. City Representative, Citizens Advisory Committee, 1992. *Member:* New London County, Connecticut (Member, General Practice Section) and American Bar Associations; New London County Womens Bar Association. ***PRACTICE AREAS:*** Commercial Law; Litigation; Landlord and Tenant Law; Foreclosure Law; Family Law; Personal Injury; Real Estate.

JONATHAN A. PECK, born Hartford, Connecticut, March 26, 1959; admitted to bar, 1985, Massachusetts and U.S. District Court, District of Massachusetts; 1987, Connecticut and U.S. District Court, District of Connecticut. *Education:* Clark University (B.A., 1981); Suffolk University (J.D., 1984). Instructor, Law and Banking Application and Principles, American Institute of Banking, 1988—. Member, Board of Directors, 1988 and Adjunct Board Member, 1989—, Big Brothers/Big Sisters. Member, Board of Directors, CONTACT, 1990—. *Member:* Hampden County, New London County, Massachusetts, Connecticut (Member, Sections on: Commercial Law; Banking Law) and American (Member, Law Practice Management Section) Bar Associations; Commercial Law League of America; Connecticut Trial Lawyers Association; New London County Young Lawyers (President, 1990-1991). ***PRACTICE AREAS:*** Commercial Law; Lender Representation Law; Loan Workouts Law; Collections; Litigation; Real Estate. ***Email:*** jon@peck-tuneski.com

OF COUNSEL

ROBERT S. TUNESKI, born New London, Connecticut, February 19, 1935; admitted to bar, 1981, Connecticut; 1982 U.S. District Court, District of Connecticut and U.S. Court of Military Appeals. *Education:* U.S. Coast Guard Academy (B.S., 1958); U.S. Naval Postgraduate School (M.S., 1966); Western New England College (J.D., 1980). Instructor, Business Law, University of New Haven, 1984-1986. Military Aide to U.S. Secretary of Transportation, 1969-1970. President, U.S. Coast Guard Academy Alumni Association, 1976-1986. Member, Board of Directors: Community Service Credit Union, 1977-1980; New London Visiting Nurse Association, 1985-1989; Niantic Rotary, 1987—. Chairman, Republican Town Committee, East Lyme, Connecticut, 1984-1986. *Member:* New London County, Connecticut (Member, Estate and Probate Tax Section) and American Bar Associations (Member, Real Property, Probate and Trust Law Section) Bar Associations. [CDR (Ret), U.S. Coast Guard, 1958-1978]. (Retired).

REPRESENTATIVE CLIENTS: Shawmut Bank, N.A.; The Bank of Southeastern Connecticut; Fleet Bank, N.A.; Commonwealth United Mortgage Co., Inc.; Navy Federal Credit Union; Boston Five Mortgage Co.; Citicorp Leasing Co.; Citicorp Mortgage Co.; Baybank of Connecticut; Levine Distributing Co.; First Eastern Mortgage Corp.; Meridian Mortgage Corp.; New London Motors.
REFERENCES: Shawmut Bank, Connecticut, N.A., New London; The Bank of Southeastern Connecticut; Waterford; Fleet Bank, N.A., New London.

THE REARDON LAW FIRM, P.C.

Established in 1920
160 HEMPSTEAD STREET
DRAWER 1430
NEW LONDON, CONNECTICUT 06320
Telephone: 860-442-0444
Telecopier: 860-444-6445
Email: reardonlaw@aol.com
URL: http://www.reardonlaw.com

Civil Trial Practice limited to Personal Injury, Wrongful Death, Medical Malpractice, Product Liability, Aviation Accidents, Admiralty Claims, Military, and Governmental Liability.

FIRM PROFILE: The Reardon Law Firm, P.C. traces its beginnings to the 1920's. The firm has always been recognized for its work in litigation, representing plaintiffs in personal injury and wrongful death claims involving automobile accidents, malpractice, product liability, premises liability and aviation accidents. Members of the firm are actively involved in professional organizations in this field and regularly lecture to attorneys and professional groups.

ROBERT I. REARDON, JR., born New York, N.Y., November 28, 1945; admitted to bar, 1970, Connecticut; 1971, U.S. Court of Military Appeals; 1974, U.S. District Court, District of Connecticut, U.S. Court of Federal Claims, U.S. Court of Appeals, Second and Eleventh Circuits and U.S. Supreme Court. *Education:* Boston College (B.S., 1967); Fordham University (J.D., 1970). Phi Alpha Delta. Co-Author: "After The Dust Settles: Other Modes of Relief," 10 The Advocate, Military Defense Journal 274, 1978. Recipient: American Bar Association Young Lawyers Award of Achievement, 1976. Lecturer, Connecticut Trial Lawyers Association Continuing Legal Education, 1986—, (Insurance, Bad Faith Law, Product Liability Law, Medical Malpractice). Town Attorney, Town of East Lyme, Connecticut, 1989-1994. Chairman, Board of Finance, Town of Waterford, Connecticut, 1974-1979. Member, East Lyme Board of Education, 1981-1985. Trustee, Eugene O'Neill Memorial Theater, Inc., 1978-1985. *Member:* New London County (Member, Executive Committee, 1975-1979) and Connecticut (Member: House of Delegates, 1975-1981; Board of Governors, 1979-1981) Bar Associations; Connecticut Trial Lawyers Association (President, 1997-1998; Officer, 1992-1998 and Member, 1987—, Board of Governors; Member, Executive Committee, 1989—; Chairman, Membership Committee, 1989-1993); The Association of Trial Lawyers of America (Member, Board of Governors, 1999—; Chairman, Litigation Group, 1991-1994); Trial Lawyers for Public Justice (Connecticut Coordinator, 1995—). [Capt., JAGC, USMC, 1970-1973]. (Board Certified as a Civil Trial Attorney by the National Board of Trial Advocacy). ***REPORTED CASES:*** Clohessy v. Bachelor, 237 Conn. 31 (1996); Fisher v. Nichols, 81 F.3d 319 (2nd Cir. 1996); Pool v. Bell, 209 Conn. 536 (1989); Sportsmen's Boating Corporation v. Hensley, 192 Conn. 747 (1984). ***PRACTICE AREAS:*** Personal Injury; Wrongful Death; Medical Malpractice; Products Liability; Aviation; Admiralty and Maritime Law. ***Email:*** reardonlaw@aol.com

SCOTT D. CAMASSAR, born New London, Connecticut, August 13, 1970; admitted to bar, 1995, Connecticut; 1996, U.S. District Court, District of Connecticut; 1999, U.S. Court of Appeals, Eleventh Circuit. *Education:* University of Connecticut (B.A., magna cum laude, 1992); Western New England College (J.D., 1995). Phi Beta Kappa. Note Editor, Western New England Law Review, 1994-1995. *Member:* New London and Connecticut Bar Associations; Connecticut Trial Lawyers Association; The Association of Trial Lawyers of America. ***PRACTICE AREAS:*** Personal Injury; Wrongful Death; Products Liability; Appellate Practice. ***Email:*** reardonlaw@aol.com

TRACEY E. HARDMAN, born Kalamazoo, Michigan, May 22, 1970; admitted to bar, 2000, Connecticut. *Education:* Colby College (B.A., cum laude, 1992); University of Connecticut, School of Law (J.D., with honors, 1999). Member, Moot Court Board. Recipient: Cali Excellence for the Future Awards in Evidence and Poverty Law, Aspen Law and Business, Award in

(This Listing Continued)

THE REARDON LAW FIRM, P.C., New London—Continued

Evidence. *Member:* Connecticut Bar Association; Connecticut Trial Lawyers Association; The Association of Trial Lawyers of America. ***PRACTICE AREAS:*** Personal Injury; Wrongful Death; Products Liability; Medical Malpractice; Appellate Practice. ***Email:*** reardonlaw@aol.com

OF COUNSEL

MARK A. DUBOIS, born Hartford, Connecticut, October 10, 1950; admitted to bar, 1978, Connecticut; 1980, U.S. District Court, District of Connecticut. *Education:* College of the Holy Cross (A.B., 1972); University of Connecticut (J.D., 1977). Member, Haddam, Ct. Planning and Zoning Commission, 1987-1997; 1999—; Chair, 1991-1997; Second Selectman, 1997-1999; Commission to Study Attorney Discipline, appointed by Chief Justice Connecticut Supreme Court, 1999-2000. *Member:* New Britain and Connecticut (Member, Committees on Legal Discipline, Court Visitation, Panel Chair, Fee Dispute Panel, and Co-Editor Professional Discipline Digest) Bar Associations; Connecticut Trial Lawyers Association (Member, Board of Governors); The Association of Trial Lawyers of America. (Board Certified as Civil Trial Attorney by the National Board of Trial Advocacy). ***PRACTICE AREAS:*** Personal Injury; Wrongful Death; Medical Malpractice; Products Liability. ***Email:*** reardonlaw@aol.com

LEGAL SUPPORT PERSONNEL

GERALD E. KING (Office Adminstrator).

KIMBERLY J. FRIEDEL (Senior Paralegal).

KYLE E. WININGER (Paralegal).

KRISTI L. ANDERSON (Paralegal).

ROBINSON & COLE LLP

Established in 1845

75 EUGENE O'NEILL DRIVE

NEW LONDON, CONNECTICUT 06320-6306

Telephone: 860-437-5000

Fax: 860-437-5099

Email: rc.com

URL: http://www.rc.com

Other Offices: Hartford, CT, Stamford, CT, Greenwich, CT, New York, NY, Boston, MA and Manchester, NH.

General Practice including Admiralty, Antitrust and Trade Regulation, Appellate, Banking and Institutional Finance, Bankruptcy and Creditors' Rights, Business Litigation, Business Workouts, Construction, Corporate and Closely Held Business, Criminal Litigation, E-Commerce and Intellectual Property, Employee Benefits and ERISA Litigation, Employment Litigation and Counseling, Environmental, Estate Planning and Probate, Government Relations, Healthcare, Immigration, Insurance, International, Labor Relations and Collective Bargaining, Land Use and Zoning, Personal Injury, Product Liability, Professional Liability, Public Finance, Real Estate Finance, Development and Leasing, Securities, Tax-Exempt Organizations, Tax Planning and Representation, Utilities and Telecommunications.

RESIDENT ATTORNEY

TIMOTHY D. BATES, admitted to bar, 1973, Connecticut; 1974, U.S. District Court, District of Connecticut; 1982, U.S. Court of Appeals, Second Circuit; 1986, U.S. Supreme Court; 1994, U.S. Court of Federal Claims. *Education:* Yale University (B.A., cum laude, 1970); Columbia University (J.D., 1973). City Attorney, Groton, 1981-1988; Borough Attorney, Stonington, 1998-2001. Member, Planning and Zoning Section, Connecticut Bar Association (Chairman, 2000—). ***PRACTICE AREAS:*** Zoning, Planning and Land Use.

Lawyers are members of local, state and national bar associations.

(For biographical data on other personnel, see Professional Biographies at Hartford, Stamford and Greenwich, CT, Boston, MA, New York, NY and Manchester, NH)

STEVENS, HARRIS & GUERNSEY, P.C.

NEW LONDON, CONNECTICUT

(See Niantic)

General Civil and Criminal Practice before State and Federal Courts. Personal Injury, Wrongful Death, Real Estate, Probate, Corporation, Domestic Relations, Environmental and Workers Compensation Law. Trials and Appeals.

SUISMAN, SHAPIRO, WOOL, BRENNAN, GRAY & GREENBERG, P.C.

SUITE 200 THE COURTNEY BUILDING

2 UNION PLAZA

P.O. BOX 1591

NEW LONDON, CONNECTICUT 06320

Telephone: 860-442-4416

Fax: 860-442-0495

Email: sswbgg@aol.com

URL: http://www.sswbgg.com

Administrative Law, Aged and Aging, Appellate Practice, Asset Protection, Business Law, Civil Practice, Civil Rights, Commercial Law, Commercial Real Estate, Constitutional Law, Contracts, Corporate Law, Criminal Law, Debtor and Creditor, Family Law, Finance, Health Care, Indians and Native Populations, Insurance, Intellectual Property, Labor and Employment, Leases and Leasing, Litigation, Medical Malpractice, Municipal Law, Partnership Law, Personal Injury, Probate, Products Liability, Property Law, Real Estate, Regulatory Law, Social Security, Taxation, Torts, Trusts and Estates, Workers Compensation, Zoning, Planning and Land Use.

JAMES F. BRENNAN, born Hartford, Connecticut, January 27, 1930; admitted to bar, 1955, Connecticut; 1959, U.S. District Court, District of Connecticut. *Education:* College of the Holy Cross (A.B., with honors, 1952); University of Connecticut (LL.B., 1955). Editor-in-Chief, University of Connecticut Law Review, 1954-1955. Town Attorney, Town of Groton, 1983—. *Member:* New London County (President, 1982), Connecticut and American Bar Associations; Connecticut Association of Municipal Attorneys (Director, 1979-1985); The Association of Trial Lawyers of America. [1st Lt., U.S. Marine Corps, 1955-1958]. ***PRACTICE AREAS:*** Civil Litigation; Municipal Law.

S. JOEL SUISMAN, born New London, Connecticut, February 9, 1935; admitted to bar, 1960, Connecticut and U.S. District Court, District of Connecticut; 1962, Florida and U.S. District Court, Southern District of Florida; 1964, U.S. Tax Court and U.S. Court of Appeals, Second Circuit. *Education:* Cornell University and Babson College (B.S., 1957); New York University (LL.B., 1960; LL.M., Taxation, 1961). Accredited Estate Planner (AEP). *Member:* New London County, Connecticut and American (Member, Section of Taxation) Bar Associations; The Florida Bar. ***PRACTICE AREAS:*** Asset Protection; Business Law; Banking; Finance; Corporate. ***Email:*** jsuisman@sswbgg.com

LAWRENCE J. GREENBERG, born Windber, Pennsylvania, August 8, 1930; admitted to bar, 1955, Connecticut. *Education:* Yale University (B.A., magna cum laude, 1952); Harvard University (J.D., 1955). Phi Beta Kappa. *Member:* New London County, Connecticut (Member, Sections on: Taxation and Corporation; Business Law) and American (Member, Sections on: Real Property, Probate and Trust Law; Taxation) Bar Associations. ***PRACTICE AREAS:*** Corporate Law; Commercial Transactions; Business and Estate Planning. ***Email:*** lgreenberg@sswbgg.com

THOMAS B. WILSON, born Hartford, Connecticut, November 25, 1939; admitted to bar, 1967, Connecticut and U.S. District Court, District of Connecticut; 1973, U.S. Supreme Court; 1975, U.S. Court of Appeals, Second Circuit. *Education:* Trinity College (B.A., 1961); University of Connecticut (J.D., with honors, 1967). Comment and Note Editor, University of Connecticut Law Review, 1966-1967. President, The University of Connecticut Law School Alumni Association, 1983-1984. Editorial Board, Connecticut Bar Journal, 1974-1978. Town Attorney, Town of Ledyard, 1971-1979, 1983-1991 and 1995—. Attorney State Trial Referee, 1988—. Judge, Mohegan Tribal Gaming Disputes Court. *Member:* New London County (Standing Committee on Recommendations for Admissions to the Bar, 1995—), Connecticut and American Bar Associations. [1st Lt., U.S.A.F., 1961-1964]. ***PRACTICE AREAS:*** Municipal Law; Land Use and Planning Law; Indian Law. ***Email:*** twilson@sswbgg.com

ANDREW BRAND, born Bronx, New York, October 15, 1941; admitted to bar, 1966, Connecticut; 1968, U.S. Court of Appeals, Second Circuit. *Education:* Wharton School, University of Pennsylvania (B.S., 1963); University of Pennsylvania (LL.B., 1966). Member, McKean Law Club. Law Clerk to Hon. William Hastie, United States Court of Appeals, Third Circuit, 1966-1967. ***PRACTICE AREAS:*** Civil Litigation. ***Email:*** abrand@sswbgg.com

JOHN A. COLLINS, III, born Boston, Massachusetts, January 30, 1956; admitted to bar, 1981, Connecticut and U.S. District Court, District of Connecticut. *Education:* College of the Holy Cross (A.B., 1978); Case Western Reserve University (J.D., 1981). Member, 1978-1981, and Notes Editor, 1980-1981, Case Western Reserve Journal of International Law. Author: "Self Determination in International Law: The Palestinians," 12 Case Western Reserve Journal of International Law 137, 1981. *Member:* New London County, Connecticut and American Bar Associations; Connecticut Trial Lawyers Association; The Association of Trial Lawyers of America; National Association of

(This Listing Continued)

Criminal Defense Lawyers; Connecticut Association of Criminal Defense Lawyers (Member, Board of Governors, 1988-1996). ***PRACTICE AREAS:*** Personal Injury Law; Criminal Law. ***Email:*** jcollins@sswbgg.com

JEFFREY W. HILL, born New London, Connecticut, December 2, 1955; admitted to bar, 1983, Connecticut and U.S. District Court, District of Connecticut. *Education:* Harvard University (B.A., 1977); University of Connecticut (J.D., 1983). *Member:* New London County (Chairman, Family Law Section), Connecticut and American (Member, Family Law Section) Bar Associations; The Association of Trial Lawyers of America; Raymond Baldwin American Inns of the Court. ***PRACTICE AREAS:*** Family Law; Marital Law. ***Email:*** jhill@sswbgg.com

JAMES P. BERRYMAN, born New York, N.Y., October 22, 1957; admitted to bar, 1983, Connecticut. *Education:* University of Notre Dame (B.A., 1979); Columbus School of Law (J.D., 1982). *Member:* New London, Connecticut (Member, Workers Compensation Section) and American Bar Associations; Connecticut Trial Lawyers Association; The Association of Trial Lawyers of America; National Organization of Social Security Claimants Representatives; National Association of Criminal Defense Lawyers; Connecticut Association of Criminal Defense Lawyers. ***PRACTICE AREAS:*** Workers Compensation Law; Social Security and Disability. ***Email:*** jberryman@sswbgg.com

HARRY E. CALMAR, born Bristol, Connecticut, August 25, 1958; admitted to bar, 1985, Connecticut; 1987, U.S. District Court, District of Connecticut; 1989, U.S. Court of Appeals, Second Circuit, U.S. Court of Appeals for the District of Columbia Circuit; 1994, Mashantucker Pequot Tribal Court. *Education:* Tufts University (B.A., cum laude, 1980); Albany Law School of Union University (J.D., 1984). *Member:* New London County (Co-Chair, Labor and Employment Law Subcommittee), Connecticut and American (Member, Labor and Employment Law Section) Bar Associations; The District of Columbia Bar; Connecticut Trial Lawyers Association. [Capt., U.S. Army Reserves, Medical Service Corps, 1981-1995]. ***PRACTICE AREAS:*** Labor and Employment; Administrative; Municipal; School Law; Civil Rights; Civil Litigation. ***Email:*** hcalmar@sswbgg.com

MATTHEW E. AUGER, born San Diego, California, February 14, 1958; admitted to bar, 1984, Pennsylvania; 1988, Connecticut; 1989, U.S. District Court, District of Connecticut. *Education:* Georgetown University (B.A., cum laude, 1980); State University of New York at Buffalo (J.D., 1984). Pi Sigma Alpha. Recipient, Birzon Award, 1984. Board Certified Civil Trial Lawyer. *Member:* New London County (Past President), Connecticut and American (Member, Litigation Section) Bar Associations; Connecticut Trial Lawyers Association. [CDR., USNR, 1984—.]. ***PRACTICE AREAS:*** Personal Injury; Arbitration; Mediation; Commercial Litigation; Breach of Contract; Federal Tort Claims; Hospital Negligence; Automobile Insurance Defense; Labor and Employment; Psychiatric Negligence; Obstetric Negligence; Medical Negligence; Negligence Defense; Premise Liability; Products Liability. ***Email:*** mauger@sswbgg.com

RAYMOND L. BARIBEAULT, JR., born Norwich, Connecticut, January 21, 1964; admitted to bar, 1989, Connecticut; 1990, U.S. District Court, District of Connecticut; 1991, Rhode Island and U.S. Court of Appeals, Second Circuit. *Education:* University of Connecticut (B.S., magna cum laude, 1986); Vermont Law School (J.D., magna cum laude, 1989). Beta Gamma Sigma; Delta Sigma Pi. Member, Moot Court Board. Recipient, School of Business Finance Award. Editor, Vermont Law Review Author: Note, "Insider Trading: The Current Move Toward Increasing Civil and Criminal Liability for An Ill-Defined Crime and the Need for a Definition," 14 Vt. L. Rev. 79 (1989). Member, Norwich Notary Club. President, Norwich Heritage Discovery Center, Inc., Norwich CT. Vice President, Madonna Place, Norwich, CT. *Member:* New London County (Member, Business Section), Connecticut (Member, Business and Corporate Sections) and American (Member, Business and Corporate Sections and Technology Subcommittee, Norwich, CT) Bar Associations. ***LANGUAGES:*** French. ***PRACTICE AREAS:*** Contracts Law; Corporate Law; Business Law; Commercial Transactions; Bankruptcy. ***Email:*** rlblaw@counsellor.com

ROBERT B. KEVILLE, born Boston, Massachusetts, February 27, 1958; admitted to bar, 1990, Connecticut; 1991, U.S. District Court, District of Connecticut. *Education:* Springfield College (B.S., 1980); University of Connecticut; University of Bridgeport (J.D., with honors, 1990). Phi Delta Phi. Member, University of Bridgeport Law Review, 1989-1990. *Member:* New London County, Connecticut and American Bar Associations; Connecticut Trial Lawyers Association; Association of Trial Lawyers of America. ***PRACTICE AREAS:*** Workers Compensation Law; Personal Injury; Civil Litigation. ***Email:*** rkeville@sswbgg.com

FRANK J. LIBERTY, born Stamford, Connecticut, February 7, 1958; admitted to bar, 1990, Connecticut and New York; 1993, U.S. District Court, Southern and Eastern Districts of New York; 1994, U.S. District Court, District of Connecticut. *Education:* University of Chicago (B.A., 1980); Brooklyn Law School (J.D., cum laude, 1989). *Member:* New London County, Connecticut, New York State and American (Member, Litigation Section) Bar Associations. ***PRACTICE AREAS:*** Intellectual Property; Personal Injury; Civil Trial Law; Commercial Litigation; Business Arbitration; Civil Litigation; NASD Arbitration; ERISA Litigation; Automotive Franchise Dealerships. ***Email:*** fliberty@sswbgg.com

EILEEN C. DUGGAN, born Derby, Connecticut, May 17, 1968; admitted to bar, 1993, Connecticut; 1994, U.S. District Court, District of Connecticut. *Education:* Yale University (B.A., summa cum laude, 1990); University of Virginia (J.D., 1993). Law Clerk, The Honorable Barry R. Schaller, Connecticut Appellate Court. *Member:* New London County, Connecticut and American Bar Associations and National Employment Lawyers Association. ***PRACTICE AREAS:*** Labor and Employment Law; Litigation. ***Email:*** eduggan@sswbgg.com

HINDA K. KIMMEL, born Waterbury, Connecticut, September 16, 1949; admitted to bar, 1994, Connecticut; 1995, U.S. District Court, District of Connecticut, Mashantucket Peguot Tribal Court and Mohegan Tribe Gaming Disputes Court. *Education:* Mills College (B.A., 1971); California State University, San Francisco (M.A., 1973); New England School of Law (J.D., magna cum laude, 1994). Member, New England Law Review, 1992-1994, Case Note Editor, 1993-1994. New England Scholar. Author: "In Re Valerie D.: Prenatal Conduct is and Insufficient Basis to Terminate Parental Rights," 28 New England Law Review 483, 1993. *Member:* New London County, Connecticut (Member, Women in the Law and Labor and Employment Sections and Education Law) and American Bar Associations. ***PRACTICE AREAS:*** Labor and Employment; Civil Rights; Special Education of Handicapped Law. ***Email:*** hkimmel@sswbgg.com

SUSAN MARA PHILLIPS, born Keene, New Hampshire, March 23, 1968; admitted to bar, 1995, Connecticut and Massachusetts. *Education:* Simon's Rock of Bard College (1984-1985); Hampshire College (B.A., 1990); University of Connecticut (J.D., 1994). Connecticut Moot Court Board. Recipient: The Honorable M. Joseph Blumfeld Prize, 1994. Clerk, The Honorable Francis X. Hennessy Connecticut Appellate Court, 1994-1995. ***PRACTICE AREAS:*** Labor and Employment; Municipal; Appellate. ***Email:*** sphillips@sswbgg.com

JEANETTE M. DOSTIE, born Boston, Massachusetts, June 1, 1964; admitted to bar, 1995, Connecticut; 1998, Rhode Island. *Education:* Brown University (B.A., 1986); University of Connecticut (J.D., with honors, 1995). Recipient: American Jurisprudence Awards, Trusts and Estates and Evidence; Little, Brown and Co. Book Awards, Trusts and Estates and Evidence. ***PRACTICE AREAS:*** Medicaid Planning; Wills, Trusts and Probate; Real Estate. ***Email:*** jdostie@sswbgg.com

MARTIN W. SCHOEPFER, born New York, N.Y., December 5, 1948; admitted to bar, 1997, Connecticut. *Education:* Boston University (B.S., 1971; M.Ed., 1976); Quinnipiac College (J.D., 1997). Founding Member and Notes and Comments Editor, Quinnipiac Health Law Journal, 1996-1997. *Member:* New London County, Connecticut and American Bar Associations. ***PRACTICE AREAS:*** Family; Criminal. ***Email:*** mschoepfer@sswbgg.com

ROBERT G. TUKEY, born New London, Connecticut, June 9, 1971; admitted to bar, 1996, Massachusetts; 1997, Connecticut; 1998, Mashantucket Pequot Tribal Court. *Education:* Fairfield University (B.A., 1993); Western New England College (J.D., 1996). *Member:* New London, Connecticut and American Bar Associations; Connecticut Trial Lawyers Association; Association of Trial Lawyers of America; Oliver Ellsworth Inn of Court. ***PRACTICE AREAS:*** Civil Litigation; Personal Injury Law. ***Email:*** rtukey@sswbgg.com

CYNTHIA L. DESMOND, born Stamford, Connecticut, October 16, 1967; admitted to bar, 1993, Massachusetts; 1994, Connecticut; 1996, Mashantucket. *Education:* Boston College (B.A., 1989); Western New England College (J.D., 1993). *Member:* Connecticut Bar Association (Member, Family Law Section). ***PRACTICE AREAS:*** Marital. ***Email:*** cdesmond@sswbgg.com

MICHAEL P. CAREY, born Hartford, Connecticut, October 14, 1955; admitted to bar, 1980, Connecticut; 1981, U.S. District Court, District of Connecticut; Mashantucket Pequot Tribal Court; 1997, Mohegan Gaming Disputes Court. *Education:* University of Rochester (B.A., cum laude, 1977); University of Connecticut (J.D., 1980). Former Member of Faculty, Institute of Public Service, University of Connecticut, 1984-1989. Counsel to and Member of Board of Directors, Catholic Charities, Diocese of Norwich, 1995—; Member, Town of Colchester Economic Development Commission, 1998—. *Member:* New London County and Connecticut (Former Member, Board of Governors and House of Delegates) Bar Associations; Connecticut Trial Lawyers Association. ***PRACTICE AREAS:*** Civil Litigation; Workers Compensation; Zoning and Planning; Land Use; Municipal Law. ***Email:*** mcarey@sswbgg.com

MICHAEL A. BLANCHARD, born Anchorage, Alaska, December 15, 1957; admitted to bar, 1982, Connecticut; 1985, Massachusetts; 1992, Mashantucket Pequot Tribal Court. *Education:* Assumption College (B.A. in Math., 1979); Western New England College (J.D., 1982). *Member:* New London County, Connecticut and Massachusetts Bar Associations; Connecticut Trial Lawyers Association; The Association of Trial Lawyers of America. ***PRACTICE AREAS:*** Family Law; Criminal Law; Personal Injury. ***Email:*** mblanchard@sswbgg.com

(This Listing Continued)

(This Listing Continued)

SUISMAN, SHAPIRO, WOOL, BRENNAN, GRAY & GREENBERG, P.C., New London—Continued

SANTA MENDOZA, born Bethlehem, Pennsylvania, January 13, 1957; admitted to bar, 1984, Connecticut. *Education:* Fairfield University (B.A., 1978); University of Connecticut School of Law (J.D., 1984). Member, Board of Tax Review, West Hartford Board of Assessment Appeals, 1994-2000. *Member Connecticut Hispanic Bar Association (Member, Board of Directors, 1999-2001).* ***PRACTICE AREAS:*** Taxation; Business Transactions; Commercial Transactions; Real Estate. ***Email:*** smendoza@sswbgg.com

OF COUNSEL

CHARLES SUISMAN, born Hartford, Connecticut, November 7, 1906; admitted to bar, 1930, Connecticut; 1936, U.S. District Court, District of Connecticut; 1964, U.S. Court of Appeals, Second Circuit. *Education:* Boston University (B.B.A., 1927); Yale University (LL.B., 1930). *Member:* New London County (President, 1963-1964), Connecticut (Chairman, Committee on Commercial Law and Bankruptcy, 1955) and American Bar Associations.

MARILYNNE GRABOYS WOOL, born Fall River, Massachusetts, July 17, 1926; admitted to bar, 1950, Rhode Island; 1951, U.S. District Court, District of Rhode Island; 1956, Connecticut. *Education:* St. Lawrence University (LL.B., 1948). Attorney Advisor, Officer of Solicitor, U.S. Department of Agriculture, Washington, D.C., 1954-1955. *Member:* Connecticut and Rhode Island Bar Associations.

LOUIS PATRICK GRAY, III, born July 18, 1916; admitted to bar, 1949, District of Columbia; 1958, Connecticut; 1970, U.S. Supreme Court; 1975, U.S. District Court, District of Connecticut and U.S. Court of Appeals, Second Circuit. *Education:* United States Naval Academy (B.S., 1940); George Washington University (J.D., with honors, 1949). Order of the Coif. Member, George Washington Law Review, 1948-1949. *Member:* New London County and Connecticut Bar Associations. [Capt., USN (Ret)]

RICHARD A. SCHATZ, born Hartford, Connecticut, October 24, 1929; admitted to bar, 1954, Connecticut and U.S. Court of Military Appeals; 1962, U.S. District Court, District of Connecticut. *Education:* Amherst College (B.A., 1951); Yale University (J.D., 1954). Member, Moot Court, 1952-1954. Assistant State's Attorney: Hartford, County, 1965-1982; New London County, 1983-1986. Director, Mt. Sinai Hospital, Hartford, Connecticut, 1970-1975. *Member:* Connecticut and American Bar Associations; National District Attorneys Association; American Board of Trial Advocates (Advocate). [1st Lt., U.S. Army, JAGC, 1954-1957]. ***LANGUAGES:*** French. ***PRACTICE AREAS:*** Personal Injury; Insurance Defense; Civil Litigation; Criminal.

REPRESENTATIVE CLIENTS: First New London Savings & Loan Assn., Inc.; Mitchell College; The Connecticut Bricklayer's International Pension Fund; Town of Groton; Town of Ledyard; Town of Stonington; Town of North Stonington, Planning and Zoning Commission; Volvo City, Milford, Inc.; New London Security Federal Credit Union; New London Flying Service, Inc.; Groton Shoppers Mart; Reeves Air, Inc.; Boats, Inc.; Sharp Electric Co., Inc.; Grover Insurance Agency; Sacred Heart Church; Lyman Allyn Art Museum, Inc.; Vines Restaurant; Spicer Gas Co.; USA Fuel; Blackburn Janitorial, L.L.C.; Yardney Technical Products, Inc.; The New London Day; KofKoff Egg Farm, L.L.C.
LOCAL COUNSEL FOR: Suisse Chalet; Holiday Inns, Inc.; Insurance Company of America; Kemper Insurance Co.; Pizza Hut; AFL-CIO; Local Union No. l2, Connecticut, of the International Union of Bricklayers and Allied Craftsmen; NICO Construction Co., Inc.; Pearson Yachts; Advest Bank; Scottsdale Insurance Co.; State Street Boston Leasing Co.; Hellogramme America, Inc.
SPECIAL LABOR COUNSEL FOR: City of New London; Town of Lyme; Town of Montville; Town of Stonington; Town of Waterford.

TOBIN, CARBERRY, O'MALLEY, RILEY & SELINGER, P.C.

Established in 1963

43 BROAD STREET
P.O. BOX 58
NEW LONDON, CONNECTICUT 06320
Telephone: 860-447-0335
Fax: 860-442-3469
Email: attorneys@tcors.com
URL: http://www.tcors.com

Hartford, Connecticut Office: 3rd Floor, 330 Main Street, 06106. Telephone: 860-541-6438. Fax: 860-541-6484.

General Civil and Criminal Practice, Trials and Appeals in all Courts, Administrative Law, Banking and Commercial Law, Commercial Real Estate, Contract Law, Corporate Law, Business Law, Employment Law, Government Relations, Public Finance, Public Utility Law, Health Care Law, Land Use Law, Personal Injury, Product Liability, Estate Planning and Probate, Elder Law, Immigration, Federal, State and Local Tax Law.

ROBERT D. TOBIN, born Boston, Massachusetts, September 15, 1942; admitted to bar, 1968, Connecticut; 1969, U.S. District Court, District of Connecticut and U.S. Court of Appeals, Second Circuit. *Education:* Boston College (B.A., cum laude, 1964; J.D., 1968). Author: "Teacher Negotiations Into the Seventies," 12 William & Mary Law Quarterly 711, 1971; "Section 9-103 and the Interstate Movement of Goods," Boston College Industrial and Commercial Law Review, Vol. IX, p. 72, 1968. Staff, Boston College Industrial and Commercial Law Review, 1967-1968. Lecturer, "Preparation for Trial: From Opening the File Through Starting the Case," Connecticut Bar Association Seminar on Estate Practice, 1983. Member, Connecticut General Assembly, 37th District, 1975-1976. State of Connecticut Trial Referee, 1985—. *Member:* New London County (Member, Board of Directors, 1984-1985), The Connecticut and American Bar Associations; Connecticut Trial Lawyers Association; The Association of Trial Lawyers of America. ***REPORTED CASES:*** Simond v. Board of Education, 473 F.2d 988 (2d Cir. 1973); Sanderson v. Banigai, 690 F.2d 337 (2d Cir. 1982); Tinnerello and Sons, Inc. v. Town of Stonington, 141 F.3d 46 (2d Cir. 1998); In re: Election for Second Congressional Districts, 231 Conn. 602 (1994); Washington Trust Co. v. Smith, 42 Conn. App. 300 (1666), rev'd 241 Conn. 734 (1997). ***PRACTICE AREAS:*** Commercial Law; Litigation; Real Estate; Zoning; Administrative Law. ***Email:*** rdtobin@tcors.com

GLENN T. CARBERRY, born Norwich, Connecticut, January 29, 1955; admitted to bar, 1979, District of Columbia; 1982, Connecticut. *Education:* Gettysburg College (B.A., summa cum laude, 1976); University of Pennsylvania (J.D., 1979). Phi Beta Kappa. Comment Editor, University of Pennsylvania Law Review, 1978-1979. Recipient: Citizen of the Year, Eastern Connecticut Chamber of Commerce, 1995; Distinguished Service Award, Chamber of Commerce of Southeastern Connecticut, 1996. Author: "Laetrile: Statutory and Constitutional Limitations on the Regulation of Ineffective Drugs," 127 University of Pennsylvania Law Review 233, 1978; "Ex Parte Communications in Off-the-Record Administrative Proceedings: A Proposed Limitation on Judicial Innovation," 1980 Duke Law Journal, 130. Co-Author: "Government Contract Bidders Should be Permitted to Extend Short Bid Acceptance Periods," Public Contract Law Journal, Volume 13, No. 2, February, 1983; "Waiver of the Government's Right to Terminate for Default in Defense Contracts," Public Contract Law Journal, Vol. 17, No. 2, June 1988. Associate, Hogan & Hartson, Washington, D.C., 1979-1982. Candidate, United States House of Representatives, 1988 and 1992. *Member:* New London County, Connecticut and American Bar Associations. ***SPECIAL AGENCIES:*** Connecticut Development Authority; Connecticut Department of Public Utility Control. ***PRACTICE AREAS:*** Banking Law; Corporate Law; Land Use; Administrative Law; Telecommunications Law. ***Email:*** gtcarberry@tcors.com

F. JEROME O'MALLEY, born Scranton, Pennsylvania, February 28, 1952; admitted to bar, 1978, Connecticut and U.S. District Court, District of Connecticut; 1983, U.S. Court of Appeals, Second Circuit. *Education:* College of the Holy Cross (B.A., cum laude, 1975); University of Connecticut (J.D., 1978). Phi Beta Kappa. Assistant States Attorney, Chief States Attorney's Office, 1978-1983. Secretary, Connecticut Association of Prosecutors, 1980-1983. Author: "FMC Corp v. Holliday: A Health Insurer's Right to Reimbursement Revisited," CTLA Forum, Vol. 9 No. 2, April, 1991; "Health Care in the U.S.: A System In Crisis," CTLA Forum, Vol. 10 No. 6, December, 1992. Member, Board of Directors: American Heart Association, 1986-1988; Mystic Marine Life Aquarium, 1986-1992; Mystic Community Center, 1994-2001. Member, Stonington Charter Commission, 1987-1988. *Member:* New London County, Connecticut and American Bar Associations; Connecticut Trial Lawyers Association; The Association of Trial Lawyers of America. ***REPORTED CASES:*** Boline v. Albert 23 Conn. App. 688 (1991); Middlesex Hospital v. North Haven, 206 Conn. (1988); State v. Ferguson, 185 Conn. 904 (1981); Thomsen v. AMI, Inc., 51 Conn. App. 201 (1998). ***PRACTICE AREAS:*** Personal Injury Law; Criminal Defense Law; Civil Litigation; Workers Compensation; Municipal Labor Law. ***Email:*** fjomalley@tcors.com

THOMAS J. RILEY, born New York, N.Y., April 3, 1953; admitted to bar, 1977, Connecticut; 1979, U.S. District Court, District of Connecticut; 1980, District of Columbia and U.S. District Court for the District of Columbia; 1982, U.S. Court of Federal Claims, U.S. Court of Appeals, Second Circuit and U.S. Court of Appeals for the Federal Circuit; 1988, U.S. District Court, Southern District of New York; 1998, U.S. Supreme Court. *Education:* College of the Holy Cross (B.A., cum laude, 1974); University of Connecticut (J.D., with high honors, 1977). Recipient: Cornelius J. Wickersham Award for Constitutional Law; American Jurisprudence Book Awards in Contracts and Constitutional Law. Member, University of Connecticut Law Review, 1975-1976. Trial Attorney, U.S. Department of Justice, Land and Natural Resources Division, Washington, D.C., 1977-1982. Assistant U.S. Attorney, District of Connecticut, 1982-1986. *Member:* Connecticut and American Bar Associations; Connecticut Trial Lawyers Association; The Association of Trial Lawyers of America; National Employment Lawyers Association; Connecticut Employment Lawyers Association. ***REPORTED CASES:*** Branch v. Occhionero, 239 Conn. 199 (1996); In re: Election for Second Congressional District, 231 Conn 602, (1994); Water Street Assoc. Ltd. Prtn. v. Innopak Plastics, 230 Conn. 764, (1994); Burge v. Stonington, 219 Conn 581, (1991); Middlesex Hospital v. Hamden, 33 Conn App 247, (1993), cert denied, 228 Conn 922, (1994); Sal Tinnerello & Sons, Inc. v. Town of Stonington, 141 F3d 46 (2nd Cir), cert. denied 525 US 923

(This Listing Continued)

(1998); Poulos v. Pfizer, Inc., 244 Conn 598 (1998). ***PRACTICE AREAS:*** Litigation; Employment Law; Waterfront Development. ***Email:*** tjriley@tcors.com

JOSEPH J. SELINGER, JR., born Rockville Center, New York, March 10, 1952; admitted to bar, 1978, Connecticut. *Education:* Amherst College (B.A., 1974); University of Connecticut (J.D., 1978). Member, National Moot Court Team, 1978. Author: "The Use of Real Estate Rehabilitation Credits by Limited Partnership," The Journal of Real Estate Taxation, Winter, 1983; "TEFRA: High Bracket Tax Payers in the Wake of the AMT," Connecticut Law Tribune, October, 1982. Co-Author: "How to Negotiate PCTV Agreements," Private Cable, March/April 1984; "Napoletano vs. Cigna: An Evolving Standard of MCO Legal Compliance?" Connecticut Medicine, The Journal of the Connecticut State Medical Society, 1996. Lecturer: "Evaluating Client Suitability for a Real Estate Limited Partnership Investment," Connecticut Bar Association Annual Tax Planning Institute, 1985; "Tax Treatment of Vacation Homes," National Institute of Real Estate Taxation, Washington, D.C., 1989; "Annual Survey of Connecticut Law: Current Developments in Business and Banking," Section on Corporations and Other Business Organizations, Connecticut Bar Association, 1991; "Risks and Benefits of Medicaid Managed Care to Long Term Care Providers," Health Care Financial Management Association, 1995; "Legal Issues Update Medicaid Managed Care," Health Care Financial Management Association and Connecticut Health Lawyers Association, 1996; "Choice of Business Entity in Connecticut: How to do it Right," National Business Institute, 1998. State of Connecticut Small Claims Court Commissioner, 1989-1995. Member, State of Connecticut Law Review Commission, 1997. *Member:* Connecticut and American Bar Associations; American Bankruptcy Institute; National Association of Health Care Lawyers; National Association of Bond Lawyers. ***PRACTICE AREAS:*** Corporate Finance; Public Finance; Health Care Law. ***Email:*** jjselinger@tcors.com

KATHLEEN A. McNAMARA, born New Haven, Connecticut, October 30, 1962; admitted to bar, 1988, Connecticut; 1989, U.S. District Court, District of Connecticut. *Education:* Boston College (B.A., Honors Program, 1985); Syracuse University (J.D., 1988). Omicron Delta Epsilon; Economics Honor Society. Member, Board of Directors: The Retired Senior Volunteer Program of Southern New London County, 1990-1996; Contact of Southeastern Connecticut, 1991-1996. Lecturer: "Connecticut Elder Law: Taking Control of the Planning Process," National Business Institute, 1994; "A Practical Guide to Estate Administration in Ct.," National Business Institute, 1994; "Basic Probate Procedures and Practice in Ct.," National Business Institute, 1995-1997. Lecturer and Contributing Author: "Peoples Law School," Connecticut Trial Lawyers Association, 1993—. Member, Town of Waterford Senior Citizen's Commission, 1997—. Corporate Secretary and Member, Board of Directors, U.S.S. Connecticut Commissioning Committee, 1997—. *Member:* New London, Connecticut (Member, Estates and Probate Committee on Legal Problems of the Elderly, 1991—) and American Bar Associations; National Academy of Elder Law Attorneys. ***PRACTICE AREAS:*** Estate Planning Law; Probate; Administrative Law; Liquor Licensing; Real Estate Law; Elder Law. ***Email:*** kamcnamara@tcors.com

RITA PROVATAS, born New London, Connecticut, May 30, 1961; admitted to bar, 1988, New York and Virginia; 1989, U.S. Court of Appeals, Fourth Circuit, U.S. District Court, Eastern District of Virginia and District of Connecticut, and U.S. Bankruptcy Court; 1990, Connecticut. *Education:* Bates College (B.A., 1983); University of Bridgeport (J.D., 1986). Writer, 1984-1985 and Executive Managing Editor, 1985-1986, University of Bridgeport Law Review. Recipient, American Jurisprudence Award for Excellence in Domestic Relations. Member, Who's Who in American Universities, 1986. Author: "In Re McLinn: De Novo Review of District Court Decisions," University of Bridgeport School of Law Review, Vol. 1, 1986. Lecturer: "Peoples Law School," Connecticut Trial Lawyers Association, 1998—. Member: Town of Waterford Board of Education; Women's Network of Southeastern Connecticut; Democrat Town Committee; Waterford Rotary Club (Board Member, 2001). *Member:* New London County, Connecticut, New York State, Virginia and American (Member, Section on Litigation) Bar Associations; The Association of Trial Lawyers of America; Connecticut Trial Lawyers Association; American Immigration Lawyer's Association. ***LANGUAGES:*** Greek. ***REPORTED CASES:*** In re Damach, Inc., 235 B.R. 727 (Bkrtcy.D.Conn. 1999); Washington Trust Co. v. Marie D. Smith, 241 Conn. 734 (1997); Drabik v. East Lyne, 234 Conn. 390 (1995); Poulos v. Pfizer, 244 Conn. 598 (1996). ***PRACTICE AREAS:*** Civil Litigation; Immigration Law; Negligence; Personal Injury. ***Email:*** rprovatas@tcors.com

---

ROBERT R. STATCHEN, born Burlington, Connecticut, June 14, 1968; admitted to bar, 1993, Illinois; 1994, Connecticut; 1998, U.S. District Court, District of Connecticut. *Education:* Clark University (B.A., with honors, 1990); Chicago-Kent College of Law (J.D., 1993); University of Connecticut (M.B.A., 2001). *Member:* Connecticut and American Bar Associations; National Association of Bond Lawyers. [JAG, U.S. Air Force, 1993-1997; Major, Connecticut Air National Guard, 1997—]. ***PRACTICE AREAS:*** Corporate Law; Business Law; Public Finance; Federal Taxation; State Taxation; Local Taxation; Intellectual Property. ***Email:*** rstatchen@tcors.com

(This Listing Continued)

REPRESENTATIVE CLIENTS: Adelphi Communications Corporation; Autotote Corp; Boston Capital Housing, LLC; Connecticut Resources Recovery Authority; Corcoran Jennison Company; Cross Sound Ferry Service, Inc.; Fleet Bank; INNCOM International, Inc.; JY Sailboats, Inc.; Levine Distributing Company, Inc.; Meristar Investment Partners, L.P.; New London Development Corporation; Norwich Navigators; Poqonnock Bridge Fire District; Rhythms Net Connections, Inc.; Southeast Area Regional Economic Development Corporation; Westport Country Playhouse; Wyman Gordon Investment Castings, Inc.
SPECIAL COUNSEL FOR: Bridgeport Hospital; City of New London; Day Kimball Hospital; Gaylord Hospital; Griffin Hospital; Hartford Hospital; Lawrence & Memorial Hospital; Manchester Memorial Hospital; Middlesex Hospital; New Britain General Hospital; Norwalk Hospital; St. Joseph's Hospital; Stamford Hospital; Town of Killingly; Veterans Memorial Medical Center; Waterbury Hospital; Windham Community Memorial Hospital; Yale-New Haven Hospital.
REFERENCES: Autotote Corporation, New York, NY; Fleet Bank, New London, Connecticut.

WALLER, SMITH & PALMER, P.C.

Established in 1885

52 EUGENE O'NEILL DRIVE

P.O. BOX 88

NEW LONDON, CONNECTICUT 06320

Telephone: 860-442-0367
Telecopier: 860-447-9915
Email: wspmain@snet.net
URL: http://www.snetyp.com/wallersmithpalmer

Old Lyme Office: 103 Halls Road. Telephone: 860-434-8063. Telecopier: 860-434-9452. Email: wspol@snet.net

General Practice. Corporation, Commercial, Estate Planning, Probate, Real Estate, Personal Injury, Municipal, Banking and Trials in all Courts.

FIRM PROFILE: Waller, Smith & Palmer, P.C. is a Connecticut firm engaged in a general law practice. The firm was formed in 1885 by Thomas W. Waller and his son, Tracy Waller. Thomas Waller had previously served as Governor of Connecticut from 1883-1885 and as United States Counsel General to London. Since its founding the firm has continuously maintained an office in New London, Connecticut.

Attorneys from the firm appear in all Connecticut courts, including probate courts, and all federal courts.

The attorneys at Waller, Smith & Palmer, P.C. are members of the New London County Bar Association, Connecticut Bar Association and American Bar Association. They maintain active memberships in professional associations specializing in particular areas of the law such as the American College of Trust and Estate Counsel, the Estate and Tax Planning Council of Eastern Connecticut, The American Association of Trial Lawyers, the Connecticut Association of Municipal Attorneys and the American Arbitration Association.

Attorneys of the firm attend professional seminars to continue their legal education.

Waller & Waller	(1885-1903)
Waller, Waller, Avery & Gallup	(1904-1934)
Waller, Gallup & Anderson	(1935-1942)
Waller, Troland, Anderson & Smith	(1943-1945)
Waller, Anderson & Smith	(1946-1952)
Waller, Smith & Palmer	(1953-1979)

TRACY WALLER (1862-1947).

J. RODNEY SMITH (1906-1979).

BIRDSEY G. PALMER (Retired).

WILLIAM W. MINER, born New London, Connecticut, April 16, 1930; admitted to bar, 1957, Connecticut. *Education:* Phillips Academy; Yale University (B.A., 1952); University of Virginia (LL.B., 1957). Associate, Shearman & Sterling & Wright, New York, N.Y., 1957-1958. Trustee: Lawrence and Memorial Hospitals, 1968-1998; Connecticut College, 1977-1988; Mystic Seaport Museum, 1986—. *Member:* New London County, Connecticut and American Bar Associations. Fellow, American College of Trust and Estate Counsel. ***PRACTICE AREAS:*** Estate Planning; Estate Administration; Real Estate.

ROBERT P. ANDERSON, JR., born New London, Connecticut, November 15, 1935; admitted to bar, 1960, Connecticut. *Education:* Phillips Academy; Yale University (B.A., 1957; LL.B., 1960). Trustee: Charles B. Allyn Foundation, Inc., 1964—; Connecticut Early Music Society, Inc., 1982—; Chairman of the Board, Waterford Country School, Inc., 1976—; and Treasurer, Mystic River Homes, Inc., 1976—. Arbitrator, American Arbitration Association. *Member:* New London County, Connecticut and American Bar Associations. ***PRACTICE AREAS:*** Trust Law; Estate Planning; Estate Administration; Real Estate.

(This Listing Continued)

WALLER, SMITH & PALMER, P.C., New London—Continued

ROBERT W. MARRION, born Winthrop, Massachusetts, February 24, 1931; admitted to bar, 1958, Connecticut; 1966, U.S. District Court, District of Connecticut. *Education:* College of the Holy Cross (A.B., 1952); Harvard University (LL.B., 1958). Town Counsel, Town of East Lyme, 1965-1990, 1994-1998. Member, Connecticut Bar Examining Committee, 1974-1996. Chairman: Board of Trustees, Mitchell College, 1976-1988; Pequot Community Foundation, 1981-1987. Trial Referee, Superior Court, 1984-1987. *Member:* New London County and Connecticut Bar Associations. Fellow, American College of Trust and Estate Counsel. ***PRACTICE AREAS:*** Corporate Law; Business Organization; Commercial Real Estate; Estate Planning; Estate Administration. ***Email:*** rwmwsp@snet.net

HUGHES GRIFFIS, born New York, N.Y., October 17, 1944; admitted to bar, 1972, Connecticut. *Education:* Choate School; Yale University (B.A., 1967); Cornell University (J.D., 1972). Probate Judge, District of Lyme, 1979-1983. Former Faculty Member, Real Estate Law, Division of Continuing Education, University of Connecticut. General Counsel and Lecturer, Eastern Connecticut Association of Realtors. Chairman, Bank Bar Committee of Southeastern Connecticut Bar Association. Trustee, Griffis Art Center. Member, American Banking Association (Banking Law). President, Thames Club, 1987. Former Chairman: Lyme Elderly Housing, Inc.; Lyme Public Library, Inc. Former Trustee, Lawrence and Memorial Hospitals. *Member:* New London County and Connecticut Bar Associations. ***PRACTICE AREAS:*** Real Estate; Banking Law; Commercial Law.

EDWARD B. O'CONNELL, born New York, N.Y., October 18, 1943; admitted to bar, 1968, Connecticut, 1969, U.S. District Court, District of Connecticut. *Education:* College of the Holy Cross (B.S., 1965); University of Connecticut (J.D., 1968). Vice Chairman, Connecticut Legal Services, Inc., 1978-1981. Superior Court Attorney Trial Referee, 1986-1989. Judge, Mashantucket Pequot Tribal Court, 1992—. Arbitrator, American Arbitration Association; Town Attorney General, Town of East Lyme; Land Use Counsel, Town of Lebanon. *Member:* New London County (President, 1989-1990), Connecticut and American Bar Associations. ***PRACTICE AREAS:*** Commercial Transactions; Commercial Litigation; Real Estate Litigation; Municipal Law; Zoning, Planning and Land Use Law.

FREDERICK B. GAHAGAN, born New York, N.Y., July 10, 1952; admitted to bar, 1980, Connecticut; 1982, U.S. District Court, District of Connecticut. *Education:* Lenox School; Kenyon College (B.A., 1974); University of Connecticut (J.D., 1980). Trustee, 1981-1985 and Vice President, 1982-1985, Lyme Land Conservation Trust. Member, 1982-1993 and Chairman, 1991-1993, Regional District #18 Board of Education. Member, Tidelands Committee of the Nature Conservancy; Director, Southeastern Connecticut Committee on Foreign Relations. *Member:* New London County, Connecticut and American Bar Associations. ***PRACTICE AREAS:*** Corporate Law; Business Organization; Land Conservation; Zoning, Planning and Land Use; Real Estate; Charitable Organizations Law.

TRACY M. COLLINS, born New Rochelle, New York, August 25, 1960; admitted to bar, 1987, Massachusetts; 1988, Connecticut; 1989, U.S. District Court, District of Connecticut. *Education:* Stonehill College (B.A., cum laude, 1982); New England School of Law (J.D., with honors, 1986). *Member:* Boston, New London County, Connecticut, Massachusetts and American Bar Associations; Connecticut Trial Lawyers Association. ***PRACTICE AREAS:*** Personal Injury; Commercial Litigation; Real Estate Litigation; Family Law; Litigation.

PHILIP M. JOHNSTONE, born Sharon, Connecticut, March 24, 1961; admitted to bar, 1986, Massachusetts; 1987, Connecticut; 1988, U.S. District Court, District of Connecticut; 1998, Rhode Island. *Education:* Duke University (B.A., magna cum laude, 1983); University of Pennsylvania (J.D., 1986). Co-Author, "Waiver of the Government's Rights to Terminate for Default in Government Defense Contracts," Public Contract Law Journal, Vol. 17, No. 2, June 1988. Director, J Boats, Inc., 1987—; Trustee, Denison Pequotsepas Nature Center, 1998—. *Member:* New London County, Connecticut, Massachusetts, Rhode Island and American Bar Associations. ***PRACTICE AREAS:*** Estate Planning; Probate; Real Estate; Corporate Law; Commercial Transactions.

DAVID P. CONDON, born New London, Connecticut, December 31, 1963; admitted to bar, 1991, Connecticut; 1992, U.S. District Court, District of Connecticut. *Education:* University of Connecticut (B.A., 1988; J.D., with high honors, 1991). Second Prize (Connecticut), Nathan Burkam Memorial Competition. Law Clerk, Judges of the Superior Court, State of Connecticut, 1991-1992. Chairman, Court Visitation Program, G.A. 21, 1994—. Trustee, James P. and Mary E. Shea Perpetual Trust, 1998—. Trustee, New London Public Library, 1999—. *Member:* New London County, Connecticut and American Bar Associations; Connecticut Trial Lawyers Association; The Association of Trial Lawyers of America. ***PRACTICE AREAS:*** Litigation; Commercial Litigation; Real Estate Litigation; Municipal Law; Family Law; Personal Injury.

VALERIE ANN VOTTO, born New Haven, Connecticut, August 7, 1961; admitted to bar, 1987, Connecticut and New York; 1991, U.S. District Court,

(This Listing Continued)

District of Connecticut. *Education:* Lehigh University (B.A., cum laude, 1983); Catholic University of America (J.D., 1986). Association of Realtors; Connecticut Association of Realtors Agency Law Work Group, 1998 —; Connecticut Law Revision Commission: Mortgage Study Committee 1997-1998; Certified Relocation Professional 1991-1997; Lecturer, Eastern Connecticut Association of Realtors; Graduate Realtors Institute; Three Rivers Community College; Norwalk Community College. Assistant Town Attorney, Town of Westport, 1987-1989. Loss Mitigation Task Force 1996 —. *Member:* New London County, Middlesex County, Connecticut (Member: Real Property, Probate and Trust Law Section; Real Property Executive Committee; Affordable Housing Committee) and American Bar Associations; Connecticut Mortgage Bankers Association (Member: Fair Housing Committee; Loss Mitigation Committee). ***PRACTICE AREAS:*** Real Estate; Land Use Law; Municipal Law.

CHARLES C. ANDERSON, born New London, Connecticut, May 30, 1964; admitted to bar, 1992, Connecticut; 1994, U.S. District Court, District of Connecticut. *Education:* The Williams School; Oberlin College (B.A., 1987); University of Connecticut (J.D., 1991). Trustee: Science Center of Eastern Connecticut, 1997—; Secretary 1999 —. *Member:* Connecticut Bar Association. ***PRACTICE AREAS:*** Estate Planning; Real Estate; Probate.

JAMES F. SPALLONE, born New Haven, Connecticut, March 3, 1965; admitted to bar, 1992, Connecticut; 1994, U.S. District Court, District of Connecticut; 1996, U.S. Court of Appeals, Second Circuit; 1998, Rhode Island. *Education:* Williams College (B.A., 1987); University of Connecticut (J.D., 1992). Member, 1990-1992 and Associate Editor, 1991-1992, Connecticut Journal of International Law. Law Clerk to the Hon. William J. Lavery, Connecticut Appellate Court, 1992-1993. Chairman, Deep River Democratic Town Committee, 1996-1999. *Member:* New Haven County, Middlesex County, Connecticut, Rhode Island and American Bar Associations. ***PRACTICE AREAS:*** Civil Litigation; Municipal Law; Criminal Law; Appellate Practice.

ELISA VALENTIN, born New Haven, Connecticut, April 15, 1971; admitted to bar, 1998, Connecticut. *Education:* Bryant College (B.S., 1993); University of Connecticut (J.D., 1998). Vice Justice, Phi Alpha Delta Law Fraternity, 1996-1997. *Member:* New London County and Connecticut Bar Associations. ***LANGUAGES:*** Spanish. ***PRACTICE AREAS:*** Real Estate; Civil Litigation.

GENERAL COUNSEL FOR: Town of East Lyme.
COUNSEL FOR: Citizens Bank of Connecticut; Soneco/Northeastern, Inc.; The Nature Conservancy; Fleet Bank.
LOCAL COUNSEL FOR: McCue Mortgage Co.; Citicorp Mortgage; U.S. Department of Housing and Urban Development.

ALLINGHAM & SPILLANE

11 SOUTH MAIN STREET
NEW MILFORD, CONNECTICUT 06776
Telephone: 860-350-5454
Fax: 860-350-5457

Criminal Litigation, Personal Injury, Workers Compensation, Real Estate, Civil Litigation.

MEMBERS OF THE FIRM

THOMAS J. ALLINGHAM, born Bridgeport, Connecticut, November 15, 1965; admitted to bar, 1991, Connecticut; 1992, U.S. District Court, District of Connecticut. *Education:* Boston University (B.S./B.A., 1987); University of Bridgeport (J.D., 1991). *Member:* New Milford (Vice President, 2000; Secretary, 1998—), Connecticut and American Bar Associations; Connecticut Trial Lawyers Association; Connecticut Criminal Defense Lawyers Association. ***PRACTICE AREAS:*** Criminal Litigation; Personal Injury Litigation; Civil Litigation; Workers Compensation Law; Real Estate. ***Email:*** tallingham@allinghamlegal.com

PHILIP F. SPILLANE, born Hartford, Connecticut, February 6, 1952; admitted to bar, 1978, Connecticut; 1979, U.S. District Court, District of Connecticut; 1980, U.S. District Court, Southern District of New York. *Education:* University of Connecticut (B.A., 1975); Western New England College School of Law (J.D., cum laude, 1978). Editor, Western New England Law Review, 1977-1978. Author: "The Inventory Search: The Aftermath of South Dakota v. Opperman," 1 Western New England Law Review 101, 1978. *Member:* New Milford (Vice President, 1987-1988; President, 1988-1989), Litchfield County, Connecticut and American (Member, Litigation Section) Bar Associations; Connecticut Trial Lawyers Association; The Association of Trial Lawyers of America. ***PRACTICE AREAS:*** Personal Injury Law; Workers Compensation Law.

BAKER LAW FIRM, P.C.

BAKER FIELDS
4 MINE HILL ROAD
NEW MILFORD, CONNECTICUT 06776
Telephone: 860-354-9100
Email: Fred@Baker-Law.com
URL: http://www.lawyers.com/blaw

Danbury Office: 24 Delay Street. Telephone: 203-792-8765. Fax: 203-791-1892.

Taxation, Estate Planning, Probate, Business and Corporate, Real Estate.

FIRM PROFILE: Baker Law Firm is dedicated to providing companies, entrepreneurs and high net worth individuals with sophisticated and timely business and legal advice, including estate and financial planning, corporate and real property transactions and related services.

(For Complete Biographical data on all personnel, See Professional Biographies at Danbury, Connecticut)

LAW OFFICES OF DAVID F. BENNETT

NEW MILFORD, CONNECTICUT

(See Danbury)

Civil Litigation, Personal Injury, Wrongful Death, Commercial, Real Estate, Trusts and Estates Law. Aviation.

LAW OFFICE OF CECILIA BUCK-TAYLOR, P.C.

Established in 1994
6 MAIN STREET
P.O. BOX 1121
NEW MILFORD, CONNECTICUT 06776
Telephone: 860-355-9191
Fax: 860-355-3061

Family Law, Divorce, Adoption, Guardianship, Probate, Estates & Wills, Juvenile Law, Criminal Law, Real Estate.

CECILIA BUCK-TAYLOR, born Brooklyn, New York, 1953; admitted to bar, 1991, Connecticut; 1992, U.S. District Court, District of Connecticut. *Education:* State University of New York at Albany (B.A., cum laude, 1985); Fordham University (J.D., 1991). New Milford Board of Education, elected 1999—. Local Grievance Panel of Danbury Superior Court, 1998-2004. Family Masters at Litchfield Superior Court, 1995—. Special Public Defender in Danbury and Litchfield Superior Courts, 1994—. *Member:* New Milford (President, 1999-2001), Danbury, Litchfield County and Connecticut Bar Associations; National Association of Counsel for Children; Connecticut Criminal Defense Lawyers Association.

CRAMER & ANDERSON LLP

51 MAIN STREET
NEW MILFORD, CONNECTICUT 06776
Telephone: 860-355-2631
Fax: 860-355-9460
Email: newmilford@crameranderson.com
URL: http://www.cramer-anderson.com

Danbury, Connecticut Office: 68 North Street. Telephone: 203-790-7747. Email: danbury@crameranderson.com
Litchfield, Connecticut Office: 46 West Street. P.O. Box 278. Telephone: 860-567-8718. Email: litchfield@cramer-anderson.com
Kent, Connecticut Office: Kent Green, P.O. Box 333. Telephone: 860-927-3568. Email: gnelson@cramer-anderson.com
Washington Depot, Connecticut Office: 2 Green Hill Road, P.O. Box 321. Telephone: 860-868-0527. Email: wfairbairn@cramer-anderson.com

General Practice. Probate, Estate Planning, Taxation, Municipal, Family, Real Estate, Negligence and Bankruptcy Law. Civil and Criminal Trials. Planning and Zoning, Corporate, Banking, Securities.

FIRM PROFILE: Cramer & Anderson, founded over one-hundred years ago, is a firm of diversely qualified attorneys that offers a wide range of sophisticated legal services to individual and business clients. In the past decade, Cramer & Anderson has grown to become the largest law firm in Litchfield County, with offices in Kent, Litchfield, New Milford and Washington, as well as an office in Danbury, Fairfield County. Listed in Martindale-Hubbell's Bar Register of Preeminent Lawyers, Cramer & Anderson's principal areas of practice include: general business, corporate and commercial law; estate planning, trusts, probate administration and elder law; litigation in all courts, ranging from commercial litigation to personal injury and family law; planning and zoning, residential and commercial real estate law. Our attorneys regularly appear in Connecticut's Superior and Appellate Courts, as well as in the Federal District Court, Second Circuit Court of Appeals, and bankruptcy courts. The firm has expanded into new areas of the law as its client base has diversified. Cramer & Anderson takes pride in its long tradition of commitment by our attorneys to professional excellence, and to public service with community, charitable and civic organizations. Using the resources of our experienced attorneys, paralegals and staff, together with our advanced technological resources, we are committed to serving our clients personally and professionally.

MEMBERS OF FIRM

DAVID CRAMER (1902-1981).

RANDALL J. BREECKNER, born Yonkers, New York, January 31, 1948; admitted to bar, 1973, Connecticut, U.S. District Court, District of Connecticut and U.S. Court of Appeals, Second Circuit. *Education:* University of Rochester (B.A., 1970); University of Connecticut (J.D., 1973). Special Public Defender, Superior Court, 1973—. Court Advocate, Juvenile Division, Superior Court, 1982. Family Relations Masters Program, Superior Court, 1991—. Small Claims Hearing Commissioner, 1983-1988. Superior Court Appointed Fact Finder, 1992—. Superior Court Appointed Trial Referee, 1992—. Superior Court Attorney Arbitrator, 1998—. *Member:* Litchfield, New Milford (Vice President, 1985-1986; President, 1986-1987) and Connecticut Bar Associations; Connecticut Trial Lawyers Association. (Resident). ***PRACTICE AREAS:*** Real Estate Law; Criminal Law; Motor Vehicle Defense Law; Business Law; Family Law. ***Email:*** newmilford@crameranderson.com

ARTHUR C. WEINSHANK, born Brooklyn, New York, November 14, 1950; admitted to bar, 1975, Florida; 1976, New York; 1980, Connecticut. *Education:* Pace University (B.B.A., 1972); University of Miami (J.D., 1974); New York University (LL.M. in Taxation, 1980). Author: "Stock Sold by an Underwriter in Connection with Transfer to Controlled Corporation," The Tax Advisor, March, 1979. Former Director, Western Connecticut Estate and Tax Planning Council. Co-Chairman, Legacy Committee of the American Cancer Society, Danbury Chapter. *Member:* Connecticut (Former Executive Committee Member, Tax Section), New York State and American (Member, Taxation Section) Bar Associations; The Florida Bar. (Resident). ***PRACTICE AREAS:*** Taxation Law; Trust Planning; Estate Planning; Probate; Administrative Law; Elder Law; Trusts and Estates; IRS Representation; General Business Law. ***Email:*** aweinshank@crameranderson.com

D. RANDALL DiBELLA, born Danbury, Connecticut, May 4, 1953; admitted to bar, 1980, Virginia, U.S. District Court, Eastern District of Virginia and U.S. Court of Appeals, Fourth Circuit; 1981, Connecticut. *Education:* Western Connecticut State College (B.A., 1975); George Mason University School of Law (J.D., 1980). Counsel, Town of Sherman, Connecticut. Member, 1988-1994 and Chairman, 1992-1994, Grievance Panel, Judicial District of Danbury. *Member:* Litchfield (Member, CLE Committee), New Milford (President, 1991-1992; Member, Litigation Committee) and Connecticut Bar Associations; Virginia State Bar; Connecticut Trial Lawyers Association. Connecticut Bar Foundation, James W. Cooper Fellow, 2000—. (Resident). ***REPORTED CASES:*** Ash v. New Milford, 207 Conn. 665 (1988). ***PRACTICE AREAS:*** Personal Injury Law; Civil Litigation; Uninsured Motorist; Uninsured Motorist Arbitration; Mediation. ***Email:*** drdibella@crameranderson,com

MITCHELL J. MELNICK, born Hartford, Connecticut, September 1, 1959; admitted to bar, 1984, Florida; 1985, District of Columbia; 1986, U.S. District Court, Southern District of Florida; 1995, Connecticut. *Education:* University of Rochester (B.A., 1981); University of Miami (J.D., 1984). *Member:* New Milford and Connecticut (Member, Sections on: Banking Law; Business Law) Bar Associations; The Florida Bar (Member, Sections on: Corporation Finance and Securities Law). (Resident). ***PRACTICE AREAS:*** Corporate Law; Banking Law; Health Care Law; Securities Law. ***Email:*** mmelnick@crameranderson.com

JOHN D. TOWER, born Greenwich, Connecticut, October 3, 1963; admitted to bar, 1989, Connecticut; 1994, U.S. District Court, District of Connecticut. *Education:* Cornell University (B.A., magna cum laude, 1985); University of Michigan (J.D., cum laude, 1989). *Member:* New Milford and Connecticut Bar Associations; Connecticut Trial Lawyers Association. (Resident). ***PRACTICE AREAS:*** Civil Litigation. ***Email:*** jtower@crameranderson.com

LISA L. BUZAID, born Danbury, Connecticut, August 13, 1959; admitted to bar, 1988, Connecticut; 1990, U.S. District Court, District of Connecticut. *Education:* Western Connecticut State University (B.A., magna cum laude, 1985); University of Bridgeport (J.D., summa cum laude, 1988). *Member:* Greater Danbury, New Milford, Connecticut and American Bar Associations. (Resident). ***PRACTICE AREAS:*** Commercial and Residential Real Estate; Landlord and Tenant Law. ***Email:*** lbuzaid@crameranderson.com

(This Listing Continued)

CRAMER & ANDERSON LLP, New Milford—Continued

CLAYTON L. BLICK (for complete biographical data, See Professional Biographies at Litchfield, CT).

GRANT J. NELSON (for complete biographical date, See Professional Biographies at Kent, CT).

PERLEY H. GRIMES, JR. (for complete biographical data, See Professional Biographies at Litchfield, CT).

ROBERT L. FISHER, JR. (for complete biographical data, See Professional Biographies at Litchfield, CT).

REGINALD WILLIAM H. FAIRBAIRN (for complete biographical data, See Professional Biographies at Washington Depot, CT).

WILLIAM C. FRANKLIN (for complete biographical data, See Professional Biographies at Litchfield, CT).

DAVID P. BURKE (for complete biographical data, See Professional Biographies at Danbury, CT).

JOSEPH A. SAFFI (for complete biographical data, See Professional Biographies at Danbury, CT).

BARRY S. MOLLER (for complete biographical data, See Professional Biographies at Litchfield, CT).

JAMES D. HIRSCHFIELD (for complete biographical data, See Professional Biographies at Litchfield, CT).

ASSOCIATES

DENISE M. CLOUTIER (for complete biographical data, See Professional Biographies at Litchfield, CT).

ROSEMARY B. JONES, born Hartford, Connecticut, April 21, 1965; admitted to bar, 1992, Connecticut; 1995, U.S. District Court, District of Connecticut. *Education:* University of Chicago (B.A., with honors, 1987); University of Connecticut (J.D., with honors, 1992). Administrative Editor, Connecticut Journal of International Law, 1991-1992. Contributor, Connecticut Environmental Practice, Butterworths, 1993. Author: "The Canadian Administrative Process for Evaluating the Transboundary Environmental Impact of Energy Exports," Connecticut Journal of International Law, Spring 1992; "Expedited Redevelopment under Connecticut's Revised Transfer Act and Licensed Environmental Professional Programs," Environmental Law & Practice, January/February 1996. *Member:* Connecticut Bar Association (Member, Executive Committee, Environmental Law Section, 1994—). (Resident). ***PRACTICE AREAS:*** Elder Law; Real Estate; Environmental Law. ***Email:*** rjones@crameranderson.com

OF COUNSEL

HENRY B. ANDERSON, born Wilkinsburg, Pennsylvania, May 30, 1918; admitted to bar, 1948, Connecticut. *Education:* Wesleyan University (B.A., 1940; M.A., 1948); University of Connecticut (LL.B., cum laude, 1948). Member, Board of Student Editors, Connecticut Bar Journal, 1947-48. Judge of Probate, Town of Sherman, 1951-59; Counsel for Town of Sherman, 1949-1976. Member, 1964-1982 and Chairman, 1977-1980, Bar Examining Committee. *Member:* Connecticut and American Bar Associations.

STEPHEN N. HUME, born Danbury, Connecticut, December 15, 1925; admitted to bar, 1951, New York; 1958, Connecticut; 1961, U.S. District Court, District of Connecticut. *Education:* College of the Holy Cross (B.N.S., 1945); Yale University (B.A., 1947); Columbia University (LL.B., 1950). Phi Delta Phi. County Counsel, Litchfield County, 1960-1961.

PAUL B. ALTERMATT, born New Haven, Connecticut, April 18, 1930; admitted to bar, 1956, District of Columbia; 1957, Connecticut and Indiana. *Education:* Wesleyan University (B.A., 1951); Georgetown University (LL.B., 1956). Insurance Commissioner, State of Connecticut, 1971-1973. Vice Chairman, Statewide Grievance Committee, 1981. Member, Governor's Task Force on Insurance, 1985-1986. *Member:* New Milford, Litchfield County and Connecticut (President, 1986-1987, Member, House of Delegates, Board of Governors and Chairman, Legislative Liaison Committee, 1980-1986) Bar Associations. Fellow, American Bar Foundation. (Resident). ***Email:*** newmilford@crameranderson.com

ROBERT M. FITZGERALD (for complete biographical data, See Professional Biographies at Litchfield, CT).

COUNSEL FOR: Town of Cornwall; First National Bank of Litchfield; New Milford Hospital, Inc.; Canterbury School; New Mil Bank; South Kent School; Marvelwood School.

MOOTS, PELLEGRINI, MANNION, MARTINDALE & DRATCH, P.C.

FORTY SIX MAIN STREET
NEW MILFORD, CONNECTICUT 06776
Telephone: 860-355-4191
Fax: 860-355-8487
URL: http://www.mpsmlaw.com

Mailing Address: P.O. Box 1319, New Milford, Connecticut 06776

Estate Planning, Probate, Business and Corporate, Real Estate, Domestic Relations, Personal Injury, Workers Compensation, Criminal and Civil Litigation. Planning Zoning and Land Use.

ROLAND F. MOOTS, JR., born Little Rock, Arkansas, July 14, 1944; admitted to bar, 1969, Connecticut; 1971, U.S. District Court, District of Connecticut; 1980, U.S. Supreme Court. *Education:* University of Miami (A.B., 1966); Boston University (J.D., 1969). Public Defender, Third Circuit Court, 1971-1973. Town Counsel, New Milford, 1973-1977. Commissioner, Small Claims Session, Superior Court, Litchfield Judicial District, 1981-1988. *Member:* Danbury, Litchfield County, Connecticut (Member, Sections on: Criminal Justice; Family Law) and American (Member, Family Law Section) Bar Associations; The Association of Trial Lawyers of America; Connecticut Trial Lawyers Association; National Association of Criminal Defense Lawyers. ***PRACTICE AREAS:*** Family Law; Criminal Law; Litigation; Personal Injury. ***Email:*** rmoots@mootslaw.com

TERRY C. PELLEGRINI, born Bristol, Connecticut, September 10, 1943; admitted to bar, 1969, Connecticut. *Education:* St. Francis College (A.B., 1966); Villanova University (J.D., 1969). Town Attorney, 1971-1973; Selectman, 1973-1975, New Milford. General Counsel, New Milford Board of Realtors and Multiple Listing Service, 1973—. Trustee, New Milford Hospital 1986—. Chairman, Board of Trustees, New Milford Hospital, 1993-1998. *Member:* Litchfield County, Connecticut Bar Associations. ***PRACTICE AREAS:*** Real Estate Law; Zoning, Planning and Land Use. ***Email:*** tpellegrini@mootslaw.com

MICHAEL J. MANNION, born Ft. Pierce, Florida, April 25, 1945; admitted to bar, 1974, Connecticut and U.S. District Court, District of Connecticut; 1980, U.S. Supreme Court; 1994, U.S. Court of Appeals, Second Circuit. *Education:* Boston College (B.A., 1967); St. John's University (J.D., 1974). Recipient, Lawyer's Cooperative Awards for Excellence in Contracts and Real Estate, 1974. Commissioner and Chairman, Bethel Planning and Zoning Commission, 1987—. *Member:* Danbury (President, 1984-1985), New Milford, Litchfield County, Connecticut (Member, Sections on: Criminal Justice; Real Property; Domestic Relations) and American Bar Associations; Connecticut Trial Lawyers Association. [1st Lt., AGC, U.S. Army, 1969-1972]. ***PRACTICE AREAS:*** Civil Litigation; Criminal Litigation; Domestic Relations Law; Zoning, Planning and Land Use. ***Email:*** mmannion@mootslaw.com

ANN MARTINDALE, born Newport News, Virginia, July 9, 1947; admitted to bar, 1988, Connecticut. *Education:* University of Michigan (B.A., 1969); University of Missouri, School of Journalism (M.A., 1972); University of Connecticut (J.D., 1988). Member and Administrative Editor, Connecticut Law Review. *Member:* New Milford, Litchfield County and Connecticut (Member, Sections on: Real Property; Planning & Zoning Law; Environmental; Estates & Probate) Bar Associations. ***PRACTICE AREAS:*** Real Estate; Commercial Lending; Environmental Law; Business Law; Estates; Probate; Zoning; Land Use. ***Email:*** amartindale@mootslaw.com

BARBARA MCMAHON DRATCH, born New Milford, Connecticut, July 15, 1942; admitted to bar, 1991, Connecticut and U.S. District Court, District of Connecticut. *Education:* Charter Oak College (B.A., 1984); University of Bridgeport (J.D., 1990). Recipient, American Jurisprudence Award in Ethics. Affiliate Member, Society of Fire Protection Engineers, 1984—. Member, National Fire Protection Association, 1982—. *Member:* Connecticut and American Bar Association. ***PRACTICE AREAS:*** Family Law; Civil Litigation; Personal Injury Law; Real Estate; Probate; Estates. ***Email:*** bdratch@mootslaw.com

---

LYNDA LEE ARNOLD, born New Milford, Connecticut, January 2, 1963; admitted to bar, 1996, Connecticut and New York. *Education:* Western Connecticut State University (B.A., 1985); Pace University School of Law (J.D., 1995). *Member:* Danbury and New Milford Bar Associations. ***PRACTICE AREAS:*** Family Law. ***Email:*** larnold@mootslaw.com

SIENKIEWICZ & McKENNA, P.C.

9 SOUTH MAIN STREET
P.O. BOX 786
NEW MILFORD, CONNECTICUT 06776
Telephone: 860-354-1583
Fax: 860-355-4439
URL: http://www.lawyers.com/smlaw

Kent, Connecticut Office: 25 North Main Street, Suite 13A. Telephone: 860-927-4640. Fax: 860-927-1909.

Civil Practice. Personal Injury, Medical Malpractice, Product Liability, Real Estate, Commercial Law, Administrative Law, Family Law, Mediation, Trusts and Estates, Wills and Probate, Zoning, Planning and Land Use, Contracts, Appellate Practice.

MEMBERS OF FIRM

NANCY SIENKIEWICZ, born Buffalo, New York, March 5, 1950; admitted to bar, 1977, Connecticut. *Education:* Syracuse University (B.S., magna cum laude, 1972); University of Connecticut (J.D., 1977). Phi Beta Kappa. Grievance Panel, Judicial District of Danbury, 1992-1998, Chairman, 1994-1998. Practitioner Member, Academy of Family Mediators. *Member:* Connecticut Bar Association. ***PRACTICE AREAS:*** Real Estate Law; Divorce Mediation; Trusts and Estates; Wills; Commercial Law.

JEFFREY B. SIENKIEWICZ, born Stamford, Connecticut, January 4, 1948; admitted to bar, 1972, Connecticut; 1975, U.S. District Court, District of Connecticut; 1985, U.S. Court of Appeals, Second Circuit. *Education:* Johns Hopkins University (B.A., 1969); Syracuse University (J.D., 1972). Town Counsel: Town of Warren, 1976-1981; Town of New Milford, 1978-1988, 1989-1992; Town of Kent, 1989—. *Member:* Connecticut Bar Association; Connecticut Trial Lawyers Association; The Association of Trial Lawyers of America; Connecticut Association of Municipal Attorneys. ***REPORTED CASES:*** Bauer v. Waste Management, 234 Conn. 221, 662 A.2d 1179 (1995); Shortt v. New Milford, 212 Conn. 294, 562 A.2d 107 (1989); Griffin Hospital v. Commission of Hospitals and Health Care, 200 Conn. 489, 512 A.2d 199 (1986); Otto Contracting Company v. S. Schinella & Son, Inc., 179 Conn. 704, 427 A.2d 856 (1980); S.C.A. Services of Connecticut, Inc. v. Town of New Milford, 174 Conn. 146, 384 A.2d 337 (1977). ***PRACTICE AREAS:*** Municipal Law; Personal Injury; Medical Malpractice; Zoning, Planning and Land Use; Products Liability; Litigation.

MICHAEL S. McKENNA, born Bainbridge, Maryland, February 23, 1957; admitted to bar, 1982, Connecticut and U.S. District Court, District of Connecticut; 1987, U.S. Court of Appeals, Second Circuit. *Education:* University of Connecticut (B.A., 1979); Villanova University (J.D., 1982). Member, Villanova Law Review, 1981-1982. Law Clerk, Superior Court Law Clerk Program, Judicial Department, State of Connecticut, 1982-1983. Superior Court: Attorney Trial Referee and Factfinder, 1998—. Member, Board of Directors, Connecticut Legal Services, Inc., 1984-1991. *Member:* Connecticut Bar Association; The Association of Trial Lawyers of America. ***REPORTED CASES:*** Mattegat v. Klopfenstein, 247 Conn. 922, 722 Atlantic 2nd 810 (1998); Bauer v. Waste Management, 239 Conn. 515, 686 A.2d 481 (1996); Dunham v. Dunham, 237 Conn. 480, 677 A.2d 436 (1996); Fair Cadillac Oldsmobile Corp. v. Allard, 41 Conn. App. 659, 677 A.2d 462 (1996); First Charter National Bank v. Ross, et al., 29 Conn. App. 667, 617 A.2d 909 (1992); Griffin Hospital v. Commission of Hospitals and Health Care, 196 Conn. 451, 493 A.2d 229 (1985). ***PRACTICE AREAS:*** Litigation; Civil Practice; Personal Injury; Administrative Law; Employment Law; Commercial Law.

THERESA BENEDICT D'ALTON, born Santa Barbara, California, July 16, 1955; admitted to bar, 1981, Massachusetts; 1982, New York and Connecticut; 1985, U.S. District Court, District of Connecticut. *Education:* Fairfield University (B.A., 1977); Suffolk University (J.D., cum laude, 1981); New York University (LL.M., 1983). (Resident, Kent). ***PRACTICE AREAS:*** Business Law; Real Estate; Commercial Law; Zoning, Planning and Land Use.

COUNSEL FOR: Town of Kent; New Milford Water Pollution Control Authority; Brookfield Water Pollution Control Authority; Ernst P. Riva & Son, Inc.; Stor-It-All, Inc.; Northeast Communications, Inc.
LOCAL AGENT FOR: Connecticut Attorney's Title Insurance Company; Commonwealth Land Title Ins. Co.
REFERENCES: Town of New Milford; Town of Kent.

MARTIN J. GERSTEN

90 BIRCH HILL ROAD
NEWTOWN, CONNECTICUT 06470-1740
Telephone: 203-364-0290
Fax: 203-364-0292
Email: MJGLAW@aol.com
URL: http://www.lawyers.com/gerstenlaw

Corporate Law, Securities, Finance, Taxation.

(This Listing Continued)

MARTIN J. GERSTEN, born New York, N.Y., March 21, 1942; admitted to bar, 1966, New York; 1975, Florida; 1978, Connecticut. *Education:* George Washington University (B.A., 1963); Columbia University (J.D., 1966). *Member:* Connecticut, New York State and American Bar Associations; The Florida Bar. ***PRACTICE AREAS:*** Corporate Law (70%); Securities (10%); Finance (10%); Taxation (10%).

HALL & SAVARESE, P.C.

43 MAIN STREET
P.O. BOX 395
NEWTOWN, CONNECTICUT 06470
Telephone: 203-426-8177; Waterbury: 203-575-9768
Fax: 203-426-6529

General Practice. Trials in all State and Federal Courts. Zoning and Land Use, Real Estate, Probate and Estate Planning, Personal Injury, Workers Compensation.

ROBERT H. HALL, born Bridgeport, Connecticut, May 23, 1939; admitted to bar, 1964, Connecticut; 1965, U.S. District Court, District of Connecticut; 1992, U.S. Court of Appeals, Second Circuit. *Education:* Yale University (B.A., 1961); Harvard University (LL.B., 1964). Town Attorney, Town of Newtown, Connecticut, 1967-1975. Member, Connecticut Public Health Council, 1971-1977. Member of Council, Town of Newtown, 1976-1978. Member, Board of Trustees, Cyrenius H. Booth Library, 1978-1992. Trustee and Secretary, Charles Ives Center for the Arts, 1984-1995. Member, Panel of Arbitrators, American Arbitration Association, 1977—. *Member:* Waterbury, Connecticut and American Bar Associations; Connecticut Trial Lawyers Association. ***PRACTICE AREAS:*** Civil and Commercial Litigation; Zoning and Land Use; Estate Planning.

STEPHEN L. SAVARESE, born South Bend, Indiana, June 4, 1960; admitted to bar, 1986, Connecticut; 1988, U.S. District Court, District of Connecticut. *Education:* University of Notre Dame (B.A., 1982); Washington College of Law, American University (J.D., 1985). Assistant Town Attorney, Town of Westport, 1986-1988. *Member:* Connecticut (Member, Sections on: Real Property; Young Lawyers) and American (Member, Sections on: Real Property, Probate and Trust Law; Torts and Insurance Practice) Bar Associations. ***PRACTICE AREAS:*** Real Estate; Personal Injury; Workers Compensation.

JACOBS PARTNERS LLC

NEWTOWN, CONNECTICUT

(See Norwalk)

Business and Personal Bankruptcy, Workouts, Debtor Creditor's Rights, Commercial Litigation, Contracts and Business Disputes.

HARVEY J. KULAWITZ, LLC

NEWTOWN, CONNECTICUT

(See Ridgefield)

All Personal Injury Cases, including Car Accident cases, Aircraft & Boating accidents, Slip & Fall accidents, Dog Bite attacks, and Wrongful Death accidents & claims.

MURPHY & MURPHY LLP

38 CHURCH HILL ROAD
NEWTOWN, CONNECTICUT 06470
Telephone: 203-270-0805
Facsimile: 203-270-8239
URL: http://www.lawyers.com/murphy&murphy

Elder Law, Probate, Estate Planning, Conservatorships, Medicare and Medicaid and Nursing Home Regulation.

MICHELE F. MURPHY, born Philadelphia, Pennsylvania, August 21, 1960; admitted to bar, 1988, Connecticut. *Education:* University of Pennsylvania (B.S., 1982); Pace University (J.D., 1988). *Member:* Danbury and Connecticut Bar Associations. ***PRACTICE AREAS:*** Elder Law; Probate; Real Estate; Medicare and Medicaid.

THOMAS E. MURPHY, born Yonkers, New York, March 7, 1960; admitted to bar, 1996, Connecticut. *Education:* University of Pennsylvania (B.S., 1982); Pace University (J.D., cum laude, 1996). ***PRACTICE AREAS:*** Elder Law; Probate; Real Estate; Medicare and Medicaid.

WILLIAM F. L. RODGERS

Established in 1993
SUGARBROOK LAW CENTER
4 HI BARLOW ROAD
NEWTOWN, CONNECTICUT 06470
Telephone: 203-270-8879
FAX: 203-270-3415;
URL: http://www.sugarbrooklaw.com
Email: wflr@sugarbrooklaw.com
URL: http://www.lawyers.com/sugarbrooklaw

General Practice, Probate, Wills, Trusts and Estate Planning, Matrimonial and Family Law, Elder Law, Corporate Law, Personal Injury, Trials.

WILLIAM F. L. RODGERS, born Winchester, Massachusetts, June 28, 1960; admitted to bar, 1985, Connecticut; 1986, New York; 1988, District of Columbia. *Education:* Phillips Academy (cum laude, 1978); University of Pennsylvania (B.A., A.M., 1982); Boston University (J.D., 1985). Phi Alpha Delta. *Member:* Danbury, Connecticut (Member, Sections on: Elder Law; Estates and Probate; Tax), New York State (Member, Trusts and Estates Section) and American Bar Associations; District of Columbia Bar. [Captain and Judge Advocate, USMC, 1986-1989; Lieutenant Colonel and Judge Advocate, USMCR]. ***REPORTED CASES:*** *Reported Cases:* Connecticut National Bank & Trust Co. v. Chadwick, 217 Conn. 260 (1991); United States v. Kohut, 44 M.J. 245 (C.A.A.F., 1996); United States v. Rosendahl, 47 M.J. 689 (N.M.C.C.A., 1997).

STEVENS, HARRIS & GUERNSEY, P.C.

Established in 1967
351 MAIN STREET
P.O. BOX P.O.DRAWER 660
NIANTIC, CONNECTICUT 06357
Telephone: 860-739-6906
Fax: 860-739-2997
Email: SHG@CTOL.net
URL: http://www.lawyers.com/stevensharrisguernseylaw

General Civil and Criminal Practice before State and Federal Courts. Personal Injury, Wrongful Death, Real Estate, Probate, Corporation, Domestic Relations, Environmental and Workers Compensation Law. Trials and Appeals.

RONALD F. STEVENS, born Hartford, Connecticut, August 29, 1945; admitted to bar, 1972, Connecticut. *Education:* Georgetown University (BSBA, 1969); Boston College School of Law (J.D., 1972). Member, East Lyme Board of Education, 1977-1987. *Member:* New London County, Connecticut and American Bar Associations; Association of Trial Lawyers of America; Connecticut Trial Lawyers Association. ***PRACTICE AREAS:*** Criminal Law; Civil Litigation.

THEODORE A. HARRIS, born New London, Connecticut, November 2, 1949; admitted to bar, 1975, Connecticut and U.S. District Court, District of Connecticut. *Education:* Drexel University (B.S., 1972); University of Connecticut (J.D., with high honors, 1975). Beta Gamma Sigma. *Member:* New London County, Connecticut and American Bar Associations. ***PRACTICE AREAS:*** Planning and Zoning Law; Real Estate Law; Commercial Law.

PAUL M. GUERNSEY, born Stamford, Connecticut, February 9, 1950; admitted to bar, 1975, Connecticut and U.S. Court of Appeals, 2nd Circuit; 1976, U.S. District Court, District of Connecticut. *Education:* University of Notre Dame (B.A., 1972); University of Connecticut (J.D., 1975). Editor, Connecticut Law Review, 1974-1975. Author: "Governmental Law Breaking and Contrived Jurisdiction Under the Travel Act," 6 Connecticut Law Review 577, 1974. Attorney State Trial Referee, Judicial District of New London, 1992—. Judge, Mohegan Gaming Disputes Court, 1996—. Chief Judge, Mohegan Gaming Disputes Court, 2000—; Arbitrator, Judicial Department Court-Annexed Arbitration Program, 1999—. Fact Finder, New London Judicial District, 1990—. Special Master, Special Masters Pre-Trial Conference Program, 1985. *Member:* New London County (Chairman, Criminal Law and Public Defender Committee, 1987—), Connecticut and American (Member, Section of Litigation) Bar Associations; Association of Trial Lawyers of America; Connecticut Trial Lawyers Association. ***REPORTED CASES:*** National Fire and Marine Ins. Co. v. Piczaio, 583 F. Supp. 624 (D. Conn 1983). ***PRACTICE AREAS:*** Civil and Criminal Litigation; Personal Injury; Wrongful Death; Motor Vehicle Accidents and Injuries.

PAIGE STEVENS QUILLIAM, born Goshen, New York, March 9, 1973; admitted to bar, 1999, Connecticut. *Education:* Saint Michael's College (B.A., magna cum laude, 1995); Quinnipiac College School of Law (J.D., 1998). Co-Editor, Sandbar, New London County Bar Newsletter. *Member:* Connecticut Bar Association. ***PRACTICE AREAS:*** Family Law; Probate Law. ***Email:*** paigeprs@aol.com

REPRESENTATIVE CLIENTS: Bayliner Marine Corp.; First American Title Insurance Company; Hoffman Tire Co. d/b/a Jetzon Tire Co.; Norwich Savings Society; Chelsea Groton Savings Bank; People's Savings Bank; Secor Auto Group; Gold's Gym of Waterford; Kidsports of Waterford.

CELLA, McKEON & WILLIAMS, P.C.

Established in 1976
SUITE A, 21 WASHINGTON AVENUE
P.O. BOX 221
NORTH HAVEN, CONNECTICUT 06473
Telephone: 203-239-5851
Fax: 203-234-2974
Email: carlc@cmwlawyers.com

General Practice. Trials in all Courts. Personal Injury, Products Liability, Medical Malpractice, Insurance, Workers Compensation, Real Estate, Municipal, Zoning, Family Law, Estates and Probate.

CARL E. CELLA, born New Haven, Connecticut, April 2, 1941; admitted to bar, 1966, Connecticut; 1976, U.S. Supreme Court and U.S. Court of Appeals, 2nd Circuit. *Education:* Georgetown University (A.B., 1963); University of Connecticut (J.D., 1966). Co-Author: "Products Liability in Connecticut," Connecticut Bar Journal, September, 1966. *Member:* New Haven County, Connecticut and American Bar Associations; Defense Research Institute; Connecticut Trial Lawyers Association. ***PRACTICE AREAS:*** Medical Malpractice; Personal Injury; Arbitration; Mediation; Automobile Liability; Uninsured and Underinsured Motorists; Products Liability. ***Email:*** carlc@cmwlawyers.com

JAMES G. WILLIAMS, born Meriden, Connecticut, January 30, 1961; admitted to bar, 1986, Connecticut; 1998, U.S. Court of Appeals, 2nd Circuit. *Education:* Providence College (B.A., 1983); Quinnipiac College School of Law (J.D., 1986). Recipient, American Jurisprudence Awards in Evidence and in Administrative Law. *Member:* New Haven, Connecticut and American Bar Associations; Defense Research Institute. ***PRACTICE AREAS:*** Personal Injury; Products Liability; Medical Malpractice; Municipal Law; Public School Law. ***Email:*** jamesw@cmwlawyers.com

KEVIN P. WALSH, born Waterbury, Connecticut, April 6, 1961; admitted to bar, 1986, Connecticut; 1987, Maine and Massachusetts; 1994, U.S. Supreme Court. *Education:* Providence College (B.A., 1983); Suffolk University (J.D., 1986). *Member:* New Haven County, Connecticut and American Bar Associations; Defense Research Institute; Connecticut Defense Research Institute. (Certified as a Civil Trial Advocate by the National Board of Trial Advocacy). ***PRACTICE AREAS:*** Medical Malpractice; Products Liability; Commercial Litigation; Personal Injury. ***Email:*** kevinw@cmwlawyers.com

MICHAEL F. O'CONNOR, born New Haven, Connecticut, November 26, 1964; admitted to bar, 1990, Connecticut; 1991, U.S. District Court, District of Connecticut. *Education:* Villanova University (B.A., 1987); University of Bridgeport (J.D., 1990). Pi Sigma Alpha. Listed in Who's Who In American Universities. *Member:* New Haven, Connecticut and American Bar Associations. ***PRACTICE AREAS:*** Products Liability; Personal Injury; Criminal Law. ***Email:*** michaelo@cmwlawyers.com

LISA D. GALATI, born Wallingford, Connecticut, April 29, 1966; admitted to bar, 1991, Connecticut; 1992, New York. *Education:* Union College (B.A., 1988); University of Bridgeport (J.D., 1991). *Member:* Connecticut, New York State and American Bar Associations. ***LANGUAGES:*** Italian and French. ***PRACTICE AREAS:*** Divorce; Real Estate; Wills; Probate; Zoning; Collections. ***Email:*** lisag@cmwlawyers.com

ROBERT J. FLANAGAN, JR., born New Haven, Connecticut, August 21, 1969; admitted to bar, 1994, Connecticut. *Education:* University of Notre Dame (B.A., magna cum laude, 1991; J.D., cum laude, 1994). Phi Alpha Delta; Phi Beta Kappa; Phi Alpha Theta. *Member:* New Haven County, Connecticut and American Bar Associations. ***PRACTICE AREAS:*** Litigation; Workers' Compensation. ***Email:*** robertf@cmwlawyers.com

ROBERT J. WEBER, III, born New Haven, Connecticut, January 22, 1966; admitted to bar, 1997, Connecticut; 1998, U.S. District Court, District of Connecticut. *Education:* Southern Connecticut State University (B.S., 1989); University of Bridgeport (A.S., 1991); Quinnipiac College School of Law (J.D., cum laude, 1997). Member, 1995-1887 and Associate Editor, 1997, National Probate Law Journal. ***PRACTICE AREAS:*** Personal Injury; Medical Malpractice; Products Liability. ***Email:*** rjweber@cmwlawyers.com

REPRESENTATIVE CLIENTS: Fleet Bank; Hubco Bank; Amex Assurance Company; American States Insurance Co.; Nationwide Insurance Co.; Peerless Insurance Co.; St. Paul Insurance Co.; International Surplus Lines Insurance Co.; Mutual of Omaha Insurance Co.; United National Ins. Co.; Hartford A&I; Montgomery

(This Listing Continued)

Ward; Housing Authority Ins. Co.; Connecticut Interlocal Risk Management; Zurich American Ins. Co.; Providence Washington Ins. Co.; AIG Speciality; Jefferson Ins. Co.; Worcester Ins. Co.
REFERENCES: Fleet Bank; Amex Assurance Company.

CIULLA & DONOFRIO, LLP

Established in 1996

127 WASHINGTON AVENUE
NORTH HAVEN, CONNECTICUT 06473
Telephone: 203-239-9828
Fax: 203-234-0379

Civil Litigation in all State and Federal Courts, Commercial Litigation, Business Law, Municipal and Governmental Law, Construction and Surety Law, Product Liability, Personal Injury, Employment Law, Insurance Litigation, Tax and Zoning Appeals, Antitrust, Securities, Tax and Corporate Law.

FIRM PROFILE: Ciulla & Donofrio, LLP was formed on November 1, 1996, by Robert K. Ciulla, formerly a partner at Tyler Cooper & Alcorn in New Haven for 25 years, and Jeffrey M. Donofrio, also a former a litigation attorney at Tyler Cooper & Alcorn. The firm has a general practice with an emphasis on civil litigation, commercial litigation and municipal law. Ciulla & Donofrio, LLP provides "big firm" expertise and personal, cost-effective service.

ROBERT K. CIULLA, born Brooklyn, New York, August 19, 1941; admitted to bar, 1967, New York; 1968, Connecticut, U.S. District Court, District of Connecticut, U.S. Court of Appeals, Second Circuit and U.S. Supreme Court. *Education:* Williams College (B.A., 1963); Yale University (LL.B., 1966). Town Counsel, Town of North Haven, 1979—. Member, Connecticut Legal Specialization Screening Committee, 1981-1991. Co-chairman, U.S. District Court Panel of Special Masters, 1986-1989. Member, Connecticut Statewide Grievance Committee, 1987-1990. Director, Connecticut Motor Club (AAA), New Haven Symphony Orchestra. *Member:* New Haven County, Connecticut (Chairman, Federal Judiciary Committee) and American (Member, Sections on: Litigation; Business Law) Bar Associations. Fellow, Connecticut and American Bar Foundations. ***PRACTICE AREAS:*** Civil Litigation; Commercial Litigation; Product Liability; Personal Injury; Municipal Law; Governmental Law; Employment Law. ***Email:*** RCiulla@cd-llp.com

JEFFREY M. DONOFRIO, born Derby, Connecticut, January 18, 1965; admitted to bar, 1990, Connecticut; U.S. District Court, District of Connecticut, U.S. Court of Appeals, Second Circuit and U.S. Court of Federal Claims. *Education:* Boston College (B.A., 1987); Catholic University of America (J.D., 1990). Speaker and Panelist: "Advance Construction Law," "Connecticut Construction Law: What Do You Do When....?" and "Construction Payment Remedies in Connecticut," National Business Institute Seminars, October 1997, April 1998, March 1999, September 1999, March 2000, March 2001 and November 2001; "Construction Claims in Connecticut," Lorman Educational Services, August 2001; Bank Compliance Association of Connecticut Commercial Litigation Seminar, August 1995. Speaker, Year 2000 Problem Seminars, Connecticut Bar Association, November 1998, February 1999, June 1999 and November 1999. Author: "Legal Technology Review," Connecticut Law Journal, March 2001; "Get the Bug Spray Ready: a Y2K Primer" and "Highlights of the Y2K Act," Connecticut Lawyer, October 1998 and October 1999; "Legal Sources on the Internet," New Haven County Bar Association, CLE Seminar, March 2000; "Legal Sources on the Internet, "Connecticut Bar Association, January 2001 and October 2001. *Member:* New Haven, Connecticut (Member: Litigation and Construction Sections; Web Site Advisory Committee and Chairman, Legal Technology Committee) and American (Member: Business Law and Litigation Sections; Forum on the Construction Industry and Construction Litigation) Bar Associations. ***PRACTICE AREAS:*** Commercial Litigation; Construction Law; Municipal; Tax Appeals; Insurance Litigation; ERISA; Business Law; Creditors Rights; Foreclosures; Collections; Lender Liability; Commercial Finance; Government Contracts. ***Email:*** JDonofrio@cd-llp.com

JENNIFER N. COPPOLA, born Derby, Connecticut, November 21, 1970; admitted to bar, 1996, Connecticut; 1998, U.S. District Court, District of Connecticut. *Education:* Trinity College (B.A., 1992); Vermont Law School (J.D., 1995). ***PRACTICE AREAS:*** Personal Injury; Collection Litigation; Commercial Litigation; Contracts; Zoning Law; Probate. ***Email:*** JCoppola@cd-llp.com

GLENN L. FORMICA, born New Haven, Connecticut, September 24, 1969; admitted to bar, 1997, Maryland; 1999, Connecticut; 2000, U.S. District Court, District of Connecticut. *Education:* Boston University (B.A., Classical Studies and English, cum laude, 1992); The Catholic University of America (J.D., 1997). *Member:* Connecticut and American Bar Associations; The Association of Trial Lawyers of America (Member, Commercial Litigation Committee; Newsletter Editor, 2000). ***PRACTICE AREAS:*** Commercial Litigation; Employment Litigation; Construction Litigation. ***Email:*** GFormica@cd-llp.com

(This Listing Continued)

OF COUNSEL

RICHARD F. CONNORS, born New Haven, Connecticut, June 20, 1942; admitted to bar, 1967, Connecticut; 1969, U.S. District Court, District of Connecticut; 1975, U.S. Court of Appeals, Second Circuit. *Education:* Villanova University (A.B., 1964); Columbia University (LL.B., 1967). *Member:* New Haven County, Connecticut and American Bar Associations. (Also practicing individually at same address). ***PRACTICE AREAS:*** Personal Injury Law; Commercial Law; Bankruptcy; Estate Planning; General Practice. ***Email:*** RConnors@cd-llp.com

PAUL E. MONAGHAN, JR., born Manhasset, New York, April 8, 1971; admitted to bar, 1996, Connecticut; 1997, U.S. Tax Court. *Education:* State University of New York at New Paltz (B.A., 1993); Yale University (J.D., 1996). Pi Sigma Alpha. Editor, 1994-1995 and Senior Editor, 1995-1996, Yale Law Journal. Co-Author: "Invetigating the Licensing or Brokerage Agreement: A Checklist for Lenders," The Practical Lawyer, January 1999; "Assessing the Uses of the Electing Small Business Trust," Estate Planning, October 1998; "Internet Solicitation and State Law Restrictions," Fundraising Regulation Report, December 1997. *Member:* Connecticut and American (Member, Business Law Section, 1998—) Bar Associations. ***PRACTICE AREAS:*** Mergers and Acquisitions; Securities; Tax Planning; Tax Controversies; Contracts; Corporate Law. ***Email:*** monaghan@shorelinelegal.com

DONALD S. HENDEL, LLC

116 WASHINGTON AVENUE, 4TH FLOOR
NORTH HAVEN, CONNECTICUT 06473-1723
Telephone: 203-234-6321
Facsimile: 203-234-6322
Email: taxlawyer@prodigy.net
URL: http://www.lawyers.com/dhendel

Tax, Business and Estate Planning.

DONALD S. HENDEL, born New Haven, Connecticut, September 3, 1956; admitted to bar, 1983, Connecticut; 1984, U.S. Tax Court; 1985, Court of Federal Claims; 1992, New York. *Education:* University of Rochester (B.A., 1978); Cornell University (M.B.A., 1980); University of Connecticut (J.D., with honors, 1983). Certified Public Accountant, Connecticut, 1982. *Member:* Connecticut (Member, Tax Section) New York State and American (Member, Sections on: Real Property, Probate and Trust Law; Taxation) Bar Associations; Connecticut Society of Certified Public Accountants. ***Email:*** taxlawyer@prodigy.net

ALBERT, WARD & JOHNSON, P.C.

NORWALK, CONNECTICUT

(See Greenwich)

General Practice. Real Estate, Zoning, Corporation, Litigation, Probate, Taxation, Construction, Environmental and Family Law.

BARR & LACAVA

NORWALK, CONNECTICUT

(See Stamford)

General Practice, Franchising and Franchise Law, Litigation in all State and Federal Courts, Real Estate, Probate, Corporate, Estate Planning, Family, Immigration, Petroleum Marketing Practices, Environmental Law, Workers Compensation, Appellate Practice, Personal Injury and Automobile Accidents.

ANDREW B. BOWMAN

NORWALK, CONNECTICUT

(See Westport)

General Civil and Criminal Litigation before all Federal and State Courts. Trials and Appeals. Criminal Defense, Tax Litigation, Employment Law, Construction Litigation, Civil Rights, Environmental Law, Personal Injury, Commercial Litigation and Negligence Law.

BRODY, WILKINSON AND OBER, P.C.

NORWALK, CONNECTICUT

(See Southport)

General Civil Practice, Corporation, Probate, Estate Planning, Trusts and Estates, Real Estate, Employment, Commercial, Environmental, Creditors Rights, Tax, Pension, Profit Sharing, Entertainment Law, Banking, General Business, Municipal,

(This Listing Continued)

BRODY, WILKINSON AND OBER, P.C., Norwalk—Continued

Freedom of Information Matters, Telecommunications, Public Utilities, Commercial Litigation.

ANDREW G. BRUCKER

Established in 1988

11 BELDEN AVENUE, 2ND FLOOR
NORWALK, CONNECTICUT 06850
Telephone: 203-840-1133
Fax: 203-846-3551
Email: AGBESQ@AOL.COM
URL: http://www.lawyers.com/bruckerlaw

Corporate, Real Estate, Probate, and Non-Profit Charitable Law.

ANDREW G. BRUCKER, born Brooklyn, New York, April 22, 1943; admitted to bar, 1967, Connecticut and American Samoa; 1969, U.S. District Court, District of Connecticut; 1971, U.S. Tax Court; 1973, U.S. District Court, Southern District of New York. *Education:* University of Rochester (A.B., with honors, 1964); Yale Law School (LL.B., 1967). Assistant Attorney General of American Samoa, 1967-1969. Acting Attorney General of American Samoa, 1969. Member, Governor's Task Force on Full Employment, 1972-1973. Trustee, 1976—, Counsel, 1997—, Florence & Edgar Leslie Charitable Trust. Vice President and General Counsel, The Arm Group, 1988-1997. Corporate Counsel, Norwalk Economic Opportunity Now (NEON), 1981-1996. Secretary & Counsel Strive/ Fairfield County, Inc. *Member:* Stamford-Norwalk Regional, Connecticut (Member, Executive Committee, Commercial Law and Bankruptcy Section, 1977, 1981-1983; Executive Committee, Real Property Section, 1994—, and Member, 1983—) and American (Member, Sections on: Real Property, Probate and Trust Law) Bar Associations; The Corporate Bar of Fairfield and Westchester Counties.

CANTOR COLBURN LLP

101 MERRITT 7
NORWALK, CONNECTICUT 06856
Telephone: 203-849-8266
Fax: 203-849-8292
Email: iplaw@cantorcolburn.com
URL: http://www.cantorcolburn.com

Bloomfield, Connecticut Office: 55 Griffin Road South, 06002. Telephone: 860-286-0115. Fax: 860-286-0115.

Patent, Trademark and Copyright Law, Unfair Competition, Computer and Related Intellectual Property Law including Litigation in all Courts.

FIRM PROFILE: In a world of corporate takeovers and merger mania, it's easy for a law firm to try to be everything to everyone. Few succeed. That's why, at Cantor Colburn LLP, intellectual property law is the only type of law we practice. And why we have gained a reputation as a leader in our field.

Our greatest strength is our focus. A focus on managing and protecting the products, processes, systems and inventions of our clients. A focus that extends to all phases of patent, trademark, copyright, unfair competition, computer and trade secret law, and related licensing and litigation. And expertise that includes a wide range of areas such as semiconductors, software, ceramics, polymeric materials, computers, chemical processing, automotive, optical imaging, biotechnology, and oil and gas wells.

MICHAEL CANTOR, born Hartford, Connecticut, July 10, 1958; admitted to bar, 1984, Connecticut and U.S. District Court, District of Connecticut; 1984, U.S. Court of Appeals for the Federal Circuit; registered to practice before U.S. Patent and Trademark Office. *Education:* University of Connecticut (B.S., with honors, Chemical Engineering/Materials Engineering, 1980; J.D., 1983). Tau Beta Pi. Adjunct Professor in Patent Law, University of Connecticut School of Law, 1993—. *Member:* Connecticut and American Bar Associations; Connecticut Patent Law Association; American Intellectual Property Law Association; International Trademark Association. ***PRACTICE AREAS:*** Patent Law; Trademark and Copyright Law; Unfair Competition; Intellectual Property Law. ***Email:*** mcantor@cantorcolburn.com

PHILMORE H. COLBURN, II, born Springfield, Massachusetts, August 2, 1959; admitted to bar, 1991, Connecticut and U.S. District Court District of Connecticut; 1992, Massachusetts and New York; 1993, U.S. District Court, District of Massachusetts; 1994, U.S. Court for the Federal Circuit 8th Circuit; registered to practice before U.S. Patent and Trademark Office. *Education:* Northeastern University (B.S.E.E., with honors, 1982); University of Massachusetts (M.B.A., 1986); Western New England College School of Law (J.D., 1991). Eta Kappa Nu. Design Engineer, Hamilton Standard division of United Technologies Corporation. *Member:* Hampden County, Connecticut and American Bar Associations; Connecticut Patent Law Association. ***PRACTICE AREAS:*** Patent Law; Trademark and Copyright Law; Unfair Competition; Intellectual Property Law. ***Email:*** pcolburn@cantorcolburn.com

MICHAEL J. KELLY, born New York City, New York, August 9, 1943; admitted to bar, 1976, New Jersey; 1988, Connecticut; registered to practice before the U.S. Patent and Trademark Office. *Education:* Fairleigh Dickinson University (B.S., Chemistry, 1969); Seton Hall University (J.D., 1976). *Member:* New York Intellectual Property Law Association (Member, Board of Directors, 1995-1997). ***PRACTICE AREAS:*** Intellectual Property Law. ***Email:*** mkelly@cantorcolburn.com

ASSOCIATES

CHRISTOPHER C. BOEHM, born Yonkers, New York, March 4, 1965; admitted to bar, 1996, Connecticut and U.S. District Court; 1997, New York and U.S. District Court, Southern District of New York; registered to practice before U.S. Patent and Trademark Office. *Education:* University of Rhode Island (B.S., Civil Engineering, 1989); Quinnipiac College (J.D., 1996). (Resident). ***PRACTICE AREAS:*** Intellectual Property. ***Email:*** cboehm@cantorcolburn.com

ROSS J. CHRISTIE, born Bridgeport, Connecticut, January 28, 1972; admitted to bar, 1997, Connecticut; 1999, New York. *Education:* Grove City College (B.S., in Chemistry, 1994); University of Dayton (J.D., 1997). Co-Chairman, National Administrative Law Moot Court Competition, 1996-1997. Town Council, Monroe, Connecticut, 1999—. *Member:* American Bar Association (Member, Intellectual Property Section, 1997—). (Resident). ***PRACTICE AREAS:*** Intellectual Property. ***Email:*** rchristie@cantorcolburn.com

MARK L. COOPER, born St. Louis, Missouri, December 22, 1965; admitted to bar, 2001, Connecticut. *Education:* University of Missouri at St. Louis (B.S., with honors in Chemistry, 1990); University of Houston (J.D., 2000).

NED McMAHON, born Tuscaloosa, Alabama, June 21, 1969; admitted to bar, 1997, Maryland (Not admitted in Connecticut). *Education:* Villanova University (B.S., 1991); University of Baltimore (J.D., 1997). ***PRACTICE AREAS:*** Patent Law (90%); Trademarks (10%). ***Email:*** nmcmahon@cantorcolburn.com

CHRISTOPHER J. PALESTRO, JR., admitted to bar, 2001, Connecticut. *Education:* Fordham University (B.S., 1998; J.D., 2001). Appointed, Honors Intern, Federal Bureau of Investigation, 1999. *Member:* New York State and American Bar Associations. ***PRACTICE AREAS:*** :Patents; Copyrights; Trademarks. ***Email:*** cpalestro@cantorcolburn.com

REPRESENTATIVE CLIENTS: General Motors Corp.; General Electric Co.; Rogers Corp.; Raymond Engineering; Baker Hughes, Inc.; The Siemon Co.; American Distilling & Mfg. Co., Inc.; Villeroy & Boch S.a.r.l.; American Optical Corp.; Kaman Corp.; University of Connecticut; JPS Elastomerics Corp.; AEARO Co.; Standard-Knapp, Inc.; Konica Corp.; International Business Machines; Bic Corporation; United States Surgical Corp.; Delphi Technologies Inc.; Jeneric Pentron Inc.; Proton Energy Systems; Sanyo Electric Co., Inc.; Macrovision Corp.

CASPER & DE TOLEDO LLC

NORWALK, CONNECTICUT

(See Stamford)

Civil Trial and Appellate Practice in all State and Federal Courts. Personal Injury, Medical Malpractice, Product Liability, Workers' Compensation, Employment Discrimination, Employee Rights and Benefits, Civil Rights, Contracts and Family Law.

COUSINS, JOHNSON & DESROSIERS, P.C.

NORWALK, CONNECTICUT

(See Stratford)

Workers' Compensation, Personal Injury, Trials, Real Estate, Probate.

CUDDY & FEDER & WORBY LLP

ONE MARSHALL STREET, SUITE 201
NORWALK, CONNECTICUT 06854
Telephone: 203-853-8001
Telecopier: 203-831-8250
URL: http://www.cfwlaw.com

White Plains, New York Office: 90 Maple Avenue. Telephone: 914-761-1300. Telecopier: 914-761-5372.

New York, N.Y. Office: 500 Fifth Avenue, Suite 2900. Telephone: 212-944-2841. Telecopier: 212-944-2843.

Hudson Valley Office: Westage Business Center, 300 South Lake Drive, Fishkill, NY, 12524. Telephone: 845-896-2229. Telecopier: 845-896-3672.

Stamford, Connecticut Office: 733 Summer Street. Telephone: 203-348-4780.

(This Listing Continued)

General Practice. Corporate, Real Estate, Zoning, Environmental, Historic Preservation, Housing and Urban Development, Condominium, Municipal, Trusts, Estates, Probate, Estate Planning and Taxation, Elder, Commercial Litigation, Industrial Development Bond Financing and Secured Lending Law.

(For complete biographical data on all personnel, see Professional Biographies at White Plains, New York)

CURTIS, BRINCKERHOFF & BARRETT, P.C.

NORWALK, CONNECTICUT

(See Stamford)

General Practice, Real Estate, Commercial Real Estate Acquisitions, Municipal Law, Zoning, Planning and Land Use, Banking, Administrative Law, Litigation, Civil Litigation, Commercial Litigation, Tax Appeals, Eminent Domain, Federal Taxation, International Taxation, State Taxation, Estate Planning, Trust and Estate, Probate, Elder Law, Family Law, Domestic Relations, Closely Held Corporations, Business Law, Corporate Law, Commercial Law, Commercial Leasing, Leases and Leasing, Employment Law, Non-Competition and Non-Solicitation Agreements, Commercial Arbitration, Construction Law, Landlord and Tenant Law, Personal Injury and Negligence, Product Liability, Bankruptcy, Civil Trial and Appellate Practice in all State and Federal Courts.

DEPANFILIS & VALLERIE, LLC

Established in 1977

25 BELDEN AVENUE

P.O. BOX 699

NORWALK, CONNECTICUT 06852-0699

Telephone: 203-846-9585

FAX: 203-847-2849

General Civil and Criminal Litigation Practice in all Courts. Negligence, Medical Malpractice, Taxation, Corporation, Estate Planning, Probate, Real Estate, Workers Compensation, Family and Landlord and Tenant Law.

ANTHONY J. DEPANFILIS, born Norwalk, Connecticut, January 7, 1949; admitted to bar, 1974, Connecticut; 1975, U.S. District Court, District of Connecticut; 1978, U.S. Supreme Court; 1980, U.S. District Court, Southern and Eastern Districts of New York; 1992, New York. *Education:* Fairfield University (B.A., 1971); Georgetown University (J.D., 1974). Judge of Probate for Norwalk-Wilton District. *Member:* Norwalk-Wilton, Connecticut and American Bar Associations; The Association of Trial Lawyers of America; Connecticut Trial Lawyers Association. ***PRACTICE AREAS:*** Criminal Law; Real Estate; Personal Injury Law; Litigation; Probate.

JOHN E. VALLERIE, JR. (1930-1997).

DAVID W. STERGAS, born Cooperstown, New York, November 5, 1947; admitted to bar, 1976, Mississippi and U.S. District Court, Northern District of Mississippi; 1978, Connecticut; 1980, U.S. District Court, District of Connecticut. *Education:* Mississippi State University (B.S., 1972); University of Mississippi (J.D., 1976); New York University (LL.M. in Taxation, 1977). *Member:* Norwalk-Wilton and Connecticut Bar Associations. ***PRACTICE AREAS:*** Commercial Law; Corporate; Estate Planning; Real Estate; Probate.

DEBORAH J. LINDSTROM, born Joliet, Illinois, September 23, 1947; admitted to bar, 1981, Connecticut; 1983, U.S. District Court, District of Connecticut. *Education:* University of Illinois (B.S., cum laude, 1969); University of Bridgeport (M.S., 1975; J.D., 1981). Delta Theta Phi. President, Women's Bar Association of Fairfield County, 1988-1989. *Member:* Norwalk-Wilton (Member, Executive Board), Connecticut (Member, House of Delegates, 1990-1993) and American Bar Associations. ***PRACTICE AREAS:*** Domestic Litigation; Family Law; Employment Law.

MARC J. GRENIER, born Norwalk, Connecticut, August 5, 1966; admitted to bar, 1991, Connecticut; 1992, U.S. District Court, District of Connecticut; 1996, U.S. Supreme Court. *Education:* Providence College (B.S., cum laude, 1988); New England School of Law (J.D., cum laude, 1991). *Member:* Regional Bar Association of Stamford, Norwalk, Darien and Wilton; Connecticut and American Bar Associations; Connecticut Trial Lawyers Association. ***PRACTICE AREAS:*** Civil Litigation; Real Estate; Matrimonial; Zoning.

CAROLYN GENTILE COLANGELO, born New Haven, Connecticut, October 14, 1969; admitted to bar, 1994, Connecticut; 1995, U.S. District Court, District of Connecticut. *Education:* Southern Connecticut State College (B.A., cum laude, 1990); Quinnipiac College School of Law (J.D., cum laude, 1993). Recipient: American Jurisprudence Book Award in Contracts, Professional Responsibility. Symposium Editor, Quinnipiac Law Review. ***PRACTICE AREAS:*** Civil Litigation; Workers Compensation; Criminal Law; Personal Injury.

(This Listing Continued)

JOHN P. THYGERSON, born Port Chester, New York, September 18, 1966; admitted to bar, 1996, Connecticut; 2000, U.S. District Court, District of Connecticut. *Education:* Fairfield University (B.A., cum laude, 1992); Yeshiva University (J.D., 1995). Member, Criminal Appeals Clinic. *Member:* Regional Bar Association of Stamford, Norwalk; The Association of Trial Lawyers of America; Connecticut Trial Lawyers Association; Connecticut Criminal Defense Lawyers Association. ***PRACTICE AREAS:*** Criminal Defense; Criminal Appeals; Workers Compensation; Civil Litigation; Personal Injury.

MARILYN F. DAVIDSON, born Boston, Massachusetts, November 9, 1963; admitted to bar, 1991, Connecticut; 1992, New York; 1999, Massachusetts. *Education:* University of Massachusetts; University of South Florida (B.A., 1985); University of Bridgeport (J.D., cum laude, 1991). Executive Managing Editor of the Connecticut Probate Law Journal. Author: Note, Tortious Interference with Inheritance. 5 Conn. Prob. L.J., 297 (1991). *Member:* Connecticut and American Bar Associations. ***PRACTICE AREAS:*** Personal Injury; Real Estate.

NEAL P. ROGAN, born New York, New York, November 9, 1958; admitted to bar, 1993, Connecticut; 1994, U.S. District Court, District of Connecticut. *Education:* Post College (B.S., Business Administration, 1987); Bridgeport University (J.D., 1993). Recipient: American Jurisprudence Awards in Legal Skills I, Legal Skills II and Federal Courts; Best Speaker Award, Bridgeport School of Law Moot Court Competition, 1991; First Place, 1992 American Bar Association National Appellate Advocacy Competition; Zeldes, Needle & Cooper Award for Excellence in Legal Writing; 1993 Arnold J. Bai Litigation Award. ***PRACTICE AREAS:*** Civil Litigation; Criminal Law; Commercial Real Estate.

APPROVED ATTORNEYS FOR: Stewart Title Guaranty Co.; First American Title Insurance Co.; Connecticut Attorney's Title Insurance Co.; Fidelity National Title Insurance Company; Lawyers Title Insurance Corp.; New Milford Savings Bank; Fairfield County Savings Bank.
REFERENCES: People's Bank; Northwestern Mutual Life Insurance Co.

DISERIO MARTIN O'CONNOR & CASTIGLIONI LLP

NORWALK, CONNECTICUT

(See Stamford)

General Practice. Litigation and Trials in all Courts. Corporate, Commercial Finance, Securities, Taxation, Banking, Foreclosure and Workout, Real Estate Law, Personal Injury and Negligence, Employment Law, Wrongful Termination, Workers Compensation, Insurance Coverage and Defense, Family, Creditors Rights and Bankruptcy, Trusts, Probate, Estate and Tax Planning.

DOUGHERTY, DOUGHERTY & VECCHIOLLA

NORWALK, CONNECTICUT

(See Greenwich)

General Practice. Estate Planning and Probate Law. Real Estate, Taxation and Corporate Law, Business Law, Trusts and Estates.

CARL A. FERRARO, JR.

21 ISAACS STREET

NORWALK, CONNECTICUT 06850

Telephone: 203-866-6503

Fax: 203-866-6002

URL: http://www.connecticutattorney.cc

Email: ferrarocar@aol.com

URL: http://www.lawyers.com/caferraro

Family Law, Residential Real Estate, Commercial Real Estate, Personal Injury, Criminal Law, Domestic Relations.

CARL A. FERRARO, JR., born Elizabeth, New Jersey, October 20, 1964; admitted to bar, 1990, Connecticut and U.S. District Court, District of Connecticut. *Education:* Rutgers University (B.A., Economics, 1987); University of Bridgeport (J.D., 1990). *Member:* Connecticut Bar Association. ***PRACTICE AREAS:*** Personal Injury; Divorce; Family Law; Real Estate; Probate; Corporate Law; General Practice.

FINN DIXON & HERLING LLP

NORWALK, CONNECTICUT

(See Stamford)

Corporate Law, Mergers and Acquisitions, Securities Law, Venture Capital Financing, Corporate Finance and Restructuring, Commercial Litigation, Banking and Lending Law, Bankruptcy and Workouts, Employee Benefits and the Federal and State Taxation of Businesses and Business Transactions.

FOGARTY COHEN SELBY & NEMIROFF LLC

NORWALK, CONNECTICUT

(See Greenwich)

Litigation in all Courts, Real Estate and Land Use, Estate Planning and Probate, Corporate, Matrimonial, Administrative and Environmental, Appellate Practice, Business, Civil Trial, Commercial Litigation, Construction, Family, Labor and Employment, Medical Malpractice, Trust and Product Liability.

GENUARIO & CONOVER

94 EAST AVENUE
P.O. BOX 2044
NORWALK, CONNECTICUT 06852
Telephone: 203-849-9292
Fax: 203-855-0370
URL: http://www.lawyers.com/genuario&conover

General Civil Practice. Trials in all State and Federal Courts. Real Estate, Probate, Employment, Construction, Personal Injury, Foreclosures, Commercial and Zoning Law.

ROBERT L. GENUARIO, born Norwalk, Connecticut, March 31, 1952; admitted to bar, 1977, Connecticut and U.S. District Court, District of Connecticut; 1986, U.S. Supreme Court. *Education:* Villanova University (B.A., 1974; J.D., cum laude, 1977). Business and Research Editor, Villanova Law Review, 1976-1977. Author: "In re Middle Atlantic Stud Welding Company," Villanova Law Review, Vol. 21, page 605, 1976; Case Note, "DeFilipo v. Ford Motor Company—Conserted Refusal To Deal," Villanova Law Review, Vol. 21, page 530, 1976. Member, 1981-1991 and Chairman, 1983, 1984 and 1991, Norwalk Board of Education. Member, Fire District Task Force Committee, 1980. Director: Norwalk Red Cross, 1984-1985; Mid Fairfield Hospice Program, 1984-1985. State Senator, Connecticut, 1991-1994; 1995—. *Member:* Stamford-Norwalk Regional, Connecticut and American Bar Associations. ***PRACTICE AREAS:*** Planning and Zoning Law; Land Use Law; Real Estate Law; Civil Litigation.

STEPHEN J. CONOVER, born Pittsburgh, Pennsylvania, January 20, 1956; admitted to bar, 1982, Connecticut, New York and U.S. District Court, District of Connecticut; 1984, U.S. District Court, Southern District of New York; 1986, U.S. Court of Appeals, Second Circuit; 1992, U.S. Supreme Court. *Education:* University of Notre Dame (B.A., 1978); St. John's University (J.D., 1981). Connecticut Superior Court Special Master, 1997—. *Member:* Stamford/Norwalk Regional (Chairman, Bench-Bar Committee; Board of Directors, 1997—), Connecticut (Construction Law Section, Professional Ethics Committee & Professional Discipline Committee) and New York State Bar Associations; Association of Trial Lawyers of America; Connecticut Trial Lawyers Association; American Arbitration Association (Panel of Arbitrators); National Employment Lawyers Association; Association of Professional Responsibility Lawyers. ***PRACTICE AREAS:*** Civil Litigation.

ASSOCIATE

AMY J. LIVOLSI, born Stamford, Connecticut, September 13, 1969; admitted to bar, 1994, Connecticut; 1996, U.S. District Court, District of Connecticut. *Education:* Boston College (B.A., 1991); Widener University School of Law (J.D., 1994). Recipient, Outstanding Law Day Activity Award, American Bar Association, 1997. Member, 1996— and Chairman, 1997—, Board of Ethics, City of Stamford. *Member:* Connecticut Bar Association (Member, 1997— and Secretary, 1998—, Executive Committee of Young Lawyers of Lower Fairfield County); The Regional Bar Association (Member, Board of Directors, 1998—; Co-Chair, Litigation Section, 2000—; Co-Chair, Young Lawyers Section, 1997-1999; Co-Chair, Law Day Committee, 1996-1997); Connecticut Trial Lawyers Association; Women's Bankruptcy Bar Association. ***PRACTICE AREAS:*** Real Estate Law; Civil Litigation.

OF COUNSEL

SHERWIN A. RODIN, born New York, N.Y., September 25, 1923; admitted to bar, 1948, New York; 1949 U.S. District Court, Southern District of New York; 1954, U.S. District Court, Eastern District of New York; 1961, U.S. Court of Appeals, Second Circuit; 1989, Connecticut and U.S. District Court, District of Connecticut. *Education:* Columbia University (B.A., 1943; LL.B., 1948). Member, Norwalk Human Relations Commission, 1966-1973. *Member:* Stamford-Norwalk Regional, New York State and American Bar Associations; New York County Lawyers Association. ***PRACTICE AREAS:*** Probate; Trust Administration; Estate Planning.

LOCAL COUNSEL FOR: Stop & Shop; Price Costo.
REPRESENTATIVE CLIENTS: Norwalk Marine Contractors, Inc.; Logical Communications; Action Housing, Inc.; Andrews Construction, Inc.; Admiral Temps Inc.; Excel Personnel Inc.; City of Norwalk.

(This Listing Continued)

APPROVED ATTORNEYS FOR: First American Title Insurance Co.; Commonwealth Title Insurance Co.
REFERENCES: Fleet Bank, N.A.; Summit Bank.

ROBERT W. GREEN

NORWALK, CONNECTICUT

(See Stamford)

Real Estate, Probate and Estate, Elder Law, Zoning, Planning and Land Use, Administrative Law, Financial Law and Legislative Practice.

GRIMES & BATTERSBY L.L.P.

NORWALK, CONNECTICUT

(See Stamford)

Patents, Trademarks, Copyrights, Unfair Competition, Trade Secrets, Multimedia, Licensing, Franchising, Litigation and Antitrust.

HARRIS & HARRIS

A Professional Limited Liability Company
11 BELDEN AVENUE, SECOND FLOOR
NORWALK, CONNECTICUT 06850
Telephone: 203-838-7111
Fax: 203-845-0772
URL: http://www.lawyers.com/harris&harris
URL: http://www.harrisharris.com

General Practice, Trials in all State and Federal Courts and Agencies, Civil Litigation, Family Law, Probate, Administrative Law, Estate Planning, Special Education, Representation of Minors before Juvenile Court, Real Estate.

ARTHUR B. HARRIS, born Paterson, New Jersey, June 3, 1926; admitted to bar, 1952, Connecticut; 1964, U.S. District Court, District of Connecticut; 1968, U.S. Tax Court; U.S. Court of Appeals, Second Circuit. *Education:* Dartmouth College; Middlebury College; Tufts University (B.S., 1946; B.A., 1948); Northwestern University; Yale University (LL.B., 1951). Chairman, Conservation Commission, City of Norwalk, 1975-1978. *Member:* Connecticut and American (Member, Sections on: Corporation, Banking and Business Law; Taxation) Bar Associations; American Judicature Society. [LTJG, U.S. Navy, 1944-1947]. ***PRACTICE AREAS:*** Estate Law (50%); Criminal Law (25%); Litigation (10%); Business Law (15%).

CHARLES S. HARRIS, born Norwalk, Connecticut, February 21, 1962; admitted to bar, 1990, Connecticut. *Education:* Hampshire College (B.A., 1984); American University (J.D., 1990). *Member:* Stanford, Norwalk and American Bar Associations. ***PRACTICE AREAS:*** Civil Litigation; Family Law; Personal Injury; Workers Compensation; Commercial Litigation.

SUZANNE D'ORSI KOETSCH, born Hartford, Connecticut, May 22, 1964; admitted to bar, 1998, Connecticut. *Education:* Southern Connecticut State College (B.S.M.S., 1991); Quinnipiac College (J.D., 1997). Member: Special Education Advocacy Network, 1998-2001; Rotary International, 1999-2001. ***LANGUAGES:*** Portuguese. ***PRACTICE AREAS:*** Juvenile Law; Special Education; Family Law; Real Estate Transactions. ***Email:*** attykoetsch@hotmail.com

AUNEMETTA SCHMID, born Scarborough Toronto Canada, September 7, 1967; admitted to bar, 2001, Connecticut. *Education:* Southern Connecticut State College (B.S., 1998); Quinnipiac College (J.D., 2001). Recipient: Quinnipiac College Service to the Community Award, 2001. Active in: Volunteer Income Tax Assistance Program; Environmental Law Society; Tax Law Society; Women's Law Society; Juvenile and Family Law Society. ***PRACTICE AREAS:*** Family Law; Tax Law; Civil Litigation; Criminal Defense.

LEGAL SUPPORT PERSONNEL

SUZANNE SMYTHE, born Carmel, California, February 22, 1958. *Education:* Mills College (B.A., 1979). Phi Beta Kappa. (Paralegal). ***LANGUAGES:*** Spanish. ***PRACTICE AREAS:*** Legal Research; Draft Legal Pleadings; State and Federal Courts; State and Federal Agencies.

HEALY & BAILLIE, LLP

Established in 1948

THE LOCK BUILDING

20 MARSHALL STREET, SUITE 104 (SOUTH NORWALK)

NORWALK, CONNECTICUT 06854-2282

Telephone: 203-354-1360

Fax: 203-354-1363

Email: mmarion@healy.com

URL: http://www.healy.com

New York, New York Office: 29 Broadway, 10006-3293. Telephone: 212-943-3980. Fax: 212-425-0131. Email: reception@healy.com. Telex: 422089. Cable "Mainbrace New York".

Hong Kong Office: Healy & Baillie, Suite 1303, Dina House, Ruttonjee Centre, 11 Duddell Street, Central. Telephone: 852-2537-8628. Fax: 852-2521-9072. Email: recpt@healy.com.hk.

Millburn, New Jersey Office: Healy & Baillie, 374 Millburn Avenue, P.O. Box 599, 07041-0599. Telephone: 973-912-8955. Fax: 973-912-9767. Email: llambert@healy.com.

Admiralty, Corporate, Insurance, Reinsurance and General Practice.

RESIDENT PARTNERS

MATTHEW A. MARION, born New York, N.Y., November 22, 1957; admitted to bar, 1988, New York and Massachusetts; 1989, District of Columbia; 2000, Connecticut. *Education:* Columbia College (B.A., 1979); Washington College of Law of American University (J.D., 1987). ***PRACTICE AREAS:*** Maritime Law; Environmental Law; Insurance Law; Commercial Law; International Practice.

PETER G. DRAKOS, born Greenwich, Connecticut, January 29, 1956; admitted to bar, 1984, New York; 2000, Connecticut. *Education:* University of Vermont (B.A., 1978); Gonzaga University (J.D., 1983). ***PRACTICE AREAS:*** Maritime Law; Maritime Arbitration; Commercial Law; Corporate Law.

(For Complete Biographical Data on all Personnel see Professional Biographies in New York, New York)

HOHN AND DULBERG

11 ISAAC STREET

P.O. BOX 127

NORWALK, CONNECTICUT 06852-0127

Telephone: 203-866-4457

URL: http://www.lawyers.com/hohnanddulberg

General Practice. Probate, Negligence, Real Estate, Criminal and Family Law. Trials in all Courts.

JAY M. DULBERG, born Norwalk, Connecticut, July 16, 1942; admitted to bar, 1971, Colorado; 1972, Connecticut; 1975, U.S. District Court, District of Connecticut. *Education:* Brown University (B.A., 1964); University of Denver (J.D., 1971). Assistant Corporation Counsel, City of Norwalk, 1977-1980. Vice President, Norwalk Land Trust, Inc., 1981—. Member, Legal Assistant Advisory Council, Norwalk Community College, 1979—. *Member:* Norwalk-Wilton and Connecticut Bar Associations. [Lt., USNR, 1965-1968]. ***PRACTICE AREAS:*** General Practice.

APPROVED ATTORNEYS FOR: Commonwealth Land Title Insurance Co.; First American Title Insurance Co.; Chicago Title Insurance Co.
REPRESENTATIVE CLIENTS: Norwalk Excavating Co.; Riverside Cemetery Assn.; Norwalk Land Trust, Inc.; Architectural Builders of Westport, Inc.
REFERENCES: Merchants Bank and Trust Co.; Fairfield County Savings Bank; Union Trust Co.; Gateway Bank.

IVEY, BARNUM & O'MARA, LLC

NORWALK, CONNECTICUT

(See Greenwich)

General Practice. E-Commerce, Litigation in all Courts. Corporate, Commercial, Finance, Taxation, Trusts, Probate, Estate Planning, Family Law, Zoning, Environmental, Real Estate, Employment Law and Elder Law.

JACOBS PARTNERS LLC

383 MAIN AVENUE

NORWALK, CONNECTICUT 06851

Telephone: 203-846-6622

Fax: 203-846-6621

Business and Personal Bankruptcy, Workouts, Debtor Creditor's Rights, Commercial Litigation, Contracts and Business Disputes.

(This Listing Continued)

MEMBERS OF FIRM

MARK R. JACOBS, born Columbus, Ohio, June 7, 1953; admitted to bar, 1983, New York; 1984, U.S. District Court, Southern and Eastern Districts of New York, U.S. District Court, District of Connecticut and U.S. District Court, District of Colorado; 1998, Connecticut. *Education:* Yale University (B.A., cum laude, 1979); New York University (J.D., 1982). Law Clerk to the Hon. S.W. Kram, U.S. District Judge, Southern District of New York. Trustee, Association of Bankruptcy Professionals, 1990—. *Member:* American (Member, Business Bankruptcy Committee, Business Law Section, 1991—) and International Bar Associations; American Bankruptcy Institute. ***LANGUAGES:*** French. ***PRACTICE AREAS:*** Bankruptcy; Insolvency; Commercial Law. ***Email:*** MRJACOBS@sprynet.com

ASSOCIATES

ROBERT M. FLEISCHER, born Stamford, Connecticut, May 24, 1962; admitted to bar, 1992, Connecticut; 1993, New York and U.S. District Court, District of Connecticut. *Education:* Northeastern University (B.S., 1985); Pace University (J.D., 1992). *Member:* Connecticut and New York State Bar Associations; Connecticut Trial Lawyers Association. ***PRACTICE AREAS:*** Litigation; Bankruptcy. ***Email:*** fleischr@sprynet.com

LESLIE L. LANE, born Rolla, Missouri, February 18, 1968; (admission pending). *Education:* Drury College (B.S., 1992); Quinnipiac College (J.D., cum laude, 1998). Recipient, Distinguished Academic Achievement Awards in Commercial Law, Business Organizations and Advanced Contracts. Managing Editor, Quinnipiac Law Review, 1997-1998. ***PRACTICE AREAS:*** Bankruptcy; Commercial Litigation; Taxation. ***Email:*** lllane@sprynet.com

KEOGH, BURKHART & VETTER

34 WALL STREET

P.O. BOX 126

NORWALK, CONNECTICUT 06852

Telephone: 203-866-2535, 866-2536

Fax: 203-855-9016

General Practice. Insurance, Real Estate, Probate, Corporation and Commercial Law, Elder Law. Trials in all Courts.

MEMBERS OF FIRM

JOHN KEOGH (1871-1960).

JOHN KEOGH, JR. (1910-1992).

ALFRED W. BURKHART, born Athens, Pennsylvania, September 12, 1923; admitted to bar, 1951, New York; 1953, Connecticut. *Education:* Cornell University (A.B., 1948; LL.B., 1951). Phi Delta Phi. City Councilman, 1961-1967; Council President, 1965-1967, Norwalk. *Member:* Norwalk-Wilton (President, 1982-1983), Stamford/Norwalk Regional (Director, 1991-1992) and Connecticut Bar Associations. [Lt. Col., U.S.A.F. Res., 1943-1946]. ***PRACTICE AREAS:*** Litigation; Probate Law; Elder Law; Real Estate Law.

THOMAS J. VETTER, born Norwalk, Connecticut, November 23, 1954; admitted to bar, 1979, Connecticut. *Education:* Nasson College (B.A., 1976); Western New England College (J.D., 1979). Author: "Liability of the Water Purveyor," Journal of New England Waterworks Association, Vol. 105, No. 4, December, 1991. Commissioner, First Taxing District, 1985-1991, Chairman, 1989-1991. Member, Norwalk Board of Education, 1992—. *Member:* Norwalk-Wilton (Member, Executive Committee, 1989-1991), Stamford/Norwalk Regional, Connecticut and American Bar Associations. ***PRACTICE AREAS:*** Real Estate Law; Probate Law; Litigation.

STEPHEN B. KEOGH, born Norwalk, Connecticut, January 8, 1960; admitted to bar, 1985, Connecticut; 1986, U.S. District Court, District of Connecticut. *Education:* Yale University (B.A., magna cum laude, 1982); Université de Poitiers, France; Columbia University (J.D., 1985). Harlan Fiske Stone Scholar. Managing Editor, Columbia Human Rights Law Review, 1984-1985. Recipient: Robert Noxon Toppan Prize for Constitutional Law, 1984; Charles Evans Hughes Public Interest Law Fellow, 1985. Member, Public Interest Law Foundation at Columbia, Inc. (Treasurer, 1984-1985). Author: "Formal and Informal Constitutional Lawmaking in the United States in the Winter of 1860-1861," The Journal of Legal History, Vol. 8, No. 3, December, 1987. *Member:* Norwalk-Wilton (Member, Executive Committee, 1988-1989), Stamford/Norwalk Regional, Connecticut and American Bar Associations; The Association of Trial Lawyers of America; Connecticut Trial Lawyers Association; National Academy of Elder Law Attorneys. ***LANGUAGES:*** French. ***PRACTICE AREAS:*** Elder Law; Probate Law; Litigation.

GENERAL COUNSEL FOR: Sono Village Condominium Associations, Inc.; Park Towers Condominium Association, Inc.
LOCAL COUNSEL FOR: Metropolitan Life Insurance Co.; Underwriters at Lloyds, England; Grange Mutual Cos.; Insurance Company of the State of Pennsylvania; Albany Insurance Co.; Provident Life & Casualty Insurance Co.; Preferred Risk

(This Listing Continued)

KEOGH, BURKHART & VETTER, Norwalk—Continued

Mutual Insurance Co.; National American Insurance Co.; Integon Insurance; CSC Insurance Services; Wausau Insurance Cos.; Utica First Insurance Co.

KOSKOFF, KOSKOFF & BIEDER, P.C.

NORWALK, CONNECTICUT

(See Bridgeport)

Litigation in all State and Federal Courts. Medical Malpractice, Equal Opportunity, Negligence, Products Liability, Civil Rights, and Class Actions.

LEV & BERLIN, P.C.

535 CONNECTICUT AVENUE
NORWALK, CONNECTICUT 06854
Telephone: 203-838-8500
Telecopier: 203-854-1652
URL: http://www.lawyers.com/levberlin
Email: dberlin@levberlin.com
URL: http://www.levberlin.com

New York Office: 420 Lexington Avenue, Suite 300, 10170. Telephone: 212-297-6166. Telecopier: 212-986-1952.

Corporation, Securities, Commercial and Investment Banking, Tax, Real Estate, Estate Planning, Intellectual Property and Civil Litigation in all State and Federal Courts.

DUANE L. BERLIN, born Norwalk, Connecticut, November 17, 1958; admitted to bar, 1984, Connecticut and U.S. District Court, District of Connecticut. *Education:* Brandeis University (A.B., 1980); University of Miami (J.D., cum laude, 1983). Member, Society of Wig and Robe. Member, University of Miami Law Review, 1981-1983. Director, Norwalk Jewish Community Center, 1988-1989. Member, Board of Trustees, Fairfield County Chapter, Leukemia Society of America, 1994. Series 7 General Securities Representative, National Association of Securities Dealers, 1999—. *Member:* Connecticut (Member, Stamford/Norwalk Regional Bar Association Internet Law Committee, 2000—) and American (Member, Sections on: Corporation, Banking and Business Law) Bar Associations. ***PRACTICE AREAS:*** Corporate Finance and Securities; Real Estate; General Corporate. ***Email:*** dberlin@levberlin.com

---

DONNA M. LATTARULO, born Bronx, New York, January, 1962; admitted to bar, 1986, Massachusetts; 1987, New York, Connecticut and U.S. District Court, District of Connecticut; 1997, U.S. District Court, District of Massachusetts and Southern District of New York. *Education:* Boston College (A.B., 1983); Pace University (J.D., 1986). Factfinder/Arbitrator, Judicial District of Stamford/Norwalk, 1999—. *Member:* Stamford/Norwalk Regional, Connecticut, New York State and American Bar Associations; Connecticut Trial Lawyers Association. ***REPORTED CASES:*** Housing Authority v. Harris, 225 Conn. 600 (1993); Housing Authority v. Harris 28 Conn. App. 684 (1992); Staudinger v. Barrett, 208 Conn. 94 (1988). ***PRACTICE AREAS:*** Civil Litigation; Landlord/Tenant Law; Personal Injury Litigation; Bankruptcy; Real Estate. ***Email:*** dlattarulo@levberlin.com

STEPHEN J. VELIE, born Concord, Massachusetts, July 1967; admitted to bar, 1998, Massachusetts and Oregon; 2001 Connecticut. *Education:* Occidental College (A.B., International Affairs, 1990); Vermont Law School (J.D., 1997); Boston University (LL.M., Financial and Banking Law, 2000). ***PRACTICE AREAS:*** Securities; Corporate Law. ***Email:*** svelie@levberlin.com

OF COUNSEL

BRUCE L. LEV, born New Haven, Connecticut, September 13, 1943; admitted to bar, 1968, Connecticut and Virginia; 1972, U.S. Supreme Court. *Education:* Wesleyan University (B.A., with honors, 1965); University of Virginia (J.D., 1968). Phi Alpha Delta (Marshal, Jefferson Chapter). Chairman, Citizens Action Committee, City of Norwalk (advisory to the Mayor), 1972-1974. Counsel to Housing Authority of The City of Norwalk, 1974-1995. Vice President and General Counsel, Micro Warehouse, Inc., April, 1995; October, 2000. Vice Chairman, USCO Logistics, November, 2000—. Member, Board of Directors, Norwalk Community Technical College. Member, National Panel of Arbitrators, American Arbitration Association. *Member:* Stamford/Norwalk Regional, Connecticut and American Bar Associations; Virginia State Bar. (Also, Chairman, USCO Logistics). ***PRACTICE AREAS:*** Corporations; Securities; Investment Banking.

DONALD M. KLEBAN, born New York, N.Y., November, 16, 1940; admitted to bar, 1968, Connecticut; 1970, New York. *Education:* Alfred University (B.A., 1965); New York University (J.D., 1968). (Resident, New York Office). ***Email:*** dkleban@levberlin.com

(This Listing Continued)

LEGAL SUPPORT PERSONNEL

SHARI SALTARELLI, (Legal Assistant). ***Email:*** ssaltarelli@levberlin.com

REFERENCES: Summit Bank; Stewart Title Guaranty Company.

LOVEJOY AND RIMER, P.C.

65 EAST AVENUE
P.O. BOX 390
NORWALK, CONNECTICUT 06852-0390
Telephone: 203-853-4400
Fax: 203-866-3386
URL: http://www.lovejoyrimer.com

General Practice. Real Estate, Probate, Estate and Tax Planning, Corporate, Municipal, Planning and Zoning, Wetlands, Family, Condominium, Collection, Litigation and Health and Hospital Law.

LAWRENCE P. DENNIN, JR., born Norwalk, Connecticut, August 17, 1939; admitted to bar, 1964, Connecticut; 1965, U.S. District Court, District of Connecticut; 1969, U.S. Supreme Court; 1973, U.S. Court of Appeals, Second Circuit. *Education:* College of the Holy Cross (A.B., 1961); University of Connecticut (LL.B., 1964). Councilman, City of Norwalk, 1967-1969. *Member:* Stamford/Norwalk Regional (President, 1994), Connecticut (Chairman, Law Office Management Committee, 1982-1984) and American Bar Associations. ***PRACTICE AREAS:*** Commercial Law; Corporate Law; Real Estate. ***Email:*** ldennin@lovejoyrimer.com

LOUIS S. CICCARELLO, born Middletown, Connecticut, October 26, 1938; admitted to bar, 1965, Connecticut and U.S. District Court, District of Connecticut; 1971, U.S. Supreme Court; 1973, U.S. Court of Appeals, Second Circuit. *Education:* University of Connecticut; Wesleyan University (B.A., 1961); Stanford University (LL.B., 1964). Instructor, Litigation and Business Law, Norwalk Community Technical College, 1984—. Member: Board of Estimate and Taxation, Norwalk, 1967-1973; Norwalk Board of Education, 1982-1989. State Senator, Connecticut, 1975-1976. *Member:* Norwalk-Wilton, Connecticut and American Bar Associations; Connecticut Trial Lawyers Association. ***PRACTICE AREAS:*** Personal Injury; Municipal Law; Zoning Law; Litigation. ***Email:*** lciccarello@lovejoyrimer.com

WILLIAM R. PASCUCCI, born Bridgeport, Connecticut, July 12, 1939; admitted to bar, 1965, Connecticut and U.S. District Court, District of Connecticut; 1969, U.S. Supreme Court; 1973, U.S. Court of Appeals, Second Circuit. *Education:* Fairfield University (B.A., 1961); Georgetown University (LL.B., 1965). Author, *Report by Committee on Condemnation and Condemnation Procedure,* American Bar Association, 1965. *Member:* Stamford/Norwalk Regional, Connecticut (Member: Executive Committee, Tax Section, 1981-1983; Executive Committee, Estates and Probate Section, 1990-1993) and American Bar Associations. ***PRACTICE AREAS:*** Probate; Federal Income Tax; Federal Estate and Gift Taxation; Estate Planning. ***Email:*** wpascucci@lovejoyrimer.com

CHRISTOPHER J. JARBOE, born Norwalk, Connecticut, August 21, 1964; admitted to bar, 1989, Connecticut; 1990, U.S. District Court, District of Connecticut; 1991, U.S. Court of Appeals, Second Circuit; 1996, U.S. Supreme Court. *Education:* American University; University of Connecticut (B.A., 1986; J.D., 1989). *Member:* Stamford/Norwalk Regional and Connecticut Bar Associations; Connecticut Trial Lawyers Association; The Association of Trial Lawyers of America. ***PRACTICE AREAS:*** Personal Injury; Collections; Litigation; Landlord and Tenant Law; Real Estate; Land Use. ***Email:*** cjarboe@lovejoyrimer.com

STEVEN DANIEL SMITH, born New Haven, Connecticut, April 9, 1966; admitted to bar, 1992, New Jersey; 1993, Connecticut. *Education:* University of Richmond (B.S.B.A., 1988); T.C. Williams School of Law, University of Richmond (J.D., 1992). Editor, Regional Bar News. *Member:* Stamford/Norwalk Regional (Co-Chair, Probate and Estates Committee), Connecticut and American Bar Associations. ***PRACTICE AREAS:*** Probate; Real Estate; Estate Administration; Trust Administration; Elder Law. ***Email:*** ssmith@lovejoyrimer.com

---

NEIL P. PHILLIPS, born New York, N.Y., May 1, 1967; admitted to bar, 1996, Connecticut; 1997, U.S. District Court, District of Connecticut and District of Columbia. *Education:* Muhlenberg College (B.A., 1989), Syracuse University (J.D., 1995). *Member:* Stamford/Norwalk Regional, Connecticut and American Bar Associations. ***PRACTICE AREAS:*** Estate Planning; Probate; Real Estate; Elder Law. ***Email:*** nphillips@lovejoyrimer.com

OF COUNSEL

JONATHAN LOVEJOY, born Norwalk, Connecticut, August 2, 1931; admitted to bar, 1956, Connecticut. *Education:* Wesleyan University (B.A.,

(This Listing Continued)

1953); Yale University (LL.B., 1956). Phi Delta Phi. Member, New Canaan Zoning Board of Appeals, 1975-1983. Chairman, Norwalk Harbor Management Commission, 1985-1990. Judge of Probate, Town of Westbrook, 1993-1995. *Member:* Connecticut (Member, Executive Committee, Probate and Estate Section, 1980) Bar Associations. ***PRACTICE AREAS:*** Estate Planning; Real Estate; Trust Law.

GENERAL COUNSEL FOR: Norwalk Hospital; Town of New Canaan.
LOCAL COUNSEL FOR: The Wilton Bank.

MARTIN, LUCAS & CHIOFFI, LLP

NORWALK, CONNECTICUT

(See Stamford)

Business Law, Corporate Finance, Mergers and Acquisitions, Internet Law, Venture Capital, Commercial and Employment Litigation; Securities, Employment, Commercial Litigation, Real Estate, Commercial Leasing, Estate and Tax Planning, Estate Settlement and Trust Administration.

McGOVERN & ASSOCIATES

NORWALK, CONNECTICUT

(See Greenwich)

General Commercial Practice. Corporate (Foreign and Domestic), Mergers and Acquisitions, Securities, Venture Capital, Taxation, Litigation in all Courts. International, Joint Ventures, Admiralty, Sports, Commercial and Residential Real Estate Law. Estates and Trusts.

ROY W. MOSS

102 HIGHLAND AVENUE
NORWALK, CONNECTICUT 06852
Telephone: 203-852-1907
Fax: 203-852-9174
Email: roywmoss@prodigy.net
URL: http://www.lawyers.com/roymosslaw

Bankruptcy.

ROY W. MOSS, born Stamford, Connecticut, March 16, 1954; admitted to bar, 1981, Connecticut. *Education:* University of Pennsylvania (A.B., 1977); University of Connecticut (J.D., 1981). Member, University of Connecticut Moot Court Board, 1980-1981. *Member:* Bridgeport and Connecticut Bar Associations. ***PRACTICE AREAS:*** Bankruptcy Law.

WILLIAM A. PELLETREAU, L.L.C.

5 MOTT AVENUE
P.O. BOX 270
NORWALK, CONNECTICUT 06850-0270
Telephone: 203-838-0529
Fax: 203-831-8285
Email: WPelleLLC@aol.com
URL: http://www.lawyers.com/pelletreau

Criminal, Divorce, Personal Injury, Real Estate and General Practice.

WILLIAM A. PELLETREAU, born Norwalk, Connecticut, February 1, 1951; admitted to bar, 1980, Connecticut, U.S. District Court and District of Connecticut; 1981, U.S. District Court, Southern District of New York. *Education:* University of New Hampshire (B.A., 1973); University of Bridgeport (J.D., 1980). Former Deputy Assistant State's Attorney, State of Connecticut, 1980-1983. *Member:* Stamford Norwalk Regional Bar Association. ***REPORTED CASES:*** Ganim v. Roberts, 204 Conn. 760, 529 A 2d. 194 (1987); State v. Morelli, 25 Conn. App. 605, 595 A 2d. 932 (1991) Trial Counsel, on brief in appeal. ***PRACTICE AREAS:*** Criminal Law; Divorce; Personal Injury; Real Estate; General Practice.

PIAZZA & PICKEL

NORWALK, CONNECTICUT

(See Stamford)

Trials and Appeals in State and Federal Courts, Negligence, Medical Malpractice, Divorce and Personal Injury Law, Wrongful Death, Legal Malpractice, Child Custody, Automobile Accidents, Product Liability, Adoption, Family Law.

ROBERTS, ROSE & BATES, P.C.

NORWALK, CONNECTICUT

(See Stamford)

General Practice, Litigation, Real Estate, Leasing, Banking, Matrimonial, Probate, Estate Planning and Trusts, International Business, Employment Law.

RUBENSTEIN, GREEN & BASS, LLC

NORWALK, CONNECTICUT

(See Westport)

General Civil Practice before State and Federal Courts, Real Estate, Corporation, Commercial and Banking, Personal Injury, Medical Malpractice, Estate Planning and Probate, Planning and Zoning Trials and Appeals, Banking Litigation.

SANDAK FRIEDMAN HENNESSEY & GRECO, LLP

NORWALK, CONNECTICUT

(See Stamford)

Trials and Appeals in all Connecticut and Federal Courts and Administrative Agencies. Personal Injury, Medical Malpractice, Commercial, Environmental Litigation, Real Estate, Zoning and Land Use, Property Tax Appeals.

STEPHEN N. SCHAFFER

9 MOTT AVENUE, SUITE 208
NORWALK, CONNECTICUT 06850
Telephone: 203-853-7711
Fax: 203-853-0448
URL: http://www.lawyers.com/stephenschaffer

General Civil Practice, Family Law, Divorce, Child Custody, Child Support, Real Estate, Personal Injury, Auto Accidents, Corporate, Business, Commercial and Litigation in all Courts.

STEPHEN N. SCHAFFER, born Stamford, Connecticut, September 25, 1937; admitted to bar, 1962, Connecticut and U.S. District Court, District of Connecticut; 1966, U.S. Court of Appeals, 2nd Circuit; 1971, U.S. Supreme Court. *Education:* Lehigh University (B.S., 1959); Boston University (J.D., 1962); New York University Graduate School of Law. Chairman, Citizens Action Committee of Norwalk, 1969-1970. Member, Mayors Committee on Planning and Zoning for the City of Norwalk, 1972; President, Jewish Federation of Greater Norwalk, Inc., 1982-1984. *Member:* Stamford-Norwalk Regional (President, Lower Fairfield County Junior Bar Association, 1968-1969); Norwalk/Wilton (President, 1999-2001); Connecticut and American Bar Associations.

SCHOONMAKER, GEORGE & COLIN, P.C.

NORWALK, CONNECTICUT

(See Greenwich)

Matrimonial and Family Law.

SILVER, GOLUB & TEITELL LLP

NORWALK, CONNECTICUT

(See Stamford)

Trial Practice in all State and Federal Courts. Medical Malpractice, Negligence, Commercial Litigation, Family and Criminal Law.

SLAVITT, CONNERY & VARDAMIS

Established in 1945
618 WEST AVENUE
P.O. BOX 2129
NORWALK, CONNECTICUT 06852-2129
Telephone: 203-838-7555
Telecopier: 203-866-9724

General Practice. Commercial Law, Condemnation, Real Estate, Estate Planning, Probate, Family and Personal Injury Law. Civil and Criminal Trial Practice in all Courts. Agency and Distributorships, Alternative Dispute Resolution, Bankruptcy, Banks and Banking, Business Law, Civil Practice, Debtor and Creditor, Eminent Domain, Inverse Condemnation, Land Annexation, Commercial Real Estate, Construction Law, Contracts, Corporate Law, Equipment Finance and Leasing, Family

(This Listing Continued)

SLAVITT, CONNERY & VARDAMIS, Norwalk—Continued

Law, Finance, Franchises and Franchising, Fire Insurance Subrogation, Uninsured and Underinsured Motorists, Uninsured and Underinsured Motorists Arbitration, Commercial Leasing, Evictions, Landlord and Tenant Law, Lease Finance, Leasing, Office Leasing, Retail Leasing, Shopping Center Leasing, Legal Malpractice, Civil Litigation, Business Acquisitions, Business Divestitures, Mortgages, Negligence, Negligence Defense, Partnership Law, Torts, Civil Liability, Tort Liability, Trusts and Estates, Wills, Workers' Compensation, Zoning, Planning and Land Use.

MEMBERS OF FIRM

ABRAHAM D. SLAVITT (1900-1994).

PAUL R. CONNERY (1897-1953).

ROBERT A. SLAVITT, born New York, N.Y., July 15, 1928; admitted to bar, 1952, Connecticut; 1957, U.S. District Court, District of Connecticut; 1962, U.S. Court of Appeals, 2nd Circuit; 1973, U.S. Tax Court; 1975, U.S. Claims Court. *Education:* Colby College (B.A., 1949); New York University (LL.B., 1952). Phi Delta Phi. Author/Editor, Revision Chapters 14A, B, C, Nichols Law of Eminent Domain, Consequential Damages, 1992. Lecturer, The School For Bank Administration, Madison, WI, 1991. ABA Conv. 1999 - Eminent Domain. Director, State of Connecticut Long Lane School, 1965-1969. Trustee, New York University Law School Alumni Association. Member, 1978-1991 and Vice President, 1985-1989, Connecticut Law Revision Committee - Law of Eminent Domain. Special Trial Referee, appointed by Chief Court Administrator, January 1, 1984-June 30, 1984; reappointed, July 1, 1984-June 30, 1999. Panel, Construction Industry, American Arbitration Association. *Member:* Norwalk-Wilton (President, 1986) and Connecticut (Member: House of Delegates, 1987-1989) Bar Associations; The Association of Trial Lawyers of America. ***PRACTICE AREAS:*** Eminent Domain Law; Real Estate Law; Civil Litigation; Business Law; Construction Law.

GEORGE A. VARDAMIS, born Bangor, Maine, September 6, 1923; admitted to bar, 1952, Maine; 1953, Connecticut; 1959, U.S. District Court, District of Connecticut. *Education:* University of Maine (B.A., with honors, 1949); Harvard University (LL.B., 1952). Phi Beta Kappa; Phi Kappa Phi. Member: Advisory Board, Paralegal Studies, Norwalk Community College, 1979; Board of Governors, Harvard Law School Association of Connecticut, 1982. *Member:* Norwalk-Wilton (President, 1980), Connecticut (Member: Legal Ethics Committee, 1969-1985; Executive Committee, Real Property Section, 1970—; Board of Governors, 1983-1985; House of Delegates, 1981—) and American Bar Associations; New England Land Title Association. ***PRACTICE AREAS:*** Real Estate Law; Corporate Law; Business Organization Law.

STEPHEN A. HABETZ, born Bridgeport, Connecticut, May 19, 1938; admitted to bar, 1964, District of Columbia, Connecticut, U.S. District Court, District of Columbia and U.S. Court of Appeals for the District of Columbia Circuit; 1968, U.S. District Court, District of Connecticut; 1973, U.S. Tax Court. *Education:* Fairfield University (B.A., with honors, 1960); Georgetown University (LL.B., 1963). Phi Delta Phi. *Member:* Norwalk-Wilton and Connecticut (Member, Executive Committee, Estates and Probate Section, 1988-1990) Bar Associations. ***PRACTICE AREAS:*** Estate Planning Law; Probate Law; Real Estate Law.

MICHAEL P. SWEENEY, born Hartford, Connecticut, June 3, 1958; admitted to bar, 1983, Connecticut; 1984, U.S. District Court, District of Connecticut. *Education:* Fairfield University (A.B., 1980); Suffolk University (J.D., 1983). Omicron Delta Epsilon; Phi Alpha Delta. *Member:* Stamford/Norwalk, Hartford County, Connecticut (Member, Executive Committee, Planning and Zoning Section, 1991—) and American Bar Associations. ***PRACTICE AREAS:*** Real Estate Law; Land Use Law; Corporate Law.

ASSOCIATES

S. ANTOINETTE MORTON, born Kansas City, Kansas, November 21, 1947; admitted to bar, 1983, Connecticut; 1984, U.S. District Court, District of Connecticut. *Education:* University of Kansas (B.S., summa cum laude, 1969); Purdue University (M.A., 1971); University of Kansas (J.D., 1983). Phi Beta Kappa. Wesport Town Representative, 1985-1987. State Attorney Trial Referee. *Member:* Bridgeport, Connecticut and American Bar Associations; Connecticut Trial Lawyers Association; Fairfield County Women's Bar Association (President, 1984-1986). ***PRACTICE AREAS:*** Probate; Real Estate Law; Family Law; Litigation.

TRICIA L. PINTO, born Patchogue, New York, September 21, 1970; admitted to bar, 1997, Connecticut; 1998, New York. *Education:* Pace University (B.S., 1992); Quinnipiac College (J.D., cum laude, 1997). Quinnipiac Probate Law Journal (Member, 1995-1996; Business Managing Editor, 1996-1997). *Member:* Connecticut and American Bar Associations. ***PRACTICE AREAS:*** General Practice.

KENNETH R. SOSNOSKI, JR., born Lakewood, New Jersey; admitted to bar, 1995, Connecticut; 1997, U.S. District Court, District of Connecticut; 1998, Colorado, U.S. District Court, District of Connecticut and Colorado and U.S. District Court, Southern District of New York. *Education:* Pennsylvania State University (B.S., 1986); University of Baltimore (J.D., 1995). Phi Beta Kappa, Lambda Chapter. Golden Key National Honor Society. Recipient: Senatorial Scholarship; House of Delegates Scholarship. Member, Board of Education, City of Danbury, 1991-1992. *Member:* Connecticut Bar Association; Connecticut Trial Lawyers Association. ***PRACTICE AREAS:*** Commercial Litigation; Civil Litigation; Real Estate.

OF COUNSEL

HARRY M. LESSIN (1909-1990).

R. E. VAN NORSTRAND (1937-1995).

TIERNEY, ZULLO, FLAHERTY & MURPHY, P.C.

Established in 1970

134 EAST AVENUE

P.O. BOX 2028-BELDEN STATION

NORWALK, CONNECTICUT 06852

Telephone: 203-853-7000

Fax: 203-838-4829

Email: tierneyzulloflaherty@snet.net

General Practice. Real Estate, Probate, Administrative, Condemnation, Employment, Healthcare, Municipal, Land Use, Planning, Zoning and Family Law. Civil Litigation, State and Federal Courts.

THOMAS TIERNEY, born Norwalk, Connecticut, January 8, 1930; admitted to bar, 1956, Connecticut. *Education:* Fairfield University (A.B., 1951); Fordham University (J.D., 1956). Minority Leader, Common Council, City of Norwalk, 1959-1961. President, Lower Fairfield Junior Bar Association, 1960. Government Appeal Agent, Local Board 17, Connecticut Selective Service, 1967-1972. Representative, State of Connecticut, 147th District, 1967-1968. *Member:* Stamford/Norwalk Regional, Norwalk-Wilton (President, 1988-1989), Connecticut and American Bar Associations. [U.S. Army Engineers, 1951-1953]. ***PRACTICE AREAS:*** Probate; Real Estate; Estate Planning.

FRANK N. ZULLO, born Norwalk, Connecticut, June 3, 1932; admitted to bar, 1957, Connecticut. *Education:* Fordham University (B.S.S., 1954; J.D., 1957). Recipient, Young Man of the Year Award, Norwalk Junior Chamber of Commerce, 1958, 1963. Prosecutor, Norwalk City Court, 1959-1960. Minority Leader, Common Council, City of Norwalk, 1963-1965. Chairman: United Fund Drive, 1963-1964, 1964-1965; Chairman, Board of Trustees, Y.M.C.A., 1987-1999; Board of Trustees, Vitam, 1990-1992. President, United Fund, 1965-1966, 1973-1974. Mayor, City of Norwalk, 1965-1971. Member, Executive Committee, 1966-1971 and President, 1968-1969, Connecticut Conference of Mayors. Member, Board of Trustees, 1971-1995, Chairman, Board of Trustees, 1979-1982 and Counsel, 1987—, Norwalk Hospital. State Trial Referee, 1984-1991. Member: Board of Trustees, Maritime Center, 1986—; Tri-State Regional Planning Association, 1988-1995; Selection Committee, Ettinger Scholarship Program, 1989—; Board of Trustees, Five Town Foundation, 1990-1997. Member, 1991— and Vice-Chairman, 1994-1999, Chairman, 1999—, Board of Trustees, Bridgeport University. Vice-Chairman, Board of Directors, Honey Hill Care Center, 1993—. *Member:* Stamford/Norwalk Regional, Norwalk-Wilton (President, 1996-1997) and American Bar Associations. ***LANGUAGES:*** Italian. ***PRACTICE AREAS:*** Zoning, Planning and Land Use; Health Law; Real Estate.

THOMAS A. FLAHERTY, born Chicago, Illinois, July 28, 1929; admitted to bar, 1956, Connecticut. *Education:* Fairfield University (B.A., 1951); Columbia University (J.D., 1956). Corporation Counsel, City of Norwalk, 1965-1968. Member: Redevelopment Agency, City of Norwalk, 1968; Board of Education, City of Norwalk, 1973-1976; Executive Committee and Board of Directors, Greater Norwalk Chamber of Commerce, 1984-1986, 1988-1991, 1997—. Chairman, Fairfield Judicial District Grievance Panel, 1992-1993. *Member:* Stamford/Norwalk Regional and Connecticut Bar Associations. ***PRACTICE AREAS:*** Health Care; Corporate Law; Administrative Law.

FRANK W. MURPHY, born Darien, Connecticut, May 31, 1937; admitted to bar, 1962, Connecticut; 1963, U.S. District Court, District of Connecticut; 1969, U.S. District Court, Southern and Eastern Districts of New York, U.S. Court of Appeals, 2nd Circuit; 1970, U.S. Supreme Court; 1973, U.S. Tax Court. *Education:* Lafayette College (A.B., 1959); University of Pennsylvania (J.D., cum laude, 1962). Phi Alpha Theta. Recipient, Connecticut Jaycee Young Man of the Year, 1970. Corporation Counsel, City of Norwalk, 1969-1978. Member: Norwalk Board of Estimate and Taxation, 1972-1978; Charter Revision Commission, 1978; Norwalk Conservation Commission, 1968-1970; Southwest Regional Planning Agency, 1968-1973; Connecticut Department of Education Arbitration Panel, 1987-1999; Connecticut Employees Review Board, 1989-1995. Counsel to: Norwalk Housing Authority, 1968-1969; New Canaan Board of Education, 1974-2000; Norwalk Board of Education, 1979-1989; Norwalk

(This Listing Continued)

Maritime Authority, 1986-1988. Special Counsel: New Canaan Police Commission, 1974—; City of Norwalk, 1981-1993; City of Stamford, 1990-1992. Arbitrator, American Arbitration Association. *Member:* Stamford/Norwalk Regional (Treasurer, 1992-1993; Secretary, 1993-1994; Vice President, 1994-1996; President-Elect, 1996-1997; President, 1997-1998), Connecticut (Member: House of Delegates, 1996—; Sections on: Litigation; Executive Committee; Labor and Employment) and American (Member, Sections on: Litigation; Urban State and Local Government; Labor and Employment; Committee on Condemnation, Planning and Zoning) Bar Associations; Defense Research Institute; National Institute of Municipal Law Officers (Secretary, Personnel and Labor Section, 1985-1989); Norwalk Community College Foundation (Member, Board of Trustees, 1989-1995; Member, Fairfield Judicial District Grievance Committee, 1996—). ***PRACTICE AREAS:*** Civil Litigation; Employment Law; Municipal Law; Health Law.

REUBEN S. MIDLER, born Paterson, New Jersey, March 20, 1949; admitted to bar, 1973, New Jersey and U.S. District Court, District of New Jersey; 1974, Connecticut; 1975, U.S. District Court, District of Connecticut. *Education:* University of Bridgeport (B.A., 1970); Rutgers University Law School (J.D., 1973). Assistant Public Defender, State of Connecticut, 1974-1977. *Member:* Stamford/Norwalk Regional, Norwalk-Wilton, Connecticut and American Bar Associations; Connecticut Trial Lawyers Association; The Association of Trial Lawyers of America. ***PRACTICE AREAS:*** Civil Litigation; Criminal Law; Domestic Relations.

GARY LORUSSO, born Norwalk, Connecticut, February 17, 1948; admitted to bar, 1975, Connecticut. *Education:* College of the Holy Cross (A.B., 1970); St. John's University (J.D., 1974). Member, Board of Directors, Keystone House, Inc., 1995—. Board of Directors Lockwood-Mathews Mansion Museum, 1999—. *Member:* Stamford/Norwalk Regional, Norwalk-Wilton and American Bar Associations. ***PRACTICE AREAS:*** Real Estate.

ANDREW F. KORDAS, born Greenwich, Connecticut, September 23, 1953; admitted to bar, 1979, Connecticut and U.S. District Court, District of Connecticut; 1980, U.S. Tax Court; 1988, U.S. Supreme Court. *Education:* Pace University (B.S., magna cum laude, 1975; J.D., 1979); New York University (LL.M., Taxation, 1981). Articles Editor, Pace Law Review, 1978-1979. Counsel, Connecticut Association of Theatre Owners, Inc. ("CATO"), 1997—. Member, Planned Giving Committee, Norwalk Hospital Foundation, 1991—. *Member:* Stamford/Norwalk Regional, Connecticut and American (Member, Forum on Entertainment and Sports Industries Section) Bar Associations. ***LANGUAGES:*** Spanish. ***PRACTICE AREAS:*** Corporate Law; Tax Law; Real Estate.

BARBARA COUGHLAN, born Bourne, Massachusetts, June 24, 1959; admitted to bar, 1984, Connecticut; 1985, New York; 1987, U.S. District Court, Eastern District of New York; 1989, U.S. District Court, District of Connecticut; 1996, U.S. District Court, Southern District of New York and U.S. Supreme Court. *Education:* Boston College (B.A., magna cum laude, 1981; J.D., 1984). Member, Jessup Moot Court Team. Counsel, The Norwalk Emergency Shelter, 1994—. Counsel, The Maritime Aquarium at Norwalk, 1995—. *Member:* Stamford-Norwalk and Connecticut (Member, Executive Committee, Planning & Zoning Section) Bar Associations. ***PRACTICE AREAS:*** Civil Litigation; Zoning, Planning and Land Use; Employment Law.

ELIZABETH A.B. SUCHY, born New York, New York, February 15, 1962; admitted to bar, 1992, Connecticut; 1993, New York; 1994, U.S. District Court, District of Connecticut. *Education:* Boston College (A.B., magna cum laude, 1983); New York University (M.A., 1985); Fordham University (J.D., 1992). Order of the Cross and Crown. Member, Boston College Alumni Interview Council, 1983—. Member, Board of Directors, VITAM, Inc., 1993-1999; Member, Board of Directors, United Way of Norwalk and Wilton, 1999—. . *Member:* Stamford/Norwalk Regional, Connecticut and American Bar Associations. ***LANGUAGES:*** French. ***PRACTICE AREAS:*** Zoning.

KARA A.T. MURPHY, born Stamford, Connecticut, June 18, 1970; admitted to bar, 1996, Connecticut; 1998, U.S. District Court, District of Connecticut. *Education:* Lafayette College (B.A., cum laude, with honors, 1992); University of Connecticut (J.D., 1996). Phi Alpha Theta. Pi Sigma Alpha. Member, McKelvy Honors Program. Author: "Pleading the Policy Limit as A Special Defense," 1 Connecticut Insurance Law Journal 167, 1995. *Member:* Samford/Norwalk Regional, Connecticut and American Bar Associations. ***PRACTICE AREAS:*** Civil Litigation.

OF COUNSEL

THOMAS A. KEATING, JR., born Danbury, Connecticut, June 21, 1915; admitted to bar, 1939, Connecticut. *Education:* Yale University (B.A., 1936; LL.B., 1939). ***PRACTICE AREAS:*** Real Estate.

VINCENT GALLOGLY, born New York, N.Y., August 18, 1938; admitted to bar, 1968, New York; 1990, Connecticut. *Education:* City College of the City University of New York (B.C.E., 1962); New York University (J.D., 1968). Licensed Professional Engineer, New York, 1966. Adjunct Professor, Pace University Law School, 1995-1998. *Member:* Connecticut, New York State and American Bar Associations; American Society of Professional Engineers. ***PRACTICE AREAS:*** Environmental Law; Real Estate. ***Email:*** frang@aol.com

(This Listing Continued)

LOCAL COUNSEL FOR: The Purdue/Frederick Co.; Hewitt Associates.
REPRESENTATIVE CLIENTS: Merritt Seven Corporate Park; Beiersdorf, Inc.; Trans-Lux, Inc.; Framatome Connectors USA, Inc.; Stew Leonard's; Cablevision of Connecticut; Norwalk Hospital; Maritime Center; Second Taxing District, City of Norwalk; Sixth Taxing District, City of Norwalk; Stanley M. Seligson Properties, Inc.; Crown Theatres, L.P.; Conair, Inc.; S.N.E.T.
APPROVED ATTORNEYS FOR: Lawyers Title Insurance Corp.; First American Title Insurance Co.
REFERENCES: First Union Bank of Connecticut; Fleet Bank; Summit Bank.

WAKE, SEE, DIMES & BRYNICZKA

NORWALK, CONNECTICUT

(See Westport)

Business and Corporate Law, Real Estate, Trusts and Probate, Estate Planning, Municipal, Zoning and Land Use Law, Litigation in all Federal and State Courts. Federal, State and Foreign Taxation, Pension and Profit Sharing, and Family Law.

ELLIOT R. WARREN

NORWALK, CONNECTICUT

(See Westport)

General Civil and Criminal Litigation before all State and Federal Courts. Trials and Appeals. Criminal Defense, Commercial and Tax Litigation, Personal Injury, Employment and Negligence Law.

WILLINGER, WILLINGER & BUCCI, P.C.

NORWALK, CONNECTICUT

(See Bridgeport)

General Practice. Real Estate, Corporate, Commercial, Foreclosure, Bankruptcy, Secured Financing, Zoning, Labor, Probate, Condemnation, Workers Compensation, Financial, Banking, Personal Injury and Criminal Law. Trials in all Courts.

BEEBE AND O'NEIL

Established in 1976

335 WASHINGTON STREET
NORWICH, CONNECTICUT 06360
Telephone: 860-889-5266
Fax: 860-887-1378
URL: http://www.lawyers.com/beebeandoneil

General Civil and Criminal Practice before State and Federal Courts. Corporation, Personal Injury, Medical Malpractice, Family Law, Commercial, Workers Compensation, Real Estate, Zoning, Wills, Probate, Bankruptcy, Collections and Taxation Law. Trials and Appeals. Banking, Lender Liability, FDIC, Governmental Bank Acquisitions.

DONALD R. BEEBE, born Norwich, Connecticut, January 4, 1950; admitted to bar, 1975, Connecticut; 1976, U.S. District Court, District of Connecticut; U.S. Court of Appeals, Second Circuit; U.S. Supreme Court; Mashantucket Pequot Tribal Court; Mohegan Gaming Disputes Court. *Education:* Harvard University (B.A., cum laude, 1972); University of Virginia (J.D., 1975). Recipient, 4-H Alumni Award. Director, Harvard Club of Southern Connecticut. Regional Director, Harvard Alumni Association. President, 4-H Foundation, Inc., New London County. *Member:* New London County and Connecticut Bar Associations. ***PRACTICE AREAS:*** Personal Injury; Medical Malpractice; Criminal Law; Civil Litigation; Commercial Litigation.

NANCY M. O'NEIL, born Norwich, Connecticut, May 26, 1951; admitted to bar, 1976, Connecticut and U.S. District Court, District of Connecticut; Mashantucket Pequot Tribal Court; Mohegan Gaming Disputes Court. *Education:* Newton College of the Sacred Heart (B.A., cum laude, 1973); University of Virginia (J.D., 1976). Law Clerk to Appellate Session of the Superior Court, Hartford, Connecticut, 1976-1977. Member, Norwich Historic District Commission. *Member:* New London County and Connecticut Bar Associations. ***PRACTICE AREAS:*** Personal Injury; Family Law; Commercial Litigation; Medical Malpractice; Civil Litigation.

OF COUNSEL

JANIS M. SMALL, born Meriden, Connecticut, October 3, 1958; admitted to bar, 1983, Connecticut.

REFERENCES: Fleet Bank, NA; Chelsea-Groton Savings Bank; Citizens Mortgage Corp. f/k/a; Boston Five Mortgage Co.; Savings Institute; Dime Savings Bank; Eastern Savings & Loan Association.

BROWN JACOBSON P.C.

Established in 1965
UNCAS-MERCHANTS NATIONAL BANK BUILDING
22 COURTHOUSE SQUARE
NORWICH, CONNECTICUT 06360
Telephone: 860-889-3321
Fax: 860-886-0673
Email: bjtlk@snet.net
URL: http://www.brownjacobson.com

General Practice in all Courts. Trials, Probate, Insurance, Real Estate, Corporate, Commercial and Administrative Law.

MILTON L. JACOBSON, born Hartford, Connecticut, May 18, 1920; admitted to bar, 1949, Connecticut and U.S. District Court, District of Connecticut. *Education:* University of Michigan (B.S., 1942; J.D., 1948). Town Counsel, Town of Norwich, 1951. Member, Norwich Board of Education, 1965-1971. *Member:* New London County (President, 1970-1971) and Connecticut Bar Associations; Society of Barristers. ***PRACTICE AREAS:*** Corporate Law; Real Estate. ***Email:*** mjacobson@brownjacobson.com

WAYNE G. TILLINGHAST, born Norwich, Connecticut, December 21, 1935; admitted to bar, 1960, Connecticut; 1961, U.S. District Court for Connecticut; 1967, U.S. Supreme Court. *Education:* University of Connecticut (B.S., 1957; LL.B., with honors, 1960). Associate Editor, University of Connecticut Law Review, 1958-1960. Adjunct Professor, Trial Practice, University of Connecticut School of Law, 1979-1999. Superior Court Attorney Trial Referee, 1984—. Listed Best Lawyers in America, 1982—. *Member:* New London County and The Connecticut (Member: House of Delegates, 1978-1981; Board of Governors, 1978-1981; Executive Committee, Civil Justice Section, 1981-1984; Federal Judiciary Committee, 1988-1994) Bar Associations; The Association of Trial Lawyers of America; Connecticut Defense Lawyers Association (1st Vice President, 1981-1982; President, 1982-1983); Connecticut Medical Defense Lawyers Association; Connecticut Academy of Certified Trial Lawyers (President, 1989-1990); Member, Federal Grievance Committee, 2000—. Advocate, American Board of Trial Advocates. Fellow: American College of Trial Lawyers and Connecticut Bar Foundation. Certified as a Civil Trial Specialist by the National Board of Tri al Advocacy. ***PRACTICE AREAS:*** Civil Litigation; Medical Malpractice Defense; Personal Injury. ***Email:*** wtillinghast@brownjacobson.com

MICHAEL E. DRISCOLL, born Norwich, Connecticut, August 26, 1948; admitted to bar, 1973, Connecticut; 1975, U.S. District Court, District of Connecticut; 1997, Mohegan Gaming Disputes Court. *Education:* Georgetown University (B.S., 1970); Georgetown University Law Center (J.D., 1973). *Member:* New London County (Treasurer, 1990-1992; President, 1993-1994) and The Connecticut (Member: House of Delegates, 1987-1990; Board of Governors, 1987-1991) Bar Associations; Connecticut Trial Lawyers Association; Connecticut Defense Lawyers Association (President, 1992-1993); The Association of Trial Lawyers of America. Associate, American Board of Trial Advocates. ***PRACTICE AREAS:*** Civil Litigation; Medical Malpractice Defense; Personal Injury. ***Email:*** mdriscoll@brownjacobson.com

DAVID S. WILLIAMS, born Turlock, California, November 15, 1951; admitted to bar, 1978, California; 1979, Connecticut; 1980, U.S. District Court, District of Connecticut; 1992, Mashantucket Pequot Tribal Court; 1996, U.S. Court of Appeals, 2nd Circuit; 1997, Mohegan Gaming Disputes Court. *Education:* University of California at Santa Barbara (B.A., 1973); University of the Pacific, McGeorge College of the Law (J.D., 1978). *Member:* New London County and The Connecticut Bar Associations; Connecticut Defense Lawyers Association; The Association of Trial Lawyers of America. ***PRACTICE AREAS:*** Civil Litigation; Defense Litigation; Personal Injury. ***Email:*** dwilliams@brownjacobson.com

JOHN C. WIRZBICKI, born Hartford, Connecticut, June 25, 1950; admitted to bar, 1975, Connecticut; 1976, U.S. District Court, District of Connecticut. *Education:* Bowdoin College (A.B., 1972); University of Connecticut (J.D., 1975). Member: Groton Board of Education, 1992-1993; Groton Town Council, 2001—. *Member:* New London County and Connecticut Bar Associations. ***PRACTICE AREAS:*** Civil Litigation; Social Security Disability; Indian Law. ***Email:*** jwirzbicki@brownjacobson.com

MICHAEL D. COLONESE, born New Haven, Connecticut, December 30, 1959; admitted to bar, 1985, Connecticut. *Education:* University of Connecticut (B.A., magna cum laude, 1982; J.D., cum laude, 1985). Omicron Delta Epsilon. Board Certified, Worker's Compensation Specialist. Recipient: American Jurisprudence Book Awards for Excellence in Evidence and Criminal Procedure; Little, Brown & Company Book Award for Excellence in Evidence; Mitchie Company Book Award for Outstanding Achievement and Improvement in the Second Year of Law School. *Member:* New London County and Connecticut Bar Associations. ***PRACTICE AREAS:*** Civil Litigation; Personal Injury; Workers Compensation. ***Email:*** mcolonese@brownjacobson.com

(This Listing Continued)

KARL-ERIK STERNLOF, born Baltimore, Maryland, June 30, 1958; admitted to bar, 1983, Connecticut. *Education:* Trinity College (B.A., 1979); University of Connecticut School of Law (J.D., 1983). Note and Comment Editor, Connecticut Law Review, 1982-1983. Board Member: New London Development Corp., 1998—; First Vice President, 2001—. Summer Music, Inc., 1997—; Treasurer, 1999—. *Member:* Mashantucket, New London County, Connecticut and American Bar Associations. ***PRACTICE AREAS:*** Commercial Real Estate; Commercial Transactions; Banking Law; Indian Law. ***Email:*** ksternlof@brownjacobson.com

JEFFREY R. GODLEY, born Putnam, Connecticut, March 21, 1962; admitted to bar, 1987, Connecticut and U.S. District Court, District of Connecticut; 1992, Mashantucket Pequot Tribal Court; 1997, Mohegan Gaming Disputes Court. *Education:* University of Connecticut (B.A., 1984); Western New England College School of Law (J.D., 1987). Staff Member, 1985-1986 and Managing Editor, 1986-1987, Western New England Law Review. Author: "Defining the CIA's 'Intelligence Sources' as an Exemption to the Freedom of Information Act—CIA v. Sims, 471 U.S. 159 (1985)," 9 W. New Eng. L. Rev. 333 (1987). *Member:* New London County and Connecticut Bar Associations (Member, House of Delegates, Board of Governors); International Association of Gaming Attorneys. ***PRACTICE AREAS:*** Commercial Transactions; Real Estate Law; Indian Law and Gaming. ***Email:*** jgodley@brownjacobson.com

JOHN F. DUGGAN, born New Haven, Connecticut, August 31, 1964; admitted to bar, 1990, Connecticut; 1994, Massachusetts, U.S. Tax Court; Mashantucket Pequot Tribal Court; 1996, U.S. District Court, District of Connecticut; 1997, Mohegan Gaming Disputes Court. *Education:* Trinity College (B.A., 1987); Pepperdine University (J.D., 1990); Boston University (LL.M., in Taxation, 1993). *Member:* New London County, Connecticut, Massachusetts and American Bar Associations. ***PRACTICE AREAS:*** Estate Planning; Probate; Taxation; Elder Law. ***Email:*** jduggan@brownjacobson.com

JEFFREY F. BUEBENDORF, born New Haven, Connecticut, March 28, 1961; admitted to bar, 1994, Connecticut and U.S. District Court, District of Connecticut; 1995, Mashantucket Pequot Tribal Court; 1997, Mohegan Gaming Disputes Court. *Education:* Hamilton College (B.A., 1983); University of Connecticut (J.D., cum laude, 1994). Phi Delta Phi (Province President). Recipient, American Jurisprudence Award for Excellence in the Study of Comparative Law. Member, 1992-1994 and Executive Director, 1993-1994, Connecticut Moot Court Board. *Member:* New London County, Connecticut and American Bar Associations. ***REPORTED CASES:*** New England Savings Bank v. Meadow Lakes Realty Co., 243 Conn. 601, 706 A 2nd 465 (1998); New England Savings Bank v. Meadow Lakes Realty Co., 44 Conn. App. 240, 688 A. 2nd 345 (1997); Plikus v. Connecticut Light and Power Co., 42 Conn. App. 299, 679 A. 2nd 401 (1996); New England Savings Bank v. Meadow Lakes Realty Co., 235 Conn. 663, 668 A. 2nd 712 (1996). ***PRACTICE AREAS:*** Civil Litigation; Personal Injury; Products Liability; Employment Law. ***Email:*** jbuebendorf@brownjacobson.com

---

DANA M. BESSETTE, born Providence, Rhode Island, April 5, 1972; admitted to bar, 1999, Massachusetts, Connecticut and U.S. District Court, District of Massachusetts; 2000, Rhode Island and U.S. District Court, District of Connecticut. *Education:* University of Rhode Island (B.A., 1994); New England School of Law (J.D., magna cum laude, 1998). New England Scholar. Recipient, CALI Award for Excellence in Wills and Estates. Lead Article Editor, New England Journal on Civil and Criminal Confinement, 1997-1998. Author: "Reinterpreting the ADA: Finding a Right to Treatment in the Least Restrictive Environment," New England Journal on Civil and Criminal Confinement, Winter 1998, Vol. 24. *Member:* New London County, Connecticut and Rhode Island Bar Associations. ***PRACTICE AREAS:*** Civil Litigation; Personal Injury; Insurance Defense. ***Email:*** dbessette@brownjacobson.com

OF COUNSEL

ALLYN L. BROWN, JR., born Norwich, Connecticut, May 21, 1915; admitted to bar, 1940, Connecticut; 1946, Federal District Court, Connecticut. *Education:* Brown University (A.B., 1937); Yale University (LL.B., 1940). Deputy Judge, City Court of Norwich, 1946-1948. State's Attorney, New London County, Connecticut, 1953-1965. Superior Court Trial Referee, 1984—. Fellow, American College of Trial Lawyers. *Member:* New London County, The Connecticut (Member, Council, 1948-1951; Second Vice President, 1952-1953; First Vice President, 1953-1954; President, 1954-1955) Bar Associations. ***Email:*** bjtlk@snet.net

VINCENT A. LAUDONE, born Norwich, Connecticut, May 14, 1918; admitted to bar, 1949, Connecticut, U.S. District Court, District of Connecticut and Massachusetts. *Education:* Wesleyan University (B.A., 1940); Boston University (LL.B., 1949). Assistant Prosecutor and Assistant Clerk, City Court of Norwich, 1951-1953. State Representative, Connecticut General Assembly, 1967-1969. *Member:* New London County (Treasurer, 1952) Bar Association. ***PRACTICE AREAS:*** Criminal Law; Motor Vehicle Accidents and Injuries. ***Email:*** bjtlk@snet.net

(This Listing Continued)

JAMES J. DUTTON, JR., born Norwich, Connecticut, November 24, 1914; admitted to bar, 1942, Connecticut; 1948, U.S. District Court for the District of Connecticut and U.S. Tax Court. *Education:* University of Notre Dame (B.C.S., 1936); Hartford College of Law (LL.B., 1941). Judge, City Court of Norwich, 1955-1961. *Member:* New London County Bar Association. ***PRACTICE AREAS:*** Estate Planning; Probate; Taxation. ***Email:*** bjtlk@snet.net

FIRM IS COUNSEL FOR: Chelsea-Groton Savings Bank; Peoples Bank; New London County Mutual Insurance Co.; Norwich Community Development Co.; Norwich Roman Catholic Diocese; The William W. Backus Hospital; Lawrence and Memorial Hospitals; Norwichtown Convalescent Home, Inc.; Franklin Mushroom Farms; Mashantucket Pequot Tribe; Foxwoods Resort and Casino; Seymour's Sand & Stone, Inc.
FIRM IS LOCAL COUNSEL FOR: Vermont Mutual Insurance Co.; Burlington Insurance Group; American Bankers Insurance Co.; American Equity Insurance Co.; National Grange Insurance Co.; Catholic Mutual Insurance Co.; Empire Mutual Insurance Companies; Travelers Insurance Co.; Nationwide Insurance Co.; Connecticut Medical Insurance Co.; EMC Insurance Companies; Phelps Dodge Copper Products; A.E.S. Thames, Inc.; Southern New England Telephone Co.; Pequot River Shipworks, LLC.
REFERENCES: Fleet Bank of Connecticut, N.A.; Chelsea-Groton Savings Bank, Norwich, Connecticut; People's Bank; Dime Savings Bank of Norwich; Liberty Bank.

DiFRANCESCA & STEELE, P.C.

811 BOSWELL AVENUE
P.O. BOX 548
NORWICH, CONNECTICUT 06360
Telephone: 860-889-3871
Fax: 860-889-7156
Email: difrancescasteele.pc@snet.net
URL: http://www.lawyers.com/difrancescasteele

General Civil and Criminal Practice, Real Estate, Probate, Negligence, Domestic Relations and Corporation Law, Trials and Workers Compensation, Bankruptcy.

DONALD J. DiFRANCESCA, born Westerly, Rhode Island, January 26, 1945; admitted to bar, 1969, Connecticut and U.S. District Court, District of Connecticut. *Education:* Providence College (A.B., 1966); Villanova University (J.D., 1969). *Member:* New London County, Connecticut (Member, Sections on: Family Law; Estates and Probate; Real Property; Planning and Zoning) and American (Member, Sections on: Family Law; Real Property; Probate and Trust Law) Bar Associations. ***PRACTICE AREAS:*** Real Estate Law; Family Law; Probate; Elder Law; Bankruptcy; Personal Injury; Wills; Trusts. ***Email:*** difrancescasteele.pc@snet.net

BETH A. STEELE, born Norwich, Connecticut, August 16, 1969; admitted to bar, 1994, Connecticut; 1995, Massachusetts. *Education:* Providence College (B.A., 1991); Villanova University School of Law (J.D., 1994). *Member:* New London, Connecticut and American Bar Associations; Connecticut Trial Lawyers Association. ***PRACTICE AREAS:*** Personal Injury; Workers Compensation; Criminal Defense; Zoning Law; Land Use. ***Email:*** bsteele@snet.net

REPRESENTATIVE CLIENTS: The McCue Mortgage Co.; Chicago Title Insurance Co.; Holmgren Subaru, Inc.; W.R. Allen & Co., Inc.; WRACO, Inc.; Hawthorne Woodworking Co., Inc.; Manafort Brothers, Inc.
APPROVED ATTORNEYS FOR: Chicago Title Insurance Co.; Farmers Home Administration.
REFERENCE: Dime Savings Bank.

HORVITZ & CAISSE

208 OTROBANDO AVENUE
NORWICH, CONNECTICUT 06360
Telephone: 860-889-5529
Fax: 860-889-1319
Email: sshesq@99main.com
Email: kecesq@99main.com

Practice Limited to Matrimonial Law.

MEMBERS OF FIRM

SHEILA S. HORVITZ, born New York, N.Y., July 11, 1944; admitted to bar, 1977, Connecticut; 1985, U.S. District Court, District of Connecticut. *Education:* Queens College of the City University of New York (B.A., cum laude, 1965); Northeastern University (M.A., in History, with honors, 1969); University of Connecticut (J.D., with honors, 1977). Phi Beta Kappa; Phi Alpha Theta;. Kappa Delta Pi. Author: "Postmajority Support in Connecticut and Views from other Jurisdictions," 4 Conn. Family L.J. 71, 1986; "Charges of Sexual Abuse in Custody and Visitation Disputes," 5 Conn. Family L.J. 96, 1987. Special Master, Matrimonial Cases, Judicial Districts of New London, Hartford, New Haven, 1985—. Fact Finder, Judicial District of New London, 1990—. Certified Mediator, American Arbitration Association, 1982. Certified Arbitrator, American Academy of Matrimonial Lawyers, 1992—. *Member:* New London County (Chairman, Family Law Committee, 1982-1986), Connecticut and American

(This Listing Continued)

(Member, Family Law Section) Bar Associations; Connecticut Trial Lawyers Association; The Association of Trial Lawyers of America. Fellow, American Academy of Matrimonial Lawyers (President, Connecticut Chapter, 2001—). ***Email:*** sshesq@99main.com

KENNETH E. CAISSE, born Norwich, Connecticut, August 25, 1966; admitted to bar, 1991, Connecticut; 1992, U.S. District Court, District of Connecticut. *Education:* Fairfield University (B.A., 1988); Western New England College School of Law (J.D., 1991). Special Master, Judicial District of New London. *Member:* New London County (Chairman, Family Law Committee, 1998—), Connecticut (Member, Family Law Section) and American Bar Associations. ***Email:*** kecesq@99main.com

REFERENCES: People's Bank; Dime Savings Bank.

O'BRIEN, SHAFNER, STUART, KELLY & MORRIS, P.C.

Established in 1966
138 MAIN STREET
P.O. BOX 310
NORWICH, CONNECTICUT 06360
Telephone: 860-889-3855
Fax: 860-886-6352
Email: osskm@snet.net
URL: http://www.obrienshafner.com

Groton, Connecticut Office: 475 Bridge Street. Telephone: 860-445-2463. Fax: 860-445-4539.

Trials in all Courts. Personal Injury, Products Liability, Workers Compensation, Medical Malpractice, Corporations, Estate Planning, Probate, Trust Law, Real Estate, General Practice, Family and Labor Law, Administrative and Admiralty Law.

FIRM PROFILE: Established in 1966, we are a general practice law firm focusing on advocacy, counseling and caring. We can handle almost every type of legal work that a family or business may require. We take great pride in our team approach of lawyers, legal assistants and staff. Each lawyer and legal assistant concentrates their talents in one or more fields. This expertise allows us to provide superior legal services in a number of fields of law as one of southeast Connecticut's most capable and experienced law firms. We emphasize trial work in Personal Injury, Workers Compensation, Probate Appeals and Commercial Litigation. In addition we have expertise in Municipal Law, Estate Planning and Elder Law, Estate and Trust Administration, Business (Corporate) and Real Estate Law.

MARK E. BLOCK, born New York, New York, December 15, 1948; admitted to bar, 1973, Connecticut, U.S. District Court, District of Connecticut and U.S. District Court, Southern District of New York, U.S. Court of Appeals, Second Circuit and U.S. Supreme Court. *Education:* Ithaca College (B.A., 1970); Brooklyn Law School (J.D., 1973). Advisory Board Member, First American Title Insurance Co. *Member:* New London County (President, 1988-1989) , Connecticut (Member: Section on Commercial Law and Bankruptcy, Real Property; Council of Bar Presidents, 1988-1989) and American Bar Associations. (Resident). ***PRACTICE AREAS:*** Real Estate; Commercial Law; Bankruptcy; Construction Law.

LLOYD L. LANGHAMMER, born Concord, New Hampshire, July 20, 1961; admitted to bar, 1986, Connecticut; 1987, U.S. District Court, District of Connecticut; 1991, U.S. Court of Appeals, Second Circuit. *Education:* Middlebury College (B.A., 1983); University of Connecticut; California Western School of Law (J.D., 1986). Member, Waterford Flood and Erosion Control Board, 1989—. *Member:* New London County, Connecticut and American Bar Associations; The Association of Trial Lawyers of America. (Resident). ***PRACTICE AREAS:*** Commercial Litigation; Bankruptcy.

RICHARD J. PASCAL, born Washington, D.C., June 22, 1959; admitted to bar, 1988, Connecticut; 1989, U.S. District Court, District of Connecticut; 1994, U.S. Supreme Court, 1995, U.S. Tax Court. *Education:* University of Pennsylvania, Wharton School (B.S., magna cum laude, 1981); George Washington University, National Law Center (J.D., 1987). Adjunct Professor, Three Rivers Community College, 1989—. Certified Public Accountant, Maryland, 1982—. Vice President, ECSU Foundation. (Resident). ***PRACTICE AREAS:*** Commercial and General Litigation; Corporate Law; Employment Law.

LESTER "L.J." ARNOLD, III, born New London, Connecticut, November 19, 1958; admitted to bar, 1994, Connecticut; 1997, U.S. District Court, District of Connecticut and U.S. Bankruptcy Court. *Education:* Dartmouth College (A.B., 1980); University of Connecticut (J.D., 1994). President, Thames Area Citizens' Advocacy Program, Inc. *Member:* New London County, Con-

(This Listing Continued)

O'BRIEN, SHAFNER, STUART, KELLY & MORRIS, P.C., Norwich—Continued

necticut and American Bar Associations (Member, Commercial Law and Bankruptcy Section). (Resident). ***PRACTICE AREAS:*** Commercial Litigation; Foreclosure; Bankruptcy; Construction Law; Real Estate Law.

(For Complete Biographical Data on all Personnel, see Professional Biographies at Groton, Connecticut)

THE REARDON LAW FIRM, P.C.

NORWICH, CONNECTICUT

(See New London)

Civil Trial Practice limited to Personal Injury, Wrongful Death, Medical Malpractice, Product Liability, Aviation Accidents, Admiralty Claims, Military, and Governmental Liability.

SUISMAN, SHAPIRO, WOOL, BRENNAN, GRAY & GREENBERG, P.C.

NORWICH, CONNECTICUT

(See New London)

Administrative Law, Aged and Aging, Appellate Practice, Asset Protection, Business Law, Civil Practice, Civil Rights, Commercial Law, Commercial Real Estate, Constitutional Law, Contracts, Corporate Law, Criminal Law, Debtor and Creditor, Family Law, Finance, Health Care, Indians and Native Populations, Insurance, Intellectual Property, Labor and Employment, Leases and Leasing, Litigation, Medical Malpractice, Municipal Law, Partnership Law, Personal Injury, Probate, Products Liability, Property Law, Real Estate, Regulatory Law, Social Security, Taxation, Torts, Trusts and Estates, Workers Compensation, Zoning, Planning and Land Use.

TOBIN, CARBERRY, O'MALLEY, RILEY & SELINGER, P.C.

NORWICH, CONNECTICUT

(See New London)

General Civil and Criminal Practice, Trials and Appeals in all Courts, Administrative Law, Banking and Commercial Law, Commercial Real Estate, Contract Law, Corporate Law, Business Law, Employment Law, Government Relations, Public Finance, Public Utility Law, Health Care Law, Land Use Law, Personal Injury, Product Liability, Estate Planning and Probate, Elder Law, Immigration, Federal, State and Local Tax Law.

WELBY, BRADY & GREENBLATT, LLP

200 SOUND BEACH AVENUE
P.O. BOX 622
OLD GREENWICH, CONNECTICUT 06870
Telephone: 203-637-1044
URL: http://www.wbgllp.com

White Plains, New York Office: Westchester Financial Center, 50 Main Street. Telephone: 914-428-2100. Fax: 914-428-2172.
Cranford, New Jersey Office: 123 North Union Avenue, Suite 103. Telephone: 908-272-7870. Fax: 908-272-7901.

Construction Law and Litigation, Public and Private Construction Contracts, Construction Claims, Mechanics Liens, Surety Law, Arbitration, Mediation, Architect and Engineers Liability, Environmental Law.

THOMAS H. WELBY, born New York, New York, December 13, 1949; admitted to bar, 1986, New York, U.S. District Court, Southern and Eastern Districts of New York and U.S. Court of Appeals for the Federal Circuits 1994, U.S. Court of Appeals, Second Circuit; 1995, Connecticut; 1996, U.S. District Court, District of Connecticut; 1997, U.S. District Court, Northern District of New York; 1998 U.S. Supreme Court. *Education:* Manhattan College (B.E., 1971); New York University (M.S.C.E., 1973); New Mexico Highlands University (M.A., Bus. Admin., 1976); Polytechnic Institute of New York (M.S., and Certificate in Construction Management, 1981); Pace University (J.D., 1985). Licensed Professional Engineer: New Jersey and New Mexico, 1976; New York, 1977. Adjunct Professor, Civil Engineering, Manhattan College. Member, Construction Panel of Arbitrators and Mediators, American Arbitration Association. *Member:* Suffolk County, Westchester County (Chairman, Construction Law Committee; Member, Alternate Dispute Resolution Committee), New York State, Connecticut (Member: Construction Law Committee; ADR Committee)

(This Listing Continued)

and American (Forum on the Construction Industry; Member, Sections on: Public Contract Law; Tort and Insurance Practice; Law Practice Mgt.) Bar Associations; Construction Industry Council of Westchester (Special Counsel) and Hudson Valley; National Society of Professional Engineers. ***REPORTED CASES:*** West-Fair Electric v. Aetna 87 NY 2d 148 (Pay-if-Paid Clause); Waltech Construction v. Town of Thompson 237 A.D. 2d 716 (Unit price where quantity far exceeds estimate); Beninati Roofing v. Gelco Builders, 279 A.D. 2d 412 (recovery of legal fees on payment bond claim under state finance law § 137). ***PRACTICE AREAS:*** Construction Law; Arbitration; Mediation; Contract Disputes; Public Bidding; Mechanics Liens; Construction Claims. ***Email:*** twelby@wbgllp.com

MICHAEL E. GREENBLATT, born Bronx, New York, March 16, 1963; admitted to bar, 1991, New York, U.S. District Court, Southern, Northern and Eastern Districts of New York and U.S. Court of Appeals, Second Circuit; 1996, New Jersey, U.S. District Court, District of New Jersey and U.S. Supreme Court; 2001, Connecticut and U.S. District Court, District of Connecticut. *Education:* Dutchess Community College; State University of New York at New Paltz (B.A., 1985); St. John's University (J.D., 1990). *Member:* Westchester County and New Jersey State Bar Associations; Builders Institute of Westchester and Mid-Hudson Region. ***REPORTED CASES:*** West-Fair Elect. v. Aetna, 78 F.3d 61 (2d Cir., 1996)(Pay-if-Paid Clause); Atlas Building systems v. Rende, 653 NYS 2d 694 (2nd Dept. 1997)(Certification of Plaintiff Class in Lein Law Trust Fund Diversion Action). ***PRACTICE AREAS:*** Construction Contracts; Mechanics Liens. ***Email:*** mgreenblatt@wbgllp.com

MICHAEL J. BARNABY, born Flushing, New York, January 8, 1963; admitted to bar, 1994, New York and U.S. District Court, Southern and Eastern Districts of New York; 1995, Connecticut; 1997, U.S. District Court, District of Connecticut; 1998, U.S. Court of Appeals, Second Circuit. *Education:* Lehigh University (B.A., 1986); Pace University (J.D., Environmental Law Certificate, 1993). Member, Construction Industry Panel of Arbitrators, American Arbitration Association. *Member:* Greenwich, New York State, Connecticut (Member, Executive Committee, Construction Law Section) and American (Forum on the Construction Industry) Bar Associations. ***PRACTICE AREAS:*** Construction Law; Mechanics Liens; Environmental Law; Arbitration. ***Email:*** mjbarnaby@wbgllp.com

ASSOCIATE

GREGORY G. DICARLO, born Tarrytown, New York, April 25, 1966; admitted to bar, 1996, Connecticut; 1997, New York; 1998, U.S. District Court, Southern and Eastern Districts of New York and U.S. District Court, District of Connecticut; 1999, U.S. District Court, Northern District of New York. *Education:* Northeastern University (B.S.E.E., 1990); St. John's University (J.D., 1996). Articles and Notes Editor, St. John's Law Review, 1995-1996. ***PRACTICE AREAS:*** Construction and Design Law; Mechanics Liens; Surety Law. ***Email:*** gdicarlo@wbgllp.com

(For complete biographical data on all personnel, see Professional Biographies at White Plains, New York)

KITCHINGS & POTTER, LLC

7 HALLS ROAD
P.O. BOX 187
OLD LYME, CONNECTICUT 06371
Telephone: 860-434-5333
Fax: 860-434-5447
Email: kitchpot@ctol.net

Trusts and Estates, Wills, Probate and Real Estate.

SUZANNE DONNELLY KITCHINGS, born Portland, Oregon, July 9, 1946; admitted to bar, 1975, District of Columbia; 1977, Connecticut; 1999, U.S. Supreme Court. *Education:* Stanford University (B.A., with distinction, 1968); Georgetown University (J.D., 1974). Member, Georgetown Law Journal, 1973-1974. ***Email:*** skitchings@biz.ctol.net

EDWARD B. POTTER, born Summit, New Jersey, October 11, 1958; admitted to bar, 1983, New York; 1985, Connecticut. *Education:* Rensselaer Polytechnic Institute (B.S., 1980); Columbia University (J.D., 1982). Harlan Fiske Stone Scholar. ***Email:*** epotter@biz.ctol.net

McGARRY, PRINCE, McGARRY, P.C.

OLD LYME, CONNECTICUT

(See New London)

General Practice. Probate, Estate Planning, Real Estate, Corporation, Municipal, Banking and Commercial Law, Zoning and Condominium Law. Trials in all Courts.

WALLER, SMITH & PALMER, P.C.

Established in 1885

103 HALLS ROAD

OLD LYME, CONNECTICUT 06371

Telephone: 860-434-8063

Telecopier: 860-434-9452

Email: wspol@snet.net

URL: http://www.snetyp.com/wallersmithpalmer

New London Office: 52 Eugene O'Neill Drive. Telephone: 860-442-0367. Telecopier: 860-447-9915. Email: wspmain@snet.net

General Practice. Corporation, Commercial, Estate Planning, Probate, Real Estate, Personal Injury, Municipal, Banking and Trials in all Courts.

ROBERT W. MARRION, born Winthrop, Massachusetts, February 24, 1931; admitted to bar, 1958, Connecticut; 1966, U.S. District Court, District of Connecticut. *Education:* College of the Holy Cross (A.B., 1952); Harvard University (LL.B., 1958). Town Counsel, Town of East Lyme, 1965-1990, 1994-1998. Chairman: Board of Trustees, Mitchell College, 1976-1988; Pequot Community Foundation, 1981-1987. Member, Connecticut Bar Examining Committee, 1974-1996. Trial Referee, Superior Court, 1984-1987. *Member:* New London County and Connecticut Bar Associations. Fellow, American College of Trust and Estate Counsel. ***PRACTICE AREAS:*** Corporate Law; Business Organization; Commercial Real Estate; Estate Planning; Administration Law. ***Email:*** rwmwsp@snet.net

FREDERICK B. GAHAGAN, born New York, N.Y., July 10, 1952; admitted to bar, 1980, Connecticut. *Education:* Lenox School; Kenyon College (B.A., 1974); University of Connecticut (J.D., 1980). Trustee, 1981-1985 and Vice President, 1982-1985, Lyme Land Conservation Trust. Member, 1982-1993 and Chairman, 1991-1993, Regional District #18 Board of Education. *Member:* New London County, Connecticut and American Bar Associations. ***PRACTICE AREAS:*** Corporate Law; Business Organization; Land Conservation; Zoning, Planning and Land Use.

VALERIE ANN VOTTO, born New Haven, Connecticut, August 7, 1961; admitted to bar, 1987, Connecticut and New York; 1991, U.S. District Court, District of Columbia. *Education:* Lehigh University (B.A., cum laude, 1983); Catholic University of America (J.D., 1986). Lecturer, Connecticut Association of Realtors. Assistant Town Attorney, Town of Westport, 1987-1989. Member, State of Connecticut Loss Mitigation Task Force. *Member:* New London County, Middlesex County, Connecticut (Member: Real Property, Probate and Trust Law Section; Real Property Committee) and American Bar Associations; Connecticut Mortgage Bankers Association (Member: Closing Compliance Committee; Fair Housing Committee; Loss Mitigation Committee). ***PRACTICE AREAS:*** Real Estate; Land Use Law; Municipal Law.

GENERAL COUNSEL FOR: Town of East Lyme; Town of Lebanon.
COUNSEL FOR: Citizens Savings Bank; Soneco/Northeastern, Inc.; The Nature Conservancy; Fleet National Bank.
LOCAL COUNSEL FOR: McCue Mortgage Co.; Citicorp Mortgage; U.S. Department of Housing and Urban Development.

(For complete Biographical data on all Personnel, see Professional Biographies at New London, Connecticut)

CLOUTIER & EDDY

29 ELM STREET

P.O. BOX 831

OLD SAYBROOK, CONNECTICUT 06475-1101

Telephone: 860-388-3456

Fax: 860-388-6374

Email: c-e@celaw.org

URL: http://www.lawyers.com/cloutier&eddy

Personal Injury and Negligence Law, Criminal and Civil Trials in all Courts. Domestic Relations, Probate, Real Estate, Commercial, Corporation, Zoning Law, Business Transactions, Estate Planning and Elder Law.

MEMBERS OF FIRM

THOMAS A. CLOUTIER, born Norwich, Connecticut, December 10, 1946; admitted to bar, 1973, Connecticut; 1974, U.S. District Court, District of Connecticut; 1979, U.S. Supreme Court. *Education:* Providence College (A.B., 1968); Boston University (J.D., 1973). Assistant Town Counsel, Town of Old Saybrook, 1985-1989. Member, 1974-1988 and Vice Chairman, 1976-1988, Westbrook Board of Education. *Member:* Middlesex County (Secretary, 1975-1977 and Director, 1982-1986; Member, 1982-1994, 1996-2001 and Chairman, 1987-1994, Practice and Procedure Committee; Member: Medical Legal Committee, 1982-1990) and Connecticut (Member: Fee Arbitration Panel, 1983-1992and Chairman, 1989-1992; New London Judicial District Grievance Panel, 1985-1990; Statewide Grievance Committee, 1993-1999 and Vice Chairman, 1995-1999) Bar Associations; The Association of Trial Lawyers of America (Member, Council of Presidents, 2000—); Connecticut Trial Lawyers Association (Member, Board of Governors, 1987—; President, Elect, 2000); Connecticut Association of Certified Trial Lawyers; Certified as a Civil Trial Advocate by the National Board of Trial Advocacy. [With U.S. Army, 1968-1970]. ***PRACTICE AREAS:*** Personal Injury; Wrongful Death; Negligence Law; Zoning. ***Email:*** tcloutier@celaw.org

JEFFREY C. EDDY, born Manchester, Connecticut, July 24, 1956; admitted to bar, 1981, Connecticut; 1984, U.S. District Court, District of Connecticut. *Education:* University of Connecticut (B.A., 1978; J.D., 1981). *Member:* Middlesex County, Connecticut (Member, Estates and Probate Section) and American (Member, Real Property, Probate and Trust Law Sections) Bar Associations. ***PRACTICE AREAS:*** Elder Law; Business Transactions; Corporate Law; Probate; Trusts and Estates; Real Estate; Business Organization. ***Email:*** jeddy@celaw.org

ASSOCIATE

RICHARD R. HANRATTY, JR., born Bronx, New York, November 13, 1965; admitted to bar, 1996, Connecticut and U.S. District Court, District of Connecticut. *Education:* University of Rhode Island (B.A., 1987); Widener University School of Law (J.D., 1995). Legislative Liaison, Pennsylvania Department of State, 1994-1995. Law Clerk, Hon. John D. Brennan, Connecticut Superior Court, 1996. Director, Old Saybrook Land Trust. *Member:* Middlesex County and Connecticut Bar Associations. [USMC, Reserve, 1985-1988]. ***PRACTICE AREAS:*** Business Law; Civil Litigation; Real Estate; Commercial Transactions. ***Email:*** rhanratty@celaw.org

REPRESENTATIVE CLIENTS: Webster Bank; Liberty Bank; Sprint PCS; Sub Carrier Communications; Westbrook Factory Stores; Mount Saint John; Saybrook Fish House Restaurants; Essex Island Marina, Inc.; The Lee Company.
APPROVED ATTORNEYS FOR: Chicago Title Insurance Company and Connecticut Attorneys Title Insurance Company; Lawyers Title Insurance Corporation.

MICHAEL E. CRONIN, JR.

201 MAIN STREET

P.O. BOX 454

OLD SAYBROOK, CONNECTICUT 06475

Telephone: 860-388-5728

Fax: 860-388-4981

General Civil Practice before State and Federal Courts. Municipal, Personal Injury, Domestic Relations, Real Estate, Zoning, Estate Planning and Probate, Corporation, Workmen's Compensation and Environmental Law. Trials and Appeals. General Litigation.

MICHAEL E. CRONIN, JR., born New London, Connecticut, June 12, 1937; admitted to bar, 1964, Connecticut. *Education:* Dartmouth College (B.A., 1959); University of Connecticut (LL.B., 1963). Town Attorney, Town of Old Saybrook, 1973-1989, 1999—. *Member:* Middlesex County and Connecticut Bar Associations. ***PRACTICE AREAS:*** Municipal Law; Zoning, Planning and Land Use; Personal Injury Law; Real Estate Law; Probate; Environmental Law.

REFERENCES: Fleet Bank; Essex Savings Bank.

GOULD, LARSON, BENNET, WELLS & McDONNELL, P.C.

OLD SAYBROOK, CONNECTICUT

(See Essex)

General Practice in all Courts. Real Estate, Zoning, Family, Bankruptcy, Banking, Probate, Corporation Law, Estate Planning and Taxation, and Personal Injury Law, Trials, Appeals, Domestic Relations, Municipal Law and Land Use Law, Insurance Defense, Elder Law, Arbitration and Mediation.

SCHINE, JULIANELLE & ANTONUCCI, P.C.

Established in 1967

35 OLD TAVERN ROAD

P.O. BOX 905

ORANGE, CONNECTICUT 06477-0905

Telephone: 203-795-3563

Fax: 203-799-9655

Email: sjalaw1@snet.net

Westport, Connecticut Office: Suite 100, 830 Post Road East. Telephone: 203-226-6861. Fax: 203-226-6866.

General Civil and Trial Practice. Corporate, Commercial and Business Law, Probate, Personal Injury, Administrative, Estate Planning, Commercial and Residential Real Estate, Higher Education Law.

LEONARD A. SCHINE (1917-1982).

(This Listing Continued)

SCHINE, JULIANELLE & ANTONUCCI, P.C., Orange—Continued

ROBERT L. JULIANELLE, born New Haven, Connecticut, February 8, 1940; admitted to bar, 1964, Connecticut and U.S. District Court, District of Connecticut; 1970, U.S. Court of Appeals, Second Circuit; 1972, U.S. Tax Court; 1973, U.S. Supreme Court. *Education:* Fairfield University (B.S.S., 1961); Georgetown University (J.D., 1964). Phi Delta Phi. Member, Georgetown University Law Journal, 1963-1964. Secretary, General Counsel, Executive Committee, Chairman, Board Affairs Committee and Member, Board of Trustees, 1982—, Sacred Heart University, Fairfield, CT. Attorney Trial Referee and Arbitrator, Superior Court of Connecticut, Ansonia/Milford J.D. Member, Board of Trustees, Natural Science for Youth Foundation, 1982-1985. State Senator, Connecticut, 1975-1977. Editorial Associate, Connecticut Bar Journal, 1978-1979. Trustee, Connecticut Public Expenditures Council, Inc., 1987-1989. Board of Directors, 1990-1996 and Chairman, 1994-1996, Notre Dame High School, West Haven, CT. Service as Arbitrator, American Arbitration Association. *Member:* New Haven, Greater Bridgeport, Connecticut (Member, Sections on: Corporate/Business Organization; Estates and Probate; Litigation) and American (Member, Sections on: Business Law; Real Property, Probate and Trust Law) Bar Associations; Connecticut Trial Lawyers Association; The Association of Trial Lawyers of America; National Association of College and University Attorneys. ***PRACTICE AREAS:*** Litigation; Estate Planning; Wills, Trusts and Probate Law; Business Law; Real Estate; Higher Education Law.

FRANCIS J. ANTONUCCI, born Cleveland, Ohio, November 7, 1947; admitted to bar, 1974, Massachusetts; 1975, Connecticut, U.S. Tax Court and U.S. District Court, District of Massachusetts; 1976, U.S. Court of Appeals, First Circuit; 1978, U.S. District Court, District of Connecticut. *Education:* Boston College (B.S., 1969); University of Toledo (J.D., 1974); Boston University (LL.M. in Taxation, 1975). *Member:* Connecticut (Member, Section on Taxation, Estate and Probate), Massachusetts (Member, Section on Taxation) and American (Member, Sections on: Taxation; Real Property, Probate and Trust Law; Corporation, Banking and Business Law) Bar Associations. [With U.S. Army, 1970-1972]. ***PRACTICE AREAS:*** Taxation Law; Estate Planning Law; Corporate Law; Probate Law; Employee Benefits Law.

OF COUNSEL

LAWRENCE W. KANAGA, born Chicago, Illinois, December 25, 1940; admitted to bar, 1965, Connecticut and U.S. District Court, District of Connecticut; 1968, U.S. Court of Appeals, Second Circuit. *Education:* Williams College (A.B., magna cum laude, 1962); Harvard University (LL.B., 1965). Phi Beta Kappa. (Also practicing individually at Westport, Connecticut).

REPRESENTATIVE CLIENTS: Sacred Heart University, Incorporated; Unimin Corporation; Mariano Brothers, Inc.; Star Distributors, Inc.; General Electric Employees Federal Credit Union; Prime Bank; Slocum & Sons Inc.; Ocean Air Transportation, Inc.; South Central Regional Water Authority; Sonitrol Security Systems of Bridgeport; Bread Basket, Inc.; Safety Marking, Inc.
APPROVED COUNSEL FOR: Connecticut Attorney's Title Insurance Co.; People's Bank; New Haven Savings Bank; Hudson United Bank; Prime Bank; The Milford Bank; Fleet Bank, N.A.; First Union National Bank; Webster Bank; Summit Bank.
REFERENCE: Fleet Bank, N.A.

THEODORE M. LADWIG

HTP BUILDING
185 SOUTH BROAD STREET
PAWCATUCK, CONNECTICUT 06379
Telephone: 860-599-1165
FAX: 860-599-1172
Email: email/atty.tedladwig@worldnet.att.net

General Civil Practice. Residential and Commercial Real Estate and Zoning Family, Estate Planning, Probate, Corporation, Municipal, Personal Injury, Family and Equine Law. Trials and Appeals.

THEODORE M. LADWIG, born Newton, Massachusetts, November 22, 1943; admitted to bar, 1971, Connecticut; 1980, U.S. Supreme Court. *Education:* University of Connecticut (B.A., 1965); Boston University (J.D., 1971). Editor, Boston University Law Review, 1969-1971. Faculty Member, University of Connecticut, Division of Continuing Legal Education, Real Estate Law, 1986-1989. Town Counsel, Town of Stonington, 1979-1985. Charter Commission, Town of Stonington, 1977-1978. *Member:* New London County, Connecticut and American Bar Associations. [U.S. Army Intelligence, 1965-1968; Capt., USAR]

BACHAND, LONGO & HIGGINS

Established in 1935
168 MAIN STREET
P.O. BOX 528
PUTNAM, CONNECTICUT 06260-0528
Telephone: 860-928-6549
Fax: 860-928-1684
Email: ehiggins@baclh.com

General Civil Practice. Real Estate, Probate, Corporation Law and Civil Litigation.

MEMBERS OF FIRM

JEAN M. BACHAND (1935-1969).

NICHOLAS A. LONGO, born Norwich, Connecticut, February 26, 1935; admitted to bar, 1959, Connecticut; 1980, U.S. District Court, District of Connecticut. *Education:* Clark University (B.A., 1956); University of Michigan (J.D., 1959). Recipient, Vocational Service Award, Putnam Rotary Club, 1990. Assistant Prosecuting Attorney, Eleventh Circuit Court, 1961-1965. Deputy Coroner, Windham County, 1965-1972. Chairman, Zoning Board of Appeals, Town of Putnam, 1961-1964. Member: Putman Board of Education, 1968-1970; State Board of Education, 1970-1973; Windham County Grievance Committee, 1985-1990; Tolland County Grievance Committee, 1990-1995; State-Wide Grievance Committee, 1980-1985. *Member:* Windham County (President, 1982-1984) and Connecticut (Member: Judiciary Committee, 1982-1984; Sections on: Banking Law; Probate and Estate Planning) Bar Associations. ***PRACTICE AREAS:*** Real Estate (65%, 500); Probate and Estate Planning (25%, 100); Banking and Corporation Law (10%, 50).

EDWIN C. HIGGINS, III, born New London, Connecticut, July 18, 1954; admitted to bar, 1979, Connecticut. *Education:* Norwich University (B.A., 1976); Western New England College School of Law (J.D., 1979). Town Counsel, Town of Putnam, 1984-1987. Chairman: Woodstock Zoning Study Committee, 1990-1991; Woodstock Planning and Zoning Commission, 1991—. *Member:* Windham County and Connecticut (Member, Sections on: Banking Law; Elder Law; Planning and Zoning) Bar Associations. ***PRACTICE AREAS:*** Real Estate; Land Use and Zoning; Probate and Estate Planning; Commercial Law. ***Email:*** ehiggins@baclh.com

REPRESENTATIVE CLIENTS: Citizens National Bank; Putnam Savings Bank; Webster Five Cents Savings Bank; Webster First Federal Credit Union; Southbridge Savings Bank; Citizens Mortgage Corp.; New London Trust Co.; Day Kimball Hospital; Bay Finance Co.
REFERENCES: Citizens National Bank; Putnam Savings Bank; Webster Five Cent Savings Bank; Webster First Federal Credit Union.

BOLAND, ST. ONGE & BROUILLARD

Established in 1983
50 ROUTE 171 (WOODSTOCK)
PUTNAM, CONNECTICUT 06260
Telephone: 860-928-0481
Telecopier: 860-928-9950
Email: bsb.law@snet.net
URL: http://www.lawyers.com/boblaw

Mailing Address: P.O. Box 550, Putnam, Connecticut 06260

General Civil and Criminal Practice before all Courts. Corporation, Banking, Leasing, Real Estate, Divorce, Custody, Mediation, Municipal, Personal Injury, Workers Compensation and Estate Planning, Probate Law. Trials and Appeals.

MEMBERS OF FIRM

JOHN D. BOLAND, born Carbondale, Pennsylvania, June 8, 1948; admitted to bar, 1977, Connecticut; 1978, Massachusetts. *Education:* University of Connecticut (B.A., magna cum laude, 1971; M.A., 1975; Mediator Certificate, 1996); Georgetown University (J.D., 1977). Member, Advisory Board of BNA Civil Trial Manual, 1989-1995. Member, State Bar Examining Committee; State Child Support Guideline Commission, 1998-1999; Chairman, Pomfret Board of Finance, 1993—. State Attorney Trial Referee, 1991—. Town Counsel: Town of Chaplin, Connecticut, 1980—; Town of Ashford, 1986-1996; Town of Brooklyn, 1986-1996; Town of Canterbury, Connecticut, 1987—. Member, Peace Corps, Bolivia, 1968-1969. ***LANGUAGES:*** Spanish. ***PRACTICE AREAS:*** Civil Litigation; Municipal Law; Real Estate Law; Mediation; Family Law.

WILLIAM H. ST. ONGE, born Hartford, Connecticut, June 1, 1947; admitted to bar, 1974, Connecticut. *Education:* Georgetown University (A.B., 1969); University of Connecticut (J.D., 1974). First Selectman, Town of Putnam, 1975-1984. Town Counsel: Town of Killingly, 1978-1995; Town of Thompson, 1983—; Town of Putnam, 1987—; Town of Windham, 1984-1986.

(This Listing Continued)

Member: Windham County and Connecticut Bar Associations; Connecticut Association of Municipal Attorneys. ***PRACTICE AREAS:*** Wills Law; Estates Law; Municipal Law; Real Estate Law.

MARK R. BROUILLARD, born Putnam, Connecticut, May 9, 1953; admitted to bar, 1979, Connecticut and U.S. District Court, District of Connecticut. *Education:* Providence College (B.A., 1975); Loyola University (J.D., 1979). Member: Board of Directors, Northeast Connecticut Civil Liberties Union, 1980-1984; Town Counsel: Borough of Danielson, 1983-1987; Town of Eastford, 1987-1993. State Attorney Trial Referee, 1991—. Special Master, Windham Judicial District and Regional Family Trial Docket. *Member:* Connecticut Trial Lawyers Association (Board of Governors, 1992-1999); The Association of Trial Lawyers of America. ***PRACTICE AREAS:*** Family Law; Workers Compensation Law; Personal Injury; Civil and Criminal Trials.

ASSOCIATES

DOUGLAS J. WILLIAMS, born Cincinnati, Ohio, August 3, 1963; admitted to bar, 1988, Connecticut and U.S. District Court, District of Connecticut. *Education:* Trinity College (B.A., with honors in History, 1985); Washington & Lee University (J.D., 1988). Burks Scholar Teaching Fellow, 1987-1988. Selectman, Town of Thompson, 1993-1995; Treasurer, Town of Thompson, 1997—. *Member:* Windham County and Connecticut Bar Associations. ***PRACTICE AREAS:*** Real Estate; Criminal Law; Workers Compensation.

COLLEEN CREEVY CORDING, born Chicago, Illinois, August 3, 1956; admitted to bar, 1986, Massachusetts; 1987, U.S. District Court, District of Massachusetts; 1993, Connecticut. *Education:* Holy Cross College (B.A., 1978); Boston College (J.D., cum laude, 1986). *Member:* Windham County, Connecticut, Massachusetts and American Bar Associations; Connecticut Trial Lawyers Association; Association of Trial Lawyers of America. ***PRACTICE AREAS:*** Litigation; Administrative Law; Education Law.

REPRESENTATIVE CLIENTS: Town of Chaplin; Northeastern Connecticut Community Development Corp.; Town of Thompson; Town of Putnam; East Killingly Fire District; Killingly Building Products, Inc.; J. Gibson McIlvain & Co.; Town of Canterbury; Putnam Savings Bank; Providence & Worcester Railroad; Cornucopia Natural Foods, Inc. Rural Homes Ltd.; Sunnyside Farm, Inc.; Johnson Corrugated, Inc.
REFERENCES: Putnam Savings Bank; Citizens National Bank; Fleet Bank.

BROWN JACOBSON P.C.

PUTNAM, CONNECTICUT

(See Norwich)

General Practice in all Courts. Trials, Probate, Insurance, Real Estate, Corporate, Commercial and Administrative Law.

HORVITZ & CAISSE

PUTNAM, CONNECTICUT

(See Norwich)

Practice Limited to Matrimonial Law.

MAHER AND COTNOIR

Established in 1980

163 PROVIDENCE STREET
P.O. BOX 187
PUTNAM, CONNECTICUT 06260
Telephone: 860-928-9694
Fax: 860-928-9459
Email: maher.and.cotnoir@snet.net

General Practice, Real Estate, Probate, Estate Planning, Civil Litigation.

JOHN J. MAHER, born 1934; admitted to bar, 1960, Connecticut. *Education:* College of the Holy Cross (A.B., 1956); University of Connecticut (J.D., 1960). Chairman, Cargill Bank Board of Directors. Former Town Counsel, City of Putnam. ***PRACTICE AREAS:*** Real Estate; Probate; Estate Planning.

ERNEST J. COTNOIR, born Putnam, Connecticut, October 11, 1961; admitted to bar, 1986, Connecticut; 1988, U.S. District Court, District of Connecticut. *Education:* University of Connecticut at Storrs (B.A., with honors, 1983); University of Connecticut at Hartford (J.D., 1986). Member: Putnam Board of Education, 1989-1997; Town of Putnam Special Services District, 1999—. *Member:* Windham County and Connecticut Bar Associations. ***PRACTICE AREAS:*** Litigation; Real Estate; Probate and Estate Planning; Zoning, Planning and Land Use; Appellate Practice; Family Law; Administrative Law.

REFERENCE: Cargill Bank; Windham Container Corp.

TRACY B. AMBLER

9 CHURCH HILL ROAD
REDDING, CONNECTICUT 06896
Telephone: 203-938-4000
Telecopier: 203-938-4008
Email: tbambler@msn.com

Business Formation, Buying and Selling of Businesses, Closely Held Business Law, Marketing Law.

TRACY B. AMBLER, born Hartford, Connecticut, September 8, 1949; admitted to bar, 1974, Connecticut; 1981, New York. *Education:* Johns Hopkins University (B.A., 1972); University of Connecticut (J.D., with high honors, 1974). Partner, 1983-1993, Kelley Drye & Warren. *Member:* Connecticut Bar Association. ***PRACTICE AREAS:*** General Business; Advertising and Sales Promotion.

REPRESENTATIVE CLIENTS: Reach Marketing, Inc.; Vision Rx., Inc.; Alarm Capital Alliance.

HARVEY J. KULAWITZ, LLC

REDDING, CONNECTICUT

(See Ridgefield)

All Personal Injury Cases, including Car Accident cases, Aircraft & Boating accidents, Slip & Fall accidents, Dog Bite attacks, and Wrongful Death accidents & claims.

COLLINS, HANNAFIN, GARAMELLA, JABER & TUOZZOLO

PROFESSIOINAL CORPORATION

24 BAILEY AVENUE
RIDGEFIELD, CONNECTICUT 06877
Telephone: 203-438-7403
Fax: 203-438-7425
URL: http://www.chgjtlaw.com

Danbury, Connecticut Office: 148 Deer Hill Avenue, P.O. Box 440, 06810. Telephone: 203-744-2150; Fax: 203-791-1126.

General Practice. Real Estate, Estate Planning, Probate, Zoning and Land Use, Tax, Corporation, Commercial, Banking, Family Law, Criminal Law, Negligence, and Civil Trials in all Courts.

(For complete Biographical data on all personnel, see professional biographies at Danbury, Connecticut)

GILL LAW PRACTICE

38-B GROVE STREET
RIDGEFIELD, CONNECTICUT 06877
Telephone: 203-438-4449
Fax: 203-431-7839
URL: http://www.gillpractice.com
Email: gill1law@aol.com
URL: http://www.lawyers.com/gillaw

Family Law, Real Estate, Business Law, Litigation, Divorce, Child Support, Child Custody.

FIRM PROFILE: Harry Gill received a Master of Laws degree from Tulane University School of Law in 1969. He practiced thereafter at Davis Polk & Wardwell, and then was Vice President & General Counsel of various divisions of General Electric, United Technologies and US West. Gill Law Practice focuses in the family law, divorce mediation, real estate, business law and litigation areas. Mr. Gill is a graduate of Coast to Coast Mediation Center, and is a member of the Family Law Section of the Connecticut Bar Association.

HARRY GILL, admitted to bar, 1977, New York; 1985, Connecticut. *Education:* St. Xavier's College, Bombay, India (B.A., Political Science, summa cum laude, 1961); Tulane University School of Law (LL.M., 1969). Recipient: Political Science Trophy; Sir Charles Sergeant Conflict of Laws Scholarship, St. Xavier's College. *Member:* Connecticut Bar Association (Member, Family Law Section, 1994—). ***PRACTICE AREAS:*** Family Law; Real Estate; Business Law; Civil Litigation; Divorce; Child Custody; Child Support. ***Email:*** gill1law@aol.com

HARVEY J. KULAWITZ, LLC

Established in 1980

402 MAIN STREET

RIDGEFIELD, CONNECTICUT 06877

Telephone: 203-438-9663 Ext. 2

FAX: 203-431-6178

URL: http://www.lawyers.com/HarveyKulawitz

All Personal Injury Cases, including Car Accident cases, Aircraft & Boating accidents, Slip & Fall accidents, Dog Bite attacks, and Wrongful Death accidents & claims.

MEMBERS OF FIRM

HARVEY J. KULAWITZ, born Brooklyn, New York, February 6, 1953; admitted to bar, 1979, Connecticut. *Education:* Syracuse University (B.S., cum laude, 1975); Temple University (J.D., 1978). *Member:* Connecticut and American Bar Associations. ***PRACTICE AREAS:*** Personal Injury; Automobile Accidents and Injuries; Aircraft & Boating Accidents; Slip and Fall; Dog Bites; Wrongful Death.

LAURA K. MANDEL

11 EVERGREEN PLACE

RIDGEFIELD, CONNECTICUT 06877-1129

Telephone: 203-778-9662

General Practice.

LAURA K. MANDEL, born Bronx, New York, November 6, 1967; admitted to bar, 1993, New York (Not admitted in Connecticut). *Education:* University of Michigan (B.A., 1989); Brooklyn Law School (J.D., 1992). *Member:* American Bar Association.

REESE, HIRSCH, DIAMOND & SHOULTS

470 MAIN STREET

P.O. BOX 1048

RIDGEFIELD, CONNECTICUT 06877

Telephone: 203-431-2302

Telecopier: 203-438-1576

Email: general@rhdslaw.com

URL: http://www.lawyers.com/rhds

New Canaan, Connecticut Office: 51 Locust Avenue. P.O. Box 1147. 06840. Telephone: 203-966-1618. Telecopier: 203-972-5192.

Probate, Trust and Estate Planning, Real Property, Business Law, Criminal Law, Civil Litigation.

JOHN R. REESE, born Gloversville, New York, October 20, 1940; admitted to bar, 1965, Connecticut. *Education:* Dartmouth College (B.A., 1962); Yale University (LL.B., 1965). Member, Estate Planning Council of Lower-Fairfield County and Western Connecticut Estate Planning Council; Incorporator, Union Savings Bank; Trustee, Keeler Tavern Museum. *Member:* New Canaan, Connecticut and American Bar Associations. ***PRACTICE AREAS:*** Estate and Trust Planning; Real Property; Business Law. **Email:** JRR@rhdslaw.com

LAWRENCE HIRSCH, born New York, N.Y., June 23, 1937; admitted to bar, 1963, Connecticut. *Education:* Hofstra University (B.A., 1960); University of Michigan (J.D., with distinction, 1963). William Fitzgerald Scholar. Phi Gamma Mu. Member, Michigan Law Review, 1962-1963. Author: "The Airlines and the Noshows," Michigan Law Review, 1962; "The Duty of the Executor to Invest in Equities," Michigan Law Review, 1963. Member, Board of Finance, Town of New Canaan, Connecticut, 1975-1980. Counsel to Ridgefield, Connecticut Planning and Zoning Commission, 1973-1978. Member, National Panel of Arbitrators, American Arbitration Association. *Member:* Norwalk-Wilton, Connecticut and American Bar Associations. ***PRACTICE AREAS:*** Real Property. **Email:** lhirsch@rhdslaw.com

JAMES D. DIAMOND, born Brooklyn, New York, June 9, 1959; admitted to bar, 1988, Connecticut; 1989, Wisconsin. *Education:* State University of New York, Albany (B.A., 1981); Brooklyn Law School (J.D., 1988). Executive Director, N.Y.S. Common Cause, 1981-1983; Executive Staff, N.Y.S. Department of Law, 1985-1988; Assistant State's Attorney, 1988-1994. Adjunct Faculty, Western Connecticut State University, 1991—. *Member:* Connecticut and American Bar Associations. ***PRACTICE AREAS:*** Criminal Law; Personal Injury; Civil Litigation. **Email:** jdd@rhdslaw.com

TAMSIN A.S. SHOULTS, born London, England, June 30, 1966; admitted to bar, 1994, Georgia; 1995, Connecticut. *Education:* Bates College (B.A., 1988); University of Connecticut (J.D., 1994). Member, Board of Directors, Girl Scout Council of Southwestern Connecticut. *Member:* Connecticut Bar Association (Member, Estate and Probate and Elder Law Section). ***PRACTICE AREAS:*** Probate; Trusts and Estates; Real Property. **Email:** tshoults@rhdslaw.com

(This Listing Continued)

THOMAS C. HEALEY, born New Haven, Connecticut, November 27, 1954; admitted to bar, 1988, Connecticut. *Education:* Southern Connecticut State University (B.S., 1986); Quinnipiac School of Law, formerly University of Bridgeport School of Law (J.D., 1988). Phi Delta Phi; Member, Editorial Board, Bridgeport Law Review, 1987-1988. Author: Note, "Connecticut Lender Liability Under Federal and State Environmental Law," 9 U.B.L Rev. 175 (1988). Commissioner, Planning and Zoning Commission, Town of Wilton, 1999-2000. Member, Board of Trustees, Wilton Congregational Church, 1998-1999. President, Darien Rotary Club, 1996. Commissioner, Inland/Wetland Commission, Town of Wilton, 1990-1992. *Member:* Connecticut and American Bar Associations. ***PRACTICE AREAS:*** Real Property. **Email:** tchealey@rhdslaw.com

FLAHERTY, MEISLER & COURTNEY, LLC

ROCKVILLE, CONNECTICUT

(See Vernon)

General Practice, Criminal, Real Estate, Estate Planning, Probate, Administrative, Workers Compensation, Municipal and Zoning, Family and Personal Injury Law. Civil and Criminal Trial Practice.

BAIO & ASSOCIATES, P.C.

15 ELM STREET

ROCKY HILL, CONNECTICUT 06067

Telephone: 860-571-8880

Facsimile: 860-571-8853

Insurance Defense and Coverage, Liability Defense Including Municipalities and Workers' Compensation Defense.

CLAUDIA A. BAIO, born Hartford, Connecticut, July 27, 1964; admitted to bar, 1989, Connecticut; 1990, U.S. District Court, District of Connecticut; 1991, Massachusetts; 1998, U.S. Supreme Court. *Education:* Trinity College (B.A., 1986); University of Hartford (State Certification, Secondary Education); University of Connecticut School of Law (J.D., 1989). Trinity College President's Fellow, 1988. Judicial Clerk to the Hon. Flemming L. Norcott Jr. of the Connecticut Appellate Court, 1989-1990. Who's Who in American Law Students, 1991. Adjunct Professor, University of Connecticut Law School, 1999—. Factfinder/Arbitrator, Superior Court, J.D. Hartford. Associate, 1990-1997, Partner, 1998-1999, Gordon, Muir & Foley LLP. *Member:* Hartford County (Board of Directors, 1999—) and Connecticut Bar Associations; Connecticut Trial Lawyers Association; Defense Research Institute; Connecticut Defense Lawyers Association; Oliver Ellsworth Inn of Court, 1991-1994 (Secretary, 1993-1994). ***PRACTICE AREAS:*** Civil Litigation; Insurance Coverage Liability. **Email:** cbaio@baiolaw.com

ASSOCIATE

ANDREW M. DEWEY, born Newark, New Jersey, June 5, 1964; admitted to bar, 1989, Connecticut; 1990, U.S. District Court, District of Connecticut. *Education:* University of Connecticut (B.A., 1986); University of Connecticut School of Law (J.D., 1989). Phi Beta Kappa; Phi Kappa Phi. *Member:* Hartford County and Connecticut Bar Associations; Connecticut Trial Lawyers Association. ***PRACTICE AREAS:*** Workers Compensation Defense; General Liability; Personal Injury Defense. **Email:** adewey@baiolaw.com

MAYO, GILLIGAN & ZITO, LLP

ROCKY HILL, CONNECTICUT

(See Wethersfield)

Trials in all Courts, Real Estate, Banking and Commercial Finance, Creditors' Rights and Bankruptcy, Employment, Business Law, Zoning, Environmental, Estate Planning, Elder Law, Probate and Personal Injury Law.

PERELMUTTER, POTASH & GINZBERG, P.C.

11 BANK STREET

SEYMOUR, CONNECTICUT 06483

Telephone: 203-888-2501

Fax: 203-888-7928

URL: http://www.lawyers.com/perelmutterpotash&ginzber

Family Law, Personal Injury Litigation, Criminal Litigation, Jury Trials, Consumer Law, Negligence Law, Products Liability, Automobile Dealership Liability, Unfair Trade Practice Litigation, Probate, Real Estate, General Practice. Trials in all Courts, Appellate Practice.

(This Listing Continued)

JOSEPH N. PERELMUTTER (1909-1982).

ARNOLD M. POTASH, born Bridgeport, Connecticut, March 15, 1936; admitted to bar, 1961, Connecticut. *Education:* Cornell University (A.B., 1958; LL.B., 1961). Phi Delta Phi. President, Cornell Club of New Haven, 1968-1970. General Counsel, Ballantine Beer, 1971-1974. Member, Board of Directors: New Haven Jewish Community Center, 1965-1975; Jewish Home for the Aged, 1977-1980; Milford Preparatory School, 1977—. *Member:* New Haven County and Connecticut Bar Associations. ***PRACTICE AREAS:*** Family Law; Personal Injury; Criminal Litigation; General Practice; Appellate Practice.

JEFFREY D. GINZBERG, born Bridgeport, Connecticut, February 18, 1955; admitted to bar, 1980, Connecticut; 1981, U.S. District Court, District of Connecticut; 1992, U.S. Supreme Court. *Education:* University of North Carolina at Chapel Hill; Brandeis University (B.A., cum laude, 1977); Boston College (J.D., 1980). Student Editor, Family Law Quarterly, 1979-1980. Author: *Child Custody and Visitation in Connecticut* Law Practice Handbooks, Inc., 1996. Lecturer: The Peoples's Law School, Connecticut Trial Lawyers Association, 1995 (topic: "Family Law") and panelist at University of Connecticut School of Law, Litigation Week (topic "Meet the Masters"). Family Court Master, 1995—. Partner, Perelmutter, Potash & Ginzberg, P.C. *Member:* Westport (Chairman, Law Day, 1981), Bridgeport, Milford, Connecticut (Member, Family Law Section) and American (Member, Family Law Section) Bar Associations; Connecticut Trial Lawyers Association. (Board Certified Family Law Trial Specialist by the National Board of Trial Advocacy). ***REPORTED CASES:*** Jacobs v. Healey Ford, 231 Conn. 705, A2d (1995) (Unfair Trade Practices); Tyers v. Coma, 214 Conn. 8, 570 A2d 196 (1990) (Fraudulent Conveyance); Chute v. Mobil Shipping & Transportation, 32 Conn. App. 16, 627 A2d 956 (1993) (Workers Compensation); In Re Jennifer P., 17 Conn. App. 427, 553 A2d 196 (1989) (Foster Parent Visitation Rights); Skolnick & Sons v. Heyman, 7 Conn. App. 175, 508 A2d 64 (1986) (Arbitration); Bayone v. Calabrese, Waterbury Judicial District, CV 93-0113272 (1995) (Personal Injury Verdict (Auto Accident)). ***PRACTICE AREAS:*** Personal Injury; Family Law; Divorce; Child Custody; Retail Collections; General Practice; Sexual Abuse; Unfair Trade; Automotive Franchises and Dealerships; Real Estate; Sexual Abuse Litigation; Unfair Trade Practices; Creditor-Debtor Liability; Civil Practice; Criminal Law; Appellate Practice; State and Federal Litigation.

KENNETH POTASH, born Woodbridge, Connecticut, February 21, 1970; admitted to bar, 1996, Connecticut; 1997, New York. *Education:* Cornell University (B.A., 1992; J.D., 1996). ***PRACTICE AREAS:*** Personal Injury; Family Law; Criminal Law; Real Estate; General Practice.

REFERENCE: Shawmut National Bank.

ANDREW C. COTÉ, P.C.

11 GAY STREET
P.O. BOX 1294
SHARON, CONNECTICUT 06069
Telephone: 860-435-4721
Fax: 860-364-0496
Email: acclegal@aol.com
URL: http://www.lawyers.com/andrewcotelaw

FIRM PROFILE: We represent public investors and securities industry professionals in disputes which involve Securities and Exchange Commission, National Association of Securities Dealers, New York Stock Exchange and state regulatory investigations and enforcement proceedings, arbitration, litigation and mediation.

ANDREW C. COTÉ, born Melbourne, Australia, November 8, 1947; admitted to bar, 1980, Connecticut and U.S. District Court, District of Connecticut. *Education:* Clark University (B.A., 1975); University of Connecticut (J.D., 1980). Formerly President of Coté & Stewart, Ltd., a Registered Investment Adviser and NASD broker-dealer. Vice President, Director of Financial Services for Northeast Savings, F.A. Consultant, Securities Compliance and Marketing for Marketing One, Inc., an NASD Broker-Dealer. Member, Panel of Arbitrators, National Association of Securities Dealers. *Member:* Connecticut and American Bar Associations. ***PRACTICE AREAS:*** Securities Litigation, Arbitration and Mediation; Business Litigation; Arbitration and Mediation; Broker-Dealer Regulation; Securities Regulation; Securities and Business Law. ***Email:*** acclegal@aol.com

GAGER & PETERSON, LLP

Established in 1917
25 WEST MAIN STREET
P.O. BOX 158
SHARON, CONNECTICUT 06069-0158
Telephone: 860-364-5531
Telecopier: 860-364-5805

Waterbury, Connecticut Office: One Exchange Place, P. O. Box 2480. Telephone: 203-597-5100. Telecopier: 203-757-7888.

(This Listing Continued)

Bethel, Connecticut Office: 2 Stony Hill Road. Telephone: 203-207-5400. Telecopier: 203-207-5407.

Litchfield, Connecticut Office: 782 Bantam Road. Telephone: 860-567-0828. Telecopier: 860-567-5844.

Southbury, Connecticut Office: 325 Main Street South. Telephone: 203-262-6600. Telecopier: 203-262-6780.

General Practice. Corporate Law, Banks and Banking, Securities, Administrative Law, Litigation, Insurance, Estate Planning, Probate, Real Estate, Family Law, Taxation, Patents, Trademarks, Copyrights, Consumer Law, Environmental, Computers and Software, Labor and Employment Law.

LOUISE F. BROWN, born Bronxville, New York, August 28, 1943; admitted to bar, 1972, Massachusetts; 1973, Connecticut. *Education:* Harvard University (B.A., cum laude, 1965); Columbia University (M.A., 1966); Boston University (J.D., cum laude, 1972). *Member:* Litchfield County (President, 1986-1988), Connecticut and American Bar Associations. (Resident). ***PRACTICE AREAS:*** Real Estate Law; Estate Planning; Estate Administration; Probate Law. ***Email:*** LFBrown@snet.net

JO E. FRIDAY, born Punta Gorda, Florida, January 2, 1950; admitted to bar, 1981, Connecticut and Florida; 1982, U.S. District Court, District of Connecticut. *Education:* University of Florida; Florida State University (B.A., Humanities, with honors, 1972; J.D., with honors, 1981). *Member:* Litchfield County, Connecticut and American Bar Associations; The Florida Bar. (Also at Litchfield Office). ***LANGUAGES:*** Spanish and Italian. ***PRACTICE AREAS:*** Real Estate Law; Family Law; Probate Law; Estate Planning; Family Mediation; Contracts. ***Email:*** Fridaylaw@snet.net

J. MICHAEL SCONYERS (See Litchfield listing).

REPRESENTATIVE CLIENTS: Sharon Hospital; Salisbury Bank & Trust Co.; National Audubon Society; Mount Riga, Inc.; Northwest Lumber & Hardware, Inc.; Naromi Land Trust, Inc.; Indian Mountain School; Salisbury School.

EDWARD R. GIACCI, P.C.

375 BRIDGEPORT AVENUE
SHELTON, CONNECTICUT 06484
Telephone: 203-925-0442
Facsimile: 203-925-3003
URL: http://www.lawyers.com/gizcci

General Practice.

EDWARD R. GIACCI, born New Haven, Connecticut, September 11, 1945; admitted to bar, 1974, Connecticut; 1978, U.S. Supreme Court. *Education:* Norwich University (B.A., 1967); Syracuse University (J.D., 1973). Phi Alpha Delta. *Member:* New Haven, Connecticut (Member, Sections on: Litigation; Criminal Law) and American (Member, Family Law Section) Bar Associations. [Capt., U.S. Army, 1968-1970]

McKINNIS & LAPERA

1077 BRIDGEPORT AVE
SHELTON, CONNECTICUT 06484
Telephone: 203-925-8799
Fax: 203-925-8780
Email: lapera@mlawtek.com
Email: mckinnis@mlawtech.com
URL: http://www.mlawtek.com

New York, N.Y. Office: 445 Park Avenue, 10022. Telephone: 212-371-5400. Fax: 212-688-8036.

Westchester County Office: 40 Oriole Avenue, Bronxville, N.Y. 10708. Telephone: 914-793-9215. Fax: 914-793-9433.

Emerging Growth Companies including Telecommunications and Electronics, Information Systems and Semiconductor Industries, Entrepreneurial Business Law, International Business Law, Capital Formation, Telecommunications Contracts and Licensing, Computer Contracts, International Commercial Contracts, Corporate Commercial Law, Strategic Associations, Semiconductor Technology, Business Startups, Technology Finance and Licensing.

PATRICK J. LAPERA, born Carbondale, Pennsylvania, May 24, 1954; admitted to bar, 1981, New York; 1982, Connecticut. *Education:* University of Scranton (B.S., cum laude, 1976); University of Chicago (M.B.A., 1980); Syracuse University (J.D., cum laude, 1980). Phi Alpha Delta. Member, Justinian Honor Society. Managing Editor, Syracuse Journal of International Law and Commerce, 1979-1980. *Member:* New York State, Connecticut and American Bar Associations. ***PRACTICE AREAS:*** Corporate Law; Business Law; Municipal Finance; Commercial Law; Finance; Real Estate.

GEORGE C. McKINNIS, born Shawnee, Oklahoma, August 4, 1937; admitted to bar, 1965, Missouri; 1968, New York; 1997, Connecticut. *Education:* Oklahoma University (B.A., 1959); University of Michigan (LL.B., 1964).

(This Listing Continued)

McKINNIS & LAPERA, Shelton—Continued

Parker School of Comparative and International Law, Columbia Law School, 1973. Phi Delta Phi. Justice for the Justice Court of the Village of Bronxville, Westchester County, N.Y., 1994. *Member:* Association of the Bar of the City of New York; Missouri and American Bar Associations; New York Magistrates Association; Westchester County Magistrates Association; Computer Law Association; The Corporate Bar Association of Westchester and Fairfield, Inc.; Licensing Executives Society; Rotary Club of Bronxville, New York. ***PRACTICE AREAS:*** Emerging Growth Companies; Entrepreneurial Business Law; International Business Law; Telecommunications Contracts; Telecommunications Licensing; Computer Contracts; International Computer Law; Corporate Commercial Law; High Technology; International High Technology; Semiconductor Technology; Technology Finance; Technology Law; Technology Licensing.

McNAMARA AND KENNEY

375 BRIDGEPORT AVENUE
SHELTON, CONNECTICUT 06484-3844
Telephone: 203-366-5661
Fax: 203-366-5335

General and Trial Practice in all State and Federal Courts. Real Estate, Probate, Corporation, Family, Insurance, Medical and Legal Malpractice, Negligence, Products Liability, Workers Compensation and Zoning.

JAMES F. KENNEY (1921-1997).

THOMAS A. MULLIGAN, JR., born New Haven, Connecticut, October 11, 1945; admitted to bar, 1970, Connecticut and U.S. Claims Court; 1971, California; 1973, District of Columbia; 1974, U.S. Supreme Court, U.S. District Court, District of Connecticut and U.S. Court of Appeals, 2nd Circuit. *Education:* Fairfield University (A.B., 1967); Catholic University of America (J.D., 1970). *Member:* International Association of Industrial Accident Boards and Commissions; Connecticut Defense Lawyers Association.

GREGORY P. LYNCH, born Bridgeport, Connecticut, November 19, 1946; admitted to bar, 1974, Connecticut, U.S. District Court, District of Connecticut, U.S. Court of Appeals, Second Circuit and U.S. Supreme Court. *Education:* University of Bridgeport (B.A., cum laude, 1970); St. John's University (J.D., 1974).

GEORGE L. HOLMES, JR., born Bridgeport, Connecticut, December 3, 1947; admitted to bar, 1972, U.S District Court, District of Connecticut; 1973, Connecticut; 1974, U.S. Court of Appeals, Second Circuit; 1990, U.S. Supreme Court. *Education:* Fairfield University (B.A:, 1969); University of Connecticut (J.D., 1973). *Member:* Federation of Insurance and Corporate Counsel; Connecticut Defense Lawyers Association.

J. KEVIN GOLGER, born Bridgeport, Connecticut, September 24, 1957; admitted to bar, 1983, Connecticut and Missouri; 1984, U.S. District Court, District of Connecticut. *Education:* Tufts University (B.A., 1979); St. Louis University (J.D., 1982). Law Clerk to the Honorable John Karns, Illinois Appellate Court, 1982-1983.

ASSOCIATE

JAMES M. HUGHES, born Newark, New Jersey, October 6, 1951; admitted to bar, 1982, Connecticut and U.S. District Court, District of Connecticut. *Education:* Providence College (B.A., 1973); Montclair State College; University of Bridgeport (J.D., 1981). Certified Teacher of the Deaf, New Jersey, 1976. ***LANGUAGES:*** Sign.

THOMAS R. ROWE, born Bridgeport, Connecticut, August 5, 1969; admitted to bar, 1995, Connecticut. *Education:* Catholic University (B.A., 1992); Quinnipiac College of Law (J.D., 1995).

BRIAN E. BRIONES, born Jamaica, New York, May 5, 1965; admitted to bar, 1990, Connecticut; 1991, New York; 1992, U.S. District Court, Southern and Eastern Districts of New York; 1999, U.S. District Court, District of Connecticut. *Education:* Fairfield University (B.S., 1987); Hofstra University (J.D., 1990). ***Email:*** bbriones@mcnamaraandkenney.com

ANN MARIE DE VIVO, born New Haven, Connecticut, October 1, 1973; admitted to bar, 1999, Connecticut. *Education:* Marist College (Political Science, 1995); Quinnipiac College (J.D., 1999). ***Email:*** office@mcnamaraandkenney.com

REPRESENTATIVE CLIENTS: Allstate Insurance Company; American International Company; The Atlantic Companies; Crawford & Company; Gates McDonald of New York; General Accident Group; Government Employees Insurance Company; Lexington Insurance Company; Lovell Safety Management; National Car Rental Claim Services; Old Dominion Freight Lines; Prudential Property & Casualty Insurance Company; Royal Insurance; Safeco Insurance Companies; Shelby Mutual Insurance Company; Pathmark Corporation; Home Depot; National General Ins. Co..

GLENN M. REISMAN

Established in 1993
TWO CORPORATE DRIVE, SUITE 650
P.O. BOX 861
SHELTON, CONNECTICUT 06484-0861
Telephone: 203-944-3040
Fax: 203-944-3044
URL: http://www.ReismanLaw.com
URL: http://www.CreditCollectionLaw.com
Email: Glenn.Reisman@corporate.ge.com
URL: http://www.lawyers.com/reisman

Creditors' Rights, Bankruptcy, Risk Management, Workouts.

FIRM PROFILE: Mr. Reisman was in-house counsel for General Electric Company's credit and collection operations. He left G.E. in 1993 to open his own practice. He continues to provide in-house type services on a nationwide basis as a consultant on: credit/security devices; collections; retain and supervise local trial counsel; and bankruptcy strategy and tactics.

GLENN M. REISMAN, born New York, New York, September 20, 1950; admitted to bar, 1976, New York; 1988, Connecticut; U.S. District Court, Eastern, Northern and Southern Districts of New York. *Education:* Hamilton College (A.B., 1972); Albany Law School of Union University (J.D., 1975). Member, Albany Law Review, 1973-1975, Comments Editor, 1974-1975. Lecturer: "Dealing with Deadbeats". Author: "The War Against Record Piracy," Albany Law Review (1974); "Measurement of Damages," Albany Law Review (1974). Counsel-Creditors' Rights/Bankruptcy/Workouts (credit and collections), General Electric Company, 1980-1992. Law Clerk to Chief Judge James T. Foley, U.S. District Court, Northern District of New York, 1975-1976. *Member:* New York State, Connecticut and American Bar Associations; American Bankruptcy Institute; American Corporate Counsel Association; The Corporate Bar (of Westchester and Fairfield Counties); Commercial Law League of America. ***TRANSACTIONS:*** Represented General Electric in the following bankruptcy proceedings: Manville Corp.; LTV Corp.; Columbia Gas System; R.H. Macy & Co.; Lone Star; Walter Industries; Trans World Airlines; Public Service Co. of NH; Pan Am Corp.; Federated Dept. Stores; Charter Co.; America West Airlines; El Paso Electric Co.; Global Marine, Inc.; Eagle-Picher Industries; Storage Technology Corp.; Wheeling-Pittsburgh Steel; Green Coal; St. Johnsbury Trucking; CF&I Steel Corp.; Sharon Steel; Tacoma Boatbuilding Co.; Kaiser Steel Corp.; Servam Corp.; Allis-Chalmers Corp.; Allegheny Intl. ***PRACTICE AREAS:*** Creditors' Rights Law; Bankruptcy Law; Workouts Law.

J. MICHELLE REISMAN, born Poughkeepsie, N.Y., May 26, 1951; admitted to bar, 1977, New York (Not admitted in Connecticut). *Education:* Boston University (B.A., 1973); Albany Law School of Union University (J.D., 1976). General Counsel, North American Leasing Corporation, 1980-1981. Counsel, New York Life Insurance Company, 1977-1980. ***PRACTICE AREAS:*** Creditor's Rights Law; Bankruptcy; Workouts.

REPRESENTATIVE CLIENTS: General Electric Company; General Electric Capital Corp.; GE Fanuc Automation North America, Inc.; Mitsubishi Imaging (MC), Inc.; Morton International; Bush Boake Allen, Inc.; J.M. Huber Corp.

SILVER, GOLUB & TEITELL LLP

SHELTON, CONNECTICUT

(See Stamford)

Trial Practice in all State and Federal Courts. Medical Malpractice, Negligence, Commercial Litigation, Family and Criminal Law.

HASSETT & GEORGE, P.C.

SIMSBURY, CONNECTICUT

(See Hartford)

Civil Litigation, Commercial Law, Real Estate, Commercial Real Estate, Internet Law, PACA Litigation, Family Law, Criminal Law, Appellate Practice.

CHARLES D. HOULIHAN, JR.

1276 HOPMEADOW STREET
SIMSBURY, CONNECTICUT 06070-0582
Telephone: 860-658-9668
Facsimile: 860-658-1339
Email: CDHatty@aol.com
URL: http://www.lawyers.com/houlihanlaw

General Civil Trials and Appellate Practice in all State and Federal Courts. Business Litigation, Construction, Mediation. Employment Law.

(This Listing Continued)

CHARLES D. HOULIHAN, JR., born Boston, Massachusetts, June 15, 1953; admitted to bar, 1979, Texas; 1993, Connecticut. *Education:* University of Massachusetts at Amherst (B.A., magna cum laude, 1975); Syracuse University (J.D., magna cum laude, 1978). Phi Beta Kappa; Order of the Coif. American Inns of Court, Texas and Connecticut, 1985—. Law Clerk, Chief Judge James C. Turk of U.S. District Court, Western District of Virginia, 1978-1979. Director, Hartford Symphony Orchestra, 1996—. *Member:* State Bar of Texas; Connecticut and American Bar Associations (Vice Chair, Committee on Liability of Charitable, Religious and Non-Profit Organizations, 1990-1994). (Board Certified, Civil Trial Law, Texas Board of Legal Specialization).

LIBERT & ASSOCIATES

Established in 1984

3 MILL POND LANE
POWDER FOREST BUSINESS PARK
P.O. BOX 538
SIMSBURY, CONNECTICUT 06070-0538
Telephone: 860-651-9321
Fax: 860-651-5735
Email: libert.i.p.law@snet.net

Patent, Trademark, Copyright, Intellectual Property and Related Matters.

FIRM PROFILE: The Law Office of Victor E. Libert was founded in 1984 and serves a clientele which includes major U.S. corporations. The firm specializes exclusively in intellectual property law including the procurement of patents and of trademark and copyright registrations both in the U.S. and overseas, the rendering of patentability, validity and infringement opinions, the negotiation and preparation of agreements in the field of intellectual property and consultation and contested matters in that field. Long-established contacts are maintained with foreign intellectual property law firms to enable the firm to serve its clients' foreign as well as domestic needs.

VICTOR E. LIBERT, born New York, N.Y., November 25, 1936; admitted to bar, 1969, New York; 1971, U.S. District Court, Northern District of Ohio; 1972, Ohio; 1977, U.S. District Court, Eastern and Southern Districts of New York and U.S. District Court, District of Connecticut; 1982, U.S. Court of Appeals, Federal Circuit; 1983, Connecticut; 1997, U.S. District Court, Central District of Illinois; registered to practice before U.S. Patent and Trademark Office. *Education:* Polytechnic Institute of Brooklyn (B.Ch.E., 1958); Brooklyn Law School (J.D., cum laude, 1968). Member, Brooklyn Law Review, 1967-1968. *Member:* Hartford County and Connecticut Bar Associations; Connecticut Patent Law Association; American Intellectual Property Law Association. [1st Lieut., Corps of Engineers, U.S. Army, 1959-1962]. ***PRACTICE AREAS:*** Intellectual Property; Patents; Trademarks; Copyrights; Trade Secrets; Intellectual Property Licensing; International Intellectual Property.

ASSOCIATES

FREDERICK A. SPAETH, born Boston, Massachusetts, May 14, 1959; admitted to bar, 1986, Connecticut; registered to practice before U.S. Patent and Trademark Office. *Education:* Boston University; University of Connecticut (B.S., 1981); Quinnipiac College (J.D., 1986); University of Bridgeport (M.B.A., 1987). Phi Delta Phi. Associate Editor, University of Bridgeport Law Review, 1985-1986. Author: "Genetic Engineering Research: An Analysis of the Government's Role in Regulation," 7 Univ. of Bridgeport L.R. 71 (1986); "'Equivalents Thereof' v. The Doctrine of Equilalents in the Interpretation of U.S. Patent Claims," 20 Quinnipiac Law Review, No. 3, Winter 2001, pp. 487-526. *Member:* Connecticut (Member, Executive Committee, Intellectual Property Law Section) and American Bar Associations; Connecticut Patent Law Association. ***PRACTICE AREAS:*** Patents; Trademarks; Copyrights; Intellectual Property.

MELINDA ANN ALDEN, born Worcester Massachusetts, January 8, 1974; admitted to bar, 2001, Connecticut. *Education:* Elms College (B.A., 1996); Western New England College School of Law (J.D., 2001). ***PRACTICE AREAS:*** Patents; Trademarks; Copyrights.

PULLMAN & COMLEY, L.L.C.

Established in 1919

(Formerly Pullman, Comley, Bradley & Reeves)

720 HOPMEADOW STREET
SIMSBURY, CONNECTICUT 06070-2225
Telephone: 860-651-9348
Fax: 860-651-1431
URL: http://www.pullcom.com

Bridgeport, Connecticut Office: 850 Main Street, P.O. Box 7006, Telephone: 203-330-2000. Telecopier: 203-576-8888.

(This Listing Continued)

Hartford, Connecticut Office: 90 State House Square. Telephone: 860-424-4300. Telecopier: 860-424-4370.

New Haven, Connecticut Office: One Century Tower, 265 Church Street. Telephone: 203-773-3006. Telecopier: 203-776-7075.

Southport, Connecticut Office: 200 Pequot Avenue, P.O. Box 510. Telephone: 203-254-5000. Telecopier: 203-254-5070.

Stamford, Connecticut Office: 350 Bedford Street. Telephone: 203-324-5000. Telecopier: 203-363-8659.

General Practice including Administrative, Antitrust, Banking, Bankruptcy and Creditors Rights, Bonds, Business and Commercial, Corporate, Education, Employee Benefits, Environmental, Hospital and Health Care, Labor and Employment, Municipal Finance, Real Estate, Securities, Tax, Trusts and Estates, and Zoning. Energy and Utilities, Litigation in all Courts.

MEMBERS OF THE FIRM

ANDREW C. GLASSMAN, born Hartford, Connecticut, May 26, 1960; admitted to bar, 1985, Connecticut; 1986, U.S. District Court, District of Connecticut. *Education:* Cornell University (B.S., 1982); University of Connecticut School of Law (J.D., 1985). Member, 1983-1985, and Editor, 1984-1985, University of Connecticut Law Review. Frequent lecturer: business acquisition topics; issues involving management of employees, human resource functions. Author: "A Future for Cogeneration: FERC v. American Electric Power Service Corporation," 16 Connecticut Law Review, 1984; "A Summary of the Americans With Disabilities Act," and "Substance Abuse in The Workplace and Employee Assistance Programs". Adjunct Faculty Member: Labor and Personnel Relations, Hartford Graduate Center, 1989-1990; Employee Relations, Teikyo Post University, 1993-1994. Member: Simsbury Rotary; Simsbury Democratic Town Committee, 1988—; Simsbury Main Street Partnership, 1999—. Simsbury Charter Revision Commission, 1990-1991. *Member:* Connecticut and American Bar Associations. (Also at Hartford Office). ***PRACTICE AREAS:*** Corporate Law; Mergers and Acquisitions; Employment Law; Commercial Transactions. ***Email:*** AXG@PULLCOM.COM

ALAN S. PARKER, born Far Rockaway, New York, January 29, 1955; admitted to bar, 1980, New York and Connecticut. *Education:* State University of New York at Binghamton (B.A., 1976); University of Toledo (J.D., cum laude, 1979); New York University (LL.M. in Taxation, 1988). Articles Editor, University of Toledo Law Review, 1979. *Member:* Connecticut (Member, Sections on Taxation and Estates and Probate), New York State and American Bar Associations. (Also at Hartford Office). ***PRACTICE AREAS:*** Probate and Estate Planning; Tax Law. ***Email:*** ASP@PULLCOM.COM

(For Complete Biographical Data on all Personnel, See Bridgeport, Connecticut Professional Biographies)

CARMODY & TORRANCE LLP

900 MAIN STREET SOUTH
P.O. BOX 410
SOUTHBURY, CONNECTICUT 06488-0410
Telephone: 203-264-7882
Facsimile: 203-264-7847
Email: contactus@carmodylaw.com
URL: http://www.carmodylaw.com

Waterbury, Connecticut Office: 50 Leavenworth Street. P.O. Box 1110, 06721-1110. Telephone: 203-573-1200. Facsimile: 203-575-2600.

New Haven, Connecticut Office: 195 Church Street, P.O. Box 1950, 06509-1950. Telephone: 203-777-5501. Facsimile: 203-784-3199.

General Practice including Administrative, Alternative Dispute Resolution, Antitrust and Trade Regulation, Arbitration, Banking, Bankruptcy, Bond Finance, Closely Held Business, Commercial Real Estate, Commercial Litigation, Complex Litigation, Construction, Contracts, Corporate, Creditors' Rights, Employment Benefits, Employer Defense, Energy, Environmental, ERISA, Estate Planning, Family Business Successions, Finance, Freedom of Information, Government (State and Municipal Contracts), Health Care, Insurance, Intellectual Property, Patents and Trademarks, Labor and Employment, Land Use, Management Counseling, Medical Malpractice Defense, Municipal, Nonprofit Organizations, Pension, Privatization, Probate, Products Liability, Professional Liability Defense, Profit Sharing, Public-Private Finance, Public Utility, Securities, Tax, Toxic Torts, Zoning Law. General Civil, Criminal and Appellate Practice in all Courts.

FIRM PROFILE: 62 Attorneys Firmwide.

PARTNERS

MICHAEL J. REARDON, born Torrington, Connecticut, October 10, 1956; admitted to bar, 1984, Connecticut; 1985, U.S. District Court, District of Connecticut. *Education:* Connecticut College (B.A., 1978); University of Bridgeport School of Law (J.D., magna cum laude, 1984). Member, University of Bridgeport Law Review, 1982-1984. Law Clerk to the Hon. Peter C. Dorsey, U.S. District Court, District of Connecticut, 1984-1986. *Member:* Connecticut

(This Listing Continued)

CARMODY & TORRANCE LLP, Southbury—Continued

Estate and Tax Planning Council. (Also at Waterbury Office). ***PRACTICE AREAS:*** Estate Planning; Business Succession; Trust Administration; Taxation; Probate; Elder Law. ***Email:*** mreardon@carmodylaw.com

DAVID L. SFARA, born Washington, Pennsylvania, March 3, 1952; admitted to bar, 1977, Connecticut and U.S. District Court, District of Connecticut. *Education:* Princeton University (A.B., 1974); University of Virginia (J.D., 1977). President, Connecticut Estate and Tax Planning Council, 2000-2001. *Member:* Connecticut Bar Association (Member, Executive Committee, Estates and Probate, 1983-2000); Attorneys for Family Held Enterprises. ***PRACTICE AREAS:*** Estate Planning; Trust Administration; Probate; Elder Law. ***Email:*** dsfara@carmodylaw.com

(For complete biographical data on all personnel, see Professional Biographies at Waterbury, Connecticut)

ENGELMAN & ENGELMAN

800 MAIN STREET SOUTH
SUITE 122
SOUTHBURY, CONNECTICUT 06488
Telephone: 203-264-1441
Fax: 203-264-1443
URL: http://www.lawyers.com/engelman&engelman

Elder Law, Estate Planning, Probate, Taxation, Wills, Trusts, Title XIX and Medicaid Hearings.

MORTON H. ENGELMAN (1924-1998).

LAWRENCE H. ENGELMAN, born Middlebury, Connecticut, May 31, 1954; admitted to bar, 1980, Florida; 1981, Connecticut. *Education:* Duke University (B.A., 1976); University of Miami (J.D., cum laude, 1980; LL.M., in Estate Planning, 1981). *Member:* The Florida Bar; Waterbury, Connecticut (Member Executive Committee, Elder Law Section, 1994-1999) and American (Member, Section on Real Property, Probate and Trust) Bar Associations. ***PRACTICE AREAS:*** Estate Planning; Wills; Trust Law; Probate; Title XIX; Elder Law.

MICHAEL R. POHL, born Brooklyn, New York, August 12, 1942; admitted to bar, 1970, Virginia; 1987, Connecticut. *Education:* University of Steubenville (B.S. in Accounting, 1965); University of Richmond (J.D., 1971). *Member:* Connecticut Bar Association (Member, Estate and Probate Section and Elder Law Section); Connecticut Estate and Tax Planning Council. ***PRACTICE AREAS:*** Estate Planning; Wills; Trust Law; Probate; Title XIX; Elder Law. ***Email:*** mrpohl2@excite.com

GAGER & PETERSON, LLP

Established in 1917

325 MAIN STREET SOUTH
SOUTHBURY, CONNECTICUT 06488
Telephone: 203-262-6600
Telecopier: 203-262-6780

Waterbury, Connecticut Office: One Exchange Place, P.O. Box 2480. Telephone: 203-597-5100. Telecopier: 203-757-7888.
Bethel, Connecticut Office: 2 Stony Hill Road. Telephone: 203-207-5400. Telecopier: 203-207-5407.
Litchfield, Connecticut Office: 782 Bantam Road. Telephone: 860-567-0828. Telecopier: 860-567-5844.
Sharon, Connecticut Office: 25 West Main Street, P.O. Box 158. Telephone: 860-364-5531. Telecopier: 860-364-5805.

General Practice. Corporate Law, Banks and Banking, Securities, Administrative, Litigation in all Courts, Insurance, Estate Planning, Probate, Real Estate, Commercial Transactions, Taxation, Patents, Trademarks, Copyrights, Consumer, Computers and Software, Family Law, Environmental Law, Employment Law, Personal Injury.

KATHY S. BOWER, born Jamestown, New York, January 16, 1963; admitted to bar, 1988, New York and New Jersey; 1989, Connecticut; 1991, U.S. District Court, District of Connecticut. *Education:* State University of New York at Oswego (B.A., magna cum laude, 1985); Hofstra University (J.D., 1988). *Member:* Connecticut and American Bar Associations. (Also at Waterbury & Bethel Offices). ***PRACTICE AREAS:*** Personal Injury; Family Law; Litigation. ***Email:*** bower@gplaw.com

THOMAS M. RICKART (See Bethel Listing).

CHRISTIAN LAWRENCE DIPENTIMA, born New Haven, Connecticut, August 21, 1971; admitted to bar, 1997, Connecticut; 1998, New York and

(This Listing Continued)

District of Columbia. *Education:* Boston College (B.A., 1994); Quinnipiac College School of Law (J.D., 1996). Editor, National Probate Journal. *Member:* Connecticut, New York State and American Bar Associations; Connecticut Trial Lawyers Association. ***REPORTED CASES:*** Espowood v. Connecticut Light & Power; Espowood v. City of Bristol. ***PRACTICE AREAS:*** Insurance Defense (45%); Plaintiffs Personal Injury (45%); Workers Compensation (5%); Family Law (3%); Labor and Employment (2%). ***Email:*** dipentima@gplaw.com

SECOR, CASSIDY & McPARTLAND, P.C.

Established in 1865

Successors to Bronson, Lewis, Upson & Secor; Lewis, Hart, Upson & Secor; Upson, Secor, Greene & Cassidy and Upson, Secor, Cassidy & McPartland, P.C.

900 MAIN STREET SOUTH
SOUTHBURY, CONNECTICUT 06488
Telephone: 203-264-8223
Fax: 203-264-6730
Email: scm@ctlawyers.com
URL: http://www.ctlawyers.com

Waterbury, Connecticut Office: 41 Church Street, P.O. Box 2818. Telephone: 203-757-9261. Fax: 203-756-5762.

General Practice. Probate, Corporation, Negligence, Real Estate, Land Use, Banking, Municipal, Commercial and Taxation Law. Criminal and Civil Trials in all Courts.

JAMES R. HEALEY, born Waterbury, Connecticut, December 11, 1929; admitted to bar, 1955, Connecticut. *Education:* Northwestern University (B.S., 1952); Cornell University (J.D., 1955). Public Defender, Superior Court of Waterbury, 1965-1969. *Member:* Waterbury (President, 1983), Connecticut and American Bar Associations. [Law Specialist, USNR, 1956-1959]. (Resident). ***PRACTICE AREAS:*** Real Estate; Estate Planning; Estate Administration. ***Email:*** jrh@ctlawyers.com

ATTORNEYS FOR: The Mattatuck Museum; American Republican, Inc.; Hubbard-Hall, Inc.; The Siemon Co.; Engineered Sinterings and Plastics, Inc.; Boutin Industries; County Line Buick-Nissan, Inc.; Taft School.

(For Complete Personnel and Biographical data, see Professional Biographies at Waterbury, Connecticut)

ROSENBLATT & SHEFFY, L.L.P.

35 NORTH MAIN STREET
SOUTHINGTON, CONNECTICUT 06489
Telephone: 860-620-9460
Fax: 860-620-9348
Email: ed@randslaw.com
URL: http://www.randslaw.com

General Practice, Real Estate, Insurance Defense, Municipal Law, Personal Injury, Litigation, Commercial Lending, Asset Recovery Law, Construction Law, Family law, Employment Law, Estate Planning, Trials in State and Federal Courts.

EDWARD M. ROSENBLATT, born New York, New York, April 30, 1952; admitted to bar, 1981, Connecticut; 1984, U.S. District Court, District of Connecticut. *Education:* State University of New York at Binghamton (B.A., 1974); University of Hartford (M.A., 1977); University of Connecticut (J.D., 1981). *Member:* Connecticut (Chair, Executive Committee, Real Property Section) and American Bar Associations. ***PRACTICE AREAS:*** Real Estate; Commercial Lending; Asset Recovery Law; Family Law. ***Email:*** ed@randslaw.com

A. ALAN SHEFFY, born Lebanon, Pennsylvania, August 11, 1963; admitted to bar, 1988, Connecticut; 1989, U.S. District Court, District of Connecticut. *Education:* Lebanon Valley College (B.S., 1985); Western New England School of Law (J.D., magna cum laude, 1988). Member, Western New England Law Review, 1986-1987. *Member:* Connecticut and American Bar Associations; Connecticut Defense Lawyers Association; Certified National Institute of Trial Advocacy. ***PRACTICE AREAS:*** Insurance Defense; Personal Injury; Construction Law; Trials in State and Federal Courts. ***Email:*** alan@randslaw.com

BRODY, WILKINSON AND OBER, P.C.

2507 POST ROAD
SOUTHPORT, CONNECTICUT 06490
Telephone: 203-319-7100
Fax: 203-254-1772
URL: http://www.brodywilk.com

General Civil Practice, Corporation, Probate, Estate Planning, Trusts and Estates, Real Estate, Employment, Commercial, Environmental, Creditors Rights, Tax, Pension, Profit Sharing, Entertainment Law, Banking, General Business, Municipal, Freedom of Information Matters, Telecommunications, Public Utilities, Commercial Litigation.

(This Listing Continued)

SETH O. L. BRODY, born Bridgeport, Connecticut, September 27, 1927; admitted to bar, 1955, Connecticut. *Education:* Bassick High School; Phillips Academy; Yale University (B.A., 1950; LL.B., 1955). Phi Alpha Delta; Corbey Court. Town Counsel of Newtown, Connecticut, 1957-1964. *Member:* Bridgeport, Connecticut and American (Member, Real Property, Probate and Trust Law Section) Bar Associations. [With U.S. Army, 1946-1947; 1950-1951]. ***PRACTICE AREAS:*** Corporate Law; Mergers and Acquisitions; Estate Planning; Trusts and Estates; Entertainment Law. ***Email:*** sbrody@brodywilk.com

PETER WILKINSON, born Cleveland, Ohio, October 18, 1930; admitted to bar, 1955, Connecticut; 1956, New York; 1957, U.S. District Courts, Southern and Eastern Districts of New York. *Education:* Yale University (B.A., 1952); Harvard University (LL.B., 1955). *Member:* Bridgeport, Connecticut and American Bar Associations. Fellow, American College of Trust and Estate Counsel. ***PRACTICE AREAS:*** Probate Law; Trusts; Estate Planning.

FRANK FRITZ OBER, born Burlington, Iowa, September 14, 1937; admitted to bar, 1962, Connecticut. *Education:* Yale University (A.B., 1959); University of Chicago (J.D., 1962). Phi Delta Phi. *Member:* Bridgeport, Connecticut (Member, Real Estate Standards Committee, 1997-1999) and American Bar Associations. ***PRACTICE AREAS:*** Real Estate; Debtor and Creditor; Contracts; Employment Law; Entertainment Law; Corporate Law. ***Email:*** fober@brodywilk.com

S. GILES PAYNE, born Bridgeport, Connecticut, August 16, 1941; admitted to bar, 1966, Connecticut; 1967, Certified to practice before General Courts Martial, U.S. Armed Forces; 1972, U.S. District Court, District of Connecticut; 1974, U.S. Court of Appeals, Second Circuit. *Education:* Phillips Academy; Yale University (B.S., 1963); University of Pennsylvania (LL.B., 1966). *Member:* Fairfield, Bridgeport, Connecticut and American Bar Associations. ***PRACTICE AREAS:*** Estate Planning; Probate; Corporate Law; Real Estate; Entertainment Law; Trusts. ***Email:*** sgpayne@brodywilk.com

JAMES E. RICE, born Cohoes, New York, November 15, 1943; admitted to bar, 1969, Michigan; 1971, Connecticut. *Education:* Fordham University (B.S., 1965); University of Michigan (J.D., 1968). Member and Vice Chairman, Town of Fairfield Historic District Commission, 1991-1994. Assistant Town Attorney, Town of Fairfield, 1994-1997. *Member:* Bridgeport, Connecticut and American Bar Associations. ***PRACTICE AREAS:*** Administrative Law; Public Utilities; Telecommunications Law; Commercial and Banking Law. ***Email:*** jrice@brodywilk.com

WILLIAM J. BRITT, born Hartford, Connecticut, March 15, 1948; admitted to bar, 1973, Connecticut. *Education:* Fairfield University (B.A., 1970); Columbus School of Law of Catholic University of America (J.D., 1973). Member, Catholic University Law Review, 1971-1973. *Member:* Bridgeport, Connecticut (Member, Executive Committee Estate and Probate Section) and American (Member, Real Property, Probate and Trust Law Section) Bar Associations. [Capt., U.S. Army, 1976-1980]. ***PRACTICE AREAS:*** Corporate Law; Mergers and Acquisitions; Estate Planning; Trusts and Estates; Real Estate. ***Email:*** wbritt@brodywilk.com

BARBARA S. MILLER, born Brooklyn, New York, February 24, 1950; admitted to bar, 1977, Connecticut; 1980, Massachusetts. *Education:* Yale University (B.A., 1972); University of Connecticut (J.D., with high honors, 1977). *Member:* Bridgeport, Connecticut (Member, Conservation and Environmental Quality Section, 1985—) and American Bar Associations; Connecticut Trial Lawyers Association. ***REPORTED CASES:*** Bank of Boston Connecticut v. Brewster, 42 Conn. Supp. 474 (1992), affd. 32 Conn.App. 215 (1993); Rosenfeld v. Franks, 208 Conn. 562 (1988). ***PRACTICE AREAS:*** Environmental Law; Employment Law; Commercial Litigation; Probate Litigation. ***Email:*** bmiller@brodywilk.com

RONALD B. NOREN, born Bridgeport, Connecticut, April 15, 1953; admitted to bar, 1978, Connecticut. *Education:* Tufts University (B.A., 1975); Suffolk University (J.D., 1978). Member, Suffolk University Law Review, 1978. *Member:* Bridgeport, Connecticut and American Bar Associations. ***PRACTICE AREAS:*** Probate; Trust Law; Estate Planning. ***Email:*** rnoren@brodywilk.com

ROBERT L. TEICHER, born New York, N.Y., February 18, 1951; admitted to bar, 1977, New York; 1980, Connecticut. *Education:* Yale University (B.A., 1972); Vanderbilt University (J.D., 1976); Quinnipiac University School of Law (LL.M., in Taxation, 1990). Research Editor, Vanderbilt Law Review, 1975-1976. Adjunct Professor, Quinnipiac University School of Law, 1991-1993. *Member:* Bridgeport, Connecticut (Member, Executive Committee, Tax Section, 1994—) and American Bar Associations. ***PRACTICE AREAS:*** Taxation; Business Law; Trusts and Estates. ***Email:*** rteicher@brodywilk.com

PETER T. MOTT, born Bridgeport, Connecticut, March 17, 1956; admitted to bar, 1983, Connecticut. *Education:* Trinity College (B.A., 1978); University of Connecticut (J.D., 1983). Associate Editor, Connecticut Law Review, 1982-1983. *Member:* Bridgeport, Connecticut (Member, Executive Committee, Estates and Probate Section) and American Bar Associations. Fellow, American College of Trust and Estate Counsel. ***PRACTICE AREAS:*** Probate Law; Trusts; Tax Law. ***Email:*** pmott@brodywilk.com

(This Listing Continued)

THOMAS J. WALSH, JR., born Newark, New Jersey, January 23, 1961; admitted to bar, 1986, Connecticut. *Education:* University of Connecticut (B.A., cum laude, 1983; J.D., 1986). Trustee, University of Connecticut, 1984-1986. Town Attorney, Fairfield, Connecticut, 1993-1997. Assistant Town Attorney, Fairfield, Connecticut, 1999—. *Member:* Bridgeport (Chair, Business Law Committee), Connecticut (Executive Committee Business Law Section) and American Bar Associations; Connecticut Secretary of State Business Advisory Committee (Member, 2000—). ***PRACTICE AREAS:*** Commercial Transactions; Business Law; Real Estate Law; Municipal Law. ***Email:*** twalsh@brodywilk.com

DIANE F. MARTUCCI, born Elmont, New York, April 4, 1951; admitted to bar, 1984, Connecticut. *Education:* University of Rochester (B.A., 1973); Fordham University (J.D., cum laude, 1984). Member, Fordham Law Review, 1983-1984. *Member:* Connecticut and American Bar Associations. ***PRACTICE AREAS:*** Employee Benefits; ERISA; Taxation; Trusts and Estates. ***Email:*** dmartucci@brodywilk.com

SETH L. COOPER, born New Haven, Connecticut, December 4, 1962; admitted to bar, 1991, Connecticut. *Education:* University of Richmond (B.A., 1985); New England School of Law (J.D., cum laude, 1991). Managing Literary Editor, New England Journal on Criminal and Civil Confinement, 1990-1991. Author: Note, "The Impact of Thornburgh v. Abbott on Prisoners' Access to the Media and on the Media's Access to Prisoners," 16 New England Journal on Criminal and Civil Confinement, 1990. *Member:* Connecticut and American (Member, CBA Section on Commercial Law and Bankruptcy) Bar Associations. ***PRACTICE AREAS:*** Commercial Law; Business Law; Debtor and Creditor; Real Estate. ***Email:*** scooper@brodywilk.com

DOUGLAS R. BROWN, born Allentown, Pennsylvania, May 21, 1965; admitted to bar, 1994, Connecticut; 1995, U.S. District Court, District of Connecticut. *Education:* Duke University (B.A., 1987); Washington University School of Law (J.D., 1994). Articles Editor, Washington University Journal of Urban and Contemporary Law. Author: Comment, "Panacea or Pandora's Box: The Two Schools of Medical Thought Doctrine After Jones v. Chidester, 610 A.2d 964 (Pa.1992)," 44 Wash. U.J. Urb. & Contemp. L. 223 (1993). *Member:* Bridgeport, Stamford/Norwalk, Connecticut and American Bar Associations. [Lt., USN, 1987-1991]. ***PRACTICE AREAS:*** Probate; Trusts and Estates; Probate Litigation; Trust Litigation; Zoning. ***Email:*** dbrown@brodywilk.com

WILLIAM A. HARRISON, born Attleboro, Massachusetts, May 8, 1968; admitted to bar, 1995, Connecticut; 1996, Rhode Island. *Education:* University of Virginia (B.A., 1990); University of Connecticut (J.D., 1994). Member, Connecticut Journal of International Law. *Member:* Bridgeport and Connecticut Bar Associations; Bridgeport Chamber of Commerce (Member, Board of Directors, 2001—); Fairfield Chamber of Commerce (Member, Board of Directors, 2001—). ***PRACTICE AREAS:*** Real Estate; Corporate Law; Commercial Lending; Entertainment Law. ***Email:*** wharrison@brodywilk.com

JENNIFER A. BASCIANO, born Bronx, New York, June 8, 1975; admitted to bar, 2000, Connecticut. *Education:* Lehigh University (B.A., 1997); University of Connecticut (J.D., 2000). Associate Editor, Insurance Law Journal. ***PRACTICE AREAS:*** Trusts and Estates. ***Email:*** jbasciano@brodywilk.com

CHARLES S. BRODY (1894-1976).

OF COUNSEL

BRUCE E. DILLINGHAM, born Medford, Massachusetts, September 18, 1925; admitted to bar, 1957, Connecticut. *Education:* Colgate University (A.B., 1947); Columbia University and Yale University (LL.B., 1957). *Member:* Bridgeport (President, 1984-1985), Connecticut and American Bar Associations.

ROY W. MOORE, III, born Atlanta, Georgia, September 6, 1941; admitted to bar, 1966, Connecticut; 1970, U.S. District Court, District of Connecticut and U.S. Court of Appeals, Second Circuit. *Education:* Harvard University (B.A., 1963); Duke University (LL.B., 1966). *Member:* Bridgeport, Connecticut and American Bar Associations. [Lt., U.S. Navy, 1966-1969]

REPRESENTATIVE CLIENTS: General Electric Co.; Horberg Industries; Preferred Tool & Die, Inc.; Electrodes, Inc.; Fleet National Bank; Wire Works, Inc.; ETW Corp.; Tiger Woods Foundation, Inc.; The Chase Manhattan Bank; New Milford Savings Bank; Acme United Corp.; Sturm Ruger & Co., Inc.; Energy East Corporation; Centrix Corp.; Seymour-Sheridan, Inc.; Town of Fairfield; Color Film Corporation; Shoemart.

COBB & EISENBERG LLC

2600 POST ROAD
SOUTHPORT, CONNECTICUT 06490
Telephone: 203-254-0000
Fax: 203-254-6060
URL: http://www.cobbeisenberg.com
Email: info@cobbeisenberg.com
URL: http://www.lawyers.com/cobbeisenberg

Securities, Corporate Law, Venture Capital, Public Offerings, Domestic and Offshore Hedge Funds and other investment vehicles, Investment Adviser Regulation; Broker-Dealer Regulation.

JEFFREY B. COBB, born Los Angeles, California, January 3, 1945; admitted to bar, 1969, New York; 1970, U.S. District Court, Southern District of New York (Not admitted in Connecticut). *Education:* Harvard University (A.B., cum laude, 1966); New York University (J.D., 1969). ***PRACTICE AREAS:*** Securities; Corporate Law; Venture Capital; Public Offerings; Investments; Investment Regulation; Broker-Dealer Regulation. ***Email:*** jcobb@cobbeisenberg.com

MATTHEW S. EISENBERG, born Bronxville, New York, August 28, 1965; admitted to bar, 1990, Connecticut; 1991, New York. *Education:* State University of New York at Binghamton (B.A., cum laude, 1987); New York University (J.D., 1990). Pi Sigma Alpha. Recipient, Harpur College Academic Honors. *Member:* Connecticut Bar Association. ***PRACTICE AREAS:*** Securities; Corporate Law; Venture Capital; Public Offerings; Investments; Investment Regulation; Broker-Dealer Regulation. ***Email:*** matthewe@cobbeisenberg.com

DALY & PAVLIS, LLC

107 JOHN STREET
SOUTHPORT, CONNECTICUT 06490
Telephone: 203-255-6700
Fax: 203-255-1953
Email: info@dalypavlis.com
URL: http://www.dalypavlis.com

Civil and Criminal Litigation, Corporate, Internal Investigations and Monitoring.

ALFRED U. PAVLIS, born Greenwich, Connecticut, March 30, 1958; admitted to bar, 1983, Connecticut; 1985, U.S. District Court, District of Connecticut; 1987, U.S. Court of Appeals, Second Circuit; 1989, U.S. District Court, Southern and Eastern Districts of New York; 1996, New York. *Education:* University of Pennsylvania (B.A., cum laude, 1980); University of Virginia School of Law (J.D., 1983). Law Clerk to Honorable T.F. Gilroy Daly, U.S. District Court, District of Connecticut, 1983-1985. Assistant United States Attorney, Criminal Division, Southern District of New York, 1985-1990. *Member:* Association of the Bar of the City of New York; Connecticut, New York State and American (Member: Sections on Litigation and Criminal Justice; Committee on White Collar Crime) Bar Associations. ***PRACTICE AREAS:*** Civil Litigation; Criminal Litigation.

DEIRDRE M. DALY, born Dublin, Ireland, June 17, 1959; admitted to bar, 1985, New York; 2001, Connecticut. *Education:* Dartmouth College (B.A., cum laude, 1981); Georgetown University (J.D., 1984). Law Clerk to Honorable Lloyd F. MacMahon, U.S. District Court, Southern District of New York, 1984-1985. Assistant United States Attorney, Criminal Division, Southern District of New York, 1985-1997; Assistant-In-Charge, White Plains Branch, 1995-1997. *Member:* Association of the Bar of the City of New York; American Bar Association. ***PRACTICE AREAS:*** Civil Litigation; Criminal Litigation.

FATTIBENE & FATTIBENE

Established in 1970
2480 POST ROAD
SOUTHPORT, CONNECTICUT 06490
Telephone: 203-255-4400
Fax: 203-259-0033
URL: http://www.fattibene.com

Patent, Trademark, Copyright and other Intellectual Property Law.

ARTHUR T. FATTIBENE, born Bridgeport, Connecticut, April 23, 1923; admitted to bar, 1952, District of Columbia; 1953, Connecticut; 1971, U.S. Supreme Court; 1982, U.S. Court of Appeals for the Federal Circuit; registered to practice before U.S. Patent and Trademark Office. *Education:* Ohio University (B.S.I.E., 1948); Georgetown University (J. D., 1952). ***PRACTICE AREAS:*** Intellectual Property; Patent; Trademark; Copyright.

PAUL A. FATTIBENE, born Bridgeport, Connecticut, November 5, 1957; admitted to bar, 1983, Connecticut; 1984, U.S. District Court, District of Connecticut; 1989, U.S. Court of Appeals for the Federal Circuit; registered to practice before U.S. Patent and Trademark Office. *Education:* University of Vermont (B.S., Engineering, 1979); University of Bridgeport School of Law (J.D., 1983). Patent Attorney: Department of the Army, Communications and Electronics Command, Fort Monmouth, New Jersey, 1984-1987; Perkin Elmer Corp., 1987-1990. Elected, Town of Fairfield, Representative Town Meeting, 1997-2001. *Member:* Connecticut Patent Law Association; The Corporate Bar Association. ***PRACTICE AREAS:*** Patent; Trademark; Copyright; Intellectual Property. ***Email:*** paul@fattibene.com

KLEBAN & SAMOR, P.C.

Established in 1978
2425 POST ROAD
P.O. BOX 763
SOUTHPORT, CONNECTICUT 06490
Telephone: 203-255-4646
Fax: 203-259-9617
Email: info@kleban-samor.com
URL: http://www.kleban-samor.com

New York, New York Office: 900 Third Avenue, 13th Floor, 10022. Telephone: 212-826-6755. Fax: 212-371-1084.

General Practice. Corporation, Federal, State and Foreign Taxation, Relocation, Residential and Commercial Real Estate, Civil Litigation in Federal and State Courts. Negligence, Estate Planning, Probate, Pension and Profit Sharing, Foreclosure, Banking, Regulatory and Financing, Securities, Zoning, Workers Compensation and Public Utilities Law.

JEROME GOLDMAN (1936-1991).

ALBERT J. KLEBAN, born Bridgeport, Connecticut, March 8, 1931; admitted to bar, 1956, Connecticut; 1962, U.S. District Court, District of Connecticut; 1967, U.S. Court of Appeals, Second Circuit and U.S. Supreme Court. *Education:* University of Connecticut (B.A., 1953; J.D., 1956). Member, University of Connecticut Law Review, 1955-1956. Chairman, Connecticut Public Utilities Control Authority, 1975-1978. Member, Connecticut Public Utilities Commission, 1974-1975. Trustee, University of Connecticut, 1973-1994. Advisor, Federal Energy Administration, 1977. Member, National Association of Regulatory Utilities Commissioners, 1974-1980. President New England Conference of Public Utilities Commissioners, 1976-1977. Energy Advisor to Governor Ella Grasso, 1978. Trustee: Park City Hospital, 1973-1980; John Dempsey Hospital, 1974-1994; St. Vincent's Medical Center Foundation, 1978—. Member, Executive Committee, Fairfield County Area, National Conference of Christians and Jews, Inc., 1982—. *Member:* Greater Bridgeport, Connecticut and American Bar Associations. ***PRACTICE AREAS:*** Public Utilities Law; Commercial Real Estate Law; Corporation Law.

ALLAN J. ROSEN, born New Haven, Connecticut, June 9, 1936; admitted to bar, 1961, Connecticut. *Education:* University of Pennsylvania (B.A., 1958); University of Connecticut (LL.B., 1961). Member, 1973— and Chairman, 1984—, Zoning Board of Appeals, Easton, Connecticut. Member, National Panel of Arbitrators, American Arbitration Association. Member, Board of Trustees and Vice President, 1998, Housatonic Community Technical College Foundation. *Member:* Bridgeport, Connecticut (Member, Executive Committee on Banking Law) and American Bar Associations. ***PRACTICE AREAS:*** Banking Law; Regulatory Law; Financing Law; Commercial Law; Real Estate Law; Loan Workouts and Restructure Law. ***Email:*** arosen@kleban-samor.com

ALEXANDER W. SAMOR, born Bridgeport, Connecticut, August 27, 1939; admitted to bar, 1964, Connecticut; 1965, U.S. District Court, District of Connecticut; 1970, U.S. Court of Appeals, Second Circuit; 1971, U.S. Supreme Court. *Education:* Fairfield University (A.B., 1961); University of Connecticut (LL.B., 1964). Law Clerk to Justice Howard W. Alcorn, Connecticut Supreme Court, 1964-1965. *Member:* Greater Bridgeport, Connecticut (Member, Sections: on Corporations and Other Business Organizations; Construction Law) and American Bar Associations. ***PRACTICE AREAS:*** Corporation Law; Securities Law. ***Email:*** asamor@kleban-samor.com

THOMAS E. MINOGUE, JR., born Bridgeport, Connecticut, May 24, 1939; admitted to bar, 1966, Connecticut. *Education:* Georgetown University (B.A., 1962); University of Connecticut (LL.B., 1965). Assistant States Attorney, Fairfield County, 1969-1978. *Member:* Connecticut and American Bar Associations. ***PRACTICE AREAS:*** Civil Litigation; Criminal Litigation. ***Email:*** tminogue@kleban-samor.com

HENRY A. PERLES, born New York, N.Y., December 12, 1942; admitted to bar, 1967, Connecticut and New York; 1969, U.S. District Court, District of Connecticut; 1984, U.S. Supreme Court. *Education:* Amherst College (B.A., 1964); Fordham University (LL.B., 1967). Chair, Colgate Society of Families, 1995-1998. *Member:* Greater Bridgeport, Fairfield, Connecticut (Member, Sections on: Real Estate; Family Law) and American (Member, Sections on: Real Property, Probate and Trust Law; Family Law) Bar Associations. ***PRACTICE AREAS:*** Commercial Real Estate Law; Family Litigation; Residential Real Estate Law. ***Email:*** hperles@kleban-samor.com

(This Listing Continued)

THOMAS E. DARDANI, born Bridgeport, Connecticut, October 7, 1943; admitted to bar, 1968, Connecticut; 1969, U.S. District Court, District of Connecticut; 1970, U.S. Court of Appeals, Second Circuit; 1977, U.S. Supreme Court. *Education:* Wesleyan University (B.A., 1965); Vanderbilt University (J.D., 1968). *Member:* Greater Bridgeport, Connecticut and American Bar Associations. ***PRACTICE AREAS:*** Commercial Law; Corporation Law; Personal Injury Law. ***Email:*** tdardani@kleban-samor.com

STEPHEN J. SAFT, born New York, N.Y., July 21, 1944; admitted to bar, 1970, New York; 1973, U.S. Tax Court; 1981, Connecticut. *Education:* University of Rhode Island (B.S., 1966); Brooklyn Law School (J.D., 1969); New York University (LL.M. in Taxation, 1970). Certified Public Accountant: New York, 1972; Connecticut, 1974. *Member:* Greater Bridgeport (Chairman, Federal Tax Committee, 1984-1986), Connecticut, New York State and American (Member, Sections on: Taxation; Economics of Law Practice) Bar Associations; Connecticut Society of Certified Public Accountants (Chairman, Committee on State Taxation, 1979; Member, Committee on Federal Taxation, 1982-1987); New York State Society of Certified Public Accountants; American Institute of Certified Public Accountants. ***PRACTICE AREAS:*** Taxation Law; Estate Planning Law; Corporation Law. ***Email:*** ssaft@kleban-samor.com

BRIAN T. SILVESTRO, born Chicago, Illinois, January 14, 1949; admitted to bar, 1974, Connecticut and U.S. District Court, District of Connecticut; 1977, U.S. Court of Appeals, Second Circuit; 1982, U.S. Supreme Court. *Education:* Wesleyan University (B.A., 1970); Suffolk University (J.D., 1974). Author: "Public Utility Law," Suffolk University Law Review, Fall, 1974. Member, Employee Relocation Council, 1978—. CRP Designation from ERC, 1999. Member, Board of Directors, 1979— and Vice President, 1986—, Wakeman Boys/Girls Club. Chairman, Fairfield Parks and Recreation Commission, 1995—. *Member:* Fairfield, Greater Bridgeport, Connecticut (Member, Real Estate Law Section) and American Bar Associations; Connecticut Young Lawyers Association (Chairman, Real Estate Section, 1977). ***PRACTICE AREAS:*** Residential Real Estate Law; Zoning Law; Relocation Real Estate; Environmental Law; Estate Planning Law. ***Email:*** bsilvestro@kleban-samor.com

STEPHEN F. DONAHUE, born Washington, D.C., March 29, 1945; admitted to bar, 1973, Connecticut, U.S. District Court, District of Connecticut and U.S. Court of Appeals, Second Circuit; 1981, U.S. Supreme Court. *Education:* College of the Holy Cross (A.B., 1966); Cornell University (J.D., 1972). Past Chairman, Connecticut Commission on Sports Violence. Member: Trumbull Task Force on Health Services, 1985-1987; Fairfield County Human Rights Commission, 1987—. Chairman, Connecticut Senior Olympic Board, 1988—. Member, Police Activities Board, 1987—. *Member:* Bridgeport and Connecticut Bar Associations; Connecticut Trial Lawyers Association (Member, Statewide Bar Grievance Committee, 1991-1995); The Association of Trial Lawyers of America. [Lt., U.S. Navy, 1966-1969]. ***PRACTICE AREAS:*** Civil; Personal Injury; Health Service Law; Commercial Litigation. ***Email:*** sdonahue@kleban-samor.com

JONATHAN D. ELLIOT, born New York, N.Y., April 13, 1955; admitted to bar, 1980, Connecticut and U.S. District Court, District of Connecticut; 1984, U.S. District Court, Southern District of New York; 1986, U.S. District Court, Eastern District of New York; 1997, U.S. Court of Appeals, Second Circuit. *Education:* Yale University (B.A., 1977); University of Michigan (J.D., 1980). *Member:* Greater Bridgeport, Connecticut (Member: Family Law Section; Consumer Law Section; Federal Practice Section) and American (Member, Sections on: Litigation, Employment Law and Family Law) Bar Associations; American Collectors' Association. ***PRACTICE AREAS:*** Civil Litigation; Family Law; Consumer Law; Collections. ***Email:*** jelliot@kleban-samor.com

THEODORE R. TYMA, born Derby, Connecticut, March 18, 1960; admitted to bar, 1985, Connecticut; 1986, U.S. District Court, District of Connecticut; 1987, U.S. Court of Appeals, Second Circuit. *Education:* Fairfield University (B.A., 1982); Suffolk University (J.D., cum laude, 1985). Law Clerk, Superior Court, Legal Research Program, Connecticut Judicial Department, 1985-1986. *Member:* Valley, Greater Bridgeport, Connecticut and American Bar Associations; Connecticut Trial Lawyers Association; The Association of Trial Lawyers of America. ***PRACTICE AREAS:*** Civil Litigation. ***Email:*** ttyma@kleban-samor.com

DAVID M. LEHN, born Cincinnati, Ohio, January 16, 1956; admitted to bar, 1982, Connecticut; 1984, U.S. District Court, District of Connecticut; 1986, U.S. Tax Court; 1990, U.S. Claims Court. *Education:* Fairfield University (B.S., cum laude, 1978); Georgetown University Law Center (J.D., 1982); New York University (LL.M. in Taxation, 1986). *Member:* Connecticut and American (Member, Taxation Section) Bar Associations. ***PRACTICE AREAS:*** Taxation; Estates and Trusts; Probate; Business and Estate Planning. ***Email:*** dlehn@kleban-samor.com

OF COUNSEL

ELLIOT I. MILLER, born Brooklyn, New York, June 4, 1934; admitted to bar, 1958, New York; 1992, Connecticut. *Education:* Tufts University (B.A., 1955); Columbia University (LL.B., 1958). Harlan Fiske Stone Scholar, Columbia Law School, 1956, 1958. *Member:* New York State and American (Member, Sections on: Taxation; Corporation, Banking and Business Law) Bar Associations; New York County Lawyers Association. ***PRACTICE AREAS:*** Tax Law; Business Related Transactions; Work-outs; Complex Litigation. ***Email:*** emiller@kleban-samor.com

LEONARD C. BLUM, born Brooklyn, New York, June 4, 1941; admitted to bar, 1966, Connecticut and U.S. District Court, District of Connecticut. *Education:* Wharton School, University of Pennsylvania (B.S., 1963); University of Connecticut (J.D., 1966). Member, Fairfield, Connecticut, Representative Town Meeting, 1969-1977. Chairman, Legislation & Administration Committee, 1973-1977. Chairman, Conservation Commission, Inland Wetlands Agency, 1978-1986. Member: Board of Directors, The Bridgeport Regional Business Council, 1987—; Fairfield Water Pollution Control Authority, 1996-1997; Fairfield Board of Assessment Appeals, 1998—. *Member:* Fairfield, Bridgeport, Connecticut and American Bar Associations. ***PRACTICE AREAS:*** Real Estate Law; Zoning Law; Land Use; Condominium Law. ***Email:*** lblum@kleban-samor.com

THERESE A. FITZMAURICE, born Stamford, Connecticut, May 12, 1961; admitted to bar, 1989, Connecticut and New York. *Education:* College of New Rochelle (B.A., cum laude, 1983); University of Bridgeport School of Law (J.D., with honors, 1989). Phi Delta Phi. *Member:* Connecticut (Member, Labor and Employment Law Section) and American (Member, Labor and Employment Law Section) Bar Associations; Connecticut Trial Lawyers Association. ***PRACTICE AREAS:*** Employment Law; Employment and Business Litigation. ***Email:*** tfitzmaurice@kleban-samor.com

JOHN J. NOVAK, JR., born New York, N.Y., February 27, 1947; admitted to bar, 1972, New York; 2001, Connecticut. *Education:* Fairfield University (B.A., cum laude, 1968); Columbia University (J.D., 1971). Editor, Columbia Law Review, 1970-1971. *Member:* New York State, Connecticut and American (Member, Sections on: Corporation, Banking and Business Law; Taxation) Bar Associations. ***PRACTICE AREAS:*** Corporate; Securities; Mergers and Acquisitions; Commercial Law. ***Email:*** jnovak@kleban-samor.com

---

SABATO P. FIANO, born Bridgeport, Connecticut, August 29, 1972; admitted to bar, 1997, Connecticut; 1998, U.S. District Court, District of Connecticut. *Education:* Fairfield University (B.A., 1994); University of Connecticut School of Law (J.D., 1997). *Member:* Connecticut Bar Association; Connecticut Trial Lawyers Association (Member, Federal Practice Section, 1998—). ***PRACTICE AREAS:*** Civil Litigation. ***Email:*** sfiano@kleban-samor.com

JENNYANN CARLES, born New York, N.Y., November 12, 1969; admitted to bar, 1997, New York and U.S. District Court, Southern and Eastern Districts of New York; 2001, Connecticut. *Education:* New York University (B.A., magna cum laude, 1992); New York Law School (J.D., 1995). *Member:* Association of the Bar of the City of New York; New York State, Connecticut and American Bar Associations; American Bankruptcy Institute. ***LANGUAGES:*** Spanish. ***PRACTICE AREAS:*** Corporate Law; Bankruptcy; Debtor and Creditor Rights. ***Email:*** jcarles@kleban-samor.com

MAUREEN DEWAN, born Teaneck, New Jersey, May 17, 1947; admitted to bar, 1973, Vermont and U.S. District Court, District of Vermont; 1973, Massachusetts and U.S. District Court, District of Massachusetts; 1976, U.S. Court of Appeals, 1st Circuit; 1978, U.S. District Court, District of Connecticut; 1982, Connecticut; U.S. Court of Appeals, First and Second Circuits. *Education:* Douglass College (B.A., 1969); Suffolk University School of Law (J.D., 1973); Yale University (M.A., 1998). *Member:* Connecticut Bar Association; Connecticut Trial Lawyers Association; Association of Trial Lawyers of America. ***PRACTICE AREAS:*** Medical Malpractice. ***Email:*** mdewan@kleban-samor.com

JANICE M. McGRATH, born New Haven, Connecticut, July 5, 1957; admitted to bar, 1983, Connecticut; 1984, Florida and U.S. District Court, District of Connecticut. *Education:* Fairfield University (B.S., summa cum laude, 1979); Georgetown University (J.D., 1983). *Member:* Connecticut and American (Member, Taxation Section) Bar Associations. ***PRACTICE AREAS:*** Taxation; Estate Planning; Trusts and Estates. ***Email:*** jmcgrath@kleban-samor.com

CHRISTOPHER J. GALUPPO, born Brooklyn, New York, May 9, 1967; admitted to bar, 1993, Connecticut and New York; 1994, Florida. *Education:* University of Miami (B.B.A., 1989; J.D., cum laude, 1992). Certified Public Accountant, New York, 1995. Member, Connecticut Society of Certified Public Accountants. *Member:* New York State, Connecticut and American Bar Associations; The Florida Bar. ***PRACTICE AREAS:*** Federal Taxation; Estate Planning; State and Local Taxation; Business. ***Email:*** cgaluppo@kleban-samor.com

REPRESENTATIVE CLIENTS: Amhealth Group, Inc.; American Bank of Connecticut; American Yacht Harbor; Ashland Management Incorporated; Baker-Firestone Inc.; Baker Properties; Black Rock Column, Inc.; Cendant Mobility Services, Inc.; Chancellor Media; Colbert Shipping Corp.; Credit Bureau of Connecticut, Inc.; D'Addario Buick-Nissan-GMC Inc.; Dailey & Partners, L.P.; Dailey Capital Management, L.P.; Eurosystems International, Inc.; European American Bank; Fidelity National Title Insurance Co.; First American Title Insurance Co.; Fairways International Clubs, LLC; HealthCapital Financial Group, LLC; The Hudson National

(This Listing Continued)

KLEBAN & SAMOR, P.C., Southport—Continued

Golf Club, Inc.; Hudson United Bank; International Scientific Communications, Inc.; JJ Brennan Construction Co., Inc.; The Kennedy Center; Lamar Communications; Media/Professional Insurance Co.; Millenium Insurance Fund, L.P.; Miller Buick/ Ford/Nissan; N.F.Shops.com, LLC; The NIA/UIA Group, LLC; National Fairways, Inc.; NeoStrata, Inc.; New Milford Savings Bank; Norfield Corp.; Nutmeg Bowl, Inc.; 1.2.1 e-marketing, Inc.; OSS, Inc.; Paraco Gas; Paragrene Ventures; Paramount Stone Company; Patriot National Bank; Phelps Engineered Plastics Corp.; Photobition Bonded Services, Inc.; Rehabilitation Center of Eastern Fairfield County; Retrieval-Masters Creditors Bureau, Inc.; SBS Group, Inc.; Summit ResidentiaL LLC; TVI Strata; UBS/Swiss Bank Corp.; U.S. Internetworking; Vero International Software (UK) Limited; V.I. Group plc; VoiceWare Technology LLC; Wakeman Memorial Association, Inc.; Weichert Relocation Co.; Wells Fargo Bank; William B. Meyer, Inc.; Yankelovich Partners, Inc.

NEUBERT, PEPE & MONTEITH, P.C.

30 JELLIFF LANE

SOUTHPORT, CONNECTICUT 06490

Telephone: 203-254-9332

New Haven, Connecticut Office: 195 Church Street, 13th Floor, 06510-2026. Telephone: 203-821-2009. Fax: 821-203-821-2009.

General Civil and Appellate Practice before State and Federal Courts. Commercial and Banking Litigation, Product Liability, Hospital Liability, Medical Malpractice, Lawyer Malpractice, Design Professional Malpractice, Employment Discrimination and Wrongful Discharge, Health Care Law, Bankruptcy, Creditor's Rights, Real Estate, Corporations, Business, Banking, Trials and Appeals.

(For Complete Biographical Data on all Personnel, see Professional Biographies at New Haven, Connecticut)

PEPE & HAZARD LLP

30 JELLIFF LANE

SOUTHPORT, CONNECTICUT 06490-1436

Telephone: 203-319-4000

FAX: 203-259-0251

URL: http://www.pepehazard.com

Hartford, Connecticut Office: Goodwin Square, 06103-4302. Telephone: 860-522-5175. Fax: 860-522-2796.

Boston, Massachusetts Office: 150 Federal Street, 02110-1745. Telephone: 617-695-9090. Fax: 617-695-9255.

Commercial, Construction, Corporations, Taxation, Finance and Real Estate, Commercial and Asset Based Finance, Environmental Health/Safety, Fidelity and Surety, Securities, Labor/Employment and Education, Municipal, Administrative, Health Care, Intellectual Property, Patent, International Trade, Estate Planning, Probate, White Collar Crime, and Bankruptcy. Trials in all Courts.

FIRM PROFILE: At Pepe & Hazard LLP, we believe that today's profound social and economic changes affect what a law firm must contribute to its clients' services. There are new problems and new opportunities. There must, then, be new solutions - addressed with traditional skills, tempered by cold, hard experience - leavened with a contemporary perspective. Established in 1983, Pepe & Hazard brings this perspective to the intricate and evolving needs of business. That we have remained relevant to our clients through more than a decade and a half of economic change is testimony to the innovative and progressive practice of law that we embrace.

MEMBERS OF FIRM

SUZANNE E. BALDASARE, born Danbury, Connecticut, April 21, 1956; admitted to bar, 1981, Connecticut; 1982, U.S. District Court, District of Connecticut and U.S. Court of Appeals, Second Circuit. *Education:* Fairfield University (B.A., magna cum laude, 1978); Suffolk University (J.D., cum laude, 1981). Phi Delta Phi. Member, National Moot Court Team, 1980-1981. *Member:* Bridgeport, Connecticut and American Bar Associations. ***PRACTICE AREAS:*** Real Estate Finance; Loan Workouts; Asset Based Lending. ***Email:*** sbaldasare@pepehazard.com

MARK I. FISHMAN, born New York, N.Y., September 25, 1945; admitted to bar, 1970, Massachusetts; 1971, U.S. District Court, District of Massachusetts; 1972, New York, U.S. District Court, Southern and Eastern Districts of New York; 1974, U.S. Supreme Court; 1979, U.S. District Court, District of Connecticut; 1980, Connecticut. *Education:* Harvard University (A.B., magna cum laude, 1967; J.D., 1970). Law Clerk, Supreme Judicial Court of Massachusetts, 1970-1971. Member, Connecticut Law Revision Commission Advisory Committee on Article 6 of the Uniform Commercial Code. Director, New Haven Jewish Federation, 1996—. *Member:* Bridgeport (Chairman, Commercial Law Committee, 1997-1998) and Connecticut (Member, Executive Committee, Commercial Law and Bankruptcy Section, 1986-1996, 1999—) Bar Associations; Commercial Law League of America; Association of Commercial Finance Attorneys. (Certified Specialist, Business Bankruptcy Law, American

(This Listing Continued)

Board of Certification). ***REPORTED CASES:*** In re Cuisinarts, Inc., 115 B.R. 744 (Bkrptcy. D. Conn. 1990). ***PRACTICE AREAS:*** Bankruptcy Law; Commercial Litigation. ***Email:*** mfishman@pepehazard.com

JAMES C. GRAHAM, born Far Rockaway, N.Y., September 2, 1955; admitted to bar, 1980, District of Columbia; 1981, Virginia; 1982, U.S. Court of Appeals, District of Columbia Circuit, U.S. District Court, District of Columbia; 1984, Connecticut and U.S. District Court, District of Connecticut. *Education:* Yale University (B.A., cum laude, 1977); University of Virginia (J.D., 1980). Author: "Lien Stripping Causes Confusion for Lenders in Chapter 13 Bankruptcy Cases," The Commercial Record, January, 1992; "Lien Stripping Revisited," The Commercial Record, April, 1993; "Bankruptcy Puts a New Spin on Environmental Claims," Connecticut Environmental Compliance Update, July, 1993; "Bankruptcy," Chapter, Connecticut Lawyers' Deskbook: A Reference Manual (Connecticut Bar Association, 1998). *Member:* Connecticut (Executive Committee, Commercial Law and Bankruptcy Section; Member, Litigation and Federal Practice Sections) and American (Member, Sections on: Business Law; Federal Practice; Litigation) Bar Associations; American Bankruptcy Institute. ***PRACTICE AREAS:*** Bankruptcy; Litigation; Commercial Law; Legal Ethics and Professional Responsibility; Debtor and Creditor. ***Email:*** jgraham@pepehazard.com

JOSEPH W. MARTINI, born Rockville Centre, New York, November 12, 1960; admitted to bar, 1986, New York; 1998, District of Columbia; U.S. District Court, Southern and Eastern Districts of New York and District of Connecticut; U.S. Court of Appeals, Second Circuit (Not admitted in Connecticut). *Education:* Gettysburg College (B.A., cum laude, 1982); Brooklyn Law School (J.D., cum laude, 1985). Moot Court Honor Society. Assistant U.S. Attorney, U.S. Attorney's Office, District of Connecticut, 1989-1998. *Member:* American Bar Association; National Association of Criminal Defense Lawyers. ***REPORTED CASES:*** United States v. Diaz , 176 F. 3d 52 (2nd Cir. 1999); United States v. Barnes, 158 F. 3rd 662 (2d Cir. 1998); Morales v. United States, 143 F. 3d 94 (2d Cir. 1998); United States v. Hernandez-Santiago, 92 F.3d 97 (2d Cir. 1996); United States v. Anderson, 15 F.3d 278 (2d Cir. 1994); United States v. Juvenile Male, 1996 WL 633402 (2d Cir. 1996); United States v. Telesco, 962 F.2d 165 (Cir. 1992); United States v. Schuler, 907 F.2d 294 (2d Cir. 1990); Schuster v. Drajane Classic Motor Cars, Inc., 67 F. Supp. 2d 288 (S.D.N.Y. 1999); Baskin v. United States, 998 F. Supp. 188 (D. Conn. 1998); United States v. Perez, 1997 U.S. Dist. Lexis 21486 (D. Conn. Dec. 30, 1997); United States v. Ortega, 1996 U.S. Dist. Lexis 20181 (D. Conn. Oct. 4, 1996); United States v. Roman, 1997 U.S. Dist. Lexis 17719 (D. Conn. Oct. 23, 1997); Mercuri v. United States, 952 F.Supp. 98 (D. Conn. 1996); United States v. Rios, 881 F.Supp. 772 (D. Conn. 1995); United States v. Morales, 881 F.Supp. 769 (D. Conn. 1995); United States v. Ortega, 842 F.Supp. 48 (D. Conn. 1994). ***PRACTICE AREAS:*** Complex Civil Litigation; White Collar Crime. ***Email:*** jmartini@pepehazard.com

HAROLD JAMES PICKERSTEIN, born Bridgeport, Connecticut, July 9, 1946; admitted to bar, 1970, Connecticut and U.S. Tax Court; 1971, U.S. Court of Appeals, 2nd, 8th, 9th and 10th Circuits; 1972, U.S. District Court, District of Connecticut; 1973, U.S. Supreme Court; 1992, District of Columbia and U.S. Court of Appeals for the District of Columbia and Federal Circuits; 1997, U.S. District Court, District of Arizona. *Education:* University of Pennsylvania (A.B., 1967); Boston University (J.D., cum laude, 1970). Member, Boston University Law Review, 1969-1970. Attorney Generals Honors Program, 1970-1972. Trial Attorney, U.S. Department of Justice, Criminal Division, 1970-1972. Assistant U.S. Attorney, 1972-1986; Chief Assistant U.S. Attorney, 1973-1986; Court Appointed U.S. Attorney, 1974; Acting U.S. Attorney, 1973-1974, District of Connecticut. Member, Panel of Special Masters, U.S. District Court, District of Connecticut. *Member:* Greater Bridgeport, Connecticut and American Bar Associations; National Association of Criminal Defense Lawyers; Federal Bar Council. Fellow, American College of Trial Lawyers. ***REPORTED CASES:*** County Produce, Inc. v. U.S. Dept. of Agriculture, 103 F.3d 263 (2d Cir. 1997); United States vs. Construction Products Research, Inc., 73 F.3d 464 (2nd Cir 1995); United States vs. Rice, 954 F2d 40 (2nd Cir. 1992);United States vs. Tolla, 781 F2d 29 (2d Cir. 1984); United States vs. Mandanici, 729 F2d 914 (2d Cir 1984); United States vs. Bifield, 702 F2d 342 (2d Cir. 1982); United States vs Mowad, 641 F2d 1067 (2d Cir. 1980); United States vs Palter, 575 F2d 1050 (2d Cir. 1978); United States vs. Bifield, 498 F. Supp. 497 (D. Conn. 1980); United States v. Turner, 558 F.2d 46 (2nd Cir. 1977); United States vs. Robinson, 544 F2d 110 (2d Cir., 1976); City National Bank vs. United States, 78-1 U.S.T.C. Par 13,219 (D. Conn. 1977); Kliban vs. United States, 65 F.R.D. 6 (D. Conn. 1974); Kennedy v. Bureau of Narcotics and Dangerous Drugs, 459 F.2d 415 (9th 1976); Baughman v. United States, 450 F.2d 1217 (8th Cir. 1971). ***PRACTICE AREAS:*** Civil Litigation; Criminal Litigation. ***Email:*** hpickerstein@pepehazard.com

REED D. RUBINSTEIN, born East Lansing, Michigan, July 5, 1960; admitted to bar, 1985, Virginia; 1986, District of Columbia; 1987, Michigan; 1992, Connecticut. *Education:* The University of Michigan (A.B., high honors and distinction in Political Science, 1982; M.A., 1985; J.D., 1985). Recipient, Scribes Award. Author: "The First Step: The Asset Conservation, Lender, and Deposit Insurance Protection Act of 1996," 22 Conn. Law Trib. p. 20 (Oct. 21,

(This Listing Continued)

1996); "Financing Vehicles for Brownfield Development," Pennsylvania's Environment, p. 10 (Feb. 1996); "Shortening the 10-Foot Pole: Changes in CRA Should Stimulate Brownfield Lending," 21 Conn. Law Trib. 25 (May 15, 1995); "Rethinking Environmental Justice," Conn. Law Trib. (Supp. Dec. 1994; "Innocent Owner Liability For Environmental Contamination Under Connecticut Law," 67 Conn. Bar J. 398 (1993); "Clean Up Superfund Or Write Off Urban Redevelopment," 19 Conn. L. Trib. 20 (May 3, 1993); "Coaxing the Phoenix: Environmental Remediation Industrial Redevelopment and Municipal Control," 10 Conn. Real Est. L.J. 69 (1993); "Walking The Line: Integrating The Requirements of OSHA's Bloodborne Pathogen Regulation and the Mandates of the ADA," 66 Conn. Bar J. 451 (1992); "Using David's Slingshot: Handling the Plaintiff's Cost Recovery Suit," 6 Toxics L. Rep. (BNA) 1283 (1992); "A Survey of Recent Environmental Law Developments," 38 Wayne L. Rev. 977 (1992); "A Practical Guide to the National Environmental Policy Act," *Michigan ICLE Environmental Deskbook* (1992); "Environmental Law and Foreign Investment in the United States and in the EEC: A Practitioner's Guide," 69 Mich. B. J. 642 (1990); "A New Export Policy: The Foreign Sales Corporation and State Unitary Taxation of Foreign Source Income," 6 Mich. Y.B. Intl. Legal Stud. 61 (1986). Adjunct Professor of Environmental Law: Western New England College School of Law, Springfield, Mass.; Thomas Cooley Law School, Lansing, Mich., 1991. *Member:* Connecticut and American (Member, Sections of: International; Litigation) Bar Associations; State Bar of Michigan; District of Columbia Bar; Virginia State Bar. ***PRACTICE AREAS:*** Environmental Liability; Real Estate Finance; Land Use and Zoning. ***Email:*** rrubinstein@pepehazard.com

ASSOCIATES

JAMES J. FLAHERTY, JR., born Rockville Centre, New York, January 31, 1960; admitted to bar, 1995, Connecticut; 1998, U.S. Tax Court, U.S. District Court, District of Connecticut and U.S. Court of Federal Claims; 1999, U.S. Supreme Court. *Education:* Fairfield University (B.S. Finance, cum laude, 1991); University of Connecticut School of Law (J.D., 1995). Associate Editor, Connecticut Journal of International Law, 1993-1995. Member, Board of Directors, Morris Foundation, 1995—. Lecturer, Naugatuck Valley Community College, 1999—. *Member:* Connecticut (Member: Probate and Trust Section; Elder Law Section; Tax Section) and American (Member: Real Property, Probate and Trust Section; Tax Section) Bar Associations; National Academy of Elder Law Attorneys; Connecticut Estate and Tax Planning Council. ***Email:*** jflaherty@pepehazard.com

STEPHAN B. GROZINGER, born Montreal, Quebec, Canada, September 23, 1969; admitted to bar, 1995, Connecticut; 1996, New York. *Education:* University of Toronto, Toronto, Ontario, Canada (B.A., 1992); University of Connecticut (J.D., 1995). Articles Editor, Connecticut Journal of International Law, 1994-1995. *Member:* Greenwich, Connecticut, New York State and American Bar Associations. ***Email:*** sgrozinger@pepehazard.com

KRISTIN B. MAYHEW, born Philadelphia, Pennsylvania, August 29, 1970; admitted to bar, 1995, Pennsylvania and New Jersey; 1999, Connecticut. *Education:* Lafayette College (B.A., 1992); Dickinson School of Law (J.D., magna cum laude, 1995). Member: Appellate Moot Court Board; Woolsack Honor Society. Marketing Manager, Dickinson Law Review. Author: "Silicone Breast Implants and Hospital Liability, A New Forum For Hybrid Transactions," 99 Dickinson Law Review 439, 1995. *Member:* Pennsylvania, New Jersey State, Connecticut and American Bar Associations. ***Email:*** kmayhew@pepehazard.com

COUNSEL

JENNIFER L. COX, born New Haven, CT, May 11, 1968; admitted to bar, 1993, CT; 1994, U.S. District Court, District of CT. *Education:* Univ. of Connecticut (B.A., 1990; J.D., 1993). Member: CT Moot Court Board, 1991-1993; National Moot Court Competition. *Member:* American Bar Assn. (Health Law Section); American Health Lawyers Assn; CT Health Lawyers Assn. ***Email:*** jcox@pepehazard.com

(For biographical data on other firm personnel, see Professional Biographies at Hartford, Connecticut and Boston, Massachusetts)

PULLMAN & COMLEY, L.L.C.

Established in 1919

(Formerly Pullman, Comley, Bradley & Reeves)

200 PEQUOT AVENUE

P.O. BOX 510

SOUTHPORT, CONNECTICUT 06490-0510

Telephone: 203-254-5000

Telecopier: 203-254-5070

URL: http://www.pullcom.com

Bridgeport, Connecticut Office: 850 Main Street. Telephone: 203-330-2000. Telecopier: 203-576-8888.

(This Listing Continued)

Hartford, Connecticut Office: 90 State House Square. Telephone: 860-424-4300. Telecopier: 860-424-4370.

New Haven, Connecticut Office: One Century Tower, 265 Church Street. Telephone: 203-773-3006. Telecopier: 203-776-7075.

Simsbury, Connecticut Office: 720 Hopmeadow Street. Telephone: 860-651-9348. Fax: 860-651-1431.

Stamford, Connecticut Office: 350 Bedford Street. Telephone: 203-324-5000. Telecopier: 203-363-8659.

General Practice including Administrative, Antitrust, Banking, Bankruptcy and Creditors Rights, Bonds, Business and Commercial, Corporate, Education, Employee Benefits, Environmental, Hospital and Health Care, Labor and Employment, Municipal Finance, Real Estate, Securities, Tax, Trusts and Estates, and Zoning. Energy and Utilities, Litigation in all Courts.

JOHN S. PULLMAN (1871-1943).

ARTHUR M. COMLEY (1883-1969).

J. KENNETH BRADLEY (1903-1969).

WILLIAM REEVES (1906-1967).

MEMBERS OF FIRM

RAYMOND E. BALDWIN, JR., born New Haven, Connecticut, August 10, 1927; admitted to bar, 1956, Connecticut. *Education:* Kent School; Williams College (B.A., 1950); Yale University (LL.B., 1956). Phi Delta Phi. *Member:* Bridgeport, Connecticut and American Bar Associations; National Association of Bond Lawyers. [USNR, 1945-1946, 1950-1953]. (Also at Bridgeport Office). ***PRACTICE AREAS:*** Public Finance Law; Bond Finance; Estates and Trusts; Real Estate. ***Email:*** REB@PULLCOM.COM

DEBORAH S. BRECK, born Aurora, Colorado, April 14, 1953; admitted to bar, 1983, Connecticut; 2000, U.S. Tax Court. *Education:* Kingswood-Oxford School; Syracuse University; Southern Connecticut State University (B.A., 1975); University of Connecticut (J.D., with honors, 1982). Associate Editor, Connecticut Law Review, 1981-1982. *Member:* Bridgeport, Connecticut (Member: Estates and Probate Section; Legal Problems of the Elderly Section) and American (Member, Real Property, Probate and Trust Section) Bar Associations. (Also at Bridgeport and Stamford Offices). ***PRACTICE AREAS:*** Estates and Trusts; Elder Law; Trust and Probate Litigation. ***Email:*** DSB@PULLCOM.COM

JAMES B. STEWART, born Rockville Centre, New York, May 30, 1943; admitted to bar, 1968, Connecticut. *Education:* Wesleyan University (B.A., 1965); Vanderbilt University (J.D., 1968). *Member:* Bridgeport, Connecticut (Member, Executive Committee, Estates and Probate Section, 1990—) and American Bar Associations. (Also at Bridgeport Office). ***PRACTICE AREAS:*** Estates and Trusts; Real Estate. ***Email:*** JBS@PULLCOM.COM

ASSOCIATES

KATHERINE E. CAULFIELD, born Arlington, Massachusetts, September 5, 1966; admitted to bar, 1991, Connecticut; 1994, Florida. *Education:* Boston College (B.S., cum laude, 1988); University of Connecticut (J.D., 1991). *Member:* Greater Bridgeport, Connecticut and American (Member, Sections on: Probate; Taxation; Real Estate) Bar Associations; The Florida Bar. (Also at Bridgeport Office). ***PRACTICE AREAS:*** Estate and Gift Planning; Estate and Trust Administration; Elder Law. ***Email:*** KEC@PULLCOM.COM

RICHARD S. DiPRETA, born Greenwich, Connecticut, November 9, 1968; admitted to bar, 1998, Connecticut. *Education:* Trinity College (B.A., 1991); University of Connecticut (M.B.A., J.D., 1997). *Member:* Greenwich, Connecticut (Co-Chair, Estates-Probate Committee, Young Lawyer Section, 1998-2001; President, Young Lawyers of Lower Fairfield County, 1999-2001) and American (Vice-Chair, Real Property, Probate and Trust, Young Lawyers Division) Bar Associations. ***PRACTICE AREAS:*** Estate Administration; Estate Planning; Probate. ***Email:*** RSD@PULLCOM.COM

TRACY WHEELER LENNON, born Yonkers, New York, December 30, 1963; admitted to bar, 1992, Connecticut. *Education:* Bowdoin College (B.A., English and Government, with honors in Government, 1986); University of Bridgeport n/n/a Quinnipiac University (J.D., with honors, 1992). *Member:* Connecticut Bar Association (Member, Probate Section). ***PRACTICE AREAS:*** Estate Planning; Estate Administration; Nonprofit Organizations Law. ***Email:*** TWL@PULLCOM.COM

JENNIFER T. McGRATH, born Simsbury, Connecticut, November 12, 1971; admitted to bar, 1998, Connecticut. *Education:* University of Connecticut (B.A., magna cum laude, Phi Beta Kappa, 1993); Trinity College (M.A., 1995); University of Connecticut School of Law (J.D., with honors, 1998). *Member:* Greater Bridgeport, Connecticut and American Bar Associations. ***PRACTICE AREAS:*** Estate and Gift Planning; Estate and Trust Administration. ***Email:*** JRT@PULLCOM.COM

(For Complete Biographical Data on all Personnel, See Bridgeport, Connecticut Professional Biographies).

SHEA & SHEA

181 OLD POST ROAD
P.O. BOX 577
SOUTHPORT, CONNECTICUT 06490
Telephone: 203-259-7522
Fax: 203-259-0864
URL: http://www.shea.com

New York, New York Office: 300 Park Avenue, Seventeenth Floor. Telephone: 212-572-6269. Fax: 212-935-1377.

International and Domestic Taxation, Corporate, Trusts and Estates, Civil and Criminal Tax Litigation, Personal Injury Law, Family Law, Probate, Private and Public Foundations.

GERALD C. SHEA, born Washington, D.C., March 9, 1959; admitted to bar, 1985, Connecticut; 1989, U.S. Tax Court; 1991, New York; 1992, U.S. District Court, District of Connecticut. *Education:* Duke University (B.A., magna cum laude, 1981); University of Connecticut (J.D., cum laude, 1985); New York University (LL.M., Taxation, 1990). Clerk for the Hon. William M. Drennen, U.S. Tax Court, 1988-1989. Author: "APA's May Effectively Address Income and Expense Allocation Problems Faced by Global Trading Businesses," Tax Notes International, May 18, 1992. *Member:* New York State and Connecticut Bar Associations.

ROBERT N. SHEA (1932-1995).

TISDALE & LENNON, LLC

10 SPRUCE STREET
SOUTHPORT, CONNECTICUT 06490
Telephone: 203-254-8474
Fax: 203-254-1641
URL: http://www.lawyers.com/tisdalelennon
Email: tl@tisdale-lennon.com
URL: http://www.tisdale-lennon.com

New York, N.Y. Office: 36 West 44th Street, Suite 1111, 10036. Telephone: 212-354-0025.

Admiralty, Maritime, Insurance, Commercial, Products Liability, Bankruptcy Litigation and Personal Injury Litigation in all Courts.

PARTNERS

THOMAS L. TISDALE, born Glen Head, New York, April 27, 1956; admitted to bar, 1981, Connecticut and U.S. District Court, Southern and Eastern Districts of New York; 1982, New York, U.S. District Court, District of Connecticut and U.S. Court of Appeals, Second and Third Circuits; 1997, U.S. Supreme Court; 2000, U.S. Court of Appeals, First Circuit. *Education:* Fairfield University (B.S., 1978); St. John's University (J.D., 1981). Who's Who in American Colleges and Universities, 1978. *Member:* Connecticut Bar Association; Maritime Law Association of the United States (Proctor); Connecticut Maritime Association.

PATRICK F. LENNON, born Port Jefferson, New York, July 1, 1965; admitted to bar, 1992, Connecticut; 1993, New York; U.S. District Court, Southern and Eastern Districts of New York; U.S. District Court, District of Connecticut; 2001, U.S. Court of Appeals, Second Circuit. *Education:* West Chester University (B.S., 1987); Quinnipiac College School of Law (J.D., magna cum laude, 1992). Phi Delta Phi; Burns Honors Inn; Historian 1991-1992. University of Bridgeport Law Review, Research Editor, 1991-1992. Recipient, American Jurisprudence Awards: Criminal Law; Jurisprudence. Author: Comment, "Connecticut's Dram Shop Act: Pro Happy Hour," 11 U. Bridgeport L. Rev. 751 (1991). Adjunct Professor of Law (Admiralty) Quinnipiac College School of Law, 1998—. *Member:* Connecticut, New York State and American Bar Associations; Maritime Law Association of the United States; Connecticut Maritime Association.

ASSOCIATES

CHARLES E. MURPHY, born Portsmouth, Virginia, June 1, 1971; admitted to bar, 1997, Connecticut; 1998, U.S. District Court, District of Connecticut; U.S. District Court, Southern and Eastern Districts of New York. *Education:* Denison University (B.A., 1993); Syracuse University College of Law (J.D., 1997). Recipient: Corpus Juris Secundum Award for Criminal Law. *Member:* Connecticut, New York State and American Bar Associations; Maritime Law Association of the United States; Connecticut Maritime Association.

KEVIN J. LENNON, born Port Jefferson, New York, February 2, 1970; admitted to bar, 1997, New York and U.S. District Court, Eastern and Southern Districts of New York; 1999, U.S. District Court, District of Connecticut (Not admitted in Connecticut). *Education:* West Chester University (B.A., cum laude, 1992); Albany Law School of Union College (J.D., cum laude, 1996). Member, The Justinian Society. *Member:* New York State and American Bar Associations; Maritime Law Association of the United States; Connecticut Maritime Association.

(This Listing Continued)

PARADISO & MUSKA

Established in 1961
2 EAST MAIN STREET
P.O. BOX 22
STAFFORD SPRINGS, CONNECTICUT 06076
Telephone: 860-684-4221
Fax: 860-684-4181

General Civil and Criminal Practice before State and Federal Courts. Real Estate, Probate, Zoning, Corporation, Family, Workers Compensation, Personal Injury and Municipal Law. Trials in all Courts.

MEMBERS OF FIRM

F. JOSEPH PARADISO, born Stafford Springs, Connecticut, January 17, 1935; admitted to bar, 1960, Connecticut. *Education:* College of the Holy Cross (B.S., 1956); Georgetown University (J.D., 1959). Delta Theta Phi. Deputy Assistant States Attorney, 1963—. *Member:* Tolland County (President, 1968-1969), Connecticut and American Bar Associations; Connecticut Association of Municipal Attorneys. [With U.S. Army, 1959-1960; Reserve, 1960-1965]. ***PRACTICE AREAS:*** Criminal; Estate; Real Estate; Family; Personal Injury.

EDWARD M. MUSKA, born Hartford, Connecticut, February 28, 1949; admitted to bar, 1974, Connecticut; 1982, U.S. Supreme Court. *Education:* Cornell University (B.A., 1971); University of Connecticut (J.D., 1974). Chairman, Stafford Planning & Zoning Commission, 1977-1984. *Member:* Connecticut Bar Association (Member, Commercial Law Section); Connecticut Trial Lawyers Association. ***PRACTICE AREAS:*** Real Estate; Zoning; Municipal; Workers Compensation; Corporation.

REPRESENTATIVE CLIENTS: Stafford Savings Bank; St. Edward's Church; Elm Water Co.; Borough of Stafford Springs; Goodhall's Garage, Inc.; Farmers Home Administration; Aqua Treatment & Service Co.; Workers Federal Credit Union; Glenville Development Corp.

ABATE & ABATE LLC

607 BEDFORD STREET
STAMFORD, CONNECTICUT 06901
Telephone: 203-348-7770
Fax: 203-324-0057
URL: http://www.lawyers.com/abate&abate

Real Estate, Wills and Probate, Business Law, Estate Planning, Zoning, Divorce, Criminal Law and Civil Litigation, Personal Injury.

ERNEST N. ABATE, born New Haven, Connecticut, August 10, 1943; admitted to bar, 1969, Connecticut; 1972, U.S. District Court, District of Connecticut; 1990, U.S. Supreme Court. *Education:* Villanova University (B.S., 1965); University of Notre Dame (J.D., 1968). Member, City Committee, Stamford, Connecticut, 1973-1978. Member, House of Representatives, Connecticut Legislature, 1975-1983. Designated "Best Legislator" in Polls conducted by Connecticut Magazine, 1982. Chairman, House Judiciary Committee, 1977-1978. Speaker of the House, 1979-1983. Chairman, Legislative Management Committee. Connecticut Gubernatorial Candidate, 1982. Delegate for Senator Edward M. Kennedy 1980 National Convention. Chairman: Connecticut Bar Association Law Day Committee, 1975-1976; Legislative Liaison Committee, 1976. Member, Connecticut Law Revision Commission, 1983-1985. Counsel to Stamford Board of Realtors, 1989-1994. Member, Special Civilian Conference with Secretary of U.S. Department of Defense, 1984. Member, Board of Trustees, Ferguson Library, 1989-1993; 1995-2001; Chairman, 1993, 2000; President, State of Connecticut Regional Action Council, 1992-1993. Member, Board of Directors: Senior Services of Stamford, Inc., 1991—; Kids In Crisis, Inc., 1999—. Member, Board of Trustees, Connecticut Public Television and Radio, 1978-1983. Member, Mayor's Ethics Panel, City of Stamford, 1993. Past Member, Board of Trustees: Federal Health Systems Agency; Child Guidance Center. *Member:* Stamford, Connecticut and American (Member Sections on: Real Estate; Probate and Estate Planning) Bar Associations. [Capt., USMC, 1969-1972]. (Also Of Counsel to Updike, Kelly and Spellacy, Hartford, Connecticut). ***PRACTICE AREAS:*** Business; Trusts and Estates; Wills; Real Estate; Zoning. ***Email:*** ernestabate@msn.com

CHARLES P. ABATE, born Twenty-Nine Palms (Marine Corps Base), California, April 19, 1970; admitted to bar, 1995, Connecticut. *Education:* University of Richmond (B.S., in Finance, cum laude, 1992); Western New England College School of Law (J.D., cum laude, 1995). *Member:* Stamford, Connecticut and American Bar Associations. ***PRACTICE AREAS:*** Commercial; Real Estate; Litigation; Personal Injury; Criminal Law; Workers Compensation; Trusts and Estates; Wills. ***Email:*** charlesabate@msn.com

ALBERT, WARD & JOHNSON, P.C.

STAMFORD, CONNECTICUT

(See Greenwich)

General Practice. Real Estate, Zoning, Corporation, Litigation, Probate, Taxation, Construction, Environmental and Family Law.

AMENDOLA & AMENDOLA

STAMFORD, CONNECTICUT

(See Fairfield)

JOHN LLOYD ANNER, III

STAMFORD, CONNECTICUT

(See Greenwich)

Arbitration, Corporate, Commercial, International, Labor and Benefits Law, Litigation in all Courts, Real Estate, Trusts and Estates.

LAW OFFICES OF SETH J. ARNOWITZ

733 SUMMER STREET, SUITE 202
STAMFORD, CONNECTICUT 06901
Telephone: 203-348-7722
Fax: 203-978-1951
URL: http://www.ctattorney.com
Email: sja@ctattorney.com
URL: http://www.lawyers.com/arnowitz

Residential Real Estate, Real Estate Litigation, Real Estate Foreclosure, Civil Litigation, Family Law.

SETH J. ARNOWITZ, born Brooklyn, New York, June 17, 1965; admitted to bar, 1989, Connecticut; 1990, U.S. District Court, District of Connecticut; 1991, U.S. District Court, Eastern and Southern Districts of New York; 1995, New York. *Education:* New York University (B.A., 1986); Hofstra University (J.D., 1989). Phi Alpha Delta. Notes and Comments Editor, Hofstra Law Review, 1988-1989. Recipient, Pre-Trial Litigation Award. Author: "Denying a Natural Parent the Right to Visitation," Family Law Review, Vol. 20, No. 2, June, 1988; "Expert Evidence in Connecticut State Courts," American Bar Association Scientific Evidence Review, Monograph No. 4 (1999). *Member:* Stamford Regional and Connecticut Bar Associations.

ASSOCIATE

JULIET M. NOLTA, born Livonia, Michigan, August 23, 1970; admitted to bar, 1999, Connecticut; 2000, U.S. District Court, District of Connecticut. *Education:* University of Michigan (B.A., cum laude, 1993); Pace University School of Law (J.D., 1998). *Member:* Stamford Regional, Connecticut and American Bar Associations. **Email:** jmn@ctattorney.com

BAINTON McCARTHY & SIEGEL, LLC

THREE STAMFORD LANDING
46 SOUTHFIELD AVENUE
STAMFORD, CONNECTICUT 06902-7236
Telephone: 203-323-8080
Facsimile: 203-325-9716
Email: info@baintonlaw.com
URL: http://www.baintonlaw.com

New York, N.Y. Office: 26 Broadway. Telephone: 212-480-3500. Facsimile: 212-480-9557.

Central Islip, New York Office: 320 Carleton Avenue. Telephone: 631-234-4900. Facsimile: 631-234-2886.

Commercial Litigation, Intellectual Property, Product Liability, Trial Practice, Bankruptcy.

(For Complete Biographical data on all Personnel, see Professional Biographies at New York, New York)

BARNETT & ASSOCIATES

STAMFORD, CONNECTICUT

(See Greenwich)

Legal Consulting, Securities, Mergers and Acquisitions, Venture Capital, General Corporate, Business Law, Contracts.

STEVEN J. BARON

600 SUMMER STREET
STAMFORD, CONNECTICUT 06901
Telephone: 203-353-0052
Fax: 203-357-7208
Email: SJBaron23@aol.com

Real Estate, Residential Closings, Mortgage Closings, Commercial Real Estate. Family Law. Personal Injury and Criminal Law.

STEVEN J. BARON, born Stamford, Connecticut, February 4, 1956; admitted to bar, 1984, Connecticut. *Education:* University of Connecticut (B.A., 1978); New England School of Law (J.D., 1983). Teacher: Continuing Education for Real Estate Brokers, 1995-1997. *Member:* Connecticut Bar Association (Member, Real Estate Section); Stamford Regional Bar Association. ***PRACTICE AREAS:*** Real Estate; Criminal Law; Personal Injury; Family Law.

BARR & LaCAVA

22 FIFTH STREET
STAMFORD, CONNECTICUT 06905
Telephone: 203-356-1505
Fax: 203-357-8397
URL: http://www.infolaw.com
Email: B&L@infolaw.com
URL: http://www.lawyers.com/barr&lacava

General Practice, Franchising and Franchise Law, Litigation in all State and Federal Courts, Real Estate, Probate, Corporate, Estate Planning, Family, Immigration, Petroleum Marketing Practices, Environmental Law, Workers Compensation, Appellate Practice, Personal Injury and Automobile Accidents.

MEMBERS OF FIRM

ALBERT J. BARR, born Reading, Pennsylvania, March 31, 1949; admitted to bar, 1974, Connecticut. *Education:* Villanova University (B.S., 1971); Seton Hall University (J.D., 1974). President, West Norwalk Association, 1985-1987. Vice President, Stamford Child Care Center, 1985-1987. Member, Board of Directors, New Canaan Community Nursery School, 1987—. President, Midtown Club, 1999—. Member, Board of Directors, Midtown Club-Stamford, 1990—. Member, Board of Directors, Midtown Little League, 1996-1998. Treasurer, Midtown Youth Football, 1998—. Member, Advisory Board, Salvation Army, Stamford. Member, State of Connecticut Underground Storage Tank Petroleum Clean Up Fund Review Board. *Member:* Stamford, Connecticut and American Bar Associations. ***PRACTICE AREAS:*** Franchising Law (50%); Real Estate Law (20%); Family Law (10%); Environmental Law (10%). **Email:** abarr@infolaw.com

JOHN J. LaCAVA, born New Britain, Connecticut, July 18, 1952; admitted to bar, 1980, Connecticut; 1982, New York; 1983, Florida. *Education:* Tufts University (B.A., 1975); University of Connecticut (J.D., cum laude, 1980). Associate Editor, Connecticut Law Review, 1979-1980. Author: "Federal Statutory Remedy Rejected for Religious Kidnapping Victim: Baer v. Baer," 11 Connecticut Law Review, 773, 1979; "The 1986 Marriage Fraud Amendments," The Massachusetts Family Law Journal, Vol. 5, No. 1, May, 1987. Member, 1990-1999, and President, 2000-2001, Board of Directors, International Institute, Bridgeport, CT. Listed in "Best Lawyers in America," by Woodward White. *Member:* Connecticut and American Bar Associations; The Florida Bar; American Immigration Lawyers Association (Chairperson, Connecticut Chapter, 1985-1987). ***LANGUAGES:*** Spanish. ***PRACTICE AREAS:*** Civil Litigation Law; Personal Injury Law; Immigration Law. **Email:** jlacava@infolaw.com

JOHN J. MORGAN, born New York, New York, February 17, 1967; admitted to bar, 1992, Connecticut; 1993, New York; 1994, U.S. District Court, District of Connecticut. *Education:* State University of New York at Albany (B.A., cum laude, 1989); Villanova University (J.D., 1992). *Member:* Stamford/Norwalk Regional, Connecticut and American Bar Associations. ***PRACTICE AREAS:*** Litigation; Insurance; Franchise Law; Personal Injury; Products Liability. **Email:** jmorgan456@aol.com

ASSOCIATES

DOUGLAS R. PENN, born Santa Fe, New Mexico, September 30, 1966; admitted to bar, 1995, Colorado; 2000, Connecticut. *Education:* University of Denver (B.A., 1989; M.A., 1994; J.D., 1994). *Member:* Colorado and American Bar Associations; American Immigration Lawyers Association. ***LANGUAGES:*** Spanish. ***PRACTICE AREAS:*** Immigration and Naturalization. **Email:** dpenn@infolaw.com

REPRESENTATIVE CLIENTS: First County Bank; City of Stamford; Farrel Corp.; Service Station Dealers of America, Inc.; Rudy's Limousine Service, Inc.; Chicago Title Insurance Co.; Gasoline and Automative Service Dealers of America, Inc.; Corporate Branding, LLC.

BELLO, LAPINE & CASSONE, L.L.P.

600 SUMMER STREET
STAMFORD, CONNECTICUT 06901
Telephone: 203-348-4244
Fax: 203-357-7208
Email: blclaw@lawyers.com
URL: http://www.lawyers.com/bl&cllp

Ridgefield, Connecticut Office: 369 North Street. 06877. Telephone: 203 438-3974.

Personal Injury, Medical Malpractice, Product Liability, Auto Accidents and Injuries, Professional Negligence, Legal Malpractice, Real Estate, Criminal.

ROBERT S. BELLO, born Stamford, Connecticut, February 23, 1937; admitted to bar, 1961, Connecticut. *Education:* Fairfield University (B.S., 1958); St. John's University (LL.B., 1961). *Member:* Stamford Regional and Connecticut Bar Associations; Connecticut Trial Lawyers Association; The Association of Trial Lawyers of America. **PRACTICE AREAS:** Criminal Litigation; Real Estate; Family Law. **Email:** blclaw@lawyers.com

LAWRENCE M. LAPINE, born Mansfield, Connecticut, March 2, 1944; admitted to bar, 1969, Connecticut; U.S. District Court, District of Connecticut. *Education:* Brown University (B.A., 1966); University of Connecticut (J.D., 1969). Special Master, Connecticut Superior Court. *Member:* Stamford Regional and Connecticut Bar Associations; National Board of Trial Advocacy; Connecticut Trial Lawyers Association; The Association of Trial Lawyers of America. (Certified as a Civil Trial Advocacy Specialist by the National Board of Trial Advocacy). **PRACTICE AREAS:** Civil Litigation; Medical Malpractice; Dental Malpractice; Legal Malpractice; Personal Injury; Products Liability; Commercial Litigation; Divorce. **Email:** blclaw@lawyers.com

THOMAS M. CASSONE, born Stamford, Connecticut, May 11, 1956; admitted to bar, 1981, Michigan; 1982 Connecticut; U.S. District Court, District of Connecticut; U.S. Bankruptcy Court. *Education:* Lehigh University (B.A., 1978); Western New England College (J.D., 1981). Corporation Counsel and Director of Legal Affairs, City of Stamford, Connecticut, 1995-1999. Trustee and Treasurer, Ferguson Library, Inc., 1997—. Counsel and Founding Member, Stamford Water Pollution Control Authority, 1997-1999. Counsel, Stamford Downtown Special Services District. Special Master, Connecticut Superior Court. Director, Public Safety, Health and Welfare, City of Stamford, Connecticut. *Member:* Stamford Regional and Connecticut Bar Associations; Connecticut Trial Lawyers Association; The Association of Trial Lawyers of America. **PRACTICE AREAS:** Civil Litigation; Products Liability; Personal Injury; Medical Malpractice; Negligence Defense; Commercial Litigation; Appellate Practice; Municipal Law; Family Law. **Email:** blclaw@lawyers.com

---

PATRICK D. McCABE, born Houston, Texas, January 18, 1971; admitted to bar, 2000, New York (Not admitted in Connecticut). *Education:* University of Texas at Austin (B.A., 1993); New York University School of Law (J.D., 1999). Member, Order of the Coif. **PRACTICE AREAS:** Litigation.

BENTLEY, MOSHER, BABSON & LAMBERT, P.C.

STAMFORD, CONNECTICUT
(See Greenwich)

General Practice. Estates and Trusts, Corporate, Tax, Real Estate, Mortgage and Banking, Consumer Lending. State and Federal Litigation including Domestic Relations.

BERKOWITZ, MALOWITZ & MULLIN

CENTURY PLAZA SOUTH TOWER
100 PROSPECT STREET
STAMFORD, CONNECTICUT 06901-1207
Telephone: 203-324-7909
Fax: 203-324-5067
URL: http://www.lawyers.com/bm&m

Personal Injury Litigation, Medical Malpractice, Products Liability Law, Workers' Compensation, and Complex Civil Litigation.

MEMBERS OF FIRM

RUSSELL J. BERKOWITZ, born Brooklyn, New York, April 23, 1958; admitted to bar, 1985, Connecticut; 1986, U.S. District Court, District of Connecticut. *Education:* Drake University (B.S., 1980; J.D., 1985). Delta Theta Phi. Member, Order of Barristers. Recipient, Who's Who Award by Strathmore's Who's Who Registry of Business Leaders. Faculty Member and Chairman, Peoples Law School Program, Connecticut Trial Lawyers Association, 1989—. Lecturer: "Brass Tacks of Civil Litigation," Stamford/Darien Bar Association, 1989—. Special Master, Superior Court, State of Connecticut, 1992. Mediator, Dispute Resolution Inc., 1989—. Diplomate, Connecticut Board of Trial Advocates. *Member:* Stamford Regional, Connecticut (Member, Civil Justice Section) and American Bar Associations; Connecticut Trial Lawyers Association; New York State Trial Lawyers Association; The Association of Trial Lawyers of America; Million Dollar Advocates Forum. Fellow, Roscoe Pound Foundation. (Certified as a Civil Trial Specialist by the National Board of Trial Advocacy). **PRACTICE AREAS:** Personal Injury; Medical Malpractice; Wrongful Deaths. **Email:** berki@disvovernet.net

WESLEY M. MALOWITZ, born Rochester, New York, April 12, 1964; admitted to bar, 1991, Connecticut; 1992, New York and District of Columbia; 1996, U.S. District Court, District of Connecticut. *Education:* Ohio University (B.A., summa cum laude, 1988); American University (J.D., summa cum laude, 1991). Phi Beta Kappa. Member, American University Law Review. *Member:* The District of Columbia Bar; Stamford/Norwalk, Connecticut, New York State and American Bar Associations; Connecticut Trial Lawyers Association. **PRACTICE AREAS:** Personal Injury; Medical Malpractice; Workers Compensation; Products Liability. **Email:** wmals@discovernet.net

CARYN L. MULLIN, born Hartford, Connecticut, October 2, 1961; admitted to bar, 1992, Connecticut; 1993, U.S. District Court, District of Connecticut. *Education:* Southern Connecticut State University (B.S.R.N., 1983); University of Bridgeport (J.D., 1992). Licensed Registered Nurse, Connecticut. *Member:* Greater Bridgeport, Stamford and Connecticut Bar Associations; Connecticut Trial Lawyers Association; The Association of Trial Lawyers of America; Million Dollar Advocates Forum. **PRACTICE AREAS:** Medical Malpractice; Personal Injury; Products Liability; Workers Compensation. **Email:** cmullin@discovernet.net

STEVEN G. M. BIRO

291 VINE ROAD
STAMFORD, CONNECTICUT 06905-2106
Telephone: 203-329-9664
Fax: 203-329-1640
Email: SBIRO@optonline.NET
URL: http://www.lawyers.com/stevenbiro

New York Office: 61 Broadway, 18th Floor, 10006, Telephone: 212-797-9100.

Personal Injuries, Divorce and Family, Accidents, Real Estate Transactions, Wills and Estates, Business Affairs, International and Domestic, Landlord-Tenant, Worker's Compensation, Collection.

STEVEN G. M. BIRO, born Anakra, Turkey, August 17, 1943; admitted to bar, 1974, Connecticut; 1975, New York, U.S. Court of Appeals 2nd Circuit; 1976, Court of International Trade; 1978, Florida and U.S. Supreme Court, U.S. District Court, District of Connecticut and U.S. District Court, Eastern and Southern Districts of New York. *Education:* Columbia College (B.A., 1965); University of Washington (M.A., 1966); Fordham University (J.D., 1974). Recipient: Law School Scholarship; New York State Scholarship Award. Case Notes Editor, 1973- 1974. Author: "Doing Business" Middle East Economic Digest Special Report on Oman (1980). Lecturer: "Coordinated Legal Research the Big Antitrust Case" (Continuing legal education program sponsored by the New York Law Journal (1978). Law Clerk: Justice Joseph S. Longo, 1975; Justice Louis Shapiro, 1974; Justice Joseph S. Longo and Honorable T.J. Meskil, U.S. Court of Appeals, 2nd Circuit. *Member:* New York and Connecticut Bar Associations; The Florida Bar. **LANGUAGES:** Hungarian, French, Turkish.

BLAIR & POTTS

TWO STAMFORD PLAZA
P.O. BOX 1214
STAMFORD, CONNECTICUT 06904
Telephone: 203-327-2333
Fax: 203-327-1731
Email: administrator@blairandpotts.com
URL: http://www.lawyers.com/blair&potts

Estate and Tax Planning and Estate Settlement and Trust Administration.

NANCY E. BLAIR, born Barbourville, Kentucky, May 6, 1953; admitted to bar, 1981, Connecticut; 1982, Massachusetts. *Education:* University of California at San Diego; Vassar College (B.A., cum laude, 1976); Boston University (J.D., 1981). Listed in: The Best Lawyers in America. Author: "Connecticut Probate Deskbook," Lawyers Cooperative Publishing Company, 1988; "Chapter 25: Planning for Disposition of Tax Shelter Investments," Estate and Personal Financial Planning, Callaghan and Company, 1988; "Connecticut Estate Planning," "Connecticut Estate Settlement," "Connecticut Will Drafting," and

(This Listing Continued)

"Connecticut Trust Drafting," for American Legal Education Foundation, 1989-1995. Adjunct Professor of Law, University of Bridgeport, LL.M. Program in Taxation, 1988-1990. *Member:* Connecticut, Massachusetts and American Bar Associations. Fellow, American College of Trust and Estate Counsel. ***PRACTICE AREAS:*** Estate Planning; Tax Planning; Estate Settlements; Trust Administration.

ARTHUR G. POTTS, JR., born Bridgeport, Connecticut, April 15, 1949; admitted to bar, 1974, Connecticut; 1977, Florida. *Education:* Williams College (B.A., magna cum laude, 1971); University of Virginia (J.D., 1974). Phi Beta Kappa. *Member:* New Canaan, Stamford Regional (Director and Chairman, Probate and Estates Committee, 1989-1991), Connecticut and American (Member, Real Property, Probate and Trust Law Section) Bar Associations; The Florida Bar. ***PRACTICE AREAS:*** Estate Litigation; Tax Planning; Estate Settlements; Trust Administration; Executive Compensation Taxation.

ASSOCIATES

KIMBERLY M. ARPAIA, born New Haven, Connecticut, January 16, 1958; admitted to bar, 1987, Connecticut. *Education:* University of Vermont (A.S., 1978; B.A., cum laude, 1984); University of Connecticut (J.D., with high honors, 1987). Recipient: Corpus Juris Secundum Award; American Jurisprudence Book Awards in Property and Family Law. Associate Editor, Connecticut Law Review, 1986-1987. Adjunct Professor, Trusts and Estates, University of Connecticut School of Law, Fall 1991. Judicial Law Clerk to the Honorable Antoinette L. Dupont, Chief Presiding Judge, Connecticut Appellate Court, 1987-1988. ***PRACTICE AREAS:*** Estate Planning; Estate Settlements; Trust Administration.

JOAN M. O'BRIEN, born Bayonne, New Jersey, June 5, 1942; admitted to bar, 1995, Connecticut; 1996, New York; 1997, U.S. District Court, Southern District of New York. *Education:* Notre Dame College (B.A., 1964); Rutgers University (M.S., 1967); Pace University (J.D., 1995). Recipient: Julian H. Hyman Scholarship Award for Excellence in Trusts and Estates; Environmental Law Certificate, Pace University; American Jurisprudence Award in Contracts. Articles Editor, Pace Law Review, 1994-1995. Judicial Law Clerk to the Honorable William B. Lewis, Stamford Superior Court, Stamford, Connecticut, Summer 1993. Author, "The Connecticut Recreational Use Statute: Should a Municipality Be Immune from Tort Liability?" 15:3 Pace Law Review, Spring 1995. *Member:* Connecticut (Member, Sections on: Elder Law, Probate and Trust Law), New York State and American Bar Associations; National Academy of Elder Law Attorneys (NAELA). ***LANGUAGES:*** French. ***PRACTICE AREAS:*** Estate Planning; Estate Settlements; Trust Administration.

ROBERT A. DEVELLIS, born Bridgeport, Connecticut, May 17, 1969; admitted to bar, 1995, Connecticut; 1996, New York. *Education:* Fordham University (B.A., 1991); Quinnipiac College (J.D., cum laude, 1995); New York University (LL.M., Taxation, 1996). Recipient, American Jurisprudence Award, Federal Income Taxation and Trusts and Estates. Member, 1993-1994, and Executive Managing Editor, 1994-1995, Connecticut Probate Law Journal. ***PRACTICE AREAS:*** Estate Planning; Estate Settlements; Trust Administration.

CATHERINE VANCE PERUSSE, born District of Columbia, February 28, 1958; admitted to bar, 1989, New York; 2000, Connecticut. *Education:* Harvard University (A.B., cum laude, 1980); Fordham University (J.D., 1988). Recipient: Walter R. Kennedy Award; American Jurisprudence Award, Patents. Member, 1986-1987, and Editor-in-Chief, 1987-1988, Fordham Law Review. Judicial Law Clerk to the Honorable John J. Gibbons, Chief Judge, United States Court of Appeals for the Third Circuit. Author: "Secondary Picketing in Railway Labor Disputes: A Right Preserved Under the Norris-La Guardia Act," 55 Fordham L. Rev. 203 (1986). *Member:* New York State Bar Association. ***PRACTICE AREAS:*** Estate Planning; Estate Settlements; Trust Administration.

MOIRA A. SPOLLEN, born New Rochelle, New York, October 10, 1974; admitted to bar, 2000, New York; 2001, Connecticut. *Education:* Fairfield University (B.A., 1996); Fordham University (J.D., 1999). Member, 1997-1998, Notes and Articles Editor, 1998-1999, Fordham Environmental Law Journal. Recipient, Archibald Murray Public Service Award. *Member:* Association of the Bar of the City of New York; New York County Lawyers Association. ***PRACTICE AREAS:*** Estate Planning; Estate Settlements; Trust Administration.

MICHAEL L. WOLF, born Port Chester, New York, May 21, 1972; admitted to bar, 2000, Connecticut and New York. *Education:* Union College (B.A., summa cum laude, 1994); University of Hawaii (J.D., 1999). Phi Beta Kappa. Phi Delta Phi. Member, University of Hawaii Law Review, 1999. Articles Editor, Asian-Pacific Law and Policy Journal. *Member:* New York State and American Bar Associations. ***LANGUAGES:*** Japanese. ***PRACTICE AREAS:*** Estate Planning; Estate Settlements; Trust Administration.

ANTHONY G. DIMARIA, born Rockville Centre, New York, August 1, 1973; admitted to bar, 1998, Connecticut; 1999, New York. *Education:* Fairfield University (B.A., magna cum laude, 1995); New York Law School (J.D., 1998); Boston University (LL.M., Taxation, 1999). Phi Beta Kappa. *Member,* New York State Bar Association (Member, Tax & Trusts & Estates Sections). ***PRACTICE AREAS:*** Estate Planning; Estate Settlements; Trust Administration.

(This Listing Continued)

MELVIN LEE BLOOMENTHAL

600 SUMMER STREET, 5TH FLOOR
STAMFORD, CONNECTICUT 06901
Telephone: 203-348-9595
Fax: 203-357-7208
Email: mlshot@aol.com

General Practice, Domestic Relations, Personal Injury.

MELVIN LEE BLOOMENTHAL, born Burlington, Vermont, December 28, 1944; admitted to bar, 1969, Vermont and U.S. District Court, District of Vermont; 1973, Connecticut and U.S. District Court, District of Connecticut. *Education:* University of Vermont (B.A., 1966); University of Maine (J.D., 1969). *Member:* Vermont, Connecticut and American Bar Associations. Regional Bar Association of Greater Stamford (Member, Board of Directors); American Trial Lawyers Association; Connecticut Trial Lawyers Association. [U.S. Army, 1970-1971, Capt. Vietnam]. ***PRACTICE AREAS:*** Workers Compensation; Products Liability; Medical Malpractice; Uninsured and Underinsured Motorists; Real Estate; Personal Injury Law; Domestic Relations Law; Divorce; Custody; General Practice.

BOEGGEMAN, GEORGE, HODGES & CORDE, P.C.

STAMFORD, CONNECTICUT
(See White Plains)

General Civil Trial Practice. Casualty Insurance, Personal Injury, Negligence, Medical Malpractice, Products Liability, Municipal Law, Commercial Litigation and Employment Law.

ANDREW B. BOWMAN

STAMFORD, CONNECTICUT
(See Westport)

General Civil and Criminal Litigation before all Federal and State Courts. Trials and Appeals. Criminal Defense, Tax Litigation, Employment Law, Construction Litigation, Civil Rights, Environmental Law, Personal Injury, Commercial Litigation and Negligence Law.

BRANDNER & PONZINI

Established in 1987
24 HOYT STREET
STAMFORD, CONNECTICUT 06905
Telephone: 203-327-6913; 203-327-5609
Fax: 203-327-6702
Email: BPLwyers@aol.com
URL: http://www.lawyers.com/brandner&ponzini

General Civil and Criminal Litigation. Driving While Intoxicated, Personal Injury, Product Liability, Automobile Accidents, Domestic Relations, Commercial, Corporate, Real Estate and Estate Planning.

GEOFFREY S. BRANDNER, born Hartford, Connecticut, June 3, 1948; admitted to bar, 1975, Connecticut; 1978, U.S. District Court, District of Connecticut. *Education:* University of Bridgeport (B.A., 1970); University of Connecticut (J.D., 1975). *Member:* Connecticut Trial Lawyers Association; The Association of Trial Lawyers of America. ***SPECIAL AGENCIES:*** Internal Revenue Service. ***PRACTICE AREAS:*** Bankruptcy; Landlord and Tenant Law; Commercial Litigation; Real Estate; Probate. **Email:** GBrandner2@excite.com

JOHN LINO PONZINI, born Queens, New York, August 29, 1953; admitted to bar, 1981, Connecticut; 1982, U.S. District Court, District of Connecticut; 1984, U.S. District Court, Southern District of New York; 1988, U.S. Court of Appeals, Second Circuit; 1989, New York. *Education:* Iona College (B.A.; 1977); Yeshiva University (J.D., 1980). Counsel: Attorney General State of Connecticut; Second Injury Fund State of Connecticut, 1997-2000. Former Representative, City of Stamford, 1995-1997. Former Vice Chair, Finance Committee City of Stamford. Former Special Public Defender, 1985-1990. Former Legal Assistant, Olin Corp. *Member:* Stamford/Norwalk Regional and Connecticut (Former Delegate; Member, Executive Committee, Criminal Justice Section, 1990-1991 and Committe On Foreclosures Superior Court, State od Connecticut) Bar Associations; Connecticut Trial Lawyers Association (Member, Unauthorized Practice of Law Committee, 1991-1993); Connecticut Crimi-

(This Listing Continued)

BRANDNER & PONZINI, Stamford—Continued

nal Defense Association. ***LANGUAGES:*** Spanish. ***SPECIAL AGENCIES:*** Federal Criminal Justice Panel. ***REPORTED CASES:*** Marsh, Day & Calhoun v. Solomon, 204 Conn. 639 (1987); Cahill v. Carella, 43 Conn. Sup. 168 (1994). ***PRACTICE AREAS:*** Civil Litigation; Criminal Law; Matrimonial Law; Personal Injury; Real Estate; Bankruptcy; Civil Litigation; Landlord and Tenant Law; Real Estate. ***Email:*** BPLwyers@aol.com

LEGAL SUPPORT PERSONNEL

CHRISTINE SMITH (Legal Administrator/Paralegal).

BRODY, WILKINSON AND OBER, P.C.

STAMFORD, CONNECTICUT

(See Southport)

General Civil Practice, Corporation, Probate, Estate Planning, Trusts and Estates, Real Estate, Employment, Commercial, Environmental, Creditors Rights, Tax, Pension, Profit Sharing, Entertainment Law, Banking, General Business, Municipal, Freedom of Information Matters, Telecommunications, Public Utilities, Commercial Litigation.

CHRISTOPHER G. BROWN

SUITE 200
999 SUMMER STREET
STAMFORD, CONNECTICUT 06905-5513
Telephone: 203-964-9794
Fax: 203-964-9795
URL: http://www.cgbrown.com
Email: cgbrown@cgbrown.com
URL: http://www.lawyers.com/cbrownlaw

Civil Litigation in all Courts, Business Law, Estate Planning, Real Estate and General Practice.

CHRISTOPHER G. BROWN, born Queens, New York, February 23, 1967; admitted to bar, 1992, Connecticut; 1993, New York and New Jersey; 1995, U.S. District Court, Southern, Eastern and Northern Districts of New York; 1996, U.S. District Court, District of New Jersey; 2001, U.S. District Court, District of Connecticut. *Education:* University of Pennsylvania (B.A., 1989); St. John's University (J.D. cum laude, 1992). Recipient, American Jurisprudence Awards for Excellence in Contracts and Property, 1990. Member, St. John's Law Review, 1990-1992. *Member:* Connecticut (Member, Sections on: Business Law; Estates and Probate) New York State and American (Sections on: Litigation; Business Law; Real Property, Health Care, Practice Management; General Practice, Solo and Small Firms) Bar Associations.

LAW OFFICES OF CHRISTOPHER C. BURDETT, P.C.

777 SUMMER STREET
STAMFORD, CONNECTICUT 06901
Telephone: 203-327-6767
Fax: 203-353-3392
Email: ccbesq@aol.com
URL: http://www.lawyers.com/christopherburdett

Civil Litigation, Personal Injury, Automobile Accidents, Malpractice, Family, Divorce and Matrimonial Litigation.

CHRISTOPHER C. BURDETT, born Bridgeport, Connecticut, September 29, 1943; admitted to bar, 1969, New York; 1972, U.S. District Court, Southern District of New York; 1975, U.S. Court of Appeals, 2nd Circuit; 1976, Connecticut, U.S. District Court, District of Connecticut and U.S. Supreme Court. *Education:* Drew University (B.A., 1965); Rutgers University (J.D., cum laude, 1968). Recipient, J. Skelley Wright Award for Civil Rights & Liberties. Editor, Rutgers Law Review, 1967-1968. Member, Board of Associates, University of Bridgeport, 1977-1986. Chairman and Chief Negotiator, Association of Legal Aid Attorneys of the City of New York, 1971-1972. Special Master, Superior Court of the State of Connecticut, 1979—. Special Counsel for Litigation, City of Norwalk, 1986-1988. *Member:* Stamford Regional and Connecticut Bar Associations; Connecticut Trial Lawyers Association; The Association of Trial Lawyers of America.

LESLIE BYELAS

STAMFORD, CONNECTICUT

(See Westport)

General Civil Trial and Appellate Practice in all State and Federal Courts. Matrimonial, Real Estate.

CACACE, TUSCH & SANTAGATA

777 SUMMER STREET
P.O. BOX 15859
STAMFORD, CONNECTICUT 06901-0859
Telephone: 203-327-2000
Telecopier: 203-353-3392
Email: lawcts@lawcts.com

General Civil and Criminal Trial Practice in State and Federal Courts, Administrative Law, Elder Law, Probate, Civil Appeals, Business Law, Creditor and Collections, Commercial Law, Telecommunications Law, Entertainment and the Arts, Contracts, Government, Construction Law, Land Use Litigation, Commercial Litigation, Personal Injury, Domestic Relations, Real Estate, Corporation, Estate Planning, Commercial Leasing, Planning and Zoning, Land Use, Environmental, Eminent Domain and Real Estate Tax Appeals.

MEMBERS OF FIRM

MICHAEL J. CACACE, born Mount Vernon, New York, April 20, 1952; admitted to bar, 1978, Connecticut; 1979, New York and U.S. District Court, District of Connecticut; 1982, U.S. District Court, Southern District of New York and U.S. Court of Appeals, Second Circuit. *Education:* Fordham University (B.A., 1974); New York Law School (J.D., 1978). Recipient: Dr. Max Reich Award, New York Law School, 1978; Community Leader of the Year, 1986 Stamford Advocate Humanitarian Award, Southern Connecticut Association of Life Underwriters, 1987-1988; Citizen of the Year, Jewish War Veterans, 1995. Author, Chapter, "Elderly Law Desk Manual," Age Discrimination Law, 1981; "Developments in Connecticut Zoning Case Law from 1992 through 1995," Feb, 1996 Connecticut Bar Journal; "Developments in Connecticut Zoning Case Law from 1996 through 1997," Oct. 1998 Connecticut Bar Journal. Instructor, Administrative Law, Norwalk Community College, 1980-1981. Member, 1975-1981 and Chairman, 1979-1981, Stamford Commission on Aging. Co-Chairman, Stamford 13th Charter Revision Commission, 1982-1983. Member, Board of Directors, 1985—, Vice President, 1989-1999 and President, 1999—, Stamford Center for the Arts. Member: Stamford Economic Assistance Corp., 1984-1985; Connecticut Committee of the Regional Plan, Inc., 1987—; Board of Directors, Senior Service, 1998—. Member, 1988-1995, Vice President, 1989-1992 and President, 1992-1994, United Way of Stamford. Member, 1988-1993 and President, 1990-1993, United Way of Connecticut. Chairman, Stamford Reappertionment Commission, 1991, 2001; Member, Board of Directors, Stanford Chamber of Commerce, 1998—. Member, Board of Directors, Senior Services, 1998—. *Member:* Stamford/Norwalk Regional (Member, Executive Committee, 1981-1992; Treasurer, 1986; Secretary, 1987; 2nd Vice President, 1988; 1st Vice President, 1989; President, 1990-1991) and Connecticut (Member, Vice Chairman, 1991-1992 and Chairman, 1994-1997, Planning and Zoning Section) Bar Associations. ***PRACTICE AREAS:*** Zoning, Planning and Land Use; Administrative Law; Real Property; Litigation; Commercial Law; Construction Law; Tax Valuation; Tax Appeals.

MARK P. SANTAGATA, born New Haven, Connecticut, January 26, 1958; admitted to bar, 1984, Connecticut; 1985, U.S. District Court, District of Connecticut. *Education:* University of Connecticut (B.A., 1979); Western New England College (J.D., 1984). Phi Alpha Delta. Member, 1985-1987 and Secretary, 1986-1987, Board of Directors, Catholic Family Services. Member, Board of Directors, 1987-1998, Chairman, Personnel Committee, 1988-1998, Member, Finance Committee, 1991-1998, Member, Executive Committee, 1992-1998, 1st Vice-Chair, 1993-1995 and Chair, 1995-1998, Hospice Care, Inc. Member, Board of Directors, 1998-2000, Chair, 1998-2000 and Director Emeritus 2000—, VNA Hospice Care of Southeastern Connecticut, Inc. Member, Board of Directors, 1986—, Secretary, 1986-1987, Vice-President, 1988, President 1989-1991 and Director Emeritus, 1992—, Senior Employment Services. Member: Board of Directors, Stamford Health Foundation, 1997—; Tangible Benefits Committee, Stamford Chamber of Commerce; Research Advisory Committee, Trends and Issues Sub-Committee, Fairfield County Information Exchange, SACIA; Kids in Crisis, Member, Personal Committee, 2001—. *Member:* Stamford/Norwalk Regional (Member: Bench Bar Committee; Medical/Legal Committee; Employment Committee; Litigation Committee) and Connecticut (Member, Sections on: Litigation; Labor and Employment; Construction Law; Executive Committee, Litigation Section) Bar Associations. ***PRACTICE AREAS:*** Litigation; Personal Injury; Torts; Labor and Employment; Real Estate; Leases and Leasing; Telecommunications Law.

PAUL T. TUSCH, born Bridgeport, Connecticut, August 30, 1960; admitted to bar, 1985, Connecticut; 1986, U.S. District Court, District of Connecticut.

(This Listing Continued)

Education: Fairfield University (B.A., 1982); University of Bridgeport (J.D., 1985). Recipient, Moot Court Award, 1983. Staff Member, 1983-1984 and Notes and Comments Editor, 1984-1985, University of Bridgeport Law Review. Author: "Equitable Estoppel, Laches and Waiver Defenses in Alimony and Support Arrearage Proceedings," Connecticut Family Lawyer, Summer 1995. "Meaningful Relief for Taxpayers Selling Real Estate," Connecticut Law Tribune, March 2, 1998; "The Art of Appraising the Marital Residence," Connecticut Law Tribune, April 6, 1998. Corporate Secretary and Board Member, First Night Stamford, 1987-1991. Member, Board of Directors: Stamford Federal Little League, 1992-1995. Member, Board of Directors, 1993-1999, Vice Chairman, 1994-1996 and Chairman, 1996-1999, Stamford Chapter, American Red Cross. Member, Board of Directors and Secretary, Teen Life Center, 1994-2001. Special Master, Connecticut Superior Court Regional Family Trial Docket, 1995—. Member, Board of Directors, 1996— and Vice President, 2000—, The Volunteer Center. *Member:* Stamford/Norwalk Regional (Member, Executive Committee, 1990-1994; Co-Chairman, 1994-1999, Real Estate Committee; Chairman, Law Day Committee, 1990) and Connecticut (Vice Chairman, Lower Fairfield County Young Lawyers Section, 1988-1989; Member, 1993—, Executive Committee and Treasurer, 2000—, Family Law Section; Member, Real Property Section) Bar Associations. ***PRACTICE AREAS:*** Real Property; Telecommunications Law; Zoning, Planning and Land Use; Family Law; Litigation.

RICHARD S. FISHER, born Brooklyn, New York, October 1, 1937; admitted to bar, 1965, Pennsylvania; 1970, U.S. Tax Court; 1971, Connecticut. *Education:* Pennsylvania State University (B.S., 1959); Cornell University (J.D., 1962); George Washington University (LL.M., Taxation, 1968). Phi Delta Phi. Tax Law Specialist, Corporation Tax Branch, Internal Revenue Service, Washington, D.C., 1965-1968. Tax Attorney, Colt Industries Inc., 1968-1970. Co-Author: "Gift Registration Regs, A Guide to Gift Taxes," Connecticut Law Tribune, June 28, 1999. Member, Board of Directors, 1991— and President, Alzheimer's Association, Fairfield County Chapter, 1996-1998. Member, Board of Directors, Jewish Home for the Elderly of Fairfield County, 1991—. President, Estate Planning Council of Lower Fairfield County, 1993-1994. *Member:* Stamford-Norwalk Regional (Chair, Senior Citizens Committee, 1989-1990; Member: Tax Committee; Business Law Committee; Elder Law Committee), Connecticut (Vice Chair, 1991-1994, Chair, 1994-1996 and Member, 1974-1998, Executive Committee, Tax Section; Member: Corporation Section; Executive Committee, Elder Law Section, 1991—; Executive Committee, Estates and Probate Section, 1998—) and American (Vice Chairman, Committee on Tax Accounting Problems, Taxation Section, 1976-1979; Member, Real Property, Probate and Trust Law Section) Bar Associations; National Academy of Elder Law Attorneys. [Capt., U.S. Army, 1962-1964]. ***PRACTICE AREAS:*** Trusts and Estates; Elder Law; Taxation; Business Law.

RONALD E. KOWALSKI II, born Malden, Massachusetts, May 24, 1966; admitted to bar, 1991, Connecticut; 1992, U.S. District Court, District of Connecticut; 1999, U.S. District Court, Southern and Eastern Districts of New York. *Education:* Fairfield University (B.A., 1988); Suffolk University (J.D., cum laude, 1991). Staff Member, 1989-1990 and Executive Board Member, 1990-1991, Moot Court, Suffolk University Law School. Recipient, American Jurisprudence Award in Administrative Law, 1990. Listed in Who's Who in American Law. Life Member, National Registry of Who's Who. Law Clerk to the Hon. William J. Lavery, Connecticut Appellate Court, 1991-1992. Member, Stamford Rotary Club, 1996—. Member: Child Care Committee, 1997—; Board of Directors, 1998—; Ad Hoc Children's Corner Committee, 1997-1998, Ad Hoc Child Care Committee, 1999 and Chair, Legal Committee, 1999—, Norwalk YMCA. Alternate Member, Easton Connecticut Planning and Zoning Commission, 2000—. Affiliate Member, Appraisal Institute, 1998—. Member, Easton Democratic Town Committee, 1999—. Volunteer, Eastern Little League, 2001—. *Member:* Stamford/Norwalk Regional (Member, Appellate Practice Committee) and Connecticut (Member, Sections on: Litigation; Franchise Law; General Practice) Bar Associations. ***PRACTICE AREAS:*** Litigation; Appellate Practice; Tax Certiorari; Tax Valuation; Tax Appeals; Property Tax. **Email:** rkowalski@lawcts.com

OF COUNSEL

KENNETH A. DELLAROCCO, born Bridgeport, Connecticut, September 5, 1952; admitted to bar, 1983, Connecticut and U.S. District Court, District of Connecticut; 1988, New York; 1991, U.S. Supreme Court. *Education:* Sacred Heart University (B.A., 1974); University of Bridgeport (J.D., 1982). Listed in: Who's Who in American Law; Who's Who in American Business; Who's Who Among Young Leaders of America. Previous Employment: Cummings & Lockwood, Stamford, Connecticut, Associate Attorney, 1982-1988; Melville Corporation, New York, Assistant General Counsel, 1988-1993; Assistant Corporate Secretary, 1988-1995, Vice President and Chief Legal Officer, 1993-1995. *Member:* Stamford/Norwalk Regional and Connecticut Bar Associations. ***PRACTICE AREAS:*** Business Law; Real Estate; Commercial Real Estate; Leases and Leasing; Corporate Law.

SHERWOOD R. SPELKE, born Stamford, Connecticut, August 6, 1941; admitted to bar, 1967, Connecticut; 1968, U.S. District Court, District of Connecticut. *Education:* Columbia University (A.B., 1963); Boston University (LL.D., 1966). Assistant Corporation Counsel, city of Stamford, 1972-1987, Stamford Personnel Commission. Attorney Trial Referee, Stamford Superior Court, 1998. *Member:* Stamford/Norwalk Regional and Connecticut Bar Association. [U.S. Army Reserve, 1966-1972)]. ***PRACTICE AREAS:*** Real Estate Law; Probate; Municipal Law. **Email:** lawcts@aol.com

JANE W. FREEMAN, born Hartford, Connecticut, December 6, 1950; admitted to bar, 1976, Connecticut; 1977, U.S. District Court, District of Connecticut. *Education:* Goucher College (B.A., cum laude, 1972); University of Connecticut (J.D., 1976). Author, "Federal Class Actions in Environmental Litigation," 51 Connecticut Bar Journal No. 2 (June 1977). Connecticut Attorney Trial Referee, 1988—. *Member:* Stamford/Norwalk Regional and Connecticut Bar Associations. ***PRACTICE AREAS:*** Land Use; Litigation; Real Estate. **Email:** jfreeman@lawcts.com

ERIC D. GRAYSON (Also practicing individually, Greenwich, CT).

ASSOCIATES

EDWARD F. NEMCHEK, born Stamford, Connecticut, April 8, 1957; admitted to bar, 1991, Connecticut; 1992, New York. *Education:* Manhattanville College (B.A., summa cum laude, 1988); Fordham University (J.D., 1991). Phi Alpha Delta (President, 1990-1991). Secretary, Metcalf House, Inc.; Advisory Board Member, Liberation-Meridian-Guenster. Trustee, Stamford Youth Hockey Association. Member, Board of Directors, Stamford Babe Ruth World Series '99 Committee. *Member:* Stamford/Norwalk Regional (Member, Sections on: Real Property; Criminal Law), Connecticut (Member, Sections on: Real Property; Criminal Law) and New York State Bar Associations; Lower Fairfield County Young Lawyers Association (Member, Criminal Law Section); Connecticut Criminal Defense Lawyers Association. ***PRACTICE AREAS:*** Real Estate; Criminal Defense.

ALICE ANN FITZPATRICK, born Bridgeport, Connecticut, April 2, 1955; admitted to bar, 1980, Connecticut and U.S. Tax Court; 1984, U.S. District Court, District of Connecticut. *Education:* Smith College (A.B., 1977); University of Connecticut (J.D., cum laude, 1980). Member, 1993-2000 and Co-Chair, 1994-1995, St. Brigid Scholarship Committee, Mercy Learning Center. Member, Board of Directors, St. Thomas Aquinas Home School Association, 2000—. *Member:* Stamford/Norwalk Regional (Member: Elder Law Section; Estate and Probate Section) and Connecticut (Member, Estates and Probate Section) Bar Associations. ***PRACTICE AREAS:*** Probate; Trusts and Estates; Estate Administration; Estate Planning. **Email:** afitzpatrick@lawcts.com

PATRICK L. POESCHL, born Brooklyn, New York, March 8, 1966; admitted to bar, 1995, Connecticut; 1996, New York; 1997, U.S. District Court, Eastern and Southern Districts of New York. *Education:* St. John's University (B.A., 1989); Queens College of the City University of New York (J.D., 1995). Phi Delta Phi, Tedone, 1995. Co-Author: "Gift Registration Regs, A Guide to Gift Taxes," Connecticut Law Tribune, June 28, 1999. Instructor, "Basic Estate Administration for the Connecticut Paralegal," Institute for Paralegal Education. *Member:* Stamford/Norwalk Regional, Connecticut (Member, Sections on: Estates and Probate; Elder Law), New York State (Member, Sections on: Trusts and Estates; Elder Law) and American (Member, Real Property, Probate and Trust Law Section) Bar Associations; National Academy of Elder Law Attorneys. ***PRACTICE AREAS:*** Estate Planning; Estate Administration; Elder Law; Estate Litigation; Conservatorship; Guardianship. **Email:** ppoeschl@lawcts.com

LAURA MORRISON ALLEN, born Greenwich, Connecticut, December 8, 1966; admitted to bar, 1996, Connecticut; 1997, New York and U.S District Court, Southern District of New York; 1998, U.S. District Court, Eastern District of New York. *Education:* Northeastern University (B.S., 1989); Pace University School of Law (J.D., 1996). Recipient, American Jurisprudence Award, Civil Practice. *Member:* Stamford/Norwalk Regional (Member, Community Services Committee), Connecticut (Member, Planning and Zoning Sections) and American Bar Associations. ***PRACTICE AREAS:*** Zoning, Planning and Land Use; Telecommunications Law; Litigation. **Email:** lallen@lawcts.com

DAVID J. COVIELLO, born Waterbury, Connecticut, December 28, 1972; admitted to bar, 2000, Connecticut. *Education:* University of Connecticut (B.S., 1996); Vermont Law School (J.D., 1999). Law Clerk to Chief Justice Francis M. McDonald, Connecticut Supreme Court. *Member:* Stamford/Norwalk Reginal, Connecticut (Member, Planning and Zoning Sections) and American Bar Associations. ***PRACTICE AREAS:*** Zoning, Planning and Land Use; Litigation. **Email:** dcoviello@lawcts.com

JOSEPH TODD PUHEKKER, born Mahopac, New York, September 22, 1972; admitted to bar, 1998, Connecticut and Louisiana; 2000, New York. *Education:* Fairfield University (B.A., 1994); New York Law School (J.D., cum laude, 1997). Executive Editor, New York Law School Moot Court Association, 1996-1997; Associate Editor, New York Law School Journal of Human Rights, 1996-1997. *Member:* Stamford/Norwalk Regional, Louisiana State, Connecti-

(This Listing Continued)

CACACE, TUSCH & SANTAGATA, Stamford—Continued

cut and American (Member, Labor and Employment Sections) Bar Associations. ***PRACTICE AREAS:*** Litigation; Zoning Law; Labor and Employment. ***Email:*** jpuhekker@lawcts.com

BARBARA S. KOTEEN, born Stamford, Connecticut, July 14, 1970; admitted to bar, 1996, New York; 1998, U.S. District Court, District of Connecticut (Not admitted in Connecticut). *Education:* University of Massachusetts (B.A., cum laude, 1992); Pace University (J.D., cum laude, 1995). Author: Kleeman v. Rheingold: There Are No Small Mistakes, 15 Pace Law Review 871 (1995). *Member:* Stamford/Norwalk Regional and Connecticut Bar Associations. ***PRACTICE AREAS:*** Probate; Estate Planning; Conservatorship; Elder Law. ***Email:*** bkoteen@lawcts.com

LEGAL SUPPORT PERSONNEL

EVA L. CHAN

CYNTHIA L. MAMMONE

GLEN A. CANNER

112 PROSPECT STREET
STAMFORD, CONNECTICUT 06901
Telephone: 203-961-1080
Fax: 203-964-9509
URL: http://www.lawyers.com/canner

Trials and Appeals in State and Federal Courts. Employment Law, Personal Injury, Divorce, Real Estate and Probate.

GLEN A. CANNER, born Stamford, Connecticut, August 12, 1953; admitted to bar, 1979, Connecticut and U.S. District Court, District of Connecticut; 1981, U.S. Tax Court; 1991, U.S. Court of Appeals, 2nd Circuit and U.S. Supreme Court. *Education:* Tufts University (B.A., magna cum laude, 1975); University of Connecticut (J.D., 1979). Phi Beta Kappa. *Member:* Greenwich, Connecticut and American Bar Associations; Connecticut Trial Lawyers Association; The Association of Trial Lawyers of America.

J. MICHAEL CANTORE, JR.

Established in 1974

1172 BEDFORD STREET
STAMFORD, CONNECTICUT 06905
Telephone: 203-327-5040
Fax: 203-348-9220
URL: http://www.lawyers.com/cantorelaw

Medical Malpractice, Personal Injury, Auto Accident, Product Liability, Civil and Commercial Litigation, Divorce, Family, Child Custody, Real Estate, Wills and Trust, Criminal Defense, DWI, Bankruptcy.

FIRM PROFILE: Making the law a more human experience J. Michael Cantore, Jr. has 29 years experience in the legal field. He is also a licensed CT Broker with 30 years experiènce, servicing the State of Connecticut for over 30 years.

J. MICHAEL CANTORE, JR., born Greenwich, Connecticut, March 16, 1943; admitted to bar, 1971, Connecticut; 1972, U.S. District Court, District of Connecticut. *Education:* C.W. Post College (B.A., 1967); Suffolk University (J.D., 1971). Phi Alpha Delta. President: New York Metropolitan Area Alumni Association; Suffolk University School of Law, 1986-1989. *Member:* Connecticut and American Bar Associations; Connecticut Trial Lawyers Association; The Association of Trial Lawyers of America. ***PRACTICE AREAS:*** Medical Malpractice; Personal Injury; Auto Accident; Product Liability; Civil Litigation; Commercial Litigation; Divorce; Family Law; Child Custody; Real Estate; Wills; Trusts; Criminal Defense; Driving While Intoxicated; Bankruptcy.

CASPER & DE TOLEDO LLC

1111 SUMMER STREET
STAMFORD, CONNECTICUT 06905
Telephone: 203-325-8600
Fax: 203-323-5970
URL: http://www.lawyers.com/casperdetoledo
Email: info@casperdetoledo.com
URL: http://www.casperdetoledo.com

Civil Trial and Appellate Practice in all State and Federal Courts. Personal Injury, Medical Malpractice, Product Liability, Workers' Compensation, Employment Discrimination, Employee Rights and Benefits, Civil Rights, Contracts and Family Law.

(This Listing Continued)

FIRM PROFILE: The practice is limited to litigation and related matters and with respect to tort and employment litigation, the firm represents plaintiffs only. All partners and associates participate on a regular basis in continuing legal education programs and the firm's partners have lectured extensively in their fields.

STEWART M. CASPER, born Fitchburg, Massachusetts, January 12, 1953; admitted to bar, 1978, Connecticut and U.S. District Court, District of Connecticut; 1985, New York; 1987, U.S. District Court, Southern District of New York, U.S. Court of Appeals, Second Circuit and U.S. Supreme Court. *Education:* University of Massachusetts (B.A., summa cum laude, 1975); Hofstra University (J.D., 1978). Phi Beta Kappa. Associate Editor, Hofstra Law Review, 1977-1978. Author: "Uninsured/Underinsured Motorist Coverage: The Claimant's Approach," Connecticut Bar Journal Vol. #58, No. 6, December 1984; "The Death of Joint and Several Liability-Have the Reports Been Exaggerated?," CTLA Forum, Vol. 8, No. 3, May/June 1990; "Litigating Stairway Liability Cases," Personal Injury Handbook, James Publishing Group, 1991; "Looking Fraudulent Surveillance In The Eye," Trial Magazine, January 1993. Co-Author: "The Changing Landscape of Uninsured/Underinsured Motor Insurance Law in Connecticut," Connecticut Bar Journal, Vol. 68, No. 2, April 1994; "Demonstrative and Documentary Evidence", Damages in Tort Actions, Matthew Bender Publishing Co., 1995; "The Crisis in Disclosure of Insurance Coverage," CTLA Forum, Vol. 15, No. 1, January/February 1997. Lecturer: Uninsured/Underinsured Motorist Cases - Determining Coverage, Connecticut Trial Lawyers Association, 1985-1990; Investigation for Auto and Premises Liability Cases, Connecticut Trial Lawyers Association, 1990; Municipal Liability vs. Immunity Under The Tort Reform Act, Connecticut Trial Lawyers Association, 1991; Conflicts of Law Issues in Uninsured & Underinsured Motorist Cases, Connecticut Trial Lawyers Association, 1991; Summation-The Finishing Touch, Connecticut Trial Lawyers Association, 1991; Automobile Insurance Reform Act of 1993, Connecticut Trial Lawyers Association, 1993; Bad Faith, No Faith or Incompetence-Claims Against Insurance Companies and Independent Agents, Connecticut Trial Lawyers Association, 1994; Consumer Remedies for Inadequate Insurance Coverage-Suing The Insurance Agent, Association of Trial Lawyers of America, 1995. Speaker, The Million Dollar Verdict - Theory & Theme in the Age of Tort Reform, Connecticut Trial Lawyers Association, 1988; Looking Fraudulent Surveillance in the Eye, The Association of Trial Lawyers of America, 1996; Cross Examination of the Defense Medical Expert, Connecticut Trial Lawyers Association, 1998-1999. Special Master: U.S. District Court, 1990—; Superior Court - Judicial District of Stamford/Norwalk, 1992—. Listed in "The Best Lawyers in America." Certified as a Civil Trial Advocate by the National Board of Trial Advocacy. *Member:* The Regional and Connecticut (Member, Sections on: Civil Justice; Workers' Compensation) Bar Associations; The Association of Trial Lawyers of America (State Delegate, 1999—; Member, Motor Vehicle Insurance Coordination Committee, 1998-2000; Member and Co-Chairperson, Insurance Committee, 1998—; Member, Traumatic Brain Injury Group); Connecticut Trial Lawyers Association (Member, 1984-1992 and Co-Chairperson, 1991, Continuing Legal Education Committee; Member, 1995-1998, and Chairperson, 1995-1996, Public Relations Committee, 1995—; Member: Board of Governors, 1984-1985, 1987-1999; Executive Committee, 1990—; Legislative Committee, 1992—; Amicus Curiae Committee, 1992—; Medical Malpractice Committee, 1996—; Parliamentarian, 1991-1992; Secretary, 1992-1993; Treasurer, 1993-1994; Vice President, 1994-1995; President-Elect, 1995-1996; President, 1996-1997; Immediate Past President, 1997-1998); Trial Lawyers for Public Justice. Fellow, Rosco Pound Institute. ***PRACTICE AREAS:*** Personal Injury; Medical Malpractice; Product Liability; Workers' Compensation. ***Email:*** scasper@casperdetoledo.com

VICTORIA DE TOLEDO, born Oceanside, N.Y., October 10, 1956; admitted to bar, 1981, Connecticut; 1982, U.S. District Court, District of Connecticut; 1985, U.S. Court of Appeals, Second Circuit; 1986, U.S. Supreme Court; 1988, U.S. District Court, Southern District of New York. *Education:* University of Pennsylvania (B.A., magna cum laude, 1978; M.A., 1978); New York University (J.D., 1981). Author: "Sexual Harassment in the Workplace: A Growing Legal Awareness," 12 Connecticut Law Tribune 31, p. 2, August 11, 1986; "Sexual Harassment: Perspectives and Damages," 19 Conn. Law Tribune 46, p. 13. Lecturer: Sexual Harassment in the Workplace, Employer Liability, Connecticut Bar Association, 1985; Termination and Partial Termination of Employee Benefit Plans, Connecticut Bar Association, 1988; Age Discrimination & Sexual Harassment, Greater Hartford/Springfield Employers Liaison Group, 1990; Tax Considerations in Litigation and Settlement of Employment Cases, Connecticut Trial Lawyers Association, 1990; Employment Claims Against Governmental Entities, Connecticut Trial Lawyers Association, 1991; Cross Examination, Connecticut Trial Lawyers Association, 1992; Alcohol and Drug Abuse Under the Americans with Disabilities Act, 1992, Council on Education in Management; Damages for Common Law Employment Claims, Connecticut Bar Association, 1993; Litigation Techniques, National Employment Lawyers Association, 1994; Settling ERISA Claims, National Employment Lawyers Association, 1994; Americans with Disabilities Act and Family and Medical Leave Act, Lorman Education Services, 1995; Sexual Harassment: Perspectives and Damages, Association of Trial Lawyers of America, 1995; Maximizing Damages in

(This Listing Continued)

Employment Cases, Connecticut Trial Lawyers Association, 1996; Using An Expert in Employment Cases, National Employment Lawyers Association, 1998; Sexual Harassment in the Workplace, American Bar Association, 1999. Special Master, U.S. District Court, District of Connecticut. Listed in "The Best Lawyers in America." *Member:* The Regional and Connecticut (Member, Family Law Section; Member, Executive Committee, 1986-1993, Vice Chairperson, 1987-1989, 1992, Secretary, 1991 and Chairperson, 1993, Women and the Law Section; Chairperson: Executive Committee, Labor and Employment Law Section, 1984-1997; Connecticut Commission on Human Rights and Opportunities Subcommittee, 1985-1988; Employment At Will Subcommittee, 1989-1991) Bar Associations; Connecticut Trial Lawyers Association; The Association of Trial Lawyers of America; The Women Trial Lawyers Caucus; National Employment Lawyers Association (Chairperson, Common Law Committee, 1994-1997; Member: Nominating Committee, 1995-1997; Affiliates Committee, 1998—); Connecticut Employment Lawyers Association (Chairperson, Executive Committee, 1993—). ***PRACTICE AREAS:*** Employment Law; Labor Law. ***Email:*** vdetoledo@casperdetoledo.com

---

ANASTASIOS T. SAVVAIDES, born Norwalk, Connecticut, August 14, 1967; admitted to bar, 1992, Connecticut; 1993, New York and U.S. District Court, District of Connecticut. *Education:* Hartwick College (B.A.,, cum laude, 1989); Suffolk University (J.D., 1992). Phi Delta Phi. Dean's List. *Member:* Connecticut Bar Association; Connecticut Trial Lawyers Association (Member, 2001—, Continuing Legal Education Committee; Member & Regional Chairperson, 2000—; Membership Committee) The Association of Trial Lawyers of America. ***LANGUAGES:*** Greek. ***PRACTICE AREAS:*** Personal Injury Litigation. ***Email:*** asavvaides@casperdetoledo.com

RHONNA W. ROGOL, born 1955; admitted to bar, 1979, Connecticut and U.S. District Court, District of Connecticut; U.S Court of Appeals, Second Circuit. *Education:* Brandeis University (B.A., magna cum laude, 1976); New York University (J.D., summa cum laude, 1979). Recipient, John Norton Pomeroy Prize. Member, Order of the Coif. Phi Beta Kappa. Advisor, 1979-1980, Judge, 2000-2001, Connecticut Mock Trial Advocacy Program. *Member:* Connecticut Bar Association; Brandeis University Alumni Lawyers Association; Connecticut Trial Lawyers Association (Member, Women's Caucus Executive Board); The Association of Trial Lawyers of America; Connecticut Employment Lawyers Association; National Employment Lawyers Association; Connecticut Women's Education & Legal Fund; Regional Bar Association (Co-Chair, Employment Law Committee). ***LANGUAGES:*** French and Hebrew. ***PRACTICE AREAS:*** Employment Law; Labor Law. ***Email:*** rrogol@casperdetoledo.com

---

VICTOR J. CAVALLO

750 SUMMER STREET
STAMFORD, CONNECTICUT 06901
Telephone: 203-602-0260
Fax: 203-602-0259
Email: victorjcavallo@lawyers.com
URL: http://www.lawyers.com/victorcavallo

Practice limited to Family Law for Husbands and Fathers. Divorce, Child Support, Child Custody, Alimony and Domestic Violence.

VICTOR J. CAVALLO, born Brooklyn, New York, April 7, 1951; admitted to bar, 1991, Connecticut; 1992, U.S. District Court, District of Connecticut. *Education:* George Washington University (B.A., 1974); University of Bridgeport Law School (J.D., 1984).

STEVEN A. CERTILMAN, P.C.

Established in 1991
350 BEDFORD STREET
STAMFORD, CONNECTICUT 06901
Telephone: 203-977-7800
Fax: 203-425-8600
URL: http://www.lawyers.com/certilman
Email: sac@certilman.com
URL: http://www.certilman.com

New York, New York Office: 640 Fifth Avenue, 4th Floor. Telephone: 212-956-3425.

Corporation and Commercial Law, Alternative Dispute Resolution, Commercial Litigation, Computer Law, Trademark, Copyright and Licensing Law, Real Estate and Condominium Law.

STEVEN A. CERTILMAN, born New York, September, 1956; admitted to bar, 1982, New York, U.S. District Court, Southern and Eastern Districts of New York and U.S. Court of Appeals, Second Circuit; 1984, District of Columbia; 1986, U.S. District Court, District of Connecticut; 1988, Connecticut. *Education:* Connecticut College (B.A., 1978); Hofstra University (J.D., 1981). Managing Editor, International Property Investment Journal, 1980-1981. Speaker: Connecticut Bar Association; Community Association Institute. Commissioner, 1987-1990 and Secretary-Treasurer, 1988-1990, Greater Stamford Transit District. Member, Board of Directors, Stamford, Connecticut Chapter, American Red Cross, 1987-1992. Attorney Trial Referee and Fact Finder/Arbitrator, Superior Court of the State of Connecticut. Arbitrator, Supreme Court of the State of New York. Mediator, U.S. District Court, Southern District of New York. Member: Connecticut Volunteer Lawyers for the Arts, 1988—. Member, National Panel of Arbitrators, Commercial and National Technology Panels, American Arbitration Association. *Member:* The Association of the Bar of the City of New York; Connecticut (Executive Committee, Computer Law Section), New York State and American Bar Associations; The District of Columbia Bar; The Regional Bar. ***Email:*** sac@certilman.com

ISSUING AGENT FOR: Chicago Title Insurance Company; CATIC.

LAW OFFICES OF MICHAEL GENE CLEAR

184 ATLANTIC STREET
P.O. BOX 3292
STAMFORD, CONNECTICUT 06905
Telephone: 203-973-0240
Facsimile: 203-973-0244
Email: MCLEAR9948@aol.com
URL: http://www.lawyers.com/michaelclear

General Civil Trial Practice in State and Federal Courts. Personal Injury, Negligence, Environmental Law and Hazardous Waste Litigation, Insurance Coverage Litigation, Complex Litigation, Commercial Litigation, Alternative Dispute Resolution, Mediation, Municipal Law, Environmental Insurance Defense, Insurance Coverage, Probate Litigation, Wills, Elder Law, Incapacity Planning, Probate Administration.

MICHAEL GENE CLEAR, born Stamford, Connecticut, March 20, 1944; admitted to bar, 1969, Connecticut; 1974, U.S. District Court, District of Connecticut; 1975, U.S. Supreme Court; 1980, U.S. District Courts, Southern and Eastern Districts of New York. *Education:* St. Anselm College (B.A., 1966); University of Connecticut (J.D., 1969). Lecturer, "Connecticut Discovery: Rules and Practice," Connecticut Bar Association, 1987 . Special Master: United States District Court, 1987—; Connecticut Superior Court, 1981—. Arbitrator and Fact Finder, Connecticut Superior Court, 1984—. Corporation Counsel, City of Stamford, 1985-1986. Member, Stamford Fire Commission, 1987-1991. *Member:* Stamford/Norwalk Regional (President, 1984-1985), Connecticut (Member, Sections on: Litigation and Elder Law) and American (Member, Sections on: Litigation, Tort and Insurance Practice) Bar Associations; The Association of Trial Lawyers of America; Connecticut Defense Lawyers Association (President, 1988-1989); Connecticut Trial Lawyers Association. ***PRACTICE AREAS:*** Automobile Accidents and Injuries; Personal Injury; Wills; Elder Law; Insurance Coverage.

GARY I. COHEN

STAMFORD, CONNECTICUT
(See Greenwich)
Practice Limited to Family and Matrimonial Law.

COHEN AND WOLF, P.C.

112 PROSPECT STREET
STAMFORD, CONNECTICUT 06904
Telephone: 203-964-9907
Facsimile: 203-576-8504
Email: cw@cohenandwolf.com
URL: http://www.cohenandwolf.com

Bridgeport, Connecticut Office: 1115 Broad Street. Telephone: 203-368-0211. Facsimile: 203-394-9901.
Danbury, Connecticut Office: 158 Deer Hill Avenue. Telephone: 203-792-2771. Facsimile: 203-791-8149.
Westport, Connecticut Office: 190 Main Street. Telephone: 203-222-1034.

General Practice. Business Transactions, Commercial Litigation, Employment and Labor, Family and Matrimonial, Land Use, Municipal, Personal Injury, Physicians Practice, Real Estate, Securities, Tax, Trusts and Estates. Litigation in all Courts.

Richard L. Albrecht	***Stewart I. Edelstein***
Jonathan S. Bowman	***Richard G. Kent***
Irving J. Kern	***Richard Slavin***
Martin J. Albert	***Richard J. Di Marco***

(This Listing Continued)

COHEN AND WOLF, P.C., Stamford—Continued

David B. Zabel ***Jocelyn B. Hurwitz***

OF COUNSEL

Stuart A. Epstein ***Jack E. McGregor***

(For complete biographical data on all personnel, see Professional Biographies at Bridgeport, Connecticut)

COLLINS, HANNAFIN, GARAMELLA, JABER & TUOZZOLO

PROFESSIONAL CORPORATION

STAMFORD, CONNECTICUT

(See Danbury)

General Practice. Real Estate, Estate Planning, Probate, Zoning and Land Use, Tax, Corporation, Commercial, Banking, Family Law, Criminal Law, Negligence, and Civil Trials in all Courts.

COUSINS, JOHNSON & DESROSIERS, P.C.

STAMFORD, CONNECTICUT

(See Stratford)

Workers' Compensation, Personal Injury, Trials, Real Estate, Probate.

CRAMER & AHERN

STAMFORD, CONNECTICUT

(See Westport)

General Civil Practice. Real Estate, Negligence, Probate, Estate Planning, Business Law, Corporate Law, Art Law. Trials.

CUDDY & FEDER & WORBY LLP

733 SUMMER STREET

STAMFORD, CONNECTICUT 06901

Telephone: 203-348-4780

URL: http://www.cfwlaw.com

White Plains, New York Office: 90 Maple Avenue. Telephone: 914-761-1300. Telecopier: 914-761-5372.

New York, N.Y. Office: 500 Fifth Avenue, Suite 2900. Telephone: 212-944-2841. Telecopier: 212-944-2843.

Hudson Valley Office: Westage Business Center, 300 South Lake Drive, Fishkill, NY, 12524. Telephone: 845-896-2229. Telecopier: 845-896-3672.

Norwalk, Connecticut Office: One Marshall Street. Telephone: 203-853-8001. Telecopier: 203-831-8250.

General Practice. Corporate, Real Estate, Zoning, Environmental, Historic Preservation, Housing and Urban Development, Condominium, Municipal, Trusts, Estates, Probate, Estate Planning and Taxation, Elder, Commercial Litigation, Industrial Development Bond Financing and Secured Lending Law.

(For complete biographical data on all personnel, see Professional Biographies at White Plains, New York)

CUMMINGS & LOCKWOOD

Established in 1909

FOUR STAMFORD PLAZA

P.O. BOX 120

STAMFORD, CONNECTICUT 06904-0120

Telephone: (203) 327-1700

Telecopier: (203) 351-4535

Email: info@cl-law.com

URL: http://www.cl-law.com

Greenwich, Connecticut Office: Two Greenwich Plaza, P.O. Box 2505, 06836. Telephone: (203) 869-1200. Telecopier: (203) 869-3120.

Hartford, Connecticut Office: CityPlace I, 185 Asylum Street, 36th Floor, 06103-3495. Telephone: (860) 275-6700. Telecopier: (860) 724-3397.

New Haven, Connecticut Office: 700 State Street, P.O. Box 1960. 06509-1960. Telephone: (203) 782-3000. Telecopier: (203) 777-3347.

West Hartford, Connecticut Office: Town Center, 29 South Main Street, Suite 208, 06107. Telephone: (860) 275-6700. Telecopier: (860) 313-0293.

Bonita Springs, Florida Office: 24311 Walden Center, Suite 201, 34134. Telephone: (941) 947-8811. Telecopier: (941) 947-8025.

(This Listing Continued)

Naples, Florida Office: 3001 Tamiami Trail North, P.O. Box 413032, 34101-3032. Telephone: (941) 262-8311. Telecopier: (941) 263-0703.

General Practice. National and Regional Litigation Counsel, Corporate Law, Patent and Intellectual Property, Trusts and Estates, Labor and Employment, Mergers and Acquisitions, Partnerships and Joint Ventures, Commercial Lending, Corporate Finance, Creditors' Rights, Bankruptcy and Workouts, Securities Regulation and Litigation, Tax, Insurance, Banking and Financial Services, Leasing, Commercial and Residential Real Estate, Construction, Environmental, Toxic Torts, Health Law, Products Liability Litigation, Probate Litigation, Family Law, International Business.

FIRM PROFILE: Cummings & Lockwood caters both to commercial entities and individual clients, serves as local, regional and national counsel in Corporate, Litigation, Creditors' Rights matters, and has one of the largest groups of Estate Planning professionals in the country.

Cummings & Lockwood attorneys answer questions and solve problems by having specialists in multiple disciplines practice together from eight offices to address the broad concerns of our diverse clientele. The firm guides corporate transactions and resolves complex business disputes for emerging, middle-market and Fortune 500 businesses, including high tech companies, financial services providers and industrial manufacturers. We are also uniquely positioned to assist affluent families and entrepreneurs in designing wealth preserving estate plans and developing business succession strategies.

MEMBERS OF FIRM

GLENN J. ANGIOLILLO, born Brooklyn, New York, September 30, 1953; admitted to bar, 1979, Connecticut; 1981, Florida. *Education:* University of Pennsylvania (B.S., 1975; M.B.A., 1976); Georgetown University (J.D., 1979). Member, Georgetown University Law Journal, 1977-1978. ***PRACTICE AREAS:*** Corporate Law; Mergers and Acquisitions; Banking and Finance. ***Email:*** gangiolillo@cl-law.com

FOSTER BAM (Resident, Greenwich, Connecticut Office).

ROBERT ALEXANDER BEER, born Waterbury, Connecticut, September 10, 1936; admitted to bar, 1964, Connecticut. *Education:* Valparaiso University (B.A., 1959; J.D., 1963); Indiana University (M.B.A., 1960); Harvard University (LL.M., 1964). Phi Alpha Delta. ***PRACTICE AREAS:*** Estate Settlement Law; Trust Administration Law; Fiduciary Accounting Law; Taxation Law; Individual Tax Planning Law; Taxation Law. ***Email:*** rbeer@cl-law.com

DONALD L. BOROD (Resident, Hartford, Connecticut Office).

PAUL L. BOURDEAU (Resident, Hartford, Connecticut Office).

MATTHEW A. BOVINO, born Waterbury, Connecticut, March 27, 1962; admitted to bar, 1987, Connecticut; 1988, U.S. District Court, District of Connecticut. *Education:* Fordham University (B.A., magna cum laude, 1984); New York University (J.D., 1987). *Member:* Connecticut and American Bar Associations. ***PRACTICE AREAS:*** Estate Planning Law; Estate Administration. ***Email:*** mbovino@cl-law.com

LISA M. BOYLE (Resident, Hartford, Connecticut Office).

WILLIAM H. BRIGHT, JR. (Resident, Hartford, Connecticut Office).

JOHN W. CANNAVINO, born San Antonio, Texas, August 10, 1951; admitted to bar, 1977, Connecticut. *Education:* State University of New York at Binghamton (B.A., 1973); Syracuse University (J.D., summa cum laude, 1977). Phi Beta Kappa; Phi Sigma Alpha. Member, Order of the Coif; Inns of Court. ***PRACTICE AREAS:*** Trial Practice; Civil Litigation; Commercial Law. ***Email:*** jcannavino@cl-law.com

JOHN F. CARBERRY, born New York, N.Y., March 18, 1957; admitted to bar, 1984, New York, U.S. District Court, Southern and Eastern Districts of New York; 1988, Connecticut and U.S. District Court, District of Connecticut; 1994, U.S. Court of Appeals, Second Circuit. *Education:* Fordham University (B.A., 1979); New York Law School (J.D., cum laude, 1983). Articles Editor, New York Law School Law Review, 1982-1983. Connecticut Superior Court Attorney Trial Referee. *Member:* Connecticut Bar Association (Member, Executive Committee, Commercial Law and Bankruptcy Section). ***PRACTICE AREAS:*** Bankruptcy Law; Creditors' Rights; Debtor and Creditor; Commercial Litigation. ***Email:*** jcarberry@cl-law.com

DEBORAH S. CHANG, born Man, West Virginia, February 15, 1960; admitted to bar, 1986, Connecticut; 1987, U.S. District Court, District of Connecticut; 1991, Arizona. *Education:* Kansas University (B.A., 1983); Drake University (J.D., cum laude, 1986). Order of the Barristers. Case Note Editor, Drake Law Review, 1985-1986. Author: "Connecticut's New AIDS Related Testing and Confidentiality Statute," Hartford County Medical Association, 1989; Law Clerk to The Hon. Chief Judge Antoinette Dupont, Connecticut Appellate Court, 1986-1987. Instructor, University of Connecticut School of Law, 1987-1991. ***PRACTICE AREAS:*** Product Liability Litigation; Medical Malpractice Law. ***Email:*** dchang@cl-law.com

(This Listing Continued)

DANIEL F. COUGHLIN, born Boston, Massachusetts, April 29, 1950; admitted to bar, 1992, Illinois; 1995, Minnesota; registered to practice before U.S. Patent and Trademark Office (Not admitted in Connecticut). *Education:* Tufts University (B.A., 1972); Bridgewater State College (M.A., 1980); University of Connecticut (Ph.D., 1985); Illinois Institute of Technology/Chicago-Kent College of Law (J.D., 1991). Phi Kappa Phi; Phi Alpha Delta; Sigma XI; Phi Lambda Upsilon. Winner, Midwest Regional ABA National Moot Court Competition, ITT/Chicago-Kent College of Law, 1990. Instructor, Polytechnic University, 2000—. Member, American Chemical Society. *Member:* Minnesota State Bar Association; Chicago Intellectual Property Law Association; American Intellectual Property Law Association; Minnesota Intellectual Property Law Association. ***LANGUAGES:*** Russian. ***PRACTICE AREAS:*** Patents. ***Email:*** dcoughlin@cl-law.com

FRANK J. COYLE (Resident, Greenwich, Connecticut Office).

DANIEL L. DANIELS, born New Milford, Connecticut, November 17, 1962; admitted to bar, 1988, New York; 1991, Connecticut. *Education:* Dartmouth College (A.B., summa cum laude, 1984); Harvard University (J.D., cum laude, 1987). Author: "Estate Planning for the 401(k) Account," in *The 401(k) Plan Handbook* Prentice Hall, 1997, ed. J. Jason. Member: Connecticut Estate and Business Planning Counsel, 1995—. ***PRACTICE AREAS:*** Estate Planning; Tax Planning; Estate Administration; Trust Administration; Probate Litigation. ***Email:*** ddaniels@cl-law.com

B. CORT DELANY (Resident, Greenwich, Connecticut Office).

MICHAEL N. DELGASS, born Berkeley, California, May 16, 1969; admitted to bar, 1995, Illinois; 1999, Florida and Connecticut; 2000, New York. *Education:* Indiana University (B.S., Geology, 1992; B.S., Biology, 1992; B.A., Chemistry, 1992); University of Chicago (J.D., 1995). Phi Beta Kappa. Author: *Pecuniary Dynastic Offshore Trusts: New Offshore Opportunities for U.S. Citizens,* 138 Trusts & Estates 12 (July 1999); *Financial Reporting for the Family Office, Reducing Fiduciary Exposure,* 135 Trust & Estates 12 (April 1999). Contributing Editor (1998 Update), *Illinois Estate Planning, Will Drafting and Estate Administration Forms,* Michie, 2d ed. (1996). Adjunct Professor, Northwestern University School of Law, Chicago, Illinois, 1999. Instructor: American Bankers Association, National Trust School, 1998; American Bankers Association, National Graduate Trust School, 1998. *Member:* Chicago (Probate Practice Committee: Member, Executive Committee, 1998-1999; Vice-Chairman, 1998-1999; Secretary, 1997-1998), Connecticut (Estates and Probate Section, Member, Executive Committee; Business Law Section) and American (Member, Sections on: Taxation and Real Property; Probate and Trust Law) Bar Associations; Family Firm Institute. ***PRACTICE AREAS:*** Trusts and Estates. ***Email:*** mdelgass@cl-law.com

ROBERT P. DOLIAN, born Terre Haute, Indiana, January 11, 1948; admitted to bar, 1975, Connecticut. *Education:* Duke University (B.A., 1969); Harvard University (J.D., cum laude, 1975). Phi Beta Kappa. Special Master: U.S. District Court, District of Connecticut, 1989—; Connecticut Superior Court, 1992. Attorney Trial Referee, Connecticut Superior Court, 1989—. ***PRACTICE AREAS:*** Commercial Litigation; Construction Litigation; Probate Litigation. ***Email:*** rdolian@cl-law.com

ALISON K. DOUGLAS (Resident, Naples, Florida Office).

PHILIP M. DRAKE (Resident, Greenwich, Connecticut Office).

LAWRENCE A. FARESE (Resident, Naples, Florida Office).

GEOFFREY F. FAY, born Yonkers, New York, December 4, 1952; admitted to bar, 1982, Connecticut and U.S. District Court, District of Connecticut. *Education:* Boston College (B.A., magna cum laude, 1975; J.D., cum laude, 1982). ***PRACTICE AREAS:*** Commercial Real Estate; Construction Law. ***Email:*** gfay@cl-law.com

CHARLES J. FILARDI, JR., born New Haven, Connecticut, April 8, 1956; admitted to bar, 1991, Connecticut; 1992, U.S. District Court, District of Connecticut. *Education:* Lafayette College (A.B., 1978); University of Bridgeport School of Law (J.D., magna cum laude, 1991). Recipient, American Jurisprudence Award, Commercial Law. *Member:* New Haven County, Connecticut and American Bar Associations; The Association of Trial Lawyers of America; Connecticut Trial Lawyers Association. [with U.S. Navy, 1980-1985; CDR, U.S. Naval Reserve, 1985—]. (Also at New Haven, Connecticut Office). ***PRACTICE AREAS:*** Bankruptcy; Debtor and Creditor; Commercial Litigation; Creditors Rights.

TIMOTHY S. FISHER (Resident, Hartford, Connecticut Office).

JAMIE JOHNSON FITZGERALD (Resident, New Haven, Connecticut Office).

JOHN A. FLAHERTY, born Norwalk, Connecticut, March 27, 1962; admitted to bar, 199l, Illinois; 1994, Connecticut. *Education:* Columbia College (A.B., 1984); University of Chicago (J.D., 1991). ***PRACTICE AREAS:*** Corporate Law; Securities. ***Email:*** jflahey@cl-law.com

THOMAS J. FREED, born Brooklyn, New York, May 22, 1963; admitted to bar, 1988, Connecticut. *Education:* State University of New York at Binghamton (B.S., 1985); State University of New York at Buffalo (J.D., cum laude, 1988). ***PRACTICE AREAS:*** Corporate Law; Mergers and Acquisitions; Venture Capital; Securities Law. ***Email:*** tfreed@cl-law.com

JOHN R. FRENCH (Resident, Greenwich, Connecticut Office).

STEVEN I. FRENKEL, born Cleveland, Ohio, January 1, 1964; admitted to bar, 1990, Connecticut and U.S. District Court, District of Connecticut; 1991, U.S. District Court, Southern and Eastern Districts of New York. *Education:* Yeshiva University (B.A., cum laude, 1986); Columbia University School of Law (J.D., 1989). Recipient, Public Speaking and Rhetoric Award. ***PRACTICE AREAS:*** Litigation; Creditors' Rights; Bankruptcy Law. ***Email:*** sfrenkel@cl-law.com

KEITH BRADOC GALLANT (Resident, New Haven, Connecticut Office).

CHARLES R. GEHRKE (Resident, Bonita Springs, Florida Office).

MARK D. GIARRATANA (Resident, Hartford, Connecticut Office).

JESSIE A. GILBERT (Resident, Greenwich, Connecticut Office).

ROBERT T. GILHULY (Resident, Greenwich, Connecticut Office).

ROBERT F. GRELE (Resident, Greenwich, Connecticut Office).

WILLIAM O'C. HARNISCH, born New York, N.Y., August 16, 1940; admitted to bar, 1966, District of Columbia; 1967, New York (Not admitted in Connecticut). *Education:* University of Notre Dame (B.B.A., 1962); Georgetown University (LL.B., 1965); New York University (LL.M. in Taxation, 1966). *Member:* Association of the Bar of the City of New York; New York State and American (Chairman, Financial Transactions Committee, 1988-1990; Vice Chairman, Sales and Financial Transactions Committee, 1986-1988; Chairman, Securities Dealers and Investors Subcommittee, 1979-1986, Section of Taxation) Bar Associations. Fellow, American Bar Foundation. ***PRACTICE AREAS:*** Taxation Law; Corporate Law; International Law. ***Email:*** wharnisch@cl-law.com

MICHAEL J. HINTON, born Brooklyn, New York, October 28, 1951; admitted to bar, 1976, Connecticut; 1978, Florida. *Education:* Georgetown University (A.B., summa cum laude, 1973); Cornell University (J.D., cum laude, 1976). Phi Beta Kappa. General Counsel: Investment Capital Associates, 1983-1987. ***PRACTICE AREAS:*** Environmental Law; Commercial Real Estate Law; Construction Law; Franchise Law; Partnership Law. ***Email:*** mhinton@cl-law.com

WILLIAM N. HOROWITZ (Resident, Bonita Springs, Florida Office) (Board Certified Taxation Lawyer, Florida Bar Board of Legal Specialization and Education).

PAUL G. HUGHES, born New York, N.Y., March 25, 1947; admitted to bar, 1973, New York; 1977, Connecticut. *Education:* Villanova University (B.A., summa cum laude, 1969); Cornell University (J.D., with distinction, 1972). Order of the Coif; Phi Kappa Phi; Delta Epsilon Sigma. ***PRACTICE AREAS:*** Corporate Law; Securities Law; Banking Regulatory. ***Email:*** phughes@cl-law.com

HOWARD M. HUJSA (Resident, Naples, Florida Office).

ROBERT B. KATZ (Resident, Hartford, Connecticut Office).

WENDI J. KEMP (Resident, Hartford, Connecticut Office).

DAVID W. KESNER (Resident, New Haven, Connecticut Office).

VINCENT M. KIERNAN, born Bronx, New York, February 8, 1956; admitted to bar, 1982, New York; 1983, New Jersey; 1991, Connecticut. *Education:* New York University (B.A., cum laude, 1977; J.D., 1981). ***PRACTICE AREAS:*** Corporate Law; Securities Law; Mergers and Acquisitions; Emerging Technologies. ***Email:*** vkiernan@cl-law.com

THAD D. KIRKPATRICK (Resident, Naples, Florida Office).

PAUL E. KNAG, born New York, N.Y., February 26, 1948; admitted to bar, 1971, New York and Connecticut. *Education:* Queens College of the City University of New York (B.A., magna cum laude, 1967); Harvard University (J.D., cum laude, 1970). Phi Beta Kappa; Pi Sigma Alpha; Phi Alpha Theta. Clerk to Judge Leonard P. Moore, U.S. Court of Appeals, Second Circuit, 1970-1971. President, Connecticut Health Lawyers' Association. ***PRACTICE AREAS:*** Litigation; Bankruptcy Law; Health Law. ***Email:*** pknag@cl-law.com

JASON HUNTER KORN (Resident, Naples, Florida Office).

BARRY KRAMER, born New York, N.Y., February 21, 1939; admitted to bar, 1966, New York; 1970, Connecticut, U.S. District Court, District of Connecticut and U.S. District Court, Southern and Eastern Districts of New York; 1979, U.S. Court of Appeals, Second Circuit; 1982, U.S. Court of Appeals for the Federal Circuit; registered to practice before U.S. Patent and Trademark Office; 1991 U.S. Supreme Court. *Education:* Rensselaer Polytechnic Institute (B.Ch.E., cum laude, 1961); New York University (J.D., cum laude, 1965). Tau Beta Pi; Phi Lambda Upsilon. Co-Author: "Patent Law Practice Forms," Clark Boardman Company, Ltd., 1985, 1989; "Trademark Law Practice Forms," Clark Boardman Company, Ltd., 1986, 1989. Editor, "Intellectual Property Law Re-

(This Listing Continued)

CUMMINGS & LOCKWOOD, Stamford—Continued

view," Clark Boardman Company, Ltd., 1984-1987. ***PRACTICE AREAS:*** Biotechnology; Intellectual Property; Patent; Trademark; Copyright. ***Email:*** bkramer@cl-law.com

KENNETH D. KRIER (Resident, Naples, Florida Office).

GINA S. LINSTONE (Resident, West Hartford, Connecticut Office).

JAMES I. LOTSTEIN (Resident, Hartford, Connecticut Office).

WILLIAM R. LYNCH (Resident, Greenwich, Connecticut Office).

JOHN R. MALLIN (Resident, Hartford, Connecticut Office).

STEPHEN MARCOVICH, born Bridgeport, Connecticut, December 21, 1953; admitted to bar, 1983, Connecticut. *Education:* Rutgers University (A.B., with high distinction, 1975); University of Bridgeport (M.B.A., 1978; J.D., summa cum laude, 1982). Henry Rutgers Scholar. Associate Editor, University of Bridgeport Law Review, 1981-1982. ***PRACTICE AREAS:*** Corporate; Securities; Venture Capital. ***Email:*** smarcovich@cl-law.com

NANCY P. MARX, born Houston, Texas, December 22, 1952; admitted to bar, 1984, Connecticut; 1985, New York. *Education:* University of Texas (B.F.A., 1975; J.D., 1984). Law Clerk, Hon. William H. Timbers, U.S. Court of Appeals, Second Circuit, 1984-1985. ***PRACTICE AREAS:*** Trusts and Estates Law and Tax Planning; Closely-Held Business Planning.

RICHARD P. McGRATH, born Chicago, Illinois, August 10, 1929; admitted to bar, 1954, District of Columbia; 1955, New York; 1960, Connecticut. *Education:* Georgetown University (A.B., magna cum laude, 1951); Harvard Law School (LL.B., cum laude, 1954). Editor of Harvard Law Review, 1953-1954. Editor, Matthew Bender "Proxy Regulation." General Counsel and Corporate Secretary, International Executive Service Corps., 1990—. ***PRACTICE AREAS:*** Corporate Law; Securities Law; Mergers and Acquisitions. ***Email:*** rmcgrath@cl-law.com

JONATHAN B. MILLS (Resident, Greenwich, Connecticut Office).

JOHN R. MUSICARO, JR., born Rockville Centre, New York, March 3, 1949; admitted to bar, 1974, New York; 1982, Connecticut. *Education:* University of Rochester (B.A., 1971); Columbia University (J.D., 1974). Phi Beta Kappa. *Member:* American College of Trust and Estate Counsel; Estate Planning Council of Lower Fairfield County. ***PRACTICE AREAS:*** Estate and Trust Administration; Estate and Tax Planning; Probate Litigation.

BASAM E. NABULSI, born St. Louis, Missouri, March 2, 1959; admitted to bar, 1986, Connecticut; 1987, New York; 1988, U.S. District Court, Southern and Eastern Districts of New York; registered to practice before U.S. Patent and Trademark Office. *Education:* Stevens Institute of Technology (B.E., Chem. Eng., 1979; M.E., Chem. Eng., 1983); Fordham University School of Law (J.D., 1986). Member, Fordham Urban Law Journal, 1985-1986. *Member:* New York Intellectual Property Law Association. ***PRACTICE AREAS:*** Intellectual Property; Patent Licensing; Biotechnology; Emerging Technologies. ***Email:*** bnabul@cl-law.com

WILLIAM H. NARWOLD, born Miami, Oklahoma, September 11, 1952; admitted to bar, 1979, Connecticut and U.S. District Court, District of Connecticut; 1984, U.S. Court of Appeals, First, Second, Fourth, Fifth, Tenth, Eleventh and Federal Circuits and U.S. Supreme Court; 1985, U.S. District Court, Southern and Eastern Districts of New York. *Education:* Colby College (B.A., 1974); University of Connecticut (J.D., cum laude, 1979). Member, 1977-1978 and Managing Editor, 1978-1979 University of Connecticut Law Review. Law Clerk, Honorable Warren W. Eginton, U.S. District Judge, District of Connecticut, 1979-1981. (Firm Managing Partner) (Also at Hartford, Connecticut Office). ***PRACTICE AREAS:*** Appellate; Products and Professional Liability; Environmental Litigation. ***Email:*** wnarwold@cl-law.com

RALPH A. NICHOLS, born Clinton, New York, January 27, 1919; admitted to bar, 1947, New York; 1949, Connecticut. *Education:* Hamilton College (A.B., 1940); Yale Law School (LL.B., 1947). *Member:* American College of Trust and Estate Counsel. ***PRACTICE AREAS:*** Trust and Estate Administration, Estate Planning. ***Email:*** rnichols@cl-law.com

GREGORY B. NOKES, born Hartford, Connecticut, September 4, 1951; admitted to bar, 1980, Connecticut. *Education:* University of Vermont (B.S., summa cum laude, 1973); University of Connecticut (J.D., with honors, 1980). Member, 1978-1980 and Articles Editor, 1979-1980, Connecticut Law Review. (Also at Hartford, Connecticut Office). ***PRACTICE AREAS:*** Labor Law; Employment Law; Civil Litigation. ***Email:*** gnokes@cl-law.com

KEVIN D. O'LEARY (Resident, Hartford, Connecticut Office).

DOUGLAS H. OLIN (Resident, Greenwich, Connecticut Office).

MARGARET A. O'NEAL, born Bronxville, New York, March 11, 1961; admitted to bar, 1990, New York and Connecticut. *Education:* Franklin and Marshall College (B.A., 1983); Fordham University (J.D., 1989). *Member:* Westchester, Regional and Connecticut Bar Associations. ***PRACTICE AREAS:*** Real Estate Law; Estate Planning; Administration. ***Email:*** moneal@cl-law.com

(This Listing Continued)

WILLARD J. OVERLOCK, born Chicago, Illinois, April 25, 1922; admitted to bar, 1949, Connecticut. *Education:* The Hotchkiss School, Yale University (B.A., 1946); Cornell University (LL.B., 1948). Phi Delta Phi. ***PRACTICE AREAS:*** Trusts and Estates. ***Email:*** woverlock@cl-law.com

R. THOMAS PAYNE, born Keyser, West Virginia, November 13, 1945; admitted to bar, 1981, Ohio; 1992, U.S. Court of Appeals, Federal Circuit and U.S. Court of Military Appeals; U.S. District Court, Southern District of Ohio; registered to practice before the U.S. Patent and Trademark Office (Not admitted in Connecticut). *Education:* United States Military Academy (B.S., 1971); University of Dayton (J.D., 1981). Phi Delta Phi. Formerly with: General Electric Company; Essex Group; John Deere & Company; Biebel French & Nauman; Kinney & Schenk; Fliet & Jacobson. *Member:* American Intellectual Property Law Association. [U.S. Army, 1965-1967; Capt., U.S. Army, 1971-1976; Maj., USAR, 1976-1993]. ***PRACTICE AREAS:*** Patents; Intellectual Property. ***Email:*** tpayne@cl-law.com

KELLEY G. PRICE (Resident, Naples, Florida Office).

CHARLES D. RAY (Resident, Hartford, Connecticut Office).

ROBERT W. REEVES, born Buffalo, New York, April 1, 1951; admitted to bar, 1976, Connecticut. *Education:* Yale University (B.A., cum laude, 1973); Columbia University (J.D., 1976). ***PRACTICE AREAS:*** Corporate Law; Banking Law; Bankruptcy Law. ***Email:*** rreeves@cl-law.com

DAVID A. REIF (Resident, New Haven, Connecticut Office).

CATHY S. REIMAN (Resident, Naples, Florida Office).

RICHARD R. RENDEIRO (Resident, Hartford, Connecticut Office).

EDWARD F. RODENBACH (Resident, Greenwich, Connecticut Office).

TIMOTHY G. RONAN, born Jamaica, New York, June 23, 1953; admitted to bar, 1984, Connecticut; 1985, U.S. District Court, District of Connecticut; U.S. District Court, Southern and Eastern Districts of New York. *Education:* College of the Holy Cross (B.A., 1975); New York Law School (J.D., magna cum laude, 1984). Editor, New York Law School Law Review, 1983-1984. ***PRACTICE AREAS:*** Commercial Litigation; Alternative Dispute Resolution; Construction Law; Probate Litigation. ***Email:*** tronan@cl-law.com

JOEL H. SCHECHTER (Resident, Naples, Florida Office).

RICHARD A. SIEGAL, born Hartford, Connecticut, January 1, 1947; admitted to bar, 1972, Pennsylvania; 1976, New Jersey; 1978, Connecticut. *Education:* Wharton School, University of Pennsylvania (B.S., cum laude, 1969); University of Pennsylvania (J.D., cum laude, 1972). Editor, University of Pennsylvania Law Review, 1971-1972. ***PRACTICE AREAS:*** Federal and State Income Taxation; ERISA. ***Email:*** rsiegal@cl-law.com

THOMAS P. SKIDD, JR., born Norwalk, Connecticut, July 2, 1936; admitted to bar, 1961, Connecticut. *Education:* Georgetown University (A.B., 1958); Yale University (LL.B., 1961). Director and Member Executive Committee, Connecticut Attorneys Title Insurance Company, 1978—. ***PRACTICE AREAS:*** Real Estate Law; Land Use Law; Zoning and Planning Law. ***Email:*** tskidd@cl-law.com

MARK G. SKLARZ (Resident, New Haven, Connecticut Office).

RICHARD M. SOLAZZO, born White Plains, New York, October 10, 1958; admitted to bar, 1984, Connecticut; 1985, New York; 1986, U.S. District Court, Southern and Eastern Districts of New York; 1988, U.S. District Court, District of Connecticut; 1992, Hawaii; 1995, U.S. Court of Appeals, Second Circuit; 1996. U.S. Court of Appeals, Third Circuit. *Education:* Cornell University (B.S., 1980); Georgetown University (J.D., cum laude, 1984). Recipient: American Jurisprudence Award in Criminal Law. Instructor, Fordham University School of Law, Continuing Legal Education, 1993. *Member:* Hawaii State and Connecticut Bar Associations. ***PRACTICE AREAS:*** Labor and Employment Litigation. ***Email:*** rsolazzo@cl-law.com

JOHN F. SPINDLER, born Milwaukee, Wisconsin, August 23, 1929; admitted to bar, 1953, Michigan; 1954, Pennsylvania; 1956, Connecticut; 1977, Florida. *Education:* University of Michigan (A.B., 1951; J.D., 1953). Delta Theta Phi; Order of the Coif. ***PRACTICE AREAS:*** Fiduciary Law; Corporate Litigation; Legal Ethics. ***Email:*** jspindler@cl-law.com

IRA B. STECHEL, born New York, N.Y., 1947; admitted to bar, 1973, New York; 1974, U.S. District Court, Southern and Eastern Districts of New York and U.S. Tax Court; 1975, U.S. Court of Appeals, 2nd Circuit; 1976, U.S. Supreme Court; 1977, U.S. Claims Court (Not admitted in Connecticut). *Education:* City College of the City University of New York (B.A., magna cum laude, 1969); Cornell University (J.D., 1972); New York University (LL.M., in Taxation, 1976). Note Editor, Cornell International Law Journal, 1971-1972. Phi Beta Kappa. Author: "Entertainment and Gifts, Meals and Lodging-Deduction and Recordkeeping Requirements, B.N.A. Tax Management Portfolio No. 520, 1999; "Structure Pay to Avoid Reasonable Compensation Attack," 56 Taxation for Accountants 93 (1996); "Effective Deferred Compensation and Equity Programs for the Closely Held Corporation," Proceedings of the N.Y.U. 49th An-

(This Listing Continued)

nual Institute on Federal Taxation, 1990. Member, Advisory Board Tax Management Real Estate Journal. *Member:* New York State and American (Member, Taxation Section) Bar Associations.

CHARLES M. TATELBAUM (See Biography at Naples, Florida).

CONRAD TEITELL, born New York, N.Y., November 8, 1932; admitted to bar, 1958, New York; 1960, U.S. District Court, Southern and Eastern Districts of New York; 1961, U.S. Tax Court and U.S. Claims Court; 1964, U.S. Supreme Court and U.S. Court of Military Appeals; 1968, District of Columbia (Not admitted in Connecticut). *Education:* University of Michigan (A.B., 1954); Columbia University (LL.B., 1957); New York University (LL.M., 1968). Adjunct Visiting Professor of Law, University of Miami School of Law, 1980—. Author: Philanthropy & Taxation (5 volumes). *Member:* American Bar Association (Member, Sections on: Taxation; Real Property, Probate and Trust Law; Member, Committee on Exempt Organizations, 1970—; Chairman, Committee on Charitable Giving, Trusts and Foundations, 1975-1981); National Association of College and University Attorneys. Fellow, The American College of Trust and Estate Counsel. ***PRACTICE AREAS:*** Charitable Giving; Tax Exempt Organizations; Estate Planning. ***Email:*** cteitell@cl-law.com

HOWARD S. TUTHILL, born September 30, 1918; admitted to bar, 1941, New York; 1951, Connecticut. *Education:* University of Virginia (B.S., 1939; J.D., 1941). Editor-in-Chief, Virginia Law Review, 1940-1941. Fellow, American College of Trust and Estate Counsel. (Also at Naples, Florida Office). ***PRACTICE AREAS:*** Estate Settlement Law; Trust Administration Law; Executive Tax Planning Law; Post-Mortem Tax Planning Law. ***Email:*** htuthill@cl-law.com

HOWARD S. TUTHILL III, born Mount Vernon, New York, March 31, 1947; admitted to bar, 1972, Connecticut; 1980, New York. *Education:* St. Lawrence University (B.A., 1969); University of Virginia (J.D., 1972). *Member:* Connecticut (Member, Executive Committee, Estates and Probate Section, 1975—) and American Bar Associations. Fellow, American College of Trust and Estate Counsel. ***PRACTICE AREAS:*** Estate Planning; Probate Law; Taxation; Trust and Estate Administration. ***Email:*** ttuthill@cl-law.com

RICHARD VOIGT (Resident, Hartford, Connecticut Office).

JANE KIMBALL WARREN (Resident at Hartford, Connecticut Office).

WILLIAM C. WEITZEL, JR., born Washington, D.C., February 6, 1935; admitted to bar, 1961, District of Columbia (Not admitted in Connecticut). *Education:* Harvard College (A.B., magna cum laude, 1956); Harvard Law School (LL.B., 1959). Assistant U.S. Attorney for District of Columbia, 1961-1966. Senior Vice President and General Counsel, Texaco Inc., 1977-1989. Trustee, Southwestern Legal Foundation. ***PRACTICE AREAS:*** Litigation. ***Email:*** wweitzel@cl-law.com

ERIC WATT WIECHMANN (Resident, Hartford, Connecticut Office).

GAYLE BRIAN WILHELM, born Springfield, Massachusetts, September 1, 1936; admitted to bar, 1964, Connecticut. *Education:* Harvard University (A.B., magna cum laude, 1957; LL.B., cum laude, 1964). Author: "Connecticut Estates Practice-Death Taxes," 1971; "Connecticut Estates Practice-Settlement of Estates," 1974; "Connecticut Estates Practice - Wills," 1986; "Connecticut Estate Practice-Trusts", 1991 all published by Lawyers Co-Operative Publishing Company. Fellow, American College of Trust and Estate Counsel. ***PRACTICE AREAS:*** Estate Settlement; Trust Administration; Probate Litigation; Estate Planning; Tax Planning. ***Email:*** gwilhelm@cl-law.com

HOLLY J. WINGER (Resident, Hartford, Connecticut Office).

SCOTT D. WOFSY, born Brooklyn, New York, December 7, 1967; admitted to bar, 1992, Connecticut; 1993, New York; registered to practice before U .S. Patent and Trademark Office. *Education:* George Washington University (B.S.M.E., 1989); New York Law School (J.D., 1992). Articles Editor, New York Law School Journal of International and Comparative Law, 1992. Member, American Society of Mechanical Engineers, 1988-1992. ***PRACTICE AREAS:*** Patent Prosecution; Patent Litigation; Intellectual Property.

MARC L. ZAKEN, born New York, N.Y., February 20, 1958; admitted to bar, 1983, New York; 1985, U.S. District Court, Southern and Eastern Districts of New York; 1988, U.S. District Court, District of Connecticut; 1989, Connecticut; 1991, U.S. Court of Appeals, Second Circuit. *Education:* Cornell University (B.S., 1979); New York University (J.D., 1982). *Member:* Stamford/Norwalk Regional (Chairman, Employment Law Committee, 1990-1991) Connecticut and American (Chair, Employer/Employee Relations Committee, Torts and Insurance Section, 1997-1998) Bar Associations. ***PRACTICE AREAS:*** Labor Law; Employment Law. ***Email:*** mzaken@cl-law.com

RESIDENT COUNSEL

VERA M. CRADDOCK-LEE, born Yorkshire, England, January 15, 1943; admitted to bar, 1987, New York; 1989, Connecticut. *Education:* University of London, England (B.A., Hons., 1965); New York University (J.D., 1985). *Member:* Stamford, Connecticut (Member, Estates and Probate Section) and American Bar Associations. ***PRACTICE AREAS:*** Estate Planning; Estate Administration. ***Email:*** vcraddocklee@cl-law.com

(This Listing Continued)

SANFORD J. DAVIS, born Glen Cove, New York, November 24, 1957; admitted to bar, 1985, New York; 1996, Florida (Not admitted in Connecticut). *Education:* University of Pennsylvania (B.S., 1980); American University (J.D., M.B.A., 1983); Georgetown University (LL.M., 1984). *Member:* New York State Bar Association. ***PRACTICE AREAS:*** Corporate Law; Corporate Taxation; Mergers and Acquisitions; Partnership Taxation; International Taxation; Individual Taxation.

JOHN D. FREEMAN, born Ohio, November 30, 1964; admitted to bar, 1990, Connecticut. *Education:* College of Wooster (B.A., 1987); Columbia University (J.D., 1989). *Member:* Connecticut (Member, Conservation and Environmental Quality Section) and American (Member, Section of Natural Resources, Energy and Environmental Law). ***PRACTICE AREAS:*** Environmental Law; Land Use Planning Law; Commercial Real Estate Law. ***Email:*** jfreeman@cl-law.com

HARRIS S. JAFFE, born Jersey City, New Jersey, June 21, 1942; admitted to bar, 1967, Illinois; 1969, New York (Not admitted in Connecticut). *Education:* University of Chicago (B.A., 1964; J.D., 1967). Phi Delta Phi. *Member:* New York State and American Bar Associations; New York County Lawyers Association (Member, Corporation Law Committee, 1991—). ***PRACTICE AREAS:*** Finance (25%); Corporate Law (25%); Securities (25%); Mergers and Acquisitions (25%). ***Email:*** hjaffe@cl-law.com

EVELYN M. SOMMER, born New York, NY, October 26, 1925; admitted to bar, 1956, New York and U.S. District Court Southern and Eastern Districts of New York; registered to practice before the U.S. Patent and Trademark Office (Not admitted in Connecticut). *Education:* Hunter College of the City University of New York (A.B., 1945); New York University; Brooklyn Law School (LL.B., 1955). Special Master, U.S. District Court, District of Connecticut, 1994—. Adjunct Professor, Intellectual Property Quinnipiac University School of Law, 1986—. Director, New York Patent, Trademark, Copyright Association, 1990-1992. Director, National Inventors Hall of Fame, 1999 . ***PRACTICE AREAS:*** Patents; Trademarks; Unfair Competition; Copyrights; Licensing; Franchise Law; Transactional.

RESIDENT ASSOCIATES

Roxana Aleali
Meghan H. Alger (admission pending)
Karen L. Allison
Amanda E. Balog (admission pending)
M. Juliet Bonazzoli
David A. Bradley
Christopher M. Cerrito
Thomas G. Ciarlone, Jr. (admission pending)
Martin A. Clarke
Jacquelyn A. Conlon
Jennifer M. Coyne
Tracy C. Daugherty
Margaret A. DeLuca
Ryan Charles Fisher
Thomas C. Frost (admission pending)
Daniel G. Johnson
Michael J. Kearney, Jr.
Andrew D. Kupinse
David T. Leibell
James J. Lillie (Not admitted in CT)
Cassandra B. McDonald
Richard Newman
Carrie Webb Olson
Bart F. Peters
Yusef Poole
Carolyn Reers (Not admitted in CT)
Lori A. Reid (admission pending)
Elisa Shevlin Rizzo (Not admitted in CT)
Claire E. Ryan
Joshua J. Sarner
Evan S. Seideman
Rachel B. Sherman
Robert J. Sickinger
David J. Silvia
Heather V. Taylor
Courtenay L. Tischer
Karen Wagshul
Mary Ellen C. Whiteman
Alison Jacobs Wice

STAFF ATTORNEY

Mady McSweeney

(For complete biographical information on personnel, see Professional Biographies at Greenwich, CT, Hartford, CT, West Hartford, CT, New Haven, CT, Bonita Springs, FL, Naples, FL and Palm Beach, FL)

CURTIS, BRINCKERHOFF & BARRETT, P.C.

Established in 1864

666 SUMMER STREET
STAMFORD, CONNECTICUT 06901-1416
Telephone: 203-324-6777
Telecopier: 203-324-9621

General Practice, Real Estate, Commercial Real Estate Acquisitions, Municipal Law, Zoning, Planning and Land Use, Banking, Administrative Law, Litigation, Civil Litigation, Commercial Litigation, Tax Appeals, Eminent Domain, Federal Taxation, International Taxation, State Taxation, Estate Planning, Trust and Estate, Probate, Elder Law, Family Law, Domestic Relations, Closely Held Corporations, Business Law, Corporate Law, Commercial Law, Commercial Leasing, Employ-

(This Listing Continued)

CURTIS, BRINCKERHOFF & BARRETT, P.C., Stamford—Continued

ment Law, Commercial Arbitration, Construction Law, Landlord and Tenant Law, Personal Injury and Negligence, Product Liability, Bankruptcy, Civil Trial and Appellate Practice in all State and Federal Courts.

FIRM PROFILE: Curtis, Brinckerhoff & Barrett, P.C., founded in 1864, is the oldest law firm in Fairfield County. The firm has a distinguished history of service to the legal profession, its clients and the public. Its present members include two former Presidents of the Stamford Bar Association, a member of the Board of Governors of the Connecticut Bar Association, past President of the Stamford Board of Representatives, Chairman of the General Law Committee in the Connecticut General Assembly and a member and Officer of the Board of the Directors of the Regional Bar Association. The firm encourages continuing professional development and all attorneys participate in civic affairs, professional association activities and continuing legal education programs.

T. WARD CLEARY (1916-1988).

JOHN WAYNE FOX, born Stamford, Connecticut, February 1, 1947; admitted to bar, 1971, Connecticut, U.S. District Court, District of Connecticut, U.S. Court of Appeals, Second Circuit; U.S. Supreme Court and U.S. Tax Court. *Education:* Fairfield University (B.A., 1968); Georgetown University (J.D., 1971). Member, Stamford Board of Representatives, 1975-1979. Chairman, Legislative and Rules Committee, 1975-1977 and President, 1977-1979. Member, House of Representatives, Connecticut General Assembly, 1981—, Judiciary Committee, and Chairman, General Law Committee. Town Counsel, Town of Darien, 1999—. *Member:* Regional and Connecticut Bar Associations; The Association of Trial Lawyers of America; Connecticut Trial Lawyers Association. ***PRACTICE AREAS:*** Litigation; Commercial Law; Family Law; Municipal Law; Tax Appeals; Eminent Domain. ***Email:*** fox@curtisbb.com

WARD FRANK CLEARY, born Stamford, Connecticut, September 29, 1943; admitted to bar, 1970, Connecticut; 1971, U.S. Tax Court. *Education:* Fordham University (B.A., 1966; J.D., 1969). Attorney, Office of Chief Counsel, Internal Revenue Service, Tax Court Litigation Division, Washington, D.C., 1969-1973. Chairman, Wilton Charter Revision Commission, 1980-1981. Member, 1981-1986 and Chairman, 1985-1986, Wilton Planning and Zoning Commission. *Member:* American Bar Association (Member, Section on Taxation). ***PRACTICE AREAS:*** Federal Taxation; International Taxation; Closely Held Corporations; Estate Planning; Commercial Real Estate Acquisitions. ***Email:*** cleary@curtisbb.com

JAMES D'ALTON MURPHY, born New Rochelle, New York, January 4, 1952; admitted to bar, 1978, Connecticut and U.S. District Court, District of Connecticut; 1979, New York; 1989, U.S. Supreme Court; 1995, U.S. Court of Appeals, Second Circuit. *Education:* Manhattanville College (B.A., 1975); Fordham Law School (J.D., 1978). Counsel, Darien Planning and Zoning Commission, Environmental Protection Commission and Zoning Board of Appeals, 1980—. Member, Weston Planning and Zoning Commission, 1989-1993. *Member:* Regional (Treasurer, 1999-2000; Secretary, 2000-2001; Second Vice President, 2001— Chairman, Land Use Committee, 1997—), Westchester County, Connecticut (Member, Executive Committee Section on Planning and Zoning, 1998—) and New York State Bar Associations; The Association of Trial Lawyers of America; Connecticut Trial Lawyers Association. ***PRACTICE AREAS:*** Zoning, Planning and Land Use; Commercial Real Estate; Commercial Litigation; Construction Law. ***Email:*** murphy@curtisbb.com

RANDOLPH T. LOVALLO, born Torrington, Connecticut, June 27, 1956; admitted to bar, 1981, Connecticut; 1983, U.S. District Court, District of Connecticut; 1991, U.S. Court of Appeals, Second Circuit. *Education:* The Johns Hopkins University (B.A., 1978); New England School of Law (J.D., 1981). Counsel to Assessor, Town of Darien, 1988-1990, 1992—. Superior Court Fact Finder/Arbitrator, 1999—. *Member:* Regional, Connecticut and American Bar Associations; The Association of Trial Lawyers of America; Connecticut Trial Lawyers Association. ***PRACTICE AREAS:*** Civil Litigation; Commercial Litigation; Landlord and Tenant Law; Corporate Law; Municipal Law; Real Estate; Personal Injury; Commercial Leasing. ***Email:*** lovallo@curtisbb.com

MICHAEL P. MURRAY, born Stamford, Connecticut, March 26, 1965; admitted to bar, 1991, Connecticut, New York, U.S. District Court, District of Connecticut and U.S. District Court, Southern District of New York; 1996, U.S. Supreme Court. *Education:* Villanova University (B.A., 1987); Fordham University (J.D., 1990). *Member:* Connecticut and New York State Bar Associations. ***PRACTICE AREAS:*** General Practice; Real Estate; Trust and Estate; Civil Litigation; Business Law. ***Email:*** murray@curtisbb.com

SUSAN L. STRATTON, born Pittsburgh, Pennsylvania, June 24, 1944; admitted to bar, 1979, Connecticut; 1989, U.S. District Court, District of Connecticut; 1990, U.S. Supreme Court. *Education:* University of Connecticut (B.A., summa cum laude, 1976; J.D., 1979). Stamford Urban Redevelopment Commission, 1993. *Member:* Regional, Connecticut and American Bar Associations; Women's Bar Association of Fairfield County (Member, Executive Committee). ***PRACTICE AREAS:*** Trusts and Estates; Probate; Elder Law; Real Estate. ***Email:*** stratton@curtisbb.com

OF COUNSEL

RICHARD L. BRINCKERHOFF, born Stamford, Connecticut, March 5, 1919; admitted to bar, 1949, Connecticut. *Education:* Williams College (B.A., 1940); Columbia University (LL.B., 1949). Member, New Canaan Zoning Commission, 1952-1954. Associate Judge, Town Court, New Canaan, 1957-1960. Representative, Connecticut General Assembly, 1961-1971. Member: Compensation Commission for Elected State Officials and Judges, 1973-1979; Town Counsel, New Canaan, 1980-1990. *Member:* Regional (Secretary, 1952-1953), Connecticut and American Bar Associations.

JOHN D. HERTZ, born Stamford, Connecticut, November 1, 1929; admitted to bar, 1955, Connecticut. *Education:* Franklin-Marshall College (B.A., 1952); Fordham University (LL.B., 1955). Book Review Editor, Fordham Law Review, 1954-1955. Member, Zoning Board of Appeals, Town of Darien, 1960-1962. Town Counsel, Town of Darien, 1974-1990, and 1992-1999. Chairman of the Board, Stamford Y.M.C.A., 1976-1981. Chairman of the Board of Trustees, Stamford Y.M.C.A., 1982—. Managing Director, William Pitt Foundation, 1991—). *Member:* Regional and Connecticut Bar Associations. [Trial Counsel, General Court-Martial, U.S. Marine Corps, 1956-1957]. ***PRACTICE AREAS:*** Real Estate; Administrative Law; Municipal Law; Commercial Law.

JANE F. DONOVAN, born Providence, Rhode Island, April 6, 1929; admitted to bar, 1967, Connecticut. *Education:* Pembroke College of Brown University (A.B., 1950); George Washington University and Fordham University (J.D., 1967). Superior Court Attorney Trial Referee, 1985—. *Member:* Regional (Treasurer, 1984; Vice President, 1988; President, 1989), Connecticut (Treasurer, 1994-1995) and American Bar Associations.

FREDERICK M. TOBIN, born New Haven, Connecticut, February 15, 1936; admitted to bar, 1964, Connecticut, U.S. District Court, District of Connecticut, U.S. Court of Appeals, Second Circuit, U.S. Supreme Court and U.S. Tax Court. *Education:* Trinity College (B.A., 1957); New York University; University of Connecticut (J.D., 1964). Member, Board of Editors, 1962-1963 and Associate Editor, 1963-1964, University of Connecticut Law Review. Author: "The Law of Defamation in Connecticut," 38 Connecticut Bar Journal 420, September, 1964; Case Comment, "State v. Doe," 37 Connecticut Bar Journal 504, September, 1963. Law Clerk to Hon. James B. Murphy, Justice, Connecticut Supreme Court, 1964-1965. President, Alumni Association, University of Connecticut, 1984-1985. Special Master, U.S. District Court, District of Connecticut, 1985—. Member, Panel of Arbitrators, American Arbitration Association. General Counsel, F. A. Bartlett Tree Expert Company. *Member:* Regional (President, 1977-1979), Connecticut (Member: House of Delegates, 1978—; Board of Governors, 1982-1984, 1990—) and American Bar Associations; Law Society of England and Wales (Affiliate Member). [Capt., U.S. Air Force Reserve, 1958-1960 and 1962]. ***PRACTICE AREAS:*** Corporate Law; Commercial Real Estate; Leases and Leasing; Real Estate; Business Law; Commercial Arbitration.

PATRICIA M. GAUG, born Bronx, New York, January 18, 1959; admitted to bar, 1985, Connecticut; 1986, U.S. District Court, District of Connecticut; 1987, New York and Massachusetts; 1989, U.S. Court of Appeals, Second Circuit; 1993, U.S. District Court, Eastern District of New York; 1996, U.S. District Court, Southern District of New York. *Education:* State University of New York at Albany (B.A., summa cum laude, 1981); Boston University (J.D., 1985). *Member:* Regional and Connecticut Bar Associations. ***PRACTICE AREAS:*** Civil Litigation; General Practice.

JOHN J. LOUIZOS, born Athens, Greece, April 7, 1972; admitted to bar, 1997, Virginia; 1999, Connecticut; 2000, U.S. District court, District of Connecticut. *Education:* University of New Hampshire (B.A., magna cum laude, 1994); Washington & Lee University (J.D., 1997). Burks Scholar. Class President, 1996-1997. Author: "Que, Ya No Hablan Ingles En Este Pais?: A Look at the Constitutionality of English Only Provisions Under the Free Speech Clause of the First Amendment," 3 Race & Ethnic Ancestry Law Digest 14 (1997). Law Clerk, Supreme Court of Virginia Office of the Chief Staff Attorney, 1997-1999. *Member:* Regional and Connecticut Bar Associations. ***LANGUAGES:*** Greek. ***PRACTICE AREAS:*** Commercial Law; Civil Litigation; Real Estate. ***Email:*** louizos@curtisbb.com

JOSEPH P. SARGENT, born Norwalk, Connecticut, November 24, 1966; admitted to bar, 1994, Louisiana; 1995, Connecticut; 1997, U.S. District Court, District of Connecticut; 1998, U.S. Court of Appeals, Second Circuit. *Education:* Fairfield University (B.A., 1989); Wake Forest University (J.D., 1994). Member, Wake Forest University Law Review, 1992-1993; Editorial Staff, 1993-1994. Recipient: North Carolina Academy of Trial Lawyers Award; American Jurisprudence Awards for Contracts I, Contracts II Taxation Policy and Trial Practice. Author: "The Standard of Proof Under the Federal Sentencing Guidelines: Raising the Standard to Beyond a Reasonable Doubt," 8 Wake

(This Listing Continued)

Forest Law Review 463 (1993); "Comparative Fault and Common Law Apportionment," Vol. 9, No. 7, Connecticut Lawyer (1999). Adjunct Professor, Fairfield University. Member, Board of Directors and Associate Chairperson, Alpha Home. *Member:* Connecticut and Louisiana State Bar Associations; Connecticut Trial Lawyers Association; Association of Trial Lawyers of America. ***PRACTICE AREAS:*** Commercial Litigation. ***Email:*** sargent@curtisbb.com

COUNSEL FOR: Town of Darien; The F.A. Bartlett Tree Expert Co.; Bartlett Realty Co.; Manulife Wood Logan, Inc.; Miller Automobile Corp.; Audiocom, Inc.; Suburban Cadillac Pontiac Corp.; Bolliger, Inc.; Triad Installation and Moving Services, Inc.; First Union Bank, N.A.; William Pitt Foundation; Bartlett Tree Foundation; Cornerstone Bank; Qwest Communications Corp.
LOCAL REAL ESTATE AND TRUST COUNSEL FOR: People's Bank, Bridgeport; First County Bank, N.A.; Cornerstone Bank; Manulife Financial; First Union Bank, N.A.

CURTIS, MALLET-PREVOST, COLT & MOSLE LLP

Established in 1830
FINANCIAL CENTRE
695 EAST MAIN STREET
STAMFORD, CONNECTICUT 06901
Telephone: 203-359-6200
Telecopier: 203-328-2617
Email: info@cm-p.com
URL: http://www.cm-p.com

REVISERS OF THE ARGENTINA, BOLIVIA, BRAZIL, CHILE, COLOMBIA, COSTA RICA, DOMINICAN REPUBLIC, ECUADOR, EL SALVADOR, GUATEMALA, HONDURAS, MEXICO, NICARAGUA, PERU, URUGUAY AND VENEZUELA LAW DIGESTS FOR THIS DIRECTORY.

New York, N.Y. Office: 101 Park Avenue. Telephone: 212-696-6000. Telecopier: 212-697-1559.
Washington, D.C. Office: Suite 1205L, 1801 K Street, N.W. Telephone: 202-452-7373. Telecopier: 202-452-7333.
Newark, New Jersey Office: One Gateway Center, Suite 403. Telephone: 973-622-0605. Telecopier: 973-622-5646.
Houston, Texas Office: 2 Houston Center, 909 Fannin Street, Suite 3725. Telephone: 713-759-9555. Telecopier: 713-759-0712.
Mexico City, D.F., Mexico Office: Curtis, Mallet-Prevost, Colt & Mosle, Ruben Dario 281, Pisos 8 & 9, Col. Bosque de Chapultepec, 11530 Mexico, D.F. Telephone: 52-55-5282-0444. Telecopier: 52-55-5282-0637.
Paris, France Office: 15 rue d'Astorg, 75008. Telephone: +33-1 42-66-39-10. Telecopier: +33-1 42-66-39-62.
London, England Office: One Cornhill, EC3V 3ND. Telephone: 0207-743-6310. Telecopier: 0207-743-6311.
Frankfurt am Main 1, Germany Office: Staufenstrasse 42. Telephone: +49-69-971-4420. Telecopier: +49-69-17 33 99.
Muscat, Sultanate of Oman Office: Jewel Beach-134. Telephone: 968-564-495. Telecopier: 968-564-497.
Milan, Italy Office: Curtis, Mallet-Prevost & Gilioli, Piazzale Principessa Clotilde 8, 20121. Telephone: +(39) 02 29 00 29 32. Telefax: +(39) 02 65 75 969.

General Practice, including the Laws of Latin American Countries.

RESIDENT PARTNER

VICTOR L. ZIMMERMANN, JR., born New York, N.Y., November 22, 1952; admitted to bar, 1978, New York; 1979, U.S. District Court, Southern District of New York; 1982, Connecticut; 1983, U.S. District Court, District of Connecticut; 1996, U.S. Court of Appeals, Second Circuit. *Education:* College of the Holy Cross (B.A., 1974); Fordham University (J.D., 1977). Member, National Moot Court Team. A Member, Enforcement Division, Securities & Exchange Commission, Washington, D.C., 1980-1982. Member, Board of Arbitrators: National Association of Securities Dealers, 1987—; New York Stock Exchange, 1988—. *Member:* The Association of the Bar of the City of New York; Connecticut and American Bar Associations. ***PRACTICE AREAS:*** Emerging Company Financings; Securities Litigation; Investment Partnerships; Financial Services Regulation. ***Email:*** vzimmerman@cm-p.com

COUNSEL

PETER E. FLEMING, III, born New York, N.Y., August 28, 1957; admitted to bar, 1986, Connecticut and Pennsylvania; 1988, Florida; 1992, New York; U.S. District Court, District of Connecticut, Middle District of Florida and Southern District of New York. *Education:* University of Vermont (B.A., 1980); Georgetown University Law Center (J.D., 1985). Editor, Law and Policy in International Business Journal. Associate, Law Offices of Richard Bennett, Jr., Washington, D.C. (representation of professional athletes), 1984-1987; Associate, Rumberger, Kirk & Caldwell, Orlando, Florida (representation of General Motors in product liability matters nationally), 1987-1990; Assistant District Attorney, New York County, 1990-1996. ***PRACTICE AREAS:*** Civil Litigation; Criminal Litigation; Securities Arbitration; Litigation. ***Email:*** p3fleming@cm-p.com

REMY A. RODAS, born La Paz, Bolivia, June 4, 1956; admitted to bar, 1982, New York; 1986, Connecticut. *Education:* Georgetown University, School of Foreign Service (B.S.F.S., 1978); Catholic University Law School (J.D., 1981). Phi Alpha Theta. *Member:* Greenwich, Stamford Regional, Connecticut, New York State and American Bar Associations. ***LANGUAGES:*** Spanish. ***PRACTICE AREAS:*** Corporate Law; Commercial Law; Transportation; Joint Ventures; Mergers and Acquisitions; International Transactions. ***Email:*** rrodas@cm-p.com

MICHAEL K. STANTON, JR., born New York, N.Y., March 16, 1961; admitted to bar, 1986, Connecticut; 1987, New York; 1988, U.S. District Courts, Southern and Eastern Districts of New York; 1991, U.S. District Court, District of Connecticut and U.S. Supreme Court. *Education:* College of the Holy Cross (B.A., 1983); Fordham University (J.D., 1986). *Member:* New York State Bar Association (Member, Executive Committee, Young Lawyers Section, 1990-1991). ***PRACTICE AREAS:*** Civil Litigation; Commercial Litigation; Construction Litigation; Probate Litigation; Torts. ***Email:*** mstanton@cm-p.com

ASSOCIATES

JERROLD A. SISKIN, born Brooklyn, New York, February 26, 1950; admitted to bar, 1976, New York and U.S. District Court, Southern and Eastern Districts of New York (Not admitted in Connecticut). *Education:* Brandeis University (B.A., History, 1972); Brooklyn Law School (J.D., 1975). *Member:* American Immigration Lawyers Association. ***PRACTICE AREAS:*** Immigration and Nationality Law. ***Email:*** jsiskin@cm-p.com

D. CHRISTINE WOODHOUSE, born Washington, D.C., August 31, 1963; admitted to bar, 1991, New York (Not admitted in Connecticut). *Education:* Stanford University (B.A., 1985); University of Virginia at Charlottesville (J.D., 1990). *Member:* New York State Bar Association; American Society of International Law. ***LANGUAGES:*** French. ***PRACTICE AREAS:*** International Finance. ***Email:*** cwoodhouse@cm-p.com

REVISERS OF THE ARGENTINA, BOLIVIA, BRAZIL, CHILE, COLOMBIA, COSTA RICA, DOMINICAN REPUBLIC, ECUADOR, EL SALVADOR, GUATEMALA, HONDURAS, MEXICO, NICARAGUA, PERU, URUGUAY AND VENEZUELA LAW DIGESTS FOR THIS DIRECTORY.

DAY, BERRY & HOWARD LLP

Established in 1919
ONE CANTERBURY GREEN
STAMFORD, CONNECTICUT 06901
Telephone: 203-977-7300
Telecopier: 203-977-7301
Email: postmaster@dbh.com
URL: http://www.dbh.com

Greenwich, Connecticut Office: One East Putnam Avenue. Telephone: 203-862-7800. Telecopier: 203-862-7801.
Hartford, Connecticut Office: CityPlace I. Telephone: 860-275-0100. Telecopier: 860-275-0343.
Boston, Massachusetts Office: 260 Franklin Street. Telephone: 617-345-4600. Telecopier: 617-439-4453.

Antitrust, Banking, Bank Lending, Bankruptcy, Bankruptcy Counseling, Benefits and Executive Compensation, Business Succession Planning, Business Transactions and Counseling, Closely Held Businesses, Credit Tenant Lease Financing, Commercial Litigation, Commercial Leasing, Construction, Direct Liability and Casualty Insurance, Disability, Emerging Companies, Energy, Environmental and Land Use, Equipment Finance and Leasing, Employment Law and Litigation, Environmental Law and Litigation, Executive Planning, Family Law, Finance and Investments, First Party Insurance, Franchise and Distributorship Litigation, Government Investigations, Health Care, Insurance Regulation and Proceedings, Insurance Litigation, International Tax, International Transactions, Life Insurance and Annuities, Low Income Housing Tax Credits, Medical and Professional Malpractice, Mergers and Acquisitions, Multi-Property Transactions, Municipal Finance, Negligence Defense, Planning for Entrepreneurs, Private Equity Funds, Product Liability, Real Estate Development, Real Estate Equity Investors, Real Estate Finance, Real Estate Workouts and Restructuring, Regulatory Insurance Proceedings and Litigation, Reinsurance, Securities Law, Securities Litigation, Strategic Joint Ventures, Structured Finance, Tax, Tax Litigation Group, Tax Exempt and Charity Giving, Tax Exempt Organizations, Technology and Intellectual Property Business and Litigation, Torts Litigation, Telecommunications, Trusts and Estates Administration, Trusts and Estates Litigation, Water Companies.

MEMBERS OF FIRM IN STAMFORD

JEROME BERKMAN, born Brooklyn, NY, 1941; admitted to bar, 1965, New York; 1970, Connecticut. *Education:* Cornell University (B.A., 1963; LL.B., 1965). ***PRACTICE AREAS:*** Real Estate Development; Commercial Leasing; Real Estate Finance. ***Email:*** jberkman@dbh.com

(This Listing Continued)

DAY, BERRY & HOWARD LLP, Stamford—Continued

MARTIN L. BUDD, born Brooklyn, NY, 1940; admitted to bar, 1969, New York; 1979, Connecticut. *Education:* Dartmouth College (A.B., summa cum laude, 1960); Oxford University, England (B.A., 1963); Harvard Law School (LL.B., magna cum laude, 1968). ***PRACTICE AREAS:*** Private Equity Funds; Mergers and Acquisitions; Strategic Joint Ventures; International Transactions; Securities Law. ***Email:*** mlbudd@dbh.com

MICHAEL P. BYRNE, born Passaic, NJ, 1960; admitted to bar, 1987, Connecticut. *Education:* Boston College (B.S., 1983); Boston College Law School (J.D., 1987). ***PRACTICE AREAS:*** Real Estate Finance; Commercial Leasing; Real Estate Development; Real Estate Workouts and Restructuring. ***Email:*** mpbyrne@dbh.com

PATRICIA A. CARPENTER, born Delhi, NY, 1952; admitted to bar, 1981, Pennsylvania; 1984, Connecticut. *Education:* Gettysburg College (B.A., 1974); Cornell University (J.D., 1981). ***PRACTICE AREAS:*** Trust and Estate Litigation; Commercial Litigation. ***Email:*** pacarpenter@dbh.com

MICHAEL G. CONSIDINE, born New York, NY., 1958; admitted to bar, 1985, New York and U.S. District Court, Southern and Eastern Districts of New York; 1986, New Jersey; 1990, U.S. Court of Appeals, Second Circuit; 1996, U.S. District Court, District of Connecticut; 1998, Connecticut. *Education:* Boston College (B.A., magna cum laude, 1980); Georgetown University (J.D., 1984). ***PRACTICE AREAS:*** Government Investigations; Commercial Litigation. ***Email:*** mgconsidine@dbh.com

KENNETH W. GAGE, born Endicott, NY, 1966; admitted to bar, 1992, New York; 1993, Connecticut, U.S. District Court, District of Connecticut and Northern and Southern Districts of New York. *Education:* University of Buffalo (B.A., 1988; J.D., 1991). ***PRACTICE AREAS:*** Employment Law; Employment Litigation; Government Investigations. ***Email:*** kwgage@dbh.com

ANDREW P. GAILLARD, born New York, NY, 1960; admitted to bar, 1985, Connecticut; 1986, New York. *Education:* Dartmouth College (A.B., cum laude, 1982); University of Pennsylvania (J.D., 1985). ***PRACTICE AREAS:*** Commercial Litigation; Government Investigations. ***Email:*** apgaillard@dbh.com

THOMAS D. GOLDBERG, born Columbus, OH, 1954; admitted to bar, 1980, New York; 1982, District of Columbia; 1990, Connecticut. *Education:* Brown University (A.B., with honors, 1976); Columbia University (J.D., 1979). ***PRACTICE AREAS:*** Bankruptcy; Commercial Litigation; Securities Litigation; Bankruptcy Counseling. ***Email:*** tdgoldberg@dbh.com

GREGORY A. HAYES, born Hartford, CT, 1962; admitted to bar, 1988, Connecticut. *Education:* Yale University (B.S., cum laude, 1984); University of Virginia (J.D., 1988). ***PRACTICE AREAS:*** Estate Planning; Trust Administration; Estate Administration; Trust Litigation; Estate Litigation. ***Email:*** gahayes@dbh.com

ROBERT J. MILLER, born Bridgeport, CT, 1945; admitted to bar, 1971, New York; 1980, Connecticut. *Education:* Amherst College (B.A., 1967); University of Virginia (J.D., 1970). ***PRACTICE AREAS:*** Trusts and Estate Administration; Planning for Entrepreneurs; Tax-Exempt Organizations; Estate Planning; Executive Planning. ***Email:*** rjmiller@dbh.com

KENNETH W. RITT, born Philadelphia, PA, 1952; admitted to bar, 1977, Connecticut; U.S. District Court, District of Connecticut and Southern, Eastern and Northern Districts of New York; U.S. Court of Appeals, First and Second Circuits. *Education:* Brown University (A.B., magna cum laude, 1974); Harvard Law School (J.D., 1977). ***PRACTICE AREAS:*** Commercial Litigation; Franchise and Distributorship Litigation; Antitrust. ***Email:*** kwritt@dbh.com

SABINO RODRIGUEZ III, born Yonkers, NY, 1953; admitted to bar, 1979, New York; 1985, Connecticut; U.S. District Court, Southern and Eastern Districts of New York; U.S. Court of Appeals, Federal Circuit; U.S. Claims Court; U.S. Tax Court. *Education:* Harvard University (A.B., magna cum laude, 1975; J.D., 1978). ***LANGUAGES:*** Spanish. ***PRACTICE AREAS:*** Strategic Joint Ventures; Tax; Benefits and Executive Compensation; Mergers and Acquisitions; Emerging Companies. ***Email:*** srodriguez@dbh.com

BONNIE J. ROE, born New York, NY, 1953; admitted to bar, 1983, New York; 1992, Tennessee (Not admitted in Connecticut). *Education:* Smith College (A.B., magna cum laude, 1975); University of California at Berkeley (M.A., 1977); New York University School of Law (J.D., 1982). ***PRACTICE AREAS:*** Mergers and Acquisitions; Private Equity Funds; Benefit and Executive Compensation; Securities Law. ***Email:*** bjroe@dbh.com

DANIEL L. SCHWARTZ, born Chicago, IL, 1963; admitted to bar, 1989, California; 1991, Connecticut; 1992, New York and U.S. District Court, District of Connecticut; 1997, U.S. Court of Appeals, Second Circuit; 1998, U.S. District Court, Southern and Eastern Districts of New York. *Education:* Princeton University (B.A., cum laude, 1985); Boalt Hall School of Law, University of California (J.D., 1988). ***PRACTICE AREAS:*** Employment Law; Employment Litigation; Securities Litigation. ***Email:*** dlschwartz@dbh.com

JAMES F. STAPLETON, born Bridgeport, CT, 1932; admitted to bar, 1957, Connecticut and Massachusetts; 1958, District of Columbia. *Education:* Fairfield University (B.S.S., 1954); Boston College (LL.B., 1957); Georgetown University (LL.M., 1958). ***PRACTICE AREAS:*** Commercial Litigation. ***Email:*** jfstapleton@dbh.com

DAVID A. SWERDLOFF, born Buffalo, NY, 1948; admitted to bar, 1979, Connecticut. *Education:* Brown University (A.B., cum laude, 1970); Medill School of Journalism, Northwestern University (M.S., 1974); University of Connecticut (J.D., magna cum laude, 1979). ***PRACTICE AREAS:*** Emerging Companies; Technology and Intellectual Property - Business; Strategic Joint Ventures; Mergers and Acquisitions; Closely Held Businesses. ***Email:*** daswerdloff@dbh.com

STANLEY A. TWARDY, JR., born Trenton, NJ, 1951; admitted to bar, 1976, Connecticut and U.S. District Court for District of Connecticut; 1977, U.S. District Court for the Southern District of New York; 1978, District of Columbia; 1979, U.S. Supreme Court and U.S. District Court for the District of Columbia; 1983, U.S. Court of Appeals, Second Circuit. *Education:* Trinity College (B.A., with honors, 1973) Phi Beta Kappa; University of Virginia (J.D., 1976); Georgetown University Law Center (LL.M., 1980). ***PRACTICE AREAS:*** Government Investigation; Commercial Litigation. ***Email:*** satwardy@dbh.com

ASSOCIATES OF FIRM IN STAMFORD

Tricia S. Begg
Melissa L. Bellavia
Ann Lisa Braun
Rob Roy Buckingham, Jr.
David Y. Choi
Richard P. Colbert
Elizabeth Corwin
Catherine R. Critton (admission pending)
Jamal M. Dawkins
Sarah Moore Fass
Kelly E. P. Flatt
Deborah S. Gordon
Joli Lyn Gross
Lorey Rives Leddy
Natasha M. Lipcan
Margaret A. McComish
Catherine Dugan O'Connor
Thomas J. O'Neill
Brian D. Porch, Jr. (admission pending)
Allen J. Roberts, III
Mark B. Robinson (Not admitted in CT)
Jennifer L. Sachs (Not admitted in CT)
Fritz Strohmeyer
Ray A. Wynter

OF COUNSEL IN STAMFORD

Emil H. Frankel

COUNSEL IN STAMFORD

Stacey B. Babson-Smith (Not admitted in CT)
Patricia M. Canavan
Terence J. Gallagher III (Not admitted in CT)
Derek Gilman
Benedicta S. McGrath
Roland A. Paul
Jonathan B. Tropp
Kathleen D. Warner
Paulette Wunsch

(For Biographical Data on other firm personnel, see Professional Biographies at Hartford and Greenwich, Connecticut and Boston, Massachusetts)

DEPANFILIS & VALLERIE, LLC

STAMFORD, CONNECTICUT

(See Norwalk)

General Civil and Criminal Litigation Practice in all Courts. Negligence, Medical Malpractice, Taxation, Corporation, Estate Planning, Probate, Real Estate, Workers Compensation, Family and Landlord and Tenant Law.

DISERIO MARTIN O'CONNOR & CASTIGLIONI LLP

Established in 1983

ONE ATLANTIC STREET
STAMFORD, CONNECTICUT 06901-2402
Telephone: 203-358-0800
Telecopier: 203-348-2321
Email: dmoc@dmoc.com

General Practice. Litigation and Trials in all Courts. Corporate, Commercial Finance, Securities, Taxation, Banking, Foreclosure and Workout, Real Estate Law, Personal Injury and Negligence, Employment Law, Wrongful Termination, Workers Compensation, Insurance Coverage and Defense, Family, Creditors Rights and Bankruptcy, Trusts, Probate, Estate and Tax Planning.

(This Listing Continued)

(This Listing Continued)

MEMBERS OF FIRM

BRIAN T. O'CONNOR, born New Haven, Connecticut, July 5, 1942; admitted to bar, 1968, Connecticut. *Education:* Providence College (B.A., cum laude, 1965); University of Connecticut (LL.B., with honors, 1968). Managing Editor, University of Connecticut Law Review, 1967-1968. Law Clerk for Justice John R. Thim of Connecticut Supreme Court, 1968-1969. *Member:* Greenwich, Regional and Connecticut Bar Associations. ***PRACTICE AREAS:*** Corporate Law; Taxation; Securities Regulation. ***Email:*** boconnor@dmoc.com

RICHARD E. CASTIGLIONI, born New Haven, Connecticut, March 4, 1952; admitted to bar, 1977, Connecticut, U.S. District Court, District of Connecticut; 1979, Florida; 1980, U.S. District Court, Southern and Eastern Districts of New York and U.S. Court of Appeals, 2nd Circuit. *Education:* University of Connecticut (B.A., magna cum laude, 1974; J.D., with honors, 1977). Phi Beta Kappa; Phi Kappa Phi. Special Pretrial Master, Superior Court, 1984, 1986—. Lecturer, Connecticut Bar Association, "Advanced Civil Procedure," 1993. Moderator, Alternative Dispute Resolution Forum, 1995. Member, Commercial Panel of Arbitrators, American Arbitration Association. *Member:* Regional (Member, Executive Committee, 1988-1997; Treasurer, 1990; Secretary, 1991; Co-Chairman, Bench-Bar Committee, 1990-1993; First Vice President, 1993; President-Elect, 1994; President, 1995-1996) and Connecticut (Member: House of Delegates, 1990-1993, 1998—; Committee on Lawyers in the Community, 1979-1983; Young Lawyers Executive Committee, 1981-1984; Executive Committee, Litigation, 1985—; Chairman, Fairfield County Corporation, Banking and Business Law Committee of the Young Lawyers Section, 1981-1984; Counsel of Bar Presidents, 1994-1997) Bar Associations; The Florida Bar; The Association of Trial Lawyers of America; Connecticut Trial Lawyers Association. ***PRACTICE AREAS:*** Commercial Litigation; Personal Injury Litigation; Labor Litigation. ***Email:*** rcastiglioni@dmoc.com

WILLIAM A. DURKIN III, born Bronxville, New York, November 1, 1954; admitted to bar, 1980, Connecticut, U.S. District Court, District of Connecticut and U.S. Court of Appeals, 2nd Circuit. *Education:* St. Lawrence University (B.A., 1976); Syracuse University (J.D., 1980). *Member:* Regional (Member, Executive Committee, 1997—; Co-Chair, Business Law Committee, 1995-1996), Connecticut (Member, Section on Corporations and other Business Organizations; Member, Young Lawyers Executive Committee, 1984-1985; Chairman, Fairfield County Corporation, Banking and Business Law Committee of the Young Lawyers Section, 1984-1985) and American Bar Associations; National Association of Industrial and Office Properties (NAIOP), (Board Member, 1999-2000). ***PRACTICE AREAS:*** Corporate Law; Commercial Finance; Commercial Real Estate. ***Email:*** wdurkin@dmoc.com

SCOTT S. CENTRELLA, born Sarasota, Florida, October 14, 1958; admitted to bar, 1983, Connecticut and U.S. District Court, District of Connecticut; 1997, U.S. District Court, Southern District of New York. *Education:* Fairfield University (B.A., cum laude, 1980); University of Connecticut (J.D., 1983). Omicron Delta Epsilon. *Member:* Regional (Co-Chair, Litigation Committee, 1995-1998) and Connecticut (Treasurer, Young Lawyers Section, 1986-1987; Member: Labor and Employment Law Section, 1987—; Federal Practice Section, 1988—; Workers Compensation Section, 1988—) Bar Associations; The American Inns of Court; The Association of Trial Lawyers of America; Connecticut Trial Lawyers Association. ***PRACTICE AREAS:*** Employment Law; Employment Litigation; Commercial Litigation; Family Law; Workers Compensation. ***Email:*** scentrella@dmoc.com

ROBERT E. MURRAY, JR., born Philadelphia, Pennsylvania, January 26, 1958; admitted to bar, 1984, Connecticut. *Education:* University of Massachusetts (B.A., summa cum laude, 1980); University of Connecticut (J.D., 1983). *Member:* Regional and Connecticut Bar Associations (Member, Real Property Section). ***PRACTICE AREAS:*** Commercial Real Estate; Residential Real Estate; Banking Law. ***Email:*** rmurray@dmoc.com

SCOTT M. HARRINGTON, born Meriden, Connecticut, December 21, 1962; admitted to bar, 1987, Connecticut; 1988, U.S. District Court, District of Connecticut; 1997, U.S. District Court, Southern District of New York. *Education:* Colgate University (B.A., cum laude, 1984); University of Connecticut (J.D., 1987). Phi Alpha Theta. *Member:* Regional and Connecticut (Member: Executive Committee, Construction Law Section, 1993 —; Litigation Section, 1993—; Commercial Law and Bankruptcy Section, 1992—; Computer Law Section, 1999—) Bar Associations; The Association of Trial Lawyers of America; Connecticut Trial Lawyers Association. ***PRACTICE AREAS:*** Commercial Litigation; Construction Litigation; Bankruptcy. ***Email:*** sharrington@dmoc.com

KEVIN T. KATSKE, born Norwich, Connecticut, April 15, 1960; admitted to bar, 1987, Connecticut. *Education:* Emory University (B.A., 1982); University of Bridgeport School of Law (J.D., 1987). Phi Delta Phi. Recipient: American Jurisprudence Awards in the Study of Real Estate Transactions and U.C.C. Article 9 Secured Transactions; Award for Superior Class Room Performance, 1987. Executive Managing Editor, The Connecticut Probate Law Journal, 1987. Author: Note, "Sterilization of the Mentally Retarded: An Analysis of Judicial and Legislative Standards," Vol. 1, No. 2, Connecticut Probate Law Journal 217. *Member:* Regional and Connecticut (Member, Real Property Section and Business Section) Bar Associations. ***PRACTICE AREAS:*** Commercial Finance; Corporate Law; Real Estate. ***Email:*** kkatske@dmoc.com

JONATHAN P. WHITCOMB, born Stamford, Connecticut, September 19, 1964; admitted to bar, 1990, Connecticut; 1991, New York; 1995, U.S. District Court, Southern District of New York; U.S. District Court, District of Connecticut. *Education:* Hobart College (B.A., 1987); New England School of Law (J.D., 1990). Dean's List. *Member:* Regional and Connecticut Bar Associations. ***PRACTICE AREAS:*** Commercial Litigation; Insurance Coverage; Insurance Defense; Intellectual Property; Personal Injury. ***Email:*** jwhitcomb@dmoc.com

DAVID L. DUFORT, born Malone, New York, June 12, 1965; admitted to bar, 1991, New York and Connecticut. *Education:* Siena College (B.B.A., magna cum laude, 1987); Albany Law School of Union University (J.D., cum laude, 1990). Member, Justinian Society. Note and Comment Editor, Albany Law Review. *Member:* Connecticut (Member, Estates and Probate Section) New York State (Member, Sections on: Trusts and Estates; Elder Law) and Regional Bar Associations. ***PRACTICE AREAS:*** Trusts and Estates; Probate; Commercial Law; Corporate Law. ***Email:*** ddufort@dmoc.com

ASSOCIATES

JASON A. MARSH, born New Haven, Connecticut, July 22, 1974; admitted to bar, 1999, Connecticut; 2000, New York. *Education:* Tufts University (B.A., 1996); University of Connecticut (J.D., 1999). Omicron Delta Epsilon. Member, University of Connecticut Moot Court Board. Associate Editor, University of Connecticut Law Review, 1998-1999. ***PRACTICE AREAS:*** Corporate Law; Commercial Leasing; Commercial Finance; Taxation; Trusts and Estates; Commercial Real Estate; Residential Real Estate. ***Email:*** jmarsh@dmoc.com

LAURA R. SHATTUCK, born Norwalk, Connecticut, May 26, 1969; admitted to bar, 1999, Connecticut. *Education:* Loyola University (B.A., 1991); Quinnipiac College School of Law (J.D., cum laude, 1999). Phi Delta Phi. Recipient: Distinguished Academic Achievement Award; Service to the Community Award. ***PRACTICE AREAS:*** Litigation. ***Email:*** lshattuck@dmoc.com

MERRIE FEDOR HAWLEY, born Bridgeport, Connecticut, July 23, 1965; admitted to bar, 1999, Connecticut; 2000, U.S. District Court, District of Connecticut and New York. *Education:* Fairfield University (B.A., 1996); Quinnipiac College School of Law (J.D., magna cum laude, 1999). Recipient: Distinguished Academic Achievement Awards in Property and Legal Research Writing II; Corpus Juris Secundum Award for Scholastic Excellence; Superior Classroom Performance Award; Award for Academic Excellence. Member, 1997-1998 and Lead Articles Editor, 1998-1999, Quinnipiac Law Review, 1998-1999. *Member:* Connecticut and American Bar Associations. ***PRACTICE AREAS:*** Litigation. ***Email:*** mhawley@dmoc.com

JAMES P. CARLON, born Plantation, Florida, August 30, 1974; admitted to bar, 1999, Connecticut; 2000, New York. *Education:* Fairfield University (B.A., 1996); New York Law School (J.D., 1999). Articles Editor, New York Law School Law Review, 1998-1999. Recipient, New York Law School Academic Scholarship. *Member:* Connecticut and American Bar Associations. ***PRACTICE AREAS:*** Corporate Law. ***Email:*** jcarlon@dmoc.com

KEVIN R. BRADY, born Hartford, Connecticut, December 10, 1971; admitted to bar, 2000, Connecticut; 2001, New York. *Education:* University of Connecticut (B.A., 1994); Quinnipiac University School of Law (J.D., 1999). Member, Moot Court. Recipient, Outstanding Brief Award, Albert R. Mugel, National Tax Moot Court Competition, 1999. Law Clerk, Superior Court, State of Connecticut, 1999. ***PRACTICE AREAS:*** Commercial Litigation; Complex Litigation. ***Email:*** kbrady@dmoc.com

ALICIA B. BROMFIELD, born Hartford, Connecticut, May 17, 1974; admitted to bar, 1999, Connecticut; 2000, New York. *Education:* The Johns Hopkins University (B.A., 1996); Quinnipiac University, School of Law (J.D., 1999). Recipient: Distinguished Academic Achievement Award, Legal Skills; Dean's Scholarship Outstanding Legal Scholarship Award. Author: "The Florida Bar v. American Senior Citizens Alliance: Is Gathering the Necessary Information the Unlicensed Practice of Law?" Quinnipiac Probate Law Journal, Vol. 12 #4 (1998). *Member:* Connecticut Bar Association; Connecticut Trial Lawyers Association. ***PRACTICE AREAS:*** Litigation; Commercial Litigation. ***Email:*** aliciab@DMOC.com

OF COUNSEL

EUGENE A. DISERIO, born New York, N.Y., May 14, 1927; admitted to bar, 1953, New York; 1969, U.S. District Court, Southern and Eastern Districts of New York; 1970, Connecticut. *Education:* Fordham University (B.A., 1948; LL.B., 1951). Phi Alpha Delta. *Member:* The Association of the Bar of the City of New York; Stamford Regional (Member, Executive Committee, 1984-1988), New Canaan and Connecticut Bar Associations.

GARRY H. MORTON, born Hartford, Connecticut, May 19, 1952; admitted to bar, 1977, Connecticut; 1978, U.S. District Court, District of Connecticut

(This Listing Continued)

DISERIO MARTIN O'CONNOR & CASTIGLIONI LLP, Stamford—Continued

and U.S. District Court, Southern District of New York; 1980, U.S. Tax Court. *Education:* Dartmouth College (A.B., summa cum laude, 1974); Columbia University (J.D., 1977). Harlan Fiske Stone Scholar. Co-author: "Significant Developments in Probate Law," Connecticut Bar Journal, February, 1981. *Member:* Stamford Regional, Connecticut (Member, Estates and Probate Section) and American (Member, Real Property, Probate and Trust Law Section) Bar Associations. (Also practicing individually). ***PRACTICE AREAS:*** Estate Planning; Estate Administration; Trust Administration; Fiduciary Taxation. ***Email:*** gmorton@dmoc.com

JOHN V. A. MURRAY, born New York, N.Y., July 26, 1952; admitted to bar, 1977, Connecticut. *Education:* Brown University (A.B., 1974); University of Connecticut (J.D., with honors, 1977). *Member:* Greenwich, Connecticut and American Bar Associations. ***PRACTICE AREAS:*** Estate Planning; Estate Administration; Real Estate Law; Commercial Transactions. ***Email:*** jvam@dmoc.com

REPRESENTATIVE CLIENTS: Fortune Brands; A.T. Clayton & Co., Inc.; Gulf Insurance; Kemper Insurance; Town of Greenwich; Chase Manhattan Automotive Finance Corp.; Subaru Leasing Corp.; BMW Financial Services of North America; Interliant, Inc.; Thorsen, Brown & Plunkett; Mees Pierson Holding Inc.; First American Title Insurance Company; Washington Mutual; Summit Bank; The Mutual Life Insurance Company of New York; Mercedes Benz Credit Corp.; Trizec Hahn Office Properties, Inc.; The Triarc Corp.; Book Automation, Inc.; Newsbank; Federal Deposit Insurance Corp.; AZ Marketing Services, Inc.; Thule, Inc.; Fleet National Bank; The Chase Manhattan Bank, N.A.; People's Bank; Citibank, N.A.; State Street Bank and Trust Company; Navigator Communications; Seaboard Properties; Home Federal Savings Bank; Cognitronics Corp.; The Perkin-Elmer Corporation; Avon Products, Inc.; MemberWorks Incorporated; Brown Brothers Harriman & Co.; Capital Access Network.

DOUGHERTY, DOUGHERTY & VECCHIOLLA

STAMFORD, CONNECTICUT

(See Greenwich)

General Practice. Estate Planning and Probate Law. Real Estate, Taxation and Corporate Law, Business Law, Trusts and Estates.

DUPONT AND RADLAUER, L.L.P.

STAMFORD, CONNECTICUT

(See New London)

Litigation, Probate, Business Organization.

DURKIN & POLERA, P.C.

Established in 1991

970 SUMMER STREET, FIRST FLOOR

STAMFORD, CONNECTICUT 06905

Telephone: 203-327-0044

Fax: 203-327-0088

URL: http://www.lawyers.com/durkin&polera

Tarrytown, New York Office: 14 North Broadway, 10591. Telephone: 914-631-1176.

General Civil, Business, Litigation and Estates Practice. Business Transactions, Trusts and Estate Planning/Administration, Tax Planning and Compliance, Real Estate and Civil Litigation at the Trial and Appellate Levels in all Courts in the Personal Injury, Negligence, Contract, Commercial, Real Estate and Employment areas of the law, NASD and NYSE Arbitrations.

MARK C. DURKIN, born Tuckahoe, New York, April 10, 1959; admitted to bar, 1984, Connecticut; 1985, U.S. District Court, District of Connecticut; 1988, New York; 1989, U.S. District Court, Southern and Eastern Districts of New York; 1994, U.S. Supreme Court. *Education:* University of Maryland (B.A., 1981); Pace University (J.D., 1984). Phi Beta Kappa. Law Clerk to Associate Justice Robert Callahan, Connecticut Supreme Court, 1987-1988. *Member:* Stamford/Norwalk Regional, New York State, Connecticut and American Bar Associations; Connecticut Trial Lawyers Association; Connecticut Attorneys Title Insurance Company. ***PRACTICE AREAS:*** Civil Litigation; Appellate Litigation; Personal Injury; Negligence; Commercial Law; Employment Law; Real Estate; NASD Arbitration; New York Stock Exchange Arbitration. ***Email:*** mdurkin@ntplx.net

JOHN C. POLERA, born White Plains, New York, April 16, 1960; admitted to bar, 1986, New York and Connecticut; 1989, U.S. District Court, Southern District of New York; 1992, U.S. District Court, District of Connecticut and U.S. Tax Court; 1993, U.S. Supreme Court. *Education:* Tulane University (B.S.M., cum laude, 1982); University of Miami (J.D., 1985); Boston University (LL.M., 1986). Certified Public Accountant, Connecticut, 1990. *Member:* Connecticut

(This Listing Continued)

and New York State Bar Associations. ***PRACTICE AREAS:*** Tax Planning; Trusts and Estates and Probate; Real Estate; Business Planning. ***Email:*** jpolera@ntplx.net

WAYNE D. EFFRON, P.C.

STAMFORD, CONNECTICUT

(See Greenwich)

Matrimonial Law and Civil Litigation including Personal Injury and Commercial Law at the Trial and Appellate Levels.

EMMET, MARVIN & MARTIN, LLP

Established in 1806

1351 WASHINGTON BOULEVARD

STAMFORD, CONNECTICUT 06902

Telephone: 203-425-1400

Fax: 203-425-1410

Email: postmaster@emmetmarvin.com

URL: http://www.emmetmarvin.com

New York, New York Office: 120 Broadway. Telephone: 212-238-3000. Fax: 212-238-3100.

Morristown, New Jersey Office: 177 Madison Avenue. Telephone: 973-538-5600. Fax: 973-538-6448.

General Practice, including Banking and Finance, Real Estate, Corporate, Securities, Tax, Employee Benefits, Trusts, Estates, Commercial Litigation, Employment Law, Creditors Rights and Bankruptcy Law.

MEMBERS OF THE FIRM

JOHN F. BARTLETT, admitted to bar, 1967, Virginia; 1976, District of Columbia; 1981, New York; 1984, Connecticut. *Education:* Washington & Lee University (B.A., 1964; LL.B., 1967). Assistant General Counsel, National Corporation for Housing Partnerships, Washington, D.C., 1972-1977. ***Email:*** jbartlett@emmetmarvin.com

BENJAMIN H. GREEN, admitted to bar, 1978, New York; 1985, Connecticut. *Education:* Brandeis University (B.A., magna cum laude, 1974); Cornell University School of Law (J.D., magna cum laude, 1977). Order of the Coif. Member, Board of Editors, Cornell Law Review, 1976-1977. Assistant District Attorney, New York County, 1977-1980. ***Email:*** bgreen@emmetmarvin.com

EMMETT & GLANDER

Established in 1989

45 FRANKLIN STREET

STAMFORD, CONNECTICUT 06901

Telephone: 203-324-7744

Facsimile: 203-969-1319

URL: http://www.emmettandglander.com

Email: offices@emmettandglander.com

URL: http://www.lawyers.com/emmett&glander

Newtown, Connecticut Office: 17 Pond Brook Road, P.O. Box 724, 06470. Telephone: 203-270-9272. Facsimile: 203-426-1270.

Litigation, Employee Rights and Benefits, Personal Injury, Professional Negligence, Products Liability, Discrimination, Civil Rights, Workers Compensation, Small Business and Corporate, Banking, Family, Real Estate, Probate and Estate Planning, Education, Arbitration and Mediation.

MEMBERS OF FIRM

KATHRYN EMMETT, born Los Angeles, California, December 13, 1944; admitted to bar, 1970, Connecticut and U.S. District Court, District of Connecticut; 1971, U.S. Court of Appeals, Second Circuit; 1979, U.S. Court of Appeals, Fifth Circuit; 1980, U.S. Court of Appeals, Fourth Circuit; 1981, U.S. Court of Appeals, Eleventh Circuit; 1975, U.S. Supreme Court; 1976, California. *Education:* Radcliffe College (B.A., magna cum laude, 1966); Yale University School of Law (J.D., 1970). Co-Author, "Stephenson's Connecticut Civil Procedure," 3rd Edition, The Atlantic Law Book Company (1997). Member, Board of Governors, Connecticut Trial Lawyers Association. Charter Fellow, Connecticut Bar Foundation. President of Board, Center for Children's Advocacy. Superior Court Judge, State of Connecticut, 1982-1988. Visiting Scholar, Yale Law School, 1988-1989. Instructor, Clinical Studies (Trial Practice), Yale Law School, 1989. Special Master, District of Connecticut; Attorney Trial Referee, 1990—. *Member:* Stamford/Norwalk and Connecticut Bar Associations; The Association of Trial Lawyers of America; Connecticut Trial Lawyers Association; National Employment Lawyers Association; Connecticut Employment Lawyers Association. ***PRACTICE AREAS:*** Litigation; Employee Rights

(This Listing Continued)

and Benefits; Professional Negligence; Product Liability; Personal Injury; Discrimination; Civil Rights; Small Business Transactions and Litigation; Arbitration; Mediation. **Email:** kemmett@emmettandglander.com

JANE W. GLANDER, born Utica, New York, December 16, 1954; admitted to bar, 1989, Connecticut; 1990, U.S. District Court, District of Connecticut. *Education:* Fairfield University (B.A., 1976; M.A., 1980); St. John's University School of Law (J.D., 1988). *Member:* Connecticut Bar Association; Connecticut Trial Lawyers Association; The Association of Trial Lawyers of America. ***PRACTICE AREAS:*** Civil Litigation; Personal Injury; Workers Compensation; Corporate Law; Small Business Law; Family; Juvenile Criminal Law; Real Estate; Foreclosures; Probate; Estate Planning. **Email:** jglander@emmettandglander.com

ASSOCIATE

CHRISTINE CAULFIELD, born Middletown, Connecticut, December 25, 1969; admitted to bar, 1996, Connecticut; 1997, New York; 1998, U.S. District Court, District of Connecticut. *Education:* Rhode Island College (B.A., summa cum laude, 1993); University of Connecticut (J.D., 1996). *Member:* Stamford/Norwalk and Connecticut Bar Associations; Connecticut Trial Lawyers Association; The Association of Trial Lawyers of America. **Email:** ccaulfield@emmettandglander.com

EPSTEIN BECKER & GREEN, P.C.

SUITE 1800, ONE LANDMARK SQUARE

STAMFORD, CONNECTICUT 06901-2601

Telephone: 203-348-3737
Facsimile: 203-324-9291
Email: mail@ebglaw.com
URL: http://www.ebglaw.com

New York, N.Y. Office: 250 Park Avenue. Telephone: 212-351-4500.
Washington, D.C. Office: 1227 25th Street, N.W., Suite 700. Telephone: 202-861-0900.
San Francisco, California Office: Epstein Becker & Green, Two Embarcadero Center, Suite 1650. Telephone: 415-398-3500.
Los Angeles, California Office: Epstein Becker & Green, Suite 500, 1875 Century Park, East. Telephone: 310-556-8861.
Dallas, Texas Office: Park Central VII, 12750 Merit Drive, Suite 1320. Telephone: 972-628-2450.
Newark, New Jersey Office: Two Gateway Center, 12th Floor. Telephone: 973-642-1900.
Boston, Massachusetts Office: 75 State Street. Telephone: 617-342-4000.
Chicago, Illinois Office: 150 North Michigan Avenue, Suite 420. Telephone: 312-499-1400.
Atlanta, Georgia Office: Suite 1400, The Lenox Building, 3399 Peachtree Road, N.E. Telephone: 404-812-5680.

General Practice. Corporation, Securities and Commercial Law. Health Care and Hospital Law. Management Labor Relations and Employee Benefits Law. Equal Employment Opportunity and Affirmative Action Law and Practice. Taxation, Insurance, Government Procurement, Municipal Finance, Real Estate, Political Activities, Legislation and Election Law. Arbitration, Administrative Proceedings, State and Federal Civil and Appellate Practice.

MEMBERS OF THE FIRM

PETER L. ALTIERI, born Norwalk, Connecticut, December 7, 1955; admitted to bar, 1981, New York and U.S. District Court, Southern and Eastern Districts of New York; 1983, U.S. District Court, District Court of Connecticut and U.S. District Court, Western and Northern Districts of New York; 1984, U.S. Supreme Court; 1986, U.S. Court of Appeals, 2nd Circuit; 1988, Connecticut. *Education:* Georgetown University (A.B., 1977); Fordham University (J.D., 1980). (Also at New York, N.Y. Office). **Email:** paltieri@ebglaw.com

DAVID S. POPPICK, born Keyport, New Jersey, February 6, 1954; admitted to bar, 1981, New York; 1982, U.S. District Court, Southern and Eastern Districts of New York; 1989, U.S. Supreme Court and U.S. Court of Appeals, 2nd Circuit; 1992, U.S. Court of Appeals, 1st Circuit; 1994, Connecticut and U.S. District Court, District of Connecticut; 1996, U.S. District Court, Western District of New York; 1997, U.S. District Court, Northern District of New York; 1999, U.S. Court of Appeals, 5th Circuit. *Education:* Northwestern University (B.S.J., 1976); Western New England College (J.D., 1980). Editor-in-Chief, Western New England Law Review, 1979-1980. Author: "Educational Malpractice," 1 Western New England Law Review 759, 1979. *Member:* New York State (Member, Employment and Labor Relations Committee) and American (Member, Litigation Section) Bar Associations. ***PRACTICE AREAS:*** Employment Law and Litigation. **Email:** dpoppick@ebglaw.com

PETER M. STEIN, born New York, N.Y., May 9, 1950; admitted to bar, 1976, New York; 1977, District of Columbia; 1987, Connecticut and U.S. District Court, District of Connecticut. *Education:* Bucknell University (B.A., 1972); George Washington University (J.D., 1975). Associate General Counsel, Health Industries, Inc., 1975-1981. Labor Counsel, U.S. Industries, Inc., 1981-1984. Instructor, Cornell Univ. School of Industrial and Labor Relations, EEO Studies Program. *Member:* The District of Columbia Bar. ***PRACTICE AREAS:*** Labor and Employment Law. **Email:** pstein@ebglaw.com

(This Listing Continued)

MICHAEL R. ZELLER, born Bronx, New York, April 28, 1946; admitted to bar, 1975, New Jersey and U.S. District Court, District of New Jersey; 1976, New York; 1977, U.S. District Court, Southern District of New York; 1978, U.S. District Court, Eastern District of New York; 1981, U.S. Court of Appeals, Third Circuit; 1987, Connecticut; 1988, U.S. District Court, District of Connecticut and U.S. District Court, Eastern District of Wisconsin; 1993, U.S. Court of Appeals, Second Circuit; 1996, U.S. District Court, Northern District of New York. *Education:* Queens College of the City University of New York (B.S., 1969); St. John's University (J.D., 1975). *Member:* The Association of the Bar of the City of New York; New York State, New Jersey State and Connecticut Bar Associations. (Also at New York, N.Y. Office). ***PRACTICE AREAS:*** Labor and Employment Law. **Email:** mzeller@ebglaw.com

SENIOR ATTORNEY

MARY A. GAMBARDELLA, born New Haven, Connecticut, October 14, 1958; admitted to bar, 1983, Connecticut and U.S. District Court, District of Connecticut; 1987, New York; 1992, U.S. Court of Appeals, Second Circuit; 1993, U.S. District Court, Southern District of New York; 1997, U.S. District Court, Eastern District of New York. *Education:* Albertus Magnus College (B.A., cum laude, 1980); Quinnipiac College School of Law (J.D., cum laude, 1983). Managing Editor, Quinnipiac College School of Law Law Review, 1982-1983. Author: "Another Victory for the Consumer: Hinchliffe, UB Law Review, 1982. Instructor, University of Bridgeport Paralegal Program, 1984-1990. ***PRACTICE AREAS:*** Employment Law; Commercial Litigation; Contracts; Sports; Entertainment. **Email:** mgambard@ebglaw.com

ASSOCIATES

JONATHAN M. PLISSNER, born New York, N.Y., June 10, 1964; admitted to bar, 1989, California and U.S. Court of Appeals, Ninth Circuit; 1990, U.S. District Court, Central District of California; 1992, U.S. District Court, Southern and Northern Districts of California; 1995, New York, New Jersey and U.S. District Court, District of New Jersey; 1996, U.S. District Court, Southern District of New York; 1999, District of Columbia; 2001, Connecticut. *Education:* State University of New York at Binghamton (B.A., 1986); University of California at Los Angeles (J.D., 1989). Phi Beta Kappa. *Member:* State Bar of California; The District of Columbia Bar. ***PRACTICE AREAS:*** Commercial Litigation; Labor and Employment; First Amendment Law; Defamation; Privacy Law. **Email:** jplissner@ebglaw.com

BRADFORD J. SULLIVAN, born New Bedford, Massachusetts, December 8, 1969; admitted to bar, 2001, Connecticut. *Education:* University of Massachusetts (B.A., History, 1993); Quinnipiac College (J.D., 2001). Phi Alpha Delta. *Member: Member:* Connecticut and American Bar Associations. ***PRACTICE AREAS:*** Labor and Employment; Litigation. **Email:** bsulliva@ebglaw.com

ELIZABETH STEBBINS TORKELSEN, admitted to bar, 1992, Massachusetts; 1994, New York and Connecticut; 1995, U.S. District Court, District of Massachusetts and U.S. District Court, Southern, Eastern and Northern Districts of New York and U.S. District Court, District of Connecticut; 1996, U.S. Court of Appeals, Second Circuit. *Education:* Bates College (B.A., cum laude, 1987); Boston College Law School (J.D., cum laude, 1992). Phi Beta Kappa. ***PRACTICE AREAS:*** Labor and Employment Law; Litigation. **Email:** etorkels@ebglaw.com

STEVEN J. YOUNES, born Allentown, Pennsylvania, March 13, 1966; admitted to bar, 1991, Connecticut; 1992, New York; 1994, U.S. District Court, District of Connecticut and U.S. District Court, Southern and Eastern Districts of New York. *Education:* Moravian College (B.A., cum laude, 1988); Quinnipiac College School of Law, formerly known as the University of Bridgeport (J.D., 1991); Oxford University. ***PRACTICE AREAS:*** Labor and Employment Law; Litigation. **Email:** syounes@ebglaw.com

(For other Personnel and Biographical Data, see Professional Biographies at Los Angeles and San Francisco, California, Washington, D.C., Miami, Florida, Chicago, Illinois, Boston, Massachusetts, Newark, New Jersey, New York, New York and Dallas, Texas Offices)

FINN DIXON & HERLING LLP

Established in 1987

ONE LANDMARK SQUARE, SUITE 1400

STAMFORD, CONNECTICUT 06901-2689

Telephone: 203-325-5000

Telecopier: 203-348-5777

Corporate Law, Mergers and Acquisitions, Securities Law, Venture Capital Financing, Corporate Finance and Restructuring, Commercial Litigation, Banking and Lending Law, Bankruptcy and Workouts, Employee Benefits and the Federal and State Taxation of Businesses and Business Transactions.

HAROLD B. FINN III, born Bronxville, New York, November 7, 1938; admitted to bar, 1967, New York; 1968, District of Columbia; 1974, Connecticut and U.S. Tax Court; U.S. District Court, Southern District of New York; U.S. District Court, District of Connecticut; U.S. Supreme Court. *Education:* Yale University (B.A., 1960); Columbia University (LL.B., magna cum laude, 1966). Articles Editor, Columbia Law Review, 1965-1966. Law Clerk, Justice Stanley F. Reed (Ret.) and Chief Justice Earl Warren, U.S. Supreme Court, 1966-1967. Chairman, Securities, Advisory Committee to Connecticut Banking Commissioner, 1999—, Member, 1979—. Member, Advisory Committee on Revision of Banking Laws of Connecticut, 1993-1994. Member, Blue Ribbon Commission of Connecticut Attorney General, 1982-1983. *Member:* Connecticut (Chairman, Executive Committee, 1992-1994; Task Force on Connecticut Business Corporation Act, Co-Chair, 1994-1997, Member, 1976—, Business Law Section) and American (Member, Federal Regulation of Securities Committee, 1979—; Chair, 1996-1998, Co-Chair, 1994-1996, Vice-Chair, 1992-1994 and Member, 1979—, Banking Law Committee; Chair, 1981— and Member of Council, 2000—, Banking Law Subcommittee on Securities; Business Law Section) Bar Associations; American Law Institute (Member, Consultative Group for Restatement Third, Trusts). Fellow, James W. Cooper Fellows Program, Connecticut Bar Foundation. ***PRACTICE AREAS:*** Securities Law; Banking Law; Corporate Law. ***Email:*** hfinn@fdh.com

BRETT W. DIXON, born Joliet, Illinois, March 2, 1955; admitted to bar, 1982, Connecticut; 1987, U.S. Tax Court. *Education:* Williams College (B.A., magna cum laude, 1977); Cornell University (M.B.A., with distinction, 1981; J.D., magna cum laude, 1982). Phi Beta Kappa; Order of the Coif. Member, Cornell International Law Journal, 1980-1982. *Member:* Connecticut (Member: Executive Committee, 1993—; Federal Business Taxes Subcommittee, 1993—; Limited Liability Company Subcommittee, 1993—; Corporation Business Tax, 1993—, Tax Section) and American (Member: Corporate Tax Committee, 1989—; Taxable Acquisitions Subcommittee, 1991—, Tax Law Section) Bar Associations. ***PRACTICE AREAS:*** Taxation Law; Corporate Law. ***Email:*** bdixon@fdh.com

MICHAEL J. HERLING, born Bay Shore, New York, August 29, 1957; admitted to bar, 1982, Connecticut. *Education:* Colgate University (A.B., magna cum laude, 1979); Stanford University (J.D., 1982). Phi Beta Kappa; Phi Alpha Theta. *Member:* Connecticut (Member, Executive Committee, Business Law Section; Reporter, Model Business Corporation Act Task Force) and American (Member, Business Law Section) Bar Associations. ***PRACTICE AREAS:*** Corporate Law; Mergers and Acquisitions Law; Corporate Finance; Securities; Venture Capital Financing Law. ***Email:*** mherling@fdh.com

DAVID I. ALBIN, born New York, New York, February 25, 1959; admitted to bar, 1984, Connecticut. *Education:* Trinity College (B.A., with honors in Political Science, 1981); Yale University (J.D., 1984). Phi Beta Kappa; Pi Gamma Mu. *Member:* Stamford/Norwalk, Connecticut (Member, Executive Committee, Business Law Section) and American (Member: Negotiated Acquisitions Committee, 1996—; Model Asset Acquisition Agreement Task Force, 1996—; Business Law Section) Bar Associations. ***PRACTICE AREAS:*** Corporate Law; Mergers and Acquisitions Law; Securities Law; Corporate Finance; Venture Capital Financing Law. ***Email:*** dalbin@fdh.com

CHARLES J. DOWNEY III, born Boston, Massachusetts, July 14, 1964; admitted to bar, 1990, New York; 1994, Connecticut. *Education:* University of Pennsylvania, Wharton Undergraduate Division (B.S., cum laude, 1986); New York University School of Law (J.D., 1989). Member, 1987-1988, and Executive Editor, 1988-1989, Annual Survey of American Law. Author: "Federalism in the Era of Michigan v. Long - Delaware v. Van Arsdall and the Continued Need for Coherent State Adjudication," 1988 Ann. Surv. Am. L., Vol. 2. Member, State Board of Directors and Secretary, Connecticut Venture Group. *Member:* Connecticut (Member, Business Law Section) and American (Member, Business Law Section) Bar Associations. ***PRACTICE AREAS:*** Corporate Law; Mergers and Acquisitions Law; Securities Law; Venture Capital Financing Law. ***Email:*** cdowney@fdh.com

JAMES R. HAWKINS, II, born Brooklyn, New York, December 14, 1941; admitted to bar, 1967, New York; 1976, Connecticut; U.S. Tax Court; U.S. District Court, Southern and Eastern Districts of New York; U.S. District Court, District of Connecticut; U.S. Court of Appeals, Second Circuit; U.S. Supreme Court. *Education:* Fordham College (A.B., 1963); Syracuse University (LL.B., 1966). Syracuse Law Review, 1965-1966. Co-Author: "Annual Survey of Broker-Dealer Litigation," Securities Industry Association and Litigation Section, American Bar Association, 1991-1998, Moderator and Co-Chair; "Review of Developments in Business and Corporate Litigation, Federal Securities Litigation," Business Law Section, American Bar Association, 1995—. Co-chair, Securities Litigation Subcommittee. Chair, Small Firms Subcommittee, Business and Corporate Litigation Committee, Business Law Section, American Bar Association. *Member:* The Association of the Bar of the City of New York; Connecticut and American Bar Associations; Federal Bar Council; Securities Industry Association. ***PRACTICE AREAS:*** Commercial Litigation; Securities; Antitrust; Alternative Dispute Resolution. ***Email:*** jhawkins@fdh.com

DONNA NELSON HELLER, born Brockton, Massachusetts, October 6, 1954; admitted to bar, 1981, New York; 1985, Connecticut; U.S. District Court, Southern and Eastern Districts of New York; U.S. District Court, District of Connecticut; U.S. Court of Appeals, Second Circuit; U.S. Supreme Court. *Education:* Bryn Mawr College (A.B., magna cum laude with honors in Fine Arts, 1976); University of Pennsylvania, Wharton Graduate Division (M.B.A., with distinction, 1980); University of Pennsylvania Law School (J.D., cum laude, 1980). Arthur Littleton Legal Writing Fellow, 1979-1980. Connecticut Superior Court Attorney Trial Referee, 1998—. *Member:* The Association of the Bar of the City of New York; Stamford Regional (Member, Committees on: Employment; Bench and Bar; Litigation), Connecticut (Member, Executive Committee Commercial Law and Bankruptcy Section, 1998—; Member, Sections on: Labor and Employment Law; Litigation; Federal Practice) and American (Member, Sections on: Labor and Employment Law; Litigation) Bar Associations; Federal Bar Council. American Inns of Court. ***PRACTICE AREAS:*** Commercial Litigation; Business Torts; Employment Law; Creditors' Rights Law; Bankruptcy Law. ***Email:*** dheller@fdh.com

ERNEST M. LORIMER, born Niagara Falls, New York, January 13, 1952; admitted to bar, 1979, New York; 1984, Connecticut. *Education:* Princeton University (A.B., 1974); Yale Law School (J.D., 1977). Senior Topic Editor, Business Law, Connecticut Bar Journal, 1997—. Co-Editor, *Connecticut Business Corporation Act Sourcebook,* 1997. Co-Author: "Business Entities," Connecticut Legal Deskbook, 1998. *Member:* Connecticut (Member, Sections on: Business Law (Vice Chairman, 1998-2000; Chairman, 2000—); Banking Law), New York State and American (Member, Sections on: Business Law; International Law) Bar Associations. ***PRACTICE AREAS:*** Public and Corporate Finance; Securities; Mergers and Acquisitions. ***Email:*** elorimer@fdh.com

PATRICK J. McHUGH, born Lynbrook, New York, March 13, 1965; admitted to bar, 1990, New York; 1995, Connecticut; U.S. District Court, Eastern and Southern Districts of New York; U.S. District Court, District of Connecticut. *Education:* Fordham University (B.A., summa cum laude, in cursu honorum, 1986) Phi Beta Kappa; Cornell University (J.D., cum laude, 1989). Editor, Cornell Law Review, 1987-1989. Law Clerk, Hon. Joseph M. McLaughlin, U.S. District Court, Eastern District of New York, 1989-1990, U.S. Court of Appeals, Second Circuit, 1990-1991. *Member:* The Association of the Bar of the City of New York; Connecticut (Member, Sections on: Litigation; Consumer Law; Commercial Law; Federal Practice) and American (Member, Sections on: Business Law; Litigation; Committee on Consumer Financial Services) Bar Associations; The Regional Bar Association of Stamford, Norwalk, Darien and Wilton, Inc. (Member, Sections on: Litigation and Business Law). ***PRACTICE AREAS:*** Commercial Litigation. ***Email:*** pmchugh@fdh.com

EDMUND M. REMONDINO, born Queens Village, New York, August 28, 1961; admitted to bar, 1987, New York; 1990, Connecticut. *Education:* State University of New York at Binghamton (B.A., 1983); New York University (J.D., 1986). Phi Beta Kappa; Phi Alpha Delta. *Member:* Stamford/Norwalk, Connecticut (Member, Financial Institutions Section) and American (Member, Business Law Section) Bar Associations. ***PRACTICE AREAS:*** Banking Law; Corporate Law; Mergers and Acquisitions; Securities Law. ***Email:*** eremondi@fdh.com

EDWARD A. WEISS, born New Hyde Park, New York, August 17, 1956; admitted to bar, 1982, Connecticut. *Education:* Swarthmore College (B.A., 1979); Stanford University (J.D., 1982). Author: "Connecticut Fraudulent Conveyance Law," 11 Bridgeport Law Review 3, 1991; "Connecticut Adopts Uniform Fraudulent Transfer Act," 2 Connecticut Lawyer 4, 1991-1992. *Member:* Stamford/Norwalk (Vice Chairman, Business Law Committee, 1989-1991; Chairman, 1991-1993) and Connecticut (Member: Banking Law Section; Commercial Law and Bankruptcy Section) Bar Associations; Association of Commercial Finance Attorneys. ***PRACTICE AREAS:*** Banking Law; Lending Law; Corporate Law. ***Email:*** eweiss@fdh.com

ASSOCIATES

ERIK A. BERGMAN, born New York, New York, November 5, 1964; admitted to bar, 1995, Connecticut. *Education:* Rutgers University (B.A., with highest honors, 1990); Yale Law School (J.D., 1993). Phi Beta Kappa. ***PRACTICE AREAS:*** Corporate Law; Mergers and Acquisitions; Venture Capital; Corporate Finance; Securities. ***Email:*** ebergman@fdh.com

JEFFREY A. BLOMBERG, born Stamford, Connecticut, December 23, 1971; admitted to bar, 1996, Connecticut; 1997, New York. *Education:* Colgate

(This Listing Continued)

University (B.A., 1993); Fordham School of Law (J.D., 1996). Associate Editor, Fordham Law Review, 1995-1996. Author, "Protecting the Right Not to Vote From Voter Purge Statutes," Fordham Law Review, December 1995. ***PRACTICE AREAS:*** Mergers and Acquisitions; Venture Capital; Corporate Finance Law; Corporate Securities. ***Email:*** jblomber@fdh.com

KRISTIN L. CHACH, born Danbury, Connecticut, March 26, 1972; admitted to bar, 1998, Connecticut; 1999, New York. *Education:* Western Connecticut State University (B.A., summa cum laude, 1994); University of North Carolina School of Law (J.D., 1998). ***PRACTICE AREAS:*** Corporate Law; Mergers and Acquisitions; Securities; Venture Capital. ***Email:*** kchach@fdh.com

NANCY L. LOMAZZO, born New York, New York, July 21, 1965; admitted to bar, 1994, New York; 1998, Connecticut. *Education:* Dartmouth College (A.B., magna cum laude, 1987); University of Chicago (J.D., 1993). ***PRACTICE AREAS:*** Real Estate; Corporate Finance; Mergers and Acquisitions. ***Email:*** nlomazzo@fdh.com

LAURA J. LUTJEN, born New York, New York, November 14, 1968; admitted to bar, 1996, New York; 1999, Connecticut. *Education:* Baruch College (B.B.A., summa cum laude, 1990); Yale University (J.D., 1993). Beta Gamma Sigma. ***PRACTICE AREAS:*** Taxation. ***Email:*** llutjen@fdh.com

SUSAN POWELL, born Los Angeles, California; admitted to bar, 1997, New York; 2001, Connecticut. *Education:* New York University (B.S., cum laude, 1989); Columbia University (J.D., 1996). Stone Scholar. ***PRACTICE AREAS:*** Executive Compensation; ERISA; Employee Benefits. ***Email:*** spowell@fdh.com

MARCIA C. SUGRUE, born Glasgow, Scotland, June 17, 1973; admitted to bar, 1998, Pennsylvania; 2001, Connecticut. *Education:* Johns Hopkins University (B.A., with honors, 1994); George Washington University (J.D., with high honors, 1998). Order of the Coif. ***LANGUAGES:*** French, Spanish. ***PRACTICE AREAS:*** Corporate Law; Securities; Mergers and Acquisitions; Venture Capital. ***Email:*** msugrue@fdh.com

GRANT S. THOMPSON, born 1970; admitted to bar, 1999, California; 2001, Connecticut. *Education:* University of North Carolina at Chapel Hill (B.A., 1992); Columbia University School of Law (J.D., 1998). James Kent Scholar, Columbia University School of Law. Senior Notes Editor, Columbia Business Law Review. Law Clerk to the Honorable Milton Pollack, U.S. District Court, Southern District of New York, 1998-1999. (New York City Office). ***PRACTICE AREAS:*** Corporate Law.

SHERYL A. YOUNG, born East Meadow, New York, August 1, 1967; admitted to bar, 1994, New York; 1995, Connecticut. *Education:* Colgate University (B.A., cum laude, with honors in psychology, 1989); New York University (J.D., 1993). Member, Review of Law and Social Change, 1991-1992. ***PRACTICE AREAS:*** Corporate Law; Mergers and Acquisitions; Securities. ***Email:*** syoung@fdh.com

SENIOR ATTORNEY

CHERYL GABES RICE, born New Britain, Connecticut, August 27, 1961; admitted to bar, 1986, Connecticut; 1987, New York. *Education:* Providence College (B.A., Economics, 1983); Hofstra University School of Law (J.D., 1986). Omicron Delta Epsilon (Providence College Chapter, 1980-1983). Member, 1983-1986 and Director, 1985-1986, Moot Court Board, Hofstra University School of Law. *Member:* Connecticut (Member: Commercial Law Section, 1987—; Business Law Section, 1987—), New York State (Member: Commercial Law Section, 1987-1998; Business Law Section, 1987-1998) and American (Member, Commercial Law Sections, 1987-1999; Business Law Section, 1987-1999) Bar Associations. ***PRACTICE AREAS:*** Asset Based Finance; Commercial Finance; Secured Finance; Unsecured Finance; Loan Workouts; Creditors Rights. ***Email:*** crice@fdn.com

JOYCE H. YOUNG, born Kansas City, Missouri, March 31, 1955; admitted to bar, 1984, New York, U.S. District Court, Southern and Eastern Districts of New York; 1991, Connecticut; 1992, U.S. Court of Appeals, Second Circuit; 1994, U.S. District Court, District of Connecticut and U.S. Supreme Court. *Education:* University of Colorado (B.A., 1977; B.S., 1977); Fordham University School of Law (J.D., 1983). Adjunct Professor, New York Law School, 1987-1993. ***PRACTICE AREAS:*** Commercial Litigation. ***Email:*** jyoung@fdh.com

OF COUNSEL

WILFORD R. YOUNG, born Rathdrum, Idaho, July 19, 1910; admitted to bar, 1941, New York; 1942, U.S. Tax Court; 1965, U.S. Supreme Court (Not admitted in Connecticut). *Education:* University of Idaho (B.S., Business, 1931; LL.D., with honors, 1975); Columbia University (M.S., 1935); Fordham University (J.D., 1940). General Counsel, Texaco, Inc., 1971-1976. *Member:* American Bar Association (Member, Taxation Section).

TIMOTHY A. BIRCH, born Cowansville, Quebec, Canada, June 16, 1958; admitted to bar, 1983, Connecticut; U.S. Supreme Court. *Education:* Muhlenberg College (A.B., 1980); Boston University (J.D., 1983). Omicron Delta Kappa; Phi Alpha Theta. Paul J. Liacos Scholar. Formerly with: Birch & Bush, P.C.; Cummings & Lockwood. ***PRACTICE AREAS:*** Mergers and Acquisitions; Corporate Finance; Corporate Law. ***Email:*** tbirch@fdh.com

FOGARTY COHEN SELBY & NEMIROFF LLC

STAMFORD, CONNECTICUT

(See Greenwich)

Litigation in all Courts, Real Estate and Land Use, Estate Planning and Probate, Corporate, Matrimonial, Administrative and Environmental, Appellate Practice, Business, Civil Trial, Commercial Litigation, Construction, Family, Labor and Employment, Medical Malpractice, Trust and Product Liability.

FOX & FOX, L.L.P.

607 BEDFORD STREET
STAMFORD, CONNECTICUT 06901
Telephone: 203-348-7773
Fax: 203-324-0057
URL: http://www.lawyers.com/foxlaw

Real Estate, Probate, Estate Planning, Family Law, Criminal and Civil Litigation, Wills, Elder Law.

GERALD M. FOX, JR., born West Orange, New Jersey, June 23, 1944; admitted to bar, 1970, Connecticut and U.S. District Court, District of Connecticut. *Education:* St. Michael's College (A.B., 1965); University of Connecticut (J.D., 1970). Member, 1971-1973, Chairman, Legislative and Rules Committee, Stamford Board of Representatives. Member, Board of Directors, Stamford Economic Assistance Corporation, 1975-1977. Member, Stamford Board of Finance, 1973-1977; Member, Democratic State Central Committee, 1978-1980. Member, Connecticut Board of Higher Education, 1980-1983. Chairman, Stamford Charter Revision Commission, 1981. Member, Panel of Arbitrators, American Arbitration Association. Judge of Probate, District of Stamford (1990—). Member, Connecticut Probate Assembly (1990—). Member, National College of Probate Judges (1990—). Member, Board of Trustees, Stamford Police Pension Fund. *Member:* Stamford (Chairman, Real Estate Committee), Connecticut (Member, Real Property, Probate and Family Law Committees; Lecturer, Estate Administration and Conservatorship) and American Bar Associations. ***PRACTICE AREAS:*** Real Estate; Family Law; Estate Planning; Probate Law; Domestic Relations; Child Custody.

GERALD M. FOX, III, born New York, New York, June 22, 1966; admitted to bar, 1992, Connecticut and New York; 1993, Illinois, U.S. District Court, Southern District of New York and U.S. District Court, District of Connecticut. *Education:* Providence College (B.A., 1988); The John Marshall Law School (J.D., 1992). Member, Stamford Board of Representatives, 1995-1999. Member, Stamford Board of Finance, 1999—. *Member:* Connecticut, New York State, Illinois State and American Bar Associations. ***PRACTICE AREAS:*** Litigation; Civil Practice; Family Law; Domestic Relations.

FRAGOMEN, DEL REY, BERNSEN & LOEWY, P.C.

ONE ATLANTIC STREET
STAMFORD, CONNECTICUT 06901
Telephone: 203-352-1871
Facsimile: 203-352-1874
URL: http://www.fragomen.com

New York, New York Office: 515 Madison Avenue. Telephone: 212-688-8555. Facsimile: 212-758-7215; 212-319-5236.

Buffalo, New York Office: 50 Fountain Plaza, Suite 1320. Telephone: 716-856-5444. Facsimile: 716-856-5151.

Washington, D.C. Office: 1212 New York Avenue, N.W., Suite 850. Telephone: 202-223-5515. Facsimile: 202-371-2898.

Coral Gables, Florida Office: 241 Sevilla Avenue, Suite 802. Telephone: 305-774-5800. Facsimile: 305-774-6666.

Chicago, Illinois Office: 150 North Wacker Drive, Suite 1120. Telephone: 312-263-6101. Facsimile: 312-346-1970.

San Francisco, California Office: 100 Pine Street, Suite 1575. Telephone: 415-986-1446. Facsimile: 415-986-7964.

Los Angeles, California Office: 12121 Wilshire Boulevard, Suite 1001. Telephone: 310-820-3322. Facsimile: 310-820-2702.

Santa Clara, California Office: 2804 Mission College Boulevard, 2nd Floor. Telephone: 408-919-0600. Facsimile: 408-919-0615.

Irvine, California Office: 18401 Von Karman Avenue, Suite 255. Telephone: 949-261-0209. Facsimile: 949-261-2821.

(This Listing Continued)

FRAGOMEN, DEL REY, BERNSEN & LOEWY, P.C., Stamford—Continued

Sacramento, California Office: 2399 Gateway Oaks Drive, Suite 200. Telephone: 916-564-6900. Facsimile: 916-564-5015.

Oakland, California Office: 1999 Harrison Street, Suite 1400. Telephone: 510-444-4208. Facsimile: 510-444-4873.

San Diego, California Office: 11512 El Camino Real, Suite 300. Telephone: 858-847-9060. Facsimile: 858-847-9119.

Iselin, New Jersey Office: Fragomen, Del Rey, Bernsen & Loewy, 99 Wood Avenue South. Telephone: 732-906-1230. Facsimile: 732-906-9190.

Troy, Michigan Office: Fragomen, Del Rey, Bernsen and Loewy, P.L.L.C., 2301 West Big Beaver Road, Suite 225. Telephone: 248-649-5404. Facsimile: 248-649-5121.

Atlanta, Georgia Office: 1175 Peachtree Street, N.E., 100 Colony Square, Suite 700. Telephone: 404-249-9300. Facsimile: 404-249-9291.

Dallas, Texas Office: 5000 Quorum Drive, Suite 215. Telephone: 972-233-6646. Facsimile: 972-233-3134.

Phoenix, Arizona Office: 3101 North Central Avenue, Suite 1470. Telephone: 602-631-9200. Facsimile: 602-631-9300.

Vienna, Virginia Office: 1595 Spring Hill Road, Suite 320. Telephone: 703-748-2380. Facsimile: 703-748-2387.

Brussels, Belgium Office: Vossendreef 6-B.I-Dreve Des Renards, 1180 Brussels, Belgium. Telephone: 011-322-374-7-37. Facsimile: 011-322-374-90-45.

U.S. and Foreign Immigration and Nationality Law.

NOREEN QUIRK, born New York, N.Y., September 14, 1953; admitted to bar, 1979, New York and U.S. District Court, Southern and Eastern Districts of New York; 1980, U.S. Court of Appeals, Second Circuit; 1989, Connecticut. *Education:* New York University (B.A., cum laude, 1975); Rutgers University (J.D., 1978). *Member:* American Bar Association; American Immigration Lawyers Association; Regional Bar Association of Stamford, Norwalk, Darien and Wilton. ***Email:*** nquirk@fragomen.com

KARIN C. LESTELLE, born New York, N.Y., October 18, 1958; admitted to bar, 1983, New York (Not admitted in Connecticut). *Education:* New York University (B.A., magna cum laude, 1979); George Washington University (J.D., with honors, 1982). Phi Beta Kappa. ***LANGUAGES:*** French. ***Email:*** klestelle@fragomen.com

PETER D. ROBERTS, born Halifax, Nova Scotia, Canada, December 6, 1960; admitted to bar, 1991, Massachusetts; 1993, Georgia (Not admitted in Connecticut). *Education:* Brown University (B.A., 1983); Northeastern University (J.D., 1990). Clerk, Honorable Marvin H. Shoob, U.S. District Court, Northern District Of Georgia, 1990-1992. *Member:* State Bar of Georgia; Massachusetts Bar Association (Recipient, Nobel Prize in Literature). ***Email:*** proberts@fragomen.com

(For complete biographical data on Personnel at New York, New York and Buffalo, New York, Washington, D.C., Coral Gables, Florida, Chicago, Illinois, San Francisco, Los Angeles, Santa Clara, Irvine, Sacramento, Oakland and San Diego, California, Iselin, New Jersey, Troy, Michigan, Atlanta, Georgia, Dallas, Texas, Phoenix, Arizona, Vienna, Virginia and Brussels, Belgium, see Professional Biographies at those locations)

FRANCO & ASSOCIATES

STAMFORD, CONNECTICUT

(See New Canaan)

Real Estate, Real Estate Development, Zoning, Planning and Land Use, Corporate Law, Commercial Law, Partnership Law, Securities Law, Trusts and Estates.

LAW OFFICES OF STEPHEN L. GANIS

1234 SUMMER STREET

STAMFORD, CONNECTICUT 06905-5532

Telephone: 203-977-2465; Fax: 203-348-0196

Email: sganis@lawyers.com

URL: http://www.lawyers.com/ganislaw

General Civil Practice, Business Law, Business Acquisitions and Sales, Contracts, Partnership, Family Business, Job Termination, Individuals with Disabilities, Wills and Probate, Estate Planning, Corporate Law, Intellectual Property, Labor and Employment and Trusts and Estates. Elder Law, Investments.

STEPHEN L. GANIS, born New York, N.Y., September 24, 1951; admitted to bar, 1982, New York and U.S. District Court, Southern and Eastern Districts of New York; 1991, Connecticut; 1994, U.S. District Court, District of Connecticut. *Education:* Syracuse University, Newhouse School of Communication (B.S., Journalism, 1973); Brooklyn Law School (J.D., 1981). Notes Editor, Brooklyn Law Review, 1980-1981. Author: Comment, "Crane: The Second Circuit Follows the Tune of Piper," 46 Brooklyn Law Rev. 1135 (1980); "Director-Protection Scheme May Drive Business Elsewhere," Ct. Law Tribune, March 26, 1990. *Member:* Connecticut and American Bar Associations.

(This Listing Continued)

REPRESENTATIVE CLIENTS: Frymaster L.L.C.; Garland Commercial Industries; Seabury Securities; Enodis Corp.; The Delfield Co.

GENUARIO & CONOVER

STAMFORD, CONNECTICUT

(See Norwalk)

General Civil Practice. Trials in all State and Federal Courts. Real Estate, Probate, Employment, Construction, Personal Injury, Foreclosures, Commercial and Zoning Law.

GILBRIDE, TUSA, LAST & SPELLANE, LLC

STAMFORD, CONNECTICUT

(See Greenwich)

General Practice. Real Estate, Corporation, Securities, Federal and State Courts, Litigation, Franchise Law, Taxation, Admiralty, International, Trademark, Probate, Zoning, Land Use, Family Law and Aviation.

GOLDBERG & ASSOCIATES

30 OAK STREET, SUITE 102

STAMFORD, CONNECTICUT 06905

Telephone: 212-968-2300

Fax: 212-968-2400

Email: kgoldberg@g-alaw.com

URL: http://www.g-alaw.com

New York, N.Y. Office: 39 Broadway, 10006. Telephone: 212-968-2300. Fax: 212-968-2400.

Hoboken, New Jersey Office: 20 Hudson Place, 07030. Telephone: 201-420-1771. Fax: 201-420-7778.

Corporate, Commercial and Insurance Law. Trial and Appellate practice in State Federal Courts; Mediation and Arbitration.

(For Complete Biographical Data on all personnel, see Professional Biographies at New York, New York)

HENRY L. GOLDSTEIN

STAMFORD, CONNECTICUT

(See New Canaan)

Estate Planning, Probate, Real Estate and Corporate Law.

MYRA L. GRAUBARD

1200 SUMMER STREET, SUITE 107

STAMFORD, CONNECTICUT 06905

Telephone: 203-327-6720

Fax: 203-358-9904

Email: mgraubardesq@aol.com

URL: http://www.lawyers.com/graubard

Commercial Law, Commercial Collections, Retail Collections, Enforcement of Judgements, Post Judgment Collections, Civil Litigation, General Civil Practice, Family Law, Divorce, Probate, Wills, Real Estate.

MYRA L. GRAUBARD, born New York, N.Y., November 23, 1943; admitted to bar, 1968, New York; 1970, U.S. District Court, Southern and Eastern Districts of New York; 1971, Connecticut; 1972, U.S. Supreme Court; 1973, U.S. District Court, District of Connecticut; 1975, U.S. Court of Appeals, Second Circuit. *Education:* Syracuse University and New York University (B.A., 1965); New York University (J.D., 1968). Phi Beta Kappa. Fact Finder and Arbitrator, Superior Court, Connecticut, 1985—. *Member:* Regional, Connecticut (Member, Sections on: Commercial Law; Family Law) and American (Member, Sections on: General Practice; Family Law) Bar Associations; Commercial Law League of America (Member, Sections on Creditors' Rights; Bankruptcy); The American Law Institute (Member, Model Peer Review Advisory Committee, 1978-1980).

ROBERT W. GREEN

30 OAK STREET, SUITE 102
STAMFORD, CONNECTICUT 06905-5313
Telephone: 203-356-1399
Fax: 203-357-0908
http://www.bobgreenlaw.com
URL: http://www.lawyers.com/bobgreen

Washington, D.C. Office: Eighth Floor, 1090 Vermont Avenue, N.W. Telephone: 202-682-9000. Fax: 203-682-0168.

Real Estate, Probate and Estate, Elder Law, Zoning, Planning and Land Use, Administrative Law, Financial Law and Legislative Practice.

ROBERT W. GREEN, born Haverhill, Massachusetts, July 31, 1941; admitted to bar, 1971, District of Columbia and U.S. Court of Appeals for the District of Columbia Circuit; 1975, U.S. Supreme Court; 1979, U.S. Court of Appeals, Fourth Circuit; 1988, Connecticut; 1991, U.S. District Court, District of Connecticut. *Education:* Wesleyan University; Indiana University (A.B., magna cum laude, 1968); University of Chicago (J.D., 1971). Phi Beta Kappa. Author: "The Legislative History of the Clayton Act," Vols. 2-3 of The Legislative History of The Federal Antitrust Law and Regulated Statutes, Earl Kinter, Ed. Chelsea House Publishers, New York, 1978; "Federal Regulation of Consumer Credit," Salinger & Green, Executive Enterprises, New York, 1989. Arent, Fox, Kintner, Plotkin & Kahn, 1971-1979. Associate General Counsel Legislature and Government Affair for General Electric Credit Corporation, Stanford Connecticut. *Member:* The District of Columbia Bar; American Bar Association. [U.S. Army Intelligence, Special Agent, 1964-1967, Sgt. E-5]. ***PRACTICE AREAS:*** Probate (30%); Trusts and Estates (30%); Zoning, Planning and Land Use (15%); Administrative Law (15%); Appellate Practice (10%).

GREEN AND GROSS, P.C.

STAMFORD, CONNECTICUT

(See Bridgeport)

Bankruptcy Law, Commercial and Construction Claims.

GRIMES & BATTERSBY L.L.P.

Established in 1980
3 LANDMARK SQUARE, SUITE 405
P.O. BOX 1311
STAMFORD, CONNECTICUT 06904-1311
Telephone: 203-324-2828
Telecopy: 203-348-2720
URL: http://www.gandb.com

Patents, Trademarks, Copyrights, Unfair Competition, Trade Secrets, Multimedia, Licensing, Franchising, Litigation and Antitrust.

CHARLES W. GRIMES, born Pittsburgh, Pennsylvania, October 24, 1951; admitted to bar, 1975, Illinois; 1978, New York; 1982, Connecticut; registered to practice before U.S. Patent and Trademark Office. *Education:* Pennsylvania State University (B.S., 1972); University of Denver (J.D., 1974). Executive Editor: The Licensing Journal; Multimedia and Technology Licensing Law Report; IP Litigator. Co-Author: "The Law of Merchandise and Character Licensing," Clark Boardman; *Licensing Law Handbook,* Clark Boardman, 1985; "Toy & Game Inventor's Guide," Kent Press, 1995; "Essential Guide to Merchandising Forms," Kent Press, 1995; "Multimedia & Technology Licensing Forms Annotated," Warren, Gorham & Lamont, 1995. Adjunct Professor, Intellectual Property, Sacred Heart University, 1991—. *Member:* New York Intellectual Property Law Association. ***LANGUAGES:*** German. ***Email:*** GRIMES@GandB.com

GREGORY J. BATTERSBY, born Brooklyn, New York, March 22, 1947; admitted to bar, 1973, New York; 1984, Connecticut; registered to practice before U.S. Patent and Trademark Office. *Education:* Seton Hall University (A.B., 1968); Fordham University (J.D., 1972). Editor, Fordham Urban Law Journal, 1971-1972. Executive Editor: The Licensing Journal; Multimedia and Technology Licensing Law Report; IP Litigator. Co-author: "The Law of Merchandise and Character Licensing," Clark Boardman, 1985; *Licensing Law Handbook,* Clark Boardman, 1985; "Toy & Game Inventor's Guide," Kent Press, 1995; "Essential Guide to Merchandising Forms," Kent Press, 1995; "Multimedia & Technology Licensing Forms Annotated," Warren, Gorham & Lamont, 1995. Editor, New York Intellectual Property Law Association Bulletin and Yearbook, 1986—. Editor-in-Chief, New York Intellectual Property Law Annual, 1994. Member, Advisory Board and Columnist, The Intellectual Property Strategist, 1994—. Lecturer, Franklin Pierce Law School Licensing Institute, 1992—. *Member:* New York Intellectual Property Law Association (Treasurer, 1995—; Chairman, 1986—, Publications Committee; Member, Board of Directors, 1992-1995); Licensing Executives Society; American Intellectual Property Law Association (Chairman, Publications Committee, 1993-1995). ***Email:*** BATTERSBY@GandB.com

GEORGE W. COOPER, born Elizabeth, New Jersey, November 27, 1927; admitted to bar, 1951, New York (Not admitted in Connecticut). *Education:* Columbia University (A.B., 1947; J.D., 1950). *Member:* American, Inter-American and International Bar Associations; International Trademark Association; New York Intellectual Property Law Association; International Association for the Protection of Industrial Property; Direct Selling Association. ***LANGUAGES:*** Spanish, French and German. ***Email:*** COOPER@GandB.com

LEORA HERRMANN, born New York, New York, November 10, 1953; admitted to bar, 1979, New York 1981, Connecticut. *Education:* University of California at Berkeley (B.A., with great distinction, 1975); Yale University (J.D., 1978). Phi Beta Kappa. Adjunct Professor of Trial Practice, University of Bridgeport School of Law, 1987-1989. *Member:* Stamford Norwalk Regional (Member, Intellectual Property Law Committee) and Connecticut Bar Associations. ***PRACTICE AREAS:*** Trademarks; Copyright; Intellectual Property Licensing; Intellectual Property Litigation. ***Email:*** HERRMANN@GandB.com

MELISSA T. ROSSE, born New York, New York, October 15, 1959; admitted to bar, 1986, New York; 1994, Connecticut. *Education:* Cornell University (A.B., cum laude, 1981); Fordham University School of Law (J.D., 1985). Staff Member, Fordham Urban Law Journal, 1984-1985. National Champion, The Association of Trial Lawyers of America, Trial Advocacy Competition, 1985. *Member:* Connecticut, New York State and American Bar Associations; New York County Lawyers Association (Member, Special Committee on Communications and Entertainment Law, 1986-1987); The Association of Trial Lawyers of America. ***Email:*** rosse@gandb.com

JAMES G. COPLIT, born New York, New York, October 11, 1968; admitted to bar, 1994, New York; registered to practice before U.S. Patent and Trademark Office (Not admitted in Connecticut). *Education:* Cornell University (B.S., 1990); Boston University (J.D., 1993). ***LANGUAGES:*** Spanish. ***Email:*** coplit@gandb.com

EDMUND J. FERDINAND, III, born New York, New York, 1967; admitted to bar, 1994, New York and U.S. District Court, Southern and Eastern Districts of New York; 1995, District of Columbia and U.S. Court of Appeals, Fourth Circuit; 1997, U.S. Court of Appeals, Second Circuit and U.S. Court of Appeals for the Federal Circuit; 2000, U.S. District Court, District of Connecticut; 2001, Connecticut. *Education:* Union College (B.A., with honors, 1989); Tulane University (J.D., cum laude, 1993). ***LANGUAGES:*** Spanish. ***PRACTICE AREAS:*** Intellectual Property Litigation; Internet Law.

GENE J. RICCOBONI, born New York, New York, November 25, 1963; admitted to bar, 2001, Massachusetts and New York (Not admitted in Connecticut). *Education:* Iona College (B.B.A.; M.B.A.); Pace University (J.D.). ***PRACTICE AREAS:*** Domain Names; Computer Contracts; Internet Law. ***Email:*** riccoboni@gandb.com

RUSSELL D. DIZE, born Easton, Maryland, September 4, 1971; admitted to bar, 2000, Connecticut. *Education:* James Madison University (B.B.A., 1993); University of Baltimore (J.D., cum laude, 1999). ***PRACTICE AREAS:*** Litigation; Intellectual Property. ***Email:*** dize@gandb.com

OF COUNSEL

EDWARD L. JUSTIN, born New York, New York, June 1, 1912; admitted to bar, 1934, New York (Not admitted in Connecticut). *Education:* New York University (B.S., 1932); New York University Law School (J.D., 1934).

LAW OFFICES OF
CHARLES W. GRINNELL

41 BANK STREET
STAMFORD, CONNECTICUT 06901
Telephone: 203-363-7106
Fax: 203-363-7108
Email: grinlaw@aol.com
URL: http://www.lawyers.com/grinnelllaw

General Business, Corporate and Tax Law, Mergers and Acquisitions, Business Succession Planning, Commercial Leasing, Licensing, Executive Compensation and Benefits, Estate Planning, Probate and Administration of Estates.

CHARLES W. GRINNELL, born Boston, Massachusetts, March 25, 1937; admitted to bar, 1966, New York; 1970, Connecticut. *Education:* Boston College (A.B.,1959); Columbia University (J.D., 1966); University of Bridgeport (LL.M. in Taxation, 1992). Associate, Dewey, Ballantine, Bushby, Palmer & Wood, New York, New York, 1966-1970. Associate, Lane, Jacques & Mosher, Greenwich, Connecticut, 1970-1971. Assistant General Counsel, Conoco, Inc.,

(This Listing Continued)

LAW OFFICES OF CHARLES W. GRINNELL, Stamford—Continued

Stamford, Connecticut, 1971-1982. General Counsel, Abex Corporation, New York, N.Y., 1982-1986. General Counsel, IC Industries, Inc., Chicago, Illinois, 1986. Director and General Counsel, Fuel Tech, Inc., A Clean Diesel Technologies, Inc., Stamford, Connecticut, 1986—. Member, South Western Regional Planning Agency of Connecticut, 1973-1976. Member, Charter Revision Commission of the City of Stamford, Connecticut, 1981-1982, 1994-1995. *Member:* Association of the Bar of the City of New York; Stamford/Norwalk Regional, Connecticut, New York State and American (Member: Taxation Section; Partnerships Committee) Bar Associations; Westchester and Fairfield County Corporate Counsel Association. ***PRACTICE AREAS:*** General Corporate; Tax and Finance Law; Mergers and Acquisitions; Commercial Leasing; Executive Compensation; Estate Planning.

JOHN R. HARNESS

1200 SUMMER STREET
STAMFORD, CONNECTICUT 06908
Telephone: 203-356-9975
Fax: 203-967-3028

Real Estate, Litigation, Family Law.

JOHN R. HARNESS, born Washington, D.C., September 23, 1956; admitted to bar, 1988, Connecticut; 1989, U.S. District Court, District of Connecticut and U.S. Court of Appeals, Second Circuit; 1992, U.S. Supreme Court. *Education:* Boston College (B.S., cum laude, 1978); University of Bridgeport (J.D., cum laude, 1988). Phi Delta Phi. Academic Invitee, University of Bridgeport Law Review, 1988. Recipient: American Jurisprudence Awards in Contract Law, Property Law, Federal Income Taxation and Excellence in Clinical Work. Barrister, Raymond E. Baldwin American Inn of Court, Bridgeport, 1989—. Member, Panel of Arbitrators, American Arbitration Association. *Member:* Board of Directors and Arbitration Committee Chairman of the Stamford Board of Realtors', Inc., 1991—. Stamford Regional, Connecticut and American Bar Associations; Connecticut Trial Lawyers Association; Association of Trial Lawyers of America. ***PRACTICE AREAS:*** Real Estate; Litigation; Family Law.

HEAGNEY, LENNON & SLANE LLP

STAMFORD, CONNECTICUT

(See Greenwich)

General Practice, Real Estate, Trusts and Estates, Probate, Corporation and Business Law, Civil and Criminal Litigation, Zoning and Family Law.

HEALY & BAILLIE, LLP

STAMFORD, CONNECTICUT

(See Norwalk)

Admiralty, Corporate, Insurance, Reinsurance and General Practice.

HEIDELL, PITTONI, MURPHY & BACH, LLP

30 OAK STREET
STAMFORD, CONNECTICUT 06905
Telephone: 203-327-1800
Email: hpmb@hpmb.com

New York, New York Office: 99 Park Avenue. Telephone: 212-286-8585. Telecopier: 212-490-8966.

Trial and Appellate Practice in all Courts; Medical and Non-Medical Professional Liability; Health Care Law including Managed Care, Physician Licensing and Credentialing; Products Liability; Directors and Officers and Employment Practice Litigation; Toxic Tort and Environmental Litigation.

LUKE M. PITTONI, born Rockville Centre, New York, May 14, 1945; admitted to bar, 1972, New York; 1975, U.S. District Court, Southern and Eastern Districts of New York and U.S. Court of Appeals, Second Circuit; 1976, U.S. Supreme Court; 1977, U.S. District Court, District of Connecticut; 1985, Connecticut. *Education:* College of the Holy Cross (B.A., 1967); Fordham University (J.D., 1971). Listed in: Best Lawyers in America; Who's Who in American Law; Best Lawyers in New York, New York Magazine. Voted in 1985 as one of the top twenty Medical Malpractice Defense Lawyers in America in a poll of plaintiffs' and defense lawyers by *Medical Economics.* Lecturer for Law Journal Press, PLI and American Conference Institute. Member, Faculty of Practicing Law Institute and Law Journal Press-Seminars. *Member:* New York State, Connecticut and American Bar Associations; Defense Research Institute; American Board of Trial Advocates; American Board of Professional Liability

(This Listing Continued)

Attorneys; American Society of Law and Medicine; Association of Hospital Risk Management of New York, Inc.; New York State Medical Defense Bar Association (Founder and Former President). ***PRACTICE AREAS:*** Trial Practice; Medical Malpractice; Products Liability; Professional Liability; Insurance Defense. ***Email:*** lpittoni@hpmb.com

ELIZABETH CORNACCHIO, born Stamford, Connecticut, November 29, 1951; admitted to bar, 1982, New York and U.S. District Court, Eastern and Southern Districts of New York; 1985, Connecticut and U.S. District Court, District of Connecticut; 1994, U.S. Court of Appeals, Second Circuit. *Education:* Ithaca College (B.Mus.Ed., cum laude, 1973); St. John's University (J.D., 1981). Member, Connecticut Society for Health Care Risk Management. *Member:* New York State and American Bar Associations; Defense Research Institute; Federation of Insurance and Corporate Counsel. ***PRACTICE AREAS:*** Medical Malpractice; Complex Litigation; Trial Practice; Professional Liability. ***Email:*** ecornacchio@hpmb.com

JOHN F. COSTA, born Bridgeport, Connecticut, November 5, 1960; admitted to bar, 1985, Connecticut; 1986, New York, U.S. District Court, Southern and Eastern Districts of New York, U.S. District Court, District of Connecticut. *Education:* College of the Holy Cross (B.A., 1982); Brooklyn Law School (J.D., 1985). Member, Connecticut Society for Health Care Risk Management. ***PRACTICE AREAS:*** Trial Practice; Appellate Practice; Medical Malpractice; Products Liability; Professional Liability. ***Email:*** jcosta@hpmb.com

DANIEL S. RATNER, born Forest Hills, New York, September 8, 1964; admitted to bar, 1989, Connecticut; 1990, New York, U.S. District Court, Southern and Eastern Districts of New York and U.S. Court of Appeals, Second Circuit. *Education:* Dickinson College (B.A., 1986); Fordham University (J.D., 1989). Assistant District Attorney, Bronx District Attorney's Office, 1989-1994. *Member:* New York State Bar Association. ***PRACTICE AREAS:*** Civil and Criminal Appellate Practice; Products Liability; Professional Liability; Medical Malpractice. ***Email:*** dratner@hpmb.com

Marian E. Courtney	***Carol L. Morris-Fox***
Janice Kirsten Lunde	***Geraldine Koeneke Russell***

(For Complete Biographical Date on all Personnel, see Professional Biographies at New York, New York)

LAW OFFICES OF DONALD A. HERNER

Established in 1991

ONE LANDMARK SQUARE, 4TH FLOOR
STAMFORD, CONNECTICUT 06901
Telephone: 203-351-1020
Fax: 203-351-1029
Email: herner@erols.com
URL: http://www.lawyers.com/herner

Corporation, Finance and Securities, Venture Capital and International, Business Law, Mergers and Acquisitions.

FIRM PROFILE: The firm specializes in serving as outside general counsel to corporations ranging from established manufacturing companies to newly formed ventures, offering a variety of services and products. Its activities are split roughly evenly between transactions (acquisitions, financings and venture capital) and more traditional corporate counseling. For clients primarily based in the New York metropolitan region, the firm is involved throughout the United States and in international cross border transactions. The firm was started in 1991 after over 20 years of practice by Mr. Herner with Anderson Kill & Olick, P.C. in New York City and Cummings & Lockwood in Stamford, CT.

DONALD A. HERNER, born Rochester, New York, August 2, 1943; admitted to bar, 1969, New York; 1970, U.S. District Court, Southern and Eastern Districts of New York; 1982, U.S. Supreme Court; 1991, Connecticut. *Education:* American University; Cornell University (A.B., 1965); Harvard University (LL.B., 1968). Lecturer, Drafting and Negotiating Commercial Agreements, Practicing Law Institute, 1980, 1981. *Member:* Connecticut, New York State and American Bar Associations. ***PRACTICE AREAS:*** General Corporate Law; Securities; Financing (Banking, Loans); International Law.

REPRESENTATIVE CLIENTS: JJI Lighting Group, Inc.; Networld, Inc.; Blume Worldwide Services, Inc.; TSI International Software, Ltd.; York Services Corp.; American Insurance Consortium, Inc.

BURT M. HOFFMAN

1234 SUMMER STREET, SUITE 400
STAMFORD, CONNECTICUT 06905
Telephone: 203-977-2490
Fax: 203-357-7669
Email: bhoffman@stamford-lawyer.com
URL: http://www.lawyers.com/ctlawyer

Civil Practice emphasizing Commercial and Residential Real Estate, Corporate Law, Sports Law, and including Zoning Subdivisions Land Use and Debtor Creditor Rights, Real Estate Finance, Mortgage Financing and Refinancing.

FIRM PROFILE: Offering 25 years of professional legal experience in Stamford and surrounding communities. His emphasis is on personalized attention for each client. His knowledgeable staff includes real estate paralegals to pre and post closing assistants.

BURT M. HOFFMAN, born Newark, New Jersey, June 2, 1942; admitted to bar, 1970, Connecticut; 1973, U.S. District Court, District of Connecticut; 1975, U.S. Supreme Court. *Education:* University of North Carolina (A.B., 1964); Seton Hall University (J.D., 1968). *Member:* Stamford/ Norwalk Regional (Member, Real Estate) and Connecticut (Member, Real Estate) Bar Associations. ***PRACTICE AREAS:*** Civil Practice; Real Estate; Corporate Law; Sports Law; Zoning and Land Use Law; Debtor Creditor Rights.

REFERENCES: Corner Stone Bank; First County Bank; First Union; Dime Savings Bank.

KEVIN T. HOFFMAN

STAMFORD, CONNECTICUT

(See Greenwich)

Commercial Litigation. Securities Arbitration, Employment and Litigation.

STACEY WEINSHEIMER HOIN

1600 SUMMER STREET
STAMFORD, CONNECTICUT 06905-5125
Telephone: 818-346-2072
Fax: 818-346-1935
Email: staceyhoin@email.msn.com

Employment Law.

STACEY WEINSHEIMER HOIN, admitted to bar, 1987, Virginia (Not admitted in Connecticut). *Education:* St. Mary's College (B.A.); Georgetown University (J.D., 1987).

HOLLAND KAUFMANN & BARTELS, LLC

STAMFORD, CONNECTICUT

(See Greenwich)

General Practice. Business and Corporate Law, Employment Law, Estate Planning and Probate Law, Family and Matrimonial Law, Litigation, Residential and Commercial Real Estate and Taxation.

HOPPER & HOPPER

STAMFORD, CONNECTICUT

(See Greenwich)

Probate and Estate Planning, Wills, Trusts and Real Estate Law.

IVEY, BARNUM & O'MARA, LLC

STAMFORD, CONNECTICUT

(See Greenwich)

General Practice. E-Commerce, Litigation in all Courts. Corporate, Commercial, Finance, Taxation, Trusts, Probate, Estate Planning, Family Law, Zoning, Environmental, Real Estate, Employment Law and Elder Law.

MICHAEL C. JACHIMCZYK

706 BEDFORD STREET
P.O. BOX 2442
STAMFORD, CONNECTICUT 06906-0442
Telephone: 203-353-1769
Fax: 203-348-8092
Email: mcjesq@excite.com
URL: http://www.lawyers.com/mcjesq

Real Estate, Zoning and Land Use Planning, Criminal Defense.

(This Listing Continued)

MICHAEL C. JACHIMCZYK, born Stamford, Connecticut, April 22, 1952; admitted to bar, 1990, New York, Connecticut, U.S. Court of International Trade; 1992, District of Columbia; 1993, U.S. District Court, Southern and Eastern Districts of New York. *Education:* Kenyon College (A.B., 1974); University of Bridgeport (J.D., 1989). *Member:* Greater Bridgeport Area, Stamford and Norwalk Area, Connecticut, New York State and American Bar Associations; The District of Columbia Bar; The Federalist Society for Law and Public Policy Studies. ***LANGUAGES:*** Spanish. ***PRACTICE AREAS:*** Real Estate; Zoning, Planning and Land Use; Criminal Defense; Probate.

JACKSON LEWIS SCHNITZLER & KRUPMAN

177 BROAD STREET, 8TH FLOOR
P.O. BOX 251
STAMFORD, CONNECTICUT 06904-0251
Telephone: 203-961-0404
Facsimile: 203-324-4704
Email: stamford@jacksonlewis.com
URL: http://www.jacksonlewis.com

Other offices located in: Atlanta, Georgia; Boston, Massachusetts; Chicago, Illinois; Dallas, Texas; Greenville, South Carolina; Hartford, Connecticut; Long Island, New York; Los Angeles, California; Miami, Florida; Minneapolis, Minnesota; Morristown, New Jersey; New York, New York; Orlando, Florida; Pittsburgh, Pennsylvania; Sacramento, California; San Francisco, California; Seattle, Washington; Washington, D.C.; White Plains, New York.

Labor Relations, Employment Discrimination, Wrongful Discharge and Other Employment-Related Litigation, Employee Benefits and Pension Law, Wage and Hour, OSHA, Immigration Law, Public Sector and State Labor Relations Law, On Behalf of Management.

FRANCIS P. ALVAREZ, born Brooklyn, New York, October 8, 1963; admitted to bar, 1990, Connecticut; 1991, New York. *Education:* Cornell University, School of Industrial and Labor Relations (B.S., 1985); Fordham University (J.D., 1990).

A. ROBERT FISCHER, born Greenwich, Connecticut, April 21, 1957; admitted to bar, 1984, Texas and New York; 1987, Connecticut. *Education:* University of Texas at El Paso (B.B.A., cum laude, 1980); University of Texas School of Law (J.D., 1983). Member, Executive Committee, Labor and Employment Section, Connecticut Bar Association, 1988-1990 and 1992-1994. Chairman, Employment Law Committee, Stamford-Norwalk Regional Bar Association, 1991-1993.

ROGER P. GILSON, JR., born Cleveland, Ohio, July 15, 1952; admitted to bar, 1979, New York; 1981, U.S. District Court, Southern and Eastern Districts of New York; 1992, Connecticut; U.S. District Court, District of Connecticut. *Education:* Syracuse University (B.A., 1974; M.P.A., 1976; J.D., cum laude, 1978). Member, 1976-1978 and Comments Editor, 1977-1978, Syracuse Law Review. *Member:* American Bar Association (Member, Labor and Employment Law Section).

CONRAD SHAWN KEE, born East St. Louis, Illinois, May 11, 1962; admitted to bar, 1987, Illinois; 1996, Connecticut. *Education:* Washington University, St. Louis, MO (B.A., 1984; J.D., 1987); McGeorge School of Law, AU, Diploma of Advanced International Legal Studies (1987).

MICHAEL J. SOLTIS, born Bridgeport, Connecticut, February 16, 1953; admitted to bar, 1979, New York; 1991, Connecticut. *Education:* University of Connecticut (B.A., 1975); New York Law School (J.D., magna cum laude, 1978); New York University (LL.M., 1986). Co-author: "The Americans With Disabilities Act: A Comprehensive Guide to Title I," Milt Wright & Associates, Inc., 1992.

ASSOCIATES

SETH F. EISENBERG, born Bridgeport, Connecticut, December 10, 1969; admitted to bar, 1996, New York; 1998, Colorado; 2001, U.S. District Court, Northern District of New York (Not admitted in Connecticut). *Education:* Union College (B.A., 1990; M.B.A., 1995); Albany Law School (J.D., cum laude, 1995). Law Clerk to the Hon. Thomas J. McAvoy, Chief Judge, U.S. District Court, Northern District of New York, 1998-2001. ***LANGUAGES:*** Spanish. **Email:** eisenbes@jacksonlewis.com

CHRISTINA CALISE FEENY, born Brooklyn, New York, February 23, 1971; admitted to bar, 1996, Connecticut; 1999, New York. *Education:* State University of New York at Albany (B.A., 1993); Fordham Law School (J.D., 1996).

JOSHUA E. GREENBERG (1970-1998).

CHRISTIAN A. GRENIER, born Providence, Rhode Island, September 20, 1968; admitted to bar, 1997, Connecticut; 1998, New York; 1999, U.S.

(This Listing Continued)

JACKSON LEWIS SCHNITZLER & KRUPMAN, Stamford—Continued

District Court, Southern District of New York. *Education:* Fordham University (B.A., 1990); St. John's University (J.D., 1997). Recipient, BNA/AB Labor and Employment Award. Member, St. John's Law Review. *Member:* Connecticut and New York State Bar Associations. ***PRACTICE AREAS:*** Labor and Employment.

EDWARD V. JEFFREY, admitted to bar, 1996, New York; 1999, Connecticut. *Education:* State University of New York at Stony Brook (B.A., Philosophy, 1992); University of Buffalo School of Law (J.D., 1995).

DAVID P. POWILATIS, born Dorchester, Massachusetts, August 18, 1972; admitted to bar, 1998, Massachusetts; 1999, U.S. District Court, District of Massachusetts and U.S. Court of Appeals, First Circuit; 2000, Connecticut. *Education:* Georgetown University (A.B., 1994); Boston College (J.D., magna cum laude, 1998). Member, Order of the Coif. *Member:* Boston and Massachusetts Bar Associations. ***PRACTICE AREAS:*** Employment Law; Labor Law.

MICHELLE H. RIORDAN, born Boston, Massachusetts, December 7, 1974; admitted to bar, 2000, Massachusetts and New York (Not admitted in Connecticut). *Education:* Boston College (B.A., magna cum laude, 1997); University of Southern California (J.D., 2000). *Member:* Boston, Massachusetts, New York State and American Bar Associations. ***LANGUAGES:*** French. ***PRACTICE AREAS:*** Labor and Employment; Benefits Law; Litigation. **Email:** riordanm@jacksonlewis.com

JEFFREY M. VONA, born Albany, New York, May 11, 1967; admitted to bar, 1998, Pennsylvania and New Jersey; 1999, New York and Connecticut. *Education:* Pennsylvania State University (B.S.C.E., 1989); Villanova University (M.B.A./J.D., 1998). Member, Moot Court Executive Board. ***PRACTICE AREAS:*** Employment Law; Labor Law.

JACOBS PARTNERS LLC

STAMFORD, CONNECTICUT

(See Norwalk)

Business and Personal Bankruptcy, Workouts, Debtor Creditor's Rights, Commercial Litigation, Contracts and Business Disputes.

JON E. JESSEN

800 SUMMER STREET, SUITE 305
STAMFORD, CONNECTICUT 06901
Telephone: 203-348-3262
Fax: 203-348-3264
Email: jonjessenlaw@aol.com
URL: http://www.lawyers.com/usimmigrationlaw

Immigration and Naturalization, Civil Litigation, Civil Rights, Personal Injury, Automobile Accidents, Wrongful Death, Criminal, DUI, Felonies, Homicides, Misdemeanors, Juvenile Crimes, Traffic Violations, Drug Crimes.

JON E. JESSEN, born Passaic, New Jersey, September 21, 1963; admitted to bar, 1991, Connecticut and Federal District Court. *Education:* Northeastern University (B.S., 1987); Quinnipiac College (J.D., 1990). *Member:* Connecticut and American Bar Associations. ***PRACTICE AREAS:*** Immigration and Naturalization.

SCOTT A. JUNKIN, P.C.

ONE STAMFORD LANDING
62 SOUTHFIELD AVENUE, SUITE 206
STAMFORD, CONNECTICUT 06902-7229
Telephone: 203-356-9005
Fax: 203-967-3923
Email: SAJPC@aol.com
URL: http://www.lawyers.com/scottjunkin

Corporate, Business, Contracts.

SCOTT A. JUNKIN, born New York, N.Y., February 6, 1946; admitted to bar, 1973, Connecticut and U.S. District Court, District of Connecticut. *Education:* Yale University (B.A., 1968); University of Pennsylvania (J.D., 1973). *Member:* New Haven County, Connecticut and American Bar Associations. ***LANGUAGES:*** Spanish. ***PRACTICE AREAS:*** Business Law; Contracts; Corporate Law; Finance; Mergers, Acquisitions and Divestitures; Securities.

KAYE AND HENNESSEY, LLC

STAMFORD, CONNECTICUT

(See Greenwich)

Real Estate, Probate, Estate Planning.

KELLEY DRYE & WARREN LLP

TWO STAMFORD PLAZA
281 TRESSER BOULEVARD
STAMFORD, CONNECTICUT 06901-3229
Telephone: 203-324-1400
Fax: (203) 327-2669; (203) 964-3188
Email: info@kelleydrye.com
URL: http://www.kelleydrye.com

New York, N.Y. Office: 101 Park Avenue. Telephone: 212-808-7800. Fax: (212) 808-7897.
Los Angeles, California Office: 777 South Figueroa Street, Suite 2700. Telephone: 213-689-1300. Fax: (213) 688-8150.
Washington, D.C. Office: 1200 19th Street, N.W., Suite 500. Telephone: 202-955-9600. Fax: (202) 955-9792.
Parsippany, New Jersey Office: 5 Sylvan Way. Telephone: 973-539-0099. Fax: (973) 539-3167.
Chicago, Illinois Office: 303 West Madison Street, Suite 1400. Telephone: 312-346-6350. Fax: (312) 346-8982.
Vienna, Virginia Office: 8000 Towers Crescent Drive, Suite 1200. Telephone: 703-918-2300. Fax: 703-918-2450.
Brussels, Belgium Office: 106 Avenue Louise, 1050. Telephone: (011) (32-2) 646-1110. Fax: (011) (32-2) 640-0589.
Hong Kong Office: Suite 1602, Fairmont House, 8 Cotton Tree Drive. Telephone: (011) (852) 2869-0821. Fax: (011) (852) 2869-0049.
Affiliated Offices:
Jakarta, Indonesia: Soebagjo, Jatim, Djarot, Plaza DM, 17th Floor, Jalan Jend. Sudirman Kav. 25, Jakarta 12920, Indonesia. Telephone: (011) (62-21) 5229765. Fax: (011) (62-21) 5229752.
Tokyo, Japan: Yumoto & Ota, Kioi Royal Heights, 3-29, Kioi-Cho, Chiyoda-Ku, Tokyo 102, Japan. Telephone: (011) (81-3) 3234-2441. Fax: (011) (81-3) 3262-2729.
Manila, Philippines: Oporto Reyes Suarez & Associates, 2111 BSA Suites, 103 C. Palanca Street, Legaspi Village, Makati City, Metro Manila. Telephone: (011) (63-2) 888-6951; 888-6953. Fax: (011) (63-2) 888-6945. E-Mail: oporto@pacific.net.ph.
Bangkok, Thailand: Dej-Udom & Associates, Charn Issara Tower, 9th Floor, 942/142-3 Rama IV Road, Bangkok 10500 Thailand. Telephone: (011) (66-2) 233-0055. Fax: (011) (66-2) 236-6681. E-Mail: dejudom@loxinfo.co.th.
Mumbai (Bombay) India: Wakhariya & Wakhariya, 41 Bajaj Bhawan, 226 Nariman Point, Mumbai 400021. Telephone: (91-22) 281-0336; 91-22-285-9820. Fax: (91-22) 281-0337. E-Mail: shabbirw@counsellor.com.

Litigation, Commercial Litigation, Emerging Growth Companies, Employee Benefits, Executive Compensation, Environmental Law, Financial Institutions, Health Care, Immigration, Insurance, Intellectual Property, Technology Litigation, International Law, Labor and Employment Law, Mergers and Acquisitions, Private Clients, Products Liability, Project Finance, Infrastructure, Real Estate Law, Restructuring, Creditors Rights, Securities, Securities Industry, Securities Litigation, Telecommunications, Trade Regulation, Antitrust, White Collar Crime, Corporate Investigations, Year 2000, Y2K.

CONNECTICUT PARTNERS

M. RIDGWAY BARKER, born Derby, Connecticut, May 28, 1955; admitted to bar, 1980, Pennsylvania; 1985, Connecticut. *Education:* Yale University (B.A., 1977); Boston University (J.D.,1980). ***PRACTICE AREAS:*** Joint Ventures; Mergers, Acquisitions and Divestitures; Securities; Public Offerings. **Email:** mrbarker@kelleydrye.com

RICHARD G. BRODRICK, born Claremont, New Hampshire, November 27, 1932; admitted to bar, 1959, New York; 1964, Connecticut. *Education:* Brown University (A.B., 1954); Harvard University (LL.B., 1958). ***PRACTICE AREAS:*** Securities; Closely Held Business Law; Business Acquisitions; Business Divestitures. **Email:** rbrodrick@kelleydrye.com

JOHN M. CALLAGY, born New York City, 1944; admitted to bar, 1969, N.Y.; 1977, Conn. *Education:* Georgetown University (A.B., 1966); New York University (J.D., 1969). ***PRACTICE AREAS:*** Business Torts; Complex Litigation; Contract Law. **Email:** jcallagy@kelleydrye.com

BRIAN J. CALVEY, born New York City, 1949; admitted to bar, 1974, N.Y. (Not admitted in Connecticut). *Education:* University of Notre Dame (A.B., magna cum laude, 1970); University of Virginia (J.D., 1973). ***PRACTICE AREAS:*** Corporate Law; Mergers, Acquisitions and Divestitures; Securities. **Email:** bcalvey@kelleydrye.com

(This Listing Continued)

JOHN T. CAPETTA, born Hartford, Connecticut, January 16, 1955; admitted to bar, 1980, Connecticut. *Education:* Providence College (B.S., 1977); University of Connecticut (J.D., 1980). ***PRACTICE AREAS:*** Corporate Law. ***Email:*** jcapetta@kelleydrye.com

RICHARD S. CHARGAR, born Brooklyn, New York, May 26, 1950; admitted to bar, 1976, New York; 1978, Connecticut. *Education:* Wharton School; University of Pennsylvania (B.S., 1972); Syracuse University (M.S. in Accounting, 1975; J.D., 1975); New York University (LL.M. in Taxation, 1980). Certified Public Accountant, Connecticut, 1978. ***PRACTICE AREAS:*** Employee Benefits; Taxation. ***Email:*** rchargar@kelleydrye.com

MARK S. GREGORY, born Washington, D.C., April 17, 1961; admitted to bar, 1986, Connecticut. *Education:* Brown University (A.B., 1983); Boston University (J.D., cum laude, 1986). Editor, American Journal of Law and Medicine. ***PRACTICE AREAS:*** Commercial Litigation; Securities Litigation; Intellectual Property Litigation; Antitrust Class Actions. ***Email:*** mgregory@kelleydrye.com

RANDI-JEAN G. HEDIN, born Downey, California, March 27, 1961; admitted to bar, 1988, New York; 1989, District of Columbia; 1997, Connecticut. *Education:* Barnard College (B.A., 1982); Brooklyn Law School (J.D., 1987). Research Editor, Brooklyn Journal of International Law. *Member:* Connecticut and American Bar Associations. ***PRACTICE AREAS:*** Securities Law; Corporate Law. ***Email:*** rhedin@kelleydrye.com

PAUL F. McCURDY, born Rockville Centre, New York, August 29, 1960; admitted to bar, 1985, Connecticut; 1986, New York, U.S. Dist. Court, Southern and Eastern Districts of N.Y. and U.S. Dist. Court, District of Conn.; 1991, U.S. Supreme Court and U.S. Court of Appeals, Second Circuit. *Education:* Lafayette College (A.B., 1982); Albany Law School of Union University (J.D., 1985). *Member:* Stamford/Norwalk, New York State, Connecticut and American Bar Associations. ***PRACTICE AREAS:*** Corporate Law; Arbitration; Securities; Broker-Dealer Arbitration. ***Email:*** pmccurdy@kelleydrye.com

SPECIAL COUNSEL

MICHAEL J. PALMIERI, born New Haven, CT., 1966; admitted to bar, 1991, Connecticut. *Education:* University of Pennsylvania (B.A., cum laude, 1988); Duke University (J.D., 1991). ***PRACTICE AREAS:*** Securities; Corporate Law. ***Email:*** mpalmieri@kelleydrye.com

CONNECTICUT ASSOCIATES

JOHN F. BEGGS, born Queens, N.Y., 1971; admitted to bar, 1996, N.Y. (Not admitted in Connecticut). *Education:* Hofstra University (B.A., magna cum laude, 1992); Fordham University School of Law (J.D., 1995). Phi Beta Kappa; Pi Sigma Alpha. Author: "Combatting Biospheric Degradation International Environmental Impact Assessment and the Transboundary Pollution Dilemma," 6 Fordham Envtl. L.J. 379, 1995; "The Theoretical Foundation of the Takings Clause and the Utilization of Historical Conceptions of Property in the Ecological Age," 6 Fordham Envtl. L.J. 867, 1995. ***PRACTICE AREAS:*** Securities; Broker-Dealer. ***Email:*** jbeggs@kelleydrye.com

MICHAEL P. BUCK, born Port Chester, New York, September 3, 1970; admitted to bar, 1996, New York; 1997, New Jersey and Connecticut. *Education:* Providence College (B.A., cum laude, 1992); Brooklyn Law School (J.D., 1995). ***PRACTICE AREAS:*** Securities Law; Corporate Law. ***Email:*** mbuck@kelleydrye.com

GRETCHEN A. CARROLL, born Stamford, Connecticut, January 21, 1970; admitted to bar, 2000, Connecticut. *Education:* Bucknell University (B.A., 1992); Syracuse University (J.D., summa cum laude, 2000). Member, Syracuse Law Review. ***LANGUAGES:*** French. ***PRACTICE AREAS:*** Securities. ***Email:*** gcarroll@kelleydrye.com

JAMES A. CORDONE, born Bridgeport, Connecticut, April 4, 1972; admitted to bar, 1997, Connecticut. *Education:* Mary Washington College (B.A., with honors, 1994); University of Connecticut School of Law (J.D., with honors, 1997). Phi Beta Kappa. Member, Connecticut Insurance Law Journal, 1995-1997. Author: "Health Care Reform in the 1990's," Connecticut Insurance Law Journal, Vol. 3, p. 193, 1997. Member, Greater Bridgeport Business Council Leadership Program, 1998-1999. ***PRACTICE AREAS:*** Real Estate. ***Email:*** jcordone@kelleydrye.com

TROY FICARRA, born New York, N.Y., September 1, 1970; admitted to bar, 1995, Connecticut; 1996, New York. *Education:* New York University (B.A., 1992; LL.M., Taxation, 1996)); Benjamin N. Cardozo School of Law, Yeshiva University (J.D., cum laude, 1995). *Member:* American Bar Association. ***PRACTICE AREAS:*** Employee Benefits. ***Email:*** tficarra@kelleydrye.com

LAUREL GIBALDI, born Cincinnati, Ohio, November 9, 1961; admitted to bar, 1989, New York (Not admitted in Connecticut). *Education:* Georgetown University (B.A., 1984); Syracuse University (J.D., 1988). ***PRACTICE AREAS:*** Real Estate. ***Email:*** lgibaldi@kelleydrye.com

(This Listing Continued)

SCOTT E. GOTTLIEB, admitted to bar, 1996, Connecticut. *Education:* Tufts University (B.A., cum laude, 1984); University of Connecticut School of Law (J.D., with honors, 1996). Member, Connecticut Journal of International Law. *Member:* Connecticut (Member, Sections on Business Law and Taxation) and American Bar Associations. ***PRACTICE AREAS:*** Corporate Law; Taxation; E-Commerce. ***Email:*** sgottlieb@kelleydrye.com

KATHRYN L. HUNTER, born New London, Connecticut, 1959; admitted to bar, 1987, New York and New Jersey; 1998, Connecticut. *Education:* Brandeis University (B.A., cum laude, 1981); Rutgers University-Newark (J.D., with honors, 1986). ***PRACTICE AREAS:*** Real Estate. ***Email:*** khunter@kelleydrye.com

THOMAS M. KELLY, born Englewood, New Jersey, March 5, 1971; admitted to bar, 1997, New Jersey; 1998, New York; 2000, Connecticut. *Education:* Syracuse University (B.A., 1993); Seton Hall University (J.D., 1997). ***PRACTICE AREAS:*** Securities. ***Email:*** tkelly@kelleydrye.com

DELPHINE W. KNIGHT-BROWN, born Manhasset, N.Y., June 24, 1964; admitted to bar, 1990, New York, U.S. District Court, Southern and Eastern Districts of New York and U.S. Court of Appeals, Eighth Circuit; 2000, U.S. District Court, District of Connecticut; 2001, Connecticut. *Education:* Princeton University (A.B., 1985); St. John's University (J.D., 1989). Law Clerk to the Honorable Frank J. Magill U.S. Court of Appeals for the Eighth Circuit. *Member:* Association of the Bar of the City of New York; New York State and American Bar Associations. ***PRACTICE AREAS:*** Litigation. ***Email:*** dkbrown@kelleydrye.com

NICHELLE MAYNARD-ELLIOTT, born Brooklyn, New York, December 13, 1968; admitted to bar, 1995, New York; 2001, Connecticut. *Education:* Brown University (B.A., 1990); Columbia University (J.D., 1994). ***PRACTICE AREAS:*** Venture Capital; Emerging Growth Companies; Mergers and Acquisitions; Corporate Law. ***Email:*** NMaynard@KelleyDrye.com

JAMES M. MORIARTY, born Bronx, New York, January 27, 1969; admitted to bar, 1999, Connecticut; 2000, New York. *Education:* Marist College (B.A., 1996); Pace University (J.D., magna cum laude, 1999). ***PRACTICE AREAS:*** Litigation; Securities Arbitration. ***Email:*** jmoriarty@kelleydrye.com

JAMES E. NEALON, born Waltham, Massachusetts, August 27, 1964; admitted to bar, 1991, New York and Connecticut; U.S. Supreme Court, U.S. Court of Appeals, Second Circuit, U.S. District Court, District of Connecticut and Southern and Eastern Districts of New York. *Education:* Fairfield University (B.A., 1986); Boston University School of Law (J.D., 1990). Editor, American Journal of Law and Medicine, 1988-1990. ***PRACTICE AREAS:*** Commercial Litigation; Securities Litigation; Employment Litigation; Bankruptcy. ***Email:*** jnealon@kelleydrye.com

CHRISTOPHER M. PARENT, born Danbury, Connecticut, July 6, 1971; admitted to bar, 2000, Connecticut. *Education:* University of Notre Dame (B.A., cum laude, 1993; J.D., 2000); The George Washington University (M.A., International Affairs, 1995). ***PRACTICE AREAS:*** Corporate; Securities; Litigation; International. ***Email:*** cparent@kelleydrye.com

CHRISTINE E. QUIER-SHETH, admitted to bar, 1999, New York (Not admitted in Connecticut). *Education:* University of West Alabama (B.S., 1989); RPI (M.B.A., 1992); New York University (J.D., 1998). ***PRACTICE AREAS:*** Employee Benefits; Executive Compensation. ***Email:*** csheth@kelleydrye.com

CAROL WEISS SHERMAN, born New York, N.Y., June 10, 1963; admitted to bar, 1989, New York; 1990, U.S. District Court, Southern and Eastern Districts of New York (Not admitted in Connecticut). *Education:* University of Virginia (B.A., 1985); University of Pennsylvania (J.D., 1988). *Member:* Association of the Bar of the City of New York. ***PRACTICE AREAS:*** Corporate Law; Securities. ***Email:*** csherman@kelleydrye.com

CHRISTOPHER J. TWOMEY, born Paterson, New Jersey, October 25, 1972; admitted to bar, 1998, New Jersey; 1999, Connecticut. *Education:* Boston College (B.A., 1995); University of Connecticut (J.D., 1998). ***PRACTICE AREAS:*** Corporate; Litigation. ***Email:*** ctwomey@kelleydrye.com

(For Complete Biographical Data of all Personnel, see New York, N.Y. Professional Biographies).

KIDAMBI & ASSOCIATES, P.C.

800 SUMMER STREET, SUITE 209
STAMFORD, CONNECTICUT 06901
Telephone: 203-961-1886
Fax: 203-961-1872
URL: http://www.lawyers.com/kidambi
Email: info@kidambi.com
URL: http://www.kidambi.com

Corporate Law, Immigration and Naturalization.

FIRM PROFILE: Kidambi & Associates, P.C. is a full-service business immigration law firm. Attorney Kidambi has successfully represented businesses internationally and in the U.S. The Firm specializes in transfer of personnel on I and H

(This Listing Continued)

KIDAMBI & ASSOCIATES, P.C., Stamford—Continued

Visas. The office is equipped with state-of-the-art technology, including a customized database that tracks client cases with the INS. The Firm offers clients a service guarantee that includes:

a. Accessibility

b. Reliable Service

c. Efficiency

d. Expeditious handling of all cases.

Besides constantly updating clients about various immigration related matters, Attorney Kidambi writes extensively though the Firm's website at http://www.kidambi.com and on the largest online Indian Newspaper in the U.S. "India Abroad" at http://immigration.indiaabroad.com/usa. The Firm also circulates a monthly newsletter titled "Business Immigration" for corporate clients. The Firm's website contains an archive of past newsletters. Attorney Kidambi travels internationally and conducts workshops on the 'Immigration Aspects of Doing Business in the U.S.' Write to him today at info@kidambi.com.

VAMAN B. KIDAMBI, born Coimbatore, India, August 12, 1970; admitted to bar, 1995, India, (Tamil Nadu); 1997, New York (Not admitted in Connecticut). *Education:* PSG College of Arts and Science, Coimbatore, India (B.Com., 1991); Bharathiyar University, India (B.L., 1994); George Washington University (LL.M., 1995). Recipent: Best Outstanding Student, PSG College of Arts and Science; Outstanding Young Advocate, Kerala Law Academy, India. *Member:* American Immigration Lawyers Association. ***LANGUAGES:*** Tamil, Telugu and Hindi. ***PRACTICE AREAS:*** Business Immigration; Corporate Law; Immigration and Naturalization; Employment Immigration; Employment Visas; Permanent Visas. ***Email:*** info@kidambi.com

---

DONALD R. KIEFER

STAMFORD, CONNECTICUT

(See Greenwich)

General Civil and Taxation, Practice with emphasis in Litigation, Family, Divorce, Domestic Relations, Real Estate, Commercial, Corporate, International, Admiralty; Probate Law & Litigation.

KOSKOFF, KOSKOFF & BIEDER, P.C.

1172 BEDFORD STREET
STAMFORD, CONNECTICUT 06905
Telephone: 203-325-3686
Email: kkb@koskoff.com
URL: http://www.koskoff.com

Bridgeport, Connecticut Office: 350 Fairfield Avenue. Telephone: 203-336-4421.
Danbury, Connecticut Office: 1 Moss Avenue. Telephone: 203-792-7100.

Litigation in all State and Federal Courts. Medical Malpractice, Equal Opportunity, Negligence, Products Liability, Civil Rights, Criminal Law and Class Actions.

(For biographical data on all personnel, see Professional Biographies at Bridgeport, Connecticut)

ROBERT M. LANE

STAMFORD, CONNECTICUT

(See Greenwich)

General Practice. Probate, Taxation, Real Estate, Estate Planning.

LAW OFFICES OF PAUL A. LANGE

STAMFORD, CONNECTICUT

(see Stratford)

Litigation and Transactions involving Aviation and Commercial Matters, Administrative Law, Insurance Defense and Coverage, Personal Injury, Products Liability, FAA Enforcement Defense and D.O.T. Regulatory Matters, General Civil Trial and Appellate Practice.

LEV & BERLIN, P.C.

STAMFORD, CONNECTICUT

(See Norwalk)

Corporation, Securities, Commercial and Investment Banking, Tax, Real Estate, Estate Planning, Intellectual Property and Civil Litigation in all State and Federal Courts.

MICHAEL J. LEVENTHAL

STAMFORD, CONNECTICUT

(See Westport)

Civil Litigation, Personal Injury, Family Law, Construction, Workers Compensation, Real Estate, Landlord Tenant; Collections.

LAW OFFICES OF LINNEA J. LEVINE, P.C.

970 SUMMER STREET
STAMFORD, CONNECTICUT 06905
Telephone: 203-348-8631
Fax: 203-359-0202
Email: linnealaw@aol.com
URL: http://www.lawyers.com/linneajlevinelaw

Purchase, New York Office: 3000 Westchester Avenue, 10577. Telephone: 914-251-1750; 800-828-1277. Fax: 914-251-1746.

Elder Law, Health Law, Family Law, Estate and Probate Law, Social Security Disability, Medicare, Medicaid, Conservator Proceedings.

FIRM PROFILE: The Law Offices of Linnea J. Levine, P.C. is concerned with solving the legal problems of families, with emphasis on the special problems of the elderly, minor children and the disabled. We comprehensively review the facts presented and resulting legal issues to anticipate and counsel our clients as to all potential problems, including financial, tax, health care and quality of life issues. Our estate plans provide for asset preservation and contingency plans in the event of catastrophic illness.

LINNEA J. LEVINE, born New York, N.Y., September 3, 1947; admitted to bar, 1991, New York and Connecticut; 1996, U.S. District Court, Southern and Eastern Districts of New York and U.S. District Court, District of Connecticut. *Education:* State University of New York at New Paltz (B.A., 1968; M.S., 1971; C.A.S., 1985); New York Law School (J.D., 1990). Certified, Elder Law Attorney, National Elder Law Foundation. *Member:* Westchester County, Fairfield County (Member, Board of Directors and Elder Law Committee), Connecticut (Member, Sections on: Family Law; Estates and Probate; Elder Law) and New York State (Member, Sections on: Family Law; Estate and Probate; Elder Law, Employment Law and Health Law) Bar Associations; National Academy of Elder Law Attorneys. ***PRACTICE AREAS:*** Elder Care; Health Care; Medicare and Medicaid; Family Law; Estate and Probate Law; Conservation Proceedings. ***Email:*** linnealaw@aol.com

ELLEN SIEV BELSON, born New York, N.Y., January 15, 1946; admitted to bar, 1994, Connecticut; 1995, New York; 1996, U.S. District Court, Southern and Eastern Districts of New York and U.S. District Court, District of Connecticut. *Education:* Brandeis University (B.A., 1967); Pace University (J.D., 1994). Recipient, President's Pro Bono Award, New York State Bar Association, 1996. *Member:* Westchester County, New York State and Connecticut Bar Associations; Women's Westchester Bar Association. ***PRACTICE AREAS:*** Elder Law; Real Property; Trusts and Estates; Probate Law; Medicaid. ***Email:*** linnealaw@aol.com

---

JACK S. LIPSON

STAMFORD, CONNECTICUT

(See Westport)

Real Estate, Mortgage Finance, Estate Planning.

LAW OFFICES OF JOHN T. LOFORESE LLC

STAMFORD, CONNECTICUT

(See Greenwich)

Civil Litigation, Real Estate, Wills and Probate, Personal Injury, Family Law, Collections.

GORDON M. LUCEY

Established in 1970

1177 SUMMER STREET

STAMFORD, CONNECTICUT 06905

Telephone: 203-325-4448

Telefax: 203-359-2994

New York, N.Y. Office: 122 East 42nd Street, Suite 1611, 10168-1699. Telephone: 212-557-9577. Telefax: 212-557-9580.

General Practice. Corporate, International, Maritime, Environmental, Litigation, Federal Agencies and Real Estate.

GORDON M. LUCEY, born New York, N.Y., April 14, 1932; admitted to bar, 1958, New York; 1962, U.S. District Court, Southern and Eastern Districts of New York; 1963, U.S. Court of Appeals, Second Circuit; 1968, Connecticut and U.S. District Court, District of Connecticut. *Education:* Hampden-Sydney College (B.A., 1954); Harvard University (J.D., 1957). Attorney-Adviser, Office of the General Counsel, Agency for International Development, Department of State, Washington, D.C., 1963-1966. *Member:* Connecticut (Member, Executive Committee, Section on International Law, 1982-1990) and American (Chairman, Committee on Export Control and Promotion, Section of International Law, 1971-1976; Chairman, Subcommittee on Exports of Agricultural Equipment and Services, 1976-1977) Bar Associations. [Lieut., U.S. Navy, Legal Officer, Germany, 1957-1960]

OF COUNSEL

KATHERINE M. SORTOR, born New London, Connecticut, March 20, 1934; admitted to bar, 1961, Connecticut; 1963, New York. *Education:* University of Geneva (Smith College Program 1953-1954); Smith College (A.B., 1955); University of Virginia (LL.B., 1959); New York University (LL.M., Corporation Law, 1969). *Member:* Association of the Bar of the City of New York; Connecticut Bar Association (Member, Executive Committee, Section on Corporations and Other Business Organizations, 1979-1983). ***LANGUAGES:*** French. ***PRACTICE AREAS:*** Corporate Law.

BARBARA H. McWHIRTER, born Cincinnati, Ohio, November 3, 1952; admitted to bar, 1984, Connecticut. *Education:* University of Georgia (B.S.A., 1975); University of Connecticut (J.D., 1982). Legal Assistant to Counsel to the Governor, State of Connecticut, 1982. Member, Board of Directors, Hazardous Waste Management Service, State of Connecticut, 1986—. *Member:* Connecticut Bar Association (Section on Conservation and Environmental Quality, 1986—). ***PRACTICE AREAS:*** Environmental Law.

LUSTIG & BROWN, LLP

1150 SUMMER STREET

STAMFORD, CONNECTICUT 06905

Telephone: 203-977-7840

Fax: 203-977-8649

Email: firm@lustigbrown.com

URL: http://www.lustigbrown.com

Buffalo, New York Office: Centerpointe Corporate Park, 400 Essjay Road, Suite 200, 14221-8228. Telephone: 716-626-2600. Fax: 716-626-2601.
New York, New York Office: 641 Lexington Avenue, 28th Floor, 10022. Telephone: 212-832-3235. Fax: 212-832-3155.
Newark, New Jersey Office: One Gateway Center, Suite 2600, 07102. Telephone: 973-645-9459. Fax: 973-645-0570.

General Insurance and Insurance Litigation, Casualty and Property Insurance, Professional Liability including Insurance Agents and Brokers Errors and Omissions, Insurance Coverage Analysis and Litigation including First and Third Party, Excess Coverage, Insurance Bad Faith, Insurance Products, Insurance Contracts, Civil Litigation, Trials and Appeals.

FIRM PROFILE: Lustig & Brown is a firm with a statewide, regional and national practice which maintains four offices in New York, Connecticut and New Jersey strictly limited to several insurance-related specialties. These include representation of insurance agents and brokers in errors and omissions claims and litigation, commercial and personal lines insurance coverage analysis and declaratory litigation, umbrella/excess representation and drafting insurance policy language.

MEMBER OF FIRM

JAMES C. KEIDEL, born Far Rockaway, N.Y., December 21, 1962; admitted to bar, 1988, New Jersey; 1989, New York, U.S. District Court, District of New Jersey and U.S. District Court, Southern and Eastern Districts of New York; 1995, North Carolina; 1999, Connecticut. *Education:* Hofstra University (B.A., 1985); Brooklyn Law School (J.D., 1988). *Member:* The Association of the Bar of the City of New York; Nassau County, New York State and American Bar Associations. ***PRACTICE AREAS:*** Insurance Agents and Brokers Errors and Omissions; Litigation. ***Email:*** jkeidel@lustigbrown.com

CHRISTOPHER B. WELDON, born Watertown, New York, December 8, 1964; admitted to bar, 1990, Connecticut; 1991, New York; 1992, U.S. District Court. Northern District of New York; 1994, U.S. District Court, District of Connecticut; 1995, U.S. District Court, Southern and Eastern Districts of New York. *Education:* The Catholic University of America (B.A., 1987); The Columbus School of Law of the Catholic University of America (J.D., 1990). Assistant District Attorney, Westchester County, New York, 1990-1992. *Member:* Connecticut and New York State Bar Associations; New York Trial Lawyers Institute. ***PRACTICE AREAS:*** Insurance Agents and Brokers Errors and Omissions; Civil Litigation and Trials. ***Email:*** cweldon@lustigbrown.com

DARREN P. RENNER, born Manhasset, New York, June 7, 1966; admitted to bar, 1995, Connecticut; 1996, New York and U.S. District Court, District of Connecticut; 1997, U.S. District Court, Southern and Eastern Districts of New York. *Education:* State University of New York at Binghamton (B.A., 1989); Franklin Pierce Law Center (J.D., 1995). *Member:* Stamford/Norwalk Regional, Connecticut, New York State and American Bar Associations; Connecticut Trial Lawyers Association. ***PRACTICE AREAS:*** Insurance Agents and Brokers Errors and Omissions; Insurance Litigation. ***Email:*** drenner@lustigbrown.com

(For Complete Biographical Data on Other Personnel, see Professional Biographies at Buffalo, New York and New York, New York)

MAHER AND WILLIAMS

STAMFORD, CONNECTICUT

(See Fairfield)

General and Federal Practice. Workers Compensation, Probate, Insurance, Subrogation, Estate Planning and Administrative Law. Trials.

MANCUSO, RUBIN & FUFIDIO

STAMFORD, CONNECTICUT

(See White Plains, New York)

Criminal Trial and Appellate Practice in State and Federal Courts, Personal Injury and Real Estate.

MARTIN, LUCAS & CHIOFFI, LLP

Established in 1996

1177 SUMMER STREET

STAMFORD, CONNECTICUT 06905

Telephone: 203-324-4200

Fax: 203-324-8649

URL: http://www.mlc-law.com

Email: admin@mlc-law.com

URL: http://www.lawyers.com/martinlucas&chioffi

New York, N.Y. Office: 90 Park Avenue, Suite 1700, 10016. Telephone: 212-569-3300. Facsimile: 212-569-3700.

Business Law, Corporate Finance, Mergers and Acquisitions, Internet Law, Venture Capital, Commercial and Employment Litigation; Securities, Employment, Commercial Litigation, Real Estate, Commercial Leasing, Estate and Tax Planning, Estate Settlement and Trust Administration.

PARTNERS

CHRISTOPHER G. MARTIN, born Bridgeport, Connecticut, 1961; admitted to bar, 1988, Connecticut and New York. *Education:* Sacred Heart University (B.S., 1983); Pace University (J.D., 1988). Certified Public Accountant, 1983. Previous Employment: Whitman, Breed, Abbott & Morgan; Marsh Day & Calhoun. Founding Member, Board of Directors, Brazelton Foundation. *Member:* Stamford/Norwalk Regional, Connecticut (Chairman; Liaison, Accountants Committee, 1992-1994) and American Bar Associations. ***PRACTICE AREAS:*** Business Law; Mergers and Acquisitions; Internet Law; Venture Capital; Taxation; Contracts; International Contracts; Loans; Securities Offerings; Estate Planning. ***Email:*** cmartin@mlc-law.com

SCOTT R. LUCAS, born Norwalk, Connecticut, 1960; admitted to bar, 1985, Connecticut; 1986, U.S. District Court, District of Connecticut; 1987, U.S. District Court, Southern and Eastern Districts of New York; 1989, U.S. Court of Appeals, Second Circuit; 1998, U.S. District Court, District of Colorado; 1999, U.S. Court of Appeals, Tenth Circuit. *Education:* Rensselaer Polytechnic Institute (B.S., 1982); Albany Law School of Union University (J.D., cum laude, 1985). The Justinian Society. Managing Editor, Albany Law Review,

(This Listing Continued)

MARTIN, LUCAS & CHIOFFI, LLP, Stamford—Continued

1984-1985. Co-Author: "After Acquired Evidence in Employment Litigation," 2 Labor and Employment Law Quarterly 1 (Spring 1995); "Unresolved Issues In The Development of Connecticut Employment Contract Law," 64 Connecticut Bar Journal 297 (1990). Author: "Monopolization and the Protection of Innovation: The Call for an Intent Standard," 48 Albany Law Review 982, 1984. Speaker: "Handling the Difficult Judge," NELA New England Regional Conference, 1999; "Plaintiff's Discovery in Employment Cases," Stamford/Norwalk Regional Bar Association, 1995. *Member:* Stamford/Norwalk Regional, Connecticut and American Bar Associations; American Trial Lawyers Association; Connecticut Trial Lawyers Association; Connecticut Employment Lawyers Association. ***PRACTICE AREAS:*** Commercial; Employment; Civil Litigation. ***Email:*** slucas@mlc-law.com

MARK P. CHIOFFI, born New Haven, Connecticut, May 5, 1966; admitted to bar, 1991, Connecticut; 1992, New York. *Education:* University of Connecticut (B.S., cum laude, 1988; J.D., cum laude, 1991); New York University (LL.M., Taxation, 1994). Recipient: American Jurisprudence Award, Trusts and Estates; Little Brown & Company Award, Trusts and Estates. Associate Editor, Connecticut Law Review, 1990-1991. Previous Employment: Blair & Potts, Stamford, CT; Mudge Rose Guthrie Alexander & Ferdon LLP and Chadbourne & Parke LLP, New York, NY. *Member:* Stamford/Norwalk Regional, Connecticut and New York State Bar Associations. ***PRACTICE AREAS:*** Estate Planning; Tax Planning; Estate Settlement; Trust Administration. ***Email:*** mchioffi@mlc-law.com

OF COUNSEL

GARY A. MACMILLAN, born Nova Scotia, Canada, 1947; admitted to bar, 1972, Connecticut; 1974, U.S. District Court, District of Connecticut; 1975, U.S. District Court, Southern District of New York and U.S. Court of Appeals, Second Circuit; 1979, U.S. Supreme Court; 1991, New York; 1998, U.S. District Court, District of Colorado; 1999, U.S. Court of Appeals, Tenth Circuit. *Education:* Cornell University (A.B., 1969); Harvard University (J.D., cum laude, 1972). Phi Beta Kappa. Co-Author: "After-Acquired Evidence in Employment Litigation," 2 Labor & Employment Law Quarterly 1 (Spring 1995); "Unresolved Issues in the Development of Connecticut Employment Contract Law," 64 Connecticut Bar Journal 297, 1990; "Breaking up is hard to do: Remedies for Management Misconduct In the Family Business," Connecticut Bar Journal, 1986; Author: "In Search of Evidentiary Standards in Environmental Litigation," University of Bridgeport Law Review, 1981; "Litigation and Personal Computers," Connecticut Law Tribune, 1984. State Attorney Trial Referee, 1985—. *Member:* Connecticut (Chairman: Unauthorized Practice of Law Committee, 1979-1985; Federal Practice Committee, 1987—; Executive Committee, Civil Justice Section, 1982-1985; Executive Committee, Labor and Employment Law Section, 1994-1995) and American Bar Associations; American Trial Lawyers Association; Connecticut Trial Lawyers Association; Stamford/Norwalk Regional Bar Association (Vice Chairman, Employment Law Committee, 1993-1995); National Employment Lawyers Association; Connecticut Employment Lawyers Association. ***PRACTICE AREAS:*** Commercial; Employment; Civil Litigation. ***Email:*** gmacmillan@mlc-law.com

ROBERT M. STEPHAN, born Milwaukee, Wisconsin, 1942; admitted to bar, 1967, Wisconsin; 1971, Connecticut; 1975, Minnesota, U.S. District Court, District of Connecticut, U.S. Court of Appeals, Second Circuit and U.S. Supreme Court. *Education:* Lawrence University (B.A., Political Science and Economics, 1964); University of Wisconsin-Madison (J.D., 1967). Previous Employment: American Maize-Products Company, Vice President, General Counsel and Secretary, 1992-1996; Erbamont N.V., Stamford, Connecticut, Vice President, General Counsel and Secretary, 1983-1992; United States Surgical Corporation, Norwalk, Connecticut, Vice President and Associate General Counsel, 1982-1983; General Mills, Inc., Staff Attorney, 1976-1977, Associate Counsel, 1977-1979, Senior Associate Counsel, Non-foods Groups, 1979-1980 and Vice President and Group General Counsel, 1980-1982; Day Berry & Howard, Hartford, Connecticut, Associate, 1971-1975; Office of the General Counsel, Securities and Exchange Commission, Washington, D.C., Attorney, 1967-1968. Assistant Attorney General, State of Wisconsin, Madison, Wisconsin, 1967. *Member:* Connecticut and American Bar Associations; Westchester Fairfield Corporate Counsel Association; Licensing Executives Society. [Capt., Judge Advocate and Military Judge, U.S. Marine Corps, 1969-1971]. (Also Practicing Individually). ***PRACTICE AREAS:*** Corporate Law; Acquisitions; Securities Regulation; Licensing; Joint Ventures; Corporate Governance; International Law. ***Email:*** rstephan@mlc-law.com

ASSOCIATES

MARY ALICE S. CANADAY, born Stamford, Connecticut, May 7, 1965; admitted to bar, 1994, Connecticut, New York, U.S. District Court, Southern and Eastern Districts of New York and U.S. Court of Appeals for the Federal Circuit; 1997, U.S. District Court, District of Connecticut. *Education:* Denison University (B.A., 1987); Pace University (J.D., cum laude, 1994). Ranking Scholar, 1992-1993. Recipient: American Jurisprudence Awards for: Civil Procedure, Corporations and Partnerships and Labor Law; Environmental Certificate, 1994. Law Clerk for U.S. Magistrate Judge Mark D. Fox in the Southern District of New York (1995-1997). *Member:* Stamford/Norwalk Regional and Connecticut Bar Associations. ***PRACTICE AREAS:*** Commercial; Employment; Civil Litigation. ***Email:*** mcanaday@mlc-law.com

JENNIFER A. HAUHUTH, born Tarrytown, New York, 1961; admitted to bar, 1994, Connecticut. *Education:* University of Bridgeport (B.A., 1989); Quinnipiac College (J.D., 1993). Phi Beta Kappa. Member, Probate Law Journal, 1991-1993. Recipient, National Association Women Lawyers Award, 1993. *Member:* Stamford/Norwalk Regional, Connecticut and American Bar Associations;. ***PRACTICE AREAS:*** Real Estate; Corporate Law; Commercial Finance; Zoning. ***Email:*** jhauhuth@mlc-law.com

GEORGE M. MELO, born New Rochelle, New York, February 23, 1973; admitted to bar, 2000, Connecticut; 2001, New York. *Education:* State University of New York at Oneonta (B.S., 1995); Pace University School of Law (J.D., cum laude, 2000). Executive Editor, Pace International Law Review, 1999-2000. Author: "Taxation in the Global Arena: Preventing the Erosion of National Tax Bases or Impinging on Territorial Sovereignty? (A Critique of the OECD's Report: 'Harmful Tax Competition: An Emerging Global Issue')," XII Pace Int'l Rev. 183 (Spring 2000). *Member:* New Rochelle, Stamford/Norwalk Regional, Connecticut and New York State Bar Associations. ***LANGUAGES:*** Portuguese/Brazilian. ***PRACTICE AREAS:*** Corporate Law; Commercial Law. ***Email:*** gmelo@mlc-law.com

AMY L. MEYERSON, born New Orleans, Louisiana, May 26, 1967; admitted to bar, 1994, Georgia; 1995, U.S. District Court, Northern District of Georgia; 1997, District of Columbia; 2000, Connecticut. *Education:* Duke University (A.B., with distinction, 1989); University of Connecticut (J.D., 1994). Member, 1992-1993 and Administrative Editor, 1993-1994, Connecticut Journal of International Law. Author: "Telecommunications Competition in the European Union After *France v. Commission*— The Terminal Equipment Case," 9 Conn. J. Intl. L. 355 (1994); "Addressing Federal, State and Local Telecommunications Regulatory Compliance Issues Arising in Seller's Representations and Warranties in Merger and Acquisition Agreements," 1060 PLI 141 (1998). Co-Author: "State Regulation of Telecommunications Mergers and Acquisitions," The M&A Lawyer, Glasser Legal Works, May 1998; "Negotiation and State Public Service Commission Review of Interconnection Agreements," in Telecommunications Law, Regulation and Policy, Ablex Publishing Corporation, 1998. *Member:* Connecticut and American (Chair, YLD Public Utilities, Communications and Transportation Law Committee) Bar Associations; State Bar of Georgia; District of Columbia Bar; Federal Communications Bar Association; Connecticut Asian Pacific American Bar Association (President and Director); National Asian Pacific American Bar Association. ***LANGUAGES:*** Mandarin Chinese. ***PRACTICE AREAS:*** Internet Law; Computer Law; Corporate Law; Commercial Law; Telecommunications Law. ***Email:*** ameyerson@mlc-law.com

LAW OFFICES OF ROBERT K. MARZIK, P.C.

STAMFORD, CONNECTICUT

(See Stratford)

General Practice, Civil Litigation, Admiralty, Maritime, Aviation, Probate and Real Estate Law.

MCGOVERN & ASSOCIATES

STAMFORD, CONNECTICUT

(See Greenwich)

General Commercial Practice. Corporate (Foreign and Domestic), Mergers and Acquisitions, Securities, Venture Capital, Taxation, Litigation in all Courts. International, Joint Ventures, Admiralty, Sports, Commercial and Residential Real Estate Law. Estates and Trusts.

MEAD, BROMLEY & BISHOP

Established in 1909

MEAD BUILDING

41 BANK STREET

STAMFORD, CONNECTICUT 06901-3066

Telephone: 203-325-4477

Telefax: 203-323-3834

URL: http://www.lawyers.com/mb&b

General Practice. Probate, Estate Planning, Real Estate, Negligence, Family, Commercial Law and Workers Compensation. Trials in all Courts.

(This Listing Continued)

(This Listing Continued)

FIRM PROFILE: Mead, Bromley & Bishop was founded in 1909 by Benjamin H. Mead and its offices have been at their present location since 1915. The firm has long been active in civic and legal affairs in the Stamford area.

MEMBERS OF FIRM

BENJAMIN H. MEAD (1883-1971).

STEPHEN L. BISHOP, born Stamford, Connecticut, June 2, 1949; admitted to bar, 1978, Connecticut; 1980, U.S. District Court, District of Connecticut. *Education:* University of Connecticut (B.A., 1972); Drake University Law School (J.D., 1977). *Member:* Stamford Regional and Connecticut Bar Associations. ***PRACTICE AREAS:*** Real Estate Law; Commercial Law; Estate Planning; Administrative Law.

DONALD B. POWERS, JR., born Schenectady, New York, June ll, 1952; admitted to bar, 1979, Connecticut; 1980, U.S. District Court, District of Connecticut. *Education:* Villanova University; Tufts University (B.A., 1975); Suffolk University (J.D., 1979). Instructor, Business Law, Fairfield University, 1982-1983. Member, Municipal Property Review Board, Town of Ridgefield, 1985-1987. *Member:* Stamford Regional and Connecticut Bar Associations. ***PRACTICE AREAS:*** Litigation; Real Estate Law; Estate Settlement Law; Family Law; Business Law.

STEVEN E. AYRES, born Decatur, Illinois, September 12, 1945; admitted to bar, 1978, Connecticut. *Education:* Dartmouth College (A.B., magna cum laude, 1967); Syracuse University (M.A., 1969); Cornell Law School (J.D., cum laude, 1978). Phi Beta Kappa. Recipient, Public Service Award, Connecticut Probate Assembly, 1999. Adjunct Professor, University of Bridgeport School of Law, Bridgeport, Ct., 1986. *Member:* Stamford Regional (Member, Board of Directors, 1991-1992; Co-Chair, Probate and Estate Committee, 1991-1992), Connecticut (Member, Executive Committee, Estates and Probate Section, 1983—) and American Bar Associations. [Lieut., USN, 1969-1975; Capt., USNR, 1975-1989, Ret.]. ***LANGUAGES:*** German and Vietnamese. ***PRACTICE AREAS:*** Trusts and Estates Law; Estate Settlement Law; Trust Administration Law; Probate Law; Tax Planning Law; Real Estate Law.

OF COUNSEL

J. ROBERT BROMLEY, born Stamford, Connecticut, April 9, 1936; admitted to bar, 1962, Connecticut. *Education:* Yale University (B.A., 1958; LL.B., 1962). Assistant Majority Leader and Chairman of Legislative and Rules Committee Board of Representatives, Stamford, 1965-1970. Member, Urban Redevelopment Commission of Stamford, 1970-1971. Corporation Counsel, City of Stamford, 1971-1973. *Member:* Stamford Regional and Connecticut Bar Associations. ***PRACTICE AREAS:*** Estate Settlement Law.

MEEHAN, MEEHAN & GAVIN

STAMFORD, CONNECTICUT

(See Bridgeport)

Criminal Law, Personal Injury, Medical Malpractice, Dental Malpractice, Legal Malpractice, Wrongful Death, Labor Law, Commercial Litigation, Appellate.

HILARY B. MILLER

STAMFORD, CONNECTICUT

(See Greenwich)

Litigation and Corporate Law. Family Law.

MORE PHILLIPS & DUNCAN, P.C.

STAMFORD, CONNECTICUT

(See Greenwich)

General Civil Practice, Trials and Appeals in Federal and State Courts, Corporate, Probate.

MURPHY AND KARPIE, LLC

STAMFORD, CONNECTICUT

(See Bridgeport)

General Civil Practice before State and Federal Courts. Insurance Defense, Personal Injury, Negligence, Products Liability, Medical Malpractice, Professional Liability, Employment Litigation, Commercial and Civil Rights Law, Appellate Practice, Toxic Torts.

ALAN NEIGHER

STAMFORD, CONNECTICUT

(See Westport)

General Civil Practice before State and Federal Courts. Antitrust, Trade Regulation, Libel and Slander, Sports, Entertainment, Communications and Copyright Law.

NEVILLE SHAVER HUBBARD & McLEAN

ONE LANDMARK SQUARE
STAMFORD, CONNECTICUT 06901
Telephone: 203-363-5300
Telecopier: 203-363-5323
Email: firm@nevillaw.com
URL: http://www.lawyers.com/nevillaw

New York, N.Y. Office: 477 Madison Avenue, 21st Floor. Telephone: 212-989-5300; Telecopier: 212-989-5323.

General Practice, Corporate, Securities, Financing, Commercial and General Litigation, Government Contracts and Taxation.

RICHARD M. NEVILLE, born New York, N.Y., April 14, 1942; admitted to bar, 1966, New York; 1973, France, Conseil Juridique (Not admitted in Connecticut). *Education:* Columbia University (A.B., 1963; J.D., cum laude, 1966). Harlan Fiske Stone Scholar. *Member:* Association of the Bar of the City of New York; New York State and American Bar Associations. ***PRACTICE AREAS:*** Securities; Corporate Finance; Corporate Law; Commercial Law; Business Law; Venture Capital; International Law. ***Email:*** neville@nevillaw.com

ALAN H. McLEAN, born New York, N.Y., April 13, 1938; admitted to bar, 1967, New York; 1992, Connecticut. *Education:* Princeton University (B.A., cum laude, 1960); Harvard University (M.A., 1963); Columbia University (LL.B., 1967). *Member:* The Association of the Bar of the City of New York; Connecticut and New York State Bar Associations. ***PRACTICE AREAS:*** Commercial Litigation; Litigation; Environmental Law; Employment Law. ***Email:*** mclean@nevillaw.com

D. SEELEY HUBBARD, born Coronado, California, January 8, 1945; admitted to bar, 1971, New York; 1972, Connecticut, U.S. District Court, Southern and Eastern Districts of New York, U.S. Court of Appeals, 2nd Circuit and U.S. Supreme Court. *Education:* Trinity College, Connecticut (B.A., 1967); University of Connecticut (J.D., 1970). Member and Vice Chairman: Darien Inland Wetlands Commission, 1974-1980; Darien Conservation Commission, Executive Committee, Conservation and Environmental Quality Section, 1978-1980. Chairman, Republican Town Committee, 1988-1990. Chairman, Darian Advisory Commission on Costal Waters. Lecturer, Connecticut Bar Association Annual Meeting, "Coastal Area Management," 1980. Faculty Member, Seminars sponsored by the Conservation and Environmental Quality Section, Connecticut Bar Association, "Coast Waters Regulation," 1985, and "Coastal Land Use Regulation," 1989. *Member:* Stamford/Norwalk Regional and Connecticut (Member, Executive Committee, Conservation and Environmental Quality Section) Bar Associations; The Association of Trial Lawyers of America. ***PRACTICE AREAS:*** Commercial Real Estate; Computers and Software; Commercial Law; Business Law; Environmental Law. ***Email:*** hubbard@nevillaw.com

---

ALAN M. SHAVER, born Detroit, Michigan, July 11, 1938; admitted to bar, 1964, Michigan; 1972, Massachusetts; 1977, New York; 1990, Connecticut and Maine. *Education:* Dartmouth College (A.B., 1960); Yale University (LL.B., 1963). *Member:* Westchester County, Massachusetts and American Bar Associations; The Corporate Bar. ***PRACTICE AREAS:*** Corporate Law; Business Law; Partnership Law; Limited Liability Company Law.

JOHN P. MALONEY, born New York, N.Y., March 16, 1939; admitted to bar, 1968, New York; 1969, U.S. Tax Court (Not admitted in Connecticut). *Education:* St. John's University (B.B.A., 1964; J.D., 1968). *Member:* New York State and American Bar Associations. ***PRACTICE AREAS:*** Taxation; Trusts and Estates.

NUSBAUM & PARRINO, P.C.

STAMFORD, CONNECTICUT

(See Westport)

Trials in all Courts. Family, Negligence, Medical Malpractice, Criminal, Real Estate, Business and Commercial Law.

OHLANDT, GREELEY, RUGGIERO & PERLE

SUITE 903
ONE LANDMARK SQUARE
STAMFORD, CONNECTICUT 06901
Telephone: 203-327-4500
Facsimile: 203-327-6401
Email: 102001.3251@compuserve.com

Practice Limited to Intellectual Property Law and Related Matters.

PAUL D. GREELEY, born Elizabeth, New Jersey, July 19, 1957; admitted to bar, 1982, District of Columbia; 1984, U.S. Court of Appeals for the Federal Circuit and U.S. District Court for the District of Columbia; 1988, Connecticut; U.S. District Court, District of Connecticut; registered to practice before U.S. Patent and Trademark Office. *Education:* Connecticut College (B.A., Chemistry, 1979); Gonzaga University (J.D., 1982). Phi Alpha Delta. Associate Editor, Canadian-American Law Journal, 1981-1982. *Member:* The Corporate Bar (Co-chair, Intellectual Property Committee).

CHARLES N. J. RUGGIERO, born Brooklyn, New York, September 28, 1949; admitted to bar, 1976, New York and U.S. District Court, Southern and Eastern Districts of New York; 1988, Connecticut and U.S. District Court, District of Connecticut; registered to practice before U.S. Patent and Trademark Office. *Education:* City College of the City University of New York (B.M.E., 1972); The John Marshall Law School (J.D., 1975). Member, John Marshall Law Review, 1973-1975. Gavel Society. Instructor, Patent Bar Review Course, Practicing Law Institute, 1985—.

TERRENCE J. McALLISTER, born Buffalo, New York, August 4, 1955; admitted to bar, 1984, New York; 1985, New Jersey (Not admitted in Connecticut). *Education:* State University of New York at Cortland (B.A., 1977); Pace University (J.D., 1983).

ASSOCIATES

JOHN YANKOVICH, born Tarrytown, New York, December 24, 1957; admitted to bar, 1996, New York; registered to practice before U.S. Patent and Trademark Office (Not admitted in Connecticut). *Education:* Polytechnic Institute of New York (M.S.E.E., 1991); Pace University (J.D., 1995).

JOSEPH V. GAMBERDELL, JR., born Baltimore, Maryland, March 31, 1954; admitted to bar, 1995, Connecticut. *Education:* University of Bridgeport (B.S.E.E., 1978); Quinnipiac College School of Law (J.D., 1994). *Member:* Connecticut and American Bar Associations. (Corporate Attorney). ***PRACTICE AREAS:*** Patents, Trademarks and Copyrights.

KARIN DAI KELLY, born Ithaca, New York, July 9, 1971; admitted to bar, 1999, Connecticut. *Education:* Trinity University (B.S., 1993); University of Florida (M.S.T., 1995); Catholic University of America (J.D., 1998). Member, Giles Sutherland Rich American Inn of Court, 1997. Recipient: Herndon Music Scholarship; Jewell H. Osborn Storey Music Scholarship; Dean's Award; Extra Mile Award for Outstanding Service to Community. Member, American Chemical Society. *Member:* American Intellectual Property Law Association; Connecticut Patent Law Association. ***PRACTICE AREAS:*** Patent Law.

SENIOR COUNSEL

JOHN F. OHLANDT, born Brooklyn, New York, February 21, 1923; admitted to bar, 1956, New York; 1964, U.S. District Court, Southern District of New York; 1975, U.S. Court of Customs and Patent Appeals (Not admitted in Connecticut). *Education:* Manhattan College (B.E.E., 1949); St. John's University School of Law (LL.B., 1955).

E. GABRIEL PERLE, born New York, N.Y., December 21, 1922; admitted to bar, 1950, New York; 1994, Connecticut. *Education:* Queens College (B.A., 1943); Yale University (LL.B., 1949). Co-author: "Publishing Law Guide," Prentice Hall Law & Business, 1989. ***PRACTICE AREAS:*** Publishing Law; Entertainment; Intellectual Property.

OF COUNSEL

GEORGE W. RAUCHFUSS, JR., born Beaver Falls, Pennsylvania, September 22, 1938; admitted to bar, 1968, District of Columbia; registered to practice before U.S. Patent and Trademark Office (Not admitted in Connecticut). *Education:* Pennsylvania State University (B.S.Ch.E., 1960); Washington College of Law, American University (J.D., 1967). Patent Examiner, 1963-1967.

ROBERT R. HUBBARD, born Erie, Pennsylvania, May 13, 1937; admitted to bar, 1965, District of Columbia; 1971, New Hampshire (Not admitted in Connecticut). *Education:* The Ohio State University (B.E.E., 1960); George Washington University (LL.B., 1964).

PATENT AGENTS

VAZKEN A. ALEXANIAN, born Aleppo, Syria, November 6, 1943. registered to practice before U.S. Patent and Trademark Office. *Education:* University of Alabama (Ph.D., 1975).

(This Listing Continued)

KRISTINA M. GRASSO
DAVID L. BARNES
MARK L. COOPER

PAUL, HASTINGS, JANOFSKY & WALKER LLP

A Limited Liability Partnership including Professional Corporations
Established in 1951
1055 WASHINGTON BOULEVARD
STAMFORD, CONNECTICUT 06901-2217
Telephone: 203-961-7400
Fax: 203-359-3031
URL: http://www.paulhastings.com

Atlanta, Georgia Office: 24th Floor, 600 Peachtree Street, N.E. Telephone: 404-815-2400.
Los Angeles, California Office: 555 South Flower Street. Telephone: 213-683-6000.
New York, New York Offices: 399 Park Avenue. Telephone: 212-318-6000 and 75 East 55th Street. Telephone: 212-318-6000.
Orange County, California Office: 695 Town Center Drive, Costa Mesa. Telephone: 714-668-6200.
San Francisco, California Office: 345 California Street. Telephone: 415-835-1600.
Washington, D.C. Office: 1299 Pennsylvania Avenue, N.W. Telephone: 202-508-9500.
Tokyo, Japan Office: 27F Ark Mori Building, 12-32, Minato-Ku, Akasaka 1-Chome, P.O. Box 577 . Telephone: (03) 3556-4711.
London, England Office: Tower 42, 25 Old Broad Street. Telephone: +44 (0) 20 7562-4000.

Aircraft Finance Practice, Asia-Pacific, Banking and Financial Services, Computer Law, Creditor's Rights and Bankruptcy, Customs, International Trade and Export Control, Emerging Growth and Technology, Energy, Federal Legislative, Healthcare, Energy, Project Finance, International Trade, Internet and Electronic Commerce, Investment Management, Japan Practice for United States-Based Clients, Latin America, Lease and Asset-Based Finance, Mergers and Acquisitions, Structured Finance and Asset Securitization, Telecommunications and Media, Timber, Paper and Packaging, Trade Regulation and Proprietary Rights, Year 2000, Employee Benefits, Executive Practice, Immigration, Railroad Labor and Employment Law, Accountant's Liability, Alternative Dispute Resolution (ADR), Antidumping, Countervailing Duty and Related Trade Proceedings, Antitrust Litigation and Government Enforcement, Appellate, Entertainment, Environmental, Government Contracts, Insurance Coverage, Intellectual Property, Technology Licensing and Litigation, Trade Secret, Patent Litigation, Securities and Corporate Finance Litigation, White Collar Corporate Criminal Defense, Affordable Housing, Land Use, Real Estate Acquisition and Disposition, Resort, Restaurant and Recreation, Retail Leasing, International Tax and Tax Litigation.

MEMBERS OF FIRM

JONATHAN BIRENBAUM, born Waterbury, Connecticut, September 12, 1953; admitted to bar, 1979, New York; 1996, Connecticut. *Education:* Colgate University (A.B., with honors, 1975); Albany Law School of Union University (J.D., cum laude, 1978). Articles Editor, Albany Law Review, 1977-1978. ***PRACTICE AREAS:*** Project Finance; Energy; Capital Markets Financing; Domestic and International Energy and Industrial Projects.

DOUGLAS C. CONROY, born Laconia, New Hampshire, May 15, 1942; admitted to bar, 1969, California; 1991, Nebraska and New York; 1994, Connecticut. *Education:* Harvard College (A.B., cum laude, 1965); University of Pennsylvania (LL.B., cum laude, 1968). Comment Editor, University of Pennsylvania Law Review, 1967-1968. Member, Board of Managers, University of Pennsylvania Law Alumni Society, 1986-1988. ***PRACTICE AREAS:*** Securities Litigation; Antitrust Litigation; Commercial Litigation; Class Actions; RICO; Trade Secret; Unfair Competition; Libel; ERISA; Derivative Actions.

CHRISTOPHER H. CRAIG, born Wilmington, Ohio, July 26, 1961; admitted to bar, 1990, New York; 1997, Connecticut. *Education:* Hamilton College (B.A., 1984); Boston University (J.D., magna cum laude, 1987). ***PRACTICE AREAS:*** Banking; Financial Institutions; Asset-Based Financial Transactions; Letters of Credit; Restructurings; Leveraged Financial Transactions; Secured Credit Facilities; Loan Sales.

MARY C. DOLLARHIDE, born Long Beach, California, January 28, 1957; admitted to bar, 1988, California; 1991, District of Columbia; 1996, Connecticut. *Education:* Occidental College (A.B., cum laude, with distinction, 1979); Circle-In-The-Square Theatre Professional Training Program (Graduate, 1981); University of Southern California (J.D., 1988). Editor-in-Chief, Southern California Law Review, 1987-1988. Co-Author: "Downsizing," by Ethan Lipsig, Bureau of National Affairs, 1996; "What Business Must Know About

(This Listing Continued)

the Americans With Disabilities Act," United States Chamber of Commerce, 1991, 2001-2002. Management Chair of the National Planning Committee for the Equal Employment Opportunity Basics Program, American Bar Association. ***PRACTICE AREAS:*** Sexual Harassment; Disability Discrimination; Employment Law; Reductions in Force; Employee Drug Testing.

ESTEBAN A. FERRER, III, born Havana, Cuba, November 2, 1950; admitted to bar, 1976, New York; 1992, Connecticut. *Education:* Dickinson College (B.A., cum laude, 1972); Columbia University (J.D., with high honors, Parker Program in Foreign and International Law, 1975). Member, Board of Directors, Goodwill Industries of Western Connecticut. ***PRACTICE AREAS:*** Emerging Growth Capital; Corporate Governance; Securities Law and Compliance; Mergers and Acquisitions; Corporate Finance; Cross-Border Transactions (Latin America); Executive Employment and Compensation Arrangements.

KURT W. HANSSON, born Mt. Kisco, New York, June 8, 1957; admitted to bar, 1986, Connecticut; 1988, District of Columbia. *Education:* Tufts University (B.A., 1980); American University (J.D., 1986). ***PRACTICE AREAS:*** Commercial Litigation; Tax Litigation; Intellectual Property Litigation; Employment Litigation; Alternative Dispute Resolution; Appellate Practice; Administrative Law; Lender Liability; Financial Services; Consumer Fraud; Insurance Coverage; Patent; Copyright; Trade Secret.

JOHN D. HAWKINS, JR., born Bronxville, New York, December 30, 1956; admitted to bar, 1980, New York; 1998, Connecticut. *Education:* Lehigh University (B.A., cum laude, 1977); University of North Carolina (J.D., with honors, 1980). Phi Beta Kappa. Member, University of North Carolina Law Review, 1979-1980. ***PRACTICE AREAS:*** Project Finance; Equipment Leasing; Asset-Based Finance.

MARIO J. IPPOLITO, born St. Louis, Missouri, February 11, 1958; admitted to bar, 1984, Connecticut and New York. *Education:* Georgetown University (B.S.B.A., magna cum laude, 1980); Columbia University (J.D., 1984). ***PRACTICE AREAS:*** Lending and Secured Transactions; Structured Finance; Asset-Based and Equipment Finance; Workouts; Bankruptcy.

CHARLES T. LEE, born New York, New York, February 20, 1950; admitted to bar, 1977, New York; 1983, Connecticut. *Education:* Harvard College (A.B., cum laude, 1972); Columbia University (J.D., 1976). Chairman, Stamford Urban Redevelopment Commission, 1984-1991. Special Master, Connecticut Superior Court, 1997—. ***PRACTICE AREAS:*** Trade Regulation; Insurance Coverage; Telecommunications; Environmental Law.

JOHN S. McGEENEY, born Woodhaven, New York, December 22, 1934; admitted to bar, 1960, Connecticut and New York. *Education:* Amherst College (A.B., 1956); Harvard University (LL.B., 1959). Fellow, American College of Trial Lawyers. ***PRACTICE AREAS:*** Commercial Litigation; Employment Law.

LESLIE A. PLASKON, born Bayonne, New Jersey, November 1, 1963; admitted to bar, 1988, California; 1991, New York and New Jersey; 1996, Connecticut. *Education:* Newcomb College (B.A., cum laude, 1985); University of Virginia (J.D., 1988). Phi Beta Kappa. ***PRACTICE AREAS:*** Creditors Rights; Bankruptcy; Commercial Lending; Foreclosure; Insolvency; Real Estate Workouts; Fraudulent Transfer; Secured Transactions; Trade Creditor Representation; Financial Institutions Representation; Commercial Matters; Debt Restructuring.

DAVID E. RABIN, born Long Island, New York, January 21, 1962; admitted to bar, 1987, New York; 1997, Connecticut. *Education:* Binghamton University (B.A., 1983); Harvard University (J.D., 1986). Phi Beta Kappa. ***PRACTICE AREAS:*** Commercial Real Estate; Real Estate Securitization; Real Estate Outsourcing; Asset Management; Mortgage Financing; Loan Workouts.

PATRICK W. SHEA, born Lakewood, Ohio, June ll, 1957; admitted to bar, 1981, District of Columbia; 1991, Connecticut. *Education:* University of Scranton (B.A., summa cum laude, 1978); Yale University (J.D., 1981). Member, Editorial Board, Yale Law Journal, 1980-1981. ***PRACTICE AREAS:*** Employment Law; Employee Benefits; Employment Discrimination; Age Discrimination; Wrongful Termination; Class Action Litigation Defense; EEOC.

DAVID E. SNEDIKER, born Chicago, Illinois, October 2, 1947; admitted to bar, 1976, New York; 1983, Connecticut. *Education:* University of Notre Dame (B.S., 1969); St. John's University (J.D., 1975). ***PRACTICE AREAS:*** Commercial Real Estate; Pension Fund Investments; Real Estate Investment; Real Estate Finance; Mortgage Finance; Real Estate Workouts; Project Finance; Joint Ventures; Loan Restructuring.

JOHN N. TURITZIN, born Manhasset, N.Y., September 5, 1955; admitted to bar, 1982, New York (Not admitted in Connecticut). *Education:* Earlham College (B.A., 1977); Princeton University (M.P.A., 1981); New York University (J.D., 1981). Phi Beta Kappa. (Also at New York, N.Y. 399 Park Avenue Office). ***PRACTICE AREAS:*** Corporate.

CARLA R. WALWORTH, born Lubec, Maine, March 7, 1957; admitted to bar, 1985, Connecticut. *Education:* Yale University (B.S., cum laude, 1979); University of Connecticut (J.D., with honors, 1985). ***PRACTICE AREAS:*** Employment Law; Employee Benefits; Employment Discrimination; Age Discrimination; Wrongful Termination; Class Action Litigation Defense; EEOC.

(This Listing Continued)

SENIOR COUNSEL

CHRISTOPHER A. BARRECA, born Pittsfield, Massachusetts, September 15, 1928; admitted to bar, 1954, Massachusetts; 1969, Kentucky; 1988, Connecticut. *Education:* Boston University (A.A., 1950; J.D., 1953); Northwestern University (LL.M., 1968). Author: "Labor Arbitrator Development," (BNA, 1983); "Labor Arbitration: A Practical Guide for Advocates," (BNA, 1990); "Labor Arbitration: Case and Materials for Advocates," (BNA, 1997). Secretary, Boston University Board of Trustees, Chair, Committee on Legal Affairs, 1980—. Chair, Labor and Employment Law Section, American Bar Association, 1997-1998. ***PRACTICE AREAS:*** Labor and Employment Law; Alternative Dispute Resolution; Bargaining Unit Certification Issues; Collective Bargaining; NLRB; EEOC; Wrongful Termination; Discrimination; Compliance Programs.

OF COUNSEL

ELIZABETH ADOLFF BROWER, born New York, New York, October 18, 1961; admitted to bar, 1990, New York; 1991, Connecticut. *Education:* Molloy College (B.S., cum laude, 1983); St. John's University (J.D., 1989). Member, St. John's University Law Review. ***PRACTICE AREAS:*** Securities Law; Corporate Finance; Mergers and Acquisitions; Venture Capital; Emerging Growth Companies; Compliance; Executive Employment Compensation Arrangements.

JOHN W. HAMLIN, born Buffalo, New York, August 18, 1954; admitted to bar, 1989, Connecticut; 1998, New York. *Education:* College of Wooster (B.A., 1976); University of Connecticut (M.A., 1984; J.D., with honors, 1988). Member: Executive Committee and Editor, Quarterly Newsletter; Labor and Employment Section, Connecticut Bar Association. ***PRACTICE AREAS:*** Labor and Employment Law; Discrimination; Wrongful Termination; Executive Employment Contracts; Severance Agreements; FMLA; ADA; EEOC; NLRB; Employee Benefits; Sexual Harassment; Investigation of Employee Misconduct.

ANDREW S. HOLMES, born Orange, New Jersey, January 10, 1955; admitted to bar, 1982, New York; 1983, Connecticut. *Education:* Princeton University (A.B., with distinction, 1977); University of Virginia (J.D., 1981). Senior Editor, Virginia Law Journal of International Law. ***PRACTICE AREAS:*** Asset Based Finance including; Equipment Leasing; Project Finance; Securitization of Transportation and Industrial Equipment; Co-Generation Power; Waste-to-Energy and Fuel Production Facilities.

BONNIE PIERSON-MURPHY, born Los Angeles, California, January 22, 1967; admitted to bar, 1992, Connecticut; 2001, Massachusetts. *Education:* Colgate University (B.A., 1989); Boston University (J.D., cum laude, 1992). Paul J. Liacos Distinguished Scholar. ***PRACTICE AREAS:*** Employment Law; Employment Discrimination; Sexual Harassment; Wrongful Termination; Class Action Litigation Defense.

ARTHUR D. RHEINGOLD, born Albany, New York, June 6, 1942; admitted to bar, 1967, New York (Not admitted in Connecticut). *Education:* Union College (B.A., 1964); New York University School of Law (LL.B., 1967). ***PRACTICE AREAS:*** Environmental Law.

ASSOCIATES

EDUARDO N. T. ANDRADE, born New York, N.Y., June 2, 1969; admitted to bar, 1999, New York (Not admitted in Connecticut). *Education:* Trinity College (B.A., 1991); Georgetown University (J.D., 1998; M.B.A., 1998). ***PRACTICE AREAS:*** Corporate Law.

MATTHEW S. ANTONETTI, born New Haven, Connecticut, September 25, 1971; admitted to bar, 1997, New York; 1998, Connecticut. *Education:* Boston College (B.A., magna cum laude, 1993); New York University (J.D., 1996). Articles Editor, Annual Survey of American Law.

RAYMOND WILLIAM BERTRAND, born Brooklyn, New York; admitted to bar, 1995, New Hampshire; 1998, New York (Not admitted in Connecticut). *Education:* Binghamton University (B.A., 1992); Albany Law School of Union University (J.D., 1995). ***PRACTICE AREAS:*** Employment; Litigation.

JAMES R. BLISS, born Rochester, New York, April 6, 1969; admitted to bar, 1995, Connecticut and New York. *Education:* New York University (B.A., magna cum laude, 1991); Fordham University (J.D., 1995).

JENIFER MAGYAR BOLOGNA, born Stamford, Connecticut, September 18, 1967; admitted to bar, 1994, Connecticut and New York. *Education:* Hamilton College (B.A., 1989); Boston University (J.D., magna cum laude, 1993). Editor, Boston University Law Review, 1991-1993. ***PRACTICE AREAS:*** Employment Law; Labor Law.

ADAM S. BOZEK, born Westerly, Rhode Island, February 7, 1967; admitted to bar, 1993, New York; 1998, Connecticut. *Education:* Boston University (B.S., summa cum laude, 1989); New York University (J.D., 1993). ***PRACTICE AREAS:*** Employment Law.

ELIZABETH A. BYRNE, born Saratoga, New York, September 17, 1975; admitted to bar, 2000, Connecticut. *Education:* Cornell University (B.S., 1997);

(This Listing Continued)

PAUL, HASTINGS, JANOFSKY & WALKER LLP, Stamford—Continued

University of Connecticut (J.D., 2000). Formerly with Connecticut Supreme Court. ***PRACTICE AREAS:*** Commercial Litigation. ***Email:*** elizabethbyrne@paulhastings.com

PAUL R. DEHMEL, born New York, N.Y., March 16, 1969; admitted to bar, 1998, New York; 2001, Connecticut. *Education:* Williams College (B.A., 1991); St. John's University (J.D., cum laude, 1997). Executive Notes and Comments Editor, St. John's Law Review. Author: "United States v. Lopez: Reevaluating Congressional Authority Under the Commerce Clause," 69 St. John's Law Review 579 (1995). ***PRACTICE AREAS:*** Commercial Litigation.

MATTHEW M. DONAHER, born Pittsburgh, Pennsylvania, October 5, 1964; admitted to bar, 1992, Connecticut; 1993, New York. *Education:* University of Notre Dame (B.B.A., 1986); Case Western Reserve University (J.D., cum laude, 1992). Recipient, American Jurisprudence Award in Contracts. Member, Case Western Reserve Law Review, 1991-1992. ***PRACTICE AREAS:*** Secured Lending; Securitization; Corporate.

THOMAS P. FRIEDMAN, born Norwalk, Connecticut, July 15, 1972; admitted to bar, 1999, California (Not admitted in Connecticut). *Education:* Tufts University (B.A., 1995); University of California School of Law, Los Angeles (J.D., 1999). ***PRACTICE AREAS:*** Litigation. ***Email:*** thomasfriedman@paulhastings.com

DAVID GALLUZZI, born Livingston, New Jersey, April 23, 1974; admitted to bar, 1999, Connecticut; 2000, New York and Rhode Island; 2001, New Jersey. *Education:* Brown University (B.A., 1996); Harvard University (J.D., 1999). ***PRACTICE AREAS:*** Corporate Law. ***Email:*** davidgalluzzi@paulhastings.com

JOSHUA D. GOODMAN, born Brooklyn, New York, June 19, 1963; admitted to bar, 1991, Pennsylvania (inactive); 1992, New Jersey; 1998, New York and Connecticut. *Education:* Swarthmore College (B.A., with honors, 1985); University of Pennsylvania (J.D., 1991). ***PRACTICE AREAS:*** Employment Law; Labor Law.

SARAH E. GRAVES, born London, England, March 28, 1967; admitted to bar, 1992, Nova Scotia; 1993, New York; 1995, Connecticut. *Education:* Acadia University (B.A., 1988); Dalhousie University (LL.B., 1991); New York University (LL.M., 1995). ***PRACTICE AREAS:*** Employment and Labor Law.

JOSEPH A. GUAY, born Putnam, Connecticut, March 10, 1968; admitted to bar, 1994, Maryland; 1996, District of Columbia (Not admitted in Connecticut). *Education:* University of Connecticut (B.S., summa cum laude, 1991); Catholic University (J.D., 1994).

KELLY WARRICK HODGES, born Pittsburgh, Pennsylvania, May 20, 1973; admitted to bar, 1998, Connecticut; 1999, New York. *Education:* Boston College (B.A., 1995); Georgetown University (J.D., 1998). ***PRACTICE AREAS:*** Corporate.

DEBORAH HRYB, born Hanover, Pennsylvania, September 7, 1951; admitted to bar, 1977, District of Columbia (Not admitted in Connecticut). *Education:* College of William & Mary (B.A., 1973); University of Virginia (J.D., 1977). ***PRACTICE AREAS:*** Employment Law. ***Email:*** deborahhryb@paulhastings.com

GREGORY F. LANG, born White Plains, New York, March 15, 1965; admitted to bar, 1993, Connecticut; 1995, New York. *Education:* Williams College (B.A., 1987); University of Connecticut (J.D., 1993).

ERIC T. LEVINE, born Hartford, Connecticut, March 3, 1969; admitted to bar, 1995, Connecticut. *Education:* Brown University (B.A., 1991); University of Connecticut (J.D., 1995). Member, Moot Court Board. Notes and Comments Editor, The Connecticut Journal of International Law. Author: "Violence in the Workplace: Potential Claims and Precautions," Connecticut Law Tribune Labor and Employment Law Magazine, November, 1999. Co-Author: "Computer Misuse," California Law Business, June, 1999; "The Termination Challenge: Practical Tips for Terminating Today's Better-Armed Employee," Corporate Legal Times, April, 1999; "From Monica to Microsoft: The Pitfalls of E-Mail and The Internet," Connecticut Law Tribune, March, 1999; "Layoffs, Employment Termination," BNA, 1998; "Practical Tips for Preparing and Negotiating Employment Arbitration Agreements," Conflict Management (Committee on Alternative Dispute Resolution, Litigation Section, American Bar Association, 1998); "Developments in Arbitration of Employment Claims/Cases," Labor Law Developments, Bender, 1997, 1996.

W. ANDREW P. LOGAN, III, born Lexington, Virginia, September 14, 1966; admitted to bar, 1995, Connecticut; 1996, New York. *Education:* College of William & Mary (A.B., 1988); St. John's University School of Law (J.D., cum laude, 1995).

MICHAEL J. MADDEN, born Poughkeepsie, New York, August 8, 1970; admitted to bar, 1995, Connecticut; 1997, New York. *Education:* Providence College (B.A., 1992); St. John's University (J.D., cum laude, 1995). Member, St. John's Journal of Legal Commentary, 1993-1994. ***PRACTICE AREAS:*** Corporate.

DIANE L. MATT, born October 27, 1969; admitted to bar, 1998, Connecticut; 2001, New York. *Education:* University of Pennsylvania (B.A., 1991); Boston University (J.D., 1998).

KAREN E. McARTHUR, born New Rochelle, New York, April 20, 1968; admitted to bar, 1996, Connecticut; 1997, New York. *Education:* State University of New York at Albany (B.A., cum laude, 1990); New York Law School (J.D., cum laude, 1996). Editor, New York Law School Law Review, 1994-1996.

FIROUZEH NUR-VACCARO, born Tehran, Iran, October 28, 1972; admitted to bar, 1997, Texas and U.S. District Court, Northern District of Texas (Not admitted in Connecticut). *Education:* Vanderbilt University (B.A., summa cum laude, 1994; J.D., 1997). Phi Beta Kappa. Member, 1995-1997 and Research Editor, 1996-1997, Vanderbilt Journal of Transnational Law. *Member:* Dallas and American Bar Associations; State Bar of Texas; American Immigration Lawyers Association. ***LANGUAGES:*** Farsi and Russian. ***PRACTICE AREAS:*** Litigation. ***Email:*** firouzehnurvaccaro@paulhastings.com

ZACHARY R. OSBORNE, born Sacramento, California, August 3, 1972; admitted to bar, 1998, Connecticut; 1999, Massachusetts. *Education:* University of California at Berkeley (B.A., 1994); Cornell University Law School (J.D., 1998). Phi Beta Kappa. ***PRACTICE AREAS:*** Employment Law; Reductions in Force Programs; Employee Benefit Litigation; Employment Discrimination Litigation.

MATTHEW R. PAUL, born Wilmington, Delaware, March 22, 1972; admitted to bar, 1998, Connecticut; 1999, New York. *Education:* Trinity College (B.A., 1994); University of Connecticut (J.D., 1998).

MARIO A. PENA, admitted to bar, 2000, Connecticut; 2001, New York. *Education:* Cornell University (B.A., 1993); New York University (M.B.A., 1999; J.D., 2000). ***PRACTICE AREAS:*** Corporate; Securities.

SUZANNE MARIE PEPE-ROBBINS, born Lynbrook, New York, July 18, 1966; admitted to bar, 1991, Connecticut; 1992, New York. *Education:* University of Southern California (B.S., 1988); New York University (J.D., 1991; LL.M., 1992). ***PRACTICE AREAS:*** Tax.

PETER M. SCHULTZ, born Queens, New York, February 26, 1968; admitted to bar, 1994, New Jersey; 1999, Connecticut. *Education:* Carleton College (B.A., cum laude, 1990); Rutgers University, Camden (J.D., with honors, 1994). ***PRACTICE AREAS:*** Employment Law.

YOLANDA SEALS-COFFIELD, born Hartford, Connecticut, June 21, 1971; admitted to bar, 1996, Connecticut. *Education:* Howard University (B.A., cum laude, 1993); Boston University School of Law (J.D., 1996). Law Clerk to Chief U.S. Magistrate Judge Joyce London Alexander, District of Massachusetts. ***PRACTICE AREAS:*** Employment Law.

BRIT K. SEIFERT, born Berea, Ohio, October 23, 1968; admitted to bar, 1995, Ohio; 2000, Connecticut. *Education:* Baldwin-Wallace College (B.A., summa cum laude, 1991); Cleveland Marshall College of Law (J.D., 1995). Executive Editor, Cleveland State Law Review, 1994-1995. ***PRACTICE AREAS:*** Employment Law; Litigation.

H. WILLIAM SMITH III, born Schenectady, New York, January 7, 1963; admitted to bar, 1992, Pennsylvania; 1993, New Jersey; 1995, Connecticut and New York. *Education:* University of Rochester (B.A., 1985; M.S., 1986); Case Western Reserve University (J.D., 1992). Articles Editor, Case Western Reserve Law Review. ***PRACTICE AREAS:*** Corporate; Corporate Finance.

JOHN P. STAIKOS, born Mt. Kisco, New York, February 14, 1970; admitted to bar, 1998, Connecticut; 1999, New York. *Education:* State University of New York at Oswego (B.A., 1992); Union University (J.D., cum laude, 1998). Executive Editor, Symposia, Albany Law Review, 1997-1998. ***PRACTICE AREAS:*** Corporate Law; Project Finance.

NEIL B. STEKLOFF, born Derby, Connecticut, August 16, 1972; admitted to bar, 1998, Connecticut; 1999, New York. *Education:* George Washington University (B.A., magna cum laude, 1995); University of Connecticut (J.D., with high honors, 1998). Commentary Editor, Connecticut Law Review, 1997-1998. ***PRACTICE AREAS:*** Employment Law.

JESSICA L. SYLVESTER, born New London, Connecticut, December 30,1971; admitted to bar, 1999, Connecticut; 2000, New York. *Education:* University of Connecticut (B.A., cum laude, 1994; J.D., with honors, 1999). ***PRACTICE AREAS:*** Corporate Law.

DINA A. TOLIA-GUPTA, born Nairobi, Kenya, October 10, 1973; admitted to bar, 1996, United Kingdom; 2000, New York (Not admitted in Connecticut). *Education:* University of Warwick, U.K. (B.A., with honors, 1995); BPP Law School, U.K. (J.D., 1996). ***PRACTICE AREAS:*** Real Estate; Real Estate Finance.

JOSHUA W. VAN HULST, born Utrecht, The Netherlands, April 3, 1966; admitted to bar, 1992, New York; 1993, Connecticut. *Education:* College of the

(This Listing Continued)

Holy Cross (A.B., 1988); Washington & Lee University (J.D., 1991). **LANGUAGES:** Dutch. **PRACTICE AREAS:** Commercial Litigation.

PEARL PROFESSIONAL CORPORATION

STAMFORD, CONNECTICUT

(See Westport)

Business, Corporate and Commercial, Aviation, Tax, Commercial Real Estate.

THOMAS J. PERKOWSKI, ESQ., P.C.

SOUNDVIEW PLAZA
1266 EAST MAIN STREET
STAMFORD, CONNECTICUT 06902
Telephone: 203-357-1950
Fax: 203-357-1959
Email: info@tjpatlaw.com
URL: http://www.tjpatlaw.com

Patent, Intellectual Property, Trademarks, Copyrights, Trade Secrets.

THOMAS J. PERKOWSKI, born Huntington, New York, January 17, 1958; admitted to bar, 1986, Connecticut; 1987, New York, New Jersey and U.S. District Court, District of New Jersey; registered to practice before U.S. Patent and Trademark Office. *Education:* Clarkson College of Technology (B.S.E.E., with distinction, 1980); Franklin Pierce Law Center (J.D., 1985). *Member:* New York State and American (Member, Section of Patent, Trademark and Copyright Law, 1989) Bar Associations.

JAY P. SBROLLINI, born Hartford, Connecticut, August 19, 1965; admitted to bar, 1992, Massachusetts; 1993, New York; 1994, District of Columbia; registered to practice before U.S. Patent and Trademark Office (Not admitted in Connecticut). *Education:* Cornell University (B.S., 1987); Boston University (M.S.E.E., 1993); Suffolk University Law School (J.D., cum laude, 1992). *Member:* American Intellectual Property Law Association. **PRACTICE AREAS:** Electrical Patent Prosecution; Computer and Software Patents; Patent Licensing.

PIAZZA & PICKEL

112 PROSPECT STREET
P.O. BOX 15390
STAMFORD, CONNECTICUT 06901
Telephone: 203-348-2465
Fax: 203-964-9509
Email: Anthony.Piazza@piazza-pickel.com
URL: http://www.lawyers.com/piazza&pickel

Trials and Appeals in State and Federal Courts, Negligence, Medical Malpractice, Divorce and Personal Injury Law, Wrongful Death, Legal Malpractice, Child Custody, Automobile Accidents, Product Liability, Adoption, Family Law.

FIRM PROFILE: The firm has achieved for clients in wrongful death and malpractice cases, seven figure recoveries.

ANTHONY A. PIAZZA, born Bridgeport, Connecticut, July 8, 1942; admitted to bar, 1972, Connecticut; 1974, U.S. Court of Appeals, Second Circuit; 1975, U.S. Supreme Court. *Education:* Seton Hall University (A.B., 1964); Fordham University (J.D., 1972). Listed in: The Best Lawyers in America, 1995—. Member, Fordham Urban Law Journal, 1972. Author: "Wanted More Judges for Swifter Justice," New York Times, 3-4-84; "Justice Delayed Is Not Justice," New York Times, 9-11-83; Various articles, Connecticut Trial Lawyer's Magazine, "The Forum," 1983—; "Being an Expert in Presenting an Expert," The Connecticut Family Law Journal, 7-87; "Sue, Settle or Be Silent," Published 1993. Lecturer: "Discovery/Depositions," Connecticut Trial Lawyers Association Seminar, Cromwell, Connecticut, 1983-1984; "How To Try A Negligence Case," Connecticut Trial Lawyers Association Seminar, New Haven, Connecticut, 1983-1984; "Pendente Lite Hearings," Connecticut Bar Association, Family Law Section, New Haven, Connecticut, 1984-1985; "Cross Examination of the Opposing Spouse and Other Key Witnesses," Connecticut Bar Association, Cromwell, Connecticut, 1985; "Discovery and Depositions: The First Step in a Proper Cross Examination," Connecticut Trial Lawyers Association, Bermuda, 1986; "A 'How To' Series On Basic Local Practice In The Areas of Civil and Family Litigation For New Admittees to the Bar," Stamford-Darien Bar Association, Stamford, Connecticut, 1986; "What You Should Know Before Calling An Expert Witness," American Academy of Matrimonial Lawyers, Mystic, Connecticut, 1987; Evidence Seminar, American Academy of Matrimonial Lawyers, Mystic, Connecticut, 1987; "How to Maximize Damages in a Wrongful Death Action," Connecticut Trial Lawyers Association Seminar, Meriden, Connecticut, 1988; "Attorney-Client Privilege Is Not All It Appears," Connecticut Trial Lawyers Association Seminar, Dublin, Ireland, 1988; "Product Liability Under Connecticut Law," The Cambridge Institute at Hartford, Connecticut, 1988, 1989; "How To Handle Common Courtroom Problems Including Thirty-Five Semi-Common Objections," Connecticut Bar Association, New Haven, Connecticut, 1989; "How to Prove Liability In A Product Liability Action," Connecticut Trial Lawyers Association, Waterbury, Connecticut, 1989; "How To Keep The Judge Awake During Most Of Your Case," American Academy of Matrimonial Lawyers, Trumbull, Connecticut, 1989; "How to Meet the Challenge of Cross-examining the Defenses's Medical Expert," Connecticut Trial Lawyers Association, Cromwell, Connecticut, 1991; "How to Cross Examine the Defenses," Medical Expert, 1994; "Trial of a Custody Case," Demonstration, Connecticut Trial Lawyers Association, 1994. Lecturer: "How to Make A Jury Hear, See and Feel Your Opening Statement," Connecticut Trial Lawyers Association, Florida, 1995; "20 Ways to Leave Your Lover/10 Informal Ways to Get Discovery," American Academy of Matrimonial Lawyers, April, 1995. Connecticut Trial Lawyers Association, Bridgeport, Connecticut. "Practical Divorce Practice," American Bar Association, Boston, Massachusetts, October, 1998. Special Master, Superior Court, State of Connecticut, 1979—. Trial Referee, 1984—. Special Master, U.S. District Court, District of Connecticut, 1990—. Member, Board of Directors, Stamford-Norwalk-Danbury Legal Services, 1974-1975. Member, Panel of Arbitrators, American Arbitration Association, 1985. *Member:* Stamford Regional (Member, Executive Committee, 1978-1979), Connecticut (Member, Civil Justice and Family Law Section) and American Bar Associations; Connecticut Trial Lawyers Association (Member, Board of Governors, 1976—; Secretary-Treasurer, 1977-1979; Vice President, 1979-1982; President Elect, 1982-1983; President, 1983-1984; Member, Executive Committee, 1985—); The Association of Trial Lawyers of America (State Delegate for Connecticut, 1985-1999); American Board of Trial Advocates; American Academy of Matrimonial Lawyers (Connecticut Chapter, President). Fellow: Roscoe Pound Foundation. **PRACTICE AREAS:** Family Law; Personal Injury; Wrongful Death. **Email:** tpiazza@spiderink.com

ALAN SCOTT PICKEL, born Cleveland, Ohio, September 28, 1965; admitted to bar, 1990, Connecticut; 1991, New York, U.S. District Court, Southern and Eastern Districts of New York and District of Connecticut. *Education:* Syracuse University (B.S., 1987; J.D., cum laude, 1990). Andrews Scholar. Justinian Society. Associate Editor, Syracuse Law Review, 1989-1990. Special Master in several judicial districts. *Member:* Stamford/Norwalk, Westchester County, Connecticut (Member: Executive Committee, Family Law Section; Litigation Section) and New York State Bar Associations; Connecticut Trial Lawyers Association; The Association of Trial Lawyers of America. **PRACTICE AREAS:** Family Law; Personal Injury Litigation; Commercial Litigation; Real Estate. **Email:** aspickel@aol.com

ASSOCIATES

TARA C.F. RYAN, born Washington, D.C., May 24, 1967; admitted to bar, 1995, Connecticut; 1996, U.S. District Court, District of Connecticut. *Education:* Denison University (B.A., 1989); Quinnipiac College School of Law (J.D., 1995). *Member:* Stamford/Norwalk and Connecticut (Member, Sections on: Litigation; Family Law) Bar Associations; Connecticut Trial Lawyers Association; The Association of Trial Lawyers of America. **PRACTICE AREAS:** Family Law; Personal Injury Litigation. **Email:** tcfryan@aol.com

MICHELLE M. NAPOLI, born Waterbury, Connecticut, June 5, 1971; admitted to bar, 1997, Connecticut; 1998, U.S. District Court, District of Connecticut; 1999, U.S. Court of Appeals, Second Circuit. *Education:* Fairfield University (B.S., 1993); University of Connecticut School of Law (J.D., 1997). Phi Delta Phi. Listed in *Who's Who Among American Law Students*, 1997. Recipient: Fairfield University Staff Association Scholarship, 1992; Outstanding Young Women of America, 1997. *Member:* Waterbury, Connecticut and American Bar Associations; Connecticut Criminal Defense Lawyers Association; Connecticut Trial Lawyers Association; Association of Trial Lawyers of America. **PRACTICE AREAS:** Criminal Litigation; Civil Litigation; Appellate Practice.

PILLSBURY WINTHROP LLP

FINANCIAL CENTRE
695 EAST MAIN STREET
P.O. BOX 6760
STAMFORD, CONNECTICUT 06904-6760
Telephone: 203-348-2300
Fax: 203-965-8226
URL: http://www.pillsburywinthrop.com

San Francisco, California Office: 50 Fremont Street, 94105-2228. Telephone: 415-983-1000. Fax: 415-983-1200.
New York, New York Office: One Battery Park Plaza, 10004-1490. Telephone: 212-858-1000. Fax: 212-858-1500.
Los Angeles, California Office: 725 South Figueroa Street, Suite 2800, 90017-5406. Telephone: 213-488-7100. Fax: 213-629-1033.

(This Listing Continued)

(This Listing Continued)

PILLSBURY WINTHROP LLP, Stamford—Continued

Other Los Angeles, California Office: Century City, 10100 Santa Monica Boulevard, Suite 2300.

Orange County, California Office: 650 Town Center Drive, Seventh Floor, Costa Mesa, California 92626-7122. Telephone: 714-436-6800. Fax: 714-436-2800.

McLean, Virginia Office: 1600 Tysons Boulevard, 22102. Telephone: 703-905-2000. Fax: 703-905-2500.

Palm Beach, Florida Office: 125 Worth Avenue, 33480. Telephone: 561-655-7297. Fax: 561-833-6726.

Sacramento, California Office: 400 Capitol Mall, Suite 1700, 95814-4419. Telephone: 916-329-4700. Fax: 916-441-3583.

San Diego, California Office: 101 West Broadway, Suite 1800, 92101-8219. Telephone: 619-234-5000. Fax: 619-236-1995.

Other San Diego, California Office: 11975 El Camino Real, Suite 200, 92130-5000. Telephone: 619-234-5000. Fax: 858-509-4010.

Silicon Valley, California Office: 2550 Hanover Street, Palo Alto, California 94304-1115. Telephone: 650-233-4500. Fax: 650-233-4545.

Washington, D.C. Office: 1133 Connecticut Avenue, N.W., 20036. Telephone: 202-775-9800. Fax: 202-833-8491.

London, England Office: 54 Lombard Street, EC3V 9DH. Telephone: +44-171-648-9200. Fax: +44-171-283-1656.

Sydney, Australia Office: Level 10, 7 Macquarie Place, NSW2000. Telephone: +612-8214-2200. Fax: 612-8214-2211.

Tokyo, Japan Office: Fuerte Kojimachi Building, 5th Floor, 1-7-25 Kojimachi, Chiyoda-ku, 102-0083. Telephone: +011-81-3-5226-7260. Fax: +011-81-3-5226-7261.

Other Tokyo, Japan Office: 6 Gaikokuho Jimu Bengoshi Jimusho, Fifth Floor, Samon Eleven Building, 3-1, Samon-cho, Shinjuku-ku, 160. Telephone: +813-3354-3531. Fax: +813-3354-3534.

Hong Kong, China Office: 2504-6 Asia Pacific Finance Tower, Citibank Plaza, 3 Garden Road, Central Hong Kong. Telephone: +852-2530-3400. Fax: +852-2530-3355.

Singapore Office: 6 Battery Road #38-01B, 049909. Telephone: +65-227-4700. Fax: +65-227-4711.

General Practice with an emphasis on Administrative, Admiralty and Maritime, Alternative Dispute Resolution, Antitrust and Trade Regulation, Appellate Practice, Art, Aviation and Aerospace, Bankruptcy, Banking, Biotechnology, Business, Civil, Class Actions, Commerce & Technology, Commercial, Communications and Media, Complex and Multi-District Litigation, Construction, Contracts, Corporate, Creditor's Rights, E-Commerce, Emerging Companies, Employee Benefits, Energy, Environmental, Equipment Finance and Leasing, Executive Compensation, Finance, Guardianship and Conservatorship, Health Care and Hospital, International, International Trade, Internet, Labor and Employment, Leases and Leasing, Licensing, Life Sciences, Litigation, Medicare and Medicaid, Mergers, Acquisitions and Divestitures, Natural Resources, Nonprofit and Charitable Organizations, Partnership, Patents, Planning and Land Use, Political, Probate, Products Liability, Project Finance, Real Estate, Regulatory, RICO, Securities, Taxation, Torts, Toxic Torts, Trademark, Trust and Estates, Utility, White Collar Crime, Wills and Zoning Law.

FIRM PROFILE: Formed in 2001 by the merger of Pillsbury Madison & Sutro and Winthrop, Stimson, Putnam & Roberts, our experience spans three centuries. Today, Pillsbury Winthrop has more than 860 lawyers in 16 locations, including 350 corporate and securities lawyers, 250 intellectual property and technology lawyers and 250 lawyers in complex and international litigation. With 16 locations in major capital finance and technology centers throughout the world, Pillsbury Winthrop is uniquely positioned to counsel clients on all aspects of global business, technology transactions, and intellectual property protection.

MEMBERS OF FIRM

THOMAS F. CLAUSS, JR., born November 26, 1953; admitted to bar, 1980, New Jersey; 1981, New York; 1986, District of Columbia; 1994, Connecticut. *Education:* Yale University (B.A., 1975); Rutgers University (J.D., 1980). Research Editor, Rutgers Law Review, 1979-1980. Law Clerk to Hon. Thomas C. Platt, U.S. District Judge, Eastern District of New York. Member, Committee on Civil Litigation, Eastern District of New York, 1990—. Member, Civil Justice Reform Act Advisory Group, Eastern District of New York, 1991-1997. ***PRACTICE AREAS:*** Corporate Litigation; Arbitration; Corporate Governance; Life Sciences and Technology. ***Email:*** tclauss@pillsburywinthrop.com

FRODE JENSEN, born May 30, 1950; admitted to bar, 1977, New York; 1985, Connecticut. *Education:* Phillips Academy, Andover; Williams College (B.A., cum laude, 1972); Columbia University (J.D., 1976). Harlan Fiske Stone Scholar, 1974-1975. Law Clerk, Hon. E.D. Steel, Jr., U.S. District Court, District of Delaware, 1976-1977. ***PRACTICE AREAS:*** Mergers, Acquisitions and Divestitures; Corporate Finance; Securities; Venture Capital; Corporate Governance. ***Email:*** fjensen@pillsburywinthrop.com

(This Listing Continued)

KELLY J. McCLURE, born October 4, 1966; admitted to bar, 1991, Connecticut. *Education:* University of Arizona (B.A., cum laude, 1988); University of Bridgeport (J.D., cum laude, 1991). Member and Managing Editor, Bridgeport Law Review, 1989-1991. ***Email:*** kmcclure@pillsburywinthrop.com

KENT S. NEVINS, born July 13, 1960; admitted to bar, 1985, Connecticut; 1986, New York and New Jersey. *Education:* Pace University (B.B.A., summa cum laude, 1982; J.D., magna cum laude, 1985). Member, Pace Law Review. ***PRACTICE AREAS:*** Real Estate; Leasing; Business Law; Banking Law. ***Email:*** knevins@pillsburywinthrop.com

KRISTAN L. PETERS, born Pensacola, Florida, 1960; admitted to bar, 1987, Pennsylvania; 1988, District of Columbia; 1991, U.S. District Court, District of Columbia and U.S. Court of Appeals for the D.C. Circuit; 1996, U.S. District Court, District of Maryland; 1997, Maryland and U.S. Court of Appeals, 4th Circuit; 1998, U.S. Supreme Court and U.S. District Court, District of Connecticut; 1999, U.S. District Court, District of Colorado; 2000, Connecticut, New York and U.S. District Court, Southern and Eastern Districts of New York. *Education:* Cornell University (B.S., Industrial and Labor Relations, 1982); Universita d'Urbino, Italy; Wellthon Academy, Barcelona, Spain; University of Texas (J.D., 1987). Symposium Editor, Texas International Law Journal. Author: "AT&T's Family-Care Union Agreement: A Harbinger of Change in Corporate America?" Employment Relations Today, Autumn 1989; "The Impact of Islamic Revivalism on Contract and Riba Law in Iran, Saudi Arabia and Egypt," 23:2 Tex. Int'l L.J., 1987. Co-Author: "Disparate Impact After Wards Cove," Advanced Conference in Employees Relations Law, IAML, April 1990. Litigated cases in: New York, Connecticut, Washington, D.C., Maryland, Virginia, Kentucky, Florida, California, Utah, Missouri, Colorado, Rhode Island and Indiana. Assistant United States Attorney, Washington, D.C., 1991-1996. ***LANGUAGES:*** Spanish, French and Italian. ***REPORTED CASES:*** Johnson v. Albright, 992 F. Supp.37 (D.D.C. 1998); Gonzalez v. U.S. 697 A.2d 819 (D.C. 1997); Passarell v. Glickman, 1997 WL 118407 (D.D.C. 1997); Strategic Analysis, Inc. v. U.S. Dept. of Navy, 939 F. Supp. 18, (D.D.C. 1996); Zellers v. U.S., 682 A.2d 1118 (D.C. 1996); Summers v. U.S. Dept. of Justice, 934 F. Supp. 458 (D.D.C. 1996); U.S. v. Bruce, 89 F.3d 886 (D.C. Cir., 1996); U.S. v. Sanchez, 88 F.3d 1243 (D.C. Cir. 1996); Deters v. U.S. Parole Com'n, 85 F.3d 655 (D.C. Cir. 1996); Davis v. Dalton, 929 F. Supp. 467 (D.D.C. 1996); U.S. v. Sammoury, 74 F. 3d 1341 (D.C. Cir. 1996); Hillard v. U.S., 638 A.2d 698 (D.C. 1994); Gray v. U.S., 617 A.2d 521 (D.C. 1992); U.S. v. Olibrices, 979 F.2d 1557 (D.C. Cir. 1992); U.S. v. Boney, 977 F.2d 624 (D.C. Cir. 1992); Earle v. U.S., 612 A. 2d 1258 (D.C. 1992); Portillo v. U.S., 609 A.2d 687 (D.C. 1992); Moore v. U.S., 608 A.2d 144 (D.C. 1992); Minnick v. U.S., 607 A.2d 519 (D.C. 1992); Williamson v. U.S., 607 A.2d 471 (D.C. 1992); U.S. v. Allen, 960 F.2d 1055 (D.C. Cir. 1992); U.S. v. Montague, 958 F.2d 1094 (D.C. Cir. 1991); Colbert v. U.S., 601 A.2d 603 (D.C. 1992); U.S. v. Johnson, 952 F.2d 1407 (D.C. Cir. 1992); Judge v. U.S., 599 A.2d 417 (D.C. 1991). ***PRACTICE AREAS:*** Employment Law; Commercial Litigation; Torts; Criminal Law.

ROBERT J. RAWN, born March 2, 1965; admitted to bar, 1991, New York; 1993, Connecticut. *Education:* Princeton University (A.B., cum laude, 1987); New York University (J.D., 1990). ***Email:*** rrawn@pillsburywinthrop.com

G. WILLIAM SISLEY, born February 25, 1944; admitted to bar, 1970, New York and New Jersey 1984, Connecticut. *Education:* Princeton University (A.B., 1966); New York University (J.D., 1969). Associate Editor, Annual Survey of American Law, 1968-1969. Law Clerk, Superior Court of New Jersey, 1969-1970. Corporate Secretary and Associate General Counsel, The Continental Group, Inc., 1981-1985. *Member:* The Association of the Bar of the City of New York; The Corporate Bar Association. ***PRACTICE AREAS:*** Mergers, Acquisitions and Divestitures; Corporate Law; Business Law; Securities. ***Email:*** gsisley@pillsburywinthrop.com

COUNSEL

ARTHUR W. HOOPER, JR., born March 30, 1944; admitted to bar, 1970, New York; 1971, Connecticut. *Education:* Franklin & Marshall College (A.B., 1966); Cornell Law School (J.D., 1969). ***PRACTICE AREAS:*** Commercial Real Estate, Leasing, Banking and Lending. ***Email:*** ahooper@pillsburywinthrop.com

SHEILA ANNMARIE MOELLER, born July 15, 1956; admitted to bar, 1984, Wisconsin; 1988, New York (Not admitted in Connecticut). *Education:* University of California at Davis; Loyola Marymount University (B.A., 1980); Pepperdine University School of Law (J.D., 1984). Phi Delta Phi. Member, Pepperdine Board of Professional Standards, 1982-1983. Intern for Justice William G. Callow, Wisconsin Supreme Court, 1983. *Member:* State Bar of Wisconsin; American Bar Association (Litigation Section); Products Liability Advisory Council. ***PRACTICE AREAS:*** Products Liability; Insurance; Commercial Litigation; Toxic Torts. ***Email:*** smoeller@pillsburywinthrop.com

ASSOCIATES

GEORGE P. BARBARESI, born September 13, 1954; admitted to bar, 1992, New York; 1998, District of Columbia (Not admitted in Connecticut). *Education:* Yale University; Stanford University (B.S., 1978); J. Reuben Clark

(This Listing Continued)

School of Law, Brigham Young University (J.D., magna cum laude, 1991). Member, 1989-1990 and Managing Editor, 1990-1991, Brigham Young University Law Review. Order of the Coif. ***PRACTICE AREAS:*** Mergers and Acquisitions; Securities; Corporate Law. ***Email:*** gbarbaresi@pillsburywinthrop.com

J. CHRISTOPHER CLIFTON, admitted to bar, 2000, New York, Indiana (inactive) and U.S. District Court, Northern and Southern Districts of Indiana; 2001, Connecticut. *Education:* The University of the State of New York (B.S., 1994); Vanderbilt University (M.B.A./J.D., 1999). Beta Gamma Sigma. Associate Editor, Vanderbilt Journal of Transnational Law. Certified Public Accountant, Maryland, 1995. *Member:* American Bar Association; American Institute of Certified Public Accountants; American Association of Attorney-Certified Public Accountants. ***PRACTICE AREAS:*** Corporate Law; Mergers and Acquisitions; Private Equity; Securities. ***Email:*** jclifton@pillsburywinthrop.com

STEPHEN J. CURLEY, born April 25, 1967; admitted to bar, 1991, Connecticut; 1992, U.S. District Court, District of Connecticut and Southern and Eastern Districts of New York; 1993, U.S. Court of Appeals, Second Circuit; 1994, U.S. Court of Appeals, Fourth and Seventh Circuits; 2001, District of Columbia. *Education:* Bowdoin College (A.B., cum laude, 1988); Boston College (J.D., cum laude, 1991). Staff Writer, 1989-1990 and Executive Editor, 1990-1991, Uniform Commercial Code Reporter-Digest. *Member:* Stamford/Norwalk, Connecticut and American Bar Associations. ***LANGUAGES:*** Russian. ***PRACTICE AREAS:*** Commercial Litigation. ***Email:*** scurley@pillsburywinthrop.com

POLLY DEVEAU DAVIS, born Manhattan, New York, June 19, 1963; admitted to bar, 1991, Connecticut. *Education:* Saint Michael's College (B.A., 1985); Vermont Law School (J.D., cum laude, 1991). *Member:* American Bar Association. ***PRACTICE AREAS:*** Commercial Real Estate; Property Law; Corporate Law. ***Email:*** pdavis@pillsburywinthrop.com

MICHAEL FORREST, admitted to bar, 1996, New York and New Jersey (Not admitted in Connecticut). *Education:* Binghamton University (B.A., 1993); George Washington University (J.D., 1996). Alan Dershowitz Fellow. *Member:* New York State Bar Association. (General Counsel). ***PRACTICE AREAS:*** Real Estate. ***Email:*** mforrest@pillsburywinthrop.com

MATTHEW C. FROST, born Torrington, Connecticut, June 16, 1967; admitted to bar, 1997, New York (Not admitted in Connecticut). *Education:* Colgate University (B.A., 1989); William & Mary Law School (J.D., 1996). Senior Professional Articles Editor, William & Mary Law Review. ***Email:*** mfrost@pillsburywinthrop.com

DONALD J. RICCITELLI, born August 17, 1964; admitted to bar, 1999, Connecticut; 2000, New York. *Education:* Yale University (B.A., History, 1996); Boston University (J.D., 1999). ***Email:*** driccitelli@pillsburywinthrop.com

VAYA SINHA, born Palina, Bihar, India, February 16, 1972; admitted to bar, 2001, New York (Not admitted in Connecticut). *Education:* The University of Delhi (B.A., with honors, 1993); University of Virginia (LL.M., 1999). ***LANGUAGES:*** Hindi. ***Email:*** jaya_kumea@hotmail.com

HENRY K. SNYDER, born February 18, 1967; admitted to bar, 1996, Connecticut; 1997, New York and U.S. District Court, District of Connecticut; 1998, U.S. District Court, Southern District of New York. *Education:* University of Pennsylvania (B.A., with honors, 1989); University of Connecticut (J.D., 1996). Member, 1994-1995, Editor, 1995-1996, Connecticut Law Review. Legislative Assistant, United States Senate, 1989-1993. *Member:* New York State and Connecticut Bar Associations. ***PRACTICE AREAS:*** Litigation; Life Sciences and Technology. ***Email:*** hsnyder@pillsburywinthrop.com

COZATA SOLLOWAY, born September 13, 1972; admitted to bar, 1997, Connecticut; 1998, New York. *Education:* Pace University (B.A., summa cum laude, 1994); Pace University School of Law (J.D., summa cum laude, 1997). Managing Editor, Pace Law Review, 1996-1997. Co-Author (with Sean F. Nolon), "Preserving Our Heritage: Tools to Cultivate Agricultural Preservation in New York State," Pace Law Review, Spring, 1997. ***PRACTICE AREAS:*** Real Estate; Corporate Law; Capital Markets. ***Email:*** csolloway@pillsburywinthrop.com

VICKI E. VOLPER, born June 24, 1955; admitted to bar, 1982, Massachusetts; 1983, New York; 1990, Connecticut. *Education:* State University of New York at Binghamton (B.A., 1977); Boston University School of Law (J.D., cum laude, 1982); New York University School of Law (LL.M., Taxation, 1987). ***Email:*** vvolper@pillsburywinthrop.com

LORI IANNOTTI ZYSKOWSKI, born April 21, 1971; admitted to bar, 1996, Connecticut; 1998, New York. *Education:* Harvard University (A.B., cum laude, 1993); Columbia University School of Law (J.D., 1996). Harlan Fiske Stone Scholar. Member and Managing Editor, Columbia-VLA Journal of Law and the Arts. ***Email:*** lzyskowski@pillsburywinthrop.com

(For biographical data on San Francisco, CA, New York, NY, Los Angeles, CA, Vienna, VA, Costa Mesa, CA, Palm Beach, FL, Sacramento, CA, San Diego, CA, Palo Alto, CA, Washington, DC, London, England, Sydney, Australia, Tokyo, Japan, Hong Kong, China and Singapore personnel, see Professional Biographies at each of those cities)

ROBERT B. POTASH

STAMFORD, CONNECTICUT

(See Greenwich)

General Practice, Real Estate, Probate and Estate Planning.

PULLMAN & COMLEY, L.L.C.

Established in 1919

(Formerly Pullman, Comley, Bradley & Reeves)

350 BEDFORD STREET

STAMFORD, CONNECTICUT 06901-1743

Telephone: 203-324-5000

Telecopier: 203-363-8659

URL: http://www.pullcom.com

Bridgeport, Connecticut Office: 850 Main Street. Telephone: 203-330-2000. Telecopier: 203-576-8888.

Hartford, Connecticut Office: 90 State House Square. Telephone: 860-424-4300. Telecopier: 860-424-4370.

New Haven, Connecticut Office: One Century Tower, 265 Church Street. Telephone: 203-773-3006. Telecopier: 203-776-7075.

Simsbury, Connecticut Office: 720 Hopmeadow Street. Telephone: 860-651-9348. Fax: 860-651-1431.

Southport, Connecticut Office: 200 Pequot Avenue, P.O. Box 510. Telephone: 203-254-5000. Telecopier: 203-254-5070.

General Practice including Administrative, Antitrust, Banking, Bankruptcy and Creditors Rights, Bonds, Business and Commercial, Corporate, Education, Employee Benefits, Environmental, Hospital and Health Care, Labor and Employment, Municipal Finance, Real Estate, Securities, Tax, Trusts and Estates, and Zoning. Energy and Utilities, Litigation in all Courts.

JOHN S. PULLMAN (1871-1943).

ARTHUR M. COMLEY (1883-1969).

J. KENNETH BRADLEY (1903-1969).

WILLIAM REEVES (1906-1967).

MEMBERS OF FIRM

ELIZABETH J. AUSTIN, born New York, N.Y., February 19, 1957; admitted to bar, 1983, Texas, Nebraska and U.S. District Court, Northern District of Texas; 1988, U.S. District Court, Eastern District of Texas; 1989, U.S. District Court, Western District of Texas and District of Connecticut; 1990, Connecticut; 1999, U.S. District Court, Southern District of New York. *Education:* University of Nebraska (B.A., 1979; J.D., 1982). *Member:* Bridgeport (Chairperson, Commercial Law Committee), Connecticut (Chair, Commercial Law and Bankruptcy Section), Nebraska State and American Bar Associations; State Bar of Texas; Commercial Law League of America; American Bankruptcy Institute; International Women's Insolvency and Restructuring Confederation; Women's Bankruptcy Bar Association (Founding Member; Executive Committee Member). (Also at New Haven, Hartford and Bridgeport Offices). ***PRACTICE AREAS:*** Insolvency Law; Bankruptcy Litigation; Commercial Litigation. ***Email:*** EA@PULLCOM.COM

DEBORAH S. BRECK, born Aurora, Colorado, April 14, 1953; admitted to bar, 1983, Connecticut; 2000, U.S. Tax Court. *Education:* Kingswood-Oxford School; Syracuse University; Southern Connecticut State University (B.A., 1975); University of Connecticut (J.D., with honors, 1982). Associate Editor, Connecticut Law Review, 1981-1982. *Member:* Bridgeport, Connecticut (Member: Estates and Probate Section; Legal Problems of the Elderly Section) and American (Member, Real Property, Probate and Trust Law Section) Bar Associations. (Also at Bridgeport and Southport Offices). ***PRACTICE AREAS:*** Estates and Trusts; Elder Law; Trust and Probate Litigation. ***Email:*** DSB@PULLCOM.COM

CHARLES K. CAMPBELL, JR., born Evanston, Illinois, May 13, 1949; admitted to bar, 1976, Connecticut. *Education:* Brown University (A.B., 1971); Vanderbilt University (J.D., 1976). Associate Editor, Vanderbilt Law Review, 1975-1976. *Member:* Greenwich, Connecticut (Officer, Executive Committee, Conservation and Environmental Quality Section, 1980-1991) and American Bar Associations. ***PRACTICE AREAS:*** Environmental Law; Land Use Planning; Real Estate Law. ***Email:*** CKC@PULLCOM.COM

JOSEPH M. LODATO, born Greenwich, Connecticut, July 12, 1964; admitted to bar, 1989, Connecticut. *Education:* Georgetown University (B.S.B.A., 1986); Georgetown University Law Center (J.D., 1989). Board of Directors, Sound View Community Media, Inc.; Board of Directors and Vice President, Business Legal Services, Inc. *Member:* Bridgeport, Stamford/Norwalk Regional (Co-Chair, Business Law Committee), Connecticut and American Bar Associa-

(This Listing Continued)

PULLMAN & COMLEY, L.L.C., Stamford—Continued

tions. ***PRACTICE AREAS:*** Corporate Law; Partnership Law; Commercial Law; Nonprofit and Charitable Organizations; Securities Law. ***Email:*** JML@PULLCOM.COM

ANDREW J. McDONALD, born Stamford, Connecticut, March 11, 1966; admitted to bar, 1991, Connecticut; 1992, U.S. District Court, District of Connecticut; 1997, U.S. Court of Appeals, Second Circuit. *Education:* Cornell University (A.B., 1988); University of Connecticut School of Law (J.D., with honors, 1991). Phi Delta Phi. Recipient, George and Lorraine Schatzki Award for Service. Managing Editor, Connecticut Journal of International Law, 1990-1991. Member, Stamford Board of Representatives, 1993-1995. Member, 1995-1999, and Chairman, 1997-1999, Stamford Board of Finance. Member, Board of Directors, Stamford Partnership, 1997—; Member, Board of Directors, Women's Business Development Center, 2000—. Trustee, Certified Employees Retirement Fund, 1997-1999; Director of Legal Affairs and Corporation Counsel, City of Stamford, 1999—. *Member:* Bridgeport, Stamford/Norwalk Regional (Co-Chairman, Municipal Law Section, 2000—), Connecticut and American Bar Associations; Connecticut Trial Lawyers Association. ***PRACTICE AREAS:*** Commercial Litigation; Municipal Law; Property Valuation. ***Email:*** AM@PULLCOM.COM

ROBERT B. MITCHELL, born Bremerton, Washington, March 27, 1953; admitted to bar, 1979, New York and U.S. District Court, Southern District of New York; 1980, Louisiana; 1981, U.S. Court of Appeals, Fifth and Eleventh Circuits; 1987, U.S. District Court, Western District of Louisiana; 1988, Connecticut and U.S. District Court, District of Connecticut; 1989, U.S. Court of Appeals, Second Circuit and U.S. Supreme Court. *Education:* Ohio Wesleyan University (B.A., 1975); Tulane University School of Law (J.D., 1978). Order of the Coif. Member, Board of Student Editors, 1976-1978, and Comments Editor, 1977-1978, Tulane Law Review. Member Monroe, Connecticut Economic Development Commission, 1990-1993; Member Monroe, Connecticut Town Council, 1993-1999. Special Master, United States District Court, District of Connecticut, 1993—. Connecticut State Court Arbitrator and Trial Referee, Connecticut Superior Court, Judicial District of Fairfield at Bridgeport. *Member:* Bridgeport (Member, Sections on: Civil, Labor and Employment, Chair, 1994-1995), Louisiana State, Connecticut (Member: Federal Practice Section; Member, Executive Board, Labor Section, 1997-1999) and American (Member, Sections on Labor and Tort and Insurance Practice) Bar Associations. (Also at Bridgeport Office). ***PRACTICE AREAS:*** General Civil Litigation; Trial Practice; Labor Law; Employment Law; Civil Rights Law; Insurance Defense. ***Email:*** RXM@PULLCOM.COM

D. ROBERT MORRIS, born Rochester, New York, August 23, 1950; admitted to bar, 1975, Connecticut; 1976, New York; 1977, Florida. *Education:* Cornell University (B.A., cum laude, 1972; J.D., 1975); New York University (LL.M., in Taxation, 1976). Co-Author: "Annual Reporting Requirements for Welfare Benefit Plans and Fringe Benefit Plans," Connecticut CPA Quarterly, September 1990. *Member:* Bridgeport, Connecticut (Member, Executive Committee, Tax Section) and American (Member, Sections on: Taxation; Business Law) Bar Associations; The Florida Bar. (Also at Bridgeport Office). ***PRACTICE AREAS:*** Taxation Law; Corporate Law; Employee Benefits Law; Estate Planning; Computer Law. ***Email:*** DRM@PULLCOM.COM

ELLIOTT B. POLLACK, born Brooklyn, New York, January 20, 1943; admitted to bar, 1965, Connecticut; 1966, U.S. District Court, District of Connecticut; 1969, U.S. Court of Appeals, Second Circuit and U.S. Supreme Court. *Education:* Columbia College (A.B., 1962); Columbia University (LL.B., 1965). Law Clerk to Associate Justice Howard W. Alcorn, Supreme Court of Connecticut, 1965-1966. Town Councilman, West Hartford, 1975-1977. Board of Directors, Hartford Dispensary, 1988—. President, Hartford Dispensary, 1991-1996; Board of Directors, Solomon Schechter Day School of Greater Hartford, 1990-1996, 1997-1999. Member, State of Connecticut Medical Examining Board, 1991-1994; Board of Directors, Hartford Stage Company, 1991-1999; Board of Directors, 1993—; Vice President, 1999-2001; President, 2001—; Capitol Area Foundation for Equal Justice. Member, Board of Directors and Secretary, Connecticut Health Lawyers Association, 1999—. *Member:* Hartford County, Connecticut (Member: Administrative Law Section; Health Law Section) and American (Member, Sections of: Health Law; Antitrust) Bar Associations; American Health Lawyers Association; Healthcare Financial Management Association; Institute for Professionals in Taxation (Legal Committee); International Association of Assessing Officers; American Property Tax Counsel. James W. Cooper Fellow, Connecticut Bar Foundation. (Also at Bridgeport and Hartford Offices). ***PRACTICE AREAS:*** Health Care; Tax Appeal and Condemnation Law; Commercial Litigation. ***Email:*** EBP@PULLCOM.COM

MARGARET M. SHEAHAN, born Bronx, New York, August 10, 1954; admitted to bar, 1980, New York and Connecticut; 1981, U.S. District Court, District of Connecticut, 1987, U.S. Court of Appeals, Second Circuit. *Education:* Fordham University (B.A., magna cum laude, 1976); New York University (J.D., 1980). *Member:* Bridgeport, Connecticut and American (Member, Section

(This Listing Continued)

on Labor and Employment Law) Bar Associations. (Also at Bridgeport Office). ***PRACTICE AREAS:*** Labor Law; Employment Law; Civil Litigation. ***Email:*** MMS@PULLCOM.COM

JAMES T. SHEARIN, born Staunton, Virginia, March 11, 1961; admitted to bar, 1986, Connecticut; 1987, U.S. District Court, District of Connecticut; 1988, U.S. Court of Appeals, Second Circuit; 1995, U.S. Supreme Court; 1997, U.S. Court of Federal Claims. *Education:* University of Connecticut (B.A., summa cum laude, 1983; J.D.; with high honors, 1986). Recipient, William F. Starr Outstanding Student Award. Administrative Editor, Connecticut Law Review, 1985-1986. Author: "The Discrimination Statutes and the Supreme Court's Program for Confusion," 17 Conn. L. Rev. 3 (1985). Co-author: "What to do When the Feds Grab for Collateral," ABA Banking Journal, Vol. LXXX16, No. 2; Commentary: "Working for Which Side," The Record, No. 175 (September 10, 1993). Author: "The Expert Witness and Mandatory Disclosure: Comply or Suffer the Consequences," Vol. 14, No. 2, CTLA Forum 136 (March/April, 1996); "Lawyering from the *John*," Vol. 6, No. 7, Connecticut Lawyer 28 (April 1996); "Protecting Your Eventual Judgment for Money Damages," The Banking Law Journal (October, 1998). Co-author: "Zealousness and Honesty in Settlement Discussion," Connecticut Law Tribune Magazine (August 9, 1999); "Medical Malpractice Liability: It's Not Just For Doctors Anymore," Vol. 11, No. 5. Connecticut Lawyer 4 (February 2001). Law Clerk, Hon. Peter C. Dorsey, District of Connecticut, 1986-1988. Member, Raymond E. Baldwin Inn of Courts, 1989—. Appointed Co-Counsel to Federal Grievance Committee (D.Conn.) 1997—. Member and Chairman, Connecticut Legal Services. President, UConn Law School Foundation, Inc. James W. Cooper Fellow, Connecticut Bar Foundation. *Member:* Bridgeport (President), Connecticut (Member: Federal Practice and Intellectual Property Sections, Executive Committees) and American Bar Associations; The Association of Trial Lawyers of America; Connecticut Trial Lawyers Association. (Also at Bridgeport and Hartford Offices). ***PRACTICE AREAS:*** Litigation; Intellectual Property; Admiralty; Securities. ***Email:*** JTS@PULLCOM.COM

(For Complete Biographical Data on all Personnel, See Bridgeport, Connecticut Professional Biographies).

QUATRELLA & RIZIO, LLC

STAMFORD, CONNECTICUT

(See Fairfield)

General Civil Practice, Real Estate, Commercial, Corporate, Probate, Commercial and Residential Landlord and Tenant, Financial, Partnership and Negligence Law.

STUART B. RATNER, P.C.

111 PROSPECT STREET
STAMFORD, CONNECTICUT 06901-1208
Telephone: 203-323-4900
Fax: 203-323-4141
Email: sbratner@hotmail.com
URL: http://www.lawyers.com/stuartratner

Federal and State Tax Law, Estate Planning and General Corporate.

STUART B. RATNER, born Hartford, Connecticut, October 17, 1956; admitted to bar, 1981, Connecticut; 1982, New York; 1986, U.S. Tax Court; 1994, U.S District Court, District of Connecticut. *Education:* University of Connecticut (B.S., 1978); Syracuse University (J.D., 1981); New York University (LL.M. in Taxation, 1982). Certified Public Accountant, Connecticut, 1982. Lecturer: The Accountants Role in Bankruptcy; Selected Bankruptcy Tax Issues. *Member:* Connecticut and American (Member, Sections on: Taxation; Economics of Law Practice) Bar Associations; American Institute of Certified Public Accountants; Connecticut Society of Certified Public Accountants. ***PRACTICE AREAS:*** Tax Controversies (50%, 200); Criminal Taxation; Estate Planning (30%, 100); Corporate Law (20%, 90).

JOHN P. REGAN

1200 SUMMER STREET, SUITE 103
STAMFORD, CONNECTICUT 06905
Telephone: 203-324-4661
Fax: 203-359-4397
Email: jpreganesq@aol.com
URL: http://www.lawyers.com/jprlaw

General Civil and Criminal Trial Practice, Commercial Litigation, Landlord Tenant, Family, Personal Injury, Real Estate, Estates, Probate Law, Wills and Medical Malpractice.

JOHN P. REGAN, born New York City, New York, June 23, 1961; admitted to bar, 1989, Connecticut and U.S. District Court, District of Connecticut. *Education:* Siena College (B.A., 1983); University of Bridgeport (J.D., 1987).

(This Listing Continued)

Law Clerk to the Judges, Stamford/Norwalk Judicial Districts, Connecticut Superior Court, 1988-1989. *Member:* Stamford Regional, Connecticut and American Bar Associations. ***LANGUAGES:*** French. ***PRACTICE AREAS:*** Commercial Law; Collections; Corporate Law; Business Law; Real Estate; Accidents; Criminal Law; White Collar Crime; Driving While Intoxicated; Personal Injury; Child Custody; Divorce; Bankruptcy; Automobile Accidents and Injuries.

REFERENCES: Fleet Bank: Patriot National Bank.

ROBERTS, ROSE & BATES, P.C.

Established in 1973

1055 WASHINGTON BOULEVARD
EIGHTH FLOOR
P.O. BOX 15630
STAMFORD, CONNECTICUT 06901
Telephone: 203-324-6755
Telecopier: 203-348-5802
URL: http://www.lawyers.com/robertsrosebates

General Practice, Litigation, Real Estate, Leasing, Banking, Matrimonial, Probate, Estate Planning and Trusts, International Business, Employment Law.

JOHN W. ROBERTS, born Stamford, Connecticut, 1932; admitted to bar, 1958, Connecticut; 1960, U.S. District Court, District of Connecticut; 1963, U.S. Supreme Court; 1965, U.S. District Court, Southern District of New York; 1966, U.S. Court of Appeals, Second Circuit. *Education:* Yale University (B.A., 1954); University of Pennsylvania (LL.B., 1958). Law Clerk to Hon. Irving Ben Cooper, U.S. District Court, Southern District of New York, 1962. Trial Attorney, U.S. Department of Justice, 1958-1959. Chairman, Greenwich, Connecticut, Housing Authority, 1978-1982. Special Pre-Trial Master, Connecticut Superior Court, 1983—. *Member:* Greenwich, Stamford/Norwalk Regional, Connecticut and American Bar Associations; Federal Bar Council. ***PRACTICE AREAS:*** Trusts and Estates; Probate; Real Estate; Civil Litigation; Matrimonial; Employment Law.

RICHARD L. ROSE, born Long Branch, New Jersey, 1936; admitted to bar, 1964, New York; 1966, Connecticut. *Education:* Cornell University (A.B., 1958); Washington & Lee University (J.D., 1963). Chairman, Advisory Committee to the Mayor of the City of Bridgeport, for the Bridgeport Foreign Trade Zone, 1989-1990. Member, United States Department of Commerce, Connecticut District Export Council, 1989-1991. General Counsel, Bridgeport Port Authority. *Member:* New York State, Connecticut (Member: Special Advisory Committee to the Connecticut Banking Commissioner on the Connecticut Securities Law, 1978—) and American Bar Associations; Connecticut World Trade Association (Director, 1989—). ***PRACTICE AREAS:*** Banking Law; Corporate Law; Securities; International Business Law.

ELIZABETH LEWIS BATES, born New London, Connecticut, 1953; admitted to bar, 1978, Massachusetts; 1979, U.S. District Court, District of Massachusetts; 1982, Connecticut. *Education:* Smith College (A.B., 1975); Northeastern University (J.D., 1978). *Member:* Stamford/Norwalk Regional, Greenwich, Connecticut and American Bar Associations. ***LANGUAGES:*** French. ***PRACTICE AREAS:*** Real Estate; Zoning, Planning and Land Use; Trusts and Estates; Probate.

COUNSEL

WILLIAM D. GAILLARD, born New York, N.Y., 1931; admitted to bar, 1956, New York; 1972, Connecticut; 1978, U.S. Supreme Court; 1989, U.S. District Court, Southern District of New York; 1990, U.S. District Court, District of Connecticut. *Education:* Princeton University (A.B., 1953); Harvard University (LL.B., 1956). ***PRACTICE AREAS:*** Corporate Law; Commercial Law.

MARY-ELIZABETH JACQUES, born New York, N.Y.; admitted to bar, 1953, Connecticut. *Education:* Vassar College (A.B., with honors, 1943) Phi Beta Kappa; Harvard University (J.D., cum laude, 1953). President, Harvard Law School Association of Connecticut, 1978-1980. *Member:* Greenwich, Stamford/Norwalk Regional, Connecticut (Member, Executive Committee, Estates and Probate Section, 1980—) and American Bar Associations; American Society of Law, Medicine and Ethics. ***PRACTICE AREAS:*** Probate; Trusts and Estates.

JOSEPH A. IZZILLO, born New York, N.Y., 1924; admitted to bar, 1951, New York; 1952, Connecticut; 1954, U.S. District Court, District of Connecticut; 1958, U.S. District Court, Southern and Eastern Districts of New York; 1960, U.S. Supreme Court. *Education:* Fordham University (1948); St. John's University (J.D., 1951). *Member:* Greenwich and Connecticut Bar Associations; National Academy of Elder Law Attorneys. ***PRACTICE AREAS:*** Guardianship and Conservatorship; Trusts and Estates.

AMY L. STAROBIN, born Brookline, Massachusetts, 1960; admitted to bar, 1986, Connecticut; 1987, New York. *Education:* Hobart and William Smith Colleges (B.A., 1982); University of Denver (J.D., 1986). Member, Administrative Law Review. ***PRACTICE AREAS:*** Civil Litigation; Employment Law; Matrimonial.

(This Listing Continued)

REPRESENTATIVE CLIENTS: Fort James Corp.; Connecticut World Trade Association; Care Technologies, Inc.; Mobil Oil Corp.; Sun Oil Co.; Index Corp.; Bridgeport Port Authority; First Union Bank; Cornerstone Bank.

ROBINSON & COLE LLP

Established in 1845

FINANCIAL CENTRE
695 EAST MAIN STREET
P.O. BOX 10305
STAMFORD, CONNECTICUT 06904-2305
Telephone: 203-462-7500
Fax: 203-462-7599
Email: stam.rc.com
URL: http://www.rc.com

Other Offices: Hartford CT, Greenwich, CT, New London, CT, Boston, MA, New York, NY, and Manchester, NH.

General Practice including Admiralty, Antitrust and Trade Regulation, Appellate, Banking and Institutional Finance, Bankruptcy and Creditors' Rights, Business Litigation, Business Workouts, Construction, Corporate and Closely Held Business, Criminal Litigation, E-Commerce and Intellectual Property, Employee Benefits and ERISA Litigation, Employment Litigation and Counseling, Environmental, Estate Planning and Probate, Government Relations, Healthcare, Immigration, Insurance, International, Labor Relations and Collective Bargaining, Land Use and Zoning, Personal Injury, Product Liability, Professional Liability, Public Finance, Real Estate Finance, Development and Leasing, Securities, Tax-Exempt Organizations, Tax Planning and Representation, Utilities and Telecommunications.

PARTNERS

FRANK LEWIS BAKER, III, admitted to bar, 1973, Connecticut; 1988, New York. *Education:* Yale University (B.A., with honors, 1968); University of Virginia (J.D., 1973). Member, University of Virginia Law Review. [U.S. Army Military Police Corps, 1970-1972]. ***PRACTICE AREAS:*** Real Estate; Finance; Taxation. ***Email:*** fbaker@stam.rc.com

DAVID W. BOGAN, admitted to bar, 1986, Connecticut; U.S. District Court, District of Connecticut. *Education:* University of Bridgeport (B.S., cum laude, 1982; J.D., 1985). Board of Directors, Connecticut Bar Foundation, 2000—; Staff Attorney: Connecticut Office of the Consumer Counsel; Connecticut Department of Public Utility Control; Connecticut Office of the Chief State's Attorney. Treasurer, 1995-1996, Chair, Public Service Committee, 1998—, Public Utility Section, 1992—, Litigation Section, 1996—and Member, House of Delegates, 1996—, Connecticut Bar Association. ***PRACTICE AREAS:*** Administrative Law; Telecommunications; Energy. ***Email:*** dbogan@stam.rc.com

ELIZABETH L. BRENNAN, admitted to bar, 1987, Connecticut; 1988, U.S. District Court, District of Connecticut; 1999, New York. *Education:* Trinity College (B.A., 1984); University of Connecticut School of Law (J.D., 1987). (Resident). ***PRACTICE AREAS:*** Real Estate; Finance; Construction Law; Commercial Leasing. ***Email:*** ebrennan@stam.rc.com

JOSEPH L. CLASEN, admitted to bar, 1981, New York; 1990, Connecticut; U.S. District Court, Eastern and Southern Districts of New York; U.S. District Court, District of Connecticut; U.S. Court of Appeals, Second and Seventh Circuits. *Education:* Boston College (A.B., magna cum laude, 1977); University of Virginia (J.D., 1980). Order of the Coif. Member, University of Virginia Law Review. ***PRACTICE AREAS:*** Litigation; Creditors' Rights; Bankruptcy. ***Email:*** jclasen@stam.rc.com

STUART R. DEANS, admitted to bar, 1982, New Jersey; 1988, Connecticut. *Education:* The Lawrenceville School; Williams College (B.A., cum laude, 1978); Vermont Law School (1978-1980); Rutgers University (J.D., 1981). Assistant Regional Counsel, U.S. Environmental Protection Agency, Region II, 1985-1987. ***PRACTICE AREAS:*** Environmental Law; Zoning, Planning and Land Use. ***Email:*** sdeans@stam.rc.com

STEVEN L. ELBAUM, admitted to bar, 1992, Connecticut; 1993, U.S. District Court, District of Connecticut. *Education:* Wesleyan University (B.A., 1986); Boston University (J.D., 1992). Editor in Chief, Probate Law Journal, 1991-1992. Law Clerk, Hon. Thomas F. Fay, Chief Justice of the Supreme Court of Rhode Island, 1992-1993. ***PRACTICE AREAS:*** Real Estate; Finance; Commercial Leasing. ***Email:*** selbaum@stam.rc.com

GREGORY E. HARMER, admitted to bar, 1981, Pennsylvania; 1983, New Jersey; 1985, Connecticut. *Education:* Fairfield University (B.A., 1977); John Marshall School of Law (J.D., with distinction, 1981). *Member:* Association of Commercial Finance Attorneys. ***PRACTICE AREAS:*** Corporate; Finance; Bankruptcy; Banking Law; Corporate Law. ***Email:*** gharmer@stam.rc.com

(This Listing Continued)

ROBINSON & COLE LLP, Stamford—Continued

STEVEN R. HUMPHREY, admitted to bar, 1966, Massachusetts; 1967, Connecticut; U.S. Court of Appeals, Second Circuit; U.S. District Court, Districts of Connecticut and Massachusetts; U.S. Supreme Court. *Education:* Wesleyan University (B.A., 1963); Vanderbilt University (J.D., 1966). Phi Alpha Delta. ***PRACTICE AREAS:*** Energy; Litigation; Telecommunications. ***Email:*** shumphrey@stam.rc.com

RICHARD A. KRANTZ, admitted to bar, 1975, Massachusetts; 1976, U.S. District Court, District of Massachusetts and U.S. Court of Appeals, First Circuit; 1979, New York and U.S. Supreme Court; 1989, Connecticut. *Education:* Johns Hopkins University (B.A., 1970); Harvard University (J.D., 1974). Phi Beta Kappa. Member, Harvard Legal Aid Bureau, 1972-1973. ***PRACTICE AREAS:*** Corporate Law; Securities. ***Email:*** rkrantz@stam.rc.com

GREGORY J. LIGELIS, admitted to bar, 1976, New York; 1989, Connecticut; U.S. Court of Appeals for the Federal Circuit; U.S. Court of International Trade; U.S. Court of Appeals, Second Circuit; U.S. District Court, Southern, Eastern, Western and Northern Districts of New York; U.S. District Court, District of Connecticut. *Education:* Hofstra University (B.A., magna cum laude, 1972); University of Pennsylvania (J.D., 1975). Adjunct Law Professor, Admiralty and Marine Insurance, University of Connecticut Law School. *Member:* Connecticut World Trade Association; International Bar Association (Member, Committee on Maritime Law and Transport). ***PRACTICE AREAS:*** Admiralty and Maritime Law; Litigation; Arbitration; Insurance. ***Email:*** gligelis@stam.rc.com

BRIAN E. MORAN, admitted to bar, 1978, Virginia and District of Columbia; 1987, Connecticut. *Education:* University of Virginia (B.A., with distinction, 1975); University of Richmond (J.D., 1978). National Moot Court Team. Editor, e-counsel: The Executive's Guide to Doing Business on the Internet (2000 Edition). *Member:* Connecticut Intellectual Property Law Association; Computer Law Association; The Regional Bar Association (Member, Internet Law Committee). ***PRACTICE AREAS:*** Litigation; Antitrust and Trade Regulation; Intellectual Property; Technology and Science. ***Email:*** bmoran@stam.rc.com

COUNSEL

DAVID J. BURKE, admitted to bar, 1988, Connecticut; 1989, New York and U.S. District Court, District of Connecticut; U.S. District Court, Southern, Northern and Eastern Districts of New York. *Education:* College of the Holy Cross (B.A., 1966); Wagner College (M.B.A., magna cum laude, 1974); Pace University School of Law (J.D., cum laude, 1988). Member, Pace University Law Review, 1987-1988. President, Board of Stamford Emergency Medical Services, Inc.; Chairperson, Health Law Section, Connecticut Bar Association. Member, Health Law Advisory Board, Pace Law School. ***PRACTICE AREAS:*** Labor and Employment; Litigation; Health Care. ***Email:*** dburke@stam.rc.com

PAMELA K. ELKOW, admitted to bar, 1989, Connecticut. *Education:* Colgate University (B.A., cum laude, 1986); George Washington University (J.D., with honors, 1989). Member, George Washington Law Review, 1988-1989. Editor, Environmental Regulation Essentials. Founder and Chair, Society of Women Environmental Professionals, Connecticut Chapter. ***PRACTICE AREAS:*** Environmental Law. ***Email:*** pelkow@stam.rc.com

CHARLES E. JANSON, born 1955; admitted to bar, 1981, Connecticut; 1982, U.S. District Court, District of Connecticut. *Education:* Williams College (B.A., cum laude, 1977); University of Connecticut School of Law (J.D., cum laude, 1981). Director, Regional Bar Association, Stamford, 2000; Advisory Board, Dahesh Museum, 2000; Board, Fairfield/Westchester County, NACORE, 1998; Trustee, Weir Farm Heritage Trust, 1997—, Director, Secretary, Fairfield 2000 Homes Corporation, 1988—. ***REPORTED CASES:*** Weiman v. Weiman 188 Conn. 232, 449 A.2d 151 (1982). ***PRACTICE AREAS:*** Real Estate; Zoning, Planning and Land Use; Environmental Law; Museum Law; Affordable Housing. ***Email:*** cjanson@stam.rc.com

JOHN F. X. PELOSO, JR., admitted to bar, 1989, Connecticut; 1990, New York and U.S. District Court, Southern District of New York; U.S. District Court, District of Connecticut. *Education:* Williams College (B.A., 1985); Fordham University (J.D., 1989). (Resident). ***PRACTICE AREAS:*** Environmental Law; Taxation; Litigation. ***Email:*** jpeloso@stam.rc.com

ASSOCIATES

JOSEPH CAREY, admitted to bar, 1975, New York and U.S. District Court, Northern District of New York; 1980, U.S. Supreme Court; 1996, Connecticut. *Education:* State University of New York at New Paltz (B.S., 1968); Albany Law School of Union University (J.D., 1974). ***Email:*** jcarey@stam.rc.com

THOMAS J. DONLON, admitted to bar, 1978, Michigan and U.S. Court of Military Appeals; 1981, U.S. Supreme Court and U.S. Court of International Trade; 1982, U.S. District Court, District of Hawaii; 1988, U.S. Court of Appeals, Fifth Circuit; 1996, New York and U.S. District Court, Southern and Eastern Districts of New York; 2001, Connecticut. *Education:* U.S. Coast Guard Academy (B.S., with high honors, 1973); University of Michigan (M.A., magna cum laude, 1977; J.D., 1978). [Comdr. U.S.Coast Guard, 1973-1996]. ***Email:*** tdonlon@stam.rc.com

KATHERINE DOWD, admitted to bar, 1992, Connecticut; 1997, California. *Education:* Smith College (B.A., 1983); College of William & Mary (J.D., 1992). ***Email:*** kdowd@stam.rc.com

ARTHUR K. ENGLE, admitted to bar, 1994, Georgia and U.S. District Court, Northern District of Georgia; 1995, U.S. District Court, Middle District of Georgia; 1999, Connecticut; 2000, U.S. District Court, District of Connecticut. *Education:* Harvard University (B.A., cum laude, 1988); Fordham University School of Law (J.D., 1994). Member, International Law Journal, 1993-1994. ***Email:*** aengle@stam.rc.com

R. KELLEY FRANCO, admitted to bar, 1995, Connecticut; 1996, New York; U.S. District Court, District of Connecticut; U.S. District Court, Southern and Eastern Districts of New York. *Education:* Institut d'Etudes Politiques de Paris (Certificat d'Etudes Politiques, 1991); Georgetown University (B.A., Government, cum laude, 1992); University of Connecticut School of Law (J.D., 1995). ***LANGUAGES:*** French. ***Email:*** rkfranco@stam.rc.com

SARAH M. HURLEY, admitted to bar, 2000, Connecticut. *Education:* Sarah Lawrence College (B.A., 1994); Pace University (J.D., 2000). ***Email:*** shurley@stam.rc.com

JOHN H. KANE, admitted to bar, 1992, Connecticut; 1993, New York and U.S. District Court, District of Connecticut; 1999, U.S. District Court, Eastern, Southern, Northern and Western Districts of New York. *Education:* Fairfield University (B.S., 1989); Fordham University (J.D., 1992). ***Email:*** jkane@stam.rc.com

STEVEN J. KOO, admitted to bar, 1998, Connecticut; 1999, New York. *Education:* University of Pennsylvania (B.S., 1995); Brooklyn Law School (J.D., 1998). ***Email:*** skoo@stam.rc.com

HIROKO MURAKI, admitted to bar, 2000, Connecticut. *Education:* Syracuse University (B.A., with honors, 1994); Pace University (J.D., 1999). ***LANGUAGES:*** Japanese. ***Email:*** hmuraki@stam.rc.com

CHRISTINA CHEN PAUL, admitted to bar, 1998, Connecticut; 1999, New York. *Education:* Colgate University (A.B., 1994); University of Connecticut (J.D., 1998). ***Email:*** cpaul@stam.rc.com

JAMES M. RUEL, admitted to bar, 1999, Connecticut; 2000, U.S. District Court, District of Connecticut. *Education:* Boston College (B.S., 1996); University of Connecticut School of Law. ***Email:*** jruel@stam.rc.com

REGINA M. SWEENEY, admitted to bar, 1994, Ireland; 1998, New York; 1999, Connecticut. *Education:* Trinity College, University of Dublin (LL.B., 1990); Georgetown University Law Center (LL.M., 1996). ***Email:*** rsweeney@stam.rc.com

Lawyers are members of local, state and national bar associations.

(For biographical data on other personnel, see Professional Biographies at Hartford, Greenwich and New London, CT, Boston, MA, New York, NY and Manchester, NH)

ROSENSTEIN & BARNES

STAMFORD, CONNECTICUT

(See Fairfield)

General Civil and Criminal Practice before State and Federal Courts. Civil Litigation, Employment Litigation, Commercial Litigation and Family Law. Domestic Relations and Child Custody Law, Covenants Not to Compete Litigation, Trials and Appeals.

RUBENSTEIN, GREEN & BASS, LLC

STAMFORD, CONNECTICUT

(See Westport)

General Civil Practice before State and Federal Courts, Real Estate, Corporation, Commercial and Banking, Personal Injury, Medical Malpractice, Estate Planning and Probate, Planning and Zoning Trials and Appeals, Banking Litigation.

JAMES M. RUBINO

1100 SUMMER STREET

STAMFORD, CONNECTICUT 06905

Telephone: 203-327-4212

Fax: 203-973-0441

URL: http://www.lawyers.com/rubinolaw

Probate and Estate Planning and Administration, Corporations, Business and Real Estate Law. Federal and State Taxation. Landlord Tenant Law.

(This Listing Continued)

JAMES M. RUBINO, born Stamford, Connecticut, April 5, 1956; admitted to bar, 1982, Connecticut and U.S. Tax Court; 1983, U.S. District Court, District of Connecticut. *Education:* Fairfield University (B.S., Accounting, 1978); University of Bridgeport (J. D., summa cum laude, 1982); New York University (LL.M., Taxation, 1987). Phi Kappa Phi; Phi Delta Phi. Member, 1993— and Chairman, 1995, Stamford Board of Finance; Stamford Board of Representatives, 1985-1993, Minority Leader, 1987-1993. Chairman, Ethics Committee, 1991-1993. Recipient: American Jurisprudence Book Awards for Excellent Achievement in the study of Business Organizations and Uniform Commercial Code, Distinguished Scholastic Performance Award, 1982; Award of The American Bar Association, Section of Urban, State and Local Government Law, 1982. Member, 1980-1981 and Managing Editor, 1981-1982, University of Bridgeport Law Review. Author, "The One Man Professional Corporation Under Fire," 2 University of Bridgeport Law Review 115 (1981). *Member:* Stamford/Norwalk Regional and Connecticut (Member, Steering Committee, Connecticut Lawyers Clearinghouse on Affordable Housing and Homeless) Bar Associations.

RUCCI, BURNHAM, CARTA & EDELBERG, LLP

Established in 1978

6 LANDMARK SQUARE, SUITE 470
STAMFORD, CONNECTICUT 06901
Telephone: 203-359-5637
URL: http://www.rbce.com

Darien, Connecticut Office: 800 Post Road, P.O. Box 1107. Telephone: 203-655-7695.

New Canaan, Connecticut Office: 71 Elm Street, P.O. Box 1680. Telephone: 203-966-6500.

Commercial and Residential Real Estate, Trusts and Estates, Estate Planning, Civil Trial Practice including Fiduciary Disputes, Employment, Commercial, Construction and Personal Injury Litigation, Corporate, Commercial, Information Technology, Banking, Workouts and Bankruptcy, Business Law, Environmental Law, Pre-Nuptial Agreements, State, Local and Federal Taxation, Zoning, Pensions, ERISA Matters and Charitable Organizations.

(For biographical data on all personnel, see Professional Biographies at Darien, Connecticut)

PHILIP RUSSELL, P.C.

STAMFORD, CONNECTICUT

(See Greenwich)

Civil and Criminal Litigation in all State and Federal Courts. Traffic, Automobile Accidents, DWI, DUI, White Collar Crimes.

RYAN, RYAN, JOHNSON & DELUCA, LLP

Established in 1954

80 FOURTH STREET
P.O. BOX 3057
STAMFORD, CONNECTICUT 06905
Telephone: 203-357-9200
FAX: 203-357-7915
Email: info@rrjd-law.com

General and Trial Practice in all State and Federal Courts. Business and Corporate, Employment, Environmental and Hazardous Waste Law, Estate Planning, Family, Health and Hospital Law, Insurance, Litigation, Medical and Legal Malpractice, Negligence, Probate, Products Liability, Railroad, Real Estate, Wills, Zoning.

MEMBERS OF FIRM

J. PAUL JOHNSON, born Jersey City, New Jersey, July 2, 1940; admitted to bar, 1966, New York; 1967, Connecticut; 1975, U.S. District Court, District of Connecticut. *Education:* Yale University (B.A., 1962); Harvard University (J.D., 1965). President, Darien United Way, 1978. Member, Darien Board of Selectmen, 1979-1985. Member, Darien Police Commission, 1987—. *Member:* Stamford/Norwalk Regional, Connecticut (Member, Family Law Section) and American (Member, Family Law Section) Bar Associations. ***PRACTICE AREAS:*** Family Law; Real Estate Law; Estate Planning; Estate Administration; Probate Litigation; Civil Litigation; Business Law. ***Email:*** jpjohnson@rrjd-law.com

CHARLES A. DELUCA, born Stamford, Connecticut, September 29, 1950; admitted to bar, 1977, Connecticut; 1978, U.S. District Court, District of Connecticut; 1980, U.S. District Court, Southern and Eastern Districts of New York; 1985, U.S. Court of Appeals, Second Circuit. *Education:* University of Connecticut (B.A., 1973); Brooklyn Law School (J.D., cum laude, 1977). Recipient: American Jurisprudence Award on Conflicts of Laws, 1977; Kenneth B. Keating Memorial Prize, 1977. Arbitrator and Fact Finder, Connecticut Superior Court, 1984—. Moderator, "What Carriers/Clients Want from Counsel Today," Connecticut Defense Lawyers Association, 2001. Lecturer: "Examination of Medical Experts," Connecticut Trial Lawyers Association, 2001; "Advanced Trial Advocacy," Yale Law School, 1991-1994. Depositions: "Plaintiff Strategies for Defense Tactic," Connecticut Trial Lawyers Association, 1997; "Masters in Trial," American Board of Trial Advocates, 1977; "The Complete Trial from Jury Selection to Deliberation," Connecticut Trial Lawyers Association, 1995-1996. Panelist, "The New 1993 Auto Insurance Reform Act," Stamford/Norwalk Regional Bar Association, 1993. Member, Chief Justice's Civil Commission. *Member:* Stamford/Norwalk Regional (President, 1993-1994), Connecticut (Member: Committee on the Courts, 2001—; Committee on Professional Ethics, 1997-2000; Task Force on Grievance Procedures, 1997) and American (Member, Sections on: Litigation; Tort and Insurance Practice Law) Bar Associations; National Association of Railroad Trial Counsel; Connecticut Defense Lawyers Association (President, 1998-1999); Defense Research Institute; Connecticut Trial Lawyers Association; International Association of Defense Counsel; American Board of Trial Advocates; Fellow, American College of Trial Lawyers. (Certified Civil Trial Advocate, National Board of Trial Advocacy). ***PRACTICE AREAS:*** Complex and Multi-District Litigation; Professional Liability; Commercial Liability; Federal Practice. ***Email:*** cdeluca@rrjd-law.com

DANIEL E. RYAN, III, born Stamford, Connecticut, November 29, 1955; admitted to bar, 1981, Connecticut; 1983, U.S. District Court, District of Connecticut; 1984, U.S. District Court, Southern and Eastern Districts of New York; 1992, New York. *Education:* Boston College (A.B., 1977); Fordham University (J.D., 1980). Instructor, Connecticut Trial Advocacy Institute, 1999—. Special Master, Connecticut Superior Court. *Member:* Stamford/Norwalk Regional, Connecticut and American Bar Associations; Defense Research Institute; Connecticut Defense Lawyers Association; Connecticut Medical Defense Lawyers Association; Raymond E. Baldwin American Inns of Court; Connecticut Society for Healthcare Risk Management; Professional Liability Underwriting Society. (Certified Civil Trial Advocate, National Board of Trial Advocacy). ***PRACTICE AREAS:*** Civil Litigation; Medical and Hospital Liability; Appeals. ***Email:*** deryan@rrjd-law.com

MICHAEL T. RYAN, born Stamford, Connecticut, October 4, 1957; admitted to bar, 1982, Connecticut; 1983, U.S. District Court, District of Connecticut; 1984, U.S. District Court, Southern and Eastern Districts of New York; 1985, Florida; 1987, U.S. Court of Appeals, Second Circuit. *Education:* Boston College (A.B., magna cum laude, 1979; J.D., 1982). Omicron Delta Epsilon. *Member:* Stamford/Norwalk Regional, Connecticut and American Bar Associations; The Florida Bar; National Association of Railroad Trial Counsel; Connecticut Defense Lawyers Association (Member, Board of Directors, 2000—); Defense Research Institute; Connecticut Trial Lawyers Association; The Association of Trial Lawyers of America. (Certified Civil Trial Advocate, National Board of Trial Advocacy). ***PRACTICE AREAS:*** Civil Litigation; Federal Practice; Professional Liability. ***Email:*** mtryan@rrjd-law.com

KEVIN M. TEPAS, born Buffalo, New York, July 23, 1947; admitted to bar, 1972, Connecticut and U.S. District Court, District of Connecticut. *Education:* Holy Cross College (B.S., 1969); University of Connecticut (J.D., 1972). State Trial Referee Attorney. State Special Masters. *Member:* Stamford/Norwalk Regional, Bridgeport, Connecticut and American Bar Associations; Connecticut Trial Lawyers Association; Connecticut Medical Lawyers Association; Connecticut Defense Lawyers Association; Defense Research Institute. [Capt., USAF, 1972-1977]. ***PRACTICE AREAS:*** Professional Malpractice; Products Liability; Personal Injury; Litigation. ***Email:*** kmtepas@rrjd-law.com

ROBERT C.E. LANEY, born Portsmouth, Virginia, November 21, 1962; admitted to bar, 1988, Virginia and U.S. District Court, Eastern District of Virginia; 1990, North Carolina and U.S. District Court, Eastern District of North Carolina; 1992, Connecticut and U.S. District Court, District of Connecticut. *Education:* College of William & Mary (B.A., 1985; J.D., 1988). Member, National Moot Court Team. *Member:* Stamford/Norwalk Regional (Co-Chair, Civil Litigation Section, 1998-2000), North Carolina, Connecticut and American (Member, Litigation Section) Bar Associations; The Association of Trial Lawyers of America; Connecticut Trial Lawyers Association; Connecticut Defense Lawyers Association; Defense Research Institute. ***PRACTICE AREAS:*** Civil Litigation. ***Email:*** roblaney@rrjmd.com

JOHN F. LEYDON, JR., born Stamford, Connecticut, December 15, 1964; admitted to bar, 1991, Connecticut, New York , U.S. District Court, District of Connecticut and U.S. District Court, Southern and Eastern Districts of New York. *Education:* Harvard College (A.B., cum laude, 1987); Fordham University (J.D., 1990). Member, Board of Representatives, City of Stamford, 12th District, 1991-1997. Member, Board of Education, City of Stamford, 1997—. *Member:* Stamford/Norwalk Regional (Co-Chair, Real Estate Committee, 2001) and Connecticut Bar Associations. ***PRACTICE AREAS:*** Business Law; Land Use; Real Estate; Trusts and Estates. ***Email:*** jfleydon@rrjd-law.com

(This Listing Continued)

RYAN, RYAN, JOHNSON & DELUCA, LLP, Stamford—Continued

CATHERINE S. NIETZEL, born Summit, New Jersey, May 22, 1964; admitted to bar, 1992, New Jersey; 1996, Connecticut; 1998, U.S. District Court, District of Connecticut. *Education:* Georgetown University (B.S.F.S., 1986); Fordham University (J.D., 1992). Legal Writing Teaching Assistant, Fordham University, 1990-1991. *Member:* Stamford, Norwalk Regional, Connecticut and American Bar Associations. ***LANGUAGES:*** French. ***PRACTICE AREAS:*** Civil Litigation; Professional Liability; Products Liability; Appellate Practice. **Email:** cnietzel@rrjd-law.com

OF COUNSEL

DANIEL E. RYAN, JR., born Stamford, Connecticut, January 26, 1928; admitted to bar, 1953, Connecticut; 1960, U.S. District Court, District of Connecticut. *Education:* Fordham University (A.B., 1950); New York University (J.D., 1953; LL.M. in Taxation, 1958). Vice Chairman, Commission to Study the Connecticut Probate Laws, 1967-1971. *Member:* Stamford/Norwalk Regional, Connecticut and American Bar Associations. ***PRACTICE AREAS:*** Estate Administration; Probate Litigation.

W. PATRICK RYAN, born Stamford, Connecticut, May 2, 1930; admitted to bar, 1957, Connecticut; 1960, U.S. District Court, District of Connecticut; 1983, U.S. District Court, Southern District of New York and U.S. Court of Appeals, Second Circuit; 1984, New York; 1986, U.S. Supreme Court. *Education:* Fordham University (B.S., 1952; J.D., 1957). Case Note Editor, Fordham Law Review, 1956-1957. Law Clerk for Honorable John W. Clancy, Chief Judge of the U.S. District Court, Southern District of New York, 1957-1958. Corporation Counsel for City of Stamford, 1964-1967. Chairman, Standing Committee on Admission to the Bar for Fairfield County, 1967—. State Attorney Trial Referee, 1985—. *Member:* Stamford/Norwalk Regional (President, 1975-1976), Connecticut and American Bar Associations; Federal Bar Council; American Society of Hospital Attorneys. Fellow: American College of Trial Lawyers; American Board of Trial Advocates; Connecticut Health Lawyers Association. ***PRACTICE AREAS:*** Civil Litigation; Professional Liability; Hospital Law; Commercial Litigation.

CHARLES M. McCAGHEY, born New York, New York, March 9, 1940; admitted to bar, 1965, New York; 1968, U.S. District Court, Southern District of New York; 1972, U.S. Court of Appeals, Second Circuit; 1978, U.S. District Court, Eastern District of New York; 1985, U.S. Court of Appeals, Eighth and Tenth Circuits; 1988, U.S. District Court, Western District of New York; 1991, Connecticut; 1992, U.S. District Court, District of Connecticut. *Education:* Manhattan College (B.A., 1962); Cornell University (LL.B., 1965). Member, Olwine, Connelly, Chase, O'Donnell & Weyher, New York, N.Y., 1974-1991. *Member:* Connecticut and American Bar Associations. ***PRACTICE AREAS:*** Commercial and Product Liability Litigation; Trials and Appeals. **Email:** cmm@rrjd-law.com

ASSOCIATES

BEVERLY J. HUNT, born Port Chester, New York, May 12, 1945; admitted to bar, 1988, Connecticut; 1989, U.S. District Court, District of Connecticut. *Education:* Long Island University (B.S., magna cum laude, 1969); Teachers College, Columbia University (M.Ed., 1972); University of Connecticut (J.D., 1988). Registered Nurse: New York, 1966; Connecticut, 1969. President, American Diabetes Association, Connecticut Affiliate, 1982-1984. Member, Board of Directors and Chair (2000—), Visiting Nurse and Hospice Care of Southwestern Connecticut. *Member:* Stamford/Norwalk Regional, Connecticut and American Bar Associations. ***PRACTICE AREAS:*** Medical Malpractice. **Email:** bjhunt@rrjd-law.com

JANINE M. KELLY, born New York, New York, August 7, 1969; admitted to bar, 1994, Connecticut; 1995, U.S. Court of Appeals, Federal Circuit; 1997, U.S. District Court, District of Connecticut. *Education:* College of the Holy Cross (B.A., 1991); Vermont Law School (J.D., 1994). *Member:* Stamford, Norwalk Regional and Connecticut Bar Associations. ***PRACTICE AREAS:*** Litigation. **Email:** jmkelly@rrjd-law.com

ROBERT O. HICKEY, born Norwalk, Connecticut, August 17, 1964; admitted to bar, 1997, Connecticut and U.S. District Court, Distrct of Connecticut. *Education:* University of Connecticut (B.A., 1986); Quinnipiac College School of Law (J.D., cum laude, 1997). President, Moot Court Honor Society, 1996. *Member:* Stamford, Norwalk Regional and Connecticut Bar Associations; Connecticut Trial Lawyers Association; National Association of Railroad Trial Counsel. ***PRACTICE AREAS:*** Civil Litigation. **Email:** rohickey@rrjd-law.com

DANIELLE DiBERARDINI-ALBRECHT, born St. Paul, Minnesota, February 15, 1970; admitted to bar, 1997, Connecticut. *Education:* Gustavus Adolphus College (B.A., 1992); Quinnipiac College (J.D., cum laude, 1997). Member, 1994-1997 and Associate Editor, 1996-1997, Quinnipiac Probate Law Journal. *Member:* Bridgeport, Stamford, Norwalk Regional, Connecticut and American Bar Associations; Young Lawyers Association. ***PRACTICE AREAS:*** Civil Litigation; Real Estate. **Email:** ddalbrecht@rrjd-law.com

JENNIFER R. MAZZELLA, born Bronx, New York, July 1, 1970; admitted to bar, 1995, Connecticut; 1996, New York and U.S. District Court, Southern and Eastern Districts of New York. *Education:* Fairfield University (B.A., 1992); St. John's University School of Law (J.D., 1995). *Member:* Connecticut Bar Association; Connecticut Defense Lawyers Association. ***PRACTICE AREAS:*** Civil Litigation. **Email:** jrmazzella@rrjd-law.com

CYNTHIA ANDREWS-DI PRETA, born White Plains, New York, June 20, 1971; admitted to bar, 1997, Connecticut. *Education:* Ohio Wesleyan University (B.A., 1993); Quinnipiac College (J.D., 1997). *Member:* Stamford/Norwalk Regional, Connecticut and American Bar Associations; The Association of Trial Lawyers of America. ***PRACTICE AREAS:*** Civil Litigation. **Email:** clandrews@rrjd-law.com

NANCY A. MEEHAN, born New Haven, Connecticut, August 17, 1963; admitted to bar, 1999, Connecticut. *Education:* Quinnipiac College (B.A., 1985); University of Arkansas at Little Rock (J.D., 1998). *Member:* Stamford/Norwalk Regional, Connecticut and American Bar Associations; Connecticut Defense Lawyers Association. ***PRACTICE AREAS:*** Civil Litigation. **Email:** nameehan@rrjd-law.com

JOHN B. GAFFNEY, born New Britain, Connecticut, September 20, 1968; admitted to bar, 1996, Connecticut; 1997, New Jersey, U.S. District Court, District of New Jersey; 1998, U.S. District Court, Eastern and Southern Districts of New York. *Education:* Providence College (B.S., 1991); Fordham University (J.D., 1996). *Member:* Stamford/Norwalk Regional, Connecticut and American Bar Associations. ***PRACTICE AREAS:*** Business Law. **Email:** jbgaffney@rrjd-law.com

ANTHONY D. SUTTON, born White Plains, New York, July 6, 1971; admitted to bar, 1998, Connecticut; 1999, U.S. District Court, District of Connecticut. *Education:* New York University (B.A., 1993); Quinnipiac College (J.D., 1998). Recipient, Distinguished Academic Achievement Award, Quinnipiac College, 1998. President, Student Bar Association, 1997-1998. Member, City of Stamford Board of Assessment Appeals, 2000—. *Member:* Connecticut Defense Lawyers Association. ***PRACTICE AREAS:*** Civil Litigation. **Email:** adsutton@rrjd-jaw.com

DEIRDRE A. MURRAY, born Cristobal, Canal Zone, Panama, February 25, 1971; admitted to bar, 1997, Tennessee; 2000, Connecticut. *Education:* College of William & Mary (B.A., 1993); Vanderbilt University (J.D., 1997). ***PRACTICE AREAS:*** Civil Litigation. **Email:** damurray@rrjd-law.com

JOSEPH C. VALDES, born New York, New York, January 6, 1963; admitted to bar, 1993, Connecticut. *Education:* University of Connecticut at Storrs (B.A., 1989); Quinnipiac College (J.D., 1992). *Member:* Stamford/Norwalk Regional Bar Association; Connecticut Trial Lawyers Association; Connecticut Hispanic Bar Association (Member, Board of Directors, 1995—). ***LANGUAGES:*** Spanish. **Email:** jcvaldes@rrjd-law.com

JONATHON CIOTTONE, born Worcester, Massachusetts, February 6, 1974; admitted to bar, 1999, Connecticut, U.S. District Court, District of Connecticut and U.S. Court of Appeals, Federal Circuit. *Education:* University of Massachusetts at Amherst (B.A., Philosophy, 1996); Quinnipiac University Law School (J.D., 1999). President, Mock Trial Honors Society. Recipient: Deans Award, Quinnipiac University Law School; Arnold J. Bai Litigation Award. National Finalist, American Trial Lawyers Association Trial Advocacy Competition. *Member:* Connecticut Bar Association. ***PRACTICE AREAS:*** Insurance Defense.

JANE B. CALLAHAN, born Norwalk, Connecticut, June 2, 1969; admitted to bar, 2000, Connecticut. *Education:* Mount St. Mary's College (B.A., 1991); Quinnipiac College (J.D., 2000). Phi Alpha Delta; Moot Court Honor Society. *Member:* Connecticut Bar Association. **Email:** jbcallahan@rrjd-law.com

REPRESENTATIVE CLIENTS: AIG; American Healthcare Inc.; Ascension Health; Boyle & Company; Atlantic Mutual Insurance Company; AXA Global Risks; Bristol West Insurance Co.; Central Vermont Railway; Chubb Group; Circon Corp.; C.N.A.; Connecticut Life and Casualty; Connecticut Medical Insurance Company; Connecticut Southern Railroad; Continental Casualty Company; Country Wide Insurance Co.; Crawford & Company; Crum & Forster Insurance; Dyson, Kissner & Moran; Electric Insurance Co.; Finast Supermarkets; First County Bank; Fuji Medical Systems; Hall-Brooke Hospital; Liberty Mutual Insurance Company; The Medical Protective Company; Metro-North Commuter Railroad; Metropolitan Property & Casualty Insurance Company; National Railroad Passenger Corporation; Nationwide Insurance Company; New England Central Railroad; New London County Mutual Insurance; Northland Insurance Company; Norwalk Hospital; Ophthalmic Mutual Ins. Co.; Professional Risk Management Services; Progressive Casualty Insurance Company; St. Paul Fire & Marine; St. Vincent's Medical Center; Stamford Health Systems; Stamford Hospital; Toys "R" Us; Travelers Property & Casualty Company; USAA; Utica National Ins. Group; Zurich American Insurance Company.

(This Listing Continued)

ST. JOHN, PARK & SCOTT

STAMFORD, CONNECTICUT

(See Greenwich)

General Practice. Wills and Estate Planning, Probate and Taxation, Trust and Estate Administration, Real Estate, Corporate, Family and Zoning Law. Civil Litigation.

ST. ONGE STEWARD JOHNSTON & REENS, LLC

Established in 1955

986 BEDFORD STREET

STAMFORD, CONNECTICUT 06905

Telephone: 203-324-6155

Telecopier: 203-327-1096

Email: info@ssjr.com

URL: http://www.ssjr.com

New Haven, Connecticut Office: 88 Prospect Street. Telephone: 203-562-4043.

Patent, Trademark, Copyright, Computer, Antitrust, Unfair Competition Law and Litigation.

FIRM PROFILE: St. Onge Steward Johnston & Reens, and its predecessor firms, was founded in Stamford in 1955 and specializes in patent, trade-mark and copyright law and related fields. The firm represents clients throughout The United States and Europe in litigation, counselling and licensing as well as in acquiring and protection of patents and intellectual property rights, ranging from food, chemicals and biologicals to automotive products, electronics, computer technology and machinery of all kinds. The attorneys in the firm have degrees in all major technical disciplines.

LOUIS H. REENS, born Amsterdam, The Netherlands, 1933; admitted to bar, 1964, Connecticut and U.S. District Court, District of Connecticut; 1975, U.S. Court of Appeals, Second Circuit; 1979, U.S. District Court, Southern District of New York; 1982, U.S. Court of Appeals for the Federal Circuit; registered to practice before U.S. Patent and Trademark Office. *Education:* Dickinson College (B.Sc., 1954); Polytechnic Institute of Brooklyn (B.E.E., 1956); University of Connecticut (LL.B., 1964). Zoning Commissioner, 1969-1971; Selectman, 1979-1989, Wilton, Connecticut. *Member:* Stamford and The Connecticut Bar Associations; Connecticut Patent Law Association (President, 1982); American Intellectual Property Law Association; New York Patent, Trademark and Copyright Law Association. ***LANGUAGES:*** Dutch, German. ***PRACTICE AREAS:*** Patent Law; Trademark Law; Copyright Law; Antitrust Law; Unfair Competition Law.

GENE S. WINTER, born White Plains, New York, April 4, 1950; admitted to bar, 1975, Pennsylvania and U.S. District Court, Eastern District of Pennsylvania; 1979, Connecticut and U.S. District Court, District of Connecticut; 1982, U.S. Court of Appeals for the Federal Circuit; 1985, U.S. Supreme Court; registered to practice before U.S. Patent and Trademark Office. *Education:* University of California at Los Angeles (B.S., summa cum laude, 1972); University of Pennsylvania; Cornell University (J.D., 1975). Tau Beta Pi. Author: "Checklist for Trademark and Service Mark Licensing," USTA Publications, 1989. Co-Author: "The Merely Descriptive Term: Is It a Trademark, A Description Protected by the First Amendment, or Both," Idea, Vol. 31, 1991. *Member:* Connecticut Patent Law Association (President, 1986-1987). ***PRACTICE AREAS:*** Patent Law; Trademark Law; Copyright Law; Antitrust Law; Unfair Competition Law; Litigation. ***Email:*** gsw@ssjr.com

STEPHEN P. McNAMARA, born Los Angeles, California, January 1, 1958; admitted to bar, 1986, Connecticut and U.S. District Court, District of Connecticut; 1987, New York; 1989, U.S. Court of Appeals for the Federal Circuit and U.S. Court of Appeals, Ninth Circuit; registered to practice before U.S. Patent and Trademark Office. *Education:* Massachusetts Institute of Technology (B.S.Ch. E., 1980); University of Connecticut (J.D., with high honors, 1986). Articles Editor, Connecticut Journal of International Law, 1985-1986. *Member:* Connecticut and American Bar Associations; Connecticut Patent Law Association (President, 1994-1995); American Intellectual Property Law Association. ***PRACTICE AREAS:*** Patent Law; Trademark Law; Copyright Law; Antitrust Law; Unfair Competition Law; Litigation. ***Email:*** spm@ssjr.com

WESLEY W. WHITMYER, JR., born Columbus, Ohio, October 1, 1963; admitted to bar, 1988, Connecticut; 1989, U.S. District Court, District of Connecticut; 1990, U.S. Court of Appeals for the Federal Circuit; registered to practice before U.S. Patent and Trademark Office. *Education:* Ohio Wesleyan University (B.A., in Physics, magna cum laude, 1985); The Ohio State University (J.D., 1988). Phi Beta Kappa. Author: "The Patent and Trademark Office's Refusal to Follow *In Re Bond,*" 74 J.P.T.O.S. 397, 1992. *Member:* Connecticut and American Bar Associations; Connecticut Patent Law Association; American Intellectual Property Law Association. ***PRACTICE AREAS:*** Patent Law; Computer Law; Litigation. ***Email:*** wwwjr@ssjr.com

MARY M. KRINSKY, born Oklahoma City, Oklahoma, December 12, 1946; admitted to bar, 1977, Montana; 1978, Connecticut; 1991, U.S. Court of Appeals for the Federal Circuit; registered to practice before U.S. Patent and Trademark Office. *Education:* Iowa State University (B.S., Chemistry, with distinction, 1967); Yale University (M.Phil., 1969; Ph.D., in Biochemistry, 1971); University of Montana (J.D., with honors, 1977). Recipient: American Jurisprudence Award in Constitutional Law and Remedies; Emmett C. Angland Memorial Award. Author: "Regulation of Food Additives Never Added: An Odd Mixture of Science and Law," 37 Montana Law Review 198, 1976. *Member:* American Judicature Society; American Intellectual Property Law Association; Connecticut Patent Law Association. ***PRACTICE AREAS:*** Patent Law; Biotechnology.

ARLANA S. COHEN, born Brooklyn, New York, December 13, 1957; admitted to bar, 1982, New York; 1984, U.S. District Court, Southern District of New York; 1988, U.S. Supreme Court (Not admitted in Connecticut). *Education:* State University of New York at Buffalo (B.A., cum laude, 1978); Benjamin N. Cardozo School of Law (J.D., 1981). *Member:* International Trademark Association (Member, Meeting Committee); New York Intellectual Property Law. ***PRACTICE AREAS:*** Litigation; Trademark; Unfair Competition; Copyrights. ***Email:*** asc@ssjr.com

EUGENE L. FLANAGAN III, born Glen Cove, New York, 1950; admitted to bar, 1976, New York; registered to practice before U.S. Patent and Trademark Office (Not admitted in Connecticut). *Education:* Manhattan College (B.E.E., with honors, 1972); St. John's University (J.D., 1975); New York University (LL.M., 1982). Tau Beta Pi; Phi Delta Phi. ***PRACTICE AREAS:*** Intellectual Property.

TODD M. OBERDICK, born New Haven, Connecticut, June 15, 1971; admitted to bar, 1997, Connecticut; 1998, U.S. District Court, District of Connecticut; registered to practice before U.S. Patent and Trademark Office. *Education:* Lehigh University (B.S.M.E., 1994); John Marshall Law School (J.D., magna cum laude, 1997). Phi Alpha Delta. Recipient, Biro Scholarship for Academic Achievement, John Marshall Law School. Staff Editor, John Marshall Law Review, 1996-1997. *Member:* Connecticut and American Bar Associations; Connecticut Patent Law Association. ***PRACTICE AREAS:*** Intellectual Property; Litigation; Patent Prosecution; Mechanical Patents; Electrical Patents. ***Email:*** tmo@ssjr.com

KATHRYN G. BELLEAU, born New York, N.Y., July 6, 1954; admitted to bar, 1990, New York (Not admitted in Connecticut). *Education:* McGill University (B.A., 1975); Brooklyn Law School (J.D., 1983). Former Corporate Counsel, American Tool Companies, Inc. ***LANGUAGES:*** German, French, Spanish, Italian, Russian, Japanese and Portuguese. ***PRACTICE AREAS:*** International Trademarks; International Copyright Law; International Intellectual Property.

RICHARD J. BASILE, born Providence, Rhode Island, March 18, 1963; admitted to bar, 1995, New York; 1996, U.S. District Court, Southern and Northern Districts of New York; registered to practice before U.S. Patent and Trademark Office (Not admitted in Connecticut). *Education:* Union College (B.S.M.E., 1985); Chicago-Kent College of Law (J.D., 1994). Member, Moot Court Honor Society. ***PRACTICE AREAS:*** Intellectual Property; Patent Litigation; Trademark Litigation.

DAVID CHEN, born Bridgeport, Connecticut, November 26, 1970; admitted to bar, 2000, Connecticut, U.S.District Court, District of Connecticut, U.S., Superior Court of Connecticut; registered to practice before U.S. Patent and Trademark Office. *Education:* University of Connecticut (B.S., 1993); New York Law School (J.D., cum laude, 1999). ***PRACTICE AREAS:*** Patent Prosecution; Patent Litigation; Trademark Prosecution; Trademark Litigation; Copyright Prosecution; Copyright Litigation.

J. BRADLEY WRIGHT, born Damariscotta, Maine, October 26, 1973; (admission pending). *Education:* Worcester Polytechnic Institute (B.S., 1996); Franklin Pierce Law Center (J.D., 1999; M.I.P., 1999). ***PRACTICE AREAS:*** Patent Prosecution; Patent Litigation; Mechanical Patents; Electrical Patents.

OF COUNSEL

RONALD J. ST. ONGE, born Kingsport, Tennessee, 1930; admitted to bar, 1960, Connecticut; 1962, U.S. District Court, District of Connecticut; 1966, U.S. District Court, Southern and Eastern Districts of New York; 1967, U.S. Court of Appeals, Second Circuit; 1968, U.S. Supreme Court; 1982, U.S. Court of Appeals for the Federal Circuit; registered to practice before U.S. Patent and Trademark Office. *Education:* Michigan State University (B.S., 1953); University of Michigan Law School (J.D., 1959). President, Connecticut Patent Law Association, 1971-1972. Member, Computer Science Accreditation Commission. *Member:* Stamford (President, 1968-1969), Connecticut (Chairman,

(This Listing Continued)

ST. ONGE STEWARD JOHNSTON & REENS, LLC, Stamford—Continued

Patent Law Section, 1967-1968) and American Bar Associations; American Intellectual Property Law Association. [Electronics Officer, U.S. Air Force]. ***PRACTICE AREAS:*** Patent Law; Trademark Law; Copyright Law; Antitrust Law; Unfair Competition; Litigation.

SANDAK FRIEDMAN HENNESSEY & GRECO, LLP

970 SUMMER STREET
STAMFORD, CONNECTICUT 06905
Telephone: 203-425-4200
Facsimile: 203-325-8608
URL: http://www.lawyers.com/sfh&g

Trials and Appeals in all Connecticut and Federal Courts and Administrative Agencies. Personal Injury, Medical Malpractice, Commercial, Environmental Litigation, Real Estate, Zoning and Land Use, Property Tax Appeals.

MEMBERS OF FIRM

KEVIN M. GRECO, born New London, Connecticut; July 25, 1957; admitted to bar, 1989, Connecticut; 1994, U.S. District Court, District of Connecticut. *Education:* Central Connecticut State University (B.S., Industrial Technology, 1984); University of Bridgeport (J.D., 1989). Epsilon Pi Tau. Member, National Honor Society. Associate Editor, University of Bridgeport Law Review, 1988-1989. Law Clerk, Connecticut Judicial Department, 1989. Author, "Phillips Petroleum Co. v. Mississippi: The Expansion of the Public Trust Doctrine," University of Bridgeport Law Review, Vol 11, No. 1. *Member:* Stamford/Norwalk Regional, Connecticut and American Bar Associations; American Inns of Court; Raymond E. Baldwin Inn of Court; Connecticut Trial Lawyers Association; Association of Trial Lawyers of America. ***PRACTICE AREAS:*** Personal Injury; Medical Malpractice; Civil Litigation; Labor Law. ***Email:*** kgreco@sfhglaw.com

WILLIAM J. HENNESSEY, JR., born Danbury, Conn., March 18, 1955; admitted to bar, 1981 Connecticut. *Education:* Fairfield University (B.A., 1977); Pace University (J.D., 1981). Assistant Corporation Counsel, City of Stamford, 1981-1986. Special Master, Connecticut Superior Court, 1987—. *Member:* Stamford Regional, Connecticut (Member, Executive Committee, Planning and Zoning Section) and American (Member, Real Property, Probate and Trust Law Section) Bar Associations. ***PRACTICE AREAS:*** Real Estate Law; Zoning Law; Land Use Law; Property Tax Appeals; Municipal Law; Civil Practice. ***Email:*** whennessey@sfhglaw.com

GARY S. KLEIN, born Stamford, Connecticut, January 25, 1967; admitted to bar, 1991, Connecticut; 1992, U.S. District Court, District of Connecticut; 1993, U.S. District Court, Southern District of New York and U.S. Court of Appeals, First and Second Circuits; 1996, U.S. District Court, Eastern District of New York. *Education:* University of Virginia (B.A., Distinguished Majors Program, 1988); Center of International Studies, Madrid, Spain; University of Miami (J.D., cum laude, 1991). Moot Court Instructor, 1991. Member, 1990 and Articles and Comments Editor, 1991, University of Miami Law Review. Member, City of Stamford Environmental Protection Board, 1996-1998. Adjunct Professor, Fairfield University, 1999—. Author: "Illegality Defense in Commercial Landlord/Tenant Actions," 42 Am. Jur. Proof of Facts, 3d, 413 (1997); "Plaintiffs' Offers of Judgement," 6 Connecticut Lawyer No. 9 at 20 (1996). Hearing Officer, Connecticut Commission on Human Rights and Opportunities, 1997-1998. Special Master, U.S. District Court, District of Connecticut, 1999—. ***REPORTED CASES:*** LoSacco v. F.D. Rich Construction Co, 992 F.2d 382 (1st Cir. 1993); Lavin v. Emery Air Freight Corp., 980 F. Supp. 93 (D. Conn. 1997); Bernbach v. Timex Corp., 989 F. Supp. 304 (D. Conn. 1996); Uniroyal Chemical Co. v. Drexel Chemical Co., Inc., 931 F. Supp. 132 (D. Conn. 1996); Stone v. Frederick Hobby Assoc. II, LLC, 2001 WL 861822 (Conn. Super. Ct. 2001); Starwood Capital Group, L.P. v. Kukral, 1995 WL 371060 (Conn. Super. Ct. 1995); Borges v. Greenwich Fed. Sav. & Loan Assn, 1993 WL 29107 (Conn. Super. Ct 1993); Town of Darien v. D'Addario, 1999 WL 1293360 (Conn. Super. Ct. 1999); King Conn. Enterprises, Inc. v. ZBA, 2000 WL 1977973 (Conn. Super. Ct. 2000); West Broad Street Company v. ZBA, 2001 WL 219699 (Conn. Super. Ct. 2001); Gateway Bank v. Mandanici, 1994 WL 320241 (Conn. Super. Ct. 1994); Pitney Bowes Credit Corp. v. Barry, 1997 WL 781840 (Conn. Super Ct. 1997); Morrill v. Kennedy Funding Capital Corp., 1994 WL 728803 (Conn. Super. Ct. 1994); Cadle Co. v. Probate Court Appeal-Trumbull, 2000 WL 739674 (Conn. Super. Ct. 2000); Cadle Co. v. Probate Court-Trumbull, 2000 WL 1701865 (Conn. Super. Ct. 2000). ***PRACTICE AREAS:*** Environmental Litigation; Commercial Litigation. ***Email:*** gklein@sfhglaw.com

PETER M. NOLIN, born Stamford, Connecticut, 1956; admitted to bar, 1981, Connecticut; 1982, U.S. District Court, District of Connecticut; 1993,

(This Listing Continued)

U.S. District Court, Southern District of New York; 1996, U.S. Court of Appeals, Second Circuit. *Education:* College of the Holy Cross (B.A., 1978); University of Connecticut (J.D., with high honors, 1981). Associate Editor, Connecticut Law Review, 1980-1981. Elected: Norwalk Common Council, 1993—; Connecticut Judicial Selection Commission, 1995-1999. Member, Norwalk Planning Commission, 1990-1993. Norwalk Representative, Southwestern Connecticut Regional Planning Association, 1990-1993. Special Master, U.S. District Court, Connecticut, 1997—. *Member:* Stamford/Norwalk Regional, Connecticut (Member, Federal Practice and Conservation and Environmental Quality Sections) and American (Member, Litigation and Natural Resources, Energy and the Environment Sections) Bar Associations; Federal Bar Council. ***REPORTED CASES:*** Finley Associates, Inc., v. Crossroads Investment Co., LLP, 2001 WL 861743 (Conn. Super July 10, 2001) (X03CV990499388s); Sealy Connecticut Inc., v. Litton Industries, Inc., 93 F. Supp. 2d 177 (2000); Connecticut National Bank v. Lorenzato, 221 Conn. 77 (1992); Crepeau v. Gronager, 41 Conn. App. 302 (1996); Gateway Bank v. Mandanici, 1994 WL 320241 (Conn. Super. Ct. 1994); Morrill v. Kennedy Funding Capital Corp., 1994 WL 728803 (Conn. Super. Ct. 1994); Kowolsky Properties v. Sherwin Williams Co. Inc., 7 Conn. App. 136 (1986). ***PRACTICE AREAS:*** Civil Litigation; Commercial Litigation; Insurance Coverage; Environmental Law. ***Email:*** pnolin@sfhglaw.com

JAY H. SANDAK, born Stamford, Connecticut, February 12, 1946; admitted to bar, 1971, Connecticut; 1972, District of Columbia and U.S. Court of Federal Claims; 1976, U.S. Supreme Court. *Education:* Colby College (A.B., 1968); Syracuse University (J.D., 1971). Member, Justinian Society. Symposium Editor, Syracuse Law Review, 1970-1971. Law Clerk to Judge R.L. Kunzig, U.S. Court of Claims, 1972-1973. Corporation Counsel, City of Stamford, 1984-1985. Lecturer: College of Evidence, Connecticut Trial Lawyers Association, "Use of Expert Witnesses, Loss of Earning Capacity," 1990; "Government Liability - Recreation Torts," 1991. Panelist, "Product Liability," Connecticut Bar Association, 1995. Special Master, U.S. District Court, 1993—. *Member:* Stamford/Norwalk Regional (Member, Executive Committee, 1983-1986), Connecticut and American Bar Associations; The Association of Trial Lawyers of America; Connecticut Trial Lawyers Association; American Inns of Court; Raymond E. Baldwin Inn of Court (Vice President, 1993-1995; President, 1995-1997). ***PRACTICE AREAS:*** Civil Litigation; Municipal Taxation; Mediation; Arbitration; Commercial Litigation; Personal Injury; Tax Appeals. ***Email:*** jsandak@sfhglaw.com

MARY E. SOMMER, born Syracuse, New York, June 17, 1949; admitted to bar, 1976, Connecticut and U.S. District Court, District of Connecticut; 1977, U.S. Court of Appeals, Second Circuit. *Education:* College of New Rochelle (B.A., 1971); University of Notre Dame (J.D., 1975). Adjunct Professor: Civil Trial Practice, University of Bridgeport School of Law, 1984-1986; College of New Rochelle Center for Entrepreneurial Studies, 1988-1992; Business Law, College of New Rochelle, 1995-1999; University of Connecticut, School of Business, Business Law and Ethics, 1997-1998. State Trial Referee, 1985—. Corporation Counsel, City of Stamford, 1986-1990. Special Master, United States Federal District Court, 1987—. *Member:* Stamford/Norwalk Regional (Chair, Community Service Committee, 1996—; Director, 1997; Treasurer, 2000-2001), Connecticut and American Bar Associations. ***PRACTICE AREAS:*** Civil Litigation; Commercial Litigation; Personal Injury. ***Email:*** msommer@sfhglaw.com

ASSOCIATES

ROBERT C. DeDONA, born Yonkers, New York, December 6, 1968; admitted to bar, 2000, Connecticut; 2001, New York and U.S. District Court, District of Connecticut. *Education:* Pace University (B.B.A., Dean's List Second Honors, 1997); Pace University School of Law (J.D., 2000). Managing Editor, Pace Law Review, 1999-2000. Member: Pace Trial Advocacy Team, 1999-2000; Pace Moot Court Board, 2000; Jessup International Moot Court Team, 1999. Author: "Simply 'Too Tenuous' McCoy v. American Suzuki Motor Corporation: The Application of the Rescue Doctrine to a Products Liability Claim," 20 Pace L. Rev. 497 (2000). *Member:* Stamford/Norwalk Regional, New York State, Connecticut and American Bar Associations. ***PRACTICE AREAS:*** Land Use; Zoning Law; Real Estate. ***Email:*** rdedona@sfhglaw.com

JEFFREY M. KNICKERBOCKER, born Hartford, Connecticut, November 7, 1966; admitted to bar, 1997, Connecticut. *Education:* University of Connecticut (B.A., 1988; M.P.A., 1989); Western New England College (J.D., cum laude, 1997). [Captain, U.S.A.F., 1997-2001.]

STEPHANIE A. McLAUGHLIN, born October 3, 1972; admitted to bar, 2000, Connecticut; 2001, New York and U.S. District Court, District of Connecticut. *Education:* American University (B.A., 1995); De Paul University College of Law (J.D., 2000). ***Email:*** smclaughlin@sfhglaw.com

LAW OFFICES OF RICHARD A. SARNER

184 ATLANTIC STREET
STAMFORD, CONNECTICUT 06901
Telephone: 203-967-8899
Fax: 203-967-8886
Email: rsarner@aol.com

New York, New York Office: 465 Park Avenue, Suite 10C. Telephone: 800-392-8550.

Estate Planning, Tax Planning, Trust Administration, Business Planning, Real Estate, Wealth Preservation, Family Wealth Transfer, Retirement Planning.

RICHARD A. SARNER, born Stamford, Connecticut, August 6, 1955; admitted to bar, 1982, New York and U.S. District Courts, Southern and Eastern Districts of New York; 1985, U.S. Court of Appeals, Second Circuit; 1989, U.S. District Court, Northern District of New York; 1990, Connecticut; 1991, U.S. District Court, District of Connecticut and U.S. Supreme Court; 1997, U.S. Tax Court. *Education:* Dartmouth College (B.A., 1977); Hofstra University (J.D., 1980). *Member:* The Association of the Bar of the City of New York; Stamford/Norwalk Regional (Member, Committee on Probate and Estates), New York State (Member, Trusts and Estates Law Section), Connecticut (Member, Estates and Probate Section) and American (Member, Real Property, Probate and Trusts Section) Bar Associations; National Network of Estate Planning Attorneys; Dartmouth Lawyers Association.

STEPHEN N. SCHAFFER

STAMFORD, CONNECTICUT
(See Norwalk)

General Civil Practice, Family Law, Divorce, Child Custody, Child Support, Real Estate, Personal Injury, Auto Accidents, Corporate, Business, Commercial and Litigation in all Courts.

WILLIAM L. SCHEFFLER & ASSOCIATES

STAMFORD, CONNECTICUT
(See Westport)

Corporate, Business Transactions, Real Estate Development, Zoning, Licensing, Administrative, Not For Profit Corporations.

SCHOONMAKER, GEORGE & COLIN, P.C.

STAMFORD, CONNECTICUT
(See Greenwich)

Matrimonial and Family Law.

SCHWARTZMAN GARELIK WALKER KAPILOFF & TROY, P.C.

777 SUMMER STREET
STAMFORD, CONNECTICUT 06901
Telephone: 203-325-1118
Fax: 203-353-3392

New York, N.Y. Office: 335 Lexington Avenue. Telephone: 212-557-2900. Fax: 212-983-4193; 599-5067.
Hollywood, Florida Office: 2021 Tyler Street 33022. Telephone: 954-921-5500. Fax: 954-925-7013.

General Civil Practice. Construction, Real Estate, Taxation, Estates, Trusts and Probate, Commercial and Tax Litigation.

ARNOLD Y. KAPILOFF, born Winston-Salem, North Carolina, November 9, 1935; admitted to bar, 1961, Virginia; 1962, New York; 1975, Florida; 1992, Connecticut and U.S. District Court, Southern and Eastern Districts of New York; U.S. Tax Court and U.S. Court of Appeals, Second Circuit; U.S. Claims Court and U.S. Supreme Court. *Education:* University of North Carolina (B.S., 1957); Georgetown University (J.D., 1961); New York University (LL.M. in Taxation, 1965). Author: "Collateral Estoppel and the Civil Fraud Penalty," Bulletin of the Section on Taxation, American Bar Association, January, 1967. Co-author: "The Bankrupt Estate, Taxable Income and the Trustee in Bankruptcy," Fordham Law Review March, 1966. Lecturer, Practising Law Institute, New York City: "Operating Losses and Tax Considerations in Insolvency," 1977-1978; "Operating Losses, Tax Problems of the Going Concern and the Failing Business," 1978-1979; "Bankruptcy Reform Act of 1978," 1978-1979. Adjunct Lecturer, Taxation, Bernard M. Baruch College of the City University of New York, Graduate Accounting Department, 1989—. *Member:* New York State (Co-Chair, Committee on Compliance Practice and Procedure, Tax Section, 1991—), Connecticut (Member, Tax Section Executive Committee) and American Bar Associations; Virginia State Bar; The Florida Bar; New York County Lawyers Association; American College of Tax Counsel. ***Email:*** akapiloff@sgwkt.com

(This Listing Continued)

WILLIAM SELSBERG

970 SUMMER STREET
STAMFORD, CONNECTICUT 06905-5518
Telephone: 203-353-1700
Fax: 203-352-1792
URL: http://www.earthlink.net/~wsels
Email: csels@earthlink.net

General Practice including Real Estate, Commercial and Residential, Corporate Law, Common Interest Community Law, Zoning and Subdivision Law, Environmental Law, Commercial and Residential Leases.

WILLIAM SELSBERG, born Lynn, Massachusetts, September 24, 1937; admitted to bar, 1962, Connecticut. *Education:* University of Connecticut (B.S., 1959; J.D., 1962). Lecturer, Real Estate Law, Norwalk Community College, 1984—. Editor/Advisor, Current Real Estate Law Textbook. *Member:* Stamford/Norwalk Regional and Connecticut Bar Associations.

REPRESENTATIVE CLIENTS: First County Bank; Joerman Realty Co.; Frank Mercede & Sons, Inc.; Kematt LLC; John Vikstrom; Waterford Builders.
APPROVED COUNSEL FOR: First County Bank; People's Bank; Fleet Bank; New Haven Savings Bank; First Union; Commonwealth Land Title Insurance Co.; Lawyers Title; Stewart Title Guaranty Co.; First American Title Insurance Co.; Chase Manhattan Bank; Citicorp Mortgage; Washington Mutual; Wells Fargo.
A List of References will be furnished upon request.

LAW OFFICE OF THOMAS M. SHANLEY

STAMFORD, CONNECTICUT
(See Greenwich)

Matrimonial, Family, Divorce, Paternity, Custody, Appeals and all areas of Domestic Relations Law.

SHIPMAN & GOODWIN LLP

ONE LANDMARK SQUARE
STAMFORD, CONNECTICUT 06901
Telephone: 203-324-8100
Telecopier: 203-324-8199
Email: www@goodwin.com
URL: http://shipman-goodwin.com

Greenwich, Connecticut Office: 43 Arch Street. Telephone: 203-869-6222.
Hartford, Connecticut Office: One American Row. Telephone: 203-251-5000.
Lakeville, Connecticut Office: 12 Porter Street. Telephone: 203-435-2539.

General Practice. Banking, Corporation, Tax, Antitrust, Trade Regulation, Finance and Securities, Venture Capital, Labor and Employment, Health Care, Environmental, Professional Liability, Pension and Profit Sharing, Estate Planning, Probate, Trust Administration and Financial Management, Municipal Law. Trials in all Courts.

PARTNERS

ROBIN G. FREDERICK, born Brooklyn, NY, 1963; admitted to bar, 1988, Connecticut; 1989, New York and U.S. District Court, Southern and Eastern Districts of New York; 1992, U.S. District Court, District of Connecticut; 1995, U.S. Court of Appeals, Second Circuit. *Education:* Cornell University (B.A., cum laude, 1985); New York University (J.D., 1988). Note Editor, Journal of International Law and Politics. *Member:* The Regional, Connecticut and American Bar Associations. ***LANGUAGES:*** French. ***PRACTICE AREAS:*** Employment Law; Civil Litigation. ***Email:*** rfrederick@goodwin.com

FREDERICK S. GOLD, born Newark, NJ, 1952; admitted to bar, 1979, New York, U.S. District Court, Eastern and Southern Districts of New York; 1980, U.S. District Court, Northern and Western Districts of New York and U.S. Court of Appeals, Second Circuit; 1985, U.S. Court of Appeals, Third Circuit; 1989, Connecticut and U.S. District Court, District of Connecticut. *Education:* Tufts University (B.A., summa cum laude, 1974); Columbia University (J.D., 1977). Phi Beta Kappa. Author: "Preparing Your Client For Deposition: Half A Loaf Is As Bad As None," Trial Magazine, February, 1993. Instructor in Trial Practice, Yale Law School, 1996—. Chair, Connecticut Trial Advocacy Institute, 1994—. Faculty Member, National Institute For Trial Advocacy, 1993—. *Member:* The Association of the Bar of the City of New York; Bridgeport, The

(This Listing Continued)

SHIPMAN & GOODWIN LLP, Stamford—Continued

Regional, Connecticut (Vice-Chair, Section of Litigation) and American (Member, Sections of Litigation and Antitrust) Bar Associations; Connecticut Trial Lawyers Association; The Association of Trial Lawyers of America. ***PRACTICE AREAS:*** Business Litigation; Commercial Litigation; Business Torts; Real Estate Litigation. ***Email:*** fgold@goodwin.com

STEVEN M. GOLD, born Brooklyn, NY, 1953; admitted to bar, 1979, New York and Connecticut. *Education:* Hobart College (B.A., 1975); Cornell University (J.D., 1978). Phi Delta Phi; Pi Gamma Mu. Confidential Law Assistant, New York Supreme Court, Appellate Division, 3rd Department, 1978-1979. *Member:* Stamford/Norwalk Regional, New York State, Connecticut and American Bar Associations; Association of Commercial Finance Attorneys. ***PRACTICE AREAS:*** Corporate Law; Commercial Finance; Computer Law. ***Email:*** sgold@goodwin.com

SHARI M. GOODSTEIN, born Canton, OH, 1959; admitted to bar, 1988, Connecticut; 1989, New York and U.S. District Court, Southern and Eastern Districts of New York; 1997, U.S. District Court, District of Connecticut. *Education:* Brandeis University (B.A., cum laude, 1981); New York University School of Law (J.D., 1988). Recipient, American Jurisprudence Award for Antitrust and Regulatory Alternatives, 1988. Member, Editorial Staff, New York University Journal of International Law and Politics, 1979-1980. Assistant Corporation Counsel, New York City Corporation Counsel's Office, 1993-1997. *Member:* The Regional, Connecticut and American Bar Associations. ***PRACTICE AREAS:*** Employment Law; Business Litigation; Commercial Litigation. ***Email:*** sgoodstein@goodwin.com

DONALD R. GUSTAFSON, born Norwalk, CT, 1953; admitted to bar, 1979, Connecticut; 1980, U.S. District Court, District of Connecticut. *Education:* Catholic University (B.A., cum laude, 1975); John Marshall Law School (J.D., with high distinction, 1979). Member, The Gavel Society. Editor-in-Chief, The John Marshall Journal of Practice and Procedure, 1978. *Member:* Stamford/Norwalk Regional, Connecticut (Member, Real Property Section) and American Bar Associations; Community Associations Institute. ***PRACTICE AREAS:*** Real Estate Development; Commercial Leasing; Commercial Financing; Loan Workouts; Land Use. ***Email:*** dgustafson@goodwin.com

BARRY C. HAWKINS, born Portland, ME, 1943; admitted to bar, 1968, Connecticut. *Education:* Bowdoin College (A.B., with honors, 1965); University of Virginia (J.D., 1968). Member: Connecticut Uniform Laws Commissioners, 1999— NCCUSL Drafting Committee for Revised Uniform Arbitration Act; Governor, 1994-1997 and Member, American College of Real Estate Lawyers. Director, 1994-1999 and Member, Stamford Regional Bar Association; Chairman, Real Property Section, 1993-1995 and Member, Executive Committee, 1978—, Connecticut Bar Association. Director, Connecticut Chapter, Community Associations Institute, 1998— Member, Gallivan Foundation Advisory Board, 1992— Trustee, Housatonic Community College Foundation, 1996—. Author: "Can Rent Receivers Be Liable Under Environmental Laws?", The Practical Real Estate Lawyers, Vol. 12, No. 2, March, 1996; "The 1995 Amendments to the Connecticut Transfer Act", Connecticut Real Estate law Journal, Vol. 13 no. 3 (1995); "Alternative Dispute Resolution in Real Estate Litigation," American Bar Association, ACREL Papers; (1994). *Member:* Connecticut and American (Real Property, Probate and Trust Law Section) Bar Associations. ***PRACTICE AREAS:*** Real Estate; Land Use Regulation; Community Association Law; Environmental Law; Business Litigation; Commercial Litigation. ***Email:*** bhawkins@goodwin.com

EDWARD M. KANE, born Glen Ridge, NJ, 1961; admitted to bar, 1987, New York; 1997, Connecticut. *Education:* University of Chicago (A.B., 1983); Fordham University (J.D., 1986); New York University (LL.M., in Taxation, 1995). Staff, Fordham Law Review, 1984-1985. *Member:* The Association of the Bar of the City of New York; New York State and American Bar Associations. ***PRACTICE AREAS:*** Corporate Law; Taxation; Securities Law. ***Email:*** ekane@goodwin.com

WILLIAM A. RUSKIN, born New Rochelle, NY, 1952; admitted to bar, 1978, New York; 1979, U.S. District Court, Southern and Eastern Districts of New York; 1981, District of Columbia; 1990, U.S. District Court, Northern District of New York; 1993, U.S. District Court, Western District of New York; 1996, U.S. District Court, Eastern District of Wisconsin; 1999, U.S. District Court, District of Connecticut (Not admitted in Connecticut). *Education:* Cornell University (B.A., 1974; J.D., 1977). Associate Products Liability Counsel, CIBA-GEIGY Corporation, 1982-1987. Author: "The Use of 'Principled Negotiation' in Resolving Environmental Disputes," American Journal of Trial Advocacy, Vol. 17, No. 1, 1993; "Value Protection: An Alternative to Litigation," BNA Toxics Law Reporter, Vol, Vol. 5, No. 14, 1990; "The Threat of Toxic Torts," Management Review, June, 1990. Mediation Panel: U.S. District Court for the Southern District of New York. *Member:* New York State and American Bar Associations; Defense Research Institute; New York Conservation Education Fund (Board Member, 1996—; Vice-Chairman of the Board, 1997—). ***PRACTICE AREAS:*** Environmental Law; Toxic Torts; Alternative Dispute Resolution; Environmental Litigation; Mediation; Product Liability Litigation. ***Email:*** wruskin@goodwin.com

(This Listing Continued)

MICHAEL L. WIDLAND, born Springfield, MA, 1940; admitted to bar, 1965, Massachusetts; 1966, Connecticut. *Education:* American International College (B.A., 1962); Boston University (LL.B., 1965). Vice-Chairman, Planning and Zoning Commission, Town of Weston, Connecticut, 1990—. Member: Executive Committee, and Board of Trustees, Stamford Center for Arts, 1991—; and Board of Directors, Connecticut Legal Services, 1994—. Trustee, Maritime Aquarium at Norwalk, 1997—. *Member:* Stamford/Norwalk Regional, Hartford County, Connecticut and American (Former Connecticut Chairman, Public Contract Section) Bar Associations; Association of Commercial Finance Attorneys; American Bankruptcy Institute; Association for Transportation Law. ***PRACTICE AREAS:*** Business Reorganizations; Corporate Law and Commercial Financing; Public Transportation; Public Contract Law. ***Email:*** mwidland@goodwin.com

ROBERT M. WONNEBERGER, born Bridgeport, CT, 1959; admitted to bar, 1984, Connecticut. *Education:* University of Connecticut (B.A., magna cum laude, 1981); University of Pennsylvania (J.D., 1984). Associate Editor, University of Pennsylvania Law Review, 1983-1984. Author: "Exploring the Limits of a Limited Guaranty," The Journal of Commercial Lending, July 1995; "Interest Rate Swaps: Does Your Borrower Understand the True Nature of the Arrangement," The Journal of Lending and Credit Risk Management, June 2000; "Loan Workouts: A Different Perspective," The Journal of Corporate Renewal, September 2000. *Member:* Connecticut and American Bar Associations; The Association of Commercial Finance Attorneys; Real Estate Finance Association; Turnaround Management Association. ***PRACTICE AREAS:*** Commercial Law; Commercial and Mortgage Lending; Loan Workouts and Debt Restructures; Real Estate. ***Email:*** rwonneberger@goodwin.com

COUNSEL

RAYMOND M. BERNSTEIN, born New York, NY, 1951; admitted to bar, 1976, North Carolina; 1977, District of Columbia; 1992, Connecticut. *Education:* Cornell University (B.S., 1973); University of North Carolina School of Law (J.D., 1976). Articles Editor, North Carolina Law Review. Law Clerk to Judge H.E. Widener, Jr., U.S. Court of Appeals, Fourth Circuit, 1976-1977. ***PRACTICE AREAS:*** Intellectual Property; Trademarks; Copyrights; Entertainment Law; Employment Law. ***Email:*** rbernstein@goodwin.com

OF COUNSEL

GEORGE C. JEPSEN, born Hattiesburg, MS, 1954; admitted to bar, 1982, Connecticut. *Education:* Dartmouth College (B.A., summa cum laude, 1976); Kennedy School of Government, Harvard University (M.P.P., 1982); Harvard Law School (J.D., cum laude, 1982). Phi Beta Kappa. Teaching Fellow, Constitutional Law, Harvard College, 1981. State Representative, Connecticut General Assembly, 1987-1991. State Senator, Connecticut General Assembly, 1991—; Co-Chairman, Judiciary Committee, 1993. ***LANGUAGES:*** French, Spanish and Chinese. ***PRACTICE AREAS:*** General Practice; Tax Law; Estate Planning. ***Email:*** gjepsen@goodwin.com

ASSOCIATES

ANDREANA R. BELLACH, born San Francisco, CA, 1974; admitted to bar, 1999, Connecticut; 2000, New York. *Education:* State University of New York College at Geneseo (B.A., summa cum laude, 1996); Vanderbilt University (J.D., 1999). Phi Alpha Delta. Member, Moot Court Board. ***PRACTICE AREAS:*** Litigation; Employment Litigation; Commercial Litigation. ***Email:*** asinigiani@goodwin.com

CATHERINE M. BRENNAN, born Greenwich, CT, 1968; admitted to bar, 1994, New York, Connecticut and U.S. District Court, Southern and Eastern Districts of New York; 1995, New Jersey and U.S. District Court, District of New Jersey. *Education:* College of the Holy Cross (A.B., 1990); Pace University (J.D., cum laude, 1993); New York University (LL.M., Taxation, 1996). Casenote and Comment Editor, Pace Law Review, 1992-1993. *Member:* Greenwich and Regional Bar Associations. ***PRACTICE AREAS:*** Estate Planning; Trust Administration; Estate Settlements. ***Email:*** cbrennan@goodwin.com

CATHY L. BROMBERG, born Houston, TX, 1953; admitted to bar, 1983, New York; 1998, Connecticut. *Education:* Baylor University (B.A., summa cum laude, 1975); University of Chicago (J.D., 1982). *Member:* New York State, Connecticut and American Bar Associations; Regional Bar Association. ***LANGUAGES:*** Spanish, French and German. ***PRACTICE AREAS:*** Corporate Law; Commercial Finance; Securities Law. ***Email:*** cbromberg@goodwin.com

LEE A. DUVAL, born St. Petersburg, FL, 1975; admitted to bar, 2001, California (Not admitted in Connecticut). *Education:* Duke University (B.S.E., 1997); University of Virginia (J.D., 2000). ***PRACTICE AREAS:*** Litigation. ***Email:*** lduval@goodwin.com

FREDERICK T. FORSTER, born Woodside, NY, 1972; admitted to bar, 2000, Connecticut and New York. *Education:* St. John's University (B.S., Management, 1996); Fordham University (M.B.A., Finance, 2000; J.D., 2000).

(This Listing Continued)

Member, Moot Court Board. *Member:* American Bar Association. ***PRACTICE AREAS:*** Corporate Law; Corporate Finance; Securities; Real Estate. ***Email:*** fforster@goodwin.com

DANIEL P. FOX, (admission pending). *Education:* West Chester University (B.A., 1995); Northeastern University School of law (J.D., 2001). References to Publications: "Structured Barriers in Authorship Measures", The Sports Lawyer Journal (Spring, 2001, vol. 8). ***Email:*** dfox@goodwin.com

CLARE ATTURA KRETZMAN, born Long Island, NY, 1953; admitted to bar, 1980, New York; 1986, Connecticut. *Education:* St. John's University at Jamaica (B.S., Accounting, 1975; J.D., 1979). Notes and Comments Editor, St. John's Law Review. *Member:* New York State and Connecticut Bar Associations. ***PRACTICE AREAS:*** Corporate Law; Business Law; Mergers and Acquisitions; Securities. ***Email:*** ckretzman@goodwin.com

MARYBETH C. McPADDEN, born Worcester, MA, 1969; admitted to bar, 1996, Connecticut. *Education:* College of the Holy Cross (B.A., English, 1990); University of Connecticut (J.D., with honors, 1996). Sigma Tau Delta; National English Honor Society. Member, 1994-1996 and Intramural Director, 1996, Connecticut Moot Court Board. First Place: Alva P. Loiselle Moot Court Competition, 1994; RisCassi & Davis Mock Trial Competition, 1996. Recipient, American Jurisprudence Award - Moot Court. *Member:* Connecticut and American Bar Associations. ***PRACTICE AREAS:*** Litigation. ***Email:*** mmcpadden@goodwin.com

R. MICHAEL MEO, JR., born Newton, MA, 1971; admitted to bar, 1995, Connecticut; 1996, U.S. District Court, District of Connecticut; 1999, U.S. District Court, Eastern and Southern Districts of New York; 2000, U.S. District Court, District of Columbia. *Education:* Trinity College (B.A., with honors, 1992); University of Pennsylvania (J.D., 1995). *Member:* Regional, Hartford County, Connecticut and American Bar Associations. ***PRACTICE AREAS:*** Commercial Litigation. ***Email:*** rmeo@goodwin.com

PIYUSH SHARMA, born New Delhi, India, 1975; (admission pending). *Education:* Brown University (B.A., magna cum laude, with honors, 1997); Fordham University (J.D., 2001). Phi Beta Kappa. Fordham Law: Moot Court Board. ***Email:*** psharma@goodwin.com

STEVEN WEINBERGER, born Brooklyn, NY, 1964; admitted to bar, 1994, Connecticut; 1996, New York. *Education:* Wesleyan University (B.A., 1985); Benjamin N. Cardozo School of Law (J.D., 1994). Editor-in-Chief, Cardozo Arts & Entertainment Law Journal, 1993-1994. Author: "Perfection of Security Interests in Copyrights: The Peregrine Effect on the Orion Pictures Plan of Reorganization," Cardozo Art & Entertainment Law Journal, Vol. 11, Page 959, 1993-1994. ***PRACTICE AREAS:*** Real Estate. ***Email:*** sweinberger@goodwin.com

CAROLYN J. ZAMBELLI, born Norwalk, CT, 1974; admitted to bar, 1999, Connecticut; 2000, U.S. District Court, District of Connecticut. *Education:* Boston College (B.A., magna cum laude, 1996); University of Connecticut (J.D., 1999). Phi Beta Kappa. Articles Editor, Connecticut Law Review, 1998-1999. Executive Director, Connecticut Moot Court Board. Law Clerk to the Honorable Thomas P. Smith, U.S. Magistrate Judge, District of Connecticut, 1999-2000. Author: "A Band-Aid for the Fourth Amendment: Knowles v. Iowa and the Supreme Court," 31 C.L.R. 1217. ***PRACTICE AREAS:*** Real Estate; Corporate Law. ***Email:*** czambelli@goodwin.com

ANDREW M. ZEITLIN, born Philadelphia, PA, 1968; admitted to bar, 1994, New Jersey; 1995, New York; 1996, U.S. District Court, Eastern and Southern Districts of New York; 2000, Connecticut and U.S. District Court, District of Columbia. *Education:* Cambridge University, England (1988-1989); Brandeis University (B.A., magna cum laude, 1990); University of Pennsylvania (J.D., 1994). Editor-in-Chief, Comparative Labor Law Journal, 1993-1994. Author: "A Test of Faith: Accommodating Religious Employees' 'Work-Related Misconduct' in the U.S. and Canada," Comparative Labor Law Journal 15:2; "Reforming Foreclosures," New York Law Journal, 1994. ***PRACTICE AREAS:*** Commercial Litigation. ***Email:*** azeitlin@goodwin.com

(For complete biographical data on all personnel, see Professional Biographies at Hartford, Connecticut)

SILVER, GOLUB & TEITELL LLP

184 ATLANTIC STREET
P.O. BOX 389
STAMFORD, CONNECTICUT 06904
Telephone: 203-325-4491
Fax: 203-325-3769
URL: http://www.sgtlaw.com

Trial Practice in all State and Federal Courts. Medical Malpractice, Negligence, Commercial Litigation, Family and Criminal Law.

FIRM PROFILE: Begun by Richard A. Silver in the early 1960s, Silver, Golub & Teitell has grown into an eleven lawyer firm dedicated solely to litigation.

(This Listing Continued)

Regularly obtaining some of the most substantial and significant verdicts in Connecticut, Silver, Golub & Teitell is recognized as one of the premier trial firms in the state.

MEMBERS OF FIRM

RICHARD A. SILVER, born Stamford, Connecticut, January 10, 1936; admitted to bar, 1960, Connecticut and Virginia; 1961, U.S. District Court, Southern District of New York and U.S. Court of Appeals, Second Circuit. *Education:* University of Pennsylvania (B.A., 1957); University of Virginia (LL.B., 1960). Senior Topical Editor, Civil Litigation, Connecticut Bar Journal, 1980—. Author: "The Connecticut Bar Journal, Vol. 57 No. 3, June, 1983 "Survey of Recent Developments Relating to Medical Malpractice," Connecticut Law Tribune, Vol. 3 No. 43, October 24, 1977; *Pisel v. Stamford Hospital,* Million Dollar Arguments, Professional Techniques Library, 1983. Lecturer and Tutor in Law, Trial Practice, Yale Law School, 1978-1984. Lecturer: Interstate Custody Disputes, 1977; Preparation, Pleading and Trial of a Medical Malpractice Case in Connecticut, Connecticut Bar Association, 1978; Evaluating Marital Assets and Drafting Separation Agreements, Connecticut Bar Association, 1979; Structured Settlements in Personal Injury Cases, 1980; Trial of Custody Cases, Connecticut Trial Lawyers Association, 1980, 1994; Matrimonial Taxation, 1980; Tax Strategy in Divorce, 1982; Trial Techniques in Matrimonial Law, American Academy of Matrimonial Lawyers, 1983; Products Liability Apportionment of Damages, Advanced, Connecticut Bar Association, 1983; Preparation for Trial and Personal Injury Action, University of Bridgeport Law School, 1983; Civil Trial Advocacy, Connecticut Bar Association, 1984, 1990; The Trial of a Medical Malpractice Case, 1985, 1986, 1988, Trial Techniques for Business Torts and Commercial Litigation, 1989, 1992 and Bankruptcy for Trial Lawyers, 1991, Connecticut Trial Lawyers Association; Commentator, Court TV Civil Litigation, 1992—. Arbitrator, Federal Court, District of Connecticut, 1980—. Member, Advisory Board, University of Quinnipiac Law School, 1982—. Chairman, Judicial Selection Committee, State of Connecticut, 1992-1995. *Member:* Stamford (President, 1982) and Connecticut (Member: House of Delegates, 1979-1992; Board of Governors, 1980-1982) Bar Associations; Virginia State Bar; Connecticut Trial Association Board (President); Trial Attorneys of America (Member, Board of Governors, 1977—; Board Member and Vice President, 1994—); American Board of Trial Advocates (Advocate, 1984—and President, Connecticut Chapter, 1994). Fellow: American Academy of Matrimonial Lawyers; The Association of Trial Lawyers of America. ***PRACTICE AREAS:*** Medical Malpractice; Personal Injury; Negligence; Business Litigation; Family Law.

DAVID S. GOLUB, born New York, N.Y., January 26, 1949; admitted to bar, 1973, Connecticut and U.S. District Court, District of Connecticut; 1974, U.S. Court of Appeals, Second Circuit; 1976, U.S. Supreme Court; 1979, U.S. District Court, Southern District of New York; 1980, U.S. District Court, Eastern District of New York; 1981, U.S. Court of Appeals, Fourth and Fifth Circuits; 1984, U.S. Court of Appeals, Eleventh Circuit; 1985, U.S. Tax Court; 1998, U.S. Court of Appeals, Sixth Circuit. *Education:* Yale University (B.A., 1970; J.D., 1973). Recipient, 1987 NLADA Arthur Von Briesen Award. Author, Article, "Human Rights Commentator," Connecticut Bar Journal, April 1981. Lecturer in Law and Supervising Attorney, Criminal Trial Clinic, University of Connecticut School of Law, 1973-1975. Lecturer and Panelist, Insanity Law, Connecticut Bar Association, 1976. Lecturer: Trial Practice Seminar, Yale Law School, 1976-1984; Conspiracy, Severance and Hearsay, Connecticut Trial Lawyers Association, 1977; Pretrial Motions in Criminal Proceedings, 1978 and Identification Law, 1979, 1981, 1983, Connecticut Bar Association; Principles of Cross-Examination, Connecticut Trial Lawyers Association, 1981; Prosecutorial Disqualification, New Jersey Trial Lawyers Association, 1981; Identification Law, Connecticut Public Defenders, 1986; Employment Contract Law, Damages in Employment Litigation, Connecticut Trial Lawyers Association, 1987; Cross-Examination of Defendant's Expert, Connecticut Trial Lawyers Association, 1989; Pleadings and Proving Employer Fraud Cases, Connecticut Trial Lawyers Association, 1990; Methods of Proving Damages, Connecticut Trial Lawyers Association, 1992; Preparing and Winning the Medical Malpractice Case Seminar, Connecticut Trial Lawyers Association, 1994; Trial Practice Workshop, Direct Examination of Experts, Connecticut Trial Lawyers Association, 1995. Guest Lecturer, Seminars on the United States Constitution, Stamford Board of Education, 1987. Moderator, Search and Seizure Panel, Connecticut Bar Association/Connecticut Trial Lawyers Association, 1980. Panelist: Federal Criminal Defense Practice and Procedure, Connecticut Bar Association, 1981; Implementation of Connecticut Sentencing Act, Connecticut Bar Association, 1981. Speaker and Panelist: How To Try An Employment Case In Federal Court, Employment Law Committee of the Stamford-Norwalk Regional Bar Association, 1997; Representing Employees Under the False Claims Act, National Employment Lawyers Association, 1997. Guest Speaker, Firearm Legislation, Stamford Exchange Club, 1982; First Amendment Principles, Greenwich Public Schools, 1992. Speaker, Liability of Search Consultants in the Recruiting Process, National Association of Corporate & Professional Recruiters, 1988. Instructor: Trial Advocacy Workshop, 1977, 1978; Video Presentation, Introduction of Evidence, Connecticut Bar Association, 1981. Special

(This Listing Continued)

SILVER, GOLUB & TEITELL LLP, Stamford—Continued

Master: Connecticut Superior Court, 1982; U.S. District Court, 1986. Member, Stamford BiCentennial Commission on the U.S. Constitution, 1986-1987. *Member:* Connecticut Bar Association; Connecticut Trial Lawyers Association; ; American Board of Trial Advocates (Advocate); Connecticut Civil Liberties Union; The Initiative for Public Interest Law (Director, 1992-1994). ***PRACTICE AREAS:*** Civil Litigation; Criminal Litigation; Civil Appeals; Criminal Appeals; Employment Litigation; Commercial Litigation; False Claims Act; Medical Malpractice; Personal Injury; Civil Rights; Criminal. ***Email:*** dgolub@sgtlaw.com

ERNEST F. TEITELL, born Philadelphia, Pennsylvania, December 4, 1952; admitted to bar, 1977, Pennsylvania; 1978, Connecticut; 1979, U.S. District Court, District of Connecticut and U.S. District Court, Southern District of New York; 1984, U.S. District Court, Eastern District of New York; 1985, U.S. Court of Appeals, Second Circuit; 1986, U.S. Supreme Court; 1993, U.S. Claims Court. *Education:* Bethany College (B.A., cum laude, 1974); Loyola University (J.D., 1977). Adjunct Professor, Trial Practice and Advanced Trial Practice, Quinnipiac University School of Law, formerly University of Bridgeport School of Law, 1987—. Editor-at-Large, Connecticut Bar Journal, 1999—. Member: Committee for Appointment of Connecticut Superior Court-Special Public Defenders, 1996—. Chairman: Development Committee, Quinnipiac College School of Law, 1995—; State of Connecticut Public Defender Services Commission, 1994-1995. Author: "Production of Documents and Tangible Things, Civil Discovery Practice in Connecticut," Law Practice Handbooks, Inc., 1995. Lecturer: Current Issues in the Psychiatrist-Patient Relationship, Pace University School of Law and Albert Einstein College of Medicine, 1999; Evidence in Connecticut, Connecticut Bar Association, 1992, 1993, 1994, 1995, 1996, 1997, 1998, 1999, 2000; Connecticut Trial Practice Institute, Connecticut Bar Association, National Institute of Trial Advocacy, 1994, 1995, 1996, 1997, 1998, 1999, 2000, 2001. Lecturer and Co-Chair, Trial Practice Workshop, Connecticut Trial Lawyers, Cross Examination, 1993, 1994, 1995, 1996, 1997, 2000. Lecturer: Expert Witnesses, 1995, "Presenting Your Case," 1998, Jury Selection, 1999, "Mastering Medical Malpractice," Connecticut Trial Lawyers, 2000; Trial Demonstration, Connecticut Trial Lawyers, 1996, 1997, 1999; Trial Techniques for Law Students, Demonstrative Evidence, American Trial Lawyers Association, 1996; College of Evidence, Connecticut Trial Lawyers, 1993; Case Evaluation Clinic, Connecticut Trial Lawyers, 1992, 1999; Order of Proof, Connecticut Trial Lawyers, 1992; Trial Techniques for Business Torts and Commercial Litigation, Connecticut Trial Lawyers, 1992; Tort Reform, Stamford-Norwalk Regional Bar Association, 1992; Direct Examination, Connecticut Legal Aid Training Seminar, 1991; Civil Discovery, New England Legal Aid Training Seminar, 1987; Criminal Law, Connecticut Bar Association, 1982; Special Master, Connecticut Superior Court, 1992—. Member, Board of Directors, Connecticut Legal Services Corp., 1985-1990. Bencher, Raymond E. Baldwin American Inn of Court, 1990-1997. Member, President's Club. Member, Rosco Pound Institute. *Member:* Stamford Regional (Director, 1986-1990), Pennsylvania, Connecticut (Member: Executive Committee, Section of Criminal Justice, 1983-1990; Judiciary Committee, 1992-1997) and American (Member, Litigation Section) Bar Associations; Connecticut Trial Lawyers Association (Member: Board of Governors, 1992—; Parliamentarian, 2001-2002; Committee on Continuing Legal Education, 1992—; Diversity Committee, 1994-1997); The Association of Trial Lawyers of America (Fellow); Trial Lawyers for Public Justice; National Association of Criminal Defense Lawyers. ***PRACTICE AREAS:*** Medical Malpractice; Negligence; Criminal Law; Products Liability. ***Email:*** eteitell@sgtlaw.com

PATRICIA M. HAUGH (1942-1988).

JOHN D. JOSEL, born Hartford, Connecticut, February 10, 1960; admitted to bar, 1986, Connecticut; 1987, New York; 1992, U.S. District Court, District of Connecticut. *Education:* Trinity College (B.A., 1982); New York Law School (J.D., cum laude, 1986). Assistant District Attorney, Manhattan District Attorney's Office, 1986-1992. *Member:* Connecticut, New York State and American Bar Associations; Connecticut Trial Lawyers Association; The Association of Trial Lawyers of America. ***PRACTICE AREAS:*** Medical Malpractice; Negligence; Criminal Law. ***Email:*** jjosel@sgtlaw.com

MARIO DiNATALE, born Bronx, New York, April 3, 1954; admitted to bar, 1980, New York; 1984, U.S. District Court, Southern and Eastern Districts of New York and U.S. Court of Appeals, Second Circuit; 1990, U.S. Court of Appeals, Third Circuit; 1993, Connecticut and U.S. District Court, District of Connecticut; 1995, U.S. Court of Appeals, Federal Circuit. *Education:* Columbia University (B.A., 1976); New York University (J.D., 1979). Assistant District Attorney, New York County, 1979-1984. Special Attorney, U.S. Department of Justice, Brooklyn Organized Crime Strike Force, 1984-1989. *Member:* Stamford-Norwalk Regional (Member, Board of Directors), New York State, Connecticut and American Bar Associations; The Association of Trial Lawyers of America; Connecticut Trial Lawyers Association; New York Council of Defense Lawyers. ***LANGUAGES:*** Italian. ***PRACTICE AREAS:*** Personal Injury; Medical Malpractice; Products Liability; Commercial Litigation; Criminal Defense. ***Email:*** mdinatale@sgtlaw.com

(This Listing Continued)

JONATHAN M. LEVINE, born Washington, D.C., September 25, 1964; admitted to bar, 1990, Connecticut; 1991, U.S. District Court, District of Connecticut; 1998, U.S. District Court, Southern District of New York and U.S. Court of Appeals, Second Circuit. *Education:* Harvard University (B.A., 1986); Yale University (J.D., 1990). Phi Beta Kappa. *Member:* Connecticut Bar Association. ***LANGUAGES:*** French and Hebrew. ***REPORTED CASES:*** Sharkey v. Ultramar Energy Limited et al.; Sheff v. O'Neill; Westport Taxi Service, Inc. v. Westport Transit Dist. State v. Sedrick Cobb; Third Taxing Dist. of City of Norwalk v. Lyons; O'Shea v. Mignone; State v. Michael Ross; Pergament v. Green; Yitanza v. Upjohn Company. ***PRACTICE AREAS:*** Medical Malpractice; Negligence; Commercial Litigation; Employment Law. ***Email:*** jlevine@sgtlaw.com

---

MARILYN J. RAMOS, born Norwich, Connecticut; admitted to bar, 1989, Connecticut; 1990, New York and U.S. District Court, Northern District of New York; 1993, U.S. District Court, District of Connecticut. *Education:* University of Madrid, Madrid, Spain; University of Connecticut (B.A., 1967; M.A., 1969); Pace University (J.D., magna cum laude, 1989). Recipient: Fishman Award; Westchester Women's Bar Association Award. Case Note and Comment Editor, Pace Law Review, 1988-1989. *Member:* Stamford-Norwalk and Connecticut Bar Associations; Connecticut Trial Lawyers Association. ***LANGUAGES:*** Spanish. ***PRACTICE AREAS:*** Personal Injury Litigation. ***Email:*** mramos@sgtlaw.com

MARY G. CURRY, born Hartford, Connecticut, December 31, 1961; admitted to bar, 1998, California, Connecticut and U.S. District Court, District of Connecticut. *Education:* Barnard College, Columbia University (B.A., 1984); Yale University (MPH, 1991); University of California (J.D., 1996). ***LANGUAGES:*** Spanish. ***PRACTICE AREAS:*** Medical Malpractice; Negligence; Commercial Litigation; Employment Law. ***Email:*** mcurry@sgtlaw.com

KATHLEEN L. BRANDT, born Cleveland, Ohio, December 7, 1949; admitted to bar, 1996, Connecticut; 1997, New York and U.S. District Court, Southern District of New York. *Education:* Western Connecticut State University (B.S.N., magna cum laude, 1990); Pace University (J.D., magna cum laude, 1996). Sigma Theta Tau (Kappa Alpha Section, 1990—). Member, Pace Law Review. Licensed R.N., New York, 1976 and Connecticut, 1987. Member, New York Trial Lawyers Association, 1997-1999. *Member:* Connecticut Bar Association; Connecticut Trial Lawyers Association; The American Association of Nurse Attorneys; American Trial Lawyers Association. ***PRACTICE AREAS:*** Medical Malpractice. ***Email:*** kbrandt@sgtlaw.com

PAUL A. SLAGER, admitted to bar, 1993, Illinois and U.S. District Court, Northern District of Illinois, including Trial Bar; 1997, U.S. Court of Appeals, Seventh Circuit; 1999, Connecticut, U.S. District Court, District of Connecticut and U.S. Court of Appeals, Second Circuit; 2000, New York. *Education:* University of Michigan (B.A., 1990; J.D., 1992). *Member:* Connecticut and American Bar Associations. ***PRACTICE AREAS:*** Civil Litigation; Medical Malpractice; Negligence; Products Liability. ***Email:*** pslager@sgtlaw.com

ANGELO A. ZIOTAS, born New Britain, Connecticut, April 4, 1964; admitted to bar, 1991, Connecticut; 1992, U.S. District Court, District of Connecticut; 1994, Rhode Island; 1996, U.S. Supreme Court; 1997, U.S. Court of Appeals, Second Circuit. *Education:* Connecticut College (B.A., 1986); University of Connecticut (J.D., cum laude, 1991). Author: "A Personal Injury Round Table," 1999-2001, "Organizing a Trial Practice for the 21st Century," 1995, "Winning Automobile Collisions," 1997, "Inadequate Security Cases: Representing the Crime Victim," 1998 and "Mild Head Injury," 2000, Connecticut Trial Lawyers Association. *Member:* Stamford-Norwalk and Connecticut Bar Associations; Connecticut Trial Lawyers Association (Member, Committee On: Continuing Legal Education); The Association of Trial Lawyers of America (Chairman, Litigation Group, 1993-1997). ***REPORTED CASES:*** Zuchowicz v. United States, 140 F. 3d 381 (1998); Rosales v. Lupien, 50 Conn. App. 405, 717 A. 2d 821 (1998); Cook v. City of Groton, 129 F. 3d 113 (1997); Scovish v. Upjohn, 237 Conn. 911; 675 A.2d 113 (1996); Geyer v. Danasi, 40 Conn. App. 919, 669 A, 2d 636 (1996); cert denied, 236 Conn. 914. 673 A. 2d 113 (1996). ***PRACTICE AREAS:*** Medical Malpractice; Product Liability; Negligence. ***Email:*** aziotas@sgtlaw.com

PETER MASON DREYER, born Bronx, New York, September 19, 1971; admitted to bar, 1996, Connecticut; 1997, New York and U.S. District Court, District of Connecticut. *Education:* Lehigh University (B.S., 1993); University of California at Los Angeles (J.D., 1996). Assistant District Attorney, Bronx County, 1997-2001. *Member:* Connecticut and American Bar Associations; Connecticut Trial Lawyers Association. ***Email:*** pdreyer@sgtlaw.com

LAW OFFICES OF
FRANK E. SISSON, III

6 LANDMARK SQUARE
STAMFORD, CONNECTICUT 06901
Telephone: 203-965-5965
Email: fsisson@compuserve.com
URL: http://www.lawyers.com/frankesisson

Westport, Connecticut Office: 180 Post Road East, 06881. Telephone: 203-965-5965. Telefax: 203-222-4869.

Business Transactions, Corporate, Commercial, Probate, Estate Planning, Elder Law, Tax Law, Real Estate.

FIRM PROFILE: The firm practices extensively in areas of business tax and estate planning. The firm maintains a high degree of technical expertise in many areas of the law, and the firm has a commitment to fulfill the needs of its' clients.

FRANK E. SISSON, III, born Enid, Oklahoma, May 19, 1952; admitted to bar, 1976, New Jersey; 1977, New York; 1979, Connecticut; 1980, Florida. *Education:* Colgate University (B.A., magna cum laude, 1973); Harvard University (J.D., cum laude, 1976). Phi Beta Kappa. Recipient, Alumni Senior History Prize. President, Harvard Law School Association of Connecticut, 1992—. *Member:* Association of the Bar of the City of New York; New Canaan (Vice President, 1988-1989; President, 1989-1991), Connecticut and New York State Bar Associations; The Florida Bar.

SLAVITT, CONNERY & VARDAMIS

STAMFORD, CONNECTICUT
(See Norwalk)

General Practice. Commercial Law, Condemnation, Real Estate, Estate Planning, Probate, Family and Personal Injury Law. Civil and Criminal Trial Practice in all Courts. Agency and Distributorships, Alternative Dispute Resolution, Bankruptcy, Banks and Banking, Business Law, Civil Practice, Debtor and Creditor, Eminent Domain, Inverse Condemnation, Land Annexation, Commercial Real Estate, Construction Law, Contracts, Corporate Law, Equipment Finance and Leasing, Family Law, Finance, Franchises and Franchising, Fire Insurance Subrogation, Uninsured and Underinsured Motorists, Uninsured and Underinsured Motorists Arbitration, Commercial Leasing, Evictions, Landlord and Tenant Law, Lease Finance, Leasing, Office Leasing, Retail Leasing, Shopping Center Leasing, Legal Malpractice, Civil Litigation, Business Acquisitions, Business Divestitures, Mortgages, Negligence, Negligence Defense, Partnership Law, Torts, Civil Liability, Tort Liability, Trusts and Estates, Wills, Workers' Compensation, Zoning, Planning and Land Use.

SMITH, RANSCHT, CONNORS, NORDELL & MUTINO, P.C.

STAMFORD, CONNECTICUT
(See White Plains, New York)

General Practice in all Courts. Probate, Real Estate, Tax, Corporation, Trials, Banking, Estate Planning, Commercial, Municipal and Zoning Law, Foreclosures.

SPITZER SUNDHEIM & BREY LLC

CENTURY BUILDING
350 BEDFORD STREET, 4TH FLOOR
STAMFORD, CONNECTICUT 06901
Telephone: 203-316-8422
Fax: 203-357-7856
URL: http://www.lawyers.com/ss&bllc

White Plains, New York Office: 123 Main Street, Suite 1700, 10601. Telephone: 914-949-5322. Fax: 914-946-5422.

Labor and Employment, Insurance Defense.

VLAD G. SPITZER, born Bucharest, Romania, March 3, 1956; admitted to bar, 1988, New York and U.S. District Court, Southern and Eastern Districts of New York; 1994, U.S. Court of Appeals, 2nd Circuit; 1995, U.S. Supreme Court; 1996, Connecticut; 1997, U.S. District Court, District of Connecticut. *Education:* New York University (B.A., with honors, 1978); Benjamin N. Cardozo School of Law, Yeshiva University (J.D., 1981). *Member:* The Association of the Bar of the City of New York; Connecticut Bar Association (Member, Labor and Employment Law Section, 1996—); National Employment Lawyers Association; National Employee Rights Institute (Member, Advisory Board, 1995—); The Association of Trial Lawyers Of America; New York County Lawyers

(This Listing Continued)

Association (Member, Civil Rights Committee, 1992-1995). ***PRACTICE AREAS:*** Labor and Employment; Commercial Litigation. ***Email:*** vgspitzer@ssbllc.com

STEVEN R. SUNDHEIM, born New York, N.Y., January 31, 1958; admitted to bar, 1985, New York and U.S. District Court, Southern and Eastern Districts of New York; 1991, U.S. District Court, Northern District of New York; 1997, Connecticut; 2000, U.S. District Court, District of Connecticut. *Education:* New York University (B.A., with honors, 1980); Benjamin N. Cardozo School of Law, Yeshiva University (J.D., 1984). Member, Benjamin N. Cardozo Law Review. Speaker, "Practical Skills for Expert Witnesses in Pre-Trial Discovery and also Trial Testimony," New York State Bar Association Continuing Legal Education. *Member:* Westchester, New York State and American Bar Associations; National Employment Lawyers Association. (Also at White Plains, New York Office). ***PRACTICE AREAS:*** Insurance Defense; Torts Litigation; Commercial Contracts; Insurance Coverage; Labor and Employment Law. ***Email:*** srsundheim@ssbllc.com

LEWIS BREY, born Saint Louis Park, Minnesota, September 5, 1968; admitted to bar, 1995, Connecticut; 1996, New York and U.S. District Court, District of Connecticut. *Education:* Emory University (B.A., 1991); Pace University School of Law (J.D., 1995). Chairman, Employee Compensation Committee, Westport, Connecticut Representative Town Meeting, 1997-1999. Member, Board of Finance, Town of Westport, Connecticut, 2000—. *Member:* Connecticut (Member, Labor and Employment Law Section) and New York State (Member, Labor and Employment Law Section) Bar Associations. ***PRACTICE AREAS:*** Labor and Employment Litigation; Commercial Contracts Litigation; Employment Arbitration. ***Email:*** ldbrey@ssbllc.com

HUMA KHAN, born Bridgeport, Connecticut, March 24, 1970; admitted to bar, 1997, Connecticut; 1998, U.S. District Court, District of Connecticut. *Education:* University of Connecticut (B.A., English Literature, cum laude, 1992; J.D., 1996). ***PRACTICE AREAS:*** Labor and Employment; Litigation; Civil Rights. ***Email:*** hkhan@ssbllc.com

SCOTT P. BENJAMIN, born Bronx, New York, September 27, 1958; admitted to bar, 1985, New York; U.S. District Court, Southern and Eastern Districts of New York (Not admitted in Connecticut). *Education:* State University of New York at Albany (B.A., 1980); Benjamin N. Cardozo School of Law, Yeshiva University (J.D., 1984). *Member:* New York State Bar Association. ***PRACTICE AREAS:*** Civil Practice; Criminal Defense; Litigation.

TARA E. SMITH, born March 5, 1974; admitted to bar, 2000, New York. *Education:* Manhattan College (B.S., Finance, magna cum laude, 1996); Albany Law School of Union University (J.D., 1999). *Member:* New York State and American Bar Associations. (Resident, White Plains, New York Office). ***PRACTICE AREAS:*** Insurance Defense; Torts Litigation. ***Email:*** tsmith@ssbllc.com

SAMUEL J. STARKS

1100 SUMMER STREET
STAMFORD, CONNECTICUT 06905
Telephone: 203-348-0441
Fax: 203-973-0441
Email: capjustice@aol.com
URL: http://www.lawyers.com/samueljstarks

Elder Law, Health Law, Estate Administration and Probate.

SAMUEL J. STARKS, born Muskegon, Michigan, February 6, 1951; admitted to bar, 1977, Illinois; 1981, Connecticut and U.S. District Court, District of Connecticut; 1987, U.S. District Court, Eastern and Southern Districts of New York. *Education:* Michigan State University (B.A., 1973); Loyola University (J.D., 1977). Author: "Elder Law: A Subjective Approach," Connecticut Lawyer, May, 1993. Lecturer: "Health Law," New Haven County Medical Association, October, 1992; Fairfield County Medical Association, October, 1991, 1993; "Medicare Issues for Psychologists," Connecticut Psychological Association, April, 1991. Adjunct Professor, Health Law, Pace University Law School, 1990-1991. Adjunct Assistant Professor, Business Law, Sacred Heart University, 1986-1988. Member, Board of Tax Review, City of Stamford, 1986-1989. Chairperson, Board of Directors, Smith House Health Care Center. Member, Board of Directors, Southwestern Connecticut Area Agency on Aging. *Member:* New Canaan, Stamford-Norwalk Regional (Chair, Elder Law Section, 1992-1993) and Connecticut Bar Associations; National Association of Elder Law Attorneys. ***PRACTICE AREAS:*** Health Law; Elder Law; Trusts and Estates.

STEEFEL, LEVITT & WEISS

A PROFESSIONAL CORPORATION

SIX LANDMARK SQUARE, FOURTH FLOOR

STAMFORD, CONNECTICUT 06901-2792

Telephone: 203-359-5662

Fax: 203-359-5805

Email: slw@steefel.com

URL: http://www.steefel.com

San Francisco, California Office: 30th Floor, One Embarcadero Center. Telephone: 415-788-0900. Fax: 415-788-2019.

General Civil and Trial Practice. Antitrust, Banking, Business, Corporate Financing, Reorganization, Corporation, Estate Planning and Probate Law, Public Utility, Real Estate, Taxation.

RICHARD J. TANNENBAUM, born Brooklyn, New York, December 8, 1954; admitted to bar, 1980, New York and U.S. District Courts, Southern and Eastern Districts of New York; 1981, Connecticut and U.S. District Court, District of Connecticut. *Education:* Temple University (B.A., 1976); Brooklyn Law School (J.D., 1979). Co-author: "Bankruptcy Commentary," 45 Brooklyn Law Review 827. Law Clerk, Hon. Howard Schwartzberg, U.S. Bankruptcy Judge, S.D.N.Y., 1979-1981. Director and Counsel to the Jackie Robinson Park of Fame, Inc. *Member:* Connecticut, New York State and American (Member: Business Bankruptcy Subcommittee on Bankruptcy Aspects of Business Transactions; Commercial Financial Services Committee; Commercial Financial Services Subcommittee on Loan Documents and Secured Lending) Bar Associations. ***PRACTICE AREAS:*** Commercial Bankruptcy; Equipment Finance; Real Estate Finance; Loan Workouts. **Email:** tannenbaumr@steefel.com

THOMAS A. BANAHAN, born Brooklyn, New York, September 15, 1955; admitted to bar, 1980, New York; 1988, Connecticut. *Education:* St. John's University (B.S., magna cum laude, 1976; J.D., 1979). Phi Delta Phi. Who's Who in the Real Estate & Development Industries. Recipient, Silver Key for Criminal Justice. *Member:* New York State Bar Association (Member, Real Property Law Section). ***PRACTICE AREAS:*** Real Estate; Banking. ***Email:*** banahant@steefel.com

(For Biographical data on all Personnel, see Professional Biographies at San Francisco, California)

RICHARD H. STEIN LLC

2777 SUMMER STREET

STAMFORD, CONNECTICUT 06905

Telephone: 203-352-8300

Fax: 203-352-8303

URL: http://www.rhstein.com

Estate Planning, Taxation, Business Law, Corporate Law.

RICHARD H. STEIN, born Cincinnati, Ohio, July 6, 1950; admitted to bar, 1975, Massachusetts; 1976, U.S. Tax Court and U.S. Court of Appeals, 1st Circuit; 1978, Connecticut; 1980, U.S. District Court, District of Connecticut; 1990, U.S. Supreme Court. *Education:* University of Cincinnati (B.A., 1972; J.D., 1975); Boston University (LL.M. in Taxation, 1977). Certified Public Accountant, Connecticut, 1978. Author: "Freedom of the Press vs. The Public's Right to Know: Newspaper Right of Reply Statutes," 43 University of Cincinnati Law Review 164, 1974; "Capitalization of Depreciation under Commissioner vs. Idaho Power Co.," 43 University of Cincinnati Law Review 948, 1974. Instructor, University of New Haven Master of Taxation Program, 1980-1981. Member, Executive Committee, Southern Fairfield County Estate Planning Council, 1996—; President, 2000-2001. Secretary, JCEF Community Foundation. *Member:* Stamford-Norwalk Regional (Member, Executive Committee, 1988-1990 and 1993-1997; Chairman, Tax Committee, 1986-1988), Connecticut (Chairman, Young Lawyers Division Tax Committee, 1982-1985; Member, Executive Committee, Tax Section, 1983-1985) and American (Member, Sections on: Real Property, Probate and Trust Law; Economics of Law Practice) Bar Associations; American Institute of Certified Public Accountants; Connecticut Society of Certified Public Accountants (Member: Federal Tax Committee, 1983-1985; Publications Committee, 1984-1985). ***PRACTICE AREAS:*** Taxation; Estate Planning; Corporate; Business Law.

TELLALIAN & TELLALIAN

STAMFORD, CONNECTICUT

(See Bridgeport)

General Practice. Probate, Corporation and Real Estate Law.

TIBBETTS KEATING & BUTLER, LLC

STAMFORD, CONNECTICUT

(See Darien)

General Practice. Residential Real Estate, Civil Litigation, State and Federal, Bankruptcy Chapter 7, Bankruptcy Litigation, Civil Appeals, Estate Planning, Estate Administration, Family Trusts, Living Trusts, Personal Injury, Commercial Real Estate, Corporate Law, Computer Law, Criminal Law.

TIERNEY, ZULLO, FLAHERTY & MURPHY, P.C.

STAMFORD, CONNECTICUT

(See Norwalk)

General Practice. Real Estate, Probate, Administrative, Condemnation, Employment, Healthcare, Municipal, Land Use, Planning, Zoning and Family Law. Civil Litigation, State and Federal Courts.

JOHN W. TIMBERS

P.O. BOX 3085

STAMFORD, CONNECTICUT 06905

Telephone: 203-322-9553

Facsimile: 203-322-4505

Civil Litigation, Criminal Litigation.

JOHN W. TIMBERS, born New York, N.Y., September 8, 1942; admitted to bar, 1969, New York; 1973, U.S. Supreme Court; 1981, Connecticut. *Education:* Dartmouth College (B.A., cum laude, 1964); University of Edinburgh, Edinburgh, Scotland; Harvard University (LL.B., cum laude, 1968). Author, "Monopolist's 'Predatory' Pricing: The Second Circuit's Approach," New York Law Journal, July 17, 1981. Law Clerk to Hon. Inzer B. Wyatt, U.S. District Court, Southern District of New York, 1968-1969. Associate, Sullivan & Cromwell, New York, N.Y., 1969-1973. Assistant U.S. Attorney, Office of the U.S. Attorney for the Southern District of New York, 1973-1976. Member, Stamford Charter Revision Commission, 1982-1983; Southwestern (Connecticut) Regional Planning Agency, 1981—. *Member:* The Association of the Bar of the City of New York (Member: Committee on Trade Regulation, 1980-1983; Committee on Federal Courts, 1987-1990); Stamford and Connecticut (Member: Executive Committee, Section on Corporations and Other Business Organizations, 1985-1990; Antitrust Law Section) Bar Associations. ***REPORTED CASES:*** Valspar Corporation v. Lukken Color Corp., 495 NW 2d 408 (Minn. 1992); Silitschanu v. Groesbeck, 208 Conn. 312, 543 A.2d 737 (1988); Hayden Publishing Co., Inc. v. Cox Broadcasting Corp., 730 F.2d 64 (2 Cir. 1984); United States v. Pastor, 557 F.2d 930 (2 Cir. 1977); United States v. Lam Lek Chong, 544 F.2d 58 (2 Cir. 1976); United States v. Lubrano, 529 F.2d 633 (2 Cir. 1975); Cinerama Inc. v. Sweet Music, S.A., 482 F.2d 66 (2 Cir. 1973). ***PRACTICE AREAS:*** Civil Litigation; Criminal Litigation.

TISDALE & LENNON, LLC

STAMFORD, CONNECTICUT

(See Southport)

Admiralty, Maritime, Insurance, Commercial, Products Liability, Bankruptcy Litigation and Personal Injury Litigation in all Courts.

TROW & SANK, P.C.

30 OAK STREET

STAMFORD, CONNECTICUT 06905

Telephone: 203-357-1190

Fax: 203-356-1383

Email: trow.sank.pc@snet.net

URL: http://www.lawyers.com/trow&sank

White Plains, New York Office: 50 Main Street, Suite 1000. Telephone: 914-682-2611. Fax: 914-682-7784.

Trials in all Courts, Personal Injury, Collections, Negligence, Commercial Litigation, Landlord Tenant, Real Estate, Probate, Estate Planning, Tax, Commercial and Corporate Law, Workers Compensation.

GRIFFITH H. TROW, born New York, N.Y., September 11, 1951; admitted to bar, 1977, Connecticut; 1978, U.S. District Court, District of Connecticut; 1981, U.S. Supreme Court; 1983, U.S. Court of Appeals, Second Circuit. *Education:* University of Rochester (B.A., with distinction, 1973); Syracuse University (J.D., 1977). Instructor in Banking Law, American Institute of Banking, 1980-1984. Special Pre-Trial Master, Superior Court, 1982-1983. *Member:*

(This Listing Continued)

Stamford, Connecticut and American Bar Associations; Connecticut Trial Lawyers Association; Regional Bar Association (Director). ***PRACTICE AREAS:*** Negligence; Personal Injury; Commercial Law; Real Estate; Civil Litigation; Workers Compensation.

MARK A. SANK, born New York, N.Y., March 20, 1959; admitted to bar, 1984, Connecticut; 1985, New York and U.S. District Court, District of Connecticut; 1990, U.S. Supreme Court. *Education:* State University of New York College at Oneonta (B.S., 1981); Vermont Law School (J.D., 1984). Certified Public Accountant, New York, 1988. Lecturer, Collections and Estate Planning. *Member:* Stamford, Connecticut, New York State and American Bar Associations; American Institute of Certified Public Accountants; Rotary Club of Stamford (Past President, 1992-1993). ***PRACTICE AREAS:*** Collections; Estate Planning; Probate; Landlord and Tenant Law; Real Estate; Civil Litigation; Corporate Law. ***Email:*** marksank@snet.net

---

CHRISTOPHER LAGANO, born Port Chester, New York, July 15, 1966; admitted to bar, 1992, Connecticut; 1993, District of Columbia; 1994, New York, U.S. District Court, District of Connecticut, U.S. District Court, Southern District of New York and U.S. Court of Appeals, District of Columbia Circuit. *Education:* John Jay College of Criminal Justice of the City University of New York (B.S./M.A., magna cum laude, 1989); Temple University (J.D., 1992). Phi Alpha Delta. *Member:* Stamford, Connecticut, New York State and American Bar Associations; District of Columbia Bar. ***PRACTICE AREAS:*** Commercial Law; Collections; Landlord and Tenant Law; Civil Litigation; Personal Injury; Foreclosures.

REPRESENTATIVE CLIENTS: Meineke Discount Muffler Shops, Inc.; Stamford Hospital, Inc.; Webster Bank; Toronto Dominion Bank; Silver Hill Hospital; EMC-Mortgage Corp.; Patriot National Bank.
APPROVED ATTORNEYS FOR: First American Title Insurance Co.
REFERENCES: Stamford Hospital; Webster Bank; Mont Management; Toronto Dominion Bank; Silver Hill Hospital; Patriot National Bank.

PETER L. TRUEBNER

111 PROSPECT STREET, SUITE 206
STAMFORD, CONNECTICUT 06901
Telephone: 203-323-4540
FAX: 203-323-4920
URL: http://www.lawyers.com/petertruebner

General Practice. Civil and Criminal Litigation, DUI, Juvenile, Personal Injury, Slip and Fall, Divorce and Family Law. Trials in all State and Federal Courts.

PETER L. TRUEBNER, born New York, N.Y., May 29, 1941; admitted to bar, 1967, Connecticut and District of Columbia; 1969, U.S. District Court, Southern District of New York and U.S. Court of Appeals, Second Circuit. *Education:* Yale University (B.A., 1964); University of Michigan (J.D., 1967); Georgetown University (LL.M., 1969). Assistant U.S. Attorney, Southern District of New York, 1969-1974. *Member:* Stamford, Connecticut and American Bar Associations; Federal Bar Council; The Association of Trial Lawyers of America; Connecticut Trial Lawyers Association.

TYLER COOPER & ALCORN, LLP

Established in 1847
ONE LANDMARK SQUARE
STAMFORD, CONNECTICUT 06901-2501
Telephone: 203-348-5555
Telecopier: 203-348-3875
URL: http://www.tylercooper.com

Hartford, Connecticut Office: CityPlace. Telephone: 860-725-6200. Telecopier: 860-278-3802.
New Haven, Connecticut Office: 205 Church Street. Telephone: 203-784-8200. Telecopier: 203-789-2133.
Greenwich, Connecticut Office: 675 Steamboat Road. Telephone: 203-869-2000. Telecopier: 203-869-2001.
Madison, Connecticut Office: 23 Woodland Road. Telephone: 203-318-3600. Telecopier: 203-318-3609.

Administrative Law, Alternative Dispute Resolution, Antitrust and Trade Regulation, Banking, Bankruptcy and Reorganization, Business Crimes, Business Organizations and Securities Law, Computer Law, Domestic Relations, Environmental Law, Financial Services, Franchising, Health Care, Immigration, Insurance Defense and Insurance Coverage Defense, Intellectual Property, Labor and Employment, Legislative Lawyering, Litigation, Media Law, Medical Malpractice Defense, Pension and Employee Benefits, Public Utilities, Real Estate, Taxation, Trusts and Estates and Workers' Compensation.

(This Listing Continued)

MEMBERS OF FIRM

EMMETT E. BROWN III, born Olean, New York, August 29, 1947; admitted to bar, 1978, New York; 1985, Connecticut. *Education:* Wharton School, University of Pennsylvania (B.S., 1972); Cornell University (M.B.A., 1976; J.D., 1977). [Capt., U.S. Army Special Forces, 1967-1971]. (Resident). ***PRACTICE AREAS:*** Corporate Law; Intellectual Property; Emerging Growth Companies; Licensing Law; Franchise Law. ***Email:*** browne@tylercooper.com

CHRISTOPHER L. ULRICH, born Chicago, Illinois, June 27, 1953; admitted to bar, 1979, New York; 1990, Connecticut. *Education:* Georgetown University (A.B., 1975); Boston College (J.D., 1978). Senior Trial Attorney, District Attorney's Office, Kings County, New York, 1978-1986. Special Attorney, Organized Crime Strike Force, Eastern District of New York, U.S. Department of Justice, 1986-1989. (Resident). ***Email:*** ulrich@tylercooper.com

COUNSEL

NAN BUDDE CHEQUER, born New York, N.Y., August 19, 1938; admitted to bar, 1986, Connecticut. *Education:* Vassar College (A.B., 1960); Yale University (J.D., 1986). (Resident). ***PRACTICE AREAS:*** Real Estate; Trusts and Estates; Corporate. ***Email:*** chequer@tylercooper.com

DEBORAH D. CANNAVINO, born Aurora, Illinois, May 29, 1965; admitted to bar, 1990, Connecticut. *Education:* Northwestern University (B.A., 1987); University of California, Hastings College of Law (J.D., 1990). ***PRACTICE AREAS:*** Employment Law; Civil Litigation.

All Partners and Associates are Members of the Connecticut and American Bar Associations

(For all personnel, see Professional Biographies at New Haven)

JULIA VON SCHILLING

832 BEDFORD STREET
STAMFORD, CONNECTICUT 06901
Telephone: 203-356-0011
Fax: 203-363-0199
Email: attyjvs@aol.com
URL: http://www.lawyers.com/family_law

Family Law, Divorce, Child Custody, Domestic Relations, Alimony, Child Support, Commercial Litigation, Estate Planning, Wills and Trusts.

JULIA VON SCHILLING, born Brooklyn, New York, July 27, 1951; admitted to bar, 1978, New York; 1984, U.S. District Court, Southern District of New York; 1991, Connecticut; 1996, U.S. District Court, District of Connecticut. *Education:* William Smith College (B.A., 1973); Syracuse University (J.D., 1977). Editor, Syracuse University Law Review, 1976-1977. *Member:* Connecticut and New York State Bar Associations. ***LANGUAGES:*** German, Spanish.

WAKE, SEE, DIMES & BRYNICZKA

STAMFORD, CONNECTICUT

(See Westport)

Business and Corporate Law, Real Estate, Trusts and Probate, Estate Planning, Municipal, Zoning and Land Use Law, Litigation in all Federal and State Courts. Federal, State and Foreign Taxation, Pension and Profit Sharing, and Family Law.

DAVID M. WALLMAN

750 SUMMER STREET
STAMFORD, CONNECTICUT 06901-1020
Telephone: 203-348-7709
Fax: 203-357-1445
Email: wallmanlaw1@aol.com
URL: http://www.lawyers.com/wallmanlaw

Affiliate Office: Studio Legale Penta Ed Associati, via G. Puccini, 2, 1-20121, Milan, Italy. Telephone: +39-02-72020070.

Business Litigation, Shareholder Lawsuits, Partnership Dissolution, Bankruptcy Litigation, Loan Workouts, Trials and Appeals in all State and Federal Courts.

DAVID M. WALLMAN, born Concord, Massachusetts, September 26, 1945; admitted to bar, 1970, Connecticut; 1972, U.S. District Court, District of Connecticut; 1975, U.S. Court of Appeals, 2nd Circuit. *Education:* University of Pennsylvania (B.A., 1967); University of Connecticut (J.D., 1970). Law Clerk to Honorable Jay E. Rubinow, Judge of the Connecticut Superior Court and Probate Court Administrator, 1970-1971. Pretrial Special Master, Connecticut Superior Court, 1995. *Member:* Stamford and Connecticut Bar Associations; Connecticut Trial Lawyers Association; American Trial Lawyers Association.

(This Listing Continued)

DAVID M. WALLMAN, Stamford—Continued

REPORTED CASES: Karp v. Urban Redevelopment Commission of the City of Stamford, 162 Conn. 525, 294 A.2d 633 (1972) (Eminent Domain); Allen v. Nissley, 176 Conn. 88, 405 A.2d 231 (1981) (Contract; Specific Performance); Phares v. Phares, 1 Conn. App. 172, 469 A.2d 791 (1984) (Domestic Relations); Garwood & Sons Construction Company, Inc. v. Centos Associates Limited Partnership, 8 Conn. App. 185, 511 A.2d 377 (1986) (Construction; Unjust Enrichment); CMG Realty of Connecticut, Inc. v. Colonnade One At Old Greenwich Ltd. Partnership (Contracts; Corporations) Desalle v. Appelberg, 36 Conn. App. 323, 688 A.2d 1356 (1997) (Contracts; Civil Procedure).

OF COUNSEL

SALLY J. BOYNTON, born Bethel, Maine, November 19, 1951; admitted to bar, 1984, New York; 1985, Connecticut. *Education:* Eisenhower College (B.A., 1973); Yeshiva University (J.D., 1983). *Member:* New York State Bar Association and New York County Lawyers Association; Connecticut Bar Association. ***PRACTICE AREAS:*** Matrimonial Law; Estate Planning; Estate Administration; Real Estate.

ELLIOT R. WARREN

STAMFORD, CONNECTICUT

(See Westport)

General Civil and Criminal Litigation before all State and Federal Courts. Trials and Appeals. Criminal Defense, Commercial and Tax Litigation, Personal Injury, Employment and Negligence Law.

WEINSTEIN, WEINER, IGNAL, NAPOLITANO & SHAPIRO, P.C.

STAMFORD, CONNECTICUT

(See Bridgeport)

General Practice including Personal Injury, Negligence, Commercial, Reorganization, Bankruptcy, Foreclosures, Criminal, Civil Rights, Employee Rights and Benefits, Employment Discrimination, Family, Workers Compensation, Real Estate. Trial and Appellate Practice in all State and Federal Courts and Administrative Agencies.

WELBY, BRADY & GREENBLATT, LLP

STAMFORD, CONNECTICUT

(See White Plains, New York)

Construction Law and Litigation, Public and Private Construction Contracts, Construction Claims, Mechanics Liens, Surety Law, Arbitration, Mediation, Architect and Engineers Liability, Environmental Law.

WIGGIN & DANA LLP

400 ATLANTIC STREET
P.O. BOX 110325
STAMFORD, CONNECTICUT 06901-3234
Telephone: 203-363-7600
Telefax: 203-363-7676
URL: http://www.wiggin.com

New Haven, Connecticut Office: One Century Tower, P.O. Box 1832. Telephone: 203-498-4400. Telefax: 203-782-2889.

Hartford, Connecticut Office: One CityPlace. Telephone: 860-297-3700. Telefax: 860-525-9380.

Berwyn, Pennsylvania Office: 1055 Westlake Drive. Telephone: 610-727-4153. Telefax: 610-727-4085.

Cherry Hill, New Jersey Office: 402 Park Boulevard North, 08802. Telephone: 856-662-3331. Telefax: 856-662-1783.

Antitrust and Trade Regulation, Appellate, Automotive Industry Law, Banking and Financial Services, Bankruptcy Law, Biotechnology Law, Civil Litigation, Closely Held Business, Cogeneration, Construction Law, Employee Benefits and ERISA Law, Environmental Law, Estate Planning and Settlement Law, Franchise Law, Governmental Affairs, Health Care, Hospital Law, Institutional Finance, Insurance Coverage Litigation, Intellectual Property, Internal Corporate Investigations and White Collar Criminal Defense Law, International Transactions, Labor Law, Litigation, Long Term Care Facilities and Financing, Mental Health Law, Mergers and Acquisitions, National and Regional Litigation Counsel, Partnerships and Joint Ventures, Patent Prosecution and Litigation, Professional Malpractice Litigation, Public Finance, Public Utilities, Real Estate Leasing, Development and Finance, Secured Transactions, Securities Regulation, State and Federal Tax Law, Tax Exempt Organizations, Technology Licensing, Telecommunications, Trademarks and Copyright, Trust and Estates Administration, Venture Capital and Zoning.

MEMBERS OF FIRM

JAMES F. FARRINGTON, JR., born Waterbury, Connecticut, 1952; admitted to bar, 1984, Connecticut; 1985, New York. *Education:* University of Notre Dame (B.Ch.E., 1974); Quinnipiac University School of Law (J.D., magna cum laude, 1984). Associate Editor, University of Bridgeport Law Review, 1981-1984. Author: "Product and Process Patent Confusion under Antitrust Analysis," 4 Bridgeport L. Rev. 109 (1982); "Piercing the Connecticut Corporate Veil," 5 Bridgeport L. Rev. 109 (1983). Member, Mannheimer Swartling Advokatbyrå, 1991-1995. Associate and Partner, Reid & Priest, 1985-1991. (Resident). ***PRACTICE AREAS:*** International Corporate; Pharmaceutical Strategic Alliances; Technology Transfer. ***Email:*** jfarrington@wiggin.com

LEONARD LEADER, born New York, N.Y., 1950; admitted to bar, 1974, New York; 1975, U.S. Court of Appeals, Second Circuit and U.S. District Court, Southern District of New York; 1983, Connecticut. *Education:* City College of the City University of New York (B.A., cum laude, 1970); Fordham Law School (J.D., cum laude, 1973); New York University Graduate School of Law (LL.M. in Taxation, 1982). Phi Beta Kappa. Member, Fordham Urban Law Journal, 1972-1973. Author: "Excluded Gifts Are Not Necessarily GST-Exempt," Probate & Property, November/December 1991; "Review of Recent Developments in Estate & Gift Taxation," The Tax Lawyer, 1975-1981. Estate Planning Instructor, Westport School of Continuing Education, 1983. Associate, Parker Chapin Flattau & Klimpl., LLP, New York, NY, 1973-1981. Member, Kleban & Samor, P.C., Southport, CT, 1981-1996. *Member:* Greater Bridgeport (Member, Probate Section), Connecticut (Member, Estates and Probate Section), New York State (Member, Trusts and Estates Section) and American (Member, Sections on: Taxation, Estate and Gift Taxes Committee, Chairman, Task Force on Charitable Easements, 1982; Real Property and Trust Law, Generation Skipping Trusts Committee of the Estate Planning and Drafting Group) Bar Associations. (Resident). ***PRACTICE AREAS:*** Trusts and Estates. ***Email:*** lleader@wiggin.com

DAVID B. FEIN, born New York, N.Y., 1960; admitted to bar, 1987, New York, Connecticut and U.S. District Court, Southern and Eastern Districts of New York; 1990, U.S. Court of Appeals, Second Circuit; 2000, U.S. Supreme Court. *Education:* Dartmouth College (A.B., cum laude, 1982); New York University School of Law (J.D., cum laude, 1985). Order of the Coif. Senior Board Member, New York University Law Review. Clerkship, Judge Frank M. Coffin, U.S. Court of Appeals for the First Circuit, 1986. Former White House Associate Counsel to the President, 1995-1996. U.S. Attorney's Office, Southern District of New York, 1989-1995: Deputy Chief of the Criminal Division; Counsel to the U.S. Attorney. Visiting Professor of Law, Yale Law School, 1999—. *Member:* Federal Bar Council (Trustee, 1999—); American Bar Association (Criminal Litigation Committee). (Resident). ***PRACTICE AREAS:*** White Collar Defense; Internal and External Investigations; Corporate Compliance; Appellate; First Amendment. ***Email:*** dfein@wiggin.com

WILLIAM A. PERRONE, born New York, N.Y., 1952; admitted to bar, 1979, Connecticut; 1981, U.S. District Court, District of Connecticut. *Education:* Brooklyn College of the City University of New York (B.A., cum laude, 1974); Western New England College School of Law (J.D., cum laude, 1979). (Resident). ***PRACTICE AREAS:*** Corporate; Emerging Growth Companies; Information Technology; Mergers and Acquisitions; Securities. ***Email:*** wperrone@wiggin.com

MICHAEL GRUNDEI, born New York, N.Y., 1964; admitted to bar, 1990, New York; 1996, Connecticut. *Education:* University of Pennsylvania (B.A., magna cum laude, 1986); Duke University School of Law (J.D., 1989). (Resident). ***LANGUAGES:*** German. ***PRACTICE AREAS:*** Corporate Finance; Securities; Venture Capital; Public Offerings; Mergers and Acquisitions. ***Email:*** mgrundei@wiggin.com

PATRICIA KAVEE MELICK, born New York, N.Y., 1962; admitted to bar, 1988, New York; 1997, Connecticut. *Education:* Lehigh University (B.A., summa cum laude, 1984); University of Chicago Law School (J.D., 1987). Phi Beta Kappa. (Resident). ***PRACTICE AREAS:*** Mergers, Acquisitions and Divestitures; Biotechnology Licensing; Commercial Transactions; Contracts; Corporate Law. ***Email:*** pmelick@wiggin.com

WILLIAM J. SPERANZA, born Poughkeepsie, New York, 1949; admitted to bar, 1976, New York; 1977, U.S. District Court, Southern and Eastern Districts of New York and U.S. Court of Appeals, Fifth Circuit; 1984, U.S. Court of Appeals for the Federal Circuit; 1985, Connecticut; 1986, U.S. District Court, District of Connecticut; 1989, U.S. Court of Appeals, Third Circuit; 1993, U.S. Supreme Court; 1997, U.S. Court of Appeals, Sixth Circuit; registered to practice before U.S. Patent and Trademark Office. *Education:* University of Notre Dame (B.S.Ch.E., cum laude, 1971); Fordham University (J.D., cum laude, 1975). Member, Fordham Law Review, 1973-1975. Author: "Re-examination - The Patent Challenger's View," 15 A.I.P.L.A. Q.J. 85, 1987. *Member:* American

(This Listing Continued)

Bar Association; Connecticut Patent Law Association. (Resident). ***PRACTICE AREAS:*** Patent Law; Intellectual Property; Litigation. ***Email:*** wsperanza@wiggin.com

MARK E. HARANZO, born Wheeling, West Virginia, September 8, 1959; admitted to bar, 1986, West Virginia, Massachusetts and U.S. District Court, Southern District of West Virginia; 1987, Florida and New York; 1989, New Jersey and U.S. District Court, District of New Jersey; 1990, Connecticut. *Education:* Wittenberg University; University of South Florida (B.A., 1981); Stetson University (J.D., 1985). Attorney, Internal Revenue Service, 1986-1988. Co-Author: "Harris Estates Practice Guide, 4th Edition," 1994 Annual Supplements; "Harris 5th Edition New York Estates," West Group, 1996 Edition, 1997-2000 Annual Supplements. Member, Archdiocese of New York, Planned Giving Committee (Co-Chair, Education Committee). *Member:* The Association of the Bar of the City of New York (Member, Estate and Gift Taxation Committee, 1993-1995); New York State (Member, Trusts and Estates Law Section), Massachusetts (Member, Probate Law Section), Connecticut (Member, Estates and Probate Section), Stamford Norwalk Regional and American (Member, Sections on: International Law and Practice; Real Property, Probate and Trust Law) Bar Associations; The West Virginia State Bar; The Florida Bar (Member: Real Property, Probate and Trust Law Section; Tax Section, Federal Estate and Gift Taxation Committee); New York County Lawyers Association (Member, Section on Estates, Trusts and Surrogate's Court Practice; Co-Chair, Committee on Surrogate's Court Practice and Trust and Estate Administration, 1992-1994). Fellow, The American College of Trust and Estate Counsel. ***PRACTICE AREAS:*** Trusts Law; Estates Law; Estate Planning Law; Estate Litigation; Taxation of Trusts and Estates; Not-For-Profit Institutions Law. ***Email:*** mharanzo@wiggin.com

LAWRENCE PEIKES, admitted to bar, 1987, California; 1990, Connecticut; 1996, New York. *Education:* University of Maryland (B.A., 1984); The National Law Center, George Washington University (J.D., with honors, 1987). *Member:* American Bar Association (Member, Section of Labor and Employment Law, 1993—). ***PRACTICE AREAS:*** Labor and Employment Law; Alternative Dispute Resolution; Employee Benefits; Trade Secrets. ***Email:*** LPeikes@wiggin.com

JAMES H. BICKS, born 1962; admitted to bar, 1989, New York; 1999, Connecticut. *Education:* Pomona College (B.A., cum laude, 1984); New York University (J.D., 1988). Editor, Moot Court Board. (Resident). ***Email:*** jbicks@wiggin.com

RESIDENT SENIOR COUNSEL

ROBERT M. MCANERNEY, born Greenwich, Connecticut, January 29, 1924; admitted to bar, 1954, Connecticut; 1959, U.S. District Court, District of Connecticut; 1969, U.S. Supreme Court. *Education:* Williams College (B.A., 1947); University of Virginia (J.D., 1953). Associated with Sullivan & Cromwell, New York, N.Y., 1953. Partner, Durey & Pierson, Stamford, Connecticut, 1954-1963. Founder and Senior Partner, McAnerney & Miller, Darien, Connecticut, 1963-1995. Major Contributing Author: "Proposal for Revision of Connecticut Statutes Relative to Divorce," 44 Connecticut Bar Journal 411 (1970). Co-Author: "Connecticut's New Approach to Marriage Dissolution," 47 Connecticut Bar Journal 375 (1973). Director and Member, Executive Committee, Connecticut Attorneys Title Insurance Company, 1970-1994. *Member:* Connecticut (Member, Board of Governors, 1964-1967; Chairman, Family Law Committee, 1967-1971; Vice Chairman, Family Law Section, 1971-1973; Chairman, Law Office Economics Committee, 1973-1975; Chairman, Special Committee on Legislative Liaison, 1977-1978; Vice-Chairman, Commission on the Legal Profession, 1978-1980, Vice-President, 1978-1979, President-Elect, 1979-1980 and President, 1980-1981) and American (Member, House of Delegates, 1978-1982) Bar Associations; New England Bar Association (Director, 1980-1984); Connecticut Bar Foundation (Director, 1978-1979). Life Fellow, American Bar Foundation. (Resident). ***PRACTICE AREAS:*** Estate Planning; Trusts and Estates; Family Law; Real Estate.

ASSOCIATES

ELIZABETH ANNE BLOOMFIELD, born Greenville, Pennsylvania, 1971; admitted to bar, 2000, New York; 2001, Connecticut. *Education:* Vassar College (A.B., 1993); New York University. Member, Order of Barristers. Casebook Editor, Moot Court Board, 1998. (Resident). ***Email:*** ebloomfield@wiggin.com

JULIE MIN CHAYET, born Bay Shore, New York, 1969; admitted to bar, 1999, Connecticut and New York. *Education:* Haverford College (B.A., 1991); Columbia University (M.P.A., 1995); Fordham University (J.D., 1998). Associate Editor, 1996-1997 and Staff Member, Environmental Law Journal. (Resident). ***LANGUAGES:*** Korean and Spanish. ***Email:*** jminchayet@wiggin.com

JEFFREY JOHN DANILE, born New York, N.Y., 1975; admitted to bar, 2000, Connecticut. *Education:* New York University (B.A., Political Science, cum laude, 1996); St. John's University (J.D., 2000). Executive Publications Editor, St. John's Law Review. Author: "Recent Developments in NY Law," 73 St. John's L. Rev. 613, 1999. (Resident). ***Email:*** jdanile@wiggin.com

(This Listing Continued)

W. BRUCE DELMONICO, born New Haven, Connecticut, 1969; admitted to bar, 1997, Connecticut; 1998, U.S. District Court, District of Connecticut; 1999, Georgia and U.S. District Court, Northern District of Georgia. *Education:* Brown University (B.A., in Honors English, 1991); University of Texas at Austin (M.A., in English, 1994, Phi Kappa Phi); University of Virginia (J.D., 1997). Dillard Fellow, 1995-1996. Essays Editor, Virginia Journal of Social Policy & The Law, 1996-1997. (Resident). ***Email:*** bdelmonico@wiggin.com

JODY L. DESTEFANIS, born Bronx, New York, 1970; admitted to bar, 1999, Connecticut; registered to practice before U.S. Patent and Trademark Office. *Education:* University of Connecticut (B.S.E., 1992); Quinnipiac College (M.B.A., 1998; J.D., 1998). (Resident). ***Email:*** jdestefanis@wiggin.com

JESSE M. FURMAN, born New York, N.Y., June 7, 1972; admitted to bar, 1999, New York; 2000, U.S. District Court, Southern District of New York (Not admitted in Connecticut). *Education:* Harvard University (A.B., summa cum laude, 1994); Oxford University, England (1995); Yale University (J.D., 1998). Phi Beta Kappa. Henry Fellow. Executive Editor, Yale Law Journal, 1997-1998; Articles Editor, Yale Law and Policy Review, 1996-1997. Law Clerk to: Judge Michael B. Mukasey, U.S. District Court, Southern District of New York, 1998-1999; Judge José A. Cabranes, U.S. Court of Appeals, Second Circuit, 1999-2000. Prospective Clerk to Justice David H. Souter, U.S. Supreme Court, 2002-2003. Author: Note, "Political Illiberalism: The Paradox of Disenfranchisement and the Ambivalences of Rawlsian Justice," 106 Yale Law Journal 1157, 1997. *Member:* New York State and American Bar Associations; Federal Bar Council. ***Email:*** jfurman@wiggin.com

SARA A. GOLDBERG, born Miami, Florida, 1970; admitted to bar, 1996, New York (Not admitted in Connecticut). *Education:* Princeton University (A.B., History, magna cum laude, 1992); New York University (J.D., cum laude, 1995). Developments Editor, New York University Environmental Law Journal, 1994-1995. Law Clerk to the Honorable Michael H. Dolinger, U.S. Magistrate Judge, U.S. District Court, Southern District of New York, 1995-1996. Author, "Lender Liability Under CERCLA: Shaping a New Legal Rule," N.Y.U. Environmental Law Journal, reprinted in Banking Law Anthology. ***LANGUAGES:*** Hebrew. ***Email:*** sgoldberg@wiggin.com

NAOMI B. GRAUBARD, born New York, N.Y., 1971; admitted to bar, 1996, Connecticut; 1997, New York; U.S. District Court, District of Connecticut. *Education:* Washington University (B.A., 1993); Boston University (J.D., cum laude, 1996). Editor-in-Chief, Boston University Probate Law Journal, 1995-1996. ***Email:*** ngraubard@wiggin.com

RUSSELL G. KAUFF, born New York, N.Y., 1969; admitted to bar, 1997, Connecticut. *Education:* Trinity College (B.A. with faculty honors in Economics, 1991); University of Connecticut (J.D., 1997). Director, Intramural Competition, Connecticut Moot Court Board, 1996-1997. Symposium Editor, Connecticut Law Review, 1996-1997. (Resident). ***LANGUAGES:*** French. ***Email:*** rkauff@wiggin.com

WILLIAM JAMES KELLEHER, III, born Flushing, New York, 1970; admitted to bar, 1996, New York and U.S. District Court, Southern and Eastern Districts of New York; 2001, Connecticut. *Education:* Fairfield University (B.A., 1992); St. John's University (J.D., 1995). Executive Publications Editor, 1994-1995, Staff Member, 1993-1994, American Bankruptcy Institute Law Review. Staff Member, New York International Law Review, 1993-1994. Author: Note, "Jury Trials in Bankruptcy Court," 2 Am. Bankr. Inst. L. Rev. 477, 1994; Recent Decision, "United World Trade v. Mangyshlakneft Oil Production Assn.," 7 N.Y. Int'l L. Rev. 75, 1994. Law Clerk to Hon. Dorothy Eisenberg, U.S. Bankruptcy Court, Eastern District of New York, 1995-1996. (Resident). ***Email:*** wkelleher@wiggin.com

CLEMENT J. NAPLES, admitted to bar, 2000, Connecticut. *Education:* Southern Connecticut State College (B.S., 1994); Quinnipiac University School of Law (J.D., 2000). Phi Delta Phi. Member, Quinnipiac Law Review. ***Email:*** cnaples@wiggin.com

JANIE L. TREANOR, born San Antonio, Texas, 1973; admitted to bar, 1998, Texas; 2001, Connecticut. *Education:* University of Texas (B.A., 1994); Southern Methodist University (J.D., 1998). Member, Moot Court Board, 1996-1977. Moot Court Board, Director of Education, 1997-1998. Moot Court Board Best Brief Nominee, 1996. Editor of the SMU Law Review, 1998. Author: Comment, "Privatization v. Corporatization of the Federal Aviation Administration: Revamping Air Traffic Control," Journal of Air Law and Commerce, Vol. 63, Feb-March, 1998. (Resident). ***Email:*** jtreanor@wiggin.com

SUZANNE E. WACHSSTOCK, born Long Beach, New York, 1969; admitted to bar, 1994, Connecticut; 1995, New York; 1996, U.S. District Court, Southern and Eastern Districts of New York and U.S. Court of Federal Claims. *Education:* Harvard University (A.B., magna cum laude, 1990; (J.D., cum laude, 1994). Phi Beta Kappa. (Resident). ***LANGUAGES:*** Hebrew. ***Email:*** swachsstock@wiggin.com

WILLINGER, WILLINGER & BUCCI, P.C.

STAMFORD, CONNECTICUT

(See Bridgeport)

General Practice. Real Estate, Corporate, Commercial, Foreclosure, Bankruptcy, Secured Financing, Zoning, Labor, Probate, Condemnation, Workers Compensation, Financial, Banking, Personal Injury and Criminal Law. Trials in all Courts.

WOFSEY, ROSEN, KWESKIN & KURIANSKY, LLP

Established in 1917

600 SUMMER STREET

STAMFORD, CONNECTICUT 06901

Telephone: 203-327-2300

Fax: 203-967-9273

URL: http://www.wrkk.com

General Practice in all Courts. Civil and Criminal Litigation, Real Estate, Corporation, Family, Bankruptcy, Taxation, Estate Planning and Probate Law.

MEMBERS OF FIRM

ABRAHAM WOFSEY (1915-1944).

MICHAEL WOFSEY (1927-1951).

DAVID M. ROSEN (1926-1967).

JULIUS B. KURIANSKY (1952-1992).

SYDNEY C. KWESKIN (1946-1998).

MONROE SILVERMAN, born Brooklyn, New York, April 5, 1931; admitted to bar, 1955, Connecticut; 1957, U.S. District Court, District of Connecticut; 1970, U.S. Court of Appeals, Second Circuit and U.S. Supreme Court. *Education:* Union College (B.S., 1952); Yale University (LL.B., 1955). Phi Beta Kappa. Member, Editorial Board, Yale Law Journal, 1953-1955. Member: City of Stamford Charter Revision Commission, 1958-1959; Board of Directors, Health Systems Agency (HSA-1), 1977-1983; Board of Directors, Connecticut Civil Liberties Union, 1987-1996. Member, Board of Directors, 1977—, Secretary, 1983-1988, Vice President, 1988-1991 and President, 1991-1993, Stamford Museum and Nature Center, Inc. Chairman, Fairfield County Chapter, Connecticut Civil Liberties Union, 1977-1983. *Member:* Stamford and Connecticut Bar Associations; The Connecticut Trial Lawyers Association. ***PRACTICE AREAS:*** Personal Injury; Contracts; Civil Litigation; Real Estate. ***Email:*** msilverman@wrkk.com

HOWARD C. KAPLAN, born New York, N.Y., May 23, 1935; admitted to bar, 1960, New York and Connecticut; 1961, U.S. District Court, District of Connecticut; 1973, U.S. Supreme Court; 1975, U.S. Court of Appeals, Second Circuit. *Education:* University of Michigan (A.B., 1956); Yale University (LL.B., 1959). Phi Beta Kappa. Author, "Selected Connecticut Business Law Cases," Collection of Connecticut Cases developed as instructional material at Yale University and University of Connecticut, revised annually. Visiting Lecturer and Guest Fellow, Yale University, 1983-1990. Instructor, Business Law, University of Connecticut Graduate School of Business, 1977-1995. Member, 1965-1969 and Majority Leader, 1967-1969, Stamford Board of Representatives. Member, Stamford Board of Ethics, 1996—. *Member:* Stamford and Connecticut Bar Associations; The Connecticut Trial Lawyers Association. ***PRACTICE AREAS:*** Construction Law; Business Law; Real Estate; Civil Litigation. ***Email:*** hkaplan@wrkk.com

EDWARD M. KWESKIN, born Stamford, Connecticut, June 26, 1946; admitted to bar, 1971, Connecticut, Pennsylvania, U.S. District Court, District of Connecticut, U.S. District Court, Eastern District of Pennsylvania and U.S. Court of Appeals, Second Circuit; 1973, U.S. Supreme Court. *Education:* University of Pennsylvania (A.B., 1968); George Washington University (J.D., with honors, 1971). Listed in: International Who's Who of Professionals, 1995—; Who's Who in American Law, 1996—; Who's Who in America, 1997—. Attorney, Community Legal Services, Inc., Philadelphia, Pennsylvania, 1971-1973. Chairman, 1999—, and Commissioner, Sixth Taxing District of Norwalk, 1992—. President, 1994-1996 and Director, 1990—, Temple Sinai, Inc. President, Director, 1973— and Secondary School Chairperson, 1992—, University of Pennsylvania Alumni Club of Fairfield County. *Member:* Stamford (Chairman: Legal Referral Committee, 1974-1979; Family Law Committee, 1984-1986; Member, Executive Committee, 1980-1989; Treasurer, 1983-1984; Secretary, 1984-1985; Vice-President, 1985-1987; President, 1987-1988; Co-Chairman, Pro Bono Committee, 1989-1990), Connecticut (Member, Executive Committee, Family Law Section, 1997-1999) and American (Member, Sections on: Family Law; Litigation) Bar Associations; Connecticut Trial Lawyers Association. ***PRACTICE AREAS:*** Divorce; Real Estate; Family Law; Wills; Estate Planning. ***Email:*** ekweskin@wrkk.com

(This Listing Continued)

DAVID M. COHEN, born Chicago, Illinois, September 13, 1948; admitted to bar, 1973, Connecticut; 1975, U.S. District Court, District of Connecticut and U.S. Court of Appeals, Second Circuit. *Education:* Harvard University (A.B., magna cum laude, 1970); Yale University (J.D., 1973). Phi Beta Kappa. Recipient, Francis E. Wayland Prize. Member, Legal Internship Committee, Connecticut Supreme Court, 1971-1973. Law Clerk to Judge Caleb Wright, U.S. District Court, District of Delaware, 1973-1975. Trial Referee, Connecticut Superior Court, 1990—; Special Master, United States District Court 1998—; James Cooper Fellow, Connecticut Bar Foundation; Director, Jewish Family Service of Stamford. *Member:* Stamford and Connecticut Bar Associations; Connecticut Trial Lawyers Association; American Immigration Lawyers Association. ***PRACTICE AREAS:*** Litigation; Employment Law; Civil Rights; Immigration and Naturalization. ***Email:*** dcohen@wrkk.com

MARSHALL GOLDBERG, born Norwich, Connecticut, January 31, 1945; admitted to bar, 1976, Connecticut; 1977, U.S. District Court, District of Connecticut; 1981, U.S. Court of Appeals, Second Circuit; 1982, U.S. Supreme Court. *Education:* Brown University (A.B., cum laude, 1967); University of Michigan (M.A., 1970); University of Connecticut (J.D., magna cum laude, 1976). Recipient: Danforth Teaching Fellowship, University of Michigan; Corpus Juris Secundum Award; Hornbook Award, University of Connecticut; American Jurisprudence Awards in: Property II; Constitutional Law. Director, Aid for Retarded, Inc. (ARI). Director and President, Stamford Jewish Community Center. *Member:* Stamford and Connecticut Bar Associations; North Stamford Association (Director). ***PRACTICE AREAS:*** Commercial Law; Creditors Rights; Creditor Bankruptcy; Real Estate. ***Email:*** mgoldberg@wrkk.com

STEPHEN A. FINN, born New York, N.Y., September 23, 1953; admitted to bar, 1979, Rhode Island; 1980, U.S. District Court, District of Rhode Island; 1981, U.S. Court of Appeals, First Circuit; 1982, U.S. District Court, District of Connecticut; 1983, Connecticut; 1995, U.S. Court of Appeals, Second Circuit. *Education:* Washington University (A.B., magna cum laude, 1975); University of Virginia (J.D., 1979). Phi Beta Kappa; Sigma Xi. *Member:* Stamford, Connecticut and American (Member, Sections on: Litigation; Tort and Insurance Practice) Bar Associations; Master, American Inns of Court; The Association of Trial Lawyers of America; Connecticut Trial Lawyers Association (Member, Court Rules Committee, 1992—) Million Dollar Advocates Forum. ***PRACTICE AREAS:*** Civil Litigation; Personal Injury; Commercial Law. ***Email:*** sfinn@wrkk.com

JUDITH ROSENBERG, born New York, N.Y., January 17, 1943; admitted to bar, 1980, Connecticut and U.S. District Court, District of Connecticut; 1981, U.S. Court of Appeals, Second Circuit; 1985, U.S. Supreme Court. *Education:* State University of New York at Stony Brook (B.S., 1964); Hofstra University (M.S., 1968); Pace University (J.D., cum laude, 1980). Member, Editorial Board, Pace Law Review, 1978-1980. Author, "Moore v. Sims: A Further Expansion of the Younger Abstention Doctrine," 1 Pace Law Review 149, 1980. *Member:* Stamford and Connecticut (Member: Executive Committee, Workers' Compensation Section; Labor and Employment Law Section) Bar Associations; Connecticut Trial Lawyers Association (Member, Workers Compensation Committee). ***PRACTICE AREAS:*** Employment Law; Workers Compensation; Accidents; Personal Injury; Discrimination. ***Email:*** jrosenberg@wrkk.com

MARK H. HENDERSON, born Greenwich, Connecticut, August 29, 1954; admitted to bar, 1985, Connecticut; 1986, New York and U.S. District Court, District of Connecticut. *Education:* Trinity College (B.S., 1976); Pace University (J.D., cum laude, 1985). Recipient, American Jurisprudence Awards in: Criminal Procedure I; Commercial Transactions II. Notes and Comment Editor, Pace Environmental Law Review, 1984-1985. Best Brief, Advanced Moot Court Competition. Author, "United States v. County of Westchester: Invalidation of an Airport Curfew," 2 Pace Envtl. L. Rev. 83. Former Director: Domestic Violence Services, Inc., Stamford, Connecticut. Former Director and Co-President, 1993-1994, Old Greenwich Riverside Community Center. Special Master: Connecticut Superior Courts, Family and Housing; Regional Family Trial Docket. *Member:* Stamford/Darien, Connecticut (Member, Family Law Section; Fee Arbitration Committee) and American (Member, Family Law Section) Bar Associations. ***PRACTICE AREAS:*** Litigation; Family Law; Criminal Law; Landlord and Tenant Law. ***Email:*** mhenderson@wrkk.com

STEVEN D. GRUSHKIN, born Greenport, Long Island, New York, April 3, 1947; admitted to bar, 1972, Connecticut; 1973, U.S. District Court, District of Connecticut and U.S. Court of Appeals, 2nd Circuit. *Education:* University of Connecticut (B.A., 1969); Suffolk University (J.D., 1972). Member, Board of Directors, Stamford Partnership, formerly Stamford Economic Assistance Corporation, 1986-1994. Past Director: Stamford Jewish Community Center; Agudath Shalom. *Member:* Stamford/ Norwalk Regional (Member, Executive Committee, 1983-1984; Vice Chairman, 1996-1997 and Co-Chairman, 1998-2000, Real Estate Committee) and Connecticut (Member, Sections on: Real Estate; Land Use Regulation; Business Law) Bar Associations. ***PRACTICE AREAS:*** Real Estate; Business Law; Commercial Law; Finance. ***Email:*** sdgrush@wrkk.com

MATTHEW J. FORSTADT, born Savannah, Georgia, February 27, 1946; admitted to bar, 1970, Connecticut and U.S. District Court, District of Con-

(This Listing Continued)

necticut; 1971, U.S. Court of Appeals, 2nd Circuit; 1975, U.S. Supreme Court; 1978, U.S. District Court, Eastern District of Wisconsin; 1981, U.S. Court of Appeals, 7th Circuit. *Education:* University of North Carolina (A.B., 1968; J.D., 1970). Member, Connecticut Advisory Committee, U.S. Commission on Civil Rights, 1975-1980. Attorney Trial Referee, State of Connecticut, 1984—. Special Master, Federal Bar, 1998—. Special Counsel to Ohio Attorney General, 1996—. Member, Panel of Arbitrators, American Arbitration Association. *Member:* Stamford/Norwalk Regional (Chairman, Bench/Bar Committee, 1984-1985; Member, Board of Directors, 1988-1989) and Connecticut Bar Associations. ***PRACTICE AREAS:*** Commercial Litigation; Financial Law; Real Estate Litigation; Business Litigation; Construction Law; Loan Workouts. ***Email:*** m4stadt@wrkk.com

STEVEN M. FREDERICK, born Brooklyn, New York, September 15, 1964; admitted to bar, 1989, Connecticut; 1990, New York and U.S. District Court, Southern and Eastern Districts of New York; 1991, District of Columbia and U.S. District Court, District of Connecticut; 1994, U.S. Court of Federal Claims; 1995, U.S. Court of Appeals, Second Circuit; 1996, U.S. Tax Court. *Education:* Tufts University (B.S., magna cum laude, 1986); New York University (J.D., 1989). Phi Beta Kappa; Psi Chi National Honor Society. Recipient, Moot Court Advocacy Award, New York University. Vice Chairman, 1996-1997 and Chairman, 1998-2000, Education Committee and Member, Board of Directors, 1999—, Stamford Chamber of Commerce. Chairman, Advisory Committee, Senior Employment Service, Inc., 1997—. Member, Board of Directors, Jewish Family Service, 1999—. *Member:* Stamford Regional, Connecticut and American Bar Associations; American Inns of Court; Connecticut Employment Lawyers Association; National Employment Lawyers Association. ***PRACTICE AREAS:*** Civil Litigation; Commercial Law; Employment Law; Civil Rights Law. ***Email:*** sfrederick@wrkk.com

ERIC M. HIGGINS, born Presque Isle, Maine, October 28, 1963; admitted to bar, 1991, Connecticut; 1992, U.S. District Court, District of Connecticut. *Education:* Dickinson College (B.A., cum laude, 1986); University of Connecticut (J.D., with honors, 1991). Law Clerk to the Honorable Maxwell Heiman, Connecticut Appellate Court, 1991-1992. Adjunct Professor, University of Connecticut School of Law, 1995. *Member:* Stamford/Norwalk Regional and Connecticut (Member, Litigation Section) Bar Associations. ***PRACTICE AREAS:*** Civil Litigation; Commercial Litigation; Real Estate Litigation; Business Litigation; Landlord and Tenant Law. ***Email:*** ehiggins@wrkk.com

OF COUNSEL

SAUL KWARTIN, born Brooklyn, New York, August 24, 1927; admitted to bar, 1952, Connecticut and New York; 1953, U.S. District Court, District of Connecticut; 1975, U.S. Court of Appeals, Second Circuit. *Education:* Dartmouth College (A.B., 1948); Cornell University (LL.B., 1951). Phi Delta Phi. Author, "Tacking of Adverse Possession," Cornell Law Quarterly, 1950. Chairman, Stamford Rent Commission, 1955-1958. Member, 1962-1965 and Chairman, 1964-1965, Stamford Planning Board. Member: Stamford Finance Board, 1965-1969; Bar Examining Committee, 1982-1992. *Member:* Stamford (President, 1979-1980) and Connecticut (Member, House of Delegates, 1980-1986) Bar Associations. ***PRACTICE AREAS:*** Real Estate; Zoning, Planning and Land Use; Litigation.

EMANUEL MARGOLIS, born Brooklyn, New York, March 18, 1926; admitted to bar, 1957, Connecticut; 1958, U.S. District Court, District of Connecticut; 1968, U.S. Court of Appeals, Second Circuit; 1969, U.S. Supreme Court. *Education:* University of North Carolina (B.A., 1947); Harvard University (Ph.D., 1951); Yale University (LL.B., 1956). Phi Beta Kappa. Listed in: Who's Who in America; The Best Lawyers in America. Author: "The Plea of Privilege Against Self-Incrimination by United Nations Employees," 40 Virginia Law Review 283-309, 1954; "The Hydrogen Bomb Experiments and International Law," 64 Yale Law Journal 629-647, 1955; "Medical Malpractice in Connecticut: Landon v. Humphrey Revisited," 32 Connecticut Bar Journal 51-69, 1958; "Questionable Status of Charitable Immunity: A Different View," 33 Connecticut Bar Journal 23-54, 1959; "A Uniform Motion for Disclosure in Negligence Cases," 38 Connecticut Bar Journal 127-150, 1963; "New Frontiers in Criminal Procedure," 41 Connecticut Bar Journal 603-625, 1967; "Corpus Delicti: State of the Disunion," II Suffolk University Law Review 44-57, 1968; "Escalating the Viet Nam Debate: A Reply to Professor Moore," 42 Connecticut Bar Journal 23-54, 1968; "Criminal Appeals in Motion," 45 Connecticut Bar Journal 114-145, 1971: "No More Prison Reform!," 46 Connecticut Bar Journal 448-482, 1972; "The Aching Bakke: Is There a Cure?" 51 Connecticut Bar Journal 417-434, 1977; "In Defense of the Insanity Defense," 58 Connecticut Bar Journal 389-409, 1984; "The War on Drugs: The Constitution Under Siege," 63 Connecticut Bar Journal 306-328, 1989; "Habeas Corpus: The No-Longer Great Writ," 98 Dick. L. Rev. 557, 1994; "State v. Ross: New Life for Connecticut's Death Penalty," 68 Connecticut Bar Journal 262, 1994. "Connecticut's War on Drugs: A Peace Proposal," Connecticut Bar Journal, 372-384, 1996; "Affirmative Action: Déja Vu All Over Again," 27 Southwestern University L. Rev. 1-72, 1997. Senior Editor, 1970-1979, 1983— and Editor-in Chief, 1980-1983, Connecticut Bar Journal. Adjunct Professor, Quinnipiac College School of Law, 1986—. Counsel to Norwalk Branch, NAACP, 1963-1980.

(This Listing Continued)

Member: Westport Planning & Zoning Commission, 1971-1975; National Board, American Civil Liberties Union, 1975-1979. Chairman, Connecticut Civil Liberties Union, 1987-1994. Legal Advisor, Connecticut Civil Liberties Union, 1995—. Member; Yale Law School Executive Committee, 2001. *Member:* Connecticut (Chairman: Section on Human Rights & Responsibilities, 1971-1975; Judiciary Committee, 1985-1991; Federal Judiciary Committee, 1991-1998) and American Bar Associations; National Association of Criminal Defense Lawyers; Connecticut Attorney Trial Referee. Fellow, James W. Cooper, Connecticut Bar Foundation. ***REPORTED CASES:*** Breen v. Selective Service Local Board No. 16, Bridgeport 396 U.S. 460 (1970); Delgado v. Connecticut, 408 U.S. 940 (1972); State v. Mooney, 218 Conn. 85, 1991. ***PRACTICE AREAS:*** Civil Litigation; Discrimination; Criminal Law. ***Email:*** e.margolis@snet.net

ANTHONY R. LORENZO, born Jersey City, New Jersey, June 18, 1926; admitted to bar, 1961, Connecticut; 1962, U.S. Tax Court; 1965, U.S. District Court, District of Connecticut; 1967, U.S. Court of Appeals, Second Circuit; 1968, U.S. Supreme Court. *Education:* New York University (B.S., 1950; J.D., 1960; LL.M., 1964). Beta Gamma Sigma. Certified Public Accountant, Connecticut, 1954. Author, "Connecticut Uniform Gifts to Minors Act," 43 The Connecticut CPA 2, December, 1979. Editor, Tax Roundtable Column for quarterly publication "THE CONNECTICUT CPA", 1967-1973. Connecticut Society of Certified Public Accountants (President, 1977-1978; President, Educational Trust Fund, 1983-1984); American Institute of Certified Public Accountants; American Association of Attorney-Certified Public Accountants (Member, National Board of Directors, 1970-1990); American Arbitration Association Panelist, New England Business Development Group Federal Tax Expert Panelist. *Member:* Stamford, Connecticut and American Bar Associations (Member, Sections on: Taxation; Corporation, Banking and Business Law; Real Property, Probate and Trust Law) Bar Associations. ***PRACTICE AREAS:*** Taxation; Corporate Law; Trusts and Estates. ***Email:*** alorenzo@wrkk.com

COUNSEL

JOSEPH M. PANKOWSKI, JR., born Gainesville, Florida, March 14, 1964; admitted to bar, 1990, Connecticut; 1991, New York. *Education:* Florida State University (B.S., summa cum laude, 1986); University of Virginia (J.D., 1990); New York University (LL.M. in Taxation, 1996); Yale University (M.A. in Religion, 1996). Justice of the Peace, Darien, Connecticut, 1996—. Vice Chair, , Darien Commission on Aging. *Member:* Stamford/Norwalk and Connecticut Bar Associations. ***PRACTICE AREAS:*** Estate Planning; Estate Settlement; Trust Administration; Guardianship and Conservatorship; Charitable Giving. ***Email:*** jpankowski@wrkk.com

DAY R. SHIELDS, born Cleveland, Ohio, September 14, 1947; admitted to bar, 1973, New York; 1982, Connecticut. *Education:* Yale University (B.A., magna cum laude, 1969; J.D., 1972). Associate, Milbank, Tweed, Hadley & McCloy, New York, NY, 1972-1979. Associate and Partner, Holland Kaufmann & Bartels (formerly Duel & Holland), Greenwich, Connecticut, 1980-1996). *Member:* Greenwich, Connecticut (Member, Estates and Probate Section), Stamford/Norwalk Regional and New York State (Member, Trusts and Estates Law Section) Bar Associations. ***LANGUAGES:*** French and Spanish. ***PRACTICE AREAS:*** Estate Planning; Probate; Trust Law; Taxation. ***Email:*** dshields@wrkk.com

ASSOCIATES

WILLIAM M. DAVOREN, admitted to bar, 1992, Connecticut; 1993, New York and U.S. District Court, District of Connecticut. *Education:* Fairfield University (B.S., 1989); Albany Law School of Union University (J.D., 1992). ***PRACTICE AREAS:*** Personal Injury; Medical Malpractice; Products Liability. ***Email:*** wdavoren@wrkk.com

JOHN A. FARNSWORTH, born Arlington, Massachusetts, March 16, 1972; admitted to bar, 1998, Massachusetts and Connecticut; 1999, U.S. District Court, District of Connecticut. *Education:* Brandeis University (B.A., cum laude, high honors in philosophy, 1994); Suffolk University (J.D., magna cum laude, 1997). Phi Delta Phi. Dean's List. Editor in Chief, "Suffolk Transnational Law Review," 1996-1997. Law Clerk: Judge Maxwell Heiman, 1997-1998; Francis X. Hennessy, 1997-1998 and E. Eugene Spear, 1998-1999 of the Connecticut Appellate Court. *Member:* Stamford/Norwalk Regional (Member, Appellate Practice Section), Connecticut and Massachusetts Bar Association. ***PRACTICE AREAS:*** Commercial Litigation; Criminal Defense. ***Email:*** jfarnsworth@wrkk.com

DANIEL M. YOUNG, born Syracuse, New York, June 20, 1970; admitted to bar, 1995, Connecticut; 1996, New York and U.S. District Court, District of Connecticut; 2000, U.S. District Court, Southern District of New York. *Education:* Cornell University (B.S., with honors, 1992); New York University (J.D., magna cum laude, 1995). Order of the Coif. Recipient, Sol D. Kapolsohn Labor Law Prize, 1995. Associate Editor, 1993-1994 and Executive Editor, 1994-1995, Annual Survey of American Law. Law Clerk to U.S. District Judge Gerald L. Goettel, District of Connecticut, 1995-1997. Author, "Employer-Union Coop-

(This Listing Continued)

WOFSEY, ROSEN, KWESKIN & KURIANSKY, LLP, Stamford—Continued

eration During the Initial Stages of Plant Development," Annual Survey of American Law, Issue 1, 1995. ***PRACTICE AREAS:*** Civil Litigation; Employment Law. ***Email:*** dyoung@wrkk.com

CHRISTIAN ROLLOW HAAVE, born Ada, Oklahoma, December 5, 1971; admitted to bar, 1999, Connecticut; 2000, U.S. District Court, District of Connecticut. *Education:* Barnard College (B.A., 1994); Georgetown University (J.D., 1998). Phi Delta Phi. Member, Board of Social Services, Greenwich, Connecticut. Associate Member, Republican Town Committee. *Member:* Stamford-Norwalk Regional Bar Association. ***PRACTICE AREAS:*** Landlord and Tenant Law; Family Law; Employment Law; Criminal Defense. ***Email:*** jhaave@wrkk.com

ALEX K. SHERMAN, born Atlanta, Georgia, February 9, 1975; admitted to bar, 2000, Maryland; 2001, District of Columbia (Not admitted in Connecticut). *Education:* Skidmore College (B.A., magna cum laude, 1997); Washington College of Law, American University (J.D., summa cum laude, 2000). Phi Beta Kappa. ***PRACTICE AREAS:*** Litigation. ***Email:*** asherman@wrkk.com

REPRESENTATIVE CLIENTS: Alexandra Realty Corp.; Allied International Corporation; Banque Paribas; Benenson Realty Corp.; BCJ Management, L.P.; Boston Land Management, Inc.; Bridgeport Housing Authority; The Chase Manhattan Bank; Child Care Center of Stamford, Inc.; Cornerstone Bank; Cost Plus Furniture Rentals; Dress Barn, Inc.; Fairbanks Capital Corp.; First County Bank; Fleet Bank; General Maritime Corp.; The Hartford Provision Co.; Hospice Care, Inc.; Jewish Family Service of Stamford, Inc.; Louis Dreyfus Corp.; Marquardt & Roche / Meditz & Hackett; MBI Inc.; Midland Property Management Co., Inc.; Norwalk Congregate Homes for the Elderly; Norwalk Federation of Teachers; Ocwen Federal Bank, FSB; Patient Care, Inc.; Peoples Bank; Pyramid Real Estate & Management Co.; Obstetrics & Gynecology Associates of Stamford, P.C.; Ridgeway Shopping Center; Rippawam Park Associates, L.P.; Samuel Lotstein Realty Co.; Schroeder Real Estate; Stamford Anesthesiology Services, P.C.; Stamford Computer Group, Inc.; Stamford Federal Savings Bank; Stamford Housing Authority; Stamford Land Trust; Stamford Jewish Community Center; Stamford Medical Group, P.C.; Temple Sinai, Inc.; Warehouse Wines & Liquors, Inc.

MARY ELLEN WYNN

1150 SUMMER STREET
STAMFORD, CONNECTICUT 06905-5530
Telephone: 203-356-1355
Fax: 203-356-9412
Email: mew1150@aol.com
URL: http://www.lawyers.com/maryellenwynn

Domestic Relations, Matrimonial Law, Family Law, Divorce, Child Custody.

MARY ELLEN WYNN, born Cleveland, Ohio, November 25, 1946; admitted to bar, 1973, Connecticut; 1974, U.S. District Court, District of Connecticut; 1975, U.S. Court of Appeals, Second Circuit; 1980, U.S. Supreme Court. *Education:* Western College for Women; The Ohio State University (B.A., 1968; J.D., 1973). Phi Delta Phi. Helen Peabody Scholar. Co-Author: "Handbook of Forms for The Connecticut Family Lawyer," Conn. Law Tribune Publ. Co., 1991. Author: "Handling the Sex Discrimination in Employment Case," 4 Connecticut Law Tribune 31, p. 11, July 24, 1978. Member, Board of Directors: The Tower School, Stamford, Connecticut, 1982-1985; Stamford YWCA, 1985-1988; Stamford/Darien Bar Association, 1986-1990; Stamford/Norwalk Regional Bar Association, 1992—(President, 2000—); Member, State of Connecticut Grievance Panel, Fairfield Judicial District, 1993-1996; Special Pre-Trial Master: Connecticut Superior Court, 1982—; U.S. District Court, 1986—. State Trial Referee, 1985—. Commissioner, Governor's Commission on Child Support, 1985-1986. Fellow, Connecticut Bar Foundation, 1997—; Member, Board of Editors, Connecticut Law Tribune, 1986-1999. Bencher, 1988-1991, Treasurer, 1988-1990 and Vice President, 1990-1991, American Inn of Court-Bridgeport. *Member:* Connecticut (Member, Executive Committee, 1979—; Secretary-Treasurer, 1979-1981, Vice Chairperson, 1981-1983 and Chairperson, 1983-1985, Family Law Section; Member, Committees on: Ethics, 1975-1985; Status of Women, 1975-1983; Federal Practice, 1982-1985; Member: Executive Committee, Women and the Law Section, 1983-1996. Task Force on Association Headquarters, 1980-1982; Committee to Review Evaluation and Retention of Judges, 1986-1987), Stamford/Darien (Chair: Family Law Committee, 1986-1988; Women and The Law Committee, 1990-1992), Stamford/Norwalk Regional (President, 2000—; Vice President, 1998-1999; Secretary, 1997-1998; Treasurer, 1996-1997; Member, Board of Directors, 1989—) and American Bar Associations; Connecticut Trial Lawyers Association; Plaintiff Employment Lawyers Association (Member, Executive Committee, 1988-1991). ***REPORTED CASES:*** Johnson v. University of Bridgeport, 629 F.2d 828, 24 Fair Empl. Prac. Cases (BNA) 1608, 24 Empl. Prac. Dec. 31,230; Williams v. Wallace Siversmiths, Inc., 566 F.2d 364, (2d. Cir. 1977); 14 Fair Empl. Prac. Cas. (BNA) 809, 13 Empl. Prac. Dec. 11,556; Kennedy v. Conn. Dept. of Public Safety, Div. of State Police, 115 F.R.D. 497 (D.Conn., 1987); Stryker v. Reg. Publ. Co., 423 F.Supp. 476, (D.Conn., 1976); 14 Fair Empl. Prac. Cases (BNA) 748, 14 Empl. Prac. Dec. 7503; In Re Grusse, 402 F.Supp 1232 (D.Conn, 1975); Seymour v. Seymour, 180 Conn. 705, 433 A.2d 1005 (1980); McPhee v. McPhee, 186 Conn. 167, 440 A.2d 274 (1982); Hawkins v. Hawkins, 11 Conn. App. 195, 526 A.2d 872 (1987); Wilkes v. Wilkes, 55 Conn. App. 313 (1999).

(This Listing Continued)

ASSOCIATE

LEAH PAVETTI HOGAN, born New London, Connecticut, January 3, 1964; admitted to bar, 1992, Connecticut; 1993, New York. *Education:* Barnard College (B.A., with distinction, 1986); Suffolk University (J.D., 1991). Recipient, American Bar Association Outstanding Law Day Activity Award, 1997. *Member:* Stamford/Norwalk Regional Bar (Member, Board of Directors 1998—; Co-chair, Young Lawyers Section, 1997-1999; Co-Chair, Law Day Committee, 1996-1997; Co-Chair, Family Law Section, 1999—), Connecticut (Vice President, Executive Committee of Young Lawyers of Lower Fairfield County 1998—; Member, Family Law Section) and American (Member, Family Law Section) Bar Associations. ***REPORTED CASES:*** Wilkes v. Wilkes, 55 Conn. App. 313 (1999). ***PRACTICE AREAS:*** Family Law; Matrimonial Law. ***Email:*** mew1150@aol.com

XYLAS & ASSOCIATES, LLP

CLEARWATER HOUSE
2187 ATLANTIC STREET, 9TH FLOOR
STAMFORD, CONNECTICUT 06902
Telephone: 203-348-5433
203-961-1183
Email: xylaslaw@mindspring.com
URL: http://www.lawyers.com/xylaslaw

New York Office: 11 East 44th Street, Suite 901, 10017. Telephone: 212-490-9352. Fax: 212-490-0502. E Mail: mail@xylaslaw.com.

Real Estate, Business Law, Corporate Law, Loans, Mortgages, Admiralty and Maritime Law.

(For complete biographical data on all personnel, see Professional Biographies at New York)

YULES & YULES, LLC

P.O. BOX 522
STAMFORD, CONNECTICUT 06904-0522
Telephone: 203-327-9200
Email: yuleslaw@yuleslaw.com

Hartford, Connecticut Office: P.O. Box 230278, 06123-0278. Telephone: 860-724-5815.
New Haven, Connecticut Office: 195 Church Street, Seventeenth Floor. 06510. Telephone: 203-789-1000. Fax: 203-789-6320.
New York, N.Y. Office: Grand Central Station, P.O. Box 4419. 10163-4419. Telephone: 203-327-9200.

Trial Practice, Automobile, Mobile Carrier, Bad Faith, Corporate Business Torts, Drug and Medical Device Litigation, Fraud, Insurance, Products Liability, Professional Malpractice, Transportation, Workers' Compensation Law, Securities Arbitration and Financial Institutions Litigation.

REPRESENTATIVE CLIENTS: Allstate Insurance Co.; The Atlantic Cos.; Nationwide Insurance Co.; Transamerica Insurance Group; Zurich-American Insurance Cos.; Chubb Group of Insurance Cos.; Dow Corning Corp.; Chrysler Corp.; Air Products & Chemicals, Inc.; Kellogg Co.; Orion Group; American Medical Systems, Inc.; United Farm Bureau Mut. Ins. Co.; National Freight Trucklines, Inc.; Pfizer Inc.; Brethren Mut. Ins. Co.

(For complete biographical data on all personnel, see Professional Biographies at New Haven, Connecticut)

KURT M. AHLBERG

2885 MAIN STREET
STRATFORD, CONNECTICUT 06614
Telephone: 203-377-1311
Fax: 203-378-6756

Real Estate, Probate, Trusts and Estates, Wills, Personal Injury, Zoning, Planning and Land Use.

KURT M. AHLBERG, born Bridgeport, Connecticut, March 1, 1952; admitted to bar, 1978, Connecticut and U.S. District Court, District of Connecticut. *Education:* Fairfield University (B.A., 1974); University of Connecticut (J.D., 1977). Assistant Town Attorney, Town of Stratford, Connecticut, 1981-1987, 1989—. *Member:* Bridgeport and Connecticut Bar Associations. ***PRACTICE AREAS:*** Aged and Aging; Trusts and Estates; Probate; Real Estate; Wills; Personal Injury.

(This Listing Continued)

REPRESENTATIVE CLIENTS: Fidelity National Title Insurance; Lawyers Title Insurance Co.; Home Building Construction Co., Inc.; Town of Stratford, Connecticut; Caselli Real Estate; People's Bank; Gilbert Builders.
REFERENCES: Hudson United Bank; People's Bank.

BECK AND BECK, LLC

83 BOOTH STREET
STRATFORD, CONNECTICUT 06614
Telephone: 203-375-2222
Fax: 203-378-5263
URL: http://www.ctbecklaw.com

New York, New York Office: 67 Will Street, Suite 2211, 10005-3198.

General Civil Litigation.

MEMBERS OF FIRM

DANA K. BECK, born 1965; admitted to bar, 1992, Connecticut; 1999, U.S. District Court, District of Connecticut. *Education:* State University of New York at Albany (B.A., 1987); Quinnipiac College (J.D., 1991). ***PRACTICE AREAS:*** Business Law. ***Email:*** dkbeck@prodigy.net

KENNETH A. BECK, born New York City, New York, January 9, 1965; admitted to bar, 1990, Connecticut; 1991, New York. *Education:* State University of New York at Oswego (B.A, 1987), University of Bridgeport (J.D., 1990). *Member:* Westchester County, New York State, Connecticut and American Bar Associations. ***PRACTICE AREAS:*** Civil Litigation; Intellectual Properties Law; Business Law. ***Email:*** kabeck@prodigy.net

COUSINS, JOHNSON & DESROSIERS, P.C.

2563 MAIN STREET
STRATFORD, CONNECTICUT 06615
Telephone: 203-386-1433
Fax: 203-386-9714
URL: http://www.lawyers.com/cousins&johnson

Workers' Compensation, Personal Injury, Trials, Real Estate, Probate.

FIRM PROFILE: The law firm of Cousins, Johnson & Desrosiers, P.C. was originally founded by Donald C. Cousins as a general practice, gradually becoming more devoted to the areas of claimant's Workers' Compensation and other medically oriented areas. Donald Cousins has been a two-term Chairman of the Workers' Compensation Section of the Connecticut Bar Association. Norma Johnson has been appointed an attorney trial referee for the Bridgeport Superior Court and is Vice-Chair of the Workers' Compensation Section of the Connecticut Bar Association. The firm concentrates in the areas of personal injury and claimant's Workers' Compensation matters, including traumatic injuries, repetitive trauma, and occupational disease and arbitration. The firm encourages continuing legal education seminars and professional association activities, particularly in the workers' compensation and personal injury areas.

DONALD C. COUSINS, born New Haven, Connecticut, October 19, 1930; admitted to bar, 1955, Connecticut; 1957, U.S. District Court, District of Connecticut; 1971, U.S. Supreme Court. *Education:* Trinity College (B.A., 1952); Harvard University (J.D., 1955). Delegate, Connecticut House of Delegates, 1975-1976. Member, CBA Special Advisory Committee on Workers' Compensation Review Division Regulations, 1979—. Seminar on Workers' Compensation, "Preparation and Presentation of Complex Cases," Connecticut Trial Lawyers Association, 1987; Seminar on Stress Claims in Workers' Compensation, IntraCorp, 1988; Seminar given by the Connecticut Bar Association, CLE Program on Connecticut Workers' Compensation, January 1989; Seminar given by the Connecticut Trial Lawyers Association on Workers' Compensation, April 1989; "Motions to Preclude: What's In and What's Out," 1989; "The Notice of Claim; Disclaimers and Motion to Preclude," Seminar of Connecticut Bar Association, Bridgeport, Connecticut, September 1989. Member, Panel of Arbitrators, American Arbitration Association. Member and Vice Chairperson, Executive Committee, 1987-1989, and Chairperson, 1989-1990, Workers' Compensation Section, Connecticut Bar Association. Advisor, Workers' Compensation Advisory Committee, to the Law Revision Commission, 1989. Co-Chair and Lecturer, CBA Seminars: "The Cardiac Stress Case in Formal Hearings," Feb. 21, 1992; "Workers' Compensation After Reform," Oct. 21, 1993. Lecturer, Greater Bridgeport Bar Association, March 1992, "Evolution of the Back Claim in Workers' Compensation." Lecturer, Conn. Bar Association Seminar. "Workers' Compensations Issues and Strategies Formal Hearings," Dec. 1994. Lecturer and Moderator "Traumatic Brain Injury and Beyond" Greater Bridgeport Bar Association Seminar, March 2001. Seminar Co-Chair, American Association of Disability Evaluating Physicians, Aug. 1994. Appointed to Serve on Legal Advisory Committee to Worker' Compensation Commission, 1992-1998. Listed in The Best Lawyers in America, Workers Compensation Law Section, 1995—. *Member:* Greater Bridgeport Bar (Chairman, Workers Compensation

(This Listing Continued)

Section), Bridgeport, Connecticut and American Bar Associations; Connecticut Trial Lawyers Association. ***LANGUAGES:*** Spanish. ***PRACTICE AREAS:*** Workers' Compensation Law; Personal Injury Law; Trials Law.

NORMA S. JOHNSON, born White Plains, New York, June 13, 1947; admitted to bar, 1983, Connecticut; 1984, U.S. District Court, District of Connecticut. *Education:* Denison University (B.A., 1969); University of Bridgeport (J.D., 1983). Phi Delta Phi; Psi Chi; Kappa Delta Pi. Family Law Clerk, Superior Court, Connecticut, 1983-1984. Appointed to ADR Program at Bridgeport Superior Court to serve as Attorney Trial Referee, Fact Finder and Arbitrator, 1990-1997. Appointed to serve on Legal Advisory Committee to the Workers' Compensation Commission, 1999, 2000, 2001. Seminar on Workers' Compensation Sacred Heart University, 1992. Peoples Law School Lecturer on Workers Compensation, 1993—. Member, Editorial Board, Compensation Quarterly, 1990-1999. Co-Chair, CBA Seminar: "Workers' Compensation Issues and Strategies at Formal Proceedings," Dec. 1994. Co-Chair, CBA Workers' Compensation Seminar, Naples, Florida, March, 2000. Member, Executive Committee, Workers' Compensation Section, Connecticut Bar Association, 1994—; Vice-Chair, 2000. Listed in The Best Lawyers in America, Workers Compensation Law Section, 1995—. *Member:* Bridgeport and Connecticut Bar Associations; Connecticut Trial Lawyers Association. ***PRACTICE AREAS:*** Workers' Compensation Law; Personal Injury Law.

ALBERT E. DESROSIERS, born Windham, Connecticut, June 8, 1954; admitted to bar, 1984, Connecticut and U.S. District Court, District of Connecticut; 1998, U.S. Supreme Court. *Education:* University of Connecticut (B.A., 1977); University of New Haven (M.S., 1979); Western New England School of Law (J.D., 1984). Phi Alpha Delta. Author: "Healthcare Plans: Stacked Deck Against Claimant?" Compensation Quarterly, Fall, 1994. Seminar Speaker: "Workers' Compensation," The Connecticut Bar Association, Annual Meeting, 1994; "Pitfalls and Practice in the Managed Care Environment," Greater Bridgeport Bar Association, March, 1996; "The Workers' Compensation Offset Against SSD Benefits," Greater Bridgeport Bar Association, April, 1998; "Managed Care and Workers' Compensation," Greater Bridgeport Bar Association, March, 2000; "Exploring Concepts of Compensability and Ethics in Workers' Compensation," Connecticut Bar Association, December 1, 2000; "Traumatic Brain Injury in Workers' Compensation and Beyond" Greater Bridgeport Bar Association, March 2001. Lecturer, Workers' Compensation, Peoples Law School, 2001. *Member:* Greater Bridgeport, Connecticut and American Bar Associations; Connecticut Trial Lawyers Association. (Board Certified Workers' Compensation Specialist, Connecticut Bar Association Standing Committee on Workers' Compensation Certification). ***PRACTICE AREAS:*** Workers' Compensation Law; Personal Injury Law; Trial Law.

PATRICIA A. MORRISSEY, born Bridgeport, Connecticut, April 23, 1963; admitted to bar, 1990, Connecticut. *Education:* University of New Haven (B.S., 1987); University of Bridgeport School of Law (J.D., 1990). Adjunct Instructor, University of New Haven, School of Public Safety and Professional Studies. Researcher, Advisor and Administrative Assistant: "Private Security Law: Case Studies," Publisher, Butterworth-Heinemann, Stoneham, Mass., October, 1992; "Risk Reduction," Vol. 37, Security Management, No. 10, 1993. Member, Board of Trustees, Sterling House Community Center, American Red Cross Stratford Community Fund. Volunteer, Emergency Medical Technician. *Member:* Bridgeport and Connecticut Bar Associations. ***PRACTICE AREAS:*** Real Estate; Probate; Personal Injury; Premises Liability.

LAWRENCE F. MORIZIO, born New York, N.Y., November 2, 1971; admitted to bar, 1998, Connecticut; 2000, New York and U.S. District Court, District of Connecticut. *Education:* Rutgers University (B.A., 1994); Quinnipiac College (J.D., with honors, 1998). Rutgers College, Dean's List, 1991-1993. Quinnipiac College School of Law, Civil Clinic Honors. *Member:* Greater Bridgeport and Connecticut (Member, Sections on: Workers Compensation and Young Lawyers Section Executive Committee, Co-Chair of the Workers' Compensation Section) Bar Associations. ***PRACTICE AREAS:*** Workers Compensation; Labor and Employment; Personal Injury.

Language: Spanish

REFERENCES: People's Bank-Bridgeport; Chase Manhattan Bank of Connecticut, N.A., Stratford, Connecticut. Hudson United Bank, Stratford, Connecticut.

COYNE, VON KUHN, BRADY & FRIES, L.L.C.

999 ORONOQUE LANE
STRATFORD, CONNECTICUT 06614
Telephone: 203-378-7100
Fax: 203-378-7711
Email: coynevkbf@snet.net
URL: http://www.lawyers.com/coynevkbf

Civil Litigation Practice including Personal Injury, Products Liability, Municipal Liability, Real Estate.

(This Listing Continued)

COYNE, VON KUHN, BRADY & FRIES, L.L.C., Stratford—Continued

JAMES E. COYNE, born Chicago, Illinois, February 15, 1949; admitted to bar, 1974, Connecticut; 1975, U.S. District Court, District of Connecticut; 1981, U.S. Court of Appeals, Second Circuit. *Education:* Tufts University (B.A., 1971); Suffolk University (J.D., cum laude, 1974). Member, Suffolk University Law Review, 1972-1974. Author: "Waiving the Right to a Jury Trial in Federal Courts: The Burden of Prejudice," 7 Suffolk University Law Review 973, Summer 1973; "Constitutional Criminal Law," 8 Suffolk University Law Review 863, Spring 1974. Senior Law Clerk to Hon. Richard H. Levet, U.S. District Court, Southern District of New York, 1974-1975. *Member:* The Connecticut and American Bar Associations. ***PRACTICE AREAS:*** Products Liability Litigation; Professional Liability Litigation; Municipal Liability; Commercial Law; Professional Injury Claims.

PHILIP F. VON KUHN, born Norwalk, Connecticut, August 6, 1959; admitted to bar, 1985, Connecticut; 1987, U.S. District Court, District of Connecticut; 1992, U.S. Court of Appeals, Second Circuit. *Education:* Fairfield University (B.A., magna cum laude, 1982), Recipient, Wall Street Journal Award in Economics; University of Connecticut (J.D., with honors, 1985).

EDWARD P. BRADY III, born New Rochelle, New York, September 19, 1964; admitted to bar, 1989, Connecticut, U.S. District Court, District of Connecticut and U.S. Court of Appeals, Second Circuit. *Education:* University of Connecticut (B.S., 1986); Suffolk University (J.D., cum laude, 1989). Author: "Compatibility of the Hague Service Convention with Service Upon a Foreign Corporation's Domestic Subsidiary," 13 Suffolk Transnational Law Journal 520, 1989. *Member:* Connecticut Bar Association. ***PRACTICE AREAS:*** Litigation.

COLLEEN D. FRIES, born Lancaster, Pennsylvania, November 26, 1956; admitted to bar, 1993, Connecticut and U.S. District Court, District of Connecticut. *Education:* Brandywine College (A.S., 1976); Fairfield University (B.S., 1985); University of Connecticut (J.D., 1992). Town Counsel, Seymour, 1993—. *Member:* Connecticut Bar Association. ***PRACTICE AREAS:*** Civil Litigation; Municipal Law.

KEVIN S. COYNE, born Norwalk, Connecticut, May 22, 1964; admitted to bar, 1992, Connecticut; 1993, U.S. District Court, District of Connecticut; 1999, U.S. Court of Appeals, Second Circuit. *Education:* University of Connecticut (B.A., 1986); University of Bridgeport (J.D., cum laude, 1992). Member, Phi Delta Phi. Recipient, American Jurisprudence Award, Products Liability. Connecticut Probate Law Journal, 1991-1992. *Member:* Connecticut Bar Association. ***PRACTICE AREAS:*** Civil Litigation; Real Estate.

ROBERT PHILIP MURPHY, born New Britain, Connecticut, May 24, 1970; admitted to bar, 1997, Connecticut; 1999, U.S. District Court, District of Connecticut. *Education:* University of Connecticut (B.A., summa cum laude, 1992; J.D., 1997); Southern Connecticut State University (M.A., Library Science, 2000). Phi Beta Kappa; Phi Kappa Phi. *Member:* Hartford County and American Bar Associations. ***PRACTICE AREAS:*** Products Liability Litigation; Professional Liability Litigation; Commercial Law; Municipal Liability.

DISERIO MARTIN O'CONNOR & CASTIGLIONI LLP

STRATFORD, CONNECTICUT

(See Stamford)

General Practice. Litigation and Trials in all Courts. Corporate, Commercial Finance, Securities, Taxation, Banking, Foreclosure and Workout, Real Estate Law, Personal Injury and Negligence, Employment Law, Wrongful Termination, Workers Compensation, Insurance Coverage and Defense, Family, Creditors Rights and Bankruptcy, Trusts, Probate, Estate and Tax Planning.

HARLOW, ADAMS & FRIEDMAN, P.C.

STRATFORD, CONNECTICUT

(See Milford)

General Civil Practice, General Civil Litigation in State and Federal Courts, Real Estate Conveyancing, Financing and Development, Zoning, Probate, Personal Injury, Commercial Litigation, Construction Law, Bankruptcy, Business Formations, Landlord and Tenant, Title Opinions, Trials and Appeals.

KNOTT & KNOTT

Established in 1953

1656 MAIN STREET

STRATFORD, CONNECTICUT 06615

Telephone: 203-375-1433

Fax: 203-378-7192

URL: http://www.lawyers.com/knott&knott

General Practice. Civil and Criminal Litigation. Real Estate Development, Zoning, Summary Process, Probate, Personal Injury, Workers Compensation, Domestic Relations, Commercial Litigation, Title Opinions. Trials.

BARRY C. KNOTT, born Bridgeport, Connecticut, September 4, 1947; admitted to bar, 1974, Connecticut; 1975, U.S. District Court for District of Connecticut; 1982, U.S. Supreme Court. *Education:* Georgetown University (B.S.B.A., 1969); St. John's University (J.D., 1974). Councilman, Town of Stratford, 1979-1987. Attorney, Stratford Housing Authority, 1990—. *Member:* Bridgeport (Member, Executive Committee, 1988—), Connecticut and American Bar Associations; Connecticut Trial Lawyers Association. ***PRACTICE AREAS:*** Real Estate; Zoning Law; Personal Injury. **Email:** barryknott@aol.com

ASSOCIATE

KATHLEEN M. KRYGIER, born Derby, Connecticut, 1971; admitted to bar, 1996, Connecticut; 1997, Maryland; 1998, District of Columbia. *Education:* Boston College (B.A., 1993); Catholic University of America (J.D., 1996). *Member:* Bridgeport (Member, Family Law and Litigation Sections) and Connecticut (Member, Family Law and Litigation Sections) Bar Associations; Young Lawyers Association. ***PRACTICE AREAS:*** Personal Injury; Domestic Relations; Civil Litigation; Workers Compensation. **Email:** kmkrygier@aol.com

APPROVED ATTORNEYS FOR: Lawyers Title Insurance Corp.; Chicago Title Insurance Co.
REFERENCES: Peoples Bank; Mechanics and Farmers Savings Bank.

LAW OFFICES OF PAUL A. LANGE

2296 MAIN STREET, SUITE 2000

STRATFORD, CONNECTICUT 06615-5938

Telephone: 203-375-7724

FAX: 203-375-9397

Email: pal@lopal.com

URL: http://www.lopal.com

New York, N.Y. Office: 885 Third Avenue, Suite 2900. Telephone: 212-385-1215. FAX: 212-608-1215.

Litigation and Transactions involving Aviation and Commercial Matters, Administrative Law, Insurance Defense and Coverage, Personal Injury, Products Liability, FAA Enforcement Defense and D.O.T. Regulatory Matters, General Civil Trial and Appellate Practice.

PAUL A. LANGE, born Mineola, New York, July 14, 1961; admitted to bar, 1986, Connecticut; 1987, New York; U.S. District Court, Southern, Northern, Western and Eastern Districts of New York; U.S. District Court, District of Connecticut; U.S. District Court, District of Massachusetts; U.S. Court of Appeals, Armed Forces, First, Second, Third, Districts of Columbia and Federal Circuits; 1996, U.S. Supreme Court; 1999, Massachusetts. *Education:* Long Island University (B.A., 1982; M.B.A., 1988); University of Bridgeport (J.D., 1986). Author, "Tort Liability Surrounding Homebuilt, Amateur-Built and Experimental Aircraft," Journal of Air Law and Commerce, 60 JALC 575, 1994-1995. *Member:* American Bar Association (Member: Forum Committee on Air and Space Law; Tort and Insurance Practice Section; Litigation Section; Chair, FAA Subcommittee, 1992-1997); National Transportation Safety Board Bar Association (Vice President, N.E. Region); Lawyer-Pilots Bar Association; Defense Research Institute. ***REPORTED CASES:*** Ranger Insurance Co. v. Kovach, 63 F.Supp 2d 174 (D.Conn. 1999).

LAW OFFICES OF ROBERT K. MARZIK, P.C.

1512 MAIN STREET

STRATFORD, CONNECTICUT 06615-7097

Telephone: 203-375-4803

Telecopier: 203-386-0136

Email: marzikr@aol.com

New York, New York Office: 380 Lexington Avenue, Suite 1700, 10168-1700. Telephone: 212-683-2805. Fax: 203-386-0136.

(This Listing Continued)

General Practice, Civil Litigation, Admiralty, Maritime, Aviation, Probate and Real Estate Law.

ROBERT K. MARZIK, born Bridgeport, Connecticut, 1936; admitted to bar, 1961, Connecticut and U.S. District Court, District of Connecticut; 1962, New York and U.S. District Court, Southern and Eastern Districts of New York; 1966, U.S. Court of Appeals, Second Circuit; 1984, U.S. Supreme Court. *Education:* College of the Holy Cross (B.A., 1958); Georgetown University (LL.B., 1961). Phi Delta Phi. Member, Georgetown Law Journal, 1960-1961. Associate, Haight, Gardner, Poor and Havens, New York, New York 1961-1969. *Member:* The Association of the Bar of the City of New York; Greater Bridgeport, New York State, Connecticut (Member, Federal Bench-Bar Relations Committee, 1974-1979) and American Bar Associations; Maritime Law Association of the United States; The Association of Trial Lawyers of America. ***PRACTICE AREAS:*** Admiralty Law; Civil Litigation; Probate Law.

KENT M. MILLER

250 ROCKWELL AVENUE
STRATFORD, CONNECTICUT 06615
Telephone: 203-380-2161
Fax: 203-386-0432
Email: lexkantiae@aol.com
URL: http://www.lawyers.com/kentmillerlaw

Landlord and Tenant Law, Mortgages, Collections.

KENT M. MILLER, born Greenwich, Connecticut, August 9, 1963; admitted to bar, 1990, Connecticut and U.S. District Court, District of Connecticut. *Education:* Ohio Wesleyan University (B.A., 1986); University of Bridgeport (J.D., 1990). Councilman, Fourth District, Bridgeport, Connecticut, 1994—. *Member:* Connecticut and American Bar Associations. ***PRACTICE AREAS:*** Landlord and Tenant Law; Mortgages; Collections.

JAMES R. MIRON

125 FERRY BOULEVARD
STRATFORD, CONNECTICUT 06615
Telephone: 203-377-4554

Arbitration.

JAMES R. MIRON, born Bridgeport, Connecticut, July 7, 1965; admitted to bar, 1994, Connecticut; 1995, Florida. *Education:* Central Connecticut State College (B.A., 1990); Western New England College (J.D., 1994).

PIAZZA & PICKEL

STRATFORD, CONNECTICUT

(See Stamford)

Trials and Appeals in State and Federal Courts, Negligence, Medical Malpractice, Divorce and Personal Injury Law, Wrongful Death, Legal Malpractice, Child Custody, Automobile Accidents, Product Liability, Adoption, Family Law.

RODIE & CONNOLLY, P.C.

3380 MAIN STREET
STRATFORD, CONNECTICUT 06614
Telephone: 203-377-1010
Fax: 203-375-0203
Email: cons3380@aol.com
URL: http://www.lawyers.com/rodie&connolly

Personal Injury, Death Claims, Auto Accidents and Medical Malpractice.

WILFRED J. RODIE, JR., born Bridgeport, Connecticut, September 2, 1961; admitted to bar, 1986, Connecticut. *Education:* Georgetown University (A.B., magna cum laude, 1983; J.D., 1986). Jesuit Honor Society. *Member:* Connecticut and American Bar Associations.

JAMES M. CONNOLLY, born Bridgeport, Connecticut, April 16, 1951; admitted to bar, 1982, Connecticut. *Education:* University of Bridgeport (B.A., 1973; J.D., 1982). Recipient: Outstanding Legal Scholarship Award; American Jurisprudence Award-Insurance. *Member:* Bridgeport and Connecticut Bar Associations; Connecticut Trial Lawyers Association; The Association of Trial Lawyers of America.

REPRESENTATIVE CLIENTS: New Haven Savings Bank; Safeco Insurance Co.; Southern Connecticut Federal Credit Union; Middlesex Mutual Assurance Co.
APPROVED ATTORNEYS FOR: Title U.S.A.; Chicago Title Insurance Co.; Commonwealth Land Title Insurance Co.; Stewart Title Insurance Co.
REFERENCES: Citytrust Co.; Paradise Green, Stratford, Connecticut.

SANDAK FRIEDMAN HENNESSEY & GRECO, LLP

STRATFORD, CONNECTICUT

(See Stamford)

Trials and Appeals in all Connecticut and Federal Courts and Administrative Agencies. Personal Injury, Medical Malpractice, Commercial, Environmental Litigation, Real Estate, Zoning and Land Use, Property Tax Appeals.

ALFANO & FLYNN, LLC

53 MOUNTAIN ROAD
SUFFIELD, CONNECTICUT 06078
Telephone: 860-668-0221
Fax: 860-668-5413
Email: afsuffield@aol.com

General Practice. Trials, Negligence, Workers Compensation, Real Estate, Probate, Municipal and Corporation Law, Personal Injury and Domestic Law.

MEMBERS OF FIRM

JOSEPH W. FLYNN, born Hartford, Connecticut, June 4, 1955; admitted to bar, 1981, Connecticut. *Education:* University of Connecticut (B.A., cum laude, 1977); St. Louis University (J.D., 1980). Phi Delta Phi; Pi Sigma Alpha. Member, Editorial Board, St. Louis University Law Journal, 1979-1980; President, Student Bar Association, 1979-1980. Member: Windsor Locks Board of Education, 1981-1985; Windsor Locks Board of Finance, 1987—, Chairman, 1990-1996. *Member:* Hartford County, Connecticut and American Bar Associations; Connecticut Trial Lawyers Association. ***PRACTICE AREAS:*** Real Estate Law; Personal Injury; Probate; Estate Administration; Planning.

CHARLES T. ALFANO, JR., born Hartford, Connecticut, April 1, 1959; admitted to bar, 1984, Connecticut. *Education:* Tufts University (B.A., 1981); University of Louisville (J.D., 1984). Phi Alpha Delta (Marshall, 1983-1984). Member, Ethics Committee, Town of Suffield, 1985; Member, Suffield Board of Finance, 1985-1989; Town Attorney, Town of Suffield, December 1989-December 1991; Member, Town of Suffield Economic Redevelopment Commission, 1991—; Member, Charter Revision Commission, Town of Suffield. Member, Board of Directors, Suffield Visiting Nurse & Emergency Aid Association. *Member:* Hartford County, Connecticut and American Bar Associations; Connecticut Trial Lawyers Association; The Association of Trial Lawyers of America. ***PRACTICE AREAS:*** Real Estate; Personal Injury; Criminal Law; Domestic Law; Probate; Estate Administration; Planning.

OF COUNSEL

CHARLES T. ALFANO, born Suffield, Connecticut, June 21, 1920; admitted to bar, 1948, Connecticut. *Education:* Illinois College and University of Connecticut (B.A., 1943); University of Michigan (J.D., 1948). Judge, Municipal Court, 1949-1951, 1955-1959. State Senator, 1959-1977; President Pro Tem, 1967-1972. Assistant Majority Leader, State Senate, 1966-1967. Minority Leader, 1972-1974; Vice President Pro Tem, 1975-1977, State Senate. Member, 1965-1977 and Chairman, 1967-1969, Legislative Council, State of Connecticut. Chairman, Legislative Management Committee, 1969-1972. Former Director & Chairman of the Board of Suffield Bank. Former Director of Connecticut Water Co. and Crown Public T.V. *Member:* Hartford County, Connecticut and American Bar Associations; Connecticut Trial Lawyers Association (Member, Board of Governors, 1965-1988). ***PRACTICE AREAS:*** Probate; Estate Administration; Planning; Real Estate Law; Corporate Law.

REPRESENTATIVE CLIENTS: First Federal Bank; Kentucky Fried Chicken, Hartford Franchise; New England Bank & Trust; Fleet Real Estate Funding Corp.; Boston Five Mtge. Corp.; Countrywide Funding Corp.; AB Massa Paper Co.; Addressing Service Company, Inc.; Laureno Lumber Company, Inc.; Citizens Mortgage Corp.; Columbia National Mortgage Corp.; North American Mortgage.

BROWER & ORGANSCHI

445 PROSPECT STREET
TORRINGTON, CONNECTICUT 06790
Telephone: 860-482-4979
Fax: 860-482-4701
URL: http://www.browerorganschi.com
Email: info@browerorganschi.com
URL: http://www.lawyers.com/browerorganschi

FIRM PROFILE: Brower & Organschi is a litigation-oriented law firm in Torrington, Connecticut. We represent civil litigation clients in cases involving personal injury, contract, property, environmental and family law. We also represent clients in non-litigation matters, including real estate transactions, incorporation, limited liability company formation and workers' compensation issues. Many of

(This Listing Continued)

BROWER & ORGANSCHI, Torrington—Continued

our clients are referred to us by out-of-state or area attorneys who do not practice civil litigation. Members of our office spend many hours keeping current in the latest developments in areas such as class actions, unfair trade practices, domestic law, personal injury litigation and uninsured motorist law. Our philosophy is to apply our expertise to move our cases through the court system and to obtain effective results for our clients.

CHARLES F. BROWER, born Syracuse, New York, May 28, 1938; admitted to bar, 1964, Connecticut and U.S. District Court, District of Connecticut; 1998, U.S. District Court, Northern District of Illinois; 2000, U.S. Court of Appeals, Seventh Circuit. *Education:* Dartmouth College (A.B., 1960); Columbia University (LL.B., 1963). Chairman, City of Torrington Charter Revision Commission, 1966-1967. Member, Civil Justice Executive Committee, 1982-1992. *Member:* Connecticut Bar Association (Member, Civil Justice Section); Association of Trial Lawyers of America; Connecticut Trial Lawyers Association. Certified as a Civil Trial Advocate by the National Board of Trial Advocacy. ***REPORTED CASES:*** Marr v. WMX Technologies, Inc., 244 Conn. 676 (1998); Jenks v. Jenks, 39 Conn. App. 139 (1995); Cook v. Cook, 38 Conn. App. 499 (1995); Lurie & Associates v. Tomik Corp., 37 Conn. App. 865 (1995); Miller v. Bourgoin, 28 Conn. App. 491 (1992); Cummings & Lockwood v. Gray, 26 Conn. App. 293 (1991); Mitchell v. Mitchell, 24 Conn. App. 343 (1991); Marron & Sipe Building & Contracting v. Flor, 22 Conn. App. 689; Zeller v. Mark, 14 Conn. App. 651 (1988); Alfano v. Insurance Center of Torrington, 203 Conn. 607 (1987); Paletsky v. Paletsky, 3 Conn. App. 587 (1985); Deer Island Assn. v. Trolle, 181 Conn. 201 (1980). ***PRACTICE AREAS:*** Civil Litigation; Copyright Infringement; Elder Law; Personal Injury. ***Email:*** chuck@browerorganschi.com

MARCUS G. ORGANSCHI, born London, England, September 12, 1952; admitted to bar, 1989, Connecticut; 1990, U.S. District Court, District of Connecticut. *Education:* University of Hartford (B.A., magna cum laude, 1977); Cornell University (J.D., 1989). President, 1997-1999 and Board Member, 1995—, Litchfield Land Trust. *Member:* Connecticut Bar Association. ***REPORTED CASES:*** Marr v. WMX Technologies; Mulla v. Maguire; Lurie v. Tomik Corp.; Summit Hydropower v. Comm'r of Environmental. ***PRACTICE AREAS:*** Civil Litigation; Family Law; Environmental Law; Real Estate; Personal Injury. ***Email:*** marc@browerorganschi.com

---

EBERSOL & McCORMICK, LLC

24 MASON STREET
P.O. BOX 598
TORRINGTON, CONNECTICUT 06790
Telephone: 860-482-8557
FAX: 860-482-8089
Email: attys.ebersol@snet.net

General Practice. Estate Planning, Corporation, Real Estate and Banking Law. Trials in all Courts.

MEMBERS OF FIRM

CHARLES R. EBERSOL, born Pittsburgh, Pennsylvania, September 18, 1916; admitted to bar, 1941, Connecticut. *Education:* Haverford College (B.A., 1938); Yale Law School (LL.B., 1941). Phi Beta Kappa. Prosecuting Attorney, City Court of Torrington, 1947-1949. Judge, City Court of Torrington, 1951-1955. Chairman of the Board of Directors, American Cancer Society, 1975-1979. *Member:* Litchfield County, Connecticut (Member of Council, 1955-1958) and American Bar Associations. ***PRACTICE AREAS:*** Estate Planning Law; Probate Law; Banking Law.

CHARLES R. EBERSOL, JR., born Torrington, Connecticut, June 21, 1952; admitted to bar, 1977, Connecticut. *Education:* Haverford College (B.A., 1974); Vanderbilt University (J.D., 1977). President, Connecticut Junior Republic, 1994-1997. *Member:* Litchfield County and Connecticut Bar Associations. ***PRACTICE AREAS:*** Real Estate Law; Planning and Zoning Law; Estate Planning Law. ***Email:*** peter.ebersol@snet.net

BRIAN McCORMICK, born Bronxville, New York, February 14, 1951; admitted to bar, 1978, Connecticut. *Education:* Georgetown University (B.S., 1973); Case Western Reserve University (J.D., 1978). President, Torrington United Way, 1994-1997. *Member:* Litchfield County, Connecticut and American Bar Associations; Connecticut Trial Lawyers Association; The Association of Trial Lawyers of America. ***PRACTICE AREAS:*** Personal Injury Law; Family Law; Civil Litigation. ***Email:*** brian.mccormick@snet.net

ASSOCIATE

MICHAEL KEILTY, born Torrington, Connecticut, June 9, 1967; admitted to bar, 1992, Connecticut. *Education:* University of Connecticut (B.A., 1989); University of Bridgeport School of Law (J.D., 1992). *Member:* Litchfield County and Connecticut Bar Associations. ***PRACTICE AREAS:*** Civil Litigation; Real Estate Law; Planning and Zoning; Environmental.

(This Listing Continued)

REPRESENTATIVE CLIENTS: Town of Warren; Torrington Honda; Ivan Lendl.
TITLE INSURANCE CO.: Connecticut Attorneys Title Insurance Co.; Chicago Title Insurance Co.
REFERENCES: Paul Hirshauer; PNC Mortgage Co.; Webster Bank; Litchfield Bancorp.

LAW OFFICES OF PETER C. HERBST

365 PROSPECT STREET
TORRINGTON, CONNECTICUT 06790
Telephone: 860-489-9495
Fax: 860-489-5977
Email: pcherbst@imagine.com
URL: http://www.lawyers.com/lawofficesofpetercherbst

Land Use Law, Land Development Law, Zoning Law, Wetlands Law, Real Estate Transactions.

PETER C. HERBST, born Northampton, Massachusetts, March 21, 1948; admitted to bar, 1973, Connecticut; 1975, U.S. District Court, District of Connecticut; 1978, U.S. Supreme Court. *Education:* Washington College (B.A., 1970); University of Maine, School of Law (J.D., 1973). Member, University of Maine Law Review, 1972-1973. Connecticut Bar Association Continuing Legal Education Faculty , 1991—. *Member:* Litchfield County and Connecticut Bar Associations.

REPRESENTATIVE CLIENTS: Shawmut Bank; Winsted Savings Bank; City of Torrington; Litchfield Bancorp, Center Bank.
APPROVED ATTORNEY FOR: Lawyers Title Insurance Corp.; Chicago Title Insurance Corp.; Connecticut Attorneys Title Insurance Co.
REFERENCES: Shawmut Bank; Northwest Bank for Savings; Winsted Savings Bank.

JOSEPH F. KEEFE

179 WATER STREET
TORRINGTON, CONNECTICUT 06790
Telephone: 860-482-7651
Fax: 860-482-7845
Email: email@skmwlaw.com
URL: http://www.snetyp.com/skmw

Civil Litigation, Criminal Litigation, Personal Injury, Commercial Litigation and Probate Litigation.

FIRM PROFILE: Mr. Keefe has been a practicing attorney for over thirty years, primarily involved in litigation, handling matters in all state and federal courts. Mr. Keefe has also taught criminal law and criminal procedure for the Connecticut Bar review courses and lectured frequently on criminal law for county, state and national organizations and trial lawyer associations. He also represents professionals before Disciplinary Authorities. Mr. Keefe has had many reported decisions and has been counsel in numerous high profile cases, including the Woody Allen defense, which can be produced upon request.

JOSEPH F. KEEFE, born Hartford, Connecticut, August 6, 1942; admitted to bar, 1967, Connecticut; 1968, U.S. District Court, District of Connecticut; 1970, U.S. Supreme Court; 1971, U.S. Court of Appeals, Second Circuit; 1972, U.S. District Court, Eastern District of Wisconsin. *Education:* Fairfield University (B.A., cum laude, 1964); University of Connecticut (J.D., 1967). Member, Editor, University of Connecticut Law Review, 1966-1967. Senior Topical Editor, Criminal Law, 1980-1985. Board of Editors, Connecticut Bar Journal, 1980-1986. Co-Author: "Practice and Procedure of Juvenile Court for the State of Connecticut," 41 Connecticut Bar Journal 201 (1967);l "Contesting Searches & Seizures After the 1972-74 Terms of the U.S. Supreme Court," 49 Connecticut Bar Journal (March 1975); "Confessions, Admissions and Recent Curtailment of the Fifth Amendments' Protection," 51 Connecticut Bar Journal (September 1977); "Forensic Sciences Service and the Criminal Justice System as Viewed by Defense," 24 Journal of Forensic Sciences No. 3 (July 1979). Fellow, American Academy of Forensic Sciences, 1977; Chairman, Jurisprudence Section, 1979-1980. Connecticut State Trial Referee, 1984—. Vice Chairman, State Grievance Committee, 1984-1986. Member, Smith, Keefe, Moraghan & Waterfall. *Member:* Connecticut (Member, Federal Judiciary Committee, 1994—) and American Bar Associations; Connecticut Trial Lawyers Association (Board of Governors, 1970-1987; President, 1979-1981); Connecticut Association of Criminal Defense Lawyers (President, 1988; Board of Directors, 1987—). ***REPORTED CASES:*** State v. Bernier, 246 Conn. 63, 717 A.2d 652 (1998). ***PRACTICE AREAS:*** Civil Litigation; Criminal Litigation.

RORABACK & RORABACK

24 MASON STREET
P.O. BOX 925
TORRINGTON, CONNECTICUT 06790
Telephone: 860-489-6880
Fax: 860-489-5301

General Practice, Real Estate and Zoning, Corporate and Commercial Law, Civil and Commercial Litigation, Administrative Law, Banking Law, Municipal Law, Estate Planning and Probate Law.

MEMBERS OF FIRM

CHARLES W. RORABACK, born Hartford, Connecticut, August 9, 1933; admitted to bar, 1958, Connecticut. *Education:* Yale University (B.A., 1955; LL.B., 1958). Phi Delta Phi. City Attorney, 1961-1963. *Member:* Litchfield County (President, 1982-1985), Connecticut and American Bar Associations. ***PRACTICE AREAS:*** Estate Planning; Probate Law; Banking Law; Municipal Law; Real Estate Law.

CHARLES E. RORABACK, born Torrington, Connecticut, February 19, 1958; admitted to bar, 1985, Connecticut. *Education:* Yale University (B.A., 1981); University of Connecticut (J.D., with honors, 1985). *Member:* Litchfield County and Connecticut Bar Associations. ***PRACTICE AREAS:*** Corporate Law; Commercial Finance Law; Municipal Law; Real Estate Law; Zoning Law; Administrative Law.

MARGARET P. RORABACK, born Torrington, Connecticut, July 24, 1961; admitted to bar, 1987, Connecticut. *Education:* Yale University (B.A., 1983); Vermont Law School (J.D., cum laude, 1987). *Member:* Litchfield County and Connecticut Bar Associations. ***PRACTICE AREAS:*** Elder Law; Estate Planning; Probate Law; Real Estate Law.

ANDREW W. RORABACK, born Torrington, Connecticut, March 29, 1960; admitted to bar, 1987, Connecticut. *Education:* Yale University (B.A., cum laude, 1983); University of Virginia (J.D., 1987). State Representative, 1995-2001; State Cenator, 2001—. *Member:* Litchfield County and Connecticut Bar Associations. ***PRACTICE AREAS:*** Civil Litigation; Commercial Litigation; Municipal Law; Banking Law; Administrative Law.

APPROVED ATTORNEY FOR: Connecticut Attorneys Title Insurance Co.
REPRESENTATIVE CLIENTS: Torrington Water Co.; Lime Rock Associates, Inc.; Town of Goshen; Town of Morris; Town of New Hartford; Torrington Savings Bank.
REFERENCE: Torrington Savings Bank.

THE LAW OFFICES OF ALLISON J. BLOOM

35 CORPORATE DRIVE
SUITE 1155
TRUMBULL, CONNECTICUT 06611
Telephone: 203-452-8000
Fax: 203-452-7594
Email: emsatty@aol.com

Contracts, Corporate Law, Emergency Medical Services Law, Taxation, Wills, Trusts and Estates, Business Law.

ALLISON J. BLOOM, born New York, N.Y., July 12, 1968; admitted to bar, 1995, Connecticut; 1996, U.S. District Court, District of Connecticut; 1997, District of Columbia; 1999, U.S. Supreme Court. *Education:* Fairfield University (B.A., 1991); Quinnipiac College (J.D., 1994). Phi Alpha Delta. Member: National Association of Emergency Medical Technicians; National Association of Emergency Medical Service Educators. *Member:* District of Columbia Bar; Connecticut Bar Association; American Health Lawyers Association. ***PRACTICE AREAS:*** Emergency Medical Services Law; Business Law; Wills; Trusts and Estates; Taxation; Corporate Law; Contracts.

BRAUNSTEIN & TODISCO, LLC

TRUMBULL, CONNECTICUT
(See Fairfield)

Taxation, Business Law, Estate Planning, Elder Law, Trusts, Probate Administration and Probate Proceedings, Commercial Transactions and Real Estate, Criminal and Civil Litigation, Bankruptcy, Trial and Appellate Practice.

HARLOW, ADAMS & FRIEDMAN, P.C.

TRUMBULL, CONNECTICUT
(See Milford)

General Civil Practice, General Civil Litigation in State and Federal Courts, Real Estate Conveyancing, Financing and Development, Zoning, Probate, Personal Injury, Commercial Litigation, Construction Law, Bankruptcy, Business Formations, Landlord and Tenant, Title Opinions, Trials and Appeals.

ARTHUR C. LASKE, III

8 DANIELS FARM ROAD
TRUMBULL, CONNECTICUT 06611
Telephone: 203-452-9987
Fax: 203-452-7680
Email: laskelaw@aol.com
URL: http://www.lawyers.com/aclaskelaw

Personal Injury, Contract Disputes, Criminal, Civil Trial Practice, Municipal Liability, Product Liability, Arbitration and Uninsured/Underinsured Motorists.

ARTHUR C. LASKE, III, born Bridgeport, Connecticut, September 29, 1962; admitted to bar, 1988, Connecticut; 1989, U.S. District Court, District of Connecticut. *Education:* Boston College (B.A., 1984); University of Connecticut (J.D., 1988). Member, National Moot Court Team, 1986-1987. Faculty Member, Connecticut Bar Association, "Connecticut Trial Advocacy Institute," 1994—, National Institute for Trial Advocacy, (NITA), National Program, Boulder Colorado (1992). Assistant City Attorney, City of Bridgeport, CT., (1993—); Trial Counsel with Marsh, Day and Calhoun (1988-1993). Elected Town Council, Town of Trumbull, 1991-1992. Board of Finance, Town of Easton (2000—). *Member:* Greater Bridgeport, Connecticut and American Bar Associations; Connecticut Trial Lawyers Association. (Board Certified, Civil Trial Advocate, National Board of Trial Advocacy). ***REPORTED CASES:*** Hamilton Moore Et Al. v. Joseph Ganim Et Al., 233 Conn. 557 (1995); Gajewski v. Pavelo, 36 Conn. App. 601 (1995); Jolly, Inc. v. Zoning Board of Appeals, 237 Conn. 184 (1996); Community Collaborative of Bridgeport, Inc. v. Joseph P. Ganim, Et.Al., 241 Conn. 546 (1997); Fanneron v. Baird, 39 Conn.App. 921 (1995).

DANA P. LONERGAN

4154 MADISON AVENUE
TRUMBULL, CONNECTICUT 06611
Telephone: 203-371-7023
Fax: 203-371-4452
Email: dloner1066@aol.com
URL: http://www.lawyers.com/personalinjuryct

Personal Injury.

DANA P. LONERGAN, born Port Chester, N.Y., May 27, 1955; admitted to bar, 1983, Connecticut. *Education:* University of Massachusetts (B.S., 1980); University of Bridgeport (J.D., 1983). *Member:* Connecticut and American Bar Associations. ***PRACTICE AREAS:*** Personal Injury Law.

JOHANNA S. MALINOWSKI

8 DANIELS FARM ROAD
TRUMBULL, CONNECTICUT 06611
Telephone: 203-268-8600
FAX: 203-261-4660
URL: http://www.lawyers.com/malinowskilaw

Real Estate, Probate, Elder Law, Real Property, Estate Planning, Business.

JOHANNA S. MALINOWSKI, born Allentown, Pennsylvania, June 17, 1940; admitted to bar, 1983, Connecticut and U.S. District Court, District of Connecticut. *Education:* Gwynedd-Mercy College (A.A., 1960); Sacred Heart University (B.S., 1979); University of Bridgeport (J.D., 1982). Member, Board of Directors, 1984— and Vice Chair, 1990—, Action for Bridgeport Community Development, Inc. Member, Family Services, Woodfield, 1984-1992. President, Bridgeport Area Branch, 1987-1989, Board Member, 1982-1991 and Chair, State Education Foundation, 1990-1994, American Association of University Women (AAUW). Assistant Adjunct Professor of Law, Real Property, Conveyancing and Estates and Probate, Sacred Heart University, 1984—. Chairman, Town of Trumbull, School Code Compliance Building Committee, 1984—. *Member:* Bridgeport, Connecticut and American Bar Associations. ***PRACTICE AREAS:*** Real Property Law; Landlord and Tenant Law; Elder Law; Probate.

MIHALY & KASCAK

925 WHITE PLAINS ROAD
TRUMBULL, CONNECTICUT 06611
Telephone: 203-452-9077
Fax: 203-452-9087
URL: http://www.snetyp.com/mihaly-kascak

Bethel, Connecticut Office: 93 Greenwood Avenue, 06801. Telephone: 203-748-9098.

(This Listing Continued)

MIHALY & KASCAK, Trumbull—Continued

General Civil and Criminal Practice before State and Federal Courts. Negligence, Insurance, Workers Compensation, Real Estate, Probate, Zoning, Criminal Defense, Appellate, Domestic Relations Law and Divorce. Trials and Appeals.

MEMBERS OF FIRM

SERGE G. MIHALY, born Stratford, Connecticut, October 29, 1933; admitted to bar, 1956, Connecticut, New York State and U.S. District Court, Southern District of New York; 1979, U.S. District Court, District of Connecticut and U.S. Court of Appeals, Second Circuit. *Education:* New York University (B.A., 1954; LL.B., 1956). Member, Justinian Society. Town Representative, Trumbull Town Meeting, 1961-1965. Majority Leader of Town Meeting, 1961-1963. Minority Leader of Town Meeting, 1963-1965. Appointed: Trumbull Police Commission, 1976-1992; State Veterans Home and Hospital Commission, 1979-1990. *Member:* Bridgeport and Connecticut Bar Associations; The Association of Trial Lawyers of America; American Judicature Society. ***PRACTICE AREAS:*** Insurance; Workers Compensation; Negligence; Probate; Trials and Appeals.

RICHARD G. KASCAK, JR., born Bridgeport, Connecticut, July 18, 1951; admitted to bar, 1983, Connecticut; 1984, U.S. District Court, District of Connecticut. *Education:* University of Connecticut (B.A., 1976); University of Bridgeport (J.D., 1983). *Member:* Bridgeport and Connecticut Bar Associations; Connecticut Trial Lawyers Association; The Association of Trial Lawyers of America. ***PRACTICE AREAS:*** Insurance; Negligence; Workers Compensation; Real Estate; Probate; Wills; Trusts; Trials and Appeals.

ASSOCIATES

JEAN Z. MAGUIRE, born Stamford, Connecticut, May 7, 1957; admitted to bar, 1982, Connecticut; 1983, U.S. District Court, District of Connecticut. *Education:* University of Connecticut (B.A., 1979); Syracuse University; University of Connecticut (J.D., 1982). *Member:* Connecticut Bar Association. ***PRACTICE AREAS:*** Commercial Real Estate; Residential Real Estate; Estate Planning; Probate; Wills; Trusts.

TIMOTHY P. KENNEDY, born Omaha, Nebraska, May 10, 1969; admitted to bar, 1998, Connecticut. *Education:* Salve Regina College (B.A., 1991; M.S., 1992); Quinnipiac College (J.D., 1997). Sigma Phi Sigma Scholastic National Honor Society. Member: Connecticut Probate Law Journal; Quinnipiac Probate Law Journal. *Member:* Connecticut and American Bar Associations. ***PRACTICE AREAS:*** Insurance; Workers Compensation; Personal Injury; Negligence; Probate; Real Estate.

OWENS, SCHINE & NICOLA, P.C.

Established in 1928

799 SILVER LANE

P.O. BOX 753

TRUMBULL, CONNECTICUT 06611-0753

Telephone: 203-375-0600

FAX: 203-375-5003

Fairfield, Connecticut Office: 53 Sherman Street, 06430. Telephone: 203-259-6612. Fax: 203-256-8796.

General Trial Practice in all Courts. Real Estate, Land Use and Planning, Environmental, Corporate, Probate, Personal Injury, Criminal, Family, Workers Compensation, Education Law, Labor Law, Foreclosures, Bankruptcy. Administrative Agency Proceedings and Appeals, Real Estate, Commercial Litigation, Construction Law, Arbitration.

FIRM PROFILE: Owens, Schine & Nicola, P.C., ("Owens & Schine") was established in 1926 by Howard T. Owens and Edward Schine. After more than 60 years in downtown Bridgeport, the firm moved to its new facility on Silver Lane in Trumbull, Connecticut, on October 1, 1990.

Owens, Schine & Nicola is a general practice law firm with 12 attorneys. The firm represents individuals, corporate clients and various lending institutions. It has developed expertise in many areas of the law including personal injury litigation, zoning, inland wetlands, criminal, wills and estate planning, tax litigation, civil litigation, divorce, bankruptcy and worker's compensation. A significant portion of Owens, Schine & Nicola's practice is devoted to businesses, corporations, commercial and residential real estate, foreclosures, loan workouts and commercial litigation.

HOWARD T. OWENS (1897-1986).

EDWARD SCHINE (1928-1983).

ROBERT M. OWENS (1935-1997).

(This Listing Continued)

ROBERT J. NICOLA, born Bridgeport, Connecticut, October 16, 1942; admitted to bar, 1967, Connecticut; 1968, U.S. District Court, District of Connecticut; 1969, U.S. Court of Appeals, Second Circuit; 1971, U.S. Supreme Court. *Education:* Franklin & Marshall College (B.A., 1964); University of Connecticut (J.D., 1967). Member, President's Circle, Franklin & Marshall College. Member, Connecticut Indian Affairs Council, 1973-1982. Member, 1976-1980 and Chairman, 1978-1980, Easton Conservation Commission. Town Attorney, Easton, Connecticut, 1980-1983. Member, Board of Associates, University of Bridgeport, 1984—. Member, 1993-1997 and Chairman, 1997—, Easton Police Commission. Member, Board of Associates, First American Title Insurance Company. *Member:* Bridgeport, Connecticut and American Bar Associations; Connecticut Trial Lawyers Association; The Association of Trial Lawyers of America. ***LANGUAGES:*** Aruman. ***PRACTICE AREAS:*** Matrimonial Law; Commercial Litigation; Workers Compensation; Personal Injury. ***Email:*** RJN@OSN-PC.com

KEVIN L. BURNS, born Bridgeport, Connecticut, December 8, 1952; admitted to bar, 1977, Connecticut and U.S. District Court, District of Connecticut; 1979, U.S. Tax Court. *Education:* Boston University (B.A., 1974); Catholic University of America (J.D., 1977). Member, 1985-1991, Secretary, 1988-1990 and Chairman, 1990-1991, Newtown Conservation Commission. Arbitrator, American Arbitration Association. *Member:* Bridgeport and Connecticut Bar Associations. ***PRACTICE AREAS:*** Probate; Estate Planning; Business Law; Bankruptcy; Commercial Litigation. ***Email:*** KLB@OSN-PC.com

CAROLYN R. LINSEY, born Rochester, New York, May 6, 1953; admitted to bar, 1977, Georgia; 1981, New Jersey; 1982, Connecticut. *Education:* University of Georgia (B.A., 1973; J.D., 1977); New York University School of Law (LL.M., Labor Law, 1981). Attorney State Trial Referee, Judicial District of Fairfield, 1990-1995. Member, Panel of Neutral Arbitrators for the State of Connecticut, 1992-1996. *Member:* Bridgeport and Connecticut Bar Associations; Connecticut Trial Lawyers Association. [Capt., U.S. Air Force Judge Advocate, 1978-1981]. ***PRACTICE AREAS:*** Civil Litigation; Employment Law; Education Law. ***Email:*** CRL@OSN-PC.com

---

ROBERT J. BERTA, born Derby, Connecticut, July 20, 1939; admitted to bar, 1964, Connecticut. *Education:* College of the Holy Cross (B.A., 1961); University of Virginia (LL.B., 1964). Delta Theta Phi. *Member:* Bridgeport, Connecticut and American Bar Associations. ***PRACTICE AREAS:*** Business Law; Tax and Estate Planning. ***Email:*** RJB@OSN-PC.com

DANIEL F. CARUSO, born Greenwich, Connecticut, December 12, 1957; admitted to bar, 1983, Connecticut; 1984, U.S. District Court, District of Connecticut. *Education:* University of Connecticut (B.A., 1980); Vermont Law School (J.D., 1983). Member, Connecticut Probate Assembly, 1995—. Member, National College of Probate Judges, Fairfield, 1995—. State Representative, 1989-1994. Treasurer, Town of Fairfield, 1993-1995. *Member:* Fairfield, Connecticut (Member, Section of Probate and Trust Law; Superintendent, Probate of Estates, Adoptions and Parental Rights Matters) and American Bar Associations. ***PRACTICE AREAS:*** Trusts and Estates; Real Estate; Small Business Law; General Practice. ***Email:*** DFC@OSN-PC.com

MICHAEL C. JANKOVSKY, born Bridgeport, Connecticut, September 8, 1969; admitted to bar, 1996, Connecticut and U.S. District Court, District of Connecticut. *Education:* St. Lawrence University (B.A., 1991); Tulane University of Louisiana (J.D., 1996). Senior Editor, Tulane Environmental Law Journal. Fairfield County Fish & Game Protective Association. *Member:* Greater Bridgeport and Connecticut Bar Associations; Connecticut Trial Lawyers Association. ***PRACTICE AREAS:*** Civil Litigation; Criminal Litigation; Workers' Compensation. ***Email:*** MCJ@OSN-PC.COM

SUSAN E. FATSE, born Washington, D.C., November 25, 1960; admitted to bar, 1993, Connecticut; 1994, U.S. District Court, District of Connecticut. *Education:* University of Connecticut (B.S., 1982); Quinnipiac College (J.D., 1993). Recipient, American Jurisprudence Award, Torts Law. Member, Quinnipiac College Law Review. Member, Inland Wetlands and Watercourses Commission, Town of New Milford, 1996-1998. ***PRACTICE AREAS:*** Litigation; Commercial Litigation; Family Law; Zoning Law; Land Use. ***Email:*** SES@OSN-PC.COM

OF COUNSEL

J. BRIAN FATSE, born Bridgeport, Connecticut, October 22, 1958; admitted to bar, 1988, Connecticut. *Education:* Franklin & Marshall College (B.A., 1980); Western New England College (J.D., cum laude, 1988). Recipient, American Jurisprudence Book Award in Criminal Law. Member, Western New England Law Review. Member, Zoning Board of Appeals, Town of Easton, 1989—. Member, Trumbull Town Attorney, 2000—. ***PRACTICE AREAS:*** Corporate Law; Bankruptcy; Real Estate. ***Email:*** JBF@OSN-PC.com

JOHN F. FALLON, born White Plains, New York, January 16, 1950; admitted to bar, 1976, Connecticut and U.S. District Court, District of Connecticut. *Education:* Fairfield University (B.A., 1971); Fordham University (J.D.,

(This Listing Continued)

1976). Member, Board of Education, Town of Fairfield, 1978-1983. Legal Counsel, Connecticut General Assembly: Judiciary Committee, 1979; Senate Majority, 1980. Chairman, Board of Police Commissioners, Town of Fairfield, 1985-1990. Connecticut State Attorney Trial Referee, 1988—. Member, State of Connecticut Judicial Review Council, 1992 —. Member, Trumbull Town Attorney, 2000—. *Member:* Fairfield, Greater Bridgeport, Connecticut (Member, House of Delegates, 1993—) and American Bar Associations. ***PRACTICE AREAS:*** Litigation; Zoning Law; Administrative Law.

KATHLEEN N. MAXHAM, born Bridgeport, Connecticut, January 3, 1955; admitted to bar, 1983, Connecticut; 1984, U.S. District Court, District of Connecticut. *Education:* Rosemont College (B.A., 1976); University of Bridgeport (J.D., 1983). *Member:* Fairfield, Greater Bridgeport, Connecticut and American Bar Associations. ***PRACTICE AREAS:*** Real Estate (residential, commercial, zoning); Estate Planning; Probate.

REPRESENTATIVE CLIENTS: Fairfield University; Bridgeport Public Schools; Town of Trumbull; Main Enterprises, Inc.; Neumade Products Corporation.
REFERENCES: J.P. Morgan Chase & Co.

LAURI GILES WATSON

5415 MAIN STREET
TRUMBULL, CONNECTICUT 06611
Telephone: 203-452-8030
Fax: 203-445-1900
Email: lawatson@aol.com
URL: http://www.lawyers.com/lgwatson

Family Law, Divorce, Child Custody, Employment Discrimination.

LAURI GILES WATSON, born Bridgeport, Connecticut, March 5, 1962; admitted to bar, 1989, Connecticut. *Education:* Springfield College (B.S., 1984); Rutgers University (J.D., 1988). *Trumbull, Connecticut and National Bar Association.* ***SPECIAL AGENCIES:*** Co-chair, Community Task Force, Trumbull. Connecticut; U.S. Justice Department; Former Associate General Counsel, Connecticut State Conference of N.A.A.C.P. ***PRACTICE AREAS:*** Family Law; Labor and Employment; Civil Rights; Education Law; Entertainment Law.

WILLIAMS, COONEY & SHEEHY

799 SILVER LANE
TRUMBULL, CONNECTICUT 06611-0753
Telephone: 203-331-0888
Telecopier: 203-380-2327
Email: wilcooshee@aol.com
URL: http://www.lawyers.com/wcs

General Civil Practice with emphasis on Civil Litigation including Commercial Litigation, Insurance Defense, Personal Injury, Malpractice and Products Liability, Civil Rights, Zoning and Employment Litigation in State and Federal Courts. Trials and Appeals, OSHA, Environmental, Banking and Municipal.

FIRM PROFILE: Williams, Cooney & Sheehy is a litigation law firm that was founded in December of 1988 by seven partners who specialize in trial work and for many years had practiced with an old-line firm in Bridgeport, Connecticut. Although the firm was founded in December of 1988, the partners have many years of experience in the trial of cases in the Federal and State Courts throughout Connecticut and are active in all phases of trial practice including the defense of professional malpractice actions and products liability cases. One of the partners is a past president of the Connecticut Bar Association. Three of the partners are past presidents of the Bridgeport Bar Association and are Fellows in the American College of Trial Lawyers.

MEMBERS OF FIRM

RONALD D. WILLIAMS, born New Haven, Connecticut, April 6, 1927; admitted to bar, 1954, Connecticut; 1955, U.S. District Court, District of Connecticut; 1962, U.S. Court of Appeals, Second Circuit; 1971, U.S. Supreme Court. *Education:* University of Virginia (B.A., 1951; LL.B., 1954). Delta Theta Phi. Justice of the Peace, 1977—. Director, Bridgeport Area Foundation, 1977-1991. Member, Advisory Committee of University of Bridgeport Law School, 1982-1992. Selectman, Town of Easton, 1975-1985. Attorney State Trial Referee, 1984-1990. Town Counsel, Town of Easton, 1985-2000. Appointed by Chief Justice of Connecticut Supreme Court as Member of Committee to Study the Rules of Civil Practice and Procedure, 1984-1985. Member, Panel of Arbitrators, American Arbitration Association. *Member:* Bridgeport (President, 1975-1976; Member, Executive Board, 1976-1979; Chairman, Medical-Legal Relations Committee, 1978-1979; Law Day Chairman, 1975), The Connecticut (Member: Board of Governors, 1975-1978; Medical-Legal Committee, 1975-1979; Special Committee on The Administration of Criminal and Civil Justice, 1977; Member, 1977-1979, and Chairman, 1977-1979, Unauthorized Practice of Law Committee; Member, 1985-1991 and Chairman, 1989-1991, Statewide Grievance Committee; Chairman, House of Delegates Rules Committee, 1978;

(This Listing Continued)

Member: Federal Judiciary Committee, 1988-1991; Central Office Committee, 1975-1978; State Bench/Bar Relations Committee; Nominating Committee, 1976-1979) and American Bar Associations; Connecticut Bar Foundation (Member, Board of Directors, 1976-1979); American Board of Trial Advocates; Connecticut Defense Lawyers Association (President, 1984-1985). Fellow: American College of Trial Lawyers. ***PRACTICE AREAS:*** Litigation; Defense.

ROBERT J. COONEY, born Bridgeport, Connecticut, January 7, 1934; admitted to bar, 1960, Connecticut; 1963, U.S. District Court, District of Connecticut; 1968, U.S. Court of Appeals, Second Circuit; 1971, U.S. Supreme Court. *Education:* Fairfield University (B.S.S., 1957); Georgetown University (LL.B., 1960). Law Clerk, Connecticut Supreme Court of Errors, 1960-1961. *Member:* Bridgeport (President, 1983-1984), The Connecticut and American (Member, Civil Justice Committee) Bar Associations; Connecticut Defense Lawyers Association (Member, Board of Directors, 1988-1990). Raymond E. Baldwin, American Inn of Court. Fellow: American College of Trial Lawyers. ***PRACTICE AREAS:*** Litigation; Defense; Environmental.

EDWARD MAUM SHEEHY, born New Haven, Connecticut, April 1, 1940; admitted to bar, 1967, Connecticut; 1968, U.S. District Court, District of Connecticut; 1970, U.S. Court of Appeals, Second Circuit; 1974, U.S. Supreme Court. *Education:* Yale University (B.A., 1961); University of Connecticut (LL.B., 1967). Editor-in-Chief, Connecticut Law Review, 1966-1967. President, University of Connecticut Law School Alumni Association, 1979-1980. Member: Board of Selectmen, Town of Woodbridge, 1979—; Deputy First Selectman, 1991-2001. Board of Directors, University of Connecticut Law School Foundation, Inc., 1979-1980, 1994-1996. Member, Task Force on the Commission of Legal Ethics, 1990. Co-Chairman, United States District Court Special Masters Program, Bridgeport, 1988-1997. Appointed by Chief Justice of Connecticut Supreme Court as Member of Civil Commission, 2000—. *Member:* The Greater Bridgeport Bar Association, Inc. (President, 1989-1990), The Connecticut (Chairman, Young Lawyers Section, 1975-1976; Assistant Treasurer, 1976-1977; Vice President, 1994-1995; President Elect, 1995; President, 1996-1997; Member: Judicial Appointment Recommendation Committee, 1977-1980; Client's Security Fund Committee, 1977-1994; Judiciary Committee, 1979-1989) and American (Member, House of Delegates, 1994-1998) Bar Associations; American Judicature Society (Member, Board of Directors, 1992-1996); Advocate, American Board of Trial Advocates. Fellow: Connecticut Bar Foundation (Member, Executive Committee, 1979; Treasurer, 1980-1982); Fellow: American College of Trial Lawyers; American Bar Foundation (Vice Chair, Connecticut, 1998). ***PRACTICE AREAS:*** Litigation.

DION W. MOORE, born Brooklyn, New York, February 9, 1939; admitted to bar, 1967, Connecticut and U.S. District Court, District of Connecticut; 1969, U.S. Court of Appeals, Second Circuit; 1970, U.S. Supreme Court; 1982, U.S. Tax Court. *Education:* Denison University (A.B., 1962); University of Connecticut; The Ohio State University (J.D., 1967). U.S. Magistrate, District of Connecticut, 1971-1975. Chairman, Ethics Study Commission, Trumbull, Connecticut, 1986—. Vice Chairman, Trumbull Planning and Zoning Commission, 1989—. *Member:* Bridgeport, The Connecticut and American Bar Associations. ***PRACTICE AREAS:*** Litigation.

RONALD D. WILLIAMS, JR., born Bridgeport, Connecticut, November 3, 1955; admitted to bar, 1982, Connecticut and U.S. District Court, District of Connecticut. *Education:* University of Connecticut (B.A., 1976); University of Bridgeport (J.D., 1982). Recipient: Faculty Award for Excellence in Legal Writing; American Jurisprudence Award for Excellent Achievement in the Study of Trusts and Estates. Associate Editor, Bridgeport Law Review, 1980-1982. Author: "Lesser Offense in Connecticut: A Critical Analysis," 3 U. Bridgeport L. Rev. 105 (1982); "Statutory Construction in Connecticut: An Overview and Analysis," 62 Conn. Bar J. 307 (1988). Assistant Public Defender, State of Connecticut, 1984-1989. *Member:* Bridgeport, Connecticut and American Bar Associations; Connecticut Defense Lawyers Association. ***PRACTICE AREAS:*** Litigation.

FRANCIS A. SMITH, JR. (1951-1989).

SUZANNAH KIM NIGRO, born Stamford, Connecticut, April 13, 1969; admitted to bar, 1994, Connecticut; 1995, U.S. District Court, District of Connecticut; 1997, U.S. Court of Appeals, Second Circuit. *Education:* Hamilton College (B.A., 1991); University of Connecticut (J.D., with honors, 1994). Member, 1992-1993, Associate Editor, 1993-1994, University of Connecticut Law Review. Law Clerk, Chief Judge Antoinette L. Dupont, 1994-1995. ***PRACTICE AREAS:*** Litigation; Appellate Practice.

REPRESENTATIVE CLIENTS: The Stop & Shop Companies, Inc.; Fleet Bank; Town of Easton; Utica Mutual Insurance Co.; Connecticut Medical Insurance Co.; Pennsylvania National Insurance; Podiatry Insurance Company of America; People's Bank; Catholic Mutual Group; Preferred Physicians Mutual; Medical Liability Mutual Insurance Company; Coldwell Banker; Royal Insurance; Avis-A-Car Systems, Inc.; Reliance Insurance Company; The Atlantic Casualty Companies; Hubbell Inc.

BURTON S. YAFFIE

925 WHITE PLAINS ROAD
TRUMBULL, CONNECTICUT 06611
Telephone: 203-261-0551
Fax: 203-459-0392
Email: bylawct@aol.com
URL: http://www.lawyers.com/yaffielaw

General Practice. Real Estate, Zoning, Corporation, Probate, Administrative, Commercial, Negligence, Family and Estate Planning Law. Trials in all Courts.

BURTON S. YAFFIE, born Bridgeport, Connecticut, July 15, 1940; admitted to bar, 1965, Connecticut; 1971, U.S. Tax Court. *Education:* The Wharton School, University of Pennsylvania (B.S. in Economics, 1962); University of Connecticut (J.D., 1965). Member, Panel of Arbitrators, American Arbitration Association, 1976—. Estate and Gift Tax Examiner, Internal Revenue Service, Bridgeport, Connecticut, 1965-1967. Commissioner, Trumbull Development Commission, 1972-1973. Town Attorney, Town of Trumbull, Connecticut, 1973-1987, 1989—. Counsel, Trumbull Sewer Commission, Trumbull, Connecticut, 1974-1981. Secretary, Connecticut Board of Pardons, 1977—. Affiliate, Greater Bridgeport Board of Realtors, 1977—. Member, Connecticut Federation of Planning and Zoning Commissions, 1973—. *Member:* Bridgeport, Connecticut and American Bar Associations; Connecticut Association of Municipal Attorneys.

APPROVED CLOSING ATTORNEY FOR: People's Bank; Hudson United Bank; Washington Mutual Bank; Wells Fargo Bank; Cendant Mortgage; Homeside Lending, Inc.; M&T Mortgage; Anchor Mortgage Co.; Fleet Bank N.A.; Derby Savings Bank; New Haven Savings Bank; Great Country Bank; Norwich Savings Society; Shelton Savings & Loan; Lomas & Nettleton Co.; The Banking Center; Milford Savings Bank; Norwalk Savings Society; Danbury Savings & Loan Association; Fidelity Savings & Loan Association; Bank of Boston, CT; Ulster Savings Bank; ARC Mortgage; Directors Mortgage Co.; Huntington Mortgage Co.; Countrywide Funding Corporation; Chase Manhattan Bank of Connecticut; Medallion Mortgage Company; Sikorsky Federal Credit Union; GMAC Mortgage Corporation; Columbia National Mortgage Corp.; First Union Mortgage Services; Household Mortgage Services; Newtown Savings Bank; Chicago Title Insurance Co.; Fidelity National Title Insurance Company; Old Republic National Title Insurance Company; First American Title Insurance Co.; Commonwealth Title Insurance Co.
REFERENCES: Hudson United Bank; Peoples Bank.

SCULLY, NICKSA, MARTIN & REEVE, LLP

79 MAIN STREET
P.O. BOX 278
UNIONVILLE, CONNECTICUT 06085-0278
Telephone: 860-673-7141
Telecopier: 860-675-8955
Email: scully.nicksa@snet.net

General Practice. Business Law, Negligence, Personal Injury, Real Estate, Commercial Law, Zoning, Planning and Land Use, Trusts and Estates, Probate, Estate Planning, Family Law and Mediation.

MEMBERS OF FIRM

EDWARD F. SCULLY, born Hartford, Connecticut, February 13, 1940; admitted to bar, 1969, Connecticut; 1970, U.S. District Court, District of Connecticut. *Education:* Fairfield University (B.S., 1962); University of Connecticut (J.D., 1969). *Member:* Hartford County, Connecticut and American Bar Associations. ***PRACTICE AREAS:*** Personal Injury; Litigation; Real Estate; General Practice; Business Law. ***Email:*** scully.nicksa@snet.net

WALTER C. NICKSA, JR., born Hartford, Connecticut, December 17, 1944; admitted to bar, 1969, Connecticut. *Education:* Yale University (B.A., 1966); University of Connecticut (J.D., 1969). *Member:* Hartford County, Connecticut and American Bar Associations. ***PRACTICE AREAS:*** Real Estate; Trusts and Estates; Probate; Corporate Law. ***Email:*** scully.nicksa@snet.net

KATHLEEN B. MARTIN, born Waterbury, Connecticut; January 11, 1944; admitted to bar, 1982, Connecticut; 1984, U.S. District Court, District of Connecticut. *Education:* University of Connecticut (B.S., 1965); Western New England College (J.D., 1982). *Member:* Hartford County, Connecticut and American Bar Associations. ***PRACTICE AREAS:*** Family Law; Mediation; Trusts and Estates; Probate; Real Estate. ***Email:*** scully.nicksa@snet.net

ROBERT J. REEVE, born Hartford, Connecticut, October 8, 1958; admitted to bar, 1983, Connecticut. *Education:* Bryant College (B.S., 1980); Western New England College (J.D., 1983). *Member:* Hartford County, Connecticut and American Bar Associations. ***PRACTICE AREAS:*** General Practice; Land Use; Real Estate; Personal Injury; Business Law; Automotive Franchises and Dealerships. ***Email:*** scully.nicksa@snet.net

PATRICK E. SCULLY, born March 25, 1967; admitted to bar, 1995, Connecticut. *Education:* Fairfield University (B.A., 1989); Western New England College (J.D., 1995). *Member:* Hartford County and Connecticut Bar Associations. ***PRACTICE AREAS:*** Personal Injury; Litigation; Real Estate; Criminal Law; Probate; Estates. ***Email:*** scully.nicksa@snet.net

(This Listing Continued)

OF COUNSEL

ROBERT G. GILLESPIE, born September 27, 1920; admitted to bar, 1949, Connecticut. *Education:* University of Connecticut (B.A.; LL.B., 1949). *Member:* Hartford County and Connecticut Bar Associations. ***PRACTICE AREAS:*** Real Estate; Wills; Probate. ***Email:*** scully.nicksa@snet.net

JOHN K. HANRAHAN, born Elizabeth, New Jersey, April 16, 1916; admitted to bar, 1946, Connecticut. *Education:* Yale University (B.A., 1939); University of Pennsylvania (LL.B., 1946). *Member:* Hartford County, Connecticut and American Bar Associations. [U.S. Navy, 1941-1946]. ***PRACTICE AREAS:*** Real Estate; Probate. ***Email:*** scully.nicksa@snet.net

FLAHERTY, MEISLER & COURTNEY, LLC

Established in 1956
62 HYDE AVENUE
VERNON, CONNECTICUT 06066-4503
Telephone: 860-872-7200
Fax: 860-875-6594
Email: FMACATTY@aol.com

General Practice, Criminal, Real Estate, Estate Planning, Probate, Administrative, Workers Compensation, Municipal and Zoning, Family and Personal Injury Law. Civil and Criminal Trial Practice.

MEMBERS OF FIRM

LEO B. FLAHERTY JR. (1923-1998).

ARTHUR P. MEISLER (1945-2001).

JOSEPH D. COURTNEY, born Hartford, Connecticut, April 6, 1953; admitted to bar, 1978, Connecticut; 1980, U.S. District Court, District of Connecticut; 1999, U.S. Court of Appeals, Second Circuit. *Education:* Tufts University (B.A., 1975); University of Connecticut (J.D., 1978). Assistant Public Defender, Tolland County, 1979-1981. State Representative, 56th Assembly District, 1987-1994. Member and Chairman, 1989-1991, Joint Human Services Committee. Member and Chairman, 1991-1994, Joint Committee on Public Health. Member: Government Administration and Elections Committee, 1985-1987; Appropriations Committee, 1989-1994. Associate Counsel, Connecticut House Speakers Office, 1995-1996. Legislative Counsel. Connecticut Secretary of State, 1997—. Town Attorney, Vernon Connecticut, 1999—. *Member:* Tolland County, Hartford County and Connecticut Bar Associations; National Association of Criminal Defense Lawyers; Connecticut Criminal Defense Lawyers Association. ***PRACTICE AREAS:*** Criminal Law; Personal Injury; Workers Compensation; Civil Practice; Real Estate.

ASSOCIATE

ELIZABETH C. FORAN, born Hartford, Connecticut, September 14, 1955; admitted to bar, 1990, Connecticut; 1991, Massachusetts. *Education:* Westfield State College (B.A., 1977); Western New England School of Law (J.D., 1990). *Member:* Connecticut Criminal Defense Lawyers Association. ***PRACTICE AREAS:*** Criminal Law; Personal Injury; Civil Practice; Real Estate.

APPROVED TITLE ATTORNEYS FOR: Connecticut Attorney's Title Insurance Co.; Chicago Title.
REFERENCES: Rockville Bank.

FORD, OBERG, MANION & HOUCK, P.C.

220 HARTFORD TURNPIKE
VERNON, CONNECTICUT 06066
Telephone: 860-646-3141
Fax: 860-649-3532

General Practice. Real Estate, Negligence, Divorce, Probate, Criminal, Commercial, Corporation and Zoning Law. Trials in all Courts.

STEVEN M. FORD, born Hartford, Connecticut, May 24, 1951; admitted to bar, 1978, Connecticut. *Education:* American University (B.S., 1973); Western New England College School of Law (J.D., 1978). Connecticut State Court Trial Referee. *Member:* Tolland County (President, 1992—) and Connecticut (Charter Member, Academy of Continuing Professional Development, 1982—) Bar Associations; Connecticut Trial Lawyers Association. ***PRACTICE AREAS:*** Commercial Law; Corporation Law; Personal Injury; Litigation; Criminal Law. ***Email:*** sford@fomhlaw.com

MARY C. OBERG, born Hartford, Connecticut, January 14, 1956; admitted to bar, 1981, Connecticut. *Education:* University of Connecticut (B.A., cum laude, 1978; J.D., 1981). ***PRACTICE AREAS:*** Divorce Law; Probate Law. ***Email:*** moberg@fomhlaw.com

DOUGLAS KEVIN MANION, born Teaneck, New Jersey, October 29, 1957; admitted to bar, 1983, Connecticut. *Education:* University of Notre Dame

(This Listing Continued)

(B.A., 1979); Washburn University (J.D., 1982). *Member:* Connecticut Bar Association; Connecticut Trial Lawyers Association. ***PRACTICE AREAS:*** Personal Injury Law; Real Estate Law; Divorce; Litigation; Criminal Law. ***Email:*** dmanion@fomhlaw.com

CYNTHIA D. HOUCK, born Philadelphia, Pennsylvania, November 13, 1950; admitted to bar, 1977, Vermont; 1979, Connecticut; 1981, U.S. District Court, District of Connecticut. *Education:* Ohio University (B.A., 1972); Vermont Law School (J.D., 1977). Phi Alpha Theta; Pi Gamma Mu; Phi Delta Phi (Officer, 1976-1977). Instructor, Family Law, People's Law School, 1989—. Connecticut State Court Trial Referee, 1993. *Member:* Tolland and Connecticut Bar Associations. ***PRACTICE AREAS:*** Family Law; Real Estate Transactions. ***Email:*** chouck@fomhlaw.com

REPRESENTATIVE CLIENTS: First Federal Savings & Loan Association of East Hartford, Conn.; Bolles Motors, Inc.; Countrywide Home Loans, Inc.
APPROVED ATTORNEYS FOR: Connecticut Attorney's Title Insurance Co.; Fidelity National Title Insurance Co.; Stewart Title Guaranty Company.

KAHAN, KERENSKY & CAPOSSELA, L.L.P.

Established in 1964

45 HARTFORD TURNPIKE
P.O. BOX K
VERNON, CONNECTICUT 06066
Telephone: 860-646-1974
Fax: 860-647-8302
Email: attorneys@kkc-law.com
URL: http://www.kkc-law.com

Business Law, Corporate Law, Elder Law, Estate Planning, Wills, Trusts and Estates, Family Law, Litigation, Personal Injury, Probate and Fiduciary Administration, Zoning, Planning and Land Use, Residential Real Estate, Commercial Real Estate, Taxation and Taxpayer Representation.

FIRM PROFILE: Located in Vernon, Connecticut, Kahan, Kerensky & Capossela, LLP was founded in 1964. Since then, the firm has grown into a modern full-service practice with sophisticated capabilities. The firm services a diverse clientele ranging from individuals to "Fortune 500" companies. Attorneys within the firm concentrate in one or more areas of law in order to remain on top of rapidly changing and growing areas of practice. The firm is able to assign one or more lawyers with particular experience and expertise to the problem at hand, and when necessary, assemble a team of lawyers in order to provide effective representation at reasonable cost.

MEMBERS OF FIRM

Solomon Kerensky
Joseph P. Capossela
William E. Breslau
Michael A. Bars
William J. Dakin
Michael J. Kopsick
Suzanne E. Caron
Jeffrey M. Winnick

ASSOCIATES

Mark W. Dietz
Dorian L. Reiser
Laurel D. Mangan
Stephen F. Sutton

DELANEY, ZEMETIS, DONAHUE, DURHAM & NOONAN, P.C.

Established in 1952

111 SOUTH MAIN STREET
P.O. BOX 747
WALLINGFORD, CONNECTICUT 06492
Telephone: 203-269-1441
Fax: 203-284-9428
Email: dzddn@worldnet.att.net

Guilford, Connecticut Office: 741 Boston Post Road, 06437. Telephone: 203-458-9168. Fax: 203-458-4424.

Practice Primarily Limited to Professional Malpractice, Products Liability, Insurance Defense, Personal Injury, Employment and Commercial Litigation in all Courts.

JOSEPH M. DELANEY, born July 8, 1924; admitted to bar, 1952, Connecticut. *Education:* Catholic University of America (A.B., magna cum laude, 1949); Harvard University (LL.B., 1952). Phi Beta Kappa. Prosecutor, 1955-1957, and Judge, 1958-1960, Wallingford Municipal Court. Assistant Town Attorney, Wallingford, 1970-1973. Deputy Coroner, New Haven County, 1976-1980. *Member:* Meriden-Wallingford and Southington (President, 1970-1971) Bar Associations. Fellow, American College of Trial Lawyers. ***PRACTICE AREAS:*** Plaintiffs Trial Practice; Personal Injury Law; Negligence Tort Law; Litigation; Trial Practice. ***Email:*** dzddn@worldnet.att.net

(This Listing Continued)

TERENCE A. ZEMETIS, born Meriden, Connecticut, March 14, 1952; admitted to bar, 1977, Connecticut. *Education:* University of Connecticut (B.A., cum laude, 1974); Albany Law School (J.D., 1977). *Member:* Meriden-Wallingford and Connecticut Bar Associations; Connecticut Trial Lawyers Association; The Association of Trial Lawyers of American; Defense Research Institute; Lawyer Pilot Bar Association; American Inns of Court. ***PRACTICE AREAS:*** Arbitration Law; Construction Law; Negligence Law; Insurance Law; Personal Injury Law; Products Liability Trial Practice; Insurance Defense Law. ***Email:*** terence.zemetis@worldnet.att.net

TIMOTHY W. DONAHUE, born New Haven, Connecticut, July 23, 1952; admitted to bar, 1978, Connecticut. *Education:* Wesleyan University (B.A., cum laude, 1974); Boston College (J.D., 1978). Law Clerk to Chief Judge T. Emmet Clarie, U.S. District Court, District of Connecticut, 1978-1979. Special Master, U.S. District Court, 1987—. *Member:* New Haven County and Connecticut Bar Associations; Defense Research Institute; Connecticut Trial Lawyers Association; The Association of Trial Lawyers of America. ***PRACTICE AREAS:*** Plaintiffs Trial Practice; Health Care Law; Drug Law; General Negligence Law; Trials and Appeals; Medical Malpractice Law; Pharmaceutical Law. ***Email:*** dzddn@worldnet.att.net

MICHAEL G. DURHAM, born Boston, Massachusetts, September 4, 1957; admitted to bar, 1982, Connecticut and U.S. District Court, District of Connecticut. *Education:* Dartmouth College (B.A., with distinction in History, 1979); University of Connecticut (J.D., 1982). Special Master, U.S. District Court, 1999—. Arbitrator, Connecticut Superior Court, 1999—. *Member:* New Haven County, New London County and Connecticut Bar Associations; American Arbitration Association; Defense Research Institute; Connecticut Defense Lawyers Association; Connecticut Trial Lawyers Association. (Resident Guilford) (Board Certified Civil Trial Specialist by the National Board of Trial Advocacy). ***PRACTICE AREAS:*** Negligence Law; Products Liability Law; Arbitration Law; Insurance Coverage; Health Care Law; Employment Law; Trial Practice. ***Email:*** mgdurham@snet.net

PATRICK M. NOONAN, born Bainbridge, Maryland, 1952; admitted to bar, 1977, Connecticut. *Education:* Yale University (B.A., magna cum laude, with distinction in English, 1974); University of Virginia (J.D., 1977). Order of the Coif. Listed in the Best Lawyers in America. Law Clerk to Chief Judge T. Emmet Clarie, U.S. District Court, 1977-1979. Reporter of Local Rules, U.S. District Court, 1981—. President, Meriden-Wallingford Young Lawyers, 1980-1982. Special Master, U.S. District Court, 1984—. Executive Board, Connecticut Defense Lawyers Association, 1994-1997. *Member:* New Haven County, Connecticut and American Bar Associations; Lawyer-Pilot Bar Association; The Association of Trial Lawyers of America. Fellow, American College of Trial Lawyers. (Resident Guilford). ***PRACTICE AREAS:*** Civil Litigation; Aviation Law; Medical Malpractice; Products Liability; Professional Liability; Commercial Litigation; Labor and Employment; Litigation. ***Email:*** patnoonan@snet.net

EDWARD W. MAYER, JR., born Pittsburgh, Pennsylvania, October 10, 1964; admitted to bar, 1989, Connecticut. *Education:* Northern Illinois University (B.S., 1986); University of Bridgeport (J.D., cum laude, 1989). Notes & Comments Editor, University of Bridgeport Law Review, 1988-1989. Author: "Anderson v. Creighton: Is Good Faith All That Is Required?," 10 Univ. of Bpt. L. Rev. 1989. President-Elect, Waterbury Young Lawyers, 1991-1992. Section Committee, Tort and Employment Law Sections, Young Lawyers Division, American Bar Association, 1992-1993. *Member:* Connecticut and American Bar Associations; The Association of Trial Lawyers of America; Connecticut Trial Lawyers Association; Connecticut Defense Lawyers Association; American Inns of Court (Associate Member). ***PRACTICE AREAS:*** Litigation; Medical Malpractice; Insurance Defense Law; Employment Litigation. ***Email:*** dzddn@worldnet.att.net

STEVEN M. BARRY, born Hartford, Connecticut, September 9, 1964; admitted to bar, 1990, Connecticut; 1991, U.S. District Court, District of Connecticut. *Education:* College of the Holy Cross (A.B., 1986); Fordham University School of Law (J.D., 1990). Law Clerk to the Honorable F. Owen Eagan, United States Magistrate Judge, 1991-1993. *Member:* Connecticut Bar Association. ***PRACTICE AREAS:*** Litigation; Insurance Defense; Personal Injury Law; Products Liability; Employment Litigation. ***Email:*** stevenbarry@snet.net

BARBARA M. DUNHAM, born Meriden, Connecticut, December 4, 1954; admitted to bar, 1995, Connecticut. *Education:* University of Connecticut (B.S., 1976); Mattatuck Community College (A.S., Nursing, 1980); Northeastern University (J.D., 1995). Law Clerk Intern, Hon. Alfred D. Covello, U.S. District Court, 1994. *Member:* New London County, New Haven County and Connecticut Bar Associations; Connecticut Nurse/Attorney Association; Connecticut Trial Lawyers Association. ***PRACTICE AREAS:*** Civil Litigation; Medical Malpractice; Personal Injury. ***Email:*** bdunham@snet.net

ANDREW P. DWYER, II, born New Haven, Connecticut, October 11, 1965; admitted to bar, 1990, Connecticut. *Education:* Providence College (B.A., 1987); University of Bridgeport School of Law (J.D., 1990). *Member:* Hartford County and Connecticut Bar Associations. ***Email:*** dzddn@worldnet.att.net

(This Listing Continued)

DELANEY, ZEMETIS, DONAHUE, DURHAM & NOONAN, P.C., Wallingford—Continued

TRACEY M. LANE, born Murfreesboro, Tennessee, May 28, 1971; admitted to bar, 1997, Connecticut; 1998, U.S. District Court, District of Connecticut. *Education:* New York University (B.A., cum laude, 1993); University of Connecticut School of Law (J.D., 1997). Member, Executive Board, Connecticut Moot Court Board. Recipient: Founders Day Award, New York University; Presidential Service Award for Programming, New York University; 1991 Chancellor's Service Award, New York University. Associate Editor, Connecticut Insurance Law Journal, 1996-1997. Law Clerk to The Honorable Judge Francis X. Henessy, Appellate Court, State of Connecticut, 1997-1998. *Member:* New Haven, Hartford County, Connecticut and American Bar Associations; Connecticut Criminal Defense Lawyers Association; Connecticut Trial Lawyers Association. ***PRACTICE AREAS:*** Civil Litigation; Appellate Practice; Criminal Appeals. ***Email:*** traceylane@snet.net

REPRESENTATIVE CLIENTS: AlliedSignal Inc.; Allstate Insurance Company; American Airlines; American Telephone and Telegraph Company; Anthem Blue Cross/Blue Shield; Associated Aviation Underwriters; Boston Mutual Life Insurance Company; Canal Insurance Company; Community Healthcare Plan, Inc.; Connecticare, Inc.; Constitution Healthcare, Inc.; Electric Insurance Company; Hartford Life & Annuity Insurance Company; The Hartford Insurance Group; ITT Sheraton Corporation; Johnson & Johnson; Maccabees Life Insurance Company; McGhan Medical Corporation; Merck & Co., Inc.; Minnesota Mining and Manufacturing Company; National Casualty Company; New York Life Insurance Company; Orkin Exterminating Corporation; Otis Elevator Company; Pharmacia & Upjohn Risk Enterprise Management; Safeco Insurance Company; Sikorsky Aircraft, Division of United Technologies Corp.; Travelers Insurance Company; Universal Underwriters Insurance Co.; United Financial Adjusting Co.; Western World Insurance Company, Inc.; Xpect Discount Stores; Yale-New Haven Hospital; Yale University.

DEL SOLE & DEL SOLE, L.L.P.

46 SOUTH WHITTLESEY AVENUE
WALLINGFORD, CONNECTICUT 06492
Telephone: 203-284-8000
Fax: 203-284-9800
Email: delsole@delsoledelsole.com
URL: http://www.lawyers.com/delsoledelsole

New Haven, Connecticut Office: 27 Elm Street, 06510. Telephone: 203-785-8500. Fax: 203-777-4485.

Trials and Appeals in all Courts. General, Tort and Malpractice, Litigation, Probate, Workers Compensation, Corporate, Real Estate Law and Insurance Law.

(For Complete Biographical Data on all personnel, see Professional Biographies at New Haven, Connecticut)

FARRELL, LESLIE & GROCHOWSKI

Established in 1967
375 CENTER STREET
P.O. BOX 369
WALLINGFORD, CONNECTICUT 06492
Telephone: 203-269-7756
Fax: 203-269-1927
Email: info@wallingfordlawyers.com
URL: http://www.lawyers.com/flglaw

General Civil and Criminal Practice before State and Federal Courts. Personal Injury, Probate, Family, Real Estate, Land Use, Immigration, Employment, Criminal Defense, Social Security, Bankruptcy, Corporate, Commercial and General Litigation. Trials and Appeals.

FIRM PROFILE: In practice since 1967, the firm of Farrell, Leslie & Grochowski offers clients in Wallingford and the surrounding area a litigation practice including civil and criminal trials and appeals in state and federal courts. The firm concentrates on social security, employment law, criminal defense as well as personal injury, family law/probate matters, bankruptcy and real estate transactions and immigration. Corporation law and commercial matters are represented as well. Members of the firm are active participants in state and national lawyer and criminal defense associations and in local government.

MEMBER OF FIRM

GERALD E. FARRELL, SR., born West Haven, Connecticut, January 17, 1942; admitted to bar, 1966, Connecticut. *Education:* Boston College (A.B., 1963; LL.B., 1966). Order of the Coif. Editorial Staff, Boston College Law Review, 1965-1966. Law Clerk to the Honorable T. Emmet Clarie, Chief Judge United States District Court, Connecticut, 1966-1967. Assistant Town Attorney, Town of Wallingford, 1984—. *Member:* New Haven County, Meriden-Wallingford-Southington and Connecticut (Chairman, Executive Committee, Criminal Justice Section, 1988-1991) Bar Associations. ***PRACTICE AREAS:*** Probate; Criminal; Real Estate; Personal Injury; Corporate Law; Bankruptcy. ***Email:*** gfarrellsr@wallingfordlawyers.com

---

GERALD E. FARRELL, JR., born Wallingford, Connecticut, January 10, 1968; admitted to bar, 1993, Connecticut. *Education:* College of the Holy Cross (B.A., cum laude, 1990); Villanova University Law School (J.D., 1993). Member, Wallingford, Connecticut, Legislature, 1996—. Secretary, Wallingford, Connecticut Republican Town Committee, 1994-1998. President, Wallingford Historic Preservation Trust, 1991—. ***PRACTICE AREAS:*** Probate; Real Estate; Land Use. ***Email:*** gfarrelljr@wallingfordlawyers.com

ANN FARRELL LESLIE, born Wallingford, Connecticut, December 26, 1968; admitted to bar, 1994, Connecticut. *Education:* Holy Cross College (B.A., with honors, 1991); Boston College Law School (J.D., cum laude, 1994). Member, 1995— and President, 1999-2000, Wallingford Business Professional Woman's Association. Member, American Immigration Lawyer's Association. ***REPORTED CASES:*** Homecare v. Acquarulo, 38 Conn.App.772 (1995). ***PRACTICE AREAS:*** Family Law; Probate; Personal Injury; Real Estate; Social Security; Immigration Law. ***Email:*** aleslie@wallingfordlawyers.com

CHRISTINE FARRELL GROCHOWSKI, born Wallingford, Connecticut, December 26, 1968; admitted to bar, 1994, Connecticut; 1995, U.S. District Court, District of Connecticut. *Education:* College of the Holy Cross (B.A., cum laude, 1991); Boston College (J.D., magna cum laude, 1994). Phi Beta Kappa; Alpha Sigma Nu. Order of the Coif. Note Editor, Boston College Law Review. Member, American Immigration Lawyers Association. ***PRACTICE AREAS:*** Employment Law; Family Law; Immigration; Personal Injury; Litigation. ***Email:*** cgrochowski@wallingfordlawyers.com

LYNNE S. FARRELL, born West Haven, Connecticut, June 9, 1938; admitted to bar, 2001, Connecticut. *Education:* Albertus Magnus (B.A., 1960); Southern Connecticut State University (M.S., Education, 1966); Fairfield University (C.A.S., 1969); Fordham University (Ph.D., 1989); Quinnipiac College School of Law (J.D., 2000). Phi Delta Kappa. Member: Elementary and Middle School Principals' Association of Connecticut; National Association of Elementary Principals. Recipient: Noonan Award for Excellence in Immigration Law, 1999 (Quinnipiac Law School); President's Award, Elementary and Middle School Principals' Association of Connecticut, 1990-1995. Educational Administrator for thirty years prior to attending law school. Adjunct Professor, Fordham University and University of New Haven. ***PRACTICE AREAS:*** Education Law; Family Law. ***Email:*** lfarrell@wallingfordlawyers.com

REPRESENTATIVE CLIENTS: Saas, Mezzanotte, and Associates, CPAs, Wallingford, Connecticut; Prime Equities Inc.; Main Line New England Realty; 21st Century Van Lines.
REFERENCES: Liberty Bank (Wallingford Office); First Union (Wallingford).

LOUGHLIN FITZGERALD

150 SOUTH MAIN STREET
WALLINGFORD, CONNECTICUT 06492
Telephone: 203-265-2035
Fax: 203-269-3487

Hamden, Connecticut Office: 1960 Whitney Avenue, 06517. Telephone: 203-288-2847.

General Practice. Litigation, Real Estate, Insurance Defense, Corporation, Labor, Probate, Condominium, Municipal and Zoning, Family, Commercial, Products Liability, Negligence, Estate Planning, Contract and Criminal Law. Trials in all Courts.

MEMBERS OF FIRM

EDWARD P. LOUGHLIN, born Wallingford, Connecticut, May 20, 1936; admitted to bar, 1962, Connecticut. *Education:* Yale University (B.A., 1958); University of Connecticut (LL.B., 1962). *Member:* Meriden-Wallingford and Connecticut Bar Associations. ***PRACTICE AREAS:*** Real Estate; Probate; Corporate Law. ***Email:*** eloughlin@lflaw.com

EDWARD B. FITZGERALD, born New Haven, Connecticut, October 30, 1934; admitted to bar, 1959, Connecticut; 1975, U.S. District Court, District of Connecticut; 1987, U.S. Court of Appeals, Second Circuit. *Education:* Cornell University (A.B., 1956); University of Connecticut (LL.B., 1959). University of Connecticut Law Review, 1958-1959. Assistant Prosecuting Attorney, Seventh Circuit Court, 1961-1970. Biographee, "Who's Who in American Law," 1983—. Member, Board of Directors, Quinnipiac Valley Health District, 1980-1986. Member, National Panel of Arbitrators, American Arbitration Association. *Member:* New Haven County, The Connecticut and American Bar Associations; Association of Defense Trial Attorneys; Defense Research Institute; Connecticut Defense Lawyers Association. ***PRACTICE AREAS:*** Civil Litigation; Insurance Defense; Personal Injury; Product Liability. ***Email:*** efitzgerald@lflaw.com

(This Listing Continued)

MICHAEL P. KAMP, born New Haven, Connecticut, March 15, 1958; admitted to bar, 1984, Virginia; 1985, Connecticut and U.S. District Court, District of Connecticut; 1985, U.S. Court of Appeals, Second Circuit. *Education:* Boston College (B.A., magna cum laude, 1981); Emory University (J.D., 1984). Member, Hamden Legislative Council, 1989-1991. Assistant Corporation Counsel, Town of Hamden, 1991-1997. Special Master: Judicial District of New Haven; Judicial District of Meriden; Federal District Court. Hamden Chamber of Commerce, President, 1992-1993. *Member:* Virginia State Bar; New Haven County, Connecticut and American Bar Associations. ***PRACTICE AREAS:*** Insurance Defense; Civil Litigation; Municipal Law. ***Email:*** mkamp@lflaw.com

CRAIG B. HENRICI, born New Haven, Connecticut, July 18, 1953; admitted to bar, 1981, Connecticut. *Education:* Middlebury College (B.A., 1975); University of Bridgeport School of Law (J.D., cum laude, 1981). Member: University of Bridgeport Law Review, 1979-1980. Member, 1983-1997 and President, 1987-1997, Legislative Council, Hamden, Connecticut. Member, Connecticut House of Representatives, 1997-1999. *Member:* New Haven County Bar Association. ***PRACTICE AREAS:*** Real Estate; Plaintiffs Personal Injury; Probate; Municipal Law; Landlord and Tenant Law. ***Email:*** chenrici@lflaw.com

JOAN C. MOLLOY, born New Haven, Connecticut, January 15, 1949; admitted to bar, 1983, Connecticut; 1985, U.S. District Court, District of Connecticut. *Education:* University of Connecticut (B.A., cum laude, 1971); Southern Connecticut State College (M.S., 1976); University of Connecticut (J.D., 1983). Superior Court Small Claims Commissioner. Member, Board of Directors, Connecticut Attorneys Title Insurance Company. *Member:* Connecticut Bar Association. ***PRACTICE AREAS:*** Real Estate; Land Use and Development; Environmental Law; Family. ***Email:*** jmolloy@lflaw.com

KATE L. RIZZO, born Meriden, Connecticut, January 22, 1960; admitted to bar, 1988, Connecticut. *Education:* University of Connecticut (B.A., 1982); University of Bridgeport (J.D., 1987). Phi Delta Phi. Member, Law Review. Special Master: New Haven Judicial District; Meriden Judicial District. *Member:* Meriden-Wallingford and Connecticut Bar Associations. ***PRACTICE AREAS:*** Domestic; Family Law; Real Estate. ***Email:*** krizzo@lflaw.com

CHARLES P. REED, born New Haven, Connecticut, February 10, 1964; admitted to bar, 1990, Connecticut and U.S. District Court, District of Connecticut. *Education:* Northwestern University (B.A., 1986); University of Notre Dame (J.D., 1990). Member, Journal of College and University Law, 1988-1989, Editor, 1989-1990. Co-Author: "Fox v. Board of Trustees of the State Univ. of New York: University Regulation Faces the First Amendment," 15 Journal of College and University Law 443 (1989). ***PRACTICE AREAS:*** Personal Injury Litigation; Commercial Litigation; Insurance Defense. ***Email:*** creed@lflaw.com

E. JAMES LOUGHLIN, born New Haven, Connecticut, April 7, 1964; admitted to bar, 1993, Connecticut; 1994, U.S. District Court, District of Connecticut. *Education:* Trinity College (B.A., 1987); Vermont Law School (J.D., 1993). *Member:* Meriden-Wallingford and Connecticut (Member, Elder Law Section) Bar Associations.. ***PRACTICE AREAS:*** Litigation; Real Estate; Zoning Law; Landlord and Tenant Law; Estates; Probate; General Practice. ***Email:*** jloughlin@lflaw.com

JOHN F. CONWAY, born Ridgewood, New Jersey, May 13, 1963; admitted to bar, 1989, Connecticut and U.S. District Court, District of Connecticut. *Education:* Lehigh University (B.S., cum laude, 1985); Fordham University School of Law (J.D., 1988). Associate Editor, Fordham Law Review, 1987-1988. Law Clerk, Honorable J. Daniel Mahoney, U.S. Court of Appeals, Second Circuit, 1988-1989. ***PRACTICE AREAS:*** Commercial Litigation; Municipal Law; Election Law; Insurance Defense. ***Email:*** jconway@lflaw.com

W. GLEN PIERSON, born Cambridge, Massachusetts, 1969; admitted to bar, 1996, New York and Connecticut. *Education:* Princeton University (A.B., cum laude, 1990); Georgetown University (J.D., 1995). Member, The Tax Lawyer, 1993-1995. ***LANGUAGES:*** French.

REPRESENTATIVE CLIENTS: Liberty Bank; New Haven Savings Bank; People's Bank; Connecticut Attorney's Title Insurance Company; Wallingford Housing Authority; Southern New England Telephone Company; United Illuminating Company; Connecticut Life & Casualty Company; Middlesex Mutual Assurance Company; Southern Aviation Underwriters; TIG Insurance; The Rockbestos Company; Utica First Insurance Company; Union Mutual Fire Insurance Company; Electric Insurance.

CRAMER & ANDERSON LLP

VAN SINDEREN BUILDING
2 GREEN HILL ROAD
P.O. BOX 321
WASHINGTON DEPOT, CONNECTICUT 06794
Telephone: 860-868-0527
Fax: 860-868-9342
Email: wfairbairn@cramer-anderson.com
URL: http://www.cramer-anderson.com

Danbury, Connecticut Office: 68 North Street. Telephone: 203-790-7747. Email: danbury@crameranderson
Litchfield, Connecticut Office: 46 West Street. P.O. Box 278. Telephone: 860-567-8718. Email: litchfield@cramer-anderson.com
Kent, Connecticut Office: Kent Green, P.O. Box 333. Telephone: 860-927-3568. Email: gnelson@cramer-anderson.com
New Milford, Connecticut Office: 51 Main Street. Telephone: 860-355-2631. Email: newmilford@crameranderson.com

General Practice. Probate, Estate Planning, Municipal, Family and Real Estate. Trials. Planning and Zoning, Corporate, Banking, Securities.

REGINALD WILLIAM H. FAIRBAIRN, born New York, N.Y., March 9, 1949; admitted to bar, 1975, Connecticut and Oklahoma. *Education:* Monmouth College (B.A., 1972); University of Tulsa (J.D., 1974). Member, Shepaug Valley Regional Board of Education, 1978-1987 and 1991-1999. Town Counsel, Washington, 1978-1980. *Member:* Litchfield County and Connecticut Bar Associations. (Resident). ***PRACTICE AREAS:*** Estate Planning; Probate Administration; Planning and Zoning; Elder Law; Real Estate. ***Email:*** wfairbairn@crameranderson.com

COUNSEL FOR: Town of Cornwall; First National Bank of Litchfield; New Milford Hospital, Inc.; Canterbury School; NewMil Bank; South Kent School; Marvelwood School.

(For Complete Personnel and Biographical Data, see Professional Biographies at New Milford, Connecticut).

CARMODY & TORRANCE LLP

50 LEAVENWORTH STREET
P.O. BOX 1110
WATERBURY, CONNECTICUT 06721-1110
Telephone: 203-573-1200
Facsimile: 203-575-2600
Email: contactus@carmodylaw.com
URL: http://www.carmodylaw.com

New Haven, Connecticut Office: 195 Church Street, P.O. Box 1950, 06509-1950. Telephone: 203-777-5501. Facsimile: 203-784-3199.
Southbury, Connecticut Office: 900 Main Street South. P.O. Box 410, 06488-0410. Telephone: 203-264-7882. Facsimile: 203-264-7847.

General Practice including Administrative, Alternative Dispute Resolution, Antitrust and Trade Regulation, Arbitration, Banking, Bankruptcy, Bond Finance, Closely Held Business, Commercial Real Estate, Commercial Litigation, Complex Litigation, Construction, Contracts, Corporate, Creditors' Rights, Employment Benefits, Employer Defense, Energy, Environmental, ERISA, Estate Planning, Family Business Successions, Finance, Freedom of Information, Government (State and Municipal Contracts), Health Care, Insurance, Intellectual Property, Patents and Trademarks, Labor and Employment, Land Use, Management Counseling, Medical Malpractice Defense, Municipal, Nonprofit Organizations, Pension, Privatization, Probate, Products Liability, Professional Liability Defense, Profit Sharing, Public-Private Finance, Public Utility, Securities, Tax, Toxic Torts, Zoning Law. General Civil, Criminal and Appellate Practice in all Courts.

FIRM PROFILE: 61 Attorneys Firmwide.

PARTNERS

TIMOTHY R. CARMODY, born Waterbury, Connecticut, June 24, 1938; admitted to bar, 1963, Connecticut. *Education:* Fairfield University (B.A., 1960); University of Connecticut (LL.B., 1963). Managing Partner of Carmody & Torrance, 1972-1994. ***PRACTICE AREAS:*** Commercial Real Estate; Construction; Public Utilities. ***Email:*** tcarmody@carmodylaw.com

JOSEPH F. BUDNY, born Erie, Pennsylvania, October 10, 1941; admitted to bar, 1967, District of Columbia and U.S. Court of Appeals, District of Columbia Circuit; 1969, Connecticut. *Education:* Gannon University (B.A., 1963); Georgetown University (J.D., 1966). *Member:* American Health Lawyers Association. ***PRACTICE AREAS:*** Health Care; Corporate Law; Commercial Law. ***Email:*** jbudny@carmodylaw.com

ANTHONY M. FITZGERALD, born Waterbury, Connecticut, May 16, 1944; admitted to bar, 1969, Connecticut; 1972, District Court, District of Connecticut; 1975, U.S. Supreme Court; 1978, U.S. Court of Appeals, Second

(This Listing Continued)

CARMODY & TORRANCE LLP, Waterbury—Continued

Circuit; 1994, U.S. District Court, Southern District of New York. *Education:* Yale University (A.B., cum laude, 1966); Columbia University (J.D., cum laude, 1969). Stone Scholar. Listed in "The Best Lawyers in America," 1995—. *Member:* Connecticut Bar Association (Member, Board of Governors, 1984-1987); American Board of Trial Advocates. Fellow, American College of Trial Lawyers. Certified as a Civil Trial Advocate by the National Board of Trial Advocacy. (Resident, New Haven Office). ***PRACTICE AREAS:*** Civil Litigation; Business Torts; Public Utilities. ***Email:*** afitzgerald@carmodylaw.com

NORMAN K. JELLINGHAUS, born Darby, Pennsylvania, June 28, 1939; admitted to bar, 1969, Connecticut and District of Columbia. *Education:* Yale University (B.A., 1961); Georgetown University (J.D., 1968). ***PRACTICE AREAS:*** Corporate Law; Taxation; Project Finance. ***Email:*** njellinghaus@carmodylaw.com

KENNETH J. POCIUS, born Waterbury, Connecticut, July 19, 1942; admitted to bar, 1970, Connecticut; 1972, U.S. District Court, District of Connecticut. *Education:* University of Connecticut (B.A., 1965); University of Connecticut School of Law (J.D., 1970). *Member:* New England Land Title Association; Real Estate Finance Association. ***PRACTICE AREAS:*** Banking; Commercial Real Estate; Zoning; Land Use; Municipal Law. ***Email:*** kpocius@carmodylaw.com

BURTON Z. ALTER, born New York, New York, July 11, 1940; admitted to bar, 1967, New York; 1991, Connecticut; U.S. District Court, Southern District of New York. *Education:* Princeton University (A.B., cum laude, 1962); Columbia University (J.D., 1965). Phi Delta Phi. Contributing Editor: *New York Corporate Handbook,* New York State Bar Association, 1983. Consultant: *New York Practice Guide,* Matthew Bender, 1987. Member, Securities Advisory Council, Office of the Banking Commissioner, State of Connecticut, 1995—. *Member:* The Association of the Bar of the City of New York; American Law Institute. (Resident, New Haven Office). ***PRACTICE AREAS:*** Corporate Law; Mergers and Acquisitions; International Mergers and Acquisitions. ***Email:*** balter@carmodylaw.com

CHARLES F. CORCORAN, III, born Westfield, Massachusetts, July 26, 1945; admitted to bar, 1971, Connecticut; U.S. District Court, District of Connecticut; 1973, U.S. Court of Appeals, Second Circuit; 1989, U.S. Supreme Court. *Education:* Yale University (A.B., magna cum laude, 1967; J.D., 1971); Gonville & Caius College, Cambridge University, England. Phi Beta Kappa. Member, Connecticut Commission to Study Alternate Methods of Sentencing, 1977-1978. Member, Board of Governors, 1987-1992 and Legal Counsel, 1988-1990, University of Hartford Construction Institute. Adjunct Professor, Trial Methods, Western New England College School of Law, 1990-1994; Author: "Reinsurance Litigation: A Primer," 16 Western New England Law Review 41, 1994, and Volume 7, National Insurance Law Review, No. 2. Member, Panel of Arbitrators, American Arbitration Association. *Member:* Connecticut Trial Lawyers Association. (Resident, New Haven Office). ***LANGUAGES:*** French, Italian, Spanish and Czech. ***PRACTICE AREAS:*** Trials and Appeals; Environmental Law; Professional Malpractice Law; Labor and Employment; Commercial and Contract Law; Insurance, Reinsurance and Surety Bond Law; Construction Litigation. ***Email:*** ccorcoran@carmodylaw.com

JAMES K. ROBERTSON, JR., born Waterbury, Connecticut, May 9, 1947; admitted to bar, 1974, Connecticut; 1975, U.S. District Court, District of Connecticut. *Education:* Yale University (B.A., with honors, 1970); University of Connecticut (J.D., with honors, 1974); Hartford Seminary (M.A., with highest honors, 1998). Managing Partner, 1994-2000. Listed in, "The Best Lawyers in America." Chairman: State of Connecticut Judicial Selection Commission, 1997—. President, Connecticut Defense Lawyers Association, 1983-1984. *Member:* Fellow: American College of Trial Lawyers; James W. Cooper, Connecticut Bar Foundation; American Board of Trial Advocates (Associate). Certified as a Civil Trial Specialist by the National Board of Trial Advocacy. ***PRACTICE AREAS:*** Civil Litigation; Arbitration; Mediation. ***Email:*** jrobertson@carmodylaw.com

THOMAS R. CANDRICK, JR., born Lewisburg, Pennsylvania, November 14, 1947; admitted to bar, 1975, Connecticut; 1978, U.S. District Court, District of Connecticut. *Education:* Cornell University (A.B., 1969); University of Pennsylvania (M.B.A., 1975; J.D., 1975). Beta Sigma Gamma. *Member:* Connecticut Bar Association (Member, Executive Committee, Business Law Section, 1987—); American Arbitration Association. (Resident, New Haven Office). ***PRACTICE AREAS:*** Corporate Law; Commercial Law; Bankruptcy; Banking. ***Email:*** tcandrick@carmodylaw.com

TRUDIE ROSS HAMILTON, born Glasgow, Scotland, December 28, 1944; admitted to bar, 1980, Connecticut and U.S. District Court, District of Connecticut; U.S. Court of Appeals, Second Circuit. *Education:* University of Dundee, Scotland (M.A., Honors 1st Class, 1973; LL.B., 1975); University of Connecticut (J.D., cum laude, 1980). Chairman, Medical Legal Committee, Connecticut Bar Association, 1983-1987. Connecticut Attorney State Trial Referee, 1987. Listed in: "The Best Lawyers in America," 1995—. *Member:* Connecticut Bar Association (Chairman, Litchfield Grievance Committee, 1988-

(This Listing Continued)

1994); American Board of Trial Advocates (Associate). Fellow, American College of Trial Lawyers. Certified as a Civil Trial Specialist by the National Board of Trial Advocacy. ***PRACTICE AREAS:*** Civil Litigation; Medical Malpractice Defense; Products Liability Defense; Health Care; Professional Liability Defense. ***Email:*** thamilton@carmodylaw.com

AUGUSTUS R. SOUTHWORTH III, born East Orange, New Jersey, November 11, 1944; admitted to bar, 1973, Connecticut and U.S. District Court, Southern and Eastern Districts of New York; 1975, U.S. Court of Appeals, Second Circuit. *Education:* Dartmouth College (B.A., 1966); Boston University (M.A., 1970; J.D., cum laude, 1973). Listed in "The Best Lawyers in America." Member, Hartford County Grievance Committee, 1987-1992. *Member:* International Association of Defense Counsel; The Association of Trial Lawyers of America; American Health Lawyers Association; Connecticut Medical Defense Lawyers Association; Oliver Ellsworth Inn of Court. ***PRACTICE AREAS:*** Civil Litigation; Health Care; Professional Liability Defense; Medical Malpractice Defense; Products Liability Defense. ***Email:*** asouthworth@carmodylaw.com

DAVID L. SFARA, born Washington, Pennsylvania, March 3, 1952; admitted to bar, 1977, Connecticut and U.S. District Court, District of Connecticut. *Education:* Princeton University (A.B., 1974); University of Virginia (J.D., 1977). President, Connecticut Estate and Tax Planning Council, 2000-2001. *Member:* Connecticut Bar Association (Member, Executive Committee, Estates and Probate, 1983-2000); Attorneys for Family Held Enterprises. (Also at Southbury Office). ***PRACTICE AREAS:*** Estate Planning; Business Succession; Taxation; Trust Administration; Probate; Elder Law. ***Email:*** dsfara@carmodylaw.com

JOHN D. YARBROUGH, JR., born Washington, D.C., October 24, 1950; admitted to bar, 1979, Connecticut; 1980, U.S. District Court, District of Connecticut. *Education:* Swarthmore College (B.A., with high honors, 1973); University of Virginia (J.D., 1979). *Member:* Connecticut Bar Association (Member: Executive Committee, Municipal and Governmental Services, 1981-1983; 1996—; Executive Committee, Planning and Zoning, 1983-1986, 1988—). ***PRACTICE AREAS:*** Public Finance; Bond Finance; Zoning and Land Use; Commercial Real Estate; Municipal Law; Environmental Law. ***Email:*** jyarbrough@carmodylaw.com

MAUREEN DANEHY COX, born New Haven, Connecticut, May 9, 1954; admitted to bar, 1980, Connecticut and U.S. District Court, District of Connecticut; 1995, U.S. Court of Appeals, Second Circuit; 2000, U.S. District Court, Eastern and Southern Districts of New York. *Education:* College of the Holy Cross (B.A., magna cum laude, 1976); University of Connecticut (J.D., with honors, 1980). Phi Beta Kappa. Recipient, Neiditz Professional Writing Award for Appellate Advocacy, 1997. Connecticut Attorney Trial Referee, 1991—; Member, Hartford County Grievance Committee, 1997—; Co-Chair, U.S. District Court, District of Connecticut Special Masters Program, 1997—. *Member:* Connecticut Defense Lawyers Association (President, 1990-1991). ***PRACTICE AREAS:*** Civil Litigation; Public Utilities; Insurance; Freedom of Information; Insurance Defense; Employer Defense. ***Email:*** mcox@carmodylaw.com

MARK J. MALASPINA, born Waterbury, Connecticut, October 7, 1957; admitted to bar, 1982, Connecticut. *Education:* Fairfield University (B.A., summa cum laude, 1979); Yale University (J.D., 1982). Director and Secretary-Treasurer, Governor Rowland Transition Team and Inauguration Committee, 1994-1995. Director and Secretary, Governor's Executive Chambers Conservancy, 1995—. ***PRACTICE AREAS:*** State Government; Municipal Government; Corporate; Commercial; Commercial Real Estate; Project Development and Finance; Privatization; Energy. ***Email:*** mmalaspina@carmodylaw.com

SUSAN SEIDLER CHAMBERS, born New York, New York, February 9, 1955; admitted to bar, 1980, Connecticut, U.S. District Court, District of Connecticut and U.S. Court of Appeals, Second Circuit. *Education:* Cornell University (B.A., 1977); University of Edinburgh, Edinburgh, Scotland; University of Connecticut (J.D., cum laude, 1980). *Member:* Connecticut Bar Association (Chair, Federal Practice Section, 2000—); The Association of Trial Lawyers of America. (Resident, New Haven Office). ***PRACTICE AREAS:*** Construction; Contract Litigation; Insurance Litigation; Employer Defense. ***Email:*** schambers@carmodylaw.com

D. CHARLES STOHLER, born Harrisburg, Pennsylvania, February 8, 1956; admitted to bar, 1981, Pennsylvania and U.S. District Court, Eastern District of Pennsylvania; 1982, Connecticut, U.S. District Court, District of Connecticut and U.S. Court of Appeals, Third Circuit. *Education:* Muhlenberg College (A.B., summa cum laude, 1978); Duke University (J.D., 1981). Phi Beta Kappa. *Member:* Connecticut Bar Association (Member, Labor and Employment Law Section). ***PRACTICE AREAS:*** Labor and Employment; Employee Benefits; ERISA. ***Email:*** cstohler@carmodylaw.com

ANN HARRIS RUBIN, born Hartford, Connecticut, April 4, 1957; admitted to bar, 1983, Connecticut and U.S. District Court, District of Connecticut; 2001, U.S. Court of Appeals, Second Circuit. *Education:* Wellesley College; Cornell University (B.A., 1979); University of Connecticut School of Law (J.D., 1983). Special Master, U.S. District Court, District of Connecticut, 1992—.

(This Listing Continued)

Arbitrator-Fact Finder, Connecticut Superior Court, 1992—. *Member:* Theodore I. Koskoff American Inn of Court. (Resident, New Haven Office). ***PRACTICE AREAS:*** Civil Litigation; Business Litigation; Insurance Law; Banking; Creditors Rights Law; Arbitration; Mediation. ***Email:*** arubin@carmodylaw.com

MARIANNE BARBINO DUBUQUE, born Waterbury, Connecticut, March 23, 1958; admitted to bar, 1983, Connecticut. *Education:* University of Connecticut (B.A., summa cum laude, 1980; J.D., with honors, 1983). Phi Beta Kappa; Phi Kappa Phi; Pi Sigma Alpha. *Member:* Connecticut Association of Municipal Attorneys; American Planning Association. ***PRACTICE AREAS:*** Municipal Law; Zoning and Land Use; Real Estate; Public Utilities. ***Email:*** mdubuque@carmodylaw.com

THOMAS J. SANSONE, born Danbury, Connecticut, December 31, 1960; admitted to bar, 1985, Connecticut; 1986, U.S. District Court, District of Connecticut; U.S. Tax Court; 1993, U.S. District Court, Southern and Eastern Districts of New York. *Education:* Boston University (B.A., magna cum laude, 1982; J.D., 1985). Member, Mortar Board. Instructor, American Institute of Banking (Waterbury Chapter), 1987-1991. *Member:* Connecticut Bar Association (Chairman, Commercial Litigation Committee, 1994-1996 and Member, Executive Committee, 1994—, Commercial Law and Bankruptcy Section); Waterbury Young Lawyers Association (President, 1991-1992); Connecticut Young Lawyers Association (Member, Executive Committee, 1991-1992). (Resident, New Haven Office). ***PRACTICE AREAS:*** Civil Litigation; Creditors Rights Law; Bankruptcy. ***Email:*** tsansone@carmodylaw.com

JOSEPH A. WELLINGTON, born Oswego, New York, September 30, 1947; admitted to bar, 1978, Massachusetts; 1991, Connecticut and U.S. District Court, District of Connecticut; 1993, U.S. District Court, District of Massachusetts. *Education:* United States Naval Academy (B.S., 1969); Suffolk University (J.D., 1978); George Washington University (LL.M., with highest honors, Environmental Law, 1987). Phi Delta Phi. Author: "A Primer on Environmental Law For the Naval Services," Naval Law Review, Vol. 38, 1989. [U.S. Marine Corps, 1969-1990; Judge Advocate, 1978-1990; Military Trial Judge, 1982-1985]. ***PRACTICE AREAS:*** Environmental; OSHA. ***Email:*** jwellington@carmodylaw.com

JOSEPH L. KINSELLA, born Auburn, New York, July 21, 1959; admitted to bar, 1984, Texas; 1991, Connecticut. *Education:* Hobart College (B.A., 1981); Syracuse University (M.B.A., 1984; J.D., 1984). Business Editor, Syracuse Law Review, 1983-1984. ***PRACTICE AREAS:*** Banking; Bankruptcy; Commercial Law. ***Email:*** jkinsella@carmodylaw.com

ANN HEDGES ZUCKER, born Columbus, Ohio, May 23, 1959; admitted to bar, 1985, Connecticut; 1986, U.S. District Court, District of Connecticut and New York. *Education:* Yale University (B.A., 1981); Fordham University (J.D., 1985). *Member:* American Health Lawyers Association; National Association of Bond Lawyers. (Resident, New Haven Office). ***PRACTICE AREAS:*** Banking; Public Finance; Health Care; Corporate Law; Commercial Real Estate. ***Email:*** azucker@carmodylaw.com

KATHLEEN LENEHAN NASTRI, born New York, New York, August 14, 1961; admitted to bar, 1986, Connecticut; 1987, U.S. District Court, District of Connecticut; 1997, U.S. Court of Appeals, Second Circuit; 2000, U.S. District Court, Southern District of New York. *Education:* University of Connecticut (B.S., 1983; J.D., with honors, 1986). *Member:* Connecticut Trial Lawyers Association (Member, Executive Committee, Board of Governors; Vice President, 2001-2002); The Association of Trial Lawyers of America; American Board of Trial Advocates. ***PRACTICE AREAS:*** Civil Litigation; Personal Injury. ***Email:*** knastri@carmodylaw.com

CHRISTOPHER ROONEY, born Argentia, Newfoundland, Canada, November 1, 1955; admitted to bar, 1984, Pennsylvania and U.S. District Court, Eastern District of Pennsylvania; 1988, Connecticut; 1989, U.S. District Court, District of Connecticut. *Education:* University of Virginia (B.A., 1977); University of Connecticut School of Law (J.D., 1984). Assistant District Attorney, Philadelphia, 1984-1989. *Member:* Connecticut Defense Lawyers Association. (Resident, New Haven Office). ***PRACTICE AREAS:*** Commercial Litigation; Land Use; Environmental Law; Criminal Law; Antitrust; Civil Rights; Health Care. ***Email:*** crooney@carmodylaw.com

JOSEPH E. DORNFRIED, born New Britain, Connecticut, December 28, 1962; admitted to bar, 1987, Connecticut; 1988, U.S. District Court, District of Connecticut. *Education:* Fairfield University (B.A., magna cum laude, 1984); University of North Carolina (J.D., with high honors, 1987). Order of the Coif. Member, North Carolina Law Review, 1986-1987. ***PRACTICE AREAS:*** Corporate Law; Commercial Law; Energy; International Law; Project Finance. ***Email:*** jdornfried@carmodylaw.com

M. ANNE PETERS, born McKeesport, Pennsylvania, May 21, 1952; admitted to bar, 1983, Arizona; 1984, Connecticut. *Education:* Wellesley College (B.A., 1974); Yale School of Forestry and Environmental Studies (M.F.S., 1976); Boston College (J.D., 1983). Solicitations and Book Review Editor, Boston College Environmental Affairs Law Review, 1982-1983. *Member:* State Bar of Arizona; Independent Connecticut Petroleum Association. ***PRACTICE AREAS:*** Environmental Law; Underground Storage Tanks. ***Email:*** apeters@carmodylaw.com

(This Listing Continued)

MICHAEL J. REARDON, born Torrington, Connecticut, October 10, 1956; admitted to bar, 1984, Connecticut; 1985, U.S. District Court, District of Connecticut. *Education:* Connecticut College (B.A., 1978); University of Bridgeport School of Law (J.D., magna cum laude, 1984). Member, University of Bridgeport Law Review, 1982-1984. Law Clerk to the Hon. Peter C. Dorsey, U.S. District Court, District of Connecticut, 1984-1986. *Member:* Connecticut Estate and Tax Planning Council. (Also at Southbury Office). ***PRACTICE AREAS:*** Estate Planning; Business Succession; Trust Administration; Taxation; Probate; Elder Law. ***Email:*** mreardon@carmodylaw.com

BRIAN T. HENEBRY, born Waterbury, Connecticut, April 2, 1962; admitted to bar, 1990, Connecticut; 1992, U.S. District Court, District of Connecticut. *Education:* University of Pennsylvania, Wharton School (B.S., 1984); University of Virginia (J.D., 1990). Phi Beta Kappa. Order of the Coif. Recipient, Neiditz Professional Writing Award, Appellate Advocacy, 1997. Member, Virginia Law Review. *Member:* Connecticut Defense Lawyers Association. ***PRACTICE AREAS:*** Civil Litigation; Public Utility Regulation. ***Email:*** bhenebry@carmodylaw.com

ARTHUR G. SCHAIER, born Brooklyn, New York, September 23, 1965; admitted to bar, 1993, New York; 2000, Connecticut; registered to practice before U.S. Patent and Trademark Office. *Education:* University of Buffalo (B.S., cum laude, 1987); New York University (J.D., 1992). ***PRACTICE AREAS:*** Patents; Trademarks; Copyrights; Intellectual Property. ***Email:*** aschaier@carmodylaw.com

GIOVANNA TIBERII WELLER, born Derby, Connecticut, February 7, 1965; admitted to bar, 1991, Connecticut; 1992, U.S. District Court, District of Connecticut; 1993, U.S. District Court, Southern and Eastern Districts of New York. *Education:* University of Connecticut (B.A., with honors, 1987; J.D., with honors, 1991). Law Clerk to the Hon. Robert I. Berdon, Connecticut Supreme Court, 1991-1992. Adjunct Professor, University of Connecticut - Law, 1995-1998. ***PRACTICE AREAS:*** Civil Litigation; Employer Defense; Labor and Employment; Appellate Practice. ***Email:*** gweller@carmodylaw.com

JOHN L. CORDANI, born Waterbury, Connecticut, May 27, 1963; admitted to bar, 1993, Connecticut; U.S. District court, District of Connecticut; registered to practice before the U.S. Patent and Trademark Office. *Education:* Texas A & M University (B.S., chemical Engineering, 1986); Rensselaer Polytechnic Institute (M.S., materials science, 1988); Qunnipiac College School of Law (J.D., summa cum laude, 1992). Professional Engineer (EIT, State of Connecticut, 1988). Intellectual Property Attorney, Executive Vice President and General Counsel, International Chemical Manufacturer, 1992-2000. ***PRACTICE AREAS:*** Patents; Trademarks; Copyrights; Intellectual Property; Chemical Intellectual Property; Intellectual Property Litigation. ***Email:*** jcordani@carmodylaw.com

HOWARD K. LEVINE, born New York, New York, September 30, 1964; admitted to bar, 1990, Connecticut; 1991, New York; 1992, U.S. District Court, District of Connecticut; 1993, U.S. Tax Court; 1994, U.S. Court of Appeals, Second Circuit; 1998, U.S. District Court, Southern and Eastern Districts of New York. *Education:* University of Connecticut (B.S., magna cum laude, 1986); University of Bridgeport (J.D., magna cum laude, 1990). (Resident, New Haven Office). ***PRACTICE AREAS:*** Civil Litigation; Labor and Employment. ***Email:*** hlevine@carmodylaw.com

JOHN R. HORVACK, JR., born Bridgeport, Connecticut, May 31, 1967; admitted to bar, 1992, Connecticut and U.S. District Court, District of Connecticut. *Education:* Boston College (B.S., Finance, cum laude, 1989); Quinnipiac College (J.D., magna cum laude, 1992). Notes and Comments Editor, Quinnipiac Law Review, 1991-1992. ***PRACTICE AREAS:*** Commercial Litigation; Intellectual Property Litigation; Personal Injury Litigation. ***Email:*** jhorvack@carmodylaw.com

KRISTIN CONNORS, born New Haven, Connecticut, June 12, 1966; admitted to bar, 1993, Connecticut and U.S. District Court, District of Connecticut. *Education:* Villanova University (B.A., 1988); University of Connecticut (J.D., 1992). *Member:* Connecticut Trial Lawyers Association. ***PRACTICE AREAS:*** Civil Litigation; Medical Malpractice Defense. ***Email:*** kconnors@carmodylaw.com

RICHARD L. STREET, born Danbury, Connecticut, May 25, 1968; admitted to bar, 1993, Connecticut; 1994, U.S. District Court, District of Connecticut; 1995, U.S. District Court, Southern and Eastern Districts of New York. *Education:* Hamilton College (A.B., cum laude, 1990); Duke University (J.D., 1993). ***PRACTICE AREAS:*** Civil Litigation; Public Utility; Land Use; Administrative Law; Municipal Law. ***Email:*** rstreet@carmodylaw.com

OF COUNSEL

G. BRADFORD PALMER, born Orange, New Jersey, July 1, 1924; admitted to bar, 1952, New York; 1956, U.S. Court of Appeals, Second Circuit; 1957, Connecticut; 1961, U.S. District Court, District of Connecticut. *Education:* Princeton University (A.B., 1948); Yale Law School (LL.B., 1951). *Member:* The Association of the Bar of the City of New York. ***Email:*** gpalmer@carmodylaw.com

(This Listing Continued)

CARMODY & TORRANCE LLP, Waterbury—Continued

WALTER F. TORRANCE, JR., born Waterbury, Connecticut, July 12, 1927; admitted to bar, 1951, Connecticut; 1954, U.S. District Court, District of Connecticut; 1955, U.S. Court of Appeals, Second Circuit. *Education:* Yale University (B.S., 1948; LL.B., 1951). Senior Vice President, Secretary and General Counsel, Northeast Utilities, Hartford, 1978-1992. ***Email:*** wtorrance@carmodylaw.com

THOMAS L. BRAYTON, born Waterbury, Connecticut, April 28, 1932; admitted to bar, 1961, Connecticut and U.S. District Court, District of Connecticut; 1972, U.S. Court of Appeals, 2nd Circuit; 1976, U.S. Supreme Court; 1977, U.S. District Court, District of Vermont. *Education:* Providence College (B.S., 1955); University of Connecticut (LL.B., 1961). *Member:* American Arbitration Association; American Board of Trial Advocates. Fellow, American College of Trial Lawyers. [Lieutenant USMC, Retired]. Certified as a Civil Trial Specialist by the National Board of Trial Advocacy. ***Email:*** tbrayton@carmodylaw.com

JEAN B. MAURO, born New Haven, Connecticut, April 18, 1936; admitted to bar, 1973, District of Columbia; 1974, Connecticut; 1982, U.S. Court of Appeals for the Federal Circuit; registered to practice before U.S. Patent and Trademark Office. *Education:* Yale University (B.E., Chemical Engineering, 1958); New York University (M.B.A., 1966); University of Maryland (J.D., 1972). Chief Patent Counsel and Trademark Counsel, Loctite Corporation, 1977-1982. Patent Counsel, 1982-1989 and Managing Patent Counsel, 1989-1998, Union Carbide Corporation. *Member:* Federal Circuit and American Bar Associations; American Intellectual Property Law Association; Connecticut Patent Law Association. ***PRACTICE AREAS:*** Corporate Law; Intellectual Property. ***Email:*** jmauro@carmodylaw.com

COUNSEL

J. ALLEN KERR, JR., born Yonkers, New York, September 2, 1944; admitted to bar, 1969, Connecticut; 1974, U.S. District Court, District of Connecticut. *Education:* DePauw University (B.A., 1966); University of Connecticut School of Law (J.D., 1969). ***PRACTICE AREAS:*** Municipal Law; Land Use; Commercial Real Estate. ***Email:*** jkerr@carmodylaw.com

ASSOCIATES

RONA C. LYNCH, born Waterbury, Connecticut, February 13, 1957; admitted to bar, 1983, Connecticut; 1984, U.S. District Court, District of Connecticut. *Education:* University of Connecticut (B.S., 1979); Western New England College School of Law (J.D., 1983). ***PRACTICE AREAS:*** Civil Litigation. ***Email:*** rlynch@carmodylaw.com

CHRISTINE I. ANDREW, born Stamford, Connecticut, October 5, 1942; admitted to bar, 1984, Connecticut; 1985, U.S. District Court, District of Connecticut. *Education:* Middlebury College (A.B., 1964); Simmons College (M.S., 1966); Cornell Law School, Cornell University (J.D., 1984). *Member:* National Academy of Elder Law Attorneys. ***PRACTICE AREAS:*** Corporate Law; Commercial Law; Elder Law. ***Email:*** candrew@carmodylaw.com

JENNIFER E. SILLS, born Hartford, Connecticut, May 11, 1965; admitted to bar, 1993, Connecticut; 1994, U.S. District Court, District of Connecticut. *Education:* Williams College (B.A., with honors, 1987); University of Connecticut (J.D., with honors, 1993). Associate Editor, Connecticut Law Review. Recipient: Gerald F. Stevens Award for Excellence in Environmental Law; American Bar Association's Section of Urban, State and Local Government Law Prize for Excellence in the Study of Land Use and Government Law. Author: "The Connecticut Environmental Protection Act ("CEPA"): Enabling Citizens to Speak for the Environment," Volume 70, No. 5, Connecticut Bar Journal; "SLAPPs: How Can the Legal System Eliminate Their Appeal," Volume 25 Connecticut Law Review. ***PRACTICE AREAS:*** Environmental; OSHA; Commercial Real Estate; Municipal Law; Land Use. ***Email:*** jsills@carmodylaw.com

MARIELLA LaROSA, born Meriden, Connecticut, December 14, 1962; admitted to bar, 1994, Connecticut. *Education:* Wheaton College (B.A., 1984) Phi Beta Kappa; Yale University School of Medicine (Physician Associate Degree, 1987); University of Connecticut School of Law (J.D., 1994). Recipient, American Jurisprudence Award for Torts. *Member:* Connecticut Health Lawyers Association; American Health Lawyers Association. ***LANGUAGES:*** Italian. ***PRACTICE AREAS:*** Health Care. ***Email:*** mlarosa@carmodylaw.com

WILLIAM M. O'DONNELL, III, born Waterbury, Connecticut, October 10, 1969; admitted to bar, 1995, Connecticut; 1996, U.S. District Court, District of Connecticut. *Education:* Yale University (B.A., 1992); University of Connecticut School of Law (J.D., 1995). ***PRACTICE AREAS:*** Civil Litigation. ***Email:*** wodonnell@carmodylaw.com

LESLIE GOLD McPADDEN, born New Haven, Connecticut, February 2, 1969; admitted to bar, 1996, Connecticut and New York; 1998, Massachusetts. *Education:* Boston University (B.S., 1991); Albany Law School of Union College (J.D., 1995). *Member:* American Health Lawyers Association; Connecticut Health Lawyers Association. ***PRACTICE AREAS:*** Insurance Defense; Health Law. ***Email:*** lmcpadden@carmodylaw.com

DOMENICO ZAINO, JR., born Hartford, Connecticut, April 18, 1971; admitted to bar, 1996, Connecticut. *Education:* Trinity College (B.A., 1993); University of Connecticut (J.D., 1996). Connecticut Insurance Law Journal. ***LANGUAGES:*** Italian. ***PRACTICE AREAS:*** Labor and Employment. ***Email:*** dzaino@carmodylaw.com

MICHAEL L. FERGUSON, born Waterbury, Connecticut, 1963; admitted to bar, 1998, Connecticut. *Education:* Central Connecticut State College (B.S., Management Information Systems, 1993); University of Connecticut (J.D., 1997). *Member:* National Bar Association. ***PRACTICE AREAS:*** Corporate law; Litigation. ***Email:*** mferguson@carmodylaw.com

MATTHEW R. PETERSON, born Nashville, Tennessee, 1971; admitted to bar, 1998, Connecticut. *Education:* Trinity College (B.A., honors, 1994); University of Connecticut (J.D., 1998). ***PRACTICE AREAS:*** Civil Litigation; Intellectual Property Licensing. ***Email:*** mpeterson@carmodylaw.com

SUSAN LoFASO HENEBRY, born 1964; admitted to bar, 1992, Connecticut. *Education:* Syracuse University (B.S., cum laude, 1986); Fordham University (J.D., 1992). ***PRACTICE AREAS:*** Public Finance; Bond Finance. ***Email:*** shenebry@carmodylaw.com

DAVID S. HARDY, born New Haven, Connecticut, 1973; admitted to bar, 1999, Connecticut. *Education:* Colgate University (A.B., 1996); University of Connecticut (J.D., 1999). (Resident, New Haven Office). ***PRACTICE AREAS:*** Civil Litigation. ***Email:*** dhardy@carmodylaw.com

ISABELLA S. MURRAY, born New Britain, Connecticut, 1973; admitted to bar, 1999, Connecticut. *Education:* College of Holy Cross (B.A., 1995); University of Connecticut School of Law (J.D., 1999). ***PRACTICE AREAS:*** Civil Litigation; Medical Malpractice Defense; Public Utilities. ***Email:*** isquicciarini@carmodylaw.com

PAMELA LEVIN COSTA, born Washington, D.C., November 3, 1958; admitted to bar, 2000, Connecticut. *Education:* Boston University (B.S., 1980); University of New Haven (M.P.A., 1993); Quinnipiac College (J.D., magna cum laude, 2000). Recipient: Distinguished Academic Achievement, Advanced Torts/Medical Malpractice, 1997; Speziale Award for Excellence in Written Advocacy, 1996. ***PRACTICE AREAS:*** Civil Litigation; Medical Malpractice Defense. ***Email:*** pcosta@carmodylaw.com

RUSSELL A. GREEN, born White Plains, New York, July 29, 1967; admitted to bar, 1994, Connecticut; 1995, U.S. District Court, District of Connecticut; 1996, New York. *Education:* University of Connecticut (B.A., cum laude, 1989; J.D., 1994). Recipient: Thomas F. Gallivan and Dean's Fellowships, 1993. *Member:* Stamford/Norwalk Regional and Connecticut (Member, Sections on: Litigation; Planning; Zoning and Environmental) Bar Associations. ***PRACTICE AREAS:*** Civil Litigation. ***Email:*** rgreen@carmodylaw.com

WILLIAM G. LEWIS, born Bronx, New York, September 18, 1964; admitted to bar, 1998, Connecticut. *Education:* Ithaca College (B.A., 1986); University of Connecticut (J.D., 1998). (Resident, New Haven Office). ***PRACTICE AREAS:*** Corporate Law; Commercial Law; Intellectual Property. ***Email:*** wlewis@carmodylaw.com

DAVID T. PAYNE, born Knoxville, Tennessee, July 26, 1971; admitted to bar, 1996, Alabama (Not admitted in Connecticut). *Education:* University of Alabama (B.S., 1993); Washington & Lee University (J.D., cum laude, 1996). ***PRACTICE AREAS:*** Corporate Law; Commercial Law; Bankruptcy. ***Email:*** dpayne@carmodylaw.com

ANNE D. PETERSON, born Nashville, Tennessee, June 27, 1969; admitted to bar, 1998, Connecticut. *Education:* Bates College (B.A., 1991); University of Connecticut School of Law (J.D., 1998). (Resident, New Haven Office). ***PRACTICE AREAS:*** Civil Litigation; Commercial Real Estate; Construction Law. ***Email:*** apeterson@carmodylaw.com

ALEXANDER G. SNYDER, born Bristol, Connecticut, June 23, 1969; admitted to bar, 1999, Connecticut. *Education:* Daniel Webster College (B.S., 1994); Quinnipiac College (J.D., magna cum laude, 1999). ***PRACTICE AREAS:*** Civil Litigation; Intellectual Property; Utilities. ***Email:*** asnyder@carmodylaw.com

DOUGLAS W. ROYCE, admitted to bar, 2000, New York (Not admitted in Connecticut). *Education:* Syracuse University (B.S., 1989); The Ohio State University (M.A., 1993); Fordham University (J.D., 1999). Member, Fordham Law Review, Fordham University, 1998-1999. ***PRACTICE AREAS:*** Corporate Law; Commercial Law. ***Email:*** droyce@carmodylaw.com

LUCY M. ROMEO, born Greenwich, Connecticut, September 5, 1973; admitted to bar, 1998, Connecticut; 1999, New York. *Education:* Yale University (B.A., cum laude, 1995); University of Connecticut (J.D., 1998). Member, Connecticut Law Review, University of Connecticut School of Law, 1997-1998. (Resident, New Haven Office). ***PRACTICE AREAS:*** Civil Litigation; Products Liability Defense; Insurance Defense. ***Email:*** lromeo@carmodylaw.com

(This Listing Continued)

(This Listing Continued)

REPRESENTATIVE CLIENTS: Algonquin Gas Transmission Co.; Anthem Blue Cross & Blue Shield of Connecticut, Inc.; Capital City Economic Development Authority; City of Waterbury; Clear Channel Communications Connecticut Development Authority; Connecticut Health and Educational Facilities Authority; Connecticut Housing Finance Authority; Connecticut Housing Finance Authority; ConnectiCare, Inc.; Connecticut Innovations, Inc.; Connecticut Lottery Corporation; Crompton Corporation; Fleet Boston Financial Co.; Hospital for Special Care; Iroquois Gas Transmission System; MacDermid, Inc.; Mercator Software, Inc.; Middlebury Water Pollution Authority; New Haven Savings Bank; New Opportunities for Waterbury, Inc.; Northeast Utilities; People's Bank; State of Connecticut; Teleflex Incorporated; Timex Corporation; Town of New Hartford; Town of Prospect; Town of Watertown; Town of Woodbury; Transwitch, Inc.; USCO Logistics; Verizon Wireless; Waterbury Companies; Waterbury Foundation; Waterbury Hospital; Waterbury Republican-American; Waterbury Spirit Professional Baseball Club; Webster Bank.
TRIAL COUNSEL FOR: Aetna Life and Casualty; Attorney's Liability Assurance Society, Inc.; Professional Risk Management Services, Inc.; Reliance National Insurance Co.; St. Paul Fire & Marine Insurance.

CICCHETTI & TANSLEY

Established in 1978
500 CHASE PARKWAY
WATERBURY, CONNECTICUT 06708
Telephone: 203-574-4700
Fax: 203-574-2902
Email: cicchetti-tansley-law.com
URL: http://www.lawyers.com/cicchetti-tansley

General Civil and Criminal Practice before State and Federal Courts; Trial and Appeals, Real Estate, Residential and Commercial, Real Estate Development, Planning and Zoning, Corporate/Business Law, Municipal Law, Commercial Litigation, Personal Injury, Domestic Relations, Workers Compensation Law, Criminal Law, Probate.

MEMBERS OF FIRM

MICHAEL H. CICCHETTI, born Waterbury, Connecticut, January 27, 1946; admitted to bar, 1972, Connecticut; 1973, U.S. District Court, District of Connecticut; 1976, U.S. Supreme Court. *Education:* Central Connecticut State University (B.A., 1968); University of Connecticut (J.D., 1972). Member, Board of Trustees, University of Connecticut, 1995—. *Member:* Waterbury, Connecticut and American Bar Associations; Connecticut Trial Lawyers Association. ***PRACTICE AREAS:*** Real Estate; Planning and Zoning; Corporate/Business Law; Personal Injury; Municipal Law; Probate. ***Email:*** mhc@cicchetti-tansley-law.com

MICHAEL G. TANSLEY, born Waterbury, Connecticut, May 19, 1957; admitted to bar, 1983, Pennsylvania; 1984, Connecticut; 1985, U.S. District Court, District of Connecticut. *Education:* University of Connecticut (B.A., magna cum laude, with distinction in Political Science, 1979); Rutgers University Law School (J.D., 1983). Judicial Clerkship, Superior Court, State of Connecticut, 1983-1984. *Member:* Waterbury and Connecticut Bar Associations; Connecticut Trial Lawyers Association; Association of Trial Lawyers of America; Connecticut Association of Municipal Attorneys. ***PRACTICE AREAS:*** Personal Injury; Commercial Litigation; Municipal Law; Workers Compensation; Criminal Law. ***Email:*** mgt@cicchetti-tansley-law.com

ASSOCIATE

PATRICK J. McGRATH, born Waterbury, Connecticut, December 14, 1972; admitted to bar, 1998, Connecticut. *Education:* Providence College (B.A., Political Science, cum laude, 1995); Suffolk University Law School (J.D., cum laude, 1998). Member, Moot Court Honor Board. Recipient, Waterbury Bar Association President's Scholarship, 1996. Member and Production Editor, Suffolk Journal of Trial and Appellate Advocacy, 1996-1998. Author: "Ambiguity Surrounding Individual Liability for Sexual Harassment Under State and Federal Law in Massachusetts, 3 Suffolk Journal of Trial and Appellate Advocacy 29 (1998). *Member:* Waterbury and Connecticut Bar Associations. ***PRACTICE AREAS:*** Land Use; Municipal Law; Personal Injury; Civil Litigation. ***Email:*** pjm@cicchetti-tansley-law.com

MARY BARILE PIERCE, born New York, N.Y., November 21, 1966; admitted to bar, 1991, Florida; 1992, District of Columbia and Alabama; 1995, Connecticut. *Education:* Bucknell University (B.A., Political Science and Biology, 1988); Catholic University of America (J.D., 1991). Moot Court Associate. *Member:* The Florida Bar; Alabama State Bar; District of Columbia Bar. ***PRACTICE AREAS:*** General Civil Litigation; Products Liability; Corporate Law. ***Email:*** mbp@cicchetti-tansley-law.com

REPRESENTATIVE CLIENTS: First Union Bank of Connecticut; American Bank of Connecticut; Connecticut Housing Finance Authority; Connecticut Resources Recovery Authority; Town of Wolcott; City of Waterbury; O & G Industries, Inc.; Montagno Construction Company, Inc.; Alliance Energy Corp.; Eastern Awning Systems, Inc.; The Robinson Company; InterWire Products, Inc.
REFERENCES: First Union Bank of Connecticut; American Bank of Connecticut.
APPROVED ATTORNEYS FOR: Connecticut Attorneys Title Insurance Company (Issuing Agent); Lawyers Title Insurance Corp. (Issuing Agent).

ANDREW C. COTÉ, P.C.

WATERBURY, CONNECTICUT

(See Sharon)

DODD, LESSACK, RANANDO & DALTON, L.L.C.

WATERBURY, CONNECTICUT

(See Cheshire)

Trials in all State and Federal Courts. Personal Injury, Products Liability, Social Security Disability, Workers Compensation and Negligence. Appellate Practice.

DRUBNER, HARTLEY, O'CONNOR & MENGACCI

500 CHASE PARKWAY
WATERBURY, CONNECTICUT 06708
Telephone: 203-753-9291
FAX: 203-753-6373
Email: drubner@dhom.com

Securities Litigation, Commercial and Business Litigation, Class Actions, Commercial Financing, Corporate Law, Mergers and Acquisitions, Commercial Law, Bonding Transactions, Administrative Law, Health Care Law, Real Estate, Condemnation, Tax Appeals, Zoning, Eminent Domain. General Civil Trial Practice in State and Federal Courts. Personal Injury, Product Liability, Medical Malpractice, Appellate Practice, Family Law.

MEMBERS OF FIRM

NORMAN S. DRUBNER, born Waterbury, Connecticut, December 28, 1939; admitted to bar, 1963, Connecticut, U.S. District Court, District of Connecticut. *Education:* Boston University (B.S., 1960); Columbia University (LL.B., 1963). *Member:* Waterbury and The Connecticut Bar Associations. ***PRACTICE AREAS:*** Finance; Real Estate Law; Commercial Transfers; Corporate Law; Zoning Law.

JAMES E. HARTLEY, JR., born Waterbury, Connecticut, April 18, 1950; admitted to bar, 1975, Connecticut; 1976, U.S. District Court, District of Connecticut; 1978, U.S. Court of Appeals, Second Circuit; 1979, U.S. Supreme Court. *Education:* Boston College (B.S., 1972); Columbia University (J.D., 1975). *Member:* Waterbury and The Connecticut Bar Associations. ***PRACTICE AREAS:*** Commercial Litigation; Class Actions; Securities Litigation.

GARY B. O'CONNOR, born Waterbury, Connecticut, April 29, 1955; admitted to bar, 1980, Connecticut; 1982, U.S. District Court, District of Connecticut. *Education:* Boston College (B.A., summa cum laude, 1977; J.D., cum laude, 1980). Phi Beta Kappa. *Member:* Waterbury and Connecticut Bar Associations. ***PRACTICE AREAS:*** Commercial and Business Litigation; Administrative Law; Class Actions; Health Care Law.

JOSEPH A. MENGACCI, born Waterbury, Connecticut, April 13, 1950; admitted to bar, 1976, Connecticut and U.S. District Court, District of Connecticut. *Education:* LaSalle College (B.S., 1972); Loyola University (J.D., 1976). Phi Alpha Delta. Member, National Championship Moot Court Team, 1974. *Member:* Waterbury and Connecticut (Member, Medical-Legal Committees, 1982—) Bar Associations; Connecticut Trial Lawyers Association (Member, Board of Directors, 1985—); The Association of Trial Lawyers of America. ***PRACTICE AREAS:*** Civil Litigation; Appellate Practice; Administrative Law.

GARY D. JONES, born St. John's, Newfoundland, Canada, March 31, 1955; admitted to bar, 1980, Connecticut; 1981, Massachusetts. *Education:* Brandeis University (B.A., magna cum laude, 1977); New York University (J.D., 1980). ***PRACTICE AREAS:*** Commercial Financing; Corporate Law; Bond Finance; Mergers and Acquisitions; Administrative Law; Communications Law.

ASSOCIATES

LINDA T. WIHBEY, born Waterbury, Connecticut, May 11, 1964; admitted to bar, 1989, Massachusetts; 1990, U.S. District Court, District of Massachusetts; 1993, Connecticut and U.S. Court of Appeals, First Circuit. *Education:* Regis College (B.A., 1986); Suffolk University (J.D., 1989). *Member:* Connecticut and American Bar Associations; Association of Trial Lawyers of America. ***PRACTICE AREAS:*** Health Care Law; Family Law; Litigation; Insurance Defense.

ENGELMAN & ENGELMAN

WATERBURY, CONNECTICUT

(See Southbury)

Elder Law, Estate Planning, Probate, Taxation, Wills, Trusts, Title XIX and Medicaid Hearings.

GAGER & PETERSON, LLP

Established in 1917

ONE EXCHANGE PLACE

P.O. BOX 2480

WATERBURY, CONNECTICUT 06722-2480

Telephone: 203-597-5100

Telecopier: 203-757-7888

Bethel, Connecticut Office: 2 Stony Hill Road. Telephone: 203-207-5400. Telecopier: 203-207-5407.

Litchfield, Connecticut Office: 782 Bantam Road. Telephone: 860-567-0828. Telecopier: 860-567-5844.

Sharon, Connecticut Office: 25 West Main Street, P.O. Box 158. Telephone: 860-364-5531. Telecopier: 860-364-5805.

Southbury, Connecticut Office: 325 Main Street South. Telephone: 203-262-6600. Telecopier: 203-262-6780.

General Practice. Corporate Law, Mergers, Acquisitions and Divestitures, Business Law, Banks and Banking, Securities, Administrative Law, Litigation in all Courts, Insurance, Trusts and Estates, Probate, Health Care, Real Estate, Commercial Real Estate, Taxation, Zoning, Planning and Land Use, Patents, Trademarks, Copyrights, Intellectual Property, Consumer Law, Computers and Software, Information Technology, Electronic Commerce, Family Law, Environmental Law, Labor and Employment, Debtor and Creditor, Personal Injury.

WILLIAM W. GAGER (1892-1967).

CARL A. PETERSON, born Hartford, Connecticut, May 13, 1935; admitted to bar, 1960, Connecticut. *Education:* Yale University (A.B., 1957); New York University (LL.B., 1960). Phi Delta Phi. *Member:* Connecticut and American Bar Associations; American Counsel Association. ***PRACTICE AREAS:*** Real Estate Law; Corporate Law; Banking Law; Commercial Lending. ***Email:*** peterson@gplaw.com

CURTIS V. TITUS, born New Haven, Connecticut, January 4, 1933; admitted to bar, 1957, Connecticut; 1958, U.S. District Court, District of Connecticut; 1966, U.S. Court of Appeals, Second Circuit; 1980, U.S. Supreme Court. *Education:* The Gunnery School; Williams College (A.B., 1954); Harvard University (LL.B., 1957). *Member:* Connecticut (Member, Executive Committee, Business Law Section, 1979—) and American Bar Associations. ***PRACTICE AREAS:*** Corporate Law; Land Use Law; Health Care Law. ***Email:*** titus@gplaw.com

WILLIAM C. CRUTCHER, born Richmond, Kentucky, February 26, 1929; admitted to bar, 1958, District of Columbia; 1959, New York, 1986, Connecticut; registered to practice before U.S. Patent and Trademark Office. *Education:* Georgia Institute of Technology (B.M.E., summa cum laude, 1950); Union College (M.I.A., cum laude, 1972); University of Louisville (J.D., 1957). General Electric Co., 1957-1973; Timex Corporation, 1973-1984. *Member:* Connecticut and American Bar Associations; Connecticut Patent Law Association; American Intellectual Property Law Association; International Trademark Association. ***PRACTICE AREAS:*** Patent; Trademarks; Copyrights; Intellectual Property. ***Email:*** crutcher@gplaw.com

THOMAS J. McHALE, born Waterbury, Connecticut, December 11, 1941; admitted to bar, 1967, Connecticut. *Education:* St. Michael's College (B.A., cum laude, 1964); Catholic University of America (J.D., 1967). Research Editor, Catholic University Law Review, 1966-1967. *Member:* Connecticut (Member, Executive Committee, Computer Law Section) and American Bar Associations. (Also at Bethel Office). ***PRACTICE AREAS:*** Banking Law; Computer Law; Labor and Employment Law. ***Email:*** mchale@gplaw.com

FRANK J. SCINTO, born San Juan, Puerto Rico, March 22, 1953; admitted to bar, 1983, Connecticut; 1984, U.S. District Court, District of Connecticut; 1991, U.S. District Court, Eastern District of Michigan; 1992, U.S. Court of Appeals, Second Circuit; 2000, U.S. Supreme Court. *Education:* Georgetown University (B.S., 1975); University of California at Los Angeles (M.B.A., 1980); Boston College (J.D., 1983). Case Editor, Boston College Uniform Commercial Code Reporter-Digest, 1982-1983. *Member:* Connecticut and American Bar Associations. ***LANGUAGES:*** Spanish. ***PRACTICE AREAS:*** Business Law; Intellectual Property; Commercial Litigation; Employment Law. ***Email:*** scinto@gplaw.com

REPRESENTATIVE CLIENTS: First Union National Bank; People's Bank; Webster Bank; Salisbury Bank Bank & Trust Co.; American Bank of Connecticut; Family Home Mortgage; Heitkamp, Inc.; Truelove & McLean, Inc.; Mirage Studios; The Platt Brothers & Co.; Heritage Village Master Assn.; Heritage Development Group; Rafferty-Brown Steel Co., Inc.; Waterbury Hospital; Greater Waterbury Health Network; Photronics, Inc.; Wentworth Laboratories, Inc.; Cadi Company, Inc.; REM Chemicals, Inc.; Shaw's Supermarkets, Inc.; Universal Data Interface Corp.; Omega River Bend Center.

(This Listing Continued)

KERNAN & HENRY

Established in 1990

207 BANK STREET

WATERBURY, CONNECTICUT 06702

Telephone: 203-756-8961

FAX: 203-754-2353

Email: kernanandhenry@email.msn.com

Mailing Address: P.O. Box 2156, Waterbury, Connecticut 06722

Southbury Office: 9 Heritage Road. Telephone: 203-264-5606. Fax: 203-264-4409.

Civil Trial Litigation, Estate Planning and Probate.

MEMBERS OF FIRM

JAMES E. KERNAN, born Waterbury, Connecticut, January 27, 1947; admitted to bar, 1971, Connecticut. *Education:* Boston College (A.B., 1968); George Washington University (J.D., with honors, 1971). *Member:* Waterbury and Connecticut Bar Associations. ***PRACTICE AREAS:*** Civil Litigation. ***Email:*** jkernan@kernanhenry.com

CHARLES W. HENRY, born Waterbury, Connecticut, August 9, 1949; admitted to bar, 1975, Connecticut. *Education:* Lake Forest College (B.A., 1971); Suffolk University (J.D., 1975). *Member:* Waterbury, Connecticut and American Bar Associations. ***PRACTICE AREAS:*** Trust Law; Estate Planning; Estate Administration; Probate. ***Email:*** cwhenry@snet.net

DAVID J. SCULLY, born New Haven, Connecticut, January 27, 1959; admitted to bar, 1985, Connecticut. *Education:* University of Connecticut (B.A., magna cum laude, 1981); American University (J.D., 1985). Phi Beta Kappa; Phi Kappa Phi; Phi Alpha Theta; Omicron Delta Epsilon. *Member:* New Haven County, Waterbury, Connecticut and American Bar Associations. ***PRACTICE AREAS:*** Civil Litigation. ***Email:*** dscully@kernanhenry.com

JOHN K. McDONALD, born Waterbury, Connecticut, June 1, 1960; admitted to bar, 1987, New Hampshire; 1991, Connecticut. *Education:* Hobart College (B.A., 1983); Case Western Reserve University (J.D., 1987). Delta Theta Phi. *Member:* Waterbury, Connecticut and New Hampshire Bar Associations. ***PRACTICE AREAS:*** Civil Litigation. ***Email:*** jmcdonald@kernanhenry.com

WENDY R. FEDERER, born Boston, Massachusetts, July 26, 1955; admitted to bar, 1992, Connecticut. *Education:* George Washington University (B.A., 1978); University of Bridgeport (J.D., 1991). *Member:* Waterbury, Connecticut and American (Member, Sections on: Estates and Probate; Real Estate) Bar Associations. ***PRACTICE AREAS:*** Trust Law; Estate Planning; Estate Administration; Probate. ***Email:*** wfederer@snet.net

ASSOCIATES

GIOVANNA TROCCHI GIARDINA, born Waterbury, Connecticut, June 24, 1969; admitted to bar, 1997, Connecticut. *Education:* University of Connecticut (B.A., 1991); Quinnipiac College (J.D., 1997). *Member:* Waterbury and Connecticut Bar Associations. ***LANGUAGES:*** Italian. ***PRACTICE AREAS:*** Civil Litigation. ***Email:*** gtgiardina@kernanhenry.com

MICHAEL A. GIARDINA, born Clifton, New Jersey, August 5, 1971; admitted to bar, 1997, Connecticut; 1998, New York. *Education:* Montclair State University (B.S., 1994); Quinnipiac College (J.D., cum laude, 1997). Phi Delta Phi. Founding Member, Quinnipiac Health Law Journal. (Resident, Southbury Office). ***PRACTICE AREAS:*** Trust Planning; Estate Planning; Administrative Law. ***Email:*** mgiardina@snet.net

JOHN P. CALABRESE, born Waterbury, Connecticut, September 22, 1965; admitted to bar, 1992, Connecticut; 1993, U.S. District Court, District of Connecticut. *Education:* University of Hartford (B.S.B.A., magna cum laude, Regents Honor, 1987); Syracuse University (J.D., cum laude, 1992). Senior Editor, Legislative Research Bureau, Syracuse University College of Law, 1991-1992. *Member:* Waterbury and Connecticut (Member, Executive Committee, Young Lawyers Section) Bar Associations. ***LANGUAGES:*** Italian. ***PRACTICE AREAS:*** Civil Litigation; General Practice; Real Estate. ***Email:*** jcalabrese@kernanhenry.com

JONATHAN KOCIENDA, born Hartford, Connecticut, April 21, 1972; admitted to bar, 1997, Connecticut; 1998, Massachusetts; 1999, U.S. Court of Appeals, Second Circuit. *Education:* College of the Holy Cross (B.A., 1994); University of Connecticut Law School (J.D., 1997). Recipient, Michie Company Book Award for Excellence. ***PRACTICE AREAS:*** Litigation; General Practice. ***Email:*** jkocienda@kernanhenry.com

(This Listing Continued)

OF COUNSEL

DONALD W. HENRY, born New York City, February 1, 1917; admitted to bar, 1946, Connecticut. *Education:* Yale University (A.B., 1939; LL.B., 1942). *Member:* Connecticut and American Bar Associations. **Email:** dwhenry@snet.net

REPRESENTATIVE CLIENTS: The Hartford; Liberty Mutual Insurance Co.; Connecticut Life & Casualty Insurance Co.; Shelby Insurance Companies; Great American Insurance Companies; Anthem Insurance Company; National Transportation Adjusters, Inc.; Prudential Insurance Company.

McCORMICK, PAULDING & HUBER, LLP

WATERBURY, CONNECTICUT

(See Hartford)

Patent, Trademark, Copyright, Unfair Competition, Franchise, Computer and Related Intellectual Property Law including Litigation in all Courts.

PHILIP H. MONAGAN

61 HOLMES AVENUE
P.O. BOX 1817
WATERBURY, CONNECTICUT 06722
Telephone: 203-754-7893
Fax: 203-754-3806
Email: monaganlaw@aol.com
URL: http://www.lawyers.com/phmonagan

Personal Injury, Commercial Litigation, Family Law, Collection Law, Real Estate, Probate, Elder Law.

PHILIP H. MONAGAN, born Waterbury, Connecticut, September 17, 1959; admitted to bar, 1985, Massachusetts; 1986, Connecticut; 1988, U.S. District Court, District of Connecticut; 1992, U.S. Supreme Court; 1993, U.S. District Court, District of Massachusetts. *Education:* University of Connecticut (B.S., 1981); University of Miami (J.D., 1985). *Member:* Waterbury, Connecticut (Member, Sections on: Elder Law; Probate and Estate Law) and American Bar Associations; The Association of Trial Lawyers of America; Connecticut Trial Lawyers Association; Connecticut Creditors Rights Attorneys Association. ***PRACTICE AREAS:*** Personal Injury; Real Estate Settlements; Probate Administration; Elder Law; Commercial Litigation; Commercial Collections; Garnishments; Post Judgment Collections; Professional Collections; Retail Collections; Secured Collections.

ANDREW J. PIANKA

86 BUCKINGHAM STREET
WATERBURY, CONNECTICUT 06710
Telephone: 203-575-1131
Fax: 203-754-1675
Email: ajpianka@snet.net
URL: http://www.attorneypianka.com

Personal Injury, Commercial Litigation, Real Estate, Collections, Debtor Creditor, Foreclosure, Landlord/Tenant, Contracts.

ANDREW J. PIANKA, born Suffern, New York, May 18, 1963; admitted to bar, 1996, Connecticut and U.S. District Court, District of Connecticut; 1997, New York; 2000, U.S. Supreme Court. *Education:* Johnson & Wales University (B.A., 1986); Quinnipiac College School of Law (J.D., cum laude, 1995). Author: "The Probate Courts Power to Probe You," The Connecticut Probate Law Journal, Vol. 10, No. 1. *Member:* Waterbury, Connecticut and New York State Bar Associations. ***PRACTICE AREAS:*** Commercial Collections; Bank Collections; Foreclosures; Commercial Litigation; Contracts; Insurance; Landlord and Tenant Law; Litigation; Municipal Taxation; Personal Injury; Automobile Accidents and Injuries; Slip and Fall; Wrongful Death; Real Estate; Workers Compensation; Family Law.

JOHN P. SANTUCCI, P.C.

Established in 1982
35 FIELD STREET
P.O. BOX 2331
WATERBURY, CONNECTICUT 06722-2331
Telephone: 203-574-5059; 574-5008
Facsimile: 203-574-3225
Email: John.P.Santucci.pc@snet.net

General Practice including Alternative Dispute Resolution, Civil Trial Practice including Family Practice, Divorce, Juvenile Neglect, Juvenile Delinquency, Landlord-Tenant, Foreclosure, Real Estate Management Issues, Arbitration, Commercial Real Estate, Insurance, Torts and General Criminal Practice.

(This Listing Continued)

JOHN P. SANTUCCI, born Waterbury, Connecticut, July 24, 1949; admitted to bar, 1974, Connecticut; 1975, U.S. District Court, District of Connecticut and U.S. Court of Appeals, Second Circuit. *Education:* Georgetown University (B.S.F.S., magna cum laude, 1971; J.D., 1974). Phi Beta Kappa; Phi Eta Sigma; Phi Alpha Theta; Pi Sigma Alpha. Appointed Chairman, Charter Revision Commission, 1977. Appointed State Trial Referee Hearing Non-Jury Civil Trial Cases, 1988. Appointed Fact Finder-Arbitrator, Connecticut Superior Court, 1992—. *Member:* Waterbury and Connecticut (Chairman, Continuing Legal Education Committee for New Haven, 1975 and Administration of Civil Justice Committee, 1976, Young Lawyers Section; Member, Committee for Professional Responsibility, 1992-1996) Bar Associations; Connecticut Trial Lawyers Association. [With U.S. Army, 1971-1977; U.S. Army Reserve]. ***PRACTICE AREAS:*** Real Estate; Torts; Civil Practice; Family Law; Criminal Law. ***Email:*** john.p.santucci.pc@snet.net

SECOR, CASSIDY & McPARTLAND, P.C.

Established in 1865

Successors to Bronson, Lewis, Upson & Secor; Lewis, Hart, Upson & Secor; Upson, Secor, Greene & Cassidy and Upson, Secor, Cassidy & McPartland, P.C.

41 CHURCH STREET
P.O. BOX 2818
WATERBURY, CONNECTICUT 06723-2818
Telephone: 203-757-9261
Fax: 203-756-5762
Email: scm@ctlawyers.com
URL: http://www.ctlawyers.com

Southbury, Connecticut Office: 900 Main Street South. Telephone: 203-264-8223. Fax: 203-264-6730.

General Practice. Estate Planning, Probate, Corporation, Negligence, Real Estate, Land Use, Banking, Municipal, Commercial and Taxation Law. Criminal and Civil Trials in all Courts.

FIRM PROFILE: Tracing its history back to the close of the Civil War in 1865, the preeminent firm of Secor, Cassidy & McPartland, P.C., with a satellite office in Southbury, offers clients a comprehensive General Practice which includes Civil and Criminal Trials in State and Federal Courts. In addition to Medical Malpractice, Personal Injury and Workers Compensation matters, the firm concentrates on Estate Planning and Administration; Corporation, Banking, Taxation and Business Law; Real Estate, Foreclosures, Municipal Law and Land Use. Attorneys Associated with the firm are active members of State and National Lawyers and Trial Lawyers Associations and the Connecticut Association of Municipal Attorneys.

NATH'L R. BRONSON (1860-1949).

LAWRENCE L. LEWIS (1881-1965).

CHARLES E. HART (1884-1972).

J. WARREN UPSON (1903-1992).

JOHN H. CASSIDY, JR., born Waterbury, Connecticut, April 26, 1924; admitted to bar, 1951, Connecticut. *Education:* Taft School (cum laude, 1941); Georgetown University (A.B., cum laude, 1948); Columbia University (LL.B., 1951). Attorney State Trial Referee, State Bar Examining Committee, 1964-1988. *Member:* Waterbury, Litchfield County and Connecticut Bar Associations. ***PRACTICE AREAS:*** Civil Litigation; Probate; Corporate Law; Real Estate. ***Email:*** jhc@ctlawyers.com

DONALD McPARTLAND, born New Haven, Connecticut, January 3, 1938; admitted to bar, 1962, Connecticut. *Education:* Yale University (B.A., 1959); Yale Law School (LL.B., 1962). Attorney State Trial Referee, 1986—. *Member:* Waterbury and Connecticut Bar Associations. ***PRACTICE AREAS:*** Civil Litigation; Medical Malpractice; Corporate Law; Real Estate. ***Email:*** mcp@ctlawyers.com

W. FIELDING SECOR, born Waterbury, Connecticut, September 8, 1942; admitted to bar, 1967, Connecticut. *Education:* Hotchkiss School; Yale University (B.A., 1964); Cornell University (LL.B., 1967). *Member:* Waterbury and Connecticut Bar Associations. [CAPT., JAGC, USNR]. ***PRACTICE AREAS:*** Commercial Law; Banking Law; Real Estate. ***Email:*** wfs@ctlawyers.com

JAMES R. HEALEY, born Waterbury, Connecticut, December 11, 1929; admitted to bar, 1955, Connecticut. *Education:* Northwestern University (B.S., 1952); Cornell University (J.D., 1955). Public Defender, Superior Court of Waterbury, 1965-1969. *Member:* Waterbury (President, 1983), Connecticut and American Bar Associations. [Law Specialist, USNR, 1956-1959]. (Resident, Southbury Office). ***PRACTICE AREAS:*** Real Estate; Estate Planning; Estate Administration. ***Email:*** jrh@ctlawyers.com

GAIL E. McTAGGART, born Fresno, California, March 5, 1944; admitted to bar, 1981, Connecticut and U.S. District Court, District of Connecticut. *Education:* California State University at Fresno (B.A., cum laude, 1966); University of Connecticut (J.D., 1981). Member, Connecticut Bar Examining

(This Listing Continued)

SECOR, CASSIDY & McPARTLAND, P.C., Waterbury—Continued

Committee. *Member:* Waterbury, Connecticut (Member, Sections on: Planning and Zoning; Commercial Law; Environmental Law) and American Bar Associations; Connecticut Association of Municipal Attorneys (Member, Board of Directors). ***PRACTICE AREAS:*** Commercial Law; Real Estate; Municipal Law; Land Use; Banking. ***Email:*** gem@ctlawyers.com

THOMAS G. PARISOT, born Waterbury, Connecticut, March 14, 1956; admitted to bar, 1981, Connecticut; 1982, U.S. District Court, District of Connecticut; 1992, U.S. Supreme Court; 1993, U.S. Court of Appeals, Second Circuit; U.S. Tax Court. *Education:* University of Scranton (B.S., cum laude, 1978); Western New England College (J.D., 1981). Assistant Corporation Counsel, City of Waterbury, 1981-1984. State Attorney Trial Referee, 1999—. *Member:* Waterbury, Connecticut and American Bar Associations; Defense Research Institute; Connecticut Trial Lawyers Association. ***PRACTICE AREAS:*** Civil Litigation; Workers Compensation. ***Email:*** tgp@ctlawyers.com

PATRICK W. FINN, born Albany, New York, July 16, 1963; admitted to bar, 1989, Connecticut. *Education:* Trinity College (B.A., 1985); Western New England College (J.D., magna cum laude, 1989). Recipient: American Jurisprudence Awards: Criminal Procedure; Legal Professions; Commercial Paper; Abraham Kamberg Award. *Member:* Litchfield, Connecticut and American Bar Associations; Connecticut Trial Lawyers Association. ***PRACTICE AREAS:*** Civil Litigation; Foreclosures; Commercial Litigation. ***Email:*** pwf@ctlawyers.com

DAVID J. BOZZUTO, born Waterbury, Connecticut, January 14, 1948; admitted to bar, 1981, Connecticut. *Education:* Hobart College (B.A., 1969); Southern Connecticut State College (M.S., 1976); Western New England College (J.D., 1981). *Member:* Waterbury (President, 1995), Connecticut and American Bar Associations; Connecticut Trial Lawyers Association. ***PRACTICE AREAS:*** Civil Litigation; Criminal Law; Personal Injury; Workers Compensation; Divorce; Family Law; Real Estate; Probate; Bankruptcy. ***Email:*** djb@ctlawyers.com

---

DONALD C. McPARTLAND, born Cheshire, Connecticut, January 15, 1969; admitted to bar, 1997, Rhode Island; 1998, Connecticut. *Education:* Emerson College (B.A., 1994); Thomas M. Cooley Law School (J.D., cum laude, 1997). Recipient: American Jurisprudence Awards for Advocacy, Trial Workshop and Law Management. *Member:* Connecticut, Rhode Island and American Bar Association. ***PRACTICE AREAS:*** Personal Injury; Insurance Defense; Criminal Law; Land Use. ***Email:*** dcm@ctlawyers.com

SPECIAL TAX COUNSEL

JOHN J. PALMERI, born Brooklyn, New York, 1957; admitted to bar, 1984, Connecticut and New York. *Education:* Brooklyn College of the City University of New York (B.S. in accounting, 1979); Brooklyn Law School (J.D., 1984); Quinnipiac College Graduate School of Law (LL.M. in Taxation, 1987). Certified Public Accountant: New York, 1984; Connecticut, 1984. *Member:* Connecticut (Member, Tax Section) and American (Member, Tax Section) Bar Associations; American Institute of Certified Public Accountants (Member, Tax Section); Connecticut Society of Certified Public Accountants; Connecticut Society Public Accountants' Trust (Member, Board of Governors; Chair, Federal Tax Division Steering Committee; Member, Estate and Gift Taxation Committee). ***PRACTICE AREAS:*** Estate Planning; Estate Administration; Commercial Transactions; Business Planning. ***Email:*** jjp@ctlawyers.com

COUNSEL

WILLIAM J. SECOR, JR., born Waterbury, Connecticut, June 22, 1914; admitted to bar, 1939, Connecticut. *Education:* Crosby High School; Yale College (A.B., 1936); Yale Law School (LL.B., 1939). Member, Thomas Swan Barrister's Union. Special Agent, Federal Bureau of Investigation, 1943-1946.

ATTORNEYS FOR: The Mattatuck Museum; American Republican, Inc.; Hubbard-Hall, Inc.; The Siemon Co.; Engineered Sinterings and Plastics, Inc.; Boutin Industries; County Line Buick-Nissan, Inc.; County Line BMW, Inc.; Ceco Buildings Division; Hamilton Development Corp.; Jamieson Manufacturing Company; Thomaston Savings Bank; American Bank of Connecticut; People's Bank; Chase Manhattan Bank of Connecticut, N.A.; The Taubman Cos.; Federal Deposit Insurance Corp.; The Taft School; Town of Middlebury; Town of Roxbury; Town of New Fairfield; Watertown Fire District; The CNA Insurance Cos.; National Grange Mutual Insurance Co.; Connecticut Interlocal Risk Management Agency; General Heat Treatment Co.; Lighting Services, Inc.

MERYL A. SPAT

182 GRAND STREET
WATERBURY, CONNECTICUT 06722-2476
Telephone: 203-754-0732
Fax: 203-754-2404
Email: maspat1@yahoo.com
URL: http://www.lawyers.com/maspat

Social Security, Workers Compensation, Family Law, Bankruptcy, Consumer Protection.

MERYL A. SPAT, born Stamford, Connecticut, April 10, 1963; admitted to bar, 1989, Connecticut, U.S. District Court, District of Connecticut and U.S. Court of Appeals, Second Circuit. *Education:* Grinnell College (B.A., 1984); University of Connecticut School of Law (J.D., 1989). Member, Board of Directors, Visiting Nurse Association, 1999-2000. *Member:* Connecticut Bar Association (Secretary, Consumer Law Section, 1999—); National Organization of Social Security Claimants Representatives. [U.S.N.R., 2000—]. ***PRACTICE AREAS:*** Social Security; Workers Compensation; Family Law; Bankruptcy; Consumer Law; Real Estate.

SUMMA & RYAN, P.C.

Established in 1988

19-21 HOLMES AVENUE
WATERBURY, CONNECTICUT 06710
Telephone: 203-755-0390
Fax: 203-756-8746
URL: http://www.lawyers.com/summa&ryanpc

Management, Labor and Employment Law, Labor Relation, Equal Employment Opportunity.

FIRM PROFILE: Summa & Ryan P.C. was founded in 1988. The focus of the firm's practice is the representation of management in labor and employment law. The firm represents both public and private sector clients in federal and state court and before federal, state, and local administrative agencies. In addition, the firm emphasizes preventive aspects of labor and employment law by providing advice to clients on laws and regulation affecting the employer/employee relationship.

JOSEPH B. SUMMA, born Waterbury, Connecticut, October 11, 1949; admitted to bar, 1978, Connecticut; 1979, U.S. District Court, District of Connecticut; 1980, U.S. Court of Appeals, Second Circuit. *Education:* Wesleyan University (B.A., 1971); Cornell University, School of Industrial and Labor Relations (M.S., with high honors, 1975); University of Connecticut (J.D., with honors, 1978). Author: "Criteria for Safety and Health Arbitration," Labor Law Journal, June, 1975. Managing Editor, Labor and Employment Law Briefs, 1982-1988. *Member:* Connecticut (Member, Labor and Employment Law Section) and American (Member, Sections on: Labor and Employment Law; Litigation) Bar Associations. ***PRACTICE AREAS:*** Labor and Employment Law. ***Email:*** jbs@summaryan.com

MARY JANE RYAN, born Brooklyn, New York, August 15, 1945; admitted to bar, 1978, Connecticut; 1980, U.S. District Court, District of Connecticut. *Education:* St. Joseph's College for Women (B.A., 1967); University of Connecticut (J.D., with honors, 1978). *Member:* Connecticut (Member, Labor and Employment Law Section) and American (Member, Labor and Employment Law Section) Bar Associations. ***PRACTICE AREAS:*** Labor and Employment Law. ***Email:*** mjane@summaryan.com

---

WILLIAM A. RYAN, born New Haven, Connecticut, November 11, 1965; admitted to bar, 1992, Connecticut. *Education:* Williams College (B.A., 1988); Hofstra University School of Law (J.D., 1992). Recipient, Labor Law Award, Hofstra University. *Member:* Connecticut (Member, Labor and Employment Law Section) and American (Member, Labor and Employment Law Section) Bar Associations. ***PRACTICE AREAS:*** Labor and Employment Law. ***Email:*** war@summaryan.com

REPRESENTATIVE CLIENTS: Alco Standard; Anamet, Inc.; American Cancer Society; Apple Health Care; Atlantic Foods, Ltd.; BKM Total Office; Barnes Group; Bernie's Audio Video; Continental Plastic Containers, Inc.; Data Documents, Inc.; Envirotest Systems Corp.; Hubbard Hall Inc.; Manufacturing Alliance of Connecticut (MAC); Monarch Brass & Copper Corp.; Moore Medical Corp.; New Haven Copper Co.; North American Bank; Pepsi-Cola Bottling Co.; Pitney Bowes; Rice Packaging; Risdon Corp.; Rostra Vernatherm, Inc.; Teikyo Post University; Teledyne Adams; Theis Precision Steel; Timex Corp.; State of Connecticut; United Community Services; Waltec American Forging; Waterbury Rolling Mills; Wilshire Corp.; Boards of Education and/or towns in: Avon, Branford, Canton, East Haven, Naugatuck, New Milford, Orange, Simsbury, West Haven and Watertown.

TINLEY, NASTRI, RENEHAN & DOST, LLP

Established in 1990

60 NORTH MAIN STREET, 2ND FLOOR

WATERBURY, CONNECTICUT 06702

Telephone: 203-596-9030
Fax: 203-596-9036
URL: http://www.tnrdlaw.com
Email: thrdlaw@cs.com
URL: http://www.lawyers.com/tnrd-attys

Trial Practice in State and Federal Courts. Commercial Litigation, Bankruptcy, Employment Law, Personal Injury, Workers Compensation, Collections, Elder Law, Estate Planning, Probate.

JEFFREY J. TINLEY, born East Northport, New York, July 4, 1955; admitted to bar, 1980, Connecticut and U.S. District Court, District of Connecticut; 1982, New York; 1983, Florida and U.S. Court of Appeals, Eleventh Circuit; 1986, U.S. Court of Appeals, Second Circuit and U.S. District Court, Middle District of Florida. *Education:* State University of New York at Stony Brook (B.A., 1977); St. John's University (J.D., with honors, 1980). Assistant U.S. Attorney, Middle District of Florida, 1983-1986. *Member:* Connecticut (Editor, Federal Practice Section Newsletter, 1998-2000) and American Bar Associations; The Florida Bar. ***PRACTICE AREAS:*** Commercial Litigation. ***Email:*** tnrd@tnrdlaw.com

ROBERT NASTRI, JR., born Waterbury, Connecticut, May 15, 1955; admitted to bar, 1985, Connecticut; 1986, U.S. District Court, District of Connecticut; 1989, U.S. District Court, Southern and Eastern Districts of New York; 1992, U.S. Supreme Court. *Education:* Wesleyan University (B.A., 1977); University of Connecticut (J.D., with honors, 1985). Statewide Legal Services of Connecticut, Inc. (Director). *Member:* Connecticut (Member, House of Delegates, 1987— and Board of Governors, 1995—) and American Bar Associations; Connecticut Trial Lawyers Association; National Employment Lawyers Association; National Association of College and University Attorneys; Connecticut Association of Municipal Attorneys. (Certified as a Civil Trial Advocate by the National Board of Trial Advocacy). ***PRACTICE AREAS:*** Personal Injury; Employment Litigation; Probate Litigation.

RICHARD P. RENEHAN, born New London, Connecticut, April 16, 1960; admitted to bar, 1985, Connecticut and U.S. District Court, District of Connecticut; 1989, U.S. District Court, Southern and Eastern Districts of New York. *Education:* College of the Holy Cross (B.A., magna cum laude, 1982) Phi Beta Kappa; University of Connecticut (J.D., 1985). Author: "Voir Dire in Connecticut," CLTA Forum, April, 1986. Arbitrator: Dispute Resolution, Inc.; National Arbitration and Mediation, Inc. *Member:* Connecticut Bar Association; The Association of Trial Lawyers of America; Connecticut Trial Lawyers Association. ***LANGUAGES:*** Spanish. ***PRACTICE AREAS:*** Personal Injury; Workers Compensation. ***Email:*** tnrd@tnrdlaw.com

MARK W. DOST, born Attleboro, Massachusetts, May 22, 1955; admitted to bar, 1981, Connecticut; 1985, U.S. Tax Court; 1986, U.S. District Court, District of Connecticut. *Education:* University of Massachusetts (A.B., summa cum laude, 1978); Boston College (J.D., cum laude, 1981). Member, Boston College Law Review, 1979-1980. Co-Author: "Estate Planning with Retirement Benefit Distributions," with J. Galiette, published by Little, Brown & Co., 1995, Aspen Law & Business, 1999. *Member:* Connecticut (Member, Executive Committee, Estates and Probate Section, 1991—; Member, Executive Committee, 1991— and Chairman, Elder Law Section, 1994-1996; Chairman, Publications Committee, 1997-2000) and American Bar Associations. Fellow, American College of Trust and Estate Counsel. ***PRACTICE AREAS:*** Estate Planning; Probate; Taxation; Elder Law. ***Email:*** mdosti@tnrdlaw.com

ASSOCIATES

MARILYN N. TOLAND, born Tuskegee, Alabama, October 12, 1955; admitted to bar, 1992, Connecticut; 1994, U.S. District Court, District of Connecticut. *Education:* Fisk University (B.A., summa cum laude, 1976); Yale University Law School (J.D., 1990). *Member:* Connecticut (Member: Executive Committee, Estates and Probate Section, 1997—) and American Bar Associations. ***PRACTICE AREAS:*** Elder Law; Medicaid Planning; Estate Administration. ***Email:*** mtoland@tnrdlaw.com

STEPHEN E. PLIAKAS, born Providence, Rhode Island, December 13, 1959; admitted to bar, 1996, New York, Massachusetts and Connecticut. *Education:* Providence College (B.A., summa cum laude, 1992); University of Connecticut (J.D., 1995). *Member:* Connecticut Bar Association. ***Email:*** tnrd@tnrdlaw.com

MARGARET M. DOHERTY, born Washington, D.C., January 23, 1960; admitted to bar, 1999, Connecticut. *Education:* California State University (B.A., 1987); Southwestern University, School of Law (J.D., 1997); San Francisco Law School (M.A., 1993). *Member:* Connecticut (Member, Litigation Section) and American Bar Associations. ***PRACTICE AREAS:*** Personal Injury; Commercial Litigation. ***Email:*** tnrd@tnrdlaw.com

(This Listing Continued)

REPRESENTATIVE CLIENTS: Gar-San Corp.; General Electric Capital Commercial Automotive Finance, Inc.; Mobil Oil Corp.; Teikyo Post University; The May Department Stores Company; Watertown Construction Company, Inc.; Town of Seymour; e-one hundred Group; West Chevrolet; Sodamate; Ledgebrook, LLC.

D'AMICO, GRIFFIN & PETTINICCHI, L.L.C.

Established in 1990

465 STRAITS TURNPIKE
P.O. BOX 670

WATERTOWN, CONNECTICUT 06798

Telephone: 860-945-6600
Fax: 860-945-6668
URL: http://www.dgplaw.com

Personal Injury, Medical Malpractice, Products liability, Family Law & Divorce Mediation.

FIRM PROFILE: Since 1990, the highly rated firm of D'Amico, Griffin & Pettinicchi LLC has offered clients throughout Connecticut a trial practice in state court and federal court concentrating in the fields of Personal Injury and Family Law. The firm also handles Family Law, Divorce Mediation and Workers Compensation matters.

MICHAEL A. D'AMICO, born Dallas, Texas, February 24, 1962; admitted to bar, 1986, Connecticut; U.S. Court of Appeals, Second Circuit; U.S. Supreme Court. *Education:* University of Connecticut (B.A., with honors, 1983); Quinnipiac College School of Law (J.D., 1986). Board of Examiners for the National Board of Trial Advocacy. Connecticut Academy of Certified Trial Lawyers. Court Appointed Arbitrator/Fact-Finder in Civil Litigation and Special Settlement Master for Personal Injury Claims. Member, Million-Dollar Advocates Forum. *Member:* Connecticut Trial Lawyers Association (Legislative and Public Relation Committees); The Association of Trial Lawyers of America. (Board Certified Civil Trial Specialist by the National Board of Advocacy). ***PRACTICE AREAS:*** Personal Injury; Medical Negligence; Products Liability; Workers Compensation. ***Email:*** m.damico@dgplaw.com

MARK F. GRIFFIN, born Torrington, Connecticut, September 5, 1958; admitted to bar, 1985, Connecticut, U.S. District Court, District of Connecticut; 1986, New York. *Education:* Providence College (B.S., with honors, Accounting, 1980); Albany Law School of Union College (J.D., 1985). *Member:* Connecticut and New York Bar Associations; Connecticut Trial Lawyers Association. ***PRACTICE AREAS:*** Personal Injury; Workers Compensation. ***Email:*** m.griffin@dgplaw.com

THOMAS P. PETTINICCHI, born Waterbury, Connecticut, November 13, 1961; admitted to bar, 1986, Connecticut, U.S. District Court, District of Connecticut. *Education:* Providence College (B.A., 1983); Western New England College (J.D., 1986). Member, Connecticut Council of Divorce Mediation; The Academy of Family Mediators. Family Special Master in the Alternative Dispute Resolution Program for Family Matters in State of Connecticut Superior Court. *Member:* Connecticut (Member, Family Law Section) Bar Association; Connecticut Trial Lawyers Association (Member, Executive Committee, Family Law Section). ***PRACTICE AREAS:*** Matrimonial Law; Divorce Mediation; Personal Injury. ***Email:*** t.pettinicchi@dgplaw.com

JONATHAN HOYT

WESTBROOK, CONNECTICUT

(See Clinton)

Real Estate both Residential and Commercial, Probate, Estate Planning, Business and Corporate Law, Commercial Transactions.

ATLAS & HUDON, LLP

95 SOUTH MAIN STREET
P.O. BOX 270670

WEST HARTFORD, CONNECTICUT 06127-0670

Telephone: 860-521-7800
Telecopier: 860-521-4783
URL: http://www.atlashudon.com

General Practice. Commercial, Banking, Corporate, Real Estate, Trust, Probate, Estate and Business Planning Law, Arbitration, Litigation.

NEIL E. ATLAS, born New Rochelle, New York, March 5, 1944; admitted to bar, 1971, Connecticut and U.S. District Court, District of Connecticut; 1972, U.S. Court of Appeals, Second Circuit; 1974, U.S. Supreme Court. *Education:* Syracuse University (B.S., 1966); University of Connecticut (J.D., 1971). ***PRACTICE AREAS:*** Commercial Law; Business Law; Real Estate.

PAUL A. HUDON, born Hartford, Connecticut, June 29, 1945; admitted to bar, 1970, Connecticut; 1971, U.S. District Court, District of Connecticut. *Edu-*

(This Listing Continued)

ATLAS & HUDON, LLP, West Hartford—Continued

cation: University of Rochester (B.A., 1967); University of Connecticut (J.D., 1970). Advisor, State of Connecticut Law Revision Commission, Probate Revision Committee, 1984—. ***PRACTICE AREAS:*** Trusts and Estates; Probate; Estate Planning; Business Planning.

WILLIAM C. DORAN, born New York, N.Y., February 26, 1945; admitted to bar, 1972, Connecticut; 1973, U.S. District Court, District of Connecticut. *Education:* Dartmouth College (A.B., 1967); Yale University (J.D., 1972). ***PRACTICE AREAS:*** Estate Planning; Business Planning; Trusts and Estates; Probate.

BEIZER & WEINTRAUB

345 NORTH MAIN STREET
WEST HARTFORD, CONNECTICUT 06117
Telephone: 860-236-5491
Fax: 860-236-5494
Email: beizerweintraub@mindspring.com
URL: http://www.lawyers.com/beizerweintraub

General Civil and Criminal Practice before State and Federal Courts. Personal Injury, Professional Malpractice, Workers Compensation, Employer/Employee Relations, Probate, Estate Planning, Real Estate, Business Entities, Commercial Loans, Domestic Relations, Foreclosures/Collections, Trials and Appeals.

MEMBERS OF FIRM

DAVID B. BEIZER, born Hartford, Connecticut, May 24, 1938; admitted to bar, 1964, Connecticut; 1965, U.S. District Court, District of Connecticut; 1967, U.S. Court of Appeals, Second Circuit. *Education:* Harvard University (A.B., magna cum laude, 1960); Columbia University (LL.B., 1963). Russell Sage Research Fellow in Law and Sociology, Columbia University, 1963-1964. Lecturer in Law, Brief Writing, University of Connecticut School of Law, 1970-1975. Attorney, Federal Communication Commission, 1964-1965. Assistant Attorney General, State of Connecticut, 1965-1971. Executive Director, Connecticut Action Now, 1971-1972. Executive Secretary and House Counsel, Connecticut Bankers Association, 1972-1978. Member, Board of Education, Town of Avon, 1975-1985. Member, Zoning Board of Appeals, Town of Avon, 1994—. *Member:* Hartford County and Connecticut Bar Associations. ***PRACTICE AREAS:*** Civil Litigation; Personal Injury and Torts; Workers Compensation; Employment Law; Wrongful Termination. ***Email:*** dbbeizer@mindspring.com

JAY B. WEINTRAUB, born Hartford, Connecticut, November 18, 1946; admitted to bar, 1971, Connecticut; 1975, U.S. District Court, District of Connecticut and U.S. Court of Appeals, Second Circuit. *Education:* University of Vermont (B.A., 1968); Georgetown University Law Center (J.D., 1971). Special Counsel, Town of Granby, 1978-1984. Commissioner, Canton Zoning Commission, 1988—. Director, Vice President and Counsel, Canton Land Trust, 1988—; Trustee, Science Center of Connecticut, 1991-1995; Director, Secretary, Rivers Alliance of Connecticut, 1992—; Special Master, Superior Court Special Masters Program, 1995—. *Member:* Hartford County and Connecticut (Member, Sections on: Real Estate; Business Law; Commercial Law and Bankruptcy; Elder Law) Bar Associations. ***PRACTICE AREAS:*** Real Estate; Business Law; Commercial Law; Bankruptcy; Debtor and Creditor; Probate; Trusts and Estates; Wills and Probate. ***Email:*** jbweintraub@mindspring.com

REPRESENTATIVE CLIENTS: Hudson United Bank; Savings Bank of Manchester; Webster Bank; Fleet Bank; Mitchell Auto Group, Inc.; The Petit Tool Co.; Capitol Cleaning Contractors, Inc.; Pyramid Communications Corporation.

BERMAN, BOURNS, AARON & DEMBO, LLC

970 FARMINGTON AVENUE
WEST HARTFORD, CONNECTICUT 06107
Telephone: 860-232-4471
Fax: 860-523-4605

Family Law, Personal Injury, Litigation, Probate, Estate Planning, Real Estate, Corporate and General Practice.

JOHN A. BERMAN, born Hartford, Connecticut, February 29, 1932; admitted to bar, 1957, Connecticut. *Education:* Wheaton College, Wheaton, Illinois (A.B., 1954); University of Connecticut (J.D., 1957). Author: "Contracts for Unmarrieds," Connecticut Law Tribune, May 4, 1981; "Compensation in Probate," Connecticut Probate Law Journal, Spring, 1986. Co-Author: "Alternate Dispute Resolution in Connecticut Probate Courts," Quinnipiac Probate Law Journal, Volume 11, Number 1, 1997. State Representative, 1977-1981, Connecticut General Assembly (Member, Judiciary Committee, 1976-1981; Ranking Member, 1978-1981). Member, Judge Judicate, Inc. Corporation Counsel, Town of West Hartford, Connecticut, 1981-1983. Probate Judge, District of West Hartford, 1983—. Member, Continuing Education Committee of

(This Listing Continued)

The Connecticut Probate Assembly, 1994—. Member, Panel of Arbitrators, American Arbitration Association. Special Master, Hartford Superior Court Mediation Panelist. President, Watkinson Prisoners Aid Society, 1996—. Director, Connecticut Council for Philanthropy, 1999—. *Member:* Hartford County (Member, Bench-Bar Relations Committee, 1972-1976), Connecticut (Member: Family Law Committee, 1969—; Executive Committee, 1971-1977; 1981-1986; Executive Committee, Estates and Probate Section, 1985-1991) and American (Member, Sections on: Family Law; General Practice) Bar Associations; The Association of Trial Lawyers of America; Connecticut Trial Lawyers Association. Fellow, American Bar Foundation Member, Board of Editors, Quinnipiac Probate Law Journal 1991—, (formerly Connecticut Probate Law Journal). ***PRACTICE AREAS:*** Family Law; Probate Law; General Practice; Mediation. ***Email:*** jberman@bermanbourns.com

COURTNEY B. BOURNS, born Cleveland, Ohio, January 4, 1936; admitted to bar, 1964, Connecticut. *Education:* Tufts University (B.S., 1958); University of Connecticut and Duke University (LL.B., 1964). Editor, Duke Law Journal, 1963-1964. Member: Board of Directors, Child and Family Services of Connecticut, Inc., 1974-1979; Supervisory Council, State Deinstitutionalization of Status Offender Project, 1976-1979; Legal Aid Society of Hartford County, Inc., 1979-1981. Vice Chairman, State Legislature's Human Services Reorganization Commission, 1977-1979. Chairman, Connecticut Task Force for Foster Children, 1979-1981. Special Master, Hartford Superior Court Family Mediation Panel. *Member:* Hartford County, Connecticut (Member, Family Law Section) and American (Member, Family Law Section) Bar Associations; Academy of Family Mediators. ***PRACTICE AREAS:*** Family Law; Mediation. ***Email:*** cbourns@bermanbourns.com

BARBARA D. AARON, born West Hartford, Connecticut, April 10, 1957; admitted to bar, 1984, Connecticut and New York. *Education:* American University (B.A., 1979); Brooklyn Law School (J.D., 1984). Moot Court Honor Society. Magistrate and Small Claims Commissioner, 1997—. Board of Directors, YWCA of Greater Hartford, 1996-1998. Co-Founder, Connecticut Council on Divorce Mediation; Family Law Special Master in Hartford, New Britain and Middletown Jurisdictions, 1995—. Instructor and Co-Trainer of Family Mediation workshops and seminars, 1995-1998. *Member:* Hartford County (Former Co-Chair, Family Law Committee, 1996-1998), Connecticut (Member: Family Law Section - Executive Committee, 1998-1999; ADR Section; Committee on Fee Arbitration; Former Chair, Committee on Alternative Dispute Resolution, 1992-1994) and American Bar Associations; Academy of Family Mediators (Practitioner Member); American Association of Conciliation Courts. ***PRACTICE AREAS:*** Family Law; Alternative Dispute Resolution; Mediation. ***Email:*** baaron@bermanbourns.com

STEVEN R. DEMBO, born Queens, New York, March 5, 1965; admitted to bar, 1990, Connecticut. *Education:* State University of New York at Binghamton (B.S., 1987); Western New England College of Law (J.D., 1990). *Member:* Hartford County, Connecticut and American Bar Associations. ***PRACTICE AREAS:*** Litigation; Personal Injury; Family Law; Criminal Law; General Practice. ***Email:*** sdembo@bermanbourns.com

ASSOCIATE

JO-ELLEN ZERESKI, born Worcester, Massachusetts, December 5, 1971; admitted to bar, 1998, Connecticut. *Education:* University of Massachusetts, Amherst (B.A., 1993); University of Connecticut (J.D., 1998). Former, Staff Attorney, West Hartford Probate Court. *Member:* Connecticut Bar Association. ***PRACTICE AREAS:*** Estate Planning; Probate; Real Estate; Corporate Law. ***Email:*** jzereski@bermanbourns.com

OF COUNSEL

JOHN K. CURRIE, born Wyandotte, Michigan, July 23, 1950; admitted to bar, 1977, Connecticut. *Education:* University of Michigan (B.G.S., 1972); State University of New York at Buffalo (J.D., 1975). *Member:* Connecticut Bar Association. ***PRACTICE AREAS:*** Litigation; Real Estate Law; General Practice.

REPRESENTATIVE CLIENTS: Otis Elevator Co.; American Lung Assn., Inc.; Hartford Insurance Group; Presbytery of Southern New England; East Coast Conference; West Hartford Fellowship Housing, Inc.; Junior League of Hartford; Klingberg Family Centers, Inc.
APPROVED ATTORNEYS FOR: Connecticut Attorneys Title Insurance Co.; Fleet Bank; People's Bank; New Haven Savings Bank; Glastonbury Bank & Trust Company; Mechanics Savings Bank; American Savings Bank; Savings Bank of Manchester.
REFERENCES: Fleet Bank, N.A.; New England Bank; Eagle Bank; Farmington Savings Bank.

LAW OFFICE OF MARTHA CROOG, LLC

Established in 1989
740 NORTH MAIN STREET, SUITE N
WEST HARTFORD, CONNECTICUT 06117
Telephone: 860-236-9651
Fax: 860-233-9927
Email: martha.croog@mcroogllc.com
URL: http://www.lawyers.com/crooglaw

Creditor's Foreclosure, Bankruptcy and Eviction, Securities Compliance, related Corporate and Banking Law.

FIRM PROFILE: The firm has three in-house attorneys and four of counsel attorneys from various judicial districts in Connecticut. The firm is devoted to the state-wide representation of creditors in the areas of foreclosure, bankruptcy and evictions; securities compliance and related corporate and banking law.

MARTHA E. CROOG, born Washington, D.C., November 27, 1956; admitted to bar, 1982, New York; 1991, Connecticut; 1992, U.S. District Court, District of Connecticut. *Education:* University of Michigan (B.A., cum laude, 1976); Recipient, Residential College Fellowship; Hofstra Law School (J.D., 1981). Editor, Hofstra Law Review, 1979-1981. Coordinator, National Institute of Trial Advocacy, 1980-1981. Author: "Private Placement Sweeteners for Connecticut Development Stage Issuers," Conn. Bar J., V. 70, No. 6 (Dec. 1996). Formerly associated with: Baer Marks & Upham; Gordon Altman Butowsky, New York, New York. Lecturer, National Business Institute, 1998. Lecturer, Lorman Business Institute, 1999. *Member:* Connecticut Bar Association (Member, Executive Committee, Business Law Section; Treasurer, 1998—; Real Estate Section). ***PRACTICE AREAS:*** Creditors Rights; Foreclosures; Bankruptcy; Corporate Law; Securities Law.

CUMMINGS & LOCKWOOD

Established in 1909
TOWN CENTER
29 SOUTH MAIN STREET
SUITE 205
WEST HARTFORD, CONNECTICUT 06107
Telephone: (860) 275-6700
Telecopier: (860) 313-0293
Email: info@cl-law.com
URL: http://www.cl-law.com

Stamford, Connecticut Office: Four Stamford Plaza, P.O. Box 120, 06904-0120. Telephone: (203) 327-1700. Telecopier: (203) 351-4535.
Greenwich, Connecticut Office: Two Greenwich Plaza, P.O. Box 2505, 06836. Telephone: (203) 869-1200. Telecopier: (203) 869-3120.
Hartford, Connecticut Office: CityPlace I, 185 Asylum Street, 36th Floor, 06103-3495. Telephone: (860) 275-6700. Telecopier: (860) 724-3397.
New Haven, Connecticut Office: 700 State Street, P.O. Box 1960. 06509-1960. Telephone: (203) 782-3000. Telecopier: (203) 777-3347.
Bonita Springs, Florida Office: 24311 Walden Center, Suite 201, 34134. Telephone: (941) 947-8811. Telecopier: (941) 947-8025.
Naples, Florida Office: 3001 Tamiami Trail North, P.O. Box 413032, 34101-3032. Telephone: (941) 262-8311. Telecopier: (941) 263-0703.

General Practice. National and Regional Litigation Counsel, Corporate Law, Patent and Intellectual Property, Trusts and Estates, Labor and Employment, Mergers and Acquisitions, Partnerships and Joint Ventures, Commercial Lending, Corporate Finance, Creditors' Rights, Bankruptcy and Workouts, Securities Regulation and Litigation, Tax, Insurance, Banking and Financial Services, Leasing, Commercial and Residential Real Estate, Construction, Environmental, Toxic Torts, Health Law, Products Liability Litigation, Probate Litigation, Family Law, International Business.

FIRM PROFILE: Cummings & Lockwood caters both to commercial entities and individual clients, serves as local, regional and national counsel in Corporate, Litigation, and Creditors' Rights matters, and has one of the largest groups of Estate Planning professionals in the country.

Cummings & Lockwood attorneys answer questions and solve problems by having specialists in multiple disciplines practice together from eight offices to address the broad concerns of our diverse clientele. The firm guides corporate transactions and resolves complex business disputes for emerging, middle-market and Fortune 500 businesses, including high tech companies, financial services providers and industrial manufacturers. We are also uniquely positioned to assist affluent families and entrepreneurs in designing wealth preserving estate plans and developing business succession strategies.

PARTNERS

GINA S. LINSTONE, born Norwalk, Connecticut, February 19, 1964; admitted to bar, 1990, Connecticut. *Education:* Northwestern University (B.A., 1986); University of Southern California (J.D., 1989). Phi Delta Phi. Chair, Greater Hartford Probate Forum, 1991. *Member:* Hartford (Chair, Membership Committee of Young Lawyers Section, 1991-1992), Connecticut (Chair, Estate and Probate Committee of Young Lawyers Section; Member, Estates and Probate Section) and American (Chair, Greater Hartford Probate Forum, 1991) Bar Associations; Estate and Tax Planning Council. ***LANGUAGES:*** Italian. ***PRACTICE AREAS:*** Estate Law; Tax Planning Law; Estate Settlement Law; Trust Administration Law. ***Email:*** glinstone@cl-law.com

PAUL L. BOURDEAU (Resident, Hartford, Connecticut Office).

SENIOR ATTORNEY

ROBERT B. FAWBER, born Hershey, Pennsylvania, February 7, 1949; admitted to bar, 1975, Connecticut. *Education:* Trinity College (B.A., 1971); Georgetown University (J.D., 1975). Phi Beta Kappa. *Member:* Hartford County, Connecticut (Member: Real Property, Estates and Probate, and Planning and Zoning Law Sections; Common Interest Ownership Manual Revision Committee) and American (Member, Real Property, Probate and Trust Law and Business Law Sections) Bar Associations. ***PRACTICE AREAS:*** Real Estate Law; Estate Planning Law; Probate Practice; Business Law. ***Email:*** rfawber@cl-law.com

RESIDENT ASSOCIATE

Kelley M. Galica Peck

(For complete biographical information on personnel, see Professional Biographies at Stamford, CT, Greenwich, CT, Hartford, CT, New Haven, CT, Bonita Springs, FL and Naples, FL)

FINK & HIGHMARK

8 CROSSROADS PLAZA
P.O. BOX 370038
WEST HARTFORD, CONNECTICUT 06137
Telephone: 860-236-6858
Fax: 860-236-6850
URL: http://www.lawyers.com/finkandhighmark

Civil Trial and Appellate Practice in State and Federal Courts. Insurance, Subrogation, Fidelity and Surety, Products Liability, Environmental, Personal Injury, Business, Commercial, Probate, Estate Planning, Corporation, Real Estate, Construction and Workers Compensation.

MEMBERS OF FIRM

EVERETT F. FINK (1923-1993).

LOUIS A. HIGHMARK, JR., born Indianapolis, Indiana, February 21, 1946; admitted to bar, 1974, Connecticut; 1975, U.S. District Court, District of Connecticut and U.S. Court of Appeals, Second Circuit. *Education:* Dartmouth College (A.B., cum laude, 1968); University of Michigan (J.D., magna cum laude, 1974). Member, West Hartford Community Planning Advisory Committee, 1984-1988. *Member:* Connecticut and American Bar Associations.

REPRESENTATIVE CLIENTS: Royal Insurance Cos.; The Connecticut Light and Power Co.; BankAmerica Mortgage; Fidelity and Deposit Company of Maryland; North American Specialty Insurance Co.; Northeast Utilities; Colonial Spring Co.; Tribune Company.
APPROVED ATTORNEY FOR: Connecticut Attorneys Title Insurance Co.

CEIL SARETTA GERSTEN

10 NORTH MAIN STREET, SUITE 204
WEST HARTFORD, CONNECTICUT 06107
Telephone: 860-231-7455
Fax: 860-231-7461
URL: http://www.lawyers.com/ceilgersten

Family, Divorce, Custody, Child Support, Criminal, DUI, DWI, Misdemeanors, Personal Injury, Automobile Accidents, Slip and Fall, Dog Bites.

CEIL SARETTA GERSTEN, born Brockton, Massachusetts, July 4, 1959; admitted to bar, 1988, Connecticut; 1989, U.S. District Court, District of Connecticut. *Education:* Wheaton College (B.S., 1981); Western New England College (J.D., 1988). *Member:* American Bar Association.

GOODMAN, ROSENTHAL & McKENNA, P.C.

Established in 1977
68 SOUTH MAIN STREET
WEST HARTFORD, CONNECTICUT 06106
Telephone: 860-231-2800
Fax: 860-523-9235
Email: grm@connix.com

Corporation, Real Estate, Pension, Employment, Antitrust, Litigation, Estate Planning.

(This Listing Continued)

GOODMAN, ROSENTHAL & McKENNA, P.C., West Hartford—Continued

EDWARD F. ROSENTHAL, born Hartford, Connecticut, July 29, 1945; admitted to bar, 1970, Connecticut; 1981, U.S. Court of International Trade; 1984, U.S. Tax Court. *Education:* Brown University (B.A., cum laude, 1967); University of Connecticut (J.D., 1970). Corporator, The Hartford Hospital, 1985—. *Member:* Hartford County and Connecticut Bar Associations. ***PRACTICE AREAS:*** Business Law; Employment; Real Estate; ERISA; Business Estate Planning; Probate.

RICHARD GOODMAN, born Hartford, Connecticut, September 24, 1939; admitted to bar, 1964, Connecticut. *Education:* Oberlin College (B.A., cum laude, 1961); Harvard University (LL.B., cum laude, 1964). Law Clerk, U.S. District Court of Connecticut, 1964-1965. Mayor, Bloomfield, Connecticut, 1975-1983. Chairman, Capitol Region Council of Governments, 1978-1979. *Member:* Connecticut Bar Association. ***PRACTICE AREAS:*** Business Law; Real Estate; Estate Planning; Divorce.

JOHN F. McKENNA, born Hartford, Connecticut, October 10, 1938; admitted to bar, 1970, Connecticut. *Education:* College of the Holy Cross (cum laude, 1962); University of Connecticut (J.D., 1970). Lecturer, University of Connecticut: Constitutional Law and Antitrust Law, MBA Program, 1977—; General Counsel, University of Connecticut, 1977-1982. [Lt., U.S. Navy, Aviator, 1962-1967]. ***PRACTICE AREAS:*** Personal Injury; Insurance Defense; Criminal; Employment; Labor Relations; Antitrust; Higher Education.

REBECCA B. LAMONT, born Glens Falls, New York, May 9, 1945; admitted to bar, 1987, Connecticut. *Education:* University of Vermont (A.B., 1968); Western New England College (J.D., cum laude, 1987). *Member:* Connecticut Bar Association. ***PRACTICE AREAS:*** Personal Injury; Divorce; Bankruptcy; Real Estate; Housing; Probate.

LEE B. ROSS, born Hartford, Connecticut, May 15, 1964; admitted to bar, 1996, Connecticut. *Education:* Union College (B.A., 1986); University of Connecticut School of Law (J.D., 1996). *Member:* Greater Hartford and Connecticut Bar Associations. ***PRACTICE AREAS:*** Personal Injury; Business Law; Real Estate; Elder; Regulatory.

HENRY B. HURVITZ

924 FARMINGTON AVENUE, 3RD FLOOR
WEST HARTFORD, CONNECTICUT 06107
Telephone: 860-232-8300
Fax: 860-232-2672
Email: hhurvitz@aol.com
URL: http://www.lawyers.com/hhurvitz

Real Estate, Family Law, Personal Injury, Wills, Probate.

HENRY B. HURVITZ, born Hartford, Connecticut, February 19, 1948; admitted to bar, 1974, Connecticut and U.S. District Court, District of Connecticut; 1975, U.S. Court of Appeals, Second Circuit; 1978, U.S. Supreme Court. *Education:* University of Wisconsin-Madison (B.A., 1970); University of Connecticut (J.D., 1973). Member, West Hartford Chamber of Commerce. *Member:* Hartford County (Member, Family Law Committee) and Connecticut Bar Associations. ***PRACTICE AREAS:*** Personal Injury; Real Estate; Family Law.

REPRESENTATIVE CLIENTS: Peoples Bank; Preferred Investment Associates, Inc.; Continental Funding Corp.; Landtect New England, Inc.; The Investors Center, Inc.
TITLE AGENT FOR: Connecticut Attorney Title Insurance Co.

KEARNS & KEARNS, P.C.

Established in 1985
1121 NEW BRITAIN AVENUE
WEST HARTFORD, CONNECTICUT 06110
Telephone: 860-233-1281
Fax: 860-523-5774
Email: attorney@ctelderlaw.com
URL: http://www.ctelderlaw.com

Elder Law, Estate Planning Administration and Probate.

FIRM PROFILE: John F. Kearns III has practiced elder law for the past 16 years. Mr. Kearns is board-certified by the National Elder Law Foundation (governing board for certification of elder law attorneys under accreditation by the American Bar Association).

JOHN F. KEARNS, JR. (1930-1985).

JOHN F. III KEARNS, born 1957; admitted to bar, 1982, Connecticut, U.S. District Court, District of Connecticut and U.S. Court of Appeals, Second Circuit; 1988, U.S. Supreme Court. *Education:* Fordham University (B.A., cum laude, 1979); Syracuse University (J.D., 1982). Phi Beta Kappa. President, 1997 and Member, Board of Directors, 1989-1997, Northern Connecticut Chapter of the Alzheimer's Association. Member, Board of Directors, 1988-1997, Alzheimer's Coalition of Connecticut, Inc., formerly known as Governor's Task Force on Alzheimer's Disease. Member: Board of Directors, National Academy of Elder Law Attorneys, 1995-2001; Board of Directors, National Elder Law Foundation, 1997— (Chairman, Standards Committee); Board of Advisors, GE Center for Financial Learning@financiallearning.com, 1999—. Certified Elder Law Attorney by National Elder Law Foundation under accreditation by the American Bar Association, 1995. *Member:* Connecticut Bar Association (Member, Executive Committee, Elder Law Section; Member, Estates and Probate Section). ***PRACTICE AREAS:*** Elder Law; Probate; Estate Planning; Estate Planning for Parents of Handicapped Children; Estate Planning for the Disabled; Estate Planning for the Elderly; Trust Administration; Trust Planning. ***Email:*** attorney@ctelderlaw.com

(This Listing Continued)

LISA M. VOZZELLA COURSER, born Hartford, Connecticut; admitted to bar, 1993, Connecticut. *Education:* Fairfield University (B.A., 1985); Western New England College (J.D., 1993). Member, Board of Directors, Alzheimer's Association, Northern Connecticut Chapter, 1997-2001. Member: Executive Committee, Alzheimer's Coalition of Connecticut, Inc.; Greater Hartford Elder Network; Greater Hartford Probate Forum. *Member:* Connecticut Bar Association (Member, Sections on: Elder Law; Estates and Probate); National Academy of Elder Law Attorneys. ***PRACTICE AREAS:*** Elder Law; Probate; Estate Planning; Estate Planning for Parents of Handicapped Children; Estate Planning for the Disabled; Estate Planning for the Elderly; Trust Administration; Trust Planning. ***Email:*** attorney@ctelderlaw.com

PAUL A. KEILY

12 NORTH MAIN STREET
WEST HARTFORD, CONNECTICUT 06107
Telephone: 860-561-9866
Fax: 860-561-9870
Email: pkeily@keilylaw.com
URL: http://www.lawyers.com/keilylaw

Civil Litigation. Commercial Real Estate, Residential Real Estate, Landlord and Tenant Law, Bankruptcy, Probate and Family Law, Divorce, Child Custody, Child Support, Adoptions.

PAUL A. KEILY, born Hartford, Connecticut, October 27, 1955; admitted to bar, 1986, Connecticut and U.S. District Court, District of Connecticut. *Education:* Bryant College (B.S., 1978); Quinnipiac College (J.D., cum laude, 1986). Recipient, Quinnipiac College School of Law Outstanding Legal Scholarship Award. Member, 1985 and Associate Editor, 1986, Law Review. *Member:* Hartford County and Connecticut Bar Associations.

REPRESENTATIVE CLIENTS: Bank America Mortgage; Chase Manhattan Mortgage; CTX Mortgage; Fleet Bank; Wells Fargo Mortgage; Peoples Bank; Webster Bank; RLMCO; Capitol Builders, Inc.; R & R Precision Tool, Inc.; Star Silk & Woolen Co; Hartford Fidelity and Bonding Co.; The Hartford Fire Insurance Co.; Countrywide Home Loans.
AGENT FOR: First American Title Insurance Co.; Connecticut Attorneys Title Insurance Co.; Fidelity National Title Insurance Co. of New York.

KOSLOFF & HARDING

28 NORTH MAIN STREET
WEST HARTFORD, CONNECTICUT 06107
Telephone: 860-521-7004
Fax: 860-521-3352
Email: amkandnjh@aol.com
URL: http://www.lawyers.com/kosloff&harding

Environmental Law.

ALAN M. KOSLOFF, born Waterbury, Connecticut, December 11, 1946; admitted to bar, 1971, Virginia; 1973, Connecticut. *Education:* University of Connecticut (B.A., 1968); George Washington University (J.D., with honors, 1971). Co-Author, Connecticut Environmental Practice. Adjunct Professor, Environmental Law, University of Connecticut Law School. Staff Attorney, Office of Enforcement and General Counsel, United States Environmental Protection Agency, Washington, D.C., 1971-1973. General Counsel, Connecticut Department of Environmental Protection, 1973-1975. Assistant Attorney General, State of Connecticut, 1975-1980. *Member:* Connecticut Bar Association (Chairman, Environmental Protection Committee, Young Lawyers Section, 1974-1976); Virginia State Bar. ***SPECIAL AGENCIES:*** Practice before US EPA, Army Corps of Engineers, Conn. DEP and Siting Council. ***PRACTICE AREAS:*** Environmental Law.

NICHOLAS J. HARDING, born Cleveland, Ohio, January 19, 1947; admitted to bar, 1978, Massachusetts; 1979, Connecticut and U.S. Tax Court;

(This Listing Continued)

1996, U.S. Court of Appeals, Second Circuit; 1997, U.S. Supreme Court. *Education:* Thomas A. Edison College (B.A., 1978); Franklin Pierce Law Center (J.D., 1978); Boston University (LL.M., Taxation, 1979). Author: "A Primer on the Environmental Problems of the Fiduciary and Heir with an Interest in Contaminated Property," The Connecticut Probate Law Journal, Volume 8, No. 1, 1993. Co-Author: "Estate Freezing Techniques for the Small Business Owner," Estate Planning Quarterly, Spring, 1983. Director, Madison Land Conservation Trust, 1983-1990. *Member:* Connecticut (Member, Environmental Law Section Executive Committee) and American (Member, Sections on: Natural Resources, Energy, Environmental, Business and Tax Law) Bar Associations. [Capt., U.S. Army, Infantry, 1966-1975]. ***LANGUAGES:*** Chinese (Mandarin). ***SPECIAL AGENCIES:*** Practice before US EPA, Army Corps of Engineers, Conn. DEP and Siting Council. ***REPORTED CASES:*** Holbrook, Comm'r DEP v. Birken Manufacturing et al 2000 Conn. Supr 2043 (Aug 3, 2000). ***PRACTICE AREAS:*** Environmental Law; Civil Litigation; Tax Litigation. ***Email:*** njharding@aol.com

ASSOCIATE

MARY McQUEENEY, born Hamden, Massachusetts, December 4, 1967; admitted to bar, 1998, Connecticut; 1999, U.S. District Court, District of Connecticut. *Education:* Central Connecticut State University (B.A., 1990); University of Connecticut (J.D., 1998). *Member:* Hartford County and Connecticut (Member, Environmental Section) Bar Associations. ***PRACTICE AREAS:*** Environmental Law; Civil Litigation. ***Email:*** AMKandNJH@aol.com

KREVOLIN, ROTH & CONNORS LLC

433 SOUTH MAIN STREET, SUITE 303
WEST HARTFORD, CONNECTICUT 06110
Telephone: 860-561-7282
Fax: 860-561-7283

Middletown, Connecticut Office: 100 Main Street, Suite 201, 06457. Telephone: 860-343-7260.

General Civil Litigation, Personal Injury, Medical Malpractice, Products Liability, Workers Compensation, Commercial Litigation, Matrimonial and Insurance.

MEMBERS OF FIRM

ANDREW W. KREVOLIN, born Hartford, Connecticut, November 22, 1955; admitted to bar, 1980, Connecticut and U.S. District Court, District of Connecticut. *Education:* Connecticut College (B.A., with honors, 1977); University of Connecticut (J.D., cum laude, 1980). *Member:* Hartford County, Connecticut and American Bar Associations; Connecticut Trial Lawyers Association; The Association of Trial Lawyers of America. ***PRACTICE AREAS:*** Personal Injury; Medical Malpractice; Products Liability; Insurance Coverage. ***Email:*** AndrewKrevolin@msn.com

STUART M. ROTH, born Hartford, Connecticut, June 8, 1945; admitted to bar, 1971, Connecticut. *Education:* University of Connecticut (B.S., 1967; J.D., cum laude, 1971). Editor, University of Connecticut Law Review, 1970-1971. *Member:* Hartford County, Connecticut and American Bar Associations; Connecticut Trial Lawyers Association; The Association of Trial Lawyers of America. ***PRACTICE AREAS:*** Products Liability; Medical Malpractice; Personal Injury; Family Law; Divorce. ***Email:*** StuartRoth_239@msn.com

SUSAN A. CONNORS, born Middletown, Connecticut February 20, 1966; admitted to bar, 1991, Connecticut; 1992, U.S. District Court, District of Connecticut. *Education:* University of Connecticut (B.A., 1988; J.D., cum laude, 1991). CT Home Inspection Licensing Board appointed, 2000. *Member:* Connecticut Bar Association (Member, Sections on: Litigation, Workers Compensation, Family Law); Connecticut Trial Lawyers Association; The Association of Trial Lawyers of America; Hartford Association of Women Attorneys (Past-President; Board Member). ***PRACTICE AREAS:*** Insurance; Personal Injury; Family Law; Divorce; Workers Compensation. ***Email:*** SusanConnors@msn.com

OF COUNSEL

WALTER B. SCHATZ, born Hartford, Connecticut, February 12, 1922; admitted to bar, 1949, Connecticut. *Education:* Cornell University (A.B., 1947; LL.B., 1949). Parajudicial Officer, U.S. District Court, District of Connecticut. Special Faculty Member, Suffolk University Law School, 1972-1991. *Member:* Hartford County, Connecticut (Chairman, Antitrust Committee, 1970-1971 and 1976-1977) and American Bar Associations. ***PRACTICE AREAS:*** Litigation.

KROLL, McNAMARA & EVANS, LLP

29 SOUTH MAIN STREET
WEST HARTFORD, CONNECTICUT 06107
Telephone: 860-561-7070
Facsimile: 860-561-7075
URL: http://www.kmelaw.com

General Practice, Commercial Real Estate, Commercial Litigation, Real Estate Development, Property Management, Real Estate Leasing, Real Estate Acquisitions and Dispositions, Real Estate Construction and Asset Management, Hotels, Real Estate Finance, Zoning, Planning and Land Use, Civil Litigation, Trial Practice, Appeals, Foreclosures, Creditors Rights, Bankruptcy, Contracts, Commercial Collections, Real Estate Litigation, Lender Liability, Landlord and Tenant Law, Trusts and Estates, Probate.

SHELLEY A. KROLL, born Queens, New York, August 14, 1957; admitted to bar, 1984, Connecticut. *Education:* Bucknell University (B.A., 1979); University of North Carolina (M. Ed., 1981); Syracuse University (J.D., cum laude, 1984). Lead Articles Editor, Syracuse Law Review, 1983-1984. Author: "Defining an Appropriate Education for Handicapped Children," Syracuse Law Review, 1983. Member, International Council of Shopping Centers. ***PRACTICE AREAS:*** Commercial Leasing; Real Estate Acquisitions; Real Estate Sales; Commercial Finance; Loan Workouts; Loan Restructuring; Construction. ***Email:*** skroll@kmelaw.com

EDWARD J. McNAMARA, III, born Teaneck, New Jersey, August 22, 1961; admitted to bar, 1989, New York; 1992, Connecticut. *Education:* Rutgers University (B.A., summa cum laude, 1985); Columbia University (J.D., 1988). Co-Author, "Leasehold Mortgages in Bankruptcy: Look Before You Leasehold," Real Estate Workouts and Bankruptcies, Vol. 2, p. 151, Prac. L. Inst., 1993. Member: Connecticut Mortgage Bankers Association; International Council of Shopping Centers. *Member:* Connecticut and American Bar Associations. ***PRACTICE AREAS:*** Real Estate Finance; Real Estate Acquisitions; Commercial Leasing; Construction; Loan Workouts. ***Email:*** emcnamara@kmelaw.com

DOUGLAS M. EVANS, born Burlington, Vermont, August 8, 1963; admitted to bar, 1989, Connecticut; 1990, U.S. District Court, District of Connecticut. *Education:* Connecticut College (B.A., 1985); Suffolk University (J.D., cum laude, 1989). Comment Editor, Suffolk Transnational Law Review, 1988-1989. *Member:* Hartford County and Connecticut (Member, Commercial Law and Bankruptcy Section) Bar Associations. ***PRACTICE AREAS:*** Commercial Litigation; Real Estate Litigation; Contracts; Bankruptcy; Creditors' Rights; Foreclosures. ***Email:*** devans@kmelaw.com

GARRETT J. DELEHANTY, JR., born Boston, Massachusetts, 1952; admitted to bar, 1976, California; 1978, U.S. Court of Appeals, Ninth Circuit and U.S. District Court, Central District of California; 1980, U.S. Supreme Court; 1989, Georgia; 1991, Connecticut. *Education:* Wesleyan University (B.A., cum laude, 1973); Columbia University (J.D., 1976). Harlan Fiske Stone Scholar. Author: "The WARN Act in Hotel Transactions," Probate and Property, March/April, 1998. *Member:* State Bar of California; State Bar of Georgia; Hartford County, Connecticut and American (Member, Hospitality Committee, Section of Real Property, Probate and Trust Law) Bar Associations. ***PRACTICE AREAS:*** Hotel Acquisitions, Sales; Finance, Management and Franchising; Real Estate Finance; Real Estate Acquisitions and Sales; Loan Workouts and Restructurings; Land Use and Zoning; Commercial Leasing. ***Email:*** gdelehanty@kmelaw.com

---

STEVEN J. MEIS, born Frankfurt, Germany, May 8, 1961; admitted to bar, 1986, Connecticut. *Education:* University of North Carolina (B.A., 1983); University of Virginia Law School (J.D., 1986). ***PRACTICE AREAS:*** Real Estate Acquisitions; Real Estate Sales; Commercial Leasing; Commercial Finance; Loan Workouts; Loan Restructuring; Construction Law. ***Email:*** smeis@kmelaw.com

RICHARD M. LEVY, born Hartford, Connecticut, September 19, 1965; admitted to bar, 1991, Connecticut; 1992, U.S. District Court, District of Connecticut; 1998, Massachusetts. *Education:* University of Connecticut (B.A., 1986; J.D., with honors, 1991). Executive Editor, Connecticut Law Review, 1990-1991. *Member:* Connecticut (Member, Sections on: Commercial Law; Bankruptcy; Litigation; Estates and Probate) and American Bar Associations. ***PRACTICE AREAS:*** Commercial Litigation; Real Estate Litigation; Foreclosure; Estate Planning; Probate; Land Use and Zoning. ***Email:*** rlevy@kmelaw.com

OF COUNSEL

ERIC W. JOHNSON, born Omaha, Nebraska, 1952; admitted to bar, 1977, Connecticut. *Education:* University of Nebraska (B.A., 1974); Cornell University (J.D., 1977). Resource Editor, Cornell International Law Journal, 1976-1977. Co-author: "Assignments of Rents: Drafting Considerations in Light of

(This Listing Continued)

KROLL, McNAMARA & EVANS, LLP, West Hartford—Continued

Bankruptcy Risks," A.B.A. Section of Real Property, Probate & Trust Law, Real Property Programs, 1991, Spring CLE Meeting, Vol. III, 1991; "Leasehold Mortgages in Bankruptcy: Look Before You Leasehold," PLI, Real Estate Workouts and Bankruptcies, No. 390, 1993, No. 402, 1994. *Member:* Hartford County, Connecticut and American (Member, Hospitality Committee, Section of Real Property, Probate and Trust Law) Bar Associations.

REPRESENTATIVE CLIENTS: Aetna, Inc.; Archon Financial, L.P.; Berkshire Development, LLC; Casual Corner Group, Inc.; Chase Enterprises; Connecticut Constitution Associates LLC; Cornerstone Real Estate Advisors, Inc.; EMC Mortgage Corporation; General Electric Capital Corp.; Healthtrax International, Inc.; Jackson Capital Partners; JDA Development Co., LLC; J & S Development and Management Corp.; Maxi Drug, Inc.; Mayfair Super Markets, Inc.; Northeast Development Corp., LLC; Oakleaf Waste Management, LLC; Royal Ahold, n.v.; Sierra Management Corp.; The Cadle Company; The Stop & Shop Supermarket Company, Inc.; Town Fair Tire Centers, Inc.; UBS Realty Investors LLC; Wal-Mart Stores, Inc.; Westfield Bank; Woodbridge Sterling Capital, LLC.

LEWIS, LEWIS & FERRARO, L.L.C.

28 NORTH MAIN STREET
WEST HARTFORD, CONNECTICUT 06107
Telephone: 860-521-1500
Telecopier: 860-521-4500
URL: http://www.lewislewisferraro.com
Email: attorneys@lewislewisferraro.com
URL: http://www.lawyers.com/lewislewisferraro

Bristol, Connecticut Office: 5 Maple Street. Telephone: 860-585-1500. Telecopier: Available Upon Request.

Family Law, Divorce, Personal Injury, Automobile Accidents, Real Estate, Medical Malpractice, Bankruptcy, Wills, Probate, Estate Planning, Trusts and Estates.

MEMBERS OF FIRM

SCOTT FOSTER LEWIS, born Hartford, Connecticut, January 9, 1954; admitted to bar, 1981, Connecticut and U.S. District Court, District of Connecticut. *Education:* Trinity College (B.A., 1976); Suffolk University (J.D., 1981); National Institute of Trial Advocacy. ***Email:*** sfl@lewislewisferraro.com

MARK J. FERRARO, born Hartford, Connecticut, February 9, 1960; admitted to bar, 1986, Florida and Connecticut. *Education:* Taylor University (B.S., summa cum laude, 1982); Stetson University College of Law (J.D., cum laude, 1985); Boston University (LL.M. Taxation Law, 1996). Publications: "The Empirical Challenge to Death Qualified Juries: on Further Examination," Nebraska Law Review, Vol. 65 (1986), Quoted at length in Lockhart v. McCree, 476 U.S. 162 (1986). ***Email:*** mjf@lewislewisferraro.com

NANCY McLUCAS

29 SOUTH MAIN STREET
WEST HARTFORD, CONNECTICUT 06107
Telephone: 860-561-5621
Fax: 860-561-4204
URL: http://www.lawyers.com/mclucas

Estate, Probate, Wills and Trusts.

NANCY McLUCAS, born Detroit, Michigan, February 27, 1950; admitted to bar, 1987, Connecticut. *Education:* Harvard University (A.B., cum laude, 1972); University of Connecticut (J.D., with high honors, 1987). *Member:* Hartford County, Connecticut and American Bar Associations. ***PRACTICE AREAS:*** Probate; Wills; Trusts and Estates.

LAW OFFICES OF ELIOT J. NERENBERG

10 NORTH MAIN STREET, SUITE 214
WEST HARTFORD, CONNECTICUT 06107
Telephone: 860-232-4881
Fax: 860-233-5478
Email: enerenberg@rcn.com

Family Law, Divorce, Child Custody, Divorce Mediation.

ELIOT J. NERENBERG, born Bronx, New York, May 15, 1949; admitted to bar, 1973, Connecticut and U.S. District Court, District of Connecticut; 1975, U.S. Court of Appeals, 2nd Circuit. *Education:* City College of the City University of New York (B.S., cum laude, 1970); New York University (J.D., 1973). Lecturer, Family Law Topics, in Connecticut and nationally. *Member:* Hartford County (Chair, Family Law Section, 1990-1992), Connecticut (Member, Task Force on the Structure of Connecticut Bar Association; Chair, Family Law

(This Listing Continued)

Section, 1998-1999) and American (Member, Family Law Section; Board Member, Publications Development Board, 1991-1999) Bar Associations. ***PRACTICE AREAS:*** Matrimonial Law (90%, 40); Real Estate (10%, 50).

ASSOCIATE

ROBERT D. ZASLOW, born New Rochelle, New York, May 21, 1968; admitted to bar, 1994, Connecticut; 1997, U.S. District Court, District of Connecticut; 1999, U.S. Supreme Court. *Education:* University of Connecticut (B.A., 1990); Ohio Northern University (J.D., 1994). Special Master, Hartford Superior Court Family Division, 2000—. *Member:* Collaborative Divorce Lawyers Association, National Association of Counsel for Children; Barrister, Oliver Ellsworth Inn of Court. ***PRACTICE AREAS:*** Family Law (80%); Juvenile Law (10%); Real Estate (10%). ***Email:*** rzaslow@rcn.com

REID AND RIEGE, P.C.

65 LA SALLE ROAD
WEST HARTFORD, CONNECTICUT 06107
Telephone: 860-232-6565
FAX: 860-232-6066
URL: http://www.reidriege.com

Hartford, Connecticut Office: One State Street. Telephone: 860-278-1150. FAX: 860-240-1002.

Lakeville, Connecticut Office: 322 Main Street. Telephone: 860-435-9894. FAX: 860-240-1002.

Woodbury, Connecticut Office: 47 Sherman Hill Road. Telephone: 203-267-6680. FAX: 860-240-1002.

Alternative Dispute Resolution. Antitrust & Trade Regulation. Bankruptcy. Business Law. Commercial Law. Commercial Real Estate/Finance. Corporate Law. Employee Benefits/Pension Plans. Employee Benefits/Taft-Hartley Plans. Environmental Law. Health Care. Labor and Employment. Litigation. Mergers and Acquisitions. Nonprofit and Charitable Organizations. Occupational Safety & Health. Probate. Real Estate. Securities. Taxation. Trade and Professional Associations. Trusts & Estates. Zoning, Planning and Land Use.

TRAVERS T. AUBURN, born Winsted, Connecticut, April 10, 1946; admitted to bar, 1972, Connecticut. *Education:* Williams College (B.A., 1968); University of Connecticut (J.D., 1972). *Member:* Litchfield County, Connecticut and American Bar Associations. ***PRACTICE AREAS:*** Probate; Real Estate; Trusts and Estates. ***Email:*** tauburn@reidandriege.com

SUZANNE S. BOCCHINI, born Chicago, Illinois, February 24, 1947; admitted to bar, 1973, Missouri; 1974, Connecticut. *Education:* The Catholic University of America (B.A., 1969); St. Louis University (J.D., cum laude, 1973). *Member:* Connecticut and American Bar Associations; Connecticut Estate and Tax Planning Council (President, 1996-1997); Hartford Estate and Business Planning Council. Fellow, American College of Probate Counsel. ***PRACTICE AREAS:*** Probate; Trusts and Estates. ***Email:*** sbocchini@reidandriege.com

FREDERICK J. MULLEN, JR., born Providence, Rhode Island, December 30, 1951; admitted to bar, 1977, Connecticut. *Education:* Yale University (B.A., 1974); University of Virginia (J.D., 1977). Articles Editor, Virginia Journal of International Law, 1976-1977. *Member:* Connecticut (Member, Executive Committee, Probate Section) and American Bar Associations; Hartford Estate and Business Planning Council; Connecticut Estate and Tax Planning Council. Fellow, American College of Trust and Estate Counsel. ***PRACTICE AREAS:*** Probate; Trusts and Estates. ***Email:*** fmullen@reidandriege.com

ALAN BIRMINGHAM, born Hartford, Connecticut, June 3, 1943; admitted to bar, 1969, Connecticut and U.S. District Court, District of Connecticut. *Education:* Tufts University (B.A., 1966); Georgetown University (J.D., 1969). *Member:* Connecticut (Member, Executive Committee, Estates and Probate Section, 1984—; Chairman, Legal Problems of the Elderly Committee, 1985-1988 and Member, Executive Committee, Elder Law Section, 1991—); American Bar Associations; Connecticut Estate and Tax Planning Council, Inc. (Director, 1985-1993; President, 1992-1993). Fellow, American College of Trust and Estate Counsel. ***PRACTICE AREAS:*** Probate; Real Estate; Trusts and Estates. ***Email:*** abirmingham@reidandriege.com

JOHN R. IVIMEY, born Teaneck, New Jersey, April 12, 1963; admitted to bar, 1991, Connecticut. *Education:* Colgate University (B.A., 1985); University of Connecticut (J.D., with high honors, 1991). *Member:* Connecticut and American Bar Associations. ***PRACTICE AREAS:*** Probate; Trusts and Estates. ***Email:*** jivimey@reidandriege.com

SACK, SPECTOR & KARSTEN, LLP

Established in 1984

836 FARMINGTON AVENUE
WEST HARTFORD, CONNECTICUT 06119
Telephone: 860-233-8251
FAX: 860-232-8736

Personal Injury, Insurance Defense, Law Enforcement Liability, Municipal Liability. General Civil Trial and Appellate Practice, Commercial Litigation, Risk Management Consulting.

MEMBERS OF FIRM

GERALD S. SACK, born Hartford, Connecticut, January 27, 1953; admitted to bar, 1977, Connecticut and U.S. District Court, District of Connecticut; 1979, U.S. Court of Appeals, Second Circuit. *Education:* Yale University (B.A., 1974); University of Connecticut (J.D., high honors, 1977). *Member:* Hartford County and Connecticut Bar Associations. ***Email:*** gsack@sackspec.com

ELLIOT B. SPECTOR, born New Britain, Connecticut, June 9, 1947; admitted to bar, 1979, U.S. Court of Appeals, Second Circuit; 1981, Connecticut and U.S. District Court, District of Connecticut. *Education:* University of Connecticut (B.A., 1969; J.D., 1981); University of Hartford (B.A., 1975). *Member:* Hartford County and Connecticut Bar Associations. ***Email:*** espector@sackspec.com

SCOTT M. KARSTEN, born Oklahoma City, Oklahoma, October 2, 1951; admitted to bar, 1982, Connecticut and U.S. District Court, District of Connecticut; 1983, U.S. Court of Appeals, Second Circuit; 1986, U.S. District Court, District of Vermont; 1992, U.S. District Court, Eastern and Southern Districts of New York. *Education:* Wesleyan University (B.A., 1974); University of Connecticut (J.D., high honors, 1982). *Member:* Hartford County and Connecticut Bar Associations. ***Email:*** skarsten@sackspec.com

MARCIA J. GLEESON, born New Britain, Connecticut, June 30, 1951; admitted to bar, 1980, Connecticut; 1981, U.S. District Court, District of Connecticut; 1991, U.S. Court of Appeals, Second Circuit; 1998, U.S. Supreme Court. *Education:* University of Connecticut (B.A., cum laude, 1973; J.D., 1980). Vice Chairwoman, City of New Britain Charter Revision Commission, 1988-1989. Fact Finder and Arbitrator, Superior Court of Connecticut, 1999—. *Member:* Hartford County and Connecticut Bar Associations. ***Email:*** mgleeson@sackspec.com

WILLIAM C. BERRY, born New York, N.Y., July 28, 1947; admitted to bar, 1980, Connecticut; 1989 U.S, District Court, District of Connecticut. *Education:* Colgate University (B.A., 1969); Toledo University; University of Connecticut (J.D., 1980). *Member:* Connecticut Bar Association. ***Email:*** wberry@sackspec.com

NICOLE D. DORMAN, born North Hollywood, California, February 13, 1953; admitted to bar, 1988, Connecticut; 1990, U.S. District Court, District of Connecticut. *Education:* St. Joseph College (B.A., magna cum laude, 1974); Catholic University of America (M.S.W., 1976); University of Connecticut (J.D., with high honors, 1988). *Member:* Connecticut Bar Association. ***Email:*** ndorman@sackspec.com

CHRISTOPHER G. ARCIERO, born New York, N.Y., August 8, 1959; admitted to bar, 1990, Connecticut; 1991, U.S. District Court, District of Connecticut. *Education:* Saint Anselm College (B.S., 1981); Western New England College School of Law (J.D., 1990). *Member:* Connecticut Bar Association. ***Email:*** carciero@sackspec.com

ASSOCIATE

MARC VIDONE, born New Haven, Connecticut, January 15, 1969; admitted to bar, 1998, Connecticut; 1999, New York and Washington D.C. *Education:* Villanova University (B.A./M.A., 1993); Thomas M. Cooley Law School (J.D., 1997). Thomas M. Cooley Law School Law Review, 1996-1997. ***PRACTICE AREAS:*** Personal Injury. ***Email:*** mvidone@sackspec.com

REPRESENTATIVE CLIENTS: Connecticut Interlocal Risk Management Agency; ESIS, Inc.; The Tribune Company; Housing Authority Risk Retention Group; Imperial Casualty & Indemnity Co.; JWF Specialty Co., Inc.; Liability Reduction, Inc.; Liberty Industries; National Casualty Co.; Nationwide Insurance Companies; Nobel Insurance Co.; Scottsdale Insurance Co.; Southern Connecticut Newspapers; Gulf Insurance Co.; Reliance Ins. Co.; Coregis Ins. Co.; Great American Ins. Co.; AESIC; Firemans Fund Life Ins. Co.; Woodland Group, LTD; Summit Risk Services, Inc.; ACE/USA; Constitution State Service Co.; Professional Claims Managers, Inc.

ROBERT F. SCHATZ

1007 FARMINGTON AVENUE
WEST HARTFORD, CONNECTICUT 06107
Telephone: 860-231-1050
Fax: 860-231-1052
Email: schatzlaw@aol.com

Corporate Law, Commercial Finance, Commercial Mortgages, Mortgage Finance, Mortgage Workouts, Asset Based Finance, Credit Enhancement, Debt and Equity Finance, Secured Finance, Structured Finance, Unsecured Finance, Employee Stock Ownership Plans (ESOP), Employee Stock Ownership Trusts, ERISA, Nonqualified Benefits, Fiduciary Law, Employee Benefits, Mergers, Acquisitions and Divestitures, Business Acquisitions, Business Divestitures, Leveraged Acquisitions, Leveraged Buyouts, Venture Capital.

ROBERT F. SCHATZ, born Hartford, Connecticut, March 17, 1951; admitted to bar, 1977, Connecticut and U.S. District Court, District of Connecticut. *Education:* Cornell University (B.A., 1974); Suffolk University (J.D., cum laude, 1977). Member, Suffolk University Law Review, 1975-1976. Author: "ESOPs: Are They As Great As Everyone Says?" 47 N.Y.C. Institute on Federal Taxation 10-1, 1989. Contributing Author: "ESOPs: The Handbook of Employee Stock Ownership Plans," Probus Publishing Company, Chicago, Illinois, October 1989; "Selling to an ESOP," National Center for Employee Ownership (1st-6th Editions, 1996-2001). Member: State of Connecticut Job Protection Advisory Board, 1984-1990; ESOP Association (Financial Institutions and Legislative Advisory Committees, 1986—). *Member:* Hartford County, Connecticut (Member, Commercial Law and Bankruptcy and Banking Law Sections) and American (Member, Banking Committee and Finlaw Section) Bar Associations.

RALPH D. SHERMAN

1001 FARMINGTON AVENUE, SUITE 300
WEST HARTFORD, CONNECTICUT 06107
Telephone: 860-561-0695
Fax: 860-561-0896
Email: atty@ralphdsherman.com
URL: http://www.ralphdsherman.com

Criminal and Civil Litigation. Civil Rights, Second Amendment Law, Firearms, Pistol Permits, Pardons, Landlord Tenant, Collections and Real Estate.

RALPH D. SHERMAN, born New Haven, Connecticut, June 22, 1957; admitted to bar, 1991, Connecticut. *Education:* Western Connecticut State University (B.A., magna cum laude, 1983); University of Connecticut (J.D., 1991). Chairman, Gunsafe, 1998—. Member, Connecticut State Police Firearms Advisory Council, 2000— *Member:* Connecticut Bar Association (Chairman, Firearms Law Committee, 1995-1999).

BRUCE H. STANGER

29 SOUTH MAIN STREET
WEST HARTFORD, CONNECTICUT 06107
Telephone: 1-888-782-6437; 860-561-0650
Fax: 860-561-0646
URL: http://www.lawyers.com/bstangerlaw
Email: bstanger@stangerlaw.com
URL: http://www.stangerlaw.com

Legal Malpractice, Medical Malpractice, Construction, Business, Civil Litigation, Commercial Litigation, Personal Injury, Corporate Law, Automobile Accidents.

BRUCE H. STANGER, born New York, N.Y., September 11, 1951; admitted to bar, 1977, Connecticut. *Education:* University of Hartford (B.S.E.E., 1974); Western New England College (J.D., cum laude, 1977). Teaching Assistant, Legal Research and Writing, Western New England Law College School of Law, 1976-1977. Law Clerk to the Judges of Appellate Session, Superior Court, 1977-1978. Member, Probus Club, Jewish Federation of Greater Hartford, Committee on Jewish Education, Solomon Shechter Day School (President, 1997-1999). Treasurer, Camp Ramah New England. *Member:* Hartford County (Member: Civil Litigation Committee, 1997-2002; Legal Technology Committee, 1998-2002; Ethics Committee), Connecticut (Member: Professional Discipline Committee, 1998-2002; Professional Responsibility Committee, 1998-2002; Professional Ethics Committee; Civil Litigation Committee) and American Bar Associations; Connecticut Trial Lawyers Association (Member, 1200 Club, 1998-1999); The Association of Trial Lawyers of America. (Also Member, Stanger & Arnold, LLP). ***PRACTICE AREAS:*** Legal Malpractice; Medical Malpractice; Construction Law; Business Law; Civil Litigation.

JEFFREY W. STEIN

28 NORTH MAIN STREET, SUITE G-01
WEST HARTFORD, CONNECTICUT 06107
Telephone: 860-561-5671
Fax: 860-561-5681
Email: jeffrey.stein@usa.net

Estate Planning, Estate Administration, Wills, Trusts, Estate Litigation, Trust Litigation, Individual Taxation, Pensions.

JEFFREY W. STEIN, born Brooklyn, New York, January 10, 1950; admitted to bar, 1975, New York; 1976, New Jersey; 1984, Connecticut; 1985, U.S. Tax Court. *Education:* State University of New York at Binghamton (B.A., 1971); St. John's University (J.D., 1974). Certified Financial Planner, 1997—. *Member:* Connecticut, New York State and American Bar Associations.

THE LAW OFFICES OF MARK J. SVONKIN, P.C.

18 NORTH MAIN STREET
WEST HARTFORD, CONNECTICUT 06107
Telephone: 860-521-2811
Fax: 860-521-6448
Email: svonk@aol.com
URL: http://www.lawyers.com/svonkin&godgelaw

Commercial Real Estate, Condominium Law, Financing, Zoning, Commercial Leasing, Corporate and LLC Law.

MARK J. SVONKIN, born 1939; admitted to bar, 1968, Connecticut. *Education:* Franklin & Marshall College (B.A., 1961); University of Connecticut (J.D., 1968). Member and Chairman, Winchester Planning and Zoning Commission, 1987-1990. Town Attorney, Town of Winchester, 1990-1991. *Member:* Hartford County, Connecticut (Member, Real Property Section) and American Bar Associations. [1st Lt., USAF, 1962-1965]. ***PRACTICE AREAS:*** Commercial Real Estate; Zoning; Commercial Leasing Law; Condominium Law. ***Email:*** svonk@aol.com

THIER LAW OFFICES, LLC

1007 FARMINGTON AVENUE
WEST HARTFORD, CONNECTICUT 06107
Telephone: 860-236-2600
Facsimile: 860-231-1052
Email: cliffthier@thierlaw.com

Commercial Law, Business Law, Corporate Law and Real Estate Law.

CLIFFORD S. THIER, born New York, N.Y., July 7, 1951; admitted to bar, 1975, New York; 1994, Connecticut; 2000, U.S. District Court, District of Connecticut. *Education:* State University of New York at Stony Brook (B.A., 1972); Widener University School of Law (J.D., 1975). *Member:* Hartford County, Connecticut and American Bar Associations; American Health Lawyers Association. ***PRACTICE AREAS:*** Commercial Law; Business Law; Corporate Law; Real Estate Law; Wills; Trusts and Estates.

WEINSTEIN & WISSER, P.C.

Established in 1991

29 SOUTH MAIN STREET
WEST HARTFORD, CONNECTICUT 06107-2103
Telephone: 860-561-2628
Telecopier: 860-521-6150
Email: weinstein&wisser@dtg.net

Litigation Practice including Commercial Specializing in Debtors Rights, Corporation, Personal Injury, Professional Malpractice, Real Estate and Bad Faith Law. Trials and Appeals in State and Federal Courts.

RICHARD P. WEINSTEIN, born New Haven, Connecticut, October 19, 1946; admitted to bar, 1970, Connecticut; 1971, U.S. Supreme Court; 1990, U.S. District Court, District of Connecticut and U.S. Court of Appeals, Second Circuit. *Education:* Washington & Jefferson College (B.A., 1968); University of Connecticut (J.D., 1970). *Member:* Hartford County, Connecticut and American Bar Associations; The Association of Trial Lawyers of America; Connecticut Trial Lawyers Association. ***PRACTICE AREAS:*** Civil Litigation; Bank Litigation; Lender Liability Law; Debtor Rights Law. ***Email:*** attyrpweinstein@dtg.net

KERRY MARC WISSER, born New York, New York, November 16, 1960; admitted to bar, 1985, Connecticut and Pennsylvania; 1986, U.S. District Court, District of Connecticut; 1992, U.S. Court of Appeals, Second Circuit; 2000, U.S. Supreme Court. *Education:* Connecticut College (B.A., 1982); University of Bridgeport (J.D., 1985). Recipient, American Jurisprudence Award for Evidence. Member, 1983-1985 and Associate Editor, 1984-1985, University of Bridgeport Law Review. *Member:* Connecticut (Member, House of Delegates), Pennsylvania and American Bar Associations; The Association of Trial Lawyers of America; Connecticut Trial Lawyers Association. ***PRACTICE AREAS:*** Civil Litigation; Personal Injury Litigation; Medical Malpractice; Commercial Litigation; Banking Litigation. ***Email:*** kmw@dtg.net

(This Listing Continued)

NATHAN A. SCHATZ, born Hartford, Connecticut, November 7, 1958; admitted to bar, 1986, Connecticut; 1988, U.S. District Court, District of Connecticut. *Education:* Emory University (B.A., 1980); University of Pennsylvania (J.D., 1984). Phi Beta Kappa; Order of the Coif. Deep River Board of Education, 1991—. *Member:* Connecticut Bar Association. ***Email:*** nschatz@dtg.net

UMEUGO & ASSOCIATES, P.C.

Established in 1996

840 ORANGE AVENUE
2ND FLOOR
P.O. BOX 26373
WEST HAVEN, CONNECTICUT 06516
Telephone: 203-931-2680
Fax: 203-931-2682
Email: umeugo@justice.com

General Practice, Debt Collections, International Law, Personal Injury, Subrogation, Insurance Law and Civil Litigation, Automobile Accidents, Workers Compensation, Medical Malpractice, Commercial Collections, Employment Law, Immigration Law, Incorporation, Wills and Trusts, Landlord and Tenant Law, Business Law, Real Estate Closings and Trademarks and Copyrights.

IKECHUKWU UMEUGO, born Onitsha, Nigeria, May 4, 1960; admitted to bar, 1989, Connecticut; 1990, U.S. District Court, District of Connecticut. *Education:* University of New Haven (B.S., magna cum laude, 1982; M.B.A., 1984); Washburn University of Topeka School of Law (J.D., with honors, 1988). *Member:* New Haven County, Connecticut and American Bar Associations. ***LANGUAGES:*** Igbo. ***PRACTICE AREAS:*** Collections; International Law; Medical Malpractice Law; Personal Injury Law; Workers Compensation; Subrogation; Insurance Law; Civil Litigation. ***Email:*** umeugo@justice.com

---

MARIA A. DABREO-EVANS, born Brooklyn, New York, October 6, 1971; admitted to bar, 1999, Connecticut; 2000, U.S. District Court, District of Connecticut. *Education:* Spelman College (B.A., cum laude, 1993); New York Law School (J.D., 1997). Psi Chi. Departmental Honors, Spelman College. *Member:* Connecticut and American Bar Associations; Association of Trial Lawyers of America; American Business Women's Association; National Trial Lawyers Association; National Bar Association. ***PRACTICE AREAS:*** Family Law; Employment Law; Debt Collection; Personal Injury; Real Estate Closings. ***Email:*** umeugo@justice.com

CHRISTINE BENHAM, born Providence, Rhode Island, March 28, 1969; admitted to bar, 2001, Connecticut. *Education:* Community College of Rhode Island (A.S., 1990); Charter Oak State College (B.S., 1998); Quinnipiac University (J.D., 2001). Member, American Registry of Radiologic Technologists, 1990-2001. Recipient, Distinguished Academic Achievement Award for Trial Practice. Radiographer's License, Connecticut, 1995-2001. *Member:* Connecticut Bar Association. ***PRACTICE AREAS:*** Medical Malpractice; Personal Injury; Environmental Law. ***Email:*** umeugo@justice.com

LAW OFFICES OF GEORGE C. GUIDERA

177 WESTON ROAD
WESTON, CONNECTICUT 06883-2113
Telephone: 203-227-5748
Fax: 203-227-0852
Email: westonlawfirm@aol.com
URL: http://www.lawyers.com/guidera

Civil Practice, Criminal Law, Real Estate, Zoning, Planning and Land Use, Probate, Trusts and Estates, Corporate Law, Family Law, Personal Injury, Commercial Law, Mortgages and Wills.

GEORGE C. GUIDERA, born Norwalk, Connecticut, July 14, 1942; admitted to bar, 1967, Connecticut; 1972, U.S. District Court, District of Connecticut. *Education:* Colgate University (B.A., 1964); Georgetown University (J.D., 1967). Adjunct Professor of Probate Law, Fairfield University, 1981-1984 and Norwalk Community College, 1982-1986. Member, Connecticut House of Representatives, 162nd Assembly District, 1971-1973. Member, Connecticut State Senate, 26th Senatorial District, 1973-1979. Legislative Commissioner,

(This Listing Continued)

State of Connecticut, 1979-1991. Chairman, Senate Judiciary Committee, 1973-1975. Member, Governor's Commission on the Age of Majority, 1971-1972. First Selectman (Mayor), Town of Weston, Connecticut, 1987-1999. Chairman, Board of Directors, Columbia Federal Savings Bank, 1987-1989. Member, Community Advisory Board of Wilton Bank, 1999—. *Member:* Westport Bar Association. ***SPECIAL AGENCIES:*** Agent for Chicago Title Insurance Company and First American Title Insurance Co. ***PRACTICE AREAS:*** Civil Practice; Criminal Law; Real Estate; Zoning, Planning and Land Use; Trusts and Estates; Corporate Law; Family Law; Personal Injury; Commercial Law; Mortgages; Wills.

ASSOCIATE

SUZANNE K. GUIDERA, born Norwalk, Connecticut, March 2, 1972; admitted to bar, 1999, Connecticut. *Education:* Arizona State University (B.S., 1994); Quinnipiac College (J.D., 1999). Member, 1997-1998, and Exchequer, 1998-1999, Phi Delta Phi. Recipient, Outstanding Legal Scholarship, Quinnipiac College. Member, 1997-1998 and Supervising Editor, 1998-1999, Quinnipiac Probate Law Journal. Author, 12 QUINNIPIAC PROB. L.J. 343 (1998). Secretary, Westport Bar Association. *Member:* Westport, Connecticut and American Bar Associations. ***SPECIAL AGENCIES:*** Agent for Chicago Title Insurance Company and First American Title Insurance Co. ***PRACTICE AREAS:*** Real Estate; Probate; Trusts and Estates; Family Law; Zoning, Planning and Land Use. ***Email:*** skgesq@aol.com

REFERENCES: First Union Bank, Wilton Office; Hudson United Bank, Weston Branch; Peoples Bank; Wilton Bank.

ALBERT, WARD & JOHNSON, P.C.

WESTPORT, CONNECTICUT

(See Greenwich)

General Practice. Real Estate, Zoning, Corporation, Litigation, Probate, Taxation, Construction, Environmental and Family Law.

AVIROM & ASSOCIATES, LLP

38 POST ROAD WEST
WESTPORT, CONNECTICUT 06880
Telephone: 203-222-9355
Email: info@avirom.com

New York, N.Y. Office: 42 Broadway, Suite 1220. Telephone: 212-747-8787. Fax: 212-747-0857.

Immigration and Nationality Law, Criminal and Matrimonial Law.

(For Complete Biographical Data on all Personnel, see Professional Biographies at New York, New York)

BERKOWITZ, TRAGER & TRAGER, LLC

Established in 1961
253 POST ROAD WEST
P.O. BOX 808
WESTPORT, CONNECTICUT 06881
Telephone: 203-226-1001
Fax: 203-226-3801
Email: btt@bertralaw.com
URL: http://www.lawyers.com/berkowitztrager&tragerllc

General Business Practice. Executive Compensation and Contracts, Sports Law, Corporations, Commercial and Residential Real Estate, Banking Law, Estate Planning, Probate, Commercial and Business Law. Tax and Tax Planning Law, Creditors Rights and Bankruptcy Law.

RICHARD BERKOWITZ, born New Haven, Connecticut, June 28, 1941; admitted to bar, 1966, Connecticut and U.S. District Court, District of Connecticut. *Education:* Dartmouth College (B.A., 1963); University of Connecticut (J.D., 1966). Member, Westport Representative Town Meeting, 1967-1971. Member, Westport Planning and Zoning Commission, 1978-1981. *Member:* Westport (President, 1978-1979), Connecticut (Member, Real Estate, Corporate, Sports and Entertainment Law Sections, 1966) and American Bar Associations. ***PRACTICE AREAS:*** Executive Compensation and Contracts; Business Law; Real Estate Law; Sports Law; Corporate Law. ***Email:*** rb@bertralaw.com

PAUL M. BERG, born New Haven, Connecticut, September 29, 1950; admitted to bar, 1977, Connecticut and U.S. District Court, District of Connecticut. *Education:* Beloit College (B.A., 1972); University of Connecticut (J.D., with high honors, 1977). Member, University of Connecticut Law Review, 1975-1977. Author: "Attorneys Fees and the Defaulting Debtor," Connecticut Law Review, Spring, 1976. *Member:* Greater Bridgeport, Connecticut (Chairman, Committee on Arts and the Law, 1985-1986; Member, Sections on: Antitrust; Taxation) and American (Member, Sections on: Taxation; Entertainment) Bar Associations. ***PRACTICE AREAS:*** Taxation Law; Intellectual Property; Antitrust Law. ***Email:*** pb@bertralaw.com

SAMUEL FEBBRAIO, JR., born Westport, Connecticut, March 5, 1958; admitted to bar, 1984, Connecticut. *Education:* Fairfield University (B.S., 1981); University of Bridgeport (J.D., magna cum laude, 1984). Executive Managing Editor, University of Bridgeport Law Review, 1983-1984. Author: "Tribal Severance Taxes: An Uncertain Sovereign Function," 4 University of Bridgeport Law Review, 1984. *Member:* Greater Bridgeport, Connecticut (Member, Sections on: Corporation; Tax) and American (Member, Taxation Section) Bar Associations. ***PRACTICE AREAS:*** Corporate Law; Securities; Taxation. ***Email:*** sf@bertralaw.com

JAY L. GOLDSTEIN, born New Bedford, Massachusetts, October 23, 1956; admitted to bar, 1986, Massachusetts; 1987, Connecticut, U.S. District Court, District of Connecticut and U.S. Tax Court. *Education:* Northeastern University (B.S., with honors, 1979); New England School of Law (J.D., 1986); Boston University (LL.M. in Taxation, 1987). Member, N.Y.U. Tax Studies Group, ILC. *Member:* Westport, Fairfield County (Member, Estate Tax Planning Council), Connecticut (Member, Estate Tax Planning Council), Massachusetts and American Bar Associations. ***PRACTICE AREAS:*** Taxation; Estate Planning; Trusts and Estates; ERISA; Pension and Profit Sharing Plans; Business Law. ***Email:*** jg@bertralaw.com

DAVID A. GREENBERG, born New York, N.Y., October 24, 1958; admitted to bar, 1983, Connecticut and U.S. District Court, District of Connecticut. *Education:* George Washington University (B.A., with distinction, 1980; J.D., with honors, 1983). Omicron Delta Epsilon. Notes Editor, The George Washington Journal of International Law and Economics Development, 1982-1983. Author: "Joint Ventures in Poland: Polish Proposals Before the Joint American-Polish Trade Commission," The George Washington Journal of International Law and Economics, Vol. 16, No. 2, 1982. *Member:* Bridgeport, Connecticut and American Bar Associations. ***PRACTICE AREAS:*** Commercial Law; Creditors Rights and Bankruptcy Law; Real Estate Law; Corporate Compliance; Banking Law. ***Email:*** dag@bertralaw.com

HOWARD D. KOMISAR, born New Haven, Connecticut, October 13, 1955; admitted to bar, 1980, Florida; 1981, U.S. District Court, Southern District of Florida; 1982, Connecticut; 1989, New York. *Education:* Wharton School, University of Pennsylvania (B.S. in Economics, 1977); University of Miami (J.D., 1980). Phi Delta Phi. *Member:* Connecticut and American Bar Associations; The Florida Bar. ***PRACTICE AREAS:*** Commercial Real Estate Finance, Leasing and Development; Corporate Law. ***Email:*** hk@bertralaw.com

RICHARD J. PREMINGER, born Brooklyn, New York, July 12, 1957; admitted to bar, 1981, California; 1983, New York; 1988, Connecticut and U.S. District Court, District of Connecticut. *Education:* State University of New York at Albany (B.A., cum laude, 1978); California Western School of Law (J.D., magna cum laude, 1981); New York University (LL.M., in Taxation, 1983). Lead Articles Editor, California Western Law Review, 1980-1981. Recipient, American Jurisprudence Awards in: Contracts; Civil Procedure; Commercial Papers and Secured Transactions. ***PRACTICE AREAS:*** Taxation; Estate Planning; Trusts and Estates; Corporate Law. ***Email:*** rjp@bertralaw.com

ROBERT H. RUBIN, born New York, N.Y., December 25, 1932; admitted to bar, 1959, Connecticut; 1961, U.S. District Court, District of Connecticut; 1966, U.S. Court of Appeals, Second Circuit; 1968, U.S. Supreme Court. *Education:* Yale University (B.A., with honors, 1954); University of Pennsylvania (J.D., cum laude, 1959). Instructor in Real Estate Law, Probate Law and Probate Administration, Connecticut Center for Continuing Education, Fairfield University, 1975-1978. Member, Norwalk Redevelopment Agency, 1966-1968. Special Corporation Counsel, City of Norwalk, 1966-1968. Corporation Counsel, City of Norwalk, 1968-1969. Member, Board of Directors, Neon (Equal Opportunity Board), 1968. Member of Advisory Council on Community Affairs, State of Connecticut, 1974-1978. *Member:* Westport (Secretary, 1980-1981; Treasurer, 1981-1982; Vice-President, 1982-1983; President, 1983-1984) and The Connecticut (Member, Executive Committee, Planning and Zoning Section, 1978—) Bar Associations; The Connecticut Trial Lawyers Association (Member, Federal Grievance Committee, U.S. District Court, District of Connecticut, 1989-1998). [Army Artillery, First Lt., 1954-1956]. ***PRACTICE AREAS:*** Land Use Law; Commercial Law; Real Estate Law; Litigation. ***Email:*** rr@bertralaw.com

DORIS B. SHILLER, born New York, N.Y., May 9, 1933; admitted to bar, 1979, Connecticut and U.S. District Court, District of Connecticut; 1982, U.S. Court of Appeals, Second Circuit. *Education:* Barnard College (B.A., cum laude, 1954); Yale University (J.D., 1979). Member, Board of Education, Westport, Connecticut, 1971-1978. Member, Board of Directors, Westport Arts Center, 1983-1995. *Member:* Westport and Connecticut (Member: Executive Committees; Business Law, Banking Law and Real Property Sections) Bar Associations. ***PRACTICE AREAS:*** Banking Law; Real Estate Law; Corporate and Related Business Law. ***Email:*** ds@bertralaw.com

(This Listing Continued)

BERKOWITZ, TRAGER & TRAGER, LLC, Westport—Continued

OF COUNSEL

ARTHUR E. BALBIRER, born New York, N.Y., November 2, 1940; admitted to bar, 1966, Connecticut and U.S. District Court, District of Connecticut; 1969, U.S. Court of Appeals, Second Circuit. *Education:* Union University (B.S., 1962); New York University (J.D., 1966). Senior Topical Editor, Family Law, Connecticut Bar Journal, 1979—. Co-author: "Annual Survey of Family Law in Connecticut," Vol. 49, pg. 1, 1975, Vol. 50, pg. 67, 1976, Vol. 51, pg. 2, 1977, Vol. 53, pg. 391, 1979, Vol. 55, pg. 29, 1981, Vol. 56, pg. 26, 1982, Vol. 57, pg. 20, 1983, Vol. 58, pg. 33, 1984, Vol. 59, pg. 115, 1985, Vol. 60. pg. 83, 1986, Vol. 61, pg. 231, 1987, Vol. 62, pg. 111, 1988, Vol. 64, pg. 81, 1990, Vol. 65, pg. 103, 1991, Vol. 66, pg. 40, 1992, Vol. 68, pg. 53, 1994, Vol. 69, pg. 115, 1995, Connecticut Bar Journal. *Member:* Westport, Connecticut (President, 1977-1978 and Member, Executive Committee, 1975-1985, Family Law Section; Member: Bench and Bar Committee, 1977-1978; Judicial Appointment Recommendation Committee, 1978-1980) and American (Member, Section on Family Law; Co-Chairman, Marital Property Committee, 1982-1983) Bar Associations. Fellow: American Academy of Matrimonial Lawyers (National Vice President, 1987-1991; President-Elect, 1991-1992; President, 1992-1993; Vice President, 1976-1979 and President, 1979-1981, Board of Managers, Connecticut Chapter; Member, National Board of Governors, 1984-1987); International Academy of Matrimonial Lawyers (Founding Fellow and Counsel, 1987; Vice President, U.S.A. Chapter, 1989-1992; President-Elect, 1992). ***PRACTICE AREAS:*** Domestic Relations Law. ***Email:*** ab@bertralaw.com

REFERENCES: Westport National Bank; Peoples Bank.

BERSHTEIN, LIPPMAN, BACHMAN & McKEON, P.C.

WESTPORT, CONNECTICUT

(See New Haven)

General Practice including Real Estate, Federal and State Court Litigation, Public and Private Finance, Banking, Leasing, Business, Municipal Tax Law, Health Care, Creditors and Debtors Rights including Workouts, Collections and Foreclosures, Landlord and Tenant, Estate Planning, Probate and Personal Injury.

BLAZZARD, GRODD & HASENAUER, P.C.

Established in 1974

943 POST ROAD EAST

P.O. BOX 5108

WESTPORT, CONNECTICUT 06881

Telephone: 203-226-7866

Telecopier: 203-454-4855

Email: BGHCT@mindspring.com

Lauderdale-By-the-Sea Office: Suite 207, W. Tradewinds Avenue, 33308. Telephone: 954-771-6667. Facsimile: 954-771-7689. E-Mail: BGHFL@AOL.COM

Administrative, Corporation, Estate Planning, Insurance, Probate, Real Estate, Taxation and Securities Law.

NORSE N. BLAZZARD, born St. Johns, Arizona, July 8, 1937; admitted to bar, 1963, California; 1966, U.S. District Court, Northern District of California; 1974, Connecticut; 1975, U.S. District Court, District of Connecticut; 1977, District of Columbia; 1978, U.S. Supreme Court and U.S. Court of Appeals, Second Circuit; 1993, Florida. *Education:* Stanford University (A.B., 1959); Hastings College of Law, University of California (J.D., 1962). Delta Theta Phi. Instructor in Business Law, University of Maryland Overseas Program in Bremerhaven, Germany, 1963-1965. Chartered Life Underwriter, The American College, 1971. Chairman, National Association for Variable Annuities, 1995. *Member:* The District of Columbia Bar; Connecticut (Chairman: Committee on Competition in Banking, Banking Law Section, 1980-1981; Committee on Trade Regulation, Consumer Law Section, 1976-1979), Federal and American (Member, Sections of: Corporation, Banking and Business Law; Science and Technology; Tort and Insurance Practice) Bar Associations; State Bar of California; The Florida Bar. [Capt., JAGC, U.S. Army, 1962-1966]. ***PRACTICE AREAS:*** Life Insurance Products; Securities Law; Corporations; Insurance Taxation; Employee Benefits; Banking Law; Administrative Law. ***Email:*** norse.blazzard@bghpc.com

LESLIE E. GRODD, born New York, N.Y., February 18, 1946; admitted to bar, 1969, New York; 1974, Connecticut; 1975, U.S. District Court, District of Connecticut and U.S. Supreme Court; 1980, U.S. Tax Court; 1982, District of Columbia. *Education:* University of Vermont (B.A., 1966); New York University (M.B.A., 1971); St. John's University (J.D., 1969). Delta Theta Phi. Member, Senior Moot Court Board. Certified Public Accountant, Connecticut, 1973. *Member:* Connecticut (Member, Sections on: Estates; Probate; Member, Executive Committee, Section of Taxation, 1981—, Vice Chairman, 1988-1991; Chairman, 1991-1994), New York State and American (Member: Estate and Gift Tax Committee, Taxation Section, 1977-1994; Committee on Insurance Company Taxation, Section of Taxation, 1982-1994; Closely Held Business Committee, Taxation Section, 1994—; Vice Chair, 2000-2001; Chair, 2001—) Bar Associations; Connecticut Society of Certified Public Accountants (Member, Federal Taxation Executive Committee, 1976-1981, 1982-1998, Chairman, 1988-1989); American Institute of Certified Public Accountants. ***PRACTICE AREAS:*** Income and Estate Taxation and Planning; Individuals; Corporations; Real Estate. ***Email:*** leslie.grodd@BGHPC.com

JUDITH A. HASENAUER, born Rochester, New York, September 28, 1946; admitted to bar, 1974, California and Connecticut; 1975, U.S. District Court, District of Connecticut; 1982, New York and District of Columbia; 1993, Florida. *Education:* University of Rochester (A.B., 1969); Golden Gate University (J.D., 1973). Member, Golden Gate Law Review, 1972-1973. Chartered Life Underwriter, The American College, 1978. *Member:* The District of Columbia Bar; The Florida Bar; State Bar of California; Connecticut and American (Member, Section on Corporation, Banking and Business Law) Bar Associations; National Association for Variable Annuities (Co-Chair, Regulatory Affairs Committee). ***PRACTICE AREAS:*** Life Insurance Products; Securities Law; Corporations; Insurance Taxation. ***Email:*** Judith.Hasenauer@BGHPC.com

WILLIAM E. HASENAUER, born Rochester, New York, June 2, 1949; admitted to bar, 1976, New York; 1978, U.S. District Court, Western District of New York and U.S. Court of Appeals, Second Circuit; 1979, Connecticut. *Education:* St. John Fisher College (B.A., 1971); John Marshall Law School (J.D., with distinction, 1975). *Member:* Westport (Member, Executive Committee, 1983-1984), Connecticut (Member: Sections on: Consumer Law; Corporations), New York State and American Bar Associations. ***PRACTICE AREAS:*** Life Insurance Products; Securities Law; Corporations; Insurance Taxation; Employee Benefits. ***Email:*** wehbgh@mindspring.com

RAYMOND A. O'HARA, III, born Norwalk, Connecticut, September 19, 1955; admitted to bar, 1981, Connecticut and U.S. District Court, District of Connecticut. *Education:* University of Bridgeport (B.A., magna cum laude, 1977); New York Law School (J.D., 1980). *Member:* Westport, Connecticut and American Bar Associations. ***PRACTICE AREAS:*** Life Insurance Products; Securities Law; Corporations; Insurance Taxation. ***Email:*** Raymond.OHara@BGHPC.com

LYNN KORMAN STONE, born New Haven, Connecticut, February 25, 1959; admitted to bar, 1985, Connecticut; 1987, U.S. District Court, District of Connecticut. *Education:* The American University (B.A., 1981); University of Bridgeport School of Law (J.D., cum laude, 1985). *Member:* Westport, Connecticut and American Bar Associations. ***PRACTICE AREAS:*** Life Insurance Products; Securities Law. ***Email:*** Lynn.Stone@bghpc.com

TINA L. LEWERT, born South Plainfield, New Jersey, July 21, 1974; admitted to bar, 2000, Florida (Not admitted in Connecticut). *Education:* Florida Atlantic University (B.S., 1997); Nova Southeastern University (J.D., 2000). *Member:* The Florida Bar (Member, Sections on: Business Law; Taxation); American Bar Association. ***PRACTICE AREAS:*** Life Insurance; Securities. ***Email:*** Tina.Lewert@bghpc.com

ELLEN MECHLIN-LEVITT, born Brooklyn, New York, June 10, 1960; admitted to bar, 1986, New York; 1995, Florida (Not admitted in Connecticut). *Education:* Cornell University (B.S., 1982); State University of New York at Buffalo Law School (J.D., 1985); New York University (LL.M., Taxation, 1993). *Member:* The Florida Bar. ***PRACTICE AREAS:*** Taxation; Insurance.

REPRESENTATIVE CLIENTS: R.B. Benson & Co., Inc; Sentry Life Insurance Co.; SunAmerica Life Companies; The New England Financial Corp.; BMA Financial Group; Peoples Bank; Chicago Title Insurance Company; Lawyers Title Insurance Company; Monarch Life Insurance Co.; First Variable Life Insurance Co.; Jackson National Life Insurance Company; Conseco; K III Holdings, Inc.; Morningside Capital Group, L.L.C.; International Pipe & Steel Corp.; Independent Jewelers Organization, Inc.; London Pacific Life & Annuity Co.; LPT Variable Insurance Series Trust; The Prudential Insurance Company of America; Metropolitan Life Insurance Company; CNA/Valley Forge; Lincoln National Life Insurance Company; MetLife Investors Insurance Company; Phoenix Home Life Mutual Insurance Company; Sage Life Assurance of America, Inc.

(This Listing Continued)

PAMELA D. BOCHINSKI

25 FORD ROAD

WESTPORT, CONNECTICUT 06880

Telephone: 203-227-4484

Fax: 203-222-4833

Email: pamela.d.bochinski@snet.net

Trusts and Estates, Probate, Wills, Taxation.

(This Listing Continued)

FIRM PROFILE: Pamela D. Bochinski has more than twenty years of experience serving clients throughout Fairfield County. She practices solely in the areas of estate planning, estate and trust administration, fiduciary and personal income tax and related matters.

PAMELA D. BOCHINSKI, born Mt. Vernon, New York, October 27, 1941; admitted to bar, 1977, Connecticut; 1990, New York. *Education:* University of Edinburgh, Edinburgh, Scotland; Bucknell University (B.A., 1963); University of Connecticut (J.D., 1977). Justice of the Peace, 1985—. *Member:* Westport, Connecticut (Member: Executive Committee, Estates and Probate Section, 1982—; Board of Editors, Connecticut Bar Journal, 1992—), New York State and American Bar Associations. (Also of Counsel to Hopper & Krause, Greenwich).

ANDREW B. BOWMAN

Established in 1982

1804 POST ROAD EAST

WESTPORT, CONNECTICUT 06880

Telephone: 203-259-0599

Fax: 203-255-2570

Email: andrew.bowman@snet.net

URL: http://www.lawyers.com/bowmanlaw

General Civil and Criminal Litigation before all Federal and State Courts. Trials and Appeals. Criminal Defense, Tax Litigation, Employment Law, Construction Litigation, Civil Rights, Environmental Law, Personal Injury, Commercial Litigation and Negligence Law.

ANDREW B. BOWMAN, born Bridgeport, Connecticut, February 1, 1945; admitted to bar, 1970, Connecticut; 1971, U.S. District Court, District of Connecticut and U.S. Court of Appeals, Second Circuit; 1973; U.S. Supreme Court; 1983, U.S. Tax Court; 1996, U.S. District Court, Southern and Eastern Districts of New York. *Education:* University of Connecticut (B.S., 1967; J.D., 1970). Instructor: Trial Practice, Yale Law School, 1977-1983; Trial Advocacy, Connecticut Bar Association, 1976, 1978 and 1979. Assistant U.S. Attorney, District of Connecticut, 1971-1974. The Federal Public Defender, District of Connecticut, 1976-1979. Member: Grievance Committee, U.S. District Court, District of Connecticut, 1984-1987; Committee on Rules and Operating Procedures, U.S. Court of Appeals, Second Circuit, 1982—. *Member:* Greater Bridgeport, Westport, Connecticut (Member, 1978— and Chairman, 1981-1984, Federal Practice Section; Chairman, Sub-Committee on Criminal Justice, 1987-1990; Member, Criminal Justice Section) and American Bar Associations; The Association of Trial Lawyers of America; Connecticut Criminal Defense Lawyers Association; American College of Trial Lawyers. [With U.S. Army, 1963-1965]

REFERENCE: Peoples Bank.

BRODY, WILKINSON AND OBER, P.C.

WESTPORT, CONNECTICUT

(See Southport)

General Civil Practice, Corporation, Probate, Estate Planning, Trusts and Estates, Real Estate, Employment, Commercial, Environmental, Creditors Rights, Tax, Pension, Profit Sharing, Entertainment Law, Banking, General Business, Municipal, Freedom of Information Matters, Telecommunications, Public Utilities, Commercial Litigation.

LAWRENCE I. BROWN

611 RIVERSIDE AVENUE

P.O. BOX 2117

WESTPORT, CONNECTICUT 06880

Telephone: 203-222-9099

Fax: 203-222-9008

Email: larrybrown@snet.net

Admiralty, Maritime and International Law.

LAWRENCE I. BROWN, born Brooklyn, N.Y., April 18, 1931; admitted to bar, 1956, Michigan and New York; 1984, Connecticut. *Education:* New York University (B.A., 1953); University of Michigan (J.D., 1955). *Member:* Connecticut and American Bar Associations; Maritime Law Association of the United States (Proctor).

REFERENCES: Bank of Westport; Chase Manhattan Bank, Westport, CT.; Mitsubishi Logistics; Mitsui Soko of Tokyo, Japan; Unique Shipping of Hong Kong; Vroon Shipping, Netherlands; Sincere Steamship of Taiwan; Seaarland Shipping Management, Villach, Austria; Denholm Shipping, Glasgow, Scotland, Isle of Man; Ehlermann & Jeschonnek, Leonhardt & Blumberg; Toepfer Transport; Cyrus Makowski; Ernst Russ GMBH & Co., Hamburg, Germany; Reederei F. Laeisz, Rostock, Germany.

LESLIE BYELAS

Established in 1962

1804 POST ROAD EAST

WESTPORT, CONNECTICUT 06880

Telephone: 203-259-0599

Fax: 203-255-2570

General Civil Trial and Appellate Practice in all State and Federal Courts. Matrimonial, Real Estate.

FIRM PROFILE: Leslie Byelas has been dedicated to serving clients throughout Fairfield and surrounding counties for over thirty-seven years. Mr. Byelas practices primarily in the area of civil litigation law.

Mr. *LESLIE BYELAS,* born Bridgeport, Connecticut, September 20, 1936; admitted to bar, 1961, Connecticut. *Education:* Boston University (B.S.B.A., 1958; LL.B., 1961). Assistant U.S. Attorney, District of Connecticut, 1969-1972. Chief Counsel, Liquor Price Fixing Investigation Commission, State of Connecticut, 1977-1978. *Member:* Bridgeport (Chairman, Federal Courts and Procedure Committee, 1973-1974), Westport, Connecticut and American Bar Associations; The Association of Trial Lawyers of America.

CASPER & DE TOLEDO LLC

WESTPORT, CONNECTICUT

(See Stamford)

Civil Trial and Appellate Practice in all State and Federal Courts. Personal Injury, Medical Malpractice, Product Liability, Workers' Compensation, Employment Discrimination, Employee Rights and Benefits, Civil Rights, Contracts and Family Law.

LAW OFFICES OF MICHAEL GENE CLEAR

WESTPORT, CONNECTICUT

(See Stamford)

General Civil Trial Practice in State and Federal Courts. Personal Injury, Negligence, Environmental Law and Hazardous Waste Litigation, Insurance Coverage Litigation, Complex Litigation, Commercial Litigation, Alternative Dispute Resolution, Mediation, Municipal Law, Environmental Insurance Defense, Insurance Coverage, Probate Litigation, Wills, Elder Law, Incapacity Planning, Probate Administration.

COBB & EISENBERG LLC

WESTPORT, CONNECTICUT

(See Westport)

Securities, Corporate Law, Venture Capital, Public Offerings, Domestic and Offshore Hedge Funds and other investment vehicles, Investment Adviser Regulation; Broker-Dealer Regulation.

COHEN AND WOLF, P.C.

190 MAIN STREET

WESTPORT, CONNECTICUT 06880

Telephone: 203-222-1034

Email: cw@cohenandwolf.com

URL: http://www.cohenandwolf.com

Bridgeport, Connecticut Office: 1115 Broad Street. Telephone: 203-368-0211. Facsimile: 203-394-9901.

Danbury, Connecticut Office: 158 Deer Hill Avenue. Telephone: 203-792-2771. Facsimile: 203-791-8149.

Stamford, Connecticut Office: 112 Prospect Street. Telephone: 203-964-9907. Facsimile: 203-576-8504.

General Practice. Business Transactions, Commercial Litigation, Employment and Labor, Family and Matrimonial, Land Use, Municipal, Personal Injury, Physicians Practice, Real Estate, Securities, Tax, Trusts and Estates. Litigation in all Courts.

Richard L. Albrecht
Jonathan S. Bowman
Martin J. Albert
Stewart I. Edelstein
G. Kenneth Bernhard
Greta E. Solomon
Richard G. Kent
Richard Slavin
Richard J. Di Marco
David B. Zabel
David M. Levine
Jocelyn B. Hurwitz
Patricia C. Sullivan

(This Listing Continued)

COHEN AND WOLF, P.C., Westport—Continued

(For complete biographical data on all personnel, see Professional Biographies at Bridgeport, Connecticut)

COHN BIRNBAUM & SHEA P.C.

Established in 1976

830 POST ROAD EAST, 2ND FLOOR

WESTPORT, CONNECTICUT 06880

Telephone: 203-341-9595

Fax: 203-341-9696

New York, New York Office: 67 Wall Street, Suite 2411. Telephone: 212-949-9555. Fax: 212-949-7997.

Hartford, Connecticut Office: 100 Pearl Street. Telephone: 860-493-2200. Fax: 860-727-0361.

Banking, Bankruptcy, Business, Commercial, Communications, Condominium, Construction, Contracting, Corporation, Creditors Rights, Employment, Environmental, Finance, Health Care Administrative, Joint Ventures, Land Use, Media, Municipal, Professional Liability Defense, Real Estate, Securities, Shopping Center, Taxation, Technology, Litigation in all State and Federal Courts.

FIRM PROFILE: Our success in building a comprehensive practice in business law is due in part to our demonstrated ability to attract competent legal professionals and back them up with a strong support staff. We have carefully recruited only experienced individuals whose legal expertise is complemented by a strong appreciation of the business environment and a dedication to timely, personalized legal service.

RICHARD J. SHEA, JR., born Bridgeport, Connecticut, March 26, 1957; admitted to bar, 1982, Connecticut; 1983, U.S. Tax Court; 1999, New York. *Education:* Yale University (B.A., 1979); University of Connecticut (M.B.A., 1982; J.D., 1982); Boston University (LL.M., Taxation, 1985). ***PRACTICE AREAS:*** Business Law; Commercial Real Estate; Securities; Technology Law. ***Email:*** rshea@cb-shea.com

MATTHEW FEIGENBAUM, born Brooklyn, New York, February 23, 1943; admitted to bar, 1980, New York, Florida and U.S. District Court, Southern District of New York; 1992, California; 1997, Connecticut. *Education:* Brooklyn College of the City University of New York (B.A., 1963); State University of New York at Albany (M.A., 1966); Fordham University (J.D., cum laude, 1979). *Member:* The Florida Bar; State Bar of California. (Also of Counsel, New York, NY Office). ***Email:*** mattf@cbsheawestport.com

ROBERT H. FEIGENBAUM, born Middletown, New York, February 6, 1969; admitted to bar, 1996, California; 1998, Connecticut. *Education:* State University of New York at Albany (B.A., 1991); University of San Diego (J.D., 1995). *Member:* State Bar of California. ***Email:*** robf@cbsheawestport.com

REPRESENTATIVE CLIENTS: Amphenol Corporation; American Card Technology, Inc.; Arthur A. Watson & Co., Inc.; The Balf Co.; Collins Enterprises, L.L.C.; E.A. Patten Company; Employers Reinsurance Corporation; Grove Property Trust; Guida-Seibert Dairy Co.; Hamden Plaza; The Hartford Roofing Co., Inc.; Icon International, Inc.; Konover & Associates, Inc.; Lehman Brothers Holdings, Inc.; McDonald's Corporation; New Haven Savings Bank, Inc.; People's Bank; Regency Savings Bank; Sabre Communications, Inc.; St. Francis Hospital & Medical Center; System Pros, Inc.; Tri-City Plaza; Walgreen Co.; Wasley Products, Inc.; Webster Bank; Winstanley Enterprises, L.L.C.
REFERENCE: Webster Bank.

(For Complete Biographical data on all personnel, see Professional biographies at Hartford, Connecticut).

COUSINS, JOHNSON & DESROSIERS, P.C.

WESTPORT, CONNECTICUT

(See Stratford)

Workers' Compensation, Personal Injury, Trials, Real Estate, Probate.

CRAMER & AHERN

38 POST ROAD WEST

WESTPORT, CONNECTICUT 06880

Telephone: 203-222-7000

Telecopier: 203-222-7788

Email: cramerandahern@lifeinvest.net

URL: http://www.lawyers.com/calaw

General Civil Practice. Real Estate, Negligence, Probate, Estate Planning, Business Law, Corporate Law, Art Law. Trials.

ALLAN P. CRAMER, born Norwich, Connecticut, March 8, 1937; admitted to bar, 1964, Connecticut; 1965, U.S. Court of Appeals, Second Circuit and U.S. Court of Military Appeals; 1966, U.S. District Court, District of Connecticut. *Education:* University of Pennsylvania (B.A., cum laude, 1958); University of Connecticut (J.D., 1964). Author: "International Copyright and the Soviet Union," 1965 Duke Law Journal 531. Attorney, Office of the General Counsel, U.S. Department of Health, Education and Welfare, 1964-1965. Member, 1967— and President, 1968-1972, University of Pennsylvania Club of Fairfield County. Justice of the Peace, 1973-1977. Trustee, 1975-1982 and Treasurer, 1976-1978, Westport Public Library. Member, 1983-1987 and Secretary, 1985-1987, Zoning Board of Appeals, Town of Westport. Member, Panel of Arbitrators, American Arbitration Association. *Member:* Westport and Connecticut Bar Associations. ***PRACTICE AREAS:*** Civil Practice; Real Estate; Negligence; Probate; Estate Planning; Business Law; Corporate Law; Trial Practice.

ANTHONY E. AHERN, born New Haven, Connecticut, September 8, 1949; admitted to bar, 1979, Connecticut and U.S. District Court, District of Connecticut. *Education:* Southern Connecticut State College (B.A., 1972); University of Connecticut (J.D., with honors, 1979). Recipient: American Jurisprudence Award for Evidence, 1978; Little, Brown & Company Award for Evidence, 1978. Member, Westport Representative Town Meeting, 1983-1987. *Member:* Westport and Connecticut Bar Associations; Connecticut Trial Lawyers Association. ***PRACTICE AREAS:*** Civil Practice; Real Estate; Negligence; Probate; Estate Planning; Business Law; Corporate Law; Trial Practice.

OF COUNSEL

ROBERT N. GROSBY, born New York, N.Y., January 13, 1927; admitted to bar, 1950, Connecticut and New York. *Education:* Dartmouth College; Harvard University (A.B., 1947); Cornell University (J.D., 1950). Phi Alpha Delta. Assistant Clerk, 1957-1958 and 1964; Counsel, 1965-1966, Connecticut House of Representatives. *Member:* Norwalk-Wilton (President, 1976), Connecticut and Federal (Vice President for Connecticut, 1965) Bar Associations; Lawyer-Pilots Bar Association.

REPRESENTATIVE CLIENTS: Fleet Bank, N.A.; One Danbury Road Shopping Center; Estate of Ina Balin; Keith Richards.

THE DASILVA LAW FIRM, LLC

830 POST ROAD E.

WESTPORT, CONNECTICUT 06880

Telephone: 203-226-0009

203-226-6445

Email: ericdasilva@lawyer.com

URL: http://www.lawyers.com/ericdasilva

Real Estate, Litigation, Negligence, Personal Injury.

ERIC S. DASILVA, born September 26, 1962; admitted to bar, 1987, Connecticut and U.S. District Court, District of Connecticut. *Education:* Fairfield University (B.A., 1984); Washington College of Law of American University (J.D., 1987). ***PRACTICE AREAS:*** Litigation; Personal Injury; Real Estate; Negligence. ***Email:*** ericdasilva@lawyer.com

DEPANFILIS & VALLERIE, LLC

WESTPORT, CONNECTICUT

(See Norwalk)

General Civil and Criminal Litigation Practice in all Courts. Negligence, Medical Malpractice, Taxation, Corporation, Estate Planning, Probate, Real Estate, Workers Compensation, Family and Landlord and Tenant Law.

DAVID L. DEPHTEREOS

191 POST ROAD WEST

WESTPORT, CONNECTICUT 06880

Telephone: 203-221-2852

Fax: 203-221-2853

Email: dephtereos@aol.com

General Corporate and Commercial Practice, Air Cargo, Maritime Law, Surface Transportation, International Trade and Transactions.

FIRM PROFILE: David L. Dephtereos has represented regional, national, and international clients involved in transportation and logistics, telecommunication, international transactions, mergers and acquisitions, and general corporate and commercial matters. Relying on his experience as general counsel of two publicly-held companies, he has developed practical solutions to business problems promptly, effectively, and efficiently, with a minimum of overhead.

DAVID L. DEPHTEREOS, born Ithaca, New York, April 10, 1954; admitted to bar, 1980, New York; 1983, Connecticut; U.S. District Courts, Southern, Eastern and Northern Districts of New York; U.S. District Court, District of Connecticut. *Education:* Cornell University (B.A. in Government, cum laude,

(This Listing Continued)

1976; J.D., 1979). Vice President, General Counsel and Secretary, Reeves Industries, Inc., 1991-1994; Vice President, General Counsel, and Secretary, Air Express International Corporation, 1985-1991. Corporate Attorney, Brink's, Incorporated, 1983-1985. *Member:* Connecticut Bar Association; Transportation Lawyers Association (Chairman, Computer and Technology Committee); Association for Transportation Law, Logistics and Policy.

EDWARD H. DIETRICH

Established in 1985

125 MAIN STREET
WESTPORT, CONNECTICUT 06880
Telephone: 203-222-7600
Fax: 203-222-1830
Email: ehdlaw@webquill.com
URL: http://www.lawyers.com/dietrichlaw

New York, N.Y. Office: 780 Third Avenue, 12th Floor, 10017. Telephone: 212-599-5075.

Estate Tax Planning, Estate and Gift Taxation, Wills and Trusts, Probate and Administration.

EDWARD H. DIETRICH, born New York, N.Y., January 6, 1944; admitted to bar, 1972, New York; 1976, Spain; 1979, Connecticut. *Education:* Yale University (B.A., cum laude, 1967); New York University (J.D., 1971); Universidad de Sevilla, Spain (Licenciado en Derecho, 1976). *Member:* Westport, Connecticut and American Bar Associations. ***LANGUAGES:*** Spanish.

REFERENCE: The Bank of Darien at Westport.

DISERIO MARTIN O'CONNOR & CASTIGLIONI LLP

WESTPORT, CONNECTICUT

(See Stamford)

General Practice. Litigation and Trials in all Courts. Corporate, Commercial Finance, Securities, Taxation, Banking, Foreclosure and Workout, Real Estate Law, Personal Injury and Negligence, Employment Law, Wrongful Termination, Workers Compensation, Insurance Coverage and Defense, Family, Creditors Rights and Bankruptcy, Trusts, Probate, Estate and Tax Planning.

FOGARTY COHEN SELBY & NEMIROFF LLC

WESTPORT, CONNECTICUT

(See Greenwich)

Litigation in all Courts, Real Estate and Land Use, Estate Planning and Probate, Corporate, Matrimonial, Administrative and Environmental, Appellate Practice, Business, Civil Trial, Commercial Litigation, Construction, Family, Labor and Employment, Medical Malpractice, Trust and Product Liability.

GABORIAULT & PEARSALL, P.C.

235 POST ROAD WEST
WESTPORT, CONNECTICUT 06880
Telephone: 203-454-0773
Fax: 203-454-1284
Email: info@gaboriault-pearsall.com
URL: http://www.lawyers.com/gaboriault&pearsall

Commercial Real Estate Finance, Asset Based Finance, Leasing, Loan Workouts, Loan Restructuring, Real Estate, Corporate Law, Corporate Collections.

PETER W. GABORIAULT, born Norwalk, Connecticut, March 18, 1956; admitted to bar, 1982, Connecticut; 1983, New York; 1984, U.S. District Court Southern and Eastern Districts of New York and District of Connecticut. *Education:* George Washington University (B.B.A., 1978; M.B.A., 1979); Pace University (J.D., 1982). *Member:* Westport, Connecticut and New York State Bar Associations. ***PRACTICE AREAS:*** Commercial Real Estate Acquisitions; Residential Real Estate Acquisitions; Land Use and Zoning; Commercial Real Estate Financing; Residential Real Estate Financing; Corporate Collections. ***Email:*** gaboriault@gaboriault-pearsall.com

STEVEN W. PEARSALL, born Huntington, New York, September 21, 1962; admitted to bar, 1988, New York; 1992, U.S. District Court, Southern District of New York; 1997, Connecticut. *Education:* University of Notre Dame (B.B.A., 1984); Fordham University (J.D., 1987). *Member:* American Bar Association. ***PRACTICE AREAS:*** Commercial Real Estate Financing; Commercial Real Estate Acquisitions and Sales; Leasing; Asset Based Lending; Equipment Finance and Leasing; Corporate Law. ***Email:*** pearsall@gaboriault-pearsall.com

(This Listing Continued)

DOUGLAS GILMORE

11 HARDING LANE
WESTPORT, CONNECTICUT 06880
Telephone: 203-226-6277
Fax: 203-222-0779
URL: http://www.douggatsnet.net

Criminal and Civil Litigation in the State and Federal Courts. Appellate Practice. Entertainment, Sports, Radio, TV, Communications, Trademarks, Copyrights, Unfair Competition, Corporate, Trade Regulation and Legislative Practice.

DOUGLAS GILMORE, born Oak Ridge, Tennessee, June 24, 1951; admitted to bar, 1977, Connecticut; 1978, U.S. District Court, District of Connecticut; 1979, U.S. Court of Appeals, Second Circuit; 1980, U.S. District Court, Eastern, Northern, and Western Districts of New York, U.S. Court of International Trade and U.S. Tax Court; 1981, U.S. District Court, Southern District of New York, Temporary Emergency Court of Appeals for the United States and U.S. Supreme Court; 1982, U.S. Court of Appeals for the Federal Circuit and U.S. Claims Court; 1983, New York. *Education:* Fairfield University (B.A., 1974); Villanova Law School (J.D., 1977).

ROBERT E. GRANT

8 MYRTLE AVENUE
WESTPORT, CONNECTICUT 06881
Telephone: 203-227-6769
URL: http://www.lawyers.com/robertgrant

Real Estate, Probate, Corporate, Zoning, Estate Planning and Negligence.

ROBERT E. GRANT, born Westport, Connecticut, May 18, 1948; admitted to bar, 1977, Connecticut; 1981, U.S. District Court, District of Connecticut. *Education:* Georgetown University (B.A., 1970); American University (J.D., cum laude, 1977). Lecturer, Real Estate Law, Norwalk Community College, 1984-1987. Member, 1982-1986 and Chairman, 1983-1986, Westport Conservation Commission. Member, Westport Shellfish Commission, 1983—. Member, Board of Directors, Westport Arts Center, 1984-1988. Member, Board of Directors, Westport United Way, 1990—. *Member:* Westport (Treasurer, 1989; President, 1991), Connecticut and American Bar Associations. ***PRACTICE AREAS:*** General Practice; Real Estate; Probate; Estate Planning; Zoning Law.

REPRESENTATIVE CLIENTS: Prudential Relocation; Kowalsky Brothers, Inc.; Roseville Estates, Inc.; Westport Country Estates, Inc.
REFERENCE: Fleet Bank.

GREEN AND GROSS, P.C.

WESTPORT, CONNECTICUT

(See Bridgeport)

Bankruptcy Law, Commercial and Construction Claims.

HALLORAN & SAGE LLP

315 POST ROAD WEST
WESTPORT, CONNECTICUT 06880-4739
Telephone: 203-227-2855
Fax: 203-227-6992
URL: http://www.halloran-sage.com

Hartford, Connecticut Office: One Goodwin Square, 225 Asylum Street, 06103. Telephone: 860-522-6103. Fax: 860-548-0006.

Middletown, Connecticut Office: 300 Plaza Middlesex, 06457. Telephone: 860-346-8641. Fax: 860-344-1641.

Washington, D.C. Office: 1627 I Street, N.W., Suite 610, 20006. Telephone: 202-496-9270. Fax: 202-496-9279.

Administrative Law, Administrative Hearings and Appeals, Alternative Dispute Resolution, Appellate Practice, Aviation Products Liability, Bad Faith Litigation, Banking Law, Bankruptcy, Breach of Contract, Business Disputes, Business Law, Business Litigation, Business Planning, Casualty Insurance Litigation, Civil Appeals, Civil Litigation, Civil Rights Litigation, Class Action, Commercial Litigation, Complex Civil Litigation, Construction and Design Law, Construction Litigation, Corporate Contracts, Corporate Law, Criminal Litigation, Drug and Medical Device Litigation, Employment Law, Energy and Health Law, Environmental Law, Excess Insurance, Family Business Succession, Fidelity and Surety Law, Finance, Education Law, Employment Law, Environmental, Environmental Insurance Coverage, ERISA, ERISA Litigation, Estate Administration, Estate and Gift Taxation, Estates Law, Excess Insurance, General Corporate Law, General Liability, Government Contracts, Government Finance, Government Relations, Health

(This Listing Continued)

HALLORAN & SAGE LLP, Westport—Continued

and Life Insurance Litigation, Insurance Bad Faith Litigation, Insurance Coverage, Institutional Liability Law, Insurance Litigation, Insurance Regulation, Intellectual Property Litigation, International Law, Judicial Review, Labor and Employment, Land Use Planning Law, Lead Paint Litigation, Legislative Practice, Liquor Liability, Lobbying, Marine Insurance Defense, Medical Malpractice, Mergers and Acquisitions and Divestitures, Municipal Law, Municipal Liability, Probate Law, Products Liability Litigation, Professional Liability Litigation, Professional Regulation, Premises Liability, Property Insurance, Psychological Injury Claims, Public Utilities Law, Public Utility Regulation, Real Estate Transactions, Reinsurance Law, Risk Management Consulting, Secured Lending, Securities Law, Subrogation, Taxation Law, Telecommunications Law, Torts, Trade Association, Trucking Transportation Litigation, Trust Law, Unfair Trade, Uninsured and Underinsured Motorists, University Law, Workers Compensation Law, Zoning, Planning and Land Use.

(For Biographical Data on all Personnel, See Professional Biographies at Hartford, Connecticut)

HEAGNEY, LENNON & SLANE LLP

WESTPORT, CONNECTICUT

(See Greenwich)

General Practice, Real Estate, Trusts and Estates, Probate, Corporation and Business Law, Civil and Criminal Litigation, Zoning and Family Law.

HERMENZE & MARCANTONIO

19 LUDLOW ROAD, SUITE 101
WESTPORT, CONNECTICUT 06880
Telephone: 203-226-6552
Fax: 203-226-6035

Trusts and Estates, Wills, Probate, Taxation.

DAVID R. HERMENZE, born Norwalk, Connecticut, April 28, 1960; admitted to bar, 1986, Connecticut. *Education:* Beloit College (B.A., magna cum laude, 1982); Cornell University (J.D., cum laude, 1986). Co-Author, "The Role of the Guardian Ad Litem in Probate Proceedings," 65 Conn. Bar Journal 6 (1991); "Wills and Trusts," Connecticut Lawyers Deskbook, 1998. Member, 1994— and Executive Committee Member, 1995—, Estate Planning Council of Lower Fairfield County. Member: Connecticut Estate and Tax Planning Council, 1993—. *Member:* Westport, Stamford Regional, Connecticut (Member: Estates and Probate Section; Executive Committee, 1999—; Editorial Staff, Estates and Probate Section Newsletter, 1997—) and American (Member, Real Property, Probate and Trust Law Section) Bar Associations. Fellow, American College of Trust and Estate Counsel. **PRACTICE AREAS:** Trusts and Estates; Wills; Probate; Taxation.

EDWARD MARCANTONIO, born Yonkers, New York, November 15, 1965; admitted to bar, 1991, Connecticut; 1992, New York. *Education:* Columbia College (B.A., cum laude, 1987); Fordham University (J.D., 1991). Member, Estate Planning Council of Lower Fairfield County, 1997—. *Member:* Westport (Member, Executive Committee, 1996—; Treasurer, 1998-1999; Vice President, 1999—; Co-Chairman, Estate Planning Section, 1998—), Stamford Regional (Vice-Chairman, Estate Planning Section, 1998—), Connecticut (Member, Estates and Probate Section) and New York State (Member, Estates and Probate Section) Bar Associations. **PRACTICE AREAS:** Trusts and Estates; Wills; Probate; Taxation.

JAMES D. FUNNELL, JR., born Oklahoma City, Oklahoma, January 12, 1960; admitted to bar, 1988, Connecticut and U.S. District Court, District of Connecticut; 1989, U.S. Tax Court. *Education:* Oklahoma State University (B.S., 1983); Oklahoma City University (J.D., 1986); McGeorge School of Law, University of the Pacific (LL.M., Business and Taxation, 1987). Editor, Newsletter, Estates and Probate Section, Connecticut Bar Association. *Member:* Stamford/Norwalk Regional, Connecticut (Member, Executive Committee, 1993—) and American Bar Associations. Fellow, American College of Trust and Estate Counsel (Member, Editorial Board). **PRACTICE AREAS:** Estate Planning; Estate Settlements; Probate; Trust Administration; Elder Law; Disability Planning.

IVEY, BARNUM & O'MARA, LLC

WESTPORT, CONNECTICUT

(See Greenwich)

General Practice. E-Commerce, Litigation in all Courts. Corporate, Commercial, Finance, Taxation, Trusts, Probate, Estate Planning, Family Law, Zoning, Environmental, Real Estate, Employment Law and Elder Law.

KOVE & KOSAKOW, LLC

Established in 1995
265 POST ROAD WEST
WESTPORT, CONNECTICUT 06880
Telephone: 203-454-0100
Fax: 203-454-3636
Email: jmk@kovkos.com
URL: http://www.kovkos.com

New York, New York Office: 685 Third Avenue, 30th Floor. Telephone: 212-297-0255.

Estate Planning, Probate, Estate Tax, Estate Administration.

MEMBERS OF FIRM

MYRON KOVE, admitted to bar, 1961, New York, U.S. District Court, Eastern and Southern Districts of New York; U.S. Court of Appeals Second Circuit (Not admitted in Connecticut). *Education:* New York University (A.B., cum laude with honors, 1956; LL.M., 1967); Harvard University (J.D., 1960). Phi Beta Kappa; Tau Kappa Alpha. Co-Author: "Real Estate Professionals Tax Guide," and "Handling Federal Estate and Gift Taxes," 6th Edition. Contributing author, "Real Estate Transactions," all published by West Group. Exec. Editor, "Insight & Strategies," Estate Planning News Letter for Professionals. (Resident, New York, New York Office). **PRACTICE AREAS:** Estate Planning; Tax Planning; Business Planning; Real Estate. **Email:** mkove@kovkos.com

JAMES M. KOSAKOW, admitted to bar, 1985, Connecticut, New York, District of Columbia and U.S. District Court, Southern and Eastern Districts of New York; 1991, Florida; 1993, U.S. Tax Court. *Education:* Connecticut College (B.A., 1976); Benjamin N. Cardozo School of Law, Yeshiva University (J.D., 1984). Co-Author, "Handling Federal Estate and Gift Taxes," 6th Edition. Assistant Editor, "Insights and Strategies," estate planning publication. (. **PRACTICE AREAS:** Estate Planning; Probate; Estate Taxation. **Email:** jmk@kovkos.com

ASSOCIATES

DOROTHY M. FREEBURG, admitted to bar, 1985, New York; 1991, Connecticut. *Education:* New York Institute of Technology (B.S., 1981); Fordham University School of Law (J.D., 1984). **PRACTICE AREAS:** Estate Planning; Estate Administration.

LINDA S. BROWN, admitted to bar, 1994, Connecticut; 1995, New York. *Education:* Syracuse University (B.A., with honors, 1971); Benjamin N. Cardozo School of Law, Yeshiva University (J.D., 1994). **PRACTICE AREAS:** Estate Planning; Estate Administration.

MICHAEL A. LAUX

EIGHT MYRTLE AVENUE
WESTPORT, CONNECTICUT 06880
Telephone: 203-226-3392
Fax: 203-222-8023
Email: lauxlaw@aol.com
URL: http://www.lawyers.com/michaelalaux

General Practice before State and Federal Courts. Estate Planning, Probate, Residential Real Estate, Commercial Real Estate, Personal Injury.

MICHAEL A. LAUX, born New York, New York, November 28, 1941; admitted to bar, 1967, Connecticut; 1970, U.S. District Court, District of Connecticut. *Education:* Amherst College (B.A., 1963); Fordham University (LL.B., 1967). President, United States Masters Swimming, 1981-1985. President, Projects Return, 1992-1995. Member: Board of Directors, 1985-1994; Board of Trustees, 1995—, Westport YMCA; Staples High School Tuition Grants Committee, 1988-1990; Westport Youth Commission, 1996—. *Member:* Westport (Member, Executive Committee, 1986-1987), Connecticut and American (Member, Sections on: Real Property, Probate and Trust Law; Family Law) Bar Associations. **LANGUAGES:** French.

LAW OFFICES OF ROGER J. LEIFER

Established in 1978
3 SYLVAN ROAD SOUTH
P.O. BOX 5180
WESTPORT, CONNECTICUT 06881
Telephone: 203-227-8463
Fax: 203-226-3366

Real Estate, Planning, Zoning and Corporate.

(This Listing Continued)

FIRM PROFILE: The Law Offices of Roger J. Leifer are dedicated to representing clients throughout Fairfield county with over twenty-five years of experience. Mr. Leifer practices primarily in the areas of real estate, planning and zoning law.

ROGER J. LEIFER, born New York, N.Y., May 14, 1950; admitted to bar, 1974, New York; 1975, District of Columbia; 1978, Connecticut and U.S. Tax Court; 1980, U.S. Supreme Court. *Education:* Columbia College (B.A., cum laude, 1971); London School of Economics, London, England; Harvard Law School (J.D., 1974). Trial Attorney and Recipient of Meritorious Service Award, Federal Trade Commission, 1974-1977. *Member:* Westport, Connecticut and New York State Bar Associations; District of Columbia Bar.

REPRESENTATIVE CLIENTS: Prudential Relocation Management; Prudential Realty Inc.; Morgan Stanley; General Motors Corporation—Argonaut Realty Division; Executive Relocation, Inc.; Swiss Bank, SBC Warburg (UBS); Chase Manhattan Bank of Connecticut; Fleet Bank; Peoples Bank; Emigrant Savings Bank; The Price Club, Inc.; Coldwell Banker; Intermatrix, Inc.; Jones Stroud Holdings, Inc., Coventry, England; Midland Business Machines, Inc., Northampton, England; First American Title Insurance Co.; International Management Group; American Title Insurance Co.; Investment Capital Associates; Talbots, Inc.; Lenders Services, Inc.; Appraisal & Title Management Services, Inc.; Leon Hirsch, Former Chairman U.S. Surgical Corp.; Nestle Corp.; First Matter, LLC.
APPROVED ATTORNEYS FOR: Prudential Insurance Company of America; Norwest Mortgage Co.; Peoples Bank of Bridgeport; Fidelity Title Insurance Co.; Chase Manhattan Bank; Chicago Title Insurance Co.; First American Title Insurance Co.; Fleet Bank; G.E. Capital; GMAC; Emigrant Mortgage Co.; Webster Bank; Ridgefield Bank; PNC Bank.

MICHAEL J. LEVENTHAL

Established in 1987

155 POST ROAD EAST, SUITE 6
WESTPORT, CONNECTICUT 06881
Telephone: 203-227-9751
Fax: 203-227-9753
Email: levlaw@snet.net
URL: http://www.lawyers.com/leventhallaw

Civil Litigation, Personal Injury, Family Law, Construction, Workers Compensation, Real Estate, Landlord Tenant; Collections.

MICHAEL J. LEVENTHAL, born Yonkers, New York, April 15, 1956; admitted to bar, 1987, Connecticut; 1988, New York; U.S. District Court, District of Connecticut and Southern and Eastern Districts of New York. *Education:* Berklee College of Music (B.A., cum laude, 1979); Pace University (J.D., 1987). *Member:* Connecticut and New York State Bar Associations; Connecticut Trial Lawyers Association. ***PRACTICE AREAS:*** Civil Litigation; Personal Injury; Construction; Workers Compensation; Family Law; Entertainment Law; Real Estate.

LEVETT ROCKWOOD P.C.

33 RIVERSIDE AVENUE
P.O. BOX 5116
WESTPORT, CONNECTICUT 06881
Telephone: 203-222-0885
Telecopier: 203-226-8025
URL: http://www.levettrockwood.com

Corporate, Health Care and Hospitals, Litigation, Taxation, Employment, Information Technology, Intellectual Property, Mergers and Acquisitions, Securities, Capital Formation and Financing, Advertising, Promotion, Creditors' Rights, Estate Planning, Commercial Real Estate.

ROBERT O. BARBERI, born Chelsea, Massachusetts, July 15, 1945; admitted to bar, 1972, New York; 1974, U.S. Court of Appeals, Second Circuit; 1975, U.S. Supreme Court and U.S. District Court, Southern and Eastern Districts of New York; 1988, Connecticut; 1992, U.S. District Court, District of Connecticut. *Education:* Amherst College (B.A., cum laude, 1967); Columbia University (J.D., 1970). Phi Delta Phi. Co-Author: "Environmental Issues in the Packaging Industry," Journal of Environmental Law & Practice, July/August, 1993. Member, Board of Advisors, Journal of Environmental Law and Practice, 1994-2000. *Member:* The Association of the Bar of The City of New York; Connecticut and American Bar Associations. [Capt., U.S. Army Reserve, 1970-1978]. ***PRACTICE AREAS:*** Corporate Law; Commercial Law; Mergers and Acquisitions. ***Email:*** rbarberi@levettrockwood.com

DEBRA R. CARDINALI, born Pittsburgh, Pennsylvania, October 1, 1957; admitted to bar, 1985, Connecticut; 1989, New York. *Education:* Old Dominion University (B.S., 1979); University of Virginia (J.D., 1985). Alpha Chi; Psi Chi. With Legal Adviser's Office, University of Virginia, 1983-1985. *Member:* Connecticut and American Bar Associations; American Health Lawyers; Connecticut Hospital Associations. ***PRACTICE AREAS:*** Mergers and Acquisitions; Health Care Law; Corporate Law; Commercial Finance. ***Email:*** dcardinali@levettrockwood.com

(This Listing Continued)

EDWARD B. CHANSKY, born Beverly, Massachusetts, March 17, 1960; admitted to bar, 1987, Connecticut. *Education:* Yale University (B.A., summa cum laude, 1982); University Innsbruck, Austria; Harvard University (J.D., cum laude, 1987). Phi Beta Kappa. Judicial Clerkship, Associate Justice Ruth I. Abrams, Massachusetts Supreme Judicial Court, 1987-1988. Co-Chair, Promotion Marketing Association, Westchester-Fairfield Chapter. *Member:* Connecticut (Chair, Intellectual Property Law Section, 1988-2001) and American Bar Associations. ***LANGUAGES:*** German. ***PRACTICE AREAS:*** Copyright and Trademark; Internet Law; Advertising and Promotion; Antitrust and Unfair Competition. ***Email:*** echansky@levettrockwood.com

STEPHEN M. COWHERD, born São Paulo, Brazil, November 15, 1959; admitted to bar, 1991, Connecticut; 1992, New York. *Education:* State University of New York at Stony Brook (B.A., 1982); St. John's University (J.D., with high honors, 1991). Phi Beta Kappa. Co-Author: "Case Management From the Other Side of the Bench," Anglo-American Bar Exchange, 1994. Adjunct Faculty, Fordham University School of Law, 1997-1998 and 2000-2001. *Member:* Connecticut (Member: Executive Committee; Health Law Section; Federal Practice Section) and American Bar Associations; American Health Lawyers Association. ***PRACTICE AREAS:*** Health Care Law; Hospital Law; Civil Litigation. ***Email:*** scowherd@levettrockwood.com

MADELEINE F. GROSSMAN, born New York, N.Y., September 2, 1939; admitted to bar, 1976, Connecticut and U.S. District Court, District of Connecticut; 1979, U.S. Court of Appeals, Second Circuit; 1982, U.S. District Court, Southern and Eastern Districts of New York and U.S. District Court, Eastern District of Michigan; 1984, U.S. Supreme Court. *Education:* Cornell University (B.A., 1961); Yale University (J.D., 1976). Phi Beta Kappa; Phi Kappa Phi. *Member:* Westport, Connecticut and American Bar Associations. ***REPORTED CASES:*** Bailey Employment System, Inc. v. Hahn, 655 F. 2nd 473 (2nd Cir. 1981); 545 F. Supp. 62 (D. Conn. 1982); Bergesen d.y. A/S v. Lindholm, 760 F. Supp. 976 (D. Conn. 1991); NCC Sunday Inserts, Inc. v. World Color Press, 759 F. Supp. 1004 (S.D.N.Y. 1991); Energy Factors Incorporated v. Nuevo Energy Company, §96, 883 Fed. Sec. L. Rep. (CCII) (S.D.N.Y. 1992); American Oil Co. v. Valenti, 179 Conn. 349 (1979). ***PRACTICE AREAS:*** Civil Litigation. ***Email:*** mgrossman@levettrockwood.com

DORIT SCHUTZENGEL HEIMER, born Haifa, Israel, November 25, 1953; admitted to bar, 1979, New York and U.S. District Court, Southern and Eastern Districts of New York; 1987, Connecticut; 1989, U.S. Court of Appeals, Second Circuit; 1998, U.S. Court of Appeals, First Circuit. *Education:* Wellesley College (B.A., 1975) Phi Beta Kappa; Harvard University (J.D., cum laude, 1978). *Member:* Westport, Connecticut (Member, Federal Practice Section; Executive Committee) and American Bar Associations. ***REPORTED CASES:*** Fornaro v. McManus, 187 F. 3rd 621 (1st Cir. 1998); NCC Sunday Inserts, Inc. v. World Color Press, 759 F. Supp. 1004 (S.D.N.Y. 1991); Pepsico, Inc. v. Dunlop Tire & Rubber Corp., 578 F. Supp. 196 (S.D.N.Y. 1984); Southport Manor Convalescent Center, Inc. v. Kundrath, 41 Conn. App. 747 (1996); Elisabeth Solomon v. Hall-Brooke Foundation, Inc., 30 Conn. App. 129 (1993). ***PRACTICE AREAS:*** Civil Litigation; Employment Law; Medical Malpractice. ***Email:*** dheimer@levettrockwood.com

CHERYL L. JOHNSON, born Columbus, Ohio, 1961; admitted to bar, 1987, New York; 1991, U.S. Tax Court; 1993, Connecticut. *Education:* Lafayette College (B.A., magna cum laude, with honors, 1983); State University of New York at Buffalo (J.D., cum laude, 1986); New York University (LL.M., Taxation, 1990). Phi Beta Kappa. Member, State University of New York at Buffalo Law Review, 1984-1986. *Member:* New York State (Member: Section on Tax; Committee on Pass-through Entities), Connecticut (Member, Tax Section) and American (Member, Section on Tax and Exempt Organizations) Bar Associations. ***PRACTICE AREAS:*** Tax Law; Corporate Law; Securities; Emerging Growth Companies. ***Email:*** cjohnson@levettrockwood.com

MARC J. KURZMAN, born Petersburg, Virginia, August 17, 1958; admitted to bar, 1984, New York; 1985, U.S. District Court, Southern and Eastern Districts of New York; 1987, Connecticut and U.S. District Court, District of Connecticut. *Education:* Cornell University (B.S., 1980); Stanford University; Columbia University (J.D., 1983). Member, Mortar Board National Honor Society. *Member:* The Association of the Bar of the City of New York; Connecticut and American Bar Associations; Connecticut Trial Lawyers Association. ***REPORTED CASES:*** Gateway Co. v. DiNoia, 232 Conn. 223, 1995; In re M&R Apparel, Inc.; Include: 92 B.R.565 (Bkrptcy. D. Conn. 1988). ***PRACTICE AREAS:*** Civil Litigation; Commercial Real Estate Law; Health Law; Hospital Law. ***Email:*** mkurzman@levettrockwood.com

DAVID R. LEVETT, born New Haven, Connecticut, April 14, 1938; admitted to bar, 1962, Connecticut; 1969, U.S. Tax Court; 1980, U.S. District Court, District of Connecticut; 1981, U.S. Court of Appeals, Second Circuit; 1982, U.S. District Court, Southern District of New York. *Education:* Yale University (B.A., 1959; LL.B., 1962). Author: "Treatment of Monetary Fringe Benefits and Post Termination Survival of the Right to Job Security," 72 Yale Law Journal 162, 1962. *Member:* Connecticut and American Bar Associations; American Academy of Healthcare Attorneys. [Captain, J.A.G.C., U.S. Army, 1962-1966]. ***PRACTICE AREAS:*** Corporate Law; Civil Litigation; Health Law; Hospital Law. ***Email:*** dlevett@levettrockwood.com

(This Listing Continued)

LEVETT ROCKWOOD P.C., Westport—Continued

JUDY A. RABKIN, born Brooklyn, New York, September 20, 1944; admitted to bar, 1977, Connecticut and U.S. District Court, District of Connecticut; 1988, U.S. District Court, Southern District of New York. *Education:* Brown University (A.B., magna cum laude, 1966); Yale University (M.A.T., 1967); University of Connecticut (J.D., with high honors, 1977). Phi Beta Kappa. Executive Editor, University of Connecticut Law Review, 1976-1977. Clerk, Justice John Speziale, Connecticut Supreme Court, 1977-1978. *Member:* Connecticut and American Bar Associations. ***PRACTICE AREAS:*** Commercial Real Estate Law; Creditors Rights Law; Bankruptcy Law. ***Email:*** jrabkin@levettrockwood.com

SHARON M. SCHWEITZER, born Hazleton, Pennsylvania, November 18, 1952; admitted to bar, 1977, Connecticut. *Education:* University of Pennsylvania (B.A., magna cum laude, 1974; J.D., 1977). Phi Beta Kappa. *Member:* Connecticut and American Bar Associations. ***PRACTICE AREAS:*** Tax Law; Estate Planning Law. ***Email:*** sschweitzer@levettrockwood.com

STEVEN M. SIEGELAUB, born New York, N.Y., April 5, 1956; admitted to bar, 1983, New York; 1984, Connecticut. *Education:* Wesleyan University (B.A., summa cum laude, Phi Beta Kappa, 1978); Columbia University (J.D., 1982). Harlan Fiske Stone Scholar. *Member:* Connecticut (Member, Real Property Section) and American (Member, Commercial Leasing Committee, Real Property, Probate and Trust Law Section) Bar Associations. ***PRACTICE AREAS:*** Commercial Real Estate Law. ***Email:*** ssiegelaub@levettrockwood.com

PETER H. STRUZZI, born Washington, D.C., August 6, 1960; admitted to bar, 1986, New York; 1989, Connecticut. *Education:* Williams College (B.A., magna cum laude, 1982); University of Pennsylvania (J.D., 1985). Phi Beta Kappa. Articles Editor, Journal of Comparative Business and Capital Market Law, 1984-1985. Instructor, Arthur D. Littleton Legal Writing, University of Pennsylvania Law School, 1984-1985. *Member:* Connecticut, New York State and American (Member, Section on Business Law) Bar Associations. ***PRACTICE AREAS:*** Corporate Law; Securities. ***Email:*** pstruzzi@levettrockwood.com

BARBARA A. YOUNG, born Cincinnati, Ohio, October 23, 1954; admitted to bar, 1980, Maryland; 1982, Connecticut. *Education:* Carleton College (B.A., cum laude, 1976); University of Virginia (J.D., 1980). Member, 1978-1980 and Managing Editor, 1979-1980, Virginia Journal of International Law. *Member:* Connecticut (Member, Business Law Section; Corporate Counsel) and American (Member, Business Law Section; Law of Commerce in Cyberspace) Bar Associations. ***PRACTICE AREAS:*** Corporate Law; Business Law; Securities Law; Mergers and Acquisitions; Commercial Finance Law. ***Email:*** byoung@levettrockwood.com

OF COUNSEL

SUZANNE B. ALBANI, born Albany, New York, September 28, 1943; admitted to bar, 1978, Connecticut. *Education:* Smith College (B.A., 1965); St. John's University (J.D., 1978). Member, St. John's University Law Review, 1976-1978. Author: "Rehabilitating Campus Buildings With Investment Tax Credits," Business Officer Magazine, March, 1983; "Conservation Easements Provide Incentive for Rehabilitation," The National Law Journal, June 30, 1986. *Member:* Connecticut and American Bar Associations; Connecticut Health Lawyers Association. ***PRACTICE AREAS:*** Health Law; Hospital Law; Commercial Real Estate Law; Corporate Law. ***Email:*** salbani@levettrockwood.com

---

MARY CHANG, born Kaohsiung, Taiwan, March 20, 1970; admitted to bar, 1995, Connecticut; 1996, New York and U.S. District Court, Southern District of New York; 1998, U.S. Tax Court. *Education:* State University of New York at Binghamton (B.A., 1991); St. John's University (J.D., cum laude, 1995); New York University (LL.M. in Taxation, 1999). *Member:* Connecticut, New York State and American Bar Associations. ***PRACTICE AREAS:*** Tax Law; Estate Planning; Corporate Law. ***Email:*** mchang@levettrockwood.com

KRISTINE M. CUNNANE, born Belleville, New Jersey, August 22, 1975; admitted to bar, 2000, Connecticut. *Education:* Boston University (B.A., M.A., magna cum laude, 1997); University of Connecticut (J.D., with honors, 2000). Executive Editor, Connecticut Law Review, 1999-2000. *Member:* Connecticut and American Bar Associations. ***PRACTICE AREAS:*** Corporate Law; Securities; Health Care Law; Mergers and Acquisitions. ***Email:*** kcunnane@levettrockwood.com

CHRISTOPHER M. GRAHAM, born Bridgeport, Connecticut, September 14, 1964; admitted to bar, 1992, Connecticut; 1993, New York and U.S. District Court, District of Connecticut. *Education:* Lehigh University (B.S., 1986); University of Connecticut (J.D., with honors, 1992). Associate Editor, University of Connecticut Law Review, 1991-1992. *Member:* Connecticut and

(This Listing Continued)

American Bar Associations. ***PRACTICE AREAS:*** Corporate Law; Mergers and Acquisitions; Securities Law; Emerging Growth Companies; Internet Law. ***Email:*** cgraham@levettrockwood.com

TRACEY C. HAMMER, born Norwalk, Connecticut, November 10, 1965; admitted to bar, 1998, New York and Connecticut. *Education:* University of Connecticut (B.A., 1986); Cornell University (J.D., 1997). *Member:* Connecticut and American Bar Associations. ***PRACTICE AREAS:*** Mergers, Acquisitions and Divestitures; Securities; Corporate Law. ***Email:*** thammer@levettrockwood.com

ROBERT LAPLACA, born Pottsville, Pennsylvania, June 15, 1967; admitted to bar, 1994 New York, Connecticut, U.S. District Court, Southern and Eastern Districts of New York; 2000, U.S. District Court, District of Connecticut. *Education:* Columbia University (B.A., 1989); Brooklyn Law School (J.D., 1993). *Member:* Connecticut and American Bar Associations. ***PRACTICE AREAS:*** Commercial Litigation; Bankruptcy; Health Care Law; Advertising Law. ***Email:*** rlaplaca@levettrockwood.com

JOHN T. SHABAN, born New York, N.Y., June 9, 1964; admitted to bar, 1993, Connecticut and U.S. District Court, District of Connecticut; 1994, New York; 1995, U.S. District Court, Southern, Eastern, and Western Districts of New York; 1996, U.S. Court of Appeals, Second Circuit. *Education:* University of Colorado at Boulder (B.A., 1988); Pace University School of Law (J.D., cum laude, 1993; Environmental Law Certificate, 1993). Member, National Moot Court Team. Member, Pace Law Review. *Member:* Connecticut, New York State and American Bar Associations. ***PRACTICE AREAS:*** Commercial Litigation; Employment Law; Sports Law. ***Email:*** jshaban@levettrockwood.com

PATRICIA D. WEITZMAN, born Bridgeport, Connecticut, February 28, 1953; admitted to bar, 1994, Connecticut. *Education:* University of Connecticut (B.S., magna cum laude, 1974; J.D., with high honors, 1994). Note and Comment Editor, Connecticut Law Review, 1993-1994. Dean's Fellow, 1993. *Member:* Connecticut and American Bar Associations; American Health Lawyers' Association; Connecticut Health Lawyers Association (Director). ***PRACTICE AREAS:*** Health Care; Hospital Law; Corporate Law; Employment Law. ***Email:*** pweitzman@levettrockwood.com

REPRESENTATIVE CLIENTS: Arch Chemicals, Inc.; BenefitPort (BLC Holdings, L.L.C.); Bolt Technology Corporation; Cannondale Corporation; Colt Capital Group; Data Viz, Inc.; FamiliyTime.com, Inc., Farrel Corporation; FKI Industries, Inc.; Greenfield Consulting Group, LLC; Hall-Brooke Behavorial Health Services; Heyman Properties; Hospital of Saint Raphael; ICX Corporation; International Speciality Products, Inc.; JP Technologies, Ltd.; Lamorte Burns & Co., Inc.; Micro Warehouse, Inc.; NewsBank, Inc.; Novar Inc.; Olin Corporation; Pomellato USA, Inc.; St. Vincent's Medical Center; Terex Corporation; The Gillette Company; The Stamford Hospital; TBM Holdings Inc., Trafalgar/Ghurka; Welch Foods, Inc.; Yue-Sai Kan Cosmetics, Ltd. (USA).

JACK S. LIPSON

Established in 1990

830 POST ROAD EAST

WESTPORT, CONNECTICUT 06880

Telephone: 203-222-8775

Fax: 203-222-3872

Email: jlipson@mindspring.com

URL: http://www.lawyers.com/lipsonlaw

Real Estate, Mortgage Finance, Estate Planning.

JACK S. LIPSON, born Bronx, New York, October 31, 1948; admitted to bar, 1975, New York and Connecticut and U.S. District Courts, Southern and Eastern Districts of New York. *Education:* University of Bridgeport (B.A., 1970); University of Miami (J.D., 1973). Assistant District Attorney, Bronx County, New York, 1973-1975. *Member:* Westport, Connecticut (Member, Commercial Law, Real Estate and Bankruptcy Section) and American Bar Associations.

LYNCH, TREMBICKI, MARTELON AND BOYNTON

Established in 1947

225 MAIN STREET, SUITE 103

WESTPORT, CONNECTICUT 06880

Telephone: 203-227-6808

Fax: 203-226-6215

URL: http://www.lawyers.com/llmtblaw

Milford, Connecticut Office: 63 Cherry Street. P.O. Box 453. Telephone: 203-878-4669. Fax: 203-876-0644.

General Practice. Probate, Real Estate, Zoning, Negligence, Workers' Compensation and Labor Relations, Domestic Relations and Municipal Law. Trials in all Courts.

(This Listing Continued)

MEMBERS OF FIRM

ALEXANDER J. TREMBICKI, born Bridgeport, Connecticut, June 10, 1955; admitted to bar, 1980, Connecticut and U.S. District Court, District of Connecticut. *Education:* University of Connecticut (B.A., cum laude, 1977; J.D., 1980). Chairman, Milford Board of Finance, 1983-1984. Member: Fairfield Representative Town Meeting, 1997—; Connecticut Judicial Department - Attorney Trial Referee/Fact Finder, 1999—; Million Dollar Advocates Forum, 1999—. *Member:* Westport, Bridgeport and Connecticut Bar Associations; Connecticut Trial Lawyers Association; The Association of Trial Lawyers of America. ***PRACTICE AREAS:*** Civil Litigation; Personal Injury; Commercial Litigation; Employment Law; Family Law; Product Liability; Aviation Accidents; Wrongful Death; Medical Malpractice; Uninsured and Underinsured Motorist; Covenants Not To Compete; Collections; Corporate Litigation; Theft of Trade Secrets; Contract Litigation; Construction Litigation; Creditors Rights; Restrictive Covenant; Deceptive Trade Practices; Business Litigation; Federal Civil Practice; Alternative Dispute Resolution.

REPRESENTATIVE CLIENTS: Lafayette American Bank & Trust Company; Holiday Inns; General Electrict Capital Corp.; ITT/Shearton Corp.; RPM, Inc.; Label Systems Corporation; TSSI, Inc.; Zivco, Inc.; Neoterizs, Inc.; Star Distibutors, Inc.; Charter Personnel Services; Multi Unit Services, Inc.

(For Complete Biographical Data on all Personnel, See Professional Biographies at Milford, Connecticut)

McGOVERN & ASSOCIATES

WESTPORT, CONNECTICUT

(See Greenwich)

General Commercial Practice. Corporate (Foreign and Domestic), Mergers and Acquisitions, Securities, Venture Capital, Taxation, Litigation in all Courts. International, Joint Ventures, Admiralty, Sports, Commercial and Residential Real Estate Law. Estates and Trusts.

ALAN NEIGHER

Established in 1980

1804 POST ROAD EAST

WESTPORT, CONNECTICUT 06880

Telephone: 203-259-0599

Fax: 203-255-2570

Email: aneigher@snet.net

URL: http://www.lawyers.com/neigherlaw

General Civil Practice before State and Federal Courts. Antitrust, Trade Regulation, Libel and Slander, Sports, Entertainment, Communications and Copyright Law.

FIRM PROFILE: Alan Neigher has for the past 28 years represented clients in sports, entertainment, news media, marketing and advertising matters. His experience runs from first amendment protection, intellectual property matters, media finance and trademark and merchandising and licensing agreements.

ALAN NEIGHER, born Bridgeport, Connecticut, July 5, 1941; admitted to bar, 1965, Connecticut; 1969, U.S. Supreme Court and U.S. District Court, District of Connecticut; 1974, U.S. Court of Appeals, Second, Fifth, Ninth and Eleventh Circuits. *Education:* Colby College (A.B., with distinction, 1962); Boston College (J.D., 1965). Author: "The Gault Decision: Due Process and the Juvenile Courts," Federal Probation, December 1967; "The Connecticut Unfair Trade Practices Act," 4 Connecticut Law Tribune 30, 1978. Co-Author: "The Connecticut Law of Tortious Invasion of Privacy," 56 Connecticut Bar Journal, 397. Adjunct Professor, Communications Law, University of Bridgeport School of Law, 1977-1985. Member, 1988— and Chair, 1990-1993, Board of Directors, Fairfield County Chapter, March of Dimes. Vice Chair, Connecticut Film Commission, 1992-1995. *Member:* Connecticut Bar Association.

OF COUNSEL

JUDITH M. TRUTT, born New York, N.Y., March 16, 1946; admitted to bar, 1981, Connecticut; 1982, U.S. District Court, District of Connecticut. *Education:* Barnard College (B.A., magna cum laude, 1967); Columbia University (M.A., 1968; M.Ph., 1975); University of Bridgeport (J.D., magna cum laude, 1981). Phi Beta Kappa. Co-Author: "The Connecticut Law of Tortious Invasion of Privacy," 56 Connecticut Bar Journal 397, 1982. Adjunct Professor, Communications Law, University of Bridgeport School of Law, 1985-1994. *Member:* Danbury and Connecticut Bar Associations. ***LANGUAGES:*** Yiddish and Spanish.

REPRESENTATIVE CLIENTS: Connecticut Magazine; Connecticut-Post; Cablevision News 12; WVIT Channel 30; Brodax Film Group; Jim Miller and the Jimmy Dorsey Orchestra; Phoenix Communications.

ANDREW B. NEVAS

120 POST ROAD WEST, SUITE 301

P.O. BOX 2115

WESTPORT, CONNECTICUT 06880

Telephone: 203-454-3843

Fax: 203-226-6077

Email: abn@iconn.net

General Practice.

ANDREW B. NEVAS, born Norwalk, Connecticut, March 26, 1961; admitted to bar, 1990, Connecticut and U.S. District Court, District of Connecticut; 1992, U.S. District Court, Southern and Eastern Districts of New York; 2001, U.S. Court of Appeals, 2nd Circuit. *Education:* Union College (B.A., 1983); Georgetown University (J.D., 1989). Member;, American Inns of Court; Member, American Criminal Law Review, 1987-1989. Director, Bank of Westport, 1997—. Member, Westport Charter Revision Commission, 1999-2000. *Member:* Westport, Connecticut (President, Young Lawyers Division, Lower Fairfield County, 1993-1994) and American Bar Associations. (Also Of Counsel to Laurence Sarezky). ***REPORTED CASES:*** Grieco v. Zoning Commission, 627 A.2d 432 (1993); Kramer v. Petisi, 728 A.2d 1097 (1999). ***PRACTICE AREAS:*** Litigation; Appellate Practice.

NUSBAUM & PARRINO, P.C.

212 POST ROAD WEST

WESTPORT, CONNECTICUT 06880

Telephone: 203-226-8181

Fax: 203-454-9937

URL: http://www.lawyers.com/nusbaum&parrino

Trials in all Courts. Family, Negligence, Medical Malpractice, Criminal, Real Estate, Business and Commercial Law.

EDWARD NUSBAUM, born Newark, New Jersey, October 16, 1948; admitted to bar, 1973, Connecticut; 1974, U.S. District Court, District of Connecticut and U.S. Court of Appeals, Second Circuit; 1980, U.S. District Court, Southern and Eastern Districts of New York. *Education:* University of Connecticut (B.A., cum laude, 1970); Rutgers University (J.D., 1973). Listed in, Best Lawyers in America. Fellow: American Academy of Matrimonial Lawyers (Member, Bench and Bar Committee, 1994—; Chairperson, Bench and Bar Committee, 1998; Member: Continuing Legal Education Committee, 1998; Professionalism in the Practice Committee); Connecticut Board of Managers, 1999-2000; International Academy of Matrimonial Lawyers; Special Master (Family Cases) Stamford, Bridgeport, Ansonia/Milford, Danbury and Middletown Superior Courts, 1983—. *Member:* Westport (Vice President, 1989; President, 1990-1991), Connecticut (Member, Fee Dispute Board, 1994—; Chair, Fee Arbitration Dispute Panel, 2001—) and American (Member, Family Law Section) Bar Associations; The Association of Trial Lawyers of America; Connecticut Trial Lawyers Association; Connecticut Board of Managers/Cancer Care, Inc. (President, 1995-1997). ***PRACTICE AREAS:*** Family Law. ***Email:*** mll@nusbaumparrino.com

THOMAS P. PARRINO, born Brooklyn, New York, November 12, 1961; admitted to bar, 1987, Connecticut and U.S. District Court, District of Connecticut. *Education:* University of Connecticut (B.A., 1984); University of Bridgeport, (J.D., 1987). Lead Articles Editor, Connecticut Probate Law Journal, 1986-1987. Recipient, Academic Award - Superior Classroom Performance, 1987. Special Master, Stamford, Bridgeport, Danbury and Middletown Superior Courts (Family Cases), 1994—. *Member:* Regional Bar Association for Stamford, Norwalk, Darien and Wilton (Co-Chair, Family Law Committee, 1997-1999); Westport Bar Association; Connecticut Bar Association (Executive Committee, 1999—; Family Law Section); Connecticut Trial Lawyers Association (Membership Committee; Public Relations Committee, 1995-1998); The Association of Trial Lawyers of America; United Way of New Canaan (Vice Chairman, 1998-1999; Chairman of the Board of Directors, 2000). ***PRACTICE AREAS:*** Family Law; Personal Injury Litigation; Civil Litigation; Real Estate. ***Email:*** TParrino@nusbaumparrino.com

---

HAROLD W. HALDEMAN, born Philadelphia, Pennsylvania, October 21, 1944; admitted to bar, 1974, Connecticut. *Education:* Williams College (B.A., 1966); University of Connecticut School of Law (J.D., with honors, 1974). Recipient, American Jurisprudence Award. Author: "A History of the First One Hundred Years of the Connecticut Bar Association, 1875-1975," 49 Connecticut Law Journal 201 (1975). Navy Marine Corps Trial Judiciary Electronic Benchbook, 1989. Lecturer: "Technology and the Judiciary," 1989-1993; "Origin of the Bill of Rights, 1986-1988. Commissioner, Connecticut Pilot Commission, 1996-1999. [Judge Advocate General's Corps, Commander, U.S. Navy, 1966-1993]. ***PRACTICE AREAS:*** Family Law; Military Law. ***Email:*** HWH@nusbaumparrino.com

(This Listing Continued)

NUSBAUM & PARRINO, P.C., Westport—Continued

OF COUNSEL

SUSAN A. MOCH, born New York, N.Y., October 10, 1952; admitted to bar, 1977, Connecticut and Florida; 1980, U.S. Court of Appeals for the District of Columbia and U.S. District Court, District of Connecticut. *Education:* Amherst College; Mount Holyoke College (A.B., 1974); University of Miami School of Law (J.D., 1977). Member, Bar and Gavel (President, 1976-1977). Recipient, Roger Sorino Award. Lecturer, "Bankruptcy Issues In Dissolutions," 1992. Member, National District Attorney's Association, 1979-1986. Magistrate (Motor Vehicle and Small Claims Cases) Ansonia/Milford, Derby, Bridgeport, and Stamford Superior Courts, 1993—. Attorney Trial Referee (Civil Cases) 1990—. Special Master (Family Cases) Bridgeport Superior Court, 1990—. *Member:* Connecticut (Secretary, 1995-1996; Member: House of Delegates, 1999—. Board of Governors, 1989-1994. Membership Services Committee 1991—; Chairperson, 1997—, Criminal Justice Section, Executive Committee, 1983-1988; Family Law Section, 1987—, Executive Committee, 1987-1990; Member, 1979-1984 and Chair, 1983-1984, Status of Women Committee; Chair, Section of Women in Law, 1984-1987) and American (Member, Sections on: Litigation, Family Law) Bar Associations; The District of Columbia Bar; The Florida Bar. ***PRACTICE AREAS:*** Family Law; Civil and Criminal Litigation. ***Email:*** SAM@nusbaumparrino.com

O'DONNELL, McDONALD AND CREGEEN, L.L.C.

WESTPORT, CONNECTICUT

(See Fairfield)

General Practice. Trials in all Courts. Probate, Real Estate, Zoning and Administrative Law, Environmental.

OTTOMANO & JOHNSON, LLC

111 SAUGATUCK AVENUE
WESTPORT, CONNECTICUT 06880
Telephone: 203-222-9900
Fax: 203-222-8504
Email: p.ottomano@snet.net

Litigation in all State and Federal Courts. Personal Injury, Worker's Compensation, Real Estate, Alternative Dispute Resolution.

PETER J. OTTOMANO, born Norwalk, Connecticut, May 7, 1954; admitted to bar, 1980, Connecticut and U.S. District Court, District of Connecticut; 1987, U.S. Court of Appeals, Second Circuit. *Education:* Franklin & Marshall College (B.A., 1976); Suffolk University (J.D., 1980). Assistant Town Attorney, Town of Trumbull, 1988-1989. Appointed by: Connecticut Superior Court (Emmett, J.) 1987 to take action necessary to protect the interests of clients of an inactive attorney; Connecticut Superior Court (Lewis, J.) 1989 to take action necessary to protect the interests of clients of a resigned attorney; Connecticut Superior Court (Spear, J.) 1990 to take action necessary to protect the interests of clients of a resigned attorney; Connecticut Superior Court (Novack, J.) 1991 to take action necessary to protect the interests of clients of an inactive attorney. *Member:* Westport and Connecticut Bar Associations; Connecticut Trial Lawyers Association; The Association of Trial Lawyers of America. ***PRACTICE AREAS:*** Civil Litigation; Plaintiffs Personal Injury; Workers Compensation; Residential Real Estate.

OF COUNSEL

CHARLES SNOWDON JOHNSON, born Bryn Mawr, Pennsylvania, August 23, 1946; admitted to bar, 1978, California; 1982, District of Columbia; 1983, Connecticut; 1990, U.S. District Court, District of Connecticut and U.S. Tax Court. *Education:* Cornell University (B.A., 1968); California Western School of Law (J.D., cum laude, 1977); Georgetown University Law Center (M.L.T., 1981). *Member:* Connecticut Bar Association; State Bar of California; The District of Columbia Bar. ***PRACTICE AREAS:*** Conveyancing; Easements; Real Estate Title Examination; Residential Real Estate; Estate Planning; Decedents Estates. ***Email:*** chassjohn@worldnet.att.net

PACIFICO & FILAN, L.L.P.

25 FORD ROAD, SUITE 2
WESTPORT, CONNECTICUT 06880
Telephone: 203-221-8066
Fax: 203-222-4833

White Plains, NY Office: 81 Main Street-Suite 118, 10601. Telephone: 914-949-7226. Facsimile: 914-949-7059.

(This Listing Continued)

Trials and Appeals. Civil Litigation. Personal Injury, Medical Malpractice and Products Liability Law. General Civil Practice. Professional Licensure and Disciplinary Proceedings. Administrative Law, Medicare Fraud and Abuse.

PAUL J. PACIFICO, born Staten Island, New York, April 28, 1942; admitted to bar, 1966, Connecticut; 1967, U.S. District Court, District of Connecticut and U.S. Court of Appeals, 2nd Circuit; 1971, U.S. Supreme Court. *Education:* Fordham University (B.S., 1963; J.D. 1966). Phi Alpha Delta. Commissioner, Connecticut Criminal Justice Commission, 1979-1981. Member, Board of Directors, First County Bank, 1988-1990. *Member:* Stamford (Secretary, 1976-1977; Treasurer, 1977-1978; 2nd Vice President, 1978-1979; 1st Vice President, 1979-1980; President, 1980-1981), Westport, Connecticut and American Bar Associations; The Association of Trial Lawyers of America; Connecticut Trial Lawyers Association; National District Attorneys' Association; American Academy of Matrimonial Lawyers. [Capt., U.S. Air Force, Judge Advocate, 1966-1970; Lt. Col., USAF Reserve, Ret.]

PATRICK J. FILAN, born Toledo, Ohio, September 1, 1956; admitted to bar, 1982, Ohio; 1983, U.S. District Court, Southern District of Ohio; 1984, Connecticut and U.S. District Court, District of Connecticut; 1990, U.S. Supreme Court; 1991, New York; 1992, U.S. District Court, Southern and Eastern Districts of New York. *Education:* Duke University (A.B., cum laude, 1978) The Ohio State University, College of Law (J.D., 1982). Phi Alpha Delta. Member, Senior Advisor, Moot Court Governing Board. Member, Million Dollar Advocates Forum. Contributing Editor, Journal of Connecticut State Dental Association. Editor, "Medicine and Law," American Bar Association. Author: "Stein v. Katz: Rude Awakening for Slumbering Malpractice Claims," Journal of Connecticut State Dental Association, Vol. 66, No. 2, Fall 1990. Speaker, "Credentialing and Peer Review," American Bar Association, National Institute on Malpractice, 1993. Program Chair and Moderator, "Managed Care Liability," Connecticut Bar Association Annual Meeting, June 1991, 1993, 1994 New York Speech. *Member:* Stamford, Connecticut (Vice-Chairman, Medical-Legal Committee) and American (Vice Chair, Law and Medicine Committee; Member: Forum on Health Law; Member Litigation Section) Bar Associations; Connecticut Defense Lawyers Association (Executive Director); Connecticut Medical Defense Lawyers Association (Former Member); New York Medical Defense Lawyers Association. ***PRACTICE AREAS:*** Personal Injury Law; Medical Malpractice; Product Liability; Civil Litigation; Health Care Fraud and Abuse; Administrative Law. ***Email:*** pjfilan@att.net

PEARL PROFESSIONAL CORPORATION

735 POST ROAD EAST
WESTPORT, CONNECTICUT 06880
Telephone: 203-222-9000
Facsimile: 203-222-9100
Email: Thefirm@PearlPC.com
URL: http://www.lawyers.com/pearlprofessionalcorp

Business, Corporate and Commercial, Aviation, Tax, Commercial Real Estate.

STEWART W. PEARL, born Chicago, Illinois, September 17, 1951; admitted to bar, 1977, New York, U.S. Tax Court and U.S. Claims Court; 1982, U.S. District Court, Southern District of New York; 1983, U.S. District Court, District of Connecticut; 1984, Connecticut. *Education:* Colgate University (A.B., magna cum laude, 1973); Harvard University (J.D., 1976). Phi Beta Kappa. *Member:* American Bar Association (Member: Taxation Section; Section of Business Law, Aircraft Financing Subcommittee); National Business Aviation Association (Member, National Tax Committee); National Aircraft Resale Association. ***PRACTICE AREAS:*** Aviation; Corporate and Commercial; Tax; Commercial Real Estate. ***Email:*** StewartPearl@PearlPC.com

LEGAL SUPPORT PERSONNEL

PATRICIA J. TURNER, born Tacoma, Washington, December 26, 1957. *Education:* University of Washington (B.A. in History, Russian Language and Literature, 1980). (Legal Assistant). ***PRACTICE AREAS:*** Corporate and Commercial; Aviation. ***Email:*** PJTurner@PearlPC.com

ASSOCIATE ATTORNEY

ANN E. FLOCKEN, born Washington, D.C., April 4, 1958; admitted to bar, 1984, New York; 1986, Connecticut. *Education:* Williams College (B.A., magna cum laude, 1980); University of Virginia (J.D., 1983). Phi Beta Kappa. *Member:* American Bar Association. (Associate Attorney). ***PRACTICE AREAS:*** Corporate Law. ***Email:*** AnnFlocken@PearlPC.com

REPRESENTATIVE CLIENTS: Madison Square Garden, L.P.; Invensys plc; Cablevision Systems Corp.; University of Notre Dame; CBS Corporation; Omni Fitness Equipment, Inc.; Citizens Utilities Company; Jimmy Buffett; Chautauqua Airlines, Inc.; TAG Aviation, S.A.; Dow Corning Corporation; Shoreline Aviation, Inc.; Jetcraft Corporation.

PIAZZA & PICKEL

WESTPORT, CONNECTICUT

(See Stamford)

Trials and Appeals in State and Federal Courts, Negligence, Medical Malpractice, Divorce and Personal Injury Law, Wrongful Death, Legal Malpractice, Child Custody, Automobile Accidents, Product Liability, Adoption, Family Law.

ROBERTS, ROSE & BATES, P.C.

WESTPORT, CONNECTICUT

(See Stamford)

General Practice, Litigation, Real Estate, Leasing, Banking, Matrimonial, Probate, Estate Planning and Trusts, International Business, Employment Law.

RUBENSTEIN, GREEN & BASS, LLC

315 POST ROAD WEST
P.O. BOX 5143
WESTPORT, CONNECTICUT 06881-5143
Telephone: 203-222-0022
Telecopier: 203-227-0766
Email: rubengreen@rubengreen.com
URL: http://www.lawyers.com/rubensteingreen

General Civil Practice before State and Federal Courts, Real Estate, Corporation, Commercial and Banking, Personal Injury, Medical Malpractice, Estate Planning and Probate, Planning and Zoning Trials and Appeals, Banking Litigation.

MEMBERS OF FIRM

MARK A. RUBENSTEIN, born Bridgeport, Connecticut, April 12,1946; admitted to bar, 1971, Connecticut and U.S. District Court, District of Connecticut. *Education:* Boston University (B.A., 1968; J.D., 1971). Member, International Board of Directors, 1979-1985, and International Treasurer, 1981-1985, Juvenile Diabetes Foundation International. Member, Merritt Parkway Commission, 1982—. Chairman, Westport Downtown Merchants Association, 1986-1994. Chairman, Westport Chamber of Commerce, 1998-2000. *Member:* Westport, Connecticut (Member, Real Estate Section; Executive Committee, Business Law Section, 1990—) and American (Member: Commercial Leasing Committee, Real Property Section) Bar Associations; American Judicature Society. ***PRACTICE AREAS:*** Real Estate Law; Banking Law; Corporate Law; Estate Planning. ***Email:*** mrubenstein@rubengreen.com

DANIEL GREEN, born Philadelphia, Pennsylvania, February 8, 1950; admitted to bar, 1975, Connecticut. *Education:* Trinity College (B.A., 1972); Albany Law School of Union University (J.D., 1975). President, Jewish Family Service, 1988-1990, Board Member, Jewish Community Center. Board Member, Congregation B'Nai Israel. *Member:* Bridgeport and Connecticut Bar Associations; Connecticut Trial Lawyers Association. ***PRACTICE AREAS:*** Commercial Litigation; Tax Appeals; Real Estate; Personal Injury. ***Email:*** dgreen@rubengreen.com

DAVID I. BASS, born Brooklyn, New York, September 21, 1963; admitted to bar, 1995, Connecticut; 1996, New York. *Education:* New York University (B.F.A., 1985); Pace University School of Law (J.D., 1995). *Member:* Westport, Connecticut and American Bar Associations. ***PRACTICE AREAS:*** Commercial Leasing; Land Use; Zoning; Real Estate. ***Email:*** dbass@rubengreen.com

---

LISA KASDEN KENT, born New York, New York, May 5, 1950; admitted to bar, 1986, Connecticut; 1988, U.S. District Court, District of Connecticut. *Education:* University of Pennsylvania (B.A., cum laude, 1972); University of Bridgeport (J.D., with honors, 1985). Licensed Real Estate Broker, Connecticut, 1989. Associate Town Attorney, Wilton, 1995. *Member:* Westport, Bridgeport (Member, Commercial Law Section; Real Estate Committee; Foreclosure Committee) Connecticut and American Bar Associations. ***PRACTICE AREAS:*** Real Estate; Leasing; Zoning; Banking. ***Email:*** lkent@rubengreen.com

OF COUNSEL

STEVEN GLAZER, born New Haven, Connecticut, May 28, 1946; admitted to bar, 1973, New York; 1975 Connecticut. *Education:* Columbia University (B.A., 1968); Lehigh University (J.D., 1972). *Member:* New York State, Connecticut and American Bar Associations. ***PRACTICE AREAS:*** Commercial Real Estate; Zoning Law; Leasing; Corporate Law.

REPRESENTATIVE CLIENTS: Fidelity National Title Insurance Co.; First Class Driving Service, Inc.; Expressway Lubrication Centers; People's Bank; Mirbach & Co.; Chase Manhattan Bank; Westmark Industries; Medsolve.com
REFERENCES: Chase Manhattan Bank; Putnam Trust.

MORTON R. RUDEN

19 LUDLOW ROAD
WESTPORT, CONNECTICUT 06880
Telephone: 203-454-0909
Telecopier: 203-341-0793
Email: attmr@aol.com

Real Estate, Banking, Corporate Law.

MORTON R. RUDEN, born Brooklyn, New York, July 3, 1937; admitted to bar, 1962, New York; 1971, Connecticut. *Education:* Union College (B.A., 1958); New York University (LL.B., 1961). Listed in Best Lawyers in America, 1997-1998; 1999-2000, 2001-2002. Chairman, CLE Seminar on Construction Lending, 1974. Co-Chairman, CLE Seminar on WOE, Wreckage and Workouts, Today's Unreal Real Estate, 1976. *Member:* Association of the Bar of the City of New York; Westport, Connecticut (Chairman, Real Property Section, 1976-1979) and American Bar Associations; American College of Real Estate Lawyers.

REFERENCES: First Union National Bank; Peoples Bank.

RUTKIN AND OLDHAM, L.L.C.

5 IMPERIAL AVENUE
P.O. BOX 295
WESTPORT, CONNECTICUT 06881
Telephone: 203-227-7301
Fax: 203-222-9295
Email: law@rutkinoldham.com
URL: http://www.lawyers.com/rutkinoldham

Greenwich Office: 125 Mason Street, 06830. Telephone: 203-869-7277.

Family, Trials and Appeals.

ARNOLD H. RUTKIN, born Bridgeport, Connecticut, July 19, 1939; admitted to bar, 1965, Massachusetts; 1966, Connecticut; 1973, U.S. Supreme Court; 1985, New York. *Education:* University of Pennsylvania (B.S., in Economics, 1961); Boston University (LL.B., 1964). Executive Editor, Connecticut Family Lawyer, 1986—. Author: "Tax Aspects in Domestic Relations Cases," Trial Magazine, June, 1980; "When Prenuptial Contracts are Challenged in Court," The Family Advocate, Winter, 1984; "Valuation of Closely Held Corporations" *Valuation & Distribution of Marital Property,* Matthew Bender Publishing Co., 1984. Co-Author: "Lay Witnesses Can Value Assets," Trial Magazine, Vol. 22, No. 6, p. 33, June, 1986. General Editor, Family Law and Practice, Matthew Bender Publishing Co., 1985; Connecticut Practice Series, Co-Author: Family Law and Practice (3 vols.) West Publishing Co., 2000-2001. Lecturer, Virginia Law Foundation on Continuing Legal Education, "Top Lawyers Trying Tough Cases," Apr. 29, 1999. Lecturer, College of Advocacy, The Association of Trial Lawyers of America, 1983-1987. Member and Director, Bridgeport Legal Services, Inc., 1969-1971. Chairman, Greater Bridgeport Housing Council, 1970-1973. Majority Leader and Councilman, Town of Trumbull, Connecticut, 1973-1975. Member, Board of Directors, Cold Spring School, New Haven, Connecticut. Founder, Member of Board of Editors and Editor-in-Chief (1999) Connecticut Family Lawyer. *Member:* Westport, Connecticut (Member, Executive Committee, Family Law Section, 1981—; Secretary-Treasurer, Family Law Committee, 1981-1982; Vice-Chairman, 1983; Chairman, 1985-1986) and American (Member, Taxation Committee, 1982; Member, 1984— and Chairman, 1985—, Continuing Legal Education Committee; Member, 1984-1995 and Editor-in-Chief, 1987-1997, The Family Advocate; Chairperson, Bylaw Committee Revision, 1984, Family Law Section) Bar Associations; Connecticut Trial Lawyers Association (Secretary-Treasurer and Second Vice President, 1970-1972; Member, Board of Governors, 1979-1984); The Association of Trial Lawyers of America (Member, 1973-1999; Vice-Chairman, 1981-1984 and Chairman, 1985-1987, Family Law Section). Fellow: American Academy of Matrimonial Lawyers; International Academy of Matrimonial Lawyers. ***REPORTED CASES:*** Wendt v. Wendt, 59 Conn. App. 656 (2000), cert. denied 255 Conn. 918 (2000); Burns v. Burns, 41 Conn. App. 716 (1996); Fiddelman v. Redmon, 31 Conn. App. 201 (1993); Knock v. Knock, 224 Conn. 776 (1993); Gross v. Latimer, 1 Conn. App. 501 (1984); Guss v. Guss, 1 Conn. App. 356, 472 A.2d 790 (1984); Grier v. Grier, 24 Conn. App. 801 (1991). ***PRACTICE AREAS:*** Family Law; Litigation. ***Email:*** law@rutkinoldham.com

SARAH S. OLDHAM, born Mineola, NY, March 5, 1951; admitted to bar, 1988, Connecticut; 1989 U.S. District Court, Southern District of New York. *Education:* Wesleyan University (B.S., cum laude, 1972); Southern Connecticut State College (M.S., School Psychology, 1974); University of Connecticut School of Law (J .D., cum laude, 1988). Member, Connecticut Law Review, 1986-1988. Board of Editors, Connecticut Family Lawyer, 1994—. Author: "Post-Majority Support: The Statute Explained," Connecticut Family Lawyer, Fall, 1993; "Recent Appellate Developments," Connecticut Family Lawyer, Spring, 1995; "Recent Appellate Decisions," Connecticut Family Lawyer, Fall, 1997; "Distributing Executive Compensation Benefits," The Family Advocate,

(This Listing Continued)

RUTKIN AND OLDHAM, L.L.C., Westport—Continued

Winter, 2001. Connecticut Practice Series, Co-Author: "Family Law and Practice," (2 vols.) West Publishing Co., 1999-2000. Lecturer, Connecticut Bar Association, "Relocation Issues After Ireland v. Ireland," September 10, 1999. *Member:* Connecticut (Member, Executive Committee of the Family Law Section, 1993—, Treasurer, 1999-2000; Secretary, 2000-2001; Co-Chair, Post-Majority Support Committee, Family Law Section, 1993-1994), Stamford-Norwalk Regional (Co-Chair, Family Law Section, 1993-1998) and American Bar Associations. ***REPORTED CASES:*** Wendt v. Wendt, 59 Conn. App. 656 (2000), cert. denied 255 Conn. 918 (2000); Ireland v. Ireland, 246 Conn. 413 (1998); Hines v. St. Vincent's Medical Center 232 Conn. 632, 657 A2d 578 (1995). ***PRACTICE AREAS:*** Family Law; Litigation. ***Email:*** law@rutkinoldham.com

OF COUNSEL

KATHLEEN A. HOGAN, born Oakland, California, February 18, 1952; admitted to bar, 1977, Tennessee; 1981, New York; 1983, Connecticut; 1989, Colorado. *Education:* College of Santa Fe (B.A., magna cum laude, 1973); University of Tennessee at Knoxville (J.D. 1977). Pi Gamma Mu. Associate Editor, Tennessee Law Review, 1976-1977. Managing Editor, Connecticut Family Lawyer, 1986-1991. Member, Board of Editors, Family Advocate, 1993—. Author: "Retirement Benefits for County Officials" and "County Correctional Facilities," University of Tennessee Press, 1978; "Involuntary Confinement of Mental Patients," 43 Tennessee Law Review 366, 1976; "Pretrial Proceedings-Exclusive Use of Marital Residence," Matrimonial and Family Law Practice, Matthew Bender Publishing Co., 1985; "Pendente Lite Exclusive Possession of the Matrimonial Home-Grounds for Relief," Connecticut Family Law Journal, Vol. 3, No. 5, July, 1985; "A Look at the Psychotherapist-Patient Privilege," The Family Advocate, Fall 1991; "Hearsay-A Rule of Exceptions," The Family Advocate, Summer 1996; "Illegal Evidence," The Family Advocate, Summer 1996. Co-Author: "Lay Witnesses Can Value Assets," Trial Magazine, June, 1986, Vol. 22, No. 6, p. 33; "Appointment of Counsel for Pre-Verbal Children," Connecticut Family Lawyer, Summer, 1988; Colorado Family Law and Practice (2 vols.) West Publishing Co., 1999; Connecticut Practice Series - Family Law and Practice 2d ed (2 vols.) West Publishing Co., 1991. *Member:* The Colorado, Connecticut and American Bar Associations. (Also Partner, McGuane and Hogan, LLP, Denver, Colorado). ***REPORTED CASES:*** Wendt v. Wendt, 59 Conn. App. 656 (2000), cert. denied 255 Conn. 918 (2000); Issler v. Issler, 250 Conn. 226 (1998); Ireland v. Ireland, 246 Conn. 413 (1998); Burns v. Burns, 41 Conn. App. 716 (1996); Fiddelman v. Redmon, 37 Conn. App. 397 (1995); Fiddelman v. Redmon, 31 Conn. App. 201 (1993); Knock v. Knock, 224 Conn. 776 (1993); Ottaviani v. Pechi, 16 Conn. App. 705 (1988); Gross v. Latimer, 1 Conn. App. 501 (1984); Bartha v. Simmons, 15 Conn. App. 801 (1988); In re Marriage of Nussbeck, 899 P.2d 347 (1995); Grier v. Grier, 24 Conn. App. 801 (1991). ***PRACTICE AREAS:*** Family Law; Litigation; Appeals. ***Email:*** law@rutkinoldham.com

HEIDI E. OPINSKY, born Hartford, Connecticut, January 10, 1959; admitted to bar, 1985, Connecticut; 1986, New York and District of Columbia;1988, U.S. District Court, Southern and Eastern Districts of New York. *Education:* St. Lawrence University (B.A., cum laude, 1981); Hofstra University School of Law (J.D., 1985). Hofstra University Representative, Executive Committee, New York State Bar Association, Law Student Division, 1983-1985. Legal Intern, Honorable Chief Justice J. Chesoni, and Magistrate Effy O'Wor, Supreme Court, Nairobi, Kenya, 1980; Appointed Guardian Ad Litem and Special Attorney by the Honorable Samuel G. Fredman, Supreme Court, Westchester County, 1999; Mediator in family law cases, State of New York; Legislative Intern, Congressman William R. Cotter, House Office Building, Washington, D.C., 1981; Legislative Liaison to Governor William O'Neill, State of Connecticut, and Office of Policy and Management, 1981-1982. Teaching Assistant, Department of Philosophy, St. Lawrence University, 1980. Lecturer: Nassau County Bar Association, State of New York; New York State Society of Certified Public Accountants, Litigation Committee. Consultant, Nationally based Accounting Firm on litigation and related family law matters, 1992—Special Counsel to major New York State Law firm, heading Matrimonial Department and Connecticut based litigation practice, 1992-1994. Participant: Legal Treatise, Aged and Mental Hygiene Law Reforms of New York, Hofstra University School of Law, 1984; New York Trial Lawyers, Trial Skills, 2000. Operated Family and Matrimonial Law and Litigation, Practice New York City, 1994-2001. *Member:* Westchester County (Member, Domestic Relations Law Review Case Updates, 1994) Connecticut, New York State and American Bar Associations; The District of Columbia Bar; Association of the Bar of the City of New York. ***REPORTED CASES:*** Fink v. Fink, 582 N.Y.S.2d 726, 182 A.D.2d 669 (2d Dept., 1992); Bicknell v. Bicknell, 631 N.Y.S.2d 78 (2d Dept., 1995); Faranda v. Dolan, New York Law Journal, Front Page, November 24, 1997, "Support Obligation Terminates, as Boys Moved to Non-Custodial Parent" (Lifson, Justice, Suffolk County, State of New York). ***PRACTICE AREAS:*** Matrimonial Law; Divorce; Family Law; Alimony; Custody; Litigation. ***Email:*** law@rutkinoldham.com

(This Listing Continued)

NORA A. BELANGER, born Hartford, Connecticut, July 27, 1953; admitted to bar, 2001, Connecticut. *Education:* Southern Connecticut State University (B.S., 1975); University of Connecticut (M.B.A., 1995); Pace University (J.D., cum laude, 2001). Member, Pace Law Review, 1999-2001; Executive Editor, Pace Law Review, 2000-2001. Author: "The Americans with Disabilities Act: A Practioner's Guide in the Aftermath of Sutton," Pace Law Review, Fall, 2001. *Member:* Connecticut and American Bar Associations. ***PRACTICE AREAS:*** Family Law; Litigation.

REFERENCES: Lafayette American Bank and Trust Co.

SACKS, MONTGOMERY, PASTORE & LEVINE, P.C.

1071 POST ROAD EAST, SUITE 3
WESTPORT, CONNECTICUT
Telephone: 203-291-6844

New York, N.Y. Office: Sacks Montgomery, P.C., 800 Third Avenue. Telephone: 212-355-4660.

Construction, Government Contract and Surety Law, Commercial Litigation.

STUART M. LEVINE, born Suffern, New York, February 9, 1938; admitted to bar, 1964, Pennsylvania; 1967, New York; 1990, Connecticut. *Education:* Princeton University (B.A., 1960); University of Pennsylvania (LL.B., 1963). Lecturer and Author: "The Construction Manager," "Fast Track Construction," and "Connecticut Construction Law," Federal Publications, Inc., 1991. *Member:* The Association of the Bar of the City of New York; New York State and American Bar Associations; The Association of Trial Lawyers of America. (Resident).

STEPHEN A. STALLINGS, born Evansville, Indiana, May 16, 1958; admitted to bar, 1990, New York; 1993, Connecticut. *Education:* University of Kentucky (B.A., 1980); St. John's University (J.D., cum laude, 1989). Staff Member, St. John's Law Review, 1987-1989. *Member:* The Association of the Bar of the City of New York; New York State Bar Association. ***Email:*** sstallings@sacksmontgomery.com

---

THOMAS F. GIORDANO, born Bronx, New York, September 18, 1964; admitted to bar, 1995, Connecticut; 1996, New York. *Education:* Columbia College, Columbia University (B.A., 1986); Columbia University Graduate School of Architecture, Planning & Preservation (M.S., 1989); Fordham Law School (J.D., cum laude, 1995). Order of the Coif. *Member:* Association of the Bar of the City of New York (Secretary, Construction Law Committee); American Bar Association. ***Email:*** tgiordano@sacksmontgomery.com

AMY S. COHEN, born New York, N.Y., September 18, 1965; admitted to bar, 1997, New York; 2000, Connecticut. *Education:* University of Vermont (B.A., cum laude, 1987); Fordham University (J.D., 1994). Phi Beta Kappa. *Member:* New York State Bar Association; The Association of the Bar of the City of New York. ***LANGUAGES:*** Spanish. ***Email:*** acohen@sacksmontgomery.com

(For Biographical data on all Personnel, see Professional Biographies at New York, New York)

SANDAK FRIEDMAN HENNESSEY & GRECO, LLP

WESTPORT, CONNECTICUT

(See Stamford)

Trials and Appeals in all Connecticut and Federal Courts and Administrative Agencies. Personal Injury, Medical Malpractice, Commercial, Environmental Litigation, Real Estate, Zoning and Land Use, Property Tax Appeals.

WILLIAM L. SCHEFFLER & ASSOCIATES

P.O. BOX 2773
WESTPORT, CONNECTICUT 06880-0773
Telephone: 203-226-6600; 1-800-429-4480
Telecopier: 203-227-1873
Email: scheff@optonline.net
URL: http://www.lawyers.com/williamscheffler&assoc

Corporate, Business Transactions, Real Estate Development, Zoning, Licensing, Administrative, Not For Profit Corporations.

WILLIAM L. SCHEFFLER, born Rockville Centre, New York, December 27, 1948; admitted to bar, 1976, Connecticut and U.S. District Court, District of Connecticut; 1977, New York and U.S. District Court, Southern District of New

(This Listing Continued)

York; 1978, U.S. District Court, Eastern District of New York; 1981, U.S. Supreme Court. *Education:* Bucknell University (B.A., 1970); Syracuse University (J.D., 1974). Managing Editor, Syracuse Journal of International Law and Commerce, 1973-1974. Author: "The Politicization and Death of Rebus Sic Stantibus," 2 Syracuse Journal of International Law and Commerce 67, 1974; "Developments in Zoning - 1991," 66 Conn Bar J. 132, 1992. Legislative Counsel, City of New York, 1974-1977. Associate Attorney, Shea & Gould, 1977-1982. Member, 1982-1989 and Of Counsel, 1990-1993, Scheffler Karlinsky & Stein. Member, 1990-1993, Scheffler & Johansen. Member, 1987-1992 and Chairman, 1989-1992, Zoning Board of Appeals, Town of Westport, Connecticut. Member, Representative Town Meeting, Westport, Connecticut, 1994—. *Member:* Westport, New York State, Connecticut and American Bar Associations. ***SPECIAL AGENCIES:*** Westport Education Foundation; Betty R. Sheffer Foundation. ***PRACTICE AREAS:*** Corporate and Business Transactions involving non-publicly traded entities; Real Estate Development; Restaurant, Club and Hotel Licensing; Leasing and Zoning Law; Administrative; Municipal; Not For Profit Corporations.

SCHINE, JULIANELLE & ANTONUCCI, P.C.

Established in 1967

SUITE 100, 830 POST ROAD EAST
WESTPORT, CONNECTICUT 06880
Telephone: 203-226-6861
Fax: 203-226-6866
Email: sjalaw2@snet.net

Orange, Connecticut Office: 35 Old Tavern Road, P.O. Box 905. Telephone: 203-795-3563. Fax: 203-799-9655.

General Civil and Trial Practice in State and Federal Courts. Corporate, Commercial and Business Law, Probate, Personal Injury, Administrative, Estate Planning, Commercial and Residential Real Estate, Higher Education Law.

(For Biographical Data on all Personnel, see Professional Biographies at Orange, Connecticut).

SCHOONMAKER, GEORGE & COLIN, P.C.

WESTPORT, CONNECTICUT

(See Greenwich)

Matrimonial and Family Law.

NANCY SEGORE-FRESHMAN

120 POST ROAD WEST
WESTPORT, CONNECTICUT 06880
Telephone: 203-222-8686
Fax: 203-222-8857
Email: nesflaw@aol.com
URL: http://www.lawyers.com/nancyfreshman

Family Law, Divorce Mediation, Collaborative Law, Estate Planning, Estate Administration.

NANCY SEGORE-FRESHMAN, born Albany, New York; admitted to bar, 1981, Connecticut, New York and U.S. District Court, District of Connecticut. *Education:* University of Rochester (B.A., 1977); Albany Law School of Union University (J.D., 1980). Phi Beta Kappa. Co-Author, "Divorce Mediation Model," Connecticut Bar Association Ethics Opinion #35. *Member:* Connecticut, New York State and American (Member, Family Law Section) Bar Associations; American Academy of Family Mediators; Connecticut Council of Divorce Mediators. ***PRACTICE AREAS:*** Family Law; Mediation; Real Estate.

RONALD L. SHEIMAN

1804 POST ROAD EAST
WESTPORT, CONNECTICUT 06880
Telephone: 203-259-0599
Telecopier: 203-255-2570
URL: http://www.lawyers.com/ronaldsheiman

Federal Income, Estate and Gift Taxation. Partnership and Corporate Law. Probate and Estate Planning. International Business Law.

RONALD L. SHEIMAN, born Bridgeport, Connecticut, April 26, 1948; admitted to bar, 1973, Connecticut; 1974, U.S. Tax Court; 1975, U.S. Court of Appeals, Second Circuit; 1977, U.S. Supreme Court; 1978, District of Columbia and U.S. District Court, District of Connecticut; 1981, New York. *Education:* University of Michigan (B.A., 1970); University of Connecticut (J.D., with honors, 1973); New York University (LL.M. in Taxation, 1974). Phi Eta Sigma. *Member:* Connecticut (Member, Taxation Section), Federal and American (Member, Sections on: Taxation; Real Property, Probate and Trust Law) Bar Associations.

REFERENCE: Peoples Bank (Greens Farms Office, Westport, Connecticut).

(This Listing Continued)

SHERWOOD & GARLICK, P.C.

Established in 1899

65 JESUP ROAD
P.O. BOX 390
WESTPORT, CONNECTICUT 06881-0390
Telephone: 203-227-9585
Fax: 203-227-7777
URL: http://www.lawyers.com/sherwoodgarlick

General Practice in all Courts. Real Property, Estate Planning, Probate, Municipal and Zoning Law, Aviation Law, Civil Litigation, and Appeals.

FIRM PROFILE: Sherwood & Garlick, P.C. continues a general law practice established in 1899 by Harry R. Sherwood following his studies under the tutelage of Honorable Wilbur Cross and graduation from Yale Law School. The firm offers a wide variety of legal services to individuals and businesses both locally and throughout the state, in all courts. The principals participate in continuing legal education seminars, professional association activities and community affairs.

HARRY R. SHERWOOD (1873-1966).

THADDEUS G. COWELL, JR. (1912-1991).

STANLEY P. ATWOOD (1937-2000).

RICHARD J. DIVINEY, born New York, N.Y., October 1, 1941; admitted to bar, 1967, New York and Connecticut. *Education:* Washington University and Quincy College (A.B., 1963); St. John's University (LL.B., 1966). Instructor, Probate Law, Fairfield University, 1978-1981. Member, Connecticut Commission on Courts Reorganization, 1974-1978. Member, Legislative Liaison Committee, Aircraft Owners and Pilots Association, 1978. *Member:* Westport (President, 1974), Connecticut and American (Member, Sections on: Economics of Law Practice; Real Property, Probate and Trust Law) Bar Associations; Lawyers-Pilots Bar Association. ***PRACTICE AREAS:*** Estate and Trust Administration; Banking Law; Real Estate; Civil Litigation; Aviation. ***Email:*** N6423Q@ATT.NET

W. GLENN MAJOR, born Weston, Connecticut, July 14, 1959; admitted to bar, 1983, Connecticut; U.S. District Court, District of Connecticut. *Education:* College of the Holy Cross (B.A., 1980); Creighton University (J.D., 1983). *Member:* Westport and Connecticut Bar Associations. ***PRACTICE AREAS:*** Residential and Commercial Real Estate; Zoning; Estate and Estate Planning; Probate. ***Email:*** w.glenn.major@att.net

CHARLES W. FLEISCHMANN, born New York, N.Y., January 21, 1945; admitted to bar, 1977, Connecticut and U.S. District Court, District of Connecticut; 1981, U.S. Court of Appeals, 2nd Circuit and U.S. Supreme Court. *Education:* Princeton University (B.A., 1967); University of Connecticut (J.D., with honors, 1977). State Trial Referee, 1984—. Special Master, U.S. District Court, 1994—. Member, Board of Directors, Connecticut Legal Services Inc., 1988-1993. Assistant Town Attorney, Town of Fairfield, 1997-1999. *Member:* Bridgeport (Member, Executive Committee, 1988-1994; Treasurer, 1994-1995; Secretary, 1995-1996; Vice President, 1996-1997; President-Elect, 1997-1998; President, 1998-1999) and Connecticut Bar Associations. [With U.S. Navy, 1968-1972]. ***PRACTICE AREAS:*** Civil Litigation.

EDWARD E. GARLICK (Retired).

COUNSEL FOR: North American Aviation, Inc.; Ogden Flight Services Group, Inc.; Turnkey Associates Inc.; Canfield Development, LLC; SpotHawk International, Ltd.
APPROVED ATTORNEYS FOR: Hudson United Bank; People's Bank; Fleet Bank; Westport National Bank; Citibank; PNC Mortgage; Threshold Mortgage; Webster Bank; Ridgefield Bank; The Wilton Bank; Ladd Financial Center; New Milford Savings Bank; Chicago Title Insurance Company; Connecticut Attorney Title Insurance Company.
REFERENCE: Webster Bank; Ladd Financial Center; Westport National Bank.

SHRADER AND KNAPP

A PROFESSIONAL CORPORATION

25 FORD ROAD
WESTPORT, CONNECTICUT 06880
Telephone: 203-227-6628
Fax: 203-227-6922
Email: shrader.knapp@erols.com
URL: http://www.lawyers.com/shraderknapplaw

Civil Trial and Appellate Practice in all State and Federal Courts. Medical Malpractice, Personal Injury, Securities and Investment Frauds, Fine Arts Claims, Commercial and Real Property Litigation.

(This Listing Continued)

SHRADER AND KNAPP, A PROFESSIONAL CORPORATION, Westport—Continued

L. DOUGLAS SHRADER, born Bowling Green, Kentucky, November 6, 1935; admitted to bar, 1964, Connecticut; 1965, U.S. District Court, District of Connecticut; 1967, U.S. Court of Appeals, 2nd Circuit. *Education:* Yale University (B.A., 1961; LL.B., 1964). Irving M. Engel Fellow, Yale Law School, 1964. Recipient, Francis Weyland Prize, Yale Law School, 1964. Law Clerk, Hon. Robert C. Zampano, U.S. District Court, District of Connecticut, 1964-1965. *Member:* Association of Trial Lawyers of America; Connecticut Trial Lawyers Association (Member, Board of Governors, 1988-1993). Fellow, American College of Trial Lawyers. [1st Lt., U.S. Army Airborne, 1953-1957]. ***PRACTICE AREAS:*** Civil Litigation; Appellate Practice; Personal Injury; Medical Malpractice; Securities and Investment Fraud; Commercial and Real Property Litigation.

BEVERLY STAUFFER KNAPP, born New Haven, Connecticut, January 11, 1959; admitted to bar, 1984, Connecticut and U.S. District Court, District of Connecticut; 1992, U.S. Court of Appeals, Second Circuit. *Education:* Sacred Heart University (B.S., summa cum laude, 1980); University of Connecticut (J.D., with high honors, 1984). Delta Epsilon Sigma. Recipient, American Jurisprudence Award for Creditors' Rights and Bankruptcy. Member and Notes and Comments Editor, Connecticut Law Review, 1983-1984. Author: "Official Responsibility and its Implications on Municipal Liability: Shore v. Town of Stonington," 15 Connecticut Law Review, No. 3, 1984. Law Clerk, Hon. Warren W. Eginton, U.S. District Court, District of Connecticut, 1984-1985. *Member:* Connecticut and American Bar Associations; The Association of Trial Lawyers of America. ***REPORTED CASES:*** Babcock v. Bridgeport Hospital, 251 Conn. 790(1999); Barretta v. Otis Elevator Co., 242 Conn. 169(1997); Baxter v. Sturm, Ruger & Co., 230 Conn. 335(1994). ***PRACTICE AREAS:*** Securities Litigation; Civil Litigation; Appellate Practice.

LEGAL SUPPORT PERSONNEL

Susan Fortuna

LAW OFFICES OF FRANK E. SISSON, III

180 POST ROAD EAST, SUITE 202
WESTPORT, CONNECTICUT 06881
Telephone: 203-222-4844
Telefax: 203-222-4869
Email: fesisson3d@cs.com
URL: http://www.lawyers.com/sisson

Stamford, Connecticut Office: 6 Landmark Square, 06901. Telephone: 203-965-5965.

Estate Planning, Probate, Corporate, Commercial, Elder Law, Tax Law, Real Estate.

FIRM PROFILE: The firm practices extensively in areas of business tax and estate planning. The firm maintains a high degree of technical expertise in many areas of the law, and the firm has a commitment to fulfill the needs of its' clients.

FRANK E. SISSON, III, born Enid, Oklahoma, May 19, 1952; admitted to bar, 1976, New Jersey; 1977, New York; 1979, Connecticut; 1980, Florida. *Education:* Colgate University (B.A., magna cum laude, 1973); Harvard University (J.D., cum laude, 1976). Phi Beta Kappa. Recipient, Alumni Senior History Prize. President, Harvard Law School Association of Connecticut, 1992—. *Member:* Association of the Bar of the City of New York; New Canaan (Vice President, 1988-1989; President, 1989-1991), Connecticut and New York State Bar Associations; The Florida Bar.

LEGAL SUPPORT PERSONNEL

AMY MITCHELL (Legal Assistant).

SPIRER & COTT

830 POST ROAD EAST
P.O. BOX 5201
WESTPORT, CONNECTICUT 06880
Telephone: 203-454-1999
Fax:203- 454-9749
Email: arspirer@yahoo.com
URL: http://www.lawyers.com/spirer

General Civil Practice before State and Federal Courts. Commercial Law, Appellate Practice, Litigation, Construction Law, Contracts, Zoning, Planning and Land Use, Environmental Law. Personal Injury, Family Law, Real Estate, Corporate Law, Business Law.

(This Listing Continued)

MEMBERS OF FIRM

ALAN R. SPIRER, born New York, N.Y., December 25, 1946; admitted to bar, 1972 Connecticut; 1974, U.S. District Court, District of Connecticut. *Education:* Johns Hopkins University (B.A., 1968); George Washington University (J.D., 1971; LL.M., 1972). Order of the Coif. Recipient, Environmental Law Fellowship. Member, George Washington University Law Review, 1970-1971. Member, 1977-1985 and Chairman, 1980-1981, Wilton Planning and Zoning Commission. Member, Wilton Inland Wetlands Agency, 1977-1985. Assistant Town Attorney, Town of Westport, 1981-1985. *Member:* Westport and The Connecticut (Member, Sections on: Environmental Quality; Planning and Zoning) Bar Associations. ***REPORTED CASES:*** Paulus v. LaSala, 56 Conn App 139 (1999); Wright Brothers Builders, Inc. v. Dowling, 247 Conn 218 (1998); Gibson v. Capano, 241 Conn 725 (1997) affirming 41 Conn App 548 (1997); Forbes v. Ballaro, 31 Conn App 235 (1993); McNally v. Zoning Commission of the City of Norwalk, 225 Conn 1 (1993); Paine Webber Jackson & Curtis v. Winters, 22 Conn App 640 (1990); Edward DeNike Tree Co. v. Butler, 21 Conn App 366 (1990); Burnstein v. Nemeyer, 213 Conn 665 (1990); Bound Brook Association v. City of Norwalk, 198 Conn 660 (1986); Shapiro v. Coney Island Restaurant, 4 Conn App 336 (1985); Arnold Bernhard & Co., Inc. v. P&Z Commission of the Town of Westport, 194 Conn 152 (1984); Pointina Beach Assn., Inc. v. Stella, 1 Conn App 341 (1984); Taylor v. Sugar Hollow Park, Inc., 1 Conn App 38 (1983); Coburn v. Lenox Homes, Inc., 186 Conn 370 (1982).

DOUGLAS M. COTT, born Port Chester, New York, April 9, 1946; admitted to bar, 1972, Connecticut; 1973, U.S. District Court, District of Connecticut. *Education:* Bucknell University; Syracuse University (A.B., 1968); Fordham University (J.D., 1972). *Member:* Connecticut and American Bar Associations.

JUDITH B. SPORN

125 MAIN STREET
WESTPORT, CONNECTICUT 06880-3303
Telephone: 203-226-6171
Fax: 203-227-5959
Email: jsporn@snet.net

Practice Limited to Immigration, Naturalization and Consular Law.

FIRM PROFILE: Judith B. Sporn is a highly specialized attorney offering legal representation in many various areas related to Immigration and Naturalization Law. She prides herself in treating every case with the utmost care. She maximizes her two decades of experience to protect the rights and privileges of all her clients.

JUDITH B. SPORN, born New York, N.Y., March 3, 1951; admitted to bar, 1980, New York; 1982, Connecticut and U.S. District Court, Southern and Eastern Districts of New York. *Education:* State University of New York at Buffalo (B.A., magna cum laude, 1973); Loyola Law School of Los Angeles (J.D., 1979). Member, Volunteer Lawyers for the Arts, 1980-1982. Member, Pro Bono Immigration Project, Los Angeles County Bar Association, 1983-1985. *Member:* Westport and Federal Bar Associations; Fairfield Women's Bar Association; American Immigration Lawyers Association.

LAW OFFICES OF ROBERT SULLIVAN

190 MAIN STREET
WESTPORT, CONNECTICUT 06880
Telephone: 203-227-1404 V/TDD
Facsimile: 203-226-6403
From San Francisco Bay Area: 510-820-0307

Danville, California Office: 375 Diablo Road, Suite 200. Telephone: 510-820-4141. Facsimile: 510-831-0155.

Business Transactions, Litigation, Criminal Law.

ROBERT J. SULLIVAN, born 1952; admitted to bar, 1983, California; 1992, Connecticut; U.S. District Court, District of Connecticut, U.S. District Court, Northern and Eastern Districts of California and U.S. District Court, Eastern District of New York. *Education:* Sacred Heart University (B.S., Accounting, 1979); Golden Gate University (J.D., 1982). *Member:* Greater Bridgeport (Member: Civil Trial Committee; Criminal Law Committee), Connecticut (Member: Criminal Justice Section; Corporate Counsel Section) and American Bar Associations; State Bar of California (Member, Litigation Section); Connecticut Criminal Defense Lawyers Association; National Association of Criminal Defense Lawyers; Connecticut Trial Lawyers Association. ***PRACTICE AREAS:*** Business Law; Litigation; Criminal Law.

TIROLA & HERRING

Established in 1967
1555 POST ROAD EAST
P.O. BOX 631
WESTPORT, CONNECTICUT 06881
Telephone: 203-255-5144
Fax: 203-255-5177
Email: tirolalaw@aol.com
URL: http://www.lawyers.com/tirolalaw

Affiliated Office: Twomey, Hoppe and Gallanty, LLP, 757 Third Avenue, New York, New York. 10017. Telephone: 212-688-0400. Fax: 212-688-1929.

General Practice, Banking and Financial, Corporate, Executive Compensation, Real Estate, Land Use and Environmental Law, Family, Estate Planning and Probate and Litigation in all Courts.

MEMBERS OF FIRM

VINCENT S. TIROLA, born New York, New York, 1937; admitted to bar, 1962, District of Columbia; 1964, Connecticut; 1969, U.S. Court of Appeals, Second Circuit and U.S. Supreme Court;. *Education:* Miami University (A.B., 1959); New York University (LL.B., 1962; LL.M., 1966). Phi Delta Phi. Professor, The Legal Environment, Sacred Heart University Graduate School, 1972-1983. Lecturer, Real Property, New York University School of Law, 1974. Justice of the Peace, Town of Westport, 1970-1974. Board Member, Connecticut Theatre Foundation, 1976-1986. Board Member, County Federal Savings, 1966-1974. Member: The Federalist Society; Fairfield Judicial District Panel; Westport Zoning Board of Appeals, 1968-1970; National Panel of Arbitrators, American Arbitration Association, 1975—. (Also Of Counsel to Twomey, Hoppe and Gallanty, LLP, New York). ***PRACTICE AREAS:*** Business Law; Executive Compensation; Real Property; Banking Law; Family Law. ***Email:*** tirolalaw@aol.com

CHARLES FREDERICKS, JR., born New York, New York, 1926; admitted to bar, 1949, New York; 1950, U.S. District Court, Southern District of New York; 1989, Connecticut. *Education:* Princeton University (A.B., 1946); Harvard University (LL.B., 1948). Lecturer, School of Organization and Management, Yale University, 1982. (Also at New York Office). ***LANGUAGES:*** French. ***PRACTICE AREAS:*** Commercial Law; Probate; Advertising Law; Corporate Real Estate; Trademarks. ***Email:*** tirolalaw@aol.com

ELIZABETH C. SEELEY, born Little Rock, Arkansas, 1938; admitted to bar, 1963, Connecticut; 1978, U.S. District Court, District of Connecticut. *Education:* Wharton School, University of Pennsylvania (B.S. in Economics, 1960); University of Virginia (LL.B., 1963). *Member:* Connecticut (Member, Executive Committee, Corporations and Business Organizations Section, 1987—) and American (Member, Committee on Commercial Leasing, 1989—) Bar Associations. ***LANGUAGES:*** French. ***PRACTICE AREAS:*** Corporate Law; Business Law; Banking Law; Commercial Real Estate. ***Email:*** tirolalaw@aol.com

BUDDY O. H. HERRING, born Kansas City, Missouri, 1946; admitted to bar, 1971, Connecticut and U.S. District Court, District of Connecticut; 1975, North Carolina and U.S. Court of Appeals, Fourth Circuit. *Education:* Wake Forest University (B.A., 1968; J.D., cum laude, 1971). Phi Alpha Delta. Editor, Wake Forest Law Review, 1970-1971. Author: *North Carolina Family Practice Manual,* 1981; "Equal Distribution in North Carolina," Fairshare, February, 1983; "An Advanced Degree—Where Is It Anyway?" American Bar Association Journal, December, 1984. Professor, Wake Forest Law School, 1975—. Associate Dean, Wake Forest Law School, 1975-1994. *Member:* North Carolina State Bar. (Also at New York Office). ***LANGUAGES:*** French. ***PRACTICE AREAS:*** Family Law; Real Property; Estate Planning; Sports Law; Entertainment Law; Civil Litigation. ***Email:*** tirolalaw@aol.com

---

THOMAS C. CUSA, born New York, New York, March 13, 1969; admitted to bar, 1999, Connecticut and New York. *Education:* Gettysburg College (B.A., Economic, 1991); Quinnipiac College School of Law2 (J.D., 1998). ***LANGUAGES:*** Spanish. ***PRACTICE AREAS:*** Real Estate; Taxation. ***Email:*** tirolalaw@aol.com

OF COUNSEL

SUSANNAH JACOBSON, born New York, N.Y., October 5, 1968; admitted to bar, 1993, Connecticut. *Education:* Hartwick College (B.A., 1990); John Marshall School of Law (J.D., 1993). Pi Sigma Alpha. Recipient, Best Oralist Award in Torts. ***LANGUAGES:*** Spanish. ***Email:*** tirolalaw@aol.com

C. MICHAEL CARTER, born Boston, Massachusetts, 1943; admitted to bar, 1974, New York; 1978, Connecticut. *Education:* University of California at Berkeley (B.S., 1967); George Washington University (J.D., with honors, 1973). (Also Senior Vice President and General Counsel, Concurrent Computer Corporation, Oceanport, New Jersey). ***PRACTICE AREAS:*** Taxation; Corporate Law. ***Email:*** tirolalaw@aol.com

(This Listing Continued)

MICHAEL E. TWOMEY, born New York, N.Y., 1949; admitted to bar, 1975, New York; U.S. District Court, Southern and Eastern Districts of New York; U.S. Court of Appeals, Second and Fourth Circuits; U.S. Supreme Court. *Education:* Princeton University (A.B., magna cum laude, 1971); Fordham University (J.D., 1974). Notes Editor, Fordham University Law Review, 1973-1974. *Member:* Association of the Bar of the City of New York; Westchester County and American Bar Associations; Federal Bar Council. (Also Member of Twomey, Hoppe & Gallanty LLP, New York City). ***PRACTICE AREAS:*** Commercial Litigation; Insurance Coverage; Products Liability; Employment Law. ***Email:*** TWOMEY@THGLLP.COM

GARY HOPPE, born Rochester, New York, 1952; admitted to bar, 1978, New York; U.S. District Court, Southern, Eastern, Northern and Western Districts of New York; U.S. Court of Appeals, Second, Sixth and Eleventh Circuits; 2001, Washington. *Education:* State University of New York College at Oswego (B.A., summa cum laude, 1974); Harvard University (J.D., cum laude, 1977). Clerk to Hon. Judith S. Kaye, New York Court of Appeals, 1983-1984. Member, The Litigators Club. *Member:* Association of the Bar of the City of New York (Member: Committee on State Courts, 1981-1983; Committee on Professional Discipline, 1988-1991; Committee on Professional and Judicial Ethics, 1985-1987, 1993-1996; Committee on Litigation, 1996-1999). (Also Member of Twomey, Hoppe & Gallanty LLP, New York City). ***PRACTICE AREAS:*** Commercial Litigation; Insurance Coverage; Directors and Officers Liability; Employment Law. ***Email:*** HOPPE@THGLLP.COM

ALAN T. GALLANTY, born Brooklyn, New York, 1959; admitted to bar, 1983, New York; U.S. District Court, Southern and Eastern Districts of New York; U.S. Court of Appeals, Second and Fourth Circuits. *Education:* State University of New York at Binghamton (B.A., 1979); Duke University (J.D., 1982). Author: "A Rule 43(e) Hearing: An Alternative Approach to Summary Judgment in Complex Commercial Litigation," New York Law Journal, October 10, 1991. Faculty, Practicing Law Institute, Basics of Accounting and Finance: What Every Practicing Lawyer Needs to Know, "Year 2000 Issues Relevant to the Deal," 1999. *Member:* Association of the Bar of the City of New York (Member, Committee on Sports Law, 1993-1995); American Bar Association (Member: Litigation, Business Law and Antitrust Sections; Committee on Professional Liability Litigation). (Also Member of Twomey, Hoppe & Gallanty LLP, New York City). ***PRACTICE AREAS:*** Commercial Litigation; Directors and Officers Liability; Employment Law. ***Email:*** GALLANTY@THGLLP.COM

GUS DIMOPOULOS, born New York, N.Y., 1975; admitted to bar, 2001, New York. *Education:* New York University (B.A., magna cum laude, 1997); Fordham Law School (J.D., 2000). *Member:* New York Bar Association. (Also Associate with Twomey, Hoppe & Gallanty LLP, New York City). ***Email:*** dimopoulos@THGLLP.com

JOHN LOGAN O'DONNELL, born Chicago, Illinois, 1914; admitted to bar, 1937, Illinois; 1943, New York; 1977, District of Columbia. *Education:* Williams College (A.B., 1934); Northwestern University (J.D., 1937). Case Editor, Illinois Law Review, 1936-1937. Member, General Counsel's Staff, Securities and Exchange Commission, Washington, D.C., 1938-1941. Instructor, Catholic University of American Law School, 1938-1941. Member, 1952-1991 and Of Counsel, 1991, Olwine, Connelly, Chase, O'Donnell & Weyher. Fellow, American College of Trial Lawyers. America Arbitration Association, Commercial Arbitration Panel. *Member:* Association of the Bar of the City of New York; American Bar Association (Member, Sections on: Litigation; Class Actions; Antitrust). (Also Of Counsel to Twomey, Hoppe & Gallanty LLP, New York City).

DIANE K. FERNBACH, born Queens, New York, May 30, 1967; admitted to bar, 1992, New Jersey and U.S. District Court, District of New Jersey; 1993, New York and U.S. District Court, Eastern and Southern Districts. *Education:* Johns Hopkins University (B.A., 1989); Tulane University (J.D., cum laude, 1992). *Member:* American Bar Association; The Association of the Bar of the City of New York. (Also Of Counsel to Twomey, Hoppe & Gallanty LLP, New York City). ***PRACTICE AREAS:*** Commercial Litigation; Professional Liability; Directors and Officers Liability; Banking Law. ***Email:*** FERNBACH@THGLLP.COM

ANTHONY DEL VECCHIO, born Bronx, New York, 1967; admitted to bar, 1994, New Jersey and U.S. District Court, District of New Jersey; 1995, New York and U.S. District Court, Southern and Eastern Districts of New York. *Education:* Binghamton University (B.A., 1989); Hofstra University (J.D., 1993). Member, Pro Bono Panel for the U.S. District Court, Southern District of New York. *Member:* Association of the Bar of the City of New York; American and Columbian Bar Associations; Volunteer Lawyers for the Arts. (Also Of Counsel to Twomey, Hoppe & Gallanty LLP, New York City). ***Email:*** DELVECCHIO@THGLLP.COM

REFERENCE: U.S. Trust Co.

URY & MOSKOW

A Limited Liability Company
518 RIVERSIDE AVENUE
P.O. BOX 231
WESTPORT, CONNECTICUT 06881
Telephone: 203-226-8088
Fax: 203-226-8437
URL: http://www.urymoskow.com
Email: law@UryMoskow.com
URL: http://www.lawyers.com/ury&moskow

General Civil and Criminal Practice before State and Federal Courts. Real Estate, Corporation, Commercial and Banking Litigation, Personal Injury, Medical Malpractice, Construction Law and Litigation, Employment Law, Toxic Tort, Pharmaceutical and Devise Litigation, Trials and Appeals.

MEMBERS OF FIRM

FREDERIC S. URY, born Zanesville, Ohio, September 11, 1952; admitted to bar, 1977, Connecticut and U.S. District Court, District of Connecticut; 1982, U.S. Supreme Court; 1989, New York. *Education:* Babson College (B.S., with highest distinction, 1974); Suffolk University (J.D., 1977). Beta Gamma Sigma. Editor-in-Chief of *The Advocate,* The Suffolk University Law School Journal, 1976-1977. Author: "Euthanasia: The Courts Struggle to find a Solution," Volume 7, No. 2, The Advocates. Instructor: Public Speaking and General Law, Westport Continuing Education, 1992-1993; Real Estate and Legal Research, Fairfield University, 1979-1988. Member, Board of Trustees, 1975-1981 and Corporation Member, 1975-1985, Babson College. President, Community Council, Westport-Weston, Inc., 1982-1984. Member, 1985-1994, President, 1988-1991, and Vice President, 1992-1993, Board of Directors, United Way, Westport-Weston, Inc. President, Congregation For Humanistic Judaism, 1997-2000. Court Appointed Arbitrator, Connecticut Bar Association, 1998—. *Member:* Westport (Secretary, 1987-1988), Connecticut (Vice-Chair, 1992-1993, Chairman, 1993-1996 and Member, Executive Committee, Litigation Section, 1987—; Chair, Continuing Education Committee, 1998; Founding Editor and Editor-in-Chief of Sidebar - The Litigation Section Newsletter, 1992-1993, Associate Editor 1993—; Bench/Bar Committee, 1995—; Court Rules Committee, 1995—), New York State and American (Member, Committee on Commercial and Banking Litigation, Litigation Section) Bar Associations; Connecticut Trial Lawyers Association; The Association of Trial Lawyers of America. (Board Certified Civil Trial Specialist by the National Board of Trial Advocacy). ***REPORTED CASES:*** Paige v. Town and Zoning Comm. of Town of Fairfield, 235 Comm. 448, 668 A.2d 340 (Conn., Nov. 21, 1995) (No. 15092); Paige v. Town and Zoning Comm. of the Town of Fairfield, 231 Conn. 934, 649 A.2d 256 (Conn., Oct 20, 1994); Manndorff v. Dax, 13 Conn. App. 282, 535 A.2d (Conn. App., Jan 19, 1988) (No. 5287); Marion Road Ass'n v. Harlow, 1 Conn. App. 329, 472 A.2d 785 (Conn. App., Mar 06, 1984) (No. 2381); National Loan Investors, L.P. v. Heritage Square Associates (1999 WL 417870). ***PRACTICE AREAS:*** Trials and Appeals in all Courts; Banking and Commercial Law; Personal Injury Law; Medical Malpractice; Real Estate; Criminal Law. ***Email:*** FRED@URYMOSKOW.COM

NEAL L. MOSKOW, born Boston, Massachusetts, May 14, 1964; admitted to bar, 1989, Connecticut; 1990, U.S. District Court, District of Connecticut; U.S. District Court, Southern and Eastern Districts of New York; U.S. Court of Appeals, Second Circuit. *Education:* Cornell University; State University of New York at Albany (B.A., magna cum laude, 1986); Boston University School of Law (J.D., 1989). Member, Board of Directors, Temple B'Nai Chaim. Author, "Connecticut's PJR After Pinsky," Sidebar, Fall 1997. Instructor: Motion Practice in Connecticut, Automobile Accidents and Insurance, and Foreclosure Law, Lorman Institute Seminar on Construction Law, Connecticut Bar Association. *Member:* Westport, Stamford, Connecticut (Member, Executive Board, Commercial Law Section; Construction Law Section; Litigation Section; Associate Editor, Sidebar, Litigation Section Newsletter, 1994—) and American Bar Associations; Connecticut Trial Lawyers Association; The Association of Trial Lawyers of America. ***REPORTED CASES:*** Distasio v. Perkin Elmer Corp., 157 F.3d 55 (2nd Cir. 1998). ***PRACTICE AREAS:*** Construction Law; Construction Litigation; Commercial, Bank and Civil Litigation; Personal Injury; Employment Law; Real Estate. ***Email:*** NEAL@URYMOSKOW.COM

ASSOCIATES

DEBORAH M. GARSKOF, born Hempstead, New York, April 5, 1969; admitted to bar, 1994, Massachusetts; 1995, U.S. District Court, District of Massachusetts; 1997, Connecticut; 1998, U.S. District Court, District of Connecticut; 2000, New York. *Education:* University of Connecticut (B.A., 1991); Suffolk University (J.D., 1994). Phi Beta Kappa. *Member:* Connecticut Bar Association; Connecticut Trial Lawyers Association. ***PRACTICE AREAS:*** Commercial Law; Banking Litigation; Civil Litigation; Employment Law; Construction Law; Real Estate. ***Email:*** DEBORAH@URYMOSKOW.COM

(This Listing Continued)

BETTY ANN ROGERS, born Boston, Massachusetts, June 20, 1954; admitted to bar, 1991, Connecticut. *Education:* Fairfield University (B.A., 1976); University of Bridgeport School of Law (J.D., magna cum laude, 1990). Phi Delta Phi. Member, Connecticut Trial Lawyers Association, 1991. Court appointed Arbitratrix/Factfinder, 2000. Recipient: Jurisprudence Awards in: Trial Practice, Evidence, Civil Procedure, Family Law, Trusts and Estates; Kristen Ann Carveth Memorial Book Award in Family Law. Research Editor, Law Review, 1988-1990. ***PRACTICE AREAS:*** Personal Injury; Medical Malpractice; Civil Litigation. ***Email:*** BettyAnn@urymoskow.com

PATRICIA WHITING WELCH, born Bridgeport, Connecticut, May 16, 1969; admitted to bar, 1999, Connecticut; 2000, U.S. District Court, District of Connecticut. *Education:* Sacred Heart University (B.S., 1993); Quinnipiac College School of Law (J.D., 1998). Member, Advisory Board, Connecticut Law Tribune, March 2000—. *Member:* Stamford and Connecticut Bar Associations; Connecticut Trial Lawyers Association. ***PRACTICE AREAS:*** Personal Injury; Medical Malpractice; Products Liability; Wrongful Death. ***Email:*** TRISH@URYMOSKOW.COM

ANTHONY J. LaBELLA, born Islip, New York, August 19, 1964; admitted to bar, 2000, Connecticut. *Education:* Vassar College (B.A., 1986); Quinnipiac College School of Law (J.D., cum laude, 1994). Phi Delta Phi. *Member:* Connecticut Bar Association. ***PRACTICE AREAS:*** Civil Litigation; Construction Law; Commercial Law; Personal Injury; Professional Malpractice; Real Estate; Products Liability. ***Email:*** Anthony@urymoskow.com

SPECIAL COUNSEL

JULIA CREMIN WYMAN, born Hartford, Connecticut, September 9, 1964; admitted to bar, 1997, Connecticut; 1998, New York. *Education:* Central Connecticut State University (B.S., 1992); Western New England College School of Law (J.D., 1997). *Member:* Hartford County Bar Associations; American and New York State Bar Associations; Connecticut Trial and Lawyers Association; The Association of Trial Lawyers of America. ***PRACTICE AREAS:*** Drug and Medical Device Litigation; Medical Malpractice; Personal Injury. ***Email:*** Julia@urymoskow.com

REPRESENTATIVE CLIENTS: A.M. Realty Co.; Banc One Asset Solutions Corporation; Bosque Asset Corp.; Chase Manhattan Bank; Coolidge-Connecticut Equities, L.P.; Connecticut Attorneys Title Insurance Company; EDGAR Online, Inc.; FirstCity Servicing Corp.; First Union National Bank; Franklin Financial; Lawyers Title Insurance Company; MacKenzie Service Corp.; National Loan Investors, L.P.; Original Grasso Construction, Inc.; Pacific Northwest Capital, Inc.; Standard Demolition, Inc.; Security National, L.P.; Viking Construction, Inc.

WAKE, SEE, DIMES & BRYNICZKA

Established in 1946
27 IMPERIAL AVENUE
P.O. BOX 777
WESTPORT, CONNECTICUT 06881
Telephone: 203-227-9545
Telecopier: 203-226-1641
Email: wsdb@wsdb.com
URL: http://www.wsdb.com

Business and Corporate Law, Real Estate, Trusts and Probate, Estate Planning, Municipal, Zoning and Land Use Law, Litigation in all Federal and State Courts. Federal, State and Foreign Taxation, Pension and Profit Sharing, and Family Law.

FIRM PROFILE: The law firm of Wake, See, Dimes & Bryniczka has been providing legal counsel to clients since 1946. Although originally a small, general practice firm, the law firm has expanded significantly during its fifty-five history in order to meet the increasing complexities of the practice of law. Yet Wake, See, Dimes & Bryniczka remains committed to providing legal services which are personally responsive to clients and their needs. The hallmark of Wake, See, Dimes & Bryniczka has been the ability to provide clients with the expertise of a large firm, with the intimacy of a small firm.

MEMBERS OF FIRM

HEREWARD WAKE (1905-1977).

EDGAR T. SEE, born Brooklyn, New York, January 31, 1916; admitted to bar, 1941, Connecticut. *Education:* Wesleyan University, Middletown, Connecticut (B.A., 1938); Yale Law School (LL.B., 1941). Town Attorney, Town of Westport, 1946-1948, 1949-1954; 1957-1966. Member, Westport Representative Town Meeting, 1955-1957; 1967-1969. Chairman, 1955-1957 and Member, 1985-1986, Westport Charter Revision Commission. Chairman, Westport-Weston Servicemen's Council, 1946-1947. Member, Board of Editors, Connecticut Bar Journal, 1945-1954. President: Westport-Weston Community Council, 1971-1976; Westport-Weston United Fund, 1979-1980. *Member:* Westport, Connecticut (Chairman, Real Property Section, 1954-1955; Member of Council, 1955-1958; Member, Board of Governors, 1973-1976; Member and Chairman, 1979-1981, Section on International Law and World Peace) and

(This Listing Continued)

American Bar Associations. Fellow, American College of Trust and Estate Counsel. Fellow: American Bar Foundation; Connecticut Bar Foundation. ***PRACTICE AREAS:*** Estate Planning; Trust Law; Probate; Real Estate. ***Email:*** esee@wsdb.com

EDWIN K. DIMES, born Hartford, Connecticut, April 13, 1923; admitted to bar, 1950, Connecticut. *Education:* Wesleyan University (B.A., 1947); Yale Law School (LL.B., 1950). Phi Beta Kappa; Phi Delta Phi. Director, Connecticut Federation of Planning and Zoning Agencies, 1955-1956; Alternate, Planning and Zoning Commission, Town of Westport, 1954-1955. Member, Westport Recreation Commission, 1969-1973. Deputy Harbormaster, Harbor of Westport, 1973-1975. Member, 1979-1997 and Chairman, 1984-1997, Board of Finance, Town of Westport. *Member:* Westport, Connecticut (Member: House of Delegates, 1955-1956, 1957-1958 and 1991—and Board of Governors, 1996—, Real Property Section and Estates and Probate Section) and American (Member, Sections of: Family Law; Antitrust Law) Bar Associations. ***PRACTICE AREAS:*** Real Estate; Family Law; Estate Planning; Probate. ***Email:*** edimes@wsbd.com

JACOB P. BRYNICZKA, born Washington, D.C., March 5, 1945; admitted to bar, 1971, Connecticut; 1975, U.S. Tax Court. *Education:* Wesleyan University (B.A., 1967); Universität Köln; University of Connecticut (J.D., 1970); University of New Haven (M.S., Taxation, 1985). Author: "The Bankruptcy Laws of Sweden," *European Bankruptcy Laws,* (I. Arnold Ross, Editor) American Bar Association Section of International Law Publication, 1974. Co-Author: "Getting to Market in the U.S.A.,"; "*Getting to Market:* From the Factory Floor to the Customer's Hands," Ontario Bar Association, 1995. Special Lecturer, Graduate Tax Program, University of New Haven, 1986-1988. Member; First Selectman's Public Welfare Advisory Committee, 1974-1975; Representative Town Meeting of Westport, 1975-1977; Recreation Commission of Westport, 1978-1981; Staples High School Tuition Grants Committee, 1995-1998. *Member:* Westport (Member, Executive Committee, 1988-1993; President, 1992-1993), Connecticut (Member, House of Delegates, 1985-1988) and American (Member: Section of Taxation; European Law Committee, 1972-1982, Section of International Law) Bar Associations. ***LANGUAGES:*** German; Swedish. ***PRACTICE AREAS:*** Business Law; Taxation; Marketing Law; Promotion Law; Estate Planning; Real Estate Law. ***Email:*** jbryniczka@wsdb.com

AMY L. Y. DAY, born Bronxville, New York, March 16, 1952; admitted to bar, 1977, Connecticut. *Education:* Smith College (A.B., 1974); Dartmouth College; University of Connecticut (J.D., 1977). Phi Beta Kappa; Phi Alpha Delta (Vice Justice, Starr Chapter, 1976-1977). Clerk, Westport Board of Finance, 1979-1983. Member, Town of Westport Social Services Advisory Board, 1985-1990. Member, Board of Directors: Westport-Weston United Way, 1982-1988; Child Care Council of Westport-Weston, 1978-1981, 1986-1989 (President, 1986-1989); Family Center: Affiliated Community Services of Westport-Weston, Inc., 1991-1992; Staples High School Tuition Grants Committee, Inc., 1992-1995. *Member:* Westport (Member, Executive Committee, 1980-1987; President, 1985-1986), Connecticut (Member, Executive Committee, Estates and Probate Section, 1986—; Member, Advisory Committee, Connecticut Lawyer, 1992—) and American Bar Associations. ***PRACTICE AREAS:*** Trust Law; Probate; Estate Planning; Real Estate. ***Email:*** alyday@wsdb.com

IRA W. BLOOM, born New Haven, Connecticut, November 18, 1953; admitted to bar, 1978, Connecticut. *Education:* Clark University (B.A., magna cum laude, high honors in Government, 1975); University of Connecticut (J.D., 1978). Phi Beta Kappa. Town Attorney, Town of Westport, 1998—; Member, Westport Representative Town Meeting, 1981-1989; Elected Deputy Moderator, 1986. Member, Vice Chairman and Chairman, Westport Board of Education, 1989-1997. Member, First Selectman's Downtown Finance Advisory Committee, 1982. Instructor, Fairfield University, Paralegal Studies Program, 1981-1982. *Member:* Westport (President, 1998-1999), Connecticut (Member: Executive Committee, Planning and Zoning Section, 1988-1991, 1994-1999; Conservation and Environmental Quality Section) and American Bar Associations. ***PRACTICE AREAS:*** Municipal Law; Zoning, Planning and Land Use; Commercial Real Estate; Residential Real Estate; Civil Litigation. ***Email:*** ibloom@wsdb.com

MARK J. KOVACK, born Kenmore, New York, October 18, 1959; admitted to bar, 1985, Connecticut; 1986, U.S. District Court, District of Connecticut. *Education:* St. Lawrence University (B.A., magna cum laude, 1982); Albany Law School of Union University (J.D., cum laude, 1985). Phi Beta Kappa; Pi Sigma Alpha. Member, Justinian Society. Member, Albany Law Review, 1983-1984. *Member:* Westport, Connecticut and American Bar Associations. ***REPORTED CASES:*** Vincent Builders Inc. v. American Application Systems Inc., 16 Conn App. 486, 1988. ***PRACTICE AREAS:*** Commercial Litigation (50%); Employment Law (15%); Real Estate Litigation (15%); Product Liability (15%); Personal Injury (5%). ***Email:*** mkovack@wsdb.com

DOUGLAS E. LoMONTE, born Riverhead, New York, October 21, 1966; admitted to bar, 1991, Connecticut; 1992, U.S. District Court, District of Connecticut. *Education:* Cesare Barbieri Center, Trinity College, Rome (1987); Trinity College, Hartford (B.A., 1988); University of Connecticut (J.D., 1991); University of New Haven (M.S., Taxation, 1999). Clerk, Westport Board of Finance, 1992-2000. *Member:* Westport, Connecticut and American Bar Associations. ***LANGUAGES:*** Italian. ***PRACTICE AREAS:*** Business Law; Taxation; Employment Law; Retirement Benefit Plans. ***Email:*** dlomonte@wsdb.com

ASSOCIATES

MICHAEL STEVEN TOMA, born Waterbury, Connecticut, February 10, 1970; admitted to bar, 1995, Connecticut. *Education:* Cornell University (B.A., 1992); University of Connecticut School of Law (J.D., 1995). Associate Editor, Connecticut Journal of International Law. Assistant to Corporation Counsel, Waterbury, 1996-1998. Assistant Town Attorney, Westport, 1998—. *Member:* Westport, Connecticut and American Bar Associations. ***PRACTICE AREAS:*** Municipal Law; Land Use Law; Real Estate; Civil Litigation. ***Email:*** mtoma@wsdb.com

LISA M. LEVY, born New Haven, Connecticut, May 10, 1971; admitted to bar, 1997, Connecticut. *Education:* Lehigh University (B.A., 1993); Quinnipiac College, School of Law (J.D., 1997). *Member:* Westport and Connecticut (Member, Estates and Probate Section) Bar Associations. ***PRACTICE AREAS:*** Estate Planning; Probate; Real Estate. ***Email:*** llevy@wsdb.com

RUSSELL S. FERGUSON, born Hartford, Connecticut, September 25, 1971; admitted to bar, 1999, Connecticut. *Education:* Providence College (B.A., 1993); University of Connecticut (J.D., 1998). *Member:* Westport, Connecticut and American Bar Associations. ***PRACTICE AREAS:*** Business Law; Marketing Law; Litigation. ***Email:*** rferguson@wsdb.com

SPECIAL COUNSEL

EUGENE E. CEDERBAUM, born Brooklyn, New York, April 16, 1942; admitted to bar, 1968, District of Columbia; 1969, U.S. Court of Appeals for the District of Columbia Circuit and U.S. Court of Military Appeals; 1974, Connecticut; 1975, U.S. District Court, District of Connecticut; 1978, U.S. Tax Court. *Education:* New York University (B.S., 1964); Columbia University (J.D., 1967). Beta Gamma Sigma. Member, Representative Town Meeting, Town of Westport, Connecticut, 1981-1985, 1989-1991. Chairman, Westport Advisory Committee, Diversity in Public Schools, 1993-1994. Member: Board of Directors, United Way of Westport-Weston, 1981-1987; Fair Housing Agent, Town of Westport, 1985—. Member, Board of Directors, Westport Arts Center, 1984-1989. Member, Staples High School Tuition Grants Committee, 1989-1992. Member, Board of Education, Town of Westport, 1995-1999. *Member:* Westport (President, 1986-1987), and The Connecticut (Member, House of Delegates, 1980-1983) and American Bar Associations; Westport Historical Society (Counsel). [JAGC, Army, 1969-1973]. ***PRACTICE AREAS:*** Business Law; Commercial Real Estate; Residential Real Estate; Commercial Litigation; Personal Injury Litigation; Municipal Law. ***Email:*** ecederbaum@wsdb.com

OF COUNSEL

RICHARD S. GIBBONS, born Norwalk, Connecticut, February 19, 1947; admitted to bar, 1972, Connecticut. *Education:* Ursinus College (B.A., 1969); Dickinson School of Law (J.D., 1972). Clerk, Westport Board of Finance, 1974-1977. Member, Charter Revision Commission, City of Norwalk, 1977-1980. Chairman, Charter Review Committee, City of Norwalk, 1979-1982. *Member:* Westport (Member, Executive Committee, 1979-1980) and Connecticut (Member, Sections on: Environmental Law; Real Property and Zoning) Bar Associations. [Capt., USAR, Ret.]. ***PRACTICE AREAS:*** Zoning Law; Real Estate; Corporate Law. ***Email:*** rgibbons@wsdb.com

WALTER M. ANDREW, JR., born New York, N.Y., May 18, 1932; admitted to bar, 1962, Connecticut; 1967, U.S. Court of Appeals, Second Circuit. *Education:* Syracuse University (A.B., 1954); University of Michigan (J.D., 1961). Member, Planning Commission, Town of Redding, 1966-1968. Member, Committee to Compile Connecticut Probate Practice Book, 1968-1969. Instructor, Real Estate Law, Fairfield University, 1976-1978. Advisory Counsel, Legal Assistant Program, Norwalk Community College, 1979-1984. *Member:* Westport (President, 1981-1982) and Connecticut (Member: Family Law Section) Bar Associations. [Capt., USAFR]. ***PRACTICE AREAS:*** Family Law; Trust Law; Estate Litigation; Wills; Probate.

LOCAL COUNSEL FOR: IMA Fin S.P.A. (Italy); Bindomatic A.B. (Sweden); Greenfield Online, Inc.
APPROVED ATTORNEYS FOR: Lawyers Title Insurance Corporation of Richmond, Va.; Chicago Title Insurance Co.; Connecticut Attorneys Title Insurance Co.; Old Republic National Title Insurance Co.; First American Title Insurance Co.; Fidelity National Title Insurance Co.
GENERAL COUNSEL FOR: L.H. Gault & Son, Inc.; Beta Shim Co.; IMA North America Inc.; Coverbind Corp.; D. L. Ryan Companies, Ltd.

(This Listing Continued)

ELLIOT R. WARREN

1555 POST ROAD EAST
WESTPORT, CONNECTICUT 06880
Telephone: 203-254-9570
Fax: 203-255-5177
Email: ewarrenlaw@aol.com
URL: http://www.lawyers.com/elliotrwarren

General Civil and Criminal Litigation before all State and Federal Courts. Trials and Appeals. Criminal Defense, Commercial and Tax Litigation, Personal Injury, Employment and Negligence Law.

ELLIOT R. WARREN, born New York, N.Y., January 8, 1950; admitted to bar, 1975, New York; 1977, District of Columbia; 1979, U.S. Court of Appeals for the District of Columbia Circuit; 1980, U.S. District Court for the District of Columbia; 1983, U.S. District Court, District of Connecticut and U.S. District Court, Southern District of New York; 1985, Connecticut and U.S. Court of Appeals, Second Circuit; 1989, U.S. Tax Court; 1990, U.S. Claims Court. *Education:* University of Rochester (B.A., with distinction, 1970); George Washington University (J.D., with honors, 1974). Trial Attorney, Antitrust Division, Department of Justice, 1974-1977. Assistant U.S. Attorney: District of Columbia, 1977-1983; District of Connecticut, 1983-1987 (Chief Fraud Counsel, 1985-1987). *Member:* Westport, Connecticut (Member, Sections on: Criminal Law; Federal Practice) and American (Member, Sections on: Criminal Law; Litigation) Bar Associations; The District of Columbia Bar; Connecticut Trial Lawyers Association; Connecticut Criminal Defense Lawyers Association.

REFERENCE: Peoples Bank.

WEISMAN & LUBELL

5 SYLVAN ROAD SOUTH
P.O. BOX 3184
WESTPORT, CONNECTICUT 06880
Telephone: 203-226-8307
Telecopier: 203-221-7279

General Civil Practice. Litigation, Family, Appeals, Real Estate, Zoning and Land Use Regulation.

MEMBERS OF FIRM

LAWRENCE P. WEISMAN, born Philadelphia, Pennsylvania, May 6, 1939; admitted to bar, 1963, Connecticut and U.S. District Court, District of Connecticut; 1966, U.S. Court of Appeals, Second Circuit; 1969, U.S. Supreme Court. *Education:* Brandeis University (B.A., 1960); Columbia University (J.D., 1963). Member, Board of Editors, Connecticut Bar Journal, 1971-1975. Author: "Planning and Zoning Law," Connecticut Bar Journal, Vol. 56, No. 2, April, 1982; "Planning and Zoning Law," Connecticut Bar Journal, Vol. 57, No. 1, February, 1983; "Planning and Zoning Law," Connecticut Bar Journal, Vol. 58, No. 1, 1984; "Planning and Zoning Law," Connecticut Bar Journal, Vol. 59, No. 2, 1985; "Planning and Zoning Law," Connecticut Bar Journal, Vol. 60, No. 2, 1986; "Planning and Zoning Law," Connecticut Bar Journal, Vol. 62, No. 4, August, 1988; "Determination of Validity of Ante Nuptial Agreements," Connecticut Family Law Journal, Vol. 2, No. 3, March, 1984; "Disclosure vs. Discovery: New Limits on Advocacy," Connecticut Family Law Journal, Vol. 3, No. 2, January, 1985. Counsel, Town of Westport, 1974-1975. Member, Governor's Advisory Council for Housing Matters, 1982-1985. Vice President, Board of Trustees, Westport Public Library. Member, Panel of Arbitrators, American Arbitration Association. Raymond E. Baldwin American Inn of Court. U.S. District Court Grievance Panel. *Member:* Westport, Connecticut (Member: Executive Committee, Planning and Zoning Section, 1979—; Family Relations Section; Judiciary Committee, 1985-1991) and American Bar Associations; Connecticut Trial Lawyers Association; The Association of Trial Lawyers of America. Fellow, American Academy of Matrimonial Lawyers. ***LANGUAGES:*** French. ***PRACTICE AREAS:*** General Civil Practice; Zoning and Land Use Regulation; Family. ***Email:*** weislaw@snet.net

ELLEN B. LUBELL, born New York, N.Y., October 7, 1947; admitted to bar, 1972, Connecticut; 1974, U.S. District Court, District of Connecticut; 1975, U.S. Court of Appeals, Second Circuit; 1979, U.S. Supreme Court; 1981, New York. *Education:* New York University (B.A., 1969); University of Connecticut (J.D., with honors, 1972). Author: "Handbook of Forms for the Connecticut Family Lawyer," 1991; "Planning and Zoning Law," Connecticut Bar Journal, Vol. 56, No. 2, April, 1982; "Planning and Zoning Law," Connecticut Bar Journal, Vol. 57, No. 1 , February, 1983; "Ethical, Courteous Advocacy, What is it? Is it possible?" Conn. Family Lawyer, Vol. 10 No. 4 (Winter 1996); "How to find the right divorce lawyer," Minuteman Newspaper, 4/21/94; "Planning and Zoning Law," Connecticut Bar Journal, Vol. 58, No. 1, 1984; "Planning and Zoning Law," Connecticut Bar Journal, Vol. 59, No. 2, 1985; "Planning and Zoning Law," Connecticut Bar Journal, Vol. 60, No. 2, 1986; "Zoning Law," Connecticut Bar Journal, Vol. 62, No. 4, 1988. Lecturer, Trial Practice, Yale University, 1981. Treasurer, Board of Directors, New Haven Legal Assistance Association, 1979-1981. Hearing Examiner, Commission on Human Rights and Opportunities, 1980-1982. State Trial Referee, 1984-1995. Associate Fellow, Timothy Dwight College, Yale University, 1980—. Member, Board of Directors, 1987— and President, 1990-1994, Women's Crisis Center. Raymond E. Baldwin American Inn of Court Bencher, 1989—. . *Member:* Westport (Member, Executive Committee, 1983-1984), Connecticut (Member: Status of Woman Committee, 1976-1986; Executive Committee, Human Rights and Responsibilities Section, 1977—; Executive Committee, Criminal Justice Section, 1978-1986; Executive Committee, Family Law Section, 1984-1996) and American Bar Associations; Fellow, American Academy of Matrimonial Lawyers. ***PRACTICE AREAS:*** Family; Appellate Practice. ***Email:*** ellenlubell@snet.net

OF COUNSEL

LIVIA D. BARNDOLLAR, born Stamford, Connecticut, August 10, 1956; admitted to bar, 1981, Connecticut; 1983, U.S. District Court, District of Connecticut; 1990, U.S. Supreme Court. *Education:* Trinity College (B.A., Intensive History, with high honors, 1978); Villanova University (J.D., 1981). Phi Beta Kappa. Member, Moot Court Board. Member, Board of Editors, 1985—, Survey Editor, 1988-1994, Editor-in-Chief, 1994-1997 and Senior Topical Editor, Family Law, 1999—, Connecticut Bar Journal. *Member:* Stamford Regional, Connecticut (Member, Family Law Executive Committee, 1995—; Co-Chair, Solo and Small Firm Practice Section, 1994-2001) and American Bar Associations. ***REPORTED CASES:*** Mitchell v. Mitchell, 194 Conn. 312 (1984); Walshon v. Walshon, 42 Conn.App. 651 (1996). ***PRACTICE AREAS:*** Family Law; Appellate Practice.

WILLINGER, WILLINGER & BUCCI, P.C.

WESTPORT, CONNECTICUT
(See Bridgeport)

General Practice. Real Estate, Corporate, Commercial, Foreclosure, Bankruptcy, Secured Financing, Zoning, Labor, Probate, Condemnation, Workers Compensation, Financial, Banking, Personal Injury and Criminal Law. Trials in all Courts.

BAKER O'SULLIVAN & BLISS PC

PUTNAM PARK
SUITE 100
100 GREAT MEADOW ROAD
WETHERSFIELD, CONNECTICUT 06109-2371
Telephone: 860-258-1993
Telecopier: 860-258-1991
Email: info@boblawyers.com

Litigation, Bankruptcy and Creditors' Rights.

ALAN ROBERT BAKER, born Markham, Ontario, January 13, 1945; admitted to bar, 1974, Connecticut, U.S. District Court, District of Connecticut and U.S. Court of Appeals, Second Circuit. *Education:* Haverford College (B.A., 1966); University of Connecticut (J.D., with honors, 1974). Law Clerk to Hon. Joseph W. Bogdanski, Associate Justice, Supreme Court of Connecticut, 1974-1975. Author: *Mechanics Liens in Connecticut Lawyers Deskbook XIII* (Connecticut Bar Association, 1998). *Member:* Hartford County (Chairman, Commercial Law Committee, 1995—), Connecticut and American Bar Associations. [Capt., USAF Intelligence, active duty, 1967-1971]. ***REPORTED CASES:*** Wards Co., Inc. v. Stamford Ridgeway Associates, 761 F.2d 117 (2d Cir. 1985); Community Savings Bank v. Federal Ins. Co., 960 F.Supp. 16 (D.Conn. 1997); Orsi v. Suhshine Art Studios, Inc. 874 F.Supp. 471 (D.Mass. 1995); First Union Caesar Corp. v. U.S. Machine Tools, Inc., 1982 WL 1586 (D.Conn. 1982); In re: Dazic Controls Corp., 178 B.R. 328, 26 Bankr. Ct. Dec. 960 (Bankr.D.Conn. 1995); In re: First Connecticut Small Business Inv. Co., 118 B.R. 179 (Bkrptcy.D.Conn. 1990); Matter of Marshall, 33 B.R. 42 (Bankr.D.Conn. 1983); Conference Center Ltd. v. TRC-The Research Corp. of New England, 189 Conn. 212, 455 A.2d 857 (1983); Connecticut Bank and Trust Co. v. Brody, 174 Conn. 616, 392 A.2d 445 (1978); Baker v. Sun Refining and Marketing Co., 14 Conn.App. 804, 539 A.2d 1043 (1988). ***PRACTICE AREAS:*** Litigation; Bankruptcy. ***Email:*** baker@boblawyers.com

WILLIAM J. O'SULLIVAN, born Queens, New York, November 21, 1959; admitted to bar, 1990, Connecticut; 1991, U.S. District Court, District of Connecticut; 1996, U.S. Court of Appeals, Second Circuit. *Education:* University of Connecticut (B.A., magna cum laude, 1982; J.D., with honors, 1990). Author: "Implied Strict Foreclosure Under Article 9 of the Connecticut UCC," Connecticut Lawyer, February 1998; "Consideration for Covenant Not to Compete: Is it Enough to Say, You're Not Fired"?, Connecticut Lawyer, February 1999. *Member:* Hartford County and Connecticut (Member, Commercial Law and Bankruptcy Section) Bar Associations. ***REPORTED CASES:*** PPG Industries, Inc. v. Webster Auto Parts Inc., 128 F.3d 103 (2d.Cir. 1997); Pettola v. Nissan Motor Acceptance Corp., 44 F.Supp.2d (D.Conn. 1999); Bhinder v. Sun Company, Inc., 246 Conn. 223 (Conn. 1998); Yost v. Seaboard Surety Company,

(This Listing Continued)

182 B.R. 375 (Bkrptcy.D.Conn. 1995). ***PRACTICE AREAS:*** Business Litigation; Commercial Litigation; Creditors Rights. ***Email:*** o'sullivan@boblawyers.com

RAYMOND C. BLISS, born Saginaw, Michigan, July 15, 1954; admitted to bar, 1984, Connecticut and U.S. District Court, District of Connecticut. *Education:* Williams College (B.A., cum laude, 1976); New York State School of Industrial and Labor Relations at Cornell University (M.I.L.R., 1978); Catholic University of America (J.D., 1984). *Member:* Hartford County and Connecticut Bar Associations. ***REPORTED CASES:*** Bainer v. Citicorp Mortgage Inc., 236 Conn. 212, 672 A.2d 500 (1996); In re Martin, 176 B.R. 675, 26 Bkrptcy.Ct-.Dec. 643 (Bankr.D.Conn. 1995); Matter of Dydo, 163 B.R. 663 (Bankr.D.Conn. 1994); Matter of DeMaio, 158 B.R. 890, 29 Collier Bkrptcy.Cas.2d 1352, 27 Fed.R.Serv.3d 1503 (Bankr.D.Conn. 1993); Matter of DeMaio, 159 B.R. 383 (Bankr.D.Conn. 1993); In re City of Bridgeport,128 B.R. 686 (Bankr. D.Conn. 1991). ***PRACTICE AREAS:*** Commercial Law; Bankruptcy; Creditors Rights. ***Email:*** bliss@boblawyers.com

---

GALE S. DWYER, born Bethesda, Maryland, January 29, 1970; admitted to bar, 1996, Washington; 1999, U.S. District Court, Western District of Washington and U.S. District Court, District of Connecticut; 2000, Connecticut. *Education:* Whitman College (B.A., 1992); Gonzaga University School of Law (J.D., cum laude, 1995); Georgetown Law School (LL.M., International and Comparative Law, 1996). Phi Delta Phi. Exchequer, 1994-1995. Licensed Insurance Adjuster. *Member:* Hartford County, Washington State and Connecticut Bar Associations. ***LANGUAGES:*** Japanese. ***PRACTICE AREAS:*** Products Liability; Commercial Litigation; Bankruptcy. ***Email:*** dwyer@boblawyers.com

DENISE R. POLIVY, born New York, NY, 1953; admitted to bar, 1997, Connecticut; 1998, U.S. District Court, District of Connecticut; 2000, U.S. Court of Appeals, Eleventh Circuit. *Education:* Wesleyan University (B.A., 1975); Dartmouth College (M.S., 1982); University of Connecticut (J.D., with high honors, 1997). Member, 1995-1996, Commentary Editor, 1996-1997, Connecticut Law Review. Author: "Unfair Discrimination in Chapter 11: A Comprehensive Compilation of Current Case Law," 72 Am. Bankr.L.J. 191 (1998); "Feist Applied: Imagination Protects, But Perspiration Persists-The Bases of Copyright Protection for Factual Complications," 8 Fordhams Intell. Prop. Media & Ent. L.J. 773 (1998); "Unfair Discrimination Under Section 1129(b)(1): A Primer," Norton Bankruptcy Law Advisor, Jan. 1998, at 5; Comment, "Virtue by Machine: A First Amendment Analysis of the V-Chip Provisions of the Telecommunications Act of 1996," 29 Conn. L. Rev. 1749 (1997). Co-Author: with Tina L. Brozmans, "Concurrent, Same Entity, Cross-Border Proceedings," 804 PLI/Comm. 853 (2000). Editor, "Commentary on the Telecommunications Act of 996," 29 Conn.L.Rev. 117 (1996). Law Clerk to the Hon. Robert L. Krechevsky, U.S. Bankruptcy Judge, District of Connecticut, 1997-1998. *Member:* Hartford County and Connecticut Bar Associations. ***PRACTICE AREAS:*** Bankruptcy; Creditors Rights. ***Email:*** polivy@boblawyers.com

REPRESENTATIVE CLIENTS: Chubb Insurance Group; Travelers Casualty & Surety Company; Crown, Cork & Seal Company, Inc.; GE Capital Corporation; Nissan Motor Acceptance Corporation; Sunoco, Inc. (R&M); Tolland Bank.

CHORCHES & NOVAK, P.C.

1260 SILAS DEANE HIGHWAY

WETHERSFIELD, CONNECTICUT 06109-4331

Telephone: 860-257-1980
Telecopier: 860-257-1988

Bankruptcy, Asset Protection, Commercial Transactions and Corporate. Civil Litigation in all State and Federal Courts. Representation before Internal Revenue Service.

MARTIN CHORCHES, born Hartford, Connecticut, October 13, 1935; admitted to bar, 1961, Connecticut, U.S. District Court, District of Connecticut, and U.S. Supreme Court. *Education:* University of Connecticut (B.S., 1958); Boston University (J.D., 1961). U.S. Trustee in Bankruptcy, U.S. District Court, District of Connecticut, 1963-1978. *Member:* Hartford County, Connecticut (Member, Executive Committee, Commercial Law and Bankruptcy Section, 1982—) and American (Member, Committee on Commercial Law, 1982—) Bar Associations; Commercial Law League of America (Member, Bankruptcy and Insolvency Section). ***PRACTICE AREAS:*** Bankruptcy; Asset Protection; Commercial Law; Real Estate; Foreclosure; Business Planning; Workouts; Representation before Internal Revenue Service.

ANTHONY S. NOVAK, born Hartford, Connecticut, January 17, 1952; admitted to bar, 1982, Connecticut and U.S. District Court, District of Connecticut; 1983, Florida; 1984, U.S. Court of Appeals, Second Circuit. *Education:* University of Connecticut (B.A., 1975; M.A., 1979); Western New England School of Law (J.D., cum laude, 1982). Phi Alpha Theta. Member, Panel of Standing Bankruptcy Trustees, Chapter 7, U.S. Bankruptcy Court, U.S. District of Connecticut, 1991—. *Member:* Hartford County, Connecticut (Member, Commercial Law Section) and American Bar Associations; The Florida Bar. ***PRACTICE AREAS:*** Bankruptcy Law; Commercial Law; Workouts; Representation before Internal Revenue Service.

TERESA A. FONTAINE, born Norwich, Connecticut, December 20, 1966; admitted to bar, 1997, Connecticut. *Education:* University of Connecticut (B.S., 1988); Quinnipiac College School of Law (J.D., 1997). Phi Delta Phi. Member and Associate Editor, Quinnipiac Law Review, 1995-1997. *Member:* Connecticut, Hartford County and American Bar Associations. ***PRACTICE AREAS:*** Bankruptcy.

MAYO, GILLIGAN & ZITO, LLP

PUTNAM PARK

100 GREAT MEADOW ROAD

WETHERSFIELD, CONNECTICUT 06109-2396

Telephone: 860-721-7725
Fax: 860-529-0493
URL: http://www.mayogilligan.com

Trials in all Courts, Real Estate, Banking and Commercial Finance, Creditors' Rights and Bankruptcy, Employment, Business Law, Zoning, Environmental, Estate Planning, Elder Law, Probate and Personal Injury Law.

MEMBERS OF FIRM

EDWARD A. ZITO, born Bloomfield, Connecticut, November 9, 1930; admitted to bar, 1959, Connecticut; 1960, U.S. District Court, District of Connecticut; 1971, U.S. Court of Appeals, Second Circuit. *Education:* Trinity College (B.A., 1955); University of Connecticut (J.D., 1959). Member: Interstate Banking Task Force, Connecticut, 1989; Charter Revision Commission, Town of Wethersfield, 1986 and 1992. President, Board of Trustees, University of Connecticut Law School Foundation, 1993. *Member:* Hartford County, Connecticut (Member, Sections on: General Practice; Probate; Real Estate; Elder Law) and American Bar Associations; National Academy of Elder Law Attorneys;. ***PRACTICE AREAS:*** General Practice; Probate; Elder Law; Real Estate. ***Email:*** ezito@mayogilligan.com

ROBERT G. GILLIGAN, born Hartford, Connecticut, July 8, 1942; admitted to bar, 1972, Connecticut. *Education:* University of Hartford (B.A., cum laude, 1970); University of Connecticut (J.D., with honors, 1972). Omicron Delta Epsilon. State Representative, 1975-1995; Assistant Majority Leader, 1977-1981; 1983-1995, House of Representatives. Director, Connecticut Resources Recovery Authority, 1975-1983. Director, Riverfront Recapture, Inc., 1983-1986. House Chairman, Banks Committee, 1981-1982; House Chairman, Insurance and Real Estate Committee; Legislative Commissioner, 1995—. Director, MetroHartford Chamber of Commerce, 1996—. *Member:* Hartford County, Connecticut (Member, Sections on: Commercial Law and Bankruptcy; Banking Law; Real Estate) and American Bar Associations. ***PRACTICE AREAS:*** Real Estate; Commercial Law; Secured Finance; Banking; Estate Planning and Settlement. ***Email:*** rgilligan@mayogilligan.com

JOHN J. MURPHY, born Troy, New York, March 6, 1955; admitted to bar, 1981, New York; 1984, Connecticut. *Education:* Hamilton College (A.B., 1977); Fordham University (J.D., 1980). *Member:* Connecticut (Member, Sections on: Banking Law; Commercial Law and Bankruptcy; Consumer Law), New York State Bar Association. ***PRACTICE AREAS:*** Commercial Finance; Banking; Corporate Law; Business Law. ***Email:*** jmurphy@mayogilligan.com

DAVID S. HOOPES, born Philadelphia, Pennsylvania, December 19, 1957; admitted to bar, 1984, Connecticut and U.S. District Court, District of Connecticut; 1994, U.S. Court of Appeals, Second Circuit; 1995, Massachusetts. *Education:* University of Massachusetts at Amherst (B.A., summa cum laude, 1981); University of Connecticut (J.D., with honors, 1984). Phi Beta Kappa; Phi Kappa Phi. Co-Author: "The Confidential Relationship in Will Contests," Trusts and Estates, Feb., 1985. *Member:* Connecticut Bar Association (Member, Commercial Law and Bankruptcy Section). ***PRACTICE AREAS:*** Commercial Litigation; Land Use; Real Estate. ***Email:*** dhoopes@mayogilligan.com

WILLIAM R. CROWE, born New York, N.Y., September 16, 1959; admitted to bar, 1985, New York; 1988, Connecticut; 1990, U.S. District Court, District of Connecticut. *Education:* Dartmouth College (A.B., with distinction in history, 1981); Fordham University (J.D., 1984). Member, Fordham Law Review, 1982-1984. Adjunct Associate Professor of Law, Fordham Law School, 1985-1988. ***PRACTICE AREAS:*** Commercial Real Estate; Business Law. ***Email:*** wcrowe@mayogilligan.com

JAMES M. SCARAMOZZA, born New Haven, Connecticut, October 15, 1959; admitted to bar, 1987, Connecticut. *Education:* Fairfield University (B.A., cum laude, 1982); Vermont Law School (J.D., magna cum laude, 1987). Member, Vermont Law Review, 1985-1987. *Member:* Connecticut (Member, Sections on: Real Property; Commercial Law), Rhode Island, Federal and American (Member, Section on: Real Property, Probate and Trusts) Bar Associations.

(This Listing Continued)

(This Listing Continued)

MAYO, GILLIGAN & ZITO, LLP, Wethersfield—Continued

PRACTICE AREAS: Commercial and Real Estate Finance; Affordable Housing; Nonprofit and Charitable Organizations; Corporate; Business Law; Problem Loan Restructurings. ***Email:*** jscaramozza@mayogilligan.com

GREGORY F. DeMANCHE, born Hartford, Connecticut, August 5, 1952; admitted to bar, 1983, Connecticut; 1984, U.S. District Court, District of Connecticut; 1993, U.S. Supreme Court. *Education:* Hofstra University (B.A., 1974); Trinity College (M.A., 1976); Indiana University (J.D., 1983). *Member:* Connecticut Bar Association (Member, Consumer Law Section). ***PRACTICE AREAS:*** Real Estate; Mortgage Lending; Consumer Lending; Regulatory Compliance; Business Law. ***Email:*** gdemanche@mayogilligan.com

GLENN POWELL, born Queens, New York, August 16, 1953; admitted to bar, 1978, Connecticut; 1979, U.S. District Court, District of Connecticut. *Education:* Hofstra University (B.A., magna cum laude, 1975) Phi Beta Kappa; Kappa Mu Epsilon, Omicron Delta Epsilon; Cornell University (J.D., 1978); Phi Delta Phi. *Member:* Connecticut Bar Association (Member, Labor and Employment Law Section); American Arbitration Association (Member, Panel of Employment Arbitrators; Panel of Employment Mediators). ***PRACTICE AREAS:*** Labor and Employment; Arbitration; Mediation; Alternative Dispute Resolution; Employment Litigation. ***Email:*** gpowell@mayogilligan.com

SEAN P. CLARK, born Cincinnati, Ohio, August 4, 1965; admitted to bar, 1990, Connecticut; 1991, U.S. District Court, District of Connecticut. *Education:* Siena College (B.S., in Finance, cum laude, 1987); Pennsylvania State University, The Dickinson School of Law (J.D., 1990). Alpha Kappa Alpha. Member, J. Braxton Craven Constitutional Appellate Moot Court Team, 1989. Who's Who Among American Law Students, 1990. *Member:* Hartford County, Connecticut and American Bar Associations. ***PRACTICE AREAS:*** Civil Litigation; Commercial Litigation; Personal Injury; Real Estate; Bankruptcy. ***Email:*** sclark@mayogilligan.com

ASSOCIATES

DEAN F. RADKE, born Hartford, Connecticut, May 3, 1950; admitted to bar, 1975, Connecticut and U.S. District Court, District of Connecticut; 1980, Maine and U.S. District Court, District of Maine. *Education:* Rensselaer Polytechnic Institute (B.S., 1972); University of Connecticut (J.D., with honors, 1975). *Member:* Connecticut Bar Association. ***REPORTED CASES:*** Burritt Mutual Savings Bank v. Tucker, 183 Conn. 369 (1981). ***PRACTICE AREAS:*** Commercial Real Estate; Commercial Transactions; Loan Workouts; Foreclosures; Banking Law; Residential Real Estate. ***Email:*** dradke@mayogilligan.com

NOREEN A. DILLMAN, born New Haven, Connecticut, October 10, 1961; admitted to bar, 1991, Connecticut. *Education:* Boston University; Southern Connecticut State University (B.A., 1983); Quinnipiac College (J.D., 1991). Certified Public Accountant, Connecticut. Formerly with Internal Revenue Service as Estate Tax Attorney. *Member:* Connecticut Bar Association; Connecticut Society of Certified Public Accountants; Estate and Business Planning Council of Hartford, Inc.; Central Connecticut Estate Planning Council (Vice President). ***PRACTICE AREAS:*** Estate Planning and Administration; Elder Law; Taxation. ***Email:*** ndillman@mayogilligan.com

J. MARTIN ACEVEDO, born San Jose, Costa Rica, March 2, 1969; admitted to bar, 1992, Republic of Costa Rica; 1997, Connecticut and U.S. District Court, District of Connecticut;. *Education:* Autonomous University of Central America (B.A., Jurisprudence, cum laude, 1990; Lic. Jurisprudence, summa cum laude, 1992); University of Connecticut School of Law (J.D., 1997). Phi Delta Phi International Honor Society. Author: "The Emerging Cause of Action for Compelled Self-Publication Defamation in the Employment Context: Should Connecticut Follow Suit?" 72 Conn. B.J. 297 (1998). *Member:* Connecticut, American, Inter-American and Costa Rican Bar Associations; Connecticut Hispanic Bar Association (Member, Board of Directors, 1999-2001). ***LANGUAGES:*** Spanish and French. ***PRACTICE AREAS:*** Real Estate Litigation; Employment Defense Litigation; Public Housing Litigation. ***Email:*** macevedo@mayogilligan.com

OF COUNSEL

WALTER H. MAYO, born St. Paul, Minnesota, October 30, 1936; admitted to bar, 1961, Minnesota; 1965, U.S. Supreme Court; 1969, Connecticut. *Education:* Princeton University (A.B., cum laude, 1958); Harvard University (LL.B., 1961). *Member:* Connecticut and American Bar Associations.

BARBARA J. RUHE

415 SILAS DEANE HIGHWAY, SUITE 304
WETHERSFIELD, CONNECTICUT 06109
Telephone: 860-513-5650
Fax: 860-513-5654
Email: rusoetal@courant.infi.net

Adoption, Matrimonial, Juvenile and Custody Law.

(This Listing Continued)

BARBARA J. RUHE, born Jersey City, New Jersey, November 25, 1948; admitted to bar, 1976, Connecticut. *Education:* Valparaiso University (B.A., 1970; J.D., 1976). Board Member: Association for Treatment and Training in the Attachment of Children; Charter Oak Preparatory Academy. Member, Connecticut Association of Foster and Adoptive Parents, Inc. *Member:* Hartford County, Connecticut and American Bar Associations. ***LANGUAGES:*** German. ***PRACTICE AREAS:*** Adoption; Matrimonial; Juvenile; Custody.

ASSOCIATE

JONATHAN W. A. RUHE, born New Brunswick, New Jersey, March 4, 1962; admitted to bar, 1987, Connecticut; 1988, U.S. District Court, District of Connecticut. *Education:* Valparaiso University (B.S., 1984; J.D., 1987). *Member:* Hartford County, Connecticut and American Bar Associations. ***PRACTICE AREAS:*** Real Estate; Juvenile; Matrimonial; Custody. ***Email:*** guar@usa.pipeline.com

OF COUNSEL

MILAGROS S. CRUZ, born New York, N.Y., August 24, 1965; admitted to bar, 1992, Connecticut; 1993, U.S. District Court, District of Connecticut. *Education:* Mount Holyoke College (B.A., 1987); University of Connecticut (J.D., 1990). Co-Author: "Nursing Home Care," Legal Aid Resource Center of Connecticut, 1992. Lecturer: "Living Wills and Other Advanced Directives," 1991; "Nursing Home Rights," 1991. Author: "Language Barriers to Justice", Connecticut Lawyer, vol. 19, #6, March, 1999. *Member:* Connecticut (Member, General Practice Committee, 1996—) Bar Association; Connecticut Hispanic Bar Association (President, 1997-1998); American Leadership Forum Class 16. American Inns of Court. ***LANGUAGES:*** Spanish. ***PRACTICE AREAS:*** General Practice; Civil Practice; Probate Litigation. ***Email:*** Milascrz@aol.com

---

SABATINI AND ASSOCIATES, LLC

WETHERSFIELD, CONNECTICUT

(See Newington)

General Civil Practice. Trials in all State and Federal Courts. Litigation, Probate, Corporate, Personal Injury, Commercial, Zoning.

LAW OFFICES OF
ALAN B. SILVER, LLC

274 SILAS DEAN HIGHWAY
WETHERSFIELD, CONNECTICUT 06109
Telephone: 860-257-9327
Fax: 860-257-9324
Email: attyalansilver@cyberzone.net

Bankruptcy, Business Law, Commercial Law, Real Estate, Personal Injury.

ALAN B. SILVER, born Hartford, Connecticut, October 27, 1947; admitted to bar, 1973, Connecticut; 1974, U.S. District Court, District of Connecticut. *Education:* University of Connecticut (B.A., 1969); Suffolk University (J.D., 1973). President: Tunxis Community College Foundation, 1984-1985; Tower Ridge Country Club, 1996—. Member: U.S. Bankruptcy Court, Panel of Trustees, District of Connecticut, 1974-1988; Advisory Board, Bank of Boston Connecticut, 1983-1987. *Member:* Hartford County (Member, Commercial Law Section), Connecticut (Member, Commercial Law Section) and American Bar Associations.

PATRICIA M. STRONG

415 SILAS DEANE HIGHWAY
SUITE 220
WETHERSFIELD, CONNECTICUT 06109-1735
Telephone: 860-571-7440
Fax: 860-571-7436
Email: pstronglaw@aol.com
URL: http://www.lawyers.com/pstronglaw

Employment and Labor Law, Civil Litigation in all State and Federal Courts, Administrative Law, Workers Compensation, Collections, Social Security Law.

PATRICIA M. STRONG, born Hartford, Connecticut, April 15, 1950; admitted to bar, 1977, Connecticut; 1980, U.S. District Court, District of Connecticut; 1982, U.S. Court of Appeals, Second Circuit; 1991, U.S. Supreme Court. *Education:* Connecticut College (A.B., cum laude, 1972); University of Connecticut School of Law (J.D., 1977). Assistant Reporter of Judicial Decisions, Connecticut Supreme Court, 1977-1981. Connecticut Assistant Attorney General, 1981-1991. *Member:* Hartford County, Connecticut (Member, Executive Committee, Sections on: Labor; Women in the Law; Chair, Retirement &

(This Listing Continued)

Employment Benefits Committee) and American (Member, Litigation Section) Bar Associations; National Employment Lawyers Associations; Connecticut Employment Lawyers Associations.

BOLAND, ST. ONGE & BROUILLARD

WILLIMANTIC, CONNECTICUT

(See Putnam)

General Civil and Criminal Practice before all Courts. Corporation, Banking, Leasing, Real Estate, Divorce, Custody, Mediation, Municipal, Personal Injury, Workers Compensation and Estate Planning, Probate Law. Trials and Appeals.

PARADISO & MUSKA

WILLIMANTIC, CONNECTICUT

(See Stafford Springs)

General Civil and Criminal Practice before State and Federal Courts. Real Estate, Probate, Zoning, Corporation, Family, Workers Compensation, Personal Injury and Municipal Law. Trials in all Courts.

TREIBER, GUARNACCIA & CONNORS

Established in 1978

25 CHURCH STREET
P.O. BOX 44
WILLIMANTIC, CONNECTICUT 06226
Telephone: 860-423-6308
Fax: 860-423-6344
Email: TGCLAW@NECA.COM

General Practice. Real Estate, Probate, Estate Planning, Commercial, Corporation, Personal Injury, Construction, Domestic Relations and Municipal Law. Civil and Criminal Trials in all Courts. Practice before Administrative Agencies.

MEMBERS OF FIRM

DAVID C. TREIBER, born Hartford, Connecticut, May 4, 1945; admitted to bar, 1970, Connecticut; 1974, U.S. District Court, District of Connecticut. *Education:* St. Michael's College (B.A., 1967); University of Connecticut (J.D., 1970). Corporation Counsel, City of Willimantic, 1977-1983. President, Willimantic YMCA, 1980-1981. Director: Greater Willimantic Chapter, American Red Cross, 1994; The Governor Samuel Huntington Trust, Inc., 1994-1998; Habitat for Humanity for the Windham Area, Inc., 1997—; Windham Federated Services for Older Americans Inc., 1997—; Chamber of Commerce, 1999—. *Member:* Windham, Connecticut and American Bar Associations; Connecticut Trial Lawyers Association; The Association of Trial Lawyers of America. ***PRACTICE AREAS:*** Real Estate; Probate and Wills; Elder Law; Civil Litigation; Personal Injury. ***Email:*** tgclaw@neca.com

GIACOMO J. GUARNACCIA, JR., born Willimantic, Connecticut, July 7, 1948; admitted to bar, 1974, Connecticut; 1975, U.S. Court of Appeals, Second Circuit; 1976, U.S. District Court, District of Connecticut. *Education:* Gannon University (B.A., 1970); College of William & Mary (J.D., 1973). Chairman, Younger Lawyers Section, Connecticut Bar Association for Tolland and Windham Counties, 1978-1983. Chairman, Charter Revision Commission, City of Willimantic, 1980. President, Greater Willimantic Chamber of Commerce, 1987. Director and Chairperson, Northeast Connecticut Economic Alliance, Inc. Director, Connecticut Attorneys Title Insurance Company. *Member:* Windham, Connecticut and American Bar Associations. ***PRACTICE AREAS:*** Real Estate; Business Law; Corporate Law; Probate and Wills; Elder Law. ***Email:*** tgclaw@neca.com

KEVIN C. CONNORS, born New Haven, Connecticut, January 1, 1954; admitted to bar, 1979, Connecticut; 1983, U.S. District Court, District of Connecticut; 2000, U.S. Supreme Court. *Education:* University of Connecticut (B.A., magna cum laude, 1974; J.D., 1979). Phi Beta Kappa; Phi Kappa Phi. Hearing Officer, State of Ct. Claims Commissioner, 1987-1995. Member: Hebron, Board of Education, 1983-1985; Hebron Board of Selectman, 1985-1987, 1989-1995. Probate Judge, District of Hebron, 1996—. *Member:* Windham County and Connecticut Bar Associations; Connecticut Criminal Defense Lawyers Association; The Association of Trial Lawyers of America. ***PRACTICE AREAS:*** Personal Injury Law; Civil Litigation; Criminal Law; Administrative Law; Probate; Wills. ***Email:*** tgclaw@neca.com

GREGORY AND ADAMS, P.C.

190 OLD RIDGEFIELD ROAD
WILTON, CONNECTICUT 06897
Telephone: 203-762-9000
Telefacsimile: 203-834-1628

New York, N.Y. Office: 156 West 56th Street, 10019. Telephone: 212-757-0434. Telefacsimile: 212-977-9583.

(This Listing Continued)

General Practice. Zoning, Planning and Land Use. Litigation. Commercial, Corporate/Transactional Law. Consumer Regulatory Matters. E-Commerce. General Counsel Services. Trusts and Estates. Taxation.

THOMAS T. ADAMS, born Orchard Park, New York, October 9, 1929; admitted to bar, 1957, New York; 1962, U.S. Supreme Court and U.S. Court of Appeals, 2nd Circuit; 1964, Connecticut. *Education:* University of Buffalo (A.B., 1951); Cornell University (J.D., 1957). Phi Delta Phi. Contributor, Cornell Law Quarterly, 1956-1957. Visiting Lecturer, Cornell Law School, 1962-1965. Author: Articles, ABA Journal, 1972. Adjunct Associate Professor of Law, Fordham University, School of Law, 1973-1976. Town Attorney, Wilton, 1966-1971. Distinguished Alumnus Award, Cornell Law School, 1990. Director, American Judicature Society, 1991-1992. Advisor, The Dana Fund for International and Comparative Legal Studies, 1976-1987. Member Emeritus, Advisory Council of Cornell Law School, 1989—. Trustee-President, The Five Town Foundation, Inc., 1981-1986, 1989-1990. *Member:* Stamford/Norwalk Regional Bar (Director); The Association of the Bar of the City of New York; Norwalk-Wilton (President, 1989-1990), Connecticut (Member: Council of Bar Presidents, 1989-1990; Ethics Committee, 1970-1975), New York State and American Bar Associations. [Capt., USAF, active duty, Korea, 1951-1953]. ***PRACTICE AREAS:*** Trusts and Estates; Probate; Real Estate; Zoning.

ANNE E. CRANE, born New York, N.Y., September 16, 1956; admitted to bar, 1988, New York; 1992, Connecticut. *Education:* State University of New York at Binghamton (B.A., cum laude, 1978); New York University School of Law (J.D., cum laude, 1987). Phi Beta Kappa; Order of the Coif. Associate Editor, Annual Survey of American Law, 1984-1985. Author: "Unsealing Adoption Records: The Right to Privacy vs. the Right to Know," Annual Survey of American Law, 1987. *Member:* New York State, Connecticut (Member, Estates and Probate Executive Committee, 1995-1998) and American Bar Associations. ***PRACTICE AREAS:*** Estate Planning; Trusts and Estates; Probate. ***Email:*** acrane@gregoryandadams.com

SUSAN LACY GOLDMAN, born Hartford, Connecticut, August 3, 1957; admitted to bar, 1985, Connecticut and Pennsylvania. *Education:* University of Colorado (B.A., 1979); Western New England College (J.D., 1985). Member, Western New England Law Review, 1984-1985. Author: "The Duty to Disclose Under The Securities and Exchange Commission's Section 10(b) and Rule 10b-5," Western New England Law Review, Vol. 7-1, 1984. *Member:* Stamford/Norwalk Regional, Connecticut, Pennsylvania and American Bar Associations. ***PRACTICE AREAS:*** Real Estate; Zoning; Planning; Land Use. ***Email:*** sgoldman@gregoryandadams.com

J. CASEY HEALY, born Washington, D.C., February 19, 1956; admitted to bar, 1983, Georgia and Connecticut; 1984, U.S. District Court, District of Connecticut and U.S. Tax Court; 1987, U.S. Supreme Court. *Education:* Spring Hill College (B.S. in Commerce, 1978); Emory University (J.D., 1982). Recent Decisions Editor, 1982 Annual Survey of Bankruptcy Law. Author: "Involuntary Cases-General Nonpayment of Debts," Annual Survey of Bankruptcy Law, 1982. Special Counsel, Wilton Police Commission, 1986-1989. Commissioner, Wilton Parks and Recreation Commission, 1991— (Secretary, 1991-1993, Chairman, 1997—). Member, Board of Directors, Connecticut Legal Services, Inc., 1989-1990. Corporator, Ridgefield Bank, 1997—. *Member:* Stamford/Norwalk Regional (Co-Chairperson: Law Office Management Committee, 1996; Land Use Committee, 1996—), Connecticut (Member, Executive Committee, Planning and Zoning Section, 1992-1994, 1998—) and American Bar Associations; State Bar of Georgia. ***PRACTICE AREAS:*** Real Estate; Zoning; Planning; Land Use. ***Email:*** jhealy@gregoryandadams.com

MICHAEL P. KAELIN, born New York, N.Y., August 8, 1959; admitted to bar, 1985, New York and U.S. District Court, Southern and Eastern Districts of New York; 1987, U.S. District Court, District of Connecticut; 1988, Connecticut; 1999, U.S. Court of Appeals, Second Circuit; 2000, U.S. Supreme Court. *Education:* Duke University (A.B., cum laude, 1981; J.D., 1984). Member: American Inns of Court; Securities Industry Association, Compliance and Legal Division. *Member:* Connecticut, New York State and American Bar Associations. ***PRACTICE AREAS:*** Litigation; Employment Law. ***Email:*** mkaelin@gregoryandadams.com

MARYANN D. LALLY, born Mt. Vernon, New York, October 22, 1960; admitted to bar, 1995, Connecticut and New York. *Education:* Lafayette College (B.A., 1982); Pace University (J.D., 1995). *Member:* New York State, Connecticut and American Bar Associations. ***PRACTICE AREAS:*** Corporate; Zoning; Planning; Land Use; Real Estate. ***Email:*** mlally@gregoryandadams.com

DERREL M. MASON, born New York, N.Y., June 14, 1960; admitted to bar, 1986, New York; 2000, Connecticut. *Education:* Georgetown University (B.S.B.A., cum laude, 1982; J.D., cum laude, 1985). Member, 1983-1984 and Associate Editor, 1984-1985, The Tax Lawyer. *Member:* New York State Bar Association. ***PRACTICE AREAS:*** Corporate Law; Lending. ***Email:*** dmason@gregoryandadams.com

MATTHEW C. MASON, born Bangor, Maine, 1956; admitted to bar, 1982, Connecticut; 1984, New York; 1994, U.S. District Court, Southern and Eastern Districts of New York; 1995, U.S. District Court, District of Connecti-

(This Listing Continued)

GREGORY AND ADAMS, P.C., Wilton—Continued

cut; 1997, U.S. Court of Appeals, 2nd Circuit. *Education:* Bucknell University (B.A., 1977); New York Law School (J.D., cum laude, 1982). Articles Editor, New York Law Review, 1980-1982. *Member:* The Association of the Bar of the City of New York; Stamford/Norwalk Regional, Connecticut and American Bar Associations. ***PRACTICE AREAS:*** Litigation; Commercial Litigation; Employment Litigation; Securities Litigation. ***Email:*** mmason@gregoryandadams.com

RALPH E. SLATER, born Brooklyn, New York, July 14, 1948; admitted to bar, 1973, Connecticut; 1983, U.S. Tax Court; 1984, U.S. District Court, District of Connecticut; 1987, U.S. Supreme Court. *Education:* Princeton University (A.B., 1970); University of Pennsylvania (J.D., 1973). Counsel, Ridgefield, Connecticut Planning and Zoning Commission and Zoning Board of Appeals, 1979-1981. Chairman, Board of Directors, The Wilton Bank, 1985—. Director, The Western Connecticut Estate and Tax Planning Council, Inc. (1992-1998). *Member:* Stamford/Norwalk Regional, Connecticut (Member, Executive Committee, Estate and Probate Section, 1984-1986, 1992-1998) and American Bar Associations. ***PRACTICE AREAS:*** Estate Planning; Trusts and Estates; Probate; Taxation. ***Email:*** rslater@gregoryandadams.com

JULIE S. SCHECHTER, born Austin, Texas, October 31, 1958; admitted to bar, 1985, New York; 1988, New Jersey; 2000 Connecticut. *Education:* Brown University (B.A., 1980); University of Texas (J.D., 1984). Associated with: American Express Travel Related Services Company, New York, N.Y., 1987-1995; GE Capital Corporation (1995-1998); Compass International Services Corp. ***PRACTICE AREAS:*** Consumer Regulatory; Corporate; E-Commerce. ***Email:*** jschechter@gregoryandadams.com

SENIOR COUNSEL

JULIAN A. GREGORY, born East Orange, New Jersey, December 16, 1912; admitted to bar, 1939, New York; 1947, Connecticut; 1960, U.S. Supreme Court; 1964, U.S. District Court, District of Connecticut; 1971, U.S. Tax Court. *Education:* Princeton University (A.B., 1935); University of Michigan (J.D., 1938). Phi Delta Phi. Member, Board of Selectmen, Wilton, 1949-1953; 1955-1957. Member, Wilton Zoning Commission, 1953-1955. Prosecuting Grand Juror, Wilton, 1957-1959. Associate Director, Union Trust Company, 1980-1986. Founder of Gregory and Adams and Senior Partner, 1963-1990. *Member:* Stamford/Norwalk Regional, Connecticut and American Bar Associations; The Association of the Bar of the City of New York. [Capt. U.S.A., 1942-1946]. ***PRACTICE AREAS:*** Trusts and Estates.

REPRESENTATIVE CLIENTS: Cannondale Associates, Inc.; Eagle Hill Foundation, Inc.; General Electric Capital Corporation; Gerber Cheese Co., Inc.; H. Muehlstein & Co.; Independent Jewelers Organization, Inc.; Louis Dreyfus Property Group; The Marshall-Qualtec Group; Navios Corp.; Bob Sharp Nissan; The Procter & Gamble Company; Stop'n Shop, Inc.; Ridgefield Bank; The Wilton Bank; Wilton Motors Buick Chevrolet Geo.

HARVEY J. KULAWITZ, LLC

WILTON, CONNECTICUT

(See Ridgefield)

All Personal Injury Cases, including Car Accident cases, Aircraft & Boating accidents, Slip & Fall accidents, Dog Bite attacks, and Wrongful Death accidents & claims.

PERRY AND McKENDRY

44 OLD RIDGEFIELD ROAD
P.O. BOX 517
WILTON, CONNECTICUT 06897
Telephone: 203-762-3301
Fax: 203-762-3631

General Practice. Probate, Trusts, Estate Planning and Real Estate.

MEMBERS OF FIRM

ALBERT L. PERRY (1907-1992).

GEORGE F. McKENDRY (1917-1997).

GREGORY M. PERRY, born New York, N.Y., February 28, 1943; admitted to bar, 1968, New York; 1976, Connecticut. *Education:* Princeton University (A.B., 1965); Cornell Law School (J.D., 1968). Order of the Coif. *Member:* Connecticut and American Bar Associations. [1st Lt., USAR, 1969-1971]. ***PRACTICE AREAS:*** General Practice; Probate; Trusts; Estates; Real Estate.

REFERENCE: The Wilton Bank, Wilton, Connecticut.

SINCHAK & BENNETT

Established in 1982
120 OLD RIDGEFIELD ROAD
P.O. BOX 460
WILTON, CONNECTICUT 06897
Telephone: 203-762-0741
Fax: 203-762-3827

General Practice. Real Estate, Corporate, Probate, Family and Personal Injury and Criminal Law.

THOMAS M. SINCHAK, born Bordentown, New Jersey, August 6, 1954; admitted to bar, 1979, Connecticut and U.S. District Court, District of Connecticut. *Education:* Boston College (B.S., cum laude, 1976); Syracuse University (J.D., cum laude, 1979). *Member:* Connecticut and American Bar Associations. ***PRACTICE AREAS:*** Residential Real Estate; Commercial Real Estate; Probate; Trusts and Estates; Corporate Law.

KIRK A. BENNETT, born Norwalk, Connecticut, May 11, 1953; admitted to bar, 1979, District of Columbia and New York; 1980, U.S. District Court, Eastern District of New York; 1982, Connecticut. *Education:* Syracuse University (B.A., 1975); George Washington University (J.D., 1978). Phi Beta Kappa. Senior Trial Assistant District Attorney, King's County, New York District Attorney, Homicide Bureau, 1980-1983. *Member:* Connecticut and American Bar Associations; The District of Columbia Bar; Connecticut Trial Lawyers Association. ***PRACTICE AREAS:*** Domestic Relations; Litigation; Trial Practice; Criminal and Civil.

REFERENCE: Union Trust Co.

SINGEWALD AND VALKENBURGH

Established in 1984
87 OLD RIDGEFIELD ROAD
P.O. BOX 796
WILTON, CONNECTICUT 06897
Telephone: 203-762-0042
Telecopier: 203-762-2095 v
Email: assist@svlaw.com
URL: http://www.lawyers.com/sandvlaw

General Practice. Real Estate and Zoning Law, Probate, Estate Planning, Federal and State Tax, Corporate and Commercial Matters. Litigation.

ROBERT A. SINGEWALD, born Norwalk, Connecticut, February 11, 1943; admitted to bar, 1967, Virginia and Connecticut; 1971, U.S. Supreme Court. *Education:* University of Notre Dame (B.A., 1964); George Washington University (J.D., with honors, 1967). Delta Theta Phi. Member, Council on Social Services, Wilton, 1971-1973. Wilton Police Commissioner, 1973-1975. Counsel to Wilton Charter Revision Commission, 1981. Member, Fairfield Judicial District Grievance Panel. *Member:* The Stamford-Norwalk, Connecticut, Virginia and American Bar Associations. ***PRACTICE AREAS:*** Real Estate; Zoning Law; Administrative Law; Corporate and Commercial Law; Estate Planning. ***Email:*** ras@svlaw.com

ROGER R. VALKENBURGH, born Boston, Massachusetts, February 15, 1947; admitted to bar, 1976, New York and U.S. District Court, Southern and Eastern Districts of New York; 1977, Connecticut; 1984, U.S. District Court, District of Connecticut and U.S. Tax Court. *Education:* University of Rochester (B.A., 1969); Cornell University (J.D., 1975). Estate Planning Council, Lower Fairfield County. Justice of the Peace, 1994—. Former Warden, St. Matthew's Episcopal Church. Former President, Wilton Chamber of Commerce. *Member:* The Association of the Bar of the City of New York; The Stamford-Norwalk, Connecticut and American Bar Associations. ***LANGUAGES:*** French. ***PRACTICE AREAS:*** Probate Matters; Real Estate; Estate Planning. ***Email:*** rrv@svlaw.com

REFERENCE: The Wilton Bank.

JOHNSON, DOWE & BROWN, LLC

Established in 1990
22 ELM STREET
WINDSOR, CONNECTICUT 06095
Telephone: 860-688-6060
Fax: 860-688-8787
Email: steveb@portone.com

Probate, Estate Planning, Real Estate, Zoning, Corporations and Elder Law.

WARREN P. JOHNSON, born Hartford, Connecticut, February 5, 1939; admitted to bar, 1965, Connecticut. *Education:* Trinity College (B.A., 1961); University of Connecticut (J.D., 1965). Recipient, Distinguished Service Award, Connecticut Probate Assembly, 1990. Mayor, Town of Windsor, Connecticut,

(This Listing Continued)

1977-1981. *Member:* Connecticut Bar Association. Fellow: American College of Trust and Estate Counsel. ***PRACTICE AREAS:*** Probate; Estate Planning. ***Email:*** warren@portone.com

EVERETT B. DOWE, III, born New York, N.Y., August 29, 1953; admitted to bar, 1985, Connecticut. *Education:* University of Connecticut (B.A. in English, 1975); Northern Michigan University (M.A. in History, 1981); Campbell University School of Law (J.D., 1985). Phi Alpha Theta. Adjunct Professor, University of Hartford, Real Property Law, 1988-1989. President, Windsor Rotary Club, 1995-1996. *Member:* Windsor, Connecticut and American Bar Associations. [Capt., U.S. Air Force, 1975-1982]. ***PRACTICE AREAS:*** Real Estate; Zoning; Corporations. ***Email:*** bend@portone.com

STEPHEN C. BROWN, born Rochester, New York, January 16, 1959; admitted to bar, 1987, Connecticut. *Education:* University of Rochester (B.A., 1981); Franklin Pierce Law Center (J.D., 1986). *Member:* Windsor, Connecticut (Member, Elder Law Section) and American (Member, Section on Real Property, Probate and Trust Law) Bar Associations. ***PRACTICE AREAS:*** Probate; Estate Planning; Medicaid; Elder Law. ***Email:*** steveb@portone.com

KENNETH B. LERMAN, P.C.

Established in 1988

651 DAY HILL ROAD
WINDSOR, CONNECTICUT 06095-0040
Telephone: 860-285-0700
Telecopier: 860-285-0139

Corporate, Securities, Real Estate, Mergers/Acquisitions, Business, Venture Capital Financing and Commercial Law.

KENNETH B. LERMAN, born New York, N.Y., March 3, 1961; admitted to bar, 1987, Connecticut and U.S. District Court, District of Connecticut; 1997, Florida. *Education:* Clark University (B.A., Business Management, and Government, 1983); Emory University (J.D., 1986). Phi Delta Phi (Lamar Inn). *Member:* Hartford County, Connecticut and American Bar Associations; The Corporate Bar.

BACON & WILSON, P.C.

Established in 1895

334 ELLA GRASSO TURNPIKE
WINDSOR LOCKS, CONNECTICUT 06096
Telephone: 860-623-6482
Fax: 860-654-1948
Email: bacon-wilson@bacon-wilson.com

Springfield, Massachusetts Office: 33 State Street, 01103. Telephone: 413-781-0560. Fax: 413-739-7740.
Westfield, Massachusetts Office: 9 Chapel Street, 01085. Telephone: 413-562-9607. Fax: 413-562-7589.
Northampton, Massachusetts Office: 351 Pleasant Street, 01060. Telephone: 413-584-3280. Fax: 413-586-5959.

General Civil and Business Practice. Trials in all courts. Trust and Estate Planning, Elder Law, Product Liability, Personal Injury, Employment Law, Employers' Rights, Medical Negligence, Mergers and Acquisitions, Banking, Real Estate, Franchise Law, Bankruptcy and Commercial Reorganization, Health Care Law, Probate, Family Law, Immigration Law, OSHA Compliance, Criminal Law, Domestic Relations.

FIRM PROFILE: Founded in 1895, Bacon & Wilson, PC offers its clients well-established and recognized expertise in many areas of the law. For over one hundred years, Bacon & Wilson has been committed to providing personal attention and service in a prompt, efficient and cost-effective manner. Quality is our standard.

(For complete biographical data on all personnel, see Professional Biographies at Springfield, Massachusetts.)

LAVIERI & DOUGHERTY, LLC

51 ELM STREET
P.O. BOX 983
WINSTED, CONNECTICUT 06098-0983
Telephone: 860-379-4343
Fax: 860-379-9279
Email: rlavieri@snet.net
URL: http://www.lawyers.com/lavieri&doughertyllc

Civil and Criminal Litigation, Zoning and Land Use, Real Estate, Domestic Litigation, Business, Corporate Law, Estate Planning, Estate Administration.

(This Listing Continued)

RICHARD R. LAVIERI, born Hartford, Connecticut, August 4, 1952; admitted to bar, 1981, Connecticut; 2000, U.S. District Court, District of Connecticut. *Education:* Northwestern Connecticut Community College (A.S., 1975); Marquette University (B.A.,1978); Tulane University of Louisiana (J.D., 1981). *Member:* Litchfield County and Connecticut Bar Association; Connecticut Criminal Defense Lawyers' Association.

MARLENE A. DOUGHERTY (Retired).

WILLIAM O. RIISKA

23 UNION STREET
WINSTED, CONNECTICUT 06098
Telephone: 860-379-7898
Fax: 860-379-3220
Email: woriiska@snet.net

Real Estate, Civil Litigation, Zoning and Land Use, Environmental Law, General Practice.

WILLIAM O. RIISKA, born Winsted, Connecticut, October 24, 1952; admitted to bar, 1977, Connecticut. *Education:* St. Lawrence University (B.A., 1974); Albany Law School of Union University (J.D., 1977). Member, Law Review. Board of Directors, Northwest Center for Family Service and Mental Health (President, 1997-2000). Board of Directors and Chair of Government Relations Committee, Northwest Connecticut Chamber of Commerce. Member, Norfolk Planning and Zoning Commission. *Member:* Litchfield County, Connecticut (Environmental Law Section Executive Committee; Media & The Law Committee) and American Bar Associations.

CARTER & CIVITELLO

Established in 1987

ONE BRADLEY ROAD, SUITE 301
WOODBRIDGE, CONNECTICUT 06525
Telephone: 203-389-7000
Fax: 203-389-7004
Email: cartercivitello@bigplanet.com
URL: http://www.lawyers.com/carter&civitellolaw

Workers Compensation, Social Security, Disability Law, Personal Injury.

MEMBERS OF FIRM

ROBERT F. CARTER, admitted to bar, 1974, Connecticut; 1978, U.S. District Court, District of Connecticut. *Education:* Harvard University (A.B., magna cum laude, Phi Beta Kappa, 1967); Yale University (M.A., 1968; J.D., 1971); University of Connecticut School of Medicine. Member, 1969-1971, Note and Comment Editor, 1970-1971, Yale Law Journal. Law Clerk to Hon. M. Joseph Blumenfeld, U.S. District Court, District of Connecticut, 1971-1972. Assistant Professor, University of Connecticut Law School, 1972-1974. Co-Author: "Legal and Scientific Probability of Causation of Cancer and Other Environmental Disease in Individuals," 10 Journal of Health Politics, Policy and Law, No. 1, 33, 1985 (with T. Brennan). Visiting Lecturer, Occupational Disease, Yale Law School, 1980-1983. Member, Legal Advisory Committee to Connecticut Workers' Compensation Commission, 1992-1998. *Member:* Connecticut Bar Association (Chairman, Worker's Compensation Section, 1993-1996; Member, Examining Committee, Workers' Compensation Certification Committee); Connecticut Trial Lawyers Forum (Associate Editor, Workers' Compensation Column). ***PRACTICE AREAS:*** Workers Compensation Law; Occupational Disease Law; Personal Injury.

DONNA CIVITELLO, admitted to bar, 1986, Connecticut; 1988, U.S. District Court, District of Connecticut; 1994, U.S. Court of Appeals, Third Circuit. *Education:* Yale University (B.A., 1978); University of Connecticut (J.D., 1986). Author, "Injured on The Job," A Handbook for the Connecticut Workers, 1992. *Member:* Connecticut Bar Association (Member: Standing Committee on Workers' Compensation Certification, 1997—; Legal Advisory Committee, Connecticut Workers' Compensation Commission, 1999—). ***PRACTICE AREAS:*** Workers Compensation Law; Disabilities; Personal Injury; Social Security.

REFERENCES: Town of Beacon Falls; Yale School of Medicine, Occupational Medicine Clinic; ConnectiCosH.

PETER M. CLARK

40 MAIN STREET
WOODBURY, CONNECTICUT 06798
Telephone: 203-263-2131
Fax: 203-263-3858
Email: pmclaw@imagine.com
URL: http://www.lawyers.com/pmclark

Real Estate, Estate Planning, Estate Administration, Commercial, Land Use, Municipal and Zoning.

(This Listing Continued)

PETER M. CLARK, Woodbury—Continued

PETER M. CLARK, born Waterbury, Connecticut, November 18, 1957; admitted to bar, 1983, New York; 1984, Connecticut. *Education:* Hamilton College (A.B., 1979); Washington College of Law, American University (J.D., 1982). Member, Lions Club. *Member:* Waterbury, Litchfield County, Connecticut (Member, Real Property Section) and American (Member, Real Property, Probate and Trust Law Section) Bar Associations. (Also with Sturges & Mathes). ***PRACTICE AREAS:*** Real Estate; Estate Planning; Wills; Probate; Land Use; Commercial Law.

REID AND RIEGE, P.C.

47 SHERMAN HILL ROAD

WOODBURY, CONNECTICUT 06798

Telephone: 203-267-6680

FAX: 860-240-1002

URL: http://www.reidriege.com

Hartford, Connecticut Office: One State Street. Telephone: 860-278-1150. FAX: 860-240-1002.

West Hartford, Connecticut Office: 65 LaSalle Road. Telephone: 860-232-6565. FAX: 860-232-6066.

(This Listing Continued)

Lakeville, Connecticut Office: 322 Main Street. Telephone: 860-435-9894. FAX: 860-240-1002.

Alternative Dispute Resolution. Antitrust & Trade Regulation. Bankruptcy. Business Law. Commercial Law. Commercial Real Estate/Finance. Corporate Law. Employee Benefits/Pension Plans. Employee Benefits/Taft-Hartley Plans. Environmental Law. Health Care. Labor and Employment. Litigation. Mergers and Acquisitions. Nonprofit and Charitable Organizations. Occupational Safety & Health. Probate. Real Estate. Securities. Taxation. Trade and Professional Associations. Trusts & Estates. Zoning, Planning and Land Use.

ALAN BIRMINGHAM, born Hartford, Connecticut, June 3, 1943; admitted to bar, 1969, Connecticut and U.S. District Court, District of Connecticut. *Education:* Tufts University (B.A., 1966); Georgetown University (J.D., 1969). *Member:* Connecticut (Member, Executive Committee, Estates and Probate Section, 1984—; Chairman, Legal Problems of the Elderly Committee, 1985-1988 and Member, Executive Committee, Elder Law Section, 1991—); American Bar Associations; Connecticut Estate and Tax Planning Council, Inc. (Director, 1985-1993; President, 1992-1993). Fellow, American College of Trust and Estate Counsel. ***PRACTICE AREAS:*** Probate Law; Real Estate; Trusts and Estates. ***Email:*** abirmingham@reidandriege.com

ERIC G. MOONEY, P.A.

BETHANY BEACH, DELAWARE

(See Georgetown)

Criminal Defense, Driving Under the Influence, Personal Injury.

SCHAB & BARNETT, P.A.

BETHANY BEACH, DELAWARE

(See Georgetown)

Commercial Collections, Commercial Law, Probate and Estates, Real Estate, Mortgage Foreclosures, Personal Injury, Commercial Insurance Claims and Defense, Products Liability, Admiralty, Maritime.

ERIC G. MOONEY, P.A.

DEWEY BEACH, DELAWARE

(See Georgetown)

Criminal Defense, Driving Under the Influence, Personal Injury.

BAILEY & WETZEL, P.A.

DOVER, DELAWARE

(See Wilmington)

General Insurance Defense, Insurance Coverage, Corporate Law, Workers' Compensation, Professional Liability, Medical Malpractice, Social Security Disability, Product Liability, Personal Injury, Subrogation, Asbestos, Environmental and Toxic Substance Defense, Computer and Bankruptcy Law.

BARROS, McNAMARA, SCANLON, MALKIEWICZ & TAYLOR

PROFESSIONAL ASSOCIATION

Established in 1981

STATE & LOOCKERMAN STREETS

P.O. BOX 1298

DOVER, DELAWARE 19903-1298

Telephone: 302-734-8400

Telefax: 302-734-4349; 302-734-8969

Email: bmsmt@dol.net

Lewes, Delaware Office: 1143 Savannah Road, 19958. Telephone: 302-644-8510.

Personal Injury, Medical Malpractice, Work Place Injury, Civil and Criminal Trial Practice. Family, Bankruptcy, Probate, Estate Planning and Corporate Law. Commercial Law. Litigation, Administrative, Zoning, Collections.

A. RICHARD BARROS, born Philadelphia, Pennsylvania, July 31, 1938; admitted to bar, 1965, Delaware. *Education:* University of Virginia (1956-1958); University of Delaware (B.A., 1961); Dickinson School of Law (J.D., 1964); Delaware State University (Honorary Doctor of Laws, 1991). Recipient, Delaware Bar Association Public Services Award, 1992. Author of numerous articles on personal injury litigation. Delaware State University Board of Trustees, 1977. President of the Board, Modern Maturity Center, 1980-2000. Comptroller, Kent County, Delaware, 1968-1972. *Member:* American Board of Trial Advocates (Advocate; President, 1998-1999); American Trial Lawyers Association (Sustaining Member); Delaware Trial Lawyers Association (President, 1998-1999). ***PRACTICE AREAS:*** Personal Injury Law; Medical Malpractice; Workplace Injuries. ***Email:*** arb@dol.net

EDWARD R. McNAMARA, born Wilmington, Delaware, January 18, 1947; admitted to bar, 1971, Delaware; 1994, U.S. Tax Court. *Education:* University of Delaware (A.B., 1968); Villanova University (J.D., 1971; LL.M., Taxation, 1985). Kent County Public Defender, 1973-1974. First President and Charter Member, Colonial Rotary Club of Dover, 1990-1991. President, Irish Society of Delmarva, Inc., 1990-1991. Member: Local Civil Practice Advisory Committee, 1991-1996, Superior Court, Kent County, State of Delaware. *Member:* Delaware (Vice President and Member, Executive Committee, 1982-1983; Member, Estates and Trust Section; Chairman, 2000-2001) and American (Member, Estates and Trust Section) Bar Associations; Delaware Trial Lawyers Association. ***PRACTICE AREAS:*** Personal Injury Law; Estate Planning Law. ***Email:*** erm@dol.net

PATRICK SCANLON, born Pittsburgh, Pennsylvania, February 27, 1943; admitted to bar, 1975, Delaware. *Education:* Duquesne University (B.A., 1966; M.A., 1968); Rutgers University at Camden (J.D., 1974). Member, Panel of Interim Bankruptcy Trustees, District of Delaware, 1979-1985. *Member:* Kent County and Delaware Bar Associations. ***PRACTICE AREAS:*** Bankruptcy Collections; Retail Collections. ***Email:*** pjs@dol.net

MICHAEL J. MALKIEWICZ, born Iowa Falls, Iowa, December 7, 1948; admitted to bar, 1981, Delaware and Pennsylvania. *Education:* Delaware State University (B.A., 1975); University of Notre Dame School of Law (J.D., 1978). Author: "A Preliminary Hearing Can Improve Final Results," DE Bar Magazine, January, 1990. Deputy Attorney General, 1981-1986. Counsel to Department of Insurance, 1985-1986, Department of Natural Resources and Environmental Control, 1981-1983 and Criminal Prosecutor, Kent County, 1984-1985. Adjunct Professor of Law, Wesley College, 1981-1991. President: Greater Dover Committee, 2000-2001; Colonial Rotary Club, 1995-1996. *Member:* Kent County, Delaware, Federal and American Bar Associations; The Association of Trial Lawyers of America; Delaware Trial Lawyers Association; National Association of Criminal Defense Lawyers. [With USMC, 1967-1971]. ***PRACTICE AREAS:*** Criminal Defense Law; Medical Malpractice; Personal Injury Law; Land Use Law; Administrative Law. ***Email:*** mjm@dol.net

ROBERT J. TAYLOR, born Hinton, West Virginia, October 7, 1957; admitted to bar, 1983, Delaware. *Education:* Concord College (B.A., History, magna cum laude, 1980); Delaware Law School of Widener University (J.D., 1983). Alpha Chi; Phi Alpha Delta (Marshal, George Read Chapter, 1981-1983). Member, Criminal Advisory Committee, Kent County Superior Court. *Member:* Kent County and Delaware Bar Associations; Delaware Trial Lawyers Association; National Association of Criminal Defense Lawyers. ***PRACTICE AREAS:*** Criminal Defense Law; Personal Injury Law; Domestic Relations Law. ***Email:*** JAY@DOL.net

JAMES J. LAZZERI, born Wilmington, Delaware, August 15, 1951; admitted to bar, 1977, Delaware and Pennsylvania. *Education:* Swarthmore College (B.A., 1973); Villanova University (J.D., 1976). *Member:* Kent County (President, 1992-1993) and Delaware State (Vice-President, 1993-1994) Bar Associations. ***PRACTICE AREAS:*** Workers' Compensation Law; Personal Injury Law. ***Email:*** jay@dol.net

BRADLEY S. EABY, born Ephrata, Pennsylvania, October 3, 1961; admitted to bar, 1989, Delaware; 1999, Pennsvylania. *Education:* Shippensburg University (B.A., 1984); Delaware Law School of Widener University (J.D., 1989). Member, Delaware Volunteer Legal Services, Inc. Member, Terry-Carey AIC. Member, Philadelphia Volunteer Lawyers for the Arts; Director, Dover Community YMCA. Past President, Dover Downtown Rotary Club. Past President, Kent County Bar Association. Past Director and Treasurer, Community Legal Aid Society, Inc. Director, Ecarte Dance Directions. *Member:* Kent County, Delaware and American Bar Associations; Delaware Trial Lawyers Association. ***REPORTED CASES:*** Forest Grove, Inc. v. Andrews, Miller & Assoc., Del. Supr. 655 A.2d 307 (1995); Lehman v. Schaefer, Del. Supr. 719 A.2d 948 (1998); Ingram v. Thorpe, Del. Supr., 747 2d 545 (2000). ***PRACTICE AREAS:*** Bankruptcy Law; Business Law; Collections; Commercial Law; Civil Litigation; Personal Injury. ***Email:*** bse@dol.net

---

ELIZABETH Y. OLSEN, born Baltimore, Maryland, February 20, 1963; admitted to bar, 1993, Maryland and Delaware. *Education:* Skidmore University (B.A., 1986); Widener University School of Law (J.D., 1992). Co-Editor for Delaware State Bar Association IN RE (1995-1998). Editor, "The Advocate," Delaware Trial Lawyers Association Magazine, 1997—. Member and Joint Program Chair Person, 1995-1996; Member and Secretary, 1996—Terry-Carey, AIC. *Member:* Kent County, Delaware and American Bar Associations; Delaware Trial Lawyers Association; Delaware Volunteer Legal Services, Inc. ***SPECIAL AGENCIES:*** Past President, Dover Downtown Rotary Club. President, American Heart Association, Kent Division, 1998-1999. Chairman, U.S. Olympic Committee of Delaware, 1998. President, Committee on Massage and Bodywork. Board Member, Advisory Council for Children, Youth and Their Families. Board Member, Red Cross of Delaware; Member on Board of the Unauthorized Practice of Law; Board Member of the Delaware Bar Foundation. ***PRACTICE AREAS:*** Domestic Relations; Criminal Law; Domestic Violence. ***Email:*** eyo@dol.net

REPRESENTATIVE CLIENTS: Delaware State Music Teachers Assn.; Sears Roebuck & Co.; Second National Federal Savings Bank; Great West Life & Annuity Insurance Company; Featherlite Credit Corporation; Mercury Finance Company.

THE BAYARD FIRM

306 SOUTH STATE STREET

DOVER, DELAWARE 19901

Telephone: 302-678-8787

URL: http://www.bayardfirm.com

Wilmington, Delaware Office: 222 Delaware Avenue, Suite 900, P.O. Box 25130. Telephone: 302-655-5000. Telecopier: 302-658-6395.

Tax, Estate Planning, Corporation, Real Estate, Securities and Bankruptcy Law. Litigation, Administrative Law.

(This Listing Continued)

THE BAYARD FIRM, Dover—Continued

Curtis P. Bounds (Also at Wilmington, Delaware Office)

(For Complete Biographical Data on all Personnel, see Wilmington, Delaware Professional Biographies).

CONNOLLY BOVE LODGE & HUTZ LLP

DOVER, DELAWARE

(See Wilmington)

General Practice, Corporations, Partnerships and Other Business Organizations, Intellectual Property, Antitrust, Commercial Transactions, Real Estate, Bankruptcy, Wills, Estates and Trusts, Taxation, Personal Injury, Family, Environmental and Construction Law, Labor and Employee Relations, Product Liability and Criminal Defense.

GRADY & HAMPTON, P.A.

Established in 1980

6 NORTH BRADFORD STREET

DOVER, DELAWARE 19901

Telephone: 302-678-1265

Fax: 302-678-3544

General Practice. Medical Malpractice, Negligence, Personal Injury, Social Security Disability, Family, Real Estate Law, Employment Law.

JOHN S. GRADY, born Wilmington, Delaware, January 17, 1944; admitted to bar, 1969, Delaware; 1970, U.S. District Court, District of Delaware; 1971, U.S. Court of Appeals, Third Circuit; 1974, U.S. Supreme Court. *Education:* St. Joseph's University (B.A., 1966), Alpha Sigma Nu; Georgetown University (J.D., 1969). Author: "Evidence and Intent in a Fourteenth Amendment Employment Discrimination Case," published in Labor Law Journal, February, 1978; "An Analysis of the Evidentiary Standard Under the Employment Discrimination Statutes," published in Equal Employment Practice Guide by Federal Bar Association, 1978; "Statistics in Employment Discrimination," published in Labor Law Journal, December, 1979; "Social Security and the Disabled Patient," published in Delaware Medical Journal, August, 1986. Instructor, Trial Advocacy, Delaware Law School, 1974. Staff Attorney, 1969-1972 and Board Member, 1980-1983, Community Legal Aid Society, Inc. Member, Preliminary Review Committee, Delaware Board of Professional Responsibility, 1988-1991. *Member:* Kent County and Delaware State Bar Associations; The Association of Trial Lawyers of America; Delaware Trial Lawyers Association (Member, Board of Governors, 1990-1992, 1997—). ***PRACTICE AREAS:*** Personal Injury Law; Real Estate Law; Employment Law.

STEPHEN A. HAMPTON, born Lancaster, Pennsylvania, June 18, 1956; admitted to bar, 1987, Delaware and U.S. District Court, District of Delaware; 1994, U.S. Court of Appeals, Third Circuit. *Education:* Pennsylvania State University (B.A., 1983); Dickinson School of Law (J.D., 1986). *Member:* Kent County, Delaware and American Bar Associations; Delaware Trial Lawyers Association; The Association of Trial Lawyers of America. ***PRACTICE AREAS:*** Medical Dental Malpractice; Personal Injury Law; Social Security Disability Law.

APPROVED ATTORNEYS FOR: Stewart Title Insurance Co.; Ticor Title Insurance Co.

LAW OFFICE OF BRUCE L. HUDSON

DOVER, DELAWARE

(See Wilmington)

Personal Injury Litigation, Medical/Dental Malpractice, Products Liability.

HUDSON, JONES, JAYWORK & FISHER

Established in 1978

225 SOUTH STATE STREET

DOVER, DELAWARE 19901

Telephone: 302-734-7401

Facsimile: 302-734-5532

URL: http://www.delawarelaw.com

Rehoboth Beach, Delaware Office: 309 Rehoboth Avenue, 19971. Telephone: 302-227-9441.

Georgetown, Delaware Office: 100 North Bedford Street, 19947. Telephone: 302-856-2256.

(This Listing Continued)

General Civil and Criminal Practice. Real Estate, Corporation, Probate, Municipal, Zoning, Personal Injury, Family Law, Public Utilities Regulation.

PARTNERS OF FIRM

WILLIAM S. HUDSON, born Philadelphia, Pennsylvania, September 12, 1934; admitted to bar, 1962, Delaware. *Education:* Dickinson College (B.A., 1956); Dickinson School of Law (J.D., 1960). *Member:* Kent County and Delaware Bar Associations. [With U.S. Army, 1956-1957]. ***PRACTICE AREAS:*** Family Law; Real Estate Law; Corporations Law; Foreign Investments in U.S. Real Estate.

R. BRANDON JONES, born Deming, New Mexico, October 21, 1944; admitted to bar, 1970, Delaware; 1973, U.S. District Court, District of Delaware. *Education:* University of Delaware (B.A., 1966); University of Virginia (J.D., 1969). *Member:* Kent County (President, 1979-1980) and Delaware Bar Associations. ***PRACTICE AREAS:*** Estates Law; Real Estate Law; Commercial Law; Corporate Law; Personal Injury.

JOHN TERENCE JAYWORK, born Philadelphia, Pennsylvania, August 3, 1947; admitted to bar, 1975, Delaware; 1976, U.S. District Court, District of Delaware; 1990, U.S. Court of Appeals, Third Circuit. *Education:* St. Andrews Presbyterian College (B.A., 1969); Emory University; University of Baltimore (J.D., cum laude, 1975). Heuisler Honor Society. Chairman, Delaware Local Records Commission. *Member:* Kent County (President, 1988) and Delaware Bar Associations. ***PRACTICE AREAS:*** Municipal Law; Zoning Law; Real Estate; Public Utility Law. ***Email:*** jtj@delawarelaw.com

HARRY M. FISHER, III, born Pensacola, Florida, October 31, 1952; admitted to bar, 1977, Delaware and Florida. *Education:* University of Delaware (B.A., 1974); Stetson University (J.D., 1977). State Coastal Zone Industrial Control Board, 1982-1992. *Member:* Kent County (Secretary, 1982-1983; Treasurer, 1983-1984) and Delaware Bar Associations; The Florida Bar; National Council of School Board Attorneys; National Organization of Legal Problems on Education. ***PRACTICE AREAS:*** Real Estate Law; School Law; Wills; Estates.

RONALD D. SMITH, born Washington, D. C., July 28, 1951; admitted to bar, 1979, Delaware; 1981, U.S. District Court, District of Delaware. *Education:* University of Delaware (B.A., 1973); Delaware Law School of Widener University (J.D., 1979). Attorney to Delaware House of Representatives, 1982—. Member, Kent County Levy Court, (President, 1993-1994). Chairman, Kent County Legislative & Legal Committee. Member: National Association of Counties, Tax and Finance Committee, 1991—. *Member:* Kent County and Delaware State Bar Associations. ***PRACTICE AREAS:*** Bankruptcy Law; Domestic Relations Law.

THOMAS I. BARROWS, born Gainesville, Florida, December 22, 1949; admitted to bar, 1975, North Carolina; 1982, Maryland; 1984, Delaware. *Education:* Wake Forest University (J.D., 1975). Phi Alpha Delta. Assistant District Attorney, 25th Judicial District of North Carolina, 1975-1982. Clerk of the Delaware Supreme Court, 1984-1985. *Member:* Kent County (President, 1991-1992), North Carolina and Delaware Bar Associations; Delaware Trial Lawyers Association. ***PRACTICE AREAS:*** Civil Litigation; Automobile Personal Injury; Landlord-Tenant Law; Premises Liability.

DANIEL P. MYERS, II, born Fairmont, West Virginia, May 17, 1962; admitted to bar, 1988, Delaware. *Education:* Millersville University (B.A., 1984); Dickinson School of Law (J.D., 1988). *Sussex County and Delaware State Bar Associations.* (Resident, Rehoboth Beach Office). ***PRACTICE AREAS:*** Real Estate; Foreclosures; Workouts; Collections; Wills; Estate Planning; Civil Litigation; Chancery Practice.

DAVID J. WEIDMAN, born Fairfax, Virginia, May 3, 1967; admitted to bar, 1997, Delaware and U.S. District Court, District of Delaware. *Education:* University of Virginia (B.A., 1989); George Mason University (M.P.A., 1992); University of Tennessee (J.D., 1996). Phi Kappa Phi; Order of Barristers. Member, Tennessee Law Review. Author: "Torts—Design Defect Analysis For Simple Tools In Michigan—No Duty To Design Child-Resistant Cigarette Lighters," Tennessee Law Review, 425 (1995); "The Real Truth About Campaign Finance: Rejecting The Hysterical Call For Publicly Financed Congressional Campaigns," Tennessee Law Review, 775 (1996). Law Clerk, Honorable William S. Lee and T. Henley Graves, Superior Court, Sussex County, Delaware, 1996-1997. *Member:* Sussex County, Delaware State and American Bar Associations. (Resident, Georgetown Office). ***PRACTICE AREAS:*** Family Law; Civil Litigation; Zoning Law.

JOSEPH A. HURLEY, P.A.

DOVER, DELAWARE

(See Wilmington)

Criminal Trial Practice Only.

KNEPPER & STRATTON

DOVER, DELAWARE

(See Wilmington)

General Civil and Trial Practice in all State and Federal Courts, Personal Injury, Automobile Accidents and Injuries, Workers Compensation, Criminal Law, Sexual Harassment, Employment Law, Employment Discrimination, Driving While Intoxicated, Traffic Violations, Wrongful Termination, Americans with Disabilities Act.

LAW OFFICE OF KATHRYN J. LAFFEY

DOVER, DELAWARE

(See Wilmington)

Family Law, Civil Litigation, Divorce and Family Mediation.

MACANANNY & GIOIA, LLP

1126 SOUTH STATE STREET

DOVER, DELAWARE 19901

Telephone: 302-730-3500
Fax: 302-730-0505
Email: glynis@erols.com
URL: http://www.lawyers.com/macanannylaw

Family Law including Child Custody, Child Support, Divorce, Adoptions. Real Estate (Residential and Commercial), Landlord and Tenant, Creditors Rights, Collection, Personal Injury, Automobile Accidents, Business Law, Business Start-Ups, Contracts, Trusts and Estates, Wills and Probate. Worker's Compensation.

GLYNIS A. MACANANNY, born Washington, D.C., July 18, 1957; admitted to bar, 1985, Maryland; 1987, U.S. District Court, District of Maryland; 1993, Delaware and U.S. District Court, District of Delaware. *Education:* University of Maryland (B.A., 1978); University of Baltimore Law School (J.D., 1984). *Member:* Maryland State and Delaware Bar Associations (Member, Family Law Sections); Terry-Carey Inns of Court. ***PRACTICE AREAS:*** Family Law; Child Custody; Child Support; Marital Property Law; Divorce; Adoption Law; Real Estate; Collections; Personal Injury; Leases and Leasing; Business Law; Trusts and Estates; Wills; Probate.

JENNIFER L. GIOIA, born Mississippi, 1971; admitted to bar, 1998, Delaware and New Jersey; 1999, Pennsylvania. *Education:* University of Delaware (B.S., 1994); Widener University School of Law (J.D., 1998). *Member:* Delaware and American Bar Associations. ***PRACTICE AREAS:*** Family Law; Workers Compensation; Personal Injury; Real Estate.

JOHN S. MALIK

DOVER, DELAWARE

(See Wilmington)

Criminal Trial and Appellate Practice in all State and Federal Courts.

MORRIS, JAMES, HITCHENS & WILLIAMS, LLP

Established in 1932

SUITE 202, 32 WEST LOOCKERMAN STREET

DOVER, DELAWARE 19904-7356

Telephone: 302-678-8815
Telecopier: 302-678-9063
URL: http://www.morrisjames.com

Wilmington, Delaware Offices: 222 Delaware Avenue, P.O. Box 2306, 19899-2306. Telephone: 302-888-6800. Telecopier: 302-571-1750 and 1010 North Bancroft Parkway, Suite 11, P.O. Box 2328, 19899-2328. Telephone: 302-655-2599. Fax: 302-655-8831.

Newark, Delaware Office: 16 Polly Drummond Hill Road, 19711-5703. Telephone: 302-368-4200. Fax: 302-368-6259.

Litigation, Corporate Law, Commercial Law, Business Law, Administrative Law, Alternative Dispute Resolution, Bankruptcy, Commercial Real Estate, Computers and Software, Education Law, Environmental Law, Family Law, Health Care, Insurance, Insurance Defense, Intellectual Property, Labor and Employment, Medical Malpractice, Partnership Law, Personal Injury, Probate, Products Liability, Real Estate, Taxation, Torts, Trusts and Estates and Wills.

(This Listing Continued)

RESIDENT PARTNER

GLENN E. HITCHENS, born Milford, Delaware, March 7, 1942; admitted to bar, 1967, Delaware. *Education:* Dickinson College (B.A., 1964); Dickinson School of Law (J.D., 1967). Member, Delaware Code Revisors, State of Delaware, 1971-1973. *Member:* Kent County, Delaware State and American Bar Associations. ***PRACTICE AREAS:*** General Practice. ***Email:*** ghitchens@morrisjames.com

(For Complete Biographical Data on all Personnel, see Professional Biographies at Wilmington)

PARKOWSKI & GUERKE

PROFESSIONAL ASSOCIATION

Established in 1975

116 WEST WATER STREET
P.O. BOX 598

DOVER, DELAWARE 19903

Telephone: 302-678-3262
Telecopier: 302-678-9415
Email: png@dol.net
URL: http://www.pnglaw.com

General Civil and Trial Practice in all Courts. Environmental, Administrative, Public Contract, Utility, Employment, Education, Real Estate, Personal Injury, Estate Planning, Commercial Law, Criminal and Family Law.

F. MICHAEL PARKOWSKI, born Williamstown, Pennsylvania, July 13, 1945; admitted to bar, 1973, Delaware; 1974, U.S. District Court, District of Delaware; 1982, U.S. Court of Appeals, Third Circuit. *Education:* Villanova University (B.E., 1968); Temple University (J.D., 1973). Assistant Professor, Environmental Law, University of Delaware, 1975-1977. Instructor, Delaware Realtors Institute, 1985-1990. Counsel: Department of Natural Resources and Environmental Control, 1973-1975; Delaware Senate Natural Resources Committee, 1978-1980, 1986-1988; Delaware Solid Waste Authority, 1976-2001; Delaware Lottery Office, 1995-2001; Delaware Department of Transportation, 1997-2001; Delaware Economic Development Office, 1999-2001; Delaware Civic Center Corp., 1999-2001. Member: Delaware Energy Commission, 1975-1976; Governor's Freshwater Wetlands Roundtable, 1989. Chairman, Governor's Magistrate Screening Committee, 1993-1994; Board of Trustees and Treasurer, Delaware State University, 1993-2001. Chair, Task Force on Citizen Involvement in the Judicial System, 1996-1999 and Vice-Chair, Family Court Internal Operation Procedures Committee, 1998-1999, Supreme Court. *Member:* Kent County (Vice President, 1982-1983; President, 1983-1984; Chairman, Governor's Judicial Nominating Commission, 2000-2001), Delaware (Chairman: Administrative Law Committee, 1980, 1981, 1987; 1989-1992; Chairman: 1989, 1990, Vice Chairman: 1991-1993, Judicial Appointment Committee; Co-Chair, Judicial Compensation Committee, 2000; Assistant Secretary, 1978; Secretary, 1979; Vice President, 1980, 1985; Member, Executive Committee, 1991-1992; Vice President at Large, 1993; President-Elect, 1994; President, 1995-1996) and American Bar Associations; Delaware Trial Lawyers Association; Terry Carey Inns of the Courts. ***PRACTICE AREAS:*** Environmental Law; Administrative Law; Real Estate Development Law; Public Works Contract Law. ***Email:*** mparkowski@dol.net

I. BARRY GUERKE, born Wilmington, Delaware, October 1, 1948; admitted to bar, 1974, Delaware and U.S. District Court, District of Delaware; 1982, U.S. Court of Appeals, Third Circuit. *Education:* University of Delaware (B.A., 1970); Dickinson School of Law (J.D., 1973). Omicron Delta Kappa. Law Clerk, Delaware Supreme Court, 1973-1974. Chairman, Governor's Magistrate Screening Committee, 1985-1987. Associate Member, Delaware Board of Bar Examiners, 1975-1979. Member: Delaware Supreme Court Advisory Committee on Rules, 1981-1987; Delaware Judicial Nominating Commission, 1987-1992; Secretary, 1989-1992; Delaware Supreme Court IOLTA Committee, 1990-1995. *Member:* Kent County (Secretary, 1979-1980; Treasurer, 1980-1981; Vice President, 1984-1985; President, 1985-1986), Delaware (Chairman, Specialization Committee, 1989-1991; Vice Chair, 2000-2001 and Co-Chair, 2001—, Professional Guidance Committee; Assistant Secretary, 1981-1982; Secretary, 1982-1983; Member-at-Large, 1983-1984; 1985-1986; Vice President, For Kent County, 1986-1987) and American Bar Associations; The Association of Trial Lawyers of America; Delaware Trial Lawyers Association (Member, Board of Governors, 1986-1990 and 1995—; President, 1999-2000); Terry-Carey American Inns of Court. ***PRACTICE AREAS:*** Personal Injury Law. ***Email:*** bguerke@dol.net

CLAY T. JESTER, born Milford, Delaware, November 16, 1950; admitted to bar, 1980, Delaware; 1983, U.S. District Court, District of Delaware. *Education:* University of Massachusetts (B.A. in Pol.Sc., 1972); Delaware Law School of Widener University (J.D., 1979). Law Clerk, Family Court of Delaware, 1976. Director, 1985-1990; President, 1987-1988, Community Legal Aid Society, Inc. *Member:* Kent County (Vice President, 1992-1993; President,

(This Listing Continued)

PARKOWSKI & GUERKE, PROFESSIONAL ASSOCIATION, Dover—Continued

1993-1994), Delaware (Member, Executive Committee, 1988-1989, 1994-1995; Section on Family Law, 1980—; Estates and Trusts Section, 1999—) and American (Member, Sections on: Family Law; Real Property Section; Probate and Trust Law Section) Bar Associations; The Association of Trial Lawyers of America; Delaware Trial Lawyers Association; Terry-Carey Inn of Courts. ***PRACTICE AREAS:*** Family Law; Personal Injury Law; Estate Planning. ***Email:*** png@dol.net

JEREMY W. HOMER, born Jamestown, New York, June 22, 1947; admitted to bar, 1975, New York; 1976, Delaware; 1979, Pennsylvania; 1981, U.S. District Court, District of Delaware. *Education:* Tulane University of Louisiana (B.A., 1970); Albany Law School of Union University (J.D., 1974); University of Delaware (M.A., 1976). Deputy Attorney General: Delaware, 1976-1978; Pennsylvania, 1981-1982. ***PRACTICE AREAS:*** Employment Law; Environmental Law; Administrative Law. ***Email:*** png3@dol.net

JOHN C. ANDRADE, born New Haven, Connecticut, August 27, 1951; admitted to bar, 1979, Connecticut; 1980, Delaware; 1981, U.S. District Court, District of Delaware; registered to practice before U.S. Patent and Trademark Office. *Education:* University of Connecticut (B.S.Ch.E., 1973); University of Delaware (M.B.A., 1978); Delaware Law School of Widener University (J.D., summa cum laude, 1978). Author: Comment, "Passing-On in Antitrust: Was Hanover Shoe 'Turned on its Head' to decide Illinois Brick?," 3 Del. J. Corp. L. 452, 1978; Andrade and Andrade, "Malpractice of Psychiatric Nurse," 26 Am. Jur. Proof of Facts 2d 53, 1981. Adjunct Professor, Products Liability, Widener University School of Law, Wilmington, Delaware, August 1983—. *Member:* Delaware and American Bar Associations; Delaware Trial Lawyers Association; The Association of Trial Lawyers of America; American Intellectual Property Law Association. ***PRACTICE AREAS:*** Patent Law; Product Liability Law; Environmental Law. ***Email:*** jandrade@dol.net

MARK F. DUNKLE, born Bellefonte, Pennsylvania, September 21, 1960; admitted to bar, 1985, Georgia; 1988, Delaware; 1989, U.S. District Court, District of Delaware; 1994, U.S. Supreme Court. *Education:* University of Virginia (B.A., with distinction, 1982); Emory University (J.D., 1985). Member, Moot Court Society, 1984-1985. Presenter: "Municipal Annexation Law in Delaware," Delaware Urban Studies Institute, 1997; "Delaware Land Use Law," National Business Institute, 1999 and 2001. Special Counsel: Delaware Department of Transportation, 1998—; Delaware Economic Development Office, 1999—; Kent County Levy Court, 1995-1996. Chairman, Governor's Magistrate Screening Committee, 1999—. Attorney Member, State Board of Accountancy, 1995-1997. Associate Member, State Board of Bar Examiners, 1992-1995. Kent County Transfer of Development Rights Committee, 1997-1998. Special Master, Family Court. Secretary, Terry-Carey Inn of Court, 1993-1996. Insurance Commissioner's Arbitration Panel, 1993-1996. *Member:* Kent County (Secretary 1991-1992; Treasurer, 1992-1993; Vice-President, 1993-1994; President, 1994-1995) and Delaware State (Nominating Committee, 1998-2000; Executive Committee, 1995-1996; Real Property Committee, 1998-2000; Editor, In Re, The Journal of the Delaware State Bar Association, 1999-2000) Bar Association. ***PRACTICE AREAS:*** Commercial Real Estate Finance; Commercial Real Estate Development; Hotel and Resort Law; Hotel and Resort Development; Commercial Litigation; Eminent Domain; Zoning Law; Land Use; Environmental Litigation. ***Email:*** mdunkle@dol.net

---

ANNE E. HARTNETT, born Dover, Delaware, July 17, 1966; admitted to bar, 1993, Delaware and Pennsylvania; 1994, U.S. District Court, District of Delaware; 1997, U.S. Supreme Court. *Education:* University of Delaware (B.A., 1988); Widener University School of Law (J.D., 1992). Judicial Law Clerk to the Honorable Vincent A. Bifferato, Delaware Superior Court, 1992-1994. Deputy Attorney General, Department of Justice, State of Delaware, 1994-1998. *Member:* Kent County and Delaware State Bar Associations; Terry-Carey American Inns of Court. ***PRACTICE AREAS:*** Governmental Law; Collections; Wills. ***Email:*** png@dol.net

MICHAEL W. ARRINGTON, born Lower Merion Twp., Pennsylvania, June 30, 1957; admitted to bar, 1997, Delaware and U.S. District Court, District of Delaware; 1998, Maryland; 1999, District of Columbia. *Education:* St. Joseph's University (B.S., 1978); Villanova University (M.A., 1980); Widener University (J.D., cum laude, 1997). Phi Kappa Phi. Phi Delta Phi. Alpha Sigma Nu. *Member:* Delaware (Member, Family Law Section), Maryland State and American Bar Associations; Richard S. Rodney Inn of Court. ***PRACTICE AREAS:*** Domestic Relations; Environmental Law; Litigation; Transactional; Eminent Domain; Wills. ***Email:*** michaela@delanet.com

BASIL C. KOLLIAS, born Wilmington, Delaware, February 16, 1962; admitted to bar, 1999, New Jersey and U.S. District Court, District of New Jersey; 2001, Delaware. *Education:* Ursinus College (B.S., Chemistry, 1983); Widener University School of Law (J.D., 1999). Phi Delta Phi. Member: American Chemical Society, 1989—; Environmental Assessment Association, 1994—; International Who's Who of Professionals, 1998. Recipient, Certificate of Achievement: Regulation of Toxic and Hazardous Substances, Widener University School of Law. Member, Executive Board, Holy Trinity Greek Orthodox Church, Willimington, Delaware, 1999-2000. *Member:* New Jersey State (Member, Environmental Law Section), Delaware State and American (Member, Environmental Law Section) Bar Associations. ***LANGUAGES:*** Greek. ***PRACTICE AREAS:*** Environmental Law; Real Estate Law; Patent Law; Administrative Law; Contracts. ***Email:*** bckollias@aol.com

OF COUNSEL

GEORGE F. GARDNER, III, born Wilmington, Delaware, October 12, 1938; admitted to bar, 1963, Delaware; 1964, District of Columbia; 1970, U.S. District Court, District of Delaware; 1981, U.S. Court of Appeals, Third Circuit. *Education:* Dickinson College (B.A., 1960); George Washington University (LL.B., 1963). Phi Delta Phi. Member, American College of Real Estate Lawyers, 1984—. *Member:* Kent County (Vice President, 1976-1977, President, 1977-1978), Delaware (Chairman, Real and Personal Property Committee, 1983-1987) and American Bar Associations. [Capt., JAGC, U.S. Army, 1964-1967]. ***PRACTICE AREAS:*** Land Use Planning; Commercial Litigation; Commercial Real Estate. ***Email:*** realestate@dol.net

REPRESENTATIVE CLIENTS: E.I. duPont de Nemours & Co.; ICI Americas; Ciba Geigy; Playtex Family Products; Hanover Foods Corp.; U.S. Borax; Chesapeake Utilities; Public Water Supply Co.; Perdue, Incorporated; Mountaire Poultry Company; J.G. Townsends, Inc.; Rodel, Inc.; Frank Robino & Sons; Wyoming Concrete Industries, Inc.; Tilcon; Chemical Industry Council of Delaware; Delaware Solid Waste Authority; Delaware Lottery Office; Delaware Department of Transportation; Delaware Agricultural Lands Preservation Foundation; Capital School District; Sussex County; University of Delaware; Wilmington Trust Company; Occidental Chemical Co.
APPROVED ATTORNEYS FOR: Ticor Title Insurance Co.; Lawyers Title Insurance Corp.; First American Title Insurance Co.; Old Republic Title Insurance Co.
REFERENCE: First National Bank of Wyoming.

PRICKETT, JONES & ELLIOTT, P.A.

Established in 1888

11 NORTH STATE STREET
DOVER, DELAWARE 19901
Telephone: 302-674-3841
Telecopier: 302-674-5864
Email: attorneys@prickett.com
URL: http://www.prickett.com

Wilmington, Delaware Office: 1310 King Street. Telephone: 302-888-6500.
Kennett Square, Pennsylvania Office: 217 West State Street. Telephone: 610-444-1573.

General Civil and Criminal Practice including: Commercial Law, Corporation Law, Estate Planning, Government Affairs, Insurance Defense, Personal Injury, Real Estate.

WAYNE N. ELLIOTT, born Laurel, Delaware, April 6, 1942; admitted to bar, 1967, Delaware. *Education:* Harvard College (A.B., magna cum laude, 1964); University of Virginia (LL.B., 1967). *Member:* Delaware State and American Bar Associations; Advocate, American Board of Trial Advocates. (Also at Wilmington Office). ***PRACTICE AREAS:*** General Litigation; Personal Injury Litigation. ***Email:*** wnelliott@prickett.com

GARY F. TRAYNOR, born Dover, Delaware, August 25, 1956; admitted to bar, 1982, Delaware. *Education:* Dartmouth College (A.B., 1978); Delaware Law School of Widener University (J.D., 1982). Phi Delta Phi. Staff Member, Delaware Journal of Corporate Law, 1981-1982. *Member:* Kent County, Delaware State and American Bar Associations; Terry-Carey Inn of Court. (Resident). ***PRACTICE AREAS:*** Corporate Litigation; Commercial Litigation; Federal Litigation; Complex Criminal Defense.

JOHN W. PARADEE, born Rockledge, Florida, February 1, 1963; admitted to bar, 1989, Delaware; 1990, U.S. District Court, District of Delaware; 1997, U.S. Supreme Court. *Education:* University of Virginia (B.A., 1985); University of Richmond (J.D./M.B.A., 1989). Pi Sigma Alpha; Phi Alpha Theta; Phi Alpha Delta. Counsel to the Minority Caucus of the House of Representatives, State of Delaware General Assembly, 1991-1993. Counsel to the Majority Caucus of the Senate, State of Delaware General Assembly, 1993-1995. Counsel to the Levy Court of Kent County, Delaware, 1995-1999. Member, Board on the Unauthorized Practice of Law, Supreme Court of Delaware, 1991—. Terry-Carey Inn of Court. Member, Delaware Heritage Commission, 1996—. President, Kent County Bar Association, 2000-2001. *Member:* Delaware State and American Bar Associations; Delaware Trial Lawyers Association; Association of Trial Lawyers of America. (Resident). ***PRACTICE AREAS:*** Commercial Litigation; Real Estate Law.

D. BENJAMIN SNYDER, born Dover, Delaware, December 23, 1974; admitted to bar, 2001, Delaware and Pennsylvania. *Education:* James Madison

(This Listing Continued)

University (B.B.A., 1997); Dickinson School of Law of the Pennsylvania State University (J.D., 2000). Senior Editor, Dickinson Journal of International Law. Recipient, Richard Reeve Baxtor Award. ***PRACTICE AREAS:*** Commercial Litigation; Commercial and Residential Real Estate Transactions; General Business; Corporate Practice; Administrative Law; Bankruptcy. ***Email:*** dsnyder@prickett.com

(For complete biographical data on all personnel, see Professional Biographies at Wilmington, Delaware)

SCHMITTINGER & RODRIGUEZ, P.A.

414 SOUTH STATE STREET
DOVER, DELAWARE 19901
Telephone: 302-674-0140
FAX: 302-674-1830
Email: attorneys@schmittrod.com
URL: http://www.schmittrod.com

Wilmington, Delaware Office: 1300 North Market Street, Suite 205. Telephone: 302-652-3676. Fax: 302-652-8788.

Rehoboth Beach, Delaware Office: 4602 Highway One. Telephone: 302-227-1400. Fax: 302-645-1843.

Odessa, Delaware Office: Odessa Professional Park, P.O. Box 626. Telephone: 302-378-1697. Fax: 302-378-1659.

General Civil Practice. Personal Injury, Workers Compensation, Federal Practice, Corporation, Estate Planning, Real Estate and Commercial Law, Litigation, Criminal and Domestic Law.

HAROLD SCHMITTINGER, born Philadelphia, Pennsylvania, July 17, 1928; admitted to bar, 1954, District of Columbia; 1955, Delaware; 1956, U.S. Tax Court. *Education:* University of Delaware (B.S., 1952); American University (LL.B., 1954); Georgetown University (LL.M., 1956). Member, 1958-1995 and President, 1990-1995, Lawyers Fund for Client Protection. *Member:* Delaware State Bar Association (President, 1980-1981). Fellow: American College of Trial Lawyers. (Also at Rehoboth Beach and Wilmington, Delaware Offices). ***PRACTICE AREAS:*** Personal Injury Law. ***Email:*** hs@schmittrod.com

NICHOLAS H. RODRIGUEZ, born Dover, Delaware, December 28, 1934; admitted to bar, 1961, Delaware. *Education:* Pennsylvania State University (B.S., 1957); Washington & Lee University (J.D., summa cum laude, 1961). Order of the Coif; Phi Beta Kappa; Phi Alpha Delta; Xi Sigma Pi. Author: Comment, 17 Washington & Lee Law Review 260 (160). U.S. Commissioner, Judicial District of Delaware, 1961-1966. City Solicitor, City of Dover, 1969—. *Member:* Kent County (President, 1971-1972), Delaware State (First Vice-President, 1971-1972) and American Bar Associations; Delaware Trial Lawyers Association; The Association of Trial Lawyers of America. Fellow: American College of Trial Lawyers. (Also at Rehoboth Beach and Wilmington, Delaware Offices). ***PRACTICE AREAS:*** Personal Injury Law. ***Email:*** nrodriguez@schmittrod.com

PAUL H. BOSWELL, born Wilmington, Delaware, July 30, 1938; admitted to bar, 1966, Delaware. *Education:* University of Delaware (B.A., 1960); Washington & Lee University (LL.B., 1963); Temple University (LL.M. in Taxation, 1980). Phi Alpha Delta. Member, Washington & Lee Law Review, 1963. Author: Comment, "Reconciliation Period, Divorces," 20 Washington & Lee Law Review 335, 1963. U.S. Magistrate, 1967-1972. *Member:* Kent County (President, 1975-1976) and Delaware State (Member, 1975— and Chairman, 1983-1984, Decedent's Trust and Estates Section) Bar Associations. Fellow, The American College of Trust and Estate Counsel. (Also at Rehoboth Beach and Wilmington, Delaware Offices). ***PRACTICE AREAS:*** Corporate Law; Estate Planning; Estate Settlements; Taxation. ***Email:*** pboswell@schmittrod.com

JOHN J. SCHMITTINGER, born Atlantic City, New Jersey, March 19, 1941; admitted to bar, 1966, Delaware. *Education:* Drew University; University of Delaware (B.A., 1963); Temple University (J.D., 1966). Phi Alpha Delta. Editor, Temple Law Quarterly, 1965-1966. Listed in: Best Lawyers in America, 1995-1996; 1996-1997; 1997-1998; 1998-1999; 1999-2000. Past President, Kent County Bar Association. *Member:* Delaware State (Past-Chairman, General Legislation Committee) and American Bar Associations; Delaware Trial Lawyers Association (Vice-President, 1979-1981); The Association of Trial Lawyers of America (Past Secretary, Board on Professional Responsibility). (Also at Rehoboth Beach and Wilmington, Delaware Offices). ***PRACTICE AREAS:*** Workers Compensation Law; Personal Injury. ***Email:*** jschmittinger@schmittrod.com

BRUCE C. ENNIS, born Dover, Delaware, March 22, 1941; admitted to bar, 1969, Delaware. *Education:* West Virginia Wesleyan College (B.A., 1963); Dickinson School of Law (J.D., 1966). *Member:* Kent County, Delaware State and American Bar Associations. (Also at Odessa, Delaware Office). ***PRACTICE AREAS:*** Real Estate. ***Email:*** bennis@schmittrod.com

DOUGLAS B. CATTS, born Lewes, Delaware, August 17, 1947; admitted to bar, 1975, Delaware. *Education:* George Washington University (B.A., 1969; J.D., 1974). Deputy City Solicitor, City of Dover, 1982-1989. Member, Advisory Committee on Delaware Uniform Rules of Evidence, 2000—. *Member:* Kent County, Delaware State (Member, Board of Directors, 1987-1988; Member, Committee on: Judicial Appointments, 1995—) and American Bar Associations; Delaware Trial Lawyers Association (Member, Board of Governors, 1980-1993; Vice-President, 1986-1987 and Legislative Chairman, 1987-1988, 1989-1990; President-Elect, 1990-1991; President, 1991-1992); American Board of Trial Advocates (1991—); The Association of Trial Lawyers of America (ATLAPAC, 1999-2000). ***PRACTICE AREAS:*** Personal Injury Law; Litigation; Labor Law. ***Email:*** dcatts@schmittrod.com

WILLIAM D. FLETCHER, JR., born Philadelphia, Pennsylvania, September 27, 1949; admitted to bar, 1975, Delaware; 1980, U.S. Supreme Court. *Education:* University of Delaware (B.A., 1972); University of Tulsa; Washington & Lee University (J.D., 1975). Assistant City Solicitor, City of Dover, 1977-1981. *Member:* Kent County, Delaware State and American Bar Associations; Delaware Trial Lawyers Association; The Association of Trial Lawyers of America. (Also at Wilmington, Delaware Office). ***PRACTICE AREAS:*** Personal Injury Law; Employment Law. ***Email:*** wfletcher@schmittrod.com

WILLIAM A. DENMAN, born Wilmington, Delaware, January 1, 1952; admitted to bar, 1977, Delaware. *Education:* University of Delaware (B.S., with honors); Catholic University of America (J.D., 1976). Phi Kappa Phi; Beta Gamma Sigma. Member, Catholic University Law Review, 1975-1976. Author: "Judicial Review of Federal Employee Discrimination Complaints," 25 Catholic University Law Review 299, 1976. *Member:* Kent County (President, 1987-1988), Delaware State and American Bar Associations; Delaware Trial Lawyers Association; The Association of Trial Lawyers of America. ***PRACTICE AREAS:*** Litigation; Corporate Law; Commercial Law; Public Utility Law. ***Email:*** wdenman@schmittrod.com

CATHERINE T. HICKEY, born Wilmington, Delaware, June 16, 1949; admitted to bar, 1978, Delaware; 1980, U.S. Court of Appeals, Third Circuit; 1981, U.S. District Court, District of Delaware. *Education:* University of Delaware (B.A., 1971); Washington College of Law of American University (J.D., 1978). Deputy City Solicitor, City of Dover, 1981. Member: Permanent Lawyers Advisory Committee, U.S. District Court for District of Delaware, 1988-1992; Delaware Insurance Authority, 1988-1993; Delaware Department of Education Due Process Hearing Panel Array, 1991-2000; Delaware Board of Medical Practice, 1994—; President, 2000—; Vice-President, 1999-2000. *Member:* Kent County, Delaware State and American Bar Associations; Terry-Carey American Inn of Courts; National School Board Association Council of School Attorneys; Delaware Council of School Board Attorneys. ***PRACTICE AREAS:*** Employment Law; Administrative Law; Education Law; Litigation. ***Email:*** chickey@schmittrod.com

CRAIG T. ELIASSEN, born Dover, Delaware, August 14, 1958; admitted to bar, 1984, Delaware. *Education:* St. Andrews University, Scotland; St. Andrews Presbyterian College (B.A., with honors, 1980); Wake Forest University (J.D., 1984). Phi Delta Phi. Law Clerk, Superior Court, Kent County, State of Delaware, 1984. Counsel to House of Representatives, State of Delaware, 1993-1995. Attorney, Kent County Row Offices, 1995-1999. Director, St. Thomas More Academy, 1997-2001. Chair, Governor's Magistrate Screening Committee, 1999. Trustee, Delaware Technical and Community College, 1999—. *Member:* Kent County, Delaware State (Member, Sections on: Family Law and Workers' Compensation) and American Bar Associations; Delaware Trial Lawyers Association (Legislative Agent, 1991-1992; LAW-PAC Trustee and Treasurer, 1994-2001; Legislative Committee, 1999—); The Association of Trial Lawyers of America (State Delegate, 1995-1999). ***PRACTICE AREAS:*** Domestic Relations Law; Workers Compensation Law; Litigation. ***Email:*** celiassen@schmittrod.com

WILLIAM W. PEPPER SR., born Salisbury, Maryland, December 3, 1959; admitted to bar, 1985, Delaware; 1986, U.S. District Court, District of Delaware; 1988, U.S. Court of Appeals, Third Circuit. *Education:* Clemson University (B.A., magna cum laude, 1982); Wake Forest University (J.D., magna cum laude, 1985). Phi Alpha Delta (Chapter Clerk, Timberlake Chapter, 1984-1985). Member, 1983-1985 and Notes and Comments Editor, 1984-1985, Wake Forest Law Review. Abney Scholar, Clemson University. Wake Forest Law Faculty Scholar. Author: "Civil Procedure-North Carolina Adopts the Stream of Commerce Theory of Jurisdiction: A Step in the Right Direction," 20 Wake Forest Law Review, 737, 1984. Deputy Solicitor, City of Dover, 1989—. City Solicitor: City of Harrington, 2001—; Town of Leipsic, 1989—. *Member:* Delaware State and American Bar Associations; The Association of Trial Lawyers of America; Delaware Trial Lawyers Association; Terry-Carey American Inn of Court. ***PRACTICE AREAS:*** Municipal Law; Employment Law; Litigation; Personal Injury; Appellate Practice. ***Email:*** wpepper@schmittrod.com

CRYSTAL L. CAREY, born Dover, Delaware, February 6, 1962; admitted to bar, 1988, Delaware, Maryland, District of Columbia, U.S. Court of Appeals, Third Circuit, U.S. District Court, District of Delaware, U.S. District Court, District of Maryland, U.S. Court of Appeals, Fourth Circuit and U.S. Supreme Court. *Education:* University of Delaware (B.S., cum laude, 1984); University of Maryland (J.D., 1987). Phi Kappa Theta. Member, Terry-Carey American Inn of Court Executive Committee. Member, State Board of Chiropractic. Attorney, Kent County Row Offices, 1999—. *Member:* Kent County (President, 1995-

(This Listing Continued)

SCHMITTINGER & RODRIGUEZ, P.A., Dover—Continued

1996), Delaware State (Member, Executive Committee, 1996-1997; 1998-1999; 2000-2001) and American Bar Associations; Maryland State Bar Association, Inc.; Bar Association of the District of Columbia; Delaware Trial Lawyers Association. (Also at Odessa, Delaware Office). ***PRACTICE AREAS:*** Domestic Relations Law; Real Property Law. ***Email:*** ccarey@schmittrod.com

SCOTT E. CHAMBERS, born Wilmington, Delaware, November 26, 1962; admitted to bar, 1988, Delaware and U.S. District Court, District of Delaware; 1989, Maryland, District of Columbia, U.S. District Court, District of Maryland, U.S. Court of Appeals, Third and Fourth Circuits, U.S. Supreme Court, U.S. Court of Military Appeals, U.S. Court of Veterans Appeals and U.S. Army Court of Military Review. *Education:* University of Delaware (B.S., 1984); Widener University (J.D., cum laude, 1988). Phi Delta Phi. Recipient, American Jurisprudence Award. Law Clerk to the Honorable Sue L. Robinson, U.S. Magistrate for the District of Delaware, 1988-1989. Attorney, Delaware House of Representatives, 1990-1993. *Member:* Kent County, Delaware State and Federal Bar Associations; Maryland State Bar Association, Inc.; The Association of Trial Lawyers of America; The National Association of Criminal Defense Lawyers; Delaware Trial Lawyers Association. [Lt. Col., Delaware Army National Guard, 1980—]. (Also at Odessa, Delaware Office). ***PRACTICE AREAS:*** Criminal Law; Personal Injury Law; Real Estate; Veterans Law. ***Email:*** schambers@schmittrod.com

FREDERICK A. TOWNSEND III, born Dover, Delaware, April 19, 1962; admitted to bar, 1990, Pennsylvania and Delaware. *Education:* University of Delaware (B.A., 1985); Widener University School of Law (J.D., 1988). Deputy Insurance Commissioner, 1994-2000. *Member:* Kent County and Delaware State Bar Associations. ***PRACTICE AREAS:*** Insurance Regulation; Real Estate. ***Email:*** ftownsend@schmittrod.com

NOEL E. PRIMOS, born Jackson, Mississippi, February 17, 1964; admitted to bar, 1990, Mississippi, U.S. District Court, Northern and Southern Districts of Mississippi and U.S. Court of Appeals, Fifth Circuit; 1992, Delaware; 1993, U.S. District Court, District of Delaware and U.S. Court of Appeals, Third Circuit; 1997, U.S. Supreme Court. *Education:* Vanderbilt University (B.A., 1986); Yale University (J.D., 1989). Phi Beta Kappa. Recipient: First Prize, Student Articles, Center for Public Resources Legal Program Awards, 1987. Harold Stirling Vanderbilt Scholar, 1982-1986. John M. Olin Scholar, 1988 and John M. Olin Fellow, 1989. Law Clerk to the Honorable William H. Barbour, Chief Judge, U.S. District Court, Southern District of Mississippi, 1989-1990. Skadden Fellow, 1990-1991. Associate Member, Delaware Supreme Court Board of Bar Examiners, 1996-2000. Member, Preliminary Review Committee, 1998—. *Member:* Kent County, Delaware State and Federal Bar Associations; The Mississippi Bar; Delaware Trial Lawyers Association; Terry-Carey American Inn of Court. ***PRACTICE AREAS:*** Civil Litigation; Employment Law. ***Email:*** nprimos@schmittrod.com

DAVID A. BOSWELL, admitted to bar, 1993, Delaware; 1994, U.S. District Court, District of Delaware; 1996, U.S. Court of Appeals, Third Circuit. *Education:* College of William & Mary (B.A., English, with honors, 1988); University of Pennsylvania (J.D., 1992). Associate Editor, 1990-1991 and Senior Editor, 1991-1992, Comparative Labor Law Journal. Judicial Law Clerk, to the Honorable Carl Goldstein, Delaware Superior Court, 1992-1993. House Attorney, House of Representatives, General Assembly of Delaware, 1994-1996. *Member:* Delaware State Bar Association; Delaware Trial Lawyers Association. (Resident, Rehoboth Beach, Delaware Office). ***PRACTICE AREAS:*** Personal Injury; Labor and Employment Litigation; Criminal Law.

WALT F. SCHMITTINGER, born Dover, Delaware, September 16, 1970; admitted to bar, 1995, Delaware. *Education:* Dickinson College (B.A., English, 1992); Widener University (J.D., 1995). Phi Delta Phi. Member, Harrington Inn. Member of Staff, Delaware Journal of Corporate Law, 1993. *Member:* Kent County, Delaware State and American Bar Associations. ***PRACTICE AREAS:*** Personal Injury Law; Litigation; Workers Compensation Law. ***Email:*** wschmittinger@schmittrod.com

R. SCOTT KAPPES, born South Boston, Virginia, October 24, 1966; admitted to bar, 1995, Pennsylvania and New Jersey; 1996, Delaware. *Education:* Towson State University (B.S., 1989); Widener University (J.D., 1994). Phi Delta Phi. (Resident, Wilmington, Delaware Office). ***PRACTICE AREAS:*** Workers Compensation; Personal Injury; Employment Law. ***Email:*** rkappes@schmittrod.com

JEFFREY J. CLARK, born Dover, Delaware, March 30, 1968; admitted to bar, 1996, Delaware; 1997, U.S. District Court, District of Delaware; 2000, U.S. Court of Appeals, Third Circuit. *Education:* United States Military Academy (B.S., 1990); Widener University (J.D., summa cum laude, 1996). Recipient, American Jurisprudence Award. Member, Delaware Journal of Corporate Law, 1994-1996. Member, Editorial Board, Delaware State Bar Association Law Review, 1996—. Author: Recent Development: "Kahn v. Lynch Communication Systems, Inc.: A Major Step Toward Clarifying the Role of Independent Committees," 20 Del. J. Corp. L. 564, 1995; "Compaq Computer Corp. v. Horton: A Straight Forward, Clarifying, Statutory Interpretation of Section 220 (b) and (c)," 20 Del. J. Corp. L. 622, 1995. Co-Author: "The Need for the Uniform Adoption of the Loss of Chance Doctrine In Delaware," 1 Del. L. Rev. 241, 1998. Wolcott Law Clerk, Honorable Maurice A. Hartnett, III, Delaware Supreme Court, 1995-1996. Counsel to Senate, State of Delaware General Assembly, 1997—. *Member:* Kent County, Delaware State and American Bar Associations; Delaware Trial Lawyers Association; Delaware Association of Criminal Defense Lawyers; Terry-Carey American Inn of Court. [with U.S. Army, 1990-1993; Capt., U.S. Army Reserves, 1993-1999]. ***PRACTICE AREAS:*** Criminal Law; Personal Injury Law; Commercial Litigation. ***Email:*** jclark@schmittrod.com

BETH BUZZELL MILLER, born Methuen, Massachusetts, April 28, 1964; admitted to bar, 1993, California; 1995, Oregon; 1997, Delaware. *Education:* University of New Hampshire (B.S., 1990); California Western School of Law (J.D., cum laude, 1993); Georgetown University (LL.M., Taxation, with distinction, 1995). *Member:* Kent County, Delaware and American Bar Associations; State Bar of California; Oregon State Bar. ***PRACTICE AREAS:*** Corporate Law; Estate Planning; Estate Settlements; Probate Litigation; Trust Litigation; Taxation. ***Email:*** bmiller@schmittrod.com

KYLE KEMMER, born East Meadow, New York, July 1, 1970; admitted to bar, 1997, Delaware; 1998, Pennsylvania. *Education:* Pennsylvania State University (B.A., 1992); Widener University School of Law (J.D., 1997). Phi Delta Phi. *Member:* Deleware State and American Bar Associations; Association of Trial Lawyers of America; Deleware Trial Lawyers Association. (Resident, Wilmington, Delaware Office). ***PRACTICE AREAS:*** Workers Compensation; Personal Injury. ***Email:*** kkemmer@schmittrod.com

REPRESENTATIVE CLIENTS: Chesapeake Utilities Corp.; Delaware State University; Eastern Shore Natural Gas Co.; New Plan Realty Trust.
APPROVED AGENT FOR: Chicago Title Insurance Co.; Ticor Title Insurance Co.; Lawyers Title Insurance Corp.; Transamerica Title Insurance Co.

WELCH & ASSOCIATES

DOVER, DELAWARE

(See Wilmington)

Commercial Litigation, Banking and Bankruptcy Litigation, Creditor's Rights, General Litigation, Corporate Litigation, Real Estate, Insurance Defense and Insurance Coverage.

YOUNG CONAWAY STARGATT & TAYLOR, LLP

DOVER, DELAWARE

(See Wilmington)

General Practice.

YOUNG & YOUNG

300 SOUTH STATE STREET
P.O. BOX 1191
DOVER, DELAWARE 19903
Telephone: 302-674-8822
Fax: 302-674-8251
Email: younglaw@intercom.net
URL: http://www.lawyers.com/young-young

Insurance Defense, Civil and Criminal Practice, Personal Injury.

MEMBERS OF FIRM

ROBERT B. YOUNG, born Philadelphia, Pennsylvania, May 18, 1943; admitted to bar, 1969, Ohio; 1970, U.S. District Court, Southern District of Ohio; 1975, Delaware; 1976, U.S. District Court, District of Delaware; 1978, U.S. Supreme Court; 1986, U.S. Court of Appeals. *Education:* Denison University (B.A., 1965); Ohio State University College of Law (J.D., 1969). Delaware Law Revisor, *Best's.* Adjunct Professor: Business Law, Delaware Technical and Community College, 1975-1977; Insurance Law, Wesley College, 1995, 1997. Acting Judge, Oakwood Municipal Court, 1971-1974. Member, Delaware Superior Court Select Committee for Effective Use of Juries, 1997-1998. Member, Delaware Supreme Court Rules Committee. Judge, Delaware high school mock trial competition. *Member:* Delaware (Member, Executive Committee) and American Bar Associations; American Board of Trial Advocates (Delaware Chapter President, 1993-1995); American Inns of Court (Chapter Counselor, 1993-1995); International Association of Defense Counsel; Association of Defense Trial Attorneys; Defense Research Institute. ***PRACTICE AREAS:*** Insurance Defense. ***Email:*** ryounglaw@hotmail.com

JEFFREY A. YOUNG, born Columbus, Ohio, December 14, 1968; admitted to bar, 1995, Delaware. *Education:* Swarthmore College (B.A., 1991); Villanova University School of Law (J.D., 1995). Member, Editorial Board, Dela-

(This Listing Continued)

ware Law Review. Law Clerk, Delaware Superior Court, 1995-1996. Adjunct Professor, Insurance Law, Wesley College, 1997. *Member:* Delaware and American Bar Associations; American Inns of Court; Association of Defense Trial Attorneys; Defense Research Institute. ***PRACTICE AREAS:*** Insurance Defense; Criminal Law; Personal Injury. ***Email:*** jyounglaw@hotmail.com

REPRESENTATIVE CLIENTS: State Farm; USAA Prop. & Cas. Ins Co.; Farm Family Mutual; Goodville Mutual Casualty; Erie Insurance Group; Ranger Insurance Company; Millers Mutual Ins.

BUCHANAN & BOLTE

FENWICK ISLAND, DELAWARE

(See Ocean City, Maryland)

Real Estate, Corporations, Criminal, DWI, Traffic and Estate Planning Law, Mediation.

ERIC G. MOONEY, P.A.

FENWICK ISLAND, DELAWARE

(See Georgetown)

Criminal Defense, Driving Under the Influence, Personal Injury.

STUMPF, VICKERS & SANDY, P.A.

FENWICK ISLAND, DELAWARE

(See Georgetown)

General Civil and Trial Practice. Personal Injury, Criminal Law, Workers' Compensation and Family Law.

RAYMOND E. TOMASETTI, JR.

1209 COASTAL HIGHWAY

FENWICK ISLAND, DELAWARE 19944

Telephone: 302-539-3041

Fax: 302-537-9986

Email: tomasetti@aol.com

Newport, Delaware Office: 16 West Market Street, P.O. Box 3058, 19804. Telephone: 302-995-2840. Fax: 302-995-9160.

General Civil and Trial Practice. Real Estate, Estate Planning, and Personal Injury.

RAYMOND E. TOMASETTI, JR., born Wilmington, Delaware, July 4, 1954; admitted to bar, 1980, Pennsylvania, Delaware, U.S. Tax Court and U.S. Court of Appeals, Third Circuit. *Education:* University of Delaware (B.S., 1976); Delaware Law School of Widener University (J.D., 1979). *Member:* Pennsylvania and Delaware Bar Associations. ***PRACTICE AREAS:*** General Civil Law; Trial Practice; Real Estate Law; Estate Planning Law; Personal Injury Law.

BAILEY & WETZEL, P.A.

GEORGETOWN, DELAWARE

(See Wilmington)

General Insurance Defense, Insurance Coverage, Corporate Law, Workers' Compensation, Professional Liability, Medical Malpractice, Social Security Disability, Product Liability, Personal Injury, Subrogation, Asbestos, Environmental and Toxic Substance Defense, Computer and Bankruptcy Law.

LAW OFFICE OF EDWARD C. GILL

16 NORTH BEDFORD STREET

GEORGETOWN, DELAWARE 19947

Telephone: 302-854-5400

Fax: 302-854-5409

Email: egill@dmv.com

General Practice.

EDWARD C. GILL, born 1957; admitted to bar, 1983, Delaware. *Education:* Tulane University of Louisiana (B.A., 1979; J.D., 1982). *Member:* American Bar Association. ***PRACTICE AREAS:*** Criminal Law; Driving While Intoxicated; Drug Crimes; Automobile Accidents and Injuries; Workers Compensation; Medical Malpractice; Personal Injury.

(This Listing Continued)

ASSOCIATES

THERESA McQUAID HAYES, born 1967; admitted to bar, 1993, Virginia; 1995, Delaware. *Education:* University of Richmond (B.A., 1989); Widener University School of Law (J.D., 1993). ***PRACTICE AREAS:*** Criminal Law; Family Law; Divorce; Child Custody; Child Support.

LORRAINE K. PHILLIPS, born Warren, Ohio, May 7, 1956; admitted to bar, 1982, Ohio and U.S. District Court, Southern District of Ohio; 1993, District of Columbia and U.S. District Court for the District of Columbia; 1994, U.S. District Court, District of Maryland; 1998, Delaware. *Education:* University of Michigan (B.A., with high distinction, 1977); University of Toledo (J.D., 1981); Georgetown University Law Center (LL.M., Labor, with distinction, 1991). Phi Beta Kappa. Recipient, James B. Angell Scholar, 1977-1978. Research Editor, University of Toledo Law Review, 1980-1981. Member, The University of Toledo College of Law Law Review, 1979-1980 and Research Editor, 1980-1981. Author: "The Legal Chokehold: Professional Employment in Ohio under the-at-Will Doctrine," 24 AKRON L. REV. 581 (1991). Assistant Solicitor, Attorney/Advisor, National Labor Relations Board, Washington, D.C., 1991-1993. Bond Claims Attorney: American Druggists' Insurance Company and Northwestern National Insurance Company, Cincinnati, Ohio, 1982-1985. *Member:* Sussex County Bar Association; District of Columbia Bar (Member, Labor Relations Section); Ohio State Bar Association (Member, Labor and Employment Section); National Employment Lawyers Association; Metropolitan Washington Lawyers Association (Member, Board of Directors); Trial Lawyers Association of Metropolitan Washington. (Also of Counsel to Cashdan and Golden, Washington, D.C.). ***PRACTICE AREAS:*** Family Law; Divorce; Child Custody; Child Support; Labor and Employment; Sexual Harassment; Landlord and Tenant Law.

JOSEPH B. GREEN

GEORGETOWN, DELAWARE

(See Wilmington)

Personal Injury, Bankruptcy and Real Estate.

GRIFFIN & HACKETT, P.A.

Established in 1976

116 WEST MARKET STREET

P.O. BOX 612

GEORGETOWN, DELAWARE 19947

Telephone: 302-856-9066

Fax: 302-856-9016

Email: gandh@ce.net

URL: http://www.gandh.baweb.com

General Civil and Trial Practice. Corporate, Business, Banking, Real Estate, Probate, Family, Estate Planning, Personal Injury, Health Care, Zoning and Education Law.

FIRM PROFILE: Griffin & Hackett was founded in 1976. The firm services the Sussex County area in general civil and trial practice, corporate, business, banking, real estate, probate, family, estate planning, personal injury, health care, labor and employment law, zoning and education law. Griffin & Hackett is the only firm in Georgetown practicing health care and education law.

JAMES D. GRIFFIN, born Atlanta, Texas, May 22, 1939; admitted to bar, 1969, Delaware; U.S. District Court, District of Delaware; U.S. Supreme Court. *Education:* University of Arkansas (B.S., 1962); University of New Mexico (J.D., 1969). Research Editor, Natural Resources Journal, 1968-1969. Member, Board of Bar Examiners, 1979-1987. Trustee, Lawyer's Fund for Client Protection, 2000—. *Member:* Sussex County (President, 1981-1983) and Delaware (Vice President, 1984-1985) Bar Associations; Delaware Trial Lawyers Association; Delaware Council of School Board Attorneys. ***PRACTICE AREAS:*** General Civil and Trial Practice; Business Law; Real Estate Law; Wills, Trusts and Estates; Personal Injury; Banking; Zoning, Planning and Land Use Law; Education Law; Elder Law; Labor and Employment Law. ***Email:*** gandh@ce.net

DAVID R. HACKETT, born Dover, Delaware, December 11, 1944; admitted to bar, 1969, Virginia; 1971, Delaware; 1972, U.S. District Court, District of Delaware. *Education:* Emory and Henry College (B.A., 1966); Washington & Lee University (J.D., 1969); Wilmington College (M.B.A., 1988). Member, Governor's Magistrate Screening Committee, 1981-1984. *Member:* Sussex County and Delaware (Health Law Committee) Bar Associations; Virginia State Bar (Health Law Section); American Health Lawyers Association. ***PRACTICE AREAS:*** Business Law; Real Estate Law; Health Care and Hospital Law; Commercial Loans; Corporate Law. ***Email:*** gandh@ce.net

(This Listing Continued)

GRIFFIN & HACKETT, P.A., Georgetown—Continued

VINCENT G. ROBERTSON, born Springfield, Virginia, February 18, 1969; admitted to bar, 1994, Delaware. *Education:* University of Delaware (B.A., 1991); University of Louisville School of Law (J.D., 1994). Member, Journal of Family Law, 1992-1993. *Member:* Sussex County (Secretary, 2000-2001) and Delaware (Associate Member, Board of Bar Examiners, 1996-2000) Bar Associations. ***PRACTICE AREAS:*** Commercial Law; Real Estate Law; Education Law; Estate Planning; Landlord/Tenant Law; Zoning, Planning and Land Use Law.

OF COUNSEL

ANNE L. NACZI, born Wilmington, Delaware, November 30, 1957; admitted to bar, 1982, Delaware. *Education:* Georgetown University (B.A., 1979); Villanova University School of Law (J.D., 1982; LL.M., 1987). Assistant Disciplinary Counsel, Board of Professional Responsibility of Delaware, Supreme Court, 1987-1994; Board of Professional Responsibility of Delaware, Supreme Court, 1994-2000. Member, Governor's Council on Long-Term Care Facilities, 1990-1996. *Member:* Delaware State (President, 1996-1997) and American Bar Associations; American Judicature Society; Defense Counsel of Delaware. ***PRACTICE AREAS:*** Negligence; Insurance; Workers Compensation; Products Liability; Medical Malpractice. ***Email:*** gandh@ce.net

REPRESENTATIVE CLIENTS INCLUDE: Mellon Bank Delaware; Marine Associates, Inc.; North Shores, Inc.; Mid-Sussex Medical Center, Inc.; Milford School District; Woodbridge School District; Laurel School District; Indian River School District; Nanticoke Health Services, Inc.; Home Health Care, Inc.; Sussex Shores Water Co.; County Bank; Nanticoke Memorial Hospital, Inc.; Delaware National Bank; Nanticoke Alternative Care, Inc.
APPROVED ATTORNEYS FOR: Chicago Title Insurance Co.; Lawyers Title Insurance Corp.; Old Republic Title Insurance Company; Penn Title Co.; TICOR Title Insurance Company of California; Marva Production Credit Assn.; Federal Land Bank of Baltimore; Delaware National Bank; Mellon Bank Delaware; County Bank; Farmers Home Administration.
REFERENCES: Mellon Bank Delaware, The Circle, Georgetown, Delaware.

LAW OFFICE OF BRUCE L. HUDSON

GEORGETOWN, DELAWARE

(See Wilmington)

Personal Injury Litigation, Medical/Dental Malpractice, Products Liability.

JOSEPH A. HURLEY, P.A.

GEORGETOWN, DELAWARE

(See Wilmington)

Criminal Trial Practice Only.

JACOBS & CRUMPLAR, P.A.

GEORGETOWN, DELAWARE

(See Wilmington)

Personal Injury, Automobile Accidents, Medical Malpractice, Social Security Disability, Products Liability and Toxic Substance, Worker Compensation, Business Litigation, Bankruptcy, Patent and Copyright Law.

JOHN S. MALIK

GEORGETOWN, DELAWARE

(See Wilmington)

Criminal Trial and Appellate Practice in all State and Federal Courts.

ERIC G. MOONEY, P.A.

11 SOUTH RACE STREET
GEORGETOWN, DELAWARE 19947
Telephone: 302-856-3070
Fax: 302-856-2177
Email: ericgmooney@aol.com
URL: http://www.lawyers.com/ericgmooney

Criminal Defense, Driving Under the Influence, Personal Injury.

ERIC G. MOONEY, born Wilmington, Delaware, May 22, 1968; admitted to bar, 1996, Delaware. *Education:* University of Delaware (B.S., 1991); Quinnipiac College (J.D., 1996). *Member:* Sussex County, Delaware State and American Bar Associations; National Association of Criminal Defense Lawyers; The Association of Trial Lawyers of America; Delaware Trial Lawyers Association. ***PRACTICE AREAS:*** Criminal Defense; Driving While Intoxicated; Personal Injury. ***Email:*** ericgmooney@aol.com

(This Listing Continued)

MOORE & RUTT, P.A.

122 WEST MARKET STREET
P.O. BOX 554
GEORGETOWN, DELAWARE 19947
Telephone: 302-856-9568
Fax: 302-855-9803
URL: http://www.mooreandrutt.com
Email: drutt@mooreandrutt.com
URL: http://www.lawyers.com/moore&rutt

Milford, Delaware Office: 109 North Walnut Street, 19963-1447. Telephone: 302-424-2240.

General, Civil and Trial Practice. Real Estate, Planning and Zoning, Personal Injury, Automobile Accidents, Commercial Law, Wills and Probate, Construction Law, Family Law, Child Support, Child Custody, Divorce, Adoption, Trusts and Estates, Estate Planning, Landlord/Tenant Litigation.

J. EVERETT MOORE, JR., admitted to bar, 1976, District of Columbia and Delaware. *Education:* University of Delaware (B.A., 1972); College of William & Mary (J.D., 1975). Alpha Phi Omega; Phi Alpha Delta; Omicron Delta Kappa. Member, National Leadership Honor Society William and Mary Chapter. Recipient, University of Delaware Presidential Citation for Outstanding Achievement. Listed in: Who's Who of Emerging Leaders in America, Second Edition; Who's Who in American Law; Who's Who in Practicing Attorneys; Who's Who Among Rising Young Americans, 1992 Edition. Member: BPOE #2173 (ELKS); Franklin Lodge #12 A.F. & A.M.; Ducks Unlimited. Sussex County Coordinator, Delaware Sportsman Against Hunger, 1994—. Delegate to State G.O.P. Convention in 1976, 1985-1998, 2000. Board of Directors, Georgetown Little League, 1992. Board of Directors, American Cancer Society, 1989. Chairman, Sussex County Republican Executive Committee, 1985-1993. Vice Chairman, State of Delaware Republican Committee, 1993-1998. Delegate to National G.O.P. Convention, 1988-1992. Buckmasters, Delaware President, Indian River School Board Member, 1994-1995. Chairman, Delaware Technical and Community College, Southern Campus Foundation. *Member:* Sussex County and Delaware State Bar Associations; The District of Columbia Bar. ***PRACTICE AREAS:*** Real Estate; Business Law. ***Email:*** jemoore@mooreandrutt.com

DAVID N. RUTT, born Milford, Delaware, May 2, 1952; admitted to bar, 1978, Pennsylvania and U.S. District Court, Western District of Pennsylvania; U.S. Court of Appeals, Third Circuit; 1988, Delaware; 1989, U.S. District Court, District of Delaware. *Education:* Washington & Jefferson College (B.A., cum laude, 1974); University of Pittsburgh (J.D., 1978). Seminar Speaker, "Land Use," Sussex County Bar Association, 1998. Member, State of Delaware Board of Bar Examiners. *Member:* Sussex County, Delaware (Member, Estates and Trusts Section) and Pennsylvania Bar Associations; Delaware Trial Lawyers Association; Terry Carey Inns of Court. ***PRACTICE AREAS:*** Residential Real Estate; Commercial Real Estate; Real Estate Litigation; Construction Law; Estate Litigation; Business Law; Commercial Law; Personal Injury Litigation; Zoning, Planning and Land Use. ***Email:*** dnrutt@mooreandrutt.com

DEAN A. CAMPBELL, born Seaford, Delaware, November 27, 1960; admitted to bar, 1997, Delaware and New Jersey; 2000, U.S. District Court, District of Delaware. *Education:* University of Delaware, Newark (B.A., 1982); Delaware State College (B.S., 1993); Widener University School of Law (J.D., magna cum laude, 1997). Phi Delta Phi. Moot Court. Member: Law Review; State of Delaware Board of Examiners. *Member:* Delaware Bar Association; Delaware Trial Lawyers Association. ***PRACTICE AREAS:*** Litigation; Real Estate Litigation; Landlord and Tenant Law; Collections; Construction Litigation; Employment Law. ***Email:*** decampbell@mooreandrutt.com

PATRICK E. VANDERSLICE, born Bridgeton, New Jersey, October 21, 1967; admitted to bar, 1999, Delaware; 2000, Maryland. *Education:* University of Delaware (B.S., 1990); Widener University School of Law (J.D., 1999). Delaware Volunteer Legal Services, 1999. Superior Court Clerk, 1999-2000. Legal Intern, Delaware Civil Clinic, 1998-1999. Research, Family Law, Protection from Abuse Statues. *Member:* Sussex County, Delaware State, Maryland State and American (Member, Family Law Section) Bar Associations. ***PRACTICE AREAS:*** Family Law; Civil Litigation; Wills; Contracts. ***Email:*** pevanderslice@mooreandrutt.com

SCHAB & BARNETT, P.A.

Established in 1982
9 CHESTNUT STREET
P.O. BOX 755
GEORGETOWN, DELAWARE 19947
Telephone: 302-856-9024
Fax: 302-856-6360

Mailing Address: P.O. Box 755, Georgetown, Delaware 19947

Lewes, Delaware Office: 1322 Kings Highway. Telephone: 302-645-6626.

Commercial Collections, Commercial Law, Probate and Estates, Real Estate, Mortgage Foreclosures, Personal Injury, Commercial Insurance Claims and Defense, Products Liability, Admiralty, Maritime.

WILLIAM SCHAB, born Baltimore, Maryland, February 25, 1949; admitted to bar, 1975, Maryland; 1977, Delaware. *Education:* St. Joseph's University (B.A., 1971); University of Maryland (J.D., 1974). Legal Aid Attorney, 1974-1981. *Member:* Sussex County, Delaware State, Maryland State and American Bar Associations; The Association of Trial Lawyers of America. ***PRACTICE AREAS:*** Real Estate; Collections; Probate and Estates.

NORMAN C. BARNETT, born Helena, Montana, May 18, 1942; admitted to bar, 1969, District of Columbia; 1981, Delaware; 1998, Montana. *Education:* University of Maryland (B.S., 1965); Howard University (J.D., 1968). Member, Howard University Law Review, 1967-1968. Solicitor, U.S. Consumer Product Safety Commission, 1977-1981. Assistant Solicitor, Federal Maritime Commission, 1969-1970. *Member:* Sussex County, Delaware State and American Bar Associations; The District of Columbia Bar; State Bar of Montana; Delaware Trial Lawyers Association. ***PRACTICE AREAS:*** Collections; Personal Injury; Real Estate; Mediation; Commercial Insurance Claims; Commercial Insurance Defense.

APPROVED ATTORNEYS FOR: First American Title Insurance Co.; Baltimore Trust Co.; County Bank; Wells Fargo Mortgage Corp.

SERGOVIC, ELLIS & SHIREY, P.A.

Established in 1988
9 NORTH FRONT STREET
P.O. BOX 875
GEORGETOWN, DELAWARE 19947-0875
Telephone: 302-855-9500
FAX: 302-855-9509
Email: serg.ellis@dol.net

General Civil Practice. Real Property, Business, Probate, Taxation, Estate Planning and Corporate Law.

FIRM PROFILE: Sergovic & Ellis was established in 1988. The firm has a general Civil Trial practice including real property, business, probate, taxation, estate planning and corporate law serving the entire Sussex County area.

JOHN A. SERGOVIC, JR., born Montclair, New Jersey, September 16, 1948; admitted to bar, 1973, Maryland; 1974, Delaware. *Education:* Villanova University (B.S., 1970); University of Maryland (J.D., 1973). *Member:* Sussex County and Delaware Bar Associations. ***PRACTICE AREAS:*** Real Property Law; Corporate Law. ***Email:*** serg.ellis@dol.net

STEPHEN P. ELLIS, born Washington, D.C., May 20, 1945; admitted to bar, 1972, Maryland; 1973, District of Columbia; 1978, Delaware. *Education:* Wheeling College (B.S., Accounting, 1967); Catholic University of America (J.D., 1972); Georgetown University (LL.M., Taxation, 1978). Certified Public Accountant, Maryland, 1976. *Member:* Maryland State Bar Association, Inc.; Delaware Bar Association; Bar Association of the District of Columbia. ***PRACTICE AREAS:*** Taxation Law; Probate Law; Estate Planning. ***Email:*** serg.ellis@dol.net

BRIAN D. SHIREY, born Dover, Delaware, October 19, 1963; admitted to bar, 1990, Delaware. *Education:* Delaware State College (B.S., magna cum laude, 1986); Widener University (J.D., 1990). Phi Delta Phi. *Member:* Delaware Bar Association (Member Sections on: Commercial Law; Labor and Employment Law; Torts and Insurance). ***PRACTICE AREAS:*** Commercial Law; General Business Law; Health Law.

SMITH O'DONNELL PROCINO & BERL, LLP

406 SOUTH BEDFORD STREET
P.O. BOX 588
GEORGETOWN, DELAWARE 19947
Telephone: 302-855-0551
Fax: 302-855-0553

Corporate, Business Law, Probate and Estate Planning, Administrative, Tax, Real Estate, Elder Law, Personal Injury, Domestic Relations, Civil Litigation.

(This Listing Continued)

GEORGE B. SMITH, born Washington, D.C., March 16, 1948; admitted to bar, 1982, Delaware; 1983, U.S. District Court, District of Delaware and U.S. Tax Court; 1993, U.S. Court of Appeals, Third Circuit. *Education:* University of Delaware (B.Sc., 1972); Delaware Law School of Widener University (J.D., 1982). Certified Public Accountant, Maryland, 1977. Vice President and Division Manager, Wilmington Trust Company, 1994-1996. Agent, District Conferee, Appeals Officer, Internal Revenue Service, 1971-1982. Member, Young, Conaway, Stargatt & Taylor, 1982-1994. *Member:* Delaware (Member: Commercial Law, Estates and Trusts, Real and Personal Property and Taxation Sections) and American (Member, Sections on: Real Property and Probate; Taxation) Bar Associations; National Academy of Elder Law Attorneys. ***PRACTICE AREAS:*** Elder Law; Guardianship; Real Estate; Estate Planning; Estate Administration; Taxation; Business Formation. ***Email:*** buck@del.net

LYNN R. O'DONNELL, born Philadelphia, Pennsylvania, June 19, 1957; admitted to bar, 1992, Delaware. *Education:* University of Delaware (B.A., magna cum laude, 1982); Villanova University (J.D., 1991). Phi Beta Kappa. Member, Villanova Environmental Law Journal, 1991-1992. Member, Terry-Carey Inns of Court, 1992-1994. Author: Casenote: "New Restrictions in Environmental Litigation: Standing and Final Agency Action After Lujan v. National Wildlife Federation," 2 Villanova Env. L.J. 227, 1991. *Member:* Delaware Bar Association; National Academy of Elder Law Attorneys. ***PRACTICE AREAS:*** Estate Planning; Estate Administration; Elder Law; Guardianship; Real Estate. ***Email:*** LOdon52980@aol.com

MICHELE L. PROCINO, born Milford, Delaware, September 23, 1969; admitted to bar, 1995, Delaware; 1996, U.S. District Court, District of Delaware; 1998, U.S. Tax Court. *Education:* Pennsylvania State University (B.A., 1991); Widener University School of Law (J.D., cum laude, 1995); Villanova University School of Law (LL.M., Taxation, 1998). Phi Kappa Phi; Phi Delta Phi. Recipient, Certificate of Achievement, Federal Income Tax, Widener University School of Law. Author: Note, "The Death of Health Care Reform In 1994: Another Example of Congress' Inability to Enact Major Reform," 1 The Widener Law Symposium Journal, 547, 1996. Member of Staff, The Widener Law Symposium Journal, 1994-1995. *Member:* Delaware (Member, Estates and Trusts and Taxation Sections) and American (Member, Real Property, Probate and Trusts, and Taxation Sections) Bar Associations. ***PRACTICE AREAS:*** Taxation; Estate Planning; Estate Administration; Liquor Licensing; Guardianship; Real Estate; Business Formation. ***Email:*** mlprocino@del.net

RICHARD E. W. BERL, JR., born Wilmington, Delaware, July 4, 1954; admitted to bar, 1979, Delaware and U.S. District Court, District of Delaware. *Education:* University of Delaware (B.A., 1976); Delaware Law School of Widener University (J.D., 1979). Law Clerk, Superior Court of Delaware, 1979-1980. Deputy Attorney General, State of Delaware, 1980-1981. *Member:* Sussex County and Delaware Bar Associations; Delaware Trial Lawyers Association. ***PRACTICE AREAS:*** Personal Injury Law; Family Law; Business Law; Real Estate.

STUMPF, VICKERS & SANDY, P.A.

Established in 1987
8 WEST MARKET STREET
GEORGETOWN, DELAWARE 19947
Telephone: 302-856-3561
FAX: 302-856-0956

General Civil and Trial Practice. Personal Injury, Criminal Law, Workers' Compensation and Family Law.

THOMAS J. STUMPF, born Buffalo, New York, July 18, 1948; admitted to bar, 1974, Tennessee and Delaware. *Education:* Allegheny College (B.A., 1970); University of Tennessee (J.D., 1973). *Member:* Sussex County and Delaware Bar Associations; Delaware Trial Lawyers Association; The Association of Trial Lawyers of America. ***PRACTICE AREAS:*** Personal Injury; Probate Law; Estate Planning Law; Litigation. ***Email:*** tstumpf@ce.net

VINCENT H. VICKERS, II, born Salisbury, Maryland, April 27, 1952; admitted to bar, 1983, Delaware. *Education:* University of Delaware (B.A., Pol.Sc., B.S., Bus. Adm., with honors, 1980); The College of William & Mary (J.D., 1983). Deputy Attorney General, Delaware Department of Justice, 1983-1987. *Member:* Sussex County and Delaware Bar Associations; Delaware Trial Lawyers Association; Delaware Association of Criminal Defense Lawyers; The Association of Trial Lawyers of America; National College for DUI Defense. ***PRACTICE AREAS:*** Criminal Law; Personal Injury; Civil and Criminal Litigation. ***Email:*** vvickers@ce.net

JOHN P. M. SANDY, born Knoxville, Tennessee, October 8, 1951; admitted to bar, 1977, Delaware. *Education:* University of Delaware (B.A., 1974); University of Baltimore (J.D., 1977). Criminal Justice Instructor, Delaware Technical and Community College, 1985—. Deputy Attorney General, 1977-1980, Chief Deputy Attorney General, 1980-1987, Sussex County. *Member:* Sussex County and Delaware Bar Associations; Delaware Trial Lawyers Association; Delaware Association of Criminal Defense Lawyers; The Association of

(This Listing Continued)

STUMPF, VICKERS & SANDY, P.A., Georgetown—Continued

Trial Lawyers of America; National Association of Criminal Defense Lawyers; National College for DUI Defense. ***PRACTICE AREAS:*** Criminal Law; Personal Injury; Civil and Criminal Litigation. ***Email:*** jsandy@ce.net

THOMAS E. GAY, born Lewes, Delaware, March 31, 1965; admitted to bar, 1992, Maine; 1994, Delaware. *Education:* University of Delaware (B.A., B.S., 1987); Widener University (J.D., 1991). *Member:* Sussex County, Delaware State and American (Member, Family Law Section) Bar Associations. Terry Carey Inn of Court. ***PRACTICE AREAS:*** Family Law. ***Email:*** tgay@ce.net

BRIAN F. DOLAN, born Wilmington, Delaware, September 24, 1958; admitted to bar, 1993, Pennsylvania and Delaware; 1994, U.S. District Court, District of Delaware. *Education:* University of Delaware (B.A., 1980; M.A., 1989); Dickinson School of Law (J.D., 1992). Member, Moot Court, 1991-1992. Member, Naval Reserve Association. *Member:* Sussex County, Delaware and American Bar Associations; Delaware Trial Lawyers Association; Terry-Carey Inn of Court. [Lt., U.S. Navy, 1981-1986; U.S. Naval Reserves, 1986—]. ***PRACTICE AREAS:*** General Civil and Trial Practice; Workman's Compensation; Personal Injury. ***Email:*** bdolan@ce.net

---

KIM DeBONTE, born Glen Ridge, New Jersey, November 16, 1968; admitted to bar, 1997, New Jersey and Delaware. *Education:* St. Joseph's University (B.S., 1990); Widener University School of Law (J.D., 1997). Phi Delta Phi. Moe Levine Trial Advocacy Honor Society. Member, Delaware Journal of Corporate Law (Law Review- #2). Adjunct Professor, Delaware Technical and Community College, 2001—. *Member:* Delaware and American Bar Associations. ***PRACTICE AREAS:*** Family Law; Criminal Law. ***Email:*** kdebonte@ce.net

TUNNELL & RAYSOR, P.A.

30 E. PINE STREET
P.O. BOX 151
GEORGETOWN, DELAWARE 19947
Telephone: 302-856-7313; 1-800-533-2897
Fax: 302-856-7329; 856-3186
Email: info@tunnellraysor.com

Bethany Beach, Delaware Office: Ocean Highway, P.O. Box 156. Telephone: 302-539-8222. Fax: 302-539-1089.
Rehoboth Beach, Delaware Office: Plaza Five, 323 East Rehoboth Avenue. Telephone: 302-227-1314. Fax: 302-227-5829.
Seaford, Delaware Office: 809 Norman Eskridge Highway. Telephone: 302-628-0123. Fax: 302-628-0125.

General Civil and Trial Practice. Labor and Employment Law, Corporate, Banking, Business, Commercial, Real Estate, Probate, Family, Tax and Estate Planning, Municipal, Negligence, Personal Injury and Criminal Law.

JOHN E. MESSICK (1959-1994).

HAROLD E. DUKES, JR., born Lewes, Delaware, October 16, 1948; admitted to bar, 1974, Delaware. *Education:* Furman University (B.A., 1971); University of South Carolina (J.D., 1973). *Member:* Sussex County, Delaware and American Bar Associations. (Resident, Rehoboth Beach Office). ***PRACTICE AREAS:*** Real Estate Law. ***Email:*** hal@tunnellraysor.com

JAMES F. WAEHLER, born Jersey City, New Jersey, June 20, 1945; admitted to bar, 1970, Virginia; 1971, Delaware; 1972, New Jersey. *Education:* Virginia Military Institute (B.A., 1967); Georgetown University (J.D., 1970). *Member:* Sussex County (President, 1991-1993) and Delaware (Vice President, 1991-1994) Bar Associations. [LTC, SJA, Delaware Air National Guard, 1980-1996]. ***PRACTICE AREAS:*** Civil Litigation; Real Estate Law; Banking Law; Corporate Law; Commercial Law. ***Email:*** jwaehler@tunnellraysor.com

HAROLD W. T. PURNELL, II, born Lewes, Delaware, February 19, 1955; admitted to bar, 1980, Delaware and U.S. District Court, District of Delaware; 1981, Pennsylvania; 1989, U.S. Tax Court. *Education:* Gettysburg College (B.A., 1977); Delaware Law School (J.D., 1980); Villanova Law School (LL.M., Taxation, 1983). Deputy Attorney General of Delaware, 1981-1984. *Member:* Sussex County, Delaware (Member, Sections on: Tax; Estates and Trusts) and American Bar Associations; Delaware Trial Lawyers Association. ***PRACTICE AREAS:*** Trusts and Estates; Real Estate; Tax; Business Organization. ***Email:*** bill@tunnellraysor.com

TEMPE BROWNELL STEEN, born Pennsylvania, May 12, 1943; admitted to bar, 1983, Delaware. *Education:* Duke University (A.B., 1965); George Washington University (M.A., 1967); Delaware Law School of Widener University (J.D., magna cum laude, 1983). Phi Delta Kappa; Phi Kappa Phi; Phi

(This Listing Continued)

Delta Phi. Clerk, Superior Court, State of Delaware, 1983-1984. *Member:* Sussex County, Delaware and American Bar Associations. (Resident, Bethany Beach Office). ***PRACTICE AREAS:*** Municipal Law (80%); Condominium Law (10%); Corporate (5%). ***Email:*** tempe@tunnellraysor.com

---

KELLY DUNN GELOF, born Warwick, Rhode Island, December 23, 1969; admitted to bar, 1994, Pennsylvania; 1996, New Jersey and Delaware. *Education:* Syracuse University (B.S., 1991); Widener University School of Law (J.D., 1994). *Member:* Sussex County, Delaware and American Bar Associations; The Association of Trial Lawyers of America; Delaware Trial Lawyers Association. ***PRACTICE AREAS:*** Personal Injury; Medical Malpractice; Criminal Law; General Civil Litigation. ***Email:*** kelly@tunnellraysor.com

MARY ROBIN SCHRIDER, born Grand Forks, North Dakota, July 16, 1974; admitted to bar, 1999, Delaware. *Education:* Washington College (B.A., 1996); College of William & Mary School of Law (J.D., 1999). Phi Delta Phi. *Member:* Sussex County and Delaware State Bar Associations. ***PRACTICE AREAS:*** Civil Litigation; Debtor and Creditor; Homeowners Association Law. ***Email:*** mary@tunnellraysor.com

HEIDI A. BALLIET, born Pennsylvania, December 24, 1969; admitted to bar, 1998, Delaware. *Education:* University of Baltimore (B.A., 1993; J.D., 1998). *Member:*, Sussex County, Delaware State and American Bar Associations; Maryland State Bar Association, Inc. ***PRACTICE AREAS:*** Real Estate. ***Email:*** heidi@tunnellraysor.com

REPRESENTATIVE CLIENTS: Wilmington Trust Company (Sussex County); Towns of Laurel, Lewes, Millsboro, Fenwick Island, Greenwood, and Delmar; Perdue, Inc. (Georgetown); Stewart Title Insurance Co.; Bank of Delmarva, N.A.; Peninsula Bank; GMAC; County Bank; Chesapeake Utilities Corp.; Artesian Water Co.

JAMES B. TYLER, III

211 EAST MARKET STREET
P.O. BOX 555
GEORGETOWN, DELAWARE 19947
Telephone: 302-856-6397; 1-800-758-0077
Fax: 302-856-6398
Email: jbtyler3@compuserve.com
URL: http://www.lawyers.com/tylerlaw

General, Civil, Trial and Appellate Litigation. Business and Estate Planning. Debtor-Creditor and Commercial Transactions, Collection and Real Estate Matters.

JAMES B. TYLER, III, born Wilmington, Delaware, August 25, 1947; admitted to bar, 1974, Delaware. *Education:* Trinity College (B.A., 1969); University of Virginia (J.D., 1974). Member, Panel of Standing Bankruptcy Trustees, District of Delaware, 1980-1983. *Member:* Sussex County, Delaware and American Bar Associations. ***PRACTICE AREAS:*** General Civil Trial; Appellate Litigation; Business Law; Estate Planning Law; Bankruptcy; Collections; Real Estate.

WALSH MONZACK AND MONACO, P.A.

GEORGETOWN, DELAWARE

(See Wilmington)

Taxation, Commercial Transactions, Business Reorganization, Commercial Bankruptcy, General Corporate, Real Estate. Civil Litigation in all Courts.

WELCH & ASSOCIATES

GEORGETOWN, DELAWARE

(See Wilmington)

Commercial Litigation, Banking and Bankruptcy Litigation, Creditor's Rights, General Litigation, Corporate Litigation, Real Estate, Insurance Defense and Insurance Coverage.

WILSON, HALBROOK & BAYARD

PROFESSIONAL ASSOCIATION

Established in 1935

107 WEST MARKET STREET
P.O. BOX 690
GEORGETOWN, DELAWARE 19947
Telephone: 302-856-0015
Telecopier: 302-856-7116
Email: whbadmin@whblaw.com

General Practice. Personal Injury, Workers Compensation, Real Estate, Banks and Banking, Commercial Law, Civil Litigation, Municipal Law, Administrative Law, Construction Law, Estate Planning, Estate Administration and Taxation.

(This Listing Continued)

HOUSTON WILSON (1910-1980).

EUGENE H. BAYARD, born Charlottesville, Virginia, June 19, 1946; admitted to bar, 1974, Delaware. *Education:* Princeton University (B.A., 1969); University of Virginia (J.D., 1974). Sussex County Attorney, 1991—. *Member:* Sussex County and Delaware Bar Associations. ***PRACTICE AREAS:*** General Practice; Litigation. ***Email:*** ehbayard@whblaw.com

CLAYTON E. BUNTING, born Lewes, Delaware, September 21, 1950; admitted to bar, 1976, Delaware. *Education:* University of Richmond, School of Business Administration (B.S., 1972); University of Baltimore School of Law (J.D., 1976). National Moot Court Representative, 1975-1976. Member, Master Terry-Carey Inns of Court. Legal Consultant, Kappa Alpha Order. Member, Board on Unauthorized Practice of Law, Delaware Supreme Court, 1997-2000. *Member:* Sussex County and Delaware State (Member, Workers Compensation Section) Bar Associations; Delaware Trial Lawyers Association (former Member, Board of Governors); The Association of Trial Lawyers of America (sustaining Member). ***PRACTICE AREAS:*** Personal Injury Law; Workers Compensation Law; Insurance; Premises Liability; Litigation. ***Email:*** cebunting@whblaw.com

DENNIS L. SCHRADER, born Charleston, West Virginia, July 6, 1947; admitted to bar, 1972, West Virginia; 1973, Delaware. *Education:* West Virginia University (B.A., 1969; J.D., 1972). Phi Delta Phi. Member: Board of Trustees, Community Legal Aid Society, Inc., 1979-1986; Long Range Courts Planning Committee, 1985-1999; Board of Professional Responsibility, 1986-1992; Board of Directors, Delaware Bar Foundation, 1987-1994; Judicial Nominating Commission, State of Delaware, 1990-1991. *Member:* Sussex County (President, 1983-1985), Delaware (President, 2000-2001; Member: Judicial Appointments Committee, 1981—; Executive Committee, 1983-1986, 1995—; Professional Guidance Committee, 1983—; National Conference of Bar Presidents, 1999—) and American Bar Associations; West Virginia State Bar; American Judicature Society. ***PRACTICE AREAS:*** Municipal Law; Construction Law; Civil Litigation; Family Law. ***Email:*** dlschrader@whblaw.com

ROBERT G. GIBBS, born Washington, D.C., June 19, 1952; admitted to bar, 1985, Maryland and District of Columbia; 1986, Delaware. *Education:* Drew University (B.A., in Economics, with honors, 1974); University of Baltimore (J.D., 1984). Phi Alpha Delta (Vice Justice, 1984-1985). Real Estate Broker, Maryland, 1981-1985. Member of Board, Unauthorized Practice of Law, Delaware Supreme Court, 1991-1997. Member, Board on Professional Responsibility, Delaware Supreme Court, 2000—. *Member:* Bar Association of Baltimore City; The District of Columbia Bar; Maryland State, Delaware State and American Bar Associations. ***PRACTICE AREAS:*** Banks and Banking; Business Law; Commercial Law; Civil Litigation; Real Estate. ***Email:*** rggibbs@whblaw.com

ERIC C. HOWARD, born San Antonio, Texas, February 24, 1956; admitted to bar, 1981, Delaware. *Education:* University of Delaware (B.A. with honors, 1978); Duke University (J.D., 1981). Phi Beta Kappa. *Member:* Delaware and American Bar Associations. ***PRACTICE AREAS:*** Civil Litigation; Business Law; Construction Law. ***Email:*** echoward@whblaw.com

MARK D. OLSON, born Johnson City, New York, April 3, 1945; admitted to bar, 1976, Delaware; 1985, U.S. Tax Court. *Education:* State University of New York (B.A., 1973); University of Pennsylvania (J.D., 1976). Phi Beta Kappa. Member, Preliminary Review Committee, Delaware Supreme Court, 1997—. *Member:* Delaware State (Member, Sections on: Tax; Estates and Trusts) and American (Member, Sections on: Taxation; Real Property, Probate and Trust) Bar Associations. ***PRACTICE AREAS:*** Taxation; Like Kind Exchanges; Estate Planning; Estate Administration; Family Business Planning; Business Succession Planning.

RETIRED

ROBERT L. HALBROOK, born Detroit, Michigan, July 25, 1929; admitted to bar, 1957, Michigan; 1968, Delaware; 1969, U.S. Supreme Court. *Education:* University of Michigan (B.A., 1952; J.D., 1956).

COUNSEL FOR: Delaware National Bank; Towns of Bridgeville, Ocean View; Town of Frankford; O.A. Newton & Son Company; Allen Family Foods; Buntings Nurseries of Selbyville, Inc.; Townsends', Inc.; J.G. Townsend, Jr. & Co.; Sussex County, Delaware; Nanticoke Homes, Inc.; Burris Foods, Inc.; First State Packaging, Inc.; Pep-up, Inc.; Sayre-Baldwin, Inc.; Sigma Industries, Inc.; Wilson Baker, Inc..

YOUNG CONAWAY STARGATT & TAYLOR, LLP

110 WEST PINE STREET
GEORGETOWN, DELAWARE 19947
Telephone: 302-856-3571
Telecopy: 302-856-9338
Email: ycst@ycst.com
URL: http://www.ycst.com

Wilmington, Delaware Office: Eleventh Floor, Wilmington Trust Center, 1100 North Market Street, P.O. Box 391. Telephone: 302-571-6600. Telecopy: 302-571-1253.

General Practice.

MEMBERS OF FIRM

H. JAMES CONAWAY, JR. (1922-1990).

CRAIG A. KARSNITZ, born Lebanon, Pennsylvania, March 30, 1952; admitted to bar, 1978, Delaware. *Education:* University of Delaware (B.A., 1974); Villanova University (J.D., 1977). Law Clerk to the Honorable John J. McNeilly, Delaware Supreme Court, 1977-1978. Member, Superior Court Rules Committee. *Member:* Delaware and American Bar Associations; Delaware Trial Lawyers Association; The Association of Trial Lawyers of America. (Resident). ***PRACTICE AREAS:*** Personal Injury; Workers' Compensation. ***Email:*** ckarsnitz@ycst.com

ASSOCIATE

VIVIAN MEDINILLA LONGO, born Guatemala City, Guatemala, July 4, 1966; admitted to bar, 1993, Delaware; 1994, Pennsylvania and U.S. District Court, District of Delaware; 1999, U.S. Supreme Court. *Education:* University of Delaware (B.S., 1988); Widener University School of Law (J.D., cum laude, 1993). Visiting Assistant Professor of Law, Widener University School of Law, 1995-1996. Member: Board of Directors, CLASI, 1997-1999; Judicial Appointments Nominating Committee, 1999-2000; Delaware Commission for Women. *Member:* Delaware State (Member, Executive Committee, 1996-1999) and American Bar Associations. Fellow: Delaware Bar Foundation. (Resident). ***LANGUAGES:*** Spanish. ***PRACTICE AREAS:*** Personal Injury; Workers' Compensation; Criminal Defense; Medical Malpractice. ***Email:*** vlongo@ycst.com

(For Complete Biographical Data on all Personnel, see Wilmington, Delaware Professional Biographies).

GARY A. BRYDE, P.A.

STONE MILL OFFICE PARK
724 YORKLYN ROAD, SUITE 100
HOCKESSIN, DELAWARE 19707
Telephone: 302-239-3700
Fax: 302-239-4015
Email: brydex4@aol.com
URL: http://www.garybryde.homepage.com

Commercial and Residential Real Estate, Real Estate Development and Financing, Zoning and Subdivision, Transactional Law, Probate, Estate Planning, Corporate Law, Personal Injury and Business Law.

GARY A. BRYDE, born Hattiesburg, Mississippi, July 14, 1950; admitted to bar, 1976, Delaware; 1977, U.S. District Court, District of Delaware. *Education:* University of Tennessee (B.S., with honors, 1972; J.D., 1976). Phi Alpha Delta. Instructor, New Castle County Board of Realtors, 1988. Law Clerk, Delaware Superior Court, 1976-1977. Adjunct Professor, University of Delaware. Deputy Attorney General, State of Delaware, 1977-1979. Attorney for: Delaware Alcoholic Beverage Control Commission, 1978-1979; New Castle County Council, 1985-1986. *Member:* Delaware Bar Association (Member, Real Property Section). ***PRACTICE AREAS:*** Commercial Real Estate; Residential Real Estate; Business Law; Personal Injury; Real Estate Development; Zoning Law; Subdivisions; Probate Law; Estate Planning; Corporate Law. ***Email:*** brydex4@aol.com

OF COUNSEL

CHARLES GRUVER, III, born Kingston, Pennsylvania, May 4, 1952; admitted to bar, 1977, Delaware, U.S. District Court, District of Delaware, U.S. Court of Appeals, Third Circuit and U.S. Tax Court; 1981, U.S. Supreme Court. *Education:* University of Buffalo (B.S.B.A., cum laude, 1974); Dickinson School of Law (J.D., 1977); Georgetown University (LL.M. in Taxation, 1981). Adjunct Professor, University of Delaware, 1988-1993. Deputy Attorney General, Civil Division, Delaware Department of Justice, 1977-1980. Acting Delaware Securities Commissioner, 1979-1980. *Member:* Delaware and American

(This Listing Continued)

GARY A. BRYDE, P.A., Hockessin—Continued

Bar Associations. [LTC., Delaware Army National Guard, 1979—]. ***PRACTICE AREAS:*** Personal Injury; Probate Law; Commercial Law; Collection Law; Estate Planning.

HARTNETT & HARTNETT

7301 LANCASTER PIKE
P.O. BOX 220
HOCKESSIN, DELAWARE 19707
Telephone: 302-239-4220
URL: http://www.lawyers.com/hartnett&hartnett

Family Law, Criminal Law.

JENNIFER ANNE HARTNETT, born 1968; admitted to bar, 1994, Delaware and U.S. District Court, District of Delaware. *Education:* University of Virginia (B.A., 1990); Columbia University (J.D., 1993). ***PRACTICE AREAS:*** Family Law; Criminal Law. **Email:** jah239@aol.com

LAWRENCE F. HARTNETT, born 1930; admitted to bar, 1959, Delaware. *Education:* University of Delaware (B.A.); Dickinson School of Law.

LAW OFFICE OF ALLAN WENDELBURG

722 YORKLYN ROAD, SUITE 300
HOCKESSIN, DELAWARE 19707
Telephone: 302-235-0900
Fax: 302-235-2710
Email: awendelburg@wendelburglaw.com
URL: http://www.lawyers.com/wendelburg

Civil Litigation, Criminal Litigation, Personal Injury, Professional Malpractice, Insurance Defense, Construction Law, Insurance, Probate, Estate Planning, Business Law, Commercial Law.

ALLAN WENDELBURG, born Oakland, California, September 7, 1954; admitted to bar, 1979, Delaware; 1993, Maryland. *Education:* University of Delaware (B.A., 1976); Widener University School of Law (J.D., 1979). Deputy Attorney General, State of Delaware, 1981-1986. *Member:* Delaware State and Maryland State Bar Associations; Defense Counsel of Delaware.

BARROS, McNAMARA, SCANLON, MALKIEWICZ & TAYLOR

PROFESSIONAL ASSOCIATION
Established in 1981
1143 SAVANNAH ROAD
LEWES, DELAWARE 19958
Telephone: 302-644-8510

Dover, Delaware Office: State & Loockerman Streets, P.O. Box 1298, 19903-1298. Telephone: 302-734-8400. Telefax: 302-734-4349.

Personal Injury, Medical Malpractice, Work Place Injury, Civil and Criminal Trial Practice. Family, Bankruptcy, Probate, Estate Planning and Corporate Law. Commercial Law. Litigation, Administrative, Zoning, Collections.

REPRESENTATIVE CLIENTS: Delaware Manufactured Housing Association, Inc.; Delaware State Music Teachers Assn.; Sears Roebuck & Co.

(For Complete Biographical Data on Personnel see Dover, Delaware)

ERIC G. MOONEY, P.A.

LEWES, DELAWARE

(See Georgetown)

Criminal Defense, Driving Under the Influence, Personal Injury.

SCHAB & BARNETT, P.A.

Established in 1982
1322 KINGS HIGHWAY
LEWES, DELAWARE 19958
Telephone: 302-645-6626

Georgetown, Delaware Office: 9 Chestnut Street, P.O. Box 755. Telephone: 302-856-9024. Fax: 302-856-6360.

Commercial Collections, Commercial Law, Probate and Estates, Real Estate, Mortgage Foreclosures, Personal Injury, Workers Compensation, Commercial Insurance Claims and Defense, Admiralty, Maritime, Beach Law.

(For Complete Biographical Data on all Personnel, see Professional Biographies at Georgetown)

COOCH AND TAYLOR

Established in 1960
51 EAST MAIN STREET, SUITE B
P.O. BOX 672
NEWARK, DELAWARE 19715-0672
Telephone: 302-368-7200
Telecopier: 302-368-7491
URL: http://www/coochandtaylor.com

Wilmington Office: Suite 1000, 824 Market Street Mall, P.O. Box 1680. Telephone: 302-652-3641. Telecopier: 302-652-5379.

Kennett Square, Pennsylvania Office: 502 West Cypress Street, P.O. Box 909. Telephone: 610-444-3700. Telecopier: 610-444-5446.

General Practice, Banking, Litigation. Corporation, Real Estate, Environmental, Land Use and Development, Trial Practice in all Federal and Delaware Courts, Family, Personal Injury, Probate, Estate Planning, Taxation, Commercial, Bankruptcy and Changery Court Practice.

(For Biographical information on all Members and Associates See Professional Biographies at Wilmington, Delaware).

KIMMEL, CARTER, ROMAN & PELTZ, P.A.

Established in 1973
1400 PEOPLES PLAZA, SUITE 100
NEWARK, DELAWARE 19702
Telephone: 302-838-5970

Wilmington, Delaware Office: 913 Market Street, 12th Floor, P.O. Box 272, 19899-0272. Telephone: 302-571-0800. Fax: 302-571-8155.

General Civil and Trial Practice in all Courts. Insurance, Negligence, Construction Accidents, Workers Compensation. Federal Practice.

FIRM PROFILE: Kimmel, Carter, Roman & Peltz, P.A. has served the citizens of Delaware for over 30 years. The firm specializes in plaintiffs' litigation and is probably the most unique law firm of its size in Delaware because its practice is confined solely to automobile accidents, workers' compensation, insurance, products liability and construction accidents. The firm's biggest asset is constant communication with clients. Telephone calls are never screened and the clients have instant access to the attorneys. There are 2 offices centrally located: 1 in downtown Wilmington in the heart of the business district and the other in suburban New Castle County located at People's Plaza. Serving Newark, Middletown, Bear, Smyrna and Dover, the firm annually receives the highest rankings in all legal publications. There are 7 attorneys servicing the public.

REFERENCES: PNC Bank; Wilmington Trust Co.

(See Wilmington)

KNEPPER & STRATTON

NEWARK, DELAWARE

(See Wilmington)

General Civil and Trial Practice in all State and Federal Courts, Personal Injury, Automobile Accidents and Injuries, Workers Compensation, Criminal Law, Sexual Harassment, Employment Law, Employment Discrimination, Driving While Intoxicated, Traffic Violations, Wrongful Termination, Americans with Disabilities Act.

MONTGOMERY, McCRACKEN, WALKER & RHOADS, LLP

CHRISTIANA EXECUTIVE CAMPUS
131 CONTINENTAL DRIVE, SUITE 304
NEWARK, DELAWARE 19713
Telephone: 302-894-7000
Fax: 302-733-7937
URL: http://www.mmwr.com

Cherry Hill, New Jersey Office: LibertyView, Suite 600, 457 Haddonfield Road. Telephone: 856-488-7700. Facsimile: 856-488-7720.

Philadelphia, Pennsylvania Office: 123 South Broad Street. Telephone: 215-772-1500. Fax: 215-772-7620.

(This Listing Continued)

Litigation (including complex, class action and multi-district litigation, professional malpractice defense for all learned professions and healthcare institutions; products liability; toxic tort defense, insurance defense, First Amendment and media law); Intellectual Property; Information Technology; E-Commerce and Web-Based Businesses; Environmental Law; Antitrust; Government Investigations & White Collar Crime; Employment Law (including NLRB, Title VII, age discrimination, ADA, public employee labor relations, and workers' compensation); Government Relations; Business and Personal Counseling (including mergers and acquisitions; corporate, securities, corporate criminal investigations and computer law); Bankruptcy/Reorganization; Health Care; Nonprofit Corporations Law; Employee Benefits; Executive Compensation and Immigration; Taxation; Trusts and Estates; Real Estate; Sports Law.

FIRM PROFILE: Founded in 1912, Montgomery, McCracken, Walker & Rhoads, LLP has developed a reputation as the "law firm's law firm." The firm focuses on quality and responsiveness. Its experience in handling multi-jurisdictional matters has established its reputation regionally, nationally, and internationally. Montgomery, McCracken, Walker & Rhoads, LLP prides itself on effectively managing complex matters and responding rapidly when clients confront unexpected problems. The Firm has offices in Philadelphia, Pennsylvania; Cherry Hill, New Jersey; and Newark, Delaware.

PARTNER

JOHN M. BLOXOM, IV, born Salisbury, Md., June 12, 1956; admitted to bar, 1983, Del. *Education:* University of Virginia (B.A., 1980); Washington & Lee University (J.D., cum laude, 1983). Phi Delta Phi; Order of the Coif. Member, 1981-1983 and Managing Editor, 1982-1983, Washington & Lee Law Review. *Member:* Delaware State and American Bar Associations. ***PRACTICE AREAS:*** Real Estate-Commercial Law; Real Estate (Property) Law; Real Estate Development and Syndications Law; Commercial Lending; Mortgage Law. **Email:** jbloxom@mmwr.com

ASSOCIATE

JOHN H. NEWCOMER, JR., born Phoenixville, Pa., July 23, 1959; admitted to bar, 1984, Del.; 1985, U.S. District Court, District of Del.; 1991, U.S. Court of Appeals, Third Circuit. *Education:* Dickinson College (B.A., cum laude, 1981); Wake Forest University (J.D., 1984). Certified Mediator for the Delaware Superior Court. *Member:* Delaware State and American Bar Associations. ***PRACTICE AREAS:*** Chancery Practice; Litigation; Mechanics Lien Law; Residential Real Estate. ***Email:*** jnewcomer@mmwr.com

(For Complete Data on all Personnel, See Professional Biographies at Philadelphia, Pennsylvania)

MORGAN SHELSBY & LEONI

A PROFESSIONAL ASSOCIATION

131 CONTINENTAL DRIVE, SUITE 206

NEWARK, DELAWARE 19713

Telephone: 302-454-7430

Fax: 302-454-7437

Affiliated Office: Morgan Shelsby Carlo Downs & Everton, P.A., 4 North Park Drive, 21031, Hunt Valley, Maryland. Telephone: 410-584-2800. Fax: 410-584-2020.

Civil and Criminal Trial Practice in all State and Federal Courts. Personal Injury, Medical Malpractice, Products Liability, Workers Compensation, Insurance and Health Care, Corporate and Commercial Litigation.

FIRM PROFILE: Morgan Shelsby & Leoni has a significant insurance defense practice including medical malpractice defense. In addition, the firm handles general business litigation and workers' compensation matters. The firm has a growing health care practice, corporate, real estate and estate planning practice and has handled a number of mergers and acquisitions for its corporate clients. The firm's significant growth since its inception in 1991 can be attributed to the strength and diversity of its attorneys. The firm consistently provides the client with high quality representation maintaining a commitment to control costs.

ROBERT C. MORGAN, born Evergreen Park, Illinois, March 2, 1955; admitted to bar, 1981, Maryland; 1982, District of Columbia (Not admitted in Delaware). *Education:* University of Maryland (B.A., 1977); University of Baltimore (J.D., 1981). *Member:* The Bar Association of Baltimore City; Maryland State and American Bar Associations; The District of Columbia Bar; Defense Research Institute; Maryland Society of Health Care Risk Managers; Maryland Association of Defense Trial Counsel; National Health Lawyers Association. (Also Member of Morgan, Shelsby, Carlo, Downs & Everton, Hunt Valley, Maryland). ***PRACTICE AREAS:*** Civil Litigation; Insurance Defense; Health Care Law; Employment Discrimination; Officers and Directors Liability.

GILBERT F. SHELSBY, JR., born Baltimore, Maryland, May 28, 1959; admitted to bar, 1985, Maryland and District of Columbia; 1987, U.S. Court of Appeals, Fourth Circuit; 1990, Delaware. *Education:* University of Maryland (B.A., cum laude, 1981); University of Maryland Law School (J.D., 1984). Phi Kappa Phi. Law Clerk to Honorable Joseph H. H. Kaplan, Administrative Judge Circuit Court for Baltimore City, 1984. Defense Counsel of Delaware. *Member:* The Bar Association of Baltimore City; Maryland State and Delaware State Bar Associations; The District of Columbia Bar; Rodney American Inn of Court. (Also Member of Morgan, Shelsby, Carlo, Downs & Everton, Huntsville, Maryland). ***PRACTICE AREAS:*** Civil Litigation; Medical Malpractice; Insurance Defense.

ROBERT J. LEONI, born Wilmington, Delaware, August 1, 1964; admitted to bar, 1990, Delaware. *Education:* University of Delaware (B.A., 1986); Widener University School of Law (J.D., 1990). *Member:* Delaware State and American Bar Associations; Defense Counsel of Delaware. (Also Member, Morgan Shelsby Carlo Downs & Everton, P.A., Hunt Valley, Maryland). ***PRACTICE AREAS:*** Civil Trial Litigation.

DOUGLASS LEE MOWREY, born Baltimore, Maryland, January 12, 1959; admitted to bar, 1985, Delaware. *Education:* Gettysburg College (1977-1979); University of Delaware (B.A.A.S., 1981); Dickinson School of Law (J.D., 1984). Rodney Inns of Court, 1994. ***PRACTICE AREAS:*** Personal Injury Defense; Medical Malpractice Defense.

MARK H. CONNER, born Wilmington, Delaware, September 21, 1964; admitted to bar, 1990, Delaware and U.S. District Court, District of Delaware. *Education:* Dickinson College (B.A., 1987); Delaware Law School of Widener University (J.D., 1990). Law Clerk, Hon. Charles H. Toliver, IV, Superior Court, New Castle County, 1990-1991. Author: "The Work Place Rights of Public Employees in Delaware," Delaware Lawyer, Vol. 10, No. 2, Summer 1992. Deputy Attorney General, Department of Justice, Delaware, 1991-1999. *Member:* Delaware State Bar Association. ***REPORTED CASES:*** State v. Varis Aizupitis, 699 A.2d 1098. ***PRACTICE AREAS:*** Civil Litigation; Criminal Law; Workers Compensation; Family Law.

LEGAL SUPPORT PERSONNEL

STEPHANIE MEYERS

LORI PYLE

REPRESENTATIVE CLIENTS: Atlantic Mutual Insurance Co.; Chubb & Son, Inc.; Fireman's Fund Insurance Cos.; Harleysville Insurance Co.; Maryland Casualty Co.; Medical Mutual Liability Society of Maryland; Nationwide Insurance Co.; Pennsylvania Casualty Co.; Phico Insurance Co.; Progressive Casualty Insurance Co.; Royal Insurance Co.; St. Paul Fire & Marine Insurance Co.; United States Fidelity & Deposit Co.; Zurich-American; Princeton Insurance Co.; Erie Insurance Co.; Property and Casualty Insurance Co.; Crawford and Co.; Crum and Forster Insurance Co.; John Hancock Property & Casualty Insurance Co.; Davco Food, Inc.; Professional Risk Management Insurance Co.; Aaoms Mutual Insurance Co.; First Financial Insurance Co.; Great Central Insurance Co.; Burlington Insurance Co.; Coopervision Pharmaceutical Co.; B. Green & Co.; AT&T Network Systems; Universal Underwriters; ITT Hartford Insurance Co.; Sentry Insurance Co.; Kemper National Insurance Co.; Hertz Corp.; Browning-Ferris Industries.

(This Listing Continued)

MORRIS, JAMES, HITCHENS & WILLIAMS, LLP

16 POLLY DRUMMOND HILL ROAD

NEWARK, DELAWARE 19711-5703

Telephone: 302-368-4200

Telecopier: 302-368-6259

URL: http://www.morrisjames.com

Wilmington, Delaware Offices: 222 Delaware Avenue, P.O. Box 2306, 19899-2306. Telephone: 302-888-6800. Telecopier: 302-571-1750 and 1010 North Bancroft Parkway, Suite 11, P.O. Box 2328, 19899-2328. Telephone: 302-655-2599. Fax: 302-655-8831.

Dover, Delaware Office: Suite 202, 32 West Loockerman Street, 19904-7356. Telephone: 302-678-8815. Telecopier: 302-678-9063.

Litigation, Corporate Law, Commercial Law, Business Law. Administrative Law, Alternative Dispute Resolution, Bankruptcy, Commercial Real Estate, Computers and Software, Education Law, Environmental Law, Family Law, Health Care, Insurance, Insurance Defense, Intellectual Property, Labor and Employment, Medical Malpractice, Partnership Law, Personal Injury, Probate, Products Liability, Real Estate, Taxation, Torts, Trusts and Estates and Wills.

RESIDENT PARTNERS

KEVIN G. HEALY, born Wilmington, Delaware, October 23, 1958; admitted to bar, 1986, Delaware; 1987, New Jersey and Pennsylvania. *Education:* University of Delaware (B.A., cum laude, 1981); Boston College; Delaware Law School of Widener University (J.D., cum laude, 1986). Member, Moot

(This Listing Continued)

MORRIS, JAMES, HITCHENS & WILLIAMS, LLP, Newark—Continued

Court. Law Clerk, Delaware Superior Court, 1985-1987. *Member:* Delaware State and American Bar Associations. **PRACTICE AREAS:** Civil Litigation; Construction Law; Personal Injury Litigation. **Email:** khealy@morrisjames.com

FRANCIS J. JONES, JR., born Wilmington, Delaware, January 4, 1957; admitted to bar, 1983, Delaware and U.S. District Court, District of Delaware. *Education:* Catholic University of America (B.A., 1979; J.D., 1982). Law Clerk to Hon. John J. McNeilly, Associate Justice, Supreme Court of Delaware, 1982-1983. *Member:* Delaware State (Chairman, Torts and Insurance Practice Section, 1990-1992) and American Bar Associations; Defense Research Institute and Defense Council of Delaware. Associate Member, Delaware Supreme Court Board of Bar Examiners. **PRACTICE AREAS:** Insurance Defense; Personal Injury; Litigation; Products Liability. **Email:** pjones@morrisjames.com

BRIAN T. MURRAY, P.A.

903 SOUTH COLLEGE AVENUE
NEWARK, DELAWARE 19713
Telephone: 302-731-1776
Fax: 302-731-1730

Commercial and Residential Real Estate, Landlord and Tenant Law, Leases and Leasing, Real Estate Development and Financing, Land Use and Zoning.

BRIAN T. MURRAY, born Hoboken, New Jersey, May 20, 1957; admitted to bar, 1983, Pennsylvania; 1986, Delaware; 1987, U.S. District Court, District of Delaware. *Education:* University of Delaware (B.A., 1979); Western New England School of Law (J.D., 1982). Assistant City Solicitor, City of Wilmington, 1988-1993. *Member:* Pennsylvania, Delaware State (Past Chair, 1992-1993; Member, Sections on: Real Estate and Personal Property) and American (Member, Sections on: Real Property, Probate and Trust Law) Bar Associations. **PRACTICE AREAS:** Real Estate; Leases and Leasing; Commercial Law; Residential Real Estate.

LEGAL SUPPORT PERSONNEL

CHRISTINE D. ALEXANDER

ELIZABETH HACKNEY

APPROVED ATTORNEY FOR: First American Title Insurance Co.; Ticor Insurance Co.; Lawyers Title Insurance Co.

RAYMOND J. OTLOWSKI

224 EAST DELAWARE AVENUE
NEWARK, DELAWARE 19711
Telephone: 302-368-8595
Fax: 302-368-8597

Personal Injury, Workers Compensation, Real Estate, Wills and Estates.

RAYMOND J. OTLOWSKI, born Perth Amboy, New Jersey, April 27, 1940; admitted to bar, 1974, Delaware and U.S. District Court, District of Delaware. *Education:* University of Delaware (B.A., 1962); University of Baltimore School of Law (J.D., 1974). Instructor, Criminal Justice, Delaware Technical and Community College, 1974-1976. Deputy Attorney General, State of Delaware, 1973-1974. Assistant Public Defender, State of Delaware, 1980. Member, Governor's Investigative Strike Force, 1975. *Member:* Delaware Bar Association; Delaware Trial Lawyers Association; Delaware Criminal Defense Attorney's Association. [Capt., U.S. Marine Corp, 1962-1966]

TRZUSKOWSKI, KIPP, KELLEHER & PEARCE, P.A.

Established in 1974

273 EAST MAIN STREET
NEWARK, DELAWARE 19711
Telephone: 302-368-2561
Telefax: 302-368-9729

Wilmington, Delaware Office: 1020 N. Bancroft Parkway, P.O. Box 429, 198999-0429. Telephone: 302-571-1782. Telefax: 302-571-1638.

General Practice. Civil Litigation, Personal Injury, Medical Malpractice, Commercial and Corporate, Real Estate, Estate Planning, Probate, Family, Matrimonial, Pension (ERISA).

(For Complete Biographical Data on All Personnel, see Professional Biographies at Wilmington, Delaware)

ERIC G. MOONEY, P.A.

OCEAN VIEW, DELAWARE

(See Georgetown)

Criminal Defense, Driving Under the Influence, Personal Injury.

SCHMITTINGER & RODRIGUEZ, P.A.

ODESSA PROFESSIONAL PARK
P.O. BOX 626
ODESSA, DELAWARE 19730-0626
Telephone: 302-378-1697
FAX: 302-378-1659
Email: attorneys@schmittrod.com
URL: http://www.schmittrod.com

Dover, Delaware Office: 414 South State Street. Telephone: 302-674-0140. Fax: 302-674-1830.
Wilmington, Delaware Office: 1300 North Market Street, Suite 205. Telephone: 302-652-3676. Fax: 302-652-8788.
Rehoboth Beach, Delaware Office: 4602 Highway One. Telephone: 302-227-1400. Fax: 302-645-1843.

General Civil Practice. Personal Injury, Workers Compensation, Federal Practice, Corporation, Estate Planning, Real Estate and Commercial Law. Litigation.

Bruce C. Ennis (Also at Dover, Delaware)
Crystal L. Carey (Also at Dover, Delaware)
Scott E. Chambers (Also at Dover, Delaware)

(For Complete Biographical Data on all Personnel, see Professional Biographies at Dover, Delaware)

GRIFFIN & HACKETT, P.A.

REHOBOTH BEACH, DELAWARE

(See Georgetown)

General Civil and Trial Practice. Corporate, Business, Banking, Real Estate, Probate, Family, Estate Planning, Personal Injury, Health Care, Zoning and Education Law.

ERIC G. MOONEY, P.A.

REHOBOTH BEACH, DELAWARE

(See Georgetown)

Criminal Defense, Driving Under the Influence, Personal Injury.

SCHMITTINGER & RODRIGUEZ, P.A.

4602 HIGHWAY ONE
REHOBOTH BEACH, DELAWARE 19971
Telephone: 302-227-1400
FAX: 302-645-1843
Email: attorneys@schmittrod.com
URL: http://www.schmittrod.com

Dover, Delaware Office: 414 South State Street. Telephone: 302-674-0140. Fax: 302-674-1830.
Wilmington, Delaware Office: 1300 North Market Street, Suite 205. Telephone: 302-652-3676. Fax: 302-652-8788.
Odessa, Delaware Office: Odessa Professional Park, P.O. Box 626. Telephone: 302-378-1697. Fax: 302-378-1659.

General Civil Practice. Personal Injury, Workers Compensation, Federal Practice. Corporation, Estate Planning, Real Estate and Commercial Law. Litigation.

Harold Schmittinger (Also at Dover and Wilmington, Delaware Offices)
Paul H. Boswell (Also at Dover and Wilmington, Delaware Offices)
Nicholas H. Rodriguez (Also at Dover and Wilmington, Delaware Offices)
John J. Schmittinger (Also at Dover and Wilmington, Delaware Offices)
David A. Boswell (Resident)

(For Complete Biographical Data on all Personnel, see Professional Biographies at Dover).

STUMPF, VICKERS & SANDY, P.A.

REHOBOTH BEACH, DELAWARE

(See Georgetown)

General Civil and Trial Practice. Personal Injury, Criminal Law, Workers' Compensation and Family Law.

JAMES B. TYLER, III

REHOBOTH BEACH, DELAWARE

(See Georgetown)

General, Civil, Trial and Appellate Litigation. Business and Estate Planning. Debtor-Creditor and Commercial Transactions, Collection and Real Estate Matters.

ERIC G. MOONEY, P.A.

SEAFORD, DELAWARE

(See Georgetown)

Criminal Defense, Driving Under the Influence, Personal Injury.

STUMPF, VICKERS & SANDY, P.A.

SEAFORD, DELAWARE

(See Georgetown)

General Civil and Trial Practice. Personal Injury, Criminal Law, Workers' Compensation and Family Law.

AGOSTINI, LEVITSKY, ISAACS & KULESZA

824 MARKET STREET, SUITE 810
P.O. BOX 2323
WILMINGTON, DELAWARE 19899-2323
Telephone: 302-654-7444
Telecopier: 302-656-8920

Commercial, Corporate and Civil Litigation. Bankruptcy, Personal Injury Law, Real Estate, Domestic Relations and Criminal Law, Collection.

CARL A. AGOSTINI (1946-1994).

NEAL J. LEVITSKY, born Wilmington, Delaware, February 28, 1956; admitted to bar, 1981, Delaware and U.S. District Court, District of Delaware. *Education:* University of Delaware (B.A., cum laude, 1978); University of Miami (J.D., cum laude, 1981). Member, University of Miami Law Review, 1979-1981. Legal Intern for the U.S. District Court for the Southern District of Florida, 1980-1981. *Member:* Delaware State and American Bar Associations. (Also Of Counsel to Farr, Burke, Gambacorta & Wright, Bellmawr, New Jersey and Wilmington, Delaware). ***PRACTICE AREAS:*** Civil Trial; Commercial Litigation; Bankruptcy; Personal Injury. ***Email:*** NLevitsky@aol.com

MICHAEL J. ISAACS, born Wilmington, Delaware, April 2, 1960; admitted to bar, 1986, California and U.S. District Court, Southern District of California; 1989, Delaware. *Education:* James Madison University (B.S., 1982); University of San Diego School of Law (J.D., 1985). *Member:* Delaware State and American Bar Associations; State Bar of California; The Defense Research Institute; Defense Counsel of Delaware. ***PRACTICE AREAS:*** Personal Injury; Real Estate.

JOSEPH D. KULESZA, JR., born Wilmington, Delaware, October 18, 1961; admitted to bar, 1987, Delaware. *Education:* St. Joseph's University (B.A., 1983); University of Delaware (Paralegal Cert., 1985); Delaware Law School (J.D., 1987). Delta Theta Phi. News Editor, The Delaware Law Forum, 1986. *Member:* Delaware State and American Bar Associations; Delaware Trial Lawyers Association; The Association of Trial Lawyers of America. ***PRACTICE AREAS:*** Domestic Law; Personal Injury; Criminal and Civil Litigation; Wills and Estates. ***Email:*** JAYKUL2@AOL.COM

L. JASON CORNELL, born Orlando, Florida; admitted to bar, 1999, Delaware; 2000, U.S. District Court, District of Delaware. *Education:* Florida State University (B.A., Political Science, 1993); Widener University (J.D., 1999). Recipient, Certificate of Achievement, Criminal Law. *Member:* Delaware State and American Bar Associations; Delaware Trial Lawyers Association. ***PRACTICE AREAS:*** Trial Practice; Commercial Litigation; Bankruptcy; Personal Injury.

LAW OFFICES OF PETER G. ANGELOS

A PROFESSIONAL CORPORATION
1300 NORTH MARKET STREET, SUITE 212
WILMINGTON, DELAWARE 19801
Telephone: 302-658-3301
Toll Free: 800-283-8193
Fax: 302-658-3319

Baltimore, Maryland Office: 100 North Charles Street, 22nd Floor, 21201. Telephone: 410-649-2000. Toll Free: 800-252-6622. Fax: 410-659-1780, 1781, 1782; 410-649-2111, 2112.

Asbestos Litigation, Tobacco Litigation, Fen-Phen Litigation, Products Liability, Medical Malpractice, Negligence, Workers Compensation, Commercial and Business Law, Real Estate, Criminal Law, Tax, Estates, Probate and Health Care.

(For biographical data on all Personnel, see Professional Biographies at Baltimore, Maryland)

DANIEL J. ANKER

1100 LOVERING AVENUE, SUITE 20
WILMINGTON, DELAWARE 19806
Telephone: 302-655-6263
Fax: 302-655-7138
Email: djankerlaw@aol.com
URL: http://www.lawyers.com/djankerlaw

Creditors Rights, Collections, Business Law, Business Startups, Business Planning, Bankruptcy, Foreclosures, Condominium Law, Landlord and Tenant Law, Administrative Law.

DANIEL J. ANKER, born Wilmington, Delaware, January 22, 1955; admitted to bar, 1988, Delaware; 1989, U.S. District Court, District of Delaware; 1999, U.S. Supreme Court. *Education:* University of Delaware (B.A.A.S., 1980); Delaware Law School of Widener University (J.D., cum laude, 1988). Phi Delta Phi. Counsel, New Castle County Ethics Commission, 1991-1992. *Member:* Delaware State Bar Association (Member: Real and Personal Property Section; Business Law Section). ***PRACTICE AREAS:*** Bankruptcy; Personal Injury; Real Estate; General Commercial Transactional Law and Litigation; Administrative Law.

REPRESENTATIVE CLIENTS: Associates Financial Services Company, Inc.; Gilpin, Van Trump & Montgomery, Inc.; Trammel Crow Company; Agent-Conestoga Title Insurance Co.; The Devon Condominium; Park Plaza Condominium; Ashton COndominium; Ford Consumer Finance.

ASHBY & GEDDES

222 DELAWARE AVENUE, 17TH FLOOR
P.O. BOX 1150
WILMINGTON, DELAWARE 19899
Telephone: 302-654-1888
Fax: 302-654-2067

General Practice and Civil Litigation, including Corporate, Commercial, Bankruptcy, and Intellectual Property Law.

MEMBERS OF FIRM

LAWRENCE C. ASHBY, born Philadelphia, Pennsylvania, August 24, 1945; admitted to bar, 1970, Delaware. *Education:* Williams College (B.A., 1967); Vanderbilt University (J.D., 1970). Order of the Coif; Phi Delta Phi. Case and Note Editor, Vanderbilt Law Review, 1969-1970. Member, Board of Bar Examiners, 1983-1990 and Delaware Supreme Court Rules Advisory Committee, 1987-1993. Member, Permanent Lawyers Advisory Committee for the United States District Court for the District of Delaware, 1985-1988, 1995—. *Member:* Delaware State (Council, Corporate Law Section, Chairman, 1996-1998) and American Bar Associations. ***Email:*** lashby@ashby-geddes.com

JAMES McC. GEDDES, born Pittsburgh, Pennsylvania, February 24, 1949; admitted to bar, 1976, Virginia; 1977, Delaware. *Education:* University of North Carolina (B.A., 1971); American Graduate School of International Management (M.I.M., 1972); Marshall-Wythe School of Law, College of William & Mary (J.D., 1975). Special Rate Counsel, Delaware Public Service Commission, 1981—. *Member:* Virginia State Bar; Delaware State and American Bar Associations; The Association of Trial Lawyers of America; Delaware Trial Lawyers Association. ***Email:*** jgeddes@ashby-geddes.com

STEPHEN E. JENKINS, born Wilmington, Delaware, August 26, 1954; admitted to bar, 1982, Delaware. *Education:* Georgetown University (A.B., 1976; J.D., magna cum laude, 1982). Member, 1980-1981 and Executive Editor, 1981-1982, Georgetown Law Journal. Articles Editor, Delaware Law Review.

(This Listing Continued)

ASHBY & GEDDES, Wilmington—Continued

Member, Delaware Court of Chancery Rules Advisory Committee. *Member:* Delaware State Bar Association (Co-Chair, Committee on Professional Ethics). [1st. Lt. U.S. Army, 1976-1979]. ***Email:*** sjenkins@ashby-geddes.com

RANDALL E. ROBBINS, born Wilmington, Delaware, May 8, 1956; admitted to bar, 1981, Virginia; 1982, Delaware. *Education:* University of Richmond (B.A., magna cum laude, 1978; J.D., 1981). Deputy Attorney General, State of Delaware, 1981-1984. *Member:* Virginia State Bar; Delaware State and American Bar Associations; The Association of Trial Lawyers of America; Delaware Trial Lawyers Association. ***Email:*** rrobbins@ashby-geddes.com

STEVEN J. BALICK, born Wilmington, Delaware, August 18, 1956; admitted to bar, 1982, Delaware. *Education:* University of Delaware (B.A., 1978); Boston University (J.D., 1981). Judicial Clerkship, Delaware Superior Court, 1981-1982. Deputy Attorney General, State of Delaware, 1982-1986. Member, Permanent Lawyers Advisory Committee, U.S. District Court, District of Delaware, 1992-1995. *Member:* Delaware State and American Bar Associations; Delaware Trial Lawyers Association; The Association of Trial Lawyers of America. ***Email:*** sbalick@ashby-geddes.com

REGINA A. IORII, born Wilmington, Delaware, August 26, 1961; admitted to bar, 1987, Delaware. *Education:* University of Delaware (B.S., magna cum laude, 1983); Widener University School of Law (J.D., magna cum laude, 1987). Phi Beta Kappa. Articles Editor, The Delaware Journal of Corporate Law, 1986-1987. *Member:* Delaware State Bar Association. ***Email:*** riorii@ashby-geddes.com

WILLIAM P. BOWDEN, born Wilmington, Delaware, October 7, 1957; admitted to bar, 1989, Delaware. *Education:* University of Delaware (B.S., 1985); Brooklyn Law School (J.D., 1988). Member, Moot Court Honor Society. *Member:* Delaware State Bar Association. ***Email:*** wbowden@ashby-geddes.com

RICHARD D. HEINS, born Rockville Center, New York, July 1, 1964; admitted to bar, 1989, New York; 1991, Delaware. *Education:* St. Johns University (B.S., summa cum laude, 1985); University of Pennsylvania (J.D., cum laude, 1988). Associate Editor, 1986-1987 and Editor, 1987-1988, University of Pennsylvania Law Review. Judicial Clerkship, Honorable William T. Allen, Delaware Court of Chancery, 1989-1990. *Member:* Delaware State Bar Association (Member of Council, General Corporation Law Section, 1999—). ***Email:*** rheins@ashby-geddes.com

PHILIP TRAINER, JR., born Bryn Mawr, Pennsylvania, February 1, 1960; admitted to bar, 1989, Delaware. *Education:* College of William & Mary (B.A., 1982); Widener University School of Law (J.D., cum laude, 1989). Staff, The Delaware Journal of Corporate Law, 1988-1989. *Member:* Delaware State Bar Association. ***Email:*** ptrainer@ashby-geddes.com

STEVEN T. MARGOLIN, born Wilmington, Delaware, July 10, 1967; admitted to bar, 1992, Delaware. *Education:* University of Delaware, (B.S., magna cum laude, 1989); Dickinson School of Law (J.D., 1992). Order of the Barristers; Woolsack Honor Society. Editor, Dickinson Law Review, 1991-1992. *Member:* Delaware State and American Bar Associations; Delaware Trial Lawyers Association. ***Email:*** smargolin@ashby-geddes.com

CHRISTOPHER S. SONTCHI, born Fort Wayne, Indiana, December 28, 1966; admitted to bar, 1993, Delaware. *Education:* University of North Carolina at Chapel Hill (B.A., with distinction, 1989); University of Chicago (J.D., 1992). Phi Beta Kappa. Judicial Clerkship, Honorable Joseph T. Walsh, Delaware Supreme Court, 1992-1993. *Member:* Delaware State Bar Association. ***Email:*** csontchi@ashby-geddes.com

ASSOCIATES

RICHARD I. G. JONES, JR., born Wilmington, Delaware, January 1, 1964; admitted to bar, 1994, Delaware. *Education:* University of Delaware (B.A., 1989); Widener University School of Law (J.D., cum laude, 1994). Phi Kappa Phi. External Managing Editor, Delaware Journal of Corporate Law, 1993-1994. Legal Intern to The Honorable Walter S. Stapleton, U.S. Court of Appeals, Third Circuit, 1994. *Member:* Delaware State and American Bar Associations. ***Email:*** rjones@ashby-geddes.com

RAFAEL X. ZAHRALDDIN-ARAVENA, born Bogóta, Colombia, May 6, 1967; admitted to bar, 1994, Pennsylvania; 1999, California; 2001, U.S. Court of Appeals, Third Circuit (Not admitted in Delaware). *Education:* University of Virginia (B.S., 1989); Widener University (J.D., 1993); Georgetown University Law Center (LL.M., 1995). Phi Kappa Phi. Harrison Inn; Dean's Scholar. Senior Writing Fellow, Georgetown University Law Center, 1994-1995. Articles Editor, The Law Review of Widener University School of Law (Delaware Journal of Corporate Law). Judicial Clerkship, Honorable Samuel L. Bufford, U.S. Bankruptcy Court, Central District of California, 1999-2000. Assistant Professor of Law, 1995-2000, Associate Professor of Law, 1998-2000, Chapman University School of Law. Secretary of State, United States of America Private International Law Advisory Committee. Member, Study Group on International Insolvency, 2000-2001. *Member:* American Bar Association (Member, Sections On: International Law & Practice, 1992-2000; Business Law, 1992-2000); Hispanic National Bar Association (1998-2001); Inter-American Bar Association (1995-1998); American Society of International Law; American Bankruptcy Institute (1999-2001). ***LANGUAGES:*** Spanish. ***Email:*** rxza@ashby-geddes.com

(This Listing Continued)

RICARDO PALACIO, born Wilmington, Delaware, September 4, 1971; admitted to bar, 1998, Delaware. *Education:* University of Delaware (B.A., 1994); Villanova University (J.D., 1998). *Member:* Delaware State and American Bar Associations. ***LANGUAGES:*** Spanish. ***Email:*** rpalacio@ashby-geddes.com

CAROLYN S. HAKE, born Carmichael, California, February 20, 1974; admitted to bar, 1999, Delaware. *Education:* University of Delaware (B.A.A.S., cum laude, 1996); Widener University School of Law (J.D., summa cum laude, 1999). Phi Beta Kappa. Staff Member, The Delaware Journal of Corporate Law, 1997-1998. Research Editor, The Delaware Journal of Corporate Law, 1998-1999. Wolcott Law Clerk to the Honorable Randy J. Holland, Delaware Supreme Court, 1998-1999. *Member:* Delaware State and American Bar Associations; Delaware Trial Lawyers Association. ***Email:*** chake@ashby-geddes.com

JOSEPH CLEMENT HANDLON, born Darby, Pennsylvania, February 25, 1974; admitted to bar, 1999, Pennsylvania; 2000, Delaware; 2001, New Jersey. *Education:* West Chester University (B.S., cum laude, 1996); Widener University School of Law (J.D., magna cum laude, 1999). Law Clerk to the Honorable Rochelle S. Friedman, Commonwealth Court of Pennsylvania, August 1999-May 2000. Associate Editor, 1997-1998 and Staff Member, 1998-1999, Widener Law Symposium. *Member:* Philadelphia, Delaware State, Pennsylvania and American Bar Associations. ***Email:*** jhandlon@ashby-geddes.com

TIFFANY L. GEYER, born Lock Haven, Pennsylvania, January 11, 1975; admitted to bar, 2000, Delaware. *Education:* Dickinson College (B.A., cum laude, 1997); Widener University School of Law (J.D., magna cum laude, 2000). Phi Kappa Phi. Staff Member, 1998-1999 and Research Editor, 1999-2000, The Delaware Journal of Corporate Law. Wolcott Law Clerk to the Honorable Carolyn Berger, Delaware Supreme Court, 1999-2000. *Member:* Delaware State and American Bar Associations. ***Email:*** tgeyer@ashby-geddes.com

GREGORY ALAN TAYLOR, born Johnson City, New York, August 25, 1975; admitted to bar, 2000, Delaware. *Education:* University of Delaware (B.A., 1997); Widener University School of Law (J.D., cum laude, 2000). Staff Member, 1998-1990 and Articles Editor, Delaware Journal of Corporate Law, 1999-2000. Legal Intern to the Honorable E. Norman Veasey, Delaware Supreme Court, 1999. *Member:* Delaware State and American Bar Associations; Delaware Trial Lawyers Association. ***Email:*** gtaylor@ashby-geddes.com

---

BAILEY & WETZEL, P.A.

Established in 1983

716 TATNALL STREET
P.O. BOX 2034
WILMINGTON, DELAWARE 19899-2034
Telephone: 302-658-5686
Telefax: 302-594-0612
URL: http://www.baileywetzel.com
Email: JBAILEY102@AOL.COM
URL: http://www.lawyers.com/baileywetzel

General Insurance Defense, Insurance Coverage, Corporate Law, Workers' Compensation, Professional Liability, Medical Malpractice, Social Security Disability, Product Liability, Personal Injury, Subrogation, Asbestos, Environmental and Toxic Substance Defense, Computer and Bankruptcy Law.

FIRM PROFILE: Firm founded in 1983. Lawyers bring a strong litigation background from both government and the private sector. Operations are conducted from our new four story building with private parking just 5 blocks from Court.

JAMES F. BAILEY, born 1950; admitted to bar, 1975, Delaware; 1976, U.S. District Court, District of Delaware. *Education:* Wake Forest University (B.A., 1972); Wake Forest Law School (J.D., 1975). Who's Who Among American Lawyers. *Member:* Delaware State (Member, Corporate Law Committee) and American Bar Associations; Delaware Claims Association; Delaware Trial Lawyers Association; Defense Research Institute; Association of Trial Lawyers of America. ***PRACTICE AREAS:*** Insurance Defense; Environmental Law; Toxic Tort; Insurance Coverage; Asbestos; Product Liability; Personal Injury. ***Email:*** jbailey102@aol.com

BENJAMIN C. WETZEL, III, born 1954; admitted to bar, 1979, Delaware and U.S. District Court, District of Delaware. *Education:* West Virginia University (B.A., cum laude, 1975); Villanova University (J.D., 1979). Member, Moot Court Board. *Member:* Delaware State and American Bar Associations; Delaware Trial Lawyers Association; The Association of Trial Lawyers of America; American Insurance Attorneys. ***PRACTICE AREAS:*** General Insurance Defense; Product Liability; Personal Injury; Subrogation.

(This Listing Continued)

CHRISTOPHER J. SIPE, born Ridgewood, New Jersey, April 14, 1970; admitted to bar, 1995, Delaware; 1996, U.S. District Court, District of Delaware; 1998, U.S. Court of Appeals, Third Circuit. *Education:* University of Delaware (B.A., summa cum laude, 1992); Widener University School of Law (J.D., 1995). Phi Beta Kappa. Phi Delta Phi. Member, Moot Court Honor Society, 1994-1995. Recipient: Friends of Widener University Scholarship; Harry S. Truman Scholarship, AmJur Constitutional Law Award. *Member:* Delaware and American Bar Associations; Delaware Trial Lawyers Association; Rodney In of Court; Saint Thomas More Society; The Federalist Society. **LANGUAGES:** Latin. **PRACTICE AREAS:** Insurance Defense; Plaintiffs' Personal Injury; Insurance Subrogation; Collections. **Email:** AXNJ66A@PRODIGY.COM

NATALIE M. IPPOLITO, admitted to bar, 1999, Delaware; 2000, U.S. District Court, District of Delaware. *Education:* Widener University (B.A., 1996; J.D., 1999). Vice Magister, Phi Delta Phi; Vice President, Sigma Sigma Sigma; National Order of Omega. Staff, The Delaware Journal of Corporate Law, 1998-1999. Law Clerk to The Honorable Susan C. Del Pesco, Superior Court of Delaware, 1999—; Extern to The Honorable Mary Pat Thynge, U.S. District Court, District of Delaware, 1998-1999. Law Clerk, Delaware Department of Justice, Office of the Attorney General, 1998. Volunteer, Delaware County Special Olympics, 1998—.

OF COUNSEL

ALAN T. BOYD, born Swedesboro, New Jersey, November 28, 1946; admitted to bar, 1973, District of Columbia; 1974, Delaware. *Education:* Bucknell University (B.S., 1968); Syracuse University (J.D., 1973). Associate Editor, Syracuse Law Review, 1972-1973. *Member:* Delaware State (Member, Insurance Committee, 1979—) and American Bar Associations; District of Columbia Bar; Delaware Trial Lawyers Association; The Association of Trial Lawyers of America. **PRACTICE AREAS:** Personal Injury.

REPRESENTATIVE CLIENTS: Aetna Casualty & Surety Co.; Aetna Life & Casualty Company; All Risk Claims Services, Inc.; AIG Insurance Companies; Allied Fidelity Insurance Co.; American Druggist's Insurance Co.; American Home Ins. Co.; American International Adjustment Co.; American Life Insurance Co.; American Universal Insurance Co.; Amica Mutual Insurance Co.; Bear, Stearns & Co.; Blue Hen Adjustment Co.; Central National Insurance Company of Omaha; Colonial Insurance Company of California; Continental Cos.; Continental Insurance Co.; County Insulation Co.; Cravens, Dargan & Co.; Crawford & Co.; Crum & Foster Management; Curley Adjustment Bureau; Del Monte Fresh Fruit Co.; Ennia Insurance Co.; Erie Insurance Co.; Fireman's Fund; Foremost Insurance Co.; Gallagher Bassett Insurance Adjusters; GEICO; Great Southwestern Insurance Co.; Harbor Insurance Co.; Hartford Insurance Co.; Highlands Insurance Co.; Home Indemnity Insurance Co.; Insurance Corporation of America; International Underwriters; The Kemper Group; Lexington Insurance Co.; Liberty Mutual Insurance Co.; Lloyds of London; London Guarantee & Accident Company of New York; Metropolitan Insurance Co.; Multiple Adjustment Bureau; National Freight Insurance Co.; National Grange Mutual Insurance Co.; National Union Fire Insurance Co.; New Castle County, Delaware; New Hampshire Group; New Jersey Manufacturers Insurance Co.; Old Dominion Freight Lines, Inc.; Pacific Reinsurance; Providers Network of America, Inc.; Prudential Insurance Co.; Reliance National Insurance Co.; Republic Wester Insurance Co.; Regis Insurance Co.; Reliance Insurance Co.; Republic Insurance Co.; Ron Coleman & Associates Adjustment Service; Schottenstein Stores; Sentry Mutual Insurance Co.; Toys-R-Us; The Travelers; Underwriters Reinsurance Co.; Wackenhut Co.; Waste Management; York Claims Service; Zurich American.

BALICK & BALICK

Established in 1957

SUITE 710 MELLON BANK CENTER
919 MARKET STREET
WILMINGTON, DELAWARE 19801
Telephone: 302-658-4265
Fax: 302-658-1682
Email: sbalick@balick.com
Email: abalick@balick.com

General Trial Practice with emphasis on Personal Injury, Workers' Compensation, Employment Law, Criminal Law, Commercial Litigation, Trials and Appeals.

SIDNEY BALICK, born Wilmington, Delaware, May 6, 1932; admitted to bar, 1956, Delaware; 1969, U.S. Supreme Court. *Education:* University of Delaware (A.B., 1953); Dickinson School of Law (J.D., 1956). Listed in Best Lawyers in America, 1999-2001. Attorney, State Senate, 1960-1966. Elected to State House of Representatives, 1970. Chairman, Professional Guidance Committee, 1975-1994. *Member:* American Bar Association; The Association of Trial Lawyers of America; Delaware Trial Lawyers Association; American Judicature Society (Member, Delaware Supreme Court Board on Professional Responsibility, 1986-1993); National Association of Criminal Defense Lawyers; American Board of Trial Advocates. Fellow, American College of Trial Lawyers. **REPORTED CASES:** Standard Distributing Co. Through Pennsylvania Mfrs. Assn. Ins. Co. v. Nally, 630 A.2d 640 (Del. Supr. 1993); Duvall v. Charles Connell Roofing 564 A.2d 1132 (Del. Supr. 1989); Berl, Matter of 560 A.2d

(This Listing Continued)

1009 (Del. Supr. 1989); Mooney v. Benson Management Co. 466 A.2d 1209 (Del. Supr. 1983); Keeler v. Harford Insurance Co. Del. Supr., 672 A.2d 1012 (1996). **PRACTICE AREAS:** Personal Injury; Medical Malpractice; Workers Compensation; Criminal Law; Employment Law. **Email:** sbalick@balick.com

ADAM BALICK, born Wilmington, Delaware, March, 30, 1963; admitted to bar, 1988, Pennsylvania; 1989, Delaware and U.S. District Court, District of Delaware. *Education:* University of Delaware (B.A.A.S., 1985); Dickinson School of Law (J.D. 1988). Member, Inns of Court, 1992-1994. Instructor: New Castle County Police Academy, 1990-1994; Delaware State Police, 1990-1994. Deputy Attorney General, 1989-1995. Judicial Law Clerk, Delaware Superior Court, 1988-1989. Chairman, Alcoholic Beverage Control Commission. *Member:* Delaware State and American Bar Associations; Delaware Trial Lawyers Association (Member, Board of Governors); National Association of Criminal Defense Lawyers. **PRACTICE AREAS:** White Collar Criminal Defense; Health Care; Commercial Litigation. **Email:** abalick@balick.com

REFERENCES: PNC Bank of Delaware; Mellon Bank.

THE BAYARD FIRM

222 DELAWARE AVENUE
SUITE 900
P.O. BOX 25130
WILMINGTON, DELAWARE 19899
Telephone: 302-655-5000
Telecopier: 302-658-6395
Email: bayardfirm.com
URL: http://www.bayardfirm.com

Dover, Delaware Office: 306 South State Street. Telephone: 302-678-8787.

General Practice which includes Administrative, Regulatory, Legislative and Government Law, Bankruptcy and Creditor's Rights, Civil Rights Litigation, Commercial and Residential Real Estate, Commercial Transactions and Litigation, Corporate Litigation, Delaware Corporation, Partnership, Limited Liability Company and Business Trust Law, Employee Benefits Planning, Employment Law and Litigation, Environmental Law, Estate Planning and Administration, Family Law, Health Care Law, Holding Companies, Intellectual Property Protection, Mergers and Acquisitions, Personal Injury, Products Liability, Taxation, Toxic Tort Litigation, Utility Regulation, White Collar Crime, Zoning, Condemnation and Land Use Planning.

FIRM PROFILE: The Bayard Firm is one of Delaware's premier law firms. The original members of the firm included former Delaware Supreme Court Chief Justice Daniel L. Herrmann, Associate Justice William Duffy and Alexis I. DuPont Bayard. The firm has a national practice in the areas of commercial bankruptcy, corporate litigation, corporate law and partnership, business trust and limited liability company law. The firm also offers a full service local practice in many other areas, including trial and appellate litigation in state and federal courts; real estate and land use; commercial transactions; intellectual property; federal and state taxation; employee benefits planning; estate planning; family law; employment law; insurance law; regulatory and administrative law; personal injury; products liability; toxic tort law and white collar crime. Attorneys at the firm are active in numerous professional, business, charitable and political activities.

The firm is the sole Delaware member of Commercial Law Affiliates, the largest association of national and international business law firms throughout the world.

The firm's subsidiary, The Delaware Corporation Agency, Inc., is a registered agent of the Office of the Secretary of State of Delaware, enabling the firm to provide a full range of services relating to new and existing Delaware entities. Another subsidiary, BHM Insurance Services, LLC, publishes regulatory information and other materials for lawyers, the insurance industry and municipalities in several states.

ALEXIS I. DUPONT BAYARD (1918-1985).
CONVERSE MURDOCH (1919-1985).
J. CALEB BOGGS (1909-1993).

PARTNERS

WILLIAM D. BAILEY, JR., born Newburgh, New York, December 12, 1935; admitted to bar, 1960, Delaware. *Education:* University of Notre Dame (A.B., 1956; J.D., 1959). Member, Gray's Inn. Member, Editorial Board, Notre Dame Lawyer, 1958-1959. Parliamentarian, Delaware State House of Representatives, 1965-1966. Special Rate Counsel, Delaware Public Service Commission, 1973-1983. Member: Delaware Supreme Court Rules Advisory Committee, 1978-1988; Appellate Handbook Committee, 1984—. Vice-Chairman, Governor's Public Utility Regulatory Task Force, 1993-1995. *Member:* The Association of the Bar of the City of New York; Delaware State (Chairman, Committees on: Continuing Legal Education, 1969-1971; Fee Dispute Resolu-

(This Listing Continued)

THE BAYARD FIRM, Wilmington—Continued

tion, 1984-1987; Member, Joint Committee on Medico-Legal Affairs, 1971-1992) and American Bar Associations. ***PRACTICE AREAS:*** Litigation; Public Utility Law; Administrative Hearings and Appeals; Eminent Domain; Condemnation Law. ***Email:*** wbailey@bayardfirm.com

VERNON R. PROCTOR, born Bryn Mawr, Pennsylvania, June 24, 1954; admitted to bar, 1979, Delaware. *Education:* Harvard College (A.B., 1976); Harvard Law School (J.D., 1979). Phi Beta Kappa. *Member:* Delaware State (Member, 1981— and Council, 1994—, Corporation Law Section) and American (Member, Section of Business Law, 1982—; Chair, Partnerships and Alternative Business Entities Subcommittee, Business and Corporate Litigation Committee, 1997—) Bar Associations. ***PRACTICE AREAS:*** Corporate and Commercial Litigation; Corporate Law; Partnership Law. ***Email:*** vproctor@bayardfirm.com

NEIL B. GLASSMAN, born Philadelphia, Pennsylvania, October 14, 1952; admitted to bar, 1982, Delaware. *Education:* Trinity College (B.A., 1974); University of Connecticut (M.B.A., 1978); Case Western Reserve University (J.D., 1981). Order of the Coif. Staff Member, Case Western Reserve Law Review, 1979-1980. Author: "Awarding Attorneys' Fees From Class Action Judgments," Case Western Reserve Law Review, Vol. 30, 1979. *Member:* Delaware State (Chairman, Commercial Law Section, 1987-1989; Member: Bankruptcy Section; Uniform Commercial Code Committee; Committee on Business Trusts) and American Bar Associations. ***PRACTICE AREAS:*** Commercial Law; Insolvency and Bankruptcy Law; Law of Corporations; Partnerships; Business Trusts; Limited Liability Companies. ***Email:*** nglassman@bayardfirm.com

BEVERLY J. WIK, born Arlington, Virginia, February 28, 1952; admitted to bar, 1981, Delaware. *Education:* University of Delaware (B.A., summa cum laude, 1974); Georgetown University (J.D., 1981; LL.M., Taxation, 1993). Phi Beta Kappa. Adjunct Professor, Widener University School of Law, 1986-1987. *Member:* Delaware State (Member and Chair, 1989-1990, Estates and Trusts Section; Member and Chair, Women and the Law, 1983-1984; Member, Sections on: Taxation; General Corporation Law) and American (Member, Sections on: Taxation; Real Property, Probate and Trust Law) Bar Associations. Fellow, American College of Trust and Estate Counsel. ***PRACTICE AREAS:*** Estate Planning; Trust Law; Local and Personal Property Taxation; Federal Income, Estate and Gift Taxation Law; Closely Held Businesses; Charitable Trusts and Foundations. ***Email:*** bwik@bayardfirm.com

EDMOND D. JOHNSON, born Boston, Massachusetts, December 12, 1941; admitted to bar, 1983, Delaware. *Education:* Harvard University (B.A., 1965); University of Florida (J.D., with high honors, 1983). Phi Kappa Phi; Order of the Coif. *Member:* Delaware State and American (Member, Sections on: Intellectual Property and Law Practice Management) Bar Associations. ***PRACTICE AREAS:*** Complex Commercial and Corporate Litigation; Class Action; Derivatives; Patent Matters. ***Email:*** ejohnson@bayardfirm.com

CHARLENE D. DAVIS, born Salem, New Jersey, July 18, 1946; admitted to bar, 1984, Delaware and U.S. District Court, District of Delaware; 1991, U.S. Court of Appeals, 3rd Circuit and U.S. Supreme Court. *Education:* Ohio Wesleyan University (B.A., cum laude, 1968); Delaware Law School (J.D., cum laude, 1984). Member: Phi Kappa Phi; Delaware Journal of Corporate Law. Recipient: American Jurisprudence Award, Contracts; First Annual Caleb R. Layton Service Award, U.S. District Court, Delaware, 1996. Author: "Responding to An Appeal and Voluntary Dismissal," Chapter 6, *Federal Practice Guide—Federal Appellate Procedure Third Circuit*, Lawyer's Cooperative Publishing, 1996. Assistant U.S. Attorney, 1984-1988. Member: Lawyers Advisory Committee, U.S. Court of Appeals, Third Circuit; Lawyers Advisory Committee and Blue Ribbon Panel, U.S. District Court, Delaware. *Member:* Delaware State, Federal (President, Delaware Chapter) and American Bar Associations; American Bankruptcy Institute; American Inns of Court. ***PRACTICE AREAS:*** Bankruptcy Law; Creditors Rights; Commercial Litigation; Business Crimes Law. ***Email:*** cdavis@bayardfirm.com

CURTIS P. BOUNDS, born Salisbury, Maryland, July 29, 1961; admitted to bar, 1990, Delaware; 1991, U.S. District Court, District of Delaware. *Education:* University of Dallas (B.A., 1983); Braniff Graduate School (1984); University of Virginia (J.D., 1990). Office of Postsecondary Education, U.S. Department of Education, 1985-1987. *Member:* Delaware State (Vice Chair, Family Law Section; Member, Labor and Employment Law Section) and American (Member: Family Law and Litigation Sections) Bar Associations. (Contact Attorney for Dover, Delaware Office). ***PRACTICE AREAS:*** Family Law; Employment Law; General Litigation. ***Email:*** cbounds@bayardfirm.com

MARLA HIRSHMAN NORTON, born Newark, New Jersey, March 24, 1962; admitted to bar, 1987, Delaware; 1989, U.S. District Court, District of Delaware; 1990, District of Columbia. *Education:* University of Delaware (B.A., 1984); George Washington University (J.D., with honors, 1987). Phi Delta Phi. Secretary, Marshall Inn, 1985-1986. Member, George Washington Journal of International Law and Economics, 1985-1987. *Member:* Delaware

(This Listing Continued)

State (Member, Commercial Law Section) and American Bar Associations. ***PRACTICE AREAS:*** Business Law; Commercial Law; Corporate Law; Trademark Law; Transactional Law. ***Email:*** mnorton@bayardfirm.com

MICHAEL L. VILD, born Cleveland, Ohio, February 21, 1964; admitted to bar, 1991, Delaware. *Education:* Ohio State University (B.Mus., summa cum laude, 1988); Brown University (1982-1984); Notre Dame (J.D., summa cum laude, 1991). Managing Editor, Notre Dame Law Review, 1990-1991. Law Clerk to the Honorable Walter K. Stapleton, U.S. Court of Appeals, Third Circuit, 1991-1992. *Member:* Delaware State and American Bar Associations. ***PRACTICE AREAS:*** Bankruptcy Law; Corporate Litigation; Commercial Litigation; Equine Law. ***Email:*** mvild@bayardfirm.com

KURT M. HEYMAN, born Chicago, Illinois, May 20, 1966; admitted to bar, 1992, Delaware and U.S. District Court, District of Delaware. *Education:* University of Michigan (A.B., with high distinction, 1988); University of Chicago (J.D., 1991). Phi Beta Kappa. Harry S. Truman Scholar. Law Clerk to The Honorable Jack B. Jacobs, Delaware Court of Chancery, 1991-1992. Author: "Expedited Proceedings in the Delaware Court of Chancery: Things of the Past?" 23 Del.J.Corp.L. 145 (1998). Co-Author: "The Disappearing Distinction Between Derivative and Direct Actions," 4 De.L.Rev. (2001). *Member:* Delaware State and American Bar Associations. ***LANGUAGES:*** Spanish. ***PRACTICE AREAS:*** Corporate Governance Litigation; Partnership and Limited Liability Company Litigation; Securities Litigation; Commercial Litigation; Class and Derivative Actions; Trade Secrets; Deceptive Trade Practices; Consumer Fraud. ***Email:*** kheyman@bayardfirm.com

JEFFREY M. SCHLERF, born Philadelphia, Pennsylvania, February 6, 1959; admitted to bar, 1992, Delaware, Pennsylvania and U.S. District Court, District of Delaware. *Education:* University of Pennsylvania (B.A., Economics, 1982); University of Delaware (M.A., Economics, 1983); William & Mary (J.D., 1991). Judicial Law Clerk, Superior Court, State of Delaware, 1991-1992. Member, Board of Editors, Delaware Lawyer. *Member:* Delaware State, Pennsylvania and American Bar Associations. ***PRACTICE AREAS:*** Bankruptcy; Commercial Transactions; Creditors Rights; Business Law; Administrative Law. ***Email:*** jschlerf@bayardfirm.com

DOUGLAS M. HERSHMAN, born Queens, New York, September 28, 1961; admitted to bar, 1987, New York; 1988, Delaware; 1995, Pennsylvania. *Education:* University of Delaware (B.A., 1983); Syracuse University (J.D., magna cum laude, 1986). Order of the Coif; Justinian Society. *Member:* Delaware State (Member, Real and Personal Property Law Section, 1988—; Chairman, 1998-2001), New York State and American Bar Associations; Home Builders Association of Delaware (Director, 1998—). ***PRACTICE AREAS:*** Real Estate; Zoning, Planning and Land Use; Leases and Leasing; Business Law; Mortgages; Alcoholic Beverages. ***Email:*** dhershman@bayardfirm.com

ASSOCIATES

RICHARD L. ABBOTT, born Wilmington, Delaware, March 17, 1964; admitted to bar, 1989, Delaware. *Education:* University of Delaware (B.A., 1986); The Dickinson School of Law (J.D., 1989). Deputy Attorney General, Delaware Department of Justice, 1989-1991. Special Counsel, Delaware Department of Transportation, 1991-1999. New Castle County Councilman, 3rd District. *Member:* Delaware State Bar Association. ***PRACTICE AREAS:*** Commercial Litigation; Real Estate Law. ***Email:*** rabbott@bayardfirm.com

DANIEL K. ASTIN, born Atlantic City, New Jersey, March 28, 1964; admitted to bar, 1989, Pennsylvania and New Jersey; 1996, Kentucky; 2001, Delaware. *Education:* Rutgers University (B.A., 1986); Rutgers University Law School (J.D., 1989). Phi Alpha Delta. Special Honors International Law. Member, Eastern District Pennsylvania Bankruptcy Conference, 1997—. Trial Attorney, U.S. Department of Justice, 1997-2001. [Lt. USNR, Judge Advocate General's Corps, 1989-1993]. ***PRACTICE AREAS:*** Bankruptcy Law; Creditors Rights; Commercial Litigation. ***Email:*** dastin@bayardfirm.com

FELICE GLENNON KERR, born Boston, Massachusetts, October 30, 1964; admitted to bar, 1989, Massachusetts; 1990, Delaware; 1991, U.S. District Court, District of Delaware. *Education:* Villanova University (B.A., 1986); Suffolk University (J.D., 1989). Phi Delta Phi. *Member:* Delaware State (Member, Sections on: Family Law, Chairman, 1999-2001; Women and Law; Gender Fairness, 1994-1996) and American (Member, Young Lawyers Division, Planning Committee on Women in the Law, 1995) Bar Associations; Delaware Mentor Program (Chair, Board of Directors, 1997-1999); Academy of Family Mediators; Lawyer's Fund For Client Protection of the Bar of Delaware (Trustee, 2001—). ***PRACTICE AREAS:*** Family Law; Personal Injury; Real Estate; Family Mediation; Juvenile Law. ***Email:*** fkerr@bayardfirm.com

FRANCIS J. SCHANNE, born Upper Darby, Pennsylvania, August 5, 1964; admitted to bar, 1989, Pennsylvania; 1990, Connecticut; 1994, Delaware. *Education:* University of Connecticut (B.S., 1986); Villanova University (J.D., 1989; LL.M., Taxation, 1996). *Member:* Delaware State (Member, Sections on: Taxation; Estates and Trusts), Pennsylvania (Member, Section on Taxation) and American (Member, Sections on: Taxation and Real Property; Probate and

(This Listing Continued)

Trust) Bar Associations. [U.S. Navy, Judge Advocate, Active Duty, 1990-1993]. ***PRACTICE AREAS:*** Estate Planning; Tax Planning; Commercial Law. ***Email:*** fschanne@bayardfirm.com

ASHLEY B. STITZER, born 1969; admitted to bar, 1996, Pennsylvania; 2000, Delaware and U.S. District Court, District of Delaware. *Education:* St. Mary's College of California (B.A., 1991); Temple University (J.D., 1996). *Member:* Delaware State and Pennsylvania Bar Associations. ***PRACTICE AREAS:*** Commercial Bankruptcy; Creditors Rights; Commercial Litigation. ***Email:*** astitzer@bayardfirm.com

STEVEN M. YODER, born Reading, Pennsylvania, June 30, 1967; admitted to bar, 1997, New Jersey; 1999, Delaware and U.S. District Court, District of Delaware; 2001, U.S.Court of Appeals, Third Circuit. *Education:* Miami (Ohio) University; Millersville University (B.S., magna cum laude, 1994); Temple University (J.D., 1997). President, Moot Court, 1996-1997. Judicial Law Clerk to the Honorable Thomas Twardowski, U.S. Bankruptcy Court, Eastern District of Pennsylvania. *Member:* Delaware State and American (Member, Business Law Section) Bar Associations; American Bankruptcy Institute; Delaware Board of Bar Examiners (Associate Member). ***PRACTICE AREAS:*** Corporate Bankruptcy and Restructuring; Creditors' Rights; Commercial Litigation. ***Email:*** syoder@bayardfirm.com

PATRICIA L. ENERIO, born Chestertown, Maryland, January 19, 1973; admitted to bar, 1998, Delaware; 1999, U.S. District Court, District of Delaware. *Education:* State University of New York at Stony Brook (B.A., 1995); Widener University (J.D., cum laude, 1998). Phi Kappa Phi. Law Clerk to the Honorable Leo E. Strine, Jr., Court of Chancery, 1998-1999. Co-Author: "The Disappearing Distinction Between Derivative and Direct Actions," 4 Del.L.Rev. (2001). *Member:* Delaware State and American Bar Associations. ***PRACTICE AREAS:*** Corporate Governance Litigation; Partnership and Limited Liability Company Litigation; Commercial Litigation and Class and Derivative Actions. ***Email:*** penerio@bayardfirm.com

CHRISTOPHER P. SIMON, born Birmingham, Michigan, August 7, 1970; admitted to bar, 1998, Delaware, U.S. District Court, District of Delaware and U.S. Court of Appeals, Third Circuit. *Education:* Washington and Lee University (B.A., 1992); Widener University School of Law (J.D., 1997). Member, Law Review Staff, Delaware Journal of Corporate Law. ***PRACTICE AREAS:*** Commercial Litigation; Bankruptcy Law. ***Email:*** csimon@bayardfirm.com

ELIO BATTISTA, JR., born Wilmington, Delaware, August 20, 1967; admitted to bar, 1999, Delaware. *Education:* Widener University (B.A., 1990; J.D., 1999). *Member:* Delaware State and American Bar Associations. [With U.S. Marine Corps, 1990-1995]. ***LANGUAGES:*** Italian, Spanish and Portuguese. ***PRACTICE AREAS:*** Bankruptcy; Creditors Rights; Commercial Litigation. ***Email:*** ebattista@bayard firm.com

JAMES TOBIA, born Newark, New Jersey, July 2, 1973; admitted to bar, 1999, Delaware. *Education:* Rutgers University, New Brunswick (B.A., 1995); Cornell Law School (J.D., 1998). Member, Cornell Journal of Law and Public Policy, 1996-1998. *Member:* Delaware State and American Bar Associations. ***PRACTICE AREAS:*** Commercial Litigation; Corporate Litigation. ***Email:*** jtobia@bayardfirm.com

CHRISTOPHER A. WARD, born Abington, Pennsylvania, July 18, 1973; admitted to bar, 1999, Delaware; 2000, U.S. District Court, District of Delaware. *Education:* Moravian College (B.A., 1995); Widener University School of Law (J.D., cum laude, 1999). Phi Delta Phi. President, Moot Court Honor Society. Law Clerk to the Honorable William L. Witham, Jr. *Member:* Delaware State and American Bar Associations. ***PRACTICE AREAS:*** Commercial Bankruptcy; Creditors Rights; Commercial Litigation. ***Email:*** cward@bayardfirm.com

ERIC M. SUTTY, born Silver Spring, Maryland, October 30, 1971; admitted to bar, 2000, Delaware. *Education:* College of William & Mary (B.B.A., 1994); University of Baltimore (J.D., cum laude; M.B.A., 2000). *Member:* Delaware State Bar Association. ***PRACTICE AREAS:*** Commercial Bankruptcy; Creditors Rights; Commercial Litigation. ***Email:*** esutty@bayardfirm.com

GEORGE J. DANNEMAN, admitted to bar, 2001, Pennsylvania (Not admitted in Delaware). *Education:* The George Washington University (B.A., 1996); Dickinson School of Law of the Pennsylvania State University (J.D., 2000). Member, Trial Moot Court Board. Articles Editor, Dickinson Journal of International Law. ***PRACTICE AREAS:*** Corporate Transactions; Real Estate Law. ***Email:*** gdanneman@bayardfirm.com

ANTHONY M. SACCULLO, born Queens, New York, August 20, 1976; admitted to bar, 2001, Delaware. *Education:* New York University (B.S., 1998); Fordham University (J.D., 2001). ***PRACTICE AREAS:*** Corporate Litigation; Bankruptcy. ***Email:*** asaccullo@bayardfirm.com

OF COUNSEL

RICHARD H. BAYARD, born Wilmington, Delaware, January 22, 1949; admitted to bar, 1979, Delaware and Pennsylvania. *Education:* University of North Carolina (B.A., 1970); Delaware Law School of Widener University (J.D., cum laude, 1978). Phi Kappa Phi. *Member:* Delaware State and American Bar Associations.

(This Listing Continued)

JOSEPH W. BENSON, P.A.

1701 NORTH MARKET STREET
P.O. BOX 248
WILMINGTON, DELAWARE 19802
Telephone: 302-656-8811
Fax: 302-656-4230

Criminal, Personal Injury, Family and Commercial Law.

FIRM PROFILE: Joseph W. Benson has been practicing law since 1968. He maintains a boutique practice, including three lawyers and a full legal support staff. Mr. Benson handles both criminal and civil litigation and is licensed to practice before all state and federal courts.

JOSEPH W. BENSON, born Wilmington, Delaware, June 17, 1942; admitted to bar, 1968, District of Columbia; 1969, Delaware; 1983, U.S. Tax Court. *Education:* Pennsylvania Military College (B.A., 1964); Catholic University of America (LL.B., 1967). *Member:* Delaware State (Member: Criminal Law Committee, 1982—; Domestic Relations, 1980—; Unauthorized Practice of Law, 1984—) and American Bar Associations; Delaware Trial Lawyers Association; The Association of Trial Lawyers of America. ***PRACTICE AREAS:*** Criminal Law; Personal Injury; Domestic Law.

ANDREW G. AHERN, III, born Bethlehem, Pennsylvania, April 6, 1949; admitted to bar, 1981, Delaware. *Education:* Saint Joseph's College; University of Delaware (B.A., magna cum laude, 1974); Delaware Law School of Widener University (J.D., 1981). Member, Moot Court Honor Society. Deputy Attorney General, State of Delaware, 1982-1983. *Member:* Delaware State (Board Member, Litigation Section, 1998—) and American Bar Associations; Delaware Trial Lawyers Association; The Association of Trial Lawyers of America; National and Delaware Association of Criminal Defense Lawyers. ***PRACTICE AREAS:*** Personal Injury; Criminal Defense; Business Law; General Litigation. ***Email:*** aahern@jwbpa.com

CARL W. HECKERT, born Wilmington, Delaware, August 12, 1964; admitted to bar, 1991, Pennsylvania; 1992, Delaware. *Education:* University of Delaware (B.S.B.A., 1986); Delaware Law School of Widener University (J.D., 1991). Instructor, Delaware Civil Clinic, Widener University, 1995. ***PRACTICE AREAS:*** Civil Litigation; Real Estate; Family Law; Estate Law; Business Law. ***Email:*** checkert@jwbpa.com

---

BIFFERATO, BIFFERATO & GENTILOTTI

BUCKNER BUILDING
1308 DELAWARE AVENUE
P.O. BOX 2165
WILMINGTON, DELAWARE 19899-2165
Telephone: 302-429-1900
Telecopier: 302-429-8600
URL: http://www.bbglaw.com

Commercial Bankruptcy, Personal Injury, Insurance Litigation, Commercial Transactions, Products Liability, Workers Compensation.

MEMBERS OF FIRM

VINCENT A. BIFFERATO, JR., born Wilmington, Delaware, April 9, 1961; admitted to bar, 1987, Delaware; 1988, U.S. District Court, District of Delaware. *Education:* Emory University (B.A., 1983); Villanova University School of Law (J.D., 1986). Attorney, Delaware State Senate, 135 General Assembly, 1989. *Member:* Delaware (Member, Sections on: Litigation; Tort and Insurance Practice) and American (Member, Section on Litigation) Bar Associations. ***PRACTICE AREAS:*** Personal Injury; Insurance Defense Law; Worker's Compensation Law. ***Email:*** vabjr@bbglaw.com

IAN CONNOR BIFFERATO, born Wilmington, Delaware, March 16, 1967; admitted to bar, 1994, Delaware; 1995, U.S. District Court, District of Delaware and U.S. Court of Appeals, Third Circuit. *Education:* University of Delaware (B.A., 1990); Widener University School of Law (J.D., 1994). Phi Delta Phi. *Member:* Delaware (Chairman, New Lawyers Section, 1998-1999) and American Bar Associations; American Bankruptcy Institute; Delaware Trial Lawyers Association. ***PRACTICE AREAS:*** Commercial Bankruptcy; Commercial Litigation; Insurance Litigation. ***Email:*** icb@bbglaw.com

JEFFREY M. GENTILOTTI, born Scranton, Pennsylvania, June 12, 1968; admitted to bar, 1995, Pennsylvania and Delaware. *Education:* Lehigh University (B.S., Economics, 1990); Widener University School of Law (J.D.,

(This Listing Continued)

BIFFERATO, BIFFERATO & GENTILOTTI, Wilmington—Continued

1994). *Member:* Delaware (Member, Sections on: Tort and Insurance Practices; Workers Compensation) and American Bar Associations; Delaware Trial Lawyers Association. ***PRACTICE AREAS:*** Insurance Defense; Personal Injury; Workers Compensation; Products Liability. ***Email:*** jmg@bbglaw.com

ASSOCIATE

MEGAN N. HARPER, born West Chester, Pennsylvania, January 26, 1969; admitted to bar, 1998, Pennsylvania (Not admitted in Delaware). *Education:* Boston University (B.S., Mass Communications, 1991); Widener University (J.D., 1997). Articles Editor, Widener Law Symposium Journal. *Member:* Pennsylvania Bar Association. ***PRACTICE AREAS:*** Bankruptcy; Insurance Defense; Personal Injury. ***Email:*** megan@bbglaw.com

GEORGE T. LEES, III, born Livingston, New Jersey, August 30, 1971; admitted to bar, 1997, Pennsylvania, New Jersey and Delaware. *Education:* University of Scranton (B.S., 1993); Widener University School of Law (J.D., 1997). ***PRACTICE AREAS:*** Toxic Torts; Premises Liability; Products Liability; Automobile Insurance Defense; Employment Law.

OF COUNSEL

VINCENT A. BIFFERATO, born June 12, 1937; admitted to bar, 1963, Delaware. *Education:* Villanova University (B.A., 1959; J.D., 1963). Member, State Public Defender's Staff, 1967. Chairman, Delaware Alcoholic Beverage Control Commission, 1967-1968. Appointed Associated Judge of the Delaware Superior Court by Governor Charles L. Terry, July, 1968. Reappointed Associate Judge of Delaware Superior Court by Governor Pierre S. Dupont, August, 1980. Appointed Resident Judge of the Delaware Superior Court by Governor Michael N. Castle, May, 1992. *Member:* Delaware State and American Bar Associations. ***Email:*** vab@bbglaw.com

BIGGS AND BATTAGLIA

1800 MELLON BANK CENTER
P.O. BOX 1489
WILMINGTON, DELAWARE 19899-1489
Telephone: 302-655-9677
Email: B-B@DOL.NET

General Practice. Trials. Negligence, Criminal, Insurance, Corporation, Tax, Probate, Real Estate, Products Liability and Family Law. Environmental Law.

MEMBERS OF FIRM

VICTOR F. BATTAGLIA, born Wilmington, Delaware, November 27, 1933; admitted to bar, 1958, District of Columbia; 1960, Delaware. *Education:* University of Delaware (B.S., 1955); Georgetown University (J.D., 1958; LL.M., 1959). Delta Theta Phi; Beta Beta Beta. Samuel Williston Fellow, Georgetown University, 1958-1959. Counsel, Governor's Committee to Revise the Penal Code, 1967-1972. Chairman, Board of Trustees, Delaware Technical and Community College, 1983-1993. Member, 1971— and Co-Chairman, 1978-1994, Long Range Courts Planning Committee. *Member:* Delaware State (President, 1979; Chairman, Professional Responsibility; Member, Health Law Section) and American Bar Associations; Delaware Bar Foundation (Chairman, Board of Directors, 1986-1991); American Judicature Society. Fellow: American Bar Foundation; American College of Trial Lawyers; American Board of Criminal Lawyers. ***PRACTICE AREAS:*** General Litigation; Civil and Criminal; Legal and Medical Malpractice and Discipline; Hospital Litigation; Estate Planning and Probate. ***Email:*** B-B@batlaw.com

ROBERT D. GOLDBERG, born Wilmington, Delaware, May 18, 1946; admitted to bar, 1974, Delaware. *Education:* University of Delaware (B.A., 1968); Boston College (J.D., 1974). First Assistant City Solicitor, 1977-1982 and City Solicitor, 1982-1985, Wilmington, Delaware. Regional Vice-President, National Institute of Municipal Law Officers, 1982-1985. *Member:* Delaware State and American Bar Associations. ***Email:*** GOLDBERG@batlaw.com

ROBERT K. BESTE, JR., born Wilmington, Delaware, June 11, 1950; admitted to bar, 1975, Delaware. *Education:* George Washington University (B.B.A., 1972; J.D., with honors, 1975). *Member:* Delaware State (Member: Family Law Committee, 1977-1992; Ethics Committee, 1980—; Tort and Insurance Practice Section, 1986—; Committee on Professional Guidance, 1995—) and American (Member: Section of Natural Resources Law, 1984—; Tort and Insurance Practice Section, 1989—) Bar Associations; Delaware Trial Lawyers Association. ***PRACTICE AREAS:*** General Civil Litigation; Estate Planning and Probate. ***Email:*** BESTE@batlaw.com

PHILIP B. BARTOSHESKY, born Wilmington, Delaware, March 8, 1955; admitted to bar, 1982, Delaware. *Education:* University of Notre Dame (B.S.,

(This Listing Continued)

1977); Rutgers University; Delaware Law School of Widener University (J.D., 1981). Member, Moot Court Honor Society. *Member:* Delaware State and American Bar Associations. ***Email:*** PBARTO@batlaw.com

VICTOR F. BATTAGLIA, JR., born Washington, D.C., November 1, 1958; admitted to bar, 1985, Pennsylvania; 1987, Delaware. *Education:* Syracuse University; University of Delaware (B.A., 1981); Delaware Law School of Widener University (J.D., 1985). *Member:* Pennsylvania and Delaware State Bar Associations. ***Email:*** B-B@batlaw.com

OF COUNSEL

JOHN BIGGS, III, born Philadelphia, Pennsylvania, May 19, 1927; admitted to bar, 1956, District of Columbia; 1957, Delaware. *Education:* Princeton University (A.B., 1951); Harvard University (LL.B., 1956). *Member:* Delaware State and American Bar Associations; American Law Institute. ***Email:*** B-B@batlaw.com

GERARD P. KAVANAUGH, SR., born Rochester, New York, 1916; admitted to bar, 1941, District of Columbia; 1944, U.S. Supreme Court; 1947, Delaware. *Education:* University of Toronto (A.B., 1938); Georgetown University (LL.B., 1941). *Member:* Delaware State (President, 1977-1978) and American (Member, Senior Lawyers Division) Bar Associations. ***Email:*** B-B@batlaw.com

S. BERNARD ABLEMAN, born Georgetown, Delaware, September 28, 1922; admitted to bar, 1970, Delaware and District of Columbia; 1981, U.S. Supreme Court. *Education:* University of Delaware (B.A., 1944); Princeton University; Temple University (J.D., 1970). Magistrate, Wilmington, Delaware, 1962-1966. *Member:* Delaware State (Member, Sections on: Corporation Law; Commercial Law; Litigation) and American (Member, Sections on: Corporation, Banking and Business Law; Litigation) Bar Associations; American Judicature Society. [1st Lieut., USA, active duty, Infantry and Signal Corps, 1943-1946; Signal Corps, 1950-1952]. ***PRACTICE AREAS:*** Corporate Law; Commercial Litigation. ***Email:*** B-B@batlaw.com

BLANK ROME COMISKY & McCAULEY LLP

CHASE MANHATTAN CENTRE
1201 MARKET STREET, SUITE 800
WILMINGTON, DELAWARE 19801
Telephone: 302-425-6400
FAX: 302-425-6464
Email: webmaster@blankrome.com
URL: http://www.blankrome.com

Media, Pennsylvania Office: Rose Tree Corporate Center, 1400 N. Providence Road, Building 1, Suite 301, 19063. Telephone: 610-891-7800. FAX: 610-891-7804.

Cherry Hill, New Jersey Office: Woodland Falls Corporate Park, 210 Lake Drive East, Suite 200, 08002-1164. Telephone: 856-779-3600. FAX: 856-779-7647.

Boca Raton, Florida Office: 1200 North Federal Highway, Suite 417, 33432. Telephone: 561-417-8100. FAX: 561-417-8101.

Allentown, Pennsylvania Office: 1620 Pond Road, Suite 200, 18104-2255. Telephone: 610-706-4300. FAX: 610-706-4343.

Philadelphia, Pennsylvania Office: One Logan Square, 19103-6998. Telephone: 215-569-5500. FAX: 215-569-5555.

Washington, D.C. Office: The Farragut Building, 900 17th Street, N.W., Suite 1000, 20006. Telephone: 202-530-7400. FAX: 202-463-6915.

Trenton, New Jersey Office: 200 West State Street, 08608. Telephone: 609-278-2320. FAX: 609-278-2323.

Baltimore, Maryland Office: 250 West Pratt Street, Suite 1100, 21201. Telephone: 410-659-1400. FAX: 410-659-1414.

New York, New York Office: The Chrysler Building, 405 Lexington Avenue, 10174. Telephone: 212-885-5000. FAX: 212-885-5001.

Cincinnati, Ohio Office: PNC Center, 201 East Fifth Street, Suite 1700, 45202. Telephone: 513-362-8700. Fax: 513-362-8787.

Administrative Law, Administrative Adjudications; Administrative Agency Practice, Administrative Hearings and Appeals, Administrative Litigation, Federal Administrative Law, Professional Licensing, Professional Licensing Regulation, Public Law, Admiralty and Maritime Law, Marine Law, Maritime Contracts, Maritime Finance, Maritime Law, Maritime Liens, Ship Sales and Mortgages, Aged and Aging, Age Discrimination, Elder Care, Elder Law, Agency and Distributorships, Distribution Agreements, International Distribution, Alcoholic Beverages, Liquor Licensing, Alternative Dispute Resolution, Arbitration, International Arbitration, International Dispute Resolution, Mediation, Antitrust and Trade Regulation, Antitrust, Business Combinations, Competition, Covenants Not To Compete, Deceptive Trade Practices, Noncompetition and Non-Solicitation Agreements, Price-Fixing, Restrictive Covenants, Trade Regulation, Unfair Trade, Appellate Practice, Civil Appeals, Art Law, Artists Rights, Museum Law, Asset Protection, International Asset Protection, Aviation and Aerospace, Aircraft Finance and Leasing, Aircraft Sales, Airline Labor Law, Aviation Law, Aviation Defense, Aviation Insurance, Aviation Litigation, Aviation Products Liability, Aviation Regulation, Bank-

(This Listing Continued)

ruptcy, Bankruptcy Arbitration, Bankruptcy Chapter 7, Bankruptcy Chapter 11, Bankruptcy Chapter 12, Bankruptcy Chapter 13, Bankruptcy Collections, Bankruptcy Litigation, Bankruptcy Mediation, Bankruptcy Reorganization, Bankruptcy Taxation, Bankruptcy Trustees Rights, Commercial Bankruptcy, Commercial Foreclosure, Commercial Insolvency, Commercial Recovery, Commercial Workouts, Foreclosures, Fraudulent Conveyance, Insolvency, International Bankruptcy, International Insolvency, Liquidations, Out of Court Debt Restructuring, Pre-Bankruptcy Workouts, Receiverships, Repossessions, Workouts, Workouts Taxation, Banks and Banking, ATM Networks, Bank Collections, Bank Directors and Officers Liability, Bank Foreclosures, Bank Mergers and Acquisitions, Banking Antitrust, Banking Law, Banking Litigation, Commercial Banking, Commercial Credit, Commercial Loans, Consumer Banking, Credit Card Law, Credit Finance, Credit Law, Electronic Banking, Fair Lending, Financial Law, Interest and Usury, International Banking Law, International Loans, Lender Law, Lender Liability, Lender Regulation, Lenders Rights, Letters of Credit, Loan Restructuring, Loan Workouts, Loans, Savings and Loan Law, Secured Lending, Truth in Lending, Biotechnology, Biomedical Technology, Biotechnology Licensing, Business Law, Business Arbitration, Business Associations Law, Business Crimes, Business Development, Business Dissolutions, Business Estate Planning, Business Formation, Business Fraud, Business Litigation, Business Mediation, Business Organization, Business Planning, Business Regulation, Business Reorganization, Business Sales, Business Succession Planning, Business Successions, Business Syndication, Business Taxation, Business Torts, Business Transactions, Business Transfers, Business Trusts, Business Valuation, Buying and Selling of Businesses, Capital Formation, Closely Held Business Estate Planning, Closely Held Business Law, Closely Held Business Taxation, Complex Business Litigation, Emerging Business Law, Emerging Growth Companies, Entrepreneurial Business Law, Family Business Law, Family Business Mediation, Family Business Successions, International Business Law, International Joint Ventures, Joint Ventures, Limited Liability Company Law, Privatization, Professional Practices, Small Business Law, Sole Proprietorships, Strategic Alliances, Chancery and Equity, Chancery Practice, Children, Child Custody, Child Support, Civil Practice, Federal Civil Practice, Sex Discrimination, Commercial Collections, Post Judgment Collections, Commercial Law, Commercial Litigation, Complex Commercial Litigation, Secured Transactions, Uniform Commercial Code, Commercial Real Estate, Commercial Real Estate Acquisitions, Commercial Real Estate Development, Commercial Real Estate Finance, Commercial Real Estate Foreclosure, Commercial Real Estate Sales, Commercial Real Estate Syndication, Commercial Real Estate Workouts, Industrial Real Estate Law, Shopping Center Acquisitions, Shopping Center Development, Shopping Center Law, Complex and Multi-District Litigation, Computers and Software, Computer Contracts, Computer Law, Computer Security, Computer Software Law, Computer Technology, Electronic Commerce, Information Technology, Information Technology Contracts, Information Technology Licensing, International Computer Law, Internet Law, Software Copyright, Software Licensing, Software Protection, Year 2000 Computer Conversion, Constitutional Law, First Amendment Law, Construction Law, Construction Finance, Construction Litigation, Construction Workouts, Environmental Construction Law, International Construction Law, Public Construction Law, Consumer Law, Consumer Arbitration, Consumer Class Actions, Consumer Credit, Consumer Credit Compliance, Consumer Finance, Consumer Fraud, Consumer Litigation, Consumer Protection, Consumer Rights, Fair Credit Reporting Act, Contracts, Breach of Contract, Commercial Contracts, Contract Fraud, Contract Litigation, International Commercial Contracts, International Contracts, Copyrights, Copyright Infringement, Copyright Litigation, Copyright Prosecution, Copyright Protection, Copyright Registration, International Copyright Law, Corporate Law, Closely Held Corporations, Corporate Banking Law, Corporate Commercial Law, Corporate Contracts, Corporate Control Contests, Corporate Criminal Law, Corporate Dissolutions, Corporate Ethics, Corporate Fiduciary Law, Corporate Finance, Corporate Formation, Corporate Governance, Corporate Income Tax, Corporate Insurance, Corporate Insurance Defense, Corporate Investigations, Corporate Litigation, Corporate Organization, Corporate Partnerships, Corporate Planning, Corporate Real Estate, Corporate Reorganization, Corporate Successions, Corporate Tax Controversies, Corporate Tax Planning, Corporate Taxation, Corporate Trusts, Corporate Workouts, Family Corporations, Foreign Sales Corporations, Hostile Takeovers, Incorporation, International Corporate Finance, International Corporate Law, International Corporate Taxation, Nonprofit Corporations, Offshore Corporations, Professional Corporations; Proxy Contests, Public Corporations, S Corporations, Securitization, Small Business Corporations, Takeovers, Tender Offers, Transfer Pricing, Criminal Law, Debtor and Creditor, Creditor Bankruptcy, Creditors Rights, Creditors Rights in Bankruptcy, Debtor and Creditor Bankruptcy, Debtor and Creditor Collections, Debtor and Creditor Remedies, Debtor and Creditor Reorganization, Debtor and Creditor Rights, Debtor and Creditor Workouts, Debtor Bankruptcy, International Creditors Rights, Secured Creditors Rights, Unsecured Creditors Rights, Disabilities, Americans with Disabilities Act, Academic Employment, College and University Law, Administrative Lobbying, Executive Lobbying, Legislative Lobbying, Lobbying, Eminent Domain, Employee Benefits, COBRA, Deferred Compensation, Employee Benefit Taxation, Employee Benefit Trusts, Employee Compensation, Employee Stock Ownership Plans, ERISA, Executive Compensation, Executive Compensation Taxation, Flexible Benefit Plans, Multi-Employer Benefits, Multi-Employer Pensions, Non-Qualified Benefits, Pension and Profit Sharing Plans, Pension Plans, Pension Taxation, Profit Sharing, Public Pension Plans, Qualified Retirement Plans, Retirement

(This Listing Continued)

Benefit Plans, Taft-Hartley Plans, Unemployment Compensation, Music Copyright, Environmental Law, Environmental Compliance, Environmental Liability, Environmental Litigation, Environmental Mediation, International Environmental Law, Equipment Finance and Leasing, Equipment Finance, Equipment Leasing, Vehicle Leasing, Family Law, Divorce, Matrimonial Law, Finance, Asset Based Finance, Financial Institution Reorganization, Financial Institutions Law, Financial Institutions Taxation, Financial Restructuring, International Commercial Finance, International Finance, Franchises and Franchising, Franchise Law, Franchise Licensing, Franchise Litigation, Franchise Taxation, International Franchising, General Practice, Federal Practice, Government, County Government Law, Federal Government Law, Government Affairs, Government Agency Practice, Government Relations, Legislative Practice, Local Government Law, Public Policy, Qui Tam Litigation, State Government Law, State Legislative Practice, Township Law, Government Contracts, Government Construction Contracts, Government Contract Arbitration, Government Contract Fraud, Government Procurement, International Government Contracts, Local Government Contracts, Public Bidding, Public Contract Law, Public Works Contracts, Guardianship and Conservatorship, Health Care, Alternative Health Care Delivery System, Certificates of Need, Health Care Administration, Health Care Contracts, Health Care Corporate Law, Health Care Facility Licensing, Health Care Facility Regulation, Health Care Finance, Health Care Fraud, Health Care Legislation, Health Care Licensing, Health Care Mergers and Acquisitions, Health Care Regulation, Health Care Reimbursement, Health Care Taxation, Health Insurance, Health Insurance Coverage, Health Insurance Defense, Health Insurance Trusts, Health Law, Health Maintenance Organizations, Integrated Health Care Delivery Systems, Long Term Care, Managed Care, Managed Care Contracts, Medical Antitrust, Mental Health Law, Nursing Home Regulation, Pharmacy Law, Physicians Contracts, Hospital Law, Hospital Administration, Medical Staff Contracts, Medical Staff Credentialing, Housing Law, Affordable Housing, Apartment Projects, Housing Finance, Insurance, Commercial Insurance, Insurance Company Taxation, Insurance Litigation, Insurance Defense, Intellectual Property, Artistic Property, Chemical Intellectual Property, Electrical Intellectual Property, Intellectual Property Infringement, Intellectual Property Licensing, Intellectual Property Litigation, International Intellectual Property, International Licensing, Mechanical Intellectual Property, Medical Intellectual Property, Pharmaceutical Intellectual Property, Piracy, Proprietary Rights, Taxation of Intellectual Property, International Law, International Trade, Antidumping, Countervailing Duties, Customs Law, Export Regulation, Import and Export Law, International Trade Regulation, Latin America Trade, Russia Trade, Investments, Financial Services Law, Financial Services Regulation, Foreign Investment, Foreign Investment in the United States, International Investment, Investment Banking Law, Investment Company Law, Investment Partnerships, Investment Regulation, Labor and Employment, Affirmative Action, Collective Bargaining, Employee Drug Testing, Employer Liability, Employment at Will, Employment Contracts, Employment Discrimination, Employment Litigation, Employment Mediation, Executive Employment Law, Executive Severance Contracts, Fair Labor Standards, Family and Medical Leave Act, Federal Employment Law, Harassment, International Employment Contracts, International Labor Law, Labor Arbitration, Management Labor Law, National Labor Relations Act, Personnel Policies, Public Sector Collective Bargaining, Public Sector Labor Relations, Sexual Harassment, Unfair Labor Practices, Union Contract Negotiations, Union Elections, Union Organization, Wage and Hour Law, WARN Act, Workplace Violence, Wrongful Termination Defense, Leases and Leasing, Commercial Leasing, International Leasing, Landlord and Tenant Law, Lease Finance, Leasing, Leveraged Leasing, Office Leasing, Retail Leasing, Shopping Center Leasing, Legal Ethics and Professional Responsibility, Legal Ethics, Litigation, Civil Litigation, Complex Litigation, Defense Litigation, Federal Civil Litigation, Federal Litigation, International Litigation, Long-Arm Litigation, Trial Practice, U.S. Supreme Court Litigation, Newspaper Contracts, Publishing Contracts, Medical Malpractice, Medicare and Medicaid, Medicaid Planning, Medicare and Medicaid Reimbursement, Medicare Fraud and Abuse, Mergers, Acquisitions and Divestitures, Business Acquisitions, Business Divestitures, International Mergers and Acquisitions, Leveraged Acquisitions, Leveraged Buyouts, Merger Reorganization, Mergers and Acquisitions, Mergers and Acquisitions Finance, Mortgages, Commercial Mortgages, Mortgage Banking Law, Mortgage Bankruptcy, Mortgage Finance, Mortgage Foreclosure, Mortgage Insurance, Mortgage Lien Foreclosure, Mortgage Refinancing, Mortgage Securitization, Mortgage Tax, Mortgage Workouts, Secondary Mortgage Market, Municipal Bonds, Municipal Bonds Taxation, Municipal Contracts, Municipal Corporation Law, Municipal Derivative Products, Municipal Finance, Municipal Labor Law, Municipal Leasing, Municipal Pension Law, Municipal Redevelopment, Municipal Securities, Municipal Taxation, Tax Increment Finance, Natural Resources, Nonprofit and Charitable Organizations, Charitable Limited Partnerships, Charitable Organizations Law, Charitable Trusts and Foundations, Nonprofit Organizations Law, Nonprofit Tax Law, Private Foundations, Tax Exempt Organizations, Occupational Safety and Health, OSHA, Partnership Law, Family Limited Partnerships, Family Partnerships, Limited Liability Partnerships, Limited Partnerships, Partnership Dissolution, Partnership Formation, Partnership Organization, Partnership Syndication, Partnership Taxation, Patents, Biochemical Patents, Biotechnology Patent Prosecution, Biotechnology Patents, Chemical Patent Prosecution, Chemical Patents, Computer and Software Patents, Design Patents, Electrical Patent Prosecution, Electrical Patents, Electronic Patents, International Patents, Mechanical Patent Prosecution, Mechanical Patents, Medical Patents, Metallurgi-

(This Listing Continued)

BLANK ROME COMISKY & McCAULEY LLP, Wilmington—Continued

cal Patents, Molecular Biology Patents, Patent Applications, Patent Infringement, Patent Interference Practice, Patent Licensing, Patent Litigation, Patent Prosecution, Patent Protection, Pharmaceutical Patents, Personal Injury, Premises Security, Probate, Ancillary Probate, International Probate, Probate Administration, Probate Litigation, Probate Taxation, Products Liability, Drug and Medical Device Defense, Firearms Products Liability, Professional Liability, Public Finance, Bond Finance, Economic Development, Housing and Urban Development, Industrial Development, International Economic Development, International Project Finance, Project Finance, Public Authority Finance, Public Finance Taxation, Public-Private Development, Tax Exempt Bonds, Tax Exempt Finance, Railway Labor Law, Real Estate, Condominium Association Law, Condominium Conversions, Condominium Development, Condominium Law, Conveyancing, Cooperative Association Law, Cooperative Conversions, Cooperative Housing Law, Easements, International Real Estate, Land Acquisitions, Land Sales, Land Trusts, Planned Unit Development Law, Real Estate Acquisitions, Real Estate Arbitration, Real Estate Banking Law, Real Estate Bankruptcy, Real Estate Brokers Licensing, Real Estate Contracts, Real Estate Development, Real Estate Finance, Real Estate Foreclosure, Real Estate Investment, Real Estate Investment Taxation, Real Estate Investment Trusts, Real Estate Joint Ventures, Real Estate Leasing, Real Estate Litigation, Real Estate Mediation, Real Estate Partnerships, Real Estate Restructuring, Real Estate Sales, Real Estate Secured Lending, Real Estate Securities, Real Estate Settlements, Real Estate Syndication, Real Estate Tax Appeals, Real Estate Tax Assessment, Real Estate Taxation, Real Estate Title, Real Estate Transfers, Real Estate Valuation, Real Estate Workouts, Real Property, Real Property Acquisitions, Real Property Development, Real Property Finance, Residential Real Estate, Residential Real Estate Development, Waterfront Development, Regulatory Law, Drug and Medical Device Regulation, Federal Regulatory Law, Regulated Industries, Regulatory Agency Practice, Regulatory Investigations, Religious Nonprofit Corporation Law, RICO, Securities, Bank Securities, Broker-Dealer Arbitration, Broker-Dealer Regulation, Initial Public Offerings, Private Placement, Private Placement Syndication, Public Offerings, SEC Enforcement, Securities Arbitration, Securities Litigation, Securities Offerings, Securities Registration, Securities Regulation, Shareholder Agreements, Shareholder Disputes, Tax Exempt Securities, Sports Contracts, Sports Licensing, Taxation, Employment Tax, Estate and Gift Taxation, Federal Income Tax, Federal Tax Controversies, Federal Taxation, Fiduciary Income Tax, Income Tax, Individual Taxation, International Tax Controversies, International Taxation, Like Kind Exchanges, Local Taxation, Low Income Housing Tax Credits, Property Tax Abatement, Property Tax Appeals, Sales and Use Tax, State Taxation, Tax Appeals, Tax Audits, Tax Collection, Tax Deferred Exchanges, Tax Planning, Tax Shelters, Trusts and Estates Taxation, Electronics, High Technology Contracts, Semiconductor Technology, Technology Contracts, Technology Licensing, Technology Protection, Technology Transfers, Torts, Trade Association Law, Toxic Torts, Trade Secrets, Theft of Trade Secrets, Trademarks, International Trademarks, Trade Dress, Trade Names, Trademark Arbitration, Trademark Infringement, Trademark Licensing, Trademark Litigation, Trademark Prosecution, Trademark Protection, Trademark Registration, Transportation, Common Carrier Law, Mass Transit Law, Public Transportation Law, Transit Labor, Trusts and Estates, Decedents Estates, Estate Administration, Estate Litigation, Estate Planning, Family Trusts, Family Weaith Transfer, Fiduciary Law, Fiduciary Liability, Fiduciary Litigation, Financial Planning, International Estate Planning, International Trusts, Living Trusts, Offshore Trusts, Personal Planning, Retirement Planning, Trust Administration, Trust Law, Trust Litigation, Trust Planning, Wealth Preservation, Unfair Competition, Utility Law, Utility Acquisitions, Utility Contracts, Utility Taxation, White Collar Crime, Embezzlement, White Collar Criminal Defense, White Collar Fraud, Wills, Contested Wills, Inheritance, Living Wills, Successions, Zoning, Planning and Land Use, Building and Public Safety Codes, Cemetery Law, Environmental Land Use, Fire Districts, Improvement Districts, Land Conservation, Land Development, Land Entitlement, Land Use, Land Use Litigation, Land Use Permitting, Land Use Regulation, Rezoning, Special Districts, Subdivisions, Water Districts, Zoning Law, Zoning Variances, Retail Industry Development.

FIRM PROFILE: Blank Rome Comisky & McCauley LLP is a full service law firm with regional, national and international practices. The Firm is organized into ten major departments - Business and Corporate, Financial Services, Government Relations, Intellectual Property, Labor and Employment, Litigation and Dispute Resolution, Matrimonial, Public Finance, Real Estate and Tax and Fiduciary Law.

The Firm represents both public and privately held businesses, as well as individuals and governmental entities. Its practice extends to virtually all sectors of the economy including: Agriculture; the Arts; Banking and Financial Institutions; Bankruptcy, Reorganizations and Workouts; Charitable Organizations; Communications; Developers and Construction Companies; Education; Entertainment; Health Care Providers; Hospitality; Insurance Agents and Brokers; Manufacturing; Printing and Publishing; Professionals and Professional Services; Telecommunications; Wholesale and Retail Operations; Service Companies; and Transportation Companies.

(This Listing Continued)

NEAL C. BELGAM, born Red Bank, New Jersey, December 1, 1963; admitted to bar, 1989, Delaware; 1990, U.S. District Court, District of Delaware; 1991, U.S. Court of Appeals, Third Circuit. *Education:* Albright College (B.A., 1986); Dickinson School of Law (J.D., 1989). Board Member, Delaware Superior Court Trial Practice Forum. Volunteer, Delaware Volunteers Legal Services. Liaison, Delaware State Bar Association Litigation Section to the District Court of Delaware Local Rules Committee for Most Recent Local Rules Revision, 1994-1995. *Member:* Delaware State (Chair, Litigation Section, 1997-1999), Federal (Vice Chair, Delaware Chapter) and American Bar Associations. ***PRACTICE AREAS:*** Litigation; Commercial Law; Corporate Law; Intellectual Property Litigation; Insurance Litigation. ***Email:*** belgam@blankrome.com

BENJAMIN J. BERGER, born Wilmington, Delaware, December 13, 1958; admitted to bar, 1984, Colorado; 1989, Delaware and Pennsylvania. *Education:* Boston University (B.A., magna cum laude, 1980); University of Denver College of Law (J.D., 1984). Intern, United States District Court, District of Colorado, Honorable John L. Kane, Jr., 1982-1983. Lecturer of Law, Real Estate Planning, University of Denver College of Law, 1987. *Member:* Philadelphia (Previous Member, Executive Committee, Real Property Section, 1995), Pennsylvania, Delaware State (Member, Real Estate and Commercial Law Sections) and American Bar Associations. ***PRACTICE AREAS:*** Real Estate Law; Commercial Law. ***Email:*** berger@blankrome.com

MICHAEL D. DEBAECKE, born Bristol, Pennsylvania, July 6, 1968; admitted to bar, 1993, Delaware; 1994, Pennsylvania. *Education:* Saint Joseph's University (B.S. in Criminal Justice, 1990); College of William & Mary (J.D., 1993). Law Clerk to Hon. Maurice A. Harnett, III and Hon. Myron T. Steele, Delaware Court of Chancery, 1993-1994. *Member:* Delaware State and American Bar Associations. ***PRACTICE AREAS:*** Bankruptcy; Chancery and Equity; Corporate Law; Commercial Litigation; Contracts; Business Law; Debtor and Creditor. ***Email:*** debaecke@blankrome.com

BONNIE GLANTZ FATELL, born Philadelphia, Pennsylvania, June 4, 1951; admitted to bar, 1981, Pennsylvania; 1996, Maryland and U.S. District Court, District of Maryland; 1999, Delaware. *Education:* Pennsylvania State University (B.S., 1973); Temple University (J.D., 1981). Author: "Debtors Beware: Strict Interpretation of Section 365(d)(4) Bodes Well For Landlords," ABI Business Reorganization Newsletter, 1996; "Effect of Bankruptcy on Equipment Leases," American Association for Equipment Lessors, 1988. Co-Author: "Checklist of Personal Liabilities of Corporate Fiduciaries on the Eve of Bankruptcy," Fourth Annual Business Lawyers' Institute, Pennsylvania Bar Institute, 1998; "The Chapter 11 Process: What Happens When the Company Files," JPBI, 1986. Chair Woman, Eastern District of Pennsylvania Bankruptcy Conference, 2000-2001. *Member:* Delaware State Bar Association; American Bankruptcy Institute. ***PRACTICE AREAS:*** Bankruptcy Reorganization; Bankruptcy Litigation; Out of Court Debt Restructuring; Secured Creditors Rights; Unsecured Creditors Rights. ***Email:*** fatell@blankrome.com

RICHARD K. HERRMANN, born Wilmington, Delaware, May 20, 1947; admitted to bar, 1971, Delaware; 1988, U.S. Court of Appeals, Third Circuit. *Education:* Syracuse University (B.S., 1969; J.D., cum laude, 1971). Order of the Coif. Member, Justinian Society. Survey Editor, Syracuse Law Review, 1970-1971. Author: "Millenium Lawyer," 2010 Edition; "Grimes v. Phycho Systems, Inc.," 2006; "Pinehust v. Time Travelers, Inc.," 2002; "The Effects of Technology on the Business of Law in the Beginning of the 21st Century," Advocate 2006; *Worldwide Lawnscape, Inc. v. U.S. Growers of America,* 2007; "The Blue Chair of the Twenty-First Century," Delaware Lawyer, 2002; *Dugan v. NextUp,* 1999; "Are You Master of Your Domain," PBA, March, 1998; "The Second Face of Toxic Tort Litigation: Claims for Insurance Coverage," Widener Law Symposium Journal, Fall, 1997; "Computer Basics for Lawyers, '96," DSBA; "Crossing the Virtual Line on the Internet," Delaware Lawyer, 1996; "Law Office of the 21st Century," 1992; The Delaware Book on Complex Insurance Coverage Litigation, 1990; "Lawyer's Guide to Office Computerization," 1989; "Transferring the Liability Risk to Others," ABA, 1987; "Who Should Control Litigation: A Matter of Teamwork," ABA, 1987; "Communicating with Expert Witnesses," Delaware Lawyer, 1987; "Products Liability: Commentary and Cases," Callaghan & Co.'s, 1986-1987; "Proper Care and Feeding of Your Forensic Engineer," Forensic Technologies International Corporation Publications, 1986; "The House of Cards Revisited, State Statutory Product Liability Law, a Game of Chance," ABA, 1985; "Application of Fair Settlement Acts to the Corporate and Self-Insured," ABA, 1985; "Finding the Expert: Pitfalls Associated with Locating, Interviewing and Retaining the Experts," ABA, 1984; "The Product Liability House of Cards," Risk Management Magazine, April, 1983; "An Overview of State Statutory," Trial Lawyers Guide, 1983; "Product Liability Law," Callaghan & Co., Vol. 27, No. 1, 1983; "The Ace of Spades, the Great Debate," ABA, 1983; "The House of Cards, State Statutory Product Liability Law, a Game of Chance," ABA, 1982. Editor: "The Internet Newsletter: Legal and Business Aspects," Leader Publications, 1996-1998; "Tips on Technology," In Re: DSBA; "Technology and The Law Newsletter," DSBA, 1992-1994. Co-Editor: "The Answer To: Complex Insurance Coverage Litigation in the State of Delaware," 1993. Lecturer: The Y2K Myth, American Arbitration Association, 1999; The Art of High Tech Trial Practice,

(This Listing Continued)

1999; Y2K and Your Law Practice, Delaware Trial Lawyers Association, 1999; Internet and the Law, Inns of Court, 1999; The New Strategies Conference, Delaware State Bar Association, 1999; Professionalism and the Internet, 1998; Electron Filing and the Courts, Inns of Court, 1998; Philadelphia Bar Association Conference, 1998; MABC Internet Symposium, 1998; Internet Legal and Business Aspects, 1997; Third Circuit Judicial Conference, 1997; Maryland Bar Association, 1997, Maryland Judicial Conference, 1997; Sussex Computer Tech Law, 1997; State of the Art, 1996; Computer Basics for Lawyers, 1996; Internet Legal and Business Aspects, 1996; Effect of Trial Technology of Appellate Evidentiary Issues, Maryland Court of Appeals Rules Committee, 1993; The Council of Chief Judges, 14th Annual Seminar, ABA, 1993; Technology and the Practice of Law, DSBA, 1992; Computer Assisted Jury Information System (CAJIS), U.S. District Court, 1992; Demonstrative Evidence, DSBA, 1988; Transferring Liability Risks to Others, ABA, 1987; The Lawyer and the Expert, ABA, 1987; Computers and Evidence, Defense Research Institute, 1986; Computers and Evidence, Delaware Trial Lawyers Association, 1986; Products Liability Trial Demonstration, Risk and Insurance Management Society (RIMS), 1985; Use of Experts, DSBA, 1984. Editor, Delaware State Bar Association Magazine. Adjunct Professor, William and Mary Law School. Chair: Technology and Information Services Committee, Delaware State Chamber of Commerce, 1995-1999; American Arbitration Association Year 2000 Task Force; Judicial Electronic Data Interchange Consortium; Supreme Court Delaware Technology Coordinating Committee; Delaware Superior Court Advisory Committee on Complex Litigation Rules. MCLE Commission. Senior Legal Technology Advisor, Courtroom 21 Project, William and Mary Law School. *Member:* Delaware State (Chair, Computer Law Section, 1993-1999) and American (Chair, Products, General Liability and Consumer Law Committee, Torts and Insurance Practice Section, 1987-1988) Bar Associations. ***PRACTICE AREAS:*** Internet Law; Technology Contracts; Trade Secrets; Technology Law; Commercial Litigation; Computers and Software; Intellectual Property. ***Email:*** herrmann@blankrome.com

ALAN J. HOFFMAN, born Philadelphia, Pennsylvania, August 31, 1948; admitted to bar, 1973, Pennsylvania; 1977, Delaware; 1990, District of Columbia. *Education:* Temple University (B.B.A., 1970); Villanova University (J.D., 1973). Associate Editor, Villanova Law Review. Author: "MTBE Litigation Unlikely to Include Rule 23(b)(3) Classes, BNA, Inc., Class Action Litigation," BNA's *Class Action Reporter,* Volume 1, No. 5, June 23, 2000 and BNA's *Toxic Law Reporter,* Volume 15, No. 26, July 6, 2000; Casenote, "Kastigar v. United States," 17 Vill. L. Rev. 559, (1972) (constitutionality, use immunity); Comment, "Practical Analysis of the Pennsylvania Rent Withholding Act," 17 Vill. L. Rev. 821 (1972) (empirical study of the Act). Supervising Assistant United States Attorney, District of Delaware, 1973-1978. Lecturer, Evidence Law, Widener Delaware Law School, 1973-1974. Recipient, United States Department of Justice Special Commendation Award for Outstanding Service, 1976. Instructor: Certified Public Accountant Continuing Professional Education Course, 1991-1993; MTBE's Application to Mass Tort Litigation, Class Actions and Alternative Dispute Resolution, Mealeys Toxic Tort Litigation Conference, November, 1999, Manufacturer and Supplier Liability for MTBE Contamination, Mealeys Conference, May, 2000. Member, J. Willard O'Brien Villanova Inn of Court (President, 2000—). *Member:* Delaware State and Federal (Member, Special Committee on Federal Sentencing Guidelines) Bar Associations; Delaware Trial Lawyers Association; Philadelphia Trial Lawyers Association. (Also at Philadelphia, Pennsylvania Office). ***PRACTICE AREAS:*** Trial Practice; Federal Litigation; Civil Litigation; Environmental Litigation; Litigation; Appellate Practice; Complex Business Litigation; Commercial Law; Complex Commercial Litigation; Complex and Multi District Litigation; Corporate Criminal Law; Corporate Litigation; Intellectual Property; Securities. ***Email:*** hoffman@blankrome.com

MARY B. MATTERER, born Wilmington, Delaware, January 23, 1947; admitted to bar, 1988, Delaware; 1997, U.S. District Court, District of Delaware; U.S. Court of Appeals, Third Circuit. *Education:* University of Delaware (B.A., 1971); Ohio University (M.A., 1979); Delaware Law School of Widener University (J.D., cum laude, 1988). Phi Kappa Alpha. Member, Delaware Journal of Corporate Law, 1986-1988. Law Clerk to Honorable John E. Babiarz, Jr., Delaware Superior Court, 1988-1989. *Member:* Delaware State and American Bar Associations. ***PRACTICE AREAS:*** Intellectual Property Litigation; Insurance Coverage Defense; Complex Litigation; Products Liability Defense. ***Email:*** matterer@blankrome.com

MARK J. PACKEL, born Philadelphia, Pennsylvania, April 24, 1958; admitted to bar, 1983, Pennsylvania; 2001, Delaware. *Education:* Dickinson College (B.A., 1980); Temple University (J.D., 1983). *Member:* Delaware State, Pennsylvania and American Bar Associations. ***PRACTICE AREAS:*** Bankruptcy Reorganization. ***Email:*** packel@blankrome.com

JULIAN P. RACKOW, born Philadelphia, Pennsylvania, December 16, 1941; admitted to bar, 1966, Pennsylvania (Not admitted in Delaware). *Education:* Cornell University (A.B., 1963); Harvard University (J.D., 1966). President, Central Philadelphia Development Corporation, 1996—. Pennsylvania Co-Chair, Government Relations Committee, International Council of Shopping Centers. Fellow, American College of Real Estate Lawyers. (Also at Philadelphia, Pennsylvania Office). ***PRACTICE AREAS:*** Retail Development; Commercial Real Estate Development; Commercial Real Estate Finance; Shopping Center Development; Public-Private Development; Real Estate Syndication; Hotel and Resort Development; Commercial Real Estate. ***Email:*** rackow@blankrome.com

CATHY L. REESE, born Southampton, New York, July 14, 1960; admitted to bar, 1989, Massachusetts; 1990, Delaware; U.S. District Court, District of Delaware and U.S. Court of Appeals, Third Circuit. *Education:* Columbia University (B.S., magna cum laude, 1982); George Washington University (J.D., with honors, 1989). Trustee Scholar. Associate Editor, Journal of International Law and Economics. Author: "The Right Stuff, In Some States Even Shareholders Can Inspect Corporate Books," Barron's, July 31, 1995; "Shareholder Probing of Corporate Misdeeds," Pensions and Investments, October 27, 1997; "Little Known Tool Helps Investors Shed Light on Corporate Dealings," Investors Business Daily, June 14, 1995. Law Clerk to the Honorable Philip Nichols, U.S. Court of Appeals, Federal Circuit, 1989. Appointed Special Deputy Attorney General, State of Delaware, 1992-1995. Moderator, "The Do's and Don'ts of Discovery," 1998. Guest, CNBC's Money Talk regarding Shareholder Litigation, September, 1995. ***PRACTICE AREAS:*** Corporate Litigation; Securities Litigation; Commercial Litigation; Technology Litigation. ***Email:*** reese@blankrome.com

LAWRENCE R. WISEMAN, born Hastings, Nebraska, January 25, 1952; admitted to bar, 1978, Delaware; 1979, Pennsylvania. *Education:* University of Nebraska (B.S., with distinction, 1974; J.D., with distinction, 1977). *Member:* Pennsylvania and Delaware State Bar Associations. (Also at Philadelphia, Pennsylvania Office). ***PRACTICE AREAS:*** Securities; Business Law; Contracts; Corporate Law; Mergers, Acquisitions and Divestitures; Regulatory Law; Investments. ***Email:*** wiseman@blankrome.com

OF COUNSEL

J. CALEB BOGGS III, born Washington, D.C., August 3, 1962; admitted to bar, 1987, Delaware; 1992, U.S. Supreme Court; 1997, District of Columbia. *Education:* University of Richmond (B.A., 1984); Catholic University of America (J.D., 1987); Georgetown University (M.B.A., 1996). Judicial Clerkship, Delaware Court of Chancery, 1987-1988. Legislative Counsel, U.S. Senate Governmental Affairs Committee, 1991-1995. *Member:* The District of Columbia Bar; Delaware State Bar Association; Federalist Society for Law and Public Policy; Republican National Lawyers Association. (Also at Washington, D.C. and Philadelphia, Pennsylvania Offices). ***PRACTICE AREAS:*** Government Relations; Legislative Practice. ***Email:*** boggs@blankrome.com

JULIANNE E. HAMMOND, born Anderson, South Carolina, October 12, 1949; admitted to bar, 1975, Delaware and U.S. District Court, District of Delaware. *Education:* University of Delaware (B.A. with honors in Political Science and History, Phi Kappa Phi, 1971); Dickinson School of Law (J.D., 1975). Member, Moot Court Board, 1973-1975. Counsel to New Castle County (Delaware) Council, 1991-1994. Assistant City Solicitor, City of Wilmington, 1978-1983. *Member:* Delaware State Bar Association (Real Property Committee). ***PRACTICE AREAS:*** Bankruptcy; Real Estate; Commercial Real Estate; State, County and Municipal Government Law; Government; Real Estate Tax Assessment; Zoning, Planning and Land Use. ***Email:*** hammond@blankrome.com

ASSOCIATES

A. KIMBERLY ROCKWELL BROSSEIT, born Atlanta, Georgia, March 22, 1968; admitted to bar, 1996, Florida; 1998, Delaware and District of Columbia. *Education:* Bryn Mawr College (B.A., 1990); Florida State University College of Law (J.D., with high honors, 1996). Certified Instructor, New Castle County Board of Realtors, 2000. Author: "Courts Clouding Equitable Estoppel," Tri-State Real Estate Journal, August 31, 2000; "The Fifth Amendment Implications of Including Habitat Modification in the Definition of Harm to Endangered Species (*Babbitt v. Sweet Home Chapter of Communities for a Great Oregon,* 115 S.Ct. 2407, (1995))," 11 Journal of Land Use and Environmental Law 273 (Summer 1996). Member, Board of Directors, Prevent Child Abuse, Delaware. ***PRACTICE AREAS:*** Zoning, Planning and Land Use; Real Estate; Corporate Law; Environmental Law. ***Email:*** brosseit@blankrome.com

WILLIAM J. BURNETT, born New Haven, Connecticut, September 25, 1969; admitted to bar, 1995, Pennsylvania and New Jersey (Not admitted in Delaware). *Education:* University of Connecticut (B.A., 1991); Temple University (J.D., cum laude, 1995). Member, Temple Moot Court Honor Society. Articles Editor, Temple Political and Civil Rights Law Review. ***PRACTICE AREAS:*** Bankruptcy; Bankruptcy Chapter 11; Bankruptcy Reorganization; Bankruptcy Chapter 7; Bankruptcy Litigation; Debtor and Creditor Collections; Debtor and Creditor Workouts; Bankruptcy Trustees Rights; Commercial Recovery; Creditors Rights. ***Email:*** burnett@blankrome.com

STEVEN L. CAPONI, born Haverford, Pennsylvania, July 2, 1968; admitted to bar, 1996, Delaware. *Education:* Temple University (B.A., 1992); Widener University School of Law (J.D., cum laude, 1996). Phi Kappa Phi. Editor, Delaware Journal of Corporate Law, 1994-1996. Law Clerk to the Honorable

(This Listing Continued)

BLANK ROME COMISKY & McCAULEY LLP, Wilmington—Continued

Joseph T. Walsh, Delaware Supreme Court, 1996-1997. *Member:* Delaware State and American (Member, Business Law Section) Bar Associations. ***PRACTICE AREAS:*** Corporate Governance; Corporate Litigation; Complex Litigation; Intellectual Property. ***Email:*** caponi@blankrome.com

DALE R. DUBÉ, born Leominster, Massachusetts, October 11, 1950; admitted to bar, 1990, Delaware; 1992, New Jersey; U.S. Court of Appeals, Third Circuit; U.S. Supreme Court. *Education:* St. Peter's College (B.S., summa cum laude, 1987); Widener University (J.D., cum laude, 1990). Phi Kappa Phi. Managing Editor, Law Review, The Delaware Journal of Corporate Law. *Member:* Delaware State (Member, Delaware Board of Bar Examiners), New Jersey State, Federal and American Bar Associations. ***PRACTICE AREAS:*** Intellectual Property Litigation; Employment Law; Employment Litigation; Commercial Litigation; Corporate Litigation; Creditors Rights. ***Email:*** dube@blankrome.com

ANDREA J. FARAONE, born Wilmington, Delaware, May 18, 1972; admitted to bar, 1999, Delaware; 2000, Pennsylvania and U.S. District Court, District of Delaware. *Education:* University of Delaware (B.A., magna cum laude, 1994); Pennsylvania State University (J.D., cum laude, 1999). Phi Beta Kappa. Comments Editor, Dickinson Journal of International Law, 1998-1999. Law Clerk, Superior Court of Delaware, 1999-2000. Author: "The Florida Equal Rights Amendment - Raising the Standard Applied to Gender Under the Equal Protection Clause of the Florida Constitution," Florida Coastal Law Journal, March, 2000. *Member:* Delaware and Pennsylvania Bar Associations. ***LANGUAGES:*** Italian. ***PRACTICE AREAS:*** Civil Litigation. ***Email:*** faraone@blankrome.com

DEBORAH CIRILLA SELLIS, born Rochester, New York, May 6, 1973; admitted to bar, 1998, Pennsylvania and New Jersey; 1999, Delaware, U.S. District Court, District of Delaware and U.S. District Court, Eastern District of Pennsylvania. *Education:* Villanova University (B.A., cum laude, 1994; J.D., 1998). Associate Editor, 1996-1997 and Managing Editor, 1997-1998, Villanova Law Review. Author: Villanova Law Review 42:1. *Member:* Delaware, Pennsylvania, New Jersey State and American Bar Associations. ***PRACTICE AREAS:*** Bankruptcy; Bankruptcy Litigation; Financial Services Law; Civil Litigation; Commercial Litigation; Defense Litigation; Insurance. ***Email:*** sellis@blankrome.com

ELIZABETH A. WILBURN, born Albemarle, North Carolina, March 18, 1970; admitted to bar, 1997, Delaware, New Jersey and U.S. District Court, District of New Jersey; 1998, U.S. District Court, District of Delaware. *Education:* Villanova University (B.A., cum laude, 1992); Widener University, School of Law (J.D., 1996). Editor, Delaware Journal of Corporate Law, 1995-1996. Judicial Clerk to the Hon. William C. Carpenter, Jr. Superior Court of Delaware, 1996-1998. *Member:* Delaware State (Member, Corporation Law and Women and the Law Sections; Member, Committee on Professional Ethics) and American (Member: Business Law Section; Litigation) Bar Associations. ***PRACTICE AREAS:*** Corporate Litigation; Commercial Litigation. ***Email:*** wilburn@blankrome.com

BOUCHARD MARGULES & FRIEDLANDER, P.A.

222 DELAWARE AVENUE, SUITE 1102
WILMINGTON, DELAWARE 19801
Telephone: 302-573-3500
Telecopier: 302-573-3501

Corporate and Commercial Litigation.

FIRM PROFILE: The firm concentrates its practice in the areas of commercial and corporate litigation, including stockholder class and derivative actions, partnership disputes and federal securities litigation. The firm also advises clients on Delaware corporate law and governance, performs internal investigations and serves as local counsel in bankruptcy proceedings and intellectual property disputes.

ANDRE G. BOUCHARD, born Joliette, Quebec, 1961; admitted to bar, 1986, Delaware. *Education:* Boston College (A.B., summa cum laude, 1983); Harvard Law School (J.D., 1986). Phi Beta Kappa. Truman Scholar, 1981. Member, Delaware Board of Bar Examiners. Member, Delaware Criminal Justice Council. Member, Delaware Sentencing Accountability Commission. Working Group Member, National Study and Action Plan Regarding Lawyer Conduct and Professionalism, 1997-1999. Chairman, Delaware State Human Relations Commission, 1994-1998. Member, Executive Committee, Delaware State Bar Association, 1997-1998. Recorder, Commission on Delaware Courts 2000, 1993-1994. Associate, Skadden, Arps, Slate, Meagher & Flom, 1986-1996. *Member:* Delaware State and American Bar Associations. ***PRACTICE AREAS:*** Corporate Litigation; Business Litigation; Intellectual Property Litigation. ***Email:*** abouchard@bmf-law.com

(This Listing Continued)

DAVID J. MARGULES, born Newark, New Jersey, 1956; admitted to bar, 1983, Delaware; 1984, U.S. District Court, District of Delaware and U.S. Court of Appeals, Third Circuit. *Education:* Columbia University (B.A., 1978); New York University (J.D., cum laude, 1983). Order of the Coif. Member, New York University Law Review, 1982-1983. Lecturer, Mergers and Acquisitions, University of Pennsylvania, 1995-2001. Commissioner, Delaware Judicial Nominating Commission, 1997-2001. *Member:* Delaware and American Bar Associations. ***PRACTICE AREAS:*** Corporate Litigation; Bankruptcy Litigation. ***Email:*** dmargules@bmf-law.com

JOEL FRIEDLANDER, born Stamford, Connecticut, 1966; admitted to bar, 1993, Delaware and Pennsylvania. *Education:* University of Pennsylvania (B.S., cum laude, 1988; J.D., 1992). Executive Editor, University of Pennsylvania Law Review, 1991-1992. Law Clerk to Vice Chancellor Jack B. Jacobs, Delaware Court of Chancery, 1992-1993. Author: "Corporation and Kulturkampf: Time Culture as Illegal Fiction," 29 U. Conn. L. Rev. 31 (1996); "Constitution and Kulturkampf: A Reading of the Shadow Theology of Justice Brennan," 140 U. Pa. L. Rev. 1049 (1992). Adjunct Professor of Equity, Widener University School of Law, 1998. Associate, Skadden, Arps, Slate, Meagher & Flom, 1993-1995. President, Delaware Chapter, Lawyers Division, Federalist Society for Law & Public Policy Studies, 1994-1999. Assistant to the President, Delaware State Bar Association, 1998-1999. Associate Member, Delaware Board of Bar Examiners, 1998—, Editorial Board, Delaware Lawyer, 1998—. ***PRACTICE AREAS:*** Corporate Litigation; Business Litigation. ***Email:*** jefdelaw@aol.com; jfriedlander@bmf-law.com

JOANNE PILEGGI PINCKNEY, born Upland, Pennsylvania, 1958; admitted to bar, 1994, Pennsylvania and New Jersey; 1995, Delaware and U.S. District Court, District of Delaware. *Education:* Newmann College (B.S., cum laude, 1981); Widener University School of Law (J.D., cum laude, 1993). Associate, Wolf, Block, Schorr and Solis-Cohen LLP, 1995-1999. *Member:* Delaware, Pennsylvania and American Bar Associations. ***PRACTICE AREAS:*** Corporate Litigation; Business Litigation; Bankruptcy Litigation. ***Email:*** jpinckney@bmf-law.com

KAREN L. PASCALE, born Philadelphia, Pennsylvania, 1960; admitted to bar, 1990, Delaware and U.S. District Court, District of Delaware; 1996, U.S. Court of Appeals, Third Circuit. *Education:* University of Delaware (B.S., cum laude, 1984); Villanova University (J.D., cum laude, 1990). Phi Kappa Phi. Order of the Coif. Member, 1988-1989, and Articles Editor, 1989-1990, Villanova Law Review. Author: "Pending Petition for Agency Reconsideration Bars Appellate Court Jurisdiction: West Penn Power Co. v. EPA," 34 Vill.L.Rev. 517 (1989). Associate, Morris, Nichols, Arsht & Tunnell, 1990-1998. Member, 1992— and Chair, 2000—, Editorial Board, Delaware Lawyer. *Member:* Delaware and American Bar Associations. ***PRACTICE AREAS:*** Business Litigation; Corporate Litigation; Intellectual Property. ***Email:*** kpascale@bmf-law.com

BUCHANAN INGERSOLL

PROFESSIONAL CORPORATION

Established in 1850

1201 NORTH MARKET STREET, SUITE 1501
WILMINGTON, DELAWARE 19801
Telephone: 302-428-5500
Fax: 302-428-3996

Pittsburgh, Pennsylvania Office: One Oxford Centre, 301 Grant Street, 20th Floor. Telephone: 412-562-8800. Telecopier: 412-562-1041. URL: http://www.bipc.com.

Philadelphia, Pennsylvania Office: Eleven Penn Center, 14th Floor, 1835 Market Street. Telephone: 215-665-8700.

Bryn Mawr, Pennsylvania Office: 937 East Haverford Road, Suite 201. Telephone: 610-581-7004.

Harrisburg, Pennsylvania Office: One South Market Square, 213 Market Street, 3rd Floor. Telephone: 717-237-4800.

Tampa, Florida Office: SunTrust Financial Centre, 401 East Jackson Street, Suite 2500. Telephone: 813-222-8180.

Aventura, Florida Office: One Turnberry Place, 19495 Biscayne Boulevard, Suite 606. Telephone: 305-933-5600.

Miami, Florida Office: Bank of America Tower, 100 S.E. Second Street, Suite 2100. Telephone: 305-347-4080.

Princeton, New Jersey Office: 700 Alexander Park, Suite 300. Telephone: 609-987-6800.

Buffalo, New York Office: 268 Main Street, Suite 201. Telephone: 716-853-2330.

Washington, D.C. Office: 1776 K Street, N.W., Suite 800. Telephone: 202-452-7900.

(This Listing Continued)

Other Washington, D.C. Office: Silverstein and Mullens, 1776 K Street, N.W., Suite 800. Telephone: 202-452-7900.
New York, New York Office: 140 Broadway, 35th Floor. Telephone: 646-458-2340.
McLean, Virginia Office: 8280 Greensboro Drive, Suite 601. Telephone: 703-749-6060.
San Diego, California Office: First National Bank Center, 401 West A Street, Suite 1900. Telephone: 619-578-5000.
London, England Office: Tower 42, The International Financial Centre, Old Broad Street, EC2N 1HQ. Telephone: 44-207-920-3700.
Dublin, Ireland Office: Level 1, 4 Custom House Plaza, IFSC, Dublin 1. Telephone: 011-353-1611-7266. Fax: 3531-836-9305.

Antitrust and Trade Regulation, Broadcasting and Cable TV, Commercial Transactions, Computer Law, Construction Industry Law, Corporate Law and Finance, Creditors' Rights and Bankruptcy, Energy, Environmental Law, ERISA and Employee Benefits, Family Law, Financial Institutions, Franchising, Government Relations, Healthcare, Insurance Regulation, Intellectual Property, International Transactions, Labor and Employment, Litigation, Mergers and Acquisitions, Municipal Law, Natural Resources Law, Public Finance, Real Estate, Security Alarm, Tax and Estate Planning, Technology Law, Trade Secret Litigation, Transportation Law, Trust and Estate Administration, Venture Capital.

FIRM PROFILE: Founded in 1850, Buchanan Ingersoll is one of the two oldest large commercial law firms in continuous practice in Pennsylvania, and a top 100 law firm in the nation. The Firm's level of business has grown seventeen-fold since 1980, demonstrating dramatic long-term growth.

The Firm's position as a national law firm is evidenced by its size and its wide variety of practice areas serving regional, national and international clients. Buchanan Ingersoll's clients range from individuals and start-up companies to private and publicly-held institutions and multinational conglomerates, including more than 50 of the Fortune 500 corporations.

The Firm's regional office system provides clients with cost-effective access to more than 412 lawyers through an integrated network. Buchanan Ingersoll has opened eleven new offices since 1992 and now has 16 overall -- Pittsburgh, Harrisburg, Philadelphia and Bryn Mawr, Miami, Aventura and Tampa, Princeton, Buffalo, Washington, D.C., New York City, McLean, Wilmington, San Diego, London and Dublin.

SHAREHOLDER

STUART M. BROWN, born 1963; admitted to bar, 1988, Pennsylvania and New Jersey (Not admitted in Delaware). *Education:* Boston University (B.S., cum laude, 1985); Temple University (J.D., 1988). Member, Temple University Law Review, 1987-1988. Chair, Alternative Dispute Resolution and Mediation Committee of Eastern District of Pennsylvania Bankruptcy Conference and Co-Chair, Young Members Committee. (Also at Philadelphia, Pennsylvania Office) (Certified Specialist, Business Bankruptcy Law, American Bankruptcy Board of Certification). ***PRACTICE AREAS:*** Bankruptcy; Creditors' Rights; Condominium Associations' Rights and Litigation. ***Email:*** brownsm@bipc.com

ASSOCIATES

FRANK B. HARRINGTON, born New York, New York, April 18, 1966; admitted to bar, 1992, Pennsylvania; 1997, New Jersey (Not admitted in Delaware). *Education:* University of Rochester (B.A., cum laude, 1989); Syracuse University College of Law (J.D., magna cum laude, 1992). Law Clerk to Hon. Sue L. Robinson, U.S. District Judge, District of Delaware, 1992-1994. (Also at Princeton, New Jersey Office). ***PRACTICE AREAS:*** Litigation. ***Email:*** harringtonfb@bipc.com

JAMI B. NIMEROFF, born Trenton, New Jersey, December 2, 1968; admitted to bar, 1993, New Jersey and U.S. District Court, District of New Jersey; 1994, Pennsylvania; 1995, Massachusetts; 1996, U.S. District Court, Eastern District of Pennsylvania (Not admitted in Delaware). *Education:* Boston University (B.A., magna cum laude, 1990); Boston University School of Law (J.D., cum laude, 1993). Member, Public Interest Law Journal. *Member:* Pennsylvania and New Jersey State Bar Associations. (Also at Philadelphia, Pennsylvania Office). ***PRACTICE AREAS:*** Bankruptcy; Creditors Rights; Commercial Litigation. ***Email:*** nimeroffjb@bipc.com

(See Professional Biographies at Bryn Mawr, Harrisburg, Philadelphia and Pittsburgh, Pennsylvania; Miami, Aventura and Tampa, Florida; New York City and Buffalo, New York; Princeton, New Jersey; Washington, D.C.; McLean, Virginia; San Diego, California; London, England)

CASARINO, CHRISTMAN & SHALK

Established in 1989

800 KING STREET, SUITE 200
P.O. BOX 1276
WILMINGTON, DELAWARE 19801
Telephone: 302-594-4500
Telecopier: 302-594-4509
URL: http://www.casarino.com

Civil Litigation, including Personal Injury, Products Liability and Workers Compensation in all State and Federal Courts in the State of Delaware.

FIRM PROFILE: The law firm of Casarino, Christman & Shalk was established on June 1, 1989. The firm consists of four partners and four associates. The firm specializes in civil litigation, primarily general casualty and insurance coverage litigation and worker's compensation.

The firm's attorneys practice in every State and Federal Court of the State of Delaware. Each of the firm's attorneys is committed to providing outstanding service to their clients in a timely and cost effective manner.

MEMBERS OF FIRM

STEPHEN P. CASARINO, born Wilmington, Delaware, September 2, 1941; admitted to bar, 1966, Delaware, U.S. District Court, District of Delaware,U.S. Court of Appeals, Third Circuit and U.S. Supreme Court. *Education:* University of Delaware (B.A., 1963); Catholic University of America (LL.B., 1966). Bencher, American Inns of Court (Rodney Chapter). Assistant City Solicitor, Wilmington, 1968-1969. Diplomate, American Board of Trial Advocates (President, Delaware Chapter, 1997). *Member:* Delaware and American Bar Associations; The Association of Trial Lawyers of America; Defense Research Institute; Defense Counsel of Delaware (Member, Board of Directors, 1996—; President Elect). [Capt., U.S. Army, 1966-1968]. ***PRACTICE AREAS:*** Civil Litigation; Personal Injury; Products Liability; Insurance Defense. ***Email:*** scasarino@casarino.com

COLIN M. SHALK, born Philadelphia, Pennsylvania, September 25, 1947; admitted to bar, 1978, Delaware, U.S. District Court, District of Delaware, U.S. Court of Appeals, Third Circuit and U.S. Supreme Court. *Education:* Ohio University; University of Delaware (B.A., with high honors, 1974); Dickinson School of Law (J.D., 1977). Barrister, American Inns of Court (Rodney Chapter). Law Clerk, Superior Court of the State of Delaware, 1977-1978. Associate Member, Delaware Board of Bar Examiners, 1985-1988. Associate, American Board of Trial Advocates. *Member:* Delaware Bar Association; Defense Research Institute; Defense Counsel of Delaware. [With USAF, 1967-1971]. ***PRACTICE AREAS:*** Insurance Defense; Workers' Compensation; Civil Litigation. ***Email:*** cshalk@casarino.com

BETH H. CHRISTMAN, born Utrecht, The Netherlands, November 28, 1955; admitted to bar, 1981, District of Columbia; 1982, Delaware; 1984, Pennsylvania and U.S. District Court, District of Delaware; 1992, U.S. Supreme Court. *Education:* Central College (B.A., 1977); George Washington University (J.D., 1980). Member, Delaware Superior Court, Civil Rules Committee. *Member:* District of Columbia Bar; Delaware and Pennsylvania Bar Associations; Defense Counsel of Delaware. ***PRACTICE AREAS:*** Insurance Defense; Workers' Compensation; Civil Litigation. ***Email:*** bchristman@casarino.com

DONALD M. RANSOM, born Wilmington, Delaware, April 18, 1961; admitted to bar, 1987, Delaware; 1988, Pennsylvania, U.S. District Court, District of Delaware and U.S. Court of Appeals, Third Circuit; 1992, U.S. District Court, Eastern District of Pennsylvania. *Education:* University of Delaware (B.A., 1984); Villanova University School of Law (J.D., 1987). *Member:* Delaware and American Bar Associations; Defense Counsel of Delaware; Defense Research Institute. ***PRACTICE AREAS:*** Civil Litigation; Personal Injury; Products Liability; Insurance Coverage; Arson and Insurance Fraud. ***Email:*** dransom@casarino.com

---

KENNETH M. DOSS, born Wilmington, Delaware, May 13, 1965; admitted to bar, 1990, Delaware; 1991, Pennsylvania and U.S. District Court, District of Delaware. *Education:* University of Virginia (B.A., 1987); T. C. Williams School of Law, University of Richmond (J.D., 1990). Cooperating Attorney, Delaware Trial Lawyers Association. *Member:* Pennsylvania, Delaware and American Bar Associations; Defense Research Institute; Defense Counsel of Delaware. ***PRACTICE AREAS:*** Insurance Defense; Civil Litigation; Workers' Compensation; Insurance Coverage. ***Email:*** kdoss@casarino.com

DIANE M. WILLETTE, born Staten Island, New York, July 1, 1963; admitted to bar, 1992, Delaware and U.S. District Court, District of Delaware; 1993, U.S. Court of Appeals, Third Circuit. *Education:* University of Delaware (B.A., 1986); Widener University (J.D., cum laude, 1991). Phi Delta Phi. Law Clerk, Superior Court of the State of Delaware, 1991-1992. Treasurer of De-

(This Listing Continued)

CASARINO, CHRISTMAN & SHALK, Wilmington—Continued

fence Council of Delaware, 1999-2000. *Member:* Delaware and American Bar Associations. ***PRACTICE AREAS:*** Personal Injury; Products Liability; Insurance Defense; Workers Compensation. ***Email:*** dwillette@casarino.com

STACEY L. CUMMINGS, born Kingston, New York, October 13, 1968; admitted to bar, 1993, Delaware; 1995, Pennsylvania and U.S. District Court, District of Delaware. *Education:* Union College (B.A., 1989); Widener University School of Law (J.D., cum laude, 1993). Phi Delta Phi (Magister); Phi Kappa Phi. Recipient, Academic Award in Corporate Finance, 1993. Member, Executive Board of Local Civic Association. *Member:* Delaware State and American Bar Associations; Delaware Trial Lawyers Association; Defense Counsel of Delaware; Defense Research Institute. ***PRACTICE AREAS:*** Insurance Defense; Workers' Compensation; Personal Injury; Insurance Coverage; Civil Litigation. ***Email:*** scummings@casarino.com

THOMAS P. LEFF, born Hackensack, New Jersey, August 15, 1950; admitted to bar, 1995, Maryland; 1997, Delaware; 1998, U.S. District Court, District of Delaware. *Education:* Case Western Reserve University (B.A., 1972); University of Maryland (J.D., 1995). General Editor, "Pattern Jury Instructions for Civil Practice in the Superior Court." *Member:* Delaware State and Maryland State Bar Associations. ***PRACTICE AREAS:*** Insurance Defense; Personal Injury; Civil Litigation. ***Email:*** tleff@casarino.com

REPRESENTATIVE CLIENTS: Atlantic Mutual Insurance Co.; CIGNA; CNA; Colonial Penn Insurance Co.; Commercial Union Insurance Co.; Continental Insurance Co.; Crawford & Company; Delaware American Insurance Company; Delaware Insurance Guaranty Association; Donegal Mutual Insurance Company; Employers Reinsurance Co.; First Mercury Syndicate, Inc.; Florists' Mutual Insurance Co.; GAB; Hartford Insurance Co.; Harleysville Insurance Co.; Home Insurance Co.; Independent Claims Service Delmarva; Liberty Mutual Insurance Co.; MAIF; Metropolitan Insurance Co.; Nationwide Insurance Co.; Nautilis Insurance Co.; Ohio Casualty Insurance Co.; Pennsylvania National Insurance Co.; Scott Wetzel Services; State Farm Mutual Automobile Insurance Co.; Tokio Marine Management, Inc.; Universal Underwriters Insurance Co.; USAA Property and Casualty Insurance Co.; U.S.A.A. Wausau Insurance Companies; Crum & Forster; State Farm Fire & Casualty Co.

CATTIE AND FRUEHAUF

1201 ORANGE STREET, SUITE 502
P.O. BOX 588
WILMINGTON, DELAWARE 19899-0588
Telephone: 302-778-1200
Fax: 302-778-1400

General Civil and Trial Practice. Insurance Defense, Insurance Coverage, Asbestos and Toxic Tort Litigation, Professional Malpractice.

MEMBERS OF FIRM

WILLIAM J. CATTIE, III, born Philadelphia, Pennsylvania, July 29, 1946; admitted to bar, 1974, Pennsylvania; 1978, Delaware. *Education:* Villanova University (B.A., 1968); Harvard University (J.D., 1974). Delta Epsilon Sigma. *Member:* Pennsylvania, Delaware State and American Bar Associations; Defense Counsel of Delaware; Defense Research Institute. [With U.S. Army, 1968-1971]. ***PRACTICE AREAS:*** Insurance Defense Law; Asbestos and Toxic Tort Litigation; Professional Malpractice; Civil Practice; Trial Practice. ***Email:*** wcattie@cattiefruehauf.com

BARBARA A. FRUEHAUF, born Buffalo, New York, May 11, 1951; admitted to bar, 1990, Delaware. *Education:* University of Delaware (B.A., 1986); Villanova University (J.D), 1989). *Member:* Delaware, Pennsylvania and American Bar Associations; Defense Counsel of Delaware; Defense Research Institute. ***PRACTICE AREAS:*** Insurance Defense Law; Civil Practice; Trial Practice; Subrogation Law. ***Email:*** bfruehauf@cattiefruehauf.com

CHIMICLES & TIKELLIS LLP

ONE RODNEY SQUARE
WILMINGTON, DELAWARE 19801
Telephone: 302-656-2500
Telecopier: 302-656-9053
Email: chimicles@aol.com
URL: http://www.chimicles.com

Haverford, Pennsylvania Office: One Haverford Centre, 361 West Lancaster Avenue, 19041-0100. Telephone: 610-642-8500. Telecopier: 610-649-3633.

Securities, Antitrust, Consumer, Environmental and Commercial Litigation, Mergers and Acquisitions, Class and Derivative Actions.

RESIDENT PARTNERS

PAMELA S. TIKELLIS, born Lawrence, Kansas, August 9, 1952; admitted to bar, 1982, Delaware. *Education:* Manhattanville College (B.A., 1974); New School for Social Research-The Graduate Faculty (M.A., 1976); Delaware Law School of Widener University (J.D., 1982). Phi Delta Phi. Member, Moot Court Honor Society, 1980-1982. Member, 1980-1981 and Managing Editor, 1981-1982, Law Review, Delaware Journal of Corporate Law. Judicial Law Clerk, Delaware Court of Chancery, 1982-1983. Lecturer and Author of Course Material on "Role of Directors in Hostile Battles For Corporate Control," Pennsylvania Bar Institute, 1988. Lecturer and Author, Securities Litigation, Practising Law Institute, 1996. Member, Civil Justice Reform Act Advisory Committee. Member, Delaware Board of Bar Examiners, 1995—. Co-Chair, Professional Ethics Committee, 1989-1992. Chair, Continuing Legal Education Committee. *Member:* Delaware State (Member: Corporation and Litigation Sections) and American (Member: Business, Banking and Corporation and Litigation Sections) Bar Associations. ***PRACTICE AREAS:*** Securities Litigation; Partnership Litigation; Antitrust; Mergers and Acquisitions; Class Actions; Derivative Actions.

ROBERT J. KRINER, JR., born Pottsville, Pennsylvania, June 28, 1961; admitted to bar, 1988, Delaware; 1989, U.S. District Court, District of Delaware. *Education:* University of Delaware (B.S., 1983); Delaware Law School of Widener University (J.D., cum laude, 1988). Member, 1986-1987 and Managing Editor, 1987-1988, Delaware Journal of Corporate Law. Law Clerk to The Honorable James L. Latchum, U.S. District Court, District of Delaware, 1988-1989. *Member:* American Bar Association. ***PRACTICE AREAS:*** Securities; Antitrust; Mergers and Acquisitions; Class and Derivative Actions.

CICONTE, ROSEMAN & WASSERMAN

1300 KING STREET
WILMINGTON, DELAWARE 19801
Telephone: 302-658-7101
Fax: 302-658-4982
URL: http://www.lawyers.com/crw

Litigation, Commercial, Collection, Personal Injury, Domestic Relations, Wills and Estates, Bankruptcy and Workers Compensation Law, Medical Malpractice, Products Liability.

EDWARD T. CICONTE, born Wilmington, Delaware, December 14, 1948; admitted to bar, 1973, Delaware and U.S. District Court, District of Delaware; 1975, U.S. District Court, Eastern District of Pennsylvania. *Education:* St. Joseph's University (B.S., 1970); Villanova University (J.D., 1973). Instructor, Commercial Law, Delaware Bar Association, 1985. Seminar Speaker, "Trial Practice", Delaware State Bar Association; "Commercial Law", National Business Association. *Member:* Delaware (Member, Sections on Commercial and Insurance Law) and American Bar Associations; Delaware Trial Lawyers Association; Commercial Law League of America; The Association of Trial Lawyers of America; National Association of Retail Collection Attorneys; American Board of Trial Advocates (President-Elect, 2002). [With USAF., 1973; USAFR, 1974-1980]. ***PRACTICE AREAS:*** Personal Injury; Collections; Medical Malpractice; Workers Compensation. ***Email:*** crw@dol.net

KENNETH M. ROSEMAN, born Philadelphia, Pennsylvania, February 11, 1953; admitted to bar, 1978, Delaware; 1979, Pennsylvania. *Education:* Temple University (B.A., cum laude, 1974); Delaware Law School of Widener University (J.D., summa cum laude, 1978). *Member:* Delaware State and American Bar Associations; Delaware Trial Lawyers Association; The Association of Trial Lawyers of America; American Board of Trial Advocates. ***PRACTICE AREAS:*** Personal Injury Law; Medical Malpractice.

JEFFREY P. WASSERMAN, born Brooklyn, New York, October 14, 1955; admitted to bar, 1982, Delaware; 1984, U.S. District Court, District of Delaware. *Education:* University of Rhode Island (B.A., 1977); New York University (M.P.A., 1979); Delaware Law School of Widener University (J.D., 1982). Phi Delta Phi. Moot Court Honor Society. *Member:* Delaware State Bar Association; Delaware Trial Lawyers Association; The Association of Trial Lawyers of America; Commercial Law League of America. ***PRACTICE AREAS:*** Personal Injury Law; Commercial Law; Bankruptcy; Workmens' Compensation Law. ***Email:*** jpwesq.crw@dol.net

REPRESENTATIVE CLIENTS: Mellon Bank Delaware; Dun & Bradstreet; American Express; Bank of America.

DAVID P. CLINE & ASSOCIATES

Established in 1991
1300 NORTH MARKET STREET, SUITE 700
WILMINGTON, DELAWARE 19801
Telephone: 302-529-7848
Fax: 302-654-0884

Personal Injury, Civil Litigation, Products Liability, Workers Compensation, Medical Malpractice, Bankruptcy.

(This Listing Continued)

DAVID P. CLINE, born Canton, New York, May 24, 1960; admitted to bar, 1987, Pennsylvania and New Jersey; 1988, Delaware; 1989, New York, U.S. Court of Appeals, Third Circuit and U.S. Supreme Court; 1990, Maryland. *Education:* St. Lawrence University (B.A., 1983); Clarkson College of Technology (M.B.A., 1984); Delaware Law School of Widener University (J.D., 1986). Phi Delta Phi. Member, Moot Court Honor Society. Delaware Law Forum. Recipient, American Jurisprudence Award in Civil Procedure and Property. Member, Delaware Journal Corporate Law, Law Review. Adjunct Professor, Advanced Marketing, Widener University, 1985. *Member:* New Jersey State, New York State, Maryland State, Pennsylvania and Delaware Bar Associations; Delaware Trial Lawyers Association. [U.S. Army Reserve Officer, J.A.G, (1983—)]

RAYMOND W. COBB, LLC

THREE MILL ROAD
SUITE 206
WILMINGTON, DELAWARE 19806
Telephone: 302-777-4100
Fax: 302-777-4111
Email: rwcobb@earthlink.net
URL: http://www.lawyers.com/cobblaw

Haddon Heights, New Jersey Office: 126 White Horse Pike. Telephone: 856-310-1100. Fax: 856-310-1212.

Products Liability, Admiralty and Maritime Law, Workers Compensation, Insurance Defense, Personal Injury Litigation, Medical Malpractice, Automobile Accidents.

RAYMOND W. COBB, born Wilmington, Delaware, December 2, 1957; admitted to bar, 1982, Pennsylvania, U.S. District Court, Eastern District of Pennsylvania and U.S. Court of Appeals, Third Circuit; 1983, New Jersey and U.S. District Court, District of New Jersey; 1988, Delaware and U.S. District Court, District of Delaware; U.S. Supreme Court. *Education:* University of Delaware (B.A., 1979); Villanova University (J.D., 1982). Member, Executive Committee of the Admiralty Law Committee, Young Lawyers Division, American Bar Association, 1989-1991. *Member:* Pennsylvania and Delaware (Member, Sections on: Workers Compensation; Litigation) Bar Associations; Defense Research Institute; Maritime Law Association of the United States (Member, Young Lawyers Committee, 1993-1998); Defense Council of Delaware. ***PRACTICE AREAS:*** Insurance Defense; Litigation; Products Liability; Toxic Torts; Asbestos Litigation; Medical Malpractice; Workers Compensation; Admiralty and Maritime Law.

CONNOLLY BOVE LODGE & HUTZ LLP

Established in 1944
1220 MARKET STREET
P.O. BOX 2207
WILMINGTON, DELAWARE 19899-2207
Telephone: 302-658-9141
Telecopier: 302-658-5614
Email: cblhlaw@cblhlaw.com
URL: http://www.cblhlaw.com

Washington, D.C. Office: Suite 800, 1990 M Street NW. Telephone: 202-331-7111. Facsimile: 202-293-6229.

General Practice, Corporations, Partnerships and Other Business Organizations, Intellectual Property, Antitrust, Commercial Transactions, Real Estate, Bankruptcy, Wills, Estates and Trusts, Taxation, Personal Injury, Family, Environmental and Construction Law, Labor and Employee Relations, Product Liability and Criminal Defense.

FIRM PROFILE: The firm's general practice division offers the full range of legal services in all fields, including the planning and implementation of transactions, business or personal, as well as the conduct of litigation in state or federal courts of all levels. The intellectual property division, the largest of any law firm in the state, engages in patent, trademark, copyright, trade secret, unfair competition and antitrust litigation in courts throughout the nation, and in the solicitation of patents, trademark registrations, and related counseling and licensing activities.

ARTHUR G. CONNOLLY (Retired).

JAMES M. MULLIGAN, JR., born Wilmington, Delaware, September 5, 1932; admitted to bar, 1958, Pennsylvania and Delaware; 1965, U.S. Court of Appeals, Federal, First and Third Circuits and U.S. Supreme Court. *Education:* St. Joseph's University (B.S., summa cum laude, 1954); University of Pennsylvania (J.D., 1957). Alpha Sigma Nu. Instructor, Wharton School of Finance and Commerce, University of Pennsylvania, 1955-1957. Assistant City Solicitor, Wilmington, 1958-1964. *Member:* Delaware State and American Bar Associations; National Association of College and University Attorneys. ***Email:*** jmm@cblhlaw.com

(This Listing Continued)

ARTHUR G. CONNOLLY, JR., born Wilmington, Delaware, September 5, 1937; admitted to bar, 1962, Delaware and District of Columbia. *Education:* Georgetown University (B.S.S., 1959; J.D., 1962). Adjunct Professor, Trial Practice, Delaware Law School, 1983-1988. Member, 1974-1982 and Chairman, 1980-1982, Delaware Board of Bar Examiners. Member: Lawyer Advisory Committee, U.S. Court of Appeals for the Third Circuit, 1984-1986; Georgetown University Law Alumni Board 1986-1988; Board of Directors, Delaware Volunteer Legal Services, Inc., 1990-1995; Delaware Code of Judicial Conduct Committee, 1990-1993; State Ethics Commission, 1991—; Board on Professional Responsibility of the Supreme Court of Delaware, 1992-1995. Former Member, Board of Trustees, Archmere Academy and Wilmington Friends School. *Member:* Delaware State (President, 1988-1989) and American Bar Associations; The District of Columbia Bar; American Bar Foundation. Fellow, American College of Trial Lawyers. ***Email:*** agc@cblhlaw.com

RUDOLF E. HUTZ, born New York, N.Y., February 8, 1938; admitted to bar, 1964, District of Columbia and Delaware; registered to practice before U.S. Patent and Trademark Office. *Education:* Princeton University (A.B., 1959); Georgetown University (J.D., 1963). *Member:* Delaware State (Chair, Intellectual Property Section, 1993-1995) and Federal Bar Associations; The District of Columbia Bar; American Intellectual Property Law Association; Philadelphia Patent Law Association; Federal Circuit Bar Association. Fellow, American College of Trial Lawyers. ***Email:*** reh@cblhlaw.com

HAROLD PEZZNER, born Ashley, Pennsylvania, August 12, 1936; admitted to bar, 1962, Maryland; 1964, Delaware; registered to practice before U.S. Patent and Trademark Office. *Education:* Wilkes University; Pennsylvania State University (B.S., 1958); George Washington University (J.D., with honors, 1962). Phi Delta Phi. *Member:* Delaware State, Federal and American Bar Associations; Philadelphia Intellectual Property Law Association; American Intellectual Property Law Association. ***Email:*** hp@cblhlaw.com

RICHARD M. BECK, born Yonkers, New York, May 12, 1938; admitted to bar, 1966, District of Columbia; registered to practice before U.S. Patent and Trademark Office (Not admitted in Delaware). *Education:* Rensselaer Polytechnic Institute (B.M.E., 1960); George Washington University (J.D., 1964). *Member:* The District of Columbia Bar. ***Email:*** rmb@cblhlaw.com

PAUL E. CRAWFORD, born Orange, New Jersey, April 4, 1940; admitted to bar, 1966, Pennsylvania and District of Columbia; 1967, Delaware; registered to practice before U.S. Patent and Trademark Office. *Education:* Villanova University (B.M.E., 1961; J.D., 1964). Tau Beta Pi; Pi Tau Sigma. Listed in The Best Lawyers in America, 2001-2002. Assistant City Solicitor, Wilmington, Delaware, 1969. *Member:* Delaware State Bar Association (Member, Intellectual Property Law Section); The District of Columbia Bar; American Intellectual Property Law Association; Delaware Association of Professional Engineers (Public Member, DAPE Council, 1990-1998, appointed by the governor). ***Email:*** pec@cblhlaw.com

STANLEY C. MACEL, III, born Wilmington, Delaware, December 5, 1938; admitted to bar, 1972, Delaware. *Education:* University of Delaware (B.A., 1963); Temple University (J.D., 1972). Barenkopf Scholar, 1971-1972. Court Administrator, Delaware Court of Chancery, 1968-1972. *Member:* Delaware State (Associate Member, Board of Bar Examiners, 1974-1982) and American Bar Associations; International Trademark Association. [Capt., U.S. Air Force, 1963-1967]. ***Email:*** scm@cblhlaw.com

HENRY E. GALLAGHER, JR., born Wilmington, Delaware, August 2, 1949; admitted to bar, 1975, Delaware. *Education:* Villanova University (A.B., 1971; J.D., 1975). Law Clerk, Superior Court of Delaware, 1975-1976. Member, Delaware Supreme Court Board on Professional Responsibility, 1986-1992. Member, Delaware Supreme Court Board of Bar Examiners, 1999—. *Member:* Delaware State (Member, Sections on: Litigation; Corporation Law) and American Bar Associations. ***Email:*** heg@cblhlaw.com

GEORGE PAZUNIAK, born Philadelphia, Pennsylvania, January 15, 1952; admitted to bar, 1976, Delaware. *Education:* Temple University (A.B., with honors, 1973); Duke University (J.D., with honors, 1975). Author, "Employment Discrimination Litigation," 4 Delaware Journal of Corporate Law 114, 1978. Lecturer in Law, Delaware Law School of Widener University, 1979-1980. *Member:* Delaware State and American Bar Associations; American Intellectual Property Law Association. ***Email:*** gp@cblhlaw.com

N. RICHARD POWERS, born Philadelphia, Pennsylvania, December 29, 1944; admitted to bar, 1972, Pennsylvania; 1974, Delaware. *Education:* St. Joseph's University (B.S., 1966); Villanova University (J.D., 1972). Order of the Coif. Associate Editor, Villanova Law Review, 1970-1972. Judicial Clerkship, Chief Judge James L. Latchum, United States District Court, District of Delaware, 1972-1974. United States Magistrate, District of Delaware, 1980-1988. *Member:* Delaware State and American Bar Associations. ***Email:*** nrp@cblhlaw.com

RICHARD DAVID LEVIN, born Philadelphia, Pennsylvania, June 11, 1945; admitted to bar, 1970, Delaware and U.S. District Court, District of Delaware; 1971, U.S. Court of Appeals, Third Circuit. *Education:* University of Delaware (B.A., 1967); Georgetown University (J.D., 1970). Co-Author: "Considerations in Buying or Selling a Business in Delaware," National Business

(This Listing Continued)

CONNOLLY BOVE LODGE & HUTZ LLP, Wilmington—Continued

Institute, Inc. 1985; "Basic Real Estate Law in Delaware," National Business Institute, Inc., 1990-1991. Assistant U.S. Attorney, District of Delaware, 1970-1973. Acting U.S. Attorney, District of Delaware, 1973. Assistant Public Defender, State of Delaware, 1973-1976. *Member:* Delaware (Member, Sections on: Real Estate; Intellectual Property) and American (Member, Sections on: Intellectual Property; Litigation; Real Property) Bar Associations. ***Email:*** rdl@cblhlaw.com

JOHN A. CLARK, III, born Wilmington, Delaware, December 15, 1946; admitted to bar, 1972, Delaware; 1973, U.S. District Court, District of Delaware. *Education:* Fordham University (B.A., 1968); George Washington University (J.D., 1971). Assistant Public Defender, State of Delaware, 1973-1979. *Member:* Delaware State (Member, Real Estate Section) and American Bar Associations. ***Email:*** jac3@cblhlaw.com

JEFFREY B. BOVE, born Wilmington, Delaware, March 20, 1952; admitted to bar, 1979, Delaware. *Education:* University of Delaware (B.A., with honors, 1975); New England School of Law (J.D., summa cum laude, 1979). Recipient, Amos L. Taylor Award for Scholastic Excellence, New England School of Law, 1979. Law Clerk, Superior Court of Delaware, 1979-1980. *Member:* Delaware State and American Bar Associations. ***Email:*** jbb@cblhlaw.com

JAMES J. WOODS, JR., born Phoenixville, Pennsylvania, September 14, 1956; admitted to bar, 1981, Delaware. *Education:* University of Delaware (B.S., with honors, 1978); University of Virginia (J.D. 1981). Phi Kappa Phi; Pi Mu Epsilon. Author, "Guest Statutes: Goodbye and Good Riddance," 16 Cumberland Law Review 263 (1986). *Member:* Delaware State Bar Association; Delaware Trial Lawyers Association; The Association of Trial Lawyers of America. ***Email:*** jjw@cblhlaw.com

COLLINS J. SEITZ, JR., born Wilmington, Delaware, September 14, 1957; admitted to bar, 1983, Delaware, U.S. District Court, District of Delaware and U.S. Court of Appeals, Third and Federal Circuits. *Education:* University of Delaware (B.A., 1980); Villanova University (J.D., 1983). Member, Villanova Law Review, 1982-1983. *Member:* Delaware State and American Bar Associations. ***Email:*** cjs@cblhlaw.com

EDWARD F. EATON, born Philadelphia, Pennsylvania, May 18, 1948; admitted to bar, 1975, Pennsylvania; 1976, Delaware, U.S. District Court, District of Delaware and U.S. Court of Appeals, Third Circuit. *Education:* Cornell University (A.B., 1970); Temple University (J.D., 1975). Law Clerk, Superior Court of Delaware, 1975-1976. Deputy Attorney General, Delaware, 1976-1977. Assistant City Solicitor, Wilmington, 1977-1979. Assistant Public Defender, 1979-1985. *Member:* Delaware State Bar Association (Member, Sections on: Family Law; Real Property; Torts and Insurance); Delaware Trial Lawyers Association. ***Email:*** efe@cblhlaw.com

CHARLES J. DURANTE, born Philadelphia, Pennsylvania, October 26, 1951; admitted to bar, 1977, Delaware; 1980, Pennsylvania; 1989, U.S. Tax Court. *Education:* Haverford College (B.A., with honors, 1973); Villanova University (J.D., 1977; LL.M., Taxation, 1983). Recipient, Alumni Award, Haverford College, 1998. Deputy Attorney General, Delaware, 1978-1981. Assistant City Solicitor, Wilmington, 1981-1985. Parliamentarian, Delaware Democratic State Committee, 1990—. President, Delaware Sportswriters and Broadcasters Association, 1996—. *Member:* Delaware State (Member, Sections on: Taxation; Trusts and Estates) and American (Member, Sections on: Taxation; Real Property, Probate and Trust Law; Entertainment and Sports Law) Bar Associations. ***Email:*** cjd@cblhlaw.com

MICHAEL K. NEWELL, born Wilmington, Delaware, September 29, 1952; admitted to bar, 1982, Pennsylvania and Delaware. *Education:* University of Delaware (B.A., 1975); Northeastern University (M.S., 1976); Widener University School of Law (J.D., 1981). Phi Delta Phi. Master, Family Court of Delaware, 1981-1982. Listed in Best Lawyers in America, 1988-2001. *Member:* Delaware State (Family Law Section, Secretary, 1985-1987, Vice Chairman, 1987-1989, Chairman, 1989-1991), Pennsylvania and American Bar Associations; Association of Trial Lawyers of America; Delaware Trial Lawyers Association. Fellow, American Academy of Matrimonial Lawyers. ***PRACTICE AREAS:*** Family Law; Separation Agreements; Divorce; Marital Property Distribution; Alimony; Child Custody; Child Support; Spousal Support; Premarital Agreements. ***Email:*** mkn@cblhlaw.com

PATRICIA SMINK ROGOWSKI, born Harvey, Illinois, October 3, 1962; admitted to bar, 1988, Delaware, Pennsylvania, U.S. District Court, District of Delaware and U.S. Court of Appeals, Federal Circuit; registered to practice before U.S. Patent and Trademark Office. *Education:* Lehigh University (B.S.M.E. with highest honors, 1984); University of Pennsylvania (J.D., 1987). Tau Beta Pi; Pi Tau Sigma. *Member:* Delaware, Pennsylvania and American (Chair, Delaware Intellectual Property Law Section, 1995-1996) Bar Associations; Philadelphia Intellectual Property Law Association (Board Member, 2000-2002); American Intellectual Property Association. ***Email:*** psr@cblhlaw.com

(This Listing Continued)

MARY W. BOURKE, born Pittsburgh, Pennsylvania, November 1, 1959; admitted to bar, 1985, Pennsylvania, Delaware and U.S. Court of Appeals, Federal Circuit; registered to practice before U.S. Patent and Trademark Office. *Education:* Princeton University (B.S.E., with honors, 1981); University of Pittsburgh (J.D., 1984). *Member:* Delaware State, Pennsylvania and American Bar Associations; American Intellectual Property Law Association. ***Email:*** mwb@cblhlaw.com

ROBERT G. McMORROW, JR., born Washington, D.C., January 18, 1958; admitted to bar, 1983, District of Columbia; 1984, Pennsylvania, U.S. District Court, Eastern District of Pennsylvania and U.S. Court of Appeals, Federal Circuit; registered to practice before U.S. Patent and Trademark Office (Not admitted in Delaware). *Education:* The Citadel (B.A., Chemistry, with high honors, 1980); Georgetown University (J.D., 1983); Villanova University (M.A., Biology, 1990). *Member:* Pennsylvania Bar Association; American Intellectual Property Law Association; Philadelphia Intellectual Property Law Association. ***Email:*** rgm@cblhlaw.com

R. ERIC HUTZ, born Washington, D.C. September 7, 1962; admitted to bar, 1988, Delaware, U.S. District Court, District of Delaware and U.S. Court of Appeals, Federal Circuit. *Education:* Lehigh University (B.A., magna cum laude, 1985); George Washington University (J.D., 1988). *Member:* Delaware State (Member, Intellectual Property Section) and Federal Bar Associations; Delaware Trial Lawyers Association. ***Email:*** eh@cblhlaw.com

ARTHUR G. CONNOLLY, III, born Washington, D.C., December 26, 1960; admitted to bar, 1988, Delaware; 1989, U.S. District Court, District of Delaware. *Education:* Williams College (B.A., cum laude, 1983); Georgetown University (J.D., 1988). Phi Beta Kappa. Judicial Clerkship, Delaware Court of Chancery, 1988-1989. Attorney, Delaware State Senate, 136th General Assembly, 1991-1992. *Member:* Delaware State and American Bar Associations. ***Email:*** ac3@cblhlaw.com

WILLIAM E. McSHANE, born Wilmington, Delaware, February 14, 1963; admitted to bar, 1989, Pennsylvania; registered to practice before U.S. Patent and Trademark Office (Not admitted in Delaware). *Education:* University of Delaware (B.S.Ch.E., 1985); Widener University School of Law (J.D., cum laude, 1988). *Member:* American Intellectual Property Law Association ("Composites" Subcommittee Chairperson, Special Committee on Export Control, 1990-1992); Pacific Industrial Property Association. ***Email:*** wem@cblhlaw.com

JAMES D. HEISMAN, born Philadelphia, Pennsylvania, April 27, 1961; admitted to bar, 1989, Delaware; 1990, U.S. District Court, District of Delaware. *Education:* Ithaca College (B.A., cum laude, 1983); Villanova University (J.D., 1989). *Member:* Delaware State Bar Association (Member, Intellectual Property and Litigation Section; Co-Chair, Mechanics' Lien Subcommittee). ***Email:*** jdh@cblhlaw.com

JEFFREY C. WISLER, born Wilmington, Delaware, October 28, 1963; admitted to bar, 1989, Delaware, New Jersey and U.S. District Court, District of New Jersey; 1990, U.S. District Court, District of Delaware; 1991, U.S. Court of Appeals, Third Circuit; 1995, U.S. Tax Court. *Education:* University of Delaware (B.S., 1985); Rutgers University School of Law (J.D., 1988). *Member:* Delaware and American Bar Associations; American Bankruptcy Institute. ***Email:*** jcw@cblhlaw.com

ASHLEY I. PEZZNER, born Silver Springs, Maryland, January 14, 1959; admitted to bar, 1990, Maryland; 1993, Delaware, 1994, U.S. District Court, District of Delaware and U.S. Court of Appeals, Third Circuit; registered to practice before U.S. Patent and Trademark Office. *Education:* University of South Carolina (B.S., 1981) Tau Beta Pi; Johns Hopkins University (M.A.S., 1985); University of Baltimore (J.D., 1990). *Member:* American Bar Association. ***Email:*** aip@cblhlaw.com

KAREN C. BIFFERATO, born Racine, Wisconsin, February 11, 1970; admitted to bar, 1994, Delaware and U.S. District Court, District of Delaware. *Education:* North Carolina State University (B.A., summa cum laude, 1991); Marshall-Wythe School of Law, College of William and Mary (J.D., 1994). Phi Delta Phi (President, 1993-1994); Order of the Coif. Member, William and Mary Law Review, 1992-1994. *Member:* Delaware State and American Bar Associations; American Bankruptcy Institute. ***Email:*** kcb@cblhlaw.com

BURTON A. AMERNICK, born Baltimore, Maryland, October 23, 1940; admitted to bar, 1966, Maryland; 1970, U.S. Supreme Court; 1971, U.S. District Court for the District of Maryland and U.S. Court of Appeals for the District of Columbia Circuit; 1974, District of Columbia; 1975, U.S. District Court for the District of Columbia; 1979, U.S. Court of Federal Claims; 1982, U.S. Court of Appeals for the Federal Circuit; registered to practice before U.S. Patent and Trademark Office (Not admitted in Delaware). *Education:* University of Maryland (B.S., Chem. E., 1963); University of Baltimore (J.D., magna cum laude, 1966). Nu Beta Epsilon. Member, Heuisler Honor Society. Author: Book, "*Patent Law for The Nonlawyer:* A Guide for The Engineer, Technologist and Manager," Van Nostrand Reinhold Company, New York, 1986; "Patent Law for the Nonlawyer," 2nd Edition, Chapman & Hall, 1991; Articles: "Essentials of Patent Law," Journal of the National Cancer Institute, Vol. 81, No. 19, October 4, 1989; "Protection of Intellectual Property, "Food Product Development:

(This Listing Continued)

From Concept to the Marketplace, Chapter 16, Edited by Ernst Graf and Israel Saguy, Van Nostrand Reinhold, 1990; "U.S. Patent Laws: An Overview," Proceedings of the Technical Association of the Pulp and Paper Industry, 1982. Patent Examiner, 1964-1968. Course Co-Director and Lecturer, Patent Law for Scientists and Engineers, Center for Professional Advancement, 1979—. Instructor, Patent Resources Group, 1991—. *Member:* Montgomery County, Maryland State and American Bar Associations; District of Columbia Bar; Maryland Patent Law Association; American Intellectual Property Law Association; American Institute of Chemical Engineers; Patent Lawyers Club of Washington, D.C. ***PRACTICE AREAS:*** Biotechnology Patents; Chemical Patents; Medical Patents; Metallurgical Patents; Pharmaceutical Patents.

GEORGE R. PETTIT, born Ossining, New York, June 21, 1945; admitted to bar, 1975, Indiana; 1977-1982, U.S Court of Customs and Patent Appeals; 1980, Virginia; 1982, District of Columbia and U.S. Court of Appeals for the Federal Circuit; registered to practice before U.S. Patent and Trademark Office (Not admitted in Delaware). *Education:* University of Maine (B.S.E.E., 1967); Brooklyn Law School (J.D., 1975). Member, Moot Court Board, 1974-1975. Member, Panel of Arbitrators, American Arbitration Association. Instructor, Patent Resources Group, 1995. Lecturer, Patent Law for Scientists & Engineers, Center for Professional Development, 1993. *Member:* District of Columbia Bar; Fairfax, Indiana State (Member, Patent and Trademark Section, 1975—) and American Bar Associations; Virginia State Bar; American Intellectual Property Law Association. ***PRACTICE AREAS:*** Electrical Intellectual Property; Intellectual Property Infringement; Intellectual Property Licensing; Computer and Software Patents; Electronic Patents.

MORRIS LISS, born New York, N.Y., July 3, 1940; admitted to bar, 1970, District of Columbia and U.S. Court of Appeals for the District of Columbia Circuit; U.S. Court of Appeals for the Federal Circuit; registered to practice before U.S. Patent and Trademark Office (Not admitted in Delaware). *Education:* City College of the City University of New York (B.E.E., 1963); George Washington University (M.S., 1966); Catholic University of America (J.D., 1970). *Member:* Bar Association of the District of Columbia; American Bar Association; American Intellectual Property Law Association. ***LANGUAGES:*** French. ***PRACTICE AREAS:*** Computer and Software Patents; Electrical Patents; Electronic Patents; Mechanical Patents; Patent Licensing.

STANLEY B. GREEN, born New York, N.Y., April 17, 1941; admitted to bar, 1967, District of Columbia and U.S. Court of Appeals for the District of Columbia Circuit; 1973-1982, U.S. Court of Customs and Patent Appeals; 1976, U.S. Court of Federal Claims; 1982, U.S. Court of Appeals for the Federal Circuit; registered to practice before U.S. Patent and Trademark Office (Not admitted in Delaware). *Education:* City College of the City University of New York (B.E.E., 1962); George Washington University (LL.B., 1966). Phi Alpha Delta; Order of the Coif. Member, George Washington Law Review, 1965-1966. Patent Examiner, 1962-1967. *Member:* District of Columbia Bar (Member, Steering Committee, PTC Section, 1992-1994); American Bar Association; American Intellectual Property Law Association; Institute of Electrical and Electronic Engineers (Member, Intellectual Property Committee, 1982—). ***PRACTICE AREAS:*** Patent Litigation; Patent Infringement; Electrical Patents; Electronic Patents; Computer and Software Patents. ***Email:*** sbg@cblhlaw.com

OF COUNSEL

JOHN D. FAIRCHILD, born East Orange, New Jersey, January 31, 1932; admitted to bar, 1963, Michigan; registered to practice before U.S. Patent and Trademark Office (Not admitted in Delaware). *Education:* University of Delaware; American University (B.A., 1959); University of Detroit (J.D., 1962). *Member:* State Bar of Michigan; American Bar Association; American Intellectual Property Law Association; International Trademark Association. ***Email:*** jdf@cblhlaw.com

WILLIAM E. LAMBERT, born Rumford, Maine, February 21, 1941; admitted to bar, 1969, District of Columbia; 1972, Pennsylvania; registered to practice before U.S. Patent and Trademark Office (Not admitted in Delaware). *Education:* Wesleyan University (B.A., 1962); Harvard University (LL.B., 1968). *Member:* The District of Columbia Bar; Association of Corporate Patent Counsel. ***LANGUAGES:*** Portuguese. ***Email:*** wel@cblhlaw.com

M. EDWARD DANBERG, born Washington, D.C., October 22, 1957; admitted to bar, 1982, Pennsylvania; 1984, Delaware; 1985, U.S. District Court, District of Delaware; 1996, U.S. Court of Appeals, Third Circuit. *Education:* University of Delaware (B.A., 1978); Catholic University of America (J.D., 1981). Deputy Attorney General, State of Delaware, 1984-1987. Council Attorney, New Castle County, 1987-1988. Assistant County Attorney, 1988-1993 and County Attorney, 1993-1997, New Castle County, Delaware. *Member:* Delaware (Chairman, Government Law Section, 1996-2000) and American Bar Associations. ***Email:*** med@cblhlaw.com

ANNE LOVE BARNETT, born Louisville, Kentucky, May 29, 1960; admitted to bar, 1991, New York; 1993, Delaware and U.S. District Court, District of Delaware. *Education:* Montclair State College (B.A., 1983); Fordham University (J.D., 1989). Staff Member, Fordham Urban Law Journal, 1988-1989. *Member:* New York State, Delaware State and American Bar Associations; Estate Planning Council of Delaware. ***Email:*** alb@cblhlaw.com

ASSOCIATES

MATTHEW F. BOYER, born Wilmington, Delaware, March 29, 1957; admitted to bar, 1987, Delaware; 1988, U.S. District Court, District of Delaware; 1994, U.S. Supreme Court. *Education:* Harvard University (B.A., 1980); University of Virginia (J.D., 1986). Member: Executive Committee, St. Thomas More Society of Wilmington; Office of Disciplinary Counsel, Delaware Supreme Court, 1994-1998. Associate Member, Board of Bar Examiners, Delaware Supreme Court, 1999—. *Member:* Delaware Bar Association (Member, Nominating Committee). ***PRACTICE AREAS:*** Employment Law; Business Litigation; Professional Ethics. ***Email:*** mfb@cblhlaw.com

GERARD M. O'ROURKE, born Wilmington, Delaware, December 27, 1967; admitted to bar, 1994, Delaware; registered to practice before the U.S. Patent and Trademark Office. *Education:* Johns Hopkins University (B.S., Chemical Engineering, 1990); Villanova University (J.D., cum laude, 1993). Case and Comment Editor, Villanova Law Review, 1993. Legal Counsel, 1994-1995 and President, 1995-1996, Wilmington Junior Chamber of Commerce. ***Email:*** gmo@cblhlaw.com

FRANCIS DIGIOVANNI, born Jersey City, New Jersey, July 14, 1965; admitted to bar, 1993, Delaware; registered to practice before U.S. Patent and Trademark Office. *Education:* Bucknell University (B.S.M.E., 1987); University of Pittsburgh (J.D., cum laude, 1993). Order of the Coif. Associate Editor, Journal of Law and Commerce, 1992-1993. *Member:* Delaware State, Federal and American Bar Associations. ***Email:*** fd@cblhlaw.com

SAMUEL D. BRICKLEY II, born Wilmington, Delaware, April 27, 1967; admitted to bar, 1993, New Hampshire; 1994, Pennsylvania and Delaware. *Education:* Cornell University (A.B., Economics and Government, 1989); University of San Diego (J.D., M.B.A., 1993). Cornell National Scholar. Adjunct Instructor, University of Delaware, 1997—. Deputy Attorney General, Department of Justice, State of Delaware, 1994-1997. *Member:* Delaware State and American Bar Associations.

THOMAS A. STEVENS, born Fort Madison, Iowa; admitted to bar, 1991, Delaware and Pennsylvania; 1993, U.S. District Court, District of Delaware. *Education:* University of Pennsylvania (B.A., 1974); Drexel University (MBA, 1981) Widener University School of Law (J.D., cum laude, 1990). Phi Kappa Phi. Beta Gamma Sigma. Member, Moot Court Honor Society. ***Email:*** tas@cblhlaw.com

OLEH V. BILYNSKY, born Philadelphia, Pennsylvania, February 6, 1960; admitted to bar, 1995, Pennsylvania; 1998, Delaware; 1999, U.S. District Court, District of Delaware; 2000, U.S. Court of Appeals, Federal Circuit. *Education:* University of Pennsylvania (B.S., with honors, 1981); Temple University (J.D., magna cum laude, 1994). *Member:* Pennsylvania, Delaware State and American Bar Associations. ***LANGUAGES:*** Ukrainian. ***Email:*** ovb@cblhlaw.com

JAMES M. OLSEN, born Wilmington, Delaware, January 19, 1967; admitted to bar, 1998, Delaware and New Jersey; U.S. District Court, District of New Jersey; registered to practice before U.S. Patent and Trademark Office. *Education:* University of Pennsylvania (B.S.M.E., 1989); Marist College (M.B.A., Finance, 1994); George Washington University (J.D., 1998). Member, Journal of International Law & Economics, 1997. Patent Examiner, 1993-1995. *Member:* The Federal Circuit Bar Association; American Intellectual Property Law Association. ***Email:*** jmo@cblhlaw.com

ERIC J. EVAIN, born Indianapolis, Indiana, June 2, 1960; admitted to bar, 1998, Delaware; U.S. District Court, District of Delaware; U.S. District Court, Federal Circuit and U.S. Court of Appeals, Third Circuit; registered to practice before U.S. Patent and Trademark Office. *Education:* Northland College (B.S, magna cum laude, 1982); University of Idaho (PhD, 1987); Widener University (J.D., cum laude, 1998). Wolcott Judicial Fellowship, 1997; Renfrew Graduate Research Fellowships, 1983-1987. Law Clerk to Joseph T. Walsh, Delaware Supreme Court. Recipient: Idaho Academy of Science Award, 1987; Certificates of Legal Achievement: Constitutional Law; Patent Law; Sales and Leases; Wills; Trusts and Estates. Deans Hall of Recognition for Public Service, 1981. *Member:* Delaware State and American Bar Associations. ***Email:*** eje@cblhlaw.com

MICHELLE MCMAHON, born Detroit, Michigan, June 1, 1974; admitted to bar, 2000, Delaware. *Education:* Western Michigan University (B.B.A., 1996); Georgetown University Law Center (J.D., 1999). ***Email:*** mm@cblhlaw.com

DANIEL C. MULVENY, born Wilmington, Delaware, January 21, 1969; admitted to bar, 1998, Pennsylvania; 2000, Delaware; 2001, U.S District Court, District of Delaware. *Education:* University of Delaware (B.Ch.E., 1992); Dickinson School of Law of the Pennsylvania State University (J.D., 1998). Member, Woolsack Honor Society. ***PRACTICE AREAS:*** Patent Prosecution; Patent Litigation. ***Email:*** dcm@cblhlaw.com

(This Listing Continued)

CONNOLLY BOVE LODGE & HUTZ LLP, Wilmington—Continued

CHRISTINE M. HANSEN, born Rochester, New York, January 9, 1964; admitted to bar, 1992, Delaware; 1993, U.S. District Court, District of Delaware; registered to practice before the U.S. Patent and Trademark Office. *Education:* Princeton University (A.B., 1986); University of Pennsylvania (J.D., cum laude, 1992). Fulbright Scholar, Philipps University, Marburg, Germany, 1986-1987. *Member:* Delaware and American Bar Associations. ***LANGUAGES:*** German. ***Email:*** cmh@cblhlaw.com

JUDITH M. JONES, born Waynesboro, Virginia, November 26, 1968; admitted to bar, 1996, Delaware. *Education:* James Madison University (B.A., 1991); Widener University (J.D., cum laude, 1996). Phi Kappa Phi; Phi Delta Phi; Order of Barristers. First Vice President, Moot Court, 1995-1996. Law Clerk to: the Honorable William N. Nichols and the Honorable William J. Walls, Jr., Delaware Family Court, Kent County, 1996-1997. ***Email:*** jmj@cblhlaw.com

PATRICK H. HIGGINS, born Baltimore, Maryland, June 30, 1959; admitted to bar, 1993, Pennsylvania; 1994, California and U.S. District Court, Southern District of California (Not admitted in Delaware). *Education:* University of Maryland (B.S., Biochem., 1983; M.S., Mol. Bio., 1984); Delaware Law School of Widener University (J.D., 1993). *Member:* State Bar of California; American Bar Association; American Intellectual Property Law Association (Member, Biotechnology Committee, 1992—); San Diego Patent Law Association; American Association for the Advancement of Science; Philadelphia Intellectual Property Law Association. ***PRACTICE AREAS:*** Intellectual Property. ***Email:*** phh@cblhlaw.com

CHRISTOS T. ADAMOPOULOS, born Salisbury, Maryland, September 26, 1974; admitted to bar, 2000, Delaware and Maryland; 2001, U.S. District Court, District of Delaware. *Education:* Johns Hopkins University (B.A., 1996); Georgetown University (J.D., 1999). Member, Georgetown Journal on Poverty and Public Policy. Intern to the Hon. Paul S. Sarbanes, United States Senator, Maryland, 1994. Law Clerk to: U.S. District Court, Baltimore, MD, 1997; Cawley & Company Solicitors, Dublin, Ireland, 1997; Shulman Rogers Gandal Pordy & Ecker, Rockville, MD, 1998. *Member:* Delaware, Maryland State and American Bar Associations. ***LANGUAGES:*** Greek. ***PRACTICE AREAS:*** Business Law; Commercial Law; Bankruptcy. ***Email:*** cta@cblhlaw.com

GARY ALAN BRIDGE, born St. Louis, Missouri, October 11, 1971; admitted to bar, 2001, Massachusetts (Not admitted in Delaware). *Education:* University of Missouri, Columbia (B.S,. Chem. Eng., 1994); University of Minnesota, Minneapolis (M.S., Biomed. Eng., 1998); Franklin Pierce Law Center (J.D., 2000). ***PRACTICE AREAS:*** Intellectual Property. ***Email:*** gab@cblhlaw.com

ADELE WILLIAMS GERNSROSS, born Philadelphia, Pennsylvania, July 22, 1956; admitted to bar, 2000, New Jersey (Not admitted in Delaware). *Education:* Immaculata College (B.S., cum laude, 1978); Widener University (J.D., 2000). Phi Delta Phi; Kappa Omicron Phi. Immaculata Honor Society. ***PRACTICE AREAS:*** Taxation; Estate Planning; Estate Administration; Trusts and Estates; Probate. ***Email:*** awg@cblhlaw.com

HELENA C. RYCHLICKI, born Charleston, South Carolina, May 18, 1960; admitted to bar, 2000, Delaware; 2001, U.S. District Court, District of Delaware. *Education:* Clemson University (B.S.,. 1982; M.S., 1983); Widener University (J.D., 2000). Phi Delta Phi. Wolcott Fellow. Member, American Chemical Society, 1982—. *Member:* Delaware State and American Bar Associations. ***PRACTICE AREAS:*** Intellectual Property. ***Email:*** hrc@cblhlaw.com

MAX B. WALTON, born Wilmington, Delaware, September 5, 1972; admitted to bar, 1999, Delaware; 2000, U.S. District Court, District of Delaware. *Education:* Washington College (B.a., Political Science, 1995); Widener University (J.D., 1999). Phi Kappa Phi. Internal Managing Editor, Widener Law Symposium Journal. *Member:* Delaware and American Bar Associations. ***PRACTICE AREAS:*** Commercial Litigation; Construction Law; Real Estate. ***Email:*** mbw@cblhlaw.com

REDMOND L. CLEVENGER, JR., born Chelsea, Massachusetts, June 19, 1968; admitted to bar, 2001, Massachusetts (Not admitted in Delaware). *Education:* Harvard University (ABL, 1997); Georgetown University Law Center (J.D., 2000; LLM., 2001). ***PRACTICE AREAS:*** Corporate Litigation.

THOMAS F. POCHE, born Drexel Hill, Pennsylvania, July 26, 1963; admitted to bar, 1995, Illinois; 2001, District of Columbia (Not admitted in Delaware). *Education:* University of Pennsylvania (B.A., 1985); University of Chicago (Ph.D., 1992); Boston University School of Law (J.D., 1995). (Resident, Washington, DC Office). ***PRACTICE AREAS:*** Patent Litigation. ***Email:*** tfp@cblhlaw.com

JOSEPH BARRERA, born Island Park, New York, May 24, 1962; admitted to bar, 1999, New Mexico; 2001, District of Columbia; registered to practice before U.S. Patent and Trademark Office (Not admitted in Delaware). *Education:* Potsdam College (B.A., cum laude, 1984); Dartmouth College (Ph.D., 1990); University of New Mexico (J.D., 1999). Member, American Chemical Society. (Resident, Washington, DC Office). ***PRACTICE AREAS:*** Intellectual Property. ***Email:*** jb@cblhlaw.com

ELLIOTT E. MENDELSON, born Huntsville, Alabama, April 13, 1963; admitted to bar, 2000, Delaware. *Education:* University of Virginia (B.S., Biology, 1985; PH.D., Microbiology, 1992); Georgetown Law School (J.D., 2000). ***PRACTICE AREAS:*** Intellectual Property. ***Email:*** ecm@cblhlaw.com

MICHAEL L. LOVITZ, born Philadelphia, Pennsylvania, June 26, 1964; admitted to bar, 1989, Pennsylvania; 1990, U.S. District Court, Eastern District of Pennsylvania; 1995, U.S. Court of Appeals, Third Circuit; registered to practice before the U.S. Patent and Trademark Office (Not admitted in Delaware). *Education:* University of Pennsylvania (B.A., 1986); Temple University (J.D., 1989). Author, "Copyright Protection in the United States: It's All Berned Up," Temple International and Comp. L.J., Vol. 3, No. 1 (1989); "The Implications of Hyperlaw for Secondary Publisher," published in the Newsletter of the National Federation of Abstracting and Information Services in February, 1998; The Trademark and Copyright Book, Sirus Entertainment, 2001; "Cat and Mouse: Josie and the Pussycats Creator Challenges Copyright Ownership", The Philadelphia Lawyer, Summer 2001; "Move Over.Com, Make Way for.Biz", Marketing Management, July/August 2001. *Member:* Philadelphia (Member, Executive Committee, Young Lawyers Division), Pennsylvania and American Bar Associations; American Intellectual Property Law Association; Copyright Society (Member, Philadelphia Chapter); Benjamin Franklin Inns of the Court; International Trademark Association; Philadelphia Volunteer Lawyers for the Arts (PVLA); National Lesbian and Gay Lawyers Association (Member, Board of Directors; Co-chair Elect, Co-Chair, 2001-2002) (NLGLA). ***PRACTICE AREAS:*** Trademarks; Unfair Competition; Copyrights. ***Email:*** mll@cblhlaw.com

DANIEL J. HARBISON, born Louisville, Kentucky, March 19, 1971; admitted to bar, 2000, Delaware; 2000, New Jersey; 2001, U.S. District Court, District of Delaware. *Education:* Purdue University (B.S., ChemE, with honors, 1995); Widener Law School (J.D., 2000). *Member:* Delaware and American Bar Associations. ***PRACTICE AREAS:*** Patent Litigation; Trademark; Copyright; Trade Secret; Antiboycott Compliance. ***Email:*** djh@cblhlaw.com

LARRY J. HUME, born Flint, Michigan, January 10, 1956; admitted to bar, 2001, Virginia, U.S. District Court, Eastern District of Virginia, U.S. Court of Appeals, Fourth Circuit and U.S. Court of Appeals for the Federal Circuit; registered to practice before U.S. Patent and Trademark Office (Not admitted in Delaware). *Education:* Arizona State University (B.S.E.E., 1978); Naval Postgraduate School (M.S.E.E., Elec. Eng., 1985); Hawaii Pacific University (M.B.A., 1990); George Mason University School of Law (J.D., 2000). Eta Kappa Nu; Tau Beta Pi. *Member:* Virginia State Bar Association; American Intellectual Property Law Association; Federal Circuit Bar Association; Institute of Electronics Engineers. [With U.S. Navy, 1978-1998, Commander]. (Resident, Washington, DC Office). ***PRACTICE AREAS:*** Patent; Trademark; Litigation Support; Copyright; Trade Secret. ***Email:*** ljh@cblhlaw.com

PATRICK J. WELLS, born Buffalo, New York, October 26, 1961; admitted to bar, 1999, New York; 2000, New Jersey (Not admitted in Delaware). *Education:* Marquette University (B.S., Civil Engineering, 1984); The George Washington University (M.S., Engineering Management, 1993); American University (J.D., 1998). *Member:* New York state and American Bar Associations; American Intellectual Property Law Association. (Resident, Washington, D.C. Office). ***PRACTICE AREAS:*** Intellectual Property; Patent Prosecution. ***Email:*** pjw@cblhlaw.com

MICHAEL L. DONNER, SR., born Richmond, Virginia, July 27, 1961; admitted to bar, 1997, Virginia (Not admitted in Delaware). *Education:* United States Naval Academy (B.S., 1983); George Mason University (J.D., with honors, 1996). [LT U.S. Navy, 1983-1993]. (Resident, Washington, D.C. Office). ***PRACTICE AREAS:*** Intellectual Property. ***Email:*** mld@cblhlaw.com

(This Listing Continued)

COOCH AND TAYLOR

Established in 1960

SUITE 1000, 824 MARKET STREET MALL
P.O. BOX 1680
WILMINGTON, DELAWARE 19899-1680
Telephone: 302-652-3641
Telecopier: 302-652-5379
URL: http://www.coochandtaylor.com

Newark Office: 51 E. Main Street, Suite B, P.O. Box 672. Telephone: 302-368-7200. Telecopier: 302-368-7491.

Kennett Square, Pennsylvania Office: 502 West Cypress Street, P.O. Box 909. Telephone: 610-444-3700. Telecopier: 610-444-5446.

General Practice, Banking, Litigation. Corporation, Real Estate, Environmental, Land Use and Development, Construction and Asbestos Defense, Trial Practice in all Federal and Delaware Courts, Family, Personal Injury, Probate, Estate Planning, Taxation, Commercial, Bankruptcy and Chancery Court Practice.

(This Listing Continued)

MEMBERS OF FIRM

DONALD C. TAYLOR, born Wilmington, Delaware, March 17, 1930; admitted to bar, 1954, Delaware and District of Columbia; 1955, U.S. District Court, District of Delaware; 1957, U.S. Court of Appeals, Third Circuit; 1965, U.S. Supreme Court. *Education:* Dickinson College (A.B., 1952); The Dickinson School of Law of the Pennsylvania State University (J.D., 1954). Omicron Delta Kappa. Member, Board of Editors, Dickinson Law Review, 1953-1954. Co-Author, "Delaware Fundamentals of Real Estate Law," published by Division of Continuing Legal Education, University of Delaware, 1972, revised 1978, 1979, 1987. Lecturer, Real Estate Law: Goldey Beacom College, 1967-1978; Wesley College, 1978; University of Delaware, 1979-1994. Director, 1978—, Artisans' Bank. Member, Council on Development Finance, State of Delaware, 1982-1995. Trustee, 1986—, Vice President, 1993-1998 and President, 1998—, Dickinson School of Law. Former Chairman, Red Cross, Delaware Chapter. Chancellor, Episcopal Diocese of Delaware. *Member:* Delaware State (Member, 1964— and Chairman, 1970-1974, Real and Personal Property Committee; Member: Bank Relations Committee, 1969-1970; Nominating Committee, 1970-1973; General Legislation Committee, 1974; Executive Committee, 1981; Member, 1977-1984 and Chairman, 1980, Specialization Committee) and American (Member, Committee on Federal Tax Aspects of Real Estate Transactions, 1975-1984) Bar Associations; American College of Real Estate Lawyers. ***PRACTICE AREAS:*** Real Estate; Banking Law; Business Law. **Email:** dtaylor@coochandtaylor.com

H. ALFRED TARRANT, JR., born Wilmington, Delaware, September 23, 1935; admitted to bar, 1961, Delaware. *Education:* Washington & Lee University (A.B., 1957); University of Delaware (M.A., 1959); University of Maryland (LL.B., 1961). Phi Alpha Delta. *Member:* Delaware State Bar Association (Member, 1968— and Chairman, 1978-1979, Family Law Committee). Fellow, American Academy of Matrimonial Lawyers. ***PRACTICE AREAS:*** Domestic Relations. **Email:** ftarrant@coochandtaylor.com

ROBERT W. CROWE, born Wilmington, Delaware, March 6, 1939; admitted to bar, 1965, Delaware. *Education:* Bowdoin College (A.B., 1960); The Dickinson School of Law of the Pennsylvania State University (LL.B., 1965). Member, Board of Editors, Dickinson Law Review, 1963-1965. *Member:* Delaware State (Member and Chairman, 1976-1978, 1987-1988, Estates and Trusts Section) and American (Member, Real Property, Probate and Trust Law Section) Bar Associations. Fellow, American College of Trust and Estate Counsel. ***PRACTICE AREAS:*** Estate Planning; Estate Settlements. **Email:** rcrowe@coochandtaylor.com

BONNIE H. SHEER, born Washington, D.C., July 27, 1943; admitted to bar, 1968, Virginia; 1970, Delaware. *Education:* Bucknell University (A.B., 1965); George Washington University (J.D., 1968). Kappa Beta Pi. Lecturer, Real Estate Law, Goldey Beacom College, 1974-1993. *Member:* Delaware State (Member, Real and Personal Property Section), Virginia (Associate) and American (Member, Real Property, Probate and Trust Law Section) Bar Associations; Virginia State Bar. ***PRACTICE AREAS:*** Real Estate. **Email:** bsheer@coochandtaylor.com

W. JEFFREY WHITTLE, born West Chester, Pennsylvania, May 31, 1947; admitted to bar, 1972, Delaware; 1973, U.S. District Court, District of Delaware; 1979, Pennsylvania; 1980, U.S. Supreme Court; 1981, U.S. Tax Court. *Education:* Pennsylvania State University (B.A., 1969); University of Kentucky (J.D., 1972); Temple University (LL.M., Taxation, 1978). Director, Attorneys Liability Protection Society. *Member:* Chester County, Delaware State (Member, Sections on: Real Property, Estates and Trusts; Personal Property), Pennsylvania and American (Member, Sections on: Real Property, Probate and Trust Law; Urban, State and Local Government Law; Law Practice Management) Bar Associations. ***PRACTICE AREAS:*** Real Estate; Land Use Law; Estate Planning; Estate Settlements. **Email:** jwhittle@coochandtaylor.com

MICHAEL A. FRIEDBERG, born New York, N.Y., September 6, 1947; admitted to bar, 1972, Virginia; 1976, U.S. Tax Court, U.S. Court of Federal Claims and U.S. Supreme Court; 1977, Delaware; 1979, Pennsylvania. *Education:* University of Virginia (B.A., 1969; J.D., 1972); Georgetown University (LL.M., Taxation, 1976). Attorney, Tax Court Litigation Division, Office of the Chief Counsel, Internal Revenue Service, 1972-1977. *Member:* Delaware State (Member and Chairman, 1987-1988, Tax Section; Chairman, Estates and Trusts Section, 1993), Virginia, Pennsylvania and American (Member, Taxation Section) Bar Associations; Virginia State Bar. ***PRACTICE AREAS:*** Tax Law; Estate Planning; Business Law; Corporate Law. **Email:** maf1del@aol.com

JEOFFREY L. BURTCH, born Columbus, Ohio, February 4, 1950; admitted to bar, 1978, Delaware, U.S. District Court, District of Delaware and U.S. Court of Appeals, Third Circuit. *Education:* Miami University (B.A., 1972; M.A.T., 1975); University of Toledo (J.D., 1978). Member, Panel of Chapter 7 Trustees. *Member:* Delaware State (Member, Commercial Law Section) and American (Member, Corporation, Banking and Business Law Section) Bar Associations; National Association of Bankruptcy Trustees; American Bankruptcy Institute. ***PRACTICE AREAS:*** Bankruptcy; Commercial Law; Banking Law. **Email:** jlburtch@coochandtaylor.com

(This Listing Continued)

C. SCOTT REESE, born Wilmington, Delaware, December 3, 1955; admitted to bar, 1981, Delaware and U.S. District Court, District of Delaware. *Education:* Colgate University (B.A., 1978); Widener University School of Law (J.D., 1981). Member, Moot Court Honor Society, 1980-1981. *Member:* Delaware (Member, Litigation Section) and American (Member, Litigation Section) Bar Associations; Defense Research Institute; Defense Counsel of Delaware. ***PRACTICE AREAS:*** Construction; Asbestos Defense; Products Liability; Commercial Litigation. **Email:** csreese@coochandtaylor.com

ANDREW P. TAYLOR, born Wilmington, Delaware, April 1, 1958; admitted to bar, 1982, Delaware; 1983, Pennsylvania and U.S. District Court, District of Delaware; 1999, U.S. Supreme Court. *Education:* University of Delaware (B.S., 1979); The Dickinson School of Law of Pennsylvania State University (J.D., 1982). Omicron Delta Epsilon. Legal Counsel for: Delaware Association of Realtors; New Castle County Board of Realtors. President, Board of Trustees, 1994-2000 and Trustee, Independence School, 1999-2001. Corporator, Artisans' Savings Bank. *Member:* Delaware State (Member, Vice Chairman, 1992-1994 and Chairman, 1994-1996, Real and Personal Property Section) and American (Member, Real Property, Probate and Trust Law Section) Bar Associations. (Also at Newark Office). ***PRACTICE AREAS:*** Real Estate; Real Estate Brokerage Law; Fair Housing; General Practice. **Email:** aptaylor@coochandtaylor.com

THOMAS D. SHELLENBERGER, born Wilmington, Delaware, April 14, 1959; admitted to bar, 1985, Delaware, U.S. District Court, District of Delaware and U.S. Court of Appeals, Third Circuit. *Education:* George Washington University; University of Delaware (B.A., 1982); Western New England College (J.D., cum laude, 1985). *Member:* Delaware State Bar Association (Member, Family Law Section). ***PRACTICE AREAS:*** Family Law; Foreclosures. **Email:** tdshell@coochandtaylor.com

---

PAULA C. WITHEROW, born Wilmington, Delaware, June 26, 1957; admitted to bar, 1990, Delaware; 1991, Pennsylvania and U.S. District Court, District of Delaware; 1993, U.S. Court of Appeals, Third Circuit; 1994, U.S. Supreme Court. *Education:* Pennsylvania State University (B.S., cum laude, 1979); Widener University School of Law (J.D., cum laude, 1990). Member, Moot Court Honor Society. *Member:* Chester County, Delaware and American Bar Associations; Delaware Trial Lawyers Association. (Also at Kennett Square, PA Office). ***PRACTICE AREAS:*** Personal Injury; Litigation. **Email:** pwithero@coochandtaylor.com

MARY ANN P. BAZZANO, born Chester County, Pennsylvania, February 7, 1963; admitted to bar, 1991, Pennsylvania, Delaware and U.S. Court of Appeals, Third Circuit. *Education:* St. Joseph's University (B.S., 1985); Widener University School of Law (J.D., 1990). *Member:* Chester County (Chairperson, Pro-Bono Committee), Delaware, Pennsylvania and American Bar Associations. (Resident, Kennett Square, PA Office). ***PRACTICE AREAS:*** Litigation; Personal Injury; Family Law. **Email:** mbazzano@inet.net

GREGORY J. WEINIG, born Wilmington, Delaware, May 9, 1971; admitted to bar, 1996, Delaware; 1997, Pennsylvania and U.S. District Court, District of Delaware. *Education:* Davidson College (B.A., 1993); Washington and Lee University (J.D., 1996); Villanova University. Associate Editor, 1994-1995 and Executive Editor, 1995-1996, Capital Defense Journal. ***PRACTICE AREAS:*** Estate Planning; Estate Settlements; Real Estate; Estate; Probate; Litigation; Bankruptcy Litigation; Bankruptcy Chapter 7. **Email:** gjweinig@coochandtaylor.com

ADAM SINGER, born London, England, February 27, 1960; admitted to bar, 1986, Massachusetts, New York and Delaware. *Education:* Johns Hopkins University (B.E.S. & M.S.E., 1981); Boston University (J.D., 1985). 1985 Edward F. Hennessey Scholar. *Member:* Delaware (Member, Professional Ethics Committee, 1988—; Co-Chair, 1999) Bar Association; Community Legal Aid Society, Inc. (Member, Board of Directors, 1994—); American Bankruptcy Institute. ***PRACTICE AREAS:*** Creditors Rights; Bankruptcy Chapter 11; Bankruptcy Chapter 7. **Email:** asinger@coochandtaylor.com

ROBERT W. PEDIGO, admitted to bar, 2001, Delaware. *Education:* Andrews Univerisity (B.A., 1981); Dickinson Law School (J.D., 2000).

SPECIAL COUNSEL

STEVEN H. AMICK, born Ithaca, New York, 1947; admitted to bar, 1972, Delaware; 1973, U.S. District Court, District of Delaware. *Education:* Washington College (B.A., 1969); The Dickinson School of Law of Pennsylvania State University (J.D., 1972). Counsel, Legal Department, E.I. duPont de Nemours, 1974-1996. Member: Delaware Courts Planning Committee, Delaware State House of Representatives, 1986-1994; Delaware State Senate, 1994—. Chairman: Joint Sunset Committee, 1986-1994; Judiciary Committee, 1992-1994; Rules Committee, 1992-1994. Senate Minority Whip, 1996-1998. Senate Minority Leader, 1998—. *Member:* Delaware State Bar Association (Member, Real Property Section). (Resident, Newark Office).

(This Listing Continued)

COOCH AND TAYLOR, Wilmington—Continued

OF COUNSEL

EDWARD W. COOCH, JR., born Wilmington, Delaware, March 22, 1920; admitted to bar, 1948, Delaware, U.S. District Court, District of Delaware and U.S. Court of Appeals, 3rd Circuit; 1965, U.S. Supreme Court. *Education:* University of Delaware (B.A., 1941); University of Virginia (LL.B., 1948). Assistant Attorney, Levy Court of New Castle County, 1955-1958. Member, Delaware Board of Bar Examiners, 1967-1974. Director, Wilmington Trust Co., 1974-1993. *Member:* Delaware State (Secretary, 1951-1952; Chairman: General Legislative Committee, 1968-1969; Committee on Uniform State Laws, 1970-1971; Member: Judicial Appointments Committee, 1976-1982; Estates and Trusts Section) and American (Member, Real Property, Probate and Trust Law Section) Bar Associations. ***PRACTICE AREAS:*** General Practice; Business Law; Estate Planning; Estate Settlements.

REPRESENTATIVE CLIENTS: Artisans' Bank; Trustees of the New Castle Common; Delaware Association of Realtors; Zurich-American Insurance Group; Greater New York Insurance Cos.; Ryder Truck Rental, Inc.; CNA; CIGNA Insurance Co.; Employers Insurance of Wausau; National Casualty Co.; Maryland Casualty Co.; Superior Insurance Co.; American Modern Insurance Co.; PNC Mortgage Corp. of America; Allied Industries; B.P. America; Principal Residential Mortgage; Jeoffrey L. Burtch, Chapter 7 Trustee.
APPROVED ATTORNEYS FOR: TICOR Title Insurance Co.; Lawyers Title Insurance Corp.; Transnation Title Insurance Company.
REFERENCES: PNC Bank, Delaware; Wilmington Trust Co.; Artisans' Bank.

COZEN O'CONNOR

A PROFESSIONAL CORPORATION

CHASE MANHATTAN CENTRE
1201 NORTH MARKET STREET
SUITE 1400
WILMINGTON, DELAWARE 19801
Telephone: 302-295-2000
888-207-2440
Fax: 302-295-2013
Email: postmaster@cozen.com
URL: http://www.cozen.com

Philadelphia, Pennsylvania Office: 1900 Market Street, 19103. Telephones: 215-665-2000; 800-523-2900. Fax: 215-665-2013.

West Conshohocken, Pennsylvania Office: 200 Four Falls Corporate Center, Suite 400, P.O. Box 800, 19428. Telephone: 610-941-5400; 800-379-0695. Fax: 610-941-0711.

Charlotte, North Carolina Office: One First Union Center, 301 South College Street, Suite 2100, 28202. Telephones: 704-376-3400; 800-762-3575. Fax: 704-334-3351.

Dallas, Texas Office: BankOne Center, 1717 Main Street, Suite 2300, 75201. Telephones: 214-462-3000; 800-448-1207. Fax: 214-462-3299.

New York, N.Y. Office: 45 Broadway Atrium, 16th Floor, 10006. Telephones: 212-509-9400; 800-437-7040. Fax: 212-509-9492.

San Diego, California Office: Suite 1610, 501 West Broadway, 92101. Telephones: 619-234-1700; 800-782-3366. Fax: 619-234-7831.

Los Angeles, California Office: 777 South Figueroa Street, Suite 2850, 90017. Telephones: 213-892-7900; 800-563-1027. Fax: 213-892-7999.

Seattle, Washington Office: Suite 5200, Washington Mutual Tower, 1201 Third Avenue, 98101. Telephones: 206-340-1000; 800-423-1950. Fax: 206-621-8783.

Newark, New Jersey Office: One Newark Center, Suite 1900, 07102. Telephone: 973-286-1200; 888-200-9521. Fax: 973-242-2121.

Atlanta, Georgia Office: Suite 2200, SunTrust Plaza, 303 Peachtree Street, N.E., 30308. Telephones: 404-572-2000; 800-890-1393. Fax: 404-572-2199.

London, England Office: Tower 42, Level 23, 25 Old Broad Street, London EC2N 1HQ. Telephone: 011-44-20-7864-2000. Fax: 011-44-20-7864-2013.

Las Vegas, Nevada Office (Affiliated with the Law Offices of J. Goldberg, C. Stuart, III & D. Grossman): #1, 1000 East Sahara Avenue, 89104-3231. Telephone: 800-782-3366.

San Francisco, California Office: 425 California Street, Suite 1800, 94104-2203. Telephone: 415-617-6100; 800-818-0165. Fax: 415-617-6101.

Chicago, Illinois Office: 222 South Riverside, Suite 1500, 60606. Telephone: 312-382-3100; 877-992-6036. Fax: 312-382-8910.

Washington, D.C. Office: 1667 K Street, NW, 20006. Telephone: 202-912-4800; 800-540-1355. Fax: 202-912-4830.

Cherry Hill, New Jersey Office: LibertyView, Suite 300, 457 Haddonfield Road, P.O. Box 5459, 08002-2220. Telephone: 856-910-5000; 800-989-0499. Fax: 856-910-5075.

Acquisitions and Divestitures, Admiralty and Maritime Law, Agents and Brokers Errors and Omissions, Alternative Dispute Resolution, Antitrust and Unfair Competition, Appellate Litigation, Appellate Practice, Arbitration and Alternative Dispute Resolution, Arson and Insurance Fraud, Asset Protection, Aviation Insurance, Aviation Law, Aviation Litigation, Aviation Products Liability, Bad Faith Litigation,

(This Listing Continued)

Bankruptcy, Bankruptcy, Insolvency and Restructuring, Banks and Banking, Business Law, Casualty Insurance Defense, Civil Practice, Commercial Law, Commercial Litigation, Commercial Real Estate, Complex and Multi-District Litigation, Construction Claims, Construction Law, Construction Law and Litigation, Copyrights, Corporate and Partnership Law, Corporate Law, Corporate Planning, Creditors Rights, Crisis Management, Debtor and Creditor, Directors and Officers Errors and Omissions, E-Commerce and Internet Law, Electric Utility Regulation, Emerging Business and Venture Capital, Emerging Growth Companies, Employee Benefits, Employee Benefits and Executive Compensation, Employment Defense, Employment Practices, Energy, Energy Regulation, Environmental Insurance, Environmental Insurance Claims, Environmental Law, Estate Planning, Family Law, Finance, Financial Services, First and Third Party Insurance Defense, Gas Utility Regulation, Health Law, Healthcare, Healthcare Finance, Healthcare Litigation, Healthcare Regulation, Healthcare Reimbursement, Information Technology, Insurance, Insurance Bad Faith Defense, Insurance Corporate and Regulatory, Insurance Coverage, Insurance Coverage Defense, Insurance Defense, Insurance Mergers and Acquisitions, Insurance Regulation, Intellectual Property, Intellectual Property Litigation, Intentional Torts, International Estate Planning, International Tax and Estate Planning, International Trusts, Labor and Employment, Latin America Practice Group, Litigation, Management Labor Law, Marine and Maritime Law, Medical Devices Defenses, Medical Malpractice Defense, Mergers, Partnership Law, Patent Privacy Law, Planning and Land Use, Privacy Law and Regulation, Private Wealth Services, Products Liability, Professional Liability, Project Finance, Property Insurance, Property Subrogation, Public Finance, Public Utility Regulation, Punitive Damages, Punitive Damages Reinsurance, Real Estate, Real Estate Litigation, Reinsurance, RICO, Securities, Securities Litigation, Tax Litigation, Taxation, Torts, Toxic and Other Mass Torts, Toxic Torts, Trademarks, Trusts and Estates, Utility Law, Wealth Preservation, White Collar Crime, Zoning.

FIRM PROFILE: Cozen O'Connor is a dynamic, full-service client-oriented actively engaged in a diverse business and litigation practice. Headquartered in Philadelphia, Pennsylvania, the firm consists of over 430 lawyers practicing from sixteen offices in the United States and an international office in London. The firm's practice is divided into four areas: business law, business litigation, insurance litigation, and personal wealth services.

Cozen O'Connor is dedicated to and focused on providing each client with the highest level of legal services rendered in the most efficient and cost-effective manner. Our philosophy acknowledges the paramount importance of each client's interests and we recognize that effective attorney-client relationships not only exist between institutions but with individuals as well. We endeavor to develop trust and confidence through close personal working relationships between our attorneys and the individual representatives of each client. This attention to the specific needs of each client explains our ability to represent a diverse clientele. Our clients range from individuals to corporations, including major utility companies, banks, real estate investment trusts, professional corporations, public companies, domestic insurance companies and foreign insurance syndicates.

FIRM MEMBERS IN WILMINGTON

MARK E. FELGER, born Buffalo, New York, 1963; admitted to bar, 1989, Pennsylvania; U.S. District Court, Eastern District of Pennsylvania; 1996, New Jersey and U.S. District Court, District of New Jersey; U.S. Court of Appeals, Third Circuit; 2000, Delaware, U.S. District Court, District of Delaware. *Education:* Rochester Institute of Technology (B.S., with honors, 1985); Boston University (J.D., 1989). *Member:* Philadelphia, Pennsylvania, Delaware State, New Jersey State and American (Member, Business Bankruptcy Sections) Bar Associations; Eastern District of Pennsylvania Bankruptcy Conference, Rules and Education Committees; American Bankruptcy Institute. ***PRACTICE AREAS:*** Bankruptcy Chapter 11; Insolvency; Workouts; Bankruptcy Litigation; Business Reorganization. ***Email:*** mfelger@cozen.com

DANIEL V. FOLT, born Akron, Ohio, 1957; admitted to bar, 1992, Delaware; 1993, Pennsylvania. *Education:* College of Great Falls (B.S., magna cum laude, 1979); California State University at Sacramento (M.S., 1988); McGeorge School of Law, University of the Pacific (J.D., with great distinction, 1992). Order of the Coif; Valedictorian. Law Clerk to Justice Andrew G.T. Moore, Delaware Supreme Court, 1992-1993. Special Deputy Attorney General, State of Delaware, 1993-1995. ***PRACTICE AREAS:*** Corporate Litigation; Commercial Litigation; Complex Litigation.

STEVEN L. BIENER, born 1961; admitted to bar, 1987, New York; 1990, Delaware. *Education:* Cornell University (B.S.); New York University (J.D.). ***PRACTICE AREAS:*** Corporate; Commercial; Environmental; Real Estate. ***Email:*** sbiener@cozen.com

FIRM ASSOCIATES IN WILMINGTON

GARY W. LIPKIN, born Philadelphia, Pennsylvania, November 17, 1971; admitted to bar, 1999, Pennsylvania and New Jersey; 2000, Delaware. *Educa-*

(This Listing Continued)

tion: Pennsylvania State University (B.S., 1995); Widener University School of Law (J.D., 1999). Moot Court. Widener Law Symp. Journal. ***PRACTICE AREAS:*** Complex Commercial Litigation. ***Email:*** glipkin@cozen.com

JENNIFER L. SCOLIARD, born Providence, Rhode Island, June 4, 1971; admitted to bar, 1997, Georgia (Not admitted in Delaware). *Education:* Widener University (B.A., cum laude, 1993); Mercer University (J.D., 1997). Phi Delta Phi. President, Public Interest Law Society, 1995-1996. *Member:* Atlanta Bar Association (Member, Bankruptcy Section, 1998—); State Bar of Georgia (Member, Sections on: Bankruptcy, 1997—; Creditors' Rights, 1999—); Georgia Association of Women Lawyers; American Bankruptcy Institute (Treasurer, 2000). ***PRACTICE AREAS:*** Bankruptcy Chapter 11; Bankruptcy Reorganization; Commercial Bankruptcy; Debtor Bankruptcy; Creditor Bankruptcy. ***Email:*** jscoliard@cozen.com

FIRM OF COUNSEL IN WILMINGTON

SANDRA KAUFMANN BATTAGLIA, born New York, N.Y., April 27, 1951; admitted to bar, 1977, Delaware; 1979, District of Columbia, U.S. District Court, District of Columbia and U.S. District Court, District of Delaware. *Education:* Vassar College (A.B., cum laude, 1972); Villanova University (J.D., cum laude, 1977). Order of the Coif. Law Clerk, Delaware Superior Court, 1977-1978. Author: "Managed Care or Managed Cost," Delaware Lawyer, Spring 2000; "Long Term Care and Managed Care," Delaware Medical Society Journal, October 1995. Lecturer: "Issues in Fundraising," Delaware Tax Exempt Organizations seminar, Wilmington, Delaware, June 2001; "Fundraising Issues," Delaware Tax Exempt Organizations seminar, Wilmington, Delaware, June 2000; "Legal Issues in Supportive Housing," American Association of Homes and Services for the Aging (AAHSA) Spring Conference, Washington, D.C., March 2000; "Managed Care and CCRCs," AASHA Annual Conference, New Orleans, Louisiana, October 1997; "Legal Issues for CCRCs - A View from the Inside," AAHSA Annual Conference, Philadelphia, Pennsylvania, October 1996; "Fair Housing Laws - How to Stay Out of Court," Pennsylvania Association of Not for Profit Homes for the Aging Annual Meeting, Valley Forge, Pennsylvania, May 1996; "Encouraging Diversity Through Advertising," United Methodist Association Annual Meeting, Cleveland, Ohio, April 1996; "Legal Issues Affecting CCRCs," American Health Lawyers Association Meeting on Long Term Care Issues, Orlando, Florida, February 1996; "Fair Housing Laws and Long Term Care Facilities," AAHSA Annual Meeting, San Antonio, Texas, November 1995. County Attorney, 1981-1983 and Director of Personnel, 1985-1987, New Castle County, Delaware. Attorney: ICI Americas, 1978-1981; Beneficial Corporation, Wilmington, Delaware, 1983-1987. Senior Vice President and General Counsel, Peninsula United Methodist Homes, Inc., Wilmington, Delaware, 1994-2000. Member, Legal Committee, American Association of Homes and Services for the Aging. Past President and Volunteer, CONTACT Delaware. Class Fund Co-Chair, Vassar College. *Member:* Delaware State (Vice Chair, 2000-2001 and Chair, 2001—, Health Law Section) and American Bar Associations; The District of Columbia Bar; American Health Lawyers Association. ***PRACTICE AREAS:*** Health Care; Nonprofit Organizations Law. ***Email:*** sbattaglia@cozen.com

REPRESENTATIVE CLIENTS: Available upon request.

KESTER I. H. CROSSE

1214 KING STREET
SUITE 300
WILMINGTON, DELAWARE 19801
Telephone: 302-658-3488
Fax: 302-652-3034
Email: kesterih@aol.com
URL: http://www.lawyers.com/kihcrosselaw

Civil Litigation, Personal Injury, Automobile Accidents and Injuries, Medical Malpractice, Family Law, Divorce, Child Custody, Child Support, Adoption Law, Business Law, Collections, Real Estate, Wills, Probate, Trusts and Estates, Employment Law, Discrimination.

KESTER I. H. CROSSE, born Port of Spain, Trinidad, October 17, 1945; admitted to bar, 1975, Delaware; 1976, U.S. District Court, District of Delaware. *Education:* University of Delaware (B.S., 1967); Tuck School, Dartmouth College (M.B.A., 1972); University of Virginia (J.D., 1975). Phi Delta Phi. Chairman, 1980-1982 and Secretary, 1980-1981, Wilmington Housing Authority. Assistant Public Defender, 1996—. *Member:* Delaware Bar Association (Assistant Secretary, 1979-1980; Member, Sections: Family Law; Multicultural Judges and Lawyers); Delaware Trial Lawyers Association. [1st Lt., U.S. Army, 1968-1970]

CROSSLAND, CONATY & ASSOCIATES, L.L.C.

1201 N. ORANGE STREET, SUITE 601
ONE COMMERCE CENTER
WILMINGTON, DELAWARE 19801
Telephone: 302-655-3000
Fax: 302-777-1218

General Civil Practice. Trusts and Estates, including Estate Planning, Estate Administration and Probate, Trust Planning and Wealth Preservation; Wills; Business Law and Commercial Law, including Business Start-Ups and Business Transfers; Construction Law; Contracts; Residential Real Estate and Commercial Real Estate; Civil Litigation, including Commercial Litigation, Contract Litigation, Personal Injury and Automobile Accidents and Injuries; Collections; Creditor Rights in Bankruptcy; Chancery Practice.

MEMBERS OF FIRM

DANIEL T. CROSSLAND, born Wilmington, Delaware, May 19, 1967; admitted to bar, 1992, Pennsylvania; 1993, Delaware; 1994, U.S. District Court, District of Delaware. *Education:* University of Rochester (B.A., 1989); Villanova University School of Law (J.D., 1992). *Member:* Delaware Bar Association (Member, Section on: Estates and Trusts). ***Email:*** dcrossland@cca-law.com

THOMAS P. CONATY, IV, born Dayton, Ohio, March 4, 1967; admitted to bar, 1994, Pennsylvania and Delaware; 1995, U.S. District Court, District of Delaware, District of Columbia and Colorado. *Education:* Washington College (B.A., 1989); Catholic University of America (J.D., 1992). Omicron Delta Kappa. Clerk, Hon. Haile Alford, Superior Court Judge of Delaware. Commissioner, Delaware Harness Racing Commission. *Member:* Delaware Bar Association (Member, Sections on: Litigation; Estates and Trusts). ***Email:*** tconaty@cca-law.com

COUNSEL

LISA K. W. CROSSLAND, born Corpus Christi, Texas, April 14, 1966; admitted to bar, 1992, Pennsylvania; 1996, Delaware. *Education:* Pennsylvania State University (B.A., 1987); Villanova University School of Law (J.D., magna cum laude, 1992). Order of the Coif. Member, 1990-1991 and Managing Editor of Articles, 1991-1992, Villanova Law Review. *Member:* Delaware State and American Bar Associations. ***Email:*** lcrossland@cca-law.com

ASSOCIATE

DAVID E. MATLUSKY, born Wilmington, Delaware, December 21, 1970; admitted to bar, 2000, Pennsylvania and Delaware; 2001, New Jersey and U.S. District Court, District of Delaware. *Education:* University of Delaware (B.S., 1993); Widener University School of Law (J.D., 1998). Phi Delta Phi. *Member:* Delaware, Pennsylvania and American (Member, Forum on the Construction Industry; Litigation Section) Bar Associations; Association of Trial Lawyers of America. ***Email:*** dmatlusky@cca-law.com

---

CHRISTINE K. DEMSEY

1328 KING STREET
WILMINGTON, DELAWARE 19801-3234
Telephone: 302-428-3190
Email: cdemsey@gte.com
URL: http://www.lawyers.com/dss

Family Law, Probate, Wills, Estate Administration, Guardianships and Conservatorships.

CHRISTINE K. DEMSEY, born Philadelphia, Pennsylvania, January 12, 1949; admitted to bar, 1982, Delaware and Pennsylvania. *Education:* Drexel University (B.S., 1971); Delaware Law School of Widener University (J.D., cum laude, 1981). Phi Kappa Phi; Phi Alpha Delta. Recipient, American Jurisprudence Award in Wills and Trusts. Hearing Officer, Fee Disputes, Delaware State Bar, 1991—. Special Master, Family Court, 1994—. Board Member, Legal Services Corporation of Delaware, Inc., 1996—. *Member:* Delaware State (Member, Executive Committee, 1987-1988; Chair, Family Law Section, 1997-1999; Chair, Women and Law Section, 1988-1989), Pennsylvania and American (Member, Family Law Section) Bar Associations. ***PRACTICE AREAS:*** Family Law; Probate; Wills.

DILWORTH PAXSON LLP

FIRST FEDERAL PLAZA
SUITE 500
WILMINGTON, DELAWARE 19801
Telephone: 302-571-9800
Fax: 302-571-8875
Email: lawyers@dilworthlaw.com
URL: http://www.dilworthlaw.com

Cherry Hill, New Jersey Office: Liberty View Suite 700, 457 Haddonfield Road, 08002. Telephone: 856-663-8877. Fax: 856-663-8855.
Harrisburg, Pennsylvania Office: 305 N. Front Street, Suite 403, 17101-1236. Telephone: 717-236-4812. Fax: 717-236-7811.
Newtown Square, Pennsylvania Office: 11 Campus Boulevard, Suite 150, 19073. Telephone: 610-325-3200. Fax: 610-325-3293.
Philadelphia, Pennsylvania Office: 3200 Mellon Bank Center, 1735 Market Street, 19103-7595. Telephone: 215-575-7000. Fax: 215-575-7200.
Turnersville, New Jersey Office: P.O. Box 762, University Executive Campus Suite 201, 151 Fries Mill Road, 08012. Telephone: 856-227-6100. Fax: 856-227-7373.
Washington, D.C. Office: 1200 Nineteenth Street, N.W., 20036. Telephone: 202-452-0900. Fax: 202-452-0930.

General Practice in all Courts, Corporate, Litigation, Bankruptcy and Insolvency, Criminal and Regulatory Investigations, E-Commerce, Employment and Management Labor Relations, Entertainment, Environmental, Healthcare, Insurance Regulation, Intellectual Property, International, Public Finance, Real Estate Securities, Tax, Trust and Estates.

MEMBER OF THE FIRM

ROBERT FORREST STEWART, JR., admitted to bar, 1968, District of Columbia; 1969, Delaware; 1976, Pennsylvania. *Education:* College of the Holy Cross (B.S., 1965); Georgetown University (J.D., 1968); Temple University (LL.M., Labor, 1978). Editor, *The Georgetown Law Journal,* 1967-1968. Lecturer and Author of Course Materials: Federal Publications Inc., "Personnel and Employment Law in Pennsylvania, New Jersey and Delaware" (1988) and "Sexual Harassment" (1993); Lorman Education Services, "Employee Discharge and Documentation" (1998); "Pennsylvania Unemployment Compensation" (1998) and "Pennsylvania, New Jersey and Delaware Wage and Hour Law Update" (1999). Author and Editor of Publication: Midatlantic Employers' Association, "Employer's Guide to Delaware and Federal Employee Relations Laws and Regulations" (1998). Chairman, Employee Relations Committee, Delaware State Chamber of Commerce. (Also in Philadelphia, Pennsylvania office). ***PRACTICE AREAS:*** Labor and Employment Law. ***Email:*** RStewart@dilworthlaw.com

(For all Personnel and Biographical data, see Professional Biographies at Philadelphia, Pennsylvania)

DUANE, MORRIS & HECKSCHER LLP

1100 NORTH MARKET STREET, SUITE 1200
WILMINGTON, DELAWARE 19801
Telephone: 302-657-4900
Fax: 302-657-4901
URL: http://www.duanemorris.com

Philadelphia, Pennsylvania Office: Suite 4200, One Liberty Place. Telephone: 215-979-1000. Fax: 215-979-1020.
New York, New York Office: 380 Lexington Avenue. Telephone: 212-692-1000. Fax: 212-692-1020.
London, England Office: 4 Chiswell Street, 5th Floor, EC1Y 4UP. Telephone: +44 20 7786 2100. Fax: +44 20 7786 2101.
Chicago, Illinois Office: 227 West Monroe Street, Suite 3400. Telephone: 312-499-6700. Fax: 312-499-6701.
Washington, D.C. Office: 1667 K Street, N.W., Suite 700. Telephone: 202-776-7800. Fax: 202-776-7801.
San Francisco, California Office: 100 Spear Street, Suite 1500. Telephone: 415-371-2200. Fax: 415-371-2201.
Boston, Massachusetts Office: 470 Atlantic Avenue, Suite 500. Telephone: 617-289-9200. Fax: 617-289-9201.
Atlanta, Georgia Office: 945 East Paces Ferry Road, Suite 2440. Telephone: 404-495-4900. Fax: 404-495-4901.
Miami, Florida Office: 200 South Biscayne Boulevard, Suite 3410. Telephone: 305-960-2200. Fax: 305-960-2201.
Harrisburg, Pennsylvania Office: 305 North Front Street, 5th Floor, P.O. Box 1003. Telephone: 717-237-5500. Fax: 717-232-4015.
Malvern, Pennsylvania Office: 200 Chesterfield Parkway, Suite 100. Telephone: 610-251-6900. Fax: 610-251-6901.
Cherry Hill, New Jersey Office: 51 Haddonfield Road, Suite 340. Telephone: 856-488-7300. Fax: 856-488-7021.

(This Listing Continued)

Newark, New Jersey Office: One Riverfront Plaza, 2nd Floor. Telephone: 973-424-2000. Fax: 973-424-2001.
Palm Beach, Florida Office: 249 Royal Palm Way, Suite 403. Telephone: 561-366-5400. Fax: 561-366-5401.
Allentown, Pennsylvania Office: 968 Postal Road, Suite 200, P.O. Box 90400. Telephone: 610-266-3650. Fax: 610-266-3651.
Houston, Texas Office: One Greenway Plaza, Suite 500. Telephone: 713-552-9900. Fax: 713-552-0109.
Bangor, Maine Office: 88 Hammond Street, Suite 500. Telephone: 207-262-5400. Fax: 207-262-5401.
Princeton, New Jersey Office: 100 College Road West, Suite 100. Telephone: 609-919-4400. Fax: 609-919-4401.
Westchester County, New York Office: 555 Pleasantville Road, Suite 200 North Building, Briarcliff Manor, New York. Telephone: 914-749-3700. Fax: 914-749-3701.

Alternative Dispute Resolution, Bankruptcy, Commercial Law, Corporate Law, Energy, Environmental Law, Estate and Asset Planning, Franchise Law, Health Care Law, Immigration Law, Intellectual Property, International Law, Labor and Employment, Litigation, Product Liability, Real Estate, Regulatory Compliance, Reorganization and Finance, Securities, Taxation and Telecommunications and Information Technologies.

FIRM PROFILE: Duane Morris is a full-service law firm. Founded in 1904, the firm has 19 offices in the United States. In 2000, the firm established itself in the United Kingdom with the formation of Duane, Morris & Heckscher, a law firm of solicitors and registered foreign lawyers, located in London and regulated by the Law Society in the conduct of investment business.

The firm's practice is varied and sophisticated, serving clients on local, national and international levels. A versatile and committed group of lawyers employing leading edge technologies and a strong administrative infrastructure enable Duane Morris to function cohesively and effectively in today's business climate. The firm is a member of several international networks, including Multilaw and TerraLex, to enhance client service and to support a growing international practice.

RESIDENT PARTNERS

MICHAEL R. LASTOWSKI, born Jersey City, New Jersey, December 26, 1953; admitted to bar, 1980, Pennsylvania; 2000, Delaware. *Education:* Brown University (B.A., 1976); University of Pennsylvania Law School (J.D., 1980). ***PRACTICE AREAS:*** Bankruptcy Law; Commercial Litigation. ***Email:*** mlastowski@duanemorris.com

THOMAS P. McGONIGLE, admitted to bar, 1993, Delaware and Pennsylvania. *Education:* Elizabethtown College (B.A., 1989); Dickinson School of Law (J.D., 1992). Judicial Clerk to the Honorable Richard R. Cooch, 1992-1993. Chief Legal Counsel & Policy Director to Governor Thomas R. Carper, 1998-2001, and Deputy Legal Counsel, 1995-1998, Office of the Governor, State of Delaware, Wilmington and Dover, Delaware. Deputy Attorney General, State of Delaware, Department of Justice, Wilmington, Delaware, 1992-1995. ***PRACTICE AREAS:*** Commercial Litigation; Administrative Law; Government Relations; Regulatory Law. ***Email:*** tpmcgonigle@duanemorris.com

FRANK E. NOYES, II, born Wilmington, Delaware, November 18, 1958; admitted to bar, 1986, Pennsylvania; 2000, Delaware. *Education:* University of Delaware (B.A., 1980); Boston College (J.D., 1986). Judicial Clerk to Honorable Jane R. Roth of United States District Court, District of Delaware, 1986-1987. ***PRACTICE AREAS:*** Product Liability; Civil Rights Liability; Tobacco Litigation; Insurance Coverage; Public Entity Liability; Civil Litigation; Zoning and Land Use. ***Email:*** noyes@duanemorris.com

JOHN L. REED, born Danville, Pennsylvania, November 5, 1964; admitted to bar, 1991, Delaware; 1993, Pennsylvania. *Education:* Villanova University (B.A., 1986); Widener University School of Law (J.D., 1991). Deputy Attorney General, State of Delaware, 1991-1995. President and Member, Delaware Chapter, Corporations and Securities Practice Group of The Federalist Society. ***PRACTICE AREAS:*** Litigation; Corporate; Securities; Partnership Law; Complex Commercial Litigation. ***Email:*** jlreed@duanemorris.com

RICHARD W. RILEY, born Philadelphia, Pennsylvania, January 15, 1962; admitted to bar, 1988, Pennsylvania and New Jersey; 2001, Delaware. *Education:* University of Notre Dame (B.B.A., 1984); Villanova University (J.D., 1988). ***PRACTICE AREAS:*** Bankruptcy Litigation; Civil Litigation; Commercial Litigation; Business Reorganization. ***Email:*** rwriley@duanemorris.com

CARL SCHNEE, born Philadelphia, Pennsylvania, January 2, 1936; admitted to bar, 1962, Delaware. *Education:* Muhlenberg College (B.A., 1957); Villanova University (J.D., 1961); University of Delaware (M.A., 2000). Chief Assistant Public Defender, State of Delaware, 1965-1969. United States Attorney, District of Delaware, 1999-2001. *Member:* Delaware State (Chair, Workers' Compensation Committee, 1969-1971) and American Bar Associations. (Part-

(This Listing Continued)

ner in Charge). ***PRACTICE AREAS:*** Commercial Litigation; Health Care; Professional Liability; White Collar Criminal Defense; Corporate Investigations. ***Email:*** cschnee@duanemorris.com

RESIDENT ASSOCIATES

TIMOTHY R. DUDDERAR, born Baltimore, Maryland, November 12, 1974; admitted to bar, 2000, Delaware. *Education:* University of Delaware (B.A., 1996); Villanova University (J.D., 1999). ***PRACTICE AREAS:*** Complex Commercial Litigation; Corporate Litigation; Securities Litigation; Partnership Law. ***Email:*** trdudderar@duanemorris.com

WILLIAM K. HARRINGTON, born Swampscott, Massachusetts, December 13, 1968; admitted to bar, 1996, Pennsylvania; 1998, New Jersey; 2001, Delaware. *Education:* Wharton School, University of Pennsylvania (B.S., 1990); Villanova University (J.D., 1996). ***PRACTICE AREAS:*** Reorganization; Finance Law. ***Email:*** wkharrington@duanemorris.com

RALPH N. SIANNI, born Wilmington, Delaware, January 23, 1968; admitted to bar, 1996, Pennsylvania; 2001, Delaware. *Education:* University of Pennsylvania (B.A., 1990); Yale University (M.A., 1991); Boston University (J.D., 1995). Note Editor, Boston Univ. Public Interest Law Journal. Judicial Clerk to the Hon. Stephen J. McEwen, Jr., President Judge, Pennsylvania Superior Court, 1997-1998. ***PRACTICE AREAS:*** Reorganization and Finance Law. ***Email:*** rnsianni@duanemorris.com

JOHN W. WEISS, born Abington, Pennsylvania, August 10, 1973; admitted to bar, 2001, Pennsylvania and New Jersey; 2001, Delaware. *Education:* The Ohio State University (B.A., 1996); Dickinson School of Law (J.D., 2000). ***PRACTICE AREAS:*** Reorganization and Finance. ***Email:*** jwweiss@duanemorris.com

OF COUNSEL

JUDITH NICHOLS RENZULLI, born Cambridge, Massachusetts, January 5, 1943; admitted to bar, 1980, Delaware; 1981, Pennsylvania. *Education:* Lebanon Valley College (B.S., 1963); University of Pennsylvania (J.D., 1980). ***PRACTICE AREAS:*** Commercial Litigation; Insurance Coverage Litigation; Real Estate Tax Assessment Litigation; Corporate Litigation. ***Email:*** renzulli@duanemorris.com

ELZUFON AUSTIN REARDON TARLOV & MONDELL, P.A.

Established in 1982
300 DELAWARE AVENUE
SUITE 1700
P.O. BOX 1630
WILMINGTON, DELAWARE 19899-1630
Telephone: 302-428-3181
Fax: 302-428-3180
URL: http://www.elzufon.com

General Civil and Trial Practice in all State and Federal Courts, Professional Liability Defense, Real Estate, Banking Law, Bankruptcy, Business Law, Corporate Law, Asbestos Defense, Products Liability, Workers Compensation Defense, Estate Planning and Construction Law.

FIRM PROFILE: Elzufon Austin Reardon Tarlov & Mondell is a service oriented law firm with a broad range of practice areas. Founded in 1982 by John A. Elzufon, the firm grew to its present size faster than any other Delaware firm. This was accomplished by an unwavering commitment to servicing client needs. The basic root of the firm is a general litigation practice. The firm also has an active transactional practice representing individual and corporate clients in commercial and residential real estate matters as well as corporate and business related issues.

JOHN A. ELZUFON, born Newark, New York, November 1, 1946; admitted to bar, 1974, Delaware; 1975, U.S. District Court, District of Delaware; 1977, U.S. Court of Appeals, Third Circuit; 1989, Pennsylvania and U.S. Supreme Court. *Education:* Rose-Hulman Institute of Technology (B.S.Ch.E., 1968); Georgetown University Law Center (J.D., 1974). Author: "New Members Manual to the U.S. House of Representatives," Georgetown University Law Center, 1974, 1976, 1978. Member, Superior Court Advisory Committee on Medical Malpractice, 1980—. Member, Insurance Commissioner's Task Force on Medical Malpractice, 1989-1991. *Member:* Delaware, Pennsylvania, Federal and American Bar Associations; Defense Research and Trial Lawyers Association; The Association of Trial Lawyers of America; Delaware Trial Lawyers Association. [Lieut., U.S. Army Corps of Engineers, 1969-1970]. ***PRACTICE AREAS:*** Professional Liability Defense; Products Liability Defense; Personal Injury. ***Email:*** jelzufon@elzufon.com

JEFFREY M. AUSTIN, born Wilmington, Delaware, June 19, 1957; admitted to bar, 1983, Delaware; 1989, Pennsylvania. *Education:* University of Delaware (B.S.B.A., cum laude, 1979); Boston College (J.D., 1982). Beta Gamma Sigma; Phi Kappa Phi. *Member:* Delaware (Member of Workers' Compensation, Tort and Insurance Practice Sections), Pennsylvania and American Bar Associations; Defense Counsel of Delaware; Philadelphia Workers' Compensation Claims Association. ***PRACTICE AREAS:*** Professional Liability Defense; Worker's Compensation Defense; Toxic Tort Defense. ***Email:*** jaustin@elzufon.com

MARK L. REARDON, born Wilmington, Delaware, January 12, 1960; admitted to bar, 1986, Pennsylvania; 1987, Delaware; 1988, U.S. District Court, District of Delaware; 1992, U.S. Court of Appeals, Third Circuit. *Education:* Boston College (B.S., 1982); Widener University School of Law (J.D., 1985). Counsel to Delaware State House of Representatives, 1991-1993. *Member:* Pennsylvania, Delaware and American Bar Associations; Delaware Trial Lawyers Association; The Defense Research Institute. ***PRACTICE AREAS:*** Civil Litigation; Construction Law; Torts and Insurance Law; Asbestos Litigation. ***Email:*** mreardon@elzufon.com

EDWARD A. TARLOV, born Wilmington, Delaware, February 6, 1958; admitted to bar, 1985, Pennsylvania; 1986, Delaware and U.S. District Court, District of Delaware. *Education:* Ithaca College (B.S., 1980); Drake University (J.D., 1984). Instructor: Real Estate Law, Advantage School of Real Estate 1993-1994; New Castle County Board of Realtors, 1994—; Delaware School of Real Estate, 1997—. *Member:* Pennsylvania, Delaware (Member, Real and Personal Property Sections) and American (Member, Real Property and Probate Section) Bar Associations. ***PRACTICE AREAS:*** Real Estate Law; Commercial Law; Banking Law; Civil Litigation. ***Email:*** etarlov@elzufon.com

SCOTT R. MONDELL, born Baltimore, Maryland, November 28, 1960; admitted to bar, 1985, Pennsylvania; 1987, U.S. District Court, Eastern District of Pennsylvania; 1988, Delaware; 1991, U.S. District Court, District of Delaware. *Education:* University of Delaware (B.S., 1982); Delaware Law School of Widener University (J.D., 1985). Elected as one of Delaware's Top Lawyers for Worker's Compensation Defense, 2001. *Member:* Delaware (Co-Chairman, Recent Caselaw Update Committee, Worker's Compensation Section, 1992-1994), Pennsylvania and American Bar Associations; Delaware Claims Association (Program Director, 1993-1999); Philadelphia Worker's Compensation Claims Association. ***PRACTICE AREAS:*** Worker's Compensation Defense; Bankruptcy Litigation. ***Email:*** smondell@elzufon.com

WILLIAM D. SULLIVAN, born Long Branch, New Jersey, November 29, 1962; admitted to bar, 1990, Delaware; 1990, Pennsylvania. *Education:* University of Notre Dame (B.S., 1984); Georgetown University (J.D., 1989). *Member:* Delaware State Bar Association (Member, Commercial Division); American Bankruptcy Institute. ***PRACTICE AREAS:*** Bankruptcy; Commercial Litigation. ***Email:*** bsullivan@elzufon.com

WILLIAM F. TAYLOR, JR., born Wilmington, Delaware, May 29, 1964; admitted to bar, 1991, Delaware and Pennsylvania. *Education:* University of Richmond (B.A., Intermediate honors, 1987); Dickinson School of Law (J.D., 1990). Pi Sigma Alpha. Staff Member and Business Manager, Dickinson Law Review, 1988-1990. Author: "Drafting of the Expulsion Clause in a Partnership Agreement, A Practical Approach," Dickinson Law Review, Vol. 93:3, 1989; "Designation Rights Sales," American Bankruptcy Institute, September, 2001. *Member:* Delaware, Pennsylvania and American (Member, Sections on: Bankruptcy; General Litigation) Bar Associations; American Bankruptcy Institute; Delaware Trial Lawyers Association. ***PRACTICE AREAS:*** Bankruptcy; Reorganization; Commercial Litigation. ***Email:*** wtaylor@elzufon.com

---

H. GARRETT BAKER, born Wilmington, Delaware, February 13, 1965; admitted to bar, 1990, Pennsylvania; 1992, Delaware; 1993, U.S. District Court, District of Delaware; U.S. Court of Appeals, Third Circuit; 1994, U.S. Supreme Court. *Education:* Evangel College (B.S., summa cum laude, 1986); Southern Illinois University (J.D., cum laude, 1990); University of Delaware (M.A., 1998). Phi Kappa Phi. Judicial Intern: Hon. Carol Los Mansmann, Circuit Judge, U.S. Court of Appeals, Third Circuit, 1989; Hon. Joseph T. Walsh, Associate Justice, Supreme Court of Delaware, 1992. Lead Articles Editor, Southern Illinois University Law Journal. Co-Author: "Survey of Family Law," 14 So. Ill. U.L.J. 1007 (1990). *Member:* Delaware State Bar Association. ***PRACTICE AREAS:*** Worker's Compensation; Insurance Defense; Litigation. ***Email:*** gbaker@elzufon.com

COLLEEN D. SHIELDS, born Wilmington, Delaware, December 26, 1967; admitted to bar, 1992, Delaware; 1993, U.S. District Court, District of Delaware; 1994, Pennsylvania. *Education:* University of Delaware (B.A., 1989); Widener University School of Law (J.D., cum laude, 1992). Phi Kappa Phi. *Member:* Delaware Bar Association; Delaware Defense Counsel. ***PRACTICE AREAS:*** Civil Litigation; Professional Liability Defense; Commercial Litigation; Real Estate. ***Email:*** cshields@elzufon.com

SCOTT A. SIMPSON, born Lawrence, Kansas, January 19, 1967; admitted to bar, 1997, Delaware. *Education:* University of Delaware (B.A., 1989); Widener University School of Law (J.D., 1996). *Member:* Delaware State Bar As-

(This Listing Continued)

ELZUFON AUSTIN REARDON TARLOV & MONDELL, P.A., Wilmington—Continued

sociation. ***PRACTICE AREAS:*** Workers Compensation Defense; Insurance Defense Litigation; General Liability Defense. ***Email:*** ssimpson@elzufon.com

ANN POULIOS, born Newport, New Hampshire, March 31, 1966; admitted to bar, 1992, Pennsylvania (Not admitted in Delaware). *Education:* State University of New York at Stony Brook (B.A., 1988); Widener University School of Law (J.D., 1991). ***PRACTICE AREAS:*** Worker's Compensation; Subrogation. ***Email:*** apoulios@elzufon.com

KELLY A. COSTELLO, born Wilmington, Delaware, January 13, 1965; admitted to bar, 1995, Delaware; 1996, Texas and U.S. District Court, District of Delaware. *Education:* University of Delaware (B.S., 1986); Widener University School of Law (J.D., 1994). Adjusters License, 1989. *Member:* Delaware State Bar Association; State Bar of Texas. ***PRACTICE AREAS:*** Professional Liability Defense; Insurance Defense. ***Email:*** kcostello@elzufon.com

KATHARINE L. MAYER, born Syosset, New York, November 12, 1973; admitted to bar, 1998, Delaware; 1999, U.S. District Court, District of Delaware. *Education:* University of Delaware (B.A., 1995); Widener University School of Law (J.D., cum laude, 1998). *Member:* Delaware State and American Bar Associations. ***PRACTICE AREAS:*** Bankruptcy; Real Estate; Corporate Law. ***Email:*** kmayer@elzufon.com

CHRISTIAN G. McGARRY, born Wilmington, Delaware, June 21, 1974; admitted to bar, 2000, Delaware and New Jersey. *Education:* University of Delaware (B.A., 1996); Widener School of Law (J.D., 1999). Phi Alpha Delta. Member, Republican Law Caucus, 1998. ***PRACTICE AREAS:*** Workers Compensation. ***Email:*** cmcgarry@elzufon.com

REPRESENTATIVE CLIENTS: ACE, USA; Aetna Insurance Co.; Agilent Technologies; Alexsis Insurance Co.; American International Adjustment Service; ASTRA Zeneca; Catalytic, Inc.; C. H. Hetrick Associates; Crawford and Company; Commonwealth Medical Liability Ins. Co.; Commonwealth Mutual Liability Ins. Co.; CNA Insurance Co.; Commerce Bank, N.A.; John Deere Insurance Co.; Erie Ins. Inc.; Encompanss Insurance Co.; Interstate Insurance Group; Employers Insurance of Wausau; Employers Reinsurance Co.; First American Title Ins. Co.; Friendly Ice Cream Corp.; Fireman's Fund; GAB Business Service, Inc.; Georgia Pacific Corporation; Great Central Insurance; The Harleysville Insurance Cos.; Lear Corp.; Liberty Mutual Insurance Co.; Orion Insurance Co.; Zurich Insurance Company; Risk Enterprise Management; OUM; Preferred Physician Mutual; Princeton Insurance Company; Professional Liability Insurance Co.; Prudential Insurance Co.; Raytheon Constructors and Engineers, Inc.; Reliance Insurance Co.; Royal Insurance Co.; RSKCO; Ryan Homes; St. Paul Fire and Marine; Schaefer Insurance Adjusters; Sedgwick Claims Management; Selective Insurance; Southern California Physicians Exchange; Toll Brothers, Inc.; Transamerica Title Insurance Co.; Montgomery Mutual Insurance Co.; Verizon Delaware, Inc.
APPROVED ATTORNEYS FOR: First American Title Insurance Co.; Stewart Title Guaranty Co.; Transamerica Title Insurance Co.; Ticor Title Insurance Company.

WILLIAM W. ERHART, P.A.

Established in 1992

300 DELAWARE AVENUE
SUITE 1130
P.O. BOX 234
WILMINGTON, DELAWARE 19899-0234
Telephone: 302-651-0113
Telecopier: 302-651-0331
URL: http://www.erhartlaw.com

Personal Injury, General Civil Litigation, Construction, Commercial, Creditor's Rights, Bankruptcy.

WILLIAM W. ERHART, born Wilmington, Delaware, May 8, 1951; admitted to bar, 1982, Delaware; 1983, U.S. District Court, District of Delaware; 1987, U.S. Court of Appeals, Third Circuit. *Education:* University of Delaware (B.A., 1979); Philadelphia Theology Seminary (B.D., 1979); Rutgers University (J.D., 1982). Member, Moot Court Board. Law Clerk, Superior Court 1982-1983. Deputy Attorney General, Delaware Department of Justice, 1983-1988. Lecturer: Consumer Law Seminar, Delaware State Bar Association 1989 and 1998; Construction Law, Lorman Seminars, 1999-2001. *Member:* Delaware Bar Association (Litigation Section, 1988—; Law and Technology Group 1991—); Delaware Trial Lawyers Association; The Association of Trial Lawyers of America (State Delegate; Member, Amicus Committee); St. Thomas More Society. [U.S.M.C. 1971-1973]. ***PRACTICE AREAS:*** Personal Injury; Commercial; Construction; Railroad Law; Creditors Rights; Bankruptcy. ***Email:*** billerhart@aol.com

APPROVED ATTORNEYS FOR: Chicago Title Insurance Co.; Ticor Title Insurance Co.; Lawyer's Title Insurance Co.
REPRESENTATIVE CLIENTS: Sysco Food Services Inc.; Rodel, Inc.; Onshore Construction Co.; R & T Group Inc.; L.F. Bafundo Roofing; Berman Development Co.; National Credit Company; Eastern Energy Harvesters, Inc.; TCBY, Inc. S.W. Downer Co., Inc., State of Delaware.

EVANS & ASSOCIATES

2 MILL ROAD
P.O. BOX 550
WILMINGTON, DELAWARE 19899-0550
Telephone: 302-655-8807; 302-655-5025
Telefax: 302-655-5441
Email: donaldelihuevans@evanslawonline.com
URL: http://www.lawyer.com/evans&associates

Affiliated With: Hwang & Associates, P.C., 1325 Spruce Street, Philadelphia, Pennsylvania, 19107. Telephone: 215-790-5100 x100. Fax: 215-790-8300. Email: HWANG@HWANGLAWFIRM.COM

General Civil Trial Practice in all Courts. Personal Injury, Negligence, Products Liability, Medical Malpractice, Automobile Accidents, Insurance Defense, Workers Compensation, Business Start-Ups, Commercial. Wills and Probate, Estate Planning, Trusts and Estates, Real Estate, Family Law, Child Custody, Child Support, Divorce, Bankruptcy.

MEMBER OF FIRM

DONALD ELIHU EVANS, born Kingston, Pennsylvania, January 28, 1947; admitted to bar, 1982, Delaware; 1983, Pennsylvania; U.S. District Court, District of Delaware and U.S. Court of Appeals, Third Circuit. *Education:* Boston University (B.A., 1972); Delaware Law School of Widener University (J.D., cum laude, 1982). Delta Theta Phi. Captain, Jessup International Moot Court Team, 1982. Member, Moot Court Honor Society. Recipient, American Jurisprudence Award for Excellence in Conflicts of Law. Member, Delaware Journal of Corporate Law, 1981-1982. *Member:* Delaware (Member, Litigation, Tort and Insurance Practice, Commercial Law and General Corporation Law Sections), Federal, American (Member, International Law and Practice, Tort and Insurance Practice and General Litigation Sections) and Inter-American Bar Associations; Delaware Trial Lawyers Association; The Association of Trial Lawyers of America; American Judicature Society. (Also Of Counsel, Hwang & Associates, P.C., Philadelphia, Pennsylvania). ***PRACTICE AREAS:*** Insurance Defense Law; Personal Injury Law; Worker's Compensation Law; New Business; Medical Malpractice Law.

REPRESENTATIVE CLIENTS: The Hartford Insurance Group; New York Stock Exchange.

FERRY & JOSEPH, P.A.

Established in 1990

824 MARKET STREET, SUITE 904
P.O. BOX 1351
WILMINGTON, DELAWARE 19899
Telephone: 302-575-1555
Fax: 302-575-1714
Email: info@ferryjoseph.com
URL: http://www.ferryjoseph.com

General Practice. Litigation, Bankruptcy, Probate, Probate and Guardianship Litigation, Elder Law, Negligence, Business, Commercial and Collection Law.

DAVID J. FERRY, JR., born Philadelphia, Pennsylvania, July 31, 1953; admitted to bar, 1982, Pennsylvania and Delaware; 1983, U.S. District Court, District of Delaware; 1995, U.S. Court of Appeals, Third Circuit. *Education:* St. Joseph's College (B.A., 1975); Delaware Law School of Widener University (J.D., 1981). *Member:* Pennsylvania, Delaware State (Chairman, Committee on Law and the Elderly, 1997-2000, Vice Chair, 2000-2001; and Secretary, Alternative Dispute Resolution Section, 2000—) and American Bar Associations; The Association of Trial Lawyers of America; Delaware Trial Lawyers Association. ***REPORTED CASES:*** Emmons v. Hartford Under, Ins. Co., 697 A.2d 742 (Del., 1997); Hudak v. Procek, 727 A.2d 841 (Del. 1999). ***PRACTICE AREAS:*** Litigation; Negligence; Commercial; Trusts and Estates; Probate Litigation; Guardianship Litigation; Elder Law. ***Email:*** dferry@ferryjoseph.com

MICHAEL B. JOSEPH, born Philadelphia, Pennsylvania, October 12, 1950; admitted to bar, 1976, Pennsylvania, Delaware and U.S. District Court, District of Delaware; 1977, New Jersey; U.S. District Court, District of New Jersey and U.S. Court of Appeals, Third Circuit. *Education:* Rutgers University (A.B., 1972); Delaware Law School of Widener University (J.D., 1975). Standing Chapter 13 Trustee for District of Delaware, 1987—. Member, Panel of Chapter 7 Trustees, 1982—. *Member:* Delaware State and American Bar Associations; Richard S. Rodney, Inn of Court; Commercial Law League of America; American Bankruptcy Institute; National Association of Bankruptcy Trustees; National Association of Chapter Thirteen Trustees. ***PRACTICE AREAS:*** Bankruptcy Law; Commercial Law. ***Email:*** mjoseph@ferryjoseph.com

THEODORE J. TACCONELLI, born Philadelphia, Pennsylvania, November 3, 1958; admitted to bar, 1988, Delaware; 1989, Pennsylvania, U.S. District Court, District of Delaware, U.S. District Court, Eastern District of

(This Listing Continued)

Pennsylvania; 1998, U.S. Court of Appeals, Third Circuit. *Education:* University of Delaware (B.S., 1982); Delaware Law School of Widener University (J.D., 1988). *Member:* Delaware State and American (Member, Business Law and Litigation Sections) Bar Associations; Commercial Law League of America. ***PRACTICE AREAS:*** Commercial Law; Bankruptcy Law; Litigation; Creditors Rights. ***Email:*** ttacconelli@ferryjoseph.com

JOHN D. MATTEY, born Pittsburgh, Pennsylvania, August 10, 1954; admitted to bar, 1992, Pennsylvania and Delaware; U.S. District Court, District of Delaware. *Education:* University of Delaware (B.S.B.A., 1977); Widener University School of Law (J.D., cum laude, 1991). Law Clerk, Hon. Jerome O. Herlihy, Superior Court, 1991-1992. *Member:* Delaware Bar Association. ***PRACTICE AREAS:*** Litigation; Bankruptcy; Collections. ***Email:*** jmattey@ferryjoseph.com

RICK S. MILLER, born Easton, Pennsylvania, September 14, 1965; admitted to bar, 1995, Delaware; 1996, U.S. District Court, District of Delaware; 1998, U.S. Court of Veterans Appeals. *Education:* Dickinson College (B.A., magna cum laude, Phi Beta Kappa, 1987); Widener University School of Law (J.D., magna cum laude, 1995). Member, Moot Court Honor Society. Member, Delaware Journal of Corporate Law, 1994-1995. Law Clerk to the Honorable Susan C. Del Pesco, Superior Court, 1995-1996. *Member:* Delaware State Bar Association; Delaware Trial Lawyers Association; Richard S. Rodney, Inn of Court. [U.S. Army, 1987-1991, First Lieutenant]. ***REPORTED CASES:*** Emmons v. Hartford Under. Ins. Co., 697 A.2d 742 (Del., 1997). ***PRACTICE AREAS:*** Litigation; Veterans Law; Commercial Law; Bankruptcy; Probate; Guardianship Litigation. ***Email:*** rmiller@ferryjoseph.com

JASON C. POWELL, born Salisbury, Maryland, May 16, 1972; admitted to bar, 1998, Delaware; 1999, U.S. District Court, District of Delaware. *Education:* La Salle University (B.A., 1993); Widener University School of Law (J.D., 1998). Phi Delta Phi. *Member:* Delaware and American Bar Associations. ***PRACTICE AREAS:*** Trusts and Estates; Mental Disability Law; Elder Law; Bankruptcy. ***Email:*** jpowell@ferryjoseph.com

EDWARD F. KAFADER, born Wilmington, Delaware, June 8, 1949; admitted to bar, 1976, Delaware; 1977, U.S. District Court, District of Delaware. *Education:* University of Delaware (B.S., 1971); Villanova University (J.D., 1976). Deputy Attorney General, 1977-1985. Attorney, Delaware State Senate, 2001. *Member:* Delaware Bar Association (Member, Medical-Legal Committee, 1980—). ***REPORTED CASES:*** Severns v. Wilmington Medical Center, et al., Del. Supr, 421 A2d 1334 (1980); Oakes v. Megaw, Del. Supr. 565 A2d 914 (1989); Wilmington United Neighborhoods v. Medical Center of Delaware, et al., D. Del. 458 F. Supp. 628, 615 F.2d 112 (1980); Pagano v. Hadley, et al., D. Del. 535 F. Supp. 92 (1982). ***PRACTICE AREAS:*** Insurance Defense; Wills; Estate Planning; Personal Injury; Government Affairs. ***Email:*** ekafader@ferryjoseph.com

REPRESERNTATIVE CLIENTS: First Union Bank (Trust Department); PNC Bank (Trust Department); News Journal Company.
REFERENCE: First Union Bank.

HERBERT G. FEUERHAKE

521 WEST STREET
WILMINGTON, DELAWARE 19801-2196
Telephone: 302-658-6101
Fax: 302-658-6105
Email: herblaw@verizonmail.com
URL: http://www.lawyers.com/feuerhakelaw

Employment Law, Wrongful Termination, Discrimination, Harassment, Americans with Disabilities Act, Unemployment Compensation, Civil Litigation.

HERBERT G. FEUERHAKE, born Ridgewood, New Jersey, February 22, 1956; admitted to bar, 1982, Connecticut and U.S. District Court, District of Connecticut; 1987, Delaware; 1998, U.S. District Court, District of Delaware and U.S. Court of Appeals, Third Circuit. *Education:* University of Delaware (B.A., cum laude, 1978); University of Pennsylvania (J.D., 1981). Phi Kappa Phi. Author: "Basic Civil Litigation," Glencoe-Shepard's-McGraw/Hill, 1993; "Basic Corporate Law and Business Organizations," Delaware supplement, Glenco-Shepard's-McGraw/Hill, 1996; "Scienter Requirement in Actions Under Antifraud Provision of Investment Adviser's Act, 15 U.S.C. Section 80b-6,"133 ALR Fed 549, 1996. Contributing Author, "Basic Legal Writing," Glenco-Shepard's-McGraw/Hill, 1993. Chapter Reviser, *Moore's Federal Practice,* Matthew Bender & Co., Inc., 1993-1995. Contributing Editor, Lawyers Cooperative Publishing Company (West Group), 1993—. Member, Board of Trustees, Mid-Fairfield Child Guidance Center, Norwalk, Connecticut, 1987-1996 (President, 1990-1991; Vice-President, 1989-1990, 1991-1994). Member, Board of Directors, Norwalk, Connecticut Historical Society, 1988-1991. Member, Wilmington 2000, Strategic Planning Committee and Transportation Working Group; Chairperson, Wayfinding Subcommittee, 1998. Member: Steering Committee, City of Wilmington Public Safety Strategic Planning Committee, 1998—; Westside Neighborhood Planning Council, 1997-1999; Cool Spring/Tilton Neighborhood Association, President, 1997-1999; Community Advisory Board, Horizon House, 1997-1999. *Member:* Delaware Bar Association; Delaware Employment Lawyers Association; National Employment Lawyers Association.

(This Listing Continued)

DAVID L. FINGER, P.A.

ONE COMMERCE CENTER
1201 ORANGE STREET, SUITE 725
WILMINGTON, DELAWARE 19801-1155
Telephone: 302-884-6766
Fax: 302-984-1294
URL: http://www.DavidFinger.com
Email: DLF@davidfinger.com
URL: http://www.lawyers.com/fingerlaw

Commercial Litigation, Bankruptcy Litigation, Corporate Litigation, Intellectual Property Litigation, Media/First Amendment Law, Civil Litigation.

DAVID L. FINGER, born Wilmington, Delaware, February 9, 1958; admitted to bar, 1988, Delaware; 1989, U.S. District Court, District of Delaware; 1990, U.S. Court of Appeals, Third Circuit. *Education:* University of Pennsylvania (B.A., 1980); University of Virginia (J.D., 1988). Co-Author: Delaware Trial Handbook, Lawyers Cooperative Publishing, 1994. Contributor: "Delaware's Freedom of Information Act", Reporters Committee for Freedom of the Press, 1993; Contributor: "Survey of Delaware Libel Law," *LDRC 50-State Survey* Libel Defense Resource Center, 1991-1993. *Member:* Delaware State (Former Chair, Government Law Section) and American (Member, Sections on: Business Law; Litigation; Communications Law) Bar Associations; First Amendment Lawyers Association.

FISH & RICHARDSON P.C.

919 NORTH MARKET STREET
SUITE 1000
P.O. BOX 1114
WILMINGTON, DELAWARE 19801
Telephone: 302-652-5070
Fax: 302-652-0607
Email: info@fr.com
URL: http://www.fr.com

Boston, Massachusetts Office: 225 Franklin Street. Telephone: 617-542-5070. Fax: 617-542-8906.
Washington, D.C. Office: 601 13th Street, N.W. Telephone: 202-783-5070. Fax: 202-783-2331.
Redwood City, California Office: 500 Aguello Street, Suite 500. Telephone: 650-322-5070. Fax: 650-854-0875.
Minneapolis, Minnesota Office: Fish & Richardson P.C., P.A., 60 South Sixth Street, 3300 Dain Rauscher Plaza. Telephone: 612-335-5070. Fax: 612-288-9696.
San Diego, California Office: 4350 La Jolla Village Drive, Suite 500. Telephone: 858-678-5070. Fax: 858-678-5099.
New York, New York Office: 45 Rockefeller Plaza, Suite 2800. Telephone: 212-765-5070. Fax: 212-258-2291.
Dallas, Texas Office: 5000 Bank One Center, 1717 Main Street. Telephone: 214-747-5070. Fax: 214-747-2091

Intellectual Property, Complex Litigation, Technology Law: Patents, Trademarks, Copyrights, Trade Secrets, Intellectual Property Litigation, Business Litigation, Technology Regulations, Antitrust Law, Corporate and Securities, White Collar Crime.

FIRM PROFILE: Fish & Richardson is one of the largest firms in the United States that focuses on intellectual property, complex litigation, and technology law. Fish & Richardson has a regulatory group that advises clients who seek to market products subject to FCC and FDA regulation. The firm's Corporate and Securities Section helps clients with capital structuring and financing, public equity and debt offerings and a wide range of corporate transactions.

Founded in 1878, Fish & Richardson has long represented great innovators and business entrepreneurs. The firm served pioneering inventors such as Alexander Graham Bell, Thomas Edison, and the Wright brothers. Today, the firm has over 250 attorneys and technology specialists in eight offices across the nation.

A significant component of the firm's work is litigation. Our litigation victories have appeared on the National Law Journal's biggest winners list for four straight years. In a survey published in May 2001, IP Worldwide found that in the year 2000 Fish & Richardson handled more patent litigation than any other firm. In addition to intellectual property litigation, the firm handles a wide variety of complex high-stakes, high-tech business litigation, including white collar criminal defense work.

(This Listing Continued)

FISH & RICHARDSON P.C., Wilmington—Continued

In 2000 the firm obtained over 1,300 issued patents and filed almost 4,000 new patent applications, ranking it among the most active law firms in the United States. On the trademark side, in 2000, the firm obtained over 300 registered trademarks and filed almost 900 new trademark applications. The firm also provides advice on copyrights and copyright registration and licensing.

Fish, Richardson & Neave .... (1916-1969)

FREDERICK P. FISH (1855-1930).

W. K. RICHARDSON (1859-1951).

THOMAS L. HALKOWSKI, born Milwaukee, Wisconsin, October 5, 1962; admitted to bar, 1989, Wisconsin (Not admitted in Delaware). *Education:* Marquette University (B.S., Engineering, 1985); University of Florida (M.S., Engineering, 1986); University of Wisconsin (J.D., 1989). Order of the Coif. Law Clerk to the Hon. Roger B. Andewelt, U.S. Court of Claims; Hon, Helen W. Nies, U.S. Court of Appeals. ***PRACTICE AREAS:*** Intellectual Property; Patent Litigation. ***Email:*** halkowsi@fr.com

WILLIAM J. MARSDEN, JR., born Englewood, New Jersey, October 13, 1955; admitted to bar, 1983, Delaware. *Education:* Haverford College (B.A., 1978); University of North Carolina (J.D., 1983). Member, Holderness Moot Court Bench. ***PRACTICE AREAS:*** Intellectual Property; Litigation. ***Email:*** marsden@fr.com

FRANK P. PORCELLI, admitted to bar, 1971, Massachusetts; 1972, Delaware; registered to practice before U.S. Patent and Trademark Office. *Education:* Boston College (A.B., magna cum laude, 1968); Northeastern University (M.S., Chem., 1981); Harvard University (J.D., 1971). ***PRACTICE AREAS:*** Intellectual Property; Litigation; Appellate. ***Email:*** porcelli@fr.com

ASSOCIATES

J. Andrew Huffman
John T. Meli, Jr.
Keith A. Walter, Jr. (Not admitted in DE)

(For biographical data on personnel at Boston, Massachusetts, Washington, D.C., Dallas, Texas, Menlo Park, California, Minneapolis, Minnesota, San Diego, California and New York, New York, see Professional Biographies at those locations)

THOMAS A. FOLEY

1326 KING STREET
WILMINGTON, DELAWARE 19801
Telephone: 302-658-3077
Fax: 302-656-1993
Email: taf@taf-law.com
URL: http://www.lawyers.com/foleylaw

Criminal Trial and Appellate Practice in all State and Federal Courts.

THOMAS A. FOLEY, born Rochester, New York, November 16, 1960; admitted to bar, 1990, Delaware; 1991, District of Columbia; 1994, U.S. District Court, District of Delaware; 1995, U.S. Court of Appeals, Third Circuit; 1996, U.S. Supreme Court. *Education:* Miami University (B.S., 1982); University of Detroit (J.D., cum laude, 1989). Deputy Attorney General, State of Delaware, 1989-1995. *Member:* Delaware and American Bar Associations; Delaware Trial Lawyers Association; National Association of Criminal Defense Lawyers. [First Lieutenant, U.S. Marine Corps., 1982-1986]. ***PRACTICE AREAS:*** Criminal Law (100%).

FOX, ROTHSCHILD, O'BRIEN & FRANKEL, LLP

Established in 1907
MELLON BANK CENTER
919 NORTH MARKET STREET
SUITE 1400, 14TH FLOOR
WILMINGTON, DELAWARE 19801-3046
Telephone: 302-655-7460
Cable Address: FROF
Fax: 302-655-7004
Email: attorneys@frof.com
URL: http://www.frof.com

Philadelphia, Pennsylvania Office: 2000 Market Street, Tenth Floor, 19103-3291. Telephone: 215-299-2000. Cable Address: FROF. Fax: 215-299-2150.

Atlantic City, New Jersey Office: CitiCenter Building, Suite 500, 1300 Atlantic Avenue, 08401. Telephone: 609-348-4515. Fax: 609-348-6834.

(This Listing Continued)

Doylestown, Pennsylvania Office: 102 North Main Street, P.O. Box 1589, 18901-0700. Telephone: 215-345-7500. Fax: 215-345-7507.

Exton, Pennsylvania Office: Eagleview Corporate Center, 760 Constitution Drive, Suite 104, P.O. Box 673, 19341-0673. Telephone: 610-458-7500. Fax: 610-458-7337.

Lansdale, Pennsylvania Office: 1250 South Broad Street, Suite 1000, P.O. Box 431, 19446. Telephone: 215-699-6000. Fax: 215-699-0231.

Trenton (Lawrenceville), New Jersey Office: Princeton Pike Corporate Center, 997 Lenox Drive, Building 3, 08648-2311. Telephone: 609-896-3600. Fax: 609-896-1469.

Voorhees, New Jersey Office: Laurelwood, Suite 103, 1103 Laurel Oak Road, 08043. Telephone: 856-782-6000. Fax: 856-346-9866.

Admiralty, Alternative Dispute Resolution, Antitrust, Banking, Bankruptcy, Civil Litigation, Commercial Litigation, Computer Law, Condominium Law, Construction, Corporate and Commercial, Condemnation Law, Corporate, Criminal Defense, Environmental, Estate Planning, Family Business, Family Law, Financial Services, Franchise, Governmental Affairs, Health Law, Insurance, Intellectual Property, Labor and Employment, General Litigation, Legal Malpractice Defense, Marine Finance, Municipal Finance, Nonprofit Institutions, Pension, Personal Injury, Probate, Products Liability, Professional Liability Defense, Profit Sharing and Employee Benefits, Public Utility, Real Estate, Securities, Sports Law, Taxation, Wills and Trusts, Zoning and Land Use.

FIRM PROFILE: Fox, Rothschild, O'Brien & Frankel, LLP has represented closely held businesses, public corporations, national and multinational corporations, government agencies and academic institutions, nursing homes, hospitals and other health care facilities in the areas of business, corporate and securities, financial services, labor, litigation, real estate and tax and estates for over nine decades. A full service law firm, Fox, Rothschild has eight offices located in Philadelphia, PA, Trenton (Lawrenceville), NJ, Lansdale, PA, Exton, PA, Atlantic City, NJ, Doylestown, PA, Voorhees, NJ, and Wilmington, DE.

PARTNER

FRANCIS G. X. PILEGGI, born Delaware County, Pennsylvania, February 6; admitted to bar, 1987, Pennsylvania, Delaware and New Jersey. *Education:* St. Joseph's University (B.A., 1982); Widener University (J.D., 1986). ***PRACTICE AREAS:*** Litigation; Commercial Transactions. ***Email:*** fpileggi@frof.com

ASSOCIATE

SHELDON K. RENNIE, born Trinidad, West Indies, December 24, 1971; admitted to bar, 1998, Pennsylvania and Delaware. *Education:* Long Island University, C.W. Post Campus of Brookville (M.S./B.A., Criminal Justice, magna cum laude, 1994); Villanova University (J.D., 1997). ***PRACTICE AREAS:*** Commercial Litigation; Creditors Rights in Bankruptcy; Corporate Litigation; Corporate Law. ***Email:*** srennie@frof.com

(For complete biographical data on personnel at Philadelphia, Doylestown, Exton and Lansdale, Pennsylvania and Atlantic City, Trenton (Lawrenceville) and Voorhees, New Jersey, see Professional Biographies at those locations)

JOHN F. GANGI

712 WEST STREET
WILMINGTON, DELAWARE 19801
Telephone: 302-656-4090
FAX: 302-656-4233
Email: jgangi1062@aol.com
URL: http://www.lawyers.com/gangilaw

General Civil and Trial Practice. Personal Injury, Auto Accidents and Family Law.

JOHN F. GANGI, born New York City, New York, January 2, 1947; admitted to bar, 1979, Pennsylvania; 1980, Delaware. *Education:* University of Kansas (B.S., Journalism, 1969); Widener University (J.D., 1977). *Member:* Delaware (Member, Tort Section) and American Bar Associations; Delaware Trial Lawyers Association; The Association of Trial Lawyers of America. ***PRACTICE AREAS:*** Civil Trial; Personal Injury Law; Family Law.

GOLDFEIN & HOSMER

A PROFESSIONAL CORPORATION

Established in 1985

PNC BANK CENTER, SUITE 1110
222 DELAWARE AVENUE
P.O. BOX 2206
WILMINGTON, DELAWARE 19899-2206
Telephone: 302-656-3301
FAX: 302-656-0643
Email: gkaplan@goldfeinlawde.com
URL: http://www.goldfeinlaw.com

Philadelphia, Pennsylvania Office: 1600 Market Street, 33rd Floor, 19103-7288. Telephone: 215-979-8200. Fax: 215-979-8201.

Princeton, New Jersey Office: Princeton Metro Center, Suite 115, 5 Vaughn Drive, 08540-6313. Telephone: 609-520-0400. Fax: 609-520-1450.

New York, New York Office: 5 Hanover Square, 21st Floor, 10004. Telephone: 212-791-0340. Fax: 212-791-0347.

Baltimore, Maryland Office: 217 East Redwood Street, 21st Floor, 21202. Telephone: 410-576-0200. Fax: 410-576-0887.

Civil Trial Practice, Casualty, Products Liability, Medical Malpractice, Insurance, Toxic Torts, Health Care, Subrogation, Hospital Liability, Insurance Coverage, General Corporate and Commercial Real Estate, Estate and Tax Planning.

REPRESENTATIVE CLIENTS: Aetna Casualty and Surety Co.; Pa. Medical Society Liability Insurance Co.; Alexsis, Inc.; COLTEC; The Coleman Company, Inc.; Countrywide Services; Supermarkets General Corp.; Trafalgar House Group; Mayflower Group; Asbestos Corporation Limited; Societe National D'Amiante; Claridge Hotel & Casino; Germantown Hospital and Medical Center; Allegheny Health Systems; National Freight; Liberty Mutual Insurance Co.; Phico Insurance Co.

(For Complete Biographical Data on All Personnel, See Professional Biographies at Philadelphia, Pennsylvania)

GOLLATZ, GRIFFIN & EWING, P.C.

1901 SUPERFINE LANE
SUITE 2
WILMINGTON, DELAWARE 19802
Telephone: 302-428-3761
Fax: 302-428-3766
Email: gge@ggelaw.com
URL: http://www.ggelaw.com

Philadelphia, Pennsylvania Office: 16th Floor, Two Penn Center Plaza. Telephone: 215-563-9400. Fax: 215-665-9988.

West Chester, Pennsylvania Office: 213 West Miner Street, P.O. Box 796. Telephone: 610-692-9116. Fax: 610-692-9177.

General Civil Litigation in State and Federal Courts. Business, Technology, Intellectual Property, Transportation, Non Profit Organizations, Estate Planning and Administration, Real Estate, Employment, Environmental and Equine Law.

FIRM PROFILE: Gollatz, Griffin & Ewing is founded on the belief that high-quality legal services traditionally offered by large law firms can and should be delivered more cost-effectively through a firm with a concentrated focus.

The firm members' collective experience in large law firms, in government service and with a national trial practice (which includes the supervision of work done by lawyers throughout the country) has contributed to its unique appreciation of both client needs and the type of service and organization required to meet them. The firm's Delaware Valley offices enable it to conduct a practice with specific knowledge of local issues.

J. MICHAEL JOHNSON, born Torrington, Connecticut, August 22, 1952; admitted to bar, 1977, Delaware; 1988, Pennsylvania, U.S. Court of Appeals, Third Circuit, U.S. District Court, Eastern District of Pennsylvania and U.S. District Court, District of Delaware. *Education:* Dickinson College (B.A., 1974); Villanova University (J.D., 1977). Assistant County Attorney and Complaints Officer, New Castle County, 1978-1980. *Member:* Delaware State Bar Association; American Inns of Court (Member, Richard Rodney Chapter). ***Email:*** jmj@ggelaw.com

---

NANCY E. WHINNERY, born Dayton, Ohio, March 6, 1956; admitted to bar, 1993, Delaware; 1994, U.S. District Court, District of Delaware; 1996, Pennsylvania and U.S. District Court, Eastern District of Pennsylvania. *Education:* University of Wisconsin (B.A., with academic distinction, 1978); Temple University (M.B.A., 1985); Temple University School of Law (J.D., magna cum laude, 1993). Member, Temple Law Review. Recipient, Award in Professional Responsibility. Author, "The Immigration Marriage Fraud Amendment: Substantive or Procedural Provisions? 64 TEMP.L.REV. 1084 (1992). *Member:*

(This Listing Continued)

Chester County (Member, Section On: Women in the Practice of Law) and Delaware State (Member, Sections On: Women in the Law Section; Employment Law) Bar Associations. ***PRACTICE AREAS:*** Employment Law; Civil Litigation. ***Email:*** new@ggelaw.com

(For Complete Biographical Data on All Personnel, see Professional Biographies at Philadelphia and West Chester, Pennsylvania and)

GORDON, FOURNARIS & MAMMARELLA, P.A.

1220 NORTH MARKET STREET
SUITE 700
P.O. BOX 1355
WILMINGTON, DELAWARE 19899-1355
Telephone: 302-652-2900
Fax: 302-652-1142

Estate Planning, Estate and Trust Administration and Taxation, Guardianships, Limited Partnerships, Limited Liability Companies, Corporations, Tax and Business Planning, Succession Planning, Charitable Foundations, Litigation, Real Estate, Zoning, Land Development, Alternative Dispute Resolution.

PETER S. GORDON, born Washington, D.C., March 7, 1952; admitted to bar, 1977, Delaware; 1979, Pennsylvania, District of Columbia and U.S. Tax Court. *Education:* Georgetown University (A.B., 1974); Fordham University (J.D., 1977); Georgetown University (LL.M. in Taxation, 1981). *Member:* Delaware Bar Association (Chairman, Sections on: Tax, 1985-1986; Estates and Trusts, 1986-1987). Delaware Tax Institute (Planning Committee, 1998—); Fellow, American College of Trust and Estate Counsel (State Chair, 1997-2001). ***PRACTICE AREAS:*** Taxation; Estate Planning; Probate; Commercial Law; Fiduciary Litigation. ***Email:*** pgordon@gfmlaw.com

THOMAS MAMMARELLA, born Wilmington, Delaware, June 22, 1953; admitted to bar, 1978, Delaware. *Education:* University of Delaware (B.A., with highest honors, 1975); Duke University (J.D., 1978). Assistant County Attorney, New Castle County, Department of Law, 1979-1980. *Member:* Delaware Bar Association (Member, Real and Personal Property Section). ***PRACTICE AREAS:*** Real Estate; Zoning; Land Development. ***Email:*** tmammarella@gfmlaw.com

EMMANUEL G. FOURNARIS, born Wilmington, Delaware, October 3, 1958; admitted to bar, 1984, Pennsylvania and Delaware; 1986, U.S. Tax Court. *Education:* University of Delaware (B.S., with honors, 1980); Delaware Law School of Widener University (J.D., with honors, 1983); Temple University (LL.M., in Taxation, 1985). *Member:* Delaware (Member, Tax Section) and Pennsylvania Bar Associations; Wilmington Tax Group. ***LANGUAGES:*** Greek. ***PRACTICE AREAS:*** Commercial Law; Business Law; Business Formation; Mergers and Acquisitions; Taxation. ***Email:*** efournaris@gfmlaw.com

SPECIAL COUNSEL

GROVER C. BROWN, born Milford, Delaware, June 18, 1935; admitted to bar, 1961, Delaware, District of Columbia and U.S. District Court, District of Delaware. *Education:* University of North Carolina (A.B., 1957); George Washington University (LL.B., 1960). Deputy Attorney General, 1964-1967. Judge, Delaware Family Court, 1971-1973. Vice Chancellor, 1973-1982 and Chancellor, 1982-1985, Delaware Court of Chancery. ***PRACTICE AREAS:*** Corporate Fiduciary Law. ***Email:*** gbrown@gfmlaw.com

---

ROBERT A. PENZA, born Philadelphia, Pennsylvania, June 1, 1963; admitted to bar, 1989, Delaware; 1990, U.S. District Court, District of Delaware. *Education:* Drexel University (B.S., 1986); Villanova University (J.D., 1989). Listed, Best Lawyers in Delaware, News Journal, 2001. *Member:* Delaware State and American Bar Associations; Delaware Trial Lawyers Association; National Football League Players Association; Canadian Football League Players Association; The Justinian Society. ***PRACTICE AREAS:*** Commercial Litigation; Civil Litigation; Real Estate; Sports Contracts. ***Email:*** rpenza@gfmlaw.com

BRYAN E. KEENAN, born Niagara Falls, New York, January 30, 1954; admitted to bar, 1979, Pennsylvania; 1982, U.S. Tax Court; 1986, Delaware; 1987, U.S. District Court, District of Delaware; 1988, U.S. Claims Court. *Education:* Syracuse University (B.S., cum laude, 1976; J.D., 1978); Temple University (LL.M., in Taxation, 1983). Adjunct Professor, Widener University School of Law Graduate Tax Program, 1990-1995. *Member:* Delaware State (Member, Sections on: Corporation Law; Taxation) and American (Member, Sections on: Taxation; Corporation, Banking and Business Law; Law Practice Management; Real Property, Probate, and Trust Law) Bar Associations; Wilmington Tax Group (Secretary/Treasurer, 2001-2002). ***PRACTICE AREAS:*** Taxation; Business Organization; Business Transactions; Charitable Trusts and Foundations. ***Email:*** bkeenan@gfmlaw.com

(This Listing Continued)

GORDON, FOURNARIS & MAMMARELLA, P.A., Wilmington—Continued

PETER M. SWEENEY, born Wilmington, Delaware, July 7, 1971; admitted to bar, 1997, Delaware; 1998, U.S. District Court, District of Delaware. *Education:* University of Notre Dame (B.A., 1994); Villanova University (J.D., 1997). Judicial clerkship, Delaware Superior Court, 1997-1998. *Member:* Delaware and American Bar Associations; St. Thomas More Society; Delaware Trial Lawyers Association; Notre Dame Club of Delaware (Secretary, 1999—); Judge Bifferato Superior Court Trial Practice Forum (Steering Committee Member). ***PRACTICE AREAS:*** Commercial Litigation; Civil Litigation; Creditors Rights Litigation. ***Email:*** psweeney@gfmlaw.com

STEPHEN DEL ROSSI, born Philadelphia, Pennsylvania, December 28, 1944; admitted to bar, 1974, Pennsylvania; 1977, U.S. Supreme Court (Not admitted in Delaware). *Education:* Drexel University (B.S., 1967); Temple University (J.D., 1974). Part time private practice, West Chester, Pennsylvania, 1974-1976. Estate Tax attorney with the Internal Revenue Service (Retired), 1976-2001. [Lieutenant, U.S. Navy, 1968-1971]. ***PRACTICE AREAS:*** Estate Administration; Tax Law. ***Email:*** sdelrossi@gfmlaw.com

APPROVED ATTORNEYS FOR: Ticor Title Insurance Company; Transnation Title Insurance Company; Lawyers Title Insurance Corporation.

GRANT & EISENHOFER, P.A.

1220 NORTH MARKET STREET, SUITE 500
WILMINGTON, DELAWARE 19801
Telephone: 302-622-7000
Fax: 302-622-7100
URL: http://www.gelaw.com

Litigation Boutique: Securities, Corporate, Bankruptcy, Insurance Coverage and Complex Commercial Litigation.

JAY W. EISENHOFER, born Philadelphia, Pennsylvania, November 28, 1956; admitted to bar, 1986, Pennsylvania; 1988, New Jersey; 1990, Delaware. *Education:* University of Pittsburgh (B.A., 1978); Villanova University School of Law (J.D., magna cum laude, 1986). Order of the Coif. Law Clerk to Hon. Vincent A. Cirillo, Pres. Judge, Pennsylvania Superior Court, 1986-1987. Associate, Skadden Arps Slate Meagher & Flom, 1989-1994; Partner, Blank Rome Comisky & McCauley, 1994-1997. Member, Governor of Delaware's Commission on Major Commercial Litigation Reform, May, 1993-1994. *Member:* Delaware State and American (Vice-Chairman, Business Torts Committee, Business Law Section, 1995—) Bar Associations. ***Email:*** jeisenhofer@gelaw.com

STUART M. GRANT, born Brooklyn, New York, June 22, 1960; admitted to bar, 1986, Delaware; 1987, New York and Massachusetts; 1989, U.S. Court of Appeals, First, Second and Third Circuits; 1994, Pennsylvania; 1996, District Of Columbia and U.S. Supreme Court; 2000, U.S. Court of Appeals, Eleventh Circuit. *Education:* Brandeis University (B.A., cum laude, Economics, 1982); New York University School of Law (J.D., 1986); Associate Editor, Annual Survey of American Law. Law Clerk to Hon. Naomi Reise Buchwald, SDNY. Adjunct Professor, Widener University Law School, Securities Litigation Seminar, 1994—. Instructor, NITA, 1995—. Associate, Skadden Arps Slate Meagher & Flom, 1987-1994; Partner, Blank Rome Comisky & McCauley, 1994-1997. *Member:* Delaware State (Ethics Committee, Litigation, Corporation and Labor Sections) and American (Litigation and Business Law Sections) Bar Associations. ***Email:*** sgrant@gelaw.com

MEGAN D. McINTYRE, born Wilmington, Delaware, August 10, 1969; admitted to bar, 1994, Delaware. *Education:* The Pennsylvania State University (B.S., Accounting, 1991); Dickinson School of Law (J.D., magna cum laude, 1994). Associate: Skadden Arps Slate Meagher & Flom, 1994-1995; Blank Rome Comisky & McCauley, 1995-1997. *Member:* Delaware State Bar Association. ***Email:*** mmcintyre@gelaw.com

OF COUNSEL

KURT N. SCHACHT, born Lancaster, Wisconsin, February 23, 1954; admitted to bar, 1984, Wisconsin; 1986, Ohio; 2001, New York (Not admitted in Delaware). *Education:* University of Wisconsin-Madison (B.S., in Chemistry, 1976; J.D., 1983). Chartered Financial Analyst. Legislative Assistant, Wisconsin State Senate, 1978-1983. Chief Legal Counsel, State of Wisconsin Investment Board, 1990-1999.

SPECIAL COUNSEL

DENISE T. DiPERSIO, born Haddonfield, New Jersey, June 5, 1955; admitted to bar, 1981, Pennsylvania; 1988, District of Columbia; 1993, New Jersey (Not admitted in Delaware). *Education:* Bryn Mawr College (A.B., cum laude, 1977); University of Miami (J.D., 1980). Partner, Lisitski & DiPersio, 1993-1995. Partner, 1991-1993 and Associate, 1987-1990, Foley & Lardner, Washington, D.C. Associate, Brownstein, Zeidman & Schromer, 1985-1987. Attorney Advisor, U.S. International Trade Commission, Washington, D.C., 1980-1985. ***Email:*** ddipersio@gelaw.com

(This Listing Continued)

GEOFFREY C. JARVIS, born Camden, New Jersey, July 11, 1958; admitted to bar, 1985, District of Columbia; 1995, Pennsylvania, U.S. Court of Federal Claims and U.S. Court of Appeals, Third Circuit; 2001, Delaware. *Education:* Cornell University (B.A., 1980); Harvard University (J.D., cum laude, 1984). Phi Beta Kappa. *Member:* Philadelphia and Pennsylvania Bar Associations. ***Email:*** gjarvis@gelaw.com

ABBOTT A. LEBAN, born Brooklyn, New York, August 30, 1933; admitted to bar, 1959, District of Columbia; 1962, U.S. Supreme Court; 1965, New York; 1972, Pennsylvania; 1998, Delaware. *Education:* Columbia University (A.B., 1955); Yale University (J.D., 1958). Law Clerk (Motions), U.S. Court of Appeals, D.C. Circuit, 1958-1959; General Attorney, Lit. Div., U.S. Civil. Aeronautics Bd., 1959-1960; Assistant U.S. Attorney, D.C., 1960-1962; Executive Assistant and Counsel to U.S. Senator Kenneth B. Keating, 1962-1965; Counsel, Federal Relations, Equitable Life Assurance Soc'y of U.S., 1965-1970; President, Intramerica Life Ins. Co., New York, N.Y., 1970-1972; Sr. Vice President and Secretary, Colonial Penn Group, Inc., Philadelphia, Pa., 1972-1981; Of Counsel, Wolf, Arnold & Cardoso, P.C., Washington, D.C., 1982-1983; Vice President, General Counsel and Secretary, American Homestead Mortgage Corporation, 1983-1987; Chief Counsel, Commonwealth of Pennsylvania Retirement Systems, 1987-1991; Of Counsel, Blank Rome Comisky & McCauley, 1991-1997. Chartered Life Underwriter (C.L.U.). ***Email:*** aleban@gelaw.com

DIANE T. ZILKA, born Flushing, New York, November 19, 1960; admitted to bar, 1986, New York and U.S. District Court, Southern District of New York (Not admitted in Delaware). *Education:* State University of New York at Binghamton (B.A., 1982); Fordham University School of Law (J.D., 1985). ***Email:*** dzilka@gelaw.com

MICHAEL J. BARRY, born Washington, D.C., April 16, 1970; admitted to bar, 1993, Pennsylvania (Not admitted in Delaware). *Education:* Carnegie Mellon University (B.F.A., 1990); University of Pittsburgh (J.D., summa cum laude, 1993). Order of the Coif. Staff Member, 1991-1992 and Executive Editor, 1992-1993, Univ. of Pittsburgh Law Review. ***Email:*** mbarry@gelaw.com

CHRISTINE S. BULMAN, born Philadelphia, Pennsylvania, July 30, 1966; admitted to bar, 1993, Michigan; 2001, Pennsylvania, New Jersey (Not admitted in Delaware). *Education:* James Madison University (B.S, 1988); University of Notre Dame (J.D., 1991). ***Email:*** cbulman@gelaw.com

CYNTHIA A. CALDER, born Wilmington, Delaware, September 15, 1965; admitted to bar, 1991, Delaware; 1992, Pennsylvania; 1995, U.S. Court of Appeals for the District of Columbia Circuit. *Education:* University of Delaware (B.A., cum laude, 1987); Villanova University (J.D., 1991). Law Clerk to Vice Chancellor Maurice A. Hartnett, III, Delaware Court of Chancery, 1991-1992. Associate, Chimicles, Jacobsen & Tikellis, 1992-1995; Associate, Blank Rome Comisky & McCauley, 1995-1997. ***Email:*** ccalder@gelaw.com

RICHARD M. DONALDSON, born Harrisburg, Pennsylvania, May 7, 1965; admitted to bar, 1991, Pennsylvania and New Jersey (Not admitted in Delaware). *Education:* Bucknell University (B.A., 1987); The Dickinson School of Law (J.D., 1991). Senior Editor, Dickinson Law Review. ***Email:*** rdonaldson@gelaw.com

JOHN C. KAIRIS, born Chicago, Illinois, July 5, 1962; admitted to bar, 1987, Ohio; 1989, Delaware. *Education:* University of Notre Dame (B.A., 1984); Ohio State University (J.D., 1987). Articles Editor, The Ohio State Law Journal, 1985-1987. ***Email:*** jkairis@gelaw.com

SIDNEY S. LIEBESMAN, born Wilmington, Delaware, April 9, 1964; admitted to bar, 1995, Pennsylvania and New Jersey; 1998, Delaware. *Education:* University of Delaware (B.A.A.S., 1986); Villanova University (J.D., 1995). Editor, Villanova Environmental Law Journal. ***LANGUAGES:*** Spanish. ***Email:*** sliebesman@gelaw.com

STEPHAN MATANOVIC, born Taranto, Italy, 1973; admitted to bar, 1999, Pennsylvania; 2000, U.S. Court of Appeals, Third Circuit (Not admitted in Delaware). *Education:* University of Virginia (B.A., 1995); Temple University School of Law (J.D., 1998). ***LANGUAGES:*** German, French, Spanish. ***Email:*** smatanovic@gelaw.com

MICHELLE N. PETERSON, born Media, Pennsylvania, June 3, 1972; admitted to bar, 2000, New Jersey and Pennsylvania (Not admitted in Delaware). *Education:* Temple University (B.S., 1995); Widener University School of Law (J.D., 1999). Member, The Negotiation Client Counseling Society, 1996-1999 (President, 1997-1999). ***Email:*** mpeterson@gelaw.com

C. CURTIS STAROPOLI, born Danbury, Connecticut, September 14, 1965; admitted to bar, 1992, Pennsylvania and New Jersey; 1997, Delaware. *Education:* University of Delaware (B.A.S., 1988); Villanova University (J.D., 1992). ***Email:*** cstaropoli@gelaw.com

JOSEPH B. GREEN

Established in 1972
TOWNE CENTER
4 EAST 8TH STREET
SUITE 200
WILMINGTON, DELAWARE 19801
Telephone: 302-654-4557
Fax: 302-655-5358
Email: joegreen@wserv.com
URL: http://www.lawyers.com/joegreen

Lewes, Delaware Office: 467 Highway One, 19958. Telephone: 302-644-1732.

Personal Injury, Bankruptcy and Real Estate.

JOSEPH B. GREEN, born Wilmington, Delaware, September 11, 1947; admitted to bar, 1972, Delaware; U.S. District Court, District of Delaware; U.S. Bankruptcy Court. *Education:* Dickinson College (B.A., 1969); Duquesne University School of Law (J.D., 1972). Associate Editor, Duquesne Law Review, 1972. *Member:* Delaware Bar Association; Delaware Trial Lawyers Association; National Association of Consumer Bankruptcy Attorneys. ***PRACTICE AREAS:*** Personal Injury; Bankruptcy; Real Estate.

HAASE & EVELAND

Established in 1991
824 MARKET STREET MALL, SUITE 830
P.O. BOX 393
WILMINGTON, DELAWARE 19899-0393
Telephone: 302-421-5900
Fax: 302-421-5909
Email: govbiggs@aol.com
URL: http://www.lawyers.com/haaselegal

Personal Injury and Workers' Compensation Litigation. Family Law, Wills, Estates, Real Estate Settlements, Medical and Dental Malpractice Law.

FIRM PROFILE: Frederick T. Haase, Jr. began his practice in 1991 and was joined recently by his partner, Elwood T. Eveland. The Firm maintains a general practice with a concentration in Personal Injury Litigation. Haase & Eveland services clients statewide in Delaware and also in Pennsylvania.

FREDERICK T. HAASE, JR., born Darby, Pennsylvania, October 19, 1951; admitted to bar, 1976, Delaware and U.S. District Court, District of Delaware; 1977, Pennsylvania; 1979, U.S. Court of Appeals, Third Circuit; 1980, U.S. Supreme Court; 1993, U.S. District Court, Eastern District of Pennsylvania. *Education:* Villanova University (B.A., summa cum laude, 1973; J.D., cum laude, 1976). Order of the Coif. Recipient, Arthur Clement Pulling Award, 1976. Member, Villanova Law Review, 1975-1976. Author: 20 Villanova L. Rev. 579 (1975); 21 Villanova L. Rev 72 (1976); 21 Villanova L. Rev. 617 (1976). Member, New Castle County Historic Review Board, 1988-1993. Former General Counsel for, The Friends of Rockwood, Inc., 1978-1997. *Member:* Delaware and Pennsylvania Bar Associations; Delaware Trial Lawyers Association; American Trial Lawyers Association. ***PRACTICE AREAS:*** Personal Injury; Workers' Compensation; Medical Malpractice; Dental Malpractice; Divorce; Wills; Probate; Family Law; Real Estate. ***Email:*** GOVBIGGS@AOL.COM

ELWOOD T. EVELAND, JR., born Linz, Austria, June 14, 1955; admitted to bar, 1981, Delaware and U.S. District Court, District of Delaware. *Education:* University of Delaware, Eastern Michigan University and Rutgers University (B.A., 1978); Delaware Law School of Widener University (J.D., 1981). Phi Delta Phi. *Member:* Delaware State Bar Association; Delaware Trial Lawyers Association; The Association of Trial Lawyers of America. ***PRACTICE AREAS:*** Personal Injury; Workers Compensation; Contracts; Construction Litigation.

LEGAL SUPPORT PERSONNEL

DOROTHY J. NATRIN (Office Administrator/Real Estate Paralegal).

JEANNE M. HANSON ATTORNEY AT LAW, LLC

521 WEST STREET
WILMINGTON, DELAWARE 19801
Telephone: 302-777-7989
Fax: 302-571-8354
URL: http://www.hanson-law.com
Email: jeanne@hanson-law.com
URL: http://www.lawyers.com/hanson-law

Family Law, Bankruptcy Chapter 7.

(This Listing Continued)

JEANNE M. HANSON, born Wilmington, Delaware, November 17, 1946; admitted to bar, 1991, Delaware; 1992, U.S. District Court, District of Delaware. *Education:* Antioch College (B.A. 1969); Widener University (J.D. 1990). Recipient, Jurisprudence Award. Paralegal, Community Aid Society, Inc., 1973-1974. Probation Officer, 1982-1983, Pre-Sentence Investigator, 1983-1987 and Mediator, 1988, Family Court of Delaware. Superior Court Arbitrator. Peace Corps. Volunteer, 1969-1971. *Member:* Delaware Bar Association (Member, Sections on: Family Law and Women in Law). ***LANGUAGES:*** Spanish. ***PRACTICE AREAS:*** Family Law; Bankruptcy. ***Email:*** jeanne@hanson-law.com

HARVEY, PENNINGTON, CABOT, GRIFFITH & RENNEISEN, LTD.

1509 GILPIN AVENUE
WILMINGTON, DELAWARE 19806
Telephone: 302-428-0719
Fax: 302-777-4682
URL: http://www.harvpenn.com

Philadelphia, Pennsylvania Office: 11 Penn Center, 29th Floor, 1835 Market Street. Telephone: 215-563-4470. Fax: 215-568-1044.
Bryn Mawr, Pennsylvania Office: 26 South Bryn Mawr Avenue, Suite 200. Telephone: 610-527-9200. Fax: 610-527-5402.
Cherry Hill, New Jersey Office: Harvey, Pennington, Cabot, Griffith & Renneisen, P.C. Cherry Tree Corporate Center, Suite 360, 535 Route 38 East. Telephone: 856-317-9122. Fax: 856-317-2215.
New York, N.Y. Office: Park Avenue Atrium, 237 Park Avenue, Twenty-First Floor. Telephone: 212-682-4900. Fax: 212-697-8486.

General Civil Practice in all Courts. Admiralty, Civil and Criminal Antitrust, Environmental, Negligence, Corporation, Labor, Probate, Real Estate and Insurance Law. Trial and Appellate Practice. Financial Institutions, Transactions, Insolvency and Creditors' Rights.

JEFFREY K. MARTIN, born Camden, New Jersey, July 31, 1956; admitted to bar, 1981, New Jersey; 1982, Pennsylvania; 1984, U.S. District Court, Eastern District of Pennsylvania; 1985, Delaware; 1986, U.S. District Court, District of Delaware; 1992, U.S. Court of Appeals, Third Circuit. *Education:* United States Military Academy; Lafayette College (A.B., 1978); Rutgers University (J.D., 1981). Editor, Rutgers Law Journal, 1980-1981. Law Clerk: New Jersey Superior Court, 1981; The Honorable William M. Marutani, Philadelphia Court of Common Pleas, 1982. *Member:* Delaware, Pennsylvania and American Bar Associations; Delaware Employment Lawyers Association (President); National Employment Lawyers Association. (Resident) (Also practicing individually). ***PRACTICE AREAS:*** Medical Malpractice; Personal Injury Law; Insurance Law; Product Liability. ***Email:*** jkmartin@harvpenn.com

OF COUNSEL

WILLIAM M. AUKAMP, born New York, N.Y., February 3, 1937; admitted to bar, 1963, New York; 1966, U.S. Court of Appeals, Second Circuit; 1967, U.S. Supreme Court; 1975, U.S. District Court, Southern and Eastern Districts of New York; 1984, Delaware and U.S. District Court, District of Delaware. *Education:* Lafayette College (A.B., 1958); Cornell University (LL.B., 1961). *Member:* Delaware Bankers Association (Board of Directors, 1985-1990; President, 1990-1991);. American Bankers Association (Banking Leadership Conference, 1984, 1986-1991); Government Relations Council, 1984, 1986-1989). ***PRACTICE AREAS:*** Banking Law; Corporate. ***Email:*** waukamp@harvpenn.com

J. STODDARD HAYES, JR.

WILMINGTON, DELAWARE

(See Gollatz, Griffin & Ewing, P.C., West Chester, Pennsylvania)

CLIFFORD B. HEARN, JR., P.A.

Established in 1974
606 MARKET STREET MALL
P.O. BOX 1205
WILMINGTON, DELAWARE 19899
Telephone: 302-575-0220
Fax: 302-575-0236

Odessa, Delaware Office: Odessa Professional Park, Suite 240. Telephone: 302-378-4827. FAX: 302-378-4946.

(This Listing Continued)

CLIFFORD B. HEARN, JR., P.A., Wilmington—Continued

General Civil and Trial Practice. Business, Family, Labor, Personal Injury, Real Estate, Criminal, Wills, Estates and Administrative Law. Commercial and Collection Law. Legislative and Regulatory Practice. Workers Compensation.

CLIFFORD B. HEARN, JR., born Raspeburg, Maryland, October 18, 1937; admitted to bar, 1962, Virginia; 1965, U.S. Supreme Court and U.S. Claims Court; 1966, Delaware. *Education:* University of Delaware (B.A., with distinction, 1959); University of Virginia (LL.B., 1962). Sigma Nu Phi. Assistant City Solicitor, City of Wilmington, 1966-1967. Town Solicitor: Town of Odessa, 1973-1974 and 1994—; Town of Townsend, 1994—; Town of Elsmere, 1977-1985. Member: House of Representatives, 1968-1972; Governor's Task Force on Community Schools, 1969; Revenue Study Commission of the State of Delaware, 1973; Long-Range Planning Committee of the Courts by appointment of the Chief Justice, 1974-1978; Governor's Task Force to Revise Medical Malpractice Laws, 1975; Delaware Health Care Injury Insurance Study Commission, 1976; Workmen's Compensation Commission, State of Delaware, 1978-1980. Counsel to Governor's Commission for Revision of Public Utility Laws, 1974. Chairman: Violent Crimes Compensation Board, State of Delaware, 1975-1985; Wilmington Charter Revision Commission, 1978-1983. Vice-President, National Association on Crime Victim's Compensation, 1980-1982. Member, Workers Compensation Advisory Council, 1997—. *Member:* Delaware State (Member, Professional Ethics Committee, 1968-1983) and American Bar Associations; Virginia State Bar. [Capt., Judiciary Defense Appellate Division, U.S. Army, 1962-1965]. ***PRACTICE AREAS:*** General Civil and Trial Practice; Personal Injury; Legislative and Regulatory Practice; Criminal; Family.

REPRESENTATIVE CLIENTS: Wilmington Housing Authority; American Insurance Assn.; Delaware Compensation Rating Bureau; Delaware Physical Therapist Assn.

HECKLER & FRABIZZIO

MELLON BANK CENTER
SUITE 1300
919 NORTH MARKET STREET
P.O. BOX 128
WILMINGTON, DELAWARE 19899-0128
Telephone: 302-573-4800
Fax: 302-573-4806

General Civil and Trial Practice. Insurance, Worker's Compensation, Negligence and Subrogation Law.

MEMBERS OF FIRM

GEORGE B. HECKLER, JR., born Philadelphia, Pennsylvania, February 21, 1947; admitted to bar, 1974, Delaware. *Education:* Baldwin-Wallace College (B.A., 1969); Dickinson School of Law (J.D., 1974). Omicron Delta Kappa; The Order of Barristers. *Member:* Delaware State (Past Chair, Section on Worker's Compensation) and American Bar Associations; Defense Counsel of Delaware; Defense Research Institute. [With U.S. Army, 1970-1971]. ***PRACTICE AREAS:*** Insurance Defense Law; Worker's Compensation Litigation; Asbestos and Toxic Tort Litigation; General Civil and Trial Practice. ***Email:*** gheckler@hfddel.com

ANTHONY M. FRABIZZIO, born Wilmington, Delaware, March 31, 1955; admitted to bar, 1981, Delaware. *Education:* University of Delaware (B.A., with honors, 1977); Dickinson School of Law (J.D., 1980). Pi Sigma Alpha. Deputy Attorney General, State of Delaware, Department of Justice, 1982-1984. *Member:* Delaware State (Member, Sections on: Worker's Compensation; Labor Law) and American Bar Associations; Defense Counsel of Delaware. ***PRACTICE AREAS:*** Insurance Defense Law; Worker's Compensation Litigation; General Civil and Trial Practice. ***Email:*** afrabizzio@hfddel.com

ROBERT H. RICHTER, born Wilmington, Delaware, June 21, 1953; admitted to bar, 1982, Delaware, Pennsylvania and U.S. District Court, District of Delaware. *Education:* University of Delaware (B.S., 1975); Delaware Law School of Widener University (J.D., 1981). Phi Delta Phi. Member, Moot Court Honor Society. Deputy Attorney General, State of Delaware, Department of Justice, 1982-1988. Counsel to: Delaware Industrial Accident Board, 1986-1988; Delaware Unemployment Insurance Appeals Board, 1985-1986. *Member:* Delaware State (Member, Worker's Compensation Section, 1992—) and American Bar Associations. ***PRACTICE AREAS:*** Worker's Compensation Litigation; General Civil and Trial Practice. ***Email:*** rrichter@hfddel.com

MARIA PARIS NEWILL, born Philadelphia, Pennsylvania, September 26, 1965; admitted to bar, 1991, Delaware. *Education:* University of Delaware (B.S.A.S., 1986); Oklahoma City University School of Law (J.D., 1990). *Member:* Delaware State Bar Association. ***PRACTICE AREAS:*** Worker's Compensation Litigation; General Civil and Trial Practice. ***Email:*** mnewill@hfddel.com

(This Listing Continued)

RICHARD D. ABRAMS, born Atlantic City, New Jersey, December 18, 1965; admitted to bar, 1991, Delaware. *Education:* George Washington University (B.A., 1988); Widener University School of Law (J.D., cum laude, 1991). Phi Delta Phi. *Member:* Delaware State Bar Association; Defense Counsel of Delaware. ***PRACTICE AREAS:*** Personal Injury; Insurance Defense; Products Liability; Subrogation; Construction Law; Architects and Engineers Liability; Real Estate Brokers and Agents Liability; Insurance Fraud Defense; Administrative Law. ***Email:*** rabrams@hfddel.com

WILLIAM D. RIMMER, born Englewood, New Jersey, April 3, 1965; admitted to bar, 1991, Delaware and New Jersey; 1992, Pennsylvania. *Education:* Drew University (B.A., 1987); Widener University (J.D., 1991). Member, Moot Court Honor Society. Assistant Public Defender, State of Delaware, 1993. *Member:* Delaware, Pennsylvania and American Bar Associations. ***PRACTICE AREAS:*** Worker's Compensation; Insurance Defense Litigation; General Litigation. ***Email:*** wrimmer@hfddel.com

ASSOCIATES

ERIK C. GRANDELL, born Wilmington, Delaware, October 28, 1958; admitted to bar, 1986, Pennsylvania; 1987, New Jersey; 1989, Delaware. *Education:* Widener University (B.S., 1979; M.B.A., 1985); Villanova Law School (J.D., 1985). Deputy Attorney General, Delaware Department of Justice, 1989-1990. *Member:* Delaware State Bar Association (Member, Family Law Committee, 1994—; Worker's Compensation Committee, 2000—). ***PRACTICE AREAS:*** Worker's Compensation. ***Email:*** egrandell@hfddel.com

DANIEL P. BENNETT, born Easton, Maryland, June 24, 1963; admitted to bar, 1990, Delaware and U.S. District Court, District of Delaware. *Education:* Wake Forest University (B.S., cum laude, 1985); College of William & Mary (J.D., 1990). Order of the Coif. Student Editor, Administrative Law Review, 1989-1990. Contributing Author, "Project: The Impact of Cost-Benefit Analysis on Federal Administrative Law," Administrative Law Review, 1990. *Member:* Delaware State and American Bar Associations; Delaware Trial Lawyers Association; The Association of Trial Lawyers of America. ***PRACTICE AREAS:*** Insurance Defense Law; Products Liability Law; Insurance Coverage Law. ***Email:*** dbennett@hfddel.com

JOHN W. MORGAN, born West Chester, Pennsylvania, October 30, 1959; admitted to bar, 1992, Delaware and Pennsylvania; 1993, New Jersey; 1996, U.S. District Court, District of Delaware and U.S. Court of Appeals, Third Circuit. *Education:* University of Delaware (B.A.-Econ., 1982); Widener University (J.D., 1991). *Member:* Delaware State Bar Association (Chair, Labor and Employment Section, 1994-1995). ***PRACTICE AREAS:*** Worker's Compensation; Labor and Employment. ***Email:*** jmorgan@hfddel.com

TIMOTHY H. ROHS, born Wilmington, Delaware, October 31, 1967; admitted to bar, 1996, New Jersey and U.S. District Court, District of New Jersey; 1997, Delaware. *Education:* Washington College (B.A., 1989); Virginia Commonwealth University (M.S., 1991); Widener University (J.D., magna cum laude, 1996). Psi Chi; Phi Alpha Theta; Phi Delta Phi. Recipient, Psychology Department Award, Washington College. *Member:* Delaware State Bar Association. ***PRACTICE AREAS:*** Insurance Defense; Subrogation; Personal Injury. ***Email:*** trohs@hfddel.com

REPRESENTATIVE CLIENTS: Acme Markets, Inc.; Allstate Insurance Company; Alternative Insurance Management Services, Inc.; American International Companies; Argonaut Insurance Co.; CGU Insurance Company; C.H. Hetrick Association, Inc.; Chubb Group of Insurance Companies; CIGNA; CNA Insurance Co.; Crawford & Company; Crum & Forster Commercial Insurance; Fireman's Fund Insurance Company; GAB Business Services, Inc.; The Harford Mutual Ins. Co.; Harleysville Insurance Companies; Hercules, Inc.; Kemper Group; Marriott International, Inc.; The Ohio Casualty Group; Pennsylvania Lumberman's Ins. Co.; Pennsylvania National Mutual Ins. Co.; Perdue Farms, Inc.; Progressive Companies; Prudential Property & Casualty Insurance Company; Reliance Insurance Co.; St. Paul Fire and Marine Insurance Co.; Sears, Roebuck & Co.; The Seibels Group, Inc.; Selective Ins. Co. of America; Sentry Insurance Co.; State Farm Insurance Co.; Super Fresh Food Markets, Inc.; Transamerica Ins. Group; Travelers Property Casualty Corp.; Universal Underwriters Group; Wausau Insurance Group; Zurich-US Insurance Co.

HEIMAN, ABER, GOLDLUST & BAKER

FIRST FEDERAL PLAZA
702 KING STREET
P.O. BOX 1675
WILMINGTON, DELAWARE 19899
Telephone: 302-658-1800
Fax: 302-658-1473

General Civil and Trial Practice, Corporate, Negligence, Personal Injury, Medical Malpractice, Insurance (Defense) Law. Bankruptcy, Commercial Law, Employment Law, Construction Law, Commercial Real Estate, Labor and Zoning Law.

FIRM PROFILE: The association of law practices of Heiman, Aber, Goldlust & Baker established in 1985, practices in courts, state and federal, throughout Delaware and also represents clients internationally. The firm is fully staffed and maintains a general civil and trial practice including employment discrimination, wrongful termination, and personal injury.

(This Listing Continued)

MEMBERS

HENRY A. HEIMAN, born Los Angeles, California, March 9, 1942; admitted to bar, 1968, New York; 1972, Delaware. *Education:* Cornell University (B.A., 1963); Yale University (J.D., 1966). U.S. Trustee in Bankruptcy, 1979-1982. Member, 1985 and Chairman, 1987-1992, Delaware Advisory Committee, United States Civil Rights Commission. *Member:* Delaware (Member, Commercial Law Section) and New York State Bar Associations; Delaware Trial Lawyers Association. ***PRACTICE AREAS:*** Commercial Law; Bankruptcy Law; Commercial Real Estate; Chancery Practice. ***Email:*** hheiman@hagblaw.com

GARY W. ABER, born Milford, Delaware, October 6, 1946; admitted to bar, 1972, Delaware. *Education:* University of Delaware (B.S., Finance, 1969); George Washington University (J.D., with Honors, 1972). Chairman, New Castle County Board of Adjustment, 1986-1990, Chairman, Delaware State Human Relations Commission, 1990—. Member, United States District Court Advisory Committee, 1984-1988. Selected, "Among Top Lawyers of Delaware," Delaware Today Magazine. *Member:* Delaware Bar Association (Member: Legal Ethics Committee, 1979-1983; Chairman, Continuing Legal Education Committee, 1983-1986; Sections on: Litigation; Torts and Insurance Practice); Delaware Trial Lawyers Association; Defense Research Institute; American Board of Trial Advocates (Elected Member). ***PRACTICE AREAS:*** Litigation; Employment Law; Personal Injury Law; Medical Malpractice; Insurance Defense Law; Litigation. ***Email:*** gaber@hagblaw.com

PERRY F. GOLDLUST, born New York, N.Y., May 15, 1942; admitted to bar, 1966, New York; 1973, Delaware; 1974, U.S. District Court, District of Delaware. *Education:* Bernard M. Baruch College of the City University of New York (B.B.A., 1964); Brooklyn Law School (J.D., 1966). Member, AFL-CIO Lawyers Coordinating Committee. First Assistant City Solicitor, Wilmington, Delaware, 1974-1976. *Member:* American (Member, Section on: Labor and Employment Law) Bar Association. ***PRACTICE AREAS:*** Labor (Union) Law; Commercial Law; Personal Injury; Workman's Compensation. ***Email:*** pgoldlust@hagblaw.com

DARRELL J. BAKER, born Seaford, Delaware, November 2, 1958; admitted to bar, 1983, Delaware and U.S. District Court, District of Delaware. *Education:* University of Delaware (B.A., 1980); University of Dayton (J.D., 1983). *Member:* Delaware Bar Association; Delaware Trial Lawyers Association. ***PRACTICE AREAS:*** Personal Injury; Real Estate Law; Zoning Law; Governmental Relations and Lobbying. ***Email:*** dbaker@hagblaw.com

DONALD L. GOUGE, JR., born Wilmington, Delaware, September 1, 1958; admitted to bar, 1984, Delaware; 1988, U.S. District Court, District of Delaware and U.S. Court of Appeals, Third Circuit; 2000, U.S. Supreme Court. *Education:* University of Delaware (B.A., 1980); California Western School of Law (J.D., 1983). Assistant City Solicitor, Wilmington, 1984-1989. *Member:* Delaware Bar Association; Delaware Trial Lawyers Association. ***PRACTICE AREAS:*** Personal Injury Law; Litigation; Insurance Defense Law; Real Estate Litigation. ***Email:*** dongouge@magpage.com

SUSAN CAROL OVER, born Harrisburg, Pennsylvania, December 3, 1958; admitted to bar, 1986, Pennsylvania; 1988, Delaware and U.S. District Court, District of Delaware. *Education:* Hood College; University of Delaware (B.A., cum laude, 1980); Dickinson School of Law (J.D., 1985). Psi Chi. *Member:* Delaware and American Bar Associations. ***PRACTICE AREAS:*** Personal Injury; Medical Malpractice; Family Law. ***Email:*** sover@hagblaw.com

SUSAN E. KAUFMAN, born Wilmington, Delaware, April 17, 1969; admitted to bar, 1995, Pennsylvania; 1996, Delaware and U.S. District Court, District of Delaware. *Education:* University of Delaware (B.S., 1991); Villanova University School of Law (J.D., 1994). *Member:* Pennsylvania, Delaware and American Bar Associations. ***PRACTICE AREAS:*** General Civil Practice; Bankruptcy; Contracts; Personal Injury; Real Estate. ***Email:*** skaufman@hagblaw.com

REPRESENTATIVE CLIENTS: The Travelers; Peninsula Insurance Co.; Agency Insurance Co.; Wilmington Stevedores, Inc.; Champion Construction Co.; S.T. Good Insurance Co., Inc.; E. Walter Helm Insurance Co., Inc.; O.C.A.W. Local 898-8; Owens-Corning, Inc.; Teamsters Local 326, AFSCME, FOP Locals 5, 10 & 14; Newark Housing Authority; New Castle County Sheriff; Commercial Union Insurance Co.; RE/Max Associates, Inc.

HERDEG, DU PONT & DALLE PAZZE, LLP

Established in 1986

1201 ORANGE STREET, SUITE 500
WILMINGTON, DELAWARE 19801
Telephone: 302-655-6500
Email: hdd@dellaw.com
URL: http://www.lawyers.com/dellaw

Estate and Tax Planning, Business Succession Planning, Trusts and Estates, Fiduciary Counseling, Wills and Probate, Estate Administration and Private Foundations.

(This Listing Continued)

FIRM PROFILE: Herdeg, du Pont & Dalle Pazze, LLP, specializes in helping individuals implement tax-advantaged estate plans, create private foundations and administer trusts and decedents' estates and in helping closely-held and family-held businesses implement succession plans. Attention is given to gift programs, asset realignments and federal and state transfer taxes, drawing on over seventy-five years of combined experience of the principals.

PARTNERS

JOHN A. HERDEG, born Buffalo, New York, September 15, 1937; admitted to bar, 1963, Connecticut; 1964, Delaware. *Education:* Princeton University (B.A., 1959); University of Pennsylvania (LL.B., 1962). Listed in: The Best Lawyers in America, 1995—; Who's Who in America, 1996—. *Member:* Delaware (Member, Estates and Trusts Section) and American Bar Associations. ***PRACTICE AREAS:*** Estate Planning; Estate and Gift Taxation; Trust Planning; Trust Administration; Estate Administration. ***Email:*** jherdeg@dellaw.com

WILLIAM B. DU PONT, JR., born Johnstown, Pennsylvania, January 27, 1946; admitted to bar, 1982, Pennsylvania, U.S. Tax Court and U.S. District Court, Western District of Pennsylvania; 1989, Delaware and U.S. District Court, District of Delaware. *Education:* Bethany College (B.S., 1971); University of Pittsburgh (J.D., 1982). Moot Court Competition Honors, 1980. Faculty: Pennsylvania Bar Institute Seminar, "How to Draft Estate Planning Documents" and "Drafting for the Marital Deduction". *Member:* Pennsylvania (Member, Section of Real Property, Probate and Trust Law) and Delaware (Member, Estates and Trusts Section) Bar Associations. ***PRACTICE AREAS:*** Estate Planning; Federal Estate and Gift Taxation; Trusts and Estates Taxation; Private Foundations; Estate Administration. ***Email:*** wdupont@dellaw.com

JAMES P. DALLE PAZZE, born Princeton, New Jersey, August 22, 1952; admitted to bar, 1978, New Jersey; 1979, District of Columbia; 1980, Delaware. *Education:* Rider College (B.A., cum laude, 1975); Delaware Law School of Widener University (J.D., cum laude, 1978); Georgetown University (LL.M. in Taxation, 1981). Member, 1976-1977 and Editor-in-Chief, 1977-1978, Delaware Journal of Corporate Law. Author: Comment, "The Effect of the Tax Reform Act of 1976 on Domestic International Sales Corporations," 2 Delaware Journal of Corporate Law 94, 1977. Adjunct Professor of Law, Delaware Law School, 1982-1995. Founder and Director, Attorneys for Family-Held Enterprises. *Member:* Delaware State (Member, Taxation Section) and American (Member, Section of Taxation, 1979—; Chairman, Committee on Small Business, Tax Section, 1990-1992; Member, Section of Business Law, 1983—; Chairman, Committee on Taxation, Business Law Section, 1991-1995) Bar Associations. Fellow, American College of Tax Counsel. ***PRACTICE AREAS:*** Estate Planning; Estate and Gift Taxation; Business Succession Planning; Federal and State Taxation Law. ***Email:*** jdallepazze@dellaw.com

REFERENCES: Christiana Bank and Trust Co.; First Union Bank.

LAW OFFICES OF DANIEL K. HOGAN

Established in 1993

1701 SHALLCROSS AVENUE, SUITE C
WILMINGTON, DELAWARE 19806
Telephone: 302-656-7540
Facsimile: 302-656-7604
Email: dkhogan@worldnet.att.net
URL: http://www.lawyers.com/dkhogan

Commercial Litigation, Creditor Bankruptcy, Real Estate, General Civil and Trial Practice, Personal Injury, Medical Malpractice, Products Liability and Corporate Law.

DANIEL K. HOGAN, born New York, N.Y., April 12, 1964; admitted to bar, 1990, Delaware, Pennsylvania, U.S. District Court, District of Delaware and U.S. Bankruptcy Court, District of Delaware. *Education:* Wake Forest University (B.S., Business Administration, 1986); Widener University (J.D., 1989). *Member:* Delaware (Member, Section on Real Estate, 1990—), Pennsylvania and American (Member, Sections on Probate and Real Estate, 1990—) Bar Associations; Delaware Trial Lawyers Association.

HOLLSTEIN KEATING CATTELL JOHNSON & GOLDSTEIN, P.C.

ONE COMMERCE CENTER, SUITE 730
12TH AND ORANGE STREETS
WILMINGTON, DELAWARE 19801
Telephone: 302-884-6700
Fax: 302-573-2507
Email: lmp@hkcjg.com

Philadelphia, Pennsylvania Office: 1608 Walnut Street, Suite 1602, 19103. Telephone: 215-893-9488. Fax: 215-893-9480. Email: JFJ@HKCJG.com.

(This Listing Continued)

HOLLSTEIN KEATING CATTELL JOHNSON & GOLDSTEIN, P.C., Wilmington—Continued

Marlton, New Jersey Office: Willow Ridge Executive Office Park, 750 Route 73 South, Suite 301, 08053. Telephone: 856-810-8860. Fax: 856-810-8861.

Commercial and Casualty Litigation, Maritime Law, Products Liability.

LYNNE M. PARKER, born Philadelphia, Pennsylvania, December 14, 1964; admitted to bar, 1989, New Jersey; 1990, Delaware; 1993, Pennsylvania. *Education:* Drexel University (B.S., 1986); Villanova University (J.D., 1989). (Also at Marlton, New Jersey Office). ***PRACTICE AREAS:*** Commercial and Casualty Litigation; Products Liability; Maritime Law. ***Email:*** lmp@hkcjg.com

LAW OFFICE OF BRUCE L. HUDSON

Established in 1979

300 DELAWARE AVENUE, SUITE 1130
WILMINGTON, DELAWARE 19801
Telephone: 302-656-9850
Fax: 302-656-9836
Email: delaw@aol.com
URL: http://www.lawyers.com/delaw

Personal Injury Litigation, Medical/Dental Malpractice, Products Liability.

BRUCE L. HUDSON, born Frankford, Delaware, April 10, 1945; admitted to bar, 1978, Pennsylvania; 1979, Delaware and U.S. District Court, District of Delaware; 1981, U.S. Court of Appeals, Third Circuit; 1992, U.S. Supreme Court. *Education:* University of Delaware (B.S., 1968; M.S., 1970); Delaware Law School of Widener University (J.D., 1977). Phi Delta Phi. Chief House Attorney, Delaware State Legislature, 1980-1982. *Member:* Delaware State, Pennsylvania and American Bar Associations; Delaware Trial Lawyers Association (President, 1992-1993, Board of Governors, 1990-1995, Chairman, Legislative Committee, 1999-2001, LAWPAC trustee, 1986—, Legislative Agent, 1983-1989); The Association of Trial Lawyers of America (State Delegate, 1990; M Club); Million Dollar Advocacy Forum. (Board Certified Civil Trial Specialist by the National Board of Trial Advocacy). ***PRACTICE AREAS:*** Personal Injury; Negligence; Professional Liability; Products Liability; Premises Liability; Medical Malpractice; Dental Malpractice; Litigation; Nursing Home Abuse and Neglect.

HUNTLEY & ASSOCIATES

Established in 1993

1105 NORTH MARKET STREET
P.O. BOX 948
WILMINGTON, DELAWARE 19899-0948
Telephone: 302-426-0610
Facsimile: 302-426-0612
URL: http://www.monopolize.com

Intellectual Property; Patent, Trademark and Copyright Law.

FIRM PROFILE: The firm was founded to provide high quality and cost effective service in intellectual property matters, including worldwide patent, trademark and copyright procurement, and related licensing and litigation. We represent a broad spectrum of clients ranging from individual entrepreneurs and small businesses to large corporations in the United States, Canada, the UK, Japan, Russia and Korea.

DONALD W. HUNTLEY, born Chicago, Illinois, September 22, 1942; admitted to bar, 1967, District of Columbia; 1973, U.S. Supreme Court; 1981, Delaware; registered to practice before U.S. Patent and Trademark Office. *Education:* University of Illinois (B.S., 1963; J.D., 1966). Edmund J. James Scholar. With: E.I. du Pont de Nemours & Co., 1966-1992; Remington Arms Company, 1985-1989. *Member:* District of Columbia Bar; Delaware (Counsel, Intellectual Property Law Section) and American Bar Associations; Philadelphia Intellectual Property Law; American Intellectual Property Law Association. ***REPORTED CASES:*** Keys v. Delaware, 337 A2d 18 (1975); Franks v. Delaware 337 A2d 578, 98 S Ct 2674 (1978). ***PRACTICE AREAS:*** Intellectual Property Law; Patent, Trademark and Copyright Law. ***Email:*** huntley@monopolize.com

ASSOCIATES

MARK C. GREGORY, born Akron, Ohio, February 4, 1965; admitted to bar, 1995, Delaware; 1996, U.S. District Court, District of Delaware. *Education:* Colgate University (B.A., 1989); Widener University School of Law (J.D., 1994). Phi Delta Phi. Intern to Chief Justice E. Norman Veasey, Supreme Court of Delaware, 1993-1994. *Member:* Delaware and American Bar Associations. ***PRACTICE AREAS:*** Intellectual Property; Patent, Trademark and Copyright Law; Entertainment Law; Internet Law. ***Email:*** gregory@monopolize.com

(This Listing Continued)

BRIAN A. GOMEZ, born Port Jefferson, New York, September 14, 1965; admitted to bar, 1993, New Jersey, Pennsylvania and U.S. District Court, District of New Jersey; 1994, Delaware; registered to practice before U.S. Patent and Trademark Office. *Education:* Indiana University (B.A., Psychology, 1987); Widener University School of Law (J.D., 1992); University of Delaware (B.A., Chemistry, 1998). Law Clerk to Jerome O. Herlihy, Superior Court of Delaware, 1993-1995. *Member:* Delaware State (Member, Intellectual Property Division) and American (Member, Intellectual Property Division) Bar Associations. ***PRACTICE AREAS:*** Intellectual Property; Patent; Trademark; Copyright. ***Email:*** gomez@monopolize.com

OF COUNSEL

THEODORE C. GREGORY, born Uniontown, Pennsylvania, October 28, 1926; admitted to bar, 1968, Ohio; 1978, District of Columbia; registered to practice before U.S. Patent and Trademark Office (Not admitted in Delaware). *Education:* Pennsylvania State University (B.S., 1948); University of Akron Law School (J.D., 1968). Phi Alpha Delta. Treasurer, Student Bar Association, 1964-1965. Attorney: Goodyear Tire & Rubber Co., 1950-1969; Johnson Steel & Wire, 1950-1953; Carborundum Co., 1948-1949. Member, American Chemical Society, 1948-1962. *Member:* Akron Bar Association; Cleveland Patent Law Association; Philadelphia Intellectual Property Law Association. (Senior Attorney). ***PRACTICE AREAS:*** Patent Law; Patent Applications; Litigation; Agreements.

JOSEPH A. HURLEY, P.A.

Established in 1979

1215 KING STREET
WILMINGTON, DELAWARE 19801
Telephone: 302-658-8980
Fax: 302-658-8987

Criminal Trial Practice Only.

JOSEPH A. HURLEY, born Washington, D.C., February 27, 1943; admitted to bar, 1970, Delaware; 1979, Florida. *Education:* University of Delaware (B.A., 1966); Dickinson School of Law (J.D., 1969). Guest Lecturer, University of Delaware and Widener School of Law. Deputy Attorney General, Department of Justice, State of Delaware, 1971-1974. Past Counsel, Governor's Strike Force. Nationally honored as Criminal Trial Attorney by National Directory of Criminal Lawyers. Listed in: Best Lawyers in America, 1991-2001; Martindale-Hubbell Bar Register of Preeminent Lawyers, 1994-2001. Recognized in Delaware Today Magazine as one of Delaware's best criminal lawyers, 2001. ***PRACTICE AREAS:*** Criminal Law.

MICHAEL R. IPPOLITI

824 MARKET STREET, SUITE 412
P.O. BOX 2284
WILMINGTON, DELAWARE 19899-2284
Telephone: 302-428-1400
Fax: 302-655-6827
URL: http://www.lawyers.com/ippolitilaw

Litigation, Workers Compensation, Employment Law, Personal Injury.

MICHAEL R. IPPOLITI, born Philadelphia, Pennsylvania, February 24, 1961; admitted to bar, 1987, Pennsylvania; 1988, Delaware. *Education:* Temple University (B.A., cum laude, 1983); Delaware Law School of Widener University (J.D., 1987). Phi Delta Phi; Alpha Phi Sigma. Co-author: with Fairfax Leary, Jr., "Letters of Credit: Have We Fully Recovered From Three Insolvency Shocks?" The University of Pennsylvania Journal of International Business Law, Vol. 5, No. 4, Fall, 1987. Author: "Page vs. Hercules: Closing the Chapter on the Cumulative Detrimental Effect Doctrine in Delaware's Workers Compensation," The Advocate, Pg 25, Fall, 1994. *Member:* Delaware (Member, Workers Compensation Section) and American (Member, Sections on: Labor and Employment Law; Torts and Insurance Practice; Litigation) Bar Associations; Association of Trial Lawyers of America, Associate Member (Member, Section on Workers Compensation and Workplace Injury); Defense Counsel of Delaware; Defense Research Institute; Delaware Trial Lawyers' Association. ***PRACTICE AREAS:*** Litigation; Workers Compensation; Employment Law.

JACOBS & CRUMPLAR, P.A.

Established in 1981

2 EAST 7TH STREET
P.O. BOX 1271
WILMINGTON, DELAWARE 19899
Telephone: 1-800-355-1818; 302-656-5445
FAX: 302-656-5875
Email: jcinbox@jacobsandcrumplar.com
URL: http://www.jacobsandcrumplar.com

Personal Injury, Automobile Accidents, Medical Malpractice, Social Security Disability, Products Liability and Toxic Substance, Worker Compensation, Business Litigation, Bankruptcy, Patent and Copyright Law.

FIRM PROFILE: Jacobs & Crumplar's entire operation is geared toward client service and getting the best results. We always do what is in your best interest. Jacobs and Crumplar's approach to the law involves an understanding of science and technology, the dynamics of the business profession, and the subtleties of contractual agreements. Its pursuit of information to gain advantages for clients has taken the firm throughout the world.

ROBERT JACOBS, born Brooklyn, New York, June 21, 1941; admitted to bar, 1968, District of Columbia; 1969, Delaware and U.S. Court of Appeals for the District of Columbia Circuit; 1980, U.S. Court of Customs and Patent Appeals; 1981, U.S. Court of Appeals, 3rd and 4th Circuits; 1983, U.S. Supreme Court. *Education:* City College of the City University of New York (B.S.Ch.E., 1963); Temple University (J.D., 1968). *Member:* Delaware State (Chairman, Torts and Insurance Practice Committee, 1992-2000) and American Bar Associations; The Association of Trial Lawyers of America (Member, 1978— and Vice Chairman, 1984-1986, Toxic, Tort and Environmental Litigation Committee; Board of Governors, 1988—); American Intellectual Property Law Association; Delaware Trial Lawyers Association (President-Elect, 1985-1986; President, 1986—); Trial Lawyers for Public Justice. ***PRACTICE AREAS:*** Product Liability; Asbestos Litigation; Medical Malpractice; Business Litigation; Patent Law; Trademarks; Copyright Law. ***Email:*** rjacobs@jacobsandcrumplar.com

THOMAS C. CRUMPLAR, born Detroit, Michigan, May 21, 1950; admitted to bar, 1975, Kentucky; 1978, Delaware; 1982, New Jersey. *Education:* University of Michigan (A.B., 1971); University of Virginia (J.D., 1975). Phi Beta Kappa. Co-Author: "Tax Exempt Religious Schools Under Attack: Conflicting Goals of Religious Freedom and Racial Integration," 48 Fordham Law Review 229, 1979. Author: "An Alternative to Public and Victim Enforcement of the Federal Securities and Antitrust Laws: Citizen Enforcement," 13 Harvard Journal on Legislation 76, 1975. Senior Law Clerk to Hon. John T. Copenhaver, U.S. District Court, Southern District of West Virginia, 1976-1978. *Member:* Delaware State and New Jersey State Bar Associations; The Association of Trial Lawyers of America; Christian Legal Society. ***PRACTICE AREAS:*** Asbestos Litigation; Products Liability Law; Toxic Substance Law; Negligence Law. ***Email:*** tcrumplar@jacobsandcrumplar.com

MARLA ROSOFF ESKIN, born Philadelphia, Pennsylvania, January 20, 1966; admitted to bar, 1991, Pennsylvania and Delaware; 1992, U.S. District Court, District of Delaware. *Education:* Temple University (B.A., 1987; J.D., 1990). *Member:* Delaware and American Bar Associations; Delaware Trial Lawyers Association (Member, Board of Governors, 1996—); The Association of Trial Lawyers of America (Member: Publication Committee, 1998—; Law Schools Committee, 2000—). ***PRACTICE AREAS:*** Negligence Law; Products Liability Law; Toxic Substance Law; Business Law; Bankruptcy. ***Email:*** meskin@jacobsandcrumplar.com

ELIZABETH B. LEWIS, born Wilmington, Delaware, December 27, 1956; admitted to bar, 1989, Pennsylvania and New Jersey; 1991, Delaware; U.S. District Court, District of Delaware. *Education:* College of Notre Dame; University of Delaware (B.A., 1978); Delaware Law School (J.D., 1988). *Member:* Delaware Bar Association; Delaware Trial Lawyers Association (Member, Board of Governors, 1997—); The Association of Trial Lawyers of America (Member; Academic Liason Committee, 1998—; Motor Vehicle Committee, 1998—; International Law Committee, 1998—). ***PRACTICE AREAS:*** Products Liability; Negligence Law; Toxic Substance Law; Business Law. ***Email:*** elewis@jacobsandcrumplar.com

VINCENT J. X. HEDRICK, II, born Wilmington, Delaware, December 3, 1964; admitted to bar, 1989, Delaware; 1991, U.S. District Court, District of Delaware and U.S. Court of Appeals, Federal Circuit. *Education:* University of Delaware (B.A., Honors Program, cum laude, 1986); Washington & Lee University (J.D., 1989). Phi Beta Kappa; Phi Sigma Tau. Recipient: Presidential Scholarship. Washington & Lee Law Review, 1987-1988. Author: "The Admissibility of Tape Recorded Evidence Produced by Private Individuals Under Title III of the Omnibus Crime Control Act of 1968," Vol. 45, Winter 1988, No. 1; "L. Ron Hubbard, How Much Is a Religious Service Worth, and Do Box Seats Cost Extra?: The Deductibility of Mandatory Donations Under Section 170 of the Internal Revenue Code.," Vol. 45, Fall 1988, No. 4. *Member:* Delaware State (Member, Intellectual Property Law Section) and American Bar Associations;

(This Listing Continued)

Delaware Trial Lawyers Association; The Association of Trial Lawyers of America. ***Email:*** vhedrick@jacobsandcrumplar.com

J. R. JULIAN, P.A.

Established in 1982

SUITE 1001, 824 MARKET STREET MALL
P.O. BOX 2171
WILMINGTON, DELAWARE 19899-2171
Telephone: 302-658-6700
Fax: 302-658-6708

General Civil Practice. Personal Injury, Negligence and Tort Law. Insurance Litigation. Workers Compensation Defense, Products Liability, Toxic Substances Litigation, Real Estate, Asbestos Defense.

FIRM PROFILE: J.R. Julian has engaged in complex litigation involving asbestos defense, personal injury, and property damage defense, general products liability defense and insurance coverage litigation defense on behalf of insurers, and workers' compensation defense.

The client's interest is the firm's primary concern. Accordingly, the firm is committed to the delivery of legal services in a competent, efficient and economical manner. To this end, the firm utilizes highly trained and competent support personnel who work directly with and in conjunction with the attorneys. Whenever possible, support staff performs work functions that do not require the direct involvement of an attorney; however, all work is supervised by the senior attorney.

J. R. JULIAN, born Wilmington, Delaware, April 6, 1943; admitted to bar, 1971, Delaware; U.S. District Court, District of Delaware; U.S. Court of Appeals, Third Circuit; U.S. Supreme Court. *Education:* American University (B.A., 1966); Columbus School of Law, Catholic University of America (J.D., 1970). Pi Sigma Alpha; Delta Theta Phi. Member, Board of Bar Examiners of the Supreme Court of the State of Delaware, 1985-1989. Member, Rules Committee, Delaware Industrial Accident Board. Member, Board of Directors, Historical Society of the Court of Chancery, State of Delaware. Member, Board of Advisors, Delaware Chapter, Lawyers Division, Federalist Society for Law and Public Policy Studies. *Member:* Delaware (President, 1998-1999; Vice President at Large; President-Elect; New Castle County; Former Vice-Chair, Judicial Appointments Committee; Member, Committees on: Executive; Alternative Dispute Resolution; Member, Sections on: Insurance; Litigation; Workers' Compensation) and American (Member, Sections on: Litigation; Business Law) Bar Associations; American Board of Trial Advocates; Defense Research Institute; American Judicature Society; Delaware Trial Lawyers Association; The Association of Trial Lawyers of America; St. Thomas More Society of Delaware (Past President). ***PRACTICE AREAS:*** Civil Litigation; Negligence; Insurance; Workers Compensation; Products Liability; Insurance Coverage.

SAMANTHA P. ZAZZO, born Philadelphia, Pennsylvania, January 21, 1970; admitted to bar, 1994, New Jersey, Pennsylvania and U.S. District Court, District of New Jersey (Not admitted in Delaware). *Education:* Drew University (B.A., 1991); Rutgers University at Camden (J.D., 1994). Dean's Scholar. Recipient, American Jurisprudence Award in Property and Pre-Trial Advocacy. Quarter-finalist, Hunter Advanced Moot Court. Author: "Search & Seizure", 24 Rutgers Law Journal 1316 (Summer, 1993). *Member:* Camden County, New Jersey State (Representative, Young Lawyers Division) and American Bar Associations. ***PRACTICE AREAS:*** Defense Litigation; Environmental. ***Email:*** spzazzo@earpcohn.com

JILL SPEVACK DiSCIULLO, born Laurel, Maryland, October 4, 1972; admitted to bar, 1999, Pennsylvania and New Jersey (Not admitted in Delaware). *Education:* Virginia Tech (B.A., 1994); Widener University School of Law (J.D., 1999). *Member:* Philadelphia (Member, Family Law Section) and Pennsylvania Bar Associations. ***PRACTICE AREAS:*** Family Law. ***Email:*** jspevack@dolchin.com

REPRESENTATIVE CLIENTS: Alexis; Atlantic Mutual Insurance Co.; Gallagher Bassett; Risk Enterprise Management (Home Insurance); Sedgwick; The PMA Group; Unigard Security Insurance Co.; St. Paul (USF&G); Casualty Reciprocal Exchange, Inc.; Admiral Insurance Co.; Royal Insurance Co.; Royal/SunAlliance; Ward North America, Inc.; SISCO;European Reinsurance Company of Zurich and Gerling-Konzern Globale Reuckversicherungs-Aktiengesellschaft; Verizon Delaware, Inc.; Arkansas Best; ConAgra Poultry; Georgia Gulf; ISS International Service Systems; Marmon Keystone; Penske Truck Leasing; Playtex Apparel, Inc.; Playtex Products, Inc.; Reliable roadway Express; McDonalds; State of Delaware; Westvaco; Zenith Products Corp.; du Pont Hospital for Children of the Alfred I. du Pont Institute of the Nemours Foundation; Barrett Business Services, Inc.
APPROVED ATTORNEYS FOR: Berks Title Insurance Co.; Pioneer Title of Delaware, Inc.

KELLEY, JASONS, McGUIRE & SPINELLI, L.L.P.

800 DELAWARE AVENUE
P.O. BOX 194
WILMINGTON, DELAWARE 19899
Telephone: 302-652-8560
Fax: 302-652-8405
Email: adellaporta@kjms.com
URL: http://www.KJMS.com

Philadelphia, Pennsylvania Office: Centre Square West, Suite 1500, 1500 Market Street, 19102. Telephone: 215-854-0658. Fax: 215-854-8434.
Marlton, New Jersey Office: One Greentree Centre, Suite 201, 08053. Telephone: 856-988-5543. Fax: 856-988-9165.

Civil Litigation, Personal Injury, Medical Malpractice Law, Collection Law, Products Liability Law, Environmental Law, Insurance Law, Reinsurance Law, Criminal Law, Commercial Law, Probate and Trust Law.

(For complete biographical data on all personnel, see Biographical Listing at Philadelphia, Pennsylvania).

KENT & McBRIDE, P.C.

BUCKNER
1308 DELAWARE AVENUE
P.O. BOX 2165
WILMINGTON, DELAWARE
Telephone: 302-777-5477
Fax: 302-429-8600

Cherry Hill, New Jersey Office: 1040 Kings Highway North, Suite 403, 08034. Telephone: 856-667-3113. Fax: 856-667-4003.
Philadelphia, Pennsylvania Office: Two Logan Square, Suite 600, 18th and Arch Streets. Telephone: 215-568-1800. Fax: 215-568-1830.

General Civil Practice in State and Federal Courts of Pennsylvania, Delaware and New Jersey. Arson and Insurance Fraud, Property, Admiralty and Maritime Law, Insurance Law, Casualty, Products Liability, Medical Malpractice, Toxic Tort Litigation, Subrogation, Motor Vehicle Law, Commercial Premises.

FIRM PROFILE: Kent & McBride, P.C. was established in 1994. The firm serves clients in Pennsylvania, New Jersey and Delaware.

Kent & McBride, P.C., is engaged primarily in property and casualty defense work. The firm represents both insurance carrier and self-insured clients in general civil litigation in state and federal courts of Pennsylvania, New Jersey and Delaware with emphasis in areas of insurance law, toxic tort and environmental law, workers' compensation, products liability, subrogation, professional malpractice, motor vehicle, and premises liability.

REPRESENTATIVE CLIENTS: Admiral Insurance Company; Advance Transformer Co.; Aetna Insurance Company; Alliance General Insurance Co.; American International Group; Armstrong World Industries, Inc.; Atlantic Mutual Insurance Company; Bayside Casualty; Best Buy, Inc.; Canteen Corporation; The Chubb Group of Insurance Companies; Colonial Penn Insurance Company; Constitution State Service Co.; CNA Insurance Company; Crawford & Company; Crum and Forster Insurance Company; Darden Restaurants, Inc. (Olive Garden & Red Lobster); ELCO Administrative Services; Enterprise Rent-A-Car; Esschem, Inc.; Farm Family Mutual Insurance Company; First Specialty Service Co.; Fireman's Fund Insurance Company; Flagstar; General Accident Insurance Company; Great Dane Trucking Company; The Hartford Insurance Company; Hanover Foods; Hechingers; IHDS of New Jersey; Integon Corp.; Jamesway Corporation; Kemper Insurance Company; Laneco, Inc.; Liberty Mutual Insurance Company; Limbach; Lindsey-Morden Claims Services; Metropolitan Property & Casualty; McNeil Consumer Products; Mine Safety Appliance Company; Mutual Benefit Insurance Co.; Myers Foods; Nabisco Brands; National Continental/Progressive Casualty Insurance Co.; Nationwide Insurance Co.; North American Phillips Co.; Pathmark, Inc.; Penn America Insurance Co.; Pennsylvania National Insurance Company; Pennsylvania Property & Casualty Insurance Guaranty Assn.; Pepsi-Cola Company; Regis Insurance Company; Rickel Home Centers, Inc.; Risk Enterprise Management; Save-A-Lot, Inc.; Scibal Associates; Selective Insurance Company of America; Supermarkets General Corporation; Supervalu, Inc.; The St. Paul Insurance Company; Swigart Associates, Inc.; Sysco Food Services; TNT/Red Star; Tokio Marine Insurance Co.; The Travelers Insurance Company; USF&G Insurance Company; Wausau Insurance Company; Williard, Inc; WCASC; Zurich American Insurance Company.

(For complete biographical data on all personnel, see Professional Biographies at Philadelphia, Pennsylvania).

KIMMEL, CARTER, ROMAN & PELTZ, P.A.

Established in 1973

12TH FLOOR, 913 MARKET STREET
P.O. BOX 272
WILMINGTON, DELAWARE 19899-0272
Telephone: 302-571-0800
Fax: 302-571-8155

Newark, Delaware Office: 1400 Peoples Plaza, Suite 100, 19702. Telephone: 302-838-5970.

General Civil and Trial Practice in all Courts. Insurance, Negligence, Construction Accidents, Workers Compensation. Federal Practice.

FIRM PROFILE: Kimmel, Carter, Roman & Peltz, P.A. has served the citizens of Delaware for over 30 years. The firm specializes in plaintiffs' litigation and is probably the most unique law firm of its size in Delaware because its practice is confined solely to automobile accidents, workers' compensation, insurance, products liability and construction accidents. The firm's biggest asset is constant communication with clients. Telephone calls are never screened and the clients have instant access to the attorneys. There are 2 offices centrally located: 1 in downtown Wilmington in the heart of the business district and the other in suburban New Castle County located at People's Plaza. Serving Newark, Middletown, Bear, Smyrna and Dover, the firm annually receives the highest rankings in all legal publications. There are 7 attorneys servicing the public.

MORTON RICHARD KIMMEL, born New York, N.Y., November 10, 1940; admitted to bar, 1965, Delaware; 1966, District of Columbia; U.S. District Court, District of Delaware; U.S. District Court, Eastern District of Pennsylvania; U.S. Court of Appeals, Third Circuit; U.S. Supreme Court. *Education:* Temple University (A.B., 1962); George Washington University (J.D., 1965). Phi Delta Phi. Law Clerk, Delaware Superior Court, 1965-1966. Author: "Alternative Dispute Resolution," The Delaware Bar in the 20th Century, 1994. Lecturer on Criminal Law, Insurance Law, Personal Injury Law, Law Office Management, Trial Court Practice Arbitration, Mediation, Ethics, Professionalism and the Lawyers' Fund For Client Protection. Chairman: Delaware Bar Association Committee on J.P. Reform, 1968-1970; Courts' Committee, Delaware Agency to Reduce Crime, 1971-1972; Defense Research Institute, 1976-1977. Supervisor, Delaware Justices of the Peace (Magistrates), 1970-1972. Member, Supreme Court's Long Range Courts Planning Committee, 1971-1974; 1985-1986. Trustee, Lawyers' Fund for Client Protection of Delaware Supreme Court, 1985-1997. President and Trustee, Kimmel-Spiller Charitable Foundation. Member, The Million Dollar Advocates Forum. Listed in: Who's Who in American Law; Who's Who in the World. *Member:* Delaware (Chairman: Committee on Continuing Legal Education, 1974-1980; Litigation Committee, 1980—) and American Bar Associations; Delaware Trial Lawyers Association; The Association of Trial Lawyers of America; American Judicature Society; American Board of Trial Advocates; Federation of Insurance Counsel; Mediator, Delaware Superior Court, 1993—. ***PRACTICE AREAS:*** General and Civil Trial Practice; Insurance; Negligence; Workers Compensation; Construction Accidents; Products Liability; Federal Practice. ***Email:*** MRKimmel@kcrlaw.com

EDWARD B. CARTER, JR., born Wilmington, Delaware, June 5, 1946; admitted to bar, 1977, Delaware. *Education:* Duke University (B.A., 1968); Delaware Law School of Widener University (J.D., 1976). Member, St. Thomas More Society, 1996—. Assistant to Director, Administrative Office of the Courts, State of Delaware, 1976 and Supervisor, Justice of the Peace Courts, 1977. Trustee Lawyer's Fund for Client Protection of Delaware Supreme Court, 1997—. *Member:* Delaware State (Member, Torts and Insurance Committee, 1984—; Workers Compensation Committee, Vice Chairman, 1992-1995; Chairman, 1996-1997) and American (Member, Litigation Committee, 1994) Bar Associations; Delaware Trial Lawyers Association (Co-Chairman, Continuing Legal Education Committee, 1993—; Board of Directors, 1993—). ***PRACTICE AREAS:*** General and Civil Trial Practice; Insurance; Negligence; Workers Compensation; Construction Accidents; Products Liability; Federal Practice. ***Email:*** EBCarter@kcrlaw.com

THOMAS J. ROMAN, born Wilmington, Delaware, January 9, 1942; admitted to bar, 1977, Delaware. *Education:* University of Delaware (B.A., 1971); Delaware Law School of Widener University (J.D., 1975). Captain, Delaware State Police, Retired, 1964-1983. *Member:* Delaware State and American Bar Associations; Delaware Trial Lawyers Association. ***PRACTICE AREAS:*** General and Civil Trial Practice; Insurance; Negligence; Workers Compensation; Construction Accidents; Products Liability; Federal Practice. ***Email:*** TJRoman@kcrlaw.com

WILLIAM R. PELTZ, born Wilmington, Delaware, April 22, 1962; admitted to bar, 1988, Delaware. *Education:* University of Delaware (B.A., 1985); Delaware Law School of Widener University (J.D., 1988). Member, Delaware Journal of Corporate Law, 1987-1988. *Member:* Delaware State and American Bar Associations; Delaware Trial Lawyers Association. ***PRACTICE AREAS:***

(This Listing Continued)

General and Civil Trial Practice; Insurance; Negligence; Workers Compensation; Construction Accidents; Products Liability; Federal Practice. **Email:** WRPeltz@kcrlaw.com

MICHAEL D. BEDNASH, born Wilmington, Delaware, June 14, 1964; admitted to bar, 1991, Delaware. *Education:* University of Delaware (B.S., 1986); Delaware Law School of Widener University (J.D., 1990). Phi Delta Phi. *Member:* Delaware State and American Bar Associations; Delaware Trial Lawyers Association. ***PRACTICE AREAS:*** General and Civil Trial Practice; Insurance; Negligence; Workers Compensation; Construction Accidents; Products Liability; Federal Practice. ***Email:*** MDBedash@kcrlaw.com

MATTHEW M. BARTKOWSKI, born Wilmington, Delaware, November 19, 1967; admitted to bar, 1993, Pennsylvania; 1994, Delaware. *Education:* University of Delaware (B.S., 1989); Widener University School of Law (J.D., 1992). Member, Trial Advocacy Honor Society. *Member:* Delaware and American Bar Associations; Delaware Trial Lawyers Association. ***PRACTICE AREAS:*** General and Civil Trial Practice; Insurance; Negligence; Workers Compensation; Construction Accidents; Products Liability; Federal Practice. ***Email:*** MMBartkowski@kcrlaw.com

---

WILLIAM R. BAKER, JR., born Wilmington, Delaware, November 24, 1968; admitted to bar, 1998, Maryland and Delaware; 1999, U.S. Court of Appeals, Third Circuit. *Education:* University of Delaware (B.A., 1991); Roger Williams University School of Law (J.D., 1997). ***PRACTICE AREAS:*** Civil Trial Practice; Insurance; Negligence; Workers Compensation; Construction Accidents; Products Liability; Federal Law. ***Email:*** wbaker@kcrlaw.com

REFERENCES: PNC Bank; Wilmington Trust Co.

KLEHR, HARRISON, HARVEY, BRANZBURG & ELLERS LLP

Established in 1975

MELLON BANK CENTER
919 MARKET STREET,
SUITE 1000
WILMINGTON, DELAWARE 19801
Telephone: 302-426-1189
Fax: 302-426-9193
Email: mail@klehr.com
URL: http://www.klehr.com

Philadelphia, Pennsylvania Office: 260 South Broad Street, Suite 400. Telephone: 215-568-6060. Fax: 215-568-6603.
Cherry Hill, New Jersey Office: LibertyView - Suite 510, 457 Haddonfield Road. Telephone: 856-486-7900. Fax: 856-486-4875.

Banking, Corporate, Tax, Construction, Securities, Commercial, Probate, Employment, Estate Planning, Real Estate, Bankruptcy and Creditors Rights Law. Intellectual Property, General Civil Trial Practice in all Courts. Commercial Profit Sharing and Employee Benefit Law.

FIRM PROFILE: Klehr, Harrison, Harvey, Branzburg & Ellers LLP is a young, dynamic firm. Initially organized in September of 1975, our firm was born of the concept that a medium-sized firm can deliver to its clients the kind of expert legal services generally associated with much larger firms, without the impersonalization, oppressive fee structures, tiers of lawyers and levels of responsibility normally associated with large firms. Utilizing the unique structure of our firm, our staff of over 90 attorneys strives to maintain an individual relationship with each of the firm's clients while continuing to retain the ability to react quickly and effectively to client problems. The firm recognizes that in today's highly competitive market for legal services, most clients choose lawyers, not law firms. Because of this, our firm is structured in a way that allows the most knowledgeable lawyer to handle each client's problem in the most effective manner.

MEMBERS OF FIRM

JOANNE B. WILLS, born Philadelphia, Pennsylvania, February 16, 1945; admitted to bar, 1985, Delaware; 1986, Pennsylvania. *Education:* Cornell University (B.A., 1966); Widener University School of Law (J.D., magna cum laude, 1985). Law Clerk to Honorable Helen S. Balick, U.S. Bankruptcy Court, District of Delaware, 1985-1986. *Member:* Delaware State (Member, Sections on: Litigation; Commercial Law, Bankruptcy and Medical Legal Committee; Chairperson, Medical Legal Committee, 1993-1995 and Women in Law Section, 1987-1988), Pennsylvania and American (Member, Sections on: Litigation, Hospital Law, Business Law, Torts and Insurance Law) Bar Associations; Delaware Trial Lawyers Association; Defense Research Institute. ***PRACTICE AREAS:*** Bankruptcy Law; Creditors' Rights Law; Commercial Litigation. ***Email:*** jwills@klehr.com

(This Listing Continued)

DAVID S. EAGLE, born West Islip, New York, September 14, 1960; admitted to bar, 1990, New York and Massachusetts; 1995, Delaware; U.S. District Court, District of Delaware; U.S. District Court, Southern and Eastern Districts of New York; U.S. Court of Appeals, Third Circuit. *Education:* Amherst College (B.A., 1982); Rabbinical College of America (1985); Columbia University (J.D., 1989). Formerly associated with Schulte, Roth & Zabel, New York, N.Y. *Member:* Delaware State Bar Association. ***PRACTICE AREAS:*** Commercial Litigation; Corporate Litigation. ***Email:*** deagle@klehr.com

RICHARD M. BECK, born Alexandria, Virginia, August 14, 1964; admitted to bar, 1990, Pennsylvania; 1992, New Jersey; 1995, Delaware. *Education:* Boston College (B.A., 1986); University of Notre Dame (J.D., 1990); Temple University (LL.M., Trial Advocacy, with honors, 1997). *Member:* Philadelphia and Delaware Bar Associations. (Also in Philadelphia, Pennsylvania Office). ***PRACTICE AREAS:*** Commercial Litigation; Bankruptcy Litigation. ***Email:*** rbeck@klehr.com

STEVEN K. KORTANEK, born Ithaca, New York, October 12, 1966; admitted to bar, 1992, Pennsylvania, Delaware and U.S. District Court, District of Delaware; 1998, U.S. Court of Appeals, Third Circuit. *Education:* Northwestern University (B.A., 1988); University of Pittsburgh School of Law (J.D., 1991). *Member:* Delaware and American Bar Associations; American Bankruptcy Institute (Member, Business Reorganization, Finance and Banking and Unsecured Trade Creditors Committees). . (Resident). ***PRACTICE AREAS:*** Bankruptcy Law; Creditors' Rights. ***Email:*** skortanek@klehr.com

ASSOCIATES

STEPHANIE A. FOX, born Kutztown, Pennsylvania, September 19, 1966; admitted to bar, 1991, Pennsylvania; 1993, Delaware and U.S. District Court, Eastern District of Pennsylvania; 1994, U.S. District Court, District of Delaware. *Education:* University of Delaware (B.A., cum laude, 1988); Dickinson School of Law (J.D., 1991). Dolan/Bennet Scholar. *Member:* Delaware County, Pennsylvania, Delaware, Pennsylvania and American Bar Associations. Fellow, Guy G. deFuria American Inns of Court. ***PRACTICE AREAS:*** Creditors Rights; Bankruptcy; Commercial Litigation. ***Email:*** sfox@klehr.com

JAMES E. HUGGETT, born Bryn Mawr, Pennsylvania, July 21, 1972; admitted to bar, 2000, Delaware. *Education:* Bloomsburg University (B.A., 1994); Temple University School of Law (J.D., 2000). Moot Court Appellate Advocacy Honor Society. *Member:* American Bar Association. ***REPORTED CASES:*** Acevedo v. U.S. Department of Education, BCY # 98-14508 ADV # 99-170 (E.D.P.A.). ***PRACTICE AREAS:*** Bankruptcy; Creditors Rights; Insolvency; Reorganization. ***Email:*** jhuggett@klehr.com

DENISE SEASTONE KRAFT, born Seattle, Washington, August 11, 1963; admitted to bar, 1989, Pennsylvania and Delaware. *Education:* West Virginia Wesleyan College (B.S., 1985); Catholic University of America (J.D., 1988). Member, Mortar Board. Who's Who of Students in American Universities and Colleges. American Inn of Court. Law Clerk to the Honorable Jerome O. Herlihy, Superior Court of the State of Delaware, 1988-1989. *Member:* Delaware County, Pennsylvania, Delaware State and American Bar Associations. ***PRACTICE AREAS:*** Commercial; Corporate; Securities; Bankruptcy Litigation. ***Email:*** dkraft@klehr.com

REPRESENTATIVE CLIENTS: Amerimar Enterprises; ATX Telecommunications Services, Inc.; Boscov's, Inc.; Electronics Boutique; First Union National Bank; General Electric Capital Corp.; Thomas Jefferson University; Lubert-Adler Real Estate Opportunities Fund, LP; Mellon Bank, N.A.; Net Value, Inc.; PNC Bank, N.A.; PREIT-Rubin, Inc.; Prudential Securities; Resources for Human Development, Inc.; Safeguard Scientifics, Inc.; School District of Philadelphia; SCP Private Equity Partners, L.P.; Sun Capital Partners, Inc.; Susquehanna Investment Group; Temple University; University of Pennsylvania; Visalign, LLC.

KLETT ROONEY LIEBER & SCHORLING

A PROFESSIONAL CORPORATION
THE BRANDYWINE BUILDING
1000 WEST STREET, SUITE 1410
WILMINGTON, DELAWARE 19801
Telephone: 302-552-4200
FAX: 302-552-4295
URL: http://www.klettrooney.com

Pittsburgh, Pennsylvania Office: 40th Floor, One Oxford Centre, 15219-6498. Telephone: 412-392-2000. Fax: 412-392-2128, 2129.
Harrisburg, Pennsylvania Office: 240 North Third Street, Suite 600, 17101-1503. Telephone: 717-231-7700. Fax: 717-231-7712.
Philadelphia, Pennsylvania Office: 12th Floor, Two Logan Square, 19103-2756. Telephone: 215-567-7500. Fax: 215-567-2737.
Newark, New Jersey Office: 550 Broad Street, Suite 810, 07102-4517. Telephone: 973-273-9800. Fax: 973-273-9430.
Trenton, New Jersey Office: Mountain View Office Park; Suite 301, 810 Bear Tavern Road, 08628. Telephone: 609-883-6990. Fax: 609-883-7730.
Washington, D.C. Office; 600 Pennsylvania Avenue, S.E., 20003. Telephone: 202-544-4094. Fax: 202-544-9497.

(This Listing Continued)

KLETT ROONEY LIEBER & SCHORLING, A PROFESSIONAL CORPORATION, Wilmington—Continued

General Practice: Business Immigration; Creditor's Rights and Bankruptcy; Employee Benefits - ERISA; Environmental Law; Estate Planning and Administration; Finance; Government Affairs; Health Care; Labor and Employment; Litigation; Occupational Safety and Health; Mine Safety and Health; Public Finance; Railway Labor Act ; Real Estate; Securities Law; Taxation; Technology Law.

SHAREHOLDERS

MARY F. CALOWAY, born Wilmington, Delaware, 1960; admitted to bar, 1992, Delaware. *Education:* University of Delaware (B.A.A.S., 1984); Widener University (J.D., 1990). ***PRACTICE AREAS:*** Banking Law; Commercial Law; Bankruptcy Law. ***Email:*** caloway@klettrooney.com

TERESA K. D. CURRIER, born York, Pennsylvania, 1960; admitted to bar, 1985, Pennsylvania; 1992, Delaware. *Education:* Lehigh University (B.A., 1982); The Dickinson School of Law (J.D., 1985). ***PRACTICE AREAS:*** Bankruptcy and Reorganization; Creditors' Rights; Commercial Transactions; Banking. ***Email:*** currier@klettrooney.com

ALFRED J. D'ANGELO, JR., born Philadelphia, Pennsylvania, 1948; admitted to bar, 1974, Pennsylvania; 1982, Delaware. *Education:* Princeton University (A.B., 1970); Villanova University (J.D., cum laude, 1974). ***PRACTICE AREAS:*** Labor and Employment Law. ***Email:*** ajdangelo@klettrooney.com

RICHARD A. FORSTEN, born Radford, Virginia, 1963; admitted to bar, 1988, Delaware; 1989, Pennsylvania. *Education:* University of Virginia (B.S., 1985; J.D., 1988). ***PRACTICE AREAS:*** Land Use and Land Use Litigation; Construction Law and Mechanics' Liens; Commercial and Real Estate Transactions; Environmental Law and Permitting. ***Email:*** forsten@klettrooney.com

MARK J. GUNDERSEN, born New York, New York, 1954; admitted to bar, 1979, Massachusetts; 1980, Delaware. *Education:* Cornell University (A.B., 1976); Boston University (J.D., 1979). ***PRACTICE AREAS:*** Mergers and Acquisitions; Licensing; Corporate Law. ***Email:*** mjgundersen@klettrooney.com

ADAM G. LANDIS, born New York, New York, 1963; admitted to bar, 1992, Massachusetts and New York; 1996, Delaware. *Education:* Bowdoin College (A.B., 1985); Northeastern University (J.D., 1991). ***PRACTICE AREAS:*** Bankruptcy; Commercial Litigation. ***Email:*** landis@klettrooney.com

WILLIAM E. MANNING, born Wilmington, Delaware, 1948; admitted to bar, 1976, Delaware. *Education:* University of Delaware (B.A., 1973); University of Louisville (J.D., 1976). ***PRACTICE AREAS:*** Land Use Regulation and Litigation; Commercial Law; Constitution Law; Legislative Representation and Drafting. ***Email:*** manning@klettrooney.com

BONNIE L. METZ, born Uniontown, Pennsylvania, 1964; admitted to bar, 1991, Delaware and Pennsylvania. *Education:* King's College (B.A., 1986); Villanova University (J.D., 1990). ***PRACTICE AREAS:*** Administrative Law; Public Utility Regulation; Healthcare Law; Immigration Law. ***Email:*** metz@klettrooney.com

DANIEL B. RATH, born Norristown, Pennsylvania, 1963; admitted to bar, 1991, Delaware; 1992, Pennsylvania. *Education:* Indiana University of Pennsylvania (B.S., 1985); Temple University (J.D., 1991). ***PRACTICE AREAS:*** Construction Litigation; Commercial Litigation. ***Email:*** rath@klettrooney.com

ASSOCIATES

REBECCA L. BUTCHER, born Bryn Mawr, Pennsylvania, 1974; admitted to bar, 1999, Delaware. *Education:* University of Virginia (B.A., with distinction, 1996); Vanderbilt University (J.D., 1999). ***PRACTICE AREAS:*** Litigation. ***Email:*** rlbutcher@klettrooney.com

RICHARD S. COBB, born Philadelphia, Pennsylvania, 1964; admitted to bar, 1993, Delaware. *Education:* Moravian College (B.A., 1986); Villanova University (J.D., 1992). ***PRACTICE AREAS:*** Commercial Litigation; Bankruptcy Litigation; Employment Litigation; Personal Injury Litigation. ***Email:*** cobb@klettrooney.com

FRANCES GAUTHIER, born New York, New York, 1966; admitted to bar, 1994, Pennsylvania; 1995, Delaware. *Education:* New York University (B.A., 1989); University of Pennsylvania School of Law (J.D., 1994). ***PRACTICE AREAS:*** Corporate Law; Intellectual Property Law. ***Email:*** fgauthier@klettrooney.com

FRANCIS X. GORMAN, born New York, New York, 1967; admitted to bar, 1998, Delaware. *Education:* University of Virginia (B.A., 1989; J.D., 1998). [Infantry Officer, United States Army, 1991-1994.]. ***PRACTICE AREAS:*** Commercial Transactions; Land Use Regulation; Litigation. ***Email:*** fxgorman@klettrooney.com

KATHLEEN P. MAKOWSKI, born Orlando, Florida, 1964; admitted to bar, 1996, Pennsylvania; 1997, Delaware. *Education:* University of Delaware (B.A., cum laude, 1993); Widener University (J.D., 1996). ***PRACTICE AREAS:*** Bankruptcy; Creditors' Rights. ***Email:*** kmakowski@klettrooney.com

KERRI KING MUMFORD, born Wilmington, Delaware, 1974; (admission pending). *Education:* High Point University (B.A., 1996); Catholic University of America (J.D., magna cum laude, 2001). ***PRACTICE AREAS:*** Bankruptcy. ***Email:*** kmumford@klettrooney.com

ERIC L. SCHNABEL, born Melle, Germany, 1968; admitted to bar, 1998, Delaware; 2000, New Jersey and Pennsylvania. *Education:* Grinnell College (B.A., 1991); Indiana University; Washington College of Law, American University (J.D., magna cum laude, 1997). ***PRACTICE AREAS:*** Bankruptcy; Insolvency; Creditor's Rights; Debtors' Rights. ***Email:*** elschnabel@klettrooney.com

JAMES D. TAYLOR, born Wilmington, Delaware, 1974; (admission pending). *Education:* University of Delaware (B.A., 1997); Villanova University (J.D., cum laude, 2000). ***PRACTICE AREAS:*** Corporate Law. ***Email:*** jdtaylor@klettrooney.com

KATHERINE RANDOLPH WITHERSPOON, born Camp LeJeune, North Carolina, 1967; admitted to bar, 1995, Delaware. *Education:* Duke University (A.B., cum laude, 1989); New York University (J.D., 1994). ***PRACTICE AREAS:*** Labor and Employment Law; Education Law. ***Email:*** kwitherspoon@klettrooney.com

---

KNEPPER & STRATTON

1225 KING STREET, SUITE 1000
P.O. BOX 1795
WILMINGTON, DELAWARE 19899
Telephone: 302-658-1717; 302-652-7717
Fax: 302-658-0631
Email: mknepper@lawyers.com
URL: http://www.lawyers.com/knepper

General Civil and Trial Practice in all State and Federal Courts, Personal Injury, Automobile Accidents and Injuries, Workers Compensation, Criminal Law, Sexual Harassment, Employment Law, Employment Discrimination, Driving While Intoxicated, Traffic Violations, Wrongful Termination, Americans with Disabilities Act.

MEMBERS OF FIRM

E. MARTIN KNEPPER, JR., born York, Pennsylvania, August 13, 1955; admitted to bar, 1981, Delaware and Pennsylvania and U.S. District Court, District of Delaware; U.S. District Court, Eastern District of Pennsylvania. *Education:* University of Delaware (B.A.A.S., 1977); Dickinson School of Law (J.D., 1980). Omicron Delta Kappa. Deputy Attorney General, State of Delaware, 1981-1982. *Member:* Delaware Bar Association; Delaware Trial Lawyers Association; The Association of Trial Lawyers of America. ***PRACTICE AREAS:*** Personal Injury Law; Criminal Law; Workers Compensation; Driving While Intoxicated; Traffic Violations; Automobile Accidents and Injuries.

BARBARA H. STRATTON, born Princeton, New Jersey, August 7, 1956; admitted to bar, 1981, Pennsylvania; 1989, Delaware and U.S. District Court, Eastern, Middle and Western Districts of Pennsylvania. *Education:* University of Delaware (B.A., cum laude, 1978); University of Pittsburgh (J.D., cum laude, 1981). Phi Beta Kappa; Mortar Board. Counsel to Pennsylvania Public Utility Commission, 1982-1985. *Member:* Delaware (Member, Board of Directors), Pennsylvania and American Bar Associations; Delaware Trial Lawyers Association; Delaware Employment Lawyers Association; National Employment Lawyers Association. ***PRACTICE AREAS:*** Personal Injury; Employment Law; Workers Compensation; Sexual Harassment; Automobile Accidents and Injuries; Wrongful Termination; Employment Discrimination.

CHARLES S. KNOTHE, P.A.

Established in 1981

#14 THE COMMONS
3516 SILVERSIDE ROAD
WILMINGTON, DELAWARE 19810-4932
Telephone: 302-478-8800
Fax: 302-478-8988
Email: cknothe@compuserve.com

Real Estate, Collections, Commercial Law, Wills and Estates, Patent, Trademark and Copyright Law.

CHARLES S. KNOTHE, born New York City, N.Y., October 20, 1944; admitted to bar, 1981, Delaware and U.S. District Court, District of Delaware and U.S. Supreme Court; practice before U.S. Patent and Trademark Office. *Education:* Worcester Polytechnic Institute (B.S.M.E., 1966); Drexel University (M.B.A., 1968); Delaware Law School of Widener University (J.D., 1980). *Member:* Delaware Bar Association. ***PRACTICE AREAS:*** Real Estate Law;

(This Listing Continued)

Collections; Commercial Law; Wills Law; Estates Law; Patent, Trademark and Copyright Law.

LAW OFFICE OF KATHRYN J. LAFFEY

Established in 1989

1500 SHALLCROSS AVENUE, SUITE 2-B

WILMINGTON, DELAWARE 19806-1432

Telephone: 302-651-7999

Fax: 302-651-7960

Email: KLaffeyatLK@aol.com

Family Law, Civil Litigation, Divorce and Family Mediation.

FIRM PROFILE: Kathryn J. Laffey established her practice in 1989. The firm maintains a general civil litigation practice but is most well known for its expertise in Family Law. Kathryn Laffey is an experienced and trained mediator in an associated Family Mediation Services. Kathryn Laffey and Janine Howard are admitted to practice before all state and federal courts.

KATHRYN J. LAFFEY, born Wilmington, Delaware, June 25, 1956; admitted to bar, 1983, Delaware; 1984, U.S. District Court, District of Delaware. *Education:* Longwood College (B.S., cum laude, 1978); University of Notre Dame (J.D., 1982). Phi Gamma Mu. Law Clerk, Family Court of Delaware, 1982-1983. *Member:* Delaware (Member, Family Law Section, Chairman, 1991-1993; Judicial Appointments Committee, 1993-1998) and American (Member, Family Law Section) Bar Associations; Melson-Arsht Inn of Court; Delaware Commission for Women (Chair, 1998—; Commissioner, 1995—); Academy of Family Mediators. ***PRACTICE AREAS:*** Family Law; Civil Litigation; Divorce and Family Mediation.

ASSOCIATE

JANINE N. HOWARD, born Chester, Pennsylvania, March 23, 1970; admitted to bar, 1995, Delaware; 1997, Pennsylvania. *Education:* Temple University (B.A., cum laude, 1992); Widener University (J.D., cum laude, 1995). Phi Delta Phi. Outstanding Achievement Scholar. *Member:* Delaware State (Member, Sections on: Family Law; Women and Law; Domestic Violence Subcommittee) and American (Member, Family Law Section) Bar Associations; Melson-Arsht Inn of Court. ***PRACTICE AREAS:*** Family Law; Domestic Violence. ***Email:*** JHowardat LK@aol.com

APPROVED ATTORNEYS FOR: Chicago Title Insurance Co.; Ticor Title Insurance Co.; Lawyers Title Insurance Co.

ROBERT C. LEFTON

Established in 1980

SUITE 1011, 913 MARKET STREET

P.O. BOX 506

WILMINGTON, DELAWARE 19899-0506

Telephone: 302-656-0703

Email: lefton@compuserve.com

Taxation, Business, Corporate, Real Estate, Estate Planning and Probate Law.

ROBERT C. LEFTON, born Brooklyn, New York, December 12, 1938; admitted to bar, 1964, New York; 1974, Delaware; 1977, U.S. District Court, District of Delaware; 1979, U.S. Tax Court; 1985, U.S. Court of Appeals, Third Circuit. *Education:* Yale University (A.B., 1960); Harvard University (LL.B., 1963). With: Office of Chief Counsel, Internal Revenue Service, 1966-1968; Tax Division, U.S. Department of Justice, 1968-1973. *Member:* Delaware (Member, 1978 and Chairman, 1979-1980, Tax Committee) and American (Member, Taxation Section) Bar Associations. ***PRACTICE AREAS:*** Taxation Law; Business Law; Corporate Law; Real Estate Law; Estate Planning Law; Probate Law.

LEVINE & THOMPSON

Established in 1983

1205 KING STREET

WILMINGTON, DELAWARE 19801

Telephone: 302-658-3070

Fax: 302-658-3031

Family, Civil Litigation, Real Estate, General Business, Personal Injury, Collections Law, Criminal Law.

MEMBERS OF FIRM

NORMAN E. LEVINE, born Wilmington, Delaware, June 2, 1943; admitted to bar, 1968, Delaware and U.S. District Court, District of Delaware; 1969, U.S. Court of Appeals, Third Circuit. *Education:* University of Pennsylvania (A.B., 1965; LL.B., 1968). Assistant U.S. Attorney, District of Delaware, 1968-1972. U.S. Attorney, District of Delaware, 1972-1973. Commissioner of Public Safety, City of Wilmington, Delaware, 1973-1976. President, U.S. District Court for the District of Delaware Historical Society, 1991-1992. *Member:* Delaware State (Chairman, Family Law Section, 1985-1987; Chairman, Lawyer Referral Committee, 1983-1985; Chairman, CLE Committee, 1989-1990), Federal (President, Delaware Chapter, 1972-1973, 1989-1991) and American Bar Associations. ***PRACTICE AREAS:*** Family Law; Civil Litigation.

JOHN J. THOMPSON, born Wilmington, Delaware, March 29, 1951; admitted to bar, 1976, Delaware and U.S. District Court, District of Delaware. *Education:* University of Delaware (A.B., 1973); Case Western Reserve University (J.D., 1976). Instructor, Business Law, Delaware Technical and Community College, 1985-1987. Appointed by Delaware General Assembly to the Task Force on Divorce Law Reform, 1983-1984. *Member:* Delaware State Bar Association (Legislative Liaison, 1987-1990, Secretary, 1993-1995 and Vice Chairman, 1995-1997; Public Legal Education Committee, 1984-1990; Unauthorized Practice of Law Committee, 1984-1990); Delaware Trial Lawyers Association (Member: Family Law Section; Executive Committee, 1991-1997); Federalist Society. ***PRACTICE AREAS:*** General Business Law; Family Law; Civil Litigation; Personal Injury; Collections Law; Real Estate. ***Email:*** lawman@aol.com

LAURENCE I. LEVINSON

Established in 1980

1326 KING STREET

WILMINGTON, DELAWARE 19801

Telephone: 302-656-3393

Fax: 302-656-1993

Email: planlaw@aol.com

URL: http://www.lawyers.com/planlaw

Estate Planning.

LAURENCE I. LEVINSON, born Wilmington, Delaware, August 15, 1953; admitted to bar, 1979, Delaware and U.S. District Court, District of Delaware; U.S. Supreme Court. *Education:* University of Delaware (B.A., 1975); Delaware Law School of Widener University (J.D., 1979). Recipient: American Jurisprudence Award for Contracts. *Member:* Delaware Bar Association (Member, Estates and Trusts Section); Estate Planning Council of Delaware; National Network of Estate Planning Attorneys. ***PRACTICE AREAS:*** Estate Planning; Charitable Planning; Asset Protection Planning; Family Wealth Transfers.

JEFFREY C. LEW

SILVERSIDE PROFESSIONAL PARK

1403 SILVERSIDE ROAD

WILMINGTON, DELAWARE 19810

Telephone: 302-475-7919

Fax: 302-475-7915

Email: lawoffice@jlew.com

Intellectual Property Law including: Patent, Trademark, Copyright and Related Matters.

JEFFREY C. LEW, born Bronx, New York, January 17, 1947; admitted to bar, 1981, Delaware; 1994, Pennsylvania; registered to practice before U.S. Patent and Trademark Office. *Education:* The Cooper Union (B.S.Ch.E., 1968); Northwestern University (M.S., 1970); Temple University (J.D., 1978). Tau Beta Pi. Senior Engineer in Research and Process Engineering, E.I. du Pont de Nemours & Co., 1969-1989. *Member:* Delaware State Bar Association (Member, Intellectual Property Section); American Intellectual Property Law Association; Philadelphia Intellectual Property Law Association. ***PRACTICE AREAS:*** Patents; Patent Applications; Patent Prosecution; Patent Licensing; Trademarks.

LAW OFFICE OF JOSEPH J. LONGOBARDI, III

Established in 1994

THE PLAZA, SUITE 115

1303 DELAWARE AVENUE

WILMINGTON, DELAWARE 19806

Telephone: 302-575-1502

Telecopier: 302-575-1506

Email: longobardi@delnet.com

URL: http://www.lawyers.com/longobardilaw

Personal Injury including Automobile Accident, Medical Malpractice, Products Liability, Criminal Defense. Family Law including Child Support, Child Custody, Divorce, Adoptions.

(This Listing Continued)

LAW OFFICE OF JOSEPH J. LONGOBARDI, III, Wilmington—Continued

JOSEPH J. LONGOBARDI, III, born Wilmington, Delaware, April 22, 1957; admitted to bar, 1983, Delaware, Pennsylvania, U.S. District Court, District of Delaware and U.S. Court of Appeals, Third Circuit. *Education:* Mount St. Mary's College (B.A., 1979); Delaware Law School of Widener University (J.D., 1982). Deputy Attorney General, 1983-1987. *Member:* Delaware and American Bar Associations; Delaware Trial Lawyers Association. ***PRACTICE AREAS:*** Personal Injury; Criminal Defense; Domestic Relations.

LEGAL SUPPORT PERSONNEL

MARGARET HAFTL (Paralegal).

LYONS, DOUGHTY & VELDHUIS, P.C.

1148 PULASKI HIGHWAY (BEAR)
P.O. BOX 313
WILMINGTON, DELAWARE 19701
Telephone: 302-428-1670
URL: http://www/ldvlaw.com
Email: ldvlaw@ldvlaw.com
URL: http://www.lawyers.com/ldvlaw

Mount Laurel, New Jersey Office: 1288 Route 73, Suite 310, P.O. Box 1269, 08054. Telephone: 856-802-1488. Fax: 856-802-2801.
Philadelphia, Pennsylvania Office: Telephone: 215-747-7735.
Pittsburgh, Pennsylvania Office: 7228 Baptist Road, #175, Bethel Park, 15102. Telephone: 412-765-2221.

Creditors Rights, Consumer Collections, Creditor Bankruptcy, Mortgage Foreclosure, Commercial Mortgages, Mortgage Banking Law, Mortgage Bankruptcy, Mortgage Insurance, Mortgage Lien Foreclosure, Mortgage Workouts, Secondary Mortgage Market, Creditors Rights in Bankruptcy, Debtor and Creditor Collections, Debtor and Creditor Remedies, Debtor and Creditor Rights, Debtor and Creditor Workouts, Fair Debt Collection Practices Act, Secured Creditors Rights, Unsecured Creditors Rights, Foreclosures, Fraudulent Conveyance, Repossessions, Workouts, Bank Collections, Bank Foreclosures, Commercial Loans, Loan Workouts, Commercial Collections, Garnishments, Post Judgement Collections, Professional Collections, Retail Collections, Secured Collections, Unsecured Collections, Bankruptcy Chapter 7, Bankruptcy Chapter 11, Bankruptcy Chapter 13, Commercial Bankruptcy.

(For complete Biographical data on all Personnel, see Professional Biographies at Mt. Laurel, New Jersey)

THE LYONS LAW FIRM

1526 GILPIN AVENUE
P.O. BOX 579
WILMINGTON, DELAWARE 19806
Telephone: 302-777-5698
Fax: 302-777-5051
Email: elyons@lyonslaw.com
URL: http://www.lawyers.com/lyonslaw

Personal Injury including Wrongful Death, Catastrophic Injury, Automobile Accidents and Injuries, Medical Malpractice, Workers Compensation, Social Security Disability, Nursing Home Abuse and Neglect, Social Security Disability, Criminal Defense including Felonies, Misdemeanors, Juvenile Criminal Law, Traffic Offenses and Driving While Intoxicated.

EDMUND DANIEL LYONS, born Washington, D. C., September 20, 1947; admitted to bar, 1974, Delaware; 1975, U.S. District Court, Northern District of California; 1977, U.S. Court of Appeals, Ninth Circuit; U.S. Court of Appeals, Tenth Circuit; 1978, California (inactive); 1980, U.S. District Court, District of Delaware; 1982, U.S. Court of Appeals, Third Circuit; 1991, U.S. Supreme Court. *Education:* Amherst College (B.A., 1969); Georgetown University (J.D., 1974). Editor, Georgetown Law Journal, 1972-1974. Listed, Criminal Defense Section, Best Lawyers in America, 1993-2001. Special Attorney, Organized Crime & Racketeering Section, U.S. Department of Justice, 1974-1978. Assistant U.S. Attorney: Northern District of California, 1978-1980; District of Delaware, 1980-1982. *Member:* Delaware and American Bar Associations; Delaware Trial Lawyers Association (President, 1995-1996); Association of Trial Lawyers of America. (Board Certified Civil Trial Specialist by the National Board of Trial Advocacy). ***PRACTICE AREAS:*** Personal Injury; Criminal Defense. ***Email:*** elyons@lyonslaw.com

DAVID J. LYONS, born Wilmington, Delaware, January 18, 1957; admitted to bar, 1985, Delaware; 1987, U.S. District Court, District of Delaware; 1989, U.S. Court of Appeals, Third Circuit. *Education:* George Washington University (B.A., 1980); University of Delaware; Widener University School of Law (J.D., 1984). Member, Widener University Law Review, 1982-1984. Named Ruby Vale scholar serving Superior Court of Delaware Clerkship, The Hon. Robert C. O'Hazs and The Hon. Joshua W. Martin (1983). Deputy Attorney General: State of Delaware, 1985-1986; Delaware Division of Public Health, 1987-1990. Named Best Lawyer in Americas Consumer Lawyers Guide, 2001-Worker's Compensation and Personal Injury. *Member:* Delaware (Member, Workers Compensation Section) and American Bar Associations; Delaware Trial Lawyers Association; Association of Trial Lawyers of America. ***PRACTICE AREAS:*** Personal Injury; Workers Compensation; Social Security Disability. ***Email:*** dlyons@lyonslaw.com

(This Listing Continued)

JOHN S. MALIK

Established in 1984
100 EAST 14TH STREET
WILMINGTON, DELAWARE 19801-3122
Telephone: 302-427-2247
Fax: 302-427-2414
URL: http://www.lawyers.com/johnmaliklaw

Criminal Trial and Appellate Practice in all State and Federal Courts.

JOHN S. MALIK, born Bryn Mawr, Pennsylvania, September 15, 1958; admitted to bar, 1984, Delaware and Pennsylvania; 1985, New Jersey and U.S. District Court, District of Delaware; 1989, U.S. Supreme Court; 1990, U.S. Court of Appeals, Third Circuit. *Education:* St. Joseph's University (B.A., 1980); Delaware Law School of Widener University (J.D., 1983). *Member:* Delaware Bar Association (Member, Criminal Law Section); National Association of Criminal Defense Lawyers; Association of Trial Lawyers of America; Delaware Association of Criminal Defense Lawyers. ***PRACTICE AREAS:*** Criminal.

BAYARD MARIN

521 WEST STREET
WILMINGTON, DELAWARE 19801-2196
Telephone: 302-658-4200
Fax: 302-658-9075
Email: bmarin6655@aol.com
URL: http://www.lawyers.com/bmarin

Civil Trial Practice, Personal Injury, Medical Malpractice, Products Liability, Insurance Law, Workers Compensation, Administrative Law and Historic Preservation Law.

BAYARD MARIN, born Newark, Delaware, June 2, 1941; admitted to bar, 1967, District of Columbia; 1973, Delaware. *Education:* University of Delaware (A.B., 1963); Syracuse University (J.D., 1966); University of London, London, England (Ph.D., 1980). Author: "Inside Justice," Associated University Presses, 1983. Adjunct Professor of Law: Medical Malpractice and Personal Injury, Products Liability, Corporate Law, Administrative Law, Worker's Compensation, University of Delaware, 1979-1995. Adjunct Professor, Widner University Law School, 2001. President, Quaker Hill Historic Preservation Foundation, 1992—. Member, Delaware State Review Board for Historic Preservation. *Member:* Delaware State Bar Association; District of Columbia Bar (Member, Medical Legal Relations Committee, 1980—). [Capt., JAGC, U.S. Army, 1968-1972]. ***PRACTICE AREAS:*** Civil Trial Practice; Personal Injury Law; Medical Malpractice; Products Liability Law; Insurance Law; Historical Preservation Law; Workers Compensation.

MARON & MARVEL, P.A.

1300 NORTH BROOM STREET
P.O. BOX 288
WILMINGTON, DELAWARE 19899
Telephone: 302-425-5177
Telecopier: 302-425-0180
Email: info@mm-w.com
URL: http://www.mm-w.com

Civil Trial in all State and Federal Courts, Environmental, Toxic Tort, Neighborhood Exposure, Complex Litigation, Products Liability, Commercial Litigation, Medical Malpractice, Construction Law, Internet Law, Employment Law, Local, Multi-State and Federal Tax Planning, Antitrust, Corporations and Special Purpose Entities, Delaware Investment Holding Companies, Mediation Services. This litigation, tax and corporate boutique is dedicated to the delivery of efficient legal services through the leveraging of technology and alternative fee structures.

JAMES J. MARON, born Queens, New York, November 17, 1957; admitted to bar, 1986, Delaware and Pennsylvania, U.S. District Court, District of Delaware and U.S. Court of Appeals, Third Circuit. *Education:* State University of New York at Stony Brook (B.A., cum laude, 1979); Delaware Law School of

(This Listing Continued)

Widener University (J.D., cum laude, 1985). Mediator, Superior Court of the State of Delaware, 1992—. *Member:* Delaware, Pennsylvania and American Bar Associations; Delaware Trial Lawyers Association; Defense Research Institute. ***PRACTICE AREAS:*** Toxic Tort; Environmental Litigation; Product Liability; Complex Litigation; Commercial Litigation. ***Email:*** jmaron@mm-w.com

WAYNE A. MARVEL, born Wilmington, Delaware, October 11, 1955; admitted to bar, 1981, Delaware, Pennsylvania, U.S. District Court, District of Delaware and U.S. Court of Appeals, Third Circuit. *Education:* University of Delaware (B.S., 1977); Villanova University (J.D., 1980). Clerk, Superior Court of the State of Delaware, 1980-1981. Member, Superior Court Civil Rules Committee, 1984-1992 . DCD State Representative to Defense Research Institute, 1993-1995. DRI State Representative, 1996—. Member, Superior Court CLAD Committee, 1993—. Chair, Asbestos Litigation Steering Committee. Director, Delaware Defense Medical Program. Contributing Author: History of Delaware Bar, Complex Litigation Chapter. Special Master, Family Court State of Delaware, 1992-1995. Mediator, Superior Court of the State of Delaware, 1992—. Moderator and Presenter, Civil Litigation Fundamentals Seminar, 1993-1997. Secretary, Computer Law Section, 1996—; Member, Litigation Section Council, 1991-1997 (Chair, 1993-1997). *Member:* Delaware State and Pennsylvania Bar Associations; Defense Counsel of Delaware (Board Member, 1988—; President, 1993-1995). Defense Research Institute. Barrister Richard Rodney Inns of Court, 1985-1989. ***PRACTICE AREAS:*** Toxic Tort; Medical Malpractice; Products Liability; Personal Injury; Commercial Law. ***Email:*** wmarvel@mm-w.com

KAREN S. BREHM, born North Braddock, Pennsylvania, October 6, 1955; admitted to bar, 1984, Pennsylvania; 1987, Delaware; U.S. District Court, Eastern District of Pennsylvania and Delaware and U.S. Court of Appeals, Third Circuit. *Education:* Villanova University (B.A., 1977); Delaware Law School of Widener University (J.D., 1984). Member, The Delaware Journal of Corporate Law, 1982-1984. *Member:* Pennsylvania, Delaware State and American Bar Associations; Defense Research Institute. ***PRACTICE AREAS:*** Toxic Tort; Environmental Litigation; Product Liability; Personal Injury. ***Email:*** kbrehm@mm-w.com

THOMAS C. MARTIN, born Butler, Pennsylvania, January 17, 1952; admitted to bar, 1980, Pennsylvania; 1992, U.S. Tax Court and U.S. Court of Federal Claims; 1995, U.S. Court of Appeals for the Federal Circuit; 1998, Delaware. *Education:* Tufts University (B.S., 1974); University of Pittsburgh School of Law (J.D., 1978). Former In-House Tax Counsel at two Fortune 500 Corporations. *Member:* Pennsylvania, Delaware State and American (Member, Tax Section) Bar Associations. ***LANGUAGES:*** German. ***PRACTICE AREAS:*** Taxation; Multi-State Corporate Tax Planning; State and Local Taxation; Tax Planning; Federal Tax Planning; Corporations; Limited Liability Companies. ***Email:*** tmartin@mm-w.com

BERNARD G. CONAWAY, born Darby, Pennsylvania, July 23, 1958; admitted to bar, 1990, Delaware; 1991, U.S. District Court, District of Delaware. *Education:* York College of Pennsylvania (B.A., 1983); Widener University School of Law (J.D., 1989). Member, Moot Court Honor Society. Law Clerk, Superior Court of the State of Delaware, 1989-1990. Publication, Federal Civil Procedure Before Trial, 3rd Circuit, Chapter 15, Pretrial Scheduling and Management, 1996. Facility Assistant, National Judicial College, Reno, Nevada, 1998. Member: Master, 1991-2000; Mediator, 1992—, Superior Court of Delaware. Member, Complex Litigation Committee, Superior Court, 1991—. Member, Executive Board, Delaware Journal of Corporate Law. *Member:* Delaware State (Member, Torts & Insurance Litigation, ADR) Bar Association; Delaware Federation of Dispute Resolution Professionals; Richard S Rodney Inn of Court (Member, Executive Committee, 1996—). ***PRACTICE AREAS:*** Toxic Tort; Alternative Dispute Resolution (60%); Products Liability; Personal Injury (20%); Commercial Law (20%). ***Email:*** bconaway@mm-w.com

PHILIP L. ROTHBART, born New York, New York, July 11, 1931; admitted to bar, 1986, Pennsylvania and New Jersey; 1987, District of Columbia, U. S. District Court, Eastern District of Pennsylvania and U.S. Court of Appeals, District of Columbia and Third Circuit (Not admitted in Delaware). *Education:* University of Oklahoma (B.A., 1951); University of Bonn, Germany (M.D., 1959); Delaware Law School of Widener University (J.D., magna cum laude, 1985). Member, Executive Board, Delaware Journal of Corporate Law, 1983-1985. Associate Medical Director, Squibb Institute for Medical Research, 1961-1964. Adjunct and Visiting Professor, Widener University School of Law, 1986-1994. *Member:* Pennsylvania and American Bar Associations. Fellow, American College of Legal Medicine. ***PRACTICE AREAS:*** Toxic Tort; Medical Malpractice; Personal Injury. ***Email:*** prothbart@mm-w.com

---

JOHN P. DANIELLO, born Wilmington, Delaware, February 27, 1968; admitted to bar, 1998, Delaware, New Jersey and Pennsylvania; 1999, U.S. District Court, District of Delaware. *Education:* University of Delaware (B.A., 1991); Widener University School of Law (J.D., 1997). *Member:* Delaware State, Pennsylvania and American Bar Associations. ***PRACTICE AREAS:*** Personal Injury; Commercial Litigation. ***Email:*** jdaniello@mm-w.com

(This Listing Continued)

REPRESENTATIVE CLIENTS: Amoco Oil Co.; Amoco Chemical Co.; Amoco Corp.; Amoco Pipeline Co.; NNL Industries; Diamond Chemical & Supply Co., Inc.; Pleasant Distributors, Inc.; Toll Brothers, Inc.; Zenon Environmental, Inc.; E*Healthline.com, Inc.

MARSHALL, DENNEHEY, WARNER, COLEMAN AND GOGGIN

1220 N. MARKET STREET, SUITE 202
WILMINGTON, DELAWARE 19801
Telephone: 302-552-4300
Fax: 302-651-7905
URL: http://www.marshalldennehey.com

Bethlehem, Pennsylvania Office: 651 East Market Street. Telephone: 484-895-2300. Fax: 484-895-0208.
Doylestown, Pennsylvania Office: 10 North Main Street. Telephone: 267-880-2020. Fax: 215-348-5439.
Erie, Pennsylvania Office: 1001 State Street, 14th Floor. Telephone: 814-461-7800. Fax: 814-461-7818.
Harrisburg, Pennsylvania Office: 4200 Crums Mill Road. Telephone: 717-651-3500. Fax: 717-651-9630.
Newtown Square, Pennsylvania Office: 18 Campus Boulevard, Suite 250. Telephone: 610-355-7420. Fax: 610-355-7444.
Norristown, Pennsylvania Office: One Montgomery Plaza, Suite 1002. Telephone: 610-270-8500. Fax: 610-270-7444.
Philadelphia, Pennsylvania Office: 1845 Walnut Street. Telephone: 215-575-2600. Fax: 215-575-0856; 575-0857.
Pittsburgh, Pennsylvania Office: 600 Grant Street, USX Tower, Suite 2900. Telephone: 412-803-1140. Fax: 412-803-1188.
Scranton, Pennsylvania Office: 507 Linden Street, Suite 800. Telephone: 570-342-1999. Fax: 570-342-4999.
Williamsport, Pennsylvania Office: 33 W. Third Street, Suite 200. Telephone: 570-326-9091. Fax: 570-326-5507.
Roseland, New Jersey Office: 425 Eagle Rock Avenue, Suite 302. Telephone: 973-618-4100. Fax: 973-618-0685.
Cherry Hill, New Jersey Office: Woodland Falls Corporate Park, 200 Lake Drive East, Suite 300. Telephone: 856-414-6000. Fax: 856-414-6077.
Weirton, West Virginia Office: 3173 Main Street. Telephone: 304-748-7400. Fax: 304-748-0620.
Steubenville, Ohio Office: Sinclair Building, 10th Floor, 100 North 4th Avenue. Telephone: 740-282-6705. Fax: 740-282-8667.
Tampa, Florida Office: 100 North Tampa Street, Suite 3550. Telephone: 813-472-7800. Fax: 813-472-7811.
Orlando, Florida Office: 201 East Pine Street, Suite 675. Telephone: 407-246-0668. Fax: 407-839-3008.

Defense Litigation Practice before all State and Federal Courts and Administrative Agencies. Appellate Advocacy, Arson, Fraud Litigation, Automotive Products Liability, Bad Faith, Disability, Employment Law, Commercial Litigation, Environmental and Toxic Torts, General Liability, Health Care Liability, Insurance Coverage, Insurance Law, Intellectual Property, Liquor Liability, Municipal Liability and Civil Rights, Construction Litigation, Medical Device and Pharmaceutical, Medical Malpractice, Products Liability, Professional Malpractice, Property Damage, Railroad Litigation, Retail Liability, Special Investigations Litigation, Amusement Park, Sports and Entertainment, Transportation Litigation, Workers' Compensation, Technology.

FIRM PROFILE: Marshall, Dennehey, Warner, Coleman and Goggin, founded in 1961, has realized substantial growth in response to our continually expanding client base.

We are exclusively a defense firm, and our professional practices encompass a wide spectrum of litigation matters.

We are over 270 attorneys strong and have seventeen offices strategically located in Pennsylvania, New Jersey, Delaware, West Virginia, Ohio and Florida.

This distribution of attorneys and offices provides our clients with access to statewide or regional representation coupled with strong, accessible, and experienced centralized management.

We are proud of the remarkable level of our internal stability, ensuring file handling continuity.

Surveys of the nation's largest firms consistently show our firm to be a leader in minority hiring and advancement as measured by the number of African-American partners and associates in our ranks.

Our expertise is evidenced by the fact that many of our attorneys have had books, chapter contributions, monographs, and articles published in their practice areas.

Our firm members are quite active and play leadership roles in numerous professional, charitable, community and business associations.

(This Listing Continued)

MARSHALL, DENNEHEY, WARNER, COLEMAN AND GOGGIN, Wilmington—Continued

We are on the cutting-edge of alternative billing arrangements.

Inquiries concerning our firm should be directed to our Chairman and CEO, Robert J. Coleman, Esq., whose number is (215) 575-2614. His fax number is (215) 575-0856 and his email address is rcoleman@mdwcg.com. His address is 1845 Walnut Street, Philadelphia, PA 19103.

RESIDENT MEMBERS

TIMOTHY A. CASEY, born Wilmington, Delaware, June 2, 1952; admitted to bar, 1979, Delaware. *Education:* University of Delaware (B.A., 1975); Dickinson School of Law (J.D., 1978). Deputy Attorney General of Delaware, 1979-1982. *Member:* Delaware State (Member: Board of Bar Examiners, 1983-1986; Rules Committee, Industrial Accident Board; Chairman, Workers' Compensation Section, 1994-1995) and American (Member, Workers' Compensation Section) Bar Associations; Defense Research Institute Delaware State Liaison, Workers' Compensation Section); Defense Counsel of Delaware. ***REPORTED CASES:*** Shipman v. Division of Social Services, Del. Fam. Ct., 442 A.2d 101 (1981); Doe v. Delaware, 450 U.S. 382, 101 S. Ct. 1495 (1981) (on the briefs); State of Delaware, Dept. of Labor v. Minner, Del. Supr., 448 A.2d 227 (1982); State of Delaware, Dept. of Labor v. Medical Placement Services, Inc., Del. Super., 457 A.2d 382 (1982); Brokenbrough v. Chrysler Corp., Del. Super., 460 A.2d 551 (1983); Steel Suppliers, Inc. v. Ehret, Inc., Del. Super., 486 A.2d 32 (1984); Lemon v. Brandywine Dialysis Center, Del. Super., 508 A.2d 892 (1986); Morgan v. Anchor Freight, Inc., Del. Super., 506 A.2d 185 (1986); Duvall v. Charles Connell Roofing, Del. Supr., 564 A.2d 1132 (1989); Furrowh v. Abacus Corp., Del. Supr., 559 A.2d 1258 (1989). ***PRACTICE AREAS:*** Workers Compensation. ***Email:*** tcasey@mdwcg.com

KEVIN J. CONNORS, born Wilmington, Delaware, May 18, 1955; admitted to bar, 1982, Pennsylvania and Delaware. *Education:* University of Virginia (B.A., with high distinction, 1977); Rotary International Graduate Fellow, University of Vienna, Austria (1977-1978); Villanova University (J.D., 1981). Staff Member, 1979-1980 and Articles Editor, 1980-1981, Villanova University Law Review. Law Clerk to the Honorable John J. McNeilly, Associate Justice, Supreme Court of Delaware, 1981-1982. Author, Note, "Commonwealth v. Bussey," 26 Vill. L. Rev. 205 (1981). Member, Philadelphia Chapter, German-American Chamber of Commerce. *Member:* Pennsylvania and Delaware State Bar Associations; Defense Counsel of Delaware; Delaware Claims Association. ***LANGUAGES:*** German. ***PRACTICE AREAS:*** Products Liability; General Liability Defense. ***Email:*** kconnors@mdwcg.com

RESIDENT ASSOCIATES

TRACY A. BURLEIGH, born Wilmington, Delaware, February 15, 1967; admitted to bar, 1997, Delaware. *Education:* University of Delaware (B.A. in Criminal Justice, 1989); Widener University School of Law (J.D., 1996). *Member:* Delaware State and American Bar Associations. ***PRACTICE AREAS:*** General Liability Defense. ***Email:*** tburleigh@mdwcg.com

SEAN A. DOLAN, born Wilmington, Delaware, November 3, 1958; admitted to bar, 1987, Delaware; 1988, Pennsylvania; 1989, New Jersey. *Education:* University of Delaware (B.A., 1981); Widener University School of Law (J.D., 1987). Staff Member, 1985-1986 and Managing Editor, 1986-1987, Delaware Journal of Corporate Law Review. *Member:* Delaware State and American Bar Associations. ***PRACTICE AREAS:*** General Liability Defense. ***Email:*** sdolan@mdwcg.com

THOMAS J. GERARD, born Washington, D.C., July 18, 1958; admitted to bar, 1991, Delaware and U.S. District Court, District of Delaware. *Education:* C.W. Post College (B.A., 1981); Widener University (J.D., 1991). Law Clerk to the Honorable Henry DuPont Ridgely, President Judge, and the Honorable Myron T. Steele, Delaware Superior Court, 1990-1991. Adjunct Professor, Workers' Compensation Program, Widener University School of Law, 1993. Instructor, Intensive Trial Advocacy Program, Widener University School of Law. *Member:* Delaware State (Member, Sections on: Workers' Compensation; Computer Law) and American Bar Associations; Defense Counsel of Delaware. ***PRACTICE AREAS:*** General Liability Defense. ***Email:*** tgerard@mdwcg.com

JESSICA L. JULIAN, born Guam, March 16, 1972; admitted to bar, 1998, Delaware. *Education:* University of Delaware (B.A., 1994); Widener University (J.D., 1997). Historian, Phi Kappa Phi, Harrington Inn Chapter. ***PRACTICE AREAS:*** Workers Compensation. ***Email:*** jjulian@mdwcg.com

LORENZA MANCINI, born Wilmington, Delaware, April 16, 1970; admitted to bar, 2000, Delaware. *Education:* Wilmington College (B.S.N., cum laude, 1995); Widener University School of Law (J.D., 2000). Phi Delta Phi. Staff Member, Widener Law Symposium, 1998-2000. Registered Nurse, Delaware, 1992. ***LANGUAGES:*** Italian. ***PRACTICE AREAS:*** Defense Litigation. ***Email:*** lmancini@mdwcg.com

CHRISTINE P. O'CONNOR, born Monterey, California, April 15, 1971; admitted to bar, 1999, Delaware; 2000, Pennsylvania. *Education:* West Chester University (B.S., cum laude, 1993); Widener University School of Law (J.D., 1999). Staff Member, The Delaware Journal of Corporate Law. Listed in, Who's Who in American Law Students, 1996-1997, 1997-1998, 1998-1999. *Member:* Delaware State and American Bar Associations. ***PRACTICE AREAS:*** Workers Compensation Defense. ***Email:*** coconnor@mdwcg.com

ELIZABETH A. SAURMAN, born Abington, Pennsylvania, March 4, 1968; admitted to bar, 1993, Delaware; 1994, Maryland and U.S. District Court, District of Delaware. *Education:* Ohio Wesleyan University (B.A., 1990); Widener University School of Law (J.D., magna cum laude, 1993). Member, Law Review, Widener University, 1991-1993. Executive Board Member, Delaware Journal of Corporate Law, 1992-1993. *Member:* Delaware State and American Bar Associations. ***PRACTICE AREAS:*** Casualty Defense; Workers Compensation Defense. ***Email:*** esaurman@mdwcg.com

SCOTT L. SILAR, born York, Pennsylvania, December 26, 1959; admitted to bar, 1992, Delaware; 1993, Pennsylvania; 1995, Illinois. *Education:* Susquehanna University (B.A., cum laude, 1981); Widener University (J.D., 1992). Judicial Law Clerk to the Honorable Richard A. Powers, III, Philadelphia, PA, 1990-1992. *Member:* Delaware State, Pennsylvania and American Bar Associations. ***REPORTED CASES:*** Construction By Franco v. Reed, C.A. No. 94L-09-20, Superior Court of Delaware, New Castle, 1994 Del. Super. LEXIS 637, October 14, 1994, submitted, December 12, 1994, decided, released for publication by the Court, February 6, 1995; Kaminski v. Kaminski, Civil Action No. 12781, Court of Chancery of Delaware, New Castle, 1995 Del. Ch. LEXIS 15, February 15, 1995, date submitted, February 24, 1995, date decided, released for publication by the Court, March 13, 1995; Persinger v. Daimlerchrysler Corp., C.A. No. 00A-07-011-CG, Superior Court of Delaware, New Castle, 2000 Del. Super. LEXIS 431, December 4, 2000, date submitted, December 15, 2000, date decided, released for publication by the Court, January 12, 2001. ***PRACTICE AREAS:*** Products Liability. ***Email:*** ssilar@mdwcg.com

JEFFREY K. MARTIN, P.A.

1509 GILPIN AVENUE
WILMINGTON, DELAWARE 19806
Telephone: 302-777-4680
Facsimile: 302-777-4682
Email: jkmartin@nela.org
URL: http://www.lawyers.com/jeffreykmartin

Employment Law, Wrongful Termination, Discrimination, Harassment and Americans with Disabilities Act, Severance, Unemployment Compensation, Personal Injury, General Civil Litigation.

JEFFREY K. MARTIN, born Camden, New Jersey, July 31, 1956; admitted to bar, 1981, New Jersey; 1982, Pennsylvania; 1984, U.S. District Court, Eastern District of Pennsylvania; 1985, Delaware; 1986, U.S. District Court, District of Delaware; 1992, U.S. Court of Appeals, Third Circuit. *Education:* United States Military Academy; Lafayette College (A.B., 1978); Rutgers University (J.D., 1981). Editor, Rutgers Law Journal, 1980-1981. Law Clerk: New Jersey Superior Court, 1981; The Honorable William M. Marutani, Philadelphia Court of Common Pleas, 1982. *Member:* Delaware, Pennsylvania and American Bar Associations; Delaware Employment Lawyers Association; National Employment Lawyers Association. (Also Resident Managing Attorney, Harvey, Pennington, Herting & Renneisen, Ltd.). ***PRACTICE AREAS:*** Employment Law; Personal Injury; General Liability. ***Email:*** jkmartin@nela.org

REPRESENTATIVE CLIENTS: Catholic Diocese of Wilmington; Centennial Life Insurance Company; Cherry Hill Construction Company; CNA Insurance Companies; Maryland Insurance Group; Princeton Insurance Company; Wyomissing Group; WSMW, Inc.

MATTLEMAN, WEINROTH & MILLER

A PROFESSIONAL CORPORATION
200 CONTINENTAL DRIVE
SUITE 211
WILMINGTON, DELAWARE 19713
Telephone: 302-731-8349
Fax: 302-731-8753
URL: http://www.mwm-law.com

Cherry Hill, New Jersey Office: 401 Route 70 East, 08034. Telephone: 856-429-5507. Fax: 856-429-9036.

Clifton, New Jersey Office: 1135 Broad Street, Suite 207, 07013. Telephone: 973-365-6140. Fax: 973-365-6143.

Philadelphia, Pennsylvania Office: 100 S. Broad Street, Suite 2226, 19110. Telephone: 215-923-2225. Fax: 215-567-4151.

Civil and Criminal Trial Practice in all courts. Commercial Litigation, Creditor Rights Litigation, Collections, Foreclosures, Repossessions, Workouts, Real Estate, Mortgages, Commercial Leasing, Personal Injury, Medical Malpractice, Consumer

(This Listing Continued)

Law, Premises Liability, Products Liability, Professional Liability, Family Law, Business Law, Corporate Law, Environmental Law, Superfund Litigation, Sports Law, Entertainment Law, Immigration Law, Wills, Trusts and Estates.

DELIA A. CLARK, born Washington, D.C., October 4, 1961; admitted to bar, 1988, Pennsylvania, New Jersey and Delaware; U.S. District Court, District of New Jersey; U.S. District Court, District of Delaware; U.S. District Court, Eastern District of Pennsylvania. *Education:* Ohio State University (B.A., 1984); Widener University (J.D., 1988). *Member:* Delaware State Bar Association; Delaware Trial Lawyers. (Resident). ***PRACTICE AREAS:*** Civil Litigation; Personal Injury; Medical Malpractice; Premises Liability; Products Liability; Professional Liability; Family Law; Business Law; Wills; Trusts and Estates. ***Email:*** dclark@mwm-law.com

MELANIE J. THOMPSON, born Wilmington, Delaware, April 28, 1967; admitted to bar, 1997, Delaware. *Education:* University of New Hampshire (B.A., English, 1989); Widener University (J.D., 1996). Judicial Law Clerk to: Hon. Jay P. James, New Castle Family Court, Delaware, 1997-1998; Hon. Mark D. Buckworth, New Castle Family Court, Delaware, 1997-1998; Hon. Chandlee Johnson Kuhn, New Castle Family Court, Delaware, 1998. Member: Big Brothers/Big Sisters; United States Tennis Association. Board Member, Widener Women's Network. *Member:* Delaware State (Member, Sections on: Family Law; Women in the Law) and American (Member, Family Law Section) Bar Associations. ***PRACTICE AREAS:*** Family Law; Wills; Trusts and Estates. ***Email:*** mthompson@mwm-law.com

ADAM R. ELGART, born Camp Springs, Maryland, February 6, 1965; admitted to bar, 1994, Delaware, Pennsylvania, U.S. District Court, District of Delaware and U.S. District Court, Eastern District of Pennsylvania. *Education:* Rutgers University (B.A., 1987); Widener University (J.D., 1993). Phi Beta Kappa; Delta Theta Phi. *Member:* Philadelphia County, Pennsylvania and Delaware State Bar Associations; Delaware Trial Lawyers Association. ***LANGUAGES:*** Italian. ***PRACTICE AREAS:*** Civil Litigation; Immigration Law; Family Law. ***Email:*** aelgart@mwm-law.com

JOHN G. MULFORD, born Wilmington, Delaware, May 13, 1941; admitted to bar, 1967, Delaware. *Education:* Wake Forest University (B.A., 1963); George Washington University; University of North Carolina (J.D., 1967). Deputy Attorney General, State of Delaware, 1968-1970. Attorney, State House of Representatives, 1970-1972. *Member:* Delaware State (Member, Insurance Law Committee; Environmental Law Committee) and American Bar Associations; American Judicature Society; Delaware Trial Lawyers Association (Member, Board of Governors 1988-1990). ***PRACTICE AREAS:*** Civil Litigation; Personal Injury; Business Law; Environmental Law. ***Email:*** jmulford@mwm-law.com

FELICIA M. SEATON, born Bronx, New York, December 10, 1969; admitted to bar, 1996, Ohio and U.S. District Court, Northern District of Ohio; 2000, Delaware. *Education:* Bar-Ilan University (B.A., cum laude, 1993); Case Western Reserve University School of Law (J.D., 1996). Author: "Future of the Israel Juvenile Justice System: Should It Follow in the Footsteps of the United States? In Case Western Reserve Journal of International Law, Spring 1996. *Member:* Cleveland, Cuyahoga County, Delaware (Member, Family Law Section; Secretary, Women and the Law Section, 2000-2001 Ohio State (Member, Estate Planning and Probate) and American (Member, 1996—; District 12 Representative to the Board of Governors of the Sections on: Estate Planning, Trust and Probate Law, 1997-1998; Moderator of the Website of the Elder Law Committee, Web page and Co-Moderator of the Website of the Estate Planning, Probate and Trust Law Section Web page, 1997-1998) Bar Associations; Estate Planning Council of Cleveland; Northern Ohio Planned Giving Council (Member, 1997-1998; Chairman, Topics Committee, 1998; Planned Giving Day, 1997-1998). [Israeli, 1987-1990, Private]. ***LANGUAGES:*** Hebrew and French. ***PRACTICE AREAS:*** Family Law; Traffic Law; Estate Planning.

HOLLY M. WHITNEY, born Wilmington, Delaware, September 1, 1958; admitted to bar, 1999, Delaware. *Education:* Mount Holyoke College (B.A., 1980); Widener University School of Law (J.D., 1998). *Member:* Delaware State and American (Member, Sections on: Real Property, Probate and Trust Law , 1994-1999; Member, Planned Giving, Committee, 1997) Bar Associations; Northern Ohio Planned Giving Council (Member, 1997-1998; Chairman, Topics Committee, 1998; Planned Giving Day, 1997-1998). ***PRACTICE AREAS:*** General Practice. ***Email:*** hwhitney@mum-law.com

(For Complete Biographical Data on all Personnel, see Professional Biographies at Cherry Hill, New Jersey)

EUGENE J. MAURER, JR., P.A.

Established in 1980

1201-A KING STREET

WILMINGTON, DELAWARE 19801

Telephone: 302-652-7900

Fax: 302-652-2173

URL: http://www.lawyers.com/ejmaurerjr

Criminal Trial and Appellate Practice.

EUGENE J. MAURER, JR., born Philadelphia, Pennsylvania, December 2, 1948; admitted to bar, 1975, Delaware; 1976, Pennsylvania (inactive) and U.S. District Court, District of Delaware. *Education:* Temple University (B.A., 1970; J.D., cum laude, 1975). Instructor: Criminal Practice, 1980-1982 and Mock Trial, 1983-1990, Widener School of Law; Criminal Law, University of Delaware, 1980. Lecturer, Criminal Law and Procedure, Bar Review of Delaware, 1981-1989. *Member:* Delaware State Bar Association (Chairman, Criminal Law Committee, 1981-1982 and 1997-1999); Delaware Trial Lawyers Association; National Association of Criminal Defense Lawyers; Delaware Association of Criminal Defense Lawyers.

LEGAL SUPPORT PERSONNEL

CAROL RENDE (Paralegal).

McCARTER & ENGLISH, LLP

Established in 1844

MELLON BANK CENTER

919 MARKET STREET

WILMINGTON, DELAWARE 19899

Telephone: 302-654-8010

Telecopier: 302-654-0795

URL: http://www.mccarter.com

Newark, New Jersey Office: Four Gateway Center, 100 Mulberry Street. P.O. Box 652. Telephone: 973-622-4444. Telecopier: 973-624-7070.
Cherry Hill, New Jersey Office: 1820 Chapel Avenue West, Suite 380. Telephone: 609-662-8444. Telecopier: 609-662-6203.
New York, New York Office: 300 Park Avenue, 18th Floor. Telephone: 212-466-9018. Telecopier: 212-432-6568.
Philadelphia, Pennsylvania Office: One Commerce Square, 2005 Market Street, Suite 3600. Telephone: 215-557-7700. Telecopier: 215-557-6544.
Baltimore, Maryland Office: 201 North Charles Street. Telephone: 410-385-1088.
Hartford, Connecticut Office: One Financial Plaza, 755 Main Street. Telephone: 860-493-3900.

Administrative Law, Alternative Dispute Resolution, Antitrust and Trade Regulation, Appellate Practice, Aviation and Aerospace, Bankruptcy, Banks and Banking, Business Law, Civil Practice, Class Actions, Commercial Law, Commercial Real Estate, Communications and Media, Complex and Multi-District Litigation, Computers and Software, Contracts, Copyrights, Corporate Law, Debtor and Creditor, Education Law, Eminent Domain, Employee Benefits, Environmental Law, Equipment Finance and Leasing, Finance, General Practice, Health Care, Insurance, Insurance Coverage, Intellectual Property, International Law, Investments, Labor and Employment, Leases and Leasing, Litigation, Mergers, Acquisitions and Divestitures, Natural Resources, Nonprofit and Charitable Organizations, Patents, Probate, Products Liability, Professional Liability, Public Finance, Real Estate, Taxation, Torts, Toxic Torts, Trade Secrets, Trademarks, Transportation, Trusts and Estates, Unfair Competition, White Collar Crime, Wills, Zoning, Planning and Land Use.

RESIDENT PARTNERS

PAUL A. BRADLEY, born 1955; admitted to bar, 1981, Illinois, 1983, Delaware. *Education:* St. Michael's College (B.A., cum laude, 1977); John Marshall Law School (J.D., with high distinction, 1981). *Member:* Delaware State and American Bar Associations; Defense Counsel of Delaware; Delaware Trial Lawyers Association; Defense Research Institute. ***PRACTICE AREAS:*** Litigation; Products Liability; Commercial; Life, Health and Disability Insurance; ERISA; Construction.

MICHAEL P. KELLY, born 1956; admitted to bar, 1984, Pennsylvania and Delaware. *Education:* Columbia University (B.A., 1979); McGill University; Dickinson School of Law (J.D., 1983). President, St. Thomas More Honor Society, 1997. Former Chief Environmental Counsel, Hercules Inc. Former Partner, Hasse, Kelly & Eveland. Chairman, New Castle County Zoning Board of Adjustment, 1989-1995. Treasurer, Delaware Bar Association, 1992-1994. *Member:* Delaware State, Pennsylvania and American Bar Associations; Delaware Trial Lawyers Association; Defense Counsel of Delaware (Founding Mem-

(This Listing Continued)

McCARTER & ENGLISH, LLP, Wilmington—Continued

ber); Rodney Inn of Court. ***LANGUAGES:*** French and Arabic. ***PRACTICE AREAS:*** Environmental Law; Complex Civil Litigation; Personal Injury; Bankruptcy; Criminal Defense. ***Email:*** mkelly@mccarter.com

SPECIAL COUNSEL

A. RICHARD WINCHESTER, born 1956; admitted to bar, 1982, Washington; 1987, Delaware. *Education:* Pennsylvania State University (B.A., summa cum laude, 1979); University of Pennsylvania (J.D., cum laude, 1982). Phi Beta Kappa; Phi Alpha Theta; Phi Delta Phi. *Member:* Seattle-King County, Washington State, Delaware State and American Bar Associations. ***PRACTICE AREAS:*** Litigation; Corporate Law; Commercial Law; Bankruptcy; Environmental Law. ***Email:*** rwinchester@mccarter.com

ASSOCIATES

JAMES JOSEPH FREEBERY, IV, born 1971; admitted to bar, 1996, Delaware. *Education:* University of Delaware (B.S., summa cum laude, 1993); University of Notre Dame (J.D., 1996). Former Criminal Prosecutor, Delaware Department of Justice. ***PRACTICE AREAS:*** Litigation; Corporate Law; Commercial Law; Bankruptcy; Environmental Law; Products Liability; Personal Injury; Criminal Defense. ***Email:*** jfreebery@mccarter.com

PAUL J. DOUGHERTY, III, born 1970; admitted to bar, 1999, Maryland and Delaware. *Education:* Loyola College (B.A., cum laude, 1992); Villanova University School of Law (J.D., 1998). Judicial Clerk for Jerome O. Herlihy, Delaware Superior Court, 1988-1999. ***PRACTICE AREAS:*** Bankruptcy; Creditors Rights. ***Email:*** pdougherty@mccarter.com

THOMAS D. WALSH, admitted to bar, 1998, Delaware. *Education:* University of Delaware (B.A., 1986); Widener University School of Law (J.D., 1997). ***PRACTICE AREAS:*** Commercial Bankruptcy; Complex Litigation; Criminal Defense. ***Email:*** twalsh@mccarter.com

(For Biographical data on all firm personnel, see Professional Biographies at Newark, New Jersey).

ELLEN SHAFFER MEYER

521 WEST STREET
WILMINGTON, DELAWARE 19801-2139
Telephone: 302-429-0344
Fax: 302-429-8806
Email: esmlaw@mindspring.com
URL: http://www.lawyers.com/rsmlaw

Domestic Relations, Adoption Law.

ELLEN SHAFFER MEYER, born Wilkes-Barre, Pennsylvania, December 14, 1939; admitted to bar, 1981, Delaware and Pennsylvania; 1982, U.S. District Court, District of Delaware. *Education:* Brown University (A.B., 1961); New York University (M.B.A., 1967); Delaware Law School of Widener University (J.D., 1980). Member, Moot Court Honor Society, 1980. Associate Editor, Law Review, 1978-1980. Author: "Alimony Reform: Facing Up to Reality," Delaware Lawyer, Spring 1987; "History of Women and the Law Section of the Delaware State Bar Association," Delaware Lawyer, Fall 1993. Updated sections of The Legal Handbook for Delaware Women, 1988. Provided written materials and conducted seminars on adoption law, 1997 and 1998. Seminar Speaker, "Adoptions," National Business Institute, 1996, 1997, 1998. Recipient, Distinguished Service Award, Delaware Volunteer Legal Services, Inc., 1996. Commissioner, Family Law Commission, State of Delaware, 1985—. Member, Child Support Formula Update Committee, 1993-1994. Volunteer, Special Master, Family Court, 1995—. Member, Family Court Task Force on Open Hearings, 1998. Member, Special Committee, Family Court Internal Operating Procedures, 1998-1999. *Member:* Delaware State (Member, Sections on: Family Law; Women and the Law; Chair, Preceptors Committee, 1999), Pennsylvania and American Bar Associations; American Academy of Adoption Attorneys.

MOORE & BRUCE, LLP

2 EAST 7TH STREET, SUITE 302
WILMINGTON, DELAWARE 19801
Telephone: 302-655-0582
Fax: 302-655-9321

Washington, D.C. Office: 1072 Thomas Jefferson Street, N.W. Telephone: 202-965-5300. Facsimile: 202-965-7745.
London, England Office: 43 Upper Grosvenor Street. Telephone: 011-44-207-493-4840. Fax: 011-44-207-493-4299.

Taxation, Corporate and Commercial Law, International Trade and Customs Law, Trusts and Estates, Civil and Criminal Tax Litigation.

(This Listing Continued)

OF COUNSEL

EDWARD M. LURIA, born Philadelphia, Pennsylvania, December ll, 1941; admitted to bar, 1968, Pennsylvania; 1970, District of Columbia and U.S. Tax Court; 1971, Delaware; 1982, U.S. Claims Court. *Education:* University of Pennsylvania (A.B., 1964; J.D., 1967); New York University (LL.M. in Taxation, 1968). Co-Author: "Tax Court-Trial of Case," Tax Management Portfolio No 153-3rd, 1975; "Cancellation of Indebtedness-Sections 108 and 1017," Tax Management Portfolio No. 88-4th, 1981. Law Clerk to Hon. John W. Kern, Jr., U.S. Tax Court, 1968-1970. Certified Public Accountant, Maryland, 1981. *Member:* The District of Columbia Bar (Member, Section on Taxation); Delaware State, Federal and American (Member, Estate and Gift Tax Committee, Committee on Value Added Taxes and Committee on Closely-Held Corporations, Section on Taxation, 1977—) Bar Associations. (Also, Member, Alvord and Alvord, and Of Counsel to Damico and Associates, Washington, D.C.). ***LANGUAGES:*** French and German. ***PRACTICE AREAS:*** Tax Law; Estate Planning; Probate; Employee Benefits; Asset Protection; Corporate Law. ***Email:*** eluria@compuserve.com

(For Complete Biographical Data on all Personnel, see Professional Biographies at Washington, DC)

MORGAN SHELSBY & LEONI

A PROFESSIONAL ASSOCIATION
WILMINGTON, DELAWARE
(See Newark)

Civil and Criminal Trial Practice in all State and Federal Courts. Personal Injury, Medical Malpractice, Products Liability, Workers Compensation, Insurance and Health Care, Corporate and Commercial Litigation.

MORRIS, JAMES, HITCHENS & WILLIAMS, LLP

222 DELAWARE AVENUE
P.O. BOX 2306
WILMINGTON, DELAWARE 19899-2306
Telephone: 302-888-6800
Telecopier: 302-571-1750
URL: http://www.morrisjames.com

Other Wilmington, Delaware Office: 1010 North Bancroft Parkway, Suite 11, P.O. Box 2328, 19899-2328. Telephone: 302-655-2599. Fax: 302-655-8831.
Dover, Delaware Office: Suite 202, 32 West Loockerman Street, 19904-7356. Telephone: 302-678-8815. Telecopier: 302-678-9063.
Newark, Delaware Office: 16 Polly Drummond Hill Road, 19711-5703. Telephone: 302-368-4200. Fax: 302-368-6259.

Litigation, Corporate Law, Commercial Law, Business Law. Administrative Law, Alternative Dispute Resolution, Bankruptcy, Commercial Real Estate, Computers and Software, Education Law, Environmental Law, Family Law, Health Care, Insurance, Insurance Defense, Intellectual Property, Labor and Employment, Medical Malpractice, Partnership Law, Personal Injury, Probate, Products Liability, Real Estate, Taxation, Torts, Trusts and Estates and Wills.

MEMBERS OF FIRM

HENRY N. HERNDON, JR., born San Antonio, Texas, July 27, 1930; admitted to bar, 1958, Delaware. *Education:* University of Mississippi (A.B., 1952); Columbia University (LL.B., 1958). Member, 1965-1980 and Chairman, 1978-1980, Censor Committee of the Supreme Court of Delaware. Member, 1987-1995, Delaware Supreme Court Board of Bar Examiners (Chairman, 1992-1993); Long Range Courts Planning Committee, 1983-1986. *Member:* Delaware State (President, 1983-1984) and American Bar Associations. Fellow: American Bar Foundation; American College of Trial Lawyers. ***PRACTICE AREAS:*** Litigation; Corporate Law; Alternative Dispute Resolution. ***Email:*** hherndon@morrisjames.com

RICHARD P. BECK, born Wilmington, Delaware, April 11, 1943; admitted to bar, 1969, Delaware. *Education:* Trinity College (B.A., cum laude, 1965); University of Virginia (LL.B., 1968). Judicial Clerkship, Delaware Superior Court and Court of Chancery, 1969-1970. *Member:* Delaware State and American Bar Associations. ***PRACTICE AREAS:*** Real Property; Commercial Transactions; Administration Law. ***Email:*** rbeck@morrisjames.com

GLENN E. HITCHENS, born Milford, Delaware, March 7, 1942; admitted to bar, 1967, Delaware. *Education:* Dickinson College (B.A., 1964); Dickinson School of Law (J.D., 1967). *Member:* Kent County, Delaware State and American Bar Associations. (Resident, Dover, Delaware Office). ***PRACTICE AREAS:*** General Practice. ***Email:*** ghitchens@morrisjames.com

EDWARD M. McNALLY, born Wilmington, Delaware, February 21, 1947; admitted to bar, 1972, Delaware. *Education:* Boston College (B.A., cum

(This Listing Continued)

laude, 1969); Columbia University (J.D., 1972). Solicitor, Town of Elsmere, 1989—. *Member:* Delaware State (Vice Chairman, Corporate Law Section, 1986-1988; Chairman, Corporate Law Section, 1988-1990) and American (Member, Sections on: Business Law; Litigation) Bar Associations. ***PRACTICE AREAS:*** Litigation; Corporate Law; Alternative Dispute Resolution. ***Email:*** emcnally@morrisjames.com

NORRIS P. WRIGHT, born Wilmington, Delaware, January 25, 1945; admitted to bar, 1973, Delaware. *Education:* University of Delaware (B.A., 1967); University of North Carolina (J.D., 19 72); Temple University (LL.M. in Taxation, 1977). Phi Delta Phi. Judicial Clerkship, Delaware Superior Court, 1973. *Member:* Delaware State (Chairman, Estates and Trusts Section, 1983-1984; Chairman, Taxation Section, 1984-1985) and American (Member, Taxation Section) Bar Associations. Fellow, American College of Trust and Estate Counsel (Regent). ***PRACTICE AREAS:*** Taxation; Trusts and Estates; Business Law. ***Email:*** nwright@morrisjames.com

JAMES W. SEMPLE, born Philadelphia, Pennsylvania, November 18, 1943; admitted to bar, 1974, Delaware; 1975, District of Columbia. *Education:* St. Joseph's College (A.B., 1965); Villanova University (J.D., 1974). Author: "Cross Examining Expert Witnesses," Civil Litigation Practice: A Fundamentals Program, Delaware State Bar Association and Widener School of Law, Wilmington, Delaware 1988; Michael DeMarco and James W. Semple, "The Admissibility at Trial Of The Settlement of a Tortfeasor," 41 *FICC Quarterly* 271 (1991); Janice J. Brown and James W. Semple, "Judicial Intervention in the Investigatory Process," F.I.C.C. Annual Meeting, August, 1991; David Erisman and James W. Semple, *Evidence in Trial Practice in Delaware,* National Business Institute, 1991; *Litigation Desk Reference: Torts and Insurance,* Delaware, Clark Boardman Callaghan, 1992; "Delaware Directive 92," A.I.D.A. Update, April 1994; "Francis Hannum, Somers S. Price Jr., James W. Semple, Bad Faith Insurance Litigation," NBI 1995; "The Implied Covenant of Good Faith and Fair Dealing in Insurance Contracts in Delaware," F.I.C.C. Quarterly, Vol. 46, No. 3,289-312, Spring 1996; "The Cry for ADR: Delaware's Response, Alternative Dispute Resolution Section," F.I.C.C. Winter Meeting, February 29, 1996; "Francis J. Murphy, Somers S. Pierce Jr., and James W. Semple, Bad Faith Litigation in Delaware," NBI 1997; "Enforcing the Covenant Not to Compete," Current Issues in Covenants Not to Compete, Business Torts Section, Annual Meeting, F.I.C.C., July 1997; "The Managed Care of Insurance Defense Lawyers, Ethics: Walking a Tightrope," The Delaware Lawyer, Vol. 15, No. 4, 14-20, Winter 1997/1998. Moderator, "Litigating Business Disputes in Delaware: A Roundtable Discussion," Inside Litigation, January 1999, Vol. 13, No. 1. *Member:* Delaware State (Member, Executive Committee, 1978-1980; Founding Chairman, Torts and Insurance Practice Section, 1982-1984) and American (Member, Litigation, Torts and Insurance Practice Section) Bar Associations; The District of Columbia Bar; American Board of Trial Advocates; Association Internationale de Droit d'Assurance, The International Society of Insurance Law (U.S. Chapter); American Inns of Court, Richard Rodney Inn; Federation of Insurance and Corporate Counsel; Defense Research Institute; American Society of Law and Medicine; Defense Counsel of Delaware (Founding President, 1989-1990). ***PRACTICE AREAS:*** Commercial Litigation; Insurance; Alternative Dispute Resolution. ***Email:*** jsemple@morrisjames.com

DAVID H. WILLIAMS, born Wilmington, Delaware, April 17, 1950; admitted to bar, 1975, Delaware. *Education:* Gettysburg College (B.A., 1972); Dickinson School of Law (J.D., 1975). Member: Delaware Supreme Court Board of Bar Examiners, 1989-1996. *Member:* Delaware State (Member, Labor and Employment Law Section) and American (Member, Sections on: Litigation; Labor and Employment Law) Bar Associations. ***PRACTICE AREAS:*** Labor and Employment; Education Law; Litigation. ***Email:*** dwilliams@morrisjames.com

P. CLARKSON COLLINS, JR., born Pittsburgh, Pennsylvania, January 20, 1950; admitted to bar, 1976, Delaware. *Education:* University of Virginia (B.A., 1971); Dickinson School of Law (J.D., 1975). Member, Board of Editors, Dickinson Law Review, 1974-1975, Assistant Secretary, 1987-1988 and Secretary, 1989-1990, Delaware Board of Bar Examiners. Deputy Attorney General, State of Delaware, 1975-1978. *Member:* Delaware State (Member, Sections on: Corporation Law; Litigation) and American (Member, Sections on: Litigation; Business Law) Bar Associations. ***PRACTICE AREAS:*** Business; Fiduciary; Litigation; Corporate Law; Professional Liability. ***Email:*** pcollins@morrisjames.com

RICHARD GALPERIN, born Wilmington, Delaware, September 4, 1949; admitted to bar, 1975, Delaware; 1976, U.S. District Court, District of Delaware. *Education:* University of Delaware (B.A., 1971); Villanova University (J.D., 1975). Omicron Delta Kappa. Assistant City Solicitor, Criminal Division, Wilmington, Delaware, 1976-1977. *Member:* Delaware State and American Bar Associations; American Board of Trial Advocates; Defense Counsel of Delaware (Secretary, 1989—). ***PRACTICE AREAS:*** Medical Malpractice Defense; Products Liability; Insurance. ***Email:*** rgalperin@morrisjames.com

STEVEN R. DIRECTOR, born Wilmington, Delaware, November 29, 1952; admitted to bar, 1977, Delaware; 1978, U.S. Tax Court and U.S. District Court, District of Delaware; 1982, U.S. Court of Appeals, Third Circuit; 1993, Maryland; 1994, U.S. District Court, District of Maryland. *Education:* University of Delaware; University of Colorado (B.A., with honors, 1974); Pepperdine University School of Law (J.D., 1977); New York University (LL.M. in Taxation, 1979). *Member:* Anne Arundel County, Delaware State (Member, 1978— and Chairman, 1980-1981, Vice-Chairman, 1999-2000, Taxation Section; Member, 1978—, Decedents' Estates and Trust Section), Maryland State and American (Member, Sections on: Taxation; Business Law) Bar Associations; Wilmington Tax Group (Chairman, 1986-1987); Estate Planning Council of Delaware (Secretary, 1993-1994, Vice Chairman, 1994-1995, and Director, 1986-1990); National Association of Bond Lawyers. ***PRACTICE AREAS:*** Business and Transactional Law; Taxation; Trusts, Estates and Estate Planning. ***Email:*** sdirector@morrisjames.com

RICHARD D. KIRK, born Washington, D.C., January 23, 1953; admitted to bar, 1978, Delaware; 1984, U.S. Supreme Court. *Education:* Georgetown University (A.B., magna cum laude, 1975); University of Virginia (J.D., 1978). Phi Beta Kappa. Law Clerk, Delaware Supreme Court, 1978-1979. Deputy Attorney General and Counsel, Delaware State Board of Education, 1982-1984. *Member:* Delaware State (President, 1993-1994; Chair, Environmental Law Section, 1990-1992) and American Bar Associations. ***PRACTICE AREAS:*** General Litigation; Environmental Law; Alcoholic Beverages; Licensing and Regulation. ***Email:*** rkirk@morrisjames.com

LEWIS H. LAZARUS, born Philadelphia, Pennsylvania, July 21, 1956; admitted to bar, 1982, California; 1985, Delaware; 1989, District of Columbia. *Education:* Swarthmore College (B.A., with high honors, 1978); Stanford Law School (J.D., 1982). Phi Beta Kappa. Co-Author; "Delaware, droit des sociétés: de nouvelles opportunités," Cahiers Juridiques et Fiscaux de L'exportation, 1995. *Member:* Delaware State (Member, Corporation Law Section) and American (Co-Chair, ABA Class and Derivative Litigation Sub-Committee to Review Proposed Changes to Rule 23 of the Federal Rules of Civil Procedure, 1991—) Bar Associations; State Bar of California; The District of Columbia Bar. ***LANGUAGES:*** Spanish. ***PRACTICE AREAS:*** Litigation; Business Law; Corporate Law. ***Email:*** llazarus@morrisjames.com

MICHAEL M. LEDYARD, born New York, N.Y., August 16, 1948; admitted to bar, 1982, Delaware; 1983, U.S. District Court, District of Delaware. *Education:* University of Hawaii (B.A., 1970); Delaware Law School of Widener University (J.D., cum laude, 1982). Member, 1980-1981 and Associate Editor, 1981, Delaware Journal of Corporate Law. *Member:* Delaware State (Member, Sections on: Corporate Law; Commercial Law; Past Member, Drafting Committees, Delaware Limited Liability Company Act, Delaware Revised Uniform Limited Partnership Act, Second Delaware Uniform Partnership Law; Member, Drafting Committee, Delaware Business Trust Act) and American (Member, Business Law Section) Bar Associations. ***PRACTICE AREAS:*** Business Trusts; Limited Liability Companies; Limited Partnerships; Joint Ventures; Structured Finance; Leveraged Leasing. ***Email:*** mledyard@morrisjames.com

FRANCIS J. JONES, JR., born Wilmington, Delaware, January 4, 1957; admitted to bar, 1983, Delaware and U.S. District Court, District of Delaware. *Education:* Catholic University of America (B.A., 1979; J.D., 1982). Law Clerk to Hon. John J. McNeilly, Associate Justice, Supreme Court of Delaware, 1982-1983. *Member:* Delaware State (Chairman, Torts and Insurance Practice Section, 1990-1992) and American Bar Associations; Defense Research Institute and Defense Council of Delaware. (Resident, Newark, Delaware Office). ***PRACTICE AREAS:*** Insurance Defense; Personal Injury; Litigation; Products Liability. ***Email:*** pjones@morrisjames.com

DANIEL P. McCOLLOM, born Ridgewood, New Jersey, May 7, 1958; admitted to bar, 1983, Pennsylvania and U.S. District Court, Western District of Pennsylvania; 1986, Delaware. *Education:* Franklin & Marshall College (B.A., 1980); University of Pittsburgh (J.D., cum laude, 1983). Staff Member, 1981-1982 and Business Editor, 1982-1983, University of Pittsburgh Law Review. *Member:* Pennsylvania, Delaware State and American (Member, Sections on: Taxation; Business Law; Committee on Partnerships and Unicorporated Business Organizations, Subcommittee on Limited Liability Companies, and Subcommittee on REITS, REMICS and Financing Trusts; Committee on Employee Benefits) Bar Associations. ***PRACTICE AREAS:*** Business Law; Taxation; Trusts and Estates. ***Email:*** dmccollom@morrisjames.com

ROBERT L. SYMONDS, JR., born Danbury, Connecticut, September 25, 1953; admitted to bar, 1986, Delaware. *Education:* Villanova University (B.A., 1975); University of Pennsylvania Law School; University of Pittsburgh School of Law (J.D., 1985). Managing Editor, 1984 and Associate Editor, 1983-1984, *The Journal of Law and Commerce.* Co-Author: "Delaware, droit des sociétés: de nouvelles opportunités," *Cahiers Juridiques et Fiscaux de L'exportation, 1995. Member:* Delaware State (Chairman, 1995-1997, Vice Chairman, 1993-1995 and Secretary, 1991-1993, Commercial Law Section; Member, Committees on Delaware Limited Liability Company Act, Delaware Revised Uniform Limited Partnership Act, Delaware Uniform Partnership Law, and Delaware Business Trust Act; Member, Sections on: Commercial Law; Corporation Law) and American (Member: Business Law Section; Committee on Partnerships and Unincorporated Business Organizations, Subcommittee on Limited Liability Companies and Subcommittee on REITS, REMICS and Financing Trusts; Committee on Developments in Business Financing and Subcommittee on Se-

(This Listing Continued)

MORRIS, JAMES, HITCHENS & WILLIAMS, LLP, Wilmington—Continued

curitization of Assets; Committee on Legal Opinions) Bar Associations. ***PRACTICE AREAS:*** Business Law; Limited Liability Companies; Partnerships; Trusts; Joint Ventures; Corporate Law; Commercial law. ***Email:*** rsymonds@morrisjames.com

STEPHEN M. MILLER, born Wilmington, Delaware, September 10, 1960; admitted to bar, 1987, Delaware; 1988, Pennsylvania. *Education:* Brandeis University; University of Delaware (B.S., 1982); George Washington University (J.D., with honors, 1987). Co-Author, "Delaware Limited Liability Company Practice Guide," *State Limited Liability Company & Partnership Laws,* Aspen Law & Business, 1994. *Member:* Delaware State (Member: Uniform Commercial Code Committee, Commercial Law Section; Sections on: General Corporation Law; Real and Personal Property Law) and American (Member: Franchising Committee, Antitrust Law Section; Franchising Forum Committee; Bankruptcy Committee, General Practice Section; Sections on: Business Law; Real Property, Probate and Trust) Bar Associations; American Bankruptcy Institute. ***PRACTICE AREAS:*** Commercial Law; Bankruptcy; Partnership Law; Limited Liability Company Law; Franchise Law; Corporate Law. ***Email:*** smiller@morrisjames.com

MARY M. CULLEY, born Chicago, Illinois, December 12, 1946; admitted to bar, 1985, Pennsylvania and Delaware; 1988, U.S. District Court, District of Delaware; 1989, U.S. Tax Court. *Education:* St. Mary's College (B.A., 1964); Delaware Law School of Widener University (J.D., cum laude, 1984); Temple University (LL.M. in Taxation, 1988). Phi Kappa Phi. Member, Moot Court Honor Society. Associate Editor, Delaware Journal of Corporate Law, 1983-1984. *Member:* Pennsylvania, Delaware State (Member, Taxation Section; Member and Chair, 1994-1995, Estates and Trusts Section; Member and Secretary, 1997-1999, Committee on the Law and the Elderly; Member and Chair, 1989-1990, Women's Section) and American Bar Associations. ***LANGUAGES:*** French. ***PRACTICE AREAS:*** Estate and Gift Taxation; Estate Planning; Probate; Elder Law; Guardianship; Conservatorship; Disability Benefits; Fiduciary Litigation. ***Email:*** mculley@morrisjames.com

LAURA SUNSTEIN MURPHY, born Philadelphia, Pennsylvania, August 23, 1947; admitted to bar, 1990, Pennsylvania; 1992, Delaware. *Education:* University of Pennsylvania (B.A., 1969); Villanova University (M.A., 1980; J.D., cum laude, 1989); Union Institute, Ohio (Ph.D., 1981). Order of the Coif. Recent Developments Editor, Villanova Law Review, 1988-1989. Member, 1981-1988 and Certified Member, 1982, National Association for the Advancement of Psychoanalysis. *Member:* Philadelphia, Pennsylvania, Delaware State and American (Member, Sections on: Business Law; Health Law) Bar Associations; American Health Lawyers Association; Hospital Association of Pennsylvania. ***LANGUAGES:*** French and Latin. ***PRACTICE AREAS:*** Health Care Law. ***Email:*** lmurphy@morrisjames.com

KEVIN G. HEALY, born Wilmington, Delaware, October 23, 1958; admitted to bar, 1986, Delaware; 1987, Pennsylvania. *Education:* University of Delaware (B.A., cum laude, 1981); Boston College; Delaware Law School of Widener University (J.D., cum laude, 1986). Member, Moot Court. Recipient, American Jurisprudence Award in Constitutional Law. Law Clerk, Delaware Superior Court, 1985-1987. *Member:* Delaware State and American Bar Associations; The Association of Trial Lawyers of America; Delaware Trial Lawyers Association. (Resident, Newark, Delaware Office). ***PRACTICE AREAS:*** Personal Injury Litigation. ***Email:*** khealy@morrisjames.com

NICHOLAS J. CAGGIANO, JR., born Philadelphia, Pennsylvania, January 8, 1957; admitted to bar, 1988, Delaware, Pennsylvania and U.S. District Court, District of Delaware. *Education:* Villanova University (B.Ch.E., cum laude, 1978; J.D., cum laude, 1987). Order of the Coif; Tau Beta Pi. Member, 1985-1986 and Articles Editor, 1986-1987, Villanova Law Review. Author: Note, "Handgun Manufacturers' Tort Liability to Victims of Criminal Shootings: A Summary of Recent Developments," 31 Villanova Law Review 1577, 1986. *Member:* Delaware State, Pennsylvania and American Bar Associations; Federal Energy Bar Association. ***Email:*** ncaggiano@morrisjames.com

MICHAEL J. MAIMONE, born New York, N.Y., January 4, 1962; admitted to bar, 1990, New York; 1997, Delaware. *Education:* College of Mount Saint Vincent (B.A., 1984); University of Virginia School of Law (J.D., 1987). Author: The Duty Of Loyalty And The Evolution Of The Scope Of Judicial Review, 59 Brooklyn L. Rev. 65 (1993); Derivative Litigation: Current Law Versus The American Law Institute, 48 Bus. Law. 1443 (1992); Chancellor Allen, The Business Judgment Rule, And The Shareholders' Right To Decide, 17 Del. J. Corp. L. 785 (1992). ***PRACTICE AREAS:*** Corporate Law; Corporate and Commercial Litigation. ***Email:*** mmaimone@morrisjames.com

LEWIS C. LEDYARD, III, born Jacksonville, North Carolina, April 28, 1964; admitted to bar, 1990, Delaware; 1991, U.S. District Court, District of Delaware and U.S. Court of Appeals, Third Circuit. *Education:* Tulane University (B.A., 1986); Villanova University (J.D., 1990). *Member:* Delaware State (Member, Commercial Law Section) and American (Member, Business Law Section) Bar Associations. ***PRACTICE AREAS:*** Business Trusts; Asset Secured Financing; Leveraged Leasing; Limited Liability Companies. ***Email:*** lledyard@morrisjames.com

GRETCHEN ANN BENDER, born San Francisco, California, September 14, 1960; admitted to bar, 1986, California; 1992, Ohio and Delaware. *Education:* Northwestern University (B.A. in History, 1982); University of San Francisco (J.D., cum laude, 1986). Topics Editor, University of San Francisco Law Review, 1985-1986. Author: "A Mixed Blessing for Predicting Antitrust Liability: Northwest Wholesale Stationers Inc. v. Pacific Stationery & Printing Co.," 20 USF L. Rev. 877, 1986. Law Clerk, Hon. Caleb M. Wright, U.S. District Court for the District of Delaware, 1990-1991; Hon. George H. Revercomb, U.S. District Court for the District of Columbia, 1989-1990. *Member:* State Bar of California; Delaware State and American Bar Associations. ***PRACTICE AREAS:*** Civil Litigation. ***Email:*** gbender@morrisjames.com

NORMAN M. POWELL, born Camden, New Jersey, October 16, 1963; admitted to bar, 1990, Delaware, New Jersey and Pennsylvania. *Education:* Georgetown University (B.S.B.A., cum laude, 1985); Villanova University (M.B.A., 1989; J.D., 1989). *Member:* Delaware State (Chairman, 1996-1998, Vice Chairman, 1994-1996 Real and Personal Property Section; Chairman, 1991-1992, Subcommittee on Landlord and Tenant Code; Chairman, 1991-1992, Subcommittee on Unrecorded Leases; Member, Commercial Law Section; Member, Committee on Uniform Commercial Code) and American (Member, Sections on: Real Property, Probate and Trust; Business Law) Bar Associations. ***PRACTICE AREAS:*** Real and Personal Property; Business Law; Business Trusts; Limited Liability Companies; Structured Finance. ***Email:*** npowell@morrisjames.com

MATTHEW J. O'TOOLE, born Teaneck, New Jersey, August 31, 1963; admitted to bar, 1994, Delaware. *Education:* Fordham University (B.A., summa cum laude, 1985; M.A., 1988); Marshall-Wythe School of Law, College of William and Mary (J.D., Order of the Coif, 1992). Law Clerk to Hon. Rebecca Beach Smith, United States District Judge, Eastern District of Virginia, 1992-1993. *Member:* Delaware State (Member, Sections on: Commercial Law; Corporate Law) and American (Member, Sections on: Antitrust; Business Law) Bar Associations. ***PRACTICE AREAS:*** Corporate Law; Business Law; Intellectual Property. ***Email:*** motoole@morrisjames.com

DENNIS R. SPIVACK, born Wilmington, Delaware, September 18, 1947; admitted to bar, 1976, Delaware. *Education:* University of Pennsylvania (B.A., magna cum laude, 1969); University of Michigan (J.D., 1975). Author: "Comment on Delaware Financial Development Act of 1981," Delaware Journal of Corporate Law. Deputy Attorney General for the State of Delaware, 1975-1978. *Member:* Delaware State and American (Member, Real and Personal Property Section) Bar Associations. ***PRACTICE AREAS:*** Real Estate Law; Commercial; Business Law. ***Email:*** dspivack@morrisjames.com

JOSEPH G. LISICKY, born Stroudsburg, Pennsylvania, May 19, 1961; admitted to bar, 1988, Pennsylvania and New Jersey; 1995, Delaware. *Education:* Pennsylvania State University (B.S., 1983); University of Massachusetts (M.R.P., 1985); Temple University (J.D., cum laude, 1988). Staff Member, 1986-1987 and Managing Editor, 1987-1988, Temple Law Review. Co-Author: "Pennsylvania Mortgage Foreclosure Practice," The Law of Distressed Real Estate, 1990; "The Tenant as Terminator: Constructive Eviction in Modern Commercial Leases," The Commercial Property Lease, Vol. II, 1997. *Member:* Pennsylvania, Delaware State and American Bar Associations. ***PRACTICE AREAS:*** Real Estate Law; Secured Lending Law. ***Email:*** jlisicky@morrisjames.com

DENNIS D. FERRI, born Trenton, New Jersey, June 12, 1946; admitted to bar, 1972, Delaware; 1973, Pennsylvania; 1999, Maryland; U.S. District Court, District of Delaware; U.S. Court of Appeals, Third Circuit. *Education:* LaSalle University (B.A., 1968); Villanova Law School (J.D., cum laude, 1972). Certified Mediator, Delaware Superior Court. *Member:* Delaware State (Past Chairman, Torts and Insurance Section; Member, Executive Committee) and American Bar Associations; Delaware Trial Lawyers Association; Defense Counsel of Delaware; American Board of Trial Advocates. ***PRACTICE AREAS:*** Personal Injury; Medical Malpractice Defense; Insurance Law; Products Liability; Professional Liability; Litigation. ***Email:*** dferri@morrisjames.com

BRETT D. FALLON, born Philadelphia, Pennsylvania, September 12, 1961; admitted to bar, 1986, Delaware; 1992, Pennsylvania. *Education:* Duke University (B.A., summa cum laude, 1983; J.D., with honors, 1986). Phi Beta Kappa. Editor, 1984-1985 and Administrative Editor, 1985-1986, Law and Contemporary Problems. *Member:* Delaware State (Member: Executive Committee; Sections on: Commercial Law; General Corporation Law; Litigation) and American (Fellow, Business Law Section; Member, Litigation Section) Bar Associations; American Bankruptcy Institute. ***PRACTICE AREAS:*** Bankruptcy; Corporate Litigation; Commercial Litigation. ***Email:*** bfallon@morrisjames.com

SUSAN D. AMENT, born Wilmington, Delaware, August 2, 1952; admitted to bar, 1983, Delaware, Pennsylvania, New Jersey and U.S. District Court, District of New Jersey; 1984, U.S. District Court, District of Delaware; 1987, U.S. Supreme Court. *Education:* University of Delaware (B.A., 1979); Delaware

(This Listing Continued)

Law School of Widener University (J.D., 1982). Member, Board of Bar Examiners, State of Delaware, 1994-1997. *Member:* Delaware State (Chairperson, Fee Dispute Committee, 1991-1994; Co-Chair, Medical Legal Committee, 1989-1990) and American Bar Associations; Delaware Trial Lawyers Association. (Resident, Bancroft Parkway Office). ***PRACTICE AREAS:*** Personal Injury Litigation; Insurance Law; Civil Litigation. ***Email:*** sament@morrisjames.com

GRETCHEN S. KNIGHT, born Wilmington, Delaware, March 11, 1965; admitted to bar, 1990, Delaware; 1991, U.S. District Court, District of Delaware. *Education:* University of Delaware (B.A., 1987); Villanova University (J.D., 1990). Phi Alpha Theta; Phi Delta Phi (Secretary, Villanova University School of Law Chapter, 1989-1990); Truman Scholar, 1985. *Member:* Delaware State and American Bar Associations. ***PRACTICE AREAS:*** Family Law; Education Law. ***Email:*** gknight@morrisjames.com

MICHAEL A. WEIDINGER, born Cincinnati, Ohio, March 28, 1961; admitted to bar, 1994, Delaware. *Education:* Miami University, Ohio (A.B., cum laude, 1983); George Washington University (J.D., high honors, 1994). Order of the Coif. Member: The George Washington Law Review, 1992-1994; Moot Court Board, 1992-1994. Author: Note, "Inequitable Pleading: Defendants' Particular Burden In Patent Infringement Suits," 62 George Washington Law Review 1178, 1994. *Member:* Delaware State Bar Association. ***PRACTICE AREAS:*** Corporate Litigation; Commercial Litigation; Securities Disputes; Corporate Law. ***Email:*** mweidinger@morrisjames.com

ASSOCIATES

ELLEN MARIE COOPER, born Wilmington, Delaware, January 21, 1957; admitted to bar, 1990, Delaware. *Education:* University of Delaware (B.A., Psychology, 1979); Columbia University (Ph.D., Social Psychology, 1984); Temple University (J.D., 1990). Assistant Professor, Pennsylvania State University, 1983-1987. Commissioner, Family Court of the State of Delaware, 1993-1998. Member, Delaware Board of Bar Examiners, Advisory Board of the Domestic Violence Project. *Member:* Delaware State and American Bar Associations. ***PRACTICE AREAS:*** Employment Law; Education Law; Health Law. ***Email:*** ecooper@morrisjames.com

CARL N. KUNZ, III, born Newburyport, Massachusetts, April 2, 1967; admitted to bar, 1993, Delaware; 1994, U.S. District Court, District of Delaware. *Education:* University of New Hampshire (B.A., 1988); Widener University School of Law (J.D., cum laude, 1993). *Member:* Delaware (Member, Sections on: Litigation; Tort and Insurance Practice; Labor and Employment Law) and American (Member, Sections on: Litigation; Tort and Insurance Law; Labor and Employment Law) Bar Associations; American Bankruptcy Institute; Defense Counsel of Delaware. ***PRACTICE AREAS:*** Bankruptcy; Creditor's Rights; Insurance Defense; Civil Litigation; Commercial Litigation. ***Email:*** ckunz@morrisjames.com

THOMAS E. HANSON, JR., born Philadelphia, Pennsylvania, December 7, 1971; admitted to bar, 1996, Pennsylvania, New Jersey, U.S. District Court, Eastern District of Pennsylvania and U.S. District Court, District of New Jersey; 2001, Delaware. *Education:* University of Pittsburgh (B.A., 1993); Boston College Law School (J.D., 1996). Recipient, Presidential Scholarship. Executive Editor, Boston College Third World Law Journal. *Member:* American Bar Association. ***PRACTICE AREAS:*** Corporate Litigation; Commercial Litigation. ***Email:*** thanson@morrisjames.com

JAMES E. DRNEC, born Chicago, Illinois, October 6, 1959; admitted to bar, 1998, Delaware. *Education:* University of Southern California (B.A., 1994); Temple University (J.D., 1998). Member, Moot Court Honor Society; Temple University National Trial Team. Recipient, Barristers Award for Outstanding Trial Advocacy. First Place, National Institute of Trial Advocacy Tournament of Champions; Association of Trial Lawyers of America's Student Trial Advocacy. *Member:* Delaware State and American Bar Associations. ***Email:*** jdrnec@morrisjames.com

SAMANTHA E. BALICK, admitted to bar, 1996, Delaware. *Education:* University of Delaware (B.A., 1992); Dickinson School of Law (J.D., 1995). Law Clerk, Honorable Carl Goldstein, Superior Court, Delaware. Former Attorney, Real Estate and Housing, Finance and Economic Development and former Chairperson, Zoning Board of Adjustment, City of Wilmington. *Member:* Delaware State and American Bar Associations. ***PRACTICE AREAS:*** Residential Real Estate; Commercial Real Estate; Finance. ***Email:*** sbalick@morrisjames.com

ELIZABETH A. BROWN, born Norman, Oklahoma, April 20, 1971; admitted to bar, 1996, Minnesota; 1998, Delaware. *Education:* Abilene Christian University (B.A., summa cum laude, 1993); University of Minnesota (J.D., magna cum laude, 1996). Order of the Coif. Member, Moot Court. Clerk, The Honorable James C. Harten, Minnesota Court of Appeals, 1996-1997. *Member:* Delaware State and American Bar Associations. ***Email:*** ebrown@morrisjames.com

ARLENE M. BENTON, born Dover, Delaware, 1972; admitted to bar, 1997, Maryland (Not admitted in Delaware). *Education:* University of Delaware

(This Listing Continued)

(B.A., 1994); Widener University School of Law (J.D., 1997). *Member:* Baltimore City, Maryland State and American Bar Associations. ***Email:*** abenton@morrisjames.com

ROSS E. ANTONACCI, born August 31, 1974; admitted to bar, 2000, Pennsylvania and New Jersey; 2001, Delaware. *Education:* Boston University School of Management (B.S., 1996); Villanova University School of Commerce and Finance (M.B.A., 2000); Villanova University School of Law (J.D., 2000). ***PRACTICE AREAS:*** Business Transactions. ***Email:*** rantonacci@morrisjames.com

CATHERINE A. BARRON, born May 22, 1975; admitted to bar, 2000, Delaware. *Education:* Seton Hall University (B.A., summa cum laude, 1997); Villanova University (J.D., magna cum laude, 2000). Author: "Passing the 'Operator' Buck in *United States v. Township of Brighton:* Whether Pollution-Related or General Activities Create CERCLA Liability for a Governmental Entity," Villanova Environmental Law Journal, 1999. ***PRACTICE AREAS:*** Business Transactions. ***Email:*** cbarron@morrisjames.com

PAUL H. OSTIEN, III, born Media, Pennsylvania, March 22, 1971; admitted to bar, 1999, Pennsylvania; 2000, New Jersey; 2001, Delaware. *Education:* Dickinson College (B.S., 1993); Vermont Law School (J.D., 1999); Villanova University (LL.M., 2000). *Member:* American Bar Association. ***PRACTICE AREAS:*** Business Transactions; Taxation; Trusts and Estates. ***Email:*** postien@morrisjames.com

CHRISTINA M. MAYCEN, born Fredericksburg, Virginia, December 29, 1975; admitted to bar, 2000, Delaware. *Education:* James Madison University (B.S., 1997); Widener University School of Law (J.D., cum laude, 2000). Phi Delta Phi. Staff Member, Delaware Journal of Corporate Law. *Member:* Delaware State and American Bar Associations; American Bankruptcy Institute. ***PRACTICE AREAS:*** Corporate Litigation; Commercial Litigation; Bankruptcy. ***Email:*** cmaycen@morrisjames.com

LINDA D. MARTIN, born Los Angeles, California, January 10, 1962; admitted to bar, 2000, Delaware. *Education:* University of West Los Angeles (B.S., magna cum laude, 1995); Whittier Law School (J.D., cum laude, 1999). Notes and Comments Editor, 1997-1998 and Executive Editor, 1998-1999, Whittier Law Review. Listed in Who's Who of American Law Students, 1998 and 1999. Law Clerk to: Honorable Randy Holland, Supreme Court, State of Delaware, 1999-2000; Honorable Susan C. Del Pesco, Superior Court, State of Delaware, 2000-2001. *Member:* Delaware (Member, Multicultural Judges and Lawyers Section) and American Bar Associations. ***PRACTICE AREAS:*** Corporate Litigation. ***Email:*** lmartin@morrisjames.com

JENNIFER L. BRIERLEY, born Wilmington, Delaware, April 29, 1970; admitted to bar, 2001, Delaware. *Education:* Salisbury State University (B.A., cm laude, 1992); Widener University (J.D., cum laude, 2000). Recipient, Outstanding Achievement Awards in Advanced Trial Methods and Equity, 2000. *Member:* Delaware State and American Bar Associations. ***PRACTICE AREAS:*** Employment Rights; Civil Rights; Education Law; Domestic Relations. ***Email:*** jbrierley@morrisjames.com

ALISA ERENSHTEYN, born Moscow, Russia, March 29, 1977; admitted to bar, 2001, Delaware. *Education:* University of Delaware (B.A., cum laude, 1998); Temple University (J.D., 2001). Participant, 1999-2000 and Team Coach, 2000-2001, International Jessup Moot Court Competition. *Member:* Delaware State and American (Member, Business Law Section) Bar Associations. ***PRACTICE AREAS:*** Business Transactions. ***Email:*** aerenshteyn@morrisjames.com

OF COUNSEL

William F. Lynch, II
George C. Hering, III
Barbara MacDonald
Sherry C. McReynolds

MORRIS AND MORRIS

Established in 1991

SUITE 1600
1105 NORTH MARKET STREET
P.O. BOX 2166
WILMINGTON, DELAWARE 19899-2166
Telephone: 302-426-0400
Facsimile: 302-426-0406
Email: firm@morrisandmorrislaw.com

Complex Representational Litigation, including Corporate, Securities and Consumer Law Litigation.

IRVING MORRIS, born Trenton, New Jersey, December 18, 1925; admitted to bar, 1951, Delaware. *Education:* University of Delaware (B.A., 1947); Yale University (LL.B., 1950). Law Clerk to Chief Judge Paul Leahy, U.S. District Court for the District of Delaware, 1951-1952. Deputy Attorney General, 1955. Supreme Court Advisory Committee on Litigation Ethical Problems

(This Listing Continued)

MORRIS AND MORRIS, Wilmington—Continued

(Chairman, 1974-1994; Co-Chairman, 1994—). Member, Board of Bar Examiners, 1975-1983. *Member:* Delaware State (Secretary, 1954-1958; Vice-President, 1963-1965; President, 1973-1974; Chairman, Corporation Law Committee, 1978-1982) and American (Member, Committee on Corporate Laws, 1975-1981; Member of Council, Section on Litigation, 1975-1976) Bar Associations. Fellow: American Bar Foundation; American College of Trial Lawyers. ***PRACTICE AREAS:*** Corporate Litigation; Securities Litigation.

KAREN L. MORRIS, born Wilmington, Delaware, December 10, 1958; admitted to bar, 1984, New York; 1990, Delaware; U.S. District Court, Southern and Eastern Districts of New York; U.S. District Court, District of Delaware; U.S. Court of Appeals, Third Circuit, U.S. Tax Court. *Education:* Yale University (B.A., M.A., 1980); Duke University (J.D., 1983). Law Clerk to Chief Justice Daniel L. Herrmann, Delaware Supreme Court, 1983-1984. Member, Federal Bar Council, 1996—. Member, Permanent Lawyers Advisory Committee to the U.S. District Court, District of Delaware, 1991-1993. *Member:* Association of the Bar of the City of New York; Delaware State, New York State and American Bar Associations. ***PRACTICE AREAS:*** Corporate Litigation; Securities Litigation.

PATRICK F. MORRIS, born Fort Dix, New Jersey, November 28, 1955; admitted to bar, 1984, Florida; 1991, Delaware. *Education:* United States Military Academy (B.S., 1978); Duke University (J.D., 1983). Order of the Coif. *Member:* Delaware and American Bar Associations; The Florida Bar. [Major, U.S. Army, JAC, 1984-1991]. ***LANGUAGES:*** Spanish. ***PRACTICE AREAS:*** Corporate Litigation; Securities Litigation.

SETH D. RIGRODSKY, born New York, N.Y., October 30, 1963; admitted to bar, 1991, New York, U.S. District Court, Southern District of New York and U.S. Court of Appeals, Third Circuit; 1993, Delaware and U.S. District Court, District of Delaware. *Education:* Brandeis University (B.A., magna cum laude, 1985); Georgetown University (J.D., magna cum laude, 1990). Order of the Coif. Articles Editor, Georgetown Law Journal, 1989-1990. Law Clerk to the Honorable Andrew G. T. Moore, II, Delaware Supreme Court, 1990-1991. *Member:* New York State, Delaware and American Bar Associations. ***PRACTICE AREAS:*** Corporate Litigation; Securities Litigation. ***Email:*** srigrodsky@morrisandmorrislaw.com

ASSOCIATES

JACQUELINE L. JENKIN GREEN, born Brooklyn, New York, April 29, 1966; admitted to bar, 1993, New Jersey, Pennsylvania and U.S. District Court, District of New Jersey (Not admitted in Delaware). *Education:* University of Delaware (B.A., 1988); Delaware Law School of Widener University (J.D., 1992). *Member:* Pennsylvania Bar Association. ***PRACTICE AREAS:*** Corporate Litigation; Securities Litigation.

JAMES A. McSHANE, born Wilmington, Delaware, January 23, 1966; admitted to bar, 1996, Pennsylvania, New Jersey, Delaware and U.S. District Court, District of New Jersey; 1997, U.S. District Court, District of Delaware. *Education:* University of Delaware (B.A., with distinction, 1989); Temple University School of Law (J.D., 1994). *Member:* Delaware Bar Association. ***LANGUAGES:*** German. ***PRACTICE AREAS:*** Corporate Litigation; Securities Litigation.

HERBERT W. MONDROS, born Philadelphia, Pennsylvania, October 13, 1960; admitted to bar, 1989, Pennsylvania; 1994, Delaware and U.S. Court of Appeals, Third, Fourth and Fifth Circuits. *Education:* Fairleigh Dickinson University (B.S., 1982); Tulane Law School (J.D., magna cum laude, 1989). Order of the Coif, 1989. Associate Editor, Tulane Law Review, 1988-1989. Trial Attorney, Environmental Crimes Section, U.S. Dept. of Justice, 1989-1992. Assistant U.S. Attorney, Lead Appellate Court Counsel, Eastern District of Louisiana, 1992-1994; Associate, Skadden Arps Slate Meagher & Flom, 1994-1997. *Member:* Delaware State and American Bar Associations. ***Email:*** hmondros@morrisandmorrislaw.com

---

MORRIS, NICHOLS, ARSHT & TUNNELL

1201 NORTH MARKET STREET
P.O. BOX 1347
WILMINGTON, DELAWARE 19899-1347
Telephone: 302-658-9200
Telecopier: 302-658-3989
URL: http://www.mnat.com

General Practice. Patent Litigation.

MEMBERS OF FIRM

JOHANNES R. KRAHMER, born Mannheim, Germany, February 29, 1932; admitted to bar, 1959, District of Columbia; 1965, Delaware. *Education:* Dartmouth College (A.B., magna cum laude, 1953); Harvard University (J.D., cum laude, 1959). Phi Beta Kappa. Attorney, Office of the Tax Legislative Counsel, U.S. Treasury Department, 1962-1964. Member, Tax Management Advisory Board, Estates, Gifts and Trusts, 1970—. *Member:* Delaware State (Chairman, Taxation Section, 1986-1987) and American (Secretary, Taxation Section, 1986-1988) Bar Associations. Fellow, American College of Trust and Estate Counsel; American College of Tax Counsel. ***Email:*** jkrahmer@mnat.com

LEWIS S. BLACK, JR., born Wilmington, Delaware, June 29, 1938; admitted to bar, 1964, Delaware; 1965, District of Columbia; 1966, New York. *Education:* Princeton University (A.B., 1960); Yale University (LL.B., 1963). Co-Author, "Delaware Corporation Law and Practice," Matthew Bender & Co., 1999. Associate Reporter, Lawyer's Basic Corporate Practice Manual, ALI-ABA, 1984. Member, Legal Advisory Committee, New York Stock Exchange, 1994-1997. Member, Editorial Advisory Board: The Journal of Corporation Law, 1977—; BNA Securities Regulation and Law Report, 1982—. *Member:* Delaware State (Member of Council, Corporation Law Section, 1982-1991) and American (Member of Council, Section of Corporation, Banking and Business Law, 1984-1988; Chairman, Federal Regulation of Securities Committee, 1986-1987; Member, Committee on Corporate Laws, 1983-1988) Bar Associations; American Law Institute. ***Email:*** lblack@mnat.com

WILLIAM O. LaMOTTE, III, born Bryn Mawr, Pennsylvania, July 15, 1943; admitted to bar, 1969, Delaware. *Education:* Yale University (B.A., 1965); University of Pennsylvania (LL.B., 1968). Chairman, 1998-2000 and Vice-Chairman, 1996-1997, Delaware Supreme Court Board of Bar Examiners. *Member:* Delaware State and American Bar Associations. ***Email:*** wlamotte@mnat.com

DOUGLAS E. WHITNEY, born Malden, Massachusetts, May 1, 1939; admitted to bar, 1965, New York; 1970, Massachusetts; 1973, Delaware. *Education:* Cornell University (B.Ch.E., 1962); Columbia University (J.D., 1965). *Member:* Delaware State, New York State and American Bar Associations; New York Intellectual Property Law Association; American Intellectual Property Law Association. ***Email:*** dwhitney@mnat.com

WILLIAM H. SUDELL, JR., born Philadelphia, Pennsylvania, February 9, 1943; admitted to bar, 1971, Delaware. *Education:* Brown University (B.S. and B.A., 1966); University of Pennsylvania (J.D., 1971). *Member:* Delaware State and American Bar Associations; American Bankruptcy Institute. ***Email:*** wsudell@mnat.com

MARTIN P. TULLY, born Philadelphia, Pennsylvania, August 10, 1944; admitted to bar, 1971, New York; 1974, Delaware. *Education:* Rutgers University (B.A., 1966); Northwestern University (J.D., cum laude, 1969). Articles Editor, Northwestern University Law Review, 1968-1969. Member, Chancery Court Rules Committee, 1986—. *Member:* Delaware State and American Bar Associations. ***Email:*** mtully@mnat.com

THOMAS R. HUNT, JR., born Elkton, Maryland, February 22, 1948; admitted to bar, 1972, Delaware. *Education:* Lehigh University (B.A., magna cum laude, 1969); University of Pennsylvania (J.D., cum laude, 1972). Associate Editor, 1970-1971; Editor, 1971-1972, University of Pennsylvania Law Review. *Member:* Delaware State and American Bar Associations. ***Email:*** thunt@mnat.com

A. GILCHRIST SPARKS, III, born Philadelphia, Pennsylvania, October 2, 1944; admitted to bar, 1973, Delaware. *Education:* Yale University (B.A., magna cum laude, 1966); University of Pennsylvania (J.D., magna cum laude, 1973). Order of the Coif. Associate Editor, 1971-1972; Editor, 1972-1973, University of Pennsylvania Law Review. Executive Editor, Delaware Law Review, 1998—. Co-Chairman, Tulane Corporate Law Institute, 1996-2001. Co-Author: "Delaware Corporation Law and Practice," Matthew Bender & Co., 2000. Assistant Secretary, 1977-1981; Secretary, 1982-1983; Member, 1986-1992; Vice Chairman, 1988-1989; Chairman, 1990-1992, Co-Chairman, 2000— Delaware State Board of Bar Examiners. Member, Permanent Advisory Committee on the Delaware Uniform Rules of Evidence to the Supreme Court of Delaware. *Member:* Delaware State (Vice Chairman, Corporate Law Section, 1982-1985; Chairman, 1985-1988; Member, Corporate Law Section, 1978—) and American (Co-Chairman, Committee on Professional Liability, Litigation Section, 1986-1988; Member, Committee on Corporate Laws, Section of Business Law, 1989-1996; 2000—) Bar Associations; American Law Institute. Fellow, American College of Trial Lawyers. ***Email:*** asparks@mnat.com

RICHARD D. ALLEN, born Williamsport, Pennsylvania, February 24, 1945; admitted to bar, 1974, Delaware. *Education:* Washington & Lee University (B.A., cum laude, 1967); Georgetown University (J.D., 1974). Editor, Georgetown Law Journal, 1972-1974. Member, Third Circuit Lawyers' Advisory Committee, 1987-1991. *Member:* Delaware State and American Bar Associations. ***Email:*** rallen@mnat.com

DAVID LEY HAMILTON, born Schenectady, New York, August 10, 1948; admitted to bar, 1975, Georgia; 1976, Delaware. *Education:* Haverford College (B.A., 1970); Emory University (J.D., with distinction, 1975). *Member:* Delaware State (Member, Uniform Commercial Code Subcommittee of Commercial Law Section) and American (Member, Joint Task Force on Revised Article 9 Enactment) Bar Associations. ***Email:*** dhamilton@mnat.com

(This Listing Continued)

JOHN F. JOHNSTON, born Kansas City, Missouri, September 2, 1946; admitted to bar, 1977, Delaware. *Education:* Northwestern University (B.A., 1968); Duke University (Ph.D., 1972); University of Pennsylvania (J.D., cum laude, 1977). Order of the Coif. *Member:* Delaware State (Member of Council, Corporation Law Section, 1991-1999) and American Bar Associations. ***Email:*** jjohnston@mnat.com

WALTER C. TUTHILL, born Norwalk, Connecticut, April 22, 1951; admitted to bar, 1977, Delaware. *Education:* Denison University (B.A., 1973); Northwestern University (M.M., 1977; J.D., cum laude, 1977). Co-Author: "Limited Liability Companies: Legal Aspects of Organization, Operation and Dissolution," BNA Corporate Practice Series, 1996—; Chapters 15-16, "The General Partnership, L.P. and L.L.P.: Formation and Organization; Management and Operation," New York and Delaware Business Entities, West Publishing Co., 1997—. Member: Mastercard/Visa Joint Legal and Legislative Advisory Committee, 1990-1992. *Member:* Delaware State (Member, Limited Partnership/Limited Liability Company Subcommittee of Corporate Law Section and Business Trust Subcommittee of Commercial Law Section) and American Bar Associations. ***Email:*** wtuthill@mnat.com

DONALD F. PARSONS, JR., born Philadelphia, Pennsylvania, June 28, 1948; admitted to bar, 1977, Delaware. *Education:* Lehigh University (B.S.E.E., cum laude, 1970; M.A., 1972); Georgetown University (J.D., 1977). Case and Note Editor, Georgetown Law Journal, 1976-1977. Judicial Clerkship, The Honorable James L. Latchum, U.S. District Court, District of Delaware, 1977-1979. Member, Board of Overseers, Widener University School of Law. *Member:* Delaware State (President, 1999-2000) and American Bar Associations; New York Intellectual Property Law Association; Philadelphia Patent Law Association; American Intellectual Property Law Association. Delaware Bar Foundation (Director). ***Email:*** dparsons@mnat.com

JACK B. BLUMENFELD, born Rochester, New York, July 31, 1952; admitted to bar, 1979, Delaware. *Education:* State University of New York at Albany (B.A., 1974); Yale University (J.D., 1977). Phi Beta Kappa. Judicial Clerkship, The Honorable Walter K. Stapleton, United States District Court, District of Delaware, 1977-1979. Member: Third Circuit Lawyers Advisory Committee, 1998-2001; Advisory Committee, District of Delaware Civil Justice Reform Act, 1992-1994. *Member:* Delaware State and American Bar Associations; New York Intellectual Property Law Association; American Intellectual Property Law Association. ***Email:*** jblumenfeld@mnat.com

DONALD NELSON ISKEN, born Wilmington, Delaware, October 12, 1953; admitted to bar, 1978, Delaware. *Education:* Bucknell University (B.A., 1975); University of Miami (J.D., cum laude, 1978). *Member:* Delaware State (Co-Chairman, Subcommittee on Revisions to the Delaware Unit Property Act, 1989-1992) and American Bar Associations; American College of Real Estate Lawyers. ***Email:*** disken@mnat.com

DONALD E. REID, born St. Paul, Minnesota, September 19, 1953; admitted to bar, 1979, Pennsylvania; 1980, Delaware. *Education:* University of Pennsylvania (B.A., 1975); Villanova University (J.D., 1978). Order of the Coif. Judicial Clerkship, The Honorable James L. Latchum, U.S. District Court, District of Delaware, 1978-1980. Assistant Secretary, 1992-1993, Secretary, 1994-1995, Member, 2000—, Board of Bar Examiners, Delaware Supreme Court. *Member:* Delaware State, Pennsylvania and American Bar Associations. ***Email:*** dreid@mnat.com

DENISON H. HATCH, JR., born Greenwich, Connecticut, September 7, 1949; admitted to bar, 1980, Delaware. *Education:* Cornell University (A.B., 1971); City College of the City University of New York (M.S., 1972); Northwestern University (J.D., 1980). *Member:* Delaware State and American Bar Associations. ***Email:*** dhatch@mnat.com

THOMAS C. GRIMM, born Rockville, Maryland, November 9, 1954; admitted to bar, 1980, Delaware; 1981, Pennsylvania. *Education:* University of Notre Dame (B.B.A., 1977); Villanova University (J.D., cum laude, 1980). Staff Member, 1978-1979 and Editor, 1979-1980, Villanova Law Review. Judicial Clerkship, The Honorable William Duffy, Supreme Court of Delaware, 1980-1981. *Member:* Delaware State and American Bar Associations. ***Email:*** tgrimm@mnat.com

KENNETH J. NACHBAR, born Oceanside, New York, February 23, 1956; admitted to bar, 1981, Delaware. *Education:* Haverford College (B.A., 1978); New York University (J.D. 1981). Member, New York University Review of Law and Social Change, 1980-1981. *Member:* Delaware State and American Bar Associations. ***Email:*** knachbar@mnat.com

ANDREW M. JOHNSTON, born Wausau, Wisconsin, April 26, 1957; admitted to bar, 1982, Delaware. *Education:* Kenyon College (A.B., summa cum laude, 1979); Northwestern University (J.D., cum laude, 1982). Phi Beta Kappa. *Member:* Delaware State and American Bar Associations. ***Email:*** ajohnston@mnat.com

MARY B. GRAHAM, born St. Louis, Missouri, February 6, 1952; admitted to bar, 1983, Delaware. *Education:* Stanford University (B.S., with distinction, 1974); Massachusetts Institute of Technology (M.S., 1978); Yale Law School (J.D., 1982). Phi Beta Kappa. Judicial Clerkship, The Honorable Walter K. Stapleton, U.S. District Court, District of Delaware, 1982-1983. Chair, District of Delaware Permanent Lawyers Advisory Committee, 1988-1992. Member: Board of Professional Responsibility of Delaware Supreme Court, 1999—; Preliminary Review Committee of the Board on Professional Responsibility, 1994-1999; Third Circuit Lawyers Advisory Committee, 1993-1995. *Member:* Delaware State and American Bar Associations. ***Email:*** mgraham@mnat.com

MICHAEL HOUGHTON, born Wilmington, Delaware, June 15, 1956; admitted to bar, 1982, Delaware. *Education:* University of Virginia (B.A., with high distinction, 1978; J.D., 1982). Commissioner, National Conference of Commissioners of Uniform State Laws, 1995—. Member, NCCUSL UCC Article 9 Revision Committee, 1995—. Chair, NCCUSL Legislative Committee, 1999—. *Member:* Delaware State (Former-Chairman, Commercial Law Section, 1993; Member, Banking Law Committee) and American Bar Associations. ***Email:*** mhoughton@mnat.com

THOMAS R. PULSIFER, born Boston, Massachusetts, February 19, 1958; admitted to bar, 1985, New York and Delaware. *Education:* Middlebury College (B.A., magna cum laude, 1980); New York University (J.D., 1983; LL.M., Taxation, 1985). Phi Beta Kappa. *Member:* Delaware State (Chair, Estates and Trusts Law Section, 2001-2002) and American Bar Associations. Fellow, American College of Trust and Estate Counsel. ***Email:*** tpulsifer@mnat.com

JON E. ABRAMCZYK, born Erie, Pennsylvania, August 30, 1960; admitted to bar, 1985, Pennsylvania; 1986, Delaware. *Education:* University of Pennsylvania (B.S., B.A., 1982); Tulane University (J.D., cum laude, 1985). Editor, 1983-1984 and Senior Managing Editor, 1984-1995, Tulane Law Review. Judicial Clerkship, The Honorable Joseph T. Walsh, Supreme Court of Delaware, 1985-1986. Member, Supreme Court Rules Committee, 1993—. *Member:* Delaware State and American Bar Associations. ***Email:*** jabramczyk@mnat.com

ALAN J. STONE, born Madelia, Minnesota, January 18, 1961; admitted to bar, 1988, New York and Delaware. *Education:* Tulane University (B.S.E., 1983; J.D., magna cum laude, 1987). Order of the Coif. Senior Notes and Comments Editor, 1986-1987, Editor, 1985-1986, Tulane Law Review. *Member:* Delaware State and American Bar Associations. ***LANGUAGES:*** German. ***Email:*** astone@mnat.com

LOUIS G. HERING, born New York, N.Y., May 16, 1960; admitted to bar, 1987, New York; 1989, District of Columbia; 1990, Delaware. *Education:* Cornell University (A.B., 1982; Phi Beta Kappa); University of California at Los Angeles (J.D., 1986). Judicial Clerkship, The Honorable Carolyn Berger, Delaware Court of Chancery, 1986-1987. *Member:* Delaware State (Past Chairman, Commercial Law Section and Member, Business Trust Subcommittee, Commercial Law Section, Member, Limited Partnership/Limited Liability Company Subcommittee of Corporate Law Section) and American (Member, Business Law Section Committee on Partnerships and other Unincorporated Business Associations) Bar Associations. ***Email:*** lhering@mnat.com

FREDERICK H. ALEXANDER, born Shreveport, Louisiana, April 26, 1963; admitted to bar, 1989, Delaware. *Education:* University of Maryland (B.A., 1985); Georgetown University (J.D., magna cum laude, 1988). Order of the Coif. Associate Editor, Georgetown Law Journal, 1987-1988. *Member:* Delaware State and American Bar Associations. ***Email:*** falexander@mnat.com

R. JUDSON SCAGGS, JR., born Roanoke, Virginia, August 19, 1959; admitted to bar, 1989, Delaware; 1990, Virginia. *Education:* Washington & Lee University (B.A., 1981); College of William & Mary (J.D., 1988). Order of the Coif. Member, William and Mary Law Review. *Member:* Delaware State and American Bar Associations. [Captain, U.S. Marine Corps, 1981-1985]. ***Email:*** rscaggs@mnat.com

WILLIAM M. LAFFERTY, born Springfield, Pennsylvania, July 4, 1963; admitted to bar, 1989, Delaware; 1990, Pennsylvania. *Education:* University of Delaware (B.S.B.A., 1985); The Dickinson School of Law (J. D., 1989). Member: Woolsack Honor Society; Appellate Moot Court Board. Articles Editor, Dickinson Law Review, 1988-1989. Judicial Clerkship, The Honorable Maurice A. Hartnett, III, Delaware Court of Chancery, 1989-1990. *Member:* Delaware State and American Bar Associations. ***Email:*** wlafferty@mnat.com

KAREN JACOBS LOUDEN, born Brooklyn, New York, December 29, 1965; admitted to bar, 1990, Delaware. *Education:* University of Pennsylvania (B.A., summa cum laude, 1987); Harvard Law School (J.D., cum laude, 1990). Phi Beta Kappa. Finalist, Ames Moot Court Competition. Associate Member, Delaware State Board of Bar Examiners, 1995-1999. Secretary, Delaware Volunteer Legal Services. *Member:* Delaware State (Chair, Women in Law Section, 1994-1995; Board Member, Intellectual Property Section, 1992-1994; Member, Committee for the Provision of Legal Services to Low Income People, 1997—) and American Bar Associations. ***LANGUAGES:*** Spanish and French. ***Email:*** klouden@mnat.com

DONNA L. CULVER, born Dover, Delaware, March 18, 1966; admitted to bar, 1991, Delaware. *Education:* University of Delaware (B.A., magna cum laude, 1988); Boston University (J.D., cum laude, 1991). Phi Beta Kappa; Phi Kappa Phi; Alpha Kappa Delta. *Member:* Delaware State and American Bar Associations. ***Email:*** dculver@mnat.com

(This Listing Continued)

MORRIS, NICHOLS, ARSHT & TUNNELL, Wilmington—Continued

JULIA HEANEY, born Bryn Mawr, Pennsylvania, November 12, 1966; admitted to bar, 1992, Delaware. *Education:* Johns Hopkins University (B.S., with honors, 1988); Columbia University (J.D., 1991). Harlan Fiske Stone Scholar. *Member:* Delaware State (Chair, Intellectual Property Law Section) and American Bar Associations; American Intellectual Property Law Association. ***Email:*** jheaney@mnat.com

JONATHAN I. LESSNER, born Miami Beach, Florida, December 21, 1961; admitted to bar, 1992, Delaware; 1993, Florida. *Education:* Cornell University (B.A., 1985); Ohio State University (M.A., 1986); University of Miami (J.D., magna cum laude, 1991). Order of the Coif. Recipient, Soia Mentschikoff Award. Editor-in-Chief, University of Miami Law Review, 1990-1991. *Member:* Delaware State (Co-Chairman, Banking Law Committee, Commercial Law Section) and American Bar Associations. ***Email:*** jlessner@mnat.com

ROBERT J. DEHNEY, born Brooklyn, New York, March 15, 1965; admitted to bar, 1990, Connecticut; 1995, New York; 1997, Pennsylvania and Delaware. *Education:* Dickinson College (B.A., 1987); Pace University (J.D., 1990). Member, Advanced Moot Court Kaufman Competition. Managing Editor, Pace Environmental Law Review. Judicial Clerkship, The Honorable Prudence Carter Beatty, U.S. Bankruptcy Judge, Southern District of New York, 1990-1992. *Member:* Delaware State and American Bar Associations; American Bankruptcy Institute. ***LANGUAGES:*** French. ***Email:*** rdehney@mnat.com

COLM F. CONNOLLY, born Wilmington, Delaware, October 18, 1964; admitted to bar, 1993, Delaware. *Education:* University of Notre Dame (B.A., with honors, 1986); London School of Economics (M.Sc., 1987); Duke University (J.D., with honors, 1991). Member, Moot Court Board. Finalist, National Bioethics and The Law Moot Court Competition. Editor, 1989-1990 and Senior Editor, 1990-1991, Law and Contemporary Problems. Judicial Clerkship, The Honorable Walter K. Stapleton, U.S. Court of Appeals, Third Circuit, 1991-1992. Assistant U.S. Attorney, District of Delaware, 1992-1999. Special Assistant Attorney General, State of Delaware, 1998-1999. *Member:* Delaware State and American Bar Associations. ***Email:*** cconnolly@mnat.com

JEFFREY R. WOLTERS, born Wilmington, Delaware, October 6, 1966; admitted to bar, 1994, Delaware. *Education:* University of Delaware (B.A., 1988); University of Virginia (J.D., 1992). Phi Beta Kappa. Member, 1990-1991 and Articles Editor, 1991-1992, Virginia Law Review. Judicial Clerkship, The Honorable Walter K. Stapleton, U.S. Court of Appeals, Third Circuit, 1992-1993. *Member:* Delaware State and American Bar Associations. ***Email:*** jwolters@mnat.com

MARYELLEN NOREIKA, born Pittsburgh, Pennsylvania, July 12, 1966; admitted to bar, 1993, Delaware. *Education:* Lehigh University (B.S., 1988); Columbia University (M.A., 1990); University of Pittsburgh (J.D., magna cum laude, 1993). Order of the Coif. Associate Editor, 1991-1992; Editor, 1992-1993, University of Pittsburgh Law Review. *Member:* Delaware State and American Bar Associations. ***Email:*** mnoreika@mnat.com

DAVID J. TEKLITS, born Reading, Pennsylvania, February 1, 1968; admitted to bar, 1993, Delaware. *Education:* University of Pennsylvania (B.S., magna cum laude, 1990); Georgetown University (J.D., magna cum laude, 1993). Order of the Coif. Editor, ABA Committee on Securities Litigation, Securities News. Associate Member, Delaware Supreme Court Board of Bar Examiners, 2000—. *Member:* Delaware State and American Bar Associations. ***Email:*** dteklits@mnat.com

S. MARK HURD, born Almond, New York, December 18, 1967; admitted to bar, 1994, New York and Delaware. *Education:* Georgetown University (B.S.F.S., magna cum laude, 1990; J.D., cum laude, 1993). Judicial Clerkship, The Honorable Murray M. Schwartz, U.S. District Court, District of Delaware, 1993-1994. *Member:* Delaware State and American Bar Associations. ***LANGUAGES:*** Spanish. ***Email:*** shurd@mnat.com

SPECIAL COUNSEL

RACHEL A. DWARES, born Wilmington, Delaware, May 25, 1960; admitted to bar, 1985, Illinois; 1994, Delaware. *Education:* Cornell University (A.B., 1982); Boston University (J.D., cum laude, 1985). Member, 1983-1984 and Note and Case Editor, 1984-1985, Boston University Law Review. *Member:* Delaware State and American Bar Associations. ***Email:*** rdwares@mnat.com

ASSOCIATES

RODGER D. SMITH, born Lewiston, New York, February 8, 1968; admitted to bar, 1994, New York; 1998, Delaware. *Education:* University of Pennsylvania (B.S., magna cum laude, 1990); New York University (J.D., magna cum laude, 1993). Order of the Coif. Note and Comment Editor, New York University Law Review. Judicial Clerkship, The Honorable W. Eugene Davis, U.S. Court of Appeals, Fifth Circuit, 1993-1994. *Member:* Delaware State, New York State and American Bar Associations. ***Email:*** rsmith@mnat.com

(This Listing Continued)

ERIC D. SCHWARTZ, born Princeton, New Jersey, January 16, 1962; admitted to bar, 1992, Delaware; 1993, Pennsylvania. *Education:* Georgetown University (B.S.B.A., cum laude, 1984); New York University (M.B.A., 1989); Villanova University (J.D., 1992). Member, Villanova University Environmental Law Journal. *Member:* Delaware State and American Bar Associations. ***Email:*** eschwartz@mnat.com

MONA A. LEE, born Philadelphia, Pennsylvania, October 2, 1966; admitted to bar, 1994, Delaware. *Education:* University of Pennsylvania (B.A., 1988); Westminster Theological Seminary (M.A.R., with high honors, 1990); Temple University (J.D., cum laude, 1994). Member, Temple Law Review, 1992-1994. Judicial Clerkship, The Honorable Louis C. Bechtle, U.S. District Court, Eastern District of Pennsylvania, 1996-1997. *Member:* Delaware State (Co-Chair, Multicultural Judges and Lawyers Section, 1999-2000; Chair, International Law Section, 1999-2001; Chair, Delaware Minority Job Fair, 1999-2000; Member, Committee on Nominations, 1999—) and American Bar Associations; National Asian Pacific American Bar Association; Asian American Bar Association of Delaware Valley; American Intellectual Property Law Association; Intellectual Property Owners Association. ***LANGUAGES:*** Korean. ***Email:*** mlee@mnat.com

STANFORD L. STEVENSON, III, born Abington, Pennsylvania, March 9, 1968; admitted to bar, 1995, Delaware. *Education:* College of William and Mary (B.B.A., 1990); Georgetown University Law Center (J.D., cum laude, 1994). Beta Gamma Sigma. Certified Public Accountant, Pennsylvania, 1995. *Member:* Delaware State (Chairman, Taxation Section, 2000-2001) and American Bar Associations. ***Email:*** sstevenson@mnat.com

DEREK C. ABBOTT, born Wilmington, Delaware, December 5, 1965; admitted to bar, 1995, Delaware. *Education:* United States Military Academy (B.S., 1987); University of North Carolina (J.D., with honors, 1995). Staff Member, 1993-1994 and Publication Editor, 1994-1995, North Carolina Law Review. *Member:* Delaware State and American Bar Associations. ***Email:*** dabbott@mnat.com

JESSICA ZELDIN, born Philadelphia, Pennsylvania, March 17, 1970; admitted to bar, 1996, Delaware. *Education:* Northwestern University (B.A., 1992); Washington University (M.A., East Asian Studies, 1995; J.D., 1995). Order of the Coif. Topics Editor, Washington University Law Quarterly. *Member:* Delaware State and American Bar Associations. ***Email:*** jzeldin@mnat.com

DAVID A. HARRIS, born Seaford, Delaware, February 9, 1971; admitted to bar, 1997, Delaware. *Education:* Salisbury State University (B.S., 1993); University of North Carolina (J.D., 1996). Order of the Coif. *Member:* Delaware State and American Bar Associations. ***Email:*** dharris@mnat.com

PATRICIA O'NEILL VELLA, born Milford, Delaware, April 24, 1970; admitted to bar, 1996, Delaware. *Education:* University of Delaware (B.S.B.A., magna cum laude, 1992); Villanova University (J.D., magna cum laude, 1996). Order of the Coif. Member, 1994-1995 and Executive Editor, 1995-1996, Villanova Law Review. Judicial Clerkship, The Honorable Randy J. Holland, Supreme Court, State of Delaware, 1996-1997. *Member:* Delaware State and American Bar Associations. ***Email:*** pvella@mnat.com

GREGORY W. WERKHEISER, born Easton, Pennsylvania, October 6, 1970; admitted to bar, 1996, Delaware. *Education:* Pennsylvania State University (B.S., 1992); Widener University (J.D., magna cum laude, 1996). Member, 1994-1995 and Articles Editors, 1995-1996, Delaware Journal of Corporate Law. Judicial Clerkship, The Honorable Jane R. Roth, U.S. Court of Appeals, Third Circuit, 1996-1997. *Member:* Delaware State and American Bar Associations. ***Email:*** gwerkheiser@mnat.com

WENDY L. WALTER, born Hampton, Virginia, September 25, 1971; admitted to bar, 1996, Kentucky; 1998, Delaware. *Education:* University of Virginia (B.A., 1993); College of William and Mary (J.D., 1996). Member, Moot Court, Board and Bar, 1995-1996. *Member:* Delaware State, Kentucky and American Bar Associations. ***Email:*** wwalter@mnat.com

CHRISTOPHER F. CARLTON, born New Milford, Connecticut, July 19, 1972; admitted to bar, 1998, Delaware. *Education:* University of Georgia (B.B.A., 1994); Villanova University (J.D., cum laude, 1997). Omicron Delta Kappa; Order of the Omega. Member, 1995-1996 and Managing Editor, 1996-1997, Villanova University Law Review. *Member:* Delaware State and American Bar Associations. ***Email:*** ccarlton@mnat.com

GARFIELD B. SIMMS, born Kingston, Jamaica, July 12, 1963; admitted to bar, 1998, Massachusetts (Not admitted in Delaware). *Education:* University of Delaware (M.E.E., 1989; Ph.D., 1992); Northeastern University School of Law (J.D., 1997). *Member:* Massachusetts and American Bar Associations. ***Email:*** gsimms@mnat.com

MICHAEL BUSENKELL, born Philadelphia, Pennsylvania, October 21, 1968; admitted to bar, 1995, Florida; 1998, U.S. District Court, Southern District of Florida; 2000, Delaware and U.S. District Court, District of Delaware. *Education:* Villanova University (B.S., 1990); Temple University School of Law (J.D., cum laude, 1995). Member, Temple Political and Civil Rights Law Re-

(This Listing Continued)

view, 1994-1995. Assistant State Attorney, Eleventh Judicial Circuit, Florida, 1995-1998. *Member:* Delaware State and American Bar Associations. **Email:** mbusenkell@mnat.com

RICHARD W. ELLIS, born Englewood, New Jersey, March 11, 1965; admitted to bar, 1998, Delaware. *Education:* North Carolina State University (B.S., 1988); Rutgers University (M.S., 1995); Rutgers University Law School (J.D., 1998). *Member:* Delaware State and American Bar Associations. **Email:** rellis@mnat.com

JOHN D. PIRNOT, born Lincoln, Nebraska, January 14, 1960; admitted to bar, 1998, Delaware. *Education:* Massachusetts Institute of Technology (B.S., 1981); Widener University School of Law (J.D., magna cum laude, 1998). Member, 1996-1997 and Managing Editor, 1997-1998, Delaware Journal of Corporate Law. Recipient, Herman V. Belk Award, 1997. Winner, DiBona Moot Court Competition, 1996. Winner and Best Speaker, Kaufman Securities Law Moot Court Competition, 1997. *Member:* Delaware State and American Bar Associations. **Email:** jpirnot@mnat.com

MEGAN E. WARD, born Salisbury, Maryland, June 9, 1973; admitted to bar, 1998, Delaware. *Education:* Washington College (B.A., summa cum laude, 1995); Washington & Lee University (J.D., magna cum laude, 1998). Omicron Delta Kappa; Phi Alpha Delta. Order of the Coif. Member, 1996-1997 and Articles Editor, 1997-1998, Washington & Lee Law Review. *Member:* Delaware State and American Bar Associations. **Email:** mward@mnat.com

MELISSA STONE MYERS, born Binghamton, New York, March 20, 1973; admitted to bar, 1998, Massachusetts; 1999, Pennsylvania; 2000, Delaware; 2001, U.S. District Court, District of Delaware. *Education:* State University of New York at Albany (B.S., magna cum laude, 1995); Boston University (J.D., cum laude, 1998). Phi Beta Kappa. *Member:* Delaware State, Pennsylvania and American Bar Associations. **Email:** mmyers@mnat.com

JASON W. STAIB, born Newport, Rhode Island, October 18, 1970; admitted to bar, 1998, Delaware. *Education:* University of Delaware (B.A., 1993); Widener University School of Law (J.D., cum laude, 1998). *Member:* Delaware State and American Bar Associations. **Email:** jstaib@mnat.com

DONNA L. HARRIS, born Stuttgart, Germany, January 15, 1971; admitted to bar, 1998, Delaware. *Education:* Seton Hall University (B.A., summa cum laude, 1993); Widener University School of Law (J.D., magna cum laude, 1998). *Member:* Delaware State and American Bar Associations. **Email:** donnaharris@mnat.com

TODD A. FLUBACHER, born Reading, Pennsylvania, August 16, 1969; admitted to bar, 1999, Delaware. *Education:* Drexel University (B.S., summa cum laude, 1992); University of Maryland (J.D., with honors, 1999). *Member:* Delaware State and American Bar Associations. **Email:** tflubacher@mnat.com

CHRISTIAN J. HENRICH, born Buffalo, New York, May 14, 1968; admitted to bar, 1999, Delaware. *Education:* Dartmouth College (B.A., magna cum laude, 1990); University of Pennsylvania (M.B.A., 1999; J.D., cum laude, 1999). Phi Beta Kappa; Palmer Scholar. Author, "Game Theory and Gonsalves: A Recommendation for Reforming Stockholder Appraisal Actions," The Business Lawyer, Vol. 56, No. 2 at 697. *Member:* Delaware State and American Bar Associations. [Captain, U.S. Army, 1990-1995]. **Email:** chenrich@mnat.com

YVETTE C. FITZGERALD, born New York, New York, July 5, 1974; admitted to bar, 2000, Delaware. *Education:* State University of New York at Geneseo (B.A., 1996); William and Mary School of Law (J.D., 2000). Order of the Coif. Member, William and Mary Law Review. *Member:* Delaware State and American Bar Associations. **Email:** yfitzgerald@mnat.com

JAMES G. McMILLAN, III, born Red Bank, New Jersey, November 18, 1955; admitted to bar, 2000, Delaware. *Education:* Haverford College (B.A., 1977); University of Chicago (M.A., 1978); University of Pennsylvania (J.D., 2000). *Member:* Delaware State and American Bar Associations. **Email:** jmcmillan@mnat.com

MATT NEIDERMAN, born Syracuse, New York, April 13, 1971; admitted to bar, 2001, Delaware. *Education:* Utah Valley State College (B.S., magna cum laude, 1997); University of Maryland (J.D., with honors, 2000). Order of the Coif; Order of the Barristers. Member, 1998-1999 and Notes and Comments Editor, 1999-2000, The Business Lawyer. Recipient, Bridgewater M. Arnold Award for Commercial Paper, 1999. Sam Allen Memorial Prize Finalist, Meyerowitz Moot Court Competition. Member, Meyerowitz National Moot Court Team. *Member:* Delaware State and American Bar Associations. **Email:** mneiderman@mnat.com

SCOTT SALERNI, born Rochester, New York, August 8, 1974; admitted to bar, 2000, Delaware. *Education:* State University of New York at Geneseo (B.A., 1996); State University of New York at Buffalo (J.D., 2000). Member, 1998-1999 and Articles Editor, 1999-2000, Buffalo Law Review. *Member:* Delaware State and American Bar Associations. **Email:** ssalerni@mnat.com

PATRICIA R. UHLENBROCK, born Philadelphia, Pennsylvania, March 24, 1959; admitted to bar, 2000, Delaware. *Education:* University of Pittsburgh (B.A., 1982); Widener University School of Law (J.D., magna cum laude, 2000). Widener Scholar, 1997-2000. Member, 1998-1999 and Research Editor, 1999-2000, Delaware Journal of Corporate Law. Judicial Clerkship, The Honorable E. Norman Veasey, Supreme Court, State of Delaware, 1999-2000. *Member:* Delaware State and American Bar Associations. **Email:** puhlenbrock@mnat.com

(This Listing Continued)

MICHAEL G. WILSON, born Kansas City, Missouri, October 15, 1968; admitted to bar, 2001, Delaware. *Education:* George Mason University (B.A., 1997); College of William & Mary (J.D., 2000). Phi Delta Phi. Member, William & Mary Bill of Rights Journal. *Member:* Delaware State and American Bar Associations. **Email:** mwilson@mnat.com

OF COUNSEL

ANDREW B. KIRKPATRICK, JR., born Asheville, N.C., January 16, 1929; admitted to bar, 1954, Delaware; 1955, Florida. *Education:* Davidson College, North Carolina (B.S., 1949); Harvard University (LL.B., 1954). Phi Beta Kappa. Member, Board of Editors, Harvard Law Review, 1950-1951 and 1953-1954. Chairman, Censor Committee of the Supreme Court of Delaware, 1970-1978. Member, Delaware Supreme Court Long Range Courts Planning Committee, 1978-1984. *Member:* Delaware State Bar Association (President, 1978-1979; Vice-Chairman, Corporation Law Committee, 1972-1977). Emeritus Fellow, American College of Trial Lawyers.

RICHARD L. SUTTON, born Dover, Delaware, July 4, 1935; admitted to bar, 1961, Delaware. *Education:* University of Delaware (B.A., 1957); Yale Law School (LL.B., 1960). Phi Beta Kappa. Member, Board of Editors, Yale Law Journal, 1958-1960. Judicial Clerkship, The Honorable Edwin D. Steele, Jr., U.S. District Court, District of Delaware, 1960-1961. Chairman Supreme Court Board on Professional Responsibility, 1988-1992. *Member:* Delaware State and American Bar Associations; American Law Institute. **Email:** rsutton@mnat.com

DAVID A. DREXLER, born New York, N.Y., December 25, 1930; admitted to bar, 1959, New York; 1963, Delaware. *Education:* Dartmouth College (B.A., 1952); Yale University (LL.B., 1955). Phi Beta Kappa. Member, Board of Editors, Yale Law Journal, 1953-1955. Co-Author, "Delaware Corporation Law and Practice," Matthew Bender & Co., 1988.

O. FRANCIS BIONDI, born Wilmington, Delaware, January 1, 1933; admitted to bar, 1958, Delaware. *Education:* LaSalle College (B.A., 1954); Boston College (M.A., 1955); University of Pennsylvania (LL.B., 1958). City Solicitor, City of Wilmington, 1963-1968. Member: Delaware Supreme Court Delaware Courts Planning Committee, 1972-1998; Council on Banking of the State of Delaware, 1974-1992. Chairman, Supreme Court Board on Professional Responsibility, 1983-1986. *Member:* Delaware State (President, 1984-1985) and American Bar Associations. **Email:** obiondi@mnat.com

WALTER L. PEPPERMAN, II, born Philadelphia, Pennsylvania, May 8, 1939; admitted to bar, 1967, Delaware. *Education:* University of Pennsylvania (B.S., 1961; LL.B., 1967). Vice-Chairman, Delaware Supreme Court Continuing Legal Education Commission, 1986-1993. *Member:* American Bar Association.

DECEASED PARTNERS

HUGH M. MORRIS (1878-1966).

ALEXANDER L. NICHOLS (1906-1985).

JAMES M. TUNNELL, JR. (1910-1986).

S. SAMUEL ARSHT (1910-1999).

REPRESENTATIVE CLIENTS: Artesian Water Company, Inc.; AstraZeneca Inc.; The Coca-Cola Company; Delaware River and Bay Authority; The Dow Chemical Company; Ford Motor Company; Georgia-Pacific Corporation; ICI Americas Inc.; J.P. Morgan Chase & Co., Incorporated; Longwood Foundation, Inc.; McDonald's Corporation; Merck & Co., Inc.; Merrill Lynch; Pharmacia Corporation; Phillips Petroleum Company.

MICHAEL P. MORTON, P.A.

Established in 1994

1203 NORTH ORANGE STREET

WILMINGTON, DELAWARE 19801

Telephone: 302-426-1313

Fax: 302-426-1300

Mobile Text Email: 3024206333@page.nextel.com

Email: MPMPA@aol.com

URL: http://www.lawyers.com/mpmpa

Affiliated Pennsylvania Offices:

Crawford, Wilson & Ryan L.L.C.: 220 West Gay Street, West Chester, Pennsylvania, 19380-2934. Telephone: 610-431-4500. FAX: 610-430-8718.

Business Dispute Resolution, Commercial Litigation, Complex Commercial Litigation, Corporate Law, L.L.C.'s, Partnerships, Business Organizations, Commercial Real Estate Acquisitions, Commercial Contracts, Bankruptcy, Secured Credi-

(This Listing Continued)

MICHAEL P. MORTON, P.A., Wilmington—Continued

tors Rights, Unsecured Creditors Rights, Environmental Insurance, Insurance Coverage, Commercial Leasing Evictions; Landlord and Tenant Law, Civil Litigation, Federal Civil Litigation, Mobile Home Law.

MICHAEL P. MORTON, born West Chester, Pennsylvania, December 13, 1955; admitted to bar, 1986, Pennsylvania and Delaware; 1990, U.S. Supreme Court. *Education:* West Chester State College (B.A., 1979); Widener University School of Law (J.D., 1985). Member, The Delaware Journal of Corporate Law, 1983-1985. Law Clerk to the Honorable Jane R. Roth, U.S. District Court, District of Delaware, 1985-1986. *Member:* Pennsylvania, Delaware State (Member, Real Property Section), Federal and American (Member, Sections on: Tort and Insurance Practice; Litigation; General Practice; National Chairperson, Law Student Division, 1984-1985; Young Lawyers Executive Council Member, 1985, 1989-1991; Young Lawyers Liaison to Legal Education and Admissions to the Bar, 1990-1992; Vice Chairperson, Commercial Torts Committee, 1994-1995) Bar Associations.

LEGAL SUPPORT PERSONNEL

PARALEGALS

MARYLOU REITH, born Philadelphia, Pennsylvania, September 8, 1967. *Education:* University of Delaware (B.S.A.S., 1989; ABA Approved Paralegal Certification, 1991). Alpha Kappa Delta. Registered Paralegal Designation, 2000; Delaware Paralegal Association, Program Director, 1992-1994; Membership Director, 1997-2000. Bar Activities Director 2000; Vice-President, 2001-2002.

CHRISTINE R. CREASEY, born Baltimore, Maryland, August 27, 1947. *Education:* University of Delaware (B.A., 1993); Widener University (ABA, Paralegal Certificate, 1999). Sigma Tau Delta. Member, Delaware Paralegal Association, Program Director, 2001-2002.

MURPHY SPADARO & LANDON

824 MARKET STREET, SUITE 700
P.O. BOX 8989
WILMINGTON, DELAWARE 19899
Telephone: 302-654-4600
Telecopier: 302-654-4775
Email: msl@msllaw.com

Admiralty Law, Banking Law, Commercial Law, Bankruptcy and Creditor Rights, Civil Litigation, Commercial Litigation, Corporate Litigation, Employment Law. Environmental Law, Insurance Coverage, Insurance Defense, International Law, Labor Law, Products Liability, Public Utility Regulation and Tort Litigation.

FRANCIS J. MURPHY, born Wilmington, Delaware, November 10, 1952; admitted to bar, 1977, Delaware and U.S. District Court, District of Delaware; 1978, U.S. Court of Appeals, Third Circuit. *Education:* University of Delaware (B.A., with high honors, 1974); Dickinson School of Law (J.D., 1977); National Institute for Trial Advocacy (Diploma, 1983). Judicial Clerkship, Delaware Superior Court, 1977-1978. Counsel to: Delaware State House of Representatives, 1985; Delaware State Senate, 1987-1989; 1999—. Delegate, Moscow Conference, 1990. Faculty: Delaware State Bar Association, "Insurance Coverage Litigation" (1997); Lorman Education Services, "Delaware Insurance Law" (1999); NBI, "Insurance Bad Faith Litigation in Delaware" (1997). *Member:* Delaware (Member, Sections on: Litigation; Commercial Litigation; General Legislation) and American (Member, Sections on: Insurance Practice; International Law) Bar Associations; Defense Research Institute; International Bar Association. ***PRACTICE AREAS:*** Insurance Coverage; Bankruptcy Law. ***Email:*** fmurphy@msllaw.com

JOHN S. SPADARO, born Brooklyn, New York, June 18, 1959; admitted to bar, 1987, New York, New Jersey and U.S. District Court, District of New Jersey; 1993, Delaware and U.S. District Court, District of Delaware; 1997, U.S. Court of Appeals, Third Circuit. *Education:* Mount St. Mary's College (B.A., cum laude, 1981); Fordham University (J.D., 1986). Faculty Member: Lorman Education Services, "Insurance Law," May 7, 1999; Superior Court Trial Practice Forum, "Oral Argument in the Superior Court: From Preparation to Practice," May 24, 1996; National Business Institute Seminar, "Insurance Coverage Law in Delaware," September 30, 1994; Superior Court Trial Practice Forum, "Attorney-Client Privilege and Work Product Protection: A Practical Survey on Inadvertent Production and Other Waiver Issues," April 21, 1994. Editor: "The Most Troublesome Exclusions and Endorsements in CGL Policies - Recent Developments," presented at Defense Research Institute Practice Seminar, "Self-Insurers and Risk Managers," September 22, 1988. *Member:* Delaware (Member, Sections on: Tort and Insurance Practice; International Law; Environmental Law; Committees on Insurance Coverage Litigation and Professional Officers' and Directors' Liability Law) and American (Member, Sections on: Tort and Insurance Practice; International Law) Bar Associations; Defense Research Institute; International Bar Association (Member, Sections on: Business Law; Committees on Procedures for Settling Disputes; International Environmental Law; Insurance). ***PRACTICE AREAS:*** Insurance Coverage; Commercial Litigation; Public Utility Regulation. ***Email:*** jspadaro@msllaw.com

(This Listing Continued)

ROGER D. LANDON, born Salisbury, Maryland, August 14, 1961; admitted to bar, 1986, Delaware; 1987, U.S. District Court, District of Delaware; 1988, U.S. Court of Appeals, Third Circuit. *Education:* University of Virginia (B.S., Commerce, 1983); Widener University School of Law (J.D., 1986). Phi Delta Phi. *Member:* Delaware (Member, Sections on: Litigation; Torts and Insurance Practice; Worker's Compensation) and American (Member, Section on: Torts and Insurance Practice) Bar Associations; Defense Research Institute; Defense Counsel of Delaware; American Board of Trial Advocates (Associate). ***PRACTICE AREAS:*** Insurance Defense; Subrogation; Products Liability; Torts. ***Email:*** rlandon@msllaw.com

JONATHAN L. PARSHALL, born Wilmington, Delaware, October 4, 1956; admitted to bar, 1992, Pennsylvania; 1994, Delaware and U.S. District Court, District of Delaware; 1998, U.S. District Court, Eastern District of Pennsylvania; 2001, U.S. Court of Appeals, Third Circuit. *Education:* University of Delaware (B.A., with honors, 1977); Columbia University Graduate School of Business (M.B.A., 1979); Delaware Law School of Widener University (J.D., magna cum laude, 1992). Staff Member, 1990-1991 and Note and Comment Editor, 1991-1992, Delaware Journal of Corporate Law. Law Clerk to the Honorable Maurice A. Harnett III, Delaware Court of Chancery, 1992-1993. *Member:* Delaware (Member, Section on: Corporate Law) and American (Member, Section on: Business Law) Bar Associations. ***PRACTICE AREAS:*** Insurance Coverage; Insurance Defense; Corporate Litigation; Civil Litigation. ***Email:*** jonp@msllaw.com

CHASE T. BROCKSTEDT, born Dover, Delaware, December 29, 1973; admitted to bar, 1999, Delaware; 2000, U.S. District Court, District of Delaware. *Education:* University of North Carolina at Wilmington (B.A., 1996); Widener University School of Law ((J.D., 1999). Judicial Extern to the Honorable Richard S. Gebelein, Superior Court of Delaware. Judicial Law Clerk to Honorable Richard R. Cooch, Superior Court of Delaware, 1999-2000. *Member:* Delaware (Member, Sections on: Litigation; New Lawyers; Tort and Insurance Practice) and American (Member, Sections on: Business Law Litigation; Insurance Practice) Bar Associations. ***PRACTICE AREAS:*** Commercial Litigation; Insurance Defense; Insurance Coverage; Civil Litigation. ***Email:*** chaseb@msllaw.com

REPRESENTATIVE CLIENTS: Underwriters at Lloyd's, London; Kemper National Insurance Companies; The Hartford Insurance Group; Chubb Group of Insurance Companies; Selective Insurance Company; Kmart Corporation; Bird Corporation; Penn National Insurance Company; Progressive Insurance Company; Fireman's Fund Insurance Company; Daimler-Chrysler Corporation; Canal Insurance Company; Salvation Army; Delaware Public Service Commission; Royal and SunAlliance; Admiral Insurance Company; Pawtucket Insurance Company; Federated Insurance Company; Windsor Insurance Company; Lonestar Steakhouse and Saloon of Wilmington, Inc.

NOLTE & BRODOWAY, P.A.

THREE MILL ROAD
SUITE 304
WILMINGTON, DELAWARE 19806
Telephone: 302-777-1700
Telecopier: 302-777-1705
Email: NOLBRO@AOL.COM

Employment Law, Insurance Defense, Workers Compensation, Commercial Litigation, Bankruptcy, Real Estate, Wills and Probate, Trusts and Estates, Asbestos, Toxic Torts.

R. STOKES NOLTE, born Woodbury, New Jersey, March 16, 1958; admitted to bar, 1984, Delaware; 1985, U.S. District Court, District of Delaware. *Education:* University of Delaware (B.S., 1980); California Western School of Law (J.D., 1983). Phi Alpha Delta. Member, Advocacy Honors Board, 1983. *Member:* Delaware State Bar Association; Defense Counsel of Delaware. ***PRACTICE AREAS:*** Workers Compensation; Employment Law; Bankruptcy; Insurance Defense.

BARBARA A. BRODOWAY, born Wilmington, Delaware, December 15, 1959; admitted to bar, 1985, Delaware; 1986, U.S. District Court, District of Delaware. *Education:* University of Delaware (B.A., 1981); Villanova Law School (J.D., 1985). *Member:* Delaware State Bar Association (Member, Real Estate Section). ***PRACTICE AREAS:*** Personal Injury; Real Estate; Insurance Defense; Asbestos; Toxic Torts; Wills; Probate; Incorporation.

REPRESENTATIVE CLIENTS: Blue Hen Claims Services, Inc.; Colonial Insurance Co. of California; County Insulation Co.; Crawford & Co.; First Delaware Insurance Co.; Gallagher Bassett; Helmsman Management Group; ITT Hartford; Liberty Mutual Insurance Co.; M. Davis and Sons; National Union Fire Insurance Co.; New Castle Mutual Insurance Co.; Ohio Casualty Insurance Co.; Peninsula Insurance Co.; Prudential Insurance Co.; Service Master; Universal Underwriters Group; Zurich American Insurance Co.; Westfield Group; Old Guard Insurance Co.

OBERLY & JENNINGS, P.A.

800 DELAWARE AVENUE
P.O. BOX 2054
WILMINGTON, DELAWARE 19899-2054
Telephone: 302-576-2000
Fax: 302-576-2004

General Civil Litigation, Criminal Defense, Personal Injury, Commercial, Corporate, Business, Government Relations.

CHARLES M. OBERLY, III, born Wilmington, Delaware, November 9, 1946; admitted to bar, 1971, Delaware and U.S. District Court, District of Delaware; 1978, U.S. Supreme Court; 1980, U.S. Court of Appeals, Third Circuit. *Education:* Wesley College (A.A., 1966); Pennsylvania State University (B.A., magna cum laude, 1968) Phi Beta Kappa; University of Virginia (J.D., 1971). Clerk to the Honorable James L. Latchum, U.S. District Court Judge, 1971-1972. Author: "Stop and Frisk, Pat Down Searches," Pepperdine Law Review, 1980. Deputy Attorney General, Delaware, 1975-1976 and 1979-1982. Delaware State Prosecutor, 1976-1979. Attorney General, State of Delaware, 1983-1995. Candidate, U.S. Senate, 1994. *Member:* Delaware State Bar Association; Delaware Trial Lawyers Association. ***PRACTICE AREAS:*** Commercial; Corporate; Civil Litigation; Government Relations; Corporate Investigations; Criminal Defense; Personal Injury.

KATHLEEN M. JENNINGS, born Wilmington, Delaware, April 4, 1953; admitted to bar, 1978, Delaware, U.S. Court of Appeals, Third Circuit and U.S. District Court, District of Delaware. *Education:* University of Delaware (B.A., high honors degree with distinction, 1975); Villanova University (J.D., 1978). Author: "DNA Guide to Basic Principals in the Forensic Field," The Advocate, May, 1990. Deputy Attorney General, 1978-1983 and 1984-1993. Chief Deputy Attorney General, 1994-1995. *Member:* Delaware State Bar Association; Delaware Trial Lawyers Association. ***PRACTICE AREAS:*** Criminal Law; Personal Injury; General Civil Litigation; Business.

KAREN SULLIVAN, born Hammond, Indiana, August 1, 1970; admitted to bar, 1998, Maryland; 1999, Delaware. *Education:* University of Delaware (B.A., 1992); Georgetown University (J.D., cum laude, 1998). *Member:* Delaware State Bar Association; Delaware Association of Criminal Defense Lawyers. ***PRACTICE AREAS:*** Criminal Law; Personal Injury; Civil Litigation. ***Email:*** ksullivan@ojlaw.com

---

MARK D. OLSON & COMPANY, L.L.C.

SUITE 301, LITTLE FALLS CENTRE TWO
2751 CENTERVILLE ROAD
WILMINGTON, DELAWARE 19808
Telephone: 302-995-7080
Telecopier: 302-995-7075
Email: mark@markolsonlaw.com
URL: http://www.markolsonlaw.com

Like Kind Exchanges, Taxation, Estate Planning, Estate Administration, Family Business Planning, Business Succession Planning.

MARK D. OLSON, born Johnson City, New York, April 3, 1945; admitted to bar, 1976, Delaware; 1985, U.S. Tax Court. *Education:* State University of New York (B.A., 1973); University of Pennsylvania (J.D., 1976). Phi Beta Kappa. Member, Preliminary Review Committee of Board on Professional Responsibility of Supreme Court of Delaware. *Member:* Delaware State (Member, Sections on: Tax; Estates and Trusts) and American (Member, Sections on: Taxation; Real Property, Probate and Trust) Bar Associations. (Also Member of firm Wilson, Halbrook & Bayard, Georgetown, Delaware). ***Email:*** mark@markolsonlaw.com

---

PACHULSKI, STANG, ZIEHL, YOUNG & JONES

PROFESSIONAL CORPORATION
919 NORTH MARKET STREET, 16TH FLOOR
P.O. BOX 8705
WILMINGTON, DELAWARE 19899-8705
Telephone: 302-652-4100
Telecopier: 302-652-4400
URL: http://www.pszyj.com

Los Angeles, California Office: 10100 Santa Monica Boulevard, 11th Floor. Telephone: 310-277-6910. Facsimile: 310-201-0760.
San Francisco, California Office: Three Embarcadero Center, Suite 1020. Telephone: 415-263-7000. Facsimile: 415-263-7010.

(This Listing Continued)

New York, New York Office: 461 Fifth Avenue, 25th Floor. Telephone: 212-624-9430. Facsimile: 212-624-9435.

Bankruptcy, Corporate Reorganization, Debtor-Creditor Matters, Insurance Insolvency, Civil Litigation, Business, Commercial Law, General Real Estate, and Corporate and Entertainment Transactions.

FIRM PROFILE: Pachulski, Stang, Ziehl , Young & Jones P.C. is a firm of sixty-three attorneys which specializes in corporate reorganization, bankruptcy and insolvency law, insurance insolvency, business and commercial litigation, and general real estate, corporate and transactual matters.

The Firm's bankruptcy attorneys are experienced in representing all major constituencies in out-of-court workouts and bankruptcy cases, including debtors, trustees, receivers, creditors' committees, secured creditors, bondholders, asset purchasers, and third party plan proponents, in domestic cross-border and international insolvencies.

The Firm's litigation attorneys have a wide range of experience in complex business litigation in state and federal courts, including litigating claims relating to contracts, commercial matters, business torts, insurance insolvencies, insurance coverage, reinsurance, director and officer liability, banking and real estate.

The Firm's demonstrated ability to effectively combine its bankruptcy and litigation disciplines distinguishes the firm from other firms and attorneys in the insolvency area. While our primary objective is to seek business solutions to our clients' problems, when results cannot be achieved by other means, the Firm's attorneys are highly experienced in prosecuting and defending complex litigation.

The Firm has acted as insolvency counsel for debtors and creditors in numerous industries, including extensive experience in the financial services, insurance, technology, health care, restaurant, agricultural, real estate, entertainment and retailing industries.

Debtors: Members of the Firm have represented a broad spectrum of debtors in successful out-of-court workouts and chapter 11 reorganizations. Representations by members of the firm in this area include: Sizzler International, Inc. and Related Entities; Breed Technologies, Inc.; Toni Braxton; TIE Communications, Inc.; W.R. Grace & Co.; Trans World Airlines, Inc.; Harnischfeger Industries, Inc.; Ameriserve Inc.; Zenith Electronics, Inc.; Inacom Corp and RBX Corp.; American Rice, Inc.; AgriBioTech, Inc.; Gateway Educational Products, Ltd., manufacturer of Hooked on Phonics; Penguin's Frozen Yogurt, Inc./Penguin's Place, Inc.; Imperial Hotels Corporation; TreeSweet Juice Co.; Buffums, Inc.; UniSil Corporation; Worlds of Wonder, Inc.; Sargent-Fletcher; Everex Systems, Inc.; San Fernando (Mission) Community Hospital; Sunbelt Nursery Group; Commonwealth Equity Trust and F&C International, Inc.

Creditors' Committees: Members of the Firm have represented numerous out-of-court and official bankruptcy creditors' committees comprising various creditor groups, including trade creditors, bondholders and other holders of unsecured debt. In the financial services area, the Firm has represented the official bankruptcy creditors' committees for First Executive Corporation (parent company to Executive Life Insurance Company and Executive Life Insurance Company of New York); First Capital Holdings Corp. (parent company to First Capital Life Insurance Company and Fidelity Bankers Life Insurance Company); Westwood Equities Corporation (parent company to the Ticor Title Group of Companies); and HomeFed Corp. (parent company to HomeFed Bank). The Firm has also represented numerous official creditors' committees and subcommittees in entertainment bankruptcy cases, including those formed in the matters of National Peregrine, Inc.; MCEG, Inc.; Qintex Entertainment, Inc.; Weintraub Entertainment, Inc.; and Fries Entertainment, Inc. Other significant committee representations include committees for American West Airlines, Inc.; B.U.M. International, Inc.; the employees of Orange County, California Leisure Technology, Inc. and subsidiaries; C&R Clothiers, Inc.; DAK Industries, Inc.; Specialty Restaurants Corporation; The Clothestime, Inc.; Guy F. Atkinson Company; Pannell Kerr Forster; Pizza Time Theaters, Inc. and Lynx Golf, Inc.

Special Interest Committees: The Firm has developed a particular expertise in representing specialized creditors' committees and subcommittees, such as bondholder, equity security, franchisee and membership committees. Members of the Firm have represented the Official Franchisee Committee of Pioneer Take-Out Corporation; the Official Committee of Equity Holders of Sun World Corporation; the Official Committee of Equity Holders of House of Fabrics, Inc.; the Official Committee of Marketing Representatives of FundAmerica, a multi-level international marketing organization; the Official Committee of Membership Creditors of American Adventure, a national recreational campground operator; the Official Bondholders Committee of Barry Jewelers, Inc.; and the Unofficial Bondholders Committee of Cirrus.

(This Listing Continued)

PACHULSKI, STANG, ZIEHL, YOUNG & JONES, PROFESSIONAL CORPORATION, Wilmington—Continued

Trustees: The Firm or its members have acted as general and special counsel for numerous chapter 7 and chapter 11 trustees. In particular, the Firm or its members have represented trustees for Triad America Corporation and related entities; Oppenheimer Industries, Inc.; National Lumber and Supply Co.; Rogersound Labs; Triad Healthcare; Hiuka America Corporation; First Lenders Indemnity Corporation; Magic Ford/Lincoln; 21st Century Film Corp.; and Papaho Corporation. The Firm is especially experienced in representing trustees in cases involving complicated fraud and asset misappropriation.

Secured and Major Unsecured Creditors/Bondholders: Members of the Firm routinely render advice to secured creditors and major unsecured creditors in transactions in which insolvency issues are of concern and have frequently represented such constituencies in bankruptcy proceedings. Typical secured and unsecured creditor clients of the Firm include: Heller Financial, Inc.; National Broadcasting Company, Inc.; The Hahn Company; First Nationwide Bank; Sony Pictures Entertainment, Inc.; Bass Hotels, Inc.; Hilton Hotel Corporation; Barclays Bank; and Paine Webber, Inc.

Purchasers and Investors: Members of the Firm have represented asset purchasers and outside investors regarding acquisitions of the stock or assets of troubled or insolvent companies in many matters including: Hiller Aviation Inc.; Irvine Ranch Farmer's Market; Eaton Leonard Corporation; Eastern Airlines; Hillsborough Holdings; BiCoastal Corporation; General Development Corporation; Vagabond, Inc.; Physicians Clinical Laboratory, Inc.; Sugar Bowl Corporation; and General Cellular Corporation.

Health Care: Lawyers of the firm are nationally recognized experts on the unique issues that arise in the reorganization or liquidation of health care-related entities. The firm has extensive experience in representing various constituencies in this highly regulated industry which is undergoing dynamic change. We have represented health care entities, trustees, and governmental and private creditors in some of the nation's largest health care bankruptcy cases. The firm's lawyers lecture extensively and publish in this area, and one of the firm's members presently chairs the ABA's Health Care Related Bankruptcy Issues Workgroup. Bankruptcy cases in which the firm or its lawyers have been involved include: FPA Management, Inc., First American Health Care of Georgia, Inc., St. Johns Home Health Agency, Mederi of Dade County, Inc., Virginia Manor Convalescent Home, Maxicare (aka Family Health Services), Triad Healthcare and San Fernando (Mission) Community Hospital.

Bankruptcy Litigation: The Firm prides itself on its ability to effectively litigate all matters arising in the specialized forum of the bankruptcy court. The Firm is particularly experienced in and has litigated hundreds of complicated fraudulent transfer and preference claims, having represented several major corporations and institutions. The Firm also has extensive experience in defending large national consumer credit providers in class action and other matters, including Sears Roebuck & Co. and Associates Have Equity Services. The Firm also successfully defended E.F. Hutton and Alexander Hamilton Life Insurance Companies against lender liability claims exceeding $200 million asserted by debtors in chapter 11 cases.

General Litigation: General business litigation is a significant part of the Firm's practice. The Firm has developed a number of litigation specialties, including the prosecution and defense of lender liability claims, major fraud actions, director and officer liability claims; employment matters; and hotel management; license and franchise termination disputes. Successful representations include: recovering a $9 million judgment against the largest private diagnostic laboratory in the United States and its owner based upon breach of an oral agreement; recovering a $7 million judgment arising out of a failed corporate acquisition transaction; recovering for numerous financial institutions on fidelity bond claims; successfully defending directors and officers of a number of failed financial institutions; obtaining a substantial settlement for a real estate development company in a fraud and breach of contract action brought against Bank of America; defending the developers of a major residential subdivision in litigation arising from land subsidence affecting hundreds of single-family homes; defending Imperial Bank against a $10 million claim brought by the FDIC; numerous representations of Fuji Photofilm, Bass Hotels and Hilton Hotel Corporation.

Insurance Litigation: The Firm also has extensive experience in insurance related litigation. Among other matters, members of the Firm have represented holders of over $750 million in group pension annuity contracts issued by Executive Life Insurance Company of California in one of the nation's largest life insurance conservatorships; participated on the steering committee for the pension group contract holders in the Mutual Benefit Life Insurance Company conservation proceeding; participated in the demutualization of Equitable Life Assurance Society of America representing the American Bar Retirement Association; represented pension policyholders in a trial regarding Mutual Life of New York's attempted unilateral restructuring of insurance contracts; handled liability insurance coverage issues for professional negligence claims of $250 million in conjunction with its representation of the Creditors' Committee of the Pannell Kerr Forster successor partnership; and represented Farmers Insurance Group in complex reinsurance matters.

Real Estate and Corporate: Our Firm's transactional practice includes the representation of clients in general real estate matters, including the acquisition, disposition, development and subdivision of real property; the leasing of commercial, industrial and retail space and the negotiation of acquisition, construction and permanent financing and workouts. The Firm also addresses clients regarding corporation, partnership and limited liability company matters, including SEC reporting stock plans, employment and compensation issues.

DAVID W. CARICKHOFF, JR, born Philadelphia, Pennsylvania, April 20, 1972; admitted to bar, 1998, Delaware, Pennsylvania and New Jersey. *Education:* Haverford College (B.A., 1994); Temple University (J.D., cum laude, 1998). Member, Temple Political and Civil Rights Law Review. Adjunt Professor of Law, Temple University, Spring 2000. *Member:* Delaware, Pennsylvania and American Bar Associations; American Bankruptcy Institute. ***PRACTICE AREAS:*** Bankruptcy Chapter 11; Corporate Restructuring; Corporate Reorganization; Bankruptcy Litigation. ***Email:*** dcarickhoff@pszyj.com

KATHLEEN MARSHALL DePHILLIPS, born Washington, D.C., February 19, 1970; admitted to bar, 2000, Pennsylvania and New Jersey (Not admitted in Delaware). *Education:* Catholic University of America (B.A., summa cum laude, 1992); George Washington University (J.D., 1997). ***PRACTICE AREAS:*** Bankruptcy. ***Email:*** kdephillips@pszyj.com

PETER J. DUHIG, born Neptune, New Jersey, December 28, 1972; admitted to bar, 2001, Delaware and Maryland. *Education:* University of Georgia (B.A., 1996); Catholic University of America (J.D., magna cum laude, 2000). ***PRACTICE AREAS:*** Bankruptcy. ***Email:*** pduhig@pszyj.com

BRUCE GROHSGAL, born Providence, Rhode Island, 1952; admitted to bar, 1981, New York; 1984, Pennsylvania; 1997, Delaware. *Education:* Brandeis University (B.A., magna cum laude, 1977); Columbia University (J.D., 1980). Harlan Fiske Stone Scholar. *Member:* Philadelphia, Pennsylvania and American Bar Associations; American Bankruptcy Institute. ***PRACTICE AREAS:*** Bankruptcy; Real Property. ***Email:*** bgroshgal@pszyj.com

CURTIS A. HEHN, born Panama Canal, Panama, December 19, 1969; admitted to bar, 1997, Pennsylvania and New Jersey (Not admitted in Delaware). *Education:* University of California at Berkeley (B.A., 1993); Rutgers University Law School, Camden (J.D., 1996). ***PRACTICE AREAS:*** Bankruptcy. ***Email:*** chehn@pszyj.com

LAURA DAVIS JONES, born Wilmington, Delaware, March 14, 1961; admitted to bar, 1986, Delaware; 1989, District of Columbia. *Education:* University of Delaware (B.S.B.A., magna cum laude, 1983); Dickinson School of Law (J.D., 1986). Alpha Mu Alpha; Beta Gamma Sigma; Delta Theta Phi (Officer, 1984-1985). Recipient, Presidential Achievement Award. Member, Board of Editors, 1984-1986 and Business Manager, 1985-1986, Dickinson Law Review. Member, Appellate Moot Court Board, 1984-1986. Law Clerk to the Honorable Helen S. Balick, U.S. Bankruptcy Court, District of Delaware, 1986-1987. Contributing Author, "Bankruptcy Business Acquisitions," LexMed Publishing, 1998. Member, Private Panel of Bankruptcy Trustees, District of Delaware, 1989—. *Member:* Delaware State (Member, Sections on: Commercial Law; Litigation; Member, Bankruptcy Subcommittee) and American (Member, Sections on: Business Law; Litigation; Member, Business Bankruptcy Committee; Member, Subcommittees on: Chapter 11 Bankruptcies; Bankruptcy Rules) Bar Associations; Bar Association of the District of Columbia. ***PRACTICE AREAS:*** Bankruptcy Chapter 11; Bankruptcy Litigation; Commercial Workouts; International Insolvency; Out of Court Debt Restructuring. ***Email:*** ljones@pszyj.com

CHRISTOPHER J. LHULIER, born Wilmington, Delaware, September 6, 1970; admitted to bar, 1998, Massachusetts; 1999, Pennsylvania and Delaware; 2000, U.S. District Court, District of Delaware. *Education:* University of Delaware (B.A., International Relations, 1992); Villanova University (J.D., 1998). Member, Project Bosnia. Author, "Information Access Rights Based on International Human Rights Law," 45 BUFF.L.REV. 899 (1997). ***LANGUAGES:*** French and Spanish. ***PRACTICE AREAS:*** Chapter 11 Bankruptcy; Corporate Restructuring and Reorganization. ***Email:*** clhulier@pszyj.com

RACHEL SARAH LOWY, born Raleigh, North Carolina, February 25, 1973; admitted to bar, 1998, Delaware; 1999, Pennsylvania. *Education:* University of Georgia (B.A., 1995); Widener University School of Law (J.D., 1998). Member, Delaware Journal of Corporate Law, Bluebook Editor, 1997-1998. Certificate of Achievement Federal Income Tax & Wills and Trusts. Law Clerk

(This Listing Continued)

to the Honorable Judges, Lee, Graves and Stokes, Delaware Superior Court, 1998-1999. Wolcott Fellowship with Delaware Supreme Court, 1997-1998. *Member:* Delaware State and Pennsylvania Bar Associations. ***Email:*** rlowy@pszyj.com

JAMES E. O'NEILL, III, born Devon, Pennsylvania, 1960; admitted to bar, 1985, Pennsylvania; 2001, Delaware. *Education:* Georgetown University (B.S., 1982); Villanova University (J.D., 1985). Member: Consumer Bankruptcy Assistance Project; National Association of Bankruptcy Trustees. Co-Chair: Committee on Alternative Dispute Resolution in Bankruptcy Court; Chapter 7 Trustee Panel for District of Delaware; Chapter 7 Trustee for District of New Jersey. ***PRACTICE AREAS:*** Corporate Law; Bankruptcy Law; Corporate Reorganizations; Commercial and Residential Foreclosures; Real Estate. ***Email:*** joneill@pszyj.com

MICHAEL R. SEIDL, born Baltimore, Maryland, March 22, 1966; admitted to bar, 1996, District of Columbia; 1998, U.S. Court of Veterans Appeals; 2000, Delaware. *Education:* James Madison University (B.A., 1988; M.A., magna cum laude, 1990); University of Delaware (Ph.D., 1995); Georgetown University (J.D., cum laude, 1996). Managing Editor, Journal of Law and Policy in International Business. Author: "A Tale of Two Discourses," 47 Stan L. Rev. 247, 1995; "Cross-Cultural Commerce in Shakespeare's Merchant of Venice," 10 Am.U. J. Intl. Law Rev. 859, 1995. Member, Modern Language Association, 1990—. *Member:* The District of Columbia Bar. ***PRACTICE AREAS:*** Business Litigation; Chapter 11 Bankruptcy. ***Email:*** mseidl@pszyj.com

ROSALIE SPELMAN, born Washington, D.C., December 11, 1951; admitted to bar, 1981, New York; 1998, New Jersey; 1999, Pennsylvania (Not admitted in Delaware). *Education:* University of Illinois (B.A., high honors, 1974); Northwestern University (M.A.T., 1975); Georgetown University (J.D., 1980). Member, Jessup International Law World Cup, 1980. ***PRACTICE AREAS:*** Bankruptcy. ***Email:*** rspelman@pszyj.com

PALMER BIEZUP & HENDERSON LLP

1223 FOULK ROAD
WILMINGTON, DELAWARE 19803
Telephone: 302-594-0895; 302-478-7443
FAX: 302-478-7625
Email: pbh1@pbh.com

Philadelphia, Pennsylvania Office: 956 Public Ledger Building, 620 Chestnut Street, Independence Mall West, 19106-3409. Telephone: 215-625-9900. FAX: 215-625-0185.
New York, New York Office: 140 Broadway, 46th Floor, PMB 46030, 10005. Telephone: 212-406-1855. FAX: 212-858-7651.
Camden, New Jersey Office: 200 North 5th Street, 08102-1204. Telephone: 856-428-7717. FAX: 856-338-1008.

Admiralty and Maritime, International, Insurance and Reinsurance, Commercial, Bankruptcy, Yachts and Recreational Craft, Aviation, Personal Injury, Product Liability, Professional Liability and Transportation Casualty Defense. General Civil, Trial and Appellate Practice in all Courts.

FIRM PROFILE: The firm conducts a Mid-Atlantic regional civil defense litigation practice concentrating on disputes arising from domestic and international maritime commerce, the offshore energy and insurance and reinsurance, industries, domestic insurance, petrochemical and manufacturing sectors, general casualty, and reinsurance and transportation. The firm's lawyers and staff are dedicated to providing quality legal service on a timely and cost-effective basis.

MEMBER OF FIRM

MICHAEL B. McCAULEY, born Philadelphia, Pennsylvania, September 23, 1951; admitted to bar, 1979, Florida; 1980, Pennsylvania; 1985, Delaware; 1986, New Jersey; 1991, New York; U.S. District Court, Eastern District of Pennsylvania; U.S. District Court, District of Delaware; U.S. District Court, District of New Jersey; U.S. District Court, Southern District of New York and U.S. Supreme Court; U.S. Court of Appeals, Third and Second Circuits and U.S. Tax Court. *Education:* U.S. Merchant Marine Academy (B.S., 1973); University of Miami (J.D., 1978). Licenses: U.S. Coast Guard Master of Freight and Towing Vessels up to 1,600 gross tons upon oceans, 1975; Second Officer of any vessel upon oceans, unlimited tonnage, 1976; Pilot, Single Engine Land Aircraft, 1974. Contributing Author: *8 Benedict on Admiralty,* Desk Reference, 1995. Author: "Limitation of Liability and Recreational Vessels," Tulane Maritime Law Journal, Vol. 16, No. 2, Spring, 1992; "Admiralty: The Common Law Afloat?" The Delaware Lawyer, March, 1993; "Deep Ocean Mining in Legal Perspective," U.S. Department of Commerce Publication, NMRCKP-112, 1974. Co-Author: "Admiralty Jurisdiction and the Pleasure Craft," Matthew Bender & Co., Inc., (C.P. Theut ed. 1992); "Limitation of Liability and the Pleasure Craft," Matthew Bender & Co., Inc., (C.P. Theut ed. 1992). Lecturer: "Maritime Liens and Their Enforcement," Delaware Bar Association, May 31, 1991; "Limitation of Liability and Recreational Vessels," Maritime Law Association of the United States, October 31, 1991; FPSO's Regulatory International Offshore Insurance Conference, Oslo, June 6, 2000. *Member:* Philadelphia, Pennsylvania, Delaware, New Jersey State, New York State and American Bar Associations; The Florida Bar; Association of Average Adjusters of the United States; Association of Average Adjusters of the United Kingdom; Maritime Law Association of the United States (Chairman, Committee on Recreational Boating, 1994-1998; Member: Committee on Navigation and Coast Guard, 1984—; Committee on Products Liability, 1988—); Lawyer-Pilots Bar Association; International Association of Defense Counsel. ***PRACTICE AREAS:*** Admiralty Law; Insurance Law; Aviation Law; Litigation. ***Email:*** mccauley@pbh.com

(For complete biographical data on all personnel, see Professional Biographies at Philadelphia, Pennsylvania)

PEPPER HAMILTON LLP

Established in 1890
1201 MARKET STREET, SUITE 1600
P.O. BOX 1709
WILMINGTON, DELAWARE 19899-1709
Telephone: 302-777-6500
Telecopy: 302-656-8865
Email: phinfo@pepperlaw.com
URL: http://www.pepperlaw.com

Philadelphia, Pennsylvania Office: 3000 Two Logan Square, Eighteenth and Arch Streets, 19103-2799. Telephone: 215-981-4000. Fax: 215-981-4750.
Washington, D.C. Office: Hamilton Square, 600 Fourteenth Street, N.W. 20005-2004. Telephone: 202-220-1200. Fax: 202-220-1665.
Detroit, Michigan Office: 100 Renaissance Center, 36th Floor, 48243-1157. Telephone: 313-259-7110. Fax: 313-259-7926.
New York, New York Office: 1180 Avenue of the Americas, 14th Floor, 10036-8401. Telephone: 212-899-5090. Fax: 212-899-5091.
Pittsburgh, Pennsylvania Office: 500 Grant Street, 50th Floor, 15219-2502. Telephone: 412-454-5000. Fax: 412-281-0717.
Berwyn, Pennsylvania Office: 1235 Westlakes Drive, Suite 400, 19312-2401. Telephone: 610-640-7800. Fax: 610-640-7835.
Cherry Hill, New Jersey Office: LibertyView Building, Suite 420, 457 Haddonfield Road, 08002-2220. Telephone: 856-910-7200. Fax: 856-665-7743.
Harrisburg, Pennsylvania Office: 200 One Keystone Plaza, North Front and Market Streets, P.O. Box 1181, 17108-1181. Telephone: 717-255-1155. Fax: 717-238-0575.
Princeton, New Jersey Office: 300 Alexander Park, 08543-5276. Telephone: 609-452-0808. Fax: 609-452-1147.
Tysons Corner, Virginia Office: 8280 Greensboro Drive, Suite 800, 22102-3807. Telephone: 703-748-3900. Fax: 703-356-0005.

General Practice.

PARTNERS

RICHARD P. ECKMAN, born Wilmington, DE, 1951; admitted to bar, 1977, Delaware; 1978, District of Columbia. *Education:* Hamilton College (A.B., 1973); Catholic University (J.D., 1977); Georgetown University (M.L.T., 1980). *Member:* Delaware State Bar Association (Chairman, Banking Law Committee, 1984-1992; Chairman, Commercial Law Section, 1989-1991); Delaware Entrepreneurs' Forum (President, 1994-1996); Delaware Innovation Fund (Board Member and Treasurer, 1995—). ***PRACTICE AREAS:*** Mergers and Acquisitions; Banking Law; Corporate Law; Real Estate. ***Email:*** eckmanr@pepperlaw.com

DAVID M. FOURNIER, born Whitinsville, MA, 1964; admitted to bar, 1990, Delaware; 1991, Pennsylvania. *Education:* Pennsylvania State University (B.A., 1985); Villanova University (J.D., 1989). Member, Villanova Law Review. Chair, International Law Section, Delaware State Bar Association, 1994-1995. ***PRACTICE AREAS:*** Business Reorganization; Bankruptcy. ***Email:*** fournierd@pepperlaw.com

M. DUNCAN GRANT, born Madison, WI, 1950; admitted to bar, 1975, Pennsylvania; 1991, Delaware. *Education:* Princeton University (A.B., 1972); University of Pennsylvania (J.D., 1975). Editor-in-Chief, University of Pennsylvania Law Review, 1974-1975. Law Clerk to Hon. Arlin M. Adams, U.S. Court of Appeals, Third Circuit, 1975-1976. (Also at Philadelphia, Pennsylvania Office). ***PRACTICE AREAS:*** Corporate Litigation; Commercial Litigation. ***Email:*** grantm@pepperlaw.com

CHRISTOPHER J. LAMB, born Wynnewood, PA, 1962; admitted to bar, 1988, New Jersey; 1989, Pennsylvania and Delaware. *Education:* LaSalle University (B.A., maxima cum laude, 1984); Temple University (J.D., cum laude, 1988). ***PRACTICE AREAS:*** Commercial Law; Real Estate; Bankruptcy. ***Email:*** lambc@pepperlaw.com

SEAN P. McDEVITT, born Springfield, PA, 1961; admitted to bar, 1990, Delaware; 1993, Pennsylvania. *Education:* University of Delaware (B.S., 1983);

(This Listing Continued)

PEPPER HAMILTON LLP, Wilmington—Continued

Temple University (J.D., cum laude, 1990). (Also at Berwyn, Pennsylvania Office). ***PRACTICE AREAS:*** Litigation; Labor Law. ***Email:*** mcdevitts@pepperlaw.com

DAVID B. STRATTON, born Wilmington, DE, 1953; admitted to bar, 1978, Delaware. *Education:* Gettysburg College (A.B., magna cum laude, 1975); University of Pittsburgh (J.D., cum laude, 1978). Assistant Editor, University of Pittsburgh Law Review. Member: American Bankruptcy Institute. *Member:* Delaware State Bar Association (Chairman, Commercial Law Section, 1983-1984). ***PRACTICE AREAS:*** Bankruptcy Law; Creditors Rights; Commercial Banking. ***Email:*** strattond@pepperlaw.com

BENJAMIN STRAUSS, born Haifa, Israel, 1955; admitted to bar, 1991, Delaware, Pennsylvania and New Jersey. *Education:* Bar-Ilan University, Israel (B.A., 1976; M.B.A., 1983); Widener University (J.D., magna cum laude, 1990). ***LANGUAGES:*** Danish, Hebrew. ***PRACTICE AREAS:*** Corporate Law; Commercial Law; Securities. ***Email:*** straussb@pepperlaw.com

ASSOCIATES

WILMER C. BETTINGER, born Baltimore, MD, 1940; admitted to bar, 1972, Delaware. *Education:* University of Maryland (B.A., 1966); Indiana University (J.D., 1971). ***PRACTICE AREAS:*** Banking Law; Creditors Rights. ***Email:*** bettingerw@pepperlaw.com

AARON A. GARBER, born Philadelphia, PA, 1968; admitted to bar, 1997, Pennsylvania; 1998, New Jersey; 1999, Delaware. *Education:* University of Colorado, Boulder (B.A., 1991); Temple University (J.D., cum laude, 1997). Editor, Temple Environmental Law & Technology Journal. ***PRACTICE AREAS:*** Bankruptcy. ***Email:*** garbera@pepperlaw.com

ADAM HILLER, born Baltimore, MD, 1971; admitted to bar, 1997, Maryland; 1999, District of Columbia (Not admitted in Delaware). *Education:* Claremont McKenna College (B.A., cum laude, 1993); University of Maryland (J.D., 1997). Law Clerk to Hon. E. Stephen Derby, U.S. Bankruptcy Court, District of Maryland, 1997-1998. ***PRACTICE AREAS:*** Bankruptcy. ***Email:*** hillera@pepperlaw.com

JOSEPH S. NAYLOR, born Wilmington, DE, 1973; admitted to bar, 1999, Delaware. *Education:* University of Delaware (B.A., cum laude, 1996); Widener University (J.D., 1999). Member, Delaware Journal of Corporate Law. Law Clerk to Justice Joseph T. Walsh, Supreme Court of Delaware, 1999-2000. ***PRACTICE AREAS:*** Commercial Litigation. ***Email:*** naylorj@pepperlaw.com

ANDREA BETH UNTERBERGER, born Long Island, NY, 1963; admitted to bar, 1998, Delaware. *Education:* Brown University (B.A., 1984); Widener University (J.D., magna cum laude, 1997). Editor, Delaware Journal of Corporate Law. Law Clerk to Hon. William B. Chandler, III, Delaware Court of Chancery, 1997-1998. ***LANGUAGES:*** Spanish. ***PRACTICE AREAS:*** Commercial Litigation; Corporate Litigation. ***Email:*** unterbergera@pepperlaw.com

PHILLIPS, GOLDMAN & SPENCE, P.A.

Established in 1985

1200 NORTH BROOM STREET
WILMINGTON, DELAWARE 19806
Telephone: 302-655-4200
Telecopier: 302-655-4210
Email: pgs@pgslaw.com

West Chester Office: 103 South High Street, 19382. Telephone: 610-701-9706. Telecopier: 610-701-9707.

Commercial, Corporate, Toxic Tort, Environmental, Superfund , Bankruptcy and Personal Injury Litigation, Insurance Coverage and Defense, Commercial Bankruptcy, Commercial Real Estate, Business Practice and Criminal Defense.

FIRM PROFILE: In 1990, three attorneys with 38 years of combined legal experience founded Phillips, Goldman & Spence in order to provide the highest quality legal services to our distinguished and diversified clientele. Our clients include large and small corporations and businesses, insurance companies and numerous individuals. Our attorneys, trained paralegals and superior support staff, pride themselves on understanding and satisfying each client's particularized needs.

Phillips, Goldman & Spence partners are experienced lawyers who have earned the respect of their peers and the courts. The associates are mentored by the partners in the areas of specialty best suited to their individual preferences and strengths. The law firm occupies a renovated Victorian mansion which provides an excellent working environment for the members of the firm and a professional and comfortable ambiance for our clients. Our computer network gives us the advantage of immediate access to file information, fast and effective legal research capabilities and direct electronic mail communication with our clients. The result is the ability to offer an efficient, thorough and economical work product of the highest quality by dedicated professionals whose primary concern is the satisfaction of the client.

JOHN C. PHILLIPS, JR., born Cleveland, Ohio, November 15, 1948; admitted to bar, 1974, Delaware; 1981, U.S. Court of Appeals, Third Circuit; 1983, U.S. Supreme Court. *Education:* Vanderbilt University (B.A., 1971); Dickinson School of Law (J.D., 1974). Editor, Dickinson Law Review, 1972-1974. Assistant Legal Counsel to the Governor of the State of Delaware, 1977-1981. Chairperson, Allocation Committee, Delaware Sand & Gravel PRP Defense Group. *Member:* Delaware and American Bar Associations; Defense Research Institute; Defense Counsel of Delaware. ***PRACTICE AREAS:*** Bankruptcy Litigation; Business Litigation; Toxic Torts; Environmental; Insurance Coverage; Insurance Defense. ***Email:*** jcp@pgslaw.com

ROBERT S. GOLDMAN, born Hartford, Connecticut, June 29, 1953; admitted to bar, 1979, Florida; 1980, Pennsylvania; 1981, New Jersey; 1986, Delaware; 1993, Maryland. *Education:* University of Connecticut (B.A., cum laude, 1975); University of Miami (J.D., 1978). *Member:* Philadelphia, Pennsylvania, Delaware, Maryland State and American (Subcommittee, Section on: EMF Litigation) Bar Associations; The Florida Bar; Defense Research Institute; Defense Counsel of Delaware. ***PRACTICE AREAS:*** Insurance Defense Law; Toxic Tort; Environmental; Personal Injury Litigation; Bankruptcy Litigation. ***Email:*** rsg@pgslaw.com

STEPHEN W. SPENCE, born Abington, Pennsylvania, January 19, 1953; admitted to bar, 1981, Delaware; 1982, Pennsylvania; 1986, U.S. Court of Appeals, Third Circuit. *Education:* University of Delaware (B.S., 1975); Delaware Law School of Widener University (J.D., cum laude, 1981). Member, Moot Court Honor Society. Business Manager, Delaware Journal of Corporate Law, 1980-1981. Member, Panel of Bankruptcy Trustees for the District of Delaware, 1983-1989. *Member:* Delaware (Member, Sections on: Real Estate; Commercial Law) and Pennsylvania Bar Associations; American Bankruptcy Institute; National Association of Bankruptcy Trustees. ***PRACTICE AREAS:*** Commercial Litigation; Bankruptcy; Commercial Real Estate; Small Business Practice. ***Email:*** sws@pgslaw.com

RICHARD P. S. HANNUM, born West Chester, Pennsylvania, May 7, 1944; admitted to bar, 1974, Delaware; 1979, Pennsylvania. *Education:* University of Pennsylvania (B.S., 1966); Dickinson School of Law (J.D., 1974). *Member:* Delaware State, Pennsylvania and American Bar Associations; National Board of Trial Advocacy; Civil Trial Advocates Association; John Stively Inn of Court. [U.S. Army, active duty, 1966-1969]. ***PRACTICE AREAS:*** Civil Litigation; Personal Injury Litigation; Bankruptcy Litigation. ***Email:*** rph@pgslaw.com

LISA CRESCI McLAUGHLIN, born Wilmington, Delaware, August 2, 1965; admitted to bar, 1992, Delaware and U.S. District Court, District of Delaware; 1993, Maryland and U.S. District Court, District of Maryland; 2000, U.S. Court of Appeals, 3rd Circuit. *Education:* University of Delaware (B.A., cum laude, 1987); Widener University School of Law (J.D., 1992). *Member:* Delaware, Maryland State and American Bar Associations; Defense Research Institute; Defense Counsel of Delaware. ***PRACTICE AREAS:*** Personal Injury; Toxic Tort; Insurance Defense; Bankruptcy Litigation; Collections. ***Email:*** lcm@pgslaw.com

JAMES P. HALL, born Wilmington, Delaware, February 12, 1966; admitted to bar, 1994, Delaware; 1995, U.S. District Court, District of Delaware. *Education:* University of Delaware (B.A., cum laude, 1988); Widener University School of Law at Wilmington (J.D., 1994). Richard S. Rodney Inn of Court. *Member:* Delaware and American Bar Associations; Defense Research Institute; Defense Counsel of Delaware; Delaware Trial Lawyers Association (Associate Member); The Association of Trial Lawyers of America (Associate Member). ***PRACTICE AREAS:*** Toxic Tort Litigation; Insurance Defense; Personal Injury Litigation; Bankruptcy Litigation; Business Litigation. ***Email:*** jph@pgslaw.com

ROSALIND D. WILLIAMS, born Vineland, New Jersey, February 18, 1966; admitted to bar, 1999, Delaware; 2000, U.S. District Court, District of Delaware and U.S. Court of Appeals, 3rd Circuit. *Education:* University of Delaware (B.A., 1988); Widener University School of Law (J.D., cum laude, 1999). *Member:* Delaware and American Bar Associations. ***PRACTICE AREAS:*** Commercial Real Estate; Residential Real Estate; Small Business Law; Bankruptcy; Contracts; Probate; Commercial Litigation. ***Email:*** rdw@pgslaw.com

MICHAEL F. DUGGAN, born Wilmington, Delaware, August 5, 1959; admitted to bar, 1994, Delaware and U.S. District Court, District of Delaware. *Education:* University of Delaware (B.S.M.E., 1981); Widener University School of Law (J.D., cum laude, 1993). Phi Delta Phi. American Inns of Court, 1996-1997. *Member:* Delaware State and American Bar Associations. ***Email:*** mfd@pgslaw.com

(This Listing Continued)

JOSEPH JAMES FARNAN, III, born Wilmington, Delaware, September 12, 1972; admitted to bar, 2000, Pennsylvania and Delaware. *Education:* Widener University (B.A., 1995; J.D., 1999). Pi Gama Mu; Pi Sigma Alpha. *Member:* Pennsylvania Bar Association. ***PRACTICE AREAS:*** Personal Injury; Commercial Litigation; Real Estate. ***Email:*** jjf@pgslaw.com

REPRESENTATIVE CLIENTS: E. I. du Pont de Nemours and Co.; Delmarva Power & Light Co.; Georgia Pacific Corp.; Sun Refining & Marketing Co.; Koppers Co., Inc.; Witco Corp.; Sherwin Williams; Mead Paper; Childers Products; Lyons Studio; Kemper Group; Travelers; Liberty Mutual; Home Insurance Co.; Maryland Casualty Co.; Royal Insurance Company of America; ITT Hartford Insurance Co.; Harleysville Insurance Co.; CIGNA; American International Adjustment Co., Inc.; Manville Personal Injury Settlement Trust; County Bank; Citicorp Acceptance Corp.; Nissan Acceptance Corp.; Ford Motor Acceptance Corp.; York Industries, Inc.; The Herty Foundation; Kentile Floors, Inc.; Phelps Dodge Industries, Inc.; Corning Inc.; Grant Wilson, Inc.; American Centennial Insurance Co.; Zurich Ins. Co.; Grotto Pizza, Inc.; Boulevard Ford, Inc.; W.R. Grace & Co.; Southern States Cooperative.

POTTER ANDERSON & CORROON LLP

Established in 1827

HERCULES PLAZA
1313 N. MARKET STREET
P.O. BOX 951
WILMINGTON, DELAWARE 19899-0951
Telephone: 302-984-6000
Fax: 302-658-1192
URL: http://www.potteranderson.com

General Practice. Corporation Law.

MEMBERS OF FIRM

ROBERT K. PAYSON, born Wilmington, Delaware, December 19, 1939; admitted to bar, 1964, Delaware. *Education:* Duke University (A.B., 1961; LL.B., 1964). Phi Delta Phi. Deputy Attorney General, State of Delaware, 1965-1966. Director, Delaware Bar Foundation, 1984-1987. Member, Delaware Court of Chancery Rules Committee, 1993—. *Member:* Delaware State and American Bar Associations. ***Email:*** rpayson@pacdelaware.com

LEONARD S. TOGMAN, born New York, N.Y., August 26, 1939; admitted to bar, 1964, New York; 1969, Delaware. *Education:* University of Pennsylvania (B.S.Econ., 1961); New York University (LL.B., 1964). Pomeroy Scholar. Order of the Coif. Member, New York University Law Review, 1963-1964. Trial Attorney, Tax Division, U.S. Department of Justice, 1964-1968. Chairman, Wilmington Tax Group, 1973-1974. Chairman, Delaware Investment Holding Company Committee, Delaware State Chamber of Commerce, 2000—. *Member:* Delaware State (Chairman, Taxation Section, 1978-1979, 1994-1995; Vice Chairman, 1993) and American Bar Associations. ***Email:*** ltogman@pacdelaware.com

MICHAEL D. GOLDMAN, born Jersey City, New Jersey, October 16, 1942; admitted to bar, 1968, Delaware. *Education:* Pennsylvania State University (B.A., 1964); Villanova University (J.D., 1967). Order of the Coif. Law Clerk, Delaware Court of Chancery, 1967-1968. Member, Delaware State Board of Bar Examiners, 1984-1993. Vice Chairman, Board of Bar Examiners, 1986-1987. Chairman, Board of Bar Examiners, 1988-1989. *Member:* Delaware State (Vice Chairman, Corporate Law Section, 1988-1989, Chairman, 1990-1992) and American Bar Associations. ***Email:*** mgoldman@pacdelaware.com

JAMES F. BURNETT, born Easton, Pennsylvania, April 4, 1941; admitted to bar, 1969, Delaware. *Education:* East Stroudsburg State College (B.A., with high honors, 1966); Georgetown University (J.D., 1969). Member, Executive Board, Georgetown Law Journal, 1967-1969. Member, Board of Bar Examiners, 1986-1993. *Member:* Delaware State and American Bar Associations. ***Email:*** jburnett@pacdelaware.com

DANIEL F. WOLCOTT, JR., born Wilmington, Delaware, March 31, 1946; admitted to bar, 1971, Delaware. *Education:* Bethany College (B.A., 1968); University of Virginia (J.D., 1971). Delta Theta Phi. Deputy Attorney General, State of Delaware, 1972-1973. Delaware Code Reviser, 1980—. City Solicitor, City of New Castle, 1997—. *Member:* Delaware State and American Bar Associations. ***Email:*** dwolcott@pacdelaware.com

CHARLES S. McDOWELL, born Norfolk, Virginia, June 20, 1945; admitted to bar, 1975, Delaware. *Education:* Princeton University (A.B., cum laude, 1967); University of Virginia (J.D., 1974). *Member:* Delaware State and American Bar Associations; National Association of Bond Lawyers. ***Email:*** cmcdowell@pacdelaware.com

DAVID B. BROWN, born Wilmington, Delaware, September 21, 1946; admitted to bar, 1973, Virginia; 1974, District of Columbia; 1980, Delaware. *Education:* University of North Carolina (B.A., with honors, 1968); University of Virginia (J.D., 1973). Phi Beta Kappa; Order of the Coif. Member, Editorial Board, 1971-1972; Notes Editor, 1972-1973, Virginia Law Review. *Member:* Delaware State and American Bar Associations; The District of Columbia Bar; Virginia State Bar. ***Email:*** dbrown@pacdelaware.com

(This Listing Continued)

SOMERS S. PRICE, JR., born Atlantic City, New Jersey, November 18, 1950; admitted to bar, 1975, Delaware. *Education:* Davidson College (B.A., cum laude, 1972); Cornell University (J.D., 1975). Phi Beta Kappa. *Member:* Delaware State and American Bar Associations. ***Email:*** sprice@pacdelaware.com

DONALD J. WOLFE, JR., born Wilkes-Barre, Pennsylvania, October 26, 1950; admitted to bar, 1976, Delaware. *Education:* University of Delaware (B.A., 1972); Temple University (J.D., cum laude, 1976). Co-Author: Donald J. Wolfe, Jr. and Michael A. Pittenger, "Corporate and Commercial Practice in the Delaware Court of Chancery: Procedures in Equity," Lexis Law Publishing, 1998. Assistant to President, Delaware State Bar Association, 1982-1983. Chair, New Lawyers Committee, Delaware State Bar Association, 1983-1984. Chair, Delaware Supreme Court Advisory Committee on IOLTA, 1987—. Trustee, Delaware Bar Foundation, 1994—. Member, Board of Bar Examiners of the Delaware Supreme Court, 1994—; Vice Chair, Board of Examiners, Delaware Supreme Court, 1998-2000; Chair, Board of Bar Examiners of the Delaware Supreme Court, 2000—. *Member:* Delaware State and American Bar Associations. ***Email:*** dwolfe@pacdelaware.com

GREGORY A. INSKIP, born Champaign, Illinois, May 30, 1952; admitted to bar, 1977, Delaware. *Education:* Yale University (B.A., summa cum laude, 1974); Harvard University (J.D., 1977). Phi Beta Kappa. *Member:* Delaware State Bar Association. ***Email:*** ginskip@pacdelaware.com

DAVID J. BALDWIN, born Holyoke, Massachusetts, December 28, 1951; admitted to bar, 1979, Delaware. *Education:* University of Massachusetts (B.A., magna cum laude, 1975); Georgetown University (J.D., 1979). Phi Beta Kappa. *Member:* Delaware State and American Bar Associations. ***Email:*** dbaldwin@pacdelaware.com

JOHN E. JAMES, born Salisbury, Maryland, March 17, 1950; admitted to bar, 1979, Delaware. *Education:* Davidson College (A.B., cum laude, 1972); Brown University (M.A., 1973); University of North Carolina (J.D., 1979). Phi Beta Kappa. *Member:* Delaware State and American Bar Associations. ***Email:*** jjames@pacdelaware.com

W. HARDING DRANE, JR., born Cleveland, Ohio, June 23, 1949; admitted to bar, 1978, Ohio; 1980, Delaware. *Education:* University of Pennsylvania (B.A., 1971); Case Western Reserve University (M.S.S.A., 1975); Cleveland State University (J.D., magna cum laude, 1978). Executive Editor, Cleveland State Law Review, 1977-1978. Law Clerk, Ohio Court of Appeals, 1978-1979. Deputy Attorney General, State of Delaware, 1980-1982. *Member:* Delaware State, Ohio State and American Bar Associations. ***Email:*** wdrane@pacdelaware.com

MARY E. COPPER, born Long Branch, New Jersey, April 6, 1950; admitted to bar, 1977, Massachusetts; 1985, Delaware. *Education:* Wellesley College (A.B., 1972); Boston University (J.D., 1976). *Member:* Delaware State and American Bar Associations. ***Email:*** mcopper@pacdelaware.com

RICHARD L. HORWITZ, born Bridgeton, New Jersey, April 30, 1957; admitted to bar, 1983, Delaware. *Education:* Amherst College (B.A., 1979); Duke University (J.D., with distinction, 1982). Phi Delta Phi. Note and Comment Editor, Duke Law Journal, 1981-1982. Law Clerk to Justice Robert L. Clifford, Supreme Court of the State of New Jersey, 1982-1983. *Member:* Delaware State and American Bar Associations. ***Email:*** rhorwitz@pacdelaware.com

MICHAEL B. TUMAS, born South Bend, Indiana, April 25, 1959; admitted to bar, 1984, Delaware. *Education:* State University of New York at Binghamton (B.A., Economics, 1981); University of Pennsylvania (J.D., 1984). *Member:* Delaware State and American Bar Associations. ***Email:*** mtumas@pacdelaware.com

KATHLEEN FUREY McDONOUGH, born Philadelphia, Pennsylvania, July 27, 1957; admitted to bar, 1985, Delaware. *Education:* St. Joseph's University (A.B., 1979); Temple University School of Law (J.D., 1985). *Member:* Delaware State and American Bar Associations. ***Email:*** kmcdonough@pacdelaware.com

LAURIE SELBER SILVERSTEIN, born St. Louis, Missouri, November 5, 1959; admitted to bar, 1985, Delaware. *Education:* University of Delaware (B.S., cum laude, 1982); The National Law Center, George Washington University (J.D., with honors, 1985). Phi Kappa Phi. Articles Editor, Consumer Protection Reporting Service, 1984-1985. *Member:* Delaware State and American Bar Associations. ***Email:*** lsilverstein@pacdelaware.com

PETER J. WALSH, JR., born Alexandria, Virginia, May 26, 1960; admitted to bar, 1986, Delaware. *Education:* Johns Hopkins University (B.A., 1983); Washington & Lee University (J.D., 1986). Member, 1984-1985 and Executive Editor, 1985-1986, Washington & Lee Law Review. Judicial Clerkship, Delaware Court of Chancery, 1986-1987. *Member:* Delaware State and American Bar Associations. ***Email:*** pwalsh@pacdelaware.com

STEPHEN C. NORMAN, born Philadelphia, Pennsylvania, January 23, 1961; admitted to bar, 1985, Pennsylvania; 1988, Delaware. *Education:* Indiana University of Pennsylvania (B.A., summa cum laude, 1982); Hofstra School of Law (J.D., with distinction, 1985). Society of Scholars. Notes and Comments

(This Listing Continued)

POTTER ANDERSON & CORROON LLP, Wilmington—Continued

Editor, Hofstra Law Review, 1984-1985. Law Clerk to Hon. William W. Caldwell, U.S. District Judge for the Middle District of Pennsylvania, 1985-1987. *Member:* Delaware State and American Bar Associations. **Email:** snorman@pacdelaware.com

ARTHUR L. DENT, born Camden, New Jersey, November 23, 1956; admitted to bar, 1986, Delaware. *Education:* Elizabethtown College (B.S., 1979); Delaware Law School of Widener University (J.D., 1986). Editor-in-Chief, Delaware Journal of Corporate Law, 1985-1986. Member, Moot Court Honor Society. *Member:* Delaware State and American Bar Associations. **Email:** adent@pacdelaware.com

HAROLD I. SALMONS, III, born Wilmington, Delaware, February 12, 1961; admitted to bar, 1986, Delaware. *Education:* Gettysburg College (B.A., 1983); Dickinson School of Law (J.D., 1986). Member, Dickinson Law Review, 1985-1986. *Member:* Delaware State Bar Association. **Email:** hsalmons@pacdelaware.com

WILLIAM R. DENNY, born Charlottesville, Virginia, January 11, 1961; admitted to bar, 1988, Delaware. *Education:* Princeton University (A.B., cum laude, 1983); Helsinki University; University of Virginia (J.D., 1987). Executive Editor, Journal of Law & Politics, 1986-1987. *Member:* Delaware State and American Bar Associations; Christian Legal Society. ***LANGUAGES:*** Finnish and Russian. **Email:** wdenny@pacdelaware.com

PHILIP A. ROVNER, born Bridgeton, New Jersey, August 14, 1959; admitted to bar, 1988, New York; 1993, Delaware. *Education:* University of Pennsylvania (B.A., 1981); Fordham University (J.D., 1987). *Member:* New York State, Delaware State and American Bar Associations. **Email:** provner@pacdelaware.com

JENNIFER GIMLER BRADY, born Denville, New Jersey, November 30, 1964; admitted to bar, 1990, Delaware. *Education:* College of William & Mary (B.A., Econ., 1987); Dickinson School of Law (J.D., 1990). Member, Appellate Moot Court Board. Managing Editor, Dickinson School of Law, Law Review, 1989-1990. *Member:* Delaware State and American Bar Associations. **Email:** jbrady@pacdelaware.com

SCOTT E. WAXMAN, born Columbus, Mississippi, March 10, 1966; admitted to bar, 1991, Pennsylvania; 1992, Delaware. *Education:* Johns Hopkins University (B.A., 1987); Georgetown University (J.D., 1990). Member, The Tax Lawyer, 1988-1990. Co-Author and Editor of Explanation Section, Delaware State and Local Tax Service, Prentice Hall, 1991. Co-Author, U.S. International Tax Reporting Forms, B.N.A., 1990. *Member:* Delaware State and American (Member, Taxation Section) Bar Associations. ***LANGUAGES:*** Mandarin Chinese, French and Russian. **Email:** swaxman@pacdelaware.com

MARK A. MORTON, born West Chester, Pennsylvania, December 22, 1963; admitted to bar, 1989, Delaware; 1994, Pennsylvania. *Education:* Dickinson College (B.A., cum laude, 1985); Georgetown University (J.D., 1989). The Tax Lawyer, 1990-1991. *Member:* Delaware State, Pennsylvania and American Bar Associations. **Email:** mmorton@pacdelaware.com

JOHN F. GROSSBAUER, born Allentown, Pennsylvania, June 23, 1961; admitted to bar, 1986, Delaware; 1995, North Carolina and U.S. District Court, Western District of North Carolina. *Education:* Pennsylvania State University (B.A., with highest distinction, 1983); Duke University (J.D., 1986). Phi Beta Kappa. University Scholar. *Member:* Delaware State (Member, Corporate Law Section) and American (Member: Business Section; Negotiated Acquisitions Committee, 1999—) Bar Associations; North Carolina State Bar. ***PRACTICE AREAS:*** Delaware Corporation Law/Transactions; Corporate; Acquisitions; Divestitures. **Email:** jgrossbauer@pacdelaware.com

KATHLEEN W. GEIGER, born Milwaukee, Wisconsin, 1952; admitted to bar, 1990, Delaware and U.S. District Court, District of Delaware; registered to practice before U.S. Patent and Trademark Office. *Education:* University of Wisconsin-Madison; Widener University School of Law (J.D., cum laude, 1990). Note and Comment Editor, Delaware Journal of Corporate Law, 1989-1990. Clerk to the Hon. Henry R. Horsey, Delaware Supreme Court, 1989-1990. *Member:* Delaware State Bar Association (Member, Intellectual Property Law Section); American Intellectual Property Law Association. ***PRACTICE AREAS:*** Patents; Intellectual Property. **Email:** kgeiger@pacdelaware.com

WENDY K. VOSS, born Lincoln, Nebraska, February 22, 1952; admitted to bar, 1992, Delaware. *Education:* University of Michigan (B.A., magna cum laude, 1974); College of William & Mary (J.D., 1992). Phi Beta Kappa; Order of the Coif. James B. Angell Scholar. Member, William & Mary Law Review, 1991-1992. **Email:** wvoss@pacdelaware.com

KEVIN R. SHANNON, born Danbury, Connecticut, April 9, 1963; admitted to bar, 1992, Delaware. *Education:* Villanova University (B.S.A., summa cum laude, 1985); Delaware Law School of Widener University (J.D., magna cum laude, 1992). Comment Editor, Delaware Journal of Corporate Law, 1990-1992. Certified Public Accountant, Pennsylvania, 1987 (inactive). *Member:* Delaware State and American Bar Associations; American Institute of Certified Public Accountants. **Email:** kshannon@pacdelaware.com

COUNSEL

ROBERT P. BARNETT, born Albany, Georgia, November 19, 1921; admitted to bar, 1948, Delaware. *Education:* Duke University (B.A., 1942; J.D., 1948). Chairman, New Castle County Zoning Board of Adjustment, 1955-1957. Member, State Board of Corrections, 1955-1965. President, New Castle County Economic Development Corporation, 1981—. *Member:* Delaware State and American Bar Associations.

MICHAEL B. KEEHAN, born Chicago, Illinois, May 8, 1935; admitted to bar, 1967, District of Columbia; 1980, Delaware; registered to practice before U.S. Patent and Trademark Office. *Education:* University of New Mexico (B.S., 1957); George Washington University (LL.B., 1965). Vice President and General Counsel of Hercules Incorporated, 1990-1996, retired. (Vice President-Law). **Email:** mkeehan@pacdelaware.com

HILMAR L. FRICKE, born Milwaukee, Wisconsin, May 17, 1935; admitted to bar, 1966, District of Columbia; registered to practice before U.S. Patent and Trademark Office (Not admitted in Delaware). *Education:* University of Wisconsin-Madison (B.S.Ch.E., 1958); University of Maryland (LL.B., 1966). *Member:* American Intellectual Property Law Association. [1st Lt., U.S. Army, 1958-1960]. ***PRACTICE AREAS:*** Patents; Contracts. **Email:** hfricke@pacdelaware.com

TODD L. GOODMAN, born Wilmington, Delaware, July 15, 1964; admitted to bar, 1992, Delaware. *Education:* University of Delaware (B.A., magna cum laude, 1987); Dickinson School of Law (J.D., 1992). Phi Beta Kappa; Woolsack Honor Society. Law Clerk to Justice Randy J. Holland, Supreme Court of Delaware, 1992-1993. *Member:* Delaware State and American Bar Associations. **Email:** tgoodman@pacdelaware.com

OF COUNSEL

JOHN P. SINCLAIR, born New York, N.Y., March 31, 1915; admitted to bar, 1940, Pennsylvania and Delaware. *Education:* Swarthmore College (A.B., 1936); University of Pennsylvania (LL.B., 1939). Member, State Legislature, 1947-1949, 1949-1951. *Member:* Delaware State and American Bar Associations.

BLAINE T. PHILLIPS, born Frankford, Delaware, May 3, 1930; admitted to bar, 1955, Virginia and Delaware. *Education:* University of Virginia (B.A., with honors, 1952; LL.B., 1955). Phi Beta Kappa; Phi Delta Phi. Recipient, Raven Award. Member, Board of Editors, Virginia Law Review, 1953-1955. Member, 1973-1985 and Chairman, 1984-1985, Board of Bar Examiners, Governor's Judicial Nominating Commission, 1988-1992. *Member:* Delaware State, Virginia and American Bar Associations.

HUGH CORROON, born Freeport, New York, April 14, 1929; admitted to bar, 1956, New York; 1957, Delaware. *Education:* Princeton University (A.B., 1951); Harvard Law School (LL.B., 1954). *Member:* The Association of the Bar of the City of New York; Delaware State and American Bar Associations.

JOSEPH H. GEOGHEGAN, born Wilmington, Delaware, February 29, 1928; admitted to bar, 1956, Delaware. *Education:* Yale University (A.B., 1948); Columbia University (LL.B., 1952). Phi Delta Phi. *Member:* Delaware State and American Bar Associations. Fellow, American College of Trust and Estate Counsel.

RICHARD L. McMAHON, born Wilmington, Delaware, April 15, 1932; admitted to bar, 1956, Delaware and District of Columbia. *Education:* Wesleyan University (A.B., 1953); University of Pennsylvania (LL.B., cum laude, 1956). Member, Board of Editors, University of Pennsylvania Law Review, 1954-1956. *Member:* Delaware State and American Bar Associations.

CHARLES S. CROMPTON, JR., born Wilmington, Delaware, December 30, 1936; admitted to bar, 1962, Delaware. *Education:* University of Delaware (B.A., 1958); University of Virginia (LL.B., 1961). Phi Beta Kappa; Order of the Coif; Raven Society; Omicron Delta Kappa. Member, Board of Editors, Virginia Law Review, 1959-1961. *Member:* Delaware State (President, 1985-1986) and American Bar Associations. Fellow, American College of Trial Lawyers (State Chairman, 1986-1988). **Email:** ccrompton@pacdelaware.com

RICHARD E. POOLE, born Wilmington, Delaware, November 24, 1940; admitted to bar, 1966, Delaware. *Education:* University of St. Andrews, St. Andrews, Scotland; Swarthmore College (B.A., with high honors, 1963); University of Chicago (J.D., 1966). Phi Beta Kappa. Law Clerk to Judge Collins J. Seitz, Third Circuit Court of Appeals, 1966-1967. *Member:* Delaware State and American Bar Associations. **Email:** rpoole@pacdelaware.com

ASSOCIATES

MICHAEL A. PITTENGER, born Niles, Michigan, August 13, 1968; admitted to bar, 1993, Delaware. *Education:* Miami University, Oxford, Ohio (B.A., magna cum laude, 1990); Washington & Lee University (J.D., magna

(This Listing Continued)

cum laude, 1993). Phi Beta Kappa; Order of the Coif. Notes and Comments Editor, Washington & Lee Law Review, 1992-1993. Co-Author: "Corporate and Commercial Practice in the Delaware Court of Chancery: Procedures in Equity," Lexis Law Publishing, 1998. *Member:* Delaware State and American Bar Associations. **Email:** mpittenger@pacdelaware.com

J. BRECK SMITH, born Bronxville, New York, January 11, 1958; admitted to bar, 1990, Pennsylvania; 1991, Delaware, Maryland and U.S. District Court, District of Delaware; 1992, U.S. District Court, District of Maryland. *Education:* Dartmouth College (B.A., 1980); Widener University School of Law (J.D., 1989). Contributing Author: "PA Real Estate Title Law: Problems and Solutions," National Business Institute, 1999. *Member:* Delaware State (Member, Real Property Section) and American (Member, Real Property Section) Bar Associations. ***PRACTICE AREAS:*** Real Estate Acquisitions; Real Estate Development; Real Estate Finance; Commercial Leasing. **Email:** jsmith@pacdelaware.com

MATTHEW E. FISCHER, born Pittsburgh, Pennsylvania, May 17, 1966; admitted to bar, 1992, Delaware; 1993, Pennsylvania. *Education:* James Madison University (B.A., cum laude, 1989); Wake Forest University School of Law (J.D., cum laude, 1992). Recipient, American Jurisprudence Awards in Legal Research and Writing, 1990, Real Property Security, 1991, Federal Jurisdiction, 1992. *Member:* Delaware State and American Bar Associations. **Email:** mfischer@pacdelaware.com

WILLIAM A. HAZELTINE, born Wilmington, Delaware, August 12, 1958; admitted to bar, 1994, Delaware. *Education:* Susquehanna University (B.Mus., 1980); The Ohio State University (M.A., 1984; J.D., 1994). Order of the Coif. *Member:* Delaware State and American Bar Associations; American Bankruptcy Institute; Commercial Law League of America. **Email:** whazeltine@pacdelaware.com

EMILIE R. NINAN, born Philadelphia, Pennsylvania, December 8, 1971; admitted to bar, 1995, Delaware. *Education:* Temple University (B.A., summa cum laude, 1991); Georgetown University Law Center (J.D., 1995); Georgetown University School of Business Administration (M.B.A., 1995). Member, Georgetown Journal of Legal Ethics. *Member:* Delaware State and American Bar Associations. **Email:** eninan@pacdelaware.com

MONICA LEIGH LOFTIN, born Virginia Beach, Virginia, September 7, 1965; admitted to bar, 1995, Delaware; 1996, Pennsylvania and U.S. District Court, District of Delaware. *Education:* University of Virginia (B.S., 1987); Widener University (J.D., cum laude, 1995). Phi Delta Phi. Member, Harrington Inn, Honor Chapter. Associate Editor, The Widener Law Symposium Journal, 1994-1995. Law Clerk to Hon. Richard S. Gebelein, Delaware Superior Court, 1995-1996. *Member:* Delaware State and American Bar Associations. ***PRACTICE AREAS:*** Bankruptcy; Creditors Rights. **Email:** mloftin@pacdelaware.com

JANINE M. SALOMONE, born Lima, Ohio, August 5, 1970; admitted to bar, 1996, Delaware and Pennsylvania. *Education:* Pennsylvania State University (B.S., summa cum laude, 1992); Dickinson School of Law (J.D., cum laude, 1995). Phi Beta Kappa. Member, Order of Woolsack. Member, Dickinson Law Review, 1993-1995. Author: "The Pennsylvania Worker's Compensation Reform as it Affects the Pennsylvania Motor Vehicle Financial Responsibility Law," Vol. 99, No. 4, Summer, 1995. *Member:* Delaware State and American Bar Associations. ***PRACTICE AREAS:*** Corporate Law. **Email:** jsalomone@pacdelaware.com

ANDREW T. O'NEILL, born Wilmington, Delaware, September 28, 1959; admitted to bar, 1992, Pennsylvania; 1995, Delaware. *Education:* University of Delaware (B.A.B.S., magna cum laude, 1981); Widener University (J.D., cum laude, 1992). Phi Beta Kappa. Certified Public Accountant, Delaware, 1993. *Member:* Delaware State and American Bar Associations. **Email:** aoneill@pacdelaware.com

JOHN A. CICCARONE, born Philadelphia, Pennsylvania, September 10, 1966; admitted to bar, 1994, Delaware; 1995, Pennsylvania and New Jersey. *Education:* University of Delaware (B.S., B.A., 1991); Widener University School of Law (J.D., M.B.A., 1994); Villanova University (LL.M. in Taxation, 1997). *Member:* Delaware Bar Association (Member, Sections on: Taxation, Trusts and Estates); Wilmington Tax Group; Estate Planning Council of Delaware. **Email:** jciccarone@pacdelaware.com

JOHN J. QUINN, III, born Baltimore, Maryland, May 11, 1955; admitted to bar, 1997, Delaware. *Education:* Lehigh University (B.S.Ch.E., magna cum laude, 1977); University of Pennsylvania Law School (J.D., 1997). Tau Beta Pi. Senior Editor, Journal of International Economic Law, 1995-1997. Member, American Institute of Chemical Engineers, 1993—. **Email:** jquinn@pacdelaware.com

NICHOLAS I. FROIO, born Philadelphia, Pennsylvania, March 23, 1971; (admission pending). *Education:* Temple University (B.A., 1993; J.D., 1997). Justinian Society. ***LANGUAGES:*** Italian. ***PRACTICE AREAS:*** Corporate; Commercial. **Email:** nfroio@pacdelaware.com

CATHERINE M. HAMBERGER, born New York, N.Y., June 27, 1970; admitted to bar, 1998, Pennsylvania; 2001, Delaware. *Education:* University of Colorado at Boulder (B.A., 1992); Dickinson School of Law (J.D., 1997). Recipient: CALI Award for Academic Excellence in the Field of Banking Regulation. *Member:* Philadelphia and American Bar Associations. ***PRACTICE AREAS:*** Business Law; Mergers and Acquisitions; Joint Ventures; Financial Law; Commercial Law; Technology Finance. **Email:** chamberger@potteranderson.com

JACQUELINE A. LEWIS, born New York; admitted to bar, 1996, Connecticut; 1997, Pennsylvania; 2000, Massachusetts (Not admitted in Delaware). *Education:* Wharton School, University of Pennsylvania (B.S., 1990); Pace Law School (J.D., 1995); Boston University School of Law (LL.M., Banking, 1998). Casenote and Comment Editor, Pace International Law Review. *Member:* American Bar Association (Member, Business Law Section). ***PRACTICE AREAS:*** Corporate Law; Commercial Law; Banking. **Email:** jlewis@potteranderson.com

BRIAN C. RALSTON, born Wilmington, Delaware, January 2, 1973; admitted to bar, 1998, Delaware. *Education:* Villanova University (B.A., 1995); Dickinson School of Law of the Pennsylvania State University (J.D., 1998). Woolsack Honor Society. Editor, Dickinson Law Review. **Email:** bralston@pacdelaware.com

ELIHU E. ALLINSON, III, born Baltimore, Maryland, May 8, 1962; admitted to bar, 1996, Maryland and Delaware. *Education:* Lafayette College (A.B., 1984); University of Delaware (M.A., 1990); Widener University School of Law (J.D., cum laude, 1995). Phi Delta Phi. Law Clerk to President Judge Henry duPont Ridgely, Superior Court of Delaware, 1996. *Member:* Delaware State and American Bar Associations. **Email:** eallinson@pacdelaware.com

PAUL D. GOLIAN, born Mt. Kisco, New York, February 3, 1973; admitted to bar, 1998, Delaware and New Jersey; registered to practice before the U.S. Patent and Trademark Office. *Education:* Loyola College (B.S., Chemistry/Biology, 1995); Vermont Law School (J.D., cum laude, 1998); Johns Hopkins University (M.S., Biotechnology, 2000). Member, Biotechnology Industry Organization. *Member:* Delaware State (Member, Intellectual Property Law Section) and American (Member, Intellectual Property Law Section) Bar Associations; American Intellectual Property Law Association; American Association for the Advancement of Science, American Chemical Society (Member, Section on Chemistry and the Law). ***PRACTICE AREAS:*** Intellectual Property; Patents. **Email:** pgolian@pacdelaware.com

RONALD S. GELLERT, born Yonkers, New York, July 20, 1971; admitted to bar, 1997, Pennsylvania and New Jersey (Not admitted in Delaware). *Education:* Rutgers College (B.A., with high honors, 1993); Rutgers University of Law (J.D., 1997). Law Clerk to the Honorable Judith H. Wizmur and Gloria M. Burns, U.S. Bankruptcy Court for the District of New Jersey, 1997-1998. *Member:* American Bar Association. ***PRACTICE AREAS:*** Bankruptcy (100%).

JAMES M. KRON, born Munich, Germany, November 10, 1953; admitted to bar, 2000, Delaware, Pennsylvania and U.S. District Court, District of Delaware; registered to practice before U.S. Patent and Trademark Office. *Education:* Lehigh University (B.S.M.E., 1976); University of Toledo (M.B.A. in Finance, 1982); Widener University School of Law (J.D., 1999). Member, Delaware Journal of Corporate Law, 1998-1999. Registered Professional Engineer, Ohio, 1982, Pennsylvania, 1997, Delaware, 1997 and New Jersey, 1997. *Member:* Delaware State and American Bar Associations. ***PRACTICE AREAS:*** Intellectual Property; Commercial Litigation. **Email:** jkron@pacdelaware.com

JOHN M. SEAMAN, born Norristown, Pennsylvania, October 14, 1969; admitted to bar, 1999, Delaware; 2000, U.S. District Court, District of Delaware. *Education:* Williams College (B.A., cum laude, 1991); University of Pennsylvania (J.D., 1999). Recipient, Henry C. Loughlin Prize in Legal Ethics. *Member:* Delaware State and American Bar Associations. ***PRACTICE AREAS:*** Corporate Litigation. **Email:** jseaman@pacdelaware.com

THOMAS R. MANCINI, born Abington, Pennsylvania, 1971; admitted to bar, 1999, New Jersey (Not admitted in Delaware). *Education:* Syracuse University (B.A. in Biology, 1993); Franklin Pierce Law Center (J.D., 1999). Recipient, SmithKline Beecham Director's Award and Crystal Impact Award for Exceptional and Outstanding Analytical Work. ***PRACTICE AREAS:*** Patents; Trademarks; Patent Applications; Patent Prosecution. **Email:** tmancini@pacdelaware.com

REBECCA L. SCALIO, born Liege, Belgium, April 2, 1967; admitted to bar, 2000, New Jersey; 2001, Delaware. *Education:* University of Delaware (B.A., magna cum laude, 1996); James E. Beasley School of Law of Temple University (J.D., 1999). Member, 1997-1998 and Executive Editor, 1998-1999, Temple Political and Civil Rights Law Review. Judicial Extern to the Hon. Stephen M. Orlofsky, U.S. District Court, District of New Jersey. *Member:* American Bar Association. ***PRACTICE AREAS:*** Corporate Litigation; Commercial Litigation.

ERICA L. NIEZGODA, born Madison Heights, Michigan, October 21, 1974; admitted to bar, 1999, Virginia; 2000, Delaware. *Education:* Tulane University of Louisiana (B.A., 1996); Georgetown University (J.D., 1999). ***PRACTICE AREAS:*** Litigation. **Email:** eniezgoda@pacdelaware.com

(This Listing Continued)

(This Listing Continued)

POTTER ANDERSON & CORROON LLP, Wilmington—Continued

NANCY WATERMAN, born Hampton, Virginia, December 19, 1969; admitted to bar, 2001, Delaware. *Education:* University of Texas at Austin (B.B.A., 1991); College of William & Mary (J.D., 1999). ***PRACTICE AREAS:*** Corporate. ***Email:*** nwaterman@pacdelaware.com

DAVID E. MOORE, born Virginia, March 14, 1969; admitted to bar, 2000, Delaware. *Education:* University of Virginia (B.S., Educ., 1992); Temple University (J.D., 1999). ***PRACTICE AREAS:*** Litigation. ***Email:*** dmoore@pacdelaware.com

MICHAEL W. WHITTAKER, born Charleston, South Carolina, July 26, 1971; admitted to bar, 2000, Delaware. *Education:* University of Cincinnati (B.S., 1997); Seton Hall University (J.D., 2000). Member, Moot Court. Member, Legislative Journal, 1999-2000. ***Email:*** mwhittaker@pacdelaware.com

RICHARD L. RENCK, born Lafayette, Indiana, December 16, 1970; admitted to bar, 2000, Delaware; 2001, Pennsylvania. *Education:* Presbyterian College (B.S., cum laude, 1992); University of South Carolina (J.D., 1999). Order of Wig and Robe. ***PRACTICE AREAS:*** Corporate.

TIMOTHY M. HOLLY, born Sandusky, Ohio, April 19, 1974; admitted to bar, 2001, Delaware. *Education:* Georgetown College (B.A., 1996); Xavier University (M.A., Industrial/Organizational Psychology). Professional Member, Society of Industrial Organizational Psychology. ***PRACTICE AREAS:*** Labor and Employment. ***Email:*** tholly@potteranderson.com

NATHAN J. LACOMB, born Norwood, New York, June 6, 1976; admitted to bar, 2001, Delaware. *Education:* St. Lawrence University (B.A., summa cum laude, 1998); University of Pennsylvania (J.D., 2001). Phi Beta Kappa. *Member:* American Bar Association (Member, Business Law Section). ***PRACTICE AREAS:*** Commercial Real Estate; Business Transactions; Land Use; Zoning Law. ***Email:*** nlacomb@potteranderson.com

ELIZABETH D. POWER, born Wilmington, Delaware, September 4, 1976; admitted to bar, 2001, Delaware. *Education:* University of Delaware (B.A., 1998); University of North Carolina at Chapel Hill (J.D., with honors, 2001). Phi Beta Kappa. Member, University of North Carolina Law Review. ***PRACTICE AREAS:*** Bankruptcy. ***Email:*** epower@potteranderson.com

MICHAEL J. SCALI, born Daytona Beach, Florida, February 24, 1976; admitted to bar, 2001, Delaware. *Education:* Villanova University (B.A., cum laude, 1998); Dickinson School of Law of the Pennsylvania State University (J.D., 2001). Woolsack Honor Society. ***PRACTICE AREAS:*** Corporate Opinion. ***Email:*** mscali@potteranderson.com

REPRESENTATIVE CLIENTS: The Corporation Trust Co.; Conectiv, Inc.; E.I. duPont de Nemours & Company, Inc.; General Motors Corp.; Hercules, Inc.; Mazda Motor of America, Inc.; Chrysler Corp.; Amtrak; ConRail; Winterthur Museum; University of Delaware; Equitable Life Assurance Society of U.S.; Chase Manhattan Bank (USA), N.A.; Citicorp.; Widener University School of Law; Exxon Corp.; Monsanto Co., Santa Fe Pacific Corp.; Kao Corp.; The Andrew Jergens Co.; The Williams Cos.; Chris-Craft Industries, Inc.

PRICKETT, JONES & ELLIOTT, P.A.

Established in 1888

1310 KING STREET

P.O. BOX 1328

WILMINGTON, DELAWARE 19899-1328

Telephone: 302-888-6500

Telecopier: 302-658-8111; 658-7257

Email: attorneys@prickett.com

URL: http://www.prickett.com

Dover, Delaware Office: 11 North State Street. Telephone: 302-674-3841.

Kennett Square, Pennsylvania Office: 217 West State Street. Telephone: 610-444-1573.

General Practice including: Trial and Appellate Litigation, Corporation, Partnership, Commercial, Banking, Business, Health Care Law, Personal Injury, Real Estate, Bankruptcy and Reorganization, Environmental, Probate, Trust and Estate Planning, Tax, Delaware Patent Litigation, Construction Law, Criminal Law, Medical Malpractice, Insurance Defense, Product Liability, Premises Liability, Occupational Disease Litigation, Labor and Employment, Government Affairs.

FIRM PROFILE: Prickett, Jones & Elliott, originally founded in 1888, now consists of 23 attorneys practicing in Wilmington and Dover, Delaware and nearby Kennett Square, Pennsylvania. It provides services in the following areas: (I) Delaware Corporate Litigation and Transactions, (II) General Litigation (including complex commercial litigation, bankruptcy and medical malpractice defense), (III) Trust, Estate and Tax Law, (IV) Business, Banking and Hospital Law, (V) Commercial and Residential Real Estate, and (VI) Legislative Representation before the Delaware General Assembly and State, County and Municipal Authorities. The firm acts as Delaware counsel in admiralty, patent and copyright cases. The firm represents charitable and philanthropic organizations, performs pro bono services and is a leader in committee work for the Courts and for national and local legal organizations.

WILLIAM S. PRICKETT (1862-1926).

WILLIAM PRICKETT (1894-1964).

RICHARD I. G. JONES, born West Chester, Pennsylvania, March 9, 1938; admitted to bar, 1964, Delaware; 1978, Pennsylvania. *Education:* Yale University (B.A., 1960); University of Pennsylvania (LL.B., 1963). Deputy Attorney General, 1965. *Member:* Delaware State, Pennsylvania and American Bar Associations. (Also at Kennett Square, Pennsylvania). ***PRACTICE AREAS:*** Medical Malpractice Litigation; Personal Injury Litigation; Equine Law. ***Email:*** rijones@prickett.com

WAYNE N. ELLIOTT, born Laurel, Delaware, April 6, 1942; admitted to bar, 1967, Delaware. *Education:* Harvard College (A.B., magna cum laude, 1964); University of Virginia (LL.B., 1967). Advocate, American Board of Trial Advocates. *Member:* Delaware State and American Bar Associations. (Also at Dover Office). ***PRACTICE AREAS:*** General Litigation in State and Federal Courts. ***Email:*** wnelliott@prickett.com

MASON E. TURNER, JR., born Media, Pennsylvania, October 14, 1942; admitted to bar, 1967, Virginia; 1969, Delaware. *Education:* Hamilton College (A.B., 1964); University of Virginia (LL.B., 1967). Deputy Attorney General of Delaware, 1971-1973. *Member:* Delaware State and American Bar Associations. Fellow: American College of Trial Lawyers. ***PRACTICE AREAS:*** Medical Malpractice; Products Liability; Insurance Defense Litigation. ***Email:*** meturner@prickett.com

JAMES L. HOLZMAN, born Brooklyn, New York, January 7, 1949; admitted to bar, 1973, Florida and Delaware. *Education:* Stetson University (B.A., 1970); University of Florida (J.D., 1972). Author: Annual Publication, "Review of Developments in Corporation Law," *Member:* The Association of the Bar of the City of New York; Delaware State (Member, Corporation Law Section; Member, Corporation Law Section Council; Chair, Delaware General Corporation Law Technology Committee) and American (Chair, Business and Corporate Litigation Committee, 1996-2000; Task Force on Litigation Reform and Rules Revision; Corporate Counsel Committee; Member, Council Section of Business Law, 2001—) Bar Associations; The Florida Bar. ***PRACTICE AREAS:*** Corporate Law and Litigation; Federal Litigation. ***Email:*** jlholzman@prickett.com

JOHN H. SMALL, born Minneapolis, Minnesota, September 4, 1946; admitted to bar, 1973, Pennsylvania; 1974, Delaware. *Education:* Georgetown University (B.A., 1968); University of Virginia (J.D., 1973). Law Clerk, Delaware Court of Chancery, 1973-1974. *Member:* Delaware State (Member: Corporation Law Section Council, 1982-1998, 2000—, Vice-Chair, 1992-1994 and Chair, 1994-1996; Alternative Entities Committee, 1983—, Chair, 2001—, Corporation Law Section) and American (Chair, Committee on Partnerships and Unincorporated Business Organizations, 1988-1992 and Member, Council, 1994-1998, Section of Business Law) Bar Associations; Member, Joint Editorial Board of American Bar Association and National Conference of Commissioners on Uniform State Laws on Unincorporated Business Organizations Act, 2001—. [U.S. Army, active duty, 1968-1970]. ***PRACTICE AREAS:*** Corporate Law and Litigation; Business Entity Law. ***Email:*** jhsmall@prickett.com

MICHAEL HANRAHAN, born Rockville Centre, New York, June 29, 1952; admitted to bar, 1978, Delaware. *Education:* Columbia University (B.A., 1974; M.B.A., 1978; J.D., 1978). Co-author: "*Weinberger v. UOP, Inc.:* Delaware's Effort To Preserve A Level Playing Field for Cash-Out Mergers," 8 Delaware Journal of Corporate Law 59, 1983; Co-author: "A Short History of the Delaware Court of Chancery," 18 Del. J. Corp. L. 819 (1993); Co-author: "Trustees of Equity: The Judges of the Delaware Court of Chancery," *The Delaware Bar in the Twentieth Century* (1994). *Member:* Delaware State (Member, Subcommittee on State Takeover Laws, 1981—) and American (Program Chair, Committee on Class Actions and Derivative Suits, 1993-1998) Bar Associations. ***PRACTICE AREAS:*** Corporate and Partnership Litigation; Corporate and Partnership Law. ***Email:*** mhanrahan@prickett.com

DAVID E. BRAND, born Knoxville, Tennessee, July 26, 1943; admitted to bar, 1973, Delaware. *Education:* College of Wooster (B.A., 1965); Vanderbilt University (M.A., 1971; J.D., 1973). Co-Author: "Developments in Contemporary Landlord-Tenant Law: An Annotated Bibliography," 26 Vanderbilt Law Review, 1973. *Member:* Delaware State and American (Member, Litigation, Intellectual Property and Dispute Resolution Sections) Bar Associations; The Association of Trial Lawyers of America. [U.S. Army active duty, 1966-1969]. ***PRACTICE AREAS:*** Commercial Litigation; Alternate Dispute Resolution; Insurance Coverage Litigation; Intellectual Property Litigation; Professional Liability Litigation. ***Email:*** debrand@prickett.com

WAYNE J. CAREY, born Philadelphia, Pennsylvania, January 27, 1948; admitted to bar, 1982, Delaware. *Education:* Union College, Kentucky (B.S., 1970); Delaware Law School of Widener University (J.D., 1981). Phi Alpha Delta. Member, 1979-1980 and Associate Editor, 1980-1981, Delaware Journal of Corporate Law. Member, Moot Court Honor Society. Law Clerk, Chief

(This Listing Continued)

Justice of Delaware Supreme Court, 1981-1982. Member, Board of Directors of Delaware Volunteer Legal Services, 1988-1996. Co-Author: *Delaware Limited Liability Company Forms and Practice Manual. Member:* Delaware State (Member, Corporation Law Section) and American (Chair, Subcommittee on International Transactions, 1989-1996, Member: Small Business Committee, Meetings Committee, Law and Accounting Committee and Audit Inquiry Responses Subcommittee, Section on Business Law) Bar Associations; Maritime Law Association; American Institute of Certified Public Accountants (Member, Task Force of Audit Inquiry Letters). ***PRACTICE AREAS:*** Corporate Law; Partnership; Limited Liability Companies; Delaware Investment Holding Companies; Business Trust Law; Chancery Court Litigation; Federal Court Litigation; Admiralty Law. ***Email:*** wjcarey@prickett.com

PAUL M. LUKOFF, born Houston, Texas, January 10, 1944; admitted to bar, 1970, Texas; 1972, Delaware; 2001, U.S. Court of Appeals, Second Circuit. *Education:* University of Delaware (A.B., 1965); University of Texas (LL.B., 1968). Instructor, Criminal Justice and Business Law, University of Delaware, 1980-1985. Member, Governor's Advisory Council for Exceptional Citizens, Delaware, 1984-1986. Assistant Public Defender, 1972-1976. *Member:* Delaware State and American (Member, Tort and Insurance Practice Section; Litigation Section; Business Law Section) Bar Associations; American Board of Trial Advocates; Defense Counsel of Delaware (Board of Directors, 1995-1999). [Capt., U.S. Army, 1968-1970]. ***PRACTICE AREAS:*** Premises Liability Litigation; Commercial Litigation; Product Liability Litigation; Medical Malpractice Litigation; Occupational Disease Litigation; Toxic Torts Litigation (Chemical Exposure); Intellectual Property Litigation (Local Counsel). ***Email:*** pmlukoff@prickett.com

ELIZABETH M. McGEEVER, born Waterbury, Connecticut, January 27, 1956; admitted to bar, 1981, Delaware; 1988, District of Columbia. *Education:* University of Connecticut (B.A., 1977); Villanova University (J.D., 1981). Attorney, Division of Enforcement, Securities and Exchange Commission, 1986-1988. *Member:* The District of Columbia Bar; Delaware State (Member, Corporation Law Council, 1990-1999) and American (Member: Business Law Section; Litigation Section; Division Director, 1998—; Co-Chair, Committee on Class Action and Derivative Suits, 1995-1998) Bar Associations. ***PRACTICE AREAS:*** Corporate Litigation; Commercial Litigation. ***Email:*** emmcgeever@prickett.com

WILLIAM J. MARTIN, III, born New Brunswick, New Jersey, November 30, 1953; admitted to bar, 1978, Delaware; 1979, U.S. Tax Court and U.S. District Court, District of Delaware; 1996, Pennsylvania. *Education:* University of Delaware (B.A., with high honors, 1975); Rutgers University (J.D., with honors, 1978); Georgetown University (LL.M. in Taxation, 1987). Pi Sigma Alpha. *Member:* Delaware (Member, Taxation Section; Estates and Trust Section) and American (Member, Health Law Section) Bar Associations. ***PRACTICE AREAS:*** Taxation; Health Law; Employee Benefits; Estates and Trusts; Commercial. ***Email:*** wjmartin@prickett.com

GARY F. TRAYNOR, born Dover, Delaware, August 25, 1956; admitted to bar, 1982, Delaware. *Education:* Dartmouth College (A.B., 1978); Delaware Law School of Widener University (J.D., 1982). Phi Delta Phi. Staff Member, Delaware Journal of Corporate Law, 1981-1982. *Member:* Kent County, Delaware State and American Bar Associations; Terry-Carey Inn of Court. (Resident at Dover Office). ***PRACTICE AREAS:*** Corporate Litigation; Commercial Litigation; Federal Litigation; Complex Criminal Defense. ***Email:*** gftraynor@prickett.com

JOHN W. PARADEE, born Rockledge, Florida, February 1, 1963; admitted to bar, 1989, Delaware; 1990, U.S. District Court, District of Delaware; 1997, U.S. Supreme Court. *Education:* University of Virginia (B.A., 1985); University of Richmond (J.D./M.B.A., 1989). Pi Sigma Alpha; Phi Alpha Theta; Phi Alpha Delta. Counsel to the Minority Caucus of the House of Representatives, State of Delaware General Assembly, 1991-1993. Counsel to the Majority Caucus of the Senate, State of Delaware General Assembly, 1993-1995. Counsel to the Levy Court of Kent County, Delaware, 1995-1999. Member, Board on the Unauthorized Practice of Law, Supreme Court of Delaware, 1991—. Terry-Carey Inn of Court. Member, Delaware Heritage Commission, 1996—. President, Kent County Bar Association, 2000-2001. *Member:* Delaware State and American Bar Associations; Delaware Trial Lawyers Association; Association of Trial Lawyers of America. (Resident at Dover Office). ***PRACTICE AREAS:*** Commercial Litigation; Real Estate Law. ***Email:*** jwparadee@prickett.com

RONALD A. BROWN, JR., born Philadelphia, Pennsylvania, March 1, 1965; admitted to bar, 1990, Delaware. *Education:* Bucknell University (B.S.B.A., 1987); Delaware Law School of Widener University (J.D., cum laude, 1990). Phi Delta Phi; Phi Kappa Phi. Staff, 1988-1989 and Articles Editor, 1989-1990, Delaware Journal of Corporate Law. Author: Note, "An Examination of a Board of Directors' Duty to Redeem the Rights Issued Pursuant to a Stockholder Rights Plan," 14 Del. J. Corp. L. 537, 1989; Note, "Claims of Aiding and Abetting a Director's Breach of Fiduciary Duty - Does Everybody Who Deals with a Delaware Director Owe Fiduciary Duties to that Director's Shareholders?" 15 Del. J. Corp. L. 943, 1990. Wolcott Law Clerk, Hon. Andrew G. T. Moore, II, Delaware Supreme Court, 1989-1990. *Member:* Delaware State and American Bar Associations. ***PRACTICE AREAS:*** Corporate Law; Chancery Court Litigation. ***Email:*** rabrown@prickett.com

BRUCE E. JAMESON, born Pittsburgh, Pennsylvania, December 15, 1964; admitted to bar, 1991, Delaware and Pennsylvania. *Education:* University of Pittsburgh (B.A., cum laude, 1987; J.D., 1990). Member, Order of the Barristers. *Member:* Delaware State, Pennsylvania and American (Member, Sections on: Business Law; Litigation; Law Practice Management) Bar Associations. ***PRACTICE AREAS:*** Corporate Law; Corporate and Commercial Litigation. ***Email:*** bejameson@prickett.com

THOMAS A. MULLEN, born Camden, New Jersey, July 18, 1967; admitted to bar, 1993, Delaware and U.S. District Court, District of Delaware. *Education:* Franklin and Marshall College (B.A., 1989); University of Pennsylvania Law School (J.D., 1992). Co-Author: Annual Publication, "Review of Developments in Corporation Law." *Member:* Delaware State (Member, Corporate Law Section; Commercial Law Section) and American (Member: Business Law Section) Bar Associations. ***PRACTICE AREAS:*** Corporate Law and Litigation; Partnership; Limited Liability Company; Business Trust Law. ***Email:*** tamullen@prickett.com

F. PETER CONATY, JR., born Wilmington, Delaware, February 24, 1967; admitted to bar, 1992, Delaware; 1993, U.S. District Court, District of Delaware. *Education:* University of Delaware (B.S.A.C., 1989); Temple University School of Law (J.D., cum laude, 1992); Georgetown University Law School (LL.M, Taxation, with distinction, 2001). Beta Alpha Psi. *Member:* Delaware State (Member, Estates and Trust Section) and American Bar Associations; Estate Planning Council of Delaware. ***PRACTICE AREAS:*** Estate Planning; Probate; Taxation. ***Email:*** fpconaty@prickett.com

OF COUNSEL

WILLIAM PRICKETT, born Wilmington, Delaware, November 13, 1925; admitted to bar, 1955, Delaware and District of Columbia. *Education:* Princeton University (B.A., 1949); Harvard University (LL.B., 1954). Co-author: Comment, "A Preview of Delaware's Financial Center Development Act of 1981," 6 Delaware Journal of Corporate Law 104, 1981; "*Weinberger v. UOP, Inc.:* Delaware's Effort To Preserve A Level Playing Field for Cash-Out Mergers," 8 Delaware Journal of Corporate Law 59, 1983; "An Explanation of *Trans Union* to 'Henny Penny' and Her Friends," 10 Delaware Journal of Corporate Law 451, 1985. Special Deputy Attorney General, 1962-1964. Chair, Continuing Committee on Rules of the Superior Court, 1965-1971. Trustee, Clients' Security Trust Fund of the Supreme Court of Delaware, 1981-1996. *Member:* The Association of the Bar of the City of New York; Delaware State (President, 1974; Member, Corporation Law Section; Chair, Judicial Nominating Commission, 1984-1985) and American Bar Associations; American Law Institute. Fellow: American College of Trial Lawyers; American Bar Foundation; Delaware Bar Foundation. [USNR, active duty, 1943-1946; USMCR, active duty, 1950-1952]. ***PRACTICE AREAS:*** Corporate Law; Chancery Litigation; Federal Litigation; Patent Litigation (Local Counsel). ***Email:*** wprickett@prickett.com

APRIL CASO ISHAK, born Jersey City, New Jersey, April 2, 1963; admitted to bar, 1989, Delaware. *Education:* Douglass College, Rutgers University (B.A., with high honors, 1985); Rutgers School of Law-Camden, New Jersey (J.D., 1989). Staff Member, 1987-1988, and Research Editor, 1988-1989, Rutgers Law Journal. *Member:* Delaware State Bar Association. ***PRACTICE AREAS:*** Corporate Law; Litigation. ***Email:*** acishak@prickett.com

---

WILLIAM H. LUNGER, born Oakland, California, April 28, 1969; admitted to bar, 1995, Delaware; 1998, Pennsylvania. *Education:* Dickinson College (B.A., 1991); Widener University School of Law (J.D., cum laude, 1994); Georgetown University Law Center (LL.M., Taxation, 1995). Member, Delaware Journal of Corporate Law. *Member:* Delaware State (Estates and Trusts, and Taxation Sections) and American (Real Property, Probate and Trust Law Section) Bar Associations. ***PRACTICE AREAS:*** Estate Planning; Estate Administration; Trust Administration; Family Business Planning; Tax. ***Email:*** whlunger@prickett.com

PAUL A. FIORAVANTI, JR., born Wilmington, Delaware, November 15, 1961; admitted to bar, 1997, Maryland; 1998, U.S. District Court, District of Maryland; 1999, Delaware, U.S. District Court, District of Delaware and U.S. Court of Appeals, Third Circuit. *Education:* University of Delaware (B.A., 1993); University of Maryland (J.D., with honors, 1997). Editor in Chief, Maryland Law Review, 1996-1997. Law Clerk to the Hon. Ellen L. Hollander, Court of Special Appeals, Maryland, 1997-1998. Author: Note, "Limiting the Self-Representation Right in Child Sex Abuse Cases," 55 Md. L. Rev. 1020 (1996). Associate Member, Delaware Board of Bar Examiners, 2001. *Member:* Delaware State (Member, Corporation Law and Litigation Sections), Maryland State (Member, Business Law Section) and American (Member, Business Law and Litigation Sections) Bar Associations. ***PRACTICE AREAS:*** Corporate Litigation; Corporate Law. ***Email:*** pafioravanti@prickett.com

(This Listing Continued)

PRICKETT, JONES & ELLIOTT, P.A., Wilmington—Continued

ALLYSON A. McKENZIE, born Philadelphia, Pennsylvania, April 23, 1974; admitted to bar, 2001, Pennsylvania (Not admitted in Delaware). *Education:* Ursinus College (B.A., 1996); Widener University School of Law (J.D., cum laude, 2000). Editor, Delaware Journal of Corporate Law (1999-2000). Author, Delaware Journal of Corporate Law, 309 (2000). *Member:* Pennsylvania (Member, Section on: Business Law) and American (Member, Sections on: Business Law; Litigation) Bar Associations. ***PRACTICE AREAS:*** Corporate; Commercial Litigation; Corporate Litigation; Bankruptcy. ***Email:*** aamckenzie@prickett.com

D. BENJAMIN SNYDER, born Dover, Delaware, December 23, 1974; admitted to bar, 2001, Delaware and Pennsylvania. *Education:* James Madison University (B.B.A., 1997); Dickinson School of Law of the Pennsylvania State University (J.D., 2000). Senior Editor, Dickinson Journal of International Law. Recipient, Richard Reeve Baxtor Award. (Resident, Dover, Delaware Office). ***PRACTICE AREAS:*** Commercial Litigation; Commercial and Residential Real Estate Transactions; General Business; Corporate Practice; Administrative Law; Bankruptcy. ***Email:*** dsnyder@prickett.com

REPRESENTATIVE CLIENTS: *NATIONAL/INTERNATIONAL:* AT&T Corp.; Bapell USA, Inc.; Carlton Communications Plc.; Ciba Specialty Chemicals Corporation; Computer Associates International; Credit Suisse First Boston; DaimlerChrysler; Dell Computer Corporation; DQE Financial Corp.; Electronic Data Systems; Enron Corp.; Gannett Co., Inc.; Global Motorsport Group; Hallwood Realty Partners; Henkel Corp.; Hicks, Muse, Tate & Furst; Hunt Petroleum; LLoyds; Motiva Enterprises, LLC; Novartis Corp.; Pioneer Natural Resources; The Racal Corp.; Range Resources; Remington Oil and Gas; Solutia, Inc.; Sulzer Medica; TV Guide, Inc.; United GlobalCom, Inc.; W.R. Berkley Corp.; Windfields Farm, Ltd.; World Trade Corp. *LOCAL:* Anesthesia Services, P.A.; Bayhealth Medical Center, Inc.; Christiana Stables; Conectiv (Delmarva Power & Light); CSX Transportation; Delaware Racing Assn.; Delaware Stadium Corporation; Doctors for Emergency Services; Dover Downs, Inc.; Kent General Hospital; Milford Memorial Hospital; Paradee Gas Co.; WaWa Food Markets, Inc.; Wilmington Trust Company. *INSURANCE COMPANIES:* AIG; ALAS; Amica Mutual Insurance Co.; Erie Insurance Group; Factory Mutual Insurance Company; Great American Insurance Company; Horace Mann Ins. Co.; Media/Professional Insurance; PHICO Insurance Company; Preferred Physicians Insurance Co.; Reliance National Insurance Co.; St. Paul Fire & Marine Insurance Co.; The Doctors' Company.

RATNER & PRESTIA

A PROFESSIONAL CORPORATION

Established in 1981

SUITE 209, WEBSTER BUILDING
3411 SILVERSIDE ROAD
P.O. BOX 7228
WILMINGTON, DELAWARE 19803
Telephone: 302-479-9470
Fax: 302-479-9480
Email: mail@ratnerprestia.com
URL: http://www.ratnerprestia.com

Valley Forge, Pennsylvania Office: Suite 301, One Westlakes (Berwyn), P.O. Box 980. Telephone: 610-407-0700. Facsimile: 610-407-0701.

Allentown, Pennsylvania Office: Suite 265, Commerce Plaza II, 5100 Tilghman Street. Telephone: 610-530-8100. Fax: 610-530-8200.

Domestic and International Intellectual Property Law including Patent, Trademark, Copyright, Unfair Competition, Trade Secret Matters and Related Litigation, Licensing and Antitrust, Biotechnology, Software and Computer Law, Internet Law, Protection and Entertainment Law.

FIRM PROFILE: Ratner & Prestia's clients range from a number of start-up companies to several multi-billion dollar corporations, both U.S. and non-U.S. based and from private individuals to well-known institutions and universities. Because of the highly technical nature of the firm's work, each member of its professional staff has been selected so that collectively the firm is able to provide comprehensive coverage both in breadth and in depth in substantially all technical fields. Diverse staff includes persons of substantial background and experience in litigation, licensing and patent and trademark prosecution. Technical specializations include computer hardware and software protection, biotechnology, biomedical devices, pharmaceutical chemistry, photochemistry, polymer chemistry and electric imaging science.

KEVIN W. GOLDSTEIN, born Elizabeth, New Jersey, 1958; admitted to bar, 1991, Delaware, Pennsylvania and New Jersey; U.S. District Court, District of Delaware, U.S. District Court, Eastern District of Pennsylvania, U.S. District Court, District of New Jersey and U.S. Court of Appeals, Third Circuit; registered to practice before U.S. Patent and Trademark Office. *Education:* Rensselaer Polytechnic Institute (B.S., 1980); Princeton University; Delaware Law School of Widener University (J.D., 1990). Judicial Clerk to Honorable Phyllis W. Beck, Pennsylvania Superior Court, 1990-1991. *Member:* Pennsylvania, Delaware and New Jersey State Bar Associations. ***PRACTICE AREAS:*** Intellectual Property; Intellectual Property Litigation. ***Email:*** kwgoldstein@ratnerprestia.com

(This Listing Continued)

COSTAS S. KRIKELIS, born Greece, November 26, 1937; admitted to bar, 1977, Delaware and U.S. District Court, District of Delaware; 1997, U.S. Supreme Court; 2001, U.S. Court of Appeals for the Federal Circuit; registered to practice before U.S. Patent and Trademark Office. *Education:* Rensselaer Polytechnic Institute (B.S.E.E., 1962); Ecole Nationale d'Electricite et de Mechanique, Nancy, France; Widener University School of Law (J.D., cum laude, 1975). Co-Author, "Intellectual Property: Recognizing Intellectual Property and Learning to Protect it," Lorman Educational Services, Inc., 1996. Mediator, Superior Court of Delaware. *Member:* Delaware Bar Association (Member, Intellectual Property Law Section); American Intellectual Property Law Association. (Resident Managing Partner). ***LANGUAGES:*** French and Greek. ***PRACTICE AREAS:*** Intellectual Property Law. ***Email:*** cskrikelis@ratnerprestia.com

BRUCE M. MONROE, born Indianapolis, Indiana, July 7, 1940; admitted to bar, 1996, Pennsylvania, New Jersey and Delaware; registered to practice before U.S. Patent and Trademark Office. *Education:* Wabash College (A.B., 1962); University of Illinois (M.S., 1964; Ph.D., 1967); Widener University School of Law (J.D., summa cum laude, 1995). Post Doctoral Fellow, California Institute of Technology, 1967-1969. Electronics Department, Intellectual Property Group for E.I. du Pont de Nemours & Co., Wilmington, Delaware, 1987-1993. Author, "Vicarious Liability of Trade Show Organizers for Copyright Infringement," Entertainment, Publishing and the Arts Handbook: Edition 251, 1995-1996, R. Thorne and J.D. Viera, Eds., 1995. Co-Author: "Photoinitiator Systems," Chem.Rev. 93, 435-448, 1993; "Intellectual Property: Reorganizing Intellectual Property and Learning to Protect it," Lorman Educational Services, Inc., 1996. Adjunct Professor, Patent Law, Widener University. *Member:* American Chemical Society; The Scientific Research Society; The Society for Imaging Science & Technology. ***PRACTICE AREAS:*** Intellectual Property; Chemical Intellectual Property. ***Email:*** bmmonroe@ratnerprestia.com

---

REX A. DONNELLY, IV, born Camden, New Jersey, March 3, 1966; admitted to bar, 1996, Delaware. *Education:* Virginia Polytechnic Institute and State University (B.S.M.E., 1988); Widener University School of Law (J.D., 1995). *Member:* Delaware State (Member, Intellectual Property Section) and American (Member, Intellectual Property Section) Bar Associations. ***PRACTICE AREAS:*** Intellectual Property. ***Email:*** radonnelly@ratnerprestia.com

PATENT AGENTS

WILLIAM P. HAUSER, born Cincinnati, Ohio, April 28, 1934. Registered to practice before U.S. Patent and Trademark Office. *Education:* University of Notre Dame (B.S., 1956); University of Rochester (Ph.D., Physical Chemistry, 1961). Sigma Xi. Postdoctorate Fellow, Mellon Institute and University of Notre Dame, 1962-1966. Intellectual Property Development Management for E.I. du Pont de Nemours & Co., Wilmington, Delaware, 1970-1991. *Member:* American Chemical Society (Member, Chemistry and the Law Section); Scientific Research Society; Society for Imaging Science and Technology. ***PRACTICE AREAS:*** Patent Prosecution. ***Email:*** wphauser@ratnerprestia.com

PAMELA D. POLITIS, born Chico, California; admitted to bar, registered to practice before the U.S. Patent and Trademark Office. *Education:* University of California, Santa Cruz (B.A., 1991); University of Michigan (Ph.D., 1999). *Member:* American Chemical Association; Association of Women in Science; American Association of Advancement of Science. ***PRACTICE AREAS:*** Patent Prosecution. ***Email:*** pdpolitis@ratnerprestia.com

CONSULTING ATTORNEY

PAUL F. PRESTIA, born Connellsville, Pennsylvania, October 17, 1937; admitted to bar, 1967, Pennsylvania; 1999, Delaware; U.S. Court of Appeals, Federal Circuit and U.S. Supreme Court; registered to practice before the U.S. Patent and Trademark Office. *Education:* Lehigh University (B.S.Ch.E., 1959); Georgetown University (J.D., 1967). Mediator, U.S. District Court, Eastern District Pennsylvania. *Member:* Philadelphia and American (Member, Sections on: Litigation; Antitrust Law; Patent, Trademark and Copyright Law) Bar Associations; American Intellectual Property Law Association (Chair, Antitrust Committee, 1986-1988; Economics of Law Practice, 1993-1995; Committee on Professionalism and Ethics, 1999-2001; Board of Directors, 1996-1999); Philadelphia Intellectual Property Law Association (President, 1987-1988); Benjamin Franklin Inn of Court (Founding Member; President, 1996). ***PRACTICE AREAS:*** Intellectual Property; Litigation; Dispute Resolution; Patents. ***Email:*** pprestia@ratnerprestia.com

REED SMITH LLP

1201 MARKET STREET, SUITE 1500
WILMINGTON, DELAWARE 19801
Telephone: 302-778-7500
FAX: 302-778-7575
Email: reedsmith@reedsmith.com
URL: http://www.reedsmith.com

Mailing Address: P.O. Box 2009, 15230-2009

Pittsburgh, Pennsylvania Office: 435 Sixth Avenue, 15219-1886. Telephone: 412-288-3131. FAX: 412-288-3063.

Washington, D.C. Office: Suite 1100 - East Tower, 1301 K Street, N.W., 20005-3317. Telephone: 202-414-9200. FAX: 202-414-9299.

Philadelphia, Pennsylvania Office: 2500 One Liberty Place, 19103-7301. Telephone: 215-851-8100. FAX: 215-851-1420.

Harrisburg, Pennsylvania Office: 213 Market Street, 17101-2132. Telephone: 717-234-5988, FAX: 717-236-3777.

Princeton, New Jersey Office: 136 Main Street, Suite 250, 08540-5799. Telephone: 609-987-0050. FAX: 609-951-0824.

New York, N.Y. Office: 375 Park Avenue, 17th Floor, 10152. Telephone: 212-521-5400. FAX: 212-521-5450.

Newark, New Jersey Office: The Legal Center, One Riverfront Plaza, First Floor, 07102-5400. Telephone: 973-621-3200. FAX: 973-621-3199.

Falls Church, Virginia Office: Suite 1400, 3110 Fairview Park Drive, 22042. Telephone: 703-641-4200. FAX: 703-641-4340.

Leesburg, Virginia Office: 44084 Riverside Parkway, Suite 300, 20176. Telephone: 703-729-8500. Metro: 703-478-1992. FAX: 703-478-8003.

McLean, Virginia Office: Suite 1100, 8251 Greensboro Drive, 22102-3844. Telephone: 703-734-4600. FAX: 703-734-4699.

Richmond, Virginia Office: Riverfront Plaza, West Tower, 901 East Byrd Street, Suite 1700, 23219-4069. Telephone: 804-344-3400. FAX: 804-344-3410.

London, England Office: Reed Smith Warner Cranston, Pickfords Wharf, Clink Street, SE1 9DG. Telephone: +44-20-7403-2900. FAX: +44-20-7403-4221.

Coventry, England Office: Reed Smith Warner Cranston, Park House, Station Square, CV1 2FL. Telephone: +44 24 7629 3000. FAX: +44 24 7629 3030. DX: 11203 Coventry 1.

Antitrust and Trade Regulation, Asbestos, Bank Regulatory, Bankruptcy, China/Asia, Communications, Construction, Consumer Financial Services, Corporate and Securities, E-Commerce, Eminent Domain/Condemnation, Employee Benefits, Employment Discrimination Litigation, Employment Law, Energy and Natural Resources, Environmental, Equipment Leasing, Family Business, Financial Services, Financial Services Insurance, Financial Services Litigation, First Amendment, Food, Drug & Device, Franchise, Government Contracts & Export Compliance, Government Relations, Health Care, Higher Education, Immigration, Information Technology, Insurance, Insurance Coverage, Intellectual Property, International, Land Use, Litigation, Media and Entertainment, Mergers and Acquisitions, Non-Profit Organizations, Product Liability, Professional Liability, Project Finance, Public Finance, Real Estate, Restrictive Covenants/Trade Secrets, Satellite Transactions, Tax, Technology, Telecommunications, Tissue Engineering and Biomedical Applications, Trusts & Estates, Venture, White Collar Crime, Year 2000.

FIRM PROFILE: Founded nearly 125 years ago, Reed Smith has been handling the interests of clients both large and small in a broad spectrum of areas. Our client base has expanded from some of Pittsburgh's leading companies and founding families to include a wide variety of Fortune 500 companies, privately held companies and emerging technology businesses.

From our beginnings in Pittsburgh we have expanded to 12 offices in the United States and two in the United Kingdom, and currently include the experience of more than 650 attorneys. Reed Smith is now a global top 30 law firm, and is ranked among the top 100 patent firms. We are counsel to 23 of the top 25 United States banks; 14 of the Fortune e-50 companies; seven of the top 10 pharmaceutical companies; and 50 of the world's leading drug and device manufacturers.

From pharmaceutical companies to financial institutions, from intellectual property dilemmas to complex health care issues, our clients look to us to help them navigate through changing industry environments.

Knox & Reed	1877-1902
Reed, Smith, Shaw & Beal	1902-1922
Reed Smith Shaw & McClay	1922-2000

MEMBERS OF FIRM

TOBEY M. DALUZ, admitted to bar, 1990, Pa. (Not admitted in Delaware). *Education:* University of Pennsylvania (B.A., 1987); Georgetown University (J.D., 1990). ***PRACTICE AREAS:*** Bankruptcy. ***Email:*** tdaluz@reedsmith.com

KURT F. GWYNNE, admitted to bar, 1992, Pa.; 1993, N.J.; 2000, Del. *Education:* University of Central Florida (B.A., summa cum laude, 1988); University of Pennsylvania (J.D., 1992). ***PRACTICE AREAS:*** Bankruptcy. ***Email:*** kgwynne@reedsmith.com

(This Listing Continued)

THOMAS P. PRESTON, admitted to bar, 1975, Pa.; 1988, De. *Education:* Yale University (B.A., 1968); University of Virginia (J.D., 1975). ***PRACTICE AREAS:*** Litigation. ***Email:*** tpreston@reedsmith.com

DAVID S. SWAYZE, admitted to bar, 1969, De. *Education:* Princeton University (A.B., 1966); University of Pennsylvania (LL.B., 1969). ***PRACTICE AREAS:*** Government Relations. ***Email:*** dswayze@reedsmith.com

J. RICHARD TUCKER, admitted to bar, 1969, Tx; 1977, Ca. (Not admitted in Delaware). *Education:* University of Delaware (B.A., 1965); South Texas College of Law (J.D.1969). ***PRACTICE AREAS:*** Corporate Law. ***Email:*** jtucker@reedsmith.com

ASSOCIATES

ALISSA BALOTTI ANDERSON, admitted to bar, 1997, De. *Education:* Connecticut College (B.A., 1992); Widener University School of Law (J.D., magna cum laude, 1997). ***PRACTICE AREAS:*** Corporate Law. ***Email:*** aanderson@reedsmith.com

JOHN G. HARRIS, admitted to bar, 1997, N.J.; 2000, Pa. (Not admitted in Delaware). *Education:* Seton Hall University (B.A., 1993); Widener University (J.D., 1997). ***PRACTICE AREAS:*** Litigation. ***Email:*** jharris@reedsmith.com

JENNIFER A. L. KELLEHER, admitted to bar, 1997, Md.; 1998, D.C. (Not admitted in Delaware). *Education:* University of Delaware (B.A., 1992); Widener University School of Law (J.D., cum laude, 1996). ***PRACTICE AREAS:*** Litigation. ***Email:*** jkelleher@reedsmith.com

RICHARD A. KEULER JR., admitted to bar, 1999, N.J. and Pa. (Not admitted in Delaware). *Education:* Princeton University (A.B., 1996); Georgetown University (J.D., 1999). ***PRACTICE AREAS:*** Bankruptcy. ***Email:*** rkeuler@reedsmith.com

CHRISTINE P. SCHILTZ, admitted to bar, 1993, De. *Education:* Wake Forest University (B.A., 1990); University of Richmond, T.C. Williams School of Law (J.D., 1993). ***PRACTICE AREAS:*** Government Relations. ***Email:*** cschiltz@reedsmith.com

MICHAEL W. TEICHMAN, admitted to bar, 1994, De. *Education:* Villanova University (B.A., 1986); Temple University (J.D., 1994). ***PRACTICE AREAS:*** Financial Services Law. ***Email:*** mteichman@reedsmith.com

JAN A. T. VAN AMERONGEN, JR., admitted to bar, 1990, Pa. and N.J.; 1992, D.C. and Md.; 1996, De. *Education:* University of Pennsylvania (B.A., 1987); College of William and Mary, Marshall-Wythe School of Law (J.D., 1990). ***PRACTICE AREAS:*** Litigation. ***Email:*** jvanamerongen@reedsmith.com

(For biographical data on personnel in Washington, D.C., Philadelphia, Pittsburgh and Harrisburg, Pennsylvania, Falls Church, Leesburg, McLean and Richmond, Virginia, Princeton and Newark, New Jersey, New York, New York and London, England, see Professional Biographies at those locations)

RICHARDS, LAYTON & FINGER, P.A.

ONE RODNEY SQUARE
P.O. BOX 551
WILMINGTON, DELAWARE 19899
Telephone: 302-658-6541
Telecopier: 302-658-6548

REVISERS OF THE DELAWARE LAW DIGEST FOR THIS DIRECTORY.

General Civil Trial Litigation and Appellate Practice in all State and Federal Courts and Banking, Bankruptcy, Business, Corporations, Employee Benefits, Environment, Government Relations, Health Care, Intellectual Property, Labor and Employment, Partnership, Real Estate, Securities, Tax, and Trusts and Estates.

FIRM PROFILE: Richards, Layton & Finger, founded in the early 1900s, is Delaware's largest law firm, with 105 lawyers. The firm has a full-service regional practice as well as a national practice in the areas of corporate law and litigation, partnership law, limited liability company and business trust law, bankruptcy and complex financial transactions. The firm offers a wide range of professional services, including general civil practice in state and federal courts, all aspects of Delaware corporate law, partnership, limited liability company and business trust law, federal and state taxation, estate planning, estates and trusts, real estate, business law, banking law, bankruptcy law, labor law, health law, intellectual property, environmental law, administrative law and governmental relations.

LAW FIRM ALLIANCES/ASSOCIATIONS: ***LEX MUNDI:*** *Lex Mundi is a global association of 158 independent law firms. The Member firms practice independently and not in a relationship for the joint practice of law.*

STATE CAPITAL LAW FIRM GROUP: *State Capital Law Firm Group is a global association of 100 independent law firms. The Member firms practice independently and not in a relationship for the joint practice of law.*

CHARLES F. RICHARDS, JR., born Philadelphia, Pennsylvania, November 11, 1937; admitted to bar, 1963, Delaware. *Education:* Princeton University

(This Listing Continued)

RICHARDS, LAYTON & FINGER, P.A., Wilmington—Continued

(A.B., 1959); Yale University (LL.B., 1962). Member, Board of Editors, Yale Law Journal, 1960-1962. Deputy Attorney General, State of Delaware, 1963-1964. Legal Secretary, Committee for Revision, Delaware Corporation Law, 1965-1967. Member, 1982-1988 and Chairman, 1986-1988, Board on Professional Responsibility of the Supreme Court of Delaware. Member, 1973— and Chairman, 1986—, Chancery Rules Committee. *Member:* Delaware State and American Bar Associations; American Law Institute; American Judicature Society (Director, 1991-1995). ***PRACTICE AREAS:*** Business Law; Business Litigation; Corporate Law; Corporate Control Contests; Corporate Litigation; Hostile Takeovers; Chancery Practice. ***Email:*** Richards@rlf.com

THOMAS P. SWEENEY, born Salt Lake City, Utah, September 26, 1936; admitted to bar, 1961, Colorado; 1963, Missouri; 1967, Delaware. *Education:* University of Utah (B.S., 1957); University of Denver (LL.B., 1960); New York University (LL.M., Taxation, 1962). Phi Delta Phi; Beta Gamma Sigma. *Member:* The Bar Association of Metropolitan St. Louis; The Colorado, Delaware State (Chairman, Decedents, Estates and Trust Committee, 1971-1973; Chairman, Tax Section, 1988-1989) and American (Chairman, Committee on Income of Estates and Trusts, Taxation Section, 1979-1981; Vice-Chairman, Committee on Government Submissions, Taxation Section, 1985-1987) Bar Associations; The Missouri Bar. Fellow: American College of Trust and Estate Counsel (Member, Board of Regents, 1982-1994; Treasurer, 1988-1989; Secretary, 1989-1990; Vice-President, 1990-1991; President-Elect, 1991-1992; President, 1992-1993; Immediate Past President, 1993-1994); American College of Tax Counsel; American Law Institute. ***PRACTICE AREAS:*** Estate Planning; Taxation (Local, Personal Property, State, Federal or International) Law; Federal Income, Estate and Gift Taxation Law; Trust Law. ***Email:*** Sweeney@rlf.com

PIERRE S. DU PONT, born Wilmington, Delaware, January 22, 1935; admitted to bar, 1964, Delaware. *Education:* Princeton University (LL.B., 1956); Harvard University (J.D., 1963). Winner, Ames Moot Court Competition. Member: Delaware General Assembly, 1968-1970; U.S. Congress, 1971-1977. Governor, State of Delaware, 1977-1985. *Member:* Delaware State and American Bar Associations. ***Email:*** duPont@rlf.com

ROBERT H. RICHARDS, III, born Philadelphia, Pennsylvania, January 26, 1938; admitted to bar, 1962, Delaware. *Education:* Princeton University (A.B., 1959); Harvard University (LL.B., 1962). Deputy Attorney General, State of Delaware, 1963. Member, District of Delaware Advisory Group for Federal Civil Justice Reform Act of 1990, 1991-1995. *Member:* Delaware State (Member: Corporation Law Section, 1984—; Intellectual Property Law Section, 1990—) and American Bar Associations; American Intellectual Property Law Association. ***Email:*** RRichards@rlf.com

R. FRANKLIN BALOTTI, born Louisville, Kentucky, April 19, 1942; admitted to bar, 1967, Delaware; 1994, Colorado. *Education:* Hamilton College (B.A., 1964); Cornell University (LL.B., 1967). Order of the Coif; Phi Kappa Phi. Co-Author and Editor: "The Delaware Law of Corporations and Business Organizations, Third Edition," Aspen Law & Business, Inc., 1998; "Meetings of Stockholders, Third Edition," Aspen Law & Business, Inc., 1998. Editorial Advisory Board, "Insights," 1987-1997. Executive Committee, Northwestern University School of Law Ray Garrett Institute, 1994—. Distinguished Practitioner-in-Residence, Cornell Law School, Fall 1996; Visiting Distinguished Corporate Professor, University of Miami School of Law, Spring 1998. Adjunct Professor: Widener University School of Law, 1991-1993, 1995; Adjunct Professor: University of Miami School of Law, 1999—; Adjunct Professor: The Cornell Law School, 1999—. Counsel, 1971-1974, Secretary, 1977-1981 and Member, 1974-1981; 1995; Delaware Courts Planning Committee. Member, and Secretary, 1974-1978, Supreme Court Advisory Committee on Rules. Member, 1980-1988, Vice-Chair, 1984-1986 and Chair, 1986-1988, Board of Bar Examiners of the State of Delaware. Member and Chair, 1991-1994, Board on the Unauthorized Practice of Law of the Supreme Court of Delaware. Chair, Delaware Supreme Court Committee On Family Court Internal Operating Procedures, 1997-1999. Member, The Cornell Law School Advisory Council, 1986-1992, 1997—. Member, Board of Overseers, Widener University School of Law, 1992-1999. Member, The American Law Institute. Fellow, The American College of Trial Lawyers. Director, Delaware Bar Foundation, 1997-2000. Member, Executive Committee, 1974-1976, 1989-1990 and 1991-1996, President, 1994-1995, President-Elect, 1993-1994, Vice-President, 1991-1993, Secretary, 1974-1975 and Member, Professional Guidance Committee, 2000—, Liaison, Judicial Nominating Commission/ Delaware State Bar Association's Committee on Judicial Appointments, 2000—, Delaware State Bar Association. Member, Ad Hoc Committee on Civil Justice Improvements, 1994-1997, Council Member, 1996-2000, Member, Committee on Corporate Laws, 1987-1993, Member, Ad Hoc Committee on ALI Corporate Governance Project, 1992-1993, Chair, Business and Corporate Litigation Committee, 1992-1996, Co-Chair, Committee on Business Courts, 1993-1997 and Member, Section of Business Law, 1968—, Section of Litigation, 1973—, Section of International Law & Practice, 1990— and Member, Standing Committee on Federal Judicial Improvements, 1999—, American Bar Association. ***Email:*** Balotti@rlf.com

(This Listing Continued)

RICHARD G. ELLIOTT, JR., born Wilmington, Delaware, May 28, 1940; admitted to bar, 1966, Delaware. *Education:* Washington & Lee University (B.S., Com., 1963); University of North Carolina (LL.B., 1966). Phi Delta Phi. Deputy Attorney General, State of Delaware, 1967-1968. Member, New Castle County Historic Review Board, 1992—. Member, Governor's Commission on Judicial Appointments, 1992-2001. *Member:* Delaware State (Chairman, 1994-1995, Labor and Employment Law Section) and American (Member, Committee on Corporate Counsel, First Amendment & Media Litigation Committee, Employment and Labor Relations Law Subcommittee, 1984—) Bar Associations. ***PRACTICE AREAS:*** Labor and Employment; Media Law. ***Email:*** Elliott@rlf.com

WENDELL FENTON, born Yonkers, New York, May 8, 1939; admitted to bar, 1966, New York; 1971, Delaware. *Education:* Yale University (B.A., 1961); Christ Church, Oxford, England; Harvard University (LL.B., 1965). *Member:* The Association of the Bar of the City of New York; Delaware State (Member, Corporation Law Section; Council, 1990-1994) and American (Member, Committee on Federal Regulation of Securities, Section of Business Law, 1979—) Bar Associations. ***Email:*** Fenton@rlf.com

ALLEN M. TERRELL, JR., born Atlanta, Georgia, August 5, 1943; admitted to bar, 1969, New York; 1970, Delaware. *Education:* Harvard University (A.B., 1965; LL.B., 1968). Adjunct Professor, Widener University School of Law, 1997. *Member:* Delaware State (Member, Corporation Law Section) and American (Member, Committees on Litigation and Federal Regulation of Securities, Section of Business Law, 1979—) Bar Associations. ***PRACTICE AREAS:*** Litigation; Corporate Law. ***Email:*** Terrell@rlf.com

DANIEL M. KRISTOL, born Wilmington, Delaware, July 7, 1936; admitted to bar, 1961, Delaware. *Education:* University of Pennsylvania (B.A., 1958; LL.B., 1961). Assistant City Solicitor, Wilmington, 1970-1973. *Member:* Delaware State (Chair, Committees on: Real and Personal Property, 1974-1978; World Peace Through Law, 1980-1981; Senior Lawyers, 1999—) and American Bar Associations; American College of Real Estate Lawyers. ***PRACTICE AREAS:*** Real Estate Law; Commercial Law. ***Email:*** kristol@rlf.com

GLENN C. KENTON, born Washington, D.C., December 21, 1943; admitted to bar, 1969, Delaware. *Education:* Swarthmore College (A.B., 1965); Georgetown University (J.D., 1968). Counsel: Delaware State House of Representatives, 1969-1970; U.S. Congressman Pierre S. du Pont, IV, 1971-1977. Secretary of State of Delaware, 1977-1985. *Member:* Delaware State (Member, Sections on Commercial Law and Governmental Law) and American (Member, Sections on Business Law and Public Utility, Communications and Transportation Law) Bar Associations. ***PRACTICE AREAS:*** Administrative Law; Insurance; Communications Law; Government Relations; Derivative Products; Securitization. ***Email:*** Kenton@rlf.com

RICHARD G. BACON, born Wilmington, Delaware, August 6, 1942; admitted to bar, 1968, District of Columbia; 1971, Delaware. *Education:* Villanova University (B.S. in Economics, 1964); Duke University (LL.B., 1967). Phi Delta Phi. *Member:* Delaware State (Chairman, Estate and Trust Section, 1981-1983) and American (Vice-Chairman, Administration and Distribution of Decedents' Estates Committee, Section of Real Property, Probate and Trust Law, 1983-1993; State Chairman, Property Tax Committee, Section of Real Property, Probate and Trust Law, 1995—) Bar Associations. Fellow, American College of Trust and Estate Counsel (State Chairman, 1987-1992). ***PRACTICE AREAS:*** Trust Law; Probate Law; Taxation (Local, State) Law. ***Email:*** Bacon@rlf.com

STEPHEN E. HERRMANN, born New York, N.Y., March 17, 1944; admitted to bar, 1969, Delaware and Virginia; 1970, District of Columbia. *Education:* Princeton University (A.B., 1966); University of Virginia (LL.B., 1969). Judicial Clerkship, The Honorable Daniel F. Wolcott, Delaware Supreme Court, 1969-1970. Special Assistant to the General Counsel, United States Environmental Protection Agency, 1971-1972. *Member:* Delaware State and American Bar Associations. ***Email:*** Herrmann@rlf.com

JULIAN H. BAUMANN, JR., born Ft. Leavenworth, Kansas, February 20, 1943; admitted to bar, 1968, South Carolina; 1976, Delaware. *Education:* Clemson University (B.S., 1965); University of Tennessee; University of South Carolina (J.D., 1968); New York University (LL.M., Taxation, 1975). *Member:* South Carolina Bar; Delaware State (Chairman, 1990-1991 and Vice-Chairman, 1989-1990, Section of Taxation) and American (Member, Section of Taxation) Bar Associations. Fellow, American College of Tax Counsel. [Capt., U.S. Army, JAGC, 1969-1974]. ***PRACTICE AREAS:*** Taxation Law.

DANIEL L. KLEIN, born Pittsburgh, Pennsylvania, October 10, 1946; admitted to bar, 1972, Pennsylvania; 1976, Delaware. *Education:* University of Pennsylvania (B.S., Economics, 1968); University of Pittsburgh (J.D., 1972). Member, 1970-1972 and Comment Editor, 1971-1972, University of Pittsburgh Law Review. Author: "Judicial Participation in Guilty Pleas: A Search for Standards," Volume 33, University of Pittsburgh Law Review. *Member:* Pennsylvania, Delaware State and American (Member, Real Property Section) Bar Associations; American College of Real Estate Lawyers (Member: Planning, Committee, 1987-1991, 1997—; Membership Committee, 1991-1993; Chair-

(This Listing Continued)

man, 1993; Member, Board of Governors, 1993-1997). ***PRACTICE AREAS:*** Real Estate Law; Real Estate Finance; Privatization; Land Use. ***Email:*** Klein@rlf.com

DONALD A. BUSSARD, born Wilmington, Delaware, June 7, 1951; admitted to bar, 1976, Delaware. *Education:* Williams College (B.A., 1973); Temple University (J.D., 1976). Phi Beta Kappa. *Member:* Delaware State (Member, Corporation Law Section and Chairman, Council of the Corporation Law Section) and American (Member, Section of Business Law) Bar Associations. ***Email:*** Bussard@rlf.com

WILLIAM J. WADE, born Morristown, New Jersey, November 3, 1947; admitted to bar, 1976, Delaware. *Education:* University of Delaware (B.A., 1973); University of Pennsylvania (J.D., 1976). Phi Beta Kappa; Phi Kappa Phi. Member, Supreme Court Advisory Committee on Discovery Abuse, 1981-1982. Associate Member, 1981-1987, Member, 1988-1996, Vice-Chairman, 1992-1993, Chairman, 1994-1996, Board of Bar Examiners. *Member:* Delaware State (Vice-Chair, 1996, Chair, 1997, Health Law Section) and American (Member: Business Law Section; Litigation Section; Health Law Section) Bar Associations. ***Email:*** Wade@rlf.com

JESSE A. FINKELSTEIN, born Rochester, New York, March 25, 1955; admitted to bar, 1980, Delaware. *Education:* University of Rochester (B.A., cum laude, 1977); Boston College Law School (J.D., cum laude, 1980). Executive Editor, Boston College International and Comparative Law Review, 1979-1980. Co-Author: "The Delaware Law of Corporations and Business Organizations," Aspen Law & Business, 1985; "Meetings of Stockholders," Aspen Law and Business, 1987. Series Editor, National Corporation Law Series, Aspen Law & Business. Member, BNA Corporate Practice Series Advisory Board. Chairman, Supreme Court Rules Committee, 1990-1996. Fellow, American College of Trial Lawyers. *Member:* Delaware State (Member, Council of Corporation Law Section) and American (Member: Section of Business Law; Litigation Section; International Law Section) Bar Associations. ***Email:*** Finkelstein@rlf.com

SAMUEL A. NOLEN, born Columbus, Ohio, November 18, 1954; admitted to bar, 1979, Delaware. *Education:* Vanderbilt University (B.A., cum laude, 1976); Universität Regensburg, Regensburg, Germany; Washington & Lee University (J.D., 1979). Delta Phi Alpha. Judicial Clerkship, Delaware Court of Chancery, 1979-1980. Associate Member, Board on the Unauthorized Practice of Law, 1991-1994; Member, Board on the Unauthorized Practice of Law, 1994-2001; Member, Board of Bar Examiners, 1997—. *Member:* Delaware State (Member, Corporation Law Section), American (Member: Section of Business Law; Litigation Section; International Law and Practice Section) and International (Member, Section of Business Law, Committee G) Bar Associations. ***LANGUAGES:*** German. ***PRACTICE AREAS:*** Corporate Law; Litigation; Mergers and Acquisitions; Chancery Practice. ***Email:*** Nolen@rlf.com

THOMAS A. BECK, born Louisville, Kentucky, April 6, 1956; admitted to bar, 1981, Delaware. *Education:* Dickinson College (B.A., cum laude, 1978); Cornell University (J.D., 1981). Associate Member, Delaware Board of Bar Examiners, 1988-1996. *Member:* Delaware State (Member, Corporation Law Section) and American (Member: Section of Business Law; Litigation Section) Bar Associations. ***PRACTICE AREAS:*** Litigation; Corporate Law; Chancery Practice. ***Email:*** Beck@rlf.com

GREGORY P. WILLIAMS, born Wilmington, Delaware, November 16, 1957; admitted to bar, 1982, Delaware. *Education:* University of Delaware (B.A.A.S., with honors, 1979); College of William and Mary (J.D., 1982). Member, William and Mary Law Review, 1980-1982. Co-Author: "Meetings of Stockholders," Prentice Hall, Law & Business, (3d ed. 1998). Chairman, Delaware Supreme Court Rules Committee, 1997—. Member, Chancery Court Rules Committee, 1986—. *Member:* Delaware State and American Bar Associations. ***PRACTICE AREAS:*** Litigation; Corporate Law; Corporate Litigation; Partnership Litigation. ***Email:*** Williams@rlf.com

JOHN A. PARKINS, JR., born Reading, Pennsylvania, December 28, 1946; admitted to bar, 1972, Delaware. *Education:* University of Delaware (B.A., 1969); Washington & Lee University (J.D., cum laude, 1972). Note and Comment Editor, Washington & Lee Law Review, 1971-1972. Law Clerk, Delaware Supreme Court, 1972-1973. Deputy Attorney General, State of Delaware, 1977-1985. Member, Supreme Court Rules Committee, 1984-1989. *Member:* Delaware State and American Bar Associations; American Board of Trial Advocates. ***PRACTICE AREAS:*** Litigation. ***Email:*** Parkins@rlf.com

PAUL M. ALTMAN, born Philadelphia, Pennsylvania, January 29, 1959; admitted to bar, 1983, Delaware. *Education:* Lehigh University (B.S., 1980); Villanova University (J.D., magna cum laude, 1983). Phi Beta Kappa; Order of the Coif. Member, 1981-1982 and Case and Comment Editor, 1982-1983, Villanova Law Review. Author: Casenote, "United States v. Newman: Misappropriation of Confidential Takeover Information Constitutes a Criminal Violation of Rule 10b-5," 27 Villanova Law Review 1329, 1981-1982. Co-Author: "Lubaroff & Altman on Delaware Limited Partnerships," (1995) and "Delaware Limited Partnerships" and "Delaware Limited Liability Companies," in Balotti and Finkelstein, Del. Law of Corps. & Bus. Orgs., 2d Ed., Chapter 24 and Chapter 27 (1990). Delaware State (Secretary, Commercial Law Section, 1986-1989; Vice-Chairman, 1989-1991; Chairman, 1991-1993; Member, Committee on Partnerships and Limited Liability Companies. Member, Commercial and Corporation Law Sections) and American (Member, Partnerships/Unincorporated Business Law; Member, Task Force on Revised Uniform Limited Partnership Act) Bar Associations. ***PRACTICE AREAS:*** Partnerships and Limited Liability Companies. ***Email:*** Altman@rlf.com

GREGORY V. VARALLO, born Philadelphia, Pennsylvania, March 3, 1959; admitted to bar, 1984, Delaware. *Education:* University of Pennsylvania (B.A., 1980); Temple University (J.D., 1983). President, Temple University School of Law Moot Court Board, 1982-1983. Best Oral Advocate, Albert R. Mugel National Moot Court Tax Competition, 1982. Co-Author: "Fundamentals of Corporate Governance," (ABA 1996); "The Board of Directors" (BNA Corporate Practice Series, 1994); "Action by Written Consent," in R. Balotti, J. Finkelstein & G. Williams, Meetings of Shareholders (Prentice Hall), 1989; A Process-Based Model For Analyzing Deal Protection Measures, 55 Bus. Law 1609 (2000). *Member:* Delaware State and American (Chairman, Corporate Counselling and Litigation Subcommittee, 1998-2000); (Co-Chairman, Task Force on Litigation Reform and Rules Revision, 2000—) Bar Associations. ***PRACTICE AREAS:*** Corporate Control Litigation; Complex Business Litigation. ***Email:*** Varallo@rlf.com

MARK J. GENTILE, born Buffalo, New York, October 19, 1956; admitted to bar, 1982, Massachusetts; 1983, New York; 1984, Colorado; 1987, Delaware. *Education:* State University of New York at Binghamton (B.S., 1979); Boston University School of Law (J.D., cum laude, 1982). Member, 1980-1981 and Managing Editor, 1981-1982, Boston University School of Law, Law Review. Law Clerk to Hon. John T. Elfvin, U.S. District Court, Western District of New York, 1982-1983. *Member:* Delaware State (Member, Corporation Law Section) and American (Member, Section of Business Law) Bar Associations. ***PRACTICE AREAS:*** Corporate Law; Securities. ***Email:*** Gentile@rlf.com

ROBERT J. KRAPF, born Wilmington, Delaware, July 25, 1951; admitted to bar, 1983, Delaware. *Education:* Georgetown University (B.S.F.S., 1973); University of Delaware (M.A., 1975); Delaware Law School of Widener University (J.D., cum laude, 1983). *Member:* Delaware State (Chairman, Real and Personal Property Section, 1990-1992) and American (Member, Section of Real Property, Probate and Trust Law; Chair, Land Use Regulation Committee; Member, Commercial Leasing Committee; Member, Section of State and Local Government Law, Land Use, Planning and Zoning Committee) Bar Associations; American College of Real Estate Lawyers; American College of Mortgage Attorneys (Member, Board of Regents, 2000—, State Chair, 1995-2000). ***PRACTICE AREAS:*** Real Estate Law; Zoning Law; Commercial Leasing. ***Email:*** Krapf@rlf.com

KEVIN G. ABRAMS, born Wilmington, Delaware, January 1, 1956; admitted to bar, 1985, Delaware. *Education:* University of Pennsylvania (A.B., 1978); University of Virginia (J.D., 1984). Member, 1982-1983 and Editor-in-Chief, 1983-1984, Journal of Law and Politics. Co-Author: "Suits Against Corporations, Directors, Officers or Stockholders" and "Sale of Assets, Dissolution and Winding-Up," *Delaware Law of Corporations and Business Organizations, Third Edition, Balotti and Finkelstein, 1998. Member:* Delaware State (Member, Corporate Law Section) and American (Member, Sections on: Business Law; Litigation) Bar Associations. ***PRACTICE AREAS:*** Mergers and Acquisitions; Corporate Law; Corporate Litigation; Securities Litigation. ***Email:*** Abrams@rlf.com

ERIC A. MAZIE, born Philadelphia, Pennsylvania, June 18, 1957; admitted to bar, 1984, Delaware. *Education:* Drexel University (B.S., cum laude, 1981); College of William and Mary, Marshall-Wythe School of Law (J.D., 1984). Editor-in-Chief, The Colonial Lawyer, 1983-1984. Co-Author: Chapter 25 - Delaware Business Trusts in "The Delaware Law of Corporations and Business Organizations," Law & Business, Inc., 1990; Chapter 9 - Role of the Trustee in Leasing Transactions in "Equipment Leasing-Leveraged Leasing," Practicing Law Institute, 1999. *Member:* Delaware State (Member, Commercial Law Section; Chairman, Business Trust Committee) and American (Member, Section of Business Law, Commercial Financial Services and Partnerships and Unincorporated Business Organizations Committees) Bar Associations. ***PRACTICE AREAS:*** Banks and Banking; Business Law; Commercial Law; Contracts; Corporate Law; Debtor and Creditor; Equipment Finance and Leasing; Partnership Law; Securities. ***Email:*** Mazie@rlf.com

ROBERT W. WHETZEL, born Pittsburgh, Pennsylvania, January 17, 1960; admitted to bar, 1984, Delaware; registered to practice before U.S. Patent and Trademark Office. *Education:* University of Delaware (B.Ch.E., 1981); Villanova University (J.D., cum laude, 1984). Order of the Coif. Recipient, Scribes Award, 1984. Member, 1982-1983 and Associate Editor, 1983-1984, Villanova Law Review. Author: Casenote, 28 Villanova Law Review 451, 1982-1983. Co-Author: Chapter 49 - Delaware Environmental Law in "Environmental Law Practice Guide" (Matthew Bender), 1992. Member, Advisory Committee for the U.S. District Court, District of Delaware, 1994—. *Member:* Delaware State (Chairman, Section of Environmental Law, 1994-1996) and American (Member, Section of Litigation, Section of Natural Resources, Energy and Environmental Law) Bar Associations. ***PRACTICE AREAS:*** Litigation; Environmental Law; Intellectual Property. ***Email:*** Whetzel@rlf.com

(This Listing Continued)

RICHARDS, LAYTON & FINGER, P.A., Wilmington—Continued

W. DONALD SPARKS, II, born Durham, North Carolina, April 16, 1958; admitted to bar, 1983, Pennsylvania; 1988, Delaware. *Education:* Dartmouth College (B.A., summa cum laude, 1980); Yale University (J.D., 1983). Member, 1981-1982 and Senior Editor, 1982-1983, Yale Law Journal. Law Clerk to Hon. Caleb M. Wright, U.S. District Court, District of Delaware, 1983-1984. *Member:* Pennsylvania, Delaware State and American Bar Associations. ***PRACTICE AREAS:*** Estate Planning and Estate Administration; Tax Exempt Organizations; Taxation. ***Email:*** Sparks@rlf.com

C. STEPHEN BIGLER, born Coatesville, Pennsylvania, August 23, 1959; admitted to bar, 1984, Delaware. *Education:* Washington & Lee University (B.S. Commerce, magna cum laude, 1981); University of Virginia (J.D., 1984). Phi Beta Kappa; Beta Gamma Sigma; Delta Sigma Rho-Tau Kappa Alpha. Managing Editor, Virginia Journal of International Law, 1983-1984. *Member:* Delaware State and American Bar Associations. ***PRACTICE AREAS:*** Corporate Law; Corporate Transactions; Mergers and Acquisitions. ***Email:*** Bigler@rlf.com

C. MALCOLM COCHRAN, IV, born Wilmington, Delaware, December 19, 1959; admitted to bar, 1985, Delaware. *Education:* University of Delaware (B.A., 1982); Catholic University (J.D., 1985). Member, Catholic University Law Review, 1984-1985. Attorney, Delaware House of Representatives, 1988-1991; Commissioner, Delaware Heritage Commission, 1990-1999. *Member:* Delaware State and American (Member, Sections on: Litigation; Business Law) Bar Associations. ***PRACTICE AREAS:*** Complex Business Litigation; Governmental Relations; Administrative Law. ***Email:*** Cochran@rlf.com

ANNE C. FOSTER, born Aiken, South Carolina, August 22, 1961; admitted to bar, 1986, Delaware. *Education:* College of William and Mary (B.A., 1983; J.D., 1986). Member, J. Braxton Craven Moot Court Team. Chair, Board on Professional Responsibility of the Supreme Court of Delaware. Member, Preliminary Review Committee of Board on Professional Responsibility of the Supreme Court of Delaware, 1993-1997. *Member:* Delaware State and American Bar Associations. ***PRACTICE AREAS:*** Litigation; Corporate Law. ***Email:*** Foster@rlf.com

CYNTHIA DEANS KAISER, born Norfolk, Virginia, July 3, 1959; admitted to bar, 1987, Delaware. *Education:* Duke University (B.S.E., cum laude, 1981); Delaware Law School of Widener University (J.D., cum laude, 1986). Phi Delta Phi. *Member:* Delaware State and American Bar Associations. ***PRACTICE AREAS:*** Asset Based Lending; Business Trusts; Securities Regulation Law (Blue Sky Law); Business Law; Commercial Law. ***Email:*** Kaiser@rlf.com

DANIEL A. DREISBACH, born Allentown, Pennsylvania, December 22, 1956; admitted to bar, 1988, Delaware and Pennsylvania. *Education:* Lehigh University (B.S.C.E., cum laude, 1982); Pennsylvania State University (B.S., 1979); Temple University (J.D., cum laude, 1987). Chi Epsilon; Phi Alpha Delta. Member, Temple Law Quarterly, 1986-1987. Co-Author: Fundamentals of Corporate Governance, Published by Section of Business Law, American Bar Association (1996). *Member:* Delaware State and American Bar Associations. ***PRACTICE AREAS:*** Litigation; Corporate Law; Corporate Transactions; Corporate Litigation; Business Law; Business Litigation; Corporate Control Contests; Hostile Takeovers. ***Email:*** Dreisbach@rlf.com

JAMES G. LEYDEN, JR., born Philadelphia, Pennsylvania, June 22, 1960; admitted to bar, 1988, Delaware. *Education:* Villanova University (B.S.A., magna cum laude, 1982; J.D., 1987). Beta Gamma Sigma; Gamma Phi; Phi Kappa Phi. Co-Author: Four Chapters of the book "New York and Delaware Business Entities; Choice, Formation, Operation, Financing and Acquisitions," published by West Publishing Company (1997), Chapters include: Formation and Organization of the Limited Liability Company; Management and Operation of the Limited Liability Company; Dissolution and Termination of the Limited Liability Company; Dissolution and Termination of Limited Partnerships, Limited Liability Partnerships and General Partnerships. *Member:* Delaware State (Member, Corporate and Commercial Law Sections) and American (Member, Section of Business Law and Committee on Partnerships and Unincorporated Business Organizations, Member, Subcommittee on Limited Liability Companies and Subcommittee on General Partnerships and Joint Ventures) Bar Associations. ***PRACTICE AREAS:*** Limited Liability Company Law; Limited Partnership Law; General Partnership Law; Business Law; Commercial Law. ***Email:*** Leyden@rlf.com

FREDERICK L. COTTRELL, III, born Wilmington, Delaware, April 30, 1963; admitted to bar, 1988, Delaware; 1989, Pennsylvania. *Education:* University of Delaware (B.A., magna cum laude, 1985); Dickinson School of Law (J.D., cum laude, 1988). Phi Beta Kappa; Delta Theta Phi. *Member:* Delaware State (Member, Sections on Intellectual Property, Litigation and Real Estate Law) and American (Member, Sections on Intellectual Property, Litigation and Real Estate Law) Bar Associations. ***PRACTICE AREAS:*** Litigation; Intellectual Property. ***Email:*** Cottrell@rlf.com

(This Listing Continued)

BERNARD J. KELLEY, born Pensacola, Florida, December 20, 1963; admitted to bar, 1989, Delaware. *Education:* Swarthmore College (B.A., 1986); University of Pennsylvania (J.D., 1989). Member, 1987-1988 and Executive Editor/Management, 1988-1989, University of Pennsylvania Journal of International Business Law. *Member:* Delaware State (Co-Chairman, Banking Law Committee, 1997—; Member: Business Trust Committee; Commercial Law Section) and American Bar Associations. ***PRACTICE AREAS:*** Partnership Law; Limited Liability Company Law; Business Trust Law; Banking Law. ***Email:*** Kelley@rlf.com

ROBERT J. STEARN, JR., born New Brunswick, New Jersey, October 27, 1962; admitted to bar, 1990, Delaware. *Education:* Dickinson College (B.A., magna cum laude, 1985); University of Pennsylvania (J.D., cum laude, 1990). Order of the Coif. Member, Moot Court Board, 1989-1990. *Member:* Delaware State and American Bar Associations. ***Email:*** Stearn@rlf.com

WILLIAM A. YEMC, born Red Bank, New Jersey, March 5, 1962; admitted to bar, 1990, Delaware; 1991, Pennsylvania. *Education:* University of Notre Dame (B.B.A., 1984); Villanova University (J.D., cum laude, 1990). Phi Kappa Phi. Order of the Coif. Member, 1988-1989 and Managing Editor of Student Work, 1989-1990, Villanova Law Review. Certified Public Accountant, Pennsylvania, 1986. *Member:* Delaware State and American Bar Associations. ***PRACTICE AREAS:*** Commercial Law; Secured Transactions; Business Trusts; Limited Liability Company Law; Partnership Law; Insurance. ***Email:*** Yemc@rlf.com

MARK D. COLLINS, born New Brunswick, New Jersey, July 8, 1965; admitted to bar, 1991, Delaware. *Education:* Rutgers College (B.A., 1987); American University, Washington College of Law (J.D., summa cum laude, 1991). Member, Washington College of Law Honor Society. Member, Moot Court Board, 1989-1990. *Member:* Delaware State (Member: Section on Commercial Law; Bankruptcy Subcommittee) and American (Member, Committee on Business Bankruptcy; Member, Subcommittees on Chapter 11 Bankruptcies; Secured Creditors; Publications and Public Relations Section of Business Law, 1994—) Bar Associations; American Bankruptcy Institute (Chair, Secured Creditors Subcommittee, Business Reorganization Committee, 1997-2000; Chair, Young Members' Committee, 1998-2000; Member, Editorial Board ABI Journal). ***PRACTICE AREAS:*** Bankruptcy Law; Creditors' Rights. ***Email:*** Collins@rlf.com

LISA A. SCHMIDT, born Newburgh, New York, June 15, 1966; admitted to bar, 1991, Delaware; 1993, Pennsylvania. *Education:* Drew University (B.A., 1988); Dickinson School of Law (J.D., 1991). Member: Woolsack Society; Moot Court Board, 1990-1991. Dickinson Law Review, 1989-1991. *Member:* Delaware State and American Bar Associations. ***Email:*** Schmidt@rlf.com

WILLIAM J. HAUBERT, born Bronxville, New York, April 11, 1966; admitted to bar, 1991, Delaware. *Education:* Villanova University (B.S., summa cum laude, 1988); Cornell University (J.D., cum laude, 1991). Beta Gamma Sigma; Gamma Phi; Phi Kappa Phi. Law Clerk to Vice Chancellor William B. Chandler, III, Delaware Court of Chancery, 1991-1992. Author: "Valuation of Securities in A *Revlon* Context," 12 Insights (Apr. 1998); "Disparate Treatment of Shareholders in a Merger," 28 The Review of Securities & Commodities Regulation 133 (1995); "Debt Restructuring Rules Favor the Insolvent," 10 Journal of Taxation of Investments 300 (1993). Co-Author: "Delaware Court Expounds on Director's Duty in Granting Section 203 Waiver," 9 The Corporate Governance Advisor 25 (January/February 2001); "Election of Directors by Written Consent: *Hoschett v. TSI Int'l Software, Ltd.,*" 4 The Corporate Governance Advisor 14 (Nov./Dec. 1996); "Abstentions and Broker Non-Votes in Delaware," 7 Insights 36 (Dec. 1993). *Member:* Delaware State and American Bar Associations. ***PRACTICE AREAS:*** Corporate Law; Corporate Transactions. ***Email:*** Haubert@rlf.com

DONEENE KEEMER DAMON, born Philadelphia, Pennsylvania, August 3, 1967; admitted to bar, 1992, Delaware; 1994, District of Columbia. *Education:* St. Joseph's University (B.S., accounting, cum laude, 1989); Temple University School of Law (J.D., cum laude, 1992). Member, Temple Moot Court Honor Society. *Member:* Delaware State (Member: Executive Committee; Section of Commercial Law; Multicultural Judges and Lawyers Section; Board of Bar Examiners; Editorial Board, The Delaware Law Review; Women and The Law Section) and American (Member; Section of Business Law; Uniform Commercial Code Committee: Meetings Committee; Diversity Committee) Bar Associations. ***PRACTICE AREAS:*** Business Law; Commercial Leasing; Asset-Based Lending; Business Trusts; Uniform Commercial Code. ***Email:*** Damon@rlf.com

DANIEL J. DeFRANCESCHI, born Brooklyn, New York, June 9, 1962; admitted to bar, 1989, Delaware. *Education:* Pennsylvania State University (B.S., 1985); Widener University (J.D., magna cum laude, 1989). Editor, 1988-1989 and Staff Member, 1987-1988, Delaware Journal of Corporate Law. Author: "Written Consents - a Powerful Tool in Hostile Battles for Corporate Control," 14 Del. J. Corp. L. 967 (1989). Wolcott Law Clerk to the Hon. Randy J. Holland, Justice, Supreme Court of Delaware, 1987-1989. Law Clerk to the Hon. Joseph J. Longobardi, Judge, U.S. Dist. Ct. for the District of Delaware, 1989-1990. *Member:* Delaware State (Member, Sections on Corporations and

(This Listing Continued)

Litigation) and American (Member, Sections on Business Law and Litigation) Bar Associations; American Bankruptcy Institute; Turnaround Management Association. ***PRACTICE AREAS:*** Bankruptcy. ***Email:*** Defranceschi@rlf.com

RAYMOND J. DiCAMILLO, born Wilmington, Delaware, August 24, 1968; admitted to bar, 1993, Delaware; 1994, Pennsylvania. *Education:* University of Pennsylvania (B.A., magna cum laude, 1990); Georgetown University Law Center (J.D., magna cum laude, 1993). Order of the Coif. Member, 1991-1992, and Associate Editor, 1992-1993, The Georgetown Law Journal. *Member:* Delaware State and American Bar Associations. ***PRACTICE AREAS:*** Business Law; Business Litigation; Corporate Law; Corporate Control Contests; Corporate Litigation; Hostile Takeovers; Chancery Practice. ***Email:*** DiCamillo@rlf.com

CATHERINE G. DEARLOVE, born Amityville, New York, June 21, 1969; admitted to bar, 1994, Delaware. *Education:* Georgetown University (B.S.F.S., magna cum laude, 1991); Stanford Law School (J.D., with distinction, 1994). Phi Beta Kappa. Member, 1991-1994 and Associate Managing Editor, 1992-1993, Stanford Journal of International Law. Member, Stanford Moot Court Board, 1993-1994. *Member:* Delaware State and American Bar Associations. ***Email:*** Dearlove@rlf.com

JEFFREY L. MOYER, born Chester, Pennsylvania, July 26, 1968; admitted to bar, 1994, Delaware. *Education:* University of Delaware (B.S., 1991); Temple University School of Law (J.D., 1994). *Member:* Delaware State and American Bar Associations. ***Email:*** Moyer@rlf.com

SRINIVAS M. RAJU, born Bhimavaram (A.P.), India, October 19, 1968; admitted to bar, 1994, Delaware. *Education:* Indiana University (B.S., 1990); Georgetown University Law Center (J.D., cum laude, 1994). Staff Member, 1992-1993 and Notes and Comments Editor, 1993-1994, Law and Policy in International Business. Member, Barristers' Council, 1992-1993. Certified Public Accountant, Illinois, 1990. *Member:* Delaware State and American Bar Associations. ***PRACTICE AREAS:*** Business Law. ***Email:*** Raju@rlf.com

---

JAMES R. ADAMS, born Elmer, New Jersey, March 21, 1951; admitted to bar, 2001, West Virginia (Not admitted in Delaware). *Education:* Ursinus College (B.A., Political Science, 1979); Widener University School of Law (J.D., cum laude, 2000). *Member:* West Virginia State Bar. ***Email:*** Adams@rlf.com

MICHAEL D. ALLEN, born Bethesda, Maryland, December 9, 1970; admitted to bar, 1996, Delaware. *Education:* Swarthmore College (B.A., 1992); Washington & Lee University School of Law (J.D., cum laude, 1996). Phi Delta Phi. Law Clerk to the Hon. Maurice A. Hartnett, III, Justice, Supreme Court of Delaware. 1996-1997. Member: Delaware State and American Bar Associations. ***PRACTICE AREAS:*** Corporate Law. ***Email:*** Allen@rlf.com

KELLY C. ASHBY, born Leesburg, Virginia, March 19, 1975; admitted to bar, 2001, Delaware. *Education:* Shenandoah University (B.A., summa cum laude, 1997); The College of William and Mary School of Law (J.D., 2000). Phi Delta Phi. The Bill of Rights Journal, 1999-2000. *Member:* Delaware State and American Bar Associations. ***Email:*** Ashby@rlf.com

MONICA M. AYRES, born Philadelphia, Pennsylvania, November 19, 1972; admitted to bar, 2000, Delaware. *Education:* University of Pennsylvania (B.A., 1994); William and Mary School of Law (J.D., 2000). Order of the Coif. Member, William and Mary Law Review, 1998-2000. *Member:* Delaware State and American Bar Associations. ***Email:*** Ayres@rlf.com

MARK A. BEAVER, born Philadelphia, PA, June 30, 1975; admitted to bar, 2000, Delaware. *Education:* Bucknell University (B.A., Economics and Finance, cum laude, 1997); Villanova University Law School (J.D., cum laude, 2000). *Member:* Delaware State and American Bar Associations. ***Email:*** Beaver@rlf.com

JENNIFER C. BEBKO, born Erie, Pennsylvania, January 8, 1972; admitted to bar, 1997, Delaware; 1998, Pennsylvania. *Education:* Cornell University (B.A., 1994); Villanova University School of Law (J.D., magna cum laude, 1997). Order of the Coif. Member, Villanova Law Review. Recipient, Corporate Law Award. *Member:* Delaware State and American Bar Associations. ***PRACTICE AREAS:*** Labor and Employment Law; Civil Practice; Litigation. ***Email:*** Bebko@rlf.com

REBECCA L. BOOTH, born Pittsburgh, Pennsylvania, September 30, 1975; admitted to bar, 2001, Delaware. *Education:* University of Kansas (B.A., 1997); Washington University School of Law (J.D., 2000). Golden Key National Honor Society. Staff Member, 1998-1999 and Articles Editor, 1999-2000, Washington University Journal of Law and Policy. *Member:* Delaware State and American Bar Associations. ***Email:*** Booth@rlf.com

THAD J. BRACEGIRDLE, born Bristol, Pennsylvania, January 23, 1972; admitted to bar, 1998, Delaware and Pennsylvania. *Education:* University of Pennsylvania (B.A., magna cum laude, 1994; J.D., 1997). Associate Editor, 1995-1996 and Comments Editor, 1996-1997, University of Pennsylvania Journal of International Economic Law. *Member:* Delaware State and American Bar Associations. ***Email:*** Bracegirdle@rlf.com

(This Listing Continued)

PAUL D. BROWN, born Dayton, Ohio, October 2, 1971; admitted to bar, 2000, Delaware and Pennsylvania. *Education:* University of Pennsylvania (B.A., 1995); University of Pittsburgh School of Law (J.D., magna cum laude, 1999). Staff Member, 1997-1998 and Managing Editor, 1998-1999, University of Pittsburgh Law Review. Author: "Lofty Goals, Questioned Motives, and Proffered Justifications: 'Regional Transport of Ground Level Ozone and the EPA's NOx SIP Call,'" 60 University of Pittsburgh Law Review 923, 1999. *Member:* Delaware State and American Bar Associations. ***Email:*** Pbrown@rlf.com

PETER D. CALDER, born Washington, District of Columbia, November 4, 1971; admitted to bar, 2000, Delaware. *Education:* University of Illinois, Urbana-Champaign (B.A., magna cum laude, 1995); University of Pennsylvania (J.D., 2000). Phi Beta Kappa. *Member:* Delaware State and American Bar Associations. ***Email:*** Calder@rlf.com

MATTHEW S. CRISCIMAGNA, born Fountain Valley, California, April 30, 1975; admitted to bar, 2001, Delaware. *Education:* Salisbury Sate University (B.A., 1997); University of Missouri-Columbia School of Law (J.D., Order of the Coif, 2000). Associate Member, 1998-1999 and Note and Comment Editor, 1999-2000, Missouri Law Review. Author: "The Narrow Application of Buckley v. Valeo: Is Campaign Finance Reform Possible in the Eighth Circuit," 64 Missouri Law Review 437 (1999); "Attorneys Beware: Obtaining Credit Reports on Opposing Party May Lead to Punitive Damages," 64 Missouri Law Review 1037 (1999). *Member:* Delaware State and American Bar Associations. ***Email:*** Criscimagna@rlf.com

BROCK E. CZESCHIN, born Jefferson City, Missouri, June 26, 1975; admitted to bar, 2000, Delaware. *Education:* Central Missouri State University (B.A., summa cum laude, 1997); Villanova University School of Law (J.D., magna cum laude, 2000). Order of the Coif. Staff, 1998-1999, and Editor-in-Chief, 1999-2000, Villanova Environmental Law Journal. Author: United States v. Navistar International Transportation Corp.: Seventh Circuit Bars Government's CERCLA Claim Based On Violation Of The Statute Of Limitations, 10 Vill. Envtl. L.J. 399 (1999). *Member:* Delaware State and American Bar Associations. ***Email:*** Czeschin@rlf.com

MELANIE GEORGE DAY, born Wilmington, Delaware, November 7, 1972; admitted to bar, 1997, Delaware. *Education:* University of Pennsylvania (B.A., magna cum laude, 1994); Georgetown University Law Center (J.D., 1997). Member, *The Tax Lawyer,* 1995-1997. Managing Editor, *The State and Local Tax Lawyer,* 1996-1997. Author: "*Transferee Liability for Interest: Baptiste v. Commissioner,*" 49 Tax Law. 533 (1996). *Member:* Delaware State and American Bar Associations. ***Email:*** Day@rlf.com

ELISA J. ERLENBACH, born Stevens Point, Wisconsin, July 27, 1974; admitted to bar, 1999, Delaware. *Education:* University of Wisconsin-Madison (B.A., French and Women's Studies, with distinction, 1996); Cornell Law School (J.D., 1999). Phi Delta Phi (Inn Historian, 1997-1998). Recipient, CALI Awards. *Member:* Delaware State and American Bar Associations. ***LANGUAGES:*** French. ***Email:*** Erlenbach@rlf.com

RICHARD J. FACCIOLO, born Wilmington, Delaware, February 10, 1959; admitted to bar, 1996, Maryland; 1999, Delaware. *Education:* University of Delaware (B.S.E.E., 1984); University of Maryland (J.D., with honor, 1996). Recipient, Bridgewater M. Arnold Prize, Day Division, Best Work in Commercial Paper, 1995-1996. Member, Maryland Law Review (Notes and Comments Editor, 1995-1996), 1994-1996. Author: Note, "Common-Law Tort Liability of Prior Leasees of Commercial Property," Maryland Law Review, Vol. 54 No. 3. *Member:* Maryland, Delaware State and American Bar Associations. ***PRACTICE AREAS:*** Business Law; Asset Based Finance; Business Organization. ***Email:*** Facciolo@rlf.com

ERIC N. FELDMAN, born Long Island, New York, June 26, 1971; admitted to bar, 1998, Delaware. *Education:* University of North Carolina at Chapel Hill (B.A., with distinction, 1993) Phi Beta Kappa; Georgetown University Law Center (J.D., cum laude, 1997). Georgetown Tax Lawyer, 1995-1997. Author: "Tax Crimes and Non-Tax Crimes in Fifth Amendment Protection Cases: *United States v. Troescher,*" 49 Tax Law. 961 (1996). *Member:* Delaware State and American Bar Associations. ***PRACTICE AREAS:*** Business Law; Commercial Law; Business Organization; Limited Liability Company Law; Partnership Law. ***Email:*** Feldman@rlf.com

STEVEN J. FINEMAN, born Willingboro, New Jersey, February 8, 1974; admitted to bar, 2001, Delaware. *Education:* Ursinus College (B.A., 1996); Tulane University School of Law (J.D., cum laude, 2000). *Member:* Delaware State and American Bar Associations. ***Email:*** Fineman@rlf.com

ZOE A. FORRESTER, born Kingston, Jamaica, B.W.I., January 14, 1967; admitted to bar, 2001, Delaware. *Education:* Binghamton University, SUNY (B.A., magna cum laude, 1995); Cornell Law School (J.D., 2000). Member, Cornell International Law Journal, 1998-1999. *Member:* Delaware State and American Bar Associations. ***Email:*** Forrester@rlf.com

SHANNON S. FRAZIER, born West Palm Beach, Florida, November 24, 1975; admitted to bar, 2001, Delaware. *Education:* University of Florida (B.S.,

(This Listing Continued)

RICHARDS, LAYTON & FINGER, P.A., Wilmington—Continued

Psychology, 1995), Phi Sigma Pi; Tulane University School of Law (J.D., cum laude, 2000), Phi Delta Phi. Recipient, CALI Award. *Member:* Delaware State and American Bar Associations. ***Email:*** Frazier@rlf.com

BRIGITTE V. FRESCO, born Wilmington, Delaware, December 9, 1969; admitted to bar, 1996, Delaware and Pennsylvania. *Education:* Pennsylvania State University (B.A., with high honors, 1992), Phi Beta Kappa; George Washington University National Law Center (J.D., with high honors, 1995). Order of the Coif. Member, The George Washington Law Review, 1993-1994. Author: "Ludin v. Mecham: Defining the Scope of the Equal Access to Justice Act," 62 Geo. Wash. L. Rev. 795 (1994). *Member:* Delaware State and American Bar Associations. ***Email:*** Fresco@rlf.com

DOMINICK T. GATTUSO, born Wilkes-Barre, Pennsylvania, January 1, 1970; admitted to bar, 1997, Delaware; 1998, New Jersey. *Education:* Wilkes University (B.A., magna cum laude, 1992); Widener University (J.D., cum laude, 1997). Phi Delta Phi. Member, 1995-1997 and Articles Editor, 1996-1997, Delaware Journal of Corporate Law. Member, Widener Moot Court Honor Society, 1995-1997. Law Clerk to the Honorable Henry duPont Ridgely, President Judge, Superior Court of Delaware, 1997-1998. Law Clerk to the Honorble N. Maxson Terry, Resident Judge, Superior Court of Delaware, 1997-1998. *Member:* Delaware State and American Bar Associations. ***PRACTICE AREAS:*** Corporate Litigation; Commercial Litigation. ***Email:*** Gattuso@rlf.com

ANNE SHEA GAZA, born Seoul, South Korea, February 17, 1972; admitted to bar, 1997, Pennsylvania (Not admitted in Delaware). *Education:* Moravian College (B.A., cum laude, with honors in Political Science, 1997); University of Pittsburgh School of Law (J.D., 1997). Staff Member, 1995-1996 and Associate Notes and Comments Editor, 1996-1997, University of Pittsburgh Journal of Law and Commerce. Recipient: Pennsylvania Defense Institute Theodore Flowers Scholarship, 1995-1996; University of Pittsburgh School of Law Faculty Award for Excellence in Legal Scholarship, 1997; CALI Excellence for the Future Award, 1997. Panelist: Pennsylvania Defense Institute Conference, 1996. *Member:* Pennsylvania and American Bar Associations. ***PRACTICE AREAS:*** Corporate Litigation; Commercial Litigation; Intellectual Property Litigation; Workmen's Compensation. ***Email:*** Gaza@rlf.com

D. SHANE GUNTER, born Thomasville, North Carolina, September 13, 1974; admitted to bar, 2000, Delaware. *Education:* Gardner-Webb University (B.S., magna cum laude, 1996); The Dickinson School of Law of the Pennsylvania State University (J.D., 1999). Member: Order of Woolsack; Appellate Moot Court Board, 1998-1999. Member, 1997-1998 and Comments Editor, 1998-1999, Dickinson Law Review. *Member:* Delaware State and American Bar Associations. ***Email:*** Gunter@rlf.com

PAUL N. HEATH, born Elkton, Maryland, June 12, 1968; admitted to bar, 1998, Delaware and Maryland. *Education:* University of Delaware (B.S., 1990); Widener School of Law (J.D., magna cum laude, 1997). ***PRACTICE AREAS:*** Bankruptcy. ***Email:*** Heath@rlf.com

KELLY A. HERRING, born Albany, New York, June 24, 1969; admitted to bar, 1997, Delaware. *Education:* LeMoyne College (B.A., History, magna cum laude, 1991); Cornell Law School (J.D., 1996). Administrative Editor, Journal of Law and Public Policy, 1996. *Member:* Delaware State and American Bar Associations. ***PRACTICE AREAS:*** Corporate Law; Securities. ***Email:*** Herring@rlf.com

TARA J. HOFFNER, born Stroudsburg, Pennsylvania, January 14, 1971; admitted to bar, 1996, Delaware. *Education:* Muhlenberg College (B.A., magna cum laude, 1993); Dickinson School of Law (J.D., cum laude, 1996). Member, Woolsack Society. Member, Dickinson Law Review, 1994-1996. *Member:* Delaware State and American Bar Associations. ***PRACTICE AREAS:*** Business Law; Commercial Leasing; Asset-Based Lending; Business Trusts. ***Email:*** Hoffner@rlf.com

KATHLEEN P. ITTEL, born Dayton, Ohio; admitted to bar, 1996, Pennsylvania (Not admitted in Delaware). *Education:* Miami University (B.S.); Widener University (J.D., 1995; M.B.A., 1999). Phi Delta Phi. *Member:* Delaware State Bar Association (Member, Section on Real Estate, 1997—). ***PRACTICE AREAS:*** Real Estate. ***Email:*** Ittel@rlf.com

KATHLEEN A. KELLEY, born Laguna Beach, California, July 7, 1972; admitted to bar, 2000, Delaware. *Education:* University of Virginia (B.A., 1994); Washington & Lee University (J.D., cum laude, 2000). Member and Case Notes Editor, Race and Ethnic Ancestry Law Journal, 1998-2000. *Member:* Delaware State and American Bar Associations. ***Email:*** Kkelley@rlf.com

JOHN H. KNIGHT, born Washington, D.C., November 9, 1966; admitted to bar, 1994, Maryland; 1996, New Jersey; 1999, Delaware. *Education:* University of Maryland (B.S., 1990; J.D., with honors, 1994). Recipient, American Jurisprudence Award in Torts I, Civil Procedure I, Contracts II and Civil Procedure II. Law Clerk to the Honorables Rosemary Gambordella, Noralyn Winfield, and William Tuohey, United States Bankruptcy Judges for the District of New Jersey. *Member:* Delaware State and American Bar Associations. ***PRACTICE AREAS:*** Bankruptcy; Commercial Litigation. ***Email:*** Knight@rlf.com

THOMAS H. KOVACH, born Woodbury, New Jersey, May 27, 1969; admitted to bar, 1997, New Jersey; 1998, Pennsylvania; 2000, Delaware. *Education:* University of Delaware (B.Ch.E.,B.A., 1992); Rutgers University School of Law, Camden (J.D., 1997). *Member:* Delaware State, Pennsylvania, New Jersey State and American Bar Associations. ***PRACTICE AREAS:*** Litigation; Environmental Law; Administrative Law. ***Email:*** TKovach@rlf.com

SETH HAMILTON KRAMER, born Silver Spring, Maryland, March 25, 1974; admitted to bar, 1999, Delaware. *Education:* University of Virginia (B.A., with distinction, 1995; J.D., 1998). Phi Beta Kappa. ***PRACTICE AREAS:*** Alternative Entities. ***Email:*** Kramer@rlf.com

PETER B. LADIG, born Wilmington, Delaware, November 30, 1971; admitted to bar, 1996, Delaware. *Education:* Yale University (B.A., 1993); Emory University School of Law (J.D., with distinction, 1996). Dean's Fellow, 1995-1996. Member, 1994-1995 and Notes and Comments Editor, 1995-1996, Bankruptcy Developments Journal. Author: "Net Envy and Delaware Law: Delaware Decisions Affecting Executive Compensation," Corporate Gov. Adviser, May/June 2000; Co-Author: "Attorney-Client Privilege: Potential Dangers of Having Corporate General Counsel Perform Multiple Roles," The Review of Securities Commodities Regulation, March 14, 2000. *Member:* Delaware State and American Bar Associations. ***PRACTICE AREAS:*** Corporate Litigation; Corporate Law. ***Email:*** Ladig@rlf.com

GREGORY W. LADNER, born Suffern, New York, December 30, 1964; admitted to bar, 1995, Delaware; 1996, Pennsylvania. *Education:* Sophia University, Tokyo, Japan; University of Notre Dame (B.A., 1986); Villanova University (J.D., 1995). Member, 1993-1994 and Managing Editor Articles, 1994-1995, Villanova Law Review. Author: Casenote, "Developing Uniformity in Limitations Periods for Implied Private Actions under the Securities Exchange Act of 1934 - Westinghouse Electric Corp. by Levit v. Franklin," 39 Villanova Law Review 1033, 1994. *Member:* Delaware State and American Bar Associations. ***PRACTICE AREAS:*** Partnership Law; Limited Liability Company Law; Commercial Law. ***Email:*** Ladner@rlf.com

J. TRAVIS LASTER, born Beirut, Lebanon, November 10, 1969; admitted to bar, 1995, Virginia; 1996, Delaware. *Education:* Princeton University (A.B., summa cum laude, 1991); University of Virginia School of Law (J.D., 1995); University of Virginia (M.A., 1996). Order of the Coif. Law School Alumni Association Award for Academic Excellence, Best Academic Record. Virginia Law Review, Articles Review Board (1994-1995), Editorial Board (1992-1994). Author: "Exposing a False Dichotomy: The Implication of the No-Talk Cases for the *Time/Revlon* Double Standard," 2 Del. L. Rev. 179 (2000); "Exorcising the Omnipresent Specter: The Impact of Substantial Equity Ownership on *Unocal* Analysis," 55 Bus Law. 109 (2000); "Liability of Directors of Acquiring Companies," Insights (Nov. 2000); "Can a Board Dilute a Majority Stockholder?" Corporate Counsel (Nov. 2000); "The Changing Rules of Takeover Defense," The Corporate Board (July/Aug. 2000); "An Appraiser By Any Other Name," Insights (May 1999); "Selecting A Forum To Reduce Y2K Risk," Insights (Mar. 1999); "The Line Item Veto and *Unocal:* Can a Bidder *Qua* Bidder Pursue *Unocal* Claims Against a Target Corporation's Board of Directors?" 53 Bus. Law. 767 (1998): "The Year 2000 Problem: Preparing to Defend Shareholder Derivative Suits," Corporate Gov. Advisor (Sept./Oct. 1998); "The Role of the Victim's Conduct in Assessing Fault under the Lex Aquilia," 25 Anglo-American L. Rev. 188 (1996); "Pierce v. Martin: When Two Good Rules Make Bad Law," 8 J. of Civil Litig. 9 (1996); "Pure Comparative Negligence: The Choice for Virginia," VTLA Journal 34 (Summer 1994). Co-Author: Appraisal Rights in Mergers & Consolidations (2001); "Practical Lessons for MBO Transactions," Insights (Mar. 2001); "Equity Ownership and the Duty of Care: Convergence, Revolution or Evolution," 55 Bus. Law. 661 (2000); "Professor Coates Is Right. Now Please Study Stockholder Voting," 54 U. Miami L. Rev. 819 (2000); "The Lessons of *Chesapeake Corp. v. Shore,*" Insights (Apr. 2000); "The Risk of Invoking the Attorney-Client Privilege in a Corporate Control Dispute," Insights (Mar. 1999); "A Mentor's Teachings: Lessons and Implications of the Delaware Dead Hand Decisions," M&A Lawyer (Feb. 1999). Law Clerk to The Honorable Jane R. Roth, United States Court of Appeals for the Third Circuit, 1995-1996. *Member:* Virginia, Delaware State and American Bar Associations. ***PRACTICE AREAS:*** Corporate Litigation; Corporate Law; General Litigation. ***Email:*** Laster@rlf.com

PATRICK M. LEATHEM, born Bronx, New York, November 12, 1973; admitted to bar, 2000, New York (Not admitted in Delaware). *Education:* University of Southern California (B.A., Print Journalism, International Relations, 1995); The George Washington University Law School (J.D., 1999). Member, 1997-1999, American Intellectual Property Law Association Quarterly Journal. *Member:* American Bar Association. ***Email:*** Leathem@rlf.com

KATHLEEN M. LEFEBVRE, born Lancaster, Pennsylvania, March 6, 1971; admitted to bar, 2000, Delaware. *Education:* Villanova University (B.A., magna cum laude, 1996), Phi Kappa Phi, Pi Sigma Alpha; Washington College of Law, American University (J.D., cum laude, 1999). Member, American Uni-

(This Listing Continued)

versity Journal of Gender, Social Policy and the Law, 1997-1999. *Member:* Delaware State and American Bar Associations. ***Email:*** Lefebvre@rlf.com

CHRISTOPHER D. LOIZIDES, born Poughkeepsie, New York, April 9, 1966; admitted to bar, 1991, Pennsylvania; 1992, New Jersey; 1993, New York; 1994, District of Columbia; 2000, Delaware. *Education:* Yale University (B.A., summa cum laude, 1988); University of Pennsylvania Law School (J.D., cum laude, 1991). Member, Order of the Coif. ***PRACTICE AREAS:*** Bankruptcy; Creditors Rights; Litigation. ***Email:*** Loizides@rlf.com

SCOTT L. MATTHEWS, born Fairfax, Virginia, September 12, 1973; admitted to bar, 2000, Delaware. *Education:* University of Delaware (B.A., English Literature and Political Science, cum laude, 1995); University of Virginia (M.A., English, 2000); University of Virginia School of Law (J.D., 2000). Pi Sigma Alpha; Sigma Tau Delta. Editor, 1998-1999 and Articles Review Editor, 1999-2000, Journal of Law and Politics. Federalist Society, Vice President, 1999-2000. *Member:* Delaware State and American Bar Associations. ***Email:*** Matthews@rlf.com

MICHAEL J. MERCHANT, born Springfield, Pennsylvania, April 8, 1974; admitted to bar, 1999, Delaware. *Education:* Pennsylvania State University (B.S., Environmental and Renewable Resource Economics, with high distinction, 1996); Villanova University School of Law (J.D., cum laude, 1999). Editor-in-Chief, Villanova Sports and Entertainment Law Journal, 1998-1999. Autor: Note, "Establishing the Boundaries of First Amendment Protection for Speech in the Cyberspace Frontier: Reno v. ACLU," 5 Villanova Sports and Entertainment Law Journal 429, 1998. *Member:* Delaware State and American Bar Associations. ***PRACTICE AREAS:*** Bankruptcy; Creditors Rights. ***Email:*** Merchant@rlf.com

CHRISTINE M. MORABITO, born Smithtown, New York, October 19, 1974; admitted to bar, 1999, Delaware. *Education:* Franklin and Marshall College (B.A., cum laude, 1996); Villanova University School of Law (J.D., cum laude, 1999). Phi Delta Phi (Treasurer, 1997-1998). Member, 1997-1998 and Managing Editor, Production, 1998-1999, Villanova Law Review. *Member:* Delaware State and American Bar Associations. ***Email:*** Morabito@rlf.com

CHRIS J. PIETRAFITTA, born Elkins Park, Pennsylvania, December 22, 1960; admitted to bar, 1990, Delaware; 1991, Pennsylvania. *Education:* La Salle University (B.S., magna cum laude and general college honors, 1983); Villanova University (J.D., cum laude, 1990). Order of the Coif. Member, Villanova Law Review, 1989-1990. Author: "Delaware's Omnipotent Business Judgment Rule - Who Speaks for the Shareholders," 35 Vill. L. Rev. 501 (1990). *Member:* Delaware State, Pennsylvania, and American Bar Associations. ***PRACTICE AREAS:*** Corporate Trust; Asset Based Finance; Business Organization. ***Email:*** Pietrafitta@rlf.com

MARK V. PURPURA, born Pottsville, Pennsylvania, May 8, 1973; admitted to bar, 1999, Delaware. *Education:* University of Southern California (B.S., Business Administration, magna cum laude, 1995); University of North Carolina School of Law (J.D., with honors, 1998). Recipient, Millard S. Breckenridge Award. Member, North Carolina Journal of International Law and Commercial Regulation, 1996-1997. Notes and Articles Editor, North Carolina Banking Institute, 1997-1998. Co-Author: Comment, "The Riegle-Neal Amendments Act of 1997: The Impact of Interstate Branching on the Dual Banking System," 2 North Carolina Banking Institute 230, 1998. *Member:* Delaware State and American Bar Associations. ***PRACTICE AREAS:*** Banks and Banking; Business Law. ***Email:*** Purpura@rlf.com

MICHELLE P. QUINN, born Baltimore, Maryland, May 10, 1973; admitted to bar, 2000, Delaware. *Education:* Johns Hopkins University (B.A., 1995); University of Virginia (J.D., 1999). Member, Editorial Board, 1997-1998 and Executive Editor, 1998-1999, Virginia Environmental Law Journal. *Member:* Delaware State and American Bar Associations. ***Email:*** Quinn@rlf.com

LEANNE J. REESE, born Media, Pennsylvania, March 31, 1970; admitted to bar, 1998, Delaware and Pennsylvania. *Education:* University of Pennsylvania (B.A., cum laude, 1992); University of Pennsylvania Law School (J.D., 1997). Member, Comparative Labor Law Journal, 1995-1997. *Member:* Delaware State and American Bar Associations. ***Email:*** Reese@rlf.com

MICHAEL K. REILLY, born Towanda, Pennsylvania, December 3, 1972; admitted to bar, 1998, Delaware. *Education:* Villanova University (B.A., summa cum laude, 1995); Cornell Law School (J.D., 1998). Phi Beta Kappa; Phi Kappa Phi; Pi Sigma Alpha; Phi Alpha Theta. Cornell Law Review, 1996-1998. *Member:* Delaware State and American Bar Associations. ***Email:*** Reilly@rlf.com

DEIRDRE M. RICHARDS, born Ardmore, Pennsylvania, February 12, 1962; admitted to bar, 1989, Pennsylvania (Not admitted in Delaware). *Education:* Hollins College (B.A., 1984); Temple University (J.D., 1989). Attorney, U.S. Department of Justice, Office of U.S. Trustee, Los Angeles, 1990-1994. *Member:* Pennsylvania Bar Association. ***PRACTICE AREAS:*** Bankruptcy; Creditors Rights; Litigation. ***Email:*** DRichards@rlf.com

RICHARD PHILIP ROLLO, born Ft. Bragg, North Carolina, April 2, 1972; admitted to bar, 1999, Florida (Not admitted in Delaware). *Education:* University of Florida (B.S., Psychology, 1995); University of Florida School of Law (J.D., with high honors, 1999). Staff Member and Symposium Editor, Florida Law Review, 1998-1999. Author: Casenote, "The Morass of Internet Personal Jurisdiction: It is Time for a Paradigm Shift," Florida Law Review, 667, Volume 51, Number 4, September 1999. *Member:* The Florida Bar; American Bar Association. ***PRACTICE AREAS:*** Corporate Litigation. ***Email:*** Rollo@rlf.com

(This Listing Continued)

ERIC A. SCHWARTZMAN, born Philadelphia, Pennsylvania, July 12, 1972; admitted to bar, 1999, Delaware. *Education:* Villanova University (B.A., summa cum laude, 1994); Georgetown University Law Center (J.D., 1998). Phi Beta Kappa; Phi Kappa Phi; Psi Chi; Omicron Delta Epsilon. Member, Georgetown International Environmental Law Review, 1996-1998. *Member:* Delaware State and American Bar Associations. ***Email:*** Schwartzman@rlf.com

CHAD M. SHANDLER, born Abington, Pennsylvania, May 4, 1972; admitted to bar, 1999, Delaware. *Education:* Villanova University (B.A., cum laude, 1994); Villanova University School of Law (J.D., cum laude, 1998). *Member:* Delaware State and American Bar Associations. ***Email:*** Shandler@rlf.com

ANDREA K. SHORT, born Dover, Delaware, February 2, 1973; admitted to bar, 2000, Delaware. *Education:* Davidson College (B.A., 1995); Washingtôn & Lee University School of Law (J.D., 2000). Staffwriter, 1998-1999 and Managing Editor, 1999-2000, Washington & Lee Law Review. Author: "Eradicating Discrimination Among Individuals with Disabilities: Parity in Employer-Provided, Long-Term Disability Benefit Plans," 56 Washington & Lee Law Review 1341, 1999. *Member:* Delaware State and American Bar Associations. ***Email:*** Short@rlf.com

RUSSELL C. SILBERGLIED, born New York, New York, August 24, 1970; admitted to bar, 1996, Delaware and Pennsylvania. *Education:* Cornell University (B.S., with honors, 1992); University of Pennsylvania Law School (J.D., 1995). *Member:* Delaware State and American Bar Associations. ***Email:*** Silberglied@rlf.com

JASON J. SOLOMON, born Johnstown, Pennsylvania, November 21, 1974; admitted to bar, 2001, Delaware. *Education:* University of North Carolina at Chapel Hill (B.S.B.A., 1997); Washington and Lee University School of Law (J.D., cum laude, 2000). Staff Member, 1998-1999 and Notes and Articles Editor, 1999-2000, Capital Defense Journal. Author: "A Quarter Century of Death: A Symposium on Capital Punishment in Virginia since Furman v. Georgia, Part III: Future Dangerousness Issues and Analysis" 12 Cap. Def. J. 55 (1999). *Member:* Delaware State and American Bar Associations. ***Email:*** Solomon@rlf.com

DEBORAH E. SPIVACK, born Mount Clemens, Michigan, December 12, 1965; admitted to bar, 1993, Delaware and New Jersey; 1994, Pennsylvania. *Education:* Pennsylvania State University (B.S., 1987); Widener University School of Law (J.D., 1993). Phi Kappa Phi. Staff Member, The Delaware Journal of Corporate Law. Judicial Law Clerk to the Honorable Helen S. Balick, U.S. Bankruptcy Court of the District of Delaware, 1993-1994. Publication: Dr. Jack Snyder and Deborah E. Spivack, *How Breast Implant Cases are Redefining the Concept of Soft Tissue Injury in the 1990's,* in Handling Soft Tissue Injury Cases: Medical Aspects, 434-495 (Monty L Preiser et al. eds., 2d ed. 1993). *Member:* Delaware State and American Bar Associations; American Bankruptcy Institute. ***Email:*** Spivack@rlf.com

LISA R. STARK, born Wilmington, Delaware, November 22, 1973; admitted to bar, 2001, Delaware. *Education:* Bucknell University (B.A., summa cum laude, 1997). Phi Beta Kappa. Recipient, Orin J. Oliphant Prize, highest G.P.A.; Washington and Lee School of Law (J.D., 2000). Recipient, Frederic L. Kirgis International Law Award. Author: "Abolishing the Worst Forms of Child Labor," 44 Hum. Rts. Mon. 17 (1998); "The Status of Women's Rights: 42nd Session of the Commission on the Status of Women," 44 Hum. Rts. Mon. 22 (1998); "Human Rights Committee: 63rd Session," 44 Hum. Rts. Mon. 22 (1998). *Member:* Delaware State and American Bar Associations. ***LANGUAGES:*** French. ***Email:*** Stark@rlf.com

MICHAEL R. STEIN, born Philadelphia, Pennsylvania, December 12, 1962; admitted to bar, 1989, Pennsylvania and New Jersey; 2000, Delaware. *Education:* Dickinson College (B.A., 1984); The Dickinson School of Law (J.D., 1989); Villanova University (LL.M., in Taxation, 1992). Articles Editor, Dickinson Journal of International Law, 1988-1989. Assistant Editor, 1993; Associate Editor, 1994, Montgomery County Law Reporter. *Member:* Delaware, Pennsylvania and American Bar Associations. ***PRACTICE AREAS:*** Estate Planning; Estate Administration; Taxation. ***Email:*** MStein@rlf.com

MELISSA K. STUBENBERG, born Honolulu, Hawaii, October 2, 1970; admitted to bar, 1998, Maryland; 1999, Delaware. *Education:* Mount Holyoke College (B.A., cum laude, 1993); George Washington University Law School (J.D., with honors, 1998). *Member:* Maryland State Bar Association, Inc.; Delaware State and American Bar Associations. ***Email:*** Stubenberg@rlf.com

REVISERS OF THE DELAWARE LAW DIGEST FOR THIS DIRECTORY.

ROSENTHAL, MONHAIT, GROSS & GODDESS, P.A.

Established in 1958

SUITE 1401, MELLON BANK CENTER

P.O. BOX 1070

WILMINGTON, DELAWARE 19899-1070

Telephone: 302-656-4433

Telecopier: 302-658-7567

Email: rmgg@rmgglaw.com

Corporate, Securities and Commercial Litigation, Corporate Law, Bankruptcy, Personal Injury and General Civil Litigation.

JOSEPH A. ROSENTHAL, born Middletown, Connecticut, December 29, 1931; admitted to bar, 1956, Massachusetts; 1957, Connecticut; 1959, Delaware. *Education:* Yale University (B.A., 1953); Harvard University (J.D., 1956). Trustee, Lawyers Fund for Client Protection, 1997—. *Member:* Delaware (Member of Council, General Corporation Law Section, 1983-2000; Chairperson, Delaware Volunteer Legal Services, Inc., 1981-1987; Recipient, First State Distinguished Service Award, 1986) and American Bar Associations. ***PRACTICE AREAS:*** Corporate Litigation; Securities Litigation; Business Litigation; Corporate Law. ***Email:*** jrosenthal@rmgglaw.com

KEVIN GROSS, born Wilmington, Delaware, August 7, 1952; admitted to bar, 1978, Delaware and Pennsylvania. *Education:* University of Delaware (B.A., 1974); American University (J.D., 1977). Member, American University Law Review, 1976-1977. Judicial Clerkship, Delaware Court of Chancery, 1977-1978. Chairperson: Advisory Committee, U.S. District Court, District of Delaware, 1995—; Delaware District Court Bankruptcy Rules and Practice Committee, 1999—; Delaware Supreme Court Board of Bar Examiners, Assistant Secretary, 1998-1999; Delaware Supreme Court Rules Committee, 1988-1994; Delaware Supreme Court Advisory Committee on IOLTA, 1986-1999; Delaware Supreme Court Committee on the Rules of Evidence, 1977—; Delaware Court of Chancery Rules Committee, 1986—; Court on the Judiciary Rules Committee, 1983. *Member:* Delaware State (Recipient, New Lawyer's Distinguished Service Award, 1988) and Federal Bar Associations; American Bankruptcy Institute. ***PRACTICE AREAS:*** Bankruptcy; Corporate Litigation; Securities Litigation; Commercial Litigation; Business Litigation; Civil Litigation; Corporate Law. ***Email:*** kgross@rmgglaw.com

NORMAN M. MONHAIT, born New Brunswick, New Jersey, March 26, 1948; admitted to bar, 1975, Pennsylvania; 1976, District of Columbia; 1980, Delaware. *Education:* Lehigh University (B.A., with highest honors, 1970); Harvard University (J.D., cum laude, 1975). Phi Beta Kappa; Omicron Delta Kappa. Comment Editor, Harvard Civil Rights-Civil Liberties Law Review, 1974-1975. Author: "Federal Declaratory Relief from Unconstitutional State Statutes: The Implications of Steffel v. Thompson," 9 Harvard Civil Rights-Civil Liberties Law Review 520, 1974. Law Clerk to Judge Max Rosenn, U.S. Court of Appeals, Third Circuit, 1975-1976. Assistant U.S. Attorney, District of Columbia, 1976-1979. Chairman, Mandatory Continuing Legal Education Review Committee, 1997-1999; Chairman, Delaware Commission on Continuing Legal Education, 1987-1993. *Member:* Delaware State (Member, Continuing Legal Education Committee, 1979-1987; Chairman, 1984-1985; Member of Council, General Corporation Law Section, 2000—) and American Bar Associations. [Lt., USNR, active duty, 1970-1972]. ***PRACTICE AREAS:*** Corporate Litigation; Securities Litigation; Business Litigation; Civil Litigation; Corporate Law. ***Email:*** nmonhait@rmgglaw.com

JEFFREY S. GODDESS, born Chicago, Illinois, September 18, 1945; admitted to bar, 1971, Delaware. *Education:* Brown University (B.A., 1967); University of Chicago (J.D., 1971). City Solicitor of the City of Wilmington, Delaware, 1977-1981. *Member:* Delaware State Bar Association (Chair, Administration of Justice Committee, 1995-2000); Delaware Trial Lawyers Association (Member, Board of Governors, 1996-2000). ***PRACTICE AREAS:*** Commercial Litigation; Corporate Litigation; Personal Injury; Civil Litigation. ***Email:*** jgoddess@rmgglaw.com

CARMELLA PISCOPO KEENER, born Brooklyn, New York, August 3, 1963; admitted to bar, 1988, Pennsylvania; 1990, New Jersey and Delaware. *Education:* Lafayette College (B.A., 1985); Rutgers University School of Law, Camden (J.D., with honors in Tax Law, 1988). Recipient: American Jurisprudence Award, Property, 1986; American Jurisprudence Award, Commercial Paper, 1987. Judicial Law Clerk, Superior Court, State of Delaware, 1989-1990. *Member:* Delaware State, Pennsylvania and American Bar Associations. ***PRACTICE AREAS:*** Insurance Coverage; Corporate Litigation; Securities Litigation; Business Litigation; Civil Litigation; Corporate Formation. ***Email:*** ckeener@rmgglaw.com

---

EDWARD B. ROSENTHAL, born Wilmington, Delaware, March 18, 1966; admitted to bar, 1992, Delaware. *Education:* Franklin and Marshall College (B.A., 1988); Villanova University (J.D., 1991). Phi Alpha Theta. Recipient, Philadelphia Trial Lawyers Trial Advocacy Award. ***Email:*** erosenthal@rmgglaw.com

(This Listing Continued)

COUNSEL FOR: Delaware Incorporating Co.

WALTER SPEED ROWLAND

2501 WILLARD STREET

WILMINGTON, DELAWARE 19806

Telephone: 302-654-6526

Fax: 302-654-7823

Email: wrowland1@home.com

Corporate and Commercial Litigation, Arbitration & Mediation, Historic Preservation, International Law, Criminal Law.

WALTER SPEED ROWLAND, born Fuquay Springs, North Carolina, March 29, 1939; admitted to bar, 1966, New York; 1974, Delaware; 1990, Virginia. *Education:* Harvard University (A.B., magna cum laude, 1961); University of Freiburg, Freiburg, West Germany; University of Chicago (J.D., 1965). *Member:* New York State, Delaware State and Virginia Bar Associations; American Arbitration Association. ***LANGUAGES:*** German. ***PRACTICE AREAS:*** Corporate; Commercial; Arbitrations; Mediation; International; Historic Preservation; Criminal Law.

SAUL EWING LLP

A Delaware Limited Liability Partnership

222 DELAWARE AVENUE, P.O. BOX 1266, 19899-1266

FOR COURIER DELIVERY: 222 DELAWARE AVENUE, SUITE 1200, 19801

WILMINGTON, DELAWARE

Telephone: 302-421-6800

Cable Address: "Bidsal"

TWX: 83-4798.

Telecopier: XEROX 7020 302-421-6813

Email: lawyers@saul.com

URL: http://www.saul.com

Philadelphia, Pennsylvania Office: Centre Square West, 1500 Market Street, 38th Floor, 19102-2186. Telephone: 215-972-7777. Cable Address: "Bidsal" TWX: 83-4798. Telecopier: XEROX 7020 215-972-7725.

New York, New York Office: Twenty-first Floor 237 Park Avenue, 10017. Telephone: 212-551-3502 TWX: 425170 Telecopier: 212-697-8486.

Chesterbrook, Pennsylvania Office: 1200 Liberty Ridge, Wayne, Pennsylvania 19087. Telephone: 610-251-5050. Cable Address: "BIDSAL". TWX: 83-4798. Telecopier: 610-651-5930.

Harrisburg, Pennsylvania Office: Penn National Insurance Tower, 2 North Second Street, 7th Floor, 17101. Telephone: 717-257-7500. Telecopier: 717-238-4622, 717-257-7516.

Princeton, New Jersey Office: 214 Carnegie Center, Suite 202, 08540. Telephone: 609-452-3100. Fax: 609-452-3122.

Baltimore, Maryland Office: 100 South Charles Street, Suite 1500, 21201-2773. Telephone: 410-332-8600. Fax: 410-332-8862.

Bankruptcy and Reorganization, Business, Construction, Criminal Defense and Government Enforcement, Education, Emerging Business, Employee Benefits, Environmental, Estates and Trusts, Financial Services, Golf, Government Relations and Regulatory Compliance, Health Law, Insurance, Intellectual Property, International, Labor and Employment, Litigation (Commercial and Civil), Products Liability, Public Finance, Real Estate, Securities, Tax, Technology, Telecommunications.

LAW FIRM ALLIANCES/ASSOCIATIONS: **INTERLEX**

PARTNERS

CARL B. EVERETT, born Plainfield, New Jersey, March 23, 1947; admitted to bar, 1974, Texas and Delaware; 1977, U.S. Court of Appeals, Sixth Circuit and U.S. District Court, District of Delaware; 1978, U.S. Court of Appeals, Fifth Circuit; 1979, U.S. Court of Appeals, First and for the District of Columbia Circuit; 1987, Pennsylvania and U.S. District Court, Eastern District of Pennsylvania. *Education:* Massachusetts Institute of Technology (B.S., 1969); University of Houston (J.D., 1973). Member, Order of the Barons. *Member:* Philadelphia (Member, Environmental Law Committee, Co-Chair, 1997), Pennsylvania, Delaware and American Bar Associations; State Bar of Texas. ***PRACTICE AREAS:*** Environmental. ***Email:*** ceverett@saul.com

TIMOTHY A. FREY, born Abington, Pennsylvania, July 24, 1953; admitted to bar, 1978, Pennsylvania; 1994, Delaware. *Education:* Dartmouth College (B.A., summa cum laude, 1975); University of Pennsylvania (J.D., cum laude, 1978). Phi Beta Kappa. Member, University of Pennsylvania Law Review, 1976-1978. *Member:* Philadelphia, Pennsylvania, Delaware State and American

(This Listing Continued)

Bar Associations; National Association of Bond Lawyers. Fellow, American College of Bond Counsel. ***PRACTICE AREAS:*** Public Finance. ***Email:*** tfrey@saul.com

WILLIAM S. GEE, born Wilmington, Delaware, March 23, 1951; admitted to bar, 1977, Delaware. *Education:* Yale University (B.A., 1973); Washington & Lee University (J.D., summa cum laude, 1977). Phi Alpha Delta. Order of the Coif. Member, Washington & Lee Law Review, 1976-1977. Author: "The Shifting Jurisdiction of the Antitrust Laws," Vol. XXXIII, Washington & Lee Law Review. *Member:* Delaware State (Member, Commercial Law Section; Section on Real Property) and American (Member, Business Law Section; Real Property, Probate and Trust Section) Bar Associations. ***PRACTICE AREAS:*** Real Estate; Commercial Transactions; Public Finance. ***Email:*** wgee@saul.com

STEVEN D. GOLDBERG, born Wilmington, Delaware, February 3, 1946; admitted to bar, 1971, Delaware. *Education:* University of Delaware (B.A., 1968); George Washington University (J.D., with honors, 1971). Phi Alpha Delta. Senior Associate, George Washington Law Review, 1969-1971. *Member:* Delaware (Member, Sections on: General Corporation; Real and Personal Property and Commercial Law) and American Bar Associations. ***PRACTICE AREAS:*** Real Property Law; Corporate Law; Alternate Entities; Commercial Transactions. ***Email:*** sdgoldberg@saul.com

DANIEL H. KRAPF, born Wilmington, Delaware, October 1, 1948; admitted to bar, 1976, Delaware; 1978, U.S. District Court, District of Delaware; 1992, U.S. Court of Appeals, Third Circuit. *Education:* University of Delaware (B.A., 1971); Dickinson School of Law (J.D., 1975). Law Clerk, Delaware Supreme Court, 1975-1976. Former Vice-President and General Counsel, Allied Properties Group. *Member:* Delaware State (Member, Sections on Real Property and Commercial Law) and American (Member, Sections on Business Law and Real Property) Bar Associations. ***PRACTICE AREAS:*** Real Estate; Commercial Transactions; Leasing; Construction; Finance Law. ***Email:*** dkrapf@saul.com

MARK MINUTI, born Wilmington, Delaware, August 10, 1963; admitted to bar, 1988, Delaware and U.S. District Court, District of Delaware. *Education:* University of Delaware (B.S., 1985); Delaware Law School of Widener University (J.D., cum laude, 1988). Law Clerk to the Honorable Clarence W. Taylor, Delaware Superior Court, 1988-1989. *Member:* Delaware State and American Bar Associations. ***PRACTICE AREAS:*** Bankruptcy. ***Email:*** mminuti@saul.com

DOMENIC E. PACITTI, born Philadelphia, Pennsylvania, June 8, 1962; admitted to bar, 1987, Pennsylvania and New Jersey; 2000 Delaware. *Education:* Lycoming College (B.A., 1984); University of Richmond (J.D., 1987). ***PRACTICE AREAS:*** Bankruptcy; Commercial Litigation. ***Email:*** dpacitti@saul.com

NORMAN L. PERNICK, born Wilmington, Delaware, July 13, 1959; admitted to bar, 1985, Delaware. *Education:* Brandeis University (B.A., magna cum laude, with high honors, 1981); George Washington University (J.D., with honors, 1984). Author: *Bankruptcy Deadline Checklist. Member:* Delaware State and American (Member, Business Bankruptcy and Small Business Committees, Section of Business Law) Bar Associations. ***PRACTICE AREAS:*** Bankruptcy Law. ***Email:*** npernick@saul.com

LINDA RICHENDERFER, born Kingston, Pennsylvania, March 25, 1959; admitted to bar, 1984, Pennsylvania (Not admitted in Delaware). *Education:* Villanova University (B.A., magna cum laude, 1980; J.D., cum laude, 1984). Order of the Coif. Case and Comment Editor, Villanova University Law Review, 1983-1984. *Member:* Philadelphia, Pennsylvania and American (Member, Section on Litigation) Bar Associations. ***PRACTICE AREAS:*** Environmental; White Collar Crime; Commercial Litigation. ***Email:*** lrichenderfer@saul.com

PAMELA J. SCOTT, born Wilmington, Delaware, November 25, 1958; admitted to bar, 1984, Pennsylvania and New Jersey; 1985, Delaware. *Education:* University of Delaware (B.S., 1980); Delaware Law School of Widener University (J.D., 1983). Executive Board Member, Moot Court Honor Society. Former First Assistant City Solicitor, City of Wilmington, 1991-1996. Former Director of Policy, State Department of Transportation, 1996-1998. *Member:* Pennsylvania, New Jersey State and Delaware State Bar Associations. ***PRACTICE AREAS:*** Commercial Real Estate; Real Estate; Zoning, Planning and Land Use; Administrative Law; Alcoholic Beverages; Eminent Domain; Historic Preservation. ***Email:*** pscott@saul.com

WENDIE COHEN STABLER, born Wilmington, Delaware, September 23, 1958; admitted to bar, 1983, Georgia and Delaware. *Education:* Syracuse University, Florence, Italy; Tufts University (B.A., magna cum laude, 1980); Emory University (J.D., 1983). Member, Emory National Moot Court Team, 1982-1983. *Member:* State Bar of Georgia; Delaware State (Member, Sections on: Commercial Law; Real Estate) and American (Member, Sections on: Business Law; Real Property, Probate and Trust; Public Utility, Communications and Transportation Law) Bar Associations. ***LANGUAGES:*** Italian. ***PRACTICE AREAS:*** Commercial Law; Telecommunications; Zoning and Land Use; Real Estate Law; Administrative Law. ***Email:*** wstabler@saul.com

(This Listing Continued)

SPECIAL COUNSEL

MICHAEL F. BONKOWSKI, born Wilmington, Delaware, June 7, 1956; admitted to bar, 1983, Delaware, U.S. District Court, District of Delaware, U.S. Court of Appeals, Third Circuit and U.S. Court of Appeals for the Federal Circuit. *Education:* Columbia College (A.B., 1978); Temple University (J.D., 1983). *Member:* Delaware State and American Bar Associations. ***PRACTICE AREAS:*** Commercial Litigation; Limited Partnerships; Corporate Law. ***Email:*** mbonkowski@saul.com

DONALD J. DETWEILER, born Wilmington, Delaware, October 29, 1963; admitted to bar, 1992, Delaware; 1993, Pennsylvania. *Education:* Villanova University (B.A., 1986); Widener University (J.D., 1992). Phi Delta Phi. Arbitrator and Mediator, Delaware Superior Court. *Member:* American Bar Association; American Bankruptcy Institute; Defense Research Institute; Defense Counsel of Delaware. ***PRACTICE AREAS:*** Bankruptcy Reorganization; Commercial Litigation; Personal Injury; Product Liability. ***Email:*** ddetweiler@saul.com

MARIA APRILE SAWCZUK, born Wilmington, Delaware, January 20, 1967; admitted to bar, 1993, New Jersey and U.S. District Court, District of New Jersey; 1994, Pennsylvania and Delaware; 1996, U.S. District Court, Eastern District of Pennsylvania; 1997, U.S. District Court, District of Delaware. *Education:* University of Delaware (B.A., 1987); Villanova University School of Law (J.D., 1993). Order of the Coif; Phi Kappa Phi. Co-Chair, Montgomery County Bankruptcy/Debtors' and Creditors' Rights Committee, 1998-1999. Member, Pennsylvania Bar Association, 1994-1999. *Member:* Delaware Bar Association. ***PRACTICE AREAS:*** Bankruptcy; Corporate Law. ***Email:*** msawczuk@saul.com

J. KATE STICKLES, born Hanover, Pennsylvania, October 7, 1962; admitted to bar, 1990, Pennsylvania, Delaware, U.S. District Court, District of Delaware and U.S. Court of Appeals, Third Circuit. *Education:* Western Maryland College (B.A., cum laude, 1984); Temple University (J.D., 1989). President, Moot Court Honor Society. Champion, National Civil Rights Moot Court Competition, Minneapolis, Minnesota. Recipient, Temple Law Alumni Moot Court Award. *Member:* Delaware State and American Bar Associations. ***PRACTICE AREAS:*** Bankruptcy Law; Commercial Law. ***Email:*** kstickles@saul.com

ASSOCIATES

KIMBERLY L. GATTUSO, born Wilmington, Delaware, November 2, 1973; admitted to bar, 1998, Delaware; 1999, U.S. District Court, District of Delaware. *Education:* University of Delaware (B.A., 1995); Widener University (J.D., 1998). Member, Delaware Journal of Corporate Law, 1996-1998. Law Clerk to the Honorable Henry duPont Ridgely, President Judge, Superior Court of Delaware, 1998-1999. *Member:* Delaware State and American Bar Associations. ***PRACTICE AREAS:*** Litigation. ***Email:*** kgattuso@saul.com

TARA L. LATTOMUS, born Portsmouth, England, November 27, 1970; admitted to bar, 1996, Delaware; 1997, Pennsylvania. *Education:* Wesley College (B.S., summa cum laude, 1993); Villanova University (J.D., cum laude, 1996). Editor, Villanova Law Review. *Member:* Delaware State and American Bar Associations. ***PRACTICE AREAS:*** Bankruptcy; Creditor Rights. ***Email:*** tlattomus@saul.com

JEREMY WILLIAM RYAN, born Philadelphia, Pennsylvania, May 19, 1971; admitted to bar, 1997, Pennsylvania; U.S. District Court, Eastern and Western Districts of Pennsylvania (Not admitted in Delaware). *Education:* Washington & Jefferson College (B.A., 1994); University of Pittsburgh (J.D., cum laude, 1997). Managing Editor, Journal of Law and Commerce, 1995-1997. *Member:* Philadelphia County, Pennsylvania and American Bar Associations. ***PRACTICE AREAS:*** Commercial Litigation; Corporate Governance. ***Email:*** jryan@saul.com

ROGER LEA TRUEMPER, born Marshall, Texas, November 11, 1960; admitted to bar, 1989, Pennsylvania; 1990, Delaware; 1992, U.S. District Court, District of Delaware. *Education:* University of Delaware (B.A., 1983); Delaware Law School of Widener University (J.D., cum laude, 1988). Recipient, American Jurisprudence Award for Constitutional Law. *Member:* Pennsylvania and Delaware Bar Associations; Delaware Trial Lawyers Association. ***PRACTICE AREAS:*** Real Estate Law; Commercial and Business Law; Commercial Litigation. ***Email:*** rtruemper@saul.com

(For complete biographical data on other personnel, see Professional Biographies at New York, N.Y.; Wayne, Philadelphia and Harrisburg, Pennsylvania; Princeton, New Jersey; Baltimore, Maryland).

SAWYER, AKIN & HERRON, P.A.

Established in 1978
1220 NORTH MARKET STREET
SUITE 608
P.O. BOX 25047
WILMINGTON, DELAWARE 19899
Telephone: 302-655-5552
Telecopier: 302-655-3697
Email: sah@sahlaw.com
URL: http://www.sahlaw.com

Trusts and Estates, Insurance Defense, Litigation.

H. MURRAY SAWYER, JR., born Niagara Falls, New York, January 10, 1946; admitted to bar, 1971, Delaware; 1980, Pennsylvania. *Education:* University of North Carolina (B.A., 1968); Vanderbilt University (J.D., 1971). Deputy Attorney General, Delaware Department of Justice, 1972-1973. Member, Supreme Court Board of Professional Responsibility, 1983-1996. Member Delaware Health Facilities Authority, 1983-1992. New Castle County Councilman, 1981-1983. President and CEO, Registered Agents, Ltd., Registered Agents Legal Services, LLC and American Incorporators, Ltd. Member and registered investment adviser representative, Westover Capital Advisors, LLC. *Member:* Delaware and Pennsylvania Bar Associations. ***PRACTICE AREAS:*** Estate Planning; Financial Planning; Living Trusts; Family Trusts; Family Wealth Transfer; Retirement Planning; Trust Law; Wealth Preservation; Estate Administration. ***Email:*** hms@sahlaw.com

ROGER A. AKIN, born Newark, New Jersey, July 26, 1945; admitted to bar, 1977, Delaware. *Education:* Syracuse University (B.A., 1967); University of Maryland (J.D., 1973). Publisher and Editor: *Delaware District Digest,* 1984—; Delaware Jurisprudence, 1994—. Deputy Attorney General, Delaware Department of Justice, 1977-1982. General Counsel to State Board of Education and Department of Public Instruction, 1979-1982. City Solicitor: Newark, Delaware, 1994—; Delaware City, Delaware, 1998-2000. *Member:* Delaware (Former Chair, Council of Litigation Section, 1991) and American Bar Associations; Defense Research Institute. ***PRACTICE AREAS:*** Insurance Defense; Defense Litigation; Municipal Law; Automobile Insurance Defense; General Liability Defense. ***Email:*** raa@sahlaw.com

BRUCE C. HERRON, born Pittsburgh, Pennsylvania, September 24, 1959; admitted to bar, 1985, Delaware. *Education:* University of Virginia (B.A., with high distinction, 1981); Dickinson School of Law (J.D., 1984). Member, Dickinson Law Review, 1983-1984. Author: "The NLRB Modification of the Midwest Piping Doctrine: Industrial Stability v. Employee Free Choice," Vol. 88, Dickinson Law Review, 1983. Assistant City Solicitor, Newark, Delaware, 1996—. *Member:* Delaware (Member, Torts and Insurance Section) and American (Member, Litigation Section) Bar Associations; Defense Research Institute; The Association of Trial Lawyers of America. ***PRACTICE AREAS:*** Insurance Defense; Civil Rights Defense; Defense Litigation; Municipal Law; Trial Practice; Commercial Insurance Defense. ***Email:*** bch@sahlaw.com

SCHLUSSER & REIVER, P.A.

Established in 1982
1700 WEST 14TH STREET
WILMINGTON, DELAWARE 19806
Telephone: 302-655-8181
Fax: 302-655-8190

Federal and State Income, Estate and Gift Taxation. Estate Planning. Probate, Tax and Fiduciary Litigation.

ROBERT E. SCHLUSSER, born Harrisburg, Pennsylvania, August 24, 1942; admitted to bar, 1967, Pennsylvania; 1970, U.S. Claims Court and U.S. Tax Court; 1971, Delaware; 1972, U.S. District Court, District of Delaware; 1973, U.S. Court of Appeals, Third Circuit and U.S. Supreme Court; 1991, Federal Circuit Court; 1993, New Mexico. *Education:* Dickinson College (B.A., 1964); Dickinson School of Law (J.D., 1967); George Washington University (LL.M., in Taxation, 1969). Chairman, Wilmington Tax Group, 1976-1977. *Member:* Delaware State (Chairman, Tax Section, 1989-1990) and American (Member, Tax and Litigation Sections) Bar Associations. ***PRACTICE AREAS:*** Taxation Law; Tax Controversies; Fiduciary Litigation. ***Email:*** rschlusser@schlusser-reiver.com

JOANNA REIVER, born Wilmington, Delaware, October 20, 1946; admitted to bar, 1976, Delaware; 1994, New Mexico. *Education:* University of Delaware; West Virginia University (A.B., 1968); Catholic University of America (J.D., 1976). Member and President, Estate Planning Council of Delaware, Inc., 1991-1992. Board of Directors, 1993-1999; Treasurer, 1998-1999, National Association of Estate Planners & Councils. *Member:* Delaware State (Chairman, Estates and Trusts Section, 1985-1986, Member, Tax Section) and American (Member, Section of Real Property, Probate and Trust Law) Bar Associations; State Bar of New Mexico; Wilmington Tax Group. Fellow, The American College of Trust and Estate Counsel. ***PRACTICE AREAS:*** Estate Planning; Probate Law. ***Email:*** jreiver@schlusser-reiver.com

NELL GRAHAM SALE, born Charleston, West Virginia, April 24, 1946; admitted to bar, 1990, Delaware; 1991, U.S. District Court, District of Delaware; 1992, Pennsylvania; 1993, U.S. District Court, Eastern District of Pennsylvania; 1995, U.S. Tax Court; 1997, U.S. Supreme Court. *Education:* DePauw University (B.A., with honors, 1968); University of North Carolina; Widener University School of Law (J.D., cum laude, 1990). Phi Beta Kappa; Phi Kappa Phi. Member, Moot Court Honor Society. Recipient, American Jurisprudence Awards. Certified Elder Law Attorney. *Member:* Delaware State (Former Chair, Women and the Law Section, 1992-1993; Chair, Estates and Trusts Section, 1996-1997), Pennsylvania (Member, Real Estate and Probate Section) and American Bar Associations; National Conference of Women's Bar Associations (Treasurer, 1995-1996); National Association of Elder Law Attorneys. ***PRACTICE AREAS:*** Estate Planning; Probate; Elder Law; Fiduciary Income Tax; Real Estate. ***Email:*** ngsale@schlusser-reiver.com

SCHMITTINGER & RODRIGUEZ, P.A.

1300 NORTH MARKET STREET, SUITE 205
WILMINGTON, DELAWARE 19801
Telephone: 302-652-3676
FAX: 302-652-8788
Email: attorneys@schmittrod.com
URL: http://www.schmittrod.com

Dover, Delaware Office: 414 South State Street. Telephone: 302-674-0140. Fax: 302-674-1830.
Rehoboth Beach, Delaware Office: 4602 Highway One. Telephone: 302-227-1400. Fax: 302-645-1843.
Odessa, Delaware Office: Odessa Professional Park, P.O. Box 626. Telephone: 302-378-1697. Fax: 302-378-1659.

General Civil Practice. Personal Injury, Workers Compensation, Federal Practice, Corporation, Estate Planning, Real Estate and Commercial Law. Litigation.

HAROLD SCHMITTINGER, born Philadelphia, Pennsylvania, July 17, 1928; admitted to bar, 1954, District of Columbia; 1955, Delaware; 1956, U.S. Tax Court. *Education:* University of Delaware (B.S., 1952); American University (LL.B., 1954); Georgetown University (LL.M., 1956). Member, 1958-1995 and President, 1990-1995, Lawyers Fund for Client Protection. *Member:* Delaware State Bar Association (President, 1980-1981). Fellow, American College of Trial Lawyers. (Also at Dover and Rehoboth Beach, Delaware Offices). ***PRACTICE AREAS:*** Personal Injury Law. ***Email:*** hs@schmittrod.com

NICHOLAS H. RODRIGUEZ, born Dover, Delaware, December 28, 1934; admitted to bar, 1961, Delaware. *Education:* Pennsylvania State University (B.S., 1957); Washington & Lee University (J.D., summa cum laude, 1961). Order of the Coif; Phi Beta Kappa; Phi Alpha Delta; Xi Sigma Pi. Author: Comment, 17 Washington & Lee University Law Review 260 (160). U.S. Commissioner, Judicial District of Delaware, 1961-1966. City Solicitor, City of Dover, 1969—. *Member:* Kent County (President, 1971-1972), Delaware State (First Vice-President, 1971-1972) and American Bar Associations; Delaware Trial Lawyers Association; The Association of Trial Lawyers of America. Fellow: American College of Trial Lawyers. (Also at Dover and Rehoboth Beach, Delaware Offices). ***PRACTICE AREAS:*** Personal Injury Law. ***Email:*** nrodriguez@schmittrod.com

PAUL H. BOSWELL, born Wilmington, Delaware, July 30, 1938; admitted to bar, 1966, Delaware. *Education:* University of Delaware (B.A., 1960); Washington & Lee University (LL.B., 1963); Temple University (LL.M. in Taxation, 1980). Phi Alpha Delta. Member, Washington & Lee Law Review, 1963. Author: Comment, "Reconciliation Period, Divorces," 20 Washington & Lee Law Review 335, 1963. U.S. Magistrate, 1967-1972. *Member:* Kent County (President, 1975-1976) and Delaware State (Member, 1975—and Chairman, 1983-1984, Decedent's Trust and Estates Section) Bar Associations. Fellow, American College of Trust and Estate Counsel. (Also at Dover and Rehoboth Beach, Delaware Offices). ***PRACTICE AREAS:*** Corporate Law; Estate Planning; Estate Settlements; Taxation. ***Email:*** pboswell@schmittrod.com

JOHN J. SCHMITTINGER, born Atlantic City, New Jersey, March 19, 1941; admitted to bar, 1966, Delaware. *Education:* Drew University; University of Delaware (B.A., 1963); Temple University (J.D., 1966). Phi Alpha Delta. Editor, Temple Law Quarterly, 1965-1966. Listed in: Best Lawyers in America, 1995-1996; 1996-1997; 1997-1998; 1998-1999; 1999-2000. Past President, Kent County Bar Association. *Member:* Delaware State (Past-Chairman, General Legislation Committee) and American Bar Associations; Delaware Trial Lawyers Association (Vice-President, 1979-1981); The Association of Trial Lawyers of America (Past Secretary, Board on Professional Responsibility). (Also at Dover and Rehoboth Beach, Delaware Offices). ***PRACTICE AREAS:*** Workers Compensation Law; Personal Injury. ***Email:*** jschmittinger@schmittrod.com

(This Listing Continued)

WILLIAM D. FLETCHER, JR., born Philadelphia, Pennsylvania, September 27, 1949; admitted to bar, 1975, Delaware; 1980, U.S. Supreme Court. *Education:* University of Delaware (B.A., 1972); University of Tulsa; Washington & Lee University (J.D., 1975). Assistant City Solicitor, City of Dover, 1977-1981. *Member:* Kent County, Delaware State and American Bar Associations; Delaware Trial Lawyers Association; The Association of Trial Lawyers of America. (Also at Dover, Delaware Office). ***PRACTICE AREAS:*** Personal Injury Law; Employment Law. ***Email:*** wfletcher@schmittrod.com

R. SCOTT KAPPES, born South Boston, Virginia, October 24, 1966; admitted to bar, 1995, Pennsylvania and New Jersey; 1996, Delaware. *Education:* Towson State University (B.S., 1989); Widener University (J.D., 1994). Phi Delta Phi. (Resident). ***PRACTICE AREAS:*** Workers Compensation; Personal Injury; Employment Law. ***Email:*** rkappes@schmittrod.com

KYLE KEMMER, born East Meadow, New York, July 1, 1970; admitted to bar, 1997, Delaware; 1998, Pennsylvania. *Education:* Pennsylvania State University (B.A., 1992); Widener University School of Law (J.D., 1997). Phi Delta Phi. *Member:* Deleware State and American Bar Associations; Association of Trial Lawyers of America; Deleware Trial Lawyers Association. (Resident). ***PRACTICE AREAS:*** Workers Compensation; Personal Injury. ***Email:*** kkemmer@schmittrod.com

REPRESENTATIVE CLIENTS INCLUDE: Chesapeake Utilities Corp.; Eastern Shore Natural Gas Co.; Delaware State University; New Plan Realty Trust.
APPROVED AGENT FOR: Chicago Title Insurance Co.; Ticor Title Insurance Co.; Lawyers Title Insurance Corp.; Transamerica Title Insurance Co.

(For Complete Biographical Data on all Personnel, see Professional Biographies at Dover)

SCHOENBECK & SCHOENBECK, P.A.

Established in 1987

1211 MILLTOWN ROAD, SUITE A
WILMINGTON, DELAWARE 19808
Telephone: 302-999-9316
Fax: 302-999-8387
URL: http://www.schoenbeck.com
Email: schoenbeck@schoenbeck.com
URL: http://www.lawyers.com/schoenbeck

Civil Litigation, Personal Injury, Family Law, Probate and Estate Planning, Real Estate, Bankruptcy, Business Law, Corporate Law.

MARK F. SCHOENBECK (Deceased).

DONNA L. SCHOENBECK, born Sewickley, Pennsylvania; admitted to bar, 1985, Pennsylvania; 1986, U.S. District Court, Eastern District of Pennsylvania; 1987, Delaware; 1988, U.S. District Court, District of Delaware; 1997, U.S. Supreme Court. *Education:* Temple University (B.A., cum laude, 1979); Widener University (J.D., 1985). Recipient: Pro Bono Publico Award, 1993. Invited Moot Court Competition Judge, Judge G. Fred Dibona Moot Court Competition, 1990—. Speaker: "Optimum Marital Deduction v. Maximum Marital Deduction and the use of Life Insurance"..."Grossing-up an Estate," New Castle County Life Underwriter's Association, April 19, 1990; General legal questions, Legal Line Radio Talk Show, WILM News Radio, July 17, 1990 and April 29, 1992; "How to Handle Client Bankruptcies, Accounts Receivable Collection and Small Claims Court," New Castle County Chamber of Commerce, February 24, 1993; Financial and Estate Planning, St. Francis Hospital Breast Cancer Support Network, October 1996; Pro-se Divorce, Delaware Commission for Women, 1994-1999. Instructor, Wills and Trusts, American Academy of Paralegal Studies, Fall 1990. *Member:* Delaware (Member, Sections on: Real Estate; Estate and Trust), Pennsylvania and American Bar Associations; American Trial Lawyers Association; Delaware Trial Lawyers Association; Pennsylvania Trial Lawyers Association. ***REPORTED CASES:*** Prices Corner Liquors, Inc., Plaintiff Below, Appellant v. Delaware Alcoholic Beverage Control Commission, Defendant Below, Appellee, Del.Supr., 705 A.2d 571 (1998). ***PRACTICE AREAS:*** Bankruptcy Chapters 7, 11, 13; Real Estate; Civil Litigation; Personal Injury; Probate; Estate Planning. ***Email:*** schoenbeck@schoenbeck.com

JANELL SCHOENBECK OSTROSKI, born Wilmington, Delaware; admitted to bar, 1993, Delaware, U.S. District Court, District of Delaware and U.S. Supreme Court. *Education:* University of Delaware (B.A., magna cum laude, 1990); Widener University (J.D., cum laude, 1993). Invited Moot Court Competition Judge, Widener University School of Law, April 1999 and April 2000. Pro-Se Divorce Seminar, Delaware Commission for Women, 1997-1999. Speaker: "Collection Law in Delaware," Seminar through Lorman Education Services; Women's Entrepreneurial Expo, November, 1995 and November, 1997; "Advanced Directives," St. Francis Hospital Breast Cancer Support Network, October 1996; "Collecting Account Receivables," New Castle County Chamber of Commerce, 1994, 1995 and 1996. Special Master to Family Court. Volunteer Legal Services. Due Process Panel Member for the Delaware Department of Education. *Member:* Delaware State Bar Association (Family Law Section). ***PRACTICE AREAS:*** Family Law; Probate; Bankruptcy; Collections. ***Email:*** ostroski@schoenbeck.com

(This Listing Continued)

SEITZ, VAN OGTROP & GREEN, P.A.

222 DELAWARE AVENUE, SUITE 1500
P.O. BOX 68
WILMINGTON, DELAWARE 19899
Telephone: 302-888-0600
Fax: 302-888-0606
Email: svglaw.com
URL: http://www.lawyers.com/svglaw

Bankruptcy, Construction, Corporate, Commercial, Insurance Coverage, Personal Injury, Transportation and Intellectual Property Litigation; General Civil Practice in all Courts.

BERNARD A. VAN OGTROP, born Aruba, Netherlands, December 3, 1944; admitted to bar, 1969, Delaware; 1979, U.S. Supreme Court. *Education:* Georgetown University (A.B., 1966); Catholic University of America (J.D., 1969). Special Agent, Federal Bureau of Investigation, 1969-1972. *Member:* Delaware, Federal and American Bar Associations; Delaware Trial Lawyers Association (Vice President, 1983—; President, 1988); American Board of Trial Advocates. ***PRACTICE AREAS:*** Personal Injury; Litigation. ***Email:*** bvanogtrop@svglaw.com

GEORGE H. SEITZ, III, born Wilmington, Delaware, November 25, 1945; admitted to bar, 1971, Delaware; U.S. District Court, District of Delaware; 1978, U.S. Court of Appeals, 3rd Circuit; 1992, U.S. Supreme Court. *Education:* University of Delaware (B.S., 1968); University of Virginia (J.D., 1971). Beta Gamma Sigma. Member, National Moot Court Team, 1970-1971. Publication, Delaware Chapter, Fifty State Public Construction Contracting, (John Wiley & Sons, Inc., 1996). Chief Deputy Attorney General of Delaware, 1976-1977. Chief Prosecutor, 1975-1976. Deputy Attorney General, 1972-1974. Law Clerk, Delaware Supreme Court, 1971-1972. *Member:* Delaware State and American (Member, Forum Committee on the Construction Industry) Bar Associations; American Board of Trial Advocates (Secretary/Treasurer, Delaware Chapter). ***PRACTICE AREAS:*** Civil Litigation; Commercial Law; Construction Law; Environmental Insurance Litigation; Tort Litigation; Patent Litigation. ***Email:*** gseitz@svglaw.com

JAMES S. GREEN, born Berwick, Pennsylvania, May 24, 1947; admitted to bar, 1972, Delaware; 1973, Pennsylvania. *Education:* Princeton University (A.B., cum laude, 1969); Villanova University (J.D., 1972). Member, Villanova Law Review, 1971-1972. Deputy Attorney General of Delaware, 1975-1976. Chairman, Delaware Board on Unauthorized Practice of Law, 1995-1999. *Member:* Delaware and American (Member, Forum Committee on the Construction Industry; Litigation Section) Bar Associations; American Board of Trial Advocates (National Board Member, 1991-2000). ***PRACTICE AREAS:*** Construction Litigation; Commercial Litigation; Tort Litigation; Alternative Dispute Resolution. ***Email:*** jgreen@svglaw.com

ROBERT KARL HILL, born Wilmington, Delaware, April 4, 1963; admitted to bar, 1989, Delaware; 1990, U.S. District Court, District of Delaware; 1993, U.S. Court of Appeals, Third Circuit. *Education:* University of Delaware (B.A., cum laude, 1985); The Dickinson School of Law of Pennsylvania State University (J.D., 1989). Phi Beta Kappa. Member, Appellate Moot Court Board. Member, Editorial Board, Dickinson Journal of International Law, 1988-1989. Law Clerk to the Honorable Vincent J. Poppiti, Superior Court of Delaware, 1989-1990. *Member:* Delaware Bar Association. ***PRACTICE AREAS:*** Litigation; Bankruptcy. ***Email:*** khill@svglaw.com

PATRICIA P. McGONIGLE, born Huntington, West Virginia, April 13, 1967; admitted to bar, 1992, Delaware; 1993, Pennsylvania and U.S. District Court, District of Delaware; 1997, U.S. District Court, Eastern District of Pennsylvania and U.S. Court of Appeals, Third Circuit. *Education:* James Madison University (B.S., cum laude, 1989); Dickinson School of Law (J.D., 1992). Pi Sigma Alpha. Member, Appellate Moot Court Board. Publication: Delaware Chapter, Fifty State Public Construction Contracting (John Wiley & Sons, Inc., 1996). *Member:* Pennsylvania, Delaware State and American (Member, Litigation Section; Public Contract Law Section) Bar Associations; Defense Counsel of Delaware. ***PRACTICE AREAS:*** Civil Litigation; Commercial Law; Construction Litigation; Bankruptcy; Business Torts; Patent Litigation; Transportation Litigation. ***Email:*** pmcgonigle@svglaw.com

CARRIE I. DAYTON, born Montrose, Pennsylvania, May 15, 1970; admitted to bar, 1997, Delaware; 1998, U.S. District Court, District of Delaware. *Education:* West Chester University (B.S., 1988); Widener University (J.D., 1997). *Member:* Delaware and American Bar Associations. ***PRACTICE AREAS:*** Civil Litigation. ***Email:*** cdayton@svglaw.com

SUZANNE I. SEUBERT, P.A.

1328 KING STREET
WILMINGTON, DELAWARE 19801-3234
Telephone: 302-661-0400
Fax: 302-428-3193
Email: s.seubert@worldnet.att.net
URL: http://www.lawyers.com/suzanneiseubertpa

Family Law, Divorce, Alimony, Child Support, Custody, Probate, Wills, Guardianships.

SUZANNE I. SEUBERT, born Columbus, Ohio, August 22, 1955; admitted to bar, 1981, Ohio; 1991, Pennsylvania and Delaware. *Education:* University of Cincinnati (B.B.A., summa cum laude, 1978); Ohio State University (J.D., 1981). Beta Gamma Sigma, Beta Alpha Psi. Deputy Attorney General, Delaware Department of Justice, 1990-1996. *Member:* Delaware State (Member: Family Law, 1996—; Law and the Elderly, 1996—; Women and the Law Sections and Chair, Guardianships Committees for Family Law and Law and the Elderly, and for the Legal Handbook for Older Delawareans), Pennsylvania and American Bar Associations. ***PRACTICE AREAS:*** Family Law; Divorce; Alimony; Child Support; Custody; Wills; Guardianship; Probate.

DOUGLAS A. SHACHTMAN & ASSOCIATES

SUITE 302, 1200 PENNSYLVANIA AVENUE
WILMINGTON, DELAWARE 19806
Telephone: 302-655-1800
Fax: 302-655-5244
Email: DoShack@aol.com
URL: http://www.lawyers.com/shachtman

Trial Practice in all Civil Courts. Civil Rights Law. Consumer Law and Construction Law, Commercial and Collection Law.

DOUGLAS A. SHACHTMAN, admitted to bar, 1974, Pennsylvania; 1975, U.S. District Court, District of Delaware; 1977, Delaware. *Education:* University of Florida (B.S.B.A., 1969); University of Pennsylvania (J.D., 1974). *Member:* Delaware State Bar Association. ***PRACTICE AREAS:*** Civil Rights; Consumer Law; Professional Negligence; Commercial Law; Collections.

REPRESENTATIVE CLIENTS: AVIS; Peecision Service; Mestek; Richards Paving; NuCar Connection; Murray Transportation; Accurate Office.

SKADDEN, ARPS, SLATE, MEAGHER & FLOM LLP

ONE RODNEY SQUARE
P.O. BOX 636
WILMINGTON, DELAWARE 19899
Telephone: 302-651-3000
Fax: 302-651-3001
URL: http://www.skadden.com

Firm/Affiliate Offices:
New York, New York: Four Times Square, 10036. Telephone: 212-735-3000. Fax: 212-735-2000.
Boston, Massachusetts: One Beacon Street, 02108. Telephone: 617-573-4800. Fax: 617-573-4822.
Washington, D.C.: 1440 New York Avenue, N.W., 20005. Telephone: 202-371-7000. Fax: 202-393-5760.
Los Angeles, California: 300 South Grand Avenue, 90071. Telephone: 213-687-5000. Fax: 213-687-5600.
Chicago, Illinois: Skadden, Arps, Slate, Meagher & Flom (Illinois), 333 West Wacker Drive, 60606. Telephone: 312-407-0700. Fax: 312-407-0411.
San Francisco, California: Four Embarcadero Center, 94111. Telephone: 415-984-6400. Fax: 415-984-2698.
Houston, Texas: 1600 Smith Street, Suite 4400, 77002. Telephone: 713-655-5100. Fax: 713-655-5200.
Newark, New Jersey: One Newark Center, 07102. Telephone: 973-639-6800. Fax: 973-639-6858.
Palo Alto, California: 525 University Avenue, Suite 1100, 94301. Telephone: 650-470-4500. Fax: 650-470-4570.
Reston, Virginia: 11911 Freedom Drive, Suite 550, 20190. Telephone: 703-796-2345. Fax: 703-796-2344.
Tokyo, Japan: ATT Main Tower 12F, 2-17-22, Akasaka, Minato-ku, 107-0052. Telephone: 011-813-3568-2600. Fax: 011-813-3568-2626.
London, England: One Canada Square, Canary Wharf, E14 5DS. Telephone: 011-44-20-7519-7000. Fax: 011-44-20-7519-7070.
Hong Kong, China: 30/F Tower Two, Lippo Centre, 89 Queensway, Central. Telephone: 011-852-2820-0700. Fax: 011-852-2820-0727.

(This Listing Continued)

Sydney, New South Wales 2000, Australia: Skadden, Arps, Slate, Meagher & Flom (International), Level 13, 131 Macquarie Street. Telephone: 011-61-2-9253-6000. Fax: 011-61-2-9253-6044.
Toronto, Ontario, Canada: Suite 1820, North Tower, P.O. Box 189, Royal Bank Plaza, M5J 2J4. Telephone: 416-777-4700. Fax: 416-777-4747.
Brussels, Belgium: 523 avenue Louise, Box 30, 1050. Telephone: 011-32-2-639-0300. Fax: 011-32-2-639-0339.
Frankfurt am Main, Germany: MesseTurm, 27th Floor, 60308. Telephone: 011-49-69-742200. Fax: 011-49-69-74220300.
Paris, France: 68, rue du Faubourg Saint-Honoré, 75008. Telephone: 011-331-55-27-11-00. Fax: 011-331-55-27-11-99.
Beijing, China: East Wing Office, Level 4, China World Trade Center, No. 1 Jian Guo Men Wai Avenue, 100004. Telephone: 011-86-10-6505-5511. Fax: 011-86-10-6505-5522.
Moscow, Russia: Degtyarniy Pereulok 4, Building 1, 103009. Telephone: 011-7-501-797-4600. Fax: 011-7-501-797-4601.
Singapore, Singapore: Skadden, Arps, Slate, Meagher & Flom (International), 9 Temasek Boulevard, Suite 29-01, Suntec Tower Two, 038989. Telephone: 011-65-434-2900. Fax: 011-65-434-2988.

General Practice.

PARTNERS

STEVEN J. ROTHSCHILD, born Worcester, MA, 1944; admitted to bar, 1968, District of Columbia; 1969, Delaware. *Education:* University of Vermont (B.A., 1965); Georgetown University (J.D., 1968).

RICHARD L. EASTON, born New York, NY, 1950; admitted to bar, 1976, New York; 1983, Delaware. *Education:* Wesleyan University (B.A., cum laude, 1972); Georgetown University (J.D., 1975). Editor, Georgetown Law Review, 1974-1975. (Also at New York, NY).

EDWARD P. WELCH, born Columbus, OH, 1950; admitted to bar, 1976, Delaware; 1982, New York. *Education:* Georgetown University (B.S., 1972); Villanova University (J.D., 1976). Associate Editor, Villanova Law Review, 1975-1976. Law Clerk, Chancellor William Marvel, Delaware Court of Chancery (1976-1977).

THOMAS J. ALLINGHAM, II, born New London, CT, 1953; admitted to bar, 1978, Delaware. *Education:* Williams College (B.A., cum laude, 1974); University of Pennsylvania (J.D., 1977).

ANTHONY W. CLARK, born Fort Sill, OK, 1951; admitted to bar, 1979, Pennsylvania; 1982, Delaware. *Education:* State University of New York at Cortland (B.A., 1973); Temple University (J.D., 1979). Law Clerk, Hon. Joseph J. Longobardi, Hon. Robert C. O'Hara, Superior Court of Delaware (1979-1980), Hon. John J. McNeilly, Supreme Court of Delaware (1980-1981).

ROBERT B. PINCUS, born Philadelphia, PA, 1955; admitted to bar, 1980, Pennsylvania; 1984, Delaware. *Education:* College of William & Mary (B.B.A., 1977); American University (J.D., magna cum laude, 1980); Georgetown University (LL.M., 1983).

KAREN L. VALIHURA, born Greensburg, PA, 1963; admitted to bar, 1988, Pennsylvania; 1989, Delaware and U.S. District Court, District of Delaware; U.S. Court of Appeals, Third Circuit; 1992, U.S. District Court, Eastern District of Pennsylvania. *Education:* Washington & Jefferson College (B.A., summa cum laude, 1985); University of Pennsylvania Law School (J.D., 1988). Phi Beta Kappa.

GREGG M. GALARDI, born Orange, NJ, 1957; admitted to bar, 1991, Delaware. *Education:* University of Pennsylvania (B.A., 1975; M.A., 1986; Ph.D., 1990; J.D., 1990). Special Projects Editor, University of Pennsylvania Law Review, 1988-1990.

MARK S. CHEHI, born Bethlehem, PA, 1956; admitted to bar, 1990, Delaware; 1991, U.S. Court of Appeals, Third Circuit; 1992, Pennsylvania. *Education:* Haverford College (B.A., 1980); University of Chicago (J.D., 1990).

ROBERT S. SAUNDERS, born Philadelphia, PA, 1966; admitted to bar, 1991, Delaware. *Education:* Dartmouth College (A.B., cum laude, with high honors in Philosophy, 1987); University of Virginia (J.D., 1991).

OF COUNSEL

RODMAN WARD, JR., born Wilmington, DE, 1934; admitted to bar, 1959, District of Columbia and Delaware. *Education:* Williams College (B.A., 1956); Harvard University (LL.B., 1959).

COUNSEL

ALLISON L. AMORISON, born Atlantic City, NJ, 1966; admitted to bar, 1993, Delaware. *Education:* Lehigh University (B.S., Accounting, 1988); Ohio State University (J.D., summa cum laude, 1992).

KEVIN F. BRADY, born Philadelphia, PA, 1951; admitted to bar, 1983, Delaware. *Education:* University of Delaware (B.A., 1975); Delaware Law School of Widener University (J.D., magna cum laude, 1982; M.B.A., 1983).

(This Listing Continued)

SPECIAL COUNSEL

RANDOLPH K. HERNDON, born New London, CT, 1953; admitted to bar, 1981, Delaware. *Education:* Georgia Institute of Technology; Duke University (B.A., 1975; J.D., with distinction, 1980). Law Clerk, Hon. James L. Latchum, Chief Judge, U.S. District Court of Delaware (1981-1983).

(For Biographical Data on other Personnel, see New York, N.Y. Professional Biographies).

SMITH, KATZENSTEIN & FURLOW LLP

THE CORPORATE PLAZA
800 DELAWARE AVENUE
P.O. BOX 410
WILMINGTON, DELAWARE 19899
Telephone: 302-652-8400
Fax: 302-652-8405
Email: info@skfdelaware.com
URL: http://www.SKFDelaware.com

Corporate and Commercial Litigation, Corporation, Securities, Business, Limited Partnership, Limited Liability Companies, Insurance, Bankruptcy, and Employment Law.

FIRM PROFILE: The firm maintains a corporate and commercial practice serving national, international and local clients.

The firm's attorneys litigate before federal and state trial and appellate courts. The firm represents plaintiffs and corporate and individual defendants in a variety of corporate and commercial litigation matters, including stockholder class and derivative actions. The firm defends a variety of professional malpractice, general liability and insurance coverage claims. In bankruptcy matters, the firm represents creditors, committees, debtors and others in Chapter 11 reorganizations, out of court restructurings, international insolvency situations, and bankruptcy protection planning.

The firm's attorneys work with corporations and major law firms throughout the world on a wide range of Delaware corporate law and insolvency-related matters. The firm handles a variety of matters involving commercial, franchise, employment, limited partnership, and limited liability company law.

MEMBERS OF FIRM

CRAIG B. SMITH, born Wilmington, Delaware, October 16, 1943; admitted to bar, 1975, Delaware. *Education:* Carleton College (B.A., 1966); Syracuse University (M.A., 1969; J.D., summa cum laude, 1975). Order of the Coif. Member, Justinian Society. Senior Notes and Comments Editor, Syracuse Law Review, 1974-1975. Co-Author: *Guide to the Takeover Law of Delaware,* The Bureau of National Affairs (1988); "Limited Partnerships: Legal Aspects of Organization, Operation and Dissolution," 24-3rd C.P.S. (BNA 1992); "Delaware Limited Liability Company & Partnership Practice Guide," *State Limited Liability Company Laws,* Aspen Law & Business, 1994; "The Corporation: Formation and Organization (N.Y. and Del.)," "The Corporation: Management and Operation (N.Y. and Del.)," and "The Corporation: Dissolution and Termination (N.Y. and Del.)," New York and Delaware Business Entities, West Publishing Co. (1997). Author: "Delaware Limited Partnership Practice Guide," State Limited Partnership Laws, Aspen Law and Business, 1987; "Limited Partnerships - Expanded Opportunities Under Delaware's 1988 Revised Uniform Limited Partnership Act," 15 Delaware Journal of Corporate Law 43 (1990). Member: Advisory Board, Corporate Practice Series, Bureau of National Affairs, 1988—; Securities Laws and Regulatory Affairs Committee, Investment Program Association, Washington, D.C., 1990—. *Member:* Delaware State (Advisor, Commercial Law Section, 1983—; Member, 1984—, Subcommittee on Delaware Alternative Entities; Member: Chancery Court Fiduciary Rules Advisory Committee, 1986-1989; Corporation Law Section Council, 1987-1990, 1993—and Chairman, 1998-2000) and American (Member, Committee on Partnerships and Unincorporated Business Organizations, Business Law Section, 1984—. Fellow, Litigation Section, 1985—) Bar Associations. ***PRACTICE AREAS:*** Corporate Law; Securities; Corporate Litigation.

ROBERT J. KATZENSTEIN, born Philadelphia, Pennsylvania, May 2, 1951; admitted to bar, 1976, Delaware; 1979, District of Columbia. *Education:* Yale University (B.A., cum laude, 1973); University of Pennsylvania (J.D., 1976). Member, Richard S. Rodney Inn of Court, 1993—. Trial Attorney, U.S. Department of Justice, Antitrust Division, Washington, D.C., 1976-1978. Assistant Disciplinary Counsel to Delaware Board of Professional Responsibility, 1986-1992. *Member:* Delaware State (Member: Committee on Judicial Appointments, 1991—; Co-chair, 1999—; Sections on: Litigation; Corporation Law; Alternate Dispute Resolution), Federal (Vice President, 1981-1983 and President, 1983-1984, Delaware Chapter) and American (Member, Section on, Litigation) Bar Associations; The District of Columbia Bar; International Association of Defense Counsel; Product Liability Advisory Council; Defense Counsel of Delaware (President, 1997-1999). ***PRACTICE AREAS:*** Litigation. ***Email:*** rkatzenstein@skfdelaware.com

DAVID A. JENKINS, born Wilmington, Delaware, August 29, 1953; admitted to bar, 1978, Delaware. *Education:* University of Pennsylvania (B.A., cum laude, 1975); University of Chicago (J.D., 1978). *Member:* Delaware State Bar Association (Member, General Corporation Law Section). ***PRACTICE AREAS:*** Litigation; Corporate Law. ***Email:*** djenkins@skfdelaware.com

LAURENCE V. CRONIN, born Brookline, Massachusetts, March 2, 1959; admitted to bar, 1986, Delaware. *Education:* Clark University (B.A., with high honors, 1981); Marshall-Wythe School of Law, College of William and Mary (J.D., 1985). Assistant City Solicitor, City of Wilmington, 1988-1990. Deputy Attorney General, State of Delaware, 1986-1988. *Member:* Delaware State (Member, Sections on: Labor and Employment Law; Litigation) and American (Member, Sections on: Labor and Employment Law) Bar Associations. ***PRACTICE AREAS:*** Litigation; Employment Law. ***Email:*** lcronin@skfdelaware.com

SELINDA A. MELNIK, born Fort Worth, Texas, August 22, 1951; admitted to bar, 1985, New York ; 2001, Delaware. *Education:* Temple University (B.A., 1972); Rutgers University (M.C.R.P., highest honors, 1974); New York Law School (J.D., summa cum laude, 1984). Order of the Coif. Member, New York Law Journal (1982-1983). Author: "The U.S. Bankruptcy Review Commission's Global Imperative," 27 Bankruptcy Court Decisions A5 (October 31, 1995); "U.S. Reorganization Regimes: To Err is Human. To Forgive is Divine?", INSOL International, The Americas: NAFTA and Beyond and the Nasty Nineties (March 1995); "Protecting Exporters to Customers in the United States," Finnish Foreign Trade Assn. (1994); "Cross-Border Insolvencies: The United States Perspective--A Primer," Practicing Law Institute Dealing With Foreign Workouts and Insolvencies: Practical Strategies for Lenders and Investors, A4-4423, page 31 (1993); "Commencing A Voluntary Case Under Chapter 7 or 11," Practicing Law Institute Basics of Bankruptcy And Reorganization A4-4391, page 45 (1992); "U.S. Chapter 11 Bankruptcy Reorganizations," The Euromoney Institute of Finance, London, England, Workouts, Turnaround & Bankruptcy (1992); "Caveat Creditor: Cross-Border Insolvency--Wherefore Creditor Democracy?", 2 Turnarounds & Workouts 1 (March 15, 1992). *Member:* Association of the Bar of the City of New York (Official Delegate to International Bar Association; Past Appointed Member, Committee on Bankruptcy and Corporate Reorganization) New York State (Chair, 1990-1992, Multinational Insolvency Committee), American (Member: Business Section: International Section: Business Bankruptcy Committee; International Bankruptcy Subcommittee) and International (Chair, Committee on Creditors' Rights and Insolvency, 2000—; Membership Chair, 1996-2000; Trustee, International Bar Foundation, 1999—; Appointed Member, Globalization of Law Initiative 1997—; Appointed Member, Professional Development Committee, 1997—); American Bankruptcy Institute (Member, International Insolvency Committee) INSOL International; American Foreign Lawyers Association; International Women's Insolvency & Restructuring Confederation (Founder, First President 1994-1998, Board 1994—, Official Delegate to UNCITRAL, 1994—). ***LANGUAGES:*** French. ***REPORTED CASES:*** BCCI; In re Evans Products Company; In re A.H. Robbins Corp.; In re Federated Dept. Stores, Inc. ***PRACTICE AREAS:*** Bankruptcy; Reorganization; Corporate Restructuring; Creditors Rights; International Insolvency; Commercial Litigation. ***Email:*** samelink@skdelaware.com

MICHELE C. GOTT, born Wilmington, Delaware, May 23, 1958; admitted to bar, 1988, Delaware. *Education:* University of Delaware (B.A., 1982); Widener University School of Law (J.D., cum laude, 1988). Law Clerk, Delaware Superior Court, 1988-1989. Deputy Attorney General, Department of Justice, State of Delaware, 1995-1997. *Member:* Delaware State (Member, Sections on: Corporation Law; Commercial Law) and American Bar Associations (Member, Business Law Section); American Bankruptcy Institute. ***PRACTICE AREAS:*** Corporate Litigation; Commercial Litigation. ***Email:*** mgott@skfdelaware.com

KATHLEEN M. MILLER, born Baltimore, Maryland, January 6, 1965; admitted to bar, 1990, Delaware; 1991, Pennsylvania. *Education:* Villanova University (B.S., 1987); Widener University School of Law (J.D., cum laude, 1990). Law Clerk, Delaware Court of Chancery, 1990-1991. Fellow, Richard S. Rodney Inn of Court (1996-1998). *Member:* Delaware State (Member: Litigation Section; Young Lawyers Division) and American (Member, Sections on: Litigation; Business Law) Bar Associations; American Trial Lawyers Association; Delaware Trial Lawyers Association; American Bankruptcy Institute; International Women's Insolvency and Restructuring Confederation). ***PRACTICE AREAS:*** Bankruptcy Litigation; Personal Injury; Products Liability; General Litigation. ***Email:*** kmiller@skfdelaware.com

ASSOCIATES

JOELLE E. POLESKY, born San Francisco, California, May 8, 1970; admitted to bar, 1998, Delaware. *Education:* Georgetown University (B.S.F.S., magna cum laude, 1992); University of Pennsylvania (J.D., cum laude, 1997). Phi Beta Kappa. Member, University of Pennsylvania Law Review, 1995-1997.

(This Listing Continued)

SMITH, KATZENSTEIN & FURLOW LLP, Wilmington—Continued

Law Clerk, U.S. District Court, District of Delaware, 1997-1998. *Member:* Delaware State and American Bar Associations. ***PRACTICE AREAS:*** Corporate Litigation; Commercial Litigation. ***Email:*** jpolesky@skfdelaware.com

PARANDA B. WIEDEMER, born August 25, 1970; admitted to bar, 2001, Delaware. *Education:* Northern Virginia Community College (A.S., cum laude, 1992); Goldey-Beacom College (B.S., cum laude, 1996);Widener University at Wilmington (J.D., cum laude, 2000). Phi Delta Phi. Member: Alternative Dispute Resolution Society; Honor Chapter, 1997-1998, Vice Magister, 1998-1999 and Magister, 1999—, Harrington Inn of Court. Law Clerk, Delaware Superior Court, 2000-2001. *Member:* Delaware and American Bar Associations. ***PRACTICE AREAS:*** Litigation; Bankruptcy. ***Email:*** pwiedemer@skfdelaware.com

OF COUNSEL

CLARK W. FURLOW, born Washington, D.C., April 1, 1945; admitted to bar, 1978, Florida; 1979, Delaware. *Education:* Boston University (B.A., 1973); Emory University (J.D., 1977). Member, Order of Barristers. Staff Member, 1975-1976 and Member, Board of Editors, 1976-1977, Emory Law Journal. Co-Author, *Guide to the Takeover Law of Delaware,* The Bureau of National Affairs (1988). Assistant Secretary, 1983-1987 and Secretary, 1987-1989, Board of Bar Examiners of the State of Delaware. Member, Permanent Lawyers Advisory Committee, United States District Court, District of Delaware, 1988-1992. *Member:* Delaware State (Vice Chairman, 1983-1986 and Chairman, 1986-1988, Professional Ethics Committee) and American Bar Associations; The Florida Bar. ***PRACTICE AREAS:*** Litigation; Corporate Law. ***Email:*** cfurlow@sunvalley.net

SNYDER & ASSOCIATES, P.A.

300 DELAWARE AVENUE
SUITE 1014
WILMINGTON, DELAWARE 19899
Telephone: 302-657-8300
Telecopier: 302-657-8301
Email: snyder90@aol.com

Mailing Address: P.O. Box 90, Wilmington, Delaware 19899

Personal Injury, Bankruptcy, Products Liability, Medical Malpractice, Workers Compensation, Commercial Litigation, Real Estate, Wills & Probate, Trusts & Estates, Estate Planning, Admiralty.

FIRM PROFILE: The firm of Snyder & Associates, with over twenty years of experience, specializes in serving the needs of the people of Delaware in the areas of litigation, personal injury, corporate and real estate law.

BAYARD J. SNYDER, born Wilmington, Delaware, November 27, 1951; admitted to bar, 1976, Delaware; 1977, U.S. Court of Appeals, Third Circuit; 1978, New Jersey; 1981, District of Columbia. *Education:* Lake Forest College (B.A., 1973); Washington & Lee University (J.D., 1976). *Member:* Delaware and American Bar Associations; The Association of Trial Lawyers of America (Sustaining Member). ***PRACTICE AREAS:*** Civil Litigation; Personal Injury; Corporate Law; Real Estate Law. ***Email:*** snyder90@aol.com

OF COUNSEL

RICHARD H. ALLEN, born Wilmington, Delaware, May 16, 1932; admitted to bar, 1959, Delaware and U.S. District Court, District of Delaware; 1969, Pennsylvania. *Education:* Bowdoin College (B.A., magna cum laude, Honors in History, 1954); University of Chicago (J.D., with honors, 1959). Order of the Coif; Phi Beta Kappa. Editor, University of Chicago Law Review, 1958-1959. *Member:* Delaware, Pennsylvania and American Bar Associations. ***PRACTICE AREAS:*** Corporate Law; Probate and Estate Planning. ***Email:*** snyder90@aol.com

REPRESENTATIVE CLIENTS: Commerce National Bank; Aloyius, Butler & Clark; J I Case Co.
REFERENCE: Sun National Bank.

CHARLES SNYDERMAN

5301 LIMESTONE ROAD, SUITE 214
WILMINGTON, DELAWARE 19808
Telephone: 302-239-1140
Fax: 302-239-2124
URL: http://www.lawyers.com/snyderman

Personal Injury, Birth Trauma, Obstetrical Negligence, Brain Injury, Misread Pap-Smears, Failure to Diagnose Cases, Medical Malpractice, Automobile Accidents. Business Litigation, Commercial Litigation, Business Formation, Business Planning, Incorporations, Limited Liability Corporations, Buying and Selling of Businesses, Registered Agent Services, Staffing Industry Law. Real Estate.

(This Listing Continued)

CHARLES SNYDERMAN, born Philadelphia, Pennsylvania, August 12, 1948; admitted to bar, 1973, Delaware; 1975, U.S. District Court, District of Delaware; 1981, U.S. Claims Court. *Education:* Temple University (B.A., 1970); Villanova University (J.D., 1973). Law Clerk, Delaware Supreme Court, 1973-1974. Deputy Attorney General, State of Delaware, 1974-1978. State of Delaware Securities Commissioner. Advocate, Na6ional College of Advocacy of The Association of Trial Lawyers of America, 1995. *Member:* Delaware State Bar Association; Delaware Trial Lawyers Association; The Association of Trial Lawyers of America (Member: Birth Trauma Litigation Group; Misread Pap-Smear Litigation Group; Traumatic Brain Injury Group; Medical Malpractice and Professional Negligence and Motor Vehicle Collision Highway and Premises Liability Sections).

LAW OFFICE OF DAVID STAATS, P.A.

SUITE 36, PROFESSIONAL BUILDINGS
1701 AUGUSTINE CUT-OFF
WILMINGTON, DELAWARE 19803
Telephone: 302-658-8188
Fax: 302-658-8168
Email: legal@staatslaw.com
URL: http://www.staatslaw.com

Commercial Litigation, Franchise Law, Business Transactions, Internet Law, Apellate Practice.

DAVID STAATS, born Marietta, Ohio, May 8, 1952; admitted to bar, 1982, Massachusetts; 1985, U.S. Tax Court; 1991, Delaware; 1992, U.S. District Court, District of Delaware; Pennsylvania; 1997, U.S. Supreme Court; 1999, U.S. Court of Appeals, Third Circuit; U.S. Court of Appeals, Federal Circuit. *Education:* Wesleyan University (B.A., summa cum laude, 1979); Harvard University (J.D., 1982). Phi Beta Kappa. Certified Public Accountant, Massachusetts, 1985 (Not Active). American Inns of Court, Richard S. Rodney Chapter (member, 1996-1999). *Member:* Delaware State Bar Association. [U.S. Army, 1973-1976]. ***LANGUAGES:*** German. ***PRACTICE AREAS:*** Commercial Litigation; Franchise Law; Business Transactions; Internet Law; Appellate Practice.

GEORGE RENOS TSAKATARAS, born Wilmington, Delaware, October 11, 1971; admitted to bar, 1997, Pennsylvania; 2000, Delaware; 2001, U.S. District Court, District of Delaware. *Education:* University of Delaware (B.S., Finance, 1993); Villanova University (J.D., 1996). Judicial Law Clerk to the Honorable S. Gerald Corso, Montgomery County, PA, April 1998 - July 1999. *Member:* Delaware State Bar Association. (Resident). ***PRACTICE AREAS:*** Commercial Litigation; Franchise Law; Business Transactions; Music Law.

STEVENS & LEE

A PROFESSIONAL CORPORATION
300 DELAWARE AVENUE
SUITE 800
WILMINGTON, DELAWARE 19801
Telephone: 302-654-5180
Fax: 302-654-5181
Email: attys@stevenslee.com
URL: http://www.stevenslee.com

Reading, Pennsylvania Office: 111 North Sixth Street, P.O. Box 679, 19603-0679. Telephone: 610-478-2000. Fax: 610-376-5610.

Wayne, Pennsylvania Office: One Glenhardie Corporate Center, 1275 Drummers Lane, P. O. Box 236, 19087-0236. Telephone: 610-964-1480. Fax: 610-687-1384.

Lancaster, Pennsylvania Office: 25 North Queen Street, Suite 602, P.O. Box 1594, 17608-1594. Telephone: 717-291-1031. Fax: 717-394-7726.

Allentown, Pennsylvania Office: 190 Brodhead Road, Suite 200, P.O. Box 20830, 18002-0830. Telephone: 610-691-7111. Fax: 610-691-7175.

Harrisburg, Pennsylvania Office: 208 North Third Street. Suite 310. P.O. Box 12090, 17108-2090. Telephone: 717-234-1250. Fax: 717-234-1939.

Off-Hill Harrisburg, Pennsylvania Office: 4750 Lindle Road, P.O. Box 11670, 17108-1670. Telephone: 717-561-5242. Fax: 717-561-5207.

Philadelphia, Pennsylvania Office: 1818 Market Street, 29th Floor, 19103. Telephone: 215-575-0100. Fax: 215-851-0214.

Scranton, Pennsylvania Office: Kane Building, Suite 2B, 116 North Washington Street, 18503. Telephone: 570-343-1827. Fax: 570-343-1892.

Wilkes-Barre, Pennsylvania Office: 120 South Franklin Street, 18701. Telephone: 570-823-6116. Fax: 570-823-1149.

Cherry Hill, New Jersey Office: 1415 Route 70 East, Suite 506, 08034. Telephone: 856-354-9200. Fax: 856-354-8111.

(This Listing Continued)

Antitrust, Securities, Tax-Exempt Finance, Tax, Employment Law, OSHA, ERISA, Mergers and Acquisitions, Litigation, Bankruptcy, Environmental Law, Banking, Insurance, Computer Law, Health Law, Complex Estate and Business Succession Planning, Government Affairs and Government Regulatory, Higher Education, Real Estate, International Law, Intellectual Property and e-Commerce Law.

FIRM PROFILE: Stevens & Lee is a professional services firm with over 160 lawyers, each involved in a high-end specialty area of the law, and more than 30 non-lawyer business and consulting professionals located in eleven offices in eastern and central Pennsylvania, New Jersey and Delaware. The firm has regional, national and international practices.

The firm has established a reputation as one of the preeminent providers of sophisticated legal services in the mid-Atlantic region. Our Corporate, M&A and Capital Markets practices are among the largest and most accomplished in the region and regularly handle some of the most complex and challenging transactions. The firm represents individuals and businesses, both publicly and privately held, in a variety of industries including financial services, health care, manufacturing, communications and retail. The firm also represents a significant number of emerging growth businesses in the high-tech sector, subsidiaries of foreign companies doing business in the United States and an increasing number of transnational transactions.

Stevens & Lee's trial lawyers regularly represent clients in litigation involving our areas of expertise including antitrust, white collar crime and construction litigation. In addition, each concentrates in specific areas of the law and in many cases, a limited number of industries. The firm maintains offices where bankruptcy court judges for the Eastern and Middle Districts of Pennsylvania and the District of Delaware sit, and where judges of the Federal District sit.

WALTER P. McEVILLY JR., born Wilmington, Delaware, November 10, 1945; admitted to bar, 1970, Delaware; 1979, Pennsylvania; U.S. District Court, District of Delaware. *Education:* Yale University (B.A., 1967); University of Pennsylvania (J.D., 1970). *Member:* Delaware State, Pennsylvania and American Bar Associations; Association; American Health Lawyers Association. ***PRACTICE AREAS:*** Health Care Law; Trusts and Estates. ***Email:*** wpm@stevenslee.com

JOSEPH H. HUSTON, JR., born Philadelphia, Pennsylvania, July 31, 1949; admitted to bar, 1975, Pennsylvania; 2001, Delaware and U.S. District Court, District of Delaware; U.S. Court of Appeals, Third Circuit; U.S. District Court, Eastern and Middle Districts of Pennsylvania. *Education:* Pennsylvania State University (B.A., 1971); Villanova University School of Law (J.D., cum laude, 1975). Order of the Coif. Editor-in-Chief, Villanova Law Review, 1974-1975. *Member:* Chester County, Philadelphia, Pennsylvania, Delaware and American Bar Associations; Eastern District of Pennsylvania Bankruptcy Conference; American Bankruptcy Institute; Union International des Avocats; INSOL. ***PRACTICE AREAS:*** Bankruptcy; CHII; Commercial Workouts; International Bankruptcy. ***Email:*** jhh@stevenslee.com

JOSEPH GREY, born Wilmington, Delaware, September 17, 1958; admitted to bar, 1986, Delaware and U.S. District Court, District of Delaware; 1991, U.S. Court of Appeals, Third Circuit; 1992, U.S. Supreme Court. *Education:* University of Virginia (B.A., with distinction, 1980; J.D., 1985). *Member:* Delaware (Member, Commercial Law Section) and American Bar Associations; American Bankruptcy Institute. ***PRACTICE AREAS:*** Bankruptcy Chapter 11; Bankruptcy Litigation. ***Email:*** jg@stevenslee.com

JOHN D. DEMMY, born Lancaster, Pennsylvania, June 7, 1961; admitted to bar, 1986, Pennsylvania; 1987, U.S. District Court, Eastern District of Pennsylvania; 1990, Delaware and U.S. District Court, District of Delaware. *Education:* Albright College (B.S., 1983); Villanova University (J.D., cum laude, 1986). *Member:* Delaware, Pennsylvania and American Bar Associations; American Bankruptcy Institute. ***PRACTICE AREAS:*** Bankruptcy; Commercial Litigation. ***Email:*** jdd@stevenslee.com

---

SUSAN M. GORDON, born Wilmington, Delaware, March 28, 1956; admitted to bar, 1997, Delaware. *Education:* University of Delaware (B.S.N., 1978); Widener University School of Law (J.D., magna cum laude, 1997). Phi Delta Phi. Licensed Registered Nurse, 1978. *Member:* Delaware State (Chair, Health Law Section, 2000-2001) and American Bar Associations; American Health Lawyers Association. ***PRACTICE AREAS:*** Health Law; Health Care Regulation. ***Email:*** smg@stevenslee.com

THOMAS G. WHALEN, JR., born Philadelphia, Pennsylvania, April 4, 1974; admitted to bar, 2001, Delaware, U.S. District Court for the District of Delaware and U.S. Bankruptcy Court for the District of Delaware. *Education:* Temple University (B.A.P.S., 1996) Temple University Beasley School of Law (J.D., 2000). ***PRACTICE AREAS:*** Bankruptcy Reorganization; Bankruptcy Litigation; Workouts; Foreclosures. ***Email:*** tgw@stevenslee.com

(This Listing Continued)

REPRESENTATIVE CLIENTS: Adidas-Salomon A.G.; Afro-Asian Satellite Communications; AmeriHealth; The Bachman Company; Bayhealth Medical Center; Blue Cross of Northeastern Pennsylvania; Boscov's Department Stores; Capital Blue Cross; Carnegie Mellon University; Carpenter Technology Corp.; Central PA Health Alliance; Commonwealth of Pennsylvania; Christian Dalloz, S.A.; D&E Communications; Delaware River Port Authority; Diakon Lutheran Social Ministries; EnerSys, Inc.; GPU Service, Inc.; HealthCentral, Inc.; Independence Blue Cross; Intelligent Electronics, Inc.; International Paper Corp.; John Hancock Mutual Life Insurance Company; Kiwi Brands, Inc.; Lancaster Health Alliance; Lehigh University; Marriott International, Inc.; Medcases.com; MediGo.com; Metropolitan Edison Company; Motorola, Inc.; Muhlenberg College; MuseumNetwork.com; Old Guard Group, Inc.; Pennsylvania Higher Edication Assistance Agency (PHEAA); Pennsylvania Intergovenmental Cooperation Authority; Pennsylvania Infrastructure Investment Authority; Pennsylvania Municipal Retirement System; Pennsylvania Power & Light Company (PP&L); Pennsylvania State Employees Retirement System; Pennsylvania Zoological Council; Polymer Corporation; RJ Reynolds Tobacco Company; Safeguard Scientific, Inc.; Sanchez Computer Associates; Sonepar Distribution US, Inc.; Sovereign Bancorp, Inc.; Susquehanna Health Systems; Temple University School of Podiatric Medicine Foundation; Time, Inc.; UGI Energy Corp.; USBANCORP, Inc.; Van Kampen Merritt, Inc.; Wellspan Health; Yuasa, Inc.

(For other Biographical Information see Professional Biographies at Harrisburg, Lancaster, Allentown, Philadelphia, Reading, Scranton, Wayne, Wilkes-Barre, PA and Cherry Hill, N.J)

STEWART & ASSOCIATES

A PROFESSIONAL LAW ASSOCIATION

SUITE 1400
THE NEMOURS BUILDING
1007 ORANGE STREET
WILMINGTON, DELAWARE 19801
Telephone: 302-652-5200
Telecopier: 302-652-7211
Email: info@delawarecorporatelaw.com
URL: http://www.delawarecorporatelaw.com

Las Vegas, Nevada Office: Hughes Center, Suite 460, 3993 Howard Hughes Parkway, 89109. Telephone: 702-836-3500. Fax: 702-836-0880. Email: info@nevadacorporatelaw.com

State, Local and Federal Taxation, Corporations, Limited Liability Companies, Intellectual Property Law, Commercial Law, Mergers and Acquisitions, International Transactions, General Practice.

FIRM PROFILE: Stewart & Associates' practice focuses on the use of special purpose entities in order to achieve a variety of tax and business planning goals. The firm routinely assists nationally recognized multi-state tax advisors, out-of-state law firms and commercial domicile service providers in the implementation of special purpose entity structures. Our experience in corporate transactional work, blended with the attorneys' diverse backgrounds in state tax planning, intellectual property and commercial law, offers clients a breadth of tax and business planning resources.

PRINCIPAL

GORDON W. STEWART, born Fort Kent, Maine, January 6, 1953; admitted to bar, 1984, Delaware and U.S. District Court, District of Delaware; 1994, Pennsylvania; 1996, Nevada; 1998, Maine. *Education:* Dartmouth College (A.B., 1978); Washington & Lee University School of Law (J.D., cum laude, 1983); New York University School of Law (LL.M. in Taxation, 1988). Research Editor, Washington & Lee Law Review, 1982-1983. *Member:* State Bar of Nevada; Delaware, Maine State, Pennsylvania and American (Member, Tax Section) Bar Associations. ***PRACTICE AREAS:*** Taxation; State and Local Taxation; Multi-State Corporate Tax Planning; Corporations; Property Tax Appeals; Tax Controversies. ***Email:*** gstewart@delawarecorporatelaw.com

DIRECTOR

DAWN B. KILCREASE, born St. Petersburg, Florida, February 7, 1966; admitted to bar, 1994, Pennsylvania, New Jersey and U.S. District Court, District of New Jersey; 1998, Delaware. *Education:* University of South Florida (B.A., with honors, 1988); Glasgow University, Glasgow, Scotland; Temple University School of Law (J.D., with honors, 1994). Member, Moot Court Honor Society. Recipient: Spoffard Award for Outstanding Legal Scholarship; Law Foundation Scholarship. Business Editor, Temple Law Review. *Member:* Pennsylvania, New Jersey State, Delaware State and International Bar Associations; State Bar of Nevada. ***PRACTICE AREAS:*** Corporate Law; Commercial Law. ***Email:*** dkilcrease@delawarecorporatelaw.com

COUNSEL

CARL J. FERNANDES, born Bethlehem, Pennsylvania, July 12, 1935; admitted to bar, 1964, District of Columbia; 1965, Pennsylvania; 1986, Delaware. *Education:* Rutgers University (B.A., 1958); Hastings College of the Law, University of California (J.D., 1964). Note and Comment Editor, Hastings College Law Review, 1963-1964. Former Vice President and General Counsel,

(This Listing Continued)

STEWART & ASSOCIATES, A PROFESSIONAL LAW ASSOCIATION, Wilmington—Continued

Johnson Matthey Investments Ltd. [Capt., USAF, 1958-1961]. ***PRACTICE AREAS:*** Corporate Law; Mergers and Acquisitions; Finance; Import and Export Law. ***Email:*** cfernandes@delawarecorporatelaw.com

ASSOCIATES

PETER CAMPBELL, born Mount Holly, New Jersey, November 15, 1961; admitted to bar, 1987, Delaware and U.S. District Court, District of Delaware. *Education:* Catholic University of America (B.A., cum laude, 1984; J.D., 1987). ***PRACTICE AREAS:*** Corporate Law; Litigation.

KEITH R. SATTESAHN, born Harrisburg, Pennsylvania, October 12, 1958; admitted to bar, 1985, Delaware and U.S. District Court, District of Delaware; 1987, U.S. Court of Appeals, Third Circuit; 1993, Pennsylvania; 1994, U.S. District Court, Middle District of Pennsylvania. *Education:* Juniata College (B.S., 1980); Temple University (J.D., cum laude, 1984). Member, Temple Law Quarterly, 1982-1984. ***PRACTICE AREAS:*** Information Technology; Intellectual Property. ***Email:*** KSattesahn@delawarecorporatelaw.com

TANYA M. MURRAY, born Bronx, New York, November 3, 1969; admitted to bar, 1996, New York; 1997, Delaware; 1999, Pennsylvania. *Education:* State University of New York at Binghamton (B.A., 1991); Hofstra University School of Law (J.D., 1995). Notes and Comments Editor, Hofstra Law Review, 1994-1995. Law Clerk to The Honorable Henry duPont Ridgely and The Honorable N. Maxson Terry, Jr., Delaware Superior Court, 1996-1997. *Member:* Delaware State, Pennsylvania, New York State and American Bar Associations. ***PRACTICE AREAS:*** Corporate Law. ***Email:*** tmurray@delawarecorporatelaw.com

MICHAEL J. CONALLEN, JR., born Camp Zama, Atsugi, Japan, April 21, 1970; admitted to bar, 1998, Pennsylvania, New Jersey; 2001, Delaware. *Education:* Temple University (B.A., cum laude, 1992); Temple University School of Law (J.D., cum laude, 1997). Moot Court Honor Society. Co-Author: "To Chase or Not to Chase; A Perplexing Problem." Current Topics in Defending Civil Rights Actions Against Governmental Entities and Their Officials (Defense Research Institute, Chicago, IL), Vol. 1996, No. 5, at 39. *Member:* Delaware State, Pennsylvania and American Bar Associations.

LEANNE C. McGRORY, born Stratford, New Jersey, September 3, 1973; admitted to bar, 2000, Pennsylvania and Delaware. *Education:* University of Delaware (B.A., 1995); Georgetown University Law Center (J.D., 1998). Sigma Tau Delta. Recipient, Charles Houston Lukens Fellowship. Former Law Clerk, Court of Common Pleas, Philadelphia, Pennsylvania. ***PRACTICE AREAS:*** Corporate Law. ***Email:*** lmcgrory@delawarecorporatelaw.com

ELIZABETH V. THOMPSON, born Ridley Park, Pennsylvania, June 15, 1971; admitted to bar, 1998, Colorado; 1999, District of Columbia (Not admitted in Delaware). *Education:* The College of Wooster (B.A., 1993); Franklin Pierce Law Center (J.D., 1997). Phi Alpha Delta. ***Email:*** ethompson@delawarecorporatelaw.com

OF COUNSEL

S. MAYNARD TURK, born Roanoke, Virginia, October 14, 1925; admitted to bar, 1951, Virginia; 1961, Delaware and U.S. Supreme Court; registered to practice before U.S. Patent and Trademark Office. *Education:* Roanoke College (B.A., 1949); Washington & Lee University (LL.B., 1952). Retired Vice President, General Counsel and Former Member, Board of Directors, Hercules Incorporated. ***Email:*** sturk@delawarecorporatelaw.com

JOHN J. LEARY, JR., born Chester, Pennsylvania, June 9, 1945; admitted to bar, 1987, Pennsylvania; 1988, U.S. Tax Court; 1993, U.S. Supreme Court (Not admitted in Delaware). *Education:* Widener University (B.S., 1975); Delaware Law School of Widener University (J.D., 1980). Member, Tax Executives Institute, Philadelphia Chapter, 1981-2000. *Member:* Pennsylvania, Federal (Member, Tax Committee) and American (Member, Tax Committee) Bar Associations. ***PRACTICE AREAS:*** Corporate Taxation; Corporate Law. ***Email:*** jleary@delawarecorporatelaw.com

JOHN M. STULL

SUITE 700, 1300 NORTH MARKET STREET
P.O. BOX 1947
WILMINGTON, DELAWARE 19899-1947
Telephone: 302-654-0399
Fax: 302-654-0884
Email: jstullesq@AOL.COM

ERISA, Taxation and Tax Litigation, Estate Planning, Probate, Pension and Profit Sharing and Corporate Law.

(This Listing Continued)

JOHN M. STULL, born Des Moines, Iowa, January 20, 1934; admitted to bar, 1958, Iowa; 1960, District of Columbia; 1967, Delaware; 1987, U.S. Tax Court; 1992, U.S. District Court, District of Delaware; 1995, U.S. Court of Appeals, Third Circuit; 1997, U.S. Supreme Court. *Education:* Drake University (B.S.B.A., 1955); University of Michigan Law School (LL.B., 1958). *Member:* Delaware Bar Association (Member: Estates and Trusts and Taxation Sections). ***PRACTICE AREAS:*** Employee Retirement Income Security Act (ERISA); Taxation (Federal and State); Estate Planning; Probate.

REFERENCES: Wilmington Trust Co.; Christiana Bank.

SWARTZ, CAMPBELL & DETWEILER

Established in 1921
MELLON BANK CENTER
919 MARKET STREET
P.O. BOX 330
WILMINGTON, DELAWARE 19899
Telephone: 302-656-5935
Fax: 302-656-1434
Email: webmaster@scdlaw.com
URL: http://www.scdlaw.com

Philadelphia, Pennsylvania Office: 1601 Market Street, 34th Floor. Telephone: 215-564-5190. Telefax: 215-299-4301.
Media, Pennsylvania Office: 115 North Jackson Street. Telephone: 610-566-9222. Fax: 610-566-7351.
Harrisburg, Pennsylvania Office: 1631 North Front Street. Telephone: 717-233-3515. Fax: 717-233-3468.
Allentown, Pennsylvania Office: Suite 230. 5100 Tilghman Street. Telephone: 610-395-5903. Fax: 610-395-7097.
Mount Laurel, New Jersey Office: Bloom Court, Suite 101. 1300 Route 73. Telephone: 856-727-4777. Fax: 856-727-0464.
Scranton, Pennsylvania Office: Bank Towers, 6th Floor, 321 Spruce Street. Telephone: 570-343-0029. Fax: 570-343-1534.
West Chester, Pennsylvania Office: One South Church Street, Suite 400. Telephone: 610-692-9500. Fax: 610-692-4936.
Fort Myers, Florida Office: The Huntington Plaza, 2000 Main Street, Suite 805. Telephone: 941-790-7700. Fax: 941-332-5325.
Bedminster, New Jersey Office: Bedminster Center, 90 Washington Valley Road. Telephone: 908-719-8932. Fax: 908-719-6005.

General Civil and Trial Practice in State and Federal Courts including Insurance, Workers Compensation, Product Liability, Toxic Torts, Medical Malpractice, Legal Malpractice, Commercial and Bankruptcy Defense.

(For complete biographical data on all personnel, see Professional Biographies at Philadelphia, Pennsylvania)

TAYLOR & McNEW LLP

Established in 1999
SUITE 210
3711 KENNETT PIKE
WILMINGTON, DELAWARE 19807
Telephone: 302-655-9200
Fax: 302-655-9361
Email: mail@law-tm.com
URL: http://www.taylormcnew.com

General Practice. Commercial, Corporate and Securities Law, Real Estate (Commercial and Residential) and Zoning, Litigation, Personal Injury, Consumer Rights, Wills, Probate, Estate Planning, Class Actions, Complex Litigation, Environmental and Collection Law.

FIRM PROFILE: Jonathan B. Taylor began his practice as a solo practitioner in 1986. R. Bruce McNew practiced law in Pennsylvania, Delaware and California with various firms and as sole practitioner prior to joining Jon in 1995. The Firm maintains a general practice based in Wilmington, Delaware, while working with clients throughout North America.

JONATHAN B. TAYLOR, born Wilmington, Delaware, December 31, 1950; admitted to bar, 1978, Delaware and Florida; 1982, U.S. District Court, District of Delaware; 1983, U.S. Court of Appeals, Third Circuit. *Education:* Ohio Wesleyan University (B.A., 1972); University of Miami (J.D., 1977). Assistant Public Defender, 1977-1981. First Assistant, New Castle County Attorney, 1981-1983. New Castle County Attorney, 1983-1985. *Member:* Delaware and American Bar Associations; The Florida Bar; American Judicature Society. ***PRACTICE AREAS:*** Real Estate Law; Zoning Law; Personal Injury Law; Business Law.

R. BRUCE McNEW, born Augusta, Georgia, October 13, 1953; admitted to bar, 1979, Delaware and U.S. District Court, District of Delaware; 1984, Pennsylvania; 1985, U.S. District Court, Eastern District of Pennsylvania; 1990

(This Listing Continued)

California; 1991, U.S. District Court, Northern, Eastern, Southern and Central Districts of California and U.S. Court of Appeals, Third, Ninth, Tenth and Eleventh Circuits and U.S. Supreme Court. *Education:* University of Virginia (B.A., with distinction, 1975); Marshall-Wythe School of Law of the College of William & Mary (J.D., 1979). Research Editor, William and Mary Law Review, 1978-1979. Instructor of Business Law, Delaware Technical and Community College, Georgetown, Delaware, 1979-1980. Law Clerk for the Supreme Court of Delaware, 1979-1980. *Member:* Delaware, Pennsylvania and American Bar Associations; State Bar of California. ***PRACTICE AREAS:*** Corporate; Securities; Commercial; Antitrust; Consumer; Environmental; Class Actions; Litigation.

AGENTS FOR: Old Republic National Title Insurance Company; Ticor Title Insurance Co.; Atlantic Title and Abstract Co. *Approved Attorneys For:* Ataco, Inc.

LAW OFFICES OF ROBIN L. THORNBURG, P.C.

WILMINGTON, DELAWARE

(See West Conshohocken, Pennsylvania)

Commercial Litigation, Business Transactions, Estate Planning, Probate & Trusts, Tax Law, Civil Litigation, Immigration Law, Personal Injury, Litigation.

TIGANI & HOOD LLP

1801 MELLON BANK CENTER
919 MARKET STREET
P.O. BOX 1471
WILMINGTON, DELAWARE 19899
Telephone: 302-777-1000
Telecopier: 302-777-1098
URL: http://www.tiganihoodlaw.com

Tax and Estate Planning, Business Transactions, Real Estate, Business Organization, Estate Administration, Civil Litigation, Criminal Trial Practice, Personal Injury, Administrative Law.

FIRM PROFILE: Tigani & Hood LLP maintains a regional practice, primarily representing closely-held businesses and individuals in the areas of tax, business and estate planning, general litigation, estate administration, personal injury, real estate and commercial transactions. Our national focus centers on clients outside the region who wish to benefit from the unique advantages Delaware affords trusts, corporations, limited liability companies and other business entities.

BRUCE W. TIGANI, born Wilmington, Delaware, May 10, 1956; admitted to bar, 1981, Delaware; 1982, Pennsylvania and U.S. Tax Court. *Education:* Georgetown University; University of Delaware (B.S., magna cum laude, 1978); Villanova University (J.D., 1981). Beta Gamma Sigma; Phi Kappa Phi. Delegate to Internal Revenue Service Mid-Atlantic Regional Liaison, 1989-1992. *Member:* Delaware State (Chairman, Tax Section, 1991-1992; Chairman, Estates and Trusts Section, 1997-1998), Pennsylvania and American (Member, Tax and Real Property, Probate and Trust Law Sections) Bar Associations; Estate Planning Council of Delaware (Member, Board of Directors, 1993-1995); Wilmington Tax Group (Chairman, 1994-1995); Delaware State Chamber of Commerce Tax Committee. ***PRACTICE AREAS:*** Tax Planning; Estate Planning; Business Transactions; Real Estate; Closely Held Business Law. ***Email:*** btigani@tiganihoodlaw.com

MICHAEL J. HOOD, born Wilmington, Delaware, December 29, 1956; admitted to bar, 1982, Delaware and Pennsylvania. *Education:* Marquette University (B.A., 1978); Widener University (J.D., 1981). Office of the Public Defender, 1988-1989. *Member:* Delaware Trial Lawyers Association. ***PRACTICE AREAS:*** Civil Litigation; Criminal Law; Personal Injury. ***Email:*** mhood@tiganihoodlaw.com

JANICE ROWE TIGANI, born Wilmington, Delaware, July 15, 1955; admitted to bar, 1982, Delaware; 1984, Pennsylvania; 1986, U.S. District Court, District of Delaware and U.S. Court of Appeals, Third Circuit. *Education:* University of Delaware (B.A.A.S., 1977); Villanova University (J.D., 1982). *Member:* Delaware State Bar Association (Member, Estates & Trusts Section; Vice Chair, Health Law Section, 1997-1998); Wilmington Tax Group. Estate Planning Council. ***PRACTICE AREAS:*** Estate Planning; Estate Administration; Residential Real Estate; Business Organization; Administrative Law. ***Email:*** jtigani@tiganihoodlaw.com

REPRESENTATIVE CLIENTS: ADP Atlantic, Inc.; ADP Capital Management, Inc.; American Floor Systems, Inc.; Applied Extrusion Technologies, Inc.; Brandywine Valley Caterers; Environmental Alliance, Inc.; Free Market Capital, L.P.; Global Assessments, Inc.; GoGolfTravel.com, Inc.; Maxxon, LLC; Restaurant Equipment Sales, Inc.; Simon, Master & Sidlow, P.A.; Standard Distributing Co., Inc.; T.A. Title Insurance Co.; Tangent Cable Systems, Inc.; The Equitable Cos.; The Rittenhouse Trust Company; U.S. Trust Company of Delaware; Wesley Realty Company; Wilmington Trust Company.

(This Listing Continued)

APPROVED ATTORNEYS FOR: Asset Management Group; Christiana Bank & Trust Company; Commonwealth Land Title Insurance Co.; First Union Trust Company, N.A.; The Glenmede Trust Co., N.A.; Lawyers Title Insurance Corporation; Sun Trust Delaware Trust Company; Ticor Title Insurance Co.

TIGHE, COTTRELL & LOGAN, P.A.

FIRST FEDERAL PLAZA, SUITE 500
P.O. BOX 1031
WILMINGTON, DELAWARE 19801
Telephone: 302-658-6400; 800-645-6401
Fax: 302-658-9836
Email: lawtcl@dol.net
URL: http://www.lawtcl.com

Philadelphia, Pennsylvania Office: 2017 Spring Garden Street. Telephone: 215-564-0101.

Towson, Maryland Office: 110 West Road, Suite 245, 21204. Telephone: 410-539-7341.

Woodstown, New Jersey Office: 19 West Avenue, 08098. Telephone: 800-645-6401.

Civil Practice, Commercial Law, Construction Law, Insurance Defense, Debtor & Creditor.

FIRM PROFILE: Tighe, Cottrell & Logan, P.A. is a mid-Atlantic regional law firm emphasizing all phases of litigation and various business practices. Our main office is centrally located in Wilmington, Delaware, with branch offices in Philadelphia, Pennsylvania, Towson, Maryland, and Woodstown, New Jersey.

MICHAEL K. TIGHE, born Newburgh, New York, February 7, 1947; admitted to bar, 1976, Delaware; 1988, Pennsylvania and Maryland. *Education:* Siena College, Loudonville, New York (B.A., cum laude, 1969); Catholic University of America, Columbus School of Law (J.D., 1976). Co-Author: "Winning Ways With Direct and Cross Examination," 1997; "Insurance Law: Third Party Coverage in Delaware," 1997; "Trying The Automobile Injury Case in Delaware," 1996; "Premises Liability Preparation and Trial of a Difficult Case in Delaware." *Member:* Delaware and American (Member: Litigation Committee; Medical Malpractice Subcommittee) Bar Associations; Delaware Trial Lawyers Association; The Association of Trial Lawyers of America; American Arbitration Association. [With U.S. Army, 1969-1971]. ***PRACTICE AREAS:*** Commercial Law; Insurance Defense; Litigation; Personal Injury; Products Liability. ***Email:*** m.tighe@dol.net

PAUL COTTRELL, born Penns Grove, New Jersey, November 5, 1951; admitted to bar, 1978, Illinois; 1985, Pennsylvania and Delaware; 1987, Maryland. *Education:* University of Delaware (B.A., magna cum laude, 1975); University of Chicago (J.D., 1978). Phi Kappa Phi; Omicron Delta Kappa; Pi Sigma Alpha. Editor-in-Chief, Law Practice Notes, *Barrister,* 1984-1988. Co-Editor: "Corporate Directors and Officers Liability, Insurance and Risk Management", Executive Enterprises, 1989. Author: *Architect-Engineer Liability Under Pennsylvania Law* (1986); "Claims Made: The Judicial Record," *Best's Review,* July 1986; "The Importance of Project Description," *The Construction Specifier,* July 1986; "Professional Liability for Computer Design," *The Computer Lawyer,* August 1986; "A Blueprint as to the Liability of Architects and Engineers," 60 Chi. Kent L. R. 163, (1984); "Risk Shifting Devices and Third-Party Practice," 14 Loyola U.Chi.L.J., 467 (1983); "Third-Party Liability Insurance: Protection in Case of Computer Error," April 2, 1984 *Computerworld.* Faculty Lecturer: Insurance School of Chicago, 1985 Spring Semester; Chicago Bar Association's Trial Advocacy Course, 1983-1985. Member, Commercial Panel of Arbitrators and Computer Panel, American Arbitration Association. Associate Director, Construction Law Institute, 1982-1984. *Member:* Pennsylvania, Delaware and Maryland Bar Associations. (Resident, Philadelphia, Pennsylvania Office). ***PRACTICE AREAS:*** Business Law; Construction Law; Corporate Law; Insurance; Professional Liability. ***Email:*** p.cottrell@dol.net

DONALD L. LOGAN, born Ephrata, Washington, December 1, 1949; admitted to bar, 1987, Delaware and Maryland; 1988, U.S. District Court, District of Delaware; 1990, U.S. District Court, District of Maryland. *Education:* University of Lowell (B.S., magna cum laude, 1976); Delaware Law School of Widener University (J.D., 1985). Recipient, American Bar Association Urban, State and Local Government Award, 1985. Adjunct Faculty: Widener University Paralegal Program, 1989-1990. Chairman, Delaware Vietnam Veterans Leadership Program, 1981-1983. *Member:* Delaware and American (Member: Law Practice Management and Construction Litigation Sections; Architects/Engineers Subcommittee) Bar Associations; Maryland State Bar Association; National Association of Highway Engineers (Board of Directors); Delaware Contractor's Association; Delaware Associated Builders and Contractors; Delaware Chapter, American Subcontractors Association (Member, Steering Committee, 1993); Plumbing, Heating and Cooling Contractors Association; Construction Specification Institute; Delaware Roofing Contractors Association. [With U.S. Navy, 1968-1972; Delaware Air National Guard, 1985-1990]. ***PRACTICE AREAS:*** Construction Law; Contracts; Leases and Leasing. ***Email:*** d.logan@dol.net

(This Listing Continued)

TIGHE, COTTRELL & LOGAN, P.A., Wilmington—Continued

JAMES S. YODER, born Little Falls, New Jersey, September 30, 1961; admitted to bar, 1987, Delaware, New Jersey, Pennsylvania, U.S. District Court, District of Delaware and U.S. District Court, District of New Jersey; 1997, Maryland. *Education:* University of Delaware (B.A.A.S., 1983); Widener University School of Law (J.D., 1986). Order of Omega Honor Society; Pi Sigma Alpha Political Science Honor Society; Delta Theta Phi Law Fraternity. Adjunct Faculty: University of Delaware Continuing Education Program. *Member:* Delaware State Bar Associations. ***PRACTICE AREAS:*** Bankruptcy; Medical Malpractice; Personal Injury; Products Liability; Professional Liability. ***Email:*** jim.yoder@dol.net

---

G. KEVIN FASIC, born Philadelphia, Pennsylvania, November 10, 1965; admitted to bar, 1996, Pennsylvania, Delaware and New Jersey. *Education:* Lehigh University (B.A., 1988); Widener University School of Law (J.D., 1995). *Member:* Delaware State (Member, Labor and Employment Law Section) and American Bar Associations. [1st Lieut., U.S. National Guard, Pennsylvania, 1988-1993]. ***PRACTICE AREAS:*** Labor & Employment; Construction Law; Employee Benefits; Disabilities. ***Email:*** lawtcl@dol.net

JOSEPH SCOTT SHANNON, born Seaford, Delaware, December 12, 1964; admitted to bar, 1995, Delaware. *Education:* University of Delaware (B.A.A.S., 1986); Widener University School of Law (J.D., 1994). Deputy Attorney General, 1995-1999. [USMC, 1986-1991]. ***PRACTICE AREAS:*** Criminal Law; Insurance Defense; Litigation. ***Email:*** lawtcl@dol.net

SCOTT L. MESSMORE, born New Eagle, Pennslyvania, June 3, 1947; admitted to bar, 1972, West Virginia; 1977, Virginia (Not admitted in Delaware). *Education:* West Virginia University (B.S., 1969); University of Virginia (J.D., 1972). Beta Gamma Sigma Honorary. Member, American Corporate Counsel Association, 1989—. Panel Member, American Arbitration Association. [U.S. Navy, 1965-1966; U.S. Army Reserve, 1966-1968]. ***PRACTICE AREAS:*** Corporate Law; Real Estate; General Practice. ***Email:*** s.messmore@dol.net

JULIE LYNN KOPEC, born Wilmington, Delaware, January 29, 1973; admitted to bar, 2000, New Jersey and U.S. District Court, District of New Jersey; 2001, Pennsylvania and U.S. District Court, Eastern District of Pennsylvania (Not admitted in Delaware). *Education:* University of Delaware (B.A., 1995); Widener University School of Law (J.D., 1999). Member, Widener Law Forum, 1997-1998. *Member:* Pennsylvania and American Bar Associations. ***PRACTICE AREAS:*** Insurance Defense; Contracts; Personal Injury; Construction Law; Workers Compensation. ***Email:*** j.kopec@dol.net

MICHAEL T. HOLLISTER, born Mechanicsburg, Pennslyvania, December 25, 1973; admitted to bar, 2001, Pennsylvania and U.S. District Court, Eastern District of Pennsylvania (Not admitted in Delaware). *Education:* University of Delaware (B.A., 1997); Widener University (J.D., 2000). Staff, Delaware Journal & Corporate Law.

TRZUSKOWSKI, KIPP, KELLEHER & PEARCE, P.A.

Established in 1974

1020 NORTH BANCROFT PARKWAY
P.O. BOX 429
WILMINGTON, DELAWARE 19899-0429
Telephone: 302-571-1782
Fax: 302-571-1638

Newark, Delaware Office: 273 East Main Street, 19711. Telephone: 302-368-2561. Telefax: 302-368-9729.

General Practice. Civil Litigation, Personal Injury, Medical Malpractice, Commercial and Corporate, Real Estate, Estate Planning, Probate, Family, Matrimonial, Pension (ERISA).

FRANCIS J. TRZUSKOWSKI, born Wilmington, Delaware, November 7, 1937; admitted to bar, 1962, Delaware. *Education:* LaSalle College (B.A., maxima cum laude, 1959); Georgetown University (LL.B., 1962). *Member:* Delaware State Bar Association (Executive Committee, 1998-1999); National Lawyers Association. ***PRACTICE AREAS:*** Pension Law; Commercial Law; General Litigation; Commercial Real Estate Law. ***Email:*** fjt@tkkp.com

JAMES F. KIPP, born Wilmington, Delaware, December 1, 1937; admitted to bar, 1963, Delaware. *Education:* St. Joseph's College (B.S., 1960); Villanova University (LL.B., 1963). Member, Villanova Law Review, 1962-1963. Assistant Public Defender for Delaware, 1964-1970. Regional Chairman, ATLA Moot Trial Competition, 1982. President, Villanova Law School Alumni Association, 1988-1989. Current Chair, Delaware Superior Court Civil Rules Advisory Commission. *Member:* Delaware Trial Lawyers Association (Treasurer,

(This Listing Continued)

1978-1979; President, 1980-1981). (Certified Civil Trial Specialists by the National Board of Trial Advocacy). ***PRACTICE AREAS:*** Personal Injury; Tort Litigation. ***Email:*** jkipp@tkkp.com

DANIEL F. KELLEHER, born Wilmington, Delaware, May 8, 1935; admitted to bar, 1962, District of Columbia and Delaware. *Education:* St. Mary's Seminary and University (A.B., 1958); Georgetown University (LL.B., 1961). Associate Judge, Family Court, State of Delaware, 1972-1978. Chairman, Delaware Children's Trust Fund, 1985—. *Member:* Delaware State and American Bar Associations. ***PRACTICE AREAS:*** Family Law; Litigation. ***Email:*** dkelleher@tkkp.com

ROBERT K. PEARCE, born Wilmington, Delaware, June 3, 1949; admitted to bar, 1974, Delaware. *Education:* University of Delaware (B.S., 1971); Villanova University (J.D., 1974). Beta Gamma Sigma. Assistant Public Defender, 1976-1977. Member, Supreme Court Discovery Abuse Committee, 1982. *Member:* Delaware State Bar Association; Delaware Trial Lawyers Association. ***PRACTICE AREAS:*** Tort Litigation; Insurance Law; Workers Compensation Law. ***Email:*** rpearce@tkkp.com

VANCE A. FUNK, III, born Philadelphia, Pennsylvania, December 16, 1942; admitted to bar, 1968, Delaware. *Education:* University of Delaware (B.S., 1965); Washington & Lee University (J.D., 1968). Phi Delta Phi. City of Newark Alderman, 1975—. Chief Alderman, State of Delaware, 1982—. *Member:* Delaware and American Bar Associations; American Judicature Society. [Capt., U.S. Army M.P., 1969-1971]. (Resident, Newark Office). ***Email:*** vfunk@tkkp.com

BARBARA SNAPP DANBERG, born Damascus, Maryland, July 20, 1965; admitted to bar, 1992, Delaware; 1993, Maryland; 1995, U.S. Tax Court. *Education:* University of Delaware (B.A.A.S., 1987); Widener University (J.D., 1992). Pi Sigma Alpha; Phi Alpha Theta; Phi Delta Phi. Research Editor, Delaware Journal of Corporate Law, 1991-1992. *Member:* Delaware State (Member, Sections on: Estates and Trust; Taxation), Maryland State and American (Member, Taxation Section) Bar Associations; Estate Planning Council of Delaware. ***PRACTICE AREAS:*** Taxation; Estate Planning; Estate Administration; Commercial Litigation. ***Email:*** barbaradanberg@earthlink.net

WILLIAM L. DOERLER, born Fort Dix, New Jersey, July 4, 1961; admitted to bar, 1997, Delaware; 1998, Pennsylvania, New Jersey and U.S. District Court, District of Delaware. *Education:* University of Delaware (B.S.A.C., 1983); Widener University, School of Law, Wilmington, Delaware (J.D., 1997). Phi Kappa Phi. Phi Delta Phi. Moe Levine Society. Law Clerk, Chief Justice Veasey, Supreme Court of Delaware, 1996-1997. *Member:* Delaware State Bar Association. ***PRACTICE AREAS:*** Appellate Practice; Civil Litigation; Insurance. ***Email:*** wdoerler@tkkp.com

---

TYBOUT, REDFEARN & PELL

Established in 1962

SUITE 1100, 300 DELAWARE AVENUE
P.O. BOX 2092
WILMINGTON, DELAWARE 19899
Telephone: 302-658-6901
Fax: 302-658-4018
Email: trpmail@TRPLaw.com
URL: http://www.trplaw.com

General Practice. Litigation. Workers Compensation. Products Liability, Medical Malpractice, Insurance Coverage, and Construction.

FIRM PROFILE: With more than 35 years experience, TYBOUT, REDFEARN & PELL, specializes in civil litigation and the attorneys of TYBOUT, REDFEARN & PELL are each licensed to practice before all Delaware State and Federal Courts.

TYBOUT, REDFEARN & PELL has experience in all areas of tort litigation, medical malpractice, products liability, construction problems, workmen's compensation, municipal liability (including civil rights actions pursuant to 42 USC § 1983) and litigation involving insurers directly.

PARTNERS

B. WILSON REDFEARN, born Chicago, Illinois, July 8, 1936; admitted to bar, 1962, Illinois and Delaware; 1965, U.S. Supreme Court; 1982, Hawaii. *Education:* Miami University (B.A., 1958); Northwestern University (J.D., 1961). Deputy Attorney General, Delaware, 1963-1965. Attorney for: New Castle County, 1967-1973; New Castle County Transportation Commission, 1967-1972; Insurance Guaranty Association, 1974-2001; Governor's Commission on Medical Malpractice, 1976-1977, Chairman, Governor's Commission on Criminal Justice, 1977-1980. Director, American Civil Liberties Union, 1986-1997. Member, Delaware Insurance Authority, 1988-1991. Chairman, Delaware State Workmen's Compensation Committee, 1975-1978. Chairman, Bench and Bar Committee, 1972-1977. Long-Range Planning Committee, 1975-1985, Chairman, 1995-1997. Judicial Selection Committee, 1980-1988, 1995-1997. Board of Bar Examiners, 1995-1998. Defense Counsel of Delaware,

(This Listing Continued)

President, 1999-2001. American Board of Trial Advocates. Member, The Defense Research Institute. Delaware Chairman, Trial Lawyers Association, 1988-1996. *Member:* Delaware State, Hawaii State and American Bar Associations. ***PRACTICE AREAS:*** Negligence; Insurance; Worker's Compensation; Products Liability; Medical Malpractice. ***Email:*** bwredfearn@trplaw.com

RICHARD W. PELL, born Greencastle, Indiana, April 12, 1941; admitted to bar, 1966, Delaware. *Education:* DePauw University (B.A., 1963); George Washington University (J.D., 1966). Phi Delta Phi. Assistant Public Defender, 1968-1969. Deputy Attorney General, 1969. Attorney, Delaware Alcoholic Beverage Control Commission, 1969-1970. Register of Wills, New Castle County, 1970-1974. Member, Delaware Insurance Authority, 1991-1993. Charter Member, Delaware Chapter, American Board of Trial Advocates. Chairman, New Castle County Human Resources Advisory Board. *Member:* Delaware State and American Bar Associations; Defense Research Institute (State Chairman, 1979-1988). ***PRACTICE AREAS:*** Negligence; Insurance; Products Liability; Medical Malpractice. ***Email:*** rpell@trplaw.com

DAVID G. CULLEY, born Wilmington, Delaware, July 13, 1957; admitted to bar, 1982, Delaware. *Education:* University of Delaware (B.A.A.S., magna cum laude with distinction, 1979); National Law Center of George Washington University (J.D., 1982). Phi Beta Kappa; Phi Kappa Phi; Pi Sigma Alpha. Deputy Attorney General, Delaware, 1983-1989. Board of Directors, Delaware Insurance Authority, 1993—. United States District Court Blue Ribbon Panel. Board of Directors, Association of Retarded Citizens of Delaware. *Member:* Delaware State and American Bar Associations. Inns of Court, Rodney Chapter; Delaware Trial Lawyers Association; Defense Counsel of Delaware; Defense Research Institute. ***PRACTICE AREAS:*** Negligence; Insurance; Workers Compensation; Products Liability; Medical Malpractice. ***Email:*** dculley@trplaw.com

SHERRY RUGGIERO FALLON, born Philadelphia, Pennsylvania, December 28, 1961; admitted to bar, 1986, Delaware and New Jersey. *Education:* University of Pennsylvania (B.A., 1983); Delaware Law School of Widener University (J.D., 1986). Phi Delta Phi. Member, Moot Court Honor Society. Member, Delaware Journal of Corporate Law, 1985-1986. *Member:* Delaware State, New Jersey State and American Bar Associations; Defense Counsel of Delaware (Executive Board Member, 1991-1992 and 1999—); Delaware Trial Lawyers Association. ***PRACTICE AREAS:*** Negligence; Insurance; Workers Compensation; Products Liability; Medical Malpractice. ***Email:*** sfallon@trplaw.com

FRANCIS X. NARDO, born Wilmington, Delaware, August 29, 1961; admitted to bar, 1988, Delaware. *Education:* Pennsylvania State University (B.A., 1984); Delaware Law School of Widener University (J.D., 1987). Assistant Public Defender, 1988-1990. Board Member, Defense Counsel of Delaware. *Member:* Delaware State and American Bar Associations. ***PRACTICE AREAS:*** Negligence; Insurance; Civil Litigation; Workers Compensation; Products Liability. ***Email:*** fnardo@trplaw.com

JOHN J. KLUSMAN, JR., born Shamokin, Pennsylvania, October 5, 1963; admitted to bar, 1989, Delaware and Pennsylvania. *Education:* Villanova University (B.S., 1985); Vermont Law School; Delaware Law School of Widener University (J.D., 1988). *Member:* Pennsylvania, Delaware State and American Bar Associations. ***PRACTICE AREAS:*** Workers Compensation; Civil Practice. ***Email:*** jklusman@trplaw.com

DANIELLE KATHLEEN YEARICK, born Wilmington, Delaware, November 23, 1972; admitted to bar, 1997, Delaware and U.S. District Court, District of Delaware; 1998, Pennsylvania. *Education:* Manhattan College (B.A., magna cum laude, 1994); Villanova University School of Law (J.D., 1997). Phi Beta Kappa. Member, Moot Court Executive Board, 1995-1997. *Member:* Delaware, Pennsylvania and American Bar Associations; Defense Counsel of Delaware; Defense Research Institute. ***PRACTICE AREAS:*** Workers Compensation; Insurance; Negligence; Civil Litigation; Bankruptcy; Products Liability. ***Email:*** dyearick@trplaw.com

CHARLES SLANINA, born Wilmington, Delaware, December 14, 1954; admitted to bar, 1980, Delaware; 1994, U.S. District Court, District of Delaware. *Education:* University of Delaware (B.A., 1976); Catholic University (J.D., 1979). Law Clerk: Family Court, 1979-1980; Deputy Attorney General, 1981-1989; Disciplinary Counsel, 1989-1993. *Member:* Delaware State and American Bar Associations; Defense Counsel of Delaware; Association of Professional Responsibility Lawyers. ***PRACTICE AREAS:*** Professional Responsibility; Personal Injury; Civil Litigation; Criminal Law. ***Email:*** cslanina@trplaw.com

DENNIS J. MENTON, born Wilmington Delaware, August 21, 1955; admitted to bar, 1987, Delaware. *Education:* University of Delaware (B.S., 1978); Delaware Law School of Widener University (J.D., cum laude, 1987). *Member:* Delaware State (Member, Workers Compensation Section, 1996—) and American Bar Associations. ***PRACTICE AREAS:*** Worker's Compensation Defense; Personal Injury Defense. ***Email:*** dmenton@trplaw.com

(This Listing Continued)

ASSOCIATES

SUSAN A. LIST, born Wilmington, Delaware, June 7, 1973; admitted to bar, 1998, Delaware; U.S. District Court, District of Delaware; 2000, U.S. Court of Appeals, Third Circuit. *Education:* University of Delaware (B.S., honors program, 1995); Villanova University (J.D., 1998). *Member:* Delaware and American Bar Associations; Defense Counsel of Delaware. ***PRACTICE AREAS:*** Negligence; Insurance; Workers' Compensation; Products Liability; Civil Litigation; Bankruptcy. ***Email:*** slist@trplaw.com

STEVEN DANIEL ROSEN, born 1973; admitted to bar, 1999, Delaware; 2000, U.S. District Court, District of Delaware. *Education:* University of Delaware (B.A., 1996); Western New England College (J.D., 1999). Judicial Clerk to the Honorable Jone E. Babiarz, Jr., Superior Court of Delaware, 1999-2000. ***PRACTICE AREAS:*** Negligence; Insurance; Workers Compensation; Products Liability; Bankruptcy. ***Email:*** srosen@trplaw.com

OF COUNSEL

F. ALTON TYBOUT, born Philadelphia, Pennsylvania, June 12, 1929; admitted to bar, 1956, Delaware. *Education:* Duke University (A.B., 1951); Yale University (LL.B., 1954). Deputy Attorney General of Delaware, 1957-1958. Chief Deputy Attorney General of Delaware, 1958. Member, Supreme Court Rules Revision Committee, 1976-1978. Member, Supreme Court Advisory Committee on Discovery Abuse. Member, Third Circuit Judicial Conference, 1985. Member, Delaware Supreme Court Uniform Rules of Evidence Committee, 1978-1980. Member, U.S. District Court Local Rules Committee, 1978-1983. Member, 1978-1985 and Chairman, 1986, Supreme Court Board on Professional Responsibility. Member, Governor's Judicial Nominating Commission, 1983-1991. Member: Delaware State and American Bar Associations; American Judicature Society; Defense Research Institute. Fellow: American College of Trial Lawyers; American Bar Foundation. ***PRACTICE AREAS:*** Negligence; Insurance; Products Liability; Medical Malpractice. ***Email:*** ftybout@trplaw.com

REPRESENTATIVE CLIENTS: Ace Insurance Co.; AIG Insurance Co.; American Reliance Insurance; ARA Health Services, Inc.; CCL Industries Inc.; Commercial Union; Continental Insurance Company; Correctional Medical Systems, Inc.; Donegal Insurance Company; Erie Insurance Company; Farm Family Insurance Company; Fireman's Fund Insurance Company; First Delaware Insurance Co.; GAB Robbins North America; Harleysville Insurance Company; Hartford Insurance Company; Haul Risk Management Services, Inc.; Insurance Guaranty Association; Ithica Insurance Co.; Kemper Group; Liberty Mutual Insurance Company; Maryland Casualty Company; North Carolina Farm Bureau Mutual Insurance Company; Orion Group; PMA; Penn National Insurance Company; Reliance Ins. Co.; Selected Risks Insurance Company; State of Delaware; State Farm Insurance Company; Universal Underwriters Insurance; University of Delaware; USAA Mutual Insurance Company; Utica Mutl. Insurance Co.; Worldwide Insurance Group; Wausau Insurance Group; Zurich American Insurance Company.

WALSH MONZACK AND MONACO, P.A.

Established in 1971
400 COMMERCE CENTER
TWELFTH AND ORANGE STREETS
P.O. BOX 2031
WILMINGTON, DELAWARE 19899
Telephone: 302-656-8162
Fax: 302-656-2769
URL: http://www.lawyers.com/wmmlaw

Taxation, Commercial Transactions, Business Reorganization, Commercial Bankruptcy, General Corporate, Real Estate. Civil Litigation in all Courts.

DAVID I. WALSH, born Wilmington, Delaware, February 5, 1943; admitted to bar, 1970, Maryland; 1971, U.S. Tax Court; 1975, Delaware. *Education:* Georgetown University (B.S., 1965); University of Baltimore (J.D., 1969); George Washington University (LL.M. in Taxation, 1972). Instructor, Federal Income Tax and Business Law, University of Delaware, 1973-1976. *Member:* Maryland State, Delaware State, Federal and American (Member, Sections on: Banking and Business Law; Taxation) Bar Associations. ***PRACTICE AREAS:*** Federal Taxation; International Taxation; Estate Planning; Corporate Law. ***Email:*** dwalsh@walmon.com

MELVYN I. MONZACK, born Providence, Rhode Island, November 26, 1940; admitted to bar, 1966, District of Columbia; 1970, U.S. Court of Appeals for the District of Columbia Circuit; 1971, Delaware; 1972, U.S. District Court, District of Delaware; 1982, U.S. Court of Appeals, Third Circuit; 1986, U.S. Supreme Court. *Education:* University of Rhode Island (B.S., 1962); George Washington University (LL.B., 1965; LL.M., 1968). Instructor, Business Law and Industrial Relations, University of Delaware, 1975-1977. *Member:* Delaware State and American (Member, Sections on: Business Law; General Practice; Real Property, Probate and Trust Law; Litigation; Economics of Law Practice) Bar Associations. ***PRACTICE AREAS:*** Commercial Transactions; Business Reorganization; Real Estate; Civil Litigation. ***Email:*** mmonzack@walmon.com

(This Listing Continued)

WALSH MONZACK AND MONACO, P.A., Wilmington—Continued

FRANCIS A. MONACO, JR., born Wilmington, Delaware, February 9, 1956; admitted to bar, 1981, Delaware; 1982, Pennsylvania, U.S. District Court, District of Delaware; U.S. Tax Court; U.S. Court of Appeals, Third Circuit; U.S. Supreme Court. *Education:* University of Delaware (B.A., with high honors, 1978); Villanova University (J.D., 1981). *Member:* Delaware State (Member, Section on: Commercial Law), Pennsylvania (Member, Sections on: Corporate, Business and Commercial Law) and American (Member, Section on: Business Law) Bar Associations; American Bankruptcy Institute. (Certified Specialist, Business Bankruptcy Law, American Bankruptcy Board of Certification). ***PRACTICE AREAS:*** Commercial Bankruptcy; Commercial Law. ***Email:*** fmonaco@walmon.com

RACHEL B. MERSKY, born Wilmington, Delaware, July 4, 1957; admitted to bar, 1981, Delaware, U.S. District Court, District of Delaware and U.S. Tax Court. *Education:* University of Delaware (B.A., 1978); Gonzaga University (J.D., 1981). Order of Barristers. Jessup Cup International Law Moot Court Team. Delaware Commission for Women, 1983-1986. *Member:* Delaware State Bar Association (Member, Section on Employment Law); Delaware Trial Lawyers Association. ***LANGUAGES:*** Spanish. ***PRACTICE AREAS:*** Business Litigation; Commercial Bankruptcy; Commercial Litigation; Employment Law. ***Email:*** rmersky@walmon.com

BRIAN J. McLAUGHLIN, born Wilmington, Delaware, February 27, 1960; admitted to bar, 1986, Delaware; 1987, U.S. District Court, District of Delaware. *Education:* University of Delaware (B.A., 1982); University of Dayton (J.D., 1985). Member, 1983-1985 and Case Note Editor, 1984-1985, University of Dayton Law Review. Author: "Public School Searches and the Fourth Amendment," 9 University of Dayton Law Review 521. Judicial Extern to the Honorable Michael Merz, U.S. Magistrate, U.S. District Court, Southern District of Ohio, 1985. Instructor, Commercial Law and Creditor Rights, Wesley College, 1990. *Member:* Delaware State (Member, Sections on: Environmental and Commercial Law) and American (Member, Sections on: Business Law; Natural Resources, Energy and Environmental Law) Bar Associations. ***PRACTICE AREAS:*** Business Law; Commercial Transactions; Environmental; Civil Litigation; Bankruptcy. ***Email:*** bmclaughlin@walmon.com

JOSEPH J. BODNAR, born Jersey City, New Jersey, December 28, 1957; admitted to bar, 1984, New Jersey; 1985, New York and Pennsylvania; 1986, Delaware. *Education:* Rutgers University (B.A., 1979); New York Law School (J.D., cum laude, 1984). Law Clerk to the Honorable N. Richard Powers, U.S. Magistrate, U.S. District Court, Delaware, 1984-1986. Member, 1981-1982, Comments Editor, 1982-1983 and Articles Editor, 1983-1984, New York Law School Journal of International Law. *Member:* Delaware State and American Bar Associations. ***PRACTICE AREAS:*** Bankruptcy; Corporate; Commercial; Civil Litigation. ***Email:*** jbodnar@walmon.com

EDWARD M. LILLY, born Elkhart, Indiana, May 17, 1965; admitted to bar, 1997, Indiana and U.S. District Court, Northern and Southern Districts of Indiana; 2000, Delaware; 2001, U.S. District Court, District of Delaware. *Education:* DePauw University (B.A., magna cum laude, 1987); Cornell University (J.D., 1996). Member, 1994-1995 and Editor, 1995-1996, Cornell Journal of Law and Public Policy, liibulletin-ny. *Member:* Indiana State and Delaware Bar Associations. ***PRACTICE AREAS:*** Business Law; Corporate Law; Commercial Litigation; Real Property. ***Email:*** elilly@walmon.com

MARY ELIZABETH M. BROWDER, born Washington, D.C., March 27, 1962; admitted to bar, 1987, Florida; 1988, Maryland; 1994, Delaware. *Education:* Stetson University (B.B.A., 1984); George Washington University (J.D., with honors, 1987); Georgetown University (M.L.T., 1991). Member, George Washington University Law Review, 1986-1987. *Member:* Delaware Bar Association (Member, Sections on Taxation and Estate Planning). (Also practicing individually, Plantation, Florida). ***PRACTICE AREAS:*** Taxation Law; Federal, State and International Taxation; Estate Planning; Probate Law; Corporate Law; Business Law. ***Email:*** browderm@bellsouth.net

KEVIN J. MANGAN, born Darby, Pennsylvania, October 31, 1964; admitted to bar, 1989, Pennsylvania, New Jersey, U.S. District Court, Eastern District of Pennsylvania and U.S. District Court, District of New Jersey; 1994, U.S. District Court, Western District of Pennsylvania; 1995, U.S. Court of Appeals, Third Circuit; 1999, Delaware. *Education:* University of Scranton (B.S., Computer Science, magna cum laude, 1986); Villanova University (J.D., 1989). *Member:* Delaware State and American Bar Associations; American Bankruptcy Institute. ***PRACTICE AREAS:*** Products Liability; Corporate Litigation; Civil Litigation; Bankruptcy. ***Email:*** kmangan@walmon.com

WEIK, NITSCHE & DOUGHERTY

Established in 1957
ONE COMMERCE CENTER, 3RD FLOOR
12TH AND ORANGE STREETS
P.O. BOX 2324
WILMINGTON, DELAWARE 19899
Telephone: 302-655-4040
Fax: 302-654-4892
URL: http://www.weiknitsche.com
URL: http://www.lawyers.com/czajkowski

Personal Injury, Workers Compensation, Family Law, Insurance Law, Wrongful Death, Premises Liability, Motorcycle Accidents, Motor Vehicle Accidents and Injuries, Head Injury.

JOSEPH W. WEIK, born Wilmington, Delaware, March 31, 1952; admitted to bar, 1979, Delaware and U.S. District Court, District of Delaware. *Education:* University of Delaware (B.A., 1974); Dickinson School of Law of Penn State University (J.D., 1978). Member, Richard S. Rodney Inn of Court, 1998—. *Member:* Delaware (Member, Nominating Committee, 1992-1996; Chairman, Workers Compensation Committee, 2000-2001) and American Bar Associations; The Association of Trial Lawyers of America; Delaware Trial Lawyers Association (President, 1997-1998; Member Board of Governors; Treasurer, 1991-1995; Triad Chair, 1995-1996; President-Elect, 1996-1997; Editor, Advocate Magazine; Chairman, Past President's Committee, 2000—). ***REPORTED CASES:*** Sears v. Sears, Del. Fam. Ct. 462. A.2d 1099, (1983); Cook v. A.H. Davis & Son, Inc., Del. Super., 567 A.2d 239 (1989); Streett v. State, Del. Supr., 669 A.2d 9 (1995). ***PRACTICE AREAS:*** Personal Injury; Workers Compensation; Wrongful Death; Premises Liability. ***Email:*** jwe:k@attys4u.com

GARY S. NITSCHE, born Wilmington, Delaware, October 17, 1960; admitted to bar, 1987, Pennsylvania, New Jersey; 1988, Delaware, U.S. District Court District of Delaware and U.S. Court of Appeals, Third Circuit; 1993, U.S. Supreme Court. *Education:* University of Delaware (B.A., 1982); Thomas M. Cooley Law School (J.D., 1987). Phi Alpha Delta. Recipient, American Jurisprudence Award in Business Planning I. *Member:* Delaware (Member: Litigation and Tort and Insurance Practice Sections), Pennsylvania and American Bar Associations; Delaware Trial Lawyers Association (Member, Board of Governors; President-Elect, 1999-2000; President, 2000-2001; Membership Chair, 1992-1996); The Association of Trial Lawyers of America (Member: Leadership Development Committee; Delaware Governor for New Lawyers Division, 1992—: Legislative Chair, 1996-1999); College of Advocacy (Advocate, 1992). ***REPORTED CASES:*** Frank v. Horizon Assurance Co., Del. Supr., 553 A. 2d 1199 (1989); Page v. Hercules, Inc., 637 A. 2d 29 (1994); Murrey v. Nationwide Mut. Ins. Co., D. Del. 674 F. Supp. 154 (1987); Lomax v. Nationwide Mut. Ins. Co., D. Del., 776 F. Supp. 870 (1991), Rev'd, 3rd Cir., 964 F. 2d 1343 (1992); Hurst v. Nationwide Mutual Ins. Co., Del. Supp. 652 A.2d 10 (1995). ***PRACTICE AREAS:*** Personal Injury; Workers Compensation; Wrongful Death; Premises Liability. ***Email:*** gnitsche@attys4u.com

SHAWN DOUGHERTY, born 1961; admitted to bar, 1988, Pennsylvania; 1989, Delaware. *Education:* University of Delaware (B.S.A.S.); Widener University (J.D.). Member, Richard S. Rodney Inn of Court, 1998-1999. *Member:* Delaware and Pennsylvania Bar Associations. ***PRACTICE AREAS:*** Family Law. ***Email:*** sdougherty@attys4u.com

STANLEY T. CZAJKOWSKI (SHY-KOW-SKI) (Retired).

ELIOT ALAZRAKI (Retired).

REFERENCES: Wilmington Trust Co.

TIMOTHY JOSEPH WEILER

727-B NORTH MARKET STREET
WILMINGTON, DELAWARE 19801
Telephone: 302-658-6900
Fax: 302-658-6909
Email: timweiler@aol.com
URL: http://www.lawyers.com/weilerlaw

Bankruptcy, Civil Litigation, Real Estate, Wills, Probate, Trusts and Estates, Estate Planning, Personal Injury, Automobile Accidents, Commercial Collections, Admiralty and Maritime, Business.

TIMOTHY JOSEPH WEILER, born Rockville Centre, New York, March, 5, 1958; admitted to bar, 1983, Pennsylvania and New Jersey; 1985, Delaware. *Education:* New York State University at Stony Brook (B.A., 1980); Delaware Law School of Widener University (J.D., 1983). Assistant Public Defender, 1990—. *Member:* Pennsylvania Bar Association; Delaware (Member, Admiralty and Maritime Committee) and American Bar Associations; Delaware Trial Lawyers Association; National Association of Criminal Defense Lawyers; Delaware Association of Criminal Defense Lawyers. ***PRACTICE AREAS:*** Bankruptcy;

(This Listing Continued)

Civil Litigation; Personal Injury; Medical Malpractice; Corporate Law; Business Law; Collections; Real Estate; Probate; Estate Planning.

MICHAEL WEISS, P.A.

Established in 1995

1220 MARKET STREET, SUITE 604

P.O. BOX 370

WILMINGTON, DELAWARE 19899

Telephone: 302-656-0400

Fax: 302-656-5011

General and Civil Trial Practice, Insurance, Negligence, Workers Compensation, Administrative Law, Federal Practice.

FIRM PROFILE: With 27 years in practice, Mr. Weiss began his sole operation in 1995. He had formerly been a partner in Kimmel, Weiss & Carter. Mr. Weiss services clients throughout the state and is admitted to practice before all state and federal courts. His civil practice concentrates in plaintiff's personal injury and claimants workers compensation. He is listed in Best Lawyers in America and Delaware Today's Top Lawyers.

MICHAEL WEISS, born Philadelphia, Pennsylvania, November 7, 1949; admitted to bar, 1974, Delaware. *Education:* University of Delaware (B.A., 1971); Villanova University (J.D., 1974). *Member:* Delaware State (Member: Worker's Compensation Section, 1990—; Medical-Legal and Dental Legal Relations Section; Litigation Section, 1984-1994; Industrial Accident Board Rules Committee, 1996—) and American (Member, Litigation Section, 1981—) Bar Associations; Delaware Trial Lawyers Association (Co-Chairman, Continuing Legal Education Committee, 1993-1995; Board of Directors, 1993-1995, 2001—; Nominating Committee, 1995-2000); The Association of Trial Lawyers of America. ***PRACTICE AREAS:*** Civil Practice; Insurance; Negligence; Workers Compensation; Administrative Law; Federal Practice. ***Email:*** mweiss@mweissesq.com

YVONNE TAKVORIAN SAVILLE, born Wilmington, Delaware, March 5, 1970; admitted to bar, 1995, Delaware. *Education:* University of Delaware (B.A., 1992); Widener University School of Law (J.D., 1995). Phi Delta Phi; Harrington Inn. Member, Moot Court Honor Society; Order of the Barristers. Winner, 16th Annual Judge G. Fred DiBona Widener Moot Court Competition. Recipient, 1991 Woman of Promise Award. *Member:* Delaware State (Member: Worker's Compensation Section, 1996—, Secretary, 2001—; New Lawyers Section, 1997—) and American (Member, Young Lawyers Division, 1996—) Bar Associations; Delaware Trial Lawyers Association (Co-Chairman, Continuing Legal Education Committee, 1999; Board of Governors, 1999—); The Association of Trial Lawyers of America (Board of Governors, New Lawyers Division, 2001—). ***PRACTICE AREAS:*** Civil Practice; Insurance; Negligence; Workers' Compensation; Personal Injury; Administrative Law. ***Email:*** ytsaville@mweissesq.com

WELCH & ASSOCIATES

824 MARKET ST., 8TH FL.

STE. 801

WILMINGTON, DELAWARE 19801

Telephone: 302-622-8900

Fax: 302-622-9046

Email: jwelch@welch-assoc.com

Commercial Litigation, Banking and Bankruptcy Litigation, Creditor's Rights, General Litigation, Corporate Litigation, Real Estate, Insurance Defense and Insurance Coverage.

JEFFREY S. WELCH, born Columbus, Ohio, May 1, 1953; admitted to bar, 1979, Pennsylvania; 1980, Delaware and U.S. District Court, District of Delaware; 1985, U.S. Court of Appeals, Third Circuit. *Education:* University of Delaware (B.S., 1975); Delaware Law School of Widener University (J.D., 1978). Judicial Clerkship, Delaware Court of Chancery, 1978-1979. Faculty Member: Delaware State Bar Association Bankruptcy Seminar, "Chapter 7 versus Chapter 13," February 25, 1994; National Business Institute, "How to Get Results in Collection of Delinquent Debts"; Lorman Business Institute, "Delaware Collection Law," September 18, 1997; National Business Institute, "Delaware Foreclosure and Repossession," October 22, 1997. *Member:* Delaware (Member, Sections on: Litigation; Commercial Law) and American (Member, Sections on: Banking; Business Law) Bar Associations; Delaware Trial Lawyers Association. ***PRACTICE AREAS:*** Commercial Litigation; Banking and Bankruptcy Litigation; Creditor's Rights; General Litigation; Corporate Litigation.

(This Listing Continued)

ALAN W. BEHRINGER, born Morgantown, West Virginia, July 18, 1945; admitted to bar, 1970, Delaware; 1974, U.S. Court of Appeals, Third Circuit. *Education:* University of Delaware (B.A., 1967); Dickinson School of Law (J.D., 1970). Speaker, CLE seminars on real estate and related subjects, sponsored by Delaware Bar Association and private organizations. Faculty Member, Delaware State Bar Association, Real Estate Fundamentals Seminar. *Member:* Delaware State (Chair, Real and Personal Property Committee, 1978-1980) and American (Member: Section of Real Property, Probate and Trust Law, 1974—; Real Estate Financing Committee, 1985—) Bar Associations. [Capt., U.S. Army, 1971-1972]. ***PRACTICE AREAS:*** Commercial Collection Litigation; Banking Litigation; Bankruptcy Litigation; Mortgage Foreclosure-Residential; Real Estate And Title Insurance; Wills and Estates. ***Email:*** albehringer@welch-assoc.com

REPRESENTATIVE CLIENTS: Wilmington Trust Company; PNC Bank; Wilmington Savings Fund Society; Advanta Mortgage Corporation, USA; Christiana Bank & Trust Company; Community Credit Corporation; Delaware Savings Bank; First State Community Loan Fund; First Union, N.A.; Frankford Bank, N.A.; Wells Fargo; OCWEN; Equicredit.

LAW OFFICE OF ALLAN WENDELBURG

WILMINGTON, DELAWARE

(See Hockessin)

Civil Litigation, Criminal Litigation, Personal Injury, Professional Malpractice, Insurance Defense, Construction Law, Insurance, Probate, Estate Planning, Business Law, Commercial Law.

WERB & SULLIVAN

TENTH FLOOR, 300 DELAWARE AVENUE

P.O. BOX 25046

WILMINGTON, DELAWARE 19899

Telephone: 302-652-1100

Telecopier: 302-652-1111

URL: http://www.lawyers.com/werb&sullivan

Bankruptcy and Corporate Reorganization, Business and Corporate Law, Incorporation and Business Formation under Delaware Law, Civil and Criminal Litigation in all Courts, Business Planning, Estate Planning, and Real Property.

FIRM PROFILE: Werb & Sullivan is a firm that practices in the areas of corporate reorganization, bankruptcy, business and corporate litigation, business planning, estate planning and general real estate matters. The firm's attorneys are experienced in representing secured and unsecured creditors, landlords, mortgage lenders and personal injury claimants in the major corporate reorganizations and bankruptcies administered in Delaware and related Delaware Chancery Court litigation. The firm routinely handles the incorporation of companies under Delaware law. The firm's attorneys are also experienced in representing clients in general real estate matters, including mortgage and title issues.

DUANE D. WERB, born Newark, New Jersey, October 24, 1950; admitted to bar, 1979, Pennsylvania; 1980, Delaware and U.S. District Court, District of Delaware; 2000, U.S. District Court, Eastern and Western Districts of Pennsylvania and U.S. District Court, District of Columbia. *Education:* Wilmington College (B.A., 1972); Delaware Law School (J.D., 1978). Adjunct Professor and Chairman, Criminal Justice Department, Wilmington College, 1978-1984. Adjunct Professor of Law, Widener University School of Law, 1979-1994. Deputy Attorney General, 1979-1983 and Chief Public Defender, 1983-1990, Kent County. *Member:* Delaware State, Pennsylvania and American Bar Associations. ***PRACTICE AREAS:*** Bankruptcy; Corporate Reorganization; Business Law; Corporate Law; Civil Litigation; Criminal Law; Business Planning; Estate Planning; Real Property. ***Email:*** ddwlaw@dca.net

BRIAN A. SULLIVAN, born Wilmington, Delaware, January 29, 1955; admitted to bar, 1981, Delaware. *Education:* Gettysburg College (B.A., 1977); John Marshall Law School (J.D., 1981). Assistant New Castle County Attorney (Planning and Zoning), 1982-1986. *Member:* Delaware State (Corporation, Real Property, Estate and Trust Sections) and American Bar Associations. ***PRACTICE AREAS:*** Bankruptcy; Corporate Reorganization; Business Law; Corporate Law; Real Property; Estate Planning. ***Email:*** baslaw@dca.net

ASSOCIATE

KIMBERLY E. CONNOLLY LAWSON, born Neptune, New Jersey, May 2, 1970; admitted to bar, 2000, Delaware; 2001, Maryland and U.S. District Court, District of Delaware. *Education:* Allentown College of St. Francis de Sales (B.A., 1992); Hahnemann University (M.A., 1994); Widener University School of Law (J.D., cum laude, 2000). *Member:* Delaware State and American (Member, Sections on: Business Law; Litigation; Real Property; Probate and Trust; Taxation) Bar Associations; Maryland State Bar Association, Inc.; Association of Trial Lawyers of America (Member, Sections on: Aviation

(This Listing Continued)

WERB & SULLIVAN, Wilmington—Continued

Law; Commercial Litigation). ***PRACTICE AREAS:*** Bankruptcy; Corporate Reorganization; Business Law; Corporate Law; Civil Litigation; Criminal Law; Wills; Trust Law; Commercial Real Estate; Residential Real Estate. ***Email:*** klawson@dca.net

REPRESENTATIVE CLIENTS: Am South Bank; American National Bank and Trust; First American Title Insurance Company; Goulds Pumps, Inc.; GreenPoint Credit Company; G.E. Capital Corp.; Greenville Capital Management; ITT Fluid Technology; J.R. Simplot Company; Lamb-Weston, Inc.; McCain Foods USA, Inc.; Mellon Bank, N.A.; Nestle USA, Inc.; Quaker Capital, L.P.; Republic Bank; S.W. Cole Engineering, Inc.; Wilmington Trust Company.

WHITE AND WILLIAMS LLP

824 NORTH MARKET STREET, SUITE 902
WILMINGTON, DELAWARE 19801-4938
Telephone: 302-654-0424
Fax: 302-654-0245
URL: http://www.whitewms.com

Paoli, Pennsylvania Office: 1500 Lancaster Avenue. Telephone: 610-251-0466. Fax: 610-296-4628.

Allentown, Pennsylvania Office: The Frederick Building, 3500 Winchester Road - 200. Telephone: 610-435-8414. Fax: 610-435-8420.

Westmont, New Jersey Office: 222 Haddon Avenue. Telephone: 856-858-5300. Fax: 856-858-0722.

Philadelphia, Pennsylvania Office: 18th Floor, 1650 Market Street. Telephone: 215-864-7000. Fax: 215-864-7523.

Pittsburgh, Pennsylvania Office: The Frick Building, 437 Grant Street, Suite 1001. Telephone: 412-566-3520. Fax: 412-566-3521.

New York, N.Y. Office: 11 East 44th Street, 9th Floor. Telephone: 888-458-1430.

General Practice, Civil Litigation (Business and Casualty), Computer Law, Corporate, Creditors' Rights, Director and Officers Liability, Environmental and Toxic Tort Litigation, Finance and Banking, Health Care and Medical Malpractice, Insurance Coverage and Reinsurance, Intellectual Property, Labor (Management), Products Liability, Professional Liability, Property and Subrogation Litigation, Real Estate, Securities, Taxation and Estates, Workers Compensation.

RESIDENT PARTNER

JOHN D. BALAGUER, born June 29, 1958; admitted to bar, 1985, Pennsylvania and New Jersey; 1989, Delaware. *Education:* Allegheny College; University of Delaware (B.A., 1981); Widener University (J.D., cum laude, 1985). Phi Alpha Theta. Member, Delaware Journal of Corporate Law Review, 1984-1985. *Member:* Delaware Bar Association; Delaware Trial Lawyers Association; Defense Counsel of Delaware; National Lawyers Association; Defense Research Institute. [Major, U.S. Army Reserve]. ***Email:*** balaguerj@whitewms.com

RESIDENT COUNSEL

DAVID E. WILKS, born April 21, 1964; admitted to bar, 1989, Delaware; 1996, Pennsylvania. *Education:* Colgate University (B.A., 1986); The Dickinson School of Law (J.D., 1989). ***Email:*** wilksd@whitewms.com

RESIDENT ASSOCIATES

LINDA M. CARMICHAEL, born July 21, 1958; admitted to bar, 1997, Delaware. *Education:* Widener University (B.S., cum laude, 1991; J.D., 1996). Phi Delta Phi. Recipient, Certificate of Achievement, Federal Income Tax, Widener University, 1996. Law Clerk to: The Honorable Charles H. Toliver, IV, 1996 and The Honorable Jerome O. Herlihy, 1997, Superior Court, New Castle County, Delaware. *Member:* Delaware State Bar Association; American Bankruptcy Institute.. ***Email:*** carmichaell.whitewms.com

MARC STEPHEN CASARINO, born January 21, 1972; admitted to bar, 1997, Delaware. *Education:* University of Delaware (B.S., Economics, 1994); Widener University (J.D., 1997). Phi Delta Phi. Associate Articles Editor, Widener Law SymposIum Journal, 1996-1997. Member, Harrington Inn Honor Chapter. First Vice-President, Corporate Law Society, 1994-1995. *Member:* Delaware State and American Bar Associations; Italian-American Bar Association; The Association of Trial Lawyers of America; Delaware Trial Lawyers Association. ***Email:*** casarinom@whitewms.com

CURTIS J. CROWTHER, born August 20, 1968; admitted to bar, 1994, Delaware. *Education:* Neumann College (B.A., magna cum laude, 1990); Widener University (J.D., cum laude, 1993). Phi Kappa Phi; Phi Alpha Delta. National Dean's List, 1988, 1989 and 1990. *Member:* Delaware State, Pennsylvania and American Bar Associations; Association of Trial Lawyers of America; American Bankruptcy Institute. ***Email:*** crowtherc@whitwms.com

SUSAN GRAHAM HARRON, born May 28, 1969; admitted to bar, 1995, Delaware; 1996, New Jersey and Pennsylvania. *Education:* Indiana University of Pennsylvania (B.A., cum laude, 1991); Widener University (J.D., cum laude, 1995). Member, Moot Court Honor Society. Associate Editor, Widener Law Symposium Law Journal. ***Email:*** harrons@whitewms.com

SETH J. REIDENBERG, born July 15, 1970; admitted to bar, 1997, Delaware; 1998, Pennsylvania. *Education:* Pennsylvania State University (B.S., 1992); Widener University (J.D., 1997). President, Delaware Corporate Law Journal, 1996-1997. *Member:* Delaware State Bar and Pennsylvania Bar Associations; Defense Council of Delaware. ***Email:*** reidenbergs@whitewms.com

CHRISTIAN J. SINGEWALD, born October 8, 1968; admitted to bar, 1994, Illinois and Connecticut; 1996, Delaware and District of Columbia. *Education:* University of Richmond (B.A., 1991); The John Marshall Law School (J.D., 1994). Phi Sigma Alpha. Member, The John Marshall Journal of Computer and Information Law. ***Email:*** singewaldc@whitewms.com

(For complete biographical data on all personnel, see Professional Biographies at Philadelphia, Pennsylvania)

RICHARD R. WIER, JR., P.A.

1220 MARKET STREET, SUITE 600
WILMINGTON, DELAWARE 19801
Telephone: 302-888-3222
Fax: 302-888-3225
URL: http://www.wierlaw.com
Email: rwier@wierlaw.com
URL: http://www.lawyers.com/richardrwier

Labor and Employment Law, Civil Rights, Sexual Harrassment, Discrimination, Civil and Criminal Litigation, DUI, Drug Abuse, Felonies, Homicides, Juvenile Misdemeanors, Parole and Probation, Sexual Assault, Traffic Violations, Personal Injury Law, Medical Malpractice, Auto Accidents, Sexual Abuse and Wrongful Death.

RICHARD R. WIER, JR., born Wilmington, Delaware, May 19, 1941; admitted to bar, 1967, Delaware and District of Columbia; 1980, Pennsylvania. *Education:* Hamilton College (B.A., 1963); University of Pennsylvania (LL.B., 1966); Temple University Law School (Labor Law, 1981-1982). Attorney General, 1975-1979, State Prosecutor, 1970-1974 and Deputy Attorney General, 1968-1970, State of Delaware. Listed in: Who's Who in America, 1978—; Who's Who in American Law; Who's Who in the East; Best Lawyers in America, 2001-2002. "Top Four Labor/Employment Attorneys in Delaware," Delaware Today, October, 1996—. *Member:* The District of Columbia Bar; Delaware (Member, Committees on: Criminal Law, 1980— and Labor Relations, 1981—; Vice Chairman, Labor Law Section, 1987-1988; Chairman, Labor Law Section, 1989-1990; Chairman, Criminal Law Section, 1987-1992; Chairman, Special Committee on Drug Crisis, 1993—), Pennsylvania and American (Member, Labor and Employment Law Section) Bar Associations; The Association of Trial Lawyers of America; Delaware Trial Lawyers Association; National Association of Attorneys General (Honorary Life Member). ***PRACTICE AREAS:*** Employee/Employer Labor Law; Employment Law; Civil Litigation; Criminal Litigation; Personal Injury.

DANIEL W. SCIALPI, born Jackson, New Jersey, February 27, 1976; admitted to bar, 2001, Delaware. *Education:* Villanova University (B.A., 1998); Widener University School of Law (J.D., 2001). Phi Delta Phi; Phi Kappa Phi. Widener Scholar. Recipient, Russell Levin Memorial Award. ***Email:*** dscialpi@wierlaw.com

WILBRAHAM, LAWLER & BUBA

A PROFESSIONAL CORPORATION
STONEY BATTER OFFICE BUILDING
5301 LIMESTONE ROAD, SUITE 221
WILMINGTON, DELAWARE 19808-1251
Telephone: 302-234-8217
Fax: 302-234-8218
Email: info@wlbdeflaw.com
URL: http://www.wilbrahamlawlerandbuba.com

Philadelphia, Pennsylvania Office: 1818 Market Street, Suite 3100. Telephone: 215-564-4141. Fax: 215-564-4385.

Haddonfield, New Jersey Office: 24 Kings Highway West. Telephone: 856-795-4422. Fax: 856-795-4699.

Pittsburgh, Pennsylvania Office: First & Market Building, 100 First Avenue, Suite 325. Telephone: 412-255-0500. Fax: 412-255-0505.

New York, New York Office: 140 Broadway, 46th Floor. Telephone: 212-943-9245. Fax: 212-943-9246.

Appellate Practice, Civil Trial Practice, Commercial Litigation, Insurance Defense, Product Liability Law, Toxic Torts, Workers Compensation.

(This Listing Continued)

FIRM PROFILE: For a detailed description of the firm's capabilities and biographies, refer to www.wilbrahamlawlerandbuba.com. Note: Most of the following attorney's have multiple jurisdictions to which they are admitted. Please refer to their detail in the professional listings at www.wilbrahamlawlerandbuba.com.

REPRESENTATIVE CLIENTS: GAF Corporation; Armstrong World Industries, Inc.; U.S. Gypsum Company; Georgia-Pacific Corporation; ARCO; Shell; Royal; AIG; Chubb; Keystone; Progressive; Admiral; Donegal; Rutgers Casualty; Travelers; St. Paul Casualty; Harleysville; USF&G; Allstate; Infinity; Erie Nationwide.

(For complete biographical data on all personnel, see Professional Biographies at Philadelphia, Pennsylvania)

WOLF, BLOCK, SCHORR AND SOLIS-COHEN LLP

Established in 1903

ONE RODNEY SQUARE
920 KING STREET, SUITE 300
WILMINGTON, DELAWARE 19801
Telephone: 302-777-5860
Fax: 302-777-5863
Email: wolfblock@wolfblock.com
URL: http://www.wolfblock.com

Philadelphia, Pennsylvania Office: 1650 Arch Street, 22nd Floor, 19103-2097. Telephone: 215-977-2000. Telecopier: 977-2334; 977-2346.

New York, New York Office: 250 Park Avenue, 10177. Telephone: 212-986-1116. Telecopier: 212-986-0604.

Camden, New Jersey Office: One Port Center, 2 Riverside Drive, Suite 502, 08103. Telephone: 856-225-1055. Fax: 856-225-9024.

Cherry Hill, New Jersey Office: 1940 Route 70 East, Suite 200, 08003. Telephone: 856-424-8200. Fax: 856-424-4446.

Harrisburg, Pennsylvania Office: 212 Locust Street, Suite 300, 17101. Telephone: 717-237-7160. Fax: 717-237-7161.

Newark, New Jersey Office: 744 Broad Street, Suite 1515, 07102. Telephone: 973-824-7723. Fax: 973-424-5740.

Norristown, Pennsylvania Office: 3 Penn Court, 325 Swede Street, P.O. Box 869, 19404. Telephone: 610-272-5555. Fax: 610-272-6976.

General Practice. Corporate, Real Estate, Taxation, Civil and Criminal Litigation, Estate Planning, Probate, Labor, Employment and Benefits, Antitrust, Securities, Banking, Municipal Finance, Patent, Trademark and Copyright, Bankruptcy, Family Law, Health Care, Intellectual Property and Information Technology, Communications, Financial Services, Government-Assisted and Affordable Housing, Utility Regulation, Surety, Fidelity and Liability, Mortgage Lending, Securitization and Environmental Law.

FIRM PROFILE: Wolf, Block, Schorr and Solis-Cohen LLP has been providing legal services for nearly a century. Our practice is national and international in scope and includes a broad range of clients from start-up companies to multi-billion dollar conglomerates. We have 18 practice groups which enable us to provide the skills and experience clients need, whether in traditional areas such as real estate, corporate/securities or litigation, or in newer fields such as information technology or securitizations.

Our attorneys enjoy a national reputation for successfully combining their skill with business experience and acumen.

Wolf Block is committed to our clients-we have established a tradition of innovation, proactive approach, timely response, and creativity advocacy.

MEMBERS OF FIRM

BARRY M. KLAYMAN, born Montclair, New Jersey, 1952; admitted to bar, 1977, Pennsylvania and U.S. District Court, Eastern District of Pennsylvania; 1980, U.S. Court of Appeals, Third Circuit; 1998, Delaware and U.S. District Court, District of Delaware. *Education:* Columbia University (B.A., magna cum laude, 1974); Harvard University (J.D., cum laude, 1977). Phi Beta Kappa. Congress Editor, Harvard Journal on Legislation, 1976-1977. Author: "The Definition of Torture in International Law," 51 Temple Law Quarterly 449, 1978. Member, Board of Directors, Philadelphia Region B'nai B'rith Youth Organization, 1983—; Chairman, 1991-1995. Member, B'nai B'rith Youth Commission, 1991—, Executive Board, 1996—; Member, B'nai B'rith Justice Lodge, 1992—. Member, Board of Directors, Akiba Hebrew Academy, 1991—, Secretary, 1994-1995, Vice-President, 1995-1996 and 1998-2000, Treasurer, 1996-1998, President, 2000—. Member: Jewish Federation of Greater Philadelphia Committee on National Services, 1992—; Committee on Planning and Allocations, 1998—. Vice President, B'nai B'rith Council of Greater Philadelphia, 1996-1997. Co-Author, "State and Local Developments," Journal of Environmental Regulation, 1991-1995. *Member:* Philadelphia, Pennsylvania, Delaware State and American (Litigation Section, Torts and Insurance Practice

(This Listing Continued)

Section) Bar Associations; The Association of Trial Lawyers of America. (Resident). ***PRACTICE AREAS:*** Commercial Litigation; Environmental Litigation; Toxic Torts Law. ***Email:*** bklayman@wolfblock.com

MARY M. MALONEYHUSS, born Plattsburgh, New York, 1960; admitted to bar, 1991, Delaware. *Education:* University of Rochester (B.S., Chemistry, 1982); University of Pittsburgh (M.S., Chemistry, 1984); William Mitchell College of Law (J.D., summa cum laude, 1990). Editor-In-Chief, William Mitchell Law Review, 1989-1990. Author: Limited Liability Company Act, Folk on the Delaware General Corporation Law, Alternative Business Entities; CERCLA Operator Liability: What is a Parent Corporation to do After *United States v. Bestfoods?* 2 Del. L.Rev. (1999). Law Clerk to the Honorable Joseph J. Longobardi, United States District Court, District of Delaware, 1990-1991. Associate, Skadden, Arps, Slate, Meagher & Flom, 1991-1994. Contract Attorney, Zeneca Inc., 1994-1997. Partner, Bouchard Margules Friedlander & Maloney-Huss, 1998-2000. Member, American Chemical Society, 1984—. Member, Delaware National Areas Advisory Council. *Member:* Delaware State (Member, Standing Committee for the Provision of Legal Services to Low Income People; Vice-Chair Environmental Law Section) and American Bar Associations. ***PRACTICE AREAS:*** Bankruptcy; Business Litigation; Environmental Litigation; Environmental Counseling. ***Email:*** mmaloneyhuss@wolfblock.com

MICHAEL L. TEMIN, born Philadelphia, Pennsylvania, 1933; admitted to bar, 1958, Pennsylvania; 2000, Delaware. *Education:* Yale University (B.A., magna cum laude, 1954); University of Pennsylvania (LL.B., cum laude, 1957). Order of the Coif. Editor, University of Pennsylvania Law Review, 1955-1957. Assistant United States Attorney, 1958-1959. Lecturer in Law, University of Pennsylvania Law School, 1982-1991; Adjunct Professor, University of Pennsylvania Law School, 1990-1995. Chairman, Eastern District of Pennsylvania Bankruptcy Conference, 1995-1996. Contributor, Bankruptcy Litigation Manual. *Member:* Philadelphia (Chairman: Section on Corporation, Banking and Business Law, 1988; Chairman: Bankruptcy Committee, Section on Corporation, Banking and Business Law, 1979-1986; Chairman, Professional Guidance Committee, 1985; Member, Board of Governors, 1988), Pennsylvania (Chairman: Bankruptcy Committee, 1979; House of Delegates, 1985-1989, 1990—) and American (Vice Chairman, Chapter 11 Subcommittee, 1992-1996; Chairman, Rules Subcommittee, Business Bankruptcy Committee, Business Law Section, 1982-1992) Bar Associations. Regent, American College of Bankruptcy. (Also at Philadelphia, PA Office). ***PRACTICE AREAS:*** Bankruptcy. ***Email:*** mtemin@wolfblock.com

ASSOCIATE

JENNIFER BARBER, born Woodbury, New Jersey, July 10, 1967; admitted to bar, 1995, New Jersey and Pennsylvania; 1996, Delaware. *Education:* Rutgers University (B.A., 1991); Widener University School of Law (J.D., 1995). Director of Legal Affairs, Delaware Family Court, 1998-1989. Deputy Legal Counsel, Gov. Thomas R. Carper, 1999-2000. ***PRACTICE AREAS:*** Business Litigation. ***Email:*** jbarber@wolfblock.com

TODD SCHILTZ, born Elkhart, Indiana, October 19, 1967; admitted to bar, 1994, Delaware. *Education:* DePauw University (B.A., cum laude, 1990); Northwestern University (J.D., 1993). *Member:* Delaware State and American Bar Associations. ***PRACTICE AREAS:*** Litigation. ***Email:*** tschiltz@wolfblock.com

(For a listing of all firm personnel see the main office listing at Philadelphia, Pennsylvania. Complete biographical data is available at the office listing where the attorney is resident)

YOUNG CONAWAY STARGATT & TAYLOR, LLP

ELEVENTH FLOOR, WILMINGTON TRUST CENTER
1100 NORTH MARKET STREET
P.O. BOX 391
WILMINGTON, DELAWARE 19899-0391
Telephone: 302-571-6600
Telecopy: 302-571-1253
Email: ycst@ycst.com
URL: http://www.ycst.com

Georgetown, Delaware Office: 110 West Pine Street. Telephone: 302-856-3571. Telecopy: 302-856-9338.

General Practice.

MEMBERS OF FIRM

H. ALBERT YOUNG (1904-1982).

H. JAMES CONAWAY, JR. (1922-1990).

BRUCE M. STARGATT, born New York, N.Y., July 8, 1930; admitted to bar, 1955, New York and Delaware; 1956, District of Columbia. *Education:* University of Vermont (B.A., 1951); Yale University (LL.B., 1954). Recipient:

(This Listing Continued)

YOUNG CONAWAY STARGATT & TAYLOR, LLP, Wilmington—Continued

First State Distinguished Service Award, 1991; American Judicature Society Herbert Harley Award, 1993. President, Delaware State Bar Association, 1981-1982. President, Delaware Bar Foundation, 1995—. Lawyer Chairman, Delaware Appellate Handbook Committee, 1984-1995. Chairman, Delaware Supreme Court Rules Lawyers Advisory Committee, 1986-1993. Delegate, American Bar Association House of Delegates, 1991—. *Member:* American Law Institute. Fellow: American Bar Foundation; American College of Trial Lawyers. ***PRACTICE AREAS:*** Corporate Fiduciary Law; Corporate Governance; Civil Litigation.

STUART B. YOUNG, born Wilmington, Delaware, June 6, 1935; admitted to bar, 1962, District of Columbia and Delaware. *Education:* Williams College (B.A., 1957); University of Virginia (LL.B., 1960); Graduate Business School, Columbia University. Sigma Nu Phi. *Member:* Delaware State, American and International Bar Associations. ***PRACTICE AREAS:*** Litigation; Corporate Law; Construction Law; Products Liability; Intellectual Property. ***Email:*** syoung@ycst.com

BEN T. CASTLE, born Las Vegas, New Mexico, August 6, 1938; admitted to bar, 1964, Virginia; 1965, Delaware. *Education:* University of Pennsylvania (A.B., 1960); Georgetown University Law Center (LL.B., 1964). Secretary, Board on Professional Responsibility of the Supreme Court of Delaware, 1994—. *Member:* Delaware State and American Bar Associations; Delaware Trial Lawyers Association (President, 1984-1985); The Association of Trial Lawyers of America; American Board of Trial Advocates; International Academy of Trial Lawyers; International Society of Barristers. Fellow, American College of Trial Lawyers; The Inner Circle of Advocates. ***PRACTICE AREAS:*** Medical Negligence; Surgeons Liability; Obstetric Malpractice; Catastrophic Injury; Wrongful Death. ***Email:*** bcastle@ycst.com

SHELDON A. WEINSTEIN, born Philadelphia, Pennsylvania, November 27, 1938; admitted to bar, 1964, Delaware. *Education:* University of Delaware (B.A., 1960); Dickinson School of Law (LL.B., 1963); New York University (LL.M., 1964). Member, Dickinson Law Review, 1962-1963. Co-Author: "Delaware Fundamentals of Real Estate Law," published by Division of Continuing Legal Education, University of Delaware, 1972, revised 1978, 1979 and 1987. *Member:* Delaware State (Member, Committees on Professional Ethics and Professional Guidance) and American Bar Associations. ***Email:*** sweinstein@ycst.com

SHELDON N. SANDLER, born Salem, Massachusetts, June 13, 1941; admitted to bar, 1966, Delaware. *Education:* University of Michigan (A.B., 1962); University of Pennsylvania (LL.B., 1965); Temple University (LL.M. in Labor Law, 1978). Author: "Delaware Wrongful Discharge Cases: The Imminent Flood," *Delaware Lawyer,* Spring 1992. Contributing Author: "Unionization Efforts in Banking: Is The Delaware Experience A Guide To The Future?" 43 Labor Law Journal 155 (March 1992). Contributor, "Delaware Employment Law Letter"; "Employment Law in Pennsylvania and Delaware: A River Runs Through It," Pennsylvania Bar Institute (April, 2000); "When Worlds Collide: Bankruptcy & Employment Law," Pennsylvania Bar Institute (April, 2001). Author: Delaware Supreme Court: The First Fifty Years - Chapter 10, "Labor and Employment Law" (June, 2001). Member, 1980-1983 and Chairman, 1983, Lawyers Advisory Committee to the Third Circuit. Member, Delaware Court of Chancery Litigation Rules Advisory Committee, 1986-1994. *Member:* Delaware State (Chairman, Labor and Employment Law Section, 1983-1984), Federal (President, Delaware Chapter, 1981-1983) and American (Member: Committee on Employee Rights and Responsibilities, State and Local Government Employment Law, Labor and Employment Law Section; Litigation Section) Bar Associations. ***PRACTICE AREAS:*** Employment Discrimination; Employment Law; Management Labor Law; Title VII Discrimination; Union Elections. ***Email:*** ssandler@ycst.com

RICHARD A. LEVINE, born New York, N.Y., June 22, 1947; admitted to bar, 1972, Delaware. *Education:* Boston University (B.A., 1969); University of Pennsylvania (J.D., 1972). Member, University of Pennsylvania Moot Court Board, 1971-1972. Member, 1982-1986, Assistant Secretary, 1976 and Secretary, 1977-1982, Board of Bar Examiners. *Member:* Delaware State (Member, Sections on: Real Property; Secretary, 1992-1995; Commercial Law) and American Bar Associations. ***PRACTICE AREAS:*** Commercial Law; Commercial Real Estate; Banks and Banking; Leases and Leasing; Partnership Law. ***Email:*** rlevine@ycst.com

RICHARD A. ZAPPA, born Wilmington, Delaware, July 9, 1948; admitted to bar, 1973, Delaware. *Education:* University of Delaware (B.A., 1970); American University (J.D., 1973). Associate Editor, American University Law Review, 1971-1973. Law Clerk, Delaware Superior Court, 1973-1974. *Member:* Delaware State and American Bar Associations; Delaware Trial Lawyers Association; The Association of Trial Lawyers of America (Member, Superior Court Rules Committee); American Board of Trial Advocates (President, 1999-2000). ***Email:*** rzappa@ycst.com

(This Listing Continued)

FREDERICK WILLIAM IOBST, born Bethlehem, Pennsylvania, December 30, 1945; admitted to bar, 1972, Pennsylvania; 1973, Delaware. *Education:* Duke University (B.A., 1967); Villanova University (J.D., 1972). Associate Editor, Villanova Law Review, 1971-1972. Law Clerk to the Honorable Edwin D. Steel, Jr., U.S. District Court, District of Delaware, 1972-1974. *Member:* Delaware State and American Bar Associations; Delaware Trial Lawyers Association (President, 2001-2002); American Board of Trial Advocates; The Association of Trial Lawyers of America; Defense Research Institute, Inc. ***PRACTICE AREAS:*** Personal Injury; Litigation; Insurance; Products Liability; Construction Law. ***Email:*** fiobst@ycst.com

DAVID C. McBRIDE, born Columbus, Ohio, June 10, 1948; admitted to bar, 1975, Delaware. *Education:* Georgetown University School of Foreign Service (B.S.F.S., 1971); Emory University (J.D., 1975). Member, Moot Court. Member, Board of Editors, Emory Law Journal, 1974-1975. Author: "Delaware Corporate Law: Judicial Scrutiny of Mergers-The Aftermath of Singer v. The Magnavox Company," 33 The Business Lawyer 2231, 1978; "The Financial Center Development Act: Birth of a Banking Bonanza," 1 Delaware Lawyer 32, 1982; "Conflicting Claims Remain an Issue in Delaware Cases," Nat'l. L.J., Merger and Acquisition Supplement S 14 (Feb. 20, 1989); "Paramount and QVC: An Encore for Mergers and Acquisitions," Fall 1994, Delaware Lawyer (reprinted, 26th Annual Institute on Securities Regulation); "General Comparison of Delaware Fiduciary Duty of Disclosure and Disclosure Obligations Under the Securities Exchange Act of 1934," 9th Annual Corporate Law Institute, Tulane Law School (March 1997); "The Conduct and Timing of Shareholders Meetings: Good Corporate Governance or Entrenchment," ABA Section of Business Law, Spring Meeting (April 1997); "Recent Developments in the Law of Preferred Shares," 11th Annual Corporate Law Institute, Tulane Law School (March 1999). Member, American Law Institute (1997—). Member, Board of Editors, Delaware Lawyer, 1982—. *Member:* Delaware State (Member, General Corporation Law Committee, 1978—; Member, Executive Council of General Corporation Law Committee, 1987-1992 and 1995—; Specialization Committee, 1983—) and American (Member, Section of Business Law, Business and Corporate Litigation Committee) Bar Associations. ***PRACTICE AREAS:*** Litigation; Business Law; Corporate Law; Health Care; Mergers Acquisitions and Divestitures. ***Email:*** dmcbride@ycst.com

RICHARD H. MORSE, born Hartford, Connecticut, November 7, 1948; admitted to bar, 1975, Delaware. *Education:* Cornell University (A.B., 1970); Harvard University (J.D., 1974). Law Clerk, Delaware Superior Court, 1974-1975. Adjunct Professor, Delaware Law School, 1983-1985. Member, Board of Directors, Delaware Volunteer Legal Services, 1993—. *Member:* Delaware State and American Bar Associations; Delaware Trial Lawyers Association (President, 1990-1991); The Association of Trial Lawyers of America; American Board of Trial Advocates. ***PRACTICE AREAS:*** Civil Litigation; Contract Litigation; Tort Liability; Wrongful Death; Intellectual Property Litigation. ***Email:*** rmorse@ycst.com

JOSEPH M. NICHOLSON, born Philadelphia, Pennsylvania, August 3, 1945; admitted to bar, 1972, Pennsylvania; 1975, U.S. Tax Court; 1977, New York; 1978, Delaware. *Education:* Pennsylvania State University (B.A., 1967); Temple University (J.D., 1971); New York University (LL.M. in Taxation, 1974). Member, Board of Editors, Temple Law Review, 1970-1971. Law Clerk to the Honorable Samuel B. Sterrett, U.S. Tax Court, 1974-1976. *Member:* Pennsylvania, New York State, Delaware State and American Bar Associations. ***PRACTICE AREAS:*** Business Law; Taxation; Trusts and Estates; Wills. ***Email:*** jnicholson@ycst.com

BARRY M. WILLOUGHBY, born Wilmington, Delaware, September 21, 1954; admitted to bar, 1979, Delaware. *Education:* University of Delaware (B.A., with high honors and distinction in Political Science, 1976); Dickinson School of Law (J.D., cum laude, 1979). Member, Dickinson Law Review, 1977-1979. *Member:* Delaware State (Member and Chairman, Labor and Employment Law Section, 1988-1989) and American (Member, Section on: Labor and Employment Law) Bar Associations. ***PRACTICE AREAS:*** Management Labor Law; Employment Discrimination; Union Elections; Wrongful Termination Defense; Employer Rights. ***Email:*** willoughby@ycst.com

JOSY W. INGERSOLL, born New York, N.Y.; admitted to bar, 1980, Delaware. *Education:* Douglass College (B.A.cum laude); Temple University (J.D., 1980). Phi Beta Kappa. Editor, Delaware State Bar Association Newsletter, 1984-1986. Secretary and Member, State of Delaware Board of Bar Examiners, 1991—. Member and Chair, Federal Court Rules Committee, 1992-1996. Member, CJA Blue Ribbon Panel, U.S. District Court, District of Delaware, 1992-1995. *Member:* Delaware State (Member, Executive Committee at Large, 1984-1986; Council Member, Intellectual Property Section), American, Federal and International Bar Associations; Delaware Trial Lawyers Association; Society of Insurance Receivers (Board Member). ***PRACTICE AREAS:*** Corporate Law; Corporate Litigation; Business Law; Patent Litigation; Trademark Litigation; Trade Secrets. ***Email:*** jingersoll@ycst.com

ANTHONY G. FLYNN, born Philadelphia, Pennsylvania, May 30, 1952; admitted to bar, 1977, Delaware. *Education:* University of Delaware (B.A., 1973); Catholic University of America (J.D., 1977). Author: Note, "Disqualification of Counsel for the Appearance of Impropriety," 25 Catholic University

(This Listing Continued)

Law Review 363, 1976. Law Clerk to the Honorable Caleb R. Layton, U.S. District Court, District of Delaware, 1977-1979. Counsel to the Governor of Delaware, 1983-1988. Chairman, Delaware Harness Racing Commission, 1988—. Instructor, University of Delaware Environmental Studies Program, 1993-1996. Executive Committee, Delaware Contractor's Association, 1999—. *Member:* Delaware State (Chairman, Environmental Law Section, 1996-1998) and American (Member, Environmental, Energy and Resources Law Section) Bar Associations. ***Email:*** aflynn@ycst.com

JEROME K. GROSSMAN, born St. Louis, Missouri, April 15, 1953; admitted to bar, 1977, Missouri; 1978, District of Columbia; 1980, Delaware. *Education:* Georgetown University (A.B., cum laude, 1974; J.D., 1977). Alpha Sigma Nu. Topics Editor, The Tax Lawyer, 1976-1977. Certified Public Accountant, Missouri, 1979. Author: "RRA '89 Eases Corporate Alternative Minimum Tax Somewhat," 72 J. Tax 140 (1990); "Published Indexes for LIFO - An Analysis of the Proposed Regulations," Inventory Tax Report, March, April, 1982; "Liquidations of LIFO Inventories After the Crude Oil Windfall Profit Tax Act of 1980," 58 TAXES 664, 1980; "Working Capital Requirements - A Solution to Your Accumulated Earnings Tax Problems," Broadcast Financial Journal, September, 1979. Co-Author: "Tax Reform Act of 1986," ALI-ABA Course of Study, 1986; "Tax Reform Act of 1984," ALI-ABA Course of Study, 1984; "Tax Considerations for Investment Real Property Transactions," Delaware State Bar Association Fundamentals of Real Estate Handbook (1988); "Considerations in Buying or Selling a Business in Delaware," National Business Institute, Inc. (1986, 1991-1993). Member, Council of American Institute of Certified Public Accountants, 2000—. *Member:* Delaware State (Member: Tax Section; Chair, 1996-1997; Estates and Trusts Section) and American (Chair, Tax Accounting Problems Committee, 1988-1990; Vice-Chair, 1986-1988; Chair, Inventories Subcommittee, 1982-1986) Bar Associations; Delaware Society of Certified Public Accountants (President, 2000—; President-Elect, 1999-2000; Vice-President, 1998-1999; Secretary, 1997-1998; Council Member, 1985-1988, 1993—; Chair: Tax Committee, 1980-1985; Ethics Committee, 1991-1992). Fellow: American College of Tax Counsel; Estate Planning Council of Delaware. ***PRACTICE AREAS:*** Taxation; Estate Planning; Buying and Selling of Businesses; Mergers, Acquisitions and Divestitures; Business Law. ***Email:*** jgrossman@ycst.com

EUGENE A. DiPRINZIO, born Collingdale, Pennsylvania, February 11, 1956; admitted to bar, 1981, Pennsylvania and Delaware. *Education:* Villanova University (B.S. in Accounting, 1978); Widener University School of Law (J.D., 1980). Member, Moot Court Honor Society. Member, 1979-1982 and Managing Editor, 1979-1980, Delaware Journal of Corporate Law. *Member:* Pennsylvania (Member, Real Property Section), Delaware State (Member, Real and Personal Property Section and Commercial Law Section) and American Bar Associations. Fellow and State Chair, American College of Mortgage Attorneys. ***PRACTICE AREAS:*** Commercial Real Estate; Banks and Banking; Business Law; Leases and Leasing. ***Email:*** ediprinzio@ycst.com

JAMES L. PATTON, JR., born Wilmington, Delaware, September 28, 1956; admitted to bar, 1983, Delaware. *Education:* Davidson College (B.A., 1979); Dickinson School of Law (J.D., 1983). Member, Woolsack Society. Member, Dickinson Law Review, 1981-1983. Member, Appellate Moot Court Board, 1982-1983. Author: "Coal v. Clean Air: A Transboundary Dispute," 86 Dickinson Law Review 753 (1982). Member, Private Panel of Bankruptcy Trustees for the District of Delaware, 1985-1988. Member, Board of Contributors, Fletcher Corporate Bankruptcy, Reorganization and Dissolution (1992, Clark, Boardman, Callaghan). *Member:* Delaware State (Chairman, 1986—, Bankruptcy Law Subcommittee, Commercial Law Section), Federal and American (Member, Business Law Section, Business Bankruptcy Committee, Chapter 11 Subcommittee, Rules Subcommittee) Bar Associations. ***PRACTICE AREAS:*** Bankruptcy; Commercial Workouts; Business Law. ***Email:*** jpatton@ycst.com

ROBERT L. THOMAS, born Wilmington, Delaware, February 24, 1946; admitted to bar, 1971, Delaware. *Education:* Dickinson College (A.B., 1968); Georgetown University (J.D., 1971; LL.M. in Taxation, 1973). Phi Beta Kappa; Omicron Delta Kappa; Pi Gamma Mu; Phi Mu Alpha. Associate Editor, Georgetown Law Journal, 1970-1971. Law Clerk to the Honorable Collins J. Seitz, U.S. Court of Appeals for the Third Circuit, 1971-1972. *Member:* Delaware State (Member, Sections on: Tax; Real Property) and American Bar Associations; American College of Real Estate Lawyers. ***PRACTICE AREAS:*** Closely Held Business Law; Commercial Real Estate Development; Condominium Development; Estate and Gift Taxation; Like Kind Exchanges. ***Email:*** rthomas@ycst.com

WILLIAM D. JOHNSTON, born Aberdeen, Maryland, January 31, 1957; admitted to bar, 1982, Delaware. *Education:* Colgate University (A.B., 1979); Washington & Lee University (J.D., 1982). Phi Delta Phi. Member, Jessup International Moot Court Team, 1980-1981. Member, Washington & Lee Law Review, 1981-1982. Member, Moot Court Board, 1981-1982. Law Clerk to the Honorable Daniel L. Herrmann, Delaware Supreme Court, 1982-1983. *Member:* Delaware State (President) and American (Chairman, Indemnification and Insurance Subcommittee of the Business and Corporate Litigation Committee

(This Listing Continued)

of the Business Law Section) Bar Associations; American Judicature Society. ***PRACTICE AREAS:*** Business Litigation; Chancery Practice; Mergers and Acquisitions; Limited Partnerships. ***Email:*** wjohnston@ycst.com

TIMOTHY J. SNYDER, born Allentown, Pennsylvania, September 29, 1951; admitted to bar, 1981, Pennsylvania; 1982, U.S. Tax Court; 1985, Delaware. *Education:* Widener University (B.S., 1973); Widener University School of Law (J.D., summa cum laude, 1981). Phi Delta Phi. Member: Delaware Journal of Corporate Law, 1980-1981; Member, Moot Court Honor Society, 1979-1981. Attorney Advisor, EB/EO Division, IRS Office of Chief Counsel, Washington, D.C., 1981-1982. Attorney Advisor, IRS District Counsel, Philadelphia, PA, 1982-1985. Monthly Contributor to Delaware Employment Law Letter. *Member:* Delaware State and American (Member, Sections on: Real Property, Probate and Trust Law; Taxation) Bar Associations. ***PRACTICE AREAS:*** Employee Benefits; Nonprofit and Charitable Organizations; Probate; Taxation; Wills. ***Email:*** tsnyder@ycst.com

BRUCE L. SILVERSTEIN, born Philadelphia, Pennsylvania, June 4, 1961; admitted to bar, 1986, Delaware. *Education:* Beaver College (B.A., with honors in Philosophy, 1983); Villanova University (J.D., cum laude, 1986). Order of the Coif. Research/Projects Editor and Member, Villanova Law Review, 1984-1986. Member, Editorial Advisory Board *Judges & Lawyers Business Valuation Update*". Author: "An Analysis of the Constitutional Validity of Delaware's 'Business Combination 'Statute," 13 Delaware Journal of Corporate Law 861 (1988); "Attorney Disqualification For A Conflict Of Interest In Federal Civil Litigation," 30 Villanova Law Review 463 (1985). Associate Member, Delaware Board of Bar Examiners, 1991-1993. *Member:* Delaware State (Member, Corporate Law Council) and American Bar Associations. ***PRACTICE AREAS:*** Corporate Law; Mergers, Acquisitions and Divestitures; Litigation; Appellate Practice; Chancery and Equity. ***Email:*** bsilvesq@ycst.com

WILLIAM W. BOWSER, born Chester, Pennsylvania, August 22, 1957; admitted to bar, 1983, Delaware. *Education:* University of Delaware (B.A., with honors, 1979); Villanova University (J.D., cum laude, 1983). Alpha Kappa Delta. Order of the Coif. Staff Member, Villanova Law Review, 1982-1983. Member, Moot Court Board, 1981-1982. County Attorney, New Castle County, Delaware, 1989-1993. Chair, Delaware Advisory Council on Cancer Incidence & Mortality, 2001—. Member, Gender Commission of Third Circuit Task Force on Equal Treatment in the Courts. Editor, *Delaware Employment Law Letter,* 1995—. *Member:* Delaware State (Chairman, Labor and Employment Law Section, 1997-1998) and American Bar Associations. ***PRACTICE AREAS:*** Collective Bargaining; Employee Drug Testing; Employment Disability Discrimination; Employment Discrimination; Employment Litigation. ***Email:*** wbowser@ycst.com

LARRY J. TARABICOS, born Wilmington, Delaware, March 21, 1960; admitted to bar, 1986, Delaware. *Education:* University of Delaware (B.A.-A.S., 1981); Emory University (J.D., 1985). Recipient, American Jurisprudence Awards for Excellence in Evidence and Ethics. Finalist, Jessup Cup International Law Southeast Regional Moot Court Competition, 1985. *Member:* Delaware State and American Bar Associations. ***PRACTICE AREAS:*** Real Estate Development; Zoning Law; Real Estate Acquisitions; Real Estate Contracts; Leases and Leasing. ***Email:*** ltarabicos@ycst.com

RICHARD A. DiLIBERTO, JR., born Hazleton, Pennsylvania, July 19, 1961; admitted to bar, 1986, Delaware; 1987, New Jersey and Pennsylvania. *Education:* Bloomsburg University of Pennsylvania (B.S.Ed., cum laude with concentration in Psychology, 1982); Widener University School of Law (J.D., cum laude, 1986). Phi Kappa Phi; Phi Alpha Delta. Member, Delaware Journal of Corporate Law, 1984-1986. Editor-in-Chief, Delaware Law Forum, 1985-1986. Member, Moot Court Honor Society, 1984-1986. Author: "An Apple for the Teacher: Educational Malpractice Fails Judicial Test, But Core Problem Remains," 53 Insurance Counsel Journal 215, 1986; "Premenstrual Stress Syndrome Defense: Legal, Medical and Social Aspects," 33 Medical Trial Technique Quarterly 351, 1987; "The Federal and State Constitutionality of Baccalaureate Services in the Public Schools," 15 Ohio Northern University Law Review 527, 1988. Law Clerk to the Honorable Vincent A. Bifferato, Delaware Superior Court, 1986-1987. Member, Delaware State House of Representatives, 1992—; Commission on Delaware Courts 2000 (1995-1996); Delaware Courts Planning Committee (1996—). Member, Richard S. Rodney Inn of American Inns of Court, 1985-1986. Adjunct Professor, Widener University Paralegal Program, 1987-1991. Instructor, Widener University School of Law Intensive Trial Advocacy Program, 1989—. *Member:* Delaware State (Vice-Chairman, Tort and Insurance Practice Section, 1991-1992) and American (Member, Sections on: Tort and Insurance Practice; Litigation) Bar Associations. ***PRACTICE AREAS:*** Personal Injury; Automobile Liability; Trial Practice; Medical Negligence; Medicare Fraud and Abuse. ***Email:*** rdiliberto@ycst.com

MELANIE K. SHARP, born Marlinton, West Virginia, July 31, 1960; admitted to bar, 1986, Delaware. *Education:* University of Delaware (B.A., 1983); Temple University School of Law (J.D., 1986). Law Clerk to the Honorable William T. Allen, Delaware Court of Chancery, 1986-1987. *Member:* Delaware State (Member, Sections on: Litigation and Tort and Insurance Practice) and American (Member, Section on Litigation) Bar Associations; Delaware Trial Lawyers Association; The Association of Trial Lawyers of America;

(This Listing Continued)

YOUNG CONAWAY STARGATT & TAYLOR, LLP, Wilmington—Continued

Richard Rodney Inns of Court. ***PRACTICE AREAS:*** Litigation; Trial Practice; Personal Injury; Products Liability; Medical Malpractice. ***Email:*** msharp@ycst.com

CASSANDRA FALINE KAMINSKI, born Wilmington, Delaware, February 4, 1958; admitted to bar, 1982, Delaware; 1983, Pennsylvania. *Education:* University of Delaware (B.S., magna cum laude, 1979); Dickinson School of Law (J.D., 1982). Kappa Delta Phi; Phi Kappa Phi. Law Clerk to the Honorable Joshua W. Martin and the Honorable Robert C. O'Hara, Delaware Superior Court, 1982-1983. Legal Counsel to the Delaware Claims Association, 1985-1986. *Member:* Delaware State (Member, Section on Worker's Compensation), Pennsylvania and American Bar Associations; Delaware Trial Lawyers Association (Member, Delaware Industrial Accident Board Rules Committee; Defense Counsel of Delaware). ***PRACTICE AREAS:*** Workers Compensation. ***Email:*** ckaminski@ycst.com

RICHARD J. A. POPPER, born Leeds, England, April 24, 1952; admitted to bar, 1977, District of Columbia; 1982, Delaware. *Education:* Tufts University (B.S., magna cum laude, 1974); George Washington University (J.D., with honors, 1977); Georgetown University (M.L.T., 1982). Author: "Post-mortem Planning for Closely-Held Businesses," Estate Planning, July, 1990. *Member:* Delaware State (Member, Estates and Trust Section, Chairperson, 1991-1992; Secretary, Tax Section 1999-2000) and American Bar Associations; The District of Columbia Bar. Fellow, American College of Trust and Estate Counsel. ***PRACTICE AREAS:*** Trusts and Estates; Estate Planning; Estate Administration; Employee Benefits; Taxation. ***Email:*** rpopper@ycst.com

TERESA A. CHEEK, born Havre de Grace, Maryland; admitted to bar, 1988, Delaware; 1997, Maryland. *Education:* University of Delaware (B.A., distinction and honors); Widener University School of Law (J.D., magna cum laude). Phi Kappa Phi. Member, Moot Court Honor Society. Recipient, Zelda K. Herrmann Memorial Cup Award. Research Editor, Delaware Journal of Corporate Law. Member, Industrial Relations Research Association. Board of Editors, Delaware Lawyer. *Member:* Delaware State and American (Sections of Labor and Employment Law, Litigation) Bar Associations. ***PRACTICE AREAS:*** Affirmative Action; Employee Discipline; Employment Discrimination; Employment Termination; Immigration Discrimination. ***Email:*** tcheek@ycst.com

NEILLI MULLEN WALSH, born New Brunswick, New Jersey, June 12, 1962; admitted to bar, 1987, New Jersey; 1989, Delaware. *Education:* University of Notre Dame (B.A., cum laude, 1984); Washington & Lee University (J.D., summa cum laude, 1987). Order of the Coif. Member, National Moot Court Team. Burks Scholar. *Member:* Delaware State and American Bar Associations; American Trial Lawyers Association; Delaware Trial Lawyers Association. ***PRACTICE AREAS:*** Medical Malpractice; Personal Injury; Premises Liability; Products Liability; Torts. ***Email:*** nwalsh@ycst.com

JANET Z. CHARLTON, born New York, New York, September 1, 1964; admitted to bar, 1989, Delaware; 1990, U.S. Court of Appeals, Third Circuit. *Education:* New York University (B.S., 1986); Temple University School of Law (J.D., cum laude, 1989); Temple University (M.B.A., 1991). Recipient: Robert E. Lamberton Award for Excellence in Constitutional Law. *Member:* Delaware State and American (Member, Business Law and Real Property and Probate Sections) Bar Associations. ***PRACTICE AREAS:*** Foreclosures; Workouts; Commercial Litigation; Construction Law; Landlord and Tenant Law. ***Email:*** jcharlton@ycst.com

ROBERT S. BRADY, born Salem, New Jersey, November 20, 1964; admitted to bar, 1990, Delaware. *Education:* Virginia Polytechnic Institute and State University (B.S., 1987); Dickinson School of Law (J.D., cum laude, 1990). Member, Woolsack Honor Society. Recipient, American Jurisprudence Awards in Torts and Constitutional Law. Member, Dickinson Law Review, 1989-1990. *Member:* Delaware State (Member, Sections on: General Corporation Law; Litigation), American (Member, Sections on: Business Law; Litigation) and Federal Bar Associations; American Bankruptcy Institute. ***PRACTICE AREAS:*** Debtor and Creditor Reorganization; Debtor and Creditor Workouts; Debtor and Creditor Bankruptcy. ***Email:*** rbrady@ycst.com

JOEL A. WAITE, born McConnellsburg, Pennsylvania, March 23, 1965; admitted to bar, 1990, Delaware; 1991, Pennsylvania. *Education:* Elizabethtown College (B.A., magna cum laude, 1987); Washington & Lee University School of Law (J.D., summa cum laude, 1990). Phi Alpha Delta. Member, Order of the Coif. Member, Washington & Lee Law Review, 1988-1989. *Member:* Delaware State and American Bar Associations. ***PRACTICE AREAS:*** Bankruptcy; Commercial Law. ***Email:*** jwaite@ycst.com

BRENT C. SHAFFER, born Buffalo, New York, January 6, 1962; admitted to bar, 1987, Maryland; 1995, Delaware. *Education:* Wake Forest University (B.A., magna cum laude, 1984; J.D., cum laude, 1987). Phi Beta Kappa; Omicron Delta Epsilon. Executive Editor, Wake Forest Law Review, 1986-1987. Recipient, Scribes Award, 1987. Author: Chapter 7C, "Subordination, Attornment & Non-Disturbance Agreements," in Current Leasing Law & Techniques, Matthew Bender, 1997; "Handling Assignment Clauses in an Age of Chameleon Entities (Part 1)," 15 The Practical Real Estate Lawyer, Sept. 1999, at 61; "Pre-Foreclosure Lease Defaults," 10 Prob. & Prop. Nov.-Dec. 1996 at 49; "Acquiring Public Use of Roadway by Statute and Prescriptive Easement in North Carolina -- *West v. Slick,*" 21 Wake Forest L. Rev. 807 (1986). Co-Author: "Drafting Letters of Intent for Leases (with forms)," 13 The Practical Real Estate Lawyer, Sept. 1997, at 57; "The Do's & Don'ts for Letters of Intent for Leases," in 2 The Commercial Property Lease (P. Randolph, Jr. ed. 1997). *Member:* Delaware State (Member, Real and Personal Property Section), Maryland State (Member, Section of Real Property, Planning and Zoning) and American (Member, Mortgage and Other Debt Financing Committee; Vice Chair, Commercial Leasing Group, Assignment and Subleasing Committee) Bar Associations. ***PRACTICE AREAS:*** Commercial Real Estate; Leases and Leasing; Affordable Housing; Commercial Mortgages; Real Estate Leasing. ***Email:*** bshaffer@ycst.com

DANIEL P. JOHNSON, born Palo Alto, California, May 13, 1958; admitted to bar, 1987, Pennsylvania; 1988, Delaware; 1993, U.S. Court of Appeals, Third Circuit; 1994, U.S. Supreme Court. *Education:* University of Delaware (B.S., 1981); Delaware Law School of Widener University (J.D., 1986). Phi Alpha Theta. *Member:* Delaware State Bar Association (Chairman, Real and Personal Property Section). ***PRACTICE AREAS:*** Real Estate Law; Zoning Law; Landlord Tenant; General Business. ***Email:*** djohnson@ycst.com

CRAIG D. GREAR, born Springfield, Pennsylvania, March 18, 1964; admitted to bar, 1990, Delaware and Pennsylvania. *Education:* Georgetown University (B.S., 1986; J.D., 1989). Delta Theta Phi. Member and Business Editor, Georgetown Journal of Legal Ethics, 1987-1989. *Member:* Delaware State (Member, Sections on Tax (Chairman, 1998-1999); Trusts and Estates) and American (Member, Sections of Taxation, Real Property, Probate and Trust Law) Bar Associations. ***PRACTICE AREAS:*** Taxation; Business Law; Estate Planning; Partnership Law; Corporate Law. ***Email:*** cgrear@ycst.com

TIMOTHY JAY HOUSEAL, born Erie, Pennsylvania, January 17, 1964; admitted to bar, 1990, Delaware; 1991, Pennsylvania; 1995, U.S. Supreme Court. *Education:* Messiah College (B.A., cum laude, 1986); Dickinson School of Law (J.D., cum laude, 1990). Member: Delta Theta Phi; Christian Legal Society (Director, State Membership); Regional Editor, Covered Events, Defense Research Institute. Articles Editor, Dickinson Law Review, 1989-1990. Author: "Forever A Farm: The Agricultural Conservation Easement in Pennsylvania," 94 Dickinson Law Review 527, 1990 (Cited as "Worth Reading" by the National Law Journal). *Member:* Delaware State, Pennsylvania, Federal and American (Member, Natural Resources and Environmental Law; Tort and Insurance; Litigation Sections) Bar Associations. ***PRACTICE AREAS:*** Environmental Law; Environmental Litigation; Insurance Coverage; Complex Litigation; Admiralty and Maritime Law. ***Email:*** thouseal@ycst.com

BRENDAN LINEHAN SHANNON, born Dallas, Pennsylvania, April 4, 1964; admitted to bar, 1992, Delaware; 1993, Pennsylvania. *Education:* Princeton University (A.B., 1986); William & Mary School of Law (J.D., 1992). Board Editor, William & Mary Law Review, 1991-1992. Author: "The Federal Magistrates Act: A New Article III Analysis for a New Breed of Judicial Officer," 33 Wm. & Mary L. Rev. 253 (1991); "The Administrative Freeze and The Automatic Stay," 2 Journal of Bankruptcy Law and Practice 864 (1992). *Member:* Delaware State and American Bar Associations. ***Email:*** bshannon@ycst.com

MARTIN S. LESSNER, born Wilmington, Delaware, April 15, 1963; admitted to bar, 1992, Delaware; 1993, Pennsylvania. *Education:* Wharton School of the University of Pennsylvania (B.S.E., cum laude, 1985); Villanova University School of Law (J.D., cum laude, 1992). Member, Order of the Coif. Recipient, Herman J. Obert Award for Highest Grade in Corporate Law, 1992. Editor, Villanova Environmental Law Journal, 1991-1992. Author: *General Comparison of Delaware Fiduciary Duty of Disclosure and Disclosure Obligations Under the Securities Act of 1934 (Including the Private Securities Litigation Reform Act of 1995)*, Securities Reform Act Litigation Reporter, Vol. 2, No. 6 March 1997 and Vol. 3, No. 1 April 1997; Bank and Corporate Governance Law Reporter, Vol. 18, Nos. 4 and 5, June and July, 1997, co-authored by David C. McBride; *Leslie Salt Co. v. United States:* Keep The Birds Out of Your Birdbath: It May Be Considered the Jurisdiction of the Army Corps of Engineers as a "Water of the United States," 2 Vill. Envtl. L.J. 463 (1991) (WESTLAW, Journals & Law Reviews database); *Marketable Title Cloud on Lands Containing Any Body of Water,* Performance of Title Insurance Underwriters (Corporate Development Services, Inc., 1991 ed.). Winner. Thirty-Second Annual Villanova Law School Reimel Moot Court Competition, 1992. Law Clerk to the Honorable Carolyn Berger, Delaware Court of Chancery, 1992-1993. *Member:* Delaware State (Member, Sections on: Corporate Law, Computer Law and Technology, Litigation) and American Bar Associations. ***PRACTICE AREAS:*** Corporate Litigation; Commercial Litigation; Civil Appeals; Business Law; Chancery Practice; Federal Civil Practice. ***Email:*** mlessner@ycst.com

PAULINE K. MORGAN, born Pittsburgh, Pennsylvania, September 1, 1956; admitted to bar, 1987, Pennsylvania and New Jersey; 1989, U.S. Court of Appeals, Third Circuit; 1997, Delaware. *Education:* Duquesne University (B.A., cum laude, 1978); University of Pennsylvania Law School (J.D., 1987). *Mem-*

(This Listing Continued)

ber: Philadelphia, Delaware and American Bar Associations; American Bankruptcy Institute; Commercial Law League of America. ***PRACTICE AREAS:*** Bankruptcy; Debtor and Creditor. ***Email:*** pmorgan@ycst.com

C. BARR FLINN, born New Haven, Connecticut, May 4, 1961; admitted to bar, 1993, New York (Not admitted in Delaware). *Education:* Princeton University (A.B., cum laude, 1983); Duke University (J.D./LL.M., with honors, 1991). Duke Law Journal. Moot Court Board. Winner, Irving R. Kaufman, Securities Law Moot Court Competition. Law Clerk to the Honorable William T. Allen, Chancellor, Delaware Court of Chancery, 1991-1992. Associate, Sullivan & Cromwell, New York, New York, 1992-1993, 1995-2000. ***PRACTICE AREAS:*** Corporate Governance Litigation; Commercial Litigation; Antitrust; Privacy Law. ***Email:*** bflinn@ycst.com

SPECIAL COUNSEL

JOHN D. McLAUGHLIN, JR., born Chester, Pennsylvania, July 23, 1953; admitted to bar, 1985, Pennsylvania and U.S. District Court, Eastern District of Pennsylvania; 1986, U.S. Court of Military Appeals and U.S. Court of Appeals, Third Circuit (Not admitted in Delaware). *Education:* University of Virginia (B.A., 1975); University of Southern California; Florida Institute of Technology (M.S., 1979); Widener University (J.D., cum laude, 1985). Phi Delta Phi (Magister, 1984-1985); Phi Kappa Phi. Recipient: Wapner-Newman Prize for Outstanding Pro Bono Advocacy, Authur A. Weeks Outstanding Service Award; Student Bar Association Outstanding Service Award; Executive Director's Award for Excellence in Legal Advocacy, U.S. Trustee Program (1999), Sustained Superior Performance Award, U.S. Department of Justice (1994, 1996, 1997). Co-Author: "Bankruptcy Considerations Regarding Collections of Debts," in *The Legal Issues of Problems Collection in Pennsylvania 55* (National Business Institute, 1991). Member, Bankruptcy Conference of the Eastern District of Pennsylvania. *Member:* Pennsylvania (Unauthorized Practice of Law Committee; Corporate, Banking and Business Law Section) and American Bar Associations. [Capt., U.S. Army, 1975-1988]. ***PRACTICE AREAS:*** Bankruptcy - Chapter 11 (100%, 2500). ***Email:*** jmclaughli@ycst.com

OF COUNSEL

WILLIAM F. TAYLOR, born Wilmington, Delaware, October 3, 1930; admitted to bar, 1954, Delaware and District of Columbia. *Education:* Dickinson College (A.B., 1952); Dickinson School of Law (LL.B., 1954). *Member:* Delaware State and American Bar Associations; American Judicature Society; Federation of Insurance and Corporate Counsel; Association of Defense Trial Attorneys; American Board of Trial Advocates (Advocate; President, Delaware Chapter, 1991-1993). ***PRACTICE AREAS:*** Negligence; Civil Liability; Casualty Insurance; Insurance Arbitration; Drug and Medical Device Defense. ***Email:*** wftayl@aol.com

EDWARD B. MAXWELL, 2ND, born Wilmington, Delaware, May 27, 1937; admitted to bar, 1964, Delaware. *Education:* Bowdoin College (A.B., 1959); Dickinson School of Law (J.D., 1964). Member, Board of Editors, Dickinson Law Review, 1962-1964. Associate Member, 1975-1977 and Member, 1987-1994, Board of Bar Examiners; Associate Member, Delaware Supreme Court Censor Committee, 1976-1980. *Member:* Delaware State (Member, General Corporation Law Committee, 1969-1986; Secretary, General Corporation Law Section, 1982-1985; Council, 1982-1986, 1993-1995) and American (Member, Sections on: Litigation; Business Law) Bar Associations. ***PRACTICE AREAS:*** Corporate Law; Litigation; Business Law; Chancery and Equity. ***Email:*** emaxwell@ycst.com

ASSOCIATES

SEAN M. BEACH, born Syosset, New York, December 17, 1970; admitted to bar, 2000, New Jersey (Not admitted in Delaware). *Education:* Rutgers College (B.A., 1993); Hofstra University (J.D., 2000). Member, Hofstra Labor and Employment Law Journal, 1998-2000. *Member:* New Jersey State and American Bar Associations. ***PRACTICE AREAS:*** Bankruptcy Litigation; Bankruptcy Chapter 11. ***Email:*** sbeach@ycst.com

M. BLAKE CLEARY, born Arlington, Virginia, September 12, 1966; admitted to bar, 1997, Pennsylvania and Delaware. *Education:* University of Virginia (B.A., 1989); Widener University School of Law at Wilmington (J.D., 1996). Member, Moot Court Honor Society. Law Clerk to the Honorable Maurice A. Hartnett, III, Delaware Supreme Court. *Member:* Delaware State and American Bar Associations. ***PRACTICE AREAS:*** Debtor and Creditor Reorganization; Debtor and Creditor Bankruptcy; Debtor and Creditor Workouts. ***Email:*** mbcleary@ycst.com

RICHARD H. CROSS, JR., born Smithtown, New York, December 13, 1965; admitted to bar, 1997, Delaware; 1999, U.S. Court of Appeals, Third Circuit. *Education:* State University of New York at Binghamton (B.A., 1988); College of William & Mary, Marshall-Wythe School of Law (J.D., 1996). Phi Delta Phi. Law Clerk to the Honorable Jerome O. Herlihy, Delaware Superior Court. *Member:* Delaware State and American Bar Associations. ***PRACTICE AREAS:*** Commercial Litigation. ***Email:*** rcross@ycst.com

(This Listing Continued)

DANIELLE B. GIBBS, born Rochester, New York; admitted to bar, 1998, Delaware. *Education:* University of Maryland at College Park (B.A., 1993); University of Baltimore (J.D., 1996). Editor in Chief, University of Baltimore Law Review, 1996. ***PRACTICE AREAS:*** Corporate Litigation; Chancery Practice. ***Email:*** dgibbs@ycst.com

LISA B. GOODMAN, born Wilmington, Delaware, March 12, 1963; admitted to bar, 1994, Delaware; 1995, Pennsylvania. *Education:* West Chester University (B.A., 1983); University of Delaware (M.A., 1985); Widener University School of Law (J.D., magna cum laude, 1994). Winner, Myrna B. Marshall Moot Court Competition, 1992. Delaware Harrisburg Moot Court Competition, 1992. DiBona Moot Court Competition, 1993; Ruby R. Vale Interschool Corporate Moot Court Competition, 1994. Member, Moot Court Honor Society. Recipient, Widener University School of Law Dean's Award, 1994. Research Editor, Delaware Journal of Corporate Law. 1994 Wolcott Fellow - Law Clerk to The Honorable Henry R. Horsey, Delaware Supreme Court. Adjunct Professor, Widener University School of Law, 1994—. Publications: "One Aspect of the Land Use Debate: Cellular Transmission Sites," In Re, Sept. 1996; "Preserving Urban Estates: A Case Study," Delaware Lawyer, Fall 2000. *Member:* Delaware State and American Bar Associations. ***PRACTICE AREAS:*** Zoning, Planning and Land Use; Commercial Real Estate; Leases and Leasing. ***Email:*** lgoodman@ycst.com

EDWIN J. HARRON, born Cape May, New Jersey, December 22, 1968; admitted to bar, 1995, Delaware. *Education:* Temple University (B.A., 1991); Widener University (J.D., cum laude, 1995). Editor-in-Chief, The Widener Law Symposium Journal, 1994-1995. Wolcott Fellow, 1994-1995. Law Clerk to the Honorable Maurice A. Hartnett III, Delaware Supreme Court, 1995-1996. *Member:* Delaware State and American (Member, Natural Resources, Energy and Environment Law Section) Bar Associations. ***PRACTICE AREAS:*** Bankruptcy; General Litigation. ***Email:*** eharron@ycst.com

SCOTT A. HOLT, born Watertown, NY, August 21, 1962; admitted to bar, 1995, Delaware. *Education:* Temple University (B.A., magna cum laude, 1991); Widener University (J.D., cum laude, 1995). Widener Scholar. Member, Delaware Journal of Corporate Law, 1993-1995. Wolcott Fellow - Law Clerk to The Honorable Joseph T. Walsh, Delaware Supreme Court, 1994-1995. *Member:* Delaware State (Chair, Labor and Employment Law Section) and American (Member, Labor and Employment Sections) Bar Associations. ***PRACTICE AREAS:*** Employment Law; Labor Law; Wage and Hour Law. ***Email:*** sholt@ycst.com

CHRISTOPHER C. JONES, born Newport News, Virginia, November 21, 1967; admitted to bar, 1995, Pennsylvania; 1996, North Carolina; 2000, Delaware. *Education:* University of North Carolina, Chapel Hill (B.S., Business Administration, 1990); Widener University School of Law (J.D., 1994); Villanova University School of Law (LL.M., Taxation, 1995). *Member:* Delaware State (Member, Tax Section), Pennsylvania, North Carolina and American (Member, Business and Tax Sections) Bar Associations. ***PRACTICE AREAS:*** Taxation; State Taxation; Local Taxation; Business Law; Corporate Law; Estate Planning. ***Email:*** cjones@ycst.com

EDWARD J. KOSMOWSKI, born Philadelphia, Pennsylvania, December 21, 1966; admitted to bar, 1999, Pennsylvania, New Jersey and Delaware. *Education:* Pennsylvania State University (B.S., 1989); Rutgers University - Camden (J.D., 1999). *Member; Delaware State, Pennsylvania, New Jersey and American Bar Associations.* ***PRACTICE AREAS:*** Bankruptcy. ***Email:*** ekosmowski@ycst.com

MAUREEN D. LUKE, born New York, N.Y.; admitted to bar, 1992, Delaware and Pennsylvania; 1993, U.S. District Court, Eastern District of Pennsylvania; 1994, U.S. District Court, Middle District of Pennsylvania. *Education:* Newton College of the Sacred Heart (B.A.); Villanova University (J.D., 1991). Managing Editor for Student Work, Villanova School of Law Environmental Law Journal. Law Clerk to the Honorable Helen S. Balick, U.S. Bankruptcy Judge for Delaware (retired) 1992-1993. Member, Eastern District of Pennsylvania Bankruptcy Conference, 1993—. ***PRACTICE AREAS:*** Bankruptcy. ***Email:*** mluke@ycst.com

JOSEPH A. MALFITANO, born Niagara Falls, New York, August 9, 1975; admitted to bar, 2000, Delaware. *Education:* State University of New York, College at Buffalo (B.S., 1997); The James E. Beasley School of Law of Temple University (J.D., 2000). Editor-in-Chief, Temple International and Comparative Law Journal, 1999-2000. Author: "Protecting Our Borders: The United States Supreme Court Refuses to Extend Fifth Amendment Privilege to Fear of Foreign Prosecution," 13.3 Temp. Int'l. & Comp. L.J. 1 (2000). *Member:* Delaware State and American Bar Associations. ***PRACTICE AREAS:*** Bankruptcy Chapter 11; Bankruptcy Litigation. ***Email:*** jmalfitano@ycst.com

ADRIA B. MARTINELLI, born Tulsa, Oklahoma, July 13, 1967; admitted to bar, 1998, Virginia; 1999, District of Columbia (Not admitted in Delaware). *Education:* College of William & Mary (B.A., 1989); George Mason University School of Law (J.D., 1997). ***PRACTICE AREAS:*** Labor and Employment; Litigation. ***Email:*** amartinelli@ycst.com

EDMON L. MORTON, born Vienna, Georgia, December 10, 1974; admitted to bar, 1999, Delaware. *Education:* University of Delaware (B.A., 1996);

(This Listing Continued)

YOUNG CONAWAY STARGATT & TAYLOR, LLP, Wilmington—Continued

Wake Forest University (J.D., 1999). Phi Alpha Delta. Member: Moot Court Board; ATLA National Trial Team. *Member:* Delaware State and American Bar Associations. ***PRACTICE AREAS:*** Bankruptcy; Corporate. ***Email:*** emorton@ycst.com

MICHAEL R. NESTOR, born Fayetteville, North Carolina, February 2, 1969; admitted to bar, 1995, Pennsylvania and New Jersey; 1996, Delaware. *Education:* University of Maryland (B.A., 1991); Widener University (J.D., 1995). *Member:* Philadelphia, Pennsylvania, Delaware State and American Bar Associations; American Bankruptcy Institute. ***PRACTICE AREAS:*** Bankruptcy; Debtor and Creditors Rights. ***Email:*** mnestor@ycst.com

JENNIFER R. NOEL, born Reading, Pennsylvania, May 8, 1969; admitted to bar, 2000, Delaware. *Education:* Widener University (B.S., summa cum laude, 1997); Widener University School of Law (J.D., cum laude, 2000). Phi Kappa Phi; Phi Delta Phi; Widener Scholar. Member, Delaware Journal of Corporate Law, 1998-2000. *Member:* Delaware State and American Bar Associations. ***PRACTICE AREAS:*** Taxation; Business Law; Intellectual Property Licensing; Employee Benefits; Tax Exempt Organizations. ***Email:*** jnoel@ycst.com

JOHN J. PASCHETTO, born Long Branch, New Jersey, September 18, 1959; admitted to bar, 1998, Delaware. *Education:* Rutgers University (B.A., summa cum laude, 1981); Harvard University (J.D., cum laude, 1998). Co-Author: "Judicial Interpretation of Corporate Charter Provisions Limiting Director Liability Under 8 Del. C. § 102(b)(7)" in "New Strategies in Contests for Corporate Control, 2000," Practicing Law Institute. ***PRACTICE AREAS:*** Corporate Law; Alternative Entity Law; Chancery Court Litigation. ***Email:*** jpaschetto@ycst.com

ADAM W. POFF, born York, Pennsylvania, March 8, 1975; admitted to bar, 2000, Delaware. *Education:* University of Delaware (B.A., 1997); Villanova University (J.D., 2000). Phi Delta Phi. Staff Member, Villanova Law Review, 1999-2000. Author: "A Tale of Two Curfews (and One City): What Do Two Washington, D.C. Juvenile Curfews Say About the Constitutional Interpretations of District of Columbia courts and the Confusion Over Juvenile Curfews Everywhere?" 46 Villanova Law Review (2000). *Member:* Delaware State and American Bar Associations. ***Email:*** apoff@ycst.com

JOHN W. SHAW, born Gettysburg, Pennsylvania, April 1, 1967; admitted to bar, 1995, Delaware and Pennsylvania; registered to practice before U.S. Patent and Trademark Office. *Education:* Pennsylvania State University (B.S., with honors and High Distinction, 1989); University of Pittsburgh School of Law (J.D., magna cum laude, 1994). Tau Beta Pi. Member, Order of the Coif. Staff Member, University of Pittsburgh Law Review, 1992-1993. Author: "Principled Interpretations of State Constitutional Law - Why Don't The 'Primacy' States Practice What They Preach?" 54 U. Pitt. L. Rev. 1019 (1993). Law Clerk to the Honorable Murray M. Schwartz, Senior Judge, U.S. District Court, District of Delaware, 1994-1995. *Member:* Delaware State and American (Member, Intellectual Property and Business Law) Bar Associations. ***PRACTICE AREAS:*** Intellectual Property Litigation; Federal Civil Litigation; Information Technology; Electronic Commerce. ***Email:*** jshaw@ycst.com

JOANNE C. SPRINGER-MESSICK, born Somerset, England, October 12, 1966; admitted to bar, 2000, Delaware. *Education:* Pennsylvania State University, Harrisburg (B.S., with highest distinction, 1996); Widener University School of Law, Harrisburg (J.D., magna cum laude, 2000). Order of Barristers; Widener Scholar; Phi Kappa Phi. Chief Justice, Nix Scholar. President, Moot Court Honor Society. Recipient: Widener President's Award; Outstanding Minority Scholar; Widener Outstanding Service Award. Author: "Post-Employment Restrictive Covenants and Attorneys," Journal of Individual Employment Rights," Vol. 8, No. 2 (1999-2000). *Member:* Delaware State and American (Member, Sections on: Litigation; Labor and Employment; Torts and Insurance Law and Immigration Law Committee) Bar Associations; American Immigration Lawyers Association. ***PRACTICE AREAS:*** Labor and Employment; Immigration Law. ***Email:*** jspringer@ycst.com

LEON L. VINOKUR, born Wilmington, Delaware, February 17, 1971; admitted to bar, 1997, Pennsylvania and Delaware. *Education:* University of Delaware (B.A., 1993); The Dickinson School of Law (J.D., 1996). Delta Theta Phi; Phi Sigma Pi. *Member:* Delaware State, Pennsylvania and American (Member, Real Property, Probate and Trust Law Section; Business Law Section; Affordable Housing and Community Development Law Forum; Secretary, 1997—) Bar Associations. ***PRACTICE AREAS:*** Zoning, Planning and Land Use; Commercial Real Estate Law; Real Estate Leasing. ***Email:*** lvinokur@ycst.com

NATALIE S. WOLF, born Philadelphia, Pennsylvania, April 15, 1968; admitted to bar, 1993, Delaware. *Education:* University of Delaware (B.A., 1990); Georgetown University Law Center (J.D., 1993). Member, Georgetown Journal of Legal Ethics, 1991-1993. Author: "The Ethical Dilemmas Faced By Attorneys Representing The Mentally Ill In Civil Commitment Proceedings," 6 Georgetown Journal of Legal Ethics, p. 163, 1992. *Member:* Delaware State (Member, Workers Compensation Section) and American Bar Associations; Delaware Trial Lawyers Association; The Association of Trial Lawyers of America; American College of Legal Medicine (Associate Member). ***PRACTICE AREAS:*** Health Care Fraud; Qui Tam Actions; Workers' Compensation Defense; Automobile Accidents and Injuries; Medical Negligence. ***Email:*** nwolf@ycst.com

CHRISTIAN DOUGLAS WRIGHT, born San Antonio, Texas, June 2, 1972; admitted to bar, 1996, Delaware. *Education:* University of Delaware (H.B.A., cum laude, 1993); Duke University School of Law (J.D., 1996). Phi Beta Kappa. Law Clerk to the Honorable William T. Quillen, Judge, Delaware Superior Court, 1996-1997. *Member:* Delaware State and American (Member, Sections on: Business Law, Litigation and Intellectual Property Law Sections) Bar Associations. ***PRACTICE AREAS:*** Corporate Law; Business Law; Intellectual Property; Partnership Law; Chancery Practice. ***Email:*** cwright@ycst.com

SHARON M. ZIEG, born Hartford, Connecticut, August 29, 1972; admitted to bar, 2000, North Carolina (Not admitted in Delaware). *Education:* University of North Carolina, Charlotte (B.S., History, 1994); Wake Forest University School of Law (J.D., 2000). National Moot Court Team. Recipient, American Bankruptcy Institute Certificate of Excellence in Bankruptcy, 2000. Member: Moot Court Board; Gabrielli Family Law Team. *Member:* North Carolina and American Bar Associations. ***PRACTICE AREAS:*** Bankruptcy. ***Email:*** szieg@ycst.com

GEORGETOWN, DELAWARE OFFICE

RESIDENT PARTNER

CRAIG A. KARSNITZ, born Lebanon, Pennsylvania, March 30, 1952; admitted to bar, 1978, Delaware. *Education:* University of Delaware (B.A., 1974); Villanova University (J.D., 1977). Law Clerk to the Honorable John J. McNeilly, Delaware Supreme Court, 1977-1978. Member, Superior Court Rules Committee. *Member:* Delaware State and American Bar Associations; Delaware Trial Lawyers Association; The Association of Trial Lawyers of America. ***PRACTICE AREAS:*** Personal Injury; Workers' Compensation. ***Email:*** ckarsnitz@ycst.com

RESIDENT ASSOCIATE

VIVIAN MEDINILLA LONGO, born Guatemala City, Guatemala, July 4, 1966; admitted to bar, 1993, Delaware; 1994, Pennsylvania and U.S. District Court, District of Delaware; 1999, U.S. Supreme Court. *Education:* University of Delaware (B.S., 1988); Widener University School of Law (J.D., cum laude, 1993). Visiting Assistant Professor of Law, Widener University School of Law, 1995-1996. Member: Board of Directors, CLASI, 1997-1999; Judicial Appointments Nominating Committee, 1999-2000; Delaware Commission for Women. *Member:* Delaware State (Member, Executive Committee, 1996-1999) and American Bar Associations. Fellow: Delaware Bar Foundation. (Resident). ***LANGUAGES:*** Spanish. ***PRACTICE AREAS:*** Personal Injury; Workers' Compensation; Criminal Defense; Medical Malpractice. ***Email:*** vlongo@ycst.com

ZUCKERMAN SPAEDER LLP

ONE COMMERCE CENTER
1201 ORANGE STREET, SUITE 650
P.O. BOX 1028
WILMINGTON, DELAWARE 19899
Telephone: 302-427-0400
Fax: 302-427-8242
Email: counsel@zuckerman.com

Washington, D.C. Office: 1201 Connecticut Avenue, N.W., Suite 1200. Telephone: 202-778-1800. Fax: 202-822-8106.

Miami, Florida Office: 201 South Biscayne Boulevard, Suite 900. Telephones: 305-358-5000; Broward County: 305-523-0277. Fax: 305-579-9749.

Ft. Lauderdale, Florida Office: One East Broward Boulevard, Suite 700. Telephone: 954-356-0463. Fax: 954-356-0406.

Tampa, Florida Office: East Kennedy Boulevard, Suite 3140. Telephone: 813-221-1010. Fax: 813-223-7961.

Baltimore, Maryland Office: Suite 2440, 100 East Pratt Street. Telephone: 410-332-0444. Fax: 410-659-0436.

New York, N.Y. Office: 1114 Avenue of the Americas, 27th Floor, Grace Building. Telephone: 212-479-6500. Fax: 212-479-6512.

Complex Civil Litigation, Business Restructuring and Reorganization.

FIRM PROFILE: Handling matters throughout the country and abroad, before federal and state courts and federal agencies and departments, Zuckerman Spaeder LLP has more than 70 lawyers in offices in Baltimore, Miami, New York, Tampa, Washington and Wilmington. The firm litigates white collar criminal defense and

(This Listing Continued)

federal enforcement actions, and prosecutes and defends complex civil actions, including commercial litigation, securities fraud class actions, malpractice litigation, antitrust, tax, and Native American land claims. Zuckerman Spaeder's health care lawyers handle regulatory, fraud and abuse, antitrust, compliance, and licensing issues, as well as litigation. The firm's creditor-debtor rights practice counsels troubled companies and manages major bankruptcy reorganizations and out-of-court workouts. The business and tax attorneys at the firm focus on corporate transactions including the formation, sale, and merger of business entities; real estate transactions; tax counseling; and estate planning.

RESIDENT MEMBER

THOMAS G. MACAULEY, born Bridgeport, Connecticut, August 25, 1966; admitted to bar, 1995, Delaware. *Education:* University of Virginia (B.A., 1988); Tulane Law School (J.D., magna cum laude, 1994). Editor-in-Chief, Tulane Law Review, 1993-1994. Law Clerk to Judge John M. Duhé, Jr., U.S. Court of Appeals for the Fifth Circuit, 1994-1995. Associate, Skadden, Arps, Slate, Meagher & Flom LLP, 1995-2000. *Member:* Delaware State and American Bar Associations; American Bankruptcy Institute. ***PRACTICE AREAS:*** Business Reorganization; Creditors Rights; Complex Civil Litigation; Corporate Governance. ***Email:*** tmacauley@zuckerman.com

(For complete biographical data on other personnel, see Professional Biographies at Washington, D.C. Office)

WHITTINGTON & AULGUR

Established in 1984

2979 BARLEY MILL ROAD

YORKLYN, DELAWARE 19736

Telephone: 302-235-5800; 1-800-441-9459

Telecopier: 302-235-5900

Email: wa@delawarelawyer.com

Odessa, Delaware Office: Suite 110, Odessa Professional Park, 313 North DuPont Highway, 19730. Telephone: 302-378-1661. Fax: 302-378-1645.

Real Estate, Foreclosure, Bankruptcy, Corporate, Environmental, Litigation, Zoning, Business Law, Condominium Association Law, Wills and Probate, Trust and Estates, Arbitration and Mediation.

MEMBERS OF FIRM

THOMAS D. WHITTINGTON, JR., born Wilmington, Delaware, February 14, 1943; admitted to bar, 1971, Delaware and Pennsylvania. *Education:* University of Delaware (B.S., 1969); University of Pittsburgh (J.D., 1971). Deputy Attorney General, State of Delaware, Counsel to the Coastal Zone Industrial Control Board and Department of Natural Resources and Environmental Control, 1971-1973. *Member:* Delaware (Member, Committees on: Corporation Law, 1979—; Real and Personal Property), Pennsylvania and American Bar Associations. ***PRACTICE AREAS:*** Corporate Formation; Real Estate Development; Condominium Association Law; Residential Real Estate; Residential Real Estate Development; Condemnation; Arbitration; Mediation. ***Email:*** tdw@delawarelawyer.com

(This Listing Continued)

ROBERT T. AULGUR, JR., born St. Louis, Missouri, May 10, 1951; admitted to bar, 1977, Delaware; 1978, U.S. Court of Military Appeals; 1982, U.S. Supreme Court; 1983, U.S. Court of Appeals, Third Circuit. *Education:* Defense Language Institute (Japanese, 1971); Ball State University (B.A., cum laude, 1973); Syracuse University (J.D., 1976). Law Clerk, Superior Court State of Delaware, 1976-1977. Chief Attorney for Delaware House of Representatives, 1982-1983. *Member:* Delaware Bar Association. [CDR, JAGC, USNR, 1977-1993]. (Resident, Odessa, Delaware Office). ***PRACTICE AREAS:*** Bankruptcy; Real Estate Foreclosure. ***Email:*** tiernon@msn.com

ASSOCIATE

KRISTI J. DOUGHTY, born Lexington, Nebraska, January 23, 1962; admitted to bar, 1987, New Jersey, Pennsylvania and U.S. Court of Appeals, Third Circuit; 2000, Delaware. *Education:* University of Montana (B.S., with high honors, 1984); Rutgers University Law School, Camden (J.D., 1987). Alpha Lambda Delta; Beta Gamma Sigma; Phi Alpha Delta. Best Oral Argument, Tax Moot Court. Law Clerk to the Honorable Graham T. Ross, J.S.C., Somerset County, Somerville, New Jersey, 1987-1988. ***PRACTICE AREAS:*** Bankruptcy; Foreclosures. ***Email:*** kdoughty@aulgur.com

REPRESENTATIVE CLIENTS: Home Builders Association of Delaware, Inc.; Artesian Water Company; Federal National Mortgage Association; Occidental Chemical Corp.; General Motors Corp.; Wilmington Trust Company; PNC Mortgage Servicing; Associated International Insurance Co.; Fleet Mortgage Corp.; GE Capital Mortgage Services, Inc.

APPROVED ATTORNEYS FOR: Transnation Title Insurance Co.; Atlantic Title & Abstract Company; First American Title Insurance Co.; Ticor Title Insurance Co.; Meridian Title Insurance Co.

THE ABELSON LAW FIRM

Established in 1982

1700 K STREET, N.W.

SUITE 700

WASHINGTON, D.C. 20006

Telephone: 202-331-0600

1-888-797-4242

Fax: 202-429-9088

URL: http://www.abelsonlaw.com

Email: maa@abelsonlaw.com

URL: http://www.lawyers.com/abelsonlaw

Baltimore, Maryland Office: Harbor Place Tower, 111 South Calvert Street, Suite 2700, 21202. Telephone: 1-888-797-4242.

Boston, Massachusetts Office: 77 North Washington Street, 02114-1908. Telephone: 1-888-797-4242.

Pittsburgh, Pennsylvania Office: 510 Third Avenue, 15219. Telephone: 1-888-797-4242.

Philadelphia, Pennsylvania Office: 510 Walnut Street, 19106. Telephone: 1-888-797-4242.

Plaintiffs Trial Practice. Negligence, Products Liability, Medical Malpractice, Wrongful Death, Insurance Bad Faith, Birth Trauma, Automobile Accidents.

FIRM PROFILE: Offering over twenty-five years of experience, The Abelson Law Firm has limited its practice to the victims of most serious personal injuries, medical malpractice, motor vehicle collisions, products liability and issues involving insurance bad faith.

MICHAEL A. ABELSON, born Wilkes-Barre, Pennsylvania, October 3, 1949; admitted to bar, 1974, Massachusetts; 1975, Pennsylvania and U.S. District Court, District of Massachusetts; 1977, District of Columbia, Maryland and U.S. District Court for the District of Columbia; 1984, U.S. District Court for the District of Maryland. *Education:* Pennsylvania State University (B.A., 1971); New England Law School (J.D., cum laude, 1974). Recipient, Trial Lawyer of the Year Award for Washington, D.C., 1992. Selected by Peers as one of Washington's Top Lawyers, Washingtonian Magazine, August, 1989. *Member:* The District of Columbia Bar; Maryland State, Pennsylvania and Massachusetts Bar Associations; Trial Lawyers Association of Washington, D.C. (Member, Board of Governors, 1980—); The Association of Trial Lawyers of America (State Delegate, 1982-1987; Sustaining Member). ***REPORTED CASES:*** McNeal v. Hi-Lo Powered Scaffolding, 836 F.2d 637, 266 US App. DC 473, 1988; Foshee v. Consolidated Rail Corporation, 849 F.2d 657, 270 US App. DC 326, 1988. ***PRACTICE AREAS:*** Negligence; Products Liability; Medical Malpractice. ***Email:*** maa@abelsonlaw.com

LAW OFFICE OF ADELE L. ABRAMS, P.C.

WASHINGTON, D.C.

(See Beltsville, Maryland)

National Safety Law Practice, OSHA Regulations, Employment Law, Wrongful Termination, Employment Discrimination, Government Regulations, Lobbying, Legislative Practice, Government Relations, Public Policy, Mine Safety Law, Divorce, Wills, Probate.

THE ACKERSON GROUP

CHARTERED

1666 K STREET, N.W., SUITE 1010

WASHINGTON, D.C. 20006

Telephone: 202-833-8833

202-833-8831

URL: http://www.ackersonlaw.com

Email: ackerson@ackersonlaw.com

URL: http://www.lawyers.com/ackerson

Litigation, Plaintiff Litigation, International, Legislative, Agricultural Law.

FIRM PROFILE: The Firm's strengths include complex financial, commercial and real estate litigation; class actions, international investment and contractual disputes; constitutional rights and human rights issues; property rights; federal regulatory and administrative proceedings; congressional and state legislative matters; international trade and development law; U.S. and international agricultural law, and cooperative, corporation and tax law. The Firm's attorneys have represented the interests of clients in federal and state courts throughout the United States, before international tribunals, and in more than 20 countries on four continents.

(This Listing Continued)

NELS ACKERSON, born Indianapolis, Indiana, April 12, 1944; admitted to bar, 1971, Indiana; 1989, U.S. Supreme Court; 1985, District of Columbia. *Education:* Purdue University (B.S., with distinction, 1967); Harvard University (Master in Public Policy, 1971); Harvard Law School (J.D., cum laude, 1971). Member, Board of Editors, Harvard Law Review, 1968-1970. Chief Counsel, United States Senate Subcommittee on the Constitution, Committee on the Judiciary, 1976-1979. Nominee for Congress of the United States from Indiana, 1980. Managing Partner, Sidley & Austin & Naquib, Cairo, Egypt, 1982-1984. Chairman, Board of Directors, Class Corridors, LLC. *Member:* District of Columbia Bar; American Bar Association (Member, Sections on: Business Law; International Law and Litigation); The Association of Trial Lawyers of America; International Right-of-Way Association; Center for National Policy; American Agricultural Law Association; National Policy Association (Member, Food and Agriculture Committee). ***REPORTED CASES:*** CSX Transportation Inc.v. Clark, 646 N.E.2d 1003 (Ind. Ct. App. 1995); Hefty v. All Other Memb ers of the Certified Settlemnet Class, 680 N.E.2d 843 (Ind. 1997); Consolidated Rail Corp. v. Lewellen, 682 N.E.2d 779 (Ind. 1997); Calumet National Bank v. American Tel. & Tel. Co., 682 N.E.2d 785 (Ind. 1997); Tazlan v. Cline, 686 N.E.2d 95 (ind. 1997); State ex rel. Firestone v. Parke Circuit Court, 621 N.E.2d 1113 (Ind. 1993); Becker v. Surface Transp. Bd., 132 F.3d 60 (D.C. Cir. 1997); Fritsch v. Interstate Commerce Commission, 59 F.3d 248 (1995); Consoltdated Rail Corp. v. Lewellen, 666 N.E.2d 958 (Ind. App. 1996); RLTD v. Surface Transp. Bd., 166 F.3d 808 (6th Cir. 1999); Clark v. CSX Transportation, Inc., 737 N.E.2d 752, 2000 WL 1512364 (Ind. App. 2000); Hash v. United States, 2000 WL 1460801; Schneider v. United State, 197 F.R.D. 397, 2000 WL 1481128 (D. Neb. 2000); Bywaters v. United States, 196 F.R.D. 458, 2000 WL 1481126 (E.D. Tex. 2000); Swisher v. United States, 189 F.R.D. 638 (D. Kan. 1999); Birt v. Surface Transp. Bd., 90 F.3d 580 (D.C. Cir. 1996); Jost v. Surface Transp. Bd., 194 F.3d 79 (D.C. Cir. 1999); Louisiana Federal Land Bank Association v. Farm Credit Admin., et. al. and First South Production Credit Assoc., 1:00CV1582/RU (D.D.C., filed 2001). ***PRACTICE AREAS:*** Litigation; Class Actions; International; Constitutional; Agricultural Law; Legislative. ***Email:*** nackerson@ackersonlaw.com

CECILIA FEX, born Stockholm, Sweden, December 23, 1957; admitted to bar, 1991, Maryland; 1992, District of Columbia. *Education:* Montgomery College, School of Nursing (A.A., 1982); University of Maryland (B.A., summa cum laude, 1988); Harvard University Law School (J.D., 1991). Instructor, Lawyering Skills Program, The Catholic University of America, Columbus School of Law, 1994-1996. Associate: Koonz, McKenney, Johnson & Regan, 1991-1994; Proskauer, Rose, 1996-1998. *Member:* District of Columbia Bar. ***LANGUAGES:*** Swedish. ***PRACTICE AREAS:*** Complex Litigation; Class Actions; Appellate Practice. ***Email:*** cfex@ackersonlaw.com

KATHLEEN CLUBB KAUFFMAN, born Minneapolis, Minnesota, May 19, 1954; admitted to bar, 1980, District of Columbia; 1985, Illinois; 1991, California. *Education:* University of Minnesota; University of Kansas (B.A., 1976; J.D., 1979). Clerk, Honorable John D. Butzner (U.S. Court of Appeals for the Fourth Circuit, 1979-1980). CEO, Starr Litigation, 1993-2000. *Member:* The District of Columbia Bar; American Bar Association. ***PRACTICE AREAS:*** Administrative Law; Litigation; Class Actions; Real Estate; Antitrust; Business Fraud; Complex Commercial Litigation. ***Email:*** kkauffman@ackersonlaw.com

ELAINE A. PANAGAKOS, born New York, N.Y., August 23, 1962; admitted to bar, 1988, New York; 1989, District of Columbia. *Education:* Yale University (B.A., cum laude, 1984); Duke University (J.D., with honors, 1987). Editor and Senior Editor, Law and Contemporary Problems, 1985-1987. ***PRACTICE AREAS:*** Commercial Litigation; Class Actions; Franchise Litigation. ***Email:*** epanagakos@ackersonlaw.com

WHITNEY ADAMS

WASHINGTON, D.C.

(See McLean, Virginia)

Business, Securities, Employment, Personal Injury and Crisis Management Litigation, Government Contracts and Government Relations.

ADDUCI, MASTRIANI & SCHAUMBERG, L.L.P.

Established in 1981

1200 SEVENTEENTH STREET, N.W., FIFTH FLOOR
WASHINGTON, D.C. 20036-3006
Telephone: 202-467-6300
Telefax: 202-466-2006
Email: ams@adduci.com
URL: http://www.adduci.com

International Trade, Customs, Trade Regulation, Unfair Competition, Patent, Trademark and Copyright, and Government Contract Law.

FIRM PROFILE: Since 1981, Adduci, Mastriani & Schaumberg, L.L.P. has provided thorough, expert counsel to meet clients' unique legal needs in international trade, customs, intellectual property, government contracts and federal court litigation and appeals. We specialize in pursuing clients' legal actions effectively and quickly before federal regulatory agencies and tribunals including: the U.S. International Trade Commission, the U.S. Department of Commerce, the Office of the U.S. Trade Representative, the U.S. Patent and Trademark Office, the U.S. Customs Service and the U.S. Court of Federal Claims.

Small teams of experienced partners and associates listen carefully to clients' concerns, respond promptly to client inquiries, provide substantial hands-on support, offer a realistic legal evaluation and develop cost-effective strategies and solutions.

V. JAMES ADDUCI, II, born Dayton, Ohio, July 6, 1950; admitted to bar, 1975, Illinois; 1976, District of Columbia; 1982, U.S. District Court, Eastern District of Virginia and U.S. Court of International Trade; 1993, U.S. Supreme Court and U.S. Court of Appeals for the Federal Circuit. *Education:* University of Colorado (B.A., 1972); John Marshall Law School (J.D., 1975). Author: "Unfair Import Competition: Section 337 of The Tariff Act of 1930, as Amended By The Trade Act of 1974," Law and Practice of United States Regulation of International Trade Oceana Publications, June, 1987; "Hi-Tech's New Best Friend: Section 337 and the Enforcement of the U.S. Intellectual Property Rights Against Importers of Hi-Tech Merchandise", North America Free Trade & Investment Report, Vol. 10, No. 3 (2000); "New U.S. Trade Act to Help Caribbean Nations Overcome NAFTA Disadvantages," North American Free Trade and Investment Report, Vol. 10. No. 10 (May 31, 2000). Attorney, U.S. International Trade Commission, 1975-1977. Member, U.S. Delegation to the Multilateral Trade Negotiations, Geneva, Switzerland, 1977-1978. *Member:* District of Columbia Bar; Virginia State Bar; Federal Circuit (Chairman, International Trade Section), Illinois State, Federal (Member, International Law and Customs Section) and American (Member, International Law Section) Bar Associations; American Intellectual Property Law Association. ***PRACTICE AREAS:*** International Trade Regulation; Imports and Exports; Customs; Litigation. ***Email:*** adduci@adduci.com

LOUIS S. MASTRIANI, born New York, N.Y., July 9, 1950; admitted to bar, 1976, California; 1978, Wisconsin; 1981, U.S. Court of International Trade; 1982, U.S. Court of Appeals for the Federal Circuit; 1984, District of Columbia; 1986, New York; 1990, U.S. Court of Appeals, Ninth Circuit; 1991, U.S. Claims Court; 1992, U.S. Supreme Court; 1994, U.S. Court of Appeals, Eleventh Circuit; 1995, U.S. Court of Appeals, Fourth Circuit. *Education:* Marquette University (B.A., 1972); Whittier College (J.D., 1976). Author: "Section 337 Practice: Recent Trends and Developments," New Matter, Vol. 11, No. 3, 1986-1988; "Antidumping Law: Issues and Applications in High Tech Industries," Computer Law Reporter, Vol. 13, Nos. 2 & 3, April/May, 1991; "U.S. Administrative Procedures for Protection from Unfair Import Competition: The Revitalization of Section 337," and "United States Antidumping Law and Practice: The Impact of Implementation of the GATT Uruguay Round Agreement," Symposium on U.S. Trade Regulation, Stockholm, Sweden, February 1995; "Turning the Tables: How Japanese Companies Are Using the U.S. Legal System to Their Advantage," Journal of Japanese Trade & Industry, Vol. 16, No. 2 (March 1997). Bi-National Panelist and Chairman, North American Free Trade Agreement, 1996—. Legal Advisor to Vice Chairman, 1977, Senior Investigative Attorney, U.S. International Trade Commission, 1978-1981. *Member:* The District of Columbia Bar; State Bar of California; Federal Circuit, New York State and American Bar Associations. ***PRACTICE AREAS:*** Customs Law; International Trade Regulation; Antidumping; Customs; Intellectual Property and Unfair Competition; Litigation; Appellate Practice. ***Email:*** mastriani@adduci.com

TOM M. SCHAUMBERG, born Amsterdam, Holland, May 29, 1938; admitted to bar, 1964, Ohio; 1968, District of Columbia; 1972, U.S. Supreme Court; 1975, Maryland; 1983, U.S. Court of Appeals for the Federal Circuit. *Education:* University of Paris, France and Yale University (B.A., 1960); Harvard University (LL.B., 1963). Post Graduate study, University of Frankfurt, Germany, 1963-1964. Author: "United States Prohibitions Against Unfair Imports - A Brief Overview of Practice Under Section 337," The California

(This Listing Continued)

International Practitioner, Vol. 10, No. 2, 2000; "A Revitalized Section 337 To Prohibit Unfairly Traded Imports," Journal of the Patent and Trademark Office Society, Vol. 77, No. 3, March 1995; "The ITC as a Forum for Protecting Intellectual Property Rights," American Intellectual Property Law Association Selected Legal Papers, Vol. VI, No. 2, December 1988; "Section 337 of the Tariff Act of 1930 as an Antitrust Remedy," The Antitrust Bulletin, Vol. XXVII, No. l, Spring, 1982. Attorney, Merger Division, Bureau of Restraint of Trade, Federal Trade Commission, 1964-1967; Panelist, United States-Canada Free-Trade Agreement, 1990-1995. *Member:* District of Columbia Bar; Federal and American Bar Associations; International Trade Commission Trial Lawyers Association (President, 1984-1985; Member, Executive Committee, 1987—). ***LANGUAGES:*** German, French, Dutch. ***PRACTICE AREAS:*** International Trade; Intellectual Property Litigation. ***Email:*** schaumberg@adduci.com

BARBARA A. MURPHY, born Boston, Massachusetts, September 10, 1957; admitted to bar, 1982, District of Columbia; 1984, U.S. Court of International Trade and U.S. Court of Appeals for the Federal Circuit; 1985, U.S. District Court for the District of Columbia; 1991, U.S. Court of Federal Claims. *Education:* Dartmouth College (B.A., 1979); George Washington University (J.D., 1982). Member, George Washington Journal of International Law & Economics, 1980-1982. Author: "Section 337 Practice: Recent Trends and Developments," New Matter, Vol. 11, No. 3, 1986. *Member:* District of Columbia Bar; American Bar Association; ITC Trial Lawyers Association (President, 1997-1998; Executive Committee, 1990—); International Trademark Association; Dartmouth Lawyers Association (President, 1998-2000). ***PRACTICE AREAS:*** Antidumping; International Trade Regulation; Unfair Competition; Intellectual Property. ***Email:*** murphy@adduci.com

HARVEY B. FOX, born Baltimore, Maryland, November 19, 1941; admitted to bar, 1966, Maryland; 1969, U.S. Supreme Court; 1981, U.S. Court of International Trade; 1983, District of Columbia; 1990, U.S. Court of Appeals for the Federal Circuit; 2000, U.S. District Court for the District of Columbia. *Education:* University of Baltimore School of Law (J.D., 1964). President, Customs Lawyers Association, 1989-1995. Attorney, United States Customs Service, 1966-1973. Director: Regulations and Legal Publications Division, 1973-1977; Entry Procedures and Penalties Division, 1977-1980; Classification and Value Division, 1980-1986; Office of Regulations and Rulings, 1986-1995. *Member:* District of Columbia Bar; American and Federal Bar Associations. ***PRACTICE AREAS:*** Customs and International Trade Law; Domestic and Foreign Administrative Law; International Business; Federal Practice Litigation. ***Email:*** fox@adduci.com

GREGORY C. ANTHES, born Fond Du Lac, Wisconsin, August 16, 1961; admitted to bar, 1990, Maryland and U.S. Court of Appeals for the Federal Circuit; 1991, District of Columbia and U.S. Court of International Trade; 1994, U.S. Supreme Court; 1995, U.S. District Court, District of Maryland. *Education:* Marquette University; University of Wisconsin-Oshkosh (B.S., History and English, 1984); George Washington University (J.D., 1990). ***PRACTICE AREAS:*** Antidumping; Appellate Practice; International Trade Regulation; Customs. ***Email:*** anthes@adduci.com

STEVEN E. ADKINS, born Georgia, August 30, 1962; admitted to bar, 1991, Virginia; 1993, Texas; 1999, District of Columbia; U.S. Supreme Court, U.S. Court of Appeals for the Fourth, Fifth and Federal Circuits; U.S. District Court, Eastern District of Virginia and Western District of Texas; U.S. Court of International Trade. *Education:* Georgia College (B.A., with honors, 1984); University of Cambridge, England; University of Richmond (J.D., 1991). Phi Delta Phi; Order of the Barrister. *Member:* American Bar Association; Virginia State Bar; State Bar of Texas. ***PRACTICE AREAS:*** International Trade; Intellectual Property Litigation; Insurance Coverage Litigation; Complex Commercial Litigation; Reinsurance; Appellate Litigation. ***Email:*** adkins@adduci.com

WILL E. LEONARD, born Shreveport, Louisiana, January 18, 1935; admitted to bar, 1958, Louisiana; 1962, U.S. Supreme Court; 1963, District of Columbia; 1982, U.S. Court of International Trade and U.S. Court of Appeals for the Federal Circuit. *Education:* Tulane University of Louisiana (B.A., 1956; LL.B., 1958); Harvard University (LL.M., 1966). Phi Beta Kappa; Omicron Delta Kappa. Member, Moot Court, 1958. Co-Author: "Section 337: A Familiar Road Into Strange Country," AIPLA Quarterly Journal, Vol. 12 No. 4, 1984; "The Metamorphosis of the U.S. International Trade Commission Under the Trade Act of 1974," Virginia Journal of International Law, Vol. 16, 1976. Legislative Assistant to Senator Russell B. Long, 1960-1966. Professional Staff Member, U.S. Senate Committee on Finance, 1966-1968. Commissioner, 1968-1977 and Chairman, 1975-1976, U.S. International Trade Commission. Former Chairman, Standing Committee on Customs, American Bar Association. *Member:* The District of Columbia Bar; Louisiana State Bar Association. ***PRACTICE AREAS:*** International Trade; Customs Law; Government Relations.

JAMES TAYLOR, JR., born Florence, South Carolina, 1942; admitted to bar, 1973, District of Columbia; 1977, U.S. Court of International Trade; 1978, U.S. Supreme Court; 1982, U.S. Court of Appeals for the Federal Circuit. *Education:* University of the South (B.A., cum laude, 1965); Institute for American Universities, Aix-en-Provence, France, 1963-1964; Georgetown University (J.D., 1973). Editor, Law and Policy in International Business, 1973.

(This Listing Continued)

Member: The District of Columbia Bar; Federal and American Bar Associations. ***LANGUAGES:*** French, German and Italian. ***PRACTICE AREAS:*** International Transactions; International Trade; Customs; Government Relations.

MICHAEL L. DOANE, born Columbia, Missouri, April 30, 1964; admitted to bar, 1990, Washington; 1992, Ohio; 1993, District of Columbia; 1998, U.S. Supreme Court. *Education:* Kent State University (B.A., cum laude, 1986); University of Washington (M.A., 1990; J.D., with honors, 1990); Georgetown University (LL.M., with distinction, 1994). Author: "Trips and International Intellectual Property Protection in an Age of Advancing Technology," The American University Journal of International Law and Policy, Vol. 9, No. 2 (Winter 1994); "Green Light Subsides: Technology Policy in International Trade," Syracuse Journal of International Law and Commerce, Vol. 21 (Spring 1995). *Member:* Washington State, Ohio State and American (Member, International Law and Intellectual Property Protection Sections) Bar Associations; ITC Trial Lawyers Association. ***PRACTICE AREAS:*** International Trade Regulation; Corporate and Business Transactions; Intellectual Property; Litigation. ***Email:*** doane@adduci.com

CARIDAD BERDUT, born Havana, Cuba, August 22, 1959; admitted to bar, 1987, Florida; 1991, U.S. Court of International Trade and U.S. Court of Appeals for the Federal Circuit; 2000, U.S. Supreme Court (Not admitted in District of Columbia). *Education:* Florida International University (B. A., 1983); Washington College of Law (J.D., 1986). Senior Attorney Advisor, Office of Regulation and Rulings, U.S. Customs Service. Assistant District Counsel, U.S. Immigration and Naturalization Service. *The American Journal of International Law and Policy, 1985-1986.* ***LANGUAGES:*** Spanish. ***PRACTICE AREAS:*** Customs; International Trade Regulation. ***Email:*** berdut@adduci.com

MAUREEN F. BROWNE, born Washington, D.C., July 6, 1967; admitted to bar, 1992, Maryland; 1993, U.S. District Court, District of Maryland; 1993, U.S. Court of Appeals, 4th Circuit; 1994, District of Columbia; 2000, U.S. Court of Appeals, D.C. Circuit, U.S. Court of Appeals, Federal Circuit and U.S. Court of International Trade. *Education:* College of the Holy Cross (B.A., 1989); George Washington University (J.D., 1992). Editor-in-Chief, Commercial Protection Reporting Service, 1991-1992. Intern, The Honorable James S. McAuliffe, Jr., Circuit Court for Montgomery County, 1990. Mediator, Superior Court for the District of Columbia. *Member:* Montgomery County and American Bar Associations; Maryland State sBar Association, Inc.; District of Columbia Bar; ITC Trial Lawyers Association. ***LANGUAGES:*** Spanish. ***PRACTICE AREAS:*** Intellectual Property; Commercial; Trade Regulation. ***Email:*** browne@adduci.com

MICHAEL G. McMANUS, born Long Island, New York, October 29, 1969; admitted to bar, 1994, Georgia; registered to practice before U.S. Patent and Trademark Office (Not admitted in District of Columbia). *Education:* University of Georgia (B.A., Political Science, 1991); University of Arkansas School of Law (J.D., 1993); Georgia State University (B.S., Biology, 1996; M.S., Chemistry, 1998). Former Attorney-Advisor, Office of Regulations and Rulings, United States Customs Service. *Member:* State Bar of Georgia. ***PRACTICE AREAS:*** Customs Law; International Trade Regulation; Patent Litigation.

DAVID F. NICKEL, born Washington, D.C., March 3, 1975; admitted to bar, 2000, Maryland (Not admitted in District of Columbia). *Education:* Princeton University (B.A., 1997); George Washington University (J.D., 2000). *Member:* Maryland State Bar Association, Inc.; American Bar Association. ***LANGUAGES:*** French. ***PRACTICE AREAS:*** Intellectual Property; International Trade Regulation; Litigation.

SARAH E. HAMBLIN, born Montreal, Quebec, Canada, March 28, 1969; admitted to bar, 2000, Virginia; registered to practice before U.S. Patent and Trademark Office (Not admitted in District of Columbia). *Education:* Mary Washington College (B.S., 19991); Columbus School of Law of The Catholic University of America (J.D., 2000). ***LANGUAGES:*** French. ***PRACTICE AREAS:*** Intellectual Property Litigation.

MARK R. LEVENTHAL, born Abington, Pennsylvania, March 19, 1969; admitted to bar, 1997, Maryland, New Jersey and U.S. District Court, District of New Jersey; 1998, District of Columbia and U.S. District Court, District of Maryland; 1999, U.S. District Court, District of Columbia; 2000, U.S. Court of International Trade and U.S. Court of Appeals for the Federal Circuit. *Education:* University of Pennsylvania (B.S., Economics, cum laude, 1991); Temple University (J.D., magna cum laude, 1997). Member, Temple Law Review. *Member:* Maryland State and American Bar Associations; The District of Columbia Bar. ***PRACTICE AREAS:*** International Trade; Antidumping; Unfair Competition; Trademarks. ***Email:*** leventhal@adduci.com

OF COUNSEL

ROBERT A. WESTERLUND, born Portsmouth, Virginia, December 13, 1956; admitted to bar, 1980, Louisiana; 1991, California; 1992, District of Columbia; 1997, Virginia. *Education:* Tulane University (J.D., 1980). Phi Theta Kappa. *Member:* Louisiana State and American Bar Associations; State Bar of California; Virginia State Bar; American Patent Law Association. (Also Special Counsel to Griffin & Szipl, P.C., Arlington, Virginia). ***PRACTICE AREAS:*** Patent Procurement; Patent Licensing; Litigation.

RAYMOND H. J. POWELL, JR., born Charleston, South Carolina, May 22, 1952; admitted to bar, 1988, Virginia; registered to practice before U.S. Patent and Trademark Office (Not admitted in District of Columbia). *Education:* The Citadel (B.S.E.E., 1974); George Washington University (J.D., 1988). Tau Beta Pi. *Member:* Virginia State Bar; American Bar Association. [U.S. Navy, 1974-1979, Lieutenant]. (Also Special Counsel to Griffin & Szipl, P.C., Arlington, Virginia). ***PRACTICE AREAS:*** Patent Law.

PHILIP L. ROBINS, born Brooklyn, New York, April 15, 1937; admitted to bar, 1961, Florida; 1965 U.S. Supreme Court, U.S. Court of Claims, and U.S. Court of Military Appeals; 1969, District of Columbia. *Education:* University of Miami (B.B.A., 1959; J.D., 1961). Author: Textile Rules of Origin: 1984, 1994. U.S. Customs Service, 1969-2000. ***PRACTICE AREAS:*** Customs; International Trade Regulation. ***Email:*** robins@adduci.com

REPRESENTATIVE CLIENTS: Furnished Upon Request.

THE LAW OFFICES OF ROGER M. ADELMAN

1100 CONNECTICUT AVENUE, N.W., SUITE 730
WASHINGTON, D.C. 20036
Telephone: 202-822-0600
Fax: 202-775-8702
Email: adelmarm@erols.com
URL: http://www.lawyers.com/rogeradelmanlaw

Civil Trials, Criminal Defense, White Collar Crimes, Business Fraud, Breach of Contract, Medical Malpractice, Wrongful Death, Personal Injury, Class Actions, Complex Litigation, Professional Malpractice, Arbitration, Mediation.

FIRM PROFILE: Mr. Adelman brings over 30 years of court room experience to a national plaintiff's trial law practice. His firm also provides alternative dispute resolution services.

ROGER M. ADELMAN, born Norristown, Pennsylvania, June 25, 1941; admitted to bar, 1967, District of Columbia; 1969, Pennsylvania. *Education:* Dartmouth College (A.B., 1963); University of Pennsylvania (LL.B., 1966). Recipient: Harold J. Sullivan Award, 1981; Charles Fahy Distinguished Adjunct Professor Award, 1989; James C. Eastman Award, 1990. Adjunct Professor, Evidence, Trial Practice, Georgetown University Law Center, Washington, D.C., 1975—. Co-Author, "The Securities Enforcement Manual: Tactics and Strategies," Section of Business Law, American Bar Association, 1997. Assistant U.S. Attorney, Washington, D.C., 1969-1987. Counsellor, William B. Bryant American Inn of Court, 1990—. *Member:* District of Columbia Bar (Editor, Criminal Jury Instructions, 1985-1991); American Bar Association (Editorial Board, Criminal Justice Magazine, 1984—).

AFRIDI, ANGELL & PELLETREAU LLP

1025 CONNECTICUT AVENUE, N.W., SUITE 904
WASHINGTON, D.C. 20036-5405
Telephone: 202-518-8900
Fax: 202-518-8903
Email: rpelletreau@afridi.com
URL: http://www.afridi-angell.com

New York, N.Y. Office: 599 Lexington Avenue, Suite 2806, 10022-6030. Telephone: 212-697-0300. Fax: 212-697-0385. E-mail: nangell@afridi.com.

Abu Dhabi, United Arab Emirates Office: Al Ghaith Tower, Level 8, Suite 806, Hamdan Street. P.O. Box 3961. Telephone: +971-2-6275134. Fax: +971-2-6272905. E-mail: abudhabi@afridi-angell.com

Dubai, United Arab Emirates Office: Emirates Towers, 35th Floor, Sheikh Zayed Road, P.O. Box 9371. Telephone: +971-4-330-3900. Fax: +971-4-330-3800. E-mail: dubai@afridi-angell.com.

Jebel Ali, United Arab Emirates Office: Jebel Ali Free Trade Zone, P.O. Box 61276, Jebel Ali. Telephone: +971-4-8816010. Fax: +971-4-8816774.

Sharjah, United Arab Emirates Office: Al-Boorj Avenue, P.O. Box 5925. Telephone: +971-6-5544062. Fax: +971-6-5547336. E-mail: sharjah@afridi-angell.com.

Islamabad, Pakistan Office: Afridi Angell & Khan, 94 W. Jinnah Avenue, Blue Area, Islamabad 44000. Telephone: +92-51-2823-110. Fax: +92-51-2823-009. E-mail: islamabad@afridi-angell.com

Karachi, Pakistan Office: House D-3/1, Kehkashan, Clifton, Block 7. Telephone: +92-21-583 3585/583 3595. Fax: +92-21-5833-022/327. E-mail: karachi@afridi-angell.com.

(This Listing Continued)

AFRIDI, ANGELL & PELLETREAU LLP, Washington—Continued

The firm, including the New York, United Arab Emirates and Pakistan Offices, and Baker Botts L.L.P., independent law firms, have established a Strategic Alliance for purposes of enhancing their respective client service capabilities in the Middle East-North Africa-South Asia Region. Baker Botts has offices in Houston, Dallas and Austin, Texas, Washington, D.C., New York, London, Riyadh and Baku.

FIRM PROFILE: The firm conducts a general international practice, specializing since 1975 in the Middle East, North Africa and South Asia region with offices in New York, Washington, D.C., three offices in the United Arab Emirates and two offices in Pakistan. The firm's practice involves transactional work of all kinds, including an oil and gas and project development and finance practice relating to private sector power and infrastructure projects. It also advises governments and other clients with respect to privatization programs and the regulation of developing capital markets in the Region. The firm handles dispute resolution matters and supervises litigation in all state and federal courts. The Washington, D.C. office, based on Ambassador Pelletreau's experience, represents governments in the Region with respect to their U.S. interests and advises clients with respect to their business activities, strategies and problems in the Region and their relationships with U.S. and Regional governments and leaders and multilateral institutions. The resources of the New York, Middle East and Pakistan offices, as well as the resources of Baker Botts with whom Afridi Angell has a Strategic Alliance, are fully available to the Washington, D.C. office. For a description of the practices of the Middle East offices of Afridi & Angell and the Pakistan offices of Afridi, Angell & Khan, see Abu Dhabi, Dubai and Sharjah, United Arab Emirates, and Islamabad and Karachi, Pakistan. The firm also has available the resources of a network of established relationships with law firms throughout the Middle East-South Asia-North Africa region.

PARTNER

ROBERT H. PELLETREAU, born 1935; admitted to bar, 1962, New York; 1997, District of Columbia. *Education:* Yale University (B.A., 1957); Harvard University (LL.B., 1961). Former Associations: Department of State, Assistant Secretary of State for Near Eastern Affairs, 1994-1997; Ambassador to: Egypt, 1991-1993; Tunisia, 1987-1991; Bahrain, 1979-1980. While in Tunisia, conducted U.S. Dialogue with the P.L.O., 1988-1990. Played Key Role in Development and Implementation of U.S. Policies toward North Africa, the Levant, Egypt and the Gulf, including Iraq and Iran, 1994-1997. Formerly with, Chadbourne & Parke, New York, New York. *Member:* Council on Foreign Relations; Middle East Institute; National U.S.-Arab Chamber of Commerce; American-Iranian Council; American Bar Association. (Also Of Counsel to Baker Botts, L.L.P.). ***LANGUAGES:*** French, Arabic. ***Email:*** rpelletreau@afridi.com

OF COUNSEL

A. JOHN RADSAN, born 1962; admitted to bar, 1988, Illinois; 1989, District of Columbia; 1990, New York; 1995, California. *Education:* Duke University (A.B., summa cum laude, 1983); Harvard University (J.D., cum laude, 1987). Phi Beta Kappa. Trial Attorney, Fraud Section of Criminal Division, U.S. Department of Justice, Washington, D.C.; Resident Legal Advisor, U.S. Embassy, Moscow; Assistant U.S. Attorney, Southern District of California. Corporate Associate, Baker & McKenzie, Chicago, Ill.; Sullivan & Cromwell, New York, N.Y. *Member:* Iranian-American Bar Association. (Also Of Counsel, Baker Botts, L.L.P.). ***LANGUAGES:*** French, Farsi and Spanish. ***Email:*** jradsan@afridi.com

(For Biographical data on other Firm personnel, see Professional Biographies at New York, N.Y., Abu Dhabi, Dubai and Sharjah, United Arab Emirates and Islamabad and Karachi, Pakistan).

CLARKE F. AHLERS, P.C.

WASHINGTON, D.C.

(See Columbia, Maryland)

Criminal Defense, Law Enforcement Officers Rights, Criminal Appeals.

MICHAEL M. AIN

Established in 1986

1155 15TH STREET, N.W., SUITE 502

WASHINGTON, D.C. 20005

Telephone: 202-828-9191

Fax: 202-371-9046

URL: http://www.lawyers.com/michaelainlaw

Email: info@ainlaw.com

URL: http://www.ainlaw.com

Rockville, Maryland Office: 600 Jefferson Plaza, Suite 308.

(This Listing Continued)

Medical Negligence, Automobile Accidents, Products Liability, Premises Liability, Police Brutality, Personal Injury.

FIRM PROFILE: Michael Ain is an experienced trial lawyer who represents individuals that have been injured as a result of physician, hospital or other health care provider or laboratory negligence, and injuries resulting from automobile accidents, unsafe products and premises, and police brutality.

MICHAEL M. AIN, admitted to bar, 1975, Maryland; 1976, District of Columbia. *Education:* State University of New York at Buffalo (B.A., Pol. Sci., 1971); George Washington University (J.D., with honors, 1975). Barrister, American Inns of Court. Lecturer, Medical Malpractice and Wrongful Death, District of Columbia Bar Association. Arbitrator, District of Columbia Superior Court. *Member:* District of Columbia Bar; Maryland Trial Lawyers Association; Metropolitan District of Columbia Trial Lawyers Association. (Also of Counsel, O'Reilly, Mark & Peelman, L.L.C.). ***REPORTED CASES:*** Burns vs. Bell 409 A 2nd 614; Bulin vs. Stein 668 A 2nd 810, 1995.

AITKEN IRVIN BERLIN & VROOMÁN, LLP

SUITE 315

666 ELEVENTH STREET, N.W.

WASHINGTON, D.C. 20001

Telephone: 202-331-8045; 202-331-3096

Telecopier: 202-331-8191; 202-573-8073

URL: http://www.aitkennirvinberlin&vrooman

Email: beaitken@aol.com

URL: http://www.lawyers.com/aitkenirvinberlin&vrooman

White Plains, New York Office: 2 Gannett Drive, Suite 418. Telephone: 914-694-2226. Fax: 914-694-1647.

Kyiv, Ukraine Representative Office: c/o DDM, 25 Povitrof Avenue, 03049. Telephone: +380-67-449-4802. Fax: +380-44-245-4633.

Affiliated Offices: Beijing, Buenos Aires, Tokyo.

Administrative and Commercial Practice before Federal Courts and Agencies and the U.S. Congress. International Trade Law and Policy, Customs, Export Control, Immigration, International Transactions and Project Finance, Government Affairs, Commercial Arbitration, Real Estate, Corporate Representation, Litigation, Arbitration, Maritime, Natural Resources and Energy Law.

FIRM PROFILE: The firm's attorneys are nationally and internationally recognized experts in international trade, natural resources, energy and commercial law matters and related litigation. Our principals are alumni of international firms. Our policy is to provide small-firm client attention, mid-sized firm rates with large-firm depth of legal experience. Our affiliated consulting firm affords extraordinary expertise in international development and finance and governmental representation.

MEMBERS OF FIRM

EVELYN F. COHN (1948-1998).

BRUCE AITKEN, born Abington, Pennsylvania, 1947; admitted to bar, 1977, Maryland and U.S. Court of Appeals, Fourth Circuit; 1978, District of Columbia; 1981, U.S. Supreme Court and U.S. Court of International Trade; 1982, U.S. Court of Appeals for the Federal Circuit. *Education:* Fordham University (B.A., 1969); Columbia University (M.B.A., 1971); American University (J.D., 1976). Member: U.S.-Canada, FTA (1991-1994), NAFTA (1994—), WTO (1996-1998) and WIPO (1996—), Dispute Resolution Panel Rosters. *Member:* American, Federal, International and Inter-Pacific Bar Associations. ***LANGUAGES:*** Russian. ***PRACTICE AREAS:*** Antitrust; Arbitration; Customs; International Trade Regulation and Policy; Congressional/Legislative; International Commercial Transactions; International Finance; International Transportation. ***Email:*** baitken@aol.com

BEN L. IRVIN, born Altoona, Pennsylvania, February 1, 1935; admitted to bar, 1968, Maryland and U.S. Court of International Trade; 1968-1982, U.S. Court of Customs and Patent Appeals; 1980, U.S. Court of International Trade; 1982, U.S. Court of Appeals for the Federal Circuit (Not admitted in District of Columbia). *Education:* Pennsylvania State University (B.A., 1961); University of Baltimore Law School (LL.B., 1965). Chief, Valuation Branch, 1970-1973, U.S. Customs Service. ***PRACTICE AREAS:*** Customs; International Trade; Food and Drug; Immigration Law. ***Email:*** birvin@bah2.gimli.com

ALAN D. BERLIN, born Brooklyn, New York, October 20, 1939; admitted to bar, 1963, New York (Not admitted in District of Columbia). *Education:* City College of New York (B.B.A., 1960); New York University School of Law (LL.B., 1963; LL.M., in Tax, 1968). (Also at White Plains, New York Office). ***PRACTICE AREAS:*** Natural Resources and Energy Law; Taxation; Corporate; Securities Law; International Commercial Transactions; Project Finance.

EDWARD A. VROOMÁN, born Poughkeepsie, New York, November 25, 1939; admitted to bar, 1964, New York; 1965 U.S. Tax Court (Not admitted in

(This Listing Continued)

District of Columbia). *Education:* Rensselaer Polytechnic Institute (B. Mgt. Eng., 1961); Duke University (J.D., 1964); New York University (LL.M. in Taxation, 1968). (Resident, White Plains, New York Office).

OF COUNSEL

KIERAN SHARPE, born Coaldale, Pennsylvania, July 16, 1951; admitted to bar, 1979, Pennsylvania (Not admitted in District of Columbia). *Education:* Albright College (B.A., Political Science, 1973); American University, Washington College of Law (J.D., 1976). ***Email:*** kjsharpe@aol.com

FREDERICK R. TRONCONE, born Erie, Pennsylvania, March 24, 1957; admitted to bar, 1982, Pennsylvania and U.S. District Court, Western District of Pennsylvania; 1985, District of Columbia; 1986, U.S. Court of Appeals for the Federal Circuit; 1988, Hawaii and U.S. District Court, District of Hawaii; 1990, U.S. Court of Appeals, District of Columbia Circuit. *Education:* Pennsylvania State University (B.A., 1979); University of Toledo (J.D., 1982). (Also Of Counsel, McNary, Morris & Smalley, Washington, D.C.; Also practicing individually). ***PRACTICE AREAS:*** Immigration Law; Labor and Employment. ***Email:*** frtusa@starpower.net

BRIEN E. KEHOE, born Utica, New York, June 20, 1946; admitted to bar, 1973, Pennsylvania; 1975, District of Columbia; 1980, U.S. Supreme Court; 1986, New York. *Education:* Washington College (A.B., 1963); Dickinson School of Law (J.D., 1973). General Counsel, Federal Maritime Commission, 1979-1981. *Member:* The District of Columbia Bar; Maritime Law Association of the United States. ***PRACTICE AREAS:*** Marine Transportation; Administration Law.

DANIEL OLIVER, born New York, N.Y., April 10, 1939; admitted to bar, 1967, New York (Not admitted in District of Columbia). *Education:* Harvard University (A.B., 1964); Fordham University (LL.B., 1967). General Counsel, U.S. Department of Education, 1981-1983. General Counsel, U.S. Department of Agriculture, 1983-1986. Chairman, Federal Trade Commission, 1986-1989. Member, Council of the Administrative Conference of the United States (Appointed by President Reagan), 1983-1989.

FOREIGN LAW CONSULTANTS/ASSOCIATES

VIRGINIE LECAILLON, born Paris, France, June 29, 1974; (admission pending). *Education:* University of Rouen (Master of Private Laws, 1996); University of Paris I - Sorbonne (Advanced Degree in North American Business Law, 1997); L.L.M. Candidate, American University School of Law (1999). ***LANGUAGES:*** French, German.

ELENA VOLOCHAY, born December 19, 1969; admitted to bar, 1991, Ukraine (Not admitted in the United States). *Education:* State University I.I. Mechnikov (J.D., 1991); American University (L.L.M., 1997).

JIANPING ZHANG, born Beijing, People's Republic of China; admitted to bar, 1997, People's Republic of China (Not admitted in United States). *Education:* University of Maryland (M.S., Economics, 1992). Specializes in accounting, economic analysis and PRC legal policy issues. ***LANGUAGES:*** Chinese.

REPRESENTATIVE CLIENTS: Alchevsk Iron & Steel Works, Ltd.; American Suzuki Motor Corp.; A & S Corp.; Association of International Auto Manufacturers; B.A.G. Corp.; Bernus Craffil, S.A. de C.V.; Bristol Myers Squibb Co.; Canon U.S.A., Inc.; Cappco Tubular Products, Inc.; Casio, Inc.; Chapparel Oil Co.; China Chamber of Commerce of Metals, Minerals & Chemicals; China Shangdong Foodstuffs, Ltd.; Colgate Palmolive Company; Computer & Communications Industry Association; ConvaTee, Inc.; Crisol International, S.A. de C.V.; Dastech International; Ferco Intertrade; Fujitsu America, Inc.; Hyundai Motor Co.; Ilyich Iron & Steel Works, Ltd.; International Electronics Manufacturers and Consumers of America, Inc.; The Interpublic Group; Israel Corp.; Kia North America, Inc.; Kuznetsk Ferroalloys Plant; Magnetogorsk Metallurgical Kombinat (MMK); Mannigton Mills, Inc.; Mexican Chamber of Economy of Textiles; National Silk Apparel Distributors Association; Niklor Chemical Co.; Pan American Pack, Inc.; Polytex Fibers, Inc.; Porsche Cars North America; The Pro Trade Group; Republic of Indonesia; Republic of Ukraine; Ronly Holdings, Ltd.; Royce International; Sinochem Jiangsu Suzhou, Ltd.; Stakhanov Ferroalloys Plant; State Planning Commission of China; Toshiba America, Inc.; Trans Commodities, A.G.; Zaporozhye Ferroalloys Plant; Zaporozhye Titanium and Magnesium Combine.

AKIN, GUMP, STRAUSS, HAUER & FELD, L.L.P.

A Registered Limited Liability Partnership including Professional Corporations

ROBERT S. STRAUSS BUILDING

1333 NEW HAMPSHIRE AVENUE, N.W., SUITE 400

WASHINGTON, D.C. 20036

Telephone: 202-887-4000

Fax: 202-887-4288

URL: http://www.akingump.com

Dallas, Texas Office: 1700 Pacific Avenue, Suite 4100. Telephone: 214-969-2800. Fax: 214-969-4343.

Austin, Texas Office: Frost Bank Plaza, 816 Congress Avenue, Suite 1900. Telephone: 512-499-6200. Fax: 512-499-6290.

(This Listing Continued)

Houston, Texas Office: 1900 Pennzoil Place-South Tower, 711 Louisiana Street. Telephone: 713-220-5800. Fax: 713-236-0822.

San Antonio, Texas Office: 300 Convent Street, Suite 1500. Telephone: 210-281-7000. Fax: 210-224-2035.

New York, New York Office: 590 Madison Avenue. Telephone: 212-872-1000. Fax: 212-872-1002.

Philadelphia, Pennsylvania Office: One Commerce Square, 2005 Market Street, Suite 2200. Telephone: 215-965-1200. Fax: 215-965-1210.

Los Angeles, California Office: 2029 Century Park East, Suite 2400. Telephone: 310-229-1000. Fax: 310-229-1001.

Denver, Colorado Office: 1675 Broadway, Suite 2300. Telephone: 303-825-7000. Fax: 303-825-7005.

McLean, Virginia Office: 1676 International Drive. Telephone: 703-891-7500. Fax: 703-891-7501.

Brussels, Belgium Office: 65 Avenue Louise, P.B. #7. Telephone: (011) 32-2-535-2911. Fax: (011) 32-2-535-2900.

Moscow, Russia Office: Ducat Place II, 7 Gasheka Street, P.B. 20. Telephone: (011) 7-095 974-2411. Fax: (011) 7-095-974-2412.

London, England Office: One Angel Court. Telephone: (011) 44-20 7726-9600. Fax: (011) 44-20 7726-9610.

Affiliated Office:

Law Office of Abdulaziz H. Fahad, One Commerce Square, Jarir Plaza, 4th Floor, Olaya Street, P.O. Box 15870, Riyadh, Saudi Arabia, 11454. Telephone: (011) 966-1-464-8081. Telex: 406176 LAWS SJ. Telecopier: (011)-966-1-462-4968.

Antitrust, Banking and Financial Institutions, Bankruptcy, Capital Markets, Communications, Corporate and Securities, Employee Benefits, Energy, Entertainment, Environmental, Food and Drug, Government Contracts, Health Care, Insurance, Intellectual Property and Technology, International, Labor and Employment, Litigation, Mergers and Acquisitions, Privatization, Project Finance, Public Law and Policy, Real Estate and Taxation.

MEMBERS OF FIRM

DONALD C. ALEXANDER, born Pine Bluff, Arkansas, May 22, 1921; admitted to bar, 1949, District of Columbia; 1954, Ohio; 1978, New York. *Education:* Yale University (B.A., 1942); Harvard Law School (LL.B., magna cum laude, 1948). Awarded LL.D. (hon.) by: Capital University, 1989; St. Thomas Institute, 1975. Editor, Harvard Law Review, 1947-1948. Commissioner of Internal Revenue, 1973-1977. Member, Commission on Federal Paperwork, 1975-1977 and Interior Department Coal Leasing Commission, 1983-1984. Chairman, I.R.S. Exempt Organizations Advisory Group, 1987-1989. Commissioner, The Martin Luther King, Jr. Federal Holiday Commission, 1992-1996. Member, Harvard Law School Visiting Committee, 1999—. *Member:* The District of Columbia Bar; New York State (Member, Executive Committee, Tax Section, 1979-1993) and American (Vice Chairman, Taxation Section, 1968-1969) Bar Associations; American Law Institute. Fellow, American College of Tax Counsel. ***PRACTICE AREAS:*** Taxation. ***Email:*** dalexander@akingump.com

KEITH R. ANDERSON, born Joliet, Illinois, January 28, 1957; admitted to bar, 1982, District of Columbia; 1989, U.S. Supreme Court; 1999, Illinois. *Education:* DePauw University (B.A., cum laude, 1979); George Washington University (J.D., 1982). Editor-in-Chief, George Washington Journal of International Law and Economics, 1981-1982. Law Clerk to Hon. Norma Holloway Johnson, U.S. District Court for the District of Columbia, 1984. *Member:* District of Columbia Bar; Illinois State and American Bar Associations; American Health Lawyers Association. ***PRACTICE AREAS:*** Health Care Law; Corporate Transactions; Corporate Law. ***Email:*** kranderson@akingump.com

RICHARD N. APPEL, born New York, New York, March 16, 1952; admitted to bar, 1976, Maryland; 1977, District of Columbia. *Education:* University of North Carolina (B.A., with honors, 1973); Columbus School of Law, Catholic University of America (J.D., 1976). Member, Catholic University Law Review, 1975-1976. Law Clerk to Honorable John P. Moore, Maryland Court of Special Appeals, 1976-1977. *Member:* The District of Columbia Bar; Maryland State and American Bar Associations. Fellow, College of Labor and Employment Lawyers. ***PRACTICE AREAS:*** Labor and Employment. ***Email:*** rappel@akingump.com

JAMES A. BARKER, JR., born Washington, D.C., September 29, 1953; admitted to bar, 1985, Maryland; 1987, District of Columbia. *Education:* Brown University (B.A., 1975); University of Virginia (J.D., 1985). Omicron Delta Kappa. Co-Author: With Jeffrey O'Connell, "Compensation for Injury and Illness: An Update of the Conard-Morgan Tabulations," 47 Ohio State Law Journal 913, 1987. Law Clerk to the Hon. Albert V. Bryan, Jr., U.S. District Court, Eastern District of Virginia, 1985-1986. *Member:* The District of Columbia Bar; Maryland State and American Bar Associations; American Health Lawyers Association; Libel Defense Resource Center. ***PRACTICE AREAS:*** Litigation; Libel Law; Health Care Law; Corporate Transactions; Trademarks. ***Email:*** jaybarker@akingump.com

(This Listing Continued)

AKIN, GUMP, STRAUSS, HAUER & FELD, L.L.P., Washington—Continued

PAUL A. BELVIN, born Newport News, Virginia, February 9, 1948; admitted to bar, 1973, Virginia; 1979, U.S. Supreme Court; 1985, Missouri; 1996, North Carolina; 1998, District of Columbia. *Education:* Wake Forest University (B.A., cum laude, 1970); College of William & Mary (J.D., 1973); Georgetown University (LL.M., 1978). Omicron Delta Epsilon. Member, 1971-1973 and Senior Note Editor, 1972-1973, William & Mary Law Review. Counselor to Commissioner Norman Johnson, 1996-1997, Chief, Office of Small Business Policy, 1980-1984, Securities and Exchange Commission; Counselor to Commissioner Carol T. Crawford, 1992-1995 USITC; Partner, 1986-1992, Counsel, 1984-1986, Stinson, Mag & Fizzell. *Member:* Missouri Bar; Virginia State, North Carolina and American (Member: Section on Corporation, Banking and Business Law; Federal Regulation of Securities Committee, 1985—) Bar Associations; The District of Columbia Bar. ***PRACTICE AREAS:*** Corporate Law; Securities. ***Email:*** pbelvin@akingump.com

STEPHEN S. BOOCHEVER, born Albany, New York, July 25, 1956; admitted to bar, 1983, District of Columbia; 1984, U.S. District Court for the District of Columbia; 1990, New York. *Education:* Cornell University (B.S., with honors, 1978); George Washington University (J.D., with honors, 1983). *Member:* District of Columbia Bar; New York State and American Bar Associations; Bar Association of the District of Columbia; National Health Lawyers Association; American Academy of Hospital Attorneys. ***PRACTICE AREAS:*** Health Care Law; Corporate Planning Law. ***Email:*** sboochever@akingump.com

SANJOY K. BOSE, born Bombay, India, September 2, 1964; admitted to bar, 1992, Virginia; 1994, District of Columbia; 2001, New York. *Education:* Ohio Wesleyan University (B.A., magna cum laude, 1988); College of William & Mary (J.D., 1992). Phi Beta Kappa; Phi Delta Phi. Member, 1990-1991 and Issue Editor, 1991-1992, Administrative Law Review. Co-Author: "The Case of Optometry and Federal Preemption of State Action: Reinforcing the Parker Doctrine to Protect State Sovereignty," 40 The Virginia Lawyer 22, 1992; "Project: The Role of Preemption in Administrative Law," 45 Administrative Law Review, 1993. *Member:* Virginia State Bar; District of Columbia Bar. ***PRACTICE AREAS:*** Corporate; Project Finance; Banking; Technology. ***Email:*** sbose@akingump.com

JANET C. BOYD, born Houston, Texas, September 19, 1953; admitted to bar, 1985, District of Columbia. *Education:* University of Texas (B.J., 1975); George Washington University (J.D., with honors, 1985). *Member:* The District of Columbia Bar (Member, Section on Taxation); American Bar Association (Member, Section on Taxation). ***PRACTICE AREAS:*** Public Policy; Taxation. ***Email:*** jboyd@akingump.com

RICK L. BURDICK, (P.C.), born Paso Robles, California, July 10, 1951; admitted to bar, 1976, Texas; 2001, District of Columbia. *Education:* University of Santa Clara (B.S.C., cum laude, 1973); College of William & Mary (J.D., 1976). Beta Gamma Sigma. William & Mary Law Review, 1975-1976. *Member:* Houston and American Bar Associations; The District of Columbia Bar. Fellow: Texas Bar Foundation; Houston Bar Foundation. ***PRACTICE AREAS:*** Corporate and Securities Law; International Law. ***Email:*** rburdick@akingump.com

DAVID P. CALLET, (P.C.), born Johnstown, Pennsylvania, January 5, 1949; admitted to bar, 1973, District of Columbia. *Education:* Pennsylvania State University (B.A., 1970); George Washington University (J.D., with honors, 1973). Author: "Walking a High Tightrope," 1978 Federal Bar Journal, Employment Practice Guide; "The Washington Scene Feature," Employment Relations Today. Assistant Counsel for Labor Relations, Office of the Solicitor, U.S. Department of Labor, 1973-1978. *Member:* The District of Columbia Bar; American Bar Association (Member, Sections on: Litigation; Labor Law). ***PRACTICE AREAS:*** Litigation. ***Email:*** dcallet@akingump.com

J. DAVID CARLIN, born Salina, Kansas, October 18, 1962; admitted to bar, 1988, Missouri; 1989, District of Columbia. *Education:* Kansas State University (B.A., summa cum laude, 1984); Justus Liebig Universität, Giessen, West Germany; Harvard Law School (J.D., 1988). Phi Beta Kappa. Harry S. Truman Scholar (1982). Co-Chairman, Harvard Legislative Research Bureau, 1987-1988. Chairman, Steering Committee, 1991-1992 and Member, Board of Advisors, 1992-1994, Homeless Children's Tutorial Project, Inc. Assistant Secretary, U.S. Department of Agriculture, 1995-1998. ***PRACTICE AREAS:*** Public Policy. ***Email:*** dcarlin@akingump.com

JAY G. COHEN, born Bronx, New York, 1959; admitted to bar, 1987, New York; 1988, Maryland (Not admitted in District of Columbia). *Education:* State University of New York at Albany (B.A., 1981); George Washington University (J.D., 1986). ***Email:*** jcohen@akingump.com

JOEL M. COHN, (P.C.), born Cleveland, Ohio, May 12, 1949; admitted to bar, 1976, Ohio and District of Columbia. *Education:* University of Wisconsin (B.A., with distinction, 1971); State University of New York at Stony Brook (1972-1973); Columbus School of Law; Catholic University of America (J.D., 1976). Law Clerk to the Honorable Milton D. Korman, Superior Court of the District of Columbia, 1976-1977. Attorney: Office of Representation Appeals, National Labor Relations Board, 1977-1979; Office of the General Counsel, Appellate Division, Equal Employment Opportunity Commission, 1979-1983. *Member:* Ohio State and American (Section of Labor and Employment Law) Bar Associations; The District of Columbia Bar. ***PRACTICE AREAS:*** Labor and Employment. ***Email:*** jcohn@akingump.com

BARRY CONATY, born Elliot Lake, Ontario, Canada, October 15, 1961; admitted to bar, 1989, District of Columbia; 1990, Colorado. *Education:* Yale University (B.A., cum laude, 1983); George Washington University (J.D., with high honors, 1989). Order of the Coif. Member, 1987-1988, and Notes Editor, 1988-1989, George Washington Law Review. Author: "Corporate Acquisitions/Dispositions," and Co-Author, "Environmental Audits," chapters in Environmental Compliance Desk Reference (Clark Boardman Callaghan, 1995); "Municipal Landfills on Federal Public Lands—A Growing Superfund Liability Problem," Municipal Attorney, Vol. 35, No. 4, 1994; "Landfill Regulations May Prove Costly for Municipalities," Corporate Legal Times, Vol. 3, No. 14, 1993. *Member:* District of Columbia Bar; Colorado and American Bar Associations. ***PRACTICE AREAS:*** Environmental Law. ***Email:*** bconaty@akingump.com

WARREN E. CONNELLY, born Mt. Vernon, New York, November 18, 1946; admitted to bar, 1973, District of Columbia. *Education:* Dartmouth College (B.A., cum laude, 1968); Georgetown University (J.D., 1973). Attorney, Cost of Living Council, 1973-1974. Member, NAFTA Chapter 19 Panel, 1996—. Member, Georgetown University Law Alumni Board, 1986-1993. Member, U.S./Canada Binational Panel, 1989-1992. Member, Arlington County, Virginia Police Trial Board, 1989-1991. *Member:* The District of Columbia Bar. [First Lieut., U.S. Army, 1968-1970]. ***PRACTICE AREAS:*** International Trade. ***Email:*** wconnelly@akingump.com

EILEEN M. CONSIDINE, born Englewood, New Jersey, October 8, 1955; admitted to bar, 1981, New York and U.S. District Court, Northern, Southern, Eastern and Western Districts of New York; 1984, U.S. Supreme Court and U.S. Court of Appeals, Second Circuit (Not admitted in District of Columbia). *Education:* Rutgers University (B.A., magna cum laude, 1977); Albany Law School of Union University (J.D., 1980). Member and Editor, Albany Law Review, 1979-1980. *Member:* Albany County and New York State Bar Associations; American Health Lawyers Association. ***PRACTICE AREAS:*** Health Law. ***Email:*** econsidine@akingump.com

COLLEEN M. COYLE, born Long Island, New York, January 24, 1963; admitted to bar, 1990, New York; 1991, District of Columbia. *Education:* Georgetown University (B.A., 1984); Catholic University of America (J.D., 1989). Recipient: Miriam Theresa Rooney Scholarship for Academic Excellence, 1988-1989. Lead Articles Editor, Journal of Contemporary Health Law & Policy, 1988-1989. *Member:* The District of Columbia Bar; New York State Bar Association. ***PRACTICE AREAS:*** Litigation. ***Email:*** ccoyle@akingump.com

DONALD B. CRAVEN, born Durham, North Carolina; admitted to bar, 1967, North Carolina; 1973, Virginia; 1975, District of Columbia. *Education:* University of North Carolina (A.B., 1963); Duke University (LL.B., 1967); Georgetown University. Phi Delta Phi (Magister, 1966-1967). Member, Editorial Board, Duke Law Journal, 1966-1967. Trial Attorney, Tax Division, U.S. Department of Justice, 1968-1973. Associate Assistant Administrator and Acting Assistant Administrator, Federal Energy Administration, 1974-1975. *Member:* The District of Columbia Bar; Bar Association of the District of Columbia; North Carolina, Virginia and American Bar Associations; North Carolina State Bar; Virginia State Bar. ***PRACTICE AREAS:*** Complex Litigation; Intellectual Property Litigation; Natural Resources; Appellate Practice; Administrative Law. ***Email:*** dcraven@akingump.com

JOHN J. D'ANDREA, born Saratoga Springs, New York, March 23, 1965; admitted to bar, 1991, New York and U.S. District Court, Northern District of New York (Not admitted in District of Columbia). *Education:* College of the Holy Cross (B.A., 1987); Albany Law School (J.D., 1990). ***PRACTICE AREAS:*** Health and Hospital Law; Health Insurance Law. ***Email:*** jdandrea@akingump.com

SEAN G. D'ARCY, born Worcester, Massachusetts, December 27, 1962; admitted to bar, 1992, Massachusetts; 1994, District of Columbia. *Education:* Fairfield University (B.A., 1984); Catholic University of America (J.D., 1991). Member, The Journal of Contemporary Health Law and Policy, 1989-1991. Member, Thurgood Marshall Inn of Court, 1990-1991. ***PRACTICE AREAS:*** Public Policy. ***Email:*** sdarcy@akingump.com

SMITH W. DAVIS, (P.C.), born West Chester, Pennsylvania, March 7, 1948; admitted to bar, 1978, District of Columbia. *Education:* University of Wisconsin and Yale University (B.A., magna cum laude, 1970); Yale University (J.D., 1974). Associate, Milbank, Tweed, Hadley & McCloy, 1974-1976. Clerk of the U.S. District Court, District of Columbia, Hon. Barrington D. Parker, 1977-1978. Counsel, House Judiciary Committee, Subcommittee on Crime, 1978-1979. Member: Board of Trustees, WETA, 1990-1992; Advisory Team, Bush-Cheney HUD Transition, 2000-2001. Special Counsel, National Republi-

(This Listing Continued)

can Senatorial Committee, 1991-1994. Senior Advisor, Phil Gramm for President, 1995-1996. *Member:* The District of Columbia Bar. ***PRACTICE AREAS:*** Public Policy. ***Email:*** sdavis@akingump.com

SYLVIA A. DE LEON, born Corpus Christi, Texas, March 2, 1950; admitted to bar, 1976, Texas; 1977, District of Columbia. *Education:* Briarcliff College (B.A., 1972); The University of Texas School of Law (J.D., 1976); Georgetown University Law Center. Adjunct Professor of Law, Georgetown University Law Center, 1988-1990. Member, Board of Directors, 1994— and Chair, Corporate Strategy Committee, 1996—, Amtrak, the National Passenger Railroad Corporation. Member, National Civil Aviation Review Commission. Presidential Appointee to the National Commission to Ensure a Strong Competitive Airline Industry, 1993. Clinton/Gore Presidential Transition, Coordinator of Transportation Issues, 1993. Task Force on the White House Conference on Travel and Tourism, 1995. Member, Board of Directors, The University of Texas Law School Association, 1985-1989; 1992-1994. The University of Texas Development Board, 1995—. *Member:* The District of Columbia Bar; Bar Association of the District of Columbia; State Bar of Texas (Chairman, Federal Law and Regulations Committee, 1984-1987). ***PRACTICE AREAS:*** Public Policy. ***Email:*** sdeleon@akingump.com

DAVID A. DONOHOE, (P.C.), born Wilmington, Delaware, May 15, 1937; admitted to bar, 1963, New York; 1967, Connecticut; 1969, District of Columbia. *Education:* Catholic University of America (A.B., cum laude, 1959; J.D., 1962). Phi Beta Kappa; Blue Key. Lecturer in Law, Catholic University of America, 1969-1972. Articles Editor, Catholic University of America Law Review, 1961-1962. National President, Catholic University Alumni Association, 1983-1987. Member, 1988-1996 and Vice Chairman, 1997—, Catholic University Board of Regents. Member, Catholic University Board of Trustees, 1998—. *Member:* The District of Columbia Bar; Bar Association of the District of Columbia; American Bar Association. ***PRACTICE AREAS:*** Litigation; Antitrust; Securities. ***Email:*** ddonohoe@akingump.com

MARILYN L. DORIA, born Boston, Massachusetts, January 15, 1944; admitted to bar, 1974, Pennsylvania and U.S. District Court, Eastern District of Pennsylvania; 1986, Texas and U.S. District Court, Southern District of Texas; U.S. Court of Appeals, Fifth Circuit; U.S. Court of Appeals, District of Columbia Circuit; 1993, District of Columbia. *Education:* Brandeis University (A.B., 1965); Syracuse-Maxwell School (M.I.P.A., 1967); Temple University (J.D., 1974). Deputy Assistant and Assistant General Counsel for Enforcement, F.E.R.C., 1979-1983. Acting Deputy General Counsel, Litigation and Enforcement and Assistant General Counsel, Oil and Gas Litigation, F.E.R.C., 1983-1985. ***PRACTICE AREAS:*** Energy. ***Email:*** mdoria@akingump.com

JOHN M. DOWD, born Brockton, Massachusetts, 1941; admitted to bar, 1967, District of Columbia, U.S. District Court for the District of Columbia, U.S. Court of Appeals for the District of Columbia Circuit, U.S. Court of Appeals, Third, Fourth, Fifth, Ninth, Tenth and Eleventh Circuits and U.S. Court of International Trade; 1970, U.S. Supreme Court; 1988, U.S. District Court, Southern District of Georgia. *Education:* St. Bernard College (A.B., cum laude, 1963); Emory University (J.D., 1965). Lecturer: National Institute for Trial Advocacy, Georgetown University, 1979-1981; Continuing Legal Education, Georgetown University Law Center, 1987-1988. Trial Attorney, Tax Division, 1969-1970; Prosecutor, Organized Crime and Racketeering Section, Criminal Division, 1972-1974; Chief, Organized Crime Strike Force, 1974-1978, U.S. Department of Justice. Special Counsel, Commissioner of Major League Baseball, 1989-1990. Master, Edward Bennett Williams Inn of Court, 1989—. Who's Who in America, 1993-1994. Arbitrator, International Chamber of Commerce, 1994. Member, Board of Trustees, Flint Hill School. *Member:* The District of Columbia Bar; American Bar Association. Fellow, The Fellows of the Young Lawyers of the American Bar. [Capt., U.S. Marine Corps, Judge Advocate, 1966-1969]. ***PRACTICE AREAS:*** Litigation; White Collar Criminal Defense. ***Email:*** jdowd@akingump.com

KEITH A. DUNSMORE, born Hartford, Connecticut, August 16, 1957; admitted to bar, 1982, Georgia; 1999, District of Columbia. *Education:* Williams College (B.A., 1979); Vanderbilt University (J.D., 1982); Emory University (LL.M., in Taxation, 1986). Phi Delta Phi. Member, 1980-1981 and Problems Editor, 1981-1982, Vanderbilt Moot Court Board. *Member:* Atlanta and American Bar Associations; State Bar of Georgia. (Resident). ***PRACTICE AREAS:*** Real Estate Finance (66%); Tax Law (34%). ***Email:*** kdunsmore@akingump.com

DAVID H. EISENSTAT, born Scranton, Pennsylvania, May 23, 1951; admitted to bar, 1976, District of Columbia; 1978, U.S. District Court for District of Columbia; 1980, U.S. Court of Appeals for the District of Columbia Circuit; 1982, U.S. Court of Appeals, Eleventh Circuit; 1985, U.S. Court of Appeals, Eighth Circuit. *Education:* University of Pennsylvania (B.A. and M.A., 1973); Syracuse University (J.D., 1976). Research Editor, Syracuse Law Review, 1975-1976. *Member:* The District of Columbia Bar; American Health Lawyers Association. ***PRACTICE AREAS:*** Health Care. ***Email:*** deisenstat@akingump.com

JOSEPH P. ESPOSITO, (P.C.), born Niagara Falls, New York, September 4, 1953; admitted to bar, 1979, New York; 1983, District of Columbia, U.S. Tax

(This Listing Continued)

Court, U.S. Court of Appeals, Second, Fourth, Sixth, Eleventh and for the District of Columbia Circuits and Court of International Trade. *Education:* State University of New York at Buffalo (B.A., magna cum laude, 1975); New York University School of Law (J.D., 1978). Phi Beta Kappa. Member of Staff, Annual Survey of American Law, 1977-1978. Associate Editor, Litigation News, 1988-1993. Author: Chapter on "Due Process," The Commissioners' Legal Handbook—An Introduction to Legal Topics for Housing and Redevelopment Officials, 1986; Essay, "Peer Review Privilege," Evidence in America, 1988; "First Amendment Rights," Annual Survey of American Law 135, 1978. Law Clerk to: The Honorable Paul C. Weick, U.S. Court of Appeals, Sixth Circuit, 1979-1980; The Honorable Phil M. McNagny, Jr., U.S. District Court, Northern District of Indiana, 1978-1979. *Member:* The District of Columbia Bar; American Bar Association (Member, Section of Litigation). ***PRACTICE AREAS:*** Litigation. ***Email:*** jesposito@akingump.com

ALLEN V. FARBER, born Springfield, Massachusetts, May 25, 1950; admitted to bar, 1975, District of Columbia; 1980, U.S. Tax Court and U.S. Supreme Court; 1995, Maryland. *Education:* Duke University (B.A., cum laude, 1972); George Washington University (J.D., 1975). *Member:* District of Columbia Bar; Bar Association of the District of Columbia; American Bar Association (Member, Section on Litigation). ***PRACTICE AREAS:*** Litigation; First Amendment Law; Libel Law; Commercial Leasing Law. ***Email:*** afarber@akingump.com

JEFFREY T. GANIBAN, born Philadelphia, Pennsylvania, February 19, 1964; admitted to bar, 1989, Pennsylvania and New Jersey; 1992, District of Columbia. *Education:* Tufts University (B.A., magna cum laude, 1986); National Law Center, George Washington University (J.D., with highest honors, 1989). Order of the Coif. Member, George Washington Law Review, 1988-1989. Law Clerk, Hon. Morton I. Greenberg, U.S. Court of Appeals, Third Circuit, 1989-1990. ***PRACTICE AREAS:*** Health Care Law. ***Email:*** jganiban@akingump.com

JOSEPH V. GATTI, born Fort Campbell, Kentucky, February 17, 1962; admitted to bar, 1987, Maryland; 1991, District of Columbia. *Education:* Johns Hopkins University (B.A., with honors, 1984); George Washington University (J.D., with honors, 1987). Member, George Washington Journal of International Law and Economics. Author: "Bank and Bank Holding Company Acquisitions of Thrifts," Chapter 5 in Mergers and Acquisitions of Banks and Savings Institutions, Keith R. Fisher, editor, Little, Brown & Company, 1993. *Member:* Maryland State and American Bar Associations; District of Columbia Bar. ***PRACTICE AREAS:*** Asset Securitization; Corporate Securities. ***Email:*** jgatti@akingump.com

DAVID GEANACOPOULOS, born Chicopee, Massachusetts, March 11, 1955; admitted to bar, 1983, District of Columbia. *Education:* Harvard University (A.B., 1977); Georgetown University (J.D., 1983). Legislative Assistant to U.S. Rep. Edward P. Boland, 1977-1983. Director and Counsel, Center for National Policy. *Member:* The District of Columbia Bar. ***PRACTICE AREAS:*** Public Policy. ***Email:*** dgeanacopoulos@akingump.com

RICHARD M. GITTLEMAN, born Providence, Rhode Island, 1955; admitted to bar, 1983, District of Columbia. *Education:* Brown University (A.B., 1977); American University (J.D., cum laude, 1982). ***LANGUAGES:*** French. ***PRACTICE AREAS:*** Project Finance; Infrastructure Development; International Transactions. ***Email:*** rgittleman@akingump.com

AVRUM M. GOLDBERG, born Pittsburgh, Pennsylvania, October 18, 1943; admitted to bar, 1970, District of Columbia. *Education:* Pennsylvania State University (B.S., 1965); Villanova University (J.D., 1969). Attorney, Division of Litigation, Office of the General Counsel, National Labor Relations Board, 1969-1973. Catholic University - Labor Relations in the Construction Industry, 1979-1981. *Member:* The District of Columbia Bar; Bar Association of the District of Columbia; American Bar Association. ***PRACTICE AREAS:*** Labor and Employment. ***Email:*** mgoldberg@akingump.com

LARRY S. GONDELMAN, born Pittsburgh, Pennsylvania, April 11, 1952; admitted to bar, 1977, Pennsylvania, Supreme Court of Pennsylvania and U.S. Court of Appeals for the District of Columbia Circuit; 1978, District of Columbia, District of Columbia Court of Appeals, U.S. Court of Appeals for the Third Circuit, U.S. District Court for the District of Columbia; 1981, U.S. Court of Appeals for the Second Circuit; 1982, U.S. Court of Appeals, First Circuit; 1983, U.S. Court of Appeals, Fourth Circuit; 1985, U.S. Court of Appeals, Seventh Circuit and U.S. District Court, District of Maryland; 1994, U.S. Supreme Court. *Education:* University of Michigan and Brandeis University (B.A., 1974); Georgetown University (J.D., 1977). Member of Staff, Georgetown Law Journal, 1975-1976. Author: "False Claims Against the Government: Defense Tactics in a False Claims Prosecution," 17 American Criminal Law Review 399, Winter 1980; "D.C. Vice - The Unconstitutionality of Mandatory Minimum Sentencing for Drug Offenses," 10 District Lawyer 32, March/April, 1986; "What the SEC Won't Tell You About Cease-and-Desist Orders," 28 Securities Regulation Law Journal 163, Fall 2000. Adjunct Professor, Washington College of Law, American University, 1984-1988. *Member:* The District of Columbia Bar; American Bar Association. ***PRACTICE AREAS:*** Litigation. ***Email:*** lgondelman@akingump.com

(This Listing Continued)

AKIN, GUMP, STRAUSS, HAUER & FELD, L.L.P., Washington—Continued

PHILIP D. GREEN, born Washington, D.C., June 20, 1950; admitted to bar, 1974, Pennsylvania; 1974, District of Columbia. *Education:* University of Pennsylvania (B.A., cum laude, 1971); George Washington University (J.D., 1974). Order of the Coif. Clerk, The Honorable John P. Fullam, U.S. District Court, Eastern District of Pennsylvania, 1974-1976. *Member:* District of Columbia Bar; Pennsylvania Bar Association. ***PRACTICE AREAS:*** Health Care Law; Corporate Transactional; Corporate Planning. ***Email:*** pgreen@akingump.com

SPENCER S. GRIFFITH, born Wichita, Kansas, May 9, 1956; admitted to bar, 1983, District of Columbia; 1984, U.S. District Court for the District of Columbia. *Education:* Brown University (A.B., 1978); New York University (J.D., 1982). Order of the Coif. Henry Luce Scholar. Editor, Annual Survey of American Law, 1982. Author: "China and the GATT," China Business Review, 1987; "Dumping and China," China Business Review, 1991. Attorney, Hong Kong Attorney General's Chambers, 1982-1983. *Member:* District of Columbia Bar Association; American Bar Association (Member, Sections on: Litigation and International Law). ***PRACTICE AREAS:*** International Trade. ***Email:*** sgriffith@akingump.com

PAUL E. GUTERMANN, born Springfield, Massachusetts, October 19, 1956; admitted to bar, 1981, District of Columbia; 1982, U.S. District Court, District of Columbia; 1984, U.S. Court of Appeals for the District of Columbia Circuit; 1985, U.S. Supreme Court; 1986, U.S. Court of Appeals, Fourth Circuit; 1987, U.S. Court of Appeals, Eleventh Circuit; 1989, U.S. District Court, District of Maryland and U.S. Court of Appeals, Sixth and Tenth Circuits; 1996, U.S. Court of Appeals, Third Circuit. *Education:* Clark University (A.B., cum laude, 1978); Case Western Reserve University (J.D., 1981). Psi Chi; Phi Beta Kappa; Order of the Coif. Halter Scholar. Recipient, Society of Benchers Award. Editor-in-Chief, Case Western Reserve Law Review, 1980-1981. *Member:* The District of Columbia Bar. ***PRACTICE AREAS:*** Environmental Law; Land Use; Project Finance. ***Email:*** pgutermann@akingump.com

SCOTT M. HEIMBERG, born Glen Ridge, New Jersey, September 29, 1959; admitted to bar, 1985, Maryland; 1987, District of Columbia, U.S. Court of Appeals for the Federal Circuit and U.S. Court of Federal Claims. *Education:* Franklin and Marshall College (B.A., 1981); George Washington University (J.D., with honors, 1984). Pi Gamma Mu; Phi Alpha Theta. Member, George Washington Journal of International Law and Economics, 1982. Attorney-Adviser to the Honorable E. P. Snyder, Chief Administrative Judge, Board of Contract Appeals, U.S. Department of Transportation, November 1985 to February 1987. *Member:* The District of Columbia Bar; Maryland State, Federal and American Bar Associations. ***PRACTICE AREAS:*** Government Contracts; Construction Law. ***Email:*** sheimberg@akingump.com

FRANK H. HENNEBURG, born July 13, 1949; admitted to bar, 1975, Illinois; 1978, District of Columbia. *Education:* Georgetown University (A.B., magna cum laude, 1971); University of Chicago (J.D., 1975). Phi Beta Kappa. ***PRACTICE AREAS:*** Real Estate. ***Email:*** fhenneburg@akingump.com

PAUL B. HEWITT, born St. Louis, Missouri, July 27, 1949; admitted to bar, 1974, Wisconsin; 1979, District of Columbia and U.S. Supreme Court. *Education:* Northwestern University (B.A., 1971); University of Wisconsin (J.D., cum laude, 1974). Articles Editor, Wisconsin Law Review, 1973-1974. Law Clerk to Chief Justice Horace W. Wilkie, Wisconsin Supreme Court, 1974-1975. Attorney, Federal Trade Commission Bureau of Competition, 1975-1978. *Member:* The District of Columbia Bar; State Bar of Wisconsin; American Bar Association (Member, Sections on: Antitrust Law; Litigation). ***PRACTICE AREAS:*** Antitrust; Trade Regulation; Litigation. ***Email:*** phewitt@akingump.com

WILLIAM G. HUNDLEY, born Pittsburgh, Pennsylvania, August 16, 1925; admitted to bar, 1951, New York; 1968, District of Columbia. *Education:* Fordham University (LL.B., 1950). Trial Attorney, Internal Security Division, U.S. Department of Justice, 1951-1957. Special Assistant to Attorney General Kennedy and Chief of Organized Crime and Racketeering Section, 1958-1966. *Member:* The District of Columbia Bar; Bar Association of the District of Columbia; Federal and American Bar Associations. Fellow, American College of Trial Lawyers. ***PRACTICE AREAS:*** Litigation. ***Email:*** whundley@akingump.com

HOWARD B. JACOBSON, born Detroit, Michigan, July 18, 1955; admitted to bar, 1979, District of Columbia and U.S. Tax Court. *Education:* University of Michigan (A.B., with high distinction, 1976); Harvard University (J.D., cum laude, 1979). Law Clerk to Judge Theodore Tannenwald, Jr., U.S. Tax Court, 1979-1981. *Member:* The District of Columbia Bar (Member, Tax Section); American Bar Association (Member, Tax Section). ***PRACTICE AREAS:*** Taxation. ***Email:*** hjacobson@akingump.com

JOEL JANKOWSKY, (P.C.), born Tulsa, Oklahoma, September 3, 1943; admitted to bar, 1968, Oklahoma and U.S. Court of Military Appeals; 1971, U.S. Supreme Court; 1976, District of Columbia. *Education:* University of

(This Listing Continued)

Oklahoma (B.B.A., 1965; J.D., 1968). Phi Delta Phi. Legislative Assistant to the Speaker, U.S. House of Representatives, 1972-1976. Vice Chairman, Board of Directors, Close-Up Foundation, 1983—. Secretary, Board of Directors, Cancer Research Foundation of America, 1993—. Member, Board of Advisors, Carl Albert Center, University of Oklahoma. *Member:* The District of Columbia Bar; Oklahoma and American Bar Associations. ***PRACTICE AREAS:*** Public Policy. ***Email:*** jjankowsky@akingump.com

OWEN M. JOHNSON, JR., born Belvidere, Illinois, December 19, 1936; admitted to bar, 1964, Illinois; 1972, District of Columbia; 1975, U.S. Supreme Court. *Education:* Dartmouth College (A.B., 1958); Oxford University, Oxford, England (B.A., juris, 1960); Harvard University (LL.B., cum laude, 1962); The Wharton School, University of Pennsylvania (M.B.A., 1990). Phi Beta Kappa. Marshall Scholar. Law Clerk, U.S. Court of Appeals, First Circuit, 1962-1963. Assistant Director, 1970-1972 and Director, 1975-1977, Bureau of Competition, Federal Trade Commission. *Member:* The District of Columbia Bar. ***PRACTICE AREAS:*** Antitrust and Trade Regulation. ***Email:*** ojohnson@akingump.com

RONALD M. JOHNSON, born Lyons, Kansas, November 10, 1949; admitted to bar, 1976, Kansas; 1979, District of Columbia. *Education:* Wichita State University and University of Kansas (B.A., 1973); University of Kansas (J.D., 1976). Member, 1975-1976 and Research Editor, 1976, Kansas Law Review. Co-Author: "Health Maintenance Organizations and Federal Law: Toward a Theory of Limited Reformmongering," 29 Vanderbilt Law Review 1163, 1976: "State HMO Laws and the Theory of Limited Reformmongering," 25 Kansas Law Review 21, 1976. Minority Staff Counsel, Senate Committee on Commerce, Science and Transportation, 1976-1977 and 1978. Legislative Assistant to Senator James Pearson, 1977-1978. *Member:* Kansas Bar Association; The District of Columbia Bar. ***PRACTICE AREAS:*** Labor and Employment. ***Email:*** rmjohnson@akingump.com

SHEILA D. JONES, born Washington, D.C., 1952; admitted to bar, 1978, District of Columbia; 1990, Colorado. *Education:* University of Maryland (B.A., with high honors, 1974); Harvard University (J.D., 1977). Co-author: Municipal Solid Waste LandFills - A Guide to the New EPA Regulation s on Municipal Solid Waste LandFills, 1992; "Transportation Regulation," a chapter in *Federal Regulation of the Chemical Industry,* 1980. Author: "Environment," a chapter in *Legal Environment for Foreign Direct Investment in the United States,* (1994 revised edition); "Drafting CERCLA Consent Decrees," 3 Natural Resources & Environment, Winter 1988. Assistant Chief, 1986-1989 and Staff Attorney, 1983-1986, Environmental Enforcement Section, U.S. Department of Justice, 1986-1989. *Member:* District of Columbia Bar; Colorado, American (Vice-Chair, Solid Waste and Hazardous Waste Committee, 1990-1991 and Vice-Chair, Government Policy Liaison and Vice-Chair, Government Policy Liaison Committee, 1998-2000; Section of Natural Resources, Energy and Environmental Law, 1990-1991) and National Bar Associations. ***PRACTICE AREAS:*** Environmental Law; Environmental Litigation. ***Email:*** sjones@akingump.com

DANIEL JOSEPH, born Paterson, New Jersey, August 20, 1941; admitted to bar, 1967, New Jersey; 1970, U.S. Supreme Court; 1974, District of Columbia. *Education:* Columbia University (A.B., 1963); Harvard University (LL.B., 1966). Law Clerk to the Honorable Irving L. Goldberg, U.S. Court of Appeals for the Fifth Circuit, 1966-1967. Attorney, U.S. Department of Justice, 1967-1971. Assistant General Counsel, Environmental Protection Agency, 1971-1972. Special Assistant for Environmental Affairs to General Counsel, U.S., DOT, 1972-1974. *Member:* The District of Columbia Bar (Member, Rules of Professional Conduct Review Committee, 1992-2000; Chair, 1996 -1999; Member: Committee on Multidisciplinary Practice, 1999—; Legal Ethics Committee, 2000—). ***PRACTICE AREAS:*** Litigation. ***Email:*** djoseph@akingump.com

STEPHEN H. KAPLAN, born Tulsa, Oklahoma, May 23, 1947; admitted to bar, 1973, Oklahoma; 1976, Colorado (Not admitted in District of Columbia). *Education:* Harvard University (A.B., cum laude, Government, 1969; J.D., 1973). General Counsel, U.S. Department of Transportation, 1993-1995. City Attorney, Denver, Colorado, 1983-1990. Assistant and First Assistant Attorney General, State of Colorado, 1976-1981. *Member:* Colorado Bar Association. ***PRACTICE AREAS:*** Aviation Law; Public Sector Law; Transportation Law; Public-Private Projects. ***Email:*** skaplan@akingump.com

DONALD MICHAEL KAYE, born Newark, New Jersey, January 8, 1960; admitted to bar, 1985, Hawaii; 1991, U.S. Court of International Trade and U.S. Court of Appeals for the Federal Circuit; 1992, District of Columbia. *Education:* Bucknell University (B.A., with honors, 1982); University of Hawaii (J.D., 1985). International Trade Attorney, Office of General Counsel, U.S. Department of Commerce, 1990-1992. *Member:* Federal and American (Member, Section on International Law and Practice) and Inter-American Bar Associations. [1st. Lieut., Infantry, U.S. Army Reserve, 1982-1985; Capt. JAGC, U.S. Army, 1985-1990]. ***LANGUAGES:*** Japanese and Spanish. ***PRACTICE AREAS:*** International Trade. ***Email:*** mkaye@akingump.com

SUKHAN KIM, born Seoul, Korea, November 20, 1949; admitted to bar, 1981, District of Columbia; 1985, U.S. Court of International Trade; U.S. Su-

(This Listing Continued)

preme Court. *Education:* Guilford College (B.A., summa cum laude, 1976); Columbia University (M.A., with Columbia Fellowship honor, 1978); Georgetown University (J.D., 1981). Phi Beta Kappa. Listed in National Registry of Who's Who in America, 2001. First Vice Chairman, U.S.-Asia Foreign Policy Council, 1983. Counsel, U.S.-Korean Foundation. Director, Korean Economic Institute. Director, The Korea Society, 1993-1998. Appointment of Adjunct Professorship, Georgetown University Law Center, 1994. Distinguished Writing Professor, Graduate School of International Studies, Yeonse University, Korea. *Member:* American Society of International Law; Washington Foreign Law Society; Asia Society. ***LANGUAGES:*** Korean. ***PRACTICE AREAS:*** International Trade. ***Email:*** skim@akingump.com

PETER J. KIRSCH, born Washington, D.C., June 12, 1958; admitted to bar, 1984, Washington; 1987, Maryland; 1988, District of Columbia; 1997, Colorado. *Education:* Oberlin College (A.B., with highest honors, 1979); University of Chicago (J.D., 1984). Author: "Environmental Protection Through Federal Preemption of State Water Laws," 20 Envir. Law Rep. 10438, 1990; "Defining the Scope of Alternatives in an EIS after Citizens Against Burlington," 21 Envir. Law Rep. 10701, 1991; "Court Ordered Reimbursement for Unproved Medical Technical Technology," 269 Journal of the American Medical Association, 2116, 1993. "Using Formal Agreements to Provide Certainty in Airport-Community Relations," Airports 95 (Institution of Engineers-Australia, Pub. No. 95/07), 1995; "Zoning for Airport Development," 37 Municipal Lawyer 6, 1996. "Sharing the Wealth from Airport Expansions," 1998 Urban Land 34. Assistant to the Legal Adviser, U.S. Department of State, 1980-1981. Law Clerk to Judge Alfred T. Goodwin, U.S. Court of Appeals, Ninth Circuit, 1984-1985. Trustee and Vice Chair, 1993-1999, 2001-2002 and Chair, 1999-2001, River Network. Member, Board of Trustees, Oberlin College, 2000—. President, Oberlin Alumni Association, 1997-1999. *Member:* District of Columbia Bar; Maryland State, Washington State, Colorado and American Bar Associations; International Municipal Lawyers Association (Past Chair, Transportation and Infrastructure Section). ***PRACTICE AREAS:*** Environmental Law; Land Use Law; Public Sector Law. ***Email:*** pkirsch@akingump.com

MERRILL L. KRAMER, (P.C.), born Detroit, Michigan, March 11, 1954; admitted to bar, 1978, Michigan and U.S. District Court, Eastern District of Michigan; 1988, District of Columbia. *Education:* Columbia University (B.A., 1975); Wayne State University (J.D., 1978). Senior Trial Attorney, Federal Energy Regulatory Commission, 1979-1984. Legal Advisor to the Cogeneration and Small Power Production Task Force, Federal Energy Regulatory Commission, 1982-1984. *Member:* Federal Energy Bar Association (Member, Board of Directors, 1990-1993; Chairman, Cogeneration and Independent Power Committee, 1988-1990). ***PRACTICE AREAS:*** Energy. ***Email:*** mkramer@akingump.com

LAWRENCE L. LAMADE, born New York, New York, April 12, 1947; admitted to bar, 1975, Maryland; 1976, District of Columbia. *Education:* Princeton University (A.B., 1969); Georgetown University (J.D., 1975). General Counsel, U.S. Department of the Navy, 1988-1989. ***Email:*** llamade@akingump.com

JAMES C. LANGDON, JR., born Los Angeles, California, September 20, 1945; admitted to bar, 1970, Texas; 1976, District of Columbia. *Education:* University of Texas (B.B.A., 1967; J.D., 1970). Associate Administrator, Federal Energy Office, 1972-1973, Federal Energy Administration, 1973-1974. Director, Office of Commercial Affairs, Department of Treasury, 1974-1975. *Member:* The District of Columbia Bar; State Bar of Texas; American Bar Association. ***PRACTICE AREAS:*** Energy; Project Finance. ***Email:*** jlangdon@akingump.com

MALCOLM LASSMAN, (P.C.), born Brooklyn, New York, June 9, 1938; admitted to bar, 1963, Virginia; 1965, District of Columbia. *Education:* Washington & Lee University (B.A., 1960; LL.B., cum laude, 1963). Delta Theta Phi. Member, Washington & Lee Law Review, 1962-1963. *Member:* The District of Columbia Bar; Virginia State, Federal and American Bar Associations. ***PRACTICE AREAS:*** General Law. ***Email:*** mlassman@akingump.com

VLADIMIR LECHTMAN, born St. Petersburg, Russia, October 4, 1955; admitted to bar, 1987, Pennsylvania; 1988, District of Columbia; 1996, New York. *Education:* University of St. Petersburg (Diploma/Linguistics, 1979); University of Texas at Austin (J.D., 1987). *Member:* American Bar Association (Business Law Section). ***PRACTICE AREAS:*** Corporate Law. ***Email:*** vlechtman@akingump.com

ROY P. LESSY, JR., born Philadelphia, Pennsylvania, February 27, 1944; admitted to bar, 1969, District of Columbia, U.S. District Court for the District of Columbia and U.S. Court of Appeals for the District of Columbia Circuit; 1971, U.S. Claims Court. *Education:* Franklin and Marshall College (B.A., with honors, 1966); George Washington University (J.D., with honors, 1969). Phi Delta Phi. Editor-in-Chief, Journal of Law and Economic Development, 1968-1969. Author: Casenote, Journal of Law and Economic Development, Fall, 1968. Lecturer, American Law Institute, 1984—. Senior Trial Attorney, U.S. Atomic Energy Commission and Deputy Chief Hearing Counsel, U.S. Nuclear Regulatory Commission, 1975-1983. Director, Special Task Force Group on Low-Level Radioactive Waste Litigation, 1981-1983. Member, Lawyers Steer-

(This Listing Continued)

ing Committee and Lawyers Committee, Nuclear Energy Institute, previously Atomic Industrial Forum, 1984—. *Member:* The District of Columbia Bar; Federal Energy and American Bar Associations. ***PRACTICE AREAS:*** Energy; Antitrust and Trade Regulation. ***Email:*** rlessy@akingump.com

LAWRENCE D. LEVIEN, (P.C.), born Philadelphia, Pennsylvania, February 10, 1946; admitted to bar, 1971, New York; 1974, District of Columbia. *Education:* Williams College (B.A., cum laude with honors, 1968); Harvard University (J.D., 1971). *Member:* The District of Columbia Bar; American Bar Association. ***PRACTICE AREAS:*** Labor and Employment. ***Email:*** llevien@akingump.com

DONALD R. LIVINGSTON, born Oak Ridge, Tennessee, January 11, 1952; admitted to bar, 1977, Georgia and U.S. District Court, Northern District of Georgia; 1978, U.S. District Court, Middle District of Georgia and U.S. Court of Appeals, Fifth Circuit; 1981, U.S. Court of Appeals, Fourth and Eleventh Circuits; 1983, U.S. Supreme Court; 1984, U.S. Court of Appeals, Sixth Circuit and U.S. District Court, Northern District of California; 1993, District of Columbia; 1994, U.S. District Court, Northern District of New York; 2001, U.S. Court of Appeals, Second Circuit. *Education:* University of Georgia (A.B., cum laude and with general honors, 1974; J.D., 1977). Phi Delta Phi. Author: "The Civil Rights Act of 1991," Stetson Law Review, Fall, 1993; "The Southern Public Employee Unions' Constitutional Card: Utilization of the Equal Protection Clause," 59 North Carolina Law Review, October, 1980. Co-Author, "The Court at the Crossroads: Runyon, Section 1981 & the Meaning of Precedent," 37 Emory Law Journal, Fall, 1988. General Counsel, U.S. Equal Employment Opportunity Commission, 1990-1993. Who's Who in America and Who's Who In American Law. *Member:* State Bar of Georgia (Chairman, 1986 and Member, Executive Board, 1984-1987, Labor and Employment Law Section); District of Columbia Bar; American Bar Association (Member, Labor and Employment Law Section). ***PRACTICE AREAS:*** Labor and Employment. ***Email:*** dlivingston@akingump.com

JORGE LOPEZ, JR., born Havana, Cuba, February 5, 1958; admitted to bar, 1984, District of Columbia. *Education:* Catholic University (B.A., summa cum laude, 1980; M.A., 1981); Harvard University (J.D., cum laude, 1984). Phi Beta Kappa. *Member:* The District of Columbia Bar. ***PRACTICE AREAS:*** Health Care. ***Email:*** jlopez@akingump.com

TERENCE J. LYNAM, born Dublin, Ireland, March 25, 1953; admitted to bar, 1978, District of Columbia; 1979, U.S. District Court, Eastern District of Virginia; 1980, Virginia, U.S. District Court for the District of Columbia and U.S. Court of Appeals, 5th Circuit; 1985, U.S. Supreme Court; 1987, U.S. Court of Appeals, 4th Circuit; 1988, U.S. Court of Appeals, 3rd Circuit; 1994, U.S. Court of Appeals, 8th Circuit; 1995, U.S. Court of Appeals, 2nd Circuit; 1996, U.S. District Court, District of Arizona; 1998, U.S. Court of Appeals, 9th Circuit; 2000, U.S. Court of Appeals, Federal Circuit; 2001, U.S. Court of Appeals, District of Columbia Circuit. *Education:* University of Pennsylvania (B.A., cum laude, 1975); Georgetown University Law Center (J.D., magna cum laude, 1978). Appellate Attorney, Department of Justice, 1979. Special Assistant United States Attorney, Eastern District of Virginia, 1980. Trial Attorney, Fraud Section, Criminal Division, Department of Justice, 1980-1984. Law Clerk, Honorable Fred B. Ugast, Superior Court of the District of Columbia, 1978-1979. Author, Article: "The Dilemma of Dismissing a Juror During Deliberations," Criminal Justice Magazine, Vol. 13, No. 4 (Winter 1999). *Member:* The District of Columbia Bar; Virginia State Bar; American Bar Association (Member, Sections on: Litigation; Criminal Law); Wong Sun Society. ***PRACTICE AREAS:*** Litigation; White Collar Criminal Defense. ***Email:*** tlynam@akingump.com

ALAN S. MACDONALD, born Boston, Massachusetts, November 4, 1962; admitted to bar, 1990, Maryland; 1991, District of Columbia; 1997, Massachusetts. *Education:* University of Edinburgh, Scotland; Middlebury College (B.A., 1986); Georgetown University (J.D., 1990). *Member:* Maryland State and Massachusetts Bar Associations; The District of Columbia Bar. ***PRACTICE AREAS:*** Litigation. ***Email:*** amacdonald@akingump.com

MARK J. MACDOUGALL, born Boston, Massachusetts, July 10, 1956; admitted to bar, 1985, Maryland; 1986, District of Columbia; 1988, U.S. Claims Court; 1992, U.S. Court of Appeals, Fifth Circuit; 1993, U.S. Supreme Court; 1994, U.S. District Court for the District of Columbia; 1996, U.S. District Court, District of Arizona; 1997, Massachusetts; 1998, U.S. District Court, Northern District of Illinois and U.S. District Court, Eastern District of Texas. *Education:* Bowdoin College; University of Notre Dame (B.A., 1978); Boston University (M.B.A., 1979); George Washington University (J.D., 1985). Vice President, The Riggs National Bank of Washington, D.C., 1983-1985. Trial Attorney, Criminal Division, U.S. Department of Justice, 1990-1993 (Dallas Bank Fraud Task Force). Author, Articles: "Eastern Europe Finds Fraud on Its Doorstep," 11 Journal of International Banking and Financial Law 2 (London, 1995); "U.S. Criminal Banking Law and the Legacy of the S & L Crisis," 9 Journal of International Banking and Financial Law 7 (London, July 1994); "Judicial Dilution and the Federal Bank Fraud Statute," 111 Banking Law Journal 173 (March-April 1994); "Beware the Advance Fee Scheme," 86 ABA

(This Listing Continued)

AKIN, GUMP, STRAUSS, HAUER & FELD, L.L.P., Washington—Continued

Banking Journal 68 (February 1994). *Member:* The District of Columbia Bar; American Bar Association. ***PRACTICE AREAS:*** Litigation; White Collar Criminal Defense. ***Email:*** mmacdougall@akingump.com

MICHAEL J. MADIGAN, (P.C.), born Washington, D.C., April 18, 1943; admitted to bar, 1968, District of Columbia. *Education:* University of Connecticut (B.A., 1965); Catholic University of America (J.D., 1968). Associate Editor, Catholic University Law Review, 1967-1968. Law Clerk to Judge Edward A. Tamm, U.S. Court of Appeals for the District of Columbia Circuit, 1968-1969. Assistant United States Attorney, 1969-1973. Assistant Minority Counsel, Senate Watergate Committee, 1973-1974. Chief Counsel to Senator Thompson, Campaign Finance Investigation, 1997-1998. Member, Board of Governors, The District of Columbia Bar, 1989-1995. Member, D.C. Judicial Nomination Commission, 1989-1994, Member, D.C. Federal Judicial Nominating Commission, 1993-1997. Member, D.C. Conference on Opportunities for Minorities in the Legal Profession. Vice Chair, Magistrate Judge Selection Committee, 1996-1997. Member, Board of Trustees, Public Defender Service for the District of Columbia, 1996—; Member, Board of Directors, Bar Association of the District of Columbia, 1996-2000. *Member:* The District of Columbia Bar; Washington Bar Association; Barristers, Counsellors; The Lawyers Club. ***PRACTICE AREAS:*** Complex Litigation; White Collar Crime; Congressional Investigations; Mediation; Arbitration. ***Email:*** mmadigan@akingump.om

MICHAEL S. MANDEL, born Charlotte, North Carolina, September 8, 1949; admitted to bar, 1974, North Carolina; 1975, District of Columbia. *Education:* University of North Carolina (A.B., 1971; M.R.P., 1974; J.D., 1974). Recipient, Certificate of Distinction and Merit, City of London Polytechnic, 1971. Special Assistant to the Secretary of Housing and Urban Development, 1979-1981. *Member:* The District of Columbia Bar; North Carolina State Bar. ***PRACTICE AREAS:*** Real Estate; Structured Financial Transactions; Real Estate Investment Trusts. ***Email:*** mmandel@akingump.com

MICHAEL S. MARCUS, (P.C.), born Charleston, West Virginia, July 6, 1944; admitted to bar, 1970, District of Columbia and U.S. District Court, District of Columbia; 1976, Virginia; 1977, U.S. District Court, Eastern District of Virginia; 1981, U.S. Court of Appeals, Fourth and District of Columbia Circuits; 1982, U.S. Court of Appeals, Fifth Circuit; 1984, U.S. Supreme Court. *Education:* Franklin & Marshall College (A.B., 1966); Villanova University (J.D., 1969). Law Clerk to Judge Kellam, 1969. Special Assistant to Attorney General, State of New Jersey, 1967-1968. *Member:* The District of Columbia Bar; Virginia State Bar. ***PRACTICE AREAS:*** Litigation. ***Email:*** mmarcus@akingump.com

ROBERT W. McCANN, born Evanston, Illinois, December 11, 1951; admitted to bar, 1980, Illinois; 1983, U.S. Supreme Court; 1998, District of Columbia. *Education:* Miami University (A.B., cum laude, 1973); University of Michigan (M.H.A., 1975; J.D., 1978). Phi Beta Kappa. Vice President and Associate General Counsel, American Hospital Association, 1982-1987. Author: "Recent Developments in Health Care Antitrust Law," *Health Law Handbook,* 2001; "You Say Viagra and I Sat Väegra: Legal Aspects of Health Care Marketing," *Health Law Handbook,* 2000; "Antitrust Update - 1998: Near Mergers, Non-Mergers, and New Life for *Venice Hospital,*" *Health Law Handbook,* 1999; "A Perspective on Recent Hospital Merger Cases," *Health Law Handbook,* 1998; "Theory and Reality in the Revised DOJ-FTC Entertainment Guidelines for Provider Networks," *Health Law Handbook,* 1997; "Provider Insures Joint Ventures," *Health Law Handbook,* 1996; "Ocean State Redux: Dominant Health Plans, Antitrust, and Health Reform," *Health Law Handbook,* 1994; "Sources of Capital Financing and Capital Cost Reimbursement," *Healthcare Corporate Law,* 1994; "Protecting the Confidentiality of Peer Review Information," J. Am. Health Information Soc., 1993; "Channel Surfing: Legal Risks In Downstream Diversification by Hospitals," *Health Law Handbook,* 1993; "Qui Tam Actions Under the Federal False Claims Act," *Health Law Handbook,* 1992; "Analyzing Confidentiality Problems in Large Scale Medical Information Systems," National Conference on Optical Imaging Systems, 1991; with W. Kopit, "Old Wine in New Bottles: The Increased Antitrust Risk of Hospital Diversification," 26 Wake Forest Law Rev. 601, 1991; with C. Reaves, "Corporate Restructuring Revisited—Tax Exemption and the Diminishment of Charitable Identity," *Health Law Handbook,* 1991; "The Uncertainty of Success: Recent Developments in HMO Law," *Health Law Handbook,* 1990; "Protection and Disclosure of Medical Peer Review Information," *Health Law Handbook,* 1989; with W. Kopit, "Toward A Definitive Antitrust Standard for Nonprofit Hospital Mergers," Journal of Health Politics, Policy and Law, Winter, 1988. ***PRACTICE AREAS:*** Antitrust; Public Finance; Health and Hospital Law. ***Email:*** rmccann@akingump.com

R. BRUCE McLEAN, born New York, New York, November 15, 1946; admitted to bar, 1971, Indiana; 1974, District of Columbia. *Education:* Indiana University (B.S., with honors, 1968; J.D., cum laude, 1971). Member, Indiana University Law Journal, 1969-1970. Order of the Coif; Phi Alpha Delta. Attorney, Appellate Court Branch, National Labor Relations Board, 1971-1973.

(This Listing Continued)

Member, Board of Visitors, Indiana University School of Law, 1989—. *Member:* The District of Columbia Bar; Federal and American Bar Associations. ***PRACTICE AREAS:*** Litigation. ***Email:*** bmclean@akingump.com

THOMAS P. McLISH, born Denver, Colorado, April 11, 1964; admitted to bar, 1989, New York; 1990, U.S. Court of Federal Claims; 1996, District of Columbia. *Education:* Claremont McKenna College (B.A., 1986); Columbia University (J.D., 1988). U.S. Department of Justice, 1990-1995. ***PRACTICE AREAS:*** Litigation; Government Contracts; Libel, Slander and Defamation; First Amendment Law. ***Email:*** tmclish@akingump.com

BRUCE S. MENDELSOHN, born Alexandria, Virginia, May 1, 1952; admitted to bar, 1977, Maryland; 1980, District of Columbia. *Education:* University of Maryland (B.S., with honors, 1974; J.D., with honors, 1977). Beta Gamma Sigma, national business honorary. Attorney and Special Counsel, Division of Corporation Finance, U.S. Securities and Exchange Commission, 1977-1980. Counsel to Commissioner, U.S. Securities and Exchange Commission, 1980-1982. Chief, Office of Regulatory Policy, Division of Investment Management, U.S. Securities and Exchange Commission, 1982-1983. *Member:* The District of Columbia Bar; Maryland State and American Bar Associations. ***PRACTICE AREAS:*** Corporate and Securities Law. ***Email:*** bmendelsohn@akingump.com

MICHAEL J. MUELLER, born Detroit, Michigan, April 24, 1960; admitted to bar, 1986, Illinois; 1987, District of Columbia. *Education:* University of Michigan (A.B., with highest distinction, 1982; J.D., cum laude, 1985). Phi Beta Kappa; Pi Sigma Alpha; Delta Theta Phi. Managing Editor, University of Michigan Journal of Law Reform, 1984-1985. Author: Note, "Abusive Pro Se Plaintiffs in Federal Courts: Proposals for Judicial Control," 18 University of Michigan Journal of Law Reform, No. 1 (1984); "RICO's Broad Applicability to Foreign Business Activity," 19 RICO Law Reporter 7 (Jan. 1994); "Litigation Activity Can Constitute RICO Predicate Acts," No. 19 Private Antitrust Litigation News (April 1995); "Klehr v. A.O. Smith Corp.: When Will We Learn the Accrual Rule for Civil RICO?" 26 RICO Law Reporter 8 (July 1997); "Supreme Court Broadly Interprets RICO's Conspiracy Provision," 13 Civil RICO Report 4 (Dec. 24, 1997); "Humana, Inc. v. Forsyth: The Insurance Business Is Now Subject to RICO... Is This The End of the McCarran-Ferguson Defense for Insurers?" 29 RICO Law Reporter 204 (February, 1999); "Supreme Court Announces Test for Whether Civil RICO Plaintiffs State a Conspiracy Claim," 16 Civil RICO Report No. 2 (May 24, 2000); "Can Employees Still Sue for Racketeering?" The Metropolitan Corporate Counsel, Vol. 8, No. 6, p. 4 (June 2000). Author and Chapter Editor, "RICO and Labor Law," The Developing Labor Law, 2000 One Year Supplement and Chapter 30 in 4th edition, 2001. Co-author: "Current Analogues Between RICO and the Clayton Act," 21 RICO Law Reporter 841 (May 1995); "Supreme Court Rejects Another Accrual Rule for Civil RICO Claims, But Fails Again to Provide Definitive Answer," 15 Civil RICO Report No. 20 (Mar. 29, 2000). Law Clerk to Hon. Avern Cohn, U.S. District Court, Detroit, 1985-1987. Advisory Board, RICO Law Reporter, 1995—. Editorial Advisory Board, Civil RICO Report, 1997—. Faculty Member, NITA Trial Advocacy Program, 1997—. *Member:* The Bar Association of the District of Columbia (Vice Chair, Litigation Committee, 1994-1996; Chair, 1996-1998); Illinois State and American (Vice Chair, 1998-2001 and Chair, 2001—, Antitrust Section Civil RICO Committee; Co-Chair, Labor and Employment Law Section, Antitrust, RICO and Labor Law Committee, 1998-2001) Bar Associations; The District of Columbia Bar. ***PRACTICE AREAS:*** Litigation. ***Email:*** mmueller@akingump.com

DANIEL L. NASH, born New York, New York, October 7, 1954; admitted to bar, 1983, District of Columbia. *Education:* State University of New York College at Cortland (B.S., cum laude, 1976); Hofstra University (M.S., 1978); University of California, Hastings College of Law (J.D., magna cum laude, 1983). Order of the Coif; Thurston Society. Note and Comment Editor, Hastings Law Journal, 1982-1983. Extern Law Clerk to Justice Stanley Mosk, California Supreme Court, 1983. Adjunct Faculty, American University, Washington College of Law, 1991-1993. *Member:* The District of Columbia Bar; American Bar Association (Section of Labor and Employment Law). ***PRACTICE AREAS:*** Labor and Employment. ***Email:*** dnash@akingump.com

ROBIN M. NUSCHLER, born New Orleans, Louisiana, May 14, 1963; admitted to bar, 1987, Louisiana; 1989, District of Columbia. *Education:* Tulane University (B.A., 1985; J.D., 1987). *Member:* The District of Columbia Bar; Louisiana State and Energy Bar Associations. ***PRACTICE AREAS:*** Energy. ***Email:*** rnuschler@akingump.com

NEIL S. OLDERMAN, born New Brunswick, New Jersey, June 4, 1963; admitted to bar, 1990, Pennsylvania; 1992, District of Columbia; 1993, Illinois. *Education:* Indiana University (B.A., 1985); Catholic University (J.D., 1990). Author, "Legal Aspects of Economic Credentialing," vol. 17, Physician Executive, 1991. Co-Author, "Overview of Legal Issues," Fundamental Medical Management: A Guide for the New Physician Executive, 1993. *Member:* Chicago, Illinois State, Pennsylvania and American Bar Associations; American Health Lawyers Association; Illinois Association of Healthcare Attorneys. ***PRACTICE AREAS:*** Health Care Transactions; Health Care Corporate Law. ***Email:*** nolderman@akingump.com

(This Listing Continued)

DAVID B. PALMER, born Des Moines, Iowa, October 19, 1946; admitted to bar, 1976, District of Columbia; 1983, U.S. Court of Appeals for the District of Columbia Circuit; 1984, U.S. District Court for the District of Columbia. *Education:* University of Florida (B.A., 1969); Western Washington University (M.A., 1972); Syracuse University (J.D., magna cum laude, 1975). Order of the Coif. Justinian Society. Associate Editor, Syracuse Law Review, 1974-1975. Attorney: Office of the General Counsel, Health Care Financing Division, U.S. Department of Health and Human Services, 1975-1983; Administrator's Citation for Development of Medicare Prospective Payment System, 1983. Author: "Uncertainties Surround Medicare Reimbursement for Capital," II (9) NASLI NEWS, 1987; "Pending Congressional Initiatives to Expand Home Care Benefits and Protect Consumers," III (1) NASLI NEWS, 1987; "Some Cons of PROs," 103 Arch. Ophthal. 343, 1985; "Case-Mix Errors," 39 Healthcare Financial Management 38, 1985; "Professional Review Organizations," in the Medicare System of Prospective Payment (DRGs), 1985; *Implications For Medical Education and Practice, 1985. Member:* The District of Columbia Bar; American Bar Association; National Health Lawyers Association. ***PRACTICE AREAS:*** Health Care. ***Email:*** dpalmer@akingump.com

JAEMIN PARK, born Seoul, Korea, November 9, 1964; admitted to bar, 1992, Maryland and Virginia (Not admitted in District of Columbia). *Education:* University of California, Los Angeles (B.S., 1988); University of Richmond (J.D., 1992). ***Email:*** jaeminpark@brownwoodlaw.com

RUSSELL W. PARKS, JR., born Cincinnati, Ohio, April 30, 1947; admitted to bar, 1973, New York; 1975, New Jersey; 1980, Texas; 1984, District of Columbia. *Education:* Trinity College (B.A., 1969); Duke University (J.D., 1972). *Member:* The District of Columbia Bar; State Bar of Texas; New York State and New Jersey Bar Associations. ***PRACTICE AREAS:*** Corporate Law. ***Email:*** rparks@akingump.com

J. STEVEN PATTERSON, born Fort Smith, Arkansas, August 5, 1965; admitted to bar, 1990, Virginia; 1996, District of Columbia. *Education:* University of Arkansas at Fayetteville (B.S., with honors, 1987); Washington and Lee University (J.D., magna cum laude, 1990). Phi Delta Phi; Omicron Delta Kappa; Gamma Beta Sigma; Order of the Coif. Editor in Chief, Washington and Lee Law Review, 1989-1990. Author, "Defining the Role of Defendant's Intentions Under Section 43(a) of the Lanham Act: Centaur Communications v. A/S/M Communications," 46 Washington and Lee Law Review 335, 1989. Co-Author (with Lyman Johnson), "The Reincarnation of Rule 152: False Hope on the Integration Front," 46 Washington and Lee Law Review 539, 1989. Law Clerk, Hon. Ellsworth A. Van Graafeiland, U.S. Court of Appeals for the Second Circuit, 1990-1991. *Member:* Virginia State Bar; District of Columbia Bar; American Bar Association. ***PRACTICE AREAS:*** Corporate Law; Securities. ***Email:*** spatterson@akingump.com

DONALD R. PONGRACE, born Chicopee, Massachusetts, 1957; admitted to bar, 1985, Maryland; 1995, District of Columbia. *Education:* University of New Hampshire; Bates College (B.A., magna cum laude, 1979); Washington College of Law, American University (J.D., magna cum laude, 1985). Phi Beta Kappa. Recipient, Laura Turley Prize for Outstanding Student Publication in American University Law Review, 1984- 1985. Notes and Comment Editor, American University Law Review, 1984-1985. Author: "Congressional Perspective on Balanced Budget and Emergency Deficit Control Act of 1985," 7 Pace University Law Review 675, 1987; "Jerry T. O'Brien, Inc. v. SEC: New Limitation on the Administrative Subpoena Power," 33 American University Law Review 701, 1984; "Stereotypification of the Fourth Amendment: An Opportunity for Clarity," 34 American University Law Review, 1985. Law Clerk to the Honorable H.E. Widener Jr., U.S. Court of Appeals, Fourth Circuit, 1985-1986. ***LANGUAGES:*** French and Swahili. ***PRACTICE AREAS:*** International Government Relations; Public Policy; Africa Trade; China Trade; Latin America Trade. ***Email:*** dpongrace@akingump.com

MICHAEL QUIGLEY, born Flushing, New York, September 11, 1957; admitted to bar, 1983, California; 1987, U.S. Court of Federal Claims; 1988, U.S. Tax Court; 1989, District of Columbia; 1991, U.S. Supreme Court. *Education:* University of California at Berkeley (A.B., 1980); Pepperdine University (J.D., cum laude, 1983). Trial Attorney, U.S. Department of Justice, Tax Division, 1983-1987. *Member:* Federal (Chair, Tax Section, 1993-1994, 1996-1997; Officer and Advisor, Section of Taxation) and American (Member, Section of Taxation Court Procedure Committee) Bar Associations. ***PRACTICE AREAS:*** Taxation Litigation. ***Email:*** mquigley@akingump.com

DENNIS M. RACE, born Cleveland, Ohio, March 13, 1947; admitted to bar, 1973, Ohio; 1975, District of Columbia. *Education:* Cleveland State University (B.A., 1970); Case Western Reserve University (J.D., 1973). Phi Alpha Delta. Articles Editor, Case Western Reserve Law Review, 1972-1973. Author: "Worker Notification: Viewpoint of the Employer," American Journal of Industrial Medicine, Vol. 23, No. 1 (Jan. 1993). Attorney, Solicitor's Office, U.S. Department of Labor, 1973-1975. *Member:* The District of Columbia Bar; Ohio State Bar Association. ***PRACTICE AREAS:*** Litigation. ***Email:*** drace@akingump.com

FRANZ R. RASSMAN, born Wilmington, Delaware, July 20, 1957; admitted to bar, 1982, Maryland; 1983, District of Columbia; 1984, U.S. District

(This Listing Continued)

Court, District of Maryland; 1987, U.S. District Court for the District of Columbia. *Education:* University of Delaware (B.S., 1979); American University (J.D., 1982). Pi Sigma Alpha (President, University of Delaware Chapter, 1978-1979). *Member:* Maryland State Bar Association; Bar Association of the District of Columbia. ***PRACTICE AREAS:*** Real Estate; Real Estate Finance. ***Email:*** frassman@akingump.com

SARAH M. ROCKWELL, born July 7, 1958; admitted to bar, 1985, Colorado; 1989, California (Not admitted in District of Columbia). *Education:* Stanford University (B.A., 1980); Massachusetts Institute of Technology (M.C.P., 1985); Boston University School of Law (J.D., 1985). *Member:* Colorado Bar Association; State Bar of California; American Planning Association. ***PRACTICE AREAS:*** Land Use; Environmental; Real Estate. ***Email:*** srockwell@akingump.com

PERRY M. ROSEN, born Plainview, New York, December 11, 1955; admitted to bar, 1981, Idaho; 1983, District of Columbia; 1989, Colorado. *Education:* State University of New York at Albany (B.A., 1978); University of Idaho (J.D., 1981). Editor-in-Chief, Idaho Law Review, 1981. *Member:* District of Columbia Bar; Idaho State Bar; Colorado Bar Association. ***PRACTICE AREAS:*** Environmental Litigation; Land Use; Project Litigation; Commercial Litigation. ***Email:*** prosen@akingump.com

STEVEN R. ROSS, born Brooklyn, New York, September 20, 1951; admitted to bar, 1976, District of Columbia; 1977, U.S. District Court for the District of Columbia; U.S. Court of Appeals for the District of Columbia Circuit; 1981, U.S. Court of Appeals, Fourth Circuit; 1982, U.S. Court of Appeals, Ninth Circuit and U.S. Supreme Court; 1983, U.S. Court of Appeals, Sixth and Eighth Circuits; 1990, U.S. Court of Appeals, Third, Fifth, Tenth and Eleventh Circuits. *Education:* Franklin & Marshall College (B.A., 1973); George Washington University (J.D., 1976). Adjunct Professor in Constitutional Law, George Mason University School of Law, 1991-1992. General Counsel, U.S. House of Representatives, 1983-1993. *Member:* American Bar Association (Member: Government Standards Committee; Subcommittee on Public Corruption, White Collar Crime Committee, Criminal Justice Section). ***PRACTICE AREAS:*** Public Policy; White Collar Criminal Defense. ***Email:*** sross@akingump.com

JERRY E. ROTHROCK, born Spokane, Washington, January 21, 1945; admitted to bar, 1975, District of Columbia. *Education:* Rice University (B.A., summa cum laude, 1967); Massachusetts Institute of Technology (M.S., 1971); Harvard University (J.D., 1974). Phi Beta Kappa. *Member:* The District of Columbia Bar; Federal and American Bar Associations. ***PRACTICE AREAS:*** Energy. ***Email:*** jrothrock@akingump.com

EDWARD L. RUBINOFF, (P.C.), born Pittsburgh, Pennsylvania, February 15, 1950; admitted to bar, 1975, Pennsylvania; 1976, District of Columbia. *Education:* University of Pennsylvania (B.A., with honors, 1972); George Washington University (J.D., with honors, 1975). Recipient: The Jennie Hassler Walburn Award, 1973. Author: "Export Controls, Sanctions and Antiboycott Laws," The International Lawyer's Deskbook (ABA, 1996); "Exports of Oil and Gas Equipment to the Soviet Union: A Case Study in the Use of Export Controls as Instruments of U.S. Foreign Policy," Law and Policy of Export Controls: Recent Essays on Key Export Issues (ABA, 1993). Co-Author: "Implementing The Omnibus Trade and Competitiveness Act Amendments to the Export Administration Act," 2 International Quarterly 158 (January 1990). *Member:* The District of Columbia Bar; American Bar Association (Section of International Law and Practice: Council Member, 1998-2001; Editor in Chief, International Law News, 1998-2001; Chairman, 1995-1998 and Vice Chair, 1993-1995, Committee on Export Controls and Economic Sanctions; Steering Group, 1988—, International Trade Committee); Lawyers Alliance for World Security (Member, 1994— and Director, 1996—). ***PRACTICE AREAS:*** International Trade; Technology. ***Email:*** erubinoff@akingump.com

GEORGE R. SALEM, born Jacksonville, Florida, December 24, 1953; admitted to bar, 1978, Georgia; 1979, Florida; 1981, District of Columbia. *Education:* Emory University (B.A., 1975; J.D., 1977); Georgetown University Law Center (LL.M., 1984). Delta Theta Phi; Omicron Delta Kappa. Solicitor of Labor, U.S. Department of Labor, 1985-1989. Deputy Solicitor of Labor for National Operations, April 8- December 8, 1985. Author: "The United States Department of Labor: Enforcement and Litigation," Critical Issues in Labor and Employment Law (Stetson University College of Law CCH, 1990); "Nonmajority Bargaining Orders: A Prospective View of United Dairy Farmers," 32 Labor Law Journal 145, March 1981; "Recent Developments in the Law at the Labor Department," Southwestern Legal Foundation, October, 1987, 1988, 1989, 1990, 1991, 1992, 1993, 1994, 1995, 1996, 1997, 1998, 1999, 2000, 2001. Recipient: Ellis Island Medal of Honor, 1992. *Who's Who in America, Who's Who in American Law, Who's Who in Finance and Industry, International Who's Who of Management Labor and Employment Lawyers.* Chairman, Arab American Leadership Council, 1990-1992. Chairman, Arab American Institute, 1999-2001. Member, Board of Directors, 1987-1994, and President, 1992-1994, National Association of Arab Americans. Member, Board of Directors, Overseas Private Investment Corporation, 1987-1988. Chairman, Tripartite Advisory Panel on International Labor Standards, 1986-1988. *Member:* American Bar

(This Listing Continued)

AKIN, GUMP, STRAUSS, HAUER & FELD, L.L.P., Washington—Continued

Association (Labor and Employment Law Section); State Bar of Georgia; The Florida Bar; The District of Columbia Bar. ***PRACTICE AREAS:*** Labor and Employment; Middle East. ***Email:*** gsalem@akingump.com

ROBERT SALCIDO, born Covina, California, October 19, 1962; admitted to bar, 1989, California (inactive); 1995, District of Columbia. *Education:* Claremont McKenna College (B.A., summa cum laude, 1984); Harvard Law School (J.D., 1988). Phi Beta Kappa. Trial Attorney, U.S. Department of Justice, Civil Division, Commercial Litigation Branch, Civil Fraud, 1988-1993. Recipient: Department of Health and Human Services, Office of Inspector General's Integrity Award for outstanding contributions to the mission of the Inspector General 1992, Department of Justice Special Achievement Awards 1991 and 1992. Publications: Books: "The False Claims Act and The Healthcare Industry: Counseling and Litigation," (American Health Lawyers Association); Articles: "Investigating Allegations of Fraud: Questions to Ask When Evaluating Whether Cost Report Claims Breach the False Claims Act," *Health Care Fraud Litigation Reporter* (February, 2000); "DOJ Must Reevaluate Use of False Claims Act in Medicare Disputes," *Washington Legal Foundation* (Jan. 7, 2000); "The Use of Voluntary Disclosures to Pre-Exempt Qui Tam Actions Under the False Claims Act: An Analysis of the Bank of Farmington Case and the OIG's Voluntary Disclosure Program," 27 HEALTH LAW DIGEST 3 (American Health Lawyers Association, April, 1999); "Screening Out Unworthy Whistleblower Actions: An Historical Analysis of the Jurisdictional Bar to Qui Tam Actions Under the False Claims Act," 24 Public Contract Law Journal 237 (Winter 1995); "HHS' Voluntary Disclosure Program: How To Obtain Benefits Under The Program While Minimizing Risk," The Health Lawyer (Late Summer 1995); "Application of the False Claim Act Knowledge Standard: What One Must 'Know' to be Held Liable Under the Act," The Health Lawyer (Mid-Winter 1996); "Mixing Oil and Water: The Government's Mistaken Use of the Medicare Anti-Kickback Statute in False Claims Act Prosecutions," 6 Annal's Health L. 105 (1997); "The Supreme Court Punts: The Court's Non-Ruling on the False Claims Act and Its Implications for the Health Care Industry," The Health Lawyer (Vol. 9 no. 7, 1997). *Member:* American Bar Association (Public Contract Law Section); American Health Lawyers Association. ***PRACTICE AREAS:*** Health Care. ***Email:*** rsalcido@akingump.com

STANLEY J. SAMORAJCZYK, born New Britain, Connecticut, October 1, 1942; admitted to bar, 1968, District of Columbia; 1970, Virginia and U.S. District Court for the Eastern District of Virginia; 1974, U.S. Court of Appeals, Fourth Circuit; 1985, U.S. District Court, District of Maryland; 1989, U.S. Court of Appeals, Third Circuit; 1991, U.S. District Court, Southern District of Texas. *Education:* Georgetown University (A.B., 1964); Catholic University of America (J.D., 1967). Chairman, Mid-Atlantic Institute on Bankruptcy and Reorganization Practice, 1986—; Member, Catholic University School of Law Board of Visitors, 1998—. Lecturer, International Business and Trade Summer Law Program, Jagiellonian University, Cracow, Poland, 1994. Fellow, American College of Bankruptcy. Lecturer, Business Bankruptcy and Reorganization, Joint Committee on Continuing Legal Education, Virginia Bar Foundation, 1979—. Member, Fourth Circuit Bankruptcy Merit Selection Panel, 1986-1988. *Member:* The District of Columbia Bar (Member, Committee on Bankruptcy and Reorganization, 1976—); Bar Association of the District of Columbia; Virginia State Bar (Member, Board of Governors, Bankruptcy Law Section, 1990-1998; Chairman, 1992-1993); American Bar Association (Member, Business Law Section, Business Bankruptcy Committee); American Bankruptcy Institute. ***PRACTICE AREAS:*** Business Reorganization; International Insolvency; International Bankruptcy; Commercial Insolvency. ***Email:*** ssamorajczyk@akingump.com

SANFORD M. SAUNDERS, JR., born Brooklyn, New York, August 28, 1958; admitted to bar, 1983, District of Columbia; 1985, U.S. Court of Appeals for the District of Columbia Circuit and U.S. District Court for the District of Columbia; 1988, U.S. District Court, District of Maryland; 1989, U.S. Court of Appeals, Fourth Circuit; 1991, Maryland; 1996, U.S. Court of Appeals, Tenth Circuit and U.S. Court of Appeals for the Federal Circuit; 1998, U.S. Supreme Court. *Education:* The Johns Hopkins University (B.A., with honors, 1980); Georgetown University (J.D., cum laude, 1983). Phi Sigma Alpha. *Member:* The District of Columbia Bar; Maritime Law Association of the United States (Member: Criminal Practice and Procedure Committee; Technology and E-Commerce Committee). ***PRACTICE AREAS:*** Litigation; Technology Law. ***Email:*** ssaunders@akingump.com

BARNEY J. SKLADANY, JR., born Kingston, Pennsylvania, September 2, 1945; admitted to bar, 1970, District of Columbia. *Education:* Rutgers University (B.A., 1967); George Washington University (J.D., 1970). ***PRACTICE AREAS:*** Public Policy. ***Email:*** bskladany@akingump.com

VALERIE A. SLATER, born Passaic, New Jersey, October 13, 1952; admitted to bar, 1977, District of Columbia; 1978, U.S. Court of Appeals for the District of Columbia and U.S. District Court, District of Columbia; 1982, U.S. Court of International Trade; 1984, U.S. Court of Appeals, Federal Circuit. *Education:* Allegheny College (B.A., magna cum laude, 1974) Phi Beta Kappa; Catholic University of America (J.D., 1977). Moot Court Vice Chancellor. *Member:* The District of Columbia Bar; U.S. Court of International Trade Advisory Committee. ***PRACTICE AREAS:*** International Trade. ***Email:*** vslater@akingump.com

ROXANE N. SOKOLOVE, born Newark, New Jersey, December 10, 1955; admitted to bar, 1979, Pennsylvania; 1985, District of Columbia; U.S. District Court, District of Columbia, Eastern District of Pennsylvania, Northern and Western Districts of Texas, U.S. Court of Appeals, Third, Fourth and Fifth Circuits. *Education:* American University (B.A., magna cum laude, 1976); University of Baltimore (J.D., 1979). U.S. Department of Justice Honors Program. Staff Attorney, Board of Immigration Appeals, 1979-1980. Trial Attorney, U.S. Department of Justice, Organized Crime and Racketeering Section, 1980-1983. Assistant U.S. Attorney, District of Columbia, 1983-1987. *Member:* The District of Columbia Bar; The Bar of the Commonwealth of Pennsylvania. ***PRACTICE AREAS:*** Labor and Employment Litigation. ***Email:*** rsokolove@akingump.com

JONATHAN S. SPAETH, born Washington, D.C., July 24, 1959; admitted to bar, 1984, Illinois; 1985, District of Columbia and U.S. District Court, Northern District of Illinois; 1990, U.S. District Court for The District of Columbia. *Education:* University of Michigan (B.A., 1981); University of Virginia (J.D., 1984). *Member:* The District of Columbia Bar. ***PRACTICE AREAS:*** Litigation. ***Email:*** jspaeth@akingump.com

DANIEL L. SPIEGEL, born Baltimore, Maryland, September 5, 1945; admitted to bar, 1980, District of Columbia. *Education:* Washington University (B.A., magna cum laude, 1967); Harvard University, John F. Kennedy School of Government (M.P.A., 1969); Georgetown University (J.D., 1979). U.S. Ambassador to the European Office of the United Nations, 1993-1996. Legislative Assistant to: Senator Alan Cranston, 1969-1971; Senator Hubert H. Humphrey, 1971-1976. Special Assistant to Secretary of State Cyrus Vance, 1977-1978. Member, Policy Planning Staff, Department of State, 1978-1979. *Member:* The District of Columbia Bar. ***PRACTICE AREAS:*** International Trade; Public Policy. ***Email:*** dspiegel@akingump.com

C. FAIRLEY SPILLMAN, born Winston-Salem, North Carolina, April 4, 1959; admitted to bar, 1984, District of Columbia. *Education:* Duke University (B.A., magna cum laude, 1981); Harvard University (J.D., cum laude, 1984). *Member:* The District of Columbia Bar. ***PRACTICE AREAS:*** Litigation. ***Email:*** fspillman@akingump.com

ROBERT S. STRAUSS, born Lockhart, Texas, October 19, 1918; admitted to bar, 1941, Texas; 1971, District of Columbia. *Education:* University of Texas (LL.B., 1941). Special Trade Representative of the United States, with the Rank of Ambassador, 1977-1979. Special Representative of the President to the Mid-East, August-December, 1979. Ambassador to the Soviet Union, and upon the dissolution of the Soviet Union, assumed the duties as U.S. Ambassador to the Russian Federation, 1991-1992. Awarded Medal of Freedom, 1981. *Member:* Dallas and American Bar Associations; The District of Columbia Bar. ***PRACTICE AREAS:*** General Practice.

LARRY E. TANENBAUM, born Baltimore, Maryland, December 7, 1951; admitted to bar, 1976, Maryland; 1977, District of Columbia. *Education:* Syracuse University and University of Maryland (B.A., with honors, 1973); University of Baltimore (J.D., magna cum laude, 1976). *Member:* The District of Columbia Bar; Maryland State Bar Association. ***PRACTICE AREAS:*** Litigation; Technology. ***Email:*** ltanenbaum@akingump.com

HENRY A. TERHUNE, born Hackensack, New Jersey, February 13, 1957; admitted to bar, 1987, New York; 1989, District of Columbia. *Education:* State University of New York (B.A., 1980); George Washington University (J.D., 1986). Legislative Assistant and Director to U.S. Representative Butler Derrick, 1979-1987. Associate Staff Member, Committee on Rules, U.S. House of Representatives, 1984-1987. *Member:* The District of Columbia Bar; New York State and American Bar Associations. ***PRACTICE AREAS:*** Public Policy. ***Email:*** hterhune@akingump.com

W. RANDOLPH TESLIK, (P.C.), born McKeesport, Pennsylvania, September 21, 1949; admitted to bar, 1976, District of Columbia; 1977, U.S. District Court for the District of Columbia; 1980, U.S. Supreme Court; 1987, U.S. District Court for the District of Maryland; 1989, U.S. Court of Appeals, Eighth Circuit; 1990, U.S. Court of Appeals, Second Circuit; 1992, U.S. Court of Appeals, Fourth Circuit; 1995, U.S. Court of Appeals, Ninth Circuit. *Education:* Duke University (A.B., 1971); Washington College of Law of American University (J.D., 1976). Author, *Prosecutorial Discretion: The Decision to Charge--Annotated Bibliography,* Law Enforcement Assistance Administration, GPO, 1975; Editor, *Criminal Trial Manual* Sixth Ed. United States Attorney's Office, 1977. Contributor: History of the United States Court of Appeals for the District of Columbia Circuit in the Country's Bicentennial Year, 1977; Criminal Jury Instructions for the District of Columbia, The Red Book, 1978. Assistant United States Attorney, District of Columbia, 1977-1986. Chief, Grand Jury Section, 1982-1986. Deputy Director, Superior Court Operations, 1986. *Member:* The District of Columbia Bar. ***PRACTICE AREAS:*** Litigation. ***Email:*** rteslik@akingump.com

(This Listing Continued)

(This Listing Continued)

THOMAS B. TRIMBLE, born Jacksonville, Florida, July 19, 1959; admitted to bar, 1988, New York and Connecticut; 1989, District of Columbia. *Education:* Bucknell University (B.A., 1982); Columbia University, School of International Affairs (M.I.A., 1985); The American University, Washington College of Law (J.D., 1987). Columnist, Moscow Tribune. *Member:* District of Columbia Bar; US-Russia Business Council; American Chamber of Commerce, Moscow. ***LANGUAGES:*** Russian. ***Email:*** ttrimble@akingump.com

JAMES P. TUITE, born Oneida, New York; admitted to bar, 1973, Texas; 1982, District of Columbia. *Education:* Duke University (A.B., 1970); University of Texas (J.D., 1973). Deputy Associate General Counsel, 1979-1980, and Trial Attorney, Office of the General Counsel, 1978-1979, Interstate Commerce Commission. *Member:* The District of Columbia Bar; State Bar of Texas; American Bar Association. ***PRACTICE AREAS:*** Complex Litigation; Trial Practice; Appellate Practice; Energy; Antitrust; Intellectual Property; Administrative Law; Transportation. ***Email:*** jtuite@akingump.com

LESLIE M. TURNER, born Neptune, New Jersey, October 2, 1957; admitted to bar, 1986, New York and District of Columbia. *Education:* New York University (B.S., 1980); Georgetown University Law Center (J.D., 1985). Recipient, National Competition and Best Brief Award, National Labor Law Moot Court Team. Law Clerk to Hon. William C. Pryor, Chief Judge, District of Columbia Court of Appeals, 1985-1986. Author: "Reforming CERCLA's Natural Resource Damage Provisions: A Challenge to the 105th Congress form the Clinton Administration," 27 ELR 10121-10127, March 1997. *Member:* The District of Columbia Bar (Member, Committee on Professionalism and Public Understanding About the Law); New York State and American (Member, Section on Individual Rights and Responsibilities, Vice-Chair, Environmental Justice Committee) Bar Associations. ***PRACTICE AREAS:*** Litigation. ***Email:*** lturner@akingump.com

PAUL L. UHRIG, born Port Cartier, Quebec, Canada, January 15, 1962; admitted to bar, 1986, Maryland; 1988, District of Columbia. *Education:* University of Notre Dame (B.A., 1983); American University (J.D., 1986). Associated Editor, The American University Journal of International Law and Policy, 1985-1986. Author: "An Ounce of Prevention- Getting Your Administrative Affairs in Order for a Due Diligence Review...," HMO Magazine, May/June 1992. *Member:* District of Columbia Bar; Bar Association of the District of Columbia; American Bar Association; National Health Lawyers Association. ***LANGUAGES:*** French. ***PRACTICE AREAS:*** Health Care; Corporate Planning; Mergers and Acquisitions. ***Email:*** puhrig@akingump.com

CHARLES L. WARREN, born Houston, Texas, July 12, 1949; admitted to bar, 1974, Texas; 1976, District of Columbia. *Education:* Washington University (B.S., 1971); University of Texas (J.D., 1974). Note and Comment Editor, Texas Law Review, 1973-1974. Law Clerk to Hon. Charles Clark, U.S. Court of Appeals, Fifth Circuit, 1974-1975. *Member:* The District of Columbia Bar; State Bar of Texas; American Bar Association. ***PRACTICE AREAS:*** Labor and Employment. ***Email:*** cwarren@akingump.com

S. BRUCE WILSON, born Salina, Kansas, August 27, 1948; admitted to bar, 1987, Virginia; 1988, District of Columbia. *Education:* Stanford University (B.A., 1970); Johns Hopkins University (M.A., 1972); George Washington University (M.B.A., 1979; J.D., 1986). Trade Counsel to Committee on Ways & Means, U.S. House of Representatives, 1991-1998. Office of U.S. Trade Representative, 1975-1991. I Member: American Bar Association (Member, International Section, 1987—). ***LANGUAGES:*** Portuguese, French, Spanish and Italian. ***PRACTICE AREAS:*** International Trade; Public Law and Policy. ***Email:*** bwilson@akingump.com

SAMUEL WOLFF, born Little Rock, Arkansas, October 25, 1956; admitted to bar, 1982, Arkansas; 1989, District of Columbia; 1992, Colorado. *Education:* London School of Economics, London, England; Brown University (A.B., magna cum laude, 1979); Georgetown University Law Center (J.D., 1982; LL.M., in Securities Regulation, 1983); University of Wisconsin School of Law (S.J.D., 1995). Co-Editor, *International Capital Markets and Securities Regulation,* West Group. Co-Author: *Securities and Federal Corporate Law,* West Group; *Emerging Trends in Securities Law,* West Group (nine books in annual series). Author: "Review of Global Offerings of Securities: Access to World Equity Capital Markets," 14 Wisc. Int'l. L.J. 236 (Fall 1995); "Recent Developments in International Securities Regulation," 23 Denv. J. Int'l L. & Pol. 347 (Spring 1995); "Off-Shore Distributions Under the Securities Act of 1933: An Analysis of Regulation S," 23 L. & Pol. in Int'l Bus. 101 (Wint. 1991-1992); "Securities Regulation in the European Community," 20 Denv. J. Int'l L. & Pol. 99 (Fall 1991); "Trust Indenture Act Reform: A Review of the SEC's Proposal," 17 Sec. Reg. L.J., 303 (Fall 1989); "A Study of Mexico's Capital Markets and Securities Regulation," 20 Vand. J. Transnat'l L. 385 (1987). Co-Author: "The Multijurisdictional Disclosure System and Cross-Border Offerings," 20 Denv. J. Int'l L & Pol. 551 (Spring 1992); "Securities Regulation in Central Europe: Hungary and Czechoslovakia," 21 Denv. J. Int'l L. & Pol. (1993); "The Securities Market and Regulation of Mexico," 19 Denv. J. Int'l L. & Pol. 569 (Spring 1991). Lecturer in Law, University of Denver College of Law, Spring 1992. Staff Attorney, Division of Corporation Finance, Securities and Exchange Commission, 1985-1988. Deputy Chief, Office of International Corporate Finance, Securities and Exchange Commission, 1988. ***PRACTICE AREAS:*** Corporate Law; Securities. ***Email:*** swolff@akingump.com

RICHARD L. WYATT, JR. (P.C.), born Andalusia, Alabama, March 16, 1953; admitted to bar, 1979, Georgia; 1990, District of Columbia. *Education:* Auburn University (B.A., 1975); Emory University (J.D., 1979). *Member:* The District of Columbia Bar; State Bar of Georgia. ***PRACTICE AREAS:*** Labor and Employment. ***Email:*** rwyatt@akingump.com

CLIFFORD J. ZATZ, born Boston, Massachusetts, October 13, 1954; admitted to bar, 1979, District of Columbia; 1981, U.S. Court of Appeals, Fourth Circuit; 1983, Massachusetts; 1988, U.S. Court of Appeals, Tenth Circuit; 1990, U.S. District Court, District of Columbia; 1991, U.S. Court of Appeals, District of Columbia Circuit; 1993, U.S. Court of Federal Claims; 1999, U.S. District Court, District of Arizona; U.S. District Court, Northern District of Illinois. *Education:* Boston University (B.A., summa cum laude, 1976); Duke University (J.D., 1979). Phi Beta Kappa. Author: "Taking the Offensive in the Long Toxic Tort Trial," 40 For The Defense No. 3 (March 1998) at 8; "Defenses on the Frontiers of Science," 19 Litigation No. 1 (Fall 1992) 13; "Summary Jury Trial: The Settlement of a Toxic Tort Case," 2 Toxics Law Reporter (BNA) 929 (1988), reprinted in 2 BNA's Alternative Dispute Resolution Report 145 (1988); "Painting Injury by the Numbers: The Myth of the Omniscient Laboratory," ICET Symposium III Immunotoxicology: From Lab to Law 97 (1987). Co-Author: "Defending Speculative Injury Claims," 2 Toxics Law Reporter (BNA) 76 (1987), reprinted in Birnbaum and Gross, eds., Preparation and Trial of a Toxic Tort Case 1988 (PLI). *Member:* The District of Columbia Bar; Massachusetts and American (Member, Section of Litigation) Bar Associations; The Defense Research Institute. ***PRACTICE AREAS:*** Litigation. ***Email:*** czatz@akingump.com

ASSOCIATES

CARRIE HILL ALLEN, born Rochester, New York, October 7, 1970; admitted to bar, 1995, Maryland; 1997, District of Columbia. *Education:* University of Miami (B.A., with honors, 1992); Northeastern University (J.D., 1995). *Member:* Energy and American Bar Associations. ***PRACTICE AREAS:*** Energy Law. ***Email:*** callen@akingump.com

WILLIAM F. ALLEN, born Danbury, Connecticut, December 2, 1966; admitted to bar, 1996, Connecticut; 1997, District of Columbia. *Education:* University of Virginia (B.S., 1988; M.B.A., 1992; J.D., 1996). Tau Beta Pi; Omicron Delta Kappa; Order of the Coif. Member, Raven Society. *Member:* The District of Columbia Bar. ***PRACTICE AREAS:*** Labor and Employment. ***Email:*** ballen@akingump.com

ALISON E. BARRY, born New York, N.Y., 1963; admitted to bar, 1996, Colorado (Not admitted in District of Columbia). *Education:* Yale University (B.S., 1985); University of Colorado at Boulder (J.D., 1996). ***Email:*** abarry@akingump.com

RICHARD W. BLACK, born Philadelphia, Pennsylvania, February 23, 1971; admitted to bar, 1996, Minnesota and U.S. District Court, District of Minnesota (Not admitted in District of Columbia). *Education:* Temple University; University of Iowa (B.A., with high distinction, 1992; J.D., with distinction, 1996). Omicron Delta Kappa. Recipient: Temple University Outstanding Achievement Scholar, 1988-1990; University of Iowa Collegiate Scholar, 1992; Iowa Law Foundation Scholar, 1993-1995. Teaching Assistant, Modern Fiction, University of Iowa Department of English, 1992. Member, 1994-1995 and Managing Editor, 1995-1996, Iowa Law Review. *Member:* Ramsey County, Minnesota State, Federal and American (Member, Labor and Employment Section, 1999—; Litigation Section, 1999—) Bar Associations. ***PRACTICE AREAS:*** Labor and Employment Litigation. ***Email:*** rblack@akingump.com

ROBERT T. BRADFORD, born Bellefonte, Pennsylvania, October 12, 1965; admitted to bar, 1990, Maryland; 1991, District of Columbia. *Education:* Princeton University (A.B., 1987); New York University (J.D., 1990). *Member:* The District of Columbia Bar. ***PRACTICE AREAS:*** Real Estate; Asset Backed Securities; Commercial Mortgage Backed Securities. ***Email:*** rbradford@akingump.com

MAIYSHA R. BRANCH, born Norristown, Pennsylvania, April 20, 1975; admitted to bar, 2000, Pennsylvania (Not admitted in District of Columbia). *Education:* Northwestern University (B.S., 1997); George Washington University Law School (J.D., 2000). Member, George Washington Environmental Lawyer Journal. ***PRACTICE AREAS:*** Litigation. ***Email:*** mbranch@akingump.com

KATHERINE D. BRODIE, born Madrid, Spain, January 1, 1968; admitted to bar, 1997, Maryland; 1998, District of Columbia. *Education:* Bowdoin College (A.B., cum laude, 1990); George Washington University (J.D., 1997). Managing Editor, George Washington Law Review, 1996-1997. Dean's Fellow, George Washington University Law School, 1996-1997. *Member:* The District of Columbia Bar. ***PRACTICE AREAS:*** Public Policy. ***Email:*** kbrodie@akingump.com

(This Listing Continued)

AKIN, GUMP, STRAUSS, HAUER & FELD, L.L.P., Washington—Continued

MELANIE R. BURKES, born Pittsburgh, Pennsylvania, December 29, 1974; admitted to bar, 2001, New York (Not admitted in District of Columbia). *Education:* Duke University (A.B., 1997); University of Virginia (J.D., 2000). Virginia Law Review. ***PRACTICE AREAS:*** Corporate Law. ***Email:*** mburkes@akingump.com

MICHAEL S. CALDWELL, born Salem, Ohio, August 17, 1970; admitted to bar, 2000, New York (Not admitted in District of Columbia).. *Education:* University of Norte Dame (B.A., 1992); Georgetown University (J.D., cum laude, 1999). Teaching Assistant, Legal Research and Writing Department, Georgetown University, 1996-1998. Adjunct Professor, U.S. Legal Discourse, Georgetown University, 2000-2001. ***REPORTED CASES:*** United States v. William Wise Murray, 176 F3d 476, 1999 WL 187192 (4th Cir. (S.C.)). ***PRACTICE AREAS:*** Litigation. ***Email:*** mcaldwell@akingump.com

DAVID A. CATANIA, born Kansas City, Missouri, January 16, 1968; admitted to bar, 1994, Maryland; 1995, U.S. District Court, District of Maryland; 1996, District of Columbia. *Education:* Georgetown University (B.S.F.S., magna cum laude, 1990; J.D., 1994). Phi Beta Kappa. At-Large Member, D.C. Council. Member, Board of Directors, Washington Metropolitan Area Transit Authority. *Member:* Maryland State Bar Association; The District of Columbia Bar. ***PRACTICE AREAS:*** Energy. ***Email:*** dcatania@akingump.com

RISA B. CHERRY, born Brooklyn, New York, June 1, 1971; admitted to bar, 1996, Maryland; 1997, District of Columbia. *Education:* Cornell University (B.A., 1993); University of Pennsylvania (J.D., 1996). Law Clerk, Honorable Joseph E. Irenas, U.S. District Court, District of New Jersey, 1996-1997. *Member:* The District of Columbia Bar; Maryland State Bar Association. ***PRACTICE AREAS:*** Labor and Employment. ***Email:*** rcherry@akingump.com

ALAN COHN, born 1971; admitted to bar, 1997, Maryland; 1998, District of Columbia. *Education:* Columbia University (B.A., 1993); Georgetown University (J.D., 1997). ***Email:*** acohn@akingump.com

MICHAEL L. CONVERSE, born Kansas City, Kansas, April 30, 1958; admitted to bar, 1992, Pennsylvania; 1993, District of Columbia. *Education:* Georgetown University (B.A., 1980); George Washington University (J.D., with high honors, 1991). Order of the Coif. Member, George Washington University Law Review. ***PRACTICE AREAS:*** Litigation. ***Email:*** mconverse@akingump.com

JANIS M. CRUM, born Reading, Pennsylvania, November 26, 1968; admitted to bar, 1998, California; 2000, District of Columbia. *Education:* California State University (B.A., magna cum laude, 1991); University of California, Hastings School of Law (J.D., 1998). Phi Kappa Phi. Author: "Is the Internet a Safe Haven for Corporate Political Speech?" 8 CommLaw Conspectus 193, Summer 2000. ***PRACTICE AREAS:*** Election Law; Political Compliance; Federal Ethics Compliance; State Ethics Compliance; Local Ethics Compliance. ***Email:*** jcrum@akingump.com

JILL F. DASH, born Miami, Florida, November 15, 1975; admitted to bar, 2000, Maryland (Not admitted in District of Columbia). *Education:* Cornell University (B.A., 1997); Duke University Law School (J.D., 2000). Member, Law and Contemporary Problems, Moot Court Board. Mordecai Scholar. ***LANGUAGES:*** Spanish. ***PRACTICE AREAS:*** Labor. ***Email:*** jdash@akingump.com

ERIN DOZIER, born New York, N.Y., July 22, 1970; admitted to bar, 1999, Connecticut; 2000, District of Columbia. *Education:* Hampshire College (B.A., 1992); Georgetown University (J.D., 1998). *Member:* Federal Communications Bar Association; American Bar Association. ***PRACTICE AREAS:*** Communications Law. ***Email:*** edozier@akingump.com

ANGELA M. DUSENBURY, born Tacoma, Washington, July 23, 1973; admitted to bar, 1999, New York (Not admitted in District of Columbia). *Education:* University of Massachusetts at Amherst (B.A., 1995); University of Texas (J.D., 1998). ***PRACTICE AREAS:*** Environmental Law. ***Email:*** adusenbury@akingump.com

THOMAS F. FELTON, born Richmond, Virginia, October 23, 1970; admitted to bar, 2000, Virginia (Not admitted in District of Columbia). *Education:* University of Virginia (B.A., English, 1992); Catholic University of America (J.D., suma cum laude, 2000). Executive Editor, Catholic University Law Review, 1999-2000. Author: "Sink or Swim Bilingual Education in the Wake of Calif. Prop 227," 48 Cath. U. L. Rev. 843 (sp 99). ***PRACTICE AREAS:*** Health Care. ***Email:*** tfelton@akingump.com

MICHAEL FERRANS, born Washington, D.C., September 25, 1971; admitted to bar, 1996, Maryland; 1998, District of Columbia. *Education:* Tulane University (B.A., 1992); George Washington University (J.D., with high honors, 1996). Order of the Coif. ***LANGUAGES:*** Spanish. ***PRACTICE AREAS:*** Labor and Employment. ***Email:*** mferrans@akingump.com

LAURA E. FITZRANDOLPH, born Sacramento, California, October 21, 1969; admitted to bar, 1998, California, U.S. District Court, Central District of California and U.S. Court of Appeals, Ninth Circuit; 1999, District of Columbia. *Education:* University of California at Berkeley (B.A., 1991); George Washington University (J.D., with high honors, 1997). Order of the Coif. Moot Court Board; Notes and Projects Editor, The George Washington Law Review. Casenote, Title VII - Employer Liability for Sexual Harassment, 64 Geo. Wash. L. Rev., 1168 (1996). *Member:* District of Columbia Bar. ***PRACTICE AREAS:*** Labor and Employment. ***Email:*** lfitzrandolph@akingump.com

CHARLES WILLIAM FRICK, born Maryland, 1974; admitted to bar, 2001, Maryland (Not admitted in District of Columbia). *Education:* Northwestern University (B.A., 1997); Harvard Law School (J.D., 2000). ***PRACTICE AREAS:*** Litigation. ***Email:*** bfrick@akingump.com

STEPHANIE AGLI GALLAGHER, born Rockville, Connecticut, November 24, 1972; admitted to bar, 1997, Maryland; 1999, District of Columbia. *Education:* Georgetown University (B.A., 1994); Harvard University (J.D., 1997). Law Clerk to the Hon. J. Frederick Motz, U.S. District Court, 1997-1999. ***PRACTICE AREAS:*** Litigation. ***Email:*** sgallagher@akingump.com

DIRK R. GARDNER, born South Weber, Utah, April 4, 1966; admitted to bar, 1998, Missouri; 2001, District of Columbia. *Education:* Brigham Young University (B.A., 1990); Washington University (J.D., 1998). Order of the Coif. Member, Washington University Law Quarterly. *Member:* Bar Association of Metropolitan St. Louis; The Missouri Bar; The District of Columbia Bar; American Bar Association. ***LANGUAGES:*** Japanese. ***PRACTICE AREAS:*** Corporate; Securities; Banking. ***Email:*** dgardner@akingump.com

FANI CYD GEROFF, born Philadelphia, Pennsylvania, December 11, 1974; admitted to bar, 1999, Maryland; 2000, District of Columbia. *Education:* Cornell University (B.S., 1996); University of Pennsylvania (J.D., 1999). ***PRACTICE AREAS:*** Litigation. ***Email:*** fgeroff@akingump.com

JONATHAN L. GOLD, born Silver Spring, Maryland, October 11, 1967; admitted to bar, 1994, Maryland; 1996, District of Columbia; U.S. District Court, District of Columbia; U.S. District Court, District of Maryland. *Education:* University of Maryland (B.S., 1989); University of Baltimore School of Law (J.D., magna cum laude, 1993). Associate Executive Editor, University of Baltimore School of Law, Law Review, 1992-1993. Law Clerk to the Judges of the U.S. Bankruptcy Court, District of Maryland, 1994-1995; Law Clerk, Chief Judge Paul Mannes, U.S. Bankruptcy Court, District of Maryland, 1995-1996. *Member:* Maryland State Bar Association; The District of Columbia Bar. ***PRACTICE AREAS:*** Bankruptcy. ***Email:*** jgold@akingump.com

ALISON LEIGH GRAY, born Charlotte, North Carolina, May 1, 1959; admitted to bar, 1984, North Carolina; 1988, District of Columbia. *Education:* University of North Carolina (B.A., summa cum laude; 1981; J.D., 1984). Phi Beta Kappa. Recipient, Bernard Boyd Award. Articles Editor, North Carolina Journal of International Law and Commercial Regulation, 1983-1984. Co-author: "Section 504: The State's Record in Complying with Civil Rights Legislation for Handicapped Persons," North Carolina Insight, October, 1983. *Member:* The District of Columbia Bar; North Carolina Bar Associations. ***PRACTICE AREAS:*** Labor and Employment. ***Email:*** agray@akingump.com

MICHELE S. GREIF, born Pompton Plains, New Jersey, February 23, 1969; admitted to bar, 1997, New Jersey; 1998, New York and U.S. District Court, District of New Jersey; 1999, District of Columbia. *Education:* University of Maryland (B.S., 1991); Seton Hall University School of Law (J.D., cum laude, 1997). Member, 1995-1997, Editorial Staff, 1996-1997, Seton Hall Law Review. Author: "Supreme Court Takes Affirmative Action Toward Settling Evolving Precedent," 26 Seton Hall Law Review, 1653 (1996). ***PRACTICE AREAS:*** Products Liability; General Litigation. ***Email:*** mgreif@akingump.com

GREGORY J. GRANITTO, born Youngstown, Ohio, October 16, 1959; admitted to bar, 1987, Maryland; 1992, U.S. District Court, District of Maryland and U.S. Supreme Court; 2000, Virginia; 2001, District of Columbia. *Education:* John Carroll University (B.A., History, 1982); Catholic University of America (J.D., 1986). *Member:* Virginia Bar Association. ***PRACTICE AREAS:*** Litigation. ***Email:*** ggranitto@akingump.com

NICOLE L. HAGENBUCH, born Rochester, New York, October 10, 1974; admitted to bar, 1999, Maryland; 2000, District of Columbia. *Education:* Lafayette College (A.B., 1996); Catholic University of America (J.D., cum laude, 1999). ***LANGUAGES:*** French. ***PRACTICE AREAS:*** Litigation; White Collar Crime. ***Email:*** nhagenbuch@akingump.com

KEITH A. HALPERN, born Norristown, Pennsylvania, August 18, 1970; admitted to bar, 1999, Maryland (Not admitted in District of Columbia). *Education:* Tufts University (B.A., 1993); Emory University (J.D., with honors, 1999). Order of Emory Advocates. ***PRACTICE AREAS:*** Labor and Employment. ***Email:*** khalpern@akingump.com

ANNE T. HICKEY, born Washington, D.C., July 18, 1971; admitted to bar, 1998, Maryland; 1999, District of Columbia. *Education:* Kenyon College (B.A., magna cum laude, 1993); Duke University (J.D., 1998). Phi Beta Kappa. ***Email:*** ahickey@akingump.com

BETH L. HIRSCHFELDER, born Highland Park, Illinois January 17, 1973; admitted to bar, 1998, Illinois; 1999, District of Columbia. *Education:*

(This Listing Continued)

University of Pennsylvania (B.A., magna cum laude, 1995); Harvard University (J.D., cum laude, 1998). ***PRACTICE AREAS:*** Litigation. ***Email:*** bhirschfelder@akingump.com

ELIZABETH A. HOLT, born Matthews, North Carolina, September 3, 1975; admitted to bar, 2001, Georgia (Not admitted in District of Columbia). *Education:* Furman University (B.A., magna cum laude, 1997); Duke University (J.D., 2000). Phi Beta Kappa. *Member:* State Bar of Georgia. ***PRACTICE AREAS:*** Labor and Employment. ***Email:*** eholt@akingump.com

MARY A. HOUSE, born Memphis, Tennessee, September 24, 1967; admitted to bar, 2000, Maryland (Not admitted in District of Columbia). *Education:* James Madison University (B.S., cum laude, 1989); American University (J.D., summa cum laude, 2000). *Member:* Maryland State Bar Association; Womens Bar Association, District of Columbia. ***PRACTICE AREAS:*** Civil Litigation; Products Liability; Antitrust. ***Email:*** mhouse@akingump.com

JAMES D. HUMPHREY, II, born Fairfax, Missouri, September 18, 1966; admitted to bar, 1997, New York (Not admitted in District of Columbia). *Education:* University of Missouri (B.A., 1988); Fletcher School of Law and Diplomacy (M.A.L.D., 1990); University of Michigan (J.D., 1995). ***Email:*** jhumphrey@akingump.com

BERND GUNNAR JANZEN, admitted to bar, 1997, New York (Not admitted in District of Columbia). *Education:* Bethel College (B.S., 1988); George Washington University (J.D., 1996). ***Email:*** bjanzen@akingump.com

JANINE L. JONES, born Chicago, Illinois, August 30, 1971; admitted to bar, 1996, Illinois and U.S. District Court, Northern District of Illinois; 1999, District of Columbia. *Education:* University of Illinois (B.A., 1993); University of Iowa (J.D., 1996). Managing Editor, Iowa Law Review. *Member:* Chicago, Illinois State, Federal and American (Member, Tax Section) Bar Associations. ***PRACTICE AREAS:*** Public Policy; Taxation. ***Email:*** jjones@akingump.com

SHELLEY E. JONES, born Huntington, West Virginia, April 22, 1974; admitted to bar, 2000, Virginia; 2001, District of Columbia. *Education:* University of Virginia (B.A., 1996; J.D., 1999). Phi Beta Kappa. Dillard Fellow, Legal Research and Writing Program, University of Virginia School of Law, 1997-1998. Judicial Clerk, Honorable Albert V. Bryan, Jr., U.S. District Court, Eastern District of Virginia, 1999-2000. *Member:* Virginia and American Bar Associations; The District of Columbia Bar. ***PRACTICE AREAS:*** Labor and Employment. ***Email:*** sejones@akingump.com

WENDY E. KAMENSHINE, born Nashville, Tennessee, August 11, 1972; admitted to bar, 1999, Maryland; 2000, District of Columbia. *Education:* University of Chicago (A.B., honors in Economics, 1994); Duke University (J.D., 1999). Lead Editor, Duke Journal of Comparative and International Law, 1998-1999. LL.M. Liaison, International Law Society, 1997-1999. ***PRACTICE AREAS:*** International. ***Email:*** wkamenshine@akingump.com

GLENN H. KAMINSKY, born Johnstown, Pennsylvania, March 28, 1974; admitted to bar, 2000, California (Not admitted in District of Columbia). *Education:* Pomona College (B.A., 1996); University of Michigan (J.D., 2000). *Member:* American Bar Association. ***LANGUAGES:*** Hebrew. ***PRACTICE AREAS:*** Corporate; Project Finance. ***Email:*** gkaminsky@akingump.com

KENNETH P. KAPLAN, born Boston, Massachusetts, November 4, 1972; admitted to bar, 1997, Maryland; 1998, District of Columbia. *Education:* University of Massachusetts (B.A., 1994); American University (J.D., 1997). Phi Beta Kappa; Phi Kappa Phi. Associate Executive Editor, American University Journal of International Law and Policy, 1996-1997. Member, United States Soccer Fed. National Referee Program, 1986—. ***PRACTICE AREAS:*** Litigation. ***Email:*** kkaplan@akingump.com

JEFFREY M. KING, born Long Island, New York, July 24, 1973; admitted to bar, 1998, New York; 1999, District of Columbia. *Education:* University of Michigan (B.A., with high honors, 1995; J.D., 1997). *Member:* American Bar Association. ***PRACTICE AREAS:*** Litigation; White Collar Crime. ***Email:*** jking@akingump.com

JO-ELLYN SAKOWITZ KLEIN, born Bronx, New York, November 28, 1972; admitted to bar, 1998, Virginia; 1999, District of Columbia. *Education:* Duke University (A.B., cum laude, 1994); Georgetown University (J.D., 1998). Articles Editor, The Georgetown Law Journal. Author: "The Stark Laws: Conquering Physician Conflicts of Interest?" 87 Geo. L.J. 2 (1998). ***PRACTICE AREAS:*** Health Care. ***Email:*** jsklein@akingump.com

ROBERT H. KLUGE, III, born Washington, D.C., February 1, 1969; admitted to bar, 1997, Virginia; 2000, District of Columbia (Not admitted in District of Columbia). *Education:* University of Virginia (B.A., 1991); American University (J.D., summa cum laude, 1997). ***PRACTICE AREAS:*** General Litigation; Regulatory; Administrative. ***Email:*** bkluge@akingump.com

KERRY E. KORODY, born Washington, D.C., July 8, 1973; admitted to bar, 1999, Maryland; 2000, District of Columbia. *Education:* University of Notre Dame (B.A., 1995); Duke University (J.D., 1999). ***PRACTICE AREAS:*** Labor and Employment. ***Email:*** kkorody@akingump.com

JONATHAN M. KRELL, born Boston, Massachusetts, November 23, 1970; admitted to bar, 1998, Virginia; 1999, District of Columbia. *Education:*

(This Listing Continued)

Wesleyan University (B.A., 1993); George Washington University (J.D., 1998). Production Editor, George Washington Law Review. ***PRACTICE AREAS:*** Labor and Employment; Technology. ***Email:*** jkrell@akingump.com

XANTHE M. LARSEN, admitted to bar, 1998, Utah; 2000, District of Columbia. *Education:* University of Utah (B.S., Economics; B.A., Political Science, cum laude, 1983; J.D.; M.B.A., with honors, 1997). Phi Kappa Phi. Beta Gamma Sigma. Articles Editor, Journal of Contemporary Law, 1996-1997. *Member:* Utah State Bar. ***PRACTICE AREAS:*** Corporate Law; Securities; Project Finance; Infrastructure Development. ***Email:*** xlarsen@akingump.com

THOMAS J. McCARTHY, born Silver Spring, Maryland, July 22, 1969; admitted to bar, 1999, Maryland and District of Columbia. *Education:* University of Michigan (A.B., 1991); University of Virginia (J.D., 1998). Articles Editor, University of Virginia Journal of International Law, 1997-1998. Co-Author: "Employment of Foreign Nationals: Exposure to Export Control Liabilities Under the Deemed Export Rule," Metropolitan Corporate Counsel, October 1999; "International Electronic Transactions: Ensuring Compliance with U.S. Customs and International Trade Laws," Metropolitan Corporate Counsel, May 2001. *Member:* Maryland State and American Bar Associations; The District of Columbia Bar (Member, Sections on: Arts, Entertainment and Sports Law; International Law). [Lt., U.S. Navy, 1991-1995]. ***PRACTICE AREAS:*** International Trade; Entertainment Law. ***Email:*** tmccarthy@akingump.com

SCOTT D. McKINNEY, born Chicago, Illinois, January 6, 1971; admitted to bar, 1998, Illinois; 1999, District of Columbia. *Education:* University of Chicago (A.B., with honors, 1993); University of Illinois (J.D., magna cum laude, 1998). *Member:* American Bar Association. ***PRACTICE AREAS:*** Corporate Law; Securities. ***Email:*** smckinney@akingump.com

ERIKA ESTERBROOK MEADORS, born Tampa, Florida, September 11, 1974; admitted to bar, 1999, Virginia; 2000, District of Columbia. *Education:* Duke University (B.A., 1996); Harvard University (J.D., 1999). ***LANGUAGES:*** Spanish. ***PRACTICE AREAS:*** Litigation; Immigration. ***Email:*** emeadors@akingump.com

BYUNG JOON MIN, born Bangkok, Thailand, May 29, 1971; admitted to bar, 1998, Delaware; 1999, District of Columbia. *Education:* University of Virginia (B.S., 1994; J.D., 1997). ***Email:*** bmin@akingump.com

ANNAMARIA LOCSIN NIELDS, born Boston, Massachusetts, 1973; admitted to bar, 2000, Virginia (Not admitted in District of Columbia). *Education:* Colgate University (B.A., 1994); George Mason University School of Law (J.D., magna cum laude, 2000). Member, 1998-2000 and Vice Justice, 1999-2000, Moot Court Board. Dean's Scholar, 1999-2000. ***PRACTICE AREAS:*** Labor and Employment. ***Email:*** anields@akingump.com

NATHAN J. OLESON, born Duluth, Minnesota, September 20, 1973; admitted to bar, 1999, Maryland; 2000, District of Columbia. *Education:* American University (B.A., 1996); Georgetown University (J.D., 1999). Order of the Coif. Member, Georgetown Law Journal. ***PRACTICE AREAS:*** Labor and Employment. ***Email:*** noleson@akingump.com

MICHAEL J. PARINI, born Smithtown, New York, April 18, 1974; admitted to bar, 2000, New York and District of Columbia. *Education:* Georgetown University (B.A., cum laude, 1996; J.D., cum laude, 1999). Co-Author: "Perinatal HIV: A Children's Human Rights Perspective," Children's Legal Rts. J., Loyola School of Law, Chicago. ***PRACTICE AREAS:*** Health Care. ***Email:*** mparini@akingump.com

J. DAVID PARK, born Seoul, Korea, November 28, 1971; admitted to bar, 1997, District of Columbia. *Education:* Tufts University (B.A., 1993); Boston University (J.D., 1996); Georgetown University (LL.M., 2001). ***LANGUAGES:*** Korean. ***PRACTICE AREAS:*** International Trade. ***Email:*** dpark@akingump.com

DAVID H. QUIGLEY, born Plainfield, New Jersey, June 29, 1973; admitted to bar, 1999, New Jersey; 2000, District of Columbia. *Education:* Cornell University (B.S., with distinction, 1995); Harvard University (J.D., 1998). Golden Key. Ames Moot Court Oralist. ***PRACTICE AREAS:*** Environmental Land Use; Project Finance. ***Email:*** dquigley@akingump.com

STACEY A. RECHT, born Washington, D.C., September 29, 1973; admitted to bar, 2000, Maryland (Not admitted in District of Columbia). *Education:* Emory University (B.A., 1995); University of Pennsylvania (J.D., 2000). ***PRACTICE AREAS:*** Labor and Employment. ***Email:*** srecht@akingump.com

AARON J. REED, born Miami Beach, Florida, June 8, 1971; admitted to bar, 1996, Maryland; 1999, District of Columbia. *Education:* Tufts University (B.A., 1993); University of Florida (J.D., cum laude, 1996). *Member:* Maryland State (Member, Labor and Employment Law Section) and American Bar Associations; The District of Columbia Bar. ***PRACTICE AREAS:*** Labor and Employment. ***Email:*** areed@akingump.com

DANIEL S. REIMER, born Montreal, Canada, May 13, 1970; admitted to bar, 1995, Colorado (Not admitted in District of Columbia). *Education:* University of Florida (B.A., 1992); University of Colorado (J.D., 1995). Phi Beta Kappa. ***Email:*** dreimer@akingump.com

(This Listing Continued)

AKIN, GUMP, STRAUSS, HAUER & FELD, L.L.P., Washington—Continued

JOHN M. REMY, born Teaneck, New Jersey, April 25, 1971; admitted to bar, 1997, New Jersey; 1998, New York and District of Columbia. *Education:* Northwestern University (B.S., magna cum laude, 1993); University of Michigan (J.D., cum laude, 1996). *Member:* The District of Columbia Bar. ***PRACTICE AREAS:*** Labor and Employment. ***Email:*** jremy@akingump.com

MARK E. RICARDO, born Tampa, Florida, October 26, 1969; admitted to bar, 1999, North Carolina and District of Columbia. *Education:* Wake Forest University (B.A., 1991); Syracuse University (J.D., 1997); Georgetown University (LL.M., Taxation and Securities and Financial Regulation, 2000). Justinian Honorary Law Society. Editor, Syracuse Journal of Legislation and Policy. ***PRACTICE AREAS:*** Commercial Real Estate; Federal Taxation; State Taxation; Local Taxation. ***Email:*** mricardo@akingump.com

JAMES MARTIN RIEKSE, born Grand Rapids, Michigan, June 21, 1975; (admission pending). *Education:* Hope College (B.A., 1997); George Washington University (J.D., 2000). Phi Beta Kappa. Order of the Coif. Member, George Washington Law Review, 1998. ***PRACTICE AREAS:*** Labor; Employment. ***Email:*** jriekse@akingump.com

REED L. RUSSELL, born Louisville, Kentucky, February 18, 1969; admitted to bar, 1999, Florida; 2000, District of Columbia. *Education:* Wake Forest University (B.S., 1991); Catholic University of America (J.D., 1999). Catholic University Law Review, Vol. 47:3. [Captain, U.S. Army Reserve, 1991—]. ***Email:*** rrussell@akingump.com

JEREMY R. SCHWER, born Wilmington, Delaware, April 17, 1973; admitted to bar, 1998, Delaware; 2001, District of Columbia. *Education:* Wake Forest University (B.A., cum laude, 1995); The Catholic University of America, Columbus School of Law (J.D., magna cum laude, 1998). Member, Catholic University Law Review, 1996-1998. *Member:* Delaware State and American Bar Associations; The District of Columbia Bar. ***Email:*** jschwer@akingump.com

MICHAEL P. SEAMAN, born Lockport, New York, June 14, 1973; admitted to bar, 2000, New York; 2001, District of Columbia. *Education:* University of Notre Dame (B.A., 1995); Duke University (J.D., 1999). Member, Duke Law Journal. *Member:* The District of Columbia Bar. ***PRACTICE AREAS:*** Corporate. ***Email:*** mseaman@akingump.com

SCOTT E. SEEWALD, born Pittsburgh, Pennsylvania, November 1, 1971; admitted to bar, 1998, Pennsylvania; 1999, District of Columbia. *Education:* University of Pennsylvania (B.A., magna cum laude, 1993); Duke University (J.D., cum laude, 1997). Phi Beta Kappa. Notes Editor, Duke Journal of Comparative and International Law. ***PRACTICE AREAS:*** Litigation. ***Email:*** sseewald@akingump.com

STACEY WRUBLE SEEWALD, born Miami, Florida, October 17, 1971; admitted to bar, 1996, Florida; 1998, District of Columbia. *Education:* University of Pennsylvania (B.S./B.A., 1993); Georgetown University Law Center (J.D., 1996). Law Fellow, 1994-1995. Editor in Chief, The Tax Lawyer, 1995-1996. Author, "Estimating Inventory Shrinkage for Tax Purposes," The Tax Lawyer, Volume 48, Number 4. *Member:* The Florida Bar; The District of Columbia Bar. ***PRACTICE AREAS:*** Corporate Law; Securities. ***Email:*** swseewald@akingump.com

RAJAT R. SHAH, born Scranton, Pennsylvania, May 23, 1971; admitted to bar, 1997, New York; 1998, District of Columbia. *Education:* Gettysburg College (B.A., magna cum laude, 1993); Vanderbilt University (J.D., 1996). Phi Beta Kappa. Member, Vanderbilt Law Review. ***LANGUAGES:*** Gujarati. ***PRACTICE AREAS:*** Corporate Law; Securities; Project Finance. ***Email:*** rshah@akingump.com

WILLIAM DIXON SHAY, III, born Denver, Colorado, July 24, 1971; admitted to bar, 1998, Colorado; 1999, District of Columbia. *Education:* Bucknell University (B.A., 1993); American University (J.D., magna cum laude, 1998). ***PRACTICE AREAS:*** Corporate Law. ***Email:*** dshay@akingump.com

JOHN SIM, born Fairfax, Virginia, September 10, 1974; admitted to bar, 2000, New York; 2001, District of Columbia. *Education:* University of Pennsylvania (B.A., 1996); American University (J.D., 1999). ***LANGUAGES:*** Korean. ***PRACTICE AREAS:*** International Trade; Corporate Law. ***Email:*** jsim@akingump.com

DANA E. SINGISER, born New York, N.Y., May 18, 1970; admitted to bar, 1999, Massachusetts; 2000, District of Columbia. *Education:* Brown University (B.A., 1992); Georgetown University (J.D., 1998). Special Assistant in the Office of Presidential Personnel, The White House, 1993-1995. ***PRACTICE AREAS:*** Public Law and Policy; Legislative. ***Email:*** dsingiser@akingump.com

NICOLE A. SMITH, born Norwalk, California, September 2, 1966; admitted to bar, 1999, Maryland; 2000, District of Columbia. *Education:* McKendree College (B.A., summa cum laude, 1996); Georgetown University (J.D., 1999). ***PRACTICE AREAS:*** Labor and Employment. ***Email:*** nsmith@akingump.com

(This Listing Continued)

DAVID G. SOCIE, born Buffalo, New York, March 2, 1968; admitted to bar, 1999, New York and District of Columbia. *Education:* State University of New York at Buffalo (B.A., 1991); St. John's University (J.D., 1997). ***PRACTICE AREAS:*** Labor and Employment Law. ***Email:*** dsocie@akingump.com

KIMBERLY STALLINGS SURINGA, born Okinawa, Japan, October 11, 1970; admitted to bar, 1996, Virginia; 1998, District of Columbia. *Education:* University of Virginia (B.A., with honors, 1992); Harvard University (J.D., cum laude, 1996). Clerk to the Honorable Leonie M. Brinkema, U.S. District Court, Eastern District of Virginia, 1996-1997. *Member:* American Health Lawyers Association. ***PRACTICE AREAS:*** Health Care. ***Email:*** ksuringa@akingump.com

ANDREW T. SWERS, born Malden, Massachusetts, September 13, 1972; admitted to bar, 1997, New York, U.S. District Court, Southern and Eastern Districts of New York; 1999, District of Columbia. *Education:* Johns Hopkins University (B.A., 1995); Columbia Law School (J.D., 1996). Phi Beta Kappa; Golden Key. Accelerated Interdisciplinary Legal Law Education Program, Columbia University and John Hopkins University. *Member:* The District of Columbia Bar; American Bar Association. ***Email:*** aswers@akingump.com

ESTHER G. TAMBURO, born Abington, Pennsylvania, October 11, 1968; admitted to bar, 1997, Pennsylvania; 1998, District of Columbia. *Education:* University of Pennsylvania (J.D., summa cum laude, 1997). *Member:* The District of Columbia Bar; Pennsylvania Bar Association. ***PRACTICE AREAS:*** Labor and Employment. ***Email:*** etamburo@akingump.com

JOSHUA C. TOLL, born Baltimore, Maryland, October 16, 1971; admitted to bar, 1997, Maryland; 1999, District of Columbia. *Education:* Cornell University (B.A., 1993); Harvard University (J.D., cum laude, 1997). Phi Beta Kappa. ***LANGUAGES:*** French. ***PRACTICE AREAS:*** Litigation. ***Email:*** jtoll@akingump.com

JAMES R. TUCKER, JR., born Macon, Georgia, October 21, 1969; admitted to bar, 1997, Georgia; 1999, District of Columbia. *Education:* Washington & Lee University (B.A., 1992); Mercer University (J.D., 1997). Recipient, Outstanding Achievement in Legal Writing Award. *Member:* State Bar of Georgia. ***PRACTICE AREAS:*** Public Policy. ***Email:*** jtucker@akingump.com

FRANCESCA UGOLINI, born Washington, D.C., February 26, 1976; admitted to bar, 2000, Maryland; 2001, District of Columbia. *Education:* University of Maryland at College Park (B.S., 1997); University of Virginia (J.D., 2000). *Member:* The District of Columbia Bar. ***LANGUAGES:*** Italian. ***PRACTICE AREAS:*** Tax. ***Email:*** fugolini@akingump.com

CHRISTOPHER J. VANARSDALE, born Point Pleasant, New Jersey, March 22, 1967; admitted to bar, 1997, Maryland and District of Columbia. *Education:* Harvard University (A.B., 1989); Cornell University Law School (J.D., 1996). ***LANGUAGES:*** Spanish. ***PRACTICE AREAS:*** Environmental Law; Environmental Litigation.

AURORE Y. VICTOR, born Brooklyn, New York, July 24, 1975; admitted to bar, 1999, Florida; 2001, District of Columbia. *Education:* Yale University (B.A., 1997); Harvard University (J.D., 2000). *Member:* The District of Columbia Bar. ***Email:*** avictor@akingump.com

KRISTIN J. VOLLMERS, born Grand Forks, North Dakota, March 5, 1970; admitted to bar, 1997, Minnesota and U.S. District Court, District of Minnesota; 1999, District of Columbia; 2000, North Dakota. *Education:* University of North Dakota (B.A., summa cum laude, 1991); University of Minnesota Law School (J.D., cum laude, 1997). *Member:* The District of Columbia Bar; American Bar Association. ***PRACTICE AREAS:*** Litigation; Health Care. ***Email:*** kvollmers@akingump.com

ERNEST SYLVAIN VOYARD, JR., born Suffern, New York, January 3, 1975; admitted to bar, 2000, Florida; 2001, District of Columbia. *Education:* Duke University (A.B., 1997); Harvard Law School (J.D., 2000). *Member:* The District of Columbia Bar. ***Email:*** evoyard@akingump.com

ROBIN MAHLER WEISMAN, born Boston, Massachusetts, March 17, 1968; admitted to bar, 1997, New York; 1998, District of Columbia. *Education:* Kenyon College (B.A., 1991); American University (J.D., 1997). ***PRACTICE AREAS:*** Public Law and Policy. ***Email:*** rmahler@akingump.com

COUNSEL

SAM J. ALBERTS, born New York, N.Y., August 24, 1964; admitted to bar, 1992, Washington; 1993, U.S. District Court, Western District of Washington; 1994, Virginia, U.S. District Court, District of Maryland and Eastern District of Virginia and U.S. Court of Appeals, Fourth and Ninth Circuits; 1995, District of Columbia, U.S. District Court, District of Columbia and U.S. Court of Federal Claims. *Education:* University of Massachusetts; New York University (B.A., cum laude, 1987); George Washington University (J.D., with honors, 1992). Pi Sigma Alpha. Recipient, Founders Day Award. Member, The George Washington Journal of International Law & Economics, 1990-1992. Author, "Trademarks and Gray Market Goods: Why U.S. Trademark Holders Should Be Held Strictly Liable For Defective Gray Market Goods," 25 George Washington Journal of International Law & Economics 841, 1992. *Member:* Virginia State

(This Listing Continued)

Bar; The District of Columbia Bar; Washington State Bar Association; American Bankruptcy Institute. ***PRACTICE AREAS:*** Financial Restructuring; Bankruptcy Chapter 11; Litigation. ***Email:*** salberts@akingump.com

MARGARET D. CHISHOLM, born Mt. Kisco, New York, January 1, 1966; admitted to bar, 1994, Massachusetts; 1996, District of Columbia and U.S. Court of International Trade. *Education:* Universite de Paris IV; Smith College (A.B., cum laude, 1987); Georgetown University (J.D., 1994). ***LANGUAGES:*** English, French. ***PRACTICE AREAS:*** European Union Policy; International Trade. ***Email:*** pchisholm@akingump.com

JOEL A. CHRISTIE, born Iowa City, Iowa, December 9, 1967; admitted to bar, 1992, Wisconsin; 1999, District of Columbia. *Education:* Northwestern University (B.A., 1989); University of Wisconsin at Madison (J.D., cum laude, 1992). *Member:* State Bar of Wisconsin. ***PRACTICE AREAS:*** Antitrust and Trade Regulation; Public Policy. ***Email:*** jchristie@akingump.com

TIMOTHY J. CHOPPIN, born Washington, D.C., June 25, 1963; admitted to bar, 1994, Maryland; 1995, District of Columbia. *Education:* Haverford College (B.A., 1985); University of Pennsylvania (M.C.P., with distinction, 1989); Georgetown University Law Center (J.D., cum laude, 1994). Author: "Breaking the Exclusionary Land Use Barrier," 82 Geo. L.J. 2039 (1994); "Post-Quill Due Process Analysis of Interstate Commerce Taxation," 5 State Tax Notes 1367 (1993). *Member:* District of Columbia Bar; American Bar Association; Urban Land Institute. ***PRACTICE AREAS:*** Real Estate. ***Email:*** tchoppin@akingump.com

DMITRI I. DUBOGRAEV, born Minsk, Belarus, January 10, 1967; admitted to bar, 1991, Russia; 1994, Virginia; 1996, District of Columbia. *Education:* Belorussian State University Law School (in law, diploma with excellence, 1991); Washington & Lee University (J.D., 1994). Co-author: "EC Food Regulations: Recent Developments," World Food Regulations Review, BNA, July 1993; "Securities Law Developments in the Russian Federation After the 1998 Financial Crisis," Emerging Trends in Securities Law, 2000-2001," West, 2000. Author: "A Success Story of U.S. Corporate Law," Belarussian Market Review, December 1996. ***LANGUAGES:*** Russian, English, Belarusian, Ukrainian and Polish. ***PRACTICE AREAS:*** Corporate Law. ***Email:*** ddubograev@akingump.com

SHARI L. FLEISHMAN, born Cleveland, Ohio, July 16, 1967; admitted to bar, 1993, Maryland, District of Columbia, U.S. District Court, District of Maryland and U.S. Court of Appeals, Fourth Circuit; 1995, U.S. District Court, Western District of Michigan; 1997, U.S. District Court for the District of Columbia. *Education:* Duke University (A.B., summa cum laude, 1989); Harvard University (J.D., 1992). Phi Beta Kappa. *Member:* The District of Columbia Bar; Maryland State, Federal and American Bar Associations; Women's Bar Association. ***PRACTICE AREAS:*** Litigation; Patent Litigation; Technology. ***Email:*** sfleishman@akingump.com

BRIAN S. GLEICHER, born New York, N.Y., January 24, 1970; admitted to bar, 1995, Florida, U.S. Tax Court; 1996, District of Columbia. *Education:* University of Florida (B.S., with high honors, 1992); Georgetown University (J.D., cum laude, 1995). Lead Articles Editor, The Tax Lawyer, 1994-1995. Author, "Filing Date of the S Corporation Shareholder's Return Triggers Statute of Limitations: Bufferd v. Commissioner," The Tax Lawyer, Volume 47. Editor in Chief, Federal Bar Association Section of Taxation Report. *Member:* Federal (Officer, Section of Taxation) and American (Member, Section on Taxation) Bar Associations. ***PRACTICE AREAS:*** Taxation. ***Email:*** bgleicher@akingump.com

KAREN GOLDMEIER GREEN, born Chicago, Illinois, October 4, 1965; admitted to bar, 1993, Maryland; 1995, District of Columbia. *Education:* Cornell University (B.S., 1987); University of Maryland (J.D., 1993). Law Review Notes and Comments Editor. Author: "The Right To Refuse Life-Sustaining Medical Treatment," (53 MD L. Rev. 1306) 1994; "Limits on the Power of Referendum," (51 MD L. Rev. 775) 1992. Counsel to the Hon. Robert T. Matsui, U.S. House of Reps, 1995-1998. Counsel to the White House Conference on Aging, 1995. *Member:* American Bar Association; Women in Government Relations (General Counsel, Board of Directors). ***PRACTICE AREAS:*** Legislative. ***Email:*** kgreen@akingump.com

STEFAN A. HAGERUP, born Milwaukee, Wisconsin, December 7, 1962; admitted to bar, 1991, Wisconsin; 1992, Maryland; 1995, District of Columbia. *Education:* University of Wisconsin-Madison (B.A., with honors, 1986; J.D., 1990). Law Clerk to the Honorable John L. Coffey, U.S. Court of Appeals, Seventh Circuit, 1990-1992. *Member:* Maryland State Bar Association Inc.; American Bar Association. ***PRACTICE AREAS:*** Litigation; Labor and Employment Law. ***Email:*** shagerup@akingump.com

JONATHAN H. HAMBRICK, born Syracuse, New York, April 3, 1967; admitted to bar, 1994, Virginia; 1996, U.S. District Court, Eastern District of Virginia; 1997, U.S. Court of Appeals, Fourth Circuit and U.S. Court of Appeals for the District of Columbia; 1998, District of Columbia and U.S. District Court, Western District of Virginia. *Education:* Yale University (B.A., 1989); College of William & Mary (J.D., 1994). *Member:* Virginia State Bar; The District of Columbia Bar. ***PRACTICE AREAS:*** Litigation. ***Email:*** jhambrick@akingump.com

(This Listing Continued)

GARY A. HEIMBERG, born New Brunswick, New Jersey, October 8, 1962; admitted to bar, 1992, Pennsylvania; 1994, District of Columbia. *Education:* George Washington University (B.A., 1985; M.P.A., 1987; J.D., 1992). ***PRACTICE AREAS:*** Public Policy. ***Email:*** gheimberg@akingump.com

JOHN R. JACOB, born Philadelphia, Pennsylvania, November 18, 1966; admitted to bar, 1993, Maryland; 1994, District of Columbia; 1999, U.S. District Court, District of Columbia and U.S. Court of Appeals, District of Columbia Circuit. *Education:* Colgate University (A.B., 1988); Washington College of Law, American University (J.D., cum laude, 1993). Executive Editor, The American University Law Review. *Member:* American Health Lawyers Association; District of Columbia Bar (Member, Health Law Section). ***PRACTICE AREAS:*** Health Care. ***Email:*** jjacob@akingump.com

POLLY B. JESSEN, born Casper, Wyoming, February 18, 1965; admitted to bar, 1994, Colorado (Not admitted in District of Columbia). *Education:* Princeton University (A.B., cum laude, 1987); Columbia University (J.D., 1994). Law Clerk to Hon. Mary J. Mullarkey, Colorado Supreme Court, 1994-1995. *Member:* Colorado Bar Association (Member, Environmental Law and Water Sections); Colorado Women's Bar Association. ***Email:*** pjessen@akingump.com

CHARLES W. JOHNSON, IV, born Washington, D.C., September 11, 1966; admitted to bar, 1994, Maryland; 1996, District of Columbia. *Education:* University of Maryland/University of London, London, England; Gettysburg College (B.A., 1989); Catholic University of America, Columbus School of Law (J.D., 1994). Note and Comment Editor, Catholic University Law Review. Author: Comment, "The Doctrine of Official Immunity-An Unnecessary Intrusion Into Speech or Debate Clause Jurisprudence," Catholic University Law Review, Vol. 43:2, p. 535. *Member:* Maryland State Bar Association; District of Columbia Bar. ***PRACTICE AREAS:*** Public Policy. ***Email:*** johnsonc@akingump.com

ROBERT G. LIAN, JR., born Worcester, Massachusetts, April 1, 1968; admitted to bar, 1993, Virginia; 1995, District of Columbia. *Education:* Colby College (B.A., 1990); Catholic University (J.D., 1993). Catholic University Law Review, 1991-1993. ***PRACTICE AREAS:*** Labor and Employment. ***Email:*** blian@akingump.com

ELIZABETH A. MATTHEWS, born Houston, Texas, February 17, 1970; admitted to bar, 1995, Maryland; 1996, District of Columbia. *Education:* Yale University (B.A., cum laude, with distinction in Humanities, 1992); Harvard University (J.D., 1995). General Editor, Harvard Civil Rights—Civil Liberties Law Review, 1993-1995. Vice President, Harvard Board of Student Advisors, 1993-1995. Law Clerk to Judge Edmund V. Ludwig, U.S. District Court, Eastern District of Pennsylvania, 1995-1996. *Member:* The District of Columbia Bar; Maryland State and American Bar Associations. ***PRACTICE AREAS:*** Labor and Employment. ***Email:*** ematthews@akingump.com

DANIEL F. McINNIS, born Long Branch, New Jersey, February 2, 1967; admitted to bar, 1994, Virginia; 1996, District of Columbia. *Education:* Yale University (B.A., 1989); Georgetown University (J.D., cum laude, 1994). Georgetown Law Journal. Member, Federalist Society. Author, "Ozone Layers and Oligopoly Profits" in "Environmental Politics: Public Costs, Private Rewards," (Praeger, 1992). Clerk to Hon. Jerry E. Smith, U.S. Court of Appeals for the Fifth Circuit, 1994-1995. Extern Clerk to Hon. James L. Buckley, U.S. Court of Appeals, District of Columbia Circuit, 1993-1994. ***PRACTICE AREAS:*** Antitrust and Trade Regulation; Litigation. ***Email:*** dmcinnis@akingump.com

JAMES J. MURPHY, born Methuen, Massachusetts, May 27, 1966; admitted to bar, 1994, Massachusetts; 1996, District of Columbia. *Education:* College of the Holy Cross (A.B., 1988); The Catholic University of America, Columbus School of Law (J.D., cum laude, 1994). Staff Member, 1991-1992, and Lead Articles Editor, 1992-1993, The Journal of Contemporary Health Law & Policy. Author, Comment, "Beyond Autonomy: Judicial Restraint and the Legal Limits Necessary to Uphold the Hippocratic Tradition and Preserve the Ethical Integrity of the Medical Profession," The Journal of Contemporary Health Law and Policy, Volume 9, Spring, 1993. ***PRACTICE AREAS:*** Labor and Employment. ***Email:*** jmurphy@akingump.com

MICHELE HARRINGTON MURPHY, born Washington, D.C., July 30, 1968; admitted to bar, 1993, Maryland; 1995, District of Columbia. *Education:* Virginia Polytechnic Institute and State University (B.A., summa cum laude, 1990); University of North Carolina (J.D., with honors, 1993). Phi Beta Kappa; Omicron Delta Kappa; Chancellor's Scholar. Staff Member, University of North Carolina Law Review. Author, "State v. Whittle Communications: Allowing Local School Boards to Turn on 'Channel One'," 70 North Carolina Law Review 1129, 1992. *Member:* The District of Columbia Bar; American Bar Association; Equal Employment Opportunity Committee. ***PRACTICE AREAS:*** Labor and Employment. ***Email:*** mmurphy@akingump.com

EVANGELINE C. PASCHAL, born Dallas, Texas, March 6, 1970; admitted to bar, 1995, Texas; 1996, U.S. Court of Appeals, Fifth Circuit; 1998, District of Columbia and U.S. District Court, District of Colorado. *Education:* Stanford University (B.A., with honors, 1991); University of Texas at Austin (J.D., with honors, 1995; M.P.Aff., 1995). Phi Delta Phi (President, 1993-1994). National Champion, Robert S. Wagner Moot Court Competition, 1995. Articles

(This Listing Continued)

AKIN, GUMP, STRAUSS, HAUER & FELD, L.L.P., Washington—Continued

Editor, The Review of Litigation. Author, "The Best Laid Plans May Be Costly: An Analysis of Lucas v. South Carolina Coastal Council and Its Implications for Land Use Planning," The Review of Litigation, Fall 1993. *Member:* State Bar of Texas; Women's Bar Association of the District of Columbia (Co-Chair, Judicial Endorsements Committee). ***PRACTICE AREAS:*** Litigation. ***Email:*** epaschal@akingump.com

LAURENT C. PAVAGEAU, born Montreal, Canada, May 3, 1970; admitted to bar, 1996, New York and District of Columbia. *Education:* Duke University (B.A., cum laude, 1992; J.D., with honors, 1995). Article Editor, Duke Law Journal, 1994-1995. ***LANGUAGES:*** French. ***PRACTICE AREAS:*** Corporate Law. ***Email:*** lpavageau@akingump.com

JOHN E. PUTNAM, born Westfield, Massachusetts; admitted to bar, 1993, Colorado; 1995, District of Columbia. *Education:* Williams College (B.A., magna cum laude, 1990); University of Chicago (J.D., with honors, 1993). Phi Beta Kappa; Order of the Coif. Articles Editor, University of Chicago Legal Forum. Judicial Law Clerk, Hon. David M. Ebel, U.S. Court of Appeals, Tenth Circuit, 1993-1994. ***Email:*** jputnam@akingump.com

BRUCE G. ROSEN, born Philadelphia, Pennsylvania, October 1, 1966; admitted to bar, 1992, Pennsylvania and New Jersey; 1998, District of Columbia. *Education:* Temple University (B.B.A., 1989; J.D., 1992). *Member:* The District of Columbia Bar. ***PRACTICE AREAS:*** Commercial Real Estate; Real Estate Finance. ***Email:*** brosen@akingump.com

MATTHEW A. ROSSI, born Rochester, New York, October 17, 1964; admitted to bar, 1994, New Jersey; 1995, District of Columbia; 1997, Court of International Trade; 1998, New York. *Education:* Le Moyne College (B.A., 1987); University of Chicago (M.A., 1989); Cornell University (J.D., 1994). *Member:* The District of Columbia Bar. ***PRACTICE AREAS:*** Litigation. ***Email:*** mrossi@akingump.com

WYNN H. SEGALL, born Philadelphia, Pennsylvania, February 5, 1960; admitted to bar, 1990, New York; 1991, District of Columbia, U.S. Court of International Trade and U.S. Court of Appeals for the Federal Circuit. *Education:* University of Pennsylvania (A.B., cum laude, with high honors in History, 1983); St. Antony's College, Oxford University , England (M.Phil., 1985); Hebrew University, Jerusalem (Postgraduate, 1986); University of Chicago (J.D., 1989). Thouron Fellow. *Member:* The District of Columbia Bar (Member, International Section); New York State (Member, International Section) and American (Member, International Section) Bar Associations. ***PRACTICE AREAS:*** International Government Relations; International Trade; Technology. ***Email:*** wsegall@akingump.com

TODD M. STENERSON, born Detroit, Michigan, October 5, 1969; admitted to bar, 1994, Michigan; 1995, Illinois and U.S. District Court, Eastern and Western Districts of Michigan; 1996, U.S. District Court, Northern District of Indiana and U.S. Court of Appeals, Sixth Circuit; 1997, U.S. District Court, Northern District of Texas; 1998, U.S. Supreme Court; 1999, District of Columbia, U.S. District Court, District of Maryland and U.S. Court of Appeals, Fourth Circuit; 2000, U.S. District Court, District of Columbia. *Education:* Western Michigan University (B.B.A., 1991); Notre Dame University (J.D., magna cum laude, 1994). Michigan Competitive Scholar. *Member:* State Bar of Michigan; Illinois State and American Bar Associations. ***PRACTICE AREAS:*** Complex Litigation; Commercial Litigation; Intellectual Property Litigation; Alternative Dispute Resolution. ***Email:*** tstenerson@akingump.com

ANTHONY W. SWISHER, born Spartanburg, South Carolina, March 25, 1968; admitted to bar, 1995, Virginia; 1996, District of Columbia. *Education:* University of Virginia (B.A., with distinction, 1990); George Washington University (J.D., with high honors, 1995). Order of the Coif. Managing Editor, George Washington Law Review. *Member:* Virginia State Bar; The District of Columbia Bar. ***PRACTICE AREAS:*** Antitrust and Trade Regulation; Litigation. ***Email:*** aswisher@akingump.com

MARK D. TAYLOR, born Idaho Falls, Idaho, April 8, 1958; admitted to bar, 1991, Utah; 1992, Colorado; 1993, District of Columbia; 1997, U.S. District Court, District of Maryland and U.S. District Court for the District of Columbia; 1998, Virginia, U.S. Court of Appeals, Fourth Circuit and U.S. Bankruptcy Court, Eastern and Western Districts of Virginia. *Education:* Boise State University (B.A., 1981); University of Utah (J.D., 1991). Phi Delta Phi. Order of the Coif. Clyde Fellow. Member, 1989-1990, Development Editor, 1990-1991, Utah Law Review. Faculty Member, Mongolian Insolvency Seminar (sponsored by World Bank and Mongolian Ministry of Justice) September 1998. Co-Author (Victor E. Schwartz, Mark A. Behrens and Mark D. Taylor): "Illinois Tort Law: A Rich History of Cooperation and Respect Between the Courts and the Legislature," 28 Loyola University Chicago Law Journal (Summer 1997) (Judicial Conference Issue); "The 'Overlooked' Tort Reform Debate," Lawyer to Lawyer, Ed. 7 (Summer 1997); "Who Should Decide America's Tort Law? -- The Battle Between Legislatures and Courts," Washington Legal Foundation Monograph (Fall/Winter 1996); "Stamping Out Tort Reform," Legal Times, Vol. XIX, No. 40, at S34 (February 10, 1997) (Product Liability Supplement); "Adoption of Common Law Act: Reasserting the Historical Right of State Legislatures to Make America's Tort Law," 23 Alec Civil Justice Task Force 1 (January 1997). Judicial Clerk to Judge Anderson, U.S. Senior Judge, District of Utah, Salt Lake City, Utah, 1992-1993. *Member:* American Bankruptcy Institute; INSOL. ***PRACTICE AREAS:*** Financial Restructuring. ***Email:*** mtaylor@akingump.com

KAREN BLAND TOLIVER, born Washington, D.C., October 14, 1967; admitted to bar, 1994, Maryland; 1996, District of Columbia. *Education:* University of Virginia (B.A., 1989); Washington College of Law (J.D., 1992); American University (M.A., Law and Intl. Affairs, 1993);. Recent Developments Editor, Journal of International Law and Policy. Co-Author: "Sensitivity to the World Trade Organization's Rules May Impact Your Company's Bottom Line," The Metropolitan Corporate Counsel, 2000; "Affiliated Persons Under the URAA," The Commerce Department Speaks on International Trade and Investments, Practicing Law Institute, 1998; "GATT Panels Need Restraining Principles," 24 Law & Policy in Int'l Bus. 1167 (1993); "The Chemical Diversion and Drug Trafficking Act of 1988: Stopping the Flow of Chemicals to the Andean Drug Cartels," American University Journal of Int'l Law & Policy 105 (1991). *Member:* Washington (Co-Chair, International Law Committee, Young Lawyers Division, 1997-1998) and Maryland State Bar Associations; The District of Columbia Bar. ***LANGUAGES:*** Spanish. ***PRACTICE AREAS:*** International Trade. ***Email:*** ktoliver@akingump.com

MARILYN C. VADON, born Hackensack, New Jersey, June 3, 1968; admitted to bar, 1993, New Jersey; 1994, Pennsylvania; 1996, District of Columbia. *Education:* University of Connecticut (B.S., cum laude, 1990); Widener University School of Law (J.D., cum laude, 1993); Georgetown University Law Center (LL.M., 1994). Phi Kappa Phi; Phi Delta Phi. Harrington Inn, Honor Chapter. Recipient: American Jurisprudence Awards for Legal Methods/Moot Court I, Wills and Trusts; Wapner Newman Wigrizer Award for Scholarship, Oral Advocacy and Pro Bono Publico. *Member:* New Jersey State and Pennsylvania Bar Association; The District of Columbia Bar; American Health Lawyers Association. ***PRACTICE AREAS:*** Corporate; Health Care Law; Business Transactions. ***Email:*** mvadon@akingump.com

SENIOR COUNSEL

KENNETH D. ALDERFER, born Sellersville, Pennsylvania, March 27, 1957; admitted to bar, 1986, Virginia; 1986, U.S. Court of Appeals, Fourth Circuit; 1987, U.S. Tax Court; 1988, District of Columbia. *Education:* Eastern Mennonite College (B.S., magna cum laude, 1979); University of Virginia (J.D., 1986). Research Editor, Virginia Tax Review, 1985-1986. Certified Public Accountant, Virginia, 1982. *Member:* The District of Columbia Bar; Virginia State Bar; American Bar Association (Member, Section on Taxation). ***PRACTICE AREAS:*** Taxation; Health Care. ***Email:*** kalderfer@akingump.com

RICHARD P. BONSIGNORE, born Brooklyn, New York, June 17, 1948; admitted to bar, 1975, New Jersey; 1980, New York; 1992, Maryland; 1993, Virginia; 1994, District of Columbia. *Education:* Hope College (A.B., 1969); University of Louisville (J.D., cum laude, 1975). U.S. Foreign Service Officer, 1986-1993. ***LANGUAGES:*** Spanish. ***PRACTICE AREAS:*** Real Estate. ***Email:*** rbonsignore@akingump.com

MARLENE M. COLUCCI, born New York, New York, August 29, 1962; admitted to bar, 1989, District of Columbia; 1990, California and U.S. District Court for the District of Columbia. *Education:* University of California at Los Angeles (B.A., 1984); Georgetown University (J.D., 1988). Georgetown Law Fellow. Administrative Editor, Journal of Law and Technology, 1987-1988. *Member:* The District of Columbia Bar; American Bar Association. ***PRACTICE AREAS:*** Public Policy. ***Email:*** mcolucci@akingump.com

MARYELLEN CONNOR, born Bethlehem, Pennsylvania, March 17, 1961; admitted to bar, 1990, Pennsylvania (inactive); 1991, District of Columbia. *Education:* Lehigh University (B.A., cum laude, 1983); Georgetown University (J.D., 1989). Member, The Tax Lawyer, Georgetown University. ***PRACTICE AREAS:*** Litigation. ***Email:*** mconnor@akingump.com

JOSEPH W. CORNELISON, born Maryville, Missouri, July 16, 1947; admitted to bar, 1977, District of Columbia; 1981, U.S. Supreme Court. *Education:* U.S. Military Academy (B.S., 1969); Western Kentucky University (M.P.S., 1974); Georgetown University Law Center (J.D., 1977). Managing Editor, Georgetown Law Journal. Law Clerk to the Hon. Oliver Gasch, U.S. District Court, District of Columbia, 1977-1978. Deputy Administrator, Panama Canal Commission (by appointment of President Clinton), 1995-1999. [Col., U.S. Army, 1969-1995]. ***LANGUAGES:*** Spanish. ***PRACTICE AREAS:*** International Business Law; Public Law; Public Policy; Environmental Law; Government Contracts. ***Email:*** jcornelison@akingump.com

WILLIAM J. FARAH, born Washington, D.C., November 23, 1957; admitted to bar, 1989, District of Columbia. *Education:* University of Rochester, Eastman School of Music (B.M., 1979); The American University (J.D., cum laude, 1989). Associate Editor, American University Law Review, 1987-1988. *Member:* The District of Columbia Bar. ***PRACTICE AREAS:*** Public Policy. ***Email:*** bfarah@akingump.com

(This Listing Continued)

LARS-ERIK A. HJELM, born Bryn Mawr, Pennsylvania, May 29, 1963; admitted to bar, 1989, Georgia; 1999, District of Columbia. *Education:* University of Pennsylvania (B.A., cum laude, 1985); Emory University (J.D., 1989). Member, Jessup Moot Court Team, 1989. President, International Law Society, 1985-1989. Instructor, Customs Law, The U.S. Customs Service Academy, 1991-1993. Attorney, 1989-1996 and Assistant Chief Counsel, 1996-1999, U.S. Customs Service. ***LANGUAGES:*** Swedish. ***PRACTICE AREAS:*** International Trade. ***Email:*** lhjelm@akingump.com

MICHELLE M. HSU, born Washington, D.C., January 27, 1963; admitted to bar, 1992, New York; 2001, District of Columbia. *Education:* Barnard College, Columbia University (B.A., 1985); Georgetown University (J.D./M.S.F.S., 1991). Topics Editor, Law and Policy in International Business. *Member:* The District of Columbia Bar; American Bar Association. ***Email:*** mhsu@akingump.com

BYRON KEITH HUFFMAN, JR., born Tuscaloosa, Alabama, May 23, 1941; admitted to bar, 1967, Connecticut; 1968, New York; 1976, District of Columbia. *Education:* Yale University (B.A., cum laude, 1964; LL.B., 1967). United States Department of State: Office of the Legal Adviser, 1970-1976; Assistant Legal Adviser for African Affairs, 1972-1974 and Near Eastern and South Asian Affairs, 1974-1976. *Member:* District of Columbia Bar; American Bar Association (Member, Section of Business Law). ***PRACTICE AREAS:*** Corporate Law; Environmental Law. ***Email:*** bhuffman@akingump.com

VERNON E. JORDAN, JR., born Atlanta, Georgia, August 15, 1935; admitted to bar, 1964, Arkansas; 1969, Georgia; 1984, District of Columbia. *Education:* DePauw University (A.B., 1957); Howard University (J.D., 1960). President and Chief Executive Officer, National Urban League, Incorporated, 1972-1981. Executive Director, United Negro College Fund, Incorporated, 1970-1971. *Member:* The District of Columbia Bar; Arkansas and American Bar Associations; State Bar of Georgia; National Bar Association. ***PRACTICE AREAS:*** General Practice.

SUSAN HECK LENT, born Flushing, New York, September 27, 1961; admitted to bar, 1986, Maryland; 1988, District of Columbia. *Education:* Emory University (B.A., 1983); George Washington University (J.D., 1986). Counsel to the Surface Transportation Subcommittee of the House of Representatives Committee on Transportation and Infrastructure, 1995-1998. *Member:* The District of Columbia Bar. ***PRACTICE AREAS:*** Public Policy; Transportation; Infrastructure Development. ***Email:*** slent@akingump.com

PATRICK F. J. MACRORY, born Teignmouth, Devon, England, March 21, 1941; admitted to bar, 1964, England; 1971, District of Columbia. *Education:* Oxford University (B.A., 1962; M.A., 1968); Middle Temple, London, England (Barrister-at-Law, 1964); George Washington University (LL.M., 1970). Visiting Associate Professor of International Law, International Christian University, Tokyo, Japan, 1977-1978. Co-Chairman, Committee on International Trade, International Law Section, American Bar Association, 1982-1984. Board Member, International Human Rights Law Group, Northern Ireland-U.S. Partnership; Director of Legal Studies, International Law Institute. ***PRACTICE AREAS:*** International Trade. ***Email:*** pmacrory@akingump.com

PAUL E. MIRENGOFF, born Washington, D.C., April 17, 1949; admitted to bar, 1975, District of Columbia. *Education:* Dartmouth College (B.A., summa cum laude, 1971, Phi Beta Kappa); Stanford University (J.D., 1974). Editor, Board of Editors, Stanford Law Review, 1973-1974. Attorney, Office of General Counsel, Equal Employment Opportunity Commission, 1976-1980. Contributor: Employment Discrimination Law Bureau of National Affairs, 1983, 1986; Sexual Harassment in Employment Law BNA Books, 1992; The Validity of Court Ordered Employment Quotas, 19 Urich L.Rev. 797 (1985). ***PRACTICE AREAS:*** Labor and Employment; Litigation; Telecommunications. ***Email:*** pmirengoff@akingump.com

TECLA A. MURPHY, born Lansing, Michigan, March 2, 1964; admitted to bar, 1989, Illinois; 1997, District of Columbia. *Education:* University of Illinois (B.A., magna cum laude, with highest distinction, 1986); University of Chicago (J.D., 1989). Co-Author: "Using the Emergence of Primary Health Care in Hospital Strategy and Community Reform," Journal of Health and Hospital Law, Vol. Nos. 11 & 12, November and December, 1992. *Member:* American Health Lawyers Association; American College of Healthcare Executives. ***PRACTICE AREAS:*** Health Care Law; Corporate Transactional. ***Email:*** tmurphy@akingump.com

KENNETH E. NATALE, born Hammondsport, New York, March 29, 1952; admitted to bar, 1977, Virginia; 1978, District of Columbia; 1986, New York. *Education:* University of Notre Dame (B.A., with high honors, 1974); George Washington University (J.D., 1977). ***PRACTICE AREAS:*** Project Finance; Energy; Corporate; International. ***Email:*** knatale@akingump.com

JAMES C. OSBORNE, JR., born Harlan, Kentucky, December 19, 1955; admitted to bar, 1984, District of Columbia; 1985, U.S. District Court, District of Columbia and U.S. Court of Appeals for the District of Columbia Circuit. *Education:* Guilford College (B.A., with honors, 1978); George Washington University (J.D., with high honors, 1984). Order of the Coif. Law Clerk to Hon. John L. Smith, Jr., U.S. District Court for the District of Columbia, 1984-1985.

(This Listing Continued)

Member: The District of Columbia Bar (Member, Sections on: Litigation; Criminal Law and Individual Rights). ***PRACTICE AREAS:*** Litigation. ***Email:*** josborne@akingump.com

W. ERIC PILSK, born Nashville, Tennessee, November 12, 1960; admitted to bar, 1988, Virginia; 1989, District of Columbia. *Education:* Wesleyan University (B.A., with honors, 1983); Vanderbilt University (J.D., 1988). Articles Editor, Vanderbilt Law Review. *Member:* District of Columbia Bar; Virginia State Bar. ***Email:*** epilsk@akingump.com

JAMES P. SCANLAN, born Oak Ridge, Tennessee, January 17, 1945; admitted to bar, 1969, Massachusetts; 1974, U.S. Court of Appeals, Eighth and Ninth Circuits; 1975, U.S. Court of Appeals, Second Circuit; 1985, U.S. Supreme Court; 1986, District of Columbia; 1989, U.S. District Court, District of Maryland. *Education:* John Carroll University (A.B., 1966); Harvard University (J.D., 1969). U.S. Equal Employment Opportunity Commission, 1973-1995. Legal Publications: "Both Sides Misuse Data in Credit Discrimination Debate," American Banker, July 22, 1998; "Mired in Numbers," Legal Times, Oct. 21, 1996; "Women Employees' Case Against Publix Built on Wrong Data, Doesn't Compute," Miami Daily Business Review, Aug. 2, 1996; "When Statistics Lie," Legal Times, Jan. 1, 1996; "Strictly Scrutinizing Affirmative Action," Legal Times 1994-1995 Supreme Court Review, July 31, 1995; "No Substitute for the Real Thing: Class-Based Affirmative Action Won't Achieve the Same Results," Legal Times, May 1, 1995; "Multimillion-Dollar Settlements May Cause Employers to Avoid Hiring Women and Minorities for Less Desirable Jobs to Improve the Statistical Picture," The National Law Journal, Mar. 27, 1995; "Measuring Hiring Discrimination," The Labor Law Journal, July, 1993; "Getting It Straight When Statistics Can Lie," Legal Times, June 28, 1993; "Unlucky Stores: Are They All Guilty of Discrimination?" San Francisco Daily Journal, Jan. 29, 1993; "Study Misses Mark of Discrimination in D.C." Washington Business Journal, May 18-25, 1992; "Bias Data Can Make the Good Look Bad," American Banker, Apr. 27, 1992; "The Curious Case of Affirmative Action for Women," Society, Jan.-Feb., 1992; "Slip-Up on Civil Rights Bill," Legal Times, Dec. 1, 1991; "Setbacks Ahead for Set-Asides," Legal Times, May 21, 1991; "Can Affirmative Action Survive the Struggle?" Legal Times, Jan. 21, 1991; "Double-Edged Civil Rights," The National Law Journal, Nov. 5, 1990; "The Court's Little Surprise," Legal Times 1989-90 Supreme Court Review, July 23, 1990; "Numbers Can Mislead on Race and Death," Legal Times, July 9, 1990; "Race, Color Bias Inseparable," Fulton County Daily Report, June 26, 1990; "Broadcasting Cases to Transmit Message on Racial Preferences," Legal Times, Mar. 19, 1990; "An Issue of Numbers," The National Law Journal, Mar. 5, 1990; "Patterson v. McLean and Affirmative Action," The Labor Law Journal, March, 1990; "Time Running Out on Minority Preferences," Legal Times, Dec. 11, 1990; "Affirmative Action for Women: New Twist on an Old Debate," Legal Times, Dec. 5, 1988; "Striking Down Set-Aside System, Court Tackles Complex Issue," The National Law Journal, Mar. 6, 1989; "Are Bias Statistics Nonsense?" Legal Times (Apr. 17, 1989); "Illusions of Job Segregation," The Public Interest, Fall 1988; "What Helps the Single Working Parent?" The National Law Journal, Sept. 29, 1988; "Semantic Quibbles Miss the Point in EEO Debate," Legal Times, Feb. 24, 1986; "The Bottom Line Limitation to the Rule of Griggs v. Duke Power Co.," 18 U. Mich. J.L. Ref. 705 (1985) Spring 1985; "Employment Quotas for Women?" the Public Interest, Fall 1983 (Fall, 1983). [Capt., U.S. ARMY, 1969-1971]. ***PRACTICE AREAS:*** Labor and Employment. ***Email:*** jscanlan@akingump.com

DAWN E. STARR, born Pottsville, Pennsylvania, May 19, 1954; admitted to bar, 1981, District of Columbia. *Education:* Lehigh University (B.A., 1976); Case Western Reserve University (J.D., 1981). Member, National Moot Court Team. Recipient, Tournament Award, Dunmore Moot Court. Counsel to Board Members and to Chairman, National Labor Relations Board, 1981-1985. *Member:* The District of Columbia Bar. ***PRACTICE AREAS:*** Labor and Employment. ***Email:*** dstarr@akingump.com

CHARLES V. STEWART, born Huntington, Pennsylvania, November 11, 1941; admitted to bar, 1985, Virginia; 1988, District of Columbia. *Education:* Haverford College (B.A., 1964); University of Pennsylvania (M.B.A., 1966); University of North Carolina, Chapel Hill (Ph.D., 1974); Duke University (J.D., 1985). ***PRACTICE AREAS:*** ERISA. ***Email:*** cstewart@akingump.com

JAMES K. STEWART, born Quincy, Illinois, December 14, 1943; admitted to bar, 1969, Virginia; 1973, District of Columbia and U.S. Supreme Court. *Education:* University of Illinois (B.S., 1966); College of William & Mary (J.D., 1969). Phi Delta Phi. Research Editor, 1967-68 and Notes Editor, 1968-69, William & Mary Law Review. *Member:* District of Columbia Bar; Virginia State Bar; Federal and American Bar Associations (Member, Litigation Section). [J.A.G.C., U.S. Army, 1969-73]. ***PRACTICE AREAS:*** Government Contracts Law; Construction Litigation. ***Email:*** jstewart@akingump.com

(For Biographical Data of other Firm Personnel, see Professional Biographies at Austin, Dallas, Houston and San Antonio, Texas, Los Angeles, California, New York, New York, Philadelphia, Pennsylvania, Denver, Colorado, McLean, Virginia, Brussels, Belgium, London, United Kingdom, Moscow, Russian Federation and Riyadh, Saudi Arabia)

WENDELL B. ALCORN, JR.

1201 PENNSYLVANIA AVENUE, NW
SUITE 300 PMB 300
WASHINGTON, D.C. 20004
Telephone: 202-661-4644
Fax: 202-661-4699
URL: http://www.lawyers.com/wendellalcorn
Email: walcorn@aol.com
URL: http://www.alcornlawoffice.com

Williamsburg, Virginia Office: 3107 Nathaniel's Green, 23185-7525. Telephone: 757-258-9563. Fax: 757-258-3448.

Antitrust and Trade Regulation, Deceptive Trade Practices, Unfair Trade, Counterfeiting, Noncompetition and Non-Solicitation Agreements, Complex and Multi-District Litigation, Corporate Law, Business Litigation, Small Business Law, Trademark Protection, International Trademarks, Trade Secrets, Trade Association Law, Business Law.

FIRM PROFILE: Mr. Alcorn is the former general counsel for the President's National Commission for the Review of Antitrust Laws and Procedures. He has over 30 years of trial experience and his firm represents clients from the United States and around the world.

WENDELL B. ALCORN, JR., born Wharton, Texas, December 19, 1939; admitted to bar, 1969, Texas; 1970, New York; 1974, U.S. Supreme Court and South Carolina; 1975, Georgia; 1996, District of Columbia. *Education:* Rice University; University of St. Thomas; University of Houston (J.D., magna cum laude, 1969). Editor-in-Chief, Houston Law Review, 1968-1969. General Counsel, President's National Commission for the Review of Antitrust Laws and Procedures, 1978-1979. Special Professor of Law, Hofstra University, 1980-1995. Visiting Lecturer, University of San Francisco Law School, 1991. Adjunct Professor, Adelphi University Business Graduate School, 1976-1978. Faculty, National Institute for Trial Advocacy, 1980—. *Member:* The District of Columbia Bar; South Carolina and American Bar Associations; State Bar of Georgia; New York Academy of Sciences; American Association for the Advancement of Science; American Chemical Society; Society of Environmental Toxicology and Chemistry; Defense Research Institute. ***PRACTICE AREAS:*** Agricultural Cooperatives; Antitrust and Trade Regulation; Business Law; Class Actions; Complex and Multi-District Litigation; Computer Contracts; Contracts; Copyrights; Franchises and Franchising; Litigation; Products Liability; Toxic Torts; Trade Association Law; Trademarks; Unfair Competition.

ALEXANDER & CLEAVER, P.A.

WASHINGTON, D.C.

(See Annapolis, Maryland)

General Civil Litigation. Personal Injury, Automobile Accidents, Corporate, Business, Administrative, Zoning, Family Law, Criminal Law, Traffic Violations and Public Utility Law; Lobbying and Government Relations.

FRANK D. ALLEN, JR.

923 SOUTH CAROLINA AVENUE, SE
P.O. BOX 15539
WASHINGTON, D.C. 20003
Telephone: 202-544-0242
Fax: 202-547-1320
URL: http://www.lawyers.com/capitolhillallen

Retirement Planning, Trusts, Wills, Estate Planning and Estate Administration.

FIRM PROFILE: Frank D. Allen, Jr. is a former trial attorney for the U.S. Department of Justice and the Pension Benefit Guaranty Corporation with over 30 years of legal experience, including litigating a wide variety of legal and factual issues.

FRANK D. ALLEN, JR., born Helena, Arkansas, August 30, 1937; admitted to bar, 1965, District of Columbia, U.S. Court of Appeals for the District of Columbia Circuit and U.S. Court of Appeals, First, Fourth, Fifth and Ninth Circuits; 1980, U.S. Supreme Court. *Education:* Millsaps College (B.S., 1960); Vanderbilt University (LL.B., 1964). Justice, Vanderbilt Moot Court, 1962-1964. Assistant General Counsel (1992-1994) and Senior Counsel (1987-1992, 1994-1995), Office of the General Counsel, Pension Benefit Guaranty Corporation, 1987-1995. Senior Attorney, Appellate Section, Civil Rights Division, U.S. Department of Justice, 1975-1987. Deputy Chief, Criminal Section, Civil Rights Division, U.S. Department of Justice, 1971-1975. Attorney, Civil Rights Division, U.S. Department of Justice, 1966-1971. *Member:* District of Columbia Bar; American Bar Association. [2nd Lt., Mississippi National Guard, 1955-

(This Listing Continued)

1960. U.S. Army Artillery and Missile Officers Candidate School, Fort Sill, Oklahoma, 1958. 1st Lt. U.S. Army Reserve, 1960-1966]

ALLEN, JOHNSON, ALEXANDER & KARP, P.A.

Established in 1970

2120 L STREET, N.W., SUITE 701
WASHINGTON, D.C. 20037
Telephone: 202-828-4141
Fax: 202-429-8798
Email: ajakdc@aol.com

Baltimore, Maryland Office: Suite 1540, 100 East Pratt Street. Telephone: 410-727-5000.

General Civil Trial Practice in all Courts. Insurance, Corporation, Insurance Defense, Products Liability, Civil Rights and Family Law.

FIRM PROFILE: Allen, Johnson, Alexander & Karp, P.A., was founded in 1970 to provide legal services in the defense of liability claims for the insurance, business and political communities. Areas of expertise include product liability, business operations, toxic torts and civil rights law. Allen, Johnson, Alexander & Karp practices in all federal and state courts in Maryland, the District of Columbia and Virginia. The Firm's four partners are veteran practitioners in the region, with more than 70 years of combined experience in civil litigation.

From its offices in Baltimore and Washington, Allen, Johnson, Alexander & Karp serves a client base that includes some of the nation's largest insurance carriers, businesses and municipal self-insurance pools.

D'ANA E. JOHNSON, born Henderson, Kentucky, December 12, 1947; admitted to bar, 1977, District of Columbia, U.S. District Court for the District of Columbia, U.S. Court of Appeals for the District of Columbia Circuit and U.S. District Court, District of Maryland; 1980, U.S. Supreme Court; 1983, Maryland; 1991, U.S. Court of Appeals, Fourth Circuit. *Education:* Morgan State College (B.S., 1969); Georgetown University Law Center (J.D., 1972). Voting Delegate, D.C. Court of Appeals Judicial Conference, 1985-2000. *Member:* Maryland State Bar Association; The District of Columbia Bar (Officer, Section on Injury to Person and Property); District of Columbia Defense Lawyer's Association; International Association of Defense Counsel; National Bar Association (Life Member); Defense Research Institute (Member, Steering Committee on Trial Tactics and Techniques Committee; Committee, Pattern Civil Jury Instruction). 1998 DC Defense Lawyer of the Year, The District of Columbia Bar. ***PRACTICE AREAS:*** Products Liability; General Civil Trial; Insurance Law; Premises Liability; Insurance Defense; Employment Law. ***Email:*** ajakdcdej@aol.com

REPRESENTATIVE CLIENTS: Scottsdale Insurance Co.; Nautilus Insurance Co.; Penn National; Jefferson Insurance Co.; Erie Insurance Group; Liberty Mutual Insurance Co.; Avis Rent-A-Car; United Technologies Corp.; Lexington Insurance Co.; Empire Insurance Cos.; Otis Elevator Co.; Carrier Corp.; Fireman's Ins. Co. of Washington, D.C.; Montgomery Elevator Co.; Metropolitan Life Insurance Co.; Empire Fire & Marine Insurance Co.; Admiral Insurance Co.; National General Insurance Co., GAB.

(For complete biographical data on all personnel, see Professional Biographies at Baltimore, Maryland)

ROBERT G. ALLEN, P.C.

WASHINGTON, D.C.

(See Manassas, Virginia)

Communications, International Telecommunications, FCC Licensing, FCC Regulation, Satellite Communication, Corporate and Business Law, Computer and Internet Law.

ALPER & MANN, P.C.

Established in 1958

SUITE 1107, 1730 K STREET, N.W.
WASHINGTON, D.C. 20006
Telephone: 202-298-9191
Fax: 202-298-9194
Email: Alpermann@INTR.NET
URL: http://www.lawyers.com/alpermannweisbaum

General Practice before all Courts and Government Agencies. Railroad Safety Litigation, FELA Litigation, Personal Injury, Corporate, Utility, Labor, Transportation, Securities, Probate, Employment and Family Law. Trials.

(This Listing Continued)

FIRM PROFILE: In addition to a general trial practice, for more than 30 years our firm has specialized in railroad safety matters, including legislation, rulemaking and litigation. Designated legal counsel to the United Transportation Union, the Brotherhood of Railroad Signalmen and the American Train Dispatchers Division of the Brotherhood of Locomotive Engineers.

LAWRENCE M. MANN, born Wilmington, North Carolina, January 30, 1940; admitted to bar, 1967, District of Columbia. *Education:* University of North Carolina (B.A., 1962); Georgetown University (LL.B., 1966). Special Assistant to United States Senator Vance Hartke, 1964-1965. Member, Legal Staff, U.S. House of Representatives Post Office and Civil Service Committee, 1965-1966. Counsel, Commission of Political Activity on Government Personnel, 1967. *Member:* The District of Columbia Bar; Bar Association of the District of Columbia; American Bar Association; The Association of Trial Lawyers of America. ***PRACTICE AREAS:*** Railroad Safety; Personal Injury; Family Law; Civil Litigation. ***Email:*** Alpermann@INTR.NET

ALSTON & BIRD LLP

Established in 1893

601 PENNSYLVANIA AVENUE, N.W.
NORTH BUILDING, 10TH FLOOR
WASHINGTON, D.C. 20004-2601
Telephone: 202-756-3300
Telecopier: 202-756-3333
Cable Address: AMGRAM GA
Telex: 54-2996 (AMG ATL)
Easylink: 62985848
URL: http://www.alston.com

Atlanta, Georgia Office: One Atlantic Center, 1201 West Peachtree Street 30309-3424. Telephone: 404-881-7000. Telecopier: 404-881-7777.

Charlotte, North Carolina Office: Bank of America Plaza, 101 South Tryon Street, Suite 4000, 28280-4000. Telephone: 704-444-1000. Fax: 704-444-1111.

Raleigh, North Carolina Office (Research Triangle Area): 3201 Beechleaf Court, Suite 600, 27604-1062. Telephone: 919-862-2200. Telecopier: 919-862-2260.

New York, New York Office: 90 Park Avenue, 10016-1387. Telephone: 212-210-9400. Fax: 212-210-9444.

(Liaison Office) Munich, Germany: Brienner Strasse 11/V, 80333 Munich. Telephone: (49) (89) 238-0-70. Telecopier: (49) (89) 238-0-7110.

Administrative Law, Alternative Dispute Resolution, Antitrust and Trade Regulation, Appellate Practice, Bankruptcy, Banks and Banking, Biotechnology, Business Law, Class Actions, Commercial Real Estate, FCC Licensing, FCC Regulation, Wireless Communications, Complex and Multi-District Litigation, Computers and Software, Constitutional Law, Construction Law, Copyrights, Corporate Ethics, Corporate Governance, Corporate Law, Criminal Law, Debtor and Creditor, Electronic Commerce, Emerging Growth Companies, Employee Benefits, Entertainment Law, ERISA, ERISA Litigation, Energy, Environmental Law, Environmental Litigation, Finance, Immigration Law, International Finance, Franchises and Franchising, Health Care Corporate Law, Health Care Regulation, Insurance Defense, Intellectual Property, International Law, International Trade, Internet Law, Labor and Employment, Land Use, Legislative Practice, Life Sciences, Litigation, Medical Malpractice, Mergers, Acquisitions and Divestitures, Multimedia Law, Municipal Law, Nonprofit and Charitable Organizations, Occupational Safety and Health, Partnership Law, Patents, Privacy Law, Products Liability, Professional Liability, Public Finance, Public Policy, Real Estate Finance, Regulatory Law, RICO, Securities, Securities Litigation, Taxation, Tax Litigation, Technology and Science, Trademarks, Trusts and Estates, Utility Law, Venture Capital, White Collar Crime, Zoning.

LAW FIRM ALLIANCES/ASSOCIATIONS: ***LEX MUNDI***

MEMBERS OF FIRM

HENRY J. BIRNKRANT, born Philadelphia, Pennsylvania, January 24, 1955; admitted to bar, 1979, District of Columbia; 1980, U.S. District Court for the District of Columbia and U.S. Court of Appeals for the District of Columbia Circuit; 1984, U.S. Tax Court; 1998, U.S. Court of Federal Claims. *Education:* University of Rochester (B.A., magna cum laude, 1976); Columbia University (J.D., 1979); New York University (LL.M. in Taxation, 1983). ***PRACTICE AREAS:*** Taxation Law; International Taxation; Federal Taxation. ***Email:*** hbirnkrant@alston.com

THOMAS M. BOYD, born Yorktown, Virginia, September, 10, 1946; admitted to bar, 1973, California; 1974, District of Columbia; 1990, U.S. Supreme Court. *Education:* Virginia Military Institute (B.A., in History, 1968); University of Virginia (J.D., 1971). [U.S.A.F., Capt., 1972-1973]. ***PRACTICE AREAS:*** Financial Services Law; Electronic Commerce; Legislative Advocacy. ***Email:*** tboyd@alston.com

(This Listing Continued)

DAVID E. BROWN, JR., born Washington, D.C., September 10, 1961; admitted to bar, 1986, Georgia; 2001, District of Columbia. *Education:* Princeton University (A.B., 1983); University of Kentucky (J.D., with high distinction, 1986). ***PRACTICE AREAS:*** Mergers and Acquisitions; Corporate Finance; Securities Regulation; Bank Mergers and Acquisitions; Electronic Banking; Joint Ventures; Strategic Alliances; Electronic Commerce; Information Technology; Internet Law; Corporate Fiduciary Law. ***Email:*** dbrown@alston.com

ROBERT T. COLE, born Brooklyn, New York, 1932; admitted to bar, 1956, New York; 1972, District of Columbia; 1989, U.S. Supreme Court. *Education:* Wharton School, University of Pennsylvania (B.S., Econ., 1953); Harvard Law School (LL.B., magna cum laude, 1956); London School of Economics (Academic Post Graduate Diploma in Law, 1959). Board of Editors, Harvard L. Rev., 1954-1956. International Tax Counsel and Deputy International Tax Counsel, U.S. Treas. Dept., 1967-1973. Editor and Principal Author: *Principal Guide to U.S. Transfer Pricing.* Co-Author: "Income Tax Treaties—Administrative and Competent Authority Aspects," 940 Tax Management. Founding Member, Cole Corette & Abrutyn, 1973-1996. [1st Lt., U.S. Air Force, 1957-1959]. ***LANGUAGES:*** French. ***PRACTICE AREAS:*** Transfer Pricing; International Taxation; International Tax Controversies; Corporate Taxation. ***Email:*** rcole@alston.com

FRANK M. CONNER III, born Richmond, Virginia, September 30, 1956; admitted to bar, 1981, Virginia and Georgia; 1990, District of Columbia. *Education:* University of Virginia (B.A., 1978; J.D., 1981). ***PRACTICE AREAS:*** Financial Services Law; Financial Institution Regulation; Mergers, Acquisitions and Divestitures; Securities Regulation; Electronic Commerce. ***Email:*** fconner@alston.com

PHILIP C. COOK, born Atlanta, Georgia, November 4, 1946; admitted to bar, 1972, Georgia; 1998, District of Columbia; 1984, U.S. Tax Court; 1994, U.S. Court of Federal Claims. *Education:* Georgia Institute of Technology (B.S., with honors, 1968); Harvard University (J.D., cum laude, 1971). *Member:* Atlanta (Member, Board of Directors, Taxation Section, 1996—) and American (Chair, Banking and Savings Institutions Committee, Section of Taxation, 1997-1999) Bar Associations; State Bar of Georgia (Chairman, Taxation Section, 1991); District of Columbia Bar; Southern Pension Conference (Steering Committee, 1984-1989; President, 1989); Atlanta Tax Forum (President, 1991); American Law Institute. Fellow, American College of Tax Counsel. (Also at Atlanta, Georgia Office). ***PRACTICE AREAS:*** Federal Income Tax; Federal Tax Controversies; ERISA Litigation. ***Email:*** pcook@alston.com

THOMAS E. CROCKER, JR., born Washington, D.C., June 9, 1949; admitted to bar, 1976, District of Columbia. *Education:* Princeton University (A.B., cum laude, 1971); Columbia University (J.D., 1974). ***LANGUAGES:*** Portuguese. ***PRACTICE AREAS:*** Technology Law; Foreign Asset Control; Import and Export Law; Trade Regulation; Banking Regulation. ***Email:*** tcrocker@alston.com

JAMES E. CROKER, JR., born Washington, D.C., August 3, 1957; admitted to bar, 1982, District of Columbia. *Education:* University of Maryland (B.A., 1979); University of Virginia (J.D., 1982). ***PRACTICE AREAS:*** Federal Taxation; International Taxation. ***Email:*** jcroker@alston.com

JOHN L. DOUGLAS, born Atlanta, Georgia, September 23, 1950; admitted to bar, 1977, Georgia (Not admitted in District of Columbia). *Education:* Davidson College (B.A., cum laude, 1972); University of Georgia (J.D., magna cum laude, 1977). (Also at Atlanta, Georgia Office). ***LANGUAGES:*** Spanish. ***PRACTICE AREAS:*** Mergers and Acquisitions; Banks and Banking. ***Email:*** jdouglas@alston.com

JONATHAN M. FEE, born Akron, Ohio, September 17, 1949; admitted to bar, 1974, Georgia, U.S. District Court, Northern District of Georgia, U.S. Court of International Trade and U.S. Court of Appeals, Eleventh and Federal Circuits (Not admitted in District of Columbia). *Education:* University of Pennsylvania (B.S. Econ., 1971); Emory University (J.D., 1974). *Member:* Atlanta and American Bar Associations; State Bar of Georgia. ***PRACTICE AREAS:*** Customs Law; International Trade Regulation. ***Email:*** jfee@alston.com

CHRISTOPHER D. FORD, born East Orange, New Jersey, January 25, 1965; admitted to bar, 1993, Georgia (Not admitted in District of Columbia). *Education:* University of Virginia (B.S., 1987); Emory University School of Law (J.D., 1993). ***PRACTICE AREAS:*** Information Technology; Telecommunications Contracts; Outsourcing Transactions; Strategic Alliances; Joint Ventures. ***Email:*** cford@alston.com

JAMES S. HUTCHINSON, born Detroit, Michigan, June 26, 1952; admitted to bar, 1979, Georgia and U.S. District Court, Northern District of Georgia; 2000, District of Columbia. *Education:* St. Lawrence University (B.A., 1974); Vanderbilt University (J.D., 1979). Phi Beta Kappa. Recipient, Vanderbilt Law Review Medal. Executive Articles Editor, Vanderbilt Law Review, 1978-1979. Author: "Non-Qualified Deferred Compensation Plans and Rabbi Trusts," Chapter in ERISA Compliance and Enforcement Library (BNA 2001). President, Southern Employee Benefits Conference, 1993. Leader, Alston & Bird LLP Employee Benefits and Executive Compensation Group, and Co-Chair, Alston & Bird LLP Tax Section. *Member:* American Bar Association; Southern

(This Listing Continued)

ALSTON & BIRD LLP, Washington—Continued

Employee Benefits Conference. ***PRACTICE AREAS:*** Pension and Profit Sharing Plans; Employee Stock Ownership Plans; Executive Compensation. ***Email:*** jhutchinson@alston.com

FREDERICK M. JOYCE, born Pompton Plains, New Jersey, April 18, 1958; admitted to bar, 1985, Maryland and District of Columbia; 1987, U.S. Court of Appeals, 4th Circuit; 1990, Virginia; 1999, U.S. Supreme Court and U.S. Court of Appeals, District of Columbia Circuit, 5th and 6th Circuits. *Education:* George Washington University (B.A., with distinction, 1980); Georgetown University Law Center (J.D., 1984). ***PRACTICE AREAS:*** Telecommunications Law; Electronic Commerce; Internet Law; Entertainment and the Arts. ***Email:*** rjoyce@alston.com

OSCAR N. PERSONS, born McCormick, South Carolina, January 7, 1939; admitted to bar, 1967, Georgia; 1981, U.S. Supreme Court; U.S. Court of Appeals, 5th, 6th, 8th and 11th Circuits (Not admitted in District of Columbia). *Education:* Georgia Institute of Technology (B.I.E., 1960); Emory University (J.D., 1967). (Also at Atlanta, Georgia Office). ***REPORTED CASES:*** Bryant v. Avado Brands, Inc. 187 F.3d 1271 (11th Cir., 1999); Bryant v. Avado Brands, Inc. 100 F. Supp 2d 1368 (M.D. GA 2000); In Re Millen Industries, Inc. Securities Litigation, 20 F. Supp 2d 1371 (N.D. GA 2000); Saltzberg v. TM Sterling/Austin Assoc., Ltd., 45 F.3d 399 (11th Cir., 1995). ***PRACTICE AREAS:*** Securities Fraud Class Actions; Complex Litigation; Business Torts; Federal Legislative Matters. ***Email:*** opersons@alston.com

THOMAS G. SCHENDT, born Wauwatosa, Wisconsin, June 27, 1958; admitted to bar, 1985, Wisconsin and U.S. District Court, Eastern and Western Districts of Wisconsin; 1993, U.S. Tax Court (Not admitted in District of Columbia). *Education:* Marquette University (B.A., 1980; M.B.A., 1982; J.D., 1985). ***PRACTICE AREAS:*** Taxation; Employee Benefits. ***Email:*** tschendt@alston.com

MARGARET A. SHEEHAN, born Wayne, Illinois, April 9, 1959; admitted to bar, 1988, New York; 1999, District of Columbia. *Education:* Duke University (A.B., magna cum laude, 1981); Georgetown University (J.D., magna cum laude, 1988). ***PRACTICE AREAS:*** Investment Management (30%); Broker-Dealer Regulation (30%); Investment Company Law (20%); Electronic Commerce (18%); Insurance Products (2%). ***Email:*** msheehan@alston.com

JONATHAN H. TALCOTT, born New York, N.Y., August 16, 1962; admitted to bar, 1989, Connecticut; 1990, New York; 1991, District of Columbia. *Education:* University of North Carolina at Chapel Hill (B.A., John Motley Morehead Scholar, with honors, 1984); University of Virginia (J.D., 1989). ***PRACTICE AREAS:*** Technology Law; Securities; Financial Services Law; International. ***Email:*** jtalcott@alston.com

CHARLES W. WHEELER, born July 8, 1945; admitted to bar, 1970, Wisconsin (Not admitted in District of Columbia). *Education:* University of Wisconsin (B.S., 1967; J.D., 1970); Georgetown University (LL.M., in Taxation, 1978). ***PRACTICE AREAS:*** Federal Taxation; International Taxation; Banks and Banking. ***Email:*** cwheeler@alston.com

SENIOR COUNSEL

BRIAN E. LEBOWITZ, born Waco, Texas, July 8, 1950; admitted to bar, 1981, District of Columbia; 1982, U.S. Court of Appeals for the District of Columbia Circuit; 1994, U.S. Tax Court. *Education:* Amherst College (B.A., summa cum laude, 1972); Yale University (M.A., 1974; M.Phil., 1975; Ph.D., 1977); Stanford University (J.D., 1980). ***PRACTICE AREAS:*** Federal Income Tax; International Income Taxation; International Tax Controversies; Tax Planning; Tax Valuation. ***Email:*** blebowitz@alston.com

EDWARD M. PRINCE, born Washington, D.C., May 3, 1937; admitted to bar, 1962, Virginia; 1963, District of Columbia. *Education:* Yale University (B.S., 1959); University of Virginia (LL.B., 1962). ***PRACTICE AREAS:*** Trademarks. ***Email:*** eprince@alston.com

COUNSEL

ROBERT A. BAUMAN, born New Bedford, Massachusetts, October 16, 1955; admitted to bar, 1984, Virginia; 1988, District of Columbia. *Education:* College of William & Mary (B.B.A., 1978; J.D., 1984). ***PRACTICE AREAS:*** Employee Benefit Law; ERISA; Qualified Retirement Plans. ***Email:*** rbauman@alston.com

MARY ANN CAPRIA, born Quantico, Virginia, January 18, 1958; admitted to bar, 1984, South Carolina (inactive); 1985, District of Columbia; 1998, Virginia; U.S. District Court for the District of Columbia; U.S. Court of Appeals for the Federal Circuit; registered to practice before U.S. Patent and Trademark Office. *Education:* University of South Carolina (B.S., 1979; J.D., 1984). ***PRACTICE AREAS:*** Intellectual Property; Patents; Trademarks; Technology Licensing; Litigation. ***Email:*** mcapria@alston.com

DAVID R. GODOFSKY, born New York, New York, November 3, 1958; admitted to bar, 1982, Missouri; 1992, Tennessee; 2000, District of Columbia. *Education:* The College of Insurance (B.S., Actuarial Science, summa cum laude, 1979); University of Virginia (J.D., 1982). ***PRACTICE AREAS:*** Employee Benefits. ***Email:*** dgodofsky@alston.com

CHRISTINE McLAUGHLIN, born Bronx, New York, March 24, 1965; admitted to bar, 1990, Connecticut; 1993, District of Columbia; 1997, U.S. Court of Appeals, 5th Circuit. *Education:* Fordham University (B.A., 1987); Catholic University of America, Institute for Communications Law Studies (J.D., 1990). ***PRACTICE AREAS:*** Telecommunications; Appellate Litigation. ***Email:*** cmclaughlin@alston.com

DWIGHT C. SMITH, III, born Fort Meade, Maryland, June 24, 1955; admitted to bar, 1982, District of Columbia and New York. *Education:* Yale University (B.A., 1977; J.D., 1981). ***PRACTICE AREAS:*** Banking; Electronic Banking; Privacy; Bank Mergers and Acquisitions; Bank Holding Company Regulation; Bank Holding Company Law; Banking Antitrust. ***Email:*** dcsmith@alston.com

ANNE WALLACE, born New York, New York, October 12, 1948; admitted to bar, 1973, District of Columbia; 1980, Pennsylvania (inactive). *Education:* Fordham University (B.A., 1970); Boston University (J.D., 1973). ***PRACTICE AREAS:*** Privacy Law; Consumer Banking; Banking Regulation; Electronic Banking. ***Email:*** awallace@alston.com

JONATHAN M. WINER, admitted to bar, 1981, Massachusetts; 1989, District of Columbia. *Education:* Yale University (B.A., 1976); New York University (J.D., 1981). ***PRACTICE AREAS:*** Privacy Law; Electronic Commerce; Banking Law; New Media Law; Government Relations. ***Email:*** jwiner@alston.com

ASSOCIATES

Pamela S. Ammermann
Gabrielle D. Bailey
Sara Ford Burstein (admission pending)
Jennifer L. Butler
James J. Casey
Marianne Casserly
Sarah Hatch Gerhart (admission pending)
Jonathan V. Gould (admission pending)
Lesley Ellen Hanchrow (Not admitted in DC)
Mark O. Henry
Kathryn Cole Kling
Jay Krutulis (Not admitted in DC)
Andrea Lane (Not admitted in DC)
Priscilla K. Lawson (admission pending)
Emily W. Mao
William E. Morlan
Thomas P. Newman (Not admitted in DC)
Ronald E. Quirk, Jr.
Michael P. Reed
Jason M. Waite (Not admitted in DC)

REPRESENTATIVE CLIENTS: AFLAC, Inc.; AmvesCap PLC; Arthritis Foundation; Atlantic Steel Industries, Inc.; Bank of America Corporation; Beers, Inc.; Bertelsmann AG; Borden, Inc.; Bose Corporation; CarsDirect.com; Celpage, Inc.; CGW Southeast and Affiliates; The Community Foundation for Greater Atlanta, Inc.; Dresdner Bank AG; Emory University and Emory Healthcare; eSASA; First Union Corporation; Fortis, Inc.; The Fulton-DeKalb Hospital Authority; Genuine Parts Co. Inc.; Georgia Hospital Association; Georgia-Pacific Corporation; Gold Kist Inc.; Group Bruxelles Lambert; Imerys; Industrial Developments International, Inc.; Kaiser Permanente Medical Care Program; Komatsu America International Company; MAG Mutual Insurance Co. Inc.; Mann & Hummel Gmbh Filterwerk; Mohawk Industries, Inc.; Municipal Electric Authority of Georgia (MEAG); Municipal Gas Authority of Georgia (MGAG); National Association for Stock Car Auto Racing, Inc. (NASCAR); The National Business Coalition on E-Commerce and Privacy; National Data Corporation; National Industries for the Blind; Paragon Trade Brands, Inc.; The Prudential Insurance Company of America; PTEK Holdings, Inc.; Regions Financial Corporation; Rodenstock Inst. Corp.; Charles Schwab & Co., Inc.; SunTrust Banks, Inc. and Affiliates; SunTrust Robinson Humphrey; Turner Broadcasting System, Inc.; UnumProvident Corporation; United Parcel Service; Verizon Communications; Vulcan Materials Co. Inc.; Waffle House, Inc.; Web MD; YUPI Internet, Inc.

(For complete biographical data on other personnel, see professional biographies at Atlanta, Georgia, Charlotte and Raleigh, North Carolina, New York, New York, and Munich, Germany).

ALTMANN AND VITT

Established in 1920

1616 H STREET, N.W.
WASHINGTON, D.C. 20006-4903
Telephone: 202-628-5093
Facsimile: 202-628-5932

Estate Planning, Trust, Probate Small Business Law, Business Succession Planning and Corporation Law. Litigation.

MEMBERS OF FIRM

ANDREW T. ALTMANN (1918-1988).

(This Listing Continued)

A. FRANCIS VITT, JR., born Chicago, Illinois, November 28, 1938; admitted to bar, 1964, Virginia and District of Columbia; 1992, Maryland. *Education:* Georgetown University (A.B., 1960; J.D., 1964). Delta Theta Phi. Assistant Commonwealth Attorney for Arlington County, Virginia, 1966. *Member:* Arlington County and Virginia Bar Associations; Virginia State Bar; District of Columbia Bar.

ALVORD AND ALVORD

Established in 1932

1600 K STREET

SUITE 200

WASHINGTON, D.C. 20006

Telephone: 202-393-2266

Fax: 202-393-2156

Email: alvordlaw@aol.com

Tax, Corporation, Probate Law, Railroad Equipment Financing.

MEMBERS OF FIRM

ELIAS C. ALVORD (1860-1942).

ELLSWORTH C. ALVORD (1895-1964).

ROBERT W. ALVORD, born Washington, D.C., September 24, 1933; admitted to bar, 1958, New York; 1959, District of Columbia and U.S. Court of Appeals, District of Columbia Circuit. *Education:* Dartmouth College and Haverford College (B.A., 1955); Columbia University (LL.B., 1958). Counsel, New York State Office of Transportation, 1961-1964. Member: Board of Directors, National Symphony Orchestra, Washington, D.C.; Board of Visitors, Legislative Drafting Research Fund, Columbia University School of Law, New York, New York; Board of Trustees, St. Albans School, Washington, D.C. Maret School, Washington, D.C.; American Symphony Orchestra League; Northland College, Ashland, Wisconsin. Senior Associate, The Salk Institute, San Diego, California. *Member:* The District of Columbia Bar; Bar Association of The District of Columbia; New York State and American Bar Associations. ***PRACTICE AREAS:*** Probate; Railroad Equipment Financing. ***Email:*** alvordlaw@aol.com

EDWARD M. LURIA, born Philadelphia, Pennsylvania, December 11, 1941; admitted to bar, 1968, Pennsylvania; 1970, District of Columbia and U.S. Tax Court; 1971, Delaware; 1982, U.S. Claims Court. *Education:* University of Pennsylvania (A.B., 1964; J.D., 1967); New York University (LL.M. in Taxation, 1968). Law Clerk to Hon. John W. Kern, Jr., U.S. Tax Court, 1968-1970. Certified Public Accountant, Maryland, 1981. *Member:* The District of Columbia Bar (Member, Taxation Section); Delaware State and American (Member, Estate and Gift Tax Committee, Committee on Value Added Taxes and Committee on Closely-Held Corporations, Taxation Section, 1977—) Bar Associations. (Also Of Counsel: Damico & Associates, Washington, D.C.; Moore & Bruce, Washington, D.C. and Wilmington, Delaware). ***PRACTICE AREAS:*** Tax Law; Estate Planning; Employee Benefits; Asset Protection. ***Email:*** eluria@aol.com

REPRESENTATIVE CLIENTS: Chapman and Cutler; Mayer, Brown & Platt; Thelen Reid & Priest; Miles & Stockbridge; Winston & Strawn; Union Pacific Railroad; Burlington Northern and Santa Fe Railway; Canadian Pacific Railway; CSX Transportation, Inc.; Amtrak; California Department of Transportation; New Jersey Transit Authority; ACF Industries; The Greenbrier Companies; Bombardier Capital Rail, Inc.; General Electric Railcar Service Corporation; Bank of America; Pitney Bowes Credit Corporation; Firstar Bank; Charter Financial, Inc.

THE AMERICAN LEGAL CENTER FOR ESTATE PLANNING

1155 CONNECTICUT AVENUE N.W., SUITE 400

WASHINGTON, D.C. 20036

Telephone: 202-429-6508

Fax: 202-467-4924

Litigation, Corporate Law, Business Law, Mergers and Acquisitions.

J. NELSON HAPPY, born Lawrence, Kansas, 1943; admitted to bar, 1967, Missouri; 1985, New York; 1989, Pennsylvania and District of Columbia; 1993, Virginia; U.S. District Court, Western District of Missouri; U.S. District Court, Southern and Eastern Districts of New York; U.S. District Court, Eastern District of Virginia; U.S. Court of Appeals, Second, Fourth and Eighth Circuits; U.S. Supreme Court. *Education:* Syracuse University (B.S., cum laude, 1964); Columbia University (J.D., 1967). Phi Kappa Phi; Delta Sigma Rho; Psi Chi; Kent Court. Recipient, Lawrence Greenbaum Prize, Columbia Law School. Author: "Damnum Absque Injuria, When Private Property May Be Damaged Without Compensation in Missouri," 36 Missouri Law Review 453, Fall, 1971. *Member:* The Association of the Bar of the City of New York; Newport News, Virginia, Pennsylvania and American Bar Associations; The Missouri Bar. [Major, USAR, Ret.]. ***PRACTICE AREAS:*** Litigation; Corporate Law; Business Law; Mergers and Acquisitions.

(This Listing Continued)

AMMERMAN & GOLDBERG

Established in 1980

1115 MASSACHUSETTS AVENUE, NW

WASHINGTON, D.C. 20005

Telephone: 202-638-0606

Fax: 202-638-3332

Email: hsaaba@aol.com

Bankruptcy, Chapter 7, Chapter 13, Consumer Bankruptcy, Personal Bankruptcy, Consumer Rights, Foreclosure Law, Debtors Rights, Creditors Rights, Wage Garnishments, Car Repossessions.

FIRM PROFILE: Attorneys Ammerman & Goldberg have combined over 45 years of experience to provide bankruptcy protection for individuals, families and small businesses from Maryland, D.C. and Virginia. The firm routinely stops foreclosures, wage garnishments, lawsuits, creditor calls and car reposessions.

HARRIS S. AMMERMAN, born 1945; admitted to bar, 1972, Pennsylvania; 1974, District of Columbia; 1978, Maryland. *Education:* Temple University (B.S., M.A., 1970); George Washington University (J.D., 1972). ***PRACTICE AREAS:*** Consumer Bankruptcy Law, Including: Chapters 7 and 13 Law; Commercial Bankruptcy; Foreclosure Law; Wage Garnishments; Creditors Rights; Debtors Rights.

JOSEPH M. GOLDBERG, born Boston, Massachusetts, November 29, 1947; admitted to bar, 1980, District of Columbia; 1981, Virginia, U.S. District Court for the District of Columbia; 1985, U.S. District Court for the Eastern District of Virginia, U.S. Bankruptcy Court for the Eastern District of Virginia. *Education:* Franklin & Marshall College (A.B., 1969); Georgetown University (J.D., 1980. ***PRACTICE AREAS:*** Bankruptcy Law; Bankruptcy Chapter 7; Bankruptcy Chapter 13; Foreclosures; Consumer Credit.

ASSOCIATE

STEVEN M. ASSARAF, born Washington, D.C., June 8, 1965; admitted to bar, 1990, Maryland; 1992, District of Columbia. *Education:* University of Maryland (B.S., 1987); University of Baltimore (J.D., 1990). *Member:* Maryland Bar Association, Inc.; The District of Columbia Bar; American Bar Association. ***PRACTICE AREAS:*** Bankruptcy; Bankruptcy Chapter 7; Bankruptcy Chapter 13; Foreclosures; Consumer Credit; Wage Garnishments.

CHRISTOPHER B. AMOLSCH

WASHINGTON, D.C.

(See Alexandria)

Federal Criminal Law, Criminal Law, Search and Seizure, Forensic DNA, Driving While Intoxicated, Traffic Violations, Criminal Appeals, Death Penalty Appeals, Bank Fraud, Health Care Fraud.

ANDALMAN & FLYNN, P.C.

WASHINGTON, D.C.

(See Silver Spring, Maryland)

Personal Injury, Automobile Accidents and Injury, Social Security, Disability Claims, Family Law, Collections, Employment Law, Wrongful Termination, Discrimination, Civil Rights, Criminal Law, Civil Litigation, Appellate Practice.

ALLAN W. ANDERSON, JR.

4812 W STREET, N.W.

WASHINGTON, D.C. 20007

Telephone: 202-298-6910

Fax: 202-298-6914

Email: ALLANDER@EROLS.COM

Administrative Law, Energy Law, Electric Power, Hydroelectricity, Public Utilities, Oil and Gas, Pipeline Law.

ALLAN W. ANDERSON, JR., born Marlborough, Massachusetts, September 21, 1946; admitted to bar, 1974, Maryland; 1978, District of Columbia; 1984, U.S. Court of Appeals for the Federal Circuit; 1990, U.S. Supreme Court. *Education:* University of Maryland (B.A., 1968); George Washington University (J.D., 1974). Trial Attorney Federal Power Commission and Federal Energy Regulatory Commission, 1974-1978. Former Member, Ward & Anderson, P.C., 1978-1999. *Member:* District of Columbia Bar; Maryland State, Federal Energy (Member, Board of Directors, 1992-1995) and American Bar Associations.

ANDERSON, COE & KING, L.L.P.

WASHINGTON, D.C.

(See Baltimore, Maryland)

General Civil and Criminal Trial Practice. Insurance, Products Liability, Malpractice, Commercial, Real Estate, Estate Planning and Probate Law. Environmental Law.

ANDERSON KILL & OLICK, L.L.P.

Established in 1979

1275 K STREET, N.W.

SUITE 1101

WASHINGTON, D.C. 20005

Telephone: 202-218-0040

Fax: 202-962-3966

Email: akodc@andersonkill.com

URL: http://www.andersonkill.com

New York, N.Y. Office: Anderson Kill & Olick, P.C., 1251 Avenue of the Americas. Telephone: 212-278-1000. Fax: 212-278-1733

Philadelphia, Pennsylvania Office: Anderson Kill & Olick, P.C., 1600 Market Street. Telephone: 215-568-4202. Fax: 215-568-4573.

Newark, New Jersey Office: Anderson Kill & Olick, P.C. One Gateway Center, Suite 901. Telephone: 973-642-5858. Fax: 973-621-6361.

Chicago, Illinois Office: Anderson Kill & Olick, 190 South La Salle Street, Suite 800. Telephone: 312-857-2500. Fax: 312-857-0122.

General Practice including Litigation, Insurance, Environmental, Employment and Labor, Products Liability, Trademark, Unfair Competition and Intellectual Property.

MICHELE A. GALLAGHER, born Rahway, New Jersey, September 28, 1966; admitted to bar, 1996, Maryland; 1998, District of Columbia and U.S. Court of Appeals, Fourth Circuit; 1999, U.S. District Court, District of Maryland; 2000, U.S. Court of Appeals for the District of Columbia; 2001, U.S. District Court for the District of Columbia. *Education:* The Catholic University of America (B.A., cum laude, 1989); George Washington University (J.D., 1995). *Member:* The District of Columbia Bar; Maryland and American Bar Associations. ***PRACTICE AREAS:*** General Litigation; Insurance Litigation. ***Email:*** mgallagher@andersonkill.com

DANIEL J. HEALY, born Troy, New York, September 26, 1973; admitted to bar, 1999, New York and Massachusetts (Not admitted in District of Columbia). *Education:* Siena College (B.A., 1995); Fordham University (J.D., 1998). (Also at New York, N.Y. Office). ***Email:*** dhealy@andersonkill.com

RHONDA D. ORIN, born New York, N.Y., October 19, 1957; admitted to bar, 1985, New York; 1986, New Jersey; 1987, U.S. Court of Appeals, Third and Ninth Circuits; 1988, U.S. Supreme Court and U.S. Court of Appeals, Second Circuit; 1993, District of Columbia; 2000, U.S. Court of Appeals for the District of Columbia; 2001, U.S. District Court for the District of Columbia. *Education:* University of Pennsylvania (B.A., summa cum laude, 1978); New York University (J.D., 1984). Recipient, Orison S. Marden Medal For Best Oral Argument, 1983 Moot Court Competition, NYU. Member, Review of Law and Social Change, 1982-1983. Author: "Making Them Pay: How To Get The Most From Health Insurance & Managed Care," St. Martin's Press, 2001. Representative Articles: "Claiming What's Yours," The Washington Post, June 2001; "Open Season on Consumers," The Washington Post, November 1999; "Revenge of the Insured," The New York Times, November 1998; "The Wrong War, The Wrong Time, The Wrong Enemy: Insurers' Allegations of Late Notice are Untimely When Underlying Actions are Pending," Tort and Insurance Law Journal, Spring, 1996; "Disaster Planning," ABA Journal, October, 1995; "Exclusion Confusion Over Business Risks," Best's Review, May, 1994; "Insurance May Provide Glimmer of Light for Darkened World Trade Center Businesses," New York Law Journal, March, 1993; "Home Insurance Co. v. American Home Products Corp.: It Is Not As Far Reaching As Might Be Perceived," New York State Bar Journal, February 1992; "Loss of Property Use Does Not Mean Lost Coverage," Risk Management Magazine, January, 1991; "The Meaning of Loss of Use In the Definition of Property Damage," Insurance Litigation Reporter, October, 1990. *Member:* American Bar Association; District of Columbia Bar; Association of Trial Lawyers of America. ***PRACTICE AREAS:*** Insurance Litigation; General Litigation. ***Email:*** rorin@andersonkill.com

(For complete biographical data on New York, New York personnel, Philadelphia, Pennsylvania personnel, Newark, New Jersey personnel, and Chicago, Illinois personnel, see Professional Biographies at Their Respective Offices).

ANDERSON & QUINN, LLC

WASHINGTON, D.C.

(See Rockville, Maryland)

Civil Trial and Administrative Practice before the State and Federal Courts and Agencies of Maryland and the District of Columbia with emphasis on Product Liability, Business and Commercial Matters, Workers' Compensation, Contracts, Construction and Insurance.

ANDREWS & KURTH L.L.P.

A Registered Limited Liability Partnership

SUITE 300, 1701 PENNSYLVANIA AVENUE, N.W.

WASHINGTON, D.C. 20006

Telephone: 202-662-2700

Telecopier: 202-662-2739

Email: webmaster@akllp.com

URL: http://www.akllp.com

Houston, Texas Office: Suite 4200, 600 Travis, 77002. Telephone: 713-220-4200. Telecopier: 713-220-4285. E-Mail: webmaster@andrews-kurth.com.

Other Houston, Texas Office: 700 Louisiana, Suite 1900. Telephone: 713-225-7000. Fax: 713-225-7047.

Dallas, Texas Office: 1717 Main Street, Suite 3700. Telephone: 214-659-4400. Telecopier: 214-659-4401.

The Woodlands, Texas Office: Waterway Plaza Two, Suite 200, 10001 Woodloch Forest Drive, 77380. Telephone: 713-220-4801. Telecopier: 713-220-4815.

Austin, Texas Office: 9020 I Capital of Texas Highway, Suite 250, 78759. Telephone: 512-340-1360. Fax: 214-659-4401.

Other Austin, Texas Office: 111 Congress Avenue, Suite 1700. Telephone: 512-320-9200. Fax: 512-320-9292.

Los Angeles, California Office: Suite 1725, 601 South Figueroa Street. Telephone: 213-896-3100. Telecopier: 213-896-3137.

New York, N.Y. Office: 805 Third Avenue, 10022. Telephone: 212-850-2800. Telecopier: 212-850-2929.

London, England Office: Level 16 City Tower, 40 Basinghall Street, EC2V 5DE. Telephone: 011-20-7382-0550. Telecopier: 011-44-20-7614-0012.

Administrative Law, Alternative Dispute Resolution, Antitrust and Trade Regulation, Appellate Practice, Banking Law, Bankruptcy, Business Law, Commercial Law, Construction Law, Contracts, Corporate Law, Debtor and Creditor, Education Law, Eminent Domain, Employee Benefits, Energy, Entertainment and Sports, Environmental Law, Finance, Government, Government Contracts, Health Care, Insurance, Intellectual Property International Law, International Trade, Investments, Labor and Employment, Leases and Leasing, Litigation, Mergers and Acquisitions, Natural Resources, Occupational Safety and Health, Patents, Products Liability, Professional Liability, Project Finance, Public Finance, Real Estate, Securities, Taxation, Technology and Science, Torts, Toxic Torts, Transportation, Trusts and Estates, Utility Law, White Collar Crime, Wills and Probates, Zoning, Planning and Land Use.

FIRM PROFILE: Andrews & Kurth L.L.P. is a national law firm with approximately 250 attorneys. Founded in 1902 in Houston, Texas, the firm is one of the oldest and largest law firms in Texas. The firm represents a wide variety of local, national and international concerns from its offices in New York, Washington, D.C., Los Angeles, Dallas, Houston, The Woodlands, Austin and London. Many of the attorneys of Andrews & Kurth have national and international reputations as leaders in their respective practice areas. Proud of the firm's tradition, Andrews & Kurth is strongly committed to providing quality legal services with individual attention and personal concern.

MEMBERS OF FIRM

MICHAEL J. FREMUTH, born London, England, 1947; admitted to bar, 1976, California and District of Columbia. *Education:* Princeton University (A.B., summa cum laude, 1969); Stanford University (J.D., cum laude, 1976). Phi Beta Kappa. *Member:* State Bar of California; The District of Columbia Bar; Federal Energy (Chairman, Antitrust Committee, 1983-1985) and American Bar Associations. ***PRACTICE AREAS:*** Energy; Administrative Law; Antitrust. ***Email:*** mfremuth@akllp.com

RICHARD C. GREEN, born Phoenix, Arizona, 1944; admitted to bar, 1976, Maryland; 1980, District of Columbia. *Education:* Yale University (B.A., 1966); Georgetown University (J.D., 1976). Member, Georgetown Law Journal, 1975-1976. *Member:* The District of Columbia Bar; Federal Energy and American Bar Associations. . ***PRACTICE AREAS:*** Energy Law. ***Email:*** rgreen@akllp.com

ANTHONY J. IVANCOVICH, born Santa Cruz, California, 1959; admitted to bar, 1984, District of Columbia. *Education:* University of California at Berkeley (B.A., 1981); George Washington University (J.D., 1984); National Institute of Trial Advocacy, Denver, Colorado (1985). Phi Beta Kappa; Phi

(This Listing Continued)

Alpha Delta. Member, George Washington University Journal of International Law and Economics, 1982-1984. *Member:* The District of Columbia Bar; Federal Energy Bar Association. ***PRACTICE AREAS:*** Natural Gas Pipelines; Natural Gas Regulation; Natural Gas Contracts; Public Utility Regulation; Administrative Hearings and Appeals. ***Email:*** aivancovich@akllp.com

THOMAS R. KLINE, born New York, N.Y., 1947; admitted to bar, 1976, New York and District of Columbia; 1996, Maryland. *Education:* Columbia University (B.A., 1968); Columbia Law School (J.D., 1975). James Kent Scholar. Harlan Fiske Stone Scholar. Member, Editorial Board, Columbia Law Review, 1974-1975. Trial Attorney, U.S. Department of Justice, Civil Division, Federal Programs Branch, 1979-1981. *Member:* The District of Columbia Bar; American Bar Association; Washington Council of Lawyers (Member, Board of Directors, 1984—). ***PRACTICE AREAS:*** Litigation. ***Email:*** tkline@akllp.com

SHEMIN V. PROCTOR, born Washington, D.C., 1965; admitted to bar, 1991, Texas and California; 1992, District of Columbia. *Education:* Harvard-Radcliffe (B.A., 1987); Harvard University (J.D., 1990). *Member:* State Bar of Texas; State Bar of California; The District of Columbia Bar; Federal Energy and American Bar Associations; Women's Bar Association. ***PRACTICE AREAS:*** Energy Law. ***Email:*** sproctor@akllp.com

MARK F. SUNDBACK, born Meadville, Pennsylvania, 1956; admitted to bar, 1981, District of Columbia. *Education:* Dickinson College (B.A., 1978); Columbia University (J.D., 1981). Omicron Delta Kappa. Editor, Columbia Journal of Transnational Law, Writing and Research, 1980-1981. *Member:* The District of Columbia Bar; Federal Energy Bar Association. ***PRACTICE AREAS:*** Energy Regulation; Natural Gas Pipelines; Electric Utilities; Oil and Gas Pipelines. ***Email:*** msundback@akllp.com

BRUCE A. TEMPLETON, born Detroit, Michigan, 1953; admitted to bar, 1981, Virginia; 1986, District of Columbia. *Education:* University of Michigan (A.B., 1978; J.D., 1980). *Member:* The District of Columbia Bar; Virginia State Bar; American (Member, Section on: Business Law, Committee on Legal Opinions). ***PRACTICE AREAS:*** Energy; General Corporate; International Trade. ***Email:*** btempleton@akllp.com

KENNETH L. WISEMAN, born Pittsburgh, Pennsylvania, 1949; admitted to bar, 1977, District of Columbia. *Education:* University of Wisconsin-Madison (B.A., 1971); Catholic University of America (J.D., 1977). *Member:* The District of Columbia Bar; Federal Energy Bar Association. ***PRACTICE AREAS:*** Energy Regulation; Natural Gas Pipelines; Electric Utilities; Oil and Gas Pipelines. ***Email:*** kwiseman@akllp.com

OF COUNSEL

SCOTT A. RICHIE, born St. Paul, Minnesota, 1952; admitted to bar, 1990, Pennsylvania; 1991, District of Columbia. *Education:* University of Wisconsin-Eau Claire (B.A., cum laude, with honors, 1975); William Mitchell College of Law (J.D., cum laude, 1987); George Washington University National Law Center (LL.M., 1993). Delta Omicron Honor Society, Pulliam Fellow; Jefferson Fellow. *Member:* The District of Columbia Bar (Member, Antitrust Section); American Bar Association. ***PRACTICE AREAS:*** Civil Litigation; Antitrust; Intellectual Property; Political Asylum. ***Email:*** srichie@akllp.com

DOUGLAS V. RIGLER, born Brookline, Massachusetts, 1934; admitted to bar, 1963, Maryland; 1964, District of Columbia; 1981, New York. *Education:* Johns Hopkins University; United States Naval Academy (B.S., 1956); George Washington University (J.D., 1963). Editor, George Washington Law Review, 1962-1963. Member, Atomic Safety and Licensing Board Panel, U.S. Nuclear Regulatory Commission, 1972-1977. *Member:* The District of Columbia Bar; Maryland State, New York State and American Bar Associations. ***PRACTICE AREAS:*** Commercial Litigation; Antitrust Litigation; Intellectual Property; Complex Multi-district Litigation; International. ***Email:*** drigler@akllp.com

THOMAS E. STARNES, born Kansas City, Missouri, 1957; admitted to bar, 1983, District of Columbia. *Education:* West Virginia Wesleyan College; University of Maine (B.A., with high distinction, 1980); George Washington University (J.D., with honors, 1983). *Member:* The District of Columbia Bar; American Bar Association. ***PRACTICE AREAS:*** Church and State; Ecclesiastical Law; Federal Civil Litigation; Environmental Litigation; First Amendment Law. ***Email:*** tstarnes@akllp.com

CRAIG B. YOUNG, born Boston, Massachusetts, 1949; admitted to bar, 1983, Virginia; 1984, District of Columbia. *Education:* The American University (B.A., 1971; M.S., 1973); George Mason University (J.D., 1982). Phi Delta Phi. Author: "City of Houston v. FAA: Judicial Re-Regulation of Airline Routes," 5 Geo. Mason U.L. Review 409, 1982. *Member:* The District of Columbia Bar; Virginia State Bar; American Bar Association. ***PRACTICE AREAS:*** Commercial Litigation; Bankruptcy Litigation; Fraudulent Conveyance; Business Litigation; Federal Civil Practice. ***Email:*** craigyoung@akllp.com

ASSOCIATES

CHRISTOPHER COBB, born 1973; admitted to bar, 2000, New York and New Jersey (Not admitted in District of Columbia). *Education:* Roanoke College (B.A., International Relations, 1996); The American University, Washington College of Law (J.D., cum laude, 2000). President, Sigma Chi. Associate, International Law Review. *Member:* New York State and New Jersey State Bar Associations. ***PRACTICE AREAS:*** Corporate; Securities. ***Email:*** chriscobb@akllp.com

GIA CRIBBS, born Fairfax, Virginia, 1976; (admission pending). *Education:* University of Maryland (B.A., summa cum laude, 1998); George Washington University (J.D., with honors, 2001). ***PRACTICE AREAS:*** Litigation. ***Email:*** giacribbs@akllp.com

CHARLES M. CROUT, born Santa Fe, New Mexico, 1967; admitted to bar, 1995, Maryland; 1996, U.S. District Court, District of Maryland; 1997, District of Columbia. *Education:* Vanderbilt University (B.A., cum laude, 1989); University of Texas at Austin (M.P.Aff., 1992); George Washington University (J.D., with honors, 1995). Member, George Washington University Journal of International Law and Economics, 1993-1995. *Member:* The District of Columbia Bar. ***PRACTICE AREAS:*** Litigation. ***Email:*** ccrout@akllp.com

MARVIN W. EHRLICH, admitted to bar, 1992, New York; 1998, District of Columbia. *Education:* Rutgers University (B.A., 1988); Washington College of Law, The American University (J.D., 1991). Senior Staff Member, The Administrative Law Journal. Editor, D.C. Practice Manual, Real Property Chapter, 1998. *Member:* The District of Columbia Bar. ***PRACTICE AREAS:*** Commercial Mortgage Finance; Secured Lending; Mortgage Loans; Workouts; Foreclosures; Real Estate Acquisitions; Real Estate Development; Leasing. ***Email:*** marvehrlich@akllp.com

ELAINE L. FARRIS, born Baltimore, Maryland, 1971; admitted to bar, 1997, Virginia; 1998, Maryland (Not admitted in District of Columbia). *Education:* University of Maryland (B.A., magna cum laude, 1994); College of William & Mary (J.D., 1997). ***Email:*** elainefarris@akllp.com

L. EDEN ROOD, born Northampton, Massachusetts, 1974; admitted to bar, 2000, Maryland (Not admitted in District of Columbia). *Education:* University of Virginia (B.A., 1996); George Washington University Law School (J.D., with honors, 2000). Member: GWULS Environmental Lawyer; Trial Court Board. *Member:* Maryland State Bar Association. ***PRACTICE AREAS:*** Litigation. ***Email:*** edenrood@akllp.com

DAVID S. SHAFFER, born Lincoln, Nebraska, 1967; admitted to bar, 1996, Maryland; 1998, District of Columbia. *Education:* University of Wisconsin (B.A., 1989); Washington College of Law (J.D., cum laude, 1996). Editor, The Journal of International Law & Policy, 1995-1996. *Member:* The District of Columbia Bar. ***PRACTICE AREAS:*** Energy Law. ***Email:*** davidshaffer@akllp.com

PETER J. THOMPSON, born Southampton, New York, 1962; admitted to bar, 1990, Maryland; 1992, District of Columbia. *Education:* Catholic University (B.A., 1987; J.D., 1990). Associate Editor, Journal of Contemporary Health Law, 1989-1990. *Member:* The District of Columbia Bar. ***PRACTICE AREAS:*** Federal Energy Regulation; Energy Regulation. ***Email:*** pthompson@akllp.com

SENIOR ATTORNEY

JOHANNA S. COULTER, born Bryn Mawr, Pennsylvania, 1965; admitted to bar, 1991, Texas (Not admitted in District of Columbia). *Education:* University of Virginia (B.A., English, 1987; J.D., 1991). Executive Editor, Virginia Environmental Law Journal. *Member:* State Bar of Texas. ***PRACTICE AREAS:*** Environmental Law. ***Email:*** jcoulter@akllp.com

(For Biographical data of Houston, Dallas and The Woodlands, Texas, Los Angeles, California and New York, New York Personnel see Professional Biographies at Houston, Dallas and The Woodlands, Texas, Los Angeles, California and New York, New York).

KENNETH J. ANNIS

Established in 1974

1100 CONNECTICUT AVENUE, N.W.
SUITE 800
WASHINGTON, D.C. 20036
Telephone: 202-785-2244
Fax: 202-785-2051
Email: kajannis@erols.com
URL: http://www.lawyers.com/kennethannis

Civil, Administrative and Criminal Practice before all Courts, Agencies, Departments and Commissions with special emphasis on Plaintiff Trial Practice, Personal Injury, Automobile, Torts, Product Liability and Medical Negligence.

KENNETH J. ANNIS, born Cambridge, Massachusetts, January 28, 1943; admitted to bar, 1973, District of Columbia; 1975, U.S. District Court for the District of Columbia; 1976, U.S. Supreme Court; 1980, Maryland; 1985, U.S. District Court for the District of Maryland; 1987, U.S. Court of Appeals, District of Columbia Circuit. *Education:* Harvard University (A.B., cum laude,

(This Listing Continued)

KENNETH J. ANNIS, Washington—Continued

1965); Georgetown University (J.D., 1972). Arbitrator/Mediator: American Arbitration Association; U.S. District Court and District of Columbia Superior Court. *Member:* The District of Columbia Bar; Montgomery County and Maryland State Bar Associations; Trial Lawyers Association of Washington, D.C. (Member, Board of Governors, 1986-); Maryland Trial Lawyers Association; The Association of Trial Lawyers of America; American Board of Trial Advocates; The George Washington Inn of Court (President, 1993-1994). ***LANGUAGES:*** French.

ANTONELLI, TERRY, STOUT & KRAUS, LLP

WASHINGTON, D.C.

(See Arlington, Virginia)

Patent, Trademark, Copyright, Unfair Competition and Antitrust Law. International, Patent and Trademark Practice.

ARENT FOX KINTNER PLOTKIN & KAHN, PLLC

Established in 1942

1050 CONNECTICUT AVENUE, N.W.

WASHINGTON, D.C. 20036-5339

Telephone: 202-857-6000

Fax: 202-857-6395

URL: http://www.arentfox.com

New York City Office: 1675 Broadway, 25th Floor. Telephone: 212-484-3900. Telecopier: 212-484-3990.

Bucharest Office: B-dul N. Titulescu, Nr.1 B1.A7, Sc. 1, Et. 6 Apt. 16, Sector 1, Bucharest, Romania. Telephone: 011-401-211-8797. Fax: 011-401-211-8771.

Advertising, Antitrust, Banking, Bankruptcy, Business Transactions, Construction, Electronic Commerce, Employment and Benefits, Energy, Environment, Food and Drug, Government Contracts, Health, Immigration, Intellectual Property, International, Legislation, Litigation, Municipal Finance, OHSA, Real Estate and Tax Law, Sports and Entertainment Law, Telecommunications, Telemedicine, White Collar Criminal. General Practice.

FIRM PROFILE: Arent Fox was founded in Washington, D.C. in 1942. From its beginning, two features have characterized the Firm's practice: its expertise as Washington lawyers knowledgeable in the regulations and affairs of the Government and its ties to and representation to the Washington business community. Today the Firm has offices in Washington, D.C., New York, New York, and Bucharest, Romania serving clients ranging from local businesses to foreign governments and international corporations.

FOUNDING MEMBERS OF FIRM

ALBERT E. ARENT, born Rochester, New York, August 25, 1911; admitted to bar, 1935, New York; 1940, U.S. Supreme Court; 1945, District of Columbia. *Education:* Cornell University (B.A., 1932); Cornell Law School (LL.B., 1935). Phi Beta Kappa; Phi Kappa Phi. Editor, *Cornell Law Quarterly*, 1933-35. Recipient, Cornell Law School Distinguished Alumnus Award, 1982. Professor of Federal Income Taxation, Georgetown University Law Center, 1951-73. Attorney for the U.S. Bureau of Internal Revenue, 1935-39; Special Assistant to the Attorney General of the United States, 1939-44. Trustee, Cornell University, 1978-83. Member, 1970-82 and Chairman, 1979-82, Cornell Law School Advisory Council. *Member:* American Law Institute. (Retired).

HENRY J. FOX (1911-1990).

EARL W. KINTNER (1912-1992).

HARRY M. PLOTKIN (1913-1998).

EDWIN L. KAHN, born New York, N.Y., August 1, 1918; admitted to bar, 1940, North Carolina; 1949, District of Columbia. *Education:* University of North Carolina (A.B., 1937); Harvard University (LL.B., cum laude, 1940). Phi Beta Kappa. Editor, *Harvard Law Review*, 1939-40. Attorney, 1940-49 and Assistant Head, 1949-52, Legislation and Regulations Division, Office of Chief Counsel, Internal Revenue Service. Director, Technical Planning Division, Internal Revenue Service, 1952-55. Member, Advisory Committee, N.Y.U. Institute on Federal Taxation, 1960-70. Director, National Tax Association-Tax Institute of America, 1969-73. Member, Editorial Advisory Board, *The Tax Advisor*, 1974-86. *Member:* Federal (Chairman, Taxation Committee, 1967-68) and American (Member of Council, 1963-66 and Vice-chairman, 1965-66, Section of Taxation) Bar Associations; American Law Institute; American College of Tax Counsel; J. Edgar Murdoch American Inn of Court (1989-91). Fellow: American Bar Foundation. (Retired).

(This Listing Continued)

MEMBERS OF FIRM

STANLEY H. ABRAMSON, born Woodbine, New Jersey, 1946; admitted to bar, 1973, New Jersey; 1975, District of Columbia; 1982, U.S. Supreme Court. *Education:* Drexel University (B.S., 1969); Rutgers University (J.D., 1973); University of Southern California (M.P.A., 1986). Associate General Counsel, U.S. Environmental Protection Agency, 1982-1988. Deputy Assistant Chief Counsel, Federal Highway Administration, U.S. Department of Transportation, 1979-1982. *Member:* Federal and American (Chair, Committee on Pesticides, Chemical Regulation and Right-To-Know, 1999—) Bar Associations; National Academy of Sciences (Member, Committee on Genetically Modified Plants, 1999-2000); National Society of Professional Engineers. ***PRACTICE AREAS:*** Administrative Law; Biotechnology; Chemical Regulation; Environmental Law; Environmental Auditing; Environmental Compliance; Environmental Construction Law; Environmental Corporate Law; Environmental Criminal Law; Environmental Due Diligence; Environmental Health and Safety; Environmental Land Use; Environmental Liability; Environmental Litigation; Environmental Penalties; Environmental Permitting; Environmental Risk Management; Federal Government Law; Federal Legislative Practice; Food and Agriculture; Food, Drug and Cosmetic Law; Hazardous Materials Transportation; Highways; National Environmental Policy Act (NEPA); Occupational Safety and Health; Pesticide Regulation; Products Liability; Regulatory Agency Practice; Seed Law; Toxic Substance Regulation; Toxic Torts; Trade and Professional Associations.

JEROME P. AKMAN, born Washington, D.C., July 26, 1944; admitted to bar, 1969, Maryland; 1970, District of Columbia. *Education:* Northwestern University (B.S.B.A., cum laude, 1966); Harvard University (J.D., cum laude, 1969). ***PRACTICE AREAS:*** Corporate Law; International Business (Trade and Finance); International Practice; Customs Law; Business Law; Commercial Transactions; Commercial Contracts; International Commercial Contracts; International Contracts; Antidumping; International Trade Regulation.

MARK E. ALBERTA, born Pittsburgh, Pennsylvania, October 31, 1950; admitted to bar, 1976, New York; 1982, Maryland; 1984, District of Columbia; 1989, Virginia. *Education:* Yale University (B.A., cum laude, 1972); George Washington University (J.D., with honors, 1975). Executive Editor, *George Washington Law Review*, 1974-75. ***PRACTICE AREAS:*** Real Estate-Commercial Law.

WILLIAM C. BASIL, born Buffalo, New York, January 5, 1956; admitted to bar, 1981, District of Columbia. *Education:* Union College (B.S., cum laude, 1978); Emory University (J.D., 1981). Editorial Board Member, *Emory Law Journal*, 1980-81. ***PRACTICE AREAS:*** Bond Finance; Financial Institutions Law.

RICHARD L. BRAND, born Manhasset, New York, June 22, 1959; admitted to bar, 1984, District of Columbia. *Education:* Georgetown University (B.S., 1981); University of Pennsylvania (J.D., cum laude, 1984). Member, Moot Court Board. Adjunct Professor of Law, Georgetown University Law Center, 1999—. ***PRACTICE AREAS:*** Real Estate; Electronic Commerce; Sports Law; Corporate Law; Business Law; Commercial Law.

TIMOTHY F. BROWN, born Seattle, Washington, July 27, 1956; admitted to bar, 1982, District of Columbia and Washington; 1990, Virginia. *Education:* Seattle University (B.A., 1978); Harvard University (J.D., 1981). Trial Attorney, U.S. Department of Justice, Civil Division, Commercial Branch, 1985-88. ***PRACTICE AREAS:*** Commercial Litigation; Bankruptcy Litigation; Surety; Construction; Government Contracts Law.

DOUGLAS R. BUSH, born Idaho Falls, Idaho, October 21, 1957; admitted to bar, 1986, Pennsylvania; 1987, District of Columbia. *Education:* Brigham Young University (B.S., 1982; J.D., magna cum laude, 1985). Phi Kappa Phi; Order of the Coif. Law Clerk for U.S. Court of Appeals for the District of Columbia Circuit, 1985-86. ***LANGUAGES:*** Spanish. ***PRACTICE AREAS:*** Trademarks; Copyrights.

RONALD L. CASTLE, born Paintsville, Kentucky, November 20, 1951; admitted to bar, 1982, Maryland; 1988, District of Columbia. *Education:* Wright State University (B.A., 1973); The Johns Hopkins University (M.A.,1975); George Washington University (J.D., 1982). ***PRACTICE AREAS:*** Litigation; ERISA; Health; Hospital Law.

WILLIAM R. CHARYK, born Princeton, New Jersey, October 21, 1948; admitted to bar, 1973, Virginia; 1974, District of Columbia. *Education:* Johns Hopkins University (B.A., 1970); George Washington University (J.D., 1973). Order of the Coif. Contributing Editor and Author of Partnership Corner Column, The Journal of Real Estate Taxation, Warren, Gorham & Lamont, 1978—. Adjunct Professor of Law, Georgetown University Law Center, 1979—. Co-Author, Tax Advisors Planning Series, Partnership Formation, 1994. ***PRACTICE AREAS:*** Pension and Profit Sharing Law; Taxpayer Representative Law; Professional Corporation Law; Partnership; Taxation of Individuals and Business Entities.

MATTHEW J. CLARK, born New York, N.Y., March 1, 1958; admitted to bar, 1983, District of Columbia; 1984, U.S. District Court for the District of Columbia, U.S. Court of Appeals for the District of Columbia Circuit, U.S.

(This Listing Continued)

Court of International Trade and U.S. Court of Appeals for the Federal Circuit. *Education:* Villanova University (B.A., 1980); Columbus School of Law; Catholic University of America (J.D., 1983). Staff, Industrial Policy Advisory Committee for Trade Policy Matters, 1991-1994. *Member:* The District of Columbia Bar; Bar Association of the District of Columbia (Member, Board of Directors, 1990-1992; Section on Administrative Law; Chairman, 1991-1992); American Bar Association (Member, Sections on: International Law and Practice; Administrative Law and Regulatory Practice; Vice Chair, Professional Education Committee); Customs and International Trade Bar Association. ***PRACTICE AREAS:*** International Trade Law; Import and Export Law.

RONALD H. CLARK, born South Gate, California, November 26, 1942; admitted to bar, 1977, Ohio (inactive); 1978, District of Columbia; 1979, U.S. District Court, District of Columbia; 1994, U.S. District Court, Northern District of California; U.S. District Court, District of Maryland; U.S. District Court, Eastern District of Michigan; U.S. Court of Appeals, Third, Sixth, Ninth, Tenth and Eleventh, District of Columbia and Federal Circuits. *Education:* University of California, Riverside (A.B., 1966); University of California, Santa Barbara (M.A., 1967; Ph.D., Woodrow Wilson Dissertation Fellow, 1970); Capital University (J.D., magna cum laude, 1977). Trial Attorney, Antitrust Division, U.S. Department of Justice, 1977-79. Assistant U.S. Attorney, District of New Jersey, 1982-84. Trial Attorney and Senior Trial Counsel, Civil Fraud Section, U.S. Department of Justice, 1984-95. ***PRACTICE AREAS:*** Health Care Fraud; Qui Tam Litigation; False Claims Act; Compliance Plans.

ELIZABETH H. COHEN, born Brooklyn, New York, May 14, 1966; admitted to bar, 1992, New York and New Jersey; 1994, Georgia; 1998, District of Columbia. *Education:* Goucher College (B.A., 1988); New York University School of Law (J.D., 1991). Phi Beta Kappa. Member, Journal of International Law and Politics. ***PRACTICE AREAS:*** Trademark Law; Internet Law; Copyright Law; Litigation.

EARL M. COLSON, born Brooklyn, New York, March 8, 1930; admitted to bar, 1957, New York; 1960, District of Columbia. *Education:* Syracuse University (B.S., magna cum laude, 1950); Harvard University (LL.B., magna cum laude, 1957). Co-author, *Problems of Federal Taxation of Estates-Gifts-Trusts,* American Law Institute, 1966. Author: *Capital Gains and Losses,* American Law Institute, 1975; *Nontax and Tax Aspects of Life Insurance,* American Law Institute, 1980. Editor, *The Practical Lawyer,* 1976—, Published by ALI/ABA. Adjunct Professor of Law, Georgetown University Law Center, 1968—. *Member:* Bar Association of the District of Columbia (Governor and Treasurer, 1974-76; Chairman, Committee on Taxation, 1968-69); American Bar Association (Chairman, Committee on Estate and Gift Taxes, Section of Taxation, 1970-72). ***PRACTICE AREAS:*** Business Planning Law; Corporate Law; ESOPS; Estate Planning Law; Tax Law.

JOHN C. CULVER, born Rochester, Minnesota, August 8, 1932; admitted to bar, 1963, Iowa; 1967, U.S. Supreme Court; 1978, District of Columbia. *Education:* Harvard University (A.B., cum laude, 1954; LL.B., 1962); Cambridge University, Emmanuel College (Lionel de Jersey Harvard Scholar, 1954-55). Honorary Degrees: Awarded LL.D. by Loras College, 1967; Awarded J.D. by St. Ambrose College, 1970; Awarded LL.D. by Upper Iowa University, 1971; Awarded L.H.D. by Marycrest College, 1975; Awarded D.C.L. by Westmar College, 1979; Awarded LL.D. by Grinnell College, 1981. Co-Author: "American Dreamer: The Life and Times of Henry Wallace," W.W. Norton. U.S. Representative, Iowa Second District, U.S. House of Representatives, 1965-75. U.S. Senator, Iowa, 1975-81. Overseer, Harvard University, 1975-81. Member: Council on Foreign Relations; Trilateral Commission, 1972-82. Chairman, Senior Advisory Committee, Institute of Politics, John F. Kennedy School of Government, Harvard University. Member, J. William Fulbright Foreign Scholarship Board. ***PRACTICE AREAS:*** International Law; Government Relations.

DAVID T. DEKKER, born Chagrin Falls, Ohio, August 1, 1956; admitted to bar, 1981, District of Columbia. *Education:* Denison University (B.A., with high honors, 1978); Cornell Law School (J.D., cum laude, 1981). Phi Beta Kappa. Member, 1979-81 and Research Editor, 1980-81, Cornell International Law Journal. ***PRACTICE AREAS:*** Litigation; Insurance; Construction; RICO; ERISA; Class Action; Civil Practice; Products Liability.

KENDRA L. DIMOND, born Harrisburg, Pennsylvania, October 12, 1947; admitted to bar, 1979, Pennsylvania and U.S. District Court, Middle District of Pennsylvania; 1995, District of Columbia; 2000, U.S. District Court, Eastern District of Michigan. *Education:* Gettysburg College (B.A., 1969); Pennsylvania State University (M.A., 1973); Dickinson School of Law (J.D., 1979). Deputy Attorney General, Pennsylvania, 1982-1988. Counsel, U.S. Senate Aging Committee, 1991. Director of Legislative Office, National Institutes of Health, 1992-1994. ***LANGUAGES:*** French. ***PRACTICE AREAS:*** Health Law; Health Care Fraud; Health Care Litigation; Public Health Law; Health Care Regulation; Health Care Reimbursement.

D. JEFFREY DISBROW, born Pontiac, Michigan, August 26, 1960; admitted to bar, 1985, Pennsylvania; 1988, New York; 1996, District of Columbia. *Education:* University of Michigan (A.B., 1982); George Washington (J.D., 1985); New York University (LL.M., Tax, 1987). ***PRACTICE AREAS:*** Tax Law.

(This Listing Continued)

MARY JOANNE DOWD, born Buffalo, New York, November 20, 1954; admitted to bar, 1981, New York; 1983, Florida; 1986, District of Columbia and U.S. District Court and Bankruptcy Courts, District of Maryland. *Education:* State University of New York College at Buffalo (B.A., summa cum laude, 1976); State University of New York at Buffalo (J.D., 1980). Clerk to: Hon. Beryl E. McGuire and Hon. John W. Creahan, United States Bankruptcy Court Judges, Western District of New York, Buffalo, New York, 1980-82. Adjunct Professor of Bankruptcy and Creditors' Rights, Georgetown University Law Center. Chapter 7 Panel Trustee for United States Bankruptcy Court District of Maryland. ***PRACTICE AREAS:*** Bankruptcy Law; Debtor Creditor Law.

MARK S. DREUX, SR., born April 3, 1954; admitted to bar, 1982, District of Columbia; 1983, Maryland. *Education:* Georgetown University (B.A., 1977); Catholic University of America (J.D., 1982). Law Clerk to Judge Mencher, Superior Court of the District of Columbia, 1982-1983. Assistant U.S. Attorney for the District of Columbia, Superior Court Division, U.S. Attorney's Office, 1983-1987. ***PRACTICE AREAS:*** Occupational Safety and Health; Litigation; White Collar Crime.

ALAN S. DUBIN, born Scranton, Pennsylvania, June 24, 1951; admitted to bar, 1976, Maryland; 1977, District of Columbia. *Education:* University of Rochester (B.A., with distinction, 1973); George Washington University (J.D., with high honors, 1976). Order of the Coif. ***PRACTICE AREAS:*** Business Law; Corporate Financing Law; Real Estate-Commercial Law.

DAVID L. DUBROW, born Far Rockaway, N.Y., November 17, 1951; admitted to bar, 1987, New York (Not admitted in District of Columbia). *Education:* Brown University (B.A., with honors, 1973); New York University School of Law (J.D., 1986). Author: "Chapter 9 of the Bankruptcy Code: A Viable Option for Municipalities in Fiscal Crisis?", Urban Lawyer 1991; The Urban Lawyer, Volume 24, Number 3, Summer, 1992. *Member:* American Bar Association. ***PRACTICE AREAS:*** Public Finance; Secured Lending; Structured Finance. ***Email:*** dubrowd@arentfox.com

MICHAEL M. EATON, born Chicago, Illinois, December 10, 1946; admitted to bar, 1971, Florida; 1972, District of Columbia; 1991, Virginia. *Education:* University of Virginia (B.A., with distinction, 1968); University of Chicago (J.D., 1971). Clerk, The Honorable C. Clyde Atkins, U.S. District Court, Southern District of Florida, 1971-73. *Member:* American Bar Association (Member, Franchising Committee, Antitrust Law Section, 1978—; Chairman: Legislation Subcommittee, 1978-80; Publications Subcommittee, 1980-83). ***PRACTICE AREAS:*** Antitrust; Health and Hospital Law; Franchise Law; Litigation; Covenants Not To Compete.

HAROLD J. ENGEL, born 1943; admitted to bar, 1969, Maryland; 1972, District of Columbia. *Education:* University of Maryland; Howard University (J.D., cum laude, 1969). Member, Howard University Law Journal, 1968-1969. Author: "Occupational Safety and Health Law," 1988 BNA 214 Howard Law Journal; "Toward a Less Hazardous Workplace," Volume 25, No. 2, 1998 The China Business Review, P. 49. ***PRACTICE AREAS:*** OSHA; MSHA; Toxic Torts; Labor.

ALAN GREGG FISHEL, born Baltimore, Maryland, May 29, 1959; admitted to bar, 1986, Maryland; 1987, District of Columbia. *Education:* Franklin & Marshall College (B.A., magna cum laude, 1981); Duke Law School (J.D., with honors, 1986). Phi Beta Kappa; Pi Gamma Mu. ***PRACTICE AREAS:*** Telecommunications; Litigation.

MARC L. FLEISCHAKER, born Cincinnati, Ohio, February 22, 1945; admitted to bar, 1971, District of Columbia; 1974, U.S. Supreme Court. *Education:* University of Pennsylvania (B.S., 1967); George Washington University (J.D., with honors, 1971). Member, *George Washington Law Review*, 1969-70. Listed in: Who's Who in America; Who's Who in American Law. Chairman, Executive Committee and Co-Chair, Washington Lawyer Committee For Civil Rights and Urban Affairs, 1990-92; 1999. Co-Chair, National Lawyers Committee For Civil Rights Under Law, 1996-98. *Member:* Federal Bar Association (Chairman: Administrative Law and Procedure Committee, 1974-75; Council on Federal Law, Agencies and Practice, 1975-79; Select Committee on Regulatory Reform, 1979-80; Continuing Education Board, 1981-84; Section on Energy, Environment and Natural Resources, 1984-85); American Society of Association Executives (Chairman: Technology Committee, Legal Section, 1995-97; Amicus Committee, 1998); Federal City Council; Economic Club of Washington. ***PRACTICE AREAS:*** Toxic Torts; Environmental Law; Antitrust; Trade Association Law; Civil Rights; Insurance; Litigation.

CAROL CONNOR FLOWE, born Owensboro, Kentucky, January 3, 1950; admitted to bar, 1977, Ohio; 1981, District of Columbia. *Education:* Murray State University (B.M.E., magna cum laude, 1972); Indiana University (J.D., summa cum laude, 1976). Order of the Coif. Candidacy Editor, *Indiana Law Journal*. General Counsel, 1989-95 and Deputy General Counsel, 1987-89, Pension Benefit Guaranty Corporation. ***PRACTICE AREAS:*** ERISA; Litigation; Employment Law; Employee Benefits Litigation; ERISA Litigation; Discrimination; Labor and Employment; Sexual Harassment; National Labor Relations Act; Wrongful Termination.

STEPHEN B. FORMAN, born New York, New York, June 7, 1940; admitted to bar, 1972, Virginia; 1973, District of Columbia. *Education:* Queens

(This Listing Continued)

ARENT FOX KINTNER PLOTKIN & KAHN, PLLC, Washington—Continued

College of the City University of New York (B.S., 1962); Columbia University (B.S., 1962; M.S., 1963); George Washington University (J.D., with honors, 1972). ***PRACTICE AREAS:*** Employment Law; Employment Discrimination; Wrongful Termination; Sexual Harassment; Wage and Hour Law; National Labor Relations Act; Collective Bargaining.

JEREMY B. FOX, born Boston, Massachusetts, December 13, 1959; admitted to bar, 1984, Massachusetts; 1985, District of Columbia and Maryland. *Education:* University of Massachusetts (B.B.A., Accounting, cum laude, 1981); George Washington University (J.D., with high honors, 1984). Order of the Coif. Member, *George Washington Law Review*, 1982-84. ***PRACTICE AREAS:*** Commercial Real Estate; Transactional Law; Commercial Leasing; Secured Finance.

JOSEPH M. FRIES, born Brooklyn, New York, August 21, 1937; admitted to bar, 1961, District of Columbia. *Education:* Cornell University (A.B., high honors in government, 1958); Harvard Law School (LL.B., cum laude, 1961). Adjunct Professor of Law, Georgetown University Law Center, 1977-80. Contributing Editor, Legal Times of Washington, 1978-81. *Member:* American College of Real Estate Lawyers. ***PRACTICE AREAS:*** Real Estate (Property) Law.

RICHARD N. GALE, born St. Louis, Missouri, May, 10, 1956; admitted to bar, 1981, District of Columbia. *Education:* Duke University (B.S., cum laude, 1978); Washington University School of Law; University of Virginia School of Law (J.D., 1981). ***PRACTICE AREAS:*** Health Care; Mergers and Acquisitions; Business Acquisitions; Business Law; Taxpayer Representative Law.

SEAN W. GLYNN, born Okinawa, Japan, December 8, 1964; admitted to bar, 1990, Maryland; 1992, District of Columbia. *Education:* Duke University (B.A., 1986); University of Maryland (J.D., 1990). Member, *Maryland Law Review*, 1988-1990. ***PRACTICE AREAS:*** Public Finance and Real Estate.

DOUGLAS H. GOLDHUSH, born New York, N.Y., July 22, 1962; admitted to bar, 1991, Massachusetts and New York; 1992, District of Columbia; 1995, U.S. Court of Appeals for the Federal Circuit; registered to practice before U.S. Patent and Trademark Office. *Education:* New York Institute of Technology (Bachelor of Technology in Electromechanical Computer Technology, 1985); Suffolk University (J.D., cum laude, 1990). *Member:* American Bar Association; American Intellectual Property Law Association; International Intellectual Property Association (IIPA); International Trademark Association; Kansai Patent Attorneys Study Group. ***PRACTICE AREAS:*** Intellectual Property; Electronic Commerce; Patents; Trademarks; Copyrights; Trade Secrets.

WILLIAM W. GOODRICH, born Washington, D.C., April 16, 1947; admitted to bar, 1975, Virginia; 1976, District of Columbia; 1979, U.S. Supreme Court. *Education:* Duke University (A.B., 1969); George Washington University (J.D., with honors, 1975). Order of the Coif. Clerk, The Honorable Marion T. Bennett, U.S. Court of Appeals for the Federal Circuit, 1975-76. *Member:* American Bar Association. ***PRACTICE AREAS:*** Government (Public) Contract Law; Intellectual Properties Law; Litigation.

MICHAEL A. GORDON, born New York, N.Y., July 18, 1952; admitted to bar, 1977, Maryland; 1978, District of Columbia. *Education:* Colgate University (A.B., cum laude, 1974); American University (J.D., 1977). Phi Beta Kappa. Law Clerk to Judge John P. Moore, Court of Special Appeals of Maryland, 1977-78. ***PRACTICE AREAS:*** Real Estate-Commercial Law.

HERVÉ GOURAIGE (Resident, New York, N.Y. Office).

JEFFERSON M. GRAY, born 1956; admitted to bar, 1984, DC; 1997, MD. *Education:* Yale University (B.A., 1978); London School of Economics (M.Sc., 1979); University of London (M.A., 1980); Harvard University (J.D., cum laude, 1983). Marshall Scholar. Editor, Harvard Law Review, 1981-83. Law Clerk to the Hon. Robert S. Vance, U.S. Court of Appeals, Eleventh Circuit, 1983-84. Assistant U.S. Attorney, U.S. Attorney's Office for the District of Maryland, 1989-96. Instructor, Civil and Criminal Trial Practice and Appellate Litigation, Attorney General's Advocacy Institute, 1992-95. *Member:* The District of Columbia Bar; American Bar Association. ***PRACTICE AREAS:*** White Collar Criminal Defense Litigation. **Email:** grayj@arentfox.com

MICHAEL A. GROW, born Ogden, Utah, October 29, 1947; admitted to bar, 1975, Virginia; 1976, District of Columbia. *Education:* Weber State College (B.A., cum laude, 1972); George Washington University (J.D., with honors, 1975). Phi Kappa Phi. *Member:* The District of Columbia Bar (Co-Chair, Intellectual Property Law Section, 1993-94); International Trademark Association (Member, Board of Directors, 1988-90 and Executive Committee, 1989-90); American Intellectual Property Law Association (Chair, Franchise Law Committee, 1993-95). ***LANGUAGES:*** Italian, Spanish. ***PRACTICE AREAS:*** Litigation; Trademark; Copyright; Unfair Competition.

DAVID C. GRYCE, born Danbury, Connecticut, January 16, 1955; admitted to bar, 1983, Colorado; 1989, District of Columbia and U.S. Supreme Court. *Education:* Brown University (A.B., 1977); University of Denver College of Law (J.D., 1983). Order of Saint Ives. Contributing Author, *The Franchise Trademark Handbook*, ABA Forum on Franchising, 1994. *Member:* The District of Columbia Bar (Member, Intellectual Property Law Section); American Bar Association (Member, Intellectual Property Law Section); International Trademark Associations (Chair, Corporations Subcommittee of the Alternative Dispute Resolution Committee); American Intellectual Property Law Association (Member, International Trademarks and Treaties Committee). ***PRACTICE AREAS:*** Information Technology Contracts; Software Licensing; Trademarks; International Trademarks; Unfair Competition; Licensing; Copyright.

DAVID C. HAAS, born Wilmington, Delaware, June 13, 1959; admitted to bar, 1984, District of Columbia; 1985, Maryland; 1986, Virginia. *Education:* College of William & Mary (B.B.A., 1981); Delaware Law School of Widener University (J.D., 1984); Georgetown University Law Center (M.L.T., 1988). ***PRACTICE AREAS:*** International Project Development; International Finance; Construction; Technology Joint Ventures; International Trade; Investment; Licensing and Distribution Agreements; Corporate and Commercial Law; Tax Law.

JAMES B. HALPERN, born Buffalo, New York, April 20, 1936; admitted to bar, 1961, New York; 1970, District of Columbia. *Education:* Harvard University (B.A., cum laude, 1958; J.D., 1961). Attorney, Corporation Finance Division, 1961-64 and Chief Counsel-Institutions, Institutional Investor Study, 1970, Securities and Exchange Commission. *Member:* American Law Institute. ***PRACTICE AREAS:*** Securities; Mergers, Acquisitions and Divestitures; Business Law; High Technology; Corporate Law; Insurance.

DENNIS J. HENDERSON (Not admitted in District of Columbia; Resident, New York, N.Y. Office).

LAWRENCE F. HENNEBERGER, born Princeton, Indiana, April 13, 1938; admitted to bar, 1962, Louisiana and Indiana; 1965, U.S. Supreme Court; 1966, District of Columbia. *Education:* Loyola University, New Orleans (B.B.A., cum laude, 1960); Loyola School of Law (LL.B., 1962); George Washington University (LL.M., 1968). [J.A.G.C., U.S. Army, 1962-65]. ***PRACTICE AREAS:*** Antitrust; Motor Vehicle Safety Law; Transportation Law; Trade Association Law.

ROBERT CHARLES HILL, born Greenwich, Connecticut, March 28, 1952; admitted to bar, 1980, Virginia; 1989, U.S. Court of Appeals for the District of Columbia Circuit; 1990, District of Columbia. *Education:* Herbert H. Lehman College of the City University of New York (B.A., cum laude, 1974); Georgetown University (J.D., 1980). Deputy Director and Counsel, Office of Asylum Policy and Review, U.S. Department of Justice, 1987-1989. Special Assistant and Senior Policy Adviser, U.S. Department of State, 1983-1987. Deputy Director, Presidential Correspondence, The White House, 1981-1983. Member, U.S. Commission on Immigration Reform, 1991-1997. *Member:* Virginia State Bar; The District of Columbia Bar; American Bar Association (Vice Chair, Immigration and Nationality Committee, International Law Section); American Immigration Lawyers Association. ***PRACTICE AREAS:*** Immigration and Nationality Law; Business Immigration; Employment Authorizations; Employment Visas; Labor Certifications; Consular Law.

ROBERT B. HIRSCH, born Newark, New Jersey, March 28, 1926; admitted to bar, 1950, District of Columbia. *Education:* George Washington University (LL.B., 1950); Johns Hopkins University. Nu Beta Epsilon (Chancellor, Gamma Chapter). Member, Board of Editors, *George Washington Law Review*, 1949-50. Chairman, Board of Advisors, The George Washington University Law School, 1991-97, Chairman Emeritus, 1998. ***PRACTICE AREAS:*** Mergers and Acquisitions; Securities Litigation; Corporate Law; Commercial Real Estate.

ROBERT H. HUEY, born Bay Shore, New York, 1943; admitted to bar, 1968, New York; 1971, District of Columbia. *Education:* Hobart College (B.A., cum laude, 1964); University of Virginia (LL.B., 1967). Phi Beta Kappa; Delta Theta Phi. *Member:* The District of Columbia Bar; New York State Bar Association. ***PRACTICE AREAS:*** International Trade Law; Import and Export Law; International Law.

JAMES H. HULME, born Drexel Hill, Pennsylvania, November 5, 1953; admitted to bar, 1979, Maryland; 1980, District of Columbia. *Education:* Middlebury College (B.A., 1976); The American University (J.D., summa cum laude, 1979). Member, American University Honor Society. Staff, *American University Law Review*, 1978-79. Clerk, The Honorable John P. Moore, Court of Special Appeals of Maryland, 1979-80. ***PRACTICE AREAS:*** Intellectual Property Infringement; Patent Infringement; Entertainment Litigation; Arbitration; Insurance Litigation; Commercial Litigation; Corporate Litigation.

KENNETH S. JACOB, born Manhasset, New York, June 23, 1967; admitted to bar, 1992, Virginia; 1993, District of Columbia. *Education:* Georgetown University (B.S.F.S., magna cum laude, 1989); University of Virginia (J.D., 1992). Phi Beta Kappa. Order of the Coif. Articles Review Editor, *Virginia Journal of International Law*. ***LANGUAGES:*** French. ***PRACTICE AREAS:*** Commercial Real Estate; Business Law.

MICHAEL EVAN JAFFE, born New York, N.Y., December 11, 1942; admitted to bar, 1967, Texas; 1969, District of Columbia; 1971, U.S. Supreme

(This Listing Continued)

Court; 1989, Maryland. *Education:* Rice University (B.A., 1964); Columbia University (LL.B., 1967). Clerk, The Honorable C.R. Layton, III, District of Delaware, 1967-69. ***PRACTICE AREAS:*** Litigation; International Arbitration; International Litigation; Construction Law.

BRYAN W. JARDINE (Resident, Bucharest, Romania Office).

QUANA C. JEW, admitted to bar, 1990, Pennsylvania and District of Columbia. *Education:* University of Wisconsin (B.A., 1984; M.A., 1987; J.D., 1990). Phi Beta Kappa, Phi Kappa Phi. Mortar Board. Articles Editor, *Wisconsin Law Review*, 1989-90. ***PRACTICE AREAS:*** ERISA; Deferred Compensation; Employee Benefit Law; Pension and Profit-Sharing Law; COBRA; Taxation; Employee Benefit Trusts; Executive Compensation; Flexible Benefit Plans; Fringe Benefits; Health Benefits; Non-Qualified Benefits; Qualified Retirement Plans; Employee Compensation; Stock Options.

JEFFREY E. JORDAN, born New York, N.Y., June 22, 1954; admitted to bar, 1979, Pennsylvania; 1980, District of Columbia. *Education:* Haverford College (B.A., 1976); American University (J.D., summa cum laude, 1979). Senior Editor, *American University Law Review*, 1978-79. Staff Attorney, Securities and Exchange Commission, 1979-81. ***PRACTICE AREAS:*** Securities Law; Securities Offering; Corporate Law; Mergers and Acquisitions.

STEPHEN D. KAHN, born Philadelphia, Pennsylvania, December 18, 1940; admitted to bar, 1966, District of Columbia; 1984, Pennsylvania. *Education:* Temple University (B.S., 1962; J.D., 1965); Georgetown University (LL.M., 1968). Board of Editors, *Temple University Law Quarterly*, 1963-65; Recent Decisions Editor, 1964-65. Beta Gamma Sigma. Attorney, Interpretative Division, Office of the Chief Counsel, Internal Revenue Service, 1965-69. ***PRACTICE AREAS:*** Public Finance; Real Estate Development; Structured Finance.

MARK M. KATZ, born Bronx, New York, March 12, 1957; admitted to bar, 1985, Pennsylvania; 1987, District of Columbia. *Education:* Oberlin College (B.A., 1979); University of Virginia (J.D., 1983). Judicial Clerk: Honorable Francis D. Murnaghan, Jr., U.S. Court of Appeals, Fourth Circuit, 1984-85; Honorable Murray M. Schwartz, U.S. District Court of Delaware, 1983-84. ***PRACTICE AREAS:*** Business Law; Tax Law; Real Estate.

BRADLEY A. KAUFMAN (Resident, New York, N.Y. Office).

SUSAN V. KAYSER (Resident, New York, N.Y. Office).

DAVID L. KELLEHER, born Medford, Massachusetts, October 30, 1953; admitted to bar, 1985, Massachusetts and District of Columbia; 1986, Virginia. *Education:* Boston State College (B.S., 1976); Northeastern University (M.P.A., 1980); Case Western Reserve University (J.D., 1984). Order of the Coif. ***PRACTICE AREAS:*** Litigation; First Amendment Litigation; Products Liability Law; Defective Products.

STEVEN KIMELMAN (Resident, New York, N.Y. Office).

CRAIG S. KING, born American Fork, Utah, February 4, 1953; admitted to bar, 1981, District of Columbia. *Education:* Brigham Young University (B.A., magna cum laude, 1977); Georgetown University Law Center (J.D., 1980). Editor, *Law & Policy in International Business*, 1979-80. Senior Advisor: Reagan/Bush Campaign, 1980; Bush/Quayle Campaign, 1988. General Counsel, Department of the Navy, 1989-93 (also Debarment Official, 1991-93). General Counsel and Secretary, Standard Missile Company, L.L.C., 1995 -1998. *Member:* American Bar Association (Member, Sections on: Antitrust; Public Contracts Law; Vice Chair, Committee on Debarment and Suspension). Top Secret Security Clearance. ***PRACTICE AREAS:*** Government Contracts; Electronic Commerce; Antitrust (contractor mergers, joint ventures and teaming); Corporate Investigations; Corporate Compliance.

SHELDON H. KLEIN, born Detroit, Michigan, June 22, 1956; admitted to bar, 1980, Maryland; 1981, District of Columbia; U.S. Court of Appeals, Fourth, Sixth and Ninth Circuits; U.S. Supreme Court. *Education:* University of Michigan (B.A., with high distinction, 1977); George Washington University (J.D., with honors, 1980). Editor, Consumer Protection Reporting Service, 1979-80. Legal Assistant, Bureau of Consumer Protection, Federal Trade Commission, 1978-80. Member: Editorial Board, The Trademark Reporter, 1989-92; Trademark World, 1987—. *Member:* District of Columbia Bar; Bar Association of the District of Columbia (Past Chair, Patent, Trademark and Copyright Section); Maryland State Bar Association; American Intellectual Property Law Association (Officer and Member, Board of Directors, 1996-00); International Trademark Association. ***PRACTICE AREAS:*** Intellectual Property; Trademarks; Copyrights; Unfair Competition; Advertising and Marketing; Trade Secrets; Litigation; Electronic Commerce.

ARLENE FINE KLEPPER, born New York, N.Y., May 5, 1949; admitted to bar, 1975, District of Columbia. *Education:* Beaver College (B.A., with honors, 1971); George Washington University (J.D., with honors, 1974). (Retired). ***PRACTICE AREAS:*** Public Finance; Project Finance; Banking Law; Health Care.

PAUL A. KOCHES, born New York, N.Y., October 4, 1953; admitted to bar, 1978, District of Columbia; 1983, U.S. Supreme Court. *Education:* University of Connecticut (B.A., cum laude, 1975); University of Miami (J.D., cum

(This Listing Continued)

laude, 1978). Order of the Coif. Member, University of Miami Law Review. ***PRACTICE AREAS:*** Antitrust; Litigation; Intellectual Property; International Transactions.

RICHARD J. KRAININ (Resident, New York, N.Y. Office).

GEORGE R. KUCIK, born Glen Lyon, Pennsylvania, March 28, 1937; admitted to bar, 1961, District of Columbia. *Education:* University of Detroit and Wilkes College (B.S., 1958); Villanova University (LL.B., 1961). Member, 1959-60 and Comment Editor, 1960-61, *Villanova Law Review*. Order of the Coif. Attorney, Department of Justice, Antitrust Division, 1961-65. ***PRACTICE AREAS:*** Litigation; Arbitration; Trial Practice; Appellate Practice; Antitrust; Trade Regulation.

MICHAEL J. KURMAN, born Neptune, New Jersey, September 18, 1951; admitted to bar, 1977, Virginia; 1978, District of Columbia. *Education:* The Ohio State University (B.A., cum laude, 1973); George Washington University (J.D., 1977). Phi Beta Kappa. Attorney, Solicitor's Honors Program and Division of Surface Mining, and Special Assistant to the Solicitor, U.S. Department of the Interior, 1977-81. Member, White House Domestic Policy Staff, 1979. ***PRACTICE AREAS:*** Energy Law; Hydroelectric Law; Indian Affairs Law; Legislative Practice; Campaign Finance Law.

MICHAEL H. LEAHY, born Columbus, Ohio, August 20, 1945; admitted to bar, 1970, District of Columbia; 1990, Maryland. *Education:* Yale University (B.A., cum laude, 1967); Duke University (J.D., with distinction, 1970). Member, Board of Editors, *Duke Law Journal*, 1969-70. ***PRACTICE AREAS:*** Real Estate.

BERNICE K. LEBER (Resident, New York, N.Y. Office).

GERARD LEVAL, born Chicago, Illinois, May 25, 1950; admitted to bar, 1976, Illinois; 1981, District of Columbia. *Education:* University of Chicago (B.A., 1972; J.D., 1975). General Counsel, United States Holocaust Memorial Museum. ***PRACTICE AREAS:*** Business Law; International Business Law; Real Estate; Museum Law.

LAWRENCE A. LEVIT, born Columbus, Ohio, August 18, 1945; admitted to bar, 1972, District of Columbia. *Education:* University of Chicago (B.A., 1966); Harvard University (J.D., cum laude, 1969). Phi Beta Kappa. Member, Harvard Legal Aid Bureau, 1967. *Member:* The District of Columbia Bar (Member, Steering Committee, Real Estate, Housing and Land Use Division, 1974-75; Vice-chairman, Real Estate Committee, 1975-76). ***PRACTICE AREAS:*** Commercial and Residential Lending and Closings; Real Estate Development and/or Syndications Law; Loan Workouts; Real Estate-Commercial Law; Real Estate (Property) Law; Commercial Real Estate Acquisitions; Commercial Real Estate Finance; Commercial Real Estate Sales; Asset Based Finance; Asset Sales; Commercial Leasing; Office Leasing; Retail Leasing; Commercial Mortgages; Condominium Law.

JEROME T. LEVY (Resident, New York, N.Y. Office).

ANTHONY V. LUPO, born Washington, D.C., July 21, 1964; admitted to bar, 1992, District of Columbia. *Education:* George Mason University (B.A., 1987); Howard University (J.D., cum laude, 1990); Georgetown University (LL.M., 1993). Feature Speaker: Comdex - Brazil and U.S.; Internet World Conference-Hong Kong, Singapore, Argentina, Venezuela, New York, Chicago, Los Angeles; E-Commerce Conference-Spain; Intellectual Property Owners Conference; National Managed Health Care Congress; National University Telecommunications Network; American Society of Association Executives. ***PRACTICE AREAS:*** E-Commerce; Intellectual Property; International Intellectual Property; Licensing; Distance Education.

JOHN B. MADDEN, JR. (Resident, New York, N.Y. Office).

STEWART S. MANELA, born Pittsburgh, Pennsylvania, February 29, 1952; admitted to bar, 1977, Virginia; 1978, District of Columbia; 1984, U.S. Supreme Court; 1994, Maryland. *Education:* University of Wisconsin (B.A., 1973); George Washington University (J.D., high honors, 1977). Editor, *George Washington Law Review*, 1976-77. Chair-Elect, ABA Committee on Employment Rights and Responsibilities. Adjunct Professor, George Mason University Law School. ***PRACTICE AREAS:*** Employment Litigation; Equal Opportunity Law; Labor Law; Occupational Safety and Health; Workers Compensation; Fair Housing.

WILLIAM E. MARAMES, born Flushing, New York, December 26, 1955; admitted to bar, 1981, New York; 1998, District of Columbia. *Education:* Queens College of the City University of New York (B.A., summa cum laude, 1977); Fordham University (J.D., 1980). Phi Beta Kappa. Co-Author: "Proving and Disproving Surveys in Trademark Litigation," Fundamentals of Intellectual Property Law Practice Before Agencies, Courts and in Corporations, 1987; "An Overview of Developments in Antitrust Law Relating to Intellectual Property," Antitrust Law Journal, Vol. 55, Issue 2, 1986. Joint Author: "Selling and Rebutting §102 and §112 Defenses in View of Decisions from the Court of Appeals for the Federal Circuit," Patent Litigation, 1986. *Member:* New York State and American (Member, Intellectual Property Law Section; Vice Chairman, Committee on Publications, 1985-92; Chairman, Special Committee on

(This Listing Continued)

ARENT FOX KINTNER PLOTKIN & KAHN, PLLC, Washington—Continued

Possible New Section Publications, 1987-89) Bar Associations; The District of Columbia Bar; International Trademark Association. ***PRACTICE AREAS:*** Trademark Law; Copyright Law; Electronic Commerce.

CHARLES M. MARMELSTEIN, born Washington, D.C., December 12, 1941; admitted to bar, 1970, Maryland; 1972, District of Columbia; 1973-1982, U.S. Court of Customs and Patent Appeals; 1976, U.S. Supreme Court; 1982, U.S. Court of Appeals for the Federal Circuit; registered to practice before U.S. Patent and Trademark Office. *Education:* University of Maryland (B.S.E.E., 1964); American University (J.D., 1970). Tau Beta Pi; Eta Kappa Nu; Phi Alpha Delta. Author and Contributing Editor, *World Trademark Transfers: Law and Practice*. Adjunct Professor, Capital Institute of Technology, 1979. Instructor, Patent Resources Group, 1982-98. *Member:* The District of Columbia Bar; Maryland State and American Bar Associations; American Intellectual Property Law Association; International Trademark Association. ***PRACTICE AREAS:*** Intellectual Property; Patents; Trade Secrets; Trademarks; Copyrights.

EUGENE A. MASSEY, born Hartford, Connecticut, June 15, 1942; admitted to bar, 1967, Connecticut; 1972, District of Columbia. *Education:* Fairfield University (A.B., cum laude, 1964); Harvard University (LL.B., cum laude, 1967). Member, Harvard Legal Aid Bureau, 1965-67. Attorney, Office of the Legal Adviser, Department of State, 1967-72. ***PRACTICE AREAS:*** International Infrastructure Projects; Maritime; Liquified Natural Gas; Energy Law; Health (Health Care) and Hospital Law; International Practice.

WAYNE H. MATELSKI, born Lincoln, Nebraska, March 10, 1948; admitted to bar, 1975, District of Columbia. *Education:* Pennsylvania State University (B.A., with distinction, 1970; M.A., 1974); George Washington University (J.D., with honors, 1974). Phi Beta Kappa. Law Clerk, The Honorable J. Walter Yeagley, District of Columbia Court of Appeals, 1974-76. ***PRACTICE AREAS:*** Food, Drug and Cosmetic Law; International Law; Food and Drug Regulation; Drug and Medical Device Regulation; Controlled Substances Law.

JOHN C. McCOY, born Bradford, Pennsylvania, July 22, 1947; admitted to bar, 1976, Virginia; 1977, District of Columbia; 1985, Maryland. *Education:* University of Notre Dame (B.B.A., 1969); George Washington University (J.D., with high honors, 1976). Beta Alpha Psi; Order of the Coif. Co-Author: "538 T.M. Bad Debts," Bureau of National Affairs, Inc. (1996); "527 T.M. Loss Deductions," Bureau of National Affairs, Inc. (1994). ***PRACTICE AREAS:*** Taxation Law; Business Planning Law; Tax Controversies.

DONALD C. McLEAN, born July 11, 1956; admitted to bar, 1981, Indiana; 1987, District of Columbia; 1990, Maryland. *Education:* Valparaiso University (B.A., summa cum laude, 1978); University of Notre Dame (J.D. cum laude, 1981). Trial Attorney, U.S. Department of Justice, Tax Division, Criminal Section, 1981-87. Recipient of U.S. Department of Justice Outstanding Attorney Award 1984, 1985. ***PRACTICE AREAS:*** Litigation; Environmental Law; Toxic Tort Law.

WILLIAM J. McSHERRY, JR. (Resident, New York, N.Y. Office).

EUGENE J. MEIGHER, born Oshkosh, Wisconsin, April 30, 1937; admitted to bar, 1964, Wisconsin; 1969, District of Columbia. *Education:* St. Louis University (A.B., 1961; Ph.L., 1962; LL.B., 1964); Yale University (LL.M., 1965). Member, Board of Editors, St. Louis University Law Journal, 1963-64. Attorney, Antitrust Division, U.S. Department of Justice, 1965-69. ***PRACTICE AREAS:*** Antitrust Law; Criminal Antitrust; Complex and Multi-District Litigation; Joint Ventures Law; Business Combinations; Mergers and Acquisitions Law; Intellectual Property Law.

JAMES P. MERCURIO, born St. Louis, Missouri, July 22, 1940; admitted to bar, 1964, Missouri; 1968, District of Columbia; 1989, Maryland. *Education:* University of Notre Dame (A.B., magna cum laude, 1963; LL.B., cum laude, 1964). Co-Author: "'Cable Speech' The Case for First Amendment Protection," Law and Business, Inc., 1983. Member, 1962-63 and Articles Editor, 1963-64, Notre Dame Lawyer. Law Clerk to Judge J. Skelly Wright, U.S. Court of Appeals, District of Columbia Circuit, 1964-65. Vice President, Council for Court Excellence, 1992, 1999. Member, Judicial Conference of the United States Court of Appeals for the District of Columbia Circuit, 1990, 1994. Member, Arbitration Panel, American Arbitration Association, 1992—. *Member:* American Law Institute. [J.A.G.C., U.S. Army, 1965-68]. ***PRACTICE AREAS:*** Litigation; Alternative Dispute Resolution; Legal Ethics and Discipline Law.

JOHN J. MEYER, born Oshkosh, Wisconsin, December 16, 1949; admitted to bar, 1979, Wisconsin; 1997, District of Columbia. *Education:* Princeton University (A.B., 1973); University of Wisconsin (J.D., 1978). Order of the Coif. ***PRACTICE AREAS:*** Health Law.

DONALD B. MITCHELL, JR., born New London, Connecticut, May 12, 1954; admitted to bar, 1981, District of Columbia. *Education:* Georgetown University (B.A., magna cum laude, 1976); George Washington University (J.D., with highest honors, 1981). Order of the Coif. ***PRACTICE AREAS:*** Environmental Law; Hazardous Materials Law; Litigation; Toxic Torts.

(This Listing Continued)

GERALD L. MITCHELL, born Brooklyn, New York, May 16, 1957; admitted to bar, 1985, District of Columbia and Maryland. *Education:* Yale University (B.A., magna cum laude, 1979); University of Chicago (J.D., cum laude, 1984). Order of the Coif. ***PRACTICE AREAS:*** Commercial Real Estate; Commercial Real Estate Acquisitions; Commercial Real Estate Development; Commercial Real Estate Finance; Finance; Credit Enhancement; Mortgages; Leases and Leasing; Commercial Leasing.

HENRY MORRIS, JR., born Washington, D.C., May 16, 1956; admitted to bar, 1983, District of Columbia; 1990, Virginia. *Education:* Columbia University (B.A., 1978; J.D., 1983). Harlan Fiske Stone Scholar. ***PRACTICE AREAS:*** Employment Law; Labor Law; Employee Benefits Law.

ROBERT B. MURRAY, born Duluth, Minnesota, July 18, 1935; admitted to bar, 1967, District of Columbia; 1969-1982, U.S. Court of Customs and Patent Appeals; 1972, U.S. Supreme Court; 1977, Virginia (admission limited to Patent, Trademark, Copyright and Unfair Competition Causes only); 1982, U.S. Court of Appeals for the Federal Circuit; registered to practice before U.S. Patent and Trademark Office. *Education:* University of Missouri (B.S. Ch.E., 1958); American University (J.D., 1966). Delta Theta Phi. *Member:* The District of Columbia Bar; Virginia State Bar; American Intellectual Property Law Association; International Trademark Association; International Patent and Trademark Association (AIPPI). ***PRACTICE AREAS:*** Intellectual Property; Patents; Technology Law; Chemical Patents; Medical Patents; Patent Licensing; Patent Litigation; Pharmaceutical Patents; Trade Secrets; Trademarks.

JOHN N. NASSIKAS III, born Manchester, New Hampshire, February 4, 1959; admitted to bar, 1984, Virginia; 1985, District of Columbia; U.S. District Court, Eastern District of Virginia, District of Columbia and District of Maryland; U.S. Court of Appeals, Fourth and District of Columbia Circuits; U.S. Supreme Court. *Education:* Yale University (B.A., magna cum laude, 1981); University of Virginia (J.D., 1984). Assistant U.S. Attorney, United State Attorney's Office, Eastern District of Virginia, 1991-1995. *Member:* Virginia State Bar; District of Columbia Bar; Federal and American Bar Associations. ***PRACTICE AREAS:*** White Collar Crime; Litigation; Criminal Law; Health Care Fraud; Criminal Litigation; Civil Litigation.

RICHARD A. NEWMAN, born Cleveland, Ohio, January 14, 1957; admitted to bar, 1980, District of Columbia. *Education:* New York University (B.A., cum laude, 1977); Case Western Reserve University (J.D., 1980). Member, Editorial Board, 1978-80 and Editor-in-Chief, 1979-80, Law and Housing Journal. *Member:* National Association of Bond Lawyers. ***PRACTICE AREAS:*** Municipal Bonds; Commercial Real Estate; Nonprofit Tax Law; Tax Exempt Organizations.

GEORGE E. ORAM, JR., born Mount Vernon, New York, December 18, 1947; admitted to bar, 1978, District of Columbia; registered to practice before U.S. Patent and Trademark Office. *Education:* University of Delaware (B.Ch.E., 1970); Catholic University of America (J.D., 1978). Instructor, Patent Resources Group, 1985-1998. *Member:* The District of Columbia Bar; American Bar Association; American Intellectual Property Law Association; Maryland Patent Law Association. ***PRACTICE AREAS:*** Mechanical Intellectual Property; Intellectual Property Infringement; International Intellectual Property.

DAVID M. OSNOS, born Detroit, Michigan, January 10, 1932; admitted to bar, 1956, District of Columbia. *Education:* Harvard University (A.B., summa cum laude, 1953; J.D., cum laude, 1956). Phi Beta Kappa. ***PRACTICE AREAS:*** Real Estate-Commercial Law; Taxation Law; Sports Law; Securities; Estate Planning.

DEANNE M. OTTAVIANO, born Brooklyn, New York, November 18, 1964; admitted to bar, 1992, New Jersey; 1993, New York, Maryland and District of Columbia. *Education:* Boston University (B.A., summa cum laude, with distinction, 1986); Georgetown University Law Center (J.D., cum laude, 1992). Trustee, D.C. Legal Aid Society. Member, Environmental Justice Committee of the Lawyers Committee for Civil Rights Under Law. ***PRACTICE AREAS:*** Insurance Coverage; Clean Air Act; Emerging Business Law; Electronic Commerce; Trade Association Law.

LYNN K. PEARLE, born New York, N.Y., May 13, 1943; admitted to bar, 1975, District of Columbia. *Education:* Smith College (B.A., 1965); Boston College (J.D., 1968). *Member:* The District of Columbia Bar (Member: Tax Section; Tax Policy Task Force; Chair, Estate Planning Committee); American Bar Association (Member, Real Property, Probate and Trust Law; Vice-Chair, Lifetime Transfers Committee). Fellow, The American College of Trust and Estate Counsel. ***PRACTICE AREAS:*** Estate Planning; Probate Law; Charitable Trusts and Foundations; Taxation (Local, Personal Property, State, Federal, or International) Law; Federal Income, Estate and Gift Taxation Law.

MATTHEW S. PERLMAN, born Washington, D.C., August 30, 1936; admitted to bar, 1960, District of Columbia and Maryland; 1964, U.S. Supreme Court; 1965, U.S. Claims Court. *Education:* Brown University (A.B., magna cum laude, 1957); Harvard University (LL.B., magna cum laude, 1960). Phi Beta Kappa. Editor, *Harvard Law Review*, 1959-60. Attorney, Air Force General Counsel's Office, 1960-65. Member, Armed Services Board of Contract Appeals, 1965-67. General Counsel, President's Commission on Postal Organization, 1967. Assistant General Counsel, Department of Transportation, 1967-69.

(This Listing Continued)

Member: Federal (Chairman, Government Contracts Committee, 1972-74; Vice-Chairman, Government Contracts Council, 1975-80) and American (Chairman, Contract Adjustment Board Committee, Public Contract Section, 1970-74) Bar Associations. ***PRACTICE AREAS:*** Construction Law; Government Contracts.

JEFFREY S. PETERS, born Rochester, New York, July 12, 1970; admitted to bar, 1996, Massachusetts; 1997, New York; 1998, District of Columbia. *Education:* Brandeis University (B.A., cum laude, with high honors, 1992); University of Pennsylvania (J.D., 1996). Articles Editor, Journal of Comparative Labor Laws, 1995-1996. ***PRACTICE AREAS:*** Health Care. ***Email:*** petersj@arentfox.com

ELLIOTT I. PORTNOY, born Morgantown, West Virginia, November 11, 1965; admitted to bar, 1992, Maryland; 1993, District of Columbia. *Education:* Syracuse University (B.A., summa cum laude, 1986); Rhodes Scholar (1986); Oxford University (D.Phil., 1989); Harvard Law School (J.D., cum laude, 1992). ***PRACTICE AREAS:*** Legislative Practice; Education Law; Special Education; Campaign Ethics; Election and Campaign Finance; Lobbying; Interactive Multimedia Law; Congressional Investigations; Government Relations; Government Ethics; Federal Legislative Practice; State Legislative Practice; Public Policy; Nonprofit Organizations Law; Federal Regulatory Law.

HOWARD B. POSSICK, born Boston, Massachusetts, October 15, 1948; admitted to bar, 1976, Florida; 1977, District of Columbia; 1989, Maryland. *Education:* Cornell University (B.A., 1970); Babson College (M.B.A., with highest distinction, 1973); University of Miami School of Law (J.D., magna cum laude, 1976). Member, 1974-75, and Editor-in-Chief, 1975-76, *University of Miami Law Review*. ***PRACTICE AREAS:*** Business Law; Corporate Law; Securities Law; Transactions; Litigation.

CONNIE A. RAFFA (Resident, New York, N.Y. Office).

DEBORAH A. RANDALL, born New York, N.Y., June 10, 1947; admitted to bar, 1976, Maryland and U.S. Supreme Court; 1981, District of Columbia; 1993, New York. *Education:* Harvard University/Radcliffe College (B.A., cum laude, 1968); Columbia University (J.D., 1976). Harlan Fiske Stone Scholar. Editor, *Legal Issues and the Integrated Delivery System, An Executive Guide*, American Hospital Publishing, Inc., 1996. Clerk, Honorable Joseph H. Young, U.S. District Court, District of Maryland, 1976-77. Attorney-Advisor: Federal Trade Commission, 1977-80; U.S. Department of Health and Human Services, 1980-82. General Counsel, National Association for Home Care, 1984-86. Member, Board of Directors, Alzheimer's Association of the National Capital Area. ***LANGUAGES:*** French. ***PRACTICE AREAS:*** Health and Hospital Law; Medicare; Certificates of Need; Health Care Contracts; Health Care Facility Licensing; Health Care Facility Regulation; Health Care Finance; Health Care Fraud; Health Care Licensing; Health Care Regulation; Health Care Reimbursement; Health Insurance Coverage; Health Care; Home Health Care; Long Term Care; Mental Health Law; Nursing Home Regulation.

MARC RAUCH (Resident, New York, N.Y. Office).

PETER S. REICHERTZ, born Dallas, Texas, September, 28, 1950; admitted to bar, 1976, District of Columbia. *Education:* Brown University (A.B., 1972); George Washington University (J.D., with honors, 1975). ***PRACTICE AREAS:*** Animal Drug Regulation; Administrative Law; Administrative Adjudications; Administrative Agency Practice; Administrative Hearings and Appeals; Administrative Litigation; Advertising and Marketing; Advertising and Labeling; Advertising; False Advertising; Controlled Substances Law; Copyright Law; Copyright Infringement; Copyright Licensing; Copyright Litigation; Copyright Prosecution; Copyright Protection; Copyright Registration; Drug and Medical Device Regulation; Federal Regulatory Law; Federal Administrative Law; Food, Drug and Cosmetic Law; International Copyright Law; Pharmaceutical Intellectual Property; Telemedicine; Trademarks; International Trademarks; Trade Dress; Trademark Arbitration; Trademark Infringement; Trademark Licensing; Trademark Litigation; Trade Prosecution.

ALAN E. REIDER, born New York, N.Y., July 31, 1949; admitted to bar, 1975, Massachusetts; 1976, District of Columbia. *Education:* Brown University (A.B., 1971); University of Texas (M.P.H., 1972); Boston University (J.D., 1975). Analyst, Department of Health, Education and Welfare, 1975-78. Chief, Review Policy Branch, Office of Professional Standards Review Organization, Health Care Financing Administration, U.S. Department of Health and Human Services, 1978-80. Chairman, Health and Human Services Section, Federal Bar Association, 1993-94. ***PRACTICE AREAS:*** Health Care Law; Health Care Fraud; Health Care Reimbursement; Physician Contracts; Physician Licensing; Hospital Law; Medicare Fraud and Abuse; Medicare and Medicaid Reimbursement.

PAUL JACKSON RICE, born East St. Louis, Illinois, July 15, 1938; admitted to bar, 1962, Missouri; 1969, Illinois; 1993, District of Columbia. *Education:* University of Missouri (A.B., 1960; J.D., 1962); Northwestern University (LL.M., 1970). Member, *Missouri Law Review*. Chief Counsel, National Highway Traffic Safety Administration, Department of Transportation, 1990-93. Commandant, The Judge Advocate General's School, U.S. Army, 1985-88. Listed Who's Who in America. [Judge Advocate Gen. Corp, U.S. Army, 1962-

(This Listing Continued)

1990, Retired Colonel]. ***PRACTICE AREAS:*** Motor Vehicle Safety Law; Automobile Law; Transportation Law; Hazardous Materials Transportation; Motor Carrier Law; Motor Carrier Regulation; Transportation Safety.

STEPHANIE A. RIGAUX, born Washington, D.C., August 7, 1965; admitted to bar, 1990, Maryland; 1992, District of Columbia. *Education:* Pennsylvania State University (B.A., 1985); American University, Washington College of Law (J.D., summa cum laude, 1990). Alpha Lambda Delta. ***PRACTICE AREAS:*** Litigation.

JEFFREY B. ROSEN, born White Plains, New York, January 22, 1956; admitted to bar, 1982, New York (Not admitted in District of Columbia). *Education:* Harvard College (B.A., cum laude, 1978); Yale Law School; New York University School of Law (J.D., cum laude, 1981). Order of the Coif. ***PRACTICE AREAS:*** Real Estate; Project Finance; Public Service Concessions.

CHARLES B. RUTTENBERG, born Reading, Pennsylvania; admitted to bar, 1949, District of Columbia. *Education:* Yale University; University of Virginia (B.A., 1946); University of Pennsylvania (LL.B., 1949). Phi Beta Kappa. Listed in, Who's Who in America. Editor, Treasurer and Member, Managing Board, University of Pennsylvania Law Review, 1947-49. Member, District of Columbia Bar, 1949—. General Counsel, National Foundation on the Arts and the Humanities, 1966-69. Chairman, Legislative Bureau, Member, Executive Committee and Board and General Counsel, Greater Washington Board of Trade, 1984-93. Member, Executive Committee and Board, Greater Washington Research Center, 1981-95. Member of Board, Washington Area Lawyers for the Arts, 1984-95. Member of Board and Executive Committee and General Counsel, Wolf Trap Foundation for the Performing Arts, 1982-92. Member, Executive Committee and Board of Trustees, University of the District of Columbia, 1990-93. Member, Executive Committee and Board of Directors, Iona Senior Services, 1997—. Mediator, U.S. District Court, District of Columbia, 1998— and District of Columbia Supreme Court. ***PRACTICE AREAS:*** Antitrust; Entertainment Law; Intellectual Property; Copyrights; Trademark Law.

WILLIAM A. SARRAILLE, born San Francisco, California, April 10, 1963; admitted to bar, 1989, California, 1990, U.S. District Court, Central District of California; 1991, District of Columbia; 1994, U.S. District Court for the District of Columbia; U.S. Court of Appeals for the District of Columbia and Sixth Circuits. *Education:* Yale University (B.A., cum laude, 1985); Harvard University (J.D., 1989). Law Clerk, Hon. Harry L. Hupp, U.S. District Court, Central District of California, 1989-90. ***PRACTICE AREAS:*** Civil Litigation; Health Care; White Collar Criminal Defense; Health Care Legislation.

THOMAS SCHATTENFIELD, born Cleveland, Ohio, September 6, 1926; admitted to bar, 1955, Ohio; 1961, District of Columbia. *Education:* University of Michigan (A.B., 1947); University of Grenoble, France; Western Reserve University (LL.B., 1955); Georgetown University. Phi Alpha Delta; Order of the Coif. Member, Board of Editors, *Western Reserve University Law Review*, 1954-55. Assistant U.S. Attorney, Southern District of Ohio, 1959-61. ***PRACTICE AREAS:*** Communications Law; Trial Practice; Broadcast Transactions.

JOANNE SCHEHL, born Philadelphia, Pennsylvania, February 1, 1954; admitted to bar, 1984, Virginia; 1991, District of Columbia. *Education:* University of Virginia (B.A., with distinction, 1978; J.D., 1984). ***PRACTICE AREAS:*** Finance; Real Estate; Business Law.

LARRI A. SHORT, born Charlottesville, Virginia, June 29, 1947; admitted to bar, 1992, Maryland; 1993, District of Columbia. *Education:* University of Michigan (B.S., with high distinction, 1969); Duke University (M.A., 1973); University of North Carolina (J.D., with high honors, 1992). Phi Beta Kappa; Phi Kappa Phi; Order of the Coif. Member, *University of North Carolina Law Review*. ***PRACTICE AREAS:*** Medicare and Medicaid; Health Care; Pharmacy Law; Fraud and Compliance.

ALLEN G. SIEGEL, born Chicago, Illinois, May 19, 1934; admitted to bar, 1960, Florida; 1964, U.S. Supreme Court; 1965, District of Columbia. *Education:* College of the City of New York; Duke University (LL.B., with distinction, 1960). Order of the Coif; Phi Delta Phi. First Associate Editor, *Duke Law Journal*, 1959-60. Adjunct Professor of Law, 1978-79 and Senior Lecturing Fellow in Law, 1979—, Duke Law School. Director, Private Adjudication Center of Duke University, 1985—. Member, Board of Regents, The Catholic University of America 1991-99. Member, Board of Visitors, Columbus School of Law, The Catholic University of America, 1998-99. General Counsel, Jewish Social Service Agency of Washington, 1990—. Attorney, National Labor Relations Board, 1962-64. *Member:* American Bar Association (Co-chairman, Subcommittee on the Fair Labor Standards Act, 1975-76; Subcommittee on the Equal Pay Act, 1973-74). ***PRACTICE AREAS:*** Labor and Employment; Collective Bargaining; Employment Discrimination Law; Alternative Dispute Resolution; Arbitration Law.

JOEL N. SIMON, born Chicago, Illinois, August 18, 1936; admitted to bar, 1960, District of Columbia. *Education:* University of Illinois (B.S., with high honors, 1957); University of Michigan (J.D., 1960). Order of the Coif; Tau Epsilon Rho; Beta Alpha Psi. Editor, *Michigan Law Review*, 1959-60. Attorney

(This Listing Continued)

ARENT FOX KINTNER PLOTKIN & KAHN, PLLC, Washington—Continued

Tax Division, Department of Justice, 1960-61. ***PRACTICE AREAS:*** Real Estate-Commercial Law; Real Estate (Property) Law; Real Estate Development and/or Syndications Law; Taxation.

HOWARD V. SINCLAIR, born Newburg, New York, October 23, 1952; admitted to bar, 1978, District of Columbia; 1980, Virginia; 1989, Maryland. *Education:* University of Rochester (B.A., 1974; M.B.A., 1975); George Washington University (J.D., with high honors, 1978). Member, *George Washington Law Review*, 1977. Order of the Coif. ***PRACTICE AREAS:*** Litigation; Commercial Transactions.

CHRISTOPHER SMITH, born Evanston, Illinois, November 12, 1947; admitted to bar, 1972, Kansas; 1973, District of Columbia; 1976, U.S. Supreme Court. *Education:* Wabash College (A.B., 1969); University of Kansas Law School (J.D., 1972). Order of the Coif; Phi Delta Phi. Articles Editor, *Kansas Law Review*, 1971-72. Co-Author: "The Law of Product Warranties," Warren, Gorham & Lamont, 1984. Special Assistant to the Assistant Administrator for Enforcement and General Counsel, U.S. Environmental Protection Agency, 1973-74. (Managing Partner). ***PRACTICE AREAS:*** Administrative Law; Commercial Law; Antitrust; Trade Regulation; Environmental Law.

MICHAEL L. STEVENS, born Newburgh, New York, May 13, 1959; admitted to bar, 1984, District of Columbia; 1995, U.S. Supreme Court. *Education:* Colgate University (B.A., magna cum laude, 1981); University of Pennsylvania (J.D., 1984). Phi Beta Kappa; Phi Alpha Theta. ***PRACTICE AREAS:*** Labor and Employment Law; Collective Bargaining; Employer Rights; Employment Contracts; Employment Discrimination; Harassment; Employment Litigation; Employment Practices Liability Insurance; Executive Severance Contracts; Wage and Hour Law; Wrongful Termination; Fair Housing Law.

CARTER STRONG, born Bronxville, New York, July 17, 1947; admitted to bar, 1972, Florida; 1973, District of Columbia. *Education:* Ithaca College (B.A., 1969); University of Miami (J.D., cum laude, 1972). ***PRACTICE AREAS:*** Mergers and Acquisitions; Securities Offerings; Corporate Law; Finance.

KATHY S. TAUB, born New York, N.Y., March 30, 1955; admitted to bar, 1980, Maryland; 1995, District of Columbia. *Education:* Duke University (B.A., cum laude, 1977); University of Maryland School of Law (J.D., with honors, 1980). Editor: Design/Build Contacting Handbook, Wiley Law Publications, 1992; Design/Build Contracting Formbook, Wiley Law Publications, 1997. *Member:* Maryland State and American Bar Associations; The District of Columbia Bar. ***PRACTICE AREAS:*** Construction Law. **Email:** taubk@arentfox.com

GARY C. TEPPER, born Vienna, Georgia, September 6, 1953; admitted to bar, 1981, District of Columbia. *Education:* Brandeis University (B.A., magna cum laude, with high honors in Mathematics, 1975); Yale University (J.D., 1979). Phi Beta Kappa. Editor, Yale Law Journal, 1978-79. Law Clerk to Hon. Gilbert S. Merritt, U.S. Court of Appeals, Sixth Circuit, 1979-80. ***PRACTICE AREAS:*** Franchise Litigation; Financial Institutions Litigation; Real Estate Litigation.

CARL A. VALENSTEIN, born Washington, D.C., August 9, 1957; admitted to bar, 1983, District of Columbia. *Education:* Yale University (B.A., cum laude, 1979); University of Michigan (J.D., cum laude, 1983). Articles Editor, *Michigan Yearbook of International Legal Studies*, 1982-83. ***LANGUAGES:*** Spanish, Portuguese, French, Italian. ***PRACTICE AREAS:*** Project Finance; Infrastructure Development; International Business (or Trade or Finance) Law; Import and Export Law; Maritime Law.

CHRISTOPHER VAN HOLLEN, JR., admitted to bar, 1991, Maryland; 1994, District of Columbia. *Education:* Swarthmore College (B.A., 1982); Harvard University (M.P.P., 1985); Georgetown University Law Center (J.D., 1989). Member, Maryland State Senate. ***PRACTICE AREAS:*** Litigation.

DAVID VIDAL-CORDERO, born San Juan, Puerto Rico, July 5, 1955; admitted to bar, 1982, District of Columbia and U.S. Tax Court; 1986, U.S. Supreme Court. *Education:* University of Puerto Rico (B.A., magna cum laude, 1977; J.D., 1982). Phi Delta Phi. ***LANGUAGES:*** Spanish, French and Portuguese. ***PRACTICE AREAS:*** International Project Finance; International Telecommunications; Privatizations; Corporate Law; International Business Transactions.

KIMBERLY A. WACHEN, born Washington, D.C.; admitted to bar, 1993, New York, Maryland and District of Columbia. *Education:* Duke University (B.A., cum laude, 1988) Beta Alpha Psi; University of Pennsylvania (J.D., 1992). Senior Editor, *Journal of International Business Law*. Certified Public Accountant, Maryland, 1989. ***PRACTICE AREAS:*** Corporate; Electronic Commerce; Real Estate.

BARBARA S. WAHL, born Washington, D.C., October 29, 1953; admitted to bar, 1979, District of Columbia; 1985, Virginia. *Education:* University of Maryland (B.A., with honors, 1975); Syracuse University (J.D., cum laude, 1978). Phi Beta Kappa; Phi Kappa Phi. Member, 1976-77 and Comments Editor, 1977-78, *Syracuse Law Review*. Clerk, The Honorable Albert V. Bryan, Jr., U.S. District Court, Eastern District of Virginia, 1978-79. ***PRACTICE AREAS:*** Litigation.

BRIAN P. WALDMAN, born Washington, D.C., February 14, 1964; admitted to bar, 1992, California; 1993, District of Columbia. *Education:* University of Chicago (A.B., with honors, 1986); University of Chicago Graduate School of Business (M.B.A., 1987); University of California at Los Angeles School of Law (J.D., 1992). Phi Beta Kappa. ***PRACTICE AREAS:*** Food, Drug, Cosmetic and Device Law; Advertising and Marketing.

ROBERT J. WATERS, born Carroll, Iowa, August 3, 1955; admitted to bar, 1986, District of Columbia. *Education:* Iowa State University (B.A., 1977); Harvard University (M.P.A., 1979); Georgetown University (J.D., 1984). Policy Analyst, Department of Health Education and Welfare, Health and Human Services, 1979-83. Administrative Assistant, U.S. Senator Tom Harkin, 1983-87. ***PRACTICE AREAS:*** Health (Health Care) and Hospital Law; Legislative Government Regulations; Telemedicine.

RICHARD J. WEBBER, born Minneapolis, Minnesota, July 27, 1948; admitted to bar, 1974, District of Columbia; 1991, Maryland. *Education:* Princeton University (B.A., cum laude, 1970); University of Michigan (J.D., cum laude, 1973). Law Clerk, Trial Division, U.S. Court of Claims, 1973-74. Law Clerk, the Honorable Marion T. Bennett, U.S. Court of Claims, 1974-75. Attorney, Civil Division, U.S. Department of Justice, 1975-80. Chairman, Federal Contracts Claims and Remedies Committee, ABA Section of Public Contract Law, 1986-91. Chairman, ADP Procurement Committee, FBA Government Contracts Section, 1992-94. Chairman, FBA Government Contracts Section, 1994-96. ***PRACTICE AREAS:*** Government Contracts; Litigation; Construction Law; Government Procurement.

BARBARA G. WERTHER, born Philadelphia, Pennsylvania, March 16, 1953; admitted to bar, 1979, District of Columbia; 1998, Virginia. *Education:* University of Pennsylvania (B.A., magna cum laude, 1975); George Washington University (J.D., 1978). ***PRACTICE AREAS:*** Construction Litigation; Governmental Contracts; Litigation.

MARSHA C. WERTZBERGER, born Kansas City, Missouri, November 29, 1940; admitted to bar, 1976, Maryland; 1978, District of Columbia. *Education:* University of Kansas (B.A., with honors in French, 1962); Philadelphia College of Pharmacy and Science (B.S., 1963) Rho Chi; Georgetown University Law Center (J.D., 1975). ***PRACTICE AREAS:*** Administrative Law; Food and Drug; Advertising.

ARNOLD R. WESTERMAN, born Wilmington, Delaware, April 17, 1938; admitted to bar, 1966, District of Columbia. *Education:* University of Maryland (A.B., 1962); George Washington University (J.D., with honors, 1965). Phi Delta Phi; Phi Alpha Theta; Pi Sigma Alpha. Attorney, Securities and Exchange Commission, 1965-68. ***PRACTICE AREAS:*** Corporate Financing Law; Corporate Restructuring Law; Securities Law; Banking; Savings and Thrift Institutions Law.

M. STEPHANIE WICKOUSKI, admitted to bar, 1979, Virginia.; 1983, District of Columbia; 1986, Maryland; 2000, New York. *Education:* College of William & Mary (A.B., 1973); Franklin Pierce Law Center (J.D., 1979). Judicial Law Clerk, Roger M. Whelan, U.S. Bankruptcy Court, District of Columbia, 1979-80. Author: "Bankruptcy Crimes," Beard Books, 2000. Trial Attorney, United States Department of Justice, Civil Division, 1980-85. *Member:* Virginia State Bar; The District of Columbia Bar. ***PRACTICE AREAS:*** Bankruptcy. **Email:** wickouss@arentfox.com

BRECKINRIDGE L. WILLCOX, born San Diego, California, August 2, 1944; admitted to bar, 1969, District of Columbia and Maryland; 1972, Hawaii. *Education:* Yale University (B.A., 1966); Duke University (J.D., 1969). Editorial Advisory Board, *Corporate Criminal Liability Reporter*, 1986-90. Board of Editors, *Business Crimes Bulletin*, 1999—. U.S. Attorney, District of Maryland, 1986-91. Trial Attorney, 1975-79, Branch Chief, Fraud Section, 1979-81 and Special Litigation Counsel, 1982-84, Criminal Division, Department of Justice. Board of Visitors, Duke University Law School, 1989—. [Capt., JAGC, USMCR, 1970-1973]. ***PRACTICE AREAS:*** Litigation; White Collar; Criminal Defense; Environmental Law Enforcement.

BLAIR C. WOODSIDE, III, born Canton, Ohio, February 4, 1945; admitted to bar, 1979, District of Columbia. *Education:* Kent State University (B.S., Ed., 1971; M.Ed., 1972); Catholic University of America (J.D., 1979). *Member:* The District of Columbia Bar; American Bar Association. [U.S. Army, 1967-1970]. ***PRACTICE AREAS:*** Commercial Real Estate; Finance.

DAVID N. WYNN (Resident, New York, N.Y. Office).

HARVEY A. YAMPOLSKY, born New York, N.Y., April 9, 1945; admitted to bar, 1971, New York; 1973, District of Columbia. *Education:* University of Rochester (A.B., 1966); University of Chicago (J.D., 1969); New York University (LL.M., 1971). Chief Counsel to the Inspector General, Department of Health and Human Services, 1978-90. Legislative Counsel, Department of Health, Education and Welfare, 1976-77. Special Assistant to Congressman John Brademas, Chief Deputy Majority Whip, U.S. House of Representatives,

(This Listing Continued)

1975. Counsel, The Urban Institute, Washington, D.C., 1973. Associate, White, Fine & Verville, Washington, D.C., 1973. Staff Attorney, Department of Health, Education, and Welfare, 1971-72. ***PRACTICE AREAS:*** Health Care Fraud; Health Care Reimbursement.

STEPHEN C. YOHAY, born February 3, 1946; admitted to bar, 1971, New York; 1978, District of Columbia. *Education:* Union College (B.A., 1967); Georgetown University (J.D., 1970); George Washington University (LL.M., Labor Law, 1974). Member, Editorial Staff, Georgetown Law Journal. Contributing Editor, Employee Relations Law Journal and Occupational Hazards Magazine. Attorney, Enforcement Division, National Labor Relations Board, 1971-1974. Supervisory Attorney, OSHA Division, U.S. Department of Labor, 1974-1975. Attorney, Office of Labor Law, U.S. Postal Service, 1975-1977. *Member:* American Bar Assn. (Chair, Litigation Section, OSHA Subcommittee, 1995—; Labor and Employment Committee, 1977—). ***PRACTICE AREAS:*** Occupational Safety and Health; Labor and Employment.

JOHN J. YUROW, born Washington, D.C., January 30, 1931; admitted to bar, 1958, District of Columbia; 1961, Michigan. *Education:* Marietta College and George Washington University (B.A., 1953); George Washington University (J.D., 1958). Phi Delta Phi; Order of the Coif. Editor, *George Washington Law Review*, 1956-57. Trial Attorney, Internal Revenue Service, 1958-62. Professorial Lecturer, Tax Practice and Procedure, National Law Center, George Washington University, 1973-76. *Member:* Federal Bar Association (Chairman, Taxation Committee, 1972-73); The District of Columbia Bar (Chairman, Steering Committee, Taxation Section, 1977-78). ***PRACTICE AREAS:*** Taxation Law; Taxpayer Representation Law; Tax Controversies Law; Partnership Law; Corporate Law.

GERALD ZINGONE, born New York, N.Y., April 27, 1960; admitted to bar, 1985, Virginia; 1986, District of Columbia. *Education:* Georgetown University (B.S.F.S., magna cum laude, 1982); University of Pennsylvania (J.D., 1985). Phi Beta Kappa. ***PRACTICE AREAS:*** Litigation; Antitrust.

COUNSEL

DAVID J. BARDIN, born New York, N.Y., June 2, 1933; admitted to bar, 1956, New York; 1966, District of Columbia; 1970, Israel. *Education:* Columbia College (A.B., 1954); Columbia University (J.D., 1956). Harlan Fiske Stone Scholar. Co-Author: "A.G.A. Select Use Handbook: Natural Gas For Environmental Control," American Gas Association, 1985. Administrator of the Economic Regulatory Administration in the U.S. Department of Energy, 1977-79. Deputy Administrator, Federal Energy Administration, 1977. Commissioner, New Jersey Department of Environmental Protection, 1974-77. Assistant to the Attorney General of Israel, 1970-72. Deputy General Counsel, 1967-69, Assistant General Counsel, 1965-67, Trial Attorney, 1958-65, Federal Power Commission. *Member:* Federal Energy Bar Association (Chairman, Committee on Cogeneration and Small Power Production Facilities, 1983-84; Member, Board of Directors, 1984-87; Director, Foundation for the Energy Law Journal, 1987-90; Vice Chairman, Committee on Environment, 1989-90; Chairman, Committee on Environment, 1990-91; Chairman, *Ad Hoc* Committee on Procedural and Accounting Implications of Enactment of Clean Air Act Amendments of 1990, 1991-93). ***LANGUAGES:*** Hebrew.

DALE L. BUMPERS, born Charleston, Arkansas, August 12, 1925; admitted to bar, 1952, Arkansas; 2001, District of Columbia. *Education:* University of Arkansas; Northwestern University (LL.B., 1951; J.D., 1951). *Member:* District of Columbia Bar. ***PRACTICE AREAS:*** Government Relations; Government Regulations.

SAMUEL K. CHARNOFF, born New York, N.Y., March 29, 1963; admitted to bar, 1989, Maryland; 1990, District of Columbia. *Education:* Columbia University (B.A., 1985); Georgetown University Law Center (J.D., 1989). ***PRACTICE AREAS:*** Labor and Employment Law; Civil Rights; Litigation.

SCOTT A. COHN (Resident, New York, N.Y. Office).

ABDULLAHI MASSOUD, born Umm Ruwabah, Sudan, May 18, 1940. *Education:* University of Khartoum School of Law (LL.B., with honors, 1965); University of London (1977-1979). Legal Assistant to Attorney General's Chambers of Sudan, 1965-1966. Third Secretary, Ministry of Foreign Affairs of Sudan, 1966-1970. Legal Advisor: State Trade Corporation of Sudan, 1970-1977; HRH Prince Saad Al Faisal, 1980-1993. *Member:* International Bar Association. ***LANGUAGES:*** Arabic and English. ***PRACTICE AREAS:*** Government Relations; Insurance; International Litigation; International Contracts; Shariah Law.

CARSON P. PORTER, born Bowling Green, Kentucky, September 22, 1945; admitted to bar, 1971, Kentucky; 1999, District of Columbia. *Education:* University of Kentucky (B.A., 1967; J.D., 1970). ***PRACTICE AREAS:*** Health Care; Litigation.

ASSOCIATES

SARIRA D. ALEXANDER, born Tehran, Iran, June 4, 1962; admitted to bar, 1994, California; 1999, District of Columbia. *Education:* University of California at Los Angeles (B.A., 1990); University of California, Hastings College of the Law (J.D., 1993). Phi Delta Phi. ***LANGUAGES:*** Farsi and French. ***PRACTICE AREAS:*** Intellectual Property; Copyrights; Trademarks; Electronic Commerce; Licensing; Intellectual Property Litigation.

(This Listing Continued)

MELISSA A. BAILEY, born Kansas City, Kansas, November 6, 1967; admitted to bar, 1995, Kansas; 1997, District of Columbia. *Education:* Northwestern University (B.A., 1990); University of Kansas (J.D., 1994). ***PRACTICE AREAS:*** Occupational Safety and Health; Labor and Employment; Government Relations.

RHONDA L. BARTON, born Wilmington, Delaware, December 10, 1966; admitted to bar, 1999, Maryland (Not admitted in District of Columbia). *Education:* Howard University (B.S., 1989); University of Maryland (J.D., 1998). Moot Court Board. ***PRACTICE AREAS:*** Patents.

HOLLY M. BASTIAN, born Hannibal, Missouri, December 25, 1964; admitted to bar, 1992, Virginia; 1993, District of Columbia. *Education:* William Woods College; University of Virginia (B.S., 1987); Georgetown Law Center (J.D., cum laude, 1992). Associate Editor, *Georgetown Law Journal*. Clerk, The Honorable Robert J. Yock, U.S. Court of Federal Claims, 1992-93. ***PRACTICE AREAS:*** Estate Planning; Estate and Gift Taxation; Wills; Trust Law; Corporate Law; Business Planning; Real Estate.

STEPHEN M. BELLOTTI, born Providence, Rhode Island, February 7, 1970; admitted to bar, 1995, Maryland; 1996, District of Columbia. *Education:* Boston College (B.A., 1992); American University (J.D., cum laude, 1995). ***PRACTICE AREAS:*** Commercial Real Estate; Finance; Business Planning.

CHRISTINA C. BENSON, born Fayetteville, Arkansas, October 8, 1967; admitted to bar, 1997, North Carolina; 1998, District of Columbia. *Education:* University of North Carolina (B.A., 1990; M.B.A., 1997; J.D., with honors, 1997). ***Email:*** bensonc@arentfox.com

RICHARD JASON BERMAN, born Philadelphia, Pennsylvania, October 13, 1969; admitted to bar, 1995, Pennsylvania; 1998, District of Columbia. *Education:* University of Delaware (B.A., 1991); George Washington University (J.D., 1995). Phi Beta Kappa. Member, George Washington University Law Review, 1995. Author: "Color Me Bad: A New Solution to the Debate Over Color Trademark Registration," George Washington Law Review, Vol. 63, No. 1. ***PRACTICE AREAS:*** Biochemical Patents; Biotechnology; Chemical; Pharmaceutical; Molecular Biology Patents; Medical Patents; Patent Prosecution; Patent Licensing; Patent Infringement; Intellectual Property.

ALISON J. BESUNDER, born Smithtown, New York, November 9, 1973; admitted to bar, 1999, New York and Massachusetts; 2000, U.S. District Court, Eastern and Southern Districts of New York (Not admitted in District of Columbia). *Education:* State University of New York at Buffalo (B.A., 1995); Brooklyn Law School (J.D., 1998). Dean's Merit Scholar, 1995-1998. Attorney, Lipsitz, Green, Fahringer, Roll, Salisbury & Cambria, LLP, 1998-1999; Pruzansky & Besunder, LLP, 2000-2001. CALI Award for Academic Excellence in New York Civil Practice, 1997. CALI Award for Academic Excellence in Commercial Paper and Business Transactions, 1997. Philip K. Younge Memorial Scholarship for Commercial Paper, 1998. ***LANGUAGES:*** Spanish, Hebrew. ***PRACTICE AREAS:*** Commercial Litigation; Professional Liability.

BARB L. BETTENHAUSEN, born Minneapolis, Minnesota, December 5, 1956; admitted to bar, 1996, Virginia; 1998, District of Columbia. *Education:* University of Missouri at Kansas City (B.A., with distinction, 1992); George Mason University (J.D., with distinction, 1996). Phi Kappa Phi. Phi Sigma Alpha. Phi Alpha Delta (Marshall, 1994-1995). Member, Golden Key. Articles Editor, George Mason Law Review, 1995-1996. Law Clerk to the Hon. Warren R. King, District of Columbia Court of Appeals, 1996-1997. ***PRACTICE AREAS:*** Business Law; International Law; Commercial Real Estate.

DARREN T. BINDER, born Hartford, Connecticut, December 20, 1968; admitted to bar, 1993, Massachusetts; 1995, District of Columbia and Texas. *Education:* Union College (B.S., magna cum laude, 1990); Boston College Law School (J.D., 1993). Phi Beta Kappa; Phi Alpha Delta (Vice Justice, 1991). Senior Notes and Comments Editor, *Boston College International and Comparative Law Review*. ***PRACTICE AREAS:*** Health Care Transactions; Health Care Regulation; Managed Care.

COSTINA S. BORTES (Resident, Bucharest, Romania Office).

PHILIP D. BRANDT, born Orlando, Florida, April 28, 1965; admitted to bar, 1997, Maryland; 1998, District of Columbia. *Education:* United States Naval Academy (B.S., 1987); George Washington University (J.D., 1997). Order of the Coif. Staff Member, *George Washington Law Review*. Law Clerk, Judge Robert J. Yock, U.S. Court of Federal Claims, 1997-98. [USN, 1987-95, Lieutenant]. ***PRACTICE AREAS:*** Corporate Contracts; Corporate Real Estate; Corporate Organization; Land Sales.

RANDALL A. BRATER, admitted to bar, 2000, District of Columbia. *Education:* Cornell University (B.A., 1997); Vanderbilt University (J.D., 2000).

LYNN A. BRISTOL, born Chicago, Illinois, August 20, 1958; admitted to bar, 1998, Maryland; registered to practice before the U.S. Patent and Trademark Office (Not admitted in District of Columbia). *Education:* University of

(This Listing Continued)

ARENT FOX KINTNER PLOTKIN & KAHN, PLLC, Washington—Continued

Chicago (A.B., Biological Sciences, 1980); University of North Carolina, Chapel Hill (Ph.D., Immunology, Biochemistry, 1988); University of Maryland (J.D., 1998). ***PRACTICE AREAS:*** Intellectual Property; Patents.

DIANE BUI, born Bethesda, Maryland, November 2, 1975; admitted to bar, 2001, Maryland (Not admitted in District of Columbia). *Education:* Duke University (B.A., magna cum laude, 1997); New York University School of Law (J.D., 2000). Editor in Chief, Annual Survey of American Law, New York University School of Law. Author, "Delegating Sovereignty: Constitutional and Legal Implications of US Participation in International Environmental Regimes," published as a chapter in Delegating State Powers: The effect of Treaty Regimes on Democracy and Sovereignty. ***PRACTICE AREAS:*** International Transactions; International Trade. ***Email:*** buid@arentfox.com

KAREN F. CANDREVA (Resident, New York, N.Y. Office).

ROBERT K. CARPENTER, born Washington, D.C., January 5, 1962; admitted to bar, 1989, Maryland; 1991, District of Columbia; 1992, U.S. District Court, District of Maryland; registered to practice before U.S. Patent and Trademark Office. *Education:* University of Maryland (B.S.Ch.E., 1985; J.D., 1989); Johns Hopkins University (M.S., Biotechnology, 2001). ***PRACTICE AREAS:*** Patents; Trademarks; Copyrights; Unfair Competition.

CRISTINA A. CARVALHO, born Salvador, Bahia, Brazil, February 2, 1963; admitted to bar, 1985, Rio de Janeiro; 1996, New York and U.S. District Court, Southern District of New York; 1998, U.S. Court of Appeals, Federal Circuit (Not admitted in District of Columbia). *Education:* Federal University of Rio de Janeiro (LL.B., 1985); Franklin Pierce Law Center (M.I.P., 1993). ***LANGUAGES:*** Portuguese and Spanish. ***PRACTICE AREAS:*** Intellectual Property; Trademark Litigation; Trademark Protection; Trademark Licensing; International Trademark Protection; International Trademark Litigation; Trade Dress; Trademark Enforcement; Unfair Competition; Internet Trademark Law; Copyright Protection; Copyright Litigation; Copyright Licensing; Software Licensing; Information Technology Licensing; Intellectual Property Portfolio Management.

KATHLEEN L. CARVER-CHENEY (Resident, New York, N.Y. Office).

THOMAS R. CASTIELLO, born Washington, D.C., April 21, 1972; admitted to bar, 1997, Maryland; 1998, District of Columbia. *Education:* Williams College (B.A., cum laude, 1994); Georgetown University Law Center (J.D., cum laude, 1997). ***PRACTICE AREAS:*** Business Law; Estate Planning.

STEVEN A. COHEN, born Huntington, New York, July 29, 1970; admitted to bar, 1995, Maryland; 1998, District of Columbia. *Education:* Johns Hopkins University (B.A., 1992); New York University (J.D., 1995). Phi Beta Kappa. ***PRACTICE AREAS:*** E-Commerce; Interactive Marketing and Advertising; Internet Law; Corporate Law; Securities.

KELI COLBY, born Indianapolis, Indiana, March 9, 1962; admitted to bar, 1991, Virginia; 1999, District of Columbia. *Education:* Sweet Briar College (B.A., cum laude, 1984); Washington College of Law, American University (J.D., 1990). ***PRACTICE AREAS:*** Real Estate Finance; Real Estate; Finance; Business Law.

SANA D. COLEMAN, born Queens, New York, February 9, 1973; admitted to bar, 1998, District of Columbia. *Education:* Duke University (A.B., 1994); Georgetown University (J.D., 1997). ***PRACTICE AREAS:*** Telecommunications; Intellectual Property; Trademarks.

DANIEL P. CONNEEN (Not admitted in District of Columbia; Resident, New York, N.Y. Office).

EVE CORBIN, born Gainesville, Florida, March 13, 1973; admitted to bar, 1999, Maryland; 2000, District of Columbia. *Education:* Yale University (B.A., with distinction, 1994); University of Michigan (J.D., 1999). ***PRACTICE AREAS:*** Business; Commercial Leasing; Bond Finance; Tax Exempt Bond; Real Estate Contracts.

HANS J. CROSBY, admitted to bar, 1998, Pennsylvania; 1999, New Jersey and Maryland; registered to practice before the U.S. Patent and Trademark Office (Not admitted in District of Columbia). *Education:* Virginia Polytechnic Institute and State University (B.S., in Biology, 1990); Drexel University (M.S., in Finance, 1995); Villanova Law School (J.D., 1998). ***PRACTICE AREAS:*** Intellectual Property; Biotechnology; Patents.

MICHAEL S. CRYAN (Resident, New York, N.Y. Office).

JAMES R. DAVIS, II, born Wheeling, West Virginia, February 9, 1967; admitted to bar, 1998, Virginia; 1999, District of Columbia. *Education:* James Madison University (B.B.A., 1990; M.B.A., 1992); University of Kansas (J.D., 1998). Editor-in-Chief, *Kansas Law Review* (Criminal Procedure Edition). Graduate Teaching Assistant, Legal Research and Writing, Appellate Advocacy. Author: " *BMW v. Gore* : Why the States (Not the U.S. Supreme Court) Should Review Substantive Due Process Challenges to Large Punitive Damage Awards," 46 U. Kan. L. Rev. 395. ***PRACTICE AREAS:*** Intellectual Property; Internet Law; Cyberspace Law; Trademark; Copyright; Trademark Litigation.

(This Listing Continued)

MARK R. DENICORE, born Oneonta, New York, October 4, 1962; admitted to bar, 1996, Virginia; 1997, Maryland; 1998, District of Columbia. *Education:* Clarkson University (B.S.C.E., 1985); Virginia Polytechnic Institute (M.E.A., 1989); Washington College of Law of American University (J.D., magna cum laude, 1996). Member, *American University Law Review*. Professional Engineer, Virginia. ***PRACTICE AREAS:*** Construction Counseling and Litigation.

PETER JAMES DERNBACH, born Washington, D.C., June 28, 1970; admitted to bar, 1998, California (Not admitted in District of Columbia). *Education:* George Washington University (B.A., International Affairs, 1992); University of Virginia School of Law (J.D., 1997). Co-author: "State of Play 1999: Intellectual Property Rights Protection in Taiwan", IP Profiles, 1999. ***LANGUAGES:*** English and Mandarin. ***PRACTICE AREAS:*** Intellectual Property; Trademarks; Copyrights. ***Email:*** dernbacp@arentfox.com

ARTHUR S. DI DIO, born Evanston, Illinois, January 1, 1965; admitted to bar, 1998, Virginia; 1999, District of Columbia. *Education:* University of Toledo (B.S., summa cum laude, 1986); University of Cincinnati (M.D., 1990); Georgetown University (J.D., cum laude, 1998). Medical Licensure, Virginia (inactive). ***LANGUAGES:*** Portuguese. ***PRACTICE AREAS:*** Health Care Law; Health Care Regulation; Health Care Litigation.

DANIEL J. DOWLING, born Brooklyn, New York, November 4, 1953; admitted to bar, 1990, Virginia; 1991, District of Columbia. *Education:* United States Military Academy (B.S., 1976); University of Virginia (J.D., 1990). [Capt., U.S. Army, 82nd Airborne Division Artillery, 1976-1980]

KRISTINE J. DUNNE, born Beaufort, South Carolina, December 24, 1967; admitted to bar, 2000, Virginia; 2001, District of Columbia. *Education:* Gordon College (B.A., 1989); Harvard University, Graduate School of Education (Ed.M., 1995); University of Virginia (J.D., 2000). ***PRACTICE AREAS:*** Employment Law; Civil Litigation; Education Law.

D. DANIEL DZARA, II, born Fort Wayne, Indiana, July 30, 1974; admitted to bar, 1999, Illinois; 2000, Louisiana (Not admitted in District of Columbia). *Education:* University of North Carolina at Chapel Hill (B.A., 1996); Tulane University (J.D., Certificate in Maritime Law, cum laude, 1999); The George Washington University (LL.M., Intellectual Property Law, 2000). Senior Notes and Comments Editor, Tulane Maritime Law Journal, 1998-1999. ***PRACTICE AREAS:*** Patents; Trademarks; Copyrights.

STEVEN ROBERT EBERT (Resident, New York, N.Y. Office).

LAURIE EDBERG, born New York, N.Y., April 24,1970; admitted to bar, 1996, New Jersey, 1997, New York, 1998, District of Columbia. *Education:* Barnard College (B.A., 1992); Brooklyn Law School (J.D., 1996). ***PRACTICE AREAS:*** Intellectual Property.

FELICIA EFTA (Resident, Bucharest, Romania Office).

CRAIG M. ENGLE, born Jackson, Michigan, July 19, 1960; admitted to bar, 1986, Ohio; 1988, U.S.Court of Appeals for the District of Columbia; 1999, U.S. Supreme Court (Not admitted in District of Columbia). *Education:* University of Cincinnati (B.S., summa cum laude, 1982); Georgetown University Law Center (J.D., 1985). Phi Beta Kappa. Co-Author: "Buckley Over Time," Notre Dame Journal of Legislation, Vol. 24, Nov. 2, 1998. Adjunct Faculty, Georgetown University Law Center, Advocacy, Research and Writing, 1985-87. ***PRACTICE AREAS:*** Government Relations; Election Law; Public Affairs. ***Email:*** englec@arentfox.com

CAROLINE T. ENGLISH, born Rochester, New York, August 18, 1970; admitted to bar, 1996, Virginia; 1999, District of Columbia. *Education:* Denison University (B.A., 1992) Phi Beta Kappa; George Washington University National Law Center (J.D., magna cum laude, 1996). Order of the Coif. Member, *George Washington Law Review*. Author: "Mediator Immunity," The George Washington Law Review, D.C. Circuit Review, June 1995 Vol. 63 No. 5. ***PRACTICE AREAS:*** Civil Litigation; Criminal Litigation.

LISA A. ESTRADA, born Denver, Colorado, July 15, 1966; admitted to bar, 1999, Virginia; 2000, District of Columbia. *Education:* Indiana University of Pennsylvania (B.A., 1988); George Mason University (J.D., magna cum laude, 1999). Author: "An Assessment of Qui Tam Suits by Corporate Counsel Under the False Claims Act," 7 George Mason Law Review 163; "Buying the Status Quo on Affirmative Action: The Piscataway Settlement and Its Lessons About Interest Group Path Manipulation," 9 George Mason Civil Rights Law Journal 207. ***PRACTICE AREAS:*** Health; White Collar Crime; Civil Litigation; Civil Fraud; Legislative Practice.

MUGUR FILIPESCU (Resident, Bucharest, Romania Office).

BENJAMIN I. FISHMAN, born Washington, D.C., March 4, 1967; admitted to bar, 1992, California; 1993, District of Columbia; 1998, Maryland. *Education:* Yale University (B.A., cum laude, 1989); University of Southern California (J.D., 1992). ***PRACTICE AREAS:*** Commercial Litigation; Antitrust; Construction Law; Patent; International Arbitration.

(This Listing Continued)

THERESE K. FRANCESE, born Syracuse, New York, February 23, 1964; admitted to bar, 1992, Virginia; 1994, District of Columbia. *Education:* Georgetown University (B.S.F.S., 1986); George Washington University Law School (J.D., with honors, 1992). Senior Articles Editor, The George Washington University Law Review. ***PRACTICE AREAS:*** Trademark Prosecution; Trademark Protection; Trademark Litigation; Copyright Protection.

HILLARY A. FROMMER, born Chappaqua, New York, December 2, 1972; admitted to bar, 1998, Illinois and U.S. District Court, Northern District of Illinois. *Education:* Cornell University (B.A., cum laude, 1995); Chicago-Kent College of Law (J.D., with honors, 1998). Member, 1996-98 and Notes and Comments Editor, 1997-98, Chicago-Kent Law Review. (Resident, New York, N.Y. Office). ***LANGUAGES:*** French. ***PRACTICE AREAS:*** Health Care; Litigation.

JOSEPH T. GATEWOOD, born Washington, D.C., August 15, 1969; admitted to bar, 1990, Maryland; 1991, U.S. District Court, District of Maryland; 1993, District of Columbia. *Education:* University of Maryland (B.A., 1986); American University (J.D., 1990). ***PRACTICE AREAS:*** Health Care; Administrative Law; Litigation; Health Care Fraud. ***Email:*** gatewooj@arentfox.com

CHRISTOPHER J. GIAIMO JR., born Wiesbäden, Germany, February 15, 1969; admitted to bar, 1995, New York, U.S. District Court, Southern and Eastern Districts of New York; 1998, Maryland, District of Columbia, and U.S. District Court, District of Maryland and District of Columbia. *Education:* St. Joseph's University (B.S., 1991); St. John's University (J.D., cum laude, 1995). Research Editor, American Bankruptcy Institute Law Review, 1993-95. ***PRACTICE AREAS:*** Creditors Rights; Bankruptcy; Litigation.

BARRY R. GOGEL (Resident, New York, N.Y. Office).

ROBIN FREEDMAN GONZALES, born Silver Spring, Maryland, July 29, 1964; admitted to bar, 1999, Maryland; 2000, District of Columbia. *Education:* College of William & Mary (B.A., English, 1986); George Washington University (J.D., with high honors, 1999). Order of the Coif. Member, George Washington Journal of International Law & Economics. *Member:* Maryland State Bar Association, Inc. ***PRACTICE AREAS:*** Business; Commercial Real Estate; Corporate Law; Leases and Leasing; Nonprofit and Charitable Organizations; Partnerships.

CHRISTOPHER H. GRIGORIAN, born Washington, D.C., November 4, 1964; admitted to bar, 1989, Maryland; 1991, District of Columbia. *Education:* George Washington University (B.B.A., 1986); American University, Washington College of Law (J.D., 1989). Trial Attorney, 1990-93 and Senior Trial Attorney, 1993-94, U.S. Department of Justice, Tax Division, 1990-94. Co-Author: "How Exempt Organizations Can Avoid Unrelated Debt-Financed Income on Realty," 6 J. Tax'n Investments 286 (1989). ***PRACTICE AREAS:*** Antitrust; Trade Regulation; Complex Litigation; Business Litigation; Motor Vehicle Safety Law.

LOUIS JOHN GRIMMELBEIN, IV, born Jamaica, New York, February 11, 1960; admitted to bar, 1990, California; 1998, District of Columbia. *Education:* Dartmouth College (A.B., with distinction, 1982); University of Notre Dame (J.D., 1990). ***PRACTICE AREAS:*** Commercial Transactions; Real Estate.

ELIZABETH SCHICKEDANZ HAILE, born Chicago, Illinois, January 27, 1975; admitted to bar, 1999, Illinois; 2000, District of Columbia. *Education:* Indiana University (B.S.P.A., magna cum laude, 1996); Georgetown University Law Center (J.D., 1999). Editor, *Georgetown Journal on Poverty Law and Policy*, 1998-99. ***PRACTICE AREAS:*** OSHA; Employment Law; ERISA.

E. L. HAMBRICK, born Atlanta, Georgia, June 11, 1953; admitted to bar, 1998, Virginia and Maryland; 1999, District of Columbia. *Education:* University of Pennsylvania (B.S.,B.A., 1975); Howard University College of Medicine (M.D., 1979); George Washington University School of Public Health and Health Services (M.P.H., 1998); George Washington University Law School (J.D., with honors, 1998). Associate, *George Washington Law Review*. Author: "Rehabilitation Act Mental Health Coverage Limits: Distinctions Are Allowed Between Mental and Physical Coverage," 65 Geo. Wash. L. Rev. 853 (1997). ***PRACTICE AREAS:*** Health Law; Emergency Medical Services Law.

PAMELA HAUGHTON-DENNISTON, admitted to bar, 1998, Maryland; 1999, District of Columbia. *Education:* St. Lawrence University (B.A., cum laude, 1973) Phi Beta Kappa; Georgetown University Law Center (J.D., 1998). ***PRACTICE AREAS:*** Computer and Software; Electronic Commerce; Trademarks; Copyright.

RUSTAN J. HILL, born Culbertson, Montana, September 21, 1961; admitted to bar, 1995, Washington; 1996, U.S. District Court, Western District of Washington; 1998, Ohio; 2001, District of Columbia. *Education:* University of Maryland (B.S.A.E., 1983); University of Washington School of Law (J.D., 1995). Professional Engineer, Washington, 1989. [US Navy, 1983-1988, Lt.; US Navy Reserve, 1988—, LCDR]. ***PRACTICE AREAS:*** Intellectual Property; Patents; Trademarks; Copyrights.

STEVEN F. HILL, born Keokuk, Iowa, November 13, 1968; admitted to bar, 1997, Illinois; 1998, District of Columbia. *Education:* Vanderbilt University (B.A., summa cum laude, 1991); Northwestern University (J.D., 1997). Phi Beta Kappa. Articles Editor, Northwestern Journal of International Law & Business. ***PRACTICE AREAS:*** Commercial Litigation; International Trade.

SAM HUANG, born Taipei, Taiwan, November 26, 1964; admitted to bar, 1996, New Jersey; 1999, New York (Not admitted in District of Columbia). *Education:* Syracuse University (B.S., Computer Engineering, 1991) Theta Tau; Rutgers School of Law (J.D., 1996). Managing Business Editor, Computer & Technology Law Journal. ***PRACTICE AREAS:*** Intellectual Property; Patents; Trademarks; Copyrights.

SUZY CHAN HUNG, born Taipei, Taiwan, January 1, 1957; admitted to bar, 1994, Maryland; 1997, District of Columbia. *Education:* Sophia University International College, Tokyo; University of California, Los Angeles (B.A., cum laude, 1979); University of Maryland (M.A., 1982); Georgetown University (J.D., 1994). Lecturer: "Permanent Residency and Naturalization Issues," Washington, D.C., 1998. ***LANGUAGES:*** Chinese and Japanese. ***PRACTICE AREAS:*** Immigration; International Trade.

DANA ISAROIU (Resident, Bucharest, Romania Office).

MELANYE K. JOHNSON, born Detroit, Michigan, October 31, 1971; admitted to bar, 1997, Michigan and U.S. District Court, Eastern District of Michigan; 2000, District of Columbia and U.S. District Court, District of Colorado. *Education:* University of Michigan (A.B., 1993); Ohio State University (J.D., 1996). Articles Editor, 1995-96, Staff, 1994-95, Ohio State Journal on Dispute Resolution. Law Clerk, Honorable Eric L. Clay, U.S. Court of Appeals, Sixth Circuit, 1997-98. ***PRACTICE AREAS:*** Intellectual Property; Trademarks; Copyrights; Intellectual Property Litigation.

EILEEN L. KAHANER, born New York, N.Y., January 6, 1967; admitted to bar, 1996, Maryland; 1998, District of Columbia. *Education:* Oberlin College (B.A., 1988); George Washington University School of Law (J.D., 1996). Order of the Coif. Managing Editor, *The Environmental Lawyer*, 1995-96. ***PRACTICE AREAS:*** Health Care.

JAMES A. KAMINSKI, born Gary, Indiana, March 30, 1969; admitted to bar, 1997, Illinois (Not admitted in District of Columbia). *Education:* Indiana University (B.A., 1991); Loyola University (J.D., 1997). ***LANGUAGES:*** Russian, French. ***PRACTICE AREAS:*** Trade Regulation; Consumer Protection; Advertising Law. ***Email:*** kaminski@arentfox.com

GREGORY B. KANG, born Philadelphia, Pennsylvania, October 30, 1967; admitted to bar, 1997, New Jersey; 1999, District of Columbia; registered to practice before U.S. Patent and Trademark Office. *Education:* Drexel University (B.S.E.E., 1990); Widener University (J.D., 1996). Examiner, U.S. Patent and Trademark Office. ***LANGUAGES:*** Korean. ***PRACTICE AREAS:*** Intellectual Property; Patents; Trademarks; Copyrights.

KATHERINE V. KELLEY, born St. Paul, Minnesota, October 8, 1955; admitted to bar, 1979, District of Columbia, District of Columbia, Court of Appeals and U.S. District Court, District of Columbia; 1982, Pennsylvania. *Education:* Macalester College; University of Minnesota (B.A., 1976) Phi Beta Kappa; Georgetown University (J.D., 1979). ***PRACTICE AREAS:*** Municipal Finance; Legislative Practice.

JONATHAN A. KIDNEY, born 1960; admitted to bar, 2000, Maryland (Not admitted in District of Columbia). *Education:* Clemson University (B.S.E.E., 1984; M.S.E.E., 1992); George Mason University (J.D., 1999).

JUTTA KLAPISCH, born Essen, Germany, September 9, 1960; admitted to bar, 1996, District of Columbia. *Education:* University of California, Boalt Hall School of Law (LL.M., 1986); University of Bonn (Dr.jur., magna cum laude, 1990). Author: "Der Einfluß der deutschen und österreichische Emigranten auf contracts of adhesion und bargaining in good faith im US-amerikanischen Recht," Nomos Verlagsgesellschaft, 1991. ***LANGUAGES:*** German, French. ***PRACTICE AREAS:*** International; Corporate; Finance.

SUSAN SONENSHEIN KLEIMAN, born New York, N.Y., October 3, 1966; admitted to bar, 1991, Pennsylvania; 1992, District of Columbia; 1996, Texas. *Education:* Emory University (B.A., with honors, 1988); American University, Washington College of Law (J.D., cum laude, 1991). ***PRACTICE AREAS:*** Employee Benefits; Executive Compensation.

SUNANDA KUNDRA, born Lusaka, Zambia, January 22, 1970; admitted to bar, 1997, California (Not admitted in District of Columbia). *Education:* Northern Illinois University (B.S., 1992); University of Nebraska at Lincoln (J.D., 1996). ***LANGUAGES:*** English, Hindi and Punjabi. ***PRACTICE AREAS:*** International Employment Contracts; International Agency and Distribution Agreements; International Licensing; International Corporate Law; Litigation.

ALISON L. KUTLER, born Omaha, Nebraska, February 17, 1971; admitted to bar, 1999, Nebraska; 2000, District of Columbia. *Education:* Georgetown University (B.A., 1993); Stanford Law School (J.D., 1999). ***PRACTICE AREAS:*** Government Relations; International.

JAMES F. LABOE, born Washington D.C., March 20, 1969; admitted to bar, 2000, New Hampshire (Not admitted in District of Columbia). *Education:* University of Notre Dame (B.A., 1995); Franklin Pierce Law Center (J.D., 2000). ***PRACTICE AREAS:*** OSHA; Litigation; Labor and Employment.

(This Listing Continued)

ARENT FOX KINTNER PLOTKIN & KAHN, PLLC, Washington—Continued

MARK BANCROFT LANGDON, born Ithaca, New York, January 15, 1969; admitted to bar, 1994, Maryland; 1995, District of Columbia. *Education:* Cornell University (B.A., 1991; J.D., 1994). Cornell Law School Moot Court Board. Member, Cornell Journal of Law & Public Policy. ***PRACTICE AREAS:*** Health Care Law.

BRIAN C. LANSING, born Bay Shore, New York, September 24, 1967; admitted to bar, 1992, North Carolina; 1993, U.S. Court of Military Appeals; 2000, U.S. Supreme Court; 2001, District of Columbia and U.S. Court of International Trade. *Education:* University of Richmond (B.A., 1989); Wake Forest University (J.D., 1992). ***PRACTICE AREAS:*** Federal Civil Litigation; State Civil Litigation.

JAMES M. LARKINS, III, born Oak Harbor, Washington, June 26, 1969; admitted to bar, 1995, Nebraska; 1996, Missouri and Kansas; 1999, District of Columbia. *Education:* University of Nebraska at Omaha (B.S.B.A., 1991); Creighton University (M.B.A., 1994; J.D., 1995); Georgetown University Law Center (LL.M. in Securities Regulation, 1998). Phi Delta Phi. ***PRACTICE AREAS:*** Securities; Financial Institutions Law; Corporate Law.

RACHEL G. LATTIMORE, born Shelby, North Carolina, July 9, 1967; admitted to bar, 1994, North Carolina; 1996, District of Columbia and U.S. District Court, District of Maryland. *Education:* University of North Carolina (B.A., with distinction, 1989); Victoria University (B.A., with honors, 1990); Duke University (J.D., 1994). Phi Beta Kappa. ***PRACTICE AREAS:*** Biotechnology; Environmental Law.

ANCUTA DELIA LEACH (Resident, Bucharest, Romania Office).

PATRICIA A. LEONARD, born Smithtown, New York, November 23, 1962; admitted to bar, 1994, Maryland; 1995, U.S. District Court, District of Maryland; 1996, District of Columbia. *Education:* University of Maryland (B.S., 1984); University of Baltimore (J.D., magna cum laude, 1994). Associate Editor, *University of Baltimore Law Review.* Member, Heuisler Honor Society. ***PRACTICE AREAS:*** Corporate Transactions; Corporate Finance; Entertainment Transactions.

JO AN LEONCE, born Brooklyn, New York, February 5, 1969; admitted to bar, 1997, Maryland; 1998, District of Columbia and U.S. District Court, District of Maryland. *Education:* Howard University (B.A., magna cum laude, 1991); University of Maryland (J.D., 1997). Member, *Maryland Law Review.* ***LANGUAGES:*** Spanish. ***PRACTICE AREAS:*** Health Care.

MELISSA CALLAHAN LESMES, born Olney, Maryland, February 7, 1968; admitted to bar, 1993, Maryland and U.S District Court, District of Maryland; 1995, District of Columbia; 1996, U.S. Court of Appeals, Fourth Circuit; 1997, U.S. Court of Appeals for the Federal Circuit; 1999, U.S. Court of Appeals, Fifth Circuit. *Education:* Duke University (A.B., cum laude, 1990); Marshall-Wythe School of Law, College of William and Mary (J.D., 1993). Phi Delta Phi. Member, *Administrative Law Review*, 1991-93. ***PRACTICE AREAS:*** Commercial Litigation; Products Liability; Insurance Coverage; Construction.

BRIAN MARC LOWINGER, born Massachusetts, March 13, 1970; admitted to bar, 2000, Massachusetts (Not admitted in District of Columbia). *Education:* George Washington University (B.S., 1992); Catholic University of America (J.D., 1999). Author: Commlaw Conspectus Issue 2, 1998. ***LANGUAGES:*** Spanish. ***PRACTICE AREAS:*** Telecommunications.

MICHAEL K. LOWMAN, born Brooklyn, New York, 1967; admitted to bar, 1993, New York; 1997, Virginia; 1998, Maryland and District of Columbia. *Education:* State University of New York at Buffalo (B.A., summa cum laude, 1989); Washington College of Law of American University (J.D., summa cum laude, 1992). Phi Beta Kappa. Senior Articles Editor, American University Law Review, 1992. ***PRACTICE AREAS:*** Commercial Litigation; Securities Litigation; Shareholder Litigation; Construction; Government Contracts.

KEITH R. MARINO, born Silver Spring, Maryland; admitted to bar, 1994, Virginia; 1996, District of Columbia; U.S. Court of International Trade; U.S. Court of Appeals for the Federal Circuit. *Education:* College of William and Mary (B.A., 1989; J.D., 1994). Order of the Coif. Member, Moot Court Bar. Co-Author: "The Standard of Review Applied by the United States Court of Appeals for the Federal Circuit in International Trade and Customs Cases," 45 American University Law Review 1749, 1996. Law Clerk to the Honorable James C. Turk, U.S. District Court, Western District of Virginia, 1994-95. ***PRACTICE AREAS:*** International Trade; International Finance; Customs Law; Patent Litigation.

RONAN JOSEPH McHUGH, born Manchester, England, February 19, 1967; admitted to bar, 1991, England; 1998, New York; 2000, District of Columbia. *Education:* London School of Economics (LL.B., Hons, 1988); College of Law Guilford, Surety Law Society (Finals Exam., 1989). ***PRACTICE AREAS:*** Construction Dispute Resolution; International Arbitration. ***Email:*** mchughr@arentfox.com

(This Listing Continued)

FREDERICK D. McKALIP, admitted to bar, 2000, Virginia (Not admitted in District of Columbia). *Education:* University of Virginia (B.A., 1988); Virginia Polytechnic Institute and State University (M.U.R.P., 1993); University of Virginia (J.D., 2000). ***Email:*** mckalipf@arentfox.com

AMY S. McNALLY, born Kansas City, Kansas, August 15, 1974; admitted to bar, 1999, Maryland; 2000, District of Columbia. *Education:* Drake University (B.A., 1996); University of Kansas (J.D., 1999). Note and Comment Editor, University of Kansas Law Review. ***PRACTICE AREAS:*** Corporate Transaction; Corporate Finance; Real Estate.

MICHAEL T. McNAMARA, born Kansas City, Missouri, June 26, 1969; admitted to bar, 1996, Maryland; 1997, District of Columbia. *Education:* Duke University (A.B., summa cum laude, 1990); Harvard Law School (J.D., magna cum laude, 1996). Phi Beta Kappa. ***PRACTICE AREAS:*** Electronic Commerce; Election, Campaign and Political Law; Administrative Law; Public Policy; Trade and Professional Associations.

J. MARCUS MEEKS, born Memphis, Tennessee, January 7, 1972; admitted to bar, 2000, Virginia (Not admitted in District of Columbia). *Education:* Ohio Wesleyan University (B.A., cum laude, 1994); Emory University (J.D., 2000). Phi Beta Kappa. ***PRACTICE AREAS:*** Litigation. ***Email:*** meeksm@arentfox.com

ANNE L. MILEM, born Suffern, New York, November 24, 1970; admitted to bar, 1995, Virginia; 1998, District of Columbia. *Education:* Texas Tech University (B.A., summa cum laude, 1992); Georgetown University Law Center (J.D., 1995). Law Clerk to the Honorable Stanley P. Klein, Fairfax County Circuit Court, 1995-97. ***PRACTICE AREAS:*** Civil Litigation; Employment Litigation; Construction Litigation; Business Torts; Civil Appeals.

ANDRA MUSATESCU (Resident, Bucharest, Romania Office).

JENNIFER L. MYRON, born Greensburg, Pennsylvania, September 15, 1972; admitted to bar, 1998, Pennsylvania; 2000, District of Columbia. *Education:* Dickinson College (B.A., cum laude, 1995); Dickinson School of Law of the Pennsylvania State University (J.D., 1998). Managing Editor, Dickinson Law Review. Law Clerk to the Honorable Joseph T. Doyle, Commonwealth Court of Pennsylvania. ***PRACTICE AREAS:*** Trademarks; Advertising Law; Copyright; Electronic Commerce.

JAMES R. NEWLAND, JR., born Alexandria, Virginia, December 20, 1965; admitted to bar, 1998, Virginia and U.S. Court of Appeals, Fourth Circuit (Not admitted in District of Columbia). *Education:* Virginia Polytechnic Institute and State University (B.A., Architecture, 1991); University of Pittsburgh (J.D., 1998). Licensed Architect, District of Columbia, 1993. Certified Construction Document Technologist, CSI, 1994. Author: "The Limitation of Liability Clause," The Construction Specifier, Vol. 50, No. 10, October, 1997. Instructor: Conditions of the Contract, Construction Specifications Institute, March, 1998; Construction Law and the Project, Associated Builders and Contractors, October, 1999—. Member: American Institute of Architects; Associated Builders and Contractors. ***PRACTICE AREAS:*** Construction Litigation; Construction Contracts; Construction Claims; Arbitration; Commercial Law; Litigation. ***Email:*** newlandj@arentfox.com

NANCY A. NOONAN, born Allentown, Pennsylvania, February 26, 1968; admitted to bar, 1996, New York and New Jersey; 1998, District of Columbia. *Education:* University of Richmond (B.A., 1990); Syracuse University Maxwell School of Citizenship and Public Affairs (M.A. in International Relations, 1995); Syracuse University College of Law (J.D., 1995). Recipient, International Legal Studies Award. Member: Moot Court Board; Journal of International Law and Commerce. Law Clerk to the Honorable Evan J. Wallach, U.S. Court of International Trade, 1995-98. ***LANGUAGES:*** French. ***PRACTICE AREAS:*** International Trade; Customs.

EUGENIA ORDYNSKY, born Los Angeles, California; March 21, 1960; admitted to bar, 1994, Maryland; 1995, District of Columbia; 1996, U.S. Court of Appeals, Fourth Circuit. *Education:* University of California, Berkeley (B.A., 1981); University of Baltimore (M.B.A., 1993; J.D., 1994). ***LANGUAGES:*** Russian. ***PRACTICE AREAS:*** Immigration Law.

TIMOTHY D. OSTERHAUS, born St. Charles, Illinois, April 29, 1971; admitted to bar, 1998, Florida; 1999, District of Columbia. *Education:* King College (B.A., 1993); University of Virginia (J.D., 1997). Law Clerk to Honorable Kenneth L. Ryskamp, U.S. District Court, Southern District of Florida, 1997-98. ***PRACTICE AREAS:*** International Trade; Antidumping; Customs Law.

MURAT OZGU, born Bethlehem, Pennsylvania, May 18, 1969; admitted to bar, 1997, Pennsylvania; 2000, District of Columbia; registered to practice before U.S. Patent and Trademark Office. *Education:* Lehigh University (B.S.M.E., 1991); Thomas M. Cooley Law School (J.D., 1995). ***LANGUAGES:*** Turkish. ***PRACTICE AREAS:*** Intellectual Property (100%); Electrical Intellectual Property; Intellectual Property Infringement; International Intellectual Property; Mechanical Intellectual Property.

HELENE PANGALOS (Resident, New York, N.Y. Office).

IULIAN PATRASCANU (Resident, Bucharest, Romania Office).

(This Listing Continued)

1980. *Member:* The District of Columbia Bar; Oklahoma Bar Association; American Intellectual Property Law Association. ***Email:*** bwesterman@armstrongpat.com

KEN-ICHI HATTORI, born Tokyo, Japan, February 21, 1944; admitted to bar, 1990, Virginia; 1992, District of Columbia; 1983-1990, Japan as Patent Attorney; registered to practice before U.S. Patent and Trademark Office. *Education:* Musashi Institute of Technology, Tokyo, Japan (B.A., 1966); Tokyo Metropolitan University, Tokyo, Japan; George Washington University; George Mason University School of Law (J.D., 1989). Lecturer for foreign participants on Industrial Property Rights Problems, Japanese Government Patent Office, 1973-1983. Examiner and Member, Board of Appeals, Japanese Government Patent Office, 1966-1983. Assistant Director, Policy Planning Office, Ministry of International Trade and Industry, 1972-1975. Author: "Federal Courts," 1992, "3000 Days in the Firm," 1994; "American Lawyer's Jokes," 1997; "CAFC Yearbook," 1998. *Member:* Virginia State Bar; District of Columbia Bar; American Intellectual Property Law Association. ***LANGUAGES:*** Japanese. ***Email:*** kenhattori@armstrongpat.com

WILLIAM G. KRATZ, JR., born Pittsburgh, Pennsylvania, February 24, 1936; admitted to bar, 1968, Pennsylvania and U.S. District Court, Western District of Pennsylvania; 1972, U.S. Supreme Court; registered to practice before U.S. Patent and Trademark Office. *Education:* Slippery Rock State University (B.S., 1957); Duquesne University (J.D., 1968). Phi Alpha Delta. *Member:* Allegheny County Bar Association; American Chemical Society; The Pittsburgh Intellectual Property Law Association. (Resident, Pittsburgh, Pennsylvania). ***PRACTICE AREAS:*** Intellectual Property Law. ***Email:*** wkratz@armstrongpat.com

MEL R. QUINTOS, born Manila, Philippines, September 29, 1956; admitted to bar, 1986, Ohio, District of Columbia, U.S. Court of Appeals, Sixth Circuit and U.S. Court of Appeals for the Federal Circuit; 1988, U.S. District Court for the District of Columbia; registered to practice before U.S. Patent and Trademark Office. *Education:* State University of New York at Stony Brook (B.E., 1978); The Ohio State University (J.D., 1984). Phi Alpha Delta. Recipient, Stony Brook University Materials Engineering Alumni Association Class Award. Engineer, Westinghouse Electric Corporation Nuclear Center, 1978-1981. Co-Author: "Means-Plus-Function," Patent Journal, Vol. 45, No. 2., Japan Patent Attorneys Association, 1992. Contributing Author: "Essentials of Drafting U.S. Patent Specification and Claims," (2000); U.S. Trade Related Intellectual Property Journal, Japan Machinery Export Association, 1993—. *Member:* District of Columbia Bar; Bar Association of the District of Columbia; American Bar Association; American Intellectual Property Law Association; Institute of Electrical and Electronics Engineers; American Society of Mechanical Engineers. ***LANGUAGES:*** Pilipino. ***Email:*** mquintos@armstrongpat.com

DONALD W. HANSON, born Spirit Lake, Iowa, June 10, 1946; admitted to bar, 1974, Indiana; 1977, District of Columbia; registered to practice before U.S. Patent and Trademark Office. *Education:* Iowa State University (B.S.Ch.E., 1968); University of Iowa and George Washington University (J.D., with honors, 1973). Omega Chi Epsilon. Member, Iowa Law Review, 1971. *Member:* The District of Columbia Bar. ***Email:*** dhanson@armstrongpat.com

STEPHEN G. ADRIAN, born St. Paul, Minnesota, April 1, 1963; admitted to bar, 1990, Virginia and U.S. Court of Appeals, Fourth and Federal Circuits; 1998, District of Columbia; registered to practice before U.S. Patent and Trademark Office. *Education:* University of North Carolina (B.S., Chemistry, 1985); George Washington University (J.D., 1990). *Member:* Virginia State and American Bar Associations; American Intellectual Property Law Association; American Chemical Society. ***Email:*** sadrian@armstrongpat.com

SCOTT M. DANIELS, born Bellingham, Washington, September 13, 1952; admitted to bar, 1977, District of Columbia; 1978, U.S. District Court for the District of Columbia and U.S. Court of Appeals for the District of Columbia Circuit; 1980-1982, U.S. Court of Customs and Patent Appeals; 1982, U.S. Court of Appeals for the Federal Circuit; registered to practice before U.S. Patent and Trademark Office. *Education:* Carleton College (B.A., cum laude, 1974); Cornell University (J.D., 1977). William Carleton Scholar. Author: "Intellectual Property Rights in the United States," JAMA, 1989; "Intellectual Property Rights Under the Thrift Act of 1988," The Inventor, March 1989; "Essentials of Drafting U.S. Patent Specification and Claims," (2000); Attorney, U.S. International Trade Commission, 1980-1982. *Member:* The District of Columbia Bar; International Trade Commission Trial Lawyers Association. ***PRACTICE AREAS:*** Intellectual Property Law. ***Email:*** sdaniels@armstrongpat.com

WILLIAM LEE BROOKS, born Waynesboro, Virginia, April 16, 1958; admitted to bar, 1987, California; 1988, U.S. District Court, Central District of California; 1989, Virginia; 1990, District of Columbia; U.S. Court of Appeals, Fourth and Ninth Circuits; registered to practice before U.S. Patent and Trademark Office. *Education:* University of Virginia (B.S.E.E., with highest distinction, 1980; M.E.E.E., 1982; J.D., 1987). Tau Beta Pi; Eta Kappa Nu. Member, Moot Court. *Member:* Virginia and American Bar Associations; American Intellectual Property Law Association. ***Email:*** wbrooks@armstrongpat.com

(This Listing Continued)

ASSOCIATES

JOHN P. KONG, born Hong Kong, September 18, 1966; admitted to bar, 1995, California; 1996, District of Columbia and U.S. Court of Appeals for the Federal Circuit; registered to practice before U.S. Patent and Trademark Office. *Education:* Rensselaer Polytechnic Institute; New York University (B.S., Computer Science, magna cum laude, 1988); George Washington University (J.D., 1995). Recipient, Founders Day Award, New York University. *Member:* District of Columbia Bar; State Bar of California; American Bar Association; American Intellectual Property Law Association. ***PRACTICE AREAS:*** Intellectual Property Law. ***Email:*** jkong@armstrongpat.com

JAMES ELWOOD ARMSTRONG, IV, born Silver Spring, Maryland, March 3, 1972; admitted to bar, 1997, Maryland; 1998, District of Columbia; registered to practice before U.S. Patent and Trademark Office, 1998. *Education:* The John Hopkins University (B.S., 1994); The American University (J.D., 1997). Pittsburgh Intellectual Property Law Association, 1997-1998; Law and Rule Committee, 1998. *Member:* Maryland State Bar Association, Inc.; American Intellectual Property Law Association. ***PRACTICE AREAS:*** Intellectual Property (100%). ***Email:*** jarmstrong@armstrongpat.com

SADAO KINASHI, born Toyama, Japan, August 21, 1950; admitted to bar, 1997, District of Columbia; admitted to practice before the U.S. Patent and Trademark Office. *Education:* Osaka University (B.S., 1973); IIT Chicago-Kent College of Law (J.D., 1997). *Member:* The District of Columbia Bar; American Bar Association; American Intellectual Property Law Association. ***LANGUAGES:*** Japanese. ***PRACTICE AREAS:*** Intellectual Property (100%). ***Email:*** skinashi@armstrongpat.com

NICOLAS E. SECKEL, born March 22, 1967; admitted to bar, 1996, France; 1998, New York; registered to practice before U.S. Patent and Trademark Office (Not admitted in District of Columbia). *Education:* Ecole Centrale (M.Eng., 1989); University of Paris; University of Grenoble (J.D., 1992); University of Strasbourg (CEIPI, International Intellectual Property Studies, 1996); Georgetown University Law Center (LL.M., Common Law, with distinction, 1997). Previous Employment: Metz-Patni, Strasbourg, France; Courtassol & Associates, Nice, France. C0-Author: "La confidentialite des Communications Client-Avocat (Attorney-Client Privilege) a l'Epreuve de la Phase d' Acquisition des Preuves (Discovery) dans un Proces aux Etats-Unis", Echanges ASPI, No. 56 (1999); "La Doctrine des Equivalents aux Etats-Unis," Echanges ASPI, No. 61 (2000). ***LANGUAGES:*** French and German. ***PRACTICE AREAS:*** Intellectual Property (100%). ***Email:*** nseckel@armstrongpat.com

THOMAS E. BROWN, born Queens, New York, December 6, 1967; admitted to bar, 1998, Virginia; registered to practice before U.S. Patent and Trademark Office (Not admitted in District of Columbia). *Education:* University of Buffalo (B.S.E.E., cum laude, 1990); George Mason University (J.D., 1996). Patent Examiner, U.S. Patent and Trademark Office, 1991-1998. ***PRACTICE AREAS:*** Patent Prosecution. ***Email:*** tbrown@armstrongpat.com

DANIEL A. GESELOWITZ, born Philadelphia, Pennsylvania, April 19, 1955; admitted to bar, 1982, District of Columbia. *Education:* Haverford College (B.S., in Chemistry, 1976); Stamford University (Ph.D. in Chemistry, 1982). Phi Beta Kappa. Recipient, George Price Prize in Chemistry. *Member:* American Chemical Society; Patent Users Information Group. Biotechnology Fellow: National Cancer Institute and Department of Nuclear Medicine; National Institutes of Health. ***PRACTICE AREAS:*** Preparation and Prosecution of Patent Applications; Appeals before Board of Patent Appeals and Interferences; Petitions to Commissioner of Patents and Trademarks. ***Email:*** dgeselowitz@armstrongpat.com

MICHAEL SCOTT ALPRIN, born Washington, D.C., July 2, 1970; admitted to bar, 2000, Maryland (Not admitted in District of Columbia). *Education:* Colby College (B.A., cum laude, 1992); Washington College of Law of American University (J.D., 2000). *Member:* Maryland State and American Bar Associations. ***LANGUAGES:*** Japanese. ***PRACTICE AREAS:*** Trademark; Patent Litigation; Research. ***Email:*** malprin@armstrongpat.com

JOSEPH L. FELBER, born Sacramento, California, October 31, 1961; admitted to bar, 2000, Virginia; 2001, District of Columbia; registered to practice before U.S. Patent and Trademark Office. *Education:* University of Virginia (B.S., Physics, 1984; M.S. Engineering Physics, 1986); Catholic University of America ((J.D., 2000). *Member:* American Intellectual Property Law Association; Giles S. Rich American Inn of Court. ***PRACTICE AREAS:*** Patent. ***Email:*** jfelber@armstrongpat.com

KENNETH HARRY SALEN, born Springfield, Massachusetts, May 4, 1964; admitted to bar, 2000, Virginia; registered to practice before U.S. Patent and Trademark Office (Not admitted in District of Columbia). *Education:* University of Maryland (B.S., Chemical Engineering, 1989); George Mason University School of Law (J.D., 2000). *Member:* American Bar Association (Member, Intellectual Property Law Section, 1998—); American Intellectual Property Law Association. ***PRACTICE AREAS:*** Intellectual Property; Patents. ***Email:*** ksalen@armstrongpat.com

(This Listing Continued)

ARMSTRONG, WESTERMAN, HATTORI, McLELAND & NAUGHTON, Washington—Continued

OF COUNSEL

LE-NHUNG McLELAND, born Saigon, Vietnam, June 26, 1949; admitted to bar, 1983, District of Columbia; 1999, U.S. Court of Appeals for the Federal Circuit; registered to practice before U.S. Patent and Trademark Office. *Education:* George Mason College (B.A., with distinction, Chem, 1972); George Washington University (M.S., Chem., 1976); American University (J.D., 1982). Co-author: "Patent Systems in Less Developed Countries: The Cases of India and the Andean Pact Countries," 2 The Journal of Law and Technology (I.L.I.) 229 (1987); "La confidenialite des Communications Client-Avocat (Attorney-Client Privilege) a l'Epreuve de la Phase d' Acquisition des Preuves (Discovery) dans un Proces aux Etats-Unis", Echanges ASPI, No. 56 (1999); "Nouvelle Loi sur the Brevets aux Etats-Unis: Consequences pour les Deposants Etrangers," Echanges ASPI, No. 61 (2000). *Member:* The District of Columbia Bar; The Women's Bar Association of the District of Columbia; American Chemical Society; American Intellectual Property Law Association. ***LANGUAGES:*** French. ***Email:*** lmcleland@armstrongpat.com

RONALD F. NAUGHTON, born Brackenridge, Pennsylvania, January 5, 1934; admitted to bar, 1967, Pennsylvania and U.S. District Court, Western District of Pennsylvania; 1977, U.S. Supreme Court; registered to practice before U.S. Patent and Trademark Office (Not admitted in District of Columbia). *Education:* Indiana University of Pennsylvania (B.S., 1957); Duquesne University (J.D., 1966). *Member:* Allegheny County and Pennsylvania Bar Associations; American Intellectual Property Law Association. ***Email:*** rnaughton@armstrongpat.com

JOHN F. CARNEY, born Brockton, Massachusetts, March 12, 1935; admitted to bar, 1962, Connecticut; 1968, U.S. District Court, District of Connecticut; 1975, Pennsylvania and U.S. District Court, Western District of Pennsylvania; 1982, U.S. Court of Appeals for the Federal Circuit; 1985, District of Columbia; registered to practice before U.S. Patent and Trademark Office. *Education:* Northeastern University (B.S.M.E., 1957); George Washington University (J.D., 1961). Pi Tau Sigma; Delta Theta Phi. *Member:* District of Columbia Bar; American Bar Association; American Intellectual Property Law Association; Patent Law Association of Pittsburgh (Member, Board of Governors, 1986-1987).

EDWARD F. WELSH, born Natrona, Pennsylvania, May 20, 1934; admitted to bar, 1963, Pennsylvania and U.S. District Court, Western District of Pennsylvania; 1968, U.S. Supreme Court; 1983, U.S. Court of Appeals, Federal Circuit and U.S. Court of Appeals, Third Circuit; registered to practice before U.S. Patent and Trademark Office. *Education:* U.S. Naval Academy at Annapolis (B.S., 1957); University of Pittsburgh (LL.B., 1963). Arbitrator, American Arbitration Association. *Member:* Allegheny County, Pennsylvania and American Bar Associations; Pittsburgh Intellectual Property Law Association. [1st Lt., U.S. Air Force, 1957-1960]. (Resident at Pittsburgh, Pennsylvania Office). ***PRACTICE AREAS:*** Intellectual Property; Commercial Litigation.

MICHAEL J. CARIDI, born Binghamton, New York, March 8, 1972; admitted to bar, 1997, Maryland; 1999, District of Columbia. *Education:* Catholic University of America (B.A., cum laude, 1994; J.D., 1997). Phi Eta Sigma. ***PRACTICE AREAS:*** Intellectual Property Litigation; International Trade; Commercial Litigation. ***Email:*** mcaridi@armstrongpat.com

LEGAL SUPPORT PERSONNEL

YASUHISA KUROSE, born Hyogo, Japan, September 8, 1954. *Education:* Kansai University (B.A., Electrical Engineering, 1980). 1990, Registered to practice before Japanese Government Patent Office. Lecturer: Industrial Property Right Law, Kansai University, 1990-1995. Member, Western Japan Patent Attorneys Club. *Member:* Japanese Patent Attorneys Association. ***LANGUAGES:*** Japanese. ***Email:*** ykurose@armstrongpat.com

Languages: Japanese, French and Filipino.

ARNOLD & PORTER

THURMAN ARNOLD BUILDING
555 TWELFTH STREET, N.W.
WASHINGTON, D.C. 20004-1206
Telephone: 202-942-5000
Cable Address: "Arfopo"
Telecopy: 202-942-5999
URL: http://www.arnoldporter.com

Northern Virginia Office: 1600 Tysons Boulevard, Suite 900, McLean, Virginia, 22102-4865. Telephone: 212-715-1000. Fax: 212-715-1399.
Los Angeles, California Office: 44th Floor, 777 South Figueroa Street, 90017-2513. Telephone: 213-243-4000. Fax: 213-243-4199.

(This Listing Continued)

LA-Century City Office: Seventeenth Floor, 1900 Avenue of the Stars, Los Angeles, California, 90067-4403. Telephone: 310-552-2500. Fax: 310-552-1191.
Denver, Colorado Office: 370 Seventeenth Street, Suite 4500, 80202-1370. Telephone: 303-863-1000. Fax: 303-832-0428.
New York, New York Office: 399 Park Avenue, 10022-4690. Telephone: 212-715-1000. Fax: 212-715-1399.
The United Kingdom Office: Tower 42, 25 Old Broad Street, London, England, EC2N 1HQ. Telephone: 011-44-20-7786-6100. Fax: 011-44-20-7786-6299.

Antitrust/Competition and Trade Regulation, Bankruptcy, Consumer Products Safety, Corporate and Securities, Derivatives, Employee Benefits, Environmental, Financial Institutions, Food, Drug and Medical Devices, Government Contracts, Health Care, Intellectual Property and Technology, International Litigation and Arbitration, International Trade, Life Sciences, Litigation, National Security Law and Policy, Privacy, Product Liability, Project Finance, Public Policy and Legislative, Real Estate, Tax, Telecommunications.

WASHINGTON, D.C. OFFICE

PARTNERS

BRUCE A. ADAMS, born January 14, 1954; admitted to bar, 1983, Massachusetts; 1985, District of Columbia. *Education:* Swarthmore College (B.A., 1976); Boston University (J.D., 1983). ***PRACTICE AREAS:*** Telecommunications Law. ***Email:*** Bruce_Adams@aporter.com

RICHARD M. ALEXANDER, born April 26, 1957; admitted to bar, 1982, District of Columbia; 1993, U.S. Supreme Court. *Education:* Brandeis University (B.A., magna cum laude with high honors, 1979); Syracuse University (J.D., 1982). ***PRACTICE AREAS:*** Financial Institutions. ***Email:*** Richard_Alexander@aporter.com

DAVID B. APATOFF, born September 28, 1952; admitted to bar, 1977, Illinois; 1979, District of Columbia; 1983, U.S. Claims Court. *Education:* Sarah Lawrence College (B.A., 1974); University of Chicago (J.D., 1977). ***PRACTICE AREAS:*** Intellectual Property; Government Contracts; Administrative. ***Email:*** David_Apatoff@aporter.com

GEOFFREY F. ARONOW, born January 29, 1955; admitted to bar, 1982, District of Columbia. *Education:* Yale University (B.A., summa cum laude, 1976; J.D.,1980). Board Member, ACLU/NCA, 1994—. Director, Division of Enforcement, Commodity Futures Trading Commission, 1995-1999. ***PRACTICE AREAS:*** Litigation; Legislative Practice; Commodities; Securities. ***Email:*** Geoffrey_Aronow@aporter.com

WILLIAM J. BAER, born May 31, 1950; admitted to bar, 1975, Wisconsin; 1980, District of Columbia. *Education:* Lawrence University (B.A., cum laude, 1972); Stanford Law School (J.D., 1975). Phi Beta Kappa. Hilmer Oelman Writing Award. Senior Articles Editor, Stanford University Law Review, 1974-1975. Author: "At the Turning Point: The Commission in 1978," "Marketing and Advertising Regulation, The Federal Trade Commission in the 1990's," (1990). Trial Attorney, Bureau of Consumer Protection, 1975-1977, Attorney Advisor to the Chairman, 1977-1978 and Assistant General Counsel, 1978-1980, Federal Trade Commission. Director, Bureau of Competition, Federal Trade Commission, 1995-1999. Section of Antitrust Law, 1981— and Clayton Act Committee, American Bar Association. American Judicature Society, 1997—. ***PRACTICE AREAS:*** Antitrust; Litigation. ***Email:*** William_Baer@aporter.com

GRANT P. BAGLEY, born April 20, 1941; admitted to bar, 1989, Utah and U.S. Court of Appeals, 10th Circuit; 1990, Colorado; 2000, District of Columbia and U.S. District Court, District of Columbia. *Education:* University of Utah (B.S., 1961); University of Utah College of Law (J.D., 1989). Order of the Coif. William H. Leary Scholar, University of Utah Law School. Vice Chancellor, Moot Court. Licensed Physician: District of Columbia, 1969; Utah, 1972; Colorado, 1984; Idaho, 1984; Maryland, 1990; California, 1990; Virginia, 2000. Publications: Medicare Coverage for Oncology Services, Cancer (Supp.) 82:10, 1998; FDA Sanctions for Practitioners for Violation of Clinical Trial Regulations and other Misconduct, Federation Bulletin 81:1, 1994; A Qualitative Analysis of Self Reported Difficulties with Silicone Breast Implants, Women's Health 2:2, 1993; A Descriptive Analysis of Physical Complaints from Women with Silicone Breast Implants, Women's Health 2:2, 1993; Informed Consent: An FDA Perspective, DIA Journal Vol. 27, 1993; Informed Consent, Food and Drug Law Journal 48:2, 1993; Food: Labeling Forms, American Family Physicians 45:3, 1992; Carcinoma of the Infant Vagina, Arch Path 90:473, 1970; Reliability of Cr 51 Isotope Scanning in the Diagnosis and Management of Placenta Previa, Ann D.C. Medical Society 40:1, Jan. 1971; Laparoscopy, A Modern Gynecologic Necessity. Ann D.C. Medical Society 41:165, Mar. 1971; Removal of a Mulligan Hood with the Laparoscope, Obstetrician Gynecology 59:950, June 1972; Development of Human Palmar and Digital Flexion Creases, Journal of Pediatrics 113:128, July 1998; Laparoscopic Outpatient Sterilization, Association, Voluntary Surgical Sterilization AVSC News 27:2, Oct. 1989. American Bar Association, 2000. American College of Obstetricians and Gynecologists, 1975. National Health Lawyers Association, 1990. American College of Legal Medicine, 1990. American Medical Association, 1995.

(This Listing Continued)

[U.S. Air Force, 1966-1968, Maryland Air National Guard, 1968-1970, Major]. ***PRACTICE AREAS:*** Health Care; Drug and Reimbursement; Health Policy and Practice. ***Email:*** Grant_Bagley@aporter.com

RICHARD E. BALTZ, born March 3, 1960; admitted to bar, 1985, Pennsylvania; 1991, District of Columbia. *Education:* Dickinson College (B.A., 1982); George Washington University (J.D., with honors, 1985). Attorney, 1985-1989, Deputy Chief, Office of Tender Offers, Division of Corporation Finance, 1988-1989, Securities and Exchange Commission. ***PRACTICE AREAS:*** Federal Securities Law; Corporate. ***Email:*** Richard_Baltz@aporter.com

LEONARD H. BECKER, born November 15, 1943; admitted to bar, 1969, New York; 1970, District of Columbia. *Education:* Harvard University (B.A., 1965); Yale University (LL.B., 1968). Phi Beta Kappa. District of Columbia Bar Counsel, 1992-1999. District of Columbia Bar, Multi-Disciplinary Practice Committee, 1999—. ***PRACTICE AREAS:*** Litigation; Professional Responsibility. ***Email:*** Len_Becker@aporter.com

DONALD O. BEERS, born May 28, 1949; admitted to bar, 1975, New York (resigned, 1996); 1986, District of Columbia and U.S. Supreme Court. *Education:* Dartmouth College (A.B., 1971); Columbia University (J.D., 1974). Columbia University Law Review. Law Clerk to Judge Milton Pollack, Southern District of New York, 1974-1975. Lecturer, Food and Drug Law, University of Pennsylvania School of Law, 1982-1984. Attorney, Office of Chief Counsel, FDA, 1975-1985. Associate Chief Counsel for Enforcement, FDA, 1978-1985. Associate Chief Counsel for Drugs, FDA, 1984-1985. ***PRACTICE AREAS:*** Food and Drug Regulation. ***Email:*** Donald_Beers@aporter.com

KATHLEEN A. BEHAN, born July 28, 1963; admitted to bar, 1989, Maryland; 1991, District of Columbia. *Education:* Yale University (B.A., magna cum laude, 1985); Columbia Law School (J.D., 1989). ***PRACTICE AREAS:*** Civil Litigation; Criminal Litigation. ***Email:*** Kathleen_Behan@aporter.com

ALEXANDER E. BENNETT, born August 9, 1940; admitted to bar, 1964, District of Columbia. *Education:* University of Michigan (A.B., 1961; J.D., 1963). Michigan Law Review. ***PRACTICE AREAS:*** Litigation. ***Email:*** Alexander_Bennett@aporter.com

JOHN T. BENTIVOGLIO, born October 6, 1963; admitted to bar, 1994, Maryland and District of Columbia. *Education:* University of California, Berkeley (B.A., 1988); Georgetown University Law Center (J.D., 1993). ***PRACTICE AREAS:*** Privacy; Internet Healthcare; Food, Drug and Medical Devices; Public Policy and Legislative; Health Care and Pharmaceutical Fraud; Fraud, Abuse and Compliance; Life Sciences. ***Email:*** John_Bentivoglio@aporter.com

PAUL S. BERGER, born August 25, 1932; admitted to bar, 1958, New York; 1961, District of Columbia. *Education:* University of Scranton (B.S., 1954); New York University (LL.B., 1957). New York University Law Review. Trustee, New York University Law Center Foundation, 1981—. ***PRACTICE AREAS:*** International Finance; International Transactions; Tax; Government Relations. ***Email:*** Paul_Berger@aporter.com

DAVID B. BERGMAN, born November 27, 1963; admitted to bar, 1991, Pennsylvania; 1992, District of Columbia. *Education:* Queen Mary College, London, England; Haverford College (B.A., 1986); Northwestern University (J.D., 1991). ***PRACTICE AREAS:*** Civil Litigation; International Arbitration; White Collar Criminal Litigation. ***Email:*** David_Bergman@aporter.com

MICHAEL L. BERNSTEIN, born February 29, 1964; admitted to bar, 1989, Pennsylvania; 1990, District of Columbia. *Education:* Brandeis University (B.A., cum laude, 1986); University of East Anglia, England; Northwestern University (J.D., cum laude, 1989). Journal of Criminal Law & Criminology. Law Clerk to Honorable Judith N. Keep, U.S. District Court, Southern District of California, 1989-1990. ***PRACTICE AREAS:*** Bankruptcy; Creditors' Rights. ***Email:*** Michael_Bernstein@aporter.com

JUDITH BERNSTEIN-GAETA, born November 27, 1950; admitted to bar, 1992, Connecticut; 1993, Maryland and District of Columbia. *Education:* University of North Dakota (B.S., 1976); Columbus School of Law, Catholic University of America (J.D., with high honors, 1992). ***PRACTICE AREAS:*** Commercial Litigation. ***Email:*** Judith_Bernstein-Gaeta@aporter.com

BLAKE A. BILES, born November 2, 1946; admitted to bar, 1975, Kansas; 1994, District of Columbia. *Education:* University of Kansas (B.A., 1968; J.D., 1975). Kansas Law Review. Office of Water Enforcement, 1975-1976; Office of General Enforcement (Toxic Substances), 1976-1977; Office of General Counsel (Toxic Substances), 1977; Director, Premanufacture Review Division, Office of Pesticides and Toxic Substances, 1978-1980, U.S. Environmental Protection Agency. ***PRACTICE AREAS:*** Environmental; Consumer Products; Administrative. ***Email:*** Blake_Biles@aporter.com

EDWARD E. BINTZ, born September 29, 1958; admitted to bar, 1985, New York; 1988, District of Columbia. *Education:* Fordham University (B.S., 1980); George Washington University (J.D., 1984); Georgetown University (LL.M., Tax, 1993). George Washington Law Review. ***PRACTICE AREAS:*** Benefits and Employment Law. ***Email:*** Edward_Bintz@aporter.com

PETER K. BLEAKLEY, born August 19, 1936; admitted to bar, 1962, Virginia; 1966, District of Columbia. *Education:* University of Virginia (B.A., 1958; LL.B., 1962). Trial Attorney: Federal Trade Commission, 1962-1966 and Antitrust Division, U.S. Department of Justice, 1966. Fellow, American College of Trial Lawyers. ***PRACTICE AREAS:*** Litigation; Products Liability; Antitrust and Trade Regulation. ***Email:*** Peter_Bleakley@aporter.com

BROOKSLEY BORN, born August 27, 1940; admitted to bar, 1966, District of Columbia. *Education:* Stanford University (A.B., 1961; J.D., 1964). President, Stanford Law Review. Recipient, Outstanding Senior Award, 1964. Adjunct Professor, Georgetown University Law Center, 1972-1973. Chairperson, Commodity Futures Trading Commission, 1996-1999. State Delegate for the District of Columbia American Bar Association, 1994—. ***PRACTICE AREAS:*** Derivatives; Civil Litigation. ***Email:*** Brooksley_Born@aporter.com

JEFFREY S. BROMME, born July 22, 1960; admitted to bar, 1986, Texas (inactive); 1988, District of Columbia. *Education:* University of Texas School of Law (J.D., with high honors, 1986). Order of the Coif. Articles Editor, Texas Law Review, 1985-1986. Law Clerk, Honorable Will Garwood, U.S. Court of Appeals, Fifth Circuit, 1986-1987. General Counsel, U.S. Consumer Product Safety Commission, 1997-1999. ***Email:*** Jeffrey_Bromme@aporter.com

JEFFREY A. BURT, born April 27, 1944; admitted to bar, 1971, Maryland, District of Columbia; 1983, U.S. Supreme Court. *Education:* Princeton University (A.B., magna cum laude, 1966); Yale University (M.A., 1970; LL.B., 1970). Yale Law Journal. Adjunct Professor of Law, Georgetown University Law Center, 1988-1994. Law Clerk to Judge Simon E. Sobeloff, U.S. Court of Appeals, Fourth Circuit, 1970-1971. Co-Chairperson, Committee on Newly Independent States of FSU, Section on International Law, American Bar Association, 1991-1999. ***PRACTICE AREAS:*** International; Litigation. ***Email:*** Jeffrey_Burt@aporter.com

MICHAEL CAGLIOTI, born February 17, 1958; admitted to bar, 1991, New York, Connecticut and District of Columbia. *Education:* Iona College (B.A., summa cum laude, 1980); Woodrow Wilson School (M.P.A., 1984); Princeton University (M.A., 1986); Yale University (J.D., 1990). Yale Journal of International Law. Yale Law Journal. ***PRACTICE AREAS:*** Financial Institutions; Litigation. ***Email:*** Michael_Caglioti@aporter.com

SUSAN BOOTH CASSIDY, born August 5, 1963; admitted to bar, 1989, Massachusetts; 1990, District of Columbia. *Education:* University of Lowell (B.S., magna cum laude, 1985); American University, Washington College of Law (J.D., cum laude, 1988). American University Law Review. ***PRACTICE AREAS:*** Government Contracts; Litigation. ***Email:*** Susan_Cassidy@aporter

HOWARD NEIL CAYNE, born March 11, 1954; admitted to bar, 1980, New York and District of Columbia. *Education:* University of Rochester (B.A., 1976); Washington University (J.D., 1979). Lecturer on Law in the Boston University Graduate Program in Banking Law Studies, 1991-1996. Senior Attorney, Office of the Comptroller of the Currency, 1979-1983. ***PRACTICE AREAS:*** Financial Institutions; Government Contracts; Litigation. ***Email:*** Howard_Cayne@aporter.com

BRUCE M. CHADWICK, born September 10, 1946; admitted to bar, 1973, Michigan; 1978, District of Columbia. *Education:* Oakland University (B.A., cum laude, 1968); University of Michigan (J.D., magna cum laude, 1972). University of Michigan Law Review. Attorney, Federal Trade Commission, 1972-1976. ***PRACTICE AREAS:*** Litigation; Products Liability. ***Email:*** Bruce_Chadwick@aporter.com

JEROME I. CHAPMAN, born January 15, 1939; admitted to bar, 1965, District of Columbia. *Education:* Tulane University (B.A., 1960); Universite d'Aix-Marseille (Universite de Provence), France; Harvard University (J.D., magna cum laude, 1964). Harvard Law Review. Fulbright Scholar, 1960-1961. Law Clerk to Hon. Elbert P. Tuttle, U.S. Court of Appeals, 1964-1965. Assistant to the Solicitor General, U.S. Department of Justice, 1965-1967. Office of Transition Counsel, Clinton-Gore Transition, 1992-1993. ***PRACTICE AREAS:*** Antitrust; Civil Litigation. ***Email:*** Jerome_Chapman@aporter.com

MARTHA L. COCHRAN, born August 24, 1948; admitted to bar, 1973, Florida; 1976, District of Columbia; 1987, Maryland. *Education:* University of Florida (B.S., 1970; J.D., 1973). Chief Counsel and Staff Director, U.S. Senate Committee on Banking, Housing and Urban Affairs, Subcommittee on Securities, 1989-1994. Legislative Director, U.S. Senator Christopher Dodd, 1987-1988. Senior Finance Counsel, U.S. House of Representatives, Committee on Energy and Commerce, Subcommittee on Telecommunications and Finance, 1981-1987. Special Counsel, Division of Enforcement, U.S. Securities and Exchange Commission, 1975-1981. Chair, American Bar Association Subcommittee on SEC Administration, Budget and Legislation, Federal Regulation of Securities Committee. Vice Chair, American Bar Association Committee on Legislation, Section of Business Law. Secretary-Treasurer, Federal Bar Association, Securities Law Committee, Executive Council. Board of Advisors, Securities Reform Act Litigation Reporter. National Association of Securities Dealers Legal Advisory Board. ***PRACTICE AREAS:*** Corporate; Securities; SEC Enforcement Matters; Financial Institutions; Legislative; Political Law; Ethics Counseling. ***Email:*** Martha_Cochran@aporter.com

ROBERT B. CONLEY, born September 22, 1960; admitted to bar, 1993, North Carolina; 1995, District of Columbia. *Education:* Dartmouth College

(This Listing Continued)

ARNOLD & PORTER, Washington—Continued

(B.A., cum laude, 1982); University of North Carolina Medical School (M.D., 1986); University of Virginia (J.D., 1990). Order of the Coif. Virginia Law Review. Law Clerk, Hon. J. Harvie Wilkinson, III, U.S. Court of Appeals, Fourth Circuit, 1990-1991. ***PRACTICE AREAS:*** Food and Drug Law; Products Liability. ***Email:*** Robert_Conley@aporter.com

WILLIAM EDRO COOK, JR., born February 19, 1962; admitted to bar, 1990, District of Columbia. *Education:* Duke University (A.B., magna cum laude, 1984); Harvard University (J.D., cum laude, 1987). Harvard Civil Rights-Civil Liberties Law Review. Law Clerk to Hon. Richard C. Erwin, U.S. District Court, Middle District of North Carolina, 1987-1988. ***PRACTICE AREAS:*** Telecommunications. ***Email:*** William_Cook@aporter.com

JAMES L. COOPER, born July 20, 1964; admitted to bar, 1992, Pennsylvania; 1993, District of Columbia. *Education:* University of Chicago (A.B., special honors, 1986; A.M., 1987); Indiana University School of Law (J.D., magna cum laude, 1991); Indiana University (Ph.D., 1993). Indiana Law Journal. Law Clerk, Hon. Bruce M. Selya, U.S. Court of Appeals, First Circuit, 1991-1992. ***PRACTICE AREAS:*** Litigation; Antitrust. ***Email:*** James_Cooper@aporter.com

GEORGE E. COVUCCI, born August 15, 1951; admitted to bar, 1976, Virginia; 1977, District of Columbia. *Education:* City College of New York (B.A., 1972); Georgetown University (J.D., 1976). American Criminal Law Review. ***PRACTICE AREAS:*** Real Estate; Tax and Estates; Bankruptcy. ***Email:*** George_Covucci@aporter.com

MICHAEL D. DANEKER, born June 11, 1965; admitted to bar, 1992, Maryland; 1993, District of Columbia. *Education:* Yale University (B.A., summa cum laude, 1987); Cambridge University, England (M.Phil., 1988); Vanderbilt University (J.D., 1992). Founders' Medal; John Wade Scholar. Vanderbilt Law Review. Law Clerk, Hon. Karen LeCraft Henderson, U.S. Court of Appeals for the District of Columbia Circuit, 1992-1993. ***PRACTICE AREAS:*** Environmental; Litigation. ***Email:*** Michael_Daneker@aporter.com

PATRICIA ANN DEAN, born April 11, 1949; admitted to bar, 1981, District of Columbia. *Education:* Georgetown University (B.S.B.A., cum laude, 1975; J.D., cum laude, 1981). Georgetown Law Journal. Law Clerk to: Hon. Edward A. Tamm, U.S. Court of Appeals, District of Columbia Circuit, 1981-1982; Hon. Byron R. White, U.S. Supreme Court, 1982-1983. Deputy Clerk, Supreme Court of the United States, 1981. ***PRACTICE AREAS:*** Litigation. ***Email:*** Patricia_Dean@aporter.com

ELI WHITNEY DEBEVOISE, II, born February 8, 1953; admitted to bar, 1977, District of Columbia. *Education:* Yale University (B.A., summa cum laude, 1974); Harvard University (J.D., 1977). Harvard International Law Journal. Law Clerk, Hon. William J. Holloway, Jr., U.S. Court of Appeals, Tenth Circuit, 1978-1979. ***PRACTICE AREAS:*** International Law. ***Email:*** Whitney_Debevoise@aporter.com

JACQUELINE R. DENNING, born December 16, 1948; admitted to bar, 1976, Maryland; 1980, District of Columbia and U.S. Supreme Court. *Education:* Emory University (B.S., valedictorian, 1971); College of William & Mary (J.D., 1976). William & Mary Law Review. ***PRACTICE AREAS:*** Litigation. ***Email:*** Jacqueline_Denning@aporter.com

STEVEN S. DIAMOND, born August 27, 1956; admitted to bar, 1981, District of Columbia; 1982, U.S. Court of Federal Claims. *Education:* University of Michigan (B.A., with high honors, high distinction, 1978; J.D., cum laude, 1981); Stanford University. Chair, International Procurement Committee, International Law Section, American Bar Association, 1989-1992. ***PRACTICE AREAS:*** Government Contracts; Corporate Transactions; Commercial Arbitration; Intellectual Property. ***Email:*** Steven_Diamond@aporter.com

A. PATRICK DOYLE, born September 6, 1948; admitted to bar, 1976, New York; 1985, District of Columbia. *Education:* State University of New York at Oswego (B.A., 1971); Syracuse University (J.D., 1975). Syracuse Journal of International Law and Commerce. Counsel, Multinational Banking Division, Office of the Comptroller of the Currency, 1979-1981. Deputy General Counsel and Acting General Counsel, Federal Home Loan Bank Board, 1982-1983. Adjunct Professor of Law, Morin Center for Banking Law Studies, Boston University School of Law, 1985-1993. ***PRACTICE AREAS:*** Financial Institutions; Corporate; Securities. ***Email:*** A._Patrick_Doyle@aporter.com

DOUGLAS A. DWORKIN, born June 7, 1947; admitted to bar, 1977, District of Columbia, Colorado and California. *Education:* Oberlin College (B.A., magna cum laude, 1968); Yale University (M.A., 1970; J.D., 1976). Executive Assistant to Deputy Secretary of State, 1979-1981. ***PRACTICE AREAS:*** Litigation; International; International Litigation; Arbitration; Public Policy and Legislative; National Security Law and Policy. ***Email:*** Douglas_Dworkin@aporter.com

DAVID S. EGGERT, born August 16, 1960; admitted to bar, 1984, District of Columbia. *Education:* Loyola University (B.A., 1981); Duke University (J.D., summa cum laude, 1984). Duke Law Journal. ***PRACTICE AREAS:*** Litigation; Antitrust; Products Liability; Class Actions. ***Email:*** David_Eggert@aporter.com

RICHARD S. EWING, born June 27, 1938; admitted to bar, 1965, District of Columbia. *Education:* Cornell University (B.A., 1960); New York University (LL.B., 1963). New York University Law Review. Bigelow Teaching Fellow, University of Chicago Law School, 1963-1964. Board of Governors, Court of Federal Claims Bar Association, 1998—; Member, Advisory Council to the Court of Federal Claims, 1997—; Co-Chair, Health Care Committee, 1999—, Deputy Chair or Member, Section Council, 1994—, Chair, Bid Protest Committee, 1994-1998, Government Contracts Section, Federal Bar Association. ***PRACTICE AREAS:*** Health Care; Government Contracts. ***Email:*** Richard_Ewing@aporter.com

DEBORAH L. FEINSTEIN, born December 30, 1960; admitted to bar, 1987, District of Columbia. *Education:* University of California at Berkeley (B.A., with honors, 1983); Harvard University (J.D., cum laude, 1987). Assistant to the Director, Bureau of Competition, Federal Trade Commission, 1989-1991. Attorney Adviser, Commissioner Dennis A. Yao, Federal Trade Commission, 1991. ***PRACTICE AREAS:*** Antitrust. ***Email:*** Deborah_Feinstein@aporter.com

ROGER P. FENDRICH, born December 27, 1943; admitted to bar, 1980, District of Columbia; 1987, U.S. Supreme Court. *Education:* University of Miami (A.B., 1965); University of Texas (Ph.D., 1971); Yale University (J.D., 1980). Woodrow Wilson Fellow. Yale Journal of International Law. Law Clerk to Hon. Jose A. Cabranes, U.S., District Court, District of Connecticut, 1980. Vice-Chairman, Committee on Criminal Law and the Administrative Process, Administrative Law Section, American Bar Association, 1987-1995. Consultant, Federal Courts Study Committee, 1989. Barrister, American Inns of Court. ***PRACTICE AREAS:*** Litigation. ***Email:*** Roger_Fendrich@aporter.com

RICHARD M. FIRESTONE, born May 28, 1948; admitted to bar, 1973, Ohio; 1974, Michigan; 1981, District of Columbia; 1986, U.S. Supreme Court. *Education:* University of Michigan (B.A., cum laude, 1970; J.D., cum laude, 1973). Chief, Common Carrier Bureau, Federal Communications Commission, 1989-1992. Chief Counsel, National Telecommunications and Information Administration, 1979-1989. Assistant Attorney General, Antitrust Section, Office of the Attorney General of Ohio, 1973-1979. ***PRACTICE AREAS:*** Telecommunications; International; Legislative. ***Email:*** Richard_Firestone@aporter.com

JAMES F. FITZPATRICK, born January 18, 1933; admitted to bar, 1959, Indiana; 1962, District of Columbia. *Education:* Indiana University (A.B., 1955; J.D., 1959); Corpus Christi College of University of Cambridge, Cambridge, England (1956). Indiana University Law Journal. ***PRACTICE AREAS:*** Legislation; Public Policy; Administrative Law. ***Email:*** James_Fitzpatrick@aporter.com

SAMUEL A. FLAX, born May 24, 1956; admitted to bar, 1981, Georgia; 1982, District of Columbia. *Education:* Georgia Institute of Technology (B.I.E., 1978); Washington and Lee University (J.D., 1981). Washington and Lee Law Review. Clerk to Hon. H. Emory Widener, Jr., U.S. Court of Appeals, Fourth Circuit, 1981-1982. ***PRACTICE AREAS:*** Corporate; Securities; Bankruptcy; Real Estate. ***Email:*** Samuel_Flax@aporter.com

SONIA (TURCOTTE) FOIS, born March 4, 1958; admitted to bar, 1988, New York; 1989, District of Columbia. *Education:* Colby College (A.B., summa cum laude, 1980); Georgetown University (J.D., magna cum laude, 1987). Georgetown Law Journal. ***PRACTICE AREAS:*** Public Policy; Legislative. ***Email:*** Sonia_Fois@aporter.com

THEODORE D. FRANK, born April 1, 1941; admitted to bar, 1966, Texas; 1969, District of Columbia. *Education:* Rensselaer Polytechnic Institute (B.S., 1963); University of Texas (LL.B., with honors, 1966); Harvard University (LL.M., 1969). Texas Law Review. Chancellors. Law Clerk, Honorable Walter P. Gewin, U.S. Circuit Judge, U.S. Court of Appeals, Fifth Circuit, 1966-1967. Faculty Assistant, Ames Competition, Harvard Law School, 1967-1969. Executive Committee, 1995-1998, Co-Chair, Ad Hoc Committee on National Telecommunications Moot Court Competition, 1994-1995, 1998-2000, Federal Communications Bar Association; Hearing Committee Member, Board of Professional Responsibility, District of Columbia Bar, 1997—. ***PRACTICE AREAS:*** Telecommunications; Communications; Administrative Law. ***Email:*** Theodore_Frank@aporter.com

JOEL M. FREED, born October 28, 1943; admitted to bar, 1970, Virginia and District of Columbia; registered to practice before U.S. Patent and Trademark Office. *Education:* Lehigh University (B.A., 1965; B.S.M.E., 1966); Georgetown University Law Center (J.D., 1970). Phi Delta Phi; Pi Tau Sigma. Staff Editor, Georgetown University Law Journal, 1969-1970. Adjunct Professor, Georgetown University Law Center, 1975—. Instructor, Legal Method, Advanced Training Program, U.S. Patent and Trademark Office, 1980-1990. ***PRACTICE AREAS:*** Intellectual Property; Litigation; Patent Law; Patent, Trademark and Copyright Law; Trade Secrets. ***Email:*** Joel_Freed@aporter.com

DAVID F. FREEMAN, JR., born September 10, 1959; admitted to bar, 1987, Virginia; 1988, District of Columbia; 1991, U.S. Supreme Court. *Educa-*

(This Listing Continued)

(This Listing Continued)

tion: University of Virginia (B.A., with high distinction, 1981; M.B.A., 1987; J.D., 1987). Phi Beta Kappa. Virginia Law Review. Faculty Award for Academic Excellence. ***PRACTICE AREAS:*** Financial Institutions; Securities. ***Email:*** David_Freeman@aporter.com

MELVIN C. GARBOW, born September 11, 1933; admitted to bar, 1960, District of Columbia. *Education:* Purdue University (B.S., 1955); George Washington University (J.D., 1960). George Washington Law Review. Law Clerk to Chief Judge Marvin Jones, U.S. Court of Claims, 1960-1961. ***PRACTICE AREAS:*** Antitrust; Litigation; Government Contracts; Real Estate. ***Email:*** Melvin_Garbow@aporter.com

MURRAY R. GARNICK, born September 4, 1959; admitted to bar, 1986, District of Columbia. *Education:* University of Georgia (B.A., summa cum laude, 1981; J.D., summa cum laude, 1984). Georgia Law Review. Law Clerk to, Honorable Carolyn Dineen King, U.S. Court of Appeals, Fifth Circuit, 1984-1985. ***PRACTICE AREAS:*** Litigation; Products Liability. ***Email:*** Murray_Garnick@aporter.com

ROBERT A. GARRETT, born October 6, 1948; admitted to bar, 1973, Illinois; 1977, District of Columbia. *Education:* Northwestern University (B.A., 1970; J.D., cum laude, 1973). Northwestern University Law Review. Law Clerk to Judge John Paul Stevens, U.S. Court of Appeals, Seventh Circuit, 1974-1975. Assistant to the General Counsel, Department of Army, 1975-1976. ***PRACTICE AREAS:*** Telecommunications Law; Communications; Intellectual Property; Sports and Entertainment; Litigation. ***Email:*** Robert_Garrett@aporter.com

DAVID P. GERSCH, born November 25, 1956; admitted to bar, 1982, District of Columbia. *Education:* Oberlin College (A.B., 1978); New York University (J.D., cum laude, 1982). ***PRACTICE AREAS:*** Litigation; Antitrust. ***Email:*** David_Gersch@aporter.com

JONATHAN GLEKLEN, born August 28, 1966; admitted to bar, 1993, Maryland; 1994, District of Columbia; 1996, U.S. Court of Appeals, Eleventh Circuit; 1999, U.S. Court of Appeals, Federal Circuit. *Education:* Yale University (B.A., cum laude, 1988); University of Chicago (J.D., with honors, 1993). Editorial Board, ABA Section of Antitrust Law, 1998 Annual Review of Antitrust Law Developments. ***PRACTICE AREAS:*** Antitrust; Intellectual Property. ***Email:*** Jonathan_Gleklen@aporter.com

NEIL M. GOODMAN, born May 10, 1957; admitted to bar, 1984, District of Columbia. *Education:* Brown University (A.B., 1979); Columbia University (J.D., 1983). Columbia Law Review. Law Clerk to Hon. Frank J. Battisti, Chief Judge, U.S. District Court, Northern District of Ohio, 1983-1984. ***PRACTICE AREAS:*** Corporate; International. ***Email:*** Neil_Goodman@aporter.com

MICHAEL D. GOODWIN, born May 5, 1960; admitted to bar, 1984, Virginia; 1985, District of Columbia. *Education:* The University of Chicago (B.A., with honors, 1981); Harvard University (J.D., cum laude, 1984). ***PRACTICE AREAS:*** Real Estate. ***Email:*** Michael_Goodwin@aporter.com

PATRICK J. GRANT, born August 12, 1951; admitted to bar, 1977, District of Columbia. *Education:* Georgetown University (A.B., 1973; J.D., 1977). Georgetown Law Journal. PLI Communications Law Faculty, 1987—. ***PRACTICE AREAS:*** Telecommunications; Cable Television; Litigation. ***Email:*** Patrick_Grant@aporter.com

JULIUS M. GREISMAN, born July 22, 1914; admitted to bar, 1937, New York; 1958, District of Columbia. *Education:* College of the City of New York (B.S.S., 1934); Brooklyn Law School (LL.B., cum laude, 1937). Brooklyn Law Review. Attorney, Tax Legislative Counsel, U.S. Treasury Department, 1948-1956. ***PRACTICE AREAS:*** Tax. ***Email:*** Julius_Greisman@aporter.com

PETER T. GROSSI, JR., born August 4, 1947; admitted to bar, 1974, Connecticut; 1975, District of Columbia. *Education:* Trinity College (B.A., M.A., 1969); Yale University (J.D., 1973). Yale Law Journal. Law Clerk to Hon. J. Joseph Smith, U.S. Court of Appeals, Second Circuit, 1973-1974. ***PRACTICE AREAS:*** Litigation; Products Liability; Antitrust; Food and Drug. ***Email:*** Peter_Grossi@aporter.com

DREW A. HARKER, born April 9, 1956; admitted to bar, 1986, Pennsylvania; 1988, District of Columbia. *Education:* University of California at San Diego (B.A., cum laude, 1979); Princeton University (M.P.A., 1981); Georgetown University (J.D., cum laude, 1986). Professional Staff Member, Committee on Armed Services, U.S. Senate, 1981-1986. Vice Chair, International Procurement Committee, Section on International Law, American Bar Association. ***PRACTICE AREAS:*** Government Contracts; Litigation; Legislative. ***Email:*** Drew_Harker@aporter.com

CATHY HOFFMAN, born December 10, 1959; admitted to bar, 1989, District of Columbia. *Education:* Colgate University (B.A., 1981); University of Minnesota (J.D., magna cum laude, 1987). Minnesota Law Review. Judicial Clerk, Judge Donald P. Lay, U.S. Court of Appeals, Eighth Circuit, 1987-1988. ***PRACTICE AREAS:*** Antitrust; Litigation. ***Email:*** Cathy_Hoffman@aporter.com

PHILIP W. HORTON, born April 22, 1955; admitted to bar, 1980, Massachusetts; 1983, District of Columbia. *Education:* Yale (A.B., summa cum

(This Listing Continued)

laude, 1977); Harvard (J.D., magna cum laude, 1980). Board of Directors, Washington Council of Lawyers, 1987—, Secretary, 1991-1994 and Treasurer, 1995—. Board of Trustees, Legal Aid Society of the District of Columbia, 1997—. ***PRACTICE AREAS:*** Litigation; Telecommunications. ***Email:*** Philip_Horton@aporter.com

ROBERTA LAZARUS HORTON, born February 22, 1961; admitted to bar, 1986, Illinois; 1988, District of Columbia. *Education:* Yale University (B.A., summa cum laude, with distinction, 1983; J.D., 1986). Judicial Clerk to Judge Sam J. Ervin, III, U.S. District Court of Appeals, Fourth Circuit, 1986-1987. Roberta Horton and David Rhodes, "Internet Forms & Commentary: A Practitioner's Guide to E-Commerce Contracts & the World Wide Web (Web Advertising Model Agreement)," American Bar Association Publication, (in progress); International Trademark Association (Publications Committee, 1994-1996); Computer Law Association. ***PRACTICE AREAS:*** Intellectual Property; Litigation. ***Email:*** Roberta_Horton@aporter.com

JOSEPH G. HOWE, III, born May 26, 1952; admitted to bar, 1978, Virginia; 1984, District of Columbia. *Education:* University of Virginia (B.A., 1975; J.D., 1978); Georgetown University (M.L.T., in Taxation, 1982). Author: "Tax Compliance Act of 1995: Busting Foreign Trusts," 1 Journal of Asset Protection, 1995; "The Impact of the Moynihan Legislation on Foreign Trust Busting Initiatives," 2 Journal of Asset Protection, 1996. Adjunct Law School Faculty: Washington College of Law, American University, 1988-1992; The George Washington University, National Law Center, 1996. Editorial Advisor and Regular Contributor: Real Estate Tax Digest; Journal of Asset Protection; Journal of Business Entities. *Member:* The District of Columbia Bar; Virginia State Bar. ***PRACTICE AREAS:*** International Taxation; International Joint Ventures; Real Estate Investment Taxation; Taxation Law; Real Estate Finance Law. ***Email:*** Joseph_Howe@aporter.com

RICHARD L. HUBBARD, born May 27, 1943; admitted to bar, 1968, District of Columbia. *Education:* Williams College (B.A., magna cum laude, 1964); Harvard University (LL.B., magna cum laude, 1967). Harvard Legal Aid Bureau, 1965-1967. Law Clerk to Judge Arnold Raum, U.S. Tax Court, 1967-1969. ***PRACTICE AREAS:*** Tax; Employee Benefits. ***Email:*** Richard_Hubbard@aporter.com

GARY E. HUMES, born August 2, 1950; admitted to bar, 1981, District of Columbia. *Education:* Wesleyan University (B.A., 1972); University of Chicago (S.M., 1974); Cornell Law School (J.D., 1981). Cornell Law Review. ***PRACTICE AREAS:*** Real Estate. ***Email:*** Gary_Humes@aporter.com

DARRYL W. JACKSON, born February 1, 1953; admitted to bar, 1977, Pennsylvania; 1979, District of Columbia. *Education:* Lincoln University (B.A., cum laude, 1974); The American University, Cairo Egypt; Howard University (J.D., 1977). Howard Law Journal. Assistant U.S. Attorney, Washington, D.C., 1980-1992 (Executive Assistant U.S. Attorney for Operations; Acting Chief and Deputy Chief, Special Prosecutions Section). Visiting Professor of Law, The George Washington University National Law Center, 1989-1990. Distinguished Lecturer in Law, 1990—; Lecturer in Law, 1985-1989, Catholic University of America School of Law. Assistant Defender, The Defender Association of Philadelphia, 1977-1980. Vice Chair, White Collar Crime Committee, 1993-1996, American Bar Association. President, Charles Fahy American Inn of Court, 1996-1998. ***PRACTICE AREAS:*** Litigation; White Collar Criminal Defense. ***Email:*** Darryl_Jackson@aporter.com

RICHARD A. JOHNSON, born March 23, 1950; admitted to bar, 1977, California; 1978, District of Columbia. *Education:* Brown University (A.B., 1972); Massachusetts Institute of Technology (M.S., 1973); Harvard University; Yale University (J.D., 1976). Yale Law Journal. Swedish Government Prize in Law, Economics and Public Policy, 1978. Law Clerk to Judge Eugene A. Wright, U.S. Court of Appeals, Ninth Circuit, Seattle, Washington, 1976-1977. Associate General Counsel for International Trade, U.S. Department of Commerce, 1980-1981. Executive Council and Co-Chair, Annual Meeting, 1995, American Society of International Law. MIT Corporation Visiting Committee. ***PRACTICE AREAS:*** Life Sciences; International Trade Law; Information Technology. ***Email:*** Richard_Johnson@aporter.com

ROBERT J. JONES, born October 24, 1948; admitted to bar, 1973, Kansas; 1974, District of Columbia. *Education:* University of Kansas (B.A., 1970; J.D., 1973). Kansas Law Review. Adjunct Professor, Georgetown University Law Center, 1983-1987. ***PRACTICE AREAS:*** Tax Law; Federal Income Tax. ***Email:*** Robert_Jones@aporter.com

JAMES P. JOSEPH, born August 5, 1962; admitted to bar, 1989, District of Columbia and U.S. Tax Court. *Education:* Georgetown University (B.A., cum laude, 1984; J.D., magna cum laude, 1989). Executive Board and Writing Program Director, Law and Policy in International Business, 1988-1989. ***PRACTICE AREAS:*** Tax. ***Email:*** James_Joseph@aporter.com

SARAH ELIZABETH KAHN, born February 2, 1964; admitted to bar, 1991, District of Columbia. *Education:* University of North Carolina (B.A., 1986); Georgetown University (J.D., cum laude, 1991). DePaul University Law Review. ***PRACTICE AREAS:*** Corporate; Securities.

(This Listing Continued)

ARNOLD & PORTER, Washington—Continued

STEVEN KAPLAN, born September 20, 1953; admitted to bar, 1978, District of Columbia. *Education:* New College (B.A., 1975); Georgetown University (J.D., magna cum laude, 1978). Listed in Who's Who in American Law. Georgetown Law Journal. (Responsible Partner, Corporate & Securities; Financial Institutions). ***PRACTICE AREAS:*** Corporate Law; Securities; Financial Institutions. ***Email:*** Steven_Kaplan@aporter.com

ANDREW T. KARRON, born June 1, 1956; admitted to bar, 1985, District of Columbia and New York. *Education:* Harvard University (A.B., 1979); New York University (J.D., 1984). Law Clerk to Hon. Harold H. Greene, U.S. District Court for the District of Columbia, 1984-1985. ***PRACTICE AREAS:*** Litigation; Accountants' Liability Law; Securities and Derivative Litigation. ***Email:*** Andrew_Karron@aporter.com

HADRIAN R. KATZ, born August 12, 1949; admitted to bar, 1977, Massachusetts and District of Columbia; 1983, U.S. Supreme Court. *Education:* Harvard College (A.B., magna cum laude, 1969); University of California at Berkeley (M.A., 1972); Harvard Law School (J.D., magna cum laude, 1976). Harvard Law Review. ***PRACTICE AREAS:*** Litigation; Computer; Intellectual Property. ***Email:*** Hadrian_Katz@aporter.com

DAVID R. KENTOFF, born July 26, 1937; admitted to bar, 1961, Illinois; 1966, District of Columbia. *Education:* Michigan State University; Northwestern University (B.S.L., 1959; LL.B., 1961). Northwestern University Law Review. ***PRACTICE AREAS:*** Products Liability; Litigation. ***Email:*** David_Kentoff@aporter.com

ABE KRASH, born April 26, 1927; admitted to bar, 1950, District of Columbia. *Education:* University of Chicago (B.A., 1946; J.D., 1949); Yale Law School (Graduate Fellow, 1949-1950). President, Friends of the Law Library of Congress, 1992-1997. ***PRACTICE AREAS:*** Antitrust; Competition and Trade; Regulation; Litigation. ***Email:*** Abe_Krash@aporter.com

WERNER KRONSTEIN, born December 12, 1930; admitted to bar, 1956, District of Columbia. *Education:* Georgetown University (A.B., 1953; LL.B., 1956). Law Clerk to Judge Charles E. Fahy, 1956-1957. Trustee and/or Vice Chairman, International Law Institute, 1968—. Board of Contributing Editors and Advisers, Securities Law Journal, 1980—. ***LANGUAGES:*** German. ***PRACTICE AREAS:*** Corporate; Securities; International. ***Email:*** Werner_Kronstein@aporter.com

M. SEAN LAANE, born December 18, 1961; admitted to bar, 1989, Michigan; 1990, District of Columbia. *Education:* University of Illinois (B.A., cum laude, 1983; M.A., 1985); University of Michigan (J.D., magna cum laude, 1988). Michigan Law Review. Law Clerk to Hon. Cornelia G. Kennedy, U.S. Court of Appeals, Sixth Circuit, 1988-1989. ***PRACTICE AREAS:*** Products Liability; Civil Litigation. ***Email:*** M._Sean_Laane@aporter.com

STUART J. LAND, born May 18, 1930; admitted to bar, 1954, District of Columbia. *Education:* Syracuse University (A.B., 1951); Harvard University (LL.B., 1954). Harvard Law Review. ***PRACTICE AREAS:*** Food, Drug and Medical Device; Litigation. ***Email:*** Stuart_Land@aporter.com

J. STEPHEN LAWRENCE, JR., born October 29, 1949; admitted to bar, 1978, District of Columbia. *Education:* Duke University (A.B., summa cum laude, 1972); University of Chicago (J.D., cum laude, 1977). University of Chicago Law Review. Law Clerk, Judge Malcolm R. Wilkey, U.S. Court of Appeals for the District of Columbia Circuit, 1976-1977. Visiting Professor of Law, Duke University School of Law, 1979. Assistant Professor of Law, University of Illinois College of Law, 1980-1981. Adjunct Professor of Law, Washington & Lee University School of Law, 1985-1995. Faculty Member, National Judicial College, 1979—. ***PRACTICE AREAS:*** Government Contracts; Construction Contracts; Commercial Contracts. ***Email:*** J._Stephen_Lawrence@aporter.com

RONALD D. LEE, born August 10, 1959; admitted to bar, 1986, New York; 1987, District of Columbia; 1991, California. *Education:* Princeton University (A.B., with highest honors, 1980); Oxford University (M.Phil., 1982); Yale University (J.D., 1985). Law Clerk to: Justice John Paul Stevens, United States Supreme Court, 1986-1987; Judge Abner J. Mikva, United States Court of Appeals for the District of Columbia Circuit, 1985-1986. ***PRACTICE AREAS:*** Telecommunications Law; Intellectual Property; Technology Law; Privacy Law; National Security Law and Policy; Litigation. ***Email:*** Ronald_Lee@aporter.com

SUSAN G. LEE, born October 15, 1959; admitted to bar, 1988, District of Columbia. *Education:* University of Virginia (B.A., 1982); Woodrow Wilson School, Princeton University (M.P.A., 1988); Columbia University Law School (J.D., 1988). ***PRACTICE AREAS:*** Derivatives; Litigation; International Law; International Litigation; Arbitration; International Trade. ***Email:*** Susan_Lee@aporter.com

KENNETH A. LETZLER, born October 24, 1943; admitted to bar, 1968, District of Columbia; 1975, U.S. Supreme Court. *Education:* Columbia University (A.B., magna cum laude, 1965); Harvard University (LL.B., magna cum laude, 1968). Harvard Law Review. Law Clerk, U.S. Court of Appeals, District of Columbia Circuit, 1968-1969. ***PRACTICE AREAS:*** Antitrust; Litigation. ***Email:*** Kenneth_Letzler@aporter.com

ARTHUR N. LEVINE, born October 23, 1945; admitted to bar, 1971, California; 1976, U.S. Supreme Court; 1991, District of Columbia. *Education:* University of California, Los Angeles (B.A., cum laude, 1967); University of California, Berkeley (J.D., with honors, 1970). Deputy General Counsel, Litigation, Food and Drug Administration, 1978-1991. Trial Attorney, Food and Drug Administration, 1970-1978. Instructor, George Washington University National Law Center, 1991-1995. ***PRACTICE AREAS:*** Food, Drug and Medical Device; Litigation. ***Email:*** Arthur_Levine@aporter.com

DANIEL MARTIN LEWIS, born February 3, 1944; admitted to bar, 1973, District of Columbia. *Education:* Yale University (B.A., magna cum laude, 1966; LL.B., 1969). Legislative Assistant to Senator Joseph Tydings, 1969-1970. Chief Legislative Assistant to Senator Edmund Muskie, 1971-1972. ***PRACTICE AREAS:*** Bankruptcy. ***Email:*** Daniel_Lewis@aporter.com

JACK L. LIPSON, born December 18, 1932; admitted to bar, 1958, New York; 1960, District of Columbia. *Education:* Brooklyn College (A.B., 1953); Harvard University (LL.B., 1956). Trial Attorney, Antitrust Division of the Department of Justice, Washington, D.C., 1960-1965. Practitioner in Residence, Cornell Law School, 1993. [Lt., U.S.N.R., 1956-1959]. ***PRACTICE AREAS:*** Litigation. ***Email:*** Jack_Lipson@aporter.com

ROBERT S. LITT, born December 29, 1949; admitted to bar, 1978, New York; 1980, District of Columbia; 1998, Maryland. *Education:* Harvard University (A.B., 1971); Yale University (M.A., American Studies, 1973; J.D., 1976). Law Clerk: Hon. Edward Weinfeld, Southern District of New York, 1976-1977; Hon. Potter Stewart, U.S. Supreme Court, 1977-1978. Assistant U.S. Attorney, Southern District of New York, 1978-1984. Special Advisor, U.S. Department of State, 1993-1994. Deputy Assistant Attorney General, Criminal Division, U.S. Department of Justice, 1994-1997. Principal Associate Deputy Attorney General, U.S. Department of Justice, 1997-1999. *Member:* Association of the Bar of the City of New York; American Bar Association. ***PRACTICE AREAS:*** White Collar Criminal Litigation; Civil Litigation. ***Email:*** Robert_Litt@aporter.com

RICHARD M. LUCAS, born May 23, 1965; admitted to bar, 1990, Connecticut; 1991, District of Columbia. *Education:* Georgetown University (B.S.B.A., cum laude, 1987); Yale University (J.D.,1990). Yale Law and Policy Review. ***PRACTICE AREAS:*** Real Estate; Litigation; Bankruptcy. ***Email:*** Richard_Lucas@aporter.com

DENNIS G. LYONS, born November 20, 1931; admitted to bar, 1955, District of Columbia; 1956, New York; 1960, U.S. Supreme Court. *Education:* College of the Holy Cross (A.B., summa cum laude, 1952); Harvard University (LL.B., summa cum laude, 1955). Harvard Law Review. Attorney, Office of the General Counsel, Department of the Air Force, Washington, 1955-1958. Law Clerk to Mr. Justice Brennan, U.S. Supreme Court, 1958-1960. Visiting Professor of Law, University of Virginia, 1982-1983. ***PRACTICE AREAS:*** Corporate; Securities; Litigation; Transportation Law. ***Email:*** Dennis_Lyons@aporter.com

HELENE B. MADONICK, born August 5, 1960; admitted to bar, 1987, New York; 1988, District of Columbia. *Education:* Tufts University (B.A., magna cum laude, 1982); Columbia University (J.D., 1986). Phi Beta Kappa. ***PRACTICE AREAS:*** Litigation; Food and Drug. ***Email:*** Helene_Madonick@aporter.com

ROBERT E. MANNION, born November 3, 1943; admitted to bar, 1969, District of Columbia; 1976, U.S. Supreme Court. *Education:* Georgetown University (A.B., 1965); Catholic University (J.D., 1969). Adjunct Professor, Banking Law, Columbus School of Law, Catholic University, 1988—. Assistant to Senator Walter F. Mondale, United States Senate, Washington, D.C., 1965-1970. Assistant General Counsel, 1976-1978, Associate General Counsel, 1978-1979 and Deputy General Counsel, 1979-1983, Board of Governors of the Federal Reserve System, Washington, D.C. Assistant General Counsel, Federal Open Market Committee, Washington, D.C., 1978-1983. Board of Advisers, The Bankers Magazine; Advisory Board to the Banking Attorney. ***PRACTICE AREAS:*** Financial Institutions; International. ***Email:*** Robert_Mannion@aporter.com

DAVID R. MARSH, born February 2, 1964; admitted to bar, 1996, New York and District of Columbia; U.S. District Court for the District of Columbia; U.S. Court of Appeals for the Federal Circuit; registered to practice before U.S. Patent and Trademark Office. *Education:* University College London, University of London, England (B.S., 1985); Institute of Plant Science Research, England (Ph.D., 1989); Nottingham Law School, England (C.P.E., 1992); New York University (J.D., 1995). Author: "The Preclusive Effect of Foreign Country Patent Judgments in the United States," New York University School of Law Journal of International Law and Politics, 27.2: 469-503, 1995; "A Win-Win Scenario for Natural Resource Access," Bio/Technology, 11.10, 1173, 1993; "An Ecological Look at GMOs," Bio/Technology, 11.8, 937, 1993. Co-Author: Nigel Jones, "Europe and America Say Yes to Plant Patents," Bio-Science Law Review, 3:88-92, 1999/2000; with Timothy W. Riffe, "Recent Legislation: The

(This Listing Continued)

(This Listing Continued)

American Inventors Protection Act," Bio-Science Law Review, 3:93-98, 1999/2000; with Nigel Jones, "Springtime for Patents," Legal Times II - Magazine, pp. 38-44, April 10, 2000; with Nigel Jones, "E.U., U.S. Favor Flora Inventions: Tribunals on Both Sides of the Atlantic Uphold Patents with Claims Directed to Plants," The National Law Journal, 22 (31): C1, C5-C7, March 27, 2000; with Joel M. Freed, "Enzo Biochem, Inc. v. Calgene, Inc., Bio-Science Law Review, 2:73-74, 1999/2000; with Joel M. Freed, Merck & Co., Inc. v. Mylan Pharmaceuticals, Inc., Bio-Science Law Review, 2:74-75, 1999/2000; with Joel M. Freed, "Pharmaceuticals & Upjohn Co. v. Mylar Pharmaceuticals, Inc., Bio Science Law Review, 6:238-239, 1998-1999; with Joel M. Freed, "Abbott Laboratories v. Geneva Pharmaceuticals, Inc., Bio-Science Law Review, 6:239, 1998-1999; with Joel Freed, "Delta & Pine Land Co. v. The Sinkers Corp., Bio-Science Law Review," 6:240-241, 1998-1999; "University of California v. Eli Lilly," Bio-Science Law Review, 2:76, 1997; with Joel M. Freed, "In re Mayne," Bio-Science Law Review, 2:77, 1997; with Joel M. Freed, "Genentech v. Chiron Corp," Bio-Science Law Review 2:78, 1997; with Joel M. Freed, "Genentech v. Novo Nordisk A/S," Bio-Science Law Review, 2:79, 1997; with Richard H. Kjeldgaard, "Recent Developments in the Patent Protection of Plant-Based Technology in the United States," European Intellectual Property Review, 19.1:16-20, 1997; with Richard H. Kjeldgaard, "Recent United States Developments in Plant Patents," Molecular Breeding, 2(2) 95-96, 1996; with Richard H. Kjeldgaard, "A Biotech Battle Brewing," Legal Times, XVIII Supplement 17-19, 1995; with Richard H. Kjeldgaard, Health Care Reform and Intellectual Property Bio/Technology, 12.6, 639-40, 1994, "Intellectual Property Rights for Plants, "Plant Cell," 6.11, 1524-28, 1994. U.S. Editor, Bio-Science Law Review. Adjunct Professor, Georgetown University Law Center, 2000—. *Member:* American Bar Association; American Intellectual Property Law Association (Chair, Plant Subcommittee, 1996—); International Society for Plant Molecular Biology; Crop Science Society of America.

JONATHAN S. MARTEL, born August 18, 1964; admitted to bar, 1989, Illinois; 1990, Massachusetts; 1991, District of Columbia. *Education:* Dartmouth College (A.B., summa cum laude, 1986); Yale University (J.D., 1989). Yale Law Journal. Law Clerk to Hon. Levin H. Campbell, U.S. Court of Appeals, First Circuit, 1990-1991. Staff Attorney, Office of General Counsel, U.S. Environmental Protection Agency, 1991-1994. Adjunct Professor, Georgetown University Law Center, 1995-1997. Vice Chair, Air Quality Subcommittee, Section on Natural Resources, Energy and Environmental Law, American Bar Association, 1996—. ***PRACTICE AREAS:*** Environmental; Regulatory; Litigation. ***Email:*** Jonathan_Martel@aporter.com

JOHN C. MASSARO, born July 9, 1967; admitted to bar, 1993, Connecticut and New York; 1994, District of Columbia. *Education:* Williams College (B.A., magna cum laude and with highest honors, 1989); Harvard University (J.D., magna cum laude, 1992). Law Clerk, Judge Bruce M. Selya, U.S. Court of Appeals, First Circuit, 1992-1993. ***PRACTICE AREAS:*** Litigation. ***Email:*** John_Massaro@aporter.com

MARK R. MERLEY, born November 19, 1958; admitted to bar, 1983, District of Columbia. *Education:* University of Pennsylvania (B.A./B.S. Econ., summa cum laude, 1980); Harvard University (J.D., magna cum laude, 1983). Harvard Law Review. ***PRACTICE AREAS:*** Antitrust; Litigation. ***Email:*** Mark_Merley@aporter.com

MICHAEL B. MIERZEWSKI, born September 14, 1951; admitted to bar, 1980, District of Columbia; 1984, U.S. Supreme Court. *Education:* Catholic University of America (B.A., cum laude, 1973); Howard University (J.D., magna cum laude, 1980). Howard Law Journal. Vice Chair, Financial Markets and Institutions Subcommittee, Antitrust Law Section, American Bar Association, 1997-1999. Frequent lecturer and writer on Fair Lending and other Banking issues. ***PRACTICE AREAS:*** Financial Institutions. ***Email:*** Michael_Mierzewski@aporter.com

THOMAS H. MILCH, born December 27, 1950; admitted to bar, 1976, Indiana; 1977, District of Columbia. *Education:* Yale University (B.A., summa cum laude, 1973; J.D., 1976). Yale Law Journal. Adjunct Professor, Environmental Law, Georgetown University Law Center, 1989—. Director, Environmental Law Institute, 1993-1999. Director, Resolve, Inc., 1993—. Chairman: American Bar Association Special Committee on Environmental Litigation Techniques, 1992-1994; Member, ABA Standing Committee on Environmental Law, 1996-1998; Vice Chairman, Committee on Environment Litigation, American Bar Association Litigation Section, 1994—. Director, Migrant Legal Action Project, 1991-1993. Member and Past Co-Chair, D.C. Advisory Counsel, Lawyers Committee on Human Rights, 1992—. ***PRACTICE AREAS:*** Environmental Law. ***Email:*** Thomas_Milch@aporter.com

BRUCE L. MONTGOMERY, born Houston, Texas, June 10, 1935; admitted to bar, 1960, Texas; 1963, District of Columbia; 1978, U.S. Supreme Court. *Education:* Rice University (B.A., 1957); Yale University (LL.B., 1960). Board of Editors, Yale Law Journal. Trial Attorney, Antitrust Division, Department of Justice, 1960-1962. ***PRACTICE AREAS:*** Antitrust; Litigation. ***Email:*** Bruce_Montgomery@aporter.com

SUSAN T. MORITA, born September 11, 1960; admitted to bar, 1988, District of Columbia. *Education:* Stanford University (B.A., 1982); Princeton University (M.P.A., 1987); Harvard University (J.D., 1988). Harvard Law Review. ***PRACTICE AREAS:*** International Trade; Corporate Transactions. ***Email:*** Susan_Morita@aporter.com

(This Listing Continued)

S. LEE NARROW, born October 4, 1942; admitted to bar, 1968, District of Columbia. *Education:* University of Wisconsin (B.A., 1964); Georgetown University (J.D., 1967); Harvard University. ***PRACTICE AREAS:*** Real Estate; Corporate; Finance. ***Email:*** S._Lee_Narrow@aporter.com

IRVIN B. NATHAN, born August 4, 1943; admitted to bar, 1969, District of Columbia and U.S. Supreme Court. *Education:* Johns Hopkins University (B.A., 1964); Columbia University (LL.B., 1967). Harlan Fiske Stone Scholar. Jerome Michael Award for Advocacy, 1967. Columbia Law Review. Law Clerk to Judge Simon E. Sobeloff, U.S. Court of Appeals, Fourth Circuit, 1967-1968. Deputy Assistant Attorney General for Enforcement, Criminal Division, U.S. Department of Justice, 1979-1981. Special Minority Counsel, Select Committee on Intelligence, U.S. Senate, 1981. Chairman, White Collar Crime Committee, Criminal Justice Section, American Bar Association, 1982-1984. Principal Associate Deputy Attorney General, U.S. Department of Justice, 1993-1994. Co-Chair, Corporate Criminal Liability Subcommittee, White Collar Crime, Section of Criminal Justice, 1995-1996. Adjunct Professor, Georgetown University Law Center. Chairman, Ethics Committee. *Member:* American Law Institute. Fellow: American Bar Foundation; American College of Trial Lawyers. ***PRACTICE AREAS:*** White Collar Crime Defense; Corporate Civil Litigation; Antitrust; Securities; Civil RICO. ***Email:*** Irvin_Nathan@aporter.com

ANNE J. O'BRIEN, born July 24, 1945; admitted to bar, 1988, Maryland; 1989, District of Columbia. *Education:* University of New Mexico (B.A., 1967); George Washington University (M.B.A., 1976); Washington College of Law of American University (J.D., magna cum laude, 1988). American College of Trust and Estate Counsel. Vice Chairman, Tax Management Estates, Gifts and Trusts Journal and Portfolio Series, 1989-1995. Co-Chair, Steering Committee, Estates, Trusts and Probate Law Section, 1997-1999, The District of Columbia Bar. Senior Acquisition Editor, Books and Media Committee and Chair, Post Mortem Transfer Tax Committee, American Bar Association. ***PRACTICE AREAS:*** Estate Planning; Probate; Charitable Planning; Estate and Trust Administration. ***Email:*** Anne_O'Brien@aporter.com

CHARLES D. OSSOLA, born August 3, 1953; admitted to bar, 1978, Virginia; 1979, District of Columbia. *Education:* Williams College (B.A., cum laude, 1975); Villanova University (J.D., 1978). Villanova Law Review. Law Clerk to U.S. District Judge Albert V. Bryan, Jr., Eastern District of Virginia, 1978-1979. Advisory Board, BNA's Patent, Trademark & Copyright Journal; Editorial Board, AIPLA Quarterly Journal. ***PRACTICE AREAS:*** Intellectual Property Litigation; Patent Litigation; Trademark Litigation; Copyright Litigation; Unfair Competition Litigation; False Advertising Litigation; Trade Litigation; Antitrust Litigation. ***Email:*** Charles_Ossola@aporter.com

DONNA E. PATTERSON, born March 4, 1949; admitted to bar, 1981, District of Columbia. *Education:* Yale University (B.A., 1971; J.D., 1981). ***PRACTICE AREAS:*** Antitrust; Competition and Trade; Regulation; Litigation; National Security Law and Policy. ***Email:*** Donna_Patterson@aporter.com

JENNIFER S. PERKINS, admitted to bar, 1985, Maryland and Pennsylvania;1986, District of Columbia. *Education:* Haverford College (B.A., 1982); Georgetown University Law Center (J.D., 1985). ***PRACTICE AREAS:*** Real Estate. ***Email:*** Jennifer_Perkins@aporter.com

STEPHANIE M. PHILLIPPS, born March 13, 1952; admitted to bar, 1977, Massachusetts; 1977, District of Columbia. *Education:* Radcliffe College (B.A., magna cum laude, 1973); Harvard University (J.D., 1976). ***PRACTICE AREAS:*** Telecommunications Law; Communications Law; Real Estate. ***Email:*** Stephanie_Phillipps@aporter.com

STEPHEN W. PORTER, born February 22, 1939; admitted to bar, 1966, Wisconsin, District of Columbia and U.S. Tax Court; 1970, U.S. Supreme Court. *Education:* University of Wisconsin (B.B.A., cum laude, 1960; J.D., with honors, 1966). Wisconsin Law Review. Adjunct Professor of Law, Georgetown University Law Center, 1971-1973 and Washington College of Law, American University, 1972-1976. Lecturer: on Real Estate Topics for ALI/ABA Institute, 1984-1985; Georgetown University, District of Columbia Bar, Continuing Legal Education Institute, 1984-1985; Johns Hopkins University School of Continuing Legal Studies, 1986. ***PRACTICE AREAS:*** Real Estate; Corporate; Securities. ***Email:*** Stephen_Porter@aporter.com

CLAIRE E. READE, born June 2, 1952; admitted to bar, 1980, Massachusetts; 1983, District of Columbia. *Education:* Wesleyan University (B.A., 1973); Fletcher School of Law and Diplomacy (M.A.L.D., 1979); Harvard University (J.D., 1979). Co-Chair, American Bar Association International Trade Committee, 1993-1995. ***PRACTICE AREAS:*** International. ***Email:*** Claire_Reade@aporter.com

STEVEN G. READE, born July 2, 1956; admitted to bar, 1983, District of Columbia. *Education:* Stanford University (B.A., with distinction, 1978); University of Pennsylvania (J.D., cum laude, 1981). University of Pennsylvania Law

(This Listing Continued)

ARNOLD & PORTER, Washington—Continued

Review. Law Clerk to Chief Judge Samuel P. King, U.S. District Court, District of Hawaii, 1981-1982. ***PRACTICE AREAS:*** Litigation; Employment Law. ***Email:*** Steven_Reade@aporter.com

THOMAS W. RICHARDSON, born 1963; admitted to bar, 1990, New Jersey; 1991, New York; 1993, District of Columbia. *Education:* University of Vermont (B.A., 1985); Rutgers University (J.D., 1990). ***PRACTICE AREAS:*** Trusts and Estates; Tax; International. ***Email:*** Thomas_Richardson@aporter.com

WALTER J. ROCKLER, born November 25, 1920; admitted to bar, 1946, Illinois; 1951, New York; 1954, District of Columbia. *Education:* University of Chicago (B.A., 1940); Harvard University (LL.B., 1943). Prosecutor, Nuremberg War Crimes Trials, 1947-1949. Director of Office of Special Investigations, Department of Justice, 1979-1980. ***PRACTICE AREAS:*** Federal Tax; International. ***Email:*** Walter_Rockler@aporter.com

WILLIAM D. ROGERS, born May 12, 1927; admitted to bar, 1953, District of Columbia. *Education:* Princeton University (A.B., 1948); Yale University (LL.B., 1951). Yale Law Journal. Law Clerk to: Judge Charles E. Clark, U.S. Court of Appeals, Second Circuit, 1951-1952; Justice Stanley Reed, U.S. Supreme Court, 1952-1953. Special Counsel, U.S. Coordinator, Alliance for Progress, 1962-1963. Deputy U.S. Coordinator, Alliance for Progress and Deputy Assistant Administrator, AID, 1963-1965. Alternate U.S. Representative, Inter-American Economic and Social Council, 1964-1965. President: Center for Inter-American Relations, 1965-1970; American Society of International Law, 1972-1974. Assistant Secretary of State for Inter-American Affairs, U.S. Coordinator, Alliance for Progress, 1974-1976. Under Secretary of State for Economic Affairs, 1976-1977. U.S. Alternate Governor, International Bank for Reconstruction and Development, African Development Bank, Asian Development Bank and Inter-American Development Bank, 1976-1977. Vice Chairman, Kissinger Associates, Inc., 1986—. Director, Council on Foreign Relations, 1980-1990. Co-Chairman, Bilateral Commission on United States-Mexican Relations, 1986-1989. Council on Foreign Relations, Cuba Task Force, 1998—. Member: Board of Visitors, Georgetown Foreign Service School, 1977-1984; Law Faculty, Cambridge University, 1982-1983; Advisory Council, Princeton University Woodrow Wilson School, 1987-1994. ***PRACTICE AREAS:*** International. ***Email:*** William_Rogers@aporter.com

RICHARD L. ROSEN, born June 11, 1950; admitted to bar, 1975, New York; 1980, District of Columbia and U.S. Supreme Court; 1984, Illinois. *Education:* Massachusetts Institute of Technology (S.B., 1970); St John's University (J.D., 1974). Attorney-Advisor to Chairman, 1977-1978 and Assistant Director, Bureau of Competition, 1981-1984, Federal Trade Commission. Chief, Communications and Finance Section, Antitrust Division, 1992-1994, U.S. Department of Justice. ***PRACTICE AREAS:*** Antitrust; Communications; Litigation. ***Email:*** Richard_Rosen@aporter.com

ROBERT D. ROSENBAUM, born July 19, 1943; admitted to bar, 1968, District of Columbia. *Education:* Wharton School of Finance and Commerce, University of Pennsylvania (B.S., 1965); Columbia University (LL.B., magna cum laude, 1968). Kent Scholar. Columbia Law Review. Adjunct Professor, Georgetown University Law Center. ***PRACTICE AREAS:*** Corporate; Securities; Litigation. ***Email:*** Robert_Rosenbaum@aporter.com

STANFORD G. ROSS, born October 9, 1931; admitted to bar, 1957, California; 1959, New York; 1968, U.S. Supreme Court; 1969, District of Columbia. *Education:* Washington University (B.A., 1953); Harvard University (J.D., 1956). Harvard Law Review. Teaching Fellow and Research Assistant, International Program in Taxation, Harvard Law School, 1957-1958. Professor of Law, New York University, 1963-1969. Adjunct Professor of Law: New York University, 1969-1978; Georgetown Law Center, 1986-1987. Visiting Professor of Law, University of Virginia, 1988-1989. Visiting Fellow, Hoover Institution, Stanford University, 1992-1993. Office of Tax Legislative Counsel, Treasury Department, 1961-1963. Assistant Tax Legislative Counsel, 1962-1963. White House Staff Assistant, 1967-1968. Executive Director, President's National Advisory Panel on Insurance in Riot-Affected Areas, National Advisory Commission on Civil Disorders, 1967-1968. General Counsel, Department of Transportation, 1968-1969. Chairman, Advisory Council on Social Security, 1978. Commissioner of Social Security, 1978-1979. Consultant, President's Commission on Pension Policy, 1980-1981. Public Trustee, Social Security and Medicare Trust Funds, 1990-1995. Chair, Social Security Advisory Board, 1997—. ***PRACTICE AREAS:*** Tax; Administrative Law. ***Email:*** Stanford_Ross@aporter.com

JULIE B. ROTTENBERG, born April 22, 1968; admitted to bar, 1994, California and Maryland; 1995, District of Columbia. *Education:* San Diego State University (A.B., cum laude, 1989); George Washington University (J.D., highest honors, 1993). George Washington Journal of International Law and Economics. Law Clerk: The Honorable Robert R. Beezer, U.S. Court of Appeals, Ninth Circuit, 1994-1995; The Honorable Samuel Grayson Wilson, U.S. District Court, Western District of Virginia, 1993-1994. ***PRACTICE AREAS:*** Litigation. ***Email:*** Julie_Rottenberg@aporter.com

(This Listing Continued)

ERIC A. RUBEL, born July 12, 1960; admitted to bar, 1985, Pennsylvania; 1986, District of Columbia. *Education:* Middlebury College (B.A., cum laude, 1982); George Washington University (J.D., with highest honors, 1985). George Washington University Law Review. Law Clerk to Hon. Jane A. Restani, U.S. Court of International Trade, 1985-1986. General Counsel, U.S. Consumer Product Safety Commission, 1994-1997, ABA. ***PRACTICE AREAS:*** Product Safety; Regulatory Law; Products Liability Litigation; Litigation. ***Email:*** Eric_Rubel@aporter.com

BLAKE D. RUBIN, born January 11, 1955; admitted to bar, 1980, Pennsylvania; 1988, District of Columbia. *Education:* Haverford College (B.A., 1976); Wharton School of Finance (M.B.A., with distinction, 1980); University of Pennsylvania Law School (J.D., cum laude, 1980). Beta Gamma Sigma; Beta Alpha Psi; Order of the Coif. Author: "Doing A Deal with a REIT from the Property Owner's Perspective," 27 *Journal of Real Estate Taxation* No.1 (1999); "Representing the Property Owner in REIT Acquisitions," 15 *Real Estate Tax Management Journal* No.7 (1999); "Doing a Deal With a REIT: The Property Owner's Perspective," 57 *N.Y.U. Federal Tax Institute* Ch.14, (1999); "Exploring the Outer Limits of the Section 704(c) Built-in Gain Rule," 89 *Journal of Taxation* Nos.3,4,5 (September, October, November 1998); "Creative Strategies for the Disposition of Overleveraged Real Estate 22 ALI-ABA Course Materials Journal No.3,4 (June, August 1998); "The Final Partnership Disguised Sale Regulations Under Section 707(a)(2)." *Tax Management Real Estate Journal* No.9 (September 1997); "Creative Tax Planning for the Disposition of Overleveraged Real Estate," 14 *Journal of Taxation of Investments* No.3 (Spring 1997); "The Tax Treatment of Environmental Clean-up Costs," Ch.9A, *Environmental Law Practice Guide* (Matthew Bender & Company Inc., New York, 1997); "Creative Tax Planning for the Disposition of Overleveraged Real Estate," 13 *Tax Management Real Estate Journal* No.2 (February 1997); "A Comprehensive Guide to Partnership Terminations, Including the Impact of the New Proposed Regulations," 24 *Journal of Real Estate Taxation* No.2 (Winter 1997); "Creative Tax Planning for the Disposition of Overleveraged Real Estate," 55 *N.Y.U. Federal Tax Institute* Ch.14 (1996); "The Tax Treatment of Environmental Clean-up Costs," 54 *N.Y.U. Federal Tax Institute* Ch.11 (1995); "Allocation of Nonrecourse Liabilities: IRS Takes Two Steps Forward, One Back," 83 *Journal of Taxation* No.5 (November 1995); "Tax Considerations in the Formation and Operation of Limited Liability Companies," 11 *Tax Management Real Estate Journal* No.8 (August 1995); "Revenue Procedure Leaves Unanswered Questions on Partnership Profits Interest Received for Services," 11 *Journal of Taxation of Investments* No.3 (Spring 1994); "The Tax Treatment of Environmental Clean-up Costs," 8 *The Practical Tax Lawyer* No.3 (Spring 1994); "Current Developments Affecting Real Estate: The 1993 Tax Act," 51 *N.Y.U. Federal Tax Institute* Ch.30 (1993); "The Proposed Regulations on Partnership Allocations with Respect to Contributed Property," 59 *Tax Notes* 257 (April 12, 1993); "The Likely Content of Clinton's Tax Proposals," 57 *Tax Notes* 1179 (November 23, 1992); "Tax Planning for the Debtor in Bankruptcy," 19 *Journal of Taxation of Real Estate* No.4 (Summer 1992); "Tax Planning for the Debtor in Bankruptcy," 39 *Tax Ideas* No.7 (July 15, 1992); "Congress Attacks Like-Kind Exchange Basis Strips," 1 *Real Estate Investment Journal* 35 (March 1992); "Controlling the Character of Income on Foreclosure," 9 *Journal of Taxation of Investments* No.1 (Autumn 1991); "Proposed Partnership Disguised Sale Regulations," 52 *Tax Notes* 1051 (August 26, 1991); "Controlling the Character of Income on Foreclosure," 38 *Tax Ideas* No.17 (November 20, 1991); "Controlling the Character of Income on Foreclosure," 15 *Units* Nos.5,6 and 7 (1991); "Using a Partnership Freeze to Reduce Corporate Tax," (Part Two), 8 *Journal of Partnership Taxation* No.1 (Spring 1991); "Using Partnerships to Defer Gain on Disposition of Real Estate," 8 *Journal of Taxation of Investments* No.2 (Winter 1991); "Using a Partnership Freeze to Reduce Corporate Tax," (Part One), 7 *Journal of Partnership Taxation* No.4 (Winter 1991); "Congress Targets Like-Kind Exchange Basis Strips," 7 *Journal of Taxation of Investments* No.4 (Summer 1990); "Taxable Dispositions of Real Estate: Planning Under the Passive Loss and Installment Sale Rules," 48 *N.Y.U. Federal Tax Institute* Ch.30 (1990); "Real Estate Under the Passive Loss Regulations: The Activity Definition," 14 *ALI-ABA Course Materials Journal* 31 (December 1989); "Acquisitions Involving S Corporations," 47 *N.Y.U. Federal Tax Institute* Ch.11 (1989); "Real Estate Installment Sales Under the 1987 Act," 41 *Tax Notes* 219 (October 10, 1988); "Tunneling Under the Two Percent Floor," 38 *Monthly Digest of Tax Articles* No.12 (September, 1988); "Sticking PIGs: Real Estate Under the Passive Loss Regulations," 39 *Tax Notes* 867 (May 16, 1988); "Avoiding the Two Percent Floor on Business Expenses," 1 *Business Tax Report* No.1 (February 12, 1988); "Tunneling Under the Two Percent Floor," 38 *Tax Notes* 177 (January 11, 1988); "Pro Rata Interest Allocation: The Path Not Chosen," 36 *Tax Notes* 301 (July 20, 1987); *Taxation in Common Transactions* (Pennsylvania Bar Institute Course Book, 1983); "When GAAP Goes to Court," 14 *The Practical Accountant* No.11 (November 1981). Chair, Real Estate Taxation Committee, Section of Taxation, American Bar Association, 1993-1995. Chair, Taxation Section, 1995-1998 and Chair, Pass-Through Entities and Real Estate Committee, Taxation Section, 1992-1995, District of Columbia Bar Association. Chair, New York University Institute on Federal Taxation, 1999. Co-Chair, ALI-ABA annual conference on Creative Tax Planning for Real Estate Transactions, 1997—. Real Estate and Partnership Taxation Chair, New York

(This Listing Continued)

University Annual Institute on Federal Taxation, 1998—. Past Chair of the Advisory Council of the National Institute on Real Estate Taxation. Adjunct Professor, Graduate Tax Program, Villanova University School of Law, 1982-1984. Attorney Advisor, Office of Tax Legislative Counsel, U.S. Department of Treasury, 1984-1987. Fellow, American College of Tax Counsel. Member: Tax Policy Advisory Committee of the National Realty Committee; National Association of Real Estate Investment Trusts; Advisory Board of the *Journal of Real Estate Taxation,* the *Journal Of Passthrough Entitite,* the *Tax Management Real Estate Journal,* the *Washington Tax Review* and the *Journal of Taxation of Investments.* ***PRACTICE AREAS:*** Federal Taxation; Real Estate Taxation; Partnership Taxation. ***Email:*** Blake_Rubin@aporter.com

MICHAEL J. RUFKAHR, born September 26, 1953; admitted to bar, 1980, New York; 1981, Missouri; 1983, U.S. Supreme Court; 1998, District of Columbia. *Education:* University of Michigan (A.B., 1976; J.D., 1979). ***PRACTICE AREAS:*** Taxation. ***Email:*** Michael_Rufkahr@aporter.com

STEPHEN M. SACKS, born April 12, 1942; admitted to bar, 1966, New York; 1968, District of Columbia. *Education:* Cornell University (B.S., 1963); Harvard University (LL.B., magna cum laude, 1966). Harvard Law Review. Harvard Legal Aid Bureau. Assistant to the General Counsel, Department of the Army, 1967-1970. ***PRACTICE AREAS:*** Litigation. ***Email:*** Stephen_Sacks@aporter.com

JAMES J. SANDMAN, born June 16, 1951; admitted to bar, 1976, Pennsylvania; 1977, District of Columbia; 1980, U.S. Supreme Court; 1982, Colorado. *Education:* Boston College (A.B., summa cum laude, 1973); University of Pennsylvania (J.D., cum laude, 1976). University of Pennsylvania Law Review. Law Clerk to Hon. Max Rosenn, U.S. Court of Appeals for the Third Circuit, 1976-1977. ***PRACTICE AREAS:*** Litigation; Products Liability. ***Email:*** James_Sandman@aporter.com

RONALD A. SCHECHTER, born July 2, 1950; admitted to bar, 1976, District of Columbia. *Education:* Syracuse University (B.A., magna cum laude, 1972); Georgetown University (J.D., 1976). Law Clerk to Chief Judge Greene, Superior Court of the District of Columbia, 1976-1977. Trial Attorney, Commercial Litigation, U.S. Department of Justice, 1984-1987. Chairman, District of Columbia Public Service Activities Committee, 1983-1985. Chairman, District of Columbia Bar Continuing Legal Education Committee, 1999—. ***PRACTICE AREAS:*** Government Contracts; Litigation; Intellectual Property. ***Email:*** Ronald_Schechter@aporter.com

LAWRENCE A. SCHNEIDER, born February 4, 1949; admitted to bar, 1975, District of Columbia. *Education:* Yale University (B.A., cum laude, 1971); Harvard University (J.D., cum laude, 1974). Harvard Civil Rights-Civil Liberties Law Review. ***PRACTICE AREAS:*** International; Litigation. ***Email:*** Lawrence_Schneider@aporter.com

SCOTT B. SCHREIBER, born September 10, 1948; admitted to bar, 1973, New York; 1974, District of Columbia. *Education:* Bates College (B.A., cum laude, 1970); Columbia University (J.D., 1973). Harlan Fiske Stone Scholar, 1971-1973. Columbia Law Review. Law Clerk to the Hon. William H. Timbers, United States Court of Appeals, Second Circuit, 1973-1974. Special Assistant Counsel, United States Senate Select Committee on Intelligence, 1981. Special Counsel, Congress of the United States, Committee on the Judiciary, Subcommittee on Civil and Constitutional Rights, 1983. ***PRACTICE AREAS:*** Financial Institutions; Litigation; Professional Liability; Insurance Coverage. ***Email:*** Scott_Schreiber@aporter.com

KENNETH L. SCHWARTZ, born January 27, 1965; admitted to bar, 1992, Pennsylvania; 1993, District of Columbia. *Education:* University of Pennsylvania (B.A., cum laude, 1986); George Washington University National Law Center (J.D., with highest honors, 1992). George Washington University Law Review. ***PRACTICE AREAS:*** Corporate; Securities; Real Estate. ***Email:*** Kenneth_Schwartz@aporter.com

MATTHEW J. SEIDEN, born June 14, 1948; admitted to bar, 1986, Maryland; 1987, District of Columbia; 1988, U.S. District Court, District of Maryland and U.S. District Court for the District of Columbia. *Education:* Princeton University (Critical Languages Program, 1967); Harvard University (B.A., magna cum laude, 1969); Columbia University (M.A., 1971); University of Maryland (J.D., 1986). Peace Corps, Brazil, 1970. Foreign Correspondent, Japan, 1973-1977. Baltimore Sun Columnist, 1979-1986. ***LANGUAGES:*** Japanese, Portuguese and Chinese. ***PRACTICE AREAS:*** Intellectual Property; Computer Law; Internet Law; International Trade; International Transactions. ***Email:*** Matthew_Seiden@aporter.com

MICHAEL T. SHOR, born May 1, 1958; admitted to bar, 1983, District of Columbia. *Education:* Dartmouth College (A.B., summa cum laude, 1980); Harvard University (J.D., cum laude, 1983). Harvard International Law Journal. Legal Assistant, Iran-United States Claims Tribunal, The Hague, 1984-1986. ***PRACTICE AREAS:*** International Trade. ***Email:*** Michael_Shor@aporter.com

NORMAN M. SINEL, born December 8, 1941; admitted to bar, 1967, California; 1968, District of Columbia. *Education:* Yale University (B.A., 1963); Stanford University (LL.B., 1966). Stanford Law Review. Law Clerk to Judge Stanley A. Weigel, U.S. District Judge, Northern District of California, 1966-1967. General Counsel, 1971-1973, Vice President and General Counsel, 1973-1976, Senior Vice President, Corporate Management and General Counsel, 1976-1979, Public Broadcasting Service. ***PRACTICE AREAS:*** Telecommunications. ***Email:*** Norman_Sinel@aporter.com

EDWARD H. SISSON, born May 19, 1955; admitted to bar, 1992, New York; 1993, District of Columbia, U.S. Court of Federal Claims and U.S. Court of International Trade; 1995, U.S. Supreme Court. *Education:* Pomona College; Massachusetts Institute of Technology (B.S., 1977); Georgetown University (J.D., magna cum laude, 1991). Journal of Law & Technology. Law Clerk, Judge Roger B. Andewelt, U.S. Court of Federal Claims, 1991-1992. ***PRACTICE AREAS:*** Litigation; Government Contracts. ***Email:*** Edward_Sisson@aporter.com

JEFFREY H. SMITH, born October 24, 1944; admitted to bar, 1971, Michigan; 1989, District of Columbia. *Education:* United States Military Academy (B.S., 1966); University of Michigan (J.D., 1971). Office of Legal Adviser, Department of State, 1975-1984; Armed Services Committee, U.S. Senate, 1984-1988. Chief, Clinton Transition Team, Department of Defense, 1992. Chairman, Joint Security Commission, 1993. Member: Commission of Roles and Missions, Department of Defense, 1994-1995; General Counsel, Central Intelligence Agency, 1995-1996; Board of Trustees, The Aerospace Corporation, 1990—; Board of Trustees, The Henry L. Stimson Center, 1990—; General Counsel, The Goldwater Foundation, 1989—; Council on Foreign Relations. [U.S. Army, JAGC, 1971-1975]. ***PRACTICE AREAS:*** Legislative; International. ***Email:*** Jeffrey_Smith@aporter.com

MICHAEL N. SOHN, born May 11, 1940; admitted to bar, 1964, New York; 1969, District of Columbia and U.S. Supreme Court. *Education:* Columbia College (A.B., 1960); Harvard University (LL.B., cum laude, 1963). Attorney, General Counsel's Office, National Labor Relations Board, 1964-1969. General Counsel, Federal Trade Commission, 1977-1980. Member, Executive Committee, Regulatory Council of the United States, 1978-1980. Council, 1978-1980 and Member, 1980-1983, Administrative Conference of the United States. ***PRACTICE AREAS:*** Antitrust; Trade Regulation. ***Email:*** Michael_Sohn@aporter.com

MICHAEL J. SONGER, born 1964; admitted to bar, 1990, Pennsylvania; 1992, Colorado; 1994, California; 1997, District of Columbia; registered to practice before U.S. Patent and Trademark Office. *Education:* University of Notre Dame (B.S.M.E., 1987; B.A., 1987); Duke University (J.D., 1990). ***PRACTICE AREAS:*** Intellectual Property.

LESTER SOTSKY, born April 8, 1954; admitted to bar, 1979, District of Columbia. *Education:* Brandeis University (B.A., summa cum laude, 1976); Yale Law School (J.D., 1979). ***PRACTICE AREAS:*** Environmental; Litigation. ***Email:*** Lester_Sotsky@aporter.com

MARY GABRIELLE SPRAGUE, born October 7, 1957; admitted to bar, 1984, Colorado; 1990, U.S. Supreme Court; 1992, District of Columbia. *Education:* Harvard University (A.B., summa cum laude, 1979); Yale University (J.D., 1983). Law Clerk to: Judge Jim R. Carrigan, U.S. District Court, District of Colorado, 1984-1985; Justice Byron R. White, U.S. Supreme Court, 1986-1987. ***PRACTICE AREAS:*** Environmental; Indian Law; Civil Litigation. ***Email:*** Mary_Gay_Sprague@aporter.com

MARK H. STUMPF, born January 25, 1947; admitted to bar, 1973, New York; 1977, District of Columbia. *Education:* Harvard University (A.B., magna cum laude, 1969; J.D., 1972). ***PRACTICE AREAS:*** International; Corporate; Securities. ***Email:*** Mark_Stumpf@aporter.com

BRYAN J. TOMASEK, born February 24, 1950; admitted to bar, 1976, Virginia; 1977, District of Columbia. *Education:* University of Illinois (B.A., 1973); Georgetown University (J.D., 1976). ***PRACTICE AREAS:*** Taxation; Partnership Law; Joint Ventures; Limited Liability Company Law; Real Estate Investment Trusts; Real Estate. ***Email:*** Bryan_Tomasek@aporter.com

ASIM VARMA, born September 8, 1964; admitted to bar, 1988, Massachusetts; 1989, District of Columbia. *Education:* University of Michigan (B.S., with highest honors, 1985); Harvard University (J.D., cum laude, 1988). ***PRACTICE AREAS:*** Antitrust; Intellectual Property; Litigation. ***Email:*** Asim_Varma@aporter.com

G. DUANE VIETH, born September 20, 1923; admitted to bar, 1949, Iowa and District of Columbia. *Education:* University of Iowa (A.B., 1947); University of Iowa Law School (J.D., 1949). Iowa Law Review. ***PRACTICE AREAS:*** Litigation. ***Email:*** G._Duane_Vieth@aporter.com

WILLIAM W. VODRA, born September 13, 1943; admitted to bar, 1968, Ohio (inactive); 1981, District of Columbia. *Education:* College of Wooster (B.A., 1965); Columbia University (J.D., 1968). U.S. Department of Justice, Bureau of Narcotics and Dangerous Drugs/Drug Enforcement Administration, 1971-1974; U.S. Department of Health, Education and Welfare, Office of General Counsel, Food and Drug Division, 1974-1979. Vice-Chairman, Commission on the Federal Drug Approval Process, 1981-1982. ***PRACTICE AREAS:*** Food and Drug; Products Liability. ***Email:*** William_Vodra@aporter.com

(This Listing Continued)

ARNOLD & PORTER, Washington—Continued

DOUGLAS L. WALD, born September 16, 1954; admitted to bar, 1979, District of Columbia. *Education:* Harvard University (A.B., 1975; J.D., 1979). Harvard Law Review. Law Clerk to Hon. Wm. H. Timbers, U.S. Court of Appeals, Second Circuit, 1979-1980. ***PRACTICE AREAS:*** Litigation; Antitrust. ***Email:*** Douglas_Wald@aporter.com

DANIEL WALDMAN, born October 18, 1955; admitted to bar, 1982, District of Columbia. *Education:* Harvard University (B.A., 1977); Columbia University School of Law (J.D., 1980). General Counsel of Commodity Futures Trading Commission, 1996-1999. ***PRACTICE AREAS:*** Derivatives; Litigation. ***Email:*** Dan_Waldman@aporter.com

ROBERT N. WEINER, born May 20, 1952; admitted to bar, 1979, District of Columbia; 1983, U.S. Supreme Court; 1993, New York. *Education:* Princeton University (A.B., summa cum laude, 1974); Yale University (J.D., 1977). Phi Beta Kappa. Note and Topics Editor, Yale Law Journal, 1976-1977. Law Clerk to: The Honorable Henry J. Friendly, U.S. Court of Appeals, Second Circuit, 1977-1978; Honorable Thurgood Marshall, U.S. Supreme Court, 1978-1979. Lecturer in Law, University of Virginia School of Law, 1994. Adjunct Professor of Law, Georgetown University Law Center, 1983-1986. Chair, Hearing Committee No. 2 of the D.C. Board on Professional Responsibility, 1988-1994; Associate Independent Counsel, 1986-1987. Senior Counsel to the Counsel to the President of the U.S., 1997-1998. *Member:* The District of Columbia Bar (President, 1995-1996; President-Elect, 1994-1995; General Counsel, 1992-1994; Member, Board of Governors, 1990-1992; Chair, Public Service Activities Committee, 1999—); American Bar Association (Member, Standing Committee on Pro Bono and Public Service); American Law Institute. Fellow, American Bar Foundation. ***PRACTICE AREAS:*** Commercial Litigation; Criminal Litigation; Products Liability. ***Email:*** Robert_Weiner@aporter.com

JOSEPH D. WEST, born April 18, 1949; admitted to bar, 1977, Virginia and District of Columbia. *Education:* Villanova University (B.C.E., magna cum laude, 1971); George Washington University (J.D., with high honors, 1977). The George Washington Law Review, 1976-1977. Registered Professional Engineer, Virginia. Fellow, American College of Construction Lawyers. [Lt., U.S. Navy, 1971-1975]. ***PRACTICE AREAS:*** Government Contracts; Construction Contracts; Contract Dispute Resolution; Commercial Litigation. ***Email:*** Joseph_West@aporter.com

LESLIE WHARTON, born July 7, 1951; admitted to bar, 1984, Texas; 1990, District of Columbia. *Education:* Boston University (B.A., summa cum laude, 1973); Princeton University (Ph.D., 1979); Harvard Law School (J.D., cum laude, 1984). Adjunct Faculty, Law for Artists and Law for Architects, Rhode Island School of Design, 1982-1983. ***PRACTICE AREAS:*** Litigation; Product Liability Law. ***Email:*** Leslie_Wharton@aporter.com

ROBERT H. WINTER, born September 21, 1941; admitted to bar, 1967, New York; 1970, District of Columbia. *Education:* Columbia College (A.B., 1962); Oriel College, Oxford University, Oxford, England (B.A., 1964; M.A., 1967); Harvard University (LL.B., 1967). Harvard Law Review. Law Clerk to Judge Irving R. Kaufman, U.S. Court of Appeals, Second Circuit, 1967-1968. (Also at London, England Office). ***PRACTICE AREAS:*** Corporate; Securities; International. ***Email:*** Robert_Winter@aporter.com

JAY KELLY WRIGHT, born November 9, 1943; admitted to bar, 1975, District of Columbia; 1978, U.S. Supreme Court; 1980, Virginia. *Education:* Dartmouth College (A.B., magna cum laude, 1965); Harvard University (M.P.P., 1973; J.D., cum laude, 1973). Harvard Law Review. Member, Editorial Advisory Board, RICO Litigation Reporter, 1984—. Law Clerk to: Judge Harold Leventhal, U.S. Court of Appeals for the District of Columbia Circuit, 1973-1974; Mr. Justice William O. Douglas, U.S. Supreme Court, 1974-1975. Adjunct Professor, Trial Practice, Georgetown University Law Center, 1993—. Thurgood Marshall American Inn of Court. [Lieut., U.S. Navy, active duty, 1965-1969]. ***PRACTICE AREAS:*** Securities; Professional Liability; Business; Constitutional Litigation; Administrative Litigation. ***Email:*** Jay_Kelly_Wright@aporter.com

WALTER F. ZENNER, born June 17, 1952; admitted to bar, 1991, Virginia; 1993, District of Columbia. *Education:* LaSalle University (B.A., 1974); University of Southern California (M.A., with distinction, 1982); George Mason University (J.D., with distinction, 1991). [With U.S. Navy, 1974-1982]. ***PRACTICE AREAS:*** Government Contracts. ***Email:*** Walter_Zenner@aporter.com

OF COUNSEL

ROSALIND K. ALLEN, born January 15, 1957; admitted to bar, 1982, District of Columbia and U.S. Claims Court; 1983, U.S. District Court for the District of Columbia, U.S. Court of Appeals for the District of Columbia Circuit and U.S. Court of Appeals for the Federal Circuit. *Education:* Vassar College (A.B., with honors, 1978); Georgetown University Law Center (J.D., 1981). ***PRACTICE AREAS:*** Telecommunications Law. ***Email:*** Rosalind_Allen@aporter.com

(This Listing Continued)

JOHN P. BARKER, born Elmhurst, Illinois, 1961; admitted to bar, 1988, California; 1989, District of Columbia. *Education:* Dartmouth College (A.B., cum laude, 1983); University of Michigan (J.D., 1986). ***LANGUAGES:*** French. ***PRACTICE AREAS:*** International Trade; Public Policy and Legislative; Intellectual Property; Technology Law; National Security Law and Policy. ***Email:*** John_Barker@aporter.com

J. BRADWAY BUTLER, born New Jersey, USA, 1941; admitted to bar, 1969, District of Columbia. *Education:* Harvard University (A.B., 1963); University of Minnesota (LL.B., 1966); George Washington University (LL.M., 1968). With Arnold & Porter, 1969-2001. *Member:* American Bar Association. (Also with Somay Hukuk Bürosu). ***LANGUAGES:*** English. ***PRACTICE AREAS:*** Real Estate; International; Corporate; Securities. ***Email:*** brad.butler@somaylaw.com

MICHAEL A. LEE, born June 20, 1942; admitted to bar, 1980, District of Columbia; 1986, U.S. Tax Court; 1997, U.S. Supreme Court. *Education:* University of California at Los Angeles (B.A., 1965; M.A., 1967); University of Hawaii School of Law; University of California at Berkeley (J.D., 1979). California Law Review. Law Clerk, Judge Cecil F. Poole, U.S. District Court, Northern District of California and U.S. Court of Appeals, Ninth Circuit, 1979-1980. ***PRACTICE AREAS:*** Tax; Real Estate; Non-Profit Organizations. ***Email:*** Michael_Lee@aporter.com

ROBERT PITOFSKY, born December 27, 1929; admitted to bar, 1956, New York; 1972, U.S. Supreme Court; 1973, District of Columbia. *Education:* New York University (B.A., 1951); Columbia University (LL.B., 1954). Commissioner, Federal Trade Commission, 1978-1981. ***PRACTICE AREAS:*** Antitrust; Competition and Trade; Regulation; Privacy; National Security Law and Policy. ***Email:*** Robert_Pitofsky@aporter.com

VICTOR L. REID, born 1956; admitted to bar, 1986, District of Columbia; 1991, U.S. Court of Appeals, Eleventh Circuit; 1992, U.S. Court of Appeals, Seventh Circuit and U.S. Supreme Court. *Education:* Morehouse College (B.A., 1979); Howard University (J.D., 1984). Senior Associate Editor, Howard Law Journal, 1984. *Member:* The District of Columbia Bar. ***PRACTICE AREAS:*** Corporate; Private Equity; Securities; Commercial Practice.

THOMAS E. SILFEN, born October 18, 1942; admitted to bar, 1967, Illinois; 1972, District of Columbia. *Education:* University of Michigan (B.A., 1964; J.D., cum laude, 1967). Michigan Law Review. Attorney, National Labor Relations Board, 1967-1972. ***PRACTICE AREAS:*** Litigation; Products Liability. ***Email:*** Thomas_Silfen@aporter.com

MELVIN SPAETH, born March 13, 1926; admitted to bar, 1952, District of Columbia. *Education:* University of Chicago (A.B., 1948; J.D., 1952). University of Chicago Law Review. Trial Attorney, Antitrust Division, Department of Justice, 1959-1963. Special Assistant to Assistant Attorney General, Antitrust Division, Department of Justice, 1963-1965. Assistant General Counsel, Federal Power Commission, 1965. ***PRACTICE AREAS:*** Litigation; Products Liability; Antitrust. ***Email:*** Melvin_Spaeth@aporter.com

JONATHAN L. STERN, born Summit, New Jersey, October 3, 1957; admitted to bar, 1983, District of Columbia; 1992, U.S. Supreme Court; 1998, U.S. District Court, District of Columbia and District of Maryland; 1999, U.S. Court of Appeals, District of Columbia and Fourth Circuits. *Education:* Hamilton College (B.A., cum laude, departmental honors in Philosophy, 1979); New York University School of Law (J.D., 1983); Georgetown University Law Center. Hamilton College: Babcock Prize in Philosophy and Pedagogy; Watrows Essay Prize for Literary Criticism; Harris Prize Scholarship in Philosophy. New York University School of Law: Ann Petluck Poses Memorial Prize. Visiting Professor, Georgetown University Law Center, 1991-1992. Adjunct Professor: Georgetown University Law Center, 1994—; George Washington University Law School, 1998—. Teaching Team Member, Trial Advocacy Workshop, Harvard Law School, 1991—. District of Columbia Public Defender Service, 1985-1997. ***PRACTICE AREAS:*** Complex Civil Litigation; Complex Criminal Litigation. ***Email:*** Jonathan_Stern@aporter.com

JAMES T. WALSH, born 1949; admitted to bar, 1976, Pennsylvania; 1977, District of Columbia; 1984, New York. *Education:* College of the Holy Cross (A.B., cum laude, 1971); Georgetown University Law Center (J.D., 1976). Attorney, U.S. Department of Commerce, 1976-1981. Attorney/Administrator, U.S. Patent and Trademark Office, 1981-1995. ***PRACTICE AREAS:*** Intellectual Property; Trademarks; Unfair Competition. ***Email:*** James_Walsh@aporter.com

MICHELE J. WOODS, born October 3, 1962; admitted to bar, 1990, District of Columbia. *Education:* Princeton University (B.A., 1984); Oxford University (M.St., 1987); Duke University (J.D./LL.M., 1990). ***PRACTICE AREAS:*** Intellectual Property; Technology Law. ***Email:*** Michele_Woods@aporter.com

ROBERT JONES WORRALL, born December 31, 1963; admitted to bar, 1993, Virginia; 1994, District of Columbia; registered to practice before U.S. Patent and Trademark Office. *Education:* Arizona State University (B.S.E.E., 1987); Franklin Pierce Law Center (J.D., 1993). Eta Kappa Nu. *Member:*

(This Listing Continued)

American Bar Association; American Intellectual Property Law Association; Institute of Electrical and Electronics Engineers. ***PRACTICE AREAS:*** Intellectual Property; Antitrust.

SPECIAL COUNSEL

WALTRAUT SUSANNE ADDY, born August 7, 1944; admitted to bar, 1982, District of Columbia; 1987, U.S. Supreme Court. *Education:* George Washington University (B.A., with distinction, 1979); Georgetown University (J.D., 1982). American Criminal Law Review. ***PRACTICE AREAS:*** Complex Civil Litigation; Government Contracts. ***Email:*** W._Susanne_Addy@aporter.com

THEODORE S. BOONE, born January 7, 1961; admitted to bar, 1988, New York; 1989, District of Columbia. *Education:* University of Illinois at Urbana-Champaign (B.A., 1983) Phi Beta Kappa; Ludwig Maximilians University, Munich, Germany (Fulbright Grantee and Bavarian State Grantee, 1983-1984); Columbia University (J.D., 1987) Certificate of Recognition with Honors in Foreign and Comparative Law; International Fellows Program; U.S. FLAS Fellowship for Hungary; Eötvös Loránd University School of Law, Budapest, Hungary (IREX Grantee, 1987-1988). President, American Chamber of Commerce, Hungary, 1991-1993. Vice Chair, Committee on International Investment, Development and Privatization, International Law Section, American Bar Association. ***LANGUAGES:*** German and Hungarian. ***PRACTICE AREAS:*** Commercial Transactions. ***Email:*** Theodore_Boone@aporter.com

MARY E. CASSIDY, born October 18, 1955; admitted to bar, 1987, New York; 1988, District of Columbia. *Education:* State University of New York at Binghamton (B.A., 1977; M.S., 1980); George Washington University National Law Center (J.D., 1986). ***PRACTICE AREAS:*** Tax; Employee Benefits. ***Email:*** Mary_Cassidy@aporter.com

PETER J. CINQUEGRANI, born December 3, 1959; admitted to bar, 1985, Maryland; 1986, District of Columbia. *Education:* Johns Hopkins University (B.A., with honors, 1981); Georgetown University (J.D., magna cum laude, 1984). ***PRACTICE AREAS:*** Tax. ***Email:*** Peter_Cinquegrani@aporter.com

MARCH COLEMAN, born March 12, 1942; admitted to bar, 1969, New York; 1976, U.S; Supreme Court; 1983, District of Columbia. *Education:* American University (B.A., 1965); Yale Law School (LL.B., 1968). Assistant General Counsel, U.S. Synthetic Fuels Corporation, 1983-1986. Senior Attorney, Office of General Counsel, FTC, 1979-1983. ***PRACTICE AREAS:*** Litigation; Antitrust. ***Email:*** March_Coleman@aporter.com

MARCIA ANN CRANBERG, born January 28, 1955; admitted to bar, 1980, Iowa; 1982, District of Columbia; 1992, Colorado. *Education:* Brandeis University (B.A., magna cum laude, 1977); University of Nice, Nice, France; University of Iowa (J.D., 1980). Adjunct Professor, Columbus School of Law, Catholic University, 1987-1991. ***PRACTICE AREAS:*** Telecommunications. ***Email:*** Marcia_Cranberg@aporter.com

LAWRENCE E. CULLEEN, born January 2, 1958; admitted to bar, 1983, Maryland; 1982, District of Columbia. *Education:* George Washington University (B.A., special honors, 1979; J.D., 1982). Vice Chair, Special Committee on Agricultural Management Issues, American Bar Association, 1995-2000; Vice Chair, Special Committee on Pesticides, Chemical Regulations and Community Right-to-Know, 1999-2000. Adjunct Professor, Environmental Law, George Washington University Law School. ***PRACTICE AREAS:*** Environmental; Administrative. ***Email:*** Lawrence_Culleen@aporter.com

BETH S. DESIMONE, born July 21, 1959; admitted to bar, 1984, District of Columbia; 1997, Florida. *Education:* Wheaton College (B.A., with highest honors, 1981); Marshall-Wythe School of Law, College of William & Mary (J.D., 1984). William & Mary Law Review. ***PRACTICE AREAS:*** Financial Institutions; Corporate. ***Email:*** Beth_DeSimone@aporter.com

HOLLY R. FOGLER, born August 18, 1967; admitted to bar, 1993, New York and District of Columbia. *Education:* University of Texas (B.B.A., with high honors, 1988; J.D., with honors, 1992). The University of Texas International Law Journal. ***PRACTICE AREAS:*** Antitrust. ***Email:*** Holly_Fogler@aporter.com

MICHAEL R. GESKE, born April 21, 1961; admitted to bar, 1990, Pennsylvania; 1991, District of Columbia. *Education:* St. Meinrad College (B.A., maxima cum laude, 1983); Indiana University (M.A., 1988; J.D., summa cum laude, 1989). Indiana Law Journal. Judicial Clerk to Hon. Bruce M. Selya, U.S. Court of Appeals, First Circuit, 1989-1990. ***PRACTICE AREAS:*** Antitrust; Litigation. ***Email:*** Michael_Geske@aporter.com

HOWARD L. HYDE, born September 4, 1957; admitted to bar, 1983, Massachusetts; 1987, District of Columbia. *Education:* Dartmouth College (A.B., summa cum laude, 1979); Harvard University (J.D., 1982). Law Clerk to The Honorable Justice Lawrence R. Yetka, Minnesota Supreme Court, 1982-1983. ***PRACTICE AREAS:*** Financial Institutions; Corporate; Securities. ***Email:*** Howard_Hyde@aporter.com

(This Listing Continued)

JEAN E. KALICKI, born February 29, 1964; admitted to bar, 1990, New York; 1991, District of Columbia. *Education:* Harvard University (A.B., summa cum laude, 1986); Harvard Law School (J.D., magna cum laude, 1989). Phi Beta Kappa. Harvard Law Review. Law Clerk to Judge Pierre N. Leval, U.S. District Court, Southern District of New York, 1989-1990. Author: "Enforcement of the U.S. Securities Laws," in *U.S. Regulation of the International Securities and Derivatives Markets* (3d e. 1996 and 4th ed. 1998); "U.S. Discovery for the Japanese Practitioner: Protecting Proprietary Information," 24 J. of the Japanese Inst. of Int'l Bus.L. 71 (1996) (co-author) (in Japanese); "Doing Business with the Soviets: The Sources of Policy Divergence Within the Atlantic Alliance," in *Present at the Creation: The Fortieth Anniversary of the Marshall Plan* (1990); "Foreign Policy by Indictment: Using Tools Against Foreign Officials Involved in Drug Trafficking," 8 Criminal Justice Ethics 3 (Summer/Fall 1989); Case Comment, "National Security and Preclusion of Judicial Review: Webster v. Doe," 102 Harvard L.Rev. 330 (1988). *Member:* American and International Bar Associations. ***PRACTICE AREAS:*** International Arbitration; Commercial Litigation. ***Email:*** Jean_Kalicki@aporter.com

DAVID E. KORN, born November 29, 1961; admitted to bar, 1987, Pennsylvania; 1988, District of Columbia. *Education:* Duke University (B.S., summa cum laude, 1983); Northwestern University (M.S., 1984); Harvard University (J.D., cum laude, 1987). Law Clerk to the Honorable Caleb M. Wright, U.S. District Court for the District of Delaware, 1987-1988. ***PRACTICE AREAS:*** Food and Drug; Intellectual Property. ***Email:*** David_Korn@aporter.com

ROSEMARY MAXWELL, born February 14, 1957; admitted to bar, 1987, Virginia; 1989, District of Columbia. *Education:* State University of New York, Albany (B.A., 1981; M.A., 1984); George Washington University (J.D., 1987). ***Email:*** Rosemary_Maxwell@aporter.com

JOAN G. OCHS, born July 22, 1956; admitted to bar, 1981, District of Columbia. *Education:* Northwestern University (B.A., with honors in History, 1978); George Washington University (J.D., 1981). ***PRACTICE AREAS:*** Government Contracts. ***Email:*** Joan_Ochs@aporter.com

NANCY L. PERKINS, born June 19, 1956; admitted to bar, 1988, Pennsylvania; 1989, District of Columbia; 1990, U.S. District Court for the District of Columbia; 1991, U.S. Court of International Trade; 1997, U.S. Supreme Court and U.S. Court of Appeals, District of Columbia Circuit. *Education:* Harvard University (A.B., 1979; M.P.P./J.D., 1987). Harvard Law Review. Clerk to U.S. District Judge, Eastern District of New York, 1987-1988. Co-Chair, International Law Section, District of Columbia Bar, 1994-1997. Assistant Treasurer, American Society of International Law, 1995—. ***PRACTICE AREAS:*** International; Litigation; Legislative. ***Email:*** Nancy_Perkins@aporter.com

RANDAL M. SHAHEEN, born March 29, 1960; admitted to bar, 1985, Pennsylvania; 1987, District of Columbia. *Education:* Bucknell University (B.A., 1982); Harvard University (J.D., magna cum laude, 1985). Harvard Law Review. ***PRACTICE AREAS:*** Antitrust; Consumer Protection. ***Email:*** Randal_Shaheen@aporter.com

THOMAS D. SYDNOR, II, born February 27, 1965; admitted to bar, 1994, California and District of Columbia. *Education:* The Ohio State University (B.A., English, 1987); Duke University (J.D., with high honors, 1991). ***PRACTICE AREAS:*** Products Liability; Administrative Law. ***Email:*** Thomas_Sydnor@aporter.com

SHARON L. TAYLOR, born February 21, 1954; admitted to bar, 1989, Maryland; 1990, District of Columbia. *Education:* University of Maryland (B.S., 1976; M.A., 1983); Catholic University of America (J.D., 1989). Catholic University Law Review. ***PRACTICE AREAS:*** Energy; Government Contracts. ***Email:*** Sharon_Taylor@aporter.com

ASSOCIATES

ERIC L. ALEXANDER, born November 8, 1970; admitted to bar, 1996, Maryland; 1998, District of Columbia. *Education:* Kenyon College (B.A., magna cum laude, with highest honors, 1992); Duke University (J.D., with honors, 1995). Law and Contemporary Problems. Judicial Clerk, Hon. Jon P. McCalla, Western District of Tennessee, 1995-1996. ***PRACTICE AREAS:*** Litigation. ***Email:*** Eric_Alexander@aporter.com

MICHAEL J. ALLAN, born December 24, 1972; admitted to bar, 1999, New York and U.S. District Court, Northern District of New York; 2000, District of Columbia; 2001, South Carolina. *Education:* Hamilton College (B.A., 1995); Syracuse University College of Law (J.D., cum laude, 1998). ***PRACTICE AREAS:*** Litigation. ***Email:*** Michael_Allan@aporter.com

JUSTIN S. ANTONIPILLAI, born July 9, 1972; admitted to bar, 1998, California and District of Columbia. *Education:* Cornell University (B.A., 1994); American University, Washington College of Law (J.D., summa cum laude, 1997). ***PRACTICE AREAS:*** Litigation; Products Liability; Corporate Law; Securities; Bankruptcy. ***Email:*** Justin_Antonipillai@aporter.com

MICHAEL C. AUGUSTINI, born September 28, 1967; admitted to bar, 1995, Maine; 1996, District of Columbia. *Education:* Bowdoin College (B.A., 1989); University of Maine School of Law (J.D., summa cum laude, 1995).

(This Listing Continued)

ARNOLD & PORTER, Washington—Continued

Maine Law Review. Judicial Clerk, The Honorable Conrad K. Cyr, U.S. Court of Appeals, First Circuit, 1995-1996. ***PRACTICE AREAS:*** Litigation. ***Email:*** Michael_Augustini@aporter.com

JONATHAN BATTEN, admitted to bar, 2000, Maryland; 2001, District of Columbia. *Education:* University of Maryland (B.A., 1992); Georgetown University Law Center (J.D., 2000).

JEANNA M. BECK, born September 27, 1971; admitted to bar, 1998, Illinois and U.S. District Court, Northern District of Illinois; 2001, District of Columbia. *Education:* Miami University (B.A., 1993); DePaul University College of Law (J.D., 1998). ***PRACTICE AREAS:*** Litigation. ***Email:*** Jeanna_Beck@aporter.com

KRISTEN E. BELZ, born April 4, 1972; admitted to bar, 1997, Maryland; 2001, District of Columbia. *Education:* University of Pittsburgh (B.A., summa cum laude, 1994); Washington College of Law at American University (J.D., summa cum laude, 1997). ***PRACTICE AREAS:*** Employee Benefits; Tax Law. ***Email:*** Kristen_Belz@aporter.com

TIMOTHY C. BICKHAM, born August 16, 1968; admitted to bar, 1994, Missouri; 1996, District of Columbia; registered to practice before U.S. Patent and Trademark Office. *Education:* William Jewell College (B.A., 1991); University of Missouri (J.D., 1994); George Washington University (LL.M., 1998). ***PRACTICE AREAS:*** Intellectual Property; Technology Law. ***Email:*** Timothy_Bickham@aporter.com

LAURA RESPESS BIDDLE, born April 7, 1966; admitted to bar, 1996, Virginia; 1997, District of Columbia. *Education:* College of William & Mary (B.B.A., 1988); Catholic University of America, Columbus School of Law (J.D., magna cum laude, 1996). ***PRACTICE AREAS:*** Financial Institutions. ***Email:*** Laura_Biddle@aporter.com

ARUNA K. BOPPANA, admitted to bar, 2001, New York and District of Columbia. *Education:* Cornell University (B.A., 1997); Vanderbilt University (J.D., 2000).

MONICA JAHAN BOSE, born July 1, 1964; admitted to bar, 1991, New York; 1992, District of Columbia. *Education:* Wesleyan University (B.A., 1986); Columbia University (J.D., 1990). ***PRACTICE AREAS:*** Environmental. ***Email:*** Monica_Bose@aporter.com

JENNIFER S. BRANNAN, admitted to bar, 2000, Kansas and District of Columbia Bar. *Education:* University of Kansas (B.S.J., 1996); University of Kansas School of Law (J.D., 1999). ***PRACTICE AREAS:*** Litigation. ***Email:*** Jennifer_Brannan@aporter.com

KATHRYN P. CABALLERO, admitted to bar, 2000, Maryland; 2001, District of Columbia. *Education:* University of Notre Dame (B.S., 1991); Princeton University (M.S.E., 1993); New York University School of Law (J.D., 1999). ***PRACTICE AREAS:*** Environmental Law. ***Email:*** Kathryn_Caballero@aporter.com

DANIEL A. CANTOR, born February 2, 1970; admitted to bar, 1996, Maryland; 1998, District of Columbia. *Education:* Bates College (B.A., 1992); Washington College of Law of American University (J.D., 1996). ***PRACTICE AREAS:*** Environmental; Litigation. ***Email:*** Daniel_Cantor@aporter.com

ARTURO CARABALLO, born April 27, 1971; admitted to bar, 1998, Florida; 1999, District of Columbia. *Education:* Tulane University (B.A., 1993; J.D., 1997). Journal of International and Comparative Law. ***LANGUAGES:*** Spanish. ***PRACTICE AREAS:*** Corporate; Securities; International; Capital Markets; Project Finance; Mergers and Acquisitions. ***Email:*** Arturo_Caraballo@aporter.com

W. JONATHAN CARDI, born October 5, 1969; admitted to bar, 1997, West Virginia; 1998, District of Columbia. *Education:* Harvard University (A.B., 1991); University of Iowa (J.D., 1998). Order of the Coif. HAncher-Finkbein Award for Most Outstanding Graduate Student. ***PRACTICE AREAS:*** Litigation; Intellectual Property. ***Email:*** Jonathan_Cardi@aporter.com

ERIKA R. CARMEAN, born June 5, 1969; admitted to bar, 1997, Maryland; 1998, District of Columbia. *Education:* University of Maryland (B.A., 1992; J.D., 1997). ***PRACTICE AREAS:*** Intellectual Property; Technology Law. ***Email:*** Erika_Carmean@aporter.com

WILLIAM J. CARMODY, born February 18, 1966; admitted to bar, 1994, Maryland; 1995, District of Columbia. *Education:* University of Virginia (B.A., 1988); Catholic University of America (J.D., magna cum laude, 1994). ***PRACTICE AREAS:*** Real Estate; Corporate; Securities. ***Email:*** William_Carmody@aporter.com

WILLIAM P. CEJUDO, born March 14, 1963; admitted to bar, 1989, Texas; 1998, District of Columbia. *Education:* Southern Methodist University (B.B.A., cum laude, 1986); University of Texas (J.D., with honors, 1989); Georgetown University (LL.M., Taxation, 1993). ***PRACTICE AREAS:*** Taxation. ***Email:*** William_Cejudo@aporter.com

(This Listing Continued)

SCOTT A. CHAMBERS, born May 13, 1952; admitted to bar, 1993, Virginia; 1994, District of Columbia; registered to practice before U.S. Patent and Trademark Office. *Education:* Florida State University (Ph.D., 1981); George Washington University (J.D., high honors, 1993). Order of the Coif. Member, George Washington University Law Review. William Brinks Scholarship, Excellence in Intel. Prop. Law, 1992. Adjunct Professor, Georgetown Law Center, 1999-2000; George Washington Law Center, 1995-1998. Associate Solicitor, U.S. Patent and Trademark Office, 1994-1999. Juvenile Justice Comm. of Montgomery County, Maryland. Member, American Chemical Society, 1983. ***PRACTICE AREAS:*** Intellectual Property. ***Email:*** Scott_Chambers@aporter.com

LISA ReVEAL CHAVARRIA, born January 21, 1964; admitted to bar, 1990, California; 1992, District of Columbia. *Education:* University of California at Los Angeles (B.A., 1986); University of California, Boalt Hall School of Law (J.D., 1990); Boston University (LL.M., 1992). ***PRACTICE AREAS:*** Financial Institutions; Corporate. ***Email:*** Lisa_Chavarria@aporter.com

EUGENE T. CHEN, born September 5, 1973; admitted to bar, 1999, California; 2000, District of Columbia. *Education:* Columbia University (B.A., summa cum laude, 1995); Stanford Law School (J.D., 1998). Phi Beta Kappa. Stanford Law Review. ***PRACTICE AREAS:*** Food and Drug Regulation; Litigation. ***Email:*** Eugene_Chen@aporter.com

YU CHEN, admitted to bar, 2001, New York and District of Columbia. *Education:* Dartmouth College (B.A., 1997); Georgetown University (J.D., 2000).

KWAME A. CLEMENT, born August 29, 1959; admitted to bar, 1999, New York; 2000, District of Columbia. *Education:* University of Liberia, Monrovia, Liberia (B.Sc., 1982); The George Washington University (J.D., 1998). Order of the Coif. Member, Law Review. ***PRACTICE AREAS:*** Antitrust; Litigation. ***Email:*** Kwame_Clement@aporter.com

JUNE E. COHAN, admitted to bar, 1997, Virginia and U.S. Court of Appeals, Fourth Circuit; 1998, District of Columbia; 1999, U.S. Court of Appeals, Federal Circuit; registered to practice before U.S. Patent and Trademark Office. *Education:* University of Virginia (B.A., in Biology, 1992); Georgetown University Law Center (J.D., cum laude, 1997). ***PRACTICE AREAS:*** Intellectual Property; Technology Law; Life Sciences. ***Email:*** June_Cohan@aporter.com

SHARON BETH COHN, born August 4, 1970; admitted to bar, 1997, Virginia; 1999, District of Columbia. *Education:* University of Virginia (B.A., with honors, 1992); Harvard Law School (J.D., 1997). ***PRACTICE AREAS:*** International Trade; Litigation. ***Email:*** Sharon_Cohn@aporter.com

PELAYO COLL, born March 30, 1971; admitted to bar, 1997, Maryland; 1998, Pennsylvania; 1999, District of Columbia. *Education:* University of Maryland (B.A., 1994); Washington College of Law of American University (J.D., magna cum laude, 1997). ***LANGUAGES:*** Spanish. ***PRACTICE AREAS:*** Real Estate. ***Email:*** Pelayo_Coll@aporter.com

ROBERT S. CONWAY, born November 13, 1967; admitted to bar, 1993, Missouri; 1994, Kansas; 1997, District of Columbia. *Education:* Duke University (A.B., magna cum laude, 1990); University of Pennsylvania (J.D., cum laude, 1993). ***PRACTICE AREAS:*** Corporate; International; Securities. ***Email:*** Robert_Conway@aporter.com

ANIKA S. COOPER, born January 18, 1973; admitted to bar, 1997, Georgia; 1998, District of Columbia. *Education:* Hampton University (B.A., high honors, 1994); Yale University (J.D., 1997). Yale Law and Policy Review. ***PRACTICE AREAS:*** Antitrust; Litigation. ***Email:*** Anika_Cooper@aporter.com

ROBERT M. COOPER, born September 10, 1969; admitted to bar, 1994, Georgia; 1996, District of Columbia. *Education:* Columbia University (B.A., 1991); Emory University (J.D., with distinction, 1994). Emory Law Journal. Law Clerk to the Honorable William C. O'Kelley, U.S. District Court, Northern District of Georgia, 1994-1996. ***PRACTICE AREAS:*** Telecommunications; Litigation. ***Email:*** Robert_Cooper@aporter.com

D. MICHAEL CORMANEY, born June 4, 1972; admitted to bar, 1997, District of Columbia. *Education:* University of Iowa (B.A., 1993); Moscow State Pedagogical University, Moscow, Russia (Certificate, 1994); University of Iowa (J.D., with highest distinction, 1997). Transnational Law and Contemporary Problems. ***LANGUAGES:*** Russian. ***PRACTICE AREAS:*** Export Controls; International Trade; Ethics and Campaign Finance. ***Email:*** D._Michael_Cormaney@aporter.com

KATHLEEN M. COURTIS, born November 11, 1965; admitted to bar, 1993, Virginia; 1994, District of Columbia. *Education:* Georgetown University (B.S.B.A., magna cum laude, 1987; M.S.T., 1990); New York University (J.D., magna cum laude, 1993; LL.M., 1994). Certified Public Accountant, Maryland, 1988. ***PRACTICE AREAS:*** Trusts and Estates. ***Email:*** Kathleen_Courtis@aporter.com

ANNE W. COVENTRY, born September 3, 1973; admitted to bar, 1999, District of Columbia. *Education:* Lawrence University (B.A., cum laude, 1995); College of William & Mary (J.D., 1999). Order of the Coif. Law Review.

(This Listing Continued)

Teaching License, English, Secondary School (6-12), Wisconsin, 1996. *Member:* The District of Columbia Bar. ***LANGUAGES:*** Russian, French. ***PRACTICE AREAS:*** Tax Law; Estates. ***Email:*** Anne_Coventry@aporter.com

HAROLD BRYAN CUNNINGHAM, admitted to bar, 1990, Colorado; 2001, District of Columbia. *Education:* University of Iowa (B.A., 1984); University of Virginia (J.D., 1990).

JOHN D. DALEY, admitted to bar, 2000, District of Columbia and New York. *Education:* University of Chicago (A.B. and A.M., 1996); Harvard Law School (J.D., 1999). ***PRACTICE AREAS:*** Litigation; International Law; Public Policy and Legislative. ***Email:*** John_Daley@aporter.com

DAVID G. DARGATIS, born June 21, 1964; admitted to bar, 1997, Pennsylvania; 1998, New Jersey; 1999, District of Columbia. *Education:* Pennsylvania State University (B.S., 1988); Fordham University (M.B.A., 1992); University of Iowa (J.D., with high distinction, 1997). Recipient: University of Iowa College of Law Faculty Scholar Award, 1997; Merit Scholarship, 1995-1997; Best Brief, VanOosterhout Memorial Moot Court Competition, 1996. Senior Articles Editor, Iowa Law Review. Certified Management Accountant, 1992. ***PRACTICE AREAS:*** Corporate Law; Securities. ***Email:*** David_Dargatis@aporter.com

ANNE P. DAVIS, born October 31, 1967; admitted to bar, 1997, Massachusetts; 1998, New York; 2000, District of Columbia. *Education:* Dartmouth College (A.B., 1989); University of Virginia (J.D., 1997). Notes Editor, Virginia Law Review. ***PRACTICE AREAS:*** Litigation; Antitrust. ***Email:*** Anne_Davis@aporter.com

JEFFREY R. DENMAN, born June 23, 1966; admitted to bar, 1992, California; 1996, District of Columbia; 1999, Virginia. *Education:* University of Maryland (B.A., 1989); University of California, at Los Angeles (J.D., 1992). ***PRACTICE AREAS:*** Intellectual Property; Technology Law. ***Email:*** Jeffrey_Denman@aporter.com

RANJIT S. DHINDSA, born October 12, 1969; admitted to bar, 1995, Maryland; 1997, District of Columbia. *Education:* University of Maryland (B.S., 1991; B.A., 1992; J.D., with honors, 1995). Order of the Coif. Judicial Clerk to the Honorable Lawrence F. Rodowsky, Court of Appeals, Maryland, 1995-1996. ***PRACTICE AREAS:*** Litigation. ***Email:*** Ron_Dhindsa@aporter.com

MARY M. DIXON, born 1966; admitted to bar, 1998, Maryland; 1999, District of Columbia. *Education:* University of Vermont (B.A., 1991); Vanderbilt University Law School (J.D., 1998). ***Email:*** Mary_Dixon@aporter.com

CLARE H. DOOLEY, born June 1, 1967; admitted to bar, 1997, California; 2000, District of Columbia. *Education:* Rice University (B.A., 1991); Loyola Law School (J.D., 1997). Law Review. ***PRACTICE AREAS:*** Products Liability. ***Email:*** Clare_Dooley@aporter.com

REBECCA L. DUBIN, born August 30, 1973; admitted to bar, 1999, Maryland; 2000, District of Columbia. *Education:* University of Maryland (B.A., 1995; J.D., 1999). ***PRACTICE AREAS:*** Litigation. ***Email:*** Rebecca_Dubin@aporter.com

CYDONII V. FAIRFAX, born December 23, 1972; admitted to bar, 1998, Maryland; 2000, District of Columbia. *Education:* University of Maryland at College Park (B.S., summa cum laude, 1994); Harvard Law School (J.D., 1998). Phi Beta Kappa. Harvard Negotiation Law Review. ***PRACTICE AREAS:*** Corporate Law; Securities.

PAUL SCOTT FEIRA, born March 14, 1967; admitted to bar, 1994, Pennsylvania; 1996, District of Columbia. *Education:* Harvard University (A.B., 1989); Yale University (J.D., 1993). Law Clerk, Judge Walter K. Stapleton, U.S. Court of Appeals, Third Circuit, 1993-1994. ***LANGUAGES:*** French. ***PRACTICE AREAS:*** Telecommunications; Corporate. ***Email:*** Scott_Feira@aporter.com

JUSTINE ANNE FITZGERALD, born January 17, 1969; admitted to bar, 1998, Virginia; 1999, District of Columbia. *Education:* University of Pennsylvania (B.S./B.A., 1991); Georgetown University Law Center (J.D., magna cum laude, 1998). ***PRACTICE AREAS:*** Real Estate. ***Email:*** Justine_Fitzgerald@aporter.com

JEFFREY K. FRANCER, admitted to bar, 2000, Massachusetts; 2001, District of Columbia. *Education:* Brown University (A.B., 1993); Harvard University (M.P.P., 1998); University of Virginia (J.D., 2000). ***PRACTICE AREAS:*** Food, Drug and Medical Devices. ***Email:*** Jeffrey_Francer@aporter.com

ANTHONY J. FRANZE, born April 7, 1970; admitted to bar, 1995, Ohio, U.S. Court of Appeals, Sixth Circuit and U.S. District Court, Southern and Northern Districts of Ohio; 1998, District of Columbia. *Education:* University of Nebraska (B.S., 1992); Notre Dame Law School (J.D., magna cum laude, 1995). ***PRACTICE AREAS:*** Litigation; White Collar Crime. ***Email:*** Anthony_Franze@aporter.com

JOHN A. FREEDMAN, born August 26, 1969; admitted to bar, 1995, Massachusetts; 1996, New York and District of Columbia. *Education:* Williams College (B.A., 1991); Harvard University (J.D., 1995). Law Clerk, Judge Walter Jay Skinner, U.S. District Court, District of Massachusetts, 1995-1996. ***PRACTICE AREAS:*** Litigation. ***Email:*** John_Freedman@aporter.com

MATTHEW L. GANNON, admitted to bar, 1998, Iowa; 1999, District of Columbia. *Education:* University of Notre Dame (B.A., magna cum laude, 1994); University of Iowa (J.D., with high honors, 1998). ***PRACTICE AREAS:*** Legislative Practice; Litigation. ***Email:*** Matthew_Gannon@aporter.com

CYNTHIA A. GIORDANO, born May 3, 1954; admitted to bar, 1979, District of Columbia; 1998, Maryland. *Education:* University of Wisconsin-Madison (B.A., 1976); George Washington University (J.D., with honors, 1979). ***PRACTICE AREAS:*** Zoning; Land Use; Historic Preservation; Real Property; Tax Appeals. ***Email:*** Cynthia_Giordano@aporter.com

ELEAZAR A. GONZALEZ, admitted to bar, 1999, Florida and District of Columbia. *Education:* Florida International University (B.A., 1995); Indiana University - Bloomington (J.D., 1998). [U.S. Navy, 1987-1991]. ***LANGUAGES:*** Spanish and Portuguese. ***PRACTICE AREAS:*** Corporate Law; Securities; International Law. ***Email:*** Eleazar_Gonzalez@aporter.com

JAMIE Z. GOODSON, admitted to bar, 2001, New York and District of Columbia. *Education:* Harvard University (A.B., 1997); Yale University (J.D., 2000). ***PRACTICE AREAS:*** Real Estate. ***Email:*** Jamie_Goodson@aporter.com

RONNA M. GOVAN, admitted to bar, 2000, Maryland; 2001, District of Columbia.

RANJEEV S. GULIANI, born August 8, 1974; admitted to bar, 2000, New York; 2001, District of Columbia. *Education:* University of Virginia (B.A., 1996; J.D., 1999). ***PRACTICE AREAS:*** Mergers and Acquisitions.

JOEL M. GULICK, admitted to bar, 2001, District of Columbia and New York. *Education:* Gettysburg College (B.A., cum laude, 1996); George Washington University School of Law (J.D., 2000). ***PRACTICE AREAS:*** Employee Benefits; Tax Law. ***Email:*** Joel_Gulick@aporter.com

JEFFREY L. HANDWERKER, born September 28, 1970; admitted to bar, 1995, Maryland; 1996, District of Columbia. *Education:* Rutgers College (B.A., 1992); George Washington University National Law Center (J.D., with high honors, 1995). The Environmental Lawyer. ***PRACTICE AREAS:*** Government Contracts; Litigation. ***Email:*** Jeffrey_Handwerker@aporter.com

MYLES R. HANSEN, admitted to bar, 1992, Illinois; 1995, District of Columbia. *Education:* Columbia University (A.B., 1983); University of Michigan (J.D., 1992). ***PRACTICE AREAS:*** Antitrust and Trade Regulation. ***Email:*** Myles_Hansen@aporter.com

GARRETT M. HEENAN, admitted to bar, 2000, Virginia; 2001, District of Columbia. *Education:* Boston University (B.A., 1992); American University (J.D., 1999). ***PRACTICE AREAS:*** Litigation; Intellectual Property; Technology Law. ***Email:*** Garrett_Heenan@aporter.com

SCOTT D. HELSEL, born February 1, 1970; admitted to bar, 1995, Virginia; 1997, District of Columbia; 1998, U.S. District Court, District of Columbia. *Education:* Elizabethtown College (B.A., magna cum laude, 1992); Marshall-Wythe School of Law, College of William and Mary (J.D., 1995). William & Mary Law Review. Judicial Clerk, Honorable Henry H. Whiting, Supreme Court of Virginia, 1995-1996. ***PRACTICE AREAS:*** Litigation; Legislative. ***Email:*** Scott_Helsel@aporter.com

THOMAS C. INDELICARTO, admitted to bar, 1997, Pennsylvania; 2000, District of Columbia. *Education:* Indiana University of Pennsylvania (B.S., 1985); University of Pittsburgh (J.D., 1997). [Captain, U.S. Army, 1985-1994]. ***PRACTICE AREAS:*** Litigation; Product Liability. ***Email:*** Thomas_Indelicarto@aporter.com

COURTNEY E. INGRAFFIA, born March 15, 1967; admitted to bar, 1995, Louisiana; 1997, District of Columbia. *Education:* Colby College (B.A., 1989); Tulane University (J.D., cum laude, 1995); Harvard University (M.P.H., 1997). Senior Member and Editor, Tulane Environmental Law Journal. Board of Directors, New Orleans Association of Women Attorneys, 1995-1996. ***PRACTICE AREAS:*** Toxic Tort Litigation; Environmental Litigation; Pharmaceutical; Products Liability. ***Email:*** Courtney_Ingraffia@aporter.com

BRIAN D. ISRAEL, born November 17, 1967; admitted to bar, 1997, New York; 2001, District of Columbia. *Education:* New College, University of South Florida (B.A., 1991); New York University (J.D., 1995). ***PRACTICE AREAS:*** Environmental; Litigation. ***Email:*** Brian_Israel@aporter.com

MICHAEL A. JOHNSON, born March 19, 1966; admitted to bar, 1997, Virginia; 1998, District of Columbia. *Education:* University of Pennsylvania (B.A., magna cum laude, 1990); Indiana University (M.A., 1997); Georgetown University (J.D., 1997). Order of the Coif. Recipient, John M. Olin Prize in Law and Economics. Member, Georgetown Law Review. ***PRACTICE AREAS:*** Civil Litigation Practice; Financial Institutions Litigation; Federal Claims; Asylum Law Practice. ***Email:*** Michael_Johnson@aporter.com

(This Listing Continued)

ARNOLD & PORTER, Washington—Continued

TRACY L. JOHNSON, born October 9, 1968; admitted to bar, 1997, Maryland; 2000, District of Columbia. *Education:* Franklin & Marshall College (B.A., 1990); Georgetown University (J.D., 1997). ***PRACTICE AREAS:*** Litigation. ***Email:*** Tracy_Johnson@aporter.com

STEPHEN E. JONES, born August 14, 1967; admitted to bar, 1998, Maryland; 1999, District of Columbia. *Education:* Virginia Polytechnic Institute and State University (B.A., 1989); University of Maryland (J.D., 1998). Order of the Coif. Maryland Law Review. National Moot Court Team. ***PRACTICE AREAS:*** Litigation; Legislative. ***Email:*** Stephen_Jones@aporter.com

SIMON KANN, born June 21, 1973; admitted to bar, 1998, California; 1999, District of Columbia. *Education:* University of Southern California (B.S., cum laude, 1995); Cornell University Law School (J.D., cum laude, 1998). Cornell International Law Journal. ***PRACTICE AREAS:*** Litigation. ***Email:*** Simon_Kann@aporter.com

ROBERT J. KATERBERG, born June 5, 1974; admitted to bar, 1999, Maryland; 2000, District of Columbia. *Education:* University of North Carolina at Chapel Hill (B.A., 1994; J.D., 1998). Order of the Coif. North Carolina Law Review. Law Clerk, Hon. R. Lanier Anderson, III, Chief Judge, U.S. Court of Appeals for the Eleventh Circuit. ***PRACTICE AREAS:*** Antitrust and Trade Regulation. ***Email:*** Robert_Katerberg@aporter.com

MATTHEW D. KEISER, born April 18, 1972; admitted to bar, 1996, Pennsylvania; 1997, New Jersey; 1998, District of Columbia. *Education:* University of Pennsylvania (B.A., magna cum laude, 1993); George Washington University (J.D., with honors, 1996). ***PRACTICE AREAS:*** Litigation; Employment Law. ***Email:*** Matthew_Keiser@aporter.com

TIMOTHY J. KELLY, born March 21, 1969; admitted to bar, 1998, Maryland; 1999, District of Columbia. *Education:* Duke University (A.B., cum laude, 1991); Georgetown University (J.D., 1997). American Criminal Law Review. ***PRACTICE AREAS:*** Litigation. ***Email:*** Timothy_Kelly@aporter.com

J. BENJAMIN KING, born November 20, 1968; admitted to bar, 1999, Maryland; 2000, District of Columbia. *Education:* University of Mississippi (B.A., 1990); University of Alabama (M.A., 1993); Cornell University (J.D., summa cum laude, 1998). ***PRACTICE AREAS:*** Litigation. ***Email:*** J_Benjamin_King@aporter.com

THOMAS L. KLEIN, born October 8, 1965; admitted to bar, 1996, Virginia; 1999, District of Columbia. *Education:* University of Virginia (B.S., 1988); Wake Forest University (J.D., 1995); New York University (LL.M., Taxation, 1996). Wake Forest Law Review. Law Clerk, Honorable William M. Fay, U.S. Tax Court, 1996-1998. ***PRACTICE AREAS:*** Tax Law. ***Email:*** Thomas_Klein@aporter.com

MICHAEL J. KLYCE, JR., born August 1, 1971; admitted to bar, 1996, Maryland; 1998, District of Columbia. *Education:* Emory University (B.A., 1993); Duke University School of Law (J.D., 1996). ***PRACTICE AREAS:*** Litigation; Antitrust; Insurance. ***Email:*** Michael_Klyce@aporter.com

CHRISTINE E. KOH, admitted to bar, 2000, District of Columbia. *Education:* Pomona College (B.A., 1995); Yale Law School (J.D., 1999).

SARAH B. KOTLER, born June 4, 1973; admitted to bar, 1999, New Jersey, New York and District of Columbia. *Education:* University of Pennsylvania (B.A., 1995); Harvard University (J.D., 1998). Clerk for Chief Judge William G. Young of the U.S. District Court for the District of Massachusetts, 1998-1999. ***PRACTICE AREAS:*** Litigation. ***Email:*** Sarah_Kotler@aporter.com

DAVID W. LEARY, born August 23, 1970; admitted to bar, 2000, New York and District of Columbia. *Education:* University of Virginia (B.A., 1993); Georgetown University (J.D., 1998). ***PRACTICE AREAS:*** Intellectual Property; Technology Law. ***Email:*** David_Leary@aporter.com

GORDON LEDERMAN, born Rochester, New York, December 7, 1971; admitted to bar, 1998, New York and District of Columbia. *Education:* Harvard University (A.B., magna cum laude, 1993; J.D., magna cum laude, 1997). ***PRACTICE AREAS:*** Public Policy; Legislative Practice; International; Litigation; Government Contracts. ***Email:*** Gordon_Lederman@aporter.com

WENDY J. LEVENSON, born June 15, 1971; admitted to bar, 1997, Michigan; 1998, District of Columbia. *Education:* University of Nevada (B.A., with high distinction, 1992); Vanderbilt University (J.D., 1996). 1994 Appellate Advocacy Competition Winner. Judicial Clerk to the Hon. Robert E. Rose, Supreme Court of Nevada. Associate Notes Editor, Vanderbilt Law Review. Vice Justice, Phi Alpha Delta. ***PRACTICE AREAS:*** Litigation; Products Liability. ***Email:*** Wendy_Levenson@aporter.com

GREGORY H. LEVINE, born June 28, 1968; admitted to bar, 1997, New York and District of Columbia. *Education:* Brown University (A.B., magna cum laude, 1990); Georgetown University Law Center (J.D., magna cum laude, 1996). ***LANGUAGES:*** Spanish. ***PRACTICE AREAS:*** Food and Drug Regulation; Health Care; Litigation. ***Email:*** Gregory_Levine@aporter.com

(This Listing Continued)

EMMA KELTON LEWIS, born April 16, 1967; admitted to bar, 1998, New York (Not admitted in District of Columbia). *Education:* Columbia University (A.B., summa cum laude, 1990); Yale University (J.D., 1997). Teaching Assistant, Environmental Law and Policy, Yale University, 1997. Yale Journal of International Law. ***LANGUAGES:*** French; Italian. ***PRACTICE AREAS:*** Litigation; Environmental Law. ***Email:*** Emma_Lewis@aporter.com

VIRGINIA W. LIAO, admitted to bar, 2000, New York and District of Columbia. *Education:* University of Virginia (B.A., 1996); Cornell University (J.D., 1999). ***PRACTICE AREAS:*** Corporate Law; Securities. ***Email:*** Virginia_Liao@aporter.com

JEFFREY A. LIESEMER, born November 26, 1965; admitted to bar, 1993, Virginia; 1996, District of Columbia. *Education:* Bucknell University (B.A., summa cum laude, 1988); University of Pittsburgh (J.D., magna cum laude, 1993). Phi Beta Kappa; Order of the Coif. Managing Editor, University of Pittsburgh Law Review, 1992-1993. Law Clerk to the Honorable Martin V. B. Bostetter, Jr., Chief Judge, U.S. Bankruptcy Court, Eastern District of Virginia, 1993-1995. Chair, Young Lawyers Division, Northern Virginia Chapter, Federal Bar Association, 1998-2000. ***PRACTICE AREAS:*** Bankruptcy; Civil Litigation. ***Email:*** Jeffrey_Liesemer@aporter.com

FRANKLIN R. LISS, born November 30, 1965; admitted to bar, 1993, Georgia; 1994, District of Columbia. *Education:* University of Pennsylvania (B.A., Biophysics, 1987); Emory University School of Law (J.D., with distinction, 1993). Emory Law Journal. ***PRACTICE AREAS:*** Antitrust. ***Email:*** Frank_Liss@aporter.com

KRAIG B. LONG, born December 19, 1968; admitted to bar, 1998, Maryland; 1999, U.S. District Court, District of Maryland and U.S. Court of Appeals, Fourth Circuit; 2000, District of Columbia. *Education:* Temple University (B.B.A., with honors, 1992); University of Maryland (J.D., with honors, 1998). Phi Alpha Delta; Golden Key. University of Maryland Alumni Association Award. Corpus Juris Secundum, Civil Procedure. Margaret E. Coonan Memorial Award. University of Maryland Leadership Award. Law Clerk to Honorable Alexander Williams, Jr., U.S. District Court for the District of Maryland. ***PRACTICE AREAS:*** Litigation. ***Email:*** Kraig_Long@aporter.com

NICK MALHOTRA, born December 8, 1968; admitted to bar, 1995, Massachusetts; 1997, Rhode Island; 2000, District of Columbia. *Education:* Brown University (B.A., magna cum laude, 1991); Columbia Law School (J.D., 1995). ***PRACTICE AREAS:*** Litigation. ***Email:*** Nick_Malhotra@aporter.com

LARK T. MALLORY, born Warren, Ohio, July 9, 1969; admitted to bar, 1998, Maryland; 1999, District of Columbia. *Education:* Ohio State University (B.S.B.A., 1991); Ohio State University College of Law (J.D., 1997); University of Florida College of Law, Graduate Tax Program (LL.M., 1998). ***Email:*** Lark_Mallory@aporter.com

CHRISTOPHER D. MAN, born August 16, 1970; admitted to bar, 1995, Missouri; 1997, District of Columbia, U. S. District Court for the District of Columbia; U.S. Court of Appeals, District of Columbia Circuit; U.S. Supreme Court. *Education:* University of Kansas (B.A., 1992); Washington University (J.D., 1995); George Washington University (LL.M., 1997). ***PRACTICE AREAS:*** Environmental; Litigation. ***Email:*** Christopher_Man@aporter.com

ROBERT E. MASCOLA, born September 27, 1964; admitted to bar, 1996, New York, Massachusetts and District of Columbia. *Education:* Harvard University (A.B., 1986; J.D., 1995). ***PRACTICE AREAS:*** Antitrust. ***Email:*** Robert_Mascola@aporter.com

DUANE J. MAUNEY, born March 20, 1970; admitted to bar, 1996, North Carolina; 1997, District of Columbia. *Education:* University of North Carolina (B.A., with highest honors, 1992; J.D., with high honors, 1996). North Carolina Law Review. ***PRACTICE AREAS:*** Litigation; Products Liability. ***Email:*** Duane_Mauney@aporter.com

THADDEUS R. MCBRIDE, admitted to bar, 2001, Maryland and District of Columbia. *Education:* Princeton University (B.A., 1995); Boston College (J.D., 2000). ***PRACTICE AREAS:*** Litigation; International Trade. ***Email:*** Thaddeus_McBride@aporter.com

ROBERT A. MCCARTER III, born November 12, 1972; admitted to bar, 1997, Maryland; 1998, District of Columbia. *Education:* Boston College (B.A., summa cum laude, 1994); Harvard Law School (J.D., cum laude, 1997). ***PRACTICE AREAS:*** Products Liability Litigation; Litigation. ***Email:*** Robert_A_McCarter@aporter.com

AMY L. MCGINNIS, born July 17, 1972; admitted to bar, 1998, Maryland and District of Columbia. *Education:* American University (B.A., cum laude, 1994); George Washington University Law School (J.D., high honors, 1998). ***PRACTICE AREAS:*** Litigation; Product Liability. ***Email:*** Amy_Mcginnis@aporter.com

KATHRYN C. MCGOVERN, admitted to bar, 1999, Virginia; 2000, District of Columbia. *Education:* College of William & Mary (B.S., 1992); Tulane Law School (J.D., 1999). Law Review. ***PRACTICE AREAS:*** Real Estate. ***Email:*** Kathryn_McGovern@aporter.com

(This Listing Continued)

ERICA TAYLOR McKINLEY, admitted to bar, 1998, Mississippi; 2000, District of Columbia, U.S. Court for the District of Columbia, U.S. Court of Appeals, Fifth Circuit. *Education:* Tougaloo College (B.A., 1994); University of Mississippi Law School (J.D., 1998). ***PRACTICE AREAS:*** Litigation; Product Liability. ***Email:*** Erica_Mckinley@aporter.com

MATTHEW MEISNER, born New York, N.Y.; admitted to bar, 1995, New York; 1998, District of Columbia. *Education:* University of Massachusetts (B.B.A., 1992); George Washington University (J.D., 1995). *Member:* American Bar Association (Member, Antitrust Section).

KENDALL MILLARD, born August 15, 1968; admitted to bar, 1999, District of Columbia. *Education:* Indiana University School of Law (J.D., magna cum laude, 1998). Indiana Law Journal. ***LANGUAGES:*** Japanese. ***PRACTICE AREAS:*** Antitrust Litigation; Litigation. ***Email:*** Kendall_Millard@aporter.com

RANDALL K. MILLER, born August 22, 1963; admitted to bar, 1997, Pennsylvania and New Jersey; 1998, District of Columbia. *Education:* Pennsylvania State University (B.A., with honors, 1988); George Washington University (J.D., with honors, 1996). Pennsylvania State University Scholar Medallion; John W. Oswald Leadership Award. Journal of International Law and Economics. ***PRACTICE AREAS:*** Litigation; Constitutional Law. ***Email:*** Randall_Miller@aporter.com

MARK J. MONTANO, born May 5, 1972; admitted to bar, 1998, Pennsylvania; 1999, District of Columbia. *Education:* Duke University (B.A., magna cum laude, 1994); University of Pennsylvania (J.D., cum laude, 1998). University of Pennsylvania Law Review. ***Email:*** Mark_Montano@aporter.com

AMY RALPH MUDGE, born April 7, 1969; admitted to bar, 1996, District of Columbia. *Education:* Smith College (B.A., 1990); Cornell University (J.D., cum laude, 1995). Cornell Law Review, 1995. Law Clerk to Honorable Sam C. Pointer, Jr., Chief Judge, Northern District of Alabama, 1995-1996. ***PRACTICE AREAS:*** Antitrust; Trade Regulation; Litigation. ***Email:*** Amy_Ralph@aporter.com

WILSON D. MUDGE, born January 9, 1968; admitted to bar, 1996, Maryland; 1997, District of Columbia. *Education:* Michigan State University (B.A., 1990); Washington College of Law, American University (J.D., summa cum laude, 1996). Law Review. ***PRACTICE AREAS:*** Antitrust and Trade Regulation; Litigation. ***Email:*** Wilson_Mudge@aporter.com

REBECCA NASSAB, born November 5, 1969; admitted to bar, 1995, Maryland; 1998, District of Columbia; 1999, U.S. District Court, District of Maryland. *Education:* University of Pennsylvania, Wharton School of Business (B.S., cum laude, 1991); George Washington University Law School (J.D., 1995). ***PRACTICE AREAS:*** Intellectual Property; Technology Law. ***Email:*** Rebecca_Nassab@aporter.com

BRAD NEWBERG, born August 14, 1972; admitted to bar, 1997, Maryland; 2000, District of Columbia. *Education:* University of Pennsylvania (B.A., 1994; J.D., 1997). ***PRACTICE AREAS:*** Intellectual Property Litigation. ***Email:*** Brad_Newberg@aporter.com

JEANNIE H. NGUYEN, born August 4, 1974; admitted to bar, 1999, Virginia; 2000, District of Columbia. *Education:* University of Virginia (B.A., 1996); Washington & Lee University (J.D., 1999). ***PRACTICE AREAS:*** Corporate Law; Securities. ***Email:*** jeannie_nguyen@aporter.com

SON B. NGUYEN, admitted to bar, 1999, Maryland; 2000, District of Columbia. *Education:* Carroll College (B.A., 1992); University of Maryland (J.D., 1999). ***PRACTICE AREAS:*** Antitrust; Competition and Trade; Regulation; Environmental Law. ***Email:*** Son_Nguyen@aporter.com

LESLIE A. NICKEL, born December 16, 1956; admitted to bar, 1994, Virginia; 1996, District of Columbia. *Education:* State University of New York at Binghamton (B.A., 1982); University of Virginia (J.D., 1994). Journal of Law and Politics. ***PRACTICE AREAS:*** Federal and State Legislation; Election and Campaign Finance Law; Lobbying; Government Ethics. ***Email:*** Leslie_Nickel@aporter.com

DONNA NORMAN, born December 26, 1966; admitted to bar, 1992, California; 1993, District of Columbia. *Education:* University of Wisconsin-Madison (B.A., Political Science, with honors,. 1989); Georgetown Law Center (J.D., magna cum laude, 1992). ***PRACTICE AREAS:*** Intellectual Property; Antitrust; Commercial Litigation. ***Email:*** Donna_Norman@aporter.com

KI O, admitted to bar, 2001, New York , Massachusetts and District of Columbia. *Education:* Colgate University (B.S., 1994); George Washington University (J.D., 2000). ***PRACTICE AREAS:*** Intellectual Property; Technology Law; Litigation. ***Email:*** Ki_O@aporter.com

KATHRYN E. OLSON, born June 5, 1966; admitted to bar, 1994, California (Not admitted in District of Columbia). *Education:* University of Pennsylvania (B.A., cum laude, 1988); University of California, Berkeley (M.P.P., 1993); University of California, Boalt Hall School of Law (J.D., 1994). ***Email:*** Kathryn_Olson@aporter.com

DAVID M. ORTA, born September 3, 1969; admitted to bar, 1994, Florida; 1999, District of Columbia. *Education:* Tulane University (B.A., 1991); Stetson

(This Listing Continued)

University College of Law (J.D., magna cum laude, 1994). Phi Delta Phi. Stetson Law Review. Cecil & Augusta Bailey Award; Stetson Law Academic Scholarship; Nader/Zrake Academic Scholarship. Who's Who Among Students in American Law Schools. *Member:* Broward County and Dade County Bar Associations; District of Columbia Bar; Hispanic Bar Association. ***LANGUAGES:*** Spanish. ***PRACTICE AREAS:*** Products Liability Litigation; Complex Commercial Litigation; Employment Litigation. ***Email:*** David_Orta@aporter.com

ANNE M. PACKAGE, born March 11, 1969; admitted to bar, 1995, Pennsylvania; 1997, North Carolina; 2001, District of Columbia. *Education:* University of Pennsylvania (B.A., 1991); University of Michigan Law School (J.D., cum laude, 1994). ***PRACTICE AREAS:*** Litigation. ***Email:*** Anne_Package@aporter.com

EMILY PAQUINELLI, admitted to bar, 2001, District of Columbia and New York. *Education:* Dickinson College (B.A., 1995); George Washington Law School (J.D., 2000).

AMANDA J. PARACUELLOS, born September 27, 1971; admitted to bar, 1996, Illinois; 1997, District of Columbia. *Education:* University of Michigan (A.B., 1993); University of Iowa (J.D., 1996). ***PRACTICE AREAS:*** Corporate Law; Securities. ***Email:*** paracam@aporter.com

DANIEL S. PARISER, born March 4, 1973; admitted to bar, 1999, New York and District of Columbia. *Education:* University of Pennsylvania (B.A., summa cum laude, 1994); Harvard Law School (J.D., magna cum laude, 1998). Boykin C. Wright Memorial Prize. ***PRACTICE AREAS:*** Products Liability Litigation. ***Email:*** Daniel_Pariser@aporter.com

DOUGLAS S. PELLEY, born June 19, 1970; admitted to bar, 1996, Massachusetts; 1997, District of Columbia. *Education:* Atlantic Union College (B.S., summa cum laude, 1993); Cornell University (J.D., magna cum laude, 1996). Cornell International Law Journal. ***PRACTICE AREAS:*** Employee Benefits; Taxation. ***Email:*** Douglas_Pelley@aporter.com

AMY K. PHILLIPS, born November 1, 1969; admitted to bar, 1998, New York and District of Columbia. *Education:* University of North Carolina, Chapel Hill (B.S.B.A., with distinction, 1992); Georgetown University Law Center (J.D., magna cum laude, 1997). American Criminal Law Review. Member and Coach, Moot Court. ***PRACTICE AREAS:*** Litigation. ***Email:*** Amy_Phillips@aporter.com

ANNALISA PIZZARELLO, born September 8, 1966; admitted to bar, 1993, California; 1994, Illinois and District of Columbia. *Education:* Brown University (B.A., with honors, 1988; M.A., with honors, 1990); University of Chicago (J.D., 1993). University of Chicago Legal Forum Journal. Law Clerk to Judge Harold M. Fong, U.S. District Court, District of Hawaii. ***LANGUAGES:*** Italian. ***PRACTICE AREAS:*** Food and Drug Law. ***Email:*** Annalisa_Pizzarello@aporter.com

IAN PLANT, admitted to bar, 1997, District of Columbia. *Education:* University of Michigan (J.D., 1997). ***PRACTICE AREAS:*** Antitrust. ***Email:*** Ian_Plant@aporter.com

KENNETH L. POLLACK, born December 28, 1967; admitted to bar, 1995, Maryland; 1997, District of Columbia. *Education:* Tufts University (B.A., cum laude, 1990); Vanderbilt University School of Law (J.D., 1995). Order of the Coif. Vanderbilt Law Review. ***PRACTICE AREAS:*** Real Estate; Health Care; Litigation. ***Email:*** Kenneth_Pollack@aporter.com

STACY J. POLLOCK, born December 24, 1969; admitted to bar, 1995, Pennsylvania; 1996, District of Columbia. *Education:* Allentown College of St. Francis De Sales (B.A., 1991); Universidad D Las Americas, Pueblo, Mexico; George Washington University National Law Center (J.D., high honors, 1994). George Washington Law Review. Judicial Clerk, Honorable Joel F. Dubina, U.S. Court of Appeals, Eleventh Circuit, 1995-1996. ***PRACTICE AREAS:*** Litigation. ***Email:*** Stacy_Pollock@aporter.com

NICHOLAS PORRITT, born May 29, 1968; admitted to bar, 1991, New Zealand as Barrister and Solicitor; 1997, New York; 1998, District of Columbia; 1999, U.S. District Court for the District of Columbia. *Education:* Victoria University of Wellington, Wellington, New Zealand (L.L.B. Hons.), 1990); University of Chicago (L.L.M., 1993; J.D., with honors, 1996). ***PRACTICE AREAS:*** Litigation. ***Email:*** Nicholas_Porritt@aporter.com

THORN L. POZEN, born September 18, 1965; admitted to bar, 1998, Maryland; 1999, District of Columbia, U.S. District Court, District of Maryland and U.S. District Court for the District of Columbia. *Education:* Connecticut College (B.A., honors and distinction, 1988); Washington College of Law of American University (J.D., magna cum laude, 1998). International Law Review. ***PRACTICE AREAS:*** Government Contracts; Public Policy. ***Email:*** Thorn_Pozen@aporter.com

ELISSA J. PREHEIM, born February 4, 1971; admitted to bar, 1996, Illinois; 1998, District of Columbia. *Education:* Northwestern University (B.A., with honors, 1993); Indiana University (J.D., summa cum laude, 1996). Indiana

(This Listing Continued)

ARNOLD & PORTER, Washington—Continued

Law Journal. Clerkship, Honorable Bruce M. Selya, U.S. Court of Appeals, First Circuit, 1996-1997. ***PRACTICE AREAS:*** Litigation; Intellectual Property. ***Email:*** Elissa_Preheim@aporter.com

LISA A. PRICE, born April 27, 1964; admitted to bar, 1993, Virginia; 1996, District of Columbia. *Education:* University of Virginia (B.A., 1986; J.D., 1993). Virginia Environmental Law Journal; Virginia Law Review. Law Clerk to: Honorable James P. Jones, U.S. District Court, Western District of Virginia, 1996-1997; Honorable Sven E. Holmes, U.S. District Court, Northern District of Oklahoma, 1997-1998. ***PRACTICE AREAS:*** Litigation. ***Email:*** Lisa_Price@aporter.com

MICHAEL D. RAIBMAN, admitted to bar, 1996, New Jersey; 1997, Pennsylvania; 1999, District of Columbia. *Education:* Washington University (A.B., cum laude, 1993); University of Pennsylvania (J.D., cum laude, 1996). Law Review. Law Clerk to: Honorable Jan E. DuBois, Eastern District of Pennsylvania, 1996-1997; Honorable Andrew J. Kleinfeld, U.S. Court of Appeals, Ninth Circuit, 1997-1998. ***PRACTICE AREAS:*** Litigation; Food Products Liability; Drug and Medical Device Litigation; Regulatory. ***Email:*** Michael_Raibman@aporter.com

KIM RAPPAPORT, admitted to bar, 2000, New York and District of Columbia. *Education:* Cornell University (B.Arch., 1996); American University, Washington College of Law (J.D., magna cum laude, 1999). ***PRACTICE AREAS:*** Litigation. ***Email:*** Kim_Rappaport@aporter.com

JEFF RICHMAN, born April 23, 1965; admitted to bar, 1995, Pennsylvania; 1996, District of Columbia. *Education:* University of Pennsylvania (B.S.E., 1987); University of Pennsylvania Law School (J.D., 1994). ***PRACTICE AREAS:*** Legislative. ***Email:*** Jeffrey_Richman@aporter.com

AMY B. RIFKIND, born October 6, 1967; admitted to bar, 1994, New York; 1995, Massachusetts; 1998, District of Columbia. *Education:* Yale University (B.A., 1989; J.D., 1993). Yale Law and Policy Review. Law Clerk to Hon. Douglas P. Woodlock, U.S. District Court for the District of Massachusetts, 1993-1994. ***PRACTICE AREAS:*** Real Estate. ***Email:*** Amy_Rifkind@aporter.com

RICHARD R. RODGERS, born March 18, 1969; admitted to bar, 2000, New York; 2001, District of Columbia. *Education:* Yale University (B.A., 1991); Columbia Law School (J.D., 1999). ***PRACTICE AREAS:*** Corporate Law; Securities; Real Estate. ***Email:*** Richard_Rodgers@aporter.com

JANICE M. RODRIGUEZ, admitted to bar, 1999, Maryland; 2000, District of Columbia. *Education:* University of Maryland University College (B.S., 1989); Georgetown University Law Center (J.D., 1999). ***PRACTICE AREAS:*** Civil Litigation. ***Email:*** Janice_Rodriguez@aporter.com

JAMES M. ROSENTHAL, born November 13, 1971; admitted to bar, 1996, Maryland; 1997, District of Columbia. *Education:* Pomona College (B.A., 1993); University of Michigan (J.D., magna cum laude, 1996). Michigan Law Review. ***PRACTICE AREAS:*** Litigation. ***Email:*** James_Rosenthal@aporter.com

SIDNEY A. ROSENZWEIG, born January 3, 1972; admitted to bar, 1998, New York and District of Columbia; registered to practice before U.S. Patent and Trademark Office. *Education:* Brown University (Sc.B., 1993); University of Pennsylvania (J.D., summa cum laude, 1996). ***PRACTICE AREAS:*** Intellectual Property; Technology Law. ***Email:*** Sidney_Rosenzweig@aporter.com

MICHAEL A. RUBIN, born April 30, 1973; admitted to bar, 1999, New York and District of Columbia. *Education:* Amherst College (B.A., magna cum laude, 1995); Yale Law School (J.D., 1998). Phi Beta Kappa. Amherst College Best Political Science Thesis Prize. Amherst College Fellowships in Law. ***PRACTICE AREAS:*** Litigation; Products Liability; Pro Bono. ***Email:*** Michael_Rubin@aporter.com

AMY F. RYAN, born October 4, 1966; admitted to bar, 1999, Virginia; 2000, District of Columbia. *Education:* University of Virginia (B.A., 1988); Georgetown University Law enter (J.D., 1999). Georgetown Law Journal, 1997-1999. ***PRACTICE AREAS:*** Intellectual Property. ***Email:*** Amy_Ryan@aporter.com

MICHAEL A. SACKEY, admitted to bar, 1999, Maryland; 2000, District of Columbia. *Education:* Washington & Lee University School of Law (J.D., 1997).

SHEILA B. SCHEUERMAN, admitted to bar, 1997, Michigan; 2001, District of Columbia. *Education:* College of the Holy Cross (B.A., 1993); Washington University School of Law (J.D., 1997).

PETER J. SCHILDKRAUT, born May 10, 1968; admitted to bar, 1997, Massachusetts; 1998, District of Columbia. *Education:* Harvard University (A.B., magna cum laude, 1990; J.D., magna cum laude/M.P.P., 1997). Harvard Journal. ***PRACTICE AREAS:*** Telecommunications; Communications Law. ***Email:*** Peter_Schildkraut@aporter.com

(This Listing Continued)

KAREN K. SCHWARTZ, born Washington, D.C., May 17, 1943; admitted to bar, 1975, District of Columbia. *Education:* Radcliffe College (A.B., cum laude, 1965); Yale University (J.D., 1972). ***PRACTICE AREAS:*** Trusts and Estates; Wills. ***Email:*** Karen_Schwartz@aporter.com

P. MONI SENGUPTA, born August 6, 1966; admitted to bar, 1992, Ohio; 1998, District of Columbia. *Education:* Carnegie Mellon University (B.S., 1988); The Ohio State University (J.D., 1992); Boston University (LL.M., 1993). ***PRACTICE AREAS:*** Financial Institutions; Litigation; Securities Regulation. ***Email:*** P._Moni_Sengupta@aporter.com

JULE L. SIGALL, born June 17, 1968; admitted to bar, 1996, Ohio; 1997, District of Columbia. *Education:* Duke University (A.B., 1990); Catholic University of America (J.D., summa cum laude, 1996). Catholic University Law Review, 1994-1996. ***PRACTICE AREAS:*** Intellectual Property. ***Email:*** Jule_Sigall@aporter.com

FABIO ROMAN SILVA, born December 3, 1969; admitted to bar, 1999, California and District of Columbia. *Education:* University of California, Santa Barbara (B.A., 1993); Stanford Law School (J.D., 1998). Business Manager, Stanford Law Review, 1997-1998. Boardmember, Gaylaw, 2000. Member: Gaylaw, 1999—; Hispanic Bar Association, 1999—; American Bar Association, 1999—. ***LANGUAGES:*** Spanish. ***PRACTICE AREAS:*** Consumer Product Safety; Civil Litigation; Intellectual Property Transactions. ***Email:*** Fabio_Silva@aporter.com

S. JNATEL SIMMONS, born 1972; admitted to bar, 1997, Pennsylvania; 2001, District of Columbia. *Education:* Bowdoin College (A.B., cum laude, 1994); University of Pennsylvania (J.D., 1997). ***PRACTICE AREAS:*** Litigation. ***Email:*** Jnatel_Simmons@aporter.com

DARREN C. SKINNER, born November 27, 1965; admitted to bar, 1995, Florida; 1996, District of Columbia. *Education:* University of the West Indies (LL.B., magna cum laude, 1987); London School of Economics (LL.M., 1988); Harvard University (LL.M., 1991); Georgetown University Law Center (J.D., cum laude, 1995). Legal Education Certificate, Commonwealth Caribbean, 1990. ***PRACTICE AREAS:*** International; Corporate. ***Email:*** Darren_Skinner@aporter.com

CAREY W. SMITH, born November 16, 1969; admitted to bar, 1996, Maryland; 1997, District of Columbia. *Education:* Amherst College (A.B., 1992); Yale University (J.D., 1995). Law Clerk, Judge Peter J. Messitte, U.S. District Court, District of Maryland, 1995-1996. ***PRACTICE AREAS:*** Tax; Real Estate. ***Email:*** Carey_Smith@aporter.com

SHERRESE M. SMITH, born November 28, 1971; admitted to bar, 1996, Ohio; 2000, District of Columbia. *Education:* University of South Carolina (B.A., 1993); Northwestern University (J.D., 1996). ***PRACTICE AREAS:*** Intellectual Property; Technology Law. ***Email:*** Sherrese_Smith@aporter.com

MICHAEL S. SOLENDER, born Chicago, Illinois, April 14, 1964; admitted to bar, 1990, New York; 1991, District of Columbia. *Education:* Columbia University (B.A., 1986); Yale University (J.D., 1989). ***Email:*** Michael_Solender@aporter.com

SIRAK SOLOMON, born October 20, 1970; admitted to bar, 1998, Maryland; 1999, District of Columbia. *Education:* Georgia State University (B.A., 1994); Howard University Law School (J.D., 1998). ***PRACTICE AREAS:*** Corporate Law; Securities. ***Email:*** Sirak_Solomon@aporter.com

PENNY SOMER-GREIF, admitted to bar, 1996, New York and New Jersey; 2000, District of Columbia. *Education:* State University of New York at Binghamton (B.S., 1992); Washington College of Law, The American University (J.D., 1995). ***PRACTICE AREAS:*** Corporate Law; Securities. ***Email:*** Penny_Somer-Greif@aporter.com

MICHAEL L. SOZAN, born January 2, 1969; admitted to bar, 1994, Virginia; 1997, District of Columbia. *Education:* College of William & Mary (B.A., 1991); George Washington University Law School (J.D., 1994). ***PRACTICE AREAS:*** Telecommunications Law. ***Email:*** Michael_Sozan@aporter.com

MARC A. STANISLAWCZYK, admitted to bar, 1997, Maryland; 1999, District of Columbia. *Education:* University of Pennsylvania (B.A., 1994); Catholic University of American (J.D., magna cum laude, 1997). ***PRACTICE AREAS:*** Government Contracts; Litigation; Health Care and Pharmaceutical; Fraud, Abuse and Compliance. ***Email:*** Marc_Stanislawczyk@aporter.com

TIM STELZIG, born February 25, 1966; admitted to bar, 1999, District of Columbia. *Education:* West Virginia University (B.A., magna cum laude, 1990); University of Illinois, Chicago (M.A., 1995); University of Pennsylvania (J.D., cum laude, 1998). University of Pennsylvania Law Review. ***Email:*** Tim_Stelzig@aporter.com

STEVE C. SUK, born June 6, 1969; admitted to bar, 1997, Virginia; 1998, District of Columbia. *Education:* George Mason University (B.A., 1993); Catholic University of America (J.D., magnum cum laude, 1997). Vernon X. Miller Scholarship, 1995-1996 and 1996-1997. Catholic University Law Review; Intellectual Properties. ***PRACTICE AREAS:*** Corporate Law; Securities; Financial Institutions. ***Email:*** Steve_Suk@aporter.com

(This Listing Continued)

ERIC SUTER, born October 23, 1967; admitted to bar, 1999, District of Columbia. *Education:* University of Colorado (B.A., summa cum laude, 1994; J.D., 1998). ***PRACTICE AREAS:*** Litigation. **Email:** Eric_Suter@aporter.com

JOY TAYLOR, born November 15, 1964; admitted to bar, 1993, Texas; 1995, District of Columbia. *Education:* University of Houston (B.S., 1986; J.D., 1993); New York University School of Law (LL.M., 1995). Certified Public Accountant, Texas, 1987. ***PRACTICE AREAS:*** Federal Taxation. **Email:** Joy_Taylor@aporter.com

TRENT TAYLOR, born July 28, 1973; admitted to bar, 1999, Tennessee and U.S. Court of Appeals, Sixth Circuit; 2000, District of Columbia. *Education:* Rhodes College (B.A., cum laude, 1995); Harvard University (J.D., 1998). ***PRACTICE AREAS:*** Litigation; Products Liability.

ROBERT J. WAGMAN, JR., born March 6, 1968; admitted to bar, 2000, Maryland and District of Columbia. *Education:* University of Maryland (B.S., 1992); American University (J.D., 1999). ***PRACTICE AREAS:*** Government Contracts. **Email:** Robert_Wagman@aporter.com

ANNE McBRIDE WALKER, born September 19, 1966; admitted to bar, 1991, Maryland; 1993, District of Columbia; 1996, U.S. Supreme Court. *Education:* University of Virginia (B.A., 1988); Georgetown University Law Center (J.D., cum laude, 1991). Georgetown Journal of Legal Ethics. ***PRACTICE AREAS:*** Litigation; Products Liability. **Email:** Anne_Walker@aporter.com

ANDREA MACINTOSH WHITEWAY, born June 8, 1967; admitted to bar, 1992, Maryland; 1993, District of Columbia and U.S. District Court, Districts of Maryland and District of Columbia; 1994, U.S. Tax Court. *Education:* Cornell University (B.A., 1989); University of Maryland School of Law (J.D., 1992); Georgetown University Law Center (LL.M. in Taxation, 1995). Articles Editor, Business Lawyer. Co-Author: with Blake Rubin, "Creative Tax Planning for the Disposition of Over Leveraged Real Estate," 13 Tax Mgmt. Real Est. J. 43 (1997); with Blake Rubin, "Exploring the Outer Limits of the 704(c) Partnership Built-in Gain Rule," J. Tax'n (Sept.-Nov. 1998). *Member:* Maryland State and American (Business Law and Taxation Sections) Bar Associations. **Email:** Andrea_Whiteway@aporter.com

CHRISTY C. WIEGAND, admitted to bar, 2001, Massachusetts and District of Columbia. *Education:* Princeton University (A.B., 1997); Cornell University (J.D., 2000).

ERICA Y. WILLIAMS, born December 31, 1973; admitted to bar, 1998, Virginia; 1999, District of Columbia. *Education:* University of Virginia (B.A., 1995; J.D., 1998). Golden Key. ***PRACTICE AREAS:*** Litigation.

CHRISTOPHER WINTERS, born August 25, 1972; admitted to bar, 1997, Illinois; 1999, District of Columbia. *Education:* Northern Illinois University (B.A., cum laude, 1994); Harvard Law School (J.D., cum laude, 1997). Harvard Journal of Legislation. ***PRACTICE AREAS:*** Intellectual Property Litigation; Litigation. **Email:** Christopher_Winters@aporter.com

ELIZABETH WIRICK, admitted to bar, 1999, District of Columbia. *Education:* Harvard College (B.A., 1988); Georgetown University (J.D., 1998). ***PRACTICE AREAS:*** Financial Institutions Law; Public Policy and Legislative. **Email:** Elizabeth_Wirick@aporter.com

GILLIAN C. WOOD, admitted to bar, 1999, District of Columbia.

TODD A. WYNKOOP, admitted to bar, 1995, Maryland; 2001, District of Columbia. *Education:* Fordham University (B.A., 1983); Georgetown University (J.D., cum laude, 1994). ***PRACTICE AREAS:*** Litigation. **Email:** Todd_Wynkoop@aporter.com

AMY J. YANOFF, born August 15, 1973; admitted to bar, 1998, Maryland; 1999, District of Columbia. *Education:* Brown University (A.B., magna cum laude, 1995); University of Michigan (J.D., cum laude, 1998). Michigan Law Review. Darrow Scholar. ***PRACTICE AREAS:*** Litigation. **Email:** Amy_Yanoff@aporter.com

MICHAEL D. YEH, born October 19, 1971; admitted to bar, 1998, California; 1999, District of Columbia. *Education:* Cornell University (B.S., 1994); University of Minnesota (J.D., magna cum laude, 1998; M.A., 1998). ***PRACTICE AREAS:*** Antitrust; Litigation. **Email:** Michael_Yeh@aporter.com

KEVIN A. ZAMBROWICZ, born February 4, 1970; admitted to bar, 1995, Virginia (inactive) and District of Columbia. *Education:* Catholic University of America (B.A., 1992; J.D., 1995). ***PRACTICE AREAS:*** Financial Institutions; Corporate; Securities. **Email:** Kevin_Zambrowicz@aporter.com

ELLIOTT ZENICK, born June 21, 1972; admitted to bar, 1998, North Carolina; 1999, District of Columbia. *Education:* University of North Carolina (B.A., with high distinction and honors, 1994; J.D., high honors, 1998). Phi Beta Kappa. North Carolina Law Review, North Carolina Banking Law Institute Journal. ***PRACTICE AREAS:*** Environmental. **Email:** Elliott_Zenick@aporter.com

(For biographical data of the Los Angeles personnel, see Professional Biographies at Los Angeles, California)
(For biographical data of the Denver personnel, see Professional Biographies at Denver, Colorado)
(For biographical data of the New York personnel, see Professional Biographies at New York, New York)
(For biographical data of the London personnel, see Professional Biographies at London, England)
(For biographical data of the McLean personnel, see Professional Biographies at McLean, Virginia)

ARNOLD, WHITE & DURKEE

WASHINGTON, D.C.

(See Howrey, Simon, Arnold & White, LLP)

ARTABANE & BELDEN, P.C.

818 18TH STREET, N.W., SUITE 410
WASHINGTON, D.C. 20006
Telephone: 202-861-0070
Fax: 202-861-2939
Email: lawyers@artabane-belden.com
URL: http://www.lawyers.com/artabane&belden

Complex and Multi-Jurisdictional Commercial Litigation, Government Contracts, Employment Law, Wrongful Termination, Wrongful Discharge, Age Discrimination, Equal Employment Opportunity Law, Executive Compensation; Employment Compliance, Intellectual Property Litigation, Trade Secrets, Copyright, Patent Infringement, Trademarks, Securities Fraud, Grand Jury Practice, White Collar Crime, Qui Tam Litigation and Personal Injury.

FIRM PROFILE: Artabane & Belden, P.C. is best known for its trial work involving complex legal issues, multiple parties and many jurisdictions. The firm represents a broad range of government contractors, employees and employers (both private and public sector), individuals, small and large businesses and associations.

JOSEPH A. ARTABANE, born Scranton, Pennsylvania, November 3, 1949; admitted to bar, 1975, District of Columbia, U.S. Court of Federal Claims, U.S. District Court for the District of Columbia and U.S. Court of Appeals for the District of Columbia Circuit; 1978, U.S. Court of Appeals, First, Third, Fourth and Seventh Circuits and U.S. Supreme Court; 1984, U.S. Court of Appeals for the Federal Circuit; 1986, U.S. Court of International Trade; 1991, U.S. District Court, District of Maryland. *Education:* Georgetown University (A.B., cum laude, 1971; J.D., 1974). Phi Beta Kappa; Pi Sigma Alpha. Editor, Georgetown Law Journal, 1971-1973. Co-Author: with Block "Federal Circuit Decision Eases Government Contracts Dispute Process," Legal Backgrounder, Washington Legal Foundation, 1995; "Sexual Harassment in the Workplace: Guidelines for Limiting Corporate Liability," Legal Backgrounder, Washington Legal Foundation, 1988; Co-Author: with Kauffman, "Emasculating The *Scanwell* Doctrine: The Government's Misuse Of The Termination For Convenience Clause," Critical Legal Issues, Working Paper Series No. 40, Washington Legal Foundation. *Government Contractors' Self-Governance Obligations and Employee Relations,* Lib. of Cong. No. 87-51645 Monograph, published by Washington Legal Foundation, 1988; *Defusing the Asbestos Litigation Crisis: The Responsibility of the U.S. Government,* Lib. of Cong. No. 86-061900 Monograph, published by Washington Legal Foundation, 1986. *Member:* District of Columbia Bar; American Bar Association (Member, Sections of: Litigation; Public Contract Law). ***PRACTICE AREAS:*** Civil Practice; Trial Practice; Corporate Litigation; Environmental Litigation; Employment Law. **Email:** jaartabane@artabane-belden.com

W. NEIL BELDEN, born Niagara Falls, New York, August 9, 1964; admitted to bar, 1990, New York and District of Columbia; 1995, U.S. District Court for the District of Columbia; 1998, U.S. District Court, Northern, Southern and Eastern Districts of New York. *Education:* Hamilton College (B.A., 1986); Vermont Law School (J.D., 1989). Co-Author: with Artabane, "Court Rules Against Retroactivity of Family and Medical Leave Regulations," Washington Legal Foundation-Counsel's Advisory, Vol.3 No.9, October 27, 1995; "Supreme Court Redefines Proof Needed in Age Discrimination Cases," Washington Legal Foundation-Counsel's Advisory, Vol.4 No.4, May 24, 1996. *Member:* New York State Bar Association; District of Columbia Bar. ***PRACTICE AREAS:*** Commercial Litigation; Employment Law; Intellectual Property. **Email:** wnbelden@artabane-belden.com

ROBERT F. CONDON, born Hempstead, New York, November 7, 1936; admitted to bar, 1961, New York; 1972, District of Columbia; 1973, U.S. Court of Federal Claims. *Education:* St. John's University (B.A., 1958); Georgetown University (J.D., with honors, 1961). Assistant District Attorney, New York

(This Listing Continued)

ARTABANE & BELDEN, P.C., Washington—Continued

County, 1961-1965. Counsel to Grievance Committee, Association of the Bar of the City of New York, 1965-1966. Associate Counsel for Litigation, New York Life Insurance Co., 1966-1972. Senior Counsel to Board, Member, Merit Systems Protection Board, 1998-1999. *Member:* The District of Columbia Bar; American Bar Association (Member, Sections on: Construction Law; Litigation, 1972-1992); Society of Professionals in Dispute Resolution. (Also of Counsel to Mitchell & Dunn). ***PRACTICE AREAS:*** Commercial Litigation; Employment Law; Real Estate; Construction Law; Professional Ethics; Government Contracts; Administrative Law. ***Email:*** rfcondon@artabane-belden.com

---

LUKE C. PINGEL, born Madison, Wisconsin, May 30, 1970; admitted to bar, 1998, California (Not admitted in District of Columbia). *Education:* University of Oregon (B.A., 1993); Santa Clara University School of Law (J.D., 1997). *Member:* Santa Clara County Bar Association; State Bar of California. ***LANGUAGES:*** Spanish. ***PRACTICE AREAS:*** Civil Litigation; Workers' Compensation; Employment Law. ***Email:*** lpingel@artabane-belden.com

OF COUNSEL

JOHN A. McCAHILL, born Canonsburg, Pennsylvania; admitted to bar, 1970, District of Columbia; 1974, U.S. Supreme Court; 1985, Pennsylvania; 1995, Virginia. *Education:* Columbia University (A.B., 1961); Catholic University of America (J.D., 1969). Assistant U.S. Attorney, District of Columbia, 1970-1973. Assistant Special Counsel to the President, 1973-1974. Special Assistant to the Attorney General, 1974. General Counsel, President's Commission on Olympic Sports, 1975-1977. Special Legislative Counsel to the U.S. Olympic Committee, 1977-1985. *Member:* The District of Columbia Bar; American Bar Association (Member: Criminal Justice Section; White Collar Crimes Committee, 1986—); Assistant United States Attorneys Association. (Also practicing individually). ***PRACTICE AREAS:*** Civil Litigation; Legislative Law; Criminal Law; White Collar Crime; Personal Injury. ***Email:*** jamccahill@artabane-belden.com

---

ARTER & HADDEN LLP

1801 K STREET, N.W., SUITE 400K
WASHINGTON, D.C. 20006
Telephone: 202-775-7100
Facsimile: 202-857-0172
URL: http://www.arterhadden.com

REVISERS OF THE OHIO LAW DIGEST FOR THIS DIRECTORY

In Cleveland, Ohio: 1100 Huntington Building, 925 Euclid Avenue, 44115-1475. Telephone: 216-696-1100. Fax: 216-696-2645.
In Columbus, Ohio: Suite 2100, One Columbus, 10 West Broad Street, 43215-3422. Telephone: 614-221-3155. Fax: 614-221-0479.
In Dallas, Texas: 1717 Main Street, Suite 4100, 75201-4605. Telephone: 214-761-2100. Fax: 214-741-7139.
In Dayton, Ohio: Suite 2310, 40 North Main Street, 45423. Telephone: 973-223-4701. Fax: 937-223-0170.
In Los Angeles, California: 725 South Figueroa Street, Suite 3400, 90017. Telephone: 213-430-3000. Fax: 212-617-9255.
In Irvine, California: Five Park Plaza, Suite 1000, Jamboree Center, 92714. Telephone: 949-252-7500. Fax: 949-833-9604.
In San Francisco, California: Two Embarcadero Center, 5th Floor, 94111. Telephone: 415-617-2100. Fax: 415-912-3636.
In San Diego, California: 550 West C Street, 16th Floor, 92101. Telephone: 619-238-0001. Fax: 619-595-1313.
In Woodland Hills, California: 5959 Topanga Canyon Boulevard, Suite 244, 91367. Telephone: 818-712-0036. Fax: 818-346-6502.

Appellate Litigation, Bankruptcy, Business Litigation, Commercial, Communications and Media, Construction, Corporate and Securities, Director and Officer Liability, Energy Deregulation, Employment, Environmental, Estates, Finance, Government Affairs, Health Care, Insurance Litigation, Intellectual Property, Customs, Trade and Technology, International, Professional and Product Liability, Real Estate, Tax Services and Workers' Compensation.

MEMBERS OF FIRM

CHARLES K. ARTER (1875-1957).

JOHN A. HADDEN (1886-1979).

WILLIAM K. DABAGHI, born Huntsville, Texas, July 20, 1945; admitted to bar, 1972, Texas; 1979, District of Columbia; 1994, Geneva; 1995, Brussels. *Education:* Harvard College (C' 1967); University of Texas (J.D., 1972); The Wharton School, University of Pennsylvania (M.B.A., 1996). Delta Theta Phi. Director, Office of Congressional Affairs, Office of the Secretary, U.S. Department of Transportation, 1982-1983. Federal Legislative Counsel, American Bankers Association, 1976-1982. Attorney, Office of General Counsel, Small Business Administration, 1974-1976. Of Counsel to Berger, Recordon & de Saugy in Geneva, Switzerland. *Member:* International, Inter-Pacific and American Bar Associations; Sons of the American Revolution; Sons of the Republic of Texas. [JAG Corps, U.S. Naval Reserve (ret)]. (Chair, International Practice Group). ***PRACTICE AREAS:*** Financial Services; International Trade Policy; World Trade Organization Dispute Settlement; Government Relations. ***Email:*** wdabaghi@arterhadden.com

RICHARD A. DEAN, born Greencastle, Indiana, September 26, 1948; admitted to bar, 1973, Ohio; 1980, U.S. Supreme Court; 1986, Texas; 1991, District of Columbia; 1992, Maryland. *Education:* DePauw University (A.B., 1970); Indiana University (J.D., 1973). Phi Beta Kappa; Order of the Coif. Note Editor, University of Indiana Law Journal, 1972-1973. Author: "Punitive Damages: The Immediate Aftermath of Haslip," For the Defense (May 1992); "Punitive Damages Revisited," Rx For the Defense (Fall 1994); "Relative Risk and Summary Judgement: Making Epidemiology Work for Defendants," Rx For the Defense (Fall 1996); "Perfecting Tort Design," Legal Times (Feb. 1997). Law Clerk for the Hon. Paul C. Weick, U.S. Court of Appeals, Sixth Circuit, 1973-1974. *Member:* American Bar Association (Member, Litigation and Tort and Insurance Practice Sections); District of Columbia Bar; International Association of Defense Counsel. ***PRACTICE AREAS:*** Litigation; Products Liability Law; Toxic Tort; Insurance Coverage. ***Email:*** rdean@arterhadden.com

WILLIAM L. GEHRIG, born Havre de Grace, Maryland, September 5, 1953; admitted to bar, 1981, District of Columbia; 1982, U.S. Court of Federal Claims; U.S. Tax Court, U.S. District Court for the District of Columbia and U.S. Court of Appeals for the District of Columbia Circuit. *Education:* University of Virginia (B.A., with high distinction, 1976; J.D., 1981). Echols Scholar. Executive Editor (Founding Managing Board), Virginia Tax Review, 1980-1981. Chair, Arter & Hadden Finance Group. Principal Author: "Federal Tax Aspects of Municipal Bonds," Fundamentals of Municipal Bond Law, (NABL), 1989-2001. Publishing Editor, Fundamentals of Municipal Bond Law (NABL), 1993-2001. Chair, 1992 NABL Fundamentals of Municipal Bond Law Seminar; Vice-Chair, 1991. Member, Board of Directors, National Association of Bond Lawyers (NABL), 1999-2001. Chair, NABL Education Committee, 1988 (Vice-Chair, 1995-1997); Steering Committee, Bond Attorneys' Workshop, 1993-1995 (Chair, Single Family Housing Bond Panel, 1993-1995). *Member:* The District of Columbia Bar; American Bar Association; National Association of Bond Lawyers. ***PRACTICE AREAS:*** Municipal Finance; Corporate Finance; Federal Taxation. ***Email:*** wgehrig@arterhadden.com

LAWRENCE H. GESNER, born New York, N.Y., 1958; admitted to bar, 1983, District of Columbia. *Education:* George Washington University (B.B.A., 1980); Georgetown University Law Center (J.D., cum laude, 1983). Chair, Arter & Hadden District of Columbia Real Estate Group. Senior Lead Articles Editor, Law and Policy in International Business, 1982-1983. ***Email:*** lgesner@arterhadden.com

MICHAEL R. GOODSTEIN, born Flushing, New York, May 16, 1964; admitted to bar, 1989, Maryland; 1990, District of Columbia, Virginia, U.S. District Court, District of Columbia, U.S. District Court, Eastern District of Virginia and U.S. District Court, District of Maryland; 1991, U.S. Bankruptcy Court, Eastern District of Virginia. *Education:* Brandeis University (B.A., 1986); Washington College of Law of American University (J.D., 1989). Note and Comment Editor, The Administrative Law Journal, 1988-1989. ***PRACTICE AREAS:*** Litigation. ***Email:*** mgoodste@arterhadden.com

PHILIP M. HOROWITZ, born Newark, New Jersey, 1946; admitted to bar, 1973, Virginia and District of Columbia. *Education:* City College of the City University of New York and Upsala College (A.B., magna cum laude, 1970); Georgetown University (J.D., 1973). Member, Board of Editors, Georgetown Law Journal, 1972-1973. Listed in: *The Best Lawyers in America,* 2001-2002; *Guide to the World's Leading Real Estate Lawyers.* Adjunct Professor, Real Estate Planning, American University, Washington College of Law, 1988—. Member, Anglo-American Real Property Institute. Chairman, National Real Estate Practice Group, Arter & Hadden, 1994—. ***Email:*** phorowit@arterhadden.com

JAMES GRIER HOYT, born San Francisco, California, 1958; admitted to bar, 1984, North Carolina; 1985, District of Columbia; 1986, Virginia. *Education:* University of Georgia (B.A., magna cum laude, 1980); Duke University (J.D., 1984). Phi Beta Kappa; Phi Eta Sigma. *Member:* The District of Columbia Bar; North Carolina State Bar; Virginia State Bar; District of Columbia Building Industry Association; International Council of Shopping Centers. ***Email:*** jghoyt@arterhadden.com

CHRISTOPHER H. JOHNSON, born Munich, Germany, February 24, 1951; admitted to bar, 1979, New York, District of Columbia, U.S. District Court, Southern and Eastern Districts of New York, District of Columbia, U.S. Court of Appeals, Second, Federal and District of Columbia Circuits, U.S. Court of International Trade; Court of Federal Claims; U.S. Supreme Court. *Education:* Princeton University (B.A., 1974); New York University (J.D., 1978). Recommended Arbitrator, Euro-Arab Arbitration System. Commissioner, Vint

(This Listing Continued)

Hill Economic Development Agency, Trustee, Physicians for Peace. *Member:* American and International Bar Associations. ***LANGUAGES:*** French. ***PRACTICE AREAS:*** International Commercial; Litigation; Construction. ***Email:*** johnsonc@arterhadden.com

WILLIAM K. KEANE, born Washington, D.C., August 5, 1944; admitted to bar, 1972, Virginia; 1973, District of Columbia; 1979, Maryland. *Education:* College of the Holy Cross (A.B., cum laude, 1966); University of Virginia (J.D., 1972). Author: "Achieving the Mobile Internet," Signal (March 2001); "Receiver Standards and Guardbands: Maximizing Spectrum Efficiency," Radio Resource Magazine (March 1998); "Flight Testing and the Radio Spectrum: Will Channels Be Available?" ITEA Journal (March/April 1997); "Access to the Network: Current Controversies Affecting Telephone Customer Interconnection Rights," Federal Bar News & Journal (November 1982); "Challenges to Private System Interconnection Rights," Telecommunications (September 1985). Co-Author: "A Prevention Policy: Reducing Your EEO Exposure," Radio Ink (October 3-16, 1994). Attorney, Federal Communications Commission, 1972-1979. ***PRACTICE AREAS:*** Telecommunications Law. ***Email:*** KKeane@arterhadden.com

HOWARD M. LIBERMAN, born Toledo, Ohio, June 13, 1946; admitted to bar, 1973, New York; 1974, District of Columbia; 1975, U.S. Court of Appeals for the District of Columbia Circuit and U.S. Claims Court; 1980, U.S. Supreme Court. *Education:* Emerson College (B.S., with honors, 1968); Brooklyn Law School (J.D., cum laude, 1972). Member, 1970-1972 and Notes Editor, 1971-1972, Brooklyn Law Review. Attorney, Cable Television Bureau, Federal Communications Commission, 1972-1974. Co-Editor, Cable TV Act of 1992 Sourcebook, 1993. *Member:* The District of Columbia Bar; Federal Communications Bar Association (Co-Chair, Constitution and By-Laws Committee, 1990-1992; Interactive Media Practice Committee, 1994-1996). ***PRACTICE AREAS:*** Communications Law; Communications Industry Transactions and Litigation. ***Email:*** hliberman@arterhadden.com

JOHN D. MADDOX, born Washington, D.C., August 5, 1940; admitted to bar, 1973, Virginia; 1974, Ohio; 1990, District of Columbia and Maryland. *Education:* United States Naval Academy (B.S., with distinction, 1965); University of Virginia (J.D., 1973). Public Administration for Senior State and Local Government Officials, John F. Kennedy School of Government, Harvard, 1984. Law Clerk to Justice Richard H. Poff, Supreme Court of Virginia, 1973-1974. Chief Counsel, 1982 and Director of Law, 1983-1985, City of Cleveland, Ohio. President, Ohio Municipal Attorneys Association, 1985. Recipient, Federal Bar Association, Litigation Section Award for Exceptional Achievement, 1987. *Member:* International Municipal Lawyers Association. [Commander, USNR-Ret.]. ***Email:*** jdmaddox@arterhadden.com

TOM McDONALD, born Binghamton, New York, May 23, 1954; admitted to bar, 1981, Ohio; 1987, District of Columbia; 1996, New York. *Education:* George Washington University (B.A., 1976); University of Minnesota (J.D., 1979). Special Counsel to the Ohio Attorney General, 1985—; Special Counsel to the City of Cleveland, 1991—. U.S. Ambassador to Zimbabwe, 1997-2001. Member: Council on Foreign Relations; Council of American Ambassadors; Corporate Council on Africa; Board of Visitors, University of Minnesota Law School; International Advisory Panel, George Washington University, Elliot School of International Affairs; Presidential Campaign to Observe Elections in Bosnia, Sept. 12-15, 1996; Presidential Delegation to Funeral of Felix Houphouet - Boicny, President of the Côte d'Ivoire (Ivory Coast), Feb. 6-7, 1994. *Member:* The Association of the Bar of the City of New York; Cleveland (Member, Labor Law Section), Broome County, Ohio State (Member, Labor Law Section), New York State and American (Member, Labor Law Section and Urban, State and Local Government Sections) Bar Associations; District of Columbia Bar; National Council of School Board Attorneys; Ohio Council of School Board Attorneys; Cleveland Employers Equal Opportunity Association; Cuyahoga County Law Directors Association (Associate); Eighth District of Ohio Judicial Conference (Life Member). ***PRACTICE AREAS:*** International Law; Arbitration; Government Relations; Labor and Employment Law. ***Email:*** tmcdonald@arterhadden.com

DAVID L. MILLER, born Chicago, Illinois, December 27, 1941; admitted to bar, 1968, District of Columbia; 1969, U.S. Tax Court; 1972, U.S. Claims Court; 1973, U.S. Court of Appeals, District of Columbia Circuit. *Education:* Ohio Wesleyan University; University of Michigan (A.B., 1964; LL.B., 1967). Co-Author: "Federal Arbitrage Law and Advance Refunding of Municipal Indebtedness," 271-2nd Tax Management, 1978. Tax Attorney, Chief Counsel's Office, Internal Revenue Service, 1967-1971. *Member:* The District of Columbia Bar; American Bar Association (Member, Committee on Tax-Exempt Bonds, 1977—; Vice Chairman, Subcommittee on Arbitrage, 1978-1979, Section on Taxation); National Association of Bond Lawyers (Member, Steering Committee, National Bond Attorneys' Workshop, 1983-1984 and 1992-1994; Chairman, Special Committee on Arbitrage Rebate, 1987-1988). Fellow, American College of Bond Counsel. ***Email:*** dmiller@arterhadden.com

JERRY A. MOORE III, born Washington, D.C., December 1, 1946; admitted to bar, 1975, District of Columbia; U.S. Supreme Court; U.S. Court of Appeals for the District of Columbia Circuit; 1976, U.S. District Court for the District of Columbia. *Education:* University of Minnesota (B.A., 1968); University of Wisconsin (M.A., 1970); Georgetown University (J.D., 1975). Law Clerk to Hon. Barrington D. Parker, U.S. District Judge, 1975-1976. ***PRACTICE AREAS:*** Real Estate and Zoning Law; Municipal; Litigation; Employment Discrimination Defense. ***Email:*** jmoore@arterhadden.com

MICHAEL J. POLLACK, born Cherry Point, North Carolina, May 9, 1963; admitted to bar, 1988, New York; 1990, District of Columbia. *Education:* George Washington University (B.A., 1985; J.D., 1988). ***PRACTICE AREAS:*** Product Liability; Personal Injury Litigation; Commercial Litigation; Intellectual Property Litigation. ***Email:*** mpollack@arterhadden.com

TED L. RAMIREZ, born San Antonio, Texas, August 16, 1952; admitted to bar, 1977, Ohio and U.S. District Court, Southern District of Ohio (Not admitted in District of Columbia). *Education:* Southwestern Adventist College (B.A., cum laude, 1974); The Ohio State University (J.D., 1976). Editor, Topics in Health Care Financing, Vol. 18 No. 4, 1992. Author: "Introduction to Multi-hospital Systems," Topics in Health Care Financing, Vol. 18, No. 4 (1992). Co-Author: "Contracting with Protestant Health Care Delivery Systems," Hospital Contracts Manual, Vol. 1, Supplements, Aspen Publishers, 1990—. ***LANGUAGES:*** Spanish. ***Email:*** TRamirez@arterhadden.com

PETER J. RIEBLING, born Burbank, California, November 17, 1965; admitted to bar, 1992, California; 1994, District of Columbia and Virginia. *Education:* University of California, Los Angeles (B.A., 1987); Southwestern University (J.D., 1992). *Member:* International Trademark Association. ***PRACTICE AREAS:*** Trademarks; Copyright; Software Licensing; Trade Secrets. ***Email:*** prieblin@arterhadden.com

THOMAS K. SLATTERY, born Jersey City, New Jersey, August 16, 1955; admitted to bar, 1989, Maryland; 1990, District of Columbia. *Education:* United States Air Force Academy (B.S., 1977); Louisiana Tech University (M.B.A., 1981); George Washington University (J.D., cum laude, 1989). [Major, retired USAF, 1977-1983, Reserve, 1984-1991]. ***Email:*** tslatter@arterhadden.com

FRANCIS R. SNODGRASS, born Washington, D.C., August 9, 1939; admitted to bar, 1964, Maryland; 1977, District of Columbia. *Education:* Princeton University (A.B., magna cum laude, 1961); Harvard University (LL.B., magna cum laude, 1964). Member, Board of Student Advisors, Harvard Law School, 1962-1964. Chief Counsel, 1973-1975 and Associate Director, 1975-1977, Division of Market Regulation, Securities and Exchange Commission. *Member:* The District of Columbia Bar; National Association of Bond Lawyers (Vice Chairman, Committee on Housing, 1979-1980; Secretary, 1980-1981). ***Email:*** fsnodgra@arterhadden.com

OF COUNSEL

MYLES J. AMBROSE, born New York, N.Y., July 21, 1926; admitted to bar, 1952, New York; 1969, U.S. Supreme Court; 1970, U.S. Court of International Trade; 1973, District of Columbia; 1979, U.S. Claims Court; 1982, U.S. Court of Appeals for the Federal Circuit. *Education:* Manhattan College (B.B.A., 1948); New York Law School (J.D., 1952). Awarded Honorary LL.D., Manhattan College, 1972. Phi Alpha Delta. Recipient; Decoration of Order of Merit, Republic of Italy, 1973; Order of Grimaldi, Principality of Monaco, 1999. Author: "Importing Under the U.S. Customs Law: A Primer," Journal of International Trade Association of North Virginia, 1983. Assistant U.S. Attorney, Southern District of New York, 1954-1957. Assistant to U.S. Secretary of Treasury, 1957-1960. Executive Director, Waterfront Commission of New York Harbor, 1960-1963. Chief Counsel, New York State Joint Legislative Committee, 1963-1965. U.S. Commissioner of Customs, 1969-1972. Special Assistant Attorney General and Special Consultant to the President, 1972-1973. Honorary Consul, Principality of Monaco, 1973-1999. Member, Board of Governors, University College of Dublin Graduate School of Business, 1996-2001. *Member:* The District of Columbia Bar (Member, Treasury Department Advisory Committee on Commercial Operation U.S. Customs Service, 1988-1991; Member, 1980-1988 and Chairman ABA Standing Committee on Customs Law, 1986-1988; Former Chairman of the Board, Daytop Village International); Customs and International Trade Bar Association. Fellow, American Bar Foundation. ***Email:*** MAmbrose@arterhadden.com

DEBORAH J. ARNOLD, born Morristown, New Jersey, April 26, 1963; admitted to bar, 1988, New Jersey; 1989, District of Columbia. *Education:* University of Rochester (B.A., magna cum laude, 1985); George Washington University (J.D., cum laude, 1988). ***Email:*** darnold@arterhadden.com

JEROME A. HOCHBERG, born Newark, New Jersey, January 22, 1933; admitted to bar, 1960, New York; 1963, U.S. Supreme Court; 1968, District of Columbia. *Education:* Cornell University (B.A., 1954); Harvard University (J.D., 1959). Contributor of Essays to "Revitalizing Antitrust In It's Second Century," Quorum Books, 1991. Attorney, 1961-1968 and 1971-1973, Antitrust Division, U.S. Department of Justice, Washington, D.C., and Assistant Chief, Antitrust Division, New York Office, 1968-1971. . *Member:* The District of Columbia Bar (Chairperson, Division of Antitrust, Trade Regulation and Consumer Affairs, 1974-1977); American Bar Association (Member: Judicial Administration Division; Antitrust Law Section; Chairman, Section 7 (Clayton Act) Committee, 1971-1974; Vice Chairman, Private Antitrust Litigation Com-

(This Listing Continued)

(This Listing Continued)

ARTER & HADDEN LLP, Washington—Continued

mittee, 1979-1982; Member, Executive Committee, Lawyers' Conference of Judicial Administration Division, 1975-1980; Member, 1975-1982 and Budget Officer, 1979-1982, Council of the Judicial Administration Division). ***Email:*** jhochber@arterhadden.com

JODI MINTZER KRAME, born Washington, D.C., June 2, 1956; admitted to bar, 1983, District of Columbia and New York. *Education:* Emory University (B.A., 1978); George Washington University (J.D., 1982). Co-Editor: "Federal Tax Aspects of Municipal Bonds," Fundamentals of Municipal Bond Law, National Association of Bond Lawyers, 1993-1995. *Member:* The District of Columbia Bar; Federal Communications Bar Association. ***PRACTICE AREAS:*** Communications; Corporate. ***Email:*** jkrame@arterhadden.com

JONATHAN W. LIPSHIE, born Far Rockaway, New York, 1960; admitted to bar, 1988, New York; 1989, District of Columbia; 1990, Virginia; 1991, Maryland; 1992, Colorado. *Education:* Georgetown University (B.S.F.S., cum laude, 1982); Sorbonne, Paris, France (Diplome Semestriel, 1981); Vanderbilt University (J.D., 1987). Pi Sigma Alpha. ***LANGUAGES:*** French, Spanish and Italian. ***PRACTICE AREAS:*** Litigation; Bankruptcy. ***Email:*** JLipshie@ arterhadden.com

THOMAS H. ODOM, born Jersey City, New Jersey, March 8, 1962; admitted to bar, 1988, New Jersey and Pennsylvania; 1990, District of Columbia; U.S. Supreme Court; U.S. Court of Appeals for the District of Columbia Circuit; U.S. Court of Appeals for the Federal Circuit; U.S. Court of Appeals for the First, Third, Fourth, Fifth, Sixth, Seventh, Tenth and Eleventh Circuits. *Education:* Rutgers College (B.A., magna cum laude, 1984); University of Pennsylvania (J.D., cum laude, 1988). Assistant Professor, Oklahoma City University School of Law, 1999—. Section, Judicial Review Committee). ***PRACTICE AREAS:*** Appellate Litigation; Administrative Law; Federalism; Constitutional Law; Legal Ethics and Discipline. ***Email:*** todom@arterhadden.com

MARK VAN BERGH, born New York, N.Y., November 28, 1956; admitted to bar, 1981, District of Columbia; 1988, U.S. Court of Appeals for the District of Columbia Circuit; 1991, U.S. Supreme Court. *Education:* Syracuse University (B.A., magna cum laude, 1978) Phi Beta Kappa; National Law Center, George Washington University (J.D., with honors, 1981). *Member:* The District of Columbia Bar; Federal Communications Bar Association (Executive Committee, 1990-1994; Assistant Treasurer, 1998-1999; Treasurer, 1999-2000; Co-Chair, Ad Hoc Committee on Communications Policy Options for Developing Countries, 1993-1996; Co-Chair, Young Lawyers Committee, 1989-1990). ***PRACTICE AREAS:*** Communications. ***Email:*** vanbergh@arterhadden.com

ASSOCIATES

HAROLD H. DAVIS, born Atlanta, Georgia, December 31, 1973; (admission pending). *Education:* George Washington University (B.A., 1996); University of Miami (B.S., 1999). ***Email:*** HDavis@arterhhadden.com

STEPHANIE L. DeLONG, born San Francisco, California, August 1, 1971; admitted to bar, 2000, California and District of Columbia. *Education:* University of California at Santa Barbara (B.A., cum laude, 1993); George Washington University (J.D., with honors, 1999). ***PRACTICE AREAS:*** Real Estate; Real Estate Finance; Corporate. ***Email:*** sdelong@arterhadden.com

ELIZABETH A. HAMMOND, born Reading, Pennsylvania, April 1965; admitted to bar, 1996, Maryland; 1998, District of Columbia. *Education:* University of Texas (B.B.A., 1987); George Washington University (J.D., 1996). *Member:* Federal Communications and American Bar Associations; American Women in Radio and Television. ***PRACTICE AREAS:*** Corporate; Communications; Telecommunications Law. ***Email:*** ehammond@arterhadden.com

DONELL A. HICKS, born Milford, Delaware, April 20, 1975; admitted to bar, 2000, Maryland; 2001, District of Columbia. *Education:* Cornell University (B.A., 1997); George Washington University (J.D., 2000). Phi Delta Phi. *Member:* American and National Bar Associations; Federal Communications Bar Association. ***PRACTICE AREAS:*** Communications; Telecomunications. ***Email:*** dhicks@arterhadden.com

DARREN E. POGODA, admitted to bar, 2000, New York and District of Columbia. *Education:* Trenton State College (B.A., 1996); Catholic University of America (J.D., cum laude, 1999). ***PRACTICE AREAS:*** Intellectual Property. ***Email:*** dpogoda@arterhadden.com

SARAH P. SINGLETON, born Highland Park, Illinois, April 1, 1974; admitted to bar, 2000, District of Columbia and Maryland. *Education:* University of Michigan (B.A., 1996); Emory University School of Law (J.D., 2000). Dean's Fellow, 1999-2000. ***PRACTICE AREAS:*** Real Estate. ***Email:*** ssinglet@arterhadden.com

AMY SUSKI, born Stamford, Connecticut, September 8, 1970; admitted to bar, 1998, Maryland; 1999, District of Columbia. *Education:* Wellesley College (B.A., cum laude, 1992); University of Virginia (J.D., 1998). ***PRACTICE AREAS:*** Business Litigation; Products Liability. ***Email:*** asuski@arterhadden.com

GAVIN WILLIAMS, born Chelmsford, England, August 14, 1974; (admission pending). *Education:* Southern Utah University (B.A., 1998); University of Miami (J.D., magna cum laude, 2001). ***PRACTICE AREAS:*** Real Estate; Litigation. ***Email:*** gwilliam@arterhadden.com

REVISERS OF THE OHIO LAW DIGEST FOR THIS DIRECTORY

WILLIAM E. ARTZ

A PROFESSIONAL CORPORATION

WASHINGTON, D.C.

(See Arlington, Virginia)

Medical Malpractice including Cebral Palsy, Hospital Negligence, Brain, Spinal Cord Injuries, Nursing Home Injuries, Late Cancer Diagnosis Amputation and Personal Injury, Auto, Bus and Train Accidents.

ASBILL, JUNKIN, MOFFITT & BOSS

CHARTERED

Established in 1981

THE PACIFIC HOUSE, 1615 NEW HAMPSHIRE AVENUE, N.W., SECOND FLOOR

WASHINGTON, D.C. 20009

Telephone: 202-234-9000

Facsimile: 202-332-6480

Email: ajmchtd@erols.com

URL: http://www.lawyers.com/asbill

Criminal and Civil Trials and Appeals before all Courts.

FIRM PROFILE: Based in Washington, D.C., Asbill, Junkin, Moffitt & Boss specializes in complex criminal and civil trial and appellate litigation. The firm's practice is nationwide.

HENRY W. ASBILL, born Wilmington, Delaware, June 1, 1947; admitted to bar, 1976, Pennsylvania, U.S. District Court, Eastern and Middle Districts of Pennsylvania and U.S. Court of Appeals, 3rd Circuit; 1977, District of Columbia, U.S. District Court for the District of Columbia and U.S. Court of Appeals for the District of Columbia Circuit; 1984, U.S. Court of Appeals, 4th Circuit; 1985, U.S. District Court, District of Maryland; 1986, U.S. Court of Appeals, 11th Circuit; 1988, U.S. Supreme Court; 1996, U.S. District Court, Eastern District of Michigan. *Education:* Princeton University (B.A., 1969); Georgetown University (J.D., 1974). Recipient: D.C. Association of Criminal Defense Lawyers R. Kenneth Mundy Lawyer of the Year Award, 1995; Benjamin N. Cardozo Citation of Merit, 1987, for Pro Bono work for Anti Defamation League of B'Nai B'Rith. Law Clerk, Hon. John W. Kern, III, District of Columbia Court of Appeals, 1974-1976. Author: "The Ten Commandments of Cross Examination Revisited: Should You Sin to Win?," Criminal Justice, Vol. 8, No. 4, Winter 1994; "Winning A Rico Megatrial," Complex Crimes Journal, ABA Litigation Section, 1989. Contributing Author, 1977-1981, D.C. Criminal Practice Institute Trial Manual. Adjunct Professor, Civil and Criminal Trial Practice, Georgetown University Law Center, 1990-1998. Instructor: Federal Judicial Training Center, 1995-1997; National Institute of Trial Advocacy, 1981, 1989, 1993-1998, 2000. Assistant to Governor William T. Cahill of New Jersey, 1969-1971. Associate, Ballard, Spahr, Andrews & Ingersoll, Philadelphia, Pennsylvania, 1976-1977. Staff Attorney, Public Defender Service for the District of Columbia, 1977-1981. President, 1992-1993, Vice President, 1991-1992, Governor, 1990-1991 and Fellow, 1987—, American Board of Criminal Lawyers. Director, 1996-2002 and Chair, Continuing Legal Education Committee, 1999-2000, Lawyers Assistance Strike Force Committee; Co-Chair, White Collar Crime Committee, 1996-2000, National Association of Criminal Defense Lawyers. President, 1995-1996 and Director, 1994-1995, D.C. Association of Criminal Defense Lawyers. ***PRACTICE AREAS:*** Appellate Practice; Civil Rights; Constitutional Law; Criminal Law; Drugs and Narcotics; Litigation; White Collar Crime.

TIMOTHY DeFOREST JUNKIN, born Washington, D.C., April 21, 1951; admitted to bar, 1977, District of Columbia; 1981, Maryland, U.S. District Court for the District of Columbia and U.S. Court of Appeals for the District of Columbia Circuit; 1985, U.S. District Court, District of Maryland and U.S. Court of Appeals, 4th Circuit; U.S. Supreme Court. *Education:* University of Maryland (B.A., cum laude, with departmental honors, 1973); Georgetown University (J.D., 1977). Georgetown Law Fellow, 1977. Adjunct Professor: American University, 1981-1984; Washington College of Law, American University, 1988-1989; Georgetown University Law Center, 1990-1996. Staff Attorney, Public Defender Service for the District of Columbia, 1977-1981. President, Public Defenders Service Association, 1990-1991. Member, Million Dollar Advocates Forum. *Member:* The District of Columbia Bar; Maryland State Bar Association; Washington Metropolitan Area Association of Trial Lawyers

(This Listing Continued)

(Director); The Association of Trial Lawyers of America. ***PRACTICE AREAS:*** Civil Litigation; Business Torts; Personal Injury; Professional Malpractice; Medical Malpractice; Insurance Litigation.

WILLIAM B. MOFFITT, born Bronx, New York, January 16, 1949; admitted to bar, 1975, Virginia and U.S. District Court, Eastern District of Virginia; 1976, U.S. Court of Appeals, 4th Circuit; 1980, U.S. Court of Appeals, 5th Circuit; 1981, U.S. Court of Appeals, 11th Circuit; 1982, U.S. Court of Appeals, 6th Circuit; 1988, U.S. Court of Appeals, First Circuit; 1991, U.S. Court of Appeals, Third Circuit; U.S. Court of Appeals, District of Columbia Circuit; U.S. District Court, Eastern District of Michigan (Not admitted in District of Columbia). *Education:* University of Oklahoma (B.A., 1971); Washington College of Law, American University (J .D., 1975). Virginia College of Criminal Defense Lawyers (President, 1983). CLE Lectures: "Representing a Witness Before a Grand Jury," Alex. Bar Assn., 1981; "The Use of Hypnosis in Criminal Trials," Va. State Conf. of Circuit Court Judges, 1981; "Use of Double Jeopardy as an Affirmative Defense in a Criminal Trial," Atlanta Bar Assn., 1984; "The Insanity Defense," NACDL, 1987; "Voir Dire," Tennessee Association of Criminal Defense Lawyers, 1993 and 1995; "Cross Examination," Michigan State Bar; "Subpoenas to Defense Counsel and Fee Forfeitures," La. State Bar, 1985-1986; "Use of FOIA and Discovery Techniques in a Criminal Case," NACDL, 1988; "Attorney-Fee Forfeiture and Subpoenas to Defense Attorneys," Philadelphia Bar Association, 1988; "Federal Discovery," NACDL, 1993; "Rush to Judgment: The First 90 Days in a Drug Case," Virginia Trial Lawyers Association, 1993; "Defending: Why?," Colorado Public State Defender Association, 1993; "New Frontiers in the Use of Psychiatric & Psychological Evidence," Texas Association of Criminal Defense Lawyers, 1998, "Chain Reaction: The Impact of Race, Rights and Taxes on American Politics," reviewed in the University of Cincinnati Law Review, 1992; "Cross Examination - Anatomy of a Murder," NACDL, 2000; "Role of Race Criminal Justice System," Lovera Lecture, Gonzaga University Law School, October 2000; "Attacks on the Defense Bar," Canadian Criminal Defense Lawyers, November 1, 2000. Keynote Speaker: Pennsylvania Criminal Defense Lawyers Annual Meeting, 1999; "Advocacy in 21st Century," T.J. Reddict Bar Association, September 1999; National Lawyers Guild Annual Convention, November 2000. Faculty Member: National Criminal Defense College, 1988—; Virginia State Bar Course on Professionalism, 1993-1996. Ohio Criminal Defense Superstars Conference, 1999. Author: "The Twilight of the Attorney-Client Privilege," The Champion, 1985. Member, Board of Directors: ACLU, 1981; Legal Services Board of Northern Virginia, 1982. Listed in: National Directory of Criminal Lawyers, sponsored by the California Attorneys for Criminal Justice, 2nd and 3rd Edition, 1991-1992; Best Lawyers in America, 1994—; Who's Who in American Law, 1994; Who's Who Registry of Business Leaders, 1995-1996. *Member:* Alexandria Bar Association (8th District Ethics Committee, 1980; Judicial Selection Committee, 1983; Board of Directors, 1987—); National Association of Criminal Defense Lawyers (Board of Directors, 1988-1994; Strike Force Chair, 1993; Secretary, 1994; Treasurer, 1995; 2nd Vice President, 1996; First Vice President, 1997-1998; President-Elect, 1998-1999; President, 1999-2000); American Board of Criminal Lawyers (Fellow, 1990—); International Association of Criminal Defense Lawyers. ***PRACTICE AREAS:*** Criminal Law; Civil Litigation; Constitutional Law; Appellate Litigation; Drugs and Narcotics. ***Email:*** w.b.moffitt@aol.com

LENARD B. BOSS, born Passaic, New Jersey, March 6, 1960; admitted to bar, 1985, Pennsylvania (Inactive); 1986, District of Columbia; 1995, Maryland; U.S. Supreme Court and U.S. District Court, District of Maryland and District of Columbia; U.S. Court of Appeals, 2nd, 3rd, 4th, 5th, 11th and District of Columbia Circuits. *Education:* Bates College (B.A., 1982); George Washington University (J.D., with high honors, 1985). Order of the Coif. Recipient, R. Kenneth Mundy Lawyer of the Year Award, D.C. Association of Criminal Defense Lawyers, 2000. Author: "Sentencing Manipulation and Entrapment as Defenses," The Champion, July 1995; "Do We Need to Increase the Sentences in 'White Collar' Cases? A View from the Trenches," Federal Sentencing Reporter, November/December 1997; "Downward Departures in Money Laundering Cases: The Punishment Should Fit the Real Crime," The Champion, September/October 1998; "Sentencing in White Collar Cases: Time Does Not Heal All Wounds," Federal Sentencing Reporter, 2000. Featured Speaker: National Seminar on the Federal Sentencing Guidelines, Topic: Money Laundering, 1994-1999; Winning Strategies for Defending Federal Criminal Cases, Topic: Fraud, Administrative Office of the United States Courts, 1997-1999; National Seminar on Mental Illness and the Criminal Law, Topic: Competency to Stand Trial, Administrative Office of United States Courts, 1999; National Seminar for Federal Defenders, Topic: Money Laundering, Federal Judicial Center, 2000; Criminal Justice Act Seminar, Topic: Money Laundering, Eastern District of Michigan; Symposium on Federal Sentencing Policy for Economic Crimes and New Technology Offenses, Topic: "Loss" in Fraud Cases, United States Sentencing Commission, 2000; NLADA 78th Annual Conference, Topic: Dealing with the Media in High-Profile Cases, 2000; Federal Capital Defense Strategy Session, Topics: Mental Health and Trial Strategy Issues, 2001. Adjunct Professor: Legal Research and Writing, George Washington University Law School, 1998-1999; Client Counseling and Interviewing, George Washington University Law School, 2000—. Faculty Member: Cross Examination, D.C. Bar/George Washington University Continuing Legal Education Program, 1994-2001; National Institute for Trial Advocacy and Georgetown University Law Center 21st Annual Session in Trial Advocacy Skills, 1999; The Habeas Institute: Representing a Death Sentenced Client in Federal Post-Conviction Proceedings, 2000; NLADA Life in the Balance Conference, 2000; Capital Litigation Persuasion Institute, Kentucky Department of Public Advocacy, 2000; Criminal Practice Institute, D.C. Public Defender Service, 2000; "Special Needs Offenders: White-Collar Crime," Federal Judicial Center, 2001. Assistant Federal Public Defender, Washington, D.C., 1995-2000. Associate, Asbill, Junkin, Myers & Buffone, Chtd., 1986-1991. Partner, Asbill, Junkin & Myers, Chtd., 1991-1995. Member, United States Sentencing Commission. Member, 1992— and Co-Chair, 2000—. ***PRACTICE AREAS:*** Appellate Practice; Criminal Law; Drugs and Narcotics; Litigation; White Collar Crime. ***Email:*** barry_boss@mindspring.com

OF COUNSEL

OSCAR I. DODEK, JR., born Washington, D.C., August 19, 1931; admitted to bar, 1985, Maryland and District of Columbia. *Education:* University of Michigan (B.A., 1956); George Washington University (M.D., 1956; J.D., 1985). Order of the Coif. Clinical Professor, Obstetrics and Gynecology, George Washington University, 1984—. Member, American College of Obstetrics and Gynecology, 1972—. Founding Fellow, Society of Reproductive Endocrinology. ***PRACTICE AREAS:*** Medical Malpractice.

W. LOUIS HENNESSY, born Washington, D.C., January 4, 1955; admitted to bar, 1997, Maryland; 1998, District of Columbia, U.S. District Court, District of Maryland and U.S. Court of Appeals, District of Columbia Circuit. *Education:* University of Maryland (B.A., 1995; J.D., 1997). Member: International Association of Chiefs of Police, 1995-1998; International Homicide Investigation Association, 1992-1998; Fraternal Order of Police, 1980-1998. Guest Instructor, FBI National Academy, 1997—. Adjunct Professor, Law Enforcement Administration, University of Maryland. Former Commander, D.C. Police Homicide Investigation Unit. *Member:* Charles County and Maryland State Bar Associations. ***PRACTICE AREAS:*** Criminal Law; Law Enforcement; Personal Injury; Premises Liability; Civil Rights; Constitutional Law; Drugs and Narcotics.

WILLIAM J. MERTENS, born Omaha, Nebraska, July 6, 1948; admitted to bar, 1975, District of Columbia; 1997, Maryland U.S. Supreme Court; U.S. Court of Appeals for the District of Columbia, Fourth, Sixth, Tenth and Eleventh Circuits; U.S. District Court for the District of Columbia, Maryland and the Northern District of New York. *Education:* Yale University (B.A., 1970); Georgetown University (J.D., 1975). Georgetown Law Journal, 1973-1975. Author, "The Fourth Amendment and the Control of Police Discretion," Univ. Mich. J. L. Reform (1984). Co-Author: with Wasserstrom, "The Good Faith Exception to the Evolutionary Rule," Geo. L. J. (1982); with Wasserstrom, "The Fourth Amendment on the Scaffold," Am. Crim. L. Rev. (1986). Distinguished Visitor From Practice, 1991-1992. Assistant Professor, University of Oklahoma, College of Law, 1982-1984. Testimony: U.S. Senate Judiciary Committee, on insanity defense reform, 1982; New York General Assembly, on insanity defense reform, 1986; Maryland House of Delegates, on racial profiling, 2000, 2001. Public Defender Service for the District of Columbia, 1975-1982, Chief of Appellate Division, 1981-1982, Deputy Chief, Trial Division, 1980-1981. Member, Editorial Board, BNA Civil Trial Manual, 1988-1995. Member, Board of Governors of Maryland ACLU, 1999—. *Member:* Bar Association of Montgomery County; American (Member, Sections on: Litigation; Criminal Justice; Member, Amicus Curiae Committee of the Criminal Justice Section, 1982-1986) Bar Association; The District of Columbia Bar (Member, Steering Committee Section on Criminal Law and Individual Rights, 1993-1998; Chair, 1997-1998). ***PRACTICE AREAS:*** Civil and Criminal Litigation; Commercial Litigation; Business Litigation; Torts Litigation; Contract Litigation; Police Misconduct; Civil Rights Litigation; Power Industry Litigation; Administrative Law. ***Email:*** wjmertens@aol.com

(This Listing Continued)

ASHCRAFT & GEREL, LLP

A Limited Liability Partnership including Professional Corporations

Established in 1953

SUITE 400, 2000 L STREET, N.W.

WASHINGTON, D.C. 20036

Telephone: 202-783-6400

URL: http://www.ashcraftandgerel.com

Alexandria, Virginia Office: Suite 650, 4900 Seminary Road. Telephone: 703-931-5500.

Rockville, Maryland Office: Suite 1002, One Central Plaza, 11300 Rockville Pike. Telephone: 301-770-3737.

Baltimore, Maryland Office: Suite 1212, 10 East Baltimore Street. Telephone: 410-539-1122.

Landover, Maryland Office: Suite 301, 4301 Garden City Drive. Telephone: 301-459-8400.

(This Listing Continued)

ASHCRAFT & GEREL, LLP, Washington—Continued

Boston, Massachusetts Office: 440 Commercial Street, Suite 600. Telephone: 617-723-8544.

Pharmaceutical Litigation, Negligence, Workers Compensation, Medical Malpractice, Social Security and Products Liability Law, AIDS Litigation, Asbestos Litigation, Breast Implant Litigation, Qui Tam.

MEMBERS OF FIRM

MARTIN E. GEREL, (P.C.), born New York, N.Y., October 27, 1918; admitted to bar, 1949, District of Columbia; 1958, Maryland; 1962, U.S. Supreme Court. *Education:* City College of the City University of New York (B.S.S., 1941); American University (M.A., 1947); Georgetown University (LL.B., 1949). *Member:* The District of Columbia Bar; Montgomery County, Prince George's County and Maryland State Bar Associations. (Resident, Rockville, Maryland Office). ***PRACTICE AREAS:*** Workers Compensation.

JAMES A. MANNINO, (P.C.), born Elizabeth, New Jersey, November 5, 1942; admitted to bar, 1968, District of Columbia; 1977, U.S. Supreme Court. *Education:* University of North Carolina (A.B., 1964; J.D., 1967). Member, Board of Editors, North Carolina Law Review, 1967. *Member:* The District of Columbia Bar; Bar Association of the District of Columbia; American Bar Association; Trial Lawyers Association of Metro Washington, D.C. (Resident). ***PRACTICE AREAS:*** Workers Compensation. ***Email:*** jmannino@dc.ashcraftlaw.com

MARK L. SCHAFFER, (P.C.), born Boston, Massachusetts, October 30, 1945; admitted to bar, 1972, Maryland and District of Columbia; 1978, U.S. Supreme Court. *Education:* Boston University (A.B., magna cum laude, 1967); Georgetown University Law Center (J.D., 1972). *Member:* The District of Columbia Bar; Bar Association of the District of Columbia; Maryland State and American Bar Associations; The Association of Trial Lawyers of America (2nd Vice Chair, 1990-1992, Workers Compensation and Disability Section). (Resident). ***PRACTICE AREAS:*** Workers Compensation. ***Email:*** mschaffer@dc.ashcraftlaw.com

WAYNE M. MANSULLA, born Brockton, Massachusetts, April 4, 1945; admitted to bar, 1974, Virginia; 1975, District of Columbia; 1978, U.S. Supreme Court. *Education:* Stonehill College (A.B., with honors, 1968); Georgetown University (J.D., 1974). *Member:* The District of Columbia Bar; Virginia State Bar; American Bar Association; The Association of Trial Lawyers of America; Trial Lawyers Association of Metropolitan Washington, D.C. [Capt., U.S. Marine Corps, 1969-1972]. (Resident). ***PRACTICE AREAS:*** Medical Malpractice; Personal Injury. ***Email:*** wmansulla@dc.ashcraftlaw.com

JAMES F. GREEN, born Pittsfield, Massachusetts, October 1, 1948; admitted to bar, 1973, Massachusetts; 1975, District of Columbia; 1977, U.S. Supreme Court; 1985, Virginia. *Education:* St. Anselm College (B.A., 1970); Suffolk University School of Law (J.D., 1973). *Member:* The District of Columbia Bar; Bar Association of The District of Columbia (Member, 1976— and Chairman, 1977, Prepaid Legal Services Committee; Chairman, Unauthorized Practice of Law Committee, 1982—); Boston, Massachusetts, Federal (Member, 1976—, Chairman, National Subcommittee on Workers' Compensation, 1982; Member, Board of Directors, District of Columbia Chapter, 1982-1985) and American (Member, Tort and Insurance Practice Section and Litigation Section; Vice Chairman, Committee on Liaison with the Judicial Administration, 1987-1988) Bar Associations; The Association of Trial Lawyers of America (Vice Chair, 1987-1989 and National Chairman, 1989-1990, Workers Compensation and Disability Section); The American Society of Law and Medicine; Trial Lawyers Association of Metropolitan Washington, D.C.; Virginia Trial Lawyers Association. (Resident). ***PRACTICE AREAS:*** Products Liability; Pharmaceutical & Medical Device Litigation. ***Email:*** jgreen@dc.ashcraftlaw.com

ALLEN J. LOWE, born Brooklyn, New York, March 29, 1951; admitted to bar, 1977, Maryland; 1978, District of Columbia; 1980, U.S. Supreme Court. *Education:* American University (B.A. in Political Science, 1973); Washington College of Law of American University (J.D., 1976). *Member:* The District of Columbia Bar; Maryland State and American Bar Associations; The Association of Trial Lawyers of America. (Resident). ***PRACTICE AREAS:*** Workers Compensation. ***Email:*** alowe@dc.ashcraftlaw.com

MICHAEL H. FELDMAN, born Philadelphia, Pennsylvania, April 15, 1949; admitted to bar, 1975, District of Columbia; 1980, Maryland. *Education:* American University (B.A., 1971), Pi Sigma Alpha; George Washington University (J.D., 1974). *Member:* The District of Columbia Bar; Maryland State and American Bar Associations; The Association of Trial Lawyers of America; Trial Lawyers Association of Metropolitan Washington, D.C. (President, 1998-1999); Trial Lawyers for Public Justice. (Resident). ***PRACTICE AREAS:*** Medical Malpractice; Personal Injury; Products Liability. ***Email:*** mfeldman@dc.ashcraftlaw.com

JAMES M. HANNY, born Buffalo, New York, August 30, 1942; admitted to bar, 1972, Maryland; 1976, District of Columbia; 1977, U.S. Supreme Court. *Education:* Canisius College (B.A., 1967); University of Maryland (J.D., 1971).

(This Listing Continued)

Assistant U.S. Attorney, 1972-1980. *Member:* The District of Columbia Bar; Maryland State and American Bar Associations; The Association of Trial Lawyers of America; Trial Lawyers Association of Metropolitan Washington D.C. (Resident). ***PRACTICE AREAS:*** Personal Injury. ***Email:*** jhanny@dc.ashcraftlaw.com

MICHAEL V. KOWALSKI, born Chicago, Illinois, March 17, 1945; admitted to bar, 1970, Iowa; 1971, U.S. Court of Military Appeals; 1980, District of Columbia and U.S. Supreme Court; 1989, Maryland. *Education:* John Carroll University (B.A., 1967); Northwestern University (J.D., 1970). Participant, The Veterans Consortium Pro Bono Program. *Member:* The District of Columbia Bar (Chair, Workers Compensation Committee, 1998-1999); Maryland State and American Bar Associations; The Association of Trial Lawyers of America. (Resident). ***PRACTICE AREAS:*** Workers Compensation; Social Security. ***Email:*** mkowalski@dc.ashcraftlaw.com

H. VINCENT McKNIGHT, JR., born Washington, D.C., September 23, 1953; admitted to bar, 1979, District of Columbia; 1980, U.S. Court of Appeals for the District of Columbia Circuit; 1986, U.S. Court of Appeals, Fourth Circuit. *Education:* Brown University (B.A., 1975); University of Pennsylvania (J.D., 1978). Law Clerk to the Honorable William C. Pryor of the District of Columbia Court of Appeals, 1978-1980. Delegate at the D.C. Judicial Conference, 1982-1987. Former Member, Board of Trustees, Georgetown Preparatory School. *Member:* The District of Columbia Bar; American and National Bar Associations; The Association of Trial Lawyers of America (Committee Co-Chairman, Whistleblowers Litigation Group, 1998—); Trial Lawyers Association of Metropolitan Washington, D.C. (Member, Board of Governors, 1991—); National Employment Lawyers Association; Metropolitan Washington Employment Lawyers Association. (Resident). ***PRACTICE AREAS:*** Railroad Law; Personal Injury; Whistleblower Litigation. ***Email:*** vmcknight@dc.ashcraftlaw.com

MICHELLE A. PARFITT, born Uniontown, Pennsylvania, September 1, 1954; admitted to bar, 1981, District of Columbia; 1992, Virginia. *Education:* Northeastern University (B.S., magna cum laude, 1975); Michigan State University (M.S., magna cum laude, 1977); Hofstra University (J.D., 1980). *Member:* The District of Columbia Bar (Co-Chair, Injury to Persons and Property Section, 1989-1990); Virginia State Bar; American Bar Association; The Association of Trial Lawyers of America; The Women's Bar Association of the District of Columbia (Co-Chair, Litigation Section, 1984-1986; Co-Chair, Naturalization and Immigration Section, 1992-1993; Co-Chair, Executive Endorsements, 1994-1996); Trial Lawyers Association of Metropolitan Washington, D.C. (Board of Governors-President Elect). (Resident). ***PRACTICE AREAS:*** Pharmaceutical & Medical Device Litigation; Products Liability; Medical Malpractice. ***Email:*** mparfitt@dc.ashcraftlaw.com

GEORGE E. SWEGMAN, born Pittsburgh, Pennsylvania, October 16, 1948; admitted to bar, 1975, Pennsylvania; 1981, District of Columbia and U.S. Supreme Court. *Education:* Pennsylvania State University (B.A., History, 1970; B.A., Pre-Law, 1970); Catholic University of America (J.D., 1975). *Member:* The District of Columbia Bar; American Bar Association; The Association of Trial Lawyers of America. (Resident). ***PRACTICE AREAS:*** Workers Compensation; Personal Injury. ***Email:*** gswegman@dc.ashcraftlaw.com

PETER J. VANGSNES, born New York, N.Y., August 4, 1955; admitted to bar, 1980, District of Columbia; 1984, U.S. Supreme Court. *Education:* Brown University (B.A., 1977); Cornell University (J.D., 1980). *Member:* The District of Columbia Bar; Bar Association of the District of Columbia; American Bar Association; The Association of Trial Lawyers of America. (Resident). ***PRACTICE AREAS:*** Toxic Torts; Products Liability; Personal Injury. ***Email:*** pvangsnes@dc.ashcraftlaw.com

MICHAEL W. HEAVISIDE, born Baltimore, Maryland, October 30, 1953; admitted to bar, 1980, Virginia; 1987, District of Columbia. *Education:* Georgetown University (B.A., 1975); College of William & Mary (J.D., 1980). Phi Delta Phi. *Member:* District of Columbia Bar; Virginia State and American Bar Associations; Virginia Trial Lawyers Association; The Association of Trial Lawyers of America. (Resident). ***PRACTICE AREAS:*** Pharmacy Law; Diet Drug Litigation. ***Email:*** mheaviside@dc.ashcraftlaw.com

CHRISTOPHER V. TISI, born Forest Hills, New York, August 1, 1960; admitted to bar, 1986, Maryland; 1987, U.S. Court of Appeals for the District of Columbia Circuit; 1988, District of Columbia; 1989, U.S. Court of Appeals, Fourth Circuit; 1992, U.S. Supreme Court. *Education:* State University of New York at Albany (B.A., cum laude, 1982); Wake Forest University (J.D., 1986). *Member:* The District of Columbia Bar; Maryland State and American Bar Associations; The Association of Trial Lawyers of America. (Resident). ***PRACTICE AREAS:*** Products Liability; Personal Injury; Diet Drug Litigation; Pharmacy Law. ***Email:*** ctisi@dc.ashcraftlaw.com

SIDNEY SCHUPAK, born New York, N.Y., June 6, 1967; admitted to bar, 1991, Maryland; 1993, District of Columbia. *Education:* City University of New York, Queens College (B.A., 1988); American University, Washington College of Law (J.D., cum laude, 1991). Co-Author: "Liability for HIV Transmission," Trial Magazine, Vol 28, No. 5 (May1992); "Causation in Transfusion Associated AIDS Cases," Trial Magazine, Vol. 29, No. 5 (May 1993). *Member:*

(This Listing Continued)

The District of Columbia Bar; Maryland State and American Bar Associations; The Association of Trial Lawyers of America; Trial Lawyers Association of Metropolitan Washington, D.C. (Resident). ***PRACTICE AREAS:*** Products Liability; Personal Injury; Medical Malpractice. ***Email:*** sschupak@dc.ashcraftlaw.com

MARTIN TRPIS, born Bratislava, Slovakia, December 24, 1957; admitted to bar, 1987, Maryland; 1999, District of Columbia. *Education:* University of Maryland (B.A., 1979); University of Virginia (J.D., 1986). *Member:* The District of Columbia Bar; Maryland State Bar Association; Maryland Trial Lawyers Association; The Association of Trial Lawyers of America; District of Columbia Trial Lawyers Association. (Resident). ***PRACTICE AREAS:*** Medical Malpractice; Personal Injury. ***Email:*** mtrpis@dc.ashcraftlaw.com

---

MICHAEL E. GALLANT, born New York, N.Y., June 20, 1967; admitted to bar, 1995, New York; 1996, District of Columbia; U.S. District Court, Northern District of New York. *Education:* Fordham University (B.A., 1989); Catholic University of America (J.D., 1995). *Member:* The District of Columbia Bar; New York State Bar Association; The Association of Trial Lawyers of America; District of Columbia Trial Lawyers Association. (Resident). ***PRACTICE AREAS:*** Products Liability; Personal Injury; Pharmacy Law; Diet Drug Litigation. ***Email:*** mgallant@dc.ashcraftlaw.com

REBEKAH R. ARCH, born Long Island, New York, September 16, 1959; admitted to bar, 1996, Virginia (Not admitted in District of Columbia). *Education:* Hunter College of the City University of New York (B.S.N., 1990); Catholic University of America (J.D., cum laude, 1996). *Member:* Virginia State Bar; The District of Columbia Bar; American Bar Association; Virginia Trial Lawyers Association; Trial Lawyers Association of Metropolitan Washington, D.C. (Resident). ***PRACTICE AREAS:*** Pharmacy Law; Diet Drug Litigation. ***Email:*** rarch@dc.ashcraftlaw.com

SOTIRIOS BASIL YANAKAKIS, born Boston, Massachusetts, October 5, 1967; admitted to bar, 1994, Pennsylvania; 1998, Virginia, U.S. District Court, Eastern District of Virginia and U.S. Court of Appeals, Fourth Circuit; 1999, District of Columbia. *Education:* Rollins College (B.A., 1989); Boston College (J.D., 1992); Washington College of Law, American University (LL.M., 1993). *Member:* American Bar Association; American Society of International Law. ***LANGUAGES:*** Greek. ***PRACTICE AREAS:*** Diet Drug Litigation; Products Liability. ***Email:*** syanakakis@dc.ashcraftlaw.com

JERRY DAVID SPITZ, born Somerville, New Jersey, October 15, 1961; admitted to bar, 1987, New York; 1988, District of Columbia and New Jersey; 1996, Maryland; 1997, Virginia. *Education:* University of Delaware (B.S.B.A., 1983); National Law Center, George Washington University (J.D., 1986). *Member:* Trial Lawyers Association of Metropolitan Washington, D.C. (Member, Board of Directors, 2001—); Maryland Trial Lawyers Association; District of Columbia Trial Lawyers Association. (Resident). ***PRACTICE AREAS:*** Personal Injury. ***Email:*** jspitz@dc.ashcraftlaw.com

KERI A. JONES, born Trenton, New Jersey, November 20, 1970; admitted to bar, 1995, New Jersey and U.S. District Court, District of New Jersey; 1997, District of Columbia. *Education:* University of Pittsburgh (B.A., 1992); Georgetown University Law Center (J.D., 1995). Recipient, Dean's List, University of Pittsburgh. Lecturer, Street Law Clinic, H.D. Woodson High School, Georgetown University Law Center, Washington, D.C., 1993-1994. (Resident). ***PRACTICE AREAS:*** Medical Malpractice; Personal Injury. ***Email:*** kjones@dc.ashcraftlaw.com

SUSAN E. FATTIG, born Gothenburg, Nebraska, September 16, 1955; admitted to bar, 1980, Nebraska; 1989, District of Columbia. *Education:* University of Nebraska at Kearny (B.S., magna cum laude, 1976); University of Notre Dame (J.D., 1980). *Member:* Nebraska State and American Bar Associations; The District of Columbia Bar (Member, Arts, Entertainment and Sports Law Section); American Trial Lawyers Association; Trial Lawyers Association of Metropolitan Washington, D.C. (Resident). ***Email:*** sfattig@dc.ashcraftlaw.com

MOHAMMAD A. SYED, born Karachi, Pakistan, September 16, 1974; admitted to bar, 2001, New York (Not admitted in District of Columbia). *Education:* University of Rochester (B.A., cum laude, 1997); George Washington University (J.D., 2000). *Member:* New York State and American Bar Associations; Trial Lawyers Association of Metropolitan Washington, D.C. (Resident). ***LANGUAGES:*** Urdu and Hindi. ***PRACTICE AREAS:*** Products Liability; Medical Malpractice. ***Email:*** msyed@dc.ashcraftlaw.com

OF COUNSEL

ALTOMEASE R. KENNEDY, born Cleveland, Ohio, May 2, 1949; admitted to bar, 1976, District of Columbia. *Education:* Goucher College (B.A., 1971); Georgetown University (J.D., 1975). *Member:* The District of Columbia Bar; Women's Bar Association of the District of Columbia; The Association of Trial Lawyers of America; National Association of Black Women Attorneys. (Resident). ***PRACTICE AREAS:*** False Claims Act; Products Liability; Medical Malpractice. ***Email:*** akennedy@dc.ashcraftlaw.com

(This Listing Continued)

KENNETH D. AUERBACH

WASHINGTON, D.C.

(See Silver Spring, Maryland)

Civil and Criminal Trial and Appellate Practice in State and Federal Courts. Felonies, Misdemeanors, Civil and Criminal Forfeiture, Civil Litigation, Personal Injury, Business Litigation, DWI, Narcotic Offenses, Homicide, Personal Injury and Veterans Benefits, Civil Rights, White-Collar Defense, Business Fraud, Post-Conviction Litigation.

BAACH ROBINSON & LEWIS PLLC

Established in 1996

ONE THOMAS CIRCLE, SUITE 200

WASHINGTON, D.C. 20005-5803

Telephone: 202-833-8900

Telecopier: 202-466-5738

Email: baachrob@baachrobinson.com

URL: http://www.baachrobinson.com

London, England Office: At Lloyd's Building, 1 Lime Street, Room 735, EC3M 7DQ. Telephone: +011-44-207-327-4433. Facsimile: +011-44-207-327-4024.

Litigation, International, Insurance, Employment, Banking, Government Relations, Antitrust, Trade, White Collar Crime.

SENIOR COUNSEL

ROBERT L. WALD, born Worcester, Massachusetts, 1926; admitted to bar, 1951, Massachusetts; 1957, U.S. Supreme Court; 1959, District of Columbia. *Education:* Harvard University (A.B., 1947); Yale University (LL.B., 1951). Law Clerk to Judge Irving Kaufman, U.S. District Court, Southern District of New York, 1951-1952. Assistant to General Counsel, Chief Division of Export Trade, Federal Trade Commission, 1954-1956. Partner, Wald, Harkrader & Ross, and predecessor firms, 1961-1987. Member, Judicial Conference D.C. Circuit, 1980—. Chairman, 1994-1996, and Board Member, 1994—, Romanian-American Enterprise Fund. *Member:* The District of Columbia Bar; Bar Association of the District of Columbia; Federal and American Bar Associations. ***PRACTICE AREAS:*** Antitrust; Trade Regulation; Government Regulation; Business Mergers; Business Acquisitions. ***Email:*** robert.wald@baachrobinson.com

MEMBERS OF FIRM

MARTIN R. BAACH, born Chicago, Illinois, April 18, 1948; admitted to bar, 1974, Ohio; 1975, District of Columbia. *Education:* Washington University (A.B., 1969); Indiana University (M.A., 1971); University of Cincinnati (J.D., 1974). Order of the Coif. Article Editor, University of Cincinnati Law Review, 1973-1974. Chair, Hearing Committee of D.C. Bar Board of Professional Responsibility. *Member:* The District of Columbia Bar; American Bar Association. ***PRACTICE AREAS:*** Civil Litigation; Commercial Litigation; Insurance; Reinsurance; Product Liability; International Arbitration; Arbitration. ***Email:*** martin.baach@baachrobinson.com

DWIGHT P. BOSTWICK, born Boston, Massachusetts, July 28, 1960; admitted to bar, 1989, Pennsylvania; 1990, Michigan; 1991, District of Columbia. *Education:* Stanford University (B.A., 1983); Georgetown University (J.D., 1988). Law Clerk, Chief Judge Manuel L. Real, U.S. District Court for the Central District of California, 1988-1989. Trial Attorney, Fraud Section of the U.S. Department of Justice, 1991-1994. Deputy Special Counsel for Financial Institution Fraud, Office of the Deputy Attorney General, U.S. Department of Justice, 1994-1995. ***PRACTICE AREAS:*** Litigation; White Collar Criminal. ***Email:*** dwight.bostwick@baachrobinson.com

ALAN B. CROFT, born Chicago, Illinois, April 24, 1945; admitted to bar, 1971, Virginia; 1973, U.S. District Court, Eastern District of Virginia; 1976, U.S. Court of Appeals, Fourth Circuit; 1994, District of Columbia. *Education:* Washington University (B.S.E.E., 1966); Washington College of Law, American University (J.D., 1970). Assistant Commonwealth's Attorney, Arlington County, 1972-1975. *Member:* Fairfax and American Bar Associations; Virginia State Bar; Virginia Trial Lawyers Association. ***PRACTICE AREAS:*** Commercial Litigation; Criminal Litigation; Professional Malpractice; Banking Disputes; Construction Litigation. ***Email:*** alan.croft@baachrobinson.com

JAMES P. DAVENPORT, born Raleigh, North Carolina, January 23, 1944; admitted to bar, 1971, District of Columbia. *Education:* Duke University (A.B., 1966; J.D., 1969). Court Law Clerk, U.S. Court of Appeals, District of Columbia Circuit, 1969-1970. Counsel, U.S. Senate Committee on the District of Columbia, 1970-1971. *Member:* The District of Columbia Bar; Bar Association of the District of Columbia; American Bar Association. ***PRACTICE***

(This Listing Continued)

BAACH ROBINSON & LEWIS PLLC, Washington—Continued

AREAS: Scientific and Technical Litigation; Product Liability; Medical Malpractice; Legal Malpractice; Environmental Insurance Coverage; Personal Injury Litigation. ***Email:*** james.davenport@baachrobinson.com

MARY E. FECHTIG, born Benton, Illinois, August 16, 1965; admitted to bar, 1991, Indiana and U.S. District Court, Southern and Northern Districts of Indiana; 1993, Illinois; 1999, District of Columbia. *Education:* Indiana University (B.S., magna cum laude, 1988; J.D., 1991). Blue Key Society. Academic All-American, 1988. *Member:* Indiana State and American Bar Associations. ***PRACTICE AREAS:*** Insurance Coverage Litigation; Litigation. ***Email:*** mary.fechtig@baachrobinson.com

BRUCE R. GRACE, born Thunder Bay, Ontario, Canada, July 6, 1957; admitted to bar, 1989, New York; 1990, District of Columbia. *Education:* University of Chicago (B.A., 1979); Columbia University (J.D., 1987). Articles and Book Reviews Editor, Columbia Law Review, 1986-1987. Author: Note, "Ignorance of the Law as an Excuse," 86 Columbia Law Review 1392 (1986). Law Clerk, Honorable Laurence H. Silberman, U.S. Court of Appeals for the District of Columbia, 1987-1988. ***PRACTICE AREAS:*** Civil Litigation; Commercial Litigation; Insurance Coverage Disputes; Reinsurance Coverage Disputes; Professional Malpractice. ***Email:*** bruce.grace@baachrobinson.com

PHILIP T. INGLIMA, born Ridgewood, New Jersey, June 23, 1962; admitted to bar, 1988, New Jersey and U.S. District Court, District of New Jersey; 1989, New York, District of Columbia and U.S. District Court for the District of Columbia; 1992, U.S. Court of Appeals for the District of Columbia Circuit and U.S. Supreme Court. *Education:* Georgetown University (A.B., 1984; J.D., 1988). Alpha Sigma Nu. Articles Editor, Georgetown International Environmental Law Review, 1988. Winning Team and Best Oralist, Final Round, Jessup International Law Moot Court Competition, 1987. Law Clerk to the Hon. June L. Green, U.S. District Court, District of Columbia, 1988-1989. Senior Associate Independent Counsel, *In re:* Bruce Babbitt, 1998-1999. Member, Judicial Conference of the D.C. Circuit, 1990-1992, 1994, 1996, 1998, 2000. *Member:* The District of Columbia Bar (Member, Sections of: Criminal Law and Individual Rights, and Litigation; Member, 1998—, and Co-Chair, 1990—, Criminal Law and Individual Rights Section); American Bar Association; The Barristers. ***PRACTICE AREAS:*** White Collar Crime; Criminal Defense; Civil Litigation. ***Email:*** philip.inglima@baachrobinson.com

MARK J. LEIMKUHLER, born Baltimore, Maryland, April 30, 1960; admitted to bar, 1986, Pennsylvania; 1988, District of Columbia. *Education:* University of Virginia (B.A., 1982); University of Pennsylvania (J.D., cum laude, 1986). ***PRACTICE AREAS:*** Civil Litigation; Commercial Litigation; Insurance Coverage; Reinsurance Coverage. ***Email:*** mark.leimkuhler@baachrobinson.com

ERIC L. LEWIS, born New York, N.Y., April 5, 1957; admitted to bar, 1985, New York and District of Columbia. *Education:* Princeton University (A.B., 1979); Cambridge University, Cambridge, England (M.Phil., 1980); Yale University (J.D., 1983). Fulbright Scholar to the United Kingdom, 1979-1980. Article and Book Review Editor, Yale Law Journal, 1982-1983. Author: Note, "Garnishing Graft: A Strategy for Recovering the Proceeds of Political Bribery," 92 Yale Law Journal 128, 1983. Adjunct Professor of Law, Georgetown University Law Center, 1987-1993. Faculty Member, National Institute for Trial Advocacy, 1990. Law Clerk, Honorable David L. Bazelon, U.S. Court of Appeals for the District of Columbia Circuit, 1983-1984. Member, Judicial Conference of the District of Columbia Circuit. ***PRACTICE AREAS:*** Civil Litigation; Commercial Litigation; White Collar Crime; International Insolvency; Fraud; Litigation. ***Email:*** eric.lewis@baachrobinson.com

STEPHEN H. MARCUS, born Saskatoon, Saskatchewan, September 4, 1953; admitted to bar, 1980, Ontario; 1985, District of Columbia. *Education:* University of Toronto (B.A., 1974); Queens University (LL.B., 1977); Cambridge University (LL.B., 1978); Georgetown University (LL.M., 1985). Constitutional Policy Advisor on Aboriginal Affairs, Department of Indian Affairs and Northern Development, Government of Canada, 1982-1984. *Member:* The District of Columbia Bar. ***PRACTICE AREAS:*** Civil Litigation; Commercial Litigation; International Trade; Insurance Litigation; Coverage Litigation; Environmental Dispute Resolution; US Trade Regulation. ***Email:*** stephen.marcus@baachrobinson.com

JEFFREY D. ROBINSON, born El Paso, Texas, October 13, 1958; admitted to bar, 1983, District of Columbia. *Education:* Lafayette College (A.B., summa cum laude, 1980); Yale University (J.D., 1983). Deputy Assistant Attorney General, Office of Legislative Affairs, United States Department of Justice, 1993-1994. Principal Deputy, Office of the Corporation Counsel, District of Columbia, 1992-1993. Minority Chief Counsel and Staff Director, Constitution Subcommittee, United States Senate Committee on the Judiciary, 1987-1988; Counsel, United States Senate Committee on the Judiciary, 1986-1987. *Member:* The District of Columbia Bar; American Bar Association. ***PRACTICE AREAS:*** Civil Litigation; Commercial Litigation; White Collar Crime; Government Relations; Employment; Insurance Coverage Litigation; Reinsurance Coverage Litigation. ***Email:*** jeffrey.robinson@baachrobinson.com

(This Listing Continued)

JOSEPH L. RUBY, born New York, N.Y., August 10, 1955; admitted to bar, 1985, New York; 1988, District of Columbia; 1989, U.S. District Court for the District of Columbia and U.S. Court of Appeals for the District of Columbia Circuit. *Education:* Reed College (B.A., 1978); University of Rochester (M.A., 1979); Yale Law School (J.D., 1984). Phi Beta Kappa. Law Clerk to Judge Herbert J. Stern, U.S. District Court, District of New Jersey, 1985-1986. ***PRACTICE AREAS:*** Civil Litigation; Commercial Litigation; Insurance Coverage; Bad Faith Disputes. ***Email:*** joseph.ruby@baachrobinson.com

JAMES SOTTILE, IV, born Gainesville, Florida, September 20, 1960; admitted to bar, 1986, District of Columbia; 1994, Maryland. *Education:* University of Florida (B.S., cum laude, 1982); Georgetown University (J.D., magna cum laude, 1985). Associate Editor, Georgetown Law Journal, 1984-1985. Adjunct Professor, Georgetown University Law Center, 1995—. *Member:* The District of Columbia Bar; Maryland State Bar Association. ***PRACTICE AREAS:*** Civil Litigation; Commercial Litigation; Professional Malpractice; Securities; Commercial Fraud. ***Email:*** james.sottile@baachrobinson.com

DUANE K. THOMPSON, born Washington, D.C., August 25, 1958; admitted to bar, 1984, District of Columbia and U.S. District Court for the District of Columbia; 1988, U.S. Court of International Trade; 2001, Maryland. *Education:* University of Pennsylvania (B.A., cum laude, 1980); Yale University (J.D., 1983). Sphinx & Onyx Honor Societies. Articles and Topics Editor, Yale Journal of International Law. *Member:* The District of Columbia Bar (Member, Board of Governors); American Bar Association (Co-Chair, Forum on Communications Law). ***PRACTICE AREAS:*** Insurance Coverage Litigation; Civil Litigation; Intellectual Property; Communications. ***Email:*** duane.thompson@baachrobinson.com

A. KATHERINE TOOMEY, born Detroit, Michigan, April 20, 1965; admitted to bar, 1991, District of Columbia. *Education:* Washington University (A.B., 1985); Yale University School of Law (J.D., 1989). Phi Beta Kappa. Recipient, Munson Prize for Clinical Projects. Senior Editor, The Yale Law Journal, Vol. 98, 1988-1989. Clerk to Judge James K. Logan, Tenth Circuit Court of Appeals, Olathe, Kansas. *Member:* The District of Columbia Bar. ***PRACTICE AREAS:*** Commercial Litigation; RICO Litigation; International Insolvency; Financial Fraud. ***Email:*** katherine.toomey@baachrobinson.com

GEOVETTE E. WASHINGTON, born Toccoa, Georgia; admitted to bar, 1992, Georgia; 1998, District of Columbia. *Education:* Wesleyan College (B.A., summa cum laude, 1989); Duke University (J.D., 1992). Phi Kappa Phi; Mortar Board. Notes Lead Editor, Alaska Law Review. Law Clerk to the Honorable Aubrey E. Robinson, Jr., United States District Court for the District of Columbia, 1992-1993. Office of Legal Counsel, U.S. Dept. of Justice, 1993-1996. *Member:* State Bar of Georgia; The District of Columbia Bar; American Bar Association. ***PRACTICE AREAS:*** Civil Litigation; Commercial Litigation; Insurance; Employment. ***Email:*** geovette.washington@baachrobinson.com

BENJAMIN L. ZELENKO, born New York, N.Y., May 12, 1933; admitted to bar, 1958, New York; 1970, District of Columbia. *Education:* Princeton University (A.B., cum laude, 1955); Harvard University (LL.B., 1958). General Counsel, House Judiciary Committee, 1967-1972. Adjunct Professor, Catholic University Law School, 1979-1985. Member: LEAA Task Force on Organized Crime, 1976 and Advisory Board, Justice Impact Study Project, 1979, Department of Justice. *Member:* The District of Columbia Bar (Member, Foundation Advisory Committee, 1985—); American Bar Association (Chairman, Special Committee on Coordination of Federal Judicial Improvements, 1978-1980). ***PRACTICE AREAS:*** Copyright; Defamation; Corporate; Labor Law; Federal Regulatory. ***Email:*** benjamin.zelenko@baachrobinson.com

ASSOCIATES

RANDOLPH M. COLLINS, born Audubon, New Jersey, December 6, 1956; admitted to bar, 1991, Maryland; 1994, District of Columbia. *Education:* Georgetown University (A.B., 1979; J.D., cum laude, 1991). American Inns of Court, 1990-1991. Judicial Law Clerk, U.S. District Court, District of Maryland, 1991-1993. Author: "Can Neutral Principles Protect First Amendment Values, 2F:4AM. Crim. L. Rev., 1991. Member, U.S. Senate Judicial Committee Prof. Staff, 1983-1986. Lt. Governor, Beyer Policy Director, 1996-1998. Board Member, Baltimore City Zoning Board, 1996. ***PRACTICE AREAS:*** Commercial Litigation; Employment Law; Public Policy Legislation. ***Email:*** randolph.collins@baachrobinson.com

CHARLES A. COWAN, born Ottawa, Ontario, Canada, February 9, 1966; admitted to bar, 1991, Texas; 2000, District of Columbia. *Education:* Baylor University (B.A., 1988); Harvard Law School (J.D. cum laude, 1991). Visiting Professor, Kyushu University Faculty of Law, Fukuoka, Japan, 1993-1996. ***PRACTICE AREAS:*** Litigation; Environmental. ***Email:*** charles.cowan@baachrobinson.com

THOMAS M. GLASSIC, born Washington, D.C., March 21, 1970; admitted to bar, 1997, Maryland; 1998, District of Columbia and U.S. District Court,

(This Listing Continued)

District of Maryland. *Education:* College of William & Mary (A.B., with honors, 1992); George Washington University (J.D., with honors, 1997). Member, George Washington Law Review, 1995-1997. ***PRACTICE AREAS:*** Insurance; Litigation. ***Email:*** thomas.glassic@baachrobinson.com

H. BRADFORD GLASSMAN, born Norfolk, Virginia, January 13, 1967; admitted to bar, 1994, Virginia; 2001, District of Columbia. *Education:* Brown University (B.A., 1988); University of Virginia (J.D., 1994). ***PRACTICE AREAS:*** Litigation. ***Email:*** brad.glassman@baachrobinson.com

HELEN F. HISER, born Elkins, West Virginia, December 14, 1956; admitted to bar, 1989, Maryland; 1990, District of Columbia. *Education:* College of Wooster (B.A., 1978); University of Kentucky (M.S.L.S., 1980); New York Law School; Washington College of Law (J.D., summa cum laude, 1989). ***PRACTICE AREAS:*** Insurance Law; Environmental Law. ***Email:*** helen.hiser@baachrobinson.com

SARAH LESLIE KNAPP, born Huntington, New York, June 1, 1970; admitted to bar, 1999, California (Not admitted in District of Columbia). *Education:* University of California at Santa Cruz (B.A., 1994); Georgetown University Law Center (J.D., cum laude, 1997). Law Clerk to the Hon. F.H. Weisberg, Superior Court of the District of Columbia, 1997-1998. ***Email:*** sarah.knapp@baachrobinson.com

MELISSA H. McNIVEN, born Tarrytown, New York, August 26, 1966; admitted to bar, 1991, Maryland; 1993, District of Columbia. *Education:* Tulane University (B.A., 1987); Washington College of Law of American University (J.D., summa cum laude, 1991). Member, Edward Bennett Williams American Inn of Court, 1996-1997. Author, "What if the Case Never Ends," Legal Times, 1998. Instructor, Litigation & Advocacy Skills, International Law Institute, 1997-1998. ***LANGUAGES:*** French. ***PRACTICE AREAS:*** Litigation. ***Email:*** melissa.mcniven@baachrobinson.com

GINA M. SAPORITO, born Wilkes-Barre, Pennsylvania, February 18, 1972; admitted to bar, 1998, Virginia, Maryland and District of Columbia. *Education:* American University (B.A., 1994); Washington College of Law of American University (J.D., cum laude, 1997). Author: "A Shelter for Contractors: The Year 2000 Readiness and Responsibility Act - The Construction Contractor, 1999, Vol. 23,, No. 21. *Member:* Fairfax and American Bar Associations. ***PRACTICE AREAS:*** Civil Litigation; Employment Law. ***Email:*** gina.saporito@baachrobinson.com

JULIE A. SCHROEDER, born Park Ridge, New Jersey, September 13, 1972; admitted to bar, 1997, Maryland; 1999, District of Columbia. *Education:* Franklin & Marshall College (B.A., 1994); American University, Washington College of Law (J.D., cum laude, 1997). Appellate Advocacy Clinic. Formerly with, Eccleston & Wolf PC. *Member:* Maryland State Bar Association; The District of Columbia Bar. ***REPORTED CASES:*** Knott v. Maryland (Md. 1998). ***PRACTICE AREAS:*** Civil Litigation; Commercial Litigation; Insurance. ***Email:*** julie.schroeder@baachrobinson.com

ELIZABETH TORRANT SHELDON, born Madison, Wisconsin, September 30, 1966; admitted to bar, 1996, Wisconsin; 1997, Maryland; 1998, District of Columbia. *Education:* Colorado College (B.A., 1988); George Washington University (M.A., 1992); University of Wisconsin-Madison (J.D., 1996). Moot Court Board. Co-Authored, Hard Rock Mining: State Approaches to Environmental Protection/Environmental Law Institute, 1996. Author: Wisconsin Environmental Law Journal, No. 2, Vol. 3, Comment: "Practicing Preventative Medicine: Recommendations for Financing Mining Waste Sites in Perpetuity." *Member:* Maryland State and American Bar Associations; State Bar of Wisconsin; The District of Columbia Bar. ***PRACTICE AREAS:*** Civil Litigation; Commercial Litigation. ***Email:*** elizabeth.sheldon@baachrobinson.com

JOHN L. SIMPKINS, born Columbia, South Carolina, November 15, 1970; admitted to bar, 2000, District of Columbia. *Education:* Harvard University (A.B., 1993); Duke University (J.D., 1999). Member, Moot Court. Member, South African Yearbook of International Law, 1999. ***Email:*** john.simpkins@baachrobinson.com

MANUEL S. VARELA, born Pontevedra, Spain, November 19, 1972; admitted to bar, 1997, Maryland; 1998, U.S. District Court, District of Maryland; 1999, District of Columbia. *Education:* Harvard University (A.B., cum laude, 1994); Georgetown University (J.D., 1997). ***LANGUAGES:*** Spanish, Portuguese. ***PRACTICE AREAS:*** Litigation; Insurance Litigation; Toxic Torts. ***Email:*** manuel.varela@baachrobinson.com

OF COUNSEL

RUSSELL M. FRANK, born North Arlington, New Jersey, September 3, 1949; admitted to bar, 1978, District of Columbia; 1990, Massachusetts. *Education:* Duke University (A.B., 1971); Boston University (Ed.M., 1974); Catholic University of America (J.D., 1977). ***PRACTICE AREAS:*** Civil Litigation; Commercial Litigation; Insurance Coverage Litigation. ***Email:*** russell.frank@baachrobinson.com

SALLY A. REGAL, born Boston, Massachusetts, February 5, 1953; admitted to bar, 1979, District of Columbia. *Education:* Northwestern University and

(This Listing Continued)

Georgetown University (B.A., 1975); Boston College and Georgetown University (J.D., 1979). *Member:* The District of Columbia Bar. ***PRACTICE AREAS:*** Civil Litigation. ***Email:*** sally.regal@baachrobinson.com

SHARON M. SCHROER, born Petersburg, Virginia, June 8, 1956; admitted to bar, 1985, New York; 1992, District of Columbia. *Education:* University of Virginia (B.A., 1979); University of Michigan (J.D., 1984). ***PRACTICE AREAS:*** Commercial Litigation; Insurance Coverage Litigation. ***Email:*** sharon.schroer@baachrobinson.com

BACON, THORNTON & PALMER, L.L.P.

WASHINGTON, D.C.

(See Lanham, Maryland)

General Civil Litigation in all State and Federal Courts. Personal Injury, Wrongful Death, Brain Injury, Spinal Injury, Negligence, Insurance Defense, Insurance Coverage, Construction Defects, Construction Accidents, Retail Liability, Employer Liability, Products Liability, Premises Liability, Environmental Exposure, Asbestos Litigation, Lead Poisoning, Medical Malpractice.

LAW OFFICES OF SUSAN BAHR, PC

WASHINGTON, D.C.

(See Montgomery Village, Maryland)

Telecommunications Law, Communications Common Carrier, FCC Regulation, Telecommunications Contracts, Wireless Communications.

BAILEY LAW GROUP

Established in 1998

1752 N STREET, N.W., SUITE 800
WASHINGTON, D.C. 20036
Telephone: 202-887-8040
Fax: 202-887-8044
URL: http://www.baileylawgroup.com
Email: kbailey@baileylawgroup.com

Environmental Law, Clean Air Act, Environmental Litigation, Environmental Compliance, Environmental Permitting, Environmental Legislative Practice, Environmental Regulation, Risk Management, Commercial Real Estate, Leasing, Real Estate Joint Ventures, Commercial Real Estate Development, Federal Litigation.

FIRM PROFILE: The Bailey Law Group is a D.C. based women-owned law firm. Attorneys for the firm are extremely skilled at learning the clients business and remaining flexible to their needs. The firm is involved with environmental issues that include litigation, legislative advocacy and analysis, strategy development, regulatory compliance, and enforcement defense. The firm handles commercial real estate matters, including lease negotiations and representation in administrative, state, and federal courts. The firm's clients are both small and large as well as regional, national and international. They include trade associations, corporations, manufacturers, airports, consumer product retailers and food service providers.

KATHY D. BAILEY, born Corpus Christi, Texas, July 30, 1955; admitted to bar, 1985, New York, Pennsylvania and U.S. District Court, Eastern District of Pennsylvania; 1991, U.S. Court of Appeals, Third Circuit and U.S. Supreme Court; 1992, U.S. Court of Appeals for the District of Columbia Circuit; 1996, District of Columbia. *Education:* University of Houston (B.S., 1975; M.S., 1978); American University (J.D., 1983). Publications and Presentations: "Using Environmental Insurance to Reduce Environmental Liability," (with William Gulledge), Natural Resources & Environment, Spring 1997; "EPA Considers Revising Its Economic Benefit Assessment Model Used in Environmental Enforcement Cases," (with Roy Belden), Corporate Conduct Quarterly, 1997; "Is An Environmental Audit in Your Future?" International Facilities Management Journal, June 1996; "Legislative and Legal Considerations," chapter in Handbook of Toxic Air Pollution, Van Nostrand Reinhold Co., Inc., 1994; "Enforcement Issues in the Clean Air Act Amendments," presented at the ALI-ABA program on Criminal Enforcement of Environmental Laws, September 1992; "Up to Your Eyeballs in Paper: Permitting Under the new Clean Air Act," presented at and published by the Air and Waste Management Association, June 1991; "An Industry View of the Air Toxics Provisions of the Clean Air Act of 1990," in The Clean Air Act Amendments of 1990, Prentice Hall 1991. Counsel, Chadbourne & Parke LLP. Senior Attorney, American Automobile Manufacturers Association. Senior Assistant General Counsel, Chemical Manufacturers Association. Manager, Air Quality Programs, Metropolitan Washington Council of Governments. Air Quality Manager, Houston-Galveston Area Council. *Member:* New York State, Pennsylvania and American (Vice

(This Listing Continued)

BAILEY LAW GROUP, Washington—Continued

Chair, 1990-1995 and 1999— and Chair, 1995-1997, Air Quality Committee, SONREEL); American Bar Association Air Committee. ***REPORTED CASES:*** Monroe v. Host Marriott Services Corp., 999 F.Supp. 599(D.N.J. 1988). ***PRACTICE AREAS:*** Environmental Law; Commercial Real Estate; Commercial Litigation. ***Email:*** kbailey@baileylawgroup.com

ASSOCIATES

LISA M. DAVENPORT, born Fort Leonard Wood, Missouri, May 8, 1963; admitted to bar, 1994, Maryland; 1999, District of Columbia. *Education:* University of Illinois; Indiana University (B.S., 1985); University of Colorado (J.D., 1992). ***LANGUAGES:*** German. ***PRACTICE AREAS:*** Commercial Real Estate. ***Email:*** ldavenport@baileylawgroup.com

DAMI Y. ODUJINRIN, born Lagos, Nigeria, June 16, 1975; admitted to bar, 1999, New York (Not admitted in District of Columbia). *Education:* University of Buckingham, United Kingdom (LL.B., 1996); Harvard Law School (LL.M., 1998). ***PRACTICE AREAS:*** Commercial Real Estate; Beverage Alcohol Control. ***Email:*** dodujinrin@baileylawgroup.com

ALEXA A. COLE, born Brooklyn, New York, August 9, 1971; admitted to bar, 2000, New York and District of Columbia. *Education:* McGill University, Canada (B.A., 1993); Vermont Law School (J.D., 1998). ***PRACTICE AREAS:*** Environmental Law; Commercial Litigation. ***Email:*** acole@baileylawgroup.com

BAISE & MILLER, P.C.

1020 19TH STREET NW, SUITE 400
WASHINGTON, D.C. 20036
Telephone: 202-331-9100
Fax: 202-331-9060
Email: admin@dclaw.net
URL: http://www.dclaw.net

Environmental, Defamation, General Commercial and International Law.

FIRM PROFILE: Baise & Miller, P.C. is a law firm with a national practice and an international scope. The firm primarily represents private corporations and trade associations, acting as litigation counsel and lobbyist.

Our clients have included equipment manufacturers, agriculture cooperatives and dairy farmers, chemical and steel manufacturers, electric utilities, sugar refiners, major manufacturing and personal products companies, municipalities and local government agencies, various small businesses, trade associations, water companies, shipbuilders, port authorities, hazardous and solid waste management companies, telecommunication companies, real estate developers and cooperative and condominium associations.

On behalf of our clients, we have successfully litigated extremely complex, multiple jurisdiction and multiple party matters and secured adoption of major federal policies. We are committed to serving our clients on a timely, cost-effective basis in accordance with the highest standards of the legal profession. We are proud of our reputation as responsive and tenacious advocates for our clients and have made achieving their goals our single highest priority.

GARY H. BAISE, born Concord, Illinois, May 24, 1941; admitted to bar, 1968, Indiana; 1974, District of Columbia. *Education:* Western Illinois University (B.S., 1963); Indiana University (J.D., 1968). Assistant to the Administrator, 1970-1971; Director, Office of Legislation, 1971-1973, U.S. Environmental Protection Agency. Trial Attorney, U.S. Department of Justice, 1969-1970. Associate Deputy Attorney General of the United States, 1973-1974. Acting Deputy Attorney General of the United States, 1974. Awarded Arthur S. Flemming Award for being one of ten outstanding young Americans in Federal Government Service, 1972. Member, Farm Foundation Board of Trustees and Board of Visitors, Indiana University School of Public and Environmental Affairs. ***PRACTICE AREAS:*** Environmental Law; Litigation. ***Email:*** gbaise@dclaw.net

ERIC P. BOCK, born Djakarta, Indonesia, November 14, 1957; admitted to bar, 1982, California; 1988, U.S. Court of Appeals for the District of Columbia Circuit; 1997, U.S. Court of Appeals, Ninth Circuit (Not admitted in District of Columbia). *Education:* California Polytechnic State University (B.S., 1974); University of Southern California (M.S., 1976); Southwestern University (J.D., 1981). State Legislative and Regulatory Advocate for City of Los Angeles, 1983-1984; Federal Legislative and Regulatory Advocate for City of Los Angeles, 1983-1990. Associate, Schwabe Williamson & Wyatt, 1991-1995. Solo Practitioner, 1996. *Member:* Federal Energy and American Bar Associations; Bar Association of the District of Columbia; State Bar of California; District of

(This Listing Continued)

Columbia Bar; American Society of Civil Engineers. ***LANGUAGES:*** Dutch. ***PRACTICE AREAS:*** Environmental Law; Natural Resources Law; Electric Utility Law; Public Policy.

ANSON M. KELLER, born St. Louis, Missouri, December 14, 1936; admitted to bar, 1963, New York; 1980, District of Columbia. *Education:* Brown University (A.B., 1958); University of Michigan (J.D., 1962). Phi Delta Phi. Associate General Counsel, Pesticides, Toxic Substances and Solid Waste Management, Environmental Protection Agency, 1973-1975. Special Assistant for Legal and Regulatory Policy, Occupational Safety and Health Administration, 1975-1980. Director, White House Task Force on Safety Standards, Revisions, under President Ford, 1976. *Member:* District of Columbia Bar. ***PRACTICE AREAS:*** Environmental Law; Litigation; First Amendment Law; Defamation. ***Email:*** amkeller@dclaw.net

MARSHALL LEE MILLER, born Chattanooga, Tennessee, October 18, 1942; admitted to bar, 1971, District of Columbia; 1979, Virginia; U.S. Supreme Court. *Education:* Harvard University (B.A., 1964); Oxford University, Oxford, England; Heidelberg University, Germany; Yale University (J.D.,1970). Special Assistant to Administrator of Environmental Protection Agency, Chief EPA Judicial Officer, 1971-1973. Associate Deputy Attorney General, 1973-1974. Acting Assistant Secretary of Labor for Occupational Safety and Health, 1975-1976. Director, Bulgarian-American Enterprise Fund, Electronic Warfare Associates. *Member:* Federal Bar Association. ***PRACTICE AREAS:*** Environmental Law; International Law. ***Email:*** miller@dclaw.net

MARK L. SHAFFER, born Los Angeles, California, 1947; admitted to bar, 1973, California; 1981, District of Columbia; 1992, Maryland; 1996,U.S. Court of Claims and U.S. Court of Appeals, Fourth, Fifth and Ninth Circuits. *Education:* University of California at Berkeley (B.A., cum laude, 1969; J.D., 1973). Associate Majority Counsel, U.S. House of Representatives "October Surprise Task Force," 1992. Trial Attorney and Senior Trial Attorney, U.S. Department of Justice, Civil Rights Division, Employment Litigation Section, 1978-1986. Trial Attorney and Senior Trial Attorney, Contra Costa County Public Defender's Office, California. Law Clerk, Earl Warren Legal Institute, National Housing and Economic Development Law Project, 1972-1973. Memberships: ABA Standing Committee on Law and the National Security; ABA White Collar Crime Committee, Edward Bennett Williams Inns of Court (1991-1996); District of Columbia Bar Rules Review Committee (1995-1996) and Member of the Board of Directors of Big Brothers of the National Capital Area, General Counsel (1986-1992). ***PRACTICE AREAS:*** Civil Trial Practice; Administrative Law; Corporations; Intellectual Property; Employment; White Collar Crime. ***Email:*** mlshaffer@dclaw.net

MICHAEL S. LEVY, born Yonkers, New York, April 25, 1940; admitted to bar, 1966, District of Columbia. *Education:* University of Vermont (B.A., 1962); University of Aix Marseilles, Aix-en-Province, France; George Washington University (J.D., 1965). Delta Theta Phi. Staff Attorney, District of Columbia Redevelopment Land Agency, 1971-1974. Assistant Corporation Counsel, District of Columbia Government, 1975-1979. Member, District of Columbia Alcoholic Beverage Control Board, 1984-1989. ***PRACTICE AREAS:*** Litigation; Condominium; Real Estate; Corporate. ***Email:*** admin@dclaw.net

ELIZABETH S. POLINER, born Middletown, Connecticut, January 28, 1960; admitted to bar, 1988, Virginia; 1989, District of Columbia. *Education:* Bowdoin College (B.A., magna cum laude, 1982); University of Virginia (J.D.,1988); American University (M.F.A., 1994). *Member:* District of Columbia Bar; Virginia State Bar. ***PRACTICE AREAS:*** Environmental Law; Administrative Law. ***Email:*** admin@dclaw.net

DAVID G. ZANARDI, born June 27, 1970; admitted to bar, 1998, Florida (Not admitted in District of Columbia). *Education:* Virginia Polytechnic Institute and State University (B.A., 1992); Nova Southeastern University (J.D., 1997); Georgetown University Law Center (L.L.M., 1998). *Member:* The Florida Bar. ***PRACTICE AREAS:*** Commercial Transactions; International Commercial Law. ***Email:*** zanardi@dclaw.net

STEWART D. FRIED, born New York, N.Y., May 5, 1969; admitted to bar, 1995, Florida; 1996, U.S. District Court, Southern and Middle Districts of Florida; 1998, District of Columbia and U.S. Court of Appeals, Third Circuit; 2000, U.S. District Court, District of Columbia. *Education:* Johns Hopkins University (B.A., 1990); University of Miami (J.D., cum laude, 1995). Associate Editor, University of Miami Inter-American Law Review, 1994-1995. *Member:* American Bar Association; The Florida Bar; American Trial Lawyers Association. ***PRACTICE AREAS:*** Civil Litigation; Commercial Litigation; Environmental Litigation; Personal Injury. ***Email:*** sdfried@dclaw.net

MICHAEL C. FORMICA, born Montclair, New Jersey, October 14, 1971; admitted to bar, 1999, District of Columbia. *Education:* University of Rhode Island (B.A., 1994); Vermont Law School (J.D., 1998). ***PRACTICE AREAS:*** Environmental Law; International Law; Litigation; Legislative Practice. ***Email:*** mformica@dclaw.net

(This Listing Continued)

OF COUNSEL

GUY VANDER JAGT, born Cadillac, Michigan, August 26, 1931; admitted to bar, 1961, Michigan (Not admitted in District of Columbia). *Education:* Hope College (B.A., 1953); Yale Divinity School (B.D., 1957); Georgetown Law School; University of Michigan (J.D., 1960). Blue Key. Member, U.S. Congress, 1966-1993. (Also of Counsel to Baker & Hostetler, Washington, D.C.). ***LANGUAGES:*** German. ***PRACTICE AREAS:*** Tax Law; Legislative Practice; Litigation. ***Email:*** admin@dclaw.net

ALEXANDER McMILLAN BULLOCK, born Sumter, South Carolina, February 15, 1960; admitted to bar, 1985, South Carolina; 1991, North Carolina; 1992, Georgia; 1995, District of Columbia. *Education:* Furman University (B.A., 1982), Omicron Delta Kappa; University of South Carolina (J.D., 1985); George Washington University (LL.M., 1997). Phi Delta Phi; Order of the Barrister. Member, Moot Court Board; American Bar Association Moot Court Team. *Member:* North Carolina and American Bar Associations; South Carolina Bar. (Also Of Counsel to Garrett & Von Oehsen LLC in Stamford, Connecticut). ***PRACTICE AREAS:*** Environmental Law; Litigation. ***Email:*** amcmillanb@aol.com

BAKER BOTTS, L.L.P.

A Registered Limited Liability Partnership
THE WARNER
1299 PENNSYLVANIA AVENUE, N.W.
WASHINGTON, D.C. 20004-2400
Telephone: 202-639-7700
Fax: 202-639-7832
Email: postmaster@bakerbotts.com
URL: http://www.bakerbotts.com

Houston, Texas Office: One Shell Plaza, 910 Louisiana. Telephone: 713-229-1234.
Austin, Texas Office: 1600 San Jacinto Center, 98 San Jacinto Boulevard. Telephone: 512-322-2500.
Dallas, Texas Office: 2001 Ross Avenue. Telephone: 214-953-6500.
New York, New York Office: 599 Lexington Avenue. Telephone: 212-705-5000.
London, England Office: 45 Ludgate Hill. Telephone: 0171-778-1400 (Local); 011-44-171-778-1400 (International).
Baku, Azerbaijan Office: 6-10 Vagif Mustafa-zadeh Street, Third Floor, Icheri Sheher, 370004. Telephone: 994-12-97-63-88 (Local); 011-994-12-97-63-88 (International). Fax: 994-12-97-63-91 (Local); 011-994-12-97-63-91 (International).
Associated Firm: Mohammed Bin Saud Al Rasheed, Attorneys and Legal Consultants, Le Cygne Commercial Center, No. 2, Olaya, Main Road, P.O. Box 62982, Riyadh 11595, Saudi Arabia. Telephone: (966-1) 464-3139. Facsimile: (966-1) 464-9264.

Antitrust, Corporate, Securities, Mergers and Acquisitions, Energy, Environmental, Finance, White Collar Crime, Government Contracts, Intellectual Property, Patents, Trademarks, Copyrights, Trade Secrets, International Trade, Tax, Trial, Administrative Law, Alternative Dispute Resolution, Biotechnology, Business Law, Commercial Law, Computers and Software, Criminal Law, Fraud and Deceit, Government, Insurance, Regulatory Law, Technology and Science, Utility Law.

FIRM PROFILE: Baker Botts L.L.P., founded in 1840, is one of the oldest law firms in America. Our Firm's lawyers serve clients through a network of offices in seven cities: Houston, Dallas, Austin, Washington, D.C., New York, London, and Baku.

Baker Botts L.L.P. provides services to clients in all principal areas of civil law, including corporate and securities; international; oil and gas; real estate; litigation; energy; environmental; labor and employment; banking and finance; bankruptcy and creditors' rights; intellectual property and technology; government contracts; tax; employee benefits; and business and estate planning.

MEMBERS OF FIRM

JAY L. ALEXANDER, born New Brunswick, New Jersey, July 27, 1961; admitted to bar, 1986, Pennsylvania; 1988, District of Columbia. *Education:* Dartmouth College (A.B., summa cum laude, 1983); Stanford University (J.D., with distinction, 1986). Phi Beta Kappa; Order of the Coif. Law Clerk to the Honorable Ruth Bader Ginsburg, 1986-1987. Faculty, National Institute of Trial Advocacy. *Member:* The District of Columbia Bar; Pennsylvania and American Bar Associations. ***Email:*** jay.alexander@bakerbotts.com

R. THOMAS AMIS, born New Orleans, Louisiana, June 22, 1956; admitted to bar, 1982, New York; 1998, District of Columbia. *Education:* Yale University (B.A., 1978); London School of Economics and Political Science (M.S., 1979); INSEAD (M.B.A., 1983); Columbia University (J.D., 1982). *Member:* New York State Bar Association; District of Columbia Bar. ***LANGUAGES:*** French. ***Email:*** tom.amis@bakerbotts.com

(This Listing Continued)

JAMES B. ARPIN, born Washington, D.C., February 26, 1959; admitted to bar, 1989, Massachusetts; 1990, Maryland and District of Columbia; registered to practice before U.S. Patent and Trademark Office. *Education:* University of Pennsylvania (B.A.S./B.S.E., 1981); Boston University (J.D., magna cum laude, 1989); The Johns Hopkins University (M.S.E.E., 2000). Editor-in-Chief, Probate Law Journal, 1988-1989. *Member:* The District of Columbia Bar (Member, Newsletter Committee, Intellectual Property Law Section, 1994-1999, Chair, 1994-1998); Maryland State, Massachusetts and American Bar Associations; American Intellectual Property Law Association. [Lt., US Navy, 1981-1986; Lt. Cmdr., USNR, 1986—]. ***Email:*** jim.arpin@bakerbotts.com

JAMES A. BAKER IV, born Houston, Texas, October 9, 1954; admitted to bar, 1982, Texas; 1988, District of Columbia. *Education:* Occidental College; Cornell University (B.S., 1977); University of Texas (J.D., 1981). Editorial Board, Texas International Law Journal, 1980-1981. Counsel to U.S. Senate Majority Leader, 1982-1985. *Member:* State Bar of Texas; The District of Columbia Bar; American Bar Association (Member, Sections on: Taxation; International Law and Practice). ***Email:*** jamie.baker@bakerbotts.com

JAMES ADDISON BAKER, III, born Houston, Texas, April 28, 1930; admitted to bar, 1957, Texas (Not admitted in District of Columbia). *Education:* Princeton University (B.A., 1952); University of Texas (LL.B., with honors, 1957). Phi Delta Phi. Secretary of State, 1989-1992; Secretary of the Treasury, 1985-1988; White House Chief of Staff, 1981-1985; White House Chief of Staff and Senior Counsellor to the President, 1992-1993; Under Secretary of Commerce, 1975-1976. Trustee, Princeton University, 1995-1999. Honorary Chair, James A. Baker, III Institute for Public Policy at Rice University. *Member:* Houston and American Bar Associations; State Bar of Texas. ***Email:*** jamesa.baker@bakerbotts.com

MICHAEL J. BARTA, born Morgantown, West Virginia, March 27, 1963; admitted to bar, 1989, Virginia; 1992, District of Columbia. *Education:* Princeton University (A.B., summa cum laude, 1985); Harvard University (J.D., cum laude, 1988). Phi Beta Kappa. Law Clerk, Honorable Jerome Farris, U.S. Court of Appeals, Ninth Circuit, 1988-1989. Chair: Computer Crimes Subcommittee, ABA's Business Law Section. Instructor: National Institute of Trial Advocacy; Trial Advocacy, Georgetown University Law Center. *Member:* Virginia State Bar; Virginia and American Bar Associations; The District of Columbia Bar; E.B. Williams Inn of Court; Criminal Justice Act Panel, U.S. District Court for the District of Columbia. ***Email:*** michael.barta@bakerbotts.com

J. BRADLEY BENNETT, born Miami, Florida, November 8, 1962; admitted to bar, 1989, New York; 1990, District of Columbia. *Education:* St. Lawrence University (B.A., summa cum laude, 1985); Georgetown University (J.D., magna cum laude, 1988). Phi Beta Kappa; Order of the Coif. Member, Georgetown Law Journal, 1986-1988. Chair, D.C. Bar Corporation, Finance and Securities Law Section; ABA Business Law Section's Financial Crimes Committee. Adjunct Professor of Securities Law, Catholic University of America Columbus School of Law. Attorney, 1988-1991 and Senior Attorney, 1991-1992, Division of Enforcement, U.S. Securities and Exchange Commission. *Member:* The District of Columbia Bar (Chair, D.C. Bar Corporation, Finance and Securities Law Section); New York State and American Bar Associations. ***REPORTED CASES:*** SEC v. Musella, 748 F. Supp. 1028 (S.D.N.Y. 1989). ***Email:*** brad.bennett@bakerbotts.com

ELLEN FELS BERKMAN, born Cincinnati, Ohio, June 26, 1964; admitted to bar, 1990, Pennsylvania; 1992, District of Columbia. *Education:* Harvard University (A.B., magna cum laude with highest honors, 1986); Columbia University (J.D., 1990). Harlan Fiske Stone Scholar. Notes Editor, Columbia Law Review, 1989-1990. Law Clerk to Judge Joyce Hens Green, U.S. District Court for the District of Columbia, 1990-1992. *Member:* The District of Columbia Bar; Pennsylvania and American Bar Associations; Women's Bar Association. ***Email:*** ellen.berkman@bakerbotts.com

J. PATRICK BERRY, born Canton, Mississippi, February 13, 1949; admitted to bar, 1977, District of Columbia. *Education:* Harvard University (A.B., magna cum laude, 1971; J.D., 1975). Counsel to the Committee on Energy and Natural Resources, United States Senate, 1975-1977. *Member:* The District of Columbia Bar (Environment, Energy and Natural Resources Section); American Bar Association (Section of Natural Resources, Energy and Environmental Law). ***PRACTICE AREAS:*** Environmental Law. ***Email:*** patrick.berry@bakerbotts.com

STEPHEN L. BRAGA, born Newport, Rhode Island, November 29, 1955; admitted to bar, 1982, District of Columbia. *Education:* Fairfield University (B.A., cum laude, 1978); Georgetown University Law Center (J.D., magna cum laude, 1981). Member, 1979-1980 and Editor, 1980-1981, Georgetown Law Journal. Adjunct Professor of Law, Georgetown University Law Center. Law Clerk to Judge Thomas A. Flannery, U.S. District Court for the District of Columbia, 1981-1982. Member, Practitioner's Advisory Group to the United States Sentencing Commission, 1992-1993. Member, District of Columbia Bar Legal Ethics Committee, 2000-2001. *Member:* The District of Columbia Bar (Member, Legal Ethics Committee, 2000-2001). ***Email:*** stephen.braga@bakerbotts.com

(This Listing Continued)

BAKER BOTTS, L.L.P., Washington—Continued

WILLIAM M. BUMPERS, born Charleston, Arkansas, August 4, 1955; admitted to bar, 1984, District of Columbia; 1986, U.S. District Court, District of Maryland; 1990, U.S. District Court, District of Columbia. *Education:* Hendrix College (B.A., 1977); Antioch University (M.A., 1980); University of Virginia (J.D., 1984). Editor-in-Chief, Virginia Journal of Natural Resources Law. ***LANGUAGES:*** German. ***Email:*** william.bumpers@bakerbotts.com

JOE R. CALDWELL, JR., born Jackson, Mississippi, March 27, 1949; admitted to bar, 1974, New Jersey; 1978, District of Columbia. *Education:* Syracuse University (A.B., 1971); Rutgers University (J.D., 1974); Georgetown University (LL.M., 1984); Harvard University (M.P.A., 1985). Faculty, NITA Trial Advocacy, Georgetown University Law Center, 1992—. Deputy Attorney General, Division of Criminal Justice, New Jersey, 1974-1975. Legal Officer, U.S. Supreme Court, 1980-1982. Counsel, Supreme Court of the United States, assistant to Chief Justice Warren E. Burger, 1982-1984. Chief of Staff and Legal Counsel to Mayor Sharon Pratt Kelly, Washington, D.C., 1991. *Member:* The District of Columbia Bar; New Jersey State and American Bar Associations. ***Email:*** joe.caldwell@bakerbotts.com

JOHN JOSEPH CASSIDY, born Washington, D.C., February 8, 1930; admitted to bar, 1955, District of Columbia. *Education:* Georgetown College (B.S., 1952); Georgetown University (J.D., 1955). The Judge Advocate General's Corps, U.S. Army, 1955-1958. Executive Assistant to Chairman, Board of Monitors, U.S. District Court, District of Columbia, 1958-1961. Attorney, Criminal and Tax Divisions, Department of Justice, 1961-1965. Special Assistant to the Attorney General of the United States, 1964-1965. Vice Chairman, Law Enforcement and Criminal Justice Commission, Montgomery County, Maryland, 1967-1970. *Member:* The District of Columbia Bar; Bar Association of the District of Columbia; American Bar Association. ***Email:*** john.cassidy@bakerbotts.com

CHRISTOPHER R. COOPER, born Mobile, Alabama, September 2, 1966; admitted to bar, 1994, California; 1997, District of Columbia. *Education:* Yale University (B.A., summa cum laude, 1988); Stanford University (J.D., with distinction, 1993). Phi Beta Kappa. President, Stanford Law Review, 1993. Law Clerk to Chief Judge Abner Mikva, U.S. Court of Appeals for the District of Columbia Circuit, 1993-1994. Special Assistant to the Deputy Attorney General, U.S. Department of Justice, 1994-1996. *Member:* The District of Columbia Bar; State Bar of California. ***Email:*** casey.cooper@bakerbotts.com

KELLY RILEY DONOVAN, born Burlington, Wisconsin, June 7, 1966; admitted to bar, 1991, Illinois; 1992, District of Columbia. *Education:* University of Illinois at Champaign-Urbana (B.S., 1988); Washington University School of Law, St. Louis, Missouri (J.D., 1991). Order of the Coif. Editor-in-Chief, Law Quarterly, 1990-1991. Certified Public Accountant, Illinois, 1988. ***Email:*** kelly.donovan@bakerbotts.com

JAMES R. DOTY, born Houston, Texas, May 14, 1940; admitted to bar, 1969, Texas; 1988, District of Columbia. *Education:* Rice University (B.A., summa cum laude, Phi Beta Kappa, 1962) Rhodes Scholar; Merton College, Oxford University, Oxford, England (A.B., 1964); Harvard University (M.A., 1968); Yale Law School (LL.B., 1969). General Counsel, United States Securities and Exchange Commission, 1990-1992. Member, Legal Advisory Committee, National Association of Securities Dealers, Inc., 1993-1995. Member, Executive Council, FBA Securities Committee. Task Force on Securities Market Development, U.S. Russian Joint Commission, 1997. *Member:* Houston and American Bar Associations; State Bar of Texas; The District of Columbia Bar; American Law Institute. ***Email:*** james.doty@bakerbotts.com

THOMAS J. EASTMENT, born New York, N.Y., March 3, 1950; admitted to bar, 1976, New York; 1977, District of Columbia. *Education:* Manhattan College (B.Ch.E., summa cum laude, 1972); University of Michigan (J.D., cum laude, 1975). Tau Beta Pi; Sigma Xi; Barrister's Society. *Member:* The District of Columbia Bar; New York State and Federal Energy Bar Associations. ***Email:*** tom.eastment@bakerbotts.com

PAUL F. ENZINNA, born Buffalo, New York, May 8, 1958; admitted to bar, 1989, Pennsylvania and District of Columbia. *Education:* Fordham University (B.A., magna cum laude, 1980); University of Virginia (M.A., 1983; J.D., 1987). Order of the Coif. Notes Editor, Virginia Law Review, 1986-1987. Law Clerk to The Honorable J. Harvie Wilkinson, U.S. Court of Appeals, Fourth Circuit, 1987-1988. Instructor, NITA, 1998—. *Member:* The District of Columbia Bar. ***Email:*** paul.enzinna@bakerbotts.com

MICHAEL A. GOLD, born Rantoul, Illinois, May 22, 1966; admitted to bar, 1994, New York; 1995, District of Columbia. *Education:* Wharton School of Business and College of Arts and Sciences, University of Pennsylvania (B.S.E., cum laude, 1988; B.A., cum laude, 1988); University of Chicago (J.D., with honors, 1993). Articles Editor, The University of Chicago Legal Forum. Judicial Clerk to the Hon. Lee H. Rosenthal, U.S. District Court, Southern District of Texas, 1993-1994. *Member:* The District of Columbia Bar; New York State Bar Association. ***Email:*** michael.gold@bakerbotts.com

(This Listing Continued)

JULIA E. GUTTMAN, born Washington, D.C., May 10, 1960; admitted to bar, 1985, Pennsylvania; 1988, District of Columbia. *Education:* Radcliffe College of Harvard University (B.A., magna cum laude, 1982); Yale Law School (J.D., 1985). Notes Editor, Yale Law Journal, 1984-1985. Law Clerk to Chief Judge Patricia M. Wald. U.S. Court of Appeals for the District of Columbia Circuit, 1985-1986. *Member:* Pennsylvania and American Bar Associations; The District of Columbia Bar. ***Email:*** julia.guttman@bakerbotts.com

JAMES R. HEAVNER, JR., born Henderson, North Carolina, December 6, 1959; admitted to bar, 1991, Maryland; 1993, District of Columbia. *Education:* United States Military Academy (B.S., 1982); Georgetown University (J.D., magna cum laude, 1991). Order of the Coif. Member, Georgetown Law Journal, 1990-1991. Law Clerk to the Hon. Paul V. Niemeyer, U.S. Court of Appeals, Fourth Circuit, 1991-1992. *Member:* The District of Columbia Bar; Maryland State and American Bar Associations. ***Email:*** james.heavner@bakerbotts.com

STEVEN R. HUNSICKER, born Denton, Texas, March 18, 1950; admitted to bar, 1976, California; 1977, District of Columbia. *Education:* University of Iowa (B.B.A., 1972); University of San Diego (J.D., 1975); University of Pennsylvania (LL.M., 1977). Editor, San Diego Law Review, 1974-1975. Fellow, Center for Study of Financial Institutions, University of Pennsylvania Law School, 1975-1976. *Member:* The District of Columbia Bar. ***Email:*** steve.hunsicker@bakerbotts.com

WILLIAM H. JEFFRESS, JR., born Birmingham, Alabama, July 17, 1945; admitted to bar, 1971, District of Columbia. *Education:* Washington & Lee University (B.A., summa cum laude, 1967); Yale Law School (LL.B., 1970). Phi Beta Kappa. Editor-in-Chief, Yale Law Journal, 1969-1970. Law Clerk to Judge Gerhard A. Gesell, U.S. District Court for the District of Columbia, 1970-1971; Justice Potter Stewart, U.S. Supreme Court, 1971-1972. Fellow, American College of Trial Lawyers. Member, ABA Standing Committee on Ethics and Professional Responsibility, 1996—. Chairperson, ABA Committee on Standards for Criminal Justice, 1993-1995. Vice-Chairperson, 1989-1991 and Member of Council, 1991-1994, ABA Criminal Justice Section. Chairperson, Advisory Board, American Criminal Law Review, 1984-1985. Member, Advisory Committee on Local Rules, United States District Court for the District of Columbia, 1973-1994. *Member:* The District of Columbia Bar; American Bar Association. ***Email:*** william.jeffress@bakerbotts.com

DEBRA J. JEZOUIT, born Hartford, Connecticut, April 12, 1964; admitted to bar, 1990, Virginia; 1992, District of Columbia. *Education:* George Washington University (B.A., 1986); University of Virginia (J.D., 1990). Phi Beta Kappa. *Member:* American Bar Association; Women's Bar Association. ***LANGUAGES:*** Spanish. ***PRACTICE AREAS:*** Environmental. ***Email:*** debra.jezouit@bakerbotts.com

BRUCE F. KIELY, born Oklahoma City, Oklahoma, August 25, 1944; admitted to bar, 1971, Virginia; 1976, District of Columbia. *Education:* University of Colorado (B.S., 1967); University of Texas (J.D., 1970). Member, Federal Power Commission, Office of General Counsel, 1972-1973. U.S. Army Selective Service System, Office of General Counsel, 1971-1972. *Member:* The District of Columbia Bar; The Virginia and Federal Energy Bar Associations. ***Email:*** bruce.kiely@bakerbotts.com

JODY MANIER KRIS, born Valparaiso, Indiana, September 28, 1968; admitted to bar, 1996, District of Columbia and Massachusetts. *Education:* Texas A & M University (B.A., summa cum laude, 1990); University of Chicago (J.D., with high honors, 1993). Order of the Coif. Editor in Chief, University of Chicago Law Review, 1993. Law Clerk to: Honorable Stephen F. Williams, 1993-1994, United States Court of Appeals for the D.C. Circuit; Honorable William H. Rehnquist, 1994-1995, United States Supreme Court. ***Email:*** jodi.kris@bakerbotts.com

NIKI KUCKES, born Princeton, New Jersey, October 28, 1959; admitted to bar, 1987, Pennsylvania; 1988, District of Columbia. *Education:* Cornell University (B.A., cum laude, 1981); Yale Law School (J.D., 1985). Law Clerk to Judge Antonin Scalia, U.S. Court of Appeals for the D.C. Circuit, 1985-1986. Editor and Senior Editor, Yale Law Journal (1983-1985). Chair, ABA Criminal Justice Standards Committee (1997-2000), Co-Chair and Steering Committee, D.C. Bar Criminal Law and Individual Rights Section (1994-1999). General Counsel, Fair Housing Council of Greater Washington, Inc. (1989-1991). *Member:* American Bar Association; Women's Bar Association of the District of Columbia. ***Email:*** niki.kuckes@bakerbotts.com

RAYMOND G. LARROCA, born San Juan, Puerto Rico, January 5, 1930; admitted to bar, 1957, District of Columbia. *Education:* Georgetown University (B.S.S., 1952); Georgetown University Law School (J.D., 1957). Phi Delta Phi. Member, Board of Editors, Georgetown Law Journal, 1956. *Member:* The District of Columbia Bar; Bar Association of the District of Columbia; American Bar Association (Member, Sections on: International Law; Criminal Justice; Litigation); National Association of Criminal Defense Lawyers. ***LANGUAGES:*** Spanish. ***Email:*** ray.larroca@bakerbotts.com

STEVEN L. LEIFER, born New York, N.Y., November 29, 1952; admitted to bar, 1977, District of Columbia. *Education:* Brandeis University (A.B., magna cum laude, 1974); Cornell University (J.D., 1977). Staff Attorney, U.S.

(This Listing Continued)

Environmental Protection Agency, Washington, D.C. Office, 1977-1981. Chief, Guidance Development Branch, Office of Legal and Enforcement Policy, U.S. EPA, 1982. Chief, CERCLA and National Projects Branches, Office of Enforcement and Compliance Monitoring, U.S. EPA, 1983-1985. Deputy Associate Enforcement Counsel for Waste, U.S. EPA, 1986-1987. Acting Associate Enforcement Counsel for Waste, U.S. EPA, 1987-1988. Partner, Rivkin, Radler, Dunne & Bayh, 1988-1989. Partner, Howrey & Simon, 1989-1996. *Member:* The District of Columbia Bar. **Email:** steven.leifer@bakerbotts.com

MARK K. LEWIS, born Bellmore, New York, August 8, 1965; admitted to bar, 1990, Maryland; 1991, District of Columbia. *Education:* University of Maryland (B.S., magna cum laude, 1987); Member, Mortar Board; Georgetown University (J.D., magna cum laude, 1990). Order of the Coif. Associate Editor, Law and Policy in International Business. *Member:* Energy Bar Association. **Email:** mark.lewis@bakerbotts.com

RANDOLPH QUAILE McMANUS, born Norman, Oklahoma, April 18, 1950; admitted to bar, 1975, Texas; 1976, District of Columbia. *Education:* Williams College (B.A., 1972); University of Houston (J.D., 1975). Order of the Barristers. *Member:* The District of Columbia Bar; State Bar of Texas; Federal Energy and American (Chairman, Electric Utilities Subcommittee of Energy Litigation Committee, Litigation Section, 1989—) Bar Associations. **Email:** randy.mcmanus@bakerbotts.com

HERBERT J. MILLER, JR., born Minneapolis, Minnesota, January 11, 1924; admitted to bar, 1949, District of Columbia. *Education:* George Washington University (B.A., 1948; LL.B., 1949). Order of the Coif; Phi Delta Phi. Assistant Attorney General, Criminal Division, Department of Justice, 1961-1965. Chairman, President's Commission on Crime in the District of Columbia, July, 1965-January, 1967. Adjunct Professor, Georgetown Law School, 1973-1974. Member, Advisory Committee on Criminal Rules for the Committee on Rules of Practice and Procedure of the Judicial Conference of the United States, 1983-1988. Member, 1983-1989 and Chairman, 1985-1989, Committee on Grievances for the United States District Court for the District of Columbia. *Member:* The District of Columbia Bar; Bar Association of the District of Columbia (Director, 1968-1969; Vice-President, 1969-1970; President, 1970-1971); American Bar Association; American College of Trial Lawyers. [U.S. Army 1943-1946, Private to Captain]. **Email:** herbert.miller@bakerbotts.com

MARTIN D. MINSKER, born Brooklyn, New York, December 18, 1942; admitted to bar, 1969, Massachusetts; 1972, District of Columbia. *Education:* Cornell University (B.S., 1964); Harvard Law School (J.D., magna cum laude, 1969; LL.M., 1970). Note Editor, Harvard Law Review, 1968-1969. Law Clerk to Justice John M. Harlan, United States Supreme Court, 1970-1971. *Member:* The District of Columbia Bar (Secretary, 1987-1988; Board of Governors, 1988-1994. Chair, Hearing Committee No. 1, Board on Professional Responsibility, 1986-1992; Co-Chairperson, D.C. Bar Continuing Legal Education Committee, 1986-1987; Chair, Lawyer Practice Assistance Committee, 1995—); Bar Association of the District of Columbia; Federal and American Bar Associations; American Law Institute; Women's Bar Association of the District of Columbia. Fellow, American Bar Foundation. **Email:** martin.minsker@bakerbotts.com

R. STAN MORTENSON, born Columbia, South Carolina, February 14, 1945; admitted to bar, 1972, District of Columbia. *Education:* Baylor University and Ohio University (B.A., cum laude, 1967); University of Michigan (J.D., magna cum laude, 1970). Associate Editor, Michigan Law Review, 1969-1970. Law Clerk to Judge Stanley N. Barnes, U.S. Court of Appeals, Ninth Circuit, 1970-1971. Instructor, Trial Advocacy, Harvard Law School and Georgetown University Law Center. Member, CJA Panel Selection Committee, U.S. District Court for the District of Columbia, 1991—. Recipient, R. Kenneth Mundy Lawyer of the Year Award, 1995 by NACDL, D.C. Chapter. *Member:* The District of Columbia Bar; American Bar Association; National Association of Criminal Defense Lawyers. Fellow, American College of Trial Lawyers; E.B. Williams Inn of Court (Master). **Email:** rstanmortenson@bakerbotts.com

HAROLD D. MURRY, JR., born Holdenville, Oklahoma, June 30, 1943; admitted to bar, 1968, Oklahoma; 1974, District of Columbia. *Education:* Oklahoma University (B.A., 1965; J.D., 1968). Phi Alpha Delta. Assistant to the Vice President, University of Oklahoma, 1968-1971. Legal Counsel, Research Institute, 1969-1971. Attorney, U.S. Department of Justice, 1971-1974. Special Assistant U.S. Attorney, 1972. Associate, 1974-1978; Partner, 1978-1991, Clifford & Warnke, Washington, D.C. Partner, Howrey & Simon, Washington, D.C., 1991-1998. *Member:* The District of Columbia Bar; Bar Association of the District of Columbia; Oklahoma, Federal and American Bar Associations. **Email:** hal.murry@bakerbotts.com

DAVID N. POWERS, born New York, N.Y., May 25, 1956; admitted to bar, 1982, California; 1985, District of Columbia. *Education:* Princeton University (A.B., cum laude, 1978); University of Virginia (J.D., 1982). Member, Editorial Board, 1980-1981 and Notes Editor, 1981-1982, Virginia Law Review. Counsel to the Commissioner, United States Securities and Exchange Commission, 1984-1986. *Member:* The District of Columbia Bar; State Bar of California (inactive). **Email:** david.powers@bakerbotts.com

(This Listing Continued)

DANIEL J. RILEY, born Amarillo, Texas, January 14, 1947; admitted to bar, 1972, Texas; 1999, District of Columbia. *Education:* University of Texas (B.A., cum laude, 1969; J.D., magna cum laude, 1971). Phi Beta Kappa; Pi Sigma Alpha; Phi Delta Phi; Order of the Coif. Member, Chancellors. Associate Editor, Texas Law Review, 1970-1971. Teaching Assistant in Legal Research and Writing, University of Texas School of Law, 1970-1971. Adjunct Professor, University of Dallas Graduate School of Management, 1983-1993. *Member:* The District of Columbia Bar; Dallas and American (Member, Public Contract Law and International Law Sections) Bar Associations; State Bar of Texas. **Email:** daniel.riley@bakerbotts.com

JAMES E. ROCAP, III, born Indianapolis, Indiana, February 23, 1950; admitted to bar, 1975, District of Columbia. *Education:* University of Notre Dame (B.A., magna cum laude, 1971); Georgetown University (J.D., 1975). Member, 1973-1974 and Case and Note Editor, 1974-1975, Georgetown Law Journal. Contributing Author, *Manual for Complex Insurance Coverage Litigation.* Law Clerk to Judge William B. Jones, Chief Judge of the U.S. District Court, District of Columbia, 1975-1976. *Member:* The District of Columbia Bar; American Bar Association (Member, Litigation Section Committee on Insurance Coverage). **Email:** james.rocap@bakerbotts.com

JOANNE C. RUTKOWSKI, born 1957; admitted to bar, 1983, Massachusetts; 1997, District of Columbia. *Education:* Albright College (B.S., magna cum laude, 1979); Harvard Law School (J.D., 1983). ***PRACTICE AREAS:*** Utility; Regulatory; Mergers and Acquisitions. **Email:** joanne.rutkowski@bakerbotts.com

MARY C. SPEARING, born St. Louis, Missouri, June 19, 1951; admitted to bar, 1977, New York; 2000, District of Columbia. *Education:* Vassar College (A.B., 1972); Fordham University Law School (J.D., 1976). Articles Editor, Fordham Urban Law Journal. U.S. Department of Justice, Criminal Division, Chief, Fraud Section, 1994-1998; Chief, General Litigation Section, 1991-1994; Deputy Chief, Child Exploitation Section, 1989-1991. Assistant U.S. Attorney, Middle District of Pennsylvania, 1983-1988. Assistant U.S. Attorney, Eastern District of Pennsylvania, 1981-1983. Master, Edward Bennet Williams Inn of Court. *Member:* American Bar Association (Vice Chair, White Collar Crime Committee, 1996-1998). **Email:** mary.spearing@bakerbotts.com

JEFFREY A. STONEROCK, born Dayton, Ohio, February 13, 1957; admitted to bar, 1984, North Carolina; 1992, District of Columbia. *Education:* United States Military Academy (B.S., 1979); Duke Law School (J.D., with honors, 1984); The Judge Advocate General's School of the Army (LL.M., with honors, 1989). *Member:* North Carolina State Bar; The District of Columbia Bar; American Bar Association (Member, Sections on: Public Utility, Communications and Transportation; Public Contract Law); Board of Contract Appeals Bar Association (Chairman, Attorney Registry Committee, 1993-1995). [Major, JAGC, U.S. Army, 1979-1992]. **Email:** jeffrey.stonerock@bakerbotts.com

DAVID A. SUPER, born Silver Spring, Maryland, October 3, 1964; admitted to bar, 1991, Maryland and District of Columbia. *Education:* University of Maryland (B.S., 1986; J.D., 1990). Order of the Coif. *Member:* The District of Columbia Bar; Maryland State Bar Association. **Email:** david.super@bakerbotts.com

RANDALL J. TURK, born Berwyn, Illinois, June 8, 1950; admitted to bar, 1981, Arizona; 1982, District of Columbia. *Education:* Princeton University (B.A., cum laude, 1973); Stanford University (M.A., 1975); Georgetown University Law School (J.D., magna cum laude, 1980). Case and Note Editor, Georgetown Law Journal, 1979-1980. Law Clerk to the Honorable Spottswood W. Robinson, III, U.S. Court of Appeals, District of Columbia Circuit, 1980-1981. Instructor, National Institute of Trial Advocacy, 1990—. Lead Author: D.C. Pretrial Practice Guide, Lawyers Cooperative Publishing/American Inns of Court Foundation, 1995-1997. Member: Wong Sun Society; White Collar Crime Committee, Litigation Section, American Bar Association. *Member:* District of Columbia Bar; American Bar Association; National Association of Criminal Defense Lawyers. ***PRACTICE AREAS:*** Business Crimes; White Collar Crime; Government Investigations; Complex and Multi-District Litigation; First Amendment; Corporate Compliance. **Email:** randy.turk@bakerbotts.com

SPECIAL COUNSEL

DIANA L. DIETRICH, born November 22, 1958; admitted to bar, 1986, District of Columbia; 1994, Washington. *Education:* Duke University (B.A., magna cum laude, 1980); University of Kansas (J.D., 1985). Note and Comment Editor, University of Kansas Law Review, 1984-1985.

ROBERT L. TROIKE, born Akron, Ohio, September 30, 1936; admitted to bar, 1964, Maryland; 1999, District of Columbia. *Education:* United States Merchant Marine Academy (B.S., 1960); University of Baltimore School of Law (J.D., 1964). *Member:* American Bar Association. **Email:** robert.troike@bakerbotts.com

O. KEVIN VINCENT, born Wright Patterson AFB, Ohio, September 3, 1962; admitted to bar, 1986, Alabama; 1992, Maryland; 1993, Virginia; 1995, District of Columbia. *Education:* University of Alabama (B.S.E.E., 1983; J.D.,

(This Listing Continued)

BAKER BOTTS, L.L.P., Washington—Continued

1986). Eta Kappa Nu; Tau Beta Pi. Hugo Black Scholar. Member, University of Alabama Law Review. *Member:* Alabama State Bar; American (Member, Public Contract Law Section) and Federal Bar Associations; Institute of Electrical and Electronics Engineers. [Capt., USAF, Office of the General Counsel, 1986-1990]. ***Email:*** kevin.vincent@bakerbotts.com

OF COUNSEL

EVAN R. BERLACK, born New York, N.Y., April 1, 1934; admitted to bar, 1963, New York; 1969, District of Columbia. *Education:* Phillips Academy (1952); Harvard University (A.B., magna cum laude, 1956; LL.B., 1962). U.S. Foreign Service Officer, 1963-65. Attorney, Office of the Legal Adviser, Department of State, 1965-68. ***LANGUAGES:*** French. ***Email:*** evan.berlack@bakerbotts.com

JAY M. CANTOR, born Philadelphia, Pennsylvania, September 26, 1932; admitted to bar, 1960, District of Columbia; registered to practice before U.S. Patent and Trademark Office. *Education:* University of Pennsylvania (B.S.E.E., 1956; A.B., 1957); George Washington University (J.D., 1959). *Member:* District of Columbia Bar; American Bar Association; American Intellectual Property Law Association. ***Email:*** jay.cantor@bakerbotts.com

THOMAS B. CARR, born Norfolk, Virginia, August 10, 1943; admitted to bar, 1969, Virginia; 1970, District of Columbia. *Education:* Georgetown University (B.S., 1965); Brandeis University (M.A., 1966); University of Virginia (LL.B., 1969). Order of the Coif. Member, Board of Editors, Securities Regulation Area Specialist, Virginia Law Review, 1967-1969. Member, D.C. Council Procurement Reform Task Force, Committee on Waste, Fraud and Abuse, 1995. *Member:* The District of Columbia Bar; Virginia State Bar; American Bar Association (Member, Section of Public Contract Law, Committee on Debarment and Suspension); The Barristers. ***Email:*** thomas.carr@bakerbotts.com

THEODORE C. JONAS, born Chattanooga, Tennessee, July 25, 1962; admitted to bar, 1991, Georgia (Not admitted in District of Columbia). *Education:* Cornell University (B.A., 1984); Cornell Law School (J.D., 1991). Former advisor to the Georgian Parliament under auspices of the National Democratic Institute for International Affairs. Member of Georgian Consulting Group, Inc., 1996. Articles Editor of the *Cornell International Law Journal.* Clerk, Judge Joseph W. Hatchett, United States Court of Appeals for the 11th Circuit. Legislative Assistant in the U.S. House of Representatives, 1984-1988. *Member:* State Bar of Georgia. ***LANGUAGES:*** Georgian, French. ***Email:*** ted.jonas@bakerbotts.com

ROBERT H. PELLETREAU, born 1935; admitted to bar, 1962, New York; 1997, District of Columbia. *Education:* Yale University (B.A., 1957); Harvard University (LL.B., 1961). Former Associations: Department of State, Assistant Secretary of State for Near Eastern Affairs, 1994-1997; Ambassador to: Egypt, 1991-1993; Tunisia, 1987-1991; Bahrain, 1979-1980. While in Tunisia, conducted U.S. Dialogue with the P.L.O., 1988-1990. Played Key Role in Development and Implementation of U.S. Policies toward North Africa, the Levant, Egypt and the Gulf, including Iraq and Iran, 1994-1997. Formerly with, Chadbourne & Parke, New York, New York. *Member:* Council on Foreign Relations; Middle East Institute; National U.S.-Arab Chamber of Commerce; American-Iranian Council; American Bar Association. (Also Member, Afridi, Angell & Pelletreau LLP). ***LANGUAGES:*** French, Arabic. ***Email:*** rpelletreau@afridi.com

A. JOHN RADSAN, born 1962; admitted to bar, 1988, Illinois; 1989, District of Columbia; 1990, New York; 1995, California. *Education:* Duke University (A.B., summa cum laude, 1983); Harvard University (J.D., cum laude, 1987). Phi Beta Kappa. Trial Attorney, Fraud Section of Criminal Division, U.S. Department of Justice, Washington, D.C.; Resident Legal Advisor, U.S. Embassy, Moscow; Assistant U.S. Attorney, Southern District of California. Corporate Associate, Baker & McKenzie, Chicago, Ill.; Sullivan & Cromwell, New York, N.Y. *Member:* Iranian-American Bar Association. (Also Of Counsel, Afridi, Angell & Pelletreau LLP). ***LANGUAGES:*** French, Farsi and Spanish. ***Email:*** jradsan@afridi.com

ASSOCIATES

AMA A. ADAMS, born Alexandria, Virginia, November 15, 1974; (admission pending). *Education:* Wesleyan University (B.A., 1996); University of Virginia (J.D., 2001).

DEMITRIUS M. ANTHONY, born December 20, 1966; admitted to bar, 2000, North Carolina (Not admitted in District of Columbia). *Education:* University of North Carolina (B.A., 1994); Howard University (J.D., 2000).

E. BARRETT ATWOOD, IV, born May 8, 1975; admitted to bar, 2000, Florida (Not admitted in District of Columbia). *Education:* Florida State University (B.S., cum laude, with honors, 1997); Georgetown University (J.D., cum laude, 2000). Assistant Editor, American Criminal Law Review.

(This Listing Continued)

BROOKSANY BARROWES, born St. Louis, Missouri, March 14, 1975; admitted to bar, 1999, Virginia (Not admitted in District of Columbia). *Education:* Brigham Young University (B.A., magna cum laude, with honors, 1996); University of Chicago (J.D., 1999). Editor-in-Chief, University of Chicago Legal Forum, 1998-1999. ***PRACTICE AREAS:*** Energy. ***Email:*** brooksany.barrowes@bakerbotts.com

JASON BENNETT, born November 29, 1970; admitted to bar, 2000, New York (Not admitted in District of Columbia). *Education:* University of Texas (B.A., 1993); Georgetown University (J.D., 1999).

RYAN EDWARD BULL, born Midland, Texas, July 12, 1972; admitted to bar, 2000, Texas (Not admitted in District of Columbia). *Education:* Vanderbilt University (B.A., 1994); University of Texas (J.D., with honors, 2000). Associate Editor, University of Texas Law Review, 1999-2000. Law Clerk to Judge Fortunato P. Benavides, U.S. Court of Appeals, Fifth Circuit, 2000-2001. *Member:* State Bar of Texas.

JAMES P. CALVE, born Ellwood City, Pennsylvania, November 25, 1957; admitted to bar, 1985, Massachusetts (Not admitted in District of Columbia). *Education:* U.S. Military Academy (B.S., 1980); Cornell University (J.D., 1985).

TIMOTHY J. CHURNA, born November 2, 1973; admitted to bar, 2001, Virginia (Not admitted in District of Columbia). *Education:* State University of New York at Binghamton (B.S., 1996); College of William & Mary (J.D., 2000). Eta Kappa Nu; Order of the Coif.

GLENN FREDERICK ELLIOTT, JR., born Wheeling, West Virginia, December 5, 1973; admitted to bar, 2001, Virginia (Not admitted in District of Columbia). *Education:* University of Pennsylvania (B.S., 1994); Georgetown University (J.D., cum laude, 2001). *Member:* Virginia State Bar.

REBECCA H. EWING, born Philadelphia, Pennsylvania, March 13, 1974; admitted to bar, 2000, Pennsylvania (Not admitted in District of Columbia). *Education:* Harvard University (A.B., magna cum laude, 1995; J.D., cum laude, 2000). Senior Editor, Harvard Civil Rights-Civil Liberties, 1999-2000. *Member:* Philadelphia, Pennsylvania and American Bar Associations.

JACQUELINE H. FINE, born Richfield, Minnesota, June 22, 1965; admitted to bar, 1992, California; 1994, District of Columbia. *Education:* University of Minnesota (B.S., with distinction, 1987); Cornell University (J.D., 1992). ***Email:*** jacqueline.fine@bakerbotts.com

JOSHUA B. FRANK, born New York, N.Y., December 7, 1971; admitted to bar, 1998, Illinois and District of Columbia. *Education:* Cornell University (A.B., with distinction, 1993; M.Eng., 1994); University of Michigan Law School (J.D., cum laude, 1997). ***Email:*** joshua.frank@bakerbotts.com

GREGORY J. GOLDEN, born Philadelphia, Pennsylvania, July 27, 1969; admitted to bar, 1996, Virginia; 1998, District of Columbia. *Education:* Washington & Lee University (B.A., 1991); University of Richmond, T.C. Williams School of Law (J.D., magna cum laude, 1996). Chancellor, McNeil Law Honor Society, 1995-1996. President, Client Counseling and Negotiation Board, 1995-1996. Recipient, Charles T. Norman Prize, 1996. Law Clerk, Hon. Robert R. Merhige, Jr., U.S. District Court, Eastern District of Virginia, 1996-1997. ***Email:*** greg.golden@bakerbotts.com

RENU K. GUPTA, born Minneapolis, Minnesota, October 4, 1967; admitted to bar, 1994, Texas (Not admitted in District of Columbia). *Education:* Rice University (B.A., 1989); University of Houston (J.D., magna cum laude, 1994). Order of the Coif. Research Editor, Houston Journal of International Law, 1992-1994. *Member:* State Bar of Texas. ***Email:*** renu.gupta@bakerbotts.com

JACQUELINE HABERER, born Rome, New York, February 3, 1973; admitted to bar, 2000, New York (Not admitted in District of Columbia). *Education:* University of Rochester (B.A., magna cum laude, 1995) Phi Beta Kappa; Harvard University (J.D., cum laude, 1999). ***Email:*** jacqueline.haberer@bakerbotts.com

JONATHAN S. HALE, born October 31, 1970; (admission pending). *Education:* Bates College (B.A., magna cum laude, 1993); American University (J.D., 1997; M.A., 1998). *Member:* The District of Columbia Bar (Member, International Law Section); American Bar Association.

MICHAEL R. HILL, born Bethesda, Maryland, August 19, 1971; (admission pending). *Education:* Washington & Lee University (B.A., 1993); Johns Hopkins University (M.S., 1998); University of Maryland (J.D., with honors, 2001).

THOMAS E. HOLMBERG, born Winfield, Illinois, December 26, 1971; admitted to bar, 2000, Maryland (Not admitted in District of Columbia). *Education:* University of Arizona (B.A., 1993); Georgetown University (J.D., 2000). ***LANGUAGES:*** Spanish. ***Email:*** thomas.holmberg@bakerbotts.com

JON B. JORDAN, born Jefferson City, Missouri, June 18, 1968; admitted to bar, 1994, Florida; 1997, District of Columbia. *Education:* Florida State University (B.S., 1990); Loyola University (J.D., cum laude, 1994). Alpha Sigma Nu; Phi Delta Phi. Listed in Who's Who in America. Author, "Regulation S and Offshore Capital: Will the New Amendments Rid the Safe Harbor of Pirates?" Northwestern Journal of International Law & Business, Vol. 19, No. 1 (1998);

(This Listing Continued)

"The Regulation of Pay-to-Pay and the Influence of Political Contributions in the Municipal Securities Industry," Columbia Business Law Review, Vol. 1999, No. 3 (1999); "Universal Jurisdiction in a Dangerous World: A Weapon for all Nation's Against International Crime," Journal of International Law, Vol. 9, No. 2 (2000). Senior Counsel and Staff Attorney, United States Securities and Exchange Commission, 1997-1999. *Member:* The Florida Bar; The District of Columbia Bar (Member, Steering Committee, Section on: Corporation, Finance and Securities Law; International Law); American Bar Association (Member, Sections on: Business Law; International Law). ***Email:*** jon.jordan@bakerbotts.com

RICHARD C. KING, JR., born October 30, 1968; admitted to bar, 1998, Texas (Not admitted in District of Columbia). *Education:* University of Texas at Austin (B.A., 1991; J.D., with honors, 1998). Order of the Coif. Member, Texas Law Review. Law Clerk to: Hon. John H. Hannah, Jr., U.S. District Court, Eastern District of Texas, 1998-1999; Hon. Robert M. Parker, U.S. Court of Appeals, First Circuit, 1999-2000.

STEPHANIE A. MARTZ, born Altoona, Pennsylvania, March 30, 1969; admitted to bar, 1997, Maryland; 2001, District of Columbia. *Education:* Georgetown University (A.B., magna cum laude, with highest distinction, 1991); Stanford University (J.D., with distinction, 1997). Executive Editor, Stanford Law Review, 1996-1997. Law Clerk to the Honorable Judge Patricia M. Wald, U.S. Court of Appeals for the D.C. Circuit, 1998-1999; Law Clerk to the Honorable Judge Robertson, U.S. District Court, for the District of Columbia, 1997-1998. ***Email:*** stephanie.martz@bakerbotts.com

MELISSA E. MAXWELL, born Washington, D.C., January 24, 1972; admitted to bar, 1997, Texas; 1998, U.S. District Court, Southern District of Texas; 2000, District of Columbia. *Education:* Middlebury College (B.A., cum laude, 1993); University of Texas at Austin (M.P.Aff., 1997; J.D., 1997). Executive Editor, Texas Journal of Women and the Law. *Member:* State Bar of Texas; The District of Columbia Bar. ***LANGUAGES:*** Italian. ***PRACTICE AREAS:*** Civil Litigation (80%); Civil Appeals (20%). ***Email:*** melissa.maxwell@bakerbotts.com

KELLI C. McTAGGART, born Pittsburgh, Pennsylvania, January 21, 1970; admitted to bar, 1999, Maryland; 2000, District of Columbia. *Education:* Georgetown University (A.B., cum laude, 1992; J.D., magna cum laude, 1998). Notes Editor, Georgetown Law Journal. Law Clerk to Frank J. Magill, U.S. Court of Appeals, Eighth Circuit, 1998-1999. ***Email:*** kelli.mctaggart@bakerbotts.com

MARK A. MILLER, born Clarksville, Tennessee, December 5, 1964; admitted to bar, 1999, Virginia; 2000, District of Columbia. *Education:* Vanderbilt University (B.A., 1986); University of Colorado (M.A., 1988); Georgetown University (J.D., magna cum laude, 1998). Order of the Coif. Senior Articles Editor, Georgetown Law Journal. Law Clerk to the Honorable A. Raymond Randolph, U.S. Court of Appeals for the District of Columbia Circuit, 1998-1999. ***Email:*** mark.miller@bakerbotts.com

LAURA J. NICHOLSON, born Port Jefferson, New York, January 26, 1974; (admission pending). *Education:* Cornell University (A.B., 1996); Georgetown University (J.D., magna cum laude, 2001). Order of the Coif.

LILA G. PANKEY, born Bakersfield, California, April 17, 1976; (admission pending). *Education:* University of Puget Sound (B.A., 1998); George Washington University (J.D., with honors, 2001).

SUHAIL PARTAWI, born September 1, 1967; admitted to bar, 2000, New York (Not admitted in District of Columbia). *Education:* Syracuse University (B.S., 1989); University of Michigan (J.D., 1997). *Member:* American Bar Association. ***LANGUAGES:*** Arabic and Persian. ***Email:*** suhail.partawi@bakerbotts.com

NIKESH R. PATEL, born Ottawa, Ontario, Canada, December 27, 1971; admitted to bar, 1996, Florida; 1998, District of Columbia. *Education:* Florida State University (B.S., Accounting and Finance, magna cum laude, 1993); Georgetown University Law Center (J.D., cum laude, 1996). ***Email:*** nik.patel@bakerbotts.com

CLARA M. POFFENBERGER, born Millington, Tennessee, December 27, 1964; admitted to bar, 1990, Virginia; Virginia Supreme Court; 1997, District of Columbia. *Education:* Virginia Polytechnic Institute and State University (B.A., 1986); Washington College of Law, American University (J.D., 1990); American University (M.A., 1991). Adjunct Professor, Air Pollution Law, American University, Spring 1998. *Member:* Virginia State Bar (Board of Governors, Environmental Law Section); Air and Waste Management Association; Association of American University Women; Women's Council on Energy and Environment. ***LANGUAGES:*** Spanish. ***Email:*** clara.poffenberger@bakerbotts.com

MARY ANN POIRIER, born Middletown, Ohio, June 30, 1970; admitted to bar, 1996, Tennessee; 1998, District of Columbia. *Education:* University of Dayton (B.C.M.E., magna cum laude, 1992); Vanderbilt University (J.D., 1996). Tau Beta Pi. Staff Member, 1994-1995 and Associate Editor, 1995-1996, Vanderbilt University Law Review. ***Email:*** mary.ann.poirier@bakerbotts.com

(This Listing Continued)

FRANK W. RAMBO, born Charleston, South Carolina, January 8, 1969; admitted to bar, 2001, New York (Not admitted in District of Columbia). *Education:* University of the South (B.S., 1991); New York University (J.D., 2000). Law Clerk to the Hon. William M. Acker, Jr., U.S. District Court, Northern District of Alabama.

ALMIRA P. SAENZ, born Washington, D.C., April 30, 1976; admitted to bar, 2001, Virginia (Not admitted in District of Columbia). *Education:* Rice University (B.A., 1998); University of Virginia (J.D., 2001). *Member:* Virginia State Bar.

STEPHEN M. SILVER, born Houston, Texas, January 17, 1974; admitted to bar, 1999, Maryland; 2000, District of Columbia. *Education:* Columbia University (B.A., 1996); Georgetown University (J.D., cum laude, 1999). Articles Editor, Georgetown Law Journal, 1998-1999. *Member:* Maryland State Bar Association; The District of Columbia Bar.

MARK T. STANCIL, born San Antonio, Texas, October 2, 1974; admitted to bar, 1999, Virginia (Not admitted in District of Columbia). *Education:* University of Virginia (B.A., 1996; M.A., 1999; J.D., 1999). *Member:* Virginia State Bar.

TAMAR C. STANLEY, born Patuxant, Maryland, July 19, 1970; admitted to bar, 1994, Virginia; 1996, District of Columbia. *Education:* Colby College (B.A., 1991); University of Virginia (J.D., 1994). Notes Editor, Virginia Journal of International Law, 1993-1994. ***Email:*** tamar.stanley@bakerbotts.com

RAMSEY R. TAYLOR, born October 20, 1971; admitted to bar, 1997, District of Columbia and New York. *Education:* College of William & Mary (B.A., 1993; J.D., 1996); New York University (LL.M., 1997). (Also at Riyadh, Saudi Arabia Office). ***Email:*** ramsey.taylor@bakerbotts.com

SAMUEL J. WALDON, born Montclair, New Jersey, May 21, 1967; admitted to bar, 1992, Texas; 1994, District of Columbia. *Education:* Virginia Polytechnic Institute and State University (B.A., summa cum laude, 1989); University of Texas (J.D., with honors, 1992). Order of the Coif; Phi Beta Kappa. Staff Attorney, U.S. Securities and Exchange Commission, Division of Enforcement, 1996-1998. *Member:* The District of Columbia Bar; State Bar of Texas. ***Email:*** samuel.waldon@bakerbotts.com

WENDY BARRETT WARREN, born Auburn, New York, July 16, 1966; admitted to bar, 1995, Virginia; 1997, District of Columbia. *Education:* University of Virginia (B.A., 1988); Syracuse University (M.L.S., 1991); University of Virginia (J.D., 1995). ***PRACTICE AREAS:*** Energy; Project Finance. ***Email:*** wendy.warren@bakerbotts.com

MATTHEW T. WEST, born Saginaw, Michigan, November 28, 1971; admitted to bar, 1997, Maryland; 1998, District of Columbia; 1999, U.S. Court of International Trade. *Education:* Michigan State University (B.A., magna cum laude, 1994); University of Michigan (J.D., 1997). *Member:* Maryland State Bar Association; The District of Columbia Bar; U.S. Court of International Trade Bar. ***Email:*** matt.west@bakerbotts.com

STEPHANIE L. ZUCKER, born Las Vegas, Nevada, May 28, 1974; admitted to bar, 1999, Texas (Not admitted in District of Columbia). *Education:* Vanderbilt University (B.A., magna cum laude, 1996); University of Texas at Austin (J.D., with honors, 1999). Order of the Coif. Law Clerk to the Hon. W. Royal Furgeson, Jr., U.S. District Court, Western District of Texas, 1999-2000. Member and Editor-in-Chief, The Review of Litigation, 1997-1999. *Member:* State Bar of Texas. ***Email:*** stephanie.zucker@bakerbotts.com

(For Complete Personnel and Biographical data of the Austin, Dallas, Houston, New York, Moscow, London and Baku Offices, see Professional Biographies at Austin, Dallas and Houston, Texas, New York, New York, London, England, and Baku, Azerbaijan).

BAKER & DANIELS

Established in 1863

805 15TH STREET, N.W., SUITE 700

WASHINGTON, D.C. 20005

Telephone: 202-312-7440

Fax: 202-312-7460

URL: http://www.bakerdaniels.com

Indianapolis, Indiana Office: 300 North Meridian Street, Suite 2700, 46204. Telephone: 317-237-0300. Fax: 317-237-1000.

Fort Wayne, Indiana Office: 111 East Wayne Street, Suite 800, 46802. Telephone: 219-424-8000. Fax: 219-460-1700.

South Bend, Indiana Office: First Bank Building, 205 West Jefferson Boulevard, Suite 250, 46601. Telephone: 219-234-4149. Fax: 219-239-1900.

Elkhart, Indiana Office: 317 West Franklin Street, P.O. Box 507, 46515-0507. Telephone: 219-296-6000. Fax: 219-296-6001.

Indianapolis-96th Street, Indiana Office: Parkwood Six, 600 East 96th Street, Suite 600, 46240. Telephone: 317-569-9600. Fax: 317-569-4800.

Qingdao, China Office: Room A & C, 9th Floor, Qingdao Beer Building, May 4th Square, 35 Donghai Road, 266071. Telephone: +011-86-532-575-1051. Fax: +011-86-532-575-1055.

(This Listing Continued)

BAKER & DANIELS, Washington—Continued

Antitrust, Bankruptcy, Business Planning, Commercial, Corporate Finance, Creditors Rights, Employee Benefits, Employment, Environment, Estate and Probate, Family, Financial, Food and Drug, Government Affairs, Health Care, Insurance, Intellectual Property, International, Legislative, Litigation, Medical Technology Regulation, Municipal, Nonprofit, Product Liability, Real Estate, Securities, Sports, Tax, Transportation, Utilities, Year 2000, Zoning and Land Use Law.

FIRM PROFILE: Since 1863 we have been helping clients do business throughout Indiana, across the country and around the world. From Fortune 500 corporations to regional businesses, local governments and individuals, clients look to Baker & Daniels for excellence in all areas of legal practice, for a creative and individualized approach to solving client problems, and for a deep understanding of business, law and government. More than 350 Baker and Daniels' professionals serve clients from the firm's seven offices in Indiana, Washington, D.C. and China (we are one of only 31 U.S. law firms licensed to practice in China). Our service to clients is enhanced by our Washington, D.C. government affairs consulting subsidiary, Sagamore Associates, and our exclusive Indiana membership in Lex Mundi, an association of more than 158 independent law firms around the world.

LAW FIRM ALLIANCES/ASSOCIATIONS: **TAGLAW (The Appleton Group Legal Network):** *The Firm is a member of TAGLaw, an international association of prominent law firms.*

MEMBERS OF FIRM

ALBERT R. DAWSON, born 1944; admitted to bar, 1979, New York; 1991, New Jersey; 2000, District of Columbia. *Education:* University of New Mexico (B.A., 1966): The American College (Chartered Life Underwriter, 1989; Chartered Financial Consultant, 1990); New York Law School (J.D., 1978). Member, Society of Financial Services Professionals. ***PRACTICE AREAS:*** Insurance; Regulatory. ***Email:*** ardawson@bakerd.com

JOSEPH W. KIMMELL, II, born 1947; admitted to bar, 1972, Indiana; 1981, U.S. Tax Court; U.S. District Court, Northern and Southern Districts of Indiana; 2000, Indiana (Not admitted in District of Columbia). *Education:* Duke University (B.A., 1969); University of Michigan (J.D., 1972). Member, Board of Directors, Indiana Lawyer's Commission, Inc., 1977-1978. Chairman, Board of Directors, Allen County Senior Citizens Foundation, 1984—. Corporation Counsel, City of Fort Wayne, 2000—. Vice-Chair, China Practice, 2000—. *Member:* Allen County and Indiana State Bar Associations. (Also at Fort Wayne, Indiana and Qingdao, China Offices). ***PRACTICE AREAS:*** Corporate Law; Mergers and Acquisitions; International Transactions. ***Email:*** jwkimmel@bakerd.com

JANA LEE PRUITT, born 1955; admitted to bar, 1981, Kentucky; 2001, District of Columbia. *Education:* University of Kentucky (B.A., 1977); University of Louisville (J.D., 1980). Phi Alpha Delta. The American College, Chartered Life Underwriter, 2000. *Member:* Kentucky and American Bar Associations; Association of Life Insurance Counsel. ***PRACTICE AREAS:*** Insurance; Legislative and Regulatory. ***Email:*** jlpruitt@bakerd.com

CHARLES T. RICHARDSON, born 1947; admitted to bar, 1972, Indiana; 2001, District of Columbia. *Education:* Indiana University (A.B., cum laude, 1969); University of Michigan (J.D., cum laude, 1972). Phi Beta Kappa; Beta Theta Pi (President, Indiana University Chapter, 1968-1969); Blue Key (President, Indiana University Chapter, 1968-1969). Chief Legislative Legal Counsel to Governor of Indiana, 1977-1988. Certified Independent Assessor, Insurance Marketplace Standards Association. Member, Board of Directors: Member, Vice President: Federation of Regulatory Counsel. *Member:* Indianapolis, Indiana State and American Bar Associations; District of Columbia Bar; National Organization of Life and Health Insurance Guaranty Associations (Member, Legal Committee). Fellow, Indianapolis Bar Foundation. ***PRACTICE AREAS:*** Insurance Regulation; Insurance Insolvency. ***Email:*** ctrichar@bakerd.com

FRANK S. SWAIN, born 1951; admitted to bar, 1976, New York; 1991, District of Columbia; 1993, U.S. Court of Federal Claims; 1994, U.S. District Court for the District of Columbia; 2001, U.S. Court of Appeals, Second Circuit; U.S. Court of Appeals for the District of Columbia Circuit. *Education:* Colgate University (B.A., cum laude, 1972); Georgetown University School of Law (J.D., 1975). Chief Counsel for Advocacy, U.S. Small Business Administration, 1981-1989. Senior Vice President, Sagamore Associates, Inc., 1990—. Author: "The Regulatory Flexibility Act: Orienting Federal Regulation to Small Business," Dickinson Law Review, 1989; "Privatization: an Entrepreneurial Success Story," Phi Kappa Phi National Forum, 1990. Member, Administrative Conference of U.S., 1982-1989. *Member:* The District of Columbia Bar. (Also at Qingdao, China Office). ***PRACTICE AREAS:*** Health Care Law; Financial Services Regulation; Government Privatization and Contracts. ***Email:*** fsswain@bakerd.com

MARK W. WELLER, born 1958; admitted to bar, 1983, Indiana (Not admitted in District of Columbia). *Education:* Indiana University (B.A., 1980); Indiana University School of Law (J.D., 1983). Attorney, National Republican Senatorial Committee, 1983-1984. Legislative Assistant and Legislative Director, U.S. Senator Richard G. Lugar, 1984-1989. Director of Government Affairs, Director of Washington Operations and Government Relations, Ball Corporation, 1989-1994. *Member:* Indiana State Bar Association. ***PRACTICE AREAS:*** Federal Legislative Practice; Regulatory Law; Health Care. ***Email:*** mwweller@bakerd.com

(This Listing Continued)

DAVID R. ZOOK, born 1958; admitted to bar, 1986, Indiana (Not admitted in District of Columbia). *Education:* University of North Carolina (B.A., 1980); De Paul University (J.D., 1985). Legislative Counsel, U.S. Representative Elwood Hillis; 1985-1987. Associate Counsel, Committee on Appropriations, U.S. House of Representatives; 1987-1990. Principal, Sagamore Associates; 1990-1998. Senior Vice President, Arthritis Foundation; 1998-2000. ***PRACTICE AREAS:*** Government Relations; Education; Health Care. ***Email:*** drzook@bakerd.com

COUNSEL

TED R. MANNEN, born 1950; admitted to bar, 1975, Illinois; 1977, Missouri; 1978, District of Columbia. *Education:* Southern Illinois University (B.A., with high honors, 1972); Northwestern University (J.D., cum laude, 1975). Notes and Comments Editor, Northwestern University Law Review. ***PRACTICE AREAS:*** Health Care; Legislation. ***Email:*** trmannen@bakerd.com

ASSOCIATES

THOMAS A. JENSEN, born 1962; admitted to bar, 1991, Indiana; 2000, District of Columbia. *Education:* Wabash College (B.A., summa cum laude, 1984); Indiana University, Bloomington (J.D., magna cum laude, 1991). Phi Beta Kappa. Order of the Coif. Managing Editor, Indiana Law Journal, 1990-1991. *Member:* American Immigration Lawyers Association. (Also at Qingdao, China Office). ***PRACTICE AREAS:*** Immigration. ***Email:*** tajensen@bakerd.com

KERRI M. WILLIS, born 1970; admitted to bar, 1999, Connecticut (Not admitted in District of Columbia). *Education:* Purdue University (B.A., with distinction, 1993); Georgetown University Law Center (J.D., 1999). Phi Beta Kappa. ***PRACTICE AREAS:*** Financial Services. ***Email:*** kmwillis@bakerd.com

REPRESENTATIVE CLIENTS: 1st Source Bank; American Commercial Lines, Inc.; American General Finance, Inc.; American Trans Air, Inc.; Amoco, Inc.; Anthem Insurance Companies, Inc.; ARAMark Corp.; Arvin-Meritor, Inc.; AT&T Corp.; Auburn Foundry, Inc.; Ball Corporation; Bank One, Indianapolis, NA; Bindley Western Industries, Inc.; Borg-Warner Corporation; Brightpoint Inc.; Browning Investments, Inc.; Browning-Ferris Industries, Inc.; Central Soya Company, Inc.; Chevron Chemical Company; Chubb Group of Insurance Companies; Cinergy Corporation; Citizens Gas & Coke Utility; City of Elkhart; City of Fort Wayne; City of Indianapolis; City of South Bend; Clarian Health Partners; Conseco, Inc.; CSX Transportation, Inc.; Cummins Engine Company, Inc.; Delco Electronics Corporation; Denison, Inc.; DePauw University; Dow AgroSciences LLC; Dow Brands, L.P.; DowElanco; EFP Corporation; EIG Operating Partnership; Eli Lilly and Company; Emmis Communications; Enkei America, Inc.; Ernest & Julio Gallo Winery; Essex Group, Inc.; Farm Credit Services of Mid-America; Fort Wayne News-Sentinel; Fujitsu TEN; General Electric Capital Corp.; General Electric Company/Motor Business Group; General Motors Acceptance Corporation; General Motors Corporation; Golden Rule Insurance Company; Grumman Allied Industries; Guardian Industries, Inc.; Guidant Corporation; Heartland Steel, Inc.; Heritage Environmental Services, Inc.; Hill-Rom; Hillenbrand Industries, Inc.; Hill's Pet Nutrition; Hudson Institute, Inc.; Hughes Aircraft Co.; Hughes Technical; Hurco Co., Inc.; Indiana Bond Bank; Indiana Constructors, Inc.; Indiana Dental Association; Indiana Michigan Power Company; Indiana University; Indianapolis Life Insurance Company; Indianapolis Public Schools; Inland Paperboard and Packaging, Inc.; Ispat Inland Inc.; ITT Corporation (Aerospace/Optical Division); IWC Resources Corporation; Jayco, Inc.; Jewel Cos., Inc./Osco Drug, Inc.; John Hancock Mutual Life Insurance Co.; Key Bank; Kimball International; Kraft Foods, Inc.; Lilly Endowment, Inc.; McDonald's Corporation; McDonald & Company Securities, Inc.; Meridian Financial Corporation; Meridian Mutual Insurance; Metropolitan Life Insurance Company; Miller Brewing Company; Minnesota Mining & Manufacturing; Modernfold, Inc.; MSA Realty Corporation; National City Bank; National Enterprises, Inc.; National Retail Hardware Association; National Starch & Chemical Company; New Bern Transport Corporation; NOLHGA; North American Van Lines, Inc.; Olive B. Cole Foundation, Inc.; Olive LLP; Paul Harris Stores, Inc.; Philip Morris Company; PSI Energy, Inc.; Quality Dining, Inc.; Quantum Chemical Corporation; Quorum Health Group of Indiana; R.R. Donnelley & Sons Co.; Raffensperger, Hughes & Co., Inc.; Ralston Purina Company; Rand McNally & Company; Rea Magnet Wire, Inc.; Red Ball Corporation; Roche Diagnostic Systems, Inc.; Rockwell International Corporation; Rose Acre Farms, Inc.; Saint John's Medical Center; Schult Homes Corporation; Seyfert Foods, Inc.; Shambaugh & Son, Inc.; Shoe Carnival; Simon & Schuster; Simon Property Group, Inc.; Sisters of St. Francis Health Services, Inc.; Slater Steels Corporation; Society Corporation; South Bend Community Schools Corporation; St. John's Health System; Steel Dynamics Inc.; Subaru-Isuzu; Tecumseh Compressor; Tenaska, Inc.; The Lutheran Hospital of Indiana, Inc.; The Prudential Insurance Company of America; Trammell Crow Company; Tranex Credit Corporation; U.S. Gymnastics Federation; United Airlines; Wabash College; Wal-Mart Stores, Inc.; Weaver Popcorn, Inc.; Westinghouse Electric Corporation; Wells Fargo; WSBT, Inc.; York International Corporation; Zimmer, Inc.

(For biographical data on other Members of Firm, Of Counsel and Associates, see Professional Biographies at Indianapolis, Fort Wayne, South Bend, Elkhart, Indiana and Qingdao, China)

BAKER, DONELSON, BEARMAN & CALDWELL

LINCOLN SQUARE, 6TH FLOOR
555 ELEVENTH STREET, N.W.
WASHINGTON, D.C. 20004
Telephone: 202-508-3400
Telecopier: 202-508-3402
Email: info@bdbc.com
URL: http://www.bakerdonelson.com

Memphis, Tennessee Office: 20th Floor, First Tennessee Building, 165 Madison, 38103. Telephone: 901-526-2000. Telecopier: 901-577-2303.
Nashville, Tennessee Office: Commerce Center, Suite 1000, 211 Commerce Street, 37201. Telephone: 615-726-5600. Telecopier: 615-726-0464.
Chattanooga, Tennessee Office: 1800 Republic Centre, 633 Chestnut Street, 37450-1800. Telephone: 423-756-2010. Telecopier: 423-756-3447.
Knoxville, Tennessee Office: 2200 Riverview Tower, 900 South Gay Street, 37901. Telephone: 865-549-7000. Telecopier: 865-525-8569.
Johnson City, Tennessee Office: SunTrust Bank Building, 207 Mockingbird Lane, P.O. Box 3038, 37602. Telephone: 423-928-0181. Telecopier: 423-928-5694; 423-928-3654; Kingsport: 423-246-6191.
Huntsville, Tennessee Office: 3 Courthouse Square, 37756. Telephone: 423-663-2321. Telecopier: 423-663-2111.
Jackson, Mississippi Office: 4268 I-55 North, Meadowbrook Office Park, 39211. Telephone: 601-351-2400. Telecopier: 601-351-2424.
Atlanta, Georgia Office: 5 Concourse Parkway, Suite 900, 30328. Telephone: 770-396-2244. Telecopier: 770-399-9363.
Atlanta, Georgia Office: 3490 Piedmont Road, Suite 650, 30305. Telephone: 404-812-3100. Fax: 404-812-3101.

General Practice, Civil Trial and Appellate Practice before all State and Federal Courts, Administrative Agencies and Commercial Arbitration Forums. Antitrust and Trade Regulation, Aviation, Banking and Finance, Bankruptcy, Business Compliance, Commercial Finance, Communications, Construction, Corporations, Employment and Labor, Entertainment, Environmental, Estate Planning and Administration, Family Law, Franchising, Healthcare, Immigration, Intellectual Property, International Law. Litigation including Commercial and Business, Personal Injury, Product Liability and Professional Malpractice, Mergers and Acquisitions, Municipal Finance, Municipal Law, Partnerships, Pensions and Employee Benefits, Real Estate Development, Securities, Federal, State and Local Taxation, Tax-Exempt Organizations, Transportation, Utilities, White Collar Crime, Zoning and Land Use Law.

MANAGING PARTNER

JAMES C. DUFF, born Hamilton, Ohio, July 8, 1953; admitted to bar, 1981, District of Columbia. *Education:* University of Edinburgh, Scotland; University of Kentucky (B.A., magna cum laude, Honors Program, 1975); Georgetown University Law Center (J.D., 1981). Phi Beta Kappa. Author: "Anti-Money Laundering Prosecutions Under 18 U.S.C. § 1960 - Why So Few?" Money Laundering Law Report, June 1996, Vol. 6, No. 11. Co-author of "Implications of New Wire Transfer Rules to Nonbanks." Money Laundering Law Report, Feb. 7, 1995, Vol. 5, No. 7; "Money Laundering: Congress Takes Aim at Non-Bank Financial Institutions," *Legal Times* (August 29, 1994). Adjunct Professor, Georgetown University Constitutional Law, 1998—. Administrative Assistant to Chief Justice Willliam H. Rehnquist Supreme Court of U.S., 1996-2000. Executive Director, Judicial Fellows Commission, 1996-2000. Trustee, Supreme Court Historical Society, 1996—. Assistant to Board of Regents, Smithsonian Institution, 1996—. *Member:* The District of Columbia Bar; Bar Association of the District of Columbia; American Bar Association; U.S. Claims Court Bar. **Email:** jduff@bdbc.com

PARTNERS

LEWIS R. DONELSON, III, born Memphis, Tennessee, October 9, 1917; admitted to bar, 1940, Tennessee; 1941, District of Columbia. *Education:* Rhodes College (B.A., with distinction in Political Science, 1938); Georgetown University Law Center (LL.B., 1941). Member, Board of Trustees: Southwestern at Memphis, 1958-1968; Memphis Theological Seminary, 1978-1989. Memphis City Councilman, 1968-1972. Delegate Tennessee Constitutional Convention, 1971. Commissioner, Finance and Administration, State of Tennessee, 1979-1981. Director, St. Jude's Children Research Hospital, 1986—. Chairman of the Board, Memphis Regional Medical Center, 1996—. Member, Tennessee Higher Education Commission, 1981-1990. *Member:* Memphis, Tennessee and American (Member, Taxation Section) Bar Associations; The District of Columbia Bar. Fellow, Tennessee Bar Association. (Also at Chattanooga, Huntsville, Knoxville, Memphis and Nashville, TN Offices). ***PRACTICE AREAS:*** Tax; Corporate Law; School Equal Protection. **Email:** ldonelson@bdbc.com

ROBERT F. WORTHINGTON, JR., born Knoxville, Tennessee, July 17, 1931; admitted to bar, 1957, Tennessee; 1977, District of Columbia. *Education:* University of Tennessee (J.D., 1957). Phi Delta Phi. President, Tennessee Business Roundtable. Former Member, Tennessee Higher Education Commission, 1986-1995. *Member:* Knox County, Tennessee and American Bar Associations; The District of Columbia Bar. (Also at Knoxville and Nashville, TN Offices). ***PRACTICE AREAS:*** Business Law; Corporate Law; Government Relations; Public Utility Law. **Email:** rworthington@bdbc.com

JAMES W. MCBRIDE, born Kilgore, Texas, September 12, 1938; admitted to bar, 1963, Texas; 1964, District of Columbia; 1966, U.S. Tax Court and U.S. Supreme Court. *Education:* University of Texas (B.A., 1960; J.D., 1962); Georgetown University (LL.M., 1966). Member of Faculty, Tax Executives Institute/ Michigan State University, State and Local Tax Course, 1979-1981. Author: "Telecommunications Issues in a Changing World - Will Fairness and Equity Result?" Institute of Property Taxation, 1997. Co-Author: "Choice of Valuation Methodology in Determining Whether the Value of Intangible Property is Included in Ad Valorem Tax Assessments," Proceedings of the Georgetown University Law Center's State and Local Tax Institute, 1996; "Reassessing the Standard of Injunctive Relief in 4R Discriminatory Taxation," Journal of Multi-State Taxation, 1994. *Member:* State Bar of Texas; The District of Columbia Bar; American Bar Association (Member, Taxation Section). ***PRACTICE AREAS:*** State and Local Tax; Tax Planning and Litigation. **Email:** jmcbride@bdbc.com

ROBERT ENGELBRECHT HAUBERG, JR., born Jackson, Mississippi, October 26, 1943; admitted to bar, 1971, New York; 1974, District of Columbia; 1991, Mississippi. *Education:* University of Mississippi (B.A., summa cum laude, 1965); Yale University (M.A., 1967; J.D., 1970). Trial Attorney and Senior Litigation Counsel, Fraud Section, Criminal Division, U.S. Dept. of Justice, 1986-1991; Trial Attorney and Assistant Chief, Communications and Finance Section, Antitrust Division, U.S. Dept. of Justice, 1976-1986; Assistant United States Attorney, District of Columbia, 1973-1976. Editor, Sentencing in Antitrust: A Practitioner's Handbook, A.B.A. Antitrust Sec., 1999. Author: "Standing Issues - Who is a Proper Plaintiff in Antitrust False Claims and Securities Litigation," Lorman Ed. Serv. (2001); "Internet Securities Fraud and Computer Crime Sentencing," ABA Criminal Justice Section (2000); "Recent Healthcare Fraud Legislation: New Prosecutorial Tools or Congressional Pie in the Sky?" 31 J. Health and Hospital L. 23, (1998); "Demonstrative Evidence in a White Collar Crime Case," A.B.A. Crim. Just. Sec. (1996); "How to Avoid Criminal Environmental Liability," Cambridge Inst. (1995); "Insurance Fraud-The New Financial Crime," A.B.A. Litig. Sec. (1993); "Beyond the Board of Directors: The Liability of Outside Professionals for Financial Institution Fraud," A.B.A. 7 Crim. Just. 19 (1992); "Framework for an Environmental Crimes Act for Mississippi," 61 Miss. L.J. 255 (1991). Listed in Best Lawyers in America, 2001. Member: American-Scandinavian Foundation; Danish Club of Washington, D.C. *Member:* The District of Columbia Bar; The Mississippi Bar; New York State, Federal, American (Co-Chair, Bank and Insurance Fraud Subcommittee, White Collar Crime Committee, Criminal Justice Section, 1992-1996; Co-Chair, White Collar Crime Committee, Gulf/Texas Region, 1996-2000; Program Co-Chair, Gaming Enforcement, 1996—; Chair, Financial Markets and Institutions Committee, Antitrust Law Section, 2000—; Vice-Chair, Criminal Practice and Procedure Committee, Antitrust Law Section, 1997-2000; Complex Crimes Committee, Litigation Section) and International (Member, Business Crimes Committee, Business Law Section) Bar Associations; American Health Lawyers Association; Securities Industry Association (Member, Compliance and Legal Division). (Also at Jackson, Mississippi Office). ***LANGUAGES:*** Danish. ***PRACTICE AREAS:*** Antitrust; White Collar Crime; Financial Institutions; Civil Litigation. **Email:** rhauberg@bdbc.com

GEORGE CRANWELL MONTGOMERY, born Chattanooga, Tennessee, August 24, 1944; admitted to bar, 1976, District of Columbia. *Education:* University of Virginia (B.A., 1966); Vanderbilt University (J.D., 1975). Managing Editor, Vanderbilt Journal of Transnational Law. Member, Legislative Staff, Senator Howard H. Baker, Jr., 1975-1981. Counsel to United States Senate Majority Leader, 1981-1985. United States Ambassador to the Sultanate of Oman, 1985-1989. Member: Board of Visitors, Georgetown University School of Business, 1994—; Council on Foreign Relations, 1993—. *Member:* The District of Columbia Bar; American Bar Association. ***PRACTICE AREAS:*** International Law; Corporate Law. **Email:** cmontgomery@bdbc.com

JOAN M. MCENTEE, born New York; admitted to bar, 1983, District of Columbia. *Education:* Marymount College, Tarrytown (B.A.); American University (M.A., in Government and Public Administration); Washington College of Law (J.D.). Distinguished and Honorary Fellow, The American University Chapter of Pi Alpha Alpha. Listed in: Outstanding Young Women in America, Washington Women's Forum and Who's Who of American Women. Staff Director and Chief Counsel, Senate Committee on Government Affairs, 1980-1987. Deputy to Chief of Staff, Vice- President Bush, 1985-1986. Deputy Assistant Secretary for Trade Development, (ITA), Department of Commerce, September, 1986-1988. Deputy Under Secretary for International Trade, (ITA), Department of Commerce, May 1988-1989. Deputy Under Secretary and Acting Under Secretary for Export Administration, (BXA), Department of Commerce, May 1989-1993. *Member:* The District of Columbia Bar; American Bar Association; Forum for International Policy; Council on Foreign Relations. **Email:** jmcentee@bdbc.com

(This Listing Continued)

BAKER, DONELSON, BEARMAN & CALDWELL, Washington—Continued

ANNE M. STOLEE, born Marshall, Minnesota, January 19, 1959; admitted to bar, 1984, Florida; 1988, District of Columbia. *Education:* Yale University (B.A., 1981); Duke University (J.D., 1984). Author: "Public Interest in Utility Property: Is it Taxable, and If so, to Whom?" Proceedings of the 1993 Annual Conference of the National Tax Association. Co-Author: "Choice of Valuation Methodology in Determining Whether the Value of Intangible Property is Included in Assessments," State Tax Notes, August 6, 1996. *Member:* The Florida Bar; The District of Columbia Bar; American Bar Association (Member, Sections on: Litigation; Taxation). ***PRACTICE AREAS:*** State and Local Tax; Federal Trial and Appellate Litigation. ***Email:*** astolee@bdbc.com

CHARLES RICHARD JOHNSTON, JR., born Evanston, Illinois, March 29, 1948; admitted to bar, 1975, California; 1977, District of Columbia; 1979, U.S. Court of International Trade; 1982, U.S. Court of Appeals for the Federal Circuit. *Education:* Ohio Wesleyan University (B.A., 1970); California Western School of Law (J.D., 1973); Cambridge University (Dipl. Int'l Law, 1974). Attorney-adviser to Commissioner Catherine Bedell, U.S. International Trade Commission, 1976-1978. Trade Counsel, Committee on Finance, U.S. Senate, 1978-1979. Adjunct Faculty, National Law Center of George Washington University, 1978-1992; School of Foreign Service, Georgetown University, 1979-1998. Author-Editor: Law and Practice of United States International Trade Regulation, Oceana Publications (1986 with supplements). Author: "Administrative Relief for Unfair Import Trade . . ." in International Trade Policy: The Lawyer's Perspective, American Bar Association, 1985. Advisory Board Member, American Society of International Law, International Legal Materials. *Member:* The District of Columbia Bar; State Bar of California; American Bar Association. ***SPECIAL AGENCIES:*** U.S. International Trade Comm. U.S. Trade Representative. ***PRACTICE AREAS:*** International Trade; International Transactions; Corporate; Legislative; Administrative. ***Email:*** crj@bdbc.com

OF COUNSEL

ALBERT B. RANDALL, born Takoma Park, Maryland, February 13, 1948; admitted to bar, 1974, Maryland; 1976, District of Columbia. *Education:* University of Maryland (B.S., 1969; J.D., with honors, 1974). ***SPECIAL AGENCIES:*** Assistant Chief Counsel for Legislation, Federal Aviation Administration, 1977-1997. Member, Administrative Conference of the United States, 1981. Commissioner, Vice Chairman and Chairman, Montgomery County Historic Preservation Commission, 1990-1995. ***PRACTICE AREAS:*** Aviation; Legislation; Administrative Law. ***Email:*** arandall@bdbc.com

DOREEN M. EDELMAN, born Imlaystown, New Jersey, April 26, 1963; admitted to bar, 1987, Maryland; 1988, Florida; 1989, District of Columbia. *Education:* University of Denver; George Washington University (B.A., with distinction, 1984); National Law Center, George Washington University (J.D., with honors, 1987). Phi Alpha Delta. Co-Author: Summary of the *North American Free Trade Agreement* (NAFTA), Oceana Publications Inc.; Summary of *WTO Agreement* Oceana Publications Inc. Member, Court of International Trade. *Member:* The District of Columbia Bar (Member, International Law Section); Maryland State (Member, International Law Section) and American Bar Associations; The Florida Bar (Member, International Law Section). ***PRACTICE AREAS:*** International Trade; Customs; International Transactions; Corporate; Legislative. ***Email:*** dme@bdbc.com

RAYMOND E. MABUS, JR., born Ackerman, Mississippi, October 11, 1948; admitted to bar, 1976, Texas; 1979, District of Columbia; 1982, Mississippi. *Education:* University of Mississippi (B.A., 1969); John Hopkins University (M.A., 1970); Harvard University (J.D., magna cum laude, 1976). Past Governor, Mississippi. U.S. Ambassador, Kingdom of Saudi Arabia. Recipient: U.S. Department of Defense Distinguished Public Service Award; U.S. Army's Distinguished Civilian Service Award; Martin Luther King Social Responsibility Award; the International Security Leadership Award; National Wildlife Federation Conservation Achievement Award; the King Abdul Aziz Award from the Kingdom of Saudi Arabia; Mississippi Association of Educators Friend of Education Award. (Also at Jackson, Mississippi Office). ***PRACTICE AREAS:*** International Law. ***Email:*** rmabus@bdbc.com

ASSOCIATE

ANNE V. WINTER, born Memphis, Tennessee, July 31, 1952; admitted to bar, 1982, Mississippi; 1995, Louisiana (Not admitted in District of Columbia). *Education:* Rhodes College (B.A., 1974); University of Tennessee at Knoxville (J.D., 1981). Phi Beta Kappa. Member, Order of the Coif. Member, University of Tennessee Law Review, 1980-1981. Law Clerk to Chief Justice Neville Patterson, Mississippi Supreme Court, 1981-1982. *Member:* The Mississippi Bar; Louisiana State Bar Association. (Also at Jackson, Mississippi Office). ***PRACTICE AREAS:*** Commercial Litigation. ***Email:*** awinter@bdbc.com

LEGAL SUPPORT PERSONNEL

LINDA HALL DASCHLE. *Education:* Kansas State University. Recipient: Kansas Hall of Aviation Fame Award; American Association of Airport Executives Award of Appreciation; American Association of Airport Executive President's Award; Civil Aeronautics, Board Special Achievement Award. Director, Federal Affairs, Air Transport Association of America, 1985-1997. Senior Vice-President, American Association Airport Executives, 1987-1993. Acting Administrator and Deputy Administrator, Federal Aviation Administration, 1993-1997. Areas of Responsibilities: Public Policy, Transportation and Aviation Law. (Senior Public Policy Advisor). ***Email:*** ldaschle@bdbc.com

LAWERENCE S. EAGLEBURGER, born Milwaukee, Wisconsin, August 1, 1930. *Education:* University of Wisconsin (B.S., 1952; M.S., 1957). Areas of Responsibilities: International Law. [1st. Lieut., U.S. Army, 1952-1954]. (Senior Foreign Policy Advisor). ***LANGUAGES:*** Spanish, Serbo-Croatian. ***Email:*** leagleburger@bdbc.com

KEITH KENNEDY, born Charlotte, North Carolina, April 29, 1948. *Education:* Duke University (B.A., 1970; M.Div., 1974). John C. Stennis Fellows, 1993—. Adjunct Professor, Georgetown University Graduate Public Policy Program, 1997-1998. Legislative Assistant to the Honorable Mark O. Hatfield, 1972-1977. Member, Senate Select Committee on Indian Affairs, 1977-1979. Staff Director, Senate Committee on Appropriations, 1980-1996. Areas of Responsibilities: Public Policy Law. ***Email:*** kkennedy@bdbc.com

FRANCINE LAMORIELLO, born Providence, Rhode Island. *Education:* Georgetown University (B.A., 1979); Johns Hopkins University (M.A., with high distinction, 1982). Author: "East is West: Japanese Investment in Europe," The Journal of European Business, February, 1992; "New York and the New Europe: A Guide to Business Opportunities," New York, January, 1993; "Expert's Corner, AT&T Global Response," A Newsletter for International Business, April, 1993; "Latin America: Pro-Business Climate Warms Up Down South," Site Selection, October, 1993; "Many Paths to South Business Overseas," Boardroom Reports, March, 1994; "A Current Overview of the Global Marketplace for High Tech Products and Services," Technology New York, April, 1994; "The Outlook for Foreign Direct Investment," 1994 Southeast International Business Profile, Atlanta, October, 1994; "New York and the New Western Hemisphere: A Guide to Business Opportunities," New York, April, 1995. Member, Board of Advisors, European Institute, 1991—. Member, U.S.-China Business Council. Areas of Responsibilities: Advising Clients on International Business Strategy, Economic and Commercial Developments, International Trade Policy and International Government Relations. Adjunct Fellow, Center for Strategic and International Studies. ***LANGUAGES:*** French and Italian. ***Email:*** flamoriello@bdbc.com

JANET L. POWELL, born Anderson, Indiana, June 17, 1948. *Education:* Ball State University (B.S., 1970). Areas of Responsibilities: Public Policy (Appropriations and Transportation). (Senior Public Policy Advisor). ***Email:*** jpowell@bdbc.com

JAMES D. RANGE. *Education:* Tulane University; Tennessee Tech University; University of Miami. Counsel, National Commission on Water Quality, under Vice-President Rockefeller and Senator Howard Baker, 1972. Minority Counsel, U.S. Senate Committee on Environment and Public Works, 1973-1980. Appointed Chief Counsel, U.S. Senate Majority Leader, 1980-1984. Member, 1985-1991 and Chairman, 1988, of the Board of the National Fish and Wildlife Foundation. Commissioner, Interstate Commission on the Potomac River Basin, 1990-1995. Member, Board of Directors: Trout Unlimited; Land Trust Alliance; Duck Unlimited's Wetlands America Trust; Recreational Boating and Fishing Foundation. Recipient, Great Blue Heron Award, the highest honor bestowed at the national level by the Department of Interior. Awarded "Friend of Fisheries" by American and Tennessee Fisheries Society. Areas of Responsibility: Corporate Securities and is a Senior Advisor for Environmental, Regulatory and Legislative Policies. (Senior Legislative Regulatory and Environmental Advisor). ***Email:*** jrange@bdbc.com

SENIOR FOREIGN-POLICY ADVISOR

MARK R. PARRIS, born Minneapolis, Minnesota, April 22, 1950. *Education:* Georgetown University (B.S.F.S., magan cum laude, 1972). Phi Beta Kappa. Ambassador to Turkey, 1997-2000. Special Assistant to President and Senior Director, National Security Council, 1995-1997. ***LANGUAGES:*** Portuguese, Russian and French. ***PRACTICE AREAS:*** Foreign Policy; Business Development. ***Email:*** mparris@bdbc.com

REPRESENTATIVE CLIENTS: AFG Industries, Inc.; Allied Signal; American Airlines; American Association of Airport Executives; American Standard; American Trucking Association; Bridgestone/Firestone, Inc.; Burger King Corp.; Burlington Northern/Santa Fe Railroad; Corning, Inc.; County of Prince William; Dallas/Ft. Worth Airport; Day & Zimmermann; Federal Express Corporation; Federal Judges Association; FLIR Systems, Inc.; Foothill Transit; Freedom Forum, Inc.; HAM Marine, Inc.; Hoosier Heritage Port Authority; ICF Kaiser International; L-3 Communications Corp.; Lincoln National Corp.; Lockheed Martin Corporation; Mission Energy; NAHB Research Center; National Corn Growers Association, Inc.; Newspaper Association; Northwest Airlines Corp.; PacifiCorp; Pennsylvania Turnpike Commission; Pennzoil Co.; PhRMA; Phillips Petroleum; The Pillsbury Company;

(This Listing Continued)

Puerto Rico Department of Transportation; PPG Industries; Schering-Plough Corporation; Siemens Corporation; Sprint; Tokyo Electric Power Co.; United Technologies Corporation; Ventura Port District; WMX Technologies.

(For complete biographical data on Memphis, Nashville, Chattanooga, Knoxville, Johnson City and Huntsville, Tennessee, Jackson, Mississippi and Atlanta, Georgia personnel, see Professional Biographies at those locations)

BAKER & HOSTETLER LLP

Established in 1916

WASHINGTON SQUARE

SUITE 1100, 1050 CONNECTICUT AVENUE, N.W.

WASHINGTON, D.C. 20036-5304

Telephone: 202-861-1500

Fax: 202-861-1783

To contact an attorney on the Internet use first initial and surname followed by @bakerlaw.com

URL: http://www.bakerlaw.com

In Cleveland, Ohio: 3200 National City Center, 1900 East Ninth Street. Telephone: 216-621-0200.

In Cincinnati, Ohio: 312 Walnut Street, Suite 2650. Telephone: 513-929-3400.

In Columbus, Ohio: Capitol Square, Suite 2100, 65 East State Street. Telephone: 614-228-1541.

In Costa Mesa, California: 600 Anton Boulevard, Suite 650. Telephone: 714-754-6600.

In Denver, Colorado: 303 East 17th Avenue, Suite 1100. Telephone: 303-861-0600.

In Houston, Texas: 1000 Louisiana, Suite 2000. Telephone: 713-751-1600.

In Los Angeles, California: 333 South Grand Avenue, Suite 1800. Telephone: 213-975-1600.

In Orlando, Florida: SunTrust Center, Suite 2300, 200 South Orange Avenue. Telephone: 407-649-4000.

In New York, N.Y.: 666 Fifth Avenue. Telephone: 646-496-1600.

General Practice.

OFFICE MANAGING PARTNER

WILLIAM H. SCHWEITZER, born Cleveland, Ohio, June 6, 1944; admitted to bar, 1970, District of Columbia. *Education:* Trinity College (B.A., 1966); Georgetown University (J.D., 1969). Assistant United States Attorney, Washington, D.C., 1970-1973. *Member:* The District of Columbia Bar; American Bar Association. (Managing Partner, Washington, D.C. Office). ***PRACTICE AREAS:*** Litigation; Election Law. ***Email:*** wschweitzer@bakerlaw.com

PARTNERS

MARC A. ANTONETTI, born New Haven, Connecticut, November 23, 1966; admitted to bar, 1991, Texas; 1994, District of Columbia. *Education:* University of Notre Dame (B.A., with honors, 1988); New York University (J.D., 1991). Executive Editor, Annual Survey of American Law, 1990-1991. *Member:* American Bar Association; State Bar of Texas; District of Columbia Bar. ***PRACTICE AREAS:*** Labor and Employment Law; Workers Compensation Law. ***Email:*** mantonetti@bakerlaw.com

EDWARD JAY BECKWITH, born Paterson, New Jersey, July 18, 1949; admitted to bar, 1975, District of Columbia; 1979, U.S. Supreme Court and U.S. Tax Court. *Education:* The Pennsylvania State University (B.S., 1971); Georgetown University Law Center (J.D., 1974; M.L., Taxation, 1983). Adjunct Professor, Georgetown University Law Center, 1984—. Author: "Estate and Gift Tax Charitable Deductions," "Estates Tax Deductions - Sections 2053 and 2054," and "Estate Tax Orphan's Deduction," BNA Tax Management Portfolios 261-3rd, (1991), 804 (1994); 426, (1981); Tech. App.: Tax Law and Private Foundations, "America's Wealthy and The Future of Foundations," Foundation Center (1987); together with numerous professional articles and presentations. 1998 Alumni Fellow Honoree - The Pennsylvania State University, University Park, PA. *Member:* The District of Columbia Bar (Member, Sections on: Estates, Trusts and Probate; Steering Committee, 1985-1987; Taxation); American Bar Association (Member, Sections on: Taxation; Real Property, Probate and Trust Law; Chair, Subcommittee on Charitable Giving; Vice Chair of Study Committee on Law Reform, Probate and Trust Division Committee Section of Real Property, Probate and Trust Law; Vice-Chair, A-7 Study Committee on Law Reform, Section of Real Property, Probate and Trust Law, 1999-2000); American Law Institute; American College of Trust and Estate Counsel (State Chair, D.C.). ***PRACTICE AREAS:*** Tax Law; Closely Held Business Enterprises; Tax-Exempt and Charitable Organizations; Charitable and Personal Planning Law; Trusts and Estates Law. ***Email:*** ebeckwith@bakerlaw.com

RALPH G. BLASEY, III, born Takoma Park, Maryland, November 9, 1960; admitted to bar, 1987, Pennsylvania; 1988, District of Columbia; 1996, Maryland. *Education:* Duke University (B.A., magna cum laude, 1982); University of North Carolina (M.B.A.; J.D., 1986). *Member:* The District of Columbia Bar; American Bar Association (Member, Litigation Section Committee); National Health Lawyers Association. [U.S. Naval Reserve, 1978-1980]. ***PRACTICE AREAS:*** Litigation; Health Care. ***Email:*** rblasey@bakerlaw.com

JOHN J. BURKE, born New York, N.Y., March 4, 1961; admitted to bar, 1986, Pennsylvania; 1988, District of Columbia. *Education:* Northwestern University (B.A., 1983); University of Pennsylvania Law School (J.D., 1986). Phi Beta Kappa. Associate Editor, University of Pennsylvania Law Review. ***PRACTICE AREAS:*** International Trade; Export Control; Product Safety.

LEE A. CASEY, born Grosse Pointe, Michigan, August 1, 1957; admitted to bar, 1982, Michigan; 1985, California; 1995, District of Columbia. *Education:* Oakland University (B.A, magna cum laude, 1979); Wayne State University; University of Michigan (J.D., cum laude, 1982). Co-Author: with David B. Rivkin, Jr., "Presidents and War Powers: Another View," Common Sense, Winter, 1996; with David B. Rivkin, Jr. and Lawrence J. Block, "The Senate's Pie-In-The-Sky Treaty Interpretation Power," University of Pennsylvania Law Review, 1989. Author: "Pirat Constitutionalism: An Essay in Self Government," 8 Journal of Law & Politics, 1992. Adjunct Professor of Law, Legal Research, Writing and Analysis, George Mason University School of Law, 1990-1995. Law Clerk to Chief Judge Alex Kozinski, U.S. Claims Court, 1984-1985. Office of Legal Policy, 1986-1990 and Office of Legal Counsel, 1992-1993, U.S. Department of Justice. *Member:* The District of Columbia Bar; Bar Association of the District of Columbia; State Bar of Michigan; State Bar of California. ***Email:*** lcasey@baker-hostetler.com

BRUCE J. CASINO, born Toronto, Canada, May 25, 1953; admitted to bar, 1988, Pennsylvania and U.S. District Court, Western District of Pennsylvania; 1989, District of Columbia, U.S. Court of Appeals, Third Circuit, U.S. Court of Appeals for the District of Columbia Circuit and U.S. District Court for the District of Columbia; 1995, U.S. Supreme Court and U.S. Court of Appeals, Ninth and Fourth Circuits. *Education:* University of Maryland (B.S., 1984); Georgetown University (J.D., cum laude, 1988). Phi Alpha Delta. Adjunct Professor of Law, George Washington University Law School, White Collar Crime Course, 1993—. Law Clerk, Hon. Carol Los Mansmann, U.S. Court of Appeals for the Third Circuit, 1988-1989. Author: "Mail Order Ministry Tax Fraud And The Problem Of A Constitutionally Acceptable Definition of Religion," 25 American Criminal Law Review 113, 1987; "Federal Grants-in-Aid: Evolution, Crisis, and Future," 20 Urban Lawyer, 25, 1988. Co-Author: "Joint Defense Privilege in Administrative Proceedings," ABA White Collar Crime, 1991, 411; "Sources of Legal Rights for the Homeless," ABA Journal of Affordable Housing and Community Development Law, Fall/Winter 1991, 12; "International Concerns Regarding Religious Freedom," Religious Freedom and the New Millenium, 2000. *Member:* The District of Columbia Bar; American Bar Association (Co-Chair, Fraud and Abuse Subcommittee, Health Law Committee, Litigation Section; Member: Individual Rights and Responsibilities Section; White Collar Crime Committee, Criminal Justice Section). ***Email:*** bcasino@bakerlaw.com

FREDERICK W. CHOCKLEY, III, born Lakewood, Ohio, June 16, 1954; admitted to bar, 1982, Virginia and District of Columbia. *Education:* Yale University (B.A., 1976); Georgetown University (J.D., 1982). Editor, American Criminal Law Review, 1981-1982. Young Lawyer of the Year, Young Lawyers Section, Bar Association of the District of Columbia, 1986. *Member:* The District of Columbia Bar; Virginia State Bar; American Bar Association. ***PRACTICE AREAS:*** Litigation. ***Email:*** fchockley@bakerlaw.com

WILLIAM F. CONROY, born Brooklyn, New York, August 9, 1949; admitted to bar, 1975, District of Columbia; 1976, New York; 1979, U.S. Tax Court; 1982, U.S. District Court, Southern and Eastern Districts of New York; 1984, U.S. Court of Appeals, Ninth Circuit. *Education:* Fordham University (B.A., 1971); Catholic University (J.D., 1975); New York University (LL.M., 1979). Member, Catholic University Law Review, 1974-1975. *Member:* The District of Columbia Bar; American Bar Association. ***PRACTICE AREAS:*** Tax and Personal Planning Law. ***Email:*** wconroy@bakerlaw.com

WILLIAM J. CONTI, born Brooklyn, New York, October 13, 1953; admitted to bar, 1978, District of Columbia; 1979, U.S. District Court for the District of Columbia; 1982, U.S. Claims Court; 1990, Maryland. *Education:* Georgetown University (B.A., cum laude, 1975; LL.B., 1978). *Member:* The District of Columbia Bar; Maryland State Bar Association. ***PRACTICE AREAS:*** Corporate Law; Securities; Mergers and Acquisitions. ***Email:*** wconti@bakerlaw.com

BARRY J. CUTLER, born New Haven, Connecticut, June 13, 1943; admitted to bar, 1968, New York; 1971, Connecticut; 1975, District of Columbia. *Education:* Cornell University (A.B., 1965); Columbia University (J.D., 1968). Phi Delta Epsilon. Law Clerk, U.S. Court of Appeals, Second Circuit, 1968-1970. Assistant U.S. Attorney, Connecticut, 1970-1974. Tutor-in-Law, Yale Law School, 1972-1974. Deputy Assistant Director, Federal Trade Commission, Bureau of Consumer Protection, 1974-1976. Assistant General Counsel, Federal Trade Commission, 1976-1978. Director, Federal Trade Commission, Bureau of Consumer Protection, 1990-1993. *Member:* The District of Columbia Bar; American Bar Association (Advisory Board, BNA Antitrust and Trade Regulation Reporter). ***PRACTICE AREAS:*** Litigation; Trade Regulation; Consumer Law. ***Email:*** bcutler@bakerlaw.com

(This Listing Continued)

(This Listing Continued)

BAKER & HOSTETLER LLP, Washington—Continued

MARK A. CYMROT, born New York, N.Y., October 8, 1947; admitted to bar, 1973, District of Columbia and U.S. Court of Appeals for the District of Columbia Circuit; 1974, U.S. Court of Appeals, 4th Circuit; 1977, U.S. Supreme Court; 1980, U.S. Court of Appeals, 5th Circuit; 1996, U.S. Court of Appeals, 2nd Circuit. *Education:* George Washington University (B.A., 1969); Columbia University (J.D., 1972). Co-Author: "A Case Study in Foreign Discovery: Minpeco S.A. v. Nelson Bunker Hunt," International Quarterly, Jan. 1990; "Squeezing Silver," Litigation, Summer, 1991; "Lessons," Litigation, Fall, 1991; "New U.S. Antitrust Policy Considered," Financial Times Business Law Brief, Feb. 1992; "Peru's External Debt Litigation," Suing Foreign States, April, 1992; "The Forgotten Rule," Litigation, Spring, 1992; "Friction Develops Among Regulators," *Financial Times Business Law Report,* (October 1992) (Co-Authored with Wilbur Fugate); "Beginnings," *Litigation,* Journal of the ABA Litigation Section (Fall 1993); "LDC Debt Market Mavericks Are Taking Big Risks," *LDC Debt Reporter,* American Banker Inc. Newsletter on Developing-Country Investment (Nov. 1, 1993); "US-UK Treaty Provides Weapon Against Crime," The National Law Journal, with T. Taylor (June 5, 1995); "Managing for Uncertainties in Central Bank Immunity," Seminar on Current Issues in Monetary and Financial Law, Sponsored by the Legal Department and The Institute of the International Monetary Fund, May 11, 2000. Trial Attorney, 1972-1977 and Special Litigation Counsel, 1979-1983, Civil Division, U.S. Department of Justice. Senior Litigator, Consumers Union of U.S. Inc., 1977-1979. Member, Cole Corette & Abrutyn, 1983-1991. *Member:* The District of Columbia Bar; American Bar Association (Member, Litigation and International Sections). ***PRACTICE AREAS:*** International; Litigation; Fraud Law. ***Email:*** mcymrot@bakerlaw.com

MATTHEW J. DOLAN, born Baltimore, Maryland, October 11, 1960; admitted to bar, 1986, Texas; 1989, District of Columbia; 1992, Maryland. *Education:* Yale University (B.A., cum laude, 1982); University of Virginia (J.D., 1986). ***PRACTICE AREAS:*** Corporate; Tax; Health Care. ***Email:*** mdolan@bakerlaw.com

LEE T. ELLIS, JR., born Philadelphia, Pennsylvania, April 15, 1945; admitted to bar, 1970, Maryland; 1971, District of Columbia; 1974, U.S. Supreme Court. *Education:* University of Tennessee (B.A., 1967); Georgetown University (J.D., 1970). *Member:* Bar Association of the District of Columbia; The District of Columbia Bar; Maryland State and American Bar Associations. ***PRACTICE AREAS:*** Litigation. ***Email:*** lellis@bakerlaw.com

ELLIOT J. FELDMAN, born Brookline, Massachusetts, 1947; admitted to bar, 1988, Massachusetts; 1989, District of Columbia. *Education:* University of Chicago (B.A., with honors, 1969); Massachusetts Institute of Technology (Ph.D., with distinction, 1973); Harvard University (J.D., cum laude, 1988). International Affairs Fellow, Council on Foreign Relations, 1984. German Marshall Fund Fellow, 1976-1977. Managing Editor, Canadian Law Newsletter, American Bar Association, 1989-1991. Member, Board of Directors, Canadian-American Business Council, 2000—. Director, University Corporation for Research on North America, Harvard University, 1979-1987. Special Projects Officer and Consultant to the Assistant Secretary of Defense, 1984. Councillor, Atlantic Council of the United States, 1988—. Foreign Associate, Royal Institute of International Affairs, UK, Elected, 1977. ***LANGUAGES:*** French and Italian. ***PRACTICE AREAS:*** International Trade; International Law; Intellectual Property Infringement.

DAVID J. FISCHER, born Muskegon, Michigan, June 17, 1958; admitted to bar, 1983, District of Columbia. *Education:* Michigan State University (B.A., with honors, 1980); The National Law Center, George Washington University (J.D., with high honors, 1983). Order of the Coif. Member, George Washington Law Review, 1981-1983. ***PRACTICE AREAS:*** Tax. ***Email:*** dfischer@bakerlaw.com

PEDER A. GARSKE, born Washington, D.C., January 13, 1962; admitted to bar, 1988, Virginia; 1989, District of Columbia. *Education:* University of Virginia (B.A., with high distinction, 1984; J.D., 1988). Phi Beta Kappa. *Member:* The District of Columbia Bar; Virginia and American Bar Associations. ***Email:*** pgarske@bakerlaw.com

FREDERICK H. GRAEFE, born Des Moines, Iowa, April 16, 1944; admitted to bar, 1973, Iowa; 1974, District of Columbia; 1976, U.S. Supreme Court. *Education:* Loyola University (A.B., 1966); Georgetown University (M.A., 1971; J.D., 1973). Editor, Law and Policy in International Business, Georgetown, 1972-1973. Law Clerk to Hon. Howard F. Corcoran, U.S. District Judge for the District of Columbia, 1973-1975. Co-Author: "The Shipping Industry Seeks a Safe Haven: Merger Jurisdiction for the FMC?" 5 J.L. & Political International Business 274, 1973. Member, Judicial Conference for the District of Columbia Circuit, 1983. *Member:* The District of Columbia Bar. [Capt., USMCR, 1967-1970]. ***PRACTICE AREAS:*** Health Law; Legislative Law; Telecommunications; Tax; International Trade. ***Email:*** fgraefe@bakerlaw.com

DAVID ALISTAIR GRANT, born Chicago, Illinois, September 17, 1954; admitted to bar, 1978, District of Columbia. *Education:* Bowdoin College (A.B., summa cum laude, 1975); Georgetown University (J.D., 1978). Phi Beta Kappa. Student Editor in Chief, The Tax Lawyer, 1977. Attorney, Office of the Solicitor, U.S. Department of Labor, Washington, D.C., 1978-1981. *Member:* The District of Columbia Bar; American Bar Association. ***PRACTICE AREAS:*** Employment Law; Benefits Law. ***Email:*** dgrant@bakerlaw.com

BRIAN S. HARVEY, born St. Catharines, Ontario, Canada, February 28, 1952; admitted to bar, 1979, Ohio; 1981, District of Columbia. *Education:* Marshall University (B.A., magna cum laude, 1976); Case Western Reserve University (J.D., 1979). Editor, Case Western Reserve Law Review, 1978-1979. Law Clerk: Hon. James C. Turk, Chief Judge, U.S. District Court, Western District of Virginia, 1979-1980; Hon. James M. Sprouse, U.S. Court of Appeals for the Fourth Circuit, 1980-1981. Mediator, U.S. District Court, District of Columbia, 1995—. *Member:* The District of Columbia Bar. ***PRACTICE AREAS:*** Employment and Labor Law; Litigation. ***Email:*** bharvey@bakerlaw.com

KENNETH C. HOWARD, JR., born Fort Worth, Texas, November 25, 1947; admitted to bar, 1975, Texas; 1980, District of Columbia. *Education:* University of Texas at Austin (B.A., Plan II Honors Program, 1969; M.A., 1972; J.D., 1975). Phi Delta Phi. Legal Assistant to Senior FCC Commissioner James H. Quello, 1981-1986. Staff Director, Temporary Commission on Alternative Financing for Public Telecommunications, 1982-1983. *Member:* The District of Columbia Bar; Federal Communications Bar Association (Co-Chair: Publications Committee, 1986-1987; Ad Hoc Committee on Membership Benefits, 1990-1991; Charitable Distributions Committee, 1991-1992; Chair, Law Journal Committee and Editorial Advisory Board, 1987-1989; Trustee, Bar Foundation, 1991-1992). ***PRACTICE AREAS:*** Business Law; Communications Law. ***Email:*** khoward@bakerlaw.com

ROBERT D. LYSTAD, born Washington, D.C., June 25, 1962; admitted to bar, 1990, Maryland; 1993, District of Columbia. *Education:* Northwestern University (B.S., 1984); University of Chicago (J.D., 1990). ***PRACTICE AREAS:*** Litigation; First Amendment; Libel; Media Law. ***Email:*** rlystad@bakerlaw.com

DAVID L. MARSHALL, born Newark, Ohio, February 24, 1954; admitted to bar, 1984, Ohio; 1986, District of Columbia. *Education:* Denison University (B.A., 1979, Psi Chi, Phi Beta Kappa); University of Michigan (J.D., 1984). Co-Author: with Guy Vander Jagt, and Matthew J. Dolan, "The Significance of the IRS Shift on Worker Classification," Tax Notes (June 19, 1995); with Edward J. Beckwith and John A. Edie, "Grants to Individuals by Private Foundations," Council on Foundations (1995); with William F. Conroy, "The Exemption Issues Facing HMOs May Foretell Problems Under Health Care Reform," *Journal of Taxation of Exempt Organizations (September/October 1993); with Kenneth J. Kies, "Recent Developments Affecting Timeshare Homeowners Association,"* *Developments* (August 1993); with Edward J. Beckwith and Theodore F. Rodriguez, "Company Foundations and the Self-Dealing Rules," Council on Foundations (1993); with Edward J. Beckwith, John A. Edie and Robert Edgar, "Establishing an Advised Fund Program," Council on Foundations (1992); with Edward J. Beckwith, "Community Foundation and Agency Endowments," Council on Foundations (1991). *Member:* The District of Columbia Bar (Member, Section of Taxation); American Bar Association (Member, Section of Taxation). ***PRACTICE AREAS:*** Taxation; Tax-Exempt Organizations; Employment Taxes. ***Email:*** dmarshall@bakerlaw.com

SHELBY F. MITCHELL, born Brooklyn, New York, February 1, 1940; admitted to bar, 1982, Maryland, 1985, U.S. District Court, District of Maryland; 1990, District of Columbia; 1993, U.S. District Court, District of Columbia; 1995, U.S. Court of Appeals, Fourth Circuit; 1996, U.S. Court of Appeals, Seventh Circuit; 1998, U.S. Court of International Trade. *Education:* New York City Community College (A.A.S., 1959); University of Maryland (B.S., magna cum laude, 1980; J.D., with honors, 1982). Phi Kappa Phi. Member, Moot Court Board. Law Clerk to: Hon. Rosalyn B. Bell, Circuit Court for Montgomery County, Md., 1982-1983; Hon. James F. Couch, Jr., Maryland Court of Appeals, 1983-1984. *Member:* Maryland State and American Bar Associations; District of Columbia Bar; Women's Bar Association of Maryland. ***PRACTICE AREAS:*** Family Law; Commercial Litigation; Trial. ***Email:*** smitchell@bakerlaw.com

BETTY SOUTHARD MURPHY, born East Orange, New Jersey; admitted to bar, 1958, District of Columbia. *Education:* The Ohio State University (B.A.); Sorbonne University, Paris, France; American University (J.D., 1958); Awarded LL.D. by: Eastern Michigan University, 1975; Capital University, 1976; University of Puget Sound Law School, 1986; Doctor of Humane Letters, Tusculum College, 1987. Kappa Beta Pi. Recipient: Inter-American Bar Association Silver Medal, 1967; Ohio Governor's Award. Adjunct Professor, American University Law School, 1972-1984, 1999—. Member: Health and Human Services Secretary's Committee on Rights and Responsibilities of Women, 1972-1974; Human Resources Committee, National Center for Productivity and Quality of Working Life, 1976-1977. Presidential Appointments: Administrator, Wage and Hour Division, Department of Labor, 1974-1975. Chairman and Member, National Labor Relations Board, 1975-1979. Council: Administrative Conference of the United States, 1975-1979; International Center for Settlement of Investment Disputes, 1976-1986; President's Commission on Executive

(This Listing Continued)

Exchange, 1981-1985; Commission on the Bicentennial of the United States Constitution, 1985-1992. Chairman, International Advisory Committee, 1986-1992. Received Award for Outstanding Service from United States Information Service, 1991. Vice Chairman, James Madison Memorial Fellowship Foundation, 1989-1996. Member of the Board, Union Internationale des Avocates, 1996—. Board of Directors, Friends of Department of Labor; Board of Trustees, Friends of Law Library of Congress, 1993—. Executive Committee, American Arbitration Association, 1996—. Board of Trustees, American University. Board of Trustees, George Mason University Foundation and George Mason University Education Foundation. *Member:* The District of Columbia Bar; Federal, International, American (Member, Section of Administrative Law; Chairman: Labor and Employment Law Committee, 1980-1983; International and Comparative Law Committee, 1983-1988; Chairman, Customs, Patent and Trade, 1988-1992; Chairman, International Committee, ABA Alternate Dispute Resolution Section, 1995—) and Inter-American Bar Associations. Life Fellow, American Bar Foundation. Fellow, National Academy of Human Resources. ***PRACTICE AREAS:*** Employment Law; Administrative Law; International Law. ***Email:*** bsmurphy@bakerlaw.com

ROGER A. PIES, born Lockport, New York, June 13, 1942; admitted to bar, 1967, New York; 1974, District of Columbia. *Education:* Cornell University; State University of New York at Buffalo (LL.B., cum laude 1967); New York University (LL.M. in Taxation, 1968). Author: "Why Not Court Appointed Experts?" Tax Notes, Vol. 40, No. 3, p. 303; "How Dispositions Affect Determination of Depreciation Class Life," 47 Tax Notes 85 (1990); "Reflections on the Burden of Proof in the Tax Court Section 482 Cases and Beyond," 56 Tax Notes 777 (1992); "Taxpayer Use of Collateral Estoppel," 68 Tax Notes 1239 (1995). Attorney, Internal Revenue Service, 1968-1974. ***PRACTICE AREAS:*** Tax. ***Email:*** rpies@bakerlaw.com

DAVID B. RIVKIN, born St. Petersburg, Florida, 1956; admitted to bar, 1985, District of Columbia. *Education:* Georgetown University (B.S.F.S., 1980; M.S., with highest distinction, 1984); Columbia University (J.D., 1985). Phi Alpha Theta. Adjunct Scholar, American Enterprise Institute for Public Policy Research. Law Clerk, Preston, Thorgrimson, Ellis & Holman, 1984-1985. Member, Council on Foreign Relations. Special Assistant to the Vice President and Associate Executive Director, White House's Council on Competitiveness, 1992-1993. Associate General Counsel, Department of Energy, 1990-1991. Deputy Director, Office of Policy Development, Department of Justice, 1988-1990. Legal Advisor to the White House Counsel, 1989-1990. Special Assistant to the Honorable C. Boyden Gray, Counselor to the then Vice President Bush, 1988-1989. Defense and Foreign Policy Advisor, Fund for America's Future and George Bush for President, 1988. Associate, Baker & Mckenzie, 1985-1988. Visiting Fellow, Heritage Foundation. Director, National Center for Therapeutic Riding. ***LANGUAGES:*** Russian. ***PRACTICE AREAS:*** Administrative Law; Environmental; Energy; International Law; Litigation; Government Relations. ***Email:*** drivkin@baker-hostetler.com

BRUCE W. SANFORD, born Massena, New York, August 5, 1945; admitted to bar, 1970, New York; 1971, Ohio; 1981, District of Columbia; 1985, Maryland. *Education:* Hamilton College (A.B., 1967); New York University (J.D., 1970). Author: Sanford's "Synopsis of Libel & Privacy," 1991; Funk & Wagnalls, 2d Ed; "Libel and Privacy," Aspen Law & Business (formerly Prentice Hall/Law & Business), 1991; "Don't Shoot the Messenger: How Our Growing Hatred of the Media Threatens Free Speech For All of Us," The Free Press, a division of Simon & Shuster, 1999; "Vision of The First Amendment for a New Millennium," Annenberg Washington Program, 1992; "Teaching An Old Dog New Tricks: The First Amendment in an Online World," Connecticut Law Review, Summer 1996 Vol. 28, No. 4. Chairman of Board of Trustees, Thomas Jefferson Center for the Protection of Free Expression, University of Virginia, 1991—. *Member:* The District of Columbia Bar; American Bar Association (Member, Governing Board, Forum Committee on Communications Law, 1985—; Chairman, Defamation Torts Committee, Torts and Insurance Practice Section, 1986-1987). ***PRACTICE AREAS:*** Business Litigation; First Amendment/Libel Law. ***Email:*** bsanford@bakerlaw.com

LOUIS R. SERNOFF, born Sellersville, Pennsylvania, December 23, 1940; admitted to bar, 1966, District of Columbia. *Education:* University of Pennsylvania (B.A., 1962; LL.B., 1965). With Bureau of Competition, 1966-1974 and Attorney-Adviser to a Commissioner, 1974, Federal Trade Commission. *Member:* The District of Columbia Bar; American Bar Association. ***PRACTICE AREAS:*** Litigation; Trade Regulation. ***Email:*** lsernoff@bakerlaw.com

LEE H. SIMOWITZ, born Augusta, Georgia, September 7, 1946; admitted to bar, 1973, District of Columbia. *Education:* Harvard University (B.A., cum laude, 1968); Yale University (J.D., 1972). Contributor, W.L. Fugate, *Foreign Commerce and the Antitrust Laws* (1996). Law Clerk to Hon. Harold H. Greene, Chief Judge, Superior Court of the District of Columbia, 1972-1973. Assistant to the Director, Bureau of Consumer Protection, Federal Trade Commission, 1975-1976. Attorney-Adviser to Calvin J. Collier, Chairman of the Federal Trade Commission, 1976-1977. *Member:* The District of Columbia Bar; American Bar Association (Member, Section of: Antitrust Law). ***PRACTICE AREAS:*** Litigation; Antitrust and Trade Regulation. ***Email:*** lsimowitz@bakerlaw.com

(This Listing Continued)

DAVID S. WACHEN, born New York, N.Y., December 17, 1964; admitted to bar, 1993, New York and U.S. District Court, Southern and Eastern Districts of New York; 1994, District of Columbia; 1996, U.S. District Court, District of Maryland. *Education:* Dartmouth College (A.B., 1987); University of Pennsylvania (J.D., 1992). Chair, Moot Court Board. Editor, University of Pennsylvania Law Review. Law Clerk to Honorable Jay C. Waldman, U.S. District Court, Eastern District of Pennsylvania, 1992-1993. *Member:* New York State and American Bar Associations; The District of Columbia Bar. ***PRACTICE AREAS:*** First Amendment; Media Law; General Litigation. ***Email:*** dwachen@bakerlaw.com

RONALD F. WICK, born Milwaukee, Wisconsin, December 10, 1964; admitted to bar, 1992, Maryland; 1993, District of Columbia; 1996, U.S. District Court for the District of Columbia; 1997, U.S. Court of Appeals, Eighth Circuit; 1998, U.S. District Court, District of Maryland. *Education:* Cornell University (A.B., cum laude, in English, 1986); Georgetown University Law Center (J.D., cum laude, 1992). Notes and Comments Editor, Georgetown Law Journal. Author: "Out of the Closet and Into the Headlines: 'Outing ' and the Private Facts Tort," Georgetown Law Journal, December 1991. *Member:* American Bar Association. ***Email:*** rwick@bakerlaw.com

JOANNE W. YOUNG, born Columbus, Georgia, 1949; admitted to bar, 1975, New York and District of Columbia; 1986, U.S. Court of Appeals, Seventh, Ninth, Tenth and District of Columbia Circuits; 1991, U.S. Supreme Court. *Education:* Wesleyan University (B.A., cum laude, 1971); Georgetown University (J.D., 1974). Phi Beta Kappa Award. Law Clerk, Honorable F.B. Ugast, Washington, D.C., 1974-1975. Author: "Transatlantic Airline Mergers—Still Waiting in the Wings," The Aviation Quarterly, 2000; "Building A Competitive Airline Industry—Deregulation, Antitrust Protection, and the E-Commerce Opportunity," The Aviation Quarterly, 2000; "Simplified Passenger Travel: Moving From Vision to Reality," American Bar Association Air & Space Lawyer, 2000, The Aviation Quarterly, 2000 and Asian Airlines & Aerospace, 2000; "Globalism vs. Extraterritoriality-Consensus vs. Unilateralism: Is there A Common ground? A U.S. Perspective," Air & Space Law, 1999 and The Aviation Quarterly, 1999; Asian Airlines & Aerospace, 1999; "Airline Alliances-Is Competition at the Crossroads?" Air & Space Law, 1999; IATA Legal Symposium and Airline Management Programs, 1998; "What Will be the Effects of EC Market Unification on Intercontinental Air Services after 1992?" *ICAO Journal,* 1990; "Aircraft Noise: Will it Muffle Airline and Airport Development?" *Airport Forum,* 1989; "Community-Oriented Essential Air Service: What's Best for Commuters?" *Commuter Air,* 1981; "The Aircraft Loan Guarantee Program: A Boon to Commuters and Crucial to the Success of Small Community Air Services," *CAAA Times,* 1979. Trial Attorney, Civil Aeronautics Board, 1975-1977. Chair, Associate Member Group, Regional Airline Association of America, 1983-1984. Trustee, Wesleyan University, 1983-1986. Board of Governors, 1995— and Vice President, 2000, Washington Foreign Law Society. Board of Directors, International Aviation Club, 1999—. Board of Directors, 1998— and Vice President, 2000, International Aviation Womens Association. Board of Directors, Icelandic-America Chamber of Commerce, 1987—. Board of Governors, City Club of Washington, 1991—. Co-Chair, Executive Endorsements Committee Womens Bar Association of the District of Columbia, 1997—. National Security Seminar Participant, U.S. Army War College, 1992. *Member:* The District of Columbia Bar; New York State, Federal (Member, Air Transportation Committee, Council on Transportation Law, 1976) and American Bar Associations; Womens Bar Association of the District of Columbia. ***PRACTICE AREAS:*** Transportation Law; International Law; Litigation; Administrative Law. ***Email:*** jyoung@bakerlaw.com

HENRY G. ZAPRUDER, born New York, New York, March 28, 1938; admitted to bar, 1962, Texas; 1969, District of Columbia. *Education:* University of Oklahoma (B.B.A., 1959); Oxford University, Oxford, England; Harvard Law School (LL.B., cum laude, 1962). Adjunct Professor, George Washington University Law School and American University Law School. Attorney, Tax Division, Department of Justice, 1963-1967. Office of Tax Legislative Counsel, U.S. Treasury Department, 1967-1969. ***PRACTICE AREAS:*** Tax. ***Email:*** hzapruder@bakerlaw.com

ASSOCIATES

MARK I. BAILEN, born Boston, Massachusetts, December 29, 1969; admitted to bar, 1997, Maryland and Massachusetts; 1998, District of Columbia. *Education:* Cornell University (A.B., 1992); New York University School of Law (J.D., 1997). ***PRACTICE AREAS:*** Litigation; First Amendment; Libel Law. ***Email:*** mbailen@bakerlaw.com

JOHNINE P. BARNES, born Steubenville, Ohio, July 10, 1970; admitted to bar, 1995, Ohio; 1999, District of Columbia. *Education:* Case Western Reserve University (B.A., magna cum laude, 1992; J.D., honors in Political Science, 1995). *Member:* Cleveland, Ohio State, American and National Bar Associations; The District of Columbia Bar. ***PRACTICE AREAS:*** Labor Law; Employment Law; Sports Law.

DARIN R. BARTRAM, born Buffalo, New York, September 28, 1968; admitted to bar, 1993, Maryland; 1996, District of Columbia. *Education:* Uni-

(This Listing Continued)

BAKER & HOSTETLER LLP, Washington—Continued

versity of Vermont (B.A., 1990); George Washington University (J.D., with honors, 1993). Member, George Washington University Law Review, 1992-1993. *Member:* Maryland State Bar Association (Member, Environmental Section); The District of Columbia Bar. ***PRACTICE AREAS:*** International Law; Environmental. ***Email:*** dbartram@bakerlaw.com

BRUCE D. BROWN, born Kansas City, Missouri, October 12, 1965; admitted to bar, 1996, Massachusetts; 1998, District of Columbia. *Education:* Stanford University (A.B., 1988); Harvard University (M.A., 1992); Yale University (J.D., 1995). ***PRACTICE AREAS:*** Litigation; First Amendment. ***Email:*** bbrown@bakerlaw.com

MARYLOU BROWN, born Springfield, Massachusetts, September 11, 1969; admitted to bar, 1998, Maryland; 1999, Florida (Not admitted in District of Columbia). *Education:* Tufts University (B.A., 1991); University of Virginia (J.D., 1998). Recipient, Outstanding Female Graduate Award, National Association of Women Lawyers. Articles Editor, Virginia Tax Review, 1997-1998. *Member:* Maryland State and American Bar Associations; The Florida Bar. ***PRACTICE AREAS:*** Trusts and Estates. ***Email:*** mbrown@bakerlaw.com

DAVID S. CHUNG, admitted to bar, 1999, Maryland and New Jersey; 2000, District of Columbia. *Education:* Virginia Commonwealth University (B.A., summa cum laude, 1995); University of Virginia (J.D., 1998). Member, Board of Advisors, Journal of Social Policy and the Law. *Member:* Maryland State, New Jersey State and American Bar Associations. ***Email:*** dchung@bakerlaw.com

ARLAND DiGIROLAMO, born Paterson, New Jersey, February 10, 1972; admitted to bar, 1998, New Jersey (Not admitted in District of Columbia). *Education:* Boston College (B.A., 1994); Rutgers University Law School (J.D., 1997). ***LANGUAGES:*** Spanish. ***PRACTICE AREAS:*** International Trade Law; International Law.

ROBERT M. DOHERTY, born Roanoke, Virginia, November 10, 1973; admitted to bar, 1999, Virginia; 2000, U.S. District Court, Western and Eastern Districts of Virginia (Not admitted in District of Columbia). *Education:* College of William & Mary (B.A., with highest honors, 1996); University of Richmond, T.C. Williams School of Law (J.D., 1999). Delta Theta Phi. Member, Moot Court. Member, Richmond Law Review, 1998-1999. ***PRACTICE AREAS:*** Litigation.

ANDREW J. DURKOVIC, admitted to bar, 1993, California (Not admitted in District of Columbia). *Education:* University of California, Los Angeles (B.A., 1989); Loyola Law School (J.D., 1992). *Member:* Los Angeles County and American Bar Associations; State Bar of California. ***LANGUAGES:*** Spanish. ***PRACTICE AREAS:*** Real Estate Litigation; Business Litigation. ***Email:*** adurkovic@baker-hostetler.com

ADAM GROPPER, born Miami, Florida, November 18, 1973; admitted to bar, 2000, New York and Florida (Not admitted in District of Columbia). *Education:* University of Florida (B.S., with honors, 1995); Florida Atlantic University (M.S.T., 1996); George Washington University (J.D., with honors, 1999). *Member:* New York State and American Bar Associations; American Bankruptcy Institute. ***PRACTICE AREAS:*** Tax Controversies; Tax Planning. ***Email:*** agropper@bakerlaw.com

SAMUEL L. HENDRIX, born March 4, 1970; admitted to bar, 1995, Virginia; 1997, District of Columbia. *Education:* Duke University (B.A., 1992); University of Virginia (J.D., 1995).

KAREN M. KRAMER, admitted to bar, 1995, Maryland; 1996, District of Columbia. *Education:* Stanford University (B.A., with distinction and departmental honors, 1992; J.D., with distinction, 1995). Member, Cap and Gown. Author: "Navigating the Risks of Pre-Publication Threats to Sue," Quill, September, 1999; "The Free Rider Problem and First Amendment Concerns: A Balance Upset by New Limitations in Mandatory Student Fees," 21 Journal of College and University Law 691, 1995; "Competing Trends in Setting the Limits to the 'Substantially Limits' Provision in Defining Disability," 4 Disability Law Reporter Service 3, 1995; "Obesity Discrimination in the Workplace: Protection Through a Perceived Disability Claim under the Rehabilitation Act and the Americans with Disabilities Act," 31 California Western Law Review 41, 1994; "Rule by Myth: The Social and Legal Dynamics Governing Alcohol-Related Acquaintance Rapes," 47 Stanford Law Review 115, 1994. Law Clerk, the Honorable Lewis A. Kaplan, U.S. District Court, Southern District of New York. ***LANGUAGES:*** Spanish. ***PRACTICE AREAS:*** Media and First Amendment; Internet Law; Intellectual Property; Employment Law. ***Email:*** kkramer@bakerlaw.com

MANDANA PARSAZAD, born Tehran, Iran, October 5, 1963; admitted to bar, 1992, California; 1994, District of Columbia. *Education:* University of Massachusetts (B.A., 1986); Tulane University of Louisiana (J.D., 1989); Georgetown University Law Center (LL.M. in International and Comparative Law, 1990; LL.M. in Taxation, 1997). *Member:* The District of Columbia Bar (Member, Sections on: International Law; Taxation); American Society of International Law. ***LANGUAGES:*** Persian. ***PRACTICE AREAS:*** Tax Law; International Taxation. ***Email:*** mparsazad@bakerlaw.com

JANIS M. PENMAN, born Buffalo, New York, April 27, 1972; admitted to bar, 1998, Maryland; 2000, District of Columbia. *Education:* Smith College (B.A., cum laude, 1994); George Washington University (J.D., 1998). *Member:* Maryland State and American Bar Associations. ***LANGUAGES:*** French. ***PRACTICE AREAS:*** Securities; Corporate Law. ***Email:*** jpenman@bakerlaw.com

INDIA J. PINKNEY, born May 22, 1973; admitted to bar, 1999, North Carolina (Not admitted in District of Columbia). *Education:* University of Virginia (B.A., 1995; J.D., 1998). Presiding Justice of Quarterfinal Round, Moot Court. Law Clerk, Honorable Henry E. Frye, Sr., North Carolina Supreme Court, 1998-1999. ***LANGUAGES:*** French and Arabic. ***PRACTICE AREAS:*** International; Employment. ***Email:*** ipinkney@bakerlaw.com

ELIZABETH A. SCULLY, admitted to bar, 1997, Ohio (Not admitted in District of Columbia). *Education:* Villanova University (B.A., cum laude, 1994); Ohio State University (J.D., with honors, 1997). ***Email:*** escully@bakerlaw.com

CHRISTOPHER T. STEPHEN, born Pontiac, Michigan, October 21, 1974; admitted to bar, 1999, Massachusetts; 2000, District of Columbia. *Education:* Boston College (B.A., 1996); Catholic University of America, Columbus School of Law (J.D., 1999). Phi Alpha Delta. ABA Law Student Division Vice Chair, 1998-1999. ***PRACTICE AREAS:*** Legislative Practice; Health Care; Medicare; Tax. ***Email:*** cstephen@bakerlaw.com

OF COUNSEL

E. MARK BRADEN, born Youngstown, Ohio, June 1, 1951; admitted to bar, 1976, Ohio; 1983, U.S. Supreme Court; 1989, District of Columbia. *Education:* Washington & Lee University (B.A., 1973; J.D., 1976). Author: " The Day Before Democracy," Barrister, Summer 1986. International Observer: National Endowment for Democracy, 1985 Philippines Presidential Election; International Delegation 1988 Pakistan National Elections. Consultant to the International Foundation for Elections Systems. Adjunct Faculty, George Washington University and Catholic University. *Member:* The District of Columbia Bar; American Bar Association (Member, Communication Law Forum and Administrative Law Section; Advisory Consultant to Standing Committee on Law and Electoral Process, 1985-1988); American Political Science Association (Member, Board of Directors, Committee for Party Renewal, 1984—). [U.S. Army Reserve, Captain, 1977]. ***PRACTICE AREAS:*** Election Law; Legislative Law. ***Email:*** mbraden@bakerlaw.com

JENIFER M. BROWN, born Washington, D.C., August 14, 1956; admitted to bar, 1986, Virginia, Wisconsin and U.S. Court of Appeals, Fourth and Seventh Circuits; 1988, District of Columbia. *Education:* University of Virginia (B.A., with distinction, 1978); University of Wisconsin (M.S.S.W., 1981; M.B.H.A., 1986; J.D., cum laude, 1986). Editor-in-Chief, *The Hospital Contracts Manual* (Aspen), 1987-1991. *Member:* The District of Columbia Bar; Virginia State Bar; State Bar of Wisconsin; American Bar Association. ***PRACTICE AREAS:*** Litigation; Trade Regulation Law. ***Email:*** jbrown@bakerlaw.com

LUIS A. GALLIANI, born Lima, Peru, April 25, 1956; admitted to bar, 1981, Peru (Not admitted in United States). *Education:* Universidad Nacional Federico Villarreal, Lima, Peru (Bachelor's Degree, 1980; Law Degree, 1981); University of Wales, Cardiff, Wales (LL.M., Maritime and International Trade Law, 1982). *Professional Experience:* Of Counsel, Cole Corette & Abrutyn, Washington, D.C., 1992-1995. Vice President, MINPECO (UK) Ltd., London, England, 1990-1992; General Counsel, MINPECO S.A., Lima, Peru, 1985-1989. Arbitrator in maritime and international trade matters, Lima, Peru, 1988—. Directorships: Member of the Board of Directors of MINPECO (USA), Inc., 1987-1989; Member of the Board of Directors of Agentes Navieros San Nicolas, Lima, Peru, 1985-1989. *Member:* Lima Bar Association; Peruvian Maritime Law Association (Member, Executive Committee, 1988-1990); Peruvian Law Institute of Mining and Oil (Member, Executive Committee, 1989-1991); Iberoamerican Institute of Maritime Law. ***LANGUAGES:*** Spanish, English. ***PRACTICE AREAS:*** International Business Law; International Dispute Resolution; Energy Law; Mining Law; Latin America. ***Email:*** lgalliani@bakerlaw.com

KATHLEEN M. KERRIGAN, born Springfield, Massachusetts, January 20, 1964; admitted to bar, 1991, Massachusetts; 1992, District of Columbia. *Education:* Boston College (B.S., 1985); University of Notre Dame (J.D., 1990). *Member:* The District of Columbia Bar. ***PRACTICE AREAS:*** Federal Taxation; Health Law. ***Email:*** kkerrigan@bakerlaw.com

DAVID M. KIRSTEIN, born Bethesda, Maryland, May 16, 1946; admitted to bar, 1971, Virginia; 1972, Kentucky; 1974, Tennessee; 1982, District of Columbia. *Education:* University of Connecticut (B.A., 1968); University of Virginia (J.D., 1971). Phi Beta Kappa; Phi Kappa Phi. Attorney, Legal Aid Society: Roanoke, Virginia, 1971-1972; Louisville, Kentucky, 1972-1973. Attorney-Instructor, University of Tennessee Law School Clinic, 1973-1974. Di-

(This Listing Continued)

rector, Paralegal Program, Boston College Law School, 1974-1976. Clinical Associate, Harvard Law School, 1975-1976. Civil Aeronautics Board, 1976-1982. Attorney, Office of General Counsel, 1976-1978; Special Counsel and Assistant to the Chairman, 1978-1981; General Counsel, 1981-1982. Majority Counsel, Aviation Subcommittee, Senate Committee on Commerce, Science and Transportation, 1982. *Member:* The District of Columbia Bar; Virginia State Bar; Kentucky, Tennessee and American Bar Associations. ***PRACTICE AREAS:*** Aviation; Administrative; Antitrust; Transportation; Commercial. ***Email:*** dkirstein@bakerlaw.com

JULIA A. OAS, born Kalamazoo, Michigan, April 20, 1961; admitted to bar, 1986, Wisconsin and U.S. District Court, Western District of Wisconsin; 1998, District of Columbia. *Education:* University of Michigan (B.A., 1983); University of Wisconsin (J.D., 1986). James B. Angell Scholar, 1980. Assistant to the Director of the Bureau of Consumer Protection, Federal Trade Commission, 1989-1991. Attorney Advisor to the Chairman, Federal Trade Commission, 1991-1995. *Member:* State Bar of Wisconsin; American Bar Association (Member, Antitrust Section). ***PRACTICE AREAS:*** Trade Regulation; Consumer Law; Litigation; Advertising Law. ***Email:*** joas@bakerlaw.com

MADELEINE B. SCHALLER, born 1942; admitted to bar, 1970, District of Columbia. *Education:* Miami University (B.A., 1964); George Washington University (J.D., 1969). ***PRACTICE AREAS:*** Contract Law; Administrative Law; Real Estate Transactions. ***Email:*** mschaller@bakerlaw.com

GUY VANDER JAGT, born Cadillac, Michigan, August 26, 1931; admitted to bar, 1961, District of Columbia, Michigan, U.S. Supreme Court and U.S. District Court, Western District of Michigan. *Education:* Hope College (B.A., 1953); Friedrich Wilhelm University, Germany; Yale Divinity School (B.A., 1957); Georgetown University; University of Michigan (J.D., 1960). Member, U.S. Congress, 1966-1993. Ranking Republican, U.S. House Trade Subcommittee, Select Revenues Subcommittee, Health and Human Resources Subcommittee; Second Ranking Republican Full House Ways and Means Committee; Member, House Foreign Relations Committee and House Space, Science and Astronautic Committee, House Government Operations Committee; Member of House Republican Leadership, 1974-1993; Chairman, National Republican Congressional Committee, 1974-1993; Senator, Michigan State Senate, 1965-1966. Appointed by President Nixon to serve as President's personal envoy to eight African nations and to Japan, Korea, and Taiwan in 1973; Lead Republican sponsor of the Comprehensive Multilateral Trade Agreement, Caribbean Basin Initiative, Campaign Reform Laws. Awarded a Knighthood in the House of Orange by Netherlands Queen Beatrix in 1986. Named Outstanding Dutch American of the Year, 1991. *Member:* District of Columbia Bar. ***LANGUAGES:*** German and French. ***PRACTICE AREAS:*** Government Affairs; Legislative; Tax; Trade Policy. ***Email:*** gvanderjagt@bakerlaw.com

RETIRED PARTNERS

RICHARD H. JONES, born Portsmouth, Virginia, September 2, 1930; admitted to bar, 1964, Virginia; 1969, District of Columbia. *Education:* Virginia Polytechnic Institute (B.S., 1958); American University (LL.B., 1964). Staff Editor, American University Law Review, 1963-1964. Licensed Airline Transport Pilot, 1969. President, Bar Association of Air Carrier Pilots, 1970-1972. Member, 1970-1978 and Chairman, 1976-1978, Virginia Advisory Committee on Aviation. Secretary, Flight Safety Foundation, 1973-1984. Secretary and Treasurer, Airline Pilots Association, International, 1969-1970. President, Committee for National Airport, 1978. Member, Presidential Advisory Board, Smithsonian Institution, National Air and Space Museum, 1982-1984. Deputy Administrator, Federal Aviation Administration, 1984-1986. *Member:* Arlington County, Virginia, Federal (Chairman, Aviation Law Section, 1978) and American (Chairman, Aviation Committee, Section of Public Utility, Communications and Transportation Law, 1992-1993) Bar Associations; Virginia State Bar. [Lt. Col., U.S. Marine Corps Air Reserve; active flight duty, 1953-1957; 1960-1966]. ***PRACTICE AREAS:*** Business Law; Legislative Law.

HARLAN POMEROY, born Cleveland, Ohio, May 7, 1923; admitted to bar, 1949, Connecticut; 1954, Ohio and U.S. Tax Court; 1958, U.S. Supreme Court; 1975, District of Columbia; 1981, Maryland. *Education:* Yale University (B.S., 1944); Harvard Law School (LL.B., 1948). *Member:* The District of Columbia Bar; Montgomery County, Greater Cleveland, Maryland State, Ohio State and American Bar Associations. ***PRACTICE AREAS:*** Tax Law; Personal Planning Law.

BAKER & McKENZIE

815 CONNECTICUT AVENUE, N.W.
WASHINGTON, D.C. 20006-4078
Telephone: (202) 452-7000
Intn'l. Dialing: (1-202) 452-7000
Facsimile: (1-202) 452-7074
URL: http://www.bakernet.com

Associated Offices of Baker & McKenzie in: Almaty, Amsterdam, Baku, Bangkok, Barcelona, Beijing, Berlin, Bogotá, Brasília, Brussels, Budapest,

(This Listing Continued)

Buenos Aires, Cairo, Calgary, Caracas, Chicago, Dallas, Düsseldorf, Frankfurt, Geneva, Guadalajara, Hanoi, Ho Chi Minh City, Hong Kong, Houston, Juárez, Kuala Lumpur, Kyiv, London, Madrid, Manama, Manila, Melbourne, México City, Miami, Milan, Monterrey, Moscow, Münich, New York, Palo Alto, Paris, Porto Alegre, Prague, Rio de Janeiro, Riyadh, Rome, St. Petersburg, San Diego, San Francisco, Santiago, São Paulo, Singapore, Stockholm, Sydney, Taipei, Tijuana, Tokyo, Toronto, Valencia, Warsaw and Zürich.

Correspondent Law Firm: Hadiputranto, Hadinoto & Partners, Jakarta.

Taxation. Customs, Tariff and International Trade Law. Corporate and Securities. Litigation. Practice before Governmental Departments, Commissions and Administrative Agencies. Patents and Trademark Law. Antitrust. Telecommunications. Banking.

MEMBERS OF FIRM

MARY C. BENNETT, born Milton, Massachusetts, February 26, 1954; admitted to bar, 1979, Massachusetts; 1980, New York; 1991, District of Columbia. *Education:* Radcliffe College (A.B., cum laude, 1976); Universite de Paris; Columbia University (J.D., 1979); Boston University (LL.M., Tax, 1985). Harlan Fiske Stone Scholar. Editor, Columbia Journal of Environmental Law, 1978-1979. Attorney, U.S. Treasury, Office of International Tax Counsel, 1985-1990. Deputy International Tax Counsel, 1987-1990. *Member:* Bar Association of the District of Columbia; American Bar Association (Member, Tax Section); International Fiscal Association (Member, National Council, U.S.A. Branch). ***LANGUAGES:*** French and Dutch. ***PRACTICE AREAS:*** Tax Planning and Advice (Corporate and International); Tax Controversies (Corporate and International). ***Email:*** mary.c.bennett@bakernet.com

DAVID A. CLANTON, born Santa Barbara, California, May 31, 1944; admitted to bar, 1979, Michigan; 1984, District of Columbia. *Education:* Andrews University (B.A., 1966); Wayne State University (J.D., 1969). Articles Editor, Wayne Law Review, 1968-1969. Commissioner, 1976-1983 and Acting Chairman, March-October, 1981, Federal Trade Commission. *Member:* State Bar of Michigan; The District of Columbia Bar; American Bar Association (Member, Sections on: Antitrust Law; Administrative Law; Antitrust and Trade Regulation; Member, Forum Committee on Franchising). ***PRACTICE AREAS:*** Antitrust Law; Administrative Law; Franchise Law; Civil Litigation. ***Email:*** david.a.clanton@bakernet.com

NICHOLAS F. COWARD, born Buffalo, New York, July 3, 1952; admitted to bar, 1982, District of Columbia. *Education:* Union College (B.A., 1976); George Mason University (J.D., 1981). *Member:* The District of Columbia Bar; American Bar Association. ***PRACTICE AREAS:*** Trade Regulations and Customs Law; Regulatory Law; Information Technology/Telecommunications; Administrative Law; Immigration Law. ***Email:*** nicholas.f.coward@bakernet.com

W. WARREN CROWDUS, III, born St. Louis, Missouri, November 3, 1958; admitted to bar, 1985, Illinois; 2000, District of Columbia. *Education:* Washington & Lee University (B.A., 1981); University of Chicago (J.D., 1985). Fulbright Scholar, German, 1981-1982. *Member:* American Bar Association (Member, Tax Section). ***PRACTICE AREAS:*** Tax Planning and Advice (Corporate and International); Tax Controversies (Corporate and International). ***Email:*** warren.crowdus@bakernet.com

PETER M. DAUB, born New York, N.Y., June 4, 1956; admitted to bar, 1982, New York; 1990, District of Columbia. *Education:* Harvard College (A.B., magna cum laude, 1978); Yale Law School (J.D., 1981). Phi Beta Kappa. Editor, Yale Law Journal, 1980-1981. Editor-in-Chief, Journal of International Taxation, 1997—. Associate International Tax Counsel, U.S. Treasury Department, 1988-1989. Attorney-Advisor, Office of International Tax Counsel, U.S. Treasury Department, 1984-1988. *Member:* Bar Association of the District of Columbia; American Bar Association (Member, Tax Section); International Fiscal Association. ***LANGUAGES:*** French. ***PRACTICE AREAS:*** Tax Planning and Advice (Corporate and International); Tax Controversies (Corporate and International). ***Email:*** peter.m.daub@bakernet.com

EDWARD E. DYSON, born Alexandria, Virginia, January 6, 1939; admitted to bar, 1966, Virginia; 1967, District of Columbia. *Education:* George Washington University (B.B.A., 1962); George Washington University Law School (LL.B., 1966). Delta Theta Phi. Member, George Washington University Law Review, 1965-1966. *Member:* The District of Columbia Bar; Virginia Bar Association; Bar Association of the District of Columbia; American Bar Association. ***Email:*** edward.e.dyson@bakernet.com

THOMAS J. EGAN, JR., born Washington, D.C., January 5, 1957; admitted to bar, 1983, District of Columbia; 1985, U.S. District Court, District of Columbia. *Education:* University of Virginia (B.A., with distinction, 1979); Washington & Lee University (J.D., cum laude, 1983); Georgetown University (LL.M. in Securities Regulation, 1992). Contributor, 1981-1982 and Note and Comment Editor, 1982-1983, Washington & Lee University Law Review. *Member:* Bar Association of The District of Columbia; The District of Columbia Bar (Member, Sections on: International Law; Corporate Law); American Bar Association (Member, Section on Corporation, Banking and Business Law).

(This Listing Continued)

BAKER & McKENZIE, Washington—Continued

PRACTICE AREAS: Mergers and Acquisitions; Securities; Investments; Corporate Law; Partnership Law; Communications and Media Law. ***Email:*** thomas.j.egan@bakernet.com

TERESA A. GLEASON, born Mineola, New York, June 16, 1963; admitted to bar, 1988, Pennsylvania; 1989, District of Columbia; 1990, U.S. Supreme Court of International Trade; 1991, U.S. Court of Appeals for the Federal Circuit; 1996, U.S. Supreme Court and U.S. Court of Federal Claims. *Education:* William Smith College (B.A., 1985); University of San Francisco (J.D., magna cum laude, 1988). Editor, University of San Francisco Law Review. Recipient, American Jurisprudence Award in Civil Procedure. *Member:* American Bar Association (Member, International Section). ***PRACTICE AREAS:*** Trade Regulations and Customs Law. ***Email:*** teresa.a.gleason@bakernet.com

DANIEL L. GOELZER, born Milwaukee, Wisconsin, February 14, 1947; admitted to bar, 1973, Wisconsin and U.S. District Court, Western District of Wisconsin; 1974, U.S. Court of Appeals, Seventh Circuit; 1975, U.S. Court of Appeals, Second and Ninth Circuits and U.S. Court of Appeals for the District of Columbia Circuit; 1976, U.S. Supreme Court, U.S. Court of Appeals Fourth and Eighth Circuits; 1980, District of Columbia; 1985, U.S. Court of Appeals, Tenth Circuit; 1986, U.S. Court of Appeals, Fifth, Sixth and Eleventh Circuits; 1987, U.S. Court of Appeals, Third Circuit, U.S. District Court, Eastern District of Wisconsin and U.S. District Court for the District of Columbia. *Education:* University of Wisconsin, Madison (B.B.A., 1969; J.D., 1973); George Washington University (LL.M., 1979). Beta Gamma Sigma; Beta Alpha Psi; Phi Kappa Phi; Order of the Coif. National Merit Scholar. Certified Public Accountant, Wisconsin, 1977. Adjunct Professor, Georgetown University Law Center, 1986-1993. Judicial Clerk to the Hon. Thomas E. Fairchild, U.S. Court of Appeals, Seventh Circuit, 1973-1974. General Counsel, Securities and Exchange Commission, 1983-1990. *Member:* The District of Columbia Bar; State Bar of Wisconsin; Federal (Member, Securities Law Executive Committee, 1986—) and American (Member, Committee on Federal Regulation of Securities, 1980—) Bar Associations; American Law Institute. ***PRACTICE AREAS:*** Capital Markets; Regulatory Law; Asset Management; Corporate Financings (Public and Private). ***Email:*** daniel.l.goelzer@bakernet.com

JONATHAN W. GOTTLIEB, born Washington, D.C., June 24, 1959; admitted to bar, 1986, Pennsylvania; 1989, District of Columbia; 1990, U.S. Court of Appeals. *Education:* De Paul University (B.A., 1982); New York Law School (J.D., 1985). Chairman, Legal Affairs Task Force, National Hydropower Association, 1991-1996. Contributing Editor, Project Finance Monthly, 1993—. Editor, Competitive Utility, 1995—. General Counsel, Power Markets Development Company, 1995-1996. *Member:* The District of Columbia Bar; Pennsylvania Bar Association; Federal Energy Bar Association; Southeastern Energy Society. ***PRACTICE AREAS:*** Infrastructure Development; Project Finance. ***Email:*** jonathan.w.gottlieb@bakernet.com

MARY B. HEVENER, born Charlottesville, Virginia, February 9, 1952; admitted to bar, 1978, Virginia; 1980, District of Columbia. *Education:* Wellesley College (B.A., cum laude, 1974); University of Virginia School of Law (J.D., 1978). Author: "Complying with IRS Employee Benefit Rules, and Employer's Guide to Fringe Benefit Rules," Thompson Publishing Group, 1987-2000. Attorney-Advisor, Office of Tax Legislative Counsel, U.S. Treasury Department, 1981-1984. *Member:* District of Columbia Bar; Virginia and American (Member, Taxation Section, Government Relations Committee, 1989—) Bar Associations. ***PRACTICE AREAS:*** Executive Compensation; Stock Options; Nonqualified Deferred Compensation Plans; Workforce Wide Benefits; Fringe Benefits; Health and Cafeteria Plans; Dependent Care; Educational Assistance Plans; Information Reporting; Penalty Abatements; Excise Taxes. ***Email:*** mary.b.hevener@bakernet.com

DAVID J. LAING, born Roanoke, Virginia, October 25, 1959; admitted to bar, 1988, North Carolina; 1989, District of Columbia. *Education:* University of Virginia (B.A., 1984); Duke University; University of North Carolina (J.D., 1988). *Member:* North Carolina State Bar; The District of Columbia Bar. ***LANGUAGES:*** French. ***PRACTICE AREAS:*** Antitrust and Unfair Trade Practices Law; Criminal Law; Mergers and Acquisitions. ***Email:*** david.j.laing@bakernet.com

DENNIS I. MEYER, born Dayton, Ohio, October 20, 1935; admitted to bar, 1960, Ohio; 1962, District of Columbia. *Education:* University of Dayton (B.S., 1957); Georgetown University (J.D., 1960; LL.M., 1962). Delta Theta Phi. Attorney Advisor to Chief Judge Tietjens of the U.S. Tax Court, 1960-1962. *Member:* The District of Columbia Bar; American Bar Association. ***PRACTICE AREAS:*** Tax Controversies (Corporate and International); Tax Planning and Advice (Corporate and International). ***Email:*** dennis.i.meyer@bakernet.com

KEVIN M. O'BRIEN, born New York, N.Y., July 9, 1956; admitted to bar, 1983, Illinois; 1985, District of Columbia. *Education:* Polytechnic Institute of New York (B.S.Ch.E., with honors, 1978); Loyola University, Chicago (J.D., with high honors, 1983). *Member:* The District of Columbia Bar; Illinois State and American Bar Associations; International Trade Commission Trial Lawyers Association; American Intellectual Property Law Association. ***Email:*** kevin.m.obrien@bakernet.com

WILLIAM D. OUTMAN, II, born St. Petersburg, Florida, November 10, 1940; admitted to bar, 1966, District of Columbia; 1999, New York; U.S. Court of International Trade; U.S. Court of Appeals for the Federal Circuit; U.S. Court of Appeals for the District of Columbia Circuit; U.S. Supreme Court. *Education:* Washington & Lee University (B.S., Business Administration, 1962); Georgetown University (J.D., 1965; LL.M. in Taxation, 1968). Omicron Delta Kappa. Chairman, 8th Annual Judicial Conference, U.S. Court of International Trade, 1992. *Member:* The District of Columbia Bar; Bar Association of the District of Columbia; American Bar Association; Court of International Trade (Member, Advisory Committee, 1994—; Chairman, 1998—); Customs and International Trade Bar Association (Member Board of Governors, 1994—; Secretary, 1998—). ***PRACTICE AREAS:*** Trade Regulations and Customs Law; Litigation; Appellate Practice. ***Email:*** william.d.outman@bakernet.com

MARC R. PAUL, born Baltimore, Maryland, October 3, 1960; admitted to bar, 1986, Pennsylvania; 1988, District of Columbia. *Education:* Harvard College (A.B., cum laude, 1982); University of London, School of Slavonic and East European Studies (M.A., 1984); Harvard Law School (J.D., cum laude, 1986). Phi Beta Kappa. Teaching Assistant, Foreign Investment, 1986 and Legal Writing, 1985-1986, Harvard Law School. *Member:* The District of Columbia Bar; Pennsylvania and American (Member, Sections on: Business Law; International Law) Bar Associations. ***LANGUAGES:*** Russian and French. ***PRACTICE AREAS:*** Corporate Financings (Public and Private); Mergers and Acquisitions; Bank Lending and Other Extensions of Credit (General); Corporate and Partnership Law; Information Technology/Telecommunications; Aviation and Aerospace Technology. ***Email:*** marc.r.paul@bakernet.com

B. THOMAS PEELE III, born Newport News, Virginia, July 25, 1947; admitted to bar, 1983, District of Columbia. *Education:* University of Virginia (B.A., 1969); The Rockefeller University (1969-1970); University of California at Berkeley (M.A., 1977); Harvard University (J.D., 1981). Phi Beta Kappa. Woodrow Wilson Fellow. Danforth Graduate Fellow. Judicial Clerk to Hon. Richard L. Williams, U.S. District Court, Eastern District of Virginia, 1981-1982. *Member:* The District of Columbia Bar; American Bar Association (Member, International Law and Litigation Sections); American Society of International Law; Customs and International Trade Bar Association. ***LANGUAGES:*** Chinese. ***PRACTICE AREAS:*** Trade Regulations and Customs Law; Litigation; Arbitration and Dispute Resolution; Administrative Law; China Trade. ***Email:*** thomas.peele@bakernet.com

RICHARD L. SLOWINSKI, born Washington, D.C., January 9, 1965; admitted to bar, 1991, Maryland; 1994, District of Columbia and U.S. Tax Court. *Education:* Bucknell University (B.A., 1987); Columbus School of Law, Catholic University of America (J.D., 1991); Georgetown University Law Center (LL.M., 1994). Phi Alpha Delta. Senior Lead Articles Editor, Catholic University Law Review, 1990-1991. Tokyo Office, 1995-1996. *Member:* Maryland State (Member, Taxation Section) and American (Member, Sections on: International Law; Taxation) Bar Associations; Bar Association of the District of Columbia (Member, Administrative Law Section). ***LANGUAGES:*** French (written). ***PRACTICE AREAS:*** Tax Controversies (Corporate and International); Tax Planning and Advice (Corporate and International). ***Email:*** richard.l.slowinski@bakernet.com

C. DAVID SWENSON, born Jackson, Mississippi, August 21, 1951; admitted to bar, 1978, District of Columbia. *Education:* University of Mississippi (B.A., with distinction, 1974; J.D., with honors, 1977); Georgetown University Law School (LL.M. in Taxation, 1981). Phi Kappa Phi; Omicron Delta Kappa. Editor, The Tax Lawyer, 1978-1979. Editor, Journal of Space Law, 1976-1977. Editor, Mississippi Law Journal, 1975-1977. Adjunct Professor of International Tax Law, Georgetown University Law School, 1986—. *Member:* Bar Association of the District of Columbia; American and International Bar Associations. ***PRACTICE AREAS:*** Tax Controversies (Corporate and International); Tax Planning and Advice (Corporate and International). ***Email:*** c.david.swenson@bakernet.com

LEONARD B. TERR, born Atlantic City, New Jersey, April 26, 1946; admitted to bar, 1975, Pennsylvania; 1976, District of Columbia. *Education:* LaSalle College (A.B., 1967); Brown University (A.M., 1968; Ph.D., 1971); Cornell University (J.D., 1975). Phi Beta Kappa. Law Clerk to the Chief Judge, U.S. Court of Appeals, Federal Circuit, 1975-1976 International Tax Counsel, U.S. Department of Treasury, 1987-1989. Recipient, Meritorious Service Award, U.S. Department of Treasury, 1989. Consultant, American Law Institute, Project of Tax Treaties, 1989. Member, Advisory Board, Tax Management International Journal, 1984-1987, 1989—. Correspondent, Tax Notes International, 1989—. Member, Board of Editors, Journal of Corporate Taxation, 1985-1987. *Member:* The District of Columbia Bar (Member: Tax Division, 1976—; International Law Division, 1976—; Chairman, Finance and Investment Committee, 1980-1981); Federal (Member, Tax Section, 1976—) and American (Member, Section of Taxation, Committee on Foreign Activities of U.S. Taxpayers, 1978—; Chairman, Section 367 Subcommittee, 1986-1987; Member: Insurance Companies Committee, 1979—; Section of International

(This Listing Continued)

Law, Insurance Committee, 1981—; Chairman, Tax Subcommittee, 1982-1983) Bar Associations; International Fiscal Association (U.S. National Reporter, 1986 Congress, 1990 Congress). ***PRACTICE AREAS:*** Tax Controversies (Corporate and International); Tax Planning and Advice (Corporate and International). ***Email:*** leonard.b.terr@bakernet.com

EUGENE THEROUX, born Medford, Massachusetts, April 29, 1938; admitted to bar, 1969, District of Columbia; 1977, Massachusetts; 1983, Virginia. *Education:* Harvard University and Pratt Institute (B.I.D., 1961; Ph.D. (Hon.) 1982); Georgetown University (J.D., 1968). Associate Professor of American Jurisprudence, University of Saigon Faculty of Law, 1968. Lecturer in International Law, Foreign Investment Commission of China, Peking, China, 1981. Vice Chairman, Board of Directors, U.S.-China Business Council, 1993—. Chairman and Legal Counsel, American Chamber of Commerce of the People's Republic of China, 1981-1982. Member, Advisory Board, Fletcher School of Law and Diplomacy, 1986—. Trustee, Monterey Institute of International Studies, 1994—. Visiting Professor of Law, Fudan University, Shanghai, China, 1986—. *Member:* The District of Columbia Bar; Virginia State Bar; Bar Association of the District of Columbia; American Bar Association; American Society of International Law. ***Email:*** eugene.a.theroux@bakernet.com

A. DUANE WEBBER, born Manhattan, Kansas, October 2, 1959; admitted to bar, 1985, Maryland; 1986, District of Columbia. *Education:* Kansas State University (B.A., B.S., cum laude, 1981); Georgetown University (J.D., magna cum laude, 1984). Executive Editor, Georgetown Law Journal, 1983-1984. *Member:* The District of Columbia Bar, Federal (Member, Taxation Section) and American (Member, Court Procedure Committee of the Taxation Section) Bar Associations. Fellow, J. Edgar Murdock American Inn of Court. ***PRACTICE AREAS:*** Tax Controversies (Corporate and International); Tax Planning and Advice (Corporate and International). ***Email:*** a.duane.webber@bakernet.com

LYNDA S. ZENGERLE, born White Plains, New York, May 29, 1944; admitted to bar, 1973, District of Columbia. *Education:* Smith College (B.A., 1966); University of Michigan (J.D., cum laude, 1971). Staff Assistant, U.S. Senator Russell Long, 1964. Economics Officer, U.S. Arms Control and Disarmament Agency, 1968-1969. Staff Attorney, Administrative Conference of the United States, 1972-1975. Adjunct Professor of Law, Georgetown University Law Center, 1987-1990. *Member:* The District of Columbia Bar; American Bar Association (Administrative Law and Regulatory Practice Section: Chair, Continuing Legal Education Committee, 1994-96; Chair, Committee on Immigration, Naturalization and Aliens, 1983-1996, Vice Chair, 1996-1997); Federal Bar Association (Chair, Committee on Labor Certification, Immigration Law Section, 1990-1992). ***LANGUAGES:*** French. ***PRACTICE AREAS:*** Immigration and Naturalization Law. ***Email:*** lynda.s.zengerle@bakernet.com

MICHAEL J. ZIMMER, born Washington, D.C., October 13, 1949; admitted to bar, 1975, District of Columbia; 1982, Virginia. *Education:* Providence College (B.A., cum laude, 1971); University of Maryland (J.D., cum laude, 1975). Member, Heusler Honor Society. Staff Vice-President, American Gas Association, 1977-1980. President, General Counsel: Cogeneration and Independent Power Coalition, 1980-1987; Clean Coal Coalition, 1983-1985; Counsel, Alliance for Power Privatization, 1995-1996; Member Board of Directors, Caterpillar Capital Company, Inc., 1988-1989; Federal Strategies, Inc., 1988-1989; Power Generating, Inc., 1994-1997. Contributing Editor, Independent Energy Magazine, 1986—. Editorial Board, The Energy Report, 1990—. *Member:* The District of Columbia Bar; Virginia State Bar; Federal Energy (Chairman, Cogeneration and Small Power Production Committee, 1986-1987) and American (Member, Sections on: Natural Resources Law; Public Utility Law; Law Practice Management) Bar Associations; National Academy of Sciences (Member, Committee on District Heating, 1984). ***PRACTICE AREAS:*** Infrastructure Development; Project Finance. ***Email:*** michael.j.zimmer@bakernet.com

NATIONAL PARTNERS

MARIANNA G. DYSON, born Madisonville, Kentucky, June 5, 1953; admitted to bar, 1980, Kentucky; 1981, Florida; 1990, District of Columbia. *Education:* University of Louisville (B.A., 1975; J.D., 1979); Georgetown University Law Center (LL.M., 1990). Author: "Employer's Guide to Fringe Benefits Rules and Complying with IRS Employee Benefit Rules," Thompson Publishing Group, 1995-2000; Chapter 1300, "Fringe Benefits Issues," A Guide to Federal Tax Issues for College and Universities, National Association of College and University Business Officers, 2001. ***PRACTICE AREAS:*** Litigation; Tax Controversies (Corporate and International); Tax Planning and Advice (Corporate and International); Employee Benefits. ***Email:*** marianna.g.dyson@bakernet.com

HARRY A. FRANKS, JR., born Baltimore, Maryland, March 18, 1963; admitted to bar, 1988, Virginia; 1990, District of Columbia. *Education:* University of Virginia (B.S., 1985; M.S., 1988; J.D., 1988). Beta Alpha Psi. Cohen Tax Scholar. *Member:* Virginia State Bar; The District of Columbia Bar. ***PRACTICE AREAS:*** Tax; International Tax. ***Email:*** harry.a.franks@bakernet.com

(This Listing Continued)

KENNETH R. HAYDUK, born Coral Gables, Florida, June 15, 1960; admitted to bar, 1989, Virginia; 1992, District of Columbia. *Education:* Rider University (B.S.C., 1985); George Washington University (J.D., 1989); New York University School of Law (LL.M. in Taxation, 1991). Certified Public Accountant, Maryland, 1990. Co-author: with Keith Martin, "Tax Issues and Opportunities in Contract Restructuring," Project Finance International, April 1997. *Member:* Virginia State Bar; The District of Columbia Bar; American Bar Association. ***PRACTICE AREAS:*** Taxation. ***Email:*** ken.r.hayduk@bakernet.com

RACHAEL E. SCHWARTZ, born New York, N.Y., October 2, 1957; admitted to bar, 1981, Maryland; 1984, District of Columbia. *Education:* Johns Hopkins University (B.A., with honors, 1978); Georgetown University Law Center (J.D., 1981); New York University Law School (LL.M. in Corporation Law, 1992; LL.M. in International Law, 1995). Pi Sigma Alpha. Articles and Notes Editor, American Criminal Law Review. Adjunct Professor, Catholic University, Columbus School of Law, 1998. *Member:* The District of Columbia Bar; American Bar Association (Member, Sections on: International Law; Business Law); Federal Communications Bar Association. ***PRACTICE AREAS:*** Communications and Media Law; Corporate and Partnership Law. ***Email:*** rachael.e.schwartz@bakernet.com

STUART P. SEIDEL, born Vallejo, California, December 16, 1945; admitted to bar, 1970, New York; 1974, District of Columbia. *Education:* Hunter College of the City University of New York (B.A., 1967); Brooklyn Law School (J.D., 1969). Assistant Commissioner, 1994-2001, Director, International Trade Compliance, 1989-1994, Regional Counsel, 1986-1988 and Assistant Chief Counsel, 1974-1986, U.S. Customs Service. *Member:* Customs Lawyers Association (President, 2000-2001). ***PRACTICE AREAS:*** Trade Regulations and Customs Law. ***Email:*** stuart.p.seidel@bakernet.com

MARC B. TUCKER, born Wilmington, Delaware, February 7, 1950; admitted to bar, 1977, District of Columbia; 1985, Delaware. *Education:* Trinity College (B.A., 1972); Columbia University (J.D., 1976). Phi Beta Kappa. Stone Scholar. Managing Editor, Columbia Law Review, 1975-1976. Author: "Takeover Bylaws: A Wrench in the Proxy Works," Nat'l L.J., Apr. 13, 1998, at 18. Co-Author: with Jay Eisenhofer, "Accountants' Liability," Nat'l L.J., June 25, 1990, at A20. Graduate Teaching Fellow, Sociology, George Washington University, 1976-1977. Law Clerk to Judge John Minor Wisdom, U.S. Court of Appeals, Fifth Circuit, 1976-1977. Assistant U.S. Attorney, Washington, D.C. and Miami, Florida, 1979-1985. *Member:* The District of Columbia Bar. ***PRACTICE AREAS:*** Litigation; Appellate Practice; Corporate and Partnership Law; Criminal Law; Insurance Law. ***Email:*** marc.b.tucker@bakernet.com

OF COUNSEL

HOWARD ADLER, JR., born Chicago, Illinois, January 25, 1925; admitted to bar, 1951, Illinois; 1956, District of Columbia. *Education:* University of Chicago (M.A., 1951); University of Chicago Law School (J.D., 1951). Comment Editor, University of Chicago Law Review. *Member:* The District of Columbia Bar; American Bar Association (Member, Antitrust Section; Council Member, 1972-1976; Vice Chairman, 1978). [U.S. Army Air Force, 1943-1946]. ***PRACTICE AREAS:*** Antitrust and Unfair Trade Practices Law; Litigation; Mergers and Acquisitions; Administrative Law. ***Email:*** howard.adler@bakernet.com

ANNE G. BATTER, born Washington, D.C., 1960; admitted to bar, 1985, Massachusetts; 1988, District of Columbia. *Education:* University of Maryland (B.A., summa cum laude, 1982); Harvard University Law School (J.D., 1985). ***PRACTICE AREAS:*** Tax Planning and Advice (Corporate and International). ***Email:*** anne.g.batter@bakernet.com

SUSAN G. BRADEN, born Youngstown, Ohio, November 8, 1948; admitted to bar, 1973, Ohio; 1974, U.S. District Court, Northern District of Ohio; 1980, U.S. Court of Appeals for the District of Columbia Circuit and U.S. Supreme Court; 1981, District of Columbia; 1993, U.S. Court of Appeals, Second Circuit and U.S. District Court, Northern District of Texas. *Education:* Case Western Reserve University (B.A., 1970; J.D., 1973). Special Counsel to Chairman, 1984-1985, Senior Attorney Advisor to Commissioner and Acting Chairman, 1980-1983, Federal Trade Commission. Senior Trial Attorney, Antitrust Division, U.S. Department of Justice, Energy Section, 1978-1980; Cleveland Field Office, 1973-1978. Assistant General Counsel, Republican National Convention, 1988 and 1992. Member: Board of Directors, National Republican Lawyers Association, 1987—; D.C. Republican National Committee, 1997—; Judicial Conference D.C. Circuit, 1992; Board of Directors, Washington Legal Foundation, 1992—; Citizens for Sound Economy, President's Council; Board of Editors, Computer Law Reporter, 1993—. Special Assistant Attorney General for the State of Alabama, 1990. Consultant to the Administrative Conference of the United States, 1984-1985. Federal Agency and Registered Lobbyist. *Member:* The District of Columbia Bar (Co-Chair, Intellectual Property Committee, Computer Law Section; Steering Committee Concerning Commercial and Government Contracts, 1993); American (Council Member, 1996 —; Chairman, Antitrust and Trade Regulation Committee, 1993, Vice Chairman, International Committee, 1993-1994 and Liaison to the National Association of

(This Listing Continued)

BAKER & McKENZIE, Washington—Continued

Attorneys General, Section of Administrative Law and Regulatory Practice; Section of Antitrust Law, Vice Chairman, National Institutes Committee, 1987-1992. Member, Sections of: Corporation, Banking and Business Law; International Law and Litigation) and Federal (Chairman: Federal Trade Regulation Committee, 1983-1984, Distinguished Service Award 1984) Bar Associations; Computer Law Bar Associations; American League of Lobbyists; Washington International Trade Association; Women in International Trade; Federalist Society, Madison Club (1986—). ***PRACTICE AREAS:*** Administrative Law; Antitrust Law; Computers and Technology Law; Intellectual Property Law; Civil Litigation; Regulatory Law. ***Email:*** susan.g.braden@bakernet.com

JOHN W. POLK, born Rochester, New York, October 16, 1943; admitted to bar, 1972, Virginia; 1973, District of Columbia; 1975, U.S. Court of Appeals for the District of Columbia Circuit; 1978, U.S. District Court, District of Columbia; 1987, U.S. Tax Court; 1988, U.S. Claims Court; 1989, U.S. District Court, Eastern District of Virginia; 1991, U.S. Supreme Court; 1994, U.S. Court of Appeals, Fourth Circuit. *Education:* Bucknell University (A.B., 1965); University of Michigan (M.A., 1966); Georgetown University (J.D., 1972). Phi Beta Kappa. Assistant United States Attorney, District of Columbia, 1973-1985. Attorney Advisor, Department of the Air Force, 1985-1986. *Member:* The District of Columbia Bar; Virginia State Bar; American Bar Association. ***PRACTICE AREAS:*** Litigation; Public Contracts and Utilities; Product Liability Law; Intellectual Property Law; Regulatory Law. ***Email:*** john.w.polk@bakernet.com

JOHN R. REILLY, born Dubuque, Iowa, June 4, 1928; admitted to bar, 1955, Iowa; 1962, District of Columbia. *Education:* Loras College and University of Iowa (B.A., 1953; J.D., 1955). Member, Board of Editors, Iowa Law Review, 1955. Assistant to Deputy Attorney General, Chief of Executive Office for U.S. Attorneys, 1961-1964. Commissioner, Federal Trade Commission, 1964-1967. *Member:* The District of Columbia Bar. ***PRACTICE AREAS:*** Antitrust Law; Mergers and Acquisitions; U.S. Trade. ***Email:*** john.r.reilly@bakernet.com

LEE H. SPENCE, born Midland Park, New Jersey, May 20, 1942; admitted to bar, 1969, District of Columbia; 1981, U.S. Court of Federal Claims; 1982, U.S. Supreme Court. *Education:* Brown University (B.A., 1964); Duke University (M.A., Psychology, 1966); Duke Law School (J.D., 1969). Sigma Xi. Editor, Duke Law School Legal Research Program, 1968-1969. *Member:* The District of Columbia Bar; American Bar Association (Member, Tax Section); International Fiscal Association. ***PRACTICE AREAS:*** Tax Planning and Advice. ***Email:*** lee.h.spence@bakernet.com

RESIDENT ASSOCIATES

BILL BATCHELOR, born Birmingham, United Kingdom, September 10, 1970; admitted to bar, 1998, England and Wales (Not admitted in the United States). *Education:* Bristol University (LL.B., 1995); York University (L.P.C., 1995). Co-Author: with Julian Mieztis, Issues for B2B Exchanges under EC Competition Law, Antitrust Magazine, Fall 2000. ***PRACTICE AREAS:*** EC Competition and Trade; EU Law (General); Antitrust and Unfair Trade Practices Law; Distributorship and Franchise Law; Information Technology/Telecommunications. ***Email:*** bill.batchelor@bakernet.com

ROBERT H. BETHEA, born Norman, Oklahoma, October 11, 1966; admitted to bar, 1991, Texas; 1992, Oklahoma; 2000, District of Columbia. *Education:* University of Oklahoma (B.B.A., 1988); University of Oklahoma College of Law (J.D., 1991); Georgetown University Law Center (LL.M., 1999). *Member:* American Bar Association. ***PRACTICE AREAS:*** Trade Regulations and Customs Law. ***Email:*** robert.h.bethea@bakernet.com

MARGARET R. BLAKE, born Washington, D.C., April 1, 1965; admitted to bar, 1993, Pennsylvania; 1994, District of Columbia. *Education:* Virginia Polytechnic Institute (B.A., 1988); Catholic University of America (J.D., 1992). Judicial Law Clerk, Superior Court of District of Columbia. *Member:* The District of Columbia Bar; American Bar Association; Women's Bar Association. ***LANGUAGES:*** French. ***PRACTICE AREAS:*** Securities and Financial Products; Regulatory Law; Mergers and Acquisitions; Corporate and Partnership Law. ***Email:*** margaret.r.blake@bakernet.com

GREGORY W. BOWMAN, born Landstuhl, Germany, April 6, 1967; admitted to bar, 1994, Illinois; 2000, District of Columbia. *Education:* West Virginia University (B.A., summa cum laude, 1990); University of Exeter, Exeter, England (M.A., with distinction, 1991); Northwestern University School of Law (J.D., cum laude, 1994). Adjunct Professor of Law, The John Marshall Law School, Chicago, Illinois, 1999. *Member:* American Bar Association (Vice-Chair, Customs Law Committee, 1999—); Customs and International Trade Bar Association (Member, Publications Committee, 1998—). ***LANGUAGES:*** Danish. ***PRACTICE AREAS:*** Trade Regulations; Customs Law; NAFTA Trade; Administrative Law. ***Email:*** gregory.w.bowman@bakernet.com

PHOEBE W. BROWN, born Rockville Center, New York, January 22, 1966; admitted to bar, 1997, Massachusetts; 1999, District of Columbia. *Education:* Brown University (A.B., magna cum laude, 1988); Yale University (M.A., 1993); Northeastern University (J.D., 1996). Author: "Russian Women Lawyers in Post-Soviet Russia," Georgia State Law Review, Vol. 12 (Jan. 1996). *Member:* The District of Columbia Bar. ***LANGUAGES:*** Russian and French. ***PRACTICE AREAS:*** Corporate and Partnership Law; Corporate Financings (Public and Private); Capital Markets. ***Email:*** phoebe.w.brown@bakernet.com

BRIAN F. BURKE, born Forestville, Maryland, April 1, 1972; admitted to bar, 1998, New York and District of Columbia. *Education:* James Madison University (B.A., cum laude, 1994); Georgetown University Law Center (J.D., 1997). *Member:* The District of Columbia Bar. ***LANGUAGES:*** Spanish. ***PRACTICE AREAS:*** Antitrust Law. ***Email:*** brian.f.burke@bakernet.com

JOHN A. COHEN, born Hoboken, New Jersey, June 4, 1966; admitted to bar, 1993, Maryland; 1995, District of Columbia; 1997, Florida. *Education:* The American University (B.A., 1988); University of Baltimore (J.D., 1993). Recipient, American Jurisprudence Award. *Member:* The District of Columbia Bar; The Florida Bar; Federal Energy Bar Association. ***LANGUAGES:*** French. ***PRACTICE AREAS:*** Public Contracts and Utilities; Regulatory Law; Administrative Law. ***Email:*** john.a.cohen@bakernet.com

DAVID S. COLE, born Buffalo, New York, June 1, 1968; admitted to bar, 1995, New York; 1997, District of Columbia. *Education:* University of Rochester (B.A., cum laude, 1990); George Washington University (J.D., trial advocacy honors, 1994). *Member:* New York State Bar Association; Bar Association of the District of Columbia. ***PRACTICE AREAS:*** Mergers and Acquisitions; Corporate and Partnership Law; Securities and Financial Products; Aviation and Aerospace Technology; Entertainment, the Arts and Sports Law. ***Email:*** david.s.cole@bakernet.com

THOMAS M. CRYAN, JR, born Jacksonville, Florida, October 27, 1972; admitted to bar, 1997, Virginia; 1999, District of Columbia. *Education:* Washington & Lee University (B.A., Econ., cum laude, 1994); George Mason University School of Law (J.D., with high honors, 1997); Georgetown University School of Law (LL.M., 1999). Attorney-Advisor to the Hon. Joel Gerber, U.S. Tax Court, 1997-1999. ***Email:*** thomas.cryan@bakernet.com

SAMIR S. DESAI, born Calcutta, India, May 14, 1968; admitted to bar, 1995, New York; 1997, District of Columbia. *Education:* Haverford College (B.A., 1989); Albany Law School (J.D., 1993); Washington College of Law (LL.M., 1995). Author: "India," Legal Aspects of Foreign Direct Investment, Kluwer Law International, 1999. Co-Author: "Awaiting the Tiger's Roar: Foreign Investment in India," International Business Lawyer, October 1997. Legal Research/Writing Instructor, Washington College of Law, 1995. *Member:* The District of Columbia Bar; American Bar Association. ***LANGUAGES:*** Hindi and Gujarati. ***PRACTICE AREAS:*** Project Finance; Asset Based Finance. ***Email:*** samir.desai@bakernet.com

ROGER M. GIBIAN, born New York, N.Y., September 3, 1968; admitted to bar, 1996, Minnesota; 1998, District of Columbia. *Education:* Vassar College (B.A., 1990); Case Western Reserve University (J.D., 1996). ***PRACTICE AREAS:*** Public Contracts and Utilities; Regulatory Law; Administrative Law. ***Email:*** roger.m.gibian@bakernet.com

DIRK GIFFORD, born Lebanon, New Hampshire, March 13, 1968; admitted to bar, 1993, California; 1999, District of Columbia. *Education:* University of Pennsylvania (B.S., 1990); Santa Clara University (J.D., 1993; M.B.A., 1993). *Member:* State Bar of California. [Captain, U.S. Army, 1994-1998]. ***LANGUAGES:*** Mandarin Chinese. ***PRACTICE AREAS:*** Commercial Litigation; Taxation. ***Email:*** dirk.gifford@bakernet.com

THOMAS GÖRGEMANNS, born Viersen, Germany, October 17, 1968; admitted to bar, 1997, Germany (Not admitted in the United States). *Education:* Universities of Trier, Cologne and Bonn (Referendar, 1993); Assessor Exam. (1996); University of Bonn (Dr. jur., 1998). Author: "Small and Medium-Sized Companies Under the German Act Against Restraints of Competition," 1998; "Mergers Realized Abroad Under the Merger Control of the Amended German Act Against Restraints of Competition," The International Lawyer, p. 1013-1031, Fall 2000. *Member:* Dusseldorf Bar; Association for Antitrust Studies; German-American Lawyers Association. ***LANGUAGES:*** English. ***PRACTICE AREAS:*** Mergers and Acquisitions; Corporate and Partnership Law; Antitrust and Unfair Trade Practices Law. ***Email:*** thomas.goergemanns@bakernet.com

KRISTI K. HANSEN, born Pocahontas, Iowa, October 8, 1974; admitted to bar, 2001, New York (Not admitted in District of Columbia). *Education:* University of Iowa (B.A., 1997); George Washington University (J.D., 2000). ***PRACTICE AREAS:*** Trade Regulations and Customs Law; Intellectual Property Law. ***Email:*** kris.k.hansen@bakernet.com

MARK R. HEILBRUN, born Iowa City, Iowa, March 12, 1963; admitted to bar, 1991, Georgia; 1992, District of Columbia. *Education:* Emory University (B.A., with highest honors, summa cum laude, 1986); University of Texas at Austin (J.D., summa cum laude, with honors, 1990). ***PRACTICE AREAS:*** Litigation. ***Email:*** mark.heilbrun@bakernet.com

JOSHUA J. IZENBERG, born Topeka, Kansas, February 26, 1973; admitted to bar, 2001, Massachusetts (limited to matters and proceedings before

(This Listing Continued)

federal courts and agencies) (Not admitted in District of Columbia). *Education:* McGill University (B.Sc., 1996); University of Toronto Faculty of Law (LL.B., 1999). ***LANGUAGES:*** Hebrew. ***PRACTICE AREAS:*** Information Technology/Telecommunications; Corporate and Partnership Law. ***Email:*** josh.izenberg@bakernet.com

JANET K. KIM, born Minneapolis, Minnesota, August 27, 1969; admitted to bar, 1995, New York; 1996, District of Columbia. *Education:* Georgetown University (B.S., magna cum laude, 1991); Columbia University (J.D., 1994). Phi Beta Kappa. *Member:* New York State Bar Association; The District of Columbia Bar. ***PRACTICE AREAS:*** International Trade; Administrative Law. ***Email:*** janet.k.kim@bakernet.com

JUHONG KIM, born Seoul, Korea, September 11, 1970; admitted to bar, 2000, New York (Not admitted in District of Columbia). *Education:* Dickinson College (B.A., Economics, 1994); Franklin Pierce Law Center (J.D./M.I.P., 1997). ***LANGUAGES:*** Korean, Japanese. ***PRACTICE AREAS:*** Intellectual Property Law; Administrative Law; Regulatory Law; Trade Regulations and Customs Law. ***Email:*** juhong.kim@bakernet.com

SCOTT A. KNOTT, born Providence, Rhode Island, August 20, 1972; admitted to bar, 1999, Florida; 2000, District of Columbia. *Education:* University of Rhode Island (B.S.B.A., 1994); University of Miami (J.D., cum laude, 1999). Recipient: Dean's Certificate of Achievement; Priscilla Schneller Scholarship. Articles and Comments Editor, University of Miami Business Law Review. *Member:* The Florida Bar. ***PRACTICE AREAS:*** Tax Controversies (Corporate and International); Tax Planning and Advice (Corporate and International). ***Email:*** scott.a.knott@bakernet.com

MATTHEW B. LANDON, born Kansas City, Missouri, April 27, 1971; admitted to bar, 1998, New York and District of Columbia. *Education:* Northern Illinois University (B.A., 1992); Cornell Law School (J.D., 1997). *Member:* The District of Columbia Bar. ***LANGUAGES:*** Thai. ***PRACTICE AREAS:*** Corporate and Partnership Law; Securities and Financial Products; Mergers and Acquisitions. ***Email:*** matthew.b.landon@bakernet.com

MICAH A. LEVY, born Boston, Massachusetts, July 20, 1971; admitted to bar, 1998, Massachusetts; 1999, U.S. Tax Court; 2000, District of Columbia. *Education:* University of Massachusetts (B.A., 1994); Boston University School of Law (J.D., 1997); Georgetown University Law School. Attorney Advisor to the Honorable James Halpern, U.S. Tax Court, 1998-1999. ***LANGUAGES:*** Hebrew. ***PRACTICE AREAS:*** Tax Planning and Advice (Corporate and International); Tax Controversies (Corporate and International); Employee Benefits; Bankruptcy, Insolvency and Reorganization. ***Email:*** micah.a.levy@bakernet.com

JEFFREY P. MAYDEW, born Hays, Kansas, February 26, 1970; admitted to bar, 1996, Iowa; practice limited to matters and proceedings before federal courts and agencies (Not admitted in District of Columbia). *Education:* Iowa State University (B.S., 1992); University of Iowa (J.D., with highest honors, 1996). Phi Beta Kappa; Phi Kappa Phi. Author: "Intangible Assets—The Treasury Issues New Regulations," Taxes, June 1996. ***PRACTICE AREAS:*** Taxation. ***Email:*** jeffrey.p.maydew@bakernet.com

JEAN A. MILNER, born Cape Town, South Africa, September 12, 1967; admitted to bar, 1996, New York; practice is limited to matters before federal agencies (Not admitted in District of Columbia). *Education:* University of Cape Town (B.A., 1988; LL.B., 1990); American University, Washington College of Law (LL.M. in International Law, 1995). Co-author: Chapter, "The North American Free Trade Association," Greening International Institutions, Jacob Wertman (Ed.) March 1996, Earthscan Publications Ltd., London. ***LANGUAGES:*** Afrikaans. ***PRACTICE AREAS:*** Corporate and Partnership Law; Securities and Financial Products. ***Email:*** jean.a.milner@bakernet.com

JENNIFER BARBEE MOLNAR, born Washington, D.C., May 5, 1972; admitted to bar, 2001, California (Not admitted in District of Columbia). *Education:* University of California, San Diego (B.A., Psychology, 1994)' University of San Diego School of Law (J.D, 2000); New York University School of Law (LL.M., Taxation, 2001). ***PRACTICE AREAS:*** Tax Planning and Advice (Corporate and International); Tax Controversies (Corporate and International); Estate and Personal Tax Planning. ***Email:*** jennifer.molnar@bakernet.com

MICHAEL E. MURPHY, born Newton, Massachusetts, May 4, 1971; admitted to bar, 1997, Pennsylvania; 1998, District of Columbia. *Education:* College of the Holy Cross (B.A., 1993); University of Pennsylvania (J.D., 1996). Member, Inns of Court. ***PRACTICE AREAS:*** Litigation; Regulatory Law; International Trade Regulation; Trade Regulations and Customs Law; Federal Administrative Law. ***Email:*** michael.e.murphy@bakernet.com

ALLEN ORR JR., born Valdosta, Georgia, August 5, 1973; admitted to bar, 1999, District of Columbia. *Education:* Morehouse College (B.A., 1995); Howard University School of Law (J.D., 1998). *Member:* Virginia State Bar; National Bar Association; American Immigration Lawyers Association. ***PRACTICE AREAS:*** Immigration Law; Administrative Law; Construction Law. ***Email:*** allen.orr@bakernet.com

IRENE M. RECIO, born Albany, New York, May 13, 1968; admitted to bar, 1997, Florida; 1998, U.S. District Court, Southern District of Florida; 2000,

(This Listing Continued)

U.S. Supreme Court (Not admitted in District of Columbia). *Education:* University of Miami (B.S., dual major in Economics/Journalism, cum laude, 1989; M.A., Intl Bus. Mgmt., 1991; J.D., 1995). *Member:* The Florida Bar; American Bar Association; American Immigration Lawyers Association. ***LANGUAGES:*** English, Spanish, and French. ***PRACTICE AREAS:*** Immigration Law. ***Email:*** irene.m.recio@bakernet.com

MARNI K. ROSENBLATT, born Huntington, New York, January 7, 1970; admitted to bar, 1999, New York; 2001, District of Columbia. *Education:* State University of New York at Albany (B.S., 1991); University of Miami (J.D., 1998). Iron Arrow, Society of Bar and Gavel; Omicron Delta Kappa; Alpha Epsilon Lambda. Listed in Who's Who Among Students in American Universities and Colleges - 1998 Edition. Dean's Honor Scholarship. Dean's Certificate of Achievement in "Taxation of Business Entities". Member, Tax Law Society (President, 1997-1998; Founding Vice-President, 1996-1997). Treasurer, 1996-1997 and Member, 1995-1998, Miami Law Women. Member, International Moot Court Board, 1997-1998. Certified Public Accountant, New York, 1995. ***LANGUAGES:*** French. ***PRACTICE AREAS:*** Taxation. ***Email:*** marni.k.rosenblatt@bakernet.com

WILLIAM RANDOLPH (RANDY) RUCKER, born Dover, New Jersey, May 5, 1972; admitted to bar, 2000, Illinois; 2001, Florida, U.S. Court of International Trade and U.S. Court of Appeals for the Federal Circuit (Not admitted in District of Columbia). *Education:* University of Alabama (B.S., 1994); The John Marshall Law School (J.D., cum laude, 2000). ***PRACTICE AREAS:*** Trade Regulations and Customs Law. ***Email:*** randy.rucker@bakernet.com

JENNIFER ANCONA SEMKO, born Baton Rouge, Louisiana, January 15, 1973; admitted to bar, 1998, Louisiana (Not admitted in District of Columbia). *Education:* Georgetown University (B.S.F.S., cum laude, 1995); Tulane University of Louisiana Law School (J.D., magna cum laude, 1998). Author: "The Price of Uniformity: Aasma and Third Party Rights of Direct Action in the Maritime Context," 21 Tulane Maritime Law Journal, 593, 1997. Law Clerk to Pascal F. Calogero, Jr., Chief Justice, Louisiana Supreme Court, 1998-1999. *Member:* Louisiana State and American (Member, Litigation Section, 1998—) Bar Associations. ***LANGUAGES:*** French. ***PRACTICE AREAS:*** Litigation; Arbitration and Dispute Resolution; Appellate Practice. ***Email:*** jennifer.a.semko@bakernet.com

NEIL K. SHAPIRO, born Philadelphia, Pennsylvania, January 22, 1960; admitted to bar, 1986, New York; 1987, District of Columbia. *Education:* Yale University (B.A., 1981); Stanford Graduate School of Business (M.B.A., 1985); Stanford University Law School (J.D., 1985). Policy Analyst, Office of Management and Budget, 1991-2001. ***PRACTICE AREAS:*** Litigation; Arbitration and Dispute Resolution; Criminal Law. ***Email:*** neil.k.shapiro@bakernet.com

ALISON STAFFORD, born Manchester, U.K., December 14, 1969; admitted to bar, 1998, United Kingdom (Not admitted in the United States). *Education:* Cambridge University (M.A. Hons (Oriental Studies), 1992); Hosei University, 1994; College of Law (CPE (Pass) and LPC (Distinction), 1996). Contributor to International Trade Aspects of Information Technology Law Chapter of Sweet & Maxwell's Encyclopedia of Information Technology Law (1999-2000). ***LANGUAGES:*** Japanese. ***PRACTICE AREAS:*** E-Commerce Law; EC Competition and Trade; EU Law (General); Trade (UK/EU/US); Trade Regulations and Customs Law. ***Email:*** alison.stafford@bakernet.com

RONALD DAVID TRICE, born Farmington Hills, Michigan, February 7, 1967; admitted to bar, 2001, District of Columbia; registered to practice before U.S. Patent and Trademark Office. *Education:* Michigan State University (B.S.E.E., 1990); Franklin Pierce Law Center (J.D., 1999). Patent Examiner, U.S. Patent and Trademark Office, 1990-1996. ***PRACTICE AREAS:*** Intellectual Property Law; Litigation. ***Email:*** ronald.d.trice@bakernet.com

ADAM C. UNDERWOOD, admitted to bar, 1999, Florida; registered to practice before U.S. Patent and Trademark Office (Not admitted in District of Columbia). *Education:* Florida International University (B.S.E.E., 1988); University of Florida (J.D., 1998). Recipient, Book Award, Trial Practice, Fall 1997. Delta Mu Omega; Omicron Delta Kappa. *Member:* The Florida Bar. ***PRACTICE AREAS:*** Intellectual Property. ***Email:*** adam.c.underwood@bakernet.com

STEPHEN H. WAGNER, born Chicago, Illinois, July 5, 1963; admitted to bar, 2000, Florida; 2001, District of Columbia. *Education:* University of Notre Dame (B.A., Economics, 1985; B.A., German, 1985); Georgetown University Law Center (J.D, 2000). ***LANGUAGES:*** German. ***PRACTICE AREAS:*** Corporate and Partnership Law; Mergers and Acquisitions; Derivatives/Financial Products; Corporate Financings (Public and Private); Major Projects. ***Email:*** stephen.h.wagner@bakernet.com

THOMAS EDWARD WILLIS, II, born 1972; admitted to bar, 1997, Virginia (Not admitted in District of Columbia). *Education:* University of Virginia (B.A., 1990); University of Oregon (J.D., 1997); Georgetown University Law Center (LL.M. in Taxation, with distinction, 1998). *Member:* Virginia State Bar (Member, Taxation Section); American Bar Association (Member, Taxation Section). ***LANGUAGES:*** French and Russian. ***PRACTICE AREAS:*** Litiga-

(This Listing Continued)

BAKER & McKENZIE, Washington—Continued

tion; Tax Planning and Advice (Corporate and International). ***Email:*** thomas.e.willis@bakernet.com

BAKER & MILLER PLLC

SUITE 1000, 915 FIFTEENTH STREET, N.W.

WASHINGTON, D.C. 20005-2318

Telephone: 202-637-9499

Facsimile: 202-637-9394

URL: http://www.bakerandmiller.com

Antitrust Counselling and Litigation, Government Investigations, Arbitration and Mediation, International Transactions and Disputes, Network Legal Problems, Electronic Banking Issues and Appeals.

DONALD I. BAKER, born Englewood, New Jersey, June 4, 1934; admitted to bar, 1963, Massachusetts; 1964, District of Columbia; 1970, U.S. Supreme Court. *Education:* Princeton University (A.B., 1957); Harvard University (LL.B., 1961); Cambridge University (M.A., 2000). Co-Author: with Ronald Brandel, "The Law of Electronic Funds Transfer Systems," (1980, 1988, 1996 and 1999). Co-Editor with J.W. Rowley, "International Mergers-The Antitrust Process," 1990, 1996 and 2000. Author: "Compulsory Access to Network Joint Ventures Under the Sherman Act: Rules or Roulette?" 1993, Utah L. Rev. 999. Trial Attorney, 1966-1971, Director of Policy Planning, 1971-1973, Deputy Assistant Attorney General for Regulation, International Trade and Appeals, 1973-1975, Assistant Attorney General, 1976-1977, Antitrust Division, U.S. Department of Justice. Professor of Law, 1975-1978 and Adjunct Professor of Law, 1978-1981, Cornell University. Advisor to Anti-Monopoly Committee of Ukraine, 1994-1995. Member, Center for Public Resources Panel of Distinguished Neutrals. Chairman, Banking Law Committee, Federal Bar Association, 1974-1975. Chairman, Antitrust and Corporate Law Committee, Business Law Section, American Bar Association, 1976-1981. *Member:* American (Member: Antitrust Section NAFTA Task Force, 1993-1994; Co-Chairman, International Antitrust Law Committee, ABA International Section, 1999—) and International (Secretary, Antitrust and Trade Committee, 1990-1993) Bar Associations; American Arbitration Association (Member, Panel of Arbitrators). Fellow, American Bar Foundation. ***Email:*** dbaker@bakerandmiller.com

W. TODD MILLER, born Evansville, Indiana, December 21, 1960; admitted to bar, 1986, Virginia; 1988, District of Columbia; 1992, U.S. Supreme Court. *Education:* University of Virginia (B.A., 1983); University of Michigan (J.D., 1986). Principal Author: United States chapter of "International Mergers: The Antitrust Process" (3rd ed., 2000). Adjunct Faculty, American University, Washington College of Law, International and Comparative Antitrust (1997—). *Member:* American (Member, Antitrust Section) and International Bar Associations. ***Email:*** tmiller@bakerandmiller.com

DEIRDRE L. HAY, born Melbourne, Australia, December 24, 1965; admitted to bar, 1990, Victoria, Australia; 1991, New South Wales, Australia; 1998, New York (Not admitted in District of Columbia). *Education:* University of Melbourne (LL.B., 1989); Cornell Law School Summer Program, Comparative and International Law, 1995. Donald McCredie Fellowship, 1996. Author: "A Lesson From the U.S. Hypothetical Monopolist About Market Definition: Timeframes and Thresholds and the QCMA Test," Australian Competition and Consumer Law Journal, November 1998; "Performers' Rights: The Right of Personality and the Possibility of a Proprietary Right," 6 Australian Intellectual Property Journal 92 (1995). ***Email:*** dhay@bakerandmiller.com

CHRISTINE J. SOMMER, born Naperville, Illinois, January 13, 1971; admitted to bar, 2000, New York (Not admitted in District of Columbia). *Education:* Creighton University (B.A., 1994; J.D., 1998); American University (L.L.M., 1999). ***PRACTICE AREAS:*** Antitrust; Litigation. ***Email:*** esommer@bakerandmiller.com

SPECIAL COUNSEL

ALICE G. GLASS, born Sanderson, Texas, June 8, 1955; admitted to bar, 1992, Texas; 1994, District of Columbia. *Education:* Sul Ross State University (B.S., 1979); University of Texas (J.D., 1992). ***Email:*** alice@an.hitchcock.org

BALCH & BINGHAM LLP

Established in 1922

1275 PENNSYLVANIA AVENUE, N.W., 10TH FLOOR

WASHINGTON, D.C. 20004

Telephone: 202-347-6000

Facsimile: 202-347-6001

URL: http://www.balch.com

Birmingham, Alabama Offices: 1710 Sixth Avenue North, 35203. Telephone: 205-251-8100. Facsimile: 205-226-8798. 1901 Sixth Avenue North, 35203. Telephone: 205-251-8100. Facsimile: 205-226-8799.

Montgomery, Alabama Office: The Winter Building, 2 Dexter Avenue, 36104. Telephone: 334-834-6500. Facsimile: 334-269-3115.

Huntsville, Alabama Office: 655 Gallatin Street, 35801. Telephone: 205-551-0171. Facsimile: 205-512-0119.

Gulfport, Mississippi Office: 1310 Twenty-Fifth Avenue. P.O. Box 130. Telephone: 228-864-9900. Fax: 228-864-8221.

Jackson, Mississippi Office: 200 North Congress Street, Suite 310. Telephone: 601-961-9900. Fax: 601-961-4466.

Hattiesburg, Mississippi Office: 119 Hardy Street. P.O. Box 707. Telephone: 601-544-1215. Fax: 601-582-8732.

Bay St. Louis, Mississippi Office: 841 Highway 90. Telephone: 228-466-9905. Fax: 228-467-1079.

General Practice, Corporation, Public Utilities, Banking, Public Finance, Taxation, Securities, Antitrust, Litigation, Labor and Employment, Probate, Real Estate, Insurance, Intellectual Property, Environmental, Bankruptcy, Legislative Practice, Mergers and Acquisitions, Health Care, International Business Transactions, Criminal, Education, Construction, Products Liability, Coal and Natural Gas, and Personal Injury Law. Trials in all Courts. Alternative Dispute Resolution.

COUNSEL

HALEY BARBOUR, born Yazoo City, Mississippi, October 22, 1947; admitted to bar, 1973, Mississippi (Not admitted in District of Columbia). *Education:* University of Mississippi (J.D., 1973). Phi Delta Phi; Omicron Delta Kappa. Member, Mississippi Law Journal, 1971-1973. Author: "Equal Protection in School Financing," Mississippi Law Journal, Vol. XLIII, No. 2, 1972; "Oil and Gas Well Operator's Liability to Lessor-Surface Owner for Slush Pit Overflow or Seepage," Mississippi Law Journal, Vol. XLIV, No. 5, 1973. *Member:* Yazoo County and American Bar Associations; Mississippi State Bar. (Also in Birmingham, Alabama Office).

LANNY GRIFFITH, born Akron, Ohio, August 13, 1951; admitted to bar, 1976, Mississippi (Not admitted in District of Columbia). *Education:* University of Mississippi (B.A., 1973; J.D., 1976). Omicron Delta Kappa (President). Southern Political Director, George Bush Presidential Campaign, 1988. Former Executive Director, Mississippi Republican Party. Special Assistant to the President, Intergovernmental Affairs, 1989-1991. U.S. Assistant Secretary of Education for Intergovernmental and Interagency Affairs, under President George Bush, 1991-1993. *Member:* The Mississippi Bar. (Also in Birmingham, Alabama Office).

EDWARD M. ROGERS, JR., born Birmingham, Alabama, November 22, 1958; admitted to bar, 1985, Alabama; 1987, District of Columbia. *Education:* University of Alabama (J.D., 1984). Deputy Assistant to the President and Executive Assistant to the Chief of Staff, The White House, 1989-1991. Deputy to Bush Campaign, Manager, Lee Atwater, 1987-1988. Special Assistant to the President for Political Affairs, The White House, 1985-1987. *Member:* American Bar Association; The District of Columbia Bar; Alabama State Bar. ***PRACTICE AREAS:*** Government Law; Legislative Practice.

RESIDENT MEMBERS OF FIRM

FREDERICK R. EAMES, born Warren, Pennsylvania, November 13, 1964; admitted to bar, 1994, Pennsylvania (Not admitted in District of Columbia). *Education:* Allegheny College (B.A., 1986); George Washington University (J.D., 1994). Author: "Reconstruction of Federalism: A Constitutional Amendment to Prohibit Unfunded Mandates," Harvard Journal on Legislation, Vol. 31, No. 2, Summer, 1994. Counsel, House Committee on Commerce, 1995-1998. ***PRACTICE AREAS:*** Legislative Practice; Energy; Environmental. ***Email:*** feames@balch.com

PATRICK J. McCORMICK, III, born Philadelphia, Pennsylvania, May 9, 1956; admitted to bar, 1985, Maryland and District of Columbia. *Education:* Wheeling College (B.A., 1977); Catholic University of America, Columbus School of Law (J.D., 1984). Deputy Assistant General Counsel, Electric Rates and Corporate Regulation, Federal Energy Regulatory Commission, 1989-1991. *Member:* The District of Columbia Bar; American Bar Association. ***PRACTICE AREAS:*** Public Utility Law; Environmental Law; Legislative Practice. ***Email:*** pmccormi@balch.com

BARBARA K. OLSON, born Houston, Texas, December 27, 1955; admitted to bar, 1989, Maryland; 1993, U.S. Court of Appeals for the District of

(This Listing Continued)

Columbia Circuit and U.S. Supreme Court; 1995, U.S. Court of Appeals, Fifth and Second Circuits (Not admitted in District of Columbia). *Education:* University of St. Thomas (B.A., 1978); Benjamin N. Cardozo School of Law (J.D., 1989). Author: "Legislation by Litigation," Washington Times. Member, Board of Directors, U.S. Chamber Institute for Legal Reform. Member, Advisory Board: Independent Women's Forum; Washington Legal Foundation. Member, Federalist Society Administrative Law Practice Group, 1996—. *Member:* American Bar Association (Member, Administrative Law Section). ***PRACTICE AREAS:*** Legislative Practice; Public Policy Law; Litigation; Regulatory. ***Email:*** bolson@balch.com

RESIDENT ASSOCIATE

KRISTI L. REMINGTON, born Allentown, Pennsylvania, September 20, 1970; admitted to bar, 1995, Maryland (Not admitted in District of Columbia). *Education:* Denison University (B.A., 1992); American University (J.D., 1995). *Member:* Maryland State Bar Association. ***LANGUAGES:*** Spanish. ***PRACTICE AREAS:*** Legislative Practice; Energy. ***Email:*** kremington@balch.com

COUNSEL FOR: Alabama Power Co.; Blue Cross and Blue Shield of Alabama; Brasfield & Gorrie, Inc.; Compass Bank; Compass Bancshares, Inc.; Harbert Corp.; Intergraph Corp.; Kimberly-Clark Corp.; Sears Roebuck and Co.; Southern Company Services, Inc.; Southern Nuclear Operating Co.; Southern Research Institute; Vesta Insurance Group, Inc.; AT&T Communications, Inc.; Auburn University; Alabama Bankers Assn.; Alabama Housing Finance Authority; Alabama River Pulp Co., Inc.; Amoco Corp.; Beneficial National Bank; Birmingham Budweiser Distributing Co., Inc.; The Boeing Co.; Citicorp Mortgage, Inc.; Colonial Properties, Inc.; Dan River, Inc.; Digital Equipment Corp.; The Equitable Life Assurance Society of the United States; First American Title Insurance Co.; Fluor Daniel, Inc.; Franklin Life Insurance Co.; General Electric Co.; Hartford Insurance Co.; James River Corp.; Jenkins Brick Co.; Lloyds, London; National Energy Partners; Texaco Inc.; The Advertiser Company (Montgomery Advertiser and Alabama Journal); United HealthCare South, Inc.

(For complete biographical data on all personnel, see Professional Biographies at Birmingham, Alabama)

BALL JANIK LLP

1455 F STREET, N.W., SUITE 225
WASHINGTON, D.C. 20005-1004
Telephone: 202-638-3307
Telecopy: 202-783-6947
Email: info@balljanik.com
URL: http://www.balljanik.com

Portland, Oregon Office: One Main Place, 101 S.W. Main Street, Suite 1100, 97204-3219. Telephone: 503-228-2525. Telecopy: 503-295-1058.

Bend, Oregon Office: 15 S.W. Colorado Avenue, Building 2, Suite K, 97702. Telephone: 541-617-1309. Telecopy: 541-617-8824.

Government Affairs, Legislative and Administrative Lobbying, Administrative Law, Federal Regulatory and Transportation Law.

MEMBERS OF FIRM

JAMES A. BEALL, born Corvallis, Oregon, January 30, 1950; admitted to bar, 1976, Oregon; 1981, District of Columbia. *Education:* Oregon State University (B.A., 1972); University of Oregon (J.D., 1976); Georgetown University (M.T.L., 1981). Member, Board of Editors, Oregon Law Review, 1975-1976. Legislative Coordinator to Congressman Al Ullman, 1977-1978. Professional Staff, House Committee on Ways and Means, 1979-1980. *Member:* Oregon State Bar; The District of Columbia Bar; American Bar Association (Member, Section on Taxation). (Also at Portland, Oregon Office). ***PRACTICE AREAS:*** Government Affairs; Legislative Lobbying; Administrative Lobbying Law. ***Email:*** jbeall@balljanik.com

ROBERT G. HAYES, born Boston, Massachusetts, February 8, 1946; admitted to bar, 1974, Vermont; 1985, District of Columbia. *Education:* Boston University (B.S., 1968); Catholic University (J.D., 1974). *Member:* Vermont Bar Association; The District of Columbia Bar. ***PRACTICE AREAS:*** Government Relations Law; International Trade Law; Natural Resources. ***Email:*** rhayes@balljanik.com

IRENE L. RINGWOOD, born Spokane, Washington, April 15, 1958; admitted to bar, 1984, Washington; 1990, District of Columbia. *Education:* Washington State University (B.A., cum laude, 1980); Gonzaga University (J.D., cum laude, 1984). *Member:* Washington State and American Bar Associations; The District of Columbia Bar. ***PRACTICE AREAS:*** Government Relations Law; International Trade Law. ***Email:*** iringwood@balljanik.com

OF COUNSEL

LOUIS E. GITOMER, born Baltimore, Maryland, September 23, 1951; admitted to bar, 1976, Maryland (Not admitted in District of Columbia). *Education:* University of Baltimore (B.S., summa cum laude, 1973; J.D., 1976). Deputy Director, Interstate Commerce Commission: Section of Finance, 1981-1982; Rail Section, 1982-1986; Motor Section, 1986-1987. *Member:* Federal

(This Listing Continued)

and American (Member, Sections on Antitrust and Administrative Law) Bar Associations; Association of Transportation Practitioners. ***PRACTICE AREAS:*** Transportation Law. ***Email:*** lgitomer@balljanik.com

JAY S. JOHNSON, born Waterloo, Iowa, October 22, 1943; admitted to bar, 1968, Oregon; 1973, U.S. Supreme Court (Not admitted in District of Columbia). *Education:* University of Michigan (B.A., with honors in economics, 1965); Stanford University Law School (J.D., 1968); George Washington University (M.S., 1974). National Oceanic and Atmospheric Administration (NOAA), United States Department of Commerce: Deputy General Counsel, 1988-2000, Assistant General Counsel for Fisheries, 1979-1988, Assistant General Counsel for Administration, 1976-1979. *Member:* Oregon State Bar. ***PRACTICE AREAS:*** Natural Resources; Administrative Law. ***Email:*** jjohnson@balljanik.com

KARL MORELL, born Geisingen, Germany, December 5, 1948; admitted to bar, 1976, Maryland (Not admitted in District of Columbia). *Education:* American University (B.S., 1971); Loyola University School of Law (J.D., 1976). Member, Loyola Law Review, 1975-1976. Chief of Staff to Chairman, Interstate Commerce Commission, 1984-1985. *Member:* Maryland State Bar Association; Association of Transportation Law, Logistics and Policy. ***PRACTICE AREAS:*** Transportation Law; Administrative Law; Commercial Transactions; Government Affairs. ***Email:*** kmorell@balljanik.com

GOVERNMENT RELATIONS SPECIALISTS

M. VICTORIA CRAM, born Mankato, Minnesota, August 3, 1953. *Education:* Carleton University (B.A., English Lit., History, 1975; M.A. English Lit., 1978). Lobbyist,: City of Portland, Oregon; City of Las Vegas, Nevada; City of Modesto, California; City of Bellevue, Washington; City of Whittier, California; City of Newport Beach, California; City of Spokane, Washington, 1983—. Washington Correspondent, Fenwick, Davis & West, 1985-1988. Assistant City Representative, National Center for Municipal Development, 1981-1983. Democratic Study Group, 1979-1981. Staff Assistant, Congressman John F. Seiberling, 1979. ***LANGUAGES:*** French. ***PRACTICE AREAS:*** Government Relations; Specializing in Urban, Tax and Appropriations Issues. ***Email:*** vcram@balljanik.com

MICHELLE GIGUERE, born Whittier, California, August 8, 1956. *Education:* Linfield College (1978). Legislative Director, Congressman Les AuCoin, 1979-1988. (Also at Portland, Oregon Office). ***PRACTICE AREAS:*** Government Relations; Specializing in Federal Legislative Appropriations and Authorization Issues. ***Email:*** mgiguere@balljanik.com

HAL D. HIEMSTRA, born Ontario, Oregon, December 13, 1953. *Education:* Lewis & Clark College (B.S., Political Science, 1976); University of Oregon (M.A., Urban and Regional Planning, 1979). Vice-President for National Policy, The Rails-to-Trails Conservancy, Washington, D.C., October 1991-August 1998. Member, Surface Transportation Policy Project Steering Committee, 1991-1998. Legislative Director, Scenic America, 1988-1991; President, American Land Resources Association, 1986-1988; Director, National Association of State Departments of Agriculture Research Foundation, 1981-1986; Consultant, Council on Environmental Quality, 1979-1981. ***PRACTICE AREAS:*** Government Relations; Specializing in Transportation Issues. ***Email:*** hhiemstra@balljanik.com

DANIEL M. JAMES, born Missoula, Montana, June 15, 1964. *Education:* Pacific University (B.A., 1987). Legislative Staff, Congressman Les AuCoin, Washington, D.C., 1986-1989. Director of Alumni Relations, Pacific University, 1989-1991. Federal Affairs Representative, Pacific Northwest Waterways Association, Vancouver, Washington, 1992-2000. (Also at Portland, Oregon Office). ***PRACTICE AREAS:*** Government Relations; Specializing in Federal Legislative Appropriations and Authorizations Issues. ***Email:*** djames@balljanik.com

ERIC M. MONDERO, born San Francisco, California, November 6, 1968. *Education:* San Diego State University (B.A., Political Science, 1993). Chief of Staff, Associate Staff to the House Appropriations Committee, and Legislative Director, Congressman Ron Packard, 1993-2000. Staff Assistant, U.S. Senator John Seymour, 1992. ***PRACTICE AREAS:*** Government Relations; Specializing in Federal Legislative Appropriations and Authorization Issues. ***Email:*** emondero@balljanik.com

M. RICHARDSON NOLAN, born Concord, Massachusetts, August 2, 1967. *Education:* Bates College, Lewiston, Maine (B.A., Economics, 1990). Economic Analyst, U.S. Chamber of Commerce, Washington, D.C., 1990-1992. Economist, Republican National Committee, Washington, D.C., 1992. Legislative Aide, Congressman Joe Barton, Washington, D.C., 1993. Senior Analyst, National Republican Senatorial Committee, Washington, D.C., 1993-1995. Legislative Director, Congressman Wally Herger, Washington, D.C., 1995-1998. Director, Congressional Affairs, American Forest and Paper Association, Washington, D.C., 1998-2001. ***PRACTICE AREAS:*** Federal Government Relations; Specializing in Natural Resources, Environment, Energy, Appropriations and Taxation. ***Email:*** rnolan@balljanik.com

PATRICIA C. WILSON, born Stambaugh, Michigan, January 12, 1948. *Education:* University of Puget Sound (M.B.A., 1972). Paralegal: Garvey, Schu-

(This Listing Continued)

BALL JANIK LLP, Washington—Continued

bert & Barer, 1980-1988; U.S. Interstate Commerce Commission, 1977-1980. Editorial Assistant, Traffic World, 1974-1977. ***PRACTICE AREAS:*** Government Relations. ***Email:*** pwilson@balljanik.com

(For Complete Biographical Data on Personnel at Portland, and Bend, Oregon, see Professional Biographies at those locations)

BALLARD SPAHR ANDREWS & INGERSOLL, LLP

Established in 1883

SUITE 1000 SOUTH, 601 13TH STREET, N.W.
WASHINGTON, D.C. 20005-3807
Telephone: 202-661-2200
Fax: 202-661-2299
URL: http://www.ballardspahr.com

REVISERS OF THE PENNSYLVANIA LAW DIGEST FOR THIS DIRECTORY.

Baltimore, Maryland Office: 300 East Lombard Street, 19th Floor. Telephone: 410-528-5600. Fax: 410-528-5650.

Camden, New Jersey Office: 800 Hudson Square, 5th Floor. Telephone: 856-541-5577. Fax: 856-541-8772.

Denver, Colorado Office: Seventeenth Street Plaza Building, Suite 2300, 1225 17th Street. Telephone: 303-292-2400. Fax: 303-296-3956.

Philadelphia, Pennsylvania Office: 1735 Market Street, 51st Floor. Telephone: 215-665-8500. Fax: 215-834-8999.

Salt Lake City, Utah Office: 201 South Main Street, Suite 600. Telephone: 801-531-3000. Fax: 801-531-3001.

Voorhees, New Jersey Office: Suite 500, Plaza 1000, Main Street. Telephone: 856-761-3400. Fax: 856-761-1020.

General Practice.

NANCY V. ALQUIST, born Philadelphia, Pennsylvania, July 16, 1953; admitted to bar, 1978, Pennsylvania; 1988, Illinois; 1992, Maryland (Not admitted in District of Columbia). *Education:* University of Pennsylvania (B.A., cum laude, 1975); Temple University (J.D., 1978). Co-Editor: Bankruptcy Law for Lenders, Executive Enterprises Publications, 1989. Author: *Bankruptcy Law and The Creditor,* Professional Education Systems, Inc., 1980. Co-Author, Contributor: "Defaults, Workouts and Bankruptcy," Commercial Leases: Selected Issues in Drafting and Negotiating in Troubled Times (ALI-ABA, 1992); "Confirmation of Competing Chapter 11 Plans," National Conference of Bankruptcy Judges, 1987. Author: "Confirming a Plan," *Litigation in Bankruptcy,* Chicago Bar Association, 1988; "Creditors' Attorney's Overview," *The Nuts & Bolts of Bankruptcy Practice,* Pennsylvania Bar Association, 1982. Contributing Author and Lecturer: "The New Bankruptcy Act-An Update," Villanova University, 1980. Lecturer: Pennsylvania Collection Law-Bankruptcy Aspects, Sponsored by Professional Education Systems, Inc., 1981; Course Planner: Creditor's Perspective, "1984 Bankruptcy Amendments," Villanova University, 1984. *Member:* American Bar Association (Member, Business Bankruptcy Committee; Member, Programs and Publications Subcommittee). ***PRACTICE AREAS:*** Bankruptcy Law; Creditors Rights Law; Commercial Law; Debtor and Creditor; Litigation. ***Email:*** alquist@ballardspahr.com

FREDERIC L. BALLARD, JR., born Philadelphia, Pennsylvania, September 12, 1941; admitted to bar, 1966, Pennsylvania; 1971, U.S. Tax Court; 1978, District of Columbia. *Education:* Harvard University (A.B., 1963; LL.B., 1966). Author: "ABCs of Arbitrage," 1998. *Member:* American Bar Association (Vice Chair, Section of Taxation, 1994-1997); National Association of Bond Lawyers; American College of Tax Counsel (Secretary/Treasurer, 2000—); American College of Bond Counsel. (Also at Philadelphia, Pennsylvania Office). ***PRACTICE AREAS:*** Finance; Health Care; Housing; Municipal Law; Taxation. ***Email:*** flb@ballardspahr.com

JEFFREY S. BALLARD, born Birmingham, Alabama, June 23, 1962; admitted to bar, 1990, Maryland and District of Columbia. *Education:* Stanford University (B.A., with distinction, 1984); George Washington University (J.D., 1990). Phi Beta Kappa. Member, George Washington Law Review, 1988-1990. ***PRACTICE AREAS:*** Finance; Corporate Law; Securities. ***Email:*** ballardj@ballardspahr.com

PAUL K. CASEY, born Northbridge, Massachusetts, April 27, 1948; admitted to bar, 1977, Maryland; 1989, District of Columbia. *Education:* St. Anselm College (A.B., summa cum laude, 1970); University of Virginia (M.A., 1973; J.D., 1977). Delta Sigma Rho - Tau Kappa Alpha. Hardy C. Dillard Legal Writing Fellow, University of Virginia, 1975-1977. Author, "Real Hope at HUD," Journal of Affordable Housing & Community Development Law, 1997. Co-Author: "Four Percent Tax Credits and Public Housing Development: Collateralizing Tax-Exempt Bonds with Federal Capital Funds," Journal of Affordable Housing and Community Development Law, 1999; "Public Housing, Private Development: The Lawyer's Role," Probate & Property, 1997; "Intercreditor Agreements in Affordable Housing Transactions," Probate & Property, 1996. Lecturer, Maryland Institute for Continuing Professional Education of Lawyers, 1982-1987. Assistant Attorney General, State of Maryland, 1983-1987. Counsel, Maryland Community Development Administration, 1983-1984. Principal Counsel, Maryland Department of Economic and Community Development, 1985-1987. Member, Maryland Housing Policy Commission, 1987-1994. Trustee, Maryland Affordable Housing Trust, 1992—. Chair, Committee on HUD Programs and Procedures, ABA Section of Real Property, Probate and Trust Law, 1994-1996. Group Chair, Community Development and Affordable Housing Committees, ABA Section of Real Property, Probate and Trust Law, 1996-2000. Member, Governing Committee, ABA Forum on Affordable Housing and Community Development Law, 1998—. *Member:* The District of Columbia Bar; Maryland State and American (Member, Real Property, Probate and Trusts Section) Bar Associations. ***PRACTICE AREAS:*** Housing and Community Development Law; Affordable Housing; Public Housing; Real Estate; Public Finance. ***Email:*** casey@ballardspahr.com

N. BETH EMERY, born Shawnee, Oklahoma, July 9, 1952; admitted to bar, 1977, Oklahoma (inactive); 1981, District of Columbia. *Education:* University of Oklahoma (B.A., with highest honors, 1974); Harvard University (J.D., 1977). Phi Beta Kappa. *Member:* Federal Energy and American (Member, Sections on: Public Utility; Communications & Transportation Law; Environment, Energy and Resources) Bar Associations; The District of Columbia Bar. ***PRACTICE AREAS:*** Energy Finance; Energy Project Development; Business Law; Finance. ***Email:*** bemery@ballardspahr.com

JOSEPH A. FANONE, born Sharon, Pennsylvania, April 14, 1949; admitted to bar, 1974, Pennsylvania; 1980, District of Columbia. *Education:* Georgetown University (A.B., 1971; J.D., 1974). Phi Beta Kappa; Pi Sigma Alpha. Assistant Attorney General, Pennsylvania Department of Justice, 1974-1977. *Member:* The District of Columbia Bar; American Bar Association; National Association of Bond Lawyers. ***Email:*** fanone@ballardspahr.com

MARY JO GEORGE, born Prince Edward Island, Canada, August 2, 1960; admitted to bar, 1985, Maryland (Not admitted in District of Columbia). *Education:* Georgetown University (A.B., magna cum laude, 1982); George Washington University (J.D., with honors, 1985). Phi Beta Kappa. *Member:* Maryland State and American Bar Associations. ***PRACTICE AREAS:*** Real Estate; Housing. ***Email:*** george@ballardspahr.com

W. KIMBALL GRIFFITH, born Richmond, Virginia, February 7, 1949; admitted to bar, 1974, Georgia; 1986, District of Columbia. *Education:* Davidson College (B.A., cum laude, 1971); University of North Carolina (J.D., 1974). Phi Beta Kappa; Omicron Delta Kappa. Administrative Editor, North Carolina Law Review. ***PRACTICE AREAS:*** Credit Enhancement; Structured Finance; Tax Exempt Bonds; Tax Exempt Finance. ***Email:*** griffithk@ballardspahr.com

CHARLES S. HENCK, born Knoxville, Tennessee, April 28, 1947; admitted to bar, 1975, Georgia; 1979, U.S. Tax Court; 1980, District of Columbia. *Education:* Emory University (B.A., 1969; J.D., 1975); Georgetown University (LL.M., Tax, 1979). Order of the Coif; Phi Delta Phi. *Member:* District of Columbia Bar; State Bar of Georgia; American Bar Association; American College of Bond Counsel; National Association of Bond Lawyers. ***PRACTICE AREAS:*** Taxation; Project Finance; Tax Exempt Finance. ***Email:*** henck@ballardspahr.com

THOMAS L. HOWARD, born Knoxville, Tennessee, September 14, 1946; admitted to bar, 1971, Tennessee; 1974, U.S. Claims Court; 1975, U.S. Tax Court; 1979, District of Columbia. *Education:* Washington & Lee University (B.A., 1968); Vanderbilt University (J.D., 1971); Georgetown University (LL.M., Taxation, 1975). Member, Board of Directors: Homer Hoyt Institute; StandardsWork. *Member:* The District of Columbia Bar; American Bar Association (Member, Closely Held Businesses Committee and Partnership Committee, Tax Section). ***PRACTICE AREAS:*** Tax Law. ***Email:*** howardt@ballardspahr.com

F. JOSEPH NEALON, born Scranton, Pennsylvania, March 28, 1949; admitted to bar, 1974, Pennsylvania; 1975, District of Columbia. *Education:* University of Scranton and Georgetown University (A.B., 1971); Georgetown University (J.D., 1974). Editor, Georgetown University Law Journal, 1973-1974. *Member:* The District of Columbia Bar; Pennsylvania and American Bar Associations. ***PRACTICE AREAS:*** Commercial Law; Insurance Defense; Labor and Employment; Litigation; Fidelity and Surety. ***Email:*** nealon@ballardspahr.com

CONSTANTINOS G. PANAGOPOULOS, born Stratford, Ontario, November 18, 1966; admitted to bar, 1988, Virginia; 1994, Maryland and U.S. District Court, District of Maryland; 1998, District of Columbia; U.S. Court of Appeals, Fourth Circuit. *Education:* Baylor University (B.A., 1988); George Washington University National Law Center (J.D., with honors, 1991). Senior Counsel, American Red Cross, 1997-1998. *Member:* Virginia State Bar; Maryland State and American Bar Associations. ***PRACTICE AREAS:*** Commercial Litigation; Employment Law; Insurance Defense; Fidelity and Surety. ***Email:*** panagopoulos@ballardspahr.com

PERRY D. ROBINSON, born Washington, D.C., July 20, 1953; admitted to bar, 1987, Maryland; 1995, District of Columbia; U.S. Court of Appeals, Dis-

(This Listing Continued)

trict of Columbia Circuit. *Education:* Virginia Polytechnic Institute and State University (B.S., 1975); Rutgers University (M.S., 1981); University of Baltimore (J.D., 1986). *Member:* Maryland State and American Bar Associations; The District of Columbia Bar. ***PRACTICE AREAS:*** Business Law; Energy; Project Finance. ***Email:*** robinsonp@ballardspahr.com

LINDA B. SCHAKEL, born Newton, Iowa, September 13, 1948; admitted to bar, 1986, Maryland; 1989, District of Columbia. *Education:* Iowa State University (B.S., with honors and distinction, 1970); University of South Florida (M.A., 1976; Ph.D., 1984); Georgetown University (J.D., cum laude, 1986). Attorney Advisor, Office of Tax Policy, U.S. Department of the Treasury, 1995-1997. *Member:* Maryland State and American Bar Associations; The District of Columbia Bar; National Association of Bond Lawyers. ***PRACTICE AREAS:*** Municipal Bonds Taxation; Project Finance. ***Email:*** schakel@ballardspahr.com

HOWARD H. SHAFFERMAN, born Washington, D.C., August 21, 1954; admitted to bar, 1978, District of Columbia. *Education:* Princeton University (A.B., 1975); University of Virginia (J.D., 1978). Author: Solicitor's Opinion M-36964, 96 Interior Dec. 439, 1989; "Federal Externality Initiatives," 14 Energy Law Journal 189, 1993; "Allowance Trading: Jurisdictional Issues and Wholesale Rate Making Consideration," Clean Air Act Implementation Proceedings, National Regulatory Research Institute, 1993. Deputy Solicitor, 1987-1989 and Acting Solicitor, 1989-1990, U.S. Department of the Interior. Chief of Staff and Counselor, Federal Energy Regulatory Commission, 1990-1993. Member, U.S. Delegation, Energy Consultative Mechanism, U.S.-Canada Free Trade Agreement, 1992. Member, Advisory Committee, Gas Industry Standards Board. *Member:* American Bar Association; District of Columbia Bar; Energy Bar Association. ***PRACTICE AREAS:*** Energy Regulation; Project Finance; Natural Resources; Cogeneration; Electric Power; Electric Power Joint Ventures; Energy Acquisitions; Energy Contracts; Energy Deregulation; Energy Finance; Energy Marketing; Energy Project Development; Federal Energy Regulation; Hydroelectricity; Hydroelectricity Licensing; Independent Power; Power Pooling Contracts; Renewable Energy; Wholesale Power Contracts; Electric Utilities; Electric Utility Finance; Electric Utility Regulation; Gas Utilities; Gas Utility Finance; Gas Utility Regulation; Public Utility Finance; Public Utility Law; Public Utility Rates; Public Utility Regulation; Utility Acquisitions; Utility Contracts; Utility Finance; Utility Mergers; Utility Rates; Utility Regulation. ***Email:*** hhs@ballardspahr.com

DANIEL F. STENGER, born Hammond, Indiana, April 28, 1955; admitted to bar, 1980, District of Columbia. *Education:* Purdue University (B.S., magna cum laude, 1977); George Washington University (J.D., with high honors, 1980). Order of the Coif. Co-Author, "Divided Authority: Federal vs. State Policy Roles in Decommissioning Economics," 12 The Energy Journal 73 (1991). Attorney Advisor, Administrative Law Judges, Federal Energy Regulatory Commission, 1980-1981. *Member:* The District of Columbia Bar; American Bar Association. ***PRACTICE AREAS:*** Business Law; Energy; Project Finance. ***Email:*** stengerd@ballardspahr.com

MARGO BEVIER STERN, born Ft. Wayne, Indiana; admitted to bar, 1979, District of Columbia; 1980, U.S. Claims Court. *Education:* The Principia College (B.A., 1965); Stanford University (M.A., 1971); Washington College of Law (J.D., 1979). Executive Editor, American University Law Review. *Member:* National Association of Bond Lawyers. ***PRACTICE AREAS:*** Municipal Finance; Real Estate; Housing Law; Affordable Housing; Low Income Housing; Multi-Family Housing and Assisted Living; Senior Citizen Housing; Public Finance; Tax Exempt Bonds; Real Estate Finance. ***Email:*** sternm@ballardspahr.com

ALLAN R. WINN, born Abington, Pennsylvania, April 11, 1944; admitted to bar, 1969, New York; 1974, District of Columbia. *Education:* University of Rochester (A.B., 1966); Cornell University (J.D., 1969). *Member:* The District of Columbia Bar; American Bar Association. ***PRACTICE AREAS:*** Real Estate; Finance Law; Housing and Urban Development Law; Commercial Real Estate; Commercial Real Estate Finance; Finance; Commercial Finance; Debt Finance; Equity Finance; Secured Finance; Structured Finance; Affordable Housing; Apartment Projects; Housing Development; Housing Finance; Low Income Housing; Multi-Family Housing; Subsidized Housing; Land Acquisitions; Land Sales; Real Estate Acquisitions; Real Estate Banking Law; Real Estate Finance; Real Estate Investment; Real Estate Secured Lending; Real Estate Syndication; Real Estate Title; Real Estate Workouts; Real Property Finance. ***Email:*** winn@ballardspahr.com

KELLY MITCHELL WRENN, born Royal Oak, Michigan, August 31, 1958; admitted to bar, 1984, Texas; 1990, District of Columbia; 1991, Virginia. *Education:* Wake Forest University (B.A., with honors, 1980); Washington & Lee University (J.D., 1984). Delta Phi Alpha; Phi Alpha Theta; Omicron Delta Kappa; Phi Alpha Delta. *Member:* State Bar of Texas; District of Columbia Bar; Virginia State Bar; American Bar Association. ***PRACTICE AREAS:*** Business Law; Finance; Health Care Finance; Real Estate; Debtor and Creditor. ***Email:*** wrenn@ballardspahr.com

(This Listing Continued)

OF COUNSEL

KATHERINE L. BISHOP, born Baltimore, Maryland, May 28, 1952; admitted to bar, 1977, Maryland; 1998, Massachusetts; 2001, District of Columbia. *Education:* Goucher College and Duke University (B.S.B.A., cum laude, 1974); Washington and Lee University School of Law (J.D., Burks Scholar, 1977). Contributor, Washington and Lee University Law Review, 1977. Member, 1989-1991 and Chairman, 1991-1992, Review Board, Maryland Attorney Grievance Commission. ***PRACTICE AREAS:*** Health Care Finance; Commercial Real Estate; Business Finance; Secured Transactions; Commercial Real Estate Finance; Asset Based Finance; Secured Finance; Structured Finance; Commercial Mortgages; Mortgage Finance; Mortgage Refinancing; Mortgage Securitization; Real Estate Finance; Real Estate Secured Lending; Real Property Finance. ***Email:*** bishop@ballardspahr.com

JAMES P. COOKE, born Niskayuna, New York, November 16, 1951; admitted to bar, 1981, Texas; 1993, District of Columbia. *Education:* Philadelphia College of Bible (B.S., with honors, 1973); Dallas Theological Seminary (Th.M., with honors, 1977); Southern Methodist University (J.D., cum laude, 1981). Order of the Coif. Executive Editor, Southwestern Law Journal, 1980-1981. Author: "Equity Participations in Texas - A Lender's Dream or a Usurious Nightmare?" 34 Southwestern Law Journal 877. *Member:* State Bar of Texas; District of Columbia Bar; American Bar Association (Member, Real Property, Probate and Trust Law Section). ***PRACTICE AREAS:*** Real Estate Law; Banking Law. ***Email:*** cooke@ballardspahr.com

EILEEN M. GREENBAUM, born New York, New York, 1951; admitted to bar, 1976, New York; 1991, District of Columbia. *Education:* Brandeis University (B.A., cum laude, 1972); State University of New York at Buffalo (J.D., 1975). *Member:* American Bar Association. ***PRACTICE AREAS:*** Commercial Real Estate; Affordable Housing; Commercial Conveyancing; Commercial Real Estate Acquisitions; Commercial Real Estate Development; Commercial Real Estate Finance; Commercial Real Estate Syndication; Commercial Real Estate Workouts; Shopping Center Acquisitions; Shopping Center Development; Housing Law; Housing Development; Housing Finance; Low Income Housing; Multi-Family Housing; Public Housing; Subsidized Housing; Mortgages; Commercial Mortgages; Mortgage Finance; Mortgage Workouts; Public Finance; Community Development; Economic Development; Housing and Urban Development; Public-Private Development; Real Estate; Conveyancing; Land Acquisitions; Land Sales; Real Estate Acquisitions; Real Estate Contracts; Real Estate Development; Real Estate Finance; Real Estate Joint Ventures; Real Estate Partnerships; Real Estate Restructuring; Real Estate Sales; Real Estate Secured Lending; Real Estate Workouts; Real Property Acquisitions; Real Property Development; Real Property Finance. ***Email:*** greenbaum@ballardspahr.com

CYNTHIA M. HAJOST, admitted to bar, 1985, District of Columbia. *Education:* University of Cincinnati (B.A., summa cum laude, 1982); George Washington University (J.D., with honors, 1985). Member, Moot Court Board. Editor, Moot Court National Competition Directory. *Member:* The District of Columbia Bar. ***PRACTICE AREAS:*** Real Estate Finance; Housing Law. ***Email:*** matthewsc@ballardspahr.com

B. CHERYL TERIO, born Washington, D.C., March 3, 1944; admitted to bar, 1984, Virginia; 1999, District of Columbia. *Education:* University of Maryland (B.A., 1966); George Mason School of Law (J.D., 1984). Division 2 Chair, ABA Forum on the Construction Industry, 1995-1997. ***PRACTICE AREAS:*** Construction Contracts; Construction and Design Law. ***Email:*** terio@ballardspahr.com

S. ELIZABETH WEAVER, born Toledo, Ohio, April 8, 1954; admitted to bar, 1979, Maryland; 1982, District of Columbia. *Education:* Swarthmore College (A.B., 1976); University of Toledo College of Law (J.D., cum laude, 1979); University of Virginia (Ph.D., 1997). Phi Kappa Phi. Executive Editor, University of Toledo Law Review, 1978-1979. *Member:* The District of Columbia Bar; Maryland State Bar Association. ***PRACTICE AREAS:*** Real Estate Development Law; Financing Law; Housing and Urban Development Law. ***Email:*** weaver@ballardspahr.com

---

W. LANGHORNE AMBROSE, born Norfolk, Virginia, May 29, 1970; admitted to bar, 1998, Virginia; 1999, District of Columbia. *Education:* University of Virginia (B.S., 1992); University of Richmond (J.D., cum laude, 1997). Associate Editor, University of Richmond Law Review, 1996-1997. ***PRACTICE AREAS:*** Real Estate Finance; Health Care Finance. ***Email:*** ambrosel@ballardspahr.com

RHONDA D. BOND-COLLINS, born Washington, D.C., August 1, 1960; admitted to bar, 1997, Maryland, U.S. District Court, District of Maryland and U.S. Court of Appeals, Fourth Circuit; 1998, District of Columbia; 2001, Virginia. *Education:* University of Maryland (B.S., 1991); Washington College of Law of American University (J.D., 1996). *Member:* Maryland State and American Bar Associations; Virginia State Bar. ***PRACTICE AREAS:*** Public Finance; Real Estate. ***Email:*** bondcollinsr@ballardspahr.com

(This Listing Continued)

BALLARD SPAHR ANDREWS & INGERSOLL, LLP, Washington—Continued

MARINA K. BOWSHER, born Kiev, Ukraine, October 20, 1971; admitted to bar, 1998, Illinois; 1999, District of Columbia and Maryland and U.S. District Court, Northern District of Illinois; 2000, U.S. District Court, District of Maryland and U.S. District Court, District of Columbia. *Education:* Rutgers College (B.A., with highest honors, 1994); Northwestern University (J.D., 1998). *Member:* Maryland State and American Bar Associations; The District of Columbia Bar. ***LANGUAGES:*** Russian. ***PRACTICE AREAS:*** Litigation. ***Email:*** kravets@ballardspahr.com

AMY E. CAMPBELL, born Omaha, Nebraska, August 23, 1965; admitted to bar, 1994, Arizona; 1999, Colorado; 2001, District of Columbia. *Education:* University of Kansas (B.A., 1987); William Mitchell College of Law (J.D., cum laude, 1994). Member, William Mitchell College of Law, Law Review. *Member:* State Bar of Arizona; The Colorado Bar Association; American Bar Association; The District of Columbia Bar. ***PRACTICE AREAS:*** Corporate Law; Public Securitization Finance; Securities. ***Email:*** campbella@ballardspahr.com

GWYNNE W. GUZZEAU, born Springfield, Massachusetts, October 14, 1966; admitted to bar, 1999, Virginia (Not admitted in District of Columbia). *Education:* Wellesley College (B.A., cum laude, 1989); Wheelock College (M.S., 1993); Georgetown University (J.D., 1999). Recipient, Dean's Certificate, Georgetown University Law Center. Member, Georgetown International Environmental Law Review. *Member:* Virginia State Bar; American Bar Association; Commercial Real Estate Women. ***PRACTICE AREAS:*** Real Estate Finance. ***Email:*** guzzeaug@ballardspahr.com

STEVE N. ISSER, born Philadelphia, Pennsylvania, 1955; admitted to bar, 2000, District of Columbia. *Education:* University of Pennsylvania (B.A., 1977; M.S., 1980); University of Texas at Austin (Ph.D., 1989; J.D., 1997). Author: "Economics and Politics of the U.S. Oil Industry, 1920-1990," 1996; "Texas, Oil and the New Deal," 2001. *Member:* The District of Columbia Bar; American Bar Association. ***PRACTICE AREAS:*** Business Law; Mergers and Acquisitions; Utility Law; Antitrust. ***Email:*** issers@ballardspahr.com

ROBERT A. KAPLAN, born Washington, D.C., November 17, 1969; admitted to bar, 1998, Maryland; 1999, District of Columbia, U.S. District Court, District of Maryland and U.S. Court of Appeals, District of Columbia Circuit; 2000, U.S. District Court, District of Columbia. *Education:* Duke University (A.B., 1991); Washington University (J.D., 1998); Georgetown University (LL.M., with distinction, 2001). Associate Editor, Washington University Journal, 1997-1998. *Member:* Maryland State and American Bar Associations; The District of Columbia Bar; National Association of Bond Lawyers. ***PRACTICE AREAS:*** Tax Law; Municipal Bonds. ***Email:*** kaplanr@ballardspahr.com

KIRSTEN E. KEATING, born Bethesda, Maryland, February 7, 1967; admitted to bar, 1994, Massachusetts; 1996, U.S. District Court, District of Massachusetts; 1997, District of Columbia; 1999, Virginia and U.S. District Court, Eastern District of Virginia. *Education:* Colgate University (B.A., 1989); University of Cincinnati (J.D., 1994). Delta Theta Phi (Vice Dean, 1992-1993). *Member:* District of Columbia Bar. ***PRACTICE AREAS:*** Litigation; Employment Law. ***Email:*** keating@ballardspahr.com

JEFFREY W. LARROCA, born Washington, D.C., October 9, 1964; admitted to bar, 1994, Maryland; 1997, District of Columbia. *Education:* James Madison University (B.A., 1986); LaSalle University; Catholic University (J.D., 1994). Member, Catholic University Law Review, 1991-1993. Adjunct Professor, Catholic University, 2001—. *Member:* Maryland State and American Bar Associations; The District of Columbia Bar. ***PRACTICE AREAS:*** Banks and Banking; Commercial Law; Insurance Defense; Labor and Employment Litigation; Age Discrimination in Employment; Employer Intentional Torts; Employment at Will; Employment Breach of Contract; Employment Class Actions; Employment Defense; Employment Disability Discrimination; Employment Discrimination; Employment Litigation; Equal Employment Opportunity Law; Fair Labor Standards; Family and Medical Leave Act; Harassment; Management Employment Law; Personnel Policies; Reductions in Work Force; Retaliatory Discharge; Sexual Harassment; Title VII Discrimination; Wage and Hour Law; Whistleblower Litigation; Wrongful Termination Defense. ***Email:*** larroca@ballardspahr.com

PAUL J. MILLER, born Oneida, New York, September 26, 1963; admitted to bar, 1993, Virginia; 1994, Maryland; 2000, District of Columbia. *Education:* Le Moyne College (B.A., 1986); State University of New York at Buffalo (J.D., 1993). *Member:* Fairfax County Bar Association. ***PRACTICE AREAS:*** Real Estate; Business; General Practice. ***Email:*** millerpj@ballardspahr.com

ELIZABETH G. MOULDS, born Chicago, Illinois, February 2, 1973; admitted to bar, 1999, Illinois; 2001, Virginia (Not admitted in District of Columbia). *Education:* University of Illinois (B.A., 1995); Boston College (J.D., 1999). *Member:* Chicago and American Bar Associations. ***PRACTICE AREAS:*** Commercial Litigation; Employment Litigation. ***Email:*** mouldse@ballardspahr.com

(This Listing Continued)

ANN MARIE H. PETERS, born Fort Sill, Oklahoma, July 11, 1949; admitted to bar, 1976, Virginia and District of Columbia. *Education:* Trinity College (A.B., 1971); Catholic University of America (J.D., 1976). *Member:* Virginia State Bar; District of Columbia Bar. ***PRACTICE AREAS:*** Real Estate; Commercial Real Estate Finance. ***Email:*** petersam@ballardspahr.com

VICKY TSILAS, born Athens, Greece, November 19, 1968; admitted to bar, 1993, New Jersey; 1994, New York; 1995, District of Columbia and U.S. Tax Court. *Education:* Bryn Mawr College (B.A., 1990); Fordham University (J.D., 1993); Georgetown University (LL.M., Tax, 1997). Recipient, Moore McCormack Award. Law Clerk to the Hon. Laurence J. Whalen, U.S. Tax Court, 1997-1999. Author: "An Analysis of the Phase-out Provisions of the Airport Noise and Capacity Act of 1990," 4 Fordham Environmental Law Report 83, 1992; "Whole Hospital Joint Ventures — Do Exempt Organizations Really Know What They're Getting Themselves Into?" 17 Exempt Organizations Tax Review 241, 273, 1997; "Sierra Club, Inc. v. Commissioner: Why Is the IRS Continuing to Fight a Losing Battle?" 24 Exempt Organizations Tax Review 487, 1999. Law Clerk: U.S. Tax Court; Judge Lawrence J. Whaler, 1997-1999. *Member:* New York State and New Jersey State Bar Associations; District of Columbia Bar. ***LANGUAGES:*** Greek and French. ***PRACTICE AREAS:*** Taxation; Federal Income Tax. ***Email:*** tsilas@ballardspahr.com

KURT E. VAN ENGEN, born Colorado Springs, March 5, 1964; admitted to bar, 1998, Virginia; 2000, District of Columbia. *Education:* American University (B.A., 1994); Washington College of Law, American University (J.D., 1997). Member, Administrative Law Review. ***PRACTICE AREAS:*** Real Estate; Asset Finance; Real Property Finance. ***Email:*** vanengen@ballardspahr.com

JOHN A. WASHINGTON, JR., born January 8, 1959; admitted to bar, 1990, New York; 1998, District of Columbia. *Education:* University of the South (B.A., 1981); Catholic University of America (J.D., 1989). *Member:* District of Columbia Bar; New York State and American Bar Associations; National Association of Bond Lawyers. ***PRACTICE AREAS:*** Public Finance. ***Email:*** washington@ballardspahr.com

SUSAN S. YIM, born Seoul, Korea, June 2, 1969; admitted to bar, 1996, Maryland and District of Columbia. *Education:* Smith College (B.A., 1992); Tulane University of Louisiana (J.D., 1995). Member, Tulane Journal of International and Comparative Law. *Member:* Maryland State Bar Association; The District of Columbia Bar; Asian Pacific American Bar Association (Member, Greater D.C. Area Chapter). ***LANGUAGES:*** Korean, French and Japanese. ***PRACTICE AREAS:*** Business Law; Energy; Project Finance. ***Email:*** yims@ballardspahr.com

REVISERS OF THE PENNSYLVANIA LAW DIGEST FOR THIS DIRECTORY.

(For Complete Biographical Data on Other Personnel, See Professional Biographies at Philadelphia, Pennsylvania, Denver, Colorado, Baltimore, Maryland, Camden and Voorhees, New Jersey, Salt Lake City, Utah)

THE BALLER HERBST LAW GROUP

2014 P STREET, N.W. SUITE 200
WASHINGTON, D.C. 20036
Telephone: 202-833-5300
Fax: 202-833-1180
Email: jimb@baller.com
URL: http://www.baller.com

Minneapolis, Minnesota Office: 953 East Grain Exchange Building, 400 South Fourth Street. 55415-1413.

General Practice.

FIRM PROFILE: The Baller Herbst Law Group emphasizes counseling, representation and administrative and judicial litigation in communications, energy and environmental matters. The firm represents local governments, trade associations and publicly-owned electric utilities in federal, state and local telecommunications and cable television matters. The firm assists local governments and utilities in comprehensive telecommunications planning. The firm assists local governments in cable television franchising and regulation of rights-of-way. The firm also deals regularly with environmental risk assessment, risk management and risk communication issues in the United States and abroad, working with multi-disciplinary teams of scientists and technical experts.

JAMES BALLER, born West Berlin, Germany, January 19, 1947; admitted to bar, 1973, District of Columbia, U.S. District Court, District of Columbia and U.S. Court of Appeals, District of Columbia Circuit; 1974, U.S. Claims Court; 1977, U.S. Supreme Court; 1982, U.S. Court of Appeals, Federal Circuit; 1990, U.S. Court of Appeals, Fifth Circuit. *Education:* Dartmouth College (A.B., Economics, with honors, 1969); Cornell University Law School (J.D., 1972). Member, Cornell Law Review, 1970-1971. Author or Co-Author: "Telecommunications Options," Public Power Magazine (Jan-Feb 1997); "Telecommunications: New Horizons In Service" (Tennessee Valley Public Power Association,

(This Listing Continued)

50th Annual Conference 1996); "The Essential Role of Consumer-Owned Electric Utilities In Developing the National Information Infrastructure: A Historical Perspective" (American Public Power Association, National Telecommunications Conference 1995); "Assessment of Dioxin-Related Health Risks for the Melbourne Metropolitan Area," *Australian Journal of Public Health* (June 15, 1993); "The Agency for Toxic Substances and Disease Registry: An Emerging Power in the Hazardous Waste Arena," 21 BNA Environment Reporter 1951, March 1, 1991; "New Science in Risk Assessment: Adapting to the Reforms," 3 Environmental Claims Journal 367, Spr. 1991; "The Petroleum Industry and the Environment—New Laws, New Concerns and New Strategies," Petroleum Management, June 1990; "Japan's National Recycling Plan," Waste Age Magazine, Aug. 1982; "Waste-to-Energy Projects in the United States: The Legal Considerations Involved," Clean Japan Center International Waste Recycling Symposium, Dec. 1981. *Member:* The District of Columbia Bar; American Bar Association.

ADRIAN E. HERBST, born Minneapolis, Minnesota, August 22, 1939; admitted to bar, 1965, Minnesota (Not admitted in District of Columbia). *Education:* University of Minnesota (B.S., 1961); William Mitchell College of Law (J.D., 1965). City Attorney, 1965-1972; City Council, 1975-1991, Bloomington. Director and Vice President, League of Minnesota Cities. Past President, Minnesota Trial Lawyers Association. Attorney, Bloomington, HRA, 1972-1975. Bloomington Port Authority, 1982-1987. *Member:* American Bar Association (Member, Forum Committee on Communication Law, 1981—); Minnesota Telecommunications Council; Federal Communications Bar Association; National Institute of Municipal Law Officers; National Association of Telecommunications Officers and Advisors. ***PRACTICE AREAS:*** Telecommunications Law; Cable Television; Municipal Law; Utilities; Planning & economic dev. activities (cities), incl. "Mall of America" in Bloomington, MN. ***Email:*** aherbst@baller.com

SEAN A. STOKES, born Philadelphia, Pennsylvania, October 20, 1964; admitted to bar, 1990, Pennsylvania; 1991, District of Columbia; 1992, U.S. Court of Appeals, District of Columbia Circuit. *Education:* Denison University (B.A., English and History, with honors, 1987); George Washington University (J.D., 1990). Member, National Association of Telecommunications Officers and Advisors, 1998—. Author: "Telecommunications Legislation Provides Lessons for Energy-Industry Restructuring," AMRA Magazine (Aug. 1998); "Reforming Telecommunications: How Utilities Fare on Capital Hill," Public Utilities Fortnightly (June, 1994). *Member:* District of Columbia Bar; American Bar Association; Federal Communications Bar Association. ***PRACTICE AREAS:*** Telecommunications Competition; Telecommunications Regulation; Cable Franchising; Cable TV; Wireless Communications. ***Email:*** sstokes@baller.com

BANNER & WITCOFF, LTD.

Established In 1920 - Predecessor Parent

1001 G STREET, N.W.

WASHINGTON, D.C. 20001-4597

Telephone: 202-508-9100

Facsimile: 202-508-9299

Email: cooperman@bannerwitcoff.com

URL: http://www.bannerwitcoff.com

Chicago, Illinois Office: Ten South Wacker Drive. Telephone: 312-715-1000. Facsimile: 312-715-1234.

Boston, Massachusetts Office: 28 State Street, 28th Floor. Telephone: 617-227-7111. Fax: 617-227-4399.

Portland, Oregon Office: 601 SW Second Avenue, Suite 1900. Telephone: 503-279-6330. Fax: 503-279-6328.

Intellectual Property including Procurement of Patents, Trademarks, Copyrights, Trade Secrets, Counseling & Opinions, Unfair Competition, Interferences, Licensing, Antitrust and International Trade Matters. Litigation including Trials and Appeals in Federal and State Courts and International Trade Commission.

FIRM PROFILE: Banner & Witcoff, Ltd. is dedicated to the practice of intellectual property law. The firm provides legal representation in obtaining, commercializing and litigating intellectual property rights in the United States and abroad. The practice includes counseling on the availability, validity and enforcement of intellectual property rights; patent interference proceedings; trademark opposition and cancellation proceedings; domestic and foreign patent and trademark prosecution; custom seizures of infringing products; and litigating patent, trademark and copyright infringement cases. Firm members have experience in both jury and bench trials in the Federal Courts and in proceedings before the International Trade Commission. Firm attorneys practice in all technologies, including the electrical, mechanical and chemical arts as well as computer hardware and software, internet and e-commerce, and biotechnology.

ROBERT F. ALTHERR, JR., admitted to bar, 1980, Ohio; 1986, U.S. Claims Court; 1994, District of Columbia and U.S. Court of Appeals, Federal Circuit; 1995, U.S. Supreme Court. *Education:* University of Cincinnati

(This Listing Continued)

(B.S.Ch.E.; 1974); Capital University Law School (J.D., summa cum laude, 1980); Wayne State University (LL.M., 1984); George Washington University (LL.M., with highest honors, 1989). Order of the Curia. Special Attorney to the U.S. Attorney General, 1992-1993. Trial Attorney: U.S. Department of Justice Civil Division, 1988-1992; Patent Litigation & Claims Attorney, U.S. Department of Army, 1987-1988. *Member:* American Bar Association; American Intellectual Property Law Association; Government Patent Lawyers Association. [U.S. Army 1974-1987; Major, JAG Corps, 1980-1987]. ***PRACTICE AREAS:*** Intellectual Property Litigation; Intellectual Property Law; Patents. ***Email:*** raltherr@bannerwitcoff.com

BRIAN E. BANNER, admitted to bar, 1974, Illinois; 1975, Virginia; 1978, Minnesota; 1998, District of Columbia; 2000, U.S. Supreme Court. *Education:* University of Arizona (B.S.B.A., 1969); The John Marshall Law School (J.D., 1974). Trademark Examining Attorney, United States Patent and Trademark Office. Co-Author: "Dressing Down," Special Report on Intellectual Property, Legal Times, April 1999; "Domain Name Rights and Dilution Remedies," Managing Intellectual Property, Trademark Yearbook, 1998. Guest Lecturer, WIPO Licensing Program, Colombo, Sri Lanka, 1986. Adjunct Professor, Georgetown University Law Center, 1997— and George Mason University Law School, 2000—. *Member:* American Bar Association (Co-Editor, Newsletter Committee, 1997—, Section Secretary, 1989-1991 and Council Member, 1992-1996, Section of Intellectual Property Law); International Trademark Association; Intellectual Property Owners, Inc. ***PRACTICE AREAS:*** Intellectual Property Law; Trademarks; Copyrights; Intellectual Property Licensing. ***Email:*** bbanner@bannerwitcoff.com

DONALD W. BANNER, admitted to bar, 1953, Michigan and Illinois; 1962, U.S. Supreme Court; 1979, Virginia; 1980, District of Columbia. *Education:* Purdue University (B.S.E.E., 1948); University of Detroit (J.D., 1952); The John Marshall Law School (M.P.L., 1958). Awarded LL.D., The John Marshall Law School, 1979. Tau Beta Pi; Eta Kappa Nu. Recipient: Jefferson Medal, 1984; Award of Pacific Industrial Property Association for International Cooperation, 1982; The Purdue University 1994 Outstanding Electrical Engineer Award; Distinguished Engineering Alumnus Award, 1997. Member, Advisory Board, Patent, Trademark and Copyright Journal, 1970-1978. Professor, 1959-1978 and Distinguished Professor of Law and Director of Intellectual Property Program, 1979-1989, The John Marshall Law School. General Patent Counsel, Borg-Warner Corporation, 1953-1978. Professor of Intellectual Property Law and Director, Intellectual Property Law Program, The National Law Center, George Washington University, 1989-1991. Biographee, "Guide to the World's Leading Patent Law Experts." U.S. Commissioner of Patents and Trademarks, 1978-1979. Member: Department of Commerce Technical Advisory Board, 1969-1974; U.S. Delegation, Washington Diplomatic Conference on the Patent Cooperation Treaty, 1970; ABA Delegation, Vienna Diplomatic Conference on Trademark Registration Treaty, 1973. Trustee, Licensing Executive Society, 1971-1974. Licensing Consultant of World Intellectual Property Organization to Peoples Republic of China, 1979. President, Giles S. Rich American Inns of Court, 1992-1994. *Member:* Illinois State (Chairman, Section of Patent, Trademark and Copyright Law, 1967-1968) and American (Chairman, Section of Patent, Trademark and Copyright Law, 1972-1973) Bar Associations; Intellectual Property Law Association of Chicago (Vice President, 1976-1978; 1980-1981); American Intellectual Property Law Association (President, 1977-1978); International Patent and Trademark Association (President, 1980-1983; Member, Executive Committee, 1975-1978); Association of Corporate Patent Counsel (President, 1970-1971). ***PRACTICE AREAS:*** Intellectual Property Law; Patents; Intellectual Property Litigation; Intellectual Property Licensing. ***Email:*** dbanner@bannerwitcoff.com

PAMELA I. BANNER, admitted to bar, 1987, Virginia; 1988, District of Columbia; U.S. District Court, Eastern District of Virginia; U.S. District Court, District of Columbia; U.S. Court of Appeals for the Federal Circuit; U.S. Supreme Court; registered to practice before U.S. Patent and Trademark Office. *Education:* Purdue University (B.S.E.E., 1980); George Washington University (J.D., 1987). Formerly Law Clerk to the Honorable William C. Bryson, United States Court of Appeals for the Federal Circuit. *Member:* District of Columbia Bar (Former Co-Chair for Steering Committee, Intellectual Property Law Section); Virginia State Bar; American Bar Association (Liaison, Intellectual Property Law Section and Council Member, 2001, Commission on Women in the Profession; Division Chair, Information, Intellectual Property Law Section, 1999-2000; Division Chair, Litigation, Alternative Dispute Resolution and Related Issues, Intellectual Property Law, Section, 1998-1999. Chair, Appellate Practice and Judiciary Committee, Intellectual Property Law Section, 1996-1998; Chair, Young Lawyers Committee, Intellectual Property Law Section, 1995-1996; Science and Technology Section; Vice-Chair, Proprietary Rights in Software Committee, 1994-1995; Fellow, 2001). ***PRACTICE AREAS:*** Intellectual Property Law; Patents; Intellectual Property Litigation; Appellate Practice; Electrical Intellectual Property; Computer and Software Patents; Business Methods Patents; Electronic Patents. ***Email:*** pbanner@bannerwitcoff.com

GARY D. FEDOROCHKO, admitted to bar, 1990, Virginia and U.S. Court of Appeals, Fourth Circuit; 1991 U.S. Court of Appeals for the Federal Circuit; 1996, District of Columbia; 1999, U.S. District Court, Eastern District of Vir-

(This Listing Continued)

BANNER & WITCOFF, LTD., Washington—Continued

ginia; registered to practice before U.S. Patent and Trademark Office. *Education:* Rensselaer Polytechnic Institute (B.S., Computer and Systems Eng., 1987); George Washington University (J.D., 1990). Author: "How Strong is First Inventor Defense,? National Law Journal, Vol. 22, No. 48, P.C 13, C22-23 24 July 2000. c *Member:* Virginia State Bar (Intellectual Property Law Section); American Bar Association (Intellectual Property Law Section); Licensing Executives Society; American Intellectual Property Law Association; Patent Lawyer's Club of Washington; Northern Virginia Technology Council (Associate Member). ***PRACTICE AREAS:*** Intellectual Property Law; Patents; Intellectual Property Licensing; Electrical Intellectual Property; Computer and Software Patents. ***Email:*** gfedorochko@bannerwitcoff.com

WILLIAM J. FISHER, admitted to bar, 1986, Maryland; 1988, District of Columbia; U.S. Court of Appeals for the Federal Circuit; U.S. District Court for the District of Columbia; 1996, U.S. Supreme Court. *Education:* Illinois Institute of Technology (B.S.Ch.E., cum laude, 1973; M.S.Ch.E., 1975); Seton Hall University (J.D., cum laude, 1985). Recipient, New Jersey State Bar Association Intellectual Property Award, 1985. Adjunct Professor, George Mason University School of Law, 1996, 2000-2001. *Member:* District of Columbia Bar; Maryland State and American (Member: Patent Section; Trademark and Copyright Law Section; Science and Technology Section) Bar Associations. ***PRACTICE AREAS:*** Intellectual Property Law; Patents; Intellectual Property Licensing; Chemical Intellectual Property; Pharmaceutical Intellectual Property. ***Email:*** wfisher@bannerwitcoff.com

CHRISTOPHER R. GLEMBOCKI, admitted to bar, 1995, Virginia; 1998, District of Columbia; registered to practice before U.S. Patent and Trademark Office. *Education:* University of Virginia (B.S.E.E., 1990); Washington College of Law of American University (J.D., 1995). Engineer in Training, 1990. *Member:* Virginia State Bar; American Bar Association (Director, Communications, Associate Editor of The Young Lawyer, and Former Chair, Computer and Intellectual Property Law Committee, Young Lawyers Division). ***PRACTICE AREAS:*** Intellectual Property Law; Patents; Electrical Intellectual Property; Computer and Software Patents; Electronic Patents. ***Email:*** cglembocki@bannerwitcoff.com

BRIAN E. HANLON, admitted to bar, 1995, Maryland; 1998, District of Columbia; registered to practice before U.S. Patent and Trademark Office. *Education:* Worcester Polytechnic Institute (B.S.M.E., with honors, 1990); Catholic University of America (J.D., magna cum laude, 1995). *Member:* Bar Association of the District of Columbia; Maryland State Bar Association, Inc.; American Bar Association; American Intellectual Property Law Association. ***SPECIAL AGENCIES:*** United States Patent Office, 1990-1996. ***PRACTICE AREAS:*** Intellectual Property Law; Patents; Design Patents; Mechanical Intellectual Property; Medical Intellectual Property. ***Email:*** bhanlon@bannerwitcoff.com

PATRICIA E. HONG, admitted to bar, 1993, Maryland; 1994, District of Columbia; U.S. Court of Appeals for the Federal Circuit; U.S. District Court, District of Columbia; registered to practice before U.S. Patent and Trademark Office. *Education:* Virginia Polytechnic Institute and State University (B.S.M.E., 1988); Catholic University of America (J.D., 1993). *Member:* American Bar Association (Member, Intellectual Property Law Section); American Intellectual Property Law Association; International Association for the Protection of Industrial Property (AIPPI). ***LANGUAGES:*** Korean. ***PRACTICE AREAS:*** Intellectual Property Law; Patents; Design Patents; Intellectual Property Litigation. ***Email:*** phong@bannerwitcoff.com

DALE H. HOSCHEIT, admitted to bar, 1956, Illinois; 1959, District of Columbia. *Education:* University of Illinois (B.S., 1951; J.D., 1956). Phi Delta Phi; Phi Lambda Upsilon; Sigma Tau. Lecturer in Law, George Mason University Law School. Lecturer, Graduate Program, Johns Hopkins University. *Member:* District of Columbia Bar; Bar Association of the District of Columbia; American Bar Association; American Intellectual Property Law Association; Licensing Executive Society. ***PRACTICE AREAS:*** Intellectual Property Law; Patents; Intellectual Property Licensing; Intellectual Property Litigation; Biotechnology; Pharmaceutical Intellectual Property; Chemical Intellectual Property. ***Email:*** dhoscheit@bannerwitcoff.com

THOMAS H. JACKSON, admitted to bar, 1982, New Jersey; 1985, District of Columbia; 1987, U.S. Court of Appeals, Federal Circuit. *Education:* University of Pennsylvania (B.S.E.E., 1967); George Washington University (M.E.A., 1970); Seton Hall University (J.D., 1982). Registered Professional Engineer, District of Columbia, 1972; New Jersey, 1978. *Member:* District of Columbia Bar; American Bar Association; American Intellectual Property Law Association. ***PRACTICE AREAS:*** Intellectual Property Law; Patents; Electrical Intellectual Property; Intellectual Property Litigation; Computer and Software Patents; Electronic Patents. ***Email:*** tjackson@bannerwitcoff.com

SARAH A. KAGAN, admitted to bar, 1988, Massachusetts; 1989, District of Columbia; registered to practice before U.S. Patent and Trademark Office. *Education:* Brandeis University (B.A., magna cum laude, Biology, 1976); University of Wisconsin (Ph.D., Molecular Biology, 1981); George Washington

(This Listing Continued)

University (J.D., with honors, 1988). *Member:* District of Columbia Bar; American Bar Association. ***PRACTICE AREAS:*** Intellectual Property Law; Patents; Biotechnology; Pharmaceutical Intellectual Property. ***Email:*** skagan@bannerwitcoff.com

ROBERT S. KATZ, admitted to bar, 1992, Virginia; 1993, District of Columbia; U.S. District Court, Eastern District of Virginia; U.S. Court of Appeals for the Federal Circuit. *Education:* Carnegie Mellon University (B.S., Mech. Eng., 1986); George Washington University (J.D., with honors, 1992). Patent Examiner, U.S. Patent and Trademark Office, 1988-1992. *Member:* District of Columbia Bar; Virginia State Bar; American Bar Association (Member: Patent, Trademark and Copyright Section; Committees on: Inventors; Industrial Designs); American Intellectual Property Law Association (Member, Industrial Designs Committee). ***PRACTICE AREAS:*** Intellectual Property Law; Patents; Design Patents; Mechanical Intellectual Property. ***Email:*** rkatz@bannerwitcoff.com

CHRISTOPHER L. McKEE, admitted to bar, 1988, Virginia; 1991, District of Columbia, U.S. Court of Appeals for the Federal Circuit and U.S. Supreme Court; registered to practice before U.S. Patent and Trademark Office. *Education:* Iowa State University (B.S., Industrial Engineering, 1983); George Washington University (J.D., 1988). Alpha Pi Mu. Member, The George Washington Journal of International Law and Economics, 1986; Patent Examiner, 1984-1986. Claim's Drafting Instructor, Patent Resources Group's Patent Bar Review Course, 1994-1998. *Member:* Virginia State Bar; District of Columbia Bar; Bar Association of the District of Columbia (Steering Committee Member, Patent, Trademark & Copyright Section, 1996-1998; 2000-2001); Federal Circuit and American Bar Associations; American Intellectual Property Law Association. ***PRACTICE AREAS:*** Intellectual Property Law; Intellectual Property Litigation; Appellate Practice. ***Email:*** cmckee@bannerwitcoff.com

NINA L. MEDLOCK, admitted to bar, 1980, District of Columbia; 1984, Texas. *Education:* Dillard University (B.S., magna cum laude, 1971); Johns Hopkins University (M.S.E., 1973); George Washington University (J.D., with honors, 1980; L.L.M., Taxation, with highest honors, 1988). Assistant to the Chief Technical Advisor, U.S. Court of Customs and Patent Appeals, 1980-1981. Law Clerk to Chief Judge Howard T. Markey, U.S. Court of Appeals for the Federal Circuit, 1981-1983. *Member:* American Bar Association (Counsel Member, Science & Technology Section, 1992-1997); American Intellectual Law Association. ***PRACTICE AREAS:*** Intellectual Property Law; Patents; Electrical Intellectual Property; Computer and Software Patents. ***Email:*** nmedlock@bannerwitcoff.com

FREDERIC M. MEEKER, admitted to bar, 1992, Virginia; 1993, District of Columbia. *Education:* George Mason University (B.S., Computer & Electronic Engineering, 1984; M.S., Computer & Electronic Engineering, 1988); George Mason University School of Law (J.D., with distinction, 1992); George Washington University (LL.M., Intellectual Property Law, 1998). Adjunct Professor, George Mason University School of Law, 1998—. Staff Engineer, IBM Corp., 1986-1991. *Member:* The Bar Association of the District of Columbia; The Virginia State Bar; Federal Circuit and American (Member, Intellectual Property Law Section; Chair, Patent Legislation Committee, 1999-2001; Chair, Patent System Policy Planning, Computer Related Inventions Subcommittee, Committee 108, Intellectual Property Section, 1999-2000; Chair, Special Committee to Monitor WTO, NAFTA and Other International Trade Agreements, 1998-1999; Co-Chair, Young Lawyers Committee, Intellectual Property Section, 1997-1998) Bar Associations; American Intellectual Property Law Association; International Association for the Protection of Industrial Property (AIPPI); Institute of Electrical and Electronic Engineers (IEEE); Association for Computing Machinery (ACM); The Association of Trial Lawyers of America (ATLA). ***PRACTICE AREAS:*** Intellectual Property Law; Patents; Intellectual Property Litigation; International Trade; Electrical Intellectual Property; Computer and Software Patents. ***Email:*** fmeeker@bannerwitcoff.com

HELEN HILL MINSKER, admitted to bar, 1988, District of Columbia; 1989, U.S. Court of Appeals, Federal Circuit; 1993, U.S. Supreme Court. *Education:* Vassar College (A.B., cum laude, 1982); London School of Economics & Political Science; George Washington University (J.D., 1987). Member, AIPLA Board of Directors (2000-2002). Chair, AIPLA Trademark Law Committee (1999-2000). Vice-Chair, INTA Meetings Committee (1999-2000, 2001-2002). Chair, ABA Intellectual Property Law Section Committee, 207 (Franchising) (1998-1999). Chair, Bar Association of District of Columbia PTC Section (1999-2000). *Member:* The District of Columbia Bar; American Bar Association; American Intellectual Property Law Association; International Trademark Association; European Community Trademark Association. ***PRACTICE AREAS:*** Intellectual Property Law; Trademarks; Copyrights; Intellectual Property Litigation. ***Email:*** hminsker@bannerwitcoff.com

THOMAS L. PETERSON, admitted to bar, 1985, District of Columbia and U.S. District Court, District of District of Columbia; 1986, U.S. Court of Appeals, Federal Circuit; 1993, U.S. Supreme Court; registered to practice before U.S. Patent and Trademark Office. *Education:* Kent State University (A.A. Electrical Engineering, 1973); Youngstown State University (B.S. Electrical Engineering, 1977); Cleveland Marshall College of Law (J.D., 1981). Member, Faculty Appoints Committee, Cleveland Marshall College of Law, 1980-1981.

(This Listing Continued)

Member, Moot Court Board of Governors, Cleveland Marshall College of Law, 1979-1981. Adjunct Professor of Law: George Mason University School of Law; Howard University School of Law. *Member:* The District of Columbia Bar; Bar Association of the District of Columbia; American Bar Association; American Intellectual Property Law Association; National Intellectual Property Law Association; National Bar Association. ***PRACTICE AREAS:*** Intellectual Property Law; Patents; Intellectual Property Licensing; Patent Prosecution; Computer and Software Patents. ***Email:*** tpeterson@bannerwitcoff.com

JOSEPH M. POTENZA, admitted to bar, 1975, Virginia; 1976, District of Columbia; 1976-1982, U.S. Court of Customs and Patent Appeals; 1982, U.S. Court of Appeals for the Federal Circuit. *Education:* Rochester Institute of Technology (B.S.E.E., cum laude, 1970); Georgetown University (J.D., 1975). Tau Beta Pi. U.S. Patent Office Examiner, 1970-1975. Law Clerk to the Honorable Harry Phillips, Chief Judge, U.S. Court of Appeals, Sixth Circuit, 1975-1976. Author: "Effectively Patenting E-Commerce," Corporate Counsel Magazine, March 1999; "War in Cyberspace: Battling it Out on the E-Commerce Frontier," USA Today Magazine, September 1999. Contributing Author: "Patent Litigation Strategies Handbook," BNA 2000. Adjunct Professor, Georgetown University Law Center, 1985—. Member: President and Master, Giles S. Rich, American Inns of Court, 1991—; Executive Board, Foundation for a Creative America. Member, The Brookings Institute (Member, Committee on Understanding Intangible Sources of Value). *Member:* The District of Columbia Bar; Virginia and American (Secretary; Chair, Division VI; Member and Chair of Federal Practice and Procedure Committee Sections of Intellectual Property Law; Antitrust Law; Litigation; Chairman, Patent, Trademark and Copyright Committee of Young Lawyers Division, 1977—; Liaison, ABA Patent, Trademark and Copyright Committee and Young Lawyers Division, 1978—; Member, House of Delegates, 1983—; Chair, Science and Technology Section; Technology Committee Section Officers Conference; Chair, ABA, Standing Committee on Publishing Oversight, 1996—) Bar Associations; National Institute for Trial Advocacy (Chair, Patent Trial Institute, 1995—); American Intellectual Property Law Association; Institute of Electrical and Electronics Engineers; Patent Lawyers Club of Washington (President, 1988-1989). Fellow, American Bar Foundation. ***PRACTICE AREAS:*** Intellectual Property Law; Patents; Copyrights; Intellectual Property Litigation; Intellectual Property Licensing; International Trade; Electrical Intellectual Property; Computer and Software Patents; Electronic Patents. ***Email:*** jpotenza@bannerwitcoff.com

STEVEN P. SCHAD, admitted to bar, 1987, Michigan and U.S. District Court, Western District of Michigan; 1991,U.S. Court of Appeals, Federal Circuit; 1993, District of Columbia. *Education:* Michigan Technological University (B.S.C.E., with honors, 1982); George Mason University (J.D., 1987). Examiner, U.S. Patent Office, 1982-1987. *Member:* The District of Columbia Bar (Member, Intellectual Property Law Section); State Bar of Michigan (Member, Section of Intellectual Property); American Bar Association (Member, Section of Patent, Trademark and Copyright Law); American Intellectual Property Law Association. ***PRACTICE AREAS:*** Intellectual Property Law; Patents; Intellectual Property Licensing; Mechanical Intellectual Property. ***Email:*** sschad@bannerwitcoff.com

JOSEPH M. SKERPON, admitted to bar, 1982, New York; 1983, District of Columbia; 1986, U.S. District Court, District of District of Columbia; 1988, U.S. Court of Appeals, Federal Circuit. *Education:* Princeton University (B.S.ChE., with honors, 1975); University of Buffalo (J.D., with honors, 1981). Lecturer in Law, George Mason University School of Law, 1994, 1995, 1996. *Member:* District of Columbia Bar; American Bar Association (Member, Section of Patent, Trademark and Copyright Law); American Intellectual Property Law Association. ***PRACTICE AREAS:*** Intellectual Property Law; Patents; Biotechnology; Pharmaceutical Intellectual Property; Chemical Intellectual Property. ***Email:*** jskerpon@bannerwitcoff.com

SUSAN A. WOLFFE, admitted to bar, 1990, Virginia; 1992, District of Columbia; registered to practice before U.S. Patent and Trademark Office. *Education:* University of Virginia (B.S.Ch.E., 1985); George Mason University Law School (J.D., 1990). Alpha Chi Sigma. *Member:* The District of Columbia Bar; Virginia State Bar (Member, Intellectual Property Law Section); American Bar Association; American Intellectual Property Law Association (Vice-Chair, Chemical Practice Committee). ***PRACTICE AREAS:*** Intellectual Property Law; Patents; Intellectual Property Licensing; Chemical Intellectual Property; Pharmaceutical Intellectual Property. ***Email:*** swolffe@bannerwitcoff.com

BRADLEY C. WRIGHT, admitted to bar, 1994, Virginia; 1995, District of Columbia; 1996, U.S. Court of Appeals for the Federal Circuit and U.S. Supreme Court; 1999, U.S. District Court, Eastern District of Virginia; registered to practice before U.S. Patent and Trademark Office. *Education:* Massachusetts Institute of Technology (B.S.E.E., 1984); George Mason University (J.D., with distinction, 1994). Member, George Mason University Law Review. Formerly Law Clerk to the Honorable William C. Bryson, United States Court of Appeals for the Federal Circuit, 1997-1998. Author: "Linux Users Risk Infringement," Intellectual Property & Technology Law Journal, Vol. 13, No. 8 (August 2001); "Patents That Protect Methods of Doing Business: A License to Steal?" The Licensing Journal (January 2001); "Employees May Own Key Patents," The National Law Journal (December 18, 2000); "Patent Law: Business Methods," The National Law Journal (Nov. 22, 1999); "War in Cyberspace: Battling it Out on the E-Commerce Frontier," USA Today Magazine (Sept. 1999); "Supplemental Claim Jurisdiction in the United States Court of Appeals for the Federal Circuit," 22 AIPLA Q.J. 235 (1994); "Changing the Standard for Computer Software Copyright Infringement," 14 Geo. Mason U.L. Rev. 663 (1992); "Ten Mistakes to Avoid at the Federal Circuit," ABA/IPL Newsletter, Vol. 17, No. 2 (Winter, 1999); "Beware the Patent Rights Sellout," The Recorder (January 1999); "Blueprint for Trouble: Supreme Court Decision Increases Risk of Patent Waivers by Selling Too Soon," Legal Times (December 7, 1998); "Patenting Methods of Doing Business," KM World, Vol. 8, Issue 3 (March 1999). Adjunct Professor of Law, George Mason University School of Law. Software Engineering Manager, E-Systems, Inc., 1984-1992. *Member:* Bar Association of the District of Columbia; American Bar Association (Member, Science and Technology Section and Intellectual Property Law Section); Institute of Electrical and Electronics Engineers; American Intellectual Property Law Association (Co-chair, Software Patent Subcommittee, Emerging Technologies Committee, 1996-1998). ***PRACTICE AREAS:*** Intellectual Property Law; Patents; Appellate Practice; Electrical Intellectual Property; Computer and Software Patents; Electronic Patents. ***Email:*** bwright@bannerwitcoff.com

OF COUNSEL

WILLIAM W. BECKETT, admitted to bar, 1956, District of Columbia; 1959, U.S. Supreme Court. *Education:* The Citadel (B.S., 1948); George Washington University (J.D., with distinction, 1956). Delta Theta Phi; Order of the Coif. Patent Editor, George Washington University Law Review, 1954-1955. *Member:* District of Columbia Bar; Bar Association of the District of Columbia; American Bar Association; American Intellectual Property Law Association. ***PRACTICE AREAS:*** Intellectual Property Law; Patents; Trademarks; Intellectual Property Licensing. ***Email:*** wbeckett@bannerwitcoff.com

EDWARD F. McKIE, JR., admitted to bar, 1952, District of Columbia; 1956, U.S. Supreme Court. *Education:* Rensselaer Polytechnic Institute (B.E.E., 1948); Georgetown University (LL.B., 1952). Phi Delta Phi (Magister, 1951). Associate Editor, Georgetown Law Journal, 1951-1952. Member, Advisory Board, Patent, Trademark and Copyright Journal, 1970-1990. Adjunct Professor, Georgetown University Law Center, 1963-1967 and 1985—. Chairman, National Council of Patent Law Associations, 1969-1970. Senior Advisor, U.S. Delegation to Diplomatic Conference on PCT, 1970. Member: International Industrial Property Panel, U.S. Department of State, 1976 and 1977. Advisory Committee, Patent and Trademark Office, 1976-1980. *Member:* District of Columbia Bar; Bar Association of the District of Columbia; American Bar Association (Chairman, Section of Patent, Trademark and Copyright Law, 1967-1968); American Intellectual Property Law Association (President, 1976-1977). Fellow: American College of Trial Lawyers. ***PRACTICE AREAS:*** Intellectual Property Law. ***Email:*** emckie@bannerwitcoff.com

WILLIAM F. RAUCHHOLZ, admitted to bar, 1992, District of Columbia; registered to practice before U.S. Patent and Trademark Office. *Education:* University of Michigan (B.S.E., Nuclear Engineering, magna cum laude, 1986); George Mason University (J.D., with distinction, 1992). *Member:* The District of Columbia Bar; American Bar Association; American Intellectual Property Law Association. ***PRACTICE AREAS:*** Intellectual Property; Patents; Chemical Intellectual Property. ***Email:*** wrauchholz@bannerwitcoff.com

DOUGLAS W. ROBINSON, admitted to bar, 1986, Maryland; 1988, District of Columbia; registered to practice before U.S. Patent and Trademark Office. *Education:* Rensselaer Polytechnic Institute (B. S., 1983); Benjamin Cardozo School of Law, Yeshiva University (J.D., 1986). Notes and Comments Editor, International Law Journal, 1985-1986. *Member:* Maryland State Bar Association; The District of Columbia Bar. ***PRACTICE AREAS:*** Patent; Trademark; Copyright and Unfair Competition Law. ***Email:*** drobinson@bannerwitcoff.com

FRANKLIN D. WOLFFE, admitted to bar, 1959, District of Columbia; 1967, Virginia; registered to practice before U.S. Patent and Trademark Office. *Education:* University of Maryland (B.S.Ch.E., 1954); George Washington University (LL.B., 1959). ***PRACTICE AREAS:*** Intellectual Property Law; Patents; Intellectual Property Licensing; Chemical Intellectual Property. ***Email:*** fwolffe@bannerwitcoff.com

ASSOCIATES

JORDAN N. BODNER, admitted to bar, 2000, Virginia; 2001, District of Columbia. *Education:* Washington University (B.S.E.E., 1991); University of Colorado (M.S.E.E., 1996); George Mason University School of Law (J.D., 1999). Eta Kappa Nu Engineering Honors Society. *Member:* The District of Columbia Bar. ***PRACTICE AREAS:*** Intellectual Property Law; Electrical Intellectual Property; Patent Prosecution; Intellectual Property Litigation; Patents. ***Email:*** jbodner@bannerwitcoff.com

STEVE S. CHANG, admitted to bar, 1999, District of Columbia; registered to practice before U.S. Patent and Trademark Office, 1998. *Education:* The Ohio State University (B.S.E.E., 1995); Temple University School of Law (J.D., 1998). Member, Moot Court Honor Society. *Member:* The District of Columbia

(This Listing Continued)

BANNER & WITCOFF, LTD., Washington—Continued

Bar (Member, Sections on: Intellectual Property, 1999—; Young Lawyers, 1999—). ***PRACTICE AREAS:*** Intellectual Property Law; Patents; Intellectual Property Litigation; Electrical Intellectual Property; Computer and Software Patents; Patent Prosecution. ***Email:*** schang@bannerwitcoff.com

JOSEPH P. CURTIN, admitted to bar, 1991, Maryland; 1992, District of Columbia; registered to practice before U.S. Patent and Trademark Office. *Education:* North Carolina State University (B.S.E.E., 1979); University of Maryland (J.D., 1991). *Member:* The District of Columbia Bar; American Bar Association (Member, Sections on: Patent, Trademark and Copyright Law; Science and Technology); American Intellectual Property Law Association. ***PRACTICE AREAS:*** Intellectual Property Law; Patents; Electrical Intellectual Property; Computer and Software Patents; Electronic Patents. ***Email:*** jcurtin@bannerwitcoff.com

ROSS A. DANNENBERG, (admission pending). *Education:* Georgia Institute of Technology (B.S.,, 1994); George Washington University (J.D., 2000). Member, Environmental Lawyer Journal, 1998-2000. ***PRACTICE AREAS:*** Intellectual Property Law; Intellectual Property Litigation; Computer and Software Patents; Trademarks; Entertainment Law. ***Email:*** rdannenberg@bannerwitcoff.com

MICHAEL DAVID, admitted to bar, 2000, Maryland; registered to practice before U.S. Patent and Trademark Office (Not admitted in District of Columbia). *Education:* Weizmann Institute of Science, Rehovot, Israel (Ph.D., 1984); University of Maryland (J.D., 1999). *Member:* Maryland State Bar Association, Inc.; American Bar Association; American Intellectual Property Lawyers Association. [with U.S. Army, 1970-1973]. ***LANGUAGES:*** Hebrew and Romanian. ***PRACTICE AREAS:*** Patents; Patent Licensing; Pharmaceutical Intellectual Property; Medical Intellectual Property Law. ***Email:*** mdavid@bannerwitcoff.com

CATHERINE A. FERGUSON, admitted to bar, 1993, New Jersey; 1994, Pennsylvania; 1998, Maryland; 1999, District of Columbia and U.S. Supreme Court; registered to practice before U.S. Patent and Trademark Office. *Education:* University of New Hampshire (B.A., 1970); University of Connecticut (M.S., 1975); Widener University (J.D., 1993). Phi Kappa Phi; Phi Delta Phi. Recipient: Judge J. Cullen Ganey Award in Criminal Procedure; American Jurisprudence Awards in: Civil Procedure; Criminal Procedure; Wills and Trusts. Author: "Electronic Mail and Privacy in the Corporate Environment," IEEE International Phoenix Conference on Computers and Communications," March 1993. *Member:* The District of Columbia Bar; Computer Law Association. ***LANGUAGES:*** Greek and German. ***PRACTICE AREAS:*** Intellectual Property. ***Email:*** caferguson@bannerwitcoff.com

HOLLY M. FORD, admitted to bar, 1992, U.S. Virgin Islands; 1997, District of Columbia. *Education:* Sorbonne/University of Tours, France (Diploma, 1984); Catholic University of America (B.A., with honors, 1985); Boston College Law School (J.D., 1989). Co-Author: "Domain Name Rights and Dilution Remedies Managing IP," April 1998. Previous Employment: Burns Doane Swecker & Mathis; Holland And Knight LLP. *Member:* The District of Columbia Bar; Bar Association of the District of Columbia (Chair, Trademark Section); American Bar Association; International Trademark Association (Project Team Member, Meetings Committee). ***LANGUAGES:*** French and Spanish. ***PRACTICE AREAS:*** Intellectual Property Law; Trademarks; Copyrights; Intellectual Property Licensing. ***Email:*** hford@bannerwitcoff.com

LISA M. HEMMENDINGER, admitted to bar, 1998, Maryland and District of Columbia; registered to practice before U.S. Patent and Trademark Office, 1998. *Education:* Smith College (A.B., 1976); University of Chicago (Ph.D., 1980); University of Maryland (J.D., 1997). Sigma Xi. Member, Order of the Coif. Author: Note, "Repressed Memory and the Discovery Rule," 56 Maryland Law Review 987, 1997. *Member:* American Intellectual Property Law Association; American Association for the Advancement of Science. ***PRACTICE AREAS:*** Intellectual Property Law; Patents; Biotechnology; Pharmaceutical Intellectual Property. ***Email:*** lhemmendinger@bannerwitcoff.com

LIN J. HYMEL, admitted to bar, 2001, Maryland; registered to practice before U.S. Patent and Trademark Office (Not admitted in District of Columbia). *Education:* Vanderbilt University (Ph.D., 1982); Georgetown University (J.D., 2001). *Member:* Maryland State, Federal Circuit and American Bar Associations; American Intellectual Property Law Association. ***LANGUAGES:*** German. ***PRACTICE AREAS:*** Intellectual Property; Patents; Pharmaceutical Intellectual Property; Medical Intellectual Property; Intellectual Property Litigation. ***Email:*** lhymel@bannerwitcoff.com

RICHARD C. IRVING, admitted to bar, 1993, Maryland; 1994, U.S. Court of Appeals for the Federal Circuit; 1998, District of Columbia; registered to practice before U.S. Patent and Trademark Office. *Education:* Northeastern University (B.S., Mathematics, 1975); The Johns Hopkins University (M.S., Computer Science, 1981); The George Washington University (J.D., 1993). Co-Author: "Who has the Right of Way? Intellectual Property Rights on the Internet," Barrister 25, Winter 1996. Associate Editor, *Dictionary of Computer Terms and Jargons for Judges, Jurors and Lawyers*, 1995. *Member:* The District of Columbia Bar (Member, Intellectual Property Law Section); Maryland State Bar Association, Inc.; American Bar Association (Member, Intellectual Property Law Section); American Intellectual Property Law Association. ***PRACTICE AREAS:*** Intellectual Property Law; Patents; Computer and Software Patents; Electrical Patents; Patent Prosecution. ***Email:*** rirving@bannerwitcoff.com

ANTHONY W. KANDARE, admitted to bar, 2001, Virginia; registered to practice before U.S. Patent and Trademark Office (Not admitted in District of Columbia). *Education:* Brigham Young University (B.S.M.E., 1992); Wayne State University (J.D., with honors, 2001). Delta Theta Phi. *Member:* American Bar Association (Member, Intellectual Property Section); American Society of Mechanical Engineers. [1st Lt., Army National Guard, 1987-1999]. ***PRACTICE AREAS:*** Intellectual Property. ***Email:*** akandare@bannerwitcoff.com

DAVID S. LEE, admitted to bar, 1992, Maryland; 1993, U.S. Court of Appeals for the Federal Circuit; registered to practice before U.S. Patent and Trademark Office (Not admitted in District of Columbia). *Education:* Syracuse University (B.S.E.E., 1988); Catholic University of America (J.D., 1991). *Member:* Maryland State (Past Chair, Korean Bar Committee) and American (Member, Sections on: Intellectual Property Law; Young Lawyers) Bar Associations; American Intellectual Property Law Association; International Association of Korean Lawyers. ***PRACTICE AREAS:*** Intellectual Property. ***Email:*** dlee@bannerwitcoff.com

DARRELL GILBERT MOTTLEY, admitted to bar, 2000, Virginia and New Jersey; registered to practice before U.S. Patent and Trademark Office (Not admitted in District of Columbia). *Education:* Virginia Polytechnic Institute and State University (B.S.E.S.M., Engineering Science and Mechanics, 1987; M.B.A., 1994); George Washington University (J.D., 2000). Tau Beta Phi; Phi Kappa Phi. Member, Golden Key. Student Post President, Virginia Tech Society of American Military Engineers, 1986-1987. Student Editor and Author, Public Contract Law Journal, 2000. *Member:* Virginia State Bar; American and National Bar Associations; National Society of Professional Engineers. [U.S. Air Force Reserves, 1987-2000]. ***PRACTICE AREAS:*** Intellectual Property; Design Patents; Mechanical Intellectual Property; Computer and Software Patents; Electrical Intellectual Property. ***Email:*** dmottley@bannerwitcoff.com

AJAY S. PATHAK, admitted to bar, 1993, Virginia; 2001, District of Columbia; registered to practice before U.S. Patent and Trademark Office, 1994. *Education:* Ohio Northern University (B.S., Pharmacy, 1983); Case Western Reserve University (M.S., Chemistry, 1985); Cleveland State University (J.D., 1992). Member, AIPLA, 1992-2001. *Member:* Virginia State Bar; The District of Columbia Bar; Patent Bar. ***PRACTICE AREAS:*** Intellectual Property Law; Patents; Biotechnology; Pharmaceutical Intellectual Property; Chemical Intellectual Property. ***Email:*** apathak@bannerwitcoff.com

PAUL M. RIVARD, admitted to bar, 1998, Virginia; 1999, District of Columbia; registered to practice before U.S. Patent and Trademark Office, 1999. *Education:* Clarkson University (B.S., 1992); The Catholic University of America (J.D., cum laude, 1998). Author: "Protection of Business Investments in Human Capital: Shop Right and Related Doctrines," Journal of the Patent and Trademark Office Society, Volume 79, Number 11, November 1997. *Member:* Virginia and American Bar Associations; The District of Columbia Bar (Member, Steering Committee, Intellectual Property Law Section); American Intellectual Property Law Association. ***PRACTICE AREAS:*** Intellectual Property Law; Patents; Chemical Intellectual Property; Pharmaceutical Intellectual Property. ***Email:*** privard@bannerwitcoff.com

CHRISTOPHER B. ROTH, admitted to bar, 1999, Virginia; 2001, District of Columbia. *Education:* Purdue University (B.S., 1994; M.S., 1996); University of Minnesota (J.D., 1999). *Member:* The District of Columbia Bar; American Institute of Chemical Engineers; American Chemical Society. ***PRACTICE AREAS:*** Intellectual Property Law; Intellectual Property Litigation; Chemical Intellectual Property; Patent Prosecution. ***Email:*** croth@bannerwitcoff.com

(For Complete Biographical Data on other Personnel, see Professional Biographies at Chicago, Illinois, Portland, Oregon and Boston, Massachusetts)

(This Listing Continued)

ALAN BANOV AND ASSOCIATES

Established in 1980

1400 K STREET, N.W., SUITE 1000
WASHINGTON, D.C. 20005-2403
Telephone: 202-842-9332
Fax: 202-842-9331
URL: http://www.banovlaw.com
Email: ab@banovlaw.com
URL: http://www.lawyers.com/alanbanovlaw

Labor and Employment, Employment Litigation, Wrongful Termination, Executive Compensation, Personnel Policies, Class Actions, Employment Contracts.

FIRM PROFILE: Alan Banov and Associates represents individuals and unions in employment and labor matters throughout Washington, D.C., Maryland, and Virginia. The firm provides clients with the highest quality litigation and counseling services that proudly reflect Mr. Banov's 30 years of experience.

(This Listing Continued)

ALAN BANOV, admitted to bar, 1971, District of Columbia and U.S. District Court, District of Columbia; 1980, Maryland, Court of Appeals of Maryland, U.S. District Court, Trial Bar, U.S. Supreme Court, U.S. Court of Federal Claims, U.S. Court of Appeals, First, Second Third, Fourth, Fifth, Sixth, Seventh, Eighth, Ninth, Tenth, District of Columbia and Federal Circuits. *Education:* University of North Carolina (A.B., 1967); George Washington University (J.D., with honors, 1971). Lectures: "Issues in D.C., Maryland Wrongful Discharge Cases," PELA Conference, Washington, January 17, 1987; "After-Acquired Evidence," Montgomery County Bar, Association Employment Law Committee, 1993; "EEO deferral agencies: a better, faster, cheaper way???" Metropolitan Washington Employment Lawyers Association, May 15, 1996; "A New Way For Wrongfully Discharged Employees in D.C. to recover damages: The Public Policy Tort Created by Carl v. Children's Hospital," Bar Association of District of Columbia Convention, November 2, 1998; "Preserving Your Verdict," panel at National Convention, National Employment Lawyers Association (NELA), July 3, 1999; Washington State Employment Lawyers Association, Feb. 4, 2000. Moderator and Co-Chair, NELA National Convention, July 2000. Panel Member, "The Financial Side of Human Resources," July 2001; "Wage and Hour Law Update," October 2001; "Litigating Employment Cases," October 2001; "State and Federal Personnel Laws in the District of Columbia," November 2001. Author: "When May Employees Sue States under the Federal Civil Rights Acts" 2 Employee Rights Quarterly 43 (summer 2001). National Labor Relations Board, Office of General Counsel, Regional Advice Branch, 1971-1974, Appellate Court Branch, 1974-1979. Mediator: Montgomery County Human Relations Commission, 1994—; Superior Court of District of Columbia, 1998—. *Member:* District of Columbia Bar; National Employment Lawyers Association (Co-Chairman and Moderator, NELA National Convention, June 23, 2000); Metropolitan Washington Employment Lawyers Association (Board Member, 1990—; President, 1998-2000). ***REPORTED CASES:*** Doby v. Safeway Stores, 523 F.Supp. 1162 (E.D.Va. 1981); Gilliam v. Glover, 470 A.2d 750 (D.C. App. 1983); Janet Hill v. Dept. of Health & Human Services, 27 MSPB 668 (1985); Webb v. U.S. Postal Service, 776 F.2d 1060 (Fed. Cir. 1985) (argued); Salyer v. D.C. Public Schools, 44 FEP Cases 1834 (D.D.C. 1987); Adkins v. United States, 816 F.2d 1580 (Fed. Cir. 1987); Keyes v. Secretary of the Navy, 853 F.2d 1016 (1st Cir. 1988); Stephenson v. Martin Marietta, Inc., 48 FEP Cases 37 (D. Md. 1988); Goos v. National Association of Realtors, 715 F.Supp. 2 (D.D.C. 1989); Goos v. National Assn. of Realtors, 57 FEP Cases 1531 (D.D.C. 1991); Goos v. National Assn. of Realtors, 997 F.2d 1565 (D.C. Cir. 1992); Goos v. National Assn. of Realtors, 68 F.3d 1380 (D.C. Cir. 1995); Kentucky Fried Chicken National Management Co. v. Weathersby, 326 Md. 663, 607 A.2d 8 (1991); Weathersby v. Kentucky Fried Chicken Nat. Mgt. Co., 804 F.Supp. 756 (D. Md. 1992); Albright v. United States, 26 C. Ct. 1119 (1992), aff'd, Albright v. United States, 10 F.3d 3 (Fed. Cir. 1993); Albright v. United States, 10 F.3d 3 (Fed. Cir. 1993); Green v. Howard University, C.A. No. 91-4194 (D.C. Super. Ct., Dec. 4, 1992), 121 Wash. L. Rep. 629 (Mar. 31, 1993); Howard University v. Green, 652 A.2d 41 (D.C. 1994); Johnson v. D.C. Public Schools, 1995 U.S. Dist. LEXIS 9588 (D.D.C. 1995); Halperin v. Abacus Technology, 128 F.3d 191 (4th Cir. 1997); Simpkins v. WMATA, 1997 WL 702349 (D.C. Cir. 1997) (unpublished); Stroman v. Blue Cross and Blue Shield Ass'n, 966 F.Supp. 9 (D.D.C. 1997); Freas v. Archer Services, 716 A.2d 998, 1998 D.C. App. LEXIS 163 (D.C. 1998); Guerra v. Cuomo, 176 F.3d 547 (D.C. Cir. 1999); Weigert v. Georgetown University, 43 F.Supp. 2d 5 (D.D.C. 1999); Litman v. George Mason University, 186 F.3d 544, 1999 U.S. App. LEXIS 17825 (4th Cir. 1999); George Mason University v. United States and Litman, 120 S. Ct. 1220 (2000). Co-Author, amicus briefs: Gray v. Citizens Bank of Washington, 609 A.2d 1143 (D.C. 1992) (en banc); Thigpen v. Greenpeace, Inc., 657 A.2d 770, 123 Wash. L. Rep. 953 (D.C. 1995). ***PRACTICE AREAS:*** Employment Law; Labor Law; Personal Injury; Litigation.

ASSOCIATE

NORBERTO PEREZ SALINAS, admitted to bar, 2000, Michigan; 2001, District of Columbia and U.S. Court of Federal Claims. *Education:* Wabash College (A.B., 1997); University of Michigan (J.D., 2000). *Member:* State Bar of Michigan; The District of Columbia Bar; American Bar Association; Metropolitan Washington Employment Lawyers Association. ***PRACTICE AREAS:*** Retaliatory Discharge; Employment Discrimination; Equal Employment Opportunity Law; Title VII Discrimination; Employment Law. ***Email:*** salinas@banovlaw.com

---

BAPTISTE & WILDER, P.C.

Established in 1985

SUITE 500, 1150 CONNECTICUT AVENUE, N.W.
WASHINGTON, D.C. 20036
Telephone: 202-223-0723
Fax: 202-223-9677
URL: http://www.lawyers.com/baptiste&wilder

Labor Relations, Federal Civil Litigation, Administrative, Regulatory, ERISA, Civil Rights Law, Aviation.

(This Listing Continued)

FIRM PROFILE: The law firm of Baptiste & Wilder, P.C. represents Labor organizations, Pension, Health & Welfare funds and individual employees with employment disputes. The firm has a national labor practice which includes litigation in federal courts and appearances before federal administrative agencies.

ROBERT M. BAPTISTE, born Cambridge, Massachusetts, August 5, 1941; admitted to bar, 1967, U.S. District Court for the District of Columbia, District of Columbia and U.S. Court of Appeals for the District of Columbia Circuit; 1970, U.S. Court of Appeals, lst Circuit; 1976, U.S. Court of Appeals, 4th and 5th Circuits; 1980, U.S. Court of Appeals, 3rd Circuit; 1981, U.S. Supreme Court; 1983, U.S. Court of Appeals, 6th Circuit; 1989, U.S. Court of Appeals, 2nd Circuit; 1988, U.S. District Court, District of Maryland. *Education:* Tufts University (B.A., 1963); Georgetown University (LL.B., 1966; LL.M., 1967). *Member:* The District of Columbia Bar; American Bar Association. ***PRACTICE AREAS:*** Labor Relations Law; Federal Civil Litigation; Administrative Law; Regulatory Law.

ROLAND P. WILDER, JR., born Malden, Massachusetts, June 21, 1940; admitted to bar, 1967, U.S. District Court for the District of Columbia, District of Columbia and U.S. Court of Appeals for the District of Columbia Circuit; 1972, U.S. Supreme Court; 1976, U.S. Court of Appeals, 4th, 5th and 6th Circuits; 1977, U.S. Court of Appeals, 8th and 9th Circuits; 1978, U.S. Court of Appeals, 2nd Circuit; 1981, U.S. Court of Appeals, 11th Circuit; 1994, U.S. District Court, District of Maryland; 1997, U.S. District Court, District of Colorado and U.S. Court of Appeals, Third Circuit. *Education:* Washington & Jefferson College (B.A., 1963); Vanderbilt University (J.D., 1966). Phi Alpha Theta; Pi Sigma Alpha; Phi Delta Phi. Recipient: American Jurisprudence Award; Short Articles Award. Managing Editor, Vanderbilt Law Review, 1965-1966. Author: Comment, *Minority Strikers,* 18 Vand. L. Rev. 262, 1964; Comment, *Pre-emption of State Libel Actions,* 18 Vand. L. Rev. 783, 1965; *Discharge In the "Law" of Arbitration,* 20 Vand. L. Rev. 81, 1966. Co-Author: *Affirmative Action Under Executive Order 11246,* 46 N.Y.U.L. Rev. 225, 1971; *The Reach of the Secondary Boycott Provisions Under the LMRA,* 1973 N.Y.U. 25th Annual Conference on Labor 69; *The Development of the Collyer Deferral Doctrine,* 27 Vand. L. Rev. 23, 1974; *Successorship: A Union Perspective,* Cleared for Takeoff, Cornell I.L.R. Press, September, 1988. Counsel for Civil Rights, Office of the Solicitor, U.S. Department of Labor, 1970-1971. Supervisory Attorney, Office of the General Counsel, National Labor Relations Board, 1972-1974. *Member:* The District of Columbia Bar; Bar Association of the District of Columbia; American Bar Association; Association of Trial Lawyers of America. ***PRACTICE AREAS:*** Labor Relations Law; Federal Civil Litigation; ERISA; Civil Rights Law.

PATRICK J. SZYMANSKI, born Detroit, Michigan, January 18, 1949; admitted to bar, 1976, Michigan; 1977, U.S. Court of Appeals, 1st, 2nd, 4th and District of Columbia Circuits; 1978, U.S. Court of Appeals, 9th Circuit; 1979, California, District of Columbia and U.S. District Court, Northern District of California; 1984, U.S. Court of Appeals, 10th Circuit; 1985, U.S. Supreme Court; 1987, U.S. Court of Appeals, 5th Circuit; 1988, U.S. District Court, District of Columbia and Maryland; 1991, U.S. District Court, Eastern District of Michigan; 1997, U.S. Court of Appeals, Eighth Circuit; 1999, U.S. Court of Appeals, Sixth Circuit. *Education:* Wayne State University (B.A., 1973; J.D., cum laude, 1976). Recipient: Samuel M. Kaynard Award for Excellence in the field of Labor and Employment Law, Hofstra Labor and Employment Journal, 2000. Articles Editor, Wayne Law Review, 1975-1976. Author: Note, "Constitutional Law —An Individual Legislator's Standing to Sue," 21 Wayne L. Rev. 1115, 1975. Co-Author: With Arthur J. Lombard, "Civil Procedure, 1975 Annual Survey of Michigan Law," 22 Wayne L. Rev. 263, 1976; "Constitutional Law, 1976 Annual Survey of Michigan Law," 23 Wayne L. Rev. 441, 1977; With John Kagel and Kathy Kelly, "Labor Arbitration: Cutting Cost and Time Without Cutting Quality," The Arbitration Journal, Sept. 1984. Attorney, Appellate Court Branch, Office of the General Counsel, National Labor Relations Board, 1976-1978, 1983-1988. *Member:* The District of Columbia Bar (Member, Section on Labor Relations, Co-Chair, 1984-1986, 1987-1989; Sections Council, Vice Chair, 1987-1988, Chair, 1988-1989); State Bar of California; State Bar of Michigan; American Bar Association. ***PRACTICE AREAS:*** Labor Law; Employment Law; ERISA; Federal Civil Litigation; Appellate Litigation.

CHRISTY CONCANNON, born Philadelphia, Pennsylvania, August 9, 1962; admitted to bar, 1987, Pennsylvania; 1988, District of Columbia; U.S. Court of Appeals for the District of Columbia Circuit; 1989, U.S. Court of Appeals, Second, Third, Fourth, and Sixth Circuits; 1996, U.S. Supreme Court; 1997, U.S. District Court, District of Colorado. *Education:* Franklin and Marshall College (B.A., 1984); Columbus School of Law, Catholic University of America (J.D., 1987). Associate Editor, The Catholic University of America Law Review, 1986-1987. Author: Comment, "The EAJA and the NLRB; Chilling the General Counsel's Prerogative to Issue Unfair Labor Practice Complaints?" 36 Catholic U.L. Rev. 175, 1986. *Member:* The District of Columbia Bar; Pennsylvania Bar Association. ***PRACTICE AREAS:*** Labor Relations; ERISA; Employment Law. ***Email:*** bapwild@aol.com

SUSAN BOYLE, born Jersey City, New Jersey, February 6, 1965; admitted to bar, 1992, New Jersey; 1993, District of Columbia; 1994, New York and U.S.

(This Listing Continued)

BAPTISTE & WILDER, P.C., Washington—Continued

District Court, District of Maryland; 1997, U.S. District Court, District of Columbia. *Education:* George Washington University (B.A., 1987); Fordham University (J.D., 1991). *Member:* New York State and New Jersey State Bar Associations; The District of Columbia Bar. ***PRACTICE AREAS:*** Labor Relations Law; Civil Rights Law.

JAMES F. WALLINGTON, born Philadelphia, Pennsylvania, March 16, 1953; admitted to bar, 1980, West Virginia; 1993, District of Columbia. *Education:* West Virginia University (A.B., 1975; J.D., 1980). *Member:* West Virginia State Bar; District of Columbia Bar. ***PRACTICE AREAS:*** Labor Relations Law.

WILLIAM R. WILDER, born Alexandria, Virginia, May 18, 1968; admitted to bar, 1993, Virginia; 1995, U.S. District Court, Eastern District of Virginia; 1996, District of Columbia; 1997, Texas and U.S. District Court, Western District of Virginia and Southern District of Texas; 1998, U.S. Court of Appeals for the Fourth and Fifth Circuits; 1999, U.S. District Court, Northern District of Texas; 2000, U.S. Court of Appeals for the Ninth Circuit. *Education:* Virginia Polytechnic Institute & State University (B.A., 1990); College of William & Mary (J.D., 1993). Member, Order of the Barristers (1993). American Bar Association National Appellate Advocacy Competition, 1992. *Member:* Virginia State Bar; District of Columbia Bar; State Bar of Texas; American Bar Association; Virginia Trial Lawyers Association; Association of Trial Lawyers of America. ***PRACTICE AREAS:*** Labor Relations; Federal Litigation; Employment Law; Civil Litigation.

JENSEN EGERTON BARBER II

Established in 1986

THE JENIFER BUILDING, SUITE 400
400 SEVENTH STREET, N.W.
WASHINGTON, D.C. 20004-2206
Telephone: 202-737-8511
Fax: 202-628-0249
Email: jebarber@juno.com

Federal Litigation Practice, Complex and Multi-District Civil and Criminal Litigation, Grand Jury Practice, Federal Criminal Law, Criminal Defense, Capital Criminal Defense, Criminal Conspiracy, Money Laundering, RICO, White Collar Crime, Business Fraud, Mail Fraud, Wiretapping, Electronic Surveillance, Forgery, Theft, Drug Crimes, DWI, Homicide, Post-Conviction Remedies, Search and Seizure, Personal Injury, Auto Accidents, Wrongful Death, Medical Malpractice, Orthopedic Malpractice.

FIRM PROFILE: Mr. Barber is a former national intelligence officer who was been responsible for collecting, analyzing and disseminating sensitive intelligence information to the highest levels of the government. He is now a well known courtroom trial attorney who specializes in complex federal litigation and criminal defense. He has a national reputation and practice concentrating on the representation of individuals and corporations in a diversity of federal legal matters. He is a frequently requested co-counsel by other attorneys and law firms to provide seasoned litigation experience, in-depth analysis and persuasive opening statements and closing arguments.

JENSEN EGERTON BARBER, II, born Asheville, North Carolina, May 22, 1945; admitted to bar, 1984, District of Columbia; 1987, U.S. District Court, District of Columbia; 1988, U.S. Court of Appeals, District of Columbia Circuit; 1989, U.S. Court of Appeals, Eleventh Circuit; 1990, U.S. Supreme Court; 1991, U.S. District Court, District of Maryland; 1995, U.S. Court of Appeals, Fourth Circuit; 2000, U.S. Court of Appeals, Third Circuit. *Education:* George Washington University (M.A. Special Studies: Criminal Justice, 1978); Columbus School of Law of the Catholic University of America (J.D., 1982). Recipient, Vietnam Veteran, Bronze Star for Bravery. Who's Who, 1998. Member University Club, Georgetown Club. *Member:* District of Columbia Bar; American Bar Association; D.C. Association of Criminal Defense Lawyers (Founding Member); National Association of Criminal Defense Lawyers; Association of Trial Lawyers of America; College of Barristers (2001). ***LANGUAGES:*** French. ***PRACTICE AREAS:*** Criminal Defense; Medical Malpractice; Personal Injury; Litigation.

LEGAL SUPPORT PERSONNEL

BRAD DAVIDSON (admission pending) (Legal Support Investigator).

LAW OFFICES OF CLAUDIA BARBER

WASHINGTON, D.C.

(See Laurel, MD)

Church Law, Copyrights, Trademarks, Real Estate Settlements, Corporate and Small Business Law, Automobile Accidents and Injuries, Personal Injury, Wrongful Death, Employment Law, Discrimination, Sexual Harassment, Family Law, Adoptions, Divorce, Custody, Visitation, Uncontested Divorces, Entertainment Law, Wills, Probate, EEO Investigations, General Practice, Franchises and Franchising, Environmental Law.

BARNES, RICHARDSON & COLBURN

Established in 1956

SUITE 1150, 1225 EYE STREET, N.W.
WASHINGTON, D.C. 20005
Telephone: 202-457-0300
Facsimile: 202-331-8746
Email: barnes@brc-dc.com
URL: http://www.barnesrichardson.com

New York, New York Office: 475 Park Avenue South. Telephone: 212-725-0200.
Chicago, Illinois Office: 303 East Wacker Drive, Suite 1100. Telephone: 312-565-2000.

Customs and International Trade Law, Administrative Law. General Federal Litigation and Appellate Practice.

RESIDENT MEMBERS OF FIRM

MATTHEW T. McGRATH, born New Castle, Pennsylvania, 1954; admitted to bar, 1979, District of Columbia; 1981, U.S. Court of International Trade. *Education:* Bucknell Univ. (B.A., cum laude, 1976); George Washington Univ. (J.D., 1979). Notes Editor, George Washington Journal of International Law and Economics, 1978-1979. ***PRACTICE AREAS:*** Customs; International Trade. ***Email:*** mmcgrath@brc-dc.com

ROBERT A. SHAPIRO, born Baltimore, Maryland, 1961; admitted to bar, 1997, New York; 1999, District of Columbia. *Education:* Connecticut College (B.A., 1983); Cornell Univ. (J.D., cum laude, 1996; LL.M., cum laude, 1996). Customhouse Broker, 1985—. ***PRACTICE AREAS:*** Customs; International Trade. ***Email:*** rshapiro@brc-dc.com

NON-RESIDENT MEMBERS OF FIRM

Rufus E. Jarman, Jr. (N.Y.)
James S. O'Kelly (N.Y.)
Robert E. Burke (Chicago)
Donald J. Unger (Chicago)
Sandra Liss Friedman (N.Y.)
Brian F. Walsh (Chicago)
Kazumune V. Kano (Chicago)
Frederic D. Van Arnam, Jr. (N.Y.)
Lawrence M. Friedman (Chicago)
Alan Goggins (N.Y.)

RESIDENT ASSOCIATES

STEPHEN W. BROPHY, born Carbondale, Pennsylvania, 1971; admitted to bar, 1998, Pennsylvania; 2000, District of Columbia. *Education:* Univ. of Scranton (B.S., 1993); Georgetown Univ. (J.D., 1996). Member, Georgetown International Environmental Law Review, 1994-1995. ***PRACTICE AREAS:*** International Trade; Customs. ***Email:*** sbrophy@brc-dc.com

MICHAEL J. CHESSLER, born Philadelphia, Pennsylvania, 1967; admitted to bar, 1995, Illinois; 1996, U.S. Court of Appeals for the Federal Circuit and U.S. Court of International Trade; 1997, District of Columbia. *Education:* George Washington Univ. (B.A., 1990); John Marshall Law School (J.D., 1995). ***PRACTICE AREAS:*** Customs; International Trade. ***Email:*** mchessler@brc-dc.com

JAMES B. DORAN, born Irvine, Ayrshire, Scotland, 1964; admitted to bar, 2000, Maryland (Not admitted in District of Columbia). *Education:* Univ. of Glasgow (M.A. (Hons), 1989); Georgetown Univ. (J.D., 1999). ***LANGUAGES:*** Spanish. ***PRACTICE AREAS:*** Food and Drug; International Trade; Customs. ***Email:*** jdoran@brc-dc.com

SPECIAL COUNSEL

ANSIS M. HELMANIS, born Germany, 1945; admitted to bar, 1973, New Hampshire; 1974, Massachusetts (Not admitted in District of Columbia). *Education:* Boston Univ. (B.A., 1967); Ruprecht-Karls-Univ., Heidelberg, Germany, 1967-1970; New England School of Law (J.D., 1973); Georgetown Univ., 1976. ***LANGUAGES:*** German and Latvian. ***PRACTICE AREAS:*** Food and Drug Regulation. ***Email:*** ahelmanis@brc-dc.com

(This Listing Continued)

COUNSEL

GUNTER VON CONRAD, born Cologne, Germany, 1934; admitted to bar, 1965, District of Columbia; 1980, U.S. Court of International Trade. *Education:* Bonn Univ.; Cologne Univ. (Dr. Jur., 1963); George Washington Univ. (M.C.L., 1965). ***LANGUAGES:*** German. ***PRACTICE AREAS:*** Customs; International Trade. ***Email:*** gvconrad@brc-dc.com

(For Complete Personnel and Biographical Data, see Professional Biographies at New York, N.Y. and Chicago, IL)

BARNES & THORNBURG

750 17TH STREET, N.W.
SUITE 900
WASHINGTON, D.C. 20006
Telephone: 202-289-1313
FAX: 202-289-1330
URL: http://www.btlaw.com

Indianapolis, Indiana Office: 11 South Meridian Street, 46204. Telephone: 317-236-1313. FAX: 317-231-7433.

Fort Wayne, Indiana Office: 600 One Summit Square, 46802. Telephone: 260-423-9440. FAX: 260-424-8316.

South Bend, Indiana Office: 600 1st Source Bank Center, 100 North Michigan, 46601-1632. Telephone: 574-233-1171. FAX: 574-237-1125.

Elkhart, Indiana Office: 121 West Franklin Street, Suite 200, 46516. Telephone: 574-293-0681. FAX: 574-296-2535.

Chicago, Illinois Office: 2600 Chase Plaza, 10 South LaSalle Street, 60603. Telephone: 312-357-1313. FAX: 312-759-5646.

Acquisitions and Divestitures, Ad Valorem Tax, Administrative Law, Affirmative Action, Agriculture Law, Americans with Disabilities Act, Antidumping, Antitrust, Antitrust and Trade Regulation, Appellate Practice, Attorney Grievances, Automotive Warranty Law, Aviation and Aerospace, Aviation Law, Banking Law, Banking Regulations, Bankruptcy, Bankruptcy Reorganization, Banks and Banking, Biochemical Patents, Biomedical Products Liability, Biomedical Technology, Biotechnology Patent Prosecution, Bond Law, Brain Injury, Breach of Warranty, Brown Fields Redevelopment, Business Immigration, Business Law, Business Litigation, Business Planning, Business Regulatory and Administrative, Business Start-ups, Business Succession Planning, Business Taxation, Business Torts, Business Transactions, Business Transfers, Buying and Selling of Businesses, Cable TV, Cargo Claims, Charitable Trusts and Foundations, Chemical Intellectual Property, Chemical Patent Prosecution, Chemical Patents, Chemical Products Liability, Civil Appeals, Civil Litigation, Civil Practice, Civil RICO, Class Action Defense, Clean Air Act, Clean Water Act, Closely Held Business Estate Planning, Closely Held Businesses, Closely Held Business Law, Closely Held Corporations, Collective Bargaining, Commercial Bankruptcy, Commercial Finance Law, Commercial Law, Commercial Leasing and Financing, Commercial Litigation, Commercial Conveyancing, Commercial Real Estate, Commercial Real Estate Acquisition, Commercial Real Estate Development, Commercial Real Estate Finance, Commercial Transactions, Commodities Fraud, Communications and Media, Complex Commercial Litigation, Complex Litigation, Computer and Software Patents, Computer Law, Computers and Software, Conflicts of Interest, Construction Labor Law, Construction Law, Consumer Credit, Contract Litigation, Cooperatives, Copyrights, Corporate Finance, Corporate Formation, Corporate Law, Corporate Taxation, Corporate Tax Planning, Countervailing Duties, Covenants Not To Compete, Creditors Rights, Creditors Rights in Bankruptcy, Criminal Defense, Criminal Law, Criminal Tax Audits, Customs Law, Dealer and Distributor Termination, Debt and Equity Finance, Decedents Estates, Defense Litigation, Design Patents, Disability Insurance Defense, Discrimination, Distribution, Drug and Medical Device Defense, Economic Development, Education Law, Elder Law, Election, Campaign and Political Law, Electric Power, Electric Utilities, Electrical Intellectual Property, Electrical Patents, Electro-mechanical Patents, Electronic Commerce, Electronic Patents, Eminent Domain, Employee Benefits, Employee Stock Ownership Plans, Employment Defense, Employment Discrimination, Employment Law, Employment Litigation, Energy, Energy Contracts, Energy Regulation, Environmental Administrative Law, Environmental Cleanup, Environmental Compliance, Environmental Criminal Defense, Environmental Law, Environmental Litigation, Environmental Permitting, Environmental Real Estate, Environmental Regulation, Environmental Risk Management, Equal Employment Opportunity Law, ERISA Litigation, Estate Administration, Estate and Gift Taxation, Estate Planning, Estate Planning and Taxation, Estate Planning and Administration, Estate Planning and Probate, Estate Planning for Parents of Handicapped Children, Estate Planning for Unmarried Individuals, Executive Compensation, Executive Severance Contracts, Export Regulation, Fair Employment Practices, Family and Medical Leave Act, Family Business Successions, Family Wealth Transfer, Federal and State Administrative Regulatory Practice, Federal and State Legislative Practice, Federal Civil Litigation, Federal Civil Practice, Federal Criminal Law, Federal Estate and Gift Taxation, Federal Litigation, Federal Tax Controversies, Federal Taxation, Fiduciary Income Tax, Finance, Financial Transactions, First Party Insurance, Foreign Investment in the United States, Freight Claims, Freight Loss and Damage,

(This Listing Continued)

Gaming Law, Gaming Licensing, Gas Utilities, General Litigation, Government, Government Affairs, Government Agency Practice, Government Contracts, Government Investigations, Government Relations, Groundwater Contamination, Hazardous Materials and Substances, Hazardous Waste, Hazardous Waste Liability, Head Injury, Health Care, Health Care Corporate Law, Health Care Contracts, Health Care Fraud, Health Care Licensing, Health Care Litigation, Health Care Mergers and Acquisitions, Health Care Regulation, Health Care Reimbursement, Health Law, Heavy Equipment Products Liability, Immigration Law, Industrial Revenue Bond Law, Inheritance Tax, Initial Public Offerings, Insurance, Insurance Bad Faith, Insurance Coverage, Insurance Litigation, Insurance Regulation, Integrated Health Care Delivery Systems, Intellectual Property, Intellectual Property General Prosecution, Intellectual Property Infringement, Intellectual Property Licensing, Intellectual Property Litigation, Intellectual Property Procurement, Intellectual Property Protection, Intellectual Property Rights, International Business Law, International Intellectual Property, International Law, International Patents, International Trade, International Transportation Law, Internet Law, Internet Trademark Law, Joint Ventures, Labor and Employment, Labor Arbitration, Labor Law, Labor Relations, Land Use, Lease Law, Leasing, Legal Ethics and Professional Responsibility, Legal Malpractice Defense, Legislative Practice, Licensing, Life Insurance Defense, Limited Liability Company Law, Limited Partnerships, Liquor Licensing, Litigation, Loans, Lobbying, Local Government Law, Logistics, Long Term Care, Managed Care, Managed Care Contracts, Management Employment Law, Management Labor Law, Manufacturers Liability, Maritime Regulations, Mechanical Intellectual Property, Mechanical Patents, Media Law, Mediation, Medical Antitrust, Medical Intellectual Property, Medical Patents, Mental Health Law, Mergers, Acquisitions and Divestitures, Mergers and Acquisitions, Mineral Taxation, Molecular Biology Patents, Motor Carrier Law, Motor Carrier Regulation, Multi-Employer Pensions, Municipal Bonds, Municipal Bonds Taxation, Municipal Finance, Municipal Law, Municipal Leasing, Municipal Redevelopment, Municipal Securities, Municipal Taxation, National Labor Relations Act, Neurolaw, Nonprofit and Charitable Organizations, Nonprofit Organizations Law, North American Free Trade Agreement, Occupational Safety and Health, OSHA, Partnership Law, Partnership Taxation, Patent Infringement, Patent Interference Practice, Patent Litigation, Patent Prosecution, Patents, PCT Legal Export, Personal Injury, Personal Injury Defense, Pesticide Litigation, Pharmaceutical Intellectual Property, Pharmaceutical Patents, Physician Contracts, Physician Practices, Planning and Land Use, Power Line Contact Injury, Probate, Probate Litigation, Products Liability, Products Liability Defense, Professional Liability, Property Law, Property Tax, Property Tax Abatement, Property Tax Appeals, Psychological Injury, Public Finance, Public Sector Labor Relations, Public Utility Law, Railroad Law, Real Estate, Real Estate Acquisitions, Real Estate Contracts, Real Estate Development, Real Estate Finance, Real Estate Licensing, Real Estate Secured Lending, Real Estate Title Insurance, Real Property, Real Property Acquisitions, Real Property Finance, Reorganizations, Resource Conservation and Recovery Act (RCRA), Retirement Benefit Plans, School Law, Securities, Securities Litigation, Securitization, Semiconductor Technology, Sexual Harassment, Small Business Corporations, State Government Law, State Tax Controversies, State Taxation, Structured Finance, Succession Planning, Superfund, Tax Controversies, Tax Exempt Finance, Tax Exempt Organizations, Tax Increment Finance, Tax Law, Tax Litigation, Taxation, Technology and Science, Technology Law, Technology Licensing, Technology Transfers, Telecommunications Competition, Telecommunications Law, Theft of Trade Secrets, Title VII Discrimination, Title IX Discrimination, Tort Defense, Toxic Exposure, Toxic Tort Class Actions, Toxic Torts, Toxic Tort Defense, Trade Dress, Trade Secrets, Trademark Litigation, Trademarks, Trademark Prosecution, Trademark Protection, Trademark Registration, Transportation, Transportation Safety, Trial Practice, Trusts and Estates, Unfair Competition, Unfair Trade, Uniform Commercial Codes, Union Contract Negotiations, Union Elections, Utilities, Utility Law, Wage and Hour Law, WARN Act, Water Pollution, Water Quality, Water Utilities, Wetland Regulation, White Collar Crime, White Collar Criminal Defense, Wills, Workers Compensation, Workouts, World Trade Organization, Wrongful Death, Wrongful Termination, Wrongful Termination Defense, Zoning, Planning and Land Use.

FIRM PROFILE: Quality. Service. Efficiency. Communication. These are the cornerstones of the firm's culture and the keys to its success.

Established on January 1, 1982, Barnes & Thornburg is relatively young; however, its founding date belies the firm's rich history. The firm's roots can be traced to two cities, South Bend and Indianapolis. Our northern Indiana presence began in 1926 with the establishment of Seebirt Oare & Omacht, and later grew when they merged with an Elkhart firm, Cawley and Harman. In Indianapolis, four partners opened Barnes Hickam Pantzer & Boyd on September 13, 1940. They began the firm with 13 people in an office of 13 rooms on the 13th floor of the Merchants Bank Building, the tallest building in Indiana at that time. The number 13 has proven to be a lucky number for Barnes & Thornburg.

Since 1982, the firm has opened offices in Chicago, Fort Wayne and Washington, D.C. and merged with Jenkins, Coffey, Hyland, Badger & Conard, an intellectual property firm; Roberts, Ryder, Rogers & Scism, a labor and employment law firm; Church, Nilsson & Paulen of Elkhart; and, most recently, Roemer & Mintz, LLP, of South Bend. The firm has also been joined by Gallucci, Hopkins & Theisen, P.C.,

(This Listing Continued)

BARNES & THORNBURG, Washington—Continued

a Fort Wayne firm with an extensive labor and employment practice, and Johnson Lawhead Buth & Pope, P.C., an Indianapolis firm with a concentration in estate planning. Today Barnes & Thornburg is the largest law firm in Indiana and one of the largest in the Midwest. More than 320 attorneys provide legal services to more than 11,000 international, national, regional and local clients.

With offices in Washington, D.C., Indianapolis, Fort Wayne, South Bend, Elkhart and Chicago, we are a business-minded law firm serving clients ranging from Fortune 100 companies and governmental entities to individuals and nonprofit organizations. We represent the interests of businesses in our primary practices: business, tax and real estate, creditors' rights, energy, telecommunications and utilities, environmental law, governmental services and finance, healthcare, intellectual property, labor and employment law, litigation, appellate, business and technology, construction law, e-commerce, economic development, entrepreneurial services, financial institutions, international, media, pension and benefits litigation, property tax, transportation and white collar crime. Each of our offices offers a unique blend of services which collectively make Barnes & Thornburg a diverse and dynamic legal resource for our clients and communities.

We have lawyers involved at city, state and national levels of the legal profession as officers, chairpersons and committee members in legal organizations. Others are authors, presenters and drafters of legislation. Most of our lawyers are active in their communities and provide civic leadership. Each office sponsors, contributes to, and often leads, an array of community activities.

LAW FIRM ALLIANCES/ASSOCIATIONS: **TECHLAW GROUP**
TERRALEX

PARTNERS

RANDOLPH J. STAYIN, admitted to bar, 1967, Ohio; 1976, District of Columbia. *Education:* Dartmouth College (A.B., 1964); University of Cincinnati (J.D., 1967). Administrative Assistant and Director of Legislation to Senator Robert Taft, Jr., 1973-1976. Member: Advisory Council for the U.S. and Foreign Commercial Service of the U.S. Department of Commerce. *Member:* Ohio State and American Bar Associations; District of Columbia Bar; International and Inter-American Bar Associations. ***PRACTICE AREAS:*** Antidumping; Countervailing Duties; Customs Law; Export Regulation; World Trade Organization. ***Email:*** rstayin@btlaw.com

RICHARD H. STREETER, admitted to bar, 1970, Texas; 1975, District of Columbia. *Education:* University of Texas (B.A., 1965; M.A., 1969; J.D., 1970). Office of the General Counsel, Interstate Commerce Commission, 1971-1975. Commissioner, 1978-1980 and Vice Chair, 1979-1980, District of Columbia Rental Accommodations Commission. ***PRACTICE AREAS:*** International Trade; Freight Loss and Damage; Hazardous Materials and Substances; Customs Law; Railroad Law; Antidumping. ***Email:*** rstreete@btlaw.com

OTHER PROFESSIONALS

JEFFREY L. TAYLOR. *Education:* Assumption College (B.A., 1984). (Lobbyist, Federal Relations). ***PRACTICE AREAS:*** Government; Technology; Communications and Media; Energy; Finance; Environment. ***Email:*** jtaylor@btlaw.com

JOHN R. EDGELL. *Education:* James Madison University (B.B.A., Management, 1983). Lobbyist, Federal Relations. Staff Assistant: Senator Bill Bradley (D-NJ), 1979; Rep. Tom Daschle (D-SD), 1985-1986. Legislative Assistant, Rep. Pete Stark (D-CA), 1987-1993. Special Assistant, Department of Commerce, Office of Secretary Ron Brown, 1993-1994. Professional Staff Member, Information, Justice, Transportation & Agriculture Subcommittee, House Government Operations, 1994-1995. Legislative Director: Rep. Bill Luther (D-MN), 1995; Rep. Joe Kennedy (D-MA), 1996. Chief of Staff and Press Secretary, Rep. Dennis Kucinich (D-OH), 1997-2001. (Lobbyist). ***PRACTICE AREAS:*** Government; Taxation; Agricultural Law; Transportation; Health Care; Aviation and Aerospace. ***Email:*** jedgell@btlaw.com

INTELLECTUAL PROPERTY DEPARTMENT

PARTNERS

PERRY PALAN, admitted to bar, 1970, Virginia; 1972, District of Columbia; 1978, Maryland; registered to practice before U.S. Patent and Trademark Office. *Education:* Washington University (B.S.E.E., 1965); George Washington University (J.D., 1970). ***PRACTICE AREAS:*** Patents; Trademarks; Copyrights; Technology Licensing; Technology Transfers; Joint Ventures. ***Email:*** ppalan@btlaw.com

JOSEPH D. LEWIS, admitted to bar, 1979, District of Columbia. *Education:* Hobart College (B.A., 1976); George Washington University National Law Center (J.D., with honors, 1979). Law Clerk to Hon. Francis C. Browne, U.S. Ct. of Claims. ***PRACTICE AREAS:*** Intellectual Property; Computer Law; Trademarks; Copyrights; Technology Law; Internet Law. ***Email:*** jdlewis@btlaw.com

OF COUNSEL

MARK M. NEWMAN, admitted to bar, 1962, District of Columbia; registered to practice before U.S. Patent and Trademark Office. *Education:* Wesleyan University; Antioch College (B.S., 1958); Washington College of Law, American University (J.D., 1962). Director, Trademark Examining Operation, 1982-1984 and Director, Mechanical Patent Examining Operation, 1971-1982, U.S. Patent and Trademark Office. *Member:* Government Patent Lawyers Association (President, 1975; Secretary, 1972-1973). (Limited to matters and proceedings before federal courts and agencies.). ***PRACTICE AREAS:*** Patents; Trademarks; Copyrights. ***Email:*** mnewman@btlaw.com

PAUL E. FAHRENKOPF, admitted to bar, 1980, New Jersey; U.S. Supreme Court; U.S. Court of Appeals for the Federal Circuit (Not admitted in District of Columbia). *Education:* The American University (B.A., 1974); University of Miami School of Law (J.D., 1978). *Member:* American Bar Association; Washington Area Lawyers for the Arts. ***PRACTICE AREAS:*** Trademark Protection; Trademark Registration; Trade Dress. ***Email:*** pfahrenk@btlaw.com

KAREN A. McGEE, admitted to bar, 1988, Maryland; 1990, District of Columbia. *Education:* Providence College (B.A., 1981); George Washington University (J.D., 1988). Formerly with U.S. Patent & Trademark Office, 1997-2000. *Member:* District of Columbia Bar (Member, Intellectual Property Section, 2000—); Federal American Inn of Courts. ***PRACTICE AREAS:*** Trademarks; International Trade; Intellectual Property. ***Email:*** kmcgee@btlaw.com

RICHARD PAUL KRINSKY, admitted to bar, 1982, District of Columbia; registered to practice before U.S. Patent and Trademark Office. *Education:* Alfred University (B.S., Ceramic Engineering, 1962); University of Alabama (M.A., Statistics/Operations Research, 1969); Columbus School of Law of the Catholic University of America (J.D., 1981). *Member:* The District of Columbia Bar. ***PRACTICE AREAS:*** Patents; Trademarks; Copyrights; Aviation Law; Intellectual Property; Transportation; Business Law; Regulatory Law; Administrative Law. ***Email:*** rkrinsky@btlaw.com

RICHARD B. LAZARUS, admitted to bar, 1974, Maryland; 1979, District of Columbia; registered to practice before the U.S. Patent and Trademark Office. *Education:* Purdue University (B.S.M.E., 1967); Catholic University of America (J.D., 1972). Science & Technology Fellow, U.S. Department of Commerce, 1974-1975. Manager, PCT Legal Affairs Branch, 1993-2000. Administrative Patent Judge, Board of Appeals and Interference, 2000-2001. ***PRACTICE AREAS:*** Patent Prosecution; Patents; Copyrights; Trademarks. ***Email:*** rlazarus@btlaw.com

REPRESENTATIVE CLIENTS: All Energy Marketing Co.; Arkansas Short Line Railroads, Inc.; ArvinMeritor; Amerigas, Inc.; AM General Corp.; BAX Global; Bridgestone-Firestone; Canadian Freightways Limited; Center for Employment Security Education and Research, Inc.; Consolidated Freightways Corporation; Con-Way Transportation Services, Inc.; Deutsche Post; Dispatch Management Services Corp.; El Conejo Americano of Texas Inc.; Emery Worldwide; ExCargo Services, Inc.; Food Processing Machinery and Supplies Association; Gates Corporation; Global Passenger Services, L.L.C.; Hays Home Delivery, Inc.; Hillenbrand Industries, Inc.; Indiana Glass Company; Kasgro Rail Corp.; Kistler Instrumente AG; Knorr-Bremse AG; Kyocera Corporation; Lancaster Colony Corporation; Lilly Industries, Inc.; Menlo Logistics, Inc.; National Candle Association; NATSO, Inc.; New York Air Brake Corporation; Porter Athletic Equipment Company; Process Equipment Manufacturers' Association; Paul Reed Smith Guitars; Scient Corporation; Vector SCM LLC; Water and Wastewater Equipment Manufacturers Association; Wheat Gluten Industry Council; Young & Rubicam Inc.

BARNETT & SIVON, P.C.

Established in 1968

2000 "M" STREET, N.W., SUITE 740
WASHINGTON, D.C. 20036-3113
Telephone: 202-463-6040
FAX: 202-785-5209

Financial Institutions, General Regulatory and Legislative Law.

FIRM PROFILE: The law firm of Barnett & Sivon, P.C. specializes in representing financial institutions and other parties before the U.S. Congress and Federal banking regulatory agencies, including the Federal Reserve Board, the Federal Deposit Insurance Corporation, the Office of the Comptroller of the Currency, and the Office of Thrift Supervision.

The firm's clients include domestic and foreign banks and bank holding companies, savings associations, individual and corporate investors, financial consultants, and banking trade associations.

ROBERT EUGENE BARNETT, born Lincoln, Nebraska, 1935; admitted to bar, 1963, New York; 1966, Nebraska and U.S. Supreme Court; 1977, District of Columbia. *Education:* Harvard University (A.B., 1957); University of Rajasthan, Jaipur, India; Harvard University (LL.B., 1962). Author: *"Responsibilities and Liabilities of Bank Directors,"* Commerce Clearing House, Inc., 1980;

(This Listing Continued)

Responsibilities and Liabilities of Savings Institutions Directors, Commerce Clearing House, Inc., 1984; *Responsibilities and Liabilities of Bank and Bank Holding Company Directors,* Commerce Clearing House, Inc., 1991, 1996. Commissioner of Uniform State Laws, 1969-1970. Counsel to the Governor of Nebraska, 1967-1970. Director, Nebraska Constitutional Revision Commission, 1969-1970. Chairman, Federal Deposit Insurance Corporation, 1976-1978. *Member:* The District of Columbia Bar; New York State and Nebraska State Bar Associations. ***PRACTICE AREAS:*** Banking Law; Financial Institutions.

JAMES C. SIVON, born Akron, Ohio, 1951; admitted to bar, 1982, District of Columbia. *Education:* Denison University (B.A., 1974); Georgetown University (J.D., 1980). Author: The New CRA, published by the American Bankers Association, May 1995; "Will Interstate Banking Reform in the United States Respect the Principle of National Treatment?" Butterworths Journal of International Banking and Financial Law, Volume 8, Number 10, November, 1993; "The Impact of the Federal Deposit Insurance Corporation Improvement Act on the Supervision and Regulation of Foreign Banks Operating in the United States," Butterworths Journal of International Banking and Financial Law, Volume 7, Number 2, February 1992; *Insurance Activities Permissible for Banks and Bank Holding Companies,* published by the American Bankers Association, April 1992. Co-Author: *FIRREA:* Implementation and Compliance, Warren, Gorham & Lamont, 1991. Senior Vice President and General Counsel, Association of Bank Holding Companies, 1983-1985. Minority Staff Director, U.S. House Committee on Banking, Finance and Urban Affairs, 1980-1983. Professional Staff, U.S. House Committee on Banking, Finance and Urban Affairs, 1974-1980. *Member:* The District of Columbia Bar; Federal and American Bar Associations. ***PRACTICE AREAS:*** Banking Law; Financial Institutions.

BARTON, BAKER, MCMAHON & TOLLE, L.L.P.

WASHINGTON, D.C.

(See McLean, Virginia)

General Practice. Government Contracts, Corporate, Business Law, Mergers and Acquisitions, Computer/Technology Law, Civil Litigation, Administrative and Regulatory Law. Small Business Assistance, Arbitration.

DAVID J. BARTONE

TWELFTH FLOOR, INTERNATIONAL SQUARE
1875 EYE STREET, N.W.
WASHINGTON, D.C. 20006
Telephone: 202-223-6200
Facsimile: 202-223-6220
Email: DJBARTONE@aol.com
URL: http://www.lawyers.com/davidbartone

Complex Civil and Commercial Litigation, Securities Litigation, Electronic Banking, Mortgage and Finance, White Collar Criminal Defense, Business Fraud.

DAVID J. BARTONE, born Conneaut, Ohio, February 8, 1958; admitted to bar, 1987, District of Columbia; 1988, U.S. District Court for the District of Columbia, U.S. Court of Appeals for the District of Columbia Circuit and U.S. Court of Appeals, Fourth Circuit; 1989, U.S. Claims Court, U.S. Court of Appeals for the Federal Circuit and U.S. Tax Court. *Education:* Kent State University (B.A., cum laude, 1980); Catholic University of America (J.D., 1985). Pi Sigma Alpha. Member, The Catholic University Law Review, 1984-1985. Law Clerk to the Honorable Nicholas S. Nunzio, District of Columbia Superior Court, 1985-1986. Author, "The ATM Surcharge Dispute in California: What Happens in the Wake of Judge Walker's Preliminary Ruling in Favor of National Banks," Article, Kiosk Magazine, February 2001. *Member:* District of Columbia Bar; American Bar Association. ***LANGUAGES:*** Italian. ***PRACTICE AREAS:*** Electronic Banking; White Collar Criminal Defense; Commercial Law; General Litigation; Corporation Law.

BASTIANELLI, BROWN & KELLEY

CHARTERED

Established in 1982

TWO LAFAYETTE CENTRE
1133 21ST STREET, N.W., SUITE 500
WASHINGTON, D.C. 20036
Telephone: 202-293-8815
Telecopier: 202-293-7994
Email: bbk@govconlaw.com
URL: http://www.govconlaw.com

Government Contracts and Construction Law, Environmental Remediation, Administrative and Legislative Practice, Admiralty and Maritime, Commercial, International and Corporate Law, Tax, Project Finance including U.S. and Foreign Flag Vessels and Aircraft and Litigation.

(This Listing Continued)

ADRIAN L. BASTIANELLI, III, born Huntington, West Virginia, April 6, 1943; admitted to bar, 1971, Kentucky; 1972, U.S. Court of Federal Claims; 1973, District of Columbia; 1982, U.S. Court of Appeals for the Federal Circuit. *Education:* Purdue University (B.S.C.E., 1966); University of Louisville (J.D., 1971). Licensed Professional Engineer, Kentucky, 1971. Law Clerk, Trial Judges, U.S. Court of Claims, 1971-1972. Co-Author: "Remedies for Breach of Contract," Federal Publications, Inc., Construction Briefings No. 80-5; Contributing Author: "Construction Claims Deskbook," Wiley Law Publication. Co-Author: "Contracting Officer Authority," Federal Publications, Inc., Construction Briefings No. 86-4; "Competitive Negotiation in Government Construction Contracts," Federal Publications, Inc. Construction Briefs No. 91-4; "Recovery Delay Damages for Home Offices, Overhead Edition II," Federal Publications Construction Briefings No. 97-2; "New Federal Regulations Affecting the Construction Industry," Federal Publications Construction Briefings No. 98-4; "The Proactive DRB and the Use of the Advisory DRB Process," S Foundation Forum 1 (Jan. 2001). Associate Editor, The Construction Lawyer. President, Washington Building Congress 1991-1993. Member, Construction Group Advisory Board, Federal Publications. *Member:* The District of Columbia Bar; Bar Association of the District of Columbia; Federal (Chairman, Construction Contract Subcommittee 1991-1992) and American (Member, Sections on: Public Contract Law; Litigation; Tort and Insurance Practice) Bar Associations; National Society of Professional Engineers. Fellow, American College of Construction Lawyers. ***PRACTICE AREAS:*** Construction Law; Government Contracts; Environmental Remediation; Alternative Dispute Resolution. **Email:** bastianelli@govconlaw.com

J. MITCHELL BROWN, born Asheville, North Carolina, November 11, 1930; admitted to bar, 1955, District of Columbia; 1959, U.S. Supreme Court; 1960, Virginia. *Education:* University of Georgia (B.B.A., with honors, 1953); George Washington University (J.D., with honors, 1955). Member, Board of Editors, George Washington Law Review, 1954-1955. Administrative Judge, Armed Services Board of Contract Appeals, 1974-1977. Member, National Panel of Arbitrators, American Arbitration Association. *Member:* The District of Columbia Bar; Bar Association of the District of Columbia (Chairman, Government Contracts Committee, 1966-1967; Vice Chairman, United States Claims Court Committee, 1982-1983); American Bar Association (Secretary, Section of Public Contract Law, 1974-1975; Chairman, Committee on Contract Administration and Termination, 1978-1979); Virginia State Bar (Member, Board of Governors Construction Law Section, 1987-1990). ***PRACTICE AREAS:*** Government Contracts; Litigation; Alternative Dispute Resolution.

PHILIP R. CROESSMANN, born Buffalo, New York, May 3, 1953; admitted to bar, 1981, New York and District of Columbia; 1987, Washington and Virginia. *Education:* University of Oregon (B.Arch., 1976); Syracuse University (J.D., 1980). Phi Delta Phi. Registered Architect in Maryland, 1986. Author: "Recordkeeping Guide for Design Professionals," American Consulting Engineers Council Professional Management Guidelines, 1985; "Ownership Transition," Chapter 3A, and "Record Retention Policies," Chapter 8A, The Design Professionals' Handbook of Business and Law, John Wiley & Sons; "Design Build Projects," Chapter 12, and "Partnering," Chapter 13, Construction Joint Ventures, Forums and Practice Guide, John Wiley & Sons; Co-Author, Construction Litigation Formbook, John Wiley & Sons. Deputy General Counsel and Lobbyist for the American Institute of Architects, 1982-1984. Member, Board of Directors, Northern Virginia Chapter, Virginia Society of the American Institute of Architects. *Member:* District of Columbia Bar; Washington State Bar Association; Virginia State Bar; New York State Bar; American Institute of Architects; Virginia Road and Transportation Builders Association; Associated Builders and Contractors. ***PRACTICE AREAS:*** Construction Law; Architect and Engineer Malpractice; Environmental Law; Insurance Coverage. **Email:** croessmann@govconlaw.com

JAMES A. KELLEY, born Washington, D.C., April 7, 1952; admitted to bar, 1979, Virginia; 1981, U.S. Court of Federal Claims; 1991, District of Columbia. *Education:* Randolph-Macon College (B.A., 1974); Delaware Law School of Widener University (J.D., 1979). Omicron Delta Kappa; Phi Delta Phi. With Office of General Counsel, U.S. Department of the Navy, 1980-1983. Assistant Counsel, Military Sealift Command, Washington, D.C., 1980-1983. Member, Defense Acquisition Regulation Subcommittee for Master Ship Repair Contracts, 1982-1983. *Member:* Bar Association of the District of Columbia; The Virginia State Bar; District of Columbia Bar; Virginia (Member, Construction and Public Contract Law Section), Federal (Member, Government Contracts Committee, 1981—) and American (Member, Section on Public Contract Law) Bar Associations; American Society of Navy Engineers; Society of Naval Architects and Marine Engineers; Shipbuilders Council of America; American Waterways Operators; Society for Protective Coatings. ***PRACTICE AREAS:*** Government Contracts; Maritime; Shipbuilding and Repair; Shipping Law; Construction Law. **Email:** kelley@govconlaw.com

LAWRENCE C. MELTON, born Marlinton, West Virginia, April 8, 1948; admitted to bar, 1976, Virginia; 1978, District of Columbia. *Education:* Tulane University (B.A., 1970); University of London (M Phil., 1973); Washington & Lee University (J.D., 1976). Co-Author, "State-by-State Guide to Architect, Engineer and Contractor Licensing," District of Columbia, Aspen Law Publish-

(This Listing Continued)

BASTIANELLI, BROWN & KELLEY, CHARTERED, Washington—Continued

ing, 1999. Note & Comments Editor, Washington & Lee Law Review, 1975-1976. Author: "Common Sense About Home Office Overhead," Construction Claims Monthly, May, 1985. Law Clerk to Chief Justice L.W. I'Anson, Virginia Supreme Court, 1976-1977. Adjunct Professor of Law, University of South Carolina. *Member:* The District of Columbia Bar; Virginia State Bar; South Carolina Bar; American Bar Association (Member, Public Contract and Litigation Sections). ***PRACTICE AREAS:*** Government Contracts; Litigation. ***Email:*** meltlaw@cnhs.infi.net

CHARLES M. REIFEL, born Memphis, Tennessee, September 29, 1946; admitted to bar, 1974, District of Columbia and U.S. Court of Federal Claims; 1975, U.S. District Court for the District of Columbia; 1976, U.S. Court of Appeals for the District of Columbia Circuit; 1982, U.S. Court of Appeals for the Federal Circuit. *Education:* Dartmouth College (A.B., 1968); George Washington University (J.D., with honors, 1973). Co-Author: "Contracting Officer Authority," Federal Publications, Inc. Briefing Papers, No. 86-4, March, 1986; "Construction Practicing Under 'Superfund,'" Construction Briefings No. 90-7, June 1990. *Member:* The District of Columbia Bar; Bar Association of the District of Columbia. ***PRACTICE AREAS:*** Government Contracts; Construction Law. ***Email:*** reifel@govconlaw.com

GEORGE W. STIFFLER, born East Orange, New Jersey, January 24, 1955; admitted to bar, 1981, District of Columbia; 1982, U.S. Court of Federal Claims and U.S. Court of Appeals for the Federal Circuit; 1986, U.S. District Court for the District of Columbia. *Education:* College of William and Mary (B.A., 1978); George Washington University (J.D., 1981). Phi Alpha Theta. Law Clerk to the Honorable Alex Kozinski, Chief Judge, U.S. Claims Court, Washington, D.C., 1984-1985. Co-Author: "Recovering Legal Fees Under EAJA/Edition II," Federal Publications, Inc. Briefing Paper No. 91-7, June 1991; "New Federal Regulations Affecting the Construction Industry," Federal Publications, Inc. Construction Briefings No. 98-4, March, 1998. *Member:* The District of Columbia Bar; Federal and American Bar Associations. ***PRACTICE AREAS:*** Government Contracts; Shipbuilding and Repair; Construction Law; Maritime. ***Email:*** stiffler@govconlaw.com

TINA S. TISINGER, born London, England, April 27, 1953; admitted to bar, 1988, Virginia, 1989, District of Columbia; U.S. Court of Appeals, Fourth Circuit. *Education:* George Mason University (B.S., with distinction, 1985); George Mason University School of Law (J.D., 1988). Phi Delta Phi. Member, Moot Court Board. Member, Board of Editors, George Mason University Law Review. Law Clerk to the Honorable W. Curtis Servell, U.S. Magistrate, U.S. District Court, Eastern District of Virginia, 1988-1989. Assistant Commonwealth's Attorney, 1989-1999. *Member:* District of Columbia Bar; Virginia State Bar. ***PRACTICE AREAS:*** Construction Law; Government Contracts; Civil Litigation. ***Email:*** tisinger@govconlaw.com

DONALD A. TOBIN, born Boston, Massachusetts, August 26, 1947; admitted to bar, 1973, Massachusetts; 1977, District of Columbia; 1978, U.S. Court of Federal Claims. *Education:* College of the Holy Cross (A.B., 1969); Boston College (J.D., cum laude, 1973). Member, Editorial Staff, Boston College Law Review, 1972-1973. Co-Author: "Recovering Legal Fees Under EAJA/Edition II," Federal Publications, Inc., Briefing Paper No. 91-7, June 1991. "Impossibility in Construction Contracts Basic Principles and Guidelines," Federal Publications, Inc. Construction Briefings No. 79-5, September, 1979. Attorney, Naval Air Systems Command, Office of the General Counsel, U.S. Department of the Navy, 1973-1976. *Member:* The District of Columbia Bar; Federal and American Bar Associations. ***PRACTICE AREAS:*** Government Contracts; Construction Law. ***Email:*** tobin@govconlaw.com

RONALD H. USCHER, born New York, N.Y., March 5, 1948; admitted to bar, 1973, Virginia; 1980, District of Columbia; 1982, U.S. Court of Federal Claims. *Education:* State University of New York at Albany (B.A., cum laude, 1969); George Washington University, National Law Center (J.D., with honors, 1973; LL.M., 1980). Assistant Counsel, Defense Fuel Supply Center, Defense Logistics Agency, Department of Defense, 1974-1982. Defense Logistics Agency Representative to Department of Justice, Criminal Division, Defense Procurement Fraud Unit, 1982-1985. Author: "Selling Petroleum to the U.S. Military" Hydrocarbon Engineering, September, 1999; "Selling Energy to the U.S. Military," National Petroleum and Refiners Association, March, 1999; Co-Author: "Facing A Fraud Investigation," Federal Publications, 1986. *Member:* District of Columbia Bar; Virginia State Bar. ***PRACTICE AREAS:*** Government Contracts; Energy Law. ***Email:*** uscher@govconlaw.com

---

NICK R. HOOGSTRATEN, born Hilversum, The Netherlands, July 26, 1961; admitted to bar, 1986, Maryland; 1988, District of Columbia and U.S. District Court, District of Maryland; 1990, U.S. Court of Federal Claims and U.S. District Court for the District of Columbia. *Education:* University of Kansas (B.A., with distinction, 1983); Georgetown University (J.D., 1986). Phi Beta Kappa; Pi Sigma Alpha. Co-Author: "Construction Contracting Under 'Superfund,'" Construction Briefings No. 90-7, June 1990. *Member:* District of Columbia Bar; Maryland State and American (Member, Section of Public Contract Law; Forum on the Construction Industry) Bar Associations. ***PRACTICE AREAS:*** Government Contracts; Construction. ***Email:*** hoogstraten@govconlaw.com

LORI ANN LANGE, born Poughkeepsie, New York, June 28, 1966; admitted to bar, 1991, Maryland; 1993, U.S. Court of Appeals for the Federal Circuit and U.S. Claims Court; 1996, District of Columbia. *Education:* George Washington University (B.A., 1988; J.D., 1991). Phi Delta Phi. Revision Author, Government Contracts, 1992-1995. Contributing Author: Construction Claims Deskbook and State-by-State Guide to Architect, Engineer and Contractor Licensing. Co-Author: "Recovering Delay Damages for Home Office Overhead/Edition II," Construction Briefings No. 97-3, February, 1997; "New Federal Regulations Affecting the Construction Industry," Construction Briefings No. 98-4, March, 1998; "Innovative Financing for Infrastructure Projects," Construction Briefings No. 98-8, July, 1998. *Member:* Maryland State, Federal and American (Member, Public Contracts Section, 1991) Bar Associations; District of Columbia Bar. ***PRACTICE AREAS:*** Government Contracts; Construction Law; Maritime Law. ***Email:*** lange@govconlaw.com

OF COUNSEL

H. CLAYTON COOK, JR., born Washington, D.C., March 25, 1935; admitted to bar, 1960, Colorado; 1961, New York; 1966, Pennsylvania; 1973, District of Columbia. *Education:* Princeton University (B.S., 1956); University of Virginia (LL.B., 1960). Order of the Coif. Member, The Raven Society. Executive Editor, University of Virginia Law Review, 1959-1960. Associate: Sullivan & Cromwell, 1960-1963; Holme Roberts & Owen, 1964; Pepper, Hamilton & Scheetz, 1965-1968; Partner, Pepper, Hamilton & Scheetz, 1969-1970, 1973, on assignment, Senior Tax Counsel, Sun Oil Co. Philadelphia, 1970. Partner, Cadwalader, Wickersham & Taft, 1974-1987; General Counsel, Maritime Administration, 1970-1973. Member, Maritime Subsidy Board, U.S. Department of Commerce, 1970-1973. Member, Administrative Conference of the United States, 1980-1990. Member: Reagan Administration Presidential Transition Team, 1980-1981. Member, Citizen Advisory Panels on Maritime Trade and Technology, United States Office of Technology Assessment, 1980-1985. Member, Military Sealift Command, National Defense Executive Reserve, 1983-1991. *Member:* District of Columbia Bar; American Bar Association; Maritime Law Association of the United States; American Law Institute (Life Member). (Also practicing individually). ***PRACTICE AREAS:*** Federal Administrative Law; MARAD Title XI, CCF, DOD Maritech; Capitol Construction Fund Finance. ***Email:*** PlimsollDC@aol.com

MARCUS W. SISK, JR., born Chico, California, August 1, 1940; admitted to bar, 1965, District of Columbia; 1968, American Samoa; 1974, California. *Education:* Stanford University (B.A., with great distinction, 1961); Harvard Law School (LL.B., cum laude, 1964). Member, Trial Staff, Civil Rights Division Department of Justice, 1964-1965. Appellate Attorney, National Labor Relations Board, 1965-1967. Assistant Attorney General and Legislative Counsel, American Samoa, 1967-1969. *Member:* The District of Columbia Bar; Federal and American Bar Associations. ***Email:*** msisk@govconlaw.com

(This Listing Continued)

BAUER & ZOUAOUI, LLP

2300 M STREET N.W., SUITE 800
WASHINGTON, D.C. 20037
Telephone: 202-775-9344, 202-775-9344
Fax: 202-775-9341
http://www.bauerzouaoui.com
Email: bauerlaw@verizon.net
URL: http://www.ilw.com/bauerlaw

Moscow, Russia Office: Novyi Arbat St., 2111. Telephone: 095-291-3941. Fax: 095-202-6063.

Corporate Practice, International Business, Transactions, Joint Ventures, International Taxation Law, International Investment and Banking Law, Immigration Services, Business Immigration, Arbitration and Mediation.

FIRM PROFILE: Bauer & Zouaoui, is an international law firm with offices in Washington, D.C., Moscow and Morocco. The firm provides legal and business counsel to a number of large and small corporations and other entities in the area of corporate, international transactions, administrative agency law, litigation, business reorganization and planning, sophisticated real estate transactions, immigration and nationality practice.

SERGE BAUER, born Alma Ata, Kazakhstan, July 13, 1962; admitted to bar, 1990, New Jersey; 1991, New York; 1992, District of Columbia. *Education:* Queens College of the City University of New York (B.A., 1984); Western New England College (J.D., 1990). *Member:* New York County, Federal and American (Member: International Law Section; Soviet Law Committee; Newly Independent States of Former Soviet Union Committee, 1993—) Bar Associations;

(This Listing Continued)

The District of Columbia Bar (Chairman, Investment and Finance Committee, International Law Section) Washington Foreign Law Society. ***LANGUAGES:*** Russian. ***PRACTICE AREAS:*** International Trade Law; Corporate Law; Immigration Law; Joint Ventures.

JAMIL ZOUAOUI, born Casablanca, Morocco, May 19, 1964; admitted to bar, 1990, Massachusetts; 1991, District of Columbia. *Education:* College of Wooster (B.A., 1985); Boston College Law School (J.D., 1989); Harvard Law School (LL.M., 1991). Associate Editor, Harvard International Law Journal. Private Sector Development Specialist, World Bank, 1991-1995. ***PRACTICE AREAS:*** International Commercial Law; Alternative Dispute Resolution; Project Finance; Corporate Law.

BAUM, HEDLUND, ARISTEI, GUILFORD & SCHIAVO

A PROFESSIONAL CORPORATION

Established in 1973

1250 24TH STREET, N.W., SUITE 300

WASHINGTON, D.C. 20037

Telephone: 202-466-0513; 800-827-0097

Fax: 202-466-0527

Email: info@baumhedlundlaw.com

URL: http://www.baumhedlundlaw.com

Los Angeles, California Office: Suite 950, 12100 Wilshire Boulevard. Telephones: 310-207-3233; 800-827-0087. Facsimile: 310-820-7444..

Limited only to Plaintiff's Serious Personal Injury and Wrongful Death Accident Litigation nationwide and worldwide; including Aviation Accident Litigation, Airline Accidents, Bus Accidents, Tractor-Trailer Accidents, Train Accidents, Public Transportation Accidents, Mass Disaster Litigation, Complex Multi-District Litigation and Product Liability including Antidepressant Drug Litigation.

(For Complete Biographical Information on all Personnel, See Professional Biographies at Los Angeles, California)

LAW OFFICES OF MARION E. BAURLEY, P.C.

Established in 1982

235 MASSACHUSETTS AVENUE, N.E.

WASHINGTON, D.C. 20002

Telephone: 202-544-9820

Fax: 202-544-9832

Email: baurley@erols.com

URL: http://www.baurleylaw.com

Adoption, Annulment, Child Custody, Child Visitation, Child Neglect, Child Support and Maintenance, Disability, Divorce, Domestic Relations, Father's Rights, Education, Elder Care, Employment, Estate and Probate, Legal Separation, Personal Injury, Professional Responsibility, Medical Malpractice, Small Business, Special Education.

FIRM PROFILE: The firm is dedicated to providing client's individualized legal services catering to their particular needs. For over twenty years, the firm has been an advocate for children representing them in all aspects of the law, from assuring that they receive an appropriate education to custody and neglect cases. The firm has counseled clients during the most traumatic times in their lives with compassion and exceptional legal representation. We strive to be and our clients consider us their families' lawyer.

MARION E. BAURLEY, born Bronx, New York; admitted to bar, 1979, District of Columbia; 1980, New York and Florida; 1982, U.S. District Court, District of Columbia; 1985, Virginia; 1986, Maryland; 2001, U.S. District Court, Southern and Northern Districts of Florida. *Education:* University of Miami (B.A., 1976); American University (J.D., 1979). *Member:* Prince Georges County, Maryland State and Virginia Bar Associations; District of Columbia Bar (Member, Court Administration Section; Family Law and Litigation Section); The Florida Bar; American Trial Lawyers Association. ***REPORTED CASES:*** In the Matter of Annie Williams, 471 A.2d 263 (D.C. 1984); Nelson v. Nelson, 548 A.2d 599 (D.C. 1988) rect. denied, 379 A.2d 713 (1988); In the Matter of Estate of Burton, 541 A.2d 599 (D.C. 1988); K.A.T. v. C.A.B., 645 A.2d 570 (D.C. 1994); In the Matter L.W., 613 A.2d 350 (D.C. 1992). ***PRACTICE AREAS:*** Family Law; Elder Law; School Law; Professional Licensing. ***Email:*** marionbaurley@baurleylaw.com

---

KATHY K.B. DUPUY-BRUNO, born Boston, Massachusetts; admitted to bar, 1999, Maryland; 2001, District of Columbia, U.S. District Court, District of Columbia and U.S. District Court, District of Maryland. *Education:* St. John's University (B.A., 1995); American University (J.D., 1998). Member, Golden Key National Honor Society, 1994. Listed in Who's Who Among Students in American Law Schools, 1997-1998; Who's Who Among Students in American Universities and Colleges, 1994-1995. *Member:* Prince Geourges County, Maryland State and American Bar Associations; Bar Association of the District of Columbia; American Trial Lawyers Association. ***LANGUAGES:*** French and Creole. ***PRACTICE AREAS:*** Family Law; Medical Malpractice; Employment Discrimination; Special Education. ***Email:*** kathybruno@baurleylaw.com

---

LEONARD N. BEBCHICK

Established in 1964

1101 CONNECTICUT AVENUE, N.W., SUITE 1000

WASHINGTON, D.C. 20036

Telephone: 202-822-6401

Fax: 202-822-6404

Email: beblaw@erols.com

Practice before all Federal Courts, Departments and Regulatory Agencies. Administrative Law, Civil Litigation and Appeals, Class Actions, Corporate Commercial Law.

FIRM PROFILE: We design innovative and individually tailored approaches, negotiated and litigated, for the resolution of client problems involving the range of Federal agencies and departments or arising from corporate or commercial conflicts. As required, particularly in complex litigation, leading specialist practitioners are involved to provide a fully effective team approach.

LEONARD N. BEBCHICK, born New Bedford, Massachusetts, December 11, 1932; admitted to bar, 1958, Massachusetts; 1960, District of Columbia; 1989, Maryland. *Education:* Cornell University (A.B., 1955); Yale University Law School (LL.B., 1958). Commercial Rates Section, Civil Aeronautics Board, 1958-1959. Special Counsel, D.C. Public Service Commission, 1965-1966. Special Counsel and Consultant, Virgin Islands Public Utilities Commission, 1967-1970. *Member:* District of Columbia Bar; Federal, American (Chairman, Advisory Committee on Aeronautical Law, 1982-1983) and International Bar Associations. [Capt., U.S. Army Reserve, active duty, 1959-1960]. ***REPORTED CASES:*** Pickett et al v. Holland America Line-Westours, 6 P.3d 63 (Wash.App.2000); Cruz v. American Airlines, 193 F.3d 526 (D.C.Cir. 1999); Unisys Corp. Long-Term Disability Plan ERISA Litigation, 97 F.3d 710 (3d Cir. 1996), 159 F.3d 1354 (3d Cir. 1998); Bebchick v. WMATC, 805 F.2d 396 (D.C. Cir. 1986) and the six earlier cases cited at n.l.; Democratic Central Committee v. WMATC, 988 F. 2d 1235, 988 F.2d 1239, 3 F.3d 1568 (D.C. Cir. 1993), 12 F.3d 269, 18 F.3d 938, 21 F.3d 1145, 41 F.3d 757 (D.C. Cir. 1994), 84 F.3d 451 (D.C. Cir. 1996); Scottish Air International v. British Caledonian Group, 81 F.3d 1224 (2d Cir. 1996) and the five earlier cases cited at 1231; British Caledonian Airways v. Bond, 665 F.2d 1153 (D.C. Cir. 1981); Roemer v. Hoffman, 419 F. Supp 130 (D.D.C. 1976).

REPRESENTATIVE CLIENTS: The Bank of New York; NationsBank Trust Company, N.A.; British Caledonian Group/British Airways; The Rank Organization; London Transport International; New York University Medical Center.

BECHTEL & COLE

CHARTERED

Established in 1982

SUITE 250, 1901 L STREET, N.W.

WASHINGTON, D.C. 20036

Telephone: 202-833-4190

Telecopier: 202-833-3084

Email: info@coleslaw.com

Federal Administrative and Appellate Administrative Litigation Practice. Communications, Telecommunications and Intellectual Property.

FIRM PROFILE: Bechtel & Cole has specialized in representing individual entrepreneurs and corporations in communications law matters. Among the firm's clients are radio and TV stations, program providers, broadcast owners, wireless communication companies, cable companies and telephone resellers. The firm's clients are both domestic and international and range from small companies to large corporations.

GENE A. BECHTEL, born Chicago, Illinois, December 31, 1932; admitted to bar, 1958, District of Columbia and U.S. Supreme Court. *Education:* McPherson College (B.S., magna cum laude, 1954); George Washington University (J.D., 1958). Order of the Coif. Member, Board of Editors, George Washington University Law Review, 1956-1957. Lecturer, School of Journalism, American University, 1966-1967. *Member:* The District of Columbia Bar; Bar Association of the District of Columbia; Federal and American (Member, House of Delegates, 1983-1984; Chairman, Administrative Law Judges Com-

(This Listing Continued)

BECHTEL & COLE, CHARTERED, Washington—Continued

mittee, Administrative Law Section, 1983-1986) Bar Associations; Federal Communications Bar Association (Vice President, 1984-1985; President, 1985-1986). ***PRACTICE AREAS:*** Communications Law; Telecommunications Law; Appellate Practice; Trademarks; Copyrights. ***Email:*** gabechtel@coleslaw.com

BELL, BOYD & LLOYD PLLC

1615 L STREET, N.W., SUITE 1200
WASHINGTON, D.C. 20036
Telephone: 202-466-6300
Fax: 202-463-0678
Email: dc@bellboyd.com
URL: http://www.bellboyd.com

Chicago, Illinois Office: Bell Boyd & Lloyd LLC, Three First National Plaza, Suite 3300, 70 West Madison Street. Telephone: 312-372-1121. Fax: 312-372-2098.

General Practice.

RESIDENT MEMBERS

EDWARD A. BLOOM, born May 9, 1958; admitted to bar, 1983, Maryland; 1984, District of Columbia and New York. *Education:* American University (B.S., cum laude, 1980; J.D., 1983). ***PRACTICE AREAS:*** Real Estate; Corporate Law. ***Email:*** attorneys@bellboyd.com

WILLIAM H. BUTTERFIELD, born January 22, 1943; admitted to bar, 1967, New York; 1970, District of Columbia; 1982, Virginia. *Education:* Boston College (B.S., magna cum laude, 1964); Georgetown University (J.D., 1967). ***PRACTICE AREAS:*** Government Contracts; Federal Procurement; General Civil Litigation. ***Email:*** attorneys@bellboyd.com

A. THOMAS CARROCCIO, born January 19, 1946; admitted to bar, 1971, District of Columbia; 1973, Maryland; 1974, U.S. Tax Court. *Education:* Mount St. Mary's College (B.S., 1967); Catholic University (J.D., 1970). ***PRACTICE AREAS:*** Legislative, Communications Law. ***Email:*** attorneys@bellboyd.com

BRIAN COHEN, born May 24, 1947; admitted to bar, 1972, Maryland; 1973, U.S. District Court, District of Maryland; 1995, District of Columbia. *Education:* University of Maryland (B.A., with honors, 1969; J.D., 1971). ***PRACTICE AREAS:*** Construction Law; Government Contracts Law. ***Email:*** attorneys@bellboyd.com

ANDREW N. COOK, born June 30, 1959; admitted to bar, 1987, Maryland; 1988, District of Columbia. *Education:* University of Arizona (B.A., with honors, 1982); Catholic University of America (J.D., 1987). ***PRACTICE AREAS:*** Government Contracts Law; Construction Law. ***Email:*** attorneys@bellboyd.com

RAYMOND C. FAY, born October 24, 1947; admitted to bar, 1974, District of Columbia; 1975, U.S. Court of Appeals for the District of Columbia Circuit and U.S. District Court for the District of Columbia; 1977, U.S. Court of Appeals, Second, Seventh, Ninth and Tenth Circuits; 1978, Illinois, U.S. Supreme Court and U.S. District Court, Northern District of Illinois; 1983, U.S. Court of Appeals, Fifth Circuit; 1984, U.S. Court of Appeals, Eleventh Circuit; 1990, U.S. Court of Appeals for the Federal Circuit and U.S. Tax Court; 1991, U.S. Court of Appeals, Sixth and Eighth Circuits; 1995, U.S. Court of Appeals, Fourth Circuit. *Education:* Xavier University and St. Louis University (A.B., magna cum laude, 1969); St. Louis University and Georgetown University (J.D., 1973). ***PRACTICE AREAS:*** Labor and Employment Law; Age Discrimination. ***Email:*** attorneys@bellboyd.com

THOMAS R. GIBBON, born July 9, 1948; admitted to bar, 1974, Maine and U.S. District Court, District of Maine; 1980, District of Columbia; 1984, U.S. Court of Appeals, District of Columbia Circuit and Tenth Circuit; 1985, U.S. District Court for the District of Columbia; 1987, U.S. Court of Appeals, Ninth Circuit. *Education:* Bucknell University (B.A., 1970); University of Maine (J.D., 1974). ***PRACTICE AREAS:*** Communications Law. ***Email:*** attorneys@bellboyd.com

RONALD E. GILBERTSON, born September 7, 1954; admitted to bar, 1979, Maryland; 1984, District of Columbia; 1986, U.S. Court of Federal Claims. *Education:* University of Maryland (B.A., 1976; J.D., with honors, 1979). ***PRACTICE AREAS:*** Black Lung Disability Defense; Coal; Mining Law; Government Contracts; Construction Claims. ***Email:*** attorneys@bellboyd.com

PETER M. KILCULLEN, born February 4, 1942; admitted to bar, 1966, Virginia and District of Columbia; 1970, U.S. Court of Federal Claims. *Education:* University of Virginia (B.A., 1963; LL.B., 1966). ***PRACTICE***

(This Listing Continued)

AREAS: Alternative Dispute Resolution; Computers and Software; Contracts; Construction Law; Federal Procurement; Fidelity and Surety; Government Contracts. ***Email:*** attorneys@bellboyd.com

CHRISTOPHER G. MACKARONIS, born March 16, 1952; admitted to bar, 1978, District of Columbia; 1979, U.S. Court of Appeals for the District of Columbia Circuit and U.S. District Court for the District of Columbia; 1988, U.S. Court of Appeals, Second and Third Circuits and U.S. Supreme Court; 1989, U.S. Court of Appeals, Tenth Circuit; 1994, U.S. Court of Appeals, Fourth Circuit. *Education:* Princeton University (B.A., 1974); Washington College of Law, American University (J.D., 1978). ***PRACTICE AREAS:*** Labor and Employment Law; Age Discrimination. ***Email:*** attorneys@bellboyd.com

JOEL S. RUBINSTEIN, born February 11, 1948; admitted to bar, 1973, Illinois and District of Columbia; 1976, U.S. Supreme Court; 1979, Maryland; 1982, New York. *Education:* University of Illinois (B.A., 1969; J.D., 1973). ***PRACTICE AREAS:*** Construction Law; Litigation; Government Contracts Law. ***Email:*** attorneys@bellboyd.com

DONALD E. SANTARELLI, born July 22, 1937; admitted to bar, 1962, Virginia; 1965, District of Columbia. *Education:* Mount St. Mary's College; University of Virginia (LL.B., 1962). ***PRACTICE AREAS:*** Legislative; Transportation. ***Email:*** attorneys@bellboyd.com

ROBERT J. SCIARONI, born May 28, 1945; admitted to bar, 1976, California; 1979, District of Columbia and U.S. District Court for the District of Columbia; 1985, U.S. District Court, District of Maryland and U.S. Court of Appeals for the District of Columbia Circuit; 1987, Virginia and U.S. District Court, Eastern District of Virginia; 1991, Maryland; 1992, U.S. Court of Appeals, Fourth Circuit. *Education:* University of San Francisco (B.A., 1972); Hastings College of Law (J.D., 1975). ***PRACTICE AREAS:*** Construction Law; Government Contracts Law; Surety Law. ***Email:*** attorneys@bellboyd.com

WALTER A. I. WILSON, born July 9, 1943; admitted to bar, 1968, Virginia and U.S. Court of Military Appeals; 1971, U.S. Supreme Court; 1974, District of Columbia; 1975, U.S. Court of Federal Claims. *Education:* Middlebury College (A.B., 1965); American University (J.D., 1968). ***PRACTICE AREAS:*** Alternative Dispute Resolution; Computers and Software; Government Contracts; Construction Law; Civil Litigation; Federal Procurement; Fidelity and Surety; Shipbuilding and Repair. ***Email:*** attorneys@bellboyd.com

CHARLES A. ZIELINSKI, born December 24, 1944; admitted to bar, 1970, New York; 1971, U.S. Court of Appeals for the District of Columbia Circuit; 1977, U.S. Supreme Court (Not admitted in District of Columbia). *Education:* LeMoyne College (B.A., 1966); State University of New York at Buffalo (J.D., 1969). ***PRACTICE AREAS:*** Communications; Energy and Environmental Law; Antitrust. ***Email:*** attorneys@bellboyd.com

OF COUNSEL

RICHARD E. HILL, born August 23, 1928; admitted to bar, 1955, Virginia; 1965, District of Columbia; 1968, Pennsylvania; 1971, New York. *Education:* Virginia Military Institute (B.S. Civ. Engr., 1949); Washington & Lee University (LL.B., magna cum laude, 1955). ***Email:*** attorneys@bellboyd.com

EDWARD J. SMITH, JR., born August 8, 1940; admitted to bar, 1966, Maryland; 1975, District of Columbia and U.S. Supreme Court. *Education:* Harvard University (A.B., 1963); University of Maryland (J.D., 1966). ***Email:*** attorneys@bellboyd.com

RESIDENT ASSOCIATES

LAURA C. FENTONMILLER, born January 31, 1970; admitted to bar, 1994, California; 1996, District of Columbia. *Education:* University of Michigan (B.S., Natural Resources, 1990; J.D., 1994). ***PRACTICE AREAS:*** Employment Law. ***Email:*** attorneys@bellboyd.com

STEVEN D. HITCHCOCK, born March 5, 1967; admitted to bar, 1994, New York; 1995, District of Columbia. *Education:* University of Rochester (B.A., magna cum laude, 1989) Phi Beta Kappa; University of Virginia School of Law (J.D., 1993). ***PRACTICE AREAS:*** Communication Law; Civil Litigation. ***Email:*** attorneys@bellboyd.com

LAWRENCE M. PROSEN, born September 10, 1970; admitted to bar, 1997, Maryland; 1998, U.S. Court of Federal Claims, U.S. Court of Appeals for the Federal Circuit, U.S. Court of Appeals, Fourth Circuit, U.S. Court of Appeals for the District of Columbia Circuit, U.S. District Court, District of Maryland and District of Columbia; 1999, U.S. District Court for the District of Columbia. *Education:* University of Maryland at College Park (B.S., Arch., 1994; B.A., Hist., 1994); The Columbus School of Law, Catholic University of America (J.D., 1997). ***PRACTICE AREAS:*** Construction Litigation; Government Contracts Law; Architects and Engineers Errors and Omissions; Civil Practice; Real Estate. ***Email:*** attorneys@bellboyd.com

MICHAEL J. SCHRIER, born March 14, 1968; admitted to bar, 1993, Pennsylvania (inactive) and Maryland; 1994, U.S. Court of Appeals for the District of Columbia Circuit and U.S. Court of Appeals for the Federal Circuit;

(This Listing Continued)

1995, District of Columbia and U.S. District Court for the District of Columbia; 1997, U.S. District Court, Central District of Illinois and U.S. Court of Appeals, Fourth Circuit; 1998, U.S. Court of Appeals, Seventh and Eighth Circuits. *Education:* Cornell University (B.A., 1990); George Washington University (J.D., 1993). ***PRACTICE AREAS:*** Litigation; Employment Law. ***Email:*** attorneys@bellboyd.com

(For Complete Biographical Data on Chicago, Illinois personnel, see Professional Biographies at Chicago, Illinois)

THE BELLAMY LAW FIRM, P.C.

1100 CONECTICUT AVENUE, N.W., SUITE 1000
WASHINGTON, D.C. 20036
Telephone: 202-785-5222
Fax: 202-785-5224
Email: bellamylaw@aol.com
URL: http://www.lawyers.com/bellamylawfirm

Legislative Practice, Labor and Employment, Wrongful Termination, Civil Litigation, Contracts, Corporate Law, Business Immigration, Small Business Law, Nonprofit Organizations Law, International Law, International Business Transactions.

FIRM PROFILE: Lorenzo M. Bellamy has represented a wide variety of clients that include individuals, entrepreneurs, small businesses, fortune 100 companies, coalitions, corporations, civic and non-governmental organizations. The firm provides both litigation and administrative representation as well as general business counselling.

LORENZO M. BELLAMY, born Santo Domingo, Dominican Republic, May 30, 1963; admitted to bar, 1996, Maryland; 1998, District of Columbia. *Education:* University of Virginia (B.A., 1986); Catholic University of America (J.D., 1995). *Member:* District of Columbia Bar; Maryland State and American Bar Associations; National Bar Association.

BENNER AND BILICKI

A Partnership including a Professional Corporation

1000 16TH STREET, NW, SUITE 603
WASHINGTON, D.C. 20036
Telephone: 202-546-6334
URL: http://www.bennerandbilicki.com
Email: bennerandbilicki@aol.com
URL: http://www.lawyers.com/bennerandbilicki

Farmington Hills, Michigan Office: 28116 Orchard Lake Road, 48334. Telephone: 248-737-5544. Telefax: 248-737-5545.

Geneva, Switzerland Office: 17 Pictet-De-Rochemont, 1207. Telephone: +41 22 736-9603. Telefax: +41 22 736-9703.

Personal Injury and Wrongful Death. Trial Practice in all State and Federal Courts. Automobile, Aviation, Industrial Accidents, Medical Malpractice, Premises Liability, Products Liability, Railroad, Workers Compensation.

FIRM PROFILE: Benner and Bilicki specialize in personal injury law and disability cases. Founded in 1981, the firm continues to represent clients throughout the United States and Europe. These clients range from personal injury settlements involving wrongful death suits to personal injury suits resulting in multi million dollar verdicts . The firm has recently won over 14 million dollars for an International Transportation case.

BRIAN J. BENNER, (P.C.), born Detroit, Michigan, February 9, 1947; admitted to bar, 1975, Michigan, U.S. District Court, Eastern and Western Districts of Michigan and U.S. Supreme Court (Not admitted in District of Columbia). *Education:* Olivet College (B.A., 1969); Wayne State University (J.D., 1975). Recipient of Trial Advocacy Award, Wayne State University, 1975. Author: "Should Michigan Rule of Evidence 703 Be Revised?", Michigan Bar Journal, June 1991. National Chairman of the Oaks Society for Olivet College, 1990—. Member: Institute for Injury Reduction, 1990; Attorneys Information Exchange Group, 1990. Plaintiff's Counsel: Canterbury England Coach Crash, 1993. *Member:* Oakland County, Detroit and American Bar (Member, Sections on: Aviation and Space Law; Litigation; Tort and Insurance Practice) Bar Associations; State Bar of Michigan (Member, Negligence Law Section); Michigan Trial Lawyers Association (Appointed to Executive Board, 1992); The Association of Trial Lawyers of America (Member, Presidents Club, 1999). ***REPORTED CASES:*** Cheeseman v. Huron Clinton Metropolitan Authority, 477 NW2d 700; Farwell v. May, 467 NW2d 593. ***PRACTICE AREAS:*** Personal Injury; Automobile; Aviation; Industrial Accidents; Medical Malpractice; Premises Liability; Products Liability; Railroad; Wrongful Death. ***Email:*** bennerbj@aol.com

(For complete biographical data on all personnel, see Professional Biographies at Farmington Hills, Michigan)

BENNET & BENNET, PLLC

1000 VERMONT AVENUE, NW, 10TH FLOOR
WASHINGTON, D.C. 20005
Telephone: 202-371-1500
Fax: 202-371-1558
URL: http://www.bennetlaw.com
Email: mail@benetlaw.com
URL: http://www.lawyers.com/bennet&bennetlaw

Communications Law, Telecommunications Law, Wireless Communications, Cable Communications, Cable TV, Cellular Radio, Cellular Telephone, Satellite Communications, Broadcastings Law, FCC Licensing, FCC Regulation, Digital Communications, Telecommunications Regulation, Internet Law, E-Commerce Law, Emerging Business Law, Federal Administrative Law, Communications Common Carrier, Radio Common Carrier, Telephone Utility Regulation.

FIRM PROFILE: Bennet & Bennet, PLLC is a full service communications law firm. The firm has a particular expertise in wireless companies and telecommunications matters gained through the representation of cellular carriers, wireless cable providers, paging companies, specialized mobile radio (SMR) operators, personal communications service (PCS) providers and broadband wireless companies.

CARESSA DAVISON BENNET, born Pensacola, Florida, November 4, 1961; admitted to bar, 1987, Pennsylvania; 1988, District of Columbia; 1989, U.S. Court of Appeals for the District of Columbia Circuit; U.S. Court of Appeals, Sixth and Eighth Circuits. *Education:* North Carolina State University (B.A., cum laude, 1983); Catholic University (J.D., 1987); Communications Law Institute (Certificate, 1987). Member, Catholic University Law Review, 1986-1987. Associate Member and Chair, Advisory Council, National Telephone Cooperative Association, 2000-2001. Member, Education Committee, Organization for the Promotion and Advancement of Small Telephone Companies, 1995-2001. Associate Member and Chair, Advisory Committee, United States Telecom Association, 2000-2001. Member, Personal Communications Industry Association, Wireless Broadband Alliance, 1998-2000. *Member:* District of Columbia Bar; American Bar Association (Member: Forum on Communications Law); Federal Communications Bar Association. ***PRACTICE AREAS:*** Communications Law. ***Email:*** cbennet@bennetlaw.com

MICHAEL R. BENNET, born Washington, D.C., August 1, 1960; admitted to bar, 1986, Maryland; 1988, District of Columbia; 1989, U.S. Court of Appeals for the District of Columbia Circuit. *Education:* University of Pennsylvania (B.A., cum laude, 1982); Duke University (J.D., 1986). Member, Editorial Board, Duke Law Journal, 1985-1986. Author: "Telephone Toll Fraud: Technical and Liability Issues," 5 Journal of Proprietary Rights 8, August 1993. *Member:* The District of Columbia Bar; Federal Communications Bar Association. ***PRACTICE AREAS:*** Communications Law. ***Email:*** mbennet@bennetlaw.com

GREGORY W. WHITEAKER, born Pine Bluff, Arkansas, January 1, 1962; admitted to bar, 1987, Maryland; 1989, District of Columbia; 1996, U.S. Court of Appeals, Fifth and Sixth Circuits; 1997, U.S. Court of Appeals for the District of Columbia Circuit. *Education:* University of Arkansas (B.A., 1984); Duke University (J.D., 1987). Member, Alaska Law Review. *Member:* Federal Communications Bar Association. ***PRACTICE AREAS:*** Communications Law. ***Email:*** gwhiteaker@bennetlaw.com

MARJORIE GILLER SPIVAK, born Binghamton, New York, November 7, 1963; admitted to bar, 1987, Pennsylvania; 1988, District of Columbia. *Education:* American University (B.A., 1984); Catholic University of America (J.D., 1987). *Member:* Pennsylvania Bar Association; The District of Columbia Bar; Federal Communications Bar Association. ***PRACTICE AREAS:*** Communications Law. ***Email:*** mgspivak@aol.com

BRENT WEINGARDT, born Bristol, Pennsylvania, April 29, 1957; admitted to bar, 1982, District of Columbia; 1991, Maryland; 1992, U.S. Supreme Court; 1993, U.S. Court of Appeals for the District of Columbia Circuit. *Education:* University of Pennsylvania (B.A., 1978); George Washington University National Law Center (J.D., with honors, 1981). *Member:* Federal Communications Bar Association (Member, Executive Committee, 1996-1999; Treasurer, 2000). ***PRACTICE AREAS:*** Communications Law. ***Email:*** bweingardt@bennetlaw.com

SENIOR COUNSEL

HOWARD S. SHAPIRO, born New York, New York, February 11, 1955; admitted to bar, 1981, Florida; 1982, Virginia; 1983, District of Columbia. *Education:* Florida State University (B.A., magna cum laude, 1977; J.D., with High Honors, 1980). Phi Beta Kappa; Phi Kappa Phi; Order of the Coif. *Member:* Federal Communications Bar Association. ***PRACTICE AREAS:*** Communications Law. ***Email:*** hshapiro@bennetlaw.com

(This Listing Continued)

BENNET & BENNET, PLLC, Washington—Continued

DONALD L. HERMAN, JR., born Mobile, Alabama, September 7, 1971; admitted to bar, 1996, Alabama; 1999, District of Columbia. *Education:* University of Texas at Austin (B.J., 1993); University of Alabama (J.D., 1996). Phi Delta Phi. *Member:* Federal Communications Bar Association. ***PRACTICE AREAS:*** Communications Law. ***Email:*** dherman@bennetlaw.com

KELVIN L. REAVES, born Columbus, Ohio, February 11, 1974; admitted to bar, 2000, Maryland, Connecticut and U.S. Court of Appeals for the District of Columbia Circuit; 2001, District of Columbia. *Education:* University of Maryland at College Park (B.A., 1996); American University Washington College of Law (J.D., 1999). *Member:* Maryland State Bar Association. ***PRACTICE AREAS:*** Communications Law. ***Email:*** kreaves@bennetlaw.com

REBECCA L. MURPHY, born Montclair, New Jersey, November 1, 1973; admitted to bar, 2000, Maryland; 2001, District of Columbia. *Education:* Drexel University (B.S., magna cum laude, 1997); Catholic University of America (J.D., 2000). Delta Theta Phi, 1997-2000. Degree Recipient, The Institute for Communications Law Studies, 2000. Member, Editorial Board, Communications Law Conspectus Journal of Communications Law and Policy, 1999-2000. *Member:* Federal Communications Bar Association. ***PRACTICE AREAS:*** Communications Law. ***Email:*** rmurphy@bennetlaw.com

LEGAL SUPPORT PERSONNEL

TELECOMMUNICATIONS ANALYST

KENNETH C. JOHNSON, born Lafayette, Indiana, July 29, 1965. *Education:* University of Virginia (B.A., 1987); George Mason University (M.A., 1994). Author: "Universal Service Trends: Discussion and Forecast," published by Telecommunications Reports. ***PRACTICE AREAS:*** Communications Law. ***Email:*** kjohnson@bennetlaw.com

BENNETT, TURNER & COLEMAN, LLP

Established in 1999

1900 K STREET N.W., SUITE 750
WASHINGTON, D.C. 20006
Telephone: 202-833-4500
Fax: 202-833-2859
Email: info@btclaw.com
URL: http://www.btclaw.com

General Practice, Administrative Law, Civil Litigation and Legislative Practice at the Federal, State and International Levels with emphasis on Biomedical Research, Food, Drug and Cosmetic Regulation, Health Care, Medical Device Regulation, Medical Publishing and Communications Issues, and Medicare and Medicaid Law.

ALAN R. BENNETT, born Greenwich, Connecticut, April 12, 1948; admitted to bar, 1973, New York and District of Columbia. *Education:* University of Connecticut (B.A., with honors, 1969); Columbia University (J.D., 1972). Phi Beta Kappa. Co-Author, with Allan M. Fox, "Legislative History of the Drug Price Competition and Patent Term Restoration Act of 1984," Food and Drug Law Institute, 1987. Trial Attorney, 1972-1974. Assistant Chief Counsel for Enforcement, 1974-1976. Associate Chief Counsel for Radiological Health, U.S. Food and Drug Administration, 1975-1976. Minority Counsel, Subcommittee on Energy, Nuclear Proliferation and Federal Services, U.S. Senate Committee on Governmental Affairs, 1977-1978. Special Counsel to the Minority, U.S. Senate Committee on Governmental Affairs, 1978-1981. *Member:* The District of Columbia Bar; New York State and American Bar Associations. ***PRACTICE AREAS:*** Food and Drug Regulation; Health Law; Product Safety. ***Email:*** ABennett@btclaw.com

ALBERT F. CACOZZA, JR., born Utica, New York, October 3, 1956; admitted to bar, 1982, District of Columbia. *Education:* Brown University (A.B., magna cum laude, 1978); University of Chicago (J.D., with honors, 1982). Phi Beta Kappa; Order of the Coif. Comment Editor, University of Chicago Law Review, 1981-1982. Law Clerk to the Hon. Ruth Bader Ginsburg, U.S. Court of Appeals for the District of Columbia Circuit, 1982-1983. Counsel, U.S. Senate Committee on Labor and Human Resources, 1987-1991. Adjunct Professor, National Law Center, George Washington University, 1991—. *Member:* The District of Columbia Bar. ***Email:*** ACacozza@btclaw.com

TERRY COLEMAN, born Minneapolis, Minnesota, August 26, 1947; admitted to bar, 1973, Minnesota; 1976, District of Columbia. *Education:* University of Minnesota (B.A., summa cum laude, 1968); Harvard University (J.D., magna cum laude, 1973). Author, "Legal Aspects of Medicare and Medicaid Reimbursement," National Health Lawyers Association. Attorney, Associate Chief Counsel for Food, Food and Drug Administration, 1973-1976. Deputy General Counsel, 1981-1988 and Acting General Counsel, 1984-1985, Department of Health and Human Services. Chief Counsel, 1986-1988 and Deputy

(This Listing Continued)

Administrator, 1988-1989, Health Care Financing Administration. *Member:* The District of Columbia Bar. ***PRACTICE AREAS:*** Health Law; Food and Drug Regulation. ***Email:*** TColeman@btclaw.com

SAMUEL D. TURNER, born Chattanooga, Tennessee, December 28, 1947; admitted to bar, 1976, Virginia; 1977, District of Columbia. *Education:* Vanderbilt University (B.A., 1969; M.A., 1973); University of Virginia (J.D., 1976). Order of the Coif; Phi Beta Kappa; Omicron Delta Kappa. Law Clerk to Judge Thomas Flannery, U.S. District Court, District of Columbia, 1976-1977. Deputy General Counsel, U.S. Department of Health and Human Services, 1981-1984. *Member:* The District of Columbia Bar; Virginia State Bar; American Bar Association. ***Email:*** STurner@btclaw.com

MICHAEL D. PETTY, born Greensboro, North Carolina, April 5, 1954; admitted to bar, 1987, North Carolina; 1996, District of Columbia and U.S. District Court for the District of Columbia; 1997, U.S. Court of Appeals for the District of Columbia Circuit. *Education:* University of North Carolina (B.A., 1977; M.P.H., J.D., with honors, 1987). Member, Order of the Golden Fleece. Former Associate Chief Counsel for Enforcement, Food and Drug Administration, U.S. Government. *Member:* North Carolina State Bar; The District of Columbia Bar; American Bar Association. ***LANGUAGES:*** Spanish. ***PRACTICE AREAS:*** Food and Drug Regulation. ***Email:*** MPetty@btclaw.com

JAYNE P. BULTENA, born Sioux Falls, South Dakota, March 17, 1965; admitted to bar, 1991, Pennsylvania, District of Columbia and South Dakota. *Education:* University of South Dakota (B.S., magna cum laude, 1987); Harvard University (J.D., 1991). Phi Beta Kappa; Omicron Delta Kappa. *Member:* Pennsylvania Bar Association; State Bar of South Dakota; The District of Columbia Bar; American Bar Association. ***PRACTICE AREAS:*** Food and Drug Regulation. ***Email:*** JBultena@btclaw.com

ELIZABETH GOSS, born Little Rock, Arkansas, November 8, 1956; admitted to bar, 1993, Arkansas; 1996, District of Columbia. *Education:* Radcliffe College (A.B., magna cum laude, 1979); Georgetown University (J.D., cum laude, 1993). *Member:* The District of Columbia Bar. ***Email:*** EGoss@btclaw.com

BRUCE S. MANHEIM, JR., born Westbury, New York, September 15, 1955; admitted to bar, 1988, California; 1989, District of Columbia. *Education:* Pomona College (B.A., Biology, 1977); Claremont McKenna College (M.A., 1978); Vermont Law School (M.S.L., cum laude, 1982); Georgetown University (J.D., cum laude, 1988). Phi Beta Kappa. Member, Georgetown University Law Review, 1988. Author: "Conservation and Sustainable Utilization of the Pacific Yew Tree," Proceedings of the Second National Cancer Institute on Taxol and Taxus, September 23, 1992; "Pollution Law Goes Abroad," The National Law Journal, October 14, 1991; "Antarctica: The Fragile Ast Frontier," The Christian Science Monitor, March 23, 1989; "Recovery for Natural Resource Damages Under Superfund," National Environmental Enforcement Journal, February 1988; "Annex V of the MARPOL Convention: Will it Stop Marine Plastic Pollution?," Georgetown International Environmental Law Review, Vol. 1, 71-112, 1988; "Triterpenoids and Interspecific Variation in Leaf Wax of Dudleya," Biochemical Systematix and Evolution, Vol. 7, 17-19, 1979. Instructor of Biology, Cornell University, Ithaca, New York, 1979-1981. Senior Attorney-Scientist, Environmental Defense Fund, Washington, D.C., 1983-1994. Research Biologist and Chemist, University of Malaya, Kuala Lumpur, Malaysia, 1978-1979. *Member:* State Bar of California; The District of Columbia Bar. ***REPORTED CASES:*** Environmental Defense Fund vs. Massey, 986 F.2d 528 (D.C. Cir. 1993). ***Email:*** BManheim@btclaw.com

ASSOCIATES

KRISTI ELAINE SCHRODE, born Lafayette, Indiana, December 17, 1968; admitted to bar, 1995, Texas; 1997, District of Columbia and U.S Court of Appeals, Fifth Circuit. *Education:* University of California at Los Angeles (B.S., 1991); University of Houston (J.D., magna cum laude, 1995); University of Texas (Ph.D., medical humanities, 1998). Order of the Coif. Chief Articles Editor, Houston Law Review, 1994-1995. Law Clerk to the Honorable Henry A. Politz, Chief Judge, U.S. Court of Appeals, Fifth Circuit, 1996-1997. Author, "Life in Limbo: Revising Policies for Permanently Unconscious Patients," 31 Houston Law Review 1609, 1995. *Member:* American Society for Bioethics and Humanities. ***PRACTICE AREAS:*** Food and Drug Regulation; Health Law. ***Email:*** KSchrode@btclaw.com

NATHAN SHAWN LEE, born Santa Clara, California, August 12, 1973; admitted to bar, 1998, Wisconsin; 1999, California (Not admitted in District of Columbia). *Education:* University of California, San Diego (B.A., 1995); University of Wisconsin-Madison (J.D., cum laude, 1998). Recipient, Academic Achievement Awards in: Modern American Legal History; International Law; Policing in a Free Society; State Constitutional Law; Administrative Law. *Member:* State Bar of California; State Bar of Wisconsin. [Lieutenant, U.S. Navy, Judge Advocate General's Corps, 1998-2001]. ***PRACTICE AREAS:*** Food and Drug Regulation; Health Law; Medical Technology. ***Email:*** nlee@btclaw.com

PRAVEEN D. FERNANDES, born Burton-on-Trent, England, April 18, 1972; admitted to bar, 2000, Maryland; 2001, District of Columbia. *Education:* Brown University (B.A., with honors, 1994); University of North Carolina at

(This Listing Continued)

Chapel Hill (J.D., 1998; M.P.H., in Health Policy and Administration, 1999). Inducted into the Davis Honor Society for public service. Note and Comment Editor, N.C. Journal of International Law and Commercial Regulation. *Member:* The District of Columbia Bar; American Bar Association; American Society for Bioethics and Humanities. ***PRACTICE AREAS:*** Health Law; Legislative Practice; Biomedical Technology. ***Email:*** pfernandes@btclaw.com

KIMBERLY E. McCUTCHEON, born Akron, Ohio, June 28, 1972; admitted to bar, 1998, North Carolina (Not admitted in District of Columbia). *Education:* University of North Carolina at Chapel Hill (B.A., with distinction, 1994; J.D., with honors, 1998). Member, Order of the Golden Fleece. Law Clerk to the Honorable Frank M. Hull, U.S. Court of Appeals for the Eleventh Circuit, 2000. *Member:* North Carolina State Bar. ***PRACTICE AREAS:*** Food and Drug Regulation; Health Law. ***Email:*** kmccutcheon@btclaw.com

OF COUNSEL

KENNETH P. BERKOWITZ, born New York, N.Y., July 7, 1942; admitted to bar, 1968, New York; 1974, New Jersey and U.S. District Court, District of New Jersey (Not admitted in District of Columbia). *Education:* Hunter College of the City University of New York (B.A., 1964); Brooklyn Law School (J.D., 1967); New York University Graduate School of Law (LL.M., 1969). Executive Editor, "Understanding Promotional and Educational Regulations/ Guidelines for Prescription Drugs," Healthcare Marketing & Communications Council, Inc., 2000. ***PRACTICE AREAS:*** Food and Drug Law; Trade Regulation. ***Email:*** KBerkowitz@btclaw.com

THE BERGER LAW FIRM, P.C.

1120 20TH STREET, N.W., SUITE 300 SOUTH TOWER
WASHINGTON, D.C. 20036
Telephone: 202-861-1361
Fax: 202-861-1362
Email: bergerlaw@yahoo.com
URL: http://www. bergerlaborlaw.com

Management Labor Law, Employment Litigation, Wage and Hour, Discrimination and Harassment, OSHA, NLRA, FLSA, SCA, Affirmative Action, Employment Contracts, Trade Secrets and Personnel Policies for High Technology, Government Contract, Construction, Media, Professional, Executive, and Association Clients.

JEFFREY L. BERGER, born New York, N.Y., June 28, 1948; admitted to bar, 1974, New York; 1977, District of Columbia; 1992, Maryland. *Education:* State University of New York at Buffalo (B.A., 1969); Rutgers University (J.D., 1973); Georgetown University (LL.M. in Tax and Labor Law, 1979). Contributing Author: *Flying Solo:* A Survival Guide for Lawyers, 3rd Edition, ABA, 2001. Columnist, Tech Net Magazine, 1998-1999. EEOC Mediator, 1999—. Labor Counsel to Computing Technology Industry Association, 1997—. Attorney, Solicitor's Office, U.S. Labor Department, 1974-1979. Board Member: Association for Corporate Growth; D.C. Stoddert Soccer League. Member, Board of Advisors, InfoZen, Inc. *Member:* District of Columbia Bar (Elected Member, Law Practice Management Committee, 2000—); American Bar Association (Member, Employment Law Section); High Tech Council of Maryland. (Also Of Counsel to Jackson & Campbell, PC).

BERGESON & CAMPBELL, P.C.

Established in 1990

1203 19TH STREET, N.W., SUITE 300
WASHINGTON, D.C. 20036-2401
Telephone: 202-962-8585
Fax: 202-962-8599
Email: bc@lawbc
URL: http://www.lawyers.com/bergeson&campbelllaw

General Civil Practice including Administrative Law, Civil Litigation, and Legislative Practice primarily including representation on Environmental, Chemical Regulation, and Occupational Health and Safety Law, Toxic Torts.

FIRM PROFILE: Bergeson & Campbell, P.C. is a Washington, D.C. law firm concentrating on chemical, medical device, and diagnostic product approval and regulation, and associated business issues. Bergeson & Campbell's clients are involved in many businesses, including basic, specialty, and agricultural and antimicrobial chemicals; pharmaceuticals, medical devices, and diagnostic products; fibers; mining and smelting; paints and coatings; printing and publishing; steel; plastic products; and hazardous waste remediation.

We represent and counsel individuals, business entities, trade associations, and industry coalitions. Our professionals conduct litigation before Federal and State courts and before Federal and State regulatory agencies; advocate policy positions before the Congress, OMB, EPA, FDA, OSHA, ATSDR, NTP, the Departments of State, Interior, and U.S. Special Trade Representative, State governmental bodies, and in other forums; and play active roles in business strategy development, compliance planning, toxic tort defense, acquisitions, and related activities.

Our fundamental goals are to solve our clients' existing problems, and to minimize future difficulties. Reliance on only a single set of skills often is not enough. Legislative opportunities, rulemaking, and litigation options must be coordinated and effectively implemented. We take a multi-disciplinary approach in assisting our clients, partnering with toxicological, chemical, engineering, economic, and other experts on individual matters as necessary to achieve results effectively and efficiently. Attention must be paid to the interplay of all branches of government and interest groups. Our capabilities, borne of site- and issue-specific experience, combined with our national and international view on policy and regulatory developments, position us to handle all these tasks with judgment, creativity, and efficiency.

Our activities are international in scope. They range from confidential counseling and legislative and administration representation to more traditional business, litigation, and arbitration matters. Our personnel offer extraordinary expertise in such areas as TSCA, FIFRA, FQPA, EPCRA, RCRA, CAA regulation and enforcement, CERCLA, recycling, and FIFRA data compensation arbitrations. Our personnel also practice before the FDA, CPSC, and FTC. We also are well-versed in the complex issues arising from the interactions of environmental health and safety. food and drug, insurance, trade, and bankruptcy law. We additionally offer clients a full range of services to prevent and defend law suits alleging toxic torts, product liability, and other claims for liability involving industrial, specialty, consumer, amd agricultural chemical and medical devices and diagnostic products. On all matters, our professionals offer experience, judgment, vision, and vigor.

PARTNERS

LYNN L. BERGESON, born Grosse Pointe, Michigan, August 22, 1953; admitted to bar, 1980, District of Columbia. *Education:* Michigan State University (B.A., magna cum laude, 1975); Columbus School of Law, Catholic University of America (J.D., 1979). Member, Catholic University of America Law Review, 1977-1979. Co-Author: "The TSCA Basic Practice Book," ABA (2000); "The FIFRA Basic Practice Book," ABA (2000); Chapters 3 and 4, "Pesticides Law Handbook," Government Institutes (1999); "Avoiding Liability for Hazardous Waste: RCRA, CERCLA and Related Corporate Law Issues," Bureau of National Affairs, Corporate Practice Series, 1999; "The RCRA Handbook," ABA Publications, 1994; Chapter 7 - Liability, "Environmental Law Practice Guide," Matthew Bender, 1992; "The Expanding Scope of Liability for Environmental Damage and Its Impact on Business Transactions," The Corporation Law Review, Spring, 1985. Editor-in-Chief: ABA Special Committee on Pesticides, Chemical Regulation, and Right-to-Know Newsletter, 2000—. Legal Editor, Pollution Engineering, 1987—; Contributing Editor, Pollution Prevention Review, 1990—; Contributing Editor, Corporate Legal Times, 1992—; Contributing Editor, The Environmental Corporate Counsel Report, 1994—. Editorial Board, Manufacturing Today. Chair, ABA Year-In-Review Committee, 2001-2002. Vice-Chair: ABA Special Committee on Agricultural Management; ABA Special Committee on Pesticides, Chemical Regulation and Right-to-Know; ABA Special Committee of the Environment and Environmental Resources; ABA Special Committee on Book Publications; ABA Special Committee on Newsletter Coordination; Rapid Response Committee. Member, Editorial Advisory Board: EPA Administrative Law Reporter, 1996—; Pollution Prevention Review, 1991—; Environmental Law Advisory Committee, National Chamber Litigation Center, U.S. Chamber of Commerce, 1992—; Editorial Advisory Board, The Environmental Corporate Counsel, 1994—; Founding Member and National Chair, The Society of Women Environmental Professionals. *Member:* The District of Columbia Bar; Bar Association of the District of Columbia; American Bar Association (Member, Section of Environment, Energy and Resources); Womens' Bar Association of the District of Columbia. ***PRACTICE AREAS:*** Federal Insecticide, Fungicide and Rodenticide Act (FIFRA); Toxic Substances Regulation; Clean Air Act; Resource Conservation and Recovery Act (RCRA); OSHA; Pesticide Regulation; Chemical Regulation; Environmental Compliance; Environmental Regulation; Environmental Arbitration; Federal Regulatory Law; Regulatory Agency Practice. ***Email:*** lbergeson@lawbc.com

LISA M. CAMPBELL, born New York, New York, March 31, 1960; admitted to bar, 1985, Arizona; 1988, District of Columbia. *Education:* University of Arizona (B.S., 1982); Stanford Law School (J.D., 1985). Co-Author: "The TSCA Basic Practice Book," ABA, 2000; "The FIFRA Basic Practice Book," ABA, 2000; Chapters 3 and 4, "Pesticides Law Handbook," Government Institutes, 1999; "Treated Article Exemption: Going, Going, Gone?", BNA Chemical Regulation Reporter, April 17, 1998; Chapter 7--Liability, "Environmental Law Practice Guide," Matthew Bender, 1992. *Member:* The District of Columbia Bar; State Bar of Arizona; American Bar Association. ***PRACTICE AREAS:*** Federal Insecticide, Fungicide and Rodenticide Act (FIFRA); Toxic Substances Regulation; Resource Conservation and Recovery Act (RCRA);

(This Listing Continued)

BERGESON & CAMPBELL, P.C., Washington—Continued

Pesticide Regulation; Chemical Regulation; Environmental Compliance; Environmental Regulation; Environmental Arbitration; Federal Regulatory Law; Regulatory Agency Practice. ***Email:*** lcampbell@lawbc.com

ASSOCIATES

LISA ROTHENBERG BURCHI, born Larchmont, New York, November 21, 1968; admitted to bar, 1996, New York; 1998, District of Columbia. *Education:* Tufts University (B.A., cum laude, 1990); The National Law Center, George Washington University (J.D., with honors, 1995). Member, George Washington University Journal of International Law and Economics, 1994-1995. Co-Author, "The TSCA Basic Practice Book," ABA, 2000. *Member:* The District of Columbia Bar. ***PRACTICE AREAS:*** Federal Insecticide, Fungicide and Rodenticide Act (FIFRA); Toxic Substances Regulation; Pesticide Regulation; Chemical Regulation; Environmental Compliance; Environmental Regulation; Environmental Arbitration; Federal Regulatory Law; Regulatory Agency Practice. ***Email:*** lburchi@lawbc.com

OF COUNSEL

BETHAMI AUERBACH, born Los Angeles, California, July 21, 1949; admitted to bar, 1974, California; 1975, District of Columbia. *Education:* Pomona College (B.A., magna cum laude, 1970); Stanford Law School (J.D., 1974); University of Iowa (M.F.A., 1983). Board of Editors, Stanford Law Review. Phi Beta Kappa. Law Clerk to Judge Joseph T. Sneed, U.S. Court of Appeals, Ninth Circuit, 1974-1975. Co-Author, Chapters 3 and 4, "Pesticides Law Handbook," Government Institutes, 1999. Office of General Counsel, U.S. Environmental Protection Agency, 1977-1980. Visiting Associate Professor of Law, University of Iowa College of Law, 1981-1983. Visiting Associate Professor of Law, Temple University Law School, 1984-1985. *Member:* The District of Columbia Bar; State Bar of California (inactive). ***PRACTICE AREAS:*** Clean Air Act; Resource Conservation and Recovery Act (RCRA); OSHA; Chemical Regulation; Environmental Compliance; Environmental Regulation; Federal Regulatory Law; Regulatory Agency Practice. ***Email:*** bauerbach@lawbc.com

RICHARD P. BOZOF, born Washington, D.C., December 8, 1947; admitted to bar, 1977, California; 1980, District of Columbia. *Education:* Dartmouth College (B.A., magna cum laude, 1969); Yale University School of Medicine (M.D., 1973); Boalt Hall School of Law, University of California (J.D., 1976). Phi Beta Kappa. General Editor and Principal Author: *Navigating Proposition 65 in the 1990's: A Guide to Safe Passage Through the Safe Drinking Water and Toxic Enforcement Act of 1986,* published by Nossaman, Guthner, Knox & Elliott, 1993. Office of General Counsel, U.S. Environmental Protection Agency, 1977-1985. Partner, Nossaman, Guthner, Knox & Elliott, 1987-1998. *Member:* District of Columbia Bar; State Bar of California. ***PRACTICE AREAS:*** Federal Insecticide, Fungicide and Rodenticide Act (FIFRA); Toxic Substances Regulation; Food and Drug Regulation; Food, Drug and Cosmetic Law; Pesticide Regulation; Chemical Regulation; Environmental Compliance; Environmental Regulation; Federal Regulatory Law; Regulatory Agency Practice. ***Email:*** rbozof@lawbc.com

MICHAEL F. COLE, admitted to bar, 1966, New York; 1999, District of Columbia. *Education:* Vanderbilt University (B.A., magna cum laude, with honors, 1963); New York University (LL.B., 1966). Phi Beta Kappa; Phi Eta Sigma. Root-Tilden Scholar. Research Editor, New York University Law Review. *Member:* The District of Columbia Bar; New York State Bar Association. ***PRACTICE AREAS:*** Food and Drug Regulation; Food, Drug and Cosmetic Law; Chemical Regulation; Environmental Compliance; Environmental Regulation; Federal Regulatory Law; Regulatory Agency Practice. ***Email:*** mcole@lawbc.com

CARA S. JABLON, born Brooklyn, New York, September 23, 1943; admitted to bar, 1978, District of Columbia. *Education:* Mount Holyoke College (A.B., with honors, 1965); George Washington University (J.D., 1977); Columbia University (Ph.D., Biochemistry, 1994). Contributing Author: "TSCA Inspections and Enforcement," Chapter 13, TSCA Handbook, Third Edition, McKenna & Cuneo, Government Institutes, Inc., 1997. Co-Author: "The FIFRA Basic Practice Book," ABA, 2000; "EPA Holds Chemical Manufacturers Strictly Liable For Good Laboratory Practice Violations," Bureau of National Affairs, Chemical Regulation Reporter, November 5, 1993; "EPA Interpretation of FFDCA Delaney Clause May Point The Way For Future Health and Safety Decisions," Bureau of National Affairs, Chemical Regulation Reporter, April 19, 1991. *Member:* The District of Columbia Bar. ***PRACTICE AREAS:*** Federal Insecticide, Fungicide and Rodenticide Act (FIFRA); Toxic Substances Regulation; Pesticide Regulation; Chemical Regulation; Environmental Compliance; Environmental Regulation; Federal Regulatory Law; Regulatory Agency Practice. ***Email:*** cjablon@lawbc.com

EILEEN B. SALATHÉ GERNHARD, born Attleboro, Massachusetts, October 29, 1965; admitted to bar, 1992, Connecticut; 1999, District of Columbia. *Education:* Wheaton College (B.A., cum laude, with honors, 1987); Georgetown University (J.D., 1992). Co-Author: "The FIFRA Basic Practice Book," ABA, 2000; Chapter 28 - Worker and Public Notification, "Environmental Law Practice Guide," revised edition, Matthew Bender, 2000; "Treated Article Exemption: Going, Going, Gone?" BNA Chemical Regulation Reporter, April 17, 1998; Chapter 7 - Liability, "Environmental Law Practice Guide," Matthew Bender, 1992. ***PRACTICE AREAS:*** Federal Insecticide, Fungicide and Rodenticide Act (FIFRA); Resource Conservation and Recovery Act (RCRA); Superfund; Pesticide Regulation; Chemical Regulation; Environmental Compliance; Environmental Regulation; Federal Regulatory Law; Regulatory Agency Practice. ***Email:*** esgernhard@lawbc.com

JANE C. BERGNER

SUITE 650
1615 L STREET, N.W.
WASHINGTON, D.C. 20036
Telephone: 202-626-8215
Telecopier: 202-626-8233
Email: jbergnerlaw@abanet.org
URL: http://www.lawyers.com/dctaxlaw

Federal and District of Columbia Tax Planning, Tax Controversies, Tax Litigation, Tax Collection. Tax Audits and Tax Appeals before Internal Revenue Service, Civil Litigation and Arbitration. Estate and Gift Taxation, Planning and Administration. Local Taxation.

JANE C. BERGNER, born Schenectady, New York, April 6, 1943 (Jane H. Cohen); admitted to bar, 1968, District of Columbia, U.S. Court of Appeals for the District of Columbia Circuit, U.S. District Court, District of Columbia; 1969, U.S. Court of Federal Claims and U.S. Court of Appeals for the Federal Circuit; 1979, U.S. Tax Court; 1992, U.S. Supreme Court. *Education:* Vassar College (A.B., 1964); Columbia University (LL.B., 1967). Author: "Tax Court Practice" Volume 9, and "Court of Federal Claims Practice" Chapter in Volume 8 on National Courts, West's Federal Forms (2001); "Payments Received in Lawsuits and Settlements," Kleinrock's Tax Expert (2001); "Income, Gift and Estate Tax Considerations Affecting the Ownership and Transfer of United States Savings Bonds," 19 Estates, Gifts and Trusts Journal 135, (1994); "Expanded Relief Available to Make Many Elections," 50 Taxation for Accountants 68, (1993); "IRS Using Authority to Seize Qualified Pension Plan Benefits," 2 IRS Practice & Policy Bulletin 80, 11 Tax Management Weekly Report 79, 19 BNA Pension Reporter 307, 17 Estates, Gifts and Trusts Journal 113, 2 IRS Practice & Policy Bulletin 208 (1992); "ESOPS and Other Applications of Section 6166," 10 Estates, Gifts and Trusts Journal 111 (1985). Trial Attorney, Review Section, 1967-1969, and Court of Claims Section, 1969-1974, Tax Division, U.S. Department of Justice. Chair, 1985-1991, Taxation Section, District of Columbia Bar (Award of Merit for Best Section, 1985-1986). Chair, 1991-1993, Tax Audits and Litigation Committee, Taxation Section, District of Columbia Bar (Award for Best Section Community Outreach Project, 1992-93). Chair, 1991-1993, Subcommittee on Important Developments, Committee on Civil and Criminal Tax Penalties, Chair, 1984-1987, Subcommittee on Liaison with the Tax Court, Committee on Court Procedure, Section of Taxation, American Bar Association. Fellow, American College of Tax Counsel. Founding Member, Tax Luncheon Group. Member, Judicial Conferences of the U.S. Tax Court and the U.S. Court of Federal Claims. *Member:* Federal Bar Association; Washington, D.C. Estate Planning Council; Boards of Directors, Jewish Social Service Agency of Metropolitan Washington and Jewish Council for the Aging; Womens Bar of DC; Board Secretary, WMAU-FM Radio Station of The American University, 1983-1987.

BERLINER, CANDON & JIMISON

1225 NINETEENTH STREET N.W., SUITE 800
WASHINGTON, D.C. 20036
Telephone: 202-955-6067
Telecopy: 202-822-0109
URL: http://www.bcjlaw.com

Berkeley, California Office: 2560 Ninth Street, Suite 316. Telephone: 510-549-6926. Telecopy: 510-649-9793.

Los Angeles, California Office: 1875 Century Park East, Suite 700. Telephone: 310-282-6848. Telecopy: 310-282-6841.

Administrative Law, Commercial Litigation, Appellate Advocacy, Intergovernmental Affairs, Legislative Practice, Health Policy, Maritime Law, International Trade, North American Energy Transactions, Oil and Gas Law, Public Utility Law, Pipeline Law, Telecommunications Law, Industrial Energy Use Law.

FIRM PROFILE: Berliner, Candon & Jimison, formerly Brady & Berliner continues a practice of government representation and administration law begun in 1985. The practice initially focused upon the representation of Canadian natural gas interests before state and federal regulatory agencies, and has now broadened its scope to include all aspects of North American energy trade and transactions,

(This Listing Continued)

maritime law, administrative law generally, commercial litigation, appellate advocacy, health policy and an active intergovernmental and legislative affairs practice.

MEMBERS OF FIRM

ROGER A. BERLINER, born Cincinnati, Ohio, February 12, 1951; admitted to bar, 1983, California; 1987, District of Columbia. *Education:* Dartmouth College (B.A., 1973); Catholic University of America; McGeorge School of Law, University of the Pacific (J.D., 1983). Special Assistant, Congressman Thomas Luken, 1973. Legislative Analyst, Democratic Study Group, U.S. House of Representatives, 1975-1976. Legislative Assistant, U.S. Senator Howard Metzenbaum, 1977-1978. Legislative Director, U.S. Senator Howard Metzenbaum, 1979. Director, Division of Congressional Liaison, Federal Energy Regulatory Commission, 1980. Consultant, Committee on Energy and Commerce, U.S. House of Representatives, 1981. Chief Consultant, Subcommittee on Energy, California State Assembly, 1982. Principal Consultant, Utilities and Commerce Committee, California State Assembly, 1983. *Member:* District of Columbia Bar; State Bar of California; American Bar Association; Federal Energy Bar Association. ***PRACTICE AREAS:*** Litigation; Administrative Law; North American Energy Law and Trade; Public Utility Law; Federal and State Legislation; Maritime Law. ***Email:*** rogerberliner@bcjlaw.com

JOHN W. JIMISON, born Rahway, New Jersey, January 27, 1946; admitted to bar, 1975, Virginia, 1980, District of Columbia. *Education:* College of Wooster (B.A., 1968); Georgetown University Law Center (J.D., 1975). Phi Alpha Theta. Special Assistant, Congressman Allard K. Lowenstein, 1970. Assistant General Manager, American Public Gas Association, 1971-1972. Analyst in Energy Policy, Congressional Research Service, Library of Congress, 1972-1974. Professional Staff Member, Senate Commerce Committee, 1974-1975. Head of Energy Section, Congressional Research Service, Library of Congress, 1976-1980. Counsel, Subcommittee on Fossil and Synthetic Fuels, Committee on Energy and Commerce, House of Representatives, 1981. Principal Administrator, International Energy Agency, Paris, France, 1982-1985. Executive Director, U.S. Combined Heat & Power Association. U.S. Representative, International Cogeneration Alliance. *Member:* Federal Bar Association; Federal Energy Bar Association; National Academy of Sciences (Chairman, Committee on Pipeline Transportation, Transportation Research Board, 1986-1989); International Association for Energy Economics (General Counsel, 1989—); United States Association for Energy Economics (General Counsel, 1991). ***LANGUAGES:*** French, Somali. ***PRACTICE AREAS:*** State Public Utility Proceedings; Municipal Law; Natural Gas; Telecommunications Law; Federal Legislation and Regulation. ***Email:*** johnj@bcjlaw.com

MARY EVA CANDON, born Washington, D.C., May 15, 1950; admitted to bar, 1987, District of Columbia. *Education:* Emmanuel College (B.A., 1972); Georgetown University Law Center (J.D., 1983). Co-Director, United States Youth Council, 1975-1977. Executive Director, District of Columbia Democratic Party, 1978-1984. President, Association of State Democratic Executive Directors, 1982-1985. Special Assistant to the Chairman of the Democratic National Committee, 1984-1985. Executive Director, American Council of Young Political Leaders, 1985-1988. Vice-President, Washington Resources and Strategy, Inc., 1988. Executive Director, Legal Aid Society of the District of Columbia, 1988-1994. Director, Federal City National Bank, 1990-1992. Member, District of Columbia Circuit's Judicial Conference Standing Committee on Pro Bono Legal Services, 1992-1994. Chair, The Consortium of Legal Services Providers, 1992-1993. Chairman, Alcoholic Beverage Control Board of the District of Columbia, 1991-1996. *Member:* District of Columbia Bar (Treasurer, 2000-2001); Bar Association of the District of Columbia; American Bar Association; The Women's Bar Association. ***PRACTICE AREAS:*** Intergovernmental Affairs; Administrative Law. ***Email:*** candon@bcjlaw.com

ASSOCIATES

PETER G. HIRST, born Trenton, New Jersey, April 29, 1950; admitted to bar, 1981, California; 1982, Massachusetts (Not admitted in District of Columbia). *Education:* Pomona College (B.A., 1974); Southwestern University (J.D., 1981). Editor, Southwestern University Law Review, 1980-1981. Senior Attorney, United Pipe Line Company, 1989-1991. *Member:* Massachusetts, American and Federal Energy Bar Associations; State Bar of California. ***PRACTICE AREAS:*** Commercial Litigation; Oil and Gas Law; State Public Utility Proceedings; Natural Gas Pipeline Litigation. ***Email:*** pghirst@bcjlaw.comer.com

MEGAN GRANT, born December 11, 1966; admitted to bar, 1995, Idaho; 1996, Colorado; 1997, District of Columbia. *Education:* University of San Diego (B.A., 1990); University of Idaho (J.D., 1995); Tulane University (LL.M., 1998).

MARK R. GISLER, admitted to bar, 1988, Maryland (Not admitted in District of Columbia). *Education:* Oregon State University (B.A, 1985); American University (J.D., 1988); Georgetown University Law Center (LL.M., 1993). Adjunct Professor, Legal Research and Writing, George Mason University, 1994-1995. Trial Attorney, Special Litigation Branch, National Labor Relations Board, 1988-1998. Assistant Counsel (on detail from NLRB), The White

(This Listing Continued)

House, Office of the President, 1996. Executive in Charge of Business and Legal Affairs, Maltese Falcon Productions, plc, Malta, 1998-2000. *Member:* Maryland State Bar Association, Inc.

OF COUNSEL

LUCIEN WULSIN, JR., born Cincinnati, Ohio, September 15, 1945; admitted to bar, 1970, Massachusetts; 1977, U.S. District Court, 1st Circuit; 1979, U.S. District Court, 5th Circuit; 1983, California (Not admitted in District of Columbia). *Education:* Trinity College (B.A., 1967); University of Virginia (J.D., 1970). *Member:* American Bar Association. (Also practicing individually in Santa Monica, California).

ANDY SCHNEIDER, born San Francisco, California, June 26, 1948; admitted to bar, 1995, District of Columbia. *Education:* Princeton University (A.B., 1970); University of Pennsylvania Law School (J.D., 1973). Adjunct Professor, Federal Legislation Clinic, Georgetown University Law Center and Principal, Health Policy Group. Staff Attorney: Health Law Project, 1973-1974; National Health Law Program, 1975-1978. Counsel, Subcommittee on Health and the Environment, Committee on Energy and Commerce, U.S. House of Representatives, 1979-1994. Medicaid Policy Advisor, Democratic Policy Committee, U.S. House of Representatives, 1995-1996. Health Counsel, Center on Budget and Policy Priorities, 1997. *Member:* The District of Columbia Bar. ***PRACTICE AREAS:*** Health Policy; Federal and State Legislation. ***Email:*** aschneider@hlthpolicy.com

DEBRA L. ROTH, admitted to bar, 1986, California (Not admitted in District of Columbia). *Education:* University of California at Berkeley (B.A., 1982); University of California at Davis (J.D., 1986). Co-Author, "Improving Health Care Quality: Opportunities for Intervention by Consumer Groups," a manual on shaping state and federal health care policy in both public and private sectors. Chief Counsel, California State Assembly Health Committee, 1997-1998. Consultant to several California Legislature Committees, including Senate Insurance Committee and Assembly Insurance Committee, 1990-1996.

LEGISLATIVE PROFESSIONALS

BURT MARGOLIN, born Chattanooga, Tennessee, September 28, 1950. *Education:* University of California at Los Angeles. Chief of Staff, Congressman Henry Waxman, 1975-1977, 1979-1982. Member, California State Assembly, 1982-1994. Chairman, California Assembly Health Committee, 1992-1994. Health Crisis Manager, Los Angeles County, 1995. (Resident, Los Angeles, California Office). ***PRACTICE AREAS:*** Federal and State Legislation; Health Policy. ***Email:*** burtm@bradyberliner.com

CARLA KISH, born Ann Arbor, Michigan, December 1, 1948. *Education:* University of Michigan (B.A., with honors, 1970); University of Michigan, School of Natural Resources (M.S., 1972); London School of Economics (M.A., 1975). Staff Member, Subcommittee on Energy and the Environment, House Interior Committee, 1976-1980. Regional Representative, Western Organization of Resource Councils, 1980. Legislative Assistant, Senator Carl Levin, 1981-1984. Staff Supervisor, The Wilderness Society, 1984-1986. Vice President, D&R International, 1987-1992. ***PRACTICE AREAS:*** Federal and State Legislation. ***Email:*** carlake@bradyberliner.com

LEGAL SUPPORT PERSONNEL

CONSULTANTS

R. THOMAS BEACH, born Albany, New York, February 8, 1955. *Education:* Dartmouth College (A.B., with high honors, 1977); University of California at Berkeley (M.E., 1980). Staff Engineer, California Public Utilities Commission, 1981-1984. Advisor to California Public Utilities Commissioners Priscilla C. Grew, Donald Vial and G. Mitchell Wilk, 1984-1989. (Resident, Berkeley California Office). ***PRACTICE AREAS:*** Electricity Restructuring; Public Utility Commission Prudence Reviews; Cogeneration; Interstate Pipelines; Natural Gas Pricing Indices. ***Email:*** tomb@crossborderenergy.com

PATRICK G. McGUIRE, born Berkeley, California, January 21, 1965. *Education:* University of California at Santa Cruz (B.A., 1989). Associate Mathematician, Sierra Energy and Risk Assessment, 1989-1992. (Resident, Berkeley, California Office). ***Email:*** patrickm@crossborderenergy.com

REPRESENTATIVE CLIENTS: The Territory of Guam; The County of Los Angeles; Sacramento Municipal Utility District; California Primary Care Association; Watson Cogeneration Company; Canadian Association of Petroleum Producers; Polyisocyanurate Insulation Manufacturers Association.
REFERENCES: City of Vernon, California; The Territory of Guam; The County of Los Angeles; Sacramento Municipal Utility District.

BERLINER, CORCORAN & ROWE, L.L.P.

A Partnership including a Professional Corporation

Established in 1941

1101 SEVENTEENTH STREET, N.W., SUITE 1100
WASHINGTON, D.C. 20036-4798
Telephone: 202-293-5555
FAX: 202-293-9035
Email: bcr@bcr-dc.com
URL: http://www.bcr-dc.com

General Practice before all Courts and Government Agencies. International, Litigation, Corporate, e-Commerce Law, Internet Law, Emerging Business Law, Merger and Acquisitions, Computer, Real Estate, Commercial Real Estate, Landlord and Tenant Law, Intellectual Property, Export Control, Criminal, Tax, Government Contracts, Entertainment, Family Law.

FIRM PROFILE: A Washington-based law firm which provides personalized, partner-level attention to its clients while possessing the resources, expertise and staff support to advise on a wide range of legal matters. The firm serves large corporations on specific matters, foreign governments, foreign businesses seeking to establish a presence in the U.S., small and medium size U.S. businesses and individuals. The firm provides legal representation before the District of Columbia courts, courts of the surrounding metropolitan area and the United States Supreme Court. Its international expertise and language skills assist clients in Europe, the Middle East, Asia and Canada.

THOMAS G. CORCORAN, JR., born Washington, D.C., April 13, 1942; admitted to bar, 1969, District of Columbia; 1980, U.S. Supreme Court; 1991, Maryland. *Education:* Brown University (A.B., 1964); Harvard University (LL.B., 1967). Law Clerk to Judge Gerard D. Reilly, District of Columbia Court of Appeals, 1971-1972. Assistant, U.S. Attorney, District of Columbia, 1972-1978. *Member:* District of Columbia Bar; Maryland State Bar Association. ***LANGUAGES:*** German and Spanish. ***REPORTED CASES:*** Pleasant Grove vs. U.S., 479 U.S. 462 (1987); Princz vs. Federal Republic of Germany, 26 F.3d 1166 (D.C. Cir. 1994). ***PRACTICE AREAS:*** Civil and Criminal Litigation; Appeals. ***Email:*** tgc@bcr-dc.com

WAYNE H. RUSCH, born Sandwich, Illinois, November 17, 1945; admitted to bar, 1970, Wisconsin; 1971, Illinois; 1980, District of Columbia; 1988, U.S. Supreme Court. *Education:* University of Wisconsin (B.B.A., 1967; J.D., 1970). District Attorney, Iowa County, Wisconsin, 1972-1975. Counsel, Asian Development Bank, 1977-1980. *Member:* State Bar of Wisconsin; District of Columbia Bar; American (Member, International Law and Practice Section) and International Bar Associations. ***PRACTICE AREAS:*** International; Corporate; Commercial Transactions. ***Email:*** whr@bcr-dc.com

CLEMENS KOCHINKE, born Anholt, Germany, February 7, 1952; admitted to bar, 1978, Germany; 1983, District of Columbia; 1985, U.S. Court of International Trade, U.S. Claims Court and U.S. Court of Appeals for the Federal Circuit; 1989, U.S. Supreme Court. *Education:* Bismarck G. Karlsruhe (Hum. Abitur, 1970); Heidelberg University Law School (Ref., 1975); LG Karlsruhe (Assessor, 1978); King's College, London (1978); George Washington University (M.C.L., 1983). Author: "Malta: A Base for Offshore Production and Services," Warren, Gorham & Lamont, 1995; "Source Code Escrow in U.S. Law," 8 Computer & Recht 1992, 7; "U.S. Reexport Controls and Information Technology," in Goebel (ed.), Legal and Economic Environment for the German Computer Industry, Cologne, 1990. Co-Author: "Shrinkwrap-Licenses and Data Base Protection in the U.S." CR 1997, 129; "Links, Frames and Meta Tags," CR 1999, 190; "Allfinanzunternehmen in den USA.," 46 RIW 518, 2000. Editor, German American Law Journal, 1991-1995. *Member:* District of Columbia Bar; German American Law Association (Vice-President, 1990—); IEEE Computer Society. ***LANGUAGES:*** German and English. ***PRACTICE AREAS:*** International; Internet; Computer. ***Email:*** ck@bcr-dc.com

RICHARD LANDFIELD, born Chicago, Illinois, January 16, 1941; admitted to bar, 1966, New York; 1972, District of Columbia; 1979, U.S. Supreme Court. *Education:* Amherst College (B.A., 1962); Harvard University (LL.B., cum laude, 1965). Recipient, John Woodruff Simpson Fellowship for Law. General Counsel, The European Institute. *Member:* The District of Columbia Bar; American Bar Association. [1st Lt., U.S. Army, 1966-1969]. ***PRACTICE AREAS:*** Corporate; International; Real Estate.

BENJAMIN H. FLOWE, JR., born Durham, North Carolina, February 8, 1956; admitted to bar, 1981, District of Columbia; 1990, U.S. Supreme Court. *Education:* Duke University (A.B., cum laude, 1978); University of North Carolina at Chapel Hill (J.D., with high honors, 1981). Order of the Coif. Executive Editor, North Carolina Journal of International Law and Commercial Regulation, 1980-1981. Staff, North Carolina Law Review, 1979-1981. Author: *Export Compliance Guide*, 1995. Member: Vice President, Regulations and Procedures Technical Advisory Committee. Vice Chair, Commerce Department; Steering Committee, Center for Strategic and International Studies, Export Controls in a Changing World. *Member:* The District of Columbia Bar; American Bar Association (Vice Chair, Export Controls and Economic Sanctions Committee); American Electronics Association (Member, Export Controls Committee); Washington International Trade Association. ***SPECIAL AGENCIES:*** Bureau of Export Administration, Commerce; Office of Defense Technology Controls, State; Office of Foreign Assets Controls, Treasury; Defense Threat Reduction Agency. ***PRACTICE AREAS:*** International; Corporate; Commercial Transactions; Maritime. ***Email:*** bflowe@bcr-dc.com

BRUCE ZAGARIS, born Modesto, California, September 4, 1947; admitted to bar, 1973, Oregon and Idaho; 1976, California; 1978, District of Columbia. *Education:* University of San Francisco; George Washington University (B.A., 1969; J.D., 1972; LL.M., 1973); Stockholm University, Sweden (LL.M., cum laude, 1975); Free University, Belgium (LL.M., cum laude, 1976). Law Clerk, K.K. Hall, U.S. District Court, Southern District of West Virginia, 1972-1973. Co-Editor, International Criminal Law, Carolina Academic Press, 1996. Author: "*Foreign Investment in the United States,*" (1980, Praeger Press). Co-Editor, International Criminal Law, 1996 Carolina Academic Press. Lecturer, Faculty of Law, the University of The West Indies, 1977-1978. Adjunct Professor, International White Collar Crime, Fordham University, 1990—; Washington College of Law, American University, 1993-1999. Assistant Attorney General, Idaho, 1973-1974. *Member:* District of Columbia Bar; American Bar Association (Chairman, Caribbean Law Committee, 1982-1987; Chairman, Committee on International Tax, 1987-1992; Chairman, Committee on International Criminal Law, 1989—); American Society of International Law (Executive Council, 1990-1993); Washington Foreign Law Society (President, 1990-1991); International Penal Law Association (Representative to Organization of American States, 1984—); International Fiscal Association. ***LANGUAGES:*** Spanish, Portuguese, French and Swedish. ***PRACTICE AREAS:*** International; Tax; Criminal. ***Email:*** bzagaris@bcr-dc.com

JOHN A. ORDWAY, JR., born Cincinnati, Ohio, December 3, 1956; admitted to bar, 1986, Pennsylvania; 1988, District of Columbia. *Education:* Harvard College (A.B., magna cum laude, 1980); George Washington University (J.D., with honors, 1985). Rotary Graduate Fellow, Hong Kong, Taiwan, 1981-1982. *Member:* Pennsylvania and American (Member, Sections on: Public Contract Law; International Law; Commercial Products and Services Committee; International Procurement Committee) Bar Associations; The District of Columbia Bar (Member, Section on Government Contracts and Litigation). ***PRACTICE AREAS:*** Government Procurement; Export Control; Criminal Defense; Litigation. ***Email:*** jao@bcr-dc.com

JAMES L. MARKETOS, born Utica, New York, March 24, 1954; admitted to bar, 1980, New York; 1988, District of Columbia. *Education:* Princeton University (A.B., 1976); New York University (J.D., 1979). Co-Editor-in-Chief, Annual Survey of American Law, 1978-1979. Recipient: Arthur T. Vanderbilt Medal, 1979. Law Clerk: Hon. Vincent L. Brockerick, S.D.N.Y., 1979-1980. ***LANGUAGES:*** Greek. ***PRACTICE AREAS:*** Litigation. ***Email:*** jlm@bcr-dc.com

JAY A. ROSENTHAL, born Reading, Pennsylvania, November 13, 1957; admitted to bar, 1985, Maryland and District of Columbia. *Education:* American University (B.A., 1979; M.A., 1981); Antioch School of Law (J.D., 1984); Georgetown University (LL.M., 1991). Author: "Music Industry Should Rally Against NEA Ruling," Billbroad, Guest Commentary, August 8, 1998; "The Effects of the 1996 Telecommunications Law on the Music Industry," Multimedia and Technology Law Report, Dec. 1996; "Copyright Restoration Under GANT," 3 Public Domain Report 1, January, 1995; "Legal and Political Considerations of the United States Ratification of the Genocide Convention," 3 Antioch Law Journal 117, 1985. Associate Professor of Entertainment Law, George Washington University School of Law. Vice President, Washington Area Music Association. Advisory Board, Songwriter Association of Washington. Volunteer Attorney, Washington Area Lawyers for the Arts. ***PRACTICE AREAS:*** Entertainment; Intellectual Property; Internet Law; Copyright and Trademark. ***Email:*** jrose13@aol.com

COUNSEL

THOMAS E. WILSON, born Pensacola, Florida, September 14, 1942; admitted to bar, 1968, District of Columbia; 1971, New York; 1972, U.S. Court of Appeals for the District of Columbia Circuit; 1974, U.S. Court of Appeals, Fifth Circuit; 1980, U.S Court of Appeals, Fourth and Eighth Circuits; 1984, U.S. Supreme Court. *Education:* Georgetown University (A.B., 1964; J.D., 1967); Columbia University (M.B.A., 1970). Author: "Separation Between Banking and Commerce under the Bank Holding Company Act—A Statutory Objective Under Attack," Catholic University Law Review, Vol. 33, No. 1, Fall, 1983. *Member:* District of Columbia Bar; New York State and American Bar Associations. [Capt., U.S. Army, 1967-1969]. ***PRACTICE AREAS:*** Litigation; White Collar Criminal. ***Email:*** bjones@bcr.dc.com

HENRY A. BERLINER, JR., born Washington, D.C., February 9, 1934; admitted to bar, 1965, District of Columbia. *Education:* University of Michigan (B.A., 1956); George Washington University (J.D., with honors, 1964). Associate Editor, George Washington Law Review, 1963-1964. Assistant U.S. Attorney, District of Columbia, 1966-1967. General Counsel and Corporate Secre-

(This Listing Continued)

tary, Baltimore Contractors, 1999—. Member, 1971-1979 and Chairman, 1975-1978, District of Columbia Commission on Judicial Disabilities and Tenure. President and Chairman of the Board, Pennsylvania Avenue Development Corporation, 1983-1990. Member, National Advisory Board and Chairman, Region One, Resolution Trust Corporation, 1990-1992. *Member:* The District of Columbia Bar; American Bar Association. ***LANGUAGES:*** Spanish.

NEAL E. KRUCOFF, born Washington, D.C., August 30, 1935; admitted to bar, 1962, District of Columbia. *Education:* University of Pennsylvania (A.B., 1957); Georgetown University (LL.B., 1962). *Member:* District of Columbia Bar (Member, Family Law Section, Probate Section and Real Estate Sections); American Bar Association (Member, Sections on Family Law and Real Estate Law); National Academy of Elder Law Attorneys. ***LANGUAGES:*** French. ***REPORTED CASES:*** Dunhill vs. D.C., 416 A2d 244 (1980); Joel vs. Joel, 559 A2d 759 (1989); Gore vs. Gore, 638 A2d 672 (1993); District of Columbia Housing Finance Agency vs. Charles L. Harper, 707 A2d 53 (1998); Lawrence J. Bernard, Jr. vs. Nancy C. Bernard, 730 A2d 663 (1999). ***PRACTICE AREAS:*** Real Estate; Family; Probate; Estate Planning; Litigation. ***Email:*** nekatlaw@cs.com

PETER HEIDENBERGER, born Munich, Germany, July 24, 1922; admitted to bar, 1952, Munich, Germany; 1957, Maryland; 1960, U.S. Supreme Court; 1962, District of Columbia. *Education:* Koenig Georg Gymnasium, Dresden (Abitur, 1939); University of Munich (doctor juris; Referendar and Assessor, OLG Munich); George Washington University (M.C.L., 1956). Recipient: Bundesverdienstkreuz 1. Klasse, 1976; Das grosse Bundesverdienstkreuz, 1985. Author: "Similarities and Differences in the Enforcement of Foreign Decrees and Judgments in the Federal Republic of Germany and the United States," Journal District of Columbia Bar Association, September 1966; "Forum Agreements in German - American Transnational Contracts," RIW, 1981; "The Jury Trial in U.S. Product Liability Litigation," RIW, 1982; "Deutsche Parteien vor amerikanischen Gerichten," RIW Heidelberg, 1988. Special Trial Attorney, U.S. Department of Justice, 1957-1963. Counsel to the Embassy of the Federal Republic of Germany, 1974—. Professorial Lecturer, Comparative Law, George Washington University, 1983. *Member:* The District of Columbia Bar; Bar Association of the District of Columbia; Maryland State and American Bar Associations. ***LANGUAGES:*** German.

C. RAY GOLD, born Greenville, North Carolina, July 30, 1966; admitted to bar, 1993, Pennsylvania (inactive); 1995, District of Columbia; 1996 , North Carolina. *Education:* University of North Carolina (B.A., 1988, Phi Beta Kappa, History); Georgetown University School of Foreign Service (M.S.F.S., 1992); Georgetown University (J.D., 1992). Co-Author: "The Legality of US Sanctions," Global Dialogue, Centre for World Dialogue, Summer 2000"; Little Secrets of the Auto Industry," (Moyer Bell, 1994). Member, Pennsylvania Bar Association (1993-1996). *Member:* The District of Columbia Bar (Member, Sections on: International Law; Intellectual Property); North Carolina State Bar; National Council on International Trade Development (Member, Export and E-Commerce Committees). ***PRACTICE AREAS:*** Export Controls; Trademarks. ***Email:*** raygold@bcr-dc.com

MARY-ELLEN NOONE, born Springfield, Massachusetts, April 25, 1969; admitted to bar, 1998, Maryland; 1999, District of Columbia. *Education:* The George Washington University (B.A., 1991); University of Baltimore (J.D., 1998). magna cum laude. ***PRACTICE AREAS:*** Litigation; Corporate. ***Email:*** menoone@bcr-dc.com

ALEXANDER CRAIG VINCENT, born Detroit, Michigan, May 22, 1965; admitted to bar, 1998, Virginia and U.S. Court of Appeals, Fourth Circuit; 2001, District of Columbia; U.S. District Court, Eastern and Western Districts of Virginia. *Education:* Oberlin College (B.A., 1987, History); The Catholic University of America, Columbus School of Law (J.D., 1998). ***PRACTICE AREAS:*** Complex Civil Litigation; White Collar Criminal Litigation; Corporate; Real Estate; Debtor and Creditor Collections; Export Control. ***Email:*** acv@ber-dc.com

---

BERMAN, AISENBERG & PLATT, PLLC

WASHINGTON, D.C.

(See Jacobson, Holman, PLLC)

Patent, Trademark, Unfair Competition, Copyright, Computer and Antitrust Law. International Patent and Trademark Practice. Practice before all Federal Courts, U.S. Patent and Trademark Office and other Administrative Agencies.

BERMAN, SOBIN & GROSS, LLP

WASHINGTON, D.C.

(See Gaithersburg, Maryland)

Workers Compensation, Occupational Injuries, Personal Injury, Wrongful Death, Dog Bites, Slip and Fall, Severe Burns, Auto Accidents and Injuries, Truck Accidents, Product Defects, Medical Malpractice, Birth Trauma, Oncology Law, Medical Negligence, Spinal Injury, Nursing Home Liability, Disability Insurance Litigation, Social Security Disability.

(This Listing Continued)

BERNABEI & KATZ, PLLC

Established in 1987

1773 T STREET, N.W.

WASHINGTON, D.C. 20009-7139

Telephone: 202-745-1942
Telecopier: 202-745-2627
URL: http://www.bernabeiandkatz.com
Email: berkatzlaw@aol.com
URL: http://www.lawyers.com/bernabei&katzlaw

Civil Rights Law, including sex, race, age and disability discrimination; Employment Law, Sexual Harassment Law; Whistleblower Litigation; General Civil Litigation.

FIRM PROFILE: The firm represents individual plaintiffs and groups in a nationwide civil rights and employment discrimination practice. The firm also acts as local counsel in the Washington, D.C. region.

LYNNE BERNABEI, born Highland Park, Illinois, April 11, 1950; admitted to bar, 1977, District of Columbia; U.S. District Court, District of Columbia; U.S. District Court, District of Maryland; U.S. Court of Appeals, Third Circuit; U.S. Court of Appeals, District of Columbia Circuit; U.S. Court of Appeals, Sixth Circuit; U.S. Court of Appeals for the Federal Circuit; U.S. Supreme Court. *Education:* Radcliffe College (B.A., magna cum laude, 1972); Harvard University (J.D., cum laude, 1977). Clerkship, Honorable William B. Bryant, U.S. District Court, 1977-1978. Author: "Bringing the Bar to Justice," A Comparative Study of Six Bar Associations, excerpted in Juris Doctor, Trial and Student Lawyer, August, 1977; "The High Citadel: The Influence of Harvard Law School," Houghton Mifflin, New York, NY, April, 1978; "The Case of the Co-Opted Critic: Ralph Nader and Harvard Law School," The Washington Monthly, October, 1978; "Whistleblowers Bill: For Employees Who Speak Out, a Shield," Legal Times, May, 1988; with Katz, D., "Practicing Public Interest Law In A Private Public Interest Law Firm," 96 W. Va. L. Rev. 293, Winter 1993-1994; "Are Employment Laws Doing Their Job?" A Plaintiffs Lawyer's View, The American Lawyer (September 1997) (reviewing Walter Olsen, The Excuse Factory); "Judge Needs Gag Order for Spouse," Legal Times, Feb. 16, 1998; "Blow the Whistle on Secrecy Deals: The Supreme Court Should Have Said That Buying an Employee's Silence Violates Public Policy," Legal Times, April 6, 1998; with Katz, D., "Harassment vs. The Reasonable Employer," Legal Times, July 13, 1998; "Judicial Legislation Run Amok: Court Adopts Strict Test For Harassment Liability," Legal Times, July 12, 1999; "Microsoft: Separate and Unequal Treatment of Its Employees," J. Empl. Discr. L. 205 (2000). Co-Author: "How Revisions to the Federal Discovery Rules will Increase Rather than Curb Discovery Abuse," J. Empl. Discr. L. 101 (2000) (with Kabat, A.); "Stock Options and Employment Discrimination Law," NELA 2000 Annual Convention Manual (with A. Kabat), June 2000; "Confidential Settlement Agreements and the Right to Testify," 1J. Empl. Discr. L. 81 (2000); "Reverse Litigation (SLAPP) Lawsuits and Employment Discrimination Law: Impermissible Retaliation Against Employees," 2 J. Empl. Discr. L. 269 (2000). Instructor, Georgetown Law Center, 1981-1982. Co-Designer: "Stopping Sexual Harrassment," a training CD-ROM, ABZ Incorporated, 2000. Member, Editorial Board, Journal of Employment Discrimination Law. *Member:* District of Columbia Bar; American Bar Association; The Association of Trial Lawyers of America; National Employment Lawyers Association. ***LANGUAGES:*** Italian, Spanish and French. ***PRACTICE AREAS:*** Employment Discrimination Law; Whistleblower Law; Civil Rights; Civil Liberties. ***Email:*** bernabei@bernabeiandkatz.com

DEBRA SUSAN KATZ, born Brooklyn, New York, October 26, 1958; admitted to bar, 1984, Wisconsin; 1986, New York; 1987, District of Columbia; U.S. District Court for the District of Columbia; U.S. District Court, District of Maryland; U.S. Court of Appeals for the District of Columbia Circuit; U.S. Supreme Court. *Education:* Union College (B.A., summa cum laude, 1980); University of Wisconsin-Madison (J.D., cum laude, 1984). Phi Beta Kappa. Member, Wisconsin Law Review, 1982-1983. Founder, Wisconsin Women's Law Journal, 1983-1984. Clerkship, Justice William Bablitch, Wisconsin Supreme Court, 1984-1985. Women's Law and Public Policy Fellowship, Georgetown University Law Center, 1985-1986. Author: "State v. Dean: A Compulsory Process Analysis of the Inadmissibility of Polygraph Evidence," Wisconsin Law Review 237, 1984; "Under Bail Reform Act 'Preventive Detention' Prevents Due Process," Legal Times, July 17, 1989; with Bernabei, L., "Practicing Public Interest Law In A Private Public Interest Law Firm," 96 W. Va. L. Rev. 293, Winter, 1993-1994; "Yes: There is a Duty to Air a Variety of Viewpoints," ABA Journal (June 1996); "One Round Too Many," Legal Times, Jan. 26, 1998; "Judge Needs Gag Order for Spouse," Legal Times, Feb. 16, 1998; with Bernabei, L., "Harassment vs. The Reasonable Employer," Legal Times (July 13, 1998); with Eisenberg, R., "Hiring Minds Wants to Know: Increasingly Popular Psychological Testing of Job Applicants May Violate ADA," Legal Times (Feb-

(This Listing Continued)

BERNABEI & KATZ, PLLC, Washington—Continued

ruary 8, 1999); with Kabat, A., "Electronic Discovery in Employment Discrimination Cases," TRIAL (December, 1999); "New Limits on Punitive Damages Imposed," Legal Times, July 12, 1999. Co-Designer: "Stopping Sexual Harrassment," a training CD-ROM, ABZ Incorporated, 2000. *Member:* District of Columbia Bar; New York State and American Bar Associations; National Employment Lawyers Association. ***PRACTICE AREAS:*** Employment Discrimination; Whistleblower Law; Civil Rights; Civil Liberties. ***Email:*** katz@bernabeiandkatz.com

---

LISA J. BANKS, born Boston, Massachusetts, March 28, 1968; admitted to bar, 1995, Colorado; 2001, District of Columbia. *Education:* Trinity College (B.A., 1990); University of Denver (J.D., 1995). Member, Editor Board, Denver University Law Review, 1994-1995. Law Clerk to: The Honorable Daniel M. Taubman, Colorado Court of Appeals, 1995-1996; The Honorable Gregory K. Scott, Colorado Supreme Court, 1996-1997. Author: "Bray v. Alexandria Women's Health Clinic: The Supreme Court's License for Domestic Terrorism", Denver U. L. Rev. (Spring, 1994). Appellate Attorney, Office of General Counsel of the U.S. Equal Employment Opportunity Commission, 1997-2000. *Member:* Colorado and American Bar Associations; The District of Columbia Bar. ***PRACTICE AREAS:*** Employment Discrimination; Civil Rights; Civil Liberties. ***Email:*** banks@bernabeiandkatz.com

ARI M. WILKENFELD, born Washington D.C., July 31, 1970; admitted to bar, 1998, Maryland and U.S. District Court, District of Maryland; 1999, District of Columbia and U.S. District Court, District of Columbia. *Education:* Syracuse University (B.A., 1993); University of Pennsylvania (J.D., 1997). *Member:* Maryland State and American Bar Associations; The District of Columbia Bar. ***PRACTICE AREAS:*** Employment Discrimination; Whistleblower Litigation; Civil Rights; Civil Liberties. ***Email:*** wilkenfeld@bernabeiandkatz.com

ALAN R. KABAT, born Spokane, Washington; admitted to bar, 1998, Maryland; 1999, District of Columbia, U.S. District Court, District of Maryland and U.S. District Court, District of Columbia; 2000, U.S. Court of Appeals for the District of Columbia Circuit. *Education:* University of Washington (B.S., 1983); Harvard University (Ph.D., 1990); Georgetown University (J.D., 1998). Author: J. Copyright Society USA, Spring 1998; Trial, December 1998; American Criminal Law Review, Winter 1998; Journal of Employment Discrimination Law, Winter, 2000. *Member:* The District of Columbia Bar; American Bar Association; American Association for the Advancement of Science. ***PRACTICE AREAS:*** Civil Litigation; Civil Rights; Civil Liberties; Employment Discrimination Law.

GENA E. WILTSEK, born New York, NY, March 19, 1973; admitted to bar, 2001, New York (Not admitted in District of Columbia). *Education:* Yale University (B.A., 1995); University of Michigan (J.D., 1999). *Member:* New York State Bar Association. ***PRACTICE AREAS:*** Employment Discrimination; Civil Rights; Civil Liberties; Whistleblower Law.

OF COUNSEL

DAVID J. MARSHALL, born Atlanta, Georgia, April 20, 1954; admitted to bar, 1981, Georgia; 2000, District of Columbia. *Education:* Emory University (B.A., summa cum laude, 1977); Harvard Law School (J.D., cum laude, 1980). ***PRACTICE AREAS:*** Civil Rights; Class Actions; Whistleblower Law; Employment Discrimination; Civil Liberties.

LAWRENCE BERNSTEIN

1818 N STREET, N.W., SUITE 700
WASHINGTON, D.C. 20036
Telephone: 202-296-1800; 202-331-7050
Fax: 202-331-9306
Email: LAWBERNS@erols.com
URL: http://www.lawyers.com/lawrencebernsteinlaw

Practice before Federal and Local Courts and Administrative Agencies. Telecommunication Law, Transactional and Commercial Law, Intellectual Property. Emerging Technology Law, e-Commerce Law, Internet Law.

LAWRENCE BERNSTEIN, born Detroit, Michigan, August 26, 1941; admitted to bar, 1973, Michigan; 1974, U.S. Court of Appeals for the District of Columbia Circuit; 1975, District of Columbia; 1984, U.S. Supreme Court. *Education:* Wayne State University (A.B., 1963; A.M., 1968; J.D., cum laude, 1973). Senior Trial Attorney, Federal Communications Commission, 1974-1983. Attorney-in-Charge, Special Investigations of Payola-Plugola and the PTL Television Network, 1977-1982. Author: "What You May Not Know About FCC Fines...And the Government Will Never Tell You," Radio & Records, July 18, 1997; "The Last Word (Hopefully) on FCC Forfeitures," Radio & Records,

(This Listing Continued)

Sept. 5, 1997. *Member:* District of Columbia Bar; American Bar Association; Federal Communications Bar Association; National Association of Broadcasters.

THE BERNSTEIN LAW FIRM, PLLC

1730 K STREET, N.W.
WASHINGTON, D.C. 20006
Telephone: 202-452-8010
Telecopier: 202-296-2065

New York, N.Y. Office: 30 Rockefeller Plaza. Telephone: 212-957-7634.

FIRM PROFILE: The Bernstein Law Firm is the successor to the Law Offices of George K. Bernstein, established in 1974. The practice of members of the firm includes such areas of insurance corporate, regulatory and finance law as mergers and acquisitions, licensing, insolvency, coverage, antitrust, taxation, reinsurance and international transactions. The firm represents, advises and provides expert witness testimony to investors, regulators, insurers and law firms regarding insurance and mortgage finance matters in federal and state courts and before regulatory and legislative bodies. The firm also specializes in corporate and financial transactions and acts as arbitrators and mediators in several areas, including employment.

GEORGE K. BERNSTEIN, born New York, N.Y., September 17, 1933; admitted to bar, 1957, New York; 1958, U.S. Court of Appeals, Second Circuit; 1972, U.S. Supreme Court; 1973, District of Columbia; 1979, U.S. District Court, District of Columbia Circuit. *Education:* Cornell University (B.A., 1955; LL.B., 1957). Phi Delta Phi. Moot Court Winner, 1955. Chancellor, Moot Court Board, 1956-1957. Recipient: B'nai B'rith Anti-Defamation League Torch of Liberty Award, 1974; U.S. Department of Housing and Urban Development Distinguished Service Award, 1974. Deputy Assistant Attorney General, 1957-1959 and Assistant Attorney General, 1959-1961, New York State. Deputy Superintendent and General Counsel, 1964-1967 and First Deputy Superintendent of Insurance, 1967-1969 New York State Insurance Department. Federal Insurance Administrator, Federal Insurance Administration, 1969-1974 and Interstate Land Sales Administrator, Office of Interstate Land Sales Registration, 1972-1974, U.S. Department of Housing and Urban Development. U.S. Delegate to the NATO Conference on Flood Insurance, 1970. Insurance Advisor to the Cost of Living Council and the Price Commission, 1971-1974. U.S. Government Consultant to the Japanese Government on Flood and Natural Disaster Insurance, 1972. Special Counsel to New York State Select Committee on Insurance, 1974-1976. Consultant to: Federal Retirement Thrift Investment Board, 1987; Overseas Private Investment Corporation, 1975-1977, 1983-1984; President's Commission for the Study of Ethical Problems in Medicine and Biomedical and Behavioral Research, 1979-1981; Inter-American Development Bank, 1993. Member: President's Interdepartmental Committee on All-Risk and Disaster Insurance, 1970-1971; President's Interdepartmental Committee on Medical Malpractice, 1971-1973; Committee on Medical Malpractice, National Academy of Sciences, 1972-1973; Advisory Committee to the New York State Legislature on Recodification of the Insurance Law, 1972-1974; President's Inter-Departmental Study on Workers' Compensation, 1973-1974; National Insurance Development Program Advisory Board, 1976-1977. Chairman, Expert Review Committee, National Earthquake Hazards Reduction Program, 1986-1988. Chairman, Policy Workshop, National Earthquake Hazard Reduction Program, 1990. Member, Advisory Panel, Federal Emergency Management Agency Loss Reduction-Earthquake Insurance Project, 1988-1990. Member, 1990-1991, Chairman, 1991-1993, Advisory Committee to the National Earthquake Hazards Reduction Program. Chairman, Ad Hoc Panel on a National Pre-Disaster Mitigation Plan, 1998. Chairman, America Burning Recommissioned, 1999—. Court appointed Agent to the Vermont Insurance Commissioner as Receiver and Liquidator of Ambassador Insurance Company, 1983—. Special Deputy of Insurance of the Vermont Department of Banking, Insurance and Securities in the Rehabilitation of Springfield Life Insurance Company, 1991-1993. Special Deputy of Insurance of the Vermont Department of Banking, Insurance, Securities and Health Care Administration in the liquidation of Beverage Retailers Insurance Company, Risk Retention Group, 1993—. Special Deputy of Insurance of the Vermont Department of Banking, Insurance, Securities & Health Care Administration in the Liquidation of NonProfits Mutual Risk Retention Group, 1999—. Special Deputy of Insurance of the Vermont Department of Banking, Insurance, Securities & Health Care Administration in the Rehabilitation of Offshore Marine Indemnity Company, 2001—. Presenter, People's Bank of China Conference on Insurance Regulation in Changing Markets, 1996. Associate Member, Society of Financial Examiners. Principal Member, Society of Insurance Receivers. Member, International Association of Insurance Receivers. Member, Insolvency International. Principal, Council for Excellence in Government, 1991-1995. *Member:* District of Columbia Bar; Association of the Bar of the City of New York (Member, 1965-1968, 1972-1975, 1980-1983, 1987-1990 and Chairman, 1975-1978 and 1990-1993, Committee on Insurance Law; Chairman, Subcommittee on Insurer Solvency, Com-

(This Listing Continued)

mittee on Insurance Law, 1988-1990; Member, Ad Hoc Committee on Professional Liability Insurance, 1990-1993); American Bar Association (Member: Tort and Insurance Practice Section, 1978—; Section on International Law, 1980—). ***PRACTICE AREAS:*** Insurance Regulation; Insurance Rehabilitation and Liquidation; Insurance Mergers and Acquisitions; Reinsurance; International Insurance; Property and Casualty Insurance Coverage. ***Email:*** gkblaw@aol.com

CARYL S. BERNSTEIN, born New York, N.Y., December 22, 1933; admitted to bar, 1968, District of Columbia and U.S. Court of Appeals, District of Columbia Circuit; 1971, U.S. Supreme Court; 1998, New York. *Education:* Cornell University (B.A., with honors in Government, 1955); Georgetown University (J.D., 1967). Phi Beta Kappa; Phi Kappa Phi. Member, Board of Editors, Georgetown Law Journal, 1966-1967. Executive Vice President, General Counsel and Secretary, Fannie Mae (Federal National Mortgage Association), 1981-1993. Vice President for Insurance, 1977-1981 and Assistant General Counsel for Insurance, 1974-1977, Overseas Private Investment Corporation. Co-Author: Chapter in *The Handbook of Mortgage Banking, A Guide to the Secondary Mortgage Market,* (with J. Carpenter) (ed. Kinney and Garrigan) 1985; "Assessing the Alternative Mortgage Instruments," (with J. Mansfield), *The National Law Journal* August 9, 1982. Adjunct Professor, Georgetown University Law Center. Public Member, Administrative Conference of the United States, 1992-1995. Honors: Catalyst Award for Corporate Leadership, 1984; Overseas Private Investment Corporation Distinguished Honor Award, 1981; Special Achievement Award, 1975. ADR: Member, Panel of Arbitrators: American Arbitration Association; National Association of Securities Dealers; American Stock Exchange; D.C. Bar Attorney/Client Arbitration Board. Mediator: U.S. District Court for the District of Columbia; NASD Dispute Resolution; Equal Employment Opportunities Commission, Washington Field Office. *Member:* District of Columbia Bar (Member, Board of Governors, Pro Bono Committee; Co-Chair, Landlord-Tenant Court Task Force); American Bar Association (Member, Sections on: Administrative Law; Vice Chair, Administrative Law Financial Services Committee, 1992-1996); Alternative Dispute Resolution; American Law Institute; American Arbitration Association. ***PRACTICE AREAS:*** Corporate; International; Mortgage Finance; Insurance; Arbitration; Mediation. ***Email:*** caryllaw@aol.com

ROBERT B. SHAPIRO, born New York, N.Y., September 12, 1949; admitted to bar, 1974, New York; 1978, District of Columbia. *Education:* The Ohio State University (B.S., 1970); Wharton School of Finance, University of Pennsylvania (M.B.A., 1974); Syracuse University (J.D., 1973); Georgetown University (LL.M. in Taxation, 1978). Lecturer, Insurance Products under the Securities Laws, Practising Law Institute, 1984. Attorney-Advisor, Division of Corporate Finance and Division of Investment Management, Securities and Exchange Commission, 1975-1979. *Member:* The District of Columbia Bar; American Bar Association (Member, Section on Corporation, Banking and Business Law). ***PRACTICE AREAS:*** Insurance Regulation; Financial Guaranty Insurance; Reinsurance; International Insurance; Fidelity and Surety; Insurance Mergers and Acquisitions; Insurance Products; Property and Casualty Insurance Coverage Issues; Insurance Rehabilitation and Liquidation; Insurance Brokers, Agents and Intermediaries. ***Email:*** BSHAPLAW@aol.com

BERNSTEIN & LIPSETT

Established in 1988

SUITE 602, 1920 L STREET, N.W.
WASHINGTON, D.C. 20036
Telephone: 202-296-1798
Fax: 202-296-7220
URL: http://www.lawyers.com/bernstein&lipsett

Wage and Labor Standards, Labor Relations, ERISA, Legislative, Administrative, Civil Rights and Prepaid Legal Services.

MEMBERS OF FIRM

JULES BERNSTEIN, born Brooklyn, New York, May 12, 1935; admitted to bar, 1962, District of Columbia; 1969, U.S. Supreme Court. *Education:* Brandeis University (B.A., 1957); University of Chicago (J.D., 1960); New York University (LL.M. in Labor Law, 1961). Author: "Legal Services, the Bar and the Unions," 58 American Bar Association Journal 472, 1972; "Group Legal Services as a Fringe Benefit: Lawyers for Forgotten Clients Through Collective Bargaining," 59 Virginia Law Review 410, 1973; "Union Busting: From Benign Neglect to Malignant Growth," University of California at Davis Law Review 14:1-78, Summer, 1980. Member, AFL-CIO Lawyers Coordinating Committee, 1983—. *Member:* District of Columbia Bar; American Bar Association (Member, Labor and Employment Law Section); National Resource Center for Consumers of Legal Services (Treasurer, 1975—); National Legal Aid and Defender Association (Member, Board of Directors and Executive Committee, 1975-1979). ***PRACTICE AREAS:*** Labor Law.

LINDA LIPSETT, born Buffalo, New York, August 7, 1951; admitted to bar, 1977, California; 1982, U.S. Court of Appeals, Ninth Circuit; 1983, U.S. Court of Appeals, District of Columbia Circuit; 1984, District of Columbia. *Education:* University of California at Berkeley (B.A., 1972); George Washington University (J.D., 1976). Member, AFL-CIO Lawyers Coordinating Committee, 1983—. *Member:* State Bar of California; District of Columbia Bar. ***PRACTICE AREAS:*** Labor Law.

(This Listing Continued)

BETTS & HOLT

WEST TOWER 10TH FLOOR
1333 H STREET N.W.
WASHINGTON, D.C. 20005-4707
Telephone: 202-530-3380
Fax: 202-530-3389

Practice before federal and state energy regulatory agencies, commissions, and courts representing the interests of municipal, cooperative, university and industrial consumers of electricity and industrial consumers and producers of natural gas.

KIRK HOWARD BETTS, born Jersey City, New Jersey, March 5, 1951; admitted to bar, 1980, District of Columbia, U.S. Court of Appeals, District of Columbia Circuit and 5th Circuit; 1981, U.S. Court of Appeals, 11th Circuit; 1984, U.S. Supreme Court; 1986, Maryland; 1989, U.S. Court of Appeals, 6th Circuit; 1996, U.S. District Court, District of Maryland. *Education:* George Washington University (B.A., 1973); Washington College of Law of The American University (J.D., 1979). Phi Alpha Delta. Member, American University Law Review, 1978-1979. Chairman, Moot Court, 1978-1979. *Member:* District of Columbia Bar; Maryland State and American (Member, Sections on: Law Practice Management; Public Utility Law; Real Estate, Probate and Trust Law) Bar Associations; Energy Bar Association. ***PRACTICE AREAS:*** Energy Contracts; Wholesale Electric Contracts; Hydroelectricity; Energy Regulatory Law; Administrative Law. ***Email:*** kbetts@bettsandholt.com

JAMES H. HOLT, born Galveston County, Texas, July 7, 1953; admitted to bar, 1979, District of Columbia and U.S. Court of Appeals, District of Columbia Circuit; 1980, U.S. District Court, District of Columbia. *Education:* Rice University (B.A., magna cum laude, 1975); University of Michigan (J.D., cum laude, 1978). Phi Beta Kappa. Co-Author: "Measuring the Costs of Regulation," Book Review, 59 Texas Law Review 623; "Marketing Synthetic Fuels, The Roles of Federal Regulation and the Synthetic Fuels Corporation," 2 Energy Law Journal. ***PRACTICE AREAS:*** Administrative Law; Natural Gas; Litigation. ***Email:*** jhh@bettsandholt.com

OF COUNSEL

JILL M. BARKER, born Memphis, Tennessee, May 19, 1959; admitted to bar, 1983, Florida; 1985, District of Columbia and U.S. Court of Appeals for the District of Columbia Circuit. *Education:* Florida State University (B.S., 1980); Washington College of Law of American University (J.D., 1983). Trial Attorney, U.S. Department of Energy, 1983-1985. *Member:* Energy Bar Association. ***PRACTICE AREAS:*** Energy Regulation; Energy Contracts; Hydroelectricity; Administrative Law; Public Utility. ***Email:*** jmb@bettsandholt.com

DAVID E. CRAWFORD, born Enid, Oklahoma, March 5, 1955; admitted to bar, 1983, District of Columbia and Oklahoma; 1989, Minnesota. *Education:* Oklahoma State University (B.A., with honors, 1977); George Washington University (M.A., 1982); National Law Center, George Washington University (J.D., 1982). Phi Kappa Phi; Blue Key. Co-Author: "Public/Private Partnerships for DHC (District Heating and Cooling) System Development: Models for Cooperation in an Era of Opportunity", Papers of the Eighty-Fourth Annual Meeting of the International District Heating and Cooling Association; "Team Formation," Electric Restructuring and Utilities Deregulation: A Facility Manager's Guide. *Member:* The District of Columbia Bar; Minnesota State, Oklahoma and American (Member, Sections on Public Utility and Environment, Energy and Natural Resources Law) Bar Associations. ***PRACTICE AREAS:*** Energy Contracts; Utilities. ***Email:*** dcrawford@bettsandholt.com

BEVERIDGE & DIAMOND, P.C.

Established in 1974

1350 I STREET, N.W., SUITE 700
WASHINGTON, D.C. 20005-3311
Telephone: 202-789-6000
Telecopier: 202-789-6190
URL: http://www.beveridgediamond.com

New York, N.Y. Office: 15th Floor, 477 Madison Avenue, 10022-5802. Telephone: 212-702-5400. Telecopier: 212-702-5450.
San Francisco, California Office: Suite 1800, 456 Montgomery Street, 94104-1251. Telephone: 415-262-4000. Telecopier: 415-262-4040.
Saddle Brook, New Jersey Office: Beveridge & Diamond, Park 80 West, Plaza II Suite 200, 07663-5836. Telephone: 201-585-8162. Telecopier: 201-368-1944.

(This Listing Continued)

BEVERIDGE & DIAMOND, P.C., Washington—Continued

Baltimore, Maryland Office: Suite 2210, 201 North Charles Street, 21201-4150. Telephone: 410-230-3850. Telecopier: 410-230-3868.

General Practice before Federal and State Courts, Departments and Agencies in the areas of Environmental Law, (including Clean Air Act, Clean Water Act, RCRA, solid waste, Superfund, toxic chemicals, pesticide regulation, wetlands and biotechnology), Litigation, Product Regulation, Land Use, International Environmental Law, Natural Resources, Corporate and Securities and Government Contracts.

FIRM PROFILE: Beveridge & Diamond, P.C. was founded in 1974 and now has over 70 lawyers in five offices. The firm successfully resolves complex disputes through litigation (including trials), innovative alternative dispute methods and sophisticated counseling in the following areas: Domestic and International Environmental Issues, Land Use and Natural Resources, Toxic Torts, Product Liability, Insurance Coverage, Product Introduction, Development and Defense, Intellectual Property, White Collar/Internal Investigations, Health Care and Securities Fraud and Business/Commercial Matters.

KARL S. BOURDEAU, born Greenfield, Massachusetts, June 1, 1953; admitted to bar, 1978, District of Columbia. *Education:* Muhlenberg College (B.S., summa cum laude, 1975); Harvard University (J.D., 1978). Phi Beta Kappa. Federal Developments Editor, Harvard Environmental Law Review, 1977-1978. Author: "Energy Conservation in the 94th Congress: A Solution to the Problem or Problems with the Solution?" *1 Harv. Envtl. L.Rev.* 225, 1977. Co-Author: "Investing in the USA: Environmental Compliance and Liability," Law Business Research, *The American Legal Yearbook*, 1998. Author: "Corrective Action Requirements Under the Resource Conservation and Recovery Act," *Environmental Risk Management-A Desk Reference*, 1991, RTM Communications, Inc. Co-Author: "The Extraterritorial Reach of United States Environmental Laws," *National Law Journal*, September, 1993. ***PRACTICE AREAS:*** Environmental Law; Environmental Litigation; International Environmental Law. ***Email:*** kbourdeau@bdlaw.com

ROBERT BRAGER, born New York, New York, September 16, 1954; admitted to bar, 1980, New York and District of Columbia; 1985, Maryland. *Education:* Columbia University (B.A., magna cum laude, 1975; J.D., 1979); London School of Economics (M.Sc., 1976). Phi Beta Kappa. Law Clerk to Honorable Aubrey E. Robinson, Jr., U.S. District Court, District of Columbia, 1979-1981. (Also at Baltimore, MD Office). ***PRACTICE AREAS:*** Litigation; Environmental Law; Media Law. ***Email:*** rbrager@bdlaw.com

DEAN H. CANNON, born Jasper, Alabama, March 28, 1957; admitted to bar, 1981, District of Columbia. *Education:* University of Alabama (B.S., summa cum laude, 1978); Georgetown University (J.D., cum laude, 1981). ***PRACTICE AREAS:*** Environmental Law; Corporate Law. ***Email:*** dcannon@bdlaw.com

RICHARD S. DAVIS, born Washington, D.C., October 20, 1953; admitted to bar, 1980, Maryland; 1982, District of Columbia. *Education:* Syracuse University (A.B., 1975); Catholic University of America (J.D., 1980). Member, *Catholic University Law Review*, 1978-1980. Author: "Chapter 18-Water Pollution Control," *Environmental Law Practice Guide*, Matthew Bender, 1992; "Chapter 31—Storm Water Regulation of Construction Activities," ABA, 1999. Law Clerk to Honorable H. Emory Widener, Jr., U.S. Court of Appeals, Fourth Circuit, 1980-1981. Professorial Lecturer in Law, Columbus School of Law, Catholic University of America, 1982. ***PRACTICE AREAS:*** Environmental Law; Clean Water Act; Water Quality; Litigation. ***Email:*** rdavis@bdlaw.com

HENRY L. DIAMOND, born Chattanooga, Tennessee, May 25, 1932; admitted to bar, 1959, District of Columbia; 1960, Tennessee; 1962, U.S. Supreme Court; 1972, New York. *Education:* Vanderbilt University (B.A., 1954); Georgetown University (LL.B., 1959). Co-Author: *Land Use in America*, Island Press, 1996. Assistant to U.S. Attorney General, 1962. Commissioner, New York State Department of Environmental Conservation, 1970-1973. Chairman: Board of Directors, New York State Environmental Facilities Corporation, 1970-1973; Member, 1972-1976 and Chairman, 1973-1976, President's Advisory Committee on Environmental Quality; Executive Director, Commission on Critical Choices for Americans, 1974-1975. ***PRACTICE AREAS:*** Environmental Law. ***Email:*** hdiamond@bdlaw.com

DAVID M. FRIEDLAND, born Denver, Colorado, April 13, 1957; admitted to bar, 1983, Colorado; 1988, District of Columbia and U.S. Supreme Court. *Education:* Georgetown University (B.S.F.S., magna cum laude, 1979; J.D., cum laude, 1983). Co-Author: "Transportation Planning and Air Pollution: The Search for Common Ground," The Metropolitan Corporate Counsel ("Issues and Overview" section), April 2001; "D.C. Court Strikes EPA Ozone Rules," The National Law Journal, August 2, 1999; "Harmon Industries, Inc. v. Browner: Does it Foreshadow the Demise of the EPA's Power to 'Overfile' State Enforcement Cases?," Environmental Law and Practice, Winter 1999; "NMA, CMA and "'Federal Enforceability' Under the Clean Air Act," Environmental Law and Practice, January/February 1996; "A Critical Review of the Environmental Protection Agency's Standards for Best Available Control Technology Under the Clean Air Act," Environmental Law Reporter, February 1990. Instructor, Legal Writing, 1985-1986, Director of Legal Writing Program and Adjunct Professor, 1986-1987, Vermont Law School. ***PRACTICE AREAS:*** Environmental Law; Clean Air Act; Litigation. ***Email:*** dfriedland@bdlaw.com

AARON H. GOLDBERG, born Houston, Texas, September 30, 1957; admitted to bar, 1985, District of Columbia. *Education:* Yale University (B.S., magna cum laude, 1979); California Institute of Technology (M.S., 1982); Stanford University (J.D., 1985). Phi Beta Kappa. Author: "The Federal Hazardous Waste Program: A House of Cards?," *Environment Reporter* (Analysis and Perspective), Bureau of National Affairs, June 16, 1995. ***PRACTICE AREAS:*** Environmental Law; Administrative Law; Hazardous Waste; Resource Conservation and Recovery Act (RCRA). ***Email:*** agoldberg@bdlaw.com

JOHN S. GUTTMANN, JR., born Paterson, New Jersey, July 24, 1953; admitted to bar, 1978, District of Columbia; 1984, New York and U.S. Supreme Court. *Education:* University of Pennsylvania (B.A., cum laude, 1975); Cornell University (J.D., 1978). Note and Comment Editor, *Cornell Law Review*, 1977-1978. Law Clerk to Honorable Aubrey E. Robinson, Jr., U.S. District Court, District of Columbia, 1978-1980. (Also at New York, NY Office). ***PRACTICE AREAS:*** Complex Litigation; Product Liability; Toxic Tort Defense; Environmental Law. ***Email:*** jguttmann@bdlaw.com

PAUL E. HAGEN, born Southampton, New York, April 14, 1964; admitted to bar, 1990, Maryland; 1992, District of Columbia. *Education:* Providence College (B.A., 1986); American University (J.D., 1990). Articles Editor, *The American University Journal of International Law and Policy*, 1989-1990. Author: "The Green Diplomacy Gap," *The Environmental Forum*, August 2000. Co-Author: "The Cartagena Protocol on Biosafety: New Rules for International Trade in Living Modified Organisms," *Georgetown International Environmental Law Review*, 2000. Adjunct Professor of Law, American University, 1992—. *Member:* American Bar Association (Chair: International Environmental Law Committee, International Law and Practice Section, 1994-1999; Liaison to the Standing Committee on Environmental Law); IUCN Environmental Law Commission. ***PRACTICE AREAS:*** International Environmental Law; Environmental Law. ***Email:*** phagen@bdlaw.com

JOHN N. HANSON, born Malden, Massachusetts, July 24, 1945; admitted to bar, 1970, Wisconsin; 1977, U.S. Supreme Court; 1980, District of Columbia. *Education:* George Washington University (A.B., 1967; J.D., cum laude, 1970). Professorial Lecturer in Law, Columbus School of Law, Catholic University of America, 1979-1983. Trial Attorney, 1972-1977 and Assistant Chief, Enforcement, Civil Division, 1978-1979, U.S. Department of Justice. ***PRACTICE AREAS:*** Litigation; Environmental and Administrative Law. ***Email:*** jhanson@bdlaw.com

STEVEN A. HERMAN, born Bronx, New York, September 26, 1944; admitted to bar, 1970, Arkansas; 1973, New York (Not admitted in District of Columbia). *Education:* Rutgers University, New Brunswick (B.A., 1966); Rutgers University, Newark (J.D., 1969). Assistant Administrator, Enforcement and Compliance Assurance, U.S. Environmental Protection Agency, 1993-2001. *Member:* American Bar Association. ***PRACTICE AREAS:*** Environmental; Public Land Law. ***Email:*** sherman@bdlaw.com

STEVEN M. JAWETZ, born San Francisco, California, November 8, 1956; admitted to bar, 1982, California; 1983, District of Columbia. *Education:* Stanford University (B.A., with distinction, 1978); University of California at Berkeley (M.P.P., 1982); Boalt Hall School of Law, University of California (J.D., 1982). Phi Beta Kappa. Law Clerk to Honorable John C. Mowbray, Nevada Supreme Court, 1982-1983. Attorney, Land and Natural Resources Division, U.S. Department of Justice, 1984-1987. ***PRACTICE AREAS:*** Superfund; Natural Resource Damages; Hazardous Waste. ***Email:*** sjawetz@bdlaw.com

DAVID S. KRAKOFF, born Columbus, Ohio, March 16, 1949; admitted to bar, 1976, District of Columbia; 1979, U.S. Supreme Court. *Education:* Dartmouth College (A.B., 1971); Antioch School of Law (J.D., 1975). Co-Author: "Advising Clients in the Post-Weitzenhoff Era," *Criminal Justice*, Fall 1995; "Determining Intent in Medicare Fraud—The Accidental Kickback," *Legal Times*, September 15, 1997; "The Hidden Cost to Corporate Settlements of Environmental Prosecutions—Is it Worth the Price?" *The Journal of American Corporate Counsel Association*, November/December, 1997; "Environmental Reporting: New Criminal Exposure," *The Metropolitan Corporate Counsel*, March 1998; "Environmental Crimes: Recent Trends," *1999 Wiley Environmental Law Update*, December 18, 1998; "Environmental Crimes Case—From Pretrial Proceedings to Sentencing Guidelines," American Bar Association, Criminal Justice Section, Section of Environmental, Energy and Resources, July 1999. Assistant U.S. Attorney, U.S. Attorney's Office for the District of Columbia, 1976-1986. Chief, Chronic Offender Unit, 1983-1985. *Member:* American Bar Association (Litigation Section, Complex Crimes Committee; Criminal Justice Section, White Collar Crime Committee; Chairman, Environmental Crimes Subcommittee, 1997-1999); National Association of Criminal Defense Lawyers; Edward Bennett Williams American Inn of Court. ***PRACTICE AREAS:*** White Collar Criminal Defense; Civil Litigation. ***Email:*** dkrakoff@bdlaw.com

(This Listing Continued)

CYNTHIA A. LEWIS, born Columbia, Missouri, October 11, 1953; admitted to bar, 1978, District of Columbia; 1983, U.S. Supreme Court. *Education:* College of William and Mary (B.A., with high honors, 1975); Harvard University (J.D., cum laude, 1978). Phi Beta Kappa. Editor, Harvard Civil Rights-Civil Liberties Law Review, 1977-1978. Author: "Obtaining Compensation for Use of Pesticide Data," 4 *Envtl. L. Forum* 17, 1985; "The Regulation of Pesticides Under the Federal Insecticide, Fungicide and Rodenticide Act," *Law of Environmental Protection*, 1987. Co-Author: "EPA's Pesticides in Groundwater Strategy: Will It Work?" 4 *Nat. Resources & Envir.* 16, 1989; "EPA Enforcement of TSCA Designed to Send a Message to Industry," 4 *Corporate Legal Times*, No. 26 (October, 1994); *Federal Chemical Regulation:* TSCA, EPCRA and the Pollution Prevention Act, 1997. ***PRACTICE AREAS:*** Environmental Law; Advertising and Labeling; Pesticide Regulation; International Environmental Law; Environmental Administrative Law. ***Email:*** clewis@bdlaw.com

LORELIE S. MASTERS, born Fremont, Michigan, December 5, 1954; admitted to bar, 1981, District of Columbia. *Education:* Georgetown University (A.B., cum laude, 1977); Notre Dame Law School (J.D., 1981). Pi Sigma Alpha. White Scholar, Thomas J. and Alberta White Center for Law and Public Policy. Member, Industry Advisory Board, Lt. Joseph P. Kennedy Institute. Editor-in-Chief, Journal of Legislation, 1980-1981. Co-Author: Treatise, *Insurance Coverage Litigation,* Aspen Law & Business. Author: "Covering Cyberspace and Computer Liabilities," 13 John Liner Review, No. 4, Winter 2000; "Punitive Damages: Covered or Not?" *The Business Lawyer*, Vol. 55, No. 1, November 1999; "ACE and X.L.: A New 'Batch' of Coverage Issues," *Coverage* Vol. 9, No. 1, Jan./Feb., 1999. *Member:* American Bar Association (Member, Sections on: Litigation; Science and Technology; Chair, Insurance Coverage Litigation Committee, Section of Litigation; Co-Chair, Insurance Coverage Litigation Committee). ***PRACTICE AREAS:*** Litigation; Insurance Litigation; High-Technology; Health Insurance. ***Email:*** lmasters@bdlaw.com

DONALD J. PATTERSON, JR., born Newark, New Jersey, August 3, 1957; admitted to bar, 1982, District of Columbia. *Education:* College of William and Mary (B.A., summa cum laude, 1979); University of Michigan (J.D., 1982). Phi Beta Kappa. ***PRACTICE AREAS:*** Environmental Law; Litigation. ***Email:*** dpatterson@bdlaw.com

CHRISTOPHER F. REGAN, born Buffalo, New York, November 10, 1965; admitted to bar, 1991, New York; 1992, District of Columbia. *Education:* State University of New York College at Brockport (B.S., magna cum laude, 1987); University of Michigan (J.D., 1990). Co-Author: "The Hidden Cost to Corporate Settlements of Environmental Prosecutions—Is it Worth the Price?" *The Journal of American Corporate Counsel Association*, November/December 1997. ***PRACTICE AREAS:*** White Collar Criminal Defense; Environmental Law. ***Email:*** cregan@bdlaw.com

THOMAS RICHICHI, born Des Moines, Iowa, April 20, 1953; admitted to bar, 1978, District of Columbia; 1983, U.S. Supreme Court. *Education:* University of Missouri (B.A., 1975); Georgetown University (J.D., 1978). Phi Beta Kappa. Law Clerk to Honorable John J. Sirica, U.S. District Court, District of Columbia. ***PRACTICE AREAS:*** Litigation; Environmental Law; Aviation Law; International Environmental Law. ***Email:*** trichichi@bdlaw.com

HAROLD L. SEGALL, born Bryn Mawr, Pennsylvania, January 10, 1958; admitted to bar, 1985, Pennsylvania and District of Columbia; 1992, U.S. Supreme Court. *Education:* Yale University (B.A., 1979); Hebrew University of Jerusalem, Israel (Middle East Studies, Rotary International Graduate Fellowship, 1980-1981); University of Chicago (J.D., 1984). Author: "Strategizing Cleanup Cases," *Legal Times*, June 1997; "Enhancing the Effectiveness of the Relationship Between In-House and Outside Counsel in Litigation," *The Metropolitan Corporate Counsel*, May 1999; "A Risk-Based Cleanup Regime," *Legal Times*, September 1999. Mediator for Superior Court for the District of Columbia. Arbitrator, Panel of Arbitrators, American Arbitration Association. ***PRACTICE AREAS:*** Environmental Litigation; Commercial Litigation; Environmental Real Estate; Alternative Dispute Resolution. ***Email:*** hsegall@bdlaw.com

JAMES B. SLAUGHTER, born Richmond, Virginia, September 19, 1960; admitted to bar, 1987, Virginia; 1989, District of Columbia. *Education:* Yale University (B.A., 1982); Columbia University (J.D., 1987). Staff Member, 1985-1986 and Articles Editor, 1986-1987, Columbia Journal of Law and Social Problems. Law Clerk to Honorable James M. Sprouse, U.S. Court of Appeals, Fourth Circuit, 1987-1988. Assistant Public Defender, 1988-1990 and Senior Assistant Public Defender, 1991, Office of the Public Defender, Fairfax, VA. *Member:* Fairfax County Bar Association; Environmental Law Institute; Defense Research Institute; National Association of Criminal Defense Lawyers. ***PRACTICE AREAS:*** Environmental Litigation; Toxic Tort; Superfund; Civil Litigation; Criminal Defense. ***Email:*** jslaughter@bdlaw.com

GARY J. SMITH, born Delta, Colorado, February 1, 1951; admitted to bar, 1976, District of Columbia; 1989, California; 1999, New York. *Education:* Claremont Men's College (B.A., magna cum laude, 1973); Harvard University (J.D., 1976). Staff Member, 1974-1975 and Member, Board of Editors, 1975-1976, Harvard Journal on Legislation. ***PRACTICE AREAS:*** Environmental Law; Litigation. ***Email:*** gsmith@bdlaw.com

(This Listing Continued)

KATHRYN E. SZMUSZKOVICZ, born Kalamazoo, Michigan, April 26, 1955; admitted to bar, 1984, Michigan; 1985, District of Columbia; 1991, U.S. Supreme Court. *Education:* Kalamazoo College (B.A., cum laude, 1977); University of Michigan (J.D., 1984). Member, Panel of Arbitrators, American Arbitration Association. ***LANGUAGES:*** French. ***PRACTICE AREAS:*** Biotechnology; Pesticide, Seed and Food Regulation; Alternative Dispute Resolution; Commercial Law. ***Email:*** kszmuszkovicz@bdlaw.com

MARK A. TURCO, born St. Louis, Missouri, December 7, 1950; admitted to bar, 1982, District of Columbia. *Education:* Columbia University (A.B., 1973); Georgetown University (J.D., cum laude, 1982). Staff Member, 1980-1981 and Editor, 1981-1982, *Georgetown Law Journal*. (Also at Baltimore, MD Office). ***PRACTICE AREAS:*** Environmental Law; Litigation. ***Email:*** mturco@bdlaw.com

FRED R. WAGNER, born Brooklyn, New York, March 28, 1962; admitted to bar, 1987, Pennsylvania; 1988, District of Columbia. *Education:* Tufts University (B.A., summa cum laude, 1984); University of Virginia (J.D., 1987). Phi Beta Kappa. Notes Editor, *Virginia Environmental Law Journal*, 1985-1986. Trial Attorney, Environment Division, U.S. Department of Justice, 1987-1991. Special Assistant U.S. Attorney, Misdemeanor Trial Section, D.C., U.S. Attorney's Office, 1990. Co-Chair, Environment, Energy and Natural Resources Section, District of Columbia Bar. ***PRACTICE AREAS:*** Litigation; Environmental Law. ***Email:*** fwagner@bdlaw.com

BENJAMIN F. WILSON, born Bloomington, Indiana, June 29, 1951; admitted to bar, 1976, Georgia; 1978, District of Columbia. *Education:* Dartmouth College (A.B., magna cum laude, 1973); Harvard University (J.D., 1976). Phi Beta Kappa. Trial Attorney, Civil Division, U.S. Department of Justice, 1979-1983. Chairman: District of Columbia Board of Elections and Ethics, 1990—; Energy, Environmental and Public Utilities Section, National Bar Association. ***PRACTICE AREAS:*** Commercial Litigation; Environmental Law. ***Email:*** bwilson@bdlaw.com

SENIOR COUNSEL

ALBERT J. BEVERIDGE, III, born Indianapolis, Indiana, January 26, 1935; admitted to bar, 1963, District of Columbia; 1966, U.S. Supreme Court; 1984, New York. *Education:* Princeton University (A.B., cum laude, 1957); Harvard University (J.D., cum laude, 1962). ***PRACTICE AREAS:*** Corporate; Estates and Trusts. ***Email:*** beveridgeaj@bdlaw.com

JONATHAN Z. CANNON, born Chestertown, Maryland, April 27, 1945; admitted to bar, 1975, District of Columbia. *Education:* Williams College (B.A., 1967); University of Pennsylvania (J.D., 1974). Order of the Coif. Editor-in-Chief, University of Pennsylvania Law Review, 1973-1974. Law Clerk to the Honorable David L. Bazelon, U.S. Court of Appeals, District of Columbia Circuit, 1974-1975. Partner, Beveridge & Diamond, P.C., 1980-1986, 1990-1992). Deputy General Counsel, Litigation and Regional Operations, 1987, Deputy and Acting Assistant Administrator of OSWER, 1988-1989, Assistant Administrator for Administration and Resource Management and Chief Financial Officer, 1993-1995 and General Counsel, 1995-1998, U.S. Environmental Protection Agency. Adjunct Professor, Environmental Law, Washington & Lee School of Law, 1982-1983. Law Lecturer, Environmental Law, University of Virginia School of Law, Charlottesville, Virginia, 1983-1987, 1997-1998. The John A. Ewald, Jr. Professor, Environmental Law, University of Virginia School of Law, Charlottesville, Virginia, 1999—. *Member:* American Bar Association (Member, Natural Resources Section). ***PRACTICE AREAS:*** Environmental Law; Administrative Law. ***Email:*** jcannon@bdlaw.com

HAROLD HIMMELMAN, born Mt. Vernon, New York, September 15, 1942; admitted to bar, 1967, New York; 1969, District of Columbia; 1970, U.S. Supreme Court. *Education:* Williams College (B.A., cum laude, with highest honors, 1964); New York University (LL.B., 1967). Phi Beta Kappa. Attorney, U.S. Department of Justice, Civil Rights Division, Honors Program, 1967-1969. Author: "Resolve Disputes, Get on With Business: An ADR Primer," *U.S. Business Litigation*, Vol. 2, No. 12, July 1997; "ADR Will Work if You Use it Wisely," *The Metropolitan Corporate Counsel*, Vol. 7, No. 8, August 1999. Member: Panel of Mediators/Arbitrators, JAMS; U.S. Copyright Arbitration Panel. ***PRACTICE AREAS:*** Alternative Dispute Resolution; Mediation; Arbitration; Environmental and Administrative Law; Litigation. ***Email:*** hhimmelman@bdlaw.com

OF COUNSEL

GUS BAUMAN, born Memphis, Tennessee, September 4, 1949; admitted to bar, 1975, Maryland; 1976, District of Columbia. *Education:* Clark University (A.B., cum laude, 1971); Washington University (J.D., 1974). Articles Editor, *Urban Law Annual*, 1973-1974. Associate General Counsel, Maryland-National Capital Park and Planning Commission, 1974-1978. Litigation Counsel, National Association of Home Builders, 1979-1988. Partner, Beveridge & Diamond, 1988-1989. Chairman, Maryland-National Capital Park and Planning Commission, 1989-1993. ***PRACTICE AREAS:*** Land Use; Environmental Law; Inverse Condemnation; Trade Association Law. ***Email:*** gbauman@bdlaw.com

(This Listing Continued)

BEVERIDGE & DIAMOND, P.C., Washington—Continued

LAURA K. MCAFEE, born Camden, New Jersey, February 21, 1966; admitted to bar, 1991, Maryland; 1999, Colorado (Not admitted in District of Columbia). *Education:* Carleton College (B.A, magna cum laude, 1988); University of Texas (J.D., 1991). Phi Beta Kappa. Member, Order of the Coif. Member, Texas Law Review. ***PRACTICE AREAS:*** Environmental Law; Air Pollution; Environmental Litigation; Environmental Permitting; Civil Litigation. ***Email:*** lmcafee@bdlaw.com

MICHAEL R. NEILSON, born Portsmouth, Virginia, February 18, 1960; admitted to bar, 1986, Virginia; 1988, District of Columbia; 1998, North Carolina. *Education:* The Catholic University of America (B.A., magna cum laude, 1983); University of Virginia (J.D., 1986). Phi Beta Kappa. Member, Editorial Board, *Virginia Journal of Natural Resources Law*, 1985-1986. ***PRACTICE AREAS:*** Biotechnology; Chemical Regulation; Chemical Products Liability. ***Email:*** mneilson@bdlaw.com

---

STEPHEN M. ARNER, born Alexandria, Virginia, November 19, 1970; admitted to bar, 1995, Virginia; 1997, District of Columbia. *Education:* College of William & Mary (B.A., 1992; J.D., 1995). Phi Delta Phi. Author: "AP Bites Off More Than It Can Chew," D.C. Bar Computer and Telecommunications Law Section Newsletter, September 2000, at 20; "A Compass for Travelers in the Trackless Wastes of CERCLA: A Modest Proposal to Soften CERCLA's Blow Absent Major Congressional Action," *J. Envtl. L. & Prac.*, Spring 1999, at 20. ***PRACTICE AREAS:*** Litigation; Environmental Law. ***Email:*** sarner@bdlaw.com

THOMAS A. BLASER, born Cheverly, Maryland, October 28, 1974; admitted to bar, 2000, Maryland (Not admitted in District of Columbia). *Education:* Dickinson College (B.A., cum laude, 1996); Vermont Law School (J.D., magna cum laude, 2000). Member, National Moot Court Team. Dean's Fellow. Member, Vermont Law Review. ***PRACTICE AREAS:*** Environmental Law. ***Email:*** tblaser@bdlaw.com

MICHELE A. BODDY, born Lakewood, California, May 21, 1963; admitted to bar, 2001, Massachusetts (Not admitted in District of Columbia). *Education:* California State University, Long Beach (B.S., 1987); Vermont Law School (J.D., 2000). ***PRACTICE AREAS:*** Environmental Law. ***Email:*** mboddy@bdlaw.com

CHRISTINA E. CAREY, born Ann Arbor, Michigan, February 12, 1972; admitted to bar, 2000, Michigan (Not admitted in District of Columbia). *Education:* University of Michigan (B.S., with distinction, 1994); University of Virginia (J.D., 1999). ***PRACTICE AREAS:*** Environmental Law; Litigation. ***Email:*** ccarey@bdlaw.com

SCOTT R. DAMELIN, born Malden, Massachusetts, May 26, 1969; admitted to bar, 1995, Massachusetts; 1996, District of Columbia. *Education:* Tufts University (B.A., 1991); Boston College (J.D., 1994). *Member:* The District of Columbia Bar; American Bar Association. ***PRACTICE AREAS:*** Civil Litigation; Criminal Litigation; Environmental Law. ***Email:*** sdamelin@bdlaw.com

BRIAN L. DOSTER, born Orlando, Florida, December 29, 1969; admitted to bar, 1995, Florida; 1998, District of Columbia. *Education:* Duke University (A.B., cum laude, 1992; J.D., with honors, 1995). Editorial Board, *Duke University Environmental Law and Policy Forum*, 1994-1995. ***PRACTICE AREAS:*** Environmental Law; Air Quality; Water Quality; Administrative Litigation. ***Email:*** bdoster@bdlaw.com

LEAH A. DUNDON, born Ithaca, New York, July 2, 1970; admitted to bar, 1997, Tennessee; 1998, District of Columbia. *Education:* American University (B.A., cum laude, 1993); Vanderbilt University (J.D., 1997). Golden Key National Honor Society. Recipient: Corpus Juris Secundum Book Award, Torts, University of Miami Law School. Author: "Environmental Reporting: New Criminal Exposure," *Metropolitan Corporate Counsel*, March 1998. Co-Author: "Environmental Crimes: Recent Trends," *Wiley Environmental Law Update*, Chap. 10, 1999. ***PRACTICE AREAS:*** White Collar Criminal Defense; Environmental Law. ***Email:*** lgregor@bdlaw.com

JAMES T. ESSELMAN, born Cincinnati, Ohio, June 10, 1969; admitted to bar, 2000, Virginia (Not admitted in District of Columbia). *Education:* American University (B.A., 1991); University of Virginia (J.D., 2000). ***PRACTICE AREAS:*** Environmental Law. ***Email:*** jesselman@bdlaw.com

ALESSIO D. EVANGELISTA, born Rochester, New York, September 2, 1970; admitted to bar, 1996, New York and U.S. District Court, Northern District of New York; 1997, District of Columbia. *Education:* State University of New York at Geneseo (B.A., 1991); Syracuse University (J.D., 1995). Order of the Coif. Editor-in-Chief, Syracuse Law Review, 1994-1995. *Member:* The District of Columbia Bar; American Bar Association. ***PRACTICE AREAS:*** White Collar Criminal Litigation; Civil Litigation. ***Email:*** aevangelista@bdlaw.com

(This Listing Continued)

RICHARD J. FERRIS, JR., born Boston, Massachusetts, January 18, 1962; admitted to bar, 1996, Massachusetts; 1998, District of Columbia. *Education:* Clark University (B.A., 1984); The George Washington University Elliott School of International Affairs (M.A., E. Asian Studies, with distinction, 1988); Duke University (J.D., 1994; LL.M., Comp. & Int'l Legal Studies, 1994). Editor and Articles Editor, *Duke Journal of Comparative & International Law*, 1992-1994. Author: "Implications of China's Accession to the WTO for Environmental, Health and Safety Standards: Policy and Law Considerations," *The World Bank, Policy Reform and the Environment in China,* August 31, 2000; "Shaping an Environmental Protection Regime for the New Century: Environmental Law and Policy in the People's Republic of China," *Asian J. Envtl. Mgmt*, 1998; "Aspiration and Reality in Taiwan, Hong Kong, South Korea and Singapore: An Introduction to the Environmental Regulatory Systems of Asia's Four New Dragons," 4 *Duke J. Comp. & Int'l. L.* (1993). Member: American Society of International Law, 1992—; IUCN Commission on Environmental Law, 1999—. Legal Advisor (Honorary), Qu Ge Ping, Chair, Environmental Protection and Natural Resource Conservation Committee, National People's Congress, China, 2000—. Chair, United States Council for International Business China and Environment Working Group, 1999—. Editorial Advisor, *China Environmental Review*, 1999—. *Member:* The District of Columbia Bar (Member, International Law Section, Steering Committee, 2001-2004); American Bar Association (Co-Chair, Section on Environment, Energy and Resources, International Environmental Law Committee, 2001-2002); Inter-Pacific and International Bar Associations; Hong Kong Environmental Law Association. ***LANGUAGES:*** French, Japanese, Mandarin Chinese, Taiwanese. ***PRACTICE AREAS:*** International Environmental Law; China Trade; Asia Trade; United Nations Law; International Finance; New Media Law. ***Email:*** rferris@bdlaw.com

MEREDITH L. FLAX, born Washington, DC, August 16, 1969; admitted to bar, 2001, Michigan (Not admitted in District of Columbia). *Education:* University of Michigan (B.A., 1991; J.D., 2000). *Member:* American Bar Association. ***PRACTICE AREAS:*** Environmental. ***Email:*** mflax@bdlaw.com

MATTHEW C. HOLLORAN, born Washington, D.C. January 15, 1969; admitted to bar, 1995, Maryland; 1999, District of Columbia. *Education:* Loyola College (B.A., summa cum laude, 1990); College of William & Mary, Marshall-Wythe School of Law (J.D., 1994). Order of the Barristers. Co-Author: "Determining Intent in Medicare Fraud—The Accidental Kickback," *Legal Times*, September, 1997. Law Clerk to Honorable Sidney A. Fitzwater, U.S. District Court, Northern District of Texas, 1994-1995. Co-Chair, Practice Development Subcommittee, ABA White Collar Crime Committee. ***PRACTICE AREAS:*** Litigation; White Collar Crime; Commercial Litigation. ***Email:*** mholloran@bdlaw.com

MADELEINE BOYER KADAS, born Austin, Texas, March 21, 1967; admitted to bar, 1994, Texas; 1999, District of Columbia. *Education:* University of Texas at Austin (B.A., 1988); University of Texas at Austin (J.D., 1994); Escuela Libre de Derecho, Mexico City, Mexico (LL.M., 1995). Phi Beta Kappa. Book Review Editor, *International Law Journal*. Contributor: Mexican Environmental Law Summary, NAFTA Commission on Environmental Cooperation, 1995. ***LANGUAGES:*** Spanish, Italian, French. ***PRACTICE AREAS:*** International Environmental Law; Environmental Law. ***Email:*** mkadas@bdlaw.com

DANIEL M. KRAININ, born Plainview, New York, November 28, 1969; admitted to bar, 1997, California; 1999, District of Columbia. *Education:* Wesleyan University (B.A., with high honors, 1991); University of Virginia (J.D., 1997). Articles Editor, *Virginia Environmental Law Journal*, 1996-1997. Law Clerk to Hon. Carlos Moreno, U.S. District Court, Central District of California, 1998. ***PRACTICE AREAS:*** Environmental; Litigation. ***Email:*** dkrainin@bdlaw.com

KATHLEEN LENNON, born Flushing, New York, February 27, 1973; admitted to bar, 1998, New York and New Jersey (Not admitted in District of Columbia). *Education:* State University of New York at Binghamton (B.A., magna cum laude, 1995); Vermont Law School (J.D., magna cum laude, 1998). Member, Head Note Editor, Vermont Law Review. Author: "Government's Udder Disregard for Consumer's Right to Information on RBST: Mandatory Labeling of Milk Products Should Be Allowed," Vermont Law Review, Vol. 22, Book 2. Co-Author: "Preemption Defense Cracks In Pesticide Exposure Cases," New York Law Journal, March 8, 1999. ***PRACTICE AREAS:*** Environmental Law; Environmental Litigation. ***Email:*** klennon@bdlaw.com

RUTH ANN LOWERY, born Jackson, Mississippi, July 8, 1972; admitted to bar, 1997, Maryland; 1998, District of Columbia. *Education:* Millsaps College (B.A., summa cum laude, 1994); Washington College of Law of American University (J.D., summa cum laude, 1997). Phi Beta Kappa. Member, The American University Law Review. ***PRACTICE AREAS:*** Environmental Law; Environmental Litigation. ***Email:*** rlowery@bdlaw.com

ANTHONY L. MICHAELS, born Cleveland, Ohio, 1970; admitted to bar, 1995, Virginia; 1998, Georgia and District of Columbia. *Education:* Virginia Polytechnic Institute and State University (B.S., 1992); College of William and Mary (J.D., 1995). Member, William & Mary Bill of Rights Journal, 1993-1994.

(This Listing Continued)

Staff Attorney, U.S. Court of Appeals, Eleventh Circuit, 1996-1999. ***PRACTICE AREAS:*** Environmental Law; Litigation. ***Email:*** amichaels@bdlaw.com

BRYAN J. MOORE, born Fairhope, Alabama, March 3, 1974; admitted to bar, 2000, Maryland (Not admitted in District of Columbia). *Education:* University of Alabama (B.A., 1997); Tulane Law School (J.D., 2000). Phi Beta Kappa. Phi Delta Phi. Member, Order of the Coif, 2000—. Recipient, Haber Joseph McCarthy Environmental Law Award. Editor-in-Chief, Tulane Environmental Law Journal, 1999-2000. ***PRACTICE AREAS:*** Environmental Law; Pesticide Regulation. ***Email:*** bmoore@bdlaw.com

JAMES T. PARKINSON, born New York, N.Y., August 1, 1968; admitted to bar, 1999, California (Not admitted in District of Columbia). *Education:* Gettysburg College (B.A., 1990); University of Pennsylvania (M.S., 1994); American University (J.D., 1999). Senior Recent Developments Editor, *Administrative Law Review,* 1998-1999. Author: "The National Association of Securities Dealers Should Possess Authority to Issue Temporary-Cease-and-Desist-Orders," 51 *Administrative Law Review* 301, 1999. ***PRACTICE AREAS:*** Environmental Law; White Collar Crime. ***Email:*** jparkinson@bdlaw.com

JUSTIN A. SAVAGE, born Evanston, Illinois, February 12, 1972; admitted to bar, 1997, Virginia; 2000, District of Columbia. *Education:* McNeese State University (B.A., in History, 1994); University of Virginia (J.D., 1997). Recipient, C.J.S. Award in Civil Procedure. Editorial Board Member, 1995-1996 and Executive Editor, 1996-1997, *Virginia Environmental Law Journal.* Author: Note, "Confiscation of Emission Reduction Credits: The Case for Compensation Under the Takings Clause," 16 *Va. Envtl. L.J.* 227 (1997). ***PRACTICE AREAS:*** Environmental Law; Litigation. ***Email:*** jsavage@bdlaw.com

ILANA Z. SULTAN, born Minneapolis, Minnesota, July 22, 1967; admitted to bar, 1994, Illinois; 1996, Georgia; 2000, District of Columbia. *Education:* Columbia University (B.A., 1990); University of Chicago (J.D., 1994). ***PRACTICE AREAS:*** White Collar Criminal Defense; Environmental Law. ***Email:*** isultan@bdlaw.com

DAVID W. WAGNER, born Pittsburgh, Pennsylvania, December 16, 1964; admitted to bar, 1999, Maryland (Not admitted in District of Columbia). *Education:* Pennsylvania State University (B.S., 1987); George Washington University (M.A., 1995); American University (J.D., 1997). *Member:* American Bar Association (Vice Chair, International Environmental Law Committee, 1999—). ***PRACTICE AREAS:*** International Environmental; Environmental Litigation. ***Email:*** dwagner@bdlaw.com

DAVID M. (MAX) WILLIAMSON, born Charlottesville, Virginia, July 9, 1965; admitted to bar, 1997, Rhode Island; 1999, District of Columbia. *Education:* Yale University (B.A., 1987); Vermont Law School (J.D., magna cum laude, 1997; Masters, summa cum laude, 1997). ALI-ABA Fellowship in Environmental Law, 1996. Law Clerk to the Hon. Robert G. Flanders, Jr., Rhode Island Supreme Court. Law Clerk, United States Department of Justice, Environmental and Natural Resources Division. Co-Author: "Protecting Regional Transportation Projects Against Clean Air Attacks," *Development Magazine,* 2000; "Closing the Loop: Leadership in the Legal Community Through Court-Mandated Recycled Paper Usage," D.C. Bar Environment Section, 2000; "D.C. Court Strikes EPA Ozone Rules," *The National Law Journal,* 1999. ***PRACTICE AREAS:*** Environmental Compliance; Environmental Litigation; Environmental Land Use and Transportation Planning; Appellate Practice. ***Email:*** dwilliamson@bdlaw.com

(For complete biographical data on other personnel, see Professional Biographies at San Francisco, California, New York, New York, and Baltimore, Maryland)

BHAGAT & ASSOCIATES

1001 CONNECTICUT AVENUE N.W.
SUITE 1138
WASHINGTON, D.C. 20036
Telephone: 202-293-4044
Fax: 202-293-4046
URL: http://ww.visastous.com
Email: rkbhagat@bhagatandassociates.com
URL: http://www.lawyers.com/rajbhagat

Immigration and Naturalization, Business Immigration, Family Immigration, Consular Law, Employment Visas, Permanent Visas, Citizenship, Political Asylum, Deportation, Refugee Law, Immigration Discrimination, Religious Visas, Personal Injury, Automobile Accidents and Injuries, Slip and Fall, Wrongful Death, Medical Malpractice, Bodily Injury.

FIRM PROFILE: For over 20 years Mr. Raj Bhagat has assisted a variety of companies, individuals and families through the immigration process. Clients to the firm are frequently from the Far East, India, Pakistan, the Middle East, South America and other regions around the globe. The firm has proficiency in the following languages: Hindi, Punjabi, Urdu, Russian and Spanish. Mr. Bhagat also advises, counsels and litigates in the area of personal injury.

(This Listing Continued)

RAJ K. BHAGAT, born India, August, 15, 1946; admitted to bar, 1987, District of Columbia; 1992, District of Columbia Court of Appeals. *Education:* Punjab University, India (B.A., 1969; M.A. Public Administration, 1971); Dehli University, India (LL.B., 1974); Howard University (M.A., Comparative Jurisprudence, 1983). Personnel Manager, Oberoi International Hotel. Comptroller, Embassy Suites, Washington, D.C. Legal Counsel, 1990— and Trustee, 1990-1994, Hindu Temple of Metropolitan Washington, D.C. Member, Bar of India, 1974. *Member:* American Bar Association; American Immigration Lawyers Association.

BIGHAM ENGLAR JONES & HOUSTON

818 CONNECTICUT AVENUE, N.W., SUITE 1010
WASHINGTON, D.C. 20006
Telephone: 202-293-3330
Telefax: 202-293-3515
Email: bejh.com

London, England Office: 107/112 Leadenhall Street, EC3A 4AH. Telephone: 207-891-2504. Telefax: 207-891-2401.

Newark, New Jersey Office: One Gateway Center, Suite 2600, 07102-5315. Telephone: 973-799-8545. Telefax: 973-799-8546.

General Practice. Admiralty, Insurance, Aviation, Banking, Bankruptcy, Personal Injury and Products Liability Law, Environmental and Reinsurance.

FIRM PROFILE: Bigham Englar Jones & Houston has been serving the diverse needs of its clients for over 90 years. As established in 1909, the Firm was primarily engaged in the practice of maritime and insurance law. Today we provide services in the areas of aviation, banking, bankruptcy, business organization, corporations, environmental law, estate planning, insurance law, international law, taxation, real estate, litigation, and arbitration to individual, corporate and commercial clients.

Our principal office is in New York and we maintain additional offices in Newark, New Jersey, Washington, D.C. and in London, England. We have an extensive network of correspondent counsel throughout the United States and major international commercial centers in order that we may serve our clients wherever their need arises.

DANIEL H. MURRAY, admitted to bar, 1970, New York; 1977, U.S. Supreme Court; 1981, District of Columbia; 1982, U.S. District Court, District of Columbia. *Education:* C.W. Post College (B.A., 1965); Fordham University School of Law (J.D., 1970). *Member:* District of Columbia Bar; Democratic Leadership Council; National Democratic Institute; International Law Institute. ***PRACTICE AREAS:*** State Government Law; Federal Government Law; Business Development.

BINGHAM DANA LLP

1120 20TH STREET, N.W.
WASHINGTON, D.C. 20036
Telephone: 202-778-6150
Telecopy: 202-778-6155
Email: info@bingham.com
URL: http://www.bingham.com

Boston, Massachusetts Office: 150 Federal Street. Telephone: 617-951-8000. Telecopy: 617-951-8736.

New York, New York Office: 399 Park Avenue. Telephone: 212-318-7700. Fax: 212-752-5378.

Los Angeles, California Office: 444 South Flower Street, Suite 4500. Telephone: 213-817-3700. Fax: 213-817-3701.

Hartford, Connecticut Office: One State Street. Telephone: 860-240-2700. Fax: 860-240-2800.

London, England Office: 39 Victoria Street, SWIH 0EE. Telephone: 011-44-71-799-2646. Telecopy: 011-44-71-799-2654.

Singapore Office: Level 15 Prudential Tower, 30 Cecil Street, 049712. Telephone: 65 232-2768/2769. Fax: 65 232-2888.

Corporate and Securities Law, Banking and Financial Services, Financial Restructuring, Project/Structured Finance, Technology, Private Equity, Investment Management, Commercial and Criminal Litigation, Corporate Acquisitions, Real Estate, Entrepreneurial Services, Intellectual Property, Tax, Estate Planning, Securities Litigation, Business Regulation and White Collar Defense, Product Liability, Antitrust, Distribution and Franchising, Employment Law, Environmental Law, Sports, Media, Entertainment, International Transactions including International Trade, European, Japanese and Latin American Practices and Alternative Dispute Resolution.

FIRM PROFILE: Bingham Dana LLP is a dynamic and innovative international law firm of more than 500 attorneys that provides a full complement of high-quality legal services, business/governmental consulting, and financial management and

(This Listing Continued)

BINGHAM DANA LLP, Washington—Continued

investment advisory services. We serve our clients - ranging from small and emerging entrepreneurial businesses to the world's largest corporations and financial institutions - through offices in Boston, New York, London, Washington, Hartford, Los Angeles and Singapore.

RESIDENT PARTNERS

WILLIAM H. BOGER, III, born Columbus, Ohio, October 18, 1956; admitted to bar, 1983, Ohio (Not admitted in District of Columbia). *Education:* Ohio State University (B.A., 1979); University of Toledo (J.D., 1982); Georgetown University (LL.M., 1984). ***PRACTICE AREAS:*** Legislative Practice; Financial Institutions; Internet; Communications; Telecommunications Law; Regulatory and Legislative Practice. ***Email:*** whboger@bingham.com

ROGER D. FELDMAN, born April 7, 1943; admitted to bar, 1966, New York; 1977, District of Columbia. *Education:* Brown University (B.A., summa cum laude, 1962); Harvard University (M.B.A., with distinction, 1967); Yale University (LL.B., 1965). ***Email:*** rfeldman@bingham.com

YOSHIHIDE ITO, born 1955; admitted to bar, 1991, New York (Not admitted in District of Columbia). *Education:* Hitotsubashi University, Tokyo, Japan (LL.B., 1979); Harvard University (M.P.P., 1982); Georgetown University (LL.M.). ***Email:*** yito@bingham.com

PAUL J. LAMBERT, born 1946; admitted to bar, 1970, Massachusetts; 1982, District of Columbia. *Education:* College of the Holy Cross (A.B., magna cum laude, 1967); Harvard (J.D., cum laude, 1970). ***PRACTICE AREAS:*** Commercial Litigation; Environmental Litigation; Administrative Litigation; Employment Litigation. ***Email:*** lamberpj@bingham.com

J. MICHAEL PICKETT, born 1965; admitted to bar, 1989, Maryland; 1995, District of Columbia. *Education:* DePauw University (B.A., 1986); Washington University (J.D., 1989). ***PRACTICE AREAS:*** Commercial Real Estate. ***Email:*** picketjm@bingham.com

NANCY M. PERSECHINO, born 1954; admitted to bar, 1981, New York; 1990, California; 1995, District of Columbia. *Education:* University of Chicago (B.A., with honors, 1976; J.D., 1980). ***PRACTICE AREAS:*** Energy; Corporate; Finance. ***Email:*** nmpersechino@bingham.com

PAUL S. QUINN, born Pawtucket, Rhode Island, December 24, 1934; admitted to bar, 1961, District of Columbia. *Education:* Providence College (A.B., 1956); Georgetown University (J.D., 1961). ***PRACTICE AREAS:*** Legislative Practice; Financial Institutions; Telecommunications; International Business. ***Email:*** psquinn@bingham.com

BARRY P. ROSENTHAL, born 1948; admitted to bar, 1974, Pennsylvania; 1975, District of Columbia. *Education:* University of Rochester (B.A., cum laude, 1970); University of Pennsylvania (J.D., 1974). ***PRACTICE AREAS:*** Commercial Real Estate; Real Estate Finance; Corporate Law. ***Email:*** rosentbp@bingham.com

PETER D. SCHELLIE, born 1945; admitted to bar, 1970, Indiana; 1976, District of Columbia; 1985, Maryland. *Education:* Indiana University (A.B., cum laude, 1967); University of Michigan (J.D., 1970). ***PRACTICE AREAS:*** Commercial Finance; Project Finance; Workouts; Bankruptcy. ***Email:*** schellpd@bingham.com

ROGER L. SELFE, born 1948; admitted to bar, 1973, Ohio; 1980, New York; 1990, District of Columbia. *Education:* Ohio University (B.A., 1970); The Ohio State University (J.D., 1973); New York University (LL.M., 1975). ***Email:*** selferl@bingham.com

NEAL E. SULLIVAN, born 1960; admitted to bar, 1990, Massachusetts; 1999, District of Columbia. *Education:* Stonehill College (B.A., 1982); Suffolk University (J.D., 1990). ***PRACTICE AREAS:*** Securities Litigation; Broker-Dealer; Investment Adviser Regulation; Market Regulation. ***Email:*** sullivne@bingham.com

ENID L. VERON, born 1941; admitted to bar, 1979, District of Columbia. *Education:* Brooklyn College of the City University of New York (B.A., summa cum laude, 1960); New York University (Ph.D., 1977); University of Virginia (J.D., 1979). ***PRACTICE AREAS:*** Project and Structured Finance; Energy. ***Email:*** elveron@bingham.com

ERICA H. WEISS, born 1964; admitted to bar, 1989, Maryland; 1995, District of Columbia. *Education:* The Wharton School of the University of Pennsylvania (B.S., cum laude, 1986; J.D., 1989). ***PRACTICE AREAS:*** Commercial Real Estate; Real Estate Finance; Workouts. ***Email:*** weisseh@bingham.com

OF COUNSEL

JOSEPH P. PELICAN, born 1960; admitted to bar, 1985, New York; 1988, Massachusetts; 1993, District of Columbia; 1994, Maryland. *Education:* Rensselaer Polytechnic Institute (B.S., magna cum laude, 1981); Columbia University (J.D., 1984). ***PRACTICE AREAS:*** Commercial Finance; Corporate Law; Workouts. ***Email:*** pelicajp@bingham.com

WAYNE PESTONE, born Plainview, New York, February 14, 1966; admitted to bar, 1992, New York and Connecticut; 1993, District of Columbia. *Education:* Vassar College (B.A., 1988); Georgetown University (J.D., 1991). ***Email:*** wpestone@bingham.com

BONNIE S. TEMPLE, born 1941; admitted to bar, 1975, District of Columbia. *Education:* Radcliffe College (B.A., cum laude, 1963); New York University (M.U.P., 1971); Georgetown University (J.D., 1974). ***PRACTICE AREAS:*** Corporate Law; Finance; Real Estate. ***Email:*** templebs@bingham.com

MARK C. WILLIAMS, born New York, New York, May 20, 1963; admitted to bar, 1991, New York; 1999, District of Columbia. *Education:* Columbia University (B.A., 1987); New York Law School (J.D., 1990). ***PRACTICE AREAS:*** Energy; Utility Law; Corporate; Project Finance; Federal Administrative Law. ***Email:*** mcwilliams@bingham.com

RESIDENT ASSOCIATES

MATTHEW R. BOWSHER, born 1973; admitted to bar, 1998, Ohio (Not admitted in District of Columbia). *Education:* University of Michigan (A.B., 1995); Northwestern University (J.D., 1998). ***PRACTICE AREAS:*** Commercial Real Estate. ***Email:*** bowshemr@bingham.com

CHRISTIAN J. CLAYTON, born 1973; admitted to bar, 2001, Virginia (Not admitted in District of Columbia). *Education:* University of Colorado at Boulder (B.A., 1996); American University (J.D., 2001). ***PRACTICE AREAS:*** Business Corporate; Business Finance; Litigation. ***Email:*** cjclayton@bingham.com

MARGARET KADEL ECK, born 1965; admitted to bar, 1995, California; 1999, District of Columbia. *Education:* University of Richmond (B.S., 1987); Pepperdine University School of Law (J.D., cum laude, 1995). ***PRACTICE AREAS:*** Commercial Real Estate; Real Estate Finance. ***Email:*** eckm@bingham.com

GERARD P. FINN, born 1966; admitted to bar, 1994, Pennsylvania; 1995, District of Columbia. *Education:* Bucknell University (B.A., 1988); George Washington University (J.D., 1994). ***PRACTICE AREAS:*** Environmental Law; Commercial Litigation; Bankruptcy. ***Email:*** gpfinn@bingham.com

ANDREA T. GARZA-VALE, (admission pending). *Education:* Vanderbilt University (B.A., 1998); Georgetown University (J.D., 2001). ***Email:*** atgarzavale@bingham.com

JEFFREY O. HIMSTREET, born San Diego, California, May 5, 1967; admitted to bar, 1993, Oregon and Washington; 1996, District of Columbia. *Education:* Willamette University (B.S., 1989; J.D., 1993); Georgetown University (LL.M., 1998). ***PRACTICE AREAS:*** Securities. ***Email:*** johimstreet@bingham.com

THOMAS C. KLANDERMAN, born 1970; admitted to bar, 1998, New York (Not admitted in District of Columbia). *Education:* State University of New York at Binghamton (B.A., with high honors, 1992); Georgetown University (J.D., 1996). ***PRACTICE AREAS:*** Real Estate. ***Email:*** tcklanderman@bingham.com

KARA E. McCABE, born 1970; admitted to bar, 2001, Massachusetts (Not admitted in District of Columbia). *Education:* University of Massachusetts (B.A., 1992); Suffolk University (J.D., 2000). ***PRACTICE AREAS:*** Commercial Real Estate. ***Email:*** kemccabe@bingham.com

(For Complete Biographical Data on other Personnel, See Professional Biographies at Boston, Massachusetts, Hartford, Connecticut, Los Angeles, California, New York, New York, London, England and Singapore Offices)

(This Listing Continued)

LAW OFFICES OF BINSTOCK, TORCHINSKY AND ASSOCIATES, P.C.

WASHINGTON, D.C.

(See Chevy Chase, Maryland)

Living Trusts, Estate Planning, Asset Protection, Tax Planning, Business Planning Law, Corporate, Partnerships, Elder Care, International Tax, Charitable Trusts and Private Foundations.

BIRCH, HORTON, BITTNER & CHEROT, P.C.

SUITE 1200
1155 CONNECTICUT AVENUE, N.W.
WASHINGTON, D.C. 20036
Telephone: 202-659-5800
Facsimile: 202-659-1027
Email: info@bhb.com
URL: http://www.birchhorton.com

Anchorage, Alaska Office: 1127 West 7th Avenue. Telephone: 907-276-1550.

General Practice.

FIRM PROFILE: Founded in 1971, Birch, Horton, Bittner and Cherot, P.C. maintains a national, full service law practice with offices in Anchorage, Alaska and Washington, D.C. One of the largest Alaska-based law firms in the United States, the firm has earned widespread recognition for its performance in servicing the needs of clients located in over thirty states and in several foreign countries, in all areas of corporate and individual representation. Our clients range from large multinational corporations and institutions to small business enterprises and individuals.

THOMAS L. ALBERT, admitted to bar, 1988, Maryland; 1989, District of Columbia, Virginia and U.S. District Court, District of Maryland; 1990, U.S. District Court, District of Columbia; 1991, U.S. District Court, Eastern District of Virginia; 1992, U.S. Court of Appeals for the District of Columbia; 1997, U.S. Bankruptcy Court, Eastern District of Virginia. *Education:* Hofstra University (B.A., 1985); Washington College of Law of American University (J.D., cum laude, 1988). *Member:* The District of Columbia Bar (Member, Natural Resources Section). ***Email:*** talbert@dc.bhb.com

RONALD G. BIRCH, admitted to bar, 1966, Alaska; 1970, U.S. Supreme Court; 1972, District of Columbia; 1975, U.S. District Court, District of Alaska, U.S. Court of Appeals, Ninth Circuit and U.S. District Court for the District of Columbia; 1976, U.S. Court of Appeals for the District of Columbia and U.S. Claims Court; 1997, U.S. District Court, District of Maryland. *Education:* Colgate University (B.A., 1962); Columbia University (J.D., 1965). Administrative Assistant, U.S. Senator Ted Stevens, 1968-1971. *Member:* The District of Columbia Bar; Alaska Bar Association; Corporate Counsel Institute (Chair, Anchorage Natural Resources Section, 1980-1982). ***PRACTICE AREAS:*** Litigation; Employment; Natural Resources. ***Email:*** rbirch@dc.bhb.com

WILLIAM P. HORN, admitted to bar, 1983, District of Columbia; 1990, U.S. District Court, District of Columbia; 1995, U.S. Supreme Court; 1996, U.S. Court of Appeals for the District of Columbia. *Education:* American University (B.A., 1972; J.D., 1983). Recipient, Outstanding Service Award, U.S. Department of the Interior, 1984. Author: "Private Claims and Public Resources," Natural Resources and Environment, Vol. 4, No. 4, Spring, 1990. Assistant Secretary for Fish, Wildlife and Parks, U.S. Department of the Interior, 1985-1988. Deputy Undersecretary of the U.S. Department of the Interior, 1981-1985. Republican Committee Staff, Committee on Interior and Insular Affairs, U.S. House of Representatives, 1977-1981. *Member:* The District of Columbia Bar. ***Email:*** whorn@dc.bhb.com

ROY STAPLETON JONES, JR., admitted to bar, 1974, District of Columbia and Florida. *Education:* United States Military Academy (B.S., 1964); University of Maryland (J.D., 1973). Counsel, Committee on Interior and Insular Affairs and Counsel, Chairman Morris K. Udall, U.S. House of Representatives, 1979-1991. Counsel on Oversight, Committee on Interior and Insular Affairs and Subcommittee on General Oversight and Alaska Lands, U.S. House of Representatives, 1975-1979. Legislative Assistant, U.S. Congressman James A. Haley, U.S. House of Representatives, 1970-1975. *Member:* The District of Columbia Bar; The Florida Bar. ***Email:*** rjones@dc.bhb.com

HARVEY A. LEVIN, admitted to bar, 1974, Pennsylvania; 1975, District of Columbia; 1978, U.S. Supreme Court; 1985, Maryland; U.S. Court of Appeals for the District of Columbia Circuit and U.S. Court of Appeals, Fourth, Sixth and Ninth Circuits; U.S. District Court for the District of Columbia, U.S. District Court, District of Maryland and U.S. District Court, Eastern District of Michigan. *Education:* Williams College (B.A., cum laude, 1970); Georgetown University Law Center (J.D., 1974). Law Clerk to Judge Stanley S. Harris, District of Columbia Court of Appeals, 1974-1975. Member, Judicial Conference, District of Columbia Circuit (1987, 1989). Assistant Chief Counsel, Enforcement Office of Thrift Supervision, 1991-1993. *Member:* The District of Columbia Bar; Maryland State and Pennsylvania Bar Associations. ***REPORTED CASES:*** Peterson v. Cooley, 142 F.3d 181 (4th Cir. 1998); In re Firstcorp, Inc. (RTC v. Firstcorp, Inc.), 973 F.2d 243 (4th Cir. 1992); Carleton v. Firstcorp, Inc., 967 F.2d 942 (4th Cir. 1992); OTS v. Smallwood, 925 F. 2d 894 (6th Cir. 1991); Sargent v. Paine-Webber, Inc., 882 F.2d 529 (D.C. Cir. 1989); In re Sealed Case, 856 F.2d 268 (D.C. Cir. 1988); DiStefano v. U.S., 787 F. Supp. 292 (D.R.I. 1992); Home Mortgage Bank v. Ryan, 768 F. Supp. 330 (D. Utah 1991). ***PRACTICE AREAS:*** Commercial Litigation; Banking; Commercial Transactions; Bankruptcy. ***Email:*** hlevin@dc.bhb.com

(This Listing Continued)

ELISABETH HEWITT ROSS, admitted to bar, 1978, Alaska; 1978, U.S. District Court, District of Alaska; 1983, U.S. District Court for the District of Columbia and U.S. Court of Appeals for the District of Columbia Circuit; 1984, U.S. Supreme Court; 1985, District of Columbia; 1997, U.S. Court of Appeals, Fifth Circuit. *Education:* Brown University (B.A., cum laude, 1974); Northeastern University (J.D., 1978). Assistant Attorney General, State of Alaska, 1978-1982. Author, "The Regulation of Affiliated Interests," Public Utilities Fortnightly, June 7, 1984. *Member:* The District of Columbia Bar; Alaska Bar Association; Federal Communications Bar Association; Women's Bar Association. ***REPORTED CASES:*** Re: Matanuska Telephone Ass'n, 2 APUC 432 (1979); Re: College Utilities Corp., 3 APUC 463 (1981); Re: Alascom, Inc., 81 PUR 4th 320 (1986); Re: Alascom, Inc., 10 APUC 76 (1989); Investigation of Alascom, Inc., 12 FCC Rcd 3646 (1997). ***PRACTICE AREAS:*** Communications; Public Utilities; Administrative; Energy; Legislative. ***Email:*** eross@dc.bhb.com

---

DOUGLAS SCOTT BURDIN, admitted to bar, 1991, California; 1992, District of Columbia; 1994, U.S. Court of Appeals, Ninth Circuit and U.S. District Court for the District of Columbia; 1996, U.S. Court of Appeals for the District of Columbia Circuit. *Education:* University of Colorado (B.A., with distinction, 1983); San Francisco State University (Teaching Credential, 1987); Hastings College of Law, University of California (J.D., cum laude, 1991). Note Development Editor, Hastings Communications and Entertainment Law Journal, 1990-1991. *Member:* The District of Columbia Bar (Labor Relations Section); American Bar Association (Natural Resources and Labor and Employment Law Sections). ***REPORTED CASES:*** Fund for Animals, Inc. v. Thomas, 127 F.3d 80 (D.C. Cir. 1997). ***PRACTICE AREAS:*** Natural Resources; Wildlife Litigation; Employment; Communications. ***Email:*** dburdin@dc.bhb.com

ALLISON M. ELLIS, born September 14, 1970; admitted to bar, 1996, Illinois; 1998, Maryland and District of Columbia. *Education:* University of Florida (B.A.); Loyola University (J.D., 1996). ***PRACTICE AREAS:*** Litigation; Telecommunications; Corporate; Lobbying; Child Advocacy. ***Email:*** aellis@dc.bhb.com

(For biographical data on other personnel, see Professional Biographies at Anchorage, Alaska)

BISCEGLIE & WALSH

Established in 1984

SUITE 400
1130 SEVENTEENTH STREET, N.W.
WASHINGTON, D.C. 20036
Telephone: 202-778-1160
Facsimile: 202-659-9536
Email: bisc-walsh@worldnet.att.net
URL: http://www.lawyers.com/bisceglie&walsh

Civil, Criminal Trial, Appellate and Federal Agency Practice. Corporate Law, Government Relations, Media Law, International Human Rights.

FIRM PROFILE: A Washington, D.C. based law firm with a national and international practice representing corporations, not-for-profit organizations and individuals in commercial transactions, administrative and regulatory proceedings, law enforcement investigations, civil and criminal litigation, personal injury, medical malpractice and international human rights cases in the European Court of Human Rights and international human rights fora.

MEMBERS OF FIRM

ANTHONY P. BISCEGLIE, born New York, N.Y., July 22, 1952; admitted to bar, 1978, District of Columbia; 1979, U.S. District Court, District of Columbia and U.S. Court of Appeals, District of Columbia Circuit; 1990, U.S. Supreme Court; 1991, Maryland; 2000, U.S. Court of Appeals, Fourth Circuit. *Education:* University of Colorado (B.A., magna cum laude, 1974); Antioch School of Law (J.D., 1978). Law Clerk, Honorable Robert M. Scott, 1978-1979. Member: Board of Advisors, RICO Litigation Reporter, 1984—; Board of Advisors, Corporate Counsel, Lawcast, 1994—; Editorial Advisory Board, Civil RICO Report, 1987—. Arbitrator, New York Stock Exchange, 1989—. *Member:* District of Columbia Bar; American Bar Association; National Association of Criminal Defense Lawyers; American Trial Lawyers Association. ***PRACTICE AREAS:*** Corporate Counseling; Administrative Law; Commercial Litigation; Business Crimes; White Collar Criminal Defense.

WILLIAM C. WALSH, born New York, N.Y., October 18, 1948; admitted to bar, 1976, District of Columbia; 1977, U.S. District Court, District of Columbia Circuit; 1980, U.S. Supreme Court. *Education:* La Salle College (B.A., maxima cum laude, 1970); Antioch Law School (J.D., 1976). *Member:* District of Columbia Bar; American Society for Access Professionals; Amnesty International Legal Network. ***LANGUAGES:*** Spanish. ***PRACTICE AREAS:*** Con-

(This Listing Continued)

BISCEGLIE & WALSH, Washington—Continued

stitutional Law; International Human Rights; Freedom of Information Act; Litigation. ***Email:*** wcwalsh@worldnet.att.net

LAW OFFICES OF BERT NEIL BISGYER

Established in 1981
1025 THOMAS JEFFERSON STREET, N.W.
SUITE 525 EAST
WASHINGTON, D.C. 20007
Telephone: 202-338-2172
Telecopier: 202-338-2447
Email: blsgyer@bisgyerlaw.com
URL: http://www.lawyers.com/bisgyeremploymentlaw

Labor and Employment Law for management including litigation.

BERT NEIL BISGYER, born Washington, D.C., May 25, 1947; admitted to bar, 1973, District of Columbia; 1974, U.S. Court of Appeals, 2nd, 7th and 8th Circuits; 1975, U.S. Court of Appeals, 4th and 5th Circuits; 1976, U.S. Court of Appeals for the District of Columbia and 6th Circuits; 1979, U.S. District Court, District of Maryland; 1980, Maryland; 1981, U.S. Court of Appeals, 11th Circuit; 1983, U.S. District Court for the District of Columbia; 1984, U.S. Supreme Court. *Education:* Washington University (A.B., cum laude, 1969); George Washington University (J.D., honors, 1973). Antoinette F. Dames Scholar, 1969. Author: "Training Program for Managerial and Non-Supervisory Personnel: Discharging the Employer's Duty to Identify, Prevent, Train for, Respond to, and Correct Harassment, including Sexual Harassment,: 2000; "Aids in the Workplace: Basic Issues and Considerations for the Food Industry," NAWGA 1988; "Pre-Employment Inquiry Guide," NAWGA 1987; "Employee Handbook for the Food Industry," NAWGA, 1985; "Policing Interstate Debt Collection Calls," excerpted in the "Consumer Protection Reporter," 1972. Attorney, National Labor Relations Board Appellate Court Branch, 1973-1977. *Member:* The District of Columbia Bar; Maryland State and American (Member, Section on Labor and Employment Law) Bar Associations. (Also Of Counsel to Hodes, Ulman, Pessin & Katz, P.A., Towson, MD). ***PRACTICE AREAS:*** Labor and Employment; Employment Discrimination.

OF COUNSEL

CARL S. SILVERMAN, born Wilmington, Delaware, June 29, 1946; admitted to bar, 1971, Virginia; 1972, Maryland; 1973, District of Columbia; 1981, U.S. Supreme Court. *Education:* University of Delaware (B.A., 1967); Georgetown University Law Center (J.D., 1970; LL.M., 1974). Trial Attorney for the National Labor Relations Board, 1971-1976. Contributing Editor to the ABA Labor Law Section's Committee on the Development of the Law Under the N.L.R.A., 1974-1976. Author: "The Case for the National Labor Relations Board's Use of Rulemaking in Asserting Jurisdiction," 25 Labor Law Journal 607. *Member:* Maryland State Bar Association, Inc.; American Bar Association (Member, Committee on the L Development of Law under the N.L.R.A., Labor Law Section, 1981—). ***PRACTICE AREAS:*** Labor and Employment; Employment Discrimination; Collective Bargaining.

BLANK ROME COMISKY & McCAULEY LLP

THE FARRAGUT BUILDING
900 17TH STREET, N.W., SUITE 1000
WASHINGTON, D.C. 20006
Telephone: 202-530-7400
FAX: 202-463-6915
Email: webmaster@blankrome.com
URL: http://www.blankrome.com

Media, Pennsylvania Office: Rose Tree Corporate Center, 1400 N. Providence Road, Building 1, Suite 301, 19063. Telephone: 610-891-7800. FAX: 610-891-7804.
Philadelphia, Pennsylvania Office: One Logan Square, 19103-6998. Telephone: 215-569-5500. FAX: 215-569-5555.
Cherry Hill, New Jersey Office: Woodland Falls Corporate Park, 210 Lake Drive East, Suite 200, 08002-1164. Telephone: 856-779-3600. FAX: 856-779-7647.
Boca Raton, Florida Office: 1200 North Federal Highway, Suite 417, 33432. Telephone: 561-417-8100. FAX: 561-417-8101.
Allentown, Pennsylvania Office: 1620 Pond Road, Suite 200, 18104-2255. Telephone: 610-706-4300. FAX: 610-706-4343.
Wilmington, Delaware Office: Chase Manhattan Centre, 1201 Market Street, Suite 800, 19801. Telephone: 302-425-6400. FAX: 302-425-6464.
Trenton, New Jersey Office: 200 West State Street, 08608. Telephone: 609-278-2320. FAX: 609-278-2323.

(This Listing Continued)

Baltimore, Maryland Office: 250 West Pratt Street, Suite 1100, 21201. Telephone: 410-659-1400. FAX: 410-659-1414.
New York, New York Office: The Chrysler Building, 405 Lexington Avenue, 10174. Telephone: 212-885-5000. FAX: 212-885-5001.
Cincinnati, Ohio Office: PNC Center, 201 East Fifth Street, Suite 1700, 45202. Telephone: 513-362-8700. Fax: 513-362-8787.

Administrative Law, Administrative Adjudications; Administrative Agency Practice, Administrative Hearings and Appeals, Administrative Litigation, Federal Administrative Law, Professional Licensing, Professional Licensing Regulation, Public Law, Admiralty and Maritime Law, Marine Law, Maritime Contracts, Maritime Finance, Maritime Law, Maritime Liens, Ship Sales and Mortgages, Aged and Aging, Age Discrimination, Elder Care, Elder Law, Agency and Distributorships, Distribution Agreements, International Distribution, Alcoholic Beverages, Liquor Licensing, Alternative Dispute Resolution, Arbitration, International Arbitration, International Dispute Resolution, Mediation, Antitrust and Trade Regulation, Antitrust, Business Combinations, Competition, Covenants Not To Compete, Deceptive Trade Practices, Noncompetition and Non-Solicitation Agreements, Price-Fixing, Restrictive Covenants, Trade Regulation, Unfair Trade, Appellate Practice, Civil Appeals, Art Law, Artists Rights, Museum Law, Asset Protection, International Asset Protection, Aviation and Aerospace, Aircraft Finance and Leasing, Aircraft Sales, Airline Labor Law, Aviation Law, Aviation Defense, Aviation Insurance, Aviation Litigation, Aviation Products Liability, Aviation Regulation, Bankruptcy, Bankruptcy Arbitration, Bankruptcy Chapter 7, Bankruptcy Chapter 11, Bankruptcy Chapter 12, Bankruptcy Chapter 13, Bankruptcy Collections, Bankruptcy Litigation, Bankruptcy Mediation, Bankruptcy Reorganization, Bankruptcy Taxation, Bankruptcy Trustees Rights, Commercial Bankruptcy, Commercial Foreclosure, Commercial Insolvency, Commercial Recovery, Commercial Workouts, Foreclosures, Fraudulent Conveyance, Insolvency, International Bankruptcy, International Insolvency, Liquidations, Out of Court Debt Restructuring, Pre-Bankruptcy Workouts, Receiverships, Repossessions, Workouts, Workouts Taxation, Banks and Banking, ATM Networks, Bank Collections, Bank Directors and Officers Liability, Bank Foreclosures, Bank Mergers and Acquisitions, Banking Antitrust, Banking Law, Banking Litigation, Commercial Banking, Commercial Credit, Commercial Loans, Consumer Banking, Credit Card Law, Credit Finance, Credit Law, Electronic Banking, Fair Lending, Financial Law, Interest and Usury, International Banking Law, International Loans, Lender Law, Lender Liability, Lender Regulation, Lenders Rights, Letters of Credit, Loan Restructuring, Loan Workouts, Loans, Savings and Loan Law, Secured Lending, Truth in Lending, Biotechnology, Biomedical Technology, Biotechnology Licensing, Business Law, Business Arbitration, Business Associations Law, Business Crimes, Business Development, Business Dissolutions, Business Estate Planning, Business Formation, Business Fraud, Business Litigation, Business Mediation, Business Organization, Business Planning, Business Regulation, Business Reorganization, Business Sales, Business Succession Planning, Business Successions, Business Syndication, Business Taxation, Business Torts, Business Transactions, Business Transfers, Business Trusts, Business Valuation, Buying and Selling of Businesses, Capital Formation, Closely Held Business Estate Planning, Closely Held Business Law, Closely Held Business Taxation, Complex Business Litigation, Emerging Business Law, Emerging Growth Companies, Entrepreneurial Business Law, Family Business Law, Family Business Mediation, Family Business Successions, International Business Law, International Joint Ventures, Joint Ventures, Limited Liability Company Law, Privatization, Professional Practices, Small Business Law, Sole Proprietorships, Strategic Alliances, Chancery and Equity, Chancery Practice, Children, Child Custody, Child Support, Civil Practice, Federal Civil Practice, Sex Discrimination, Commercial Collections, Post Judgment Collections, Commercial Law, Commercial Litigation, Complex Commercial Litigation, Secured Transactions, Uniform Commercial Code, Commercial Real Estate, Commercial Real Estate Acquisitions, Commercial Real Estate Development, Commercial Real Estate Finance, Commercial Real Estate Foreclosure, Commercial Real Estate Sales, Commercial Real Estate Syndication, Commercial Real Estate Workouts, Industrial Real Estate Law, Shopping Center Acquisitions, Shopping Center Development, Shopping Center Law, Complex and Multi-District Litigation, Computers and Software, Computer Contracts, Computer Law, Computer Security, Computer Software Law, Computer Technology, Electronic Commerce, Information Technology, Information Technology Contracts, Information Technology Licensing, International Computer Law, Internet Law, Software Copyright, Software Licensing, Software Protection, Year 2000 Computer Conversion, Constitutional Law, First Amendment Law, Construction Law, Construction Finance, Construction Litigation, Construction Workouts, Environmental Construction Law, International Construction Law, Public Construction Law, Consumer Law, Consumer Arbitration, Consumer Class Actions, Consumer Credit, Consumer Credit Compliance, Consumer Finance, Consumer Fraud, Consumer Litigation, Consumer Protection, Consumer Rights, Fair Credit Reporting Act, Contracts, Breach of Contract, Commercial Contracts, Contract Fraud, Contract Litigation, International Commercial Contracts, International Contracts, Copyrights, Copyright Infringement, Copyright Litigation, Copyright Prosecution, Copyright Protection, Copyright Registration, International Copyright Law, Corporate Law, Closely Held Corporations, Corporate Banking Law, Corporate Commercial Law, Corporate Contracts, Corporate Control Contests, Corporate Criminal Law, Corporate Dissolutions, Corporate Ethics, Corporate Fiduciary Law, Corporate Finance, Corporate Formation, Corporate Governance, Corporate In-

(This Listing Continued)

come Tax, Corporate Insurance, Corporate Insurance Defense, Corporate Investigations, Corporate Litigation, Corporate Organization, Corporate Partnerships, Corporate Planning, Corporate Real Estate, Corporate Reorganization, Corporate Successions, Corporate Tax Controversies, Corporate Tax Planning, Corporate Taxation, Corporate Trusts, Corporate Workouts, Family Corporations, Foreign Sales Corporations, Hostile Takeovers, Incorporation, International Corporate Finance, International Corporate Law, International Corporate Taxation, Nonprofit Corporations, Offshore Corporations, Professional Corporations; Proxy Contests, Public Corporations, S Corporations, Securitization, Small Business Corporations, Takeovers, Tender Offers, Transfer Pricing, Criminal Law, Debtor and Creditor, Creditor Bankruptcy, Creditors Rights, Creditors Rights in Bankruptcy, Debtor and Creditor Bankruptcy, Debtor and Creditor Collections, Debtor and Creditor Remedies, Debtor and Creditor Reorganization, Debtor and Creditor Rights, Debtor and Creditor Workouts, Debtor Bankruptcy, International Creditors Rights, Secured Creditors Rights, Unsecured Creditors Rights, Disabilities, Americans with Disabilities Act, Academic Employment, College and University Law, Administrative Lobbying, Executive Lobbying, Legislative Lobbying, Lobbying, Eminent Domain, Employee Benefits, COBRA, Deferred Compensation, Employee Benefit Taxation, Employee Benefit Trusts, Employee Compensation, Employee Stock Ownership Plans, ERISA, Executive Compensation, Executive Compensation Taxation, Flexible Benefit Plans, Multi-Employer Benefits, Multi-Employer Pensions, Non-Qualified Benefits, Pension and Profit Sharing Plans, Pension Plans, Pension Taxation, Profit Sharing, Public Pension Plans, Qualified Retirement Plans, Retirement Benefit Plans, Taft-Hartley Plans, Unemployment Compensation, Music Copyright, Environmental Law, Environmental Compliance, Environmental Liability, Environmental Litigation, Environmental Mediation, International Environmental Law, Equipment Finance and Leasing, Equipment Finance, Equipment Leasing, Vehicle Leasing, Family Law, Divorce, Matrimonial Law, Finance, Asset Based Finance, Financial Institution Reorganization, Financial Institutions Law, Financial Institutions Taxation, Financial Restructuring, International Commercial Finance, International Finance, Franchises and Franchising, Franchise Law, Franchise Licensing, Franchise Litigation, Franchise Taxation, International Franchising, General Practice, Federal Practice, Government, County Government Law, Federal Government Law, Government Affairs, Government Agency Practice, Government Relations, Legislative Practice, Local Government Law, Public Policy, Qui Tam Litigation, State Government Law, State Legislative Practice, Township Law, Government Contracts, Government Construction Contracts, Government Contract Arbitration, Government Contract Fraud, Government Procurement, International Government Contracts, Local Government Contracts, Public Bidding, Public Contract Law, Public Works Contracts, Guardianship and Conservatorship, Health Care, Alternative Health Care Delivery System, Certificates of Need, Health Care Administration, Health Care Contracts, Health Care Corporate Law, Health Care Facility Licensing, Health Care Facility Regulation, Health Care Finance, Health Care Fraud, Health Care Legislation, Health Care Licensing, Health Care Mergers and Acquisitions, Health Care Regulation, Health Care Reimbursement, Health Care Taxation, Health Insurance, Health Insurance Coverage, Health Insurance Defense, Health Insurance Trusts, Health Law, Health Maintenance Organizations, Integrated Health Care Delivery Systems, Long Term Care, Managed Care, Managed Care Contracts, Medical Antitrust, Mental Health Law, Nursing Home Regulation, Pharmacy Law, Physicians Contracts, Hospital Law, Hospital Administration, Medical Staff Contracts, Medical Staff Credentialing, Housing Law, Affordable Housing, Apartment Projects, Housing Finance, Insurance, Commercial Insurance, Insurance Company Taxation, Insurance Litigation, Insurance Defense, Intellectual Property, Artistic Property, Chemical Intellectual Property, Electrical Intellectual Property, Intellectual Property Infringement, Intellectual Property Licensing, Intellectual Property Litigation, International Intellectual Property, International Licensing, Mechanical Intellectual Property, Medical Intellectual Property, Pharmaceutical Intellectual Property, Piracy, Proprietary Rights, Taxation of Intellectual Property, International Law, International Trade, Antidumping, Countervailing Duties, Customs Law, Export Regulation, Import and Export Law, International Trade Regulation, Latin America Trade, Russia Trade, Investments, Financial Services Law, Financial Services Regulation, Foreign Investment, Foreign Investment in the United States, International Investment, Investment Banking Law, Investment Company Law, Investment Partnerships, Investment Regulation, Labor and Employment, Affirmative Action, Collective Bargaining, Employee Drug Testing, Employer Liability, Employment at Will, Employment Contracts, Employment Discrimination, Employment Litigation, Employment Mediation, Executive Employment Law, Executive Severance Contracts, Fair Labor Standards, Family and Medical Leave Act, Federal Employment Law, Harassment, International Employment Contracts, International Labor Law, Labor Arbitration, Management Labor Law, National Labor Relations Act, Personnel Policies, Public Sector Collective Bargaining, Public Sector Labor Relations, Sexual Harassment, Unfair Labor Practices, Union Contract Negotiations, Union Elections, Union Organization, Wage and Hour Law, WARN Act, Workplace Violence, Wrongful Termination Defense, Leases and Leasing, Commercial Leasing, International Leasing, Landlord and Tenant Law, Lease Finance, Leasing, Leveraged Leasing, Office Leasing, Retail Leasing, Shopping Center Leasing, Legal Ethics and Professional Responsibility, Legal Ethics, Litigation, Civil Litigation, Complex Litigation, Defense Litigation, Federal Civil Litigation, Federal Litigation, International Litigation, Long-Arm Litigation, Trial Practice, U.S. Supreme Court Litigation, Newspaper Contracts, Publishing Contracts, Medical Malpractice, Medicare and Medicaid,

(This Listing Continued)

Medicaid Planning, Medicare and Medicaid Reimbursement, Medicare Fraud and Abuse, Mergers, Acquisitions and Divestitures, Business Acquisitions, Business Divestitures, International Mergers and Acquisitions, Leveraged Acquisitions, Leveraged Buyouts, Merger Reorganization, Mergers and Acquisitions, Mergers and Acquisitions Finance, Mortgages, Commercial Mortgages, Mortgage Banking Law, Mortgage Bankruptcy, Mortgage Finance, Mortgage Foreclosure, Mortgage Insurance, Mortgage Lien Foreclosure, Mortgage Refinancing, Mortgage Securitization, Mortgage Tax, Mortgage Workouts, Secondary Mortgage Market, Municipal Bonds, Municipal Bonds Taxation, Municipal Contracts, Municipal Corporation Law, Municipal Derivative Products, Municipal Finance, Municipal Labor Law, Municipal Leasing, Municipal Pension Law, Municipal Redevelopment, Municipal Securities, Municipal Taxation, Tax Increment Finance, Natural Resources, Nonprofit and Charitable Organizations, Charitable Limited Partnerships, Charitable Organizations Law, Charitable Trusts and Foundations, Nonprofit Organizations Law, Nonprofit Tax Law, Private Foundations, Tax Exempt Organizations, Occupational Safety and Health, OSHA, Partnership Law, Family Limited Partnerships, Family Partnerships, Limited Liability Partnerships, Limited Partnerships, Partnership Dissolution, Partnership Formation, Partnership Organization, Partnership Syndication, Partnership Taxation, Patents, Biochemical Patents, Biotechnology Patent Prosecution, Biotechnology Patents, Chemical Patent Prosecution, Chemical Patents, Computer and Software Patents, Design Patents, Electrical Patent Prosecution, Electrical Patents, Electronic Patents, International Patents, Mechanical Patent Prosecution, Mechanical Patents, Medical Patents, Metallurgical Patents, Molecular Biology Patents, Patent Applications, Patent Infringement, Patent Interference Practice, Patent Licensing, Patent Litigation, Patent Prosecution, Patent Protection, Pharmaceutical Patents, Personal Injury, Premises Security, Probate, Ancillary Probate, International Probate, Probate Administration, Probate Litigation, Probate Taxation, Products Liability, Drug and Medical Device Defense, Firearms Products Liability, Professional Liability, Public Finance, Bond Finance, Economic Development, Housing and Urban Development, Industrial Development, International Economic Development, International Project Finance, Project Finance, Public Authority Finance, Public Finance Taxation, Public-Private Development, Tax Exempt Bonds, Tax Exempt Finance, Railway Labor Law, Real Estate, Condominium Association Law, Condominium Conversions, Condominium Development, Condominium Law, Conveyancing, Cooperative Association Law, Cooperative Conversions, Cooperative Housing Law, Easements, International Real Estate, Land Acquisitions, Land Sales, Land Trusts, Planned Unit Development Law, Real Estate Acquisitions, Real Estate Arbitration, Real Estate Banking Law, Real Estate Bankruptcy, Real Estate Brokers Licensing, Real Estate Contracts, Real Estate Development, Real Estate Finance, Real Estate Foreclosure, Real Estate Investment, Real Estate Investment Taxation, Real Estate Investment Trusts, Real Estate Joint Ventures, Real Estate Leasing, Real Estate Litigation, Real Estate Mediation, Real Estate Partnerships, Real Estate Restructuring, Real Estate Sales, Real Estate Secured Lending, Real Estate Securities, Real Estate Settlements, Real Estate Syndication, Real Estate Tax Appeals, Real Estate Tax Assessment, Real Estate Taxation, Real Estate Title, Real Estate Transfers, Real Estate Valuation, Real Estate Workouts, Real Property, Real Property Acquisitions, Real Property Development, Real Property Finance, Residential Real Estate, Residential Real Estate Development, Waterfront Development, Regulatory Law, Drug and Medical Device Regulation, Federal Regulatory Law, Regulated Industries, Regulatory Agency Practice, Regulatory Investigations, Religious Nonprofit Corporation Law, RICO, Securities, Bank Securities, Broker-Dealer Arbitration, Broker-Dealer Regulation, Initial Public Offerings, Private Placement, Private Placement Syndication, Public Offerings, SEC Enforcement, Securities Arbitration, Securities Litigation, Securities Offerings, Securities Registration, Securities Regulation, Shareholder Agreements, Shareholder Disputes, Tax Exempt Securities, Sports Contracts, Sports Licensing, Taxation, Employment Tax, Estate and Gift Taxation, Federal Income Tax, Federal Tax Controversies, Federal Taxation, Fiduciary Income Tax, Income Tax, Individual Taxation, International Tax Controversies, International Taxation, Like Kind Exchanges, Local Taxation, Low Income Housing Tax Credits, Property Tax Abatement, Property Tax Appeals, Sales and Use Tax, State Taxation, Tax Appeals, Tax Audits, Tax Collection, Tax Deferred Exchanges, Tax Planning, Tax Shelters, Trusts and Estates Taxation, Electronics, High Technology Contracts, Semiconductor Technology, Technology Contracts, Technology Licensing, Technology Protection, Technology Transfers, Torts, Trade Association Law, Toxic Torts, Trade Secrets, Theft of Trade Secrets, Trademarks, International Trademarks, Trade Dress, Trade Names, Trademark Arbitration, Trademark Infringement, Trademark Licensing, Trademark Litigation, Trademark Prosecution, Trademark Protection, Trademark Registration, Transportation, Common Carrier Law, Mass Transit Law, Public Transportation Law, Transit Labor, Trusts and Estates, Decedents Estates, Estate Administration, Estate Litigation, Estate Planning, Family Trusts, Family Wealth Transfer, Fiduciary Law, Fiduciary Liability, Fiduciary Litigation, Financial Planning, International Estate Planning, International Trusts, Living Trusts, Offshore Trusts, Personal Planning, Retirement Planning, Trust Administration, Trust Law, Trust Litigation, Trust Planning, Wealth Preservation, Unfair Competition, Utility Law, Utility Acquisitions, Utility Contracts, Utility Taxation, White Collar Crime, Embezzlement, White Collar Criminal Defense, White Collar Fraud, Wills, Contested Wills, Inheritance, Living Wills, Successions, Zoning, Planning and Land Use, Building and Public Safety Codes, Cemetery Law, Environmental Land Use, Fire Districts, Improvement Districts, Land Conservation, Land Development, Land Entitlement, Land Use, Land Use

(This Listing Continued)

BLANK ROME COMISKY & McCAULEY LLP, Washington—Continued

Litigation, Land Use Permitting, Land Use Regulation, Rezoning, Special Districts, Subdivisions, Water Districts, Zoning Law, Zoning Variances, Retail Industry Development.

FIRM PROFILE: Blank Rome Comisky & McCauley LLP is a full service law firm with regional, national and international practices. The Firm is organized into ten major departments - Business and Corporate, Financial Services, Government Relations, Intellectual Property, Labor and Employment, Litigation and Dispute Resolution, Matrimonial, Public Finance, Real Estate and Tax and Fiduciary Law.

The Firm represents both public and privately held businesses, as well as individuals and governmental entities. Its practice extends to virtually all sectors of the economy including: Agriculture; the Arts; Banking and Financial Institutions; Bankruptcy, Reorganizations and Workouts; Charitable Organizations; Communications; Developers and Construction Companies; Education; Entertainment; Health Care Providers; Hospitality; Insurance Agents and Brokers; Manufacturing; Printing and Publishing; Professionals and Professional Services; Telecommunications; Wholesale and Retail Operations; Service Companies; and Transportation Companies.

RESIDENT MEMBERS

MARK BLONDMAN, born New York, N.Y., October 15, 1954; admitted to bar, 1980, Missouri; 1983, Pennsylvania; 1987, New Jersey; 1994, Texas (Not admitted in District of Columbia). *Education:* University of Pennsylvania (B.S., cum laude, 1975); Cornell University (M.S., 1977); University of Kansas (J.D., 1980). *Member:* American Bar Association. (Also at Philadelphia, Pennsylvania Office). ***PRACTICE AREAS:*** Age Discrimination; Sex Discrimination; Americans with Disabilities Act; Harassment; Sexual Harassment; Wrongful Termination Defense; Labor and Employment. ***Email:*** blondman@blankrome.com

HERBERT COHEN, born Brooklyn, New York, August 30, 1933; admitted to bar, 1969, District of Columbia, U.S. District Court for the District of Columbia and U.S. Court of Appeals for the District of Columbia Circuit; 1973, U.S. Supreme Court; 1982, U.S. Court of Appeals for the Federal Circuit; 1989, U.S. District Court, District of Maryland; 1991, U.S. District Court, Eastern District of Virginia; registered to practice before U.S. Patent and Trademark Office. *Education:* University of Michigan (B.S.Chem.E., 1956); American University (J.D., 1968). ***PRACTICE AREAS:*** Trademarks; International Trademarks; Patents; International Patents. ***Email:*** cohen@blankrome.com

CHARLES A. CRAGIN, born Portland, Maine, October 9, 1943; admitted to bar, 1970, Maine and U.S. District Court, District of Maine; 1974, U.S. Supreme Court; 1989, District of Columbia; U.S. Tax Court and U.S. Court of Veterans Appeals. *Education:* University of Maine (B.S., cum laude, 1967; J.D., cum laude, 1970). Phi Kappa Phi. Maine Commission on Governmental Ethics and Election Practices, 1979-1982; Chairman, Board of Veterans' Appeals, U.S. Department of Veterans Affairs, 1991-1997; Principal Deputy and Acting Under Secretary of Defense (Personnel and Readiness), 1998-2001; Principal Deputy and Acting Assistant Secretary for Reserve Affairs, 1997-2001; Acting Assistant to the Secretary of Defense for Civil Support, 2000-2001. *Member:* District of Columbia Bar; Maine State (Former Chairman, Public Relations Committee, 1972-1978) and American Bar Associations; American Society of Hospital Attorneys (Former Member, Board of Directors, 1976-1978). ***PRACTICE AREAS:*** Government; Election, Campaign and Political Law; Health Care; Administrative Law; Regulatory Law. ***Email:*** cragin@blankrome.com

EDWARD J. FARRELL, born Philadelphia, Pennsylvania, July 29, 1945; admitted to bar, 1970, District of Columbia; 1971, U.S. Court of International Trade; 1982, U.S. Court of Appeals for the Federal Circuit. *Education:* Lehigh University (B.A., cum laude, 1967); Georgetown University (J.D., 1970). *Member:* Federal and American Bar Associations. ***PRACTICE AREAS:*** International Trade; Antidumping; Countervailing Duties; Customs Law; Import and Export Law; International Trade Regulation; Export Regulation. ***Email:*** farrell@blankrome.com

SUSAN B. FLOHR, born Alexandria, Virginia, March 19, 1953; admitted to bar, 1979, District of Columbia; 1985, Virginia; 1988, U.S. Court of Appeals for the Federal Circuit; 1991, U.S. Supreme Court; registered to practice before U.S. Patent and Trademark Office. *Education:* George Mason University (B.A., 1975); Washington College of Law of American University (J.D., 1979). Member, 1977-1979 and Senior Editor, 1978-1979, American University Law Review, . Author: "Funding Public Participation in Agency Proceedings," 27 American University Law Review 981, 1978. *Member:* The District of Columbia Bar; Virginia State Bar (Member, Sections on: Patent, Trademark and Copyright Law; Litigation). ***PRACTICE AREAS:*** Trademark Law; Copyright Law; Computer Law; Unfair Competition Law; Licensing; Prosecution; Litigation; Appellate Practice. ***Email:*** flohr@blankrome.com

(This Listing Continued)

MICHAEL C. GREENBAUM, born Chicago, Illinois, July 19, 1951; admitted to bar, 1976, Pennsylvania; 1978, Virginia, U.S. Court of Appeals, Fourth Circuit, U.S. District Court, Eastern District of Virginia and U.S. Tax Court; 1979, District of Columbia; 1982, U.S. Court of Appeals for the Federal Circuit; 1986, U.S. Supreme Court, U.S. District Court, District of Columbia, U.S. Court of Appeals for the District of Columbia Circuit; registered to practice before U.S. Patent and Trademark Office. *Education:* Worcester Polytechnic Institute (B.S.E.E., summa cum laude, 1973); Rutgers University (J.D., 1976). Law Clerk to the Honorable Joseph V. Colaianni, U.S. Court of Claims, Trial Division, 1978-1979. ***PRACTICE AREAS:*** Software Protection; Year 2000 Computer Conversion; Copyright Infringement; Electrical Intellectual Property; Biomedical Technology; Computer and Software Patents; Electrical Patents; Patent Infringement; Trademark Registration. ***Email:*** greenbaum@blankrome.com

KATHLEEN McDERMOTT, born Norfolk, Virginia, 1961; admitted to bar, 1986, Maryland; 1987, Massachusetts (Not admitted in District of Columbia). *Education:* Wright State University (B.A., 1982); Suffolk University (J.D., cum laude, 1986). Assistant U.S. Attorney, District of Maryland, 1991-1999, Health Care Fraud Coordinator and Affirmative Civil Enforcement Coordinator, District of Maryland. *Member:* Maryland State (Officer, Litigation Section Council) and American Bar Associations; American Health Lawyers Association; Health Care Compliance Association. ***PRACTICE AREAS:*** False Claims Act; Qui Tam Litigation; Government Investigations; Health Care Fraud; Health Care Litigation; Complex Litigation. ***Email:*** mcdermott-k@blankrome.com

DAVID A. NORCROSS, born Camden, New Jersey, March 30, 1937; admitted to bar, 1961, New Jersey; 1971, U.S. Court of Appeals, Third Circuit; 1986, U.S. Supreme Court; 1993, District of Columbia. *Education:* University of Delaware (B.A., 1958); University of Pennsylvania (LL.B., 1961). Executive Assistant to Governor of New Jersey, 1971-1973. Executive Director, New Jersey Election Law Enforcement Commission, 1973-1976. General Counsel: Republican National Committee, 1993-1997 (Counsel to Chairman, 1983-1989); International Republican Institute, 1984-1992; Center for Democracy, 1984-1995. Commissioner, Burlington County Board of Elections, 1982-2000; Secretary, 1990-2000. Member, Republican National Committee, 1977-1981; 1992—. Member, Board of Directors, International Republican Institute, 1984—. New Jersey Registered Legislative Agent. *Member:* Burlington County and New Jersey State Bar Associations; District of Columbia Bar. (Also at Trenton, New Jersey Office). ***PRACTICE AREAS:*** Federal Government Law; Federal Legislative Practice; Government Affairs; Government Relations; State Government Law; State Legislative Practice; Trade Association Law. ***Email:*** norcross@blankrome.com

VICTOR M. WIGMAN, born Philadelphia, Pennsylvania, March 2, 1940; admitted to bar, 1967, District of Columbia and U.S. District Court for the District of Columbia; 1972, Superior Court for the District of Columbia; 1981, Virginia (Admission Limited to Patent, Trademark, Copyright and Unfair Competition Causes only); 1982, U.S. Court of Appeals for the Federal Circuit; 1995, U.S. District Court, Eastern District of Virginia; registered to practice before U.S. Patent and Trademark Office. *Education:* Drexel University (B.S.M.E., 1963); University of Pennsylvania (J.D., 1966). ***PRACTICE AREAS:*** Intellectual Property Infringement; International Licensing; Mechanical Patents; Metallurgical Patents; Patent Infringement; Patent Litigation; Trademark Litigation; Trade Secret Litigation. ***Email:*** wigman@blankrome.com

CHARLES R. WOLFE, JR., born Washington, D.C., March 5, 1952; admitted to bar, 1978, Virginia; 1979, U.S. District Court, Eastern District of Virginia; 1979-1982, U.S. Court of Customs and Patent Appeals; 1981, U.S. Court of Appeals, Fourth Circuit; 1982, U.S. District Court, Western District of Virginia and U.S. Court of Appeals for the Federal Circuit; 1983, District of Columbia, U.S. District Court for the District of Columbia and U.S. Supreme Court; registered to practice before U.S. Patent and Trademark Office. *Education:* Lehigh University (B.S.Ch.E., summa cum laude, 1974); Georgetown University (J.D., 1978). Tau Beta Pi. Patent Examiner, U.S. Patent and Trademark Office, 1974-1977. *Member:* The District of Columbia Bar; Virginia State Bar (Member, Litigation and Patent, Trademark, Copyright Section). (Also at Philadelphia, Pennsylvania Office). ***PRACTICE AREAS:*** Patent Law; Trademark Law; Unfair Competition Law; Patent Litigation; Copyright Law; Licensing Law. ***Email:*** wolfe@blankrome.com

JOEL ROTHSTEIN WOLFSON, born Denver, Colorado, May 3, 1955; admitted to bar, 1980, District of Columbia and U.S. Court of Appeals for the District of Columbia Circuit; 1981, U.S. District Court for the District of Columbia and U.S. Bankruptcy Court, District of Columbia; 1987, U.S. District Court, District of Maryland and U.S. Bankruptcy Court, District of Maryland; 1988, U.S. Court of Appeals, Tenth Circuit. *Education:* University of Wisconsin-Madison (B.S., with distinction in Mathematics, 1976); Cornell University (J.D., 1980). Author: "Contracts and Copyright Are Not At War," 87 Cal. L. Rev. 79, 1999; "Electronic Mass Information Providers and Section 552 of the Restatement (Second) of Torts: The First Amendment Casts a Long Shadow," 29 Rutgers Law Journal 67, 1997; "Express Warranties and Published Information Content Under Article 2B; Does the Shoe Fit?" 16 The John Marshall Journal of Computer and Information Law 337, 1997; "A Conduct Code, An Ethics

(This Listing Continued)

Code With Bite," 1 The Journal of computing and Society 119, 1991; "Class Actions in Bankruptcy: A Clash of Policies Reconciled," Emory Bankruptcy Developments Journal, Vol. 5, No. 2, 1988. *Member:* The District of Columbia Bar (Past Co-Chair, Technical Education Committee, Computer Law Section); Bar Association of the District of Columbia (Chair, Corporation, Securities and Business Committee, 1989-1991); D.C. Computer Law Forum (Member, Board of Directors); American Law Institute; Computer Law Association. (Associate General Counsel). ***PRACTICE AREAS:*** Computers and Software; Intellectual Property; Contracts; Commercial Law; Technology and Science. ***Email:*** wolfson@blankrome.com

SENIOR, SPECIAL AND OF COUNSEL

J. CALEB BOGGS III, born Washington, D.C., August 3, 1962; admitted to bar, 1987, Delaware; 1992, U.S. Supreme Court; 1997, District of Columbia. *Education:* University of Richmond (B.A., 1984); Catholic University of America (J.D., 1987); Georgetown University (M.B.A., 1996). Judicial Clerkship, Delaware Court of Chancery, 1987-1988. Legislative Counsel, U.S. Senate Governmental Affairs Committee, 1991-1995. *Member:* The District of Columbia Bar; Delaware State Bar Association; Federalist Society for Law and Public Policy; Republican National Lawyers Association. (Also at Wilmington, Delaware and Philadelphia, Pennsylvania Offices). ***PRACTICE AREAS:*** Government Relations; Legislative Practice. ***Email:*** boggs@blankrome.com

DONALD R. GREENE, born New Haven, Connecticut, January 7, 1931; admitted to bar, 1966, District of Columbia; 1987, Texas; registered to practice before U.S. Patent and Trademark Office. *Education:* University of Miami (B.S.E.E., 1961); George Washington University (J.D., 1965). ***PRACTICE AREAS:*** Electronic Patents; Intellectual Property Licensing; Semiconductor Technology; Technology Licensing; Electronics; Computer Technology. ***Email:*** greene@blankrome.com

GEORGE C. MYERS, JR., born Laurel, Mississippi, November 19, 1938; admitted to bar, 1973, Massachusetts; 1981, U.S. Court of Appeals for the Federal Circuit and U.S. Court of Appeals, Fourth Circuit; registered to practice before U.S. Patent and Trademark Office (Not admitted in District of Columbia). *Education:* U.S. Naval Academy (B.S., 1960); Boston College (J.D., 1973). ***PRACTICE AREAS:*** Patent Litigation; Patent Prosecution; Patent Licensing. ***Email:*** myers-gc@blankrome.com

LISA J. SAVITT, born Philadelphia, Pennsylvania, June 3, 1956; admitted to bar, 1982, New York; 1984, Pennsylvania; 1992, District of Columbia. *Education:* George Washington University (B.A., 1978); New York Law School (J.D., 1981). Author: "Update on the Hague Convention on the Recognition and Enforcement of Foreign Judgments in Civil and Commercial Matters," 34 Tort and Insurance Law Journal 519, Winter, 1999; "Foreign Judgment Recognized in New York Court Even Though Assets Blocked by U.S. Sanctions," International Trade Law Quarterly, Winter, 1999; "Recent Developments in Aviation and Space Law," 30 Tort and Insurance Law Journal 249, Winter, 1995. *Member:* American Bar Association (Deputy to Chair, Public International Law Division, Section on International Law; Vice Chair, Women's Interest Network; Vice Chair, Aviation Committee, Section on Tort and Insurance Practice; Member, Aviation Litigation Committee, Section on Litigation); International Aviation Womens Association (President, 1994-1996); Aviation Insurance Association (Director, Attorneys Division). ***PRACTICE AREAS:*** Aviation Liability; Aviation Litigation; Products Liability; International Commercial Litigation; Employment Law; International Trade. ***Email:*** savitt@blankrome.com

MICHAEL D. WHITE, born Richmond, Virginia, April 21, 1952; admitted to bar, 1982, District of Columbia, Virginia and U.S. Court of Appeals, Fourth Circuit; 1983, California; 1990, U.S. Court of Appeals for the Federal Circuit; registered to practice before U.S. Patent and Trademark Office. *Education:* University of Virginia (B.S.N.E., with highest distinction, 1975; B.S., Applied Mathematics, with high distinction, 1975; M.E.N.E., 1975); University of Tennessee at Knoxville (J.D., with honors, 1981). Tau Beta Pi. Member, George Washington American Inn of Court (Master; Secretary). Author: "Publishing Without Perishing: Protecting Patent Rights in the Publication of Research Results," Medical Device Research Report, Vol. 2, No. 2, March/April, 1995; "Hippocrates Cringes: The Debate Over Medical Procedures Patents," Medical Device Research Report, Vol. 3, No. 4, July/August, 1996. Co-Author: "Experimental Investigations of Two-Phase Mixture Level Swell and Axial Void Fraction Distribution Under High Pressure, Low Heat Flux Conditions in Rod Bundle Geometry," ANS Specialists Conference on Small Break Loss of Coolant Analysis in LWRs, Monterey, California, 1981; "The Safe Use of Nuclear Power Systems in Outer Space: Current Safety Standards and a Suggested Framework for the Future," Space Technology & Applications International Forum (STAIF-2000), Albuquerque, New Mexico, February 2000. Lectures: "Patenting Your Invention, Conception to Exploitation," (co-presenter), Association for the Advancement of Medical Instrumentation, 30th Annual Meeting, Anaheim, California, May, 1995; "Considerations for the Protection of Technology Created in Eastern European Countries," NATO Advanced Research Workshop on Intellectual Property in Central and Eastern Europe: the Creation of Favorable Legal and Market Preconditions, Vilnius, Lithuania, June, 1998. *Member:* American Society of Mechanical Engineers. ***PRACTICE AREAS:***

(This Listing Continued)

Patent Litigation; Patent Validity and Infringement Opinions; Mechanical Intellectual Property; Electro-Mechanical Patents; Mechanical Patent Prosecution; Design Patents; Proprietary Rights; Copyright Protection. ***Email:*** white@blankrome.com

RESIDENT ASSOCIATES

LYN ANNE BAILEY, born Okinawa, Japan, June 7, 1969; admitted to bar, 1994, Maryland; 1995, District of Columbia; 1998, Pennsylvania. *Education:* University of Maryland (B.A., cum laude, 1991); American University (J.D., 1994). Law Clerk: Chief Judge Emeritus Louis C. Bechtle, U.S. District Court, Eastern District of Pennsylvania, 1996-1998; Chief Judge Edward N. Cahn, U.S. District Court, Eastern District of Pennsylvania, 1995-1996. ***LANGUAGES:*** Mandarin Chinese. ***PRACTICE AREAS:*** Complex Commercial Litigation. ***Email:*** bailey@blankrome.com

DAVID J. EDMONDSON, born San Diego, California, May 20, 1962; admitted to bar, 1992, Virginia; registered to practice before U.S. Patent and Trademark Office (Not admitted in District of Columbia). *Education:* Johns Hopkins University (B.A., Physics, 1983); Princeton University (M.A., Plasma Physics, 1986); University of Michigan (J.D., 1992). Phi Beta Kappa. Donald E. Kerr Medal for Outstanding Work in Physics. Former Patent Examiner, Class 359, "Optics, Systems and Elements." *Member:* Virginia State Bar; American Intellectual Property Law Association. ***PRACTICE AREAS:*** Intellectual Property; Electrical Intellectual Property; Electrical Patent Prosecution; Computer and Software Patent Protection; International Patents; Patent Applications. ***Email:*** edmondson@blankrome.com

BROOKE THOMAS ILEY, born Baltimore, Maryland, April 21, 1969; admitted to bar, 1994, Maryland; 1995, District of Columbia and U.S. District Court, District of Maryland; 1997, U.S. District Court for the District of Columbia. *Education:* University of Maryland (B.S., 1991); Catholic University of America, Columbus School of Law (J.D., 1994). *Member:* District of Columbia Bar; Maryland State, Federal and American Bar Associations. (Also at Baltimore, Maryland Office). ***PRACTICE AREAS:*** Labor and Employment Law. ***Email:*** iley@blankrome.com

BRIAN C. JONES, born Warwick, Rhode Island, October 27, 1956; admitted to bar, 1994, Maryland; 1997, District of Columbia; registered to practice before the U.S. Patent and Trademark Office. *Education:* University of Maryland (B.S., 1981); George Washington University National Law Center (J.D., 1994). ***PRACTICE AREAS:*** Chemical Intellectual Property; Pharmaceutical Intellectual Property; Mechanical Intellectual Property; International Intellectual Property; Intellectual Property Infringement; Intellectual Property Licensing; Intellectual Property Litigation; Intellectual Property Portfolio Management. ***Email:*** jones@blankrome.com

DENISE CATHERINE LANE, born Melrose, Massachusetts, August 12, 1969; admitted to bar, 1997, Massachusetts; 1999, U.S. Court of Appeals, Tenth Circuit; 2000, U.S. Court of Appeals, Federal Circuit; registered to practice before U.S. Patent and Trademark Office (Not admitted in District of Columbia). *Education:* University of Massachusetts (B.S., Chemical Engineering, 1994); Boston University (J.D., 1997). *Member:* Massachusetts and American Bar Associations; American Intellectual Property Law Association. ***PRACTICE AREAS:*** Intellectual Property Litigation; Intellectual Property Licensing; Patent Prosecution. ***Email:*** lane@blankrome.com

RAFAEL PEREZ-PINEIRO, born San Juan, Puerto Rico, February 28, 1972; admitted to bar, 2001, Florida (Not admitted in District of Columbia). *Education:* University of Puerto Rico (B.S., magna cum laude, 1994); Johns Hopkins University (M.S., 1997); George Washington University Law School (J.D., 2001). ***PRACTICE AREAS:*** Intellectual Property. ***Email:*** perez-r@blankrome.com

PETER S. WEISSMAN, born Brooklyn, New York; admitted to bar, 1996, Virginia; 1997, District of Columbia; registered to practice before U.S. Patent and Trademark Office. *Education:* State University of New York at Stony Brook (B.E., 1989); George Washington University (J.D., 1996). *Member:* American Bar Association. ***PRACTICE AREAS:*** Intellectual Property Law; Electrical Patents; Mechanical Patents; Trademarks; Fastener Quality Act. ***Email:*** weissman@blankrome.com

NEIL R. WHITE, born Norfolk, Virginia, April 13, 1970; admitted to bar, 1995, Maryland; 1996, U.S. District Court, District of Maryland (Not admitted in District of Columbia). *Education:* Northeastern University (B.S., cum laude, 1992); University of Baltimore (J.D., magna cum laude, 1995). Member, Heuisler Honor Society. Law Clerk to the Hon. Glenn T. Harrell, Court of Special Appeals of Maryland, 1995-1996. *Member:* Maryland State and American Bar Associations; Bankruptcy Bar Association. ***PRACTICE AREAS:*** Complex Litigation; Civil Litigation; Commercial Litigation; White Collar Criminal Defense; Bankruptcy Litigation. ***Email:*** white-nr@blankrome.com

JOHN YUN, born Seoul, Korea, October 22, 1970; admitted to bar, 2001, New York (Not admitted in District of Columbia). *Education:* University of Maryland, College Park (B.S., 1994); George Washington University (J.D., 2000). *Member:* American Bar Association; American Intellectual Property

(This Listing Continued)

BLANK ROME COMISKY & McCAULEY LLP, Washington—Continued

Law Association; American Society of Mechanical Engineers; Society of Automotive Engineers. ***PRACTICE AREAS:*** Intellectual Property. ***Email:*** yun@blankrome.com

THE LAW OFFICES OF BLAYLOCK AND BLEECKER

CHARTERED

WASHINGTON, D.C.

(See Bethesda, Maryland)

Personal Injury, Negligence, Medical Malpractice, Product Liability and Medical Legal Law. Trial Practice in all State and Federal Courts.

BLOOSTON, MORDKOFSKY, DICKENS, DUFFY & PRENDERGAST

Established in 1979

2120 L STREET, N.W., SUITE 300
WASHINGTON, D.C. 20037
Telephone: 202-659-0830
Fax: 202-828-5568
Email: jap@bloostonlaw.com
URL: http://www.bloostonlaw.com

Practice is Limited to Telecommunications Law.

FIRM PROFILE: Blooston, Mordkofsky, Dickens, Duffy & Prendergast (including its predecessor, the offices of Jeremiah Courtney), the oldest law firm in Washington, D.C. engaged exclusively in the practice of telecommunications law, represents its clients before the Federal Communications Commission, the courts and state regulatory commissions and in international matters. The firm's clients include several telephone companies; internet service providers (ISPs); publicly and privately held companies engaged in cellular, SMR, cable, MDS, LMDS and other wireless services, domestic and international; companies using communications facilities internally; tower owners and equipment manufacturers. The firm has an engineering department, and a legislative consultant, with expertise in finance and international transactions.

MEMBERS OF FIRM

ARTHUR BLOOSTON (1914-1999).

HAROLD MORDKOFSKY, admitted to bar, 1963, Maryland; 1968, District of Columbia and U.S. Court of Appeals for the District of Columbia. *Education:* The City College of the City University of New York (B.E.E., 1958); University of Maryland (LL.B., 1962). Eta Kappa Nu. Author: "The FCC, IMTS and Paging: Answers to your Questions," Phone Call, Vol. 20, No. 7, July, 1981; Co-Author: "Wireless Cable: An Alternative to CATV," OPASTCO Roundtable, Summer, 1990. ***PRACTICE AREAS:*** Telecommunications Law; Cellular Radio; FCC Licensing; FCC Regulation. ***Email:*** halmor@bloostonlaw.com

BENJAMIN H. DICKENS, JR., admitted to bar, 1977, Florida, District of Columbia and U.S. Court of Appeals for the District of Columbia Circuit. *Education:* Mercer University (B.A., 1974); Florida State University (J.D., 1977). Phi Delta Phi. Author: "FCC Preemption and Forbearance: Exploring the Regulatory Vacuum," Rural Telecommunications, Summer, 1985; "Fighting Hostile Takeovers: A Regulatory Rural Perspective," Rural Telecommunications, Summer, 1987; "ONA and Price Caps: Should the Commission Cap Deregulation Instead?" Rural Telecommunications, Summer, 1988. Associate Public Counsel, State of Florida, 1977-1984. ***LANGUAGES:*** Spanish. ***PRACTICE AREAS:*** Telecommunications Law; International Telecommunications.

JOHN A. PRENDERGAST, admitted to bar, 1985, Maryland and District of Columbia; 1987, U.S. Court of Appeals for the District of Columbia Circuit. *Education:* Loyola College (B.A., summa cum laude, 1981); Georgetown University (J.D., cum laude, 1985). Phi Alpha Theta. Author: "PCS Spectrum Is Going Once, Going Twice," America's Network, Feb. 15, 1994. ***PRACTICE AREAS:*** Telecommunications Law; FCC Licensing; FCC Regulation; PCS.

GERARD J. DUFFY, admitted to bar, 1976, Virginia; 1977, District of Columbia. *Education:* Villanova University (B.A., 1970); University of Illinois (M.A. in Economics, 1973); George Washington University (J.D., with honors, 1976); Virginia Tech University (M.S., Accountancy, 1988). Author: "Cellular Radio: The Whys and Hows of Joining the Network," Rural Telecommunications Winter, 1983; "Ten Commandments For Surviving CATV Rate Regulation," Rural Telecommunications, July-August 1994. ***PRACTICE AREAS:*** Telecommunications Law; Cable TV; FCC Regulation; PCS. ***Email:*** gjd@bloostonlaw.com

RICHARD D. RUBINO, admitted to bar, 1985, Oklahoma; 1988, Virginia; 1997, District of Columbia. *Education:* Old Dominion University (B.A., 1982); Oklahoma City University (J.D., 1985). Phi Delta Phi. Member, Oklahoma City University Law Review, 1984-1985. ***PRACTICE AREAS:*** Telecommunications Law; FCC Licensing; FCC Regulation. ***Email:*** rdr@bloostonlaw.com

OF COUNSEL

ROBERT M. JACKSON, admitted to bar, 1978, Maryland; 1979, District of Columbia; 1981, U.S. Supreme Court. *Education:* George Washington University (B.A., 1974); Catholic University of America (J.D., 1978). Pi Sigma Alpha. Member, Catholic University of America Law Review, 1977-1978. ***PRACTICE AREAS:*** Telecommunications Law; Cellular Communications; FCC Licensing; FCC Regulation.

LEGISLATIVE CONSULTANT

PERRY W. WOOFTER, admitted to bar, 1953, West Virginia; 1960, U.S. Supreme Court (Not admitted in District of Columbia). *Education:* West Virginia University (B.A., 1949; LL.B., 1952). Senior Vice President, Oil Capital, Ltd. Administrative Assistant and Chief of Staff, U.S. Senator Robert C. Byrd; Counsel and Chief Government Representative, American Petroleum Institute. ***PRACTICE AREAS:*** Telecommunications Law; International Transactions; Federal Legislative Practice; Energy; International Project Finance.

ASSOCIATES

DAVID CARY MITCHELL, admitted to bar, 1994, New York; 1995, District of Columbia. *Education:* Dartmouth College (A.B., 1985); Newhouse School of Public Communications (M.S., 1986); Syracuse University (J.D., 1993). ***PRACTICE AREAS:*** Telecommunications; FCC Licensing; FCC Regulation; PCS. ***Email:*** cma@bloostonlaw.com

MICHAEL B. ADAMS, JR., admitted to bar, 1995, Virginia; 1997, District of Columbia. *Education:* Williams College (B.A., 1990); George Washington University (J.D., 1995). ***PRACTICE AREAS:*** Telecommunications Law; FCC Regulation; PCS.

KATHLEEN A. KAERCHER, admitted to bar, 1992, Pennsylvania (Not admitted in District of Columbia). *Education:* LaSalle University (B.A., 1988); Syracuse University (M.S., Communications, 1990; J.D., 1991). Member, General Counsel, OPASTCO, 1999-2000. ***PRACTICE AREAS:*** Telecommunications Law; FCC Licensing. ***Email:*** kak@bloostonlaw.com

BLUESTONE LAW INTERNATIONAL

WASHINGTON, D.C.

(See Bethesda, Maryland)

Collections, Commercial Collections, International Collections, Small Business Law, Business Litigation, Professional Collections, Civil Trials, Commercial Law, Process Service and Investigations, Eills, Estates, Probate Litigation, Guardianship, Conservatorship, Power of Attorney.

BLUMENFELD & COHEN

Established in 1984

1625 MASSACHUSETTS AVENUE, N.W., SUITE 300
WASHINGTON, D.C. 20036
Telephone: 202-955-6300
Facsimile: 202-955-6460
Email: info@technologylaw.com
URL: http://www.technologylaw.com

Telecommunications, Communications Regulation, Antitrust, Economic and Business Regulation Legislation, Criminal Practice in State and Federal Courts, Trial and Appellate Litigation, Civil Litigation and Administrative Proceedings before State and Federal Agencies, Contract and Transactional Law.

FIRM PROFILE: Representing the next-generation of law firm in the United States, Blumenfeld & Cohen provides legal and strategic consulting services combining exceptional governmental and business experience with cutting-edge legal strategies. Founded in 1984 by two experienced litigators who held key Justice Department positions during the landmark United States v. AT&T antitrust trial, the firm currently serves public sector clients as well as individual and corporate clients ranging from start-up ventures to established Fortune 500 firms.

(This Listing Continued)

MEMBERS OF FIRM

JEFFREY BLUMENFELD, born New York, N.Y., May 13, 1948; admitted to bar, 1973, District of Columbia; 1980, U.S. Supreme Court. *Education:* Brown University (A.B. cum laude, Honors in Religious Thought, 1969); University of Pennsylvania (J.D., 1973). Listed in: Who's Who in American Law; Who's Who in the East. Co-Author: Chapter 30: Who's Who in America. United States Telecommunications Law And Practice, Colin D. Long, ed. (2d ed. 1995); "A New Universal Service Paradigm: Local Competition," Vol. I, Proceedings of the Ninth NARUC Biennial Regulatory Information Conference, The National Regulatory Research Institute (Sept. 7-9, 1994). Chief Legal Officer, General Counsel, Rhythms NetConnections Inc. Trial Attorney, Antitrust Division, U.S. Department of Justice, 1973-1975. Assistant U.S. Attorney for the District of Columbia, 1975-1979. Trial Attorney: Antitrust Division, U.S. Department of Justice, 1979-1984: United States v. AT&T, 1979-1982. Assistant Chief, Communications and Finance Section, 1982-1984; Chief, United States v. AT&T Staff, 1984. Adjunct Professor, Telecommunications, Adjunct Professor, Trial Practice, Georgetown University Law Center, 1983—. Instructor, National Institute for Trial Advocacy, Washington, D.C. GULC Session, 1982—. Lecturer and Instructor, Attorney General's Advocacy Institute, U.S. Department of Justice, 1982-1990; Consultant and special Trial Counsel, U.S. Department of Justice, Antitrust Division, 1995-1997. *Member:* District of Columbia Bar (Member, Steering Committee, Division on Antitrust, Trade Regulation and Consumer Affairs, 1983-1987); American Bar Association (Vice Chairman, Committee on Federal Rules of Evidence and Criminal Procedure, Criminal Justice Section, 1973-1975; White Collar Crime Committee, Criminal Justice Section, 1984—; Subcommittee on Corporate Liability, 1989—). ***SPECIAL AGENCIES:*** F.C.C.; State PUCs. ***PRACTICE AREAS:*** Antitrust; Telecommunications; Litigation. ***Email:*** jeffb@rhythms.net

GARY M. COHEN, born Buffalo, New York, December 22, 1943; admitted to bar, 1968, New York; 1984, District of Columbia. *Education:* State University of New York at Buffalo (B.A., 1965; J.D., cum laude, 1968). Articles Editor, Buffalo Law Review, 1967-1968. Trial Attorney, Antitrust Division, U.S. Department of Justice, 1968-1979; United States v. AT&T, 1982-1984. Special Assistant U.S. Attorney, Eastern District of Virginia, 1979. Counsel, Subcommittee on Antitrust, Monopoly and Business Rights, Committee on the Judiciary, U.S. Senate, 1980-1981. *Member:* The District of Columbia Bar; New York State Bar Association. ***PRACTICE AREAS:*** Criminal and Civil Antitrust Litigation and Counseling; Telecommunications Law; Civil Litigation. ***Email:*** gary@technologylaw.com

DAVID M. NASEMAN, born Lansing, Michigan, December 10, 1948; admitted to bar, 1976, New York (Not admitted in District of Columbia). *Education:* Boston University (B.A., 1971); Tulane University (J.D., 1975). Order of the Coif. Managing Editor, Tulane Law Review, 1974-1975. ***Email:*** david@technologylaw.com

CHRISTY C. KUNIN, born San Francisco, California, December 21, 1961; admitted to bar, 1993, Maryland; 1994, District of Columbia. *Education:* Bates College (B.A., 1984); Annenberg School for Communications, University of Southern California (M.A., with distinction, 1990); Catholic University of America (J.D., 1993). Recipient, Alumni Society Achievement Award. Managing Editor, Catholic University Law Review. Co-Author: Chapter 30: United States Telecommunications Law and Practice, Colin D. Long, ed. (2d ed. 1995); "A New Universal Service Paradigm: Local Competition," Vol. I, Proceedings of the Ninth NARUC Biennial Regulatory Information Conference, The National Regulatory Research Institute (Sept. 7-9, 1994). Author, "Unilateral Tariff Exculpation in the Era of Competitive Telecommunications," 41 Catholic University Law Review 907, 1992. *Member:* District of Columbia Bar; Maryland State and American Bar Associations; Federal Communications Bar Association. ***PRACTICE AREAS:*** Telecommunications Law; Communications Law; Technology Law. ***Email:*** christy@technologylaw.com

ELISE P.W. KIELY, born Baltimore, Maryland, October 16, 1968; admitted to bar, 1994, Georgia; 1995, Maryland; 1996, District of Columbia; 1997, Maine. *Education:* University of North Carolina-Chapel Hill (B.A., with distinction, 1991); Emory University (J.D., with distinction, 1994). Member, Emory International Law Review. Author: "Article V(b)(2) of the New York Convention," Emory International Law Review, 1993. *Member:* The District of Columbia Bar; State Bar of Georgia; Maryland State Bar Association; Federal Communications Bar Association. ***PRACTICE AREAS:*** Telecommunications; Antitrust; Legislation. ***Email:*** elise@technologylaw.com

SPECIAL COUNSEL

LARRY A. BLOSSER, born Wooster, Ohio, November 29, 1946; admitted to bar, 1978, Ohio; 1982, District of Columbia. *Education:* Michigan State University (B.A., with high honors, 1968); Kent State University (B.S., 1971); The University of Akron School of Law (J.D., 1978). ***PRACTICE AREAS:*** Telecommunications. ***Email:*** larrg@technologylaw.com

MICHAEL D. McNEELY, born Orange, New Jersey, October 31, 1945; admitted to bar, 1976, Oregon; 1980, District of Columbia and The U.S. Supreme Court. *Education:* Rensselaer Polytechnical Institute (B.S., 1969); Williamette University College of Law (J.D., summa cum laude, 1976). Comment Editor, Willamette Law Journal, 1975-1976. Trial Attorney, Antitrust Division, United States Department of Justice, 1976-1988. United States v. At&t., 1979-1982. Assistant Director, Bureau of Competition, United States Federal Trade Commission, 1988-1999. *Member:* District of Columbia Bar; Oregon State Bar (inactive); American Bar Association (Section of Intellectual Property Law; Section of Antitrust Law; Forum on Communications Law); Federal Communications Bar Association. ***PRACTICE AREAS:*** Antitrust Litigation and Counseling; Telecommunications Law; Civil Litigation; Administrative Litigation. ***Email:*** mike@technologylaw.com

ASSOCIATES

JEREMY D. MARCUS, born New Hyde Park, New York, October 3, 1971; admitted to bar, 1997, New York; 1998, Georgia (Not admitted in District of Columbia). *Education:* University of Pennsylvania (B.A., cum laude, 1993); Georgetown University (J.D., 1996). Author: "Educating Immigrant Children: To What End?" 10 Geo.Immigr.L.J. 485. *Member:* New York State Bar Association; State Bar of Georgia; Federal Communications Bar Association. ***PRACTICE AREAS:*** Communications Law; Telecommunications Law; Technology Law; Transactional Law. ***Email:*** jeremy@technologylaw.com

KRISTIN L. SMITH, born Indianapolis, Indiana, June 23, 1972; admitted to bar, 1999, District of Columbia. *Education:* Butler University (B.S., 1994); Indiana University School of Law-Indianapolis (J.D., 1998). *American Bar Association; Member:* Federal Communications Bar Association; Women in Cable and Telecommunications. ***PRACTICE AREAS:*** Communications Law; Technology Law. ***Email:*** kristin@technologylaw.com

PATRICK J. O'CONNOR, born Buffalo, New York, September 12, 1973; admitted to bar, 2000, Virginia (Not admitted in District of Columbia). *Education:* University of Richmond (B.A., cum laude, 1995); Georgetown University Law Center (J.D., 1999). *Member:* Virginia Bar Association; Federal Communications Bar Association; Virginia Trial Lawyers Association. ***PRACTICE AREAS:*** Telecommunications Law; Antitrust Law; International Law; Corporate Law. ***Email:*** patrick@technologylaw.com

(This Listing Continued)

LAW OFFICE OF PAUL S. BLUMENTHAL, P.A.

WASHINGTON, D.C.

(See Annapolis, Maryland)

Civil and Criminal Litigation, Personal Injury, Medical Malpractice, Products Liability, Slip and Fall, Automobile Accidents, Family Law, Divorce, Child Custody, Child Support, Adoptions, Real Estate Litigation, Criminal Defense, Driving While Intoxicated, Traffic Violations, Business Law, Contract Negotiation and Insurance Coverage.

BODE & GRENIER, L.L.P.

1150 CONNECTICUT AVENUE, N.W., NINTH FLOOR
WASHINGTON, D.C. 20036
Telephone: 202-828-4100
Fax: 202-828-4130
Fax: 202-835-3219
Email: bodegrenier@bode.com
URL: http://www.bode.com

Antitrust, Commercial, Energy, Environmental, Intellectual Property, Internet/Technology, Complex Business Litigation, Insurance, Nationwide Civil Rights, Personal Injury, Wrongful Death, Real Estate, Construction.

FIRM PROFILE: Bode & Grenier is a civil litigation boutique with a nationwide practice representing clients before state and federal courts and federal administrative bodies. The firm has enjoyed successes meriting nationwide reporting in newspaper and television, most recently in cases involving Internet law and civil rights. Mr. Bode's practice involves complex commercial litigation in such areas as environment, energy, securities and derivatives, and intellectual property law. Mr. Grenier has been a staunch advocate for the rights of individuals in leading civil rights, consumer advocacy, and wrongful death cases. The combination has been symbiotic. The commercial litigation practice has developed expanded capabilities from the demanding trial schedule of the personal injury practice, while the civil rights practice has benefited from the sophisticated business law advocacy practiced by the firm.

The firm makes wide use of top associate counsel, as well as other premier practitioners in specialized practice areas. In this manner, the firm is able to offer clients the capabilities of a large firm, with the individual attention and efficiency of a smaller firm.

(This Listing Continued)

BODE & GRENIER, L.L.P., Washington—Continued

ROBERT M. BECKMAN (1930-2000).

WILLIAM H. BODE, born El Paso, Texas, April 18, 1942; admitted to bar, 1972, District of Columbia and Virginia; 1973, U.S. District Court for the District of Columbia; 1976, U.S. Supreme Court; 1978, U.S. Temporary Emergency Court of Appeals and U.S. Court of Appeals, Ninth Circuit; 1979, U.S. Court of Appeals, Fifth Circuit; 1982, Court of International Trade; 1991, U.S. Court of Appeals for the Federal Circuit and U.S. Court of Appeals, District of Columbia Circuit. *Education:* United States Air Force Academy (B.S., 1964); Stanford University (M.S., 1966); George Washington University (J.D., 1971). Co-Author: "Opinion: Discovery in Superfund Cases," 1 Chemical Waste Litigation Reporter 654, 1986; "Crimes and Misdemeanors-Enforcement Under the 1990 Clean Air Act Amendments," Hazmat World, May, 1991. Author, "Lender Liability and CERCLA'S Security Interest Exemption," Hazmat World, September, 1991; Author, "Tort Theories Offer Revenge for Innocent LUST Buyers," Hazmat World, April, 1992: Co-Author, "Avoiding Criminal Liability for Environmental Noncompliance," Hazardous Materials Management, Spring, 1993. Lecturer: "Recovery for Environmental Response Costs Under Comprehensive General Liability Insurance Policies," Hazmat International Conference, June, 1991. ***PRACTICE AREAS:*** Environmental Law; Energy Law; Antitrust; Administrative Law; Intellectual Property; Litigation. ***Email:*** wbode@bode.com

PETER C. GRENIER, born Washington, D.C., December 7, 1963; admitted to bar, 1988, Maryland; 1989, District of Columbia; 1990, U.S. District Court, District of Columbia; 1991, U.S. District Court, District of Maryland; 1993, U.S. Court of Appeals, District of Columbia Circuit; 1997, U.S. Court of Appeals, Fourth Circuit. *Education:* University of Notre Dame (B.A., 1985; J.D., 1988). Law Clerk, the Honorable Sylvia Bacon, District of Columbia Superior Court, 1988-1989. Author: "Environmental Issues of the 1990's," Executive Update (1990). *Member:* District of Columbia Bar; Maryland State Bar Association, Incorporated; American Bar Associations. ***LANGUAGES:*** French, Latin. ***PRACTICE AREAS:*** Business Litigation; Real Estate Construction Litigation; Personal Injury; Medical Malpractice; Wrongful Death. ***Email:*** pgrenier@bode.com

JAMES M. LUDWIG, III, born Washington, D.C., August 16, 1953; admitted to bar, 1988, Virginia; 1991 District of Columbia; 1997, U.S. Court of Appeals, Ninth Circuit. *Education:* Hamilton College (B.A., 1975); University of Virginia (J.D., 1988). Phi Beta Kappa. Member, National Litigation Panel, University of Virginia School of Law, 1994-1998. *Member:* American Bar Association. ***PRACTICE AREAS:*** Civil Rights; Internet Litigation; Computer Litigation; Commercial Litigation; Product Liability. ***Email:*** jludwig@bode.com

SAUL J. SINGER, born Brooklyn, New York, October 23, 1951; admitted to bar, 1990, Maryland and U.S. District Court, District of Maryland; 1991, District of Columbia. *Education:* Brooklyn College; University of Baltimore (J.D., magna cum laude, 1989). Elected Member, Heuisler Honor Society. Author: "Flooding the Fifth Amendment: The N.F.I.P. and the Takings Clause," Boston College Environmental Affairs Law Review, Vol. 17. No. 2. 1990. ***PRACTICE AREAS:*** Litigation; Civil Litigation; Professional Discipline. ***Email:*** ssinger@bode.com

DAVID H. SAFFERN, born St. Louis, Missouri, February, 16, 1949; admitted to bar, 1975, District of Columbia; 1977, U.S. District Court for the District of Columbia and U.S. Court of Appeals for the District of Columbia Circuit; 1991, Maryland. *Education:* Washington College (B.A., cum laude, 1971); Georgetown University (J.D., 1975). Phi Alpha Theta; Omicron Delta Kappa. Law Clerk to the Hon. Bruce S. Mencher, District of Columbia Superior Court, 1975-1977. Assistant U.S. Attorney for the District of Columbia, 1978-1990. Deputy Chief, Felony Trial Division, 1989-1990. *Member:* The District of Columbia Bar; American Bar Association. ***PRACTICE AREAS:*** Real Property Tax and Assessment Appeals; Eminent Domain; Litigation. ***Email:*** dsaffern@bode.com

ASSOCIATES

CLIFTON MERRITT MOUNT, born Washington, D.C., September, 16, 1961; admitted to bar, 1988, Maryland; 1989, District of Columbia; 1991, U.S. District Court, District of Maryland and U.S. District Court, District of Columbia. *Education:* Denison University (B.A., 1983); Pepperdine University; Wake Forest University (J.D., 1988). Phi Delta Phi. Guest Lecturer, District of Columbia Labor and Employment Law, National Business Institute, 1995. Lecturer: Third Party Coverage, National Business Institute, 1996; Insurance Coverage Law, National Business Institute, 1997. Invited Panel Speaker, Emerging Trends in Workers' Compensation Law, National Council of Compensation Insurers, Annual Symposium, 1996. Maryland Health Claims Arbitration Panelist. *Member:* The District of Columbia Bar (Member, Coordinating Committee for Revision of District of Columbia Practice Manual, 3rd Ed.); Bar Association of the District of Columbia (Young Lawyers Section Newsletter Editor, 1991 and 1992; Executive Council, 1991-1994; Liaison to Young Lawyers

(This Listing Continued)

Division, ABA, 1993-1994); American Bar Association. ***LANGUAGES:*** French. ***PRACTICE AREAS:*** Insurance Litigation; Professional Malpractice; Workers' Compensation Defense; Construction Litigation; Civil Litigation; Personal Injury; Civil Rights Litigation. ***Email:*** cmount@bode.com

MARC ERIC PASEKOFF, born Miami, Florida, February 2, 1967; admitted to bar, 1992, Florida and Maryland; 1993, District of Columbia; 1997, U.S. District Court, District of Maryland; 1998, U.S. District Court, District of Columbia and U.S. Court of Appeals, Fourth Circuit. *Education:* University of Virginia (B.A., psychology, with honors, 1988); University of Florida (J.D., 1991). Member, Florida Law Review, 1989-1991. *Member:* District of Columbia Bar; Maryland State Bar Association; The Florida Bar. ***PRACTICE AREAS:*** Civil Litigation; Commercial Litigation. ***Email:*** mpasekoff@bode.com

LORI JEAN POLACHECK, born Milwaukee, Wisconsin, December 24, 1962; admitted to bar, 1989, Illinois and U.S. District Court, Northern District of Illinois; 1991, Washington; 1992, U.S. District Court, Western District of Washington; 1994, Massachusetts and U.S. District Court, District of Massachusetts (Not admitted in District of Columbia). *Education:* University of Michigan (B.A., highest distinction, 1985); University of Chicago (J.D., 1989). Phi Beta Kappa. Mechem Scholar. Edwin F. Mandel Award. Author: "Discovery of Testifying Experts," Washington State Bar News, March 1993. Clinical Lecturer, University of Chicago Law School, 1990-1991. ***PRACTICE AREAS:*** Litigation. ***Email:*** lpolacheck@bode.com

DARRIN P. SOBIN, born Long Island, New York, October 20, 1965; admitted to bar, 1994, District of Columbia; 2000, U.S. District Court, District of Columbia; 2001, Maryland. *Education:* George Washington University (B.A., 1988); District of Columbia School of Law (J.D., cum laude, 1992). Member, District of Columbia Law Review. Law Clerk to Hon. June L. Green, U.S. District Court for the District of Columbia. President, Moot Court Association, 1990-1991. ***PRACTICE AREAS:*** Intellectual Property; Internet Law; Contracts; Litigation; Appellate Practice. ***Email:*** dsobin@bode.com

BETH A. BULGERON, born Hartford, Connecticut, February 22, 1971; admitted to bar, 2000, California; 2001, District of Columbia. *Education:* University of Wisconsin-Madison (B.A., 1993); McGeorge School of Law, University of the Pacific (J.D., 2000). ***PRACTICE AREAS:*** Complex Business Litigation; Appellate Practice; Construction Law. ***Email:*** bbulgeron@bode.com

ASSOCIATE COUNSEL

WILLIAM CONRAD VON RAAB, born New York, N.Y., January 26, 1942; admitted to bar, 1966, Virginia and New York; 1982, District of Columbia; 1983, U.S. Court of International Trade. *Education:* Yale University (A.B., 1963); University of Virginia (LL.B., 1966). U.S. Commissioner of Customs, 1986-1989. (Also practicing individually Washington, D.C. and Alexandria, Virginia). ***PRACTICE AREAS:*** International Trade Law. ***Email:*** wvonraab@bode.com

JOHN UMANA, born Manhattan, New York, May 31, 1947; admitted to bar, 1977, Michigan; 1978, District of Columbia. *Education:* Manhattan College (B.A., summa cum laude, 1969); University of Michigan (M.A., 1972; Ph.D., 1975; J.D., magna cum laude, 1977). Kent Fellow, Danforth Foundation. Member, Editorial Board, Michigan Law Review, 1975-1977. *Member:* The District of Columbia Bar; State Bar of Michigan; American Bar Association. (Also Practicing Individually at Washington, D.C.). ***Email:*** jumana@bode.com

OF COUNSEL

CLARK R. SILCOX, born Los Angeles, California, April 27, 1953; admitted to bar, 1978, California; 1979, District of Columbia; 1981, U.S. Court of Appeals, District of Columbia Circuit; 1984, U.S. Supreme Court; 1996. U.S. Court of Appeals, Second Circuit. *Education:* University of California at Berkeley (B.A., with high honors, 1975); George Washington University (J.D., with honors, 1978). Author: "Economic Theory and Antitrust Law," in Federal Antitrust Laws, Appendix D, Oppenheim, Weston & McCarthy eds., 1981; "Unfair Methods of Competition: The Courts Revise Proof of Injury To Competition In Antitrust Cases Under Section 5 of FTC Act," 29 Antitrust Bulletin, Fall, 1984; "The Robinson-Patman Act and Competitive Fairness: Balancing The Economic and Social Dimensions of Antitrust," 31 Antitrust Bulletin, Fall 1986. *Member:* The District of Columbia Bar; State Bar of California; American Bar Association (Member, Sections on: Antitrust Law; Corporation, Banking and Business Law). ***PRACTICE AREAS:*** Antitrust and Trade Regulation. ***Email:*** csilcox@bode.com

REPRESENTATIVE CLIENTS: Atchison, Topeka & Santa Fe Railway Co.; Anheuser Busch Cos.; Consumers Power Co.; FFP Partners, LLP; J.D. Street & Co.; Reynolds Metals Co.; USA Petroleum Corp.; U.S. Oil & Refining Co.

BOIES, SCHILLER & FLEXNER LLP

5301 WISCONSIN AVENUE, N.W., SUITE 570
WASHINGTON, D.C. 20015
Telephone: 202-237-2727
Facsimile: 202-237-6131
URL: http://www.bsfllp.com

Armonk, New York Office: 80 Business Park Drive, Suite 110. Telephone: 914-273-9800. Facsimile: 914-273-9810.

Orlando, Florida Office: 390 North Orange Avenue, Suite 1890. Telephone: 407-425-7118. Facsimile: 407-425-7047.

Hollywood, Florida Office: 2435 Hollywood Boulevard. Telephone: 954-929-1190. Facsimile: 954-929-1185.

Hanover, New Hampshire Office: 26 South Main Street. Telephone: 603-643-9090. Facsimile: 603-643-9010.

Palm Beach Gardens, Florida Office: 11380 Prosperity Farms Road, Suite 110A. Telephone: 561-622-9700. Facsimile: 561-622-4400.

Albany, New York Office: 100 State Street, 12207. Telephone: 518-434-0600. Telecopier: 518-434-0665.

Oakland, California Office: 1970 Broadway, Suite 630, 94612. Telephone: 510-874-1000. Telecopier: 510-874-1460.

Litigation in all Federal and State Courts. Antitrust, Securities, Commercial and Banking Law, Bankruptcy, Criminal, Civil RICO, Appellate Practice, First Amendment and Civil Rights, Libel, Intellectual Property, Professional Liability, Employment, Environmental and Arbitration.

PARTNERS

DAVID R. BOYD, born Paducah, Kentucky, November 25, 1946; admitted to bar, 1973, Virginia and District of Columbia; 1974, U.S. Supreme Court. *Education:* Vanderbilt University (B.A., cum laude, 1968); University of Virginia (J.D., 1973). Fulbright Fellow to Argentina. Executive Editor, University of Virginia Law Review, 1972-1973. Law Clerk to: Hon. Carl McGowan, U.S. Court of Appeals for the District of Columbia, 1973-1974; Justice Lewis F. Powell, Jr., U.S. Supreme Court, 1974-1975. Executive Assistant to Chairman of Securities and Exchange Commission, 1975-1976. ***LANGUAGES:*** Spanish. ***PRACTICE AREAS:*** Trial Litigation; Appellate Litigation; Corporate. ***Email:*** dboyd@bsfllp.com

MICHAEL A. BRILLE, born Las Vegas, Nevada, January 18, 1968; admitted to bar, 1994, California; 1998, District of Columbia. *Education:* University of San Diego (B.B.A., 1990); Yale University (J.D., 1993). Phi Alpha Delta. Beta Gamma Sigma. Recipient, John Currier Gallagher Prize. Law Clerk to the Honorable Philip M. Pro, U.S. District Court, District of Nevada, 1993-1995. Trial Attorney, U.S. Department of Justice, Civil Division, Washington, D.C., 1995-1997. *Member:* State Bar of California; The District of Columbia Bar. [Judge Advocate General's Corp's, U.S. Army Reserve, Captain, 1995—]. ***PRACTICE AREAS:*** Antitrust; Commercial Litigation. ***Email:*** mbrille@bsfllp.com

JAMES P. DENVIR, III, born New York, N.Y., October 8, 1950; admitted to bar, 1975, Florida; 1979, District of Columbia. *Education:* Yale University (B.A., 1972); University of Florida (J.D., 1975). Order of the Coif. Articles Editor, University of Florida Law Review, 1974-1975. Trial Attorney, 1975-1984 and Chief, AT&T Trial Staff, 1982-1984, Antitrust Division, U.S. Department of Justice. ***PRACTICE AREAS:*** Antitrust; Commercial Litigation. ***Email:*** jdenvir@bsfllp.com

DONALD L. FLEXNER, born White Plains, New York, June 20, 1941; admitted to bar, 1967, New York; 1980, U.S. Supreme Court; 1981, District of Columbia. *Education:* New York University (B.A., 1964; LL.B., 1967). Trial Attorney, 1967-1975, Section Chief, 1976-1978, Deputy Assistant Attorney General, 1978-1980, Antitrust Division, U.S. Department of Justice. *Member:* New York State, District of Columbia and American (Chairman, Industry Regulation Committee, Antitrust Section; Member, Antitrust Section Task Force on Antitrust Division) Bar Associations. ***PRACTICE AREAS:*** Antitrust; Litigation. ***Email:*** dflexner@bsfllp.com

WILLIAM A. ISAACSON, born Milwaukee, Wisconsin, 1960; admitted to bar, 1987, Pennsylvania; 1988, District of Columbia. *Education:* University of Redlands (B.A., 1982); University of Virginia (J.D., 1986). Order of the Coif. Recipient, Margaret G. Hyde Award. Editor, Virginia Law Review, 1985-1986. Author, "Garcia v. San Antonio Metropolitan Transit Authority: Antifederalism Revisited," 21 University of Toledo Law Review 147, Fall 1989. Law Clerk to Chief Judge Harrison L. Winter, U.S. Court of Appeals, Fourth Circuit, 1986-1987. Member, Advisory Board, AARP National Litigation Project, 1991—. Partner, Kaye, Scholer, Fierman, Hays & Handler, LLP 1996-1997. *Member:* The District of Columbia Bar. ***PRACTICE AREAS:*** Commercial Litigation; Arbitration. ***Email:*** wisaacson@bsfllp.com

AMY J. MAUSER, born New York, N.Y., May 17, 1963; admitted to bar, 1989, Massachusetts; 1990, District of Columbia. *Education:* Mount Holyoke College (B.A., cum laude, 1985); Washington College of Law of the American University (J.D., 1988). Member and Articles Editor, American University Law

(This Listing Continued)

Review, 1986-1988. Law Clerk to the Honorable Charles R. Richey, U.S. District Court, District of Columbia, 1988-1990. ***PRACTICE AREAS:*** Commercial Litigation. ***Email:*** amauser@bsfllp.com

JONATHAN D. SCHILLER, born 1946; admitted to bar, 1973, District of Columbia. *Education:* Columbia University (B.A., 1969; J.D., 1973). Author of numerous publications and articles including: "Parallel Proceedings Involving International Arbitration," International Disputes Seminar, ICC, Los Angeles California (Oct. 1999); "Identifying and Applying the Law Governing the Arbitration Procedure: Role of the Law of the Place of Arbitration, A Commentary," ICCA Congress Series No. 9, Paris, May 1998. Co-Author: "Providing For Confidentiality In International Mediation," ICC Institute of International Business Law and Practice, October 1995; "Destruction of Grand Jury Documents," Destruction of Evidence, John Wiley & Sons, 1989; "Modification of Pension Fund Contributions During the Term of a Collective Agreement: The 1987 Employment and Economic Security Pact," 90 West Virginia Law Review 843, Spring 1988; "The Legal Liability of Private Security Guard Company for the Criminal Act of Third Parties," An Overview, The Annals 91, July 1988. Law Clerk to the Hon. Charles R. Richey, U.S. District Court, District of Columbia, 1973-1974. Member, Rogovin, Huge & Schiller, 1976-1990. Member, Judicial Conference of the District of Columbia Circuit, 1976-1981, 1983—. Member, Standing Committee on Pro Se and Pro Bono Matters of the Judicial Conference of the District of Columbia, 1984-1992. Director, Irwin Sweeney Miller Foundation, 1976—. Board Member, Washington Council of Lawyers, 1976. President, Washington Tennis and Education Foundation, 1993—. *Member:* The District of Columbia Bar; Milan Chamber of National and International Arbitration; Club of Arbitrators. Fellow, American Bar Foundation. ***PRACTICE AREAS:*** Litigation; Civil Litigation; Criminal Defense; International Arbitration. ***Email:*** jschiller@bsfllp.com

W. TODD THOMAS, born Pittsburgh, Pennsylvania, June 20, 1965; admitted to bar, 1993, Florida; 1994, U.S. District Court, Southern District of Florida; 1995, District of Columbia; 1997, U.S. District Court, Middle District of Florida. *Education:* University of Florida (B.A., 1986); Adam Mickiewic University, Poland (1987); George Washington University (M.A., National Security Studies, 1989); Yale University (J.D., 1993). Phi Beta Kappa. Recipient: Brian Piccolo Scholar-Athlete Award; School of International Affairs Graduate Fellowship (GWU), U.S. Department of State, 1989. Law Clerk to the Honorable José A. Gonzalez, Jr., U.S. District Court, Southern District of Florida, 1993-1995. Associate, Kaye, Scholar, Fierman, Hays & Handler LLP, 1995-1998. *Member:* The Florida Bar; The District of Columbia Bar. ***PRACTICE AREAS:*** Litigation; International Arbitration. ***Email:*** tthomas@bsfllp.com

OF COUNSEL

GEORGE T. FRAMPTON, JR., born Washington, D.C., August 24, 1944; admitted to bar, 1970, New York; 1971, District of Columbia; 1983, U.S. Supreme Court. *Education:* Yale College (B.A., cum laude, 1965); London School of Economics, England (M.Sc., with distinction, 1966); Harvard University (J.D., magna cum laude, 1969). Treasurer, Harvard Law Review, 1968-1969. Law Clerk to Mr. Justice Harry Blackmun, U.S. Supreme Court, 1971-1972. Assistant Special Prosecutor, Watergate Special Prosecution Force, 1973-1975. Member, Rogovin, Huge and Lenzer, 1976-1985. Deputy Director, U.S. Nuclear Regulatory Commission Special Inquiry Group on Three Mile Island, 1979-1980. Assistant Independent Counsel, Investigation into Allegations Concerned Edwin Meese III, 1984. Special Independent Counsel, State of Alaska, 1985. President, The Wilderness Society, 1986-1993. Assistant Secretary of the Interior for Fish, Wildlife and Parks, 1993-1997. Of Counsel, Boies and Schiller, 1998. Chairman, White House Council on Environmental Quality, 1998-2001. ***PRACTICE AREAS:*** Litigation; Civil Litigation; Criminal Defense; Non-Profit Law; Environmental Law. ***Email:*** gframpton@bsfllp.com

KIMBERLY J. TUCKER, born Baltimore, Maryland, November 28, 1959; admitted to bar, 1985, Florida; 1986, U.S. District Court, Middle District of Florida; 1987, U.S. Court of Appeals, Eleventh Circuit; 1990, Maine and U.S. District Court, Middle and Northern District of Florida; 2001, U.S. Supreme Court (Not admitted in District of Columbia). *Education:* Florida State University (B.S., cum laude, 1981); University of Virginia (J.D., 1985). Assistant Attorney General, 1986— and Deputy General Counsel, 1991-1993 and 1996-2001, Florida Attorney General's Office. Special Assistant Attorney General, Florida Department of Corrections, 1990-1991. Special Assistant U.S. Attorney, Northern District of Florida, 1991—. General Counsel, Florida Department of Health and Rehabilitative Services, 1993-1996. ***REPORTED CASES:*** Palm Beach County Canvassing Bd. v. Harris, 772 So.2d 1273, 25 Fla. L. Weekly S1126, 26 Fla. L. Weekly S26 (Fla., Dec. 11, 2000) (NO. SC00-2348, SC00-2349); Chiles v. State Employees Attorneys Guild, 734 So.2d 1030, 161 L.R.R.M. (BNA) 2359, 138 Lav.Cas. P 58,664, 24 Fla. L. Weekly S225 (Fla., May 20, 1999) (NO. 93,655); State v. American Tobacco Co., 723 So.2d 263, 12 Fla.L. Weekly S593 (Fla., Nov. 13, 1998) (NO.93,14893,195,93,633); Kerrigan, Estess, Rankin & McLeod v. State, 711 So.2d 1246, 23 Fla.L.Weekly D1243 (Fla.App.4 Dist., May 18, 1998) (NO. 97-4008, 97-4328, 97-42222, 97-4311); State v. Florida Police Benev. Ass'n, 688 So.2d 326, 155 L.R.R.M. (BNA) 2765, 22 Fla.L. Weekly S85, 21 Employee Benefits Cas. 1862 (Fla., Feb. 20, 1997)

(This Listing Continued)

BOIES, SCHILLER & FLEXNER LLP, Washington—Continued

(NO. 89,181); State, Dept. of Health and Rehabilitative Services v. Lee, 665 So.2d 304, 20 Fla. L. Weekly D2735 (Fla. App. 1 Dist., Dec. 13, 1995) (NO. 93-1350, 93-1411); Department of Health and Rehabilitative Services v. B.J.M., 656 So.2d 906, 20 Fla.L.Weekly S188 (Fla., Apr. 27, 1995) (NO. 83,067); State v. Family Bank of Hallandale, 623 So.2d 474, 18 Fla. L. Weekly S409, 18 Fla. L. Weekly S409, 18 Fla. L. Weekly S 504, 20 UCC Rep.Serv.2d 1273, 21 UCC Rep.Serv.2d 665 (Fla., Jul 01, 1993) (NO. 79,449); Chiles v. United Faculty of Florida, 615 So.2d 671, 143 L.R.R.M. (BNA) 2136, 143 L.R.R.M. (BNA) 286, 18 Fla.L.Weekly S143 (Fla., Mar.11, 1993) (NO. 81,252); State v. Florida Police Benev. Ass'n, Inc., 613 So.2d 415, 142 L.R.R.M. (BNA) 2224, 18 Fla. L. Weekly SI (Fla., Dec. 24, 1992) (NO. 77,842); State v. Family Bank of Hallandale, 593 So.2d 581, 17 Fla. L. Weekly D419 (Fla.App. 1 Dist., Feb 05, 1992) (NO. 91-350); State v. Florida Police Benev. Ass'n, Inc., 580 So.2d 619 (Fla.App. 1 Dist., Jan.25, 1991) (NO. 90-1236); Lane v. Kaney, 557 So.2d 210, 15 Fla. L. Weekly D509 (Fla.App. 5 Dist., Feb. 22, 1990) (NO. 89-2312); Holland v. Hainwright, 499 So.2d 21, 11 Fla. L. Weekly 2620 (Fla.App. 1 Dist., Dec 12, 1986) (NO. BM-46); Adams v. Wainwright, 875 F.2d 1536 (11th Cir.(Fla.), Jun 27, 1989) (NO. 87-3865); Card v. Dugger, 871 F.2d 1023 (11th Cir.(Fla.), Apr. 28, 1989) (NO.88-3563); Bobby M. v. Chiles, 907 F.Supp. 368 (N.D.Fla., Oct. 29, 1995) (NO.TCA 83-7003-MMP); Celestineo v. Singletary, 147 F.R.D. 258 (M.D.Fla., Mar.30, 1993) (NO. 72-109-CIV-J-14, 72-94-CIV-J-14); Wilson v. Franceschi, 735 F.Supp. 395 (M.D.Fla., Feb. 05, 1990) (NO.89-739CIV-T-17C); Card v. Dugger, 709 F.Supp. 1098 (M.D.Fla., Jun 17, 1988) (NO. 86-572-CIV-J-14); Bush v. Palm Beach County Canvassing Board, 531, U.S. 70, 121 S.Ct. 471, 148 L.Ed 2d 366 (2000) #00-836 (Counsel to Respondent Attorney General Robert A. Butterworth). ***PRACTICE AREAS:*** Litigation; Constitutional Law. ***Email:*** ktucker@bsfllp.com

RESIDENT ASSOCIATES

KEVIN R. ANTHONY, born Boston, Massachusetts, June 20, 1959; admitted to bar, 1998, Florida, U.S. District Court, Southern, Middle and Northern Districts of Florida and U.S. Court of Appeals, 11th Circuit (Not admitted in District of Columbia). *Education:* University of Florida; Barry University (B.P.S., 1994); University of Miami (J.D., magna cum laude, 1998). Order of the Coif; Phi Delta Phi. Recipient, Dean's Honor Scholarship. Member, University of Miami Law Review, 1997-1998. Associate, Morgan, Lewis & Bockius LLP, 1998-2000. ***PRACTICE AREAS:*** Complex Commercial Litigation; Antitrust Litigation; Intellectual Property Litigation; Employment Litigation. ***Email:*** kanthony@bsfllp.com

ELLEN BLANCHARD, born Greenfield, Massachusetts, March 24, 1975; admitted to bar, 2000, Virginia (Not admitted in District of Columbia). *Education:* Ohio Wesleyan University (B.A., International Business, Japanese Studies, Psychology, 1997); Washington College of Law, American University (J.D., 2000). Psi Chi. ***PRACTICE AREAS:*** International Arbitration; Antitrust. ***Email:*** eblanchard@bsfllp.com

KERRI L. BOYER, born Upper Darby, Pennsylvania, May 28, 1968; admitted to bar, 1993, Virginia; 1998, South Carolina (Not admitted in District of Columbia). *Education:* University of Virginia (B.A., 1990); Louisiana State University (J.D., 1993). *Member:* Virginia State Bar; South Carolina Bar. ***PRACTICE AREAS:*** Litigation; International Arbitration. ***Email:*** kboyer@bsfllp.com

DARA CACCIAMANI, born Scranton, Pennsylvania, April 16, 1973; admitted to bar, 2000, North Carolina (Not admitted in District of Columbia). *Education:* Bloomsburg University (B.A., 1995); North Carolina Central University (J.D., 2000). Member, North Carolina Central University Law Journal, 1998-2000. *Member:* North Carolina and American Bar Associations. ***PRACTICE AREAS:*** Copyright; Trademark; Antitrust; General Commercial Litigation. ***Email:*** dcacciamani@bsfllp.com

SCOTT E. GANT, born New York, N.Y., January 13, 1969; admitted to bar, 1995, Pennsylvania; 1997, District of Columbia. *Education:* Wesleyan University (B.A., 1991); Harvard University (J.D., 1995). Phi Beta Kappa. Law Clerk to Judge Scirica, U.S. Court of Appeals, Third Circuit, 1995-1996. Author: "The Once and Future President: Constitutional Interstices and the Twenty-Second Amendment," 83 Minnesota Law Review 565, 1999 (co-authored with Bruce G. Peabody); "Bajakajian and Excessive Fines Claims Against the United States," 8 Federal Circuit Bar Journal 39, 1999; "Judicial Supremacy and Nonjudicial Interpretation of the Constitution," 24 Hastings Constitutional Law Quarterly 359, 1997; "Musings on a Constitutional Mystery: Missing Presidents and 'Headless Monsters '?", 14 Constitutional Commentary 83, 1997 (co-authored with Bruce G. Peabody). *Member:* The District of Columbia Bar. ***PRACTICE AREAS:*** Commercial Litigation; Antitrust; Constitutional Law; Media Law. ***Email:*** sgant@bsfllp.com

SETH A. GOLDBERG, born Philadelphia, Pennsylvania, July 21, 1971; admitted to bar, 1999, Florida (Not admitted in District of Columbia). *Education:* Temple University (B.A., Political Science, 1994; J.D., 1999). Staff Member, 1997-1998 and Senior Note Comment Editor, 1998-1999, Temple Political and Civil Rights Law Review. Author: "O'Dell v. Netherland: Unconstitutional Death Sentence Affirmed on a Technicality," Temple Political and Civil Rights Law Review, Fall 1998. *Member:* The Florida Bar. ***PRACTICE AREAS:*** Antitrust; Complex Litigation. ***Email:*** sgoldberg@bsfllp.com

WILLIAM C. JACKSON, born Chelsea, Massachusetts, February 12, 1969; admitted to bar, 1998, Massachusetts; 2000, New York (Not admitted in District of Columbia). *Education:* Harvard College (B.A., cum laude, 1991); Columbia Law School (J.D., 1997). Harlan Fiske Stone Scholar; Tony Patiño Fellow. Law Clerk: Judge Norma Shapiro, U.S. District Court, Eastern District of Pennsylvania, 1997-1998; Judge Frank Coffin, U.S. Court of Appeals, First Circuit, 1998-1999. Co-Author: "Teaching the Skills of Settlement," 46 SMU L. Rev. 1985 (Summer 1993). Lecturer on Law, Stanford Law School, 1996. ***PRACTICE AREAS:*** Litigation; International Arbitration. ***Email:*** wjackson@bsfllp.com

SAMUEL C. KAPLAN, born Houston, Texas, 1971; admitted to bar, 1998, Maryland and District of Columbia. *Education:* University of Texas (B.A., summa cum laude, 1992); Harvard University (J.D., magna cum laude, 1996). Phi Beta Kappa. Law Clerk, Chief Judge Richard S. Arnold, 8th Circuit, 1996-1997. Author: "Grab Bag of Principles or Historical Grab Bag? The Constitutionalization of Common Law," 49 S.C.L. Rev. 463, 1998; "Court's Redistricting Ruling Draws Mixed Reaction," *Congressional Quarterly Weekly Report*, March 6, 1993: Vol. 51, No. 10 p. 538. Co-Author, "High Court Says State Courts Get First Shot at Remaps," *Congressional Quarterly Weekly Report*, February 27, 1993: Vol. 51, No. 9, p. 477. Instructor, University of Miami School of Law, 1997-1998. *Member:* Maryland State Bar Association. ***PRACTICE AREAS:*** General Commercial Litigation. ***Email:*** skaplan@bsfllp.com

ALFRED P. LEVITT, born Manhasset, New York, February 19, 1969; admitted to bar, 1995, New York; 2000, District of Columbia. *Education:* Roger Williams College (B.F.A., magna cum laude, 1991); Temple Law School (J.D., magna cum laude, 1994). Executive Editor, Temple Law Review, 1993-1994. Author: "Corporate Responses to Potential Illegal Conduct Identified in the Course of an Audit," INSIGHTS: The Corporate & Securities Law Advisor, Vol. 14, No. 2 (Aspen Law & Business February 2000) (Co-authored); "Recent Trends in Securities Litigation," SEC Disclosure & Accounting Conference (Glasser Legal Works 1999) (Co-authored); "Taking on a New Direction: The Rehnquist-Scalia Approach to Regulatory Takings," 66 Temp .L. Rev. 193 (1993). ***PRACTICE AREAS:*** Antitrust; Trade Regulation; Securities. ***Email:*** alevitt@bsfllp.com

NOAH MESSING, born New York, N.Y., August 12, 1974; (admission pending). *Education:* Emory University (B.A., 1996); Yale University (J.D., 2000). Phi Beta Kappa. Cokes Fellow. Recipient: Potter Stewart Prize; Benjamin N. Cordozo Prize. ***PRACTICE AREAS:*** Antitrust; Complex Civil Litigation; Arbitration; First Amendment. ***Email:*** nmessing@bsfllp.com

CARL JOHN NICHOLS, born Rhinebeck, New York, June 25, 1970; admitted to bar, 1998, Virginia and U.S. Court of Appeals, Fourth Circuit; 2000, District of Columbia; U.S. District Court, Eastern District of Virginia; U.S. District Court, District of Columbia. *Education:* Dartmouth College (B.A., cum laude, 1992); University of Chicago (J.D., with high honors, 1996). Order of the Coif. Member, University of Chicago Law Review. Law Clerk to: Honorable Laurence H. Silberman, U.S. Court of Appeals for the District of Columbia Circuit, 1996-1997; Associate Justice Clarence Thomas, U.S. Supreme Court, 1997-1998. ***PRACTICE AREAS:*** Complex Commercial Litigation; International Arbitration. ***Email:*** cnichols@bsfllp.com

ALISON E. PECK, born Columbus, Indiana, May 16, 1970; admitted to bar, 1997, Indiana (Not admitted in District of Columbia). *Education:* Butler University (B.A., summa cum laude, 1992); Yale University Law School (J.D., 1995). Senior Research Fellow, Global Constitutionalism Project, Yale Law School, 1996-1997. Editor, Yale Law Journal, 1993-1995. Law Clerk: Chief Judge Jon O. Newman, U.S. Court of Appeals, Second Circuit, 1995-1996; Judge G. Federico Mancini, Court of Justice for the European Communities, 1999. Author: "Standing for Protection of Collective Rights in the European Communities," The George Washington International Law Journal. *Member:* Indiana and American Bar Associations. ***LANGUAGES:*** Spanish and French. ***PRACTICE AREAS:*** Commercial Litigation; Arbitration; International Arbitration. ***Email:*** apeck@bsfllp.com

KENNETH F. ROSSMAN IV, born Tucson, Arizona, May 6, 1968; admitted to bar, 1996, Virginia; 1997, District of Columbia and U.S. Court of Federal Claims; 1998, Colorado and U.S. Court of Appeals, 10th Circuit; 1999, U.S. Court of Appeals, 9th Circuit; 2000, U.S. Supreme Court; U.S. District Court, Eastern District of Virginia; U.S. District Court, Eastern District of Michigan. *Education:* University of Virginia (B.A., 1990); George Mason University (J.D., with distinction, 1996). Dean's Scholar. Managing Editor, George Mason Law Review, 1995-1996. Law Clerk: Judge Weinstein, U.S. Court of Federal Claims, 1996-1997; Judge Brorby, U.S. Court of Appeals, Tenth Circuit, 1997-1998. Author: "Key Tronic v. United States: Ratifying an Inequitable Distribution of Private Party Costs Under Superfund by Refusing to Shift Attorney's Fee's," 4 Geo. Mason L. Rev. 113 (1995). *Member:* The District of

(This Listing Continued)

Columbia Bar; American Bar Association (Member: Antitrust Section; Litigation Section). ***PRACTICE AREAS:*** Complex Commercial Litigation; Antitrust. ***Email:*** krossman@bsfllp.com

ALANNA RUTHERFORD, born New York, N.Y., March 13, 1975; admitted to bar, 2001, New York (Not admitted in District of Columbia). *Education:* Goergetown University (B.S.P.S., 1997); Columbia University (J.D., 2000). Harlan Fiske Stone Scholar. ***LANGUAGES:*** French. ***PRACTICE AREAS:*** Antitrust; Commercial Litigation; Telecommunications Law. ***Email:*** arutherford@nsfllp.com

JONATHAN SHERMAN, born Washington, D.C., January 4, 1963; admitted to bar, 1992, New York; 2000, District of Columbia; U.S. Court of Appeals, Eleventh Circuit; U.S. District Court, Southern, Eastern and Western Districts of New York. *Education:* University of Rochester (B.A., Phi Beta Kappa, magna cum laude, 1984); Yale University (M.A., 1989); Stanford University (J.D., 1991). Articles Editor, Stanford Law Review, 1990-1991. Adjunct Associate Professor of Law, Fordham University, 1998-2001. Lecturer, Yale University, 1993. *Member:* Supreme Court Bar Association. ***Email:*** jsherman@bsfllp.com

HERSHEL A. WANCJER, born Southfield, Michigan, April 1, 1973; admitted to bar, 2000, Michigan (Not admitted in District of Columbia). *Education:* University of Michigan (B.A., Political Science, 1995); Case Western Reserve University (J.D., 1999). Executive Notes Editor, Case Western Reserve Journal of International Law. *Member:* State Bar of Michigan. ***LANGUAGES:*** Polish. ***PRACTICE AREAS:*** Antitrust; Complex Litigation. ***Email:*** hwancjer@bsfllp.com

(For complete biographies on other Personnel, see Professional Biographies at: Armonk, New York; Hanover, New Hampshire; Hollywood, Florida; Orlando, FLorida; Oakland, California)

BOND, CONTE & NORMAN, P.L.L.C.

SUITE 900, SOUTH TOWER
601 PENNSYLVANIA AVENUE, N.W.
WASHINGTON, D.C. 20004
Telephone: 202-638-4100
Fax: 202-638-0062
URL: http://www.bondconte&norman

Military Courts Martial, Military Administrative Law, Medical Malpractice Defense, Criminal Defense, Drug Crimes, Capital Crimes, Misdemeanors, Driving While Intoxicated, Business Fraud, White Collar Crime, Civil Practice, Small Business Law, Contracts, Wrongful Death, Personal Injury, Automobile Accidents and Injuries, Wrongful Termination, Employment Litigation, Terrorism Law, Federal Tort Claims.

FIRM PROFILE: For over 14 years the firm's central focus has remained trial work in both civil and criminal courts. Mr. Ferris Bond is a former Department of Justice trial attorney and Ms. Jane Norman is a former JAG Corp litigator. Members of the firm have very significant courtroom experience and they have successfully represented a wide variety of clients. The firm also regularly represents men and women in military courts and with military administrative issues. Law Suits against foreign government sponsored terrorism.

FERRIS R. BOND, born Camden, New Jersey, April 10, 1948; admitted to bar, 1974, Texas; 1983, District of Columbia. *Education:* University of Denver (B.A., 1970); South Texas College of Law (J.D., 1974). ***Email:*** ferrisbond@aol.com

JOSEPH R. CONTE, born Latrobe, Pennsylvania, November 13, 1948; admitted to bar, 1982, District of Columbia and Virginia. *Education:* West Virginia University (B.S., 1970); George Mason University (J.D., 1982). *Member:* Virginia State Bar Association. ***PRACTICE AREAS:*** Criminal Law; Contracts Law; General Practice.

JANE CAROL NORMAN, born Los Angeles, California, February 9, 1951; admitted to bar, 1975, California; 1979, Pennsylvania; 1981, Maryland; 1984, District of Columbia. *Education:* University of California (B.A., 1972); Loyola Marymount University, Los Angeles (J.D., 1975).

JOHN BOND

WASHINGTON, D.C.

(See Fairfax, Virginia)

Business Law, Business Litigation, Business Formation, Disputes, Corporate, Contracts, Zoning and Land Use, e-Commerce, Internet Law.

BONNER KIERNAN TREBACH & CROCIATA

Established in 2001

1250 EYE STREET, N.W.
WASHINGTON, D.C. 20005
Telephone: 202-712-7000
FAX: 202-712-7100
URL: http://www.bktc.net

Rockville, Maryland Office: 51 Monroe Street. Telephone: 301-340-9155. Fax: 301-340-1310.
Fairfax, Virginia Office: 10511 Judicial Drive. Telephone: 703-691-0500. Fax: 703-591-5082.
Boston, Massachusetts Office: One Liberty Square. Telephone: 617-426-3900. Fax: 617-426-0380.
Parsippany, New Jersey Office: 140 Littleton Road, Suite 201. Telephone: 973-335-8480. Fax: 973-299-1337.
New York, New York Office: Empire State Building, Suite 3304. Telephone: 212-268-7535. Fax: 212-268-4965.
Providence, Rhode Island Office: 55 Pine Street. Telephone: 401-273-0100. Fax: 401-273-0101.
Hartford, Connecticut Office: 44 Capitol Avenue, Suite 402. Telephone: 860-249-9900. Fax: 860-246-3727.

General Civil Defense, Appellate and Trial Practice, Civil Mediation and Arbitrations, Product Liability, Malpractice, Property, Casualty, Insurance Law, Construction Litigation, Toxic and Environmental Litigation, Insurance Coverage Disputes, Railroad and Airline Litigation, Employment Law, Commercial Litigation and Counseling, Alternative Dispute Resolutions, Aviation, Computer Law, Technology Law, Consumer Fraud, White Collar Crime.

FIRM PROFILE: Bonner Kiernan Trebach & Crociata is a progressive, specialized law firm dedicated to the practice of corporate defense litigation. The firm concentrates in the following areas: negligence, product liability, malpractice, environmental, regulation and toxic damage, transportation and aviation, employment litigation and counseling, insurance coverage and reinsurance. Bonner Kiernan Trebach & Crociata provides a full range of litigation and counseling services in all these areas of concentration, while tailoring its representation to complement the client's own in-house capabilities in litigation control. Bonner Kiernan Trebach & Crociata was founded to be, and intends to remain, a firm dedicated to providing quality litigation services through personally committed and accessible attorneys and staff. The firm is currently litigating matters in state and federal courts throughout the United States. Bonner Kiernan Trebach & Crociata's philosophy is to provide aggressive, cost-effective case management with an eye to efficiency and quality results.

MEMBERS OF FIRM

JOHN A. KIERNAN, born Boston, Massachusetts, January 24, 1948; admitted to bar, 1974, Massachusetts; 1976, U.S. District Court, District of Massachusetts and U.S. Court of Appeals, First Circuit; 1998, District of Columbia. *Education:* Harvard University (B.A., cum laude, 1970); Boston University (J.D., 1974). Adjunct Professor of Law, New England School of Law, 1987—. Member of the Faculty, National College of District Attorneys, 1982-1988. Chief, Homicide Division, Suffolk District Attorneys Office, 1980-1988. Special Prosecutor, Commonwealth of Massachusetts, 1988—. Conservation Commissioner, Town of Milton, 1993—. Member, Superior Court Commission (Redraft of Criminal Rules), 1994. Member, Massachusetts Judicial Nominating Council, Eastern Region, 1996—. *Member:* Massachusetts Bar Association; Federal Bar Association; Massachusetts District Attorneys Association; National District Attorneys Association; Defense Research Institute. (Resident, Boston, Massachusetts Office). ***PRACTICE AREAS:*** General and Products Liability; Environmental Liability; Commercial Disputes; Employment Discrimination; White Collar Crime. ***Email:*** jkiernan@bktc.net

JOSEPH S. CROCIATA, born Rochester, New York, November 30, 1951; admitted to bar, 1982, Illinois; 1983, District of Columbia and U.S. District Court for the District of Columbia; 1988, U.S. Court of Appeals, District of Columbia Circuit and U.S. Court of Appeals, Seventh Circuit; 1990, Maryland, U.S. District Court, Northern District of Illinois, Trial Bar, U.S. District Court, District of Maryland and U.S. Court of Appeals, Fourth Circuit; 1994, U.S. Court of Appeals, First Circuit. *Education:* State University of New York at Brockport (B.A., 1979); Washington College of Law of the American University (J.D., 1982). Member: National Moot Court Team, 1981; Wagner Labor Law Moot Court Team, 1981. Mediator, Superior Court of the District of Columbia, 1991—. Arbitrator, Superior Court of the District of Columbia, 1991—. Neutral Case Evaluator: Superior Court of the District of Columbia, 1992—. Member, Illinois State Bar Association, 1982-1986. *Member:* Chicago Bar Association; The District of Columbia Bar; District of Columbia Defense Lawyers Association; National Association of Railroad Trial Counsel; Lawyer-Pilots' Bar Association; National Association of College and University Attorneys; Defense Research Institute. (Also at Rockville, Maryland Office). ***PRAC-***

(This Listing Continued)

BONNER KIERNAN TREBACH & CROCIATA, Washington—Continued

TICE AREAS: Aviation Litigation; Employers Liability; Insurance; Personal Injury; Railroad Liability; Insurance Coverage Disputes. **Email:** jcrociata@bktc.net

BARRY D. TREBACH, born Brooklyn, New York, July 16, 1954; admitted to bar, 1981, District of Columbia; 1982, U.S. District Court for the District of Columbia; 1983, Maryland; 1989, U.S. District Court, District of Maryland. *Education:* Vassar College (B.A., 1976); Antioch School of Law (J.D., 1981). Law Clerk to the Honorable Frederick H. Weisberg, 1981. Mediator: Superior Court of the District of Columbia, 1988; U.S. District Court for the District of Columbia, 1990. Panel Chairman, Health Claims Arbitration Office of Maryland, 1987. *Member:* The District of Columbia Bar; Maryland State Bar Association, Inc.; Charles Fahy American Inns of Court; Delegate, D.C. Judicial Conference; D.C. Defense Lawyers Association; Trial Lawyers Association of Washington, D.C. (Also at Rockville, Maryland Office). **PRACTICE AREAS:** Alternative Dispute Resolution; Medical Malpractice; Personal Injury; Product Liability; Torts. **Email:** btrebach@bktc.net

KEITH M. BONNER, born Washington, D.C., April 14, 1954; admitted to bar, 1980, District of Columbia and U.S. Court of Appeals, District of Columbia Circuit; 1988, U.S. District Court, District of Maryland; 1990, Maryland; 1994, U.S. Court of Appeals, Fourth Circuit. *Education:* Marquette University (B.A., 1976); Georgetown University (J.D., 1979). Law Clerk to The Honorable Fred L. McIntyre, Associate Judge, Superior Court of The District of Columbia, 1979-1981. *Member:* The District of Columbia Bar (Co-Chairman, Injuries to Persons and Property Section, 1994-1996; Member, Steering Committee, 1994—; Faculty, 1995—; Editor, Standardized Civil Jury Instructions for the District of Columbia, 1998—, revised edition); Bar Association of the District of Columbia; Montgomery County and American Bar Associations; Maryland State Bar Association, Inc.; The District of Columbia Defense Lawyers Association (President, 1993-1994; Member, Executive Committee, 1991-1996); Defense Research Institute. (Also at Rockville, Maryland Office). **PRACTICE AREAS:** Medical Malpractice; Personal Injury; Product Liability; Construction; Toxic Torts; Insurance Coverage Law. **Email:** kbonner@bktc.net

MICHAEL D. CHEFITZ, born Philadelphia, Pennsylvania, March 10, 1959; admitted to bar, 1985, Massachusetts and U.S. District Court, District of Massachusetts; 1996, Rhode Island; 2000, U.S. District Court, District of Rhode Island. *Education:* Brandeis University (B.A., Politics, magna cum laude, 1981); Boston University (J.D., cum laude, 1984). Recipient, American Jurisprudence Book Award in Evidence, 1983. Instructor, Business Law, Northeastern University, 1986—. (At Boston, Massachusetts and Providence, Rhode Island Offices). **PRACTICE AREAS:** Insurance Coverage Disputes; Insurance Claims Defense; Products Liability. **Email:** mchefitz@bktc.net

BRIAN R. ADE, born Camden, New Jersey, October 20, 1954; admitted to bar, 1980, New Jersey; 1989, New York. *Education:* Rutgers College (B.A., 1976); Western New England College (J.D., 1980). *Member:* Bergen County (Member: Civil Practice Committee; ADR Committee; Product Liability Committee; Chair, Speakers Bureau, 1990-1996); New Jersey State (Member, Environmental Law Section) and American (Member, Tort and Insurance Practice Section) Bar Associations; The Defense Research Institute, Inc. (Member, Construction Law Committee and Environmental Law Committee); New Jersey Defense Association; Trial Attorneys of New Jersey. (Certified Civil Trial Attorney, Supreme Court of New Jersey, Board on Trial Attorney Certification) (At New York, N.Y. and Parsippany, New Jersey Offices). **PRACTICE AREAS:** Business Litigation; Business Mediation; Complex Business Litigation; Construction Accidents; Construction and Design Law; Construction Contracts; Construction Insurance Defense; Construction Mediation; Contractors Liability; Contract Litigation; Corporate Insurance Defense; Environmental Insurance Coverage; Environmental Litigation; Hazardous Waste Litigation; Indoor Air Quality; Toxic Substance Liability; Accident Insurance; Commercial Insurance; Excess and Reinsurance; General Liability; Insurance Arbitration; Insurance Contracts; Insurance Coverage; Insurance Litigation; Subrogation; Breach of Warranty; Food Borne Disease; Manufacturers Liability; Products Liability Defense; Warranty Law; Tort Defense; Chemical Exposure; Lead Poisoning. **Email:** bade@bktc.net

CHRISTOPHER E. HASSELL, born Philadelphia, Pennsylvania, April 5, 1954; admitted to bar, 1979, District of Columbia; 1980, U.S. District Court, District of Columbia; 1981, U.S. Court of Appeals, District of Columbia Circuit; 1989, Virginia; 1991, U.S. District Court, Eastern District of Virginia; 1992, U.S. Court of Appeals, Fourth Circuit; 1998, Maryland. *Education:* Hobart College (B.A., cum laude, 1976); Georgetown University (J.D., 1979). Law Clerk to Honorable Joseph M. Hannon, Superior Court of the District of Columbia. Counsel for Legal Affairs, Automatic Data Processing, Bethesda, Maryland, 1993-1996. Director, Legal and Regulatory Affairs, National Biosystems, Inc., Rockville; Maryland. *Member:* The District of Columbia Bar; American Bar Association; Defense Research Institute; District of Columbia Defense Lawyers Association. (Also at Rockville, Maryland and Fairfax, Virginia Offices). **PRACTICE AREAS:** Insurance Defense; Employment Discrimination; Products Liability; Medical Malpractice Law. **Email:** chassell@bktc.net

STUART L. PEACOCK, born Los Angeles, California, January 12, 1962; admitted to bar, 1987, California, District of Columbia; 1991, U.S. District Court, Northern District of California and U.S. Court of Appeals, Ninth Circuit; 1992, U.S. Court of Appeals, Fourth Circuit. *Education:* University of California at Santa Cruz (B.A., 1984); Hastings College of Law, University of California (J.D., 1987). Recipient: Oakes College Distinguished Service Award; 1066 Foundation Award. **PRACTICE AREAS:** Insurance Coverage Disputes; Commercial Litigation. **Email:** speacock@bktc.net

MICHAEL M. HICKS, born Harrisburg, Pennsylvania, June 13, 1956; admitted to bar, 1982, District of Columbia and U.S. District Court, District of Columbia; 1983, U.S. Court of Appeals, District of Columbia Circuit and U.S. Court of Appeals for the Third Circuit; 1995, U.S. District Court, District of Maryland; 1998, Maryland. *Education:* Haverford College (B.A., 1978); George Washington University (J.D., 1981). Author: "The New Liability Crisis," The Tufts University Asbestos Information Center, 1986; "The Liability of Building Owners and Contractors," The Tufts University Asbestos Information Center, 1987; "Confronting the Hazard of Asbestos; Liability of Building Owners and Contractors: Parts I and II," Insulation Outlook, 1988; "The ABC's of O&M," Asbestos Abatement, 1988. Member, Core Faculty Georgia Tech Research Institute; Asbestos Information Center, 1986. General Counsel: National Econ Corporation, 1988-1989, 1992—. Professorial Lecturer of Law, The George Washington University Law School. Member: National Institute of Trial Advocacy, 1986; U.S. District Court for the District of Columbia Committee on Pro se Litigation, 1995-1998; District of Columbia Coalition on Environmental Justice, 1995—. Delegate, U.S. Court of Appeals for the District of Columbia Circuit Judicial Conference, 1996, 1998 and 2000. Member, Board of Directors, The Frederick Abramson Memorial Foundation, 1998—. *Member:* The District of Columbia Bar (Member of 1987-1988 Admission Rules Study Committee; Conference of Minorities, 1992—; D.C. Circuit Task of Force on Gender, Race, and Ethnic Bias, 1993—; Board of Governors, 1996-1999); Washington Bar Association (Vice-President, 1986-1993; Chairman of the Board, 1991-1993; President, 1993-1995; Chairman, Law Day Committee, 1985-1987); National Asbestos Council (Member, Board of Directors, 1987-1990; Chairman, Legal and Insurance Committee, 1986-1988). (Also at Rockville, MD Office). **PRACTICE AREAS:** Bank Directors and Officers Liability; Lender Liability; Legal Malpractice Defense; Medical Malpractice Defense; Negligence Defense; Tort Defense. **Email:** mhicks@bktc.net

JOSEPH J. BOTTIGLIERI, born Brooklyn, New York, September 16, 1961; admitted to bar, 1987, New Jersey and U.S. District Court, District of New Jersey; 1989, District of Columbia; 1993, U.S. District Court, District of Maryland; 1994, Maryland and U.S. District Court for the District of Columbia. *Education:* University of Scranton (B.S., cum laude, 1984); Catholic University of America (J.D., 1987). Delta Mu Delta. *Member:* Maryland State Bar Association; The District of Columbia Bar; American Bar Association. (Also at Parsippany, New Jersey Office). **PRACTICE AREAS:** Products Liability; Medical Malpractice; Errors and Omissions. **Email:** jbottiglieri@bktc.net

KENNETH A. SCHOEN, born Newark, New Jersey, September 22, 1963; admitted to bar, 1988, New Jersey and U.S. District Court, District of New Jersey; 1989, New York and U.S. District Court, Southern and Eastern Districts of New York. *Education:* Emory University (B.A., 1985); Boston University (J.D., 1988). Case and Note Editor, Probate Law Journal, 1988. Deputy Attorney General (Tort Litigation Section and Environmental Compliance Unit), 1988-1993. Member, Justice William J. Brennan, Jr. American Inn of Court, 1991-1993. *Member:* Essex County, New Jersey State and American Bar Associations; New Jersey Defense Association. (At Parsippany, New Jersey and New York, New York Offices). **PRACTICE AREAS:** Premises Liability; Product Liability; Commercial Litigation. **Email:** kschoen@bktc.net

OF COUNSEL

ANDREW BUTZ, born Baltimore, Maryland, January 15, 1945; admitted to bar, 1976, Virginia; 1977, District of Columbia and U.S. Court of Appeals, Fourth Circuit; 1979, U.S. Court of Appeals, District of Columbia Circuit; 1980, U.S. Supreme Court; 1982, Illinois; 1983, U.S. District Court, Northern District of Illinois, including Trial Bar; 1985, U.S. District Court, Eastern District of Michigan; 1990, U.S. Court of Appeals, Sixth Circuit; 1991, U.S. Court of Appeals, Seventh Circuit. *Education:* Princeton University (A.B., 1966); Dartmouth College; Georgetown University (J.D., 1976). Editor, Georgetown Law Journal, 1974-1976. Law Clerk to Hon. Albert V. Bryan, Senior Circuit Judge, U.S. Court of Appeals, Fourth Circuit, 1976-1977. (Also at Fairfax, Virginia Office). **PRACTICE AREAS:** Insurance Coverage Law; Complex Litigation; Commercial Insurance; Excess and Reinsurance; Antitrust; Contract Litigation; Commercial Fraud; Commercial Litigation; Commercial Torts; Civil RICO; Dealer and Distributor Termination. **Email:** abutz@bktc.net

ALEXANDER H. GILLESPIE, born Princeton, New Jersey, March 16, 1959; admitted to bar, 1986, Connecticut; 1987, New York and District of

(This Listing Continued)

Columbia. *Education:* St. Michael's College (B.A., cum laude, 1981); Washington University (J.D., 1986). Recipient, Scribes Award. Honorary Member, Scribes, 1987. Staff Member, 1984-1985 and Associate Editor, 1985-1986, Washington University Law Quarterly. *Member:* American Bar Association (Member, Section on: Tort and Insurance Practice). (Also at New York, New York Office). ***PRACTICE AREAS:*** Federal Civii Practice; Insurance; Casualty Insurance; Insurance Coverage; Environmental Law; Excess Coverage; Excess and Reinsurance; Products Liability; Lead Poisoning. ***Email:*** agillespie@bktc.net

JOHN P. NOYES, born Boston, Massachusetts, November 11, 1951; admitted to bar, 1989, Massachusetts; 1990, U.S. District Court, District of Massachusetts and U.S. Court of Appeals, First Circuit; 1992, District of Columbia. *Education:* Boston University (A.B., 1973); Suffolk University (J.D., cum laude, 1989). Recipient, American Jurisprudence Awards in: Evidence, Advanced Evidence, Medical Malpractice, State Criminal Practice, Appellate Advocacy and Procedure. Legal Assistant to District Attorney, Suffolk County, 1984-1987, 1989. Special Assistant Attorney General, Commonwealth of Massachusetts, 1990-1991. *Member:* The District of Columbia Bar; Defense Research Institute (Member, Committees on: Product Liability Law; Industrywide Litigation; Trial Practice and Procedures); Massachusetts Defense Lawyers Association; Aircraft Owners and Pilots Association. (Also at Boston, Massachusetts Office). ***REPORTED CASES:*** Alexis v. McDonald's Restaurants of Massachusetts, Inc., 67 F.3d 341 (1st Cir. 1995); District Attorney for the Norfolk District v. Flatley, 419 Mass. 507 (1995); Commonwealth v. Fitzgibbons, 23 Mass. App.Ct 301 (1986). ***PRACTICE AREAS:*** Trial Practice; Appellate Practice; Product Liability; General Liability; Insurance Law. ***Email:*** jnoyes@bktc.net

RONALD G. GUZIAK, born Pittsburgh, Pennsylvania, July 5, 1946; admitted to bar, 1971, Pennsylvania; 1972, U.S. Court of Military Appeals; 1976, District of Columbia; 1989, Maryland. *Education:* Duquesne University (B.A., 1968; J.D., 1971). *Member:* The Bar Association of the District of Columbia; The District of Columbia Bar; Maryland State and American Bar Associations; District of Columbia Defense Lawyers Association; Defense Research Institute. [Capt., U.S. Army, JAGC, 1972-1976; Army Senior Trial Specialist, 1975-1976]. (Also at Rockville, Maryland Office). ***PRACTICE AREAS:*** General Litigation; Medical Malpractice; Construction Litigation; Toxic Tort Litigation; Product Liability; Insurance Law. ***Email:*** rguziak@bktc.net

ERIC A. SPACEK, born Honolulu, Hawaii, October 14, 1966; admitted to bar, 1991, Virginia, U.S. District Court, Eastern District of Virginia and U.S. Court of Appeals, Fourth Circuit; 1992, District of Columbia and U.S. District Court for the District of Columbia; 2001, U.S. Court of Appeals, District of Columbia Circuit. *Education:* Eastern College (B.A., 1988); Washington College of Law, American University (J.D., 1991). *Member:* The District of Columbia Bar; Virginia State Bar. (Also at Fairfax, Virginia Office). ***PRACTICE AREAS:*** Civil Liability; Defense Litigation; Insurance Defense; Professional Liability Defense Law. ***Email:*** espacek@bktc.net

CAROLYN ISRAEL STEIN, born Arcadia, California, May 27, 1965; admitted to bar, 1991, Maryland; 1992, District of Columbia and U.S. District Court, District of Maryland; 1995, U.S. District Court, District of Columbia. *Education:* Syracuse University (B.S., cum laude, 1987); George Washington University (J.D., with honors, 1991). Judicial Clerk, Honorable James P. Salmon, Seventh Judicial Circuit Court of Maryland, 1991-1992. *Member:* The District of Columbia Bar; District of Columbia Women's Bar Association. (Also at Rockville, Maryland Office). ***PRACTICE AREAS:*** Medical Malpractice; Construction Litigation; Product Liability; Premises Liability; Personal Injury; Torts. ***Email:*** cstein@bktc.net

MICHAEL J. SMITH, born Quantico, Virginia, April 8, 1967; admitted to bar, 1992, Massachusetts; 1993, Connecticut and Rhode Island. *Education:* Providence College (B.A., 1989); Quinnipiac College (J.D., 1992); Boston College. *Member:* Massachusetts, Rhode Island and American Bar Associations; Defense Research Institute. (At Boston, Massachusetts, Providence, Rhode Island and Hartford, Connecticut Offices). ***PRACTICE AREAS:*** Product Liability; Employment Discrimination; General Liability; Environmental Liability; Insurance Coverage Disputes. ***Email:*** msmith@bktc.net

TOD W. READ, born Miami, Florida, April 14, 1959; admitted to bar, 1988, Florida; 1990, District of Columbia. *Education:* Grinnell College (B.A., 1981); Florida State University (J.D., 1988). Member: Florida State University Law Review, 1987-1988; Florida State University Journal of Land Use and Environmental Law, 1986-1988. Author: "Environmental Permit Coordination in Florida," 3 J. Land Use and Envtl. L. 53, Spring, 1987. Co-Author: with Edward Kurent, "Use of EPA and PRP Information Sources in Defense of CERCLA Remedial Actions," 2 Envtl. Claims J. 193, Winter, 1989/1990. *Member:* The District of Columbia Bar; The Florida Bar; American Bar Association. ***PRACTICE AREAS:*** Environmental Law; Toxic Torts; Insurance Defense. ***Email:*** tread@bktc.net

HUGH R. CURRAN, born Bridgeport, Connecticut, May 24, 1962; admitted to bar, 1988, Massachusetts; 1990, Connecticut and U.S. District Court, District of Massachusetts; 1997, U.S. District Court, District of Connecticut.

(This Listing Continued)

Education: College of the Holy Cross (B.A., 1984); Suffolk University (J.D., 1988). Member, Special Faculty, Clinical Studies Program, Suffolk University Law School, 1990-1993. Assistant District Attorney, Suffolk County District Attorney's Office, 1988-1996. *Member:* Massachusetts and Connecticut Bar Associations; National District Attorneys Association; Defense Research Institute. (Also at Boston, MA and Hartford, CT Offices). ***PRACTICE AREAS:*** Trial Practice; Appellate Practice; Product Liability; General Liability; Insurance. ***Email:*** hcurran@bktc.net

ALAN S. BLOCK, born Philadelphia, Pennsylvania, February 11, 1966; admitted to bar, 1991, District of Columbia, Virginia, U.S. District Court, Eastern District of Virginia, U.S. Bankruptcy Court, Eastern District of Virginia and U.S. Court of Appeals, Fourth Circuit; 1994, U.S. District Court for the District of Columbia; 1998, U.S. District Court, District of Maryland. *Education:* George Washington University (B.A., 1987); George Mason University School of Law (J.D., 1990). Counsel, Office of the U.S. Senate Sergeant at Arms. Assistant Corporation Counsel, Office of the Corporation Counsel, District of Columbia, Civil Division, General Litigation Section. *Member:* The District of Columbia Bar; Virginia State Bar. (Also at Fairfax, Virginia Office). ***PRACTICE AREAS:*** Employment Litigation; Construction Litigation; Commercial Contracts; Commercial Litigation; Personal Injury; Hospital Liability Defense; Hospital Negligence; Civil Litigation; Federal Civil Litigation; Medical Malpractice Defense. ***Email:*** ablock@bktc.net

ASSOCIATES

ALAN G. WHITE, born Newark, New Jersey, December 13, 1945; admitted to bar, 1974, New Jersey and U.S. District Court, District of New Jersey. *Education:* Rutgers University (B.A., 1968); Suffolk University (J.D., cum laude, 1974). Managing Editor, Suffolk University Law Review, 1973-1974. Judicial Law Clerk to Superior Court Assignment Judge, Passaic County, New Jersey, 1974-1975. (Resident, Parsippany, NJ Office). ***PRACTICE AREAS:*** Insurance Coverage; Litigation; Insurance Defense. ***Email:*** awhite@bktc.net

ALAN L. KORZEN, born New York, New York, May 24, 1964; admitted to bar, 1989, Connecticut; 1990, New Jersey and New York; 1991, New York. *Education:* George Washington University (B.A., 1986); Pace University (J.D., 1989). (Also at Parsippany, NJ and New York, NY Offices). ***Email:*** akorzen@bktc.net

MARY C. COMMERTON, born Rockaway, New York, December 5, 1965; admitted to bar, 1990, New Jersey; 1991, New York. *Education:* St. John's University (B.S., 1987; J.D., 1990). Assistant District Attorney, New York County, 1990-1997. *Member:* Staten Island, Richmond County, New York State and American Bar Associations. (At Parsippany, New Jersey and New York, New York Offices). ***PRACTICE AREAS:*** Personal Injury; Premises Liability; Insurance Law; Civil Litigation; Criminal Defense Law. ***Email:*** mcommerton@bktc.net

MICHELE T. OSHMAN, born Baltimore, Maryland, February 16, 1958; admitted to bar, 1986, Maryland; 1987, Illinois and U.S. District Court, Northern District of Illinois (Not admitted in District of Columbia). *Education:* Towson University (B.A., 1981); University of Baltimore School of Law (J.D., 1986). ***PRACTICE AREAS:*** Insurance Coverage Litigation; Litigation. ***Email:*** moshman@bktc.net

DAVID C. NUMRYCH, born Chicago, Illinois, October 8, 1964; admitted to bar, 1990, Illinois; 1996, District of Columbia; 1997, Maryland; 1998, Virginia, U.S. District Court, District of Columbia, U.S. District Court, Eastern District of Virginia and U.S. District Court, District of Maryland. *Education:* University of Illinois (B.A., 1987); Chicago Kent College of Law (J.D., 1990). *Member:* The District of Columbia Bar; Maryland State Bar Association; Virginia State Bar. [Capt., USAF JAG Corps., 1991-1997]. ***REPORTED CASES:*** State Farm v. Enterprise Rent-A-Car, Volume 127 Washington Law Reporter Page 127 (1999). ***PRACTICE AREAS:*** Corporate Defense; Insurance Defense; Employer Liability; Personal Injury; Insurance Coverage Disputes; Workers Compensation; Aviation Litigation. ***Email:*** dnumrych@bktc.net

SHERI M. L. COLLINS, born Bremerton, Washington, August 4, 1966; admitted to bar, 1992, Washington; 1994, Maryland; 1996, District of Columbia and U.S. District Court, District of Maryland; 1997, U.S. Court of Appeals, Fourth Circuit; 2000, U.S. District Court, District of Columbia. *Education:* University of Chicago (B.A., 1989); Emory University School of Law (J.D., 1992). Managing Editor, Emory International Law Review, 1991-1992. (Also at Rockville, MD Office). ***PRACTICE AREAS:*** Insurance Coverage Litigation; Professional Liability Defense; General Liability Defense. ***Email:*** scollins@bktc.net

ANTHONY J. LAPORTA, born Bloomington, Illinois, January 14, 1968; admitted to bar, 1993, New Jersey; 1994, New York. *Education:* Lafayette College (B.A., 1990); St. John's University (J.D., 1993). (At Parsippany, New Jersey and New York, New York Offices). ***PRACTICE AREAS:*** Insurance Coverage; Litigation; Construction; Products Liability; Automobile; Premises Liability; General Liability Litigation. ***Email:*** alaporta@bktc.net

(This Listing Continued)

BONNER KIERNAN TREBACH & CROCIATA, Washington—Continued

JAMES MICHAEL DUNPHY, JR., born Boston, Massachusetts, 1968; admitted to bar, 1995, Massachusetts and U.S. District Court, District of Massachusetts; 1996, U.S. District Court, District of Vermont; 1997, Vermont (Not admitted in District of Columbia). *Education:* Villanova University (B.A., cum laude, 1990); New England School of Law (J.D., 1994). *Member:* Defense Research Institute; Vermont Bar Association. (Also at Boston, MA Office). ***PRACTICE AREAS:*** Premises Liability; Dram Shop Liability; Insurance Defense. ***Email:*** jdunphy@bktc.net

STEPHEN E. HUGHES, born Amityville, New York, April 27, 1953; admitted to bar, 1995, Massachusetts; 1998, U.S. District Court, District of Massachusetts; 2001, U.S. Court of Appeals, First Circuit. *Education:* Northwestern University (B.S., 1975); Boston College (M.S., 1979; J.D., magna cum laude, 1995). *Member:* Massachusetts Bar Association (Member, Labor and Employment Section and Employee Rights and Responsibilities Practice Group). (Resident, Boston, MA Office). ***PRACTICE AREAS:*** Employment Discrimination; Environmental Liability; General Liability; Construction/Contractor; FELA; Railroad; Insurance. ***Email:*** shughes@bktc.net

FELICITY A. McGRATH, born Urbana, Illinois, July 16, 1970; admitted to bar, 1995, Florida; 1996, New Jersey; 1998, Virginia and District of Columbia; 1999, Maryland and U.S. District Court, Eastern District of Virginia; 2000, U.S. District Court, District of Maryland. *Education:* University of Pennsylvania (B.A., 1992); University of Miami School of Law (J.D., cum laude, 1995); Wellesley College. Omicron Delta Kappa. Recipient, Dean's Honor Scholarship, University of Miami. Articles and Comments Editor, Interamerican Law Review, University of Miami. (Also at Rockville, MD, Fairfax, VA and Parsippany, NJ Offices). ***PRACTICE AREAS:*** Liability Litigation. ***Email:*** fmcgrath@bktc.net

WILLIAM H. WHITE JR., born Red Bank, New Jersey, December 27, 1969; admitted to bar, 1996, Florida and New Jersey; 1997, Maryland, U.S. District Court, Northern and Southern Districts of Florida and U.S. District Court, District of New Jersey; 1998, District of Columbia and U.S. District Court, District of Maryland; 1999, U.S. District Court, Eastern District of New York; 2000, U.S. District Court, District of Columbia; 2001, U.S. Court of Appeals for the District of Columbia Circuit. *Education:* Georgetown University (B.A., 1992); University of Miami (J.D., cum laude, 1996). Phi Delta Phi. Managing Editor, University of Miami Inter-American Law Review, 1995-1996. Author: "Foreign Law, Politics and Litigants in U.S. Courts: A Discussion of Issues Raised by Transportes Aereos Nacionales, S.A. v. De Brenes," 27 U. Miami Inter-Am. L. Rev. 161, Fall 1995. *Member:* The Florida Bar; Maryland State and American Bar Associations; District of Columbia Bar; The Association of Trial Lawyers of America. (Also at Parsippany, New Jersey Office). ***LANGUAGES:*** Spanish. ***PRACTICE AREAS:*** Insurance Coverage Litigation; Excess and Reinsurance; Commercial Litigation; Contracts; Commercial Torts. ***Email:*** wwhite@bktc.net

KRISTIN A. SBARRA, born Tarrytown, New York, August 26, 1971; admitted to bar, 1996, Massachusetts. *Education:* State University of New York at Binghamton (B.A., 1993); Boston University (J.D., 1996). Edward Hennessey Scholar. *Member:* The Association of Trial Lawyers of America. (Resident, Boston, MA Office). ***PRACTICE AREAS:*** Civil Litigation; Insurance Defense Law; Criminal Law. ***Email:*** ksbarra@bktc.net

CHRISTOPHER L. JEFFORD, born New Haven, Connecticut, February 20, 1970; admitted to bar, 1997, Massachusetts and Connecticut. *Education:* University of Notre Dame (B.A., 1992); Quinnipiac College (J.D., magna cum laude, 1996). *Member:* Connecticut, Massachusetts and American Bar Associations. (Also at Boston, MA and Hartford CT Offices). ***PRACTICE AREAS:*** Litigation; Civil Defense; Insurance Defence; Environmental Law; Commercial Arbitration; Products Liability. ***Email:*** cjefford@bktc.net

EWAN M. CLARK, born Pretoria, Republic of South Africa, November 15, 1968; admitted to bar, 1996, New Jersey; 2000, New York. *Education:* Edinburgh University (B.S. in Business and Economics, 1991); Seton Hall University, School of Law at Newark (J.D., 1996). *Member:* New Jersey State and New York State Bar Associations. (Also at Parsippany, NJ and New York, NY Offices). ***PRACTICE AREAS:*** Insurance; Commercial Law; Environmental Law; Products Liability; Personal Injury.

MUSA L. EUBANKS, born Boston, Massachusetts; admitted to bar, 1999, District of Columbia; 2001, Maryland. *Education:* George Mason University (B.A., 1993); George Washington University (J.D., 1996). Author: Contributor, Milton C. Lee, Jr., "Criminal Discovery: What Truth Do We Seek?" 4 D.C. L. Rev. 7, 1998. *Member:* Washington State and Maryland State (Member, Young Lawyers Division) Bar Associations; District of Columbia Bar (Member, Young Lawyers Division). (Also at Rockville, MD Office). ***PRACTICE AREAS:*** Insurance Defense; Civil Litigation. ***Email:*** meubanks@bktc.net

ALISON J. McGRIFF, born Wilmington, Delaware, March 18, 1971; admitted to bar, 1997, Maryland; 1998, District of Columbia and U.S. District Court, District of Maryland; 1999, U.S. District Court for the District of Columbia. *Education:* Spelman College (B.S., Chemistry, 1994); University of Maryland, Baltimore (J.D., 1997). Phi Alpha Delta. *Member:* Maryland State Bar Association, Inc.; The District of Columbia Bar. (Also at Rockville, MD Office). ***PRACTICE AREAS:*** Insurance Defense; Professional Liability. ***Email:*** amcgriff@bktc.net

NADINE D.Y. ADRIAN, born Germany, May 11, 1973; admitted to bar, 1997, California and U.S. District Court, Central District of California (Not admitted in District of Columbia). *Education:* American University (B.A., 1994); Pepperdine University, School of Law (J.D., 1997). Alpha Kappa Psi; Golden Key Honor Society. Member, Wagner National Labor Law Moot Court Team; Second Place Member ABA Moot Court Team and Second Place Brief; Recipient, American Jurisprudence Award in Appellate Advocacy. *Member:* State Bar of California. ***LANGUAGES:*** German. ***PRACTICE AREAS:*** Civil Litigation. ***Email:*** nadrian@bktc.net

JONATHAN E. AGIN, born Cleveland, Ohio, May 20, 1971; admitted to bar, 1999, Maryland; 2000, District of Columbia. *Education:* John Carroll University (B.A., 1993); Case Western Reserve University (J.D., 1999). Associate, 1997 and Contributing Editor, 1998, Law Review. (Also at Rockville, MD Office). ***LANGUAGES:*** Spanish. ***PRACTICE AREAS:*** Litigation. ***Email:*** jagin@bktc.net

HEATHER SHOAF DEANE, born Pittsburgh, Pennsylvania, July 19, 1972; admitted to bar, 1997, Virginia (Not admitted in District of Columbia). *Education:* The Pennsylvania State University (B.A., Political Science, 1994); Washington College of Law, The American University (J.D., 1997). Penn State Honors Scholar. Editor, Journal of Gender of the Law. *Member:* Virginia Bar Association. ***Email:*** hdeane@bktc.net

JEAN-MARIE SYLLA, JR., born New York, N.Y., 1968; admitted to bar, 1999, Maryland; 2000, District of Columbia, U.S. District Court, District of Maryland and U.S. District Court, District of Columbia. *Education:* University of Maryland (B.A., 1992; M.S., 1997; J.D., 1999). Member, National Trial Team. Managing Editor, Journal of Health Care Law and Policy, 1998-1999. Phi Alpha Delta, President, 1997-1998. *Member:* Maryland State, Federal and American Bar Associations; The Association of Trial Lawyers of America. (Also at Rockville, MD Office). ***PRACTICE AREAS:*** Business Litigation; Insurance Coverage; Insurance Liability; Products Liability. ***Email:*** jsylla@bktc.net

LUCY C. CHIU, born Boston, Massachusetts, March, 24, 1971; admitted to bar, 1999, Virginia; 2001, District of Columbia. *Education:* Tufts University (B.A., 1993); University of Notre Dame (J.D., 1998). ***LANGUAGES:*** Mandarin. ***PRACTICE AREAS:*** Civil Litigation; Trial Practice. ***Email:*** lchiu@bktc.net

SHALINI K. KEDIA, born Phoenix, Arizona, August 9, 1972; admitted to bar, 1999, California; 2001, Maryland and District of Columbia. *Education:* Arizona State University (B.A., 1995); University of California, Hastings College of the Law (J.D., 1999). ***PRACTICE AREAS:*** Litigation. ***Email:*** shalinikedia@excite.com

HEATHER L. PARENT, born Maine, May 19, 1975; admitted to bar, 2001, Massachusetts (Not admitted in District of Columbia). *Education:* Susquehanna University (B.S., 1997); Vermont Law School (M.S.E.L., 2000; J.D., 2000). *Member:* Massachusetts and American (Section on Energy and the Environment) Bar Associations. ***PRACTICE AREAS:*** Insurance Defense; Environmental Law. ***Email:*** hparent@bktc.net

DANA DENISE M. ORQUIZA, born New York, N.Y., November 11, 1971; admitted to bar, 2001, Maryland (Not admitted in District of Columbia). *Education:* Georgetown University (B.S.N., 1994); Columbus School of Law of The Catholic University of America (J.D., 2000). Sigma Theta Tau; International Honor Society of Nursing at Georgetown University, 1994. Team Member, National Moot Court, Siegal Cup (Law and Medicine), Columbus School of Law, The Catholic University of America, 2000. Registered Nurse, District of Columbia, 1994. ***PRACTICE AREAS:*** Liability. ***Email:*** dorquiza@bktc.net

LEGAL SUPPORT PERSONNEL

DANIEL W. GILL, born New York City, New York, October 8, 1945. *Education:* Assumption College (A.B., Foreign Affairs, 1967); University of So. Cal., Washington, D.C. (M.S.S.M., 1980). *Member:* Association of Legal Administrators. ***Email:*** dgill@bktc.net

(This Listing Continued)

BOROS & GAROFALO, P.C.

Established in 1966

SUITE 550
1201 CONNECTICUT AVENUE, N.W.
WASHINGTON, D.C. 20036
Telephone: 202-822-9070
Cable Address: "Airlaw"
Telecopier: 202-822-9075
Email: mail@bgairlaw.com

Administrative Practice. Aviation, International, Transportation and Litigation. Corporation Law.

FIRM PROFILE: Throughout its existence, Boros & Garofalo, P.C. has specialized in aviation law. The firm represents clients before numerous U.S. government agencies, including FAA, DOT, Department of State, Department of Defense, Customs Service, Immigration and Naturalization Service, and the Department of Commerce. Clients include scheduled and charter U.S. and foreign airlines, commuter air carriers, on-demand air taxis, aircraft brokers and leasing companies, fixed base operators, FAA-licensed repair stations, aircraft parts dealers and manufacturers, major tour operators/wholesalers, travel agents, and other aircraft owners and operators. The firm advises clients on a broad range of aviation issues, including matters affecting regulatory compliance, licenses and operations, aviation-related immigration issues, bilateral air service negotiations, aircraft purchase and sale contracts and leases, general contract matters, overflight matters, and export and import matters.

GARY B. GAROFALO, born Hartford, Connecticut, June 13, 1940; admitted to bar, 1965, Connecticut; 1969, District of Columbia; 1971, U.S. Supreme Court. *Education:* Rensselaer Polytechnic Institute (B.S.A.E., 1962); University of Virginia (LL.B., 1965). Tau Beta Pi. Co-Author: "The Aviation Drug Testing Handbook," Dow, Lohnes & Albertson, 1989. Staff Attorney, Federal Aviation Administration, 1965-1968. *Member:* The District of Columbia Bar; Connecticut, Federal and American Bar Associations. ***PRACTICE AREAS:*** Federal Aviation Regulation; Airline Regulation. ***Email:*** ggarofalo@bgairlaw.com

AARON A. GOERLICH, born Washington, D.C., August 8, 1955; admitted to bar, 1980, Florida; 1981, District of Columbia. *Education:* Tulane University of Louisiana (B.A., 1977; J.D., cum laude, 1980). Pilot's License (Instrument Rating), 1973—. *Member:* The District of Columbia Bar; The Florida Bar; Federal, American and Lawyer Pilots Bar Associations; National Transportation Safety Board Bar Association. ***PRACTICE AREAS:*** Aviation; Aeronautical Regulation. ***Email:*** agoerlich@bgairlaw.com

DON H. HAINBACH, born New York, N.Y., November 4, 1955; admitted to bar, 1980, District of Columbia and New York. *Education:* Brown University (A.B., with honors, 1976); University of Michigan (J.D., 1979). Executive Assistant to Civil Aeronautics Board Member, Diane K. Morales, 1984. *Member:* The District of Columbia Bar; New York State, Federal and American Bar Associations. ***PRACTICE AREAS:*** Transportation Regulation; International Aviation. ***Email:*** dhainbach@bgairlaw.com

ASSOCIATES

KATHERINE M. ALDRICH, born Holliston, Massachusetts, February 26, 1964; admitted to bar, 1991, Virginia and District of Columbia. *Education:* Salve Regina College (B.A., magna cum laude, 1986); Georgetown University Law Center (J.D., 1991). *Member:* District of Columbia Bar; Virginia and American Bar Associations. ***PRACTICE AREAS:*** Airline Regulation; Aviation Law. ***Email:*** kaldrich@bgairlaw.com

JOHN R. COPLEY, born High Point, North Carolina, July 3, 1963; admitted to bar, 1992, Virginia; 1999, District of Columbia. *Education:* Wake Forest University (B.A., magna cum laude, 1985); University of Virginia (M.A., 1987; J.D., 1992). Dupont Fellow. *Member:* Association for Transportation Law, Logistics and Policy. ***LANGUAGES:*** Spanish. ***PRACTICE AREAS:*** Commercial Law; Transportation Law. ***Email:*** jcopley@bgairlaw.com

VICTOR H. SMITH, born Brooklyn, New York, April 30, 1969; admitted to bar, 1996, Maryland; 2000, District of Columbia. *Education:* Swarthmore College (B.A., 1991); Washington College of Law of American University (J.D., 1996). ***PRACTICE AREAS:*** Aviation Law. ***Email:*** vsmith@bgairlaw.com

OF COUNSEL

HOWARD S. BOROS (Retired).

R. EVAN SMITH, born New York, N.Y., November 12, 1941; admitted to bar, 1967, New York; U.S. District Court, Southern District of New York (Not admitted in District of Columbia). *Education:* Swarthmore College (A.B., with honors, 1963); Columbia Law School (LL.B., with honors, 1966). Harlan Fiske Stone Scholar. Lecturer: "Noise Regulation and the Retrofit Alternative," Geneva Aviation Conference, February 1992. *Member:* The Association of the Bar of the City of New York (Member, Aeronautics Committee, 1985-1987). ***PRACTICE AREAS:*** Aircraft Finance Law; Equipment and Project Finance Law; General Corporate Law.

GREGORY S. WINTON, born New York, N.Y., May 6, 1964; admitted to bar, 1991, Connecticut and New York; 1993, District of Columbia; 1998, Maryland; 1999, Pennsylvania. *Education:* Dowling College (B.S., 1986); Jacob D. Fuchsburg Law Center of Touro College (J.D., 1991). *Member:* Lawyer Pilots Bar Association; National Transportation Safety Board Bar Association; The Association of Trial Lawyers of America. ***PRACTICE AREAS:*** Aviation; Civil Litigation; Personal Injury; Wrongful Death; Product Liability. ***Email:*** gwinton@bgairlaw.com

PIERRE E. MURPHY (Also Practicing Individually).

(This Listing Continued)

BOSE LAW FIRM, PLLC

WASHINGTON, D.C.

(See Arlington, Virginia)

General Civil and Litigation Practice in State and Federal Courts. Business Law, Corporate Law, Construction Law, Contracts, Employment Law, Sexual Harassment, Personal Injury, Automobile Accidents and Injuries, Criminal Law, Driving While Intoxicated, Traffic Violations and Immigration.

BOSE McKINNEY & EVANS LLP

700 NORTH ONE LAFAYETTE CENTRE
SUITE N 700, 1120 20TH STREET, N.W.
WASHINGTON, D.C. 20036
Telephone: 202-973-1229
Fax: 202-973-1212
URL: http://www.boselaw.com

Indianapolis, Indiana Offices: 2700 First Indiana Plaza, 135 North Pennsylvania Street, 46204. Telephone: 317-684-5000. Facsimile: 317-684-5173.

Indianapolis North Office: Suite 500, 600 East 96th Street, 46240. Telephone: 317-574-3700. Facsimile: 317-574-3716.

General Civil Practice in all Courts including Agricultural Law, Antitrust, Appellate Practice, Capital Strategies, Civil Rights, Commercial Law, Communications and Media, Constitutional Law, Corporate Law, Creditors Rights, Creditors Rights in Bankruptcy, Debtor Bankruptcy, Education Law, Employee Benefits, Entertainment and the Arts, Entrepreneurial Services, Environmental Law, Finance, Financial Institutions Law, Government Contracts, Government Relations, High Technology, Insurance, Intellectual Property, International Law, Labor and Employment, Legislative Practice, Litigation, Mergers and Acquisitions, Municipal Finance, Municipal Law, Planning and Land Use, Probate, Real Estate, Regulated Industries, Regulatory Agency Practice, Securities, Taxation, Trusts and Estates, Utility Law, Wills and Zoning.

GEORGE THOMAS PATTON, JR., born South Bend, Indiana, November 28, 1961; admitted to bar, 1987, Indiana and U.S. District Court, Northern and Southern Districts of Indiana; 1989, U.S. Court of Appeals, Seventh Circuit; 1990, U.S. Supreme Court; 2000, District of Columbia; 2001, U.S. District Court, District of Columbia and U.S. Court of Appeals for the District of Columbia Circuit. *Education:* Wabash College (A.B., cum laude, 1984); Aberdeen University, Scotland; Indiana University at Bloomington (J.D., cum laude, 1987). Order of Barristers. Barrister, Edward Coke Appellate Inn of Court, Washington D.C., 2000—. Law Clerk to Chief Justice Randall T. Shepard, Indiana Supreme Court, 1987-1989. Author: "4A Indiana Practice - Appellate Procedure," 3rd Edition, West Publishing Co. Forthcoming (2001); "Recent Developments in Indiana Appellate Procedure: Reforming the Procedural Path to the Indiana Supreme Court," 25 Indiana L. Rev. 1105 (1992); "1992, Developments in Indiana Appellate Procedure: Of Timely Praecipes, Interlocutory Appeals and Civility," 26 Indiana Law Review 799 (1993); "1993, Developments in Indiana Appellate Procedure: Changes in Original Actions, Rehearing and Transfer," 27 Indiana Law Review 843, (1994); "Recent Developments in Indiana Appellate Procedure: New Appellate Rules, A Constitutional Amendment and a Proposal 33," Indiana Law Review 1275, 2000. Co-Author: 1991 and 1993 Supplements and 1996 Revision to "Chapter 12-The Brief," The Attorneys Guide to the Seventh Circuit Court of Appeals. Chair, November 14, 1997 and Presenter, October 18, 1996, November 18, 1998 and May 4, 2000, Appellate Practice Institute, Indiana Continuing Legal Education Forum. Adjunct Assistant Professor of Appellate Advocacy and Procedure, Indiana School of Law at Bloomington, 1990-1994. Consumer Member, Hearing Officer, Administrative Law Judge and President, Indiana State Board of Nursing, 1991-1998. *Member:* Indianapolis (Co-chair, Bench-Bar Conference, 2000), Indiana State (Chair: Appellate Rules Project, 1997—; Appellate Practice Section, 1996-1997; Appellate Issues Study Committee, 1995-1996) and American (Member: Appellate Practice Committee, Litigation Section; Appellate Advocacy Committee, Tort and Insurance Practice Section) Bar Associations; Bar

(This Listing Continued)

BOSE McKINNEY & EVANS LLP, Washington—Continued

Association of the District of Columbia (Appellate Courts Committee, 2000—). ***PRACTICE AREAS:*** Litigation; Appellate Practice. ***Email:*** gpatton@boselaw.com

REPRESENTATIVE CLIENTS: Agmax, Inc.; Batteries.com; BP Amoco Corp.; Association of Indiana Life Insurance Companies; BMW Constructors, Inc.; Chicago Title Insurance Company; City of Indianapolis; Duke Realty Corporation.; Eli Lilly Federal Credit Union; Emmis Communications Corporation; Endress +Hauser, Inc.; Fall Creek Regional Waste District; First Indiana Bank; Firstar Bank, N.A.; Hillenbrand Industries, Inc.; Huntington National Bank of Indiana; Indiana Community Business Credit Corporation; Indiana Health Facility Financing Authority; Indiana Bankers Assn.; Indianapolis Colts, Inc.; Indianapolis Life Insurance Co.; Indiana Psychological Association; Indiana University Anesthesiology Associates; David Letterman Companies; Lincoln National Corporation; Worldcom; Metropolitan Life Insurance Co.; Metropolitan School District of Wayne Township, Marion County, Indiana; Midwest Natural Gas Corp.; New Boston Citimark Limited Partnership; The Prudential Insurance Company of America; Personnel Management, Inc.; Skinner & Broadbent; The Somerset Group, Inc.; TIAA/CREF; The Travelers Insurance Co.; Thomson Multimedia, Inc.; USX Corporation; Young Automotive Group.

BOSEK LAW FIRM

1090 VERMONT AVENUE, N.W.
SUITE 800
WASHINGTON, D.C. 20005
Telephone: 202-326-5256
Fax: 202-289-7624
Email: rbosek@boseklaw.com

Administrative Law Practice before the Federal Energy Commission, Oil and Natural Gas Pipeline Law, Rate Structuring and Tariff Issues.

FIRM PROFILE: The firm has a national practice representing oil and natural gas pipelines, shippers and producers.

RUTH A. BOSEK, born Rochester, New York, July 10, 1949; admitted to bar, 1985, District of Columbia. *Education:* University of Dayton (B.A., 1971); State University of New York at Albany (M.A., 1973); Georgetown University (J.D., cum laude, 1985). *Member:* District of Columbia Bar. ***PRACTICE AREAS:*** Energy Law.

BENNETT BOSKEY

1800 MASSACHUSETTS AVENUE, N.W., SUITE 600
WASHINGTON, D.C. 20036
Telephone: 202-737-6580
Fax: 202-737-6966
Email: BennettBos@aol.com

General Practice.

BENNETT BOSKEY, born New York City, August 14, 1916; admitted to bar, 1940, New York; 1943, U.S. Supreme Court; 1949, District of Columbia. *Education:* Williams College (A.B., 1935); Harvard Law School (LL.B., 1939). Phi Beta Kappa. Author: Vols. I, IA and IAA, "Supreme Court," West's Federal Forms, 1998 Revision and annual Pocket Parts; "Mechanics of the Supreme Court's Certiorari Jurisdiction," 46 Columbia L. Rev. 225. Co-Author: with Eugene Gressman, "The Supreme Court's New Rules—Model 1995," 164 F.R.D. 80; "The 1997 Restatement and Revisions of the Supreme Court's 1995 Rules," 170 F.R.D. 30; "The Supreme Court's 1999 Revisions of Its Rules," 183 F.R.D. 603. Member, Board of Editors, Harvard Law Review, 1937-1939. Law Clerk to: Judge Learned Hand, 1939-1940; Justice Stanley Reed, 1940-1941; Chief Justice Harlan F. Stone, 1941-1943. Special Assistant to the Attorney General, U.S. Department of Justice (War Division), Washington, D.C., 1943; Advisor on Enemy Property, U.S. Department of State, 1946-1947; Attorney and then Deputy General Counsel, U.S. Atomic Energy Commission, 1947-1951. Member, Volpe, Boskey & Lyons and predecessor firms, 1952-1996. Member, U.S. Delegation to London Conference on German-Owned Patents, 1946. Member, Advisory Board of the International Legal Studies Program, Washington College of Law, American University, 1987-1999. *Member:* The District of Columbia Bar; Bar Association of the District of Columbia; American Bar Association; American Law Institute (Member of Council, 1972—; Treasurer, 1975—; Member, ALI-ABA Committee on Continuing Professional Education, 1985—). [1st Lt., A.U.S., 1943-1946]

BOSLEY & HUTZELMAN, P.C.

WASHINGTON, D.C.

(See Alexandria, Virginia)

Pensions, Employee Benefits and Employment Tax Law. Litigation.

JOSH F. BOWERS, P.C.

1090 VERMONT AVENUE, N.W., SUITE 500
WASHINGTON, D.C. 20005
Telephone: 202-408-8360
Email: jbdclaw@aol.com
URL: http://www.lawyers.com/federal_employment_law

An Employment practice limited to the representation of Federal Employees: Wrongful Termination, Harassment, Employment discrimination, Employee Rights, Wage and Hour Law, Whistleblower Defense, Family Medical Leave Act, Personal Injury, Automobile Accidents, Wrongful Death, Defective Products.

FIRM PROFILE: Joshua F. Bowers, Esq. is a nationally recognized attorney representing Federal Employees across the United States for over 15 years. Mr. Bowers has represented Federal employees in courts, administrative forums available to Federal employees, testified before the U.S. Congress on behalf of Federal employees and is a frequent speaker at seminars on Federal employee issues.

JOSH F. BOWERS, born Washington, D.C., July 23, 1953; admitted to bar, 1986, Virginia; 1987, District of Columbia. *Education:* Antioch College (B.A., 1977); Antioch School of Law (M.A., 1983; J.D., 1986). Frequent speaker on Federal employee issues at public forums including the National Employment Lawyers Association, Government Training Institute, American Bar Association Committees, the White House Panel on National Security. Former Chairperson, Public Sector Committee, Labor and Employment Section, District of Columbia Bar. Former Secretary/Treasurer, Society of Federal Labor Relations Professionals, District of Columbia Chapter. *Member:* Metropolitan Washington Employment Lawyers Association (Board Member). ***PRACTICE AREAS:*** Employment Discrimination. ***Email:*** JBdcLaw@aol.com

BOWYTZ, SAVIT & SZYMKOWICZ, LLP

WASHINGTON, D.C.

(See Bethesda, Maryland)

Government Contracts, Business Planning and Transactions, Corporate Commercial Law, Contract Law, Employment Law, Technology, Estate and Probate, Litigation, Finance and Venture Capital, Internet.

BRACEWELL & PATTERSON, L.L.P.

Established in 1945

2000 K STREET, N.W., SUITE 500
WASHINGTON, D.C. 20006-1872
Telephone: 202-828-5800
Fax: 202-223-1225

Houston, Texas Office: South Tower Pennzoil Place, 711 Louisiana Street, Suite 2900, 77002-2781. Telephone: 713-223-2900. Fax: 713-221-1212.

Austin, Texas Office: 111 Congress Avenue, Suite 2300, 78701-4052. Telephone: 512-472-7800. Fax: 512 472-9123.

Other Austin Office: Lakewood on the Park, 7600 B North Capital of Texas Highway, Suite 350, 78731. Telephone: 512-343-6116. Fax: 512-343-6002.

Corpus Christi, Texas Office: 2000 One Shoreline Plaza, South Tower, 800 North Shoreline Boulevard, 78401-3700. Telephone: 361-882-6644. Fax: 361-882-6659.

Dallas, Texas Office: Lincoln Plaza, 500 N. Akard Street, Suite 4000, 75201-3387. Telephone: 214-758-1000. Fax: 214-758-1010.

Fort Worth, Texas Office: 201 Main Street, Suite 1600, 76102. Telephone: 817-332-8143. Fax: 817-332-8409.

San Antonio, Texas Office: 800 One Alamo Center, 106 S. St. Mary's Street, 78205. Telephone: 210-226-1166. Fax: 210-226-1133.

Reston, Virginia Office: 12355 Sunrise Technology Park, Fifth Floor, 20191-3458. Telephone: 703-893-4670. Fax: 703-827-0545.

London, England Office: No. 1 Cornhill, EC3V 3ND. Telephone: 011-44-207-743-6250. Fax: 011-44-207-743-6251.

Almaty, Kazakhstan Office: 65 Kazybek bi str., Suite 410, 480091. Telephone: 73272-581-400. Fax: 73272-581-444.

Astana, Kazakhstan Office: Karaotkel Compound, Office C-7-2. Telephone: 011-7-3172-222-127.

General Civil Practice, Trial and Appellate Practice in State and Federal Courts, Administrative Law, Antitrust, Bank Lending, Bankruptcy Reorganization and Creditors' Rights, Communications, Construction, Corporate and Securities, Early Stage Companies, Employee Benefits, Energy, Environmental, Financial Services, Health Care, Hospitality, Industrial Disaster, Insurance Bad Faith, Insurance Defense, Intellectual Property and Technology, International, Labor and Employment, Land Use and Zoning, Legislative and Governmental Relations, Lender Liability Litigation, Litigation and Alternative Dispute Resolution, Oil and Gas, Founda-

(This Listing Continued)

tions and Not-for-Profit Organizations, Personal Injury, Power, Products Liability, Project Finance, Public Projects, Public Utilities, Real Estate, School Law, Taxation, Telecommunications, Trademark and Copyright, Trusts and Estates.

FIRM PROFILE: Founded in Houston in 1945 as a trial and general civil practice. Today the firm has approximately 300 lawyers with U.S. offices in Houston, Texas; Austin, Texas; Corpus Christi, Texas; Dallas, Texas; Fort Worth, Texas; San Antonio, Texas; Reston, Virginia, and Washington, D.C., and foreign offices in London, England, Almaty and Astana, Kazakhstan.

Represents domestic and foreign clients in a wide variety of trade and investment transactions and litigation, including multinational commercial and financial transactions, public and private offerings of securities, organizational and structural arrangements, including joint ventures, and advises clients in matters, involving energy, natural resources, and domestic and international tax matters. Advisors to the World Bank and governments in providing assistance in the areas of capital market development, privatization, bank supervision and financial sector reform.

Assists clients in compliance with U.S. customs and import Laws, matters before the International Trade Commission and the Department of Commerce (International Trade Administration), and provides advice on establishing and operating foreign trade zones and subzones in the United States, and on the benefits of establishing operations in the U.S. or overseas foreign trade zones.

JOSEPH S. BRACEWELL (1892-1965).
HARRY W. PATTERSON (1922-1990).

FOUNDING PARTNERS AND SPECIAL COUNSEL

SEARCY BRACEWELL, born Houston, Texas, January 19, 1918; admitted to bar, 1940, Texas; 1954, U.S. Supreme Court; 1975, District of Columbia. *Education:* Agricultural and Mechanical College of Texas (B.A., 1938); Houston School of Law. Texas House of Representatives, 1946-1948. Member, Texas Senate, 1948-1958. *Member:* Houston Bar Association; The District of Columbia Bar; State Bar of Texas.

FENTRESS BRACEWELL, born Houston, Texas, November 28, 1921; admitted to bar, 1943, Texas; 1950, U.S. Supreme Court; 1975, District of Columbia. *Education:* Baylor University (LL.B., 1943). Chairman, Port of Houston Authority, 1970-1985. *Member:* Houston and American Bar Associations; The District of Columbia Bar; State Bar of Texas.

PARTNERS

MICHAEL L. PATE, born Fort Worth, Texas, July 9, 1951; admitted to bar, 1976, Texas; 1984, District of Columbia; 1986, U.S. Tax Court; 1987, U.S. Supreme Court. *Education:* Schreiner College (A.A., 1971); Texas Wesleyan College (B.S., 1973); University of Texas (J.D., 1975). Phi Delta Phi. *Member:* The District of Columbia Bar; State Bar of Texas; American Bar Association. ***PRACTICE AREAS:*** Federal and State Taxation; Energy; Environmental; Legislation.

ED BETHUNE, born Pocahontas, Arkansas, December 19, 1935; admitted to bar, 1963, Arkansas; 1989, District of Columbia. *Education:* University of Arkansas (B.S., B.A., 1961; J.D., 1963). Special Agent, Federal Bureau of Investigation, 1964-1968. Prosecuting Attorney, 1st Judicial District, 1970-1971. Chairman, Arkansas Criminal Code Revision Commission, 1971-1975. Chairman, 9th District, Federal Home Loan Bank Board, 1973-1977. Member, United States Congress, Second District of Arkansas, 1979-1985 (Committee on Budget; Committee on Banking, Finance and Urban Affairs; Committee on Small Business). Chairman, Arkansas Republican Party, 1986-1988. *Member:* Arkansas Bar Association; The District of Columbia Bar. ***PRACTICE AREAS:*** Government Relations; Government Strategies.

GENE E. GODLEY, born Houston, Texas, October 6, 1939; admitted to bar, 1963, Texas; 1970, U.S. Supreme Court; 1971, District of Columbia; 1985, Massachusetts. *Education:* Southern Methodist University (B.A., 1960); University of Chicago (J.D., 1963). Phi Delta Phi. Adjunct Professor of Law, Catholic University of America, 1972. General Counsel, U.S. Senate Labor and Public Welfare Committee, 1970. General Counsel, U.S. Senate District Committee, 1971-1972. Assistant Secretary of the Treasury for Legislative Affairs, 1977-1980. *Member:* District of Columbia Bar; State Bar of Texas; Massachusetts Bar Association. ***LANGUAGES:*** Spanish. ***PRACTICE AREAS:*** Business Law; International Trade; Energy; Government; International Law. ***Email:*** ggodley@bracepatt.com

JOHN R. COPE, born San Angelo, Texas, May 30, 1942; admitted to bar, 1966, Texas; 1969, U.S. Court of Appeals, Fifth Circuit; 1976, District of Columbia; 1977, U.S. Court of Appeals for the District of Columbia Circuit and Temporary Emergency Court of Appeals; 1980, U.S. Court of Appeals, Seventh Circuit; 1982, U.S. Supreme Court; 1985, U.S. District Court, District of Maryland; 1992, U.S. Tax Court. *Education:* University of Texas at Austin (B.B.A., 1964; LL.B., 1966); Wesley Theological Seminary (M.T.S., summa cum laude, 2001). Phi Alpha Delta. Chairman, Practising Law Institute Seminars on Litigation, 1980-1981. Member, Federal Savings and Loan Advisory Council, Federal Home Loan Bank Board, 1980-1981. Chief Judge, Wake Island Court, 1989-1990. *Member:* The District of Columbia Bar (Member, Government Contracts and Litigation Divisions); Houston and American (Member, Section on Litigation) Bar Associations; State Bar of Texas. Fellow, Houston Bar Foundation. ***PRACTICE AREAS:*** Business Litigation; Intellectual Property Litigation; Litigation; Professional Liability; Securities Litigation. ***Email:*** jcope@bracepatt.com

(This Listing Continued)

JAMES L. CHAPMAN, born Washington, D.C., March 8, 1945; admitted to bar, 1970, Texas; 1987, U.S. District Court, Eastern District of Texas; 1999, District of Columbia. *Education:* University of Texas (B.B.A., 1968); Southern Methodist University (J.D., 1970). Phi Alpha Delta. District Attorney, Eighth Judicial District, Texas, 1977-1985. U.S. Representative, Texas First District, 1985-1996. *Member:* The District of Columbia Bar; State Bar of Texas. ***PRACTICE AREAS:*** Energy; Health Care; Environmental; Government; Public Policy.

CHARLES H. SHONEMAN, born Philadelphia, Pennsylvania, June 27, 1947; admitted to bar, 1973, District of Columbia; 1974, U.S. Court of Appeals for the District of Columbia Circuit; 1980, U.S. Court of Appeals, Fourth Circuit and U.S. Supreme Court; 1981, U.S. Court of Appeals, Fifth Circuit; 1983, U.S. Court of Appeals, Tenth Circuit; 1988, U.S. Court of Appeals, Third Circuit. *Education:* Duke University (B.A., 1969); George Washington University (J.D., with honors, 1972). *Member:* The District of Columbia Bar; American Bar Association; Energy Bar Association. ***PRACTICE AREAS:*** Electric Power; Energy Regulation; Oil and Gas Pipelines; Regulated Industries; Public Utility Regulation.

MARC RACICOT, born Thompson Falls, Montana, July 24, 1948; admitted to bar, 1973, Montana and U.S. District Court, District of Montana; 1989, U.S. Supreme Court (Not admitted in District of Columbia). *Education:* Carroll College (B.A., 1970); University of Montana (J.D., 1973). ***PRACTICE AREAS:*** Government Relations and Strategy; Public Policy.

GEORGE M. FOOTE, born August 8, 1949; admitted to bar, 1975, District of Columbia; 1981, Virginia and U.S. Tax Court. *Education:* Washington & Lee University (B.A., 1971); Georgetown University Law Center (J.D., 1974; LL.M., 1978). ***PRACTICE AREAS:*** International Transactions; Telecommunications; Nonprofit Organizations.

STEPHEN F. HOGWOOD, born Delaware, Ohio, August 2, 1952; admitted to bar, 1977, Texas; 1991, District of Columbia. *Education:* Oxford University, England and University of the South (B.A., summa cum laude, 1974); Duke University (J.D., 1977). Phi Beta Kappa. Member, Brazil-U.S. Business Council and Washington, D.C. Chapter, British American Business Association. *Member:* The District of Columbia Bar; State Bar of Texas. ***PRACTICE AREAS:*** Energy Project Development; Energy Finance; Energy Acquisitions; International Transactions; International Finance; International Construction Law. ***Email:*** shogwood@bracepatt.com

NANCY MORRISON O'CONNOR, born Washington, D.C., August 25, 1951; admitted to bar, 1977, Texas; 1989, District of Columbia; 1990, Maryland. *Education:* Gettysburg College (B.A., magna cum laude, 1973); University of Notre Dame (J.D., 1976). Editor, Notre Dame Lawyer Law Review, 1975-1976. Member, Ethics Panel, Montgomery County Board of Education, 2000. Adjunct Faculty, "Employment Dispute Resolution," University of Texas, Spring 1986. *Member:* American Bar Association (Vice Chair, Section on Administrative Law and Regulatory Practice, Labor and Employment Law Committee, 1991—; Member, Sections on: Labor and Employment Law; Litigation). ***PRACTICE AREAS:*** Labor and Employment; Civil Litigation.

ANTHONY H. ANIKEEFF, born Washington, D.C., December 30, 1952; admitted to bar, 1980, Virginia; 1983, District of Columbia; 1985, U.S. Court of International Trade; 1986, U.S. District Court for the District of Columbia; 1987, U.S. Court of Federal Claims; 2000, U.S. Court of Appeals for the Federal Circuit. *Education:* University of Virginia (B.A., with distinction, 1975); College of William and Mary (J.D., 1980); London School of Economics and Political Science, University of London (LL.M., 1981). Research Editor, William and Mary Law Review, 1978-1980. Law Clerk to Hon. D. Dortch Warriner, U.S. District Court, Richmond, Virginia, 1981-1982. Associate, Kilpatrick & Lody, 1982-1987. Trial Attorney, Senior Trial Counsel and Assistant Branch Director, Commercial Litigation Branch, Civil Division, U.S. Department of Justice, 1987-1999. Vice President and General Counsel, Alliance and Automobile Manufacturers, 1999-2000. ***PRACTICE AREAS:*** Government Contracts; Commercial Litigation; International Trade. ***Email:*** aanikeeff@bracepatt.com

LUIS M. NIDO, born San Juan, Puerto Rico, November 13, 1948; admitted to bar, 1980, Puerto Rico; 1981, District of Columbia and U.S. District Court, District of Columbia; 1986, U.S. Court of Appeals, Sixth and Eleventh Circuits; 1988, U.S. Court of Appeals, Seventh and District of Columbia Circuits. *Education:* U.S. Military Academy (B.S., 1971); Georgetown University Law Center (J.D., cum laude, 1980). Member, Editorial Board, Law and Policy in International Business, 1979-1980. *Member:* The District of Columbia Bar; Bar Association of Puerto Rico; Federal and American Bar Associations. ***LAN-***

(This Listing Continued)

BRACEWELL & PATTERSON, L.L.P., Washington—Continued

GUAGES: Spanish. ***PRACTICE AREAS:*** Environmental Law; Environmental Liability; Environmental Litigation; Mergers and Acquisitions; Superfund. ***Email:*** lnido@bracepatt.com

RANDALL S. RICH, born St. Louis, Missouri, January 12, 1955; admitted to bar, 1980, Missouri; 1981, District of Columbia. *Education:* Brandeis University (B.A., magna cum laude with high honors, 1977); Washington University (J.D., 1980). Member, Washington University Law Quarterly, 1979-1980. *Member:* The District of Columbia Bar; The Missouri Bar; American and Energy (Co-Chair, Committee on Programs and Meetings, 1999-2000; Chairman, Committee on Natural Gas Rate and Accounting Regulations, 1990; Vice Chairman, 1992-1993) Bar Associations. ***SPECIAL AGENCIES:*** Federal Energy Regulatory Commission and State Public Utility Commissions. ***PRACTICE AREAS:*** Oil and Gas Pipelines; Public Utility Regulation; Energy Regulation; Electric Power.

JEFFREY D. WATKISS, born Salt Lake City, Utah, March 24, 1954; admitted to bar, 1980, District of Columbia. *Education:* Stanford University (A.B., 1975); University of Utah (J.D., 1980). Order of the Coif. Editor-in-Chief, Utah Law Review, 1979-1980. Special Assistant to Deputy General Counsel for Litigation, 1982-1985. Senior Litigation Attorney, Federal Energy Regulatory Commission, 1985-1986. *Member:* District of Columbia Bar; Energy Bar Association. ***LANGUAGES:*** French and Spanish. ***PRACTICE AREAS:*** Energy and Environmental.

ALBERT B. KRACHMAN, born Chester, Pennsylvania, November 13, 1956; admitted to bar, 1983, District of Columbia; 1984, U.S. Court of Appeals for the Federal Circuit and U.S. Claims Court; 1993, U.S. Supreme Court. *Education:* Boston University (B.A., summa cum laude, 1979); George Washington University (J.D., 1982). Phi Delta Phi; Pi Mu Epsilon. Member, George Washington University Law Review, 1981-1982. *Member:* The District of Columbia Bar (Member, Sections on: Government Contracts; Litigation). ***PRACTICE AREAS:*** Commercial Law; Litigation; Government Contracts; Construction Law; Technology. ***Email:*** akrachman@bracepatt.com

NANCY A. WODKA, born Trenton, New Jersey, December 16, 1952; admitted to bar, 1984, District of Columbia. *Education:* Clark University (B.A., 1974); George Washington University (J.D., with honors, 1984). *Member:* District of Columbia Bar. ***PRACTICE AREAS:*** Asset Based Finance; Construction Law; Energy Project Development; Energy Acquisitions; Energy Finance. ***Email:*** nwodka@bracepatt.com

NANCY JO NELSON, born Chicago, Illinois, August 10, 1955; admitted to bar, 1985, Texas; 1986, District of Columbia; 1993, New York. *Education:* Ohio State University (B.A., cum laude, 1977); Georgetown University, Center for Contemporary Arab Studies (M.A., 1980); The George Washington University, National Law Center (J.D., with honors, 1984). *Member:* State Bar of Texas; District of Columbia Bar; New York State Bar Association. ***PRACTICE AREAS:*** Project Finance; Export Finance; Loan Facilities; Letters of Credit; Structured Finance.

SCOTT H. SEGAL, born Dallas, Texas, April 29, 1964; admitted to bar, 1989, Texas; 1991, District of Columbia. *Education:* Emory University (B.A., summa cum laude, 1986); University of Texas at Austin (J.D., 1989). Phi Beta Kappa. Member, Texas Law Review, 1988-1989. Editor, Environmental Law Journal. Director of Forensics, University of Texas, Austin, 1987-1989. Executive Director, Cement Kiln Recycling Coalition, 1992. *Member:* State Bar of Texas; District of Columbia Bar. ***PRACTICE AREAS:*** Trade; Legislation; Energy; Environmental.

KEVIN A. EWING, born Washington, D.C., May 22, 1966; admitted to bar, 1992, Maryland; 1994, District of Columbia. *Education:* Yale College (B.A., cum laude, 1988); Georgetown University (J.D., 1991); University of Heidelberg, Germany (LL.M., 1993). Member, Women's Council on Energy and the Environment. ***LANGUAGES:*** German, French. ***PRACTICE AREAS:*** Environmental Law; Environmental Criminal Defense; Environmental Lender Liability; Hazardous Waste; Mergers and Acquisitions. ***Email:*** kewing@bracepatt.com

COUNSEL

RONALD N. CARROLL, born Baltimore, Maryland, November 14, 1949; admitted to bar, 1976, Pennsylvania; 1985, Maryland, U.S. Court of Appeals for the District of Columbia and Fifth Circuits; 1987, U.S. Court of Appeals, Fourth Circuit; 1992, U.S. District Court, District of Maryland; 1993, U.S. Court of Appeals, Eleventh Circuit; 1996, District of Columbia and U.S. District Court for the District of Columbia Circuit. *Education:* University of Maryland (B.A., 1972); University of Baltimore (J.D., 1975). Articles Editor, University of Baltimore Law Review. Law Clerk to Hon. James C. Morton, Jr., Maryland Court of Special Appeals, 1976-1978. Author: "Zoning Legislation for Society Aesthetic Purposes Held Not Within the Police Powers of the State with Certain Specified Exceptions," 3 U.Balt. L.R. 125 (1973). *Member:* District of Columbia Bar; Federal Energy Bar Association. ***PRACTICE AREAS:*** Energy; Administrative; Regulatory; Antitrust; Litigation; Appellate. ***Email:*** rcarroll@bracepatt.com

(This Listing Continued)

RICHARD D. HORN, born Bad Kreuznach, Germany, May 16, 1962; admitted to bar, 1989, Maryland; 1991, District of Columbia. *Education:* North Carolina State University (B.A., 1984); American University (J.D., cum laude, 1989). *Member:* The District of Columbia Bar; Maryland Bar Association.

CHARLES L. INGEBRETSON, born San Diego, California, July 1, 1955; admitted to bar, 1987, Virginia (Not admitted in District of Columbia). *Education:* Duke University (B.A., 1978); University of Notre Dame (J.D., 1987). General Counsel, Committee on Commerce, U.S. House of Representatives, 1995-1998; Counsel, Committee on Energy & Commerce, U.S. House of Representatives, 1990-1994; Legislative Director, Office of Congressman Dan Coats (R-IN), 1981-1984. ***PRACTICE AREAS:*** Public Utility Regulation; Regulated Industries; Trade Regulation. ***Email:*** cingebretson@bracepatt.com

ASSOCIATES

BRIAN W. BAKER, admitted to bar, 1999, Connecticut and District of Columbia; District of Columbia Court of Appeals. *Education:* University of Virginia (B.A., 1996); Vanderbilt University Law School (J.D., 1999). ***PRACTICE AREAS:*** Litigation; Government Contracts. ***Email:*** bbaker@bracepatt.com

CARLYN M. CAREY, admitted to bar, 2000, New York and Massachusetts (Not admitted in District of Columbia). *Education:* Ithaca College (B.A., 1992); American University (J.D., 2000). ***PRACTICE AREAS:*** Real Estate; Energy; Finance; Corporate Transactions. ***Email:*** ccarey@bracepatt.com

KIMBERLY CURRY, born Washington, D.C., July 8, 1972; admitted to bar, 2001, Maryland (Not admitted in District of Columbia). *Education:* University of Maryland (B.A., 1994); George Washington University (J.D., 2000). ***PRACTICE AREAS:*** Energy. ***Email:*** kcurry@bracepatt.com

ARYEH FISHMAN, born New York, N.Y., August 18, 1969; admitted to bar, 1997, New York; 1998, U.S. Court of Appeals for the District of Columbia Circuit and U.S. District Court, Southern and Eastern Districts of New York; 1999, District of Columbia and U.S. District Court for the District of Columbia. *Education:* Brown University (B.A., 1991); Georgetown University Law Center (J.D., 1996). Co-Author: Chapter on Natural Gas Transportation, "Energy Law and Transactions," Matthew Bender, 2000. *Member:* New York State and American Bar Associations; District of Columbia Bar; Federal Energy Bar Association. ***PRACTICE AREAS:*** Energy Law; Electricity; Natural Gas Transportation; Administrative Law; Appellate Litigation. ***Email:*** afishman@bracepatt.com

AMAURI GAUDENSI COSTA, born Jundiaí, SP, Brazil, May 20, 1968; admitted to bar, 1991, São Paulo, Brazil (Not admitted in the United States). *Education:* Universidade de São Paulo (LL.B., 1990); University McKenzie (Graduate Specialization in Corporate and Commercial Law, 1991); Queen Mary and Westfield College, University of London (LL.M., 1995). (Foreign Legal Consultant — Brazil). ***LANGUAGES:*** Portuguese, English, Spanish. ***PRACTICE AREAS:*** International Loans; International Energy Law; International Finance. ***Email:*** acosta@bracepatt.com

KEVIN B. HAWKINS, born Charlottesville, VA, 1966; admitted to bar, 1998, Connecticut; 1999, U.S. District Court, District of Connecticut (Not admitted in District of Columbia). *Education:* Bowdoin College (A.B., 1988); University of Connecticut (J.D., cum laude, 1998). Member, University of Connecticut Law Review. Certified Social Worker, New York, 1997. Co-Chair, Real Property, Young Lawyers Section, Connecticut Bar Association, 1998-2000; Chair, Hartford Local Unit, Young Lawyers Section, 2000-2001. *Member:* Connecticut, American (Vice Chair, Young Lawyers Division, Public Transportation, Energy and Communications Committee, 2001—) and Energy Bar Associations. ***LANGUAGES:*** Vietnamese. ***PRACTICE AREAS:*** Energy; Finance. ***Email:*** khawkins@bracepatt.com

MARC C. HEBERT, born Jefferson Parish, Louisiana, January 22, 1969; admitted to bar, 1994, Louisiana; 1996, Virginia; 1998, District of Columbia and U.S. Court of Appeals for the Federal Circuit, U.S. Court of Appeals, Fourth Circuit; U.S. Court of International Trade. *Education:* Southern Methodist University; Tulane University (B.A., 1991); Loyola University (J.D., 1994); George Washington University (LL.M., in Environmental, 1996). Member, St. Thomas More Inns of Court. Author: "Coastal Restoration Under CWPPRA and Property Rights Issues," Louisiana Law Review, Vol. 57, No. 4, 1997; "Unilateralism as a Defense Mechanism: An Overview of the Iran and Libyan Sanctions," Act of 1996 Vol. 5, Yearbook of International Law, University of Miami, 1997. *Member:* Louisiana State, Virginia and American Bar Associations. ***PRACTICE AREAS:*** Legislation (5%); International Law (80%); Environmental Law (10%); Election Law (5%). ***Email:*** mhebert@bracepatt.com

ROBERT HOUSMAN, born Manhasset, New York, August 13, 1965; admitted to bar, 1991, Pennsylvania; 1993, U.S. Court of Appeals for the District of Columbia Circuit (Not admitted in District of Columbia). *Education:* St. Lawrence University (B.A., 1987); Washington College of Law (J.D., 1990).

(This Listing Continued)

JASON B. HUTT, born New Haven, Connecticut, February 19, 1973; admitted to bar, 1999, District of Columbia and New York. *Education:* Colgate University (B.A., 1995); Vermont Law School (J.D., magna cum laude, 1998). Dean's Fellowship. American College of Trial Lawyers National Moot Court Competition Finalist. Associate Articles Editor, Vermont Law Review. ***LANGUAGES:*** Spanish. ***PRACTICE AREAS:*** Environmental Law; Environmental Litigation; Mergers and Acquisitions. ***Email:*** jhutt@bracepatt.com

JACQUELINE R. JAVA, born Pittsburgh, Pennsylvania, October 22, 1975; admitted to bar, 2001, Virginia and District of Columbia. *Education:* Pennsylvania State University (B.S., 1997); George Washington University (J.D., 2000). Member, International Law Review, George Washington University, 1999-2000. ***PRACTICE AREAS:*** Telecommunications; Energy.

SHELBY J. KELLEY, admitted to bar, 1999, Virginia and District of Columbia, U.S. District Court, Eastern and Western Districts of Virginia; U.S. District Court for the District of Columbia, U.S. Court of Appeals, Fourth Circuit; U.S. Supreme Court. *Education:* Georgetown University (B.A., 1995; J.D., 1999). ***PRACTICE AREAS:*** Litigation. ***Email:*** skelley@bracepatt.com

LORI H. SCHECTEL, born Edison, New Jersey, July 14, 1974; admitted to bar, 1999, Maryland (Not admitted in District of Columbia). *Education:* Emory University (B.A., 1996); University of Maryland (J.D., with concentration in Environmental Law, 1999). Omicron Delta Kappa; Phi Sigma Iota. Senior Articles Editor, Maryland Journal of International Law & Trade, 1998-1999. *Member:* Maryland State and American Bar Associations. ***LANGUAGES:*** Spanish. ***PRACTICE AREAS:*** Environmental Law. ***Email:*** lschectel@bracepatt.com

ANDREA M. SETTANNI, born Haddonfield, New Jersey, July 2, 1970; admitted to bar, 1995, Maryland; 1997, District of Columbia. *Education:* Boston College (B.A., 1992); Catholic University of America (J.D., 1995). *Member:* The District of Columbia Bar; Energy Bar Association. ***PRACTICE AREAS:*** Regulatory Law; Utility Law; Energy Law. ***Email:*** asettanni@bracepatt.com

CHARLTON C. WALKER, born Decatur, Georgia, December 16, 1969; admitted to bar, 1995, North Carolina; 2001, District of Columbia. *Education:* Oglethorpe University (B.A., 1992); Duke University (J.D., 1995). *Member:* American Bar Association (Member, Public Contract Law Section). [Captain, U.S. Air Force, 1995-2000]. ***PRACTICE AREAS:*** Government Contracts; Litigation. ***Email:*** cwalker@bracepatt.com

(For Data on all Firm Personnel see Professional Biographies at Houston, Austin, Corpus Christi, Fort Worth, Dallas, and San Antonio, Texas, McLean, Virginia and London, England)

BRADLEY ARANT ROSE & WHITE LLP

801 PENNSYLVANIA AVENUE NW, SUITE 230
WASHINGTON, D.C. 20004
Telephone: 202-393-7150
Facsimile: 202-347-1684
Email: info@bradleyarant.com
URL: http://www.bradleyarant.com

REVISERS OF THE ALABAMA LAW DIGEST FOR THIS DIRECTORY

Birmingham, Alabama Office: 2001 Park Place, Suite 1400, 35203. Telephone: 205-521-8000. Facsimile: 205-521-8800.

Huntsville, Alabama Office: 200 Clinton Avenue West, Suite 900, 35801. Telephone: 256-517-5100. Facsimile: 256-517-5200.

Montgomery, Alabama Office: RSA Union Office Building, 100 North Union Street, Suite 650, 36104. Telephone: 334-261-4211. Facsimile: 334-261-4234. and 504 South Perry Street, 36102. Telephone: 334-834-6222. Facsimile: 334-834-7080.

Jackson, Mississippi Office: 188 East Capitol Street, Suite 450, 39201. Telephone: 601-948-8000. Facsimile: 601-948-3000.

Banking and Financial Services; Competitive Practices; Intellectual Property; Construction and Procurement; Corporate Law; Securities; Mergers and Acquisitions; Compliance; Environmental Law; Toxic Torts; Labor and Employment; ERISA; Litigation; Governmental Affairs; Health Care Law; Tax Exempt Facilities; Health Care Fraud; International Law; International Transactions; Public Finance; Real Estate Law; Finance; Land Use; Leasing; Workouts; Reorganization Restructuring and Insolvency; Tax Law; Trusts and Estates; White Collar Crime.

MEMBERS OF FIRM

DOUGLAS E. ECKERT, born White Plains, New York, March 27, 1966; admitted to bar, 1993, Alabama, U.S. Court of Appeals, Eleventh Circuit and U.S. District Court, Northern, Middle and Southern Districts of Alabama (Not admitted in District of Columbia). *Education:* University of Virginia (B.A., International Relations, with honors, 1987; J.D., 1993). Executive Editor, Virginia Journal of International Law, 1991-1993. Author: "International Arbitrational Alternate Dispute Resolution," Construction Law (Matthew Bender & Company) (upcoming); "Consolidation of Multiple Arbitrations: An International Perspective on the American Approach and a Proposal for an Institution Solution," Virginia Journal of International Law, Fall, 1993. Adjunct Professor, European Community Law, University of Alabama, 1997. Senior Legislative Assistant, Sen. Trent Lott, 1987-1989. *Member:* Birmingham, American and International Bar Associations; Alabama State Bar; London Court of International Arbitration. (Also at Birmingham, Alabama Office). ***PRACTICE AREAS:*** International; Litigation; Construction; Governmental Affairs. ***Email:*** deckert@bradleyarant.com

BEN L. ERDREICH, born Birmingham, Alabama, December 9, 1938; admitted to bar, 1963, Alabama; 1984, District of Columbia. *Education:* Yale University (B.A., 1960); University of Alabama (J.D., 1963). Editor-in-Chief, Alabama Law Review. Member, Alabama House of Representatives, 1970-1974; Member, Jefferson County (Alabama) Commission, 1974-1982; Member of Congress, U.S. House of Representatives, Alabama Sixth District, 1983-1993; Chairman, U.S. Merit Systems Protection Board, 1993-2000. *Member:* Birmingham and American Bar Associations; Alabama State Bar; The District of Columbia Bar. ***PRACTICE AREAS:*** Government Affairs; Election Law; Campaign Law; Political Law. ***Email:*** berdreich@bradleyarant.com

GEORGE BRYAN HARRIS, born Columbia, South Carolina, July 8, 1964; admitted to bar, 1989, Alabama and U.S. District Court, Northern District of Alabama; 1991, District of Columbia; 1992, U.S. District Court, Middle District of Alabama; 1993, U.S. Supreme Court and U.S. District Court, Southern District of Alabama; U.S. Court of Appeals, Fifth and Eleventh Circuits; 1995, London Court of International Arbitration; 1996, U.S. District Court, Northern District of Texas; 2000, U.S. Court of Appeals, Fourth and Federal Circuits. *Education:* University of Alabama (B.A., Political Science, magna cum laude, 1986); University of Virginia (J.D., 1989). Phi Beta Kappa; Omicron Delta Kappa. Mortar Board. *Member:* Birmingham and American Bar Associations; Alabama State Bar; District of Columbia Bar. (Also at Montgomery and Birmingham, Alabama Offices). ***PRACTICE AREAS:*** Corporations; Business Litigation; Alternative Dispute Resolution. ***Email:*** gharris@bradleyarant.com

JEFFREY D. KOMAROW, born Brooklyn, New York, March 2, 1949; admitted to bar, 1975, District of Columbia, U.S. District Court, District of Columbia and U.S. Court of Appeals, District of Columbia Circuit; 1981, U.S. Court of Appeals, Fifth Circuit; 1984, U.S. Court of Appeals, Eleventh Circuit; 1988, U.S. Supreme Court and U.S. Court of Appeals, Third Circuit. *Education:* University of Michigan (A.B., with high distinction, 1971; J.D., magna cum laude, 1974). Order of the Coif. Articles Editor, Michigan Law Review, 1973-1974. Law Clerk to Judge Edward Allen Tamm, U.S. Court of Appeals for the District of Columbia Circuit, 1974-1975. *Member:* The District of Columbia Bar; Energy Bar Association (Chairman, Committee on Antitrust, 1990-1991). ***PRACTICE AREAS:*** Energy; Appellate Practice; Utility Law; Regulatory Law. ***Email:*** jkomarow@bradleyarant.com

JACK W. SELDEN, born Washington, D.C., January 8, 1955; admitted to bar, 1981, Alabama; 1982, U.S. District Court, Northern District of Alabama and U.S. Court of Appeals, Eleventh Circuit; 1993, U.S. Supreme Court (Not admitted in District of Columbia). *Education:* University of Virginia (B.A., 1978); University of Alabama (J.D., 1981). United States Attorney for Northern District of Alabama, 1992-1993. Assistant U.S. Attorney, Northern District of Alabama, 1982-1985. Member, U.S. Attorney General's Advisory Subcommittees on White Collar Crime, Financial Litigation and Sentencing Guidelines, 1992-1993. Member, National Association of Former United States Attorneys, 1993—, Member, Board of Directors. *Member:* Birmingham and American Bar Associations; Alabama State Bar. ***PRACTICE AREAS:*** Litigation; Health Care Fraud; White Collar Criminal Defense; Governmental Affairs. ***Email:*** jselden@bradleyarant.com

LUTHER J. STRANGE, III, born March 1, 1953; admitted to bar, 1979, Louisiana; 1980, Texas; 1981, Alabama; 1988, District of Columbia; U.S. Supreme Court; U.S. Court of Appeals, Fifth, Eleventh and District of Columbia Circuits; U.S. District Court, Northern District of Alabama. *Education:* Tulane University (B.A., Political Science, 1975; J.D., 1979). Author: "The Lawyer As A Lobbyist," The Alabama Lawyer, January, 1988. *Member:* Federal Energy Bar Association (Past Chairman, Legislation, Energy and Regulatory Reform Committee); Public Affairs Research Council of Alabama (Board of Directors); U.S. Oil and Gas Association, Alabama and Mississippi Division (Board of Directors); Alabama Industry and Manufacturers Association (Chairperson, Federal Affairs Committee). (Also at Montgomery, Huntsville and Birmingham, Alabama Offices). ***PRACTICE AREAS:*** Governmental. ***Email:*** lstrange@bradleyarant.com

ASSOCIATE

DAVID STEWART, admitted to bar, 2000, Alabama (Not admitted in District of Columbia). *Education:* Washington & Lee University (B.A., magna cum laude, 1996); University of Virginia School of Law (J.D., 2000). Phi Beta Kappa. Rhodes Scholar nominee. Member, Executive Committee, Student Body, Washington & Lee University. Honor Counsel, University of Virginia School of Law. Mock Covention General Chairman, Washington & Lee University. (Also in Birmingham and Montgomery, Alabama and Offices). ***PRACTICE AREAS:*** Government Affairs; Election Law; Campaign Law; Political Law; Litigation. ***Email:*** dstewart@bradleyarant.com

(This Listing Continued)

BRADLEY ARANT ROSE & WHITE LLP, Washington—Continued

FINANCIAL SERVICE COMPANIES: SouthTrust Corporation; Financial Investors of the South; Synovus Financial Corp.; SouthTrust Bank; First Commercial Bank; First National Bank of Jasper; Bank of Alabama; Aliant Bank; SOUTHBank; Retirement Systems of Alabama.
CONSTRUCTION AND ENGINEERING: BE&K; Brasfield & Gorrie; The Clark Construction Group; Bill Harbert International; EuroDisney; Robins & Morton; Beaver Construction Company; Wheelabrator Technologies; Hoar Construction Company.
EDUCATION: University of Alabama; Auburn University; University of South Alabama.
ENVIRONMENTAL: WMX Corporation; BEC-Allwaste; Birmingham Steel; Energen.
FOOD AND BEVERAGE: Associated Grocers of Alabama, Inc.; Barber Dairies, Inc.; Coca-Cola Bottling Company United, Inc.; Shoney's.
HEALTH CARE: The Children's Health System of Alabama; Eastern Health System, Inc. (including Medical Center East); University of Alabama Health Services Foundation, P.C. (The Kirklin Clinic); The DCH Health Care Authority; CACH HMO, Inc.; VIVA Health, Inc.; University of Alabama Hospital; American Medical Response (AMR); The South Baldwin County Health Care Authority (including South Baldwin Regional Medical Center); The Colbert County - Northwest Alabama Health Care Authority (including Helen Keller Hospital); The Healthcare Authority of Morgan County; City of Decatur (including Decatur General Hospital); Alacare Home Health Services, Inc.; The Heart Center, P.C.; Huntsville Lung Associates, P.C.
INSURANCE: Hartford Insurance Co.; Seaboard/St. Paul Surety Company; Torchmark; Liberty National Life Insurance Company; State Farm; The Chubb Group.
MANUFACTURING: Blount Inc.; Ciba-Geigy; Ford Motor Co.; U.S. Pipe and Foundry Co.; Kenworth Truck Company and Peterbilt; Stockham Valves & Fittings, Inc.; United Technologies Corporation; Russell Corporation; Fruit of the Loom, Inc.; Martin Industries, Inc.; WMX Corporation; Trico Steel Company, Inc.; The Goodyear Tire & Rubber Co.; Bridgestone/Firestone, Inc.; Michelin Tire Corp.
MEDIA/PUBLICATIONS/COMMUNICATIONS: The Huntsville Times; The New York Times Co.; Time Warner Cable; EBSCO Industries, Inc.; Southern Progress Corporation.
MINING, MINERALS, NATURAL RESOURCES: Jim Walter Resources, Inc.; Hunt Refining Company; Champion International Corp.; Vulcan Materials Company; Nelson Brothers, Inc.; AlaGasCo.
REAL ESTATE: Alabama Association of Homebuilders; Birmingham Association of Realtors; Birmingham Realty Company; Graham & Company; Jim Wilson & Associates; The Hays Group; Torchmark Development Corporation; Guilford Capital Corporation; Sloss Development Group.
RETAIL GASOLINE DISTRIBUTION: Chevron U.S.A., Inc.; Union Oil Company of California; BP Oil Co.
TECHNOLOGY AND BIOTECHNOLOGY: BioCryst Pharmaceuticals; Bioelastics Research, Ltd.; Southern BioSystems, Inc.; Southern Applied Technologies, Inc.
TRADE ASSOCIATIONS: Ductile Iron Pipe Research Association; Associated Builders and Contractors, Inc.

REVISERS OF THE ALABAMA LAW DIGEST FOR THIS DIRECTORY

(For biographical data on all personnel, see Professional Biographies at Birmingham, Alabama)

BRAND & FRULLA

A PROFESSIONAL CORPORATION

923 FIFTEENTH STREET, N.W.
WASHINGTON, D.C. 20005
Telephone: 202-662-9700
Facsimile: 202-737-7565
URL: http://www.lawyers.com/brand&frulla

Criminal and Civil Litigation. Practice before Congress, Federal, State and Local Agencies. Appellate and Supreme Court Practice.

FIRM PROFILE: A Washington, D.C.-based law firm with a national practice, Brand & Frulla concentrates in the areas of civil and criminal litigation. Its clients range from Fortune 100 companies to small start-ups, from non-profit organizations to national trade associations and trade unions, from individuals to state and local governments and officials.

The firm represents clients before federal and state regulatory and law enforcement agencies, the U.S. Congress in civil and criminal investigations, government contracts and government, private enterprise ethics and election law.

STANLEY M. BRAND, born New York, N.Y., November 9, 1948; admitted to bar, 1975, District of Columbia; 1976, U.S. District Court for the District of Columbia; 1978, U.S. Court of Appeals for the District of Columbia; 1981, U.S. Court of Appeals, 4th Circuit and U.S. Supreme Court. *Education:* Franklin & Marshall College (B.A., 1970); Georgetown University Law Center (J.D., 1974). Adjunct Professor, Appellate Advocacy: Separation of Powers, Administrative Law, Georgetown University Law Center, 1983-1986. Legislative Assistant to the Honorable Thomas P. O'Neill, Jr., Majority Leader, United States House of Representatives, 1971-1974. Attorney/Advisor, United States Securities and Exchange Commission, Division of Investment Management, 1974-1976. General Counsel to the United States House of Representatives, 1976-1983. Vice-President, National Association of Professional Baseball Leagues, Inc., 1992—. *Member:* The District of Columbia Bar; Federal Bar Association. ***PRACTICE AREAS:*** Criminal Law; Civil Litigation; Trade Associations; Trade Regulation; Administrative Law; Election Law. ***Email:*** sbrand@brand-frulla.com

(This Listing Continued)

DAVID E. FRULLA, born Glens Falls, New York, October 6, 1962; admitted to bar, 1987, Maryland; 1988, District of Columbia. *Education:* Dartmouth College (A.B., summa cum laude, 1984); University of Virginia (J.D., 1987). Phi Beta Kappa; Order of the Coif. Notes Editor, University of Virginia Journal of Law and Politics. Author: "Soft Money: The Outlook for Reform," U. VA. J.L. & P., 1987; "State Criminal Liability in the Boardroom," White Collar Crime Reporter (June 1992); "Who's Up First? The Clark Clifford Prosecutions and the Limits of Federal Authority," White Collar Crime Reporter (Nov./Dec. 1992); Co-Author: "Qui Tam Litigation Under the False Claims Act," (book length monograph, ABA Section of Public Contract Law, 1994). *Member:* The District of Columbia Bar; Maryland State and American Bar Associations. ***PRACTICE AREAS:*** Regulatory Litigation; Small Business Law; Natural Resources; Campaign Ethics; Criminal; Regulatory Law; Civil Litigation. ***Email:*** dfrulla@brand-frulla.com

ROSS A. NABATOFF, born New York, N.Y., November 28, 1958; admitted to bar, 1984, District of Columbia; 1985, Florida. *Education:* Duke University (B.A., 1980); Washington University (J.D., 1983). Law Clerk, Honorable Joseph W. Hatchett, Circuit Judge, U.S. Court of Appeals, Eleventh Circuit, 1983. Assistant U.S. Attorney, Northern District of Florida, Tallahassee, Florida, 1984-1987. ***PRACTICE AREAS:*** Criminal Litigation; Civil Litigation; Federal Employment Litigation. ***Email:*** rnabatoff@brand-frulla.com

---

ANDREW DEWALD HERMAN, born Washington, D.C., December 11, 1968; admitted to bar, 1997, California; 1999, District of Columbia, U.S. District Court for the District of Columbia and U.S. Court of Appeals, First, Fourth and District of Columbia Circuits. *Education:* University of Michigan (B.A., 1991); University of California, Hastings (J.D., magna cum laude, 1996). Order of the Coif; Thurston Society. Law Clerk to: Honorable Melvin Burnetti, U.S. Circuit Judge, Ninth Circuit Court of Appeals, 1996-1997; Honorable Charles R. Breyer, U.S. District Judge, Northern District of California, 1998. ***PRACTICE AREAS:*** Criminal Litigation; Civil Litigation; Administrative Law. ***Email:*** aherman@brand-frulla.com

JASON S. HADGES, born New Rochelle, New York, September 24, 1969; admitted to bar, 1995, Florida; 1999, District of Columbia. *Education:* Duke University (B.A., 1991); American University (J.D., summa cum laude, 1995). [LT. JAGC, U.S. Navy, 1995-1999]. ***PRACTICE AREAS:*** Criminal Litigation; Civil Litigation; Employment Law; Administrative Law. ***Email:*** jhadges@brand-frulla.com

COREY A. RUBIN, born Brooklyn, New York, November 26, 1969; admitted to bar, 1997, California; 1998, District of Columbia. *Education:* Sacramento State University (B.A., 1994); University of San Francisco Law School (J.D., 1997). *Member:* State Bar of California; District of Columbia Bar. ***PRACTICE AREAS:*** Election and Campaign Finance; White Collar Crime; Administrative Law. ***Email:*** crubin@brand-frulla.com

DEBORAH Y. HO, born Houston, Texas, March 22, 1969; admitted to bar, 1996, Mississippi; 1998, District of Columbia; U.S. Court of Federal Claims; U.S. District Court for the District of Columbia. *Education:* Stanford University (B.A., 1991); University of Mississippi (J.D., magna cum laude, 1996). Author: "Employment Law - Exceptions to the At-Will Doctrine," 64 Miss. L. J. 257, 1994. ***PRACTICE AREAS:*** Civil Litigation; Regulatory Law; Legislative Practice; Election Law. ***Email:*** dho@brand-frulla.com

HELEN-MARY BRIDGET McGOVERN, born Washington, D.C., June 8, 1973; admitted to bar, 2001, Massachusetts (Not admitted in District of Columbia). *Education:* Georgetown University (B.A., cum laude, 1995); University of Notre Dame (J.D., 2000). ***Email:*** bmcgovern@brand-frulla.com

OF COUNSEL

EUGENE GRESSMAN, born Lansing, Michigan, April 18, 1917; admitted to bar, 1940, Michigan; 1945, U.S. Supreme Court; 1948, District of Columbia; 1954, U.S. Court of Appeals for the District of Columbia Circuit; 1959, Maryland. *Education:* University of Michigan (A.B., 1938; J.D., 1940); Seton Hall University (LL.D., 1994). Phi Beta Kappa; Order of the Coif. Member Board of Editors, Michigan Law Review, 1939-1940. Co-Author: Stern, Gressman, Shapiro & Geller: "Supreme Court Practice," 7th edition, BNA, Inc., 1993; Crump, Gressman and Day, "Cases and Materials on Constitutional Law," 3rd edition, Matthew Bender Co., 1998; Wright, Miller, Cooper and Gressman: "Federal Practice and Procedure: Jurisdiction," Vol. 16, West Publishing Co., 1977. Visiting Professor: Ohio State Law School, Summer, 1967; Michigan Law School, Summer, 1969; Indiana Law School (Washington Program), Fall, 1975; George Washington University Law School, 1971-1977; Catholic University Law School, Summer, 1977; Fordham University Law School, 1982-1983, 1987-1988. Distinguished Visiting Professor, Seton Hall University School of Law, 1987-1994. William Rand Kenan, Jr. Professor of Law, University of North Carolina School of Law, 1977-1987, Professor Emeritus, 1987—. Attorney, Securities & Exchange Commission, 1940-1943. Law Clerk to Justice Frank Murphy, U.S. Supreme Court, 1943-1948. Judge, Appeal Tax Court, Montgomery County, Maryland, 1959-1962. Chairman, Rules Advisory Committee of the

(This Listing Continued)

Fourth Circuit, 1984-1989. *Member:* The District of Columbia Bar; Federal and American Bar Associations; American Judicature Society; American Law Institute. Honorary Fellow of the American Academy of Appellate Lawyers. ***PRACTICE AREAS:*** Constitutional Law; Federal Litigation; Professional Practice.

MARGARET COLGATE LOVE, born Baltimore, Maryland; admitted to bar, 1977, District of Columbia. *Education:* Sarah Lawrence College (B.A., 1963); Yale Law School (J.D., 1977). Author, "Of Pardons, Politics and Collar-buttons: Reflections on the President's Duty to be Merciful", 27 Fordham Urban Law Journal 1483 (2000). U.S. Pardon Attorney, 1990-1997; Associate Deputy Attorney General, 1989-1990; Deputy Associate Attorney General, 1988-1989; Special Counsel, Office of Legal Counsel, U.S. Department of Justice, 1979-1988. *Member:* District of Columbia Bar (Member: Rules of Professional Conduct Review Committee; Legal Ethics Committee, 1991-1997); American Bar Association (Member: Commission on Evaluation of the Model Rules of Professional Responsibility; Committee on Ethics and Professional Responsibility, 1991-1997 (Chair, 1995-1997); Task Force on Collateral Consequences of a Felony Conviction (Chair); American Law Institute. ***PRACTICE AREAS:*** Post-Conviction Remedies; Professional Conduct; Government Ethics. ***Email:*** mlove@brand-frulla.com

BRAUDE & MARGULIES, P.C.

Established in 1977

THE BRAWNER BUILDING
888 SEVENTEENTH STREET, N.W., SUITE 500
WASHINGTON, D.C. 20006
Telephone: 202-293-2993
Fax: 202-331-7916
Email: Braudemarg@aol.com

Practice before all State, Federal Courts and Administrative Agencies, Government, Public and Private Construction Contracts, all facets of Government Contracts, Real Estate Development, Arbitration, Civil Litigation and Construction Insurance Law.

FIRM PROFILE: Braude & Margulies, P.C. founded in 1977, limits its practice exclusively to construction litigation government contracts and alternative dispute resolution. Most of the firm's lawyers hold degrees in architecture or engineering and have practical field experience in construction. Applying this technical expertise, the firm specializes in the resolution of disputes and claims arising from terminations for default, defective design, delays, suspensions of work, changed conditions, architectural errors and omissions, bid mistakes and protests, and construction liability insurance claims on national and international projects of virtually every type.

HERMAN M. BRAUDE, born New York, N.Y., October 16, 1939; admitted to bar, 1965, District of Columbia, U.S. Court of Appeals for the District of Columbia and U.S. Claims Court; 1968, Maryland; 1970, U.S. Supreme Court; 1982, U.S. Court of Appeals for the Federal Circuit; 1993, New York; 1998, Florida. *Education:* Cooper Union (B.S. in C.E., 1961); Georgetown University (J.D., 1964). Phi Delta Phi. Editor, Georgetown Law Journal, 1963-1964. Visiting Lecturer, Construction Contracting, National Law Center, George Washington University, 1985—. Lecturer, "Forensic Engineering," American Society of Civil Engineers, 1985. Author: "Private Construction Management Contracts," Construction Briefings No. 87-7, June, 1987; "The Surety's Liability Under The Miller Act for Delay Damages," 36 Fed. B. J. 86, Spring, 1977; "Government Contracts Recent Decision—United States v. Carlo Bianchi & Co.," 52 Georgetown Law Journal 189, 1963. Co-author: "Construction Contracting," George Washington University, 1991; "Providing and Pricing Construction Claims," Wiley Law Publications, 1981; "Modern Insights on Validity and Force and Effect of Procurement Regulations—A New Slant on Standing and the Christian Doctrine," 31 Fed. B. J. 99, Spring, 1972; "Use of 'Equal' Products," Construction Briefings, No. 80-4, Federal Publications, July, 1980; " 'All' Risk Insurance," Construction Briefings, No. 81-6, Federal Publications, November, 1981; Comprehensive General Liability Insurance, Construction Briefing, No. 82-2, Federal Publications, March, 1982; "U.C.C. Problems in Construction," Construction Briefings, No. 83-6, Federal Publications, June, 1983; "Recovering Extended Home Office Overhead Costs," Construction Briefings, No. 84-6, Federal Publications, June, 1984; "Subcontract Inc. By Reference Clauses," Construction Briefings, No. 85-7, Federal Publications, July, 1985; "Private Construction Surety Bonds," Construction Briefing No. 86-6, May 1986; "Quantum Meruit Recovery in Construction Contracts," Construction Briefings No. 88-7, June 1988; "Pass-Through Claims and Liquidation Agreements," Construction Briefings No. 89-7, June 1989. Member, Commercial Panel of Arbitrators, American Arbitration Association, 1974. Law Clerk to U.S. Senior Judge Samuel E. Whitaker sitting on the U.S. Court of Claims and by designation, on the U.S. Court of Appeals for the Fifth Circuit, 1964-1965. *Member:* The District of Columbia Bar; Bar Association of the District of Columbia; The Florida Bar; Maryland State (Chairman, Special Committee on State and Local Public Contract Law, 1976-1980), Federal and American Bar Associations; American Society of Civil Engineers. ***PRACTICE AREAS:*** Construction Law; Government Contracts; Administrative Law; Civil Trial Practice Law.

SAMUEL M. MORRISON, JR., born Chattanooga, Tennessee, September 29, 1939; admitted to bar, 1978, Tennessee; 1982, Maryland; 1988, District of Columbia. *Education:* Tennessee Polytechnic Institute (B.S.C.E., 1963); Nashville Y.M.C.A. Night Law School (J.D., 1978). Tau Beta Pi. Licensed Professional Engineer: Tennessee, 1972; Maryland, 1987; Civil Engineer, 1967-1982. Member, Panel of Arbitrators, American Arbitration Association. *Member:* The District of Columbia Bar; Tennessee, Maryland State and American Bar Associations. [Capt., U.S. Army, 1963-1967]. ***PRACTICE AREAS:*** Construction Law; Administrative Law; Civil Trial Practice Law. ***Email:*** smorrison@braudemargulies.com

GERSON B. KRAMER, born New York, N.Y., June 12, 1925; admitted to bar, 1955, District of Columbia and U.S. Court of Appeals for the District of Columbia; 1956, U.S. Claims Court; 1970, U.S. Supreme Court; 1972, District of Columbia Court of Appeals; 1981, Court of Appeals of Maryland; 1982, U.S. Court of Appeals for the Federal Circuit. *Education:* Rutgers University (A.B. in Economics, with high honors, 1951); George Washington University (LL.B., 1955). Phi Beta Kappa; Phi Delta Phi. Staff Member, George Washington University Law Review, 1954-1955. Economist, U.S. Department of Labor, 1951-1955. Senior Trial Attorney, U.S. Department of Justice, 1956-1966. Member, Department of Commerce Appeals Board, 1966-1967. Member, Department of Transportation Contract Appeals Board, 1967-1979; Chairman, 1969-1979. Founding Member, 1969, Secretary-Treasurer, 1969-1972, Vice-President, 1973-1974 and President, 1976-1977, BCA Judges Association. Author: "Contract Appeals Boards and the Subpoena Power," 29 Federal Bar Journal 200, 1970; "Contract Claims Remedies: Is Proliferation of Forums the Answer?" 42 George Washington Law Review 256, 1974. ***PRACTICE AREAS:*** Federal Contracts; Litigation; Construction Law; Arbitration Mediation.

MICHAEL B. BEARD, born Cumberland, Maryland, November 5, 1963; admitted to bar, 1995, Maryland; 1996, District of Columbia and U.S. District Court, District of Maryland. *Education:* University of Maryland (B.S., 1991); University of Baltimore (J.D., 1994). ***PRACTICE AREAS:*** Complex Litigation; Environmental Law; Construction Contracts; Government Contracts.

OF COUNSEL

J. RICHARD MARGULIES, born Washington, D.C., June 17, 1945; admitted to bar, 1974, Maryland; 1975, District of Columbia; 1976, U.S. Claims Court. *Education:* Cornell University (B.S., 1967); George Washington University (Masters, Engineering Administration, 1971); Georgetown University (J.D., 1974). Visiting Lecturer, Construction Contracting, National Law Center, George Washington University, 1985. Associate Professional Lecturer in Engineering, George Washington University, 1975—. *Member:* The District of Columbia Bar; Maryland State and American (Member, Forum Committee on the Construction Industry, Administrative Law Section, 1977—) Bar Associations; American Society of Civil Engineers (Associate Member). (Also Member, Sacks & Margulies, P.C., Rockville, Maryland). ***PRACTICE AREAS:*** Construction Law; Administrative Law; Civil Trial Practice Law.

BRAULT, GRAHAM, SCOTT & BRAULT, PLLC

Established in 1952

1140 CONNECTICUT AVENUE, N.W.
SUITE 250
WASHINGTON, D.C. 20036
Telephone: 202-785-1200
Fax: 202-785-4301
Email: dcbgsb@aol.com
URL: http://www.bgsb.com

Brault, Graham, Scott & Brault, LLC:
Rockville, Maryland Office: 101 South Washington Street. Telephone: 301-424-1060. FAX: 301-424-7991.
Fairfax, Virginia Office: Suite 500, 11350 Random Hills Road, Fair Oaks Plaza, 22030-7429. Telephone: 202-785-1200.

General, Civil, Trial and Appellate practice in all State and Federal Courts. Negligence, Insurance, Medical Malpractice, Personal Injury, Products Liability and Commercial Litigation.

FIRM PROFILE: Brault, Graham, Scott & Brault, LLC was founded over 45 years ago as a general insurance defense firm and has experienced a measured growth to its present size of some 9 lawyers. The firm maintains offices in Washington, D.C. and Rockville, Maryland and Fairfax, Virginia. The firm has the capacity to litigate

(This Listing Continued)

BRAULT, GRAHAM, SCOTT & BRAULT, PLLC, Washington—Continued

throughout the State of Maryland, Northern Virginia and Washington, D.C. It has, and will, litigate in any jurisdiction required by its clients where its particular talents and expertise are needed. The firm practices all major aspects of insurance law, including policy interpretation, declaratory judgments, direct defense of insurers, excess, reinsurance, subrogation, surety and fidelity bonding, licensing, risk management consultation and general insurance defense litigation with special emphasis on professional malpractice defense. In addition the firm practices extensively in the field of commercial litigation.

REPRESENTATIVE CLIENTS: American Oil Co.; Crum & Forster Group; Donegal Mutual Insurance Co.; Fireman's Fund American Insurance Cos.; Hartford Insurance Group; Kemper Group; National Indemnity Co.; Reliance Insurance Cos.; Safeco Group; Transport Indemnity Co.; Government Employees Insurance Co.; Universal Underwriters; Electric Insurance Company Wausau Ins. Co.; PHICO; INA; Maryland Casualty; Tower Underwriters; Allstate; Colonial Penn; CIGNA; Casualty Indemnity Exchange; Auto Owners Ins. Co.; Miller National Claim Service; Seibels Bruce & Co.; Integral Ins. Co.; International Underwriters for Casualty Indemnity Exchange; Medlantic Healthcare; Medical Mutual Liability Insurance Society of Maryland; The George Washington University; Children's Hospital National Medical Center; PMA Group; Physicians National; National Interstate Transportation Company; Gallaudet University; Prudential Insurance Co.; The Paradigm Ins. Co.; Medical Mutual Insurance Society of Maryland; Legal Mutual Liability Insurance Society of Maryland; Liberty Life Insurance Company; Lerner Corporation; E.I. duPont deNemours & Company; Washington Hospital Center; Farm Bureau Insurance Companies; Bell Atlantic, MD.

(For complete biographical data on all personnel, see Professional Biographies at Rockville, Maryland)

BRAULT PALMER GROVE ZIMMERMAN WHITE & STEINHILBER LLP

WASHINGTON, D.C.

(See Fairfax, Virginia)

General Trial Practice in all State and Federal Courts. Negligence, Insurance, Workers Compensation, Products Liability, Malpractice and Construction and Related Bond Matters.

BREDHOFF & KAISER, P.L.L.C.

Established in 1953

805 FIFTEENTH STREET, N.W., SUITE 1000
WASHINGTON, D.C. 20005
Telephone: 202-842-2600
Fax: 202-842-1888
URL: http://www.bredhoff.com

General Appellate and Trial Practice, Civil and Criminal including practice before U.S. Supreme Court, Labor, Civil Rights, Constitutional Law, Bankruptcy, Occupational Safety and Health Law, Employee Benefit Law including Fiduciary and Tax Law, Antitrust, RICO, Attorney Discipline Law.

MEMBERS OF FIRM

GEORGE H. COHEN, born Brooklyn, New York, January 3, 1934; admitted to bar, 1961, District of Columbia and Virginia; U.S. Supreme Court; U.S. Court of Appeals, First, Second, Third, Fourth, Fifth, Sixth, Ninth, Tenth, Eleventh and District of Columbia Circuits. *Education:* Cornell University (B.A., 1955; LL.B., 1957); Georgetown University (LL.M., 1960). Adjunct Professor of Law, Georgetown University Law Center. General Counsel, American Federation of Musicians, 1989—. Member, Advisory Committee, United States Court of Appeals for the District of Columbia Circuit, 1993-1998. Member, Advisory Council for Environmental Health, John Hopkins University School of Hygiene and Public Health, 1981-1997. Attorney-Advisor, 1960-1963 and Appellate Court Litigation Attorney, 1963-1966, National Labor Relations Board. *Member:* Bar Association of the District of Columbia; Federal (Chairman, Labor Law Committee, 1971-1973) and American (Union Co-Chairman, Committee on Occupational Safety and Health Law, 1976-1978) Bar Associations.

ROBERT H. CHANIN, born Brooklyn, New York, December 24, 1934; admitted to bar, 1959, New York; 1969, District of Columbia; U.S. Supreme Court; U.S. Court of Appeals, First, Second, Third, Fourth, Fifth, Sixth, Seventh, Eighth, Ninth, Tenth, Eleventh and District of Columbia Circuits. *Education:* Brooklyn College (B.A., summa cum laude, 1956); Yale University (LL.B., 1959); Columbia University (M.A., Psychology, 1961). Phi Beta Kappa. Staff Attorney, Columbia University Law School, Project for Effective Justice, 1959-1962. Associate, Kaye, Scholer, Fierman, Hays & Handler, New York, N.Y., 1962-1968. General Counsel, National Education Association, 1968—. Deputy Executive Director, National Education Association, 1973-1980. Professorial Lecturer in Law, George Washington University National Law Center, 1973-1980. President, National Organization of Lawyers for Education Associations, 1969—. Member, Executive Committee of National Resource Center for Consumers of Legal Services, 1977—. Of Counsel to the National Coalition for Public Education and Religious Liberty, 1984—. Co-Author: "The Law and Practice of Teacher Negotiations," 1970 and 1973 Editions, Bureau of National Affairs. *Member:* District of Columbia Bar; American Bar Association.

ROBERT M. WEINBERG, born New York, N.Y., June 8, 1942; admitted to bar, 1969, District of Columbia; U.S. Supreme Court; U.S. Court of Appeals, Second, Third, Fourth, Fifth, Sixth, Seventh, Eighth, Ninth, Tenth, Eleventh, District of Columbia and Federal Circuits. *Education:* University of Michigan (B.A., 1965; J.D., summa cum laude, 1968). Order of the Coif. Editor-in-Chief, Michigan Law Review, 1967-1968. Law Clerk to Justice William J. Brennan, Jr., U.S. Supreme Court, 1968-1969. Associate Director, Citizens Board of Inquiry into Health Services for Americans, 1969-1970. Adjunct Professor, Constitutional Law, Catholic University Law School, 1970-1973 and Congressional Investigations, Georgetown University Law Center, 1997—. Trial Attorney, 1970-1973, and Chief, Appellate Division, 1973-1974, Public Defender Service for the District of Columbia. Member, Special Committee of the District of Columbia Bar on Criminal Code Revision, 1977-1978. Member, Advisory Committee on Procedures, U.S. Court of Appeals for the District of Columbia Circuit, 1978-1983. Member, Special Committee of the District of Columbia Bar Regarding Court Appointment of Counsel Programs in the Superior Court, 1993-1994. *Member:* District of Columbia Bar; American Bar Association.

JEFFREY L. GIBBS, born Brooklyn, New York, July 4, 1945; admitted to bar, 1973, District of Columbia; U.S. Court of Appeals, Third, Fourth, Fifth, Sixth and District of Columbia Circuits; 1992, Maryland. *Education:* Brooklyn College of the City University of New York (B.A., cum laude, 1967); University of Wisconsin (M.A., Industrial Relations, 1969); Northwestern University (J.D., cum laude, 1972). Member, Editorial Board, Northwestern Law Review, 1971-1972. Member, Board of Senior Editors, "Employee Benefits Law," Bureau of National Affairs, 1991. *Member:* District of Columbia Bar; American Bar Association (Co-Chairman, Employee Benefits Committee Section of Labor and Employment Law, 1987-1990).

JULIA PENNY CLARK, born Oak Grove, Louisiana, February 23, 1948; admitted to bar, 1976, Texas (inactive) and District of Columbia; U.S. Supreme Court; U.S. Court of Appeals, Second, Third, Fourth, Fifth, Sixth, Seventh, Eleventh, District of Columbia Circuits and U.S. District Court, District of Columbia. *Education:* University of Texas (B.A., with highest honors, 1969; J.D., with highest honors, 1973). Phi Beta Kappa; Chancellors; Order of the Coif. Note and Comment Editor, Texas Law Review, 1972. Author: Casenote, Texas Law Review, January, 1972; Note, "The Duty of Fair Representation: A Theoretical Structure," Texas Law Review, August, 1973. Law Clerk to: J. Braxton Craven, Jr., U.S. Court of Appeals, Fourth Circuit, 1973-1974; Hon. Lewis F. Powell, Jr., U.S. Supreme Court, 1974-1975. Member, Committee on Admissions and Grievances for the U.S. Court of Appeals for the District of Columbia Circuit, 1990-1996. *Member:* District of Columbia Bar; American Bar Association; Women's Bar Association of the District of Columbia.

JEFFREY R. FREUND, born Minneapolis, Minnesota, July 5, 1945; admitted to bar, 1970, California (inactive) and U.S. District Court, Northern District of California; 1972, District of Columbia; U.S. Supreme Court; U.S. Court of Appeals, First, Third, Fourth, Sixth, Eighth, Ninth, District of Columbia and Federal Circuits. *Education:* Northwestern University (B.A., 1967); Boalt Hall School of Law, University of California (J.D., 1970). Member, 1968-1970 and Executive Editor, 1969-1970, California Law Review. Author: "Neighborhood Police Districts: A Constitutional Analysis," 57 California Law Review 909, 1969. Adjunct Professor, Georgetown University Law Center, 1975-1976. Law Clerk to Hon. Alfonso Zirpoli, U.S. District Court for the Northern District of California, 1970-1971. Legal Assistant to Commissioner Nicholas Johnson, Federal Communications Commission, 1971-1972. Trial Attorney, 1972-1976 and Training Director, 1976-1977, Public Defender Service for the District of Columbia. Associate, Van Arkel, Kaiser & Rosenberg, 1977-1981. General Counsel, Bakery, Confectionery and Tobacco Workers Union, 1991—. Co-General Counsel, Bakery and Confectionery Union and Industry International Pension and Health Benefits Fund, 1991—. *Member:* District of Columbia Bar (Member, District of Columbia Board on Professional Responsibility, 1984-1991).

W. GARY KOHLMAN, born Seattle, Washington, October 10, 1946; admitted to bar, 1971, Washington (inactive); 1973, District of Columbia; 1979, U.S. Supreme Court; 1983, Maryland; U.S. District Court, District of Columbia, U.S. District Court, District of Maryland, U.S. Court of Appeals, Fourth and District of Columbia Circuits; 1992, U.S. District Court, District of Arizona. *Education:* University of Michigan (B.B.A., 1968; LL.B., 1971). Order of the Coif. Law Clerk to Justice Samuel J. Roberts, Supreme Court of Pennsylvania, 1971-1972; Trial Attorney, 1973-1976, Director of Training, 1977-1979 and Chief of the Trial Division, 1979-1982; Public Defender Service for the District of Columbia. Instructor, Trial Practice Continuing Legal Education Program; District of Columbia Bar Association, 1984-1985. Faculty, Harvard Law School Trial Advocacy Workshop, 1985. *Member:* District of Columbia Bar; American Bar Association; American Inn of Court, Charles Fahey Branch, 1988-1992.

(This Listing Continued)

JEREMIAH A. COLLINS, born New Haven, Connecticut, September 24, 1949; admitted to bar, 1976, District of Columbia; U.S. Supreme Court; U.S. Court of Appeals, First, Second, Third, Fourth, Fifth, Sixth, Seventh, Eighth, Ninth, Tenth, Eleventh and District of Columbia Circuits. *Education:* St. John's College (A.B., magna cum laude, 1971); Stanford University (J.D., 1976). Order of the Coif. Adjunct Professor of Law, Georgetown University Law Center, 1985-1987. Counsel, Foreign Service Grievance Board, U.S. State Department, 1993—. *Member:* District of Columbia Bar; American Bar Association (Co-Chairman, Committee on Occupational Safety and Health Law, 1986-1989).

MADY GILSON, born Brooklyn, N.Y., April 24, 1951; admitted to bar, 1976, District of Columbia; U.S. Court of Appeals, Second, Fourth, Fifth, Ninth, Eleventh and District of Columbia Circuits; 1980, U.S. Supreme Court. *Education:* Pembroke College, Brown University (B.A., magna cum laude, 1971); Antioch School of Law (J.D., 1976). Phi Beta Kappa. Trial Attorney, Public Defender Service for the District of Columbia, 1976-1980. *Member:* District of Columbia Bar; American Bar Association. ***LANGUAGES:*** Spanish.

BRUCE R. LERNER, born Brooklyn, New York, March 8, 1957; admitted to bar, 1984, District of Columbia; 1992, Maryland; U.S. Supreme Court, U.S. Court of Appeals for the District of Columbia, Third, Fourth, Sixth, Seventh, Eighth and Ninth Circuits, U.S. District Court, District of Columbia and District of Maryland. *Education:* Harpur College, State University of New York at Binghamton (B.A., 1978); Woodrow Wilson School of Public and International Affairs, Princeton University (M.P.A., 1982); University of Pennsylvania (J.D., summa cum laude, 1982). Phi Beta Kappa; Pi Sigma Alpha; Order of the Coif. Executive Editor, University of Pennsylvania Law Review, 1981-1982. Author: Comment, "Eliminating Sex Discrimination in Educational Institutions: Does Title IX Reach Employment?" U. Pa. L. Rev., 1980. Law Clerk to: Judge Abner J. Mikva, U.S. Court of Appeals for the District of Columbia, 1982-1983; Justice William J. Brennan, Jr., U.S. Supreme Court, 1983-1984. General Counsel, National Postal Mail Handlers Union, 1992—. *Member:* District of Columbia Bar; American Bar Association.

ANDREW D. ROTH, born New York, N.Y., March 29, 1961; admitted to bar, 1988, District of Columbia; 1994, U.S. Supreme Court; U.S. Court of Appeals, First, Third, Fourth, Sixth, Seventh, Eighth, Tenth, Eleventh and District of Columbia Circuits. *Education:* Cornell University (B.S., 1983); University of Michigan (J.D., magna cum laude, 1986). Member, Order of the Coif. Managing Editor, Michigan Law Review, 1985-1986. Law Clerk to Harry T. Edwards, U.S. Court of Appeals for the District of Columbia Circuit, 1986-1987. Author: "An Examination of Whether Incarcerated Juveniles Are Entitled by the Constitution to Rehabilitative Treatment," 85 Michigan L. Rev. 286. *Member:* District of Columbia Bar; American Bar Association.

JOHN M. WEST, born Uniontown, Pennsylvania, September 18, 1946; admitted to bar, 1989, Pennsylvania (inactive); 1990, District of Columbia; 1995, U.S. Supreme Court; U.S. Court of Appeals, Third, Fourth, Sixth, Seventh, Eighth, Eleventh and District of Columbia Circuits. *Education:* Elizabethtown College (B.A., 1970); University of Denver (M.A., 1972; Ph.D., 1976); University of Michigan (J.D., summa cum laude, 1987). Order of the Coif. Editor-in-Chief, Michigan Law Review, 1986-1987. Law Clerk to: Judge Harry T. Edwards, U.S. Court of Appeals for the District of Columbia Circuit, 1987-1988; Justice William J. Brennan, Jr., United States Supreme Court, 1988-1989. Author: "Expert Services and The Indigent Criminal Defendant: The Constitutional Mandate of Ake v. Oklahoma," 84 Michigan L. Rev. 1326 (1986). *Member:* District of Columbia Bar; American Bar Association. ***LANGUAGES:*** German, French and Swedish.

DOUGLAS L. GREENFIELD, born Philadelphia, Pennsylvania, April 24, 1959; admitted to bar, 1986, Pennsylvania (inactive) and New Jersey (inactive); 1987, U.S. Court of Appeals, Third and District of Columbia Circuits; 1988, District of Columbia. *Education:* Stanford University (B.A., 1981); Claremont Graduate School (M.A., 1983); Temple University (J.D., 1986). Associate Articles Editor, Temple Law Quarterly Review, 1985-1986. *Member:* District of Columbia Bar; American Bar Association (Co-Chair, Sub Committee on Fiduciary Responsibility of Labor Section's Employee Benefit Committee, 1995—; Member, Labor, Tax and Business Sections' Employee Benefits Committees, 1987—; Counsel, Steelworkers Health and Welfare Fund, 1997—; Member, Sections on: Tax, Labor and Business; Joint Committee on Employee Benefits, 1987).

ROGER POLLAK, born Washington, D.C., April 9, 1959; admitted to bar, 1991, Connecticut (inactive) and District of Columbia. *Education:* Dartmouth College; University of California at Berkeley, College of Natural Resources (B.S. 1983), Valedictorian; Yale University (M.P.P.M., 1990; J.D., 1990). General Counsel, Union Privilege, 1999—. *Member:* District of Columbia Bar.

ANNE RONNEL MAYERSON, born Chicago, Illinois, February 25, 1962; admitted to bar, 1988, California (inactive); 1989, District of Columbia. *Education:* Brown University (B.A., magna cum laude, 1984); Harvard University (J.D., cum laude, 1987). Phi Beta Kappa. *Member:* District of Columbia Bar; State Bar of California.

LEON DAYAN, born Van Nuys, California, July 23, 1963; admitted to bar, 1991, California (inactive); 1994, District of Columbia; U.S. Supreme Court;

(This Listing Continued)

U.S. Court of Appeals, First, Fourth, Fifth, Sixth, Seventh, Eighth, Ninth, Tenth and Federal Circuits. *Education:* Stanford University (A.B., honors, 1985); Boalt Hall School of Law, University of California (J.D., 1989). Phi Beta Kappa. Order of the Coif. Law Clerk to the Honorable Betty B. Fletcher, U.S. Court of Appeals for the Ninth Circuit, 1989-1990. Author: "Qui Tam Suits Against Public Entities Under *Stevens*," 19 TAF QR 15 (July 2000); "The Scope of Copyright in Information: An Alternative to Classic Theory," 42 Fed. Com. L.J. (1990). Adjunct Professor of Law, George Washington University. *Member:* District of Columbia Bar.

OF COUNSEL

LAURENCE GOLD, born 1936; admitted to bar, 1961, District of Columbia; 1965, U.S. Supreme Court; U.S. Court of Appeals First, Second, Third, Fourth, Fifth, Sixth, Seventh, Eighth, Ninth, Tenth, Eleventh and District of Columbia Circuits. *Education:* Princeton University (A.B., 1958); Harvard University (LLB, 1961; LLM, 1962). Law Clerk, The Honorable Joe Ingraham, United States District Court, Houston, Texas, 1962-1963; Attorney Supreme Court Branch Office of the General Counsel, National Labor Relations Board, 1963-1965; Associate, Woll & Mayer, Washington, D.C., 1965-1970; Partner Woll, Mayer & Gold, 1970-1975; Special Counsel, AFL-CIO, 1975-1980; General Counsel, AFL-CIO, 1981-1995; Executive Director, AFL-CIO Lawyers Coordinating Committee, 1983-1995; Visiting Lecturer of Law, George Washington University Law School, 1969-1975; Visiting Professor, Georgetown Law School, 1976-1977; Visiting Lecturer in Law, University of Michigan Law School, 1996; Adjunct Professor of Law, New York University Law School, 1997.

PATRICIA POLACH, born Chicago, Illinois, May 13, 1954; admitted to bar, 1985, Michigan (inactive); 1986, U.S. District Court, Eastern District of Michigan; 1988, District of Columbia; 1989, U.S. Court of Appeals, Ninth and Fifth Circuits; 1992, U.S. Court of Appeals, Tenth Circuit; 1995, U.S. Court of Appeals, District of Columbia Circuit. *Education:* Michigan State University (B.A., with high honors, 1980); University of Michigan (J.D., cum laude, 1985). Phi Beta Kappa; Phi Kappa Phi. National Merit Scholar. Law Clerk to the Honorable Horace W. Gilmore, U.S. District Judge for the Eastern District of Michigan, 1985-1987. Counsel, Regional Orchestra Players' Association. *Member:* District of Columbia Bar; American Bar Association.

CONSTANCE MARKAKIS, born Northampton, Massachusetts, April 18, 1954; admitted to bar, 1986, Michigan; 1997, District of Columbia. *Education:* University of Michigan (B.A., 1976); Wayne State University (J.D., 1983). *Member:* American Bar Association.

LAURA PAGE KENNEDY, born Syracuse, New York, September 23, 1956; admitted to bar, 1984, District of Columbia. *Education:* Hampshire College (B.A., 1979); New York University (J.D., 1984); Georgetown University Law Center (LL.M., 1988). E. Barrett Prettyman Teaching Fellow, 1984-1986. Staff Attorney, 1986-1990 and Deputy Chief, Appellate Division, 1990-1991, Public Defender Service for the District of Columbia. Assistant Federal Public Defender, Northern District of California, 1991-1992. *Member:* District of Columbia Bar.

ASSOCIATES

ALICE O'BRIEN, born Rochester, New York, June 10, 1965; admitted to bar, 1995, California (inactive); 1997, District of Columbia; U.S. Court of Appeals, Fifth, Sixth, Ninth, Tenth and Eleventh Circuits. *Education:* Yale University (B.A., 1988); Georgetown University (J.D., cum laude, 1995). Author, Countervailing Low Wage Subsidies: A Counter to the Leveling of Labor Conditions," Vol. 4, Transnational Law & Contemporary Problems (1994). *Member:* The State Bar of California; District of Columbia Bar.

DEVKI K. VIRK, born Brookline, Massachusetts, April 16, 1968; admitted to bar, 1996, California; 1998, District of Columbia. *Education:* University of Chicago (A.B., 1989); University of Illinois (J.D., summa cum laude, 1995). Order of the Coif. Member, University of Illinois Law Review, 1993-1995; Notes and Comments Editor, 1994-1995. Law Clerk to the Honorable Martin L.C. Feldman, U.S. District Court, Eastern District of Louisiana, 1995-1996. Author, Note, "Participation with Representation: Ensuring Workers' Rights in Cooperative Management," 1994 Univ. of Illinois Law Review 729.

PHILIP HOSTAK, born Passaic, New Jersey, January 23, 1964; admitted to bar, 1999, New York and U.S. Court of Appeals, Third Circuit; 2000, U.S. Court of Appeals, Sixth Circuit; 2001, District of Columbia. *Education:* University of Texas at Austin (B.A., with high honors, 1991); Cornell University Law School (J.D., magna cum laude, 1996). Order of the Coif. Managing Editor, Cornell Law Review, 1995-1996. Law Clerk to: Hon. Louis H. Pollak, U.S. District Court for the Eastern District of Pennsylvania, 1997-1998; Hon. Dolores K. Sloviter, U.S. Court of Appeals for the Third Circuit, 1998-1999. Author: Note, "International Union, United Mine Workers of America v. Bagwell: A Paradigm Shift in the Distinction Between Civil and Criminal Contempt," 81 Cornell L. Rev. 181 (1995). *Member:* The District of Columbia Bar; New York State and American Bar Associations.

(This Listing Continued)

BREDHOFF & KAISER, P.L.L.C., Washington—Continued

ROBERT W. ALEXANDER, born Chicago, Illinois, August 25, 1962; admitted to bar, 1992, Colorado; 2000, District of Columbia; U.S. Court of Appeals, Sixth, Ninth and Tenth Circuits; U.S. District Court, District of Colorado. *Education:* Grinnell College; Roosevelt University (B.A., with honors, 1989); University of Colorado (J.D., 1992); University of Michigan (LL.M., 1995). Order of the Coif. Editor-in-Chief, University of Colorado Law Review, 1991-1992. Teaching Fellow, Stanford Law School, 1997-1999. Clerk to Carlos F. Lucero, U.S. Court of Appeals, Tenth Circuit, 1995-1997. Author: "The Collision of Tribal Resource Development and State Taxation: An Economic Analysis," 27 University of New Mexico Law Review No. 2 (1997). *Member:* Colorado Bar Association; District of Columbia Bar.

PORTIA YU-JUNG WU, born New Haven, Connecticut, July 23, 1970; admitted to bar, 1999, New York; 2000, District of Columbia. *Education:* Yale College (B.A., summa cum laude, 1991); Cornell University (M.A., 1995); Yale Law School (J.D., 1998). Member: Yale Journal of International Law, 1995-1996; Yale Law Journal, 1996-1998. Law Clerk, Hon. Richard A. Paez, U.S. District Court, Central District of California, 1998-1999. ***LANGUAGES:*** Mandarin Chinese.

MICHAEL H. SAMPSON, born Tallahassee, Florida, June 13, 1974; admitted to bar, 2000, New York; 2001, District of Columbia. *Education:* University of Virginia (B.A., with high distinction, 1996); University of Chicago (J.D., with honors, 1999). *Member:* New York State and American Bar Associations.

SENIOR COUNSEL

ELLIOT BREDHOFF, born New York, N.Y., July 31, 1921; admitted to bar, 1949, New York; 1953, District of Columbia; 1958, U.S. Court of Appeals for the District of Columbia Circuit and U.S. Court of Appeals for the Sixth Circuit; 1959, U.S. Supreme Court; 1961, U.S. Court of Appeals, Third Circuit. *Education:* College of the City of New York (B.S., 1942); Yale University (LL.B., 1949). Editor, Yale Law Journal, 1948-1949. Ethical Practices Commissioner for American Federation of State, County and Municipal Employees, 1964-1965. Special Counsel: United Steelworkers of America, AFL-CIO, 1965-1991. General Counsel: Industrial Union Department, AFL-CIO, 1968-1996; General Counsel Emeritus, 1996—; Utility Workers Union of America, 1991-1994. Counsel: National Industrial Group Pension Plan, 1973-1994; Counsel Emeritus, 1994—; Foreign Service Grievance Board, State Department, 1973-1993. Public Member, Administrative Conference of the U.S., 1988-1995. Union Member, NLRB Advisory Panel, 1994—. President, National Resource Center for Consumers of Legal Services, 1979—. Member, Board of Directors, American Arbitration Association, 1983-1995. *Member:* District of Columbia Bar; American Bar Association (Member, Commission on Law and the Economy, 1977-1979; Chairman, Section of Labor and Employment Law, 1984-1985).

BREDIMUS & ASSOCIATES, P.C.

1718 "M" STREET, NORTHWEST
WASHINGTON, D.C. 20036-4505
Telephone: 202-589-1885

Leesburg, Virginia Office: 11 West Market, 20176. Telephone: 703-777-9563. Fax: 703-771-3257.

Frederick, Maryland Office: 905 West 7th Street, Suite 321, 21701-8527. Telephone: 301-228-3695.

General Business and Commercial Law, including Commercial Contracts, Taxation and Real Estate, Wills and Probate, Trusts and Estates and Estate Planning. General Civil and Criminal Trial Practice including Criminal Defense, Personal Injury and Bankruptcy.

(For complete biographical data on all personnel, see Professional Biographies at Leesburg, Virginia)

BREGMAN, BERBERT & SCHWARTZ, L.L.C.

WASHINGTON, D.C.

(See Bethesda, Maryland)

General Civil Trial and Appellate Practice, Mediation and Arbitration, Leasing, Landlord-Tenant, Real Estate Transactions, Foreclosures, Tax Appeals, Personal Injury, Computer Software Law, Licensing, and Litigation, Internet Law and Transactions, Entity Startup, Formation, Capitalization, and Funding, Wills and Trusts, Estate Planning and Administration, Business Transactions and Corporate Matters, Condominium, Co-ops and Homeowners Associations.

BRENEMAN & GEORGES

WASHINGTON, D.C.

(See Alexandria, Virginia)

Patent, Trademark, Copyright Law and related Litigation.

DIANE M. BRENNEMAN

Established in 1987

601 PENNSYLVANIA AVENUE, N.W., NINTH FLOOR
WASHINGTON, D.C. 20004
Telephone: 202-362-1161
Fax: 202-362-1171
Email: dmbrenneman46@aol.com
URL: http://www.lawyers.com/dianembrennemanlaw

Civil and Family Mediation and Arbitration, Divorce, Custody.

DIANE M. BRENNEMAN, born 1946; admitted to bar, 1980, District of Columbia; 1982, U.S. District Court, District of Columbia; 1995, U.S. Court of Appeals, for the District of Columbia; U.S. Supreme Court; 1988, Maryland. *Education:* University of Santa Clara (B.A., 1968); Georgetown University (J.D., 1979). clinical Fellow and Professor, Professor: Antioch School of Law, 1979-1988; District of Columbia School of Law, 1988-1989. Member, Peace Corps, 1968-1970. *Member:* Montgomery County, Washington,and American Bar Associations; Maryland State Bar Association, Inc.; District of Columbia Bar (Co-Chair, Family Law Representation Committee, 1997—; Assistant Chair, Family Law Task Force, 1992-1997; Member, Steering Committee and Co-Chair, 1990-1995, Family Law Section; Member, Solo and Small Firm Task Force, Civility Task Force); Womens Bar Association of the District of Columbia (Member, Board of Directors); American Trial Lawyers Association; District of Columbia Trial Lawyers. (Also Of Counsel, O'Reilly & Mark, L.L.C.). ***LANGUAGES:*** Hindi. ***PRACTICE AREAS:*** Wills, Estates and Probate Law; Mediation; Arbitration; Family Law.

BRICKFIELD BURCHETTE RITTS & STONE, P.C.

Established in 1938

8TH FLOOR, WEST TOWER
1025 THOMAS JEFFERSON STREET, N.W.
WASHINGTON, D.C. 20007-5201
Telephone: 202-342-0800
Fax: 202-342-0807
Email: bbrslaw.com
URL: http://www.bbrslaw.com

Austin, Texas Office: Suite 400, 1005 Congress Avenue. Telephone: 512-472-1081. Fax: 512-472-7473.

FIRM PROFILE: Brickfield Burchette Ritts & Stone, P.C., serves as counselor and advocate for such clients as major manufacturers, rural electric cooperatives, municipal electric utilities, public power authorities, water/irrigation districts, hydroelectric project developers, and national associations. The firm has developed, over the course of more than half a century, from a small natural resources practice to a firm of more than twenty lawyers with a broad and sophisticated regulatory, complex litigation, transactional and legislative practice focused principally on energy and public utility matters. The Firm has also developed expertise in international trade matters and in representing emerging technology companies.

Firm attorneys represent clients before independent agencies of the United States government such as the Federal Energy Regulatory Commission and the U.S. International Trade Commission, and various executive branch departments such as the Departments of Energy, Commerce, the Interior and Agriculture, as well as before state regulatory bodies and all levels of the federal courts. In addition to representation in complex administrative and court litigation, the Firm advises and represents its clients regarding business and transactional issues, and serves as general counsel to a healthcare professional association.

JAMES W. BREW, born Danbury, Connecticut, January 27, 1954; admitted to bar, 1980, New York; 1999, District of Columbia. *Education:* Georgetown University (A.B., 1976; J.D., 1979). New York State Energy Plan Task Force, 1992. Staff Counsel, New York State Public Service Commission, 1979-1991. Managing Attorney for Energy Policy & Federal Affairs, New York State Public Service Commission, 1991-1995. Author: "Moving Toward More Effective Rate Making Incentives," The Elec. Journal, Dec. 1992. **Email:** jbrew@bbrslaw.com

PETER J. P. BRICKFIELD, born New York, N.Y., September 10, 1943; admitted to bar, 1970, New York and U.S. Claims Court; 1972, U.S. Court of Appeals, 5th Circuit; 1980, District of Columbia. *Education:* State University of

(This Listing Continued)

New York (B.S., 1965); Providence College (M.A., 1966); New York Law School (J.D., 1969). Trial Attorney, Civil Division, U.S. Department of Justice, 1969-1974. Senior Trial Attorney, Bureau of Competition, Federal Trade Commission, 1974-1977. Assistant Director, Bureau of Competition, Federal Trade Commission, 1977-1979. Contributor: "International Antitrust; Fifth Annual Fordham Corporate Law Institute," Harcourt Brace Jovanovich, 1979. Author: "Competitive Issues and Alternative Energy Sources, Alternative Energy, the Federal Role," McGraw-Hill, 1982. ***SPECIAL AGENCIES:*** FERC. ***TRANSACTIONS:*** Large Plant Siting. ***PRACTICE AREAS:*** Energy; Steel. ***Email:*** pjpb@bbrslaw.com

WILLIAM H. BURCHETTE, born Orange, California, December 22, 1945; admitted to bar, 1971, North Carolina; 1972, U.S. Court of Military Appeals; 1973, U.S. Claims Court; 1978, District of Columbia. *Education:* Guilford College (B.A., 1968); Wake Forest University (J.D., 1971). Phi Alpha Delta. Trial Attorney, Land and Natural Resources Division, Department of Justice, 1974—. Trustee, Guilford College. *Member:* District of Columbia Bar; North Carolina and American (Member, Natural Resources Law Section) Bar Associations. Fellow, American Bar Foundation. [Capt., USMCR, 1966-1974]. ***Email:*** wburchette@bbrslaw.com

MARK C. DAVIS, born Crawford, Nebraska, June 8, 1959; admitted to bar, 1985, Texas (Not admitted in District of Columbia). *Education:* Nebraska Western Junior College (A.A., 1979); University of Nebraska (B.S., with honors, 1981; J.D., 1984). Phi Theta Kappa. *Member:* Travis County Bar Association; State Bar of Texas (Member, Sections on: Administrative and Public Law; Public Utility Law); Texas Young Lawyers Association. (Resident, Austin, Texas Office). ***Email:*** mdavis@bbrsaustin.com

PETER J. MATTHEIS, born Owatonna, Minnesota, August 25, 1959; admitted to bar, 1985, Virginia; 1986, District of Columbia; U.S. District Court, Eastern District of Virginia and U.S. Court of Appeals, Fourth Circuit. *Education:* Miami University (B.S., in Bus., 1982); University of Pennsylvania (J.D., 1985). *Member:* The District of Columbia Bar; Virginia State Bar. ***PRACTICE AREAS:*** Energy; Energy Regulation; Public Utility Law; Energy Contracts; Legislative Practice; Administrative Law. ***Email:*** pjm@bbrslaw.com

MICHAEL N. McCARTY, born Washington, D.C., December 10, 1953; admitted to bar, 1979, District of Columbia; 1980, U.S. Court of Appeals for the District of Columbia Circuit; 1982, U.S. District Court for the District of Columbia; 1983, U.S. Court of Appeals, Tenth Circuit; 1986, U.S. Court of Appeals, Ninth Circuit; 1987, U.S. District Court, Northern District of California; 1996, U.S. Court of Federal Claims; 1997, U.S. District Court, District of Arizona; 1999, U.S. Court of Appeals for the Federal Circuit. *Education:* University of Virginia (B.A., with distinction, 1976); Catholic University of America (J.D., 1979). Staff Member, 1977-1978 and Notes Editor, 1978-1979, Catholic University Law Review. Author: Note, "Limitation of State Prisoners' Civil Rights Suits in the Federal Courts," 27 Catholic University Law Review 115, 1977; Casenote, 27 Catholic University Law Review 653, 1978. Law Clerk to the Hon. Stanley S. Harris, Judge, District of Columbia Court of Appeals, 1979-1980. *Member:* Bar Association of the District of Columbia (Member, Executive Council, Young Lawyers Section, 1988-1990); Energy Bar Association (Chair, Hydroelectric Regulation Committee, 1993-1994); The Association of Trial Lawyers of America. ***PRACTICE AREAS:*** Energy; Hydroelectricity Licensing; Natural Resources; Endangered Species; Health Care Administration; Commercial Litigation. ***Email:*** mmccarty@bbrslaw.com

FREDERICK H. RITTS, born Chicago, Illinois, July 10, 1939; admitted to bar, 1971, Georgia; 1972, District of Columbia; 1975, U.S. Supreme Court. *Education:* Duke University (B.A., 1962); University of Georgia (J.D., 1970). Member, Board of Editors, University of Georgia Law Review, 1969-1970. Author: "Who Spiked the Prices?" Public Power, July-August 2000. [Lt. Cmdr., USNR, 1962-1968]. ***PRACTICE AREAS:*** Energy; Energy Regulation; Energy Finance; Energy Contracts; Legislative Practice. ***Email:*** fritts@bbrslaw.com

FERNANDO RODRIGUEZ, born Fort Worth, Texas, March 29, 1953; admitted to bar, 1978, Texas; 1984, U.S. Court of Appeals, Fifth Circuit; 1986, U.S. Supreme Court; 1988, U.S. District Court, Western District of Texas. *Education:* St. Louis University; University of Illinois (B.A., 1975); Baylor University (J.D., 1978). Pi Sigma Alpha; Delta Theta Phi. *Member:* Travis County Bar Association; State Bar of Texas (Member, Sections of: Environmental and Natural Resources; Computer; Public Utility; Public and Administrative Law). (Resident, Austin, Texas Office). ***Email:*** frodriguez@bbrsaustin.com

A. HEWITT ROSE, born Durham, North Carolina, 1951; admitted to bar, 1981, District of Columbia; 1986, U.S. Court of Appeals for the District of Columbia Circuit; U.S. Court of Appeals, Fifth Circuit. *Education:* University of North Carolina (B.A., Political Science, 1973); Duke University Public Policy School; University of North Carolina (J.D., 1980). Phi Beta Kappa. Captain, International Moot Court Team, 1978-1979. *Member:* District of Columbia Bar; Energy and American Bar Associations. [Lt., U.S. Navy, 1973-1976]. ***PRACTICE AREAS:*** Public Utility Law; Energy; Antitrust; Administrative Law; Litigation. ***Email:*** hrose@bbrslaw.com

(This Listing Continued)

CHRISTINE C. RYAN, born Washington, D.C., 1949; admitted to bar, 1983, District of Columbia and U.S. District Court for the District of Columbia; 1986, U.S. Court of Appeals, Fifth Circuit; U.S. Court of Appeals, District of Columbia Circuit. *Education:* Rosemont College (B.A., 1971); Georgetown University (J.D., 1982). Law Clerk to the Honorable John L. Smith, Chief Judge, U.S. District Court for the District of Columbia, 1982-1983. *Member:* District of Columbia Bar; Energy and American Bar Associations. ***Email:*** cryan@bbrslaw.com

GARRETT A. STONE, born Washington, D.C., March 5, 1958; admitted to bar, 1982, Colorado; 1986, District of Columbia. *Education:* University of North Carolina at Asheville (B.A., 1979); University of North Carolina at Chapel Hill (J.D., with honors, 1982). Member, North Carolina Law Review, 1980-1981. *Member:* American Bar Association (Member, Sections on: Administrative Law; Public Utility Law; Litigation). ***Email:*** gstone@bbrslaw.com

DAMON E. XENOPOULOS, born Johannesburg, South Africa, May 4, 1961; admitted to bar, 1985, South Africa (Advocate); 1988, New York; 1989, California (inactive);1990, U.S. Court of Appeals, Federal Circuit; 1991, U.S. Court of International Trade; 1993, District of Columbia. *Education:* University of the Witwatersrand, South Africa (B.A., 1982; LL.B., with distinction, 1985); George Washington University (M.C.L., 1986); New York University (LL.M. in International Legal Studies, 1988). Part-Time Tutor, School of Law, University of the Witwatersrand, Johannesburg, South Africa, 1984. Recipient, Syfrets Trust Ltd. Prize, Best Student in Law of Taxation and Trusts, University of the Witwatersrand, Johannesburg, South Africa, 1985. *Member:* American Bar Association. ***SPECIAL AGENCIES:*** U.S. Department of Energy; State Utility Commissions; Economic Development Agencies; U.S. Department of Commerce; U.S. International Trade Commission; U.S. Department of Treasury; U.S. Trade Representative. ***PRACTICE AREAS:*** Administrative Law; Business Law; Commercial Law; Contracts; Energy; International Trade; Litigation; Natural Resources; Regulatory Law; Technology and Science; Utility Law. ***Email:*** dex@bbrslaw.com

OF COUNSEL

STEPHEN J. KARINA, born Chicago, Illinois, August 8, 1947; admitted to bar, 1988, Maryland (Not admitted in District of Columbia). *Education:* University of Wyoming (B.A., 1969; M.A., 1973); University of Georgia (Ph.D., 1978); University of Maryland (J.D., 1988). Member, 1986-1987 and Articles Editor, 1987-1988, Maryland Law Review. Law Clerk to Honorable Alan M. Wilner, Associate Judge of Maryland Court of Special Appeals, 1988-1989. Adjunct Professor, School of Law, University of Baltimore, 1989-1992. Instructor, Department of Urban Studies and Planning, University of Maryland, 1990—. Author: Note, "Ford v. Ford: A Maryland Slayer's Statute Is Long Overdue," 46 Maryland Law Review 501, 1987. *Member:* Maryland State Bar Association. ***Email:*** skarina@bbrslaw.com

JOHN H. CONWAY, born Brooklyn, New York, July 30, 1948; admitted to bar, 1978, Wisconsin; 1985, U.S. Supreme Court; U.S. Court of Appeals for the District of Columbia, First, Fourth, Fifth, Sixth, Eighth, Ninth, Tenth and Eleventh Circuits; 2001, District of Columbia. *Education:* Tufts University (B.A., 1970); Boston University (M.B.A., cum laude, 1975); University of Wisconsin-Madison (J.D., cum laude, 1978). Managing Editor, Wisconsin Law Review, 1978. *Member:* State Bar of Wisconsin; Energy Bar Association. ***PRACTICE AREAS:*** Energy; Antitrust; Appellate Practice; Administrative Law; Litigation. ***Email:*** jconway@bbrslaw.com

---

MALCOLM A. BURKE, born New York, N.Y., January 25, 1973; admitted to bar, 2001, Virginia (Not admitted in District of Columbia). *Education:* Washington & Lee University (B.S., 1996; J.D., 2001). Certified Public Accountant, Virginia, 1999. ***Email:*** mburke@bbrslaw.com

ERIC M. DEVITO, born Canton, Ohio, March 18, 1971; admitted to bar, 1998, Maryland; 2001, District of Columbia. *Education:* Ohio State University (B.S.B.A., Accounting, summa cum laude, 1992); University of Maryland (J.D., 1998). Order of the Coif. Certified Public Accountant, 1993. Executive Editor, The Journal of Health Care Law and Policy, 1997-1998. *Member:* Maryland State, Energy and American Bar Associations. ***PRACTICE AREAS:*** Energy. ***Email:*** edevito@bbrslaw.com

MICHAEL K. LAVANGA, born Plainfield, New Jersey, August 18, 1969; admitted to bar, 2000, Virginia; 2001, District of Columbia. *Education:* Catholic University of America (B.A., 1991; M.A., 1995); University of Maryland (J.D., 2000). Manuscripts Editor, The Maryland Law Review, 1999-2000. *Member:* Virginia Bar Association; District of Columbia Bar; Energy Bar Association. ***PRACTICE AREAS:*** Energy. ***Email:*** mlavanga@bbrslaw.com

SHAUN C. MOHLER, born Washington, D.C., December 13, 1967; admitted to bar, 1995, Virginia; 1997, District of Columbia; 1999, U.S. District Court, Eastern District of Virginia. *Education:* University of Virginia (B.A., 1990); American University, Washington College of Law (J.D., 1995). Managing Editor, The American University Law Review, Vol. 44, 1994-1995. Law

(This Listing Continued)

BRICKFIELD BURCHETTE RITTS & STONE, P.C., Washington—Continued

Clerk to the Honorable Thomas S. Kenny, Nineteenth Judicial Circuit of Virginia, 1995-1996. *Member:* American Bar Association (Member, Litigation Section). ***PRACTICE AREAS:*** Energy; Litigation. ***Email:*** smohler@bbrslaw.com

KATHLEEN T. MULVILLE, born Fairfax, Virginia, December 17, 1971; admitted to bar, 1999, Virginia (Not admitted in District of Columbia). *Education:* University of Virginia (B.S.C.E., 1994); William and Mary School of Law (J.D., 1999). Phi Delta Phi. Member, American Society of Civil Engineers, 1991-1994. Articles Editor, William and Mary Environmental Law and Policy Review, 1997-1999. Author: "How the Antarctic Science, Tourism and Conservation Act of 1996 Fails Antarctica," William and Mary Environmental Law and Policy Review, Volume 23, No. 2. *Member:* Virginia State Bar; Energy Bar Association. ***PRACTICE AREAS:*** Energy Law. ***Email:*** ktmulville@bbrslaw.com

NELSON H. NEASE, born Abilene, Texas, December 1, 1967; admitted to bar, 1998, Texas. *Education:* University of Texas at Austin (B.A., 1992; J.D., 1997). *Member:* Travis County Bar Association; State Bar of Texas (Member, Sections on: Antitrust Business Legislation; Environmental & Natural Resources; Taxation Law; Administrative & Public Law; Public Utility Law); Texas Young Lawyers Association. (Resident, Austin, Texas Office). ***LANGUAGES:*** Spanish. ***Email:*** nnease@bbrsaustin.com

STACEY WALSH THOMPSON, born Washington, D.C., March 25, 1970; admitted to bar, 1998, Florida; 1999, District of Columbia. *Education:* University of Massachusetts (B.A., cum laude, 1992); George Washington University Law School (J.D., with honors, 1998). Member, George Washington Journal of International Law & Economics. *Member:* The District of Columbia Bar. ***LANGUAGES:*** Spanish. ***PRACTICE AREAS:*** Energy; Litigation. ***Email:*** sthompson@bbrslaw.com

---

BRINCEFIELD HARTNETT MALOOF & PALEOS, P.C.

WASHINGTON, D.C.

(See Alexandria, Virginia)

General Civil Practice concentrating in Civil Litigation, Real Estate, Business Law, Family Law and Personal Injury Claims, Insurance, Labor and Employment, Medical Malpractice, Wills, Probate, Professional Liability, Appellate Practice.

JOHN H. BROADLEY

1054 31ST STREET NW, SUITE 200
WASHINGTON, D.C. 20007
Telephone: 202-333-6025
Fax: 202-333-5685
Email: jbroadley@alum.mit.edu
URL: http://www.lawyers.com/broadley
Litigation, Transportation.

JOHN H. BROADLEY, born Huddersfield, England, May 25, 1945; admitted to bar, 1971, California; 1976, District of Columbia. *Education:* Massachusetts Institute of Technology (B.S., 1967); University of California at Berkeley (J.D., 1970). Special Counsel for Rail Litigation, U.S. Department of Justice, 1976-1981; Chief Counsel, Federal Railroad Administration, 1981-1982; General Counsel, Interstate Commerce Commission, 1982-1984. ***PRACTICE AREAS:*** Litigation; Transportation Law.

BROBECK, PHLEGER & HARRISON LLP

A Partnership including a Professional Corporation
1333 H STREET, N.W.
SUITE 800
WASHINGTON, D.C. 20005
Telephone: 202-220-6000
Facsimile: 202-220-5200
Email: info@brobeck.com
URL: http://www.brobeck.com

San Francisco, California Office: Spear Street Tower, One Market. Telephone: 415-442-0900. Facsimile: 415-442-0900.
Los Angeles, California Office: 550 South Hope Street. Telephone: 213-489-4060. Facsimile: 213-745-3345.
Palo Alto, California Office: Two Embarcadero Place, 2200 Geng Road. Telephone: 650-424-0160. Facsimile: 650-496-2885.

(This Listing Continued)

San Diego, California Office: 12390 El Camino Real. Telephone: 858-720-2500. Fax: 858-720-2555.
Irvine, California Office: 38 Technology Drive. Telephone: 949-790-6300. Facsimile: 949-790-6301.
Austin, Texas Office: 4801 Plaza on the Lake. Telephone: 512-330-4000. Facsimile: 512-330-4001.
Broomfield, Colorado Office: 370 Interlocken Boulevard, Suite 500. Telephone: 303-410-2000. Facsimile: 303-410-2199.
New York, N.Y. Office: 1633 Broadway, 47th Floor. Telephone: 212-581-1600. Facsimile: 212-586-7878.
Dallas, Texas Office: 300 Crescent Court, Suite 1400. Telephone: 972-715-2700. Fax: 972-715-2704.
Reston, Virginia Office: 2100 Reston Parkway, Suite 203. Telephone: 703-621-3000. Fax: 703-621-3001.
Associated International Offices:
London, England Office: Brobeck Hale and Dorr International, Hasilwood House, 60 Bishopsgate, London EC2N 4AJ. Telephone: + 44 171 638 6688. Facsimile: + 44 171 638 5888.
Oxford, England Office: Brobeck Hale and Dorr, Park Gate. 25 Milton Park. Abingdon. OX14 4RY. Telephone: +44 1235 82 30 00. Fax: +44 1235 82 30 30.
Munich, Germany Office: Brobeck Hale and Dorr, Maximilianstrasse 31. D-80539. Telephone: +49 89 24 213-0. Fax: +49 89 24 213-213.

General Practice, including Business and Technology, Business Litigation, Securities Litigation, Patent and Trademark Litigation; Technology Litigation, Environmental Litigation, Product Liability Litigation, Insurance Coverage Litigation on behalf of Policyholders, Intellectual Property (including Patent and Trademark Prosecution, Copyright, Trade Secrets and Licensing), Labor Law, Financial Services and Insolvency (including Bankruptcy and Loan Workout), Real Estate, and Tax, Executive Compensation, Employee Benefits and Estate Planning.

PARTNERS

CONO A. CARRANO, born New York, 1962; admitted to bar, 1994, New York; 1995, District of Columbia; registered to practice before U.S. Patent and Trademark Office. *Education:* State University of New York at Stony Brook (B.E.E.E., 1984); Polytechnic University (M.S.E.E., 1988); Hofstra University (J.D., 1994). ***PRACTICE AREAS:*** Intellectual Property Law. ***Email:*** ccarrano@brobeck.com

NORA E. GARROTE, born Havana, Cuba, 1958; admitted to bar, 1983, District of Columbia. *Education:* Bryn Mawr College (A.B., magna cum laude, 1980); Columbia University (J.D., 1983). Previously Partner, Piper & Marbury LLP. ***LANGUAGES:*** Spanish. ***PRACTICE AREAS:*** Intellectual Property; Technology Law; Computer Law; Telecommunications Law. ***Email:*** ngarrote@brobeck.com

JOHN B. MISSING, born Tucson, Arizona, 1956; admitted to bar, 1982, California; 1990, District of Columbia. *Education:* Cornell University (A.B., 1979; J.D., 1982). Phi Beta Kappa. ***PRACTICE AREAS:*** Securities Litigation; Commercial Litigation. ***Email:*** jmissing@brobeck.com

STEPHEN A. RIDDICK, born Norfolk, Virginia, 1963; admitted to bar, 1988, Maryland (Not admitted in District of Columbia). *Education:* University of Virginia (B.A., 1985); University of North Carolina at Chapel Hill (J.D., 1988). ***PRACTICE AREAS:*** Corporate Finance; Mergers and Acquisitions. ***Email:*** sriddick@brobeck.com

ANTHONY W. SHAW, born Rochester, New York, 1954; admitted to bar, 1981, New York; 1982, District of Columbia and U.S. Court of Appeals for the Federal Circuit; 1983, Virginia; registered to practice before U.S. Patent and Trademark Office. *Education:* Cornell University (A.B., 1976; M.Eng., 1977); Georgetown University Law Center (J.D., cum laude, 1981). Member, Georgetown Law Journal, 1979-1981. Law Clerk to Hon. Giles S. Rich, U.S. Court of Appeals for the Federal Circuit, 1981-1983. Adjunct Professor of Law, Georgetown University Law Center. *Member:* District of Columbia Bar; Virginia State Bar; New York State, Federal Circuit and American Bar Associations. ***Email:*** ashaw@brobeck.com

RODGER L. TATE, born Peoria, Illinois, 1947; admitted to bar, 1975, Maryland; 1976, District of Columbia; registered to practice before U.S. Patent and Trademark Office. *Education:* University of Cincinnati (B.S.Ch.E., with honors, 1970); Georgetown University (J.D., 1975). Omicron Delta Kappa; Tau Beta Pi; Phi Delta Phi. Editor, Georgetown Law Journal, 1975. U.S. Patent Office Examiner, 1970-1974. *Member:* The District of Columbia Bar; Maryland State and American Bar Associations; BIO Licensing Executives Society USA/Canada (Member, Intellectual Property Committee); American Intellectual Property Law Association. ***PRACTICE AREAS:*** Intellectual Property. ***Email:*** rtate@brobeck.com

OF COUNSEL

LAURENCE H. POSORSKE, born Oshkosh, Wisconsin, 1948; admitted to bar, 1992, Maryland; 1994, District of Columbia; registered to practice

(This Listing Continued)

before U.S. Patent and Trademark Office. *Education:* University of Wisconsin-Madison (B.A., honors degree, 1970); Cornell University (Ph.D., 1976); Georgetown University (J.D., 1992). *Member:* Maryland State and American Bar Associations; The District of Columbia Bar; American Intellectual Property Law Association; American Chemical Society (Biochemical Technology Division); Institute of Food Technologists; American Association for Advancement of Science. **Email:** lposorske@brobeck.com

MICHAEL C. TODD, born Miami, Florida, 1965; admitted to bar, 1991, Florida; 2000, District of Columbia. *Education:* Brown University (B.A., 1987); University of Miami School of Law (J.D., 1991). Member, 1989-1991, Articles and Comments Editor, 1990-1991, University of Miami Law Review. Senior Counsel, U.S. Securities and Exchange Commission, 1994-1996. *Member:* American Bar Association (Member, Business Law Section). ***PRACTICE AREAS:*** Corporate Law; Securities; Mergers and Acquisitions; Venture Capital; Finance; Business Law. **Email:** mtodd@brobeck.com

DOUGLAS C. BOGGS, born Washington, D.C., 1967; admitted to bar, 1995, Maryland; 1997, District of Columbia. *Education:* Duke University (B.A., 1989); Georgetown University (M.B.A., 1995; J.D., 1995). *Member:* The District of Columbia Bar; American Bar Association. ***PRACTICE AREAS:*** Corporate; Mergers and Acquisitions; Real Estate; Securities; Finance; Federal Legislation. **Email:** dboggs@brobeck.com

SENIOR ASSOCIATE

KIMBERLY B. KIEFER, born Milwaukee, Wisconsin, 1970; admitted to bar, 1996, Illinois; 1998, District of Columbia. *Education:* University of Wisconsin-Madison (B.A., 1992); Georgetown University (J.D., magna cum laude, 1996); University of Munich, Germany (LL.M., 1997). ***LANGUAGES:*** German. ***PRACTICE AREAS:*** Privacy Law; Internet Law; Digital Signatures; Export Regulation; Intellectual Property; Software Licensing. **Email:** kkiefer@brobeck.com

ASSOCIATES

ADA FERNANDEZ, born Fayetteville, Arkansas; admitted to bar, 1998, Virginia; 1999, District of Columbia. *Education:* Brown University (A.B., 1993); Georgetown University (J.D., 1998). ***LANGUAGES:*** Spanish. ***PRACTICE AREAS:*** Securities Litigation. **Email:** afernandez@brobeck.com

AKINYALE S. HARRISON, born Staten Island, New York, 1972; admitted to bar, 1999, New York; 2001, District of Columbia. *Education:* University of Virginia (B.S., 1994); University of Michigan Law School (J.D., 1997). Phi Delta Phi. *Member:* New York State and American Bar Associations. ***PRACTICE AREAS:*** Corporate Law; Venture Capital; Mergers and Acquisitions. **Email:** aharrison@brobeck.com

CECIL E. KEY, born Forrest City, Arkansas, 1959; admitted to bar, 1997, Virginia; 1998, District of Columbia; U.S. District Court, Eastern District of Virginia; U.S. Court of Appeals, Federal, First and Fourth Circuits. *Education:* University of Texas at Arlington (B.M., cum laude, 1983); Southern Methodist University (M.M., 1985); Georgetown University (J.D., cum laude, 1997). Kappa Delta Pi. Associate Editor, Law and Policy in International Business. Author: Note, "Everything Old is New Again: An Analysis of Rights of Foreign Inventors Under Section 104," 27 Law & Policy in Int'l. Bus. 755, 1996. *Member:* American Intellectual Property Law Association; International Trademark Association. ***PRACTICE AREAS:*** Intellectual Property. **Email:** ckey@brobeck.com

ROBERT A. KING, born Hartford, Connecticut, 1969; admitted to bar, 1999, Virginia; 2000, District of Columbia; registered to practice before U.S. Patent and Trademark Office. *Education:* United States Military Academy (B.S., 1991); Catholic University of America (J.D., cum laude, 1999). Member, Catholic University Law Review, 1996-1997. [Captain, U.S. Army, 1991-1995]. ***PRACTICE AREAS:*** Intellectual Property. **Email:** rking@brobeck.com

DANIEL LEE, admitted to bar, 1999, California; 2001, District of Columbia. *Education:* University of California at Los Angeles (B.A., Economics, Business, 1996); George Washington University (J.D., with honors, 1999). Managing Editor, George Washington University Law Review, 1998-1999. Law Clerk, Piper & Marbury LLP, 1998-1999. Author: Case Note, "Holding the Federal Government Liable for Current Basis Fee Enhancements Requires an Explicit Waiver of Sovereign Immunity from Interest, 66 Geo. Wash. L. Rev. 4, April 1998. ***PRACTICE AREAS:*** Venture Capital; Public Offerings; Emerging Growth Companies. **Email:** dlee@brobeck.com

MITCHELL D. LEE, admitted to bar, 1997, New York and District of Columbia. *Education:* Cornell University (B.A., 1990; J.D., 1996). ***PRACTICE AREAS:*** Corporate and Securities; Venture Capital; Mergers and Acquisitions. **Email:** milee@brobeck.com

NATALIE K. MEYER, born San Antonio, Texas, 1970; admitted to bar, 1999, New York; 2001, District of Columbia. *Education:* Birmingham-Southern College (B.A., 1992); University of Virginia Graduate School of Arts and Sciences (M.A., 1995); University of Virginia School of Law (J.D., 1998). ***PRACTICE AREAS:*** Technology Law; Intellectual Property; Corporate Law. **Email:** nmeyer@brobeck.com

DEAN S. NORDLINGER, born Washington, D.C., 1969; admitted to bar, 2000, Virginia (Not admitted in District of Columbia). *Education:* University of Michigan (B.A., Spanish Language and Literature, 1991); University of San Diego (M.I.B., 1994); Georgetown University (J.D., 2000). ***PRACTICE AREAS:*** Business and Technology Transactions. **Email:** dnordlinger@brobeck.com

STEPHANIE M. PRIES, born Bronx, New York, 1969; admitted to bar, 1998, California; 1999, District of Columbia. *Education:* Princeton University (A.B., 1991); Stanford University (M.A., 1992); Santa Clara University School of Law (J.D., 1998; Certificate, High-Technology Law). Editor-in-Chief, Santa Clara Law Review. Author, Comment, "Can Prepurchase Entrepreneurial Efforts Satisfy the Fourth Prong of the *Howey* Test? A Critique of *SEC v. Life Partners,* 38 Santa Clara Law Review 269 (1997). *Member:* State Bar of California. ***LANGUAGES:*** Spanish, Portuguese. ***PRACTICE AREAS:*** Corporate Law; Securities. **Email:** spries@brobeck.com

CRAIG L. PUCKETT, born Los Angeles, California, May 22, 1965; admitted to bar, 1999, Virginia; 2000, U.S. District Court, Eastern District of Virginia and U.S. Court of Appeals for the Federal Circuit; registered to practice before U.S. Patent and Trademark Office (Not admitted in District of Columbia). *Education:* University of California at Los Angeles (B.S., Chemistry, 1988); University of Wisconsin-Madison (Ph.D., Organic Chemistry, 1995); Franklin Pierce Law Center (J.D., 1998). ***PRACTICE AREAS:*** Intellectual Property. **Email:** cpuckett@brobeck.com

MATTHEW M. ROSINI, born Danville, Pennsylvania, 1972; admitted to bar, 1997, Pennsylvania and U.S. District Court, Western District of Pennsylvania; 1998, Massachusetts; 2001, District of Columbia. *Education:* Boston College (B.S., magna cum laude, 1994; J.D., 1997). Beta Gamma Sigma. Co-Author: "Directors' and Officers' Liability for Y2K: A Corporate Governance Litigation Bear and Securities Litigation Bull?" The Delaware Journal of Corporate Law, Volume 24, Number 3. Member, Pennsylvania Bar Association, 1997-1999. *Member:* Allegheny County Bar Association. **Email:** mrosini@brobeck.com

JADE B. VERITY, born 1971; (admission pending). *Education:* Humboldt State University (B.A., English, magna cum laude, 1993); Georgetown University Law Center (J.D., cum laude, 2001). ***PRACTICE AREAS:*** Securities Litigation. **Email:** jverity@brobeck.com

ARMAND J. ZOTTOLA, admitted to bar, 1997, Maryland; 1998, District of Columbia. *Education:* Bucknell University (B.A., 1992); Franklin Pierce Law Center, Intellectual Property Summer Institute (1995); Catholic University, Columbus School of Law (J.D., 1997). *Member:* District of Columbia Bar (Member, Sections on: Intellectual Property; Computer & Technology); American Bar Association (Member, Sections on: Intellectual Property; Science & Technology). ***PRACTICE AREAS:*** Intellectual Property (Copyright and Trademark); E-Commerce; Computer and Software; Information Technology. **Email:** azottola@brobeck.com

Brobeck, Phleger & Harrison LLP as offices in Europe through a joint venture, Brobeck Hales and Dorr. The offices are located in London and Oxford, England and Munich, Germany.

(This Listing Continued)

KIMBERLY A. BROOKS

WASHINGTON, D.C.

(See Bethesda, Maryland)

Decedent's Estates, Wills and Trusts, Probate, Elder Law, Elder Care, Living Trusts, Wealth Transfer, Powers of Attorney, Assisted Living, Long Term Care, Estates, Trusts and Gift Taxation, Small Business Formation, Qualified Retirement Plans and ERISA Compliance, Individual Income Taxation, Tax Collections, Tax Controversies.

BROWDY AND NEIMARK

Established in 1952

SUITE 300, 624 NINTH STREET, N.W.
WASHINGTON, D.C. 20001-5303
Telephone: 202-628-5197
Telecopier: 202-737- 3528
Email: pmcinnis@browdyneimark.com
URL: http://www.lawyers.com/browdyneimark

U.S. and International Intellectual Property including Patent, Trademark, Copyright and Unfair Competition Law.

(This Listing Continued)

BROWDY AND NEIMARK, Washington—Continued

FIRM PROFILE: For over forty-five years our firm has advised, counseled and represented inventors, companies and governmental agencies, both domestic and foreign, in connection with both U.S. and foreign intellectual property and related matters, and has procured domestic and foreign patents, trademarks and copyrights.

SHERIDAN NEIMARK, born Youngstown, Ohio, April 7, 1935; admitted to bar, 1962, District of Columbia; 1963-1982, U.S. Court of Customs and Patent Appeals; 1973, U.S. Supreme Court and U.S. Court of Appeals, Fifth Circuit; 1975, U.S. Court of Appeals, Fourth Circuit; 1982, U.S. Court of Appeals for the Federal Circuit. *Education:* Carnegie-Mellon University (B.S.Ch.E., 1957); George Washington University (J.D., 1961). Listed in Who's Who's in American Law. Co-Author: "Is There a Viable Doctrine of Non-Statutory Late Claiming as a Defense In Patent Litigation?" Vol. L No. 10 JPOS 677 (October, 1968). Examiner, U.S. Patent Office, 1957-1962. Member, 1972-1986 and Vice Chairman, 1976-1977, Maryland Developmental Disabilities Council. Member, Advisory Board, (ABA) Mental and Physical Disability Law Reporter. *Member:* District of Columbia Bar; American Bar Association; American Intellectual Property Law Association. ***PRACTICE AREAS:*** Patent Opinions; Patent Prosecution; Pharmaceuticals and Pesticides; Chemistry; Plastics and Moldings; Alloys; Mechanical Patents; Design Patents; Trademarks. ***Email:*** BRWDYNMRK@DIGIZEN.NET

ROGER L. BROWDY, born Washington, D.C., August 3, 1945; admitted to bar, 1972, Maryland and District of Columbia; 1973, U.S. Court of Customs and Patent Appeals; 1982, U.S. Court of Appeals for the Federal Circuit. *Education:* University of Michigan (B.S.E.Ch.E., 1967); Georgetown University (J.D., 1972). Examiner, U.S. Patent Office, 1967-1968. Patent Advisor, Frankford Arsenal, 1969-1971. *Member:* District of Columbia Bar; Maryland Patent Law Association (President, 1985-1987); American Intellectual Property Law Association. ***REPORTED CASES:*** Fiers vs. Revel, 25 UPSPQ2d 1601 (Fed Cir 1993); Ex parte Rubin, 5 USPQ2d 1461 (PTO Bd Pat. App. & Int. 1987), ASLHA vs. NHAS, 224 USPQ 798 (TTAB 1984). In re Koller, 204 USPQ 702 (CCPA 1980), In re Hirao, 188 USPQ 248 (CCPA 1975), In re Hayashibara, 188 USPQ 4, (CCPA 1975), In re Hirao, 190 USPQ 15 (CCPA 1976). ***PRACTICE AREAS:*** Pharmaceutical Intellectual Property; Medical Intellectual Property; Chemical Intellectual Property; International Intellectual Property; Intellectual Property Licensing; Biotechnology; Interferences; Trademark Proceedings. ***Email:*** BRWDYNMRK@DIGIZEN.NET

ANNE M. KORNBAU, born Baltimore, Maryland, September 7, 1944; admitted to bar, 1970, Maryland; 1976, Virginia; 1986, District of Columbia. *Education:* Drexel University (B.S. Chem., 1966); George Washington University (J.D., 1970). *Member:* District of Columbia Bar; Virginia State Bar (Inactive; Member and Chair, 1993-1994, Intellectual Property Section; Member, Board of Governors, 1988-1990); American Bar Association; American Intellectual Property Law Association (Author: "PTO Affairs," column in AIPLA Bulletin, 1985-1987; Member, Ad Hoc Committee on PTO Automation, 1983-1999; Chair: Committee on Relations with Patent and Trademark Office, 1985-1987; Chair, Public Information Committee, 1994-1996). ***LANGUAGES:*** French. ***PRACTICE AREAS:*** Intellectual Property Law; Biotechnology Law; Pharmaceuticals; Chemistry Trademark Law. ***Email:*** ANNE@BROWDYNEIMARK.COM

NORMAN J. LATKER, born Chicago, Illinois, December 19, 1931; admitted to bar, 1956, Illinois; 1979, District of Columbia; registered to practice before U.S. Patent and Trademark Office. *Education:* University of Illinois, Champaign-Urbana (B.S.C.E., 1953; J.D., 1959) Awarded honorary LL.D., by University of Illinois, 1985. Chi Epsilon. Recipient: Birch Award, Society of University Patent Administrators, for Development of Bayh-Dole Act of 1980, 1983; First Recipient, Vannevar Bush Award for Outstanding Contribution to the U.S.A. For Creating the Model for the Successful Public and Private Technology Partnerships, AFT2E, U.S. Department of Commerce Silver Medal, 1985; Bronze Medal, for development of Federal Technology Transfer Act of 1986. Author: "Utilization of Government-Owned Health and Welfare Inventions," Journal of the Patent Office Society, November, 1965; "A Win-Win Philosophy for Technology Management," Journal of the Association of University Technology Managers, Spring 1989. Guest Lecturer, "Technology Transfer and Government Intellectual Property Policy," George Washington University Procurement Law, 1980—. Chairman, Subcommittee on University Patent Policy of the Federal Council for Science, Engineering and Technology, 1971-1978. Vice-Chairman, Subcommittee on Intellectual Property of the Federal Council for Science, Engineering and Technology, 1974-1978. Patent Counsel, Department of Health, Education and Welfare and National Institutes of Health, 1965-1980. Director, Office of Federal Technology Management, Department of Commerce, 1980-1987. *Member:* District of Columbia Bar; Illinois State, Federal and American Bar Associations; American Intellectual Property Law Association; Licensing Executive Society; Society of University Patent Administrators; Maryland Patent Law Association. ***TRANSACTIONS:*** Expert witness in court cases involving government patent policy issues. Platzer et al vs. Sloan Kettering Institute, U.S. District Court Southern District of New York. Southern Research Institute vs. Griffin Corp., U.S. District Court Northern District of Alabama. Center For Neurologic Study vs. Gen. Probe inc. Superior Court of the State of California. Giese v. Pierce Chemical Co., U.S. District Court, District of Massachusetts. ***PRACTICE AREAS:*** Intellectual Property Law; Mechanical; Electro-Mechanical; Chemistry Law; Government Patent Policy; Technology Transfers. ***Email:*** BRWDYNMRK@DIGIZEN.NET

DIANA MICHELLE SOBO, born Fort Lauderdale, January 21, 1969; admitted to bar, 1998, Florida (Not admitted in District of Columbia). *Education:* University of Miami (B.S., cum laude, 1990); University of Florida (J.D., 1997). Member: Entertainment, Arts & Sports Law Society, University of Florida (President, 1996-1997); Law Association of Women, University of Florida (Vice-President, 1996). ***PRACTICE AREAS:*** Trademarks; Copyrights; Unfair Competition; Intellectual Property; Entertainment Law. ***Email:*** dmsobo@browdyneimark.com

OF COUNSEL

IVER P. COOPER, born New York, N.Y., November 10, 1953; admitted to bar, 1978, New York and U.S. Claims Court; 1980, District of Columbia; 1982, U.S. Court of Appeals for the Federal Circuit; 1984, Virginia; 1976, registered to practice before U.S. Patent and Trademark Office. *Education:* Massachusetts Institute of Technology (B.S., in Chemistry, 1974); Boston University, Boston (J.D., 1977); George Washington University (LL.M. in Patents and Trade Regulation, 1979). Contributing Editor, Medical Devices and Diagnostics Industry Magazine, 1984-1986. Recipient: First Prize, Nathan Burkan Memorial Competition at Boston University, sponsored by the American Society of Composers, Authors and Publishers, 1976; Robert C, Watson Award of the American Patent Law Association, 1979; Stephen P. Ladas Award for the U.S. Trademark Association, 1979. Author: Book, *Biotechnology and The Law,* Clark, Boardman Co., Ltd., 1982, 1985-1989, 1991-2000; Final Report to the Office of Technology Assessment, U.S. Congress on Property Rights in Cell Lines, May 23, 1986; "Patent Problem for Chemical Researchers-The Utility Requirement After Brenner v. Manson," 18 IDEA 23-37, Spring, 1976; "Patent Protection for New Forms of Life," 38 Federal Bar Journal, 34-48, Winter, 1979; "Arzberger Under the Microscope: A Critical Reexamination of the Exclusion of Bacteria From Plant Patent Protection," 7 Rutgers Journal of Computers, Technology and the Law, 367-79, February, 1980; Mapmaking and Copyright: "The Direct Observation Rule and the Public Interest," 18 Publishing, Entertainment, Advertising and Allied Fields Law Quarterly 311-33, Winter, 1980; "Trademark Aspects of Pharmaceutical Product Design," 70 Trademark Reporter 1-46, January-February, 1980; "The Patent System and the New Biology," 8 Rutgers Journal of Computers, Technology and the Law, 1-48, 1980; "Unclean Hands and Unlawful Use in Commerce: Trademarks Adrift on the Regulatory Tide," 71 Trademark Reporter, 38-58, 1981; "Preventing Inadvertent Forfeiture of Patent Rights," 5 Medical Devices and Diagnostic Industry (MDDI), 70-72, 115, March, 1983; "U.S. Export Controls on Biotechnology," 6 Recombinant DNA Technical Bulletin, 12-18, March, 1983; "Putting New Life Into Your Medical Device Patents," 8 MDDI 58-61, October, 1986. Co-author: "Final Report to the Office of Technology Assessment, U.S. Congress on Certain Laws Affecting the International Transfer of Biotechnology," April 8, 1983; *Environmental Regulation of Biotechnology,* MacMillan Press, 1989. Law Clerk to Trial Judge Joseph V. Colaianni, U.S. Court of Claims, 1977-1978. Fellow, Food and Drug Law Institute, 1978-1979. Member, Board of Editors, Biotechnology Law Reports, 1982—. Patent and Associate General Counsel, Association of Biotechnology Companies, 1984-1989. Advisor to the Board, U.S. Patent and Trademark Office, Biotechnology Institute, 1989-1991; Member, Association of Biotechnology Companies Patent Law Working Group, 1991-1993. Co-Chair, PTO Affairs Sub-Committee, 1992-1993. *Member:* District of Columbia Bar; American Intellectual Property Law Association (Member: Chemical Practice and Plant Variety Protection Committees, 1985—). ***PRACTICE AREAS:*** Biotechnology and Biomedical Patents. ***Email:*** icooper@browdyneimark.com

JAY M. FINKELSTEIN, born Philadelphia, Pennsylvania, February 23, 1937; admitted to bar, 1964, District of Columbia; 1966, U.S. Court of Appeals for the District of Columbia Circuit; 1967-1982, U.S. Court of Customs and Patent Appeals; 1970, U.S. Supreme Court; 1982, U.S. Court of Appeals for the Federal Circuit; registered to practice before U.S. Patent and Trademark Office. *Education:* Drexel University (B.S.E.E., 1959); George Washington University (J.D., with honors, 1963). Phi Alpha Delta; Tau Beta Pi; Eta Kappa Nu. Patent Examiner, U.S. Patent Office, 1959-1961. *Member:* The District of Columbia Bar; American Intellectual Property Law Association. ***PRACTICE AREAS:*** Intellectual Property. ***Email:*** jfinkelstein@browdyneimark.com

PATENT AGENT

ALLEN C. YUN, born Taipei, Taiwan, February 8, 1957. *Education:* Cornell University (B.S., 1979; Ph.D., 1986; M.Eng., 1987). Recipient, Acheson Scholar Award, School of Chemical Engineering, Cornell University, 1987.

(This Listing Continued)

Author: Expression of Beta-Galactosidase Controlled by a Nitrogenase Promoter in Stem Nodules of Aeschynomene scabra. Proc. Natl. Acad. Sci. USA 81:5806-5810., Legocki, R.P., Yun, A.C. and Szalay, A.A. (1984); Structural Genes of Dinitrogenase and Dinitrogenase Reductase An Transcribed from Two Separate Promoters in the Broad Host Range Cowpea Rhizobium Strain IRc78. Proc. Natl. Acad. Sci. USA 81:7358-7362; Yun, A.C. and Szalay, A.A. (1994); Nitrogenase Promoter-lacZ Fusion Studies of Essential Nitrogen Fixation Genes in Bradyrhizobium japonicum I110. J. Bacteriol. 167:784-791., Yun, A.C., Noti, J.D. and Szalay, A.A. (1986); Expression of the Klebsiella pneumoniae nifH Gene in Saccharomyces cerevisiae. Enzyme Microb. Technol. 9:438-443, Maina, C.V., Yun, A.C. and Szalay, A.A. (1987); A Plasmid Sequence from Rhizobium leguminosarum 300 Contains Homology to Sequences near the Octopine TL-DNA Right Border. Mol. Gen. Genet. 209:580-584, Yun, A.C., Hadley, R.G. and Szalay, A.A. (1987). *Member:* American Association For Advancement of Science. ***PRACTICE AREAS:*** Drafting and Prosecuting Patent Applications; Biotechnology; Chemical Patents. ***Email:*** ACYUN@BROWDYNEIMARK.COM

BROWN & FREESTON

3201 NEW MEXICO AVENUE, N.W.
SUITE 242
WASHINGTON, D.C. 20016
Telephone: 202-237-6008
Fax: 202-237-5259
URL: http://www.brown-freeston.com

Product Safety Law, Product Liability, Recalls, Administrative Law, Environmental Law, Expert Witnessing.

FIRM PROFILE: The firm specializes in the representation of both domestic and international manufacturing of products before the Consumer Product Safety Commission. The firm's regulatory practice includes ongoing product liability updates for its clients.

MICHAEL A. BROWN, born San Angelo, Texas, October 15, 1938; admitted to bar, 1962, Texas; 1963, U.S. Claims Court; 1968, U.S. Supreme Court; 1975, District of Columbia. *Education:* St. Mary's University (B.B.A., 1961; LL.B., magna cum laude, 1961); Georgetown University (LL.M., 1970). Delta Theta Phi (Vice-Dean, 1960-1961). General Counsel, 1973-1976 and Executive Director, 1976-1979, U.S. Consumer Product Safety Commission. Enforcement Counsel and Deputy General Counsel, United States Environmental Protection Agency, 1982-1983. *Member:* American Bar Association (Vice-Chair, Toxic and Environmental Torts Litigation Committee, National Resources, Energy and Environmental Resources Section, 1990-1992). [Col., USAR, JAGC, U.S. Army]. ***PRACTICE AREAS:*** Environmental Law; Product Safety Law. ***Email:*** mab@brown-freeston.com

MARGARET A. FREESTON, born Utica, New York, July 8, 1944; admitted to bar, 1969, Connecticut; 1972, District of Columbia; 1980, U.S. Supreme Court; 1984, Maryland. *Education:* Mount Holyoke College (B.A., 1966); Georgetown University (J.D., 1969). Acting General Counsel, 1981-1982 and 1978-1979, Executive Legal Assistant to the Chairman, 1983 and Deputy General Counsel, 1977-1984, U.S. Consumer Product Safety Commission. *Member:* The District of Columbia Bar; American Bar Association (Vice Chair, Consumer Products Regulation Committee, Section of Administrative Law and Regulatory Practice, 1999-2000); Women's Bar Association of the District of Columbia. ***PRACTICE AREAS:*** Product Safety Law; Administrative Law. ***Email:*** maf@brown-freeston.com

---

BROWN NIETERT & KAUFMAN

CHARTERED

Established in 1975

SUITE 660
1920 N STREET, N.W.
WASHINGTON, D.C. 20036
Telephone: 202-887-0600
Facsimile: 202-457-0126
Email: steve@bnkcomlaw.com
URL: http://www.bnkcomlaw.com

Practice before Federal and Local Courts, Government Departments and Commissions. Legislative and Committee Appearances. Public Utilities, State and Municipal Commissions and Agencies. Specializing in Telecommunications.

FIRM PROFILE: The firm's representation of clients has taken it before the Executive Branch, the Congress and various federal administrative bodies, including the Federal Communications Commission, Copyright Office, Justice Department, Federal Trade Commission, Commerce Department, State Department, International Trade Commission and Office of the United States Trade Representative, as well as local zoning and cable television franchising authorities.

(This Listing Continued)

Brown Nietert & Kaufman, Chartered, is a Washington, D.C. law firm providing legal, legislative, administrative law and related services including commercial transactions, primarily in the area of U.S. and foreign telecommunications. The firm was established in 1975 by Richard L. Brown. The firm has represented clients from every state and several foreign countries with a wide variety of communications interests including: commercial and private mobile radio services (including broadband and narrowband PCS, cellular telephone, paging, Specialized Mobile Radio and two-way dispatch facilities), wireless cable (MMDS, MDS and ITFS), commercial and non-commercial broadcasting, landline telephony, microwave and satellite telecommunications.

RICHARD L. BROWN, born New York, N.Y., November 9, 1944; admitted to bar, 1969, New York; 1972, District of Columbia and U.S. District Court for the District of Columbia; 1973, U.S. Court of Appeals for the District of Columbia Circuit; 1974, U.S. Claims Court; 1980, U.S. Supreme Court. *Education:* Emory University (B.A., 1966); New York University (J.D., 1969). Co-Author: with Finn, *The Satellite Earth Station Zoning Book, Questions and Answers About Satellite Earth Stations* and *The Business of Private Cable Television (SMATV),* Society for Private and Commercial Earth Stations, 1983; "Section 605 of the Communications Act: Teaching a Salty Old Sea Dog New Tricks," Catholic University Law Review, Vol. 34, Spring 1985. *Member:* District of Columbia Bar; American Bar Association; Federal Communications Bar Association. ***PRACTICE AREAS:*** Telecommunications. ***Email:*** Richard@BNKCOMLAW.COM

ROBYN G. NIETERT, born Watertown, New York, February 18, 1953; admitted to bar, 1980, District of Columbia and U.S. District Court for the District of Columbia; 1982, U.S. Court of Appeals for the Federal Circuit. *Education:* George Washington University (B.A., 1975); National Law Center, George Washington University (J.D., 1980). Winner: 1980 Nathanial Burkhan Memorial Competition Sponsored by ASCAP. Recipient, Golden Receiver Award for legal contribution of the Year for Wireless, 1993. Member, Editorial Advisory Board, National Satellite Publishing, Inc. Co-Author with Brown and Finn, *Questions and Answers About Satellite Earth Stations, Society for Private and Commercial Earth Stations,* 1983. Co-Author with Kaufman, "Twenty Questions About the 220-222 MH2 Band," 1993. *Member:* District of Columbia Bar; American Bar Association; Federal Communications Bar Association. ***PRACTICE AREAS:*** Telecommunications. ***Email:*** Robyn@BNKCOMLAW.COM

LORRETTA K. TOBIN, born St. Louis Missouri, May 11, 1959; admitted to bar, 1987, Virginia (Not admitted in District of Columbia). *Education:* James Madison University (B.A., 1981); Creighton University School of Law (J.D., 1984). *Member:* Virginia State Bar; American Bar Association (Member: Administrative Law Section; Forum Committee on Communications); Federal Communications Bar Association. ***PRACTICE AREAS:*** Telecommunications.

RHONDA L. NEIL, born Melrose, Massachusetts, June 30, 1963; admitted to bar, 1988, Maryland; 1991, District of Columbia. *Education:* Skidmore College (B.A., honors, 1985); Washington College of Law, The American University (J.D., 1988). Phi Beta Kappa. Note and Comment Editor, The American University Law Review, 1987-1988. *Member:* District of Columbia Bar; Maryland State and American Bar Association; Federal Communications Bar Association. ***PRACTICE AREAS:*** Telecommunications.

OF COUNSEL

DAVID J. KAUFMAN, born Chicago, Illinois, March 6, 1953; admitted to bar, 1977, Virginia and District of Columbia; 1979, U.S. Court of Appeals for the District of Columbia Circuit. *Education:* University of Illinois (B.A., 1973); Georgetown University (J.D., 1976). Illinois State Scholar; Edmund J. James Scholar. Co-Author with Nietert, "Twenty Questions About the 220-222 MH2 Band," 1993. Mr. Kaufman has testified as an expert appraiser of cellular properties. *Member:* District of Columbia Bar; Virginia State Bar; Federal Communications Bar Association. ***PRACTICE AREAS:*** Telecommunications. ***Email:*** David@BNKCOMLAW.COM

THOMAS P. BROWN, III

WASHINGTON, D.C.

(See Bethesda, Maryland)

General Civil Practice, Real Estate, Probate.

BROWNSTEIN HYATT & FARBER, P.C.

Established in 1968

1615 L STREET, N.W.
SUITE 450
WASHINGTON, D.C. 20036
Telephone: 202-296-7353
Telecopier: 202-296-7009
URL: http://www.bhf-law.com

Denver, Colorado Office: Twenty-Second Floor, 410 Seventeenth Street, 80202-4437. Telephone: 303-223-1100. Telecopier: 303-223-1111.
Glenwood Springs, Colorado Office: 715 Grand Avenue, Suite C, 81601. Mailing Address: P.O. Box 357, 81602-0357. Telephone: 970-945-5302. Telecopier: 970-384-2360.

Administrative, Legislative, Regulatory.

WILLIAM T. BRACK, born Butte, Montana, February 6, 1952; admitted to bar, 1982, District of Columbia and U.S. Tax Court. *Education:* University of Northern Colorado (B.A., Math., 1975; B.S., Business/Accounting, 1977); University of Tulsa (J.D., 1981); Georgetown University (Masters in Tax Law Program, 1984). Phi Delta Phi. Staff Member, University of Tulsa Law Review, 1979-1981. Certified Public Accountant, Oklahoma, 1978—. Chief of Staff to U.S. Senator Hank Brown, Colorado, 1991-1995. *Member:* Bar Association of the District of Columbia; Oklahoma Society of Certified Public Accountants. (Resident). ***PRACTICE AREAS:*** Taxation; Financial Institutions Law; Foreign Trade; Telecommunications; Health Care. ***Email:*** bbrack@bhfdc.com

THOMAS H. HUDSON, born Russellville, Arkansas, November 23, 1946; admitted to bar, 1973, Louisiana; 1974, District of Columbia. *Education:* Louisiana State University (B.A., 1968; J.D., 1971). Chief of Staff, U.S. Senator John Breaux, Louisiana, 1976-1988. Louisiana State Senate, 1976-1988. *Member:* The District of Columbia Bar. (Resident). ***PRACTICE AREAS:*** State and Federal Legislative Practice; Administrative; Regulatory. ***Email:*** thudson@bhfdc.com

OF COUNSEL

LEE COWEN, born Denver, Colorado, May 16, 1964; admitted to bar, 1989, Maryland; 1990, District of Columbia. *Education:* Brandeis University (B.A., 1986); Emory University School of Law (J.D., 1989). (Resident). ***PRACTICE AREAS:*** Legislative; Administrative. ***Email:*** lcpwen@bhfdc.com

LEGAL SUPPORT PERSONNEL

MICHAEL B. LEVY, born Baltimore, Maryland, July 12, 1947. *Education:* Rutgers University (Ph.D., 1979); Brown University (B.A., 1969). University Bevier Scholar; Outstanding Dissertation in Political Science, 1979. Author: "Political Thought in America," Dorsey Press, 1988; "The Liberal Future in America," W. Philip Abbott, Greenwood Press, 1985; "Handbook of Political Theory and the Policy Sciences," W.E.B. Portis, Greenwood Press, 1988. Associate Professor: Texas A&M University, 1978-1985; Rutgers University, 1977-1978. Staff Economist, Joint Economic Committee, U.S. Congress, 1985-1986. Chief of Staff, U.S. Senator Lloyd Benton, 1987-1992. Assistant Secretary, U.S. Treasury, 1993-1995. Senior Advisor to Secretary of Treasury, 1995. Distinguished Professor, Georgetown University School of Business, 1995. (Legislative Consultant). ***Email:*** levy@gunet.georgetown.edu

RICHARD E. MAY, born Columbus, Ohio, July 2, 1954. *Education:* Ohio University (B.S.Ed., 1976; M.A., 1982). Staff Director, U.S. House Budget Committee, 1995-1997. ***PRACTICE AREAS:*** Federal Budget Issues; Tax Policy; Telecommunications Law. ***Email:*** rmay@bhfdc.com

KATHRYN DOERR, born Los Angeles, California, November 3, 1972. *Education:* Boston College (B.A., 1995). ***Email:*** kdoerr@bhfdc.com

REPRESENTATIVE CLIENTS: American Salvage Pool Association; Apollo Real Estate Advisors, L.P.; AT&T; First Data Corp.; Global Crossing; IPWireless, Inc.; National Cable Television Association; NL Industries; Vector Group, Ltd.; Western Union Financial Services, Inc.

(For Complete Biographical Data on all Personnel see Professional Biographies at Denver, Colorado)

BRUDER, GENTILE & MARCOUX, L.L.P.

Established in 1976

1100 NEW YORK AVENUE, N.W., SUITE 510 EAST
WASHINGTON, D.C. 20005-3934
Telephone: 202-783-1350
Telecopiers: 202-737-9117; 347-2644
Email: bgmstaff@brudergentile.com
URL: http://www.brudergentile.com

General and Administrative Practice including Public Utility, Electric Power, Natural Gas, Cogeneration, Hydroelectric, Bulk Power Transmission, Energy and Antitrust. Appellate Practice.

(This Listing Continued)

FIRM PROFILE: Bruder, Gentile & Marcoux, founded in 1976, practices extensively before the Federal Energy Regulatory Commission, the Department of Energy and the Federal Courts in a variety of energy-related matters. Each of the firm's partners has substantial and diversified energy law experience. The breadth of our practice is evidenced by the diversity of our client base. Representative clients include investor- and privately-owned electric utilities and their affiliates, cooperatively-owned utilities, natural gas distribution companies, interstate natural gas pipelines, industrial companies and utility trade associations. Our staff of sixteen individuals includes nine attorneys and seven legal support personnel. The firm has conducted ratemaking litigation involving a wide range of legal, financial, economic and accounting issues. We have also conducted litigation and provided counsel on competitive issues in regulated industries, and we have experience with the antitrust laws and policies related to those industries. Our attorneys have represented clients in regulatory matters involving cogeneration/small power production, hydroelectric licensing and utility mergers and emerging issues relating to utility deregulation. We have also worked extensively with energy-related contracts (power sales, transmission, steam supply, gas supply and transportation) and in the area of market-based pricing of electricity.

GEORGE F. BRUDER (Retired).

CARMEN L. GENTILE, born Boston, Massachusetts, May 22, 1940; admitted to bar, 1968, Massachusetts; 1971, District of Columbia. *Education:* Harvard University (A.B., 1961); University of Pennsylvania (LL.B., 1967). Law Clerk to the Justices of the Massachusetts Superior Court, 1967-1968. Assistant Legal Counsel to the Governor of Massachusetts, 1968-1970. *Member:* The District of Columbia Bar; Bar Association of the District of Columbia (Member: Board of Directors, 1983-1985; Board of Trustees, Bar Associations Research Foundation, 1991-1994); Massachusetts, Federal Energy (Member: Board of Directors, 1986-1989; President, 1995-1996) and American (Member: Natural Resources, Energy and Environmental Law Section; Vice-Chair, Electric Power Committee, 1996-1997) Bar Associations. ***PRACTICE AREAS:*** Utility Law; Appellate Practice; Antitrust Law. ***Email:*** clgentile@brudergentile.com

ALBERT R. SIMONDS, JR. (Retired).

J. MICHEL MARCOUX, born Washington, D.C., January 21, 1945; admitted to bar, 1973, Virginia; 1974, District of Columbia; 1976, U.S. Supreme Court. *Education:* Washington & Lee University (A.B., 1966); The University of Virginia (LL.B., 1972); Queens' College, University of Cambridge (D.I.L., 1974). Editor, Virginia Journal of International Law, 1971-1972. Law Clerk to Circuit Judge Roger Robb, U.S. Court of Appeals for the District of Columbia Circuit, 1973-1974. *Member:* The District of Columbia Bar; Virginia State Bar; Federal Energy (Member, Board of Directors, 1991-1994; Chairman, Natural Gas Rate and Accounting Regulations Committee, 1984-1985; Chairman, Committee on Practice and Procedure, 1987-1988) and American Bar Associations. ***PRACTICE AREAS:*** Natural Gas; Appellate Practice. ***Email:*** jmmarcoux@brudergentile.com

DAVID E. GOROFF, born Quincy, Massachusetts, April 24, 1952; admitted to bar, 1977, Massachusetts; 1979, U.S. Court of Appeals, District of Columbia Circuit; 1980, District of Columbia; 1981, U.S. District Court, District of Columbia. *Education:* Tufts University (B.A., magna cum laude, 1974); Suffolk University (J.D., cum laude, 1977). Member, 1975-1976 and Comment Editor, 1976-1977, Suffolk Law Review. Trial Attorney, Deputy Assistant General Counsel and Acting Assistant General Counsel, Federal Energy Regulatory Commission, 1977-1986. *Member:* The District of Columbia Bar; American Bar Association; Federal Energy Bar Association. ***PRACTICE AREAS:*** Electric Utility; Cogeneration; Energy Contracts. ***Email:*** degoroff@brudergentile.com

JAMES H. McGREW, born Idaho Falls, Idaho, December 7, 1944; admitted to bar, 1974, California; 1981, District of Columbia and Maryland. *Education:* Harvard University (A.B., cum laude, 1965; J.D., cum laude, 1974). Author: "Let's Streamline, Not Abolish FERC," 129 Public Utilities Fortnightly No. 12, 1992; "Electric Utilities: Steering Clear on the Information Highway," 133 Public Utilities Fortnightly No. 10, 1995; "Gas Daily's Guide to FERC's Regulation of Natural Gas," Pasha Publications, 1997. Trial Attorney and Supervisory Trial Attorney, Federal Energy Regulatory Commission, 1980-1986. *Member:* Maryland State, Federal Energy (Chair, Tax Developments Committee, 1995-1996) and American Bar Associations; District of Columbia Bar. ***PRACTICE AREAS:*** Natural Gas; Electric Utility Law; Energy Law; Appellate Practice. ***Email:*** jhmcgrew@brudergentile.com

THOMAS L. BLACKBURN, born Pittsburgh, Pennsylvania, July 13, 1948; admitted to bar, 1975, District of Columbia; 1976, U.S. Court of Appeals for the District of Columbia Circuit. *Education:* Duquesne University (B.A., magna cum laude, 1970); Georgetown University (J.D., 1975). Trial Attorney and Supervisory Trial Attorney, Federal Energy Regulatory Commission, 1979-1987. *Member:* The District of Columbia Bar; Federal Energy (Chairman, Electric Utility Regulation Committee, 1997-1998; Board of Directors, 1998; Co-

(This Listing Continued)

Chairman, Committee on Alternative Dispute Resolution, 1998) and American Bar Associations. ***PRACTICE AREAS:*** Electric Utility. ***Email:*** tlblackburn@brudergentile.com

ANTONIA A. FROST, born Fairfax, Virginia, April 17, 1968; admitted to bar, 1995, District of Columbia; 1996, Pennsylvania. *Education:* George Mason University (B.A., 1990; J.D., 1993). Omnicron Delta Epsilon; Phi Delta Phi. Recipient: Presidential Merit Scholar; Weber H. Peterson Award; In Common Cause Award. Trial Attorney, Federal Energy Regulatory Commission. *Member:* Pennsylvania (Member, Public Utility Law Section), Federal Energy and American (Member, Sections on: Public Utility; Communications; Transportation Law) Bar Associations; Bar Association of the District of Columbia. ***PRACTICE AREAS:*** Electric Utilities; Administrative Law. ***Email:*** aafrost@brudergentile.com

DAVID MARTIN CONNELLY, born Philadelphia, Pennsylvania, January 30, 1970; admitted to bar, 1998, Maryland; 1999, District of Columbia, U.S. Court of Appeals for the District of Columbia Circuit and U.S. Court of Appeals, Fourth Circuit. *Education:* Albright College (B.A., 1991); Towson University (M.A., 1994); University of Baltimore (J.D., 1998). Member: Hueisler Honor Society; Daniel O'Connell Law Society. *Member:* Montgomery County, Maryland State, Federal and Federal Energy Bar Associations; The District of Columbia Bar. ***PRACTICE AREAS:*** Administrative Litigation. ***Email:*** dmconnelly@brudergentile.com

GARY D. LEVENSON, born Detroit, Michigan, June 15, 1964; admitted to bar, 1993, Pennsylvania; 1995, District of Columbia. *Education:* University of Chicago (A.B., 1986); Indiana University (J.D., 1993). Author: FRFC-SEC Overlapping Jurisdiction and the Ohio Power Litigation: A Loss for Rate Payers, 68 Indiana LJ 1417 (1993). *Member:* Federal Energy Bar Association. ***LANGUAGES:*** French. ***PRACTICE AREAS:*** Electric Utilities; Electric Cooperatives; Mergers and Acquisitions; Administrative Law. ***Email:*** gdlevenson@brudergentile.com

OF COUNSEL

PETER K. MATT, born Brooklyn, New York, June 25, 1947; admitted to bar, 1973, Virginia; 1974, District of Columbia and U.S. Court of Appeals for the District of Columbia Circuit; 1977, U.S. Court of Appeals, Seventh and Ninth Circuits; 1991, U.S. Supreme Court. *Education:* University of Pittsburgh (B.A., 1969); George Washington University (J.D., with honors, 1973). *Member:* The District of Columbia Bar; Virginia State Bar; Federal Energy and American Bar Associations. ***PRACTICE AREAS:*** Electric Utilities; Energy; Antitrust Law; Energy Project Development. ***Email:*** pkmatt@brudergentile.com

BRUNENKANT & HASKELL, LLP

Established in 1995

805 15TH STREET, N.W., SUITE 1101

WASHINGTON, D.C. 20005

Telephone: 202-408-0700

Fax: 202-408-5959

Email: brunenkant@bh-law.com

URL: http://www.bh-law.com

Energy Law, Electricity and Natural Gas Regulation, Merger and Acquisition of Energy Companies, Natural Resource and Administrative Practice, Utility Law, Appellate Practice and Representation of Clients before the Federal and State Regulatory Commissions, Environmental Issues as related to Energy Law.

JON L. BRUNENKANT, born Washington, D.C., June 17, 1950; admitted to bar, 1975, Virginia; 1978, District of Columbia, U.S. Court of Appeals for the District of Columbia Circuit and Fifth Circuit; 1979, U.S. Supreme Court. *Education:* Northwestern University (B.A., with honors, 1972); Iran Center for Management Studies, Tehran, Iran (M.B.A., with honors, 1977); George Washington University (J.D., with honors, 1975). *Member:* District of Columbia Bar; Virginia State Bar; Federal Energy and American Bar Associations. ***PRACTICE AREAS:*** Energy Law; Regulatory Law; Utility Law. ***Email:*** brunenkant@bh-law.com

MARK R. HASKELL, born Burlington, Vermont, June 24, 1960; admitted to bar, 1985, District of Columbia; 1987, Virginia (inactive). *Education:* University of Maine at Orono (B.A., in Political Science, with highest honors and highest distinction, 1982); Harvard University (J.D., 1985). Phi Beta Kappa; Phi Kappa Phi; Pi Sigma Alpha. Harry S. Truman Scholar. Executive Editor, Harvard Journal on Legislation, Vol. 22, No. 1, Winter, 1985. Notes Editor, Harvard Journal on Legislation, Vol. 22, No. 2, Spring 1985. *Member:* The District of Columbia Bar; Virginia State Bar; American Bar Association; Federal Energy Bar Association. ***PRACTICE AREAS:*** Energy Law; Environmental Law; Natural Resources; Regulatory Law; Utility Law. ***Email:*** haskell@bh-law.com

(This Listing Continued)

JAMES W. MOELLER, born Elgin, Illinois, January 21, 1958; admitted to bar, 1985, District of Columbia. *Education:* Lake Forest College (B.A., 1980); Tufts University, Fletcher School of Law and Diplomacy (M.A.L.D., 1984); Harvard University (J.D., 1984). Phi Beta Kappa. Managing Editor, Harvard International Law Journal, 1983-1984. Author: "Requiem for the Public Utility Holding Company Act of 1935: The Old Federalism and State Regulation of Inter-State Holding Companies", 17 Energy L.J. 343 (1996); "Electric Utilities and Telecommunications", 16 Energy L.J. 95 (1995); "Toward an SEC-FERC Memorandum of Understanding", 15 Energy L.J. 31 (1994); "Electric Demand-Side Management Under Federal Law", 13 Va. Envtl. L.J. 57 (1993); "U.S. Investment in Foreign Utilities Under the Public Utility Holding Company Act of 1935 and the Energy Policy Act of 1992", 24 Law & Pol'y Int'l Bus. 503 (1993); "State Regulation of Nuclear Power and National Energy Policy", 12 J. Energy Nat. Resources & Envtl. L. 1 (1992); "Nuclear Workers and Unconfirmed Positive Drug Tests: NRC Regulation of Safety and Labor", 6 Admin. L.J. 65 (1992). *Member:* District of Columbia Bar; American Bar Association; Federal Energy Bar Association; American Society of International Law. ***PRACTICE AREAS:*** Energy Law; Environmental Law; Utility Law. ***Email:*** moeller@bh-law.com

CHERYL J. WALKER, born Dayton, Ohio, October 28, 1964; admitted to bar, 1992, District of Columbia; 1994, U.S. Court of Appeals for the District of Columbia Circuit; 1996, U.S. Court of Appeals, Fifth Circuit. *Education:* GMI Engineering & Management Institute (B.S.E.E., 1988); George Washington University (J.D., with honors, 1992). Member, Moot Court Board. Senior Managing Editor, The George Washington Law Review. Member, Institute of Electrical and Electronic Engineers, 1985-1988. *Member:* District of Columbia Bar; Federal Energy Bar Association. ***PRACTICE AREAS:*** Energy Law; Utility Law. ***Email:*** walker@bh-law.com

SENIOR ATTORNEY

KENNETH M. ALBERT, born New York, N.Y., May 27, 1957; admitted to bar, 1983, New York; 1984, District of Columbia; 2000, Maryland. *Education:* Brandeis University (B.A., cum laude, 1979); Georgetown University Law Center (J.D., 1983). Associate, Goldberg, Fieldman & Letham, P.C., Washington, D.C. Attorney, American Gas Association, Arlington, Virginia. *Member:* Federal Energy Bar Association. ***PRACTICE AREAS:*** Energy Law (100%). ***Email:*** albert@bh-law.com

ASSOCIATES

MELISSA L. LAUDERDALE, born Osceola, Arkansas, November 30, 1969; admitted to bar, 1996, Texas; 1998, District of Columbia. *Education:* University of Texas (B.A., 1991; J.D., M.P. aff., 1995); University of Edinburgh (LL.M., 1995). Member, Board of Advocates, 1994-1995. *Member:* State Bar of Texas; American Bar Association. ***PRACTICE AREAS:*** Energy Law; Utility Law. ***Email:*** lauderdale@bh-law.com

CHRISTIE L. RICHART, born Urbana, Illinois, July 15, 1972; admitted to bar, 1998, Virginia; 1999, District of Columbia. *Education:* University of Illinois at Urbana-Champaign (B.A., 1994); Washington and Lee University (J.D., 1998). *Member:* Virginia State Bar; American Bar Association; Federal Energy Bar Association. ***PRACTICE AREAS:*** Energy Law; Utility Law. ***Email:*** richart@bh-law.com

REBECCA C. MOOREHEAD, born Dayton, Ohio, April 10, 1975; admitted to bar, 1998, District of Columbia. *Education:* Baylor University (B.A., 1997); Washington & Lee University (J.D., 2000). *Member:* American Bar Association; Energy Bar Association. ***PRACTICE AREAS:*** Energy. ***Email:*** moorehead@bh-law.com

BRUSTEIN & MANASEVIT

Established in 1980

3105 SOUTH STREET, N.W.

WASHINGTON, D.C. 20007

Telephone: 202-965-3652

Facsimile: 202-965-8913

Email: bruman@bruman.com

URL: http://www.bruman.com

FIRM PROFILE: Brustein & Manasevit has a nationwide administrative and legislative law practice focusing on elementary, secondary & higher education and workforce development. We represent recipients and subrecipients of federal financial assistance from the U.S. Departments of Education, Labor, Health and Human Services, and Agriculture. We counsel clients on matters related to financial as well as programmatic compliance reviews, and, specifically, we defend institutions of higher education in adverse actions and other institutional eligibility matters. Our practice includes comprehensive legislative and regulatory representation, as we

(This Listing Continued)

BRUSTEIN & MANASEVIT, Washington—Continued

monitor and analyze federal legislation and regulations for educational entities. We also provide consulting services and workshops on federal administrative matters and maintain a general civil practice, including civil rights representation.

MEMBERS OF FIRM

LEIGH M. MANASEVIT, born Bridgeport, Connecticut, November 7, 1948; admitted to bar, 1975, California; 1977, U.S. Court of Appeals, Second Circuit; 1979, District of Columbia; 1981, U.S. Supreme Court. *Education:* Columbia University (B.A., 1970); University of Southern California; University of Connecticut (J.D., with high honors, 1974). Member and Associate Editor, Connecticut Law Review, 1973-1974. Publications: Great Expectations: Understanding the New Title I; Opportunities and Challenges: An Administrator's Guide to the New IDEA. *Member:* The District of Columbia Bar; State Bar of California. ***PRACTICE AREAS:*** Education; Civil Litigation. ***Email:*** lmanasevit@bruman.com

MICHAEL L. BRUSTEIN, born Fairfield, Connecticut, May 13, 1949; admitted to bar, 1974, Connecticut; 1978, U.S. Supreme Court; 1979, District of Columbia; 1980, U.S. District Court for the District of Columbia; 1982, New York. *Education:* New York University (B.A., cum laude, 1971); University of Connecticut (J.D., 1974). Phi Beta Kappa; Pi Sigma Alpha. Publications: The AVA Audit Handbook-Avoiding Audit Liability Under The 1990 Perkins Act; The AVA Guide to Federal Funding for Tech Prep; The AVA Guide to the Perkins Act; The AVA Guide to the School-to-Work Opportunities Act; School-to-Work User's Guide: Understanding Federal Cost Principles & Avoiding Audit Liability; The One-Stop Guide to the Perkins Act of 1998; The Administrator's Guide to the Adult Education & Family Literacy Act of 1998; A Guide to the Workforce Investment Act of 1998. *Member:* The District of Columbia Bar. ***PRACTICE AREAS:*** Education; Civil Litigation. ***Email:*** mbrustein@bruman.com

KRISTEN TOSH COWAN, born Rochester, Pennsylvania, May 16, 1968; admitted to bar, 1993, Pennsylvania; 1994, District of Columbia. *Education:* Duke University (B.A., 1990); American University, Washington College of Law (J.D., 1993). Staff Member, The Administrative Law Journal of the American University, 1992-1993. Publications: Great Expectations: Understanding the New, Title I, Title I Monitor contributor. *Member:* District of Columbia Bar; Pennsylvania Bar Association. ***PRACTICE AREAS:*** Education; Administrative Litigation; Civil Litigation; Civil Rights. ***Email:*** ktoshcowan@bruman.com

ASSOCIATES

CHRISTINE M. PLAGATA-NEUBAUER, born Paterson, New Jersey, March 2, 1969; admitted to bar, 1994, Virginia; 1995, Maryland (Not admitted in District of Columbia). *Education:* College of William and Mary (B.A., 1991); American University, Washington College of Law (J.D., 1994). *Member:* Virginia State Bar. ***PRACTICE AREAS:*** Education Law; Administrative Law; Civil Rights. ***Email:*** cp-neubauer@bruman.com

CLAIRE A. MILNER, born Cleveland, Ohio, October 7, 1970; admitted to bar, 1997, California (Not admitted in District of Columbia). *Education:* Bucknell University (B.A., 1992); Catholic University of America (J.D., 1997). Author: "Gulf War Guinea Pigs," The Journal of Contemporary Health Law and Policy, Volume 13, 1997. *Member:* State Bar of California. ***PRACTICE AREAS:*** Education Law; Federal Legislative Practice; Government Relations. ***Email:*** cmilner@bruman.com

JONATHAN D. TARNOW, born Syracuse, New York, February 6, 1971; admitted to bar, 1997, Maryland; 1998, District of Columbia and U.S. District Court, District of Maryland; 1999, U.S. District Court, District of Columbia. *Education:* George Washington University (B.A., 1993; J.D., 1996). Omicron Delta Kappa. Philip C. Jessup International Moot Court Competition, 1995. President, Moot Court Board, 1995-1996. Legal Research and Writing Fellow, 1995-1996. Recipient: Judge Albert H. Grenadier Award; The George Washington Award. Member, Board of Trustees, The George Washington University (1997-2000). *Member:* The District of Columbia Bar (Member, Education Law Task Force); American Bar Association. ***PRACTICE AREAS:*** Administrative Law; Education Law; Civil Litigation. ***Email:*** jtarnow@bruman.com

MELISSA CLARRY, born Redlands, California, July 2, 1971; admitted to bar, 1996, Maryland (Not admitted in District of Columbia). *Education:* Kenyon College (B.A., magna cum laude, 1993); Washington College of Law of American University (J.D., 1996). Phi Beta Kappa. Associate Editor, American University Law Review, 1995-1996. ***PRACTICE AREAS:*** Education Law; Federal Legislative Practice; Administrative Law. ***Email:*** mclarry@bruman.com

REPRESENTATIVE CLIENTS: California Department of Education; Office for the System Director for Federal Grants, Minnesota State Colleges and Universities; New York State Education Department; Massachusetts Department of Education; Colorado Department of Education; Alabama Department of Education; District of Columbia Public Schools; Georgia Department of Education; Kentucky Department of Education; Washington State Board for Community Colleges; Arizona State Department of Education; New York City Board of Education; St. Louis Public Schools; City University of New York; University of North Carolina, Greensboro; Puerto Rico Department of Education; Allen County Community College; Butler County Community College; Clovis Unified School District; West Virginia Human Resource Investment Council; The Association of Judaic Schools; National Adult Education Professional Development Consortium, Inc.; National Association of Federal Financial Administrators; National Coordinating Council for Vocational Student Organizations; National Association of Workforce Boards.

(This Listing Continued)

BRYAN CAVE LLP

A Partnership including a Professional Corporation

Established in 1873

700 THIRTEENTH STREET, N.W.

WASHINGTON, D.C. 20005-3960

Telephone: (202) 508-6000

Facsimile: (202) 508-6200

For attorney e-mails use: First initials of first and middle names, last name, firm name, e.g., rmsmith@bryancave.com

URL: http://www.bryancave.com

St. Louis, Missouri Office: One Metropolitan Square, 211 N. Broadway, 63102-2750. Telephone: (314) 259-2000. Facsimile: (314) 259-2020.

New York, N.Y. Office: 245 Park Avenue, 10167-0034. Telephone: (212) 692-1800. Facsimile: (212) 692-1900.

Kansas City, Missouri Office: 3500 One Kansas City Place, 1200 Main Street, 64105-2100. Telephone: (816) 374-3200. Facsimile: (816) 374-3300.

Jefferson City, Missouri Office: 221 Bolivar Street, 65102-1670. Telephone: (573) 556-6620. Facsimile: (573) 556-6630.

Overland Park, Kansas Office: 7500 College Boulevard, Suite 1100, 66210-4035. Telephone: (913) 338-7700. Facsimile: (913) 338-7777.

Phoenix, Arizona Office: Two North Central Avenue, Suite 2200, 85004-4406. Telephone: (602) 364-7000. Facsimile: (602) 364-7070.

Santa Monica, California Office: 120 Broadway, Suite 300, 90401-2305. Telephone: (310) 576-2100. Facsimile: (310) 576-2200.

Irvine, California Office: 2020 Main Street, Suite 600, 92614. Telephone: (949) 223-7000. Facsimile: (949) 223-7100.

Chicago, Illinois Office: Bryan Cave (Illinois), Chicago Title and Trust Building, 161 North Clark Street, Suite 2840, 60601. Telephone: 312-602-5000. Facsimile: 312-602-5050.

London, England Office: 33 Cannon Street, EC4M 5TE. Telephone: 44-20-7246-5800. Facsimile: 44-20-7246-5858.

Riyadh, 11465 Saudi Arabia Office: In Cooperation with Kadasah Law Firm, P.O. Box 20883. Telephone: 966-1-474-0888. Facsimile: 966-1-476-2881.

Kuwait City, Kuwait Office: Mashora Advocates & Legal Consultants, Sheraton Towers, Second Floor, P.O. Box 5902 Safat, 13060. Telephone: 965-240-4470. Facsimile: 965-242-4047.

Dubai, U.A.E. Office: Al-Mehairi Legal Consultants - Bryan Cave LLP, Dubai, Holiday Centre, Suite 1103, P.O. Box 13677, UAE. Telephone: 971-4-3314-123. Facsimile: 971-4-3318-287.

Abu Dhabi, U.A.E. Office: Al-Mehairi Legal Consultants - Bryan Cave LLP, Al Otaiba Tower, Suite 804, P.O. Box 47645. Telephone: 971-2-6340-322. Facsimile: 971-2-6340-522.

Hong Kong Office: Suite 2106, Tower One, Lippo Centre, 89 Queensway. Telephone: 852-2522-2821. Facsimile: 852-2522-3830.

Shanghai 200040, People's Republic of China Office: Suite 448, Shanghai Centre, 1376 Nan Jing West Road. Telephone: 8621-6279-8166. Facsimile: 8621-6279-8165.

General Civil Practice. Administrative, Antitrust, Aviation, Communications, Computer, Copyright, Corporate Finance, Corporation, Criminal Defense, Environmental, Financial Institutions, Government Contracts, Intellectual Property, International, International Trade and Customs, Legislative Patents, Life Sciences, Real Estate, Securities, Taxation, Technology, Trademark, Transportation, Trusts and Estates. General Civil Trial and Appellate Practice.

PARTNERS

JOHN P. BARRIE, admitted to bar, 1972, California; 1975, District of Columbia and U.S. Claims Court; 1977, Missouri and U.S. Tax Court. *Education:* University of California at Los Angeles (A.B., 1969); Hastings College of Law, University of California (J.D., 1972); New York University (LL.M., in Taxation, 1973). Fellow, American College of Tax Counsel. ***PRACTICE AREAS:*** Federal and State Taxation Controversy; Transactional Matters.

WILLIAM F. BAVINGER III, admitted to bar, 1968, Michigan; 1975, U.S. Supreme Court; 1976, Missouri; 1978, District of Columbia. *Education:* Yale University (B.E., 1965); University of Michigan (J.D., cum laude, 1968). Assistant General Counsel, U.S. Securities and Exchange Commission, 1975-1976. ***PRACTICE AREAS:*** Corporate Law; Securities Regulation Law.

RICHARD A. COHN, admitted to bar, 1974, Missouri; 1975, District of Columbia. Adjunct Professor, George Mason University Law School, 1994. Lecturer: Mid-Atlantic Chapter, American Institute of Banking, 1991-1997;

(This Listing Continued)

Commercial Loan Documentation, Executive Enterprises, 1998. Faculty Member, Commercial Real Estate Lending, Practicing Law Institute, 1998. Attorney Advisor, Legal Honors Program, U.S. Department of Housing and Urban Development, Washington, D.C., 1974-1978. Assistant General Counsel, Federal Home Loan Mortgage Corporation, Washington, D.C., 1978-1979. ***PRACTICE AREAS:*** Real Estate and Real Estate Finance Law; Creditors Rights Law; Bankruptcy Law; Business Law.

JAMES M. COLE, admitted to bar, 1979, California; 1985, District of Columbia. Special Counsel, U.S. House Ethics Committee re: Speaker Newt Gingrich, 1996. Adjunct Professor, Georgetown University Law Center, 1990-1999. U.S. Department of Justice, Public Integrity Section: Deputy Chief, 1989-1992; Trial Attorney, 1980-1989; Attorney General's Honor Graduate Program, 1979. ***PRACTICE AREAS:*** White Collar Criminal Defense; Corporate Investigations.

JOHN MICHAEL COOPER, admitted to bar, 1973, Ohio; 1977, District of Columbia. *Education:* Swarthmore College (B.A., with distinction, 1970); Harvard University (J.D., magna cum laude, 1973). Phi Beta Kappa. ***PRACTICE AREAS:*** Administrative Law; Government Contracts Law; Antitrust Law; Litigation.

JOHN C. DANFORTH, admitted to bar, 1964, New York; 1966, Missouri (Not admitted in District of Columbia). *Education:* Princeton University (B.A., with honors, 1958); Yale Divinity School (Bachelor of Divinity degree, 1963); Yale Law School (J.D., 1963). United States Senator, Missouri, 1976-1994. ***PRACTICE AREAS:*** Corporate Law; Health Care Law; International Law.

ALAN J. DIXON, admitted to bar, 1949, Illinois and Missouri (Not admitted in District of Columbia). *Education:* University of Illinois (B.S., 1946); Washington University (LL.B., 1949). United States Senator, Illinois, 1981-1993. ***PRACTICE AREAS:*** Corporate Law; Government Contracts.

WILLIAM C. EDGAR, admitted to bar, 1989, District of Columbia; 1992, Maryland. *Education:* Skidmore College (B.A., with honors in Economics and Philosophy, 1984); George Washington University (J.D., with honors, 1989). ***PRACTICE AREAS:*** Commercial Litigation; Products Liability.

ROBERT M. HUBER, admitted to bar, 1982, District of Columbia. *Education:* University of Maryland (B.A., cum laude, 1978); University of Virginia (J.D., 1982). Phi Beta Kappa. Trial Attorney, U.S. Department of Justice, Antitrust Division, 1982-1987. ***PRACTICE AREAS:*** Antitrust and Trade Regulation.

KENNETH M. KASTNER, admitted to bar, 1979, District of Columbia. *Education:* University of Virginia (B.A., 1974; J.D., 1978). Assistant General Counsel, Chemical Manufacturers Association, 1982-1988. Author: "RCRA Corrective Action: Toxics Law Reporter, BNA, 1989; "RCRA Overview" and "Definition of Solid Waste," ABA, 1990 and 1994; "TCLP," "Hazardous Waste Identification Rule," "Subpart CC Air Emissions" and "Land Disposal Restrictions," Environment Reporter, BNA, 1990, 1996 and 1998.

STANLEY J. MARCUSS, admitted to bar, 1968, Connecticut; 1969, District of Columbia; 1981, New York. *Education:* Trinity College, Connecticut (B.A., summa cum laude, 1963); Cambridge University (B.A., 1965; M.A., 1968) Marshall Scholar; Harvard (J.D., 1968). Counsel, Senate International Finance Subcommittee, 1973-1977; Senior Deputy Assistant Secretary of Commerce, 1977-1980.

LADAWN NAEGLE, admitted to bar, 1984, District of Columbia. *Education:* University of San Diego (B.A., summa cum laude, 1981); George Washington University (J.D., 1984). Order of the Coif. ***PRACTICE AREAS:*** Corporate Law; Securities Regulation Law; Technology.

RODNEY F. PAGE, admitted to bar, 1971, District of Columbia; 1972, Virginia. *Education:* University of Kentucky (B.A., 1968); Harvard University (J.D., 1971). Omicron Delta Kappa. ***PRACTICE AREAS:*** Commercial Litigation; Appellate Practice.

THERESE D. PRITCHARD, born 1953; admitted to bar, 1978, Massachusetts; practice limited to matters and proceedings before Federal Courts and Agencies (Not admitted in District of Columbia). *Education:* Bryn Mawr College (A.B.); Boston College (J.D.). Deputy Chief Counsel for Enforcement, Office of Thrift Supervision, 1991-1994. Assistant Director, Enforcement, Securities and Exchange Commission, 1986-1991. ***PRACTICE AREAS:*** Banking Securities.

DANIEL C. SCHWARTZ, admitted to bar, 1969, District of Columbia. Assistant to the Director, 1973-1975, Assistant Director for Evaluation, 1975-1977 and Deputy Director, 1977-1979, Bureau of Competition, Federal Trade Commission. General Counsel, National Security Agency, 1979-1981. ***PRACTICE AREAS:*** White Collar Criminal Defense; Trade Regulation; Antitrust Law.

ERIC F. STOER, admitted to bar, 1969, Maryland; 1970, District of Columbia; 1973, U.S. Supreme Court; 1976, U.S. Court of Appeals, 3rd Circuit; 1979, U.S. Court of Appeals, 10th Circuit; 1980, U.S. Court of Appeals, 6th Circuit. *Education:* University of Maryland (B.A., 1966; J.D., 1969). ***PRACTICE AREAS:*** International Business; Licensing; Antitrust.

(This Listing Continued)

KATHLEEN E. TOPELIUS, admitted to bar, 1978, District of Columbia; 1988, U.S. Supreme Court. *Education:* University of Connecticut (B.A., 1970); Catholic University of America (J.D., 1978). ***PRACTICE AREAS:*** Banking; International Banking; Financial Institutions; Mergers and Acquisitions; Administrative Law.

ROBERT F. VAN VOORHEES, admitted to bar, 1972, Virginia; 1973, District of Columbia; 1976, U.S. Supreme Court; U.S. Court of Appeals for the District of Columbia, 5th and 11th Circuits. *Education:* George Washington University (B.A., 1969); University of Virginia (J.D., 1972). Order of the Coif. ***PRACTICE AREAS:*** Environmental Law; Occupational Safety and Health Law; Administrative Law; Litigation.

JOHN R. WILNER, admitted to bar, 1966, District of Columbia. *Education:* University of Pennsylvania (B.S.Ec., 1962); Georgetown University (J.D., 1966). ***PRACTICE AREAS:*** Communications Law.

KEVIN J. WOLF, admitted to bar, 1992, Missouri; 1993, District of Columbia. *Education:* University of Missouri (B.A., with honors, 1988); University of Minnesota (M.A., 1992; J.D., 1992). Phi Beta Kappa. Executive Editor and Co-Founder, Minnesota Journal of Global Trade, 1991-1992. ***LANGUAGES:*** German. ***PRACTICE AREAS:*** International Trade; Corporate Investigations; White Collar Criminal Defense.

OF COUNSEL

JOAN Z. BERNSTEIN, admitted to bar, 1952, New York and Illinois; 1968, District of Columbia; 1980, U.S. Supreme Court. *Education:* University of Wisconsin (B.A., 1948); Yale University (LL.B., 1951).

STEPHEN S. KAYE, admitted to bar, 1979, District of Columbia. *Education:* Colgate University (A.B., with honors, 1974); American University (J.D., magna cum laude, 1979). ***PRACTICE AREAS:*** Government Contracts Law; Litigation; Corporate Investigations.

JAMES J. MURPHY, admitted to bar, 1958, Missouri; 1969, U.S. Supreme Court; 1976, District of Columbia. *Education:* St. Louis University (B.S., 1955; LL.B., 1958). ***PRACTICE AREAS:*** Litigation; Administrative Practice; Legislation.

JOHN J. O'CONNOR III, admitted to bar, 1953, California; 1957, Arizona; 1981, District of Columbia. *Education:* Stanford University (A.B., 1951; LL.B., 1953). Phi Delta Phi. (Also at Phoenix, Arizona Office). ***PRACTICE AREAS:*** Litigation; Corporate Law.

JO ANNE PEELE, admitted to bar, 1984, Missouri; 1988, District of Columbia. *Education:* Drake University (B.A., summa cum laude, 1981); University of Iowa (J.D., with high distinction, 1984). Phi Beta Kappa. ***PRACTICE AREAS:*** Litigation; International.

ROBERT P. VISSER, admitted to bar, 1967, New York; 1969, District of Columbia and U.S. Court of Federal Claims; 1973, California; 1975, U.S. Supreme Court. *Education:* The City College of the City University of New York (B.S., Physics, 1963); The National Law Center of The George Washington University Law School (J.D., with honors, 1966). Phi Delta Phi. ***PRACTICE AREAS:*** International Investment; International Finance; International Trade; International Corporate; Corporate.

DOUGLAS E. WINTER, admitted to bar, 1975, Missouri; 1976, Illinois and District of Columbia; 1977, U.S. Court of Military Appeals. *Education:* University of Illinois (B.S., summa cum laude, 1971; M.S., 1972); Harvard University (J.D., cum laude, 1975). ***PRACTICE AREAS:*** Litigation; Products Liability; Aviation Law; Entertainment Law.

COUNSEL

SCOTT M. BADAMI, admitted to bar, 1991, Missouri and District of Columbia. *Education:* James Madison University (B.A., 1984); University of Missouri (J.D., 1991).

STUART M. GINSBERG, admitted to bar, 1985, Pennsylvania; 1987, District of Columbia. *Education:* Williams College (B.A., cum laude, 1977); University of Pennsylvania School of Dental Medicine (D.M.D., 1981); Georgetown University Law Center (J.D., 1985). ***PRACTICE AREAS:*** Real Estate; Commercial Law; Business Law.

SCOTT R. HARRISON, admitted to bar, 1986, Massachusetts; 1989, Pennsylvania; 1990, Delaware; 2001, District of Columbia. *Education:* Gordon College (B.A., 1981); Suffolk University (J.D., 1986).

DANA B. ROSENFELD, admitted to bar, 1984, Maryland; 1988, District of Columbia. *Education:* University of Maryland (B.A., 1981); Washington College of Law of American University (J.D., 1984). Attorney Advisor, Chairman Robert Pitofsky, Federal Trade Commission, 1995-1996. Senior Legal Advisor, 1996-1998 and Assistant Director, 1998-2001, Bureau of Consumer Protection, Federal Trade Commission. ***PRACTICE AREAS:*** Advertising Law; Consumer Protection; Privacy Law.

ANGELA F. WILLIAMS, admitted to bar, 1988, Virginia; 1991, District of Columbia. *Education:* University of Virginia (B.A., 1985); University of Texas

(This Listing Continued)

BRYAN CAVE LLP, Washington—Continued

at Austin (J.D., 1988). Assembly Speaker, Young Lawyers Division, American Bar Association, 1999-2000. Member, Commission on Young Women in the Profession, American Bar Association, 2000-2003. *Member:* Virginia State Bar; The District of Columbia Bar. [U.S. Air Force, 1988-1995, Capt.]. ***PRACTICE AREAS:*** White Collar Crime; Securities; Nonprofit Organizations Law.

JILL M. ZUCKER, admitted to bar, 1990, New Jersey and District of Columbia. *Education:* Cook College, Rutgers University (B.S., 1983); University of Southern California (M.M.A., 1985); University of Virginia (J.D., 1989). Alpha Zeta. ***PRACTICE AREAS:*** Environmental Law; Consumer Product Safety; Transportation; Regulatory Law.

RESIDENT ASSOCIATES

Jenifer Berger
Vanessa Y. Chandler (Not admitted in DC)
Daniel M. Fisher-Owens
Rebecca A. Ford
John Staley Heatly
Christopher C. S. Manning
Margaret G. Perl
Earl G. Pinto
Phillip A. Quatrini
Colleen M. Reddan
Heather Rheiner Badami
Sylvia A. Rhodes
Vasilios Salamandrakis
Sarah P. Swanz
Robert W. Tomilson
Tina R. Tyson
Whitney Wilson
Jami Wyatt

All Partners and Associates of the Firm are members of the American Bar Association.

REPRESENTATIVE CLIENTS: AIMCO; Air Transport Association; Baxter International; Bechtel Corp.; Benchmark Media, Inc.; Bridgestone/Firestone Inc.; Chase Manhattan Bank Chemical Manufactures Association; Chevy Chase Savings Bank, F.S.B.; CIGNA; Connecticut Yankee Atomic Power Co.; Elf Atochem N. America, Inc.; Fieldcrest Cannon, Inc.; First Data Resources, Inc.; Household, Intl.; L'Oreal, S.A.; MCG Credit Corporation; M.W. Kellogg Co.; Mobil Oil Corp.; National Guard Association of the United States; Northeast Utilities; R.J. Reynolds Tobacco International; Republic National Bank of New York; RJR Nabisco; Roche Diagnostics; Salomon Brothers International; Satellite Technology Management, Inc.; Sears, Roebuck & Company; Tandy Corp.; Time Warner Cable; Transammonia, Inc.; W.R. Grace & Company.

JAMES S. BUBAR

1667 K STREET, NW, SUITE 801
WASHINGTON, D.C. 20006
Telephone: 202-223-2060
Fax: 202-223-2061
Email: jbubar@aol.com
URL: http://www.lawyers.com/jamesbubar

Communications Law, FCC Law, Business Formations, Business Law, Securities Law, Securities Fraud, Business Transactions, Litigation, Commercial Litigation.

JAMES S. BUBAR, born 1952; admitted to bar, 1978, California; 1980, District of Columbia; 1981, U.S District Court, Northern District of California; 1983, Maryland; 1996, U.S. Court of Appeals, 4th Circuit; 1997, U.S. Supreme Court. *Education:* University of California, Santa Cruz (A.B., with honors, 1974); Hastings College of Law, University of California (J.D., 1978). *Member:* The District of Columbia Bar; The State Bar of California; Federal Communications Bar Association. ***PRACTICE AREAS:*** Communications (35%); Business Law (35%); Litigation (30%).

BUC & BEARDSLEY

919 EIGHTEENTH STREET, N.W.
SUITE 600
WASHINGTON, D.C. 20006-5503
Telephone: 202-736-3600
Fax: 202-736-3608

Food, Drug, Medical Device, Biologics and Cosmetics Law. Advertising and Marketing Law. Consumer Products Safety Law.

RESIDENT PARTNERS

KATE C. BEARDSLEY, born Rochester, New York, February 4, 1949; admitted to bar, 1975, Georgia; 1987, District of Columbia. *Education:* Smith College (B.A., 1970); Emory University (J.D., 1975). Editor, Emory Law Journal, 1974-1975. Contributor, "Personal Justice Denied: Report of the Commission on Wartime Relocation and Internment of Civilians," 1982. Special Counsel to the Executive Associate Director, Office of Management and Budget, 1976-1979; Recipient, Outstanding Service Award, Office of Management and Budget, 1978. Deputy Director, United States Regulatory Council, 1979-1980; Nixon, Hargrave, Devans & Doyle, 1987-1989; Weil, Gotshal & Manges, 1989-1994. Member, Secretary's Advisory Committee on Genetic Testing, 1999—

(This Listing Continued)

Advisory Board, Food and Drug Law Journal, 1999—. *Member:* American Association of Tissue Banks (Vice Chair, Governmental Affairs Committee, 1999—); Food and Drug Law Institute (Secretary's Advisory Committee on Genetic Testing, 1999—). ***Email:*** kbeardsley@bucbeardsley.com

NANCY L. BUC, born Orange, New Jersey, July 27, 1944; admitted to bar, 1969, Virginia; 1977, New York; 1978, District of Columbia. *Education:* Brown University (A.B., 1965; LL.D., honoris causa, 1994); University of Virginia (LL.B., 1969). Director, Agritope, Inc., 1997-2000. Fellow, 1980-1992 and Trustee, 1973-1978, 1998—, Brown University. Trustee, Virginia Law School Foundation, 1990-1998. Board Member: The Alan Guttmacher Institute, 1989-1995; National Partnership for Women and Families, 1993—. Member: National Institute of Health Recombinant DNA Advisory Committee, 1990-1994; Office of Technology Assessment Advisory Committee on New Developments in Biotechnology, 1986-1988; National Institutes of Health Consensus Development Panel on Effective Medical Treatment of Opiate Addiction, 1997; Office of Technology Assessment Advisory Panel on Government Policies and Pharmaceutical Research and Development, 1989-1993; Institute of Medicine Committees on Medications Development, Research at the National Institute of Drug Abuse, 1993-1994; Applications of Biotechnology to Contraceptive Research and Development, 1994-1996. Adjunct Professor of Law, Georgetown University Law Center, 2000—. Member, American Bar Association Antitrust Law Section Special Committee to Study the Federal Trade Commission, 1988-1989. Assistant General Counsel, Department of Health and Human Services and Chief Counsel, Food and Drug Administration, 1980-1981. Recipient, Secretary's Special Citation and FDA Award of Merit, January, 1981. Attorney, including Attorney-Adviser to Chairman Miles W. Kirkpatrick and Assistant Director, Bureau of Consumer Protection, 1969-1972, Federal Trade Commission. Partner, 1977-1980, 1981-1994 and Associate, 1972-1977, Weil, Gotshal & Manges.

JANE E. BALUSS, born Fayetteville, North Carolina, December 24, 1952; admitted to bar, 1985, District of Columbia, U.S. District Court, District of Columbia and U.S. Court of Appeals, District of Columbia Circuit. *Education:* University of North Carolina, Greensboro (B.A., summa cum laude, 1974, Phi Beta Kappa); Duke University School of Law (J.D., 1985). Associate Editor, Alaska Law Review, 1983-1985. Co-Author: "Laboratory Inspections Under CLIA '88 - Getting Ready," American Clinical Laboratory, Jan. 1993, 30. Co-Author: "HCFA's Final Clinical Regulations," 9 Health Span No. 43 (April 1992); "Mandatory Mediation of Coastal Zone Planning Disputes in Alaska - An Innovative Approach to Administrative Decisionmaking," Duke Alaska L.Rev. 349 (1984); "Legal Issues in Organ Donation," Hospital Law in North Carolina (A. Dellinger ed.) 1985. ***Email:*** jbaluss@bucbeardsley.com

ASSOCIATES

ABIGAIL E. BRANDEL, born Newton, Massachusetts, April 25, 1969; admitted to bar, 1994, Maryland; 2001, District of Columbia. *Education:* Bucknell University (B.A., 1991); University of Maryland (J.D., with honors, 1994). Associate Editor, The Business Lawyer, 1993-1994. Author: Legislating Surrogacy: A Partial Answer to Feminist Criticism," 54 Maryland Law Review 488 (1995). ***Email:*** abrandel@bucbeardsley.com

JULIA C. TIERNEY, born Boston, Massachusetts, January 20, 1976; admitted to bar, 2000, Maryland; 2001, District of Columbia and U.S. District Court, District of Columbia. *Education:* Johns Hopkins University (B.A., 1997); Georgetown University Law Center (J.D., 2000). Annual Review Section Editor, Georgetown Journal of Gender and the Law, 1999-2000. *Member:* District of Columbia Bar. ***Email:*** jtierney@bucbeardsley.com

ADAM S. BLOOM, born Pensacola, Florida, March 23, 1973; admitted to bar, 2000, Maryland; 2001, District of Columbia. *Education:* University of Michigan (B.A., 1995); George Washington University (J.D., with honors, 2000). Managing Editor, George Washington Journal of International Law and Economics, 1999-2000. ***Email:*** abloom@bucbeardsley.com

WILLIAM LAFONT HUIE, born Austin, Texas, July 8, 1973; admitted to bar, 1998, Texas (Not admitted in District of Columbia). *Education:* University of Texas (B.A., with honors, 1995; J.D., 1998). Associate Editor, Planning Forum: Dick DeGuerin Scholarship, 1998; Dedoram Scholar, 1991-1992; Plan II Honors, 1991-1995; National Merit Scholar, 1991-1995. *Member:* State Bar of Texas (Member, Health Law Section, 1998— Committee on Poverty and the Law, 2000-2001). ***LANGUAGES:*** French. ***PRACTICE AREAS:*** FDA Regulatory; Healthcare LTC Regulatory. ***Email:*** bhuie@bucbeardsley.com

BUCHANAN INGERSOLL

PROFESSIONAL CORPORATION

Established in 1850

1776 K STREET, N.W., SUITE 800

WASHINGTON, D.C. 20006-2365

Telephone: 202-452-7900

Telecopier: 202-452-7989

URL: http://www.bipc.com

Pittsburgh, Pennsylvania Office: One Oxford Centre, 301 Grant Street, 20th Floor. Telephone: 412-562-8800.

Philadelphia, Pennsylvania Office: Eleven Penn Center, 14th Floor, 1835 Market Street. Telephone: 215-665-8700.

Bryn Mawr, Pennsylvania Office: 937 East Haverford Road, Suite 201. Telephone: 610-581-7004.

Harrisburg, Pennsylvania Office: One South Market Square, 213 Market Street, 3rd Floor. Telephone: 717-237-4800.

Tampa, Florida Office: SunTrust Financial Centre, 401 East Jackson Street, Suite 2500. Telephone: 813-222-8180.

Aventura, Florida Office: One Turnberry Place, 19495 Biscayne Boulevard, Suite 606. Telephone: 305-933-5600.

Miami, Florida Office: Bank of America Tower, 100 S.E. Second Street, Suite 2100. Telephone: 305-347-4080.

Princeton, New Jersey Office: 700 Alexander Park, Suite 300. Telephone: 609-987-6800.

Buffalo, New York Office: 268 Main Street, Suite 201. Telephone: 716-853-2330.

New York, New York Office: 140 Broadway, 35th Floor. Telephone: 646-458-2340.

Other Washington, D.C. Office: Silverstein and Mullens, 1776 K Street, N.W., Suite 800. Telephone: 202-452-7900.

McLean, Virginia Office: 8280 Greensboro Drive, Suite 601. Telephone: 703-749-6060.

Wilmington, Delaware Office: 1201 North Market Street, Suite 1501. Telephone: 302-428-5500.

San Diego, California Office: First National Bank Center, 401 West A Street, Suite 1900. Telephone: 619-578-5000.

London, England Office: Tower 42, The International Financial Centre, Old Broad Street, EC2N 1HQ. Telephone: 44-207-920-3700.

Dublin, Ireland Office: Level 1, 4 Custom House Plaza, IFSC, Dublin 1. Telephone: 011-353-1611-7266. Fax: 3531-836-9305.

Antitrust and Trade Regulation, Broadcasting and Cable TV, Commercial Transactions, Computer Law, Construction Industry Law, Corporate Law and Finance, Creditors' Rights and Bankruptcy, Energy, Environmental Law, ERISA and Employee Benefits, Family Law, Financial Institutions, Franchising, Government Relations, Healthcare, Insurance Regulation, Intellectual Property, International Transactions, Labor and Employment, Litigation, Mergers and Acquisitions, Municipal Law, Natural Resources Law, Public Finance, Real Estate, Security Alarm, Tax and Estate Planning, Technology Law, Trade Secret Litigation, Transportation Law, Trust and Estate Administration, Venture Capital.

FIRM PROFILE: Founded in 1850, Buchanan Ingersoll is one of the two oldest large commercial law firms in continuous practice in Pennsylvania, and a top 100 law firm in the nation. The Firm's level of business has grown seventeen-fold since 1980, demonstrating dramatic long-term growth.

The Firm's position as a national law firm is evidenced by its size and its wide variety of practice areas serving regional, national and international clients. Buchanan Ingersoll's clients range from individuals and start-up companies to private and publicly-held institutions and multinational conglomerates, including more than 50 of the Fortune 500 corporations.

The Firm's regional office system provides clients with cost-effective access to more than 412 lawyers through an integrated network. Buchanan Ingersoll has opened eleven new offices since 1992 and now has 16 overall -- Pittsburgh, Harrisburg, Philadelphia and Bryn Mawr, Miami, Aventura and Tampa, Princeton, Buffalo, Washington, D.C., New York City, McLean, Wilmington, San Diego, London and Dublin.

Founded in 1960 by Leonard L. Silverstein and Richard A. Mullens, Silverstein and Mullens became a division of Buchanan Ingersoll in 2000 when the firms merged. Silverstein and Mullens is internationally recognized for its experience in federal taxation, employee benefits and compensation planning, nonprofit and charitable organizations and trade associations, estate planning, commercial real estate, government relations and litigation. The firm provides representation to local, national and multinational corporations, partnerships, trade associations, government entities and foreign governments.

(This Listing Continued)

Silverstein and Mullens also has overall editorial responsibility for the highly regarded Tax Management Portfolios and other products published by Tax Management, a subsidiary of the Bureau of National Affairs (BNA). The portfolios, which Leonard Silverstein originally developed and edited, have set the standard for topic-based tax research tools and cover all areas of taxation.

SHAREHOLDERS

EDWARD JOHN ALLERA, born New Kensington, Pennsylvania, October 13, 1946; admitted to bar, 1974, Pennsylvania; 1975, District of Columbia. *Education:* West Virginia University (B.S., Pharmacy, 1969); Georgetown University Law Center (J.D., 1974). Editor, Law and Policy in International Business, 1974. Assistant Chief Counsel, 1975 and Associate Chief Counsel, 1976, for Veterinary Medicine, Food and Drug Administration. Assistant Chief Counsel for Food, Food and Drug Administration, 1977-1978. *Member:* The District of Columbia Bar; Pennsylvania Bar Association. ***PRACTICE AREAS:*** Food, Drug and Cosmetic Law; Biomedical; Biotechnology. ***Email:*** allerae@bipc.com

STEVEN M. HILTON, born Philadelphia, Pennsylvania, March 7, 1958; admitted to bar, 1986, District of Columbia. *Education:* Princeton University (B.A., 1980); Georgetown University (J.D., 1985). Commissioner, American Battle Monuments Commission (Federal Commission). Deputy Assistant to the President, The White House, 1993-1995. *Member:* The District of Columbia Bar. [Major, USAR, 1980—]. ***PRACTICE AREAS:*** Government Relations. ***Email:*** hiltons@bipc.com

ANDREW P. LOEWINGER, born Washington, D.C., September 23, 1953; admitted to bar, 1984, District of Columbia. *Education:* Colorado College (B.A., magna cum laude, 1975); Columbia University (M.I.A., 1980); Georgetown University (J.D., 1983). Phi Beta Kappa. Topics and Articles Editor, Franchise Law Journal, 1990-1996. Articles and Notes Editor, American Criminal Law Review, 1982-1983. Editor, International Franchise Law Bibliography, Kluwen Publishers, 2001. Author: "Master Franchising: What Happens to Subfranchisees When A Master Franchise Agreement Is Transferred or Terminated?" International Bar Association, May 2000; "Franchising," *Doing Business in the United States,* Matthew Bender, 1995; "International Franchising Law," Introduction, Matthew Bender, 1993; "Avoiding the Long Arm of the Law in International Franchising," ABA Forum on Franchising, October 1995; "Multiple-Unit Franchise Agreements in the Pacific Rim: Problems and Solutions," Franchise Law Journal, Vol. 10, No. 1, Summer 1990. *Member:* The District of Columbia Bar; American (Forum on Franchising) and International Bar Associations. ***LANGUAGES:*** French and German. ***PRACTICE AREAS:*** Franchising; Antitrust; International Franchising; Distribution. ***Email:*** loewingerap@bipc.com

ROBERT G. PINCO, born Los Angeles, California, February 9, 1944; admitted to bar, 1969, Maryland; 1970, District of Columbia; 1971, U.S. Claims Court; 1973, U.S. Supreme Court. *Education:* University of Connecticut School of Pharmacy (B.S.Ph., 1966); Georgetown University Law School (J.D., 1969). Registered Pharmacist, District of Columbia, 1966. Co-Author: *Amphetamine Use & Misuse: A Medico-Legal View - Uppers & Downers,* Prentice Hall, 1973; "The OTC Review-A Light at the End of the Tunnel," Food Drug Cosmetic Journal, 1976; "Are Cosmetics Drugs?" Journal of Central Atlantic States Association of Food and Drug Officials, 1976; "Alternatives to Non-Incarceration for Drug Abusing Defendants," Baltimore Law Journal, Spring 1973; "OTC Internal—Analgesics: It's Time We Took Them Seriously," Hospital Formulary, December 1979; "Cosmetics/Drugs —An Evolving Resolution of an Old Issue," (2-part series), Cosmetic Technology, May-June 1982; "Prescription to Over-The-Counter Switches: An Example of the Need For New Procedures in the Post-Monograph Era," Food Drug Cosmetic Law Journal, 1984; Hurdling International Barriers to Existing and New Excipients, "World Pharmaceutical Standards Review," Vol. 1, No. 5 (February 1991) and PharmTech Japan, Vol. 8, No. 2 (February 1992); *The Medical Device Industry,* "Responding as Companies to International Issues - Using Partnerships and Other Joint Ventures," (1990); "Homeopathic Drugs: What Are They and How Are They Regulated in the United States and in the European Union," Biological Therapy, Vol. XIV, No. 1, January 1996. Co-author: "The Ambiguities of the Dietary Supplement and Health Education Act of 1994," Food and Drug Law Journal, 1996; "The FDA's Regulation of Dental Products," Journal of Clinical Dentistry, Vol. VI, No. 3, 1995. Attorney, Department of Justice, 1969-1972. Assistant General Counsel, White House Special Action Office for Drug Abuse Prevention, Executive Office of the President, 1972-1974. Director, Over-the-Counter Drugs, Food and Drug Administration, 1974-1977. Member, Food and Drug Law Institute, 1977—. Adjunct Associate Professor of Pharmacy, University of Maryland School of Pharmacy, 1978—. Member, University of Maryland School of Pharmacy Board of Advisors, 1994—. *Member:* The District of Columbia Bar; Maryland State, Federal (Vice Chairman, Food and Drug Committee, 1977) and American Bar Associations; American Society for Pharmacy Law (Recipient, 1986 President's Award). ***PRACTICE AREAS:*** Food, Drug and Cosmetic Law. ***Email:*** pincor@bipc.com

(This Listing Continued)

BUCHANAN INGERSOLL, PROFESSIONAL CORPORATION, Washington—Continued

DONALD E. SEGAL, born Houston, Texas, November 13, 1947; admitted to bar, 1972, Massachusetts; 1974, District of Columbia. *Education:* Brandeis University (B.A., with honors, 1969); Boston College (J.D., 1972). Contributor and Editor, Boston College Law Review, 1971-1972. Associate Chief Counsel, Food and Drug Administration, 1979-1991. *Member:* The District of Columbia Bar. **PRACTICE AREAS:** Food, Drug and Cosmetic Law; Regulatory Law; Biotechnology; Administrative Law. **Email:** segalde@bipc.com

MARK M. YACURA, born East Vandergrift, Pennsylvania, September 30, 1949; admitted to bar, 1985, Pennsylvania; 1986, District of Columbia. *Education:* University of Pittsburgh (B.A., cum laude, 1971; M.B.A., 1978); Duquesne University (B.S., 1978); American University (J.D., cum laude, 1985). Registered Pharmacist, Pennsylvania, 1978. Author: "Inside the PDR," Trial, June, 1984; "Regulatory & Evidentiary Ramifications of the Patient Medication Instruction," (PMI) Leaflet, Medical Trial Technique Quarterly, Spring, 1985. *Member:* The District of Columbia Bar; Pennsylvania Bar Association; American Pharmaceutical Association. **PRACTICE AREAS:** Food, Drug and Cosmetic Law; Corporate Transactions; Trade Law. **Email:** yacuramm@bipc.com

ASSOCIATES

SHANNON HAAF, born Philadelphia, Pennsylvania, June 16, 1972; admitted to bar, 1998, Pennsylvania, New Jersey and U.S. District Court, Eastern District of Pennsylvania; 2001, District of Columbia. *Education:* University of Maryland (B.A., 1994); University of Baltimore (J.D., 1997). **PRACTICE AREAS:** Franchise Law. **Email:** haafs@bipc.com

TODD H. HALPERN, born Livingston, New Jersey, June 8, 1970; admitted to bar, 1997, New York and U.S. District Court Southern and Eastern Districts of New York; 2001, District of Columbia. *Education:* University of Wisconsin-Madison (B.A., 1992); Fordham University (J.D., 1996). Member, Fordham International Law Journal. Co-Author, with Robert Pinco: "Guidelines for the Promotion of Dietary Implements: Examining Government Regulation Five Years After Enactment of the Directory Supplement Health and Education Act of 1994," 54 Food and Drug Law Journal 567, 1999. *Member:* Association of the Bar of the City of New York; New York State Bar Association (Member, Section on Food and Drug Law); The District of Columbia Bar. **PRACTICE AREAS:** Food, Drug and Cosmetics Law; Regulatory Law; Corporate Law; Biotechnology; Consumer Protection. **Email:** halpernth@bipc.com

PAUL J. LARSEN, born Lincoln, Nebraska, February 24, 1971; admitted to bar, 1997, Georgia (Not admitted in District of Columbia). *Education:* Harvard University (B.A., 1993); Vanderbilt University (J.D., 1997). Judicial Law Clerk, U.S. District Court, Dallas, Texas, 1998-1999. **PRACTICE AREAS:** Food, Drug and Cosmetic Law; Sweepstakes. **Email:** larsenpj@bipc.com

PATRICK A. NICKLER, born Olean, New York, August 3, 1974; admitted to bar, 1999, Pennsylvania; 2000, Massachusetts (Not admitted in District of Columbia). *Education:* Franklin & Marshall College (B.A., 1996); Boston College (J.D., 1999). Phi Beta Kappa. Managing Editor, Boston College Environmental Affairs Law Review. Author, "Tragedy of the Commons in Coastal Fisheries: Contending Prescriptions and the Case of the Atlantic Bluefin Tuna," Boston College Environmental Affairs Law Review, Vol. 26 No. 3. **PRACTICE AREAS:** Real Estate. **Email:** nicklerpa@bipc.com

BRADLEY K. STEINBRECHER, born Rochester, Minnesota, March 1, 1967; admitted to bar, 1995, Pennsylvania; 1999, District of Columbia. *Education:* Messiah College (B.S., 1989); University of Chicago (A.M.R.S., 1992); University of Pennsylvania (J.D., 1995). **PRACTICE AREAS:** International Franchising; Franchising. **Email:** steinbrecherbk@bipc.com

THEODORE M. SULLIVAN, born Cheverly, Maryland, January 6, 1966; admitted to bar, 1997, Illinois (Not admitted in District of Columbia). *Education:* George Mason University (B.S., 1989); Chicago-Kent College of Law, Illinois Institute of Technology (J.D., 1997). **PRACTICE AREAS:** Food, Drug and Cosmetic Law. **Email:** sullivantm@bipc.com

(See Professional Biographies at Bryn Mawr, Harrisburg, Philadelphia and Pittsburgh, Pennsylvania; Miami, Aventura and Tampa, Florida; New York City and Buffalo, New York; Princeton, New Jersey; McLean, Virginia; Wilmington, Delaware; San Diego, California; London, England)

BUCHMAN & O'BRIEN, LLP

1331 PENNSYLVANIA AVENUE, N.W., SUITE 1211
WASHINGTON, D.C. 20004
Telephone: 202-638-6854
Telecopier: 202-638-2286
Email: dco@bev-alc-law.com
URL: http://www.bev-alc-law.com

New York, New York Office: 10 East 40th Street, Suite 708. Telephone: 212-686-0440. Telecopier: 212-889-7622.

(This Listing Continued)

San Francisco, California Office: 505 Sansome Street, Suite 1500. Telephone: 415-398-0440. Telecopier: 415-394-9564.

Edison, New Jersey Office: 510 Thornall Street, Suite 200 (Metro Park). Telephone: 732-632-9463. Telecopier: 732-632-8760.

General Civil Practice. Administrative, Corporate, Labor, Alcoholic Beverage Control and Business Law. Trade Regulation. Trademark, Copyright, Unfair Competition and Licensing, Food and Drug Law.

RESIDENT PARTNER

MARK A. KOSLOWE, born New York, N.Y., 1952; admitted to bar, 1977, New York; U.S. District Court, Eastern and Southern Districts of New York; Florida; 1979, District of Columbia. *Education:* Yeshiva University (B.A., 1973); New York University (A.P.C., 1979); Fordham University (J.D., 1976). *Member:* The Florida Bar; District of Columbia Bar; New York Criminal and Civil Courts Bar Association. (Managing Partner). **PRACTICE AREAS:** Alcoholic Beverage Control Law, Licensing and Regulation. **Email:** makoslowe@bev-alc-law.com

(For Biographical data on all Personnel, see Professional Biographies at New York, New York)

BUDOW AND NOBLE, P.C.

WASHINGTON, D.C.

(See Bethesda, Maryland)

Civil Litigation, Trial and Appellate Practice in all Maryland and District of Columbia Courts, Insurance, Negligence, Workers' Compensation.

BULLOCK & ASSOCIATES, INC.

5335 WISCONSIN AVE, N.W., SUITE 440
WASHINGTON, D.C. 20015-2034
Telephone: 202-966-5006
Fax: 202-686-3681
URL: http://www.bullockassociates.com
Email: JBullock@BullockAssociates.com
URL: http://www.lawyers.com/bullockassociates

Criminal Investigations, Business Fraud, Corporate Fraud, Fraud Investigations, Computer Fraud, Computer Forensics, Internal Investigations, Due Diligence and Anti-Corruption Investigations, Litigation Intelligence, Counterfeiting, Product Diversion, Internet Fraud, Telecommunications Fraud, Information Protection.

FIRM PROFILE: Jerry Bullock is a former managing director at Pricewaterhouse Coopers Investigations in Washington, D.C. Prior to his affiliation with Pricewaterhouse, Mr. Bullock's career highlights include his presidential appointment and senate confirmation as U.S. Marshal for the District of Columbia as well as his service as assistant inspector general for investigations at the U.S. Department of Justice. The firm represents Fortune 500 companies, law firms, big five professional service firms, governments, highnet worth individuals, industry organizations and associations.

J. JEROME BULLOCK, admitted to bar, 1975, Iowa (Not admitted in District of Columbia). *Education:* Tuskegee University (B.S., distinguished military graduate, 1969); Howard University School of Law (J.D., 1975). Associate Legal Counsel, U.S. Marshals Service, 1975-1977; United States Marshal for the District of Columbia, 1977-1982; Chief, Office of Congressional and Public Affairs, 1983-1985; Chief Inspector, United States Marshals Service, 1985-1989; Assistant Inspector General for Investigations, United States Department of Justice, 1989-1994. *Member:* Iowa State, American, International and National Bar Associations. [Capt., U.S. Army, 1969-1972]. **Email:** JBullock@BullockAssociates.com

BULMAN, DUNIE, BURKE & FELD

CHARTERED

WASHINGTON, D.C.

(See Bethesda, Maryland)

General Civil Trial Practice before State and Federal Courts. Negligence, Medical Malpractice, Products Liability, Corporation, Insurance, General Commercial, Real Estate, Probate, Trusts, Estate Planning, Family Law, Children, Business Planning, Mediation and Arbitration, Franchise Law.

BUONASSISSI, HENNING & LASH

A PROFESSIONAL CORPORATION

WASHINGTON, D.C.

(See Fairfax, Virginia)

General Civil Practice in all Courts. Corporate, Commercial, Real Estate, Bankruptcy, Taxation, Family and Probate Law.

LAW OFFICES OF CATHY L. BURGESS

1767 P STREET, N.W.
FIRST FLOOR
WASHINGTON, D.C. 20036
Telephone: 202-265-5157
Fax: 202-265-5618
Email: cathy@clburgess.com
URL: http://www.lawyers.com/cathyburgesslaw

Healthcare, Food and Drug, Corporate Compliance and Legislative Advocacy.

CATHY L. BURGESS, born Birmingham, Alabama, November 25, 1958; admitted to bar, 1988, District of Columbia; 1989, U.S. District Court for the District of Columbia and U.S. Claims Court. *Education:* Georgetown University (B.S.F.S., 1982); Catholic University of America (J.D., 1988). Lead Articles Editor, The Journal of Contemporary Health Law and Policy, 1987-1988. Author: "Chapter 4, Riley, Fell and Rosanske, Validation of Methods in Pharmaceutical and Biomedical Analysis," 1996; "The Ever-Changing Standards of CGMP: United States v. Barr Laboratories, Inc.," 10 Clinical Res. and Reg. AFF. 137, 1993. *Member:* The District of Columbia Bar.

OF COUNSEL

MICHAEL O. SPIVEY, born Columbus, Georgia, August 28, 1955; admitted to bar, 1988, Pennsylvania and District of Columbia. *Education:* Birmingham-Southern College (B.A., magna cum laude, 1977); University of Chicago (M.A., Divinity, 1978; M.A., Public Policy Studies, 1979); Georgetown University (J.D., 1987). Adjunct Professor, Washington School of Law, American University. *Member:* The District of Columbia Bar; National Health Lawyers Association. ***PRACTICE AREAS:*** Healthcare.

BURNS, DOANE, SWECKER & MATHIS, L.L.P.

WASHINGTON, D.C.

(See Alexandria, Virginia)

BURT, MANER & MILLER

Established in 1987
975 EAST TOWER
1300 EYE STREET, N.W.
WASHINGTON, D.C. 20005
Telephone: 202-783-1500
Facsimile: 202-783-1523
Email: queries@bmmdc.com
URL: http://www.lawyers.com/corporatetaxlaw

London, England Office: Suite 105/106 Hamilton House, 1 Temple Avenue, EC4Y OHA. Telephone: 020-7353-4722. Facsimile: 020-7353-4723.

Tax, both domestic and international, including international transactions, controversies, and litigation.

FIRM PROFILE: Burt, Maner & Miller specializes in corporate tax, tax controversies, international tax planning and transactions, as well as structured financing. Most of the firm's work is for U.S. and European-based multinational corporations. The firm is affiliated with the United Kingdom tax firm of Paynter, Granby.

MEMBERS OF FIRM

DAN BURT, born Philadelphia, Pennsylvania, October l, 1942; admitted to bar, 1970, Pennsylvania; 1977, Massachusetts; 1986, District of Columbia. *Education:* LaSalle College (B.A., cum laude, 1964); Cambridge University, Cambridge, England (M.A., 1966); Yale University (LL.B., 1969). Author: "Abuse of Trust: A Report on Ralph Nader's Network," Regnery Gateway, Copyright, The Capital Legal Foundation, 1982. President, Capital Legal Foundation, 1980-1987. Attorney Advisor: to the International Tax Counsel, U.S. Treasury, 1971-1972; to Under Secretary of Treasury, Edwin S. Cohen, 1972-1973. *Member:* The District of Columbia Bar; Massachusetts and Pennsylvania Bar Associations. (Also at London, England Office). ***PRACTICE AREAS:*** Structured Finance; Litigation; Tax Audits. ***Email:*** dburt@bmmuk.co.uk

(This Listing Continued)

HENRY B. MILLER, born Kingsport, Tennessee, September 7, 1951; admitted to bar, 1977, District of Columbia; 1978, U.S. Tax Court; 1994, U.S. District Court, District of Columbia; 1995, U.S. Court of Appeals, Third Circuit; 1996, U.S. Court of Appeals, Seventh Circuit. *Education:* Erskine College (B.A., with honors, 1974); Georgetown University (J.D., 1977). Omicron Delta Kappa. Erskine Scholar. Member, Tax Lawyer Journal, Georgetown University, 1976-1977. Docket Attorney, Tax Litigation Division, Office of Chief Counsel IRS, 1977-1978. Trial Attorney, IRS District Counsel, Office of International Operations, 1978-1982. *Member:* The District of Columbia Bar; Federal Bar Association. ***PRACTICE AREAS:*** Tax Planning; Tax Controversy; Litigation. ***Email:*** henrymiller@bmmdc.com

FORBES MANER, born Richmond, Virginia, December 27, 1951; admitted to bar, 1977, Virginia; 1978, District of Columbia; U.S. Court of Appeals for the District of Columbia Circuit; 1981, U.S. Claims Court; 1985, U.S. Tax Court. *Education:* Harvard University (B.A., magna cum laude, 1974); University of Virginia (J.D., 1977). *Member:* The District of Columbia Bar. ***PRACTICE AREAS:*** Litigation. ***Email:*** fmaner@bmmdc.com

JONATHAN E. JACKEL, born Brooklyn, New York, October 30, 1965; admitted to bar, 1991, Maryland; 1992, U.S. Tax Court and U.S. District Court, District of Maryland; 1999, District of Columbia. *Education:* Boston University (B.S., magna cum laude, 1986); Georgetown University (J.D., cum laude, 1991). Law Clerk, Hon. Renato Beghe, U.S. Tax Court, 1991-1992. Trial Attorney, U.S. Department of Justice, Tax Division, 1992-1996. *Member:* American Bar Association (Member, Taxation Section, 1991—). ***REPORTED CASES:*** Shell Petroleum, Inc. v. United States, 996 F.Supp. 361 (D. Del. 1997); Rodek v. United States, 962 F.Supp. 34 (D. Del. 1997); Finkelstein v. United States, 943 F.Supp. 425 (D. N.J. 1996). ***PRACTICE AREAS:*** Tax Litigation; International Taxation; Taxation. ***Email:*** jjackel@bmmdc.com

OF COUNSEL

ALAN L. FELD, born New York, N.Y., February 5, 1940; admitted to bar, 1963, New York; 1974, Massachusetts (Not admitted in District of Columbia). *Education:* Columbia University (A.B., magna cum laude, 1960); Harvard University (LL.B., cum laude, 1963). Professor, Boston University School of Law, 1971—; Professor-in-Residence, Office of Chief Counsel IRS, Spring 1996. Author: "Federal Income Taxation of Corporate Transactions," 3rd edition, with William D. Andrews, Little, Brown and Co., 1994; "Patrons Despite Themselves, Taxpayers & Arts Policy," with Michael O'Hare and Mark Schuster, New York University Press, 1983; "Tax Policy and Corporate Concentration," Lexington Books, 1982. *Member:* Massachusetts and American Bar Associations; American Law Institute. ***PRACTICE AREAS:*** International Tax; Structured Finance.

ASSOCIATES

SUSAN PECORARO SEGAR, born Morgan City, Louisiana, October 5, 1967; admitted to bar, 1993, Louisiana; 1996, U.S. Tax Court; 1999, District of Columbia. *Education:* Louisiana State University and A and M College (B.S., 1989; J.D., 1993); Georgetown University (LL.M., with honors, 1994). Law Clerk, Hon. D. Irvin Couvillion, U.S. Tax Court, 1994-1996. *Member:* Louisiana State and American (Member, Tax Section) Bar Associations. ***PRACTICE AREAS:*** Federal Taxation; International Taxation; Tax Controversies. ***Email:*** ssegar@bmmdc.com

DAVID M. OLIVER JR., born Houston, Texas, February 28,1973; admitted to bar, 1998, Louisiana (Not admitted in District of Columbia). *Education:* Louisiana State University (B.S., 1995; J.D., 1998); Georgetown University Law Center (LL.M., with honors, Taxation, 1999). Omicron Delta Kappa; Beta Alpha Psi; Finalist;: Albert R. Mugel National Tax Moot Court Competition, 1998; Member: Philip C. Jessup International Law Moot Court Competition, 1998; Law Clerk, Hon. D. Irvin Couvillion, U.S. Tax Court, 1999-2000 *Member:* Louisiana State and American Bar Associations. ***PRACTICE AREAS:*** Federal Taxation; International Taxation; Tax Controversies. ***Email:*** doliver@bmmdc.com

REPRESENTATIVE CLIENTS: A.E. Staley Manufacturing Co.; Cadbury Schweppes Plc; Dover Corporation; EnviroSource, Inc.; First Continental Trading Inc.; Global Asset Management Limited, Nationwide Tradeshow Services; Racal Electronics PLC; Rolls Royce, Plc (Aerospace); Tate & Lyle North American Sugars Inc.; Tate & Lyle PLC; Vickers, Plc.

BURZIO & McLAUGHLIN

CANAL SQUARE
SUITE 540
1054 THIRTY-FIRST STREET, N.W.
WASHINGTON, D.C. 20007
Telephone: 202-965-4555
Telecopier: 202-965-4432
Email: BMLaw@erols.com

Practice Before Postal Rate Commission, U.S Postal Service and Other Federal Administrative Agencies, Federal Appellate Litigation, Postal Law and Related Litigation, Lobbying, Business and Transactional Matters, Aviation Regulatory Law.

MEMBERS OF FIRM

JOHN M. BURZIO, born Dewar, Oklahoma, January 9, 1936; admitted to bar, 1960, Oklahoma; 1968, District of Columbia; 1978, U.S. Supreme Court. *Education:* University of Oklahoma (B.B.A., 1957; LL.B., 1960). Order of the Coif. Editor-in-Chief, University of Oklahoma Law Review, 1959-1960. Counsel, Senate Aviation Subcommittee, 1964-66. Staff Director and Counsel, Senate Post Office and Civil Service Committee, 1966-68. *Member:* The District of Columbia Bar; American Bar Association. ***PRACTICE AREAS:*** Federal Administrative Law; Postal Law; Aviation Regulatory Law.

THOMAS W. McLAUGHLIN, born Manhattan, Kansas, August 10, 1947; admitted to bar, 1974, District of Columbia; 1984, Maryland. *Education:* University of Kansas (B.S., 1970); University of Michigan (J.D., 1973). Trial Attorney, Civil Aeronautics Board, 1973-76. *Member:* The District of Columbia Bar; Maryland State Bar Association. ***PRACTICE AREAS:*** Federal Administrative Law; Postal Law; Aviation Regulatory Law.

TIMOTHY L. KEEGAN, born New York, N.Y., April 9, 1949; admitted to bar, 1985, District of Columbia. *Education:* Fordham University (B.A., 1971); University of Virginia (M.A., 1972; Ph.D., 1979; J.D., 1985). *Member:* The District of Columbia Bar. ***PRACTICE AREAS:*** Federal Administrative Law; Postal Law.

OF COUNSEL

ALVIN H. GANDAL, born Cleveland, Ohio, February 8, 1932; admitted to bar, 1956, Ohio; 1961, District of Columbia. *Education:* Case Western Reserve University (A.B., 1954; LL.B., 1956). Omicron Delta Kappa. Attorney: U.S. Department of Labor, 1956; National Labor Relations Board, 1960-1961. Deputy Assistant General Counsel, U.S. Postal Service, 1969-1973. Director, Office of Contract Analysis, U.S. Postal Service, 1973-1979. Nominated by the President to be Chairman of the Postal Rate Commission, 1977. Assistant General Counsel, Federal Labor Relations Authority, 1979-1982. *Member:* District of Columbia Bar. [Office of the Judge Advocate General, U.S. Army, 1957-1960]

BUTERA & ANDREWS

1301 PENNSYLVANIA AVENUE, N.W.
WASHINGTON, D.C. 20004-1701
Telephone: 202-347-6875
Fax: 202-347-6876
URL: http://www.butera-andrews.com
Email: info@butera-andrews.com
URL: http://www.lawyers.com/butera-andrews

Banking, Other Legislative Matters, Federal Litigation.

JAMES J. BUTERA, born Philadelphia, Pennsylvania, 1944; admitted to bar, 1973, District of Columbia. *Education:* St. Joseph's University (B.A., 1966); Georgetown University (J.D., 1972). *Member:* The District of Columbia Bar; American Bar Association. [U.S.M.C., 1966-1969]. ***PRACTICE AREAS:*** Government Relations; Financial Institutions Law; Regulation Law; Real Estate; Litigation. ***Email:*** jbutera@butera-andrews.com

WRIGHT H. ANDREWS, JR., born Anderson, South Carolina, 1947; admitted to bar, 1974, District of Columbia and Georgia. *Education:* Emory University (B.A., with honors, 1970; J.D., with distinction, 1973). Order of the Coif. Chief Legislative Assistant to U.S. Senator Sam Nunn, 1973-1975. Member Editorial Board, Georgia State Bar Journal, 1979-1981. Member, American League of Lobbyists, 1985—(President, 1995-1996). *Member:* The District of Columbia Bar; State Bar of Georgia; Federal and American Bar Associations. ***PRACTICE AREAS:*** Federal Legislation; Banking Law; Mortgages; Environmental Law; Nuclear Energy; Immigration; Tax Law; Energy. ***Email:*** wandrews@butera-andrews.com

STEPHEN C. LECKAR, born Berlin, Germany, 1948; admitted to bar, 1974, Georgia; 1979, District of Columbia and Illinois; 1981, U.S. District Court, Northern District of Illinois; U.S. District Court, District of Columbia; U.S. Court of Appeals for the District of Columbia Circuit; U.S. District Court, District of Maryland; U.S. Court of Federal Claims. *Education:* Georgia State University (B.S., 1970); Duke University (J.D., 1973). Mediator, U.S. District Court for the District of Columbia. Member, Advisory Committee on Rules, U.S. Court of Appeals for the District of Columbia Circuit. *Member:* The District of Columbia Bar; State Bar of Georgia; Illinois State and American Bar Associations. ***PRACTICE AREAS:*** Federal Civil Litigation; Federal Criminal Law. ***Email:*** sleckar@butera-andrews.com

JOHN J. McINESPIE, born Glasgow, Scotland, April 4, 1948; (admission pending). *Education:* Oxford College; University of Glasgow School of Law (LL.B., 1975); Georgetown University Law Center (LL.M., 1993). ***Email:*** jmcinespie@sablaw.com

DENNIS M. HART, born Chicago, Illinois, April 26, 1949; admitted to bar, 1974, Texas; 1978, District of Columbia; 1984, Virginia. *Education:* University of Illinois (B.A., 1971); University of Houston (J.D., 1974). *Member:* State Bar of Texas; The District of Columbia Bar; Virginia State Bar. ***REPORTED CASES:*** Morton v. United States, 415 A.2d 800 (D.C. 1980); United States v. Smith, 630 F.2d 192 (3rd Cir. 1980); In re Application of National Broadcasting Co., 653 F.2d 609 (D.C.Cir. 1981); United States v. Ross, 456 U.S. 798 (1982); United States v. Jenrette, 744 F.2d 817 (D.C.Cir. 1984); Poteat v. King, 487 A.2d 215 (D.C. 1984); Baggett v. United States, 528 A.2d 444 (D.C. 1987); Briscoe v. United States, 528 A.2d 1243 (D.C. 1987); Gaston v. United States, 535 A.2d 893 (D.C. 1988); O'Donnell v. United States, 552 A.2d 503 (D.C. 1988); Chappell v. United States, 558 A.2d 348 (D.C. 1989); Tucker v. United States, 571 A.2d 797 (D.C. 1990); United States v. Doe, 903 F.2d 16 (D.C.Cir. 1990); United States v. Jones, 909 F.2d 533 (D.C.Cir. 1990); United States v. McNeil, 911 F.2d 272 (D.C.Cir. 1990); United States v. Moskal, 498 U.S. 103 (1990); United States v. Johnson, 922 F.2d 850 (D.C.Cir. 1991); Allen v. United States, 647 A.2d 1165 (D.C. 1994); United States v. Anderson, 59 F.3d 1323 (D.C.Cir. 1995)(en banc); Herbin v. United States, 683 A.2d 437 (D.C. 1996); Nixon v. United States, 730 A.2d 145 (D.C. 1999). ***PRACTICE AREAS:*** Appellate Practice; Criminal Trial; Civil Trial.

FRANK A. TILLOTSON, born West Islip, New York, June 16, 1965; admitted to bar, 1996, Georgia (Not admitted in District of Columbia). *Education:* State University of New York at Albany (B.S., 1987); University of Georgia (J.D., 1996). *Member:* State Bar of Georgia. ***PRACTICE AREAS:*** Government Relations. ***Email:*** ftillotson@butera-andrews.com

PHILIP S. CORWIN, born Brooklyn, New York, March 15, 1950; admitted to bar, 1975, Massachusetts; 1976, District of Columbia; 1994, U.S. Supreme Court. *Education:* Cornell University (B.A., 1971); Boston College (J.D., 1975). *Member:* American Bar Association (Legislative Liaison, Science and Technology Section, 1999—; Legislative Reporter, Cyberspace Law Committee, 1998—); American Bankruptcy Institute. ***PRACTICE AREAS:*** Bankruptcy; Financial Services; Intellectual Property; Electronic Commerce. ***Email:*** pcorwin@butera-andrews.com

BUTLER, SNOW, O'MARA, STEVENS & CANNADA, PLLC

SUITE 500, EOP BUILDING
819-7TH STREET N.W.
WASHINGTON, D.C. 20001
Telephone: 202-408-8668
Telecopier:202-408-8768
Email: first.last@butlersnow.com
URL: http://www.butlersnow.com

Jackson, Mississippi Office: 17th Floor, AmSouth Plaza, 210 East Capitol Street, 39201. Telephone: 601-948-5711. Telecopier: 601-985-4500.

Gulfport, Mississippi Office: Suite 204, Whitney National Bank Building, 1300 Twenty Fifth Avenue, P.O. Drawer 4248, 39502. Telephone: 601-864-1170. Telecopier: 601-868-1531.

Memphis, Tennessee Office: Suite 501, Forum I Building, 6750 Poplar Avenue, P.O. Box 171443, 38187-1443, 38187-1443. Telephone: 901-680-7200. Telecopier: 901-680-7201.

General Civil Practice. Trials and Appeals before all State and Federal Courts. State and Federal Agency Practice, Administrative Law, Alternative Dispute Resolution, Antitrust and Trade Regulation, Appellate Litigation, Banking and Financial Services, Bankruptcy and Creditors' Rights, Business Planning and Operations, Civil Rights, Commercial Lending, Commercial Litigation, Construction, Criminal Defense, Director and Officer Liability, Drug and Medical Device Litigation, Economic Development Incentives, Employee Benefits, Environmental, Estate and Trust Administration, Estate and Wealth Transfer Tax Planning, Gaming Law and Regulation, Governmental Relations, Government Litigation, Healthcare, Insurance Defense, Insurance Law and Regulation, Intellectual Property, International Law, Labor and Employment Law (Management), Medical Professional Liability, Mergers and Acquisitions, Premises Liability, Products Liability, Professional Li-

(This Listing Continued)

ability, Public Finance, Public Utilities, Real Estate, Securities, State and Municipal Bonds, Taxation, Technology and Intellectual Property, Toxic Torts, Transportation, and Workers' Compensation.

LAW FIRM ALLIANCES/ASSOCIATIONS: ***LEX MUNDI***

HARMONIE GROUP

SOUTHERN LAW NETWORK

STATE LAW RESOURCES, INC.

EMPLOYMENT LAW ALLIANCE

SPECIAL COUNSEL

MIKE ESPY, born Yazoo City, Mississippi, 1953; admitted to bar, 1978, Mississippi (Not admitted in District of Columbia). *Education:* Howard University (B.A., 1975); University of Santa Clara (J.D., 1978). Managing Attorney, Central Mississippi Legal Services, 1978-1980. Assistant Secretary of State and Director of Public Lands, 1980-1984. Assistant Attorney General and Director of the Office of Consumer Protection, 1984-1985. Member, U.S. House of Representatives, 1986-1992. Vice-Chair of the Democratic Leadership Council. U.S. Secretary of Agriculture, 1993-1994. U.S. Secretary of Energy Advisory Board. *Member:* The Mississippi Bar. (Also at Jackson, Mississippi Office). ***PRACTICE AREAS:*** International Law; Government Relations; Governmental Liability; Agribusiness; Business Planning; Economic Development; Public Finance; Products Liability. ***Email:*** mike.espy@butlersnow.com

(For biographical data on all personnel, see Professional Biographies at Jackson, Mississippi)

BUTLER & SPEARS

1250 24TH STREET, N.W., SUITE 300
WASHINGTON, D.C. 20037
Telephone: 202-467-2794
Email: butlercyn@aol.com

Employment Law, Employee Rights, Wrongful Termination, Harassment, Unfair Labor Practices, Employment Discrimination, Age Discrimination, Equal Employment Opportunity Law, Small Business Law, Complex Commercial Litigation, Breach of Contract, E-Commerce Law, High Technology and Internet Law, Employment Class Actions.

FIRM PROFILE: Butler & Spears is a versatile business and employment litigation law firm. The firm has a national practice and is best known for its very experienced analysis, development and preparation of plaintiff-side employment law cases. The firm regularly represents individual employees, executives, laborers, educators and class action groups as well as small businesses and high-tech start-up companies.

MEMBERS OF FIRM

CYNTHIA L. BUTLER, born Pittsburg, Pennsylvania, July 24, 1960; admitted to bar, 1987, California; 1988, U.S. District Court, Central District of California; 1990, Pennsylvania and New Jersey; 1991, U.S. District Court, Eastern District of Pennsylvania, District of New Jersey and Northern District of California; 1995, District of Columbia and U.S. Court of Appeals, Third Circuit. *Education:* Cornell University College of Arts and Sciences (A.B., 1982); Georgetown University Law Center (J.D., 1987). International Editor, Georgetown Immigration Law Journal, 1986-1987. Certified, Advanced Mediation, Harvard Law School, June 2001. *Member:* American Bar Association; John Carroll Society.. ***LANGUAGES:*** French.

BYRON P. SPEARS, JR., born Louisville, Kentucky, June 3, 1947; admitted to bar, 1988, District of Columbia; 1992, U.S. Supreme Court. *Education:* United States Air Force Academy; University of Maryland (B.A., 1971); Washington College of Law, American University (J.D., 1987). Partner, Butler & Spears, Washington, DC, 1996—. Senior Technical Writer, Conquest Systems Inc., Washington, DC, May 2000—. Business Decision Implementor, Systems Plus, Inc., Washington, DC, March 1999—. Senior Management Analyst, HTE-UCS, Inc., Washington, DC, March 1997-March 1999. Writer/Editor, Byron Spears Writing and Editing Services, Clinton, Maryland, October 1995—. Editor, Research Institute of America, Alexandria, Virginia, August 1994-October 1995. Vice President and General Counsel, J. Cherian Consultants, Inc., Washington, DC, September 1993-July 1994. Special Assistant to Commissioner Joy Cherian, Equal Employment Opportunity Commission (EEOC), Washington, DC, November 1987-August 1993. Senior Editor, Law Publications, American Council of Life Insurance, Washington, DC, June 1982-November 1987.Election Judge, primary and general elections, Prince George's County, Maryland, 1988-1998. Founding Member, Worship Team Member, Recording Secretary of Board of Deacons and Racial Reconciliation Forum participant, Christ Our Shepherd Church, Washington, DC, 1987—. *Member:* The District of Columbia Bar; American Bar Association (Chairman, 1992-1995 and Vice Chairman,

(This Listing Continued)

1991-1992, Committee on International Employment Law, Section of International Law and Practice).

BYRNE GOLDENBERG & HAMILTON, PLLC

1025 CONNECTICUT AVENUE NW, SUITE 1012
WASHINGTON, D.C. 20036
Telephone: 202-857-9775
Fax: 202-857-9779
URL: http://www.lawyers.com/bghlaw

General Practice.

JOHN J. BYRNE, JR., born Washington, D.C., December 10, 1953; admitted to bar, 1981, New York; 1982, U.S. District Court, Southern and Eastern Districts of New York; 1985, Maryland; 1987, District of Columbia. *Education:* Yale University (B.A., summa cum laude, 1976); University of Virginia (J.D., 1980). Phi Beta Kappa.

LLOYD P GOLDENBERG, born Milwaukee, Wisconsin, August 7, 1947; admitted to bar, 1972, California; 1975, District of Columbia. *Education:* University of Wisconsin at Madison (B.A., summa cum laude, 1969); Harvard University (J.D., cum laude,1972). Phi Beta Kappa.

THOMAS J. HAMILTON, born Washington, D.C., April 5, 1954; admitted to bar, 1979, Virginia; 1980, District of Columbia; 1987, Maryland. *Education:* Yale University (B.A., cum laude, 1976); University of Virginia (J.D., 1979); Georgetown University (LL.M., Tax, 1987). Certified Public Accountant, District of Columbia, 1989. *Member:* The District of Columbia Bar; Virginia State Bar; American Bar Association; American Institute of Certified Public Accountants; American Association of Attorney-Certified Public Accountants.

LAW OFFICES OF PLATO CACHERIS

Established in 1971
SUITE 730
1100 CONNECTICUT AVENUE, NORTH WEST
WASHINGTON, D.C. 20036
Telephone: 202-775-8700
Fax: 202-775-8702
Email: pcacheris@erols.com
URL: http://www.lawyers.com/platocacheris

Alexandria, Virginia Office: 120 North Alfred Street. Telephone: 703-549-8181.

Federal and State Criminal and Civil Trials and Appeals, International Criminal Law, including Extraditions.

FIRM PROFILE: For over twenty-five years the law firm of Plato Cacheris has represented individuals, corporations and associations seeking counsel in matters involving white collar criminal and complex civil litigation defense. The firm's criminal and civil practice extends to clients both nationally and internationally.

PLATO CACHERIS, born Pittsburgh, Pennsylvania, May 22, 1929; admitted to bar, 1956, Virginia, District of Columbia, Supreme Court of Virginia and U.S. Court of Appeals for the District of Columbia Circuit; 1959, U.S. Supreme Court; 1960, U.S. Court of Appeals, Fourth Circuit and U.S. District Court, Eastern District of Virginia; 1980, U.S. Court of Appeals, Second, Third and Fifth Circuits; 1982, U.S. Court of Appeals, Seventh, Eighth, Ninth, Tenth and Eleventh Circuits; 1985, U.S. District Court, District of Maryland; 1988, U.S. District Court, Central District of California; 1996, U.S. District Court, Eastern District of Michigan. *Education:* Georgetown University (B.S., Foreign Service, 1951; J.D., 1956). Phi Delta Phi. Trial Attorney, Foreign Agents Registration Section, 1956-1958 and Criminal Division, 1958-1960, U.S. Department of Justice. First Assistant U.S. Attorney, Eastern District of Virginia at Alexandria, 1960-1965. *Member:* The District of Columbia Bar; Bar Association of the District of Columbia; Alexandria (Virginia) and American Bar Associations; Virginia State Bar; National Association of Criminal Defense Lawyers; The Barristers; The Lawyers Club. Fellow: American College of Trial Lawyers; International Academy of Trial Lawyers; American Board of Criminal Lawyers. [1st Lt., USMCR, 1951-1953]. ***LANGUAGES:*** Greek. ***PRACTICE AREAS:*** Criminal and Civil Litigation. ***Email:*** pcacheris@erols.com

PRESTON BURTON, born Morgantown, West Virginia, November 27, 1962; admitted to bar, 1989, Virginia and Virginia Supreme Court; 1990, U.S. District Court, Eastern District of Virginia and Western District of Kentucky, and U.S. Court of Appeals, Sixth and District of Columbia Circuits; 1991, District of Columbia and U.S. Court of Appeals, Fourth Circuit; 1992, U.S. District Court, District of Columbia; 2000, U.S. Supreme Court. *Education:* Duke University (A.B., magna cum laude, 1985); University of Virginia (J.D., 1989). Law Clerk to Hon. Boyce F. Martin, Jr., United States Court of Appeals, Sixth Circuit, 1989-1990. Assistant U.S. Attorney, District of Columbia, 1994-

(This Listing Continued)

LAW OFFICES OF PLATO CACHERIS, Washington—Continued

1998. Voting Member, D.C. Judicial Conference, 1997—. Member, United States Sentencing Commission Practitioners' Advisory Group. Adjunct Professor, George Washington University School of Law. *Member:* Virginia State (Member, Section of Criminal Law) and American (Member, Section of Criminal Justice) Bar Associations; The District of Columbia Bar (Member, Sections of: Criminal Law, Individual Rights and Litigation); The Barristers; William B. Bryant Inn of Court; D.C. Association of Criminal Defense Lawyers. ***PRACTICE AREAS:*** White Collar Criminal Litigation. ***Email:*** prestonburton@erols.com

JOHN F. HUNDLEY, born Washington, D.C., April 8, 1967; admitted to bar, 1993, Virginia; 1994, U.S. District Court, Eastern District of Virginia; 1996, District of Columbia and U.S. Court of Appeals, Third Circuit; U.S. District Court, Eastern District of Michigan; 2000, U.S. Supreme Court and U.S. Court of Appeals, Fourth Circuit; 2001, U.S. District Court, District of Columbia. *Education:* University of Virginia (B.A., Lambda Pi Epsilon, 1989); Georgetown University (J.D., 1993). Law Clerk to Chief Judge James C. Cacheris, U.S. District Court, Eastern District of Virginia. Juvenile Justice Clinic, 1992-1993. *Member:* Virginia State Bar (Criminal Law Section); District of Columbia Bar (Criminal Law and Individual Rights Section); American Bar Association (Criminal Justice Section). ***PRACTICE AREAS:*** Criminal and Civil Litigation. ***Email:*** johnhundley@erols.com

ASSOCIATE

ERIK A. COX, born Rochester, New York, October 14, 1975; admitted to bar, 2001, Virginia (Not admitted in District of Columbia). *Education:* University of Rochester (B.A., cum laude, 1998); George Washington University Law School (J.D., 2001). *Member:* Virginia State Bar. ***PRACTICE AREAS:*** Criminal Litigation; Civil Litigation. ***Email:*** erikcox@rcn.com

OF COUNSEL

SYDNEY J. HOFFMANN, born Hartford, Connecticut, January 3, 1952; admitted to bar, 1986, Virginia; 1987, District of Columbia; 1988, U.S. District Court, District of Columbia and U.S. District Court, Eastern District of Virginia; U.S. Court of Appeals for the District of Columbia Circuit. *Education:* Georgetown University (B.A., magna cum laude, 1974; M.A., Philosophy, 1978; J.D., cum laude, 1986). Member: American Criminal Law Review, 1984; Appellate Litigation Clinic, 1985-1986. Fellow, Research and Writing Program, 1985-1986. Law Clerk to Chief Judge, William C. Pryor, District of Columbia Court of Appeals, 1986-1987. Assistant U.S. Attorney for the District of Columbia, 1990-1993. *Member:* District of Columbia Bar (Member, Section on: Criminal Law; Individual Rights); Virginia State Bar. ***PRACTICE AREAS:*** Criminal Litigation.

LEGAL SUPPORT PERSONNEL

DONNA M. COFFMAN, (Office Administrator). ***Email:*** dcoffman@erols.com

---

CADEAUX & TAGLIERI, P.C.

Established in 1974

1100 CONNECTICUT AVENUE, N.W., SUITE 800

WASHINGTON, D.C. 20036

Telephone: 202-785-3373

Email: jim@cadotag.com

URL: http://www.lawyers.com/cadeaux&taglieri

Personal Injury, Negligence, Medical Malpractice, Products Liability, Wrongful Death, Automobile Accidents and Injuries, Workers Compensation, Police and Firemen's Retirement Law.

ROBERT CADEAUX (1936-1994).

JAMES W. TAGLIERI, born Jersey City, New Jersey, October 16, 1950; admitted to bar, 1975, Maryland; 1976, District of Columbia; 1977, U.S. District Court for the District of Columbia and U.S. District Court, District of Maryland; 1986, U.S. Court of Appeals for the District of Columbia Circuit; 1989, U.S. Court of Appeals for the Federal Circuit. *Education:* Georgetown University (B.S.F.S., 1972); American University (J.D., 1975). Recipient, Lawyers of the Year Award, Trial Lawyers Associations of Metropolitan, Washington, D.C., 1997. Member, The Temporary Motor Vehicle Insurance Review Commission, District of Columbia, 1987. Volunteer Arbitrator, D.C. Superior Court Mandatory Arbitration Program, 1987—. Volunteer Mediator, D.C. Superior Court Settlement Week, April 1988. Voluntary Mediator, D.C. Superior Court, 1989—. Volunteer Mediator, U.S. District Court for D.C., 1989—. *Member:* The District of Columbia Bar (Member, Steering Committee Injury To Persons and Property Section, 1990-1995); The Bar Association of the District

(This Listing Continued)

of Columbia (Member, Civil Jury Instruction Committee of Young Lawyers Section); Maryland State Bar Association; Trial Lawyers Association of Metropolitan Washington, D.C. (Member, Board of Governors, 1986—; Secretary, 1987-1988; President, 1989-1990); Maryland Trial Lawyers Association (Member, Nursing Home Litigation Committee, 2001—); The Association of Trial Lawyers of America (Delegate, 1988—; Sustaining Member, 1989—); Trial Lawyers for Public Justice. ***PRACTICE AREAS:*** Personal Injury; Medical Malpractice; Nursing Home Liability; Products Liability; Workers Compensation. ***Email:*** jim@cadotag.com

JOYCE M. NOTARIUS, born New Rochelle, New York, February 24, 1950; admitted to bar, 1975, Indiana and U.S. District Court, Southern District of Indiana; 1978, District of Columbia; 1980, U.S. District Court, District of Columbia and U.S. Court of Appeals, District of Columbia Circuit; 1984, Maryland. *Education:* University of Wisconsin (B.A., 1972); Indiana University (J.D., 1975). Former Counsel, Travelers Insurance Company. Former Assistant Corporation Counsel for the District of Columbia. Law Clerk to the Honorable Charles S. White, Court of Appeals of Indiana. Volunteer Mediator, District of Columbia Superior Court, Settlement Week, 1989. Volunteer Mediator, District of Columbia Superior Court, 1989—. *Member:* The District of Columbia Bar (Member, Steering Committee, Injury to Persons and Property Section, 1988); Trial Lawyers Association of Metropolitan Washington, D.C.; The Association of Trial Lawyers of America. ***PRACTICE AREAS:*** Personal Injury; Medical Malpractice; Products Liability. ***Email:*** joyce@cadotag.com

---

NICHOLAS S. NUNZIO, JR., born Washington, D.C., October 10, 1954; admitted to bar, 1981, Maryland; 1982, District of Columbia. *Education:* George Washington University (B.A., 1977); University of Baltimore (J.D., 1981). Articles Editor, University of Baltimore Law Forum, 1980-1981. *Member:* Montgomery County, Maryland State and American Bar Associations; The District of Columbia Bar; Association of Defense Trial Counsel.

JOHN G. HARNISHFEGER, born Lima, Ohio, August 8, 1967; admitted to bar, 1993, Maryland; 1994, Virginia; 1996, District of Columbia. *Education:* Miami University (B.A., 1989); Ohio Northern University (J.D., 1992). *Member:* District of Columbia Bar Association, Maryland State Bar Association and Virginia State Bar Association. ***PRACTICE AREAS:*** Workers Compensation; Personal Injury; Products Liability. ***Email:*** john@cadotag.com

THOMAS M. WOCHOK, born Philadelphia, Pennsylvania, August 28, 1949; admitted to bar, 1975, Ohio (inactive) and U.S. District Court, Northern District of Ohio; 1980, District of Columbia and U.S. District Court, District of Columbia; 1981, Virginia and U.S. Court of Appeals, District of Columbia Circuit; 1982, U.S. District Court, Eastern District of Virginia; 1984, U.S. Court of Appeals, Fourth Circuit and U.S. Supreme Court; 1996, Maryland; 1997, U.S. District Court, District of Maryland. *Education:* Catholic University of America (B.A., magna cum laude, 1970); University of Toledo (J.D., 1974); Georgetown University (LL.M., with distinction, 1993). Phi Kappa Phi; Delta Theta Phi. Instructor, "The Legal Environment of Insurance," Society of Chartered Property & Casualty Underwriters, District of Columbia Chapter, 1986, 1989. Former Managing Attorney, Travelers Insurance Company. Former Senior Staff Attorney, The St. Paul Companies. Member: Catholic University Cardinal Club; Georgetown Club of Metropolitan Washington.Volunteer, Neutral Case Evaluator, Medical Malpractice Panelist and Motion Conciliator, Fairfax County Circuit Court. *Member:* Fairfax County Bar Association; Trial Lawyers Association of Metropolitan Washington, D.C.; The Association of Trial Lawyers of America. Certified as a Civil Trial Advocate by the National Board of Trial Advocacy. ***REPORTED CASES:*** Wilson v. Good Humor Corporation, 757 F.2d 1293 (1985); El-Meswari v. Washington Gas Light, et al., 785 F.2d 483 (1986). ***PRACTICE AREAS:*** Personal Injury; Medical Malpractice; Products Liability; Premises Liability; Construction Liability; Nursing Home Liability. ***Email:*** tom@cadotag.com

OF COUNSEL

HENRY M. LLOYD, born New York, N.Y., March 11, 1935; admitted to bar, 1973, District of Columbia; 1982, U.S. Court of Appeals, Eleventh Circuit; 1984, U.S. Court of Appeals for the District of Columbia Circuit. *Education:* Cornell University (B.A., 1956); Balliol College, Oxford University, England (B.A., 1960; M.A., 1964); Georgetown University (J.D., 1973). Professorial Lecturer in Law, George Washington Law School, 1991—. Legislative Staff Coordinator, AID, Department of State, 1967-1968. Member, Editorial Board, The Washington Star, 1968-1970. Staff Director, Subcommittee on Asian and Pacific Affairs, House Foreign Affairs Committee, 1971-1973. *Member:* District of Columbia Bar; American Bar Association (Member, Sections of: Antitrust, Tort and Insurance Practice; Litigation); The Association of Trial Lawyers of America; Trial Lawyers Association of Metropolitan Washington, D.C.; The Counsellors. [LTJG, U.S. Naval Reserve, 1956-1958]. ***LANGUAGES:*** French. ***PRACTICE AREAS:*** Litigation; Antitrust.

CADWALADER, WICKERSHAM & TAFT

1201 F STREET, N.W., SUITE 1100
WASHINGTON, D.C. 20004
Telephone: 202-862-2200
Fax: 202-862-2400
Email: cwtinfo@cwt.com
URL: http://www.cadwalader.com

New York, N.Y. Office: 100 Maiden Lane, 10038. Telephone: 212-504-6000. Fax: 212-504-6666.

Charlotte, North Carolina Office: Suite 2400, 227 West Trade Street, 28202. Telephone: 704-348-5100. Fax: 704-348-5200.

London, England Office: Gracechurch House, First Floor, 55 Gracechurch Street, EC3V OEE. Telephone 0207-456-8500. Fax: 0207-456-8600.

Capital Markets, Securitization, Corporate Law, Real Estate, Securities, Mergers, Acquisitions and Divestitures, Litigation, Finance, Project Finance, Bankruptcy, Banks and Banking, Taxation, Trusts and Estates, Health Care, Environmental Law, Nonprofit Charitable Organizations, Employee Benefits.

MEMBERS OF FIRM

FREDERICK R. ANDERSON, admitted to bar, 1969, District of Columbia; U.S. Court of Appeals, District of Columbia Circuit; 1986, U.S. Supreme Court; 1999, U.S. District Court, District of Columbia and U.S. Court of Appeals, Ninth Circuit. *Education:* University of North Carolina (B.A., summa cum laude, 1963); Oxford University, Oxford, England (B.A., Jurisp., 1965); Harvard University (J.D., 1968). Board Chairman, Center for International Environmental Law, 1991—. Member, Commission on Life Sciences, National Academy of Sciences, 1995—. Member, Harvard Group on Risk Management Reform, 1994-1996. Author: "Environmental Protection: Law and Policy," Little, Brown & Co., 1984, 2nd Ed., 1990, 3d Ed., 1999. Dean and Ann Loeb Bronfman Professor of Law, American University, 1985-1990. Professor of Law, University of Utah, 1980-1985. President, Environmental Law Institute, 1970-1980, Chairman, Advisory Council, 1992-1994. Chairman, Advisory Working Group, U.S. Sentencing Commission, 1992-1994. Member, Panel on Science, Technology and Law, National Academy of Sciences, 2000—. *Member:* American Bar Association (Member and Chairman, 1972-1984, Standing Committee on Environmental Law; Chairman, Commission on Inter-American Affairs, 1986-1989). ***PRACTICE AREAS:*** Environmental Law; Natural Resources; Administrative Law; Government; Technology and Science. ***Email:*** fred.anderson@cwt.com

JOSEPH J. ANDREW, born Indianapolis, Indiana, March 1, 1960; admitted to bar, 1985, Indiana, U.S. District Court, Southern and Northern Districts of Indiana and U.S. Court of Appeals, Seventh Circuit (Not admitted in District of Columbia). *Education:* Yale University (B.A., magna cum laude, 1982; J.D., 1985). Scholar of the House, 1982. Member, Board of Directors, Yale Moot Court Society, 1984-1985. Law Clerk to Hon. Judge Joel M. Flaum, U.S. Court of Appeals, Seventh Circuit, 1985-1986. Deputy Secretary, State of Indiana, 1989-1991. National Chairman, The Democratic National Committee, 1999-2001. *Member:* Indianapolis, Indiana State and American Bar Associations. (Also at New York, New York Office). ***PRACTICE AREAS:*** Corporate; Government Affairs; Intellectual Property Law. ***Email:*** joe.andrew@cwt.com

RAYMOND BANOUN, born June 1, 1945; admitted to bar, 1968, District of Columbia; 1980, U.S. Supreme Court. *Education:* City College of New York (B.A., 1965); George Washington University (J.D., with honors, 1968). Assistant U.S. Attorney, District of Columbia, 1970-84. Deputy Chief and Acting Chief, Fraud Division, 1981-83. Senior Litigation Counsel, 1983-84. Special Assistant to the U.S. Attorney, Central District of California, 1977-80. Clerk, The Honorable Harold H. Greene, Chief Judge, Superior Court for the District of Columbia, 1968-70. *Member:* American (Vice Chairman, 1985-1986 and Chairman, 1986-1988, Business Fraud Crime Committee, Criminal Justice Section; Member, Council of Criminal Justice, 1988-1991) and International (Vice-Chairman, 1986-1992 and Chairman, 1993-1997, Business Crimes Committee, Section of Business Law) Bar Associations. Fellow, American College of Trial Lawyers. ***PRACTICE AREAS:*** White Collar Fraud; Civil Litigation; Criminal Law; SEC Enforcement. ***Email:*** ray.banoun@cwt.com

CHARLES E. BRYAN, born Jackson, Tennessee, November 9, 1946; admitted to bar, 1975, New York, U.S. District Court, Southern District of New York and U.S. Court of Appeals, Second Circuit; 1988, District of Columbia. *Education:* University of Virginia (B.A., with highest distinction, 1970); Yale University (J.D., 1974). Phi Beta Kappa. *Member:* The District of Columbia Bar. ***PRACTICE AREAS:*** Securitization; Corporate Finance; Securities Offerings. ***Email:*** charlie.bryan@cwt.com

JAMES P. CARROLL, born Washington, D.C., August 22, 1952; admitted to bar, 1977, Maryland; 1978, District of Columbia, U.S. District Court for the District of Columbia and U.S. Court of Appeals, District of Columbia Circuit; 1996, North Carolina. *Education:* Georgetown University (B.A., with honors, 1974); Catholic University of America (J.D., with honors, 1977). Legal Adjunct Professor of Law, George Washington University, 1985-1997. *Member:* American Bar Association (Member, Real Estate and Probate Section; Vice Chairman, Real Estate Securitization Committee). (Also in Charlotte, North Carolina Office). ***PRACTICE AREAS:*** Real Estate Finance; Real Estate Secured Lending; Real Estate Securities. ***Email:*** james.carroll@cwt.com

DIANA R. DE BRITO, born New York, N.Y., November 16, 1957; admitted to bar, 1984, New York; 1986, District of Columbia. *Education:* Yale University (B.A., cum laude, 1979); Georgetown University (J.D., 1983). *Member:* American Bar Association (Member, Section of Business Law, 1987—); The District of Columbia Bar; Association of the Bar of the City of New York. ***PRACTICE AREAS:*** Corporate Law; Securities; Finance; Joint Ventures; Business Acquisitions. ***Email:*** diana.debrito@cwt.com

MARK C. ELLENBERG, born Monticello, New York, March 22, 1950; admitted to bar, 1975, District of Columbia; 1979, U.S. Supreme Court. *Education:* Cornell University (B.S., 1972); Georgetown University (J.D., 1975). Research Editor, Georgetown Law Journal, 1974-1975. Law Clerk to Hon. Thomas A. Flannery, Judge, U.S. District Court for the District of Columbia, 1975-1976. Adjunct Professor, Georgetown University Law Center, 1993—. *Member:* The District of Columbia Bar; American Bar Association. ***PRACTICE AREAS:*** Insolvency; Complex Litigation. ***Email:*** mark.ellenbeg@cwt.com

MARK P. HOWE, born Boston, Massachusetts, October 11, 1955; admitted to bar, 1987, New York; 1990, District of Columbia. *Education:* Harvard University (A.B., cum laude, 1978); Yale University (M.A.R., 1981); Georgetown University (J.D., magna cum laude, 1984). Member, Georgetown University Law Review. ***PRACTICE AREAS:*** Corporate Tax Planning; Corporate Taxation; Federal Income Tax; Federal Taxation; Income Tax. ***Email:*** mark.howe@cwt.com

LAURENCE S. KIRSCH, born Washington, D.C., July 20, 1957; admitted to bar, 1982, District of Columbia; 1983, U.S. Court of Appeals, Third Circuit; 1985, U.S. District Court for the District of Columbia and U.S. Court of Appeals for the District of Columbia; 1987, U.S. Supreme Court; 1997, U.S. Court of Appeals, Fifth Circuit; 1997, U.S. Court of Appeals, Fifth Circuit. *Education:* University of Pennsylvania (B.A.S., summa cum laude, 1979; M.S., 1979); Harvard University (J.D., 1982). Phi Beta Kappa; Hexagon Society. Member, 1979-1982 and Managing Editor, 1981-1982, Harvard Environmental Law Review. Registered Environmental Assessor, California, 1989. Visiting Assistant Professor of Law, University of Bridgeport Law School, 1983-1984. *Member:* Federal and American (Member, Natural Resources Law Section) Bar Associations; The District of Columbia Bar (Member, Environmental and Natural Resources Section); Environmental Law Institute (Associate Member); Environmental Assessment Association; American Association for the Advancement of Science; Institute of Electrical and Electronics Engineers. ***PRACTICE AREAS:*** Environmental Law; Environmental Litigation; Environmental Bankruptcy. ***Email:*** laurence.kirsch@cwt.com

KENNETH KLEIN, born Albany, New York, July 26, 1951; admitted to bar, 1977, District of Columbia. *Education:* University of Delaware (B.A., magna cum laude, 1973); Rutgers University School of Law; University of Georgia (J.D., with honors, 1976); Georgetown University (M.L.T., 1980). Articles Editor, Georgia Journal of International and Comparative Law, 1975-1976. Associate Chief Counsel (Technical), IRS, 1988-1990. Attorney, Legislation and Regulations Division, Office of Chief Counsel, IRS, 1977-1981. Member, Board of Visitors, University of Georgia School of Law, 1992-1995. Member, Board of Trustees, 1994—, Secretary, 1996-1997, Treasurer, 1997-1999, and President, 1999—, The Langley School, McLean, VA. *Member:* American Bar Association (Taxation Section); American Society of International Law (Fellow, 1976-1977; Member: Executive Council, 1982-1984; Budget Committee, 1983-1993; Chairman, Budget Committee, 1990-1993; International Taxation Correspondent-International Legal Materials, 1985—); Maritime Law Association (Tax Sub-Committee on Marine Financing, 1990—). ***PRACTICE AREAS:*** International Taxation; Tax Planning; Tax Controversies. ***Email:*** ken.klein@cwt.com

EDWIN L. LYON, born Wichita, Kansas, April 14, 1947; admitted to bar, 1972, Missouri; 1976, District of Columbia. *Education:* Southwest Missouri State University (B.S., cum laude, 1969); Washington University (J.D., 1972). Staff Attorney, Securities and Exchange Commission, 1972-1975. Chief Counsel, Division of Trading and Markets, Commodity Futures Trading Commission, 1976-1977. *Member:* The District of Columbia Bar; The Missouri Bar; American Bar Association (Member, Committee on Regulation of Futures and Derivative Instruments, Business Law Section, 1976—). ***PRACTICE AREAS:*** Commodities Regulation; Investment Partnerships; Securities Offerings. ***Email:*** ed.lyon@cwt.com

DANIEL J. MULCAHY, born Auburn, New York, October 28, 1946; admitted to bar, 1972, New York; 1989, U.S. Tax Court; 1996, District of Columbia. *Education:* Syracuse University (A.B., cum laude, 1968); University of Virginia (J.D., 1971); New York University (LL.M., Taxation, 1977). Order of the Coif. Member, Virginia Law Review, 1969-1971. *Member:* American Bar Association (Member, Tax Section). ***PRACTICE AREAS:*** Federal Income Tax; Leveraged Leasing; Aircraft Financing and Leasing. ***Email:*** daniel.mulcahy@cwt.com

(This Listing Continued)

CADWALADER, WICKERSHAM & TAFT, Washington—Continued

DAVID F. WILLIAMS, born Washington, D.C., July 7, 1952; admitted to bar, 1979, District of Columbia; 1986, U.S. Supreme Court. *Education:* Yale University (B.A., cum laude, 1974); University of Virginia (J.D., 1979). *Member:* The District of Columbia Bar; American Bar Association (Co-Chair, Business Transactions and Bankruptcy Subcommittee of Environmental Litigation Committee, Litigation Section). ***PRACTICE AREAS:*** Complex Commercial Litigation; Environmental Litigation; Bankruptcy Litigation. ***Email:*** david.williams@cwt.com

SENIOR COUNSEL

ROBERT T. LASKY, born Philadelphia, Pennsylvania, May 30, 1942; admitted to bar, 1967, Pennsylvania; 1969, District of Columbia. *Education:* Franklin & Marshall College (B.A., magna cum laude, 1964); University of Pennsylvania (LL.B., magna cum laude, 1967). Order of the Coif; Phi Beta Kappa. Comment Editor, University of Pennsylvania Law Review, 1966-1967. Lecturer in Law, University of Pennsylvania Law School, 1971. Law Clerk to Justice Samuel J. Roberts, Supreme Court of Pennsylvania, 1967-1968. Law Clerk to Chief Justice Earl Warren, U.S. Supreme Court, 1968-1969. *Member:* The District of Columbia Bar. ***PRACTICE AREAS:*** Securitization; Structured Finance; Mortgage Securitization; Mortgage Backed Securities. ***Email:*** bob.lasky@cwt.com

COUNSEL

PETER M. DODSON, born Memphis, Tennessee, April 14, 1954; admitted to bar, 1980, Virginia; 1984, New York; 1985, District of Columbia and U.S. District Court, Southern and Eastern Districts of New York; 1991, U.S. District Court for the District of Columbia. *Education:* University of Virginia (B.A., magna cum laude, 1976; M.A., 1979; J.D., 1979; M.A., 1982; Ph.D., 1985). *Member:* The District of Columbia Bar; New York State Bar Association. ***PRACTICE AREAS:*** Bankruptcy; Bankruptcy Reorganization; Insolvency. ***Email:*** pdodson@cwt.com

SPECIAL COUNSEL

Charles H. Camp; William T. Christian (Not admitted in DC); ***Robert A. Davis, Jr.; Geraldine E. Edens; Joyce J. Gorman.***

SENIOR ATTORNEY

JONATHAN R. STONE, born New York, N.Y., May 7, 1950; admitted to bar, 1989, Maryland; 1990, District of Columbia. *Education:* Queens College, City University of New York (B.A., Archeology, 1973); University of Massachusetts (B.S., Geology, 1976); George Washington University National Law Center (J.D., 1989). ***PRACTICE AREAS:*** Environmental Law. ***Email:*** jstone@cwt.com

ASSOCIATES

Elizabeth E. Aherne; Cheryl D. Barnes; Stephen Chippendale; R. Campbell Connell; John Gutowski (Not admitted in DC); ***Gregg S. Jubin; Sophie A. Kozuch*** (Not admitted in DC); ***Deana A. Labriola*** (admission pending); ***Susan A. McCarter*** (Not admitted in DC); ***D. David Parr, Jr.; Mary Randolph Sargent; Danielle K. Stinemetz*** (Not admitted in DC).

(For data on other personnel see Professional Biographies at New York City).

CAHILL GORDON & REINDEL

Established in 1919

1990 K STREET, N.W.

WASHINGTON, D.C. 20006-1103

Telephone: 202-862-8900

Facsimile: 202-862-8958

New York, N.Y. Office: 80 Pine Street. Telephone: 212-701-3000.

London, England Office: Augustine House, 6A Austin Friars, London, England EC2N 2HA. Telephone: +44-20 7920 9800. Facsimile: +44-20 7920 9825.

General Practice.

RESIDENT PARTNER

DONALD J. MULVIHILL, born Staten Island, New York, September 25, 1931; admitted to bar, 1957, New York; 1961, District of Columbia. *Education:* University of Notre Dame (A.B., cum laude, 1953); Fordham University (LL.B., 1956). Editor-in-Chief, Fordham Law Review, 1955-1956. Task Force Co-Director, President's Commission on the Causes and Prevention of Violence, 1968-1970. Trustee, The Milton S. Eisenhower Foundation. ***Email:*** mulvid@cgrdc.com

(This Listing Continued)

COUNSEL

CORYDON B. DUNHAM, born Yonkers, New York, November 14, 1927; admitted to bar, 1951, New York; 1990, District of Columbia. *Education:* Bowdoin College (B.A., cum laude, 1948); Harvard University (LL.B., 1951). General Counsel, 1971-1988, Senior Counsel to the President, 1989 and Executive Vice President, 1976-1989, National Broadcasting Company, Inc. Member, Board of Directors, American Arbitration Association, 1982—. Member, Committee on Governance, Board of Directors, American Arbitration Association, 1995-1997. Member, Executive Committee, Board of Directors, American Arbitration Association, 1982-1994. Member, Board of Directors, American Corporate Counsel Association, 1983-1987. Chairman, Legal Committee of the Board of Governors of the New York Chapter of the National Academy of Television Arts and Sciences, 1997—. The Guest Scholar on Free Press and the Information Super Highway, Woodrow Wilson International Center for Scholars, Appointment Winter, 1995, Washington, DC. Author: *Fighting for the First Amendment, Stanton of CBS Versus Congress and the Nixon White House,* 1997, Greenwood Publishing Group, Inc.

SENIOR ATTORNEY

KIRSTEN EMIGHOLZ, born Syracuse, New York, January 20, 1949; admitted to bar, 1983, New Jersey; 1984, New York (Not admitted in District of Columbia). *Education:* Syracuse University (B.A., cum laude, 1970); Purdue University (M.S., 1975); Rutgers University (J.D., with honors, 1983). Editor, Rutgers Law Review, 1982-1983. ***Email:*** emighk@cgrdc.com

RESIDENT ASSOCIATES

BARBARA O. BRINCEFIELD, born Washington, D.C., August 14, 1952; admitted to bar, 1980, District of Columbia. *Education:* Smith College (A.B., 1974); George Washington University (J.D., 1980). ***Email:*** brincb@cgrdc.com

KATHY SILBERTHAU STROM, born Providence, Rhode Island, June 1, 1956; admitted to bar, 1982, New York; 1984, District of Columbia; 1990, Maryland. *Education:* Harvard University (A.B., 1978); New York University (J.D., 1981). ***Email:*** stromk@cgrdc.com

CAHN & SAMUELS, LLP

2000 P STREET, N.W., SUITE 200

WASHINGTON, D.C. 20036

Telephone: 202-331-8777

Fax: 202-331-3838

URL: http://www.pattmcopy.com

Rockville, Maryland Office: P.O. Box 5565.

Intellectual Property including procurement and protection of Patent, Trademark and Copyright, counseling and preparation of opinions, protection of trade secrets, litigation, International Patent Prosecution and Licensing, Patent Prosecution including Electrical, Mechanical, Medical, Biotechnology, Software, Business Methods, Electronic Commerce and Chemical.

FIRM PROFILE: The Firm provides Intellectual Property counsel to a wide variety of clients both foreign and domestic. The list includes Fortune 500 companies, government agencies (including the Armed Services), mechanical equipment manufacturers, toys and games producers, bulk vendors, e-commerce companies, high technology and biotechnology start-ups and regional small businesses.

MAURICE U. CAHN, born Rochester, New York, October 31, 1955; admitted to bar, 1982, Maryland; 1984, District of Columbia. *Education:* Lehigh University (B.A., 1977; M.S., in Organic Chemistry, 1979); Catholic University of America (J.D., 1982). *Member:* District of Columbia Bar; Montgomery County and American Bar Associations; Maryland State Bar Association, Inc.; American Intellectual Property Law Association; American Chemical Society. ***PRACTICE AREAS:*** Intellectual Property Law. ***Email:*** mucpatent@pattmcopy.com

FREDERICK N. SAMUELS, born Berkeley, California, June 13, 1963; admitted to bar, 1990, Maryland; 1992, District of Columbia. *Education:* Howard University; University of Maryland (B.S.E.E., 1986); George Washington University (J.D., 1990). Member, Washington Area Lawyers for the Arts. *Member:* The District of Columbia Bar; Maryland State and American Bar Associations; National Bar Association; American Intellectual Law Association. ***PRACTICE AREAS:*** Intellectual Property Law. ***Email:*** fsamuels@pattmcopy.com

GEORGE A. METZENTHIN, born Lincoln, Nebraska, November 28, 1969; admitted to bar, 1995, Ohio; 1996, Florida; 1998, District of Columbia; registered to practice before U.S. Patent and Trademark Office. *Education:* Case Western Reserve University (B.S.E.E., cum laude, 1992; J.D., 1995). Tau Beta Pi. *Member:* Ohio State and American Bar Associations; The Florida Bar; The

(This Listing Continued)

District of Columbia Bar; American Intellectual Property Association; Institute of Electrical and Electronics Engineers. ***PRACTICE AREAS:*** Intellectual Property Law. ***Email:*** gam@pattmcopy.com

WILLIAM J. BUNDREN, born Colorado Springs, Colorado, August 20, 1956; admitted to bar, 1983, Virginia; 1992, District of Columbia. *Education:* University of Tennessee at Knoxville (B.A., with high honors, 1978); Washington & Lee University (J.D., 1981); John's Hopkins University (M.S., Biotechnology, 1994). *Member:* District of Columbia Bar; Virginia State Bar; American Bar Association (Member, Intellectual Property Law Section); American Intellectual Property Law Association. ***PRACTICE AREAS:*** Intellectual Property Law. ***Email:*** wjbundren@pattmcopy.com

---

LAW OFFICES OF CYNTHIA THOMAS CALVERT, L.L.C.

WASHINGTON, D.C.

(See Ellicott City, Maryland)

Employment Law, representing Business Owners in Maryland and the District of Columbia.

CAMERON & HORNBOSTEL LLP

Established in 1972

SUITE 700
818 CONNECTICUT AVENUE, N.W.
WASHINGTON, D.C. 20006
Telephone: 202-293-4690
Cable Address: "Continent"
Telecopier: 202-293-1877
Email: lawyersdc@cameron-hornbostel.com
URL: http://www.Cameron-Hornbostel.com

New York, N.Y. Office: Suite 249, 866 United Nations Plaza. Telephone: 646-840-6666. Cable Address: "Continents, New York." Telecopier: 646-735-3759. Email: lawyersny@cameron-hornbostel.com.

International Law, Banking, Litigation, and General Practice.

FIRM PROFILE: Cameron & Hornbostel LLP, is an American law firm that specializes in representing foreign clients in the United States and U.S. clients in international transactions, regulatory proceedings and litigation. Established in 1972, the firm's practice areas include corporate law, banking, insurance and reinsurance, employment law, real estate law, investment and contracts, customs and international trade regulation, export finance, and corporate trademarks.

LAW FIRM ALLIANCES/ASSOCIATIONS: **LAW EUROPE**

MEMBERS OF FIRM

DUNCAN H. CAMERON, born Brandon, Manitoba, Canada, May 26, 1934; admitted to bar, 1959, New York; 1967, District of Columbia; 1970, U.S. Supreme Court. *Education:* Harvard University (B.A., cum laude, 1956); Columbia University (LL.B., 1959; Ph.D., 1965). Adjunct Professor of Law, Georgetown University Law Center, 1970-1980, 1989—. Visiting Professor of Law, Victoria University, New Zealand, 1986. Office of General Counsel, AID, Department of State, 1963-1967. Legal Advisor, USAID Mission to Dominican Republic, 1966—. Chairman, Board of Trustees, Pan American School of Agriculture, 1991-1997 (Board Member, 1986—). President, Chilean American Chamber of Commerce, Washington, D.C., 1992-1996 (Board Member, 1992—). Board Member, The Historical Society of Washington, D.C., 1998—. *Member:* The District of Columbia Bar; American Bar Associations. ***LANGUAGES:*** Spanish. ***PRACTICE AREAS:*** International Business Transactions; International Banking Law. ***Email:*** dcameron@cameron-hornbostel.com

MICHELE SHERMAN DAVENPORT, born Plattsburgh, New York, June 3, 1963; admitted to bar, 1989, New York, District of Columbia, U.S. Court of International Trade and U.S. Court of Appeals for the Federal Circuit; 2000, California and U.S. District Court, Central District of California; 2001, U.S. District Court, Southern District of New York. *Education:* Georgetown University (B.S.F.S., magna cum laude, 1985); University of Kent at Canterbury, England; Columbia University (J.D., 1988). Phi Beta Kappa. Harlan Fiske Stone Scholar. Managing Editor, Columbia Journal of Transnational Law, 1987-1988. ***PRACTICE AREAS:*** International Trade Regulation; Litigation. ***Email:*** msdavenport@cameron-hornbostel.com

LUIZ CLAUDIO DUARTE, born Rio de Janeiro-RJ, Brazil, December 16, 1954; admitted to bar, 1980, Brazil (Not admitted in District of Columbia). *Education:* Federal University of Rio de Janeiro, Brazil (J.D., 1980); University of Georgia (LL.M., 1997). Associate, King & Spalding, 1997-2000. ***LANGUAGES:*** Portuguese and Spanish. ***PRACTICE AREAS:*** Corporate L... International Business Transactions; International Trade. ***Email:*** lcduart... cameron-hornbostel.com

JIM TOM HAYNES, born Eagle Pass, Texas, June 4, 1943; admitted to b... 1968, Texas; 1970, New York; 1980, U.S. Supreme Court; 1981, District... Columbia and U.S. Court of Appeals for the District of Columbia Circu... *Education:* University of Hawaii; University of Texas at Austin (B.A., 196... LL.B., 1968); University of Rio de Janeiro, Brazil. Attorney, Office of Gener... Counsel, 1978-1979, Appellate Trial Attorney, 1979-1981, U.S. Immigratic... and Naturalization Service. *Member:* The District of Columbia Bar; State Bar o... Texas; New York State Bar Association; American Immigration Lawyers Association (Member, Board of Governors, 1985-1995). ***LANGUAGES:*** Portuguese and Spanish. ***PRACTICE AREAS:*** Immigration Law. ***Email:*** jthaynes@cameron-hornbostel.com

DEAN HOLBROOK, born New York, N.Y., March 7, 1935; admitted to bar, 1960, New York; 1962, U.S. District Court, Southern District of New York; 1973, U.S. Court of Appeals, Second Circuit and U.S. Supreme Court; 1998, U.S. Court of Appeals, Eleventh Circuit. *Education:* Princeton University, Woodrow Wilson School of Public and International Affairs (A.B., 1956); Yale Law School (J.D., 1959); New York University (LL.M., in Taxation, 1967). Phi Alpha Delta. (Also practicing as Cameron, Hornbostel & Holbrook LLP) (Resident, New York, N.Y. Office). ***PRACTICE AREAS:*** International Corporate Law; Taxation. ***Email:*** DeanHolbrook@aol.com

PETER A. HORNBOSTEL, born New York, N.Y., October 29, 1936; admitted to bar, 1962, New York; 1968, District of Columbia. *Education:* Brown University (B.A., magna cum laude, Phi Beta Kappa, 1958); Columbia University (J.D., 1961). Kent Scholar. Editor, Columbia Law Review, 1959-1961. University of Vienna, Austria, 1961-1962. Office of General Counsel, AID, Department of State, 1963-1965. Legal Advisor, USAID Mission to Brazil, 1965-1968. Adjunct Professor of Law, Georgetown University Law Center, 1993—. *Member:* The District of Columbia Bar; American Bar Association; Interamerican Bar Association; Brazilian American Chamber of Commerce. ***LANGUAGES:*** Portuguese, Spanish and German. ***PRACTICE AREAS:*** International Business Transactions; International Finance; Reinsurance. ***Email:*** phornbostel@cameron-hornbostel.com

STEPHEN L. HUMPHREY, born Washington, D.C., June 10, 1949; admitted to bar, 1974, Maryland; 1975, Virginia; 1978, District of Columbia; 1979, U.S. Supreme Court. *Education:* Wisconsin State University-Oshkosh (B.S., 1971); University of Louisville (J.D., cum laude, 1974). Member, Washington Foreign Law Society. Editor-in-Chief, University of Louisville Law Review, 1973-1974. Recipient: Carl Mann Scholarship; Louis D. Brandeis Scholar; Bernard Flexner Memorial Scholarship; American Jurisprudence Book Awards in Uniform Commercial Code, Constitutional Law and Federal Taxation. Law Clerk to Hon. Roszel C. Thomsen, Senior Judge, U.S. District Court, District of Maryland, 1974-1975. *Member:* District of Columbia Bar; Bar Association of the District of Columbia; Virginia and American (Section on: Intellectual Property Law) Bar Associations; Washington Law Society. ***PRACTICE AREAS:*** International Trade; International Project Finance; International Banking; Trademark Law; Technology Transfers; International Distribution Agreements. ***Email:*** shumphrey@cameron-hornbostel.com

WILLIAM K. INCE, born New York, N.Y., August 29, 1936; admitted to bar, 1962, District of Columbia; 1966, California; 1975, U.S. Court of International Trade; 1982, U.S. Court of Appeals for the Federal Circuit. *Education:* Princeton University (A.B., cum laude, 1959); Yale University (LL.B., 1962); New York University (LL.M., 1970). Co-Editor and Author, "Manual for the Practice of United States Import Law," Kluwer Law and Taxation Publishers, 1992. Chairman, International Trade and Customs Law Committee, 1974-1980 and Chairman, International Law Section, 1990-1992, Federal Bar Association. *Member:* The District of Columbia Bar; State Bar of California; Federal and American Bar Associations. [Lt., Law Specialist, U.S. Navy, 1962-1966]. ***PRACTICE AREAS:*** International Trade Law; Customs Law. ***Email:*** wince@cameron-hornbostel.com

DENNIS JAMES, JR., born Hackensack, New Jersey, March 28, 1945; admitted to bar, 1973, District of Columbia; U.S. Supreme Court; U.S. Court of International Trade and U.S. Court of Appeals, Federal Circuit. *Education:* Lafayette College (B.A., with distinction, 1967); Georgetown University Law Center (J.D., 1972). Phi Beta Theta. National History Honor Society. Visiting Professor of History and Law, Saigon University, 1974-1975. Editor, Doing Business in Vietnam, second edition, 1974. Binational Panelist, United States-Canada Free Trade Agreement, 1990-1992. *Member:* The District of Columbia Bar; American Bar Association (Member, International Law and Practice Section); Customs and International Trade Bar Association; Washington Foreign Law Society. [U.S. Army, 1968-1970]. ***PRACTICE AREAS:*** International Trade Law. ***Email:*** djames@cameron-hornbostel.com

ALEXANDER W. SIERCK, born New York, New York, December 15, 1940; admitted to bar, 1965, New York; 1968, District of Columbia and U.S. Supreme Court; 1981, U.S. Court of International Trade. *Education:* University of Virginia (B.A., 1962; LL.B., 1965). Adjunct Professor, Georgetown Univer-

(This Listing Continued)

(This Listing Continued)

CAMERON & HORNBOSTEL LLP, Washington—Continued

sity Law Center, 1998—. Director of Trade Policy, Antitrust Division, U.S. Department of Justice, 1978-1980. Member, Alumni Council, University of Virginia School of Law, 1995-1999. *Member:* The District of Columbia Bar (Chairman, International Law Division, 1979-1980; Member, Steering Committee, 1983-1985); American Bar Association; American Society of International Law. ***PRACTICE AREAS:*** International Trade Law; Antitrust Law; Federal Regulatory Law. ***Email:*** asierck@cameron-hornbostel.com

THOMAS SILBIGER, born Amsterdam, Netherlands, April 6, 1938; admitted to bar, 1963, New York. *Education:* Columbia University (B.S., 1959); Harvard University (LL.B., 1962); Leiden University Law School, Netherlands (Drs., 1963). Recipient, Fulbright Scholarship at Leiden University Law School, 1962-1963. President, 1988-1990, and Director, 1988—, The Finnish-American Chamber of Commerce, Inc., New York. Recipient, Knight First Class of the Order of the Lion of the Republic of Finland, January, 1993. Chairman, American Foundation for Suicide Prevention, 1997—. *Member:* The Association of the Bar of the City of New York (Member, Committees on: International Law, 1969-1973; Aeronautics, 1975-1978); American Bar Association; International Bar Association. (Resident, New York, N.Y. Office). ***PRACTICE AREAS:*** Corporate Law; Commercial Law; Technology Transfers. ***Email:*** tsilbiger@cmaeron-hornbostel.com

FREDERICK SIMPICH, born Washington, D.C., September 18, 1931; admitted to bar, 1961, District of Columbia. *Education:* Stanford University (A.B., with honors in History, 1954; LL.B., 1960). Member, Board of Editors, Stanford Law Review, 1959-1960. Special Assistant to Secretary of Commerce, 1965-1968; General Counsel, Department of Commerce, 1968-1969. *Member:* The District of Columbia Bar; American Bar Association. [Lieut., U.S. Army, 1955-1956]. ***LANGUAGES:*** French. ***PRACTICE AREAS:*** International Business Law; Commercial Real Estate; Insurance; Reinsurance; Nonprofit Organizations Law. ***Email:*** fsimpich@cameron-hornbostel.com

HOWARD L. VICKERY, born Washington, D.C., August 9, 1947; admitted to bar, 1975, California; 1978, District of Columbia; 1989, New York. *Education:* Swarthmore College (B.A., with honors, 1970); University of California at Berkeley (M.A., 1971); University of Chicago (J.D., 1975). (Resident, New York, N.Y. Office). ***LANGUAGES:*** Portuguese. ***PRACTICE AREAS:*** Commercial Litigation; International Business Transactions; Banking Law. ***Email:*** hvickery@cameron-hornbostel.com

ASSOCIATES

JAYNI L. EDELSTEIN, born Elgin, Illinois, December 14, 1965; admitted to bar, 1995, New York. *Education:* University of Wisconsin-Madison (B.A., 1988); New York Law School (J.D., 1992); Columbia University (LL.M., 1995). (Resident, New York, N.Y. Office). ***LANGUAGES:*** Spanish, French and Portuguese. ***Email:*** jedelstein@cameron-hornbostel.com

VALERIE ELLIS, born Miami, Florida, November 14, 1968; admitted to bar, 2001, District of Columbia. *Education:* American University (M.P.A., 1995); Tulane Law School (J.D., 1998). ***PRACTICE AREAS:*** International Trade; International Business Law. ***Email:*** vellis@cameron-hornbostel.com

ANA V. FARACH, born Tegucigalpa, Honduras, May 15, 1969; admitted to bar, 1998, District of Columbia. *Education:* Georgetown University (B.S.B.A., cum laude, 1991); George Washington University (J.D., 1997). Associate Attorney, Baker & Hostetler, LLP, 1997-2000. Legal Assistant, Inter-American Development Bank, 1991-1997. *Member:* District of Columbia Bar; American Bar Association. ***LANGUAGES:*** Spanish, French and Portuguese. ***PRACTICE AREAS:*** Corporate Law; International Business Transactions. ***Email:*** afarach@cameron-hornbostel.com

YONG LEE, born Taejon, South Korea, June 22, 1970; admitted to bar, 1998, Illinois and New York (Not admitted in District of Columbia). *Education:* Yale University (B.A., 1992); University of Michigan Law School (J.D., 1997). Executive Editor, Michigan Journal of Race & Law, 1996-1997. *Member:* New York State and Illinois State Bar Associations. ***LANGUAGES:*** Korean, French, Spanish. ***PRACTICE AREAS:*** Business Transactions; Litigation; International Trade. ***Email:*** ylee@cameron-hornbostel.com

MATTHEW J. MARTIN, born Greenwich, Connecticut, October 16, 1968; admitted to bar, 1999, New York. *Education:* Kenyon College (B.A., 1990); The New York Law School (J.D., 1998). *Member:* New York State Bar Association. (Resident, New York, N.Y. Office). ***PRACTICE AREAS:*** Corporate Law; Trusts and Estates; Taxation; Immigration Law. ***Email:*** mmartin@cameron-hornbostel.com

LUIZA TORRESAN WILSON, born Maringá-PR Brazil, March 8, 1971; admitted to bar, 1996, Brazil; 2001, New York (Not admitted in District of Columbia). *Education:* University of Sao Paulo, USP, Sao Paulo SP Brazil (LL.B., 1995); Georgetown University Law Center (LL.M., 1998). ***LANGUAGES:*** Portuguese, German, Spanish and Italian. ***PRACTICE AREAS:*** Project Finance; Litigation; International Trade. ***Email:*** lwilson@cameron-hornbostel.com

(This Listing Continued)

FOREIGN ATTORNEY

J. A. ANTUNES MACIEL, born Rio de Janeiro, Brazil, January 1, 1961; admitted to bar, 1984, Rio de Janeiro, Brazil (Not admitted in the United States) (Legal Consultant on the Laws of Brazil). *Education:* Pontifical Catholic University of Rio de Janeiro, Brazil (J.D., 1983); New York University (LL.M./M.C.J., 1988). General Counsel, Banco Fininvest S/A, 1983/1994. Allende & Brea - Tozzini & Freire, 1995/1996. New York University Alumni Association. (Resident, New York, N.Y. Office). ***LANGUAGES:*** Portuguese, Spanish, French. ***PRACTICE AREAS:*** Corporate Law; Banking Law; Contracts; Tax Law. ***Email:*** jmaciel@cameron-hornbostel.com

OF COUNSEL

BERTRAND J. DELANNEY (Resident, New York, N.Y. Office).

RICHARD C. KATZ (Also Member, DeConcini McDonald Yetwin & Lacy, P.C., Tucson, Arizona).

CAMERON MCKENNA LLP

2175 K STREET, N.W.
FIFTH FLOOR
WASHINGTON, D.C. 20037-1850
Telephone: 202-466-0060
Fax: 202-466-0077
Email: info@cmcklaw.com
URL: http://www.cmcklaw.com

CMS offices and associated offices worldwide: Berlin, Brussels, London, Paris, Utrecht, Vienna, Zurich, Aberdeen, Amsterdam, Amhem, Beijing, Belgrade, Bratislava, Bristol, Bucharest, Budapest, Buenos Aires, Cape Town, Casablanca, Chemnitz, Dresden, Dusseldorf, Frankfort, Hamburg, Hilversum, Hong Kong, Johannesburg, Leipzig, Lyon, Madrid, Moscow, Munich, New York, Prague, Singapore, Stuttgart, Toronto, and Warsaw.

Practice focuses on Energy, Infrastructure, Environmental, Transportation, Public Utilities, Administrative, Litigation, International Trade, Transactions and Finance, and also represents clients before federal regulatory agencies and related federal appellate courts.

FIRM PROFILE: Cameron McKenna LLP is an associate office of CMS Cameron McKenna, a full service international law firm with over 800 lawyers advising businesses, governments, public sector bodies and financial institutions in over 60 countries covering Europe, Asia, Africa, and North America. Cameron McKenna LLP is also a member of CMS, a transnational legal organization, consisting of 33 offices in 21 jurisdictions with over 1,400 lawyers, combining our international expertise with strong local legal knowledge in the world's business centers.

Law Firm Alliance: CMS. CMS Members include: CMS Cameron McKenna, CMS Bureau Francis Lefebvre, CMS Derks Star Busmann Hanotiau CMS Hasche Sigle Eschenlohr Peltzer Schafer, CMS Strommer Reich-Rohiwig Karasek Hainz and CMS von Erlach Klainguti Settler White.

PARTNERS

JOEL F. ZIPP, born Cleveland, Ohio, February 12, 1948; admitted to bar, 1975, Ohio; 1976, District of Columbia, U.S. Court of Appeals for the District of Columbia Circuit and U.S. Court of Appeals, Fifth Circuit; 1983, U.S. Supreme Court. *Education:* University of Wisconsin (B.S. with distinction, 1970; M.S., 1972); Case Western Reserve University (J.D., 1975). Author: "The King Can Do Wrong," 46 Cleveland Bar Journal No. 1, 1974; "The Impact of the Great Plains Coal Gasification Decision on Coal Gas Industry," Public Utilities Fortnightly, 1980; "Exports of Natural Gas From Canada," 4 Oil and Gas Analyst, 1982. Co-author: "Risks and Uncertainties In Commercial Development of Coal-Based Fuels," 4 Western New England Law Review, 1981. Notes Editor, Energy Law Journal, 1990-1998. Attorney, Federal Power Commission and Federal Energy Regulatory Commission, 1975-1979. Partner, Morley Caskin, 1980-1998. *Member:* District of Columbia Bar (Member, Foundation of the Energy Law Journal Board of Directors, 1999-2001); Energy Bar Association (Member, Board of Directors, 1993-1996; President, 2000-2001) and American Bar Associations. ***SPECIAL AGENCIES:*** Federal Energy Regulatory Commission. ***PRACTICE AREAS:*** Energy; Public Utilities; Energy Project Development; North American Energy Trade; Administrative Law. ***Email:*** jzipp@cmcklaw.com

GEORGE H. WILLIAMS, JR., born Philadelphia, Pennsylvania, June 8, 1947; admitted to bar, 1976, Maryland; 1978, District of Columbia; 1979, U.S. Court of Appeals for the District of Columbia Circuit and U.S. Court of Appeals, Eighth Circuit; 1981, U.S. Court of Appeals, Fifth and Eleventh Circuits; 1982, U.S. Court of Appeals, Ninth Circuit; 1983, U.S. Supreme Court. *Education:* University of Virginia (B.A., 1969); University of Baltimore (J.D., 1976). Casenote Editor, University of Baltimore Law Review, 1975-1976. Attorney: Federal Power Commission, 1973-1978; Office of the Solicitor, Federal

(This Listing Continued)

Energy Regulatory Commission, 1979-1982. *Member:* District of Columbia Bar; Maryland State, Federal Energy and American Bar Associations. ***PRACTICE AREAS:*** Energy Law; Public Utilities Law; Administrative Law; Appellate Practice. **Email:** gwilliams@cmcklaw.com

AMY S. KOCH, born 1956; admitted to bar, 1982, District of Columbia; 1984, U.S. Court of Appeals, District of Columbia Circuit; 1988, U.S. Court of Appeals, Ninth and Tenth Circuits. *Education:* University of Michigan (B.A., 1978); George Washington University (J.D., 1981). Partner, McKenna LLP, 1996-1997. Counsel, LeBoeuf, Lamb, Green & MacRae LLP, 1991-1996. Associate: Chadbourne & Parke, 1987-1991; Reid & Priest, 1981-1987. *Member:* District of Columbia Bar; Federal Energy Bar Association; International Hydropower Association. ***PRACTICE AREAS:*** Energy Competition; Energy Finance; Energy Project Development; Energy Regulation; Federal Energy Regulation; Hydroelectricity; Independent Power; International Energy Law. **Email:** akoch@cmcklaw.com

ANDRZEJ M. BLACH, born Katowice, Poland, January 17, 1959; admitted to bar, 1993, New York; 1997, Poland. *Education:* Warsaw University School of Law, Poland (LL.M., 1981; Ph.D. Law, 1989); Yale Law School (LL.M., 1991). Lecturer, Warsaw University School of Law, 1981-1989. Associate, White & Case, 1992-1997. ***LANGUAGES:*** Polish and German. ***PRACTICE AREAS:*** Energy Law; Corporate Law; International Law. **Email:** andrzejb@cmcklaw.com

COUNSEL

REINIER H. J. H. LOCK, born 1942; admitted to bar, 1973, California; 1974, England; 1979, District of Columbia. *Education:* Rhodes University, South Africa (B.Com., 1964; LL.B., 1966); Oxford University, Oxford, England (B.C.L., 1969); University of California (LL.M., 1977). Author: "The Canada/United States Pre-Trade Agreement and Trade in Energy," 9 Energy Law Journal 327, 1988; "Encouraging Decentralized Generation of Electricity: Implementation of the New Statutory Scheme," 2 Solar Law Rptr. 705, 1980; "Antitrust and Regulatory Issues in a Competitive Electric Industry," Utilities Policy, Volume 1, No. 3, April 1991; "The New Clean Air Act: Compliance and Opportunity," Public Utility Reports, 1991; "Ownership and Control of Transmission Facilities and Antitrust Law: The U.S. Experience," Utilities Law Review, Vol. 2, Issue 1, Spring 1991. *Member:* State Bar of California; The District of Columbia Bar; International Bar Association (Secretary, Section on Energy and Natural Resources Law); Energy Bar Association (Formerly Chairman, Committee on International Energy Transactions). **Email:** rlock@cmcklaw.com

JOHN J. BARTUS, born New York, New York, March 12, 1949; admitted to bar, 1975, District of Columbia and New York. *Education:* Manhattan College (B.S.E.E., 1971); St. John's University (J.D., 1974); Georgetown University (L.L.M, 1978). Tau Beta PI National Engineering Honor Fraternity; Eta Kapp NU National Electrical Engineering Honor Fraternity. Associate Editor, St. John's University Law Review, 1974. Attorney, Federal Power Commission, 1974-1975. Attorney, Federal Energy Regulator Commission, 1979-1999. Legal Advisor to Commissioner Anthony G. Sausa, 1988. Special Assistant, United States Attorney, District of Columbia, 1993. *Member:* District of Columbia Bar; New York State and Federal Energy Bar Associations. [United States Air Force JAG, Captain, 1975-1979; Colonel, USAFR.]. ***PRACTICE AREAS:*** Energy Law; Public Utilities Law; Administrative Law. **Email:** jbartus@cmcklaw.com

ROBERT C. PLATT, born Chicago, Illinois, July 27, 1951; admitted to bar, 1977, New York; 1978, District of Columbia. *Education:* Cornell University (A.B., cum laude with distinction, 1973; J.D., 1976). Assistant Advisory Counsel, Federal Energy Regulatory Commission, 1978-1984. Attorney, Mesa Petroleum Co., 1984-1986. Natural Gas Counsel, Independent Petroleum Association of America, 1986-1987. *Member:* The District of Columbia Bar; New York State Bar Association; Energy Bar Association. ***PRACTICE AREAS:*** Energy Law; Administrative Law. **Email:** rplatt@cmcklaw.com

LENA S. ZEZULIN, born Glen Cove, New York, 1955; admitted to bar, 1979, District of Columbia; 1980, U.S. District Court for the District of Columbia; 1984, U.S. Court of Appeals, Fourth and Eighth Circuits; 1985, U.S. Supreme Court. *Education:* Radcliffe College; Harvard University (B.A., cum laude, 1976; J.D., 1979). Phi Beta Kappa. Recipient, Gerda Richards Crosby Memorial Prize. Contributing Author: "Employee Benefits Law," American Bar Association Section of Labor and Employment Law, 1991. Senior Manager, Price Waterhouse LLP, Moscow, Russia, 1997. Project Associate, Harvard Institute for International Development, Legal Reform Project, Moscow, Russia, 1995-1997. Partner, Slevin & Hart, P.C., 1991-1995. Thomas Hart & Associates, (Partner, 1987-1991; Associate, 1983-1987). Associate, Lippman & Hart, 1982-1983. Associate, Marshall, Bratter, Greene, Allison & Tucker, 1979-1982. *Member:* The District of Columbia Bar. ***LANGUAGES:*** Russian, French. ***PRACTICE AREAS:*** Employee Benefit Law; Employment Law; Non-Profit Organizations; International Law; Civil Litigation; Arbitration. **Email:** lzezulin@cmcklaw.com

SENIOR ASSOCIATES

BRIDGET SHAHAN, born Nashville, Tennessee, November 9, 1963; admitted to bar, 1993, Tennessee; 1996, District of Columbia and U.S. Court of Appeals for the District of Columbia. *Education:* Catholic University of America (B.S., 1986; J.D., 1992). Attorney: United Cities Gas Company, 1993-1995; Jenner & Block, 1996-1997. *Member:* District of Columbia Bar; Energy Bar Association. ***PRACTICE AREAS:*** Energy Law. **Email:** bshahan@cmcklaw.com

NONA S. PUCCIARIELLO, born Texas, 1964; admitted to bar, 1990, Texas; 1991, U.S. District Court, Southern District of Texas; 1998, England and Wales (Not admitted in District of Columbia). *Education:* University of Texas (B.B.A., 1987); Texas Tech University (J.D., 1990). *Member:* State Bar of Texas; The Law Society of England and Wales. ***PRACTICE AREAS:*** Energy; Project Finance. **Email:** nsp@cmck.com

ASSOCIATES

GUNNAR BIRGISSON, born Reykjavik, Iceland, February 2, 1964; admitted to bar, 1996, Maryland; 1998, District of Columbia; U.S. Court of Appeals for the District of Columbia and First and Fifth Circuits. *Education:* University of California, Berkeley (B.A., 1987; M.A., 1990); Duke University (J.D., 1996). *Member:* Maryland State and American Bar Associations; The District of Columbia Bar; Energy Bar Association. ***LANGUAGES:*** Icelandic. ***PRACTICE AREAS:*** Energy Law; Administrative Law; Appellate Practice; International Law. **Email:** gbirgisson@cmcklaw.com

MATTHEW E. ROSS, born New York, N.Y., March 27, 1971; admitted to bar, 1997, New York; 1999, District of Columbia. *Education:* Johns Hopkins University (B.A., 1993); Brooklyn Law School (J.D., 1996). International Business Law Fellowship. American Jurisprudence Award, Legal Writing. *Member:* District of Columbia Bar; New York State and American Bar Associations; Federal Energy Bar Association. ***LANGUAGES:*** French, Italian. ***PRACTICE AREAS:*** Energy Law; Public Utilities Law; Corporate Law; International Law. **Email:** mross@cmcklaw.com

JUDITH M. ANDRADE, born Providence, Rhode Island, October 17, 1973; admitted to bar, 1998, Massachusetts; 1999, New York and District of Columbia. *Education:* St. Joseph's University (B.A., 1995); Roger Williams University School of Law (J.D., 1998). *Member:* New York State and Federal Energy Bar Associations; The District of Columbia Bar. ***PRACTICE AREAS:*** Energy Utility Regulation; Gas Utility Regulation; Public Utility Rates.

Languages: English.

CAPLAN, BUCKNER & KOSTECKA, CHTD.

WASHINGTON, D.C.

(See Bethesda, Maryland)

General Practice with Emphasis on Civil, Commercial, Construction, Tax, Domestic and Personal Injury Litigation before all Federal and State Courts in Maryland, Virginia and the District of Columbia. Corporate and Individual Income Tax Planning, Estate and Gift Planning, Estate and Trust Administration, Pension and Profit Sharing, Plans, Employee Benefits, Business and Real Property Acquisition, Dispositions and Financing.

CAPLIN & DRYSDALE

CHARTERED

ONE THOMAS CIRCLE, N.W.

WASHINGTON, D.C. 20005

Telephone: 202-862-5000

Cable Address: "Capdale"

Telex: 904001 CAPL UR WSH

Fax: 202-429-3301

URL: http://www.caplindrysdale.com

New York, N.Y. Office: 399 Park Avenue, 36th Floor. Telephone: 212-319-7125. Fax: 212-644-6755.

Federal Tax Practice. Civil and Criminal Litigation, Corporations, Securities, International and Administrative Practice, Estate Planning.

FIRM PROFILE: Caplin & Drysdale was founded as a federal tax specialty firm in 1964 by Mortimer M. Caplin, Commissioner of Internal Revenue under Presidents Kennedy and Johnson. A substantial part of the firm's practice is now devoted to civil and criminal litigation in both state and federal courts. On the tax side, the firm assists individuals and corporations on a full range of domestic and international tax problems, including structuring business transactions, dealing with the Internal Revenue Service in tax controversies, designing employee benefit plans and executive compensation arrangements, and representing clients with an interest in tax legislation and Treasury regulations. Individual lawyers specialize in international tax, corporate tax, state and local tax, employee benefits, taxation of insurance companies and products, partnerships, leasing transactions, estate planning, and litigation of tax cases at the trial and appellate levels. Other lawyers in the firm specialize in representing foundations, public philanthropies and other

(This Listing Continued)

CAPLIN & DRYSDALE, CHARTERED, Washington—Continued

tax-exempt organizations. On the litigation side, the firm represents business entities and individuals in tax and other white collar prosecutions at all stages of the federal criminal process, both pre- and post-indictment. The civil litigation practice includes the representation of plaintiffs and defendants in litigation involving RICO, securities laws, ERISA, products liability, legal malpractice, forfeiture, bankruptcy, contract and other commercial disputes before courts, arbitration panels and regulatory agencies in the securities and banking areas. Recently, the firm added a political activity practice group which advises clients on compliance with federal, state, and local campaign finance and PAC laws, government ethics requirements, lobbying registration, and related government affairs issues. The group also represents clients in FEC proceedings and civil or criminal litigation arising from political activities.

MORTIMER M. CAPLIN, born New York, N.Y., July 11, 1916; admitted to bar, 1941, Virginia; 1942, New York; 1964, District of Columbia. *Education:* University of Virginia (B.S., 1937; LL.B., 1940); New York University (J.S.D., 1953). Phi Beta Kappa; Order of the Coif; Phi Delta Phi. Editor-in-Chief, Virginia Law Review, 1939-1940. Professor of Law, 1950-1961; Visiting Professor, 1965-1987; Professor Emeritus, 1988, University of Virginia. Commissioner of Internal Revenue, U.S. Treasury Department, 1961-1964. Board of Visitors, University of Virginia, 1992-1997. Board of Trustees, George Washington, 1966-1992. *Member:* Federal and American (Member: House of Delegates, 1980-1992; Standing Committee on Federal Judiciary, 1993-1997; ALI-ABA Committee on Continuing Professional Education) Bar Associations; American Law Institute. Fellow: American Bar Foundation; American College of Tax Counsel; American Tax Policy Institute. ***REPORTED CASES:*** Holywell Corp. vs. Smith, 503 U.S. 47 (1992); United States vs. Tenzer, 127 F3d 222 (2d Cir. 1997). ***PRACTICE AREAS:*** Federal Tax Law; Tax Controversies; Tax Procedure; Corporate Law. ***Email:*** mmc@capdale.com

DOUGLAS D. DRYSDALE, born Philadelphia, Pennsylvania, August 9, 1924; admitted to bar, 1952, Virginia; 1964, District of Columbia. *Education:* University of Virginia (B.A., 1944; LL.B., 1953). Phi Delta Phi; Order of the Coif; Phi Beta Kappa. Lecturer in Taxation, University of Virginia Law School, 1960-1981. *Member:* The District of Columbia Bar; Virginia State Bar; American Bar Association. ***Email:*** ddd@capdale.com

BERNARD S. BAILOR, born Lewistown, Pennsylvania, May 8, 1940; admitted to bar, 1970, Maryland; 1976, District of Columbia; 1987, New York. *Education:* St. Francis College (B.S., 1965); Georgetown University (J.D., 1970). Senior Trial Attorney, Criminal Section, Tax Division, U.S. Department of Justice, 1971-1977. *Member:* The District of Columbia Bar; Maryland State, American (Member, Committee on Discovery in Criminal Cases, Section of Criminal Justice, 1975-1976; Vice-Chairman, 1986-1988 and Chairman, 1988-1990, White Collar Crime Committee, Member, Council Criminal Justice Section, 1990—) and International Bar Associations; National Association of Criminal Defense Lawyers; Edward Bennett Williams Inn of Court (Master of the Bench); Wong Sun Society. ***PRACTICE AREAS:*** Criminal Litigation. ***Email:*** bsb@capdale.com

ROBERT A. BOISTURE, born Baton Rouge, Louisiana, October 22, 1952; admitted to bar, 1979, District of Columbia. *Education:* Princeton University (A.B., 1974); Oxford University, Oxford, England (B.A., 1976); Yale University (J.D., 1979). Phi Beta Kappa; Marshall Scholar. Co-Editor-in-Chief, Journal of Taxation of Exempt Organizations. Author: "Private Foundations and Choices in Giving," ALI-ABA Conference on Tax Exempt Organizations, November 1998; "Proposed Intermediate Sanctions Regulations," Journal of Taxation of Exempt Organizations, November 1998; "Current Developments in the Law of Tax-Exempt Charities," ALI-ABA Conference on Tax Exempt Organizations, November 1997; "Emphasis on Control by Exempt General Partners May Indicate Restrictive Rules on Joint Ventures," Journal of Taxation of Exempt Organizations, November/December 1997; "Intermediate Sanctions for Public Charities: Using the New Rules to Protect Your Clients and Protecting Your Clients from the New Rules," Virginia Conference on Federal Taxation, June 1997; "What the Law Allows—An Overview of the Laws that Govern What Foundations Can and Can't Do Regarding Involvement in the Public Policy Process," Foundation News, May/June 1997; "State Attorneys General's Legal Authority to Police the Sale of Nonprofit Hospitals and HMOs," Exempt Organization Tax Review, February 1996. Co-Chair, ALI-ABA Conference on Tax Exempt Charitable Organizations. Member, Board of Advisors, NYU National Center on Philanthrophy and the Law. *Member:* The District of Columbia Bar; American Bar Association (Member, Committee on Exempt Organizations, 1980—, Co-Chair, Committee on Partnerships and Joint Ventures, 1997; Member, Committee on Government Submissions, Taxation Section); American Health Lawyers Association. ***PRACTICE AREAS:*** Tax Exempt Organizations Law. ***Email:*** rab@capdale.com

HERMAN B. BOUMA, born Grand Rapids, Michigan, December 28, 1950; admitted to bar, 1979, Texas; 1991, U.S. Tax Court; 1993, District of Columbia. *Education:* Calvin College (B.A., 1972); University of Texas at Austin (J.D., with honors, 1979). Attorney, Legislation and Regulations Division (International Branch), Office of Chief Counsel, Internal Revenue Service, 1979-1983: Principal author of the final foreign tax credit regulations under sections 901/903; U.S. negotiator on income tax treaties with Sweden, Denmark, and The Netherlands Antilles; Recipient, Chief Counsel Award for Outstanding Performance. Author: *The U.S. Tax Code and Reality: Improving the Connection,* Tax Notes International (October 1999); *The Taxation of Foreign Income from 1909 to 1989: How a Tilted Playing Field Developed,* Tax Notes (June 1989, co-authored with William P. McClure); and *The Final Foreign Tax Credit Regulations,* Taxes--The Tax Magazine (August 1984). U.S. Tax Court, 1994-1997. *Member:* State Bar of Texas; District of Columbia Bar (Member, Taxation Section); American Bar Association (Member, Taxation Section); Federal Bar Association (Member, Taxation Section); International Fiscal Association, USA Branch; J. Edgar Murdock Inn of Court. ***REPORTED CASES:*** Exxon Corporation v. Commissioner, 113 T.C. No. 24 (1999); The Coca-Cola Company v. Commissioner, 106 T.C. 1 (1996). ***PRACTICE AREAS:*** International Taxation. ***Email:*** hbb@capdale.com

MILTON CERNY, born Cicero, Illinois, August 27, 1933; admitted to bar, 1988, Pennsylvania; 1989, District of Columbia. *Education:* American University (B.S., 1956); Washington College of Law of American University (J.D., 1959). Author: "Twenty Years History of Tax-Exempt Organizations (1972-1992)," Tax Notes, Special Supplement, November 4, 1992; "Your Day in Court: Actions, Options and Strategies During the Audit and/or Appeal," New York University, 20th Conference on Charitable Organizations, 1992; "Corporate Sponsorship Guidelines—Did IRS Fumble the Ball?" Tax Notes, Special Report, July 13, 1992; "IRS Intermediate Sanctions: How They Will Impact Colleges and Universities," The Journal of College University Law, Vol. 25, Number 4, Spring 1999; "Current Issues Involving Lobbying and Political Activities As They Effect Exempt Organizations," The Exempt Organizations Tax Review, Vol. 20, No. 3, June 1998; "Civil Society: A New Approach as East Meets West," Tax Notes International, Vol. 17, No. 10, September 1998; "The Heart of Europe—Government Seeks A New Role in the Emerging Civil Society," Tax Notes International, Vol. 17, No. 12, December 1998; "Private Foundations: A New Era," The Exempt Organizations Tax Review, Vol. 3, No. 7, June 1998; "U.S. Compensation for Deprivation of Rights: Justice Tax Would Be Justice Denied," Tax Notes International, December 1996. Lecturer: Georgetown University Law Center, Continuing Legal Education, 1984-1993; OECD Institutes, Ankara and Vienna; Practicing Law Institute, 1984-1989; New York University Institute on Federal Taxation, 1986-1993. Technical Advisor to the Assistant Commissioner, Exempt Organizations and Employee Plans, 1978-1984. Chief, Exempt Organizations Ruling Branch, 1985-1988. Member, Advisory Board: Exempt Organizations Tax Review; Journal of Taxation of Exempt Organizations; American University School of Law; Wesley Theological Seminary; REELI. *Member:* District of Columbia Bar (Co-Chair, Exempt Organizations Subcommittee on International Philanthrophy, 1985-1999); Pennsylvania and American (Co-Chair, Exempt Organizations Subcommittee on Private Foundations, 1993-1994; Chair, Legislative and Political Activities, 1992-1993; Project on Central and Eastern European Law Initiative) Bar Associations. ***LANGUAGES:*** Czechoslovakian. ***PRACTICE AREAS:*** Tax Law; Non-Profit Organizations Law; International Law. ***Email:*** mc@capdale.com

JULIE W. DAVIS, born Washington, D.C., May 27, 1940; admitted to bar, 1980, District of Columbia; 1981, Maryland. *Education:* Duke University (B.A., 1962); Georgetown University (J.D., magna cum laude, 1980; LL.M., Tax, 1984). Editor, Georgetown Law Journal, 1979-1980. Adjunct Professor, Georgetown University Law Center Graduate, LL.M. Tax Program, 1994—. *Member:* The District of Columbia Bar; Maryland State and American (Member, Sections on: Taxation; Litigation; Co-Chair, Tax Litigation Committee) Bar Associations; Women's Bar Association of the District of Columbia. ***PRACTICE AREAS:*** Federal Tax Controversies and Litigation; Health Care Taxation; Estate Planning. ***Email:*** jwd@capdale.com

MICHAEL DORAN, born Steubenville, Ohio, February 15, 1966; admitted to bar, 1993, Pennsylvania; 1995, District of Columbia. *Education:* Wesleyan University (B.A., 1988); Yale University (J.D., 1991). Phi Beta Kappa. Law Clerk to Hon. I. Leo Glasser, U.S. District Court, Eastern District of New York, 1991-1992. *Member:* District of Columbia Bar; American Bar Association. ***PRACTICE AREAS:*** Employee Benefits; Taxation. ***Email:*** mtd@capdale.com

NATHAN D. FINCH, born Roanoke, Virginia, August 11, 1967; admitted to bar, 1992, Virginia; 1993, District of Columbia; 1994, U.S. District Court, Eastern District of Virginia; 1996, U.S. District Court for the District of Columbia; 1998, U.S. Court of Appeals, Tenth Circuit. *Education:* University of Virginia (B.A., 1989; J.D., 1992). Order of the Coif. Member, University of Virginia Law Review. Law Clerk, The Honorable Bernard G. Barrow, Court of Appeals of Virginia, 1992-1993. ***PRACTICE AREAS:*** Commercial Litigation; Civil Litigation; Criminal Litigation; Tax Litigation. ***Email:*** ndf@capdale.com

MATTHEW W. FRANK, born St. Louis, Missouri, January 15, 1962; admitted to bar, 1987, Pennsylvania; 1988, District of Columbia; 1991, California. *Education:* Swarthmore College (B.A., 1982); University of Michigan (J.D., magna cum laude, 1986). Order of the Coif. Articles Editor, Michigan

(This Listing Continued)

Law Review, 1985-1986. Co-Author: with David Rosenbloom, "Transfers Between Commonly Controlled Persons," CCH Federal Tax Service. Law Clerk to Hon. Louis F. Oberdorfer, U.S. District Court for the District of Columbia, 1986-1987. Assistant U.S. Attorney, Criminal Division, Central District of California, 1990-1993. Recipient, John Marshall Award for Trial of Litigation, 1994. Teaching: Adjunct Professor: Georgetown University Law Center, 1997; University of Iowa College of Law, 1997, 1998; University of Michigan Law School, 1996, 1998. Columnist, CCH Journal of Global Transfer Pricing. ***PRACTICE AREAS:*** Tax Litigation; General Tax. ***Email:*** mwf@capdale.com

SETH M. GREEN, born Washington, D.C., September 5, 1967; admitted to bar, 1991, Maryland; 1992, District of Columbia. *Education:* Harvard University (A.B., 1988); University of Maryland School of Law (J.D., 1991); New York University (LL.M., 1992). Associate Tax Legislative Counsel, Office of Tax Policy, U.S. Department of Treasury, 1994-1998. ***PRACTICE AREAS:*** Federal Income Taxation; Corporate Tax; Partnership Tax. ***Email:*** smg@capdale.com

JESSICA L. KATZ, born Washington, D.C., September 9, 1966; admitted to bar, 1993, Pennsylvania; 1994, District of Columbia. *Education:* Princeton University (B.S.E., 1988); University of Bristol, Bristol, England; Columbia University (J.D., 1992). Tau Beta Pi. Member, Columbia University Law Review. Law Clerk, Stephen F. Williams, U.S. Court of Appeals for the District of Columbia Circuit, 1992-1993. *Member:* District of Columbia Bar (Member, Tax Section); American Bar Association (Member, Section on Taxation). ***PRACTICE AREAS:*** Tax Law. ***Email:*** jlk@capdale.com

BETH SHAPIRO KAUFMAN, born Phoenix, Arizona, May 18, 1959; admitted to bar, 1985, Massachusetts and District of Columbia; 1991, Maryland. *Education:* Pomona College (B.A., cum laude, 1981); Harvard University (J.D., 1984). Member, 1982-1984 and Notes Editor, 1983-1984, Harvard Law Review. Associate Professorial Lecturer in Law, George Washington University, National Law Center, 1988-1990. Law Clerk to Chief Judge Spottswood W. Robinson, III, U.S. Court of Appeals for the District of Columbia Circuit, 1984-1985. *Member:* The District of Columbia Bar; American Bar Association (Member, Section of Federal Tax Practice, Real Property, Probate and Trust Law). ***PRACTICE AREAS:*** Estate Planning. ***Email:*** bsk@capdale.com

ALBERT G. LAUBER, JR., born Bronxville, New York, January 1, 1950; admitted to bar, 1977, Connecticut; 1978, District of Columbia; 1982, U.S. Supreme Court. *Education:* Yale College (B.A., summa cum laude, 1971); Clare College, Cambridge University, Cambridge, England (M.A., 1974); Yale University (J.D., 1977). Phi Beta Kappa. Woodrow Wilson Fellow. Mellon Fellow. Note Editor, Yale Law Journal, 1976-1977. Law Clerk to: Hon. Malcolm R. Wilkey, U.S. Court of Appeals for the District of Columbia Circuit, 1977-1978; Hon. Harry A. Blackmun, U.S. Supreme Court, 1978-1979. Tax Assistant to the Solicitor General, U.S. Department of Justice, 1983-1986. Deputy Solicitor General, U.S. Department of Justice, 1986-1987. Professorial Lecturer in Law, George Washington University Law School, 1983-1989. Lecturer in Law University of Virginia Law School, 1988-1990. *Member:* American Bar Association. ***Email:*** agl@capdale.com

PATRICIA G. LEWIS, born Philadelphia, Pennsylvania, January 8, 1945; admitted to bar, 1971, Massachusetts; 1972, District of Columbia; 1974, New York. *Education:* Wellesley College (B.A., 1966); Harvard University (M.B.A., with high distinction, 1971; J.D., cum laude, 1971). Professorial Lecturer, George Washington University Law School, Washington, D.C., 1980-1983. Commissioner's Advisory Group, Internal Revenue Service, 1994-1996. *Member:* The District of Columbia Bar (Chair, Taxation Section, 1992-1995; Chair, Employee Benefits Committee, Taxation Section, 1985-1989); American Bar Association (Member, Section of Taxation). ***PRACTICE AREAS:*** Federal Tax Practice. ***Email:*** pgl@capdale.com

CATHERINE E. LIVINGSTON, born Boston, Massachusetts, November 6, 1965; admitted to bar, 1992, Massachusetts and District of Columbia. *Education:* Yale University (B.A., summa cum laude, 1987; J.D., 1991). Law Clerk to Hon. Stanley Sporkin, U.S. District Court for the District of Columbia, 1991-1992. Attorney Advisor, 1994-1997, Associate Tax Legislative Counsel, 1997-1998 and Deputy Tax Legislative Counsel, Tax Legislation, 1998, Office of Tax Policy, U.S. Department of the Treasury. *Member:* District of Columbia Bar (Chair, Exempt Organizations Committee, Section on Taxation, 1999—); American Bar Association (Secretary, Exempt Organizations Committee, Section on Taxation, 1993-1995). ***PRACTICE AREAS:*** Tax; Non Profit Organizations. ***Email:*** cel@capdale.com

PETER VAN N. LOCKWOOD, born New York, N.Y., April 23, 1940; admitted to bar, 1968, District of Columbia; 1985, New York. *Education:* Harvard University (B.A., 1963; J.D., 1966). Member, Board of Editors, Harvard Law Review, 1964-1966. Supreme Court Note and Developments Editor, 1965-1966. Law Clerk to: Chief Judge Bailey Aldrich, U.S. Court of Appeals for the First Circuit, 1966-1967; Justice Thurgood Marshall, U.S. Supreme Court, 1967-1968. *Member:* The District of Columbia Bar; American Bar Association (Member, Sections of: Business Law; Litigation; Tort and Insurance Law). ***PRACTICE AREAS:*** Civil Litigation; Corporation Law; Securities Law. ***Email:*** pvnl@capdale.com

(This Listing Continued)

KENT A. MASON, born Washington, D.C., September 15, 1954; admitted to bar, 1981, Georgia; 1987, District of Columbia. *Education:* Amherst College (B.A., magna cum laude, 1976); University of Pennsylvania (J.D., magna cum laude, 1980). Phi Beta Kappa; Order of the Coif. Member, University of Pennsylvania Law Review, 1978-1980. Law Clerk to Hon. Phyllis A. Kravitch, U.S. Court of Appeals, Eleventh Circuit, 1980-1981. Attorney-Advisor, Office of the Tax Legislative Counsel, Treasury Department, 1984-1986. Legislation Attorney, Joint Committee on Taxation, U.S. Congress, 1986-1988. *Member:* American Bar Association (Former Chair, Subcommittee on New Welfare Benefit Legislation). ***PRACTICE AREAS:*** Employee Benefits Law. ***Email:*** kam@capdale.com

SCOTT D. MICHEL, born Beaumont, Texas, July 4, 1955; admitted to bar, 1981, District of Columbia; 1993, New York. *Education:* Northwestern University (B.S., with highest distinction, 1977); University of Virginia (J.D., 1980). Order of the Coif. Managing Board, Virginia Law Review, 1979-1980. Author: *Compelled Production of Documents and Testimony in Tax Examinations,* (BNA 1987). Law Clerk to the Honorable Joyce Hens Green, U.S. District Judge, District of Columbia, 1980-1981. *Member:* The District of Columbia Bar; American Bar Association (Chair, 1997-1999 and Vice Chair, 1995-1997, Committee on Civil and Criminal Tax Penalties, Tax Section; Member: Criminal Justice and Litigation Sections). ***PRACTICE AREAS:*** Criminal Litigation; Tax Litigation. ***Email:*** sdm@capdale.com

RALPH A. MUOIO, born New York, N.Y., October 12, 1932; admitted to bar, 1962, New York; 1965, District of Columbia. *Education:* Wharton School of Finance & Commerce, University of Pennsylvania (B.S., Econ., 1955); Harvard University (LL.B., 1961). Attorney, Tax Division, Department of Justice, 1961-1965. Professorial Lecturer, George Washington University Law School, 1975-1979. *Member:* The District of Columbia Bar; New York State and American Bar Associations. ***PRACTICE AREAS:*** Federal Tax Litigation. ***Email:*** ram@capdale.com

CONO R. NAMORATO, born Brooklyn, New York, July 2, 1942; admitted to bar, 1968, New York; 1969, District of Columbia. *Education:* Iona College (B.B.A., summa cum laude, 1963); Brooklyn Law School (J.D., 1968). Attorney, 1968-1975, Chief Criminal Section, 1975-1977 and Deputy Assistant Attorney General, 1977-1978, Tax Division, U.S. Department of Justice. *Member:* The District of Columbia Bar; American Bar Association (Member: Taxation Section; Chairman, Subcommittee on Criminal Tax Policy, 1991—; Co-Chairman, Committee on Complex Crimes, Litigation Section, 1986-1987; Chairman, Tax Litigation Committee, Litigation Section, 1988-1990; Co-Chairman, Committee on Federal Legislation, Litigation Section, 1991-1992). Fellow: American Bar Foundation. ***PRACTICE AREAS:*** Criminal Litigation. ***Email:*** crn@capdale.com

MARCUS SHERMAN OWENS, born Ft. Belvoir, Virginia, September 12, 1949; admitted to bar, 1974, Florida; 1976, U.S. Tax Court and U.S. Supreme Court (Not admitted in District of Columbia). *Education:* Florida State University (B.A., 1971); Duke University (J.D., 1974). Recipient: Internal Revenue Service Commissioner's, 1992 and Assistant Commissioner's, 2000, Awards for Exemplary Service. Tax Law Specialist, IRS, 1975--1990. Director, Exempt Organizations IRS, 1990-2000. Member, American Society of Association Executives. *Member:* American Bar Association. ***PRACTICE AREAS:*** Federal Taxation; Tax Exempt Organizations. ***Email:*** mso@capdale.com

TREVOR POTTER, born Chicago, Illinois, October 24, 1955; admitted to bar, 1983, Illinois; 1988, District of Columbia. *Education:* Harvard University (A.B., 1978); University of Virginia (J.D., 1982). Order of the Coif. Editor-in-Chief, Journal of International Law. Visiting Member, Lincoln College, Oxford University, 1995; Merrill Lecturer, University of Virginia School of Law, 1996. Special Assistant, Office of Legal Policy, U.S. Department of Justice, 1982-1983. Assistant General Counsel, Federal Communications Commission, 1983-1985. Former Commissioner and Chairman, Federal Election Commission, Appointed by President Bush in 1991, Served as Vice-Chair, 1993, and Chair, 1994. Elected Member, Administrative Law Section Council, 1995-1998; Chair, Section Committee on Election Law, 1993-1995, 2000—; Chair, Section Committee on Lobbying and the Legislative Process, 1998-2000; Member, ABA Standing Committee on Election Law, 2000. Editor: Brookings Institution Campaign Finance Web site, 1998—; Political Activity, Lobbying Laws and Gift Rules Guide (Glasser Legal Works, 1999). Director, The Reform Institute, 2001—. ***PRACTICE AREAS:*** Election, Campaign and Political Law. ***Email:*** tp@capdale.com

CHRISTOPHER S. RIZEK, born New Brunswick, New Jersey, November 24, 1956; admitted to bar, 1983, District of Columbia and Maryland. *Education:* Dartmouth College (A.B., 1979); Georgetown University Law Center (J.D., 1982; LL.M., Taxation, 1997). Trial Attorney: Tax Division, U.S. Justice Department, 1984-1988; Office of Tax Legislative Counsel, U.S. Treasury Department, 1995-1998. ***PRACTICE AREAS:*** Taxation; Litigation. ***Email:*** csr@capdale.com

DANIEL B. ROSENBAUM, born Brooklyn, New York, January 14, 1944; admitted to bar, 1969, New York; 1972, U.S. Supreme Court; 1973, District of Columbia. *Education:* Brooklyn College and City College of the City Univer-

(This Listing Continued)

CAPLIN & DRYSDALE, CHARTERED, Washington—Continued

sity of New York (B.B.A., cum laude, 1965); Stanford University (J.D., 1968). Adjunct Professor of Law, Georgetown University Law Center, 1976-1980. Attorney, U.S. Department of Justice, Tax Division, 1968-1972. ***PRACTICE AREAS:*** Federal Tax Practice; Tax Controversies; Corporate Tax Planning; Employment Tax. ***Email:*** dbr@capdale.com

H. DAVID ROSENBLOOM, born New York, N.Y., May 26, 1941; admitted to bar, 1967, New York; 1968, District of Columbia and U.S. Supreme Court. *Education:* Princeton University (A.B., 1962); University of Florence; Harvard University (J.D., 1966). President, Harvard Law Review, 1966. Lecturer: Harvard Law School, 1984-1987, 1990-1993, 1995-1996, 1999; Stanford Law School, 1988; Columbia Law School, 1997; University of Pennsylvania Law School, 1998; Public Finance Training Institute, Taiwan; Instituto Tecnologico Autonomo de Mexico. Special Assistant to Arthur J. Goldberg, U.S. Ambassador to United Nations, 1966-1967. Law Clerk, Abe Fortas, U.S. Supreme Court, 1967-1968. International Tax Counsel, U.S. Treasury Department, 1978-1981. *Member:* The District of Columbia Bar. ***LANGUAGES:*** French and Italian. ***PRACTICE AREAS:*** Federal Tax Practice. ***Email:*** hdr@capdale.com

JAMES E. SALLES, born New York, N.Y., February 16, 1960; admitted to bar, 1987, Georgia; 1988, District of Columbia. *Education:* Johns Hopkins University (B.A., 1983); Emory University (M.B.A.; J.D., with distinction, 1987); New York University (LL.M., 1988). Beta Gamma Sigma; Order of the Coif. Graduate Editor, Tax Law Review, 1987-1988. Managing Editor, Emory Law Journal, 1986-1987. Author/Co-Author: "The 'Ins' and 'Outs' - and 'Overs' and 'Unders' 0 of the New 'Global Netting' Rules for IRS Interest," 18 Tax Notes Int'l 1609 (1999), 83 Tax Notes 543 (1999); "IRS Issues Revenue Procedure on 'Global Netting' of Interest," Practical U.S./International Tas Strategies (April 20, 1999); "Navigating the Global Netting Rules," Practical U.S./International Tax Strategies (Dec. 10, 1998 and Jan. 12, 1999); "The Receipt of Property for Services After the TRA," 19 Tax Adviser 325 (1988); 302 T.M., Accounting Methods-General Principles (1990); "Tiptoeing Through the Minefield: Foreign Nationals Face a New Tax Environment in Dealing with U.S. Affiliates," Foreign Investment in the U.S. News and Analysis, Dec. 1990, at 13. *Member:* The District of Columbia Bar; State Bar of Georgia; American Bar Association. ***PRACTICE AREAS:*** Taxation Law. ***Email:*** jes@capdale.com

WALTER B. SLOCOMBE, born Albuquerque, New Mexico, September 25, 1941; admitted to bar, 1970, District of Columbia. *Education:* Princeton University (A.B., 1963); Harvard University (J.D., summa cum laude, 1968). Rhodes Scholar, Oxford University, 1963-1965. U.S. Department of Defense: Under Secretary of Defense for Policy, 1994-2001; Principal Deputy Under Secretary for Policy, 1993-1994; Deputy Under Secretary for Policy Planning, 1979-1981; Principal Deputy Assistant Secretary for International Security Affairs, 1977-1979. ***PRACTICE AREAS:*** Civil Litigation; Tax Exempt Organizations. ***Email:*** wbs@capdale.com

STAFFORD SMILEY, born White Plains, New York, August 14, 1948; admitted to bar, 1976, District of Columbia; 1986, New York. *Education:* Yale University (B.A., 1970); Harvard University (J.D., 1976). Editor, Harvard Journal on Legislation, 1975-1976. Adjunct Professor: The National Law Center, George Washington University, 1982-1988; Georgetown University Law Center, 1995—. Law Clerk to Judge Arnold Raum, U.S. Tax Court, 1976-1978. *Member:* The District of Columbia Bar; American Bar Association. ***PRACTICE AREAS:*** Federal Tax Practice; Estate Planning. ***Email:*** scs@capdale.com

TREVOR W. SWETT III, born Trieste, Italy, August 14, 1953; admitted to bar, 1982, District of Columbia; 1983, Maryland; 1998, New York. *Education:* Yale University (B.A., cum laude, 1974); University of Virginia (J.D., 1981). Order of the Coif. Executive Editor, Virginia Law Review, 1980-1981. Law Clerk to Honorable Harrison L. Winter, Chief Judge, U.S. Court of Appeals, Fourth Circuit, 1981-1982. *Member:* The District of Columbia Bar; Maryland State, New York State and American Bar Associations. Overseas Member: The Commercial Bar Association (London). ***PRACTICE AREAS:*** Commercial Litigation; Tax Litigation. ***Email:*** tws@capdale.com

RICHARD E. TIMBIE, born Winchester, Massachusetts, August 22, 1946; admitted to bar, 1973, District of Columbia; 1986, New York. *Education:* Stanford University (B.S., 1968; J.D., 1971). Order of the Coif. President, Stanford Law Review, 1970-1971. Adjunct Professor: Georgetown University Law Center, 1997—; George Washington University Law School, 1979-1981. Board of Advisors, New York University Institute on Federal Taxation, 1990-1997. Instructor, Organization for Economic Co-Operation and Development, International Taxation Training Programs. Special Mission Consultant, U.S. Department of the Treasury, Office of Technical Assistance, Regional Tax Advisor in Eastern Europe and the Former Soviet Union. Consultant, Harvard Institute for International Development, Russian Tax Reform Project. *Member:* The District of Columbia Bar; New York State and American (Member, Sections on Taxation and Litigation) Bar Associations. ***PRACTICE AREAS:*** Tax; International Taxation; Litigation. ***Email:*** ret@capdale.com

(This Listing Continued)

THOMAS A. TROYER, born Omaha, Nebraska, August 15, 1933; admitted to bar, 1958, Colorado; 1967, District of Columbia. *Education:* Harvard University (A.B., 1955); University of Michigan Law School (J.D., 1958). Phi Beta Kappa; Order of the Coif. Associate Editor, Michigan Law Review, 1957-1958. Attorney: Tax Division, Department of Justice, 1962-1964; Office of Tax Legislative Counsel, Treasury Department, 1964-1966. Associate Tax Legislative Counsel, 1966-1967. Professorial Lecturer, George Washington University Law School, 1970-1975. Adjunct Professor: Georgetown University Law Center, 1971-1977; Graduate Tax Programs, University of Miami Law School, 1978-1985. *Member:* The District of Columbia Bar; American Bar Association (Chairman, Committee on Exempt Organizations, Tax Section, 1973-1975; Chairman, Committee on Low-Income Taxpayer Assistance Program, Tax Section, 1976-1978; Chairman, Committee on Technical Review, 1980-1982; Council Director, Tax Section, 1982-1985; Vice-Chairman, Government Relations, Tax Section, 1989-1991); American Law Institute. Fellow: American Bar Foundation; American College of Tax Counsel; American Tax Policy Institute. ***PRACTICE AREAS:*** Federal Tax Practice; Tax Exempt Organizations; Charitable Foundations; Public Charities; Charitable Giving. ***Email:*** tat@capdale.com

DOUGLAS N. VARLEY, born Salisbury, Maryland, July 27, 1961; admitted to bar, 1994, Virginia; 1996, District of Columbia. *Education:* University of Virginia (B.A., 1983, J.D., 1994); University of Chicago (M.A., 1988). Phi Beta Kappa. *Member:* District of Columbia Bar. ***PRACTICE AREAS:*** Tax Exempt Organizations. ***Email:*** dnv@capdale.com

DAVID N. WEBSTER, born Providence, Rhode Island, March 31, 1934; admitted to bar, 1958, District of Columbia; 1994, Maryland. *Education:* Providence College (A.B., 1955); Georgetown University (J.D., 1958). Recipient, Georgetown Alumni Club, Alumni Achievement Award, 1976. Listed in The Best Lawyers in America. Adjunct Professor: Legal and Business Ethics, University of Virginia Law School, 1999; Criminal Law, Georgetown University Law Center, 1987-1990. Lecturer, Trial Practice, Catholic University School of Law, 1971-1974. Faculty, National Institute of Trial Advocacy, 1979-1985. Member: Judicial Conference, District of Columbia Circuit, 1975-1986; District of Columbia Court of Appeals, 1976-1992. *Member:* The District of Columbia Bar (Member, Legal Ethics Committee, 1978-1983); The Bar Association of the District of Columbia (Member, Board of Directors, 1972-1975; President, 1975-1976); American Bar Association (Member, Section on Litigation); The Barristers (President, 1990-1991); American Judicature Society; The Counselors; Washington Council of Lawyers. Fellow: American Bar Foundation. Fellow, American College of Trial Lawyers. ***PRACTICE AREAS:*** Airplane Crash Litigation; Arbitration; Breach of Contract; Business Torts; Class Actions; Complex Litigation; Defense of Legal Malpractice; Drug and Medical Device Litigation; Legal Ethics Law; Partnership Dissolutions; Products Liability; Securities Litigation; Toxic Torts; Wrongful Death Law. ***Email:*** dnw@capdale.com

OF COUNSEL

ANN C. McMILLAN, born Galax, Virginia, October 7, 1959; admitted to bar, 1984, California; 1988, District of Columbia. *Education:* University of Virginia (B.A., with distinction, 1981); University of California at Los Angeles (J.D., 1984). Editor, 1983-1984 and Member, 1982-1983, UCLA Law Review. *Member:* The District of Columbia Bar; State Bar of California; American Bar Association. ***PRACTICE AREAS:*** Securities (10%); Corporate (90%). ***Email:*** acm@capdale.com

REBECCA I. ROSENBERG, admitted to bar, 1992, Pennsylvania; 1993, Massachusetts; 1999, U.S. Tax Court (Not admitted in District of Columbia). *Education:* Bryn Mawr College (A.B. in Psychology, magna cum laude, with high honors, 1989); Harvard Law School (J.D., cum laude, 1992); Georgetown Law Center (LL.M. in Taxation, with distinction, 1998). *Member:* American Bar Association (Member, Tax Section). ***REPORTED CASES:*** Compaq Computer Corp. v. Commissioner, 113 TC 214 (1999); American Air Liquide, Inc. v. Commissioner, 116 TC No. 3 (V16/2001); Riggs v. Commissioner, TC Memo 2001-12. ***PRACTICE AREAS:*** International Tax; General Tax. ***Email:*** rir@capdale.com

---

JASON K. BORTZ, born November 17, 1969; admitted to bar, 1998, New York; 1999, District of Columbia. *Education:* Hamilton College (B.A., 1991); Cornell Law School (J.D., 1997). Editor, Cornell Law Review, 1995-1997. Law Clerk to Hon. James B. Loken, U.S. Court of Appeals, Eighth Circuit, 1997-1998. ***PRACTICE AREAS:*** Employee Benefits Law; Tax. ***Email:*** jkb@capdale.com

KIMBERLY N. BROWN, born Buffalo, New York, September 4, 1968; admitted to bar, 1994, California; 1995, District of Columbia. *Education:* Cornell University (B.A., magna cum laude, 1990); University of Michigan (J.D., cum laude, 1993). Phi Beta Kappa. Note Editor, Michigan Law Review, 1992-1993. Law Clerk, Honorable Charles R. Richey, U.S. District Court for the District of Columbia, 1994-1995. Associate Independent Counsel, Office of the

(This Listing Continued)

Independent Counsel Kenneth W. Starr, 1996-1997. Assistant U.S. Attorney, 1997-1999. *Member:* American Bar Association; Women's Bar Association of the District of Columbia. ***LANGUAGES:*** French. ***PRACTICE AREAS:*** Litigation. ***Email:*** knb@capdale.com

KRISTEN M. GURDIN, born Kingston, Pennsylvania, March 11, 1974; admitted to bar, 2000, Pennsylvania (Not admitted in District of Columbia). *Education:* Brown University (A.B., magna cum laude, 1996); Temple University (J.D., magna cum laude, 2000); Trinity College Dublin (M.Litt, 2000). Fulbright Fellowship to Republic of Ireland, 1996-1997. Author: "Letter Ruling Alert: PRI Possibilities in the Age of Venture Philanthropy: Foundation's Investment in Environmental Venture-Capital Fund Qualifies as Program-Related Investment," 33 Exempt Organization Tax Review, October 2001. ***PRACTICE AREAS:*** Taxation; Tax Exempt Organizations. ***Email:*** kmg@capdale.com

DIANA R. HARTSTEIN, born Pittsburgh, Pennsylvania, February 3, 1971; admitted to bar, 1998, New York; 1999, District of Columbia. *Education:* University of Maryland (B.S., magna cum laude, 1993); Columbia University (J.D., 1998). Harlan Fiske Stone Scholar. Certified Public Accountant, Maryland, 1993. ***PRACTICE AREAS:*** Election, Campaign and Political Law; Exempt Organizations.

BETH S. HELEMAN, born Vineland, New Jersey, September 8, 1971; admitted to bar, 1996, Pennsylvania; 1997, District of Columbia; 1998, U.S. Court of Claims. *Education:* Rutgers University at New Brunswick (B.A., with honors, 1993); University of Pennsylvania (J.D., cum laude, 1996). Member, Journal of Int'l Economics Law. *Member:* District of Columbia Bar. ***PRACTICE AREAS:*** Civil Litigation. ***Email:*** bsh@capdale.com

H. CARTER HOOD, born July 26, 1969; admitted to bar, 1998, Virginia; 1999, District of Columbia. *Education:* Harvard University (A.B., 1991; J.D., 1998); George Washington University (M.T., 1995). ***PRACTICE AREAS:*** Tax. ***Email:*** hch@capdale.com

KIRK L. JOWERS, born Salt Lake City, Utah, May 8, 1967; admitted to bar, 1995, Utah; 1997, District of Columbia. *Education:* University of Utah (B.S., magna cum laude, 1992); Harvard University (J.D., cum laude, 1995). Law Clerk to: the Hon. Stephen H. Anderson, 10th Circuit Court of Appeals, 1995-1996; the Hon. Dee V. Benson, Federal District Court of Utah, 1996-1997. ***PRACTICE AREAS:*** Election, Campaign and Political Law. ***Email:*** klj@capdale.com

WILLIAM M. KLIMON, born Harvey, Illinois, September 12, 1966; admitted to bar, 1998, Maryland; 1999, District of Columbia; 2000, Virginia. *Education:* University of Pennsylvania (B.A., 1987); Cornell University (1990-1992); University of Maryland (J.D., with honor, 1998). Phi Delta Phi. Order of the Coif. Sam Allen Memorial Prize. Editor in Chief, The Business Lawyer. Law Clerk to the Honorable Raymond G. Thieme, Jr., Maryland Court of Special Appeals, 1998-1999. *Member:* Maryland State and American Bar Associations. ***PRACTICE AREAS:*** Corporate; Mergers, Acquisitions and Divestitures; Financing; Franchising. ***Email:*** wmk@capdale.com

NEAL M. KOCHMAN, born Los Angeles, California, March 10, 1950; admitted to bar, 1996, District of Columbia; 1997, U.S. Tax Court. *Education:* Cornell University (B.S., 1972); Cornell University (M.I.E., 1973); Georgetown University (J.D., cum laude, 1996). Associate Editor, The Georgetown Law Journal. *Member:* District of Columbia Bar; American Bar Association (Member, Section of Taxation). ***PRACTICE AREAS:*** Tax. ***Email:*** nmk@capdale.com

KARIN J. LUNDELL, born Los Angeles, California, March 22, 1955; admitted to bar, 2000, New York (Not admitted in District of Columbia). *Education:* University of Paris, Paris, France (B.A., 1997); New York University School of Law (J.D., 1999; LL.M. in Taxation, 2001). *Member:* American Bar Association. ***LANGUAGES:*** French and Russian. ***PRACTICE AREAS:*** Tax Exempt Organizations; Taxation. ***Email:*** kjl@capdale.com

BRIAN R. LYNN, born Deratur, Georgia, May 31, 1974; (admission pending). *Education:* University of California at Santa Barbara (B.A., 1995); Harvard University (J.D., 2001). ***PRACTICE AREAS:*** Tax Law. ***Email:*** brl@capdale.com

LLOYD H. MAYER, born Toronto, Ontario, Canada, August 18, 1967; admitted to bar, 1994, Pennsylvania; 1996, District of Columbia. *Education:* Stanford University (A.B., 1989); Yale Law School (J.D., 1994). Business Editor, Yale Law and Policy Review. Law Clerk to Judge Lowell A. Reed, Jr., U.S. District Court, Eastern District of Pennsylvania. ***PRACTICE AREAS:*** Tax; Exempt Organizations. ***Email:*** lhm@capdale.com

---

THOMAS C. CARDARO & ASSOCIATES

WASHINGTON, D.C.

(See Baltimore)

Medical Malpractice, Personal Injury, Civil Practice.

CARLIN, BRADSHAW, THOMAS & YEATMAN L.L.P.

WASHINGTON, D.C.

(See Bethesda, Maryland)

Real Estate, Estate Planning, Wills, Trusts, Estate and Trust Administration, Wealth Preservation, Family Business Successions, Probate, Guardianships, Land Use, Banking and Business Law.

CARLINER, REMES AND MIRBAGHERI-SMITH, P.C.

SUITE 903
1700 K STREET, N.W.
WASHINGTON, D.C. 20006
Telephone: 202-223-0050
Fax: 202-223-0052
URL: http://www.carliner-remes.com
Email: info@carliner-remes.com
URL: http://www.lawyers.com/carliner-remeslaw

Immigration and Nationality Law. Administrative Law. International Law.

FIRM PROFILE: David Carliner, Robert A. Remes and Ladan Mirbagheri-Smith together have a total of 75 years of the most sophisticated immigration experience.

Supported by the efforts of associates, legal assistants, law clerks and staff, we can explain the complicated details of immigration law in at least seven languages. We are especially proud of our ability to explain the complexities of U.S. immigration law in terms that are understandable to everyone and at the same time are complete and accurate. We take as much time as necessary to answer all of your questions.

We can help develop strategies to get permanent residence for employees, family members or yourself through employment, family relationships, asylum or presence in the U.S. for over ten years. In many cases, we can avoid the time-consuming process of labor certification by showing that a skill, experience or qualification is in the national interest or reflects exceptional or extraordinary ability.

DAVID CARLINER, born Washington, D.C., August 13, 1918; admitted to bar, 1940, Virginia; 1946, District of Columbia; 1953, U.S. Supreme Court. *Education:* American University; University of Virginia and National University (LL.B., 1941). Author: "The Rights of Aliens," published by Avon Press, December, 1975, (Co-author), revised edition, Southern Illinois University Press, 1990. Chairman: Washington Chapter, 1956-1957; National Board, 1955-1979. Editor of Bulletin of Association of Immigration and Nationality Lawyers, 1955-1965. General Counsel, American Civil Liberties Union, 1976-1979. Chair, International Human Rights Law Group, 1980-1986. Lecturer, Immigration and Naturalization Law, Harvard University Law School, Spring, 1985. *Member:* The District of Columbia Bar (Member, Board of Governors, 1980-1983); Virginia State Bar; Federal (Chairman, Committee on Immigration and Naturalization, 1961-1962) and American (Member, 1954— and Chair, 1979-1983, Immigration and Nationality Committee, Administrative Law Section; Member, Coordinating Committee on Immigration Law, 1984-1989) Bar Associations; American Law Institute; American Immigration Lawyers Association (Member, Board of Governors, 1954-1980). ***PRACTICE AREAS:*** Immigration Law.

ROBERT A. REMES, born New York, N.Y., August 16, 1948; admitted to bar, 1973, Massachusetts; 1974, District of Columbia. *Education:* Cornell University (B.S., 1970); Boston University (J.D., 1973). Chairman, Washington Chapter, Association of Immigration and Nationality Lawyers, 1980-1981. *Member:* Massachusetts Bar Association; The District of Columbia Bar; American Immigration Lawyers Association. ***PRACTICE AREAS:*** Immigration and Naturalization; Visas; Political Asylum. ***Email:*** raremes@carliner-remes.com

LADAN MIRBAGHERI-SMITH, born Bloomington, Indiana, October 26, 1962; admitted to bar, 1987, Pennsylvania; 1990, District of Columbia. *Education:* Chatham College (B.A., magna cum laude, 1983); University of Pittsburgh (J.D., 1986). Phi Beta Kappa. *Member:* The District of Columbia Bar; American Immigration Lawyers Association. ***LANGUAGES:*** Farsi and French. ***PRACTICE AREAS:*** Immigration Law; Visas. ***Email:*** ladan@carliner-remes.com

REFERENCES: Bank of America, N.A.; Suntrust Bank.

CARLSMITH BALL LLP

A Limited Liability Law Partnership

Established in 1857

1201 PENNSYLVANIA AVENUE, N.W.

SUITE 300

WASHINGTON, D.C. 20004-2401

Telephone: 202-628-2228

Fax: 202-628-2071

Email: execdirector@carlsmith.com

URL: http://www.carlsmith.com

REVISERS OF THE HAWAII LAW DIGEST FOR THIS DIRECTORY

Honolulu, Hawaii Office: Suite 2200, Pacific Tower, 1001 Bishop Street. P.O. Box 656, 96809-0656. Telephone: 808-523-2500. Fax: 808-523-0842.

Kapolei, Hawaii Office: Suite 318, Kapolei Building, 1001 Kamokila Boulevard, 96707. Telephone: 808-523-2500. Fax: 808-674-0850.

Wailuku, Maui Hawaii Office: Suite 400, One Main Plaza, 2200 Main Street, P.O. Box 1086, 96793-1086. Telephone: 808-242-4535. Fax: 808-244-4974.

Kailua-Kona, Hawaii Office: Suite 209, 75-1000 Henry Street, 96740. Telephone: 808-329-6464. Fax: 808-329-9450.

Hilo, Hawaii Office: 121 Waianuenue Avenue, P.O. Box 686, 96721-0686. Telephone: 808-935-6644. Fax: 808-935-7975.

Hagatna, Guam Office: Suite 401, Bank of Hawaii Building, 134 West Soledad Avenue, P.O. Box BF, 96932-5027. Telephone: 671-472-6813. Fax: 671-477-4375. Telex: 721-6445 CWCMI GM.

Saipan, Commonwealth of the Northern Mariana Islands Office: Carlsmith Building, Capitol Hill, P.O. Box 5241, 96950-5241. Telephone: 670-322-3455. Fax: 670-322-3368.

Los Angeles, California Office: 9th Floor, 444 South Flower Street, 90071-2901. Telephone: 213-955-1200. Fax: 213-623-0032.

Admiralty & Maritime, Administrative, Banking & Finance, Corporate, Environmental, Foreign Investment Interests, Hospitality, Hotel, Resort & Entertainment, Immigration, International, Labor & Employment, Litigation and Dispute Resolution, Public Utilities, Real Property and Land Use, Tax, Trusts, and Compensation Planning, Latin America Trade & Investment, Pacific Rim Trade & Investment, Energy Development & Regulations, Health Care, Medicare/Medicaid Fraud & Abuse, Telecommunications, Class Action Defense, E-Commerce, Internet Law, Intellectual Property Litigation, Construction Law, Appellate Practice, Estate Planning, Commercial Leasing, Product Liability, Professional Liability, Bank Regulatory Enforcement, Antitrust, Election and Campaign Finance, Government Contracts, Legislative Lobbying, Media Law, Franchise Law, Tax-Exempt Organizations, Foreign Sales Corporation, Project Finance.

FIRM PROFILE: The law firm of Carlsmith Ball was established in 1857 in Hilo, Hawaii. The firm currently has 110 attorneys in ten offices located throughout Hawaii and in Guam, Saipan, Los Angeles, Washington, D.C. and Mexico City, Mexico.

Our firm assists businesses in solving problems or concerns that arise in the course of business operations. The attorneys in this firm concentrate exclusively in business law and have extensive experience with the industries in the Pacific Region. In addition, our Washington, D.C. office provides essential representation when our clients have needs at the federal level and assists the Guam and Saipan offices in territorial and commonwealth matters. Our clientele includes businesses from the construction, health care, retail, real estate, transportation, maritime, media, agricultural, education, tourism, entertainment, and finance industries, amongst others. Our understanding of the Pacific Region, including extensive foreign language capabilities, allows us to provide you a distinct combination of technical skills and practical experience to serve your legal and business needs.

With more than 140 years of successful practice, we identify and anticipate obstacles to business procedures and solve problems more rapidly than less experienced firms. Our attorneys have long-established working relationships with the regulators in our jurisdictions, making us knowledgeable of the internal, informal administrative practices of government agencies, and the political forces that affect their decision making outcomes. This means more cost-effective representation for our clients.

Our goals are to:

Assist you in developing a business structure which complements the operational and financial needs of your company.

Anticipate business issues which may affect your company and guide you in efficiently resolving any problems or obstacles that arise.

Develop options to enable you to avoid or minimize potential problems.

Provide a level of client service which will ensure that you return to Carlsmith Ball time and again and recommend our firm to others.

(This Listing Continued)

RESIDENT PARTNER

NANCY M. BECKNER, born Carlisle, Pennsylvania, December 22, 1944; admitted to bar, 1979, Hawaii; 1990, California; 1992, District of Columbia. *Education:* Wilson College and University of Maryland (B.A., with high honors, 1966); Washington College of Law and University of Hawaii (J.D., 1979). Recipient: American Jurisprudence Awards in Labor Law and Criminal Justice; Dean's Award for Scholastic Excellence. Former Chair, Foreign Tax Committee, Los Angeles County Bar Association. *Member:* The District of Columbia Bar (Taxation Section). ***PRACTICE AREAS:*** International Tax; International Estate Planning; Corporate and Partnership Tax; Tax Exempt Organizations. ***Email:*** nmb@carlsmith.com

REVISERS OF THE HAWAII LAW DIGEST FOR THIS DIRECTORY

(For Complete Biographical data on all Personnel, see Professional Biographies at Honolulu, Hawaii)

CARMEL & CARMEL, P.C.

4101 RIVER ROAD NW

WASHINGTON, D.C. 20016-4617

Telephone: 202-237-1700

Fax: 202-237-1701

URL: http://www.carmeldc.com

Email: info@carmeldc.com

URL: http://www.lawyers.com/carmel&carmel

Real Estate Development, Acquisition and Finance including Resort, Hotel and Land Development, Golf Course Development, Condominiums and Timeshare Communities, Information Technology, Regulatory Law, Computers and Software, Copyrights, Trademarks, Internet Law, Domain Name Disputes, E-Commerce Issues, Entertainment and Sports Law, Immigration, Representation of clients before HUD and the FTC, Americans With Disabilities Act, Employment Law, Private Offerings, Venture Capital, Acquisitions, Divestitures and Strategic Alliances and General Counseling for Emerging Technology Companies.

FIRM PROFILE: Originally established in 1928 by Percy Carmel (1901-1984) and Judge Macy Carmel (1912-1976), Carmel & Carmel is now best known for its representation of a national base of resort and recreational real estate developers in matters involving federal and multi-state regulation before HUD, the FTC and various state real estate commissions. This involves large planned unit developments with mixed-use projects ranging from lot sales to home sales condominiums and timeshare, hotel development and assisted living facilities for a broad range of companies. Additionally, the firm has particular experience in representing both existing companies in matters relating to technology and e-commerce as well as emerging technology companies in all stages of development.

Carmel & Carmel counsels clients whose business interests range from local to international. Their clients include: land developers; national homebuilders; construction companies; hospitality industry clients; financial institutions; a variety of internet and emerging technology companies; media enterprises; and many other companies, institutions and individuals.

FRANK J. CARMEL, born Hampton, Virginia, May 11, 1954; admitted to bar, 1979, District of Columbia; 1980, Virginia. *Education:* Virginia Polytechnic Institute and State University (B.A., with distinction, 1976); University of Virginia School of Law (J.D., 1979). Phi Kappa Phi. Real Estate Agent, Virginia, 1977. Licensed Private Pilot. Author: "Marketing Resort Properties on the Internet: Legal Implications," Developments, December 1996. Listed in the National Directory of Who's Who, 1998. *Member:* District of Columbia Bar; Virginia State Bar; Federal (Liaison Committee Officer) and American (Chair, Legal Aspects of Marketing Real Estate) Bar Associations. ***PRACTICE AREAS:*** Real Estate Development; Regulatory Law; Internet Law; Information Technology; Corporate Law. ***Email:*** fcarmel@carmeldc.com

CARR GOODSON, P.C.

1667 K STREET, N.W., SUITE 1100

WASHINGTON, D.C. 20006

Telephone: 202-310-5500

Telecopier: 202-310-5555

Email: (attorney initials)@carrgoodson.com

URL: http://www.carrgoodson.com

Vienna, Virginia Office: Tycon Towers, 8000 Towers Crescent Drive, Suite 1350, 22182. Telephone: 703-691-8818.

Baltimore, Maryland Office: 401 East Pratt Street, Suite 1622, The World Trade Center, 21202. Telephone: 410-752-1570.

Rockville, Maryland Office: 31 Wood Lane, 20850. Telephone: 301-424-7024.

(This Listing Continued)

Appellate, Business Transactions, Construction, Election, Employment and Labor, Environmental, Health Care, Insurance Coverage, Intellectual Property, Litigation (Commercial and Complex), Products Liability, Professional Liability, Tax, Technology, Toxic and Mass Tort, Trusts and Estates.

LAWRENCE E. CARR, JR., born Colorado Springs, Colorado, August 10, 1923; admitted to bar, 1949, Colorado; 1952, District of Columbia; 1961, Maryland. *Education:* University of Notre Dame (B.S., 1948; LL.B., 1949); George Washington University (LL.M., 1954). Member: Judicial Conference for the District of Columbia Circuit, 1970, 1975, 1976 and 1979-1982; Advisory Council, University of Notre Dame Law School, 1984—. *Member:* District of Columbia Bar; Bar Association of the District of Columbia (Member, Board of Directors, 1969-1971; Vice President, 1973-1974; President, 1974-1975; President, Research Foundation, 1985-1986); Maryland State and American (Member, House of Delegates, 1974-1975) Bar Associations; American Judicature Society; District of Columbia Defense Lawyers Association (President, 1978-1979); The Counselors. Fellow, American Bar Foundation. [Col., USMCR, (Ret.)]. ***PRACTICE AREAS:*** Litigation; Environmental; Insurance Coverage. ***Email:*** lec@carrgoodson.com

ROBERT W. GOODSON, born Washington, D.C., November 18, 1950; admitted to bar, 1976, Maryland; 1977, District of Columbia. *Education:* University of Notre Dame (A.B., cum laude, 1972; J.D., 1976). Law Clerk to the Hon. James H. Taylor, Associate Judge, Seventh Judicial Circuit of Maryland, 1976-1977. Member of Board of Directors, 1994-1998, Franklin Square Association, Chairman, 1997-1998. Board of Directors, Executive Committee, Washington Business Improvement District. *Member:* Maryland Association of Defense Trial Counsel; Defense Research Institute; American Inns of Court (Master of the Bench). (Also at Baltimore and Rockville, Maryland Offices). ***PRACTICE AREAS:*** Professional Liability; Health Care; Litigation. ***Email:*** rwg@carrgoodson.com

WILLIAM J. CARTER, born Baltimore, Maryland, September 1, 1949; admitted to bar, 1974, Virginia and Pennsylvania; 1975, U.S. Supreme Court; 1980, District of Columbia and Maryland. *Education:* Virginia Polytechnic Institute and State University (B.S., 1971); Marshall-Wythe School of Law, College of William & Mary (J.D., 1974). Phi Delta Phi. Member, Dean's Advisory Board, College of Arts & Sciences, Virginia Polytechnic Institute and State University, 1996—. Author: "Appellate Practice Handbook for Maryland, Virginia and the District of Columbia - Civil Cases," The Harrison Company, 1996. *Member:* The Counselors. [Capt., U.S. Army, JAGC, 1974-1979]. ***PRACTICE AREAS:*** Appellate; Litigation; Insurance Coverage. ***Email:*** wjc@carrgoodson.com

CATHERINE A. HANRAHAN, born Evergreen Park, Illinois, July 3, 1959; admitted to bar, 1985, Maryland; 1994, District of Columbia. *Education:* James Madison University (B.S., 1981); University of Baltimore (J.D., 1985). Law Clerk to Hon. G. R. Hovey Johnson, Prince George's County, Circuit Court, 1985-1986. Author: "Indoor Air Quality in the Office Environment: An Expanding Area of Toxic Tort Litigation," BNA Toxics Law Reporter, 1994. (Also at Baltimore and Rockville Maryland Offices). ***PRACTICE AREAS:*** Health Care; Products Liability. ***Email:*** cah@carrgoodson.com

PAUL J. MALONEY, born Washington, D.C., March 15, 1954; admitted to bar, 1982, District of Columbia and Maryland. *Education:* Washington & Lee University (B.A., cum laude, 1976); Catholic University of America (J.D., 1981). Law Clerk to the Hon. Joseph M. Hannon, Superior Court of the District of Columbia, 1981-1982. Prince George's County Assistant State's Attorney, 1982-1984. *Member:* District of Columbia Defense Lawyers (President, 1996); Defense Research Institute; American Board of Trial Advocates; Barristers. ***PRACTICE AREAS:*** Professional Liability; Products Liability. ***Email:*** pjm@carrgoodson.com

THOMAS L. McCALLY, born Bethesda, Maryland, January 28, 1959; admitted to bar, 1984, Georgia and Maryland; 1985, District of Columbia. *Education:* University of Delaware (B.A., cum laude, 1981); Emory University (J.D., 1984). Member, Order of the Barristers. Director-in-Chief, Emory Moot Court Society, 1983-1984. Member: National Appellate Advocacy Moot Court Team; Regional Champion and National Quarter Finalist, 1983. Law Clerk to the Honorable Richard B. Latham, Circuit Court, Montgomery County, Maryland, 1984-1985. Chair of the Civil Jury Instructions Committee, 1992—and Member of the Executive Committee for the Young Lawyers Section of the District of Columbia Bar, 1992-1995. *Member:* American Inns of Court. ***PRACTICE AREAS:*** Employment Law; Labor Law; Employee Benefits. ***Email:*** tlm@carrgoodson.com

KEVIN M. MURPHY, born Washington, D.C., July 17, 1959; admitted to bar, 1984, Maryland; 1985, District of Columbia. *Education:* University of Notre Dame (B.B.A., 1981); Catholic University of America, Columbus School of Law (J.D., 1984). Co-Author, "The Application of Daubert or Frye Analysis to Expert Testimony in the Soft Sciences," The Quarterly, Vol. 47, No. 3 (1997). *Member:* Maryland Association of Defense Trial Counsel (Executive Committee, 1997-1999); Defense Research Institute; Federation of Insurance and Corporate Counsel; American Intellectual Property Law Association. (Also at Baltimore and Rockville, Maryland Offices). ***PRACTICE AREAS:*** Products Liability; Intellectual Property; Professional Liability. ***Email:*** kmm@carrgoodson.com

JAN E. SIMONSEN, born New York, N.Y., March 22, 1960; admitted to bar, 1988, Virginia; 1989, District of Columbia. *Education:* Northeastern University (B.S., 1984); Vermont Law School (J.D., 1988). Law Clerk, Superior Court of the District of Columbia, 1988-1989. *Member:* District of Columbia Bar (Chairperson, Litigation Section, Steering Committee, 1992-1994); Bar Association of the District of Columbia; District of Columbia Defense Lawyers (Member, Board of Directors, 1997; Treasurer, 1998—); Defense Research Institute. ***PRACTICE AREAS:*** Litigation; Products Liability. ***Email:*** jes@carrgoodson.com

MARK M. JONES, born Louisville, Kentucky, March 3, 1957; admitted to bar, 1984, District of Columbia; 1994, Virginia. *Education:* Connecticut College (B.S., cum laude, 1979); University of Kentucky School of Law (J.D., 1984). *Member:* The District of Columbia Bar; Virginia State Bar; Defense Research Institute. ***PRACTICE AREAS:*** Insurance Defense; Medical Malpractice. ***Email:*** mmj@carrgoodson.com

SENIOR COUNSEL

SHADONNA E. HALE, born Takoma Park, Maryland, August 20, 1956; admitted to bar, 1990, Maryland; 1993, District of Columbia. *Education:* The American University (B.S.N., 1979); The Catholic University of America (M.S.N., 1983); University of Maryland (J.D., with honors, 1990). Sigma Theta Tau. Recipient: American Jurisprudence Prize Award (Evidence); John S. Strahorn, Jr., Memorial Prize (Evidence). Member, Moot Court Board. Law Clerk to the Honorable John N. Prevas, Baltimore City Circuit Court. Registered Nurse: Washington, D.C., 1977; Maryland, 1979. *Member:* Baltimore City and Maryland State Bar Associations; The District of Columbia Bar; Maryland Association of Defense Trial Counsel; Defense Research Institute; Maryland Society of Health Care Risk Managers. ***PRACTICE AREAS:*** Professional Liability; Health Care. ***Email:*** seh@carrgoodson.com

OF COUNSEL

EDWARD J. KRILL, born Milwaukee, Wisconsin, January 21, 1941; admitted to bar, 1966 Wisconsin; 1972, District of Columbia; 1993, Maryland. *Education:* Marquette University (A.B., 1963); Georgetown University (J.D., 1966). Founding Member, American Society of Hospital Attorneys. *Member:* National Health Lawyers Association. ***PRACTICE AREAS:*** Health Care; Employment Law; Labor Law. ***Email:*** ejk@carrgoodson.com

---

JUAN M. ANDERSON, born Washington, D.C., March 29, 1967; admitted to bar, 1996, Maryland; 1999, U.S. District Court, District of Maryland, and U.S. Court of Appeals, Fourth and Federal Circuits; 2000, District of Columbia. *Education:* University of the District of Columbia (B.A., 1990); Columbus School of Law, Catholic University of America (J.D., 1996). Research Assistant, Civil Practice in the District of Columbia, 1995. Law Clerk to the Honorable Lee F. Satterfield, Superior Court of the District of Columbia, 1996-1997. *Member:* Montgomery County, Maryland State and American Bar Associations; The District of Columbia Bar. ***LANGUAGES:*** Spanish. ***Email:*** jma@carrgoodson.com

DAVID J. FINUCANE, born Long Island, New York, April 30, 1962; admitted to bar, 1994, Maryland; 1997, U.S. Court of Appeals, Fourth Circuit; 1998, District of Columbia. *Education:* Southern Illinois University (B.S., 1990); Temple University (J.D., 1994). [Hospital Corpsman, U.S. Navy, 1980-1990]. ***Email:*** djf@carrgoodson.com

PAMELA S. FOX, born Los Angeles, California, August 7, 1968; admitted to bar, 1994, Virginia; 1998, Maryland and District of Columbia. *Education:* University of California at Los Angeles (B.A., 1990); George Washington University National Law Center (J.D., 1994). Recipient, The Judge Albert H. Grenadier Award. First Place, The Jessup International Moot Court Competition, Mid-Atlantic Regional, 1993. ***Email:*** psf@carrgoodson.com

TINA M. MAIOLO, born Bridgeport, Connecticut, April 5, 1971; admitted to bar, 1996, Virginia; 1997, District of Columbia. *Education:* College of William and Mary (B.A., 1993); Marshall-Wythe School of Law (J.D., 1996). ***LANGUAGES:*** Italian, Spanish. ***Email:*** tm@carrgoodson.com

VALERIE G. PREISS, admitted to bar, 1989, Virginia; 1990, District of Columbia. *Education:* Texas A & M University (B.A., cum laude, 1986); George Washington University (J.D., cum laude, 1989). Managing Editor, George Washington Journal of International Law and Economics. Law Clerk to the Honorable Patrick J. Attridge, U.S. District Court, District of Columbia, 1989-1990. Founding Member and Secretary, George Washington Americans Inns of Court, 1989-1994. Pegasus Trust Scholar, 1991. Special Assistant U.S. Attorney, Eastern District of Virginia, 1995-1996. Assistant Commonwealth's Attorney, Arlington County, Virginia, 1996-2000.

(This Listing Continued)

CARR GOODSON, P.C., Washington—Continued

DENNIS J. QUINN, born Passaic, New Jersey, January 22, 1963; admitted to bar, 1988, Pennsylvania; 1997, Virginia, District of Columbia, U.S. District Court for the District of Columbia and Eastern District of Virginia, and U.S. Court of Appeals, Fourth Circuit. *Education:* Montclair State University (B.A., cum laude, 1985); George Washington University (J.D., 1988). Phi Delta Phi (President, 1986-1987). *Member:* Alexandria and Federal Bar Associations. [LCDR, U.S. Navy Judge Advocate General Corps, 1988-1994]. ***Email:*** djq@carrgoodson.com

ANGELA W. RUSSELL, born Shelby, North Carolina, January 19, 1964; admitted to bar, 1989, Minnesota; 1995, District of Columbia; 1996, Maryland. *Education:* Hobart and William Smith Colleges (B.A., 1985); University of Maryland (J.D., 1988). Recipient: Dean's Scholarship; Clark Scholarship. Law Clerk to the Honorable Pamela G. Alexander, Hennepin County District Court, Minneapolis, Minnesota. ***Email:*** awr@carrgoodson.com

WILLIAM B. SCHROEDER, born Philadelphia, Pennsylvania, June 27, 1970; admitted to bar, 1997, Maryland; 1998, District of Columbia, Virginia and U.S. District Court, District of Maryland. *Education:* Franklin & Marshall College (B.A., English, 1992); Washington College of Law of American University (J.D., 1997). ***PRACTICE AREAS:*** Medical Malpractice; Professional Liability; Insurance Defense. ***Email:*** wbs@carrgoodson.com

MICHAEL J. SEPANIK, born Fairfax, Virginia, November 30, 1973; admitted to bar, 1999, Maryland and U.S. District Court, District of Maryland (Not admitted in District of Columbia). *Education:* University of Chicago (B.A., 1995); Emory University (J.D., 1999). ***PRACTICE AREAS:*** Product Liability; Antitrust; Business Tort; Employment Law; Professional Liability; General Liability. ***Email:*** mjs@carrgoodson.com

JAMES P. STEELE, born Washington, D.C., August 13, 1964; admitted to bar, 1992, Maryland; 1995, District of Columbia. *Education:* University of Delaware (B.A., 1987); Catholic University of America, Columbus School of Law (J.D., 1992). ***Email:*** jps@carrgoodson.com

ANDREW J. WAGHORN, born Islip, New York, May 17, 1965; admitted to bar, 1990, New York and Connecticut (Not admitted in District of Columbia). *Education:* Catholic University of America (B.A., Politics, 1987; J.D., 1990). Recipient, Frank A. Giadano Scholarship for Legal Studies. [With JAGC, U.S. Navy, 1991-1996]. ***PRACTICE AREAS:*** Medical Malpractice Defense. ***Email:*** ajw@carrgoodson.com

CARR, MORRIS & GRAEFF, P.C.

Established in 1982

1120 G STREET, N.W., SUITE 930

WASHINGTON, D.C. 20005-3801

Telephone: 202-789-1000

Facsimile: 202-628-3834

URL: http://www.cmgpc.com

General Business and Civil Litigation Practice. Corporate, Labor and Employment, Estate Planning, Malpractice, Products Liability and Negligence Law.

LAWRENCE E. CARR III, born Bethesda, Maryland, March 24, 1951; admitted to bar, 1979, District of Columbia; 1988, Maryland. *Education:* University of Notre Dame (B.A., magna cum laude, 1973; J.D., cum laude, 1979). Staff Editor, Notre Dame Lawyer, 1978-1979. [Col., USMCR, active duty, 1973-1976]. ***PRACTICE AREAS:*** Civil Litigation; Personal Injury; Professional Liability; Products Liability; Insurance Defense. ***Email:*** lcarr@cmgpc.com

ROY R. MORRIS, born Pittsburgh, Pennsylvania, March 13, 1952; admitted to bar, 1976, Virginia; 1977, District of Columbia; 1980, U.S. Supreme Court; 1984, Maryland. *Education:* College of William and Mary (A.B., with honors, 1973); Georgetown University (J.D., 1976); George Washington University (Masters in Taxation, 1980). ***PRACTICE AREAS:*** Business Law; Corporate Law; Estate Planning. ***Email:*** rmorris@cmgpc.com

STEPHEN D. GRAEFF, born Philadelphia, Pennsylvania, January 22, 1950; admitted to bar, 1975, New Jersey; 1976, New York; 1977, District of Columbia; 1984, Maryland. *Education:* American University (B.A., cum laude, 1972); George Washington University (J.D., with honors, 1975). Phi Kappa Phi. Recipient, Guttman Foundation Scholarship. Special Assistant Attorney General, New York State Special Prosecutor's Office, 1975-1977. Trial Attorney, Criminal Division, U.S. Justice Department, 1977-1980. ***PRACTICE AREAS:*** Labor and Employment; Civil Litigation; Criminal Defense. ***Email:*** sgraeff@cmgpc.com

ADAM R. WILK, born Queens, New York, July 27, 1963; admitted to bar, 1988, Virginia; 1989, District of Columbia. *Education:* State University of New York at Albany (B.A., cum laude, 1985); George Washington University (J.D., 1988). ***PRACTICE AREAS:*** Civil Litigation; Commercial Law; Commercial Collections; Debtor and Creditor; Mortgage Foreclosure. ***Email:*** awilk@cmgpc.com

PHILIP M. SCHWARTZ, born East Meadow, New York, November 3, 1964; admitted to bar, 1989, Maryland; 1990, District of Columbia. *Education:* Indiana University (B.S., 1986); George Washington University, (J.D., 1989). Phi Alpha Delta (Treasurer, 1987-1988). ***PRACTICE AREAS:*** Labor and Employment; Civil Litigation; Corporate Law; Real Estate Finance. ***Email:*** pschwart@cmgpc.com

TIMOTHY R. FEELY, born Gainesville, Florida, October 25, 1967; admitted to bar, 1997, Virginia; 1998, District of Columbia and Maryland. *Education:* Mary Washington College (B.S., 1989); Catholic University of America, Columbus School of Law (J.D., 1997). ***PRACTICE AREAS:*** Business Law; Commercial Law; Corporate Law; Labor and Employment; Litigation. ***Email:*** tfeely@cmgpc.com

ALAN C. BOWDEN, born Newport News, Virginia, December 10, 1968; admitted to bar, 1998, Virginia; 1999, District of Columbia. *Education:* Virginia Polytechnic Institute and State University (B.S., 1991); DePaul University (J.D., 1998). *Member:* Virginia State Bar; District of Columbia Bar. ***PRACTICE AREAS:*** Business Law; Corporate Law; Civil Litigation. ***Email:*** abowden@cmgpc.com

DANA SUZANNE GLYNN, born Falls Church, Virginia, April 23, 1974; admitted to bar, 1999, Virginia; 2000, District of Columbia and Maryland. *Education:* University of Virginia (B.A., 1996); Tulane University of Louisiana (J.D., cum laude, 1999). *Member:* Virginia State Bar; The District of Columbia Bar. ***PRACTICE AREAS:*** Civil Litigation; Corporate Law; Business Law. ***Email:*** dglynn@cmgpc.com

BRENDA M. HANKINS, born Houston, Texas, July 31, 1974; admitted to bar, 2001, New York (Not admitted in District of Columbia). *Education:* Oregon State University (B.S., 1996); American University (J.D., cum laude, 2000). Senior Recent Developments Editor, Administrative Law Review, 1999-2000. ***PRACTICE AREAS:*** Business Law; Corporate Law; Estate Planning. ***Email:*** bhankins@cmgpc.com

OF COUNSEL

MELVILLE W. FELDMAN (1920-1998).

NÉSTOR ENRIQUE CRUZ, born Havana, Cuba, June 29, 1945; admitted to bar, 1972, Florida; 1975, District of Columbia; 1993, Virginia. *Education:* Villanova University (B.A., 1966); Cornell Graduate School of Management (M.B.A., 1969); Cornell Law School (J.D., 1970). Author: "Is Equal Employment Opportunity Cost Effective?" 31 Labor Law Journal 295 (1980); "Abuse of Rights in Title VII Cases," 32 Labor Law Journal 315 (1981); "Factor Analysis in N.L.R.B. Cases," 40 Labor Law Journal 654 (1989); "The Organizational Culture of the N.L.R.B.," 40 Labor Law Journal 654 (1989). Counsel to Chairman, N.L.R.B., 1974-1975, 1988-1991. Director of Review & Appeals, E.E.O.C., 1979-1988. ***LANGUAGES:*** Spanish. ***PRACTICE AREAS:*** Estate Planning; International Estate Planning; Labor and Employment; International Law; Immigration.

FRANCIS D. CARTER

SUITE 717, THE OFC BUILDING

1730 RHODE ISLAND AVENUE NW

WASHINGTON, D.C. 20036-3115

Telephone: 202-393-4330

Fax: 202-393-5657

Email: frank@fdcarter.com

General Civil and Criminal Practice, Litigation in all Courts, White Collar Criminal Defense, Business Fraud, Domestic Relations Law, Business Litigation, Employment Defense, Discrimination Defense.

FRANCIS D. CARTER, born Washington, D.C., August 20, 1946; admitted to bar, 1973, District of Columbia, U.S. District Court, District of Columbia and U.S. Court of Appeals, District of Columbia Circuit; 1980, U.S. Supreme Court. *Education:* Villanova University (A.B., 1968); George Washington University (J.D., 1972). Law Clerk, Honorable H. Carl Moultrie, I, Chief Judge, Superior Court for the District of Columbia, 1972-1973. Public Defender Service, District of Columbia (Deputy Director, 1978-1979; Director, 1979-1985). *Member:* District of Columbia Bar (Member, Board on Professional Responsibility, 1985-1993; Secretary, 1980-1981; Member, Nominating Committee, 1978; Chairman, 1998; Member, Board of Governors, 1999-2001); Bar Association of the District of Columbia (Member, Executive Council, Young Lawyers Section, 1979-1981); Washington, American (Member: Committee on Defense Services, 1984-1986; Committee on Corrections, 1983-1985) and National Bar Associations; District of Columbia Circuit Judicial Conference; Dis-

(This Listing Continued)

trict of Columbia Judicial Conference; District of Columbia Federal Judicial Nominating Commission; Edward Bennett Williams Inn of Court. Fellow, American College of Trial Lawyers. ***REPORTED CASES:*** U.S. v. Tabron, 410 A. 2d 209 (D.C. 1979); U.S. v. Coates, 482 A. 2d 1239 (D.C. 1984); U.S. v. Fawaz Yunis, 859 F. 2d 953 (D.C. Cir. 1988), 867 F. 2d 617 (D.C. Cir. 1989), 924 F.2d 1086 (D.C. Cir, 1991); U.S. v. Hani El-Sayegh, 131 F.3d 158 (D.C. Cir. 1997); U.S. v. Brown and Anderson, 766 A.2d 530 (D.C. 2001).

CARTER & COLEMAN

700 E STREET S.E.
WASHINGTON, D.C. 20003
Telephone: 202-682-7373
Fax: 202-682-7373
Email: info@cartercoleman.com
URL: http://www.cartercoleman.com

Alexandria, Virginia Office: 602 Cameron Street, 22314. Telephone: 703-739-4200. Fax: 703-739-4210.

General Civil Practice, Professional Liability Insurance Defense, Insurance and Health Care Law, Medical Malpractice, Employment Law, Medical Benefits Coverage and Reimbursement, ERISA, Creditors Bankruptcy, Corporate and Commercial Law, Franchise Law, Business Law, Trial and Appellate Litigation in State and Federal Courts.

RICHARD D. CARTER, born Newburgh, New York, February 17, 1949; admitted to bar, 1980, District of Columbia; 1981, U.S. District Court for the District of Columbia; 1987, U.S. Supreme Court; 1990, U.S. District Court, District of Maryland; 1991, Virginia, U.S. District Court, Eastern District of Virginia and U.S. Court of Appeals, Fourth Circuit, Maryland; 1992, U.S. Bankruptcy Court, Eastern District of Virginia; 1994, U.S. District Court, Eastern District of Wisconsin and U.S. District Court, District of Arizona. *Education:* Pace University (B.A., cum laude, 1977); George Washington University (J.D., 1980). Adjunct Professor, Trial Advocacy, Georgetown University Law Center, 1982-2000. Recipient, Mayor's Distinguished Public Service Award, Washington D.C., 1993. Listed, Who's Who In American Law. Author: "Too Experimental for Insurers-or Just Too Expensive?" Healthspan, Vol. 9 No. 1, p.11, January, 1992; Chapter on "Landlord & Tenant Law and Practice," D.C. Practice Manual, District of Columbia Bar, 1987, 1993; "Fundamentals of Superior Court Practice," CLE,GULC/D.C. Bar, 1982-1989; "Bridge The Gap" program, CLE, GULC/D.C. Bar, 1985-1989; Landlord and Tenant Practice," D.C./GULC, 1986-1989. Panel Member: "Health Care Reform," American Bar Association Annual Convention, N.Y., 1993; "Medico-Legal Aspects of Bone Marrow Transplantation and Health Care Reform," Keystone Symposia, 1994; "Women's Health Care & Insurance Coverage for Necessary Treatment," National Association of Women Judges, District Meeting, Washington, D.C., 1994; "The Ten Commandments of Insurance Coverage"; "Bone Marrow Transplantation for Breast Cancer," The Next Step, Western Pennsylvania Hospital, 1994; "Managed Care, Managed Competition and Physician Independence," Virginia Association of Hematologist and Oncologist Annual Meeting, 1994; "Collision Course: Managed Competition and State of the Art Healthcare," *Advances in Cancer Care:* An Update For Hematopoietic Investigators and Educators, Boston, MA, 1995; "Transplant Center Reimbursement Issues," National Marrow Donor Program Council, December, 1996; "Recent Developments in the Law Affecting Business Organizations," Virginia State Bar Annual Meeting, Virginia Beach, VA, June 1997, 1998; "When Health Care Coverage is Denied: Patient Rights and Public Policy," Virginia Bar Association Summer Meeting, The Greenbriar, July 1997; "Nuts and Bolts of ERISA," *Litigating HMO Cases,* ATLA National College of Advocacy, Atlanta, GA, September 1997; "Managed Care and Malpractice Liability," Fairfax Medical Society Meeting, October 1997; "Life Insurance-No Longer Just a Death Benefit," Blood & Marrow Transplant Newsletter, November, 1997; "ERISA Basics," *Litigating HMO and Managed Care Cases,* Pennsylvania Trial Lawyers Association, Philadelphia, PA, April 1998; "ERISA in a Nutshell," Louisiana Trial Lawyers Association Health Law Conference, New Orleans, Louisiana, April 1998; "ERISA Claims: Litigating The Denial of Payment for Treatment," Annual Meeting, Association of Trial Lawyers of America, Washington, D.C., July, 1998; "Shifting Standards of Evidence? From Coverage to Case Review to Court", "Professional Responsibility for Trial Lawyers," *Translating Evidence Into Practice '98,* Agency for Health Care Policy and Research Center for Practice and Technology Assessment, Washington, D.C., July 1998. Program Chair: "Confidentiality of Medical Records," Alexandria, VA, 1995; *National Medical Legal Symposium,* Loyola University Law School, Chicago, IL, April, 1997; "Attorneys Fees in ERISA" and "ERISA Claims and Full and Fair Review," Loyola University School of Law, Chicago, IL, April 1998; *National Medical Legal Symposium,* Loyola University Law School, Chicago, IL, April 1997. Delegate, Judicial Conference of the District of Columbia, 1985—. Executive Director, D.C. Law Students in Court, 1985-1990. Supervising Attorney, D.C. Law Students in Court, 1980-1985. *Member:* The District of Columbia Bar (Member, Sections on: Litigation; Health Law); American Bar Association (Member, Sections on: Litigation; Torts and Insurance Practice); American Inns of Court, Thurgood Marshall Chapter; Defense Research Institute. ***PRACTICE AREAS:*** Insurance Defense; Health Insurance; ERISA; Federal Litigation; Appeals. ***Email:*** rcarter@cartercoleman.com

DOUGLAS M. COLEMAN, born Indianapolis, Indiana, April 27, 1960; admitted to bar, 1985, Virginia; 1986, U.S. District Court, Eastern District of Virginia; 1988, U.S. Court of Appeals, Fourth Circuit; 1990, U.S. District Court, District of Maryland (Not admitted in District of Columbia). *Education:* University of Virginia (B.A., 1982); University of Richmond (J.D., 1985). Panel Member: "Managing Legal Liability," Northern Virginia Association of Realtors Management Series; "1133 Claims in ERISA," Current Issues in Bone Marrow Transplantation, Westchester Medical College, April 1998; "Defense of Real Estate Agents," Alexandria Bar Association, May 1998; "Current ERISA Law Issues and Case Preparation," Loyola University School of Law, Chicago, IL, April 1998. *Member:* Virginia State Bar; Alexandria Bar Association; Virginia Association of Defense Attorneys. ***PRACTICE AREAS:*** Professional Liability; Medical Malpractice; Insurance Law; Commercial Law; ERISA; Health Insurance Coverage; Civil Trials; Civil Appeals. ***Email:*** dcoleman@cartercoleman.com

JULIANE C. MILLER, born New York, N.Y., December 14, 1966; admitted to bar, 1992, Virginia; 1993, Maryland; 1996, District of Columbia; U.S. Court of Appeals, Fourth Circuit; U.S. District Court, Eastern and Western Districts of Virginia; U.S. District Court, District of Maryland. *Education:* State University of New York at Geneseo (B.A., 1988); Ohio Northern University (J.D., 1991); Georgetown University (LL.M., Health Law, 1993). ***PRACTICE AREAS:*** Health Care Litigation; ERISA; Disabilities. ***Email:*** jmiller@cartercoleman.com

GERALD F. RAGLAND, JR., born Alexandria, Virginia, May 19, 1941; admitted to bar, 1975, Pennsylvania and U.S. Court of Appeals, Third Circuit; 1980, Virginia; 1981, District of Columbia and U.S. District Court Eastern District of Virginia; U.S. District Court, Middle District of Pennsylvania; U.S. District Court, District of Columbia; U.S. Court of Appeals, Second, Fourth and District of Columbia Circuits; U.S. Supreme Court. *Education:* Longwood College (B.S., 1965); Temple University (J.D., 1975). *Member:* Alexandria and Virginia State Bar Associations; Bar Association for the District of Columbia. ***PRACTICE AREAS:*** Gneral Tort liability; Professional Liability; Medical Malpractice; Civil Trials; Civil Appeals. ***Email:*** gragland@cartercoleman.com

ASSOCIATES

PEGGY E. TAYLOR, born Ft. Belvoir, Virginia, November 19, 1974; admitted to bar, 2000, Virginia (Not admitted in District of Columbia). *Education:* University of Virginia (B.A., Foreign Affairs, 1996); Georgetown University Law Center (J.D., 1999). Student Attorney, D.C. Law Students in Court Program. *Member:* Virginia and Alexandria Bar Associations. ***PRACTICE AREAS:*** Insurance Defense; Health Law; Medical Malpractice; Federal Litigation. ***Email:*** ptaylor@cartercoleman.com

MIKHAEL D. CHARNOFF, born Fairfax, Virginia, September 28, 1973; admitted to bar, 1999, Virginia and Maryland; 2000, U.S. District Court, Eastern District of Virginia (Not admitted in District of Columbia). *Education:* Mary Washington College (B.A., 1995); University of Virginia (J.D., 1999). Law Clerk to Honorable Frank E. Schwelb, DC Court of Appeals, 2001. *Member:* Fairfax Bar Association; Virginia Trial Lawyers Association. ***PRACTICE AREAS:*** Civil Litigation; Insurance Defense. ***Email:*** mcharnoff@cartercoleman.com

REPRESENTATIVE CLIENTS: The Atlantic Company of America; Armer International; Time for Good Food Inc.; The Birchmere; CNA Insurance Company; Concord General Corporation; CIGNA; John P. Pearl & Associates, Ltd.; Journal Newspapers; Lloyd's of London; Principal Mutual Life Insurance Company; Penn-America Group, Inc.; Phyllis Wheatley YWCA, Inc.; Professional Indemnity Underwriters Corporation; St. Paul's Fire & Marine Insurance Company; TIG Insurance Company; Washington Gas Co.

CARTER, LEDYARD & MILBURN

1401 EYE STREET, NW, SUITE 300
WASHINGTON, D.C. 20005
Telephone: 202-898-1515
Fax: 202-898-1521
Email: info@clm.com
URL: http://www.clm.com

New York, N.Y. Offices: 2 Wall Street, 10005. Telephone: 212-732-3200. Fax: 212-732-3232. Cable Address: "Ledyard" New York and Midtown Office: 570 Lexington Avenue, 10022. Telephone: 212-371-2720. Fax: 212-317-4234.

General Practice.

RESIDENT MEMBERS

ROBERT L. HOEGLE, born Pittsburgh, Pennsylvania, 1952; admitted to bar, 1977, District of Columbia; 1994, New York. *Education:* Georgetown University (A.B., 1974; J.D., 1977). Phi Beta Kappa. Special Projects Editor, Law

(This Listing Continued)

CARTER, LEDYARD & MILBURN, Washington—Continued

and Policy in International Business, 1976-1977. *Member:* The District of Columbia Bar; Federal, American and Federal Communications Bar Associations. ***PRACTICE AREAS:*** Litigation; Telecommunications; Federal Agency Law. ***Email:*** hoegle@clm.com

TIMOTHY J. FITZGIBBON, born Elizabeth, New Jersey, 1955; admitted to bar, 1983, District of Columbia; 1995, New York. *Education:* Georgetown University Law Center (B.S.F.S., 1977; J.D., 1983). Recipient, Lawyers Cooperative American Jurisprudence Award for Excellence in Constitutional Law, 1982. Staff Member, American Criminal Law Review, 1981-1982. *Member:* District of Columbia Bar; American Bar Association; Federal Communications Bar Association. ***PRACTICE AREAS:*** Litigation; Telecommunications; Federal Government Law. ***Email:*** fitzgibbon@clm.com

RESIDENT OF COUNSEL

JOHN F. CAHILL, born New York, N.Y., July 20, 1952; admitted to bar, 1983, Virginia; 1985, District of Columbia; 1991, Pennsylvania. *Education:* Manhattan College (B.S., 1974); University of Virginia (M.S., 1977); Georgetown University (J.D., 1983). ***PRACTICE AREAS:*** Technology; Environmental; Insurance; Litigation. ***Email:*** cahill@clm.com

MARY S. DIEMER, born Cheverly, Maryland, 1963; admitted to bar, 1990, District of Columbia; 1990, Maryland; 1992, U.S. District Court for the District of Columbia; 1995, U.S. Court of Appeals, Third and fifth Circuits. *Education:* George Washington University (B.A., 1985), Phi Beta Kappa; Boston University (J.D., 1988). G. Joseph Tauro Scholar. *Member:* American Bar Association (Associate Editor, Litigation News). ***PRACTICE AREAS:*** Telecommunications; Litigation. ***Email:*** diemer@clm.com

INTELLECTUAL PROPERTY COUNSEL

L. LAWTON ROGERS, III, born Mullins, South Carolina, October 14, 1936; admitted to bar, 1967, Virginia and District of Columbia. *Education:* University of South Carolina (B.S.E.E., 1959); Georgetown University (J.D., 1967); George Washington University (LL.M., Patent and Trade Regulation Law, 1972). ***PRACTICE AREAS:*** Intellectual Property; Litigation. ***Email:*** rogers@clm.com

MARK CHARLES COMTOIS, born Hartford, Connecticut, June 1, 1959; admitted to bar, 1996, Virginia (Not admitted in District of Columbia). *Education:* United States Naval Academy (B.S.M.E., 1981); George Mason University School of Law (J.D., 1995). *Member:* Virginia State Bar; American Intellectual Property Law Association. [U.S. Navy, Nuclear Submarine Officer, 1981-1986]. ***PRACTICE AREAS:*** Intellectual Property; Litigation. ***Email:*** comtois@clm.com

D. JOSEPH ENGLISH, born Williamsport, Pennsylvania, November 20, 1963; admitted to bar, 1998, Virginia (Not admitted in District of Columbia). *Education:* U.S. Naval Academy (B.S.M.E., 1986); Catholic University of America (J.D., 1998). *Member:* Virginia State Bar; American Intellectual Property Law Association. [U.S. Navy, Nuclear Submarine Officer, 1986-1994]. ***PRACTICE AREAS:*** Intellectual Property; Litigation. ***Email:*** english@clm.com

PATRICK DENNIS McPHERSON, born Ridgewood, New Jersey, March 26, 1963; admitted to bar, 1995, Maryland (Not admitted in District of Columbia). *Education:* United States Naval Academy (B.S., 1985); Catholic University of America (J.D., 1995). [U.S. Navy, Nuclear Submarine Officer, 1985-1992]. ***PRACTICE AREAS:*** Intellectual Property; Litigation. ***Email:*** mcpherson@clm.com

RESIDENT ASSOCIATES

Thomas F. Bardo
Peter K. Killough
Bradley A. Farrell (Not admitted in DC)

(For Complete Biographical Data on all Personnel see Professional Biographies at New York, N.Y.)

WENDY A. CARTWRIGHT & ASSOCIATES, P.C.

WASHINGTON, D.C.

(See Bowie)

Family, Divorce, Child Custody, Bankruptcy, Debtor and Creditor, Criminal, Juvenile Law, Personal Injury, Employment Law, Civil Litigation, Business Law, Contracts. Criminal in State and Federal Courts.

CASHDAN, GOLDEN & KANE, PLLC

1150 CONNECTICUT AVENUE, N.W., 9TH FLOOR
WASHINGTON, D.C. 20036-4104
Telephone: 202-862-4330
Fax: 202-862-4331
URL: http://www.CGKLaw.com
URL: http://www.lawyers.com/cgklaw

Employment Law, Wrongful Termination, Employment Contracts, Executive Compensation, Employment Mediation, Fair Employment Practices, Discrimination, Harassment, College and University Law, Whistleblower Litigation, Employee Rights, Executive Severance Contracts, Sexual Harassment, Disability Discrimination, Federal Employment Law, Handicapped Rights and Age Discrimination.

FIRM PROFILE: Cashdan, Golden & Kane is a law firm with a national practice serving employees and management in employment law, civil rights, discrimination, harassment, termination and related matters, including policy, planning, negotiations, litigation and mediation. The firm has extensive experience in matters relating to executives, professionals and all levels of employees, including private sector, federal, state and local employees.

MEMBERS OF FIRM

DAVID R. CASHDAN, born Detroit, Michigan, October 13, 1939; admitted to bar, 1967, District of Columbia and U.S. Court of Appeals for the District of Columbia Circuit; 1968, U.S. Supreme Court, U.S. Court of Appeals, Fifth Circuit; 1970, U.S. Court of Appeals, Third Circuit and U.S. Court of Appeals, Seventh Circuit; 1977, U.S. Court of Appeals, Fourth Circuit; 1990, Maryland. *Education:* Oberlin College (B.A., 1961); University of Michigan (J.D., 1964). Recipient, Federal Bar Association's National Outstanding Younger Attorney Award, 1969. Author: "Unjust Dismissal: District of Columbia Update," The Washington Lawyer, November/December, 1989. Co-Author: "Whistle Blowers and D.C.'s Public Policy Tort," The Washington Lawyer, July/August, 1992; "Getting to Trial with a Gender Harassment Case," D.C. Bar CLE, Spring, 1995. Adjunct Professor of Law, Equal Opportunity Law, Denver College of Law, Spring Quarters, 1972-1974. Chairperson and Lecturer, Equal Employment Opportunity Law, CLE Colorado Bar, 1972 and 1973. Senior Attorney and Acting Chief, District Court Section, U.S. Equal Employment Opportunity Commission, 1965-1970. ADA Policy Law Editorial Advisory Board. Editorial Board, Bender's Labor & Employment Bulletin. *Member:* The District of Columbia Bar (Co-Chairperson, Steering Committee of Labor Law Division, 1996-1997; Member, 1972-1974, 1993-1995); American Bar Association (Member, Sections of: Labor and Employment Law; Individual Rights and Responsibilities Law; Litigation); National Employment Lawyers Association; National Employment Rights Institute (Member, Advisory Board); Metropolitan Washington Employment Lawyers Association (President, 1993-1996; Board of Directors, 1988—); District of Columbia Employment Justice Center (Board of Directors, 2000—); Chet Levitt Employment Law Fund (Co-Chair, 1997—). ***REPORTED CASES:*** Lead Counsel: Bell et al. v. Automobile Club of Michigan, 80 F.R.D. 228 (ED.Mich. 1978). ***Email:*** dcashdan@CGKLaw.com

VICKI G. GOLDEN (1942-2001).

MICHAEL G. KANE, born Hoboken, New Jersey, October 7, 1966; admitted to bar, 1992, New York and District of Columbia; 1993, Virginia; 1994, Maryland; U.S. District Court, District of Columbia; U.S. Court of Appeals, Fourth Circuit; 1995, U.S. District Court, Eastern District of Virginia; 1996, U.S. District Court, District of Maryland; 1997, U.S. Court of Appeals, District of Columbia Circuit; U.S. Supreme Court. *Education:* New York University (B.A., 1988); Fordham University (J.D., 1991). Law Clerk to the Honorable Marcel Livaudais, Jr., U.S. District Court, Eastern District of Louisiana, 1991-1992. Staff Member, Fordham International Law Journal, 1989-1990. *Member:* American Bar Association (Member, Sections on: Litigation; Labor and Employment); District of Columbia Bar (Labor and Employment Section, 1995—); Virginia Bar Association (Member, Labor and Employment Section); Metropolitan Washington Employment Lawyer's Association (1995—); Chet Levitt Employment Law Fund (Co-Chair, 1997—). ***REPORTED CASES:*** Whitbeck v. Vital Signs, Inc., 116 F. 3d 588 (D.C.Cir. 1997); Sanders, et al v. District of Columbia, 16 F. Supp. 2d 10 (D.D.C. 1998). ***Email:*** mkane@CGKLaw.com

ASSOCIATE

MEREDITH S. FRANCIS, born Bryn Mawr, Pennsylvania, August 22, 1973; admitted to bar, 1997, New Jersey; 1999, District of Columbia. *Education:* University of Pennsylvania (B.A., 1994; Graduate Certificate, Women's Studies, 1997; J.D., 1997). Co-Author: "Claims of Alleged Harassers: Enforcing The Rights of the Wrongfully Accused," 4 Lab. Empl. Bulletin 205, April 1, 2001. *Member:* New Jersey State and American Bar Associations; District of Columbia Bar; Metropolitan Washington Employment Lawyers Association; National Employment Lawyers Association. ***PRACTICE AREAS:*** Labor and Employment. ***Email:*** mfrancis@CGKLaw.com

CASTRO, BARROS, SOBRAL, VIDIGAL, GOMES ADVOGADOS

Established in 1953

801 PENNSYLVANIA AVENUE N.W.
MARKET SQUARE, SUITE 747
WASHINGTON, D.C. 20004
Telephone: (1 202) 638-7071
Facsimile: (1 202) 638-7072
Email: maildc@cbsvg.com.br

Other Offices in Brazil:
Rio de Janeiro: Praia de Botafogo, 228 - 15th Floor, 22359-900. Telephone: +(55 21) 2553-1855. Fax: +(55 21) 2552-1796. Email: mailrj@cbsvg.com.br.
São Paulo: Rua do Rocio, 291 - 11th Floor, 04552-000. Telephone: +(55 11) 3040-0908. Fax: +(55 11) 3040-0937/0938. Email: mailsp@cbsvg.com.br.
Porto Alegre: Avenida Carlos Gomes 11 6th Floor, 90480-903. Telephone: +(55 51) 328-7309. Fax: +(55 51) 328-3081. Email: mailpoa@cbsvg.com.br.
Brasília, D.F.: SQN Quadra 4, Bloco 404-A, 70714-900. Telephone: +(55 61) 326-0300. Fax: +(55 61) 328-6653. Email: maildf@cbsvg.com.br.
Offices Abroad:
Lisbon: Heron Castilho, Rua Braamcamp, 40-8° E, 1269-013, Lisbon, Portugal. Telephone: +351 21 387-5702. Fax: +351 21 387-5743.

Antitrust, Aviation, Finance and Capital Market, Civil, Entertainment, Corporate, Investment, Litigation, Environmental, Intellectual Property, International Trade, Labor, Maritime, Privatization, Tax, Infrastructure.

(For complete biographical data on all Personnel, see Rio de Janeiro, Brazil)

CHARLES I. CATE

1730 K STREET, N. W., SUITE 304
WASHINGTON, D.C. 20006
Telephone: 202-289-1006
Email: chascate@msn.com
URL: http://www.lawyers.com/irsnemesis

Arlington, Virginia Office: 2009 North 14th Street, Suite 306. 22201. Telephone: 703-522-2112. Fax: 703-522-5201.

Federal Tax Matters; Tax Controversies, Criminal Tax Litigation, Civil Tax Litigation, Income Tax Planning, Estate Tax Planning, Exempt Organizations..

CHARLES I. CATE, born Hampton, Virginia, 1944; admitted to bar, 1970, District of Columbia. *Education:* Georgetown University, Washington, D.C. (B.A., 1966; M.A., Tax, 1979); Catholic University of America (J.D., 1969). Internal Revenue Service Attorney, 1975-1979. *Member:* District of Columbia Bar (Member, Taxation Section). [Capt., U.S. Army, 1970-1971]. ***PRACTICE AREAS:*** Taxation; Tax Controversies; Probate; Wills; Exempt Organizations; Civil Litigation; Criminal Litigation; Tax Litigation; Income Tax Planning; Estate Tax Planning; Tax Returns.

CHADBOURNE & PARKE LLP

1200 NEW HAMPSHIRE AVENUE, N.W.
WASHINGTON, D.C. 20036
Telephone: 202-974-5600
Facsimile: 202-974-5602

New York, N.Y. Office: 30 Rockefeller Plaza, 10112. Telephone: 212-408-5100. Facsimile: 212-541-5369.
Los Angeles, California Office: Two California Plaza, 350 S. Grand Avenue, Suite 3300, 90071. Telephone: 213-892-1000. Facsimile: 213-622-9865.
Upper Montclair, New Jersey Office: 539 Valley Road, 07043. Telephone: 973-655-1550. Facsimile: 973-655-1558.
London, England Affiliate Office: Chadbourne & Parke, a multinational partnership of Registered Foreign Lawyers and Solicitors, Regis House, 45 King William Street, London EC4R 9AN. Telephone: 44-171-337-8000. Facsimile: 44-171-337-8001.
Moscow, Russia Office: 52/5 Kosmodamianskaya, 113054. Telephone: 7095-974-2424. Facsimile: 7095-974-2425. International satellite via US: Telephone: 212-408-1190. Facsimile: 212-408-1199.
Hong Kong, China Office: Suite 2203, Tower I, Lippo Centre, 89 Queensway. Hong Kong. Telephone: 852-2842-5400. Facsimile: 852-2521-7527.

Practice before all Federal and District of Columbia Trial and Appellate Courts, Federal Agencies and Departments.

PARTNERS

NOAM AYALI, born Haifa, Israel, August 12, 1960; admitted to bar, 1989, Israel; 1991, New York (Not admitted in District of Columbia). *Education:* Tel

(This Listing Continued)

Aviv University Law School (LL.B., 1988); Boston University - Morin Center for Banking Law Studies (LL.M., 1990). Recipient, A. John Serino Outstanding Graduate Student Prize - International Banking Law, Boston University. Senior Counsel, International Finance Corporation, 1996-1999. *Member:* New York State, American (Member, Sections on: Business Law; International Law and Practice) and Israel Bar Associations.

CAREY G. CHILD, born Ogden, Utah, January 22, 1965; admitted to bar, 1992, Virginia and District of Columbia. *Education:* University of Utah (B.A., B.A., cum laude, 1989); Georgetown University (J.D., magna cum laude, 1992). Omicron Delta Epsilon; Order of the Coif. ***LANGUAGES:*** Spanish.

WILLIAM S. D'AMICO, born New York, N.Y., October 24, 1938; admitted to bar, 1967, District of Columbia. *Education:* Boston College (B.S. in Economics, 1963; J.D., 1966). Attorney, Federal Trade Commission, 1966-1969. *Member:* American Bar Association (Member, Antitrust Law Section).

PETER F. FITZGERALD, born Morristown, New Jersey, June 16, 1956; admitted to bar, 1982, New York; 1999, District of Columbia. *Education:* University of Notre Dame (B.A., summa cum laude, 1978); Rutgers University (J.D., 1981); Notre Dame Centre for International Legal Studies. Phi Beta Kappa. Notre Dame Scholar. Essex County Bar Association Scholarship. Associate General Counsel, Overseas Private Investment Corporation, 1986-1993. *Member:* American Bar Association.

ANDREW A. GIACCIA, born Reading, Pennsylvania, August 31, 1959; admitted to bar, 1984, Pennsylvania and New Jersey; 1987, District of Columbia. *Education:* Georgetown University (A.B., magna cum laude, 1981; J.D., 1984). Phi Beta Kappa; Alpha Sigma Nu. *Member:* The District of Columbia Bar (Environmental, Energy and Natural Resources Section); American Bar Association (National Resources, Energy, and Environmental Law Section).

CORNELIUS J. GOLDEN, JR., born Montreal, Quebec, Canada, July 7, 1948; admitted to bar, 1973, California; 1975, District of Columbia; 1988, New York. *Education:* Stanford University (B.A., in Economics, 1970; J.D., 1973). Articles Editor, Stanford Law Review, 1972-1973. Research Fellow in Commercial Law, Centre National de la Recherche Scientifique, Paris, France, 1974. Author: "The United Kingdom and the European Court of Justice: An Encounter Between Common and Civil Law Traditions," 21 American Journal of Comparative Law 664 (1973) (with V. Grementieri); "The Export Trading Company Act of 1982: An American Response to Foreign Competition," 58 Notre Dame Law Review 743 (1983) (with C. Kolb); "The Export Trading Company Act of 1982," 18 Revue Suisse du Droit International de la Concurrence 3 (1983) (with C. Kolb). *Member:* The District of Columbia Bar; State Bar of California; American Bar Association (Member, Section of Business Law).

KENNETH W. HANSEN, born Columbus, Ohio, January 27, 1951; admitted to bar, 1984, Massachusetts (Not admitted in District of Columbia). *Education:* Harvard College (A.B., cum laude, 1974); Yale University (M.A., 1976); Harvard University (M.P.A., 1979); University of Pennsylvania (J.D., cum laude, 1983). General Counsel, Export-Import Bank of the United States, 1995-1999. Of Counsel, Baker & Botts, 1995. Associate General Counsel for Investment, Assistant General Counsel, Senior Commercial Counsel and Counsel, each at Overseas Private Investment Corporation, 1986-1995. Associate, Nintz, Levin, Cohn, Ferris, Glovsky and Popeo, P.C., 1983-1986. Adjunct Professor: Georgetown University Law Center, 1990—; Boston University Law School, 1992-1999; Fletcher School of Law and Diplomacy, Tufts University, 1993; George Washington University, National Law Center, 1991-1993. *Member:* Boston, Massachusetts and American Bar Associations; American Society of International Law; Washington Foreign Law Society (Boardmember).

TRACEY W. LAWS, born Clifton Forge, Virginia, January 17, 1964; admitted to bar, 1990, Texas; 1992, District of Columbia. *Education:* College of William and Mary (B.A., 1985); University of Virginia (J.D., 1990).

KEITH MARTIN, born Minneapolis, Minnesota, May 5, 1953; admitted to bar, 1977, District of Columbia; 1985, New York. *Education:* Wesleyan University (B.A., 1974); The London School of Economics, England (M.Sc., 1978); George Washington University (J.D., 1977). Legislative Assistant, Senator Henry M. Jackson, 1974-1977. Legislative Counsel, Senator Daniel Patrick Moynihan, 1979-1982. Author: "Foreign Investment in Real Property Tax Act," in Manual of Foreign Investment in the United States 537 (Shepard's/McGraw-Hill, 1984); "Financing International Projects," in Independent Energy Magazine (January 1993) (with Hugh McCrory); "Tax Issues and Incentives for Biomass Projects," in Project Finance Monthly (September and October 1993); "Tapping into Tax-Exempt Financing," in Independent Energy Magazine (November 1993); "Keeping Earnings Offshore," in Independent Energy Magazine (April 1994) (with Sheila Malkani); "Tax Strategies for Foreign Projects," in Independent Energy Magazine (November 1994) (with Sheila Malkani); "New Guidelines on Foreign Companies as Partnerships," International Corporate Law (March 1995); "India Confirms Mauritius Treaty Benefits," in Tax Notes International (September 1996); "Beware the Foreign Corrupt Practices Act, in International Commercial Litigation (October 1996); "IRS Targets Debt-Equity Swaps in Latin American Privatizations," in Latin American Finance & Capital Markets (October 1996); "Tax Issues and Opportunities in Restructuring Contracts," in Project Finance International (April 1997); "Cross Border Leasing,"

(This Listing Continued)

CHADBOURNE & PARKE LLP, Washington—Continued

in Proceedings, EEI Tax School (July 1997); "US Changes Tax Burden on International Projects," in International Financial Law Review (November 1997); "US Courts Get Tough on Schemes," in International Tax Review (November 1998); "Latest Tax Angles for Latin American Projects," in Latin American Tax Strategies (September 1999); "The Foreign Corrupt Practices Act, in Corporate Legal Departments (Practicing Law Institute, 3d ed., 2000). Editor, Project Finance NewsWire. Contributing Editor, International Tax Report, Natural Gas, Practical Latin American Tax Strategies. *Member:* The District of Columbia Bar (Member, Tax Section); New York State (Member, Tax Section), Federal (Member, Tax Section) and American (Member, Taxation Section) Bar Associations.

JOHN B. O'SULLIVAN, born Los Angeles, California, October 20, 1943; admitted to bar, 1974, New York; 1989, District of Columbia; U.S. Court of Appeals, Second, Third and District of Columbia Circuits. *Education:* Princeton University (B.A., 1965); New York University (J.D., 1970). Assistant General Counsel for Electric Rates and Corporate Regulation, 1978 and Chief Advisory Counsel, 1979-1981, Federal Energy Regulatory Commission. *Member:* The District of Columbia Bar; Federal Energy and American Bar Associations.

WILLIAM K. PERRY, born Detroit, Michigan, May 25, 1954; admitted to bar, 1984, New York and U.S. District Court, Southern and Eastern Districts of New York; 1994, U.S. Court of Appeals, Second Circuit; 1998, District of Columbia. *Education:* University of Michigan (A.B., 1976; J.D., 1983). Recipient, American Jurisprudence Award. Author: "The High Cost of Corporate Crime," Management Accounting, December, 1991; "Product Liability in The U.S.: A Risky and Costly Business" appearing in *A Guide To Investing In California: The Pacific Century,* Asia Law & Practice Publishing, Ltd. 1997 (co-author); *Compliance Programs and the Corporate Sentencing Guidelines,* Clark Boardman Callaghan 1993 (co-author of chapter on compliance programs and trials); and other publications. *Member:* New York State and American Bar Associations; Defense Research Institute; International Bar Association; London Court of International Arbitration (Representative Member).

DAVID M. RAIM, born New York, N.Y., March 11, 1953; admitted to bar, 1979, New York and U.S. District Court, Southern and Eastern Districts of New York; 1981, U.S. Court of Appeals, Second Circuit; 1982, U.S. Supreme Court; 1985, District of Columbia and U.S. District Court for the District of Columbia; 1988, U.S. Court of Appeals, Third Circuit. *Education:* Yale University (B.A., cum laude, 1975); University of Pennsylvania (J.D., cum laude, 1978). Author: "Arbitration and The Insolvent Insurer," Legal Times, January 11, 1999; "Legal and Insurance Considerations of the Year 2000 Problem," Journal of Insurance Regulation, September 1998; "Time's Up for 'Good Faith'," Legal Times, January 13, 1997; "The Case For Arbitration," Global Reinsurance, September, 1991; "Going to Arbitration," Reinsurance, March, 1990; "Arbitrating Disputes," Reinsurance Digest (January/February, 1990); "The Reinsurance Arbitration Award," American Bar Association, 1987; "Insuring the Premises," Commercial Real Estate Tenant's Handbook, John Wiley & Sons, 1987; "The Fine Art of Deciphering Insurance Provisions in Mortgage and Leases," Real Estate Finance Journal, Winter, 1986; "Passing the Buck," November, 1997; "Arbitration and the Insolvent Insurer," *Legal Times,* January 11, 1999; "Legal and Insurance Considerations of the Year 2000 Problem," *Journal of Insurance Regulation,* Spring, 1999, Volume 17, Issue No. 3. *Member:* The District of Columbia Bar (Chairman, Members Benefit Committee, 1988-1994); International Bar Association. ***LANGUAGES:*** French.

DAVID K. SCHUMACHER, born Akron, Ohio, June 23, 1964; admitted to bar, 1989, Virginia; 1990, District of Columbia. *Education:* University of Virginia (B.A., 1996); George Washington University (J.D., with honors, 1989). Author: Chapter, "Fuel Supply and Transportation Arrangements," in book *Power Project Documentation*.

ROBERT F. SHAPIRO, born New York, N.Y., May 31, 1951; admitted to bar, 1976, Maryland; 1977, District of Columbia. *Education:* Trinity College (B.A., 1973); George Washington University (J.D., 1976). Trial Attorney, 1977-1979; Assistant Advisory Counsel, 1980-1981; Attorney, Solicitors Office, 1981-1984; Federal Energy Regulatory Commission. *Member:* The District of Columbia Bar; Maryland State, Energy and American Bar Associations.

ELLEN H. WOODBURY, born Wiesbaden, Germany, December 11, 1947; admitted to bar, 1981, New York; 1984, U.S. District Court, Southern District of New York (Not admitted in District of Columbia). *Education:* Radcliffe College (B.A., cum laude, 1969); New York University (J.D., cum laude, Order of the Coif, 1980); Princeton University (M.A., 1981).

RESIDENT COUNSEL

ROY S. BELDEN, born Meriden, Connecticut, June 24, 1963; admitted to bar, 1991, Connecticut; 1992, District of Columbia; 1995, U.S. Court of Appeals for the District of Columbia Circuit. *Education:* Bates College (B.A., 1985); George Washington University (J.D., with honors, 1991). Co-author: "The Role of Private Citizens in Enforcing U.S. Environmental Laws," chapter in the *International Environmental Law and Regulation* Vol. 2, 1997. Author: *Basic Practice Series: "Clean Air Act"; "Reinvigorating the Due Process Defense:* EPA Required to Give Fair Warning of Rule Interpretations," *Environment Reporter,* The Bureau of National Affairs, April 26, 1996; "Preparing for the Onslaught of Clean Air Act Citizen Suits: A Review of Strategies and Defenses," *The Environmental Lawyer,* Vo. 1, No. 2, February 1995. *Member:* The District of Columbia Bar; American Bar Association (Air Quality Committee; Natural Resources, Energy and Environmental Law Section, Vice Chair, 1996—); Environmental Law Institute; Air and Waste Management Association.

J. CHRISTOPHER GROOBEY, born Richmond, Virginia, July 5, 1965; admitted to bar, 1991, California; 1992, District of Columbia. *Education:* Hampshire College (B.A., 1987); University of Chicago (J.D., 1991). Editor-in-Chief, University of Chicago Legal Forum, 1990-1991. ***PRACTICE AREAS:*** Project Finance; Capital Markets; Corporate Law.

LYNN N. HARGIS, born San Antonio, Texas, February 23, 1943; admitted to bar, 1975, California; 1980, District of Columbia. *Education:* Southern Methodist University (B.A., 1964); University of California at Berkeley (J.D., 1975). Assistant General Counsel for Electric Rates and Corporate Regulation, Federal Energy Regulatory Commission, 1979-1985. *Member:* The District of Columbia Bar; The State Bar of California.

DON J. MROS, born St. Louis, Missouri, May 9, 1951; admitted to bar, 1984, Missouri; 1988, District of Columbia. *Education:* University of Missouri (B.A., 1973; J.D., 1984). Member, Order of Bench and Bar. Casenote Editor, Missouri Law Review. *Member:* The District of Columbia Bar; The Missouri Bar.

ALEJANDRO SILVA, born Bogota, Colombia, September 11, 1963; admitted to bar, 1988, Colombia; 2001, District of Columbia as Special Legal Consultant. *Education:* Universidad del Rosario (Law Degree, 1988). Professor, Universidad del Rosario, Bogota D.C., Colombia, Civil Law - Obligations, 1999-2001. Counsel, International Finance Corporation, 1994-1996. Managing Partner, Silva, Pineros & Gomez, 1997-2001. ***LANGUAGES:*** Spanish.

RESIDENT OF COUNSEL

EDMUND E. HARVEY, born New York, N.Y., October 18, 1920; admitted to bar, 1948, New York; 1969, District of Columbia. *Education:* University of Notre Dame (A.B., 1941); Fordham University (LL.B., 1947). *Member:* The District of Columbia Bar; The Association of the Bar of the City of New York; American Bar Association.

RESIDENT ASSOCIATES

MARISSA L. ALCALA, born Nyack, New York, May 26, 1976; admitted to bar, 2001, New York (Not admitted in District of Columbia). *Education:* Yale University (B.A., 1997); Georgetown University (J.D., 2000).

TODD E. ALEXANDER, born Chicago, Illinois, November 14, 1969; admitted to bar, 1995, New York; 2001, District of Columbia. *Education:* University of Illinois (B.S., 1991); Georgetown University (J.D., 1994).

JOEL M. BARANOWSKI, born Milwaukee, Wisconsin, July 29, 1971; admitted to bar, 1997, Maryland; 1999, District of Columbia. *Education:* University of Pennsylvania (B.A., cum laude, 1993); Georgetown University Law Center (J.D., 1996). Lecturer, Concordia International University, Estonia, May 1997-June 1998. ***LANGUAGES:*** German.

MEAGHAN McGRATH BEAUMONT, born Denver, Colorado, October 7, 1967; admitted to bar, 1993, New York and District of Columbia. *Education:* Columbia College (B.A., cum laude, 1989) Phi Beta Kappa; Georgetown University (J.D., cum laude, 1992). Co-Chair, Energy Committee, Indo-American Chamber of Commerce, 1994-1995. *Member:* New York State and American Bar Associations; The District of Columbia Bar.

THANE BENEDICT IV, born New Haven, Connecticut, February 21, 1969; admitted to bar, 1999, New York (Not admitted in District of Columbia). *Education:* Connecticut College (B.A., 1992); Cornell Law School (J.D., 1996).

ROHIT CHAUDHRY, born New Delhi, India, September 20, 1967; admitted to bar, 1989, India, 1994, New York; 2000, England and Wales (Not admitted in District of Columbia). *Education:* Hindu College, University of Delhi, New Delhi, India (B.A. (Hons), 1989); Delhi University Faculty of Law, New Delhi, India (LL.B., 1992); Harvard Law School (LL.M., 1993). *Member:* New York State and American Bar Associations; Delhi Bar Association. ***LANGUAGES:*** Hindi.

TIMOTHY E. CURLEY, born Suffern, New York, March 23, 1970; admitted to bar, 1996, New York and New Jersey; 2000, District of Columbia. *Education:* Duke University (B.A., magna cum laude, 1992); Albany Law School of Union University (J.D., cum laude, 1995). Phi Beta Kappa. *Member:* The District of Columbia Bar; American Bar Association. [Lt., U.S. Navy, JAG Corps, 1995-2000.]

ANTHONY DANTI, born Lancaster, Wisconsin, May 12, 1970; (admission pending). *Education:* Georgetown University (B.S.F.S., 1992; J.D., 2001).

(This Listing Continued)

JENNIFER R. DEVERY, born Menomonee Falls, Wisconsin, December 13, 1973; admitted to bar, 1998, Maryland; 1999, U.S. District Court, District of Maryland; 2000, District of Columbia. *Education:* The Pennsylvania State University (B.A., 1994); University of Maryland (J.D., 1998). Order of the Coif; Order of the Barristers.

TIMOTHY J. DICINTIO, born Reading, Pennsylvania, August 8, 1968; admitted to bar, 1993, Pennsylvania; 1996, District of Columbia. *Education:* Yale University (B.A., magna cum laude, 1990); Harvard Law School (J.D., cum laude, 1993). *Member:* Bar Association of the District of Columbia; American Bar Association.

BENJAMIN T. FORD, admitted to bar, 2001, New York (Not admitted in District of Columbia). *Education:* Brigham Young University (B.A., cum laude, 1996); Harvard Law School (J.D., 2000). ***LANGUAGES:*** Cantonese.

PHILIP J. GOODMAN, born Groton, Connecticut, March 16, 1961; admitted to bar, 1992, Pennsylvania; 1993, U.S. District Court, Eastern District of Pennsylvania; 1994, District of Columbia. *Education:* United States Naval Academy (B.S., 1982); The Fuqua School of Business, Duke University (M.B.A., 1989); University of Pennsylvania (J.D., magna cum laude, 1992). Law Clerk, Hon. Norma L. Shapiro, U.S. District Judge, Eastern District of Pennsylvania, 1992-1993. [Lt., U.S. Navy, 1982-1987]

KIMBERLY J. HEIMERT, born Memphis, Tennessee, June 22, 1969; admitted to bar, 1994, New York (Not admitted in District of Columbia). *Education:* The American University (B.A., summa cum laude, with highest honors, 1991); Harvard University (J.D., cum laude, 1994). ***LANGUAGES:*** Russian.

THOMAS G. HOHENTHANER, born Yankton, South Dakota, December 17, 1959; admitted to bar, 1990, Virginia; 1992, District of Columbia. *Education:* University of South Dakota (B.A., 1982); University of Virginia (J.D., 1990). University Scholar, University of South Dakota. Chief Counsel: U.S. Senate Committee on Commerce, Science, and Transportation; U.S. Senate Committee on Small Business.

MICHELLE A. JONES, born San Salvador, El Salvador, June 10, 1974; admitted to bar, 1998, Virginia; 1998, U.S. Court of Appeals, Fourth Circuit; 1999, U.S. Court of Appeals, Eighth Circuit; 2000, District of Columbia. *Education:* Vanderbilt University (B.A., 1995); Harvard University (J.D., 1998).

HELÉNA M. KLUMPP, born Chicago, Illinois, January 12, 1971; admitted to bar, 1996, Virginia; 1998, District of Columbia. *Education:* Illinois Wesleyan University (B.A., magna cum laude, 1993); Georgetown University (J.D., 1996). American Jurisprudence Award. Corpus Juris Secundum Award.

REKA S. KOERNER, born New York, N.Y., October 23, 1972; (admission pending). *Education:* Carleton College (B.A., 1994); University of Texas School of Law (J.D., 1999). Law Clerk to U.S. District Judge Hilda G. Hagle.

SAMUEL R. KWON, born Seoul, Korea, September 23, 1974; admitted to bar, 1999, New York (Not admitted in District of Columbia). *Education:* The Wharton School, University of Pennsylvania (B.S., magna cum laude, 1996); Georgetown Law Center (J.D., cum laude, 1999).

JOY L. LANGFORD, born Meridian, Mississippi, May 27, 1969; admitted to bar, 1994, Virginia; 1996, District of Columbia and U.S. District Court, Eastern District of Virginia. *Education:* Mississippi College (B.A., special distinction with highest honors, 1991); Georgetown University (J.D., cum laude, 1994). Author, "Passing the Buck: Are Bad Faith Punitive Damages Reinsurable?" Reinsurance. Nov. 19. Moot Court/Trial Advocacy Advisor, Georgetown University Law Center, 1995—. *Member:* American Bar Association (Tort and Insurance Practice Section).

ELLEN M. MACDONALD, born Princeton, New Jersey, August 17, 1969; admitted to bar, 1994, North Carolina; 1997, District of Columbia. *Education:* Yale University (B.A., magna cum laude, with distinction, 1991); University of North Carolina, Chapel Hill (J.D., 1994). Member, University of North Carolina Law Review.

KRISTIN L. MEIKLE, born Tulsa, Oklahoma, February 27, 1967; admitted to bar, 1995, Pennsylvania; 1996, District of Columbia. *Education:* University of Florida (B.A., 1989); Georgetown University (J.D., cum laude, 1994). Phi Beta Kappa. Instructor, Legal Research and Writing for Foreign Students, Summer, 1995, 1996, 1997, 1998 and 1999. Adjunct Faculty, Georgetown University, 1998 and 1999. *Member:* American Bar Association.

W. ROBERTSON MILBOURNE JR., born Philadelphia, Pennsylvania, August 8, 1972; admitted to bar, 2000, New York (Not admitted in District of Columbia). *Education:* Dartmouth College (A.B., 1995); Duke University (J.D., 1999).

M. KATHERINE MONTGOMERY, born Jackson, Mississippi, April 3, 1974; admitted to bar, 2000, Maryland; 2001, District of Columbia. *Education:* Loyola University (B.A., 1996); Georgetown University (J.D., 1999). Barristers' Council - Trial Team Member, 1997-1999. Law Clerk to the Hon. Charles B. Kornmann, U.S. District Judge, District of South Dakota, 1999-2000. Legal Research and Writing Fellow, 1996-1997. *Member:* Maryland State Bar Association.

(This Listing Continued)

AMY E. NELSON, born Dallas, Texas, January 30, 1973; (admission pending). *Education:* Texas A & M University (B.S., 1995); George Washington University (J.D., with honors, 2001).

JAMES W. SCARROW, born Lansing, Michigan, January 24, 1961; admitted to bar, 1990, Virginia and District of Columbia; 1994, Texas. *Education:* Dartmouth College (B.A., 1983); University of Wisconsin-Madison (M.S-.C.E.E., 1985); University of Virginia (J.D., 1990).

WILLIAM H. SCHMIDT, JR., born Paramus, New Jersey, December 18, 1972; admitted to bar, 1997, Virginia; 1999, District of Columbia. *Education:* Drew University (B.A., 1994); George Washington Law School (J.D., 1997). Senior Managing Editor, The George Washington Law Review.

JOHN R. R. TORMEY, born Los Angeles, California, September 26, 1968; admitted to bar, 1996, Maryland; 1997, U.S. District Court, District of Maryland; 1998, District of Columbia. *Education:* Westmont College (B.A., Biology, 1990); George Washington University (J.D., 1996).

LUIS F. TORRES, born Denton, Texas, March 5, 1972; admitted to bar, 1998, District of Columbia and New York. *Education:* Georgetown University, Walsh School of Foreign Service (B.S.F.S., 1994); George Washington University Law School (J.D., 1998). Dean's Citation, Georgetown University. *Member:* American Bar Association (Section of Business Law). ***LANGUAGES:*** Spanish, Italian and French.

STEVEN E. WAGNER, born Alamogordo, New Mexico, July 11, 1972; admitted to bar, 1998, Maryland (Inactive); 2000, District of Columbia. *Education:* Georgetown University (B.A., 1994); University of Pennsylvania (J.D., 1998). Alpha Sigma Nu; Phi Sigma Alpha. ***LANGUAGES:*** Spanish.

STAFF ATTORNEYS

KATHRYN L. CERVON, born Quincy, Illinois, December 3, 1957; admitted to bar, 1990, Pennsylvania; 1991, Florida and District of Columbia. *Education:* Colorado College (B.A., 1980); Columbia University (M.I.A., 1983); University of Bonn, Germany; National Law Center, George Washington University (J.D., 1990). Author: "CERCLA Cleanup Costs As 'Damages' Under the CGL Policy," 41 Fed. of Ins. & Corporate Counsel Q. 391 (Summer 1991). *Member:* District of Columbia Bar; The Florida Bar; American Bar Association (Member, Tort and Insurance Practice Section). ***LANGUAGES:*** German.

CHRISTOPHER T. GALLU, JR., born Baltimore, Maryland, January 31, 1970; admitted to bar, 1997, Maryland; 1999, District of Columbia. *Education:* Pennsylvania State University (B.A., 1993); George Washington University (J.D., with honors, 1997). Associate, The George Washington University Law Review.

(For Biographical Data of other Personnel, see Professional Biographies at New York, N.Y., Los Angeles, California, Upper Montclair, New Jersey, London, England, Moscow, Russia and Hong Kong, China)

CHAIKIN & SHERMAN, P.C.

THE LAW BUILDING
1232 SEVENTEENTH STREET, N.W.
WASHINGTON, D.C. 20036
Telephone: 202-659-8600
Fax: 202-659-8680
Email: Sherman@DC.law-net
URL: http://www.lawyers.com/chaikin&sherman

Bethesda, Maryland Office: 7315 Wisconsin Avenue, Suite 220-E. 20814.

Medical Malpractice, Wrongful Death, Automobile Negligence, Serious Personal Injury, Product Liability, Premises Liability, Class Action Lawsuits, Discrimination.

FIRM PROFILE: The firm concentrates its practice in the representation of victims of medical malpractice, automobile negligence, premises liability and those who are injured due to defective products. The firm has two former presidents of the Metropolitan Washington D.C. Trial Lawyers Association and a recipient of the Trial Lawyers of the Year Award. The members of the firm also serve as arbitrators and mediators, both under court auspices as well as privately.

DONALD J. CHAIKIN, born Jersey City, New Jersey, August 12, 1933; admitted to bar, 1964, District of Columbia and Maryland. *Education:* University of Maryland (B.A., 1960); Washington College of Law of American University (LL.B., 1963). Co-Recipient, Plaintiffs Trial Lawyer of the Year Award, 1986. Commissioner, District of Columbia Baseball Commission, 1984-1986. Member, Panel of Arbitrators, American Arbitration Association. *Member:* The District of Columbia Bar; Maryland State Bar Association; Trial Lawyers Association of Metropolitan Washington, D.C. (Member, Board of Governors, 1976-1980; President, 1982-1983). ***PRACTICE AREAS:*** Auto Negligence; Premises Liability.

IRA SHERMAN, born Bronx, New York, December 6, 1945; admitted to bar, 1974, New York; 1975, District of Columbia and Maryland. *Education:*

(This Listing Continued)

CHAIKIN & SHERMAN, P.C., Washington—Continued

State University of New York at Buffalo (B.S., 1967; J.D., 1974). Senior Trial Attorney, Office of the Solicitor, Division of Civil Rights, U.S. Department of Labor, 1975-1980. Member, Judicial Conference of the District of Columbia, 1994-2000. Appointed by District of Columbia Superior Court as Arbitrator & Mediator for alternative Disputes Resolution Division, 1988-1998. Master, George Washington Inns of Court. *Member:* District of Columbia Bar; Montgomery County, Prince Georges County, Maryland State and American Bar Associations; The Association of Trial Lawyers of America; Trial Lawyers Association of Metropolitan Washington, D.C. (President, 1993-1994; Member, Board of Governors). ***PRACTICE AREAS:*** Wrongful Death; Medical Malpractice; Auto Negligence; Products Liability; Serious Personal Injury. ***Email:*** Sherman@dc-Law.net

---

JOSEPH CAMMARATA, born Brooklyn, New York, June 23, 1958; admitted to bar, 1984, New York and U.S. District Court, Eastern and Southern Districts of New York; U.S. Tax Court; 1985, District of Columbia; 1986, U.S. Court of Federal Claims; 1992, Maryland and U.S. District Court, District of Columbia; 1993, Virginia and U.S. District Court for the Eastern and Western Districts of Virginia; 1994, U.S. Court of Appeals, Fourth Circuit; 1995, U.S. Court of Appeals, Eighth and Eleventh Circuits and U.S. Supreme Court; 1996 U.S. District Court, District of Maryland; 1998, U.S. District Court, Central District of Illinois. *Education:* Georgetown University School of Foreign Service (B.S.F.S., 1980); St. John's University School of Law (J.D., 1983); Pace University Lubin Graduate School of Business (Cert. of Adv. Grad. Stdy. in Acctg., 1984); Georgetown University Law Center (M.L.T., 1987). Recipient: Department of Justice, Tax Division, Outstanding Attorney Award, 1989; Named One of the Top Fifty Lawyers in the Washington, D.C. area, Washingtonian, 1997; Named One of Top Forty Lawyers Under Forty in the Washington Legal Establishment, Washingtonian, 1998; Who's Who in American Law; Who's Who in the East; Who's Who in Emerging Leaders; the National Registry of Who's Who. Certified Public Accountant, New York, 1988. Trial Attorney, Tax Division, Department of Justice, 1986-1990. Chairman, Criminal Justice Advisory Board, Fairfax County, VA , 1995-1997. Chairman, Community Initiative to reduce Youth Violence, Fairfax County, VA, 1996-1997. *Member:* New York State, Maryland State, Virginia and American Bar Associations; The Association of Trial Lawyers of America; Trial Lawyers Association of Metropolitan Washington, D.C.; Virginia Trial Lawyers Association; American Institute of Certified Public Accounts (Tax Executive Committee). ***PRACTICE AREAS:*** Litigation; Personal Injury; Medical Malpractice; Wrongful Death; Sexual Harassment; Employment Discrimination. ***Email:*** Joe@dc-law.net

ALLAN M. SIEGEL, born Baltimore, Maryland, October 11, 1969; admitted to bar, 1994, Maryland; 1995, Virginia, District of Columbia, U.S. District Court, District of Maryland and U.S. Court of Appeals, Fourth Circuit; 1999, U.S. District Court, District of Columbia. *Education:* The George Washington University (B.B.A., magna cum laude, 1991; J.D., with honors, 1994). Board of Governors and Co-Chair Education Committee, Trial Lawyers Association of Metropolitan Washington D.C. *Member:* District of Columbia Bar; Maryland State Bar Association; Virginia State Bar Association; Bar Association of the District of Columbia;; Virginia Trial Lawyers Association; Association of Trial Lawyers of America;. ***PRACTICE AREAS:*** Medical Malpractice; Auto Negligence; Wrongful Death; Premises Liability; Product Liability. ***Email:*** Allan@dc-law.net

GARRETT V. WILLIAMS, born Wilmington, Delaware, June 16, 1969; admitted to bar, 1995, Maryland and U.S. District Court, District of Maryland; 1996, District of Columbia. *Education:* Emory University (B.A., 1991); George Washington University (J.D., 1994). Sigma Delta Tau. Moot Court Board. Judicial Clerk to Hon. Charles H. Toliver, IV, Superior Court of Delaware, 1994-1995. *Member:* Montgomery County, Mary land State, American and National Bar Associations; District of Columbia Bar; Trial Lawyers Association of Metropolitan Washington, D.C.; The Association of Trial Lawyers of America. ***PRACTICE AREAS:*** Personal Injury; Employment Discrimination; Premises Liability; Medical Malpractice; Products Liability. ***Email:*** Garrett@dc-law.net

CAMELLIA JAVADI JACOBS, born Morgantown, West Virginia, November 5, 1976; admitted to bar, 2000, Maryland; 2001, District of Columbia. *Education:* Tulane University of Louisiana (B.A., 1997); Washington College of Law, American University (J.D., 2000). Motions Clerk, D.C. Court of Appeals, 2000-2001. *Member:* Maryland State Bar Association; The District of Columbia Bar; District of Columbia Trial Lawyers Association. ***LANGUAGES:*** Farsi. ***PRACTICE AREAS:*** Wrongful Death; Medical Malpractice; Automobile Negligence; Personal Injury. ***Email:*** camellia@dc-law.net

CHRISTINE A GRAY-KNIGHT, born Washington, D.C., August 4, 1961; admitted to bar, 1987, Pennsylvania; 1992, District of Columbia. *Education:* University of Maryland (B.A., 1983); Howard University (J.D., 1986). *Member:* District of Columbia Bar. ***PRACTICE AREAS:*** Personal Injury. ***Email:*** christine@dc-law.net

(This Listing Continued)

OF COUNSEL

SILVERIO COY, born May 7, 1952; admitted to bar, 1986, Pennsylvania, District of Columbia and U. S. Count of Appeals for the District of Columbia Circuit. *Education:* Inter-American University of Puerto Rico (B.A., 1975); Columbus University (J.D., 1984). *Member:* Bar Association of the District of Columbia; Pennsylvania and American Bar Associations. ***LANGUAGES:*** Spanish. ***PRACTICE AREAS:*** International Law; Immigration Law. ***Email:*** silverio@dc-law.net

---

JOY S. CHAMBERS

WASHINGTON, D.C.

(See Alexandria, Virginia)

Estate Planning, Wills, Trusts and Probate Law, Elder Law, Guardianships, Living Wills, Powers of Attorney.

CHARAPP, DEESE & WEISS, LLP

Established in 1996

1901 PENNSYLVANIA AVENUE, N.W., SUITE 1001
WASHINGTON, D.C. 20006
Telephone: 202-463-9100
Fax: 202-463-2091
URL: http://www.cdw-law.com

Vienna, Virginia Office: 8300 Boone Boulevard, Suite 500, 22182. Telephone 703-714-9576.
Bethesda, Maryland Office: 3 Bethesda Metro Center, Suite 700, 20814. Telephone: 301-657-6258.
Richmond, Virginia Office: 2201 West Broad Street, Suite 201, 23220. Telephone: 804-358-8003. Fax: 804-358-3889.

Civil Litigation, Corporate Law and Government Contracts.

MICHAEL G. CHARAPP, born Pittsburgh, Pennsylvania, May 11, 1949; admitted to bar, 1974, Virginia; 1975, District of Columbia. *Education:* University of Pittsburgh (B.A., 1971); Georgetown University (J.D., 1974). Editor, Legislative Notes, Law & Policy in International Business, 1973-1974. *Member:* The District of Columbia Bar; Virginia State Bar; American Bar Association. ***PRACTICE AREAS:*** Corporations and Commercial Transactions; Franchises; Real Estate; Commercial Law; Litigation. ***Email:*** mike.charapp@cdw-law.com

C. MICHAEL DEESE, born Mobile, Alabama, October 6, 1951; admitted to bar, 1976, Ohio; 1978, District of Columbia. *Education:* Phillips Universitat, Marburg, Germany and Davidson College (A.B., 1973); University of Pennsylvania (M.A., 1976; J.D., 1976). Phi Eta Sigma. *Member:* The District of Columbia Bar; American Bar Association. ***PRACTICE AREAS:*** Trade Association Law; Litigation; First Amendment. ***Email:*** michael.deese@cdw-law.com

BRAD D. WEISS, born Philadelphia, Pennsylvania, November 19, 1955; admitted to bar, 1982, Virginia; 1983, District of Columbia; 1985, Maryland; 1988, Pennsylvania; 1998, New York. *Education:* George Washington University (B.A. 1978); George Mason University (J.D., 1982). Phi Delta Phi. Member, Moot Court Board, 1980-1981. Editor, George Mason University Law Review, 1981-1982. Author: "Gulf Offshore Corp. vs. Mobil Oil Corp.: Jurisdiction within the Meaning of the Outer Continental Shelf Lands Act," 5 GMU L. Rev. 478 (1982); Dr. Yeager, "Apartments: Must They be Habitable," 4 GMU L. Rev. 179 (1981); (Research Assistant and Author of Article Chapter). Member, Washington Area Lawyers for the Arts; Board of Directors, Arlington Arts Center, 1988-1989. *Member:* The District of Columbia Bar; Arlington County, Pennsylvania, Maryland State and American Bar Associations; Virginia State Bar. ***PRACTICE AREAS:*** Corporate and Commercial Transactions; Complex Litigation; Employment and Discrimination Litigation; Aviation Transactions. ***Email:*** brad.weiss@cdw-law.com

---

SARAH DALY JACKOWSKI, born Augusta, Georgia, March 21, 1968; admitted to bar, 1993, Virginia; 1994, Maryland; 1996, District of Columbia. *Education:* James Madison University (B.S., summa cum laude, 1990); Georgetown University (J.D., 1993). *Member:* Virginia State Bar; District of Columbia Bar. ***PRACTICE AREAS:*** Corporate Law; Commercial Transactions; Trade and Professional Associations Law. ***Email:*** sarah.jackowski@cdw-law.com

MICHAEL C. GARTNER, born Washington, D.C., May 30, 1971; admitted to bar, 1997, Virginia; 1999, District of Columbia. *Education:* Virginia Polytechnic Institute and State University (B.A., 1993); William Mitchell College of Law (J.D., magna cum laude, 1997). *Member:* Fairfax County and Virginia Bar Associations. ***PRACTICE AREAS:*** Civil Litigation; Employment Law; Corporate Law. ***Email:*** michael.gartner@cdw-law.com

(This Listing Continued)

JAMES B. ST. JOHN, III, born North Kingstown, Rhode Island, May 31, 1966; admitted to bar, 1998, Maryland; 1999, District of Columbia. *Education:* Washington & Lee University (B.A., 1988); Tulane University of Louisiana (J.D., 1998). *Member:* Montgomery County, Maryland State and American Bar Associations. ***PRACTICE AREAS:*** Civil Litigation; Corporate Law. ***Email:*** jay.stjohn@cdw-law.com

STEPHEN F. VARHOLY, born Arlington, Virginia, May 7, 1970; admitted to bar, 2000, Virginia (Not admitted in District of Columbia). *Education:* University of South Carolina (B.A., 1994); The Catholic University of America (J.D., cum laude, 2000). *Member:* Fairfax County Bar Association; Virginia State Bar; Federal Communications Bar. ***PRACTICE AREAS:*** Civil Litigation; Corporate Law; Employment Law. ***Email:*** stephen.varholy@cdw-law.com

OF COUNSEL

EDWARD H. KIM, born Seoul, Korea, May 9, 1966; admitted to bar, 1991, Maryland; 1993, District of Columbia. *Education:* Boston University (B.S., cum laude, 1988); George Washington University (J.D., 1991). Member: Beta Gamma Sigma, Locke Honorary Society. Government Contracts Counsel, National Lien and Bond Claim Systems. *Member:* The District of Columbia Bar (Member, Sections on: Government Contracts; Litigation; Court and Board Practice Committee), American Bar Association (Public Contract Law; Science and Technology), Asian Pacific American and Korean American Bar Associations. ***LANGUAGES:*** Korean. ***PRACTICE AREAS:*** Government Contracts; Business Litigation; Corporate. ***Email:*** edward.kim@cdw-law.com

HOLMES C. HARRISON, born Richmond, Virginia, June 25, 1941; admitted to bar, 1966, Virginia, U.S. Supreme Court, U.S. Court of Military Appeals and U.S. District Court, Western District of Virginia (Not admitted in District of Columbia). *Education:* Hampden-Sydney College (B.A., 1963); University of Richmond (J.D., 1966). Omicron Delta Kappa; Phi Delta Phi. Member, McNeill Law Society. *Member:* Harrisonburg-Rockingham Bar Association (President, 1979-1980); Virginia State Bar; Virginia Trial Lawyers Association; The Association of Trial Lawyers of America. [Capt., JAGC, U.S. Army, 1966-1972]. ***PRACTICE AREAS:*** Civil Litigation. ***Email:*** holmes.harrison@cdw-law.com

BRENDA HOUCK HARBISON, born Lancaster, Pennsylvania, April 13, 1969; admitted to bar, 1996, Delaware; 1997, Pennsylvania 1998, Virginia. *Education:* University of Pittsburgh (B.A., cum laude, 1991) Widener University School of Law (J.D., cum laude 1996; M.B.A., 1996). Research Editor, Delaware Journal Corporate Law, 1995-1996. Author: Statutory Amendments to the Delaware General Corporation Law," 20 Del. J. Corp.L. 477 (1995). *Member:* Delaware State Bar Association; Virginia State Bar; Virginia Women Attorneys Association; Metropolitan Richmond Women's Bar Association; Virginia Trial Lawyer Association. (Resident, Richmond, Virginia Office). ***PRACTICE AREAS:*** Civil Litigation; Franchise Law; Automotive Law; Administrative Law. ***Email:*** brenda.harbison@cdw-law.com

THE CHAVERS LAW FIRM, P.C.

2600 VIRGINIA AVENUE, N.W., SUITE 200
WASHINGTON, D.C. 20037
Telephone: 202-333-8575
Fax: 202-333-8226
URL: http://www.lawyers.com/chaverslaw

Corporate Diversity, Civil Rights Compliance, Women's Rights Issues, Employment Contracts, Discrimination, Sexual Harassment, Labor Law, Employment Law, Corporate Law, Commercial Transactions, Government Contracts, International Commercial Transactions, Arts and Entertainment Law, Internet Law, E-Commerce and Intellectual Property.

FIRM PROFILE: The firm's national practice includes representation of individuals, small to large businesses, organizations and nonprofit associations and foreign governments. The firm acts in many instances as general counsel to various corporations, especially in the areas of civil rights compliance, labor issues and commercial transactions.

CLAYBORNE E. CHAVERS, born Philadelphia, Pennsylvania, January 16, 1947; admitted to bar, 1976, Pennsylvania; 1978, U.S. Court of Claims; 1979, District of Columbia and U.S. District Court for the District of Columbia; 1983, U.S. Court of Appeals for the District of Columbia Circuit. *Education:* University of Pennsylvania; Pennsylvania Academy of Fine Arts; Cheyney State College; Howard University (B.F.A., cum laude, 1972; J.D., 1975). Delta Theta Phi (Vice Dean, 1973-1975). Professor, Art and Entertainment Law, Sagamon State University, University of the District of Columbia, 1979-1981. Visiting Lecturer: University of the District of Columbia, 1981-1985; Georgetown University School of Law; College of William & Mary School of Law; Howard University School of Law. Commissioner, Howard County, Maryland, Human Rights Commission, 1985-1986. *Member:* The District of Columbia Bar; American Bar Association; National Bar Association (Founder and First Chairman, Entertainment Arts & Sports Section, 1979-1980); Washington Area Lawyers for the Arts; Black Entertainment and Sports Lawyers. ***PRACTICE AREAS:*** Entertainment and Art Law; Civil Rights Law; Business Development.

(This Listing Continued)

JEAN D. META, born Baltimore, Maryland, June 3, 1974; admitted to bar, 2000, Maryland (Not admitted in District of Columbia). *Education:* The American University (B.A., 1996); University of Pittsburgh (J.D., 1999). *Member:* Maryland State (Young Lawyers Section) and American (Litigation Section) Bar Associations; Pro Bond Resource Center of Maryland. ***PRACTICE AREAS:*** Intellectual Property; Internet Law; Business Organization; Entertainment and the Arts; Sports Law.

OF COUNSEL

ELLIOTT CARL ALDERMAN, born Manhattan, New York, October 13, 1956; admitted to bar, 1983, District of Columbia; 1993, Virginia. *Education:* Rutgers University (B.A., 1978); American University (J.D., 1982). Former Senior Attorney, U.S. Copyright Office. Special Assistant U.S. Attorney for the District of Columbia. Law Clerk to Assistant Chief of Administrative Law, Judge G. Marvin Bober, U.S. Department of Labor. *Member:* The District of Columbia Bar. ***PRACTICE AREAS:*** Trademark; Copyright.

CLARE CHERKASKY

WASHINGTON, D.C.
(See Falls Church, Virginia)
Immigration and Naturalization.

CHONÉ & ASSOCIATES, PLLC

206 NINTH STREET, S.E.
P.O. BOX 15430
WASHINGTON, D.C. 20003
Telephone: 202-543-3066
Fax: 202-543-2836
URL: http://www.cabinetchone.com
Email: pchone@cabinetchone.com
URL: http://www.lawyers.com/chonemauprivezlaw

Small Business Corporate Counseling; Immigration (Business Immigration, Employment Visas, Family Immigration and Naturalization); Family Law (International Child Abductions, Prenuptial Agreements, Divorce); Estates and Trusts (International Wills); Civil Litigation.

FIRM PROFILE: The firm has a particular expertise in the representation of the French- speaking community, both individuals and businesses in the United States, and the firm has a strong presence in the Metropolitan Washington, D.C. area. Attorneys Choné and Mauprivez are especially adept at resolving international legal problems that stem from jurisdictional conflict between France and the United States. The firm is affiliated with Michel Choné, Daniel Maninetti, Pierre Grolleau et Louis-Henri Delestable, Notaires Associés ă Saint Nicolas de Port, France.

PIERRE CHONÉ, born Nancy, France, November 15, 1957; admitted to bar, 1996, Maryland; 1997, District of Columbia; 2001, U.S. Supreme Court. *Education:* University of Maryland (B.S., 1993; J.D., 1996). Member, French American Chamber of Commerce. *Member:* Maryland State and American Bar Associations; District of Columbia Bar; American Immigration Lawyers Association; Association of Trial Lawyers of America. ***LANGUAGES:*** French. ***PRACTICE AREAS:*** Immigration Law; Business Law; Family Law; Estates and Trusts; Civil Litigation. ***Email:*** pchone@cabinetchone.com

OF COUNSEL

BRUNO J. MAUPRIVEZ, born France, December 14, 1951; admitted to bar, 1986, Pennsylvania; 1987, Maryland; 1997, District of Columbia. *Education:* American University (B.A., 1981); Washington College of Law (J.D., 1986). *Member:* Pennsylvania Bar Association. ***LANGUAGES:*** French and Spanish. ***PRACTICE AREAS:*** Torts; Commercial Litigation.

CHURCH & HOUFF, P.A.

WASHINGTON, D.C.
(See Baltimore, Maryland)
General Civil Litigation. Trial and Appeals. Insurance Coverage, Casualty Torts and Negligence Litigation, Products Liability, Professional Negligence. Complex Litigation.

R. JACK CLAPP & ASSOC. CO., L.P.A.

HALL OF STATES BUILDING
444 NORTH CAPITAL STREET, N.W., SUITE 828
WASHINGTON, D.C. 20001
Telephone: 888-334-8500
Email: RJClappDC@aol.com
URL: http://www.rjackclapp.com

Cleveland, Ohio Office: One Cleveland Center, Suite 2420, 1375 East Ninth. Telephone: 216-861-1400. Fax: 216-861-1401.
Mentor, Ohio Office: 7784 Reynolds Road. Telephone: 216-946-1100. Fax: 216-946-1756.

Wrongful Death, Personal Injury, Medical Malpractice, Defective Products, Automobile Accidents and Aviation Law.

(For complete biographical data on all personnel, see Professional Biographies at Cleveland, Ohio)

CLAXTON, SALE & QUINN, P.C.

Established in 1984
FIFTH FLOOR
910 SIXTEENTH STREET, N.W.
WASHINGTON, D.C. 20006
Telephone: 202-833-4170
Fax: 202-887-5137
URL: http://www.lawyers.com/claxtonsale&quinn

Civil Litigation, Government Contracts, Energy, Telecommunication Law, Employment Law, Business Law; Business Litigation.

STEPHEN SALE, born Peru, Illinois, June 7, 1952; admitted to bar, 1977, District of Columbia; 1985, U.S. Court of Federal Claims, U.S. Court of Appeals for the Federal Circuit and U.S. Court of Appeals, First Circuit; 1991, U.S. Court of Appeals, Eighth Circuit. *Education:* University of Dallas (B.A., summa cum laude, 1974); Georgetown University (J.D., 1977). Phi Alpha Delta. *Member:* The District of Columbia Bar. **PRACTICE AREAS:** Telecommunications Law; Government Contracts; Energy; Corporate Law. **Email:** sale@dclawfirm.net

JOHN D. QUINN, born New Haven, Connecticut, August 15, 1951; admitted to bar, 1977, Pennsylvania; 1979, District of Columbia; 1981, U.S. Court of Appeals, D.C. Circuit; 1985, Virginia; 1991, U.S. Court of Appeals, Eighth Circuit and U.S. Court of Appeals, Fourth and Federal Circuits; 1997, Maryland. *Education:* Villanova University (B.S., 1973); University of Pittsburgh (J.D., 1977). *Member:* The District of Columbia Bar. **PRACTICE AREAS:** Commercial Litigation; Employment Law; Telecommunications Law; Business Law. **Email:** quinn@dclawfirm.net

CHARLES R. (RICK) CLAXTON, born Springfield, Missouri, August 2, 1949; admitted to bar, 1978, District of Columbia; 1979, U.S. District Court for the District of Columbia, U.S. Court of Appeals for the District of Columbia Circuit and U.S. Court of Appeals, Fourth Circuit; 1983, Maryland. *Education:* University of Missouri (B.J., 1972); Boston University (J.D., cum laude, 1978). Executive Editor, American Journal of Law and Medicine, 1977-1978. *Member:* District of Columbia Bar; Maryland State and American Bar Associations; Association of Trial Lawyers of America; Trial Lawyers Association of Metro D.C.; Maryland Trial Lawyers Association. **PRACTICE AREAS:** Commercial Litigation; Medical Malpractice; Legal Malpractice; Employment Law. **Email:** claxton@dclawfirm.net

MICHELE BARTOLI-CAIN, born Los Angeles, California, March 2, 1958; admitted to bar, 1984, District of Columbia and U.S. District Court for the District of Columbia. *Education:* North Carolina State University (B.A., cum laude, 1980); Wake Forest University (J.D., 1983). Pi Sigma Alpha; Sigma Kappa. Blue Key. Golden Chain; Moot Court National Team and Executive Board, 1982-1983. Member, Order of The Barristers, 1983. Editor, American Society of International Law Proceedings, 1982. *Member:* American Bar Association; The Association of Trial Lawyers of America; National Museum for Women in the Arts (Charter Member); Virginia Women's Attorney's Association; Campagna Center; Trial Lawyers of Metro District of Columbia; Virginia Trial Lawyers Association. **PRACTICE AREAS:** Commercial Litigation; Personal Injury; Medical Malpractice; Dental Malpractice; Products Liability; Automobile Accidents and Injuries. **Email:** cain@dclawfirm.net

CLEARY, GOTTLIEB, STEEN & HAMILTON

Established in 1946
2000 PENNSYLVANIA AVENUE, N.W.
SUITE 9000
WASHINGTON, D.C. 20006-1801
Telephone: 202-974-1500
Facsimile: 202-974-1999
URL: http://www.cgsh.com

New York, New York Office: One Liberty Plaza, New York, N.Y. 10006. Telephone: 212-225-2000.
Paris, France Office: 41, Avenue de Friedland, 75008 Paris, France. Telephone: 33-1-40-74-68-00.
Brussels, Belgium Office: Rue de la Loi 57, 1040 Brussels, Belgium. Telephone: 32-2-287-2000.
London, England Office: City Place House, 55 Basinghall Street, London EC2V 5EH England. Telephone: 44-71-614-2200.
Hong Kong Office: 39th Floor, Bank of China Tower, One Garden Road, Hong Kong. Telephone: 852-2521-4122.
Tokyo, Japan Office: Cleary, Gottlieb, Steen & Hamilton Gaikokuho Jimu Bengoshi Jimusho, 20th Floor, Shin Kasumigaseki Building, 3-2, Kasumigaseki 3-Chome, Chiyoda-Ku, Tokyo 100-0013, Japan. Telephone: 81-3-3595-3911.
Frankfurt, Germany Office: Main Tower, Neue Mainzer Strasse 52, 60311 Frankfurt am Main, Germany. Telephone: 49-69-971-03-0.
Rome, Italy Office: Piazza de Spagna 15, 00187 Rome, Italy. Telephone: 39-06-69-52-22-1.

Antitrust, Banking and Financial Institutions, Business Litigation, Corporate, Derivatives and Commodities, Employee Benefits, Employment and Pensions, Energy, Environmental Law, Insurance Coverage, Intellectual Property, International Litigation and Arbitration, International Trade, Investment Funds, Joint Ventures, Litigation, Mergers and Acquisitions, Privatizations, Product Liability, Project Finance, Real Estate, Securities and Derivatives, Structured Finance, Taxation, Trusts and Estates, White Collar Defense, Workouts and Bankruptcy.

OF COUNSEL

ROBERT C. BARNARD, born Portland, Oregon, October 31, 1913; admitted to bar, 1940, Washington; 1947, District of Columbia. *Education:* Reed College (A.B., 1935); Columbia Law School and Rhodes Scholar, Oxford University, England (B.A. in Jurisprudence, 1938; B.C.L., 1939; M.A., 1951). Member, Columbia Law Review, 1936. Recipient, Sterling Fellowship, Yale Law School, 1939. Attorney, Antitrust Division, U.S. Department of Justice, 1939-1941. Attorney, 1941-1947 and First Assistant, 1945-1947, Office of the Assistant Solicitor General, U.S. Department of Justice. Resident at Paris Office, 1949-1952. *Member:* The District of Columbia Bar; Washington State, Federal and American Bar Associations.

FRED D. TURNAGE, born Ayden, North Carolina, September 24, 1920; admitted to bar, 1948, North Carolina; 1965, District of Columbia. *Education:* Wake Forest College (A.B., 1942); Wake Forest College School of Law (LL.B., 1948). Trial Attorney, Antitrust Division, U.S. Department of Justice, 1948-1965. Special Assistant to the Attorney General, 1965. *Member:* The District of Columbia Bar; North Carolina State Bar; Federal and American Bar Associations.

J. EUGENE MARANS, born Butte, Montana, May 26, 1940; admitted to bar, 1966, New York; 1971, District of Columbia. *Education:* Harvard College (A.B., magna cum laude, 1962); Harvard Law School (LL.B., cum laude, 1965). Law Clerk to Judge John Minor Wisdom, U.S. Court of Appeals for the Fifth Circuit, 1965-1966. Co-Editor and Contributor: *Manual of Foreign Investment in the United States*, 1993; "Guide to Absentee Voting in Federal Elections by American Citizens Abroad," 1976. Resident at: New York Office, 1966-1970; Paris Office, 1970-1971; Hong Kong Office, 1990-1993. *Member:* The District of Columbia Bar (Chair, International Division, 1978-1979; Co-chair, International Investment and Finance Committee, 1982-1989); Association of the Bar of the City of New York; Federal, American, International and Inter-American Bar Associations; Washington Foreign Law Society (President, 1985-1986); Union Internationale des Avocats; American Society of International Law; International Fiscal Association; American Law Institute. **Email:** emarans@cgsh.com

DANIEL B. SILVER, born Philadelphia, Pennsylvania, August 14, 1941; admitted to bar, 1968, District of Columbia. *Education:* University of California at Berkeley (B.A., highest honors, 1961); Harvard University (M.A., 1965; Ph.D., 1967); Harvard Law School (LL.B., magna cum laude, 1968). General Counsel: National Security Agency, 1978-1979; Central Intelligence Agency, 1979-1981. Adjunct Professor, Georgetown University Law Center, 1981-1983, 1989-1992, 1994—, Distinguished Visitor from Practice, 1993. Resident at Brussels Office, 1983-1985. *Member:* The District of Columbia Bar; American Bar Association. **Email:** dsilver@cgsh.com

(This Listing Continued)

RICHARD DEC. HINDS, born Boston, Massachusetts, November 28, 1941; admitted to bar, 1967, New York; 1973, District of Columbia. *Education:* Tufts University (B.A., magna cum laude, 1964); Columbia University (LL.B., cum laude, 1967). Editor, Columbia Law Review, 1966-1967. Law Clerk to Judge Leonard P. Moore, U.S. Court of Appeals for the Second Circuit, 1967-1968. Special Assistant to Assistant Secretary for Tariff and Trade Affairs, U.S. Treasury Department, 1971-1973. *Member:* The District of Columbia Bar; New York State and American Bar Associations; American Law Institute. ***Email:*** rhinds@cgsh.com

WASHINGTON, D.C. PARTNERS

DONALD L. MORGAN, born Houston, Texas, January 21, 1934; admitted to bar, 1962, District of Columbia; 1992, Japan as Gaikokuho Jimu Bengoshi. *Education:* Harvard College (A.B., magna cum laude, 1956); Harvard Law School (LL.B., magna cum laude, 1962). Articles Editor, Harvard Law Review, 1961-1962. Resident at: Tokyo Office, 1992-1996. *Member:* The District of Columbia Bar; American Bar Association; The First Tokyo Bar Association. ***Email:*** dmorgan@cgsh.com

KENNETH L. BACHMAN, JR., born Washington, D.C., August 24, 1943; admitted to bar, 1968, District of Columbia. *Education:* Ohio University (A.B., summa cum laude, 1965); Harvard Law School (J.D., cum laude, 1968). Law Clerk to Judge Irving Ben Cooper, U.S. District Court, Southern District of New York, 1968-1970. *Member:* The District of Columbia Bar; American Bar Association. ***Email:*** kbachman@cgsh.com

CHARLES F. LETTOW, born Iowa Falls, Iowa, February 10, 1941; admitted to bar, 1969, California and Iowa; 1972, District of Columbia; 1991, Maryland. *Education:* Iowa State University (B.S.Ch.E., 1962); Stanford University (LL.B., 1968); Brown University (M.A., 2001). Order of the Coif. Note Editor, Stanford Law Review, 1967-1968. Law Clerk to: Judge Ben. C. Duniway, U.S. Court of Appeals for the Ninth Circuit, 1968-1969; Chief Justice Warren E. Burger, Supreme Court of the United States, 1969-1970. Counsel, Council on Environmental Quality, 1970-1973. Author: "Looking At Federal Administrative Law With A Constitutional Framework In Mind," 45 Okla. L. Rev. 5, 1992; "The Control of Marine Pollution," Federal Environmental Law, 1974. Co-Author: "Impact of Federal Institutional Arrangements," Federal Environmental Law, 1974. *Member:* The District of Columbia Bar; State Bar of California; Iowa State, Maryland State, and American (Chairman, Environmental Controls Committee, Section of Business Law, 1983-1987) Bar Associations; American Law Institute. ***Email:*** clettow@cgsh.com

SARA D. SCHOTLAND, born Washington, D.C., May 2, 1948; admitted to bar, 1971, District of Columbia. *Education:* Harvard University (A.B., magna cum laude, 1968); Georgetown University (J.D., 1971). Law Clerk to Judge Oscar H. Davis, U.S. Court of Claims, 1971-1972. Adjunct Professor, George Washington University National Law Center, 1995—. *Member:* The District of Columbia Bar; American Bar Association; Defense Research Institute. ***Email:*** sschotland@cgsh.com

JOHN S. MAGNEY, born Minneapolis, Minnesota, August 10, 1946; admitted to bar, 1973, District of Columbia. *Education:* Marquette University (B.A., 1968); Northwestern University (J.D., 1972). Trial Attorney, Antitrust Division, U.S. Department of Justice, 1972-1975. Resident at: Brussels Office, 1994-1997. *Member:* The District of Columbia Bar. ***Email:*** jmagney@cgsh.com

MARK LEDDY, born Bayonne, New Jersey, January 9, 1947; admitted to bar, 1971, Massachusetts; 1986, District of Columbia. *Education:* Boston College (B.A., 1968; J.D., 1971). Editor-in-Chief, Annual Survey of Massachusetts Law, 1970-1971. Trial Attorney, 1972-1977, Section Chief, 1977-1979, Deputy Director of Operations, 1979-1984 and Deputy Assistant Attorney General, 1984-1986, Antitrust Division, U.S. Department of Justice. Author: "Entry Issues in Merger Analysis," 54 Antitrust Law Journal, 1985; "Introduction to Criminal Antitrust Litigation," Antitrust Counseling and Litigation Techniques, 1989; "The 1992 U.S. Horizontal Merger Guidelines and Some Comparisons with EC Enforcement Policy," 14 *European Competition Law Review*, 1993. Resident at: Brussels Office, 1991-1994. *Member:* The District of Columbia Bar. ***Email:*** mleddy@cgsh.com

JOHN C. MURPHY, JR., born Minneapolis, Minnesota, May 26, 1945; admitted to bar, 1972, California; 1978, District of Columbia. *Education:* Georgetown University (A.B., cum laude, 1967); University of Pennsylvania (J.D., cum laude, 1972). Order of the Coif. Editor, University of Pennsylvania Law Review, 1970-1972. Graduate Fellow, University of Pennsylvania Law School, Center for Study of Financial Institutions, 1972. Special Counsel, Office of the Bank Study, Securities and Exchange Commission, 1975-1977. General Counsel, Federal Deposit Insurance Corporation, 1984-1987. Chairman, Legal Advisory Group, Federal Financial Institutions Examination Council, 1984-1985. Co-Author: "Foreign Investment in U.S. Banking," *Foreign Investment in the United States,* 1990; "The International Lending Supervision Act of 1983," *International Banking: U.S. Laws and Regulations,* 1984. *Member:* The District of Columbia Bar; State Bar of California; Federal (Vice Chairman, Executive Council, Banking Law Committee, 1988-1992; Chairman, 1992-1994) and

(This Listing Continued)

American (Chairman, Subcommittee on Bank and Bank Holding Company Acquisitions and Dispositions, Committee on Banking Law, Section of Business Law, 1992-1994) Bar Associations. ***Email:*** jmurphy@cgsh.com

GEORGE S. CARY, born San Francisco, California, October 2, 1951; admitted to bar, 1976, California; 1979, District of Columbia. *Education:* University of California, Santa Cruz (A.B., honors, 1973); University of California, Berkeley (J.D., 1976). Deputy Director, Bureau of Competition, U.S. Federal Trade Commission, 1995-1998. Trial Attorney, Bureau of Competition, U.S. Federal Trade Commission, 1976-1984. *Member:* The District of Columbia Bar; State Bar of California. ***Email:*** gcary@cgsh.com

JANET L. WELLER, born Boston, Massachusetts, September 17, 1953; admitted to bar, 1978, District of Columbia. *Education:* Harvard University (B.A., cum laude, 1975); University of Michigan (J.D., 1978). *Member:* The District of Columbia Bar; American Bar Association. ***Email:*** jweller@cgsh.com

MITCHELL S. DUPLER, born New York, N.Y., August 29, 1955; admitted to bar, 1979, District of Columbia. *Education:* Harvard University (A.B., cum laude, 1976); Harvard Law School (J.D., cum laude, 1979). Member, Harvard Environmental Law Review, 1976-1977. Resident at London Office, 1982-1984. *Member:* The District of Columbia Bar; American Bar Association. ***Email:*** mdupler@cgsh.com

LINDA J. SOLDO, born Albany, New York, June 13, 1950; admitted to bar, 1981, District of Columbia; 1982, Maryland. *Education:* Manhattanville College (A.B., 1972); Catholic University of America (J.D., 1981). Managing Editor, Catholic University Law Review, 1980-1981. *Member:* The District of Columbia Bar; Maryland State and American Bar Associations. ***Email:*** lsoldo@cgsh.com

GIOVANNI P. PREZIOSO, born Boston, Massachusetts, December 23, 1957; admitted to bar, 1982, District of Columbia. *Education:* Harvard University (A.B., magna cum laude, 1979); Harvard Law School (J.D., magna cum laude, 1982). *Member:* The District of Columbia Bar; American Bar Association (Chairman, Federal Securities Law Subcommittee on Municipal and Governmental Obligations, Section of Business Law). ***Email:*** gprezioso@cgsh.com

JOHN T. BYAM, born Charlotte, North Carolina, November 15, 1956; admitted to bar, 1982, District of Columbia. *Education:* College of William & Mary (A.B., A.B., 1978); Northwestern University (J.D., 1982). Executive Editor, Journal of Criminal Law and Criminology, 1981-1982. Co-Editor: *Manual of Foreign Investment in the United States*, 1993; "Structuring International Joint Ventures," Asian Investment Guide to the United States, 1996. Resident at Brussels Office, 1985-1988. *Member:* The District of Columbia Bar; American Bar Association. ***Email:*** jbyam@cgsh.com

MATTHEW D. SLATER, born New Rochelle, New York, November 6, 1957; admitted to bar, 1984, West Virginia; 1985, District of Columbia. *Education:* Harvard University (A.B., magna cum laude, 1979); University of Chicago (J.D., cum laude, 1983). Editor-in-Chief, University of Chicago Law Review, 1982-1983. Author: "Civil Rights Attorney's Fees Awards in Moot Cases," 49 U. Chi. L. Rev. 819, 1982. Law Clerk to Judge Carl McGowan, U.S. Court of Appeals for the District of Columbia Circuit, 1983-1984. Principal Deputy General Counsel, United States Air Force, 1995-1998. *Member:* The District of Columbia Bar; West Virginia and American Bar Associations; The Association of Trial Lawyers of America. ***Email:*** mslater@cgsh.com

MICHAEL R. LAZERWITZ, born Newark, New Jersey, May 25, 1958; admitted to bar, 1985, Pennsylvania; 1991, District of Columbia. *Education:* Princeton University (A.B., magna cum laude, 1980); University of Chicago (J.D., honors, 1983). Order of the Coif. Articles Editor, University of Chicago Law Review, 1982-1983. Law Clerk to: Judge Henry J. Friendly, U.S. Court of Appeals, Second Circuit, 1983-1984; Chief Justice Warren E. Burger, Supreme Court of the United States, 1984-1985. Assistant U.S. Attorney, Criminal Division, U.S. Attorney's Office, Eastern District of Pennsylvania, 1985-1988. Assistant to the Solicitor General, Office of the Solicitor General, U.S. Department of Justice, 1988-1991. Author: "The Perlman Exception: Limitation, Required by the Final Decision Rule," 49 University of Chicago L. Rev. 798, 1982. *Member:* The District of Columbia Bar; Pennsylvania Bar Association; American Society for Legal History. ***Email:*** mlazerwitz@cgsh.com

†***JAMES R. MODRALL,*** born Cambridge, Massachusetts, October 13, 1958; admitted to bar, 1987, New York. (Not admitted in District of Columbia). *Education:* Stanford University (B.A.S., 1980); University of Michigan Law School (J.D., 1986); European University Institute (LL.M., 1986). Resident at: New York Office, 1986-1988; 1992-1995; Brussels Office, 1988-1992; 1995-2000. *Member:* New York State and American Bar Associations. ***Email:*** jmodrall@cgsh.com

MICHAEL A. MAZZUCHI, born Washington, D.C., January 21, 1967; admitted to bar, 1992, Virginia; 1995, District of Columbia. *Education:* University of Michigan (B.A., highest distinction and highest honors, 1989; J.D., magna cum laude, 1992). Order of the Coif. Articles Editor, Michigan Law Review, 1991-1992. *Member:* The District of Columbia Bar; Virginia State Bar. ***Email:*** mmazzuchi@cgsh.com

(This Listing Continued)

CLEARY, GOTTLIEB, STEEN & HAMILTON, Washington—Continued

ROBERT W. COOK, born Susquehanna, Pennsylvania, August 5, 1965; admitted to bar, 1992, Pennsylvania; 1993, Massachusetts; 1994, District of Columbia. *Education:* Harvard College (A.B., magna cum laude, 1988); London School of Economics (M.Sc., 1989); Harvard Law School (J.D., cum laude, 1992). *Member:* The District of Columbia Bar. ***Email:*** rcook@cgsh.com

SPECIAL COUNSEL

W. RICHARD BIDSTRUP, born Warren, Pennsylvania, February 6, 1957; admitted to bar, 1982, District of Columbia. *Education:* Massachusetts Institute of Technology (S.B., 1979); Harvard Law School (J.D., cum laude, 1982). Editor, Harvard Environmental Law Review, 1981-1982. Editor, Harvard Journal on Legislation, 1981-1982. *Member:* The District of Columbia Bar; American Bar Association. ***Email:*** rbidstrup@cgsh.com

SCOTT N. BENEDICT, born Salem, Massachusetts, August 13, 1959; admitted to bar, 1985, District of Columbia and Maryland. *Education:* Brown University (A.B., magna cum laude, 1981); Harvard Law School (J.D., cum laude, 1984). *Member:* The District of Columbia Bar; Maryland State Bar Association. ***Email:*** sbenedict@cgsh.com

LINDA S. MATLACK, born Philadelphia, Pennsylvania, January 28, 1946; admitted to bar, 1985, District of Columbia. *Education:* University of Wisconsin (B.A., 1967; M.A., 1971); Georgetown University (J.D., magna cum laude, 1985). Associate Articles Editor, Georgetown Law Journal, 1984-1985. Co-Author: "Problems of Enforcement in the Multinational Securities Market," U. Penn. J. Int'l. Bus. Law, 1987. *Member:* The District of Columbia Bar. ***Email:*** lmatlack@cgsh.com

KEVIN A. GRIFFIN, born Los Alamos, New Mexico, October 9, 1956; admitted to bar, 1980, District of Columbia; 1988, Massachusetts. *Education:* Reed College (B.A., 1977); Harvard Law School (J.D., magna cum laude, 1980). Member, Harvard Law Review, 1979-1980. Law Clerk to Judge Frank A. Kaufman, U.S. District Court, District of Maryland, 1980-1981. *Member:* The District of Columbia Bar; Massachusetts Bar Association. ***Email:*** kgriffin@cgsh.com

SENIOR ATTORNEYS

JOYCE E. McCARTY, born Erie, Pennsylvania, November 12, 1950; admitted to bar, 1986, Hawaii; 1988, District of Columbia. *Education:* Thiel College (B.A., cum laude, 1972); Richardson School of Law (J.D., 1986). Editor-in-Chief, University of Hawaii Law Review, 1985-1986. Law Clerk to Judge Samuel P. King, U.S. District Court, District of Hawaii, 1986-1987. *Member:* The District of Columbia Bar; Hawaii State Bar Association. ***Email:*** jmccarty@cgsh.com

KAREN A. KERR, born Altoona, Pennsylvania, October 16, 1951; admitted to bar, 1989, Maryland; 1991, District of Columbia. *Education:* University of Maryland (B.A., cum laude, 1974); University of Iowa (M.A., 1978); University of Maryland (J.D., 1989). Order of the Coif. Articles Editor, University of Maryland Journal of International Law and Trade, 1988-1989. Law Clerk to Judge Edward S. Northrop, U.S. District Court, District of Maryland, 1989-1990. *Member:* The District of Columbia Bar; Maryland State and American Bar Associations. ***Email:*** kkerr@cgsh.com

SCOTT R. GOODWIN, born Boston, Massachusetts, September 22, 1957; admitted to bar, 1992, Maryland and District of Columbia. *Education:* Cornell University (B.S., with distinction, 1979); Georgetown University Law Center (J.D., magna cum laude, 1992). *Member:* The District of Columbia Bar; Maryland State Bar Association. ***Email:*** sgoodwin@cgsh.com

ASSOCIATES

REYN C. ANDERSON, born Nuremburg, Germany, September 12, 1970; admitted to bar, 2000, New York; 2001, District of Columbia. *Education:* University of Florida (B.A., cum laude, 1993); New York University (J.D., 2000). Editor, Journal of International Law and Politics, 1999-2000. *Member:* The District of Columbia Bar; New York State Bar Association. ***Email:*** randerson@cgsh.com

ROBIN M. BERGEN, born Brooklyn, New York, July 29, 1969; admitted to bar, 1995, New York and District of Columbia. *Education:* University of Virginia (B.S., distinction, 1991); New York University (J.D., cum laude, 1994). Associate Editor, New York University Review of Law and Social Change. *Member:* The District of Columbia Bar; New York State and American Bar Associations. ***Email:*** rbergen@cgsh.com

BRENT E. BINGE, born Seattle, Washington, November 4, 1970; admitted to bar, 1999, New York and District of Columbia. *Education:* University of Puget Sound (B.A., magna cum laude, 1993); Georgetown University Law

(This Listing Continued)

Center (J.D., magna cum laude, 1998). Order of the Coif. Senior Notes and Comments Editor, Georgetown Law Journal. *Member:* The District of Columbia Bar; New York State Bar Association. ***Email:*** bbinge@cgsh.com

LAURA L. BLACK, born Chambersburg, Pennsylvania, April 28, 1974; admitted to bar, 2000, New York; 2001, District of Columbia. *Education:* Bucknell University (B.A., summa cum laude, 1996); Harvard University (J.D., cum laude, 1999). Deputy Editor-in-Chief and Executive Editor, Harvard International Law Journal. *Member:* New York State Bar Association. ***Email:*** lblack@cgsh.com

DEREK M. BUSH, born New York, N.Y., June 27, 1967; admitted to bar, 1994, Illinois; 1997, District of Columbia. *Education:* Princeton University (A.B., cum laude, 1989); University of Chicago (J.D., cum laude, 1994). Comment Editor, University of Chicago Law Review, 1993-1994. Law Clerk to Judge Emilio M. Garza, U.S. Court of Appeals for the Fifth Circuit, 1994-1995. *Member:* The District of Columbia Bar; Illinois State Bar Association. ***Email:*** dbush@cgsh.com

BRIAN BYRNE, born Milwaukee, Wisconsin, May 28, 1970; admitted to bar, 1995, California; 1996, District of Columbia. *Education:* Brown University (B.A., magna cum laude, 1992); University of Michigan (J.D., magna cum laude, 1995). Order of the Coif. Executive Editor and Co-Founder, Michigan Telecommunications & Technology Law Review, 1994-1995. *Member:* The District of Columbia Bar; State Bar of California. ***Email:*** bbyrne@cgsh.com

JEREMY J. CALSYN, born Sterling, Illinois, August 20, 1973; admitted to bar, 1999, California; 2000, District of Columbia. *Education:* Southwest Missouri State University (B.S., summa cum laude, 1995); Georgetown University (J.D., magna cum laude, 1999). Law Clerk to Judge Louis F. Oberdorfer, U.S. District Court, District of Columbia, 2000-2001. *Member:* The District of Columbia Bar; State Bar of California. ***Email:*** jcalsyn@cgsh.com

KERRI J. CHASE, born Bay Shore, New York, August 30, 1970; admitted to bar, 1999, Maryland; 2000, District of Columbia. *Education:* University of Maryland (B.S. cum laude, 1992); University of Michigan (J.D., cum laude, 1999). *Member:* Maryland State Bar Association; The District of Columbia Bar. ***Email:*** kchase@cgsh.com

JANIE A. CHUANG, born Houston, Texas, June 26, 1973; admitted to bar, 1999, California; 2000, District of Columbia. *Education:* Yale University (B.A., magna cum laude, 1995); Harvard University (J.D., cum laude, 1998). *Member:* The District of Columbia Bar; State Bar of California. ***Email:*** jchuang@cgsh.com

ALEXIS L. COLLINS, born Cincinnati, Ohio, August 11, 1973; admitted to bar, 1999, Pennsylvania; 2001, District of Columbia. *Education:* Oberlin College (B.A., 1994); University of Chicago (J.D., with honors, 1999). Law Clerk to Judge John R. Padova, U.S. District Court, Eastern District of Pennsylvania, 1999-2001. *Member:* The District of Columbia Bar; Pennsylvania Bar Association. ***Email:*** acollins@cgsh.com

L. BURTON DAVIS, born Charlotte, North Carolina, March 10, 1970; admitted to bar, 1996, Maryland; 1998, District of Columbia. *Education:* University of North Carolina (B.A., with highest distinction, 1992); Yale University (J.D., 1996). Law Clerk to Judge T. S. Ellis, III, U.S. District Court, Eastern District of Virginia, 1996-1997. *Member:* The District of Columbia Bar; Maryland State Bar Association. ***Email:*** bdavis@cgsh.com

JACOB O. DAVISON, admitted to bar, 1999, New York; 2001, District of Columbia. *Education:* Georgetown University (B.A., 1995; J.D., cum laude, 1998). *Member:* New York State Bar Association; The District of Columbia Bar. ***Email:*** jdavison@cgsh.com

TANYA N. DUNNE, born Melbourne, Australia, December 28, 1968; admitted to bar, 2001, New York (Not admitted in District of Columbia). *Education:* Phillips Institute of Technology (B.S., 1990); Georgetown University (J.D., magna cum laude, 2001). *Member:* New York State Bar Association. ***Email:*** tdunne@cgsh.com

WILLIAM S. FULTZ, born Winston-Salem, North Carolina, November 23, 1971; admitted to bar, 1998, Virginia; 1999, District of Columbia. *Education:* University of North Carolina (B.A., 1994); University of Virginia (J.D., 1998). Phi Beta Kappa. Order of the Coif. Member, Virginia Law Review. Dillard Fellow. *Member:* Virginia Bar Association; The District of Columbia Bar. ***Email:*** wfultz@cgsh.com

MICHAEL HERSHAFT, born New York, New York, April 27, 1973; admitted to bar, 2000, New York; 2001, District of Columbia. *Education:* Northwestern University (B.S., M.S., 1995); University of Chicago (J.D., 1999). Top Access Editor, University of Chicago Law Review. Law Clerk to Judge John M. Duhé, Jr., U.S. Court of Appeals, for the 5th Circuit, 1999-2000. *Member:* New York State Bar Association; The District of Columbia Bar. ***Email:*** mhershaft@cgsh.com

STEVEN J. KAISER, born Morristown, New Jersey, February 22, 1970; admitted to bar, 1996, New Jersey; 1997, District of Columbia. *Education:* Princeton University (B.S., magna cum laude, 1992); Harvard University (J.D.,

(This Listing Continued)

magna cum laude, 1995). Law Clerk to Robert N. Wilentz, Chief Justice, Supreme Court of New Jersey, 1995-1996. *Member:* The District of Columbia Bar; New Jersey State Bar Association. ***Email:*** skaiser@cgsh.com

ELKE M. KRAULAND, born Hartford, Connecticut, December 28, 1971; admitted to bar, 1998, Connecticut; 1999, District of Columbia. *Education:* University of Connecticut (B.A., summa cum laude, 1993); George Washington University (J.D., 1998). Order of the Coif. Notes Editor, George Washington Journal of Law and Economics. *Member:* Connecticut Bar Association; The District of Columbia Bar. ***Email:*** ekrauland@cgsh.com

JAMES D. LIVINGSTONE, born Norwood, Massachusetts, June 3, 1973; admitted to bar, 1998, Massachusetts; 1999, District of Columbia. *Education:* University of Connecticut (B.A., 1995); George Washington University (J.D., 1998). Order of the Coif. *Member:* Massachusetts Bar Association; The District of Columbia Bar. ***Email:*** jlivingstone@cgsh.com

†MUTHEU MAITHA, born Nairobi, Kenya, December 5, 1973; admitted to bar, 2001, New York (Not admitted in District of Columbia). *Education:* James Madison University (B.A., summa cum laude, 1996); Cornell University (J.D./LL.M., cum laude, 2000). *Member:* New York State Bar Association. ***Email:*** mmaitha@cgsh.com

PAUL D. MARQUARDT, born Detroit, Michigan, August 24, 1968; admitted to bar, 1996, Michigan; 1998, District of Columbia. *Education:* University of Michigan (B.A., with highest distinction, 1990); Yale University (J.D., 1994; M.A., 1994). Law Clerk to Judge James B. Loken, U.S. Court of Appeals, Eighth Circuit, 1994-1995. Resident at Brussels Office, 1998-2001. *Member:* The District of Columbia Bar; State Bar of Michigan; American Bar Association; American Society of International Law. ***Email:*** pmarquardt@cgsh.com

PATRICIA M. McDERMOTT, born Fair Lawn, New Jersey, March 12, 1971; admitted to bar, 1997, Virginia; 1998, District of Columbia. *Education:* Tufts University (B.A., 1993); George Washington University (J.D., with honors, 1997). Law Clerk to the Hon. Judge Cameron M. Currie, U.S. District Court, District of South Carolina, 1998-1999. *Member:* The District of Columbia Bar; American Bar Association. ***Email:*** pmcdermott@cgsh.com

JOHN P. McGILL, JR., born Washington, D.C., November 15, 1966; admitted to bar, 1999, Maryland; 2000, District of Columbia. *Education:* University of Richmond (B.A., cum laude, 1988); Georgetown University (J.D., magna cum laude, 1999). Order of the Coif. *Member:* Maryland State Bar Association; The District of Columbia Bar. ***Email:*** jmcgill@cgsh.com

DIPALI B. MEHTA, born Rajkot, Gujarat, India, November 10, 1970; admitted to bar, 1993, Connecticut; 1999, District of Columbia. *Education:* Fairfield University (B.A., 1992); University of Connecticut (J.D., 1995). *Member:* Connecticut Bar Association; The District of Columbia Bar. ***Email:*** dmehta@cgsh.com

PAMELA G. MEISEL, born New York, N.Y., July 30, 1968; admitted to bar, 1995, New York; 2001, District of Columbia. *Education:* Cornell University (B.A., 1990); Columbia University (J.D., 1994). Law Clerk to the Hon. Judge Carol B. Amon, U.S. District Court, Eastern District of New York, 1992. *Member:* New York State Bar Association; The District of Columbia Bar. ***Email:*** pmeisel@cgsh.com

†MARC L. MEZEY, born Cluj, Romania, April 28, 1973; admitted to bar, 2000, New York; 2001, District of Columbia. *Education:* Johns Hopkins University (B.A., 1996); Columbia University (J.D., 1999). *Member:* New York State Bar Association. ***Email:*** mmezey@cgsh.com

MARK W. NELSON, born Chelsea, Massachusetts, July 2, 1967; admitted to bar, 1993, New York; 1994, District of Columbia. *Education:* Cornell University (B.S., 1989); Harvard Law School (J.D., magna cum laude, 1992). Law Clerk to Judge Andrew J. Kleinfeld, U.S. Court of Appeals for the Ninth Circuit, 1992-1993. Resident at: Brussels Office, 1995-1998. *Member:* The District of Columbia Bar; New York State Bar Association. ***Email:*** mnelson@cgsh.com

ANDREW K. NIEBLER, born Glen Rock, New Jersey, May 18, 1967; admitted to bar, 1998, New Jersey; 1999, New York and District of Columbia. *Education:* Princeton University (A.B., magna cum laude, 1989); Georgetown University (J.D., magna cum laude, 1998). Order of the Coif. *Member:* New Jersey State and New York State Bar Associations; The District of Columbia Bar. ***Email:*** aniebler@cgsh.com

SUZANNE B. PERRY, born Buffalo, New York, October 30, 1972; admitted to bar, 1999, New York; 2000, District of Columbia. *Education:* Cornell University (B.A., 1994); Yale University (J.D., 1998); European University Institute (LL.M., 2000). *Member:* The District of Columbia Bar; New York State and American Bar Associations. ***Email:*** sperry@cgsh.com

†STEPHEN E. POMPER, born Chicago, Illinois, August 23, 1965; admitted to bar, 1994, New York; 2001, District of Columbia. *Education:* Harvard College (A.B., summa cum laude, 1987); Yale University (J.D., 1993). *Member:* New York State Bar Association. ***Email:*** spomper@cgsh.com

MITCHELL L. RABINOWITZ, born Atlantic City, New Jersey, September 17, 1967; admitted to bar, 1993, Maryland; 1994, District of Columbia. *Education:* University of Pennsylvania (B.A., B.S., summa cum laude, 1989);

(This Listing Continued)

Harvard University, Kennedy School of Government (M.P.P., 1993); Harvard Law School (J.D., cum laude, 1993). *Member:* The District of Columbia Bar; Maryland State Bar Association. ***Email:*** mrabinowitz@cgsh.com

†MASHA SMITH, born St. Petersburg, Russia, July 9, 1975; admitted to bar, 2001, Massachusetts and District of Columbia. *Education:* Marlboro College (B.A., 1996); Cornell University (J.D., cum laude, 2000). *Member:* Massachusetts Bar Association. ***Email:*** msmith@cgsh.com

JULIE A. SOUTHFIELD, born Muncie, Indiana, April 11, 1972; admitted to bar, 2000, Virginia; 2001, District of Columbia. *Education:* Purdue University (B.A., 1995; M.S., 1997); George Washington University (J.D., highest honors, 2000). Order of the Coif. *Member:* The District of Columbia Bar; Virginia State Bar. ***Email:*** jsouthfield@cgsh.com

†ALIZA SPERLING, born New York, New York, October 11, 1974; admitted to bar, 2001, Massachusetts (Not admitted in District of Columbia). *Education:* Barnard College (B.A., magna cum laude, 1996); New York University (J.D., cum laude, 2000). *Member:* Massachusetts Bar Association. ***Email:*** asperling@cgsh.com

†PATRICK A. TILLOU, born Falls Church, Virginia, June 30, 1975; admitted to bar, 2000, Virgin Islands (Not admitted in District of Columbia). *Education:* Duke University (A.B., magna cum laude, 1997); University of Michigan (J.D., cum laude, 1999). ***Email:*** ptillou@cgsh.com

†PETIA VRETENAROVA, born Sofia, Bulgaria, August 26, 1973; admitted to bar, 2001, New York (Not admitted in District of Columbia). *Education:* American University (B.A., cum laude, 1996); Syracuse University (M.P.A., 1997; J.D., summa cum laude, 2000). Associate Notes and Comments Editor, Syracuse University Law Review. *Member:* New York State Bar Association. ***Email:*** pvretenarova@cgsh.com

PATRICIA J. WALSH, born Boston, Massachusetts, May 22, 1965; admitted to bar, 1997, Connecticut; 2000, District of Columbia. *Education:* Mount Holyoke College (B.A., cum laude, 1987); Princeton University (M.A., 1991); Yale University (J.D., 1996). Law Clerk to the Hon. Judge Janet C. Hall, U.S. District Court, District of Connecticut, 1997-1998; Law Clerk to the Hon. Judge Rosemary Barkett, U.S. Court of Appeals, Eleventh Circuit, 1996-1997. *Member:* Connecticut Bar Association; The District of Columbia Bar. ***Email:*** pwalsh@cgsh.com

WILBERT H. WATTS, JR., born Bedford, Virginia, April 14, 1974; admitted to bar, 1999, Virginia; 2000, District of Columbia. *Education:* Georgetown University (A.B., magna cum laude, 1996); Harvard University (J.D., 1999). *Member:* The District of Columbia Bar; Virginia State Bar Association. ***Email:*** wwatts@cgsh.com

† Non-admitted attorneys working under the supervision of principals of the firm resident in the Washington, †C Office

(For biographical data of the New York partners, see Professional Biographies at New York, N.Y.).

(For biographical data as to the European Offices, see Professional Biographies at Paris, France, Brussels, Belgium, London, England, Frankfurt, Germany and Rome, Italy).

(For Biographical data of the Hong Kong Partners, see Professional Biographies at Hong Kong, Hong Kong).

(For Biographical data of the Tokyo, Japan Partners, see Professional Biographies at Tokyo, Japan)

CLEARY & KOMEN, LLP

SUITE 200
600 PENNSYLVANIA AVENUE, S.E.
WASHINGTON, D.C. 20003-4304
Telephone: 202-675-4700
Fax: 202-675-4716
Email: cleary-komen@cleary-komen.com

Copyright, Trademark and Unfair Competition Law, Foreign and Domestic. Practice before Federal Courts and Government Departments.

FIRM PROFILE: The practice at Cleary & Komen, LLP encompasses a full spectrum of activities pertaining to copyrights, trademarks and trade secrets, including the clearance of trademarks and copyrighted materials, preparation and prosecution of trademark and copyright applications and licensing, as well as the protection and enforcement of these rights in the courts. The firm prides itself in fashioning creative solutions and providing cost-effective services to meet its clients' legal needs.

The firm's clients include domestic and foreign corporations and individuals which the firm represents before the Patent and Trademark Office and the Copyright Office, as well as the district and appellate courts.

The firm is committed to maintaining manageable growth to ensure personal service to all of its clients. Its senior attorneys are involved in the work of every client, with appropriate support from the firm's legal and professional staff.

(This Listing Continued)

CLEARY & KOMEN, LLP, Washington—Continued

The hallmark of the firm's copyright practice has historically been its representation of clients in the entertainment and motion picture industry. With the advent of new technology and media formats, the firm's clientele has increasingly included software, multi-media and other high technology companies.

The firm's members are each recognized leaders in the field and are frequently sought after to consult with other practitioners. The firm has a national practice, and is associated with other firms throughout the world to assist its clients in obtaining protection for their intellectual property on a worldwide basis.

MEMBERS OF FIRM

J. MICHAEL CLEARY, born Minneapolis, Minnesota, March 17, 1943; admitted to bar, 1969, Virginia; 1970, District of Columbia; 1971-1982, U.S. Court of Customs and Patent Appeals; 1981, U.S. Supreme Court; 1982, U.S. Court of Appeals for the Federal Circuit. *Education:* Catholic University of America (B.A., 1965; M.A., 1966); George Washington University (J.D., 1969). Delta Theta Phi. Co-author: "Gray Market Litigation," Trial Magazine, March 1989. Author: "Film and Television Title Clearance Problems," L.A. Lawyer, Vol. 13, No. 2, April, 1990. *Member:* District of Columbia Bar; Virginia State Bar; Bar Association of the District of Columbia (Chairman, Copyright Committee, 1976-1979; Member, Executive Council, 1979-1982 and Chairman, 1983-1984, Patent, Trademark and Copyright Section; Member, Board of Directors, 1984-1985); American Bar Association (Member: Intellectual Property Law Section; Executive Council, 1994-1998); American Intellectual Property Law Association; International Trademark Association; (Chairman, Patent and Trademark Office Committee, 1984-1986; Member, Board of Directors, 1986-1988); The Copyright Society of the U.S.A. (Member, Board of Trustees, 1983-1986). ***PRACTICE AREAS:*** Copyright Law; Trademark Law; Unfair Competition Law; Litigation. ***Email:*** mcleary@cleary-komen.com

EDWIN KOMEN, born Oak Park, Illinois, July 31, 1949; admitted to bar, 1976, Virginia; 1977, District of Columbia. *Education:* University of Southern California (B.A. in Cinema, 1971); George Washington University (J.D., with honors, 1976). Phi Beta Kappa. Member, George Washington Law Review, 1974-1976. *Member:* District of Columbia Bar (Chairman, Copyright Committee, 1982-1983); Bar Association of the District of Columbia (Chairman, Copyright Committee, 1981-1983, 1984-1986, 1991-1996, 1998—; Member, Executive Council, Young Lawyers Section, 1982-1986; Treasurer, Patent, Trademark and Copyright Law Section, 1986-1987; Member, Executive Council, Patent, Trademark and Copyright Law Section, 1987-1990, 1995-1996; Treasurer, 1990-1991; Secretary, 1996-1998); Virginia State Bar; American Bar Association (Member, Intellectual Property Law Section). ***PRACTICE AREAS:*** Copyright Law; Trademark Law; Unfair Competition Law. ***Email:*** ekomen@cleary-komen.com

ASSOCIATES

SCOTT J. MAJOR, born Newark, New Jersey, June 15, 1962; admitted to bar, 1992, Virginia; 1998, District of Columbia. *Education:* University of Notre Dame (B.B.A. in Finance, 1984); Catholic University of America (J.D., 1991). Guest Lecturer, Intelletual Property, George Mason University. Trademark Attorney, United States Trademark Office, 1994-1997. *Member:* Virginia State Bar (Member, Intellectual Property Law Section); District of Columbia Bar (Member, Intellectual Property Law Section); International Trademark Association (Member, Examination Guidelines Subcommittee). ***PRACTICE AREAS:*** Trademark Law; Unfair Competition Law; Copyright Law. ***Email:*** smajor@cleary-komen.com

HAE PARK-SUK, born Seoul, South Korea, December 12, 1970; admitted to bar, 1997, Virginia; 2000, District of Columbia. *Education:* University of Virginia (B.A., English Literature, 1992); George Mason University School of Law (J.D., 1997). Trademark Attorney, United States Trademark Office, 1997-1999. *Member:* Virginia State Bar (Member, Intellectual Property Law Section); Virginia Bar Association (Member, Intellectual Property Law Section); American Intellectual Property Law Association. ***PRACTICE AREAS:*** Trademarks; Unfair Competition Law; Copyrights. ***Email:*** hpark-suk@cleary-komen.com

OF COUNSEL

BERNARD C. DIETZ, born Bridgeport, Connecticut, November 2, 1942; admitted to bar, 1968, District of Columbia; 1969, U.S. Court of Appeals for the District of Columbia Circuit. *Education:* Fairfield University (B.S., 1964); Catholic University of America (J.D., 1967). Editor, "Copyright Registration Practice", Westgroup, 1999—. Co-Author, Compendium II, Copyright Office Practices. Author, Numerous Articles pertaining to Copyright Law. Attorney, U.S. Copyright Office, 1967-1993. Head: Visual Arts Section, Examining Division, 1969-1981; Renewals Section, Examining Division, 1981-1993. Member, Editorial Board, European Intellectual Property Review, 1977—. *District of Columbia Bar (Member, Intellectual Property Law Committee); American Intellectual Property Law Association.* ***PRACTICE AREAS:*** Copyrights; Entertainment Law; Unfair Competition Law. ***Email:*** dietzlaw@aol.com

CLIFFORD CHANCE ROGERS & WELLS LLP

Established in 1949

2001 K STREET N.W.

WASHINGTON, D.C. 20006-1001

Telephone: 202-912-5000

Facsimile: 202-912-6000

URL: http://www.cliffordchance.com

New York, N.Y. Office: Two Hundred Park Avenue, New York, N.Y. 10166-0153. Telephone: 212-878-8000. Facsimile: 212-878-8375.

Other Offices: Amsterdam, Bangkok, Barcelona, Beijing, Berlin, Brussels, Budapest, Dubai, Dusseldorf, Frankfurt, Hanoi, Ho Chi Minh City, Hong Kong, London, Madrid, Milan, Moscow, Munich, Padua, Paris, Prague, Rome, Sao Paulo, Shanghai, Singapore, Tokyo, Warsaw.

General Practice.

SENIOR PARTNER

WILLIAM P. ROGERS (1913-2001).

PARTNERS

KEVIN J. ARQUIT, born Ithaca, New York, September 11, 1954; admitted to bar, 1980, New York and U.S. District Court, Eastern and Southern Districts of New York; 1983, U.S. Court of Appeals, Third Circuit and U.S. District Court, Northern District of California; 1984, U.S. District Court, Western District of New York; 1985, U.S. Court of Appeals, Second Circuit and U.S. District Court, Northern District of New York; 1989, U.S. Supreme Court; 1993, District of Columbia. *Education:* St. Lawrence University (B.A., cum laude, 1975); Cornell Law School (J.D., cum laude, 1978). General Counsel, Federal Trade Commission, 1988-1989. Director, Bureau of Competition, Federal Trade Commission, 1989-1992. Chairman, Antitrust and Trade Regulation Committee, International Bar Association, 1996—. Member, BNA's Advisory Board on Trade Regulation, 1993—. Member, Business Law, Inc.'s Board of Advisors to the Antitrust Counselor. ***Email:*** kevin.arquit@cliffordchance.com

LEIV H. BLAD, JR., born Garden Grove, California, February 23, 1962; admitted to bar, 1990, California; 1992, District of Columbia. *Education:* University of California at Los Angeles (B.A., 1985); University of Virginia (M.A., 1987); Boston University (J.D., cum laude, 1990). Note and Comment Editor, Annual Review of Banking Law, 1988-1990. Author: "Searching for the Ideological Origins of Federal Deposit Insurance," Volume 9, Annual Review of Banking Law, 1990. *Member:* State Bar of California; The District of Columbia Bar; American Bar Association. ***PRACTICE AREAS:*** Commercial Litigation; Intellectual Property Litigation; Antitrust. ***Email:*** leiv.blad@cliffordchance.com

DAVID D. DiBARI, born Rome, New York, January 12, 1964; admitted to bar, 1990, New York; 1991, District of Columbia. *Education:* Colgate University (A.B., 1986); Albany Law School of Union College (J.D., 1989). Phi Alpha Delta; Phi Beta Kappa; Pi Sigma Alpha; Phi Eta Sigma. Lead Articles and Symposium Editor, Albany Law Review, 1988-1989. Member, Justinian Society. *Member:* The District of Columbia Bar (Member, Government Contracts Section); New York State and American (Member, Public Contracts Section) Bar Associations. ***LANGUAGES:*** Spanish and Italian. ***PRACTICE AREAS:*** Litigation; Regulatory; White Collar Defense; International Arbitration; Foreign Corrupt Practices Act; Export Control; Government Contracts. ***Email:*** david.dibari@cliffordchance.com

JEREMY A. CONNICK, born London, England; admitted to bar, 1987, England and Wales (Not admitted in United States). *Education:* Leeds University, Leeds, England; Chester Law College, Chester, England. ***PRACTICE AREAS:*** Project Finance; Energy. ***Email:*** jeremy.connick@cliffordchance.com

JAMES C. EGAN, JR., born Rockville Centre, New York, November 7, 1943; admitted to bar, 1971, Florida; 1972, New York; 1996, District of Columbia. *Education:* University of South Florida (B.A., 1966); St. John's University School of Law (J.D., 1971). Federal Trade Commission Director for Litigation, 1990-1994 (Assistant Director, 1979-1990). *Member:* The Florida Bar; The District of Columbia Bar; American Bar Association. [U.S. Army, 1966-1969 1st LT.]. ***PRACTICE AREAS:*** Antitrust; General Litigation. ***Email:*** jim.egan@cliffordchance.com

ANTHONY F. ESSAYE, born London, England, May 13, 1934; admitted to bar, 1962, New York; 1966, District of Columbia. *Education:* Georgetown University (B.S.S., 1955); Harvard University (LL.B., 1961). Office of the General Counsel, 1963-1965; Deputy General Counsel, 1965-1966, Peace Corps. Resident Partner, Paris Office, 1974-1976. Chairman, International Practice Group, 1989-1995. Managing Partner, Washington, D.C. Office, 1978-1998. Chairman, National Lawyers' Council of the Democratic National Committee, 1991-1998. *Member:* The District of Columbia Bar; New York State and

(This Listing Continued)

American (Chairman, Committee on International Courts, International Law Section, 1983-1984) Bar Associations. ***Email:*** anthony.essaye@cliffordchance.com

DAVID J. EVANS, born Boston, Massachusetts, February 16, 1953; admitted to bar, 1978, Maine; 1980, District of Columbia. *Education:* Boston University (B.S., summa cum laude, 1975); University of Maine School of Law (J.D., cum laude, 1978). Staff Counsel, Nuclear Regulatory Commission, 1978-1979. Attorney: Andrews & Kurth, 1980-1983; Pillsbury, Madison & Sutro, 1983-1988. Partner, Pillsbury, Madison & Sutro, 1988-1998. Vice President and General Counsel, KMR Power Corporation, 1994-1998. *Member:* The District of Columbia Bar. ***PRACTICE AREAS:*** Project Finance; Utility Law; Energy Law. ***Email:*** david.evans@cliffordchance.com

KENNETH A. GALLO, born Ridgewood, New Jersey, November 16, 1956; admitted to bar, 1983, District of Columbia. *Education:* University of Georgia (B.A., with honors, 1978; J.D., cum laude, 1982). Order of Barristers. Notes Editor, Georgia Law Review, 1981-1982. Law Clerk, Honorable George L. Hart, Jr., United States District Court for the District of Columbia, 1982-1983. *Member:* The District of Columbia Bar; American Bar Association (Member, Sections on: Litigation; Antitrust; Intellectual Property). ***PRACTICE AREAS:*** Antitrust Law; Complex Litigation; Intellectual Property. ***Email:*** ken.gallo@cliffordchance.com

IRA D. HAMMERMAN, born Brooklyn, New York, November 18, 1960; admitted to bar, 1986, New York and District of Columbia. *Education:* Emory University (B.A., 1982); Georgetown University (J.D., 1985). Phi Beta Kappa; Pi Sigma Alpha. Managing Partner, Washington, D.C. Office, 1998—. *Member:* The District of Columbia Bar; The Association of the Bar of the City of New York; American Bar Association; Securities Industry Association (Member, Compliance and Legal Division). ***SPECIAL AGENCIES:*** U.S. Securities and Exchange Commission; New York Stock Exchange; NASD Regulation, Inc. ***PRACTICE AREAS:*** Securities Regulation and Enforcement. ***Email:*** ira.hammerman@cliffordchance.com

SARA P. HANKS, born London, England, November 14, 1957; admitted to bar, 1984, England; 1985, District of Columbia; 1995, New York. *Education:* Oxford University, England (B.A., 1980); The College of Law, England. ***Email:*** sara.hanks@cliffordchance.com

JOHN PAUL KETELS, born New York, N.Y., December 26, 1944; admitted to bar, 1976, California; 1978, District of Columbia. *Education:* University of Michigan (B.S., 1968); University of California at Davis (J.D., 1976). Order of the Coif; Phi Kappa Phi; University of California at Davis Law Review. Counsel to Commissioner, 1977-1980 and Attorney, Division of Market Regulation, 1976-1977, U.S. Securities and Exchange Commission, Washington, D.C. *Member:* The District of Columbia Bar; State Bar of California; American Bar Association (Member, Committee on Federal Regulation of Securities, Section of Business Law). [Lt., U.S. Navy, 1969-1972]. ***Email:*** john.ketels@cliffordchance.com

STEVEN A. NEWBORN, born Brooklyn, New York, July 26, 1946; admitted to bar, 1975, New York; 1976, U.S. District Court, Southern District of New York; 1995, District of Columbia. *Education:* Long Island University (B.A., cum laude, 1971); St. John's Law School (J.D., with honors, 1974). Editorial Board, St. John's Law Review. Author: "The Growing Judicial Acceptance of the Merger Guidelines," 60 Antitrust L. J. 849 (1992); "Appellate Review of Sentencing," 47 St. John's L. Rev. 250 (1972). Co-Author: "Second Circuit Note," 47 St. John's L. Rev. 223 (1972); "Survey of New York Practice," 47 St. John's L. Rev. 146 (1972). Instructor, National Institute for Trial Advocacy. Director for Litigation, FTC, 1991-1994. Assistant Director for Litigation, FTC, 1988-1991. Special Assistant U.S. Attorney, Criminal Division, Eastern District of Virginia, 1982-1984. Vice Chair, ABA Antitrust Section, Clayton Act Committee. *Member:* The District of Columbia Bar; American Bar Association. ***REPORTED CASES:*** Administrative Trials: Reichold Chemicals, Inc. (and appeal); The Reuben Donnelley Corporation; Brunswick/Yamaha (and appeal); B.A.T.; PPG/Swedlow. Injunctions Litigated (in federal district court except as noted): FTC v. Mannesmann (defendants abandoned deal after case in chief); FTC v. Great Lakes Chemicals; FTC v. PPG (and appeal); FTC v. Imo Industries; FTC v. Harbour Group; FTC v. Wallace Silver (before Bankruptcy Court); FTC v. Appleton (defendants abandoned deal after case in chief); FTC v. Alliant Techsystems. ***PRACTICE AREAS:*** Antitrust; Litigation; International Law. ***Email:*** steve.newborn@cliffordchance.com

MICHAEL A. O'SHEA, born Brooklyn, New York, August 10, 1961; admitted to bar, 1988, New York and Massachusetts; 1989, U.S. District Court, Southern and Eastern Districts of New York; 1994, U.S. Court of Appeals for the Federal Circuit; 1998, District of Columbia; registered to practice before U.S. Patent and Trademark Office. *Education:* Northwestern University (B.S., 1983); Fordham University (J.D., 1987). *Member:* The District of Columbia Bar. ***PRACTICE AREAS:*** Civil Trial Practice; Patents; Copyrights; Trademarks. ***Email:*** michael.o'shea@cliffordchance.com

ANTHONY J. RENZI, JR., born Binghamton, New York, January 31, 1964; admitted to bar, 1989, Pennsylvania; 1991, District of Columbia. *Education:* State University of New York at Buffalo (B.S., cum laude, 1986); American University (J.D., cum laude, 1989). Executive Associate Editor, 1988-1989 and Staff Member, 1987-1988, The American University Law Review. Author: "Proxy Reform: A New Era of SEC Activism," Insights, Vol. 6, No. 11 at 2 (Nov. 1992); "Settling With The SEC: Hazards and Helpful Hints," Insights, Vol. 6, No. 1 at 13 (Jan. 1992). *Member:* The District of Columbia Bar. ***Email:*** tony.renzi@cliffordchance.com

JON RANDALL ROELLKE, born Orange, New Jersey, March 26, 1959; admitted to bar, 1987, Massachusetts; 1990, District of Columbia; 1992, U.S. District Court, District of Columbia; 1994, U.S. District Court, District of Maryland; 1997, U.S. Supreme Court. *Education:* San Francisco State University (B.A., magna cum laude, 1983); Boston College (J.D., cum laude, 1987). Advisor, Georgetown University Law Center National Trial Team, 1991-1996. *Member:* The District of Columbia Bar; American Bar Association. ***PRACTICE AREAS:*** Antitrust; Intellectual Property; Commercial Litigation. ***Email:*** jon.roellke@cliffordchance.com

JOHN E. SCRIBNER, born Oklahoma City, Oklahoma, August 26, 1964; admitted to bar, 1992, Oklahoma; 1995, District of Columbia. *Education:* Westminster College (B.A., 1986); University of Oklahoma (J.D., 1992). Note Editor, Oklahoma Law Review. Staff Attorney, Federal Trade Commission, 1992-1998. *Member:* Oklahoma and American (Member, Antitrust Section) Bar Association; The District of Columbia Bar. ***PRACTICE AREAS:*** Antitrust. ***Email:*** john.scribner@cliffordchance.com

RYAN TRAINER, born Copenhagen, Denmark, October 14, 1956; admitted to bar, 1981, District of Columbia; 1982, U.S. Court of International Trade; 1984, U.S. Court of Appeals for the Federal Circuit; 1997, U.S. District Court, District of Columbia. *Education:* University of Colorado (B.A., 1978); George Washington University (J.D., with honors, 1981). Phi Beta Kappa. Executive Editor, George Washington Journal of International Law and Economics, 1980-1981. Staff Attorney, Office of Assistant General Counsel for Import Administration, Department of Commerce, 1981-1984. ***PRACTICE AREAS:*** International Trade Regulation and Policy. ***Email:*** ryan.trainer@cliffordchance.com

DALE C. TURZA, born Boston, Massachusetts, October 22, 1949; admitted to bar, 1978, District of Columbia; 1979, U.S. District Court for the District of Columbia and U.S. Court of Appeals for the District of Columbia Circuit; 1982, U.S. Supreme Court. *Education:* Connecticut College (B.A., summa cum laude, 1971); Columbia University (M.A., 1974); Georgetown University (J.D., 1978). Phi Beta Kappa. Editor, Journal of Law and Policy in International Business, 1977-1978. *Member:* The District of Columbia Bar; American Bar Association. ***Email:*** dale.turza@cliffordchance.com

LAURA A. WILKINSON, born Brooklyn, New York, November 8, 1960; admitted to bar, 1987, New York; 1988, District of Columbia. *Education:* University of Pennsylvania (B.A., 1982); Cornell University (M.B.A., 1985; J.D., 1986). Deputy Assistant Director, 1993-1996 and Staff Attorney, 1986-1993, Federal Trade Commission. Co-author: "Mergers in the Defense Industry: Application of the 1992 Horizontal Merger Guidelines," 23 Public Contract L.J. (Fall 1993). Adjunct Professor, Howard University School of Law. *Member:* The District of Columbia Bar; American (Antitrust Section, FTC Committee) and National Bar Associations. ***PRACTICE AREAS:*** Antitrust; Litigation. ***Email:*** laura.wilkinson@cliffordchance.com

COUNSEL

MICHAEL J. KING, born Hong Kong, September 29, 1955; admitted to bar, 1981, District of Columbia; 1982, Maryland. *Education:* Boston University (B.A., cum laude, 1977); The American University (J.D., cum laude, 1981). Staff Member, The American University Law Review. National Association of Securities Dealers, Inc.: Chief Litigation Counsel, 1997-1998 and Chief Counsel, 1991-1997, Market Regulation Department; Senior Attorney, Office of General Counsel, 1989-1991. Trial Attorney, Tax Division, United States Department of Justice, 1984-1989. Attorney, Division of Market Regulation, Securities and Exchange Commission, 1982-1984. *Member:* The District of Columbia Bar; Maryland State and American Bar Associations; Securities Industry Association. ***PRACTICE AREAS:*** Securities Regulation and Enforcement; Corporate; Litigation. ***Email:*** michael.king@cliffordchance.com

GEORGE KLEINFELD, born New York, September 16, 1959; admitted to bar, 1984, Florida; 1985, District of Columbia. *Education:* Georgetown University School of Foreign Service (B.S., magna cum laude); University of Pennsylvania (J.D., 1983; M.S., 1983). Order of the Coif. Recipient: American Jurisprudence Awards; Fellowship Award, Law and Economics. Author of over 20 law review articles and other published articles on international communications, trade and investment issues. Adjunct Professor, International Finance, George Mason University School of Law. Former Attorney/Advisor, Office of the Assistant General Counsel for International Affairs, U.S. Treasury Department. Washington, D.C. Coordinator, Global Communications, Media & Tech-

(This Listing Continued)

(This Listing Continued)

CLIFFORD CHANCE ROGERS & WELLS LLP, Washington—Continued

nology Law Group of Clifford Chance. *Member:* The Florida Bar; The District of Columbia Bar; Federal Communications Bar Association. ***PRACTICE AREAS:*** Communications Law; International Trade; Investments. ***Email:*** george.kleinfeld@cliffordchance.com

FRED W. REINKE, born Hahn Air Force Base, West Germany, August 3, 1961; admitted to bar, 1988, New York; 1989, District of Columbia. *Education:* St. Olaf College (B.A., 1983); Hamburg University (Fulbright Scholar, 1984); Columbia University (J.D., 1987). Harlan Fiske Stone Scholar. *Member:* The District of Columbia Bar; American Bar Association; Council on Foreign Relations; American Council on Germany.

MICHAEL R. SILVERMAN, born New York, N.Y., May 17, 1947; admitted to bar, 1973, District of Columbia. *Education:* Syracuse University (B.A., 1969); Georgetown University (J.D., 1972; LL.M., 1975). Phi Beta Kappa. Administrative Editor, Law and Policy in International Business. *Member:* American Bar Association (Member, International Law Section). ***PRACTICE AREAS:*** International Project Finance; International Investment; International Commercial Law. ***Email:*** michael.silverman@cliffordchance.com

JOHN M. SIPPLE, JR., born Beaver Falls, Pennsylvania, October 12, 1946; admitted to bar, 1973, Maryland; 1980, District of Columbia. *Education:* University of Pittsburgh (B.A., 1969); University of Maryland School of Law (J.D., with honors, 1973). Research Editor, Maryland Law Review. Chief and Assistant Director, Premerger Notification Office, Federal Trade Commission, 1987-1997. *Member:* The District of Columbia Bar; American Bar Association (Vice Chair, Antitrust Section, Clayton Act Committee). ***PRACTICE AREAS:*** Antitrust; HSR Premerger Notification; International Merger Notification. ***Email:*** john.sipple@cliffordchance.com

KIRSTEN A. WOLFE, born Williston, North Dakota, March 14, 1964; admitted to bar, 1990, District of Columbia. *Education:* William Paterson College of New Jersey (B.M., 1987); Georgetown University (J.D., cum laude, 1990). Editor, Georgetown Immigration Law Journal. Author: Note, "U.S. v. Kungys," 3 Georgetown Immigration L.J., 387, 1989. Law Clerk, Hon. Patrick J. Atridge, Magistrate Judge for the U.S. District Court, District of Columbia. *Member:* The District of Columbia Bar; American Bar Association (Member, Antitrust Section). ***PRACTICE AREAS:*** Antitrust; Consumer Protection. ***Email:*** kirsten.wolfe@cliffordchance.com

CONSULTANT

VIRGINIA L. SNIDER, born Chicago, Illinois, July 17, 1946. *Education:* Memphis State University (B.S., 1967); Washington State University (B.A., 1971). Formerly: Director of Special Projects, United States Federal Trade Commission; Supervising Merger Analyst, Senior Merger Analyst, 1973-1994. Author: "The Growing Judicial Acceptance of the Merger Guidelines," *Antitrust Law Journal*, Volume 60, Issue 3. ***PRACTICE AREAS:*** Antitrust; Mergers, Acquisitions and Divestitures. ***Email:*** ginger.snider@cliffordchance.com

ASSOCIATES

MATTHEW D. ADLER, born Philadelphia, Pennsylvania, June 15, 1970; admitted to bar, 1996, New York; 1998, District of Columbia. *Education:* University of Michigan (A.B., 1992); Cornell Law School (J.D., 1995). Editor, Cornell Journal of Law & Public Policy. ***PRACTICE AREAS:*** Mergers and Acquisitions; Private Equity; Capital Markets. ***Email:*** matt.adler@cliffordchance.com

MICHAEL R. ALBRECHT, born St. Louis, Missouri, December 4, 1969; admitted to bar, 1996, Missouri; 1997, Illinois; 1998, District of Columbia. *Education:* St. Louis University (B.S.B.A., magna cum laude, 1992; J.D., cum laude, 1996). Editor, Saint Louis Law Journal, 1995-1996. *Member:* The Missouri Bar; The District of Columbia Bar. ***PRACTICE AREAS:*** White Collar Crime; Regulatory Law; Litigation. ***Email:*** michael.albrecht@cliffordchance.com

JULIE N. AMBROSE, born Detroit, Michigan, November 25, 1971; admitted to bar, 1997, District of Columbia; registered to practice before U.S. Patent and Trademark Office. *Education:* Purdue University (B.S., 1994); Franklin Pierce Law Center (J.D., 1997; M.I.P., 1997). Senior Editor, "Idea: Journal of Law and Technology," Franklin Pierce Law Center. *Member:* American International Property Law Association. ***PRACTICE AREAS:*** Intellectual Property; Patent Litigation. ***Email:*** julie.ambrose@cliffordchance.com

CARRIE M. ANDERSON, born Malden, Massachusetts, September 14, 1972; admitted to bar, 1997, Massachusetts; 1998, District of Columbia. *Education:* University of Miami (B.A., cum laude, 1993); Georgetown University Law Center (J.D., cum laude, 1997). Editor-in-Chief, *American Criminal Law Review Twelfth Survey of White Collar Crime*. Author: "Eleventh Survey of White Collar Crime," Antitrust Law, American Criminal Law Review, Volume

(This Listing Continued)

33, Spring 1996. *Member:* The District of Columbia Bar; American Bar Association (Member, Antitrust Section). ***PRACTICE AREAS:*** Antitrust and Trade Regulation; Litigation. ***Email:*** carrie.anderson@cliffordchance.com

HEATHER FAI AUYANG, born Santa Monica, California, October 19, 1972; admitted to bar, 1997, California; 1998, Illinois; 2000, District of Columbia; registered to practice before the U.S. Patent and Trademark Office. *Education:* University of California at San Diego (B.S., 1994); Tulane University (J.D., cum laude, 1997). *Member:* Chicago, Illinois State and American Bar Associations; State Bar of California; American Intellectual Property Law Association. ***PRACTICE AREAS:*** Patent Litigation. ***Email:*** heather.auyang@cliffordchance.com

ALLEN R. BACHMAN, born Halifax, Nova Scotia, Canada, April 14, 1972; admitted to bar, 1999, Virginia; 2000, District of Columbia. *Education:* College of William & Mary (B.A., 1994; J.D., 1999). *Member:* Virginia and American Bar Associations; The District of Columbia Bar. ***PRACTICE AREAS:*** Litigation; Antitrust. ***Email:*** allen.bachman@cliffordchance.com

ALLYSON BAKER, born Washington, D.C., September 17, 1973; admitted to bar, 2001, New York (Not admitted in District of Columbia). *Education:* Columbia University (B.A., 1995); New York University (J.D., cum laude, 2000). ***PRACTICE AREAS:*** Litigation. ***Email:*** allyson.baker@cliffordchance.com

LACY D. BERRINGTON, born Silver Spring, Maryland, January 31, 1972; admitted to bar, 1997, Maryland; 1998, District of Columbia. *Education:* American University (B.A., magna cum laude, 1994); University of Pennsylvania (J.D., 1997). Golden Key. Alpha Lambda Delta. Dean's Scholar. ***PRACTICE AREAS:*** Antitrust. ***Email:*** lacy.berrington@cliffordchance.com

JAMES J. BLACK, born Cheverly, Maryland, August 1, 1966; admitted to bar, 1998, New York and District of Columbia. *Education:* Southern Illinois University (B.A., 1990); University of Virginia (M.A., 1994; J.D., 1996). Rotary Scholar, Erlangen, Germany, 1986-1987. University Scholar, University of Regensburg, Germany, 1988-1989. Bosch Fellow, Berlin, Germany, 1996-1997. Author: "Free Speech and the Internet: The Inevitable Move Toward Governmental Regulation," Richmond Journal of Law & Technology, Vol. 4, Issue 2, Winter 1997. *Member:* The District of Columbia Bar; German-American Law Association. ***LANGUAGES:*** German. ***PRACTICE AREAS:*** Corporate; Securities; Mergers and Acquisitions; Cross-Border Finance. ***Email:*** james.black@cliffordchance.com

DANIEL T. BROWN, born Wilmington, Delaware, September 16, 1967; admitted to bar, 1994, Illinois; 2001, District of Columbia. *Education:* University of Delaware (B.A., 1991); Chicago-Kent College of Law (J.D., with high honors, 1994). Order of the Coif. Member, 1992-1993; Notes and Comments Editor, 1993-1994, Chicago-Kent Law Review. Law Clerk to the Hon. James L. Latchum, U.S. District Court, District of Delaware, 1994-1995. Attorney, 1997-1998, Senior Attorney, 1998-1999 and Branch Chief, 1999-2000, Division of Enforcement, U.S. Securities and Exchange Commission. *Member:* Federal and American Bar Associations. ***PRACTICE AREAS:*** Securities Litigation; Enforcement Defense; Regulatory Law. ***Email:*** daniel.brown@cliffordchance.com

ERIN M. BROWN, born Los Angeles, California, September 25, 1973; admitted to bar, 1999, California; 2000, District of Columbia. *Education:* University of California at Los Angeles (B.A., summa cum laude, 1995); Georgetown University Law Center (J.D., 1999). Phi Beta Kappa. Dean's list. ***LANGUAGES:*** Spanish. ***PRACTICE AREAS:*** Litigation. ***Email:*** erin.brown@cliffordchance.com

ALI HASAN BURNEY, born Karachi, Pakistan, April 2, 1974; (admission pending). *Education:* University of the South (B.A., 1994); University of London, Queen Mary & Westfield College, London, United Kingdom (LL.M., Banking and Finance Law, 1998); Albany Law School of Union University (J.D., cum laude, 2001). Summer Associate, McNamee, Lochner, TItus and Williams, Albany, New York. ***PRACTICE AREAS:*** Securities Regulation; Litigation; Alternative Dispute Resolution. ***Email:*** ali.burney@cliffordchance.com

N. SEAN BUTLER, born Hartford, Connecticut, July 23, 1974; admitted to bar, 2001, Maryland (Not admitted in District of Columbia). *Education:* Georgia Institute of Technology (B.S., Economics, 1996); Columbus School of Law of The Catholic University of America (J.D., 2001). Associate Editor, Catholic University Law Review, 2000-2001. ***PRACTICE AREAS:*** Litigation; Alternative Dispute Resolution. ***Email:*** sean.butler@cliffordchance.com

BRET A. CAMPBELL, born La Grange, Illinois, January 30, 1967; admitted to bar, 1995, Massachusetts; 1996, New York and District of Columbia; 1997, U.S. District Court, District of Columbia; 2000, U.S. Court of Appeals for the Federal Circuit. *Education:* Hobart College (B.A., with honors, 1989); Vermont Law School (J.D., cum laude, 1994). Clerk, Hon. Jerome J. Neidermeier, U.S. District Court, District of Vermont. *Member:* The District of Columbia Bar; New York State and Federal Circuit Bar Associations. ***PRACTICE AREAS:*** Antitrust Litigation; Intellectual Property Litigation; Securities Litigation. ***Email:*** bret.campbell@cliffordchance.com

(This Listing Continued)

CHRISTINE SUHMING CHEN, born Albany, New York; admitted to bar, 2000, District of Columbia. *Education:* Dartmouth College (B.A., cum laude, 1996); University of Pennsylvania (J.D., 1999). ***LANGUAGES:*** Mandarin, Taiwanese and French. ***PRACTICE AREAS:*** Corporate Banking Law; Corporate Finance. **Email:** christine.chen@cliffordchance.com

ELIZABETH CHEN, born Livonia, Michigan, January 20, 1970; admitted to bar, 2001, New York (Not admitted in District of Columbia). *Education:* University of Michigan (A.B., 1991); Columbia University (J.D., 2000). ***PRACTICE AREAS:*** Litigation. **Email:** elizabeth.chen@cliffordchance.com

GREGORY D. CHO, born New York, N.Y., June 26, 1972; admitted to bar, 2000, New York (Not admitted in District of Columbia). *Education:* University of Wisconsin- Madison (B.A., 1994); University of Iowa (J.D., with distinction, 1999). Member, Moot Court Board, University of Iowa, 1999. Managing Editor, Iowa Law Review. Law Clerk to the Hon. Judge W. Craig Broadwater, Northern District of West Virginia, 1999-2001. ***PRACTICE AREAS:*** Litigation. **Email:** gregory.cho@cliffordchance.com

FRANK C. CIMINO, JR., born Baltimore, Maryland, December 26, 1969; admitted to bar, 1996, Maryland; 1999, District of Columbia; registered to practice before U.S. Patent and Trademark Office. *Education:* Drexel University (B.S.M.E., cum laude, 1992); University of Baltimore (J.D., with honors, 1996); The Johns Hopkins University (M.S.E.E., 1999). Executive Editor, Intellectual Property Law Journal, 1996. *Member:* The District of Columbia Bar; American Bar Association; American Intellectual Property Law Association. ***PRACTICE AREAS:*** Intellectual Property Law; Patent Litigation. **Email:** frank.cimino@cliffordchance.com

BOYD TRISTAN CLOERN, born Madisonville, Kentucky, April 19, 1972; admitted to bar, 1998, Kentucky; 2000, District of Columbia. *Education:* University of Kentucky (B.A., 1995; J.D., cum laude, 1998). Member and Associate Editor, Kentucky Law Journal, University of Kentucky College of Law. *Member:* Kentucky Bar Association; The District of Columbia Bar. ***PRACTICE AREAS:*** Complex Litigation; Antitrust; Unfair Competition; Intellectual Property. **Email:** boyd.cloern@cliffordchance.com

CHARLES M. COLE, born Abington, Pennsylvania, April 7, 1963; admitted to bar, 1994, Pennsylvania, New York and Maryland; 1995, District of Columbia. *Education:* Lehigh University (B.S., 1985); American University (J.D., cum laude, 1993). Author: "Poland, Hungary and the Czech and Slovak Federal Republic: An Examination of the Evolving Legal Framework for Foreign Investment," Am. U.J. Int'l L. & Pol'y. 667 (1992). *Member:* The District of Columbia Bar. ***PRACTICE AREAS:*** Corporate. **Email:** charles.cole@cliffordchance.com

ANTHONY M. COOKE, born Philadelphia, Pennsylvania, January 17, 1968; admitted to bar, 1995, Pennsylvania (inactive) and New Jersey; 2000, District of Columbia. *Education:* University of St. Andrews, Scotland; Georgetown University (B.A., 1990); Tulane University (J.D., cum laude, 1995). Senior Articles Editor, Tulane Environmental Law Journal Student Attorney, Tulane Environmental Law Clinic. **Email:** anthony.cooke@cliffordchance.com

SHA-SHANA N. L. CRICHTON, born St. James, Jamaica, West Indies, August 24, 1971; admitted to bar, 1999, New Jersey; 2000, New York and District of Columbia. *Education:* University of the West Indies (B.A., with honors, 1994); Howard University School of Law (J.D., cum laude, 1999). Phi Alpha Delta. Howard Merit Scholar. Managing Editor, Howard Law Journal, 1998-1999. *Member:* New York State and American Bar Associations; Caribbean Bar Association. ***LANGUAGES:*** Spanish, French. ***PRACTICE AREAS:*** Litigation. **Email:** sha-shana.crichton@cliffordchance.com

PATRICIA C. CROWLEY, born Framingham, Massachusetts; admitted to bar, 1994, Maryland; 1998, District of Columbia; U.S. District Court, District of Columbia and U.S. Court of Appeals, Federal Circuit. *Education:* Trinity University (B.A., with honors, 1990); Columbus School of Law, Catholic University of America (J.D., cum laude, 1994). *Member:* American Bar Association (Member, Antitrust Division). ***PRACTICE AREAS:*** Litigation; Antitrust. **Email:** patricia.crowley@cliffordchance.com

JULIA SYMON DE KLUIVER, born Liverpool, England, July 11, 1968; admitted to bar, 1994, Louisiana; 1997, District of Columbia. *Education:* Tufts University (B.A., 1989); Tulane University of Louisiana (J.D., magna cum laude, 1994). Order of the Coif; Order of the Barristers. Administrative Justice, Tulane Moot Court Board, 1993-1994. *Member:* Louisiana State and American Bar Associations; The District of Columbia Bar. ***PRACTICE AREAS:*** Antitrust; Intellectual Property; Complex Litigation. **Email:** julia.dekluiver@cliffordchance.com

H.C. EREN, born Atlanta, Georgia, August 27, 1960; admitted to bar, 1998, Maryland; 1999, District of Columbia; 2000, New York. *Education:* University of Maryland (B.A., Economics, 1982; B.A., Political Science, 1982); American University (J.D., 1998). Formerly with Office of Foreign Assets Control, U.S. Treasury Department. Member, International Trade Law Group and Japan Business Group, Clifford Chance. *Member:* New York State, Maryland State, American (Deputy Chairman, Business Transactions and Dispute Division, 2000— and Leadership Member, International Law Section) and International Bar Associations; The District of Columbia Bar. ***LANGUAGES:*** French, Spanish and Turkish. ***PRACTICE AREAS:*** Economic Sanctions; International Public Law; International Regulatory Law; International Trade; Project Finance; Corporate Finance. **Email:** hal.eren@cliffordchance.com

BENJAMIN M. FARBER, born Tallahassee, Florida, May 30, 1974; admitted to bar, 2000, New Jersey and New York; 2001, District of Columbia. *Education:* Cornell University (B.A., 1996); Albany Law School of Union University (J.D., cum laude, 1999). Member, 1997-1998 and Executive Editor, Lead Articles, 1998-1999, Albany Law Review. ***PRACTICE AREAS:*** Corporate Law. **Email:** ben.farber@cliffordchance.com

MICHAEL FRANSELLA, born Winter Park, Florida, January 11, 1976; admitted to bar, 2001, Virginia (Not admitted in District of Columbia). *Education:* Williams College (B.A., summa cum laude, 1998); Yale University (J.D., 2001). Phi Beta Kappa. *Member:* Virginia State Bar. ***PRACTICE AREAS:*** Mergers and Acquisitions; Securities. **Email:** michael.fransella@cliffordchance.com

PAUL R. FRONTCZAK, born Chicago, Illinois, June 30, 1971; admitted to bar, 1996, New Jersey; 1998, New York; 1999, District of Columbia. *Education:* Muhlenberg College (B.A., 1993); Albany Law School (J.D., cum laude, 1996). Associate Editor, Albany Law Review, 1995-1996. *Member:* The District of Columbia Bar. ***PRACTICE AREAS:*** Antitrust; Antitrust Litigation. **Email:** paul.frontczak@cliffordchance.com

STEVEN F. GATTI, born Teaneck, New Jersey, August 26, 1968; admitted to bar, 1995, New Jersey, Maryland and U.S. District Court, District of New Jersey; 1997, District of Columbia and U.S. District Court, District of Maryland. *Education:* College of William & Mary (B.A., 1990); George Washington University (J.D., with honors, 1995). Member, George Washington Moot Court Board, 1994-1995. Author: "Rules Governing E-Mail and Other Communications with the Public," NSCP Currents (Jan. 1998). ***PRACTICE AREAS:*** Securities Regulation and Enforcement; Technology Law; E-Commerce. **Email:** steven.gatti@cliffordchance.com

JULIE A. GOLDMAN, born New York, N.Y., December 20, 1966; admitted to bar, 2000, New York and District of Columbia. *Education:* Colorado State University (B.A., 1993); Georgetown University (J.D., 1999). Dean's list. Author: Note, "Bad Lawyering or Ulterior Motive...," 30 Law & Policy Intl. Bus. 417. ***LANGUAGES:*** French, Spanish and Italian. ***PRACTICE AREAS:*** Corporate. **Email:** julie.goldman@cliffordchance.com

ALLYSON ANN GOZYCKI, born Hartford, Connecticut, June 22, 1974; admitted to bar, 2001, Maryland (Not admitted in District of Columbia). *Education:* College of the Holy Cross (B.A., 1996); Columbus School of Law of the Catholic University of America (J.D., 2001). ***PRACTICE AREAS:*** Litigation. **Email:** allyson.gozycki@cliffordchance.com

ALISSA S. HECHT, born Northbrook, Illinois, December 30, 1970; admitted to bar, 1997, New York (Not admitted in District of Columbia). *Education:* University of California at Los Angeles (B.A., 1992); University of Chicago (J.D., 1996). ***PRACTICE AREAS:*** Antitrust. **Email:** alissa.hecht@cliffordchance.com

MARC JARSULIC, born Dearborn, Michigan; admitted to bar, 1999, New York; 2001, District of Columbia. *Education:* University of Pennsylvania (Ph.D., 1978); University of Michigan (J.D., 1998). Author: "Protecting Workers from Wrongful Discharge: Montana's Experience with Tort and Statutory Regimes," 3 Employee Rights and Employment Policy Journal, 105, 1999. *Member:* American Bar Association; American Economic Association. ***PRACTICE AREAS:*** Antitrust. **Email:** marc.jarsulic@cliffordchance.com

JENNIFER M. JEANNOT, born Dearborn, Michigan, November 18, 1972; admitted to bar, 2000, Virginia; 2001, District of Columbia. *Education:* Mount Holyoke College (B.A., cum laude, 1994); American University, Washington College of Law (J.D., magna cum laude, 2000). Editor-in-Chief, American University International Law Review, 1999-2000. Author: Comment, "An International Perspective on Domestic Banking Reform," 14 Am. U. Int'l L.Rev. 1715 (1999). *Member:* Virginia Bar Association; The District of Columbia Bar. ***LANGUAGES:*** French. ***PRACTICE AREAS:*** Securities Regulation; Banking Regulation; Corporate Law. **Email:** jennifer.jeannot@cliffordchance.com

GIBBS A. JOHNSON, born April 14, 1964; admitted to bar, 1999, New York; 2001, District of Columbia. *Education:* Brigham Young University (B.S., 1987); University of South Carolina (M.I.B.S., 1993); Harvard Law School (J.D., 1998). ***PRACTICE AREAS:*** International Project Finance. **Email:** gibbs.johnson@cliffordchance.com

THOMAS C. KOONCE, born Lumberton, North Carolina, March 3, 1971; admitted to bar, 1998, North Carolina; 1999, District of Columbia. *Education:* Davidson College (B.A., 1993); College of William & Mary (J.D., 1998). Publication Editor, William & Mary Law Review. *Member:* North Carolina State Bar; The District of Columbia Bar; American Bar Association. ***PRACTICE AREAS:*** Antitrust; Litigation. **Email:** thomas.koonce@cliffordchance.com

DENISE LANDERS, born New York, N.Y., March 12, 1966; admitted to bar, 1996, Massachusetts (Not admitted in District of Columbia). *Education:* Wellesley College (B.A., cum laude, 1988); Boston University School of Law

(This Listing Continued)

CLIFFORD CHANCE ROGERS & WELLS LLP, Washington—Continued

(J.D., 1996). U.S. Securities and Exchange Commission, Market Regulation, 1996-1997. ***PRACTICE AREAS:*** Securities Law. ***Email:*** denise.landers@cliffordchance.com

AIMEE D. LATIMER, born Decatur, Georgia, August 6, 1971; admitted to bar, 1996, Illinois; 1998, Virginia (Not admitted in District of Columbia). *Education:* Northwestern University (B.S., 1993); Loyola University (J.D., cum laude, 1996). Alpha Sigma Nu. Best Oralist Award, Moot Court Competition, Illinois State Bar Association, 1995. Member, 1994 and Executive Editor of Student Articles, 1995-1996, Loyola Law Journal. Author: "Miller v. Johnson: The Supreme Court Eases the Burden of Proving Racial Gerrymandering," Loyola Law Journal, Vol. 27, No. 1. Law Clerk, Honorable Allen Hartman, Illinois Appellate Court, 1996-1998. ***PRACTICE AREAS:*** Commercial Litigation; Litigation. ***Email:*** aimee.latimer@cliffordchance.com

FRANCESCA D. LAURSEN, born New York, N.Y., May 2, 1966; admitted to bar, 2001, New York and District of Columbia. *Education:* University of Massachusetts (B.A., 1988); Schiller International University, Germany (Masters in International Business Management, 1989); American University (J.D., 2000). Formerly with Fidelity Investments. ***LANGUAGES:*** Spanish and Portuguese. ***PRACTICE AREAS:*** Project Finance; Corporate Finance; '40 Act Investment Compliance; Family Law. ***Email:*** francesca.laursen@cliffordchance.com

JULIA LEE, born Taiwan, R.O.C., June 25, 1966; admitted to bar, 1992, Pennsylvania; 2001, District of Columbia. *Education:* Washington University (B.A., 1988); George Washington University (J.D., 1991). *Member:* American Bar Association. ***LANGUAGES:*** Italian, Taiwanese. ***PRACTICE AREAS:*** Securities; Mergers and Acquisitions; Corporate Finance. ***Email:*** julia.lee@cliffordchance.com

ADAM S. LOVINGER, born Eugene, Oregon, August 16, 1971; (admission pending). *Education:* University of Pennsylvania (B.A., 1994); Georgetown University (J.D., 2001). ***PRACTICE AREAS:*** Project Finance. ***Email:*** adam.lovinger@cliffordchance.com

MELISSA A. MACGREGOR, born Glens Falls, New York, April 18, 1976; (admission pending). *Education:* St. Lawrence University (B.A., magna cum laude, 1998); American University (J.D., cum laude, 2001). Phi Beta Kappa (Member, St. Lawrence University Chapter). ***PRACTICE AREAS:*** Securities Regulation; Securities Litigation Defense; Corporate Law. ***Email:*** melissa.macgregor@cliffordchance.com

CATHERINE MCCARTHY, born Chorley, UK, January 21, 1971; admitted to bar, 1995, New York; 1997, England and Wales; 2001, District of Columbia. *Education:* Oxford University (B.A., First Class Honors, 1992; J.D.); Harvard Law School (LL.M., 1994). ***PRACTICE AREAS:*** Project Finance; Banking Law. ***Email:*** catherine.mccarthy@cliffordchance.com

PRAKASH H. MEHTA, born Boulder, Colorado, January 24, 1969; admitted to bar, 1994, Maryland; 1996, District of Columbia. *Education:* Georgetown University School of Foreign Service (B.S.F.S., summa cum laude, 1991); Georgetown University Law Center (J.D., magna cum laude, 1994). Phi Beta Kappa; Order of the Coif. Member, Georgetown Law Journal. *Member:* The District of Columbia Bar. ***LANGUAGES:*** Gujarati, Hindi, French. ***PRACTICE AREAS:*** International; Corporate Transactional; Private Equity. ***Email:*** prakash.mehta@cliffordchance.com

KATHERINE WELLS MEIGHAN, born Washington, D.C., December 18, 1970; admitted to bar, 1995, Virginia; 1996, District of Columbia. *Education:* College of William & Mary (B.A., 1992); University of Virginia (J.D., 1995). John M. Olin Fellowship. Order of the Coif. Phi Beta Kappa. Member, Virginia Journal of International Law, 1993-1994. Author: "For Better or For Worse: A Corporate Finance Approach to Evaluating Educational Degrees at Divorce," 5 Geo. Mason L. Rev. 193 (1997); "In a Similar Voice: A Unifying Economic Analysis of Gilligan's Amy and Jake," 2 American Univ. J. of Gender & Law 139 (1994); "The Israel-PLO Declaration of Principles: Prelude to a Peace?" 34 VA J. of Int'l Law 435 (1994). *Member:* Virginia State Bar; The District of Columbia Bar. ***LANGUAGES:*** French and Spanish. ***PRACTICE AREAS:*** Corporate; Banking; International Law. ***Email:*** katie.meighan@cliffordchance.com

ASHLEY ANNE MEISE, born Anchorage, Alaska, August 28, 1968; admitted to bar, 1998, New York; 1999, District of Columbia. *Education:* Vassar College (B.A., 1990); Georgetown University Law Center (J.D., 1997); Georgetown University School of Business (M.B.A., 1997). Notes and Comments Editor, Georgetown Journal on Fighting Poverty, 1995-1996. Law Clerk to Administrative Law Judge Kuhlmann, U.S. Department of Commerce, Washington, D.C., 1/95-6/95, 8/95-10/95. *Member:* The District of Columbia Bar. ***PRACTICE AREAS:*** Securities; Cross Border Finance; Mergers and Acquisitions; Emerging Markets; General Corporate Practice. ***Email:*** ashley.meise@cliffordchance.com

(This Listing Continued)

JENNIFER J. MINK, born Washington, D.C., January 18, 1971; admitted to bar, 1996, Virginia; 1997, District of Columbia. *Education:* George Mason University (B.S., summa cum laude, 1993); University of Virginia (J.D., 1996). Member, Editorial Board, 1994-1995 and Articles Review Board, 1995-1996, Virginia Journal of International Law. *Member:* Virginia State Bar; The District of Columbia Bar. ***PRACTICE AREAS:*** Corporate. ***Email:*** jennifer.mink@cliffordchance.com

HODA ATIA MOUSTAFA, born Bethesda, Maryland, July 21, 1972; admitted to bar, 1998, Illinois; 1999, District of Columbia. *Education:* University of Maryland (B.S., 1994); Georgetown University (J.D./M.S.F.S., 1998). Editor, Georgetown Environmental Law Review. Author, International Trade and Business Law Annual, Winter, 2000. ***LANGUAGES:*** Arabic, French and Spanish. ***TRANSACTIONS:*** Suez Gulf and Port Said East Power Projects, Egypt; Bujagali Hydroelectric Power Project, Uganda. ***PRACTICE AREAS:*** Project Finance. ***Email:*** hoda.moustafa@cliffordchance.com

SCOTT B. MURRAY, born East Orange, New Jersey, June 25, 1968; admitted to bar, 1994, Pennsylvania; 1995, New Jersey; 1999, District of Columbia. *Education:* Princeton University (B.S.E., 1991); Rutgers University-Camden (J.D., 1994). *Member:* The District of Columbia Bar; American Bar Association. ***PRACTICE AREAS:*** Antitrust and Trade Regulation. ***Email:*** scott.murray@cliffordchance.com

JOSEPH L. MUSELLA, born Colorado Springs, Colorado, May 31, 1973; admitted to bar, 1999, New Jersey; 2000, New York; 2001, District of Columbia. *Education:* George Washington University (B.B.A., 1995); George Mason School of Law (J.D., 1999). ***PRACTICE AREAS:*** Banking Law; Corporate Law; Securities. ***Email:*** joseph.musella@cliffordchance.com

GREGORY G. NARDINI, born Elmhurst, Illinois, July 13, 1975; admitted to bar, 2001, New York and District of Columbia. *Education:* University of Illinois (A.B., 1997; J.D., 2000). ***LANGUAGES:*** Spanish and French. ***PRACTICE AREAS:*** Corporate Law. ***Email:*** gregory.nardini@cliffordchance.com

SUSAN M. PETERSEN, born Milwaukee, Wisconsin, December 30, 1958; admitted to bar, 1997, Maryland (Not admitted in District of Columbia). *Education:* University of Wisconsin (B.A., 1981); Columbus School of Law of The Catholic University of America (J.D., 1997). USIT. ***SPECIAL AGENCIES:*** U.S. Securities and Exchange Commission. ***PRACTICE AREAS:*** Securities. ***Email:*** susan.petersen@cliffordchance.com

TIMOTHY P. PETERSON, born Ft. Leonard Wood, Missouri, August 26, 1969; admitted to bar, 1999, New York; 2000, District of Columbia. *Education:* Miami University (A.B., 1991); The Ohio State University (M.B.A., 1993); Georgetown University Law Center (J.D., 1998). Member, Editorial Board, Georgetown International Environmental Law Review. ***PRACTICE AREAS:*** Securities; Securities Litigation; White Collar Crime. ***Email:*** timothy.peterson@cliffordchance.com

CARLOS E. PROVENCIO, born Bitburg, Germany, April 5, 1968; admitted to bar, 1996, Missouri; 1998, District of Columbia. *Education:* Swarthmore College (B.A., 1990); St. Louis University (J.D., magna cum laude, 1996). Editor-in-Chief, Public Law Review, 1995-1996. *Member:* The Missouri Bar; The District of Columbia Bar. ***LANGUAGES:*** Spanish. ***PRACTICE AREAS:*** Antitrust; Commercial Litigation; Securities Litigation; Corporate Compliance; White Collar. ***Email:*** carlos.provencio@cliffordchance.com

JENEEN RAMOS, born Queens, New York, April 25, 1972; admitted to bar, 2000, New York (Not admitted in District of Columbia). *Education:* University of Central Florida (B.A., 1995); Howard University (J.D., cum laude, 1999). Member, Howard Law Journal. Author: "The Wrath of Kahn: The Impact on Minority Franchises," Volume 42, Howard Law Journal. ***PRACTICE AREAS:*** Litigation. ***Email:*** jeneen.ramos@cliffordchance.com

CHRISTOPHER D. ROBERTI, born 1971; admitted to bar, 1999, New York and District of Columbia. *Education:* University of Illinois (A.B., 1993); Northwestern University School of Law (J.D., 1998). *Member:* New York State Bar Association; The District of Columbia Bar. ***LANGUAGES:*** German and Spanish. ***PRACTICE AREAS:*** Corporate; International Private Equity; International Mergers and Acquisitions; Securities. ***Email:*** christopher.roberti@cliffordchance.com

KEVIN T. ROCHE, born Scranton, Pennsylvania, January 21, 1970; admitted to bar, 2000, New York (Not admitted in District of Columbia). *Education:* Mary Washington College (B.A., cum laude, 1993); Catholic University School of Law (J.D., 1999). Senior Associate Editor, The Journal of Contemporary Health and Law Policy, 1998-1999. ***PRACTICE AREAS:*** Financial Services Law; Technology and Science. ***Email:*** kevin.roche@cliffordchance.com

NICHOLAS M. ROEGNER, born January 19, 1967; admitted to bar, 1997, New York; 1998, District of Columbia. *Education:* Columbia University (B.A., 1990); College of William & Mary (J.D., 1996). ***PRACTICE AREAS:*** International Capital Markets; International Trade. ***Email:*** nicholas.roegner@cliffordchance.com

VINCENT SERPICO, born Brooklyn, New York, June 7, 1966; admitted to bar, 1997, New York (Not admitted in District of Columbia). *Education:* New

(This Listing Continued)

York University (B.S., 1988); Columbia Law School (J.D., 1996). Stone Scholar. ***PRACTICE AREAS:*** Technology; Internet Law. ***Email:*** vincent.serpico@cliffordchance.com

KIMBERLY L. SHAW, born Camp Lejeune MCB, North Carolina; (admission pending). *Education:* Middlebury College (B.A., magna cum laude, 1995); University of Virginia (J.D., 2001). ***LANGUAGES:*** French. ***Email:*** kimberly.shaw@cliffordchance.com

ROBYN SHIELDS, born New York, N.Y., August 8, 1953; admitted to bar, 1998, New York and District of Columbia. *Education:* New York University (B.A., 1974); Loyola University (M.Ed., 1977); Albany Law School, Union College (J.D., 1997). Note and Comment Editor, Albany Law Review, 1995-1997. Author: "Can the Feds Put Deadbeat Parents in Jail?: A Look at the Constitutionality of the Child Support Recovery Act," Albany Law Review. *Member:* The District of Columbia Bar. ***PRACTICE AREAS:*** International Banking Law; Corporate. ***Email:*** robyn.shields@cliffordchance.com

DAMON A. TERRILL, born Iowa City, Iowa, September 20, 1969; admitted to bar, 2000, New York, District of Columbia and U.S. Court of International Trade. *Education:* University of Iowa (B.A., with distinction and special honors, 1991); School of International Service, American University (M.A., International Affairs, 1995); New York University School of Law (J.D., 1999). Phi Beta Kappa; Omicron Delta Kappa. Honors Research Scholar; Lawrence Fairall Scholar; Hurst Scholar. Research and Teaching Fellow; Robert Bosch Foundation Fellow. Editor-in-Chief, New York University Journal of Legislation and Public Policy, 1998-1999. Co-Author: "Foreign-Ownership Issues: An FCC Tied in Legal Knots," Telecommunications Reports International, Feb. 16, 2001; "Global Telecomms Market Access-A Legal Perspective," International Telecommunications Quarterly, Quarterly Issue 4, 2000; "U.S. Federalism and Effective Market Access for Professional Services: Tempering Promises with Reality," 6 International Trade Law & Regulation 175, 2000. Adjunct Professor of European Union Law, George Mason University, 2000— *Member:* Bar Association of the City of New York (Member, International Security Affairs Committee, 1997-1998). ***LANGUAGES:*** German. ***PRACTICE AREAS:*** International Dispute Resolution; International Arbitration; International Litigation; Telecommunications Regulation; Data Privacy Regulation. ***Email:*** damon.terrill@cliffordchance.com

LEE K. VAN VOORHIS, born Jeannette, Pennsylvania, February 14, 1967; admitted to bar, 1997, New York; 1998, District of Columbia. *Education:* Yale University (B.A., 1989); Cornell University (J.D., 1996). *Member:* The District of Columbia Bar. ***PRACTICE AREAS:*** Antitrust. ***Email:*** lee.vanvoorhis@cliffordchance.com

PAUL VAN WAGENEN, born Bayshore, New York, August 16, 1971; (admission pending). *Education:* Harvard University (A.B., 1997); Georgetown University (J.D., 2001). ***LANGUAGES:*** Spanish. ***PRACTICE AREAS:*** Project Finance; Banking Law. ***Email:*** paul.vanwagenen@cliffordchance.com

MARY F. WALTERS, born Irving, Texas, May 31, 1970; admitted to bar, 1997, Texas; 1999, District of Columbia. *Education:* Texas A & M University (B.A., 1991; M.S., 1993); University of Texas (J.D., 1997). ***LANGUAGES:*** Spanish. ***PRACTICE AREAS:*** Commercial Litigation; Antitrust Litigation; Intellectual Property Litigation. ***Email:*** mary.walters@cliffordchance.com

JOSHUA N. WEINER, born Washington, D.C., July 23, 1972; (admission pending). *Education:* Franklin & Marshall College (B.A., 1994); Emory University School of Law (J.D., with honors, 1999). Thrower Symposium Editor, Emory Law Journal, 1998-1999. ***PRACTICE AREAS:*** Antitrust. ***Email:*** joshua.weiner@cliffordchance.com

CHRISTOPHER WILLOTT, born Frodsham, England, March 3, 1970; admitted to bar, 2000, New York (Not admitted in District of Columbia). *Education:* Georgetown University (B.A., 1993; J.D., 2000; M.S.F.S., 2000). ***PRACTICE AREAS:*** Project Finance. ***Email:*** chris.willott@cliffordchance.com

GLEN M. ZWICKER, born New Haven, Connecticut, December 8, 1971; admitted to bar, 1999, New York and District of Columbia. *Education:* Georgetown University (B.A., 1993; J.D., 1998; M.S., Foreign Service, 1998). *Member:* New York State Bar Association; The District of Columbia Bar. ***LANGUAGES:*** Spanish and Portuguese. ***PRACTICE AREAS:*** Corporate; International. ***Email:*** glen.zwicker@cliffordchance.com

(For biographical data of all partners, see Professional Biographies at New York, New York)

CLIFFORD, LYONS & GARDE

1620 L STREET, N.W.
SUITE 625
WASHINGTON, D.C. 20036-5600
Telephone: 202-289-8990
Fax: 202-289-8992
URL: http://www.lawyers.com/clg-law

Civil Litigation, Labor and Employment (Employees and Employers, Public and Private), Wrongful Termination, Employment Discrimination, Civil Rights, Administrative Law-Nuclear and Energy Issues, Employment Investigations.

FIRM PROFILE: Clifford, Lyons & Garde is a nationally-recognized trial firm that specializes in civil litigation and employment matters. The firm provides legal representation and consulting services to both individuals and corporations, plaintiffs and defendants, employees and employers. Members of the firm practice mainly in federal courts but also represent clients in state courts, and before federal and state administrative agencies and arbitration panels. Members of the firm regularly conduct on-site training and seminars concerning employment and work environment issues, provide mediation services and conduct independent investigations of employment-related disputes. The firm also represents individuals and families who have been seriously injured. Recently-litigated matters have included disputes involving race, gender, age, and disability discrimination, retaliation for raising safety concerns and other protected activity, breach of employment contracts, employers' insurance coverage, and medical malpractice.

JOHN M. CLIFFORD, born Washington, D.C., October 28, 1947; admitted to bar, 1973, Maryland; 1974, District of Columbia; 1986, U.S. Supreme Court. *Education:* Michigan State University (B.A., 1970); Catholic University of America (J.D., 1973). Member, Catholic University Law Review, 1972-1973. Author: Note, "Political Campaign Broadcasts," 22 Catholic University Law Review 171. Law Clerk to Judge John B. Doyle, District of Columbia Superior Court, 1973-1974. Assistant Corporation Counsel for the District of Columbia, 1974-1979. Board of Directors, Lab School of Washington. *Member:* District of Columbia Bar (Litigation Steering Committee, 1999—); Maryland State and American Bar Associations. ***PRACTICE AREAS:*** Civil Litigation; Employment; Commercial; Personal Injury. ***Email:*** jclifford@clg-law.com

MONA LYONS, born New York, N.Y., January 10, 1950; admitted to bar, 1975, District of Columbia. *Education:* College of the Potomac (B.A., 1972); Manhattanville College; Catholic University of America (J.D., 1975). *Member:* District of Columbia Bar. ***PRACTICE AREAS:*** Civil Litigation; Employment; Medical Malpractice; Personal Injury. ***Email:*** mlyons@clg-law.com

BILLIE PIRNER GARDE, born Neenah, Wisconsin, April 5, 1953; admitted to bar, 1986, Wisconsin; 1992, Texas; 1997, District of Columbia. *Education:* Northeastern Oklahoma State University (B.A., 1978; M.Ed., 1980); Antioch Law School (J.D., 1986). *Member:* District of Columbia Bar; State Bar of Wisconsin; State Bar of Texas; American Bar Association; Association of Trial Lawyers of America; Trial Lawyers for Public Justice. ***PRACTICE AREAS:*** Civil Litigation; Toxic Torts; Employment; Work Environment Training and Consulting. ***Email:*** bpgarde@aol.com

ASSOCIATE

PETER F. BUTCHER, born Schenectady, New York, September 4, 1962; admitted to bar, 1993, New York and Massachusetts; 1994, District of Columbia. *Education:* Temple University (B.A., 1988); Georgetown University Law Center (J.D., 1992). Senior Writing Fellow, Legal Writing Center, 1991-1992. Author: "Assessing Fear of Persecution in a War Zone," Georgetown University Law Journal, Vol. 5, No. 3. Law Clerk to the Honorable Colleen Kollar-Kotelly, Superior Court, District of Columbia, 1992-1993. ***PRACTICE AREAS:*** Civil Litigation; Employment; Medical Malpractice. ***Email:*** pbutcher@clg-law.com

COALE COOLEY LIETZ McINERNY

A PROFESSIONAL CORPORATION
Established in 1990
818 CONNECTICUT AVENUE, N.W., SUITE 857
WASHINGTON, D.C. 20006
Telephone: 202-887-4770
Facsimile: 202-887-4778

Aviation, Personal Injury, Wrongful Death, Product Liability, Mass Tort Litigation and General Litigation.

FIRM PROFILE: Coale, Cooley, Lietz, McInerny & Broadus is a law firm that specializes in representing people who have claims in Aviation, Personal Injury, Wrongful Death, Mass Disaster and Commercial Accidents. Based in Washington, D.C., Coale, Cooley, Lietz, McInerny & Broadus handles cases throughout the United States and abroad.

(This Listing Continued)

COALE COOLEY LIETZ McINERNY, A PROFESSIONAL CORPORATION, Washington—Continued

JOHN P. COALE, (A PROFESSIONAL CORPORATION), born Baltimore, Maryland, December 21, 1946; admitted to bar, 1972, Maryland; 1975, District of Columbia; 1979, U.S. Supreme Court. *Education:* University of Maryland (B.A., 1969); University of Baltimore (J.D., 1972). Member, University of Baltimore Law Review, 1971-1972. Plaintiffs Counsel: Union Carbide, Bhopal, India Disaster, 1984; Arrow Air Crash, Gander, Newfoundland, 1985; Dupont Plaza Hotel Fire, San Juan, Puerto Rico, 1986; Northwest Airlines Crash, Detroit, 1987; Continental Express Crash, Durango, Colorado, 1988; Ford Motor Company School Bus Crash, Carrollton, Kentucky, 1988; Delta Airlines Crash, Dallas, Texas, 1988; Independent Air Inc., Crash, Azores, Portugal, 1989; Hatchie River Bridge Collapse, Covington, Tennessee, 1989; Scenic Air Tours Airline Crash, Hawaii, 1989; United Airlines Crash, Sioux City, Iowa, 1989; Grand Canyon Airlines Crash, Phoenix, Arizona, 1989; Ft. Benjamin Harrison Gas Explosion, Indiana, 1989; Aeroperlas Air Crash, Panama City, Panama, 1990; L-Tryptophan Drug Litigation, 1990; U.S. Air LAX Crash, 1990; US Air West Virginia Crash, 1990; Imperial Food Company Fire, North Carolina, 1991; AC/DC Concert Tragedy, Salt Lake City, Utah, 1991; Amtrak "Sunset Limited" Train Disaster, Bayou Canot, Alabama, 1992; Waco, Texas (Branch Davidian) Fire, 1993; USAir Flight 1016 Crash, Charlotte, North Carolina, 1994; USAir Flight 427 Crash, Aliquippa (Pittsburgh), Pennsylvania, 1994; American Airlines Flight 965 Air Crash, Cali, Columbia, 1995; ValuJet Flight 592 Air Crash, Miami, Florida, 1996; Comair Flight 3272 Air Crash, Detroit, Michigan, 1997; Plaintiffs Steering Committee, Amtrak/Conrail Train Crash, Chase, Maryland, 1987; Executive Committee, Castano Tobacco Litigation, 1994; Plaintiffs Steering Committee, Norplant Class Action, 1996; Plaintiffs Steering Committee, National Gun Litigation (Representing the Cities of New Orleans, Atlanta, Cleveland, Cincinnati, Newark and Wilmington, Delaware) REPAIR Group, National HMO Class Actions. *Member:* The District of Columbia Bar. ***PRACTICE AREAS:*** Products Liability Law; Mass Disaster Litigation; Aviation Law. ***Email:*** jcoale@coalecooley.com

DIANE E. COOLEY, born Cambridge, Massachusetts, May 10, 1965; admitted to bar, 1991, Massachusetts and Connecticut; 1992, District of Columbia, U.S. District Court, District of Massachusetts and U.S. District Court for the District of Columbia and U.S. Court of Appeals, Seventh and Fifth Circuits. *Education:* Boston University (B.A., cum laude, 1987); Georgetown University (J.D., 1990). Adjunct Professor, Civil Discovery, Georgetown University Law Center, 1993—. *Member:* Massachusetts and Connecticut Bar Associations; The District of Columbia Bar. ***PRACTICE AREAS:*** Civil Litigation. ***Email:*** dcooley@coalecooley.com

DAVID K. LIETZ, born Mauston, Wisconsin, October 16, 1966; admitted to bar, 1991, District of Columbia; 1994, U.S. District Court, District of Columbia; 1995, U.S. District Court, Eastern District of Michigan; U.S. Court of Appeals, Sixth Circuit. *Education:* Luther College (B.A., cum laude, 1988); Georgetown University Law Center (J.D., 1991). Recipient: American Jurisprudence Award for Oral Advocacy, 1990-1991. Member: Cardozo/BMI Entertainment Law Moot Court Team. Winner, Best Brief, 1991. Assistant Director, Georgetown Barrister's Council, 1989-1990. *Member:* District of Columbia Bar; International Society of Air Safety Investigators (ISASI). ***PRACTICE AREAS:*** Aviation; Wrongful Death; Commercial Vehicle Liability. ***Email:*** dlietz@coalecooley.com

JULIA WERNETT McINERNY, born Jim Thorpe, Pennsylvania, March 12, 1964; admitted to bar, 1993, Maryland and U.S. District Court, District of Maryland; 1994, Pennsylvania and U.S. District Court, Eastern District of Pennsylvania; 1995, District of Columbia. *Education:* University of Maryland (B.S., 1986); University of Baltimore (J.D., 1993). Recipient: American Jurisprudence Award in Trial Advocacy; Lexis/Nexis Research Award, Best Brief, 1992. *Member:* District of Columbia Bar; American Bar Association; Association of Trial Lawyers of America. ***PRACTICE AREAS:*** Civil Litigation; Commercial Vehicle Liability. ***Email:*** jmcinerny@coalecooley.com

---

DEBORAH ST. JEAN, born Kirkland Lake, Ontario, Canada, October 16, 1957; admitted to bar, 1987, Maryland; 1989, District of Columbia. *Education:* Carlton University (B.A., 1979); Antioch School of Law (J.D., 1987). *Member:* The District of Columbia Bar. ***PRACTICE AREAS:*** Products Liability; Criminal Law.

COAN & LYONS

Established in 1979

SUITE 1000, 1100 CONNECTICUT AVENUE, N.W.
WASHINGTON, D.C. 20036
Telephone: 202-728-1070
Facsimile: 202-293-2448
URL: http://www.lawyers.com/coan&lyons

General Practice. Federal, Administrative and Legislative Practice. Real Estate, Housing and Urban Affairs, Contracts, Banking Law, Litigation, Probate, Wills, Fair Housing.

MEMBERS OF FIRM

CARL A. S. COAN, JR., born Philadelphia, Pennsylvania, September 1, 1934; admitted to bar, 1958, District of Columbia. *Education:* Georgetown University (A.B., 1954; LL.B., 1958). Delta Theta Phi. Author: "The Housing and Urban Development Act of 1968: Landmark Legislation for the Urban Crisis," The Urban Lawyer, Vol. 1 No. 1, Spring, 1969. Attorney, 1958-1969 and Assistant General Counsel, 1968-1969, Federal Housing Administration, Urban Renewal Administration and U.S. Department of Housing and Urban Development. Deputy Legislative Counsel, 1969-1971 and Vice President Government Affairs and Legislative Counsel, 1971-1977, National Association of Home Builders. Member, Advisory Committee on Uniform Land Transactions Act, Conference of Commissioners on Uniform State Laws, 1972-1975. Member, 1967-1973 and Chairman, 1969-1973, Consumer Protection and Public Utilities Commission of Fairfax County, Virginia. Member, 1975-1985, Vice Chairman, 1977-1983 and Chairman, 1983-1985, Redevelopment and Housing Authority of Fairfax County, Virginia. Commissioner, Fairfax County Planning Commission, Fairfax County, VA, 1995-1999. Public Member, Joint Committee on Alternative Mortgage Instruments of Virginia General Assembly, 1977-1980. Director, Vice President and Member, Executive Committee, National Housing Conference. Trustee, Cooperative Housing Foundation. *Member:* Federal and American (Member, Sections on: Real Property, Probate and Trust Law, Administrative Law and Regulatory Practice; Chair, Housing Subcommittee, Section of State and Local Government Law) Bar Associations. [1st Lieut., U.S. Army, 1954-1956]. ***PRACTICE AREAS:*** Housing and Urban Affairs; Real Estate; Legislative Law; Fair Housing. ***Email:*** carlcoan@coanlyons.com

WILLIAM S. MOORHEAD (1923-1987).

RAYMOND K. JAMES, born Torrington, Connecticut, September 12, 1934; admitted to bar, 1963, District of Columbia. *Education:* New York University (B.A., 1956); Harvard University (LL.B., 1963). Phi Beta Kappa. Counsel, Judiciary Committee, U.S. House of Representatives, 1963-1966. Legislative Attorney, 1967-1971 and Assistant General Counsel for Legislation, 1971-1973, U.S. Department of Housing and Urban Development. Chief Counsel, Subcommittee on Housing and Community Development, Committee on Banking, Finance and Urban Affairs, U.S. House of Representatives, 1973-1977. Chief Counsel, Federal Railroad Administration, U.S. Department of Transportation, 1977-1981. ***PRACTICE AREAS:*** Housing and Urban Affairs; Real Estate; Legislative Law. ***Email:*** rayjames@coanlyons.com

CARL A. S. COAN, III, born Shirley, Massachusetts, March 25, 1956; admitted to bar, 1981, District of Columbia; 1983, Virginia. *Education:* University of Virginia; George Mason University (B.A., with high distinction, 1978); Georgetown University (J.D., cum laude, 1981). Delta Theta Phi. Contributor, American Bar Association Journal of Affordable Housing and Community Development Law, 1994. Commissioner, Redevelopment and Housing Authority of Fairfax Co., Virginia, 1996-2000. *Member:* The District of Columbia Bar; Virginia State Bar; American Bar Association. ***REPORTED CASES:*** Kansas City v. Department of Housing and Urban Development, 861 F.2d 739 (D.C. Cir. 1988); Brighton Village Associates et al v. United States, 52 F.3rd 1056 (Fed. Cir. 1995); Trafalgar Capital Associates, Inc. v. Cuomo, 153 F.3d 21 (1st Cir. 1998). ***PRACTICE AREAS:*** Housing and Urban Affairs; Real Estate; Litigation; Wills; Probate; Corporate. ***Email:*** ccoan@coanlyons.com

ASSOCIATE

SHEILA C. SALMON, born Washington, D. C., April 8, 1963; admitted to bar, 1988, Virginia; 1989, District of Columbia. *Education:* Virginia Tech University (B.S. in Finance, 1985);Washington College of Law of American University (J.D., 1988). Contributor: American Bar Association Journal of Affordable Housing and Community Development Law, 1994; The Urban Lawyer of the Section of State and Local Government Law, Fall 1995; State and Local Law News of ABA Section of State and Local Government Law, Summer 1995. Chair, Legislative Committee, National Council on Seniors Housing, National Association of Home Builders, 1999—. *Member:* District of Columbia Bar; Virginia State Bar; American Bar Association (Member, Section of Real Property, Probate and Trust Law). ***PRACTICE AREAS:*** Housing and Urban Development; Fair Housing; Real Estate; Probate. ***Email:*** ssalmon@coanlyons.com

(This Listing Continued)

OF COUNSEL

JAMES A. LYONS, JR., born Philadelphia, Pennsylvania, June 15, 1930; admitted to bar, 1957, Pennsylvania; 1970, District of Columbia and U.S. Claims Court. *Education:* St. Joseph's University (B.S., 1953); Villanova University (J.D., 1956). Author: Section on Urban Renewal and Related Programs, *West's Federal Practice Manual,* 1970—. Contributor, Seniors' Housing News, 1989—. Attorney Adviser, Housing and Home Finance Agency, 1956-1960; Urban Renewal Coordinator, Federal Housing Administration, 1960-1965. Director: Specialized Housing Department, National Association of Home Builders, 1965-1968; National Housing Conference. Consultant, President's Committee on Urban Housing, 1967-1968. Chairman, Legislative Committee, National Council on Seniors Housing, National Association of Home Builders, 1989-1998. Member, American Bar Association Forum on Affordable Housing and Community Development Law. ***PRACTICE AREAS:*** Real Estate; Housing and Urban Affairs; Fair Housing.

COATES, DAVENPORT & GURNE, PLLC

900 NINETEENTH STREET, N.W.
WASHINGTON, D.C. 20006
Telephone: 202-778-0020
Fax: 202-778-0029
URL: http://www.lawyers.com/coates

Corporate Law, Business Law, Commercial Law, Small Business Law, Employment Law, Trade Association Law, Education Law, Merger and Acquisitions, Real Estate, Leasing, Commercial Transactions, Electronic Commerce.

FIRM PROFILE: Coates, Davenport & Gurne is a small business boutique law firm. The firm also has a major focus on trade and education association law as well as real estate and commercial transactions. Our attorneys represent clients throughout Washington, D.C., Virginia and Maryland. Among its clients are medium and small businesses, educators, high-tech companies, national associations, colleges, consultants, engineers, local entrepreneurs, physician groups, realtors, internet and e-commerce companies. The firm has received the highest possible rating from Martindale-Hubbell.

DAVID M. DAVENPORT, born Corvallis, Oregon, May 22, 1944; admitted to bar, 1968, Virginia; 1969, District of Columbia; 1970, U.S. Court of Military Appeals; 1976, U.S. Supreme Court; 1978, U.S. Tax Court; 1991, U.S. District Court, District of Maryland. *Education:* Mount St. Mary's College (B.S., 1965); George Washington University (J.D., 1968). Phi Delta Phi. Recipient, ABA— LSD Silver Key Award. Director, Atlas World Group, Inc., 1988—; President's Council, Mount St. Mary's College, 1994—. *Member:* Mclean Bar Association (President, 1990-1991); The District of Columbia Bar; Virginia State Bar. (Also Of Counsel to Coates & Davenport, Richmond, Virginia). ***PRACTICE AREAS:*** Corporate Law; Mergers and Acquisitions; Business Law; Commercial Law; Civil Litigation; Association Law; Education Law. ***Email:*** ddavenport@cdgattorneys.com

PATRICIA D. GURNE, born Philadelphia, Pennsylvania, May 25, 1941; admitted to bar, 1969, Colorado; 1971, District of Columbia; 1980, U.S. Supreme Court. *Education:* MacMurray College (A.B., 1965); George Washington University (J.D., 1969). Recipient, Women Lawyer of the Year award, 1999; Who's Who of American Woman, current edition. Member: Judicial Conference of the District of Columbia, 1979-1996, 1998; Trustee, George Washington University, 1981—. *Member:* The District of Columbia Bar (Member: Board of Governors, Secretary, 1978-1979; American Bar Association; Women's Bar Association Foundation (President, 1984-1986). ***PRACTICE AREAS:*** Association Law; Employment Law; Education Law; Corporate Law; Civil Litigation; Real Estate Law. ***Email:*** PGurne@CDGattorneys.com

JENNIFER M. PORTER, born Brisbane, Australia, 1948; admitted to bar, 1984, District of Columbia. *Education:* University of Queensland, Brisbane, Australia (B.A., 1973); George Washington University (J.D., 1983). *Member:* The District of Columbia Bar (Member, Ethics Committee, 1996-1998; District of Columbia Women's Bar Association (President, 1989-1990; Board Member, 1990-1997; President, 1994-1999, Bar Association Foundation). ***PRACTICE AREAS:*** Corporate Law; Environmental Law; Occupational Safety and Health Law; Administrative Law; Association Law. ***Email:*** jporter@cdgattorneys.com

COUNSEL

SUSAN M. GSCHWENDTNER, admitted to bar, 1983, District of Columbia and Illinois. *Education:* Illinois State University (B.A., with highest honors, 1980); Harvard University (J.D., 1983); Georgetown University (Certificate of Business Administration, 1993). Law Clerk to the Hon. Thomas Penfield Jackson, U.S. District Court for the District of Columbia, 1983-1984. Senior Vice President and General Counsel, JBG Companies, 1987-1999. President, Sugi Corporation, 1999—. *Member:* The District of Columbia Bar; International Association of Attorneys and Executives in Corporate Real Estate (Chairman of the Board, 1997-1998). ***PRACTICE AREAS:*** Real Estate Law; Corporate Law; Business Law.

STEPHEN R. YUREK, born Hastings, Minnesota, March 5, 1962; admitted to bar, 1987, Minnesota; 1996, Virginia (Not admitted in District of Columbia). *Education:* St. John's University (B.S., 1984); William Mitchell College of Law (J.D., 1987). Member, Education Law Association, 1995— American Corporate Council Association, 1998—. Associate Consultant, Dahlen, Berg & Co., a management consulting firm specializing in providing economic, engineering, financial, management, operating, and regulatory services to clients in the areas of energy procurement, environmental regulation, and electric and natural gas utility regulation. *Member:* Federal Energy Bar Association; American Society of Association Executives. ***PRACTICE AREAS:*** Education Law; Association Law; Corporate Law; Administrative Law; Energy Law.

SPECIAL COUNSEL

KATHLEEN G. GALLAGHER, born Fort Lauderdale, Florida, January 19, 1948; admitted to bar, 1973, District of Columbia; 1978, Virginia; 1985, Florida. *Education:* Manhattanville College (B.A., 1970); Suffolk University (J.D., 1973); Georgetown University (LL.M., 1982). Trial Attorney, U.S. Securities and Exchange Commission, 1975-1978. Author: "Legal and Professional Responsibility of Corporate Counsel to Employees During an Internal Investigation for Corporate Misconduct," The Corporation Law Review, Vol. 6, No. 1, Winter, 1983; Securities Regulation Law Journal, 1984-1996. Adjunct Professor, Georgetown University Law Center, Small Business Finance, 1988—. *Member:* McLean Bar Association (President, 1993-1994); American Bar Association (Member, Corporation, Banking and Business Law); Virginia State Bar; District of Columbia Bar; Florida State Bar. (Also, Member of Talbott & Gallagher, McLean, VA). ***PRACTICE AREAS:*** Business Organizations; Real Estate Finance and Acquisitions; Corporate Finance and Securities; General Corporate; Partnership Law. ***Email:*** kgg@talbottgallagher.com

SHEILA TRICE BEIL, born Pittsburgh, Pennsylvania, August 25, 1949; admitted to bar, 1974, Massachusetts; 1977, Tennessee; 1980, U.S. Court of Appeals, Sixth Circuit; 1985, Kentucky; 2000, U.S. Supreme Court (Not admitted in District of Columbia). *Education:* Wellesley College (B.A., 1971); The Harvard Law School (J.D., 1974). National Association of College and University Attorneys, 1996-2000, Executive Director and CEO; Bell & Trice Enterprises, Inc., Executive Vice President, 2000. Recipient: National Association for Women in Education, 2000 Woman of Distinction Award; 1995 Recipient, Thomas S. Biggs, Jr. Award at the National Conference on Law and Higher Education/Stetson College of Law for dedicated service to the national university community. ***PRACTICE AREAS:*** Education Law; General.

LAW OFFICES OF NICHOLAS H. COBBS

Established in 1989
1776 K STREET, N.W., SUITE 300
WASHINGTON, D.C. 20006-2304
Telephone: 202-452-8222
Facsimile: 202-452-1659
Email: ncobbs@erols.com
URL: http://www.cobbslaw.com

Administrative Law and Commercial Litigation, including Aviation, Admiralty, Insurance and Civil Appeals.

NICHOLAS H. COBBS, born New York, N.Y., June 28, 1946; admitted to bar, 1975, New York; 1982, District of Columbia and U.S. Supreme Court; 1984, Maryland; 1990, Virginia. *Education:* Amherst College (A.B., cum laude, 1968); University of Pennsylvania (J.D., 1974). Lecturer, District of Columbia Bar Legal Education, 1993—. Mediator/Arbitrator, D.C. Superior Court, 1988—. *Member:* The District of Columbia Bar(Litigation Steering Committee); Federal and American Bar Associations; Lawyer-Pilots Bar Association; National Transportation Safety Board Bar Association; Maritime Law Association. ***LANGUAGES:*** French.

GEORGE M. COBURN

Established in 1991
1661 CRESCENT PLACE, N.W., SUITE 208
WASHINGTON, D.C. 20009-4047
Telephone: 202-234-2054
Fax: 202-234-2054
Email: coburn.legalconsltg@erols.com

Government Contract Counseling and Litigation. Commercial Contract Arbitration, Neutral in Government Procurement Alternate Dispute Resolution (ADR).

(This Listing Continued)

GEORGE M. COBURN, Washington—Continued

GEORGE M. COBURN, born New York, N.Y., December 15, 1923; admitted to bar, 1949, Massachusetts; 1964, U.S. Supreme Court; 1973, District of Columbia, U.S. Court of Federal Claims; 1982, U.S. Court of Appeals, Federal Circuit. *Education:* Harvard College (A.B., 1947; LL.B., 1949). Author: "The Contract Disputes Act of 1978," PLI, 1982. Member, Procurement Planning Committee and Chair, Procurement Legal Subcommittee, National Defense Industrial Association. *Member:* The District of Columbia Bar; American Bar Association (Chairman: Section of Public Contract Law, 1978-1979; Committee on Debarment and Suspension, 1980-1984. Fellow of the Section of Public Contract Law).

COBURN & SCHERTLER

1150 18TH STREET N.W., SUITE 850
WASHINGTON, D.C. 20036
Telephone: 202-628-4199
Fax: 202-628-4177
Email: cobscher@aol.com

Criminal and Civil Litigation.

FIRM PROFILE: Coburn & Schertler is a novel law firm practicing criminal and civil litigation. We have the experience and ability to handle all types of litigation matters, including criminal defense, civil litigation and domestic litigation. We are experienced in all types of criminal defense matters, whether federal or state courts, including white collar crimes, appellate practice, congressional hearings, and death penalty cases. Our extensive background consists of litigating a wide variety of civil matters, including commercial litigation, business torts, personal injury, medical malpractice, 1983 actions, qui tam actions, as well as divorce and custody cases. The hallmark principles of our practice are aggressiveness, close client relationships and cost effectiveness. We routinely handle complex litigation and have participated in numerous high-profile civil and criminal matters throughout the country. Our commitment is to provide each client with the highest quality work product and serving the community through pro bono activities.

BARRY COBURN, born New York, N.Y., February 9, 1956; admitted to bar, 1981, District of Columbia; 1990, Maryland; 1994, Virginia. *Education:* Yale University (B.A., 1977); Harvard University (J.D., 1981). Associate, Covington & Burling, 1990-1991. Assistant U.S. Attorney, District of Columbia, 1985-1989. Special Assistant, Director of Operations, 1984-1985 and Trial Attorney, 1981-1984, Antitrust Division, United States Department of Justice. ***PRACTICE AREAS:*** Criminal Litigation; Civil Litigation.

DAVID SCHERTLER, born November 29, 1955; admitted to bar, 1982, District of Columbia; 1983, Illinois. *Education:* Amherst College (B.A., 1977); University of Virginia (J.D., 1982). Recipient, "Outstanding Advocate Award," Assistant U.S. Attorney's Association, 1990. Trial Attorney, Antitrust Division, Department of Justice, 1982-1984; Assistant U.S. Attorney, Washington, D.C., 1984-1986; Deputy Chief, Homicide Section, U.S. Attorney's Office, 1990-1992; Chief, Homicide Section, U.S. Attorney's Office, Washington, D.C., 1992-1996. *Member:* The District of Columbia Bar Association; Illinois State and American Bar Associations. ***PRACTICE AREAS:*** Criminal Litigation; Civil Litigation.

RUSSELL D. DUNCAN, born Chelsea, Massachusetts, July 22, 1956; admitted to bar, 1982, District of Columbia. *Education:* Harvard University (A.B., magna cum laude, 1978; J.D., cum laude, 1982). Law Clerk to the Hon. Neil Lynch, Associate Justice, Massachusetts Supreme Court, 1982-1983. Assistant United States Attorney, U.S. Attorney's Office, Washington, D.C., 1985-1994. ***PRACTICE AREAS:*** Litigation; Government Contracts; White Collar Crime; Insurance Fraud. ***Email:*** rduncan@wrf.com

ASSOCIATES

SANDRA L. BRICKEL, born Wilmington, Delaware, February 11, 1967; admitted to bar, 1999, Maryland and New Jersey; 2000, District of Columbia. *Education:* Pennsylvania State University (B.S., 1989); Catholic University of America (J.D., 1998). Law Clerk, The Honorable Stephanie Duncan-Peters, Superior Court of the District of Columbia, 1998-1999. *Member:* Maryland State Bar Association; The District of Columbia Bar. ***PRACTICE AREAS:*** Criminal Law; Civil Litigation.

LISA A. F. FISHBERG, born Mount Kisco, New York, July 7, 1972; admitted to bar, 1998, New York; 1999, District of Columbia. *Education:* State University of New York at Albany (B.A., 1994); George Washington University (J.D., 1997). *Member:* New York State Bar Association. ***PRACTICE AREAS:*** Criminal Litigation; Civil Litigation.

ANNE L. SALTZBERG, born Los Angeles, California, October 9, 1974; admitted to bar, 1999, California; 2001, District of Columbia. *Education:* San Diego State University (B.A., 1996); Southwestern University School of Law (J.D., magna cum laude, 1999). Law Clerk, Hon. Frank E. Schwelb, District of Columbia Court of Appeals, 1999-2000. *Member:* State Bar of California; District of Columbia Bar. ***PRACTICE AREAS:*** Criminal Defense; Civil Litigation. ***Email:*** AnneSaltzberg@aol.com

(This Listing Continued)

MARK E. SCHAMEL, born Buffalo, New York, June 6, 1973; admitted to bar, 1999, District of Columbia. *Education:* State University of New York at Brockport (B.S., 1995); Boston University (J.D., 1998). *Member:* The District of Columbia Bar. ***PRACTICE AREAS:*** Criminal Litigation; Civil Litigation. ***Email:*** markschamel@cs.com

COHEN & COHEN

1000 CONNECTICUT AVENUE, NW
SUITE 505
WASHINGTON, D.C. 20006
Telephone: 202-955-4529
Fax: 202-955-3142
http://www.lawyers.com/cohen&cohenlaw
URL: http://www.cohenandcohen.net

Personal Injury, Medical Malpractice, Automobile Accidents and Injuries, Product Liability and Criminal Defense Law.

MEMBERS OF FIRM

WAYNE R. COHEN, born Washington, D.C., August 2, 1966; admitted to bar, 1991, Florida; 1992, District of Columbia, New York and Maryland. *Education:* University of Michigan (B.B.A., with distinction, 1988); University of Miami (J.D., cum laude, 1991). Executive Editor, University of Miami Entertainment and Sports Law Review, 1991. Author: "The Relationship Between Criminal Liability and Sports: A Jurisprudential Investigation," 7 University of Miami Entertainment and Sports Law Review 31, 1990; "An Economic Analysis of the Issues Surrounding AIDS and the Workplace: In the Long Run, the Path of Truth and Reason Cannot Be Diverted," 41 American University Law Review 1199, 1992. Adjunct Professor, Trial Skills Advocacy, George Washington School of Law , 1993—. *Member:* The Florida Bar; District of Columbia Bar (Member, Steering Committee, Tort Section, 1999—); Maryland State, New York State and American Bar Associations; Association of Trial Lawyers of America (Vice President, Washington, DC, 2002-2003). ***PRACTICE AREAS:*** Personal Injury; Medical Malpractice; Criminal Defense; Product Liability. ***Email:*** wrc@cohenandcohen.net

JILL F. COHEN, born Queens, New York, April 11, 1967; admitted to bar, 1992, New York; 1993, Maryland and District of Columbia. *Education:* University of Michigan (B.A., with high distinction, 1989); University of Miami (J.D, cum laude, 1992). Visiting Student, Georgetown University Law Center, 1991-1992. Assistant District Attorney, Queens County District Attorney's Office, 1992-1994. *Member:* District of Columbia Bar; Maryland State and New York State Bar Associations. ***PRACTICE AREAS:*** Personal Injury; Medical Malpractice; Product Liability. ***Email:*** jfc@cohenandcohen.net

THOMAS J. SIMEONE, born Rochester, New York, May 2, 1964; admitted to bar, 1991, Virginia; 1992, District of Columbia; 1998, Maryland. *Education:* Syracuse University (B.S., cum laude, 1986); Columbia University (J.D., 1991). Certified Public Accountant, Maryland. Author, "Great Expectations: New York's Attempt to Eliminate Gender Preference in Child Custody Disputes," 24 Col. J. Law & Soc. Prob. 457, 1991. Editor, Columbia Journal of Law and Social Problems, 1990-1991. Associate Professional Lecturer of Law, George Washington School of Law, 1995—. *Member:* District of Columbia Bar; Virginia State Bar; Maryland State Bar Association. ***PRACTICE AREAS:*** Personal Injury; Medical Malpractice; Product Liability. ***Email:*** tjs@cohenandcohen.net

ASSOCIATE

CRAIG D MILLER, born Bethesda, Maryland, May 11, 1971; admitted to bar, 1997, Virginia; 1998, Maryland and District of Columbia. *Education:* Indiana University (B.A., with honors, 1994); George Washington University (J.D, 1997). *Member:* District of Columbia Trial Lawyers Association. ***PRACTICE AREAS:*** Personal Injury; Medical Malpractice; Products Liability; Class Actions. ***Email:*** cdm@cohenandcohen.net

ADAM R. LEIGHTON, born Cleveland, Ohio, May 27, 1971; admitted to bar, 1998, Ohio, Maine and District of Columbia. *Education:* Tulane University of Louisiana (B.A., 1993); University of Toledo (J.D., 1997). *Member:* District of Columbia Bar (Member: Injury to Persons and Property Section). ***PRACTICE AREAS:*** Medical Malpractice; Personal Injury. ***Email:*** arl@cohenandcohen.net

JAY L. COHEN, P.C.

WASHINGTON, D.C.

(See Chevy Chase, Maryland)

Government Contract Law, Appellate Law, Business Torts, Small Business, Employment Litigation, Contract Law, Negotiations, Drafting and Litigation.

COHEN, MILSTEIN, HAUSFELD & TOLL, P.L.L.C.

WEST TOWER, SUITE 500
1100 NEW YORK AVENUE, N.W.
WASHINGTON, D.C. 20005-3964
Telephone: 202-408-4600
Facsimile: 202-408-4699
Email: lawinfo@cmht.com
URL: http://www.CMHT.com

Seattle, Washington Office: 999 Third Avenue, Suite 3600, 98104. Telephone: 206-521-0080. Facsimile: 206-521-0166.

New York, New York Office: 825 Third Avenue, 30th Floor, 10022. Telephone: 212-838-7797. Fax: 212-838-7745.

General Civil Trial and Appellate Practice in State and Federal Courts. Antitrust and Unfair Trade Practices, Securities, Civil Rights and Employment Law, Consumer Product Liability, Franchising, Mass Torts, and Toxic Tort Litigation. Complex, Multi-District and Class Action Litigation.

FIRM PROFILE: The firm is one of a handful of firms in the United States litigating plaintiffs' class actions as a regular part of its business, with a specialty in antitrust, securities, civil rights and employment law, environmental toxic tort, consumer and product liability cases. The firm has been involved in many of the major complex class action cases litigated in the United States and has a national reputation in this area. Members of the firm have concluded numerous securities and antitrust class actions in which they have played a principal or lead role or served on the Executive Committee of plaintiffs' counsel.

MEMBERS OF FIRM

JERRY S. COHEN (1925-1995).

HERBERT E. MILSTEIN, born Boston, Massachusetts, 1936; admitted to bar, 1961, Massachusetts and District of Columbia. *Education:* Harvard University (A.B., cum laude, 1958); Columbia University (LL.B., 1961). Adjunct Professor, Georgetown University Law Center, 1980-1987. Attorney, 1965-1967, Special Counsel, 1968, Assistant Chief Enforcement Attorney, 1969 and Chief Enforcement Attorney, 1970, Division of Corporate Regulation, Securities and Exchange Commission. Equity Receiver, SEC v. National American Life Insurance Company, U.S. District Court for the District of Columbia, 1976-1980. ***PRACTICE AREAS:*** Complex and Multi-District Litigation; Securities Fraud Class Actions; Securities Litigation. **Email:** hmilstein@cmht.com

MICHAEL D. HAUSFELD, born Brooklyn, New York, 1946; admitted to bar, 1969, District of Columbia. *Education:* Brooklyn College (A.B., cum laude, 1966); George Washington University (J.D., with honors, 1969). Order of the Coif. Member, Board of Editors, George Washington Law Review, 1968-1969. Adjunct Professor, Georgetown University Law Center, 1980-1987. Member, Advisory Board, Institute of Law and Economics, Georgetown University Law Center, 1980—. ***PRACTICE AREAS:*** Environmental Class Actions; Antitrust; Consumer Rights; Discrimination. **Email:** mhausfeld@cmht.com

STEVEN J. TOLL, born Queens, New York, 1950; admitted to bar, 1975, Virginia; 1976, District of Columbia; 1998, Washington. *Education:* University of Pennsylvania (B.S., in Economics, cum laude, 1972); Georgetown University (J.D., 1975). Beta Gamma Sigma. Special Projects Editor, The Tax Lawyer, 1974-1975. Attorney, Enforcement and Litigation Sections of Federal Home Loan Bank Board, 1975-1978. ***PRACTICE AREAS:*** Products Liability Class Actions; Securities Fraud Class Actions. **Email:** stoll@cmht.com

ANN C. YAHNER, born Minneapolis, Minnesota, 1949; admitted to bar, 1979, District of Columbia. *Education:* Wellesley College (B.A., 1971); Harvard University (J.D., 1979). Phi Beta Kappa. Wellesley Scholar. Author: "Coastal Zone Management Act Amendments of 1976," 1 Harvard Environmental Law Review 259, 1976. Trial Attorney, Antitrust Division, U.S. Department of Justice, 1979-1982. ***PRACTICE AREAS:*** Antitrust Class Actions; Price-Fixing; Federal Litigation. **Email:** ayahner@cmht.com

LISA M. MEZZETTI, born Astoria, New York, 1956; admitted to bar, 1982, New York and District of Columbia. *Education:* Stonehill College (B.A., magna cum laude, 1977); Catholic University (J.D., 1980); Georgetown University Law Center (LL.M., Securities Regulation, 1986). Phi Alpha Delta.

(This Listing Continued)

Chancellor, Moot Court Board, 1979-1980. ***PRACTICE AREAS:*** Complex Commercial Litigation; Complex and Multi-District Litigation; Securities Arbitration; Securities Class Actions. **Email:** lmezzetti@cmht.com

ANDREW N. FRIEDMAN, born White Plains, New York, 1958; admitted to bar, 1983, District of Columbia; 1986, New York. *Education:* Tufts University (B.A., magna cum laude, 1980); George Washington University (J.D., 1983). Phi Beta Kappa. Attorney, U.S. Patent and Trademark Office, 1983-1985. *Member:* The District of Columbia Bar; New York State Bar Association. ***PRACTICE AREAS:*** Securities Litigation; Securities Fraud Class Actions; Civil Litigation. **Email:** afriedman@cmht.com

RICHARD S. LEWIS, born Buffalo, New York, March 17, 1954; admitted to bar, 1986, Pennsylvania; 1988, District of Columbia. *Education:* Tufts University (B.A., cum laude, 1976); University of Michigan (M.P.H., 1981); University of Pennsylvania (J.D., cum laude, 1986). Comments Editor, University of Pennsylvania Law Review, 1985-1986. Author: Comment, "O.C.A.W. v. American Cyanamid: The Shrinking of The Occupational Safety & Health Act," U. Pa. L. Rev., July 1985. Law Clerk to the Honorable Stanley S. Brotman, U.S. District Court, District of New Jersey. *Member:* The District of Columbia Bar; Pennsylvania Bar Association. ***PRACTICE AREAS:*** Environmental Class Actions; Antitrust; Consumer Rights. **Email:** rlewis@cmht.com

DANIEL S. SOMMERS, born New York, N.Y., December 13, 1960; admitted to bar, 1986, New Jersey; 1987, New York; 1988, District of Columbia. *Education:* Union College (B.A., magna cum laude, 1983); George Washington University, National Law Center (J.D., 1986). Pi Sigma Alpha. Member: Moot Court Board, 1984-1986; National Moot Court Team, 1985-1986. *Member:* The District of Columbia Bar; American Bar Association. ***PRACTICE AREAS:*** Securities Litigation; Class Actions. **Email:** dsommers@cmht.com

DANIEL A. SMALL, born Hartford, Connecticut, June 7, 1959; admitted to bar, 1987, Maryland; 1999, District of Columbia. *Education:* Colgate University (B.A., cum laude, 1981); Washington College of Law (J.D., 1986). Law Clerk for Roger Vinson, U.S. District Judge, Northern District of Florida, 1986-1988. *Member:* Maryland State and American Bar Associations. ***PRACTICE AREAS:*** Antitrust; Class Actions; Complex and Multi-District Litigation. **Email:** dsmall@cmht.com

GARY E. MASON, born Mineola, New York, April 17, 1962; admitted to bar, 1988, New York; 1989, District of Columbia. *Education:* Brown University (A.B., magna cum laude, with honors, 1984); Duke University (J.D., 1987). Phi Beta Kappa. Law Clerk to the Honorable Andrew J. Kleinfeld, U.S. District Judge for the District of Alaska, 1987-1988. Author: Note, "Lawrence v. Lawrence: The Use of Rule 60(6) Motions Based Upon Post Judgement Changes in Controlling Law," 1987 Alaska Law Review 153. *Member:* The District of Columbia Bar; American Bar Association. ***PRACTICE AREAS:*** Antitrust Class Actions; Consumer Class Actions; Environmental Class Actions. **Email:** gmason@cmht.com

JOSEPH M. SELLERS, born Philadelphia, Pennsylvania, November 14, 1953; admitted to bar, 1980, District of Columbia; U.S. Supreme Court; U.S. District Court, District of Columbia Circuit; U.S. Court of Appeals, Fourth and Eleventh Circuits. *Education:* Brown University (A.B., 1975); Case Western Reserve University (J.D., 1979). Research Editor, Case Western Reserve University Law Review, 1978-1979. Author: "The Impact of Intent on Equal Protection Jurisprudence," 84 Dickinson Law Review 363, 1980. Adjunct Professor: Employment Discrimination, Washington College of Law, 1993—; Professional Responsibility, Georgetown University Law Center, 1997—. *Member:* American Bar Association; Washington Council of Lawyers Board. ***PRACTICE AREAS:*** Civil Rights; Employment Law. **Email:** jsellers@cmht.com

SHARON A. SNYDER, born Buffalo, New York; admitted to bar, 1988, Florida; 1990, District of Columbia. *Education:* University of Wisconsin at Madison (B.A., 1971); University of Florida (M.A., 1974; J.D., 1988). Order of the Coif. Executive Research Editor, International Law Journal, 1986-1988. Law Clerk to Judge Susan H. Black, U.S. District Court, Middle District of Florida, 1988-1991. Instructor, Legal Research and Writing, University of Florida, 1986-1988. *Member:* The Florida Bar; District of Columbia Bar; American Bar Association. ***PRACTICE AREAS:*** Antitrust; Antitrust Class Actions; Securities Fraud Class Actions. **Email:** ssnyder@cmht.com

MARK S. WILLIS, born Mesa, Arizona, December 31, 1960; admitted to bar, 1990, Massachusetts; 1999, District of Columbia. *Education:* Brigham Young University (B.A., 1986); Pepperdine University (J.D., 1989); Georgetown University (LL.M., International Law, 1993). Regional Semi-Finalist, National Moot Court Competition, 1988. Author: "Admission of Securities to Official Listing on Stock Exchanges Within the European Union and the Subsequent Disclosure Obligations," *Securities Law Techniques,* Chapter 60, Matthew Bender, 1998; "Company Laws of the European Union," *Business Organizations with Tax Planning,* Chapter 196, Matthew Bender, 1998; "A Brief Overview of the European Union's Efforts to Harmonize the Requirements for Listing Securities," *International Law News,* Fall, 1997. Co-Author: Comment, "Corporation Code Sections 309 and 1203: California Redefines Directors'

(This Listing Continued)

COHEN, MILSTEIN, HAUSFELD & TOLL, P.L.L.C., Washington—Continued

Duties Towards Shareholders," Pepperdine Law Review, Vol. 16, No. 4, August 1989. ***PRACTICE AREAS:*** Securities Litigation; Securities Fraud Class Actions; Civil Litigation. ***Email:*** mwillis@cmht.com

STEPHEN DARLEY ANNAND, born Lynchburg, Virginia, February 20, 1948; admitted to bar, 1972, Virginia; 1973, U.S. District Court, Eastern District of Virginia; 1975, West Virginia and U.S. Court of Appeals, Fourth Circuit; 1976, U.S. Supreme Court; 1984, West Virginia and U.S. District Court, Southern District of West Virginia (Not admitted in District of Columbia). *Education:* West Virginia University (B.S., Business Administration, 1969); Washington & Lee University (J.D., cum laude, 1972); George Washington University Law Center (LL.M. Environmental Law, 1975). Omicron Delta Kappa; Phi Delta Phi. Contributor, 1970-1971 and Notes and Comments Editor, 1971-1972, Washington & Lee University Law Review. Member, National Moot Court Team, 1970. Author: "Legislative and Judicial Controls of Contingency Fees in Tort Cases," 99 W.Va. Law Rev. 81 (Fall 1996). Lecturer, Brief Writing and Appellate Advocacy, Washington and Lee University School of Law, 1995-1997. *Member:* Alexandria, Fairfax (Virginia), Kanawha County, West Virginia, Virginia and American Bar Associations; Virginia State Bar; West Virginia State Bar; Defense Research Institute; Defense Trial Counsel of West Virginia; The Association of Trial Lawyers of America. ***REPORTED CASES:*** State v. Chase Securities, Inc., 424 S.E. 2d 591 (W.Va. 1992); Belcher v. Charleston Area Medical Center, 422 S.E. 2d 827 (W.Va. 1992); Buckhannon-Upshur County Airport Authority v. R & R Coal Contracting, Inc., 413 S.E. 2d 404 (W.Va. 1991); Wetzel County Solid Waste Authority v. West Virginia Div. of Natural Resources, 401 S.E. 2d 227 (W.Va. 1990); Gilman v. Choi, 406 S.E. 2d 200 (W.Va. 1990); Evans v. Gogo, 407 S.E. 2d 361 (W.Va. 1990); Roberts v. Stevens Clinic Hosp., Inc., 345 S.E. 2d 791 (W.Va. 1986); Farish for Farish v. Courion Industries, Inc., 754 F.2d 1111 (4th Cir. 1985); Bly v. Otis Elevator Co., 713 F.2d 1040, (4th Cir. 1983); Goldstein v. Potomac Elec. Power Co., 607 F.2d 1080, (4th Cir. 1979); Ancarrow v. City of Richmond, 600 F.2d 443, (4th Cir. 1979); Goldstein v. Potomac Elec. Power Co., 578 F.2d 975 (4th Cir. 1978); Matter of Johnson, 552 F.2d 1072 (4th Cir. 1977); Virginians for Dulles v. Volpe, 541 F.2d 442 (4th Cir. 1976); Fleming v. Yamaha Corp., USA, 774 F.Supp. 992 (W.D.Va. 1991). ***PRACTICE AREAS:*** Civil Litigation; Health Care Litigation. ***Email:*** sannand@cmht.com

MARC I. MACHIZ, born Brooklyn, N. Y., November 13, 1952; admitted to bar, 1978, California; 1979, U.S. District Court, Western District of California; 1982, District of Columbia; 1983, U.S. Court of Appeals, District of Columbia Circuit; 1985, U.S. District Court for the District of Columbia. *Education:* University of Pennsylvania (B.A., 1975); Boalt Hall School of Law, University of California (J.D., magna cum laude, 1978). Member, Moot Court Board. Recipient, American Jurisprudence Award for Civil Procedure. Associate Editor, Industrial Relations Law Journal, 1977-1978. General Litigation Counsel, 1986-1988 and Associate Solicitor, 1988-2000, Plan Benefits Security Division, Office of the Solicitor of Labor. *Member:* The District of Columbia Bar; State Bar of California; American Bar Association (Member, Employee Benefits Committee, Sections on Labor and Litigation, 1988—). ***PRACTICE AREAS:*** Employee Benefits; ERISA. ***Email:*** mmachiz@cmht.com

PAUL T. GALLAGHER, born Arlington, Virginia, October 12, 1961; admitted to bar, 1992, Virginia; 1993, District of Columbia. *Education:* George Mason University (B.A., 1986); Marshall-Wythe School of Law, College of William and Mary (J.D., 1992). Member, William & Mary Law Review, 1990-1992. *Member:* Bar Association of the District of Columbia; Virginia State Bar; American Bar Association (Member, Litigation Section). ***PRACTICE AREAS:*** Antitrust Class Actions; Securities Class Actions. ***Email:*** pgallagher@cmht.com

MURRAY T. S. LEWIS, born Johannesburg, South Africa, October 14, 1958; admitted to bar, 1982, Missouri; 1983, Washington; 1987, California and U.S. District Court, Southern District of California; U.S. District Court, Eastern and Western Districts of Washington; U.S. District Court, Northern, Eastern and Central Districts of California; U.S. Court of Appeals, Ninth Circuit; U.S. District Court, Western District of Missouri. *Education:* University of Natal, Durban, South Africa (B.A., 1978); Creighton University (J.D., 1982). National Moot Court Competition Team; Phillip C. Jessup International Moot Court Competition Team; Creighton University Law Review, 1981-1982. Author: Note, "Constitutional Law, First Amendment Right of Access to Government Information: A Presumption of Open Trials," 14 CRT L. Rev. 853, 1981. Co-Author, Article, "Erosion of the Economic Loss Doctrine in Construction Litigation: Two Points of View (When Courts Should Stop the Buck at Economic Loss)," Construction Business Review, May/June 1991. *Member:* San Diego County, Washington State and American Bar Associations; The Missouri Bar; State Bar of California. (Resident, Seattle, Washington). ***LANGUAGES:*** French and Afrikaans. ***PRACTICE AREAS:*** Civil Litigation; Professional Liability; Product Liability; Commercial Litigation. ***Email:*** mlewis@cmht.com

LINDA P. NUSSBAUM, born Brooklyn, New York, April 11, 1953; admitted to bar, 1978, New York and U.S. District Court, Southern and Eastern Districts of New York (Not admitted in District of Columbia). *Education:* Brooklyn College of the City University of New York (B.A., magna cum laude, 1974); National Law Center, George Washington University (J.D., with honors, 1977); New York University School of Law (LL.M., Taxation, 1984). Phi Beta Kappa. *Member:* New York County Lawyers Association; New York State and American Bar Associations. (Resident, New York, New York). ***PRACTICE AREAS:*** Antitrust Litigation; Complex Civil Litigation. ***Email:*** lnussbaum@cmht.com

ASSOCIATES

CHRISTINE E. WEBBER, born Brockton, Massachusetts, January 23, 1967; admitted to bar, 1991, Illinois; 1993, District of Columbia. *Education:* Harvard University (A.B., magna cum laude, 1988); University of Michigan (J.D., magna cum laude, 1991). Order of the Coif. Law Clerk, Hon. Hubert L. Will, U.S. District Court, Northern District of Illinois, 1991-1993. *Member:* American Bar Association. ***PRACTICE AREAS:*** Employment Discrimination. ***Email:*** cwebber@cmht.com

ALEXANDER E. BARNETT, born New York, N.Y., August 5, 1967; admitted to bar, 1993, New York; 1994, District of Columbia. *Education:* University of Pennsylvania (B.A., 1989); St. John's University (J.D., 1992). *Member:* District of Columbia Bar; Bar Association of the District of Columbia; American Bar Association. (Resident, New York, New York). ***PRACTICE AREAS:*** Litigation; Antitrust. ***Email:*** abarnett@cmht.com

MATTHEW JAMES IDE, born Lake George, New York, February 24, 1962; admitted to bar, 1993, Virginia; 1996, Washington. *Education:* University of Washington (B.A., 1990); College of William and Mary, Marshall-Wythe School of Law (J.D., 1993). Member, College of William and Mary, Administrative Law Review, 1992-1993. Co-Author: "The Decriminalization of Administrative Law Penalties," 45 Admin. L. Rev. 367, 1993. *Member:* Virginia State Bar; Washington State Bar Association. [2d Ranger Bn., U.S. Army, 1980-1987]. (Resident, Seattle, Washington Office). ***PRACTICE AREAS:*** Securities Fraud; Antitrust. ***Email:*** mide@cmht.com

SUZETTE M. MALVEAUX, born Lansing, Michigan, December 4, 1966; admitted to bar, 1996, Maryland; 1998, U.S. Court of Appeals, Third Circuit; 1999, District of Columbia. *Education:* Harvard University (A.B., magna cum laude, 1988); New York University School of Law (J.D., 1994). Recipient, Judge Rose L. & Herbert Rubin Law Review Prize. Earl Warren Scholar, NAACP Legal Defense and Educational Fund. Root-Tilden-Snow Scholar. Vanderbilt Medal. Fellow: Center for International Studies; American Association of University Women. Associate Editor, New York University School of Law Law Review, 1993-1994. *Member:* Maryland State Bar Association, Inc. ***PRACTICE AREAS:*** Civil Rights. ***Email:*** smalveaux@cmht.com

KEELYN M. FRIESEN, born Carson City, Michigan, March 6, 1969; admitted to bar, 1994, Minnesota; U.S. District Court, District of Minnesota; U.S. District Court, Eastern and Western Districts of Wisconsin; U.S. District Court, Eastern District of Michigan; U.S. Court of Appeals, Seventh and Eighth Circuits (Not admitted in District of Columbia). *Education:* Michigan State University (B.A., with honors, 1991); Notre Dame School of Law, London, England (1992); Hamline University School of Law (J.D., 1994). Recipient: State of Michigan Competitive Scholarship; Michigan State University Award of Excellence. Author: "Non Passage of the Women's Health Equity Act: Inaction which may lead to Cancerous Results," Journal of Public Law and Policy, Fall, 1993; "Suit Claims to Uncover a Hidden Holocaust," Star Tribune, July 23, 2000. Presenter, Banja Luka, Serb Republic of Bosnia-Hercegovina, Second International Conference on "Jasenovac, System of Croatian Ustasha Camps of Genocide 1941-1945," May 2000. *Member:* Hennepin County and Minnesota State Bar Associations. (Resident, Seattle, Washington). ***PRACTICE AREAS:*** International Human Rights; Consumer Fraud Litigation; Class Actions; Complex Litigation.

MARY N. STRIMEL, born Lansing, Michigan, December 1, 1971; admitted to bar, 1994, Virginia; 1997, District of Columbia and Maryland. *Education:* Washington University (A.B., 1991); Harvard Law School (J.D., cum laude, 1994). Phi Beta Kappa. *Member:* American Bar Association; Virginia Trial Lawyers Association; Metropolitan Washington Employment Lawyers Association. ***PRACTICE AREAS:*** Antitrust; Environmental Law. ***Email:*** mstrimel@cmht.com

DOUGLAS J. McNAMARA, born Commack, New York, November 11, 1970; admitted to bar, 1996, New York (Not admitted in District of Columbia). *Education:* State University of New York at Albany (B.A., 1992); New York University School of Law (J.D., 1995). Author: Buckley, Imbler and Stare Decists: The Present Predicament of Procesutorial Immunity and An End to Its Absolute Means, 59 Alb. L. Rev. 1135 (1996); Sexual Discrimination and Sexual Midconduct: Applying New York's Gender-Specific Sexual Misconduct Law to Minors, 14 Touro L. Rev. N.2 (Winter 1998). ***PRACTICE AREAS:*** Mass Tort; Consumer Protection. ***Email:*** dmcnamara@cmht.com

AGNIESZKA M. FRYSZMAN, born Warsaw, Poland; admitted to bar, 1997, New Jersey; 1998, District of Columbia. *Education:* Brown University

(This Listing Continued)

(B.A., 1987); Georgetown University Law Center (J.D., 1996). Order of the Coif. ***LANGUAGES:*** Polish and French. ***PRACTICE AREAS:*** Antitrust. ***Email:*** afryszman@cmht.com

DEBORAH J. VAGINS, born Columbus, Ohio, June 14, 1969; admitted to bar, 1996, Maryland; 1997, District of Columbia and U.S. District Court, District of Maryland; 1998, U.S. Court of Federal Claims; 1999, U.S. Court of Appeals for the Federal Circuit. *Education:* Swarthmore College (B.A., with distinction, 1991); American University, Washington College of Law (J.D., magna cum laude, 1996). Author: "Occupational Segregation and the Male-Worker-Norm: Challenging Objective Work Requirements Under Title VII," published in Women's Rights Law Reporter, Rutgers University, 1996. *Member:* The District of Columbia Bar. ***PRACTICE AREAS:*** Civil Rights; Employment Discrimination Litigation. ***Email:*** dvagins@cmht.com

CHARLES E. TOMPKINS, born Fort Riley, Kansas, August 1, 1970; admitted to bar, 1998, New York and District of Columbia. *Education:* Colgate University (B.A., magna cum laude, 1992); University of Virginia (J.D., 1997). *Member:* The District of Columbia Bar. ***PRACTICE AREAS:*** Civil Litigation; Antitrust. ***Email:*** ctompkins@cmht.com

DONNA SOLEN, born Coral Gables, Florida, July 1, 1970; admitted to bar, 1997, Florida; 1999, District of Columbia. *Education:* Florida State University (B.S., magna cum laude, 1994); University of Florida (J.D., 1997). Phi Eta Sigma. Editor-in-Chief, Florida Journal of International Law, 1997. Appellate Advocacy Teaching Fellow, 1996-1997. Florida Journal of International Law Best Note, Fall 1996, Best Comment, Fall 1995. Author: ISO 14000: Emerging International Environmental Law, Florida Journal of International Law; Forum Non Conveniens and the International Plaintiff, Florida Journal of International Law. *Member:* The Florida Bar; American Bar Association; The District of Columbia Bar. ***PRACTICE AREAS:*** Health Care; Consumer Fraud; Products Liability; Antitrust; Environmental. ***Email:*** dsolen@cmht.com

TAMARA J. DRISCOLL, born Hamilton, Montana, June 14, 1972; admitted to bar, 1997, Montana. *Education:* University of Notre Dame (B.A., Philosophy and Theology, with honors, 1994); University of Montana (J.D., 1997). President, UM Women's Law Caucus. Member, Montana Law Review. Judicial Clerk to the Honorable Terry N. Trieweiler and Honorable Jim Regnier, Montana Supreme Court. *Member:* State Bar of Montana; Washington State and American Bar Associations. (Resident, Seattle, Washington Office). ***PRACTICE AREAS:*** Securities Fraud; Consumer Protection. ***Email:*** tdriscoll@cmht.com

ELIZABETH HAINES CRONISE, born Allentown, Pennsylvania, April 25, 1971; admitted to bar, 1997, Virginia and District of Columbia. *Education:* Carnegie Mellon University (B.A., with honors, 1992); George Washington University (J.D., with honors, 1997). Recipient, West Publishing Award for Clinical Achievement in Family Law, 1997. President, George Washington University Law School Moot Court Board, 1996-1997. Dean's Fellow in Legal Research and Writing, 1996-1997. *Member:* The District of Columbia Bar; Virginia State Bar; American Bar Association; Virginia Trial Lawyers Association; American Trial Lawyers Association; Virginia Women Attorneys Association. ***LANGUAGES:*** French. ***Email:*** ecronise@cmht.comom

JULIE GOLDSMITH, born Seattle, Washington, July 18, 1970; admitted to bar, 1997, Washington and U.S. District Court, Western District of Washington. *Education:* Vassar College (B.A., International Studies, 1992); University of Virginia (J.D., 1997). (Resident, Seattle, Washington Office). ***PRACTICE AREAS:*** Securities. ***Email:*** jgoldsmith@cmht.com

LESLI C. ESPOSITO, born Miami, Florida; admitted to bar, 1998, Maryland (Not admitted in District of Columbia). *Education:* Boston College (B.A., 1995); Case Western Reserve University (J.D., 1998). Recipient, Frederick K. Cox International Law Award. Editor-In-Chief, Journal of International Law, 1998. Author: "Regulating the Internet: The New Battle Against Child Pornography," Case Western Reserve Journal of International Law, Vol. 30, Issue 2 (1999). *Member:* Maryland State and American Bar Associations; Women's Bar Association of D.C.; Washington Foreign Law Society. ***PRACTICE AREAS:*** Antitrust. ***Email:*** lesposito@cmht.com

JESSICA GLICK LYN, born Buffalo, New York, September 6, 1968; admitted to bar, 1998, Maryland; 2001, District of Columbia. *Education:* Simon's Rock College of Bard (B.A., cum laude, 1988); New York University (M.A., 1990); Cornell University (M.P.A., 1992); American University (J.D., 1998). Federal Circuit Editor, American University Law Review. ***LANGUAGES:*** Spanish. ***PRACTICE AREAS:*** Civil Rights; Employment Discrimination; Antitrust. ***Email:*** jglick@cmht.com

VICTORIA S. NUGENT, born New Hampshire, November 9, 1969; admitted to bar, 1999, Maryland (Not admitted in District of Columbia). *Education:* Wesleyan University at Middletown, Connecticut (B.A., 1991); Georgetown University at Washington, D.C. (J.D., 1998). *Member:* Maryland State Bar Association. ***PRACTICE AREAS:*** Consumer Law; Antitrust. ***Email:*** vnugent@cmht.com

BRIAN A. RATNER, born Pittsburgh, Pennsylvania, May 10, 1974; admitted to bar, 2000, Pennsylvania and New Jersey; 2001, District of Columbia. *Education:* Indiana University (B.A., 1996); University of Pittsburgh (J.D., 1999). Managing Editor, Journal of Law and Commerce, University of Pittsburgh School of Law. Board National Honor Society, Indiana University. ***PRACTICE AREAS:*** Litigation; Antitrust. ***Email:*** bratner@cmht.com

MEGAN E. JONES, born Langdon, North Dakota, December 23, 1973; admitted to bar, 1999, North Carolina (Not admitted in District of Columbia). *Education:* North Carolina State University (B.A., 1995); University of North Carolina at Chapel Hill (J.D., 1999). Articles and Notes Editor, North Carolina Banking Institute. Member, Civil Trial Team. Computer Law Association, 2000—. Author: "Navigating the Sea of E-Business" in Global ECommerce Law & Business Report, March, 2000; "Bankers Beware: The Risks of Syndicated Credits" in N.C. Banking Institute. Member, Executive Subcommittee, the Children of the Law Committee, 2000—. *Member:* American Bar Association (Member, Section: Young Lawyers Division). ***PRACTICE AREAS:*** Litigation. ***Email:*** mjones@cmht.com

ROBERT J. WOZNIAK, JR., born Grand Rapids, Michigan, December 19, 1966; admitted to bar, 2000, Michigan (Not admitted in District of Columbia). *Education:* University of Michigan (B.A., 1988); Wayne State University (J.D., 2000). Formerly with U.S. Department of Justice, Antitrust Division, 2000-2001. ***PRACTICE AREAS:*** Antitrust. ***Email:*** rwozniak@cmht.com

JOSHUA S. DEVORE, born Englewood, New Jersey, July 21, 1975; admitted to bar, 2000, Virginia (Not admitted in District of Columbia). *Education:* Rice University (B.A., 1997); Georgetown University Law Center (J.D., 2000). ***PRACTICE AREAS:*** Securities Litigation; Consumer Protection. ***Email:*** jdevore@cmht.com

JUSTINE J. KAISER, born Pittsburgh, Pennsylvania, January 7, 1974; admitted to bar, 2000, Maryland (Not admitted in District of Columbia). *Education:* Lehigh University (B.A., 1991); Washingto College of Law - American University (J.D., 2000). *Membe:* Maryland State and American Bar Associations. ***PRACTICE AREAS:*** Civil Litigation; Antitrust. ***Email:*** jkaiser@cmht.com

R. JOSEPH BARTON, born Wellesley, Massachusetts, 1969; admitted to bar, 2001, California (Not admitted in District of Columbia). *Education:* College of William & Mary (B.A., History, 1991; J.D., 2000). Order of the Coif; Order of the Barristers. Recipient: Lawrence W. I'Anson Award, May 2000; William B. Spong Award, May 2000; Robert R. Kaplan Award for Excellence in Legal Writing, May 2000; Thomas Jefferson Award, April 2000; Gambrell Professionalism Award, May 1999. Staff Member, 1998-1999; Associate Articles Editor, William & Mary Law Review, 1999-2000; Staff Member, William & Mary Bill of Rights Journal, 1997-2000; Member, William & Mary National Trial Team. Law Clerk to Hon. Lenoce C. Nesbitt, U.S. District Court, Southern District of Florida, 2000-2001. Teaching Assistant, Legal Skills Program, College of William & Mary Law School, 1999-2000. Pupil, I'Andon-Hoffman Inn of Court, 1999-2000. Author, Note, Drowning in a Sea of Contract: Application of the Economic Loss Rule to Fraud and Negligent Misrepresentation Claims, 41 Wm. & Mary L. Rev. 1789 (2000); Note, Utilizing Statistics and Bellwether Plaintiff Trials: What do the Constitution and the Federal Rules of Civil Procedure Permit?, 8 Wm & Mary Bill Rts. J. 199 (1999). *Membr:* State Bar of California; American Bar Association; Association of Trial Lawyers of America. ***PRACTICE AREAS:*** Complex Civil Litigation; Class Action Litigation.

JAMES PIZZIRUSSO, born Memphis, Tennessee, July 8, 1975; admitted to bar, 2001, Virginia (Not admitted in District of Columbia). *Education:* University of Tennessee - Knoxville (B.A., summa cum laude, 1998); George Washington University (J.D., with honors, 2001). Torch Bearer. Author: Increased Risk, Fear of Disease and Medical Monitoring! Are Novel Damage Claims Enough to Overcome Causation Difficulties in Toxic Torts? 7 Envtl. Law, 183 (2000); Whitman v. American Trucking Associations, I. Nondelegahon Doctrine and the Clean Air Act: Putting the Brakes on American Trucking, The Environmental Lawyer, (Vol. 7-3, 2001). *Member:* American Bar Association; Association of Trial Lawyers of America; Trial Lawyers for Public Justice. ***REPORTED CASES:*** Dela Rosa v. Sec'y HHS, No. 93-433V, 2001 WL 1056928 CFed. Cl., Aug. 14, 2001). ***PRACTICE AREAS:*** Mass Torts; Consumer; Environmental. ***Email:*** jpizzirusso@cmht.com

OF COUNSEL

MARGARET G. FARRELL, born Evanston, Illinois, September 20, 1939; admitted to bar, 1965, District of Columbia; 1966, U.S. Court of Appeals, District of Columbia Circuit; 1980, U.S. Supreme Court. *Education:* Cornell University (B.A., 1961); Yale University; University of Chicago (J.D., 1964). Adjunct Professor: Yale University, 1986; University of Virginia, 1987. Visiting Professor, George Washington University, 1988; Cardozo Law School, 1988-1995; Widener University, Wilmington, Delaware, 1995-1996. *Member:* The District of Columbia Bar (Member, Health Law Section); American Bar Association, (Member, Health Law Section). ***PRACTICE AREAS:*** Health Law; Products Liability; Insurance; Employment Disability Law. ***Email:*** mfarrell@cmht.com

MARLENE F. GIBBONS, born Whittier, California, October 7, 1951; admitted to bar, 1981, District of Columbia. *Education:* California State Uni-

(This Listing Continued)

(This Listing Continued)

COHEN, MILSTEIN, HAUSFELD & TOLL, P.L.L.C., Washington—Continued

versity at Fullerton (B.A., 1974); University of Richmond (J.D., 1981). Associate Editor, University of Richmond Law Review, 1980-1981. *Member:* The District of Columbia Bar. ***PRACTICE AREAS:*** Civil Litigation; Health Care. ***Email:*** mgibbons@cmht.com

CHERYL HAMER MACKELL, born Exeter, New Hampshire, March 29, 1948; admitted to bar, 1984, California; 1989, District of Columbia; 1999, New Mexico; U.S. District Court, Northern, Southern, Eastern and Central Districts of California; U.S. Court of Appeals, Second, Third, Fourth, Seventh, Ninth, Tenth and Eleventh Circuits; U.S. Supreme Court. *Education:* Columbia University (B.S., 1973); Lincoln University (J.D., 1983). Adjunct Professor: Pace University, Dyson College of Arts and Sciences and The Graduate School of Public Administration, 1996-1998. *Member:* American Bar Association (Member, Sections: Criminal Justice); District of Columbia Bar (Member, Sections: Corporation, Finance, Securities Law, Criminal Law, Individual Rights); State Bar of California (Member, Section: Criminal Justice). ***PRACTICE AREAS:*** Securities; Business Law; Civil Rights; Criminal Law. ***Email:*** cmackell@cmht.com

SUSAN R. SCHWAIGER, born Memphis, Tennessee, July 23, 1949; admitted to bar, 1993, New York (Not admitted in District of Columbia). *Education:* Maryville College (1967-1969); University of Tennessee (B.S., 1971); University of Kentucky (M.A., 1973); Brooklyn Law School (J.D., cum laude, 1992). Member, Brooklyn Law Review. Author: "The Submission of Written Instructions and Statutory Language to New York Criminal Juries," Article in Brooklyn Law Review, Vol. 56 No. 4 Winter 1991. Associate, Shearman & Sterling. *Member:* New York State and American Bar Association. (Resident, New York, New York). ***PRACTICE AREAS:*** Complex Civil Litigation; Securities Litigation; Antitrust Litigation. ***Email:*** sschwaiger@cmht.com

---

COHEN MOHR LLP

SUITE 504, 1055 THOMAS JEFFERSON STREET, N.W.
WASHINGTON, D.C. 20007
Telephone: 202-342-2550
Facsimile: 202-342-6147
URL: http://www.cohenmohr.com

McLean, Virginia Office: 1420 Beverly Road, Suite 330, 22101. Telephone: 703-761-1100. Telecopier: 703-761-0180.

Corporate and Business Practice. Government Contracts, Computer Law, Financing Transactions, Commercial Contracts, Acquisitions, Civil Litigation, Business Law, Employment Law, Construction Law.

FIRM PROFILE: Cohen Mohr specializes in representing information technology companies in commercial, corporate, government contract and civil litigation matters. Cohen Mohr represents computer, internet, telecommunications, software, network, multimedia, training, and service companies in structuring corporate transactions, drafting and negotiating contracts, including mergers and acquisitions, distribution channels, software licensing, and lease transactions, and counseling and litigating employment matters, such as non-competition, confidentiality, compensation and discrimination suits. Cohen Mohr also represents manufacturers, suppliers and construction contractors in government and commercial matters. Cohen Mohr's government contracts practice includes bid protests, construction and contract claims, GSA Schedules, regulatory interpretation and compliance, audit defense, and small business and disadvantaged business matters. Cohen Mohr's litigation practice includes software infringement, breach of contract, unfair business practices, and employment cases in state and federal courts.

DAVID S. COHEN, born Washington, D.C., October 20, 1949; admitted to bar, 1975, District of Columbia. *Education:* University of Pennsylvania (B.A., magna cum laude, 1972; J.D., 1975). Co-Author with Andrew B. Katz: "Looking for a Partner? You May Want Uncle Sam," Washington Business Journal, Vol. 17, No. 11, July 24, 1998. *Member:* The District of Columbia Bar; American Bar Association. ***PRACTICE AREAS:*** Information Technology Contracts; Commercial Arbitration; Commercial Litigation; Information Technology Licensing; Government Contracts; Intellectual Property. ***Email:*** dcohen@cohenmohr.com

DANIEL H. DuVAL, born Washington, D.C., April 7, 1953; admitted to bar, 1979, Georgia; 1991, District of Columbia; 1993, Virginia. *Education:* Harvard University (A.B., magna cum laude, 1976); University of Virginia (J.D., 1979). Previous Employment: King & Spalding, Partner, 1988-1992. *Member:* McLean, Fairfax County and American Bar Associations. (Resident, McLean, VA Office). ***PRACTICE AREAS:*** Business Law; Corporate Law; Commercial Law; Finance. ***Email:*** dduval@cohenmohr.com

RUSSELL J. GASPAR, born Elizabeth, New Jersey, September 18, 1950; admitted to bar, 1975, Virginia; 1976, District of Columbia and U.S. Court of Appeals for the District of Columbia Circuit; 1979, U.S. Court of Appeals, Ninth Circuit; 1981, U.S. Court of Appeals, Tenth Circuit; 1985, U.S. Court of Appeals, Fourth Circuit; 2001, U.S. District Court, District of Maryland. *Education:* Georgetown University (B.S.F.S., magna cum laude, 1972; J.D., 1975). Phi Beta Kappa. Senior Case and Note Editor, Law and Policy in International Business, Georgetown Law Review, 1974-1975. Author: "Par Value Modification Act of 1973," 6 Law and Policy in International Business 267, 1974. *Member:* District of Columbia Bar; Virginia State Bar. ***PRACTICE AREAS:*** Civil Litigation and Appeals; Employment Litigation; Employment Law; Federal Administrative Litigation; Commercial Arbitration. ***Email:*** rgaspar@cohenmohr.com

VICTOR G. KLINGELHOFER, born Takoma Park, Maryland, May 18, 1951; admitted to bar, 1983, Virginia; 1988, District of Columbia; 1990, Maryland. *Education:* Randolph-Macon College (B.A., 1973); Catholic University (J.D., 1983). Member, Catholic University Law Review, 1981-1983. *Member:* Virginia State and The District of Columbia Bars; Virginia Bar Association. [1st Lt., U.S. Army, 1973-1979]. (Resident, McLean, VA, Office). ***LANGUAGES:*** German. ***PRACTICE AREAS:*** Government Contracts; Civil Litigation; Telecommunications Law; Business Law; Contracts; Commercial Law; Construction Law. ***Email:*** vklingelhofer@cohenmohr.com

ANDREW J. MOHR, born New York, N.Y., February 6, 1954; admitted to bar, 1980, District of Columbia. *Education:* Tufts University (B.A., magna cum laude, 1976); George Washington University (J.D., with honors, 1980). Washington Editor, Government Video Magazine. Regular Columnist; Government Marketing Newsletter; and World Markets Research Centre Purchasing Supersite. *Member:* The District of Columbia Bar; Federal Bar Association. ***LANGUAGES:*** Russian. ***PRACTICE AREAS:*** Corporate Law; Business Law; Computers and Software Contracts; Government Contracts; Commercial Law. ***Email:*** amohr@cohenmohr.com

WILLIAM F. SAVARINO, born Buffalo, New York, March 18, 1958; admitted to bar, 1983, Kentucky; 1984, District of Columbia; 1990, Virginia, U.S. Court of Federal Claims, U.S. District Court, Eastern District of Virginia and U.S. District Court, for the District of Columbia. *Education:* University of Maryland (B.S., 1980); University of Louisville (J.D., 1983). Co-Author: "Representing a Technology Start-Up," New York Law Journal, Vol. 2, No. 7, November, 1998; "Foreign Takeovers of High-Tech Companies: Practical Considerations and Strategies for the Defence Contractor," International Company and Commercial Law Review, Vol. 1, Issue 1, 1990; "Defense Strategies to Protect Against Foreign Investment," The National Law Journal, Vol. 12, No. 3, September 1989; "Business Strategies From the Vendors Perspective," The Computer Lawyer, Vol. 5, No. 8, August 1989. Staff Attorney, Contract Law Division, Office of the General Counsel, U.S. Department of Commerce, 1984-1986. Associate, Dickstein, Shapiro & Morin, 1986-1989; Principal, Dickstein, Shapiro & Morin, 1990-1994; Partner, Cohen & White, 1994. *Member:* District of Columbia Bar; Virginia Bar Association. ***PRACTICE AREAS:*** Litigation; Government Contracts; Business Law; Computers and Software. ***Email:*** bsavarino@cohenmohr.com

OF COUNSEL

BRIAN J. CRAIG, born Ontario, Canada, August 16, 1964; admitted to bar, 1994, Maryland; 1995, District of Columbia. *Education:* Catholic University of America (B.A., 1987); Washington College of Law, American University (J.D., 1994). Formerly Counsel, TRW, Inc., 1996-1999; Associate Attorney, McKenna and Cuneo, 1994-1996. [Capt., U.S. Army Reserve, 1987-1991]. ***PRACTICE AREAS:*** Business Law; Corporate Law; Commercial Law; Government Contracts; Computers and Software. ***Email:*** bcraig@cohenmohr.com

LAUREL ANN HOCKEY, born Amarillo, Texas, July 29, 1964; admitted to bar, 1989, Virginia; 1991, District of Columbia; U.S. Court of Federal Claims; U.S. District Court, Eastern District of Virginia. *Education:* College of William & Mary (B.A., in History & Religion, 1986); National Law Center, George Washington University (J.D., with honors, 1989). Phi Alpha Theta. *Member:* The District of Columbia Bar; Virginia State Bar. ***PRACTICE AREAS:*** Small Business Law; Business Law; Corporate Law; Government Contracts. ***Email:*** lhockey@cohenmohr.com

JOHN J. O'BRIEN, born Boston, Massachusetts, July 27, 1959; admitted to bar, 1985, Virginia; 1987, District of Columbia. *Education:* University of Virginia (B.S., 1981); Marshall Wythe School of Law, College of William & Mary (J.D., 1985). Phi Alpha Delta. ***PRACTICE AREAS:*** Government Contracts Law; Litigation; Business Law. ***Email:*** jobrien@cohenmohr.com

ASSOCIATES

C. KELLY KROLL, born Washington, D.C., February 10, 1967; admitted to bar, 2000, Virginia; 2001, District of Columbia, U.S. District Court, Eastern District of Virginia, U.S. Court of Appeals, Fourth Circuit and U.S. Court of Federal Claims. *Education:* University of Rochester (B.A., 1989); George Mason University School of Law (J.D., 2000). *Member:* Virginia State Bar; District of Columbia Bar; American Bar Association. ***PRACTICE AREAS:*** Government Contracts; Commercial Law. ***Email:*** kkroll@cohenmohr.com

(This Listing Continued)

ROWENA E. LAXA, born Des Moines, Iowa, May 27, 1959; admitted to bar, 1998, Virginia; 1999, Maryland and District of Columbia. *Education:* University of Michigan (B.A., 1986); George Mason University School of Law (J.D., with honors, 1998). *Member:* Virginia State Bar; Maryland State and American (Member, Employment and Labor Law Section) Bar Associations; District of Columbia Bar; Asian Pacific American Bar Association; Philippine American Bar Association. ***PRACTICE AREAS:*** Employment Law; Commercial Litigation; Government Contracts. ***Email:*** rlaxa@cohenmohr.com

COHN AND MARKS

Established in 1946

1920 N STREET, N.W., SUITE 300
WASHINGTON, D.C. 20036-1622
Telephone: 202-293-3860
Fax: 202-293-4827
URL: http://www.cohnmarks.com

Communications, Media, Trade Association Practice. Practice Before Federal Courts and Agencies.

MEMBERS OF FIRM

JOEL H. LEVY, born Brooklyn, N.Y., June 25, 1935; admitted to bar, 1960, New York; 1963, District of Columbia. *Education:* Dartmouth College (A.B., 1957); Harvard University (LL.B., 1960). Attorney, Rules and Standards Division, 1960-1963. Office of the General Counsel, Litigation Division, 1963-1965, Federal Communications Commission. National Vice President, American Jewish Congress, 1980-1986 and 1988-1992; Co-Chair Commission on Law and Social Action. *Member:* The District of Columbia Bar; Federal Communications Bar Association. ***SPECIAL AGENCIES:*** Federal Communications Commission. ***PRACTICE AREAS:*** Mass Media Law; Telecommunications Law; Electronic Media Mergers and Acquisitions; Administrative Litigation. ***Email:*** JHL@COHNMARKS.COM

ROBERT B. JACOBI, born Washington, D.C., May 19, 1930; admitted to bar, 1954, Virginia; 1958, District of Columbia. *Education:* Washington & Lee University (LL.B., 1954); American University (A.B., 1958); Georgetown University (LL.M., 1962). With Hearing Division, 1963-1965 and Office of the General Counsel, Litigation Division, 1965, Federal Communications Commission. *Member:* The District of Columbia Bar; Federal Communications Bar Association. ***SPECIAL AGENCIES:*** Federal Communications Commission. ***PRACTICE AREAS:*** Communications Law. ***Email:*** RBJ@COHNMARKS.COM

ROY R. RUSSO, born Utica, New York, July 26, 1936; admitted to bar, 1959, New York; 1967, District of Columbia. *Education:* Columbia University (B.A., 1956); Syracuse University (LL.B., cum laude, 1959). Order of the Coif; Phi Alpha Delta. Member, Editorial Board, Syracuse Law Review, 1958-1959. Staff Attorney, Federal Communications Commission, Office of Opinions and Review and Review Board, 1959-1966. Alumni Medalist, Columbia University, 1994. *Member:* The District of Columbia Bar; Federal Communications Bar Association (Co-Chair, Mass Media Practice Committee, 1988-1991); Computer Law Association; International Institute of Communications. ***SPECIAL AGENCIES:*** Federal Communications Commission. ***PRACTICE AREAS:*** Communications Law. ***Email:*** RRR@COHNMARKS.COM

RONALD A. SIEGEL, born Brooklyn, New York, April 6, 1940; admitted to bar, 1965, New York, District of Columbia. *Education:* University of Michigan (B.A., 1961; J.D., with distinction, 1964). With Broadcast Bureau, 1964 and Office of General Counsel, Litigation Division, 1965-1966, Federal Communications Commission. *Member:* The District of Columbia Bar; Federal Communications Bar Association (Chair, Cable Television Subcommittee, 1989-1994); Cable TV Pioneers. ***SPECIAL AGENCIES:*** Federal Communications Commission; U.S. Copyright Office; State and Local Cable Television Franchising Authorities. ***PRACTICE AREAS:*** Communications Law; Cable Television; Mass Media and New Technologies. ***Email:*** RAS@COHNMARKS.COM

LAWRENCE N. COHN, born Washington, D.C., September 3, 1943; admitted to bar, 1969, District of Columbia. *Education:* Carleton College (A.B., 1965); Cornell University (J.D., 1968). *Member:* The District of Columbia Bar; Federal Communications Bar Association. ***SPECIAL AGENCIES:*** Federal Communications Commission. ***PRACTICE AREAS:*** Communications Law; Employment Law. ***Email:*** LNC@COHNMARKS.COM

RICHARD A. HELMICK, born Cincinnati, Ohio, June 25, 1942; admitted to bar, 1971, Ohio (Inactive); 1972, District of Columbia. *Education:* Xavier University (A.B., magna cum laude, 1964); University of Cincinnati (J.D., 1971). Member, Board of Editors, Cincinnati Law Review 1970-1971. Staff Attorney, International and Satellite Communications Division, Common Carrier Bureau, Federal Communications Commission, 1971-1972. *Member:* The District of Columbia Bar; Federal Communications Bar Association. ***SPECIAL AGENCIES:*** Federal Communications Commission. ***PRACTICE AREAS:*** Communications Law. ***Email:*** RAH@COHNMARKS.COM

(This Listing Continued)

WAYNE COY, JR., born Manila, Philippines, January 21, 1938; admitted to bar, 1969, District of Columbia. *Education:* Amherst College (A.B., 1960); Catholic University (J.D., 1969). Delta Theta Phi. Member, Catholic University Law Review, 1968-1969. *Member:* The District of Columbia Bar; Federal Communications Bar Association. ***SPECIAL AGENCIES:*** Federal Communications Commission; Patent and Trademark Office and Department of Commerce: NTIA and CPB. ***PRACTICE AREAS:*** Communications Law; Intellectual Property Rights; Non-Profit Corporations. ***Email:*** WC@COHNMARKS.COM

J. BRIAN DE BOICE, born Decatur, Illinois, November 8, 1951; admitted to bar, 1979, Illinois; 1981, District of Columbia. *Education:* Kenyon College (A.B., cum laude, 1973); University of Illinois (J.D., magna cum laude, 1979). Order of the Coif. Member, 1977-1978; Managing Editor, 1978-1979, University of Illinois Law Forum. Law Clerk to the Hon. Philip W. Tone and the Hon. William J. Bauer of the U.S. Court of Appeals for the Seventh Circuit, 1979-1980. *Member:* The District of Columbia Bar; Federal Communications Bar Association. ***SPECIAL AGENCIES:*** Federal Communications Commission; State and Local Cable Television Franchising Authorities. ***PRACTICE AREAS:*** Communications Law; Broadcasting Law; Cable Television Litigation. ***Email:*** JBD@COHNMARKS.COM

JEROLD L. JACOBS, born New York, N.Y., June 12, 1943; admitted to bar, 1969, New York; 1972, District of Columbia and U.S. Court of Appeals for the District of Columbia Circuit; 1973, U.S. Supreme Court; 1988, U.S. Court of Appeals, Eleventh Circuit. *Education:* Amherst College (B.A., cum laude, 1965); Harvard University (J.D., 1968). Supervising Attorney, FCC Cable Television Bureau and Broadcast Bureau, 1973-1980. Member: Federal Communications Commission Review Board, 1980-1987; United States Senior Executive Service, 1979-1980. *Member:* The District of Columbia Bar; Federal, Federal Communications and American Bar Associations. ***SPECIAL AGENCIES:*** Federal Communications Commission. ***PRACTICE AREAS:*** Communications Law; Telecommunications Law; Cable Communications Law. ***Email:*** JLJ@COHNMARKS.COM

ASSOCIATES

SUSAN VALERIE SACHS, born Newport News, Virginia, October 8, 1960; admitted to bar, 1987, Virginia; 1988, District of Columbia. *Education:* College of William and Mary (B.A., with honors, 1982; J.D., 1987). Executive Editor, Professional Articles, William and Mary Law Review, 1986-1987. Recipient, American Jurisprudence Award in Virginia Procedure. *Member:* The District of Columbia Bar; Virginia State Bar; Federal Communications Bar Association. ***SPECIAL AGENCIES:*** Federal Communications Commission; U.S. Copyright Office. ***PRACTICE AREAS:*** Communications Law; Cable TV; Mass Media Law. ***Email:*** SVS@COHNMARKS.COM

KEVIN M. GOLDBERG, born Washington, D.C., August 26, 1971; admitted to bar, 1995, Maryland; 1996, District of Columbia. *Education:* James Madison University (B.A., magna cum laude, 1992); George Washington University (J.D., with high honors, 1995). Order of the Coif. Recipient, Imogene Williford Constitutional Law Award. Member, Virginia Coalition for Open Government. *Member:* District of Columbia Bar; Federal Communications Bar Association; Computer Law Association. ***LANGUAGES:*** Spanish. ***PRACTICE AREAS:*** Communications Law; First Amendment Law. ***Email:*** KMG@COHNMARKS.COM

JOSEPH M. DI SCIPIO, born Denver, Colorado, April 4, 1967; admitted to bar, 1996, New York; 1998, District of Columbia. *Education:* University of Denver (B.A., magna cum laude, 1989); Syracuse University (M.P.A., 1995; J.D., magna cum laude, 1995). Order of the Coif. Business Editor, Syracuse Journal of International Law, 1994-1995. Attorney-Advisor, Federal Communications Commission CIB, CCB Policy Division, 1995-1997. *Member:* Federal Communications Bar Association (Trustee, FCBA Foundation, 1999-2000; Co-Chair, Young Lawyers Committee, 1996-1998, Executive Committee Member, 1997-2000; Co-Chair, Syracuse Law Association Council, 2001—). ***SPECIAL AGENCIES:*** Federal Communications Commission. ***PRACTICE AREAS:*** Communications Law; Telecommunications Law; Common Carrier; Mass Media Law. ***Email:*** JMD@COHNMARKS.COM

OF COUNSEL

MARCUS COHN, born Omaha, Nebraska, September 20, 1913; admitted to bar, 1939, Oklahoma; 1947, District of Columbia. *Education:* University of Oklahoma and University of Chicago (B.A., 1935); University of Chicago (J.D., cum laude, 1938); Harvard University (LL.M., 1940). Phi Beta Kappa; Order of the Coif. Professorial Lecturer in Law, Graduate School of Public Law, George Washington University, 1965-1978. Member, National Council on the Humanities, National Endowment for the Humanities, 1980-1986. Member, National Executive Committee, 1963-1976, American Jewish Committee. *Member:* The District of Columbia Bar; American Bar Association (Member, Science and Technology Section; Chairman, Communications Law Committee, 1974-1976); Federal Communications Bar Association (President, 1973-1974).

LEONARD H. MARKS, born Pittsburgh, Pennsylvania, March 5, 1916; admitted to bar, 1938, Pennsylvania; 1945, District of Columbia. *Education:*

(This Listing Continued)

COHN AND MARKS, Washington—Continued

University of Pittsburgh (B.A., 1935); University of Pittsburgh Law School (LL.B., 1938). Assistant to the General Counsel, Federal Communications Commission, 1942-1945. Appointed by President Johnson, Director, United States Information Agency, 1965-1968. Ambassador and Chairman of: International Plenipotentiary Conference on Communications Satellites, Washington, D.C., 1969; The U.S. Delegation to the International Telecommunications Union Conference on High Frequency Broadcasting, 1984, 1987. *Member:* The District of Columbia Bar; American Bar Association (Member, House of Delegates, 1960-1963; Chairman, International Communications Committee, 1963-1965); Federal Communications Bar Association (President, 1959-1960; Chairman, Advisory Committee on International Communications and Information Policy, Department of State, 1988-1994). ***Email:*** LHM@COHNMARKS.COM

RICHARD M. SCHMIDT, JR., born Winfield, Kansas, August 2, 1924; admitted to bar, 1948, Colorado; 1968, District of Columbia. *Education:* University of Denver (A.B., 1945; J.D., 1948). Lecturer, Radio Law, University of Denver, 1948-1963. Deputy District Attorney, 1949-1950. Counsel, Special Investigating Subcommittee, U.S. Senate, 1959-1960. General Counsel, United States Information Agency, 1965-1968. *Member:* The District of Columbia Bar; Denver (President, 1963-1964), Colorado and American (Chairman, Committee on Association Communications, 1969-1973; Member, National Conference of Lawyers and Representatives of the Media, 1982—; Chairman, 1982-1986; Commission on Lawyer Advertising, 1994-1998) Bar Associations; Federal Communications Bar Association. ***SPECIAL AGENCIES:*** Federal Communications Commission. ***PRACTICE AREAS:*** First Amendment Law; Trade Association Law; Legislative Law. ***Email:*** RMS@COHNMARKS.COM

COLE, RAYWID & BRAVERMAN, L.L.P.

Established in 1966

1919 PENNSYLVANIA AVENUE, N.W.

WASHINGTON, D.C. 20006

Telephone: 202-659-9750
Cable Address: "Crab"
Telecopier: 202-452-0067
URL: http://www.crblaw.com

El Segundo, California Office: 2381 Rosecrans Avenue, Suite 110. Telephone: 310-643-7999. Fax: 310-643-7997.

Telecommunications, Cable Television, Telephony, Wireless and Wireline Communications, Satellite Communications, Broadcast, Programming, Copyright, Trademark, Information and Privacy, Corporate and Commercial Law, Antitrust and Constitutional Law, Civil, Administrative and Commercial Practice in all Courts, State and Federal Agencies, State and Federal Legislatures.

FIRM PROFILE: Cole, Raywid & Braverman has a nationwide commercial practice concentrated in telecommunications and related industries. Our team of seasoned telecommunications specialists, many with business backgrounds in the telecommunications industry, bring a wealth of knowledge and practical experience to bear on clients' business problems. The practice includes attorneys specializing in federal regulatory matters, local government relations, state regulatory matters, litigation, intellectual property and antitrust compliance. The firm is a member of the Association for Local Telecommunications Services.

PARTNERS

JOHN P. COLE, JR., born Washington, D.C., January 12, 1930; admitted to bar, 1956, District of Columbia and Maryland; 1961, Georgia; 1964, U.S. Supreme Court. *Education:* Auburn University (B.S., 1953); George Washington University (LL.B., 1956). Author: "Community Antenna Television, The Broadcaster Establishment and the Federal Regulator," The American University Law Review, Volume 14, No. 2, (June, 1965); "The Cable Television 'Press' and the Protection of the First Amendment--A not so 'Vexing Question'," California Western Law Review, Volume 28, No. 2, (May, 1992). Attorney, Federal Communications Commission, 1956-1957. Staff, U.S. House of Representatives, 1962-1963. *Member:* The District of Columbia Bar; American Bar Association; Federal Communications Bar Association. ***PRACTICE AREAS:*** Communications; Cable Television; Cable Franchising; Appellate Litigation; Constitutional Law. ***Email:*** jcole@crblaw.com

ALAN RAYWID (1930-1991).

BURT A. BRAVERMAN, born New York, N.Y., April 20, 1946; admitted to bar, 1969, Virginia; 1970, District of Columbia; 1973, U.S. Supreme Court. *Education:* Miami University (B.A., 1966); George Washington University (J.D., with honors, 1969). Phi Delta Phi. Editor-in-Chief, Journal of International Law and Economic Development, 1968-1969. Author: "The Technology Gap: A Problem in European Unity," III Journal of Law and Economic Development 1968; "Chrysler Corporation v. Brown: Protecting Business Secrets in the '80s," 4 Corporation Law Review 23, 1981. Co-Author: "A Practical Review of State Open Records Laws," 49 George Washington Law Review 720, 1981; "Submitters Beware: The Perils of FOIA Implementing Regulations," 12 A.I.P.L.A. J. 33, 1984; "INFORMATION LAW: Freedom of Information, Privacy, Open Meetings, Other Access Laws," PLI, 1986; "Getting and Protecting Competitive Business Information," Management Concepts, Inc. (Pub., 1997). *Member:* The District of Columbia Bar; Virginia State Bar; American Bar Association; Federal Communications Bar Association. ***PRACTICE AREAS:*** Commercial and Regulatory Litigation; Telecommunications; Antitrust; Unfair Trade; Competition; Programming Law; Cable TV; Transactional Matters; Freedom of Information; Privacy Law. ***Email:*** bbraverman@crblaw.com

(This Listing Continued)

ROBERT L. JAMES, born New York, N.Y., January 5, 1944; admitted to bar, 1969, District of Columbia and Maryland; 1974, U.S. Supreme Court. *Education:* Cornell University (A.B., 1966); George Washington University (J.D., 1969). *Member:* The District of Columbia Bar; American Bar Association; Federal Communications Bar Association. ***PRACTICE AREAS:*** Cable Television; Common Carrier; Cable Programming; Cable Franchising; Satellite Communications; Copyright Law; Administrative Law. ***Email:*** bjames@crblaw.com

JOHN D. SEIVER, born Philadelphia, Pennsylvania, July 30, 1953; admitted to bar, 1979, District of Columbia; 1982, U.S. Claims Court; 1983, U.S. Supreme Court. *Education:* University of Virginia (B.A., with distinction, 1975); Boston University (J.D., 1979). *Member:* The District of Columbia Bar; Federal and American Bar Associations; Federal Communications Bar Association. ***PRACTICE AREAS:*** Communications Law; Telecommunications Competition; Video Competition; Telecommunications Regulation; Satellite Communications; Cable Programming. ***Email:*** john.seiver@crblaw.com

WESLEY R. HEPPLER, born Battle Creek, Michigan, January 13, 1954; admitted to bar, 1979, District of Columbia; 1987, U.S. Supreme Court. *Education:* Michigan State University (B.A., with high honors, 1976); College of William & Mary (J.D., 1979). Phi Kappa Phi; Phi Alpha Delta. Staff Member, William & Mary Law Review, 1977-1979. Author, "Telecommunications Franchising," Cable Television Law 2001 PLI 2001; "The 1992 Cable Act: Rate Regulation, Must Carry and Retransmission Consent," Cable Television Law 1993, Practicing Law Institute, 1993; "A Practical Review of State Open Records Laws," 49 George Washington Law Review 720, 1981. *Member:* The District of Columbia Bar; Federal Communications Bar Association. ***PRACTICE AREAS:*** Cable Television; Communications Common Carrier; Copyright; Cable Programming; Cable Franchise Renewals and Transfers; Rate Regulation. ***Email:*** wheppler@crblaw.com

PAUL GLIST, born Seattle, Washington, September 3, 1953; admitted to bar, 1978, District of Columbia; 1986, U.S. Supreme Court. *Education:* Cornell University (A.B., with distinction, 1975); Stanford University (J.D., 1978). Phi Beta Kappa. Author: "Telecommunications Franchising," Cable Television Law 2001, PLI 2001; "Rate Regulation and Video Competition", Cable Television Law 1999, PLI 1999; "Rate Regulation 1997," Cable Television Law 1997, Implementing The 1996 Telecommunications Act, PLI 1997; "The 1992 Cable Act: Rate Regulation, Must Carry and Retransmission Consent," Cable Television Law 1994, Practicing Law Institute 1994; "Syndicated Exclusivity and Copyright," Cable Television 1989, Practising Law Institute, 1989; "Cable Must Carry—Again," 39 Federal Communications Law Journal 109, 1987; "Cable Copyright: The Role of the Copyright Office," 35 Emory Law Journal 621, 1986; "Standards of Renewal Under the Cable Communications Policy Act of 1984," A Practical Guide to the CCPA, Practising Law Institute, 1985; "Copyright and Signal Piracy," Cable Television Retrospective and Prospective, Practising Law Institute, 1985. *Member:* The District of Columbia Bar; American Bar Association; Federal Communications Bar Association. ***PRACTICE AREAS:*** Cable Communications; Telecommunications Law; Rate Regulation; Compulsory Copyrights; Cable Franchising; Renewals and Transfers; Telecommunications Legislation; Pole Attachments; Telecommunications Competition; Privacy Law. ***Email:*** pglist@crblaw.com

DAVID M. SILVERMAN, born Chicago, Illinois, May 19, 1950; admitted to bar, 1980, District of Columbia. *Education:* New College of the University of South Florida (B.A., 1973); Northwestern University (M.A., 1976; J.D., 1980). *Member:* The District of Columbia Bar (Member, Patent, Trademark and Copyright Section); American Bar Association (Member, Forum Committee on Communications Law, 1980—); Federal Communications Bar Association; International Trademark Association. ***PRACTICE AREAS:*** Intellectual Property Law, including Trademark and Copyright Registration; Licensing and Litigation; Broadcast and Cable Regulatory and Transactional Matters. ***Email:*** dsilverman@crblaw.com

JAMES F. IRELAND, III, born Yokosuka, Japan, September 27, 1954; admitted to bar, 1980, District of Columbia. *Education:* St. Lawrence University (B.A., magna cum laude, 1976); College of William & Mary (J.D., 1980). Phi Beta Kappa. Articles Editor, William & Mary Law Review, 1979-1980. *Member:* The District of Columbia Bar; American Bar Associations; Federal Communications Bar Association. ***PRACTICE AREAS:*** Telecommunications Law and Regulation; Cable Communications; Franchising; Wireless Communications; Internet Law. ***Email:*** jireland@crblaw.com

(This Listing Continued)

MAURITA K. COLEY, born Detroit, Michigan, June 18, 1956; admitted to bar, 1982, Michigan; 1989, District of Columbia. *Education:* Michigan State University (B.A., 1977); Georgetown University (J.D., 1981). Senior Vice-President, Legal Affairs, 1993-1995 and Senior Vice President, Network Operations and Programming, 1995-1999, Black Entertainment Television, Inc. *Member:* The District of Columbia Bar; State Bar of Michigan; Federal Communications Bar Association (Member, Executive Committee, 1994-1995; Foundation Board Member, 1993-1994). ***PRACTICE AREAS:*** Media Law; Internet Law; Cable TV; Entertainment Law. ***Email:*** mcoley@crblaw.com

STEVEN JAY HORVITZ, born Framingham, Massachusetts, May 18, 1959; admitted to bar, 1984, District of Columbia. *Education:* Brown University (B.A., 1981); Stanford University (J.D., 1984). Phi Beta Kappa. Associate Editor, Stanford Law Review, 1983-1984. *Member:* The District of Columbia Bar; Federal Communications Bar Association. ***PRACTICE AREAS:*** Cable Television Law, including Cable Franchising, Copyright and FCC Regulatory Matters; Home Satellite Industry Issues; Copyright and Communications Law Litigation. ***Email:*** shorvitz@crblaw.com

CHRISTOPHER W. SAVAGE, born Chicago, Illinois, April 22, 1956; admitted to bar, 1980, California; 1982, District of Columbia. *Education:* Harvard University (A.B., magna cum laude, 1977; J.D., cum laude, 1980). John Harvard Scholar. *Member:* The District of Columbia Bar. ***PRACTICE AREAS:*** Telecommunications Regulation; Wireless Communications; Internet Law; Telecommunications Competition; New Media Law. ***Email:*** chris.savage@crblaw.com

ROBERT G. SCOTT, JR., born Summit, New Jersey, June 7, 1961; admitted to bar, 1987, Virginia; 1989, District of Columbia; 1992, U.S. Supreme Court. *Education:* James Madison University (B.A., with honors, 1983); College of William & Mary (J.D., 1987). Member, William & Mary Invitational Moot Court Team, 1987. *Member:* The District of Columbia Bar; Virginia State Bar; American Bar Association; Federal Communications Bar Association. ***PRACTICE AREAS:*** FCC Regulation; Cable TV; Cable Franchising; Internet Law; Telecommunications Competition; Telecommunications Contracts; Telecommunications Regulation; Legislative Matters. ***Email:*** bscott@crblaw.com

SUSAN WHELAN WESTFALL, born Louisville, Kentucky, January 15, 1956; admitted to bar, 1988, District of Columbia; 1990, U.S. Court of Appeals for the District of Columbia; 1993, U.S. Supreme Court; 2001, Massachusetts. *Education:* Indiana University (B.A., 1977); Bellarmine College (M.B.A., 1980); Indiana University (J.D., 1987). *Member:* The District of Columbia Bar; Federal Communications Bar Association; Women's Bar Association of The District of Columbia. ***PRACTICE AREAS:*** Telecommunications; Cable Franchising Law; Equal Employment Opportunity Law; State and Local Regulatory Matters. ***Email:*** swestfall@crblaw.com

THERESA ZETERBERG CAVANAUGH, born Brooklyn, New York, July 23, 1963; admitted to bar, 1989, Pennsylvania; 1990, District of Columbia and U.S. Court of Appeals for the District of Columbia Circuit; 1993, U.S. Supreme Court. *Education:* Mary Washington College (B.A., 1985); Catholic University of America (J.D.,1988); Institute for Communications Law Studies at Catholic University School of Law (Certificate, 1988). Staff Member, 1986-1987 and Editorial Assistant, 1987-1988, The Catholic University Law Review. *Member:* District of Columbia Bar; Federal Communications Bar Association. ***PRACTICE AREAS:*** Wireless Communications; Telecommunications Regulation; FCC Regulation; FCC Licensing. ***Email:*** tzcavanaugh@crblaw.com

KARLYN D. STANLEY, born Dayton, Ohio, May 11, 1953; admitted to bar, 1983, District of Columbia; 1992, Virginia. *Education:* University of Michigan (B.A., magna cum laude, 1974); Catholic University of America (J.D., 1983). *Experience:* Federal Clerkship to Chief Judge Fred B. Ugast, D.C. Superior Court, 1983-1984; Trial Attorney, U.S. Department of Justice, Defense Procurement Fraud Unit, 1984-1987; Associate, Thelen, Marrin, Johnson & Bridges, 1987-1992; Senior Attorney, AT&T, 1992-1997. Corporate Advisory Board and Council, THE PHILLIPS COLLECTION, 1995—. Board of Directors, President (1998-2000), Vice-President (2001—) LE NEON THEATRE. *Member:* Federal Communications Bar Association (Co-chair, On-Line Committee, 1998-2000); Computer Law Association (Board Member, 1999—). ***LANGUAGES:*** French. ***PRACTICE AREAS:*** Telecommunications; Telecommunications Competition; Internet Law; International Telecommunications. ***Email:*** kstanley@crblaw.com

JOHN DAVIDSON THOMAS, born Washington, D.C., October 27, 1961; admitted to bar, 1990, District of Columbia; 1996, U.S. Supreme Court and U.S. Court of Appeals for the District of Columbia Circuit. *Education:* Cornell University (A.B., 1984); Boston University (M.S., Communications, 1987; J.D., 1990). Author: "International Aspects of Mobile Satellite Services," 43 Fed. Com. L.J. 45, 1990. ***LANGUAGES:*** Spanish. ***PRACTICE AREAS:*** Telecommunications Regulation; Telecommunications Competition; Cable Television; Pole Attachments; Satellite Communications; International Telecommunications. ***Email:*** dthomas@crblaw.com

JOHN C. DODGE, born Calais, Maine, June 21, 1960; admitted to bar, 1986, Massachusetts; 1987, District of Columbia; 1988, Maine; 1989, U.S. District Court, District of Maine. *Education:* University of Maine (B.A., 1982); Catholic University of America (J.D., 1985); Catholic University Law School Institute for Communications Law Studies (Certificate, 1985). Author: "Regulating the Baseball Monopoly: One Suggestion for Governing the Game," 5 Seton Hall Journal of Sport Law 35, 1995. Staff Attorney, Maine Office of Public Advocate, 1988-1991; District of Columbia Office of People's Counsel, 1991-1994. Member: Maine Telecommunications Relay Services Advisory Board, 1990-1991; District of Columbia Telecommunications Relay Services Advisory Board, 1993-1994. ***PRACTICE AREAS:*** Telecommunications; Administrative Law; Rate Regulation. ***Email:*** jdodge@crblaw.com

JEREMY H. STERN, born Cleveland, Ohio, October 29, 1959; admitted to bar, 1988, Michigan; 1989, District of Columbia; 2000, California. *Education:* University of Michigan (B.A., 1981); Georgetown University (J.D., 1988). Vice President, Corporate and Legal Affairs, Media One. Vice President and Corporate Counsel, Continental Cablevision. Director and Counsel, National Cable and Telecommunications Association. *Member:* The District of Columbia Bar; State Bar of California; Federal Communications Bar Association. (Also at El Segundo, California Office). ***PRACTICE AREAS:*** Cable Television; Telecommunications Regulation; Wireless Communications; Internet Law; Legislative Practice. ***Email:*** jstern@crblaw.com

MARIA T. BROWNE, born Annapolis, Maryland, October 19, 1967; admitted to bar, 1992, Virginia; 1993, District of Columbia. *Education:* University of North Carolina at Chapel Hill (B.A., Journalism, 1989); George Washington University National Law Center (J.D., 1992). *Member:* District of Columbia; Federal Communications Bar Association. ***PRACTICE AREAS:*** Cable Television; Cable Programming; Telecommunications Competition; Telecommunications Regulation; Commercial Litigation; Intellectual Property. ***Email:*** mbrowne@crblaw.com

DONNA C. RATTLEY, born District of Columbia, October 6, 1961; admitted to bar, 1991, District of Columbia. *Education:* Brandeis University (B.A., 1983); Georgetown University Law Center (J.D., 1991). *Member:* District of Columbia Bar; Federal Communications Bar. ***LANGUAGES:*** French. ***PRACTICE AREAS:*** Cable Communications; Cable Franchising Law; Telecommunications Law; Telecommunications Legislation; Telecommunications Competition. ***Email:*** drattley@crblaw.com

EDWARD L. DONOHUE, born New Britain, Connecticut, July 14, 1960; admitted to bar, 1986, Maryland; 1987, District of Columbia. *Education:* Southern Connecticut State University (B.S.,B.A., 1982); Washington College of Law of American University (J.D., 1986). *Member:* The District of Columbia Bar; Maryland State Bar Association. ***PRACTICE AREAS:*** Zoning; Land Use; Historic Preservation; Transactional Real Estate. ***Email:*** edonohue@crblaw.com

T. SCOTT THOMPSON, born Alexandria, Virginia, August 16, 1966; admitted to bar, 1993, District of Columbia. *Education:* Furman University; University of Florida (B.A., 1989); George Washington University (J.D., with honors, 1993). Notes Editor, George Washington Journal of International Law and Economics, 1993. Author: Telecommunications "Franchising," Practicing Law Institute, 2000, 2001. *Member:* The District of Columbia Bar; American Bar Association; Federal Communications Bar Association. ***PRACTICE AREAS:*** Telecommunications Competition; Cable Television Law; Telecommunications Law; Commercial Litigation. ***Email:*** sthompson@crblaw.com

MADIE D. GUSTAFSON, born Ann Arbor, Michigan, June 27, 1949; admitted to bar, 1981, Colorado (Not admitted in District of Columbia). *Education:* Northwestern University (B.S., 1971); University of Denver (M.A., 1972; J.D., 1981). Order of the Coif. Member, University of Denver Law Journal. Author: Transfers of Cable Television Systems; Regulatory Concerns at the Federal, State and Local Level, Practicing Law Institute, 1990-1992, 1994-1996; Renewal of Cable Television Franchises Under the Cable Communications Policy Act of 1984, Practicing Law Institute, 1991; Formal and Informal Renewal of Cable Television Franchises under the Cable Communication Policy Act of 1984, Practicing Law Institute, 1991-1992, 1994-1997. Previous positions include: Senior Vice President-Franchising and Local Government Affairs, AT&T Broadband; Senior Vice President, Vice President and Senior Counsel, Tele-Communications, Inc.; Senior Vice President, United Artists; Corporate Counsel, United Cable. *Member:* Denver and Colorado Bar Associations; Federal Communications Bar Association; Women in Cable & Telecommunications. (Senior Counsel). ***PRACTICE AREAS:*** Cable TV Law; Communications Law; Cable Franchising. ***Email:*** mgustafson@crblaw.com

ASSOCIATES

ADAM S. CALDWELL, born Harrisburg, Pennsylvania, August 15, 1966; admitted to bar, 1993, Maryland; 1994, Pennsylvania; 1995, District of Columbia; 1996, U.S. District Court, District of Maryland and U.S. District Court for the District of Columbia; 1997, U.S. Court of Appeals, Fourth Circuit; 1998, U.S. Court of Appeals for the District of Columbia Circuit. *Education:* Lafayette College (B.A., 1988); George Washington University National Law Center (J.D., with honors, 1993). Member, The George Washington Law Review. Editor-in-Chief, Consumer Protection Reporting Service. *Member:* The District of Columbia Bar; Pennsylvania, Maryland State and Federal Communications Bar

(This Listing Continued)

COLE, RAYWID & BRAVERMAN, L.L.P., Washington—Continued

Associations. ***REPORTED CASES:*** Kann v. Kann 690 A.2d 509 (Md. 1997). ***PRACTICE AREAS:*** Commercial Litigation; Telecommunications Law; Cable Programming; Internet Law. ***Email:*** adam.caldwell@crblaw.com

WILLIAM F. BLY, born Wilmington, Delaware, October 8, 1964; admitted to bar, 1993, Maryland; 1994, Pennsylvania; 1995, California (Not admitted in District of Columbia). *Education:* University of Delaware (B.A., 1986, B.S., 1987); George Washington University (J.D., 1993). Law Clerk to the Honorable Moody R. Tidwell, III, U.S. Court of Federal Claims, 1993-1995. (Also at El Segundo, California Office). ***PRACTICE AREAS:*** Business Litigation; Communications Law; Entertainment Law; Regulatory Law; Public Policy; Alternative Dispute Resolution. ***Email:*** bbly@crblaw.com

CHRISTIN S. McMELEY, born St. Louis, Missouri, July 28, 1970; admitted to bar, 1995, Oklahoma (practice limited to matters and proceedings before federal courts and agencies) (Not admitted in District of Columbia). *Education:* Southwest Missouri State University (B.A., cum laude, 1992); University of Tulsa (J.D., 1995). Phi Delta Phi. Notes and Comments Editor, The Energy Law Journal. *Member:* Oklahoma, Federal Communications and American Bar Associations. ***PRACTICE AREAS:*** Satellite Communications; Communications Law; Litigation; Satellite and Cable Programming. ***Email:*** cmcmeley@crblaw.com

HEIDI PEARLMAN SALOW, born Baltimore, Maryland, November 14, 1969; admitted to bar, 1995, New Jersey (inactive); 1996, Maryland; 1997, District of Columbia. *Education:* McGill University (B.A., 1991); University of Baltimore (J.D., 1995); George Washington University (LL.M. Candidate, Intellectual Property, 2002). Phi Delta Phi. Member, Philip C. Jessup International Law Moot Court Team, 1994-1995. Teaching Assistant, Legal Analysis, Research and Writing and Moot Court/Appellate Advocacy, 1994-1995. President, International Law Society, 1994-1995. Listed in Who's Who: American Law Students, 1995. Author: "Liability Immunity for Internet Service Providers-How Is It Working?" 6.1 J. Tech. L. & Pol'y 1 (2001). *Member:* Maryland State Bar Association; Federal Communications Bar Association. ***LANGUAGES:*** French. ***PRACTICE AREAS:*** Communications and Media; Intellectual Property; Computers and Software. ***Email:*** hpearlman@crblaw.com

ERIK J. CECIL, born Pittsburgh, Pennsylvania, August 24, 1965; admitted to bar, 1997, Maryland (practice limited to matters and proceedings before federal courts and agencies) (Not admitted in District of Columbia). *Education:* University of Colorado, Boulder (B.A., magna cum laude, 1989); University of Maryland (J.D., 1996). *Member:* Federal Communications Bar Association. ***PRACTICE AREAS:*** Telecommunications Law; Telecommunications Competition; Internet Law; Wireless Communications. ***Email:*** ececil@crblaw.com

BRENDA J. BOYKIN, born Arlington, Virginia, October 7, 1959; admitted to bar, 1986, Pennsylvania (inactive); 1987, District of Columbia. *Education:* University of Virginia (B.A., with high honors, 1981); University of North Carolina (J.D., with high honors, 1986). Phi Beta Kappa. Member, Order of the Coif. Editor, North Carolina Law Review, 1985-1986. *Member:* The District of Columbia Bar; Federal Communications Bar Association. ***PRACTICE AREAS:*** Telecommunications; Environmental Law. ***Email:*** bboykin@crblaw.com

ROBERT JYSTAD, born St. Louis, Missouri, June 7, 1958; admitted to bar, 1996, California (Not admitted in District of Columbia). *Education:* University of California, Irvine (B.A., 1980); Columbia University (M.I.A., 1993); University of California School of Law, Los Angeles (J.D., 1996). Principal Author, ITA Broadband Access Report (June, 1999). Author, "Privatization and Human Rights in Central Europe," 1 New Europe Law Review 21 (Winter, 1992). Telecommunications Regulatory Officer, City of Los Angeles, 1997-2000. (Also at El Segundo, California Office). ***PRACTICE AREAS:*** Cable Television; Cable Franchising; Wireless Communications; Telecommunications Law; Internet Law; Trademarks. ***Email:*** bjystad@crblaw.com

DAVID N. TOBENKIN, born Los Angeles, California, May 2, 1966; admitted to bar, 1998, California (inactive); 1999, District of Columbia; 2000, U.S. Court of Appeals for the District of Columbia Circuit. *Education:* University of California, Berkeley (B.A., with honors, 1988); University of Southern California (J.D., M.A., Communications Management, 1998). Executive Articles Editor, The Southern California Interdisciplinary Law Journal, 1997-1998. Author (with David M. Silverman): "The FCC's Main Studio Rule: Achieving Little for Localism at a Great Cost to Broadcasters," 53 Fed. Comm. L., 469 (May 2001); "The Supreme Court's Denver Nondecision and the Need for a New Media Speaker Paradigm," 7 Southern California Interdisciplinary Law Journal 205, Summer 1998. Chairman, Television and Radio Division, University of Southern California Entertainment Law Society, 1996-1997. *Member:* California State Bar; Federal Communications Bar Association. ***LANGUAGES:*** Spanish. ***PRACTICE AREAS:*** Telecommunications Law; Cable TV; Broadcast Television; Intellectual Property. ***Email:*** dtobenkin@crblaw.com

RACHAEL A. GALOOB, born Tulsa, Oklahoma, September 17, 1970; admitted to bar, 1996, Florida (practice limited to matters and proceedings before federal courts and agencies) (Not admitted in District of Columbia). *Education:* Boston College (B.A., 1992); Oklahoma City University School of Law (J.D., 1996); Georgetown University (LL.M., International and Comparative Law, 1999). Phi Delta Phi. Staff Member, Oklahoma City University School of Law Review, 1994-1996. ***LANGUAGES:*** French. ***PRACTICE AREAS:*** Regulatory Law; International Communications Law; Corporate Law; Satellite Communications. ***Email:*** rgaloob@crblaw.com

LAURA G. SCHLOSS, born Indianapolis, Indiana, January 17, 1972; admitted to bar, 1999, District of Columbia. *Education:* Princeton University (B.A., cum laude, 1994); American University (J.D., magna cum laude, 1999). Staff Member, Administrative Law Review, 1998-1999. ***PRACTICE AREAS:*** Cable Television; Telecommunications Law; Administrative Law; Litigation. ***Email:*** laura.schloss@crblaw.com

BRIAN M. JOSEF, born Syracuse, New York, January 25, 1971; admitted to bar, 1999, Maryland (practice limited to matters and proceedings before federal courts and agencies) (Not admitted in District of Columbia). *Education:* University of Pennsylvania (B.A., 1993); Catholic University of America (J.D., 1999). Note and Comment Editor, CommLaw Conspectus: Journal of Communications Law and Policy, 1998-1999. Managing Editor and Consultant, East European and Former Soviet Telecom Report, 1995-1996. *Member:* Maryland State and American Bar Associations; Federal Communications Bar Association. ***PRACTICE AREAS:*** Cable Television; Telecommunications Law; Internet Law; Federal Administrative Law; Copyrights. ***Email:*** bjosef@crblaw.com

K. C. HALM, born Washington, D.C., July 11, 1967; admitted to bar, 1999, Maryland (practice limited to matters and proceedings before federal courts and agencies) (Not admitted in District of Columbia). *Education:* Ithaca College (B.A., 1989); American University (J.D., cum laude, 1999). Articles Editor, Administrative Law Review, 1997-1999. Author: "Bechtel v. FCC: The Beginning of the End of the FCC's Comparative Hearing Process" 50 Administrative Law Review 491 (Spring 1998). ***PRACTICE AREAS:*** Telecommunications Law; Telecommunications Competition; Administrative Law; Administrative Litigation. ***Email:*** khalm@crblaw.com

ADRIENNE P. BYRD, born Rantoul, Illinois; admitted to bar, 1991, Maryland; 2001, District of Columbia. *Education:* Towson State University (B.S., 1987); George Washington University (J.D., 1991). ***PRACTICE AREAS:*** Corporate Transactions; New Media Law; Internet Law; Copyrights; Trademarks. ***Email:*** abyrd@crblaw.com

CHRISTOPHER W. HEMBREE, born Royal Oak, Michigan, April 16, 1969; admitted to bar, 1997, Maryland; 1998, U.S. District Court, District of Maryland; 2000, District of Columbia. *Education:* American University (B.A., 1994); Catholic University Columbus School of Law (J.D., 1997). Member, Colonial Athletic Association Scholar-Athlete. *Member:* The District of Columbia Bar; Maryland State and American Bar Associations; Federal Communications Bar Association. [U.S. Marine Corps, 1987-1991]. ***PRACTICE AREAS:*** Communications and Media; Zoning, Planning and Land Use; Property Law. ***Email:*** chembree@crblaw.com

FELICIA K. WATSON, born Quantico, Virginia; admitted to bar, 1996, Washington and U.S. District Court, Western District of Washington; 1999, U.S. Court of Federal Claims; 2000, District of Columbia. *Education:* Seattle University (B.S., magna cum laude, 1983); Gonzaga University School of Law (J.D., cum laude, 1996); Georgetown University Law Center (LL.M., International and Comparative Law, with distinction, 1999). ***PRACTICE AREAS:*** Commercial Litigation; Communications Law; Cable Communications. ***Email:*** fwatson@crblaw.com

GENEVIEVE D. SAPIR, born Cleveland, Ohio, November 14, 1972; admitted to bar, 1997, Maryland; 2001, District of Columbia, U.S. District Court, District of Maryland. *Education:* American University (B.A., magna cum laude, 1994); George Washington University (J.D., 1997). Member, Philip C. Jessup International Law Moot Court Team, 1995-1996. *Member:* Federal Communications Bar Association. ***PRACTICE AREAS:*** Telecommunications Law; Cable TV; Administrative Law; Litigation. ***Email:*** gsapir@crblaw.com

GERIE A. MILLER, born Flushing, New York, September 15, 1974; admitted to bar, 1999, Maryland; 2000, District of Columbia. *Education:* American University (B.A., cum laude, 1996); Washington College of Law (J.D., cum laude, 1999). *Member:* American Bar Association; Federal Communications Bar Association. ***PRACTICE AREAS:*** Telecommunications Law; Cable Communications; Administrative Law. ***Email:*** gmiller@crblaw.com

JILL M. VALENSTEIN, born Mount Kisco, New York, November 9, 1960; admitted to bar, 1995, Maryland; 1997, District of Columbia. *Education:* Emerson College (B.S., 1982); University of Baltimore (J.D., cum laude, 1995). ***PRACTICE AREAS:*** Telecommunications Law; Cable TV; Litigation. ***Email:*** jvalenstein@crblaw.com

KRISTY J. HALL, born Charleston, West Virginia, March 29, 1974; admitted to bar, 2000, Virginia (practice limited to matters and proceedings before federal courts and agencies) (Not admitted in District of Columbia). *Education:* Olivet Nazarene University (B.A., magna cum laude, 1996); George Mason

(This Listing Continued)

University (J.D., 1999). *Member:* American Bar Association. ***PRACTICE AREAS:*** Communications Law; Commercial Litigation; Antitrust. ***Email:*** khall@crblaw.com

DANIELLE FRAPPIER, born Detroit, Michigan, January 28, 1974; admitted to bar, 2000, Maryland (practice limited to matters and proceedings before federal courts and agencies) (Not admitted in District of Columbia). *Education:* University of Michigan (B.A., 1996); Institut d'études politiques, Aix-en-Provence, France (Certificate in Political Science, 1995); Washington College of Law of American University (J.D., 2000). *Member:* Maryland State and American Bar Associations; Federal Communications Bar Association. ***LANGUAGES:*** French. ***PRACTICE AREAS:*** Domestic and International Telecommunications Law; Internet Law; Telecommunications Competition. ***Email:*** dfrappier@crblaw.com

STEVEN J. GERBER, born New York, N.Y., January 6, 1969; admitted to bar, 1995, New Jersey; 1996, New York; 2001, District of Columbia. *Education:* Johns Hopkins University (B.A., 1991); The American University, Washington College of Law (J.D., cum laude, 1995); The American University School of International Service (M.A., 1996). *Member:* American Bar Association; Federal Communications Bar Association. ***PRACTICE AREAS:*** Telecommunications Law; Cable TV; CLEC Franchising; Pole Attachments. ***Email:*** sgerber@crblaw.com

CODY HARRISON, born Columbia, Tennessee, 1970; admitted to bar, 1999, Maryland (practice limited to matters and proceedings before federal courts and agencies) (Not admitted in District of Columbia). *Education:* Middle Tennessee State University (B.S., 1994); District of Columbia School of Law (J.D., cum laude, 1998); George Washington University Law Center (LL.M., Litigation and Dispute Resolution, 2000). Managing Editor, The District of Columbia Law Review. *Member:* American Bar Association (Litigation Section); Federal Communications Bar Association. ***PRACTICE AREAS:*** Cable TV; Telecommunications Law; Pole Attachments; Litigation. ***Email:*** charrison@crblaw.com

MARIA CELESTE MORAN, born Ridgewood, New Jersey, October 12, 1971; admitted to bar, 2001, Maryland (practices under the supervision of principals of the firm) (Not admitted in District of Columbia). *Education:* Swarthmore College (B.A., 1993); University of Michigan Law School (J.D., 2000). Editorial Staff Member, Michigan Journal of Gender and Law, Michigan Telecommunications and Technology Law Review, 1999-2000. *Member:* Maryland State and American Bar Associations. ***LANGUAGES:*** French, Italian. ***PRACTICE AREAS:*** Cable TV; Litigation; Antitrust; Internet Law. ***Email:*** mmoran@crblaw.com

TIMOTHY TOBIN, born Port Jefferson, New York, February 5, 1969; admitted to bar, 2001, Virginia (practices under supervision of principals of the firm) (Not admitted in District of Columbia). *Education:* Michigan State University (B.A., 1991); George Mason University School of Law (J.D., magna cum laude, 2001). *Member:* Federal Communications Bar Association; Virginia State Bar. ***PRACTICE AREAS:*** Cable TV; Telecommunications Law; Internet Law; Intellectual Property. ***Email:*** ttobin@crblaw.com

OF COUNSEL

FRANCES J. CHETWYND, born United Kingdom, April 26, 1943; admitted to bar, 1975, Virginia; 1976, District of Columbia; 1980, U.S. Supreme Court. *Education:* University of Maryland (B.A., with high honors, 1969); George Washington University (J.D., with honors, 1975). Co-Author: "INFORMATION LAW: Freedom of Information, Privacy, Open Meetings, Other Access Laws," PLI, 1986. *Member:* The District of Columbia Bar (Chair, Administrative Law Section Steering Committee, 1987-1989); Virginia and American Bar Associations. ***PRACTICE AREAS:*** Commercial and Regulatory Litigation; Communications; Administrative Law; Cable Franchising; Intellectual Property; Antitrust; Freedom of Information. ***Email:*** efchetwynd@aol.com

ELLEN S. DEUTSCH, born Brooklyn, New York, November 2, 1943; admitted to bar, 1977, District of Columbia, U.S. District Court, District of Columbia and U.S. Court of Appeals, District of Columbia Circuit. *Education:* Antioch College (B.A., 1974); Catholic University of America (J.D., 1977). Member, Catholic University Law Review, 1976-1977. *Member:* American Bar Association; Federal Communications Bar Association. ***LANGUAGES:*** French. ***PRACTICE AREAS:*** Telecommunications Regulation; Litigation; Legislative Practice. ***Email:*** esdesq@yahoo.com

ANN E. FLOWERS, born Weirton, West Virginia, December 22, 1956; admitted to bar, 1983, District of Columbia. *Education:* University of North Carolina (B.A., with honors, 1978); Georgetown University (J.D., cum laude, 1983). Member, 1981-1982 and Senior Lead Articles Editor, 1982-1983, Law and Policy in International Business. *Member:* District of Columbia Bar. ***PRACTICE AREAS:*** Transactional Matters; Acquisitions and Finance; Corporate Organization and Governance Issues. ***Email:*** ann.flowers@crblaw.com

FREDERICK W. GIROUX, born Oswego, New York, January 20, 1962; admitted to bar, 1987, Massachusetts; 1988, District of Columbia. *Education:* Providence College (B.A., cum laude, 1984); Catholic University of America (J.D., 1987). *Member:* The District of Columbia Bar; Massachusetts, Federal Communications and American Bar Associations. ***PRACTICE AREAS:*** Communications Law; Rate Regulation; Cable Franchising; Signal Carriage; Telecommunications Regulation; Telecommunications Competition; Pole Attachment Litigation. ***Email:*** fgiroux@crblaw.com

GEOFFREY C. COOK, born Boston, Massachusetts, November 20, 1963; admitted to bar, 1988, Massachusetts; 1989, U.S. District Court, District of Massachusetts and U.S. Court of Appeals, First Circuit; 1992, U.S. Court of Federal Claims, U.S. Court of Appeals for the Federal Circuit and U.S. Supreme Court; 1998, District of Columbia, U.S. District Court, District of Columbia and U.S. Court of Appeals, Eleventh Circuit and District of Columbia Circuit. *Education:* Harvard College (A.B., magna cum laude, 1985); Harvard Law School (J.D., 1988). Phi Beta Kappa. Recipient: Ferguson Prize; Hoopes Prize. Reconciling The First Amendment With The Individuals Reputation, 93 Dickinson L. Rev. 265 (1989). Trial Attorney, U.S. Department of Justice, Civil Division, 1992-1998. *Member:* American Bar Association; Federal Communications Bar. ***PRACTICE AREAS:*** Commercial Litigation; Cable TV; Communications Law; Telecommunications Law. ***Email:*** gcook@crblaw.com

TERENCE S. COOKE, born Edinburgh, Scotland, February 15, 1946; admitted to bar, 1976, Virginia; 1998, District of Columbia. *Education:* Louisiana State University (B.A., 1969); Tulane University (J.D., 1975). Counsel, Home Owners Warranty Corporation, 1981-1994. State and Local Gov't. Affairs Counsel, Pocket Communications, 1995-1998. *Member:* Federal Communications and American Bar Associations. [U.S. Army, 1969-1972]. ***PRACTICE AREAS:*** Commercial Law; Zoning and Land Use; Insurance Law; Employment Law; Corporate Law; Telecommunications Law. ***Email:*** tcooke@crblaw.com

JOEL PEARLMAN, born Brooklyn, New York, May 30, 1944; admitted to bar, 1979, Maryland; registered to practice before U.S. Patent and Trademark Office (Not admitted in District of Columbia). *Education:* Massachusetts Institute of Technology (B.S.E.E., 1966); University of Maryland (M.S.E.E., 1974); University of Maryland School of Law (J.D., with honors, 1979). Delta Theta Phi. Order of the Coif. Senior Attorney-Advisor International, Federal Communications Commission, Washington, D.C., 1979-1994. Intellectual Property Counsel, Comsat Corporation, Bethesda, Maryland, 1994-2000. U.S. Delegate to Intelsat and Inmarsat Treaty Organizations, 1985-1991. *Member:* Federal Communications Bar Association. (General Attorney) (With COMSAT Intellectual Property Office). ***Email:*** jpearlman@crblaw.com

JAMES R. J. SCHELTEMA, born Washington, D.C., March 5, 1960; admitted to bar, 1989, Maryland (Not admitted in District of Columbia). *Education:* Montgomery College (A.A., 1980); University of Maryland (B.A., 1981; B.S., 1985); Washington College of Law, American University (J.D., 1989). Certified Public Accountant, Maryland, 1986. Assistant Staff Counsel, Public Service Commission of Maryland. *Member:* Maryland State Bar Association, Inc. ***Email:*** jscheltema@home.com

SPECIAL COUNSEL

SUZANNE E. CURTIS, born Locust Valley, New York, 1964; admitted to bar, 1992, California (Not admitted in District of Columbia). *Education:* Williams College (B.A., with honors, 1986); Santa Clara University (J.D., with honors, 1992). *Member:* State Bar of California. ***PRACTICE AREAS:*** Communications Law; Cable TV; Telecommunications Law. ***Email:*** scurtis@crblaw.com

(This Listing Continued)

COLLIER SHANNON SCOTT, PLLC

SUITE 400
3050 K STREET, N.W.
WASHINGTON, D.C. 20007
Telephone: 202-342-8400
Facsimile: 202-342-8451
Email: lawyers@colliershannon.com
URL: http://www.colliershannon.com

Charlotte, North Carolina Office: 277 West Trade Street, Suite 2020.

Advertising and Marketing, Antitrust and Trade Regulation, Consumer Protection and Advertising, Energy, Environmental, Government Relations, Intellectual Property, International Trade, Labor and Employment, Litigation, Trade Associations, Taxation.

FIRM PROFILE: For over 35 years, Collier Shannon Scott has solved competitive problems for its clients. The firm represents Fortune 500 companies, privately held corporations, and trade associations in the US and abroad. With over 100 attorneys, practice areas include Advertising and Marketing, Antitrust and Trade Regulation, Business Strategies and Transactions, E-Commerce and Technology, Environmental, Government Relations and Public Policy, Intellectual Property, International Trade and Customs, Litigation, and Trade Associations.

(This Listing Continued)

COLLIER SHANNON SCOTT, PLLC, Washington—Continued

MEMBERS OF FIRM

ROBERT A. COLLIER (1917-1984).

WILLIAM W. SCOTT, born Greenwich, Connecticut, June 8, 1937; admitted to bar, 1965, District of Columbia and U.S. Court of Appeals for the District of Columbia Circuit; 1969, U.S. Supreme Court. *Education:* Brown University (A.B., 1959); Georgetown University (J.D., 1964). Member, Georgetown Law Journal, 1963-1964. Law Clerk to the Honorable Charles F. McLaughlin, U.S. District Court for the District of Columbia, 1964-1965. *Member:* The District of Columbia Bar; Bar Association of the District of Columbia; American Bar Association. [U.S. Marine Corps, 1959-1961]. ***Email:*** wscott@colliershannon.com

DAVID A. HARTQUIST, born Austin, Minnesota, June 29, 1941; admitted to bar, 1966, California; 1975, U.S. Supreme Court; 1976, District of Columbia; 1980, U.S. Court of International Trade. *Education:* University of Southern California (B.S., 1963); Harvard University (J.D., 1966). Beta Gamma Sigma. Legislative Assistant to U.S. Senator Richard S. Schweiker, 1970-1973. Assistant to the President, Overseas Private Investment Corporation, 1973-1974. General Counsel, White House Council on International Economic Policy, 1974-1976. *Member:* The District of Columbia Bar; State Bar of California; American Bar Association; Court of International Trade Bar; U.S. Supreme Court Bar. ***PRACTICE AREAS:*** International Trade. ***Email:*** dhartquist@colliershannon.com

R. TIMOTHY COLUMBUS, born West Bend, Wisconsin, March 17, 1949; admitted to bar, 1974, Virginia; 1975, District of Columbia. *Education:* Harvard University (A.B., cum laude, 1971); University of Virginia (J.D., 1974). *Member:* The District of Columbia Bar; Virginia State Bar. ***Email:*** tcolumbus@colliershannon.com

LAUREN R. HOWARD, born Norfolk, Virginia, December 26, 1945; admitted to bar, 1975, District of Columbia. *Education:* Barnard College, Columbia University (B.A., 1967); Georgetown University Law Center (J.D., 1974). Lead Articles Editor, American Criminal Law Review, 1973-1974. *Member:* The District of Columbia Bar; American Bar Association. ***PRACTICE AREAS:*** International Trade. ***Email:*** lhoward@colliershannon.com

MICHAEL D. SHERMAN, born Washington, D.C., April 22, 1950; admitted to bar, 1975, District of Columbia. *Education:* Yale University (A.B., cum laude, 1972); University of Virginia (J.D., 1975). *Member:* The District of Columbia Bar; American Bar Association. ***Email:*** msherman@colliershannon.com

MARK L. AUSTRIAN, born Paterson, New Jersey, July 17, 1945; admitted to bar, 1971, New York; 1973, U.S. District Court, Southern and Eastern Districts of New York; 1975, U.S. Supreme Court; 1981, District of Columbia and U.S. Court of Appeals for the First, Second, Third and District of Columbia Circuits. *Education:* University of Pennsylvania (B.S., 1967; J.D., cum laude, 1970). Research and Developments Editor, University of Pennsylvania Law Review, 1969-1970. Law Clerk to Hon. Orrin G. Judd, United States District Court, Eastern District of New York, 1970-1971. Master, William B. Bryant Inn of Court. Faculty, National Institute for Trial Advocacy (Advanced, Expert Computer Technology and Patent Litigation Programs). *Member:* The District of Columbia Bar; New York State and American Bar Associations; Defense Research Institute; American Law Institute; Council for Excellence (Member, Board of Directors). ***PRACTICE AREAS:*** Federal Civil Litigation; Product Liability; Intellectual Property; Antitrust; Telecommunications; Environmental Litigation; Toxic Tort. ***Email:*** maustrian@colliershannon.com

JOHN B. WILLIAMS, born Detroit, Michigan, February 24, 1952; admitted to bar, 1978, District of Columbia; 1979, U.S. District Court for the District of Columbia; 1981, U.S. Court of Appeals for the District of Columbia Circuit; 1986, U.S. Supreme Court; 1991, U.S. Court of Appeals, First and Third Circuits; 1995, U.S. Court of Appeals, Fourth and Federal Circuits. *Education:* Hamilton College (A.B., 1974); Catholic University of America (J.D., 1978). Article and Book Review Editor, Catholic University Law Review, 1977-1978. *Member:* The District of Columbia Bar; American Bar Association. ***PRACTICE AREAS:*** Litigation. ***Email:*** jwilliams@colliershannon.com

PAUL C. ROSENTHAL, born Miami Beach, Florida, December 12, 1950; admitted to bar, 1976, California and District of Columbia. *Education:* University of Florida (A.A., 1970); University of California at Berkeley (A.B., 1972); University of California at Davis (J.D., 1975). Phi Beta Kappa. Counsel, U.S. Senate Committee on Governmental Affairs, 1975-1981. Member, U.S. Court of International Trade Advisory Committee. *Member:* The District of Columbia Bar; State Bar of California; Federal (Chairman, Administrative Law Section, 1983-1985; Chairman, Regulatory Reform Committee, 1981-1983) and American (International Trade Steering Committee) Bar Associations. ***PRACTICE AREAS:*** International Trade. ***Email:*** prosenthal@colliershannon.com

JOHN L. WITTENBORN, born Chester, Illinois, August 7, 1949; admitted to bar, 1974, Indiana and Ohio; 1980, U.S. Supreme Court; 1986, District of Columbia and U.S. Court of Appeals, District of Columbia Circuit. *Education:* U.S. Air Force Academy (B.S., distinguished graduate, 1971); Indiana University (J.D., cum laude, 1974); George Washington (LL.M., with highest honors, 1980). *Member:* The District of Columbia Bar; Indiana State and American Bar Associations. ***PRACTICE AREAS:*** Environmental Law and Litigation. ***Email:*** jwittenborn@colliershannon.com

JEFFREY L. LEITER, born Marysville, California, September 3, 1953; admitted to bar, 1981, District of Columbia. *Education:* George Washington University (B.A., 1975); Catholic University of America (J.D., 1980). Omicron Delta Kappa. Editor-in-Chief: "The Underground Storage Tank Guide," 1988; "The Aboveground Storage Tank Guide," 1991. Contributing Editor: "The Guide to Used Oil Regulations," 1992. *Member:* The District of Columbia Bar; American Bar Association. ***PRACTICE AREAS:*** Energy; Petroleum Marketing; Environmental Law. ***Email:*** jleiter@colliershannon.com

JEFFREY S. BECKINGTON, born Monterey, California, August 10, 1948; admitted to bar, 1977, Virginia; 1978, District of Columbia; 1981, U.S. Court of Appeals for the Federal Circuit and U.S. Court of International Trade. *Education:* Princeton University (A.B., cum laude in History, 1970); Vanderbilt University (J.D., 1977); Georgetown University (LL.M. in International Law, 1982). Research Editor, Vanderbilt Journal of Transnational Law, 1976-1977. *Member:* The District of Columbia Bar; Virginia State Bar; American Bar Association; American Society of International Law. [U.S. Marine Corps Reserve, 1970-1973]. ***PRACTICE AREAS:*** International Trade. ***Email:*** jbeckington@colliershannon.com

JUDITH L. OLDHAM, born Detroit, Michigan, August 6, 1942; admitted to bar, 1981, District of Columbia. *Education:* Duke University; University of Michigan (B.A., cum laude, 1965); Georgetown University (J.D., cum laude, 1981). Editor, Georgetown Law Journal, 1980-1981. *Member:* The District of Columbia Bar. ***PRACTICE AREAS:*** Advertising; Trade and Professional Associations. ***Email:*** joldham@colliershannon.com

LAURENCE J. LASOFF, born Boston, Massachusetts, September 6, 1950; admitted to bar, 1982, District of Columbia; 1983, U.S. Court of International Trade; U.S. Court of Appeals for the Federal Circuit. *Education:* Columbia University (B.A., 1972); Johns Hopkins University School of Advanced International Studies (M.A., 1974); George Washington University (J.D., 1982). International Trade Specialist, Bureau of East-West Trade, U.S. Department of Commerce, 1974-1977. Executive Assistant to the Assistant Secretary of Commerce for International Trade, 1977-1979. U.S. Industry Trade Advisor, Consumer Goods, 1992—. Member, Industry Functional Advisory Committee on Customs Trade Policy, 1994—. *Member:* The District of Columbia Bar; American Bar Association (Member, Sections on: Litigation; International Law). ***PRACTICE AREAS:*** International Trade; Customs Law. ***Email:*** llasoff@colliershannon.com

PATRICK J. COYNE, born Harrisburg, Pennsylvania, March 9, 1956; admitted to bar, 1982, District of Columbia and U.S. Claims Court; 1983, U.S. Court of Appeals for the Federal Circuit and U.S. District Court for the District of Columbia; 1986, U.S. Court of Appeals, Ninth Circuit; 1987, U.S. Court of Appeals, Third Circuit; U.S. Supreme Court. *Education:* Virginia Polytechnic Institute and State University; University of Virginia (B.S.C.E., with high distinction, 1979; J.D., 1982). Tau Beta Pi; Chi Epsilon. Research and Projects Editor, Virginia Journal of Natural Resources Law, 1981-1982. Law Clerk to the Honorable Edward S. Smith, Circuit Judge, U.S. Court of Appeals for the Federal Circuit, 1982-1984. *Member:* The District of Columbia Bar; Federal and American Bar Associations; American Intellectual Property Law Association; International Trademark Association; Copyright Society of the USA. ***SPECIAL AGENCIES:*** United States Patent and Trademark Office Reg. No. 31821. ***PRACTICE AREAS:*** Federal Civil Litigation; Patent, Trademark and Copyright; Antitrust. ***Email:*** pcoyne@colliershannon.com

WILLIAM C. MACLEOD, born Chicago, Illinois, April 7, 1952; admitted to bar, 1979, Illinois and U.S. District Court, Northern District of Illinois; 1988, U.S. Court of Appeals, 7th Circuit and U.S. Supreme Court; 1992, District of Columbia. *Education:* Ripon College (B.A., cum laude, 1973); University of Virginia; University of Miami (J.D., cum laude, 1979). Society of Wig and Robe. Director, Chicago Regional Office, Federal Trade Commission (1983-1986). Director, Bureau of Consumer Protection, FTC (1986-1990). *Member:* Illinois State (Antitrust Section) and American (Member, Antitrust Section) Bar Associations. ***PRACTICE AREAS:*** Antitrust; Trade Regulation. ***Email:*** wmacleod@colliershannon.com

WILLIAM J. RODGERS, born New York, N.Y., June 19, 1943; admitted to bar, 1968, New York (Not admitted in District of Columbia). admitted to bar, 1968, New York; 1972, U.S. District Court, Northern District of New York; 1974, District of Columbia and U.S. District Court for the District of Columbia; 1976, U.S. Court of Appeals for the District of Columbia Circuit and U.S. District Court, Southern and Eastern Districts of New York; 1977, U.S. Court of Appeals, Second and Fourth Circuits and U.S. Supreme Court; 1980, U.S. Court of Appeals, Fifth Circuit; 1981, U.S. District Court, Eastern District of Michigan; 1984, U.S. Court of Appeals, Eleventh Circuit; 1985, U.S. Court of Appeals, Tenth Circuit; 1987, U.S. Court of Appeals, Sixth Circuit. *Education:*

(This Listing Continued)

Cornell University (B.S., 1965); Fordham University (J.D., 1968). Executive Assistant to Secretary of Labor, 1972-1974. President, Fordham Law Alumni Association of Washington, 1977-1979. *Member:* The District of Columbia Bar; Federal and American (Member, Committee on Development of the Law Under the National Labor Relations Act, Section on Labor and Employment Law, 1973—) Bar Associations. Fellow, American Bar Foundation. ***PRACTICE AREAS:*** Labor and Employment Law. ***Email:*** wrodgers@colliershannon.com

MICHAEL J. COURSEY, born Ramey Air Force Base, Puerto Rico, March 26, 1954; admitted to bar, 1981, Massachusetts; 1982, District of Columbia; 1989, U.S. Court of International Trade; 1991, U.S. Court of Appeals for the Federal Circuit. *Education:* College of the Holy Cross (A.B., magna cum laude, 1977) Phi Beta Kappa; University of Virginia (J.D., 1981). Editor-in-Chief, The Virginia Journal of International Law, 1980-1981. Deputy Assistant Secretary for Investigations, International Trade Administration, U.S. Department of Commerce, 1988-1989. Director, Office of Investigations, International Trade Administration, U.S. Department of Commerce, 1986-1988. *Member:* The District of Columbia Bar; Massachusetts Bar Associations; Customs and International Trade Bar Association. ***PRACTICE AREAS:*** International Trade. ***Email:*** mcoursey@colliershannon.com

ROBIN H. GILBERT, born Atlanta, Georgia, April 15, 1952; admitted to bar, 1986, District of Columbia; 1987, U.S. Court of Appeals for the Federal Circuit and U.S. Court of International Trade; 1990, U.S. Supreme Court. *Education:* George Mason University (B.A., cum laude, 1975); Georgetown University Law Center (J.D., 1986). Staff Member, 1984-1985 and Executive Editor, 1985-1986, Law and Policy in International Business. *Member:* The District of Columbia Bar; American Bar Association (Member, Section of International Law and Practice). ***PRACTICE AREAS:*** Customs Law; International Trade. ***Email:*** rgilbert@colliershannon.com

WILLIAM M. GUERRY, JR., born Norfolk, Virginia, April 3, 1961; admitted to bar, 1987, Virginia; 1988, District of Columbia. *Education:* University of Virginia (B.A., magna cum laude, 1983); Wolfson College of Cambridge University, Cambridge, England; University of Virginia (J.D., 1986). Law Clerk to Justice Charles S. Russell, Supreme Court of Virginia, 1986-1987. *Member:* The Virginia State Bar; The District of Columbia Bar; American Bar Association (Member, Natural Resources Section). ***SPECIAL AGENCIES:*** Environmental Protection Agency. ***PRACTICE AREAS:*** Environmental Law. ***Email:*** wguerry@colliershannon.com

JOHN B. BREW, born Erie, Pennsylvania, March 11, 1963; admitted to bar, 1988, Pennsylvania; 1989, U.S. Court of International Trade; 1994, District of Columbia; 1995, U.S. Court of Appeals for the Federal Circuit. *Education:* Bucknell University (B.A., 1985); City of London Polytechnic, London, England; Dickinson School of Law (J.D., 1988). Phi Eta Sigma. Staff Editor, Dickinson Law Review, 1986-1988. *Member:* The District of Columbia Bar; American Bar Association; Customs and International Trade Bar Association. ***PRACTICE AREAS:*** Customs and International Trade Law. ***Email:*** jbrew@colliershannon.com

KERRIE L. HOOK, born Leominster, Massachusetts, May 2, 1962; admitted to bar, 1987, California and U.S. Court of Appeals, Ninth Circuit; 1989, District of Columbia; 1995, U.S. Court of Appeals, Federal Circuit; 1997, U.S. District Court, District of Maryland. *Education:* George Mason University (B.A., with distinction, 1984, Alpha Chi); Washington College of Law, The American University (J.D., cum laude, 1987). Mooers Trophy Recipient, 1987. *Member:* State Bar of California; The District of Columbia Bar; American Bar Association (Member, Litigation Section). ***SPECIAL AGENCIES:*** Consumer Product Safety Commission. ***PRACTICE AREAS:*** Litigation. ***Email:*** khook@colliershannon.com

RUSSELL S. FRYE, born Dayton, Ohio, July 12, 1953; admitted to bar, 1978, Ohio; 1981, District of Columbia. *Education:* Princeton University (A.B., cum laude, 1975); University of Denver (J.D., 1978). Member, Order of St. Ives. Associate Editor, Transportation Law Journal, 1977-1978. Author: *Water Pollution:* Law & Liability, Graham & Trotman, 1993 (chapter on U.S. citizen suits); *Clean Water Act Update Compliance Handbook,* John Wiley & Sons, 1989; "The Role of Private Banks in Promoting Sustainable Development, from Outside Counsel's Perspective," 29 Law & Policy in International Business (Summer 1998); "The Role of Law and Lawyers in Protection of the Global Environment," International Business Lawyer, March 1997; "New Clean Air Act Permit Rules," 15 National Law Journal (June 28, 1993) (co-author). *Member:* The District of Columbia Bar; American (Member, Water Quality Committee, Natural Resources Law Section) and International (Committee on Environmental Law, Section on Business Law, Chairman, 1995-1998) Bar Associations. ***REPORTED CASES:*** U.S. v. Stone Container Corp., 229 F.3d 1345 (9th Cir. 2000); American Forest & Paper Ass'n v. U.S.EPA, 137 F.3d 291 (5th Cir. 1998); American Iron & Steel Institute v. EPA, 115 F.3d 979 (D.C. Cir. 1997). ***PRACTICE AREAS:*** Environmental; Administrative. ***Email:*** rfrye@colliershannon.com

SCOTT SINDER, born Akron, Ohio, May 26, 1963; admitted to bar, 1989, Colorado and District of Columbia. *Education:* University of Michigan (A.B., 1985; M.P.P., 1987; J.D., 1988). Recipient, Henry M. Campbell Moot Court Award (First Place, 1987). Law Clerk to the Honorable Zita L. Weinshienk, U.S. District Court, District of Colorado (March 1989-August 1990). Deputy General Counsel for Delegate Selection, Kerrey for President Campaign (December, 1991 - March, 1992). ***PRACTICE AREAS:*** Litigation; Government Relations; Trade Association Law; Election Law. ***Email:*** ssinder@colliershannon.com

JOHN E. VILLAFRANCO, born Bronx, New York, February 12, 1962; admitted to bar, 1991, New Jersey; 1992 New York and District of Columbia. *Education:* Wake Forest University (B.A., 1984); Tulane University Law School, International Studies Program; Catholic University, Columbus School of Law (J.D., 1991). Member, Catholic University Journal of Contemporary Health Law and Policy, 1989-1990. Commissioner, City of Alexandria Commission on Consumer Affairs, 1994-1998. *Member:* The District of Columbia Bar; New York State and American Bar Associations. ***PRACTICE AREAS:*** Antitrust; Trade Regulation; Electronic Commerce; Advertising Law. ***Email:*** jvillafranco@colliershannon.com

THOMAS W. MITCHELL, born Washington, D.C., June 6, 1963; admitted to bar, 1989, Virginia and New York; 1990, District of Columbia; 1997, Maryland. *Education:* University of Virginia (B.A., 1985); Georgetown University (J.D., 1988). Associate Editor, Georgetown Law Journal, 1987-1988. Law Clerk to Hon. Fred B. Ugast, Chief Judge, Superior Court of the District of Columbia, 1988-1989. *Member:* New York State, Virginia and Maryland State Bar Associations; District of Columbia Bar. ***PRACTICE AREAS:*** Litigation; Telecommunications. ***Email:*** tmitchell@colliershannon.com

THOMAS E. GILBERTSEN, born Georgetown, Kentucky, December 6, 1961; admitted to bar, 1989, Ohio; 1992, District of Columbia. *Education:* The Ohio State University (B.A., 1984); Cornell Law School (J.D., 1989). *Member:* American Bar Association; The Association of Trial Lawyers of America. ***PRACTICE AREAS:*** Intellectual Property; Antitrust; Litigation; Commercial Law; Employment Law. ***Email:*** tgilbertsen@colliershannon.com

RICHARD H. KJELDGAARD, born Lyons, Nebraska, June 20, 1952; admitted to bar, 1978, Wisconsin; 1980, District of Columbia; 1983, U.S. Court of Appeals for the Federal Circuit and U.S. Claims Court; registered to practice before U.S. Patent and Trademark Office. *Education:* University of Nebraska (B.A., with honors, 1975); George Washington University (J.D., 1978). Law Clerk to Associate Judge Phillip B. Baldwin, U.S. Court of Appeals for the Federal Circuit, 1982-1984. *Member:* The District of Columbia Bar; American Bar Association; American Intellectual Property Law Association. ***PRACTICE AREAS:*** Intellectual Property Law; Patent, Trademark and Copyright Law. ***Email:*** rkjeldgaard@colliershannon.com

MICHAEL H. KNIGHT, born Alexandria, Virginia, August 19, 1965; admitted to bar, 1991, Virginia; 1994, District of Columbia. *Education:* George Mason University, Fairfax (B.S., 1988); George Mason University School of Law, Arlington (J.D., 1991). Phi Delta Phi. Managing Editor, The George Mason University Law Review, 1990-1991. Law Clerk to the Hon. Douglas O. Tice, Jr., U.S. Bankruptcy Judge, Eastern District of Virginia, 1991-1992. *Member:* Virginia State Bar (inactive); The District of Columbia Bar (Member, Antitrust and Trade Regulation Section); American Bar Association (Member, Antitrust Law Section). ***PRACTICE AREAS:*** Antitrust. ***Email:*** mknight@colliershannon.com

DAVID E. JOHNSTON, born Chicago, Illinois, November 20, 1948; admitted to bar, 1975, North Carolina. *Education:* Kenyon College (B.A., cum laude, 1971); Indiana University School of Law - Bloomington (J.D., 1974). Boards of Directors: Bob Timberlake, Inc.; Charlotte World Affairs Council. Member, Executive Committee, Board of Directors: Charlotte Regional Sports Commission; Children's Law Center. Member: Economic Development Committee, North Carolina Citizens for Business and Industry; Advisory Board, Charlotte Chamber of Commerce; National Association of Corporate Directors; American Association of Bank Directors; Task Force on North Carolina Business Corporation Act, North Carolina Business Council; Business and Regulatory Advisory Board, Attorney General, North Carolina; Society of International Business Fellows; Consulegis EWIV. *Member:* Mecklenburg County (Member, Long Range Planning Committee), North Carolina (Member: Securities Regulation Committee; Corporate Law Committee; International Law and Practice Section) and American (Member: Corporate Banking and Business Law Committee; Banking Law Committee's Subcommittee on Regulatory Enforcement and Directory Liability; Federal Regulation of Securities Subcommittee; Subcommittee on Reporting Companies Under the 1934 Act: Ad Hoc Committee on Central and Eastern Europe) Bar Associations. (Resident, Charlotte, North Carolina Office). ***PRACTICE AREAS:*** Securities; Corporate; Mergers and Acquisitions. ***Email:*** djohnston@colliershannon.com

KATHLEEN E. McDERMOTT, born Cincinnati, Ohio, July 21, 1949; admitted to bar, 1975, District of Columbia; 1982, U.S. Supreme Court. *Education:* Georgetown University (B.S.F.S., cum laude, 1971); Georgetown University (J.D., 1974). Law Clerk to the Administrative Law Judges of the Federal Trade Commission, Washington, D.C., 1974-1975. Associate, 1975-1980, Partner, 1980-1993, Collier Shannon Scott. Executive Vice President, Chief Legal Officer, Member of the Executive Council, American Stores Company, Salt

(This Listing Continued)

COLLIER SHANNON SCOTT, PLLC, Washington—Continued

Lake City, Utah, 1993-1999. *Member:* The District of Columbia Bar; American Bar Association (Member, Business Law Section; Committee of Corporate General Counsel, 1997-1999; Antitrust Law Section; Chair, Federal Trade Commission Committee, 1983-1986; Features Editor, Antitrust Magazine, 1990-1993; Vice Chair, Corporate Counseling Committee, 2001—). ***PRACTICE AREAS:*** Antitrust and Trade Regulation; Corporate Law. ***Email:*** kmcdermott@colliershannon.com

ALLAN J. WEINER, born New Castle, Pennsylvania, June 29, 1948; admitted to bar, 1973, Ohio; 1978, District of Columbia. *Education:* University of Michigan (B.B.A., with distinction, 1970); Ohio State University (J.D., cum laude, 1973). Beta Alpha Psi; Beta Gamma Sigma. Member, Ohio State Law Journal, 1971-1972. Certified Public Accountant, Ohio, 1973. Attorney and Assistant Branch Chief, Interpretative Division, Office of the Chief Counsel, Internal Revenue Service, 1973-1977. *Member:* The District of Columbia Bar (Chair, Tax Section Pass-Through Entities and Real Estate Committee, 1995-1998); American Bar Association (Member, Sections of: Taxation; Real Property, Probate and Trust Law; Business Law). ***PRACTICE AREAS:*** Federal Income Tax; Business Transactions. ***Email:*** aweiner@colliershannon.com

KATHRYN McMAHON-LOHRER, born Binghamton, New York, November 5, 1962; admitted to bar, 1992, New York; 1995, District of Columbia; 1997, U.S. Court of Appeals, Fourth Circuit. *Education:* Syracuse University (B.A., 1988); Cornell Law School (J.D., 1992). *Member:* District of Columbia Bar; New York State and American (Member, Section on Natural Resources, Energy and Environmental Law) Bar Associations. ***PRACTICE AREAS:*** Environmental; Occupational Safety and Health; Employment Discrimination Law. ***Email:*** kmcmahon@colliershannon.com

LEWIS ROSE, born New York, N.Y., July 16, 1957; admitted to bar, 1982, New York; 1988, District of Columbia. *Education:* State University of New York at Buffalo (B.A., magna cum laude, 1978; J.D., 1981). Co-Author: CCH Advertising Law Guide, May 2000. Attorney, Bureau of Consumer Protection, 1981-86. Attorney Advisor to Commissioner Calvani, Federal Trade Commission, 1986-87. ***PRACTICE AREAS:*** Advertising Law; Consumer Law; Consumer Credit Law; Unfair Trade Practice; Internet Law; Trademark and Copyright Law; Telemarketing Law; Direct Marketing; Audiotext; Sweepstakes, Contests, Promotion Law. ***Email:*** lrose@colliershannon.com

JOHN P. FELDMAN, born Boston, Massachusetts, January 23, 1964; admitted to bar, 1990, Illinois; 1991, Massachusetts; 1993, District of Columbia. *Education:* Princeton University (A.B., magna cum laude, 1986); Cornell Law School (J.D., 1990). ***PRACTICE AREAS:*** Advertising and Promotion; Sweepstakes; Electronic Commerce; Trademark; Copyright. ***Email:*** jfeldman@colliershannon.com

GREGORY M. SCOTT, born Cleveland, Ohio, July 11, 1960; admitted to bar, 1993, Virginia; 2001, District of Columbia. *Education:* Colorado College (B.A., 1983); Washington College of Law (J.D., 1992). *Member:* American Bar Association. ***PRACTICE AREAS:*** Legislative; Administrative. ***Email:*** gscott@colliershannon.com

CHET M. THOMPSON, born Washington, D.C., March 23, 1968; admitted to bar, 1993, Maryland; 1995, District of Columbia; U.S. Court of Appeals for the District of Columbia Circuit. *Education:* Boston College (B.A., cum laude, 1990); Columbus School of Law, Catholic University of America (J.D., Top 5 percent, 1993). Member, Columbus Law School Law Review. *Member:* The District of Columbia Bar; Maryland State and American Bar Association (Member, Natural Resources Section). ***PRACTICE AREAS:*** Environmental Law; Litigation. ***Email:*** cthompson@colliershannon.com

D. REED FREEMAN, JR., born Arlington, Virginia, May 14, 1968; admitted to bar, 1993, Virginia and U.S. District Court, Eastern District of Virginia; 1999, District of Columbia. *Education:* University of Richmond (B.A., 1990); University of Virginia (J.D., 1993). Law Clerk to the Honorable Claude M. Hilton, U.S. District Court, Eastern District of Virginia. Co-Author: *CCH Advertising Law Guide,* 2000. Adjunct Professor of Law, George Mason University School of Law, 2000—. Member, Federal Trade Commission Bureau of Consumer Protection, 1996-1997. ***PRACTICE AREAS:*** Advertising; Electronic Commerce; Privacy and Publicity; Federal Trade Commission Investigations and Litigation; Unfair Trade Practices; Antitrust; Trade Associations. ***Email:*** rfreeman@colliershannon.com

OF COUNSEL

THOMAS F. SHANNON, born Lowell, Massachusetts, June 11, 1927; admitted to bar, 1953, New Hampshire; 1958, District of Columbia and U.S. Supreme Court. *Education:* Bowdoin College (A.B., 1950); University of Virginia (LL.B., 1953). Phi Alpha Delta. Legislative Counsel to U.S. Senator Styles Bridges, 1955-1957. Chief Republican Counsel, Committee on Appropriations, U.S. Senate, 1957-1958. *Member:* The District of Columbia Bar; Bar Association of the District of Columbia; New Hampshire and American Bar Associations. ***PRACTICE AREAS:*** International Trade. ***Email:*** tshannon@colliershannon.com

FRANK F. MURTHA, born Brooklyn, New York, February 27, 1938; admitted to bar, 1964, New York; 1965, U.S. District Court, Eastern and Southern Districts of New York and U.S. Court of Appeals, Second Circuit; 1972, U.S. Supreme Court (Not admitted in District of Columbia). *Education:* Villanova University (A.B., 1960); Columbia University (J.D., 1963). Samuel Rubin Scholarship, 1963. President, National Foundation for Occupational and Environmental Health Research, 1983-1985. Adjunct Professor, Pace University School of Law, 1987-1993. Former Labor Counsel, American Can Company. *Member:* Westchester County, New York State (Member, Labor Law Section) and American (Member, Employment Law Section) Bar Associations. ***Email:*** fmurtha@colliershannon.com

MICHAEL R. KERSHOW, born Huntington, New York, December 24, 1954; admitted to bar, 1981, District of Columbia. *Education:* Colgate University (B.A., magna cum laude, 1977); Georgetown University (J.D., 1980). Phi Beta Kappa. Law Clerk to the Hon. George R. Gallagher, Associate Judge, District of Columbia Court of Appeals, 1980-1981. *Member:* The District of Columbia Bar; American Bar Association; Customs and International Trade Bar Associations. ***PRACTICE AREAS:*** International Trade; Customs Law; Food and Drug Regulation. ***Email:*** mkershow@colliershannon.com

KATHLEEN WEAVER CANNON, born Eglin AFB, Florida, August 18, 1955; admitted to bar, 1981, District of Columbia; 1982, U.S. Court of Appeals for the Federal Circuit. *Education:* University of Maryland (B.S., magna cum laude, 1977); University of North Carolina (J.D., 1981). Editor-in-Chief, North Carolina Journal of International Law and Commercial Regulation, 1980-1981. *Member:* The District of Columbia Bar; American Bar Association. ***PRACTICE AREAS:*** International Trade. ***Email:*** kcannon@colliershannon.com

MARY TUCK STALEY, born Scarsdale, New York, August 31, 1957; admitted to bar, 1983, District of Columbia; 1984, U.S. Court of International Trade and U.S. Court of Appeals for the Federal Circuit. *Education:* Kenyon College (B.A., cum laude, 1979); American University (J.D., 1983); George Washington University (LL.M., 1987). *Member:* The District of Columbia Bar; American Bar Association. ***PRACTICE AREAS:*** International Trade Law. ***Email:*** mstaley@colliershannon.com

DAVID C. SMITH, JR., born Glastonbury, Connecticut, September 21, 1959; admitted to bar, 1987, Florida; 1989, District of Columbia; 1992, U.S. Court of International Trade and U.S. Court of Appeals for the Federal Circuit. *Education:* St. Lawrence University (B.A., Government, 1981); Georgetown University Law Center (J.D., 1987). Member and Third Year Editor, American Criminal Law Review, 1985-1987. International Trade Analyst, International Trade Administration, U.S. Department of Commerce, 1990-1992. *Member:* The District of Columbia Bar; The Florida Bar; American Bar Association (Member, International Law Section). ***PRACTICE AREAS:*** International Trade Law; Customs Law. ***Email:*** dsmith@colliershannon.com

R. ALAN LUBERDA, born Hammond, Indiana, July 12, 1959; admitted to bar, 1985, District of Columbia; U.S. Court of International Trade; U.S. Court of Appeals, Federal Circuit; U.S. District Court, District of Columbia. *Education:* George Washington University (B.A., with distinction, 1982); Cornell University (J.D., 1985). Phi Beta Kappa. ***PRACTICE AREAS:*** International Trade; Customs Law. ***Email:*** aluberda@colliershannon.com

MAUREEN ENRIGHT, born Washington, D.C., April 16, 1959; admitted to bar, 1988, Virginia and District of Columbia. *Education:* Fordham University (B.A., 1981); University of Virginia (J.D., 1988). Phi Beta Kappa. *Member:* The District of Columbia Bar; Virginia State Bar; American Bar Association. ***PRACTICE AREAS:*** Trade Regulation. ***Email:*** menright@colliershannon.com

FRANK KOSZORUS, JR., born Munsing, Germany, November 16, 1947; admitted to bar, 1977, District of Columbia; 1978, U.S. District Court, District of Columbia; 1989, U.S. District Court, District of Maryland. *Education:* American University (B.A., 1970); De Paul University (J.D., cum laude, 1976). Public Member, U.S. Delegation to the 1989 Paris Conference on the Human Dimension of the Conference on Security and Cooperation in Europe. *Member:* The District of Columbia Bar (Member, Litigation and International Sections); New York State (Member, Task Force on Simplification of Laws, 1987) and American (Member, Litigation Section) Bar Associations. ***LANGUAGES:*** Hungarian. ***PRACTICE AREAS:*** Litigation; Government Relations; International. ***Email:*** fkoszorus@colliershannon.com

MICHAEL O. HILL, born Princeton, New Jersey, July 12, 1957; admitted to bar, 1985, Vermont; 1989, District of Columbia. *Education:* Williams College (B.A., 1980); Yale University (J.D., 1984). Editor, Yale Law Journal, 1983-1984. Law Clerk to the Honorable Albert W. Coffrin, Chief Judge, U.S. District Court, District of Vermont, 1984-1985. Member, Board of Advisors, Chemical Waste Litigation Reporter, EPA Administrative Law Reporter and Environmental Solutions Trade Magazine. Recipient, Special Achievement Award and Special Commendation for Outstanding Service, U.S. Department of Justice. Trial Attorney, U.S. Department of Justice Environmental Enforcement Section,

(This Listing Continued)

1986-1990. *Member:* The District of Columbia Bar (Member, Environment, Energy and Natural Resources Section); American Bar Association (Member, Sections on: Natural Resources, Energy and Environmental Law; Litigation). ***PRACTICE AREAS:*** Environmental Law and Litigation. ***Email:*** mhill@colliershannon.com

MARY C. CRONIN, born Teaneck, New Jersey, November 16, 1957; admitted to bar, 1987, New York; 1989, U.S. District Court, Southern District of New York (Not admitted in District of Columbia). *Education:* University of Michigan (A.B., magna cum laude, 1979); Fordham University (J.D., 1986). *Member:* American Bar Association (Member, Environmental Law Section). ***PRACTICE AREAS:*** Commercial Litigation; Real Estate Transactions. ***Email:*** mcronin@colliershannon.com

THERESE MARIE WOODS, born New York, N.Y., October 27, 1964; admitted to bar, 1990, Connecticut; 1991, New York; 1992, U.S. Court of Federal Claims; 1993, District of Columbia; 1996, U.S. Supreme Court. *Education:* Fordham College of Business Administration (B.S., cum laude, 1986); Fordham Law School (J.D., 1990); Fordham Graduate School of Business Administration (M.B.A., 1990). Business and Development Editor, Fordham International Law Journal, 1989-1990. Author: Note, "The EEC-Mexican Agreement: Time for Reevaluation?" 12 Fordham Int'l L.J. 541 (1989). Law Clerk to Hon. Marian Blank Horn, U.S. Court of Federal Claims, 1990-1992. Attorney Advisor, Division of Market Regulation, U.S. Securities and Exchange Commission, 1992-1995. U.S. Attorney's Office for the District of Columbia, Assignment from SEC as Special Assistant in Criminal Division, 1994-1995. Senior Counsel, Office of Compliance Inspections and Examinations, 1996-1998. Associate, Securities and Financial Services, Clifford Chance Rogers and Wells. ***PRACTICE AREAS:*** Securities; Financial Services; Corporate. ***Email:*** twoods@colliershannon.com

LYNN DUFFY MALONEY, born Flemington, New Jersey, March 4, 1964; admitted to bar, 1992, New Jersey; 1993, District of Columbia and U.S. Court of Appeals for the Federal Circuit; 1996, U.S. Court of International Trade. *Education:* Georgetown University (B.A., 1986); Fordham University (J.D., 1992). ***LANGUAGES:*** Spanish, Italian. ***PRACTICE AREAS:*** International Trade. ***Email:*** lmaloney@colliershannon.com

ASSOCIATES

STEPHANIE SIEGEL, born Ann Arbor, Michigan, September 29, 1959; admitted to bar, 1985, District of Columbia; 1990, U.S. Supreme Court. *Education:* University of Rochester (B.A., cum laude and with distinction, 1981); Washington College of Law, American University (J.D., 1985). ***PRACTICE AREAS:*** Occupational Safety and Health; Environmental Law. ***Email:*** ssiegel@colliershannon.com

WILLIAM M. BAILEY, born Mount Holly, New Jersey, May 7, 1963; admitted to bar, 1989, Maryland; 1992, District of Columbia. *Education:* University of North Carolina at Chapel Hill (B.A., 1985; J.D., 1989). Staff Member, North Carolina Journal of International Law and Commercial Regulation. ***PRACTICE AREAS:*** Litigation. ***Email:*** wbailey@colliershannon.com

MICHAEL R. McCARTHY, born Silver Spring, Maryland, March 30, 1966; admitted to bar, 1991, Virginia; 2000, U.S. Supreme Court and U.S. District Court, Eastern District of Virginia; 2001, District of Columbia and Maryland. *Education:* University of Notre Dame (B.A., 1988); Catholic University of America (J.D., 1991). ***PRACTICE AREAS:*** Litigation. ***Email:*** mmccarthy@colliershannon.com

MICHAEL R. CARITHERS, JR., born Wilmington, Delaware, June 7, 1966; admitted to bar, 1991, Michigan; 1992, District of Columbia. *Education:* Harvard University (B.A., 1988); University of Michigan (J.D., 1991). *Member:* State Bar of Michigan; The District of Columbia Bar; American and National Bar Associations. ***PRACTICE AREAS:*** Litigation; White Collar Defense. ***Email:*** mcarithers@colliershannon.com

KATHARINE I. MATTHEWS, born Monterey, California, October 26, 1957; admitted to bar, 1992, California; 1994, District of Columbia; registered to practice before U.S. Patent and Trademark Office. *Education:* Linfield College (B.A., 1979); University of Colorado (M.A., 1987); Georgetown University Law Center (J.D., 1991). *Member:* District of Columbia Bar; American Bar Association; American Intellectual Property Law Association. ***PRACTICE AREAS:*** Patent; Trademark; Copyright; Litigation. ***Email:*** kmatthews@colliershannon.com

DAVID J. ERVIN, born Honolulu, Hawaii, 1967; admitted to bar, 1992, Virginia; 1993, U.S. District Court, Eastern District of Virginia; U.S. Bankruptcy Court, Eastern District of Virginia; U.S. Court of Appeals, Fourth Circuit; 1995, District of Columbia and U.S. District Court, District of Columbia. *Education:* American University (B.A., cum laude, 1989); Washington College of Law, American University (J.D., cum laude, 1992). Law Clerk to the Hon. Leonie M. Brinkema, U.S. District Court, Eastern District of Virginia, 1992-1993. *Member:* Fairfax and American (Member, Litigation Section) Bar Assns; Virginia State Bar; District of Columbia Bar. ***PRACTICE AREAS:*** Intellectual Property; Litigation. ***Email:*** dervin@colliershannon.com

(This Listing Continued)

ANN M. PLAZA, born Omaha, Nebraska, August 16, 1967; admitted to bar, 1993, Maryland; 1995, District of Columbia. *Education:* University of Kansas (B.S., with distinction, 1990); Georgetown University (J.D., cum laude, 1993). ***Email:*** aplaza@colliershannon.com

ADAM H. GORDON, born Pawtucket, Rhode Island, October 28, 1966; admitted to bar, 1993, Connecticut; 1994, District of Columbia; 1998, U.S. District Court for the District of Columbia. *Education:* Yale University (B.A., 1988); University of York, York, England (M.A., with honors, 1990); George Washington University (J.D., with honors, 1993). *Member:* The District of Columbia Bar; American Bar Association. ***PRACTICE AREAS:*** International Trade. ***Email:*** agordon@colliershannon.com

MARK V. WILSON, born New York, N.Y., July 17, 1963; admitted to bar, 1993, New York (Not admitted in District of Columbia). *Education:* Simon's Rock College (B.A., 1984); Wake Forest University School of Law (J.D., 1992). Member: Association of the Bar of the City of New York, 1992-1993; New York State Bar Association, 1992-1993; American Bar Association, 1992-1993. [Specialist, U.S. Army, 1986-1988; Army National Guard, 1989-1992]. ***PRACTICE AREAS:*** Corporate; Securities. ***Email:*** mwilson@colliershannon.com

MARY JEAN FELL, born Orange, New Jersey, October 22, 1963; admitted to bar, 1995, New Jersey; 1997, District of Columbia. *Education:* College of the Holy Cross (B.A., 1986); Catholic University (J.D., cum laude, 1994). Note and Comment Editor, Catholic University Law Review, 1993-1994. *Member:* American Bar Association (Member, Antitrust Section). ***PRACTICE AREAS:*** Antitrust. ***Email:*** mjfell@colliershannon.com

DAVID R. YOHANNAN, born Plainfield, New Jersey, September 19, 1966; admitted to bar, 1994, Virginia; 1996, District of Columbia. *Education:* Pennsylvania State University (B.Sc., 1988); George Mason University (J.D., 1994). *Member:* American Bar Association (Intellectual Property Section); American Intellectual Property Law Association. ***PRACTICE AREAS:*** Patent, Trademark and Copyright; Litigation. ***Email:*** dyohannan@colliershannon.com

GARRETT B.M. DUARTE, born Aberdeen, Maryland, July 11, 1968; admitted to bar, 1995, New York; 1996, District of Columbia. *Education:* Princeton University (A.B., cum laude, 1990); University of Michigan (J.D., 1994). [Capt., USAR, 1990—]. ***PRACTICE AREAS:*** Antitrust; Litigation. ***Email:*** gduarte@colliershannon.com

JAMES M. PACIOUS, born Washington, D.C., January 4, 1970; admitted to bar, 1995, Pennsylvania; 1997, Georgia (Not admitted in District of Columbia). *Education:* Duke University (B.A., 1991); Villanova University (J.D., 1994). Member, American Bar Association, 1995-1997. ***PRACTICE AREAS:*** Trademarks. ***Email:*** jpacious@colliershannon.com

CARL R. KATZ, born Los Angeles, California, December 9, 1967; admitted to bar, 1996, California; 1998, District of Columbia. *Education:* University of California, San Diego (B.A., 1990); University of Southern California (J.D., 1995). ***PRACTICE AREAS:*** Antitrust; Consumer Protection. ***Email:*** ckatz@colliershannon.com

CHRISTY HALLAM DeSANCTIS, born Montclair, New Jersey, January 2, 1970; admitted to bar, 1996, New York; 1998, New Jersey and U.S. District Court, District of New Jersey; 1999, District of Columbia; 2000, U.S. District Court for the District of Columbia. *Education:* Duke University (B.A., magna cum laude, 1992); New York University (J.D., cum laude, 1995). Law Clerk, Hon. John W. Bissell, United States Court, District of New Jersey, 1996-1998. ***PRACTICE AREAS:*** Litigation; Government Relations. ***Email:*** cdesanctis@colliershannon.com

ADAM B. CRAMER, born Detroit, Michigan, May 4, 1970; admitted to bar, 1995, Maryland; 1998, District of Columbia. *Education:* Pennsylvania State University (B.S., with honors, 1992); Boston University (J.D., 1995). ***PRACTICE AREAS:*** Environmental Law. ***Email:*** acramer@colliershannon.com

JOHN N. COULBY, III, born Easton, Maryland, January 28, 1958; admitted to bar, 1996, Maryland; 1998, District of Columbia; registered to practice before U.S. Patent and Trademark Office. *Education:* Washington College (B.S., 1980); The Catholic University of America (M.S., 1984); Widener University School of Law (J.D., 1995). *Member:* Maryland State and American Bar Associations; American Intellectual Property Law Association. ***PRACTICE AREAS:*** Intellectual Property; Litigation. ***Email:*** jcoulby@colliershannon.com

JOSEPH J. GREEN, born New York, N.Y., July 10, 1971; admitted to bar, 1996, Virginia; 1997, District of Columbia. *Education:* University of Virginia (B.A., with high honors, 1993); Harvard University (J.D., cum laude, 1996); George Washington University Law School (LL.M., 2001). ***PRACTICE AREAS:*** Environmental. ***Email:*** jgreen@colliershannon.com

ERIC R. McCLAFFERTY, born Detroit, Michigan, February 20, 1958; admitted to bar, 1996, Maryland; 1997, District of Columbia; 1998, U.S. Court of International Trade and U.S. Court of Appeals for the Federal Circuit. *Education:* University of Michigan (B.A., with distinction, 1980; M.A., 1982); University of Virginia (J.D., 1996). *Member:* The District of Columbia Bar; Maryland State and American Bar Associations. ***LANGUAGES:*** French,

(This Listing Continued)

COLLIER SHANNON SCOTT, PLLC, Washington—Continued

Dutch. ***PRACTICE AREAS:*** International Trade; Import and Export Compliance; Business Immigration; Customs; Export Controls. ***Email:*** emcclafferty@colliershannon.com

THERESA ADAMS COATZEE, born Charlottesville, Virginia, April 7, 1968; admitted to bar, 1996, Colorado; 2001, District of Columbia. *Education:* Colgate University (A.B., 1990); University of Denver College of Law (J.D., 1996). *Member:* American Bar Association (Member, Antitrust Division). ***PRACTICE AREAS:*** Antitrust; Litigation; Consumer Protection. ***Email:*** tcoatzee@colliershannon.com

JOHN M. HERRMANN, born Bellefonte, Pennsylvania, May 28, 1969; admitted to bar, 1997, New York; 1998, U.S. Court of Appeals, Second Circuit and U.S. Court of International Trade; 1999, District of Columbia and U.S. Court of Appeals, Federal Circuit. *Education:* Stanford University (A.B., with honors, 1991); University of Virginia (J.D., 1996). Law Clerk to the Hon. Gregory W. Carman, Chief Judge, U.S. Court of International Trade, 1996-1998. ***PRACTICE AREAS:*** International Trade; Customs. ***Email:*** jherrman@colliershannon.com

GRACE W. KIM, born Seoul, South Korea, June 16, 1967; admitted to bar, 1996, Maryland; 1999, District of Columbia and U.S. Court of Appeals of International Trade. *Education:* University of California at Los Angeles (B.A., 1989); Washington College of Law, American University (J.D., 1996). *Member:* Maryland State and American (Member, International Trade Section) Bar Associations. ***LANGUAGES:*** Korean. ***PRACTICE AREAS:*** International Trade; Immigration. ***Email:*** gkim@colliershannon.com

JEFFREY A. KAUFFMAN, born Harrisburg, Pennsylvania, June 6, 1970; admitted to bar, 1997, District of Columbia. *Education:* Dickinson College (B.A., 1992); Syracuse University (J.D., 1996). ***PRACTICE AREAS:*** Antitrust; Consumer Protection. ***Email:*** jkauffman@colliershannon.com

DOUGLAS S. KANTOR, born Fort Myers, Florida, January 12, 1969; admitted to bar, 1996, Maryland (Not admitted in District of Columbia). *Education:* University of Virginia (B.A., 1991); Yale University (J.D., 1996). Deputy Chief of State and Special Counsel, U.S. Department of Housing and Urban Development, 1999-2000. *Member:* Maryland State Bar Association. ***PRACTICE AREAS:*** Government Relations; Litigation; Corporate Counseling. ***Email:*** dkantor@colliershannon.com

LISA GOLDBLATT, born New Haven, Connecticut, July 29, 1969; admitted to bar, 1997, Maryland; 1998, District of Columbia. *Education:* Yale University (B.A., cum laude, 1991); George Washington University (J.D., 1997). *Member:* Federal and American Bar Associations. ***PRACTICE AREAS:*** Litigation; Securities; Banking. ***Email:*** lgoldblatt@colliershannon.com

LANA L. LEIBY, born Ft. Riley, Kansas, September 20, 1973; admitted to bar, 1998, Maryland and New Jersey; 2000, District of Columbia. *Education:* Louisiana Tech University (B.S., magna cum laude, 1994); Tulane Law School (J.D., 1997). Outstanding Senior Scholar, Louisiana Tech University. ***Email:*** lleiby@colliershannon.com

THOMAS S. CUSHING III, born Lancaster, New York, July 4, 1967; admitted to bar, 1997, Virginia (Not admitted in District of Columbia). *Education:* Vanderbilt University (B.A., 1989); George Washington University (M.P.A., 1993); George Mason University School of Law (J.D., 1997). ***PRACTICE AREAS:*** Litigation. ***Email:*** tcushing@colliershannon.com

VICTORIA L. LIPPINCOTT, born El Paso, Texas, May 3, 1971; admitted to bar, 1997, Mississippi; 2001, District of Columbia. *Education:* University of Mississippi (B.P.A., 1993; J.D., 1997). ***Email:*** vlippincott@colliershannon.com

MERCEDES K. KELLEY, born Oconomowac, Wisconsin, October 15, 1973; admitted to bar, 1999, Virginia and U.S. District Court, Eastern District of Virginia (Not admitted in District of Columbia). *Education:* DePauw University (B.M., 1995); University of Michigan (J.D., 1998). ***PRACTICE AREAS:*** Advertising Law; Marketing Law; Consumer Protection; Internet Law; Electronic Commerce. ***Email:*** mkelley@colshan.com

NICHOLAS A. WIDNELL, born Pittsburgh, Pennsylvania, May 22, 1970; admitted to bar, 1999, District of Columbia and U.S. Court of Appeals, Fifth Circuit. *Education:* University of Chicago (B.A., 1992); George Mason University School of Law (J.D., 1998). ***PRACTICE AREAS:*** Antitrust. ***Email:*** nwidnell@colliershannon.com

ALEXANDER ZELIKSON, born Kiev, Ukraine, October 19, 1973; admitted to bar, 1998, Maryland; 1999, District of Columbia. *Education:* Loyola College (B.A., 1995); George Washington University (J.D., 1998). Phi Beta Kappa; Phi Alpha Theta. *Member:* American Bar Association. ***LANGUAGES:*** Russian. ***PRACTICE AREAS:*** Corporate Law; Real Estate Law. ***Email:*** azelikson@colliershannon.com

CHRISTIE L. GRYMES, born Houston, Texas, April 19, 1972; admitted to bar, 1998, Maryland; 1999, District of Columbia. *Education:* University of Texas (B.B.A., 1994); George Washington University (J.D., with honors, 1998).

(This Listing Continued)

Executive Articles Editor, The Environmental Lawyer, 1997-1998. Author: *State Advertising Law,* Advertising Law Guide (CCH), 2000. ***PRACTICE AREAS:*** Advertising and Marketing; Consumer Protection; Promotion Law; Internet Law. ***Email:*** cgrymes@colliershannon.com

CHRISTINA BECHAK PARASCANDOLA, admitted to bar, 2000, District of Columbia; 2001, U.S. Court of Appeals, District of Columbia Circuit. *Education:* American University in Cairo, Egypt; American University (B.A., 1992); Washington College of Law of American University (J.D., 1999). Managing Editor, Administrative Law Review, 1998-1999. *Member:* American Bar Association (Member, Section on Administrative Law and Regulatory Practice). ***PRACTICE AREAS:*** Administrative Law; Environmental Law. ***Email:*** cparascandola@colliershannon.com

ANDREW M. JOHNSON, born Grand Rapids, Michigan, October 18, 1974; admitted to bar, 1999, North Carolina. *Education:* Miami University (B.A., summa cum laude, 1996); University of Virginia (J.D ., 1999). *Member:* North Carolina State Bar. (Resident, Charlotte, North Carolina Office). ***PRACTICE AREAS:*** Corporate. ***Email:*** amjohnson@colliershannon.com

ELISA A. NEMIROFF, born Camden, New Jersey, June 2, 1974; admitted to bar, 1999, Maryland; 2000, District of Columbia. *Education:* Lehigh University (B.S., magna cum laude, 1996); George Washington University (J.D., with honors, 1999). ***PRACTICE AREAS:*** Advertising; Privacy. ***Email:*** enemiroff@colliershannon.com

ROBERT T.C. VERMYLEN, born New York, N.Y., July 14, 1972; admitted to bar, 2000, New York and New Jersey; 2001, District of Columbia. *Education:* Georgetown University (B.S., 1994; J.D., 1999). *Member:* New York State Bar Association; The District of Columbia Bar. ***PRACTICE AREAS:*** International Trade; Antitrust. ***Email:*** rvermylen@colliershannon.com

SAPNA DELACOURT, born Royal Oak, Michigan, December 29, 1973; admitted to bar, 2000, Michigan; 2001, District of Columbia. *Education:* University of Michigan (B.A., Political Science, 1996); Georgetown University (J.D., 2000). Pi Sigma Alpha. Recipient: University of Michigan Class Honors, 1994-1996; Saint Thomas Moore Award for Outstanding Publication in the field of Legal Ethics. ***PRACTICE AREAS:*** Competition; Antitrust. ***Email:*** sdelacourt@colliershannon.com

KRISTIN PIERCE BARRY, born Portland, Maine, November 9, 1973; admitted to bar, 2000, Maryland; 2001, District of Columbia. *Education:* Dartmouth College (A.B., Government, cum laude, 1996); Georgetown University Law Center (J.D., 2000). ***PRACTICE AREAS:*** Litigation. ***Email:*** kpierce@colliershannon.com

HALYE SUGARMAN, born Cleveland, Ohio, February 15, 1975; admitted to bar, 2001, District of Columbia and Massachusetts. *Education:* University of Florida (B.A., 1997); George Washington University (J.D., 2000). ***PRACTICE AREAS:*** Litigation. ***Email:*** hsugarman@colliershannon.com

JENNIFER E. McCADNEY, born Denver, Colorado, April 20, 1973; admitted to bar, 2001, New York and District of Columbia. *Education:* George Washington University (B.A., magna cum laude, 1995; J.D., with honors, 2000). ***PRACTICE AREAS:*** International Trade. ***Email:*** jmccadney@colliershannon.com

JOHN H.R. LANOU, born Alexandria, Virginia, March 20, 1972; admitted to bar, 2000, Virginia; 2001, District of Columbia. *Education:* University of Virginia (B.A., 1994); College of William & Mary (J.D., 2000). Member, Society for Evolutionary Analysis in the Law (SEAL). ***PRACTICE AREAS:*** Antitrust. ***Email:*** jlanou@colliershannon.com

W. DAVID HUBBARD, born Long Island, New York, February 21, 1975; (admission pending). *Education:* University of Maryland (B.A., 1997); Georgetown University (J.D., 2000). Phi Beta Kappa; Omicron Delta Kappa. *Member:* American Bar Association. ***Email:*** whubbard@colliershannon.com

MARK W. RYGIEL, born Pittsburgh, Pennsylvania, March 8, 1973; admitted to bar, 2000, Pennsylvania; registered to practice before U.S. Patent and Trademark Office (Not admitted in District of Columbia). *Education:* University of Notre Dame (B.S.M.E., 1995); George Washington University (J.D., 2000). *Member:* American Intellectual Property Law Association. ***PRACTICE AREAS:*** Intellectual Property; Patents; Trademarks; Copyrights. ***Email:*** mrygiel@colliershannon.com

JASON EDWARD MURPHY, born Memphis, Tennessee, July 19, 1975; admitted to bar, 2000, North Carolina. *Education:* University of Tennessee at Knoxville (B.A., summa cum laude, 1997); Duke University (J.D., with honors, 2000). Phi Beta Kappa. Editor, Journal of Law & Contemporary Problems, 1999-2000. Poet Laureate, University of Tennessee, 1997. *Member:* North Carolina State Bar (Member, Business Law Section). (Resident, Charlotte, North Carolina Office). ***PRACTICE AREAS:*** Corporate. ***Email:*** jmurphy@colliershannon.com

GONZALO E. MON, born Ridgewood, New Jersey, March 23, 1973; admitted to bar, 2000, Virginia; 2001, District of Columbia. *Education:* The

(This Listing Continued)

College of New Jersey (B.A., 1996); George Washington University (J.D., 2000). ***PRACTICE AREAS:*** Promotion Law; Advertising Law. ***Email:*** gmon@colliershannon.com

JAMIE M. LARMANN, born West Chester, Pennsylvania, April 1, 1976; (admission pending). *Education:* Cornell University (B.A., 1998); George Washington University (J.D., 2001). ***PRACTICE AREAS:*** Intellectual Property. ***Email:*** jlarmann@colliershannon.com

IVA C. SMITH, born San Diego, California, July 31, 1970; (admission pending). *Education:* University of California at Los Angeles (B.A., 1994); American University, Washington College of Law (J.D., 2001). *Member:* American Bar Association. ***PRACTICE AREAS:*** Litigation. ***Email:*** ismith@colliershannon.com

REFERENCE: Riggs National Bank, Washington, D.C.

SUSAN E. COLMAN

INTERNATIONAL SQUARE, PMB 400
1825 I STREET, N.W., SUITE 400
WASHINGTON, D.C. 20006
Telephone: 202-775-4937
Fax: 301-469-7862
Email: colman@patriot.net

Information Technology and Computer Law including Software Licensing and Piracy Litigation (International and Domestic). Trademark Prosecution and Litigation, Copyrights and Intellectual Property Law.

SUSAN E. COLMAN, born Detroit, Michigan, August 29, 1946; admitted to bar, 1981, Massachusetts; 1983, District of Columbia; 1988, U.S. District Court for the District of Columbia. *Education:* University of Michigan (B.S., 1968); Franklin Pierce Law Center (J.D., 1981). Author: "Consumer Protection in E-Commerce" Computer Law Association Conference, Milan, Italy, Oct. 2000; "Privacy Laws In The United States" Computer Law Association Madrid, Spain, June 1999; "Intellectual Property Law in the United States," (in Swedish), Teknisk Utblick, August-November, 1991; "The State of Software Copyright Protection in the United States," Nordic Intellectual Property Law Review, August, 1988; Co-Author: "Keep Competitors Off Your Intellectual Property" Phone & Magazine, Sept. 1999. Member, 1988— and Member, Board of Directors, 1989-1996, Washington, D.C. Chapter, Swedish-American Chamber of Commerce. Member, International Who's Who of E-Commerce Lawyers. *Member:* District of Columbia Bar; Frederick B. Abramson Memorial Foundation, (Board of Directors, 1992-1999; 2000-2002); Massachusetts Bar Association; Computer Law Association; Women's Bar Association (Chair, 75th Anniversary Planning Committee, 1990-1991). ***LANGUAGES:*** Swedish, Norwegian, Danish.

COMISKEY & HUNT

WASHINGTON, D.C.

(See McLean, Virginia)

Personal Counsel to Individuals, Families, Closely-Held Companies and Private Foundations. Crisis Management. Internet, Media, Entertainment and Sports. General Civil and Trial Practice in all State and Federal Courts in Virginia, the District of Columbia and Maryland. Federal and State Legislative and Administrative Law Practice.

CONDON & FORSYTH LLP

1016 SIXTEENTH STREET, N.W.
WASHINGTON, D.C. 20036
Telephone: 202-289-0500
Telecopier: 202-289-4524
Email: twhalen@condonlaw.com
URL: http://www.condonlaw.com

New York, N.Y. Office: 685 Third Avenue, 14th Floor. Telephone: 212-921-5100. Telecopier: 212-370-4453; 212-370-4483; 212-370-4465.

Los Angeles, California Office: 1801 Avenue of the Stars, Suite 1450, 90067. Telephone: 310-557-2030. Telecopier: 310-557-1299.

Civil and Commercial Litigation. Aviation, Business, Employment, International Trade, Products Liability, Administrative and Insurance Law.

RESIDENT PARTNERS

THOMAS J. WHALEN, born Jersey City, New Jersey, 1938; admitted to bar, 1964, District of Columbia and New Jersey; 1968, New York, U.S. Court of Appeals, Second Circuit and U.S. Court of Appeals for the District of Columbia Circuit; U.S. District Court for the District of Columbia and U.S. District Court, Southern and Eastern Districts of New York; 1976, U.S. Supreme Court. *Education:* St. Peter's College (A.B., 1960); Georgetown University Law Center (LL.B., 1963). Law Secretary to Judge Gerald McLaughlin, U.S. Court of Appeals, Third Circuit, 1963-1964. Representative of U.S. Government to Unidroit on Proposed International Convention on the Recognition of Security Interests in Mobile Equipment. *Member:* The District of Columbia Bar; Federal and American (Member, U.C.C. Committee of Business Law Section and Tort and Insurance Practice Section) Bar Associations. [Capt., U.S. Army, 1964-1967]. ***Email:*** twhalen@condonlaw.com

OF COUNSEL

EVELYN D. SAHR, born Washington, D.C., 1958; admitted to bar, 1983, District of Columbia; 1987, U.S. Court of Appeals, District of Columbia Circuit and U.S. Court of Appeals, Sixth and Tenth Circuits; 1997, U.S. Court of Appeals, Fourth Circuit. *Education:* University of North Carolina at Chapel Hill (B.A., with honors, 1980); George Washington University (J.D., 1983). Phi Beta Kappa; Phi Eta Sigma; Kappa Tau Alpha. Trial Attorney, U.S. Department of Justice, Civil Division, 1985-1989. *Member:* The District of Columbia Bar; Federal (Chairperson for Publications, Corporate and Association Counsel Division) and American Bar Associations. ***Email:*** esahr@condonlaw.com

SENIOR ATTORNEY

DAVID G. SCHRYVER, born Warren, Ohio, 1938; admitted to bar, 1963, Ohio (inactive); 1965, New York; 1988, District of Columbia. *Education:* St. Bonaventure University (B.A., 1960); Georgetown University (LL.B., 1963). Assistant General Counsel, Republic Steel Corporation, 1972-1984. Co-author: "Foreign Investment Registration," International Financial Law Review, July, 1987. *Member:* Federal (Former Chair, Corporate and Association Counsel Division) and American Bar Associations; The District of Columbia Bar. ***Email:*** dschryver@condonlaw.com

RESIDENT ASSOCIATES

JOHN J. DELANEY, born St. Louis, Missouri, 1957; admitted to bar, 1984, Maryland; 1987, District Of Columbia; U.S. Court of Appeals, Seventh and Eighth Circuits; 1988, U.S. Court of Appeals, District of Columbia and Fourth Circuits; 1993, U.S. Supreme Court. *Education:* University of Notre Dame (B.A., 1979); Catholic University of America (J.D., 1983). *Member:* The District of Columbia Bar; Bar Association of the District of Columbia; Montgomery County, Maryland State and American Bar Associations. ***Email:*** jdelaney@condonlaw.com

BRENDA A. HEFFERNAN, born Somerville, New Jersey, 1964; admitted to bar, 1990, New York and Connecticut; 1992, U.S. District Court, Southern and Eastern Districts of New York; 1993, U.S. Court of Appeals, Second Circuit; 1995, U.S. District Court, District of Connecticut and U.S. District Court, District of Maryland; 1997, Maryland; 1998, District of Columbia, Virginia and U.S. District Court, Eastern District of Virginia. *Education:* University of Rhode Island (B.A., 1986); Pace University (J.D., 1989); Boston University (LL.M., Banking and Financial Law, 1990). Co-Author: "The Effects of the Repeal of the 30% Withholding Tax on Interest Payments to Foreign Holders of Eurobonds," B.U. Int'l L.J. 59 (1991). *Member:* Alexandria, Federal and American Bar Associations. ***Email:*** bheffernan@condonlaw.com

CONLON, FRANTZ, PHELAN & PIRES, LLP

Established in 1985

SUITE 700, 1818 N STREET, N.W.
WASHINGTON, D.C. 20036
Telephone: 202-331-7050
Fax: 202-331-9306
Email: firm@CFPPLLAW.com
URL: http://www.lawyers.com/conlonfrantzphelan&pires

General, Trial and Appellate Practice. Civil Rights, Complex Litigation, Agriculture, Real Estate, Trade Association, Government Contracts, Personal Injury, Medical Malpractice, Administrative, Antitrust, Wills and Estates and Family Law.

FIRM PROFILE: Conlon, Frantz, Phelan & Pires, LLP is a general practice law firm serving clients in Washington, D.C., Maryland, Virginia and courts throughout the country. Our five partners average 25 years of experience practice and are committed to the highest quality of legal representation. The firm offers its clients the personal attention and efficiency available only from a small law firm.

Since 1997, the firm has been co-lead counsel in Pigford v. Glickman, the largest civil rights class action in the United States, representing over 22,500 African American farmers and their families against the United States Department of Agriculture. The Pigford settlement resulted in the first court-created private system for addressing civil rights violations. Recovery will exceed $1 billion.

(This Listing Continued)

CONLON, FRANTZ, PHELAN & PIRES, LLP, Washington—Continued

In November, 1999, the firm filed Keepseagle v. Glickman, a parallel suit to Pigford, on behalf of Native American farmers and ranchers against the United States Department of Agriculture. There are over 800 named plaintiffs representing a class of 19,000 Native American farmers.

The firm is co-lead counsel in Deloach v. Philip Morris, an antitrust class action on behalf of 475,000 tobacco growers and quota holders against the four major cigarette manufacturers. The complaint includes 6,427 named plaintiffs and seeks $69 billion in damages.

PARTNERS

DAVID J. FRANTZ, born Cleveland, Ohio, November 13, 1948; admitted to bar, 1974, Virginia and U.S. District Court for the Eastern District of Virginia; 1975, District of Columbia, U.S. District Court for the District of Columbia and U.S. Court of Appeals, Fourth Circuit; 1979, U.S. Court of Appeals for the District of Columbia Circuit; 1984, U.S. Court of Appeals for the Federal Circuit; 1986, U.S. District Court, District of Maryland; 1999, U.S. Supreme Court. *Education:* Georgetown University (B.S.B.A., 1970; J.D., 1974). *Member:* The District of Columbia Bar; Virginia State Bar; American Bar Association (Member, Litigation Section); Virginia Trial Lawyers Association. ***PRACTICE AREAS:*** Litigation; Trade Association Law; Commercial Law. ***Email:*** djf@cfppllaw.com

MICHAEL J. CONLON, born Washington, D.C., October 19, 1948; admitted to bar, 1974, Maryland; 1975, District of Columbia; 1977, U.S. Tax Court and U.S. District Court for the District of Columbia; 1979, U.S. Claims Court. *Education:* University of Notre Dame (A.B., cum laude, 1970); Georgetown University (J.D., 1974). Editor, Georgetown Law Journal, 1973-1974. *Member:* District of Columbia Bar (Lecturer, Continuing Legal Education Program, 1989—). ***PRACTICE AREAS:*** Corporate Law; Trade Association Law; Real Estate Law. ***Email:*** mjc@cfppllaw.com

BRIAN P. PHELAN, born Jersey City, New Jersey, May 3, 1948; admitted to bar, 1973, Maryland and U.S. District Court for the District of Columbia; 1974, District of Columbia and U.S. District Court, District of Maryland, including Trial Bar; U.S. Court of Appeals, Fourth Circuit. *Education:* Georgetown University (A.B., 1970); Georgetown Law Center (J.D., 1973). *Member:* The District of Columbia Bar (Member, Superior Court Digest Committee); Montgomery County and Maryland State Bar Associations; The Association of Trial Lawyers of America; District of Columbia Land Title Association. ***PRACTICE AREAS:*** Commercial Litigation; Personal Injury Law; Family Law; Estate Planning; Real Estate Law. ***Email:*** bpp@cfppllaw.com

ALEXANDER J. PIRES, JR., born Easton, Massachusetts, December 26, 1947; admitted to bar, 1973, District of Columbia; 1974, U.S. Claims Court; 1977, U.S. District Court for the District of Columbia; 1978, U.S. Supreme Court; 1982, U.S Court of Appeals, Fifth Circuit; 1984, Maryland; 1985, U.S. District Court for the District of Columbia Circuit and U.S. District Court, District of Maryland; 1987, U.S. Court of Appeals, Fourth Circuit; 1990, U.S. Court of Appeals, Eleventh and Federal Circuits. *Education:* Boston University (B.S.B.A., 1969); George Washington University (J.D., with honors, 1972; LL.M., 1978). Author: "Why the U.S. Claims Court is not a Viable Venue for Farmers: The U.S. Claims Court's Handling of Agricultural Cases, 1980-1990," University of Arkansas at Little Rock Law Review, Winter, 1993; "Federal Court Jurisdiction Over USDA/ASCS Cases," Indiana Law Review, Spring 1991. Adjunct Professor of Law, Georgetown University Law School, 1999—. Attorney, Land and Natural Resources Division, U.S. Department of Justice, 1973-1977. Senior Trial Attorney, Antitrust Division, U.S. Department of Justice, 1977-1980. Deputy Assistant Secretary, Housing, U.S. Department of Housing and Urban Development, 1980. Editor, D.C. Digest, 1988-1993; *Member:* District of Columbia Bar; Bar Association of the District of Columbia; Maryland State and American Bar Associations; The Association of Trial Lawyers of America; The Agricultural Law Association. [Capt., USAR, 1973]. ***REPORTED CASES:*** Pigford v. Glickman, 206 F.3d 1212 (D.C. Cir. 2000); Veg-Mix, Inc. v. USDA, 832 F.2d 601 (D.C.Cir. 1987); Pigford v. Glickman, 185 F.R.D. 82 (D.D.C. 1999); Pigford v. Glickman 182 F.R.D. 341 (D.D.C. 1998); Guy v. Glickman, 945 F.Supp. 324 (D.D.C. 1996); Vandervelde v. Yeutter 774 F.Supp 645 (D.D.C. 1991); Brick v. J.C. Bradford & Co., Inc. 677 F. Supp. 1251 (D.D.C. 1987); Esch v. Lyng, 665 F.Supp. 6 (D.D.C. 1987); Solon Automated Services, Inc. v. U.S. 658 F.Supp. 28 (D.D.C. 1987); U.S. v. American Tel. & Tel.Co., 83 F.R.D. 323 (D.D.C. 1979); Ft. Mojave Tribe v. U.S., 546 F.2d 429 (Ct.Cl. 1976). ***PRACTICE AREAS:*** Agricultural Law; Civil Rights; Litigation. ***Email:*** farmerslawyer@aol.com

MARY JEAN FASSETT, born Roseland, New Jersey, June 25, 1962; admitted to bar, 1987, Virginia, U.S. District Court, Eastern District of Virginia and U.S. Court of Appeals, Fourth Circuit; 1988, Maryland and District of Columbia; 1990, U.S. District Court, Western District of Virginia; 1991, U.S. District Court, District of Maryland; 1998, U.S. Bankruptcy Court, Eastern District of Virginia. *Education:* Bucknell University (B.A., cum laude, 1984); Georgetown University Law Center (J.D., 1987). *Member:* The District of Columbia Bar; Virginia State Bar; Maryland State Bar Association. ***PRACTICE AREAS:*** Litigation; Agricultural Law; Probate; Guardianship Law. ***Email:*** mjf@cfppllaw.com

ASSOCIATES

ANURAG VARMA, born Calgary, Alberta, Canada, November 15, 1972; admitted to bar, 1998, Colorado; 1999, U.S. District Court, District of Colorado; 2001, District of Columbia. *Education:* University of Alberta (B.Comm., 1994); University of Denver (J.D., 1997); Georgetown University Law Center (L.L.M., 1999). *Member:* American Bar Association; South Asian Bar Association (DC). ***LANGUAGES:*** Hindi. ***PRACTICE AREAS:*** Civil Rights; Class Actions; Government Relations. ***Email:*** av@cfppllaw.com

MICHELLE A. PILGRIM, born Jamaica, New York, May 5, 1969; admitted to bar, 1997, Maryland; 1998, U.S. District Court, District of Maryland; 2001, District of Columbia. *Education:* University of Maryland (B.A., 1991; J.D., 1996). ***PRACTICE AREAS:*** Civil Rights; Class Actions. ***Email:*** map@cfppllaw.com

INGRID HUTTO, born Columbia, South Carolina, August 27, 1967; admitted to bar, 1999, New York (Not admitted in District of Columbia). *Education:* Wofford College (B.A., 1990); Georgetown University Law Center (J.D., 1999). ***LANGUAGES:*** Spanish. ***PRACTICE AREAS:*** Civil Rights; Class Actions. ***Email:*** ih@cfppllaw.com

JAMES E. FISHER, II, born Washington D.C., September 6, 1969; admitted to bar, 1999, Maryland (Not admitted in District of Columbia). *Education:* Howard University (B.B.A., 1992); University of Maryland (J.D., 1997). ***PRACTICE AREAS:*** Civil Rights; Class Actions. ***Email:*** jef@cfppllaw.com

MALCOLM C. GRACE, born Atlantic City, New Jersey, January 18, 1972; admitted to bar, 1998, New York; 1999, District of Columbia. *Education:* Syracuse University (B.A., 1994; J.D., 1997). ***PRACTICE AREAS:*** Civil Rights; Class Actions. ***Email:*** mcg@cfpplaw.com

GREG J. KIRSCHNER, born Bristol, Connecticut, August 22, 1973; admitted to bar, 1999, Virginia (Not admitted in District of Columbia). *Education:* George Washington University (B.A., cum laude, 1995); Georgetown University Law Center (J.D., 1999). ***PRACTICE AREAS:*** Civil Rights; Class Actions. ***Email:*** gjk@cfppllaw.com

CASSANDRA D. MASON, born Baltimore, Maryland, December 26, 1969; admitted to bar, 1999, California (Not admitted in District of Columbia). *Education:* Towson State University (B.S., 1992); University of Southern California (J.D., 1998). ***PRACTICE AREAS:*** Civil Rights; Class Actions. ***Email:*** cm@cfpplaw.com

JENNY CELESTIN, born New York, New York, December 15, 1970; admitted to bar, 2001, District of Columbia. *Education:* Long Island University (B.A., 1993; M.S., 1995); University of the District of Columbia School of Law (J.D., 1998). ***PRACTICE AREAS:*** Civil Rights; Class Actions. ***Email:*** jc@cfpplaw.com

JOHN P. CONNOLLY

WASHINGTON, D.C.

(See Alexandria, Virginia)

Federal and State Court Litigation. Federal and State Administrative Law. Securities and Commodities Litigation and Arbitration. Commercial Litigation. Business Law. Employment Law.

CONSTANGY, BROOKS & SMITH, LLC

WASHINGTON, D.C.

(See Arlington, Virginia)

Labor Relations, Employment Litigation, Employee Benefits, Wage and Hour, OSHA.

H. CLAYTON COOK, JR.

TWO LAFAYETTE CENTRE
1133 21ST STREET, N.W., SUITE 500
WASHINGTON, D.C. 20036
Telephone: 202-293-8815
Facsimile: 202-293-7994
Email: PlimsollDC@aol.com

Maritime Law, Maritime Finance, Shipbuilding and Repair, Project Finance, Administrative Law, Admiralty.

(This Listing Continued)

FIRM PROFILE: Formerly General Counsel of the Maritime Administration and a partner in the Cadwalader, Wickersham & Taft and Pepper, Hamilton & Scheetz law firms, Mr. Cook provides counsel to vessel owners, shipyards, banks, maritime labor, domestic and foreign corporations and law firms, on U.S. government maritime laws, rules and programs, in a vessel finance and maritime administrative agency process.

H. CLAYTON COOK, JR., born Washington, D.C., March 25, 1935; admitted to bar, 1960, Colorado; 1961, New York; 1966, Pennsylvania; 1973, District of Columbia. *Education:* Princeton University (B.S., 1956); University of Virginia (LL.B., 1960). Order of the Coif. Executive Editor, University of Virginia Law Review, 1959-1960. Partner, Pepper, Hamilton & Scheetz, 1969, 1973, on assignment, Senior Tax Counsel, Sun Oil Company, Philadelphia, 1970. Partner, Cadwalader, Wickersham & Taft, 1974-1987; General Counsel, Maritime Administration, 1970-1973. *Member:* District of Columbia Bar; American Bar Association; Maritime Law Association of the United States (Procter in Admiralty); American Law Institute (Life Member). (Also Of Counsel to Bastianelli, Brown & Kelley, Chartered).

THE LAW OFFICE OF CURTIS C. COON, LLC

WASHINGTON, D.C.

(See Towson, Maryland)

Bankruptcy, Business Law, Real Estate, Construction Law, Civil Litigation. Trusts and Estates, Wills.

COOPER & KIRK, PLLC

SUITE 200
1500 K STREET, N.W.
WASHINGTON, D.C. 20005
Telephone: 202-220-9600
Fax: 202-220-9601
Email: info@coopekirk.com
URL: http://www.cooperkirk.com

Administrative, Appellate, Constitutional, Employment, Litigation, Supreme Court, Trial.

PARTNERS

CHARLES J. COOPER, born Dayton, Ohio, March 8, 1952; admitted to bar, 1977, Alabama; 1979, District of Columbia; 1980, Georgia. *Education:* University of Alabama (B.S., 1974; J.D., 1977). Omicron Delta Kappa; Jasons; Order of the Coif. Editor-in-Chief, Alabama Law Review, 1976-1977. Law Clerk to: Justice (now Chief Justice) William H. Rehnquist, U.S. Supreme Court, 1978-1979; Judge Paul H. Roney, U.S. Court of Appeals for the Fifth (now Eleventh) Circuit, St. Petersburg, Florida, 1977-1978. Department of Justice, Assistant Attorney General, Office of Legal Counsel, 1985-1988; Deputy Assistant Attorney General, Civil Rights Division, 1982-1985; Special Assistant to the Assistant Attorney General, Civil Rights Division, 1981-1982. Commission Member: National Commission On Responsibilities For Financing Postsecondary Education (appointed by President Reagan) (1990); The National Commission On Judicial Discipline and Removal (appointed by President Bush) (1991). Public Member, The Administrative Conference of the United States (1991). Member, Standing Committee on Rules of Practice and Procedure of the Judicial Conference of the United States. *Member:* American Law Institute; American Academy of Appellate Lawyers; Federalist Society (Chairman, Civil Rights Practice Group). ***PRACTICE AREAS:*** Trial and Appellate Litigation. ***Email:*** ccooper@cooperkirk.com

VINCENT J. COLATRIANO, born Phillipsburg, New Jersey, August 6, 1965; admitted to bar, 1990, Maryland; 1991, District of Columbia, U.S. District Court, District of Maryland and U.S. District Court, District of Columbia; 1992, U.S. Court of Federal Claims and U.S. Court of Appeals, Federal Circuit; 1993, U.S. Court of Appeals, District of Columbia and U.S. Supreme Court. *Education:* George Washington University (B.A., summa cum laude, 1987); National Law Center, George Washington University (J.D., with highest honors, 1990). Member, George Washington University Law Review, 1989-1990. ***PRACTICE AREAS:*** Trial and Appellate Litigation; Administrative Law and Litigation; Litigation; Constitutional Law. ***Email:*** vcolatriano@cooperkirk.com

ROBERT J. CYNKAR, born Chicago, Illinois, April 22, 1952; admitted to bar, 1977, Illinois; 1978, District of Columbia; 1984, Virginia. *Education:* Princeton University (A.B., magna cum laude, 1974); New York University (J.D., 1977). Member, New York University Law Review, 1976-1977. Minority Counsel, Subcommittee on Improvements in Judicial Machinery, United States Senate Judiciary Committee, 1979-1981. General Counsel, Subcommittee on Regulatory Reform, United States Senate Judiciary Committee, 1981-1983. Assistant U.S. Attorney, U.S. Attorney's Office, Eastern District of Virginia, 1983-1985. Special Assistant to the Attorney General, U.S. Department of Justice, 1985. Deputy Assistant Attorney General, Civil Division, U.S. Department of Justice, 1985-1988. Chair, Committee on Government Organization, ABA Administrative Law Section, 1997-1999. ***PRACTICE AREAS:*** Trial and Appellate Litigation; Regulatory Litigation; Constitutional Litigation. ***Email:*** rcynkar@cooperkirk.com

MICHAEL W. KIRK, born Omaha, Nebraska, January 19, 1963; admitted to bar, 1989, New York; 1990, District of Columbia. *Education:* Georgetown University (A.B., cum laude, 1985); Northwestern University (J.D., cum laude, 1988). Order of the Coif. Executive Editor, Journal of Criminal Law and Criminology. Law Clerk to Hon. James L. Ryan, U.S. Court of Appeals, 6th Circuit, 1988-1989. ***PRACTICE AREAS:*** Trial and Appellate Litigation; Constitutional Litigation; Administrative Litigation. ***Email:*** mkirk@cooperkirk.com

DAVID H. THOMPSON, born New York, N.Y., November 1, 1968; admitted to bar, 1995, New York; 1996, District of Columbia. *Education:* Harvard University (A.B., magna cum laude, 1991; J.D., cum laude, 1994). Phi Beta Kappa. ***Email:*** dthompson@cooperkirk.com

ASSOCIATES

HAMISH P. M. HUME, born Oxford, United Kingdom, February 21, 1968; admitted to bar, 1995, New York; 1996, District of Columbia. *Education:* Yale University (B.A., cum laude, 1990); Oxford University (B.A., 1992); University of Virginia (J.D., 1994). Editorial Board, Virginia Law Review, 1993-1994. Author: "The Business of Learning," 81 Virginia L. Rev. 887, April 1995. *Member:* The District of Columbia Bar; New York State Bar Association. ***LANGUAGES:*** Spanish. ***PRACTICE AREAS:*** Trial and Appellate Litigation; Constitutional Litigation; Tax Litigation. ***Email:*** hhume@cooperkirk.com

VICTOR J. WOLSKI, born New Brunswick, New Jersey, November 14, 1962; admitted to bar, 1992, California; 1993, U.S. District Court, Eastern District of California; 1994, Washington; 1996, Oregon (Not admitted in District of Columbia). *Education:* University of Pennsylvania (B.A.B.S., 1984); University of Virginia (J.D., 1991). Law Clerk, Hon. Vaughn R. Walker, U.S. District Court, Northern District of California, 1991-9992. Speechwriter to Secretary of Agriculture Richard Lyng, 1988. Property rights attorney, Pacific Legal Foundation, 1992-1997. Tax Counsel to Senator Connie Mack, 1997-2000. General Counsel, Joint Economic Committee, U.S. Congress, 1999-2000. *Member:* The Federalist Society. ***PRACTICE AREAS:*** Constitutional Litigation (8); Trial Practice; Appellate Practice; Land Use; Administrative Law (5); Tax Law. ***Email:*** vwolski@cooperkirk.com

BRIAN STUART KOUKOUTCHOS, born Indianapolis, Indiana, May 20, 1958; admitted to bar, 1986, Massachusetts; 1988, U.S. Supreme Court; U.S. Court of Appeals, Fifth Circuit (Not admitted in District of Columbia). *Education:* Haverford College (B.A., History, with high honors, 1980); Harvard University (J.D., magna cum laude, 1983). Law Clerk, Hon. Judge Howard Turrentine, Southern District of California, 1983-1984. Author: "Cases in Constitutional Law," Prentice-Hall, 9th ed. 2000; "Solomon Meets Galileo (And Isn't Quite Sure What To Do With Him)," 15 Cardozo Law Review 2237, Spring 1994; "Constitutional Kinetics: The Independent Counsel Case and the Separation of Powers," 23 Wake Forest L. Rev. 635, 1988; American Constitutional Law, Vol. I, 3rd Edition (Collaborator with Laurence H. Tribe) 2000; American Constitutional Law 2d ed. (Collaborator with Laurence H. Tribe)1988; "God Save This Honorable Court: How the Choice of Supreme Court Justices Shapes our History" (Collaborator with Laurence H. Tribe) 1985. Senior Teaching Fellow, Harvard University, 1985-1986. Visiting Professor, Constitutional Law & History, Haverford College, 1996— Iran-Contra Investigation Associate Independent Counsel, 1988 and 1993. Special Assistant Attorney General, Commonwealth of Massachusetts, 1995-1998. *Member:* Massachusetts Bar Association. ***REPORTED CASES:*** Ortiz v. Fiberboard, 119 S.Ct. 2295 (1999); Unum Life Ins. Co. v. Ward, 119 S.Ct. 1380 (1999); South Dakota v. Bourland, 508 U.S. 679 (1993); Amchem Products v. Windsor, 521 U.S. 591 (1997); Daubert v. Merrell Dow Pharmaceuticals, 509 U.S. 579 (1993); Ran-Dav's Country Kosher v. New Jersey, 129 N.J. 141 (1992), cert. denied, 507 U.S. 952 (1993); Cipollone v. Liggett, 505 U.S. 504 (1992); Adams Fruit v. Barrett, 494 U.S. 638 (1990); Sable Communications v. FCC, 492 U.S. 115 (1989); Pennzoil v. Texaco, 481 U.S.1 (1987); Fisher v. City of Berkeley, 475 U.S. 260 (1986); Northeast Bancorp v. Bd. of Governors, 472 U.S. 159 (1985). ***PRACTICE AREAS:*** Constitutional Law; Appellate Practice. ***Email:*** bkoukoutchos@cooperkirk.com

(This Listing Continued)

THEODORE M. COOPERSTEIN, P.C.

1815 PENNSYLVANIA AVENUE, N.W.
SUITE 501
WASHINGTON, D.C. 20006
Telephone: 202-331-7895
Fax: 202-331-9841
800-732-5118
Email: tmc@coopersteinlaw.com
URL: http://www.coopersteinlaw.com

Commercial Litigation, Civil Litigation with International Emphasis, and Federal Constitutional and Civil Rights Litigation, in both Trial and Appeals Courts.

THEODORE M. COOPERSTEIN, born Livermore, California, March 26, 1963; admitted to bar, 1988, New Hampshire and New York; 1990, District of Columbia; 2001, U.S. District Court, District of Maryland and U.S. Court of Appeals, Third Circuit. admitted to bar, 1988, New York and New Hampshire; 1989, U.S. District Court, Eastern and Southern Districts of New York; 1990 District of Columbia; 1991, U.S. District Court, District of Columbia and U.S. Court of Appeals, District of Columbia Circuit; 1992, U.S. Court of Appeals, Second Circuit, U.S. Supreme Court and U.S. District Court, Northern District of New York; 1993, U.S. District Court, District of New Hampshire and U.S. Court of Appeals, Ninth Circuit; 1998, U.S. Court of Federal Claims and U.S. Court of Appeals, Federal Circuit; 1999, U.S. Court of Appeals, Fourth Circuit and U.S. Court of Appeals, Eighth Circuit; 2000, U.S. Court of Appeals, Fifth Circuit. *Education:* Dartmouth College (A.B., summa cum laude, 1984); Stanford University (J.D., 1987); Georgetown University (LL.M., International Law, with distinction, 1999). Phi Beta Kappa. Note Editor, Stanford Law Review. Author: "Sensing Leave for One's Takings," 7 Stanford Environmental Law Journal 49, 1988. Law Clerk to Hon. Morris S. Arnold, U.S. District Judge, Western District of Arkansas, 1987-1988. Member, Federalist Society for Law and Public Policy (New York Lawyers' Chapter, 1988-1995; Washington D.C. Lawyers' Chapter, 1995—; Vice-Chair, Civil Rights Practice Group). Vice-Chairman, International and National Security Law Practice Group, 1997-1999. Special Assistant District Attorney, New York County, New York, 1990-1992. Assistant General Counsel, Federal Bureau of Investigation, 1995-1998. Member, Army & Navy Club, Washington, D.C.; Supreme Court Historical Society, 1997—. *Member:* New Hampshire and American (Member, Sections on: Litigation; International Law; Business Torts Committee; Central and Eastern European Law Initiative) Bar Associations; The District of Columbia Bar; International Bar Association (Member, Section on Legal Practice; Section on Business Law); American Society of International Law. [Major, Military Intelligence, Civil Affairs, U.S. Army Reserve, 1983—]. ***LANGUAGES:*** German and French. ***PRACTICE AREAS:*** Federal Litigation; Appellate Practice; Civil Rights Section 1983; Foreign Sovereign Immunities Act; International Litigation; U.S. Supreme Court Litigation.

COOTER, MANGOLD, TOMPERT & WAYSON, L.L.P.

5301 WISCONSIN AVENUE, N.W., SUITE 500
WASHINGTON, D.C. 20015
Telephone: 202-537-0700
Fax: 202-364-3664
Email: edwayson@waysonlaw.com
URL: http://www.lawyers.com/cmt&w

Annapolis, Maryland Office: 191 Main Street. 21401. Telephone: 410-268-2020. Fax: 410-268-4576.

General Litigation, Commercial Transactions, Governmental Relations, Banking and Gaming Law.

DALE A. COOTER, born Syracuse, New York, August 28, 1948; admitted to bar, 1975, Maryland; 1976, District of Columbia 1984, Virginia. *Education:* State University of New York at Fredonia (B.A., cum laude, 1970); Georgetown University (J.D., 1975). Editor, Georgetown University Law Journal, 1973-1975. Adjunct Professor, Georgetown University Law Center, 1985-1994. ***Email:*** dcooter@cootermangold.com

DONNA S. MANGOLD, born Chicago, Illinois, October 1, 1956; admitted to bar, 1981, District of Columbia; 1986, Maryland. *Education:* Barat College (B.A., magna cum laude, 1978); Georgetown University Law Center (J.D., 1981). Associate Editor, Law and Policy in International Business, 1980-1981. ***Email:*** dmangold@cootermangold.com

JAMES E. TOMPERT, born Battle Creek, Michigan, July 21, 1954; admitted to bar, 1981, District of Columbia; 1985, Maryland; 1986, Virginia. *Education:* Duke University (B.A., 1976); University of Michigan (J.D., 1981). Legislative Assistant, Congressman Philip E. Ruppe, U.S. House of Representatives, Washington, D.C., 1976-1978. ***Email:*** jtompert@cootermangold.com

(This Listing Continued)

KAREN SIMONEK KARAS, born Chicago, Illinois, April 29, 1960; admitted to bar, 1985, Illinois; 1988, District of Columbia; 1994, Maryland. *Education:* Barat College (B.A., cum laude, 1982); Georgetown University (J.D., 1985). Associate Editor, The Tax Lawyer, 1984-1985. ***Email:*** kkaras@cootermangold.com

ELIZABETH A. McFARLAND, born Santa Monica, California, March 28, 1965; admitted to bar, 1993, Maryland; 1994, California and District of Columbia; 1995, Arizona and U.S. District Court, Central District of California. *Education:* University of California at Los Angeles (B.A., 1987); Georgetown University (J.D., 1993). Editor, Georgetown Immigration Law Journal, 1990-1992. Consultant to Government of Estonia regarding antitrust legislation, 1992. Adjunct Professor, Santa Barbara College of Law, 1995. ***Email:*** emcfarland@cootermangold.com

COPILEVITZ & CANTER, LLC

Established in 1977
1815 H STREET NW
SUITE 501
WASHINGTON, D.C. 20006
Telephone: 202-861-0740
Fax: 202-331-9841
Email: Copcandc@aol.com
URL: http://www.exempttaxlaw.com

Kansas City, Missouri Office: 423 West 8th Street, Suite 400, 64105. Telephone: 816-472-9000. Fax: 816-472-5000.

Federal and State Tax-Exempt Organizations, Charitable Fund-raising, Registrations of Charities and Fund-raisers, Nonprofit, Not-For-Profit and Charity Organizations Practice, Nonprofit and Tax-Exempt Organization Counsel, Charitable Giving Law, Administrative Agency Practice, Constitutional and First Amendment Practice, Telemarketer and Telemarketing Law.

FIRM PROFILE: Copilevitz & Canter, LLC, with offices in Kansas City, Missouri and Washington, D.C. provides specialized legal services to nonprofit organizations, professional fund-raisers and commercial telemarketers with legal counsel and resource publications in all areas of First Amendment law relevant to this practice.

REPRESENTATIVE CLIENTS: National Geographic Society; Reese Brothers; C.A.R.E.; Children's Wish Foundation International, Inc.; Consumers Union; DialAmerica Marketing, Inc.; Kiwanis International Foundation; National Children's Cancer Society, Inc.; Paralyzed Veterans of America; World Vision; World Wildlife Fund; APAC Customer Services; Carnival Cruise Lines; Center Financial Services; Capital One; Option One Mortgage Co.; National Foundation for Cancer Research; American Kidney Fraud; National Development Council; National Center for Public Policy Research.

(For Complete Biographical Data on All Personnel, see Professional Biographies at Kansas City, Missouri)

COUCH WHITE, LLP

700 13TH STREET N.W., SUITE 950
WASHINGTON, D.C. 20005
Telephone: 202-434-4503
Fax: 202-434-4562
Email: CouchWhiteBrenn@Global2000.net
URL: http://www.couchwhite.com

Albany, New York Office: 540 Broadway, P.O. Box 22222. Telephone: 518-426-4600. Telecopier: 518-426-0376.

Administrative and General Civil Practice before all Federal and State Courts and Administrative Agencies; Automotive Law; Construction; Surety; Energy Law; Environmental Law; Commercial; Real Estate; Probate and Bankruptcy Litigation; Appellate Practice; Labor; Health Care; Government Relations; Trusts; Estate Planning and Administration; Federal and New York Taxation; Internal Revenue Service Practice.

FIRM PROFILE: Couch White is a law firm that reflects the needs of an extensive business clientele. The firm's practice includes substantial work in the following areas: electricity and natural gas; cogeneration; health care; commercial litigation including antitrust and products liability; government relations; construction law; automotive law; commercial transactions; and private client services.

Couch White is a firm committed to service and excellence. The firm's success in representing its clients in significant matters, and the presence of Honorable Lawrence H. Cooke, Former Chief Judge of the State of New York as Senior Counsel are testaments to that commitment.

MEMBERS OF FIRM

ALGIRD F. WHITE, JR., born Hudson, New York, October 12, 1947; admitted to bar, 1973, New York and U.S. District Court, Northern District of

(This Listing Continued)

New York; 1978, U.S. Supreme Court; 1980, U.S. District Court, Eastern and Southern Districts of New York; 1981, U.S. Court of Appeals, Second Circuit; 1982, U.S. District Court, Western District of New York (Not admitted in District of Columbia). *Education:* Colgate University (A.B., 1969); Boston University (J.D., 1972). *Member:* Albany County, New York State and American Bar Associations. ***PRACTICE AREAS:*** Antitrust; Energy Law. ***Email:*** awhite@couchwhite.com

BARBARA S. BRENNER, born New York, N.Y., May 12, 1942; admitted to bar, 1979, New York and U.S. District Court, Northern District of New York; 1982, U.S. Court of Appeals, District of Columbia Circuit; 1983, U.S. Supreme Court, U.S. Court of Appeals, Second Circuit and U.S. District Court, Western District of New York (Not admitted in District of Columbia). *Education:* University of Rochester (B.A., magna cum laude, 1964) Phi Beta Kappa; Albany Law School of Union University (J.D., cum laude, 1978). Member, Justinian Society. Member, Albany Law Review, 1977. Law Assistant, New York Supreme Court, Appellate Division, Third Department, 1978-1980. *Member:* Albany County, New York State and American Bar Associations; Energy Bar Association. ***PRACTICE AREAS:*** Energy Law. ***Email:*** bbrenner@couchwhite.com

ROBERT M. LOUGHNEY, born Scranton, Pennsylvania, July 25, 1955; admitted to bar, 1981, Pennsylvania; 1987, New York; 1988, U.S. District Court, Northern District of New York (Not admitted in District of Columbia). *Education:* University of Scranton (B.S., magna cum laude, 1977); Temple University (J.D., cum laude, 1981). *Member:* Albany County, New York State (Member, Section on Environmental Law) and American (Member, Sections on: Litigation; Corporation; Natural Resources, Energy and Environmental Law) Bar Associations. ***PRACTICE AREAS:*** Energy Law; Environmental Law. ***Email:*** rloughney@couchwhite.com

LEONARD H. SINGER, born Boston, Massachusetts, June 8, 1958; admitted to bar, 1984, New York and U.S. Army Court of Military Review; 1987, Missouri and U.S. District Court, Western District of Missouri; 1988, U.S. District Court, Northern District of New York; 1995, U.S. Court of Appeals, Second Circuit (Not admitted in District of Columbia). *Education:* State University of New York at Albany (B.A., cum laude, 1980); State University of New York at Buffalo (J.D., cum laude, 1983). Member, 1982 and Senior Editor, 1983, Buffalo Law Review. *Member:* Albany County, New York State and American Bar Associations. [Captain, Judge Advocate General's Corps, U.S Army, 1983-1987]. ***PRACTICE AREAS:*** Energy Law; Telecommunications Law; Commercial Litigation. ***Email:*** lsinger@couchwhite.com

DOREEN UNIS SAIA, born North Adams, Massachusetts, November 3, 1966; admitted to bar, 1994, New York (Not admitted in District of Columbia). *Education:* Williams College (B.A., 1988); Washington & Lee University (J.D., magna cum laude, 1993). National Moot Court Team. *Member:* New York State and American Bar Associations. ***PRACTICE AREAS:*** Energy Law; Construction Law; Commercial Litigation; Appellate Practice. ***Email:*** dsaia@couchwhite.com

REPRESENTATIVE CLIENTS: Alcan Rolled Products; Anheuser-Busch, Inc.; Agvar Chemicals Inc.; Auburn Steel Corp.; Bethlehem Steel Corp.; Blue Circle Cement, Inc.; Callanan Industries, Inc.; Carrier Corp.; C.L. King & Associates, Inc.; Corning Incorporated; General Accident and Insurance Company; General Mills, Inc.; General Motors Corp.; Health Plan Association; IBM Corp.; Occidental Chemical Corp.; Praxair, Inc.; Revere Copper Products; Southern Energy, Inc.; Tougher Industries, Inc.; U.W. Marx, Inc.; Sweet Associates, Inc.; Enterprise Rent-a-car; Sprint; D&H Railroad; NYS Auto Repair Technicians Association; NYS Alliance for Children with Special Needs; NY Manufactures Housing Association; Associated of General Contractors of America, New York State Chapter, Inc.; General Building Contractors of New York State, Inc.
REFERENCE: M & T Bank.

COUDERT BROTHERS LLP

1627 I STREET, N.W.
WASHINGTON, D.C. 20006
Telephone: 202-775-5100
Telecopier: 202-775-1168
For attorney e-mails use: lastnamefirstinitial@coudert.com
URL: http://www.coudert.com

REVISERS OF THE FRANCE LAW DIGEST FOR THIS DIRECTORY.

Offices also at: New York; Los Angeles; Palo Alto; San Francisco; San Jose; Denver; Paris; London; Antwerp; Brussels; Ghent; Berlin; Frankfurt; Munich; Milan; Beijing; Hong Kong; Shanghai; Singapore; Sydney; Tokyo; Almaty; Moscow; St. Petersburg; Bangkok; Montreal.

General Practice.

MEMBERS OF THE FIRM

STEPHEN A. BEST, born Washington, DC, May 26, 1964; admitted to bar, 1989, VA; 1990, DC. *Education:* Washington & Lee University (B.A., cum laude, 1986); University of Texas at Austin (J.D., 1989). Author: "The FBI is Asking," Legal Times, October 1, 2001. Adjunct Professor of Trial Advocacy, University of Virginia Trial Advocacy Institute, 1997-2001 and George Washington University National Law Center, 1997-2000. Listed in Who's Who in American Law. Assistant Commonwealth's Attorney for Fairfax County, Virginia 1990-1995. Assistant United States Attorney for the District of Columbia, 1995-1998. *Member:* American Bar Association (Section of Litigation, Committee Chair, 1997-2001). ***PRACTICE AREAS:*** White Collar Criminal Defense; Complex Civil Litigation; Internal Investigations. ***Email:*** bests@coudert.com

MICHAEL R. CALABRESE, born Atlantic City, NJ, May 28, 1956; admitted to bar, 1982, DC. *Education:* Georgetown University (B.S.F.S., 1978); University of Virginia (J.D., 1982). Phi Beta Kappa. Executive Editor, Virginia Journal of International Law, 1981-1982. Law Clerk to the Honorable Albert V. Bryan, Circuit Judge, U.S. Court of Appeals, Fourth Circuit, 1982. *Member:* American and International Bar Associations; American Society of International Law. ***PRACTICE AREAS:*** International Corporate; Commercial Regulation; Trade Regulation. ***Email:*** calabresem@coudert.com

WILLIAM K. COULTER, born Wilmington, DL, 1946; admitted to bar, 1971, PA; 1972, DC. *Education:* Franklin & Marshall College (B.A., honors, 1968); University of Pittsburgh (J.D., honors, 1971); College of William & Mary (1975); University of Virginia (1979). Editor: FCBA Int'l. Comm. Practice Handbook (1985); ABA Public Utility Law Reports (1980). Deputy Attorney General, Dept. of Justice, Wilmington, Del. (1970). Legal Advisor, FCC, DOD and State Department. Chairman, Int'l Telecom Comm., Fed. Comm. Bar Assn. (1990). Comm. Counsel to Sen. Howard Baker (1993-1998). Vice Pres. & Gen. Counsel, COMSAT (1987-1993). ***LANGUAGES:*** French. ***PRACTICE AREAS:*** Telecommunications; International; Commercial Transactions. ***Email:*** coulterw@coudert.com

RICHARD N. DEAN, born Providence, RI, March 5, 1955; admitted to bar, 1981, NY; 1995, DC. *Education:* Vanderbilt University (B.A., 1977); University of Virginia (M.A., 1980; J.D., 1980). Senior Editor, Virginia Journal of International Law, 1979-1980. Author: "Considering Business Opportunities in the Soviet Union in the 1990"s," 24 Vanderbilt Journal of Transnational Law, No. 2, 1991; "The Russian Legal System: Ten Years Later," *Private Investments Abroad,* Matthew Bender & Co., 1997. Lecturer, University of Virginia School of Law, 1993—. ***LANGUAGES:*** Russian. ***PRACTICE AREAS:*** Russian Law; Corporate; Foreign Corrupt Practices Act. ***Email:*** deanr@coudert.com

KAY GEORGI, born Ithaca, NY, March 28, 1963; admitted to bar, 1990, NY and DC. *Education:* Cornell University (B.A., 1985; J.D., with specialization in Int'l Legal Affairs, summa cum laude, 1989). Phi Beta Kappa; Order of the Coif. Co-Author: "Treatment of Russia in Antidumping Investigations - A Call for Action;" "The Greening of Extraterritorial Jurisdiction in United States Law: What Are The Limits;" "Anti-Dumping Law: Recent Changes in U.S. and EU:" "Introduction to U.S. Section 301 Investigations, Int'l Trade Law & Reg; "Anti-Dumping Law & Prac. in Can., the EC and US After IWTO Anti-Dumping Agt." *Member:* New York State and American Bar Associations; The District of Columbia Bar. ***LANGUAGES:*** Italian. ***PRACTICE AREAS:*** International Trade. ***Email:*** georgik@coudert.com

TARA KALAGHER GIUNTA, born Cape Cod, MA, May 26, 1959; admitted to bar, 1986, PA; 1987, DC. *Education:* Tufts University (B.A.cum laude, 1981); Catholic University of America (J.D., 1986). Author: "Financing Options for Telecom Projects in U.S.," FCBA Int'l Practice Handbook (1993); "Treatment of Intellectual Property Between Developing Economies of East Asia and The Developed World," PTC 94 Proceedings; Building Blocks to Forging A Robust Telecommunications Infrastructure, Asian Pacific Telecommunications Finance & Trade Colloquium, New Delhi, India (1997), Reprinted International Law News, ABA (1998). *Member:* The District of Columbia Bar; American Bar Association; Federal Communications Bar Association. ***PRACTICE AREAS:*** Telecommunications; Satellites; Aerospace. ***Email:*** giuntat@coudert.com

JOHN M. GURLEY, born Sayre, OK, June 21, 1955; admitted to bar, 1984, KS; 1986, DC. *Education:* University of Kansas (B.A., 1977); Alliance Francaise, Paris, France (1978); International Institute of Human Rights, Strasbourg, France (1982); University of Kansas School of Law (J.D., 1983). Legal Intern, Subcommittee on Courts, United States Senate, 1982. *Member:* The District of Columbia Bar. ***LANGUAGES:*** French. ***PRACTICE AREAS:*** International Trade; Customs Law.

MARIAN M. HAGLER, born Klamath Falls, OR, July 13, 1962; admitted to bar, 1990, California; 1991, District of Columbia. *Education:* University of California at Berkeley (A.B., magna cum laude, 1984); Georgetown University (M.S.F.S., 1990; J.D., cum laude, 1990). Phi Beta Kappa. U.S. Dept. of Treasury, OGC (IA), 1999-2001. *Member:* District of Columbia Bar; State Bar of California; American Bar Association. ***LANGUAGES:*** Russian. ***PRACTICE AREAS:*** Corporate; Russia; Kazakhstan. ***Email:*** haglerm@coudert.com

JANET HERNANDEZ, born Jersey City, NJ, April 26, 1966; admitted to bar, 1992, Florida (Not admitted in District of Columbia). *Education:* Florida International University (B.A., 1988); University of Pennsylvania (J.D., 1991). Co-Author: with Tara Giunta, "Financing International Telecommunications Projects in Asia," Connect-World-Asia, First Quarter 1999. Author: "Market Access Issues confronting Satellite Ventures," Space Business International, March 1999; "Telecommunications Privatisations in Central America," Connect-World-Latin America, Third Quarter 1998; "Creation of New Regulatory

(This Listing Continued)

COUDERT BROTHERS LLP, Washington—Continued

Regimes in the African Region," African Communications, September/October 1998; Chapter Two on Africa in Volume I: General Trends in Telecommunications Reform, International Telecommunication Union, 1998. *Member:* The Florida Bar; American, Federal Communications, Hispanic and Inter-American Bar Associations. ***LANGUAGES:*** Spanish. ***PRACTICE AREAS:*** Telecommunications. ***Email:*** hernandezj@coudert.com

TEDSON J. MEYERS, born Bayonne, NJ, May 6, 1928; admitted to bar, 1953, DC; 1957, NY; 1971, U.S. Supreme Court. *Education:* The Ohio State University and New York University (A.B., 1949; M.A., 1950); Harvard Law School (J.D., 1953). Assistant to the Chairman, Federal Communications Commission, 1961-1962. *Member:* The District of Columbia Bar; American (Council Member, Section on Science and Technology, 1983—; Chairman, International Telecommunications Committee, 1983-1987; Member, Section on International Law and Practice) and Federal Communications Bar Associations. ***PRACTICE AREAS:*** Telecommunications; Aerospace. ***Email:*** tmeyers@tedson.com

ROBERT F. PIETROWSKI, JR., born Pasadena, CA, February 7, 1945; admitted to bar, 1974, DC; 1978, U.S. Supreme Court. *Education:* Stanford University (B.S., Petroleum Engineering, 1970); University of Virginia (J.D., 1973). Phi Delta Phi. Member, ICSID Panel of Arbitrators, 1988-1994. *Member:* International Law Association; Union Internationale des Avocats; International Bar Association; American Society of International Law. Fellow, American Bar Foundation. [1st Lt., U.S. Army, 1966-1969]. ***LANGUAGES:*** French. ***PRACTICE AREAS:*** International Arbitration. ***Email:*** pietrowskir@coudert.com

VERA ANN RECHSTEINER, born Puerto Armuelles, Panamá, July 21, 1957; admitted to bar, 1985, Maryland (Not admitted in District of Columbia). *Education:* Georgetown University, School of Foreign Service (B.S.F.S., 1979); George Washington University/National Law Center (J.D., 1985). *Member:* Maryland State and American Bar Associations. ***LANGUAGES:*** Spanish, German, French. ***PRACTICE AREAS:*** International Business Transactions; Project Finance; Energy; International Taxation. ***Email:*** rechsteinerv@coudert.com

ROGER D. STARK, born April 10, 1955; admitted to bar, 1985, NY; 1986, DC. *Education:* Queens College of the City University of New York (B.A., 1981); Vanderbilt University (J.D., 1984). Associate Editor, Vanderbilt Journal of Transnational Law, 1983-1984. ***LANGUAGES:*** Spanish. ***PRACTICE AREAS:*** Business Transactions; Financial Transactions; Energy; Infrastructure; International Law. ***Email:*** starkr@coudert.com

ROGER B. WAGNER, born October 9, 1954; admitted to bar, 1982, DC and MA; 1985, CA. *Education:* Yale University (B.A., cum laude, 1977); University of Virginia (J.D., 1981). Phi Delta Phi. Member, Editorial Board, Virginia Journal of Natural Resources Law, 1980-1981. ***PRACTICE AREAS:*** Corporate Law; Project Finance; Energy; Privatization. ***Email:*** wagnerr@coudert.com

COUNSEL

MATTHEW J. McCONKEY, born Flint, MI, December 31, 1965; admitted to bar, 1991, MI; 1998, DC. *Education:* University of Michigan (B.A., 1988); American University, Washington College of Law (J.D., magna cum laude, 1991). ***PRACTICE AREAS:*** Customs; International Trade.

RESIDENT ASSOCIATES

Kristen Angus (Not admitted in DC)
Lina A. Braude (Not admitted in DC)
Peter Chessick (Not admitted in DC)
Markus Dausses (Not admitted in DC)
Matthew R. Fowler (Not admitted in DC)
Cathy J. Futrowsky
Elizabeth Holowinski
H. Rosemary Jeronimides
Alexander A. Kalinov
Kevin M. King
Mark P. Lunn
Julie N. Mack (Not admitted in DC)
Kenneth E. Mack
Monica Restrepo (Not admitted in DC)
Lynn Robitaille (Not admitted in DC)
Yira Rodriguez-Creus (Not admitted in DC)
Lisa Weiss Rosaya
Nancy J. Rosenfeld
Segei Vataev
David M. Viscovich
Matthew J. Vitale

LEGAL SUPPORT PERSONNEL

TIMOTHY J. LOGUE, born Pittsburgh, Pennsylvania, June 4, 1953. *Education:* Duquesne University (B.A., magna cum laude, 1975) Kappa Tau Alpha; American University (M.A., International Communications, with distinction, 1978). Secretary/Treasurer, Arthur C. Clarke Foundation of the United States. *Member:* Society of Satellite Professionals International (President, Mid-Atlantic Chapter); Pacific Telecommunications Council (Vice-Chair, Media and Communications Committee). (Space and Telecommunications Analyst). ***PRACTICE AREAS:*** Satellite Communications; Telecommunications. ***Email:*** loguet@coudert.com

REVISERS OF THE FRANCE LAW DIGEST FOR THIS DIRECTORY.

(For complete biographical data of other Office Personnel, see Professional Biographies at Various Office Locations)

THOMAS A. COUGHLIN

Established in 1985

1750 K STREET, N.W., SUITE 1200
WASHINGTON, D.C. 20006-2305
Telephone: 202-828-4968
Telecopier: 202-828-4966
Email: tac1@erols.com

Estate planning, and business practice in the District of Columbia, Virginia and Maryland. Specialized national practice in historic preservation, conservation easements, and non-profit organizations.

THOMAS A. COUGHLIN, born Boston, Massachusetts, December 8, 1945; admitted to bar, 1970, Massachusetts; 1979, District of Columbia; 1987, U.S. Tax Court; 1991, Maryland; 1993, Virginia. *Education:* Hiram College; Brandeis University (B.A., 1967); Boston College Law School (J.D., 1970). Co-Author: "Historic Preservation Law and Taxation," Matthew Bender & Company, 3 Vols., 1986; "How the Tax Reform Act of 1986 Affects Real Estate," 2 The Practical Real Estate Lawyer 11, November, 1986; "Guidelines for the Valuation of Easements for Land Conservation and Historic Preservation," National Trust for Historic Preservation and Land Trust Exchange, Washington, D.C., 1984. Author: "Using Historic Rehabilitation and Low Income Housing Tax Credits," 2 The Practical Tax Lawyer 25, Winter 1988; "Handling Easement Valuation Disputes Before the IRS and in the Courts," 3 The Practical Real Estate Lawyer 81, January, 1987. Member, 1998—, Board of Directors, Washington, D.C. Estate Planning Council and Newsletter Editor; Member: Northern Virginia Estate Planning Council; National Network of Estate Planning Attorneys. *Member:* American Bar Association (Chair, Committee on Historic Preservation and Land Conservation, Section of Real Property, Probate and Trust Law, 1986-1990; Member: Committee on Real Estate Tax Problems, Section of Taxation). ***REPORTED CASES:*** Higgins vs. Commissioner, T.C. Memo 1990-103, CCH 1990-103, Dec 46,418(M).

COUNTS, POTTS-DUPRE & DIFEDE

CHARTERED

SUITE 444
1125 FIFTEENTH STREET, N.W.
WASHINGTON, D.C. 20005
Telephone: 202-223-0888
Telecopier: 202-223-3868

Pension and Labor Law. Real Estate, Tax and Commercial Transactions Law. Litigation.

JOHN P. COUNTS, born Wilmington, Delaware, January 2, 1948; admitted to bar, 1973, District of Columbia; 1979, U.S. Supreme Court. *Education:* University of Delaware (B.A., 1970); George Washington University (J.D., 1973). Phi Beta Kappa; Phi Kappa Phi; Order of the Coif. Author: "Financial Management of Apprenticeship Funds: Satisfying the Basic Legal Obligations," Employee Benefits Journal, Vol. 9, No. 1, March, 1984. Member, National Coordinating Committee for Multiemployer Plans. *Member:* The District of Columbia Bar; American Bar Association (Member, Sections on: Labor and Employment Law; Litigation; Former Co-Chairman, Subcommittee on ERISA Preemption, Labor and Employment Law Section; Member, National Coordinating Committee for Multiemployer Plans). Fellow, College of Labor and Employment Lawyers. ***Email:*** jphillipc@aol.com

DAVID H. POTTS-DUPRE, born Madison, Indiana, November 26, 1954; admitted to bar, 1983, California; 1985, District of Columbia; 1988, U.S. District Court for the District of Columbia; 1990, U.S. District Court, District of Maryland. *Education:* Kalamazoo College; University of California at Davis (B.S., with highest honors, 1978; J.D., 1983). Law Clerk to Hon. Allen T. Compton, Alaska Supreme Court, 1983-1984. Attorney, Office of The Chief Counsel, Federal Labor Relations Authority, 1984-1985. *Member:* The District of Columbia Bar; American Bar Association (Co-Chair, Subcommittee on Jointly Administered Plans, Committee on Employee Benefits, Section on Labor and Employment Law; Member, Committee on Employee Benefits). ***Email:*** dpotts-dupre@worldnet.att.net

JAMES R. DIFEDE, born Manhasset, New York, August 29, 1959; admitted to bar, 1986, New York; 1989, District of Columbia. *Education:* Adelphi University (B.B.A., magna cum laude, 1982); Georgetown University (J.D.,

(This Listing Continued)

magna cum laude, 1986). Delta Tau Alpha; Delta Mu Delta; Order of the Coif. Member, The Tax Lawyer, 1985-1986. *Member:* The District of Columbia Bar; American Bar Association (Member, Sections on: Real Property, Probate and Trust Law; Corporation, Banking and Business Law).

JAMES V. COLE II, born Rockville Centre, New York, May 18, 1967; admitted to bar, 1996, New York; 1998, District of Columbia. *Education:* University of Virginia (B.A., 1989); George Mason University School of Law (J.D., 1995); Georgetown University (LL.M., with distinction, Taxation, 2001). Recipient, Employee Benefits Certificate, Georgetown University, 2001. Senior Notes Editor, George Mason Law Review, 1994-1995. Author: "The Demisay Dilemma," 2 George Mason Law Review 377, 1995. *Member:* The District of Columbia Bar; American (Member, Sections on: Taxation; Labor and Employment Law; Real Property, Probate and Trust Law) Bar Association. **Email:** jvcii@worldnet.att.net

---

JENNIFER BUSH HAWKINS, born Franklin Square, New York, August 9, 1966; admitted to bar, 1994, New York and U.S. District Court, Southern and Eastern Districts of New York; 1996, District of Columbia and U.S. Court of Veterans Appeals; 1997, U.S. District Court, District of Maryland. *Education:* St. John's University (B.S., 1988); Hofstra University (J.D., 1993). Notes and Comment Editor, Hofstra Law Review, 1992-1993. *Member:* The District of Columbia Bar (Member, Labor and Employment Law Section); American Bar Association. **Email:** jbushhawkins@worldnet.att.net

SHANE N. KRAMER, born Cambridge, Massachusetts, September 17, 1973; admitted to bar, 1999, Virginia; 2001, District of Columbia. *Education:* University of Virginia (B.A., 1996); Washington & Lee University (J.D., 1999); Georgetown University Law Center (LL.M., Taxation, with distinction, 2000). *Member:* The District of Columbia Bar (Member, Taxation Section); Virginia State and American (Member, Taxation Section) Bar Associations. **Email:** snkramer@worldnet.att.net

KELLY HUCKNO GIL, born Jamestown, New York, October 25, 1970; admitted to bar, 1997, Maryland; 1998, District of Columbia and U.S. District Court, District of Maryland. *Education:* State University of New York at Binghamton (B.A., History, 1992); University of Baltimore (J.D., 1997). *Member:* The District of Columbia Bar; Maryland State Bar Association Inc.; American (Member, Sections on: Real Property, Probate and Trust Law) Bar Association. **Email:** k.h.gil@worldnet.att.net

KATHERINE L. JOUGH, born New York, New York, March 14, 1971; admitted to bar, 1998, Missouri; 1999, Illinois; 2001, District of Columbia. *Education:* Vassar College (B.A., 1993); Washington & Lee University (J.D., 1998). Phi Beta Kappa. *Member:* The District of Columbia Bar (Member, Real Estate, Housing and Land Use Section); Illinois State Bar Association; The Missouri Bar; American Bar Association (Member, Real Property, Probate and Trust Law Section). **Email:** kjough@worldnet.att.net

MELINDA L. EMCH, born Colorado Springs, Colorado, July 9, 1971; admitted to bar, 2000, Colorado (Not admitted in District of Columbia). *Education:* Creighton University (B.A., 1993; J.D., 2000); Georgetown University (LL.M., Taxation, 2001). Recipient, Employee Benefits Certificate, Georgetown University, 2001. *Member:* Colorado and American Bar Associations. **Email:** m.emch@worldnet.att.net

KEITH C. OTT, born Kansas City, Missouri, July 7, 1964; admitted to bar, 1995, Kansas; 1996, Missouri; 1998, New York; 2001, Pennsylvania (Not admitted in District of Columbia). *Education:* University of Kansas (B.S.B.A., 1987); University of Central Florida (M.B.A., 1990); University of Tulsa (J.D., 1995); Fordham University (LL.M. in Banking, Corporate and Finance, 1996); New York University (LL.M. in Taxation, 1999). Recipient, American Jurisprudence Award in Corporate Law, University of Tulsa, 1994. Senior Articles Editor, Federal Energy Bar Association Energy Law Journal, 1994-1995. Research and Writing Editor, Fordham Finance, Securities and Tax Law Forum, 1995-1996. Law Clerk to the Honorable John A. Borron, Jr., Sixteenth Judicial Circuit, Missouri, 1996-1997. Co-Author: Simes & Smith, Law of Future Interests, West Publishing Company, 1997 Pocket Parts. *Member:* Pennsylvania and American Bar Associations; The Missouri Bar. **Email:** k.c.ott@worldnet.att.net

JEANNINE R. SHAVITZ, born Teaneck, New Jersey, November 4, 1969; admitted to bar, 1995, New Jersey; 1996, New York (Not admitted in District of Columbia). *Education:* Villanova University (B.A., 1991); Pace University School of Law (J.D., cum laude, 1995). **Email:** jshavitz@worldnet.att.net

WILLIAM GRAY MITCHELL, JR., born Durham, North Carolina, February 2, 1969; admitted to bar, 1996, North Carolina (Not admitted in District of Columbia). *Education:* University of North Carolina at Chapel Hill (B.A., 1991; J.D., 1996). *Member:* North Carolina Bar Association. **Email:** gray.mitchell@worldnett.att.net

ROBERT D. COURTLAND

CHARTERED

WASHINGTON, D.C.

(See, Bethesda, Maryland)

Taxation, Corporate, Finance, Business and Estate Planning Law. Federal and International Tax Practice.

COVINGTON & BURLING

1201 PENNSYLVANIA AVENUE, N.W.
WASHINGTON, D.C. 20004-2401
Telephone: 202-662-6000
Fax: 202-662-6291
Email: postmaster@cov.com
URL: http://www.cov.com

San Francisco, California Office: 601 California Street, Suite 1900, 94108. Telephone: 415-591-6000.
New York, N.Y. Office: 1330 Avenue of the Americas, 10019-5400. Telephone: 212-841-1000. Telecopier: 212-841-1010.
London, England Office: Leconfield House, Curzon Street, W1Y 8A5. Telephone: 011-44-71-495-5655. Fax: 011-44-71-495-3101.
Brussels, Belgium Office: 44 Avenue des Arts (Bte. 8), 1040. Telephone: 011-32-2-549-5230. Fax: 011-32-2-502-1598.

General Practice, including, but not limited to: Antitrust and Competition, Appellate, Arbitration and Alternative Dispute Resolution, Banking and Financial Services, Bankruptcy and Insolvency, Business Law, Civil Rights, Communications and Media, Copyrights, Corporate, Criminal, Election and Campaign Finance, Emerging Companies, Employee Benefits, Employment, Energy, Environmental, Food, Drug and Cosmetics, Government Contracts, Health Services, Information Services, Insurance, Intellectual Property, International, Information Technology and Internet, Latin America, Legislative, Litigation, Mergers and Acquisitions, Petroleum, Products Liability, Professional Responsibility, Real Estate, Securities, Sports, Taxation, Toxic Torts, Trade Associations, Trade Regulation, Trademarks, Transportation, Trusts and Estates and Year 2000 Computer Conversion.

PARTNERS

DANA T. ACKERLY II, born September 3, 1943; admitted to bar, 1970, New York; 1971, District of Columbia. *Education:* Williams College (B.A., magna cum laude, 1965); Harvard University (J.D., 1969).

HARVEY M. APPLEBAUM, born March 1, 1937; admitted to bar, 1962, Alabama; 1964, District of Columbia. *Education:* Yale University (B.A., summa cum laude, 1959); Harvard University (LL.B., magna cum laude, 1962).

JAMES R. ATWOOD, born February 21, 1944; admitted to bar, 1970, California; 1971, District of Columbia. *Education:* Yale University (B.A., magna cum laude, 1966); Stanford University (J.D., summa cum laude, Valedictorian, 1969).

BRUCE A. BAIRD, born March 26, 1948; admitted to bar, 1976, New York; 1979, District of Columbia. *Education:* Cornell University (B.A., 1970); New York University (J.D., 1975).

PATRICIA A. BARALD, born June 26, 1948; admitted to bar, 1974, New York; 1975, District of Columbia. *Education:* Brown University (B.A., 1970; M.A., summa cum laude, 1970); Cornell University (J.D., summa cum laude, 1973).

THOMAS O. BARNETT, born August 1, 1962; admitted to bar, 1989, Maryland; 1991, District of Columbia. *Education:* Yale University (B.A., summa cum laude, 1985); London School of Economics (M.Sc., 1986); Harvard University (J.D., magna cum laude, 1989).

MICHAEL ST. PATRICK BAXTER, admitted to bar, 1981, Ontario, Canada; 1985, District of Columbia. *Education:* University of Western Ontario (LL.B., Dean's Honor List, 1979); Harvard University (LL.M., 1983).

BRUCE C. BENNETT, admitted to bar, 1984, New York. *Education:* University of California, Los Angeles (B.A., cum laude, 1979); University of Southern California (J.D., 1983). (Resident, New York, N.Y. Office).

PAUL J. BERMAN, born January 7, 1951; admitted to bar, 1975, District of Columbia; registered to practice before U.S. Patent and Trademark Office. *Education:* Harvard University (A.B., magna cum laude, 1972; J.D., cum laude, 1975).

DR. GEORG M. BERRISCH, born Düsseldorf, Germany, 1960; admitted to bar, 1991, Hamburg, Germany. *Education:* McGill University (LL.M.); University of Passau (Dr. jur.). (Resident, Brussels, Belgium Office).

JONATHAN D. BLAKE, born June 14, 1938; admitted to bar, 1965, District of Columbia. *Education:* Yale University (B.A., magna cum laude, 1960); Trinity College, Oxford, England (Rhodes Scholar, B.A.; M.A., 1962); Yale University (LL.B., 1964).

(This Listing Continued)

COVINGTON & BURLING, Washington—Continued

DORIS BLAZEK-WHITE, born November 17, 1943; admitted to bar, 1969, District of Columbia and Virgin Islands (inactive); 1978, Maryland. *Education:* Goucher College (B.A., 1965); Georgetown University (J.D., 1968).

PETER W. L. BOGAERT, born May 1, 1959; admitted to bar, 1984, Brussels; 1995, England. *Education:* Catholic University of Leuven (B.Phil., 1979; Lic.Jur., cum laude, 1982); Oxford University (B.A., first class honors, 1984). (Resident, Brussels, Belgium Office).

ERIC C. BOSSET, born September 16, 1962; admitted to bar, 1987, Florida; 1988, District of Columbia. *Education:* Carleton College (B.A., summa cum laude, 1984); Yale University (J.D., 1987).

RICHARD A. BRADY, born September 17, 1934; admitted to bar, 1960, District of Columbia. *Education:* Yale University (B.S., summa cum laude, 1956; LL.B., 1959).

LANNY A. BREUER, born 1958; admitted to bar, 1986, New York; 1988, District of Columbia. *Education:* Columbia University (B.A., 1980; J.D., 1985).

EDWARD C. BRITTON, born May 18, 1955; admitted to bar, 1985, Massachusetts (Inactive); 1987, District of Columbia. *Education:* Princeton University (A.B., 1977); Oxford University, England (B.A., with First Class Honours, 1981); Harvard University (J.D., cum laude, 1983).

CAROLINE M. BROWN, born March 14, 1962; admitted to bar, 1993, New York and District of Columbia. *Education:* Harvard College (A.B., magna cum laude, 1985); Harvard University (J.D., magna cum laude, 1990).

DAVID N. BROWN, born May 29, 1940; admitted to bar, 1967, District of Columbia. *Education:* Cornell University (A.B., 1963); University of Chicago (J.D., 1966).

E. EDWARD BRUCE, born November 23, 1938; admitted to bar, 1967, District of Columbia. *Education:* Yale University (B.A., summa cum laude, 1960; LL.B., magna cum laude, 1966).

JOHN G. BUCHANAN III, born December 7, 1950; admitted to bar, 1979, District of Columbia. *Education:* Princeton University (A.B., magna cum laude, 1972); Oxford University, England (B.A., with First Class Honors, 1974); Harvard University (J.D., 1978).

CHARLES E. BUFFON, born September 8, 1939; admitted to bar, 1965, District of Columbia. *Education:* Dartmouth College (A.B., magna cum laude, 1961); Harvard University (LL.B., cum laude, 1964).

BOBBY R. BURCHFIELD, born October 23, 1954; admitted to bar, 1980, District of Columbia. *Education:* Wake Forest University (B.A., cum laude, 1976); George Washington University (J.D., with high honors, 1979).

KURT G. CALIA, born Frederick, Maryland, June 3, 1968; admitted to bar, 1994, Pennsylvania (inactive); 1995, District of Columbia and California; registered to practice before U.S. Patent and Trademark Office. *Education:* Haverford College (B.S., 1990); Boston University (J.D., 1993). (Resident, San Francisco, California Office).

RUSSELL H. CARPENTER, JR., born May 17, 1941; admitted to bar, 1968, District of Columbia. *Education:* Princeton University (A.B., with honors, 1963); Oxford University (B.Phil., 1965); Yale University (LL.B., with honors, 1968).

WARREN G. CAYWOOD, JR., born November 30, 1951; admitted to bar, 1977, New York; 1983, U.S. District Court, Southern District of New York. *Education:* Yale University (B.A., cum laude, 1973); Columbia University (J.D., 1976). (Resident, New York, N.Y. Office).

LEONARD CHAZEN, born February 26, 1942; admitted to bar, 1971, New York. *Education:* Yale University (B.A., 1963; L.L.B., 1967). (Resident, New York, N.Y. Office).

GEORGE M. CHESTER, JR., born February 25, 1947; admitted to bar, 1976, Wisconsin; 1977, District of Columbia. *Education:* Princeton University (A.B., summa cum laude, 1969); University of Hawaii (M.A., 1972); University of Virginia (J.D., 1976); Oxford University (Trinity College), D.Phil. Program, 1972-1973.

BRICE M. CLAGETT, born July 6, 1933; admitted to bar, 1958, District of Columbia. *Education:* Princeton University (A.B., summa cum laude, 1954); Harvard University (J.D., magna cum laude, 1958).

WILLIAM R. COLLINS, born April 28, 1960; admitted to bar, 1986, New York. *Education:* University of Virginia (B.A., with honors, 1982); Albany Law School of Union University (J.D., cum laude, 1985). (Resident, New York, N.Y. Office).

RICHARD D. COPAKEN, born June 24, 1941; admitted to bar, 1966, District of Columbia. *Education:* Harvard University (B.A., summa cum laude, 1963; LL.B., magna cum laude, 1966).

CAROLYN F. CORWIN, born July 27, 1950; admitted to bar, 1977, District of Columbia. *Education:* Oberlin College (A.B., 1971); Catholic University of America (M.S.L.S., 1972); Yale University (J.D., 1977).

(This Listing Continued)

EVAN R. COX, born October 14, 1960; admitted to bar, 1987, California; 1988, District of Columbia. *Education:* Michigan State University (B.A., with honors, 1982); University of California, Berkeley (J.D., 1987). (Resident, San Francisco, California Office).

THOMAS L. CUBBAGE III, born October 24, 1966; admitted to bar, 1992, Texas (inactive); 1995, District of Columbia. *Education:* Southern Methodist University (B.A., magna cum laude, 1989); University of Texas (J.D., with high honors, 1992).

MICHAEL E. CUTLER, born November 17, 1955; admitted to bar, 1982, District of Columbia. *Education:* Vassar College (A.B., 1977); Stanford University (J.D., 1981).

RODERICK ALLEN DE ARMENT, born March 3, 1948; admitted to bar, 1973, District of Columbia. *Education:* Trinity College (B.A., honors, 1970); University of Virginia (J.D., 1973).

JOHN B. DENNISTON, born June 3, 1936; admitted to bar, 1963, District of Columbia. *Education:* Cornell University (Bachelor of Engineering Physics, 1958); Harvard University (J.D., 1962); University of Sydney.

MITCHELL F. DOLIN, born February 6, 1956; admitted to bar, 1982, District of Columbia. *Education:* Tufts University (B.A., 1978); New York University (J.D., 1981).

JOHN C. DUGAN, born June 3, 1955; admitted to bar, 1981, District of Columbia. *Education:* University of Michigan (B.A., with high distinction, 1977); Harvard University (J.D., cum laude, 1981).

JULIE M. EDMOND, born August 18, 1955; admitted to bar, 1983, District of Columbia. *Education:* Yale University (B.A., 1976); Catholic University of America (M.S.W., 1978); Harvard University (J.D., 1981).

CLAUSEN ELY, JR., born February 18, 1945; admitted to bar, 1973, Alabama (inactive) and District of Columbia. *Education:* Huntingdon College (A.B., 1967); University of Alabama (J.D., 1972).

ANNA ENGH, admitted to bar, 1989, Virginia; 1991, District of Columbia. *Education:* Davidson College (B.A., 1981); University of Virginia (M.Ed., 1982); College of William & Mary (J.D., 1989).

NICHOLAS W. FELS, born March 19, 1943; admitted to bar, 1968, New York; 1970, California; 1971, District of Columbia. *Education:* Harvard University (B.A., magna cum laude, 1964; LL.B., cum laude, 1968); University of California at Berkeley (M.A., 1965).

MATTHEW E. FISHBEIN, born November 21, 1953; admitted to bar, 1980, New York and U.S. District Court, Southern and Eastern Districts of New York; U.S. District Court, District of Rhode Island; 1984, U.S. Court of Appeals, 5th Circuit; 1985, U.S. Court of Appeals, 2nd Circuit. *Education:* Williams College (A.B., 1975); New York University (J.D., 1979). (Resident, New York, N.Y. Office).

PETER L. FLANAGAN, born Milwaukee, Wisconsin, July 16, 1965; admitted to bar, 1994, New York and District of Columbia. *Education:* University of Wisconsin (B.A., 1987); Princeton University (M.P.A., 1993); New York University (J.D., 1993).

ELLEN J. FLANNERY, born December 13, 1951; admitted to bar, 1978, Massachusetts; 1979, District of Columbia. *Education:* Mount Holyoke College (A.B., cum laude, 1973); Boston University (J.D., cum laude, 1978).

ANDREW H. FRIEDMAN, born August 19, 1955; admitted to bar, 1980, District of Columbia. *Education:* Trinity College (B.A., summa cum laude, 1977); Harvard University (J.D., cum laude, 1980).

ROBERT J. GAGE, born June 9, 1951; admitted to bar, 1977, District of Columbia. *Education:* Kent State University (B.A., summa cum laude, 1973); Harvard University (M.P.P., 1977; J.D., cum laude, 1977).

MARIALUISA S. GALLOZZI, born December 22, 1961; admitted to bar, 1987, New York; 1988, District of Columbia. *Education:* Harvard University (A.B., cum laude, National Merit Scholarship, 1982); New York University (J.D., 1986).

OSCAR M. GARIBALDI, born June 22, 1946; admitted to bar, 1973, Argentina; 1978, District of Columbia; 1990, Spain. *Education:* University of Buenos Aires (Bachiller, highest honors, 1964; J.D., Honor Diploma, 1972); Harvard University (LL.M., 1975).

THEODORE L. GARRETT, born September 4, 1943; admitted to bar, 1968, New York; 1971, District of Columbia. *Education:* Yale University (B.A., 1965); Columbia University (J.D., 1968).

CORINNE A. GOLDSTEIN, born March 2, 1951; admitted to bar, 1976, District of Columbia. *Education:* Wellesley College (B.A., with honors, 1973); University of Michigan (J.D., magna cum laude, 1976).

LINDA C. GOLDSTEIN, born April 1, 1960; admitted to bar, 1987, New York; 1988, U.S. District Court, Southern District of New York and U.S. Court of Appeals, Second Circuit. *Education:* Yale University (B.A., magna cum laude, 1981; J.D., 1985). (Resident, New York, N.Y. Office).

(This Listing Continued)

ELLEN P. GOODMAN, born September 16, 1965; admitted to bar, 1992, Pennsylvania; 1993, District of Columbia. *Education:* Harvard University (A.B., magna cum laude, 1987; J.D., cum laude, 1992).

SAUL B. GOODMAN, born April 27, 1953; admitted to bar, 1980, District of Columbia. *Education:* Yale University (B.A., cum laude, 1975); University of Virginia (J.D., 1978).

JOHN P. GOURARY, born December 30, 1957; admitted to bar, 1983, New York, U.S. District Court, Southern District of New York. *Education:* Princeton University (A.B., magna cum laude, 1979); Columbia University (J.D., 1982). (Resident, New York, N.Y. Office).

WILLIAM F. GREANEY, born June 8, 1956; admitted to bar, 1981, District of Columbia. *Education:* University of Maryland (B.A., summa cum laude, 1977); Harvard University (J.D., cum laude, 1981).

JOANNE B. GROSSMAN, born October 23, 1949; admitted to bar, 1975, California; 1976, District of Columbia. *Education:* Radcliffe College (A.B., cum laude, 1971); University of California, Boalt Hall School of Law (J.D., 1975).

EUGENE D. GULLAND, born August 27, 1947; admitted to bar, 1973, District of Columbia; 1986, Virginia. *Education:* Princeton University (A.B., 1969); Yale University (J.D., 1972).

JOHN E. HALL, born November 6, 1957; admitted to bar, 1985, California; 1987, District of Columbia; 1989, Missouri. *Education:* Harvard University (A.B., 1979; J.D., magna cum laude, 1983); University of Sydney (Post-Graduate study in economics, 1983-1984).

DAVID W. HALLER, born February 25, 1962; admitted to bar, 1988, Illinois; 1989, New York; 1990, U.S. District Court, Southern District of New York and U.S. Tax Court; 1996, U.S. Court of Appeals, Second Circuit; 1999, U.S. Court of Appeals, Ninth Circuit; 2000, U.S. Supreme Court. *Education:* Northwestern University (B.A., with highest distinction, 1984); Yale University (J.D., 1987). (Resident, New York, N.Y. Office).

NEWMAN T. HALVORSON, JR., born December 17, 1936; admitted to bar, 1962, Ohio; 1963, District of Columbia. *Education:* Princeton University (A.B., magna cum laude, 1958); Harvard University (LL.B., magna cum laude, 1961).

ROBERT P. HANEY, JR., born July 23, 1956; admitted to bar, 1984, New York; 1986, U.S. District Court, Southern and Eastern Districts of New York. *Education:* Middlebury College (B.A., summa cum laude, 1978); Harvard University (M.P.P., J.D., cum laude, 1983). (Resident, New York, N.Y. Office).

DAVID L. HARFST, born February 14, 1950; admitted to bar, 1983, District of Columbia. *Education:* Wesleyan University (B.A., magna cum laude, 1972); Yale University (J.D., 1982). (Resident, Brussels, Belgium Office).

J. MICHAEL HEMMER, born May 28, 1949; admitted to bar, 1976, California (Inactive); 1977, District of Columbia. *Education:* Stanford University (B.A., 1973); University of California, Boalt Hall School of Law (J.D., 1976).

ANTHONY HERMAN, born February 5, 1950; admitted to bar, 1989, Pennsylvania; 1990, District of Columbia. *Education:* University of South Carolina (B.A., 1983); Harvard University (J.D., magna cum laude, 1986).

TIMOTHY C. HESTER, born January 31, 1955; admitted to bar, 1983, District of Columbia. *Education:* Williams College (B.A., magna cum laude, 1977) Phi Beta Kappa; University of Michigan (J.D., cum laude, 1982).

DAVID H. HICKMAN, born September 7, 1941; admitted to bar, 1968, Maryland; 1970, District of Columbia. *Education:* Harvard University (B.A., magna cum laude, 1963; LL.B., magna cum laude, 1967).

HARRY G. HIVES, born April 7, 1947; admitted to bar, 1978, New York and U.S. Tax Court. *Education:* Princeton University (A.B., summa cum laude, 1968); Yale University (M.Phil., 1972); University of Pennsylvania (J.D., 1975). (Resident, New York, N.Y. Office).

MICHAEL B. HOPKINS, born March 11, 1948; admitted to bar, 1980, New York and U.S. District Court, Southern and Eastern Districts of New York. *Education:* Holy Cross College; New York University (B.A., 1970); City College of the City University of New York (M.A., 1972); Benjamin N. Cardozo School of Law (J.D., 1979). (Resident, New York, N.Y. Office).

MICHAEL S. HORNE, born May 10, 1938; admitted to bar, 1963, District of Columbia. *Education:* University of Minnesota (B.A., magna cum laude, 1959); Harvard University (J.D., magna cum laude, 1962).

PHILIP K. HOWARD, born October 24, 1948; admitted to bar, 1975, New York, U.S. District Court, Southern and Eastern Districts of New York and U.S. Court of Appeals, Second Circuit; 1979, U.S. Supreme Court. *Education:* Yale University (B.A., with honors, 1970); University of Virginia (J.D., 1974). (Resident, New York, N.Y. Office).

(This Listing Continued)

JOHN A. HURVITZ, born December 2, 1964; admitted to bar, 1991, Connecticut; 1992, New York; 1993, District of Columbia; registered to practice before U.S. Patent and Trademark Office. *Education:* Haverford College (B.A., 1986); Yale University (J.D., 1991).

PETER BARTON HUTT, born November 16, 1934; admitted to bar, 1959, New York; 1961, District of Columbia. *Education:* Yale University (B.A., magna cum laude, 1956); Harvard University (LL.B., 1959); New York University (LL.M., in Food and Drug Law, 1960).

JEFFREY G. HUVELLE, born February 6, 1946; admitted to bar, 1973, Massachusetts; 1976, District of Columbia. *Education:* Harvard University (B.A., cum laude, 1968); Columbia University (J.D., 1973).

MICHAEL X. IMBROSCIO, born Defiance, Ohio, June 30, 1968; admitted to bar, 1994, Pennsylvania; 1995, District of Columbia. *Education:* Ohio State University (B.A., 1990); Harvard University (J.D., 1993).

STEPHEN A. INFANTE, born December 22, 1965; admitted to bar, 1991, New York. *Education:* Tufts University (B.A., summa cum laude, 1987); Harvard University (J.D., magna cum laude, 1990). (Resident, New York, N.Y. Office).

WILLIAM D. IVERSON, born January 28, 1942; admitted to bar, 1969, District of Columbia. *Education:* University of Pennsylvania (B.S., 1963); Yale University (LL.B., magna cum laude, 1968).

O. THOMAS JOHNSON, JR., born July 3, 1946; admitted to bar, 1972, California (inactive); 1975, District of Columbia. *Education:* Stanford University (B.A., 1968; J.D., 1971).

ELIZABETH T. KESSENIDES, born August 2, 1963; admitted to bar, 1987, New York. *Education:* Barnard College (B.A., 1984); New York University (J.D., 1987). (Resident, New York, N.Y. Office).

MARK F. KIGHTLINGER, born September 14, 1959; admitted to bar, 1991, District of Columbia; U.S. Court of International Trade and U.S. Court of Appeals for the Federal Circuit. *Education:* Williams College (B.A., 1981); Cambridge University (B.A., 1983); Yale University (J.D., 1988; Ph.D., 1991); Cambridge University (M.A., 1995). (Resident, Brussels, Belgium Office).

RICHARD F. KINGHAM, born August 2, 1946; admitted to bar, 1973, District of Columbia. *Education:* George Washington University (B.A., 1968); University of Virginia (J.D., 1973). (Resident, London, England Office).

BRUCE N. KUHLIK, born September 7, 1956; admitted to bar, 1982, District of Columbia. *Education:* Harvard University (A.B., summa cum laude, 1978; J.D., magna cum laude, 1981).

EUGENE I. LAMBERT, born December 22, 1935; admitted to bar, 1960, District of Columbia. *Education:* George Washington University (A.B., with highest honors, 1957); Yale University (J.D., 1960).

D. MICHAEL LEFEVER, born December 23, 1953; admitted to bar, 1979, Pennsylvania; 1980, Massachusetts; 1986, District of Columbia. *Education:* Dickinson College (B.A., magna cum laude, 1976); Boston University (J.D., 1979).

BINGHAM B. LEVERICH, born July 31, 1937; admitted to bar, 1965, District of Columbia. *Education:* Wesleyan University (B.A., 1959); Free University of Berlin (Fulbright Scholarship, 1959-1961); Yale University (LL.B., 1964).

JACK P. LEVIN, born August 17, 1946; admitted to bar, 1972, New York, New Jersey and U.S. District Court, District of New Jersey; 1973, U.S. District Court, Southern and Eastern Districts of New York; U.S. Court of Appeals, Second Circuit; 1992, U.S. Supreme Court. *Education:* Rutgers University (B.A., with honors, 1968); University of Pennsylvania (J.D., 1971). (Resident, New York, N.Y. Office).

GREGG H. LEVY, born January 18, 1953; admitted to bar, 1977, District of Columbia. *Education:* Harvard University (A.B., 1974; J.D., cum laude, 1977).

MICHAEL R. LEVY, born August 10, 1948; admitted to bar, 1974, District of Columbia. *Education:* Yale University (B.A., magna cum laude, 1970); Harvard University (J.D., cum laude, 1973).

CHARLES E. LISTER, born June 18, 1938; admitted to bar, 1966, District of Columbia. *Education:* Harvard University (A.B., magna cum laude, 1960); Oxford University, England (B.A., 1962; B.C.L., 1963; M.A., 1966, Rhodes Scholar); George Washington University (M.C.L., 1965). (Resident, London, England Office).

S. WILLIAM LIVINGSTON, JR., born November 10, 1944; admitted to bar, 1970, District of Columbia. *Education:* Carleton College (B.A., cum laude, 1966); Harvard University (J.D., magna cum laude, 1969).

J. JAY LOBELL, born October 5, 1962; admitted to bar, 1989, New Jersey; 1990, New York. *Education:* Queens College of the City University of New York (B.A., summa cum laude, 1985); Yale University (J.D., 1988). (Resident, New York, N.Y. Office).

(This Listing Continued)

COVINGTON & BURLING, Washington—Continued

ROBERT A. LONG, JR., born March 18, 1958; admitted to bar, 1987, Pennsylvania; 1988, District of Columbia. *Education:* University of North Carolina at Chapel Hill (B.A., Morehead Scholar; Phi Beta Kappa, 1980); Oxford University, England (B.A./M.A., Rhodes Scholar, 1982); Yale University (J.D., 1985).

MARK H. LYNCH, born December 1, 1944; admitted to bar, 1974, District of Columbia. *Education:* Yale College (B.A., 1966); George Washington University (J.D., 1974).

DANIEL M. MANDIL, born April 21, 1956; admitted to bar, 1990, New York. *Education:* Harvard University (B.A., 1978; M.A., 1982); Columbia University (J.D., 1987). (Resident, New York, N.Y. Office).

AARON R. MARCU, born October 13, 1955; admitted to bar, 1981, New York and U.S. District Court, Southern and Eastern Districts of New York; 1984, U.S. Court of Appeals, Second Circuit; 1990, U.S. Supreme Court. *Education:* Northwestern University (B.S.J., with highest distinction, 1977); Harvard University (J.D., cum laude, 1980). (Resident, New York, N.Y. Office).

DAVID LAWRENCE MEYER, born September 30, 1961; admitted to bar, 1987, Maryland; 1988, District of Columbia. *Education:* Amherst College (B.A., magna cum laude, 1983); Yale University (J.D., 1986).

CHARLES A. MILLER, born February 7, 1935; admitted to bar, 1960, District of Columbia. *Education:* University of California at Berkeley (A.B., 1955); University of California, Boalt Hall School of Law (LL.B., 1958).

ALLAN B. MOORE, born July 21, 1964; admitted to bar, 1991, Massachusetts (Inactive) and District of Columbia. *Education:* Harvard University (A.B., magna cum laude, 1986; J.D., 1990). (Resident, London, England Office).

AMY N. MOORE, born September 24, 1953; admitted to bar, 1984, District of Columbia. *Education:* Mount Holyoke College (A.B., summa cum laude, 1976); University of Virginia (M.A., 1978; J.D., 1983).

PETER J. NICKLES, born September 26, 1938; admitted to bar, 1964, District of Columbia. *Education:* Princeton University (B.A., 1960); Harvard University (LL.B., 1963); University of Munich (EC and International Law Studies); University of the Sorbonne (EC and International Law Studies).

WILLIAM M. PAUL, born February 9, 1951; admitted to bar, 1978, District of Columbia. *Education:* Johns Hopkins University (B.A., 1973); University of Michigan (J.D., magna cum laude, 1977).

C. WILLIAM PHILLIPS, born July 25, 1956; admitted to bar, 1983, New York and U.S. District Court, Southern and Eastern Districts of New York; U.S. Court of Appeals, Second Circuit. *Education:* Vanderbilt University (B.A., magna cum laude, 1978); Harvard University (J.D., 1982). (Resident, New York, N.Y. Office).

MARK E. PLOTKIN, born May 30, 1961; admitted to bar, 1987, Maryland (Inactive); 1988, District of Columbia, U.S. District Court, District of Maryland and District of Columbia; U.S. Court of Appeals for the District of Columbia Circuit, Third, Fourth and Fifth Circuit. *Education:* Yale University (B.A., summa cum laude, 1983); Harvard University (J.D., magna cum laude, 1987).

ETHAN M. POSNER, born December 17, 1962; admitted to bar, 1990, New York; 1991, District of Columbia. *Education:* Wesleyan University (B.A., high honors, 1984); University of Michigan (J.D., magna cum laude, 1989).

HILARY PRESCOTT, born January 11, 1960; admitted to bar, 1985, as a solicitor in England and Wales. *Education:* University of Sussex (B.A., 1982); Guildford College of Law (1983). (Resident, London, England Office).

DAVID H. REMES, born December 22, 1954; admitted to bar, 1983, District of Columbia. *Education:* Columbia University (B.A., magna cum laude, 1976); Harvard University (J.D., 1979).

PAUL V. ROGERS, born April 15, 1957; admitted to bar, 1985, Massachusetts; 1999, District of Columbia. *Education:* Williams College (B.A., cum laude, 1979); Georgetown Law School (J.D., cum laude, 1985).

NEIL K. ROMAN, born June 6, 1958; admitted to bar, 1986, District of Columbia. *Education:* Bowdoin College (A.B., magna cum laude, 1980); Harvard University (J.D., cum laude, 1985).

STEVEN J. ROSENBAUM, born March 13, 1955; admitted to bar, 1980, District of Columbia. *Education:* University of Texas (B.A., cum laude, 1977); Harvard University (J.D., cum laude, 1980).

JOHN PETER RUPP, born December 30, 1944; admitted to bar, 1972, Maine and District of Columbia. *Education:* University of Iowa (B.A., 1967); Yale Law School (J.D., 1972).

ROBERT N. SAYLER, born June 1, 1940; admitted to bar, 1965, District of Columbia. *Education:* Stanford University (A.B., 1962); Harvard University (LL.B., 1965).

(This Listing Continued)

LAURIE C. SELF, born July 13, 1964; admitted to bar, 1992, District of Columbia. *Education:* Duke University (A.B., 1986); University of Virginia (J.D., 1989).

RICHARD C. SHEA, born December 12, 1952; admitted to bar, 1985, District of Columbia. *Education:* Amherst College (A.B., magna cum laude, 1976); Pontificia Universidad Catolica, Lima, Peru; University of Virginia (J.D., 1983).

LAURENCE A. SILVERMAN, born September 9, 1953; admitted to bar, 1978, New York; 1979, District of Columbia. *Education:* Columbia University (B.A., summa cum laude, 1974); Yale Law School (J.D., 1977). (Resident, New York, N.Y. Office).

CHRISTOPHER N. SIPES, born January 17, 1965; admitted to bar, 1992, California (Inactive); 1993, District of Columbia; registered to practice before U.S. Patent and Trademark Office. *Education:* Harvard College (A.B., 1986); California Institute of Technology (M.S., 1989); Harvard University (J.D., 1991).

WILLIAM P. SKINNER, born April 4, 1951; admitted to bar, 1976, Missouri and District of Columbia. *Education:* Harvard University (B.A., cum laude, 1972; J.D., magna cum laude, 1975).

JAY T. SMITH, born November 1, 1960; admitted to bar, 1988, New York; 1989, District of Columbia. *Education:* Harvard University (A.B., magna cum laude, 1982; J.D., magna cum laude, 1986).

JOHN THOMAS SMITH, II, born October 22, 1943; admitted to bar, 1968, District of Columbia. *Education:* Yale University (B.A., 1964; J.D., 1967).

SCOTT F. SMITH, born 1954; admitted to bar, 1981, New York and Arkansas. *Education:* Harvard University (B.A., magna cum laude, 1976); Texas University (J.D., with high honors, 1980). (Resident, New York, N.Y. Office).

JAMES C. SNIPES, born January 12, 1953; admitted to bar, 1982, District of Columbia; 1999, California. *Education:* Swarthmore College (B.A., with high honors, 1975); Oxford University (B.A., 1977); Yale University (J.D., 1980). (Resident, San Francisco, California Office).

REBECCA SNOW, born December 7, 1960; admitted to bar, 1986, Nevada; 1987, District of Columbia. *Education:* Brigham Young University (B.S., summa cum laude, 1983); Harvard University (J.D., cum laude, 1986).

STUART C. STOCK, born July 19, 1946; admitted to bar, 1971, Missouri; 1973, Indiana; 1974, District of Columbia. *Education:* Purdue University (B.S., with highest distinction, 1968); Harvard University (J.D., magna cum laude, 1971).

PHILIPP U. TAMUSSINO, born January 11, 1964; admitted to bar, 1991, New York; 1996, District of Columbia. *Education:* Karl-Franzens Universität (Mag.iur., with honors, 1987; Dr.iur., with honors, 1989); New York University (LL.M., 1990). (Resident, New York, N.Y. Office).

KEITH A. TEEL, born November 11, 1956; admitted to bar, 1981, District of Columbia; registered to practice before U.S. Patent and Trademark Office. *Education:* Washington & Lee University (B.S., magna cum laude, 1978); University of Virginia (J.D., 1981).

PHYLLIS D. THOMPSON, born October 1, 1952; admitted to bar, 1981, District of Columbia. *Education:* George Washington University (B.A., Valedictorian, 1974; J.D., with high honors, 1981); Princeton University (M.A., 1976).

LEE J. TIEDRICH, born January 19, 1966; admitted to bar, 1991, Pennsylvania; 1993, District of Columbia; 1999, California; registered to practice before U.S. Patent and Trademark Office. *Education:* Duke University (B.S.E., magna cum laude, 1988); University of Pennsylvania (J.D., cum laude, 1991).

HENRIETTE A. TIELEMANS, born May 6, 1953; admitted to bar, 1980, Brussels (Not admitted in United States). *Education:* University of Antwerp (Lic. Jur., magna cum laude, 1976); Harvard University (LL.M., Fulbright Fellow, 1978). (Resident, Brussels, Belgium Office).

ALLAN J. TOPOL, born June 16, 1941; admitted to bar, 1966, District of Columbia; registered to practice before U.S. Patent and Trademark Office. *Education:* Carnegie Mellon University (B.S., 1962); Yale University (LL.B., 1965).

PETER D. TROOBOFF, born June 22, 1942; admitted to bar, 1968, New York; 1970, District of Columbia. *Education:* Columbia University (A.B., cum laude, 1964); Institut d' Études Européennes, Paris, 1962-1963; Harvard University (LL.B., cum laude, 1967); London School of Economics, London, England (LL.M., 1968); Hague Academy of International Law (Diploma, cum laude, 1968).

SETH A. TUCKER, born August 30, 1962; admitted to bar, 1988, Illinois (Inactive); 1989, District of Columbia. *Education:* Harvard University (A.B., magna cum laude, 1984; J.D., cum laude, 1988); Ecole Normale Supérieure, Paris, France (1984-1985).

(This Listing Continued)

KELLY VANCE, born October 29, 1959; admitted to bar, 1985, New York. *Education:* University of Utah (B.S., magna cum laude, 1981; J.D., 1984). (Resident, London, England Office).

JOHN VANDERSTAR, born September 17, 1933; admitted to bar, 1961, District of Columbia. *Education:* Princeton University (B.S.E., 1954); Harvard University (J.D., cum laude, 1961).

D. JEAN VETA, born October 19, 1954; admitted to bar, 1981, District of Columbia. *Education:* Newcomb College, Tulane University (B.A., summa cum laude, 1977); Tulane University (J.D., magna cum laude, 1981).

JOHN M. VINE, born June 25, 1944; admitted to bar, 1970, District of Columbia. *Education:* Amherst College (A.B., 1966); Harvard University (J.D., magna cum laude, 1969).

RALPH C. VOLTMER, JR., born April 11, 1960; admitted to bar, 1988, New York; 1989, District of Columbia; 1996, Tennessee. *Education:* Wheaton College (B.A., 1982); University of California, Riverside (M.A., 1984); Georgetown University (J.D., magna cum laude, 1987).

THEODORE VOORHEES, JR., born May 24, 1949; admitted to bar, 1975, District of Columbia. *Education:* Harvard University (B.A., 1971); Catholic University of America (J.D., 1974).

GERARD J. WALDRON, born November 20, 1960; admitted to bar, 1990, Pennsylvania (Inactive); 1997, District of Columbia. *Education:* University of Virginia (B.A., 1982); Duke University (J.D., with high honors, 1990; M.P.P., with honors, 1991).

J. D. WEINBERG, born 1965; admitted to bar, 1991, New York. *Education:* Georgetown University School of Foreign Service (B.S.F.S., cum laude, 1987); University of London, London, England; University of Texas at Austin (J.D., with honors, 1990). (Resident, New York, N.Y. Office).

HARRIS WEINSTEIN, born May 10, 1935; admitted to bar, 1962, District of Columbia. *Education:* Massachusetts Institute of Technology (S.B., 1956; S.M., 1958); Columbia University (LL.B., 1961).

MARK A. WEISS, born June 20, 1937; admitted to bar, 1961, New York; 1962, District of Columbia. *Education:* Columbia College (A.B., 1958); Harvard University (LL.B., magna cum laude, 1961).

ELIZABETH STOTLAND WEISWASSER, born May 26, 1966; admitted to bar, 1992, Illinois; 1995, New York (Not admitted in District of Columbia). *Education:* Northwestern University (B.A., biochemistry/molecular biology, 1988); University of Chicago (J.D., 1992).

STEPHEN A. WEISWASSER, born November 21, 1940; admitted to bar, 1967, District of Columbia. *Education:* Wayne State University (B.A., 1962); Johns Hopkins University (Graduate Studies, 1962-1963); Harvard University (J.D., 1966).

ALBERT L. WELLS, born October 15, 1957; admitted to bar, 1988, New York and U.S. District Court, Southern and Eastern Districts of New York. *Education:* California Institute of Technology (B.S., M.S., with honors, 1978); Oxford University, England (D.Phil., 1982); Yale Law School (J.D., 1987). (Resident, New York, N.Y. Office).

REEVES C. WESTBROOK, born August 21, 1949; admitted to bar, 1975, District of Columbia. *Education:* Vanderbilt University (B.A., magna cum laude, 1971); Yale University (J.D., 1974).

ROBERT WICK, born November 19, 1965; admitted to bar, 1994, District of Columbia. *Education:* Dartmouth College (A.B., 1988); Harvard University (J.D., 1992).

WESLEY S. WILLIAMS, JR., born November 13, 1942; admitted to bar, 1969, New York; 1970, District of Columbia. *Education:* Harvard University (B.A., 1963; J.D., 1967); Fletcher School of Law and Diplomacy (M.A., 1964); Columbia University (LL.M., 1969).

THOMAS S. WILLIAMSON, JR., born July 14, 1946; admitted to bar, 1975, District of Columbia and California. *Education:* Harvard University (B.A., magna cum laude, 1968) Phi Beta Kappa; University of California, Boalt Hall School of Law at Berkeley (J.D., 1974).

BRUCE SANDNESS WILSON, born March 24, 1959; admitted to bar, 1988, Virginia; 1989, District of Columbia. *Education:* University of Virginia (B.A., with high distinction, 1981; J.D., 1986).

KURT A. WIMMER, born March 21, 1959; admitted to bar, 1987, Kansas (inactive); 1988, Texas (inactive); 1993, District of Columbia. *Education:* University of Missouri-Columbia (B.J., 1982); Syracuse University (M.A., 1985; J.D., magna cum laude, 1985). (Resident, London, England Office).

SONYA D. WINNER, born May 13, 1957; admitted to bar, 1983, District of Columbia; 1999, California. *Education:* Michigan State University (B.A., with honors, 1979); Harvard Law School (J.D., magna cum laude, 1982). (Resident, San Francisco, California Office).

(This Listing Continued)

SENIOR COUNSEL

EDWIN S. COHEN, born September 27, 1914; admitted to bar, 1935, Virginia; 1937, New York; 1973, District of Columbia. *Education:* University of Richmond (B.A., 1933); University of Virginia Law School (J.D., 1936).

JOHN L. ELLICOTT, born May 26, 1929; admitted to bar, 1954, Maryland (Inactive); 1957, District of Columbia. *Education:* Princeton University (A.B., summa cum laude, 1951); Harvard University (LL.B., cum laude, 1954).

DANIEL M. GRIBBON, born January 27, 1917; admitted to bar, 1942, New York; 1946, District of Columbia. *Education:* Western Reserve University (A.B., summa cum laude, 1938); Harvard University (LL.B., magna cum laude, 1941).

DAVID B. ISBELL, born February 18, 1929; admitted to bar, 1956, Connecticut; 1957, District of Columbia. *Education:* Yale University (B.A., with high honors, 1949; J.D., 1956).

JAMES C. McKAY, born February 24, 1917; admitted to bar, 1946, District of Columbia. *Education:* Cornell University (B.S., 1938); Georgetown University (LL.B., 1947); Georgetown University Law School (LL.D., 1989, honorary).

ALFRED H. MOSES, born July 24, 1929; admitted to bar, 1956, District of Columbia. *Education:* Dartmouth College (B.A., with highest distinction, 1951) Rufus Choate Scholar; Georgetown University (LL.B., 1956).

JOHN H. SCHAFER, born October 28, 1926; admitted to bar, 1955, District of Columbia. *Education:* Williams College (A.B., 1948); School of Advanced International Studies, Johns Hopkins University (M.A., 1950); University of Virginia (LL.B., 1954).

STANLEY L. TEMKO, born January 4, 1920; admitted to bar, 1943, New York; 1951, District of Columbia. *Education:* Columbia University (A.B., 1940; LL.B., 1943).

J. RANDOLPH WILSON, born August 16, 1922; admitted to bar, 1950, District of Columbia. *Education:* Virginia Polytechnic Institute (B.S., 1943); School of Advanced International Studies, Johns Hopkins University (M.A., 1947); Columbia University (LL.B., Kent Scholar, 1950).

EDWIN M. ZIMMERMAN, born June 11, 1924; admitted to bar, 1949, New York; 1969, District of Columbia. *Education:* Columbia University (A.B., with honors, 1944; LL.B., 1949).

OF COUNSEL

DAVID W. ADDIS, born March 17, 1953; admitted to bar, 1988, District of Columbia. *Education:* University of Virginia (B.A., with high distinction, 1975; M.F.A., 1982); Columbia University (J.D., 1988).

STEPHEN CALKINS, admitted to bar, 1976, New York and District of Columbia. *Education:* Yale University (B.A., magna cum laude, 1972); Harvard University (J.D., cum laude, 1975).

KIPP A. CODDINGTON, born December 15, 1963; admitted to bar, 1992, Virginia; 1993, District of Columbia. *Education:* Purdue University (B.S., 1986); Georgetown University (J.D., 1992).

PATRICK S. DAVIES, born June 25, 1961; admitted to bar, 1988, District of Columbia. *Education:* University of Scranton (B.S., summa cum laude, 1983); Universidad Catolica de Chile (Fulbright/ITT International Fellowship, 1983-1984); University of Notre Dame (J.D., magna cum laude, 1987).

EDWARD H. DIXON, born January 20, 1964; admitted to bar, 1993, Maryland; 1994, District of Columbia. *Education:* Columbia University (B.A., 1986); University of Michigan (J.D., 1993).

RONALD G. DOVE, JR., born December 31, 1964; admitted to bar, 1991, District of Columbia. *Education:* Milligan College (B.A., 1987); Harvard University (J.D., 1991).

HERBERT ESTREICHER, born September 21, 1954; admitted to bar, 1989, New York and District of Columbia. *Education:* Brandeis University (B.A., magna cum laude, 1975); Harvard University (Ph.D., 1980); New York University (J.D., cum laude, 1988).

SCOTT DAVID FELDSTEIN, born November 2, 1959; admitted to bar, 1985, New York; 1986, District of Columbia. *Education:* Cornell University (B.A., 1981); University of Pennsylvania (J.D., 1984).

KATHLEEN T. GALLAGHER-DUFF, born 1953; admitted to bar, 1985, Maryland; 1987, District of Columbia. *Education:* Merrimack College (B.A., 1975); Georgetown University (J.D., 1984).

JAMES A. GOOLD, born September 7, 1950; admitted to bar, 1976, Illinois; 1991, District of Columbia. *Education:* Wesleyan University (B.A., with high honors, 1972); University of Chicago (J.D., 1976).

DAVID R. GRACE, born September 7, 1956; admitted to bar, 1981, Illinois; 1983, District of Columbia. *Education:* Princeton University (A.B., magna cum laude, 1978); Harvard University (J.D., cum laude, 1981); Georgetown University (LL.M., 1984).

(This Listing Continued)

COVINGTON & BURLING, Washington—Continued

R. LAIRD HART, born September 11, 1953; admitted to bar, 1981, District of Columbia. *Education:* Princeton University (A.B., 1975; M.P.A., 1976); Yale University (J.D., 1980).

STUART IRVIN, born June 11, 1961; admitted to bar, 1989, Maryland; 1991, District of Columbia. *Education:* Emory University (B.A., 1984); George Washington University (J.D., with honors, 1989); Cambridge University (LL.M., with honors, 1990).

W. ANDREW JACK, born February 8, 1962; admitted to bar, 1986, Virginia (Inactive); 1987, District of Columbia. *Education:* George Washington University (B.A., 1983; J.D., with highest honors, 1986).

ANNA D. KRAUS, born October 3, 1956; admitted to bar, 1983, District of Columbia; 1985, Arizona (inactive). *Education:* University of New Mexico (B.A., 1978); Stanford Graduate School of Business (M.B.A., 1982); Stanford Law School (J.D., 1982).

BENEDICT M. LENHART, born February 9, 1963; admitted to bar, 1990, Ohio (Inactive); 1991, District of Columbia. *Education:* University of Michigan (B.A., with high honors, 1985); Harvard University (J.D., cum laude, 1989).

RICHARD A. MERRILL, born May 20, 1937; admitted to bar, 1964, New York (inactive); 1966, District of Columbia; 1980, Virginia (inactive). *Education:* Columbia University (A.B., magna cum laude, 1959; LL.B., magna cum laude, 1964); Oxford University (B.A., 1961; M.A., 1965).

ALAN A. PEMBERTON, born November 4, 1952; admitted to bar, 1982, District of Columbia. *Education:* University of Chicago (B.A., with honors, 1974); University of Michigan (M.A., 1977; J.D., magna cum laude, 1981).

DOUGLAS E. PHILLIPS, born May 6, 1955; admitted to bar, 1981, District of Columbia. *Education:* Princeton University (A.B., magna cum laude, 1977); New York University (J.D., 1980).

ANDREA G. REISTER, born November 26, 1957; admitted to bar, 1993, District of Columbia; registered to practice before U.S. Patent and Trademark Office. *Education:* University of Washington (B.S., magna cum laude, 1980; B.S., magna cum laude, 1980); George Mason University School of Law (J.D., with distinction, 1993).

JACK LEE SCHENENDORF, born May 29, 1944; admitted to bar, 1975, Maryland (Not admitted in District of Columbia). *Education:* Union College (B.S., 1966); Georgetown University Law Center (J.D., 1975).

ELLIOTT SCHULDER, born January 16, 1947; admitted to bar, 1974, New York; 1985, District of Columbia. *Education:* Yale University (B.A., 1968); New York University (J.D., Moot Court Honors, 1973).

ROBERT E. SHAW, born February 2, 1957; admitted to bar, 1984, New Jersey; 1989, District of Columbia. *Education:* Rutgers University (B.A., 1979; J.D., with honors, 1984).

ROBERT B. STEVENS, born June 8, 1933; admitted to bar, 1956, England. *Education:* Oxford University, Keble College (B.A., 1955; B.C.L., 1956; M.A., 1959; D.C.L., 1984); Yale University (LL.M., 1958). (Resident, London, England Office).

SARAH E. TAYLOR, born April 10, 1957; admitted to bar, 1989, District of Columbia. *Education:* University of Wisconsin-Madison (B.S., with honors, 1980); University of Minnesota (M.P.H., 1983); George Washington University (J.D., with high honors, 1989).

EDWARD S. WEST, born June 23, 1957; admitted to bar, 1984, Pennsylvania; 1985, District of Columbia; 1991, Maryland. *Education:* Yale University (B.A., 1979); Georgetown University (J.D., 1984).

TOGO D. WEST, JR., born June 21, 1942; admitted to bar, 1968, District of Columbia; 1969, New York and U.S. Court of Military Appeals; 1978, U.S. Supreme Court. *Education:* Howard University (B.S.E.E., 1965; J.D., cum laude, 1968).

SPECIAL COUNSEL

STEPHEN P. ANTHONY, born August 30, 1961; admitted to bar, 1989, Maryland; 1991, District of Columbia. *Education:* Dartmouth College (A.B., 1983); Columbia University (J.D., 1988).

DENNIS B. AUERBACH, born April 24, 1961; admitted to bar, 1989, District of Columbia. *Education:* Princeton University (B.A., 1984); Harvard University (J.D., 1988).

KATHLEEN L. BLANER, born August 30, 1953; admitted to bar, 1989, Maryland; 1991, District of Columbia. *Education:* American University (A.B., with honors, 1978); Catholic University Law School (J.D., 1989).

MICHAEL J. CICERO, born October 21, 1959; admitted to bar, 1991, District of Columbia. *Education:* Notre Dame University (B.A., 1981); University of South Carolina (M.S.); University of Chicago (J.D., 1989).

(This Listing Continued)

WILLIAM H. FITZ, born January 14, 1942; admitted to bar, 1968, District of Columbia. *Education:* Washington & Lee University (B.A., 1964); George Washington University (J.D., 1967).

THOMAS W. KRAUSE, born June 8, 1961; admitted to bar, 1991, District of Columbia. *Education:* University of Illinois (B.S., 1982); Harvard University (J.D., 1990).

MICHAEL GARY MICHAELSON, born July 6, 1947; admitted to bar, 1985, Pennsylvania; 1986, District of Columbia. *Education:* Johns Hopkins University (A.B., with honors, 1968); University of Pennsylvania (M.D., 1973); Harvard University (J.D., cum laude, 1984).

JULIE SIMON MILLER, born February 14, 1967; admitted to bar, 1993, New York; 1995, District of Columbia. *Education:* Vassar College (B.A., 1988); George Washington University (J.D., 1992).

JAMES S. PORTNOY, born June 30, 1960; admitted to bar, 1989, New York; 1992, Pennsylvania; 1994, District of Columbia. *Education:* University of Pennsylvania (B.A., 1982); University of Michigan (J.D., 1987).

KEVIN SHORTILL, born January 17, 1963; admitted to bar, 1989, New York; 1991, District of Columbia. *Education:* Washington University (A.B., 1985); University of Michigan (J.D., 1988).

ELAINE WINTROUB STONE, born July 2, 1953; admitted to bar, 1980, California; 1983, Texas; 1990, District of Columbia. *Education:* Barnard College (B.A., summa cum laude, 1975); New York University (J.D, with honors, 1978).

ASSOCIATES

Raymond A. Atkins; M. Stacey Bach; Karen A. Ballotta; Catherine Cloud Barre (Not admitted in DC); ***Ronald John Baumgarten, Jr.; Bryan Beier; Thomas W. Beimers; Andrew Betaque*** (Not admitted in DC); ***Hillary Brill*** (Not admitted in DC); ***P. Robert Broeren, Jr.; Eric D. Brown; Nathan A. Brown; Tyrone Anthony Brown*** (Not admitted in DC); ***Christopher Burke; Charles J. Butler; Fernando Campoamor-Sanchez; Les P. Carnegie; Michael K. Catoe; Marney L. Cheek*** (Not admitted in DC); ***George F. Cicotte; Tracey H. Cohen; Aaron Cooper*** (Not admitted in DC); ***Scott L. Cunningham*** (Not admitted in DC); ***Catherine Janine Dargan; James Robert Dean, Jr; John T. Delacourt; Christopher M. Denig; John V. Donnelly, III*** (Not admitted in DC); ***Kathleen J. Donnelly; Kenneth J. Drexler; Phillip E. Dube; Richard Dulik; Siobhan Elizabeth Dupuy; Erin M. Egan; Kimberly K. Egan; Christine E. Enemark; Juan Manuel Estrada; Michael J. Fanelli; Mark E. Feldman*** (Not admitted in DC); ***David Finkelson; Michael J. Francese; Richard L. Freuhauf; James M. Garland*** (Not admitted in DC); ***Laura B. Gasho; Jason P. Gluck; Adam W. Goldberg; Sara L. Gottovi; Eric Dodson Greenberg; Gideon Y. Grunfeld; Miriam J. Guggenheim; Michael Hadley; Stephen J. Hess; Elie Honig*** (Not admitted in DC); ***Marianna Horton; Camilla M. Jackson; Russell D. Jessee; Jennifer Anne Johnson; Julie L.B. Johnson; Emily Johnson Henn; Russell P. Kanjorski; Faith D. Kasparian; Georgia Kazakis; Timothy J. Keefer; Robert K. Kelner; Ann-Kelley Kemper; Laura M. Kim; Erika King; Karen Kizer*** (Not admitted in DC); ***Susan Koegel; Rukesh Korde; Douglas Kramer*** (Not admitted in DC); ***Karen Kramer; Joseph A. Kresse; Joan L. Kutcher*** (Legislative Counsel); ***Michael Scott Labson; Monique J. La Fleur; Marie A. Lavalleye; Amy L. Levine; Jason A. Levine; Andrew D. Levy; Jason R. Litow; Catherine E. Long; John F. C. Luedke; Robert J. Lundman; C. Cecilia Macazana Barragan*** (Not admitted in United States); ***Brooks Mackintosh; Simone Manigo-Truell*** (Not admitted in DC); ***Scott B. Markow*** (Not admitted in DC); ***Deborah J. Matties; James A. McLaughlin; C. Martin Meekins*** (Not admitted in DC); ***Nicole Jo Moss; Ralph M. Muoio; David G. Nason; Heather L. Nevin*** (Not admitted in DC); ***Robert S. Newman; Keith A. Noreika; David P. W. Orlin; Shaun M. Palmer*** (Not admitted in DC); ***Eric J. Pan; Elizabeth Pearsall; James B. Perrine; Jeannie M. Perron; Eric Phillips; Jennifer Plitsch; C. Edward Polk, Jr.*** (Not admitted in DC); ***Christopher J. Prokop; Benjamin J. Razi*** (Not admitted in DC); ***Roni R. Reed*** (Resident, San Francisco, California Office); ***Donald J. Ridings, Jr.; Edward Holden Rippey; Andrew Rittenberg; Jason F. Robinson*** (Not admitted in DC); ***Michael L. Rosenthal; Kristina Rosette; Simone Ross; Rochelle E. Rubin; Gary Rubman*** (Not admitted in DC); ***David P. Ruschke; James P. A. Ryan; Joel Samuels; John Scheib; Paul W. Schmidt; Andrew P. Schoeffler; Jennifer Schwartz*** (Not admitted in DC); ***Vijay Shanker; Fairlea Sheehy; Alexei M. Silverman; Grail Peyton Walsh Sipes; Richard W. Smith; Carl L. Spataro, Jr.*** (Not admitted in DC); ***Jalena G. Specht*** (Not admitted in DC); ***Jeremy D. Spector; Lisa J. Stevenson; Hisanari Tanaka*** (Not admitted in DC; Not admitted in United States); ***Chad Y. Tang; Cametra Thompson; Henry P. Ting; Joseph E. Topmiller*** (Not admitted in DC); ***Emin Toro*** (Not admitted in DC); ***P. Andrew Torrez*** (Not admitted in DC); ***Terry L. Turnipseed; Nancy A. Udell; Debra R. Volland; Steven M. Warshawsky; George L. Washington, Jr.; Kashi Way*** (Not admitted in DC); ***Rachel Welch*** (Not admitted in DC); ***Christopher J. Wenk*** (Not admitted in DC); ***Grady Lee White; Jeffrey L. White; Gregory M. Williams; Jarrett Williams; Mary***

(This Listing Continued)

Newcomer Williams; Elizabeth I. Winston; Joshua D. Wolson (Not admitted in DC); ***Robert E. Wone; Rebecca Woods; D. Grayson Yeargin*** (Not admitted in DC); ***Anthony S. Yoo; Peter Zern.***

(For complete biographical data on San Francisco, California, London, England and Brussels, Belgium Associates, see those offices)

COZEN O'CONNOR

A PROFESSIONAL CORPORATION

1667 K STREET, NW
WASHINGTON, D.C. 20006
Telephone: 202-912-4800; 800-540-1355
Fax: 202-912-4830
Email: postmaster@cozen.com
URL: http://www.cozen.com

Charlotte, North Carolina Office: One First Union Center, Suite 2100, 301 S. College Street, 28202. Telephones: 704-376-3400; 800-762-3575. Fax: 704-334-3351.

Dallas, Texas Office: 2300 BankOne Center, 1717 Main Street, 75201. Telephones: 214-462-3000; 800-448-1207. Fax: 214-462-3299.

New York, N.Y. Office: 45 Broadway Atrium, 16th Floor, 10006. Telephones: 212-509-9400; 800-437-7040. Fax: 212-509-9492.

West Conshohocken, Pennsylvania Office: 200 Four Falls Corporate Center, Suite 400, P.O. Box 800, 19428. Telephone: 610-941-5400; 800-379-0695. Fax: 610-941-0711.

San Diego, California Office: Suite 1610, 501 West Broadway, 92101. Telephones: 619-234-1700; 800-782-3366. Fax: 619-234-7831.

Los Angeles, California Office: 777 South Figueroa Street, Suite 2850, 90017. Telephones: 213-892-7900; 800-563-1027. Fax: 213-892-7999.

Seattle, Washington Office: Suite 5200, Washington Mutual Tower, 1201 Third Avenue, 98101. Telephones: 206-340-1000; 800-423-1950. Fax: 206-621-8783.

Newark, New Jersey Office: One Newark Center, Suite 1900, 07102. Telephone: 973-286-1200; 888-200-9521. Fax: 973-242-2121.

Atlanta, Georgia Office: Suite 2200, SunTrust Plaza, 303 Peachtree Street, N.E., 30308. Telephones: 404-572-2000; 800-890-1393. Fax: 404-572-2199.

London, England Office: Tower 42, Level 23, 25 Old Broad Street, London EC2N 1HQ. Telephone: 011-44-20-7864-2000. Fax: 011-44-20-7864-2013.

Wilmington, Delaware Office: Chase Manhattan Centre, 1201 North Market Street, Suite 1400, 19801. Telephone: 302-295-2000; 888-207-2440. Fax: 302-295-2013.

Las Vegas, Nevada Office (Affiliated with the Law Offices of J. Goldberg, C. Stuart, III & D. Grossman): #1, 1000 East Sahara Avenue, 89104-3231. Telephone: 800-782-3366.

San Francisco, California Office: 425 California Street, Suite 1800, 94104-2203. Telephone: 415-617-6100; 800-818-0165. Fax: 415-617-6101.

Chicago, Illinois Office: 222 South Riverside, Suite 1500, 60606. Telephone: 312-382-3100; 877-992-6036. Fax: 312-382-8910.

Philadelphia, Pennsylvania Office: 1900 Market Street, 19103. Telephones: 215-665-2000; 800-523-2900. Fax: 215-665-2013.

Cherry Hill, New Jersey Office: LibertyView, Suite 300, 457 Haddonfield Road, P.O. Box 5459, 08002-2220. Telephone: 856-910-5000; 800-989-0499. Fax: 856-910-5075.

Acquisitions and Divestitures, Admiralty and Maritime Law, Agents and Brokers Errors and Omissions, Alternative Dispute Resolution, Antitrust and Unfair Competition, Appellate Litigation, Appellate Practice, Arbitration and Alternative Dispute Resolution, Arson and Insurance Fraud, Asset Protection, Aviation Insurance, Aviation Law, Aviation Litigation, Aviation Products Liability, Bad Faith Litigation, Bankruptcy, Bankruptcy, Insolvency and Restructuring, Banks and Banking, Business Law, Casualty Insurance Defense, Civil Practice, Commercial Law, Commercial Litigation, Commercial Real Estate, Complex and Multi-District Litigation, Construction Claims, Construction Law, Construction Law and Litigation, Copyrights, Corporate and Partnership Law, Corporate Law, Corporate Planning, Creditors Rights, Crisis Management, Debtor and Creditor, Directors and Officers Errors and Omissions, E-Commerce and Internet Law, Electric Utility Regulation, Emerging Business and Venture Capital, Emerging Growth Companies, Employee Benefits, Employee Benefits and Executive Compensation, Employment Defense, Employment Practices, Energy, Energy Regulation, Environmental Insurance, Environmental Insurance Claims, Environmental Law, Estate Planning, Family Law, Finance, Financial Services, First and Third Party Insurance Defense, Gas Utility Regulation, Health Law, Healthcare, Healthcare Finance, Healthcare Litigation, Healthcare Regulation, Healthcare Reimbursement, Information Technology, Insurance, Insurance Bad Faith Defense, Insurance Corporate and Regulatory, Insurance Coverage, Insurance Coverage Defense, Insurance Defense, Insurance Mergers and Acquisitions, Insurance Regulation, Intellectual Property, Intellectual Property Litigation, Intentional Torts, International Estate Planning, International Tax and Estate Planning, International Trusts, Labor and Employment, Latin America Practice Group, Litigation, Management Labor Law, Marine and Maritime Law, Medical Devices Defenses, Medical Malpractice Defense, Mergers, Partnership Law, Patent Privacy Law, Planning and Land Use, Privacy Law and Regulation, Private Wealth Services, Products Liability, Professional Liability, Project Finance, Property Insurance, Property Subrogation, Public Finance, Public Utility Regulation, Punitive Damages, Punitive Damages Reinsurance, Real Estate, Real Estate Litigation, Reinsurance, RICO, Securities, Securities Litigation, Tax Litigation, Taxation, Torts, Toxic and Other Mass Torts, Toxic Torts, Trademarks, Trusts and Estates, Utility Law, Wealth Preservation, White Collar Crime, Zoning.

(This Listing Continued)

FIRM PROFILE: Cozen O'Connor is a dynamic, full-service client-oriented actively engaged in a diverse business and litigation practice. Headquartered in Philadelphia, Pennsylvania, the firm consists of over 430 lawyers practicing from sixteen offices in the United States and an international office in London. The firm's practice is divided into four areas: business law, business litigation, insurance litigation, and personal wealth services.

Cozen O'Connor is dedicated to and focused on providing each client with the highest level of legal services rendered in the most efficient and cost-effective manner. Our philosophy acknowledges the paramount importance of each client's interests and we recognize that effective attorney-client relationships not only exist between institutions but with individuals as well. We endeavor to develop trust and confidence through close personal working relationships between our attorneys and the individual representatives of each client. This attention to the specific needs of each client explains our ability to represent a diverse clientele. Our clients range from individuals to corporations, including major utility companies, banks, real estate investment trusts, professional corporations, public companies, domestic insurance companies and foreign insurance syndicates.

FIRM MEMBERS IN WASHINGTON, D.C.

ELLEN JANE ABROMSON, born 1951; admitted to bar, 1981, Massachusetts; 1982, Pennsylvania; 1984, Maryland (Not admitted in District of Columbia). *Education:* University of Massachusetts (B.A., 1973); Suffolk University (J.D., 1981). ***PRACTICE AREAS:*** Contracts; Real Estate; Government Relations; Insurance; Corporate; Mergers and Acquisitions.

EDWARD B. CROSLAND, JR., born Selma, Alabama, April 6, 1944; admitted to bar, 1971, Virginia; 1972, District of Columbia. *Education:* Washington & Lee University (B.A., 1966; B.S., 1967; J.D., 1970). Staff Attorney, Division of Corporation, Finance, Securities and Exchange Commission, 1970-1971; Securities Industry Study, U.S. Senate Committee on Banking, Housing and Urban Affairs, 1971-1973; Office of Disclosure Policy and Proceedings, Securities and Exchange Commission, 1973-1975.

MATTHEW G. ASH, born London, Ontario, Canada, September 30, 1943; admitted to bar, 1973, District of Columbia; 1981, U.S. Supreme Court. *Education:* University of Michigan (B.A., 1965); Wayne State University (M.A., with honors, 1969); Georgetown University (J.D., 1973). United States Department of Justice, Community Relations Service, 1969-1973; Office of General Counsel, Federal Home Loan Bank Board, 1973-1980; Chief, FSLIC Assistance Division, 1976-1978; Staff Member, Antitrust and Monopoly Subcommittee, United States Senate Committee on the Judiciary, 1973. ***PRACTICE AREAS:*** Banking Law; Corporate Law; Litigation.

ROBERT G. RATHBUN, born Grosse Pointe, Michigan, September 15, 1953; admitted to bar, 1982, Michigan; 1985, California; 1994, Virginia (Not admitted in District of Columbia). *Education:* Oakland University (B.S., 1977); University of Detroit (J.D., 1982). ***LANGUAGES:*** French and German. ***PRACTICE AREAS:*** Corporate Law; International Business; Mergers and Acquisitions.

ANDREW B. KATZ, born Philadelphia, Pennsylvania, April 2, 1964; admitted to bar, 1989, Pennsylvania; 1990, U.S. Court of Federal Claims, U.S. Court of Appeals, Federal Circuit; 1996, District of Columbia; registered to practice before U.S. Patent & Trademark Office. *Education:* Lafayette College (A.B., Engr., 1986); George Washington University (J.D., 1989). Co-Author: with David S. Cohen, "Looking for a Partner you may want Uncle Sam," Washington Business Journal, Vol. 17, No. 11, July 24, 1998. Author: "State Street May Place Start-Ups In Peril," New York Law Journal, Vol. 12, No. 9, January 19, 1999; "Overcoming Obstacles to Successful Technology Transfer," *Intellectual Property Today,* Oct. 1996. *Member:* The District of Columbia Bar; American Bar Association; American Intellectual Property Law Association (Head Government Intellectual Property Policy Committee); District of Columbia Patent Lawyers Association; District of Columbia Computer Law Forum. ***PRACTICE AREAS:*** Trademarks; Unfair Competition; Copyrights; Computer Law; Patents; Corporate Law; Government Contracts. ***Email:*** akatz@cozen.com

CRAIGHILL, MAYFIELD, FENWICK, CROMELIN & COBB, L.L.P.

Established in 1898

SUITE 215, 4910 MASSACHUSETTS AVENUE, N.W.
WASHINGTON, D.C. 20016-4300
Telephone: 202-364-4242
Facsimile: 202-966-1078
URL: http://www.lawyers.com/cmfcc

Estate Planning, Wills and Trusts, Probate, Living Wills, Wealth Preservation, Power of Attorney, Health Directives, Family Business Planning.

MEMBERS OF FIRM

G. BOWDOIN CRAIGHILL, JR., born Washington, D.C., February 9, 1914; admitted to bar, 1939, District of Columbia. *Education:* private schools, District of Columbia; University of the South (B.A., 1936); George Washington University (J.D., 1939). Phi Beta Kappa; Phi Delta Phi. Chancellor, Episcopal Diocese of Washington, 1973-1978. *Member:* District of Columbia Bar; Barristers Club; Lawyers' Club, D.C.; Bar Association of the District of Columbia (Director, 1951-1952). [Commander, USNR, active duty, 1941-46]. ***PRACTICE AREAS:*** Estate Planning; Probate Law; Trusts.

RICHARD H. MAYFIELD, born Washington, D.C., September 29, 1921; admitted to bar, 1948, District of Columbia; 1957, Maryland. *Education:* Swarthmore College (A.B., 1943); Harvard Law School (LL.B., 1948). *Member:* District of Columbia Bar; Barristers Club; Lawyers' Club, D.C. Fellow: American College of Trust and Estate Counsel (Regent, 1983-1986). ***PRACTICE AREAS:*** Estate Planning; Probate Law; Trusts.

FRANCIS E. FENWICK, born Rio de Janeiro, Brazil, July 4, 1945; admitted to bar, 1975, Virginia; 1980, District of Columbia; 1991, Maryland. *Education:* Georgetown University (B.A., 1967; J.D., 1975). *Member:* Maryland State Bar Association; District of Columbia Bar; Virginia State Bar; Barristers Club; Lawyers Club of Washington D.C. ***LANGUAGES:*** Portuguese. ***PRACTICE AREAS:*** Estate Planning; Probate Law; Trusts.

PAUL B. CROMELIN, III, born Washington, D.C., February 24, 1954; admitted to bar, 1979, Virginia and District of Columbia; 1985, Maryland. *Education:* Washington and Lee University (B.A., 1976); University of Richmond (J.D., 1979). *Member:* District of Columbia Bar (Member, Steering Committee, Estates, Trusts and Probate Law Section, 1988-1992); Virginia State Bar; Maryland State Bar Association; Barristers Club; Lawyers Club of Washington, D.C.; District of Columbia Estate Planning Council. ***PRACTICE AREAS:*** Estate Planning; Probate Law; Trusts.

CALVIN H. COBB, III, born Washington, D.C., January 25, 1958; admitted to bar, 1985, District of Columbia and California (inactive); 1992, Maryland. *Education:* Princeton University (A.B., 1980); Georgetown University (J.D., with honors, 1984). Barrister's Council Fellowship. Lead Articles Editor, The Tax Lawyer, Georgetown University, 1983-1984. Law Clerk, Manuel L. Real, Chief Judge, U.S. District Court for Central District of California, 1984-1985. Co-Lecturer, District of Columbia Bar Continuing Legal Education Program, Basic Estate Planning Series, "Part III: The Will and Estate Plan for the Senior Surviving Spouse with Surviving Children and Grandchildren, An Estate in Excess of $675, 000 and Who May be Contemplating Remarriage". Co-Coordinator, D.C. Practice Manual, Estates, Trusts & Probate Section. *Member:* District of Columbia Bar (Steering Committee, Estates, Trusts & Probate Section); Maryland State Bar Association; Barristers Club. ***PRACTICE AREAS:*** Estate Planning; Probate Law; Trusts.

CRESKOFF & DORAM LLP

1620 I STREET, N.W., SUITE 900
WASHINGTON, D.C. 20006
Telephone: 202-463-1300
Fax: 703-709-9246
URL: http://www.internationalaw.com

Pasadena, California Office: 1028 North Lake Avenue, Suite 202, 91104. Telephone: 626-296-9161

Customs, International Trade Law, Litigation, Trade Associations, Antidumping.

STEPHEN M. CRESKOFF, born Philadelphia, Pennsylvania, September 25, 1939; admitted to bar, 1969, Maryland; 1970, District of Columbia; 1974, U.S. Court of Appeals for the District of Columbia Circuit; 1975, U.S. Court of International Trade; 1981, U.S. Court of Appeals for the Federal Circuit. *Education:* University of Pennsylvania (A.B., 1963); University of Maryland (J.D., with honors, 1969); Georgetown University (LL.M., 1976). Notes & Comments Editor, Maryland Law Review, 1968-1969. Member, Editorial Board, The Federal Bar Journal, 1976-1980. Special Assistant to the Under Secretary, U.S. Treasury Department, 1977-1978. Deputy to the Assistant Secretary, Enforcement & Operations, U.S. Treasury Department, 1978-1980. Adjunct Professor,

(This Listing Continued)

Johns Hopkins University, 1995—. *Member:* District of Columbia Bar; Federal (Chairman, International Trade and Customs Law Committee, 1980-1982; Commendation for Outstanding Service, 1981) and American (Deputy Chair, Customs and International Trade Committee, Administrative Law Section, 1988-1990) Bar Associations. ***REPORTED CASES:*** Janini v. Kuwait University, 43 F.3d 1534 (D.C. Cir. 1995); United States v. Chow 841 F. Supp. 12 86 (CIT 1993); Babcock and Wilcox Co. v. United States, 521 F. Supp. 479 (CIT 1981). ***Email:*** screskoff@aol.com

MICHAEL R. DORAM, born Portland, Oregon, August 16, 1940; admitted to bar, 1967, District of Columbia; 1968, U.S. Tax Court and U.S. Court of Federal Claims; 1971, U.S. Supreme Court; 1973, California; 1986, U.S. District Court, Central District of California; 1987, U.S. District Court, Southern District of California and U.S. Court of International Trade; 1988, U.S. Court of Appeals, Federal Circuit. *Education:* Stanford University (B.A., 1963); Georgetown University (J.D., 1966; LL.M., 1968). Director and Secretary, Export Managers of California, 1988-1994. *Member:* Los Angeles County (Member, Customs Law Committee; Vice Chair and Chair, 1981-1984 and Member, 1984—, International Law Section) and American (Member, International Law Section) Bar Associations; State Bar of California (Member, International Law Section); Customs and International Trade Bar Association; Export Legal Assistance Network (ELAN). ***PRACTICE AREAS:*** Customs Law; International Trade.

OF COUNSEL

ROBERT M. GREEN, born Bethlehem, Pennsylvania, July 2, 1953; admitted to bar, 1981, Georgia and U.S. District Court, Northern District of Georgia; 1982, U.S. Court of Appeals, Eleventh Circuit; 1988, District of Columbia; 1993, U.S. District Court, District of Columbia; 1996, U.S. Court of Appeals, Federal Circuit. *Education:* Gettysburg College (A.B., 1975); Potomac School of Law (J.D., 1979); Tulane University (LL.M., Admiralty, 1997). Pi Lambda Sigma. Member, Potomac Law Review. Articles and Comments Editor, Law Review, Vol. 2. Consultant, Trade Services, Inc., Washington, D.C., 1996—. Executive Vice President, Washington Consular Services, Inc., Washington, D.C., 1984-1996. Attorney, Ashcraft & Gerel, Washington, D.C., 1981-1984. Registered Agent, Child Empowerment Network (Blue Knights), 1994-1996. Chair, Westmoreland Volunteer Corps, 1992-1993. *Member:* Maritime Law Association of the U.S. (Maritime Arbitration Committee); Association for Transportation Law, Logistics & Policy. ***LANGUAGES:*** Spanish.

CREWS & HANCOCK, P.L.C.

WASHINGTON, D.C.

(See Fairfax, Virginia)

Hospital, Health, Insurance, Administrative, Corporate, Safety and Security Law and Civil Litigation.

CRISPIN & BRENNER, P.L.L.C.

1156 15TH STREET, N.W.
SUITE 1105
WASHINGTON, D.C. 20005
Telephone: 202-828-0152
Fax: 202-828-0158
Email: office@crispinandbrenner.com

Communications Law, with Special Emphasis on Wireless Communications, Common Carrier Law, Cellular, Radio and TV Licensing, and Commercial Litigation, with Special Emphasis on Communications Law, Copyright and Intellectual Property Law, Environmental Law, and Professional Liability and Insurance Law.

FIRM PROFILE: Crispin & Brenner, P.L.L.C., is a law firm with a high quality practice involving a broad range of matters in the areas of communications law and litigation. Our clients range from Fortune 500 multinational corporations and financial institutions to medium and small-sized corporations, partnerships and individuals.

WILLIAM H. CRISPIN, born Boston, Massachusetts, May 21, 1946; admitted to bar, 1975, Illinois; 1982, District of Columbia; 1988, Virginia. *Education:* Dartmouth College (A.B. in History, cum laude, with highest distinction in Major, 1968); University of Chicago (J.D., 1975). *Member:* Chicago, Illinois State, Virginia and American Bar Associations; District of Columbia Bar; Federal Communications Bar Association. ***PRACTICE AREAS:*** Commercial Litigation; Communications Law.

DEAN R. BRENNER, born New York, N.Y., October 20, 1960; admitted to bar, 1985, District of Columbia; 1986, U.S. District Court for the District of Columbia; 1990, U.S. Court of Appeals, District of Columbia Circuit and Eleventh Circuit; 1991, U.S. Supreme Court; 1992, U.S. Court of Appeals, Third Circuit; 2000, Maryland. *Education:* Duke University (A.B., magna cum laude, with distinction, 1982); Georgetown University (J.D., cum laude, 1985). CBS

(This Listing Continued)

Scholarship, 1978-1982. Staff Member and Associate Editor, The Tax Lawyer, 1983-1985. Staff Assistant and Policy Analyst, U.S. House of Representatives Subcommittee on Telecommunications, Consumer Protection and Finance, 1981-1984. *Member:* Maryland State and American Bar Associations; The District of Columbia Bar; Federal Communications Bar Association. ***PRACTICE AREAS:*** Communications Law; Commercial Litigation.

KATHERINE CONNOR LINTON, born Wilmington, Delaware, March 28, 1961; admitted to bar, 1988, California; 1990, District of Columbia. *Education:* Middlebury College (B.A., magna cum laude, 1983); University of California at Los Angeles (J.D., 1988). Law Clerk to Honorable John G. Davies, U.S. District Court for the Central District of California, 1988-1989. Co-author with Ellen Vargyas, "The Legal Implications of Gender Bias in Standardized Testing," 7 Berkeley Women's Law Journal, 1992. Counsel, National Women's Law Center, Washington, D.C., 1989-1991. *Member:* District of Columbia Bar; American Bar Association; Women's Bar Association (Co-Chair, Tax and Business Forum). ***LANGUAGES:*** Spanish, French. ***PRACTICE AREAS:*** Professional Liability and Insurance Law; Commercial Litigation; Communications Law. ***Email:*** klinton@crispinandbrenner.com

JOHN L. RICHARDSON, born Pontiac, Michigan, October 31, 1940; admitted to bar, 1967, Virginia and District of Columbia; 1968, U.S. Court of Appeals for the District of Columbia Circuit; 1970, U.S. Supreme Court. *Education:* University of Michigan (B.A., 1962); University of Virginia (J.D., 1967). *Member:* The District of Columbia Bar; Virginia State Bar; American Bar Association. [Lieut., U.S. Army, 1962-1964]. ***PRACTICE AREAS:*** Corporate Law; Government; Transportation; International Commercial Law. ***Email:*** jrichardson@crispinandbrenner.com

CROSS, MURPHY, SMUCK & HOUSTON

Established in 1954

1350 CONNECTICUT AVENUE, N.W., SUITE 300
WASHINGTON, D.C. 20036
Telephone: 202-393-8668
Telecopier: 202-833-2351
Email: anwalt1350@aol.com
URL: http://www.lawyers.com/cms&hlaw

Estate Planning, Tax Planning, Tax Law, Trust Law, Trust Administration, Wills, Probate and Probate Administration.

FIRM PROFILE: The firm represents individuals, corporations and organizations seeking counsel for tax planning issues, trust and estate planning and administration and trust and probate litigation. The firm is primarily a regional firm representing clients in metropolitan Washington, D.C., northern Virginia and central and southern Maryland.

MEMBERS OF FIRM

JOHN W. CROSS (1902-1971).

JAMES RUSSELL MURPHY (1905-1986).

JOHN C. SMUCK, born Washington, D.C., December 19, 1937; admitted to bar, 1962, District of Columbia; 1970, U.S. Supreme Court; 1978, Virginia; 1991, Maryland. *Education:* University of Virginia (B.A., 1959); Harvard University (LL.D., 1962). *Member:* The District of Columbia Bar; Bar Association of the District of Columbia; Virginia and American Bar Associations. ***PRACTICE AREAS:*** Estate Planning Law; Trusts Law; Tax Law.

STUART E. HOUSTON, born Atlanta, Georgia, April 25, 1949; admitted to bar, 1974, Maryland; 1975, District of Columbia; 1978, U.S. Tax Court. *Education:* Washington & Lee University (B.A., 1971; J.D., 1974); Georgetown University (LL.M., 1976). *Member:* District of Columbia Bar; American Bar Association. (Also Member, Burwell, Hansen, Peters & Houston). ***PRACTICE AREAS:*** Estate Planning; Trust Law; Tax Law.

REFERENCE: Sun Trust Bank, N.A.

LAW OFFICES OF THOMAS K. CROWE, P.C.

2300 M STREET, N.W.
SUITE 800
WASHINGTON, D.C. 20037
Telephone: 202-973-2890
Fax: 202-973-2891
Email: tkcrowe@bellatlantic.net
URL: http://www.tkcrowe.com

Telecommunications Law, Commercial Transactions, Litigation and Legislative.

THOMAS K. CROWE, born Brooklyn, New York, August 19, 1957; admitted to bar, 1984, New Jersey; 1985, District of Columbia; 1992, New York. *Education:* New York University (B.A., magna cum laude, 1979); George Washington University (J.D., 1982). Phi Beta Kappa. Recipient, Founder's Day Award. Author: "The U.S. Pacific Territories and Federal Telecommunications Policies: A Blueprint for the Future," CommLaw Conspectus, Journal of Communications Law and Policy, Summer 1995 Edition; "Long Distance Services Theft: Who Pays?" The National Law Journal, Oct. 1992. Formerly, Partner, Hopkins & Sutter; Counsel, LeBoeuf, Lamb, Greene & MacRae, L.L.P.; Associate, Jones, Day, Reavis & Pogue. *Member:* District of Columbia Bar, American and Federal Communications Bar Associations.

CROWELL & MORING LLP

Established in 1979

1001 PENNSYLVANIA AVENUE, N.W.
WASHINGTON, D.C. 20004-2595
Telephone: 202-624-2500
Fax: 202-628-5116
URL: http://www.crowell.com

Irvine, California Office: 2010 Main Street, Suite 1200. Telephone: 949-263-8400. Fax: 949-263-8414.

London, England Office: Crowell & Moring, 180 Fleet Street, EC4A 2HG. Telephone: 44-207-413-0011. Fax: 44-207-413-0333.

Brussels, Belgium Office: Crowell & Moring, 27, Avenue Des Arts, B-1040. Telephone: 32 2 231 1799. Fax: 32 2 230 6399.

General Practice.

MEMBERS OF FIRM

BRIAN C. ELMER, born Washington, D.C., April 18, 1936; admitted to bar, 1963, Michigan and District of Columbia. *Education:* Cornell University (A.B., 1960); University of Michigan (J.D., 1962). Law Clerk successively to Chief Judges Miller and Bazelon, U.S. Court of Appeals, D.C. Circuit, 1962-1964.

PATRICK W. LEE, born Omaha, Nebraska, May 19, 1937; admitted to bar, 1962, District of Columbia. *Education:* College of St. Thomas (A.B., 1959); Georgetown University (J.D., 1962). Member, Board of Editors, Georgetown Law Journal, 1962. ***PRACTICE AREAS:*** Litigation; Products Liability Law.

W. STANFIELD JOHNSON, born Omaha, Nebraska, May 21, 1938; admitted to bar, 1964, District of Columbia. *Education:* Stanford University (A.B., 1960); Harvard University (LL.B., 1963). Phi Beta Kappa.

PETER B. WORK, born Cleveland, Ohio, October 4, 1939; admitted to bar, 1965, Colorado; 1968, District of Columbia. *Education:* DePauw University (A.B., 1961); University of Chicago (J.D., 1964).

DONALD D. EVENSON, born Blue Earth, Minnesota, January 28, 1940; admitted to bar, 1966, Minnesota; 1971, District of Columbia; registered to practice before U.S. Patent and Trademark Office. *Education:* University of Minnesota (B.A.E., 1963; LL.B., 1966). ***LANGUAGES:*** German. ***PRACTICE AREAS:*** Patents; Trademarks; Copyrights; Trade Secrets; Litigation. ***Email:*** devenson@crowell.com

RIDGWAY M. HALL, JR., born Milwaukee, Wisconsin, September 10, 1941; admitted to bar, 1966, Connecticut; 1977, District of Columbia. *Education:* Yale University (B.A., 1963); Harvard University (LL.B., 1966). Associate General Counsel, Environmental Protection Agency, 1976-1977. ***PRACTICE AREAS:*** Environmental Law; Litigation.

HAROLD J. HELTZER, born New York, N.Y., April 13, 1942; admitted to bar, 1967, New York; 1973, District of Columbia. *Education:* City College of New York (B.A., 1963); New York University (LL.B., 1966); Georgetown University (LL.M., 1970). Adjunct Professor, Georgetown University Law Center, 1973—. Attorney, Civil and Tax Divisions, U.S. Department of Justice, 1966-1972. Attorney-Advisor, Office of Tax Legislative Counsel, U.S. Department of the Treasury, 1972-1974. ***PRACTICE AREAS:*** Taxation Law.

JOHN C. LENAHAN, born Bronx, New York, March 15, 1941; admitted to bar, 1966, New York; 1971, District of Columbia and Virginia. *Education:* Niagara University (B.A., 1962); St. John's University (LL.B., 1966). Assistant United States Attorney, United States Attorney's Office for the District of Columbia, 1971-1975. ***PRACTICE AREAS:*** Litigation; Intellectual Property; Employment Law; Aviation Law; Products Liability. ***Email:*** jlenahan@crowell.com

RICHARD L. BEIZER, born Hartford, Connecticut, July 20, 1942; admitted to bar, 1967, Virginia; 1970, District of Columbia. *Education:* Harvard College (A.B., 1964); University of Virginia (LL.B., 1967). Law Clerk to Judge Bryan, Sr., U.S. Court of Appeals, Fourth Circuit, 1969-1970. Assistant United States Attorney, 1971-1983, Chief, Fraud Division, 1979-1983, United States Attorney's Office for the District of Columbia. ***PRACTICE AREAS:*** Criminal Law; Criminal Trial Practice; Business Crimes Law; Litigation; Public Contract Law.

(This Listing Continued)

CROWELL & MORING LLP, Washington—Continued

R. BRUCE KEINER, JR., born Washington, D.C., July 12, 1942; admitted to bar, 1968, District of Columbia. *Education:* Dickinson College (B.A., 1964); University of Virginia (LL.B., 1967). ***PRACTICE AREAS:*** Administrative Practice; Aviation Law; Transportation Law. ***Email:*** rbkeiner@crowell.com

STEVEN P. QUARLES, born Kansas City, Missouri, May 9, 1942; admitted to bar, 1980, New York; 1981, District of Columbia. *Education:* Princeton University (A.B., 1964); Yale University (J.D., 1968). Fulbright Scholar, Aligarh Muslim University, India, 1964-1965. Counsel, U.S. Senate Committee on Energy and Natural Resources and Subcommittee on Public Lands and Resources, 1971-1978. Director, Office of Coal Leasing, Planning and Coordination, 1978-1979, Deputy Under Secretary, 1979-1981, U.S. Department of the Interior. ***PRACTICE AREAS:*** Natural Resources Law; Forestry Law; Mineral Law; Environmental Law; Energy Law.

ROBERT P. CHARROW, born St. Louis, Missouri, October 21, 1944; admitted to bar, 1970, California; 1979, District of Columbia. *Education:* Harvey Mudd College (B.S., 1966); Stanford University (J.D., 1969). Associate Professor of Law, University of Cincinnati, 1980-1983. Deputy Chief Counsel, Reagan-Bush '84, 1984-1985. Deputy General Counsel, 1985-1988, Principal Deputy General Counsel, 1988-1989, U.S. Department of Health & Human Services. ***PRACTICE AREAS:*** Science Law; Health and Hospital Law; Food, Drug and Cosmetic Law; Tort Law; Election Law.

JEFFREY H. HOWARD, born New York, N.Y., August 23, 1944; admitted to bar, 1969, District of Columbia; 1988, Virginia. *Education:* Randolph-Macon College (B.A., 1966); University of Virginia (LL.B., 1969). Order of the Coif. Member, Editorial Board, Virginia Law Review, 1967-1969. Associate General Counsel for Pesticides, Toxics and Solid Waste, Environmental Protection Agency, 1975-1976. Lecturer on Environmental and Antitrust Law, University of Virginia School of Law, 1971—. Lecturer on Environmental Law, Beijing University, 1985. ***PRACTICE AREAS:*** Energy, Environmental and Industrial Disease; Toxic Torts; Antitrust; Litigation.

THOMAS P. HUMPHREY, born Cincinnati, Ohio, March 9, 1944; admitted to bar, 1969, Illinois; 1971, District of Columbia. *Education:* Yale University (B.A., 1966; LL.B., 1969). Assistant General Counsel, U.S. Department of Energy, 1977-1981. ***PRACTICE AREAS:*** Government Contracts Law; Natural Resources Law; Litigation.

MICHAEL M. LEVY, born St. Louis, Missouri, July 21, 1944; admitted to bar, 1969, Michigan; 1970, District of Columbia; 1985, Maryland. *Education:* Cornell University (A.B., 1966); University of Michigan (J.D., 1969). ***PRACTICE AREAS:*** Litigation.

JOHN A. MACLEOD, born Manila, Philippines, June 5, 1942; admitted to bar, 1969, District of Columbia. *Education:* University of Notre Dame (B.B.A., 1963; J.D., 1969). Editor-in-Chief, Notre Dame Lawyer, 1968-1969. ***PRACTICE AREAS:*** Natural Resources Law; Mining Law; Timber Law; Environmental Law.

KENT R. MORRISON, born Wichita, Kansas, March 28, 1944; admitted to bar, 1969, Texas; 1973, District of Columbia. *Education:* Rice University (B.A., 1966); Yale University (LL.B., 1969). Phi Beta Kappa. ***PRACTICE AREAS:*** Public Contract Law; Litigation; Criminal Law. ***Email:*** kmorrison@crowell.com

HERBERT I. CANTOR, born Brooklyn, New York, December 10, 1935; admitted to bar, 1970, Maryland; 1971, District of Columbia; registered to practice before U.S. Patent and Trademark Office and Canadian Patent Office. *Education:* New York University (B.A., Chem., 1965); Catholic University (J.D., 1970). Associate Editor, Catholic University Law Review, 1969-1970. Adjunct Professor of Law, Georgetown University Law Center, 1988-1989. Examiner, U.S. Patent and Trademark Office, 1965-1967. ***PRACTICE AREAS:*** Patent Interferences; Litigation; Counseling. ***Email:*** hcantor@crowell.com

BARRY E. COHEN, born Chicago, Illinois, June 20, 1945; admitted to bar, 1971, Illinois; 1973, District of Columbia. *Education:* University of Illinois (B.S., 1967); Northwestern University (J.D., 1970); University of London (LL.M., 1971). Order of the Coif. Member, Northwestern University Law Review, 1969-1970. Attorney, Office of the Assistant General Counsel for International Affairs, U.S. Department of Defense, 1971-1973. Adjunct Professor of Law, Legal Ethics, Georgetown University, 1991—. ***PRACTICE AREAS:*** International Business Law; Import and Export Law; Legal Ethics and Professional Responsibility.

MARC F. EFRON, born Washington, D.C., November 11, 1942; admitted to bar, 1970, District of Columbia. *Education:* Dartmouth College (A.B., 1965); Harvard University (J.D., 1970). ***PRACTICE AREAS:*** Government/Public Contract Law; Litigation; Criminal Law. ***Email:*** mefron@crowell.com

JAMES F. McKEOWN, born White Plains, New York, September 30, 1942; admitted to bar, 1970, Virginia; 1971, District of Columbia; registered to practice before U.S. Patent and Trademark Office. *Education:* City College of the City University of New York (B.E. in Mech., 1965); Catholic University

(This Listing Continued)

(J.D., 1970); George Washington University (M.L. in Patent and Trade Regulation, 1974). Associate Editor, The Catholic University Law Review, 1968-1970. ***PRACTICE AREAS:*** Patents; Trademarks; Copyrights; Trade Secrets; Litigation. ***Email:*** jmckeown@crowell.com

TIMOTHY M. BIDDLE, born San Jose, California, December 1, 1940; admitted to bar, 1971, Virginia; 1972, District of Columbia. *Education:* Georgetown University (A.B., 1962); Catholic University (J.D., 1971). Law Clerk to Judge Ryan, District of Columbia Superior Court, 1968-1970. Comment Editor, Catholic University Law Review, 1969-1970. ***PRACTICE AREAS:*** Mine Safety and Health Law; Administrative Law; OSHA Law; Coal Law; Association Law.

GARY R. EDWARDS, born Passaic, New Jersey, July 26, 1945; admitted to bar, 1971, Virginia; 1972, District of Columbia; registered to practice before the U.S. Patent and Trademark Office. *Education:* Purdue University (B.S.E.E., 1967); Georgetown University (J.D., 1971). Case and Note Editor, Executive Board, Georgetown Law Journal, 1970-1971. ***PRACTICE AREAS:*** Patents; Trademarks; Copyrights; Trade Secrets; Intellectual Property Licensing. ***Email:*** gedwards@crowell.com

HERBERT J. MARTIN, born Philadelphia, Pennsylvania, May 24, 1940; admitted to bar, 1971, Virginia; 1972, District of Columbia. *Education:* Fordham University (B.A., 1965; M.A., 1966); Catholic University (J.D., 1971). Articles Editor, Catholic University Law Review, 1970-1971. Law Clerk to Judge Jones, U.S. District Court, District of Columbia, 1971-1972. ***PRACTICE AREAS:*** Energy Law; Federal Gas Law; Interstate Commerce Law; Public Utility Law; Transportation Law.

JOSEPH I. GOLDSTEIN, born Roosevelt, New Jersey, September 21, 1942; admitted to bar, 1973, Pennsylvania; 1987, District of Columbia. *Education:* Rutgers University (B.A., 1964); University of Michigan (J.D., 1972). Adjunct Professor, Howard University Law School, 1984-1992. Branch Chief, 1982-1984, Assistant Director, 1984-1986, Executive Assistant to the Chairman, 1986-1987 and Associate Director, 1987-1995, Division of Enforcement, Securities and Exchange Commission. ***PRACTICE AREAS:*** Broker-Dealer Arbitration; Broker-Dealer Regulation; Securities Arbitration; Securities Disclosure; Securities Fraud. ***Email:*** jgoldstein@crowell.com

RICHARD McMILLAN, JR., born Opa Locka, Florida, June 16, 1944; admitted to bar, 1972, Minnesota; 1973, District of Columbia. *Education:* Princeton University (A.B., 1966); University of Minnesota (J.D., 1972). Order of the Coif. Member, Board of Editors, University of Minnesota Law Review, 1971-1972. ***PRACTICE AREAS:*** Litigation.

DANA C. CONTRATTO, born Urbana, Illinois, June 21, 1947; admitted to bar, 1973, District of Columbia. *Education:* Southern Illinois University (B.S., 1970); Washington University (J.D., 1973). Editor-in-Chief, Urban Law Annual, 1972-1973. Court Law Clerk, U.S. Court of Appeals, D.C. Circuit, 1973-1974. Law Clerk to Chief Judge Tamm, Temporary Emergency Court of Appeals and Circuit Judge, U.S. Court of Appeals, D.C. Circuit, 1974-1975.

GEORGE D. RUTTINGER, born Detroit, Michigan, January 17, 1948; admitted to bar, 1974, California; 1975, District of Columbia. *Education:* University of Michigan (A.B., 1970; J.D., 1973). Phi Beta Kappa; Order of the Coif. Managing Editor, Michigan Law Review, 1972-1973. Law Clerk to Judge Wilkey, U.S. Court of Appeals, D.C. Circuit, 1973-1974. ***PRACTICE AREAS:*** Litigation; Government (or Public) Contract Law; Contract Law; Construction Law.

RICHARD E. SCHWARTZ, born Indianapolis, Indiana, March 14, 1948; admitted to bar, 1973, District of Columbia. *Education:* Yale University (B.A., 1970); University of Michigan (J.D., 1973). ***PRACTICE AREAS:*** Environmental Law; Toxic Torts; Water Quality Law.

HOWARD M. WEINMAN, born New York, N.Y., May 6, 1947; admitted to bar, 1973, District of Columbia. *Education:* Columbia University (B.A., 1969); Harvard University (M.P.P., 1973; J.D., 1973); George Washington University (LL.M., 1981). Phi Beta Kappa. Adjunct Professor, Georgetown University Law Center, 1988, 1989. Legislation Attorney, Joint Committee on Taxation, U.S. Congress, 1978-1980. ***PRACTICE AREAS:*** Taxation Law. ***Email:*** hweinman@crowell.com

KAREN HASTIE WILLIAMS, born Washington, D.C., September 30, 1944; admitted to bar, 1973, District of Columbia. *Education:* Bates College (B.A., 1966); Tufts University (M.A., 1967); Catholic University (J.D., 1973). Associate Editor, Catholic University Law Review, 1972-1973. Law Clerk to Judge Robinson, U.S. Court of Appeals, D.C. Circuit, 1973-1974. Law Clerk to Associate Justice Marshall, U.S. Supreme Court, 1974-1975. Chief Counsel, U.S. Senate Committee on the Budget, 1977-1980. Administrator, Office of Federal Procurement Policy, U.S. Office of Management and Budget, 1980-1981. Chairman, Procurement Subcommittee, Federal Interagency Task Force on Women Business Enterprises, 1980-1981. ***PRACTICE AREAS:*** Administrative Law; Public Contract Law; Legal Ethics and Discipline Law.

TERRY L. ALBERTSON, born Montebello, California, November 15, 1946; admitted to bar, 1974, Maryland; 1975, District of Columbia. *Education:* Georgetown University (A.B., 1968); Yale University (A.M., 1969); Harvard

(This Listing Continued)

University (J.D., 1974). Phi Beta Kappa. ***PRACTICE AREAS:*** Contract Law; Government Contract Law; Public Contract Law; State and Federal Grants.

JOSEPH D. EVANS, born Ogden, Utah, July 2, 1946; admitted to bar, 1975, District of Columbia; registered to practice before U.S. Patent and Trademark Office. *Education:* Utah State University (B.S., Chemistry, 1970); George Washington University (J.D., 1974). ***LANGUAGES:*** German. ***PRACTICE AREAS:*** Patents; Trademarks; Copyrights; Trade Secrets; Litigation. ***Email:*** jdevans@crowell.com

RICHARD J. MORVILLO, born Rockville Centre, New York, March 16, 1948; admitted to bar, 1975, New York and District of Columbia. *Education:* Colgate University (A.B., 1970); Fordham University (J.D., 1974). Trial Attorney, 1974-1977, and Branch Chief, 1977-1978, Division of Enforcement, Securities and Exchange Commission. ***PRACTICE AREAS:*** SEC Enforcement Law; Litigation; White Collar Criminal Defense Law.

NANCY S. BRYSON, born Pittsfield, Massachusetts, January 17, 1951; admitted to bar, 1975, District of Columbia. *Education:* Boston University (B.A., 1972); Georgetown University (J.D., 1975). Phi Beta Kappa. Appellate Attorney, U.S. Department of Labor, 1975-1979. Trial Attorney, Lands Division, U.S. Department of Justice, 1979-1984.

JoANN E. MACBETH, born Evanston, Illinois, May 18, 1948; admitted to bar, 1976, New York; 1983, District of Columbia; 1986, Virginia; 1989, Maryland. *Education:* Wellesley College (B.A., 1970); Columbia University (J.D., 1975). Legislative Assistant to Representative Elizabeth Holtzman, 1977-1981. ***Email:*** jmacbeth@crowell.com

DAVID W. O'BRIEN, born Albany, New York, June 12, 1950; admitted to bar, 1975, Virginia; 1981, District of Columbia. *Education:* University of Notre Dame (B.A., 1972); Georgetown University (J.D., 1975). Assistant Commonwealth's Attorney, Alexandria, Virginia, 1975-1979. ***PRACTICE AREAS:*** Criminal Law; Litigation; Surety and Fidelity Bond Law; Construction Law. ***Email:*** dobrien@crowell.com

WM. RANDOLPH SMITH, born Hot Springs, Arkansas, December 25, 1951; admitted to bar, 1976, California; 1981, District of Columbia. *Education:* Tulane University (B.A., 1972); Stanford University (J.D., 1975). Phi Beta Kappa. Member, Board of Editors, Stanford Law Review, 1974-1975. General Attorney, 1975-1978, Attorney Advisor to the Chairman, 1978-1980, Assistant to the Chairman, 1980-1981, Federal Trade Commission. ***PRACTICE AREAS:*** Antitrust Law; Unfair Trade Practices; Consumer Law.

FRED S. SOUK, born Beckley, West Virginia, May 12, 1943; admitted to bar, 1975, Maryland; 1976, District of Columbia. *Education:* Massachusetts Institute of Technology (B.S., 1967); University of Maryland (M.S.W., 1969); George Washington University (J.D., 1975). Order of the Coif. Member, George Washington Law Review, 1973-1974. Law Clerk to Chief Judge Northrop, U.S. District Court, District of Maryland, 1975-1976. ***PRACTICE AREAS:*** Products Liability Law; Tort Law; Construction Law; Contract Law; Litigation. ***Email:*** fsouk@crowell.com

JOHN I. STEWART, JR., born Oklahoma City, Oklahoma, February 11, 1950; admitted to bar, 1975, District of Columbia. *Education:* University of Virginia (B.A., 1971); University of Chicago (J.D., 1975). Phi Beta Kappa. Topics and Comment Editor, University of Chicago Law Review, 1974-1975. ***PRACTICE AREAS:*** Litigation; Communications Law; Copyright Law; Insurance Coverage. ***Email:*** jstewart@crowell.com

FREDERICK W. CLAYBROOK, JR., born Houston, Texas, October 24, 1951; admitted to bar, 1976, Ohio; 1977, District of Columbia. *Education:* Wheaton College (A.B., 1973); Duke University (J.D., 1976). Member, Editorial Board, Duke Law Journal, 1975-1976. Law Clerk to Judge Tjoflat, U.S. Court of Appeals, Fifth Circuit, 1976-1977. ***PRACTICE AREAS:*** Government Contract Law; Federal Practice; Contract Law; Railroad Law; Litigation.

ROBERT T. EBERT, born Bethlehem, Pennsylvania, April 25, 1951; admitted to bar, 1976, Pennsylvania; 1979, District of Columbia. *Education:* Dickinson College (B.A., 1973); Dickinson School of Law (J.D., 1976). Member, Dickinson Law Review, 1974-1976. Attorney-Advisor, 1976-1982, Chief Legislative Counsel, 1982-1985, Deputy Associate Administrator for Congressional Affairs, 1985-1986, General Services Administration. ***PRACTICE AREAS:*** Government Contract Law.

THOMAS P. GIES, born Geneva, Illinois, October 12, 1950; admitted to bar, 1976, Illinois; 1977, District of Columbia; 1982, Florida. *Education:* University of Notre Dame (B.A., 1972); George Washington University (J.D., 1976). Member, George Washington Law Review, 1974-1976.

ARTHUR N. LERNER, born Newark, New Jersey, March 20, 1951; admitted to bar, 1977, Massachusetts; 1980, District of Columbia. *Education:* University of Michigan (A.B., 1973); Harvard University (J.D., 1976). Trial Attorney, 1976-1978, Assistant to the Director, 1978-1979, Bureau of Competition, Federal Trade Commission. Attorney Advisor to the Chairman, Federal Trade Commission, 1979-1981. Deputy Assistant Director, 1981-1982 and Assistant Director, 1982-1985, Health Care, Bureau of Competition, Federal Trade Commission. ***PRACTICE AREAS:*** Antitrust Law; Health Care Law. ***Email:*** alerner@crowell.com

(This Listing Continued)

ANDREW H. MARKS, born New York, N.Y., May 5, 1951; admitted to bar, 1976, Florida; 1977, District of Columbia; 1984, Maryland. *Education:* Harvard University (A.B., 1973); University of Michigan (J.D., 1976). Order of the Coif. Managing Editor, Michigan Law Review, 1975-1976. Law Clerk to Judge Richey, U.S. District Court, District of Columbia, 1976-1978. Executive Assistant, Ambassador Sol M. Linowitz, Personal Representative of the President to the Middle East Peace Negotiations, 1979-1981. President, District of Columbia Bar, 1998-1999. Member, Board of Directors, District of Columbia Bar Foundation, 2000—. ***PRACTICE AREAS:*** Directors and Officers Liability; Insurance Coverage; Litigation; Professional Liability Law; RICO. ***Email:*** amarks@crowell.com

JAMES J. REGAN, born Milwaukee, Wisconsin, November 28, 1951; admitted to bar, 1976, Wisconsin; 1977, District of Columbia. *Education:* Georgetown University (B.A., 1973; J.D., 1976). Chief Counsel and Hearing Examiner, General Services Administration Board of Contract Appeals, 1982-1986. ***PRACTICE AREAS:*** Government Contracts Law.

JENNIFER N. WATERS, born Bridgeport, Connecticut, December 21, 1951; admitted to bar, 1977, District of Columbia. *Education:* Radcliffe College (B.A., 1972); Harvard University (J.D., 1976). Phi Beta Kappa. Court Law Clerk, U.S. Court of Appeals, D.C. Circuit, 1976-1977. ***PRACTICE AREAS:*** Energy Law; Public Utility Law; Oil and Gas Law; Appellate Practice.

ROSEMARY M. COLLYER, born Port Chester, New York, November 19, 1945; admitted to bar, 1977, Colorado; 1990, District of Columbia. *Education:* Trinity College (B.A., 1968); University of Denver (J.D., 1977). Member, Denver Law Journal, 1975-1977. Chairman, Federal Mine Safety and Health Review Commission, 1981-1984. General Counsel, National Labor Relations Board, 1984-1989.

DAVID FLORIN, born New York, N.Y., March 31, 1952; admitted to bar, 1977, Virginia; 1980, District of Columbia. *Education:* Harpur College, State University of New York at Binghamton (B.A., 1974); George Washington University (J.D., 1977). Phi Beta Kappa. ***PRACTICE AREAS:*** Health Law; Litigation; Insurance; Antitrust Law; Association Law. ***Email:*** dflorin@crowell.com

JOHN T. BRENNAN, JR., born Schenectady, New York, November 7, 1949; admitted to bar, 1978, District of Columbia. *Education:* Union College (B.A., 1970); George Washington University (M.H.A., 1973); Georgetown University (J.D., 1978). Phi Beta Kappa. Member, American Criminal Law Review, 1976. ***PRACTICE AREAS:*** Health and Hospital Law; Fraud and Abuse; Administrative Law. ***Email:*** john.brennan@crowell.com

KENNETH M. BRUNTEL, born Yokohama, Japan, August 15, 1949; admitted to bar, 1978, District of Columbia. *Education:* Dartmouth College (A.B., 1971); Yale University; George Washington University (J.D., 1978). ***PRACTICE AREAS:*** Public Contract Law; Wage and Hour Law; Business Crimes Law.

ROBERT C. DAVIS, JR., born Huntington, West Virginia, April 1, 1952; admitted to bar, 1978, Oklahoma; 1990, District of Columbia. *Education:* University of Oklahoma (B.B.A., 1974); Oklahoma City University (J.D., 1978); George Washington University (LL.M., 1984). Trial Attorney, 1979-1986, Regional Counsel, 1986-1987, United States Air Force. ***PRACTICE AREAS:*** Environmental Law; Hazardous Materials Law; Natural Resources Law; Toxic Substances Law; Toxic Torts. ***Email:*** rdavis@crowell.com

WARREN J. DeVECCHIO, born Washington, D.C., June 12, 1952; admitted to bar, 1978, District of Columbia. *Education:* Duke University (B.A., 1974); Catholic University (J.D., 1978). Casenote Editor, Catholic University Law Review, 1977-1978. Law Clerk to Judge Harris, District of Columbia Court of Appeals, 1978-1979. ***PRACTICE AREAS:*** Government (or Public) Contract Law.

CLIFFORD B. HENDLER, born Troy, New York, October 22, 1953; admitted to bar, 1978, California; 1980, District of Columbia. *Education:* Yale University (B.A., 1975); Stanford University (J.D., 1978). Order of the Coif. Law Clerk to Judge Duniway, U.S. Court of Appeals, Ninth Circuit, 1978-1979. ***Email:*** chendler@crowell.com

MICHAEL L. MARTINEZ, born St. Louis, Missouri, April 23, 1954; admitted to bar, 1979, Pennsylvania; 1981, District of Columbia. *Education:* University of California at Davis (A.B., 1975); University of California at Berkeley (J.D., 1978). Member, Ecology Law Quarterly, 1976-1978. Honors Attorney, U.S. Department of Transportation, 1978-1979. Attorney-Advisor, Urban Mass Transportation Administration, 1979-1983. Assistant United States Attorney: Eastern District of Pennsylvania, 1983-1985; District of Columbia, 1985-1993. Deputy Chief, Civil Division, 1989-1993. Member, U.S. District Court for the District of Columbia's Local Rules Advisory Committee, 1994-1998. ***PRACTICE AREAS:*** Federal Civil Litigation; False Claims Act; Government Contract Fraud; Foreign Sovereign Immunities Act; Health Care Fraud. ***Email:*** mmartinez@crowell.com

THOMAS C. MEANS, born Charleston, South Carolina, October 3, 1947; admitted to bar, 1978, District of Columbia. *Education:* Dartmouth College (A.B., 1969); Princeton Theological Seminary; University of Colorado (M.P.A.,

(This Listing Continued)

CROWELL & MORING LLP, Washington—Continued

1975); George Washington University (J.D., 1978). Phi Beta Kappa; Order of the Coif. Member, George Washington Law Review, 1976-1978. ***PRACTICE AREAS:*** Natural Resources Law; Mining or Mineral Law; Mine Safety and Health Law; Environmental Law; Administrative Law. ***Email:*** tmeans@crowell.com

SHAUNA E. ALONGE, born Amsterdam, New York, January 26, 1956; admitted to bar, 1979, Virginia; 1987, District of Columbia. *Education:* Newcomb College of Tulane University (B.A., 1977); Tulane University (J.D., 1979). Attorney-Advisor, U.S. Department of the Navy, 1979-1986. ***PRACTICE AREAS:*** Government Contract Law; Business Crimes Law; Health Care Law.

CLIFTON S. ELGARTEN, born New York, N.Y., June 1, 1950; admitted to bar, 1980, New York; 1982, District of Columbia. *Education:* City College of the City University of New York (B.A., 1975); Cardozo School of Law (J.D., 1979). Note and Comment Editor, Cardozo Law Review, 1978-1979. Law Clerk to Judge Pollak, U.S. District Court, Eastern District of Pennsylvania, 1979-1980. Law Clerk to Associate Justice Brennan, U.S. Supreme Court, 1981-1982.

LORRAINE BERMAN HALLOWAY, born New York, N.Y., May 26, 1947; admitted to bar, 1979, District of Columbia. *Education:* University of Wisconsin (B.A., 1969); Catholic University (J.D., 1979). Member, Catholic University Law Review, 1977-1979. Law Clerk to Judge Ferren, District of Columbia Court of Appeals, 1979-1980. Trial Attorney, Civil Division, U.S. Department of Justice, 1980-1984. ***PRACTICE AREAS:*** Aviation Law; Import and Export Law; Transportation Law.

SUSAN M. HOFFMAN, born Ft. Wayne, Indiana, September 7, 1954; admitted to bar, 1980, District of Columbia. *Education:* Indiana University (B.A., 1976); George Washington University (J.D., 1979). Phi Beta Kappa; Order of the Coif. Articles Editor, George Washington Law Review, 1978-1979. Law Clerk to Judge Harold H. Greene, U.S. District Court, District of Columbia, 1979-1980. ***PRACTICE AREAS:*** Adoption Law; Child Abuse and Neglect; Child Custody; Domestic Violence; Mediation.

LAUREL PYKE MALSON, born Savannah, Georgia, June 30, 1954; admitted to bar, 1980, District of Columbia. *Education:* University of Michigan; Wesleyan University (B.A., 1976); Harvard University (J.D., 1979). Editor, Civil Rights-Civil Liberties Law Review, 1978-1979. Law Clerk to Judge Keith, U.S. Court of Appeals, Sixth Circuit, 1979-1980. Law Clerk to Judge Edwards, U.S. Court of Appeals, D.C. Circuit, 1980-1981. Attorney-Advisor, Office of Legal Counsel, U.S. Department of Justice, 1981-1985.

STUART H. NEWBERGER, born New York, N.Y., December 2, 1953; admitted to bar, 1980, District of Columbia. *Education:* George Washington University (B.A., 1974); Georgetown University (J.D., 1979). Law Clerk to Judge Harold H. Greene, U.S. District Court, District of Columbia, 1979-1980. Assistant United States Attorney for the District of Columbia, 1982-1987. Adjunct Professor, Georgetown University Law Center, 1984—. ***PRACTICE AREAS:*** Trial Practice/Litigation; Appellate Practice; Constitutional Law; Insurance Coverage; Environmental Law.

DAVID B. SIEGEL, born Lancaster, Pennsylvania, June 1, 1953; admitted to bar, 1979, District of Columbia. *Education:* University of Pennsylvania (B.A., 1975; M.A., 1975; J.D., 1979). Phi Beta Kappa. Law Clerk to Judge Newcomer, U.S. District Court, Eastern District of Pennsylvania, 1979-1981.

ROBERT M. HALPERIN, born Boston, Massachusetts, March 11, 1954; admitted to bar, 1980, District of Columbia; 1983, California (Inactive). *Education:* Harvard University (B.A., 1976); Duke University (M.A., 1980; J.D., 1980). Member, Editorial Board, Duke Law Journal, 1979-1980.

RAYMOND F. MONROE, born Jersey City, New Jersey, December 7, 1955; admitted to bar, 1980, New Jersey; 1981, District of Columbia. *Education:* Hobart College (B.A., 1977); Duke University (J.D., 1980). Phi Beta Kappa. Executive Editor, Duke Law Journal, 1979-1980. Law Clerk to Justice Pollock, Supreme Court of New Jersey, 1980-1981. ***PRACTICE AREAS:*** Government Contract Law; Business Crimes Law.

ROBERT L. WILLMORE, born West Germany, July 16, 1955; admitted to bar, 1981, District of Columbia. *Education:* Massachusetts Institute of Technology (B.S., 1977); Yale University (J.D., 1980). Phi Beta Kappa. Editor, Yale Law Journal, 1979-1980. Law Clerk to Judge Higginbotham, U.S. District Court, Northern District of Texas 1980-1981. Assistant General Counsel, U.S. Office of Management & Budget, 1982-1985. Staff Director, Legal Policy Cabinet Council Toxic Torts/Compensation Working Group, 1983-1985. Deputy Assistant Attorney General, Civil Division, U.S. Department of Justice, 1985-1988. Executive Secretary, White House Tort Policy Working Group, 1985-1988. Chairman, Task Force on Liability Insurance Availability, 1985-1988. ***PRACTICE AREAS:*** Insurance Coverage Law; Products Liability Law; Toxic Torts. ***Email:*** rwillmore@crowell.com

ALAN W.H. GOURLEY, born Charlottesville, Virginia, September 30, 1955; admitted to bar, 1981, District of Columbia. *Education:* Beloit College

(This Listing Continued)

(B.A., 1977); University of Virginia (J.D., 1981). Phi Beta Kappa. ***PRACTICE AREAS:*** Public Contract Law; Litigation; Business Crimes Law; International Law.

WILMA A. LEWIS, born Santurce, Puerto Rico, June 28, 1956; admitted to bar, 1981, District of Columbia. *Education:* Swarthmore College (B.A., 1978); Harvard University (J.D., 1981). Phi Beta Kappa. Adjunct Faculty Member, The George Washington University National Law Center, 1993—. Assistant United States Attorney, 1986-1993, Assistant Chief, 1989-1992 and Deputy Chief, 1993, Civil Division, United States Attorney's Office for the District of Columbia. Associate Solicitor, 1993-1995 and Inspector General, 1995-1998, Department of the Interior. United States Attorney, District of Columbia, 1998-2001. Fellow, American Bar Foundation. ***PRACTICE AREAS:*** Litigation. ***Email:*** wlewis@crowell.com

MARK D. PLEVIN, born Queens, New York, June 6, 1957; admitted to bar, 1981, District of Columbia; 1990, California. *Education:* State University of New York at Albany (B.A., 1978); University of Virginia (J.D., 1981). Order of the Coif. Member, Editorial Board, Virginia Law Review, 1979-1981. ***PRACTICE AREAS:*** Litigation; Insurance Coverage; RICO.

DAVID Z. BODENHEIMER, born High Point, North Carolina, December 11, 1955; admitted to bar, 1982, North Carolina; 1988, District of Columbia. *Education:* University of North Carolina at Chapel Hill (B.A., 1978; M.B.A., 1982; J.D., 1982). Phi Beta Kappa. Assistant Counsel, Office of General Counsel, U.S. Department of the Navy, 1982-1988. ***PRACTICE AREAS:*** Government Contracts Law; Business Crimes Law; Litigation.

ROBERT L. ROTH, born New Rochelle, New York, 1954; admitted to bar, 1982, Maryland; 1994, District of Columbia and Pennsylvania. *Education:* Lehigh University (B.A., 1976); Syracuse University College of Law (J.D., 1982). Adjunct Professor of Law, University of Baltimore School of Law, 1984—. Counsel, Maryland General Assembly, 1982-1983. Counsel, Commission to Revise the Annotated Code of Maryland, 1983-1985. Maryland Assistant Attorney General, 1985-1988. Attorney, Office of General Counsel, U.S. Dept. of Health and Human Services, 1988-1993. ***PRACTICE AREAS:*** Health Care; Health Insurance; Employee Benefits; Legislation; Litigation; Administrative Law. ***Email:*** rroth@crowell.com

R. TIMOTHY McCRUM, born Pittsburgh, Pennsylvania, November 4, 1958; admitted to bar, 1984, Pennsylvania; 1985, District of Columbia. *Education:* Franklin and Marshall College (B.A., 1980); Lewis and Clark College (J.D., 1983). Attorney-Advisor, Office of the Solicitor, U.S. Department of the Interior, 1984-1986. ***PRACTICE AREAS:*** Environmental Law; Mining and Mineral Law; Natural Resources Law.

KENT A. GARDINER, born Mineola, New York, December 2, 1958; admitted to bar, 1985, New York; 1992, District of Columbia. *Education:* State University of New York (B.A., 1981); Georgetown University (J.D., 1984). Phi Beta Kappa. Member and Editor, American Criminal Law Review, 1982-1984. Trial Attorney, Antitrust Division, U.S. Department of Justice, 1984-1987. ***PRACTICE AREAS:*** Litigation; Antitrust Law; Criminal Law.

PAT S. CONTI, born Brooklyn, New York, September 6, 1960; admitted to bar, 1986, New York; 1999, District of Columbia. *Education:* New York University (B.A., 1982); Brooklyn Law School (J.D., 1985). Staff Attorney, 1990-1992, Senior Counsel, 1992-1993, Branch Chief, 1993-1996, Division of Enforcement, Securities and Exchange Commission. ***PRACTICE AREAS:*** Broker-Dealer Regulation; SEC Enforcement; Investment Management; Self-Regulatory Agency Investigations.

ELLEN MORAN DWYER, born Rochester, New York, August 19, 1960; admitted to bar, 1986, Massachusetts and District of Columbia. *Education:* St. Lawrence University (B.A., 1982); Cornell University (J.D., 1985). Phi Beta Kappa.

CATHY GEBHARD, born New York, N.Y., May 23, 1952; admitted to bar, 1985, Maryland; 1987, District of Columbia; 1992, Massachusetts. *Education:* Oberlin College (B.A., 1974); George Washington University (M.A., 1978); University of Pennsylvania (J.D., 1985). ***PRACTICE AREAS:*** Biotechnology Licensing; Mergers and Acquisitions; Corporate Law.

LUTHER ZEIGLER, born Denver, Colorado, April 23, 1958; admitted to bar, 1985, California; 1986, District of Columbia. *Education:* Oberlin College (A.B., 1980); Stanford University (M.A., 1982; J.D., 1985). Phi Beta Kappa; Order of the Coif. Associate Editor, Stanford Law Review, 1984-1985. ***PRACTICE AREAS:*** Litigation; Appellate Practice. ***Email:*** lzeigler@crowell.com

PAUL WILLIAM KALISH, born Brooklyn, New York, February 23, 1962; admitted to bar, 1986, Maryland; 1988, District of Columbia. *Education:* Duke University (B.A., 1983); Northwestern University (J.D., 1986). Order of the Coif. Editor, Northwestern University Law Review, 1985-1986. ***PRACTICE AREAS:*** Contract Law; Insurance Law.

J. MICHAEL KLISE, born Evanston, Illinois, August 28, 1947; admitted to bar, 1986, Maryland; 1988, District of Columbia. *Education:* Catholic University (B.A., 1969; J.D., 1986); University of Virginia (M.A., 1971). Note

(This Listing Continued)

Editor, Catholic University Law Review, 1985-1986. ***PRACTICE AREAS:*** Administrative Law; Coal Law; Mine Safety and Health Law; Natural Resources Law.

JAMES R. STUART, III, born West Point, New York, April 6, 1961; admitted to bar, 1986, Virginia; 1988, District of Columbia. *Education:* Carnegie Mellon University (B.S., 1983); Harvard University (J.D., 1986). ***PRACTICE AREAS:*** Corporate Law; Business Law; Securities Finance; Venture Capital; Commercial Contracts. ***Email:*** jstuart@crowell.com

WILLIAM D. WALLACE, born Miami, Florida, January 7, 1950; admitted to bar, 1987, Florida; 1993, District of Columbia. *Education:* Princeton University (A.B., 1972); University of South Florida (M.A., 1976); University of Illinois (Ph.D., 1985); University of Florida (J.D., 1986). Order of the Coif. Member, 1985, Research Editor, 1986, University of Florida Law Review. Law Clerk to Judge Vinson, U.S. District Court, Northern District of Florida, 1987-1989. ***PRACTICE AREAS:*** FCC Regulation; Satellite Communications; Wireless Cable.

SCOTT L. WINKELMAN, born Detroit, Michigan, July 30, 1962; admitted to bar, 1987, Illinois; 1988, District of Columbia. *Education:* University of Michigan (B.A., 1984); Harvard University (J.D., 1987). Phi Beta Kappa. Editor, Harvard Environmental Law Review, 1985-1986. Law Clerk to Judge Pratt, U.S. District Court, District of Columbia, 1987-1988.

WILLIAM L. ANDERSON, born Ozark, Arkansas, September 20, 1953; admitted to bar, 1988, Minnesota; 1989, District of Columbia. *Education:* Hendrix College (B.A., 1975); University of Minnesota (J.D., 1988). Order of the Coif. President, Minnesota Law Review, 1987-1988.

CHARLES C. HWANG, born Seoul, Republic of Korea, November 29, 1962; admitted to bar, 1989, New York; 1991, District of Columbia. *Education:* Harvard University (A.B., 1984); Columbia University (J.D., 1988); Georgetown University (LL.M., 1998). Articles Editor, Columbia Law Review, 1987-1988. ***PRACTICE AREAS:*** Taxation.

KEITH T. SAMPSON, born 1961; admitted to bar, 1988, Massachusetts; 1989, District of Columbia; 1999, California. *Education:* London School of Economics, England (G.C., 1982); Connecticut College (B.A., 1983); George Washington University (J.D., 1988). *Member:* Federal Energy Bar Association. ***PRACTICE AREAS:*** Electricity and Natural Gas Law; Public Utility; Administrative Law.

JEFFREY D. SANOK, born Merrillville, Indiana, June 23, 1962; admitted to bar, 1988, New York; 1991, Virginia and District of Columbia; registered to practice before U.S. Patent and Trademark Office. *Education:* University of Notre Dame (B.S.E.E., 1984); Georgetown University (J.D., 1988). ***PRACTICE AREAS:*** Litigation; Patents; Trademarks; Copyrights; Trade Secrets. ***Email:*** jsanok@crowell.com

KATHRYN DEAN KIRMAYER, born Englewood, New Jersey, January 23, 1964; admitted to bar, 1989, Virginia; 1990, District of Columbia. *Education:* Williams College (B.A., 1986); Washington & Lee University (J.D., 1989). Order of the Coif. Lead and Student Articles Editor, Washington & Lee Law Review, 1988-1989. ***Email:*** kkirmayer@crowell.com

DAVID M. SCHNORRENBERG, born Chapel Hill, North Carolina, December 8, 1963; admitted to bar, 1990, New York; 1998, District of Columbia. *Education:* University of North Carolina at Chapel Hill (B.A., 1986); Columbia University (J.D., 1989). Phi Beta Kappa. ***PRACTICE AREAS:*** Civil Litigation; Complex and Multi-District Litigation; Antitrust; Securities Litigation; Products Liability.

JEANE A. THOMAS, born Columbus, Ohio, January 8, 1964; admitted to bar, 1989, Maryland; 1992, District of Columbia. *Education:* The Ohio State University (B.A., 1986); Georgetown University (J.D., 1989).

ALEXANDRE DE GRAMONT, born Cincinnati, Ohio, November 19, 1963; admitted to bar, 1990, New Jersey; 1991, District of Columbia. *Education:* Wesleyan University (B.A., 1986); New York University (J.D., 1990). Law Clerk to Justice Handler, Supreme Court of New Jersey, 1990-1991. ***PRACTICE AREAS:*** Litigation.

KATHLEEN E. KARELIS, born Pittsburgh, Pennsylvania, October 14, 1960; admitted to bar, 1990, Florida; 1991, District of Columbia. *Education:* Rollins College (B.S., 1985); Florida Institute of Technology (M.S., 1987); University of Miami (J.D., 1990). Order of the Coif. Managing Editor, University of Miami Law Review, 1989-1990.

KRIS DAVID MEADE, born Ann Arbor, Michigan, July 9, 1965; admitted to bar, 1990, Maryland; 1992, District of Columbia. *Education:* University of Michigan (B.A., 1987); George Washington University (J.D., 1990). Phi Beta Kappa. ***PRACTICE AREAS:*** Labor and Employment. ***Email:*** kmeade@crowell.com

PHILIP KATZ, born Pottstown, Pennsylvania, August 22, 1959; admitted to bar, 1992, Pennsylvania (inactive); 1993, District of Columbia. *Education:* University of Virginia (B.A., 1981); Georgetown University (J.D., 1992). Order of the Coif. ***PRACTICE AREAS:*** Drug and Medical Device Regulation; Food and Drug Regulation; Food, Drug and Cosmetic Law; Advertising and Labeling; False Advertising. ***Email:*** pkatz@crowell.com

SENIOR COUNSEL

ELDON H. CROWELL, born Middletown, Connecticut, May 15, 1924; admitted to bar, 1951, Connecticut and District of Columbia. *Education:* Princeton University (A.B., 1948); University of Virginia (LL.B., 1951). Order of the Coif. Member, Editorial Board, Virginia Law Review, 1949-1951. Visiting Lecturer in Law, University of Virginia School of Law, 1968-1982. Public Member, Administrative Conference of the U.S., 1971-1975 and 1986—. Fellow, American Bar Foundation, 1979—. ***PRACTICE AREAS:*** Public Contract Law; International Law.

RICHARD J. BEDNAR, born Omaha, Nebraska, October 30, 1931; admitted to bar, 1954, Nebraska; 1984, District of Columbia. *Education:* Creighton College; Creighton University (LL.B., 1954); George Washington University (LL.M., 1969). Assistant Judge Advocate General of the Army, Civil Law, 1979-1981. Director, Government Contracts Program, The National Law Center, George Washington University, 1984-1987. ***PRACTICE AREAS:*** Government Contract Law; Public Contract Law; Contract Law; Court Martial.

ROGER N. BOYD, born Washington, D.C., September 17, 1929; admitted to bar, 1961, Connecticut; 1962, District of Columbia. *Education:* Bowdoin College (A.B., 1951); Yale University (LL.B., 1961). Phi Beta Kappa. Fulbright Scholar, University College, North Staffordshire, England, 1951-1952. ***PRACTICE AREAS:*** Government and Public Contract Law; Contract Law.

L. GRAEME BELL, III, born Toledo, Ohio, August 13, 1944; admitted to bar, 1970, District of Columbia; 1997, Rhode Island. *Education:* Dartmouth College (A.B., 1966); Harvard University (J.D., 1969). Phi Beta Kappa. Assistant Professor, Catholic University Law School, 1969-1972. ***PRACTICE AREAS:*** Public Contract Law; Business Crimes Law; Arbitration Law.

IRVING B. YOSKOWITZ, born New York, N.Y., December 2, 1945; admitted to bar, 1970, New York; 1973, District of Columbia; 1983, Connecticut. *Education:* City College of New York (B.B.A., 1966); Harvard University (J.D., 1969). Knox Fellow, London School of Economics, 1971-1972. Editor, Harvard Law Review, 1968-1969. [Major, U.S. Army, Systems Analyst, Office of the Secretary of Defense, 1969-1971]. ***Email:*** iyoskowitz@crowell.com

JOSEPH M. OLIVER, JR., born Savannah, Georgia, July 26, 1946; admitted to bar, 1970, Georgia; 1971, District of Columbia. *Education:* University of Virginia (B.A., 1967); University of Georgia (J.D., 1970). Member, Managing Board, Georgia Law Review, 1969-1970. Law Clerk to Judge Collins, U.S. Court of Claims, 1970-1971. ***PRACTICE AREAS:*** Energy Law; Public Utility Law. ***Email:*** joliver@crowell.com

COUNSEL

WALTER J. BONNER, admitted to bar, 1955, District of Columbia; 1960, Virginia. *Education:* Catholic University of America (B.A., 1951); Georgetown University (J.D., 1955). Adjunct Professor of Criminal and Corporation Law, Georgetown University Law Center, 1957-1958. Adjunct Professor of Trial Practice, 1967-1983 and Guest Lecturer, 1984—, Georgetown University Law Center. Law Clerk to Judge Cayton, U.S. Court of Appeals, District of Columbia Circuit, 1954-1955; Judge McLaughlin, U.S. District Court, District of Columbia, 1955-1956. Assistant U.S. Attorney, District of Columbia, 1956-1960. Fellow, American College of Trial Lawyers. [Captain, USNR, Retired]. ***PRACTICE AREAS:*** Complex Civil Litigation; Criminal Law; Trial Practice. ***Email:*** wbonner@crowell.com

EDWARD M. GREEN, born Malden, Massachusetts, August 16, 1943; admitted to bar, 1968, District of Columbia. *Education:* Boston University (A.B., 1965; J.D., 1967). Attorney-Advisor, Office of the Solicitor, Division of Mine Health and Safety, 1970-1973. Counsel to Secretary of Interior for Surface Mining and Reclamation, 1973-1974. Special Assistant to Administrator, Mining Enforcement and Safety Administration, 1975-1977, U.S. Department of the Interior. ***PRACTICE AREAS:*** Mining or Mineral Law; Trade Association Law; Mine Safety and Health Law; Administrative Law; Natural Resources Law. ***Email:*** egreen@crowell.com

MICHAEL J. COOPER, born Grand Island, Nebraska, October 6, 1943; admitted to bar, 1969, Utah (inactive); 1973, New York (Not admitted in District of Columbia). *Education:* University of Washington (B.A., 1966); University of Utah (J.D., 1969); New York University (LL.M., 1972). Attorney-Advisor, 1973-1977, Assistant Branch Chief, 1978-1980, Interpretative Division, Office of Chief Counsel, Internal Revenue Service. Adjunct Professor, International Taxation, Georgetown University Law School, 1982-1983. ***PRACTICE AREAS:*** International Corporate Taxation. ***Email:*** mcooper@crowell.com

THOMAS A. GUIDOBONI, born Plymouth, Massachusetts, May 18, 1946; admitted to bar, 1972, Virginia; 1973, District of Columbia. *Education:* University of Virginia (B.A., 1968; J.D., 1971). Phi Beta Kappa. Law Clerk to Judge Braman, Superior Court of the District of Columbia, 1971-1972. Adjunct Professor of Law, Georgetown University Law Center, 1975-1976. Staff Attor-

(This Listing Continued)

CROWELL & MORING LLP, Washington—Continued

ney, 1972-1976, and Director, Appointed Counsel Program, 1976-1978, Public Defender Service for the District of Columbia. Member, District of Columbia Law Revision Commission, 1977-1978. ***PRACTICE AREAS:*** Litigation; Appellate Practice; Criminal Law. ***Email:*** tguidoboni@crowell.com

LLOYD M. WEINERMAN, born Newton, Massachusetts, October 24, 1940; admitted to bar, 1973, Maryland; 1995, District of Columbia. *Education:* Boston University (B.A., 1962); University of Baltimore (J.D., 1973). Order of the Coif. Principal Contract Advisor, Health Care Financing Administration and Social Security Administration, 1976-1996. ***PRACTICE AREAS:*** Government Contracts; Health Care.

MARK R. EATON, born Ann Arbor, Michigan, December 25, 1950; admitted to bar, 1975, Georgia; 1978, District of Columbia; 1982, Virginia. *Education:* Wesleyan University (B.A., 1973); Columbia University (J.D., 1975). Harlan Fiske Stone Scholar. ***PRACTICE AREAS:*** Corporate Law; Securities Law. ***Email:*** mark.eaton@crowell.com

THOMAS R. LUNDQUIST, born Jamestown, New York, March 11, 1952; admitted to bar, 1977, Massachusetts; 1979, District of Columbia. *Education:* Union College (B.S., 1974); Harvard University (J.D., 1977). Phi Beta Kappa. Attorney Advisor, U.S. Department of the Interior, 1977-1981. ***PRACTICE AREAS:*** Federal Administrative Law; Endangered Species; National Environmental Policy Act (NEPA); Forestry Law; Public Land Law.

VINCENT J. SUNDERDICK, born Clover Bottom, Missouri, July 3, 1947; admitted to bar, 1978, Michigan; registered to practice before the U.S. Patent and Trademark Office (Not admitted in District of Columbia). *Education:* University of Missouri at Rolla (B.S.E.E., 1969); Washington University, St. Louis (M.S., Bio-Medical Eng., 1971); Georgetown University (J.D., 1978). Tau Beta Pi. Examiner, U.S. Patent Office, 1973-1978. ***PRACTICE AREAS:*** Patent Law. ***Email:*** vsunderdick@crowell.com

LINDA S. BRUGGEMAN, born Dayton, Ohio, October 9, 1951; admitted to bar, 1979, Minnesota; 1982, District of Columbia. *Education:* Miami University (B.A., 1972); Georgetown University (J.D., 1979). Phi Beta Kappa. Attorney-Advisor, General Services Administration, 1980-1985. Attorney-Advisor, U.S. Department of Justice, 1987-1989. ***PRACTICE AREAS:*** Government Contract Law.

ANNE M. ("NANCY") WHEELER, born Plainfield, N.J., April 27, 1954; admitted to bar, 1981, District of Columbia; 1991, Maryland. *Education:* Catholic University (B.A., 1976); George Washington University (J.D., 1980). Phi Beta Kappa. ***PRACTICE AREAS:*** Health and Hospital Law; Mental Health Law; Malpractice Law.

DARYL A. LANDER, born Boston, Massachusetts, December 4, 1952; admitted to bar, 1981, Oregon; 1983, District of Columbia. *Education:* Wheaton College (B.A., 1975); Georgetown University (M.A., 1977; LL.M., 1983); Willamette University (J.D., 1981). Staff Member, 1979-1980, Comment Editor, 1980-1981, Willamette Law Review. Law Clerk to Justice Denecke, Supreme Court of Oregon, 1981-1982.

RICHARD E. MENDALES, born New York, New York, March 12, 1950; admitted to bar, 1982, New York; 2001, District of Columbia. *Education:* University of Chicago (A.B., 1969; A.M., 1980); Yale University (J.D., 1981). Order of the Coif. Associate Professor of Law, 1988-1995, Professor of Law, 1995-1999, University of Miami School of Law. ***LANGUAGES:*** French and German. ***PRACTICE AREAS:*** Corporate; Bankruptcy Reorganization; Professional Responsibility; Structured Finance; International Business Transactions. ***Email:*** rmendales@crowell.com

EILEEN M. GLEIMER, born Queens, New York, June 24, 1957; admitted to bar, 1982, District of Columbia. *Education:* American University (B.S., 1979); Emory University School of Law (J.D., 1982). Order of the Coif. Articles Editor, Emory Law Journal, 1981-1982. ***Email:*** egleimer@crowell.com

RICHARD J. MANNIX, born Brooklyn, New York, April 4, 1943; admitted to bar, 1984, New York; 1985, District of Columbia. *Education:* St. Peter's College (B.S., 1964); New York University (M.A., 1965; Ph.D., 1975); Brooklyn Law School (J.D., 1983). Member, 1980-1981, 1982-1983 and Senior Editor, 1981-1982, Brooklyn Law Review.

KATHLEEN M. STRATTON, born Detroit, Michigan, May 30, 1959; admitted to bar, 1984, Michigan; 1986, District of Columbia. *Education:* Hope College (B.A., 1981); Indiana University (J.D., 1984). Member Editorial Staff, Indiana Law Journal, 1983-1984. ***PRACTICE AREAS:*** Health and Hospital Law; Fraud and Abuse; Administrative Law. ***Email:*** kstratton@crowell.com

KATHRYN A. UNDERHILL, born Buffalo, New York, July 24, 1959; admitted to bar, 1984, District of Columbia. *Education:* University of Miami (B.A., 1981); Duke University (J.D., 1984). ***PRACTICE AREAS:*** Litigation; Insurance Law.

BARBARA H. RYLAND, born Pittsburgh, Pennsylvania, June 30, 1960; admitted to bar, 1988, Maryland; 1990, District of Columbia. *Education:* University of Virginia (B.A., 1983); Duke University (J.D., 1987). Editor, Law and

(This Listing Continued)

Contemporary Problems, 1986-1987. Law Clerk to Judge Winter, U.S. Court of Appeals, Fourth Circuit, 1987-1988. ***PRACTICE AREAS:*** Health Care Law. ***Email:*** bryland@crowell.com

STEVEN P. TAUB, born New York, N.Y., February 9, 1962; admitted to bar, 1988, New York; 1989, District of Columbia. *Education:* The Wharton School, University of Pennsylvania (B.S.E., 1984); Georgetown University (J.D., 1987).

EDWARD JACKSON, born Havre de Grace, Maryland, February 21, 1953; admitted to bar, 1988, Maryland; 1989, District of Columbia. *Education:* Southern College (B.S., 1975); University of Maryland (M.B.A., 1977; J.D., 1988). Certified Public Accountant, Maryland 1979. Certified Management Accountant, 1984.

JOHN E. McCARTHY, JR., born Washington, D.C., June 26, 1953; admitted to bar, 1989, Virginia; 1990, Maryland; 1991, District of Columbia. *Education:* Rockhurst College (B.S.E.S., 1976); Catholic University (M.E.E., 1978; J.D., 1989). ***PRACTICE AREAS:*** Information Technology; Bid Protests; Public Contract Law; Insurance Coverage; E-Commerce.

MARGIT H. NAHRA, born Evanston, Illinois, May 30, 1962; admitted to bar, 1989, Illinois (Inactive); 1990, District of Columbia. *Education:* Georgetown University (B.S.F.S., 1984); University of Virginia (J.D., 1989). Notes Editor, University of Virginia Journal of Law and Politics, 1989. Law Clerk to Judge Merhige, Jr., U.S. District Court, Eastern District of Virginia, 1989-1990. ***PRACTICE AREAS:*** Litigation; Health Care Law. ***Email:*** mnahra@crowell.com

ROBERT S. CANTERMAN, born Butler, Pennsylvania, November 22, 1958; admitted to bar, 1990, Pennsylvania; 1991, District of Columbia. *Education:* Dickinson College (B.A., 1981); American Graduate School of International Management (M.I.M., 1982); American University (J.D., 1990). Phi Beta Kappa. ***PRACTICE AREAS:*** Health Care Law; Antitrust Law. ***Email:*** rcanterman@crowell.com

TERENCE F. FLYNN, born Martinsville, Indiana, September 27, 1960; admitted to bar, 1990, Virginia; 1991, District of Columbia. *Education:* University of Maryland (B.A., 1984); Washington and Lee University (J.D., 1990). ***PRACTICE AREAS:*** Labor and Employment; Civil Litigation; Employee Benefits; Communications and Media; Corporate Law. ***Email:*** tflynn@crowell.com

GLENN D. GRANT, born Flushing, New York, May 26, 1964; admitted to bar, 1990, Pennsylvania; 1993, District of Columbia. *Education:* Bucknell University (B.A., 1986); George Washington University (J.D., 1990). Member, George Washington Law Review, 1988-1990.

JONATHAN HALE PITTMAN, born New York, New York, February 9, 1963; admitted to bar, 1991, New York and District of Columbia. *Education:* Vassar College (B.A., 1985); Vanderbilt University (J.D., 1990). Order of the Coif. Member and Authorities Editor, Vanderbilt Journal of Transnational Law, 1988-1990. Law Clerk to Judge Terry, District of Columbia Court of Appeals, 1990-1991.

ELLEN B. STEEN, born Monroe, Louisiana, February 26, 1966; admitted to bar, 1991, North Carolina; 1993, District of Columbia. *Education:* Tulane University (B.A., 1988); University of North Carolina (J.D., 1991). Articles Editor, North Carolina Journal of International Law and Commercial Regulation, 1990-1991. ***PRACTICE AREAS:*** Environmental Law; Clean Water Act; Hazardous Materials and Substances. ***Email:*** esteen@crowell.com

STEPHEN M. BYERS, born Hagerstown, Maryland, October 4, 1965; admitted to bar, 1992, Pennsylvania (inactive); 1994, District of Columbia. *Education:* Wake Forest University (B.A., 1987); University of Virginia (J.D., 1992). Editorial Board, Virginia Law Review, 1990-1992. ***PRACTICE AREAS:*** Business Crimes; False Claims Act; Federal Criminal Law; Government Contract Fraud; Grand Jury Practice. ***Email:*** sbyers@crowell.com

PETER W. PAULSEN, born New York, N.Y., March 4, 1960; admitted to bar, 1994, New York; 1995, District of Columbia. *Education:* Trinity College (B.A., 1981); Wadham College, Oxford University (B.A., 1984); Harvard University (J.D., 1992). Phi Beta Kappa. Articles Editor, Harvard Women's Law Journal, 1991-1992. ***Email:*** ppaulsen@crowell.com

TRACY A. ROMAN, born New Hartford, New York, December 18, 1965; admitted to bar, 1992, Virginia; 1994, District of Columbia. *Education:* University of Virginia (B.A., 1988; J.D., 1992). Notes Editor, Virginia Journal of International Law, 1991-1992. ***PRACTICE AREAS:*** Antitrust; Commercial Litigation; Class Action Defense; Aviation Products Liability. ***Email:*** troman@crowell.com

MONICA G. PARHAM, born Baltimore, Maryland, January 16, 1968; admitted to bar, 1993, North Carolina; 1995, District of Columbia. *Education:* University of North Carolina at Chapel Hill (B.A., 1990); Yale University (J.D., 1993). Phi Beta Kappa. Senior Editor, Yale Law and Policy Review, 1992-1993. Law Clerk to Judge Ellis, U.S. District Court, Eastern District of Virginia, 1993-1994.

(This Listing Continued)

JEFFREY F. ROBERTSON, born Jackson, Tennessee, June 28, 1968; admitted to bar, 1996, New York; 1997, District of Columbia. *Education:* University of Tennessee (B.A., 1990); Columbia University (J.D., 1994). Phi Beta Kappa. Research and Writing Editor, Columbia Human Rights Law Review, 1993-1994. ***PRACTICE AREAS:*** SEC Enforcement; Securities Litigation; Broker-Dealer Arbitration; Securities Class Actions; NASD Arbitration.

CHRISTOPHER H. WOOD, born Kanagawa, Japan, June 13, 1968; admitted to bar, 1994, Virginia; 1996, District of Columbia. *Education:* Washington & Lee University (B.A., 1990); College of William and Mary (J.D., 1994). Phi Beta Kappa.

ROBERT L. GRABAREK, JR., born Baltimore, Maryland, September 14, 1959; admitted to bar, 1995, Maryland; 1996, District of Columbia; 2001, Virginia; registered to practice before U.S. Patent and Trademark Office. *Education:* United States Naval Academy (B.S., Ocean Engineering, 1981); Virginia Polytechnic Institute and State University (Master of Engineering Administration, Industrial Engineering and Operations Research, 1990); University of Baltimore (J.D., 1995). University of Baltimore Law Review, Editorial Board/ Casenotes Editor, 1994-1995. ***Email:*** rgrabarek@crowell.com

ASSOCIATES

JODY GOODMAN, born New York, New York, September 23, 1958; admitted to bar, 1985, Florida; 1986, District of Columbia. *Education:* Yale University (B.A., 1980); University of Miami (J.D., 1985). Adjunct Professor, University of Bonn, Germany, 1991-1992. Assistant State Attorney, Miami, Florida, 1985-1986. Assistant U.S. Attorney, Washington, D.C., 1987-1989. ***Email:*** jgoodman@crowell.com

BAZIL FACCHINA, born Takoma Park, Maryland, October 29, 1960; admitted to bar, 1987, Massachusetts; 1989, District of Columbia. *Education:* Boston University (B.S.B.A., 1981); University of Virginia (J.D., 1986); New York University (LL.M., 1990). Articles Editor, Virginia Tax Review, 1985-1986. Attorney-Advisor, Judge Wells, 1990-1993, 1995-1997 and Judge Chiechi, 1993-1995, U.S. Tax Court. ***Email:*** bfacchina@crowell.com

LINN KAISER REDWAY, born Keyser, West Virginia, September 18, 1960; admitted to bar, 1986, Virginia; 1987, District of Columbia. *Education:* Roanoke College (B.A., 1982); George Washington University (J.D., 1986). Order of the Coif. Member, George Washington University Law Review, 1985-1986. ***Email:*** lredway@crowell.com

BRIAN J. WEBER, born Cleveland, Ohio, May 24, 1959; admitted to bar, 1987, Illinois; 1993, Maryland; 1995, District of Columbia. *Education:* University of Chicago (B.A., 1981; J.D., 1987). ***Email:*** bweber@crowell.com

RICHARD R. DIEFENDORF, born Schenectady, New York, October 13, 1959; admitted to bar, 1989, Virginia; 1997, District of Columbia; registered to practice before U.S. Patent and Trademark Office, 1986. *Education:* University of Rochester (B.S.M.E., 1981); George Mason University (J.D., 1989). U.S. Patent Examiner, 1981-1986. ***Email:*** rdiefendorf@crowell.com

CHRISTINE C. D'ALESSANDRO, born Watertown, New York, January 1, 1965; admitted to bar, 1991, Connecticut and New York; 1992, District of Columbia. *Education:* Syracuse University (B.A., 1988); New York University (J.D., 1991). Phi Beta Kappa. ***Email:*** cd'alessandro@crowell.com

ARIEL R. DAVID, born Milwaukee, Wisconsin, March 17, 1964; admitted to bar, 1991, Pennsylvania (inactive); 1992, District of Columbia. *Education:* University of Wisconsin at Madison (B.B.A., 1986); Temple University (J.D., 1991). Law Clerk to Judge Salzman, Superior Court of the District of Columbia, 1991-1992. Counsel, Committee on Armed Services, U.S. House of Representatives, 1992-1995. Law Clerk to Judge Merow, U.S. Court of Federal Claims, 1995-1996. ***Email:*** adavid@crowell.com

CHERYL B. GRANDY, born Wake Forest, Illinois; admitted to bar, 1992, Virginia; 1994, District of Columbia. *Education:* Georgetown University (B.S., 1979); George Mason University (J.D., 1992). ***Email:*** cgrandy@crowell.com

JEROME A. MURPHY, born Washington, D.C., December 9, 1963; admitted to bar, 1992, Maryland; 1999, District of Columbia. *Education:* Georgetown University (B.A., 1985); University of Maryland (J.D., 1992). Order of the Coif. Executive Editor, Maryland Law Review, 1991-1992. Judge Advocate General's Corps, USA, 1992-1998. ***Email:*** jmurphy@crowell.com

ELIZABETH W. NEWSOM, born Belleville, New Jersey, March 30, 1965; admitted to bar, 1992, Maryland; 1995, District of Columbia. *Education:* University of Pennsylvania (B.A., 1987); George Washington University (J.D., 1992). Member, George Washington Law Review, 1990-1992. Law Clerk to Judge Margolis, U.S. Court of Federal Claims, 1992-1993. Trial Attorney, Civil Division, Commercial Litigation Branch, Department of Justice, 1995-2001. ***Email:*** bnewsom@crowell.com

KAREN A. ROSENTHAL, born Groton, Connecticut, May 18, 1964; admitted to bar, 1993, Virginia; 1995, District of Columbia. *Education:* James Madison University (B.A., 1986); University of Virginia (J.D., 1993). Member, 1991-1992 and Executive Editor, 1992-1993, Virginia Environmental Law Journal. ***Email:*** krosenthal@crowell.com

(This Listing Continued)

GLORIA MARTINEZ TRATTLES, born New York, New York, May 21, 1967; admitted to bar, 1994, New York; 2001, District of Columbia. *Education:* Columbia University (B.A., 1989); New York University (J.D., 1993). Order of the Coif. Instructor of Law, New York University School of Law, 1998-2000. ***LANGUAGES:*** Spanish. ***Email:*** gtrattles@crowell.com

WARREN A. ZITLAU, born Wilmington, Delaware, February 3, 1968; admitted to bar, 1994, Pennsylvania, New York and District of Columbia; 1996, Virginia; registered to practice before U.S. Patent and Trademark Office. *Education:* University of Delaware (B.Ch.E., 1990); Boston University (J.D., 1993). Tau Beta Pi. ***Email:*** wzitlau@crowell.com

ANDREW W. BAGLEY, born Washington, D.C., October 31, 1963; admitted to bar, 1994, Maryland; 1995, District of Columbia. *Education:* Duke University (A.B., 1986); University of Maryland (J.D., 1994). Order of the Coif. Member, 1992-1993, Assistant Editor, 1993-1994, Maryland Law Review.

CHRISTOPHER E. KACZMAREK, born Milwaukee, Wisconsin, January 24, 1966; admitted to bar, 1994, Virginia; 1996, District of Columbia. *Education:* College of William and Mary (B.A., 1988); American University (J.D., 1994). Member, 1992-1993, Note and Comment Editor, 1993-1994, American University Law Review.

PAUL ALP, born Poughkeepsie, New York, July 25, 1969; admitted to bar, 1995, Indiana; 1998, Maryland and District of Columbia. *Education:* University of Virginia (B.S., 1991); George Washington University (J.D., 1995). *Member:* Indiana State and American Bar Associations; District of Columbia Bar; Maryland State Bar Association, Inc. ***Email:*** palp@crowell.com

TARA WEINSTOCK BLANCHARD, born Massapequa, New York, May 12, 1970; admitted to bar, 1995, Maryland; 1996, District of Columbia. *Education:* Harvard University (B.A., 1991); George Washington University (J.D., 1995). Staff Member, The Environmental Lawyer, 1994-1995. ***Email:*** tblanchard@crowell.com

KEVIN P. FORJETTE, born Worcester, Massachusetts, January 22, 1969; admitted to bar, 1996, Vermont; 1998, District of Columbia. *Education:* George Washington University (B.A., 1991); Vermont Law School (J.D., 1995). ***Email:*** kforjette@crowell.com

KIMBERLY J. GOLD, born Boston, Massachusetts, November 18, 1970; admitted to bar, 1995, Massachusetts; 1998, District of Columbia. *Education:* Brandeis University (B.A., 1992); American University (J.D., 1995). Law Clerk to Judge Wynn, Superior Court of the District of Columbia, 1995-1996. ***Email:*** kgold@crowell.com

BETH M. KRAMER, born Washington, D.C., May 2, 1968; admitted to bar, 1995, Maryland; 1997, District of Columbia. *Education:* University of Pennsylvania (B.A., 1990); George Washington University (J.D., 1995). ***Email:*** bkramer@crowell.com

ALICIA J. PALMER, born Latrobe, Pennsylvania, June 4, 1967; admitted to bar, 1995, Virginia; 1996, District of Columbia. *Education:* Indiana University of Pennsylvania (B.S., 1988); American University (J.D., 1995). ***Email:*** apalmer@crowell.com

BARRY M. PARSONS, born Wilkes-Barre, Pennsylvania, February 25, 1965; admitted to bar, 1995, Virginia; 1997, District of Columbia. *Education:* King's College (B.S., 1987); American University (M.B.A., 1990); George Mason University (J.D., 1995). Editor-in-Chief, George Mason Law Review, 1994-1995. Law Clerk to Judge Bertelsman, U.S. District Court, Eastern District of Kentucky, 1995-1996. ***Email:*** bparsons@crowell.com

FELICIA GOLDBERG SCHWEITZER, born Boston, Massachusetts, December 22, 1970; admitted to bar, 1995, Maryland and New Jersey; 1996, District of Columbia. *Education:* University of Pennsylvania (B.A., 1992); George Washington University (J.D., 1995). Member, George Washington Journal of International Law and Economics, 1993-1995.

KIMBERLY A. TOLHURST-LAPP, born Pensacola, Florida, May 25, 1970; admitted to bar, 1996, Virginia; 1998, District of Columbia. *Education:* University of Virginia (B.A., 1992); College of William & Mary (J.D., 1995). Executive Board Member, William & Mary Journal of Women and the Law, 1993-1995. ***Email:*** ktolhurstlapp@crowell.com

WILLIAM G. ACKERMAN, born Cheyenne, Wyoming, January 24, 1968; admitted to bar, 1997, Wyoming and Colorado; registered to practice before U.S. Patent and Trademark Office (Not admitted in District of Columbia). *Education:* University of Wyoming (B.S., 1991; J.D., 1996). ***Email:*** wackerman@crowell.com

THOMAS NEWTON BOLLING, born Birmingham, Alabama, November 18, 1960; admitted to bar, 1997, Connecticut; 1999, District of Columbia. *Education:* Columbia College; Columbia University (A.B., 1987); Washington University (J.D., 1996). ***Email:*** tbolling@crowell.com

BARBARA E. BUTTERWORTH, born Belleville, New Jersey, 1966; admitted to bar, 1996, Maryland (inactive); 1997, District of Columbia. *Education:* Boston College (B.A., 1988); Georgetown University (J.D., 1996; LL.M., 2001). Law Clerk to Judge Morrison, District of Columbia Superior Court,

(This Listing Continued)

CROWELL & MORING LLP, Washington—Continued

1996-1997. Visiting Associate Professor of Law, 1999-2001 and Adjunct Professor, 2001—, Georgetown University Juvenile Justice Clinic. ***Email:*** bbutterworth@crowell.com

JEFFREY E. GREENE, born Washington, D.C., February 23, 1969; admitted to bar, 1996, Maryland; 1998, District of Columbia. *Education:* Boston University (B.A., 1990); University of Maryland (J.D., 1996). Order of the Coif. Staff Member, 1994-1995 and Executive Notes and Comments Editor, 1995-1996, Maryland Law Review. ***Email:*** jgreene@crowell.com

SARAH J. ZIMMERMAN, born Hartford, Connecticut, June 16, 1967; admitted to bar, 1996, Maryland; 1998, District of Columbia. *Education:* University of Pennsylvania (B.A., 1989); George Washington University (J.D., 1996). Member, 1994-1995, Executive Notes Editor, 1995-1996, George Washington Journal of International Law and Economics. Law Clerk to Judge Salmon, Maryland Court of Special Appeals, 1996-1997.

CRAIG APPELBAUM, born Mayfield Heights, Ohio, June 9, 1970; admitted to bar, 1998, New York; 2001, District of Columbia. *Education:* Colby College (B.A., 1992); University of Pennsylvania (J.D., 1997). Phi Beta Kappa. Special Projects Editor, Journal of International Economic Law, 1996-1997.

EMMA K. BURTON, born Virginia, 1972; admitted to bar, 1997, Maryland; 1998, District of Columbia. *Education:* Brown University (B.A., 1994); Georgetown University Law Center (J.D., 1997). Member, Georgetown Journal of Legal Ethics, 1995-1997. ***Email:*** eburton@crowell.com

BENJAMIN T. BUTLER, born Stanford, California, August 7, 1972; admitted to bar, 1998, California and District of Columbia. *Education:* Duke University (A.B., 1994; J.D., 1997). Articles Editor, Duke Law Journal, 1996-1997. ***Email:*** bbutler@crowell.com

BRIDGET E. CALHOUN, born Washington, D.C., February 23, 1971; admitted to bar, 1997, Maryland; 2000, District of Columbia. *Education:* Dartmouth College (B.A., 1993); University of Maryland (J.D., 1997). Order of the Coif. Managing Editor, Maryland Law Review, 1996-1997. Law Clerk to Judge Black, U.S. District Court, District of Maryland, 1997-1999. ***Email:*** bcalhoun@crowell.com

KAREN CANAAN, born London, England, January 16, 1963; admitted to bar, 1997, California; registered to practice before U.S. Patent and Trademark Office (Not admitted in District of Columbia). *Education:* University of Texas at Austin (B.A., 1986); Whitter Law School (J.D., 1997). ***LANGUAGES:*** French. ***Email:*** kcanaan@crowell.com

MICHAEL I. COE, born Huntington, West Virginia, January 29, 1971; admitted to bar, 1997, Virginia; registered to practice before U.S. Patent and Trademark Office (Not admitted in District of Columbia). *Education:* Centre College of Kentucky (B.S., Chemical Physics, 1993); College of William & Mary (J.D., 1997). ***Email:*** mcoe@crowell.com

DANIEL R. FORMAN, born New York, New York, June 2, 1972; admitted to bar, 1998, New York; 1999, District of Columbia. *Education:* Vassar College (B.A., 1994); Benjamin N. Cardozo School of Law (J.D., 1997). Staff Member, Cardozo Law Review, 1995-1997. ***Email:*** dforman@crowell.com

L. RACHEL GERVIN, born Wheaton, Illinois, December 30, 1969; admitted to bar, 1998, Maryland; 1999, District of Columbia. *Education:* University of California at Los Angeles (B.A., 1992); Howard University (J.D., 1997). Articles Editor, Howard Law Journal, 1996-1997. ***Email:*** rgervin@crowell.com

EDWARD B. GLENNON, born Alexandria, Virginia, February 19, 1968; admitted to bar, 1997, Virginia; 1999, District of Columbia. *Education:* University of Virginia (B.A., 1990); College of William and Mary (J.D., 1997). Order of the Coif. Board Editor, William and Mary Law Review, 1996-1997. Law Clerk to Judge Wilson, U.S. District Court, Western District of Virginia, 1997-1998. ***Email:*** eglennon@crowell.com

CHRISTOPHER J. HUBER, born Fayetteville, North Carolina, March 3, 1972; admitted to bar, 1997, Maryland; 1998, District of Columbia. *Education:* Yale University (B.A., 1994); Georgetown University (J.D., 1997). Order of the Coif. Senior Project Editor, White Collar Crime Project, American Criminal Law Review, 1996-1997. ***Email:*** chuber@crowell.com

DANIEL A. SASSE, born St. Louis, Missouri, September 7, 1972; admitted to bar, 1997, Missouri; 2000, District of Columbia. *Education:* Valparaiso University (B.A., 1994); Emory University (J.D., 1997). Staff Member, Emory International Law Review, 1995-1997. Law Clerk to Judge Whipple, U.S. District Court, Western District of Missouri, 1997-1999. ***Email:*** dsasse@crowell.com

DYLANA LEIGH BLUM, born Thousand Oaks, California, August 16, 1973; admitted to bar, 1999, California; 2000, District of Columbia. *Education:* Stanford University (B.A., 1995); Harvard University (J.D., 1998). Phi Beta Kappa. Symposium Editor, Women's Law Journal, 1996-1997. Law Clerk to Judge Legg, U.S. District Court, District of Maryland, 1998-1999. ***Email:*** dblum@crowell.com

(This Listing Continued)

TEJPAL SINGH CHAWLA, born Philadelphia, Pennsylvania, September 8, 1973; admitted to bar, 1998, California; 1999, District of Columbia. *Education:* Boston University (B.A., 1995); George Washington University (J.D., 1998). Member, Public Contract Law Journal, 1996-1998. ***Email:*** tchawla@crowell.com

MIGUEL H. DEL TORO, born San Juan, Puerto Rico, February 9, 1972; admitted to bar, 1999, California and District of Columbia. *Education:* Harvard University (A.B., 1994); Stanford University (J.D., 1998). Member, Stanford Journal of International Law, 1995-1996. Member, 1996-1997 and Associate Editor, 1997-1998, Stanford Law Review. ***LANGUAGES:*** Spanish. ***Email:*** mdeltoro@crowell.com

ADAM C. GAJADHARSINGH, born Winnipeg, Canada, December 29, 1973; admitted to bar, 1998, Georgia; 1999, District of Columbia. *Education:* Tulane University (B.A., 1995); Emory University (J.D., 1998). Phi Beta Kappa. ***Email:*** agajadharsingh@crowell.com

DAVID L. HAGA, born Louisville, Kentucky, October 17, 1973; admitted to bar, 1998, Virginia; 1999, District of Columbia. *Education:* University of Virginia (B.A., 1995; J.D., 1998). ***Email:*** dhaga@crowell.com

KAY LEE KIM, born Seoul, Korea, June 25, 1971; admitted to bar, 1999, Maryland and New York (Not admitted in District of Columbia). *Education:* Colgate University (B.A., 1993); University of Maryland (J.D., 1998). Associate Editor, Maryland Law Review, 1997-1998. ***Email:*** kkim@crowell.com

DONALD J. KOCHAN, born Detroit, Michigan, 1974; admitted to bar, 2000, New York (Not admitted in District of Columbia). *Education:* Western Michigan University (B.A., 1995); Cornell University (J.D., 1998). Managing Editor, The Cornell International Law Journal, 1997-1998. Law Clerk to Judge Suhrheinrich, U.S. Court of Appeals, Sixth Circuit, 1998-1999. ***Email:*** dkochan@crowell.com

PETER G. KORYTNYK, born Buffalo, New York, January 6, 1968; admitted to bar, 1999, Virginia; registered to practice before U.S. Patent and Trademark Office (Not admitted in District of Columbia). *Education:* Syracuse University (B.S.M.E., 1990); Catholic University (J.D., 1998). Patent Examiner, U.S. Patent Office, 1990-1998. ***LANGUAGES:*** Ukrainian. ***Email:*** pkorytnyk@crowell.com

SARAH C. LINDSEY, born Alpena, Michigan, June 9, 1973; admitted to bar, 1998, Maryland; 1999, District of Columbia. *Education:* Michigan State University (B.A., 1995); American University (J.D., 1998). Articles Editor, American University Law Review, 1997-1998. ***Email:*** slindsey@crowell.com

JOSEPH P. MASTROSIMONE, born Queens, New York, January 17, 1973; admitted to bar, 1998, Virginia; 1999, District of Columbia. *Education:* University of Rochester (B.A., 1995); George Washington University (J.D., 1998). Order of the Coif. Notes Editor, George Washington Law Review, 1997-1998. ***Email:*** jmastrosimone@crowell.com

KIRSTEN L. NATHANSON, born Fairmont, West Virginia, November 27, 1970; admitted to bar, 1998, Maryland; 1999, District of Columbia. *Education:* University of Pennsylvania (B.A., 1992); George Washington University (J.D., 1998). Order of the Coif. Notes Editor, George Washington Law Review, 1997-1998. ***Email:*** knathanson@crowell.com

ARYEH S. PORTNOY, born New Rochelle, New York, November 8, 1973; admitted to bar, 1999, New York and District of Columbia. *Education:* Columbia College; Columbia University (B.A., 1995); New York University (J.D., 1998).

BRADFORD K. WATTS, admitted to bar, 1999, Massachusetts (Not admitted in District of Columbia). *Education:* Brigham Young University (B.A., 1992); Georgetown University (J.D., 1998). ***Email:*** bwatts@crowell.com

BRIDGET ALLISON, born New Haven, Connecticut, 1973; admitted to bar, 1999, Maryland; 2000, District of Columbia. *Education:* University of Connecticut (B.A., 1996); Georgetown University (J.D., 1999). Phi Beta Kappa. White Collar Crime Project Editor, American Criminal Law Review, 1998-1999. ***Email:*** ballison@crowell.com

JOHN WITHERSPOON BORCHERT, born Lancaster, Ohio, August 13, 1974; admitted to bar, 2000, Georgia; 2001, District of Columbia. *Education:* Ohio University (B.A., 1996); Emory University (J.D., 1999). Phi Beta Kappa. Note and Comment Editor, Emory International Law Review, 1998-1999. ***Email:*** jborchert@crowell.com

JENNY CHUNG SAVIDGE, born Okinawa, Japan, June 4, 1968; admitted to bar, 2000, New York (Not admitted in District of Columbia). *Education:* University of California at Berkeley (B.A., 1990); City University of New York (J.D., 1999). Staff Member, New York City Law Review, 1997-1998. Court Law Clerk, New York State Court of Appeals, 1999-2001. ***LANGUAGES:*** Hakka Chinese. ***Email:*** jchungsavidge@crowell.com

J. CHRIS HAILE, born Nashville, Tennessee, January 30, 1972; admitted to bar, 1999, Virginia; 2001, District of Columbia. *Education:* Vanderbilt University (B.A., 1994); Georgetown University (J.D., 1999). Editor in Chief, Georgetown Journal on Poverty Law & Policy, 1998-1999. *Member:* The District of Columbia Bar. ***Email:*** jhaile@crowell.com

(This Listing Continued)

MATTHEW C. HANS, born Dayton, Ohio, August 14, 1974; admitted to bar, 1999, Missouri; 2000, District of Columbia. *Education:* Xavier University (B.A., 1996); Catholic University (J.D., 1999). Production Editor, The Journal of Contemporary Health Law and Policy, 1998-1999. ***Email:*** mhans@crowell.com

KAREN C. HERMANN, born Belleville, Illinois, August 19, 1972; admitted to bar, 1999, Virginia; 2001, District of Columbia. *Education:* Fontbonne College (B.A., 1996); George Washington University (J.D., 1999). Executive Managing Editor, American Intellectual Property Law Quarterly Journal, 1998-1999. Law Clerk to Judge Margolis, U.S. Court of Federal Claims, 1999-2000. ***Email:*** khermann@crowell.com

VALERIE HINKO, born Wilkes-Barre, Pennsylvania, August 15, 1969; admitted to bar, 1999, Maryland; 2001, District of Columbia. *Education:* Yale University (B.A., 1991); George Washington University (J.D., 1999). Member, 1997-1998, Articles Editor, 1998-1999, The George Washington University Law Review. ***Email:*** vhinko@crowell.com

BURKE W. KAPPLER, born Pittsburgh, Pennsylvania, March 28, 1973; admitted to bar, 1999, Virginia; 2001, District of Columbia. *Education:* American University (B.A., 1993); Harvard University (J.D., 1999). Executive Editor, Harvard Civil Rights-Civil Liberties Law Review, 1998-1999. Pro Se Law Clerk, U.S. District Court, Eastern District of Virginia, 1999-2000. ***Email:*** bkappler@crowell.com

J. CATHERINE KUNZ, born Cincinnati, Ohio, August 26, 1971; admitted to bar, 1999, Ohio; 2000, District of Columbia. *Education:* Stanford University (B.A., 1993); Nicholas School of the Environment (M.E.M., 1999); Duke University (J.D., 1999). Editor-in-Chief, Alaska Law Review, 1997-1998. ***Email:*** ckunz@crowell.com

AMY E. LADERBERG, born Norfolk, Virginia, April 7, 1974; admitted to bar, 1999, Virginia (Not admitted in District of Columbia). *Education:* Williams College (B.A., 1996); College of William & Mary (J.D., 1999). Articles Editor, The William and Mary Journal of Women and the Law, 1996-1999. Notes Editor, The William and Mary Law Review, 1997-1999. Law Clerk to Judge Friedman, U.S. District Court, Eastern District of Virginia, 1999-2000. ***Email:*** aladerberg@crowell.com

SHARI ROSS LAHLOU, born Monterey, California, January 11, 1967; admitted to bar, 1999, Maryland (Not admitted in District of Columbia). *Education:* Dickinson College (B.A., 1989); George Washington University (J.D., 1999). Order of the Coif. Member, 1997-1998, Senior Managing Editor, 1998-1999, The George Washington Law Review. ***Email:*** slahlou@crowell.com

WILLIAM M. MANN, born Huntington, New York, January 20, 1971; admitted to bar, 1999, Virginia; 2000, District of Columbia. *Education:* University of Richmond (B.A., 1993); University of Virginia (J.D., 1999).

CHRISTINA M. MIRELES, born San Jose, California, October 18, 1971; admitted to bar, 2000, District of Columbia. *Education:* Tufts University (B.A., 1993); Georgetown University (M.P.P., 1995); Northwestern University (J.D., 1999). Articles Editor, Northwestern University Law Review, 1998-1999. ***Email:*** cmireles@crowell.com

KATHERINE NESBITT, born Summit, New Jersey, September 8, 1972; admitted to bar, 2001, North Carolina and District of Columbia. *Education:* Duke University (A.B., 1994; J.D., 1999). Contributions Editor, Duke Environmental Law & Policy Forum, 1996-1998. Law Clerk to Judge Jordan, U.S. District Court, Southern District of Florida, 1999-2000. ***Email:*** knesbitt@crowell.com

MONYA A. PHILLIP, born Annapolis, Maryland, October 28, 1970; admitted to bar, 1999, Maryland; 2000, District of Columbia. *Education:* University of Delaware (B.A., 1993); University of Maryland (J.D., 1999). ***Email:*** mphillip@crowell.com

MIGUEL E. RODRIQUEZ, born Cheverly, Maryland, February 20, 1972; admitted to bar, 1999, Maryland; 2000, District of Columbia. *Education:* University of Pennsylvania (B.A., 1994; J.D., 1999). ***Email:*** mrodriguez@crowell.com

JENNIFER KANE SCHWARTZ, born Columbus, Ohio, 1971; admitted to bar, 1999, Ohio and District of Columbia. *Education:* Carnegie Mellon University (B.S., 1993); George Washington University (M.A., 1995; J.D., 1999). Order of the Coif. Member, George Washington Law Review, 1997-1998. ***Email:*** jschwartz@crowell.com

REBECCA L. SPRINGER, born Kansas City, Missouri, November 20, 1971; admitted to bar, 1999, Virginia; 2000, District of Columbia. *Education:* Washington University (B.A., 1993); Duke University (J.D., 1999). Conference and Development Editor, Duke Journal of Gender Law and Policy, 1998-1999. ***Email:*** rspringer@crowell.com

MICHAEL G. VAN ARSDALL, born Newport, Rhode Island, July 29, 1970; admitted to bar, 1999, Virginia; 2001, District of Columbia. *Education:* University of Rhode Island (B.A., 1992); Catholic University (J.D., 1999). Note and Comment Editor, Catholic University Law Review, 1998-1999. *Member:* The District of Columbia Bar. ***Email:*** mvan.arsdall@crowell.com

(This Listing Continued)

ADAM DALEY WILSON, admitted to bar, 1999, California; 2001, District of Columbia. *Education:* University of Pennsylvania (B.A., 1994); Stanford University (J.D., 1999). Associate Editor, Stanford Law Review, 1997-1999. ***Email:*** awilson@crowell.com

MICHAEL G. ABELOW, born Lincoln, Nebraska, 1974; admitted to bar, 2000, Maryland (Not admitted in District of Columbia). *Education:* James Madison University (B.A., 1996); Washington & Lee University (J.D., 2000). Order of the Coif. Member, Washington & Lee Law Review, 1998-1999. ***Email:*** mabelow@crowell.com

JAMES CAMPBELL COOPER, born Washington, D.C., June 27, 1968; admitted to bar, 2000, Virginia; 2001, District of Columbia. *Education:* University of South Carolina (B.A., 1990; M.A., 1991); George Mason University (J.D., 2000). Member, George Mason Law Review, 1998-2000. ***Email:*** jcooper@crowell.com

PARUL P. DESAI, born Orange, New Jersey, August 21, 1974; admitted to bar, 2000, New Jersey; 2001, New York and District of Columbia. *Education:* Rutgers University (B.S., 1996); New York Law School (J.D., 2000). Member, 1998-1999, Notes and Comments Editor, 1999-2000, New York Law School Law Review. Law Clerk to Judge Lefelt, New Jersey State Appellate Division, 2000-2001. ***LANGUAGES:*** Gujarati. ***Email:*** pdesai@crowell.com

PATRICIA J. B. DEWITT, born Oakland, California, January 30, 1974; admitted to bar, 2000, California; 2001, District of Columbia. *Education:* University of California at Los Angeles (B.A., 1996); Harvard University (J.D., 2000). ***Email:*** pdewitt@crowell.com

F. RYAN KEITH, born Portsmouth, Virginia, June 19, 1974; admitted to bar, 2000, Kentucky; 2001, District of Columbia. *Education:* Centre College of Kentucky (B.A., 1996); Washington & Lee University (J.D., 2000). Staff Member, 1998-1999 and Lead Articles Editor, 1999-2000, Washington & Lee Law Review. Law Clerk to Judge Martin, U.S. Court of Appeals, Sixth Circuit, 2000-2001. ***Email:*** frkeith@crowell.com

BRIDGET E. LITTLEFIELD, born Silver Spring, Maryland, October 2, 1973; admitted to bar, 2000, Maryland (Not admitted in District of Columbia). *Education:* University of Maryland (B.A., 1995; J.D., 2000). Phi Beta Kappa. Order of the Coif. Staff Editor, 1998-1999, Notes and Comments Editor, 1999-2000, Maryland Law Review. Law Clerk to Judge Smalkin, U.S. District Court, District of Maryland, 2000-2001. ***Email:*** blittlefield@crowell.com

EDWARD R. MURRAY, born Arlington, Virginia, March 13, 1970; admitted to bar, 2000, Virginia; 2001, District of Columbia. *Education:* Virginia Polytechnic Institute and State University (B.A., 1992); George Washington University (J.D., 2000). Order of the Coif. Member, The George Washington Law Review, 1998-2000. ***Email:*** emurray@crowell.com

AMY B. NEWMAN, born Pittsburgh, Pennsylvania, January 18, 1971; admitted to bar, 2000, Maryland; 2001, District of Columbia. *Education:* Tufts University (B.A., 1993); American University (J.D., 2000). Staff Member, The American University Law Review, 1998-2000. ***Email:*** anewman@crowell.com

HEIDI PIRANIAN, born Princeton, New Jersey, September 6, 1975; admitted to bar, 2000, Pennsylvania (Not admitted in District of Columbia). *Education:* Princeton University (B.A., 1997); Harvard University (J.D., 2000). Editor, Journal of Law and Public Policy. ***Email:*** hpiranian@crowell.com

DAVID E. BELL, born Gulfport, Mississippi, December 15, 1975; admitted to bar, 2001, Virginia (Not admitted in District of Columbia). *Education:* University of Miami (B.A., 1998); University of Virginia (J.D., 2001). Phi Beta Kappa. Member, Editorial Board, Virginia Journal of Sports and the Law, 1999-2001. ***Email:*** dbell@crowell.com

JENNIFER A. GRUDA, born Concord, Massachusetts, November 29, 1976; admitted to bar, 2001, Virginia (Not admitted in District of Columbia). *Education:* Brandeis University (B.A., 1998); Georgetown University (J.D., 2001). Phi Beta Kappa; Order of the Coif. Member, 1999-2000 and Notes and Comments Primary Editor, 2000-2001, Georgetown Law Journal. ***Email:*** jgruda@crowell.com

JENNIFER E. SCHLOSSER, born Concord, New Hampshire, June 1, 1975; admitted to bar, 2001, Virginia (Not admitted in District of Columbia). *Education:* Syracuse University (B.A., 1998); George Washington University (J.D., 2001). Phi Beta Kappa; Order of the Coif. Production Editor, The George Washington Law Review, 2000-2001.

(For complete biographical data on personnel at Irvine, California and London, England, see Professional Biographies at those locations)

CROWLEY, HOGE & FEIN, P.C.

Established in 1967

1710 RHODE ISLAND AVENUE, NW, SEVENTH FLOOR

WASHINGTON, D.C. 20035-3125

Telephone: 202-483-2900

Fax: 202-483-1365

URL: http://www.chf-law.com

General Civil and Criminal Law Practice including Counselling, Negotiations, Trial and Appellate Work in Family Law, Estate Planning, Probate, Fiduciary Matters, Negligence and Small Businesses.

DANIEL H. CROWLEY, born Baltimore, Maryland, April 8, 1937; admitted to bar, 1966, Maryland; 1967, District of Columbia. *Education:* Yale University (A.B., 1960); University of Maryland (J.D., 1966). *Member:* The District of Columbia Bar; Maryland State Bar Association. ***PRACTICE AREAS:*** Probate; Estate Planning; Trust Administration.

CHRISTOPHER G. HOGE, born Katonah, New York, June 12, 1948; admitted to bar, 1975, District of Columbia and U.S. Court of Appeals for the District of Columbia Circuit; 1977, U.S. Supreme Court; 1987, Maryland. *Education:* University of North Carolina (B.A., 1970); American University (J.D., 1974). Law Clerk to Honorable George Revercomb, Judge Superior Court of the District of Columbia, 1974-1975. *Member:* The District of Columbia Bar; The Bar Association of the District of Columbia (President, 1998-1999), Maryland State and American Bar Associations; The George Washington American Inn of Court (President, 1996-1997). Fellow, American Bar Foundation (1999—). ***PRACTICE AREAS:*** Civil Law; Criminal Litigation; Professional Negligence.

LESLIE G. FEIN, born Milwaukee, Wisconsin, August 2, 1946; admitted to bar, 1971, Tennessee and District of Columbia; 1972, U.S. District Court for the District of Columbia Circuit; 1975, U.S. District Court, District of Maryland; 1980, U.S. Supreme Court; 1987, Maryland. *Education:* Tulane University (B.A., 1968); University of Tennessee (J.D., 1971). *Member:* The District of Columbia Bar; The Bar Association of the District of Columbia (Chairman, Lawyer Referral Service Committee, 1986-1988; 1998-2000); Maryland State Bar Association. ***PRACTICE AREAS:*** Family Law; Personal Injury Law; Elder Law. ***Email:*** CHFLGF@aol.com

---

CULLEN AND DYKMAN LLP

1101 FOURTEENTH STREET, N.W., SUITE 550

WASHINGTON, D.C. 20005

Telephone: 202-223-8890

Telecopier: 202-457-1405

Email: cullenanddykman.com

URL: http://www.cullendykman.com

Brooklyn, New York Office: 177 Montague Street. Telephone: 718-855-9000. Telecopier: 718-855-4282.

Garden City, New York Office: Garden City Center, 100 Quentin Roosevelt Boulevard. Telephone: 516-357-3700. Telecopier: 516-357-3792.

Newark, New Jersey Office: One Gateway Plaza, Suite 2600. Telephone: 973-353-8410. Telecopier: 973-353-8411.

General Practice.

MEMBER OF FIRM

KENNETH T. MALONEY, born Elizabeth, New Jersey, July 18, 1961; admitted to bar, 1986, New Jersey; 1988, District of Columbia and U.S. Court of Appeals, Fifth Circuit; 1989, New York and U.S. Court of Appeals, D.C. Circuit. *Education:* University of Virginia (B.A., 1983); Rutgers University at Newark (J.D., 1986). Arbitrator, District of Columbia. Member, Attorney-Client Arbitration Board. *Member:* New Jersey State and American Bar Associations; Federal Energy Bar Association; Fairfax County, Virginia Human Services Council. ***Email:*** kmaloney@cullenanddykman.com

OF COUNSEL

ROBERT G. HARDY, born Urbana, Illinois, 1944; admitted to bar, 1969, North Carolina; 1972, District of Columbia. *Education:* Duke University (B.A., 1966); University of North Carolina (J.D., 1969). *Member:* The District of Columbia Bar; North Carolina and Federal Energy Bar Associations. ***PRACTICE AREAS:*** Administrative Law; Energy Law. ***Email:*** rhardy@cullenanddykman

(For complete biographical data on all Members, Of Counsel and Counsel at Brooklyn, New York, Garden City, New York and Newark, New Jersey see Professional Biographies at those locations)

THE CULLEN LAW FIRM, PLLC

1101 30TH STREET N.W., SUITE 300

WASHINGTON, D.C. 20007

Telephone: 202-944-8600

Fax: 202-944-8611

URL: http://www.cullenlaw.com

Email: pdc@cullenlaw.com

URL: http://www.lawyers.com/cullenlaw

Class Actions, Transportation Litigation, Motor Carrier Law, Interstate Commerce, Trade Association Law, Legislative Practice, Administrative Agency Practice, International Trade Regulation, Asia Trade, Customs Law, Antidumping, False Claims Act, Whistleblower Litigation, Constitutional Law, Commercial Litigation. Civil Litigation and Appeals in all State and Federal Courts.

FIRM PROFILE: Located in the nation's capitol, The Cullen Law Firm represents over 60 years of practical legal and complex litigation experience. The firm represents clients on a nationwide basis in civil trials and appeals in all state and federal courts. The firm is best known for its class action transportation litigation, its international trade law practice and its Constitutional challenges to state taxes imposed on interstate commerce. The firm represents American corporations, multi-national corporations, trade associations (both domestic and foreign) and small businesses and individual entrepreneurs. The Cullen Law Firm is proud of its unique record of success in the representation of each of the members of its diverse client base.

PAUL D. CULLEN, SR., born Boston, Massachusetts, October 6, 1940; admitted to bar, 1965, Connecticut; 1966, New York; 1972, District of Columbia; 1974, U.S. Supreme Court; 1979, U.S. Court of Appeals for the District of Columbia Circuit; 1980, U.S. Court of International Trade; 1982, U.S. Court of Appeals for the Federal Circuit; 1999, U.S. Court of Appeals, Sixth and Eighth Circuits. *Education:* Georgetown University College of Arts and Sciences (A.B., 1962); Georgetown University Law Center (J.D., 1965). Member, Georgetown Law Center National Moot Court Team, 1965. Trial Attorney, U.S. Department of Justice, Civil Division, 1970-1972. Assistant Counsel, Corning Glass Works, 1972-1978. *Member:* District of Columbia Bar; Federal and American Bar Associations. [Capt., U.S. Army Intelligence, 1965-1967]. ***PRACTICE AREAS:*** Transportation; Class Actions; False Claims Act; International Trade Law; Whistleblower Litigation. ***Email:*** pdc@cullenlaw.com

JOSEPH A. BLACK, born Buffalo, New York, February 5, 1944; admitted to bar, 1987, Pennsylvania; 1988, District of Columbia and U.S. Court of International Trade; 1989, U.S. Court of Appeals for the Federal Circuit. *Education:* Central Missouri State University (B.A., 1968); California State University Long Beach (M.A., 1972); Catholic University of America (J.D., 1987). Member: Catholic University Law Review; U.S. Customs Service, 1971-1980; International Trade Administration, Department of Commerce, 1980-1984. *Member:* The District of Columbia Bar; American Bar Association. ***PRACTICE AREAS:*** International Trade Regulation; Customs Law; False Claims Act; Commercial Litigation; Motor Carrier Law; Transportation; Whistleblower Litigation. ***Email:*** jab@cullenlaw.com

DAVID A. COHEN, born Detroit, Michigan, August 28, 1963; admitted to bar, 1988, Pennsylvania; 1990, New Jersey (Not admitted in District of Columbia). *Education:* Wayne State University (B.A., cum laude, 1985); Rutgers University School of Law (J.D., with honors, 1988). Member, Board of Editors, Rutgers Law Journal, 1986-1988. Daily Editor: Pittsburgh Legal Journal, 1996-1998. Attorney Advisor, U.S. Department of Labor, 1988-1990. Associate, Jones, Day, Reavis & Pogue, 1995-1999. ***PRACTICE AREAS:*** Class Actions; Property Litigation; Labor and Employment. ***Email:*** dac@cullenlaw.com

PAUL D. CULLEN, JR., born White Sands, New Mexico, April 18, 1967; admitted to bar, 1999, District of Columbia. *Education:* College of William and Mary (B.A., 1989); Georgetown University (J.D., 1998). National Finalist, Saul Lefkowitz Trademark Moot Court Competition. *Member:* District of Columbia Bar. ***PRACTICE AREAS:*** Transportation Law; False Claims Act; Class Action Litigation; Partnership Law; Government Affairs. ***Email:*** pxc@cullenlaw.com

JOSEPH A. HENNESSEY, born Washington, D.C., March 11, 1965; admitted to bar, 1996, Maryland; 1997, District of Columbia. *Education:* Tufts University (B.A., magna cum laude 1989); St. John's College: The Graduate Institute (M.A., cum laude 1993); The Columbus School of Law at Catholic University (J.D., cum laude, 1995). Judicial Clerk to the Hon. John A. Terry, District of Columbia Court of Appeals. ***PRACTICE AREAS:*** International Arbitration; Commercial Law; Litigation; Privacy Law; Regulatory Law; Appellate Practice; Complex and Multi-District Litigation; Intellectual Property Litigation; Intellectual Property; Transportation. ***Email:*** jah@cullenlaw.com

JOYCE E. MAYERS, born Coral Gables, Florida, February 19, 1951; admitted to bar, 1977, Florida; 1979, District of Columbia, U.S. District Court, District of Columbia, U.S. Court of Appeals, First Circuit and U.S. Court of Federal Claims. *Education:* Wellesley College (B.A., 1973); Boston College

(This Listing Continued)

Law School (J.D., 1977). Division of Enforcement, Commodity Futures Trading Commission, 1981-1983. Special Counsel, Division of Trading and Markets, Commodity Futures Trading Commission, 1983-1984. Former Associate, Reed Smith. Former Partner, Bethel & Nicastro. *Member:* The District of Columbia Bar; The Florida Bar. ***PRACTICE AREAS:*** Securities; Commodities; Complex Litigation; False Claims Act; Telecommunications Law. ***Email:*** jem@cullenlaw.com

CLAIRE L. SHAPIRO, born Detroit, Michigan, July 10, 1953; admitted to bar, 1980, District of Columbia. *Education:* University of Michigan (A.B., with honors, 1975); Georgetown University (J.D., with honors, 1980). Administrative Editor, Georgetown University Law Journal, 1978-1979. *Member:* The District of Columbia Bar. ***PRACTICE AREAS:*** Transportation Law; Class Actions; Litigation; Insurance Coverage; Insurance Litigation. ***Email:*** cls@cullenlaw.com

JAMES J. WHITTLE, born West Islip, New York, September 30, 1963; admitted to bar, 1990, Maryland; 1991, District of Columbia. *Education:* State University of New York at Brockport (B.S., cum laude, 1986); Washington College of Law of American University (J.D., 1990). Phi Delta Phi. National Political Science Honor Society. Dean's Fellow, 1990. Executive Editor, American University Journal of International Law and Policy, 1989-1990. Author: "Juda v. United States: An Atoll's Legal Odyssey," 4 Am. U.J. Int'l. L. & Pol'y. 655 (1989). Law Clerk, Honorable Rosalyn B. Bell, Associate Judge, Maryland Court of Special Appeals, 1990-1991. *Member:* The District of Columbia Bar. ***PRACTICE AREAS:*** Insurance Coverage; Insurance Litigation; Civil Litigation; Complex Litigation; Class Actions. ***Email:*** jjw@cullenlaw.com

---

BELINDA RODRIGUEZ HARRISON, born Alice, Texas, November 24, 1971; admitted to bar, 2001, Maryland (Not admitted in District of Columbia). *Education:* Shippensburg University (B.S., magna cum laude, 1997); American University's Washington College of Law (J.D., 2001). Phi Beta Kappa. Board of Governors Scholar. ***LANGUAGES:*** Spanish. ***PRACTICE AREAS:*** Transportation; Bankruptcy; First Amendment Law. ***Email:*** brh@cullenlaw.com

---

THE CUNEO LAW GROUP, P.C.

Established in 1989

317 MASSACHUSETTS AVENUE, N.E.

SUITE 300

WASHINGTON, D.C. 20002

Telephone: 202-789-3960

Fax: 202-789-1813

Email: contact@cuneolaw.com

URL: http://www.cuneolaw.com

Civil Litigation in Federal and State Courts. General Commercial Practice. Administrative, Antitrust, Copyright, Franchise, Health Care, Civil Rights, White Collar Criminal and Securities Law. Government Relations.

JONATHAN W. CUNEO, born New York, N.Y., September 10, 1952; admitted to bar, 1977, District of Columbia; 1978, U.S. District Court, District of Columbia and U.S. Court of Appeals, District of Columbia Circuit; 1994, U.S. Supreme Court. *Education:* Columbia University (A.B., 1974); Cornell University (J.D., 1977). Law Clerk to the Honorable Edward A. Tamm, U.S. Court of Appeals for the District of Columbia Circuit, 1977-1978. Author: "Judge Tamm and the Evolution of Administrative Law: The Art of Judging," 74 Georgetown L.J. 1595, 1986; with Jerry Cohen, "Pulling the Plug on Antitrust Law," The Nation, September 26, 1986; "House Takes Up Cause of Discounters," Legal Times, Vol. X No. 30, December 1987; "Supreme Court's 'Sharp' Ruling Means Higher Prices, Fewer Choices for Consumers," Manhattan Lawyer, May 31-June 6, 1988; Chapter, "Consumer Protection -- Federal Trade Commission," as part of "Changing America: Blueprints for the New Administration," edited by Mark Green, 1992; "Antitrust and Clinton: Changes on the Horizon," The California Lawyer, February 1993; "Action on Class Actions", The Recorder, April 30, 1997. Attorney, Office of the General Counsel, Federal Trade Commission, 1978-1981. Counsel, Subcommittee on Monopolies and Commercial Law, House Committee on the Judiciary, 1981-1986. General Counsel: Committee to Support the Antitrust Laws, 1986—; National Association of Securities and Commercial Law Attorneys, 1988-1996. Legislative Counsel, National Coalition of Petroleum Retailers and Service Station Dealers of America, 1988-1994. Member: Arlington County Democratic Committee, 1983-1987; Board of Directors, Violence Policy Center, 1996—; The American Antitrust Institute, 1998—; The Appleseed Foundation, 1999—; F.I.S.T. Fighters' Initiative For Support and Training, 2000. Faculty Member, "Copyright for the Nineties: What Every Lawyer Needs to Know," a series by West Publishing Company (1990). Guest Lecturer, Southwestern Law School, 1997, 1998. *Member:* The District of Columbia Bar; American Bar Association. ***PRACTICE AREAS:*** Litigation; Government Relations.

(This Listing Continued)

JAMES J. SCHWEITZER, born New York, N.Y., May 23, 1947; admitted to bar, 1973, District of Columbia, U.S. District Court, District of Columbia and U.S. Court of Appeals, District of Columbia Circuit. *Education:* Yale University (B.A., 1969); University of Virginia (J.D., 1973). Attorney-Advisor, Department of Transportation, Federal Highway Administration, 1973-1974. Director, Legal Counsel Section, Office of the Commonwealth of Puerto Rico, D.C., 1974-1977. Legislative Assistant/Director for U.S. Representative Elizabeth Holtzman, 1977-1979. Counsel: Subcommittee on Immigration, Refugees, and International Law, House Judiciary Committee, 1979-1981; House Committee on the Judiciary, 1981-1989. Associate Staff Member, Select Committee to Investigate Covert Arms Transactions with Iran, 1987. *Member:* The District of Columbia Bar. ***PRACTICE AREAS:*** Government Relations.

DAVID W. STANLEY, born Saint Louis, Missouri, May 30, 1944; admitted to bar, 1972, Virginia; 1973, District of Columbia; 1974, U.S. District Court, District of Columbia; 1978, U.S. Court of Appeals, District of Columbia Circuit; 1980, U.S. Supreme Court. *Education:* University of Virginia (B.A., 1966; J.D., 1972). Law Clerk to the Hon. Gerard D. Reilly, Chief Judge, District of Columbia Court of Appeals, 1972-1973. Assistant U.S. Attorney for the District of Columbia (Fraud Division, 1981-1984), 1973-1984. Assistant Chief Trial Attorney, Division of Enforcement, U.S. Securities and Exchange Commission, 1984-1987. Of Counsel, Swidler & Berlin, Chartered, 1987-1992. *Member:* The District of Columbia Bar; Virginia State Bar; Assistant U.S. Attorneys Association for District of Columbia (President, 1994-1995); The Barristers-District of Columbia. ***PRACTICE AREAS:*** Litigation.

MICHAEL G. LENETT, born New York, N.Y., February 24, 1962; admitted to bar, 1988, Virginia; 1989, Maryland; 1990, District of Columbia and U.S. Court of Appeals, Ninth Circuit; 1991, U.S. Court of Appeals, Tenth Circuit; 1992, U.S. Supreme Court; 1999, U.S. District Court, District of Columbia. *Education:* Brandeis University (B.A., with honors, magna cum laude, 1984); Georgetown University (M.A., 1988; J.D., 1988; LL.M., with Distinction, 1992). Senior Articles and Notes Editor, American Criminal Law Review. Associate, McGuire, Woods, Battle and Boothe, 1988-1990. Staff Attorney, 1990-1991, Senior Counsel, 1991-1993 and Special Counsel, 1993, Office of the General Counsel, U.S. Securities and Exchange Commission. Adjunct Professor, The National Law Center, George Washington University, 1992-1993. Counsel, Subcommittee on Antitrust, Monopolies, and Business Rights, Committee on the Judiciary, United States Senate, 1993-1995. Democratic Counsel, Committee on the Judiciary, United States Senate, 1995-1996. President, Montgomery County District 19 Democratic Club, 1998-1999, 2000-2001. Chairman, Maryland Democratic Precinct 13-02, 1997—. Member, Board of Directors, Family Learning Solutions, 1998-2000. Author: "Taking a Bite Out of Violent Crime," University of Dayton Law Review (March 1995); "Fifth Amendment Limitations on Compelled Production of Evidence," 25 American Criminal Law Review 509 (Winter 1988); "Airport Searches and Seizures: The *Pulido* Court's Response to Terrorism," 25 American Criminal Law Review 549 (Winter, 1988). Co-Author: "The SEC Enters the ADR Zone," Business Law Today (ABA Jan./Feb. 1993); "Recent SEC & SRO Enforcement Initiatives Regarding Broker-Dealer Supervision & Compliance," Second Annual Supervisory & Compliance Seminar (Prentice Hall Law & Business, 1990); "Enforcement Issues Arising From the Operations of Penny Stock Broker-Dealers," Insider Trading, Fraud & Fiduciary Duty Under the Federal Securities Laws (ALI-ABA, 1990); "Compliance Officers' Supervisory Responsibilities: The *Chambers* Case," 4 Insights 1 (July 1990); "Defending SEC Insider Trading Investigations," Insider Trading, Fraud & Fiduciary Duty Under the Federal Securities Laws (ALI-ABA, 1989). *Member:* Montgomery County, Maryland State and American (Member, Sections on: Business Law; Litigation) Bar Associations; The District of Columbia Bar (Member, Sections on: Corporation, Finance and Securities Law; Litigation). ***PRACTICE AREAS:*** Litigation; Torts; Consumer Law; Securities; Government Relations.

DANIEL COHEN, born Detroit, Michigan, January 24, 1958; admitted to bar, 1989, Florida; 2000, District of Columbia. *Education:* Ithaca College (B.A., 1981); Western New England (J.D., 1988). Defense Criminal Trial Attorney, Public Defenders Office, Jacksonville, Florida, 1989-1999. Mediator, Insurance Alternative Dispute Resolution, Florida, 1999-2000. *Member:* The District of Columbia Bar; The Florida Bar. ***PRACTICE AREAS:*** Litigation; Antitrust; Insurance; Alternative Dispute Resolution; Criminal Law.

CHARLES J. LaDUCA, born Buffalo, New York, September 30, 1974; admitted to bar, 2001, New York (Not admitted in District of Columbia). *Education:* George Washington University (B.A., English, 1996); Catholic University Law School (J.D., 2000). *Member:* New York State and American Bar Associations. ***PRACTICE AREAS:*** Litigation; Torts; Consumer Law; Securities; Antitrust. ***Email:*** charlesl@cuneolaw.com

OF COUNSEL

JON ANDERS TOSTRUD, born Saint Paul, Minnesota, February 6, 1969; admitted to bar, 1994, Minnesota; 1999, California (Not admitted in District of

(This Listing Continued)

THE CUNEO LAW GROUP, P.C., Washington—Continued

Columbia). *Education:* St. Olaf College (B.A., 1991); William Mitchell College of Law (J.D., 1994). ***PRACTICE AREAS:*** Civil Rights; Class Actions; Wage and Hour Law; Antitrust Class Actions; Securities Class Actions; Privacy Law. **Email:** jont@cuneolaw.com

CURTIS, MALLET-PREVOST, COLT & MOSLE LLP

Established in 1830

SUITE 1205L, 1801 K STREET, N.W.
WASHINGTON, D.C. 20006
Telephone: 202-452-7373
Telecopier: 202-452-7333
Email: info@cm-p.com
URL: http://www.cm-p.com

REVISERS OF THE ARGENTINA, BOLIVIA, BRAZIL, CHILE, COLOMBIA, COSTA RICA, DOMINICAN REPUBLIC, ECUADOR, EL SALVADOR, GUATEMALA, HONDURAS, MEXICO, NICARAGUA, PERU, URUGUAY AND VENEZUELA LAW DIGESTS FOR THIS DIRECTORY.

New York, N.Y. Office: 101 Park Avenue. Telephone: 212-696-6000. Telecopier: 212-697-1559.
Newark, New Jersey Office: One Gateway Center, Suite 403. Telephone: 973-622-0605. Telecopier: 973-622-5646.
Houston, Texas Office: 2 Houston, Center, 909 Fannin Street, Suite 3725. Telephone: 713-759-9555. Telecopier: 713-759-0712.
Stamford, Connecticut Office: Financial Centre, 695 East Main Street. Telephone: 203-359-6200. Telecopier: 203-328-2617.
Mexico City, D.F., Mexico Office: Curtis, Mallet-Prevost, Colt & Mosle, Ruben Dario 281, Pisos 8 & 9, Col. Bosque de Chapultepec, 11530 Mexico, D.F. Telephone: 52-55-5282-0444. Telecopier: 52-55-5282-0637.
Paris, France Office: 15 rue d'Astorg, 75008. Telephone: +33-1 42-66-39-10. Telecopier: +33-1 42-66-39-62 .
London, England Office: One Cornhill, EC3V 3ND. Telephone: 0207-743-6310. Telecopier: 0207-743-6311.
Frankfurt am Main 1, Germany Office: Staufenstrasse 42. Telephone: +49-69-971-4420. Telecopier: +49-69-17 33 99.
Muscat, Sultanate of Oman Office: Jewel Beach-134. Telephone: 968-564-495. Telecopier: 968-564-497.
Milan, Italy Office: Curtis, Mallet-Prevost & Gilioli, Piazzale Principessa Clotilde 8, 20121. Telephone: +(39) 02 29 00-29 32. Telefax: +(39) 02 65 75 969.

General Corporate Practice including Securities, Investment Management, International Transactions and Finance, Antitrust and Trade Regulation, Regulation of International Transactions, Employment. Civil Trial and Appellate Practice, Criminal Defense. Consultants on Laws of Latin American Countries.

RESIDENT PARTNERS

PRESTON BROWN, born New York, N.Y., October 6, 1936; admitted to bar, 1962, New York; 1969, District of Columbia. *Education:* Harvard University (B.A., magna cum laude, 1958; LL.B., 1961). Executive Assistant to Hon. Marietta Tree, Delegate, New York State Constitutional Convention, 1967. Special Assistant to Under Secretary and Secretary, U.S. Department of Housing and Urban Development, 1967-1969. Author: "The Potential Effect of the U.S. Economic Embargo of Cuba and Related U.S. Legislation on U.S.-Mexico Transactions," Chapter 4, "Doing Business in Mexico," P. von Mehren, Ed. (1998); "U.S. Legislation Directed Against Persons Investing in Property Confiscated by Cuba," Foreign Investment Law Journal (ICSID Review, Fall 1996); "The U.N./Iraq Oil for Food Program," Middle East Commercial Law Review (1996); "Proposed U.S. Sanctions on Persons Participating in the Development of the Petroleum Resources of Iran or Libya," Oil & Gas Law and Taxation Review (1996); "The Transformation of the Maquiladora under NAFTA (with C. Karr), Martinus Nijoff (1994); "Latin American Trade Accords," (With C. Karr), N.Y. Law Journal (1993); "The Kuwait/Iraq Sanctions-U.S. Regulations in an International Setting," Practising Law Institute (1991); "The U.S. Iraq/Kuwait Sanctions Program," Journal of International Banking (1990); "Multilateral Investment Guaranty Agency," International Business Lawyer (1989); "Unfair Methods of Competition in Importation: The Expanded Role of the U.S. International Trade Commission under Section 337 of the Trade Act of 1930 as amended," Business Lawyer (1976); "The 1971 I.C.J. Advisory Opinion on South West Africa (Namibia)," Vanderbilt Journal of Transnational Law (1971). *Member:* The District of Columbia Bar; American Bar Association; American Society of International Law. ***PRACTICE AREAS:*** Corporate Law; Regulatory Agency Practice; International Regulatory Law. **Email:** pbrown@cm-p.com

SAMUEL ROSENTHAL, born New York, N.Y., December 24, 1950; admitted to bar, 1976, New Jersey and District of Columbia; 1980, U.S. Court of Appeals, Third Circuit; 1984, U.S. Supreme Court and U.S. Court of Appeals, Fourth Circuit; 1985, U.S. Court of Appeals, Second, Fifth and Tenth Circuits; 1999, New York. *Education:* Cornell University (B.S., 1973; J.D., 1976). Author: "Tips for Appellate Advocacy," BNA Criminal Practice Manual, Volume 3, No. 8, April 19, 1989; "Amicus Curiae: Judicial Lobbyist Wields Power in Appellate Courts," National Law Journal, December 5, 1988; "Whittling Away the Sixth Amendment, a Review of the Supreme Court's Last Term," ABA Criminal Justice Magazine, Winter, 1988; "Jeopardy and Termination Assessments After Laing and Hall: Jeopardizing the Fourth Amendment," 31 Tax Law Review, 317, 1976. Assistant U.S. Attorney, District of New Jersey, 1980-1984. Chief, Appellate Section, Criminal Division, Department of Justice, 1984-1988. *Member:* The District of Columbia Bar; New Jersey State Bar Association; National Association of Criminal Defense Attorneys; National Health Lawyers Association. ***PRACTICE AREAS:*** Civil Litigation; International Litigation. **Email:** srosenthal@cm-p.com

JEFFREY I. ZUCKERMAN, born New York, N.Y., January 15, 1950; admitted to bar, 1973, New York and U.S. Court of Appeals, Second Circuit; 1974, U.S. District Court, Eastern and Southern Districts of New York; 1976, U.S. Supreme Court; 1978, U.S. Court of Appeals for the District of Columbia Circuit and U.S. District Court, Northern District of New York; 1981, U.S. Court of Appeals, Tenth Circuit; 1983, U.S. District Court for the District of Columbia; 1989, District of Columbia. *Education:* City College of the City University of New York (B.A., cum laude, with honors in Economics, 1969); Yale University (J.D., 1972). Phi Beta Kappa. Member, Board of Editors, Yale Law Journal, 1971-1972. Author: "Mexico: Towards Freer Markets," International Corporate Law, March 1995, at 23 (Co-author); "USA: Proposed Changes to the Hart-Scott-Rodino Premerger Notification and Report Form," 1994 International Business Law Journal 1017; "Competing Approaches in Latin America," International Corporate Law, April 1993, at 25; Case Note (La Société Honda France), 86 Am. J. Intl. L. 561 (1992); "Courts May Not, and Should Not, Order Divestiture in Private Section 7 Cases," Antitrust, Spring 1990 at 37; "The FTC's Approach to Merger Analysis: Is Anyone Out There Paying Attention?" 57 Antitrust Law Journal 115 (1988); "'Preliminary' Relief Against Anticompetitive Mergers," 82 Yale Law Journal 155 (1972). Special Assistant to the Assistant Attorney General, Antitrust Division, U.S. Department of Justice, 1981-1984. Chief of Staff, U.S. Equal Employment Opportunity Commission, 1984-1986. Director, Bureau of Competition, Federal Trade Commission, 1986-1989. Member, Business and Industry Advisory Committee, Committee on Competition Law and Policy, Organization for Economic Cooperation and Development (OECD). Member, ICC Commission on Law and Practices Relating to Competition. *Member:* The Association of the Bar of the City of New York; The District of Columbia Bar (Treasurer, 1995-1996); New York State and American Bar Associations; New York County Lawyers Association. ***PRACTICE AREAS:*** Civil Litigation; Antitrust and Trade Regulation; Employment Law. **Email:** jzuckerman@cm-p.com

REVISERS OF THE ARGENTINA, BOLIVIA, BRAZIL, CHILE, COLOMBIA, COSTA RICA, DOMINICAN REPUBLIC, ECUADOR, EL SALVADOR, GUATEMALA, HONDURAS, MEXICO, NICARAGUA, PERU, URUGUAY AND VENEZUELA LAW DIGESTS FOR THIS DIRECTORY.

(For complete biographical data on all personnel, see Professional Biographies at New York, New York)

DAHLGREN AND CLOSE

Established in 1946

1000 CONNECTICUT AVENUE, N.W., SUITE 204
WASHINGTON, D.C. 20036
Telephone: 202-659-1440
Fax: 202-659-5755
Email: dahlgrenclose@cs.com
URL: http://www.lawyers.com/dahlgrencloselaw

General, International, Corporate and Administrative Practice, Retirement Planning, Wills, Estates, Trusts, Probate, Family Wealth Transfer, Expert Witnessing for Wills, Estates and Probate.

MEMBERS OF FIRM

JOHN O. DAHLGREN (1913-1989).

DAVID P. CLOSE, born New York, N.Y., March 16, 1915; admitted to bar, 1942, New York; 1946, District of Columbia and U.S. Supreme Court; 1946, U.S. Claims Court; 1947, U.S. Court of Appeals for the District of Columbia Circuit; 1982, U.S. Court of Appeals for the Federal Circuit. *Education:* The Hill School, Williams College (A.B., 1938); Columbia University (J.D., 1942); Mount Vernon College (L.H.D., 1998). Phi Delta Phi. Director, 1960—, Vice President, 1960-1989, President, 1989—, International Humanities, Inc. Member, Board of Directors, National Society for the Prevention of Blindness, Inc., 1961-1969 and International Eye Foundation, 1961—, President, International

(This Listing Continued)

Eye Foundation, 1986-1989. President, D.C. Society for the Prevention of Blindness, 1961-1963. Trustee, 1963-1978 and President, 1971-1974, Mt. Vernon College. Trustee, Williams College, 1963-1968. Trustee, 1965-1985, Honorary Trustee, 1985—and Chairman, 1974-1985, The Hill School. Director, 1973—, Secretary/Treasurer, 1974-1977, and Treasurer, 1991—, Marjorie Merriweather Post Foundation of D.C. Director, National Savings & Trust, Co., 1973-1988. American Council for the United Nations University, (Member, 1981—and Treasurer, 1987-1991). *Member:* The District of Columbia Bar; Bar Association of the District of Columbia; The Association of the Bar of the City of New York (Associate Member); American and Inter-American Bar Associations; The Association of Trial Lawyers of America. [U.S. Naval Intelligence, 1942-1946]. ***LANGUAGES:*** French and Spanish. ***PRACTICE AREAS:*** General Practice; International Law; Corporate Law; Administrative Law.

OF COUNSEL

JOSEPH D. CRUMLISH, born Philadelphia, Pennsylvania, August 19, 1922; admitted to bar, 1967, District of Columbia; 1968, U.S. Court of Appeals, District of Columbia Circuit; 1975, U.S. Supreme Court; 1980, U.S. Claims Court; 1982, U.S. Court of Appeals, Federal Circuit. *Education:* Georgetown University (B.S.S., 1946; Ph.D., 1954); Catholic University of America (J.D., 1966; M.A., 1948). Adjunct Professor: Legal Process, Georgetown University School of Summer and Continuing Education, 1973; Business Law, George Washington University, 1974-1975; Business Law, University of Maryland, 1975-1979; Acquisition Law, Southeastern University, 1983. Author: "A City Finds Itself, The Story of the Philadelphia Home Rule Charter Movement," Wayne State University Press, Detroit, 1959. Co-Author: with George F. Wirth "A Preliminary Study of Engineering Seismology Benefits," U.S. Department of Commerce Coast and Geodetic Survey, pp 46, August, 1967. Member, Board of Governors, Georgetown Alumni Association, 1961-1962. Member, Board of Governors, Catholic University of America Alumni Association, 1983. Vice President, International Education Association, 1983. Member: American Political Science Association, 1950-1954; American Association of Public Opinion Research, 1954-1961. Member, Board of Directors, Past President and Co-Founder, The Thomas More Society of America, 1980—. Chairman, Law Committee, The Acquisition Institute, 1983-1984. Member, Board of Advisors, Foundation for Research in Human Behavior, Ann Arbor, Michigan, 1959-1960. Member, Bar Association of the District of Columbia, 1967-1980. *Member:* District of Columbia Bar (Member, Wills and Probate Section, 1990—); Federal Bar Association (Member, Government Contracts Section, ADP Committee, 1992-1995; Senior Lawyers Division, Representation of Social Security Claimants, 1994-1995). [Sgt., USAF, 1943-1945]. ***PRACTICE AREAS:*** General; Corporate; Administrative; Government Contracts; Wills and Estates. ***Email:*** Crumlish@intr.net

REFERENCE: Crestar Bank, N.A., Washington, D.C.

G. ALLEN DALE

307 G STREET, N.W.
WASHINGTON, D.C. 20001
Telephone: 202-638-2900
Fax: 202-783-1654
Email: gallendale@aol.com
URL: http://www.lawyers.com/gallendalelaw

Criminal Defense, Drug Crimes, Sex Crimes, Domestic Violence, Assault and Battery, Homicide, Criminal Appeals, White Collar Crimes, Business Fraud, Driving While Intoxicated, Traffic Violations, Police Misconduct, Federal Criminal Defense.

FIRM PROFILE: Mr. Dale is a very experienced and well known trial attorney. For more than 20 years he has represented individuals and families from all walks of life throughout metropolitan Washington, D.C.

G. ALLEN DALE, born 1951; admitted to bar, 1978, District of Columbia. *Education:* Appalachian State University (B.A.); Georgetown University (J.D.). ***PRACTICE AREAS:*** Criminal Law (100%).

DAMICO & ASSOCIATES

Established in 1976
1101 - 17TH STREET, N.W.
SUITE 820
WASHINGTON, D.C. 20036-4704
Telephone: 202-872-1045
Fax: 202-872-1141
URL: http://www.lawyers.com/damico&associates

Employee Benefits, Pension and Profit Sharing Plans, Employee Stock Ownership Plans, Executive Compensation, Estate Planning.

(This Listing Continued)

NICHOLAS P. DAMICO, born Chester, Pennsylvania, June 29, 1937; admitted to bar, 1963, Pennsylvania; 1966, District of Columbia; 1986, Maryland. *Education:* St. Joseph's University, Philadelphia, Pennsylvania (B.S., 1960); University of Pennsylvania (LL.B., 1963); Georgetown University (LL.M. in Taxation, 1967). Tax Law Specialist, Pension Trust Branch, National Office, Internal Revenue Service, 1964-1966. Associate, 1966-1972 and Partner, 1972-1976, Silverstein & Mullens, Washington, D.C. Executive Editor, Executive Compensation Journal, 1973-1976. Author: "Qualified Plan Distributions After DEFRA," 44th Ann. N.Y.U. Institute on Federal Tax, Ch. 8, 1986; "Rollover Opportunities and Withholding on Distributions Both Expanded by New Law," Journal of Taxation, January, 1973. Adjunct Professor, Georgetown University Law Center, 1973-1975. *Member:* The District of Columbia Bar (Member, Taxation Section); Maryland State and American (Member, Committee on Employee Benefits, Section of Taxation, 1967—) Bar Associations. ***PRACTICE AREAS:*** Employee Benefits; Estate Planning; Taxation. ***Email:*** nicholas.damico@verizon.net

OF COUNSEL

EDWARD M. LURIA, born Philadelphia, Pennsylvania, December ll, 1941; admitted to bar, 1968, Pennsylvania; 1970, District of Columbia and U.S. Tax Court; 1971, Delaware; 1982, U.S. Claims Court. *Education:* University of Pennsylvania (A.B., 1964; J.D., 1967); New York University (LL.M. in Taxation, 1968). Law Clerk to Hon. John W. Kern, Jr., U.S. Tax Court, 1968-1970. Certified Public Accountant, Maryland, 1981. *Member:* The District of Columbia Bar (Member, Taxation Section); Delaware State and American (Member, Estate and Gift Tax Committee, Committee on Value Added Taxes and Committee on Closely-Held Corporations, Taxation Section, 1977—) Bar Associations. (Also with Alvord and Alvord and Of Counsel to Moore & Bruce, LLP, Wilmington, Delaware). ***PRACTICE AREAS:*** Tax Law; Estate Planning; Employee Benefits; Asset Protection. ***Email:*** eluria@aol.com

REPRESENTATIVE CLIENTS: American Systems Corp.; Boys and Girls Clubs of America; Dewberry & Davis; Ford's Theatre Society; The Johns Hopkins University Applied Physics Laboratory; Westat, Inc.
REFERENCE: United Bank.

DANZIGER, MAK AND FU, LLP

SUITE 420, 5301 WISCONSIN AVENUE, N.W.
WASHINGTON, D.C. 20015
Telephone: 202-686-9958
Fax: 202-686-9790
Email: immlaw@dmfllp.com
URL: http://www.lawyers.com/danzigermak

Immigration and Consular Matters.

MEMBERS OF FIRM

PAMELA J. MAK, born Abington, Pennsylvania, September 25, 1958; admitted to bar, 1985, Pennsylvania and District of Columbia. *Education:* Temple University (B.A., magna cum laude, 1980); Villanova University (J.D., 1984). Lecturer: "Implementing the Immigration Act of 1990," 1992; "Immigration Strategies for Human Resources Planners," 1993; "The Law and the Hiring of Foreign Nationals," Employer's Relocation Council, 1994; "Immigration and Tax Treatment of Foreign Nationals," Swiss-American Chamber of Commerce, 1997; "Optimal Strategies for a Toughening Situation," 1998; "2000 U.S. Business Immigration Workshop". *Member:* Pennsylvania Bar Association; District of Columbia Bar; American Immigration Lawyers Association. ***PRACTICE AREAS:*** Business Immigration; Citizenship; Consular Law.

K. N. MINNIE FU, born Taiwan, June 27, 1961; admitted to bar, 1998, Virginia and District of Columbia; U.S. Court of Appeals, Fourth Circuit. *Education:* National Taiwan University (B.A., 1983); University of Pennsylvania (M.S., 1985); Washington College of Law, American University (J.D., 1997). Lecturer: "U.S. Immigration Law Update - Optimal Strategies for a Toughening Situation," 1998; "2000 U.S. Business Immigration Workshop". *Member:* Virginia Bar Association; District of Columbia Bar; Asian Pacific American Lawyers Association; American Immigration Lawyers Association. ***LANGUAGES:*** Chinese. ***PRACTICE AREAS:*** Business Immigration; Citizenship; Consular Law.

ASSOCIATES

DENISE ANN THOMASSON, born Akron, Ohio, March 30, 1966; admitted to bar, 1999, New York (Not admitted in District of Columbia). *Education:* University of Akron (B.A., 1988); Washington College of Law, American University (J.D., 1996). ***LANGUAGES:*** Spanish and French. ***PRACTICE AREAS:*** Business Immigration; Citizenship; Consular Law.

MARTIN B. DANZIGER, born New York, N.Y., April 8, 1931; admitted to bar, 1958, New York; 1959, Florida; 1960, U.S. District Court, Southern and Eastern Districts of New York; 1968, U.S. Supreme Court; 1978, District of Columbia and U.S. Court of Appeals, District of Columbia Circuit. *Education:*

(This Listing Continued)

DANZIGER, MAK AND FU, LLP, Washington—Continued

New York University (B.A., 1955; LL.B., 1958). Lecturer on Immigration and Naturalization: at the United Nations, 1984; International Bank for Reconstruction and Development (World Bank), 1986; Organization of American States, 1986, 1989; Pan American Health Organization, 1986; International Monetary Fund, 1984, 1989; American Management Association, 1984. Assistant District Attorney, New York County District Attorney's Office, 1961-1967. Associate Deputy Attorney General, U.S. Department of Justice, 1973-1974. Deputy Commissioner, Immigration and Naturalization Service, U.S. Department of Justice, 1980. (Retired).

MICHAEL M. DAVIDSON

WASHINGTON, D.C.

(See Arlington, Virginia)

Labor, Employment, Termination, Executive Contracts, Small Business Law, Non-Profit Law, International Law, Corporate Law, Civil and Employment Litigation, Arbitration.

DAVIS & CAMPBELL L.L.C.

1828 L STREET, N.W., SUITE 660
WASHINGTON, D.C. 20036
Telephone: 202-293-5690
Fax: 202-296-5706
URL: http://www.dcamplaw.com

Peoria, Illinois Office: 401 Main Street, Suite 1600, 61602-1241. Telephone: 309-673-1681. Telecopier: 309-673-1690.
Chicago, Illinois Office: 135 South La Salle Street, Suite 1424, 60603. Telephone: 312-795-1681; 312-201-0999. Fax: 312-201-0749.

Management Labor Law, Corporate Law, Trial Practice, Employee Benefits, Mergers and Acquisitions, Employer Rights, Local Government Rights, Employment Law, Commercial Law, Commercial Litigation, Complex Litigation, Intellectual Property, Securities Regulation, Antitrust, Immigration and Naturalization, Real Estate, Zoning Planning and Land Use, Tax Law, Estate Planning, Probate.

OF COUNSEL

CARLOS M. RECIO, born Fairmont, West Virginia, August 10, 1952; admitted to bar, 1977, Maryland; 1981, California; 1982, District of Columbia; 1985, Virginia. *Education:* Seton Hall University (B.A., 1974); Georgetown University (J.D., 1977); Harvard University (LL.M., 1978). Editor, American Criminal Law Review, 1975-1977. Law Clerk to Damon J. Keith, U.S. Court of Appeals, Sixth Circuit, 1978-1981. Assistant Professor of Law, The Detroit College of Law, Detroit, Michigan 1980-1981. *Member:* The District of Columbia Bar; Virginia State Bar; Maryland State and American Bar Associations. ***PRACTICE AREAS:*** Immigration and Naturalization; Complex Litigation; Commercial Law. ***Email:*** CRecio@erols.com

DAVIS & HARMAN LLP

Established in 1985

SUITE 1200, 1455 PENNSYLVANIA AVENUE, N.W.
WASHINGTON, D.C. 20004
Telephone: 202-347-2230
Fax: 202-393-3310

General Practice including Administrative, Agricultural, Commodities, Insurance and Tax Law. Legislative Practice.

FIRM PROFILE: Davis & Harman LLP was founded in 1985. The firm serves clients in the areas of federal income taxation, employee benefits and legislation. A substantial portion of the firm's practice involves the financial services industry and insurance products.

MEMBERS OF FIRM

THOMAS A. DAVIS, born Birmingham, Alabama, March 20, 1938; admitted to bar, 1963, Florida; 1970, District of Columbia. *Education:* University of Florida (B.A., 1960; J.D., 1968, replaced LL.B. conferred, 1963); Georgetown University (LL.M., 1967). Pi Sigma Alpha; Phi Delta Phi. Co-Author: "Horse Owners and Breeders Tax Handbook," 1997; "Cattleman's Tax Manual," 1978. Member, University of Florida Law Center Board of Trustees. Special Assistant Attorney General, Florida, 1963. Office of the Chief Counsel, Internal Revenue Service, 1966-1970. *Member:* District of Columbia Bar; The Florida Bar. [Capt., U.S. Army Reserve, Active Duty, 1964-1966]. ***PRACTICE AREAS:*** Taxation Law; Legislation Law; Commodities Futures Law; Administrative Law. ***Email:*** tadavis@davis-harman.com

(This Listing Continued)

WILLIAM B. HARMAN, JR., born Newport News, Virginia, June 5, 1930; admitted to bar, 1956, Virginia; 1961, District of Columbia. *Education:* College of William and Mary (A.B., 1951; J.D., 1956); Georgetown University (LL.M., 1960). Phi Beta Kappa. Order of the Coif. Attorney, Legislation and Regulations Division, Office of Chief Counsel, Internal Revenue Service, 1958-1959. Attorney, Office of Tax Legislative Counsel, Department of Treasury, 1959-1961. Associate General Counsel, American Life Convention, 1962-1968. General Counsel, American Life Convention, 1968-1972. Vice President, Law, American Life Insurance Association, 1973-1975. Executive Vice President, American Council of Life Insurance, 1976-1978. *Member:* The District of Columbia Bar; Virginia State Bar; American Law Institute; Association of Life Insurance Counsel. ***PRACTICE AREAS:*** Taxation Law; Insurance Law; Legislation Law. ***Email:*** wbharman@davis-harman.com

JOHN T. ADNEY, born Wood River, Illinois, September 1, 1950; admitted to bar, 1975, Illinois; 1977, District of Columbia. *Education:* Millikin University (B.A., 1972); Yale Law School (J.D., 1975). Phi Kappa Phi. Law Clerk, Trial Division, U.S. Claims Court, 1975-1976. Law Clerk to Judge Marion T. Bennett, U.S. Claims Court, 1976-1977. *Member:* The District of Columbia Bar; Illinois State and American (Chairman, Committee on Insurance Companies, Taxation Section, 1988-1990) Bar Associations. ***PRACTICE AREAS:*** Taxation Law; Insurance Law; Legislation Law. ***Email:*** jtadney@davis-harman.com

JOSEPH F. McKEEVER, III, born Weymouth, Massachusetts, July 21, 1950; admitted to bar, 1978, District of Columbia. *Education:* George Washington University (B.A., 1972; J.D., with high honors, 1978). Order of the Coif. Law Clerk to Trial Judge Harry Wood, U.S. Court of Federal Claims, 1978-1979. Law Clerk to Senior Judge Wilson Cowen, U.S. Court of Appeals for the Federal Circuit, 1979-1980. Contributor and Co-Editor, "Annuities Answer Book," Panel Publishers. Co-Author with Kirk Van Brunt: "Insurance Contracts After TAMRA: More Questions Than Answers," 3 Insurance Tax Review 285, 1989; Co-Author with Kirk Van Brunt and Daniela Stoia: "Rev. Proc. 98-27: Some Relief for the Heartburn of Inadvertent MECS," 17 Insurance Tax Review, 283, 1999. *Member:* District of Columbia Bar; American Bar Association (Chair, Committee on Insurance Companies, Taxation Section, 2000—); National Association for Variable Annuities (Chairman, Tax Committee, 1994—). ***PRACTICE AREAS:*** Taxation Law; Insurance Law. ***Email:*** jfmckeever@davis-harman.com

RICHARD S. BELAS, born New Britain, Connecticut, April 2, 1948; admitted to bar, 1974, New York; 1975, Connecticut and U.S. Tax Court; 1993, District of Columbia. *Education:* Trinity College (A.B., 1970); University of Virginia Law School (J.D., 1973); New York University (LL.M., 1977). Member, Editorial Board, University of Virginia Law Review, 1972-1973. Lecturer, Tax Policy, Chaminade University M.B.A. program, 1989. Minority Tax Counsel, 1980; Majority Tax Counsel, 1981-1983; Deputy Chief Counsel, 1983-1984; U.S. Senate Finance Committee; Chief Counsel to U.S. Senate Majority Leader, 1985-1986. Chief Counsel to U.S. Senate Republican Leader, 1987-1989. *Member:* New York State and American (Member, Tax Section) Bar Associations; District of Columbia Bar. [U.S. Air Force Reserve, 1970-1981, Captain]. ***PRACTICE AREAS:*** Taxation Law; Legislative Issues Law. ***Email:*** rsbelas@davis-harman.com

BARBARA N. SEYMON-HIRSCH, born New Haven, Connecticut, August 14, 1953; admitted to bar, 1978, District of Columbia; 1983, New York. *Education:* Vassar College (B.A., 1974); California Western School of Law (J.D., 1977); Georgetown University Law Center (LL.M., Tax, 1978). Contributor and Co-Editor, "403 (b) Answer Book" and "Annuities Answer Book," Panel Publishers. Tax Law Specialist, Exempt Organizations Division, National Office, Internal Revenue Service, 1979-1982; Member, Internal Revenue Service Information Reporting Program Advisory Committee, 1994-1995. *Member:* American Bar Association (Tax Section, 1983—). ***PRACTICE AREAS:*** Taxation Law; Pensions Law; Employee Benefits Law; Insurance Law; Employment Tax Law. ***Email:*** bnseymon@davis-harman.com

RANDOLF HURST HARDOCK, born Rochester, New York, October 16, 1956; admitted to bar, 1981, District of Columbia. *Education:* University of Rochester (B.A., magna cum laude, 1978); University of Pennsylvania (J.D., magna cum laude, 1981). Phi Beta Kappa; Order of the Coif. Editor, University of Pennsylvania Law Review, 1979-1981. Tax Counsel (U.S. Senate Finance Committee) 1986-1993; Benefits Tax Counsel (U.S. Treasury) 1993-1995. *Member:* The District of Columbia Bar; American Bar Association. ***PRACTICE AREAS:*** Taxation Law; Pensions; Employee Benefits; Legislation; Employment Tax Law. ***Email:*** rhhardock@davis-harman.com

CRAIG R. SPRINGFIELD, born St. Petersburg, Florida, June 26, 1964; admitted to bar, 1990, Florida; 1992, District of Columbia. *Education:* University of Central Florida (B.S.B.A., magna cum laude, 1985; M.S.A., 1987); University of Florida (J.D., with honors, 1990); New York University (LL.M., Taxation, 1991). Beta Gamma Sigma; Beta Alpha Psi. Co-Author with John Adney: "The New Tax Rules Governing Long-Term Care Insurance--Parts I-III," Journal of the American Society of Chartered Life Underwriters and Chartered Financial Consultants, September and November, 1997 and January, 1999. ***PRACTICE AREAS:*** Taxation Law; Insurance Law. ***Email:*** crspringfield@davis-harman.com

(This Listing Continued)

KIRK VAN BRUNT, born Fullerton, California, February 12, 1958; admitted to bar, 1985, Massachusetts; 1987, District of Columbia. *Education:* Northwest Nazarene College (B.A., magna cum laude, 1980); Harvard Law School (J.D., cum laude, 1985). Member, Harvard Law Review, 1983-1985. Author: "The Proposed PFIC Rules for Foreign Banks and Foreign Securities Dealers," 11 TAX NOTES INT'L 453, August 1995; "Contingent Payment Debt Instruments--A Light at the End of the Tunnel," 73 TAXES 365, July 1995; "Tax Aspects of REMIC Residual Interests," 2 FLA.TAX REV. 149, 1994; "*Newark Morning Ledger*-- Taxpayers Score a Big Victory," Section of Taxation Report, Federal Bar Association, Summer 1993. Co-Author with Joseph McKeever: "Life Insurance Contracts After TAMRA: More Questions than Answers," 3 Insurance Tax Review 285, 1989. *Member:* The District of Columbia Bar; Massachusetts and American (Member, Tax Section) Bar Associations. ***PRACTICE AREAS:*** Taxation Law. ***Email:*** kvbrunt@davis-harman.com

MARK E. GRIFFIN, born Syracuse, New York, January 8, 1959; admitted to bar, 1985, New York and District of Columbia. *Education:* Hamilton College (B.A., magna cum laude, 1981); Syracuse University (J.D., cum laude, 1984); Georgetown University (LL.M. in Taxation, 1988). Attorney-Advisor to Special Trial Judge Hu S. Vandervort, Jr., U.S. Tax Court, 1986-1988. Contributor, "Annuities Answer Book," Panel Publishers. Author: "IRS Technical Advice Memorandum Sparks Debate on Split Dollar Life Insurance Arrangements," Federal Bar Association Section of Taxation Report 1 (Summer 1996); "The Federal Income Taxation of Annuities: A Success Story," 49 J. Am. Soc'y CLU & ChFC No. 3, 44 (1995); "The Taxation of Accelerated Benefits Under a Life Insurance Contract," 47 J. Am. Soc'y CLU & ChFC No. 4, 38 (1993); "Analysis of the Rollover and Withholding Provisions of Unemployment Compensation Amendments Act of 1992," 6 Ins. Tax Review 1223 (1992). Co-Author with John Adney: "Chameleon-Like Concepts in the Code's Insurance Definitions *or* When is a QAB Not a QAB?," 9 Ins. Tax Review 1013 (1995); "The Great Single Prenim Life Insurance Controversey: Past and Prologue" (parts 1-3), 43 J. Am. Soc'y CLU & ChFC No 3, 64 (1989); No. 4, 74 (1989); No. 5, 70 (1989). *Member:* District of Columbia Bar; New York State, Federal and American Bar Associations. ***PRACTICE AREAS:*** Taxation Law; Insurance Law. ***Email:*** megriffin@davis-harman.com

OF COUNSEL

THOMAS W. EWING, born Lincoln, Illinois, September 19, 1935; admitted to bar, 1968, Illinois (Not admitted in District of Columbia). *Education:* Millikin University (B.S., 1957); John Marshall Law School (J.D., 1968). Assistant State's Attorney, Livingston County, 1968-1972. Member, 1975-1991, Assistant Minority Leader, 1982-1990, Deputy Minority Leader, 1990-1991, Illinois House of Representatives. Member of Congress, U.S. House of Representatives, 1991-2000. [With U.S. Army and Army Reserve, 1957-1963]. ***PRACTICE AREAS:*** Legislative Practice; Business Law; Agricultural Law; General Practice. ***Email:*** twewing@davis-harman.com

THOMAS L. STAPLETON, born Brooklyn, New York, June 25, 1934; admitted to bar, 1959, New York; 1963, U.S. Supreme Court; 1972, District of Columbia; U.S. Court of Appeals, First, Second, Fourth, Seventh, Eighth, Ninth and Tenth Circuits; U.S. Court of Federal Claims. *Education:* Brooklyn College (B.A., 1956); University of Pennsylvania (J.D., 1959). Trial Attorney, 1964-1972, Assistant Chief, 1972-1973, Appellate Section, Tax Division, U.S. Department of Justice. Vice President, 1973-1979, Vice President and Associate General Counsel, 1979-1983, Senior Vice President and Tax Director, 1983-1999, Metropolitan Life Insurance Company. Chair, Tax Committee of the Life Insurance Council of New York (1977-1999). *Member:* Association of the Bar of the City of New York; Federal and American (Member, Tax Section) Bar Associations; Association of Life Insurance Counsel. [Capt. U.S. Army (1960-1963)]. ***PRACTICE AREAS:*** Taxation Law; Insurance Law; Legislative Practice; Tax Litigation. ***Email:*** tlstapleton@davis-harman.com

ASSOCIATES

BRYAN W. KEENE, born Tampa, Florida, November 5, 1973; admitted to bar, 2000, Florida; 2001, District of Columbia. *Education:* University of Florida (B.S., 1994; J.D., cum laude, 1998). Co-Author with William B. Hannan, Jr. and John T. Adney: "The Taxes on Starlight: A Case for the Repeal of Sections 809, 815, and 1503 (c) of the Internal Revenue Code," 20 Insurance Tax Review 31 (2001). Co-Author with William B. Harman, Jr.: "The Impact of Financial Services Reform on State Insurance Regulation," Journal of Financial Services Professionals, November 2000, at 86. *Member:* District of Columbia Bar; The Florida Bar; American Bar Association. ***PRACTICE AREAS:*** Taxation Law; Insurance Law. ***Email:*** bwkeene@davis-harman.com

DANIELA STOIA, born Lugoj, Romania, January 14, 1975; admitted to bar, 1998, Maryland; 1999, District of Columbia. *Education:* Michigan State University (B.A., 1994); Vanderbilt University (J.D., 1998). Phi Betta Kappa; Golden Key National Honor Society. *Member:* The District of Columbia Bar; American Bar Association. ***LANGUAGES:*** Romanian. ***PRACTICE AREAS:*** Taxation Law. ***Email:*** dstoia@davis-harman.com

(This Listing Continued)

JOHN J. O'NEILL, JR., born Toledo, Ohio, September 9, 1971; admitted to bar, 2000, Massachusetts (Not admitted in District of Columbia). *Education:* Skidmore College (B.A., 1994); Georgetown University (J.D., 1999). ***PRACTICE AREAS:*** Taxation Law; Pension Law; Employee Benefits Law. ***Email:*** jjoneill@davis-harman.com

JOHN J. SPINA, born Bogota, New Jersey, November 1, 1971; admitted to bar, 1999, New Jersey and District of Columbia. *Education:* Montclair State University (B.A., 1995); University of North Carolina (J.D., 1999). Author: "United States v. Albank, FSB: Is Justice Being Served in the Enforcement of Fair Lending Laws?", 2 NC Banking Institute 207 (1998). *Member:* American Bar Association. ***PRACTICE AREAS:*** Taxation Law; Insurance Law. ***Email:*** jspina@davis-harman.com

CHELSEA K. BACHRACH, born Kunsan, South Korea, September 9, 1969; admitted to bar, 2000, California (Not admitted in District of Columbia). *Education:* Barnard College, Columbia University (B.A., 1991); University of California at Los Angeles, School of Public Health (M.P.H., 1995); Georgetown University Law Center (J.D., 2000). *Member:* State Bar of California. ***PRACTICE AREAS:*** Taxation Law; Insurance Law. ***Email:*** ckbachrach@davis-harman.com

DAVIS & LEIMAN, P.C.

Established in 1994

5108 34TH STREET, N.W.

WASHINGTON, D.C. 20008

Telephone: 202-296-4790

Fax: 202-296-4791

Email: dltrade@aol.com

URL: http://www.lawyers.com/davis&leiman

International Trade Law with special emphasis in the area of U.S. Import and Export Law, Anti-Dumping, Countervailing Duties Law, W.T.O. & GATT. International Commercial Arbitration.

FIRM PROFILE: The international trade law and consulting firm of Davis & Leiman P.C. focuses on the representation of domestic and foreign companies with international trade problems. We also provide backup assistance to larger firms who need temporary help in representing their clients' trade litigation. The firm's concentrations include U.S. trade litigation, particularly antidumping and countervailing duties investigations and administrative reviews, customs compliance, international commercial arbitration, and business immigration assistance. Thanks to the unique qualifications of the firm's members, its clients enjoy the highest quality services. At the same time, the experience and specialization of the firm's members and the firm's low overhead permit Davis & Leiman to provide their services efficiently and at moderate cost.

MARK DAVID DAVIS, born Provo, Utah, April 2, 1956; admitted to bar, 1983, District of Columbia; 1984, U.S. District Court for the District of Columbia; 1985, U.S. Court of Appeals for the District of Columbia Circuit; 1991, U.S. Supreme Court. *Education:* Brigham Young University (B.A., cum laude, 1980; M.A., 1983; J.D., magna cum laude, 1983). Order of the Coif. Editor-in-Chief, Brigham Young University Law Review, 1982-1983. Adjunct Professor, Georgetown University Law Center, 1990-1995. Professorial Lecturer, American University Law School, 1995-1996. Adjunct Professor, Brigham Young University Law School, 1996—. Faculty, International Law Institute, 1989—. Legal Advisor to Arbitrators, Iran-United State Claims Tribunal, 1986-1987. *Member:* District of Columbia Bar; Utah State Bar; American Bar Association. ***LANGUAGES:*** Italian, Dutch, Russian. ***PRACTICE AREAS:*** International Trade; Commercial Arbitration; Business Immigration; Russian Legal Development. ***Email:*** dltrade@aol.com

NON-ATTORNEY MEMBER

KARMI LEIMAN, born Portland, Maine, October 2, 1960. *Education:* University of Pennsylvania (B.A., 1983); Georgetown University (M.B.A., 1988). International Trade Specialist, Steptoe & Johnson, 1991-1994. Import Compliance Specialist, U.S. Department of Commerce, 1988-1991. (International Trade Consultant). ***LANGUAGES:*** Spanish. ***PRACTICE AREAS:*** Antidumping and Countervailing Duties Proceedings; Customs Matters. ***Email:*** dltrade@aol.com

DAVIS POLK & WARDWELL

Established in 1849

1300 I STREET, N.W.

WASHINGTON, D.C. 20005

Telephone: 202-962-7000

Fax: 202-962-7111

URL: http://www.dpw.com

New York, N.Y. Office: 450 Lexington Avenue, 10017. Telephone: 212-450-4000. Fax: 212-450-3800.

(This Listing Continued)

DAVIS POLK & WARDWELL, Washington—Continued

Menlo Park, California Office: 1600 El Camino Real, Menlo Park, California, 94025. Telephone: 650-752-2111.
London, England Office: 99 Gresham Street, London, EC2V 7NG, England. Telephone: 44-171-418-1300. Fax: 44-171-418-1400.
Paris, France Office: 15, avenue Matignon, 75008 Paris, France. Telephone: 33-01-56-59-36-00. Fax: 33-01-56-59-36-90.
Frankfurt, Germany Office: MesseTurm, 60308 Frankfurt am Main, Germany. Telephone: 49-69-97-57-03-0. Fax: 49-69-74-77-44.
Tokyo, Japan Office: Akasaka Twin Tower East, 11th Floor, 17-22, Akasaka 2-Chome, Minato-ku, Tokyo 107-0052, Japan. Telephone: 81-3-5561-4421. Fax (main): 81-3-5561-4425.
Hong Kong, China Office: The Hong Kong Club Building, 3A Chater Road, Hong Kong. Telephone: 852-2533-3300. Fax: 852-2533-3388.

General Practice.

MEMBERS OF FIRM

STEPHEN H. CASE, born Trenton, New Jersey, March 1, 1942; admitted to bar, 1969, New York; 1971, U.S. District Court, Southern District of New York; 1972, United States Court of Appeals, Third Circuit; 1975, United States Court of Appeals, Second Circuit, U.S. District Court, Eastern District of New York; 1986, District of Columbia. *Education:* Columbia University (A.B., 1964; LL.B., 1968). Adjunct Professor, Georgetown University Law School, 1990-1991. *Member:* The District of Columbia Bar; The Association of the Bar of the City of New York; New York State and American Bar Associations; National Bankruptcy Conference.

SCOTT W. MULLER, born Stamford, Connecticut, February 15, 1950; admitted to bar, 1977, New York; 1986, District of Columbia, United States Court of Appeals, Second, District of Columbia and Fifth Circuits, U.S. District Court, Southern District of New York, U.S. Tax Court, U.S. Supreme Court. *Education:* Princeton University (A.B., 1971); Georgetown University (J.D., 1975). Assistant U.S. Attorney, Criminal Division, Southern District of New York, 1979-1982. *Member:* The Association of the Bar of the City of New York; New York State and American (Member, Committee on White Collar Crimes) Bar Associations; The District of Columbia Bar; Federal Bar Council; American Law Institute.

JORDAN LUKE, born New York, New York, November 28, 1944; admitted to bar, 1973, District of Columbia. *Education:* Yale University (A.B., 1967); University of Pennsylvania (J.D., 1972). Law Clerk, Justice William J. Brennan, Jr., U.S. Supreme Court, 1973. Assistant U.S. Attorney, D.C., 1974-1977. Assistant General Counsel, U.S. Treasury, 1979-1984. Deputy Chief Counsel, Office of the Comptroller of the Currency, 1984-1987. General Counsel, Federal Home Loan Bank Board, 1987-1989. Chief Counsel, Office of Thrift Supervision, 1989-1990. *Member:* The District of Columbia Bar; American Bar Association.

DANA L. TRIER, born Boulder, Colorado, 1948; admitted to bar, 1975, New York; 1978, District of Columbia. *Education:* Indiana University (1970); University of Michigan (J.D., 1974). Deputy Tax Legislative Counsel, Tax Legislative Counsel and Acting Deputy Assistant Secretary (Tax Policy), U.S. Treasury Department, 1988-1989. Adjunct Professor, Georgetown University Law Center, 1981-1984; 1990—. *Member:* The District of Columbia Bar; New York State (Executive Committee, Taxation Section) and American (Vice Chair, Corporate Tax Committee, Taxation Section) Bar Associations. ***PRACTICE AREAS:*** Tax Law.

RESIDENT COUNSEL

MARGARET M. AYRES, born Chicago, Illinois, August 10, 1943; admitted to bar, 1973, District of Columbia. *Education:* Smith College (B.A., 1965); Yale University (J.D., 1972). Chief Counsel, Urban Mass Transportation Administration, U.S. Department of Transportation, 1977-1981. *Member:* The District of Columbia Bar; Federal and American Bar Associations.

THEODORE A. DOREMUS, JR., born Long Branch, New Jersey, November 18, 1940; admitted to bar, 1969, Florida; 1972, District of Columbia and U.S. Court of Appeals, District of Columbia Circuit; 1980, U.S. Supreme Court. *Education:* Washington & Lee University (B.A., 1963); Stetson College of Law (J.D., 1969). Senior Branch Attorney, Securities and Exchange Commission, 1970-1975. General Counsel, Minority Staff, Committee on Banking, Finance and Urban Affairs, U.S. House of Representatives, 1975-1979. *Member:* The Florida Bar; Federal and American (Member, Committee on Financial Institutions, 1980—) Bar Associations.

ROBERT W. WEAVER, born Richlands, Virginia, October 28, 1951; admitted to bar, 1983, New York; 1993, District of Columbia. *Education:* University of Virginia (B.A., 1974; J.D., 1981). U.S. Treasury Department, Office of Tax Legislative Counsel, Attorney-Advisor, 1989-1992.

(This Listing Continued)

RESIDENT ASSOCIATE

MARGARET E.M. PAULSEN, born Ossining, New York, 1965; admitted to bar, 1998, New York (Not admitted in District of Columbia). *Education:* Wesleyan University (B.A., 1987); George Washington University (J.D., 1991).

(For Complete Biographical Data on all Personnel see Professional Biographies at New York City)

DAVIS WRIGHT TREMAINE LLP

1500 K STREET, N.W.
SUITE 450
WASHINGTON, D.C. 20005
Telephone: 202-508-6600
FAX: 202-508-6699
URL: http://www.dwt.com

Anchorage, Alaska Office: Suite 800, 701 West 8th Avenue. 99501-3408. Telephone: 907-257-5300. FAX: 907-257-5399.
Bellevue, Washington Office: 1800 Bellevue Place, 10500 NE 8th Street. 98004. Telephone: 425-646-6100. FAX: 425-646-6199.
Honolulu, Hawaii Office: 1360 Pauahi Tower, 1001 Bishop Street, 96813. Telephone: 808-538-3360. FAX: 808-526-0101.
Los Angeles, California Office: 865 South Figueroa Street, Suite 2400, 90017-2566. Telephone: 213-633-6800. FAX: 213-633-6899.
New York, N.Y. Office: 1740 Broadway, 10019. Telephone: 212-489-8230. FAX: 212-489-8340.
Portland, Oregon Office: 2300 First Interstate Tower, 1300 SW Fifth Avenue. 97201. Telephone: 503-241-2300. FAX: 503-778-5299.
San Francisco, California Office: One Embarcadero Center, Suite 600, 94111. Telephone: 415-276-6500. FAX: 415-276-6599.
Seattle, Washington Office: 2600 Century Square, 1501 Fourth Avenue. 98101. Telephone: 206-622-3150. FAX: 206-628-7040.
Shanghai, China Office: Suite 450 E. Tower, Shanghai Centre, 1376 Nanjing Xi Lu, 200040. Telephone: 011-8621-6279-8560. FAX: 011-8621-6279-8547.

Administrative; Banking; Communications; Corporate; Customs Law; Domestic and International Trade Regulation Law; Employee Benefits; Environmental; Government Contracts Law; Government Investigations; Labor; Legislative Practice; Litigation; Maritime; Media Law; Nuclear Energy; Securities; Tax.

FIRM PROFILE: Since its founding in the early 1900s in Seattle, Washington, Davis Wright Tremaine has continued to grow and change in response to the needs of its clients. Today the firm is organized by practice industry groups, and offers a wide range of legal services to regional, national and international clients through offices in Washington, Oregon, Alaska, California, Washington D.C., Hawaii, New York, NY, and Shanghai, China. A state-of-the-art communications network provides our clients the benefit of immediate access to shared knowledge, experience and resources of attorneys firm-wide. Dedicated to a tradition of public and professional service, the people of Davis Wright Tremaine are active in professional groups at the national, state and local levels.

PARTNERS

JAMES S. BLITZ, born Philadelphia, Pennsylvania, May 11, 1957; admitted to bar, 1982, District of Columbia. *Education:* Dickinson College (B.A., cum laude, 1978); George Washington University (J.D., 1981). Contributing Editor, Multichannel Video Compliance Guide. *Member:* Federal Communications Bar Association (Member, Executive Committee, 2000-2003, Co-Chair, State and Local Practice Committee, 1998-2000); FCBA Foundation (Member, Board of Trustees, Chairman, 1996-1997). ***PRACTICE AREAS:*** Cable Communications; Broadcast Television; Communications; Cable TV; Satellite Communications; Wireless Communications; Telephone.

PAMELA C. COOPER, born Albany, New York, March 6, 1960; admitted to bar, 1986, Virginia; 1988, District of Columbia; 1991, U.S. Supreme Court. *Education:* University of Virginia (B.A., 1982); Columbus School of Law, Catholic University of America (J.D., 1986). ***PRACTICE AREAS:*** Telecommunications; Broadcasting Transactions; FCC Regulation. ***Email:*** pamcooper@dwt.com

RICHARD L. CYS, born Boulder, Colorado, October 9, 1944; admitted to bar, 1969, District of Columbia. *Education:* University of Colorado at Boulder (B.S., with honors, 1966); Georgetown University (J.D., 1969). Law Clerk to Hon. John Pratt, U.S. District Judge for the District of Columbia, 1969-1970; Assistant U.S. Attorney for the District of Columbia, 1970-1977. *Member:* District of Columbia Bar; FCBA. ***PRACTICE AREAS:*** Communications and Media; Litigation; White Collar Criminal Defense. ***Email:*** rickcys@dwt.com

LAURA R. HANDMAN, born New York, N.Y., December 5, 1951; admitted to bar, 1977, Massachusetts; 1983, New York; 1994, District of Columbia. *Education:* Yale University (B.A., cum laude, 1973); Boston University (J.D., magna cum laude, 1977). Member, Boston University Law Review, 1975-1977.

(This Listing Continued)

Assistant United States Attorney, Eastern District of New York, 1979-1983. Law Clerk to Hon. Raymond J. Pettine, U.S. Chief District Judge, District of Rhode Island, 1977-1978. *Member:* The Association of the Bar of the City of New York (Chairman, Communications and Media Committee, 1995-1998); District of Columbia Bar (Member, Arts, Entertainment and Sports Law Section, Chair, Media Law Committee, 1999—); American Bar Association (Member, Forum on Communications Governing Board, 1998—); Libel Defense Resource Center (President, Defense Counsel Section, 1997-1998). (Also at New York, NY Office). ***PRACTICE AREAS:*** Libel Law; Privacy Law; Media Law; Intellectual Property; Litigation. ***Email:*** laurahandman@dwt.com

KEITH M. KORENCHUK, born Lyons, Illinois, February 8, 1953; admitted to bar, 1978, Washington; 1982, North Carolina (Not admitted in District of Columbia). *Education:* Duke University (B.A., 1975); Harvard University (M.P.H., 1982); University of Virginia (J.D., 1978). Phi Beta Kappa. Author: *Transforming the Delivery of Health Care: The Integration Process (1998); Medicare Managed Care: Developing Successful Provider Sponsored Organizations* (1998). ***PRACTICE AREAS:*** Health Care.

RANDALL B. LOWE, born Englewood, New Jersey, November 20, 1948; admitted to bar, 1973, Illinois; 1975, Connecticut; 1976, District of Columbia; 1977, New Jersey; 1980, New York. *Education:* University of Rhode Island (B.A., 1970); Washington University (J.D., 1973). Pi Sigma Alpha; Phi Alpha Theta. Contributor: Telecommunications Access & Public Policy (Abilex Publ. Corp., 1982); The New Investment Theory of Real Options and Its Implication for Telecommunications Economics (Kluwer Academic Publ., 1991). *Member:* Federal Communications Bar Association. ***PRACTICE AREAS:*** Communications Law. ***Email:*** randylowe@dwt.com

RICHARD D. MARKS, born New York, N.Y., June 21, 1944; admitted to bar, 1972, District of Columbia. *Education:* University of Virginia (B.A., magna cum laude, 1966); Yale University (J.D., 1969). Phi Beta Kappa; Phi Pi Theta. Chair, Computer Law Division, Section of Science and Technology, ABA. Director, Computer Law Assn. Member, ALI. [Captain, U.S. Army, Military Intelligence, 1970-1971 (Vietnam Service)]. ***PRACTICE AREAS:*** Computer; Telecommunications; HIPAA; First Amendment; Media. ***Email:*** richardmarks@dwt.com

JAMES B. VASILE, born Hackensack, New Jersey, December 14, 1944; admitted to bar, 1975, District of Columbia. *Education:* Rutgers University (B.A., 1966); Georgetown University (J.D., 1974). ***PRACTICE AREAS:*** Energy; Environmental; Natural Resources; Utilities. ***Email:*** jamesvasile@dwt.com

DANIEL WAGGONER, born New Haven, Connecticut, August 15, 1952; admitted to bar, 1979, Washington; 1989, District of Columbia. *Education:* Tufts University (B.A., summa cum laude, 1974); Yale University (J.D., 1979). Editor, Yale Law Journal, 1978-1979. Chair, Governing Committee, Forum on Communications Law. Co-Chair. LDRC/NAB/NAA Seminar on Defamation Law. (Also at Seattle, Washington Office). ***PRACTICE AREAS:*** Communications; Media; Antitrust Regulation; Litigation. ***Email:*** danwaggoner@dwt.com

RESIDENT ASSOCIATES

HOWARD A. BENOWITZ, born Freehold, New Jersey, November 10, 1966; admitted to bar, 1994, Maryland; 1995, District of Columbia. *Education:* Duke University (B.A., 1989); Washington University (J.D., 1994). National Environmental Law Moot Court. Co-Author: "Legal Implications of Electric Utility Restructuring and Deregulation for Local Governments", Municipal Lawyer, Vol. 40. No. 1, Jan/Feb 1999. *Member:* District of Columbia Bar; Federal Energy Bar Association; American Bar Association. ***PRACTICE AREAS:*** Energy Law; Administrative Law.

CONSTANCE M. PENDLETON, born Tel Aviv, Israel, April 28, 1970; admitted to bar, 1998, New York; 1999, District of Columbia. *Education:* Barnard College (B.A., cum laude, 1992); University of Virginia (J.D., 1997). ***LANGUAGES:*** French. ***PRACTICE AREAS:*** Litigation; First Amendment Law. ***Email:*** conniependleton@dwt.com

REBECCA R. REED, born Philadelphia, Pennsylvania, January 5, 1970; admitted to bar, 1996, Maryland; 1998, District of Columbia. *Education:* University of Michigan (B.A., 1991); George Washington University (J.D., 1996). ***PRACTICE AREAS:*** Communications Law; Information Technology. ***Email:*** rebeccareed@dwt.com

HOLLY RACHEL SMITH, born Philadelphia, Pennsylvania, June 13, 1973; admitted to bar, 1999, District of Columbia. *Education:* University of Colorado at Boulder (B.A., 1993); The College of William & Mary (M.P.P., 1995); University of Oregon (J.D., 1999). ***PRACTICE AREAS:*** Telecommunications; Technology; Government Regulation. ***Email:*** hollysmith@dwt.com

COUNSEL

JULIE KAMINSKI CORSIG, born St. Louis, Missouri, December 1, 1966; admitted to bar, 1993, Missouri; 1994, District of Columbia. *Education:* Boston College (B.A., magna cum laude, 1989); Washington University (J.D., 1993; M.B.A., 1993). *Member:* The Missouri Bar; District of Columbia Bar; Bar Association of the District of Columbia; American Bar Association; Women's Bar Association. ***PRACTICE AREAS:*** Telecommunications Law. ***Email:*** juliecorsig@dwt.com

MARY LAWLESS PLANTAMURA, born Washington, D.C., April 14, 1960; admitted to bar, 1985, Maryland; 1986, District of Columbia. *Education:* College of the Holy Cross (B.A., cum laude, 1982); George Washington University (J.D., with honors, 1985). *Member:* Federal Communications Bar Association. ***PRACTICE AREAS:*** Communications; Broadcast Station Transfers; Federal Communication Commission Compliance. ***Email:*** maryplantamura@dwt.com

DANIEL W. PUGH, born May 6, 1966; admitted to bar, 1994, Maryland; 1996, District of Columbia. *Education:* Massachusetts Institute of Technology (S.B., 1989); University of Maryland School of Law (J.D., 1994). Member, 1992-1994 and Executive Editor, 1993-1994, Maryland Law Review. ***Email:*** danpugh@dwt.com

REPRESENTATIVE CLIENTS: American On Line; AT&T Wireless; Black Entertainment Television; CNN and Turner Broadcasting; Discovery Communications; Eldorado Communications; Home Box Office; NEXTLINK Communications; PriCellular Corp.; Radio One; SEASAC; Wireless Broadcasting Systems.

(For Complete Biographical Data on Personnel at Anchorage, Alaska, Los Angeles and San Francisco, California, Honolulu, Hawaii, Portland, Oregon, Bellevue and Seattle, Washington, New York, NY, Charlotte, North Carolina and Shanghai, China, see Professional Biographies at those locations)

MICHAEL M. DE ANGELI, P.C.

WASHINGTON, D.C.

(See Rockville, Maryland)

Patent, Trademark, Copyright Practice including Related Patent Litigation, Computer and Software Patents, Electro-Mechanical Patents, Instrumentation, Patent Infringement.

DEBEVOISE & PLIMPTON

Established in 1931

555 13TH STREET N.W.

WASHINGTON, D.C. 20004

Telephone: 202-383-8000
Telecopier: 202-383-8118
URL: http://www.debevoise.com

New York, N.Y. Office: 919 Third Avenue, 10022-3904. Telephone: 212-909-6000. Telex: (Domestic) 148377 DEBSTEVE NYK. Telecopier: (212) 909-6836.

Paris, France Office: 21 Avenue George V 75008. Telephone: (33-1) 40 73 12 12. Telecopier: (33-1) 47 20 50 82. Telex: 648141F DPPAR.

London, England Office: Old Broad Street, EC2N 1HQ. Telephone: (44-71) 786-9000. Telex: 884569 DPLON G. Telecopier: (44-71) 588-4180.

Hong Kong Office: 13/F Entertainment Building, 30 Queen's Road Central. Telephone: 852-2160-9800. Fax: 852-2810-9828.

Moscow, Russia Representative Office: Debevoise & Plimpton, LLC, Bolshoi Palashevsky Pereulok 13/2, 4th Floor, 103104. Telephone: 7 (095 or 503) 956-3858. Fax: 7 (095 or 503) 956-3868.

Frankfurt am Main, Germany Office: Börsencenter, Taubenstrasse 7-9, 60313. Telephone: +49-69-20 97 5000. Fax: +49-69-20 97 555.

Class Actions, Commercial Law, Communications and Media, Corporate Law, Government, Intellectual Property, Litigation, Securities, White Collar Crime.

MEMBERS OF FIRM

JUDAH BEST, born September 4, 1932; admitted to bar, 1959, N.Y.; 1961, District of Columbia. *Education:* Cornell University (A.B., 1954); Columbia University (LL.B., 1959). Co-author: "Appointment of a Guardian in the Conflict of Laws," 45 Iowa Law Review 212, 1960; "Conditions of Probation: An Analysis," 51 Georgetown Law Journal 809, 1963. Author: "The Trial Lawyer's Role in the Sensational Case," Litigation Magazine, ABA, Vol. 3, No. 3, Spring, 1977; "The Foreign Corrupt Practices Act," 11 Securities Regulation 975, 1978; "The Work-Product Doctrine in Criminal Cases," Litigation Magazine, ABA, Vol. 4, Summer, 1978; "An Analysis of the New Bank Fraud Statute," Inside Litigation, Vol. 1, No. 8, June, 1987. Assistant U.S. Attorney, District of Columbia, 1961-1964. *Member:* The District of Columbia Bar; Federal and American (Member, Special Committee on Governance, 1993-1994; Standing Committee on Federal Judiciary, 1990-1993, Chair, 1996-1997; Chairman, Litigation Section, 1988-1989; Section Delegate to the House of Delegates, 1989-1997) Bar Associations; American Law Institute. Fellow, American College of Trial Lawyers. ***PRACTICE AREAS:*** Federal Criminal Law; Grand Jury Practice; Securities; Litigation; SEC Enforcement; Federal Litigation. ***Email:*** jbest@debevoise

(This Listing Continued)

DEBEVOISE & PLIMPTON, Washington—Continued

RALPH C. FERRARA, born June 16, 1945; admitted to bar, 1970, District of Columbia; 1982, N.Y.; 1990, Florida; 1993, Colorado. *Education:* Georgetown (B.S.B.A., 1967); University of Cincinnati (J.D., 1970); George Washington (LL.M. in Corporate Law, 1972). Author: Treatises: *Securities Practice: Federal and State Enforcement,* Vol. 2, Callaghan & Co., 1985; *Takeovers: Attack & Survival,* Butterworth Legal Publishers, 1987; *Redeeming Fallen Brokers: Managing the Aftermath of Broker-Dealer Enforcement Proceedings,* Butterworth Legal Publishers, 1988; *Stockbroker Supervision:* Managing Stockbrokers and Surviving Sanctions, Butterworth Legal Publishers, 1989; *Beyond Arbitration: Designing Alternatives to Securities Litigation,* Butterworth Legal Publishers, 1991; *Takeovers II: A Strategist's Manual for Business Combinations in the 1990s,* Butterworth Legal Publishers, 1993; "Shareholder Derivative Litigation: Besieging the Board," Law Journal Seminars-Press, 1995; "Ferrara on Insider Trading and The Wall," Law Journal Seminars-Press, 1995; "Managing Marketers: Supervisory Responsibilities of Broker-Dealers and Investment Advisors," CCH, 2000; "Academic and Professional Journals: Internal Corporate Investigations and the SEC's Message to Directors in Cooper Co.," University of Cincinnati Law Review, Vol. 65, No. 1 (Fall 1996); "Government Subpoenas and Attorney Files," The Review of Securities & Commodities Regulation, Vol. 27, No. 2 (January 26, 1994); "Alternative Dispute Resolution in Class Action Suits," The Review of Securities & Commodities Regulation, Vol. 26, No.19 (November 10, 1993); "Role of Investigative Committees and Special Counsel," The Corporate Analyst, Vol. 5, No. 1 (November 1992); "Securities Market Reform in the Age of Program Trading," Journal of Corporate Disclosure and Confidentiality, Vol. 3, No. 3 (September 1992). Articles: "Representing Foreign Individuals in SEC and SRO Proceedings," International Securities Regulation Report Vol. 5, No. 3 (Jan. 14, 1992); "The Institutional Investor and Corporate Ownership," Securities Regulation Law Journal (Winter 1992); "The Regulations Governing Broking," International Financial Law Review (December 1991); "Hardball! The SEC's New Arsenal of Enforcement Weapons," The Business Lawyer, Vol. 47, No. 1 (Nov. 1991); "Derivative Liability in Securities Law: Controlling Person Liability and Respondeat Superior, "part of an article published in 40 Wash. & Lee L. Rev. 1007 (1983), Securities Law Administration, Litigation and Enforcement, Selected Articles on Federal Securities Law, Volume III, Section of Business Law, American Bar Association (1991); "Legal Representation in the International Securities Market: Representing a Party or Witness in an SEC or SRO Proceeding," The Delaware Journal of Corporate Law, Vol. 14, No. 3 (1989); "Broker-Dealer Supervision of Registered Representatives and Branch Office Operations," (co-author) The Business Lawyer, Vol 44, No. 4 (August 1989); "SEC Expands Enforcement Role To the International Marketplace," The National Law Journal (April 24, 1989); "Inside Traders Face Wave of Private Litigation," The National Law Journal (September 19, 1988); "Laying Out the Basics: A Close-Up View of the Supreme Court Decision in Basic v. Levinson," American Business Law Journal, Vol. 26, No. 2 (Summer 1988); "Danger Points and Defenses for Broker-Dealers," The National Law Journal (November 9, 1987); "Immobilization of the Security Certificate: The U.S. Experience," Securities Regulation Law Journal, Vol. 15, No. 3 (Fall 1987); "Financial Planning by Insurance Companies," The Review of Financial Services Regulation, Vol. 3, No. 3 (February 4, 1987), reprinted as "Marketing Financial Planning Services: Overcoming the Regulatory Hurdles for Insurance Companies," Journal of Insurance Regulation, Vol. 5, No. 4 (June 1987); "Banks as Financial Planners," The Review of Financial Services Regulation, Vol. 2, No. 8 (April 23, 1986); "Federal Regulation of Financial Planners," The Review of Financial Services Regulation, Vol. 2, No. 2 (January 29, 1986); "Tender Offer Tactics," The Review of Securities & Commodities Regulation, Vol. 19, No. 2 (January 22, 1986); "Overview of an SEC Enforcement Action," 8 Corporation Law Review 306 (Fall 1985); "Tender Offer Developments: 1985 Midyear Review," Legal Times (August 5, 1985); "Preventing Insider Trading," The Listed Company (May 1985); "New 'Insider Trading' Act Fails to Define Liability," New York Law Journal (December 10, 1984); "Opposition to 'Poison Pill ' Warrants is Mounting," Legal Times of Washington (October 15, 1984); "Should Criminal Courts Enforce Securities Law?" Legal Times of Washington (October 8, 1984); "SEC-CFTC Accord: One Year Later, An Uneasy Peace," Legal Times of Washington (January 30, 1984); "Derivative Liability in Securities Law: Controlling Person Liability, Respondeat Superior and Aiding and Abetting," 40 Washington & Lee Review 1007 (Summer 1983); "Shelf Registration of SEC Temporary Rule 415," 5 Corporation Law Review (Fall 1982); "Legislative and Market Forces Reshape Financial Services Industry," North Carolina Bar Association Commercial, Banking and Business Law Section (August 1982); "The Interplay Between State Corporation and Federal Securities Law -- Santa Fe, Singer Burks, Maldonado, Their Progeny & Beyond," 7 Delaware Journal of Corporate Law 1 (1982); "Courts Struggle to Define 'Manipulative' Practices," Legal Times of Washington (May 3, 1982); "SEC Tests Waters with Shelf Registration Release," Legal Times of Washington (March 8, 1982); "Tender Offers 1981: Significant Legal Developments," Legal Times of Washington (January 25, 1982); "The Role of Inside Counsel in the Corporate Accountability Process," 4 Corporation Law Review 3 (1981); "Disclosure of Information Bearing on Management Integrity and Competency -- Sliding Down the Slippery Slope of Materiality," 76 Northwestern University Law Review and Washington University Law Review 555 (1981); "Corporate Governance," 36 The Business Lawyer 759 (1981); "A Reappraisal of Santa Fe: Rule 10b-5 and The New Federalism," 129 University of Pennsylvania Law Review 263 (1980); "Rule 10b-5 and the New Federalism," 53 Wisconsin Bar Bulletin 16 (November 1980); "Accountants and Bankers: Public Expectations and Professional Accountability," Journal of Commercial Bank Lending (The Robert Morris Associates, June 1978); "The Future of Federal Influence on Corporate Governance," Directors Monthly (National Association of Corporate Directors, Vol. 2, No. 5, May 1978); "Public and Private Enterprise in the United States: Co-Existence and Unsteady Equilibrium," *Public and Private Enterprise in Mixed Economies* (W. Freedman, ed., London: English Edition, Stevens and Sons, 1974), A comparative analysis treating co-existent public and private enterprise in France, Italy, Turkey, Nigeria, United Kingdom and United States, (Editions published in French, Italian and Turkish); "Administrative Proceedings Under the Securities Exchange Act of 1934," 25 Mercer Law Review 671, Lead Articles Issue, Securities Regulation Edition (Spring 1974); "Securities and Exchange Commission's Detection of Investigation, and Enforcement of Selected Practices that Impair Investor Confidences in our Capital Markets," Howard Law Review, Lead Articles Issue - Securities Regulation Edition (June 1971). Member, Advisory Board of Securities Regulation and Law Report. Faculty, National Law Center, George Washington University, 1970-1972. General Counsel, Board of Visitors, University of Cincinnati College of Law and Board of Advisors, The Center for Corporate Law, University of Cincinnati College of Law, 1987—; Securities and Exchange Commission, 1978-1981. Member: "e *Securities*" Board of Advisors, 1998—; Washington, D.C. Panel of Distinguished Neutrals, CPR Institute for Dispute Resolution, 1996—; Administrative Conference of the United States, 1982-1985; Ray Garrett Institute Advisory Committee, 1982-1984; Practising Law Institute, Securities Law Advisory Committee, 1981—, Co-Chair, Annual Institute on Securities Regulation, 1994-1998; Co-Chair, Sweeping Reform: Litigating and Bespeaking Caution Under the New Securities Law, 1996; The Review of Financial Services Regulation, Board of Advisers, 1987—. Member, Legal Advisory Committee to the New York Stock Exchange Board of Directors. Chairman, 1992-1994, Center for Public Resources, Inc., Securities Dispute Committee, 1988-1989. *Member:* Federal (Member: Executive Council, Securities Law Committee, 1978—; General Counsel Committee, 1978-1981) and American (Member: Section on Corporation, Banking and Business Law; Federal Regulation of Securities Committee; Vice-Chairman: Civil Liabilities and Litigation Subcommittee, 1981—; Chairman, Task Force on Broker-Dealer Compliance, 1988—. Chairman, Market Structures Working Group of the Task Force on Review of Federal Securities Laws. Member: Task Force on Insider Trading Controls, 1985—; Task Force SEC Settlements, 1987-1989; Task Force on Section 15 (c) (4) Proceedings, 1987—; Task Force on Securities Arbitration, 1987—; Section Planning and Review, 1986—) Bar Associations; Insurance Marketplace Standards Association (Independent Assessor Certification, Market Conduct Program, 1997); American Law Institute. ***PRACTICE AREAS:*** Corporate Financing Law; Mergers and Acquisitions; SEC Enforcement; Securities Litigation; Securities Regulation Law; Securities Offerings; Insurance; Insurance Class Action Litigation. ***Email:*** rcferrara@debevoise.com

JEFFREY P. CUNARD, born December 9, 1955; admitted to bar, 1981, Calif; 1982, District of Columbia; 1993, New York. *Education:* University of California at Los Angeles (B.A., 1977); Yale Law School (J.D., 1980). Editor, Yale Law Journal, 1979-1980. Co-author: with Robert R. Bruce and Mark D. Director: "The Telecom Mosaic: Assembling the New International Structure," Butterworths, 1988; "From Telecommunications to Electronic Services: A Global Spectrum of Definitions, Boundary Lines and Structures," Butterworths, 1986. Author: "Property of the Mind: Software and The Law," in The Future of Software, MIT, 1995; "Obscenity and Indecency," "Copyright" and "Trademark and Unfair Competition Issues," in *Internet and Online Law* (K. Stuckey, ed.) Law Journal Seminars-Press 1996-2001; "Privatization et typologie des services de telecommunication: observation de certaines tendences nationales recents (Etats-Unis, Japon, Royaume-Uni, Republique Federale d'Allemagne)," Droit de 1'Informatique 1987/2 (1987); "Freeing Public Broadcasting from Unconstitutional Restraints," 89 Yale Law Journal 719 (1980). Law Clerk to Judge William Matthew Byrne, Jr., U.S. District Court, Central District of Columbia, 1980-1981. *Member:* The District of Columbia Bar (Co-Chair, Investment and Finance Committee, International Law Section, 1989-1993); The Association of the Bar of the City of New York; The Federal Communications Bar Association. ***PRACTICE AREAS:*** Computers and Software; Technology and Science; Telecommunications Law; Communications Law; Copyright Law. ***Email:*** jpcunard@debevoise.com

COLBY A. SMITH, born May 7, 1956; admitted to bar, 1988, N.Y.; 2000, D.C. *Education:* Utah (B.S., 1979); Columbia (M.A., 1984; J.D., 1987). Senior Editor, Columbia Law Review. Co-Author: with Ralph C. Ferrara and Phillip D. Parker, "Managing Marketers: Supervisory Responsibilities of Broker-Dealers and Financial Advisors." *Member:* American Bar Association (Member, Litigation Section). ***PRACTICE AREAS:*** Securities Law; Federal and State Election Law; Intellectual Property Litigation. ***Email:*** casmith@debevoise.com

(This Listing Continued)

KENNETH J. BERMAN, born October 31, 1954; admitted to bar, 1980, New York; 2001, District of Columbia. *Education:* Dickinson College (B.A., 1976); University of Chicago (J.D., 1979). Securities and Exchange Commission, Division of Investment Management: Associate Director (Public Utility and Investment Company Regulation), 1997-2000; Assistant Director, Office of Regulatory Policy, 1995-1997; Deputy Office Chief and Special Counsel, Office of Investment Adviser and Disclosure Regulation, 1989-1995. *Member:* The Association of the Bar of the City of New York (Investment Management Regulation Subcommittee); American Bar Association. ***PRACTICE AREAS:*** Investment Management Law; Securities Regulation Law. ***Email:*** kberman@debevoise.com

JONATHAN R. TUTTLE, born May 10, 1967; admitted to bar, 1992, Virginia; 1993, District of Columbia; U.S. District Court, Eastern District of Virginia; U.S. District Court for the District of Columbia. *Education:* College of William & Mary (B.A., 1989); Harvard University (J.D., 1992). *Member:* Virginia State Bar; Virginia Bar Association; The District of Columbia Bar. ***PRACTICE AREAS:*** Securities Litigation; Securities Enforcement Defense; Commercial Litigation. ***Email:*** jrtuttle@debevoise.com

COUNSEL

ANN M. ASHTON, born March 2, 1954; admitted to bar, 1980, District of Columbia. *Education:* Catholic University of America (B.A., 1976); George Washington University (J.D., 1980). Order of the Coif. Managing Editor, The George Washington Law Review, 1979-1980. *Member:* The District of Columbia Bar; American Bar Association. ***PRACTICE AREAS:*** Complex and Multi-District Litigation; Litigation; Securities Litigation; Class Action Defense. ***Email:*** amashton@debevoise.com

PHILLIP D. PARKER, born April 16, 1947; admitted to bar, 1978, District of Columbia. *Education:* Kenyon College (A.B., 1970); University of Virginia (J.D., 1975). Phi Beta Kappa. Woodrow Wilson Fellow. Attorney, U.S. Securities and Exchange Commission, 1975-1996. Chief Counsel, Division of Enforcement, 1984-1987. Associate General Counsel, 1988-1992. Deputy General Counsel, 1992-1996. Adjunct Professor, Georgetown University Law Center, 1992-1997. Member, Administrative Conference of the United States, 1993-1995. *Member:* District of Columbia Bar. ***PRACTICE AREAS:*** Securities Regulation and Enforcement; Broker-Dealer Regulation; Securities Litigation; Corporate Investigations. ***Email:*** pdparker@debevoise.com

HERBERT THOMAS, born February 21, 1957; admitted to bar, 1991, Virginia; 1992, District of Columbia. *Education:* Colby College (B.A., 1979); Columbia University (M.A., 1986); University of Virginia (J.D., 1991). Executive Editor, Virginia Law Review, 1990-1991. Law Clerk to Hon. Larry G. Elder, Court of Appeals of Virginia. ***PRACTICE AREAS:*** General Litigation; Securities Litigation; Insurance Litigation and Regulation. ***Email:*** hcthomas@debevoise.com

RETIRED PARTNER

ROBERT J. GENIESSE, born September 16, 1929; admitted to bar, 1958, N.Y.; 1982, District of Columbia. *Education:* Williams (B.A., 1951); Harvard (LL.B., 1957). Phi Beta Kappa. Editor, Harvard Law Review, 1955-1957. Assistant U.S. Attorney, Southern District of New York, 1962-1963; Chief Appellate Attorney, 1963-1964. Former Member: The Association of the Bar of the City of New York; American Bar Association (Co-chairman, Securities Litigation Committee, Litigation Section, 1980-1983); American Law Institute. *Member:* The District of Columbia Bar; New York State Bar Association. ***PRACTICE AREAS:*** Litigation; International Trade Law; Securities Regulation Law.

ASSOCIATES

SCOTT N. AUBY, born November 26, 1968; admitted to bar, 1993, California; 1994, U.S. Court of Appeals, Ninth Circuit; 1996, District of Columbia. *Education:* Lawrence University (B.Mus., 1990); Harvard (J.D., 1993). ***PRACTICE AREAS:*** Class Actions; Litigation; Securities Litigation. ***Email:*** snauby@debevoise.com

RACHEL H. GRAHAM, born April 20, 1966; admitted to bar, 1993, North Carolina; 1995, District of Columbia. *Education:* Colby College (B.A., 1987); University of North Carolina (J.D., 1993). Phi Beta Kappa. Staff Attorney and Senior Counsel, U.S. Securities and Exchange Commission, 1995-2000. Legislative Assistant, U.S. Sen. Thomas Daschle, 1994-1995. ***PRACTICE AREAS:*** Securities Regulation; Corporate Law. ***Email:*** rhgraham@debevoise.com

ELIZABETH N. KAPLAN, born December 29, 1967; admitted to bar, 1993, Virginia; 1995, District of Columbia. *Education:* University of Washington (B.A., 1990); Georgetown University (J.D., 1993). Phi Beta Kappa. Staff Member, 1991-1992 and Articles Editor, 1992-1993, American Criminal Law Review. ***PRACTICE AREAS:*** Corporate Law; Securities Regulation Law. ***Email:*** enkaplan@debevoise.com

PHILIP S. KHINDA, born June 3, 1964; admitted to bar, 1992, Pennsylvania; 1994, District of Columbia. *Education:* Columbia University (B.A., 1986; J.D., 1992). Staff Member, Columbia Journal of Law and Social Problems, 1990-1991. Author: "Undesired Results Under *Halper* and *Grady:* Double Jeopardy Bars on Criminal RICO Actions Against Civilly-Sanctioned Defendants," 25 Colum. J.L. & Soc. Probs. 117 (1991). Adjunct Professor of Law, Georgetown University, 1999—. Staff Attorney and Senior Counsel, Division of Enforcement, U.S. Securities and Exchange Commission, 1992-1996. ***PRACTICE AREAS:*** Securities Litigation and Enforcement Defense; Commercial Litigation; Securities Regulation. ***Email:*** pskhinda@debevoise.com

(For Biographical data of other Partners, see Professional Biographies at New York, N.Y.)

DECARO, DORAN, SICILIANO, GALLAGHER & DEBLASIS, LLP

WASHINGTON, D.C.

(See Lanham, Maryland)

General Civil Trial Practice in State and Federal Courts. Insurance Defense, Insurance Coverage, Contracts Law, Construction Litigation, Mechanics Lien, Medical Malpractice, Professional Malpractice, Products Liability, Toxic Tort and Environmental Law, Worker's Compensation, Domestic and Family Law, Personal Injury, Wills, Estates and Trusts, Criminal Law, Business, Employment Law and Discrimination Law.

DECHERT

1775 EYE STREET, N.W.

WASHINGTON, D.C. 20006-2401

Telephone: 202.261.3300

Telefax: 202.261.3333

URL: http://www.dechert.com

Philadelphia, Pennsylvania: 4000 Bell Atlantic Tower, 1717 Arch Street, 19103-2793. Telephone: 215.994.4000.

New York, New York: 30 Rockefeller Plaza, 10112. Telephone: 212.698.3500.

Harrisburg, Pennsylvania: Thirty North Third Street, 17101-1603. Telephone: 717.237.2000.

Princeton, New Jersey: Princeton Pike Corporate Center, P.O. Box 5218, 08543-5218. Telephone: 609.620.3200.

Boston, Massachusetts: Ten Post Office Square South, 12th Floor, 02109-4603. Telephone: 617.728.7100.

Hartford, Connecticut: 90 State House Square, 06103-3702. Telephone: 860.524.3999.

Newport Beach, California: 4675 MacArthur Court, Suite 1400, 92660-8842. Telephone: 949.442.6000.

London, England: 2 Serjeants' Inn, EC4Y 1LT. Telephone: +44 20 7583 5353.

Brussels, Belgium: 65 Avenue Louise 1050. Telephone: +32 2 535 5411.

Paris, France: 55, avenue Kléber, 75116. Telephone: +33 1 53 65 05 00.

Luxembourg: Brucher & Seimetz in association with Dechert, Avocats a la Cour, 10 rue de Vianden B.P. 709, L-2017. Telephone: +352 45 62 62.

Antitrust, Banking, Bankruptcy and Reorganization, Business and Technology, Commercial Litigation, Complex Litigation, Copyrights, Corporate Finance, Competition, Construction, Customs and Excise, Criminal and Civil Fraud, Defamation, Domestic Taxation, Employee Benefits and Executive Compensation, Employment, Environmental, Estate Planning, EU Legislation, Financial Services, First Amendment, Government Affairs, Health Care, Immigration, Insurance, Intellectual Property, Internet and e-Commerce, Information Technology, Insurance, International Business, International Taxation, International Trade, Investment Management, Labor, Latin America, Life Sciences, Mass Torts, Media, Mergers and Acquisitions, Patent Law and Litigation, Privacy, Private Equity, Products Liability, Property Planning, Real Estate and Mortgage Finance, Retail, Securities Litigation and Enforcement, Securitization, State and Local Taxation, Tax-Exempt Organizations, Trademarks, Venture Capital.

RESIDENT PARTNERS

KAREN L. ANDERBERG, born Baldwin, New York, 1964; admitted to bar, 1992, Maryland; 1993, District of Columbia. *Education:* Colgate University (B.A., 1986); Boston University (J.D., cum laude, 1992). Notes Editor, Boston University Law Review, 1991-92. ***PRACTICE AREAS:*** Investment Management; Financial Services Law. ***Email:*** karen.anderberg@dechert.com

SANDER M. BIEBER, born Los Angeles, California, 1950; admitted to bar, 1976, District of Columbia. *Education:* Princeton University (B.A., 1972); Case Western Reserve University (J.D., 1976). Associate Editor, Case Western Reserve Law Review. Judicial Intern to the Chief Justice, Supreme Court of the United States, 1974. Co-Author: with Olivia P. Adler, "ADRs: Expanding Their Role in an International Market," Vol. 4, No. 7, Butterworths Journal of International Banking and Financial Law, July 1989. Attorney, Office of Chief Counsel, Federal Railroad Administration, U.S. Department of Transportation, 1976-78. *Member:* The District of Columbia Bar; American Bar Association (Member, Corporation, Banking and Business Law Section; Mexican Law Commit-

(This Listing Continued)

DECHERT, Washington—Continued

tee, International Law and Practice Section). ***PRACTICE AREAS:*** Securities Law; Financial Services Law; Investment Management Law; Corporate Law. ***Email:*** sander.bieber@dechert.com

CATHERINE BOTTICELLI, born New York, New York, 1963; admitted to bar, 1988, Connecticut; 1989, New York; 1994, District of Columbia. *Education:* Fordham University (B.A., magna cum laude, 1985; J.D., 1988). Notes and Comments Editor, International Law Journal, "Targets of Opportunity: Attorneys and Accountants Become Fair Game for Disgruntled Investors," co-authored with Theodore Sonde for presentation at 24th Biennial Conference of International Bar Association, September 24, 1992; "New Weapon in the SEC's Arsenal: Secondary Liability After Central Bank," co-authored with Bettina M. Lawton, ABA Journal, *Business Law Today* (July/August 1995). ***PRACTICE AREAS:*** Securities Litigation; Commercial Litigation. ***Email:*** catherine.botticelli@dechert.com

FRANK J. EISENHART, born Philadelphia, Pennsylvania, 1945; admitted to bar, 1972, Pennsylvania; 1989, District of Columbia; 2001, Maryland. *Education:* Boston College (B.S., 1968); Temple University (J.D., 1972). Mediator, District of Columbia Superior Court. Member, Committee on Unauthorized Practice of Law, District of Columbia Court of Appeals. *Member:* District of Columbia Bar (Litigation Section Steering Committee, 1994); American Bar Association (Member, Sections on: Litigation; Business Law). ***PRACTICE AREAS:*** Securities Litigation; Commercial Litigation; Product Liability Litigation. ***Email:*** frank.eisenhart@dechert.com

RUTH S. EPSTEIN, born Washington, D.C., 1952; admitted to bar, 1979, District of Columbia. *Education:* Cornell University (B.A., with distinction, 1974); Harvard University (J.D., cum laude, 1977). Phi Beta Kappa. Law Clerk to the Honorable Judge William Wayne Justice, U.S. District Court for the Eastern District of Texas, 1977-78. Securities and Exchange Commission, Division of Enforcement and Office of General Counsel, 1978-84. ***PRACTICE AREAS:*** Financial Services Law; Investment Management. ***Email:*** ruth.epstein@dechert.com

SUSAN C. ERVIN, born Aberdeen, Maryland, 1951; admitted to bar, 1977, New York; 1985, District of Columbia. *Education:* Mount Holyoke (B.A., magna cum laude, 1973); Rutgers School of Law (J.D., high honors, 1976). Staff Member, Commodity Futures Trading Commission, 1983-97. Office of the General Counsel, 1983-86; Associate Director, Division of Trading and Markets, 1987; Deputy Director/Chief Counsel, Division of Trading and Markets, 1987-97. Author: "Single Stock Futures," Review of Securities & Commodities Regulation, 2001; "Mutual Funds and Derivatives: Defining the Regulatory Boundaries," Futures & Derivatives Law Report, 1999; "Congress Liberalizes Derivatives Regulation," NSCP Currents, 2001; "The Perils of Success: Public Policy Issues Presented by Hedge Funds," 16 Futures and Derivatives Law Report 8-21, March/April 1996; "Hedge Funds in the 1990's: Private Risk Taking, Public Consequences," The Financial Services Revolution: Understanding the Changing Roles of Banks, Mutual Funds, and Insurance Companies, Irwin, 1997. Co-Author: "Maintenance of Market Strategies in Futures Broker Insolvencies: Futures Position Transfers from Troubled Firms," 44 Washington and Lee Law Review 849-915, 1987. Chairman, Committee on Futures Regulation of the Association of the Bar of the City of New York, 2000-03; Board of Editors, Futures and Derivatives Law Report; Editorial Advisory Board, Futures Industry Magazine. ***PRACTICE AREAS:*** Derivative Products; Financial Services Law; Securities Regulation; Investment Management. ***Email:*** susan.ervin@dechert.com

PAUL H. FRIEDMAN, born Pittsburgh, Pennsylvania, 1954; admitted to bar, 1978, Ohio; 1979, District of Columbia, U.S. Supreme Court, U.S. Court of Appeals for the District of Columbia, First, Sixth, and Ninth Circuits, U.S. District Court for the District of Columbia. *Education:* University of Chicago (B.A., 1975); Boston University (J.D., 1978). Author: "Private Damage Actions Under RICO: A Suggested Analysis," 14 Capital University Law Review 205, 1985. *Member:* District of Columbia Bar; American Bar Association (Member, Antitrust Law Section; Vice-Chair, Civil Practice and Procedure Committee). ***PRACTICE AREAS:*** Antitrust and Trade Regulation; Complex Litigation; Complex Commercial Litigation. ***Email:*** paul.friedman@dechert.com

DAVID J. HARRIS, born Bethesda, Maryland, 1956; admitted to bar, 1982, Pennsylvania; 1983, District of Columbia. *Education:* Purdue University (B.S., 1978; B.A., 1978) Phi Beta Kappa, Pi Kappa Phi; Georgetown University School of Foreign Service (M.S.F.S., 1982); Georgetown University Law Center (J.D., magna cum laude, 1982). Topics Editor, Law and Policy in International Business, 1980-81. ***PRACTICE AREAS:*** Financial Services Law; Investment Management. ***Email:*** david.harris@dechert.com

ROBERT W. HELM, born Akron, Ohio, 1957; admitted to bar, 1984, California; 1985, District of Columbia; 1997, New York. *Education:* Stanford University (A.B., 1979); Stanford Law School (J.D., 1982). Fulbright-Hays Direct Exchange Fellow to Italy, 1982-83; attach é de recherche, European University Institute, Florence, Italy, 1983-84. Member, Editorial Board, Villanova Journal of Investment Management Regulation. Author: "International Investment Funds," Financial Products Fundamentals, 2000; "Offshore Investment Funds," Financial Services 2000, 1996; "Self-Directed Employee Benefit Plans and Private Investment Companies: Unraveling PanAgora," The Investment Lawyer, 1995; "Private Placements of Shares of Offshore Umbrella Funds in the United States," World Fund Industry (FICOM), 1995; "European Regulation of Investment Funds," The Review of Securities and Commodities Regulation, 1989. Co-Author: "The U.S. Market for U.K. Investment Trust Companies," Journal of International Banking Law, 1995; "Buying a Fund Organization," World Fund Industry (FICOM), 1995; "Investment Funds in Luxembourg," Journal of International Banking Law, 1990; "Distributing Shares of U.S. Mutual Funds Abroad: A U.S. Securities and Tax Perspective," International Business Lawyer, 1992; "Offering Shares of Non-U.S. Investment Funds in the United States: A U.S. Securities and Tax Law Perspective," Journal of International Banking Law, 1992. Arbitrator, National Futures Association. *Member:* District of Columbia Bar; State Bar of California; New York State, American and International Bar Associations; Managed Fund Association; Luxembourg-American Chamber of Commerce. Fellow, Royal Society for the Arts. ***LANGUAGES:*** Italian. ***PRACTICE AREAS:*** Investment Management; Securities Regulation; Financial Services Law. ***Email:*** robert.helm@dechert.com

JANE A. KANTER, born New York, New York, 1949; admitted to bar, 1974, Missouri; 1996, District of Columbia. *Education:* Queens College of the City University of New York (B.A., honors, 1970); Brooklyn Law School (J.D., 1973); Washington University School of Law (LL.M. in Taxation, 1978). Member, Brooklyn Law Review, 1972-73. Attorney, Office of the Solicitor, Plan Benefits Security Division, U.S. Department of Labor, 1979-80. Attorney-Adviser, Division of Investment Management, Securities and Exchange Commission, 1981-82. Office of the General Counsel, 1982. Special Counsel, Office of Disclosure Policy, Division of Investment Management, 1982-84. ***PRACTICE AREAS:*** Financial Services Law; Investment Management. ***Email:*** jane.kanter@dechert.com

BETTINA M. LAWTON, born Albany, New York, 1954; admitted to bar, 1980, District of Columbia; 1981, New York; 1994, Virginia. *Education:* Siena College (B.B.A.; M.C.L., 1976); Georgetown University (J.D., 1980). Attorney, Securities and Exchange Commission, Division of Enforcement, 1982-84; Author, "Special Obligations and Problems of Financial Institutions and Other Regulated Industries," *Destruction of Evidence,* John Wiley & Sons, Inc., January 1989; Presenter: "Cyber Fraud and Litigation Risks," Financial Executives International, WebCast, May, 2001; "SEC Enforcement - A Checklist," 16th Midyear SEC Reporting Forum, An Update for Corporate Officers, The SEC Institute, May, 2001; "Staying Out of Trouble with the SEC," Staying Out of Trouble Conference, The SEC Institute, April, 2001; "SEC Regulation Fair Disclosure," 6th Annual Insurance Industry Update Conference, The SEC Institute, October, 2000. *Member:* American Bar Association (Member, Business Law and Litigation Sections; Council, 1996-99, Law Practice Management Section; Member, Federal Regulation of Securities Committee, Subcommittee on Civil Litigation and SEC Enforcement Matters, 1984—; Member, Federal Regulation of Securities Committee); The Women's Bar Association of the District of Columbia (President, 1986-87; Director, 1989-92); The Women's Bar Association Foundation (Director, 1987-90). ***PRACTICE AREAS:*** Securities Litigation; Financial Services Law; Investment Management; SEC Enforcement. ***Email:*** bettina.lawton@dechert.com

ALLAN S. MOSTOFF, born New York, New York, 1932; admitted to bar, 1958, New York; 1964, District of Columbia. *Education:* Cornell University (B.S., 1953); New York University (M.B.A., 1954); New York Law School (LL.B., 1957). Adjunct Professor, Georgetown University Law Center, 1971-81; Staff Member, Securities and Exchange Commission, 1962-76; Associate Director, Division of Corporate Regulation, 1968-72; Director, Division of Investment Management Regulation, 1972-76; Member, American Law Institute, Financial Accounting Standards Advisory Council, 1982-86; Advisory Board, Securities Regulation and Law Report, 1976-85; Advisory Board, Investment Lawyer, 1993—. *Member:* American (Investment Companies Subcommittee, Federal Regulation of Securities Law Committee, Corporation, Banking and Business Law Section) and Federal (Executive Council, Securities Law Committee) Bar Associations. ***PRACTICE AREAS:*** Investment Management; Financial Services Law; Securities Law; Corporate Law. ***Email:*** allan.mostoff@dechert.com

JACK W. MURPHY, born Clarkson, New York, 1958; admitted to bar, 1984, New York; 1998, District of Columbia. *Education:* State University of New York at Albany (B.A., 1980); Boston College Law School (J.D., 1983). Associate Director and Chief Counsel, Division of Investment Management, U.S. Securities and Exchange Commission, 1994-97. ***PRACTICE AREAS:*** Investment Management; Financial Services Law; Securities; Corporate Law. ***Email:*** jack.murphy@dechert.com

JEFFREY S. PURETZ, born Baltimore, Maryland, 1953; admitted to bar, 1981, District of Columbia. *Education:* University of Maryland (B.A., 1976); Catholic University of America (J.D., 1981). Attorney/Advisor, Securities and Exchange Commission, Division of Investment Management, 1982-85. ***PRACTICE AREAS:*** Corporate Securities Law; Investment Management Law; Insurance Law; Financial Services Law. ***Email:*** jeffrey.puretz@dechert.com

(This Listing Continued)

KEITH T. ROBINSON, born Des Moines, Iowa, 1965; admitted to bar, 1992, Maryland; 1994, District of Columbia. *Education:* University of Virginia (B.A., with distinction, 1988); University of North Carolina, Chapel Hill (J.D., with honors, 1991). Law Clerk to the Honorable Robert E. Maxwell, U.S. District Court, Northern District of West Virginia, 1991-92. ***PRACTICE AREAS:*** Securities Regulation; Financial Services Law; Investment Management. ***Email:*** keith.robinson@dechert.com

MELVIN A. SCHWARZ, born Cincinnati, Ohio, 1950; admitted to bar, 1975, Pennsylvania; 1980, New York; 2001, District of Columbia. *Education:* The Johns Hopkins University (B.A., 1972); University of Chicago Law School (J.D., 1975). Phi Beta Kappa; Order of the Coif. ***PRACTICE AREAS:*** Antitrust and Competition Law; Intellectual Property; Securities Fraud; International Arbitration. ***Email:*** melvin.schwarz@dechert.com

THEODORE SONDE, born New York, New York, 1940; admitted to bar, 1964, New York; 1978, District of Columbia. *Education:* City College of the City University of New York (B.A., 1961); New York University (LL.B., 1964); Georgetown University (LL.M., 1967). Faculty Member, ALI-ABA Trial Evidence and Civil Practice Programs, 1984—; Adjunct Professor: George Washington University National Law Center, 1976-82; Georgetown University School of Law, 1977-95. Director, Office of Enforcement, Federal Energy Regulatory Commission, 1980-81; Associate Director, Division of Enforcement, Securities and Exchange Commission, 1974-80. Author: "Staying Out of More Trouble," The SEC Institute, September 2001; "The Evolution of Professional Liability- Work in Progress," ALI-ABA, April 1998; "Professional Liability and the Effect of The Securities Litigation Reform Act of 1995 on Lawyers and Accountants," Business Laws, Inc., Corporate Counsel's Guide to Lawyering Laws, December 1997; "The Coming Changes in Securities Litigation (Part 2)," The Practical Litigator, Volume 8, Number 4, July 1997; "The Coming Changes in Securities Litigation (Part 1)," The Practical Litigator, Volume 8, Number 3, May 1997; "Professional Liability and the Effect of the 1995 Legislation on Outside Counsel and Accountants; Inside Counsel and Supervisors," The Corporate Analyst, Volume 9, Number 2, February 1997; "Some Traps for the Unwary," ALI-ABA Civil Practice and Litigation Techniques in the Federal Courts, Washington, D.C., December 1995, The Practical Litigator, Volume 7, Number 3, May 1996; "The SEC's 21A Report on The Cooper Companies: The Message to Directors," Insights: The Corporate & Securities Law Advisor, March/April 1995; "Central Bank and Securities Litigation Reform - What Is the Prospect for Future Professional Liability for Accountants and Lawyers?" American Conference Institute, New York, May 1995; "'Ex Parte' Interviews and 'Inadvertent' Disclosure - Some Areas with Traps for the Unwary," ALI-ABA, December 1995; "The Attorney's Dilemma: What To Do in Light of Salomon Brothers, Kaye, Scholer and Jones, Day?" American Conference Institute, June 1993; "Targets of Opportunity: Attorneys and Accountants Become Fair Game for Disgruntled Investors," International Bar Association, Cannes, France, September 24, 1992; "Supreme Court Seems to Boost SEC's International Enforcement Efforts," Financial Regulation Report, March 1990, page 7; "Developments in Canada-U.S. Securities Enforcement," Vol. XII, Canadian Law Newsletter, Fall/Winter 1988, page 4; "Seagulls on the Water: Some Ships in a Storm - A Comment on Lanza v. Drexel," 49 NYU L.Rev.1 (1974); "The Responsibilities of Professionals Under the Federal Securities Laws - Some Observations," 68 Nw.U.L.Rev. 1 (1973); "Utilizing the Federal Securities Law to 'Clear the Air', 'Clean the Sky', 'Wash the Wind'," 16 Howard Law Review 831 (1972). ***PRACTICE AREAS:*** Securities Regulation Law; Litigation; International Finance Law; White Collar Defense Law. ***Email:*** theodore.sonde@dechert.com

PAUL SCHOTT STEVENS, born New Orleans, Louisiana, 1952; admitted to bar, 1979, District of Columbia. *Education:* Yale College (B.A., magna cum laude, 1974); University of Virginia (J.D., 1978). Senior Vice President and General Counsel, Mutual Funds and International, Charles Schwab & Co., Inc., 1997-99; Senior Vice President and General Counsel, Investment Company Institute, 1993-97; Associate, 1978-85, and Partner, 1989-93, Dickstein, Shapiro & Morin; Executive Assistant, Secretary of Defense, 1989; Special Assistant to the President, National Security Affairs, The White House, 1987-89; Executive Secretary and Legal Adviser, National Security Council, 1987-89; Deputy Director and General Counsel, President's Blue Ribbon Commission on Defense Management, 1985-86; Chair, American Bar Association's Standing Committee on Law and National Security, 1995-98; Member, Quality of Markets Committee, The NASDAQ Stock Market, Inc., 1997; Investment Companies Committee, NASD Regulation, Inc. 1999; U.S.-Japan Leadership Fellow, 1989-90; Department of Defense Medal for Distinguished Public Service, 1989; Platform Committee Staff, Foreign Policy, National Defense and Intelligence, Republican National Convention, 1988 and 1992; Council on Foreign Relations. Author: "Mutual Funds, Investment Advisers and the National Securities Markets Improvement Act of 1996," The Business Lawyer, Vol. 52, No. 2, Feb. 1997; "The Reagan NSC: Before and After, Perspectives on Political Science," Vol. 19, No. 2, Spring 1990; "Room for 'Maneuver': Some Policy Issues in the Iran-Contra Affair," Houston Journal of International Law, Vol. 11, No. 1, Fall 1989. *Member:* Federal, American and International Bar Associations. ***PRACTICE AREAS:*** Securities; Financial Services Regulation; Investment Management. ***Email:*** paul.stevens@dechert.com

(This Listing Continued)

WALLACE L. TIMMENY, born Tarrytown, New York, 1937; admitted to bar, 1965, New York; 1977, District of Columbia. *Education:* Fairfield University (B.B.A., cum laude, 1961); New York University (LL.B., 1964). U.S. Securities and Exchange Commission, 1967-79; Former Deputy Director of the Division of Enforcement, 1977-79; Chairman of Executive Council, Securities Law Committee of the Federal Bar Association. Former Adjunct Professor: American University School of Law; George Mason University School of Law; Georgetown University School of Law. ***PRACTICE AREAS:*** Securities Regulation; Investment Management; Financial Services Law. ***Email:*** wallace.timmeny@dechert.com

PATRICK W.D. TURLEY, born Hudson, New York, 1961; admitted to bar, 1987, Pennsylvania; 1989, District of Columbia. *Education:* Colgate University (B.A., 1983); Catholic University of America (J.D., 1986). ***PRACTICE AREAS:*** Financial Services Law; Investment Management. ***Email:*** patrick.turley@dechert.com

DAVID A. VAUGHAN, born Toledo, Ohio, 1965; admitted to bar, 1991, New York; 1996, District of Columbia. *Education:* Bowling Green State University (B.A., cum laude, 1987); Georgetown University Law Center (J.D., cum laude, 1990). ***LANGUAGES:*** Spanish. ***PRACTICE AREAS:*** Financial Services Law; Investment Management. ***Email:*** david.vaughan@dechert.com

DONALD ZARIN, born Newark, New Jersey, 1949; admitted to bar, 1976, District of Columbia and New Jersey; 1987, U.S. Court of International Trade and U.S. Supreme Court. *Education:* Georgetown University (B.S., 1971); George Washington University (M.A. in Int'l Affairs, 1975; J.D., 1975). Notes Editor, Journal of International Law and Economics, 1974-75. "Unilateral Economic Sanctions: The Need for Reform," 1 Transnational Law Exchange, (April 1998); "Doing Business Under the Foreign Corrupt Practices Act," Practicing Law Institute, 1995; "Countertrade and The Law," 18 The George Washington J. Int'l. L. & Econ. 235, 1984; "The Export Trading Company Act: Reducing Antitrust Uncertainty in Export Trade," 17 The George Washington J. Intl. L. & Econ. 297, 1983; "Export Controls - Where Are We Going," The Journal of Commerce. Adjunct Professor of International Trade Law, Columbus School of Law, Catholic University, 1985-92. Legal Counsel to newly emerging Micronesian State (Palau) in its treaty negotiation, 1979. Attorney, Office of General Counsel, U.S. Department of Commerce, 1980-83. Legal Counsel and Member of Executive Committee, Turkish-U.S. Business Council, 1986-94. *Member:* The District of Columbia Bar; New Jersey State and American (Member, Section on International Law and Practice) Bar Associations. ***PRACTICE AREAS:*** International Trade; Transactional. ***Email:*** donald.zarin@dechert.com

RESIDENT COUNSEL

ELLIOTT ROWLES CURZON, born Bellingham, Washington, 1955; admitted to bar, 1983, District of Columbia. *Education:* San Diego State University (B.A., Political Science, 1978); University of the Pacific McGeorge School of Law (J.D., 1983). *Member:* District of Columbia Bar; American Bar Association (Federal Securities Law Committee; Market Regulation Subcommittee). ***PRACTICE AREAS:*** Securities Law; Regulatory Policy; Securities Regulation; Broker-Dealer Regulation. ***Email:*** elliott.curzon@dechert.com

EDWARD B. HORAHAN III, born Drexel Hill, Pennsylvania, 1951; admitted to bar, 1976, District of Columbia. *Education:* LaSalle College (B.A., 1973); Yale Law School (J.D., 1976). Phi Alpha Theta. Co-Author: "The SEC's Version of the Efficient Market Theory and Its Impact on Securities Law Liabilities," 39 Washington & Lee Law Review 943, 1982; "ERISA--Fiduciary Responsibility and Prohibited Transactions," Tax Management Portfolio No. 365 (BNA 1995). Staff Attorney: Office of the Solicitor, Plan Benefits Security Division, U.S. Department of Labor, 1978-80; Office of the General Counsel, U.S. Securities and Exchange Commission, 1976-78. *Member:* District of Columbia Bar; American Bar Association. ***PRACTICE AREAS:*** Civil Litigation; Securities Law; Employee Benefits Law; Administrative Law; ERISA. ***Email:*** edward.horahan@dechert.com

REID B. HORWITZ, born Cincinnati, Ohio, 1957; admitted to bar, 1982, Ohio (Not admitted in District of Columbia). *Education:* University of Cincinnati (B.A., 1979; J.D., 1982). ***PRACTICE AREAS:*** Antitrust; Competition. ***Email:*** reid.horwitz@dechert.com

ELIZABETH M. KNOBLOCK, born Quanset Point, Rhode Island, 1955; admitted to bar, 1979, District of Columbia; 1988, New York. *Education:* John B. Stetson University (B.A., 1976); Georgetown University (J.D., 1979; LL.M., 1989); Nova University of Florida (M.B.A., 1993). Attorney, Gruntal & Company, Inc., 1988; Attorney, Shearson Lehman Hutton, Inc., 1986-88; Attorney, Securities and Exchange Commission, 1984-86; Attorney, Commodity Futures Trading Commission, 1980-84; Attorney, American Bar Association Model Procurement Code Project, 1979-80; Attorney, General Counsel, Senior Vice President, Secretary, Templeton Investment Counsel, Inc., 1990-2001; Kidder, Peabody & Co. Inc., 1989-90. Speaker: "Developing Written Procedures for the Investment Adviser," National Regulatory Services, Inc., 10th Annual Investment Adviser and Broker-Dealer Compliance Conference, April, 1995; "Investment Adviser Trading Issues," National Society of Compliance Professionals, 1995 NSCP National Membership Meeting; Speaker, "Equitable Allocation of

(This Listing Continued)

DECHERT, Washington—Continued

Investment Opportunities and Trading Issues," and "Managing Problems From Complaints to Enforcement Actions," National Regulatory Services, Inc., Annual Compliance Conference for Investment Advisers & Broker Dealers, April, 1996; Speaker, "Managing Problems: Complaints to Enforcement Actions," National Society of Compliance Professionals, NSCP 1997 Southern Regional Membership Meeting, February, 1997; Speaker, "Allocation of Investment Opportunities, Cross Trading & Insider Trading," National Regulatory Services, Annual Compliance Conference, April, 1997;. Panelist: "Investment Advisory Issues for Broker-Dealers," SIA Compliance & Legal Division, Southwest Regional Compliance Seminar, November, 1995; "Error Correction Policies and Procedures," National Society of Compliance Professionals Inc., 1996 National Membership Meeting, October, 1996; "IA In-house Compliance Audits," National Society of Compliance Professionals, 1997 NSCP National Membership Meeting, Oct., 1997; "Foreign Investing - Minimizing Emerging Market Clearance, Settlement and Custody Risks," Federal Bar Association & ICI Education Foundation, Mutual Funds and Investment Management Conference, March, 1998; "IA Trading Issues: Allocation, Principal Trades, and More," National Regulatory Services, Inc., NRS Spring Compliance Conference, April, 1998; "IA Trading Issues: Allocation, Principal Trades, Errors and More," National Regulatory Services, Inc., NRS Spring 1999 Compliance Conference, April, 1999; "International Compliance Issues - Voting Non-U.S. Proxies and Protecting Shareholder Rights," ICI Mutual Fund Compliance Conference, June, 1999; "Investment Adviser and Investment Company Advertising," National Regulatory Services, 16th Annual Spring Investment Adviser & Broker-Dealer Compliance Conference, April, 2001; "Trading Issues: IPO Allocations, Principal Trades, Errors and More," and "Soft Dollar Best Practices," National Regulatory Services, Symposium on Investment Adviser Trading Practices, August, 2001; "Hedge Fund Conflicts Advanced," National Society of Compliance Professionals, National Membership Meeting, October, 2001. Author: "What Will This Bring, Managing the Transition," National Regulatory Services, Inc., Preparing for 1997: New Laws, New Opportunities, New Responsibilities for Investment Advisers and Broker-Dealers - The National Securities Markets Improvement Act of 1996, November, 1996; "IA Trading Issues: IPO Allocations, Principal Trades, Errors and More," National Regulatory Services, NRS Spring 2000, April, 2000. *Member:* District of Columbia Bar; The Florida Bar; American Bar Association; Investment Company Institute. ***PRACTICE AREAS:*** Financial Services Law; Investment Management; Securities Regulation; Broker-Dealer Regulation; Private Placement; Investment Partnerships; Mutual Funds; SEC Regulation; Initial Public Offerings; International Securities; Public Offerings; Securities Disclosure; Securities Offerings; Securities Registration; Foreign Investment; Foreign Investment Regulation; Institutional Investment Law; Investment Company Law. ***Email:*** elizabeth.knoblock@dechert.com

PAUL J. MASON, born Brooklyn, New York, 1932; admitted to bar, 1958, Maryland and District of Columbia. *Education:* Brooklyn College (B.A., summa cum laude, 1953); Harvard University (M.A., with distinction, 1954); George Washington University Law School (J.D., 1958). Executive Director, Insurance Marketplace Standards Association; Chief Counsel of Securities; Member, American Council of Life Insurance. Co-Chair, American Bar Association, Subcommittee on Securities Activities of Insurance Companies; Co-Chair, ALI-ABA Conference on Securities Products of Insurance Companies. ***PRACTICE AREAS:*** Financial Services Law; Financial Services Regulation; Investment Banking Law; Investment Company Law; Investment Management; Investment Regulation; Mutual Funds; Financial Institution Regulation; Financial Institutions Law. ***Email:*** paul.mason@dechert.com

RALPH OMAN, born Huntington, New York, 1940; admitted to bar, 1973, District of Columbia; 1974, U.S. District Court, District of Maryland and U.S. Court of Appeals, Fourth Circuit; 1976, U.S. Supreme Court. *Education:* Sorbonne University, Paris, France; Hamilton College (A.B., 1962); Georgetown University (J.D., 1973). President, Giles S. Rich Inn of Court, the Court of Appeals for the Federal Circuit. Executive Editor, Law and Policy in International Business, 1973. Member, Editorial Advisory Board, Fordham Intellectual Property Media & Entertainment Journal. Adjunct Professor, George Washington University Law School. Register of Copyrights of the United States of America, 1985-93. Chief Counsel, U.S. Senate Subcommittee on Patents, Copyrights and Trademarks, 1983-85. Staff Director and Chief Counsel, Subcommittee on Criminal Law, Committee on the Judiciary, U.S. Senate, 1981-83. Legislative Counsel to Senator Charles McC. Mathias (R-Maryland), 1977-80. Counsel to Senator Hugh Scott (R-Pennsylvania), Subcommittee on Patents, Trademarks and Copyrights, Committee on the Judiciary, U.S. Senate, 1975-77. Attorney, Antitrust Division, U.S. Department of Justice, 1974-75. Law Clerk to the Honorable Judge C. Stanley Blair, U.S. District Court, District of Maryland. *Member:* Federal (Past President, Capitol Hill Chapter) and American (Chair, International Copyright Committee) Bar Associations. ***LANGUAGES:*** French. ***PRACTICE AREAS:*** Intellectual Property. ***Email:*** ralph.oman@dechert.com

KIMBERLY DOPKIN RASEVIC, born Baltimore, Maryland, 1966; admitted to bar, 1991, Maryland; 1992, District of Columbia; 1995, Colorado. *Education:* University of Colorado at Boulder (B.A., magna cum laude, 1988); Duke University School of Law (J.D., 1991). Phi Beta Kappa. Assistant Director, Division of Investment Management; Senior Adviser to the Director, Division of Investment Management; Counsel to Commissioner Norman S. Johnson; Senior Counsel, Office of the General Counsel, U.S. Securities and Exchange Commission, 1996-2001. ***PRACTICE AREAS:*** Securities; Financial Services Law; Investment Management. ***Email:*** kimberly.rasevic@dechert.com

ROBERT A. ROBERTSON, born Los Angeles, California, 1960; admitted to bar, 1987, California (Not admitted in District of Columbia). *Education:* Claremont McKenna College (B.A., 1981); Loyola Marymount University (M.B.A., 1983); University of California at Los Angeles Law School (J.D., 1987). Counselor to the Commissioner, Securities and Exchange Commission in Washington, D.C., 1990-97. ***PRACTICE AREAS:*** Securities Law; Litigation; Financial Services Law; Investment Management. ***Email:*** robert.robertson@dechert.com

ALAN ROSENBLAT, born New York, N.Y., 1926; admitted to bar, 1955, New York; 1956, Illinois; 1988, District of Columbia. *Education:* University of Chicago (B.A., with honors, 1951; J.D., 1954). Managing Editor, University of Chicago Law Review, 1953-54. Author: Articles on securities law issues. Assistant Chief Counsel, Division of Investment Management, 1966-68, Chief Counsel, 1968-76, and Assistant General Counsel, 1976-86, Securities and Exchange Commission. ***PRACTICE AREAS:*** Investment Management; Financial Services Law. ***Email:*** alan.rosenblat@dechert.com

R. MICHAEL SMITH, born Manhattan, Kansas, 1948; admitted to bar, 1975, Washington; 1984, District of Columbia; 1990, Virginia; 1991, Maryland. *Education:* Colgate University (B.A., cum laude, 1970); University of Chicago (J.D., 1975); Georgetown University (LL.M., Labor and Employment Law, 1985). Author: "Exceptions to the Employment-At-Will Doctrine," Labor Law Journal, Dec., 1985. Attorney, Division of Enforcement Litigation, 1979-81 and Region 19, 1981-83, National Labor Relations Board. Labor Counsel, Bell Atlantic Corporation, 1983-87. Chair, ABA Employee Rights and Responsibilities Committee Continuing Legal Education Committee; Member, ABA Employee Rights and Responsibilities Committee Management Leadership Council. *Member:* Maryland State (Labor and Employment Law Section) and American (Labor and Employment Law Section) Bar Associations. Fellow, College of Labor and Employment Lawyers. ***PRACTICE AREAS:*** Labor and Employment; Employment Litigation. ***Email:*** michael.smith@dechert.com

RESIDENT ASSOCIATES

OLIVIA P. ADLER, born Moscow, Idaho, 1941; admitted to bar, 1968, District of Columbia. *Education:* Radcliffe College (A.B., magna cum laude, 1962); Harvard University (LL.B., 1967). ***PRACTICE AREAS:*** Investment Management; Financial Services Law. ***Email:*** olivia.adler@dechert.com

KAREN ASPINALL, born New York, N.Y., 1974; admitted to bar, 2001, New York (Not admitted in District of Columbia). *Education:* American University (B.A., cum laude, 1995; J.D., cum laude, 2000). ***PRACTICE AREAS:*** Investment Management; Financial Services Law. ***Email:*** karen.aspinall@dechert.com

VINCENT J. BADOLATO, born Washington, D.C., 1967; admitted to bar, 1993, Virginia; 1994, Maryland; 1996, District of Columbia. *Education:* Brown University (B.A., 1989); University of California at Los Angeles (J.D., 1993). ***PRACTICE AREAS:*** Investment Management; Financial Services Law. ***Email:*** vincent.badolato@dechert.com

DANIELE ALLISON BAKER, born Henderson, Kentucky, 1975; admitted to bar, 2001, Virginia (Not admitted in District of Columbia). *Education:* Transylvania University (B.A., Political Science, cum laude, 1998); Georgetown University Law Center (J.D., magna cum laude, 2001). Order of the Coif. Editor-in-Chief, The Georgetown Journal of Gender and the Law. ***PRACTICE AREAS:*** Financial Services Law; Investment Management; Securities Litigation; Antitrust and Trade Regulation. ***Email:*** allison.baker@dechert.com

CYNTHIA D. BAUGHMAN, born Washington, D.C., 1968; admitted to bar, 1997, Pennsylvania and New Jersey; 1999, District of Columbia. *Education:* University of Maryland (B.S., 1993); Dickinson School of Law, Pennsylvania State University (J.D., 1997). ***PRACTICE AREAS:*** Financial Services Law; Investment Management. ***Email:*** cynthia.baughman@dechert.com

ERIK BERTIN, born Washington, D.C., 1971; admitted to bar, 1997, California and District of Columbia. *Education:* Johns Hopkins University (B.A., 1993); University of Pennsylvania (J.D., 1996). ***PRACTICE AREAS:*** Intellectual Property. ***Email:*** erik.bertin@dechert.com

STEPHEN H. BIER, born Brooklyn, New York, 1963; admitted to bar, 1990, New Jersey; 1992, New York; 2000, District of Columbia. *Education:* Rutgers University (B.A., magna cum laude, 1985); Harvard University (J.D., cum laude, 1989). Executive Editor, Harvard Environmental Law Review, 1988-89. ***PRACTICE AREAS:*** Financial Services Law; Investment Management. ***Email:*** stephen.bier@dechert.com

(This Listing Continued)

THOMAS C. BOGLE, born Bala Cynwyd, Pennsylvania, 1975; (admission pending). *Education:* George Washington University (B.A., cum laude, 1998); Tulane University Law School (J.D., magna cum laude, 2001). Order of the Coif. Senior Articles Editor, Tulane Law Review. ***PRACTICE AREAS:*** Investment Management; Financial Services Law. ***Email:*** thomas.bogle@dechert.com

JULIEN M. BOURGEOIS, born Bethune, France, 1976; admitted to bar, 2001, Maryland (Not admitted in District of Columbia). *Education:* University of Paris X, Nanterre(Bi-deug, License, Maitrise, with honors, 1998); University of Richmond, T.C. Williams School of Law (J.D., 2000). ***LANGUAGES:*** French. ***PRACTICE AREAS:*** Investment Management; Financial Services Law. ***Email:*** julien.bourgeois@dechert.com

TERRI L. BOWMAN, born Madison Heights, Michigan, 1968; admitted to bar, 1993, Virginia; 1996, District of Columbia. *Education:* Michigan State University (B.A., with honors, 1990); George Washington University (J.D., 1993). Managing Editor, George Washington Journal of International Law and Economics. Adjunct Professor of Legal Research and Writing, George Washington University, 1995-96. Law Clerk to the Honorable Mary Ellen Abrecht, District of Columbia Superior Court, 1993-95. Law Clerk to the Honorable Warren R. King, District of Columbia Court of Appeals, 1995-96. *Member:* The District of Columbia Bar; Virginia State Bar. ***PRACTICE AREAS:*** Antitrust and Trade Regulation. ***Email:*** terri.bowman@dechert.com

JANET A. BROECKEL, born Spokane, Washington; admitted to bar, 1990, Connecticut; 1991, New York; 1992, U.S. District Court, Southern District of New York; 1993, U.S. District Court, Eastern District of New York; 1998, District of Columbia; 1999, U.S. Court of Appeals, Second Circuit. *Education:* University of Washington (B.A., cum laude, 1987); American University (J.D., 1990). Senior Counsel, U.S. Securities and Exchange Commission, 1990-94. *Member:* District of Columbia Bar; New York State Bar Association. ***PRACTICE AREAS:*** SEC Enforcement; Securities Litigation; Securities Regulation; Broker-Dealer Regulation; Government Investigations; Civil Fraud; Criminal Law. ***Email:*** janet.broeckel@dechert.com

DILIA M. CABALLERO, born 1971; admitted to bar, 1995, Massachusetts; 1998, District of Columbia. *Education:* Harvard and Radcliffe College (B.A., cum laude, 1992); Georgetown University Law Center (J.D., 1995). Member, Law and Policy in International Business. ***LANGUAGES:*** Spanish. ***PRACTICE AREAS:*** Financial Services Law; Investment Management. ***Email:*** dilia.caballero@dechert.com

CHRISTOPHER DAVID CHRISTIAN, born Springfield, Massachusetts, 1972; admitted to bar, 1999, Massachusetts and District of Columbia. *Education:* Brandeis University (B.A., 1995); Catholic University of America (J.D., cum laude, 1998). ***PRACTICE AREAS:*** Financial Services Law; Investment Management. ***Email:*** christopher.christian@dechert.com

ERIN DUFFY CONATON, born Washington, D.C., 1973; admitted to bar, 2000, Maryland; 2001, District of Columbia. *Education:* Georgetown University (B.A., 1995); Columbus School of Law of The Catholic University of America (J.D., cum laude, 1999). ***PRACTICE AREAS:*** Investment Management; Financial Services Law. ***Email:*** erin.duffy@dechert.com

JENNIFER E. COON, born Albany, New York, 1973; admitted to bar, 2001, New York and Massachusetts (Not admitted in District of Columbia). *Education:* Carleton College (1995); Syracuse University College of Law (J.D., magna cum laude, 2000). Order of the Coif. Editor-in-Chief, The Labor Lawyer ABA Journal. Associate Notes and Comments Editor, Syracuse Law Review. *Member:* New York State Bar Association. ***PRACTICE AREAS:*** Financial Services Law; Investment Management. ***Email:*** jennifer.coon@dechert.com

ETHAN D. COREY, born Massachusetts, 1963; admitted to bar, 1988, Massachusetts; 1991, District of Columbia. *Education:* McGill University (B.A., 1985); Boston University School of Law (J.D., magna cum laude, 1988). ***PRACTICE AREAS:*** Investment Management; Financial Services Law. ***Email:*** ethan.corey@dechert.com

CATHERINE A. COURTNEY, born San Andres Island, Columbia, 1968; admitted to bar, 2001, Maryland (Not admitted in District of Columbia). *Education:* University of Maryland, College Park (B.A., Economics and French Language and Literature, 1990); Columbus School of Law of The Catholic University of America (J.D., 2001). ***LANGUAGES:*** French, Italian and Spanish. ***PRACTICE AREAS:*** Investment Management; Financial Services Law. ***Email:*** catherine.courtney@dechert.com

RENA I. CURTIS, born Fairfax, Virginia, 1971; admitted to bar, 1999, Maryland and District of Columbia. *Education:* University of Maryland (B.A., 1994); Catholic University of America (J.D., cum laude, 1999). ***PRACTICE AREAS:*** Commercial Litigation; SEC Enforcement; Antitrust. ***Email:*** rena.curtis@dechert.com

JAMES GREGORY DYER, born Santa Monica, California, 1974; admitted to bar, 2001, California (Not admitted in District of Columbia). *Education:* Brigham Young University (B.S., Finance, magna cum laude, 1998; J.D., magna cum laude, 2001). Order of Barristers. Chair, Moot Court Board of Advocates. ***LANGUAGES:*** Spanish. ***PRACTICE AREAS:*** Civil Litigation; Complex Litigation; Defense Litigation; Trial Practice; Bank Securities; NASD Arbitration; Securities Litigation. ***Email:*** gregory.dyer@dechert.com

BRYAN ISAAC EDER, born Detroit, Michigan, 1975; admitted to bar, 2001, Maryland (Not admitted in District of Columbia). *Education:* Michigan State University (B.A., Journalism, Political Economy, 1998); University of Chicago Law School (J.D., 2001). Phi Beta Kappa. ***PRACTICE AREAS:*** Investment Management; Financial Services Law. ***Email:*** bryan.eder@dechert.com

TAYLOR VINSON EDWARDS, born Baltimore, Maryland, 1967; admitted to bar, 2000, Maryland; 2001, New Jersey (Not admitted in District of Columbia). *Education:* Morgan State University (B.S., 1992); Case Western Reserve University (J.D., 2000; M.B.A., 2000). ***PRACTICE AREAS:*** Financial Services Law; Investment Management; Corporate Law. ***Email:*** alvin.edwards@dechert.com

JENNIFER O. EPSTEIN, born Providence, Rhode Island, 1970; admitted to bar, 1997, New York; 1999, District of Columbia. *Education:* University of Iowa (B.B.A., with distinction, 1992); Columbia University (J.D., 1996). Harlan Fiske Stone Scholar. Editor-in-Chief, Columbia Business Law Review. *Member:* The District of Columbia Bar; New York State and American Bar Associations. ***PRACTICE AREAS:*** Investment Management; Financial Services Law; Securities Regulation. ***Email:*** jennifer.epstein@dechert.com

JEFFREY A. FOOR, born Miami, Florida, 1973; admitted to bar, 2001, Florida (Not admitted in District of Columbia). *Education:* University of Pennsylvania (B.A., 1995); George Washington University Law School (J.D., 2001). Recipient, Jacob Burns Award. Member, Environmental Lawyer. ***PRACTICE AREAS:*** Investment Management; Financial Services Law. ***Email:*** jeffrey.foor@dechert.com

JOHN K. FORST, born Summit, New Jersey, 1960; admitted to bar, 1991, Florida (Not admitted in District of Columbia). *Education:* The George Washington University (B.B.A., 1984); Capital University Law School (J.D., 1991); Georgetown University Law Center (LL.M., 1997). *Member:* American Bar Association. ***PRACTICE AREAS:*** Banking Regulation; Securities Regulation; Broker-Dealer Regulation; Federal Regulatory Law; Trust Administration. ***Email:*** john.forst@dechert.com

BRENDAN C. FOX, born Hartford, Connecticut, 1969; admitted to bar, 1993, Virginia; 1994, District of Columbia. *Education:* State University of New York at Albany (B.A., magna cum laude, 1990); National Law Center, George Washington University (J.D., with honors, 1993). Member, George Washington Law Review, 1991-93. ***PRACTICE AREAS:*** Financial Services Law; Investment Management. ***Email:*** brendan.fox@dechert.com

WENDY FOX, born New York, N.Y., 1951; admitted to bar, 1977, New York, U.S. District Court, Southern and Eastern Districts of New York; 1980, District of Columbia. *Education:* Williams College (B.A., 1973); Columbia University School of Law (J.D., 1976). ***PRACTICE AREAS:*** Investment Management; Financial Services Law; Securities; Corporate Law. ***Email:*** wendy.fox@dechert.com

ERIC B. GARVEY, born Milwaukee, Wisconsin, 1973; admitted to bar, 2001, Maryland (Not admitted in District of Columbia). *Education:* University of Maryland (B.A., 1995); Catholic University of America (J.D., cum laude, 2001). Associate Editor, Catholic University Law Review, 2000-01. ***PRACTICE AREAS:*** Investment Management; Financial Services Law. ***Email:*** eric.garvey@dechert.com

REGINA NICOLE GRIFFIN, born Jacksonville, Texas; (admission pending). *Education:* University of Texas at Austin (B.B.A., 1991); Marymount University (M.B.A., 1996); Columbus School of Law of The Catholic University of America (J.D., 2001). Staff Member, Catholic University Law Review. ***PRACTICE AREAS:*** Investment Management; Financial Services Law. ***Email:*** nicole.griffin@dechert.com

R. WILLIAM HAWKINS, born 1974; admitted to bar, 2001, Maryland (Not admitted in District of Columbia). *Education:* Vanderbilt University (B.A., 1996); George Washington University (J.D., 2000). ***PRACTICE AREAS:*** Financial Services Law; Investment Management. ***Email:*** william.hawkins@dechert.com

NANDITA HOGAN, born Philadelphia, Pennsylvania, 1971; admitted to bar, 1996, Pennsylvania and New Jersey (Not admitted in District of Columbia). *Education:* Franklin & Marshall College (B.A., 1993); Temple University (J.D., 1996). ***PRACTICE AREAS:*** Investment Management; Financial Services Law. ***Email:*** nandita.hogan@dechert.com

RICHARD R. HOLLEY, III, born South Kingstown, Rhode Island, 1975; admitted to bar, 2001, North Carolina (Not admitted in District of Columbia). *Education:* Bates College (B.A., Political Science, magna cum laude, 1997); University of North Carolina at Chapel Hill (J.D., with honors, 2001). Phi Beta Kappa. Editor-in-Chief, North Carolina Banking Institute Journal. ***PRACTICE AREAS:*** Investment Management; Financial Services Law. ***Email:*** richard.holley@dechert.com

(This Listing Continued)

DECHERT, Washington—Continued

HUGH HOLLMAN, born Nairobi, Kenya, 1974; admitted to bar, 1999, Cape Town, South Africa (Not admitted in the United States). *Education:* University of Cape Town (B.B.S., 1995; LL.B., 1999); Duke University (LL.M., 2000). ***PRACTICE AREAS:*** Financial Services Law; Investment Management. ***Email:*** hugh.hollman@dechert.com

JESSE KANACH, admitted to bar, 1999, Virginia; 2000, District of Columbia. *Education:* University of Virginia (B.A., 1996); Georgetown University (J.D., 1999). ***PRACTICE AREAS:*** Financial Services Law; Investment Management. ***Email:*** jesse.kanach@dechert.com

SANJAY LAMBA, born Arlington, Virginia, 1972; admitted to bar, 1997, Virginia (Not admitted in District of Columbia). *Education:* George Mason University (B.S., Finance, 1994); Boston University School of Law (J.D., 1997). ***PRACTICE AREAS:*** Financial Services Law; Investment Management. ***Email:*** sanjay.lamba@dechert.com

ROBERT S. LAMONT, JR., born Alexandria, Virginia, 1973; admitted to bar, 1998, Florida; 1999, District of Columbia. *Education:* University of Florida (B.S., 1995); Florida State University (J.D., 1998); Georgetown University (LL.M., 1999). ***PRACTICE AREAS:*** Financial Services Law; Investment Management. ***Email:*** robert.lamont@dechert.com

DENNIS J. LAWSON, born Tacoma Park, Maryland, 1966; admitted to bar, 1995, Maryland; 1996, District of Columbia. *Education:* Johns Hopkins University (B.A., 1988); George Washington University (B.B.A., summa cum laude, 1992); University of Maryland Law School (J.D., with honors, 1995). Order of the Coif. ***PRACTICE AREAS:*** Complex Litigation; Litigation; Complex Commercial Litigation. ***Email:*** dennis.lawson@dechert.com

CAROLYN S. LEE, born Reading, Pennsylvania, 1974; admitted to bar, 2000, Maryland; 2001, California and District of Columbia. *Education:* University of California at Berkeley (B.A., 1996); George Washington University (J.D., with honors, 2000). ***PRACTICE AREAS:*** Financial Services Law; Investment Management. ***Email:*** carolyn.lee@dechert.com

RANDY G. LEGG, born Offenbach, Germany, 1965; admitted to bar, 1998, Virginia; 1999, District of Columbia. *Education:* University of Maryland (B.A., 1988); Catholic University of America (J.D., 1998). ***PRACTICE AREAS:*** Financial Services Law; Investment Management. ***Email:*** randy.legg@dechert.com

J. CHRISTOPHE LEITZ, born Paris, France, 1971; admitted to bar, 2000, New York; 2001, District of Columbia. *Education:* University of California at Berkeley (B.A., with honors, 1993); Boston University School of Law (J.D., 1998); Georgetown University (LL.M., Securities Regulation, 1999). ***LANGUAGES:*** French. ***PRACTICE AREAS:*** Financial Services Law; Investment Management; Securities Regulation. ***Email:*** christophe.leitz@dechert.com

BENNETT A. MACDOUGALL, born Bellingham, Washington, 1971; admitted to bar, 1998, Washington; 2000, District of Columbia. *Education:* Evergreen State College (B.A., 1994); Drake University Law School (J.D., 1997); New York University School of Law (LL.M., 1998). ***PRACTICE AREAS:*** Financial Services Law; Investment Management. ***Email:*** bennett.macdougall@dechert.com

MAUREEN MAGNER, born Medford, Massachusetts, 1973; admitted to bar, 2001, New York and Massachusetts (Not admitted in District of Columbia). *Education:* Clark University (B.A., 1995; M.B.A., 1996); Columbus School of Law of The Catholic University of America (J.D., 2001). ***PRACTICE AREAS:*** Investment Management; Financial Services Law. ***Email:*** maureen.magner@dechert.com

ANDREA R. MANGO, born Buffalo, New York, 1972; admitted to bar, 1999, Maryland and Massachusetts (Not admitted in District of Columbia). *Education:* Miami University, Oxford, Ohio (B.A., Political Science, 1995); Columbus School of Law of The Catholic University of America (J.D., 1998). ***PRACTICE AREAS:*** Securities Litigation. ***Email:*** andrea.mango@dechert.com

REBECCA B. MARTIN, born 1972; admitted to bar, 2000, Maryland; 2001, District of Columbia. *Education:* Bryn Mawr College (B.A., 1994); Georgetown University (J.D., 2000). ***PRACTICE AREAS:*** Financial Services Law; Investment Management. ***Email:*** rebecca.martin@dechert.com

BRIAN SCOTT MASTERSON, born Orange, Texas, 1973; admitted to bar, 2001, Virginia (Not admitted in District of Columbia). *Education:* Lipscomb University (B.S., summa cum laude, 1995); University of North Carolina (J.D., with honors, 2001). Publication Editor, North Carolina Law Review. ***PRACTICE AREAS:*** Investment Management; Financial Services Law. ***Email:*** brian.masterson@dechert.com

LISA MCCREA, born Tampa, Florida, 1963; admitted to bar, 1994, California; 1996, District of Columbia. *Education:* University of California at Berkeley (B.A., magna cum laude, 1986); Washington & Lee University School of Law (J.D., 1992). ***PRACTICE AREAS:*** Securities Regulation; SEC Enforcement. ***Email:*** lisa.mccrea@dechert.com

(This Listing Continued)

MICHAEL J. MCDONOUGH, born Portsmouth, Rhode Island, 1965; admitted to bar, 1997, Maryland; 1998, District of Columbia. *Education:* Bridgewater College (B.A., cum laude, 1987); University of Virginia (M.A., 1990); George Washington University (J.D., 1997). ***PRACTICE AREAS:*** Financial Services Law; Investment Management. ***Email:*** michael.mcdonough@dechert.com

KATHRYN A. MCELROY, born 1968; admitted to bar, 1995, Massachusetts; 2000, District of Columbia. *Education:* Connecticut College (B.A., 1990); Northeastern University (J.D., 1995). *Member:* Massachusetts and American Bar Associations; Women's Bar Association. ***PRACTICE AREAS:*** Financial Services Law; Investment Management. ***Email:*** kathryn.mcelroy@dechert.com

CAROLYN M. MCPHILLIPS, admitted to bar, 2000, Virginia (Not admitted in District of Columbia). *Education:* University of North Carolina at Chapel Hill (B.S., 1996; J.D., 2000). ***PRACTICE AREAS:*** Financial Services Law; Investment Management. ***Email:*** carolyn.mcphillips@dechert.com

CHRISTIAN NATIELLO, born New York, N.Y., 1973; admitted to bar, 2000, Maryland; 2001, District of Columbia. *Education:* Bucknell University (B.A., 1995); Case Western Reserve University (J.D., 2000). ***PRACTICE AREAS:*** Litigation; Products Liability. ***Email:*** christian.natiello@dechert.com

MARIAM A. NAWABI, born 1973; admitted to bar, 1999, Virginia; 2000, District of Columbia. *Education:* George Mason University (B.A., 1995); Georgetown University (J.D., 1999). ***PRACTICE AREAS:*** Litigation. ***Email:*** mariam.nawabi@dechert.com

LAURA A. NOVACK, born Englewood, New Jersey, 1960; admitted to bar, 1986, New York; 2000, District of Columbia. *Education:* Rutgers University (B.A., with high honors, 1982); New York University (J.D., 1985). Phi Beta Kappa. Note and Comment Editor, The Journal of International Law and Politics, 1984-85. ***PRACTICE AREAS:*** Financial Services Law; Investment Management. ***Email:*** laura.novack@dechert.com

MICHAEL D. PAPPAS, born Washington, D.C., 1970; admitted to bar, 1995, Maryland; 1998, District of Columbia. *Education:* Georgetown University (B.A., 1992); University of Maryland School of Law (J.D., 1995). ***PRACTICE AREAS:*** Financial Services Law; Investment Management. ***Email:*** michael.pappas@dechert.com

REZA PISHVA, admitted to bar, 2001, New York (Not admitted in District of Columbia). *Education:* Northwestern University (B.A., 1997); Kogod School of Business (M.B.A., 2000); Washington College of Law of American University (J.D., 2000). ***PRACTICE AREAS:*** Financial Services Law; Investment Management. ***Email:*** reza.pishva@dechert.com

MARGARET RILEY, admitted to bar, 2000, Colorado; 2001, District of Columbia. *Education:* State University of New York College at Cortland (B.A., 1974); Loyola Law School (J.D., 1999). ***PRACTICE AREAS:*** Financial Services Law; Investment Management. ***Email:*** margaret.riley@dechert.com

MICHELLE C. ROBERTS, born 1969; admitted to bar, 2001, New York and District of Columbia. *Education:* Swarthmore College (B.A., 1991); Princeton University (M.A., 1994); University of Virginia (J.D., 2000). ***PRACTICE AREAS:*** Financial Services Law; Investment Management. ***Email:*** michelle.roberts@dechert.com

ROLAND ST. PAUL, born Grenada, 1962; admitted to bar, 1993, U.S. Virgin Islands; 2000, District of Columbia. *Education:* University of West Indies (B.Sc., with honors, 1984); Howard University (M.B.A., 1986); University of Virginia School of Law (J.D., 1992). ***PRACTICE AREAS:*** Securities; Corporate Law; Financial Services Law; Investment Management. ***Email:*** roland.stpaul@dechert.com

JOHN I. SAKHLEH, born Rockville, Maryland, 1973; admitted to bar, 1999, Maryland; 2000, District of Columbia. *Education:* University of Maryland (B.S., Accounting, magna cum laude, 1995); George Washington University (J.D., with honors, 1999). Certified Public Accountant, 1995. ***PRACTICE AREAS:*** Financial Services Law; Investment Management; Securities Regulation. ***Email:*** john.sakhleh@dechert.com

CAROLINE SCHAEFER, admitted to bar, 1997, California; 1998, District of Columbia. *Education:* Smith College (B.A., 1992); Washington College of Law of American University (J.D., 1996). ***LANGUAGES:*** Russian. ***PRACTICE AREAS:*** Securities; Financial Services Law; Investment Management; Corporate Law. ***Email:*** caroline.schaefer@dechert.com

PAUL F. SCHLICHTING, (admission pending). *Education:* Pace University (B.A., 1984); Fordham University (M.B.A., 1993); University of Pennsylvania (J.D., 2001). ***PRACTICE AREAS:*** Financial Services Law; Investment Management.

ADAM MATTHEW SCHOEBERLEIN, born Highland Park, Illinois, 1972; admitted to bar, 2001, Virginia (Not admitted in District of Columbia). *Education:* University of Virginia (B.A., 1996); Georgetown University Law Center (J.D., 2001). Business Editor, American Criminal Law Review. ***PRACTICE AREAS:*** Securities Litigation; SEC Enforcement. ***Email:*** adam.schoeberlein@dechert.com

(This Listing Continued)

MICHAEL LAUREN SHERMAN, born Brookville, Maryland, 1974; admitted to bar, 2001, Maryland (Not admitted in District of Columbia). *Education:* American University (B.A., Literature, cum laude, 1998); Vanderbilt University Law School (J.D., 2001). Professional Authorities Editor, Vanderbilt Journal of Transnational Law. ***PRACTICE AREAS:*** Investment Management; Financial Services Law. ***Email:*** michael.sherman@dechert.com

CHRISTOPHER SMITH, born Rice Lake, Wisconsin, 1976; admitted to bar, 2001, Virginia (Not admitted in District of Columbia). *Education:* Harvard University (A.B., Government and Economics, 1998); Georgetown University Law Center (J.D., 2001). ***PRACTICE AREAS:*** Investment Management; Financial Services Law. ***Email:*** christopher.smith@dechert.com

JANENE M. SMITH, born Washington, D.C., 1965; admitted to bar, 1996, Maryland; 1997, District of Columbia and U.S. Court of Appeals, Seventh Circuit; 1998, U.S. Court of Appeals, Ninth and Eleventh Circuits. *Education:* University of Pennsylvania - The Wharton School (B.S., 1987); Widener University School of Law (J.D., 1995). ***PRACTICE AREAS:*** Financial Services Law; Investment Management. ***Email:*** janene.smith@dechert.com

ROBERT J. SMITH, born Gorizia, Italy, 1952; admitted to bar, 1992, Maryland (Not admitted in District of Columbia). *Education:* Loyola University (B.A., 1974); Villanova University (M.A., 1980); University of Maryland (J.D., 1992). *Member:* Maryland State Bar Association, Inc.; American Bar Association. ***PRACTICE AREAS:*** Securities; Litigation; Bank Broker/Dealer. ***Email:*** robert.smith@dechert.com

CRISTINA M. SORGI, born 1976; admitted to bar, 1998, Caracas, Venezuela (Not admitted in the United States). *Education:* Catholic University Andres Bello; Georgetown University (LL.M., 2000). ***PRACTICE AREAS:*** Financial Services Law; Investment Management. ***Email:*** cristina.sorgi@dechert.com

VICTORIA M. SZYBILLO, born Plainview, New York, 1976; admitted to bar, 2001, Maryland and New Jersey (Not admitted in District of Columbia). *Education:* George Washington University (B.B.A., 1998); Columbus School of Law of The Catholic University of America (J.D., 2001). ***LANGUAGES:*** French and Spanish. ***PRACTICE AREAS:*** Investment Management; Financial Services Law. ***Email:*** victoria.szybillo@dechert.com

PETROS L. TSIRIGOTIS, born Boston, Massachusetts, 1968; admitted to bar, 1998, Maryland and District of Columbia. *Education:* Boston University (B.A., 1990); Columbus School of Law of The Catholic University of America (J.D., 1997). ***PRACTICE AREAS:*** Securities Regulation; Financial Services Law; Investment Management. ***Email:*** peter.tsirigotis@dechert.com

CLIFFORD J. TURBITT, admitted to bar, 1999, New York; 2000, District of Columbia. *Education:* Wharton School of Business, University of Pennsylvania (B.S., 1984); Fordham University School of Law (J.D., 1998). ***PRACTICE AREAS:*** Investment Management; Financial Services Law. ***Email:*** clifford.turbitt@dechert.com

ERIN GIBSON WAGNER, born Dayton, Ohio, 1974; admitted to bar, 2000, Michigan; 2001, District of Columbia. *Education:* Miami University (B.A., cum laude, 1996); Case Western University School of Law (J.D., 1999). Associate, Case Western Reserve University School of Law Journal of International Law. Co-Editor, Canada-U.S. Law Journal. ***PRACTICE AREAS:*** Financial Services Law; Investment Management. ***Email:*** erin.wagner@dechert.com

RICHARD WEI, born New York, New York, 1970; admitted to bar, 1998, Maryland; 1999, District of Columbia and U.S. District Court for the District of Columbia. *Education:* University of Maryland (B.S., 1992); University of North Carolina (J.D., 1998). ***PRACTICE AREAS:*** Securities Litigation. ***Email:*** richard.wei@dechert.com

TRAYNE S. WHEELER, admitted to bar, 2001, Massachusetts and District of Columbia. *Education:* University of Chicago (A.B., 1995); Boston University (J.D., 2000). ***PRACTICE AREAS:*** Financial Services Law; Investment Management. ***Email:*** trayne.wheeler@dechert.com

YUEYAO (GEORGE) ZHAO, born Tengzhou City, Shandong Province, People's Republic of China, 1964; admitted to bar, 1999, Maryland; 2000, New York and District of Columbia. *Education:* Shandong Teacher's University, China (B.A., 1985); Shandong University, China (M.A., 1988); Florida International University (M.A., 1993; Ph.D., 1997); State University of New York Law School (J.D., 1999). ***PRACTICE AREAS:*** Financial Services Law; Investment Management; Securities; Corporate Law; Contracts; International Business Law; Broker-Dealer Regulation; Securities Regulation; Intellectual Property. ***Email:*** george.zhao@dechert.com

JEREMY ZUBA, born Chicago, Illinois, 1973; (admission pending). *Education:* University of Illinois, Urbana-Champaign (B.A., Asian Studies, 1996); American University (M.A., International Affairs, 2001; J.D., 2001). ***LANGUAGES:*** Japanese. ***PRACTICE AREAS:*** Investment Management; Financial Services Law. ***Email:*** jeremy.zuba@dechert.com

OF COUNSEL

ARTHUR W. LEIBOLD JR., born Ottawa, Illinois, 1931; admitted to bar, 1957, Pennsylvania; 1972, District of Columbia. *Education:* Haverford College

(This Listing Continued)

(A.B., 1953); University of Pennsylvania (J.D., cum laude, 1956). Phi Beta Kappa; Order of the Coif. Member, University of Pennsylvania Law Review, 1954-56. General Counsel, Federal Home Loan Bank Board and Federal Savings and Loan Insurance Corporation, 1969-72. General Counsel, Federal Home Loan Mortgage Corporation, 1970-1972. Member, Administrative Conference of the United States, 1969-72. *Member:* The District of Columbia Bar; Philadelphia, Federal (Member, National Council, 1971-80), American (Treasurer, 1979-83; Member, House of Delegates, 1967-69; 1979-88) and International (Chairman, 1983-87, Committee U, Section of Business Law) Bar Associations. ***PRACTICE AREAS:*** Banking Law; Savings and Loan Institutions Law. ***Email:*** arthur.leibold@dechert.com

(Partners of the Firm, Counsel, Of Counsel and Associates in Harrisburg, Pennsylvania; New York, New York; Washington, D.C.; Boston, Massachusetts; Newport Beach, California; Princeton, New Jersey; Hartford, Connecticut; London, England; Brussels, Belgium; Paris, France and Luxembourg are listed in the Biographical Section respectively.)

DECKELBAUM OGENS & RAFTERY

CHARTERED

WASHINGTON, D.C.

(See Bethesda, Maryland)

Bankruptcy, Business Reorganization, Commercial Transactions and Litigation, Domestic Relations and Family Law, Contracts, Real Estate, Leasing, Landlord Tenant, Commercial and Consumer Collections, Corporate, Negligence, Medical Malpractice, Employment Law, General Civil and Trial Practice.

JANET K. DeCOSTA, P.C.

Established in 1993

601 THIRTEENTH STREET, N.W.
SUITE 500 NORTH
WASHINGTON, D.C. 20005
Telephone: 202-638-3344
Fax: 202-824-8126
Email: JanetKDC@aol.com
URL: http://www.lawyers.com/decostalaw

Securities Litigation, Securities Fraud, NASD Arbitration and Mediation, Class Action, Complex and Multijurisdictional Litigation, Commercial Litigation, Employment Law, Civil Trial and Appellate Practice.

FIRM PROFILE: Janet K. DeCosta has served as lead and defense counsel in securities fraud cases, SEC enforcement actions involving inside trading, market manipulation, accounting fraud, breach of contract and breach of fiduciary cases. Ms. DeCosta has led trial teams in complex SEC injunctive enforcement actions and complex multi-defendant criminal cases. Clients to the firms's national practice include individuals, institutional investors, corporations and broker/dealers. Ms. DeCosta has served as lead counsel in and negotiated to settlement employment discrimination actions.

JANET K. DeCOSTA, born Boston, Massachusetts, September 13, 1947; admitted to bar, 1979, Massachusetts, District of Columbia, U.S. District Court, District of Columbia, U.S. District Court, Commonwealth of Massachusetts Supreme Judicial Court and U.S. Court of Federal Claims. *Education:* University of Massachusetts (B.A., 1969); DePaul University (J.D., 1979). Notes and Comment Editor, DePaul University Law Review, 1978-1979. Author: *SEC Enforcement Developments Involving Financial Disclosure,* Texas Society of Certified Public Accountants, Securities Registration Conference, August 22, 1986. Speaker, NASD Arbitrator Skills Training Program, Chicago, Illinois, Spring, 1996. U.S. Department of Justice, Criminal Division, Honors Program, 1979-1984, 1985. Special Assistant U.S. Attorney, U.S. Department of Justice, Office of the U.S. Attorney, Eastern District of Virginia, 1984-1985. Assistant Chief Trial Counsel, Division of Enforcement, U.S. Securities and Exchange Commission, 1985-1987. National Association of Attorneys General, 1989-1992; General Counsel, State Bankruptcy Committee, 1990-1992. *Member:* District of Columbia Bar (Member, Sections on: Securities and Litigation); American Bar Association (Member, Sections on: Litigation and Alternative Dispute Resolution). ***PRACTICE AREAS:*** Securities; Arbitration; Litigation; Employment Law. ***Email:*** JanetKDC@aol.com

DEKIEFFER & HORGAN

SUITE 800
729 FIFTEENTH STREET, N.W.
WASHINGTON, D.C. 20005
Telephone: 202-783-6900; 800-787-1600
Facsimile: 202-783-6909
Email: khorgan@dhlaw.com
URL: http://www.dhlaw.com

Saarbrucken, Germany Office: Beethovenstrasse 13, D-66111. Telephone: 011 49 681379 3220. Fax: 011 496 681390 7219.

Monterey, Nuevo León, Mexico Office: Rio Mississippi 51, San Pedro, Garza Garcia, 66220. Telephone: 011-52-8-378-1990. Fax: 011-52-8-378-1991.

International Trade Law, Customs Law, Antidumping Law, Import and Export Regulation, International Commercial Transactions.

FIRM PROFILE: As counsel to numerous foreign and domestic companies involved in international trade, we advise and represent clients in matters involving international commercial transactions and U.S. government regulation of international business. By ensuring adherence to the law and promoting effective interaction with the responsible government agencies, we help clients compete successfully in the international business arena. Areas of frequent concern to our clients include the imposition of U.S. customs duties or quotas on imported merchandise, the application of U.S. export controls to shipments abroad, U.S. regulation of "unfair" foreign trade practices, such as dumping and infringement of trademarks and copyrights, embargoes on trade with hostile countries, and U.S. laws regulating the activities of U.S. companies abroad, such as the Foreign Corrupt Practices Act and U.S. anti-boycott laws.

MEMBERS OF FIRM

DONALD E. DEKIEFFER, born Newport, Rhode Island, November 8, 1945; admitted to bar, 1971, District of Columbia; 1982, U.S. Supreme Court. *Education:* University of Colorado (B.A., 1968); Georgetown University (J.D., 1971). Member, U.S.-Canada Dispute Resolution Panel, 1989—. General Counsel to the Office of the United States Trade Representative, 1981-1983. Professional Staff, U.S. Senate Republican Policy Committee, 1969-1971. ***PRACTICE AREAS:*** International Trade and Regulation; Export and Customs Law; Foreign Asset Control; Unfair Trade; Antidumping; Countervailing Duties. ***Email:*** ddekieffer@dhlaw.com

J. KEVIN HORGAN, born Pittsburgh, Pennsylvania, September 27, 1952; admitted to bar, 1982, New York and Pennsylvania; 1983, U.S. Court of International Trade and U.S. Claims Court; 1988, Illinois and U.S. Court of Appeals for the Federal Circuit; 1991, District of Columbia. *Education:* University of Pittsburgh (B.A., 1974); New York Law School (J.D., 1981). Trial Attorney, Commercial Litigation Branch, Civil Division, U.S. Department of Justice, 1983-1987. Law Clerk to Chief Judge Edward D. Re, United States Court of International Trade, 1981-1983. *Member:* District of Columbia Bar. ***PRACTICE AREAS:*** International Trade and Regulation; Export and Customs Law; Unfair Trade Practices; Antidumping; Countervailing Duties. ***Email:*** khorgan@dhlaw.com

OF COUNSEL

JOHN J. KENKEL, born 1950; admitted to bar, 1980, District of Columbia; U.S. Court of Appeals for the Federal Circuit; U.S. District Court for the District of Columbia; U.S. Court of International Trade. *Education:* Georgetown University (B.A., 1972); The Catholic University of America (M.A., 1973); George Mason University (J.D., 1977). *Member:* District of Columbia Bar; American Bar Association. ***LANGUAGES:*** French. ***PRACTICE AREAS:*** International Trade; International Trade Regulation. ***Email:*** jkenkel@dhlaw.com

MARC E. MONTALBINE, born Norfolk, Virginia, June 6, 1963; admitted to bar, 1986, Virginia; U.S. Supreme Court; U.S. Court of Appeals, Fourth and Federal Circuits; U.S. Court of International Trade; U.S. District Court, Eastern District of Virginia; U.S. Bankruptcy Court, Eastern District of Virginia; U.S. Court of Federal Claims (Not admitted in District of Columbia). *Education:* Old Dominion University (B.S., 1983); University of Virginia (J.D., 1986); Universität des Saarlandes, Europa-Institut. Certified Public Accountant, Virginia. Trial Attorney, Commercial Litigation Branch, Civil Division, U.S. Department of Justice, 1991-1994. Law Clerk to Senior Judge John A. MacKenzie, U.S. District Court, Eastern District of Virginia, 1986-1987. Member: American Institute of Certified Public Accountants; German American Business Council. *Member:* Virginia State Bar. (Resident, Saarbrücken, Germany). ***LANGUAGES:*** German, French. ***PRACTICE AREAS:*** International Trade and Regulation; International Commercial Transactions. ***Email:*** montalbine@dhlaw.com

(This Listing Continued)

KEVIN C. KENNEDY, born 1951; admitted to bar, 1977, Hawaii (Not admitted in District of Columbia). *Education:* University of Michigan (B.A.); Wayne State University (J.D.). Professor, Detroit College of Law at Michigan State University, East Lansing, Michigan.

CHARLES H. NALLS, born Bethesda, Maryland, August 20, 1956; admitted to bar, 1983, District of Columbia and U.S. Court of Federal Claims; 1984, U.S. Court of Appeals, District of Columbia Circuit, Federal Circuit and Fourth Circuit; 1985, U.S. Court of International Trade; 1992, Maryland; 1993, Pennsylvania; 1997, West Virginia and U.S. District Court, District of West Virginia. *Education:* DePauw University (B.A., summa cum laude, 1979); Georgetown University (J.D., 1982). Phi Beta Kappa; Phi Delta Phi. Editor, Journal of Law and Policy in International Business. Assistant General Counsel, U.S. International Trade Commission, 1987-1993. Advisor to U.S. Negotiators in the Uruguay Round of the GATT and NAFTA. [U.S. Naval Reserve, 1987—;LCDR]. ***LANGUAGES:*** French. ***PRACTICE AREAS:*** Intellectual Property Litigation; International Trade; Trademarks; Trademark Licensing; Commercial Law. ***Email:*** challs@dhlaw.com

FRANK A. ORBAN, III, born Johnstown, Pennsylvania, May 30, 1944; admitted to bar, 1968, Pennsylvania; 1975, District of Columbia; U.S. Supreme Court; U.S Court of International Trade; U.S. Court of Appeals, Federal Circuit and U.S. District Court, Eastern District of Pennsylvania. *Education:* Harvard University (B.A., 1966); University of Pennsylvania (J.D., 1968). Former Lecturer, Law University of Virginia Law School, 1975-1978. Senior Representative, U.S. Arms Control & Disarmament Agency, US-Soviet Nuclear Arms & Space Talks, Geneva, 1987-1989. International Counsel, Armstrong World Industries, Inc.; General Manager, Corporte and Legal Affairs, New International plc London. Assistant Attorney General , Kingdom of Swaziland. Member: International Institute of Strategic Studies, London; Pennsylvania-Russia Business Counsel. Board Member, Czech Institute for Strategic Studies. *Member:* American Bar Association (Member, Sections on: International Law; ADR); American Corporate Counsel Association (Past Director); International Institute for Strategic Affairs. (Associate Counsel) (Also Counsel to Karanović & Nikolić Law Firm, Belgrade, Yugoslavia). ***LANGUAGES:*** Russian and German. ***PRACTICE AREAS:*** International Transactions; Foreign Investment; Customs Law; Export Compliance; International Arbitration. ***Email:*** forban@dhlaw.com

FOREIGN ATTORNEYS

ALEJANDRO N. GOMEZ-STROZZI, born Saltillo Coahuila, Mexico, July 7, 1966; admitted to bar, 1990, Mexico; 2000, New York. *Education:* Universidad Autónoma de Coahuila (Licenciatura en Derecho, 1990); Mexican Supreme Court Institute (Certificated Degree, 1992); Universidad Panamericana (Certificated Degrees in Taxation, Corporate Law and International Commercial Law, 1992-1993); Georgetown University (LL.M., 1997). Law Clerk: Mexican Supreme Court, 1993-1994; Mexican Federal Judiciary Council, 1995-1996. ***LANGUAGES:*** Spanish. ***PRACTICE AREAS:*** International Trade Regulation; Mexico Trade; Customs Law; Antidumping; Import and Export Law. ***Email:*** agomez-s@dhlaw.com

JUDITH L. HOLDSWORTH, born Waterbury, Connecticut, April 23, 1949; admitted to bar, 1995, Frankfurt, Germany. *Education:* Heidelberg College (B.A., 1972); University of Saarland (First State Examination, 1992); Second State Examination, 1995. Assistant Editor: "Transnational Litigation: A Practitioner's Guide," Oceana Publications. Lecturer: University of Saarland; University of Trier, Germany, 1988-1995. (Resident, Saarbrücken, Germany). ***LANGUAGES:*** German. ***PRACTICE AREAS:*** International Commercial Law; International Law; Litigation; Arbitration. ***Email:*** holdsworth@dhlaw.de

ANDREW J. J. DELEHANTY

Established in 1983

5315 CONNECTICUT AVENUE, N.W.
WASHINGTON, D.C. 20015-1829
Telephone: 202-244-5551
Email: dfnsatty@erols.com
URL: http://www.lawyers.com/delehantylaw

Criminal Defense Practice including White Collar Crime, Drug Crimes, Major Felonies, Probate Litigation, Estate Planning & Administration.

FIRM PROFILE: The firm represents individuals in all courts throughout Northern Virginia, Washington, D.C. and Southern Maryland.

ANDREW J. J. DELEHANTY, born Albany, New York, October 10, 1946; admitted to bar, 1983, District of Columbia; 1984, U.S. District Court, District of Columbia; 1986, Virginia; 1990, U.S. Court of Appeals, Fourth Circuit; 1993, U.S. Supreme Court; 1997, Maryland. *Education:* New York University (B.S., 1972); Georgetown University (J.D., 1982). *Member:* The District of Columbia Bar Association; Virginia State Bar Association. ***PRACTICE AREAS:*** Criminal Law; Civil Law; Probate Law.

ROSS S. DELSTON

Established in 1994

3013 BEECH STREET, N.W.
WASHINGTON, D.C. 20015-2203
Telephone: 202-362-2260
Fax: 202-362-2754
Email: rdelston@delston.com
URL: http://www.delston.com

Financial Services Law, Banking Law, Banking Regulation, Electronic Banking, Bank Mergers and Acquisitions, Consumer Banking, International Banking Law, Bank Insolvency, Bank Failures, International Finance, Trade Finance.

FIRM PROFILE: Ross Delston is a former federal banking regulator who represents clients before the Federal Reserve Board, the Office of the Comptroller of the Currency, the Office of Thrift Supervision, the Federal Deposit Insurance Corporation, the National Credit Union Administration and the U.S. Export-Import Bank. His clients include major banks, high-tech companies, bank and financial holding companies, and law firms. Mr. Delston is also a consultant to the International Monetary Fund and the World Bank.

ROSS S. DELSTON, born New York, New York, August 7, 1951; admitted to bar, 1976, District of Columbia. *Education:* George Washington University (B.A., with special honors, 1973; J.D., with honors, 1976). Of Counsel, Jones, Day, Reavis & Pogue, 1991-1994. Counsel, Assistance Transactions, 1986-1988 and Assistant General Counsel - Assisted Acquisitions, 1988-1991, Federal Deposit Insurance Corporation. Counsel, Office of the General Counsel, Export-Import Bank of the U.S., 1976-1986. *Member:* District of Columbia Bar (Member, Membership Benefits Committee, 1995-2001); American Bar Association (Member, Committees on: Banking and Cyberspace Law). ***SPECIAL AGENCIES:*** Export-Import Bank of the U.S.; Federal Deposit Insurance Corporation; Federal Reserve Board; National Credit Union Administration; Office of the Comptroller of the Currency; Office of Thrift Supervision; International Monetary Fund; World Bank.

DE MARTINO FINKELSTEIN ROSEN & VIRGA

Established in 1978

SUITE 400, 1818 N STREET, N.W.
WASHINGTON, D.C. 20036
Telephone: 202-659-0494
Telecopier: 202-659-1290
Email: BUSLAW@dfrv.com
URL: http://www.demartinolaw.com

New York, N.Y. Office: Suite 1700, 90 Broad Street. Telephone: 212-363-2500. Telecopier: 212-363-2723. Email: info@DFRV-NY.com

Securities and Commodities Law. Administrative Practice. Business, Corporate, Corporate Financing. Trial Practice. Estate Administration and Planning, Real Estate, Banking Law, and Elder Law.

FIRM PROFILE: De Martino Finkelstein Rosen & Virga is a law firm with offices in Washington, D.C. and New York. The firm practices in the area of business-related matters. The firm is a member of the Martindale-Hubbell Bar Register of Preeminent Lawyers and is listed in the Securities and Business Law Sections.

The firm represents diverse clients, including public companies and closely held corporations, general and limited partnerships, and financial institutions, such as broker-dealers, investment companies, investment advisors, insurance companies, their principals and advisors as well as securities and commodities industry professionals. Its attorneys have expertise in the areas of corporate finance, securities law, commercial law, broker dealer regulation, business-related civil and administrative litigation, alternative dispute resolution, commodities law, partnership law, exchange delisting matters, mergers and acquisitions.

MEMBERS OF FIRM

RALPH V. DE MARTINO, born Jackson Heights, New York, December 16, 1954; admitted to bar, 1979, Virginia, District of Columbia, U.S. Court of Appeals for the District of Columbia Circuit and U.S. Court of Appeals, 4th Circuit; 1982, U.S. Supreme Court. *Education:* Bucknell University (B.S.B.A., cum laude, 1976); George Washington University (J.D., with honors, 1979). Delta Mu Delta (President, 1975-1976). Co-Author: Rosen, De Martino and Eaton, "Hedging by Investment Companies: Legal Implications Under the Commodity Exchange Act and Investment Company Act of 1940," Securities Regulation and Law Report (BNA), Vol. 17, No. 6, February, 1985; "Securities Dealers Aggressively Market Partnership Interests," 7 Washington Business Journal, No. 11, 21, 1988. *Member:* The District of Columbia Bar; Virginia State Bar; American Bar Association (Member, Section on Business Law). (Resident). ***PRACTICE AREAS:*** Securities Law; Corporate Financing Law; Broker Dealer Regulation. ***Email:*** rdemartino@dfrv.com

STEVEN R. FINKELSTEIN, born Brooklyn, New York, January 17, 1957; admitted to bar, 1982, New York; 1989, U.S. District Court, Southern and Eastern Districts of New York and U.S. Supreme Court (Not admitted in District of Columbia). *Education:* State University of New York at Stony Brook (B.A., magna cum laude, 1978) Phi Beta Kappa; St. Johns University (J.D., 1981). *Member:* Brooklyn and New York State (Member, Sections on: Trusts and Estates; Elder Law) Bar Associations. (Resident, New York, N.Y. Office). ***PRACTICE AREAS:*** Trusts Law; Estates Law; Elder Law. ***Email:*** sfinkelstein@dfrv-ny.com

JEFFREY S. ROSEN, born Cincinnati, Ohio, July 18, 1946; admitted to bar, 1971, Ohio (inactive); 1976, District of Columbia, U.S. Claims Court and U.S. District Court for the District of Columbia Circuit; 1977, Maryland; 1998, U.S. District Court, District of Maryland. *Education:* Columbia University (B.A., 1968; J.D., 1971). Author: "Reparation Proceedings Under the Commodity Exchange Act," 27 Emory Law Journal, P. 1005, Fall, 1978; "Regulating Commodities Futures—Should Congress Alter the CFTC?" The National Law Journal, March 15, 1982; "The Impact of the Futures Trading Act of 1982 on Commodity Regulation," BNA Securities Regulation and Law Report, pg. 142, Vol. 15, No. 2, 1983; "The Regulation of Commodity Pool Operators Under The Commodity Exchange Act," 40 Washington and Lee Law Review, p. 937, Summer, 1983; "Cauldron Still Bubbling for U.S. Precious Regulations," No. 110 Futures World, April 26, 1984. Co-Author: Rosen, De Martino and Eaton, "Hedging by Investment Companies: Legal Implications Under the Commodity Exchange Act and Investment Company Act of 1940," Author: Securities Regulation and Law Report (BNA), Vol. 17, No. 6, February, 1985; "CFTC Investigative Subpoenas," Commodities Law Letter, June 1986; "Arbitration Before the National Futures Association," Jan-Feb. 1987 Commodities Law Letter 3; "Commodity Futures Trading Commission," Administrative Practice Manual of the Bar Association of the District of Columbia, 1988 Ed.; CFTC Cases Regarding Mitigation and Rehabilitation in Registration Fitness Proceedings," Commodities Law Letter June/July 1989; "CFTC's Hammond Decision: Little Ado About Nothing," Commodities Law Letter, July/August 1990. Co-Author: Brecher and Rosen, "Securities Arbitration of Customer Claims Alleging Unsuitability, Improper Markups/Markdowns or Breach of Fiduciary Duties," Vol. 2 *Securities Arbitration,* p. 469 (PLI 1996). Trial Attorney, Division of Enforcement, U.S. Securities & Exchange Commission, 1973-1976. Lecturer, Chicago-Kent/ITT Commodities Law Institute, 1982-1983, 1985-1988. Member, Board of Editors, Commodities Law Letter, 1985-1995; Association of Securities and Exchange Commission Alumni, 1993—. Arbitrator, National Futures Association. *Member:* District of Columbia Bar; Federal and American (Member, Committee on Futures Regulation, 1978—, Sections of Business Law and Litigation) Bar Associations. (Resident). ***PRACTICE AREAS:*** Commodities Law; Securities Law; Alternative Dispute Resolution; Litigation. ***Email:*** jrosen@dfrv.com

GERARD A. VIRGA, born Bronx, New York, September 3, 1954; admitted to bar, 1980, New York and U.S. District Court, Southern and Eastern Districts of New York (Not admitted in District of Columbia). *Education:* State University of New York at Stony Brook (B.A., cum laude, 1976); State University of New York at Buffalo (J.D., cum laude, 1979). *Member:* American Bar Association (Member, Sections on: Business Law; Litigation; Real Property, Probate and Trust Law). (Resident, New York, N.Y. Office). ***PRACTICE AREAS:*** Corporate Law; Real Estate Law; Commercial Litigation. ***Email:*** gvirga@dfrv-ny.com

---

KEITH H. PETERSON, born Pasadena, California, October 14, 1954; admitted to bar, 1985, New York (Not admitted in District of Columbia). *Education:* Amherst College (B.A., 1976); Columbia University. (Resident, New York, N.Y. Office). ***PRACTICE AREAS:*** Corporate Law; Real Estate Law; Estates Law; Commercial Litigation. ***Email:*** kpeterson@dfrv-ny.com

F. ALEC ORUDJEV, born Tbilisi, Georgia, June 20, 1974; admitted to bar, 1999, New York (Not admitted in District of Columbia). *Education:* North Carolina State University (B.A., magna cum laude, 1995); Syracuse University (M.A., Economics; J.D., 1998). Omicron Delta Epsilon. *Member:* New York State and American (Member, Business Law Section) Bar Associations. ***LANGUAGES:*** Russian, Turkish, German. ***PRACTICE AREAS:*** Securities; Corporate Law; Mergers and Acquisitions. ***Email:*** aorudjev@dfrv.com

VALERIE J. PELTON, born Charleston, South Carolina, August 5, 1964; admitted to bar, 1996, Virginia and U.S. Court of Appeals, Fourth Circuit; 1997, New Jersey; 1999, U.S. Supreme Court (Not admitted in District of Columbia). *Education:* Vanderbilt University (B.A., 1986); University of Nevada at Las Vegas (M.A., 1992); Whittier College School of Law (J.D., 1995). *Member:* Virginia State, New Jersey State (inactive) and American Bar Associations; Northern Virginia Technology Council (Vice Chair, European Subcommittee). ***LANGUAGES:*** French, German, Japanese. ***PRACTICE AREAS:*** Securities; Mergers and Acquisitions; Corporate Law; Aviation Law. ***Email:*** vpelton@dfrv.com

(This Listing Continued)

DE MARTINO FINKELSTEIN ROSEN & VIRGA, Washington—Continued

LEGAL SUPPORT PERSONNEL

J. KEONI ROBINSON, born Pasco, Washington, July 25, 1952. *Education:* University of New Mexico (B.U.S., 1974). Member, National Capital Area Paralegal Association, 1989—. (Legal Assistant). ***Email:*** krobinson@dfrv.com

KAREN J. MALLAN, born Lynchburg, Virginia, March 23, 1972. *Education:* Mary Washington College (B.A., 1994); Old Dominion University (Paralegal Certification, 1994). (Legal Assistant). ***Email:*** kmallan@dfrv.com

GREGORY P. BUFITHIS, born Norwalk, Connecticut, March 2, 1952. *Education:* Sorbonne, Paris (A.A., 1973); Hartwick College (B.A., 1974); John Marshall Law School (J.D., 1979). Co-Author with Richard L. Merrick, "Chapter XII-Why Is It?", 52 American Bankruptcy Law Journal 213, Summer 1978. (Legal Assistant). ***LANGUAGES:*** French and Spanish. ***Email:*** gbufithis@dfrv.com

JAMES R. DENBO

Established in 1986

1801 K STREET, N.W., SUITE 1205L
WASHINGTON, D.C. 20006
Telephone: 202-452-7373
Facsimile: 202-452-7333
Email: denbojim@aol.com

Management Labor Law. General Practice. Representing Employers in Labor and Employment Law.

JAMES R. DENBO, born Washington, D.C., February 18, 1941; admitted to bar, 1968, District of Columbia. *Education:* University of Michigan (B.A., 1963); George Washington University (J.D., 1967). With National Labor Relations Board, Washington, D.C., 1967-1969 and Milwaukee, Wisconsin, 1969-1971. Partner, Vedder, Price, Kaufman, Kammholz & Day, 1971-1985. *Member:* District of Columbia Bar; Supreme Court Bar; American Bar Association.

LAW OFFICES OF STEPHEN G. DE NIGRIS

2117 L STREET, N.W., SUITE 283
WASHINGTON, D.C. 20037-1524
Telephone: 800-791-9908
Telecopier: 888-791-4441
Email: sgd853@aol.com
URL: http://www.lawyers.com/denigrislaw

Labor law, Employment Law, Civil Litigation, Administrative Law.

STEPHEN G. DeNIGRIS, born Albany, New York, October 18, 1952; admitted to bar, 1992, New York and Florida (Not admitted in District of Columbia). *Education:* Florida Atlantic University (B.A., 1985); Nova University (J.D., 1989); Georgetown University (LL.M., 1991). *Member:* New York State Bar Association; The Florida Bar.

ASSOCIATE

MICHAEL L. MICHETTI, JR., born Washington, D.C., December 24, 1971; admitted to bar, 1998, Maryland (Not admitted in District of Columbia). *Education:* University of Michigan (B.A., 1994); Catholic University of America (J.D., 1997). *Member:* Maryland State and American Bar Associations.

DENNING & WOHLSTETTER

Established in 1953

1700 K STREET, N.W., SUITE 301
WASHINGTON, D.C. 20006
Telephone: 202-833-8884
Fax: 202-833-8886

General Practice before Federal Courts, including U.S. Court of Federal Claims, Administrative Agencies. Motor Carrier, Maritime, Aviation, Government Contract and Trademark Law.

MEMBERS OF FIRM

WILLIAM I DENNING (1883-1977).

ALAN F. WOHLSTETTER, born New York, N.Y.; admitted to bar, 1949, New York; 1953, District of Columbia; 1958, U.S. Supreme Court and U.S. Court of Federal Claims. *Education:* Harvard University (LL.B., 1948). Trial

(This Listing Continued)

Attorney for Federal Maritime Board and Maritime Administration, 1951-52. *Member:* The District of Columbia Bar; Bar Association of the District of Columbia; Transportation Lawyers Association; Maritime Administrative Bar Association. ***PRACTICE AREAS:*** Transportation Law; Government Contracts; Maritime Law; Trademark Law.

STANLEY I. GOLDMAN, born Richmond, Virginia, September 19, 1939; admitted to bar, 1965, Virginia; 1969, U.S. Court of Federal Claims; 1972, District of Columbia; 1980, U.S. Supreme Court. *Education:* University of Virginia (B.A., 1962; LL.B., 1965). Phi Alpha Delta. Attorney-Advisor, Office of Proceedings, Interstate Commerce Commission, 1965-1967. *Member:* The District of Columbia Bar; Virginia State Bar; Transportation Lawyers Association. ***PRACTICE AREAS:*** Transportation Law; Government Contracts; Maritime Law; Trademark Law.

DEWEY BALLANTINE LLP

1775 PENNSYLVANIA AVENUE, N.W.
WASHINGTON, D.C. 20006-4605
Telephone: 202-862-1000; Telecopier: 202-862-1093
Cable Address: "Dewbalaw"
URL: http://www.deweyballantine.com

Other offices: New York, New York; Los Angeles and Menlo Park, California; Houston, Texas, London, England; Hong Kong; Budapest, Hungary; Prague, Czech Republic; and Warsaw, Poland.

General Practice.

RESIDENT PARTNERS

DONNA M. ATTANASIO, born Niskayuna, NY, February 22, 1959; admitted to bar, 1988, District of Columbia. *Education:* Smith College (A.B., with departmental honors, 1981); Harvard University (J.D., 1988). *Member:* Energy and American Bar Associations; The District of Columbia Bar. ***PRACTICE AREAS:*** Energy Law. ***Email:*** dattanasio@deweyballantine.com

JAMES F. BOWE, JR., born Portland, OR, May 17, 1955; admitted to bar, 1982, District of Columbia. *Education:* Williams College (B.A., cum laude, with honors, 1977); Northwestern University (J.D., 1982). Adjunct Professor of Oil and Gas Law, 1990-1996, Georgetown University Law Center. Vice-Chairman Committee on Natural Gas Certificate and Authorization Regulations, 1990-1992, Energy Bar Association. Vice-Chairman Committee on Natural Gas Marketing and Transportation, Section on Natural Resources, Energy and Environmental Law, 1989-1991, 1992-1995, American Bar Association. ***PRACTICE AREAS:*** Energy; Project Finance. ***Email:*** jbowe@deweyballantine.com

KEVIN M. DEMPSEY, born Seward A.F.B., TN, January 29, 1962; admitted to bar, 1987, District of Columbia. *Education:* Washington University (A.B., 1984); Harvard University (J.D., cum laude, 1987). Minority Counsel, 1989-1990, Senate Committee on Commerce, Science and Transportation. Counsel, 1990-1992, Office of Senator John C. Danforth. Minority Trade Counsel, 1992-1994, Senate Committee on Commerce, Science and Transportation. *Member:* The District of Columbia Bar (Member, International Law Section). ***PRACTICE AREAS:*** International Trade. ***Email:*** kdempsey@deweyballantine.com

JOSEPH K. DOWLEY, born Los Angeles, CA, April 23, 1946; admitted to bar, 1976, Virginia; 1981, District of Columbia. *Education:* Georgetown University (A.B., 1968; J.D., 1976). Administrative Assistant to Hon. Dan Rostenkowski, 1976-1981. Assistant Chief Counsel, 1981-1985 and Chief Counsel, 1985-1987, Committee on Ways and Means, U.S. House of Representatives. [Officer, U.S. Army, Infantry, 1969-1971]. ***PRACTICE AREAS:*** Tax; Trade; Health. ***Email:*** jdowley@deweyballantine.com

ANNA-LIZA B. HARRIS, born Milton, MA, November 11, 1961; admitted to bar, 1989, District of Columbia. *Education:* Georgetown University (B.S.F.S., 1983; J.D., 1989). *Member:* The District of Columbia Bar; American Bar Association (Chair, Subcommittee on Asset-Backed Securities, L.C., Section of Taxation). ***Email:*** aharris@deweyballantine.com

THOMAS R. HOWELL, born Milwaukee, WI, July 1, 1949; admitted to bar, 1977, District of Columbia. *Education:* Harvard University (A.B., cum laude, 1971); Boston University (J.D., cum laude, 1977). Author: "Steel and the State in Romania," 24 Comparative Economic Studies 71, 1987. Co-Author, "The U.S. Commitment to the GATT System: A Reappraisal of Basic Assumptions," 6 Michigan Yearbook of International Legal Studies, 491, 1984; "International Competition in the Information Technologies: Foreign Government Intervention and the U.S. Response," 22 Stanford Journal of International Law 215, 1986; "The Microelectronics Race: The Impact of Government Policy on International Competition," Westview Press, 1988; "Steel and the State: Government Intervention and Steel's Structural Crisis," Westview Press, 1988. *Member:* District of Columbia Bar. ***PRACTICE AREAS:*** International Trade. ***Email:*** thowell@deweyballantine.com

ANDREW W. KENTZ, born Summit, NJ, April 17, 1956; admitted to bar, 1983, District of Columbia. *Education:* Georgetown University (A.B., 1978; J.D., 1983). Judicial Clerk to: Hon. George H. Revercomb, District of Columbia

(This Listing Continued)

Superior Court; Chief of Staff and Counsel Hon. Byron L. Dorgan, U.S. House of Representatives. *Member:* The District of Columbia Bar. ***PRACTICE AREAS:*** Corporate Taxation; International Trade. ***Email:*** akentz@deweyballantine.com

FELIX B. LAUGHLIN, born New Orleans, LA, December 4, 1942; admitted to bar, 1967, Tennessee; 1972, District of Columbia. *Education:* University of Tennessee (B.S., 1967); University of Tennessee College of Law (LL.B., 1967); Georgetown Law Center (LL.M. in Taxation, 1971). Order of the Coif. Interpretative Division, Office of Chief Counsel, Internal Revenue Service, 1967-1971. *Member:* The District of Columbia Bar; Federal and American Bar Associations. ***PRACTICE AREAS:*** Corporate Tax. ***Email:*** flaughlin@deweyballantine.com

JOHN R. MAGNUS, born Cincinnati, OH, September 30, 1964; admitted to bar, 1990, California; 1991, District of Columbia. *Education:* Stanford University (A.B., 1986); University of Chicago (J.D., 1990). ***LANGUAGES:*** French and Spanish. ***PRACTICE AREAS:*** Antitrust; Communications; International Trade. ***Email:*** jmagnus@deweyballantine.com

W. CLARK McFADDEN II, born Ravenna, OH, July 28, 1946; admitted to bar, 1972, Massachusetts; 1977, District of Columbia. *Education:* Williams College (B.A., cum laude, 1968); Harvard University (M.B.A., first class honors, 1972; J.D., 1972). General Counsel, U.S. Senate Committee on Armed Services, 1974-1977 and Special Counsel, U.S. Senate Committee on Foreign Relations, 1979. General Counsel, 1986-1987, President's Special Review Board (The Tower Commission). *Member:* The District of Columbia Bar. ***PRACTICE AREAS:*** International Trade and Transactions. ***Email:*** wmcfadden@deweyballantine.com

HERBERT V. MORAIS, born Ipoh, Malaysia, April 9, 1943; admitted to bar, 1970, Malaysia; 1971, Singapore; 2001, Special Legal Consultant in the District of Columbia (Not admitted in the United States). *Education:* University of Singapore (LL.B., with honors, 1966); Harvard University (LL.M., 1967; J.D., 1972). Fulbright Scholar. Lecturer and Sub-Dean, University of Singapore. (A Legal Consultant on the Laws of the Country). ***LANGUAGES:*** Malay. ***PRACTICE AREAS:*** International Legislative Reform. ***Email:*** hmorais@deweyballantine.com

EARLE H. O'DONNELL, born Philadelphia, PA, February 2, 1949; admitted to bar, 1975, Maryland; 1977, District of Columbia. *Education:* Transylvania University (B.A., 1971); George Washington University (J.D., with high honors, 1975). Order of the Coif. Senior Associate, 1973-1975, George Washington Law Review. Co-Author, with Laurel W. Glassman, "After the EPAA: What Oil Allocation and Pricing Authorities Remain?" 2 No. 1 Energy L. Jour. 1981; "Constitutional Constraints on State Efforts to Control Oil During Emergencies," 5 No. 1 Energy L. Jour. 1984; "Industrial Opportunities to Engage in Direct Purchase of Electricity: The Purchaser's Perspective," 7 No. 2 Journal of Energy and Natural Resources Law 1989; "Taking Charge: Direct Purchases of Electricity and the Industrial Consumer," Issue Paper No. 4 Southern Regulatory Policy Institute July 1990; "Should Industrial Users Be Permitted to Make Direct Purchases of Electricity?" 5 No. 4 The Cogeneration Journal Fall 1990. Speaker, 1988, 22nd Biennial Conference International Bar Association. *Member:* Federal Energy Bar Association. ***PRACTICE AREAS:*** Energy. ***Email:*** eodonnell@deweyballantine.com

JOSEPH M. PARI, born Providence, RI, June 2, 1962; admitted to bar, 1987, Rhode Island; 1988, New York and Massachusetts; 1989, District of Columbia. *Education:* Providence College (B.S., cum laude, 1984); Boston College (J.D., magna cum laude, 1987); New York University School of Law (LL.M. in Taxation, 1988). *Member:* American Bar Association (Committee on Affiliated and Related Corporations, 1991—; Chair, Subcommittee on Consolidated Returns Committee on Corporate Tax, 1995—; Section of Taxation). ***PRACTICE AREAS:*** Corporate Taxation. ***Email:*** jpari@deweyballantine.com

JOHN A. RAGOSTA, born Sharon, PA, January 19, 1960; admitted to bar, 1984, District of Columbia. *Education:* Grove City College (B.S., magna cum laude, 1981); University of Virginia (J.D., 1984); Case Western Reserve University. Fellow, American Bar Foundation. U.S. Court of International Trade Advisory Committee. U.S. Government roster of panelists under NAFTA Chapter 19. *Member:* The District of Columbia Bar. ***PRACTICE AREAS:*** International Trade. ***Email:*** jragosta@deweyballantine.com

JOHN J. SALMON, born Worcester, MA, June 22, 1948; admitted to bar, 1975, District of Columbia. *Education:* Georgetown University (A.B., 1970; M.L.T., 1981); The National Law Center, George Washington University (J.D., with honors, 1974). Professional Staff, 1975-1981, and Chief Counsel and Staff Director, 1981-1985, Ways and Means Committee, U.S. House of Representatives. *Member:* The District of Columbia Bar; Federal and American Bar Associations. ***PRACTICE AREAS:*** Tax. ***Email:*** jsalmon@deweyballantine.com

MARTHA J. TALLEY, born Fayetteville, NC, September 7, 1950; admitted to bar, 1975, North Carolina; 1979, District of Columbia. *Education:* Queens College, Charlotte, North Carolina (B.A., 1971); University of California at Berkeley, Boalt Hall School of Law (J.D., 1975). Counsel, Select Committee on Intelligence, 1975-1977 and 1979, U.S. Senate. Committee on Standards of Official Conduct, 1977-1979 and 1982-1983, U.S. House of Representatives. Trial Attorney, 1979-1982, Criminal Division Office of Special Investigation, U.S. Department of Justice. *Member:* The District of Columbia Bar. ***PRACTICE AREAS:*** Litigation. ***Email:*** mtalley@deweyballantine.com

ALAN WM. WOLFF, born Malden, MA, June 12, 1942; admitted to bar, 1966, New York; 1967, Massachusetts; 1972, District of Columbia. *Education:* Harvard University (A.B., 1963); Columbia University (LL.B., 1966). Author of a number of papers and studies on international trade and U.S. trade law, many of which are listed in on the International Trade Practice group's Web site: www.dbtrade.com. Attorney, Office of General Counsel, International Affairs Section, 1968-1973. Deputy General Counsel, U.S. Department of the Treasury, 1973-1974. General Counsel, 1974-1976 and Deputy Special Representative for Trade Negotiations with rank of Ambassador, 1977-1979, Office of Special Representative for Trade Negotiations with rank of Ambassador, 1977-1979, Office of Special Representatives for Trade Negotiations, Executive Office of the President. Chairman, Advisory Board, International Commercial Diplomacy Project. Member: Board of Trustees, Monterey Institute of International Studies; The National Research Council's Board on Science, Technology, and Economic Policy; U.S. Department of State's Advisory Committee on International Economic Policy; Advisory Committee, Institute for International Economics; Advisory Board, Economic Strategy Institute; Board of Trustees, United States Council for International Business; Council on Foreign Relations; American Society of International Law. *Member:* The District of Columbia Bar; American Bar Association. ***PRACTICE AREAS:*** International Trade; Investment Law; Business Law. ***Email:*** awolff@deweyballantine.com

COUNSEL

HARRY LEWIS CLARK, born Wilson, NC, February 21, 1963; admitted to bar, 1989, Virginia; 1990, District of Columbia. *Education:* University of North Carolina at Chapel Hill (B.A., 1985); University of Virginia (J.D., 1989). Author: "International Mergers and Acquisitions: Liability under U.S. Economic Sanctions," International Law News, Fall 2000; "U.S. Limits on International Business in the Petroleum Sector: Oil Antidumping Suits, Trade Sanctions and Other Measures," Fifty-First Annual Institute of Oil and Gas Law and Taxation (Southwest Legal Foundation, ed. Publ. No. 640, 2000); "Dealing with U.S. Extraterritorial Sanctions and Foreign Countermeasures," 20 U. Penn. J. Int'l Econ. L. 61, (1999); "The Iraq/Kuwait Economic Sanctions: Trade Relations on a War Footing," 25 Int'l Law 391, 1991; Note, "The Free Movement of Goods and Regulation for Public Health and Consumer Protection in the EEC: The West German 'Beer A Purity' Case," 28 VA Jnl. Int'l L. 753 (1988). *Member:* The District of Columbia Bar. ***Email:*** hclark@deweyballantine.com

JULIA DRYDEN ENGLISH, born Easton, MD, 1959; admitted to bar, 1989, Virginia; 1992, District of Columbia. *Education:* University of Virginia (B.A., 1981); Georgetown University Law Center (J.D., 1989). *Member:* American Bar Association; Federal Energy Bar Association. ***PRACTICE AREAS:*** Energy Regulation. ***Email:*** jenglish@deweyballantine.com

LAUREL W. GLASSMAN, born Alexandria, VA, March 17, 1949; admitted to bar, 1974, New Jersey; 1976, Colorado; 1978, District of Columbia. *Education:* Smith College (A.B., cum laude, 1971); Rutgers University (J.D., 1974). Articles Editor, Rutgers Law Review, 1973-1974. Law Clerk to Chief Judge Almeric L. Christian, U.S. District Court for the Virgin Islands, 1974-1976. Author: "Should Industrial Users Be Permitted to Make Direct Purchases of Electricity?" The Cogeneration Journal, Volume 5, Number 4, Fall, 1990; "Industrial Opportunities to Engage in Direct Purchase of Electricity," Journal of Energy and Natural Resources Law, March, 1989; "Recent Developments in the Continuing Debate Over Standby Rates for Pennsylvania Cogenerators," Cogeneration and Small Power Monthly, November, 1987; "Constitutional Constraints on State Efforts to Control Oil During Emergencies," 5 Energy Law Journal 77, May, 1984. ***PRACTICE AREAS:*** Energy. ***Email:*** lglassman@deweyballantine.com

KEITH M. SCHWARTZ, born Brooklyn, NY, August 27, 1959; admitted to bar, 1985, New York; 1988, District of Columbia. *Education:* State University of New York at Albany (B.A., cum laude, 1981); Syracuse University College of Law (J.D., cum laude, 1984). Member, Justinian Society. *Member:* The District of Columbia Bar. ***PRACTICE AREAS:*** Project Finance; Real Estate. ***Email:*** kschwartz@deweyballantine.com

MICHAEL H. STEIN, born New Haven, CT, August 28, 1942; admitted to bar, 1971, District of Columbia. *Education:* Swarthmore College (B.A., with honors, 1964); Columbia University (LL.B., 1968). Harlan Fiske Stone Scholar, 1967. Revision Editor, Columbia Journal of Law and Social Problems, 1967-1968. Lecturer in Law, University of Botswana, Lesotho & Swaziland, 1968-1970. Trial Attorney, Appellate Section, Civil Division, U.S. Department of Justice, 1970-1977. General Counsel, U.S. International Trade Commission, 1977-1984. ***PRACTICE AREAS:*** International Trade. ***Email:*** mstein@deweyballantine.com

BRADFORD L. WARD, born Boonville, MO, December 4, 1957; admitted to bar, 1984, District of Columbia. *Education:* University of Oregon (B.S.,

(This Listing Continued)

DEWEY BALLANTINE LLP, Washington—Continued

1980); American University, Washington College of Law (J.D., 1983). *Member:* The District of Columbia Bar. ***PRACTICE AREAS:*** International Trade. ***Email:*** bward@deweyballantine.com

OF COUNSEL

ZORI G. FERKIN, born Pittsburgh, PA, November 14, 1957; admitted to bar, 1981, District of Columbia; 1982, Pennsylvania. *Education:* Colgate University (A.B., 1978); Georgetown University (J.D., 1981). Administrative Editor, Law and Policy in International Business, 1980-1981. Attorney, U.S. Nuclear Regulatory Commission, 1981-1983. Assistant Counsel, 1983-1985 and Chief Counsel, 1985-1986, Pennsylvania Governor's Energy Council. ***PRACTICE AREAS:*** Energy. ***Email:*** zferkin@deweyballantine.com

(For Biographical Data of all Partners, Counsel, Of Counsel and Office Addresses, see Professional Biographies at New York, N.Y.)

JOHN C. DIBBLE

SUITE 175, 3050 K STREET NW
WASHINGTON, D.C. 20007
Telephone: 202-944-4524
Fax: 202-944-4525
Email: jdibble@wdn.com
URL: http://www.lawyers.com/johndibble

International Trade Regulation, Export Regulation, Customs Law, Foreign Asset Control, Unfair Trade Practices, Foreign Corrupt, Practices Act, Export Compliance, Foreign Trade Sanctions.

FIRM PROFILE: John Dibble has over 25 years of experience representing corporations that are involved in international trade and subject to export regulations. Mr. Dibble has worked closely with high technology companies and defense contractors providing general business and compliance counselling.

JOHN C. DIBBLE, born Washington, D.C., May 29, 1946; admitted to bar, 1974, Indiana; U.S. Court of International Trade and U.S. Court of Appeals for the Federal Circuit; 1991, District of Columbia. *Education:* Columbia University (B.A., 1968); Indiana University (J.D., 1974). Chief Deputy Prosecuting Attorney, 23rd Judicial Circuit of Indiana, 1975. Special Assistant to U.S. Senator Birch E. Bayh, 1966-1969. *Member:* Indiana State and American Bar Associations; The District of Columbia Bar. [Lt., USNR, 1969-1971]

DICKINSON LANDMEIER LLP

1900 K STREET, N.W., SUITE 1150
WASHINGTON, D.C. 20006
Telephone: 202-457-5970
Facsimile: 202-785-1226
Email: tdickinson@dllaw.com

International Law, Foreign Corrupt Practices Act, Foreign Asset Control, Export Regulation, Export Compliance, Antiboycott Compliance, Economic Sanctions, Foreign Claims, Foreign Sales and Investment, Foreign Sovereign Immunities Act, International Arbitration, International Distribution, International Joint Ventures, Public International Law, Corporate Law, White Collar Criminal Defense, Corporate Compliance.

FIRM PROFILE: Dickinson Landmeier LLP was founded in 1997. Both founding partners were formerly with Gibson, Dunn & Crutcher's Washington, D.C. office. The firm is devoted to providing legal services of the high quality expected from large national firms, combined with the focused attention that is the hallmark of a small firm. The firm's practice includes day-to-day counseling on sanctions legislation; the implementation of foreign sales through representation, agency and distribution agreements, joint ventures, etc.; and compliance with legislation such as the Foreign Corrupt Practices Act, the Export Administration Act and the International Traffic in Arms Regulations. A large portion of the firm's practice is devoted to counseling defense contractors and other corporations on a wide variety of matters relating to sales of their products overseas, including enforcement actions, and to financial institutions in executing special workouts of sovereign debt and gaining access to foreign markets.

TIMOTHY L. DICKINSON, born April 9, 1954; admitted to bar, 1980, District of Columbia; 1987, New York; 1998, Michigan. *Education:* University of Michigan (A.B., 1975; J.D., 1979); Columbia University (LL.M., 1980). Jervey Fellow. Stagiaire, Legal Service, Commission of the European Communities, Brussels, Belgium. Adjunct Professor of Law: Georgetown University Law Center, 1984-1993; University of Michigan Law School, 1998—. Chair, ABA Section of International Law and Practice, 1997-1998. Chairman, ABA Committee on Foreign Claims, 1987-1988. Co-Chairman, ABA Committee on European Law, 1989-1992. Secretary, ABA Section of International Law and Practice, 1992-1993. Chair-Elect, ABA Section of International Law and Practice, 1996-1997. Member of Executive Council, American Society of International Law; Advisory Board, International Law Institute; ABA Central and Eastern European Law Institute; University of Michigan Center for International Legal Studies. ***LANGUAGES:*** French. ***PRACTICE AREAS:*** Foreign Corrupt Practices Act; International Joint Ventures; Foreign Asset Control; Agency and Distributorships; International Arbitration; International Commercial Transactions; Foreign Sales and Investment; Economic Sanctions and Foreign Claims; Export Regulations and Compliance; Public International Law. ***Email:*** tdickinson@dllaw.com

LISA M. LANDMEIER, born Chicago, Illinois, July 28, 1964; admitted to bar, 1993, Maryland; 1995, District of Columbia. *Education:* University of Iowa (B.S., 1986); Georgetown University Law Center (J.D., magna cum laude, 1993). Order of the Coif. Member, 1991-1993 and Notes Editor, 1992-1993, Georgetown Law Journal. *Member:* Bar Association of the District of Columbia; The District of Columbia Bar; American Bar Association (Member, Section of International Law and Practice; Co-Chair, Task Force on International Standards for Corruption, 2000—). ***PRACTICE AREAS:*** International Law; Foreign Corrupt Practices Act; Foreign Asset Control; Export Regulations and Compliance; Corporate Law; International Distribution. ***Email:*** llandmeier@dllaw.com

WILLIAM F. PENDERGAST, born Troy, New York, October 4, 1946; admitted to bar, 1973, New York and U.S. District Court, Northern District of New York; 1979, District of Columbia; 1987, U.S. District Court, District of Columbia and U.S. District Court, District of Maryland. *Education:* State University of New York at Albany (B.A., 1968); Albany Law School of Union University (J.D., 1972). Assistant District Attorney, Albany, New York, 1974-1978. Trial Attorney, U.S. Department of Justice, 1978-1986. Deputy Chief, Defense Procurement Fraud Unit, U.S. Department of Justice, 1985-1986. Seyfarth, Shaw, 1986-2000. ***PRACTICE AREAS:*** White Collar Criminal Law; Complex Business Litigation; Defense Contract Fraud; False Claims Act; Foreign Corrupt Practices Act; International Arbitration. ***Email:*** wpendergast@dllaw.com

---

NATALIA H. JORDAN, born Washington, D.C., March 11, 1966; admitted to bar, 1992, Maryland (Not admitted in District of Columbia). *Education:* Duke University (A.B., 1988); College of William and Mary (J.D., 1992). *Member:* Maryland State Bar Association. ***LANGUAGES:*** Spanish. ***PRACTICE AREAS:*** International Law; Foreign Corrupt Practices Act; Corporate Law. ***Email:*** njordan@dllaw.com

ROBIN B. FIRST, born Philadelphia, Pennsylvania, February 4, 1969; admitted to bar, 1996, New Jersey; 1997, Pennsylvania; 1998, District of Columbia. *Education:* Barnard College, Columbia University (B.A., magna cum laude, 1991); Duke University School of Law (J.D., 1996); Fletcher School of Law and Diplomacy (M.A., Law and Diplomacy, 1996). *Member:* American Bar Association (Member, International Section, 1997-1998 and 2001). ***LANGUAGES:*** French. ***PRACTICE AREAS:*** International Law; Foreign Corrupt Practices Act; International Arbitration; White Collar Crime; Export Compliance. ***Email:*** rfirst@dllaw.com

DICKINSON, MACKAMAN, TYLER & HAGEN, P.C.

SUITE 506
1660 L STREET, NW
WASHINGTON, D.C. 20036-5603
Telephone: 202-463-1260
Fax: 202-463-6328

Des Moines, Iowa Office: Suite 1600 Hub Tower, 699 Walnut Street. Telephone: 515-244-2600. Fax: 515-246-4550.

General Civil Practice. Corporation, Securities, Real Estate, Probate, Trials and Appeals, Taxation, Antitrust, Banking, Administrative, Fidelity and Surety Law, Labor and Employment Law, Casualty Insurance and Workers Compensation, Public Utility, Environmental, Energy and Telecommunications, Intellectual Property.

FIRM PROFILE: Dickinson, Mackaman, Tyler & Hagen can be traced to the year 1936 when L. Call Dickinson founded a law firm devoted primarily to tax law. He was joined in 1940 by his father, former United States Senator L.J. Dickinson and the firm quickly grew in its representation of clients in many areas of law. The firm's attorneys are a diverse group with solid academic backgrounds and significant experience in their areas of concentration. Our firm represents diverse business enterprises os all sizes, many of which operate on a national basis. We serve as Iowa counsel for numerous out-of-state corporations and routinely act as co-counsel to a variety of national law firms. Our firm also has experience representing trade industry associations and in working with governmental entities at all

(This Listing Continued)

levels. In addition to our work for businesses and organizations, we have traditionally provided a full array of personal legal services for individual clients.

REPRESENTATIVE CLIENTS: Adventure Lands of America; Associated Builders and Contractors of Iowa; Burlington Northern Railroad Co.; Central Iowa KFC; Central Tractor Farm & Country, Inc.; City of Windsor Heights; City of Johnston; Dahl's Food Markets; Des Moines Board of Water Works Trustees; Farm and City Insurance Co.; Farmers Commodities Corporation; Git-N-Go Convenience Stores, Inc.; Guide One Mutual Insurance Co.; Hills Bank and Trust Co.; Iowa Association of Business and Industry; Iowa Association of Realtors; Iowa Taxpayers Association; Life Care Retirement Communities, Inc.; MCI Telecommunications; Merchants Bonding Co. (Mutual); Norwest Bank Iowa, N.A.; Peoples Natural Gas Co.; QuikTrip Corporation; Scottsdale Insurance Co., Scottsdale, AZ; Teleconnect; Travelers Insurance Group; Texaco; Universal Outdoor Advertising, Inc.; Waukee State Bank; Wesley Retirement Services, Inc.; Williams Cos.
REFERENCE: Norwest Bank, Iowa, N.A.

(For Complete Biographical Data on All Personnel, see Professional Biographies at Des Moines, Iowa)

DICKINSON WRIGHT PLLC

Established in 1878

SUITE 800, 1901 L STREET, N.W.
WASHINGTON, D.C. 20036-3506
Telephone: 202-457-0160
Facsimile: 202-659-1559
URL: http://www.dickinson-wright.com

Detroit, Michigan Office: 500 Woodward Avenue, Suite 4000. Telephone: 313-223-3500. Facsimile: 313-223-3598.
Ann Arbor, Michigan Office: 101 North Main Street, Suite 535. Telephone: 734-623-7075. Fax: 734-623-7568.
Bloomfield Hills, Michigan Office: 38525 Woodward Avenue, Suite 2000. Telephone: 248-433-7200. Facsimile: 248-433-7274.
Grand Rapids, Michigan Office: 200 Ottawa Avenue, N.W., Suite 900. Telephone: 616-458-1300. Facsimile: 616-458-6753.
Lansing, Michigan Office: Suite 200, 215 South Washington Square. Telephone: 517-371-1730. Facsimile: 517-487-4700.

Alternative Dispute Resolution, Antitrust, Appellate Litigation, Banking and Financial Services, Bankruptcy, Business Criminal Defense and Internal Investigations, Commercial and Business Litigation, Construction Law, Corporate, Corporate Finance, Ebusiness, Education and School Law, Employee Benefits, Employment Litigation, Energy and Public Utilities, Environmental, Family and Matrimonial Law, Gaming Law, Immigration, Insurance Industry, Intellectual Property, International, Labor and Employment Relations, Mergers and Acquisitions, Municipal Law and Finance, Private Capital, Product Liability/Personal Injury Litigation, Railroads and Transportation, Real Estate, Regulatory and Administrative Law, Risk Management, Securities, Taxation, Telecommunications, Trade Regulation, Trusts and Estate Planning.

RESIDENT MEMBERS

MARC A. BERGSMAN, born Cleveland, Ohio, September 2, 1952; admitted to bar, 1977, Ohio; 1978, District of Columbia; 1980, U.S. District Court for the District of Columbia. *Education:* Miami University (B.A., 1974); Cleveland Marshall College of Law (J.D., cum laude, 1977). *Member:* The District of Columbia Bar. ***PRACTICE AREAS:*** Trademark; Copyright; Unfair Competition. ***Email:*** mbergsma@dickinson-wright.com

WILLIAM E. ELWOOD, born Woodbury, New Jersey, April 17, 1943; admitted to bar, 1969, Pennsylvania; 1971, District of Columbia and U.S. Tax Court; 1972, U.S. Court of Appeals, District of Columbia Circuit and U.S. Court of Federal Claims; 1973, U.S. Supreme Court; 1974, U.S. Court of the Armed Forces; 1982, U.S. Court of Appeals for the Federal Circuit; 1989, Michigan. *Education:* Pennsylvania State University (B.S., 1965); University of Pennsylvania (J.D., 1968); Georgetown University (LL.M., Taxation, 1974). *Member:* Detroit, Pennsylvania and American Bar Associations; The District of Columbia Bar; State Bar of Michigan. ***PRACTICE AREAS:*** Taxation Law; Partnerships; Corporate Law; Communications Law. ***Email:*** welwood@dickinson-wright.com

DAVID R. HAARZ, born Detroit, Michigan, December 18, 1950; admitted to bar, 1976, Michigan; 1990, Ohio; 1996, District of Columbia. *Education:* Oakland University (B.A., cum laude, 1973); University of Michigan (J.D., 1976). *Member:* State Bar of Michigan; The District of Columbia Bar. ***PRACTICE AREAS:*** International Trademarks; International Patents; Domestic Trademarks. ***Email:*** dhaarz@dickinson-wright.com

SAMUEL D. LITTLEPAGE, born Morgantown, West Virginia, July 10, 1947; admitted to bar, 1977, Virginia and U.S. District Court, Eastern District of Virginia; 1980, U.S. Court of Appeals, Fourth Circuit; 1982, U.S. Court of Appeals for the Federal Circuit; 1985, District of Columbia, U.S. Court of Appeals for the District of Columbia Circuit and U.S. Court of Appeals, Eleventh Circuit; 1993, U.S. Supreme Court; 1994, U.S. Court of Appeals, Sixth and Third Circuits and U.S. Court of Federal Claims; 1995, U.S. District Court for the District of Columbia. *Education:* West Virginia University (B.A., 1969; M.A., 1973); George Mason University School of Law (J.D., cum laude, 1977). *Member:* The District of Columbia Bar; Bar Association of the District of Columbia; Virginia State Bar; American Bar Association; International Trademark Association; U.S. Copyright Society; American Intellectual Property Law Association. ***PRACTICE AREAS:*** Trademark Litigation; Copyright Litigation; Unfair Competition Litigation. ***Email:*** slittlep@dickinson-wright.com

STEPHEN L. SULZER, born New York, N.Y., August 7, 1955; admitted to bar, 1980, District of Columbia; 1981, U.S. Court of Appeals for the District of Columbia Circuit and U.S. District Court for the District of Columbia; 1987, U.S. Court of Appeals, Seventh Circuit; 1989, U.S. Court of Appeals for the Federal Circuit; 1991, U.S. Court of Appeals, Ninth Circuit; 1992, U.S. District Court, Eastern District of Michigan; 1993, U.S. Supreme Court; 1996, U.S. Court of Federal Claims. *Education:* Northwestern University (B.A., 1977); Emory University (J.D., 1980). Office of Unfair Import Investigations, U.S. International Trade Commission. Adjunct Faculty, Swiss Federal Institute of Technology, Zurich, 1997—. Co-Author: "Doctrine of Equivalents Is Not Limited to Piracy," The National Law Journal, 1997; "U.S. Courts Rewrite Rules for Interpreting Patent Claims," Intellectual Property Worldwide, 1997. *Member:* The District of Columbia Bar; American Bar Association (Member, Sections of: Antitrust Law; Litigation; Patent, Trademark and Copyright Law); ITC Trial Lawyers Association (Chairman, Intellectual Property Law Developments Committee, 1990-1993; Member, Executive Committee, 1987-1988, 1990-1993). ***PRACTICE AREAS:*** Patent and Intellectual Property Litigation; Intellectual Property Licensing; Antitrust Litigation and Counseling; ITC Section 337 Litigation. ***Email:*** ssulzer@dickinson-wright.com

RESIDENT OF COUNSEL

LAURINDA L. HICKS, born Belo Horizonte M.G., Brazil, February 6, 1944; admitted to bar, 1987, Pennsylvania; 1989, Virginia; 1991, District of Columbia. *Education:* University of North Carolina (B.A., 1972); Faculdade de Direito da Pontificia Universidade Católica do Rio de Janeiro, Brazil (Bachelor of Laws, 1979); American University, Washington College of Law (LL.M., 1987). *Member:* Virginia State Bar; The District of Columbia Bar; International Trade Association. ***LANGUAGES:*** Portuguese, Spanish and French. ***PRACTICE AREAS:*** Intellectual Property; International Law. ***Email:*** lhicks@dickinson-wright.com

J. JOHN SHIMAZAKI, born Tokyo, Japan, January 30, 1959; admitted to bar, 1988, California, U.S. District Court, Northern District of California and U.S. Court of Appeals, Ninth Circuit; 1998, District of Columbia; registered to practice before the U.S. Patent and Trademark Office. *Education:* California Polytechnic State University (B.S., 1982); Brigham Young University (J.D., cum laude, 1988). *Member:* Orange County Bar Association; State Bar of California; The District of Columbia Bar. ***PRACTICE AREAS:*** Patent Law; Trademark Law; Licensing. ***Email:*** jshimazaki@dickinson-wright.com

RESIDENT ASSOCIATE

NICOLE M. MEYER, born Columbus, Ohio, January 12, 1973; admitted to bar, 1998, Virginia; 1999, U.S. Court of Appeals, Fourth Circuit (Not admitted in District of Columbia). *Education:* Amherst College (B.A., 1995); Washington College of Law of American University (J.D., 1998). Vice President, Intellectual Property Law Association, Washington College of Law. *Member:* Virginia and American Bar Associations. ***PRACTICE AREAS:*** Trademark Litigation and Prosecution; Copyright Litigation and Prosecution. ***Email:*** nmeyer@dickinson-wright.com

(This Listing Continued)

DICKSTEIN SHAPIRO MORIN & OSHINSKY LLP

Established in 1953

2101 L STREET, N.W.
WASHINGTON, D.C. 20037-1526
Telephone: 202-785-9700
Fax: 202-887-0689
URL: http://www.legalinnovators.com

New York, New York Office: 1177 Avenue of the Americas, 10036-2714. Telephone: 212-835-1400. Fax: 212-997-9880.
Correspondent Office, St. Petersburg, Russia: Russian-American Law Firm, Lermontovsky Prospect 7/12, 190008. Local Telephone: 114-5660. International Telephone: 850-1430.

General Practice, including: Antitrust, Bankruptcy and Creditors' Rights, Banking, Business Crimes/Regulatory Enforcement, Civil Litigation, Construction, Communications, Alternative Dispute Resolution, Corporate, Financial Institutions, Intellectual Property, Employee Benefits (ERISA), Energy, Environmental Law, Finance, Government Affairs, Government Contracts, Health Care, Immigration and Naturalization, Insurance, Intellectual Property, International Trade, Labor and

(This Listing Continued)

DICKSTEIN SHAPIRO MORIN & OSHINSKY LLP, Washington—Continued

Employment, Litigation, Mergers and Acquisitions, Natural Resources, Patents, Real Estate, Securities, Sports Law, Tax, Trademarks, Trusts and Estates, Utility Law, and White Collar Crime.

FIRM PROFILE: For more than 45 years, Dickstein Shapiro Morin & Oshinsky LLP's (Dickstein Shapiro) goal has been to achieve results for its clients. The firm has long served as litigation counsel in numerous cases of national importance throughout the United States. In the past two decades, Dickstein Shapiro's capabilities have branched out well beyond the litigation arena. Some of the nation's most distinguished attorneys practicing in areas such as bankruptcy, corporate, energy, environment, financial institutions, government contracts, intellectual property, international trade and public policy have joined the firm. Today, versatility and breadth of experience across legal disciplines enable Dickstein Shapiro to respond immediately and efficiently with a team approach to a client's most urgent and complex legal problems.

Through its varied achievements, Dickstein Shapiro has come to represent a broad range of clients from many different sectors of the economy. Dickstein Shapiro's more than 300 attorneys counsel business enterprises in such diverse fields as manufacturing, energy, banking, shipbuilding, electronics, aerospace and telecommunications, helping them to meet the challenges of increasingly competitive markets in the United States and elsewhere in the world. Current firm efforts span securities, tax, grand jury and other law enforcement proceedings, corporate mergers and acquisitions, energy projects, antitrust actions, labor and civil litigation, and major commercial and insurance litigation. The firm also represents trade associations, corporations, and state and local governments in Washington legislative and agency matters. Dickstein Shapiro can give clients assistance tailored to suit their particular needs, whether it be in a courtroom, a board room, an administrative proceeding, on Capitol Hill or at a State Capital.

MEMBERS OF FIRM

KENNETH L. ADAMS, born New York, N.Y., January 13, 1946; admitted to bar, 1971, District of Columbia and U.S. District Court, District of Columbia; 1974, U.S. Court of Appeals, District of Columbia Circuit; 1978, U.S. Claims Court; 1979, U.S. Court for Berlin; 1980, U.S. Supreme Court. *Education:* Yale University (A.B., 1967); University of Chicago (J.D., 1970). Legislative Assistant to Congressman Abner J. Mikva, 1970-1972. *Member:* The District of Columbia Bar; American Bar Association. ***PRACTICE AREAS:*** Litigation; Toxic Torts; Governmental Affairs. ***Email:*** AdamsK@dsmo.com

LEE A. ALEXANDER, born Pittsburgh, Pennsylvania, September 2, 1951; admitted to bar, 1976, Pennsylvania; 1979, District of Columbia; 1991, U.S. Supreme Court. *Education:* Pennsylvania State University (B.S., honors program with distinction, 1973); University of Pittsburgh (J.D., 1976). Notes Editor, University of Pittsburgh Law Review, 1975-1976. Deputy Chief of Staff to Chairman Martin L. Allday, 1989-1991, Senior Legal Advisor on Natural Gas Issues to Chairman Matha O. Hesse, 1988-1989, Attorney-Advisor, Office of the General Counsel, 1987-1988, Federal Energy Regulatory Commission. Assistant to the Director and Senior Attorney-Advisor, Office of Proceedings, 1982-1987, Assistant to the Director, Small Business Assistance Office, 1980-1982, Attorney-Advisor, Office of Proceedings, 1976-1980, Interstate Commerce Commission. *Member:* District of Columbia Bar (Member, Energy Section); Pennsylvania and American (Member, Energy Section) Bar Associations; Energy Bar Association. ***PRACTICE AREAS:*** Energy Law; Regulatory Law; Environment Law; Transportation Law. ***Email:*** AlexanderL@dsmo.com

ANGELO V. ARCADIPANE, born Trenton, New Jersey, July 31, 1941; admitted to bar, 1969, District of Columbia; 1977, U.S. Supreme Court. *Education:* Rider College (B.S., 1963); Pennsylvania State University (M.A., 1965); Georgetown University (J.D., 1968). Associate Editor, American Bar Association Annual Report on Developing Labor Law, 1972-1990. Attorney, Office of the General Counsel, National Labor Relations Board, 1968-1971. Managing Partner, 1992—. *Member:* The District of Columbia Bar; American Bar Association (Member, Labor and Employment Law Section). ***PRACTICE AREAS:*** ERISA; Labor Law; Litigation. ***Email:*** ArcadipaneA@dsmo.com

MATTHEW STEVEN BERGMAN, born New York, New York, February 17, 1966; admitted to bar, 1991, Maryland; 1993, District of Columbia. *Education:* Brandeis University (B.A., 1988); Emory Law School (1988-1989); George Washington University (J.D., 1991). ***PRACTICE AREAS:*** Banking; Real Estate; Corporate Law; Litigation. ***Email:*** BergmanM@dsmo.com

GEORGE T. BOGGS, born Charleston, South Carolina, April 17, 1947; admitted to bar, 1974, Virginia; 1975, District of Columbia. *Education:* Princeton University (A.B., cum laude, 1969); University of Virginia (J.D., 1974). Co-Author: "Foreign Corporations and Branches in the U.S.—Pricing Policies—Retention of Records—Foreign Laws—Secrecy," 6 Intl. Co. & Com. Law Rev., No. 6, 1990; "Expanded Tax Audits of Foreign-Owned Entities that Engage in U.S. Business," 18 Journal of the Japanese Institute of International Business Law, No. 6, 1990. Board of Outside Advisers, Virginia Tax Review, University of Virginia, 1986—. *Member:* The District of Columbia Bar; Virginia State Bar; Virginia, International and American (Taxation Section, Corporate Tax Committee, 1986—) Bar Associations. ***PRACTICE AREAS:*** International Business Law; International Law; Federal Taxation; International Taxation. ***Email:*** BoggsG@dsmo.com

JAMES W. BRADY, JR., born Allentown, Pennsylvania, June 30, 1957; admitted to bar, 1987, New York and U.S. District Court, Southern and Eastern Districts of New York; 1990, U.S. District Court, Northern District of New York; 1991, U.S. Court of Appeals, Federal Circuit; 1992, District of Columbia; registered to practice before U.S. Patent and Trademark Office. *Education:* The Pennsylvania State University (B.S. Env.E., with highest distinction, 1982); Cornell University (J.D., 1985); National Institute for Trial Advocacy, Georgetown University Law Center Continuing Legal Education Division (Diploma, 1998). Senior Editor, *IP Insights* Newsletter, 1995—. Author: "Protecting the Value of Chemical Patents Obtained Through Evidence of Comparative Experimental Results," IP Insights, Vol. 8, No. 4, 1998. *Member:* The District of Columbia Bar; American Bar Association; American Intellectual Property Law Association (Member, Chemical and Biotechnology Practice Committee); The Federal Circuit Bar Association (Member, Board of Directors, 1999—; Chairman, Judicial Conference, Annual Meeting Committee, 1992—; Member, Continuing Legal Education Committee, 1991—). ***PRACTICE AREAS:*** Intellectual Property; Biotechnology Law; Litigation. ***Email:*** BradyJ@dsmo.com

PAUL BENNETT BRAN, born Washington, D.C., September 10, 1958; admitted to bar, 1985, Maryland; 1986, District of Columbia, U.S. District and Bankruptcy Courts, District of Columbia, U.S. District and Bankruptcy Courts, District of Maryland, U.S. Courts of Appeal, District of Columbia and Fourth Circuit; 1987, Virginia and U.S. Court of Federal Claims; 1989, U.S. District and Bankruptcy Courts, Eastern District of Virginia and U.S. Supreme Court; 1994, U.S. Court of Appeals, Sixth Circuit. *Education:* University of Maryland (B.A., 1982); University of Miami (1983) and Georgetown University (J.D., cum laude, 1985). Member, The Tax Lawyer, 1984-1985. *Member:* The District of Columbia Bar; Virginia State Bar; Maryland State and American Bar Associations; American Bankruptcy Institute; Walter B. Chandler American Inn of Court. ***PRACTICE AREAS:*** Bankruptcy Law; Creditors Rights; Commercial Litigation. ***Email:*** BranP@dsmo.com

KENNETH W. BROTHERS, born Fall River Mills, California, August 24, 1962; admitted to bar, 1988, Colorado and U.S. District Court, District of Colorado; 1989, U.S. Court of Appeals, Tenth Circuit; 1990, U.S. District Court, District of Arizona; 1994, District of Columbia; 1996, U.S. District Court for the District of Columbia; 1997, U.S. Court of Appeals for the District of Columbia Circuit; 2000, U.S. Supreme Court. *Education:* University of Utah (B.S., 1985); George Washington University (J.D., with high honors, 1988). Order of the Coif. Member, Moot Court Board. Member, George Washington Law Review. Senior Editor, Harvard Journal of Law and Public Policy. Author: Note, "Church-Affiliated Universities and Labor Unions," 56 Geo. Wash. L. Rev. 558, 1988. Development and Review Editor, "Trademark Law and The Internet" (2d. ed. 2001). *Member:* The District of Columbia Bar; Colorado and American Bar Associations; International Trademark Association (Member, Publications Committee). ***PRACTICE AREAS:*** Complex Litigation; Intellectual Property Litigation; Commercial Litigation; Antitrust; Appellate Practice.

KAREN L. BUSH, born Denville, New Jersey, May 29, 1958; admitted to bar, 1984, California; 1988, District of Columbia; 1996, Maryland. *Education:* Bucknell University (B.A., with honors in English, cum laude, 1980); George Washington University (J.D., with honors, 1984). Co-Author: "Solid Case Law Demonstrates That There Is Insurance Coverage For Antitrust And Other Unfair Trade Practices Claims, And The Body Of That Case Law Is Growing," 13 Insurance Litigation Reporter 151, April 1991. Deputy City Attorney, Signal Hill and Laguna Beach, 1985-1986. *Member:* The District of Columbia Bar; Maryland State Bar Association. ***PRACTICE AREAS:*** General Litigation; Insurance Recovery; Insurance Litigation. ***Email:*** BushK@dsmo.com

HENRY C. CASHEN II, born Detroit, Michigan, June 25, 1939; admitted to bar, 1964, Michigan; 1969, U.S. Supreme Court; 1973, District of Columbia. *Education:* Brown University (A.B., with honors, 1961); University of Michigan (J.D., 1963). Deputy Counsel to the President of the United States, 1969-1970. Deputy Assistant to the President of the United States, 1971-1973. *Member:* The District of Columbia Bar; American Bar Association; State Bar of Michigan. ***PRACTICE AREAS:*** Administrative Law; Government Relations; Agency and Legislative Practice. ***Email:*** CashenH@dsmo.com

LESLIE R. COHEN, born Boston, Massachusetts, January 31, 1950; admitted to bar, 1975, Massachusetts and District of Columbia; 1978, U.S. Supreme Court. *Education:* Brandeis University (B.A., magna cum laude, 1971); Boston University (J.D., magna cum laude, 1974). Editor, Boston University Law Review, 1972-1974. Law Clerk to Hon. Bryan Simpson, U.S. Court of Appeals, Fifth Circuit, 1974-1975. Author: "Sex Discrimination and Sex-Based Mortality Tables," 53 B.U.L. Rev. 624, 1973. *Member:* The District of Columbia

(This Listing Continued)

Bar; Massachusetts, Federal and American Bar Associations; Women's Bar Association of District of Columbia. ***PRACTICE AREAS:*** Civil Litigation; Insurance. ***Email:*** CohenL@dsmo.com

ROBIN L. COHEN, born Philadelphia, Pennsylvania, October 27, 1961; admitted to bar, 1986, Pennsylvania; 1989, New Jersey and New York; U.S. District Court, Southern District of New York. *Education:* University of Pennsylvania (B.A., magna cum laude, 1983; J.D., 1986). (Resident, New York, N.Y. Office). ***PRACTICE AREAS:*** Litigation; Insurance Litigation; Insurance Recovery. ***Email:*** CohenR@dsmo.com

RICHARD J. CONWAY, born Boston, Massachusetts, February 22, 1948; admitted to bar, 1973, District of Columbia. *Education:* Boston College (B.S., cum laude, 1969); Georgetown University (J.D., 1972). Editor, Law and Policy in International Business, 1971-1972. Co-Author: "Foreign Takeovers of High-Tech Companies: Practical Considerations and Strategies for the Defence Contractor," 1 Int'l Co. & Com. L. Rev., No. 1, 1990; "Defence Strategies to Protect Against Foreign Investment," The National Law Journal, Mergers and Acquisitions Special, September 25, 1989; "Business Strategies from the Vendor's Perspective," 6 The Computer Lawyer, August 1989. Speaker: "Considerations Involving When and Where to File a Protest Action," Eastern Briefing Conference, Bid Protest Panel, May 13, 1987. Attorney-Adviser, Procurement Law, Office of General Counsel, U.S. General Accounting Office, 1972-1976. *Member:* The District of Columbia Bar; American Bar Association. ***PRACTICE AREAS:*** Government Contract Law. ***Email:*** ConwayR@dsmo.com

THOMAS J. D'AMICO, born New Brunswick, New Jersey, April 13, 1947; admitted to bar, 1974, Virginia; 1974-1982, U.S. Court of Customs and Patent Appeals; 1977, U.S. Claims Court; 1978, District of Columbia; 1982, U.S. Court of Appeals, Federal Circuit; registered to practice before U.S. Patent and Trademark Office. *Education:* Washington University (B.S.E.E., 1969); George Washington University (J.D., with honors, 1974). Co-Author: "E-commerce Law Report," 1998—; "Protecting Assets from Internet Fraud," Journal of Asset Protection, March/April 1998; "Sealed With a Click: Forming Enforceable On-Line Arguments," The Licensing Journal, October 1997; "Who Owns the Future? Choice of Law in Cyberspace," Outside Counsel, Spring 1996; "Recent Changes in Jury Trial Practice in the Federal Circuit," The Law Works, January 1996; "U.S. Intellectual Property Law and the Internet," English and Japanese versions in four part series, Japanese Group AIPPI Journal, June 1996 to February 1997; "Piecemeal Decisions Are Forcing On-Line Service Providers Between a Rock and a Hard Place," The Computer Lawyer, November 1995. Contributing Author: "Litigation Support Services," McGraw Hill CPE Course, November 1995. Co-Author: "Calculating Damages in Patent Infringement Actions," Journal of the Japanese Institute of International Business Law, February 1993. Author: "Reading Patent Claims from a Financial Perspective," Deloitte & Touche Hearsay, November 1999; "Downloading the Foreign Internet Defendant Into U.S. Courts," JPA Journal, April 1997; "Practical Aspects of Discovery for a Foreign Corporation Involved in U.S. Patent Litigation," European Intellectual Property Law Review, January 1993 and Japanese Group AIPPI Journal, January/February 1992; "Employer Liability for Unauthorized Copying of Software by Employees," The Computer Lawyer, February 1992; "Non-Statutory Subject Matter: The USPTO's Revamped Software Rejection of the Nineties," Japanese Group AIPPI Journal, May 1992; "Practical Aspects of Discovery for a Foreign Corporation Involved in U.S. Patent Litigation," Japan AIPPI Journal, September 1991; Founding Editor, IP Insights, the quarterly Dickstein Shapiro Morin & Oshinsky LLP intellectual property newsletter. Speaker, "Patent Infringement on the Internet," AIPLA Mid-Winter Program, February 1999; "Intellectual Property Law & the Standards Setting Process," CEMA Mid-Winter Meeting, February 1998; "Damages in U.S. Intellectual Property Law Disputes," KPMG Mid-Winter Seminar, March 1998; "Personal Jurisdiction and the Internet," Cyberlaw Law School, October 1997 and 1998. Co-Chair and Speaker, "Personal Jurisdiction and the Internet," Netlaw '97, September 1997. Speaker, "Intellectual Property Law 'The Internet', " PTC Section, ABA Spring Program, April 1997. Lecturer: "U.S. Intellectual Property Law and the Internet," AIPPI of Japan, May 1997; "Patent Litigation in U.S. Courts and the ITC," Taiwan Computer Association, May 1997; "Calculating and Minimizing Damages in Patent Infringement Actions," License Executives Society of Japan, April 1987; "Calculating Damages in Patent Infringement Actions," AIPPI of Japan, September 1987; "Views From the Outside," USPTO Academy, 1979. Patent Examiner, U.S. Patent Office, 1969-1975. Law Clerk, U.S. Patent Office Board of Appeals, 1974-1975. Technical Advisor and Law Clerk to Hon. Donald E. Lane, U.S. Court of Customs and Patent Appeals, 1975-1977. *Member:* The District of Columbia Bar (Member, Steering Committee, Patent, Trademark and Copyright Section, 1988-1990); Virginia State Bar; Virginia and American Bar Associations; American Intellectual Property Law Association; Patent Lawyers Club. ***PRACTICE AREAS:*** Intellectual Property Law. ***Email:*** DAmicoT@dsmo.com

MERLE MILLER DeLANCEY, JR., born Alexandria, Virginia, September 21, 1966; admitted to bar, 1991, Virginia; 1992, District of Columbia, U.S. Court of Appeals, Fourth Circuit; 1993, U.S. District Court for the District of Columbia, U.S. District Court, District of Maryland and U.S. District Court, Eastern District of Virginia. *Education:* Furman University (B.A., 1988); Wake

(This Listing Continued)

Forest University (J.D., 1991). Business Editor, Wake Forest University Law Review. Member, Executive Council, Moot Court. Co-Author: "Service Contracts: Allegations of 'Bait & Switch,'" Briefing Papers, Second Series, No. 97-6, May 1997; "Substantial Completion in Construction Contracts," Briefing Papers, Second Series, No. 96-4, March 1996; "Can One Unilaterally Gain the Right to Make Unilateral Changes in Working Conditions?" The Labor Lawyer, Vol. 9, No. 2, Spring 1993. *Member:* Virginia State Bar; Bar Association of the District of Columbia; American Bar Association. ***PRACTICE AREAS:*** Government Contract/Regulation; Litigation/Complex and Multi-District; ERISA/Employee Benefits; Leases and Leasing; Health Care. ***Email:*** DelanceyM@dsmo.com

IDA WURCZINGER DRAIM, born Paterson, New Jersey, December 14, 1955; admitted to bar, 1982, New York and U.S. District Court, Eastern and Southern Districts of New York; 1987, District of Columbia; 1991, U.S. District Court for the District of Columbia; 1997, U.S. Court of Appeals for the District of Columbia. *Education:* Rutgers University (B.A., 1977); Harvard University (J.D., 1981). Phi Beta Kappa. Speaker, "Internal Audit Programs for Broker-Dealers," National Regulatory Services Compliance Conferences, 1998-2000; "Variable Products," and "Broker-Dealer Sales Compensation Issues," Financial Markets Association 2000 Compliance Conference. Author: Year 2000 Supplement to "Securities Fraud: Litigating under rule 10b-5" (Matthew Bender); "A Compliance Officer's New Year's Resolutions," NSCP Currents, Jan./Feb. 1993; "SEC Faces Mandatory Arbitration Issue," The National Law Journal, Nov. 14, 1988; "Confusion Follows SEC Reaction to Stock Market Crash," The National Law Journal, Nov. 9, 1987; "A Glance at SEC's Treble Penalty Provision," New York Law Journal, July 27, 1987; "Disclosure of a Potential Change in Corporate Counsel," (co-authored with SEC Associate Director of Enforcement, Joseph I. Goldstein), The Review of Securities and Commodities Regulation, Vol. 19, June 11, 1986; "SEC Regulation of Accountants' Independence," (co-authored with former SEC Director of Enforcement, Gary Lynch), ALI-ABA Course Materials Journal, Vol. 10, Dec. 1985 and Practicing Law Institute on Legal Liability of Accountants, B4-6715 (1985); "Toward a Definition of 'Tender Offer'," Harvard Journal on Legislation, Vol. 19, 1982. Member, NASDAQ Listing Qualifications Appeals Panel. Enforcement Attorney, U.S. Securities and Exchange Commission, 1984-1985. Special Counsel to Chairman John Shad, U.S. Securities and Exchange Commission, 1986-1987. *Member:* The District of Columbia Bar (Chair, Steering Committee of Corporation, Finance and Securities Law Section, 1996-1997); New York State Bar Association; National Association of Securities Dealers (Board of Arbitrators, Board of Mediators). ***PRACTICE AREAS:*** Securities. ***Email:*** DraimI@dsmo.com

STEPHEN A. DVORKIN, born Brooklyn, New York, June 21, 1947; admitted to bar, 1974, New York and U.S. Court of Appeals, Second Circuit; 1975, U.S. District Court, Southern and Eastern Districts of New York and U.S. Court of Appeals, Second Circuit. *Education:* New York University (B.A., 1969; J.D., 1973; LL.M., 1981). Author: "Purchased Policy as Pig in Poke," 3 (2) Journal of Insurance Coverage 20, Spring, 2000; "Personal Injury, Insurance Coverage For Environmental Liability," 2 Environmental Claims Journal 333, Spring, 1990; "Categorical Waiver of an Insurance Company's Right to Receive Notice of Third-Party Claims," 3 Insurance Coverage Litigation Reporter 125, August 2, 1996. Assistant U.S. Attorney, Southern District of New York, 1981-1987. Chief, General Enforcement Branch, U.S. Environmental Protection Agency, Region II, 1976-1981. *Member:* New York State Bar Association (Member, Environmental Law Committee). (Resident, New York, N.Y. Office). ***PRACTICE AREAS:*** Civil Litigation; Insurance Law; Environmental Law. ***Email:*** DvorkinS@dsmo.com

LARRY F. EISENSTAT, born Pittsburgh, Pennsylvania, December 15, 1953; admitted to bar, 1985, Pennsylvania; 1988, U.S. District Court, Western District of Pennsylvania; 1989, District of Columbia; 1990, U.S. District Court, Eastern District of Pennsylvania; 1994, U.S. Court of Appeals for the District of Columbia Circuit. *Education:* University of Chicago (B.A., 1982; J.D., 1985). *Member:* The District of Columbia Bar; Pennsylvania and American Bar Associations; Federal Energy Bar Association. ***PRACTICE AREAS:*** Energy; Utilities; Litigation; Antitrust; Eminent Domain. ***Email:*** EisenstatL@dsmo.com

DAVID L. ELKIND, born New York, N.Y., November 2, 1957; admitted to bar, 1984, New York; 1989, District of Columbia. *Education:* George Washington University (B.A., with distinction in Journalism, 1979); Georgetown University Law Center (J.D., cum laude, 1983). Editor, Law and Policy in International Business, 1982-1983. Author: "Litigating Environmental Claims," 15 The Risk Management Letter, Issues 4-5, 1994; "Insurance Coverage for Asbestos Claims Against Foreign Corporations," 5 International Insurance Law Review 31, October 1997. *Member:* The District of Columbia Bar; New York State and American Bar Associations. ***PRACTICE AREAS:*** Insurance Litigation; Commercial Litigation. ***Email:*** ElkindD@dsmo.com

DAVID L. ENGELHARDT, born Easton, Pennsylvania, November 4, 1962; admitted to bar, 1989, Pennsylvania; 1990, District of Columbia, U.S. Court of Appeals for the District of Columbia Circuit and U.S. District Court for the District of Columbia; 1995, U.S. Court of Appeals, Ninth Circuit. *Education:* Bucknell University (B.A., summa cum laude, with honors in English, 1984); Georgetown University (J.D., cum laude, 1989). Phi Beta Kappa. ***PRAC-***

(This Listing Continued)

DICKSTEIN SHAPIRO MORIN & OSHINSKY LLP, Washington—Continued

TICE AREAS: Complex Civil Litigation; Energy; Construction; Insurance Coverage; Administrative Law; Appellate Practice. ***Email:*** EngelhardtD@dsmo.com

EMANUEL FAUST, JR., born Columbia, South Carolina, May 1, 1958; admitted to bar, 1983, District of Columbia; 1984, U.S. District Court, District of Columbia. *Education:* University of South Carolina (B.A., 1980); Duke University (J.D., 1983). Member, Duke Law Journal, 1981-1983. *Member:* The District of Columbia Bar. ***PRACTICE AREAS:*** Corporate Law; Securities Law; Corporate Finance, Mergers and Acquisitions. ***Email:*** FaustE@dsmo.com

MARGARET FEINSTEIN, born New York, N.Y., November 12, 1958; admitted to bar, 1988, Pennsylvania; 1990, District of Columbia. *Education:* Wesleyan University (B.A., 1981); American University (J.D., 1988). Editor, Law Review of The Washington College of Law, 1987-1988. Co-author: "Comparable Worth Claims-Minimizing The Risk," 12 Employment Relations Today 135, 1986. Law Clerk to Hon. Patricia C. Fawsett, U.S. District Court, Middle District of Florida. ***PRACTICE AREAS:*** Civil Litigation; Government Affairs. ***Email:*** FeinsteinM@dsmo.com

HOWARD N. FELDMAN, born New Hyde Park, New York, February 15, 1958; admitted to bar, 1983, Maryland; 1984, District of Columbia; 1986, U.S. District Court for the District of Columbia; 1995, U.S. District Court for the District of Maryland; 1997, U.S. Court of Appeals, 4th Circuit; 1998, U.S. Court of Appeals, Ninth Circuit,. *Education:* State University of New York at Stony Brook (B.A., with high honors, 1980); American University (J.D., magna cum laude, 1983). Phi Beta Kappa. Member, 1981-1982 and Assistant Editor, 1982-1983, American University Law Review. Author: "H.L. v. Matheson: Where Does the Court Stand on Abortion and Parental Notification?" 31 Am. U. L. Rev. 431, 1982; "Settling on a Division of Liability," Legal Times (July 24, 1995); "SEC Year 2000 Disclosure Requirements," Corporate Finance Reporter (June/July 1998); "SEC Requires Year 2000 Compliance From Broker-Dealers," Securities Operations Letter (February 1999), Global Custody News (February 1999). Law Clerk to Hon. Rita C. Davidson, Court of Appeals of Maryland, 1983-1984. *Member:* The District of Columbia Bar; Maryland State Bar Association; Maryland Trial Lawyers Association. ***PRACTICE AREAS:*** Litigation: Securities, Commercial, Product Liability and Intellectual Property. ***Email:*** FeldmanH@dsmo.com

BARRY J. FLEISHMAN, born New York, N.Y., October 27, 1956; admitted to bar, 1981, Pennsylvania and U.S. District Court, Eastern District of Pennsylvania; 1984, District of Columbia and U.S. Court of Appeals for the District of Columbia Circuit. *Education:* New York University (B.A., 1976; J.D., 1981). Phi Beta Kappa. Note and Comment Editor, Review of Law and Social Change. Author: "Emerging Liability Issues for the New Electric Power Industry," The Electricity Journal, March 1998; "Electric Utilities Cut Back On R & D Projects," Power Quality Assurance Magazine, January/February 1997; "The Basics of the New Customer/Supplier Electric Power Relationship," Power Quality Assurance Magazine, September/October 1996; "Using Legal Decisions To Help Prevent Products Liability—The 'Sophisticated Buyer' Defense," Power Quality Assurance Magazine, March/April 1996; "Using Legal Decisions to Help Prevent Products Liability—Design Defects," Power Quality Assurance Magazine, January/February 1996; "Whose Fault Is It?" Power Quality Assurance Magazine, November/December 1995; "Power Quality And Products Liability Law Emerging Issues," International Conference and Exhibition, Germany, Fall 1995; "Insurance Coverage for Latent Injury Claims—EMF Litigation," Power Quality Assurance Magazine," September/October 1995; "British High Court Rejects Attempt to Force Regulation on Regulation on EMF," Power Quality Assurance Magazine, July/August 1995; "Punitive Damages—What's Behind All the Commotion?" Power Quality Assurance Management, July/August 1995; "The Essential Connection Between Loss Prevention and Liability," Power Quality Assurance Magazine, March/April 1995; "Emerging Insurance Coverage Issues In the Electric Power Industry," Power Quality Assurance Magazine, January/February 1995; "Duty to Warn," Power Quality Assurance Magazine, November/December 1994. Lecturer: Coordinating Group on Energy Law/Torts and Insurance Practice Section, American Bar Association, San Antonio, TX, 1997; Insurance Coverage Committee, American Bar Association, Tucson, AZ, 1992; The Corporate Bar—Association of Westchester and Fairfield, Inc., Stamford, CT, 1997; EPRI Power Quality Interest Group Meeting, Rochester, NY, 1997; Environmental Liability Coverage, Institute of Scrap Recycling Industries, Las Vegas, NV, Chicago, IL and Philadelphia, PA, 1994; National Apartment Association, Washington, DC and Atlanta, GA, 1997; National Multi Housing Council, Laguna Niguel, CA, 1997; Power Quality Assurance National Convention Exhibition, Dallas, TX, 1994, Long Beach, CA, 1995 and Las Vegas, NV, 1996; Alberta Exposition and Conference on Power Quality, Calgary, AB, 1995; Power Quality International Conference and Exhibition, Bremen, Germany, 1995; Court TV—Insurance Coverage Instruction, Washington, DC, 1997. Member, Advisory Board, Power Quality Assurance Magazine. *Member:* The District of Columbia Bar; American Bar Association (Former Chair, Energy Resources Law Committee; Member, Professionalism

(This Listing Continued)

Committee; Chair, Coordinating Group on Energy Law, 1998-1999). ***PRACTICE AREAS:*** Insurance Litigation; Electric Power Products Liability. ***Email:*** FleishmanB@dsmo.com

LAWRENCE D. GARR, born Philadelphia, Pennsylvania, September 25, 1945; admitted to bar, 1971, Pennsylvania; 1977, U.S. Tax Court; 1980, U.S. Supreme Court; 1985, District of Columbia; 1986, U.S. Court of Appeals, Fourth Circuit; 1987, U.S. Claims Court. *Education:* University of Pennsylvania (B.A., 1967); Temple University (J.D., 1971); Georgetown University (LL.M., Taxation, 1974). Author: "The New Bank Levy Law; Impact on Bank Procedures," The Banking Law Journal, March-April, 1990. Co-Author: "Use of Summons May be Limited When Taxpayer Is In Bankruptcy Court," 3 Bankruptcy Law Reporter 629, May 23, 1991; "From the IRS, Deals for Deadbeats," The Washington Post, Outlook Section, March 22, 1992; "Cutting a Deal with the IRS in 1997: Forms Over Substance," Vol. 76, No. 4, Tax Notes 547, July 28, 1997; "The IRS—Still Going for the Jugular," The Washington Post, Op-Ed Section, January 12, 1998. Senior Tax Attorney, Office of Chief Counsel, Internal Revenue Service, 1971-1985. *Member:* The District of Columbia Bar; Federal and American (Member, Taxation Section) Bar Associations. ***PRACTICE AREAS:*** Taxation (Local, State, Federal or International) Law; Federal Income Estate and Gift Taxation Law; Taxation of Individuals and Business Entities; IRS Collection Procedures; Litigation; Criminal; Bankruptcy. ***Email:*** GarrL@dsmo.com

ALLAN B. GOLDSTEIN, born Glen Cove, New York, October 30, 1948; admitted to bar, 1974, New York; 1983, Florida; 1985, Virginia; 1989, District of Columbia. *Education:* George Washington University (B.A., 1970; LL.M, Taxation, 1978); Albany Law School of Union University (J.D., 1973). Member, Albany Law Review, 1972-1973. Trial Attorney, Tax Division, U.S. Department of Justice, 1979-1983. *Member:* The District of Columbia Bar; Virginia State Bar; The Florida Bar; New York State Bar Association. ***PRACTICE AREAS:*** Banking Law; Real Estate (Property) Law; Taxation of Individuals Law; Business Entities Law. ***Email:*** GoldsteinA@dsmo.com

HOWARD GRAFF, born New York, N.Y., July 22, 1948; admitted to bar, 1973, New York and U.S. District Court, Southern and Eastern Districts of New York; 1976, U.S. Court of Appeals, Second Circuit; 1985, U.S. Court of Appeals, Fourth, Sixth, Eleventh and Eighth Circuits. *Education:* American University (B.A., 1969); Rutgers University (J.D., 1972). *Member:* New York State and American (Member, Antitrust Section) Bar Associations. (Resident, New York, N.Y. Office). ***PRACTICE AREAS:*** Litigation. ***Email:*** graffh@dsmo.com

G. MICHAEL GREEN, born Rockville Centre, New York, September 29, 1958; admitted to bar, 1983, District of Columbia. *Education:* Georgetown University (B.S.B.A., summa cum laude, 1980; J.D., magna cum laude, 1983). Associate Editor, The Tax Lawyer, 1982-1983. Certified Public Accountant, District of Columbia, 1981. *Member:* The District of Columbia Bar. ***PRACTICE AREAS:*** Tax Law. ***Email:*** GreenM@dsmo.com

DONALD A. GREGORY, born Washington, D.C., July 26, 1951; admitted to bar, 1979, Virginia, U.S. Court of Appeals, Fourth and Fifth Circuits; 1980, U.S. Court of Appeals, Federal Circuit; 1987, District of Columbia; registered to practice before U.S. Patent and Trademark Office. *Education:* University of Virginia (B.S. Nuc. Engr., with distinction, 1973); College of William & Mary (J.D., 1979). Phi Delta Phi. Co-Author: *Introduction to Intellectual Property Law*, BNA, 1994; "The U.S. Patent Office Guidelines for Computer Implemented Inventions," I European Intellectual Property Review 56, 1996; "Patentees Can Restrict Use of Sold Items," National Law Journal May 16, 1994; "Tie-Outs—Misuse of U.S. Patents," 9 European Intellectual Property Review 317, 1992; "Patent and Data Rights under U.S. Government Contracts," The Virginia State Bar News, October 1985. Member: American Nuclear Society, 1980-1981; Engineer Club of Richmond, Virginia, 1982-1984. U.S. Correspondent, European Intellectual Property Review, 1988—. *Member:* Fairfax and Virginia Bar Associations; Virginia State Bar (Member, Intellectual Property Section); American Intellectual Property Law Association; Licensing Executives Society. ***PRACTICE AREAS:*** General Practice; Licensing Law; Patent, Trademark and Copyright Law. ***Email:*** GregoryD@dsmo.com

JON DAVID GROSSMAN, born Baltimore, Maryland, March 29, 1955; admitted to bar, 1988, Pennsylvania and District of Columbia; U.S. Supreme Court; registered to practice before U.S. Patent and Trademark Office. *Education:* University of Chicago (B.A., 1977); Johns Hopkins University (M.S., Computer Sciences, 1982); American University (J.D., 1986). Co-Author: *Introduction to Intellectual Property Law*, BNA, 1994; "Intellectual Property Legal Opinions," Aspen Law and Business, 1999; "A Step-by-Step Guide to Prosecuting Business Method Patents," The Computer Lawyer, March 2000; "Intellectual Property Licensing: The Hidden Costs of Internet Radio," E-Commerce Law Report October 1999; "Internet Basics and Copyright Law," Journal of Internet Law, June 1998; "ISP Contracts: What to Look For," Advisor Insite, June 1998; "Legal Risks Remain for On-Line Businesses," Washington Technology, July 1996; "United States v. Microsoft-A Review of the On-going Struggles?" Computer and Telecommunications Law Review, Oct/Nov. 1995; "Substantial Similarity at Issue in Software Infringement Cases," The National Law Journal; March 1990; "Protection for Computer Software," European In-

(This Listing Continued)

tellectual Property Review, November 1988 and January 1989; "Software Ideas, Expression Need A Uniform System of Protection," The National Law Journal, August 1988; "Moral Rights and Computer Software: An International Overview," The Computer Lawyer, June 1988. Adjunct Faculty, The Johns Hopkins University, 1990-1991. Patent Examiner, U.S. Patent and Trademark Office, Computer Control and Applications, 1985-1987. *Member:* The District of Columbia Bar; Pennsylvania and American Bar Associations. ***PRACTICE AREAS:*** Patent Law; Copyright Law; Computer Law. **Email:** GrossmanJ@dsmo.com

KATHERINE J. HENRY, born Purcell, Oklahoma, June 23, 1958; admitted to bar, 1990, Pennsylvania; 1991, U.S. Court of Appeals, District of Columbia and Fourth Circuits; 1992, District of Columbia and U.S. Court of Appeals, Eleventh Circuit; 1993, U.S. District Court, District of Columbia and District of Maryland; 1994, U.S. Court of Appeals, Federal Circuit and U.S. Court of Federal Claims. *Education:* Oklahoma Baptist University (B.A., magna cum laude, with honors, 1981); Baylor University; University of Oklahoma; University of Chicago (J.D., with honors, 1989). Winner, 1988 Thomas J. Mulroy Prize. Fellow, Bradley Law and Government Program. Associate Editor, University of Chicago Law Review. Champion, 1988 Hinton Moot Court. Law Intern, The Office of Solicitor General of the United States, 1989. Law Clerk to Judge Irving L. Goldberg, U.S.C.A. for the Fifth Circuit, 1989-1990. Editor, National Association of Women Lawyers Journal, 1999—. Liaison to Women in the Profession, 2000—. *Member:* District of Columbia Bar; American Bar Association; Chartered Institute of Arbitrators; National Association of Women Lawyers (Immediate Past President, 2000-2001, President, 1999-2000, President Elect, 1998-1999, Vice President, 1996-1997 and Member, Board of Directors, 1995—); Women's Bar Association of the District of Columbia. ***PRACTICE AREAS:*** Civil Litigation; Insurance Coverage Litigation; Complex Commercial Litigation; White Collar Crime; Appellate Practice; Alternative Dispute Resolution. **Email:** HenryK@dsmo.com

ROBERT J. HIGGINS, born Wilkes-Barre, Pennsylvania, June 2, 1941; admitted to bar, 1969, District of Columbia; U.S. District Court for the District of Columbia; U.S. Supreme Court; U.S. Court of Appeals for the District of Columbia Circuit; U.S. Court of Appeals, 1st, 2nd, 3rd, 4th, 5th, 7th, 9th and 11th Circuits; U.S. Tax Court. *Education:* Kings College (A.B., 1963); Pennsylvania State University (M.A., 1965); Georgetown University (J.D., 1968). Law Clerk to Hon. William B. Jones, U.S. District Court, District of Columbia, 1968-1969. Assistant U.S. Attorney, District of Columbia, 1969-1973. Advisory Committee on Rules, U.S. District Court, District of Columbia, 1973—. Member, Judicial Conference of the District of Columbia Circuit, 1972—. *Member:* The District of Columbia Bar. ***PRACTICE AREAS:*** Securities Litigation; General Commercial Litigation; ERISA; RICO; Labor Litigation. **Email:** HigginsR@dsmo.com

GARY M. HOFFMAN, born Philadelphia, Pennsylvania, February 25, 1946; admitted to bar, 1971, Virginia; 1972, District of Columbia; 1974-1982, U.S. Court of Customs and Patent Appeals; 1975, U.S. Court of Appeals, District of Columbia Circuit; 1982, U.S. Court of Appeals, Federal Circuit; registered to practice before U.S. Patent and Trademark Office. *Education:* University of Pennsylvania (B.S.E.E., 1967); George Washington University (J.D., with honors, 1971). Co-editor of "Patent Litigation Strategies Handbook," Sponsored by ABA and published by BNA, 2000. Co-Author: "Trials in Multiple Parts," IP Litigator 1998; "Paper Side of Patent Litigation," PLI 1998; "Marking of Patent Articles: Failure Can Deny You Damages," Corporate Counsel Magazine, 1998; "The Doctrine of Equivalents Goes Back to its Boots: Hilton Davis," European Intellectual Property Review, 1996; "In Opinions to Clients, Intellectual Property Lawyers Face Risks," The National Law Journal, 1993; "Substantial Similarity at Issue in Software Infringement Cases," The National Law Journal, March 1990; "Curbing International Piracy of Intellectual Property - Policy Options for a Major Exporting Country," The Annenberg Washington Program, September 1989; "Patents: Underutilized Leverage for Protecting and Licensing Software," The Computer Lawyer, May 1989. Lecturer, AIPLA, American Bar Association, Prentice Hall Law and Business Seminars, Association of Corporate Patent Counsel, ALI-ABA and Patent Resource Group. Patent Examiner, U.S. Patent Office, 1967-1972. Law Clerk to Fred Strader, Board of Appeals of U.S. Patent and Trademark Office, 1971-1972. Co-Chairman, Seminar on Virginia's Center for Innovative Technology, 1985. Member, Board of Correspondents of European Intellectual Property Review, 1987—. Member, Board of Advisors, The Computer Lawyer, 1988—. Project Director for the Annenberg Washington Program's Project on Curbing International Piracy of Intellectual Property, 1988-1989 and Forum on Computer Software Protection, 1991. *Member:* The District of Columbia Bar; Virginia State Bar (Member, Board of Governors, Patent, Trademark and Copyright Section, 1981-1983; Secretary, 1983-1984; Vice-Chairman, 1984-1985; Chairman, 1985-1986); Virginia (Chairman, Intellectual Property Committee, 1987-1988) and American Bar Associations (Chairman, Committee on Attorney's Opinions for Intellectual Property Section, 1994-1996); American Intellectual Property Law Association (Member: Patent Law Committee, 1973-1978; Publications Committee, 1977-1979; Member, 1979— and Subcommittee Chairman, 1982-1988, Federal Practice and Procedure Committee; Member and Subcommittee Chairman, 1980-1981, Young Lawyers' Committee; Chairman, Federal Litiga-

(This Listing Continued)

tion Committee, 1989-1991; Chairman, Litigation Advocacy Committee, 1987-1989; Co-Chairman of the 1999 Mid-Winter Institute on Cyberspace Law and the 1989 and 1995 Mid-Winter Institutes on the Art of Litigation Advocacy). ***PRACTICE AREAS:*** Intellectual Property Law; Computer Law; Litigation. **Email:** HoffmanG@dsmo.com

R. BRUCE HOLCOMB, born New York, N.Y., July 16, 1956; admitted to bar, 1981, District of Columbia; 1982, U.S. District Court, District of Columbia and U.S. Court of Appeals, District of Columbia Circuit. *Education:* Ithaca College (B.A., magna cum laude, 1978); George Washington University (J.D., with honors, 1981). Member, 1979-1980, and Notes Editor, 1980-1981, George Washington Law Review. *Member:* The District of Columbia Bar; American Bar Association. ***PRACTICE AREAS:*** Litigation; Antitrust Law; Securities Law; Insurance Law. **Email:** HolcombB@dsmo.com

J. ANDREW JACKSON, born Norfolk, Virginia, August 24, 1959; admitted to bar, 1984, West Virginia and U.S. District Court, Southern District of West Virginia; 1988, U.S. Claims Court; U.S. Court of Appeals, Federal Circuit; 1992, District of Columbia; 1993, Virginia. *Education:* Virginia Military Institute (B.S.E.E., with distinction, 1981); West Virginia University (J.D., 1984); George Washington University (LL.M., Government Procurement Law, 1989). Co-Author: "The Qui Tam Quagmire: Understanding the Law in an Era of Aggressive Expansion," Washington Legal Foundation; "Service Contracts: Allegations of 'Bait and Switch,'" Federal Publications Inc., Briefing Papers, Second Series, May 1997; "Expanding Contracting Opportunities Without Competition," Public Contract Law Journal, Volume 26, Number 2, Winter 1997. Author: "Lobbying Disclosure Act of 1995: Traps for Unwary Government Contractors," The American Lawyer's Corporate Counsel Magazine, August 1996. Co-Author: "Rewriting the Contract," Legal Times, June 17, 1996; "Substantial Completion in Construction Contracts," Federal Publications Inc., Briefing Papers, Second Series, March 1996. Lecturer: "The Basics of Commercial Contracting," Federal Publications Inc. Litigation Attorney, U.S. Department of the Army, 1988-1989. Special Assistant United States Attorney, U.S. Department of Justice, 1988-1989. Trial Attorney, Civil Division, U.S. Department of Justice, 1989-1990. *Member:* Bar Association of the District of Columbia; Virginia, West Virginia (inactive) and American (Member, Public Contract Section) Bar Associations. [U.S. Army JAGC, 1984-1988]. ***PRACTICE AREAS:*** Government Contract Law; Government Contract Litigation; Federal Litigation. **Email:** JacksonA@dsmo.com

HOWARD S. JATLOW, born Newark, New Jersey, December 30, 1949; admitted to bar, 1975, District of Columbia. *Education:* George Washington University (B.A., 1971); American University (J.D., 1974). Recipient: Wall Street Journal Award for Outstanding Student in Investment and Portfolio Management, Class of 1971; Faculty Award for Outstanding Graduating Law Student, Class of 1974. Co-author: "The Role of Environmental Assessments in Real Estate Transactions," Real Estate Law Journal, Spring 1990; "Assessing Liability the Environmental Review Process," Corporate Real Estate Executive, March-April 1990. *Member:* The District of Columbia Bar; American Bar Association (Member, Section on Corporation, Banking and Business Law). ***PRACTICE AREAS:*** Banking Law; Commercial Law; Real Estate Law; Sports Law. **Email:** JatlowH@dsmo.com

JEFFREY M. JOHNSON, born Roanoke, Virginia, July 16, 1954; admitted to bar, 1979, District of Columbia; 1989, Maryland. *Education:* Denison University (B.A., cum laude, 1976); Georgetown University (J.D., 1979). Editor, Georgetown Law Journal, 1978-1979. Director, Council for Court Excellence, 1984-1987. Barrister, Charles Fahy American Inn of Court, 1983-1986. Master, Giles Sutherland Rich American Inn of Court, 1997-1999. *Member:* The District of Columbia Bar; Maryland State and American (Member, Section on Litigation and Intellectual Property) Bar Associations. ***PRACTICE AREAS:*** Patent Litigation; Civil Litigation; Trial Practice. **Email:** JohnsonJeff@dsmo.com

PETER HAFNER JOST, born New Rochelle, New York, June 7, 1949; admitted to bar, 1977, Virginia and District of Columbia; 1978, U.S. District Court, District of Columbia and U.S. Tax Court; 1979, U.S. District Court, Eastern District of Virginia; 1983, U.S. Supreme Court. *Education:* University of North Carolina (A.B., with honors, 1971); University of Virginia (J.D., 1977). Phi Beta Kappa. John Motley Morehead Foundation Scholar. Co-Author: "Reforms May Increase Contractors' Liability Risks," The National Law Journal, May 19, 1997. Author: "Navigating The Global Marketplace—Political Risk in the People's Republic of China, Columbia, and Canada," Corporate Counsel Magazine, April 1997. Commissioner, 1984-1986, Chairman, 1986-1990, Alexandria Redevelopment and Housing Authority. Member, Sharon Pratt Dixon Transition-Housing Subcommittee, 1990-1991. Board Member, 1992— and President, 1993-1996, Canadian-American Business Council. *Member:* The District of Columbia Bar; Virginia State Bar; Virginia and American (Member, Committee on Affiliated and Related Corporations, Section on Taxation, 1983-1985) Bar Associations. ***PRACTICE AREAS:*** International Transactions; Commercial Law; Real Estate Law; Local, State, Federal and International Taxation Law; Federal Income Estate and Gift Taxation Law. **Email:** JostP@dsmo.com

(This Listing Continued)

DICKSTEIN SHAPIRO MORIN & OSHINSKY LLP, Washington—Continued

PETER J. KADZIK, born Kenmore, New York, November 8, 1953; admitted to bar, 1978, New York and District of Columbia. *Education:* State University of New York at Buffalo (B.A., summa cum laude, 1974); Georgetown University (J.D., 1977). Phi Beta Kappa. Articles Editor, Georgetown Law Journal, 1976-1977. Law Clerk to Hon. Thomas A. Flannery, U.S. District Court, District of Columbia, 1977-1978. Assistant United States Attorney, District of Columbia, 1978-1980. Member and Chairman, Hearing Committee No. 8, Board on Professional Responsibility, District of Columbia Bar, 1980-1987. Member, Region 2 Advisory Board, Thrift Depositor Protection Oversight Board, 1993-1995. Member, President's Advisory Committee on the Arts (John F. Kennedy Center for the Performing Arts) 1999—. *Member:* The District of Columbia Bar; Erie County, New York State and American (Member, Sections on: Litigation; Antitrust Law) Bar Associations. ***PRACTICE AREAS:*** Antitrust Law; Legislative Practice; Litigation. ***Email:*** KadzikP@dsmo.com

LESLIE A. KAPLAN, born New York, N.Y., April 12, 1947; admitted to bar, 1986, Maryland; 1987, District of Columbia. *Education:* University of Pennsylvania (B.A., 1968); Boston University (M.Ed., 1972); Georgetown University (J.D., cum laude, 1986). Editor, Georgetown Law Journal, 1985-1986. *Member:* The District of Columbia Bar; Maryland State and American Bar Associations; Women's Bar Association of the District of Columbia. ***PRACTICE AREAS:*** Real Estate; Financial Institutions; Lending. ***Email:*** KaplanL@dsmo.com

GEORGE KAUFMANN (1931-1990).

LEON B. KELLNER, born New York, N.Y., December 31, 1945; admitted to bar, 1972, New York; 1974, U.S. Court of Appeals, Second Circuit and U.S. District Court, Southern District of New York; 1985, Florida; 1992, U.S. Court of Federal Claims; 1995, U.S. Court of Appeals for the District of Columbia Circuit; 1996, District of Columbia; 1998, U.S. Court of Appeals, Eleventh Circuit and U.S. District Court, District of Columbia. *Education:* State University of New York at Buffalo (B.A., cum laude, 1967); Harvard University (J.D., 1971). Chief, Civil Division, 1982-1984, Executive Assistant U.S. Attorney, U.S. Attorneys Office, 1984-1985 and U.S. Attorney, 1985-1988, Southern District of Florida. *Member:* The Association of the Bar of the City of New York (Secretary, Administrative Law Committee, 1974-1977); Dade County, New York State and American (Member, Ad Hoc Committee on Sentencing Guidelines, 1986-1988) Bar Associations; District of Columbia Bar; Federal Bar Council; Eastern Mineral Law Foundation (Member, Coal Subcommittee, 1981-1982). ***PRACTICE AREAS:*** Civil Litigation; Insurance Coverage Litigation. ***Email:*** KellnerL@dsmo.com

DEBORAH P. KELLY, born Plainfield, New Jersey, December 25, 1952; admitted to bar, 1988, Maryland; 1989, District of Columbia; 1993, U.S. Supreme Court. *Education:* University of Vermont (B.S., magna cum laude, 1974); Johns Hopkins University (M.A., 1977; Ph.D., 1982), McCoy Prize, John Hart Fellowship; American University (J.D., summa cum laude, 1988). Mussey Prize. Author: "Harassment-Sex and Other Forms," Employment Law Desk Book for Human Resource Professionals and General Counsels, 2001; "Securities Industry Must Prepare for Arbitration's End," Corporate Legal Times, Sept. 1998; "Protecting Yourself, Guarding Against Sexual Harassment," Doing Business, Dec. 1997; "Understanding and Preventing Sexual Harassment in the Workplace," and "Interviewing - The Legal Perspective," Home Care Human Resources Manual, Aspen Publishers, Inc., June 1997; "What Should You Know About Sexual Harassment?" 4 Perspectives, July 1996; "Victims Participation in the Criminal Justice System," Skogan & Davis (eds), in Victims of Crime, Sage Publications, 2nd edition, 1996, 1st ed. 1990; "Anti-Stalking Laws: The States Respond," National Abortion Federation, Legal Clearinghouse, 1993; "Empowering Clinics: A User's Guide to Victim Impact Statutes," National Abortion Federation Legal Clearinghouse, 1992; "Have Victims Reforms Gone Too Far or Not Far Enough?" 6 ABA Criminal Justice, Fall 1991; "Reconcilable Rights to a Fair Trial and a Free Press," in A Time for Choices, First Amendment Congress, 1991. Adjunct Professor, Washington College of Law, American University, 1992-1994; Political Science Professor, 1981-1988. *Member:* The District of Columbia Bar; Maryland State Bar Association; American Bar Association (Member, Labor and Employment Section; Vice-Chair, Publications Committee, EEO Section, 1995-1996; Chair, 1991-1994, Vice Chair, 1988-1991, Criminal Justice Section, Victims Committee); American Law Firm Association (Member, Steering Committee of Labor and Employment Law Practice Group, 1998—). ***PRACTICE AREAS:*** Employment Litigation; Corporate Counseling; Civil Litigation. ***Email:*** KellyD@dsmo.com

JAMES D. KELLY, born Manhasset, New York, May 18, 1961; admitted to bar, 1989, New York; 1990, District of Columbia. *Education:* Assumption College (B.A., cum laude, 1983); University College, Ireland (1983); Fordham University (J.D., 1988). *Member:* Bar Association of the District of Columbia; Bar Association of the City of New York; New York State and American Bar Associations. ***PRACTICE AREAS:*** Commercial Transactions; Real Estate; Banking and Financial Institutions. ***Email:*** KellyJ@dsmo.com

(This Listing Continued)

WILLIAM D. KINGERY, JR., born Boston, Massachusetts, November 6, 1948; admitted to bar, 1978, New York; 1981, U.S. Tax Court; 1982, District of Columbia. *Education:* Massachusetts Institute of Technology (S.B., 1974); Syracuse University (J.D., cum laude, 1977); New York University (LL.M., Taxation, 1979). Member, 1976-1977, Technical Editor, 1977-1978, Syracuse Journal of International Law and Commerce. Attorney-Advisor, United States Tax Court, 1979-1981. *Member:* The District of Columbia Bar; New York State and American (Member, Section on Taxation) Bar Associations. ***PRACTICE AREAS:*** Tax Law. ***Email:*** KingeryW@dsmo.com

JOEL B. KLEINMAN, born New York, N.Y., August 24, 1949; admitted to bar, 1975, District of Columbia; 1989, New York. *Education:* University of Virginia (B.A., 1971); Georgetown University (J.D., 1974). *Member:* The District of Columbia Bar; New York State and American Bar Associations. ***PRACTICE AREAS:*** Insurance Coverage Law; Antitrust and Trade Regulation Law; Communications Law. ***Email:*** KleinmanJ@dsmo.com

JOSEPH E. KOLICK, JR., born Waynesburg, Pennsylvania, January 11, 1955; admitted to bar, 1979, District of Columbia; 1980, U.S. District Court, District of Columbia. *Education:* University of Pennsylvania (B.A., cum laude, 1975); Georgetown University (J.D., magna cum laude, 1979). Lecturer: "The Fruits of Internal Investigation—Are They Protected by Privilege?" 1999 National CLE Conference, Civil Litigation (LE 1, BNA). *Member:* The District of Columbia Bar; American Bar Association (Member, Sections on: Labor and Employment Law; Litigation). ***PRACTICE AREAS:*** Securities Litigation; Commercial Litigation; Employment Law. ***Email:*** KolickJ@dsmo.com

MARK H. KOLMAN, born Baltimore, Maryland, August 24, 1946; admitted to bar, 1972, Maryland; 1980, U.S. District Court, District of Maryland, U.S. Court of Appeals, Fourth Circuit and U.S. Supreme Court; 1991, District of Columbia; 1992, U.S. District Court, District of Columbia. *Education:* Bucknell University (B.A., 1968); University of Maryland (J.D., 1971). Lecturer: Presenting Litigation, Insurance Coverage and Evidence, Maryland Institute for Continuing Professional Education of Law (MICPEL). Assistant States Attorney for Baltimore City, 1971-1975. Assistant States Attorney for Baltimore County, Chief Circuit Court Division, 1975-1980. Assistant Federal Defender, District of Maryland, 1980. Assistant U.S. Attorney, District of Maryland, 1980-1984 (Chief Criminal Cases). Partner, Gordon, Feinblatt, Rothman, Hoffberger and Hollander, 1984-1991 (Chairman Litigation Department). Partner, Anderson Kill Olick & Oshinsky, 1991-1996. Partner, DSMO, 1996—. Member, Board of Directors, Maryland States Attorneys' Association, 1977-1991. Member, Board of Trustees, Maryland Chapter, Leukemia Society of America, 1986-1991. Member, Board of Directors, National Coalition for Cancer Survivorship, 1992-1996. Member, University of Maryland Cancer Center, Board of Visitors, 1993—. *Member:* Baltimore County, Maryland State, Federal (Past Chairman, Board of Governors, Maryland Chapter, 1990-1991; President, Maryland Chapter, 1994-1995; Member, Board of Governors, D.C. Chapter FBA, 1998—) and American Bar Associations; District of Columbia Bar. ***PRACTICE AREAS:*** General Litigation; Insurance Litigation. ***Email:*** KolmanM@dsmo.com

IRA L. KOTEL, born New York, New York, May 25, 1964; admitted to bar, 1990, New York. *Education:* Rutgers College, Rutgers University (B.A., summa cum laude, 1986); Columbia University (J.D., 1989). James A. Elkins Scholar. Member, Columbia Business Law Review, 1988. Formerly with Cravath, Swaine & Moore. *Member:* The Association of the Bar of the City of New York; New York State and American Bar Associations. (Resident, New York, N.Y. Office). ***PRACTICE AREAS:*** Mergers, Acquisitions and Divestitures; Business Law; Corporate Finance and Securities.

JOHN T. KOTELLY, born Detroit, Michigan, October 13, 1938; admitted to bar, 1968, District of Columbia and U.S. Court of Appeals, District of Columbia Circuit. *Education:* Rensselaer Polytechnic Institute (B.A.E., 1960); Georgetown University (J.D., 1967). Recipient, John Marshall Award for Litigation, U.S. Department of Justice, 1978. Law Clerk to Hon. Andrew M. Hood, Chief Judge, District of Columbia Court of Appeals, 1968-1969. Assistant United States Attorney, District of Columbia, 1969-1978, 1979-1981. Special Litigation Counsel, Criminal Division, Department of Justice, 1978-1979. Deputy Independent Counsel for the Alexis Herman Investigation, 1998-2000. Member, D.C. Commission on Judicial Disabilities and Tenure, 1984-1985. *Member:* The District of Columbia Bar; American Bar Association. ***PRACTICE AREAS:*** White Collar Criminal Defense Law; Civil and Criminal Litigation. ***Email:*** KotellyJ@dsmo.com

ALBERT H. KRAMER, born Los Angeles, California, August 30, 1940; admitted to bar, 1968, California and District of Columbia. *Education:* University of California at Berkeley (B.A., with honors, 1963; M.A., with honors, 1964); Stanford University (LL.B., 1967). Phi Beta Kappa. Member, Board of Editors, Stanford Law Review, 1965-1967. Director, Bureau of Consumer Protection, Federal Trade Commission, 1977-1981. *Member:* The District of Columbia Bar (Chairman, Administrative Law and Agency Practice Division, 1974-1975); State Bar of California; American Bar Association (Member: Section of Science and Technology; Forum Committee on Communications Law). ***PRACTICE AREAS:*** Communications Law; Administrative Law; Trade Regulation Law. ***Email:*** KramerA@dsmo.com

(This Listing Continued)

STEFAN M. KRANTZ, born Durham, North Carolina, October 12, 1967; admitted to bar, 1992, Pennsylvania; 1993, District of Columbia; 1996, U.S. Court of Appeals for the District of Columbia Circuit. *Education:* Cornell University (B.A., cum laude, with honors, 1989); American University (J.D., 1992). Member, Washington College of Law, Law Review. Author: "Unbundling at the State Level and the Critical Role of Marketers," National Law Journal, July 28, 1997; "Gas Contracting in the Emerging Retail Market," Natural Gas Contracts, Nov. 1997; "Retail Energy Blueprint," Independent Energy, April 1998. Co-Author: "Small Business Decisions in the New Gas Industry," Outside Counsel, Winter 1996. *Member:* American Bar Association (Member, Section on Natural Resources, Energy, and Environmental Law); Federal Energy Bar Association. ***LANGUAGES:*** French and Hebrew. ***PRACTICE AREAS:*** Energy Law; Natural Gas Transactions; Regulatory. ***Email:*** KrantzS@dsmo.com

ARTHUR J. LAFAVE III, born Cleveland, Ohio, July 30, 1954; admitted to bar, 1981, District of Columbia; 1983, U.S. Court of International Trade; 1985, U.S. Court of Appeals, Federal Circuit. *Education:* Williams College (B.A., cum laude, 1976); The Johns Hopkins School of Advanced International Studies (M.A., with distinction, 1978); University of Virginia (J.D., 1981). Order of the Coif. Director, American Hospital of Istanbul, Inc., 1990—. *Member:* The District of Columbia Bar; Bar Association of the District of Columbia; American Bar Association; Customs and International Trade Bar Association. ***PRACTICE AREAS:*** Customs Law; International Trade Law. ***Email:*** LafaveA@dsmo.com

NEIL LEFKOWITZ, born Princeton, New Jersey, August 28, 1953; admitted to bar, 1980, New York; 1984, District of Columbia. *Education:* Oberlin College (B.A., 1975); University of North Carolina (J.D., with honors, 1979). Phi Beta Kappa; Order of the Coif. Member, North Carolina Law Review, 1978-1979. *Member:* The District of Columbia Bar; New York State and American Bar Associations. ***PRACTICE AREAS:*** Emerging Company Law; Corporate Transactions; Corporate Finance. ***Email:*** LefkowitzN@dsmo.com

RICHARD J. LEVERIDGE, born Jamestown, New York, June 14, 1956; admitted to bar, 1981, District of Columbia; 1982, U.S. District Court, District of Columbia; 1986, U.S. Supreme Court; 1988, U.S. Court of Appeals, Fourth Circuit; 1990, U.S. Court of Appeals, District of Columbia; 1997, New York; 1998, U.S. District Court, Southern and Eastern Districts of New York. *Education:* Providence College (B.A., magna cum laude, 1978); Georgetown University (J.D., cum laude, 1981). Co-Author: "Using Smart Contracting To Assure Efficiency In Resolving Complex Construction Cases," 17 The Construction Contractor 3, 1993. *Member:* The District of Columbia Bar; American Bar Association. ***PRACTICE AREAS:*** Litigation. ***Email:*** LeveridgeR@dsmo.com

BARRY WM. LEVINE, born New York, N.Y., December 25, 1942; admitted to bar, 1969, New York and California; 1970, District of Columbia and U.S. Court of Appeals, District of Columbia Circuit; 1971, U.S. Tax Court; 1975, U.S. Claims Court; 1979, U.S. Court of Appeals, Third Circuit; 1980, U.S. Court of Appeals, Second and Fourth Circuits; 1982, U.S. Court of Appeals, Federal Circuit; 1988, U.S. Court of Appeals, Ninth Circuit; 1996, U.S. Court of Appeals, Eleventh Circuit. *Education:* New York University (B.S., 1964); University of California at Berkeley-Boalt Hall (J.D., 1967). Fellow, Institute Universitaire de Hautes Etudes Internationales, Geneva, Switzerland. Author: 1994 Complex Crimes Journal, "The Deprivation of 'Intangible Rights' Under the Mail Fraud Statute: Some Key Considerations," American Bar Association Section of Litigation, Criminal Litigation Committee, December 1994; Lawyers' Desk Book on White-Collar Crime, "Responding to Subpoenas," The National Legal Center for the Public Interest, December 1991. Assistant United States Attorney, District of Columbia, 1969-1975. Member, Judicial Conference of the District of Columbia Circuit, 1977—. *Member:* The District of Columbia Bar; State Bar of California; American Bar Association (Member, Sections on: Criminal Justice; Litigation); Assistant U.S. Attorney's Association of the District of Columbia (Member, Executive Committee, 1978); American Judicature Society; National Association of Criminal Defense Lawyers. ***PRACTICE AREAS:*** Criminal Law; Criminal Trial Practice; Civil Litigation; Intellectual Property Trial Practice. ***Email:*** LevineB@dsmo.com

DANIEL M. LITT, born New York, N.Y., 1952; admitted to bar, 1978, District of Columbia; 1980, Maryland. *Education:* Syracuse University (B.A., cum laude, 1974); University of Copenhagen, Copenhagen, Denmark; Georgetown University (J.D., 1978). Member, 1977 and Editor, 1978, Georgetown Law Journal. Law Clerk to Hon. Sarah T. Hughes, U.S. District Court, Northern District of Texas, 1978-1979. ***PRACTICE AREAS:*** Bankruptcy Law; Creditors Rights; Commercial Litigation. ***Email:*** LittD@dsmo.com

FREDERICK M. LOWTHER, born Sewickley, Pennsylvania, December 28, 1943; admitted to bar, 1969, New York; 1970, Pennsylvania; 1973, District of Columbia. *Education:* Brown University (A.B., magna cum laude, 1965); Yale University (J.D., 1968). Phi Beta Kappa. Author: "The Iroquois Pipeline Project: A Study in Federal/State Conflict," Alberta Law Review, Vol. XXXI, No. 1, 1993. Law Clerk, Hon. Caleb M. Wright, U.S. District Court, District of Delaware, 1968-1969. Associate, Pepper, Hamilton & Scheetz, Philadelphia, Pennsylvania, 1969-1971. Attorney, U.S. Maritime Administration, 1971-1972.

(This Listing Continued)

Director, Office of Energy Programs, U.S. Department of Commerce, 1972-1973. Member, Board of Directors: EEX Corporation; Poseidon Resources Corporation; Northeast Gas Markets; KeySpan Energy Development Corporation. General Counsel and Counsel to the Chairman, KeySpan Energy, 1998—. *Member:* The District of Columbia Bar; New York State, Pennsylvania, Federal Energy and American Bar Associations. ***PRACTICE AREAS:*** Administrative Law; Energy Law; International Practice; Water Law. ***Email:*** LowtherF@dsmo.com

PATRICK WINSTON LYNCH, born Chapel Hill, North Carolina, June 19, 1962; admitted to bar, 1988, New York and District of Columbia. *Education:* Duke University (B.A., magna cum laude, 1984); Columbia University (J.D., 1987). Phi Eta Sigma. Harlan Fiske Stone Scholar. *Member:* The District of Columbia Bar; New York State, American and Energy Bar Associations. ***PRACTICE AREAS:*** Energy; Project Finance; International Law; Water Law. ***Email:*** LynchP@dsmo.com

KENNETH M. LYONS, born Newark, New Jersey, October 24, 1955; admitted to bar, 1980, Virginia and District of Columbia. *Education:* Seton Hall University (A.B., 1977); Washington & Lee University (J.D., 1980). *Member:* The District of Columbia Bar; Virginia State Bar; American Bar Association. ***Email:*** LyonsK@dsmo.com

MATTHEW G. MALONEY, born Cleveland, Ohio, June 1, 1957; admitted to bar, 1981, Virginia and District of Columbia. *Education:* Georgetown University (B.S.F.S., cum laude, 1978); University of Virginia (J.D., 1981). Order of the Coif. Executive Editor, Virginia Journal of International Law, 1980-1981. Law Clerk to Hon. Albert V. Bryan, U.S. Court of Appeals, Fourth Circuit, 1981-1982. *Member:* The District of Columbia Bar; Virginia and American (Member, Sections on: International Law; Corporation, Banking and Business Law) Bar Associations; Virginia State Bar; American Society of International Law. ***PRACTICE AREAS:*** Securities Law; General Corporate Law. ***Email:*** MaloneyM@dsmo.com

ELAINE METLIN, born Pittsburgh, Pennsylvania, January 26, 1951; admitted to bar, 1985, Maryland and District of Columbia. *Education:* University of Pittsburgh (B.A., magna cum laude, 1972); University of Virginia (J.D., 1983). Author: "Going to Court Against Antiabortion Action: A Model Pleadings Book," NAF Legal Clearinghouse, 2d ed. 1995; "The First Amendment Book: A Guide to Abortion Providers and Their Attorneys," NAF Legal Clearinghouse, 3d ed. 1996. Staff Attorney, U.S. District Court, Jacksonville, Florida, 1983-1984. *Member:* The District of Columbia Bar; Maryland State and American Bar Associations; Women's Bar Association; National Association of Women Lawyers; American Health Lawyers; U.S. Supreme Court Bar. ***PRACTICE AREAS:*** White Collar Criminal Defense; Antitrust; Health Care; Civil Litigation. ***Email:*** MetlinE@dsmo.com

ANDREW P. MILLER, born Fairfax, Virginia, December 21, 1932; admitted to bar, 1960, Virginia; 1967, U.S. Supreme Court; 1979, District of Columbia. *Education:* Princeton University (A.B., 1954); University of Virginia (LL.B., 1960). Phi Beta Kappa; Omicron Delta Kappa. Raven Society. Editor-in-Chief, Virginia Law Review, 1959-1960. Co-Author: "The Constitutionality of Political Gerrymandering: Davis v. Bandemer and Beyond," 4 J. Law & Politics 697 (1988); "Amended Section 2 of the Voting Rights Act: What Is the Intent of the Results Test?" 36 Emory L.J. 1 (1987); "Davis v. Bandemer—Political Gerrymandering Challenged on Equal Protection Grounds," 17 Urb. Lawyer 945 (1985). Attorney General, Virginia, 1970-1977. Chairman, Southern Conference of Attorneys General, 1973-1974. President, The John Marshall Foundation, 1987-1989. Vice Chairman, Virginia Board of Corrections, 1983-1986. *Member:* The District of Columbia Bar; Bar Association of the District of Columbia; Virginia (Chairman, Young Lawyers Section, 1967-1968; Member, Executive Committee, 1985-1988) and American (House of Delegates, 1971-1976; Action Commission on Court Costs and Delay, 1979-1984; Commission on Public Understanding About the Law, 1992-1995) Bar Associations; Virginia State Bar; American Judicature Society (Member, Executive Committee, 1974-1976; Director, 1973-1976); National Association of Attorneys General (Chairman, Antitrust Committee, 1971-1976; Member, Executive Committee, 1973-1974). Fellow: American Bar Foundation. [U.S. Army, Artillery, 1955-1957, 1st Lt.]. ***PRACTICE AREAS:*** Litigation; Government Affairs. ***Email:*** MillerA@dsmo.com

G. JOSEPH MINETTI (1907-1993).

M. J. MINTZ, born Philadelphia, Pennsylvania, October 29, 1940; admitted to bar, 1969, District of Columbia. *Education:* Temple University (B.S., 1961; J.D., 1968). Executive Editor, Temple Law Quarterly. Certified Public Accountant, 1965. Adjunct Professor of Law, International School of Law, 1974-1978. Attorney Advisor to Hon. Bruce M. Forrester, U.S. Tax Court, 1968-1970. Assistant General Counsel, Cost of Living Council, Executive Office of the President, 1971-1973. Member, U.S. Secretary of Labor's ERISA Advisory Council, 1981-1985. Board of Advisors, U.S. Pension Benefit Guaranty Corporation, Appointed by President Reagan, 1987, reappointed and designated Chairman by President Bush, 1991. Appointed as Member of Virginia Public Building Authority by Governor George Allen, 1996-2001. *Member:* The Dis-

(This Listing Continued)

DICKSTEIN SHAPIRO MORIN & OSHINSKY LLP, Washington—Continued

trict of Columbia Bar; American Bar Association (Member, Section on Taxation). ***PRACTICE AREAS:*** Employee Benefit Law; ERISA; Tax Controversies Law; Business Planning. ***Email:*** MintzM@dsmo.com

IRA R. MITZNER, born Brooklyn, New York, July 24, 1947; admitted to bar, 1973, District of Columbia. *Education:* Brown University (B.A., cum laude, 1969); Georgetown University (J.D., 1973). Editor and Principal Contributor: *ERISA Litigation: A Basic Guide*, International Foundation of Employee Benefit Plans, 1993. Author: "Documents and Procedures Necessary for Effective Collection," Institute on Collection of Employer Contributions, 1982; "Litigation Under Section 303 of the LMRA," 1A West's Federal Practice Manual; "Collection of Employer Delinquencies to Multiemployer Employee Benefit Plans," Employee Benefits Annual, Vol. 27, 1985; "Collection Philosophies and Strategies That Work," International Foundation Digest, Vol. 23, No. 9, September 1986; "Conflicts of Responsibility," Employee Benefits Annual, Vol. 29, 1987; "Multiemployer Trustees Face Conflicts of Responsibilities," Pension World, February, 1988; "Trustee Pitfalls: The Need to Recognize Problem Areas," Employee Benefit Issues, Vol. 31, 1989; "The Art of Collection," Trustees Handbook, 4th Edition, 1990; "The Art of Collection," Employee Benefit Issues - The Multiemployer Perspective, Vol. 32, 1990; "Trustee Pitfalls: The Need to Recognize Fiduciary Problem Areas," employee Benefit Issues, 1991; "Collection of Employer Delinquencies," Employee Benefit Issues, 1992; "Trustee Pressures When There Is An Economic Downturn," International Foundation Digest, July 1994; "Liability Exposures of ERISA Fiduciaries," Professional Liability Insurance, published by International Risk Management Institute, November 1994; "Collection Strategies in the Construction Industry," Employee Benefit Issues, 1995; "Prohibited Transactions - A Reality Check," Employee Benefit Issues, Vol. 38; "ERISA Litigation: What Every Trustee Should Know," Employee Benefits Journal, Vol. 21, No. 4, December 1996; "Collections," Trustees Handbook, 5th Edition, 1998; "Recent Legal Decisions - Pension," Employee Benefit News, 1999; "ERISA Litigation: Up Close and Personal," Employee Benefit Issues, 1998. Adjunct Professor, George Washington University, 1994—. *Member:* The District of Columbia Bar; American Bar Association. ***PRACTICE AREAS:*** ERISA; Labor (Employees) Law; Litigation. ***Email:*** MitznerI@dsmo.com

PETER W. MORGAN, born Poughkeepsie, New York, August 14, 1951; admitted to bar, 1978, District of Columbia. *Education:* Davidson College (A.B., 1973); University of Virginia (M.A., 1974; J.D., 1978). Order of the Coif. Author: "The Appearance of Propriety: Ethics Reform and the Blifil Paradoxes," 44 Stan. L. Rev. 593, 1992; "The Undefined Crime of Lying to Congress: Ethics Reform and the Rule of Law," 86 Nw. U.L. Rev. 177, 1992; "Broader Costs of the New Prosecutorial Ethics," 11 J. Law & Politics 543, 1995. Co-Author: with Glenn Reynolds, "The Appearance of Impropriety: How the Ethics Wars Have Undermined Government, Business, and Society," The Free Press, 1997. Associate Professor of Law, University of Tennessee, 1989-1992. *Member:* The District of Columbia Bar; American Bar Association. ***PRACTICE AREAS:*** Alternative Dispute Resolution; Litigation; Government Ethics; Governmental Affairs. ***Email:*** MorganP@dsmo.com

KENNETH R. MORROW, born Selma, Alabama, July 27, 1958; admitted to bar, 1990, Maryland; 1993, District of Columbia. *Education:* University of Maryland (B.S., magna cum laude, 1980; J.D., with honor, 1990). Order of the Coif. *Member:* Maryland State and American Bar Associations; District of Columbia Bar. ***PRACTICE AREAS:*** Corporations; Mergers and Acquisitions; Securities; Business Law. ***Email:*** MorrowK@dsmo.com

DAVID M. NADLER, born Brooklyn, New York, August 22, 1956; admitted to bar, 1981, Pennsylvania; 1982, U.S. Court of Appeals, Federal Circuit; 1986, District of Columbia; 1990, Virginia. *Education:* Brooklyn College (B.A., summa cum laude, 1978); Temple University (J.D., 1981). Author or Co-Author: "SBA Proposes Contract Building Protections," *Government Technology Reseller,* May 1999; "Administration Relaxes Restrictions on Encryption Software," *E-Commerce Law Report,* November 1999; "House Passes Digital Signature Act," *Cyberspace Lawyer,* December 1999; "Resellers Face IT Accessibility Standards," *Government Technology Reseller,* November 1999; "OFPP Denies Audit-Clause Challenge," *Government Technology Reseller,* January 2000; "Congress Proposes Anticybersquatting Legislation," *Journal of Internet Law,* February 2000; "Courts Issue Key Decisions on Cyber - Ad Jurisdictions," *Cyberspace Lawyer,* April 2000; "Time is Running Out for Internet Self-Regulation," Washington Technology, July 1998; "Embedded Systems—The Real Year 2000 Problem," Corporate Counsel Magazine, July 1998; "Court Backs ISP Third Party Immunity," Washington Technology, May 1998; "Navigating the Bid Protest Process," Government Technology Reseller, May 1998; "Speeding Up Slow Payment," Government Technology Reseller, March 1998. Attorney-Advisor, Naval Sea Systems Command, 1981-1984. Trial Attorney, Litigation Division, U.S. Department of the Navy, 1984-1986. *Member:* The District of Columbia Bar; American Bar Association. ***PRACTICE AREAS:*** Computer Technology Law; Intellectual Property; Government Contracts. ***Email:*** NadlerD@dsmo.com

(This Listing Continued)

MICHAEL E. NANNES, born Detroit, Michigan, March 21, 1953; admitted to bar, 1977, District of Columbia; 1978, Florida. *Education:* University of Michigan (B.B.A., with high distinction, 1974); Georgetown University (J.D., 1977). Staff Member, 1975-1976, Topics Editor, 1976-1977, Georgetown Law Journal. Co-Author: "Using Smart Contracting To Assure Efficiency In Resolving Complex Construction Cases," 17 The Construction Contractor 3, 1993; "First of Its Kind Waste - Water Privatization - A Lesson in Teamwork," Corporate Counsel Magazine, December 1997. Law Clerk to Hon. John H. Pratt, U.S. District Court, District of Columbia, 1978. *Member:* The District of Columbia Bar; American Bar Association. ***PRACTICE AREAS:*** Energy Law; Construction Law; Arbitration Law. ***Email:*** NannesM@dsmo.com

BERNARD NASH, born New York, N.Y., September 22, 1942; admitted to bar, 1966, New York; 1977, District of Columbia and Maryland; 1987, U.S. Supreme Court. *Education:* City College of the City University of New York (B.B.A., 1963); Brooklyn Law School (J.D., cum laude, 1966). Associate Editor, Brooklyn Law Review, 1965-1966. Special Counsel, Securities and Exchange Commission, 1966-1971. Counsel, Committee on the Judiciary, Subcommittee on Antitrust and Monopoly, United States Senate, 1971-1977. *Member:* New York State, Maryland State, Federal and American (Member, Section on Antitrust Law) Bar Associations. ***PRACTICE AREAS:*** Antitrust; Complex Litigation; Alternative Dispute Resolution; State Government Law; Public Policy; Legislative Practice. ***Email:*** NashB@dsmo.com

ERIC OLIVER, born Trenton, New Jersey, April 21, 1965; admitted to bar, 1993, Pennsylvania; 1994, District of Columbia and New York; registered before U.S. Patent and Trademark Office. *Education:* Drexel University (B.S.E.E., 1988); George Washington University (J.D., 1993). Phi Eta Sigma; Eta Kappa Nu. Author: "Patentability in the Protection of Computer Program-Related Inventions," Patent World, 1993; "Beyond Patents: Alternative Forms of Protection for Computer Programs and Related Inventing in the United States," Patent World, 1993. Co-Author: "With Hilton Davis the Federal Circuit Takes the Doctrine of Equivalents Back to Its Roots (With a View to the Future)," Law Works, 1995; "Working with the Doctrine of Equivalents After Hilton Davis," Computer Lawyer, 1995; "Federal Circuit Expands Use of Patent Infringement Evidence," The Intellectual Property Strategist, 1995; "The Doctrine of Equivalents After Hilton-Davis," Computer Lawyer, 1996; "Closing Arguments in Patent Cases: Knowing Your Theory," Law Works, 1996; "Chapter 6: Formulating a Discovery Plan," *Patent Litigation Strategies Handbook,* 2000; "Prosecuting Business Method Patents," *Cyberspace Lawyer,* November 1999; "Intellectual Property Licensing: The Hidden Costs of Internet Radio," *E-commerce Law Report,* October 1999. Patent Examiner, U.S. Patent and Trademark Office, 1988-1990. ***PRACTICE AREAS:*** Intellectual Property. ***Email:*** OliverE@dsmo.com

JEROLD OSHINSKY, born Jersey City, New Jersey, July 12, 1942; admitted to bar, 1968, New York; 1969, U.S. District Court, Southern District of New York, U.S. Court of Appeals, Second Circuit and U.S. District Court, Eastern District of New York; 1971, U.S. Supreme Court; 1979, U.S. Court of Federal Claims; 1980, District of Columbia, U.S. District Court for the District of Columbia and U.S. Court of Appeals for the District of Columbia Circuit; 1987, U.S. Court of Appeals, Sixth Circuit; 1988, U.S. Court of Appeals, Fifth Circuit; 1990, U.S. Court of Appeals, Third Circuit and Eighth Circuits. *Education:* Brooklyn College of the City University of New York (B.A., 1964); Columbia University (LL.B., 1967). Harlan Fiske Stone Scholar. Editor, Columbia Journal of Law and Social Problems, 1966-1967. Member, Advisory Counsel, Lawyers Committee for Human Rights. Author: "Property Damage," Asbestos Issues '88, Vol. 1 No. 5 (1988); "NEPACCO - An Aberration: Insurance Coverage for Hazardous Waste Cleanups Far from Settled by Erroneous Eighth Circuit Ruling," The Environmental Counselor, No. 6 (1989); "The Trigger of Coverage Under the Standard Form CGL Policies for Delayed-Manifestation Bodily Injury and Property Damage Claims Arising from Asbestos, Hazardous Substances, and Environmental Impairment Litigation," The Environmental Counselor, No. 7 (1989); "Insurance Industry Documents Relating to the Pollution Exclusion Under Standard CGL Policies," The Environmental Counselor, N0. 8 (1989); "Environmental Coverage Litigation Involving the CGL Policy: What is a Suit?" Environmental Hazards, Vol. 1 No. 2 (1990); "A Funny Thing Happened on the Way to the Forum," Environmental Hazards, Vol. 1 No. 3 (1989); "The Coverage Lawyer as Indiana Jones: Finding Lost Insurance Coverage," Environmental Hazards, Vol. 2 No. 7 (1990); "Avoiding the Courtroom," Asbestos Issues, Vol. 3 No. 6 (1990); "Environmental Impairment Liability: The CGL Policyholder's Viewpoint," The John Liner Review, Vol. 4 No. 2 (1990); "Procedural Practical, Tactical and Strategic Issues in Coverage Disputes Stemming from Mass Tort Claims," Managing Complex Litigation (ABA Tort and Insurance Section 1992); "Insurance Coverage for CERCLA and other Environmental Impairment Claims," in R. Mays, CERCLA Litigation, Enforcement and Compliance (Shepard's/McGraw-Hill 1993). Co-Author and Editor, "Practitioner's Guide to Litigating Insurance Coverage Actions," Aspen Law and Business, Fall 1994; Practitioner's Guide to Litigating Insurance Coverage Actions," Second Edition, Aspen Law and Business, 1998; "Something Old, Something New: An Overview of Major Issues Facing Policyholders in Insurance Coverage Disputes," Journal of Insurance Coverage, Vol. 1, No. 2, 1998. Member, Editorial Advisory Board, Journal of Insurance Cov-

(This Listing Continued)

erage. *Member:* New York State and American Bar Associations; District of Columbia Bar. ***PRACTICE AREAS:*** Insurance Litigation; Commercial Litigation. ***Email:*** OshinskyJ@dsmo.com

RANDY PAAR, born Los Angeles, California, March 2, 1949; admitted to bar, 1976, New York and U.S. District Court, Southern and Eastern Districts of New York; 1994, U.S. Supreme Court and U.S. Court of Appeals, Second, Third and Fifth Circuits. *Education:* Harvard University (B.A. in Economics, 1971); New York University (J.D., 1975). (Resident, New York, N.Y. Office). ***PRACTICE AREAS:*** Insurance Law. ***Email:*** PaarR@dsmo.com

LEWIS J. PAPER, born Newark, New Jersey, October 13, 1946; admitted to bar, 1971, District of Columbia; 1975, New Jersey; 1984, Maryland and U.S. Supreme Court. *Education:* University of Michigan (B.A., 1968); Harvard University (J.D., 1971); Georgetown University (LL.M., 1972). Phi Beta Kappa; Pi Sigma Alpha. Note Editor, Harvard Journal on Legislation, 1970-1971. Fellow, Institute for Public Interest Representation, Georgetown Law School, 1971-1972. Legislative Counsel to Senator Gaylord Nelson, U.S. Senate, Washington, D.C., 1973-1975. Assistant General Counsel for Agenda Review and Policy, Federal Communications Commission, Washington, D.C., 1978-1979. Associate General Counsel and Chief, Administrative Law Division, FCC, Washington, D.C., 1979-1981. Adjunct Professor of Law in Communications, Georgetown University Law Center, 1983-1986. *Member:* The District of Columbia Bar; Maryland State Bar Association. ***PRACTICE AREAS:*** Communications Law; Litigation; Government Relations Law. ***Email:*** PaperL@dsmo.com

DAVID PATTON PARKER, born Florence, Alabama, January 27, 1949; admitted to bar, 1974, Virginia; 1975, District of Columbia. *Education:* University of the South (B.A., cum laude, 1971); University of Virginia (J.D., 1974). Deputy General Counsel, 1979-1985, General Counsel, 1985-1995, Secretary, 1990-1995, Allied Capital Corporation, Allied Capital Advisers, Inc. and Affiliated Funds. *Member:* Federal and American Bar Associations. ***PRACTICE AREAS:*** Finance; Venture Capital; Business Transactions; Corporate; Creditors Rights; Corporate Counseling. ***Email:*** ParkerD@dsmo.com

CORRINE PROPAS PARVER, born Montreal, Quebec, Canada, November 27, 1944; admitted to bar, 1983, District of Columbia. *Education:* McGill University, Montreal, Canada (Diploma in Physical Therapy, 1964; B.P.T., 1966); Washington College of Law, American University (J.D., cum laude, 1982). Assistant Editor, American University Law Review, 1981-1982. Licensed Physical Therapist, New York, 1970 and Maryland, 1977. Author of numerous articles in Health Care Trade Press, 1989—. Adjunct Lecturer: Health Law, Washington College of Law, The American University Summer Lecture Series, 1995—; Business Crimes and Health Care Fraud, University of Maryland School of Law. Member: American Physical Therapy Association, 1997-1998; National Family Caregivers Association (Co-Chair, Board of Directors, 1997); Foundation for Physical Therapy (Member, Board of Trustees, 1993-1997). *Member:* The District of Columbia Bar (Member, Health Law Section); American Bar Association (Member: Health Law Section; Health Law Forum, 1983—); American Health Lawyers Association. ***LANGUAGES:*** French. ***PRACTICE AREAS:*** Health Care; Administrative Government Relations. ***Email:*** ParverC@dsmo.com

WOODY N. PETERSON, born Canton, Ohio, April 19, 1948; admitted to bar, 1977, Massachusetts and U.S. Court of Appeals, Fourth Circuit; 1978, District of Columbia, U.S. District Court, District of Columbia and U.S. Court of Appeals, District of Columbia Circuit; 1982, U.S. Supreme Court; 1983, U.S. Court of Appeals, Second Circuit; 1993, U.S. Court of Appeals, Federal Circuit. *Education:* Harvard University (A.B., magna cum laude, 1970; J.D., cum laude, 1976). Phi Beta Kappa. Attorney, Office of General Counsel, National Labor Relations Board, 1976-1977. *Member:* The District of Columbia Bar; American Bar Association (Member, Sections on: Litigation; Labor and Employment Law). ***PRACTICE AREAS:*** Litigation; Civil Litigation; Appellate Practice; Employee Rights. ***Email:*** PetersonW@dsmo.com

GEORGE R. PITTS, born Williamsburg, Virginia, July 11, 1950; admitted to bar, 1983, California; 1985, Virginia; 1989, District of Columbia. *Education:* Swarthmore College (B.A., with high honors, 1972); University of Pennsylvania (M.A., 1975; Ph.D., 1977); University of Virginia (J.D., 1983). Phi Beta Kappa. Teaching Fellowship, University of Pennsylvania, 1973-1977. Research Fellowship, American Council of Learned Societies, 1980. Author: "Barratry as a Covered Risk in Marine Insurance: Problems and Perspectives," 14 Journal of Maritime Law and Commerce, April 1983; "Rights to Future Payment as Property of the Estate Under Section 541 of the Bankruptcy Code," 64 American Bankruptcy Law Journal 61 (1990). ***LANGUAGES:*** French, Latin and Greek. ***PRACTICE AREAS:*** Bankruptcy; Commercial Litigation. ***Email:*** PittsG@dsmo.com

IRA H. POLON, born New York, N.Y., March 9, 1943; admitted to bar, 1968, New York; 1971, District of Columbia; 1972, U.S. Court of Appeals, District of Columbia Circuit. *Education:* Lehigh University (B.A., cum laude, 1965); Columbia University (LL.B., 1968). Lecturer and Author of securities laws and venture capital materials for seminars sponsored by the American Law Institute, Federal Communications Bar Association, Maryland Institute for Continuing Professional Education for Lawyers, the Emerging Business Committee

(This Listing Continued)

of the Division of Corporation, Finance and Securities Law, District of Columbia Bar and other groups. Television Panelist on securities laws for "General Counsel," December 1985. *Member:* The District of Columbia Bar; The Bar Association of the District of Columbia; New York State and American (Member, Corporation, Banking and Business Law Section) Bar Associations. [1Lt., Capt., U.S. Army, 1969-1971]. ***PRACTICE AREAS:*** Mergers, Acquisitions and Divestitures Law; Business Law; Corporate Law; Finance Law. ***Email:*** PolonI@dsmo.com

CHARLES M. PRATT, born Richmond, Virginia, April 30, 1939; admitted to bar, 1968, New York. *Education:* Harvard University (A.B., 1961); University of Chicago (J.D., cum laude, 1967). Author: "Cogeneration: A Successful Response to the Energy Crisis?" IX Fordham Urban Law Journal 483 (1981). *Member:* The Association of the Bar of the City of New York (Chairman, Energy Committee, 1997-2000); New York State (Public Utility Law Section) and American (Public Utility Law Section, Council, 1992—) Bar Associations. (Resident, New York, N.Y. Office). ***PRACTICE AREAS:*** Energy. ***Email:*** PrattC@dsmo.com

ADAM PROUJANSKY, born New York, N.Y., June 9, 1963; admitted to bar, 1989, New York; 1990, District of Columbia. *Education:* Cornell University (A.B., cum laude, 1985); Harvard University (J.D., cum laude, 1988). Phi Beta Kappa. Editor, Civil Rights/Civil Liberties Law Review, 1987-1988. ***PRACTICE AREAS:*** Criminal and Civil Litigation. ***Email:*** ProujanskyA@dsmo.com

FRANK C. RAZZANO, born Brooklyn, New York, February 25, 1948; admitted to bar, 1973, New York (Not admitted in District of Columbia). admitted to bar, 1973, New York, U.S. District Court, Southern and Eastern Districts of New York and U.S. Court of Appeals, Second Circuit; 1976, New Jersey, U.S. District Court, District of New Jersey and U.S. Supreme Court; 1977, U.S. District Court, District of Maryland; 1978, U.S. District Court, Northern District of California; 1982, District of Columbia and U.S. District Court for the District of Columbia; 1983, U.S. Court of Appeals for the District of Columbia Circuit and U.S. Court of Appeals, Fifth Circuit; 1984, Virginia and U.S. Court of Appeals, Fourth Circuit; 1989, U.S. District Court, Eastern District of Virginia; 1990, U.S. Court of Appeals, Sixth Circuit; 1991, U.S. District Court, Western District of Virginia. *Education:* St. Louis University (B.A., magna cum laude, 1969); Georgetown University (J.D., 1972). Phi Beta Kappa. Editor, Georgetown Law Journal, 1971-1972. Author: "Arbitration After McMahon," 6 RICO Law Reporter 1, July, 1987; "RICO Discovery: A Defendant's Viewpoint," 7 RICO Law Reporter 707, May, 1988; "Securities and Exchange Commission Investigations," 1 Corp. Analysis 67, Nov., 1988, reprinted as a chapter in "How to Handle Government Investigations" (BLI, 1989); "Will Juries Now Define the Term Pattern of Racketeering," 9 RICO Law Reporter 414, March, 1989; "FOIA and SEC Inquiries—Part II," 1 Journal of Corporate Disclosure and Confidentiality 33, September, 1989; "RICO's Death Watch," 10 RICO Law Reporter 222, August, 1989; "Sentencing Commission Proposal, With Higher Fines, Makes Need For Corporate Codes Even More Compelling," 5 BNA Corporate Counsel Weekly 8 December 5, 1990; "Multi-factor Test Gets Top Marks," 13 RICO Law Reporter 806 May, 1991; "Can RICO Extend the Statute of Limitations for Section 10 (b) Violations?" 14 RICO Law Reporter 681, October, 1991; "A New Avenue of Approach for RICO Defendants," 15 RICO Law Reporter 675, April, 1992; "American Money Laundering Statutes: A Case For A Worldwide System of Banking Compliance Systems," 3 Journal of International Law and Practice 277, Summer, 1994 reprinted in Italian, 3 Tempi Romana 671, Sept.-Dec. 1994; "How to Achieve Securities Litigation Reform," 22 RICO Law Reporter 9, July-August 1995; "Cooperate or Fight," 4 Prevention of Corporate Liability 12, Feb. 1996; "Book Review: Insider Trading," 52 Business Lawyer 1431, August 1997; "An Unanswered Question: Who Does a Civil RICO Cause of Action Accrue?" 26 RICO Law Reporter, October 1997; "Securities and Exchange Commission Investigations," 5 Securities Reform Act Litigation Reporter 263, December 1997; "Mr. Corporate in a Pinstriped Suit - Almost," 7 Business Law Today 12, May/June 1998; "Is the Fifth Amendment Merely a Limitation on Government Power or an Affirmation of Personal Integrity," 27 RICO Law Reporter 849, June 1998; "The Dissolution of the Bill of Rights' Ideals," 28 RICO Law Reporter 8, July 1998; "The SEC's Dirty Little Secrets," 5 Securities Reform Act Litigation Reporter 792, August 1998; "Is China Entering a Free Market," 26 Securities Regulation Law Journal 317, Winter 1999; "The Litigator's Dream Come True: The Year 2000," 27 Securities Regulation Law Journal 3, Spring 1999; "So You Want to Be an International Financial Center... Are You Prepared to Spit in the Giant's Eye?" Securities Regulation Journal, Winter 2001. Contributor, "The Sobriety Test," Shark Tales, 2000. Civil Law Editor RICO Law Reporter, 1987—. Panelist: "International Financial Centers: The U.S. Response," Pacific Islands Judicial Conference, Guam, August 1999; Eighth Annual SMU Corporate Counsel Symposium, Southern Methodist University Law School, Dallas, Texas, October 2000. Adjunct Professor of Law, University of Maryland, Business Crimes Seminar, 1996—. Member, Advisory Board, Securities Reform Act Litigation Reporter, 1996—. Member, Advisory Board, Securities Regulation Law Journal, 1998—. Assistant U.S. Attorney, District of New Jersey, 1975-1978. Assistant Chief Trial Attorney, Securities and Exchange Commission, 1978-1982. *Member:* District of Columbia Bar (Chairman, Liti-

(This Listing Continued)

DICKSTEIN SHAPIRO MORIN & OSHINSKY LLP, Washington—Continued

gation Section, 1987-1989; Vice-Chairman, Council on Sections, 1988-1989); Virginia State Bar; American Bar Association (Chairman, Criminal Law Committee, Business Law Section); Virginia Trial Lawyers Association. [Capt., U.S. Army, 1972-1980]. ***PRACTICE AREAS:*** Broker Dealer Securities; White Collar Criminal Defense Litigation. ***Email:*** RazzanoF@dsmo.com

TODD M. ROBERTS, born Dawson Creek, Canada, June 20, 1964; admitted to bar, 1988, New York. *Education:* University of Alberta (Faculty of Business, 1983); McGill University (LL.B., with honors, 1986); Cambridge University, England (LL.M., with honors, 1987). Faculty Scholar; University Scholar. Formerly with Cravath, Swaine & Moore. *Member:* The Association of the Bar of the City of New York; American Bar Association. (Resident, New York, N.Y. Office).

GABRIELLE S. ROTH, born Neubruke, Germany, September 29, 1964; admitted to bar, 1990, New Jersey; 1991, New York and District of Columbia; 1994, U.S. Court of Appeals for the Federal Circuit; 1995, U.S. Supreme Court. *Education:* University of Rochester (B.A., magna cum laude, 1986) Phi Beta Kappa; The George Washington University (J.D., with honors, 1990). Judicial Clerk to Hon. Frank E. Schwelb, District of Columbia Court of Appeals, 1990-1991. Co-Author, Intellectual Property Legal Options, Treatise, (Aspen Publishing, 1999, 2000). *Member:* Bar Association of the District of Columbia; New York State and American Bar Associations; American Intellectual Property Law Association; International Trademark Association. ***PRACTICE AREAS:*** Trademark and Copyright Prosecution; Intellectual Property Litigation; Unfair Competition Litigation. ***Email:*** RothG@dsmo.com

CHARLES W. SABER, born Boston, Massachusetts, June 29, 1954; admitted to bar, 1979, District of Columbia. *Education:* University of Massachusetts (B.A., 1976); Georgetown University (J.D., 1979). Co-Author: *Introduction to Intellectual Property Law*, BNA, 1994. *Member:* The District of Columbia Bar; American Bar Association; American Intellectual Property Association; International Trademark Association. ***PRACTICE AREAS:*** Patent, Trademark and Copyright Law; Litigation. ***Email:*** SaberC@dsmo.com

FRANCIS J. SAILER, born March 27, 1953; admitted to bar, 1978, Wisconsin; 1988, District of Columbia; U.S. Court of Federal Claims; U.S. Court of International Trade; U.S. District Court, District of Columbia; U.S. Court of Appeals, District of Columbia Circuit; U.S. Court of Appeals for the Federal Circuit; U.S. District Court, Eastern and Western Districts of Wisconsin. *Education:* Marquette University (B.A., Political Science, 1975; J.D., 1978); Georgetown University Law Center (LL.M., International and Comparative Law, 1982). Member, Marquette Law Review. Managing Editor, Marquette Oyer. Author: "Antidumping Duty Overview and Application to China as a Non-Market Economy Country," *Doing Business in China,* 2nd Edition, Business Laws Inc., 1999. Law Clerk to Hon. Gordon Myse, Tenth Wisconsin Circuit, 1978-1979. Trial Attorney, U.S. Department of Justice, 1980-1985. Deputy Assistant Secretary of Commerce for Import Administration - Investigations, U.S. Department of Commerce, 1989-1992. *Member:* American Bar Association (Member: Customs Committee; International Trade Steering Committee); Customs and International Trade Bar Association; Inter Pacific Bar Association. ***PRACTICE AREAS:*** Customs Law; Import and Export Law; International Law; International Sales; Trade Regulation Law. ***Email:*** SailerF@dsmo.com

HOWARD SCHIFFMAN, born New York, N.Y., July 17, 1951; admitted to bar, 1978, New York; 1981, U.S. Court of Appeals, District of Columbia Circuit; 1982, District of Columbia; 1984, U.S. Supreme Court; 1988, U.S. District Court, Southern District of New York and U.S. Court of Appeals, Eleventh Circuit; 1995, U.S. Court of Appeals, Second Circuit and U.S. District Court, District of Maryland; 1998, U.S. Court of Appeals, Ninth Circuit. *Education:* Colgate University (B.A., cum laude, 1973); Fordham University (J.D., cum laude, 1977). Member, Fordham Law Review, 1976-1977. Adjunct Professor, Seminar on "White Collar Crime," Washington College of Law, American University, 1987-1992. Speaker: "Retail Surveillance Techniques," Securities Industries Association (SIA) Compliance and Legal Division Seminar-Orlando, FL- March/2000; Contributor for Fourth and DC Circuits, "Survey of Securities Class Actions and Derivative Suits" - (1998, 1999, 2000 & 2001); "SEC Order Handling Issues," Securities Industry Association (SIA) Compliance and Legal Division Seminar, 1999, 2000—; "Broker Dealer/Equity Trading Desk Activities," National Society of Compliance Professionals (NSCP), 1999; "Prosecuting and Defending Class Actions," Insight Conference, 1999; "Avoiding and Mitigating Potential Civil and Criminal Liability," ABA Section of Business-Compliance Law, 1998. ACI Speaker, "Overview of Current Derivatives Litigation," 1995. SIA Seminar Speaker on Class Actions/Major Liabilities, 1993 and on ERISA Obligations for Securities Professionals, 1990 and on Criminalization of Securities Activities, 1992. Derivatives Litigation Seminar, 1995. Faculty, Practicing Law Institute, 1989-1990. Trial Attorney, Division of Enforcement, Securities and Exchange Commission, Washington, D.C., 1977-1980. Faculty Co-Chairman, ABA National Institute on Enforcement Actions Against Banks and Thrifts, 1984. *Member:* The District of Columbia Bar;

(This Listing Continued)

American Bar Association (Member, Sections on: Litigation; Corporation; Finance and Securities Law); Association of Securities and Exchange Commission Alumni (President, 1997-2000; Director, 1995—). ***PRACTICE AREAS:*** Securities Litigation; Litigation; Criminal Law. ***Email:*** SchiffmanH@dsmo.com

GARY L. SCHOENBRUN, born Queens, New York, November 7, 1958; admitted to bar, 1984, New York; 1985, U.S. Tax Court. *Education:* University of Rochester (B.A., magna cum laude, 1980); Harvard University (J.D., cum laude, 1983); New York University (LL.M. in Taxation, 1987). Phi Beta Kappa. Isaac Sherman Fellowship for best work in Economics. Author: "Temporary Distribution Preferences Allocable to Non-recourse Liabilities", Journal of Partnership Taxation, Spring, 1990; "Consequences of Preferred Return Provisions in a Partnership Agreement", Journal of Partnership Taxation, Winter, 1992. *Member:* New York State Bar Association (Section on Taxation; Committee on Partnerships, 1987—). (Resident, New York, N.Y. Office).

RICHARD SCHRAMM (1941-1991).

L. KEVIN SHERIDAN, JR., born Baltimore, Maryland, October 8, 1962; admitted to bar, 1989, New York. *Education:* University of Virginia (B.A., 1984); Fordham University (J.D., 1988). Managing Editor, Fordham Law Review, 1987-1988. Law Clerk to Hon. Edward R. Korman, U.S. District Court, Eastern District of New York, 1988-1989. Formerly with Cravath, Swaine & Moore. *Member:* The Association of the Bar of the City of New York; American Bar Association. (Resident, New York, N.Y. Office).

ELIZABETH A. SHERWIN, born Coxsackie, New York, May 23, 1957; admitted to bar, 1985, New York and U.S. District Court, Southern and Eastern Districts of New York; 1986, New Jersey and U.S. District Court, District of New Jersey; 1994, U.S. Court of Appeals, Third Circuit; 1998, U.S. Court of Appeals, Fourth Circuit. *Education:* Rutgers University (B.A., with honors, 1980); New York University (J.D., with honors, 1984). Order of the Coif. Senior Note and Comment Editor, Review of Law and Social Change, 1983-1984. Speaker: "The Duty to Defend In New Jersey," New Jersey Institute of Continuing Legal Education, 1997; Insurance Coverage for Lead Liability, Second Annual Seminar on Lead Liability Litigation, 1995. *Member:* New York State and American (Member, Litigation and Dispute Resolution Management Sections) Bar Associations. (Resident, New York, N.Y. Office). ***PRACTICE AREAS:*** Insurance Litigation; Commercial Litigation. ***Email:*** SherwinE@dsmo.com

JUSTIN D. SIMON (1947-2001).

KENNETH M. SIMON, born Pittsburgh, Pennsylvania, April 25, 1952; admitted to bar, 1977, District of Columbia. *Education:* University of Pittsburgh (B.A., magna cum laude, 1974); Georgetown University (J.D., 1977). Co-Author: "Fiducia Structure Supports 144A Financing of TermoEmcali Power Project," Project Finance International, Sept. 1997; "Negotiating Gas Contracts in Colombia: The TermoEmcali Experience," Latin American Law and Business Report, August 1997; "The Evolving Generation Industry," Independent Energy, July-August 1997; "The State Road Map," Independent Energy, June 1997. Author: "Electric Restructuring Across the Country," Public Utilities Fortnightly, May 15, 1997; "Yes, Transmission Pricing Should Foster Competition," Private Power Executive, November-December 1993; "Anticompetitive Effects of Northeast Utilities' Acquisition of Public Service of New Hampshire," Wheeling & Transmission Monthly, June 1990. Director, Electric Generation Association, 1992-1996. *Member:* The District of Columbia (Chairman, Energy Committee of Section on Environment, Energy and Natural Resources, 1988-1990) Bar; Federal Energy (Chairman, 1990-1991, Vice Chairman, 1989-1990, Committee on Cogeneration and Independent Power) Bar Association; American Bar Association. ***PRACTICE AREAS:*** Project Finance; Energy Law; Cogeneration Law; International Law. ***Email:*** SimonK@dsmo.com

JAMES VANR. SPRINGER, born New York, N.Y., July 9, 1934; admitted to bar, 1962, District of Columbia; 1963, U.S. Court of Appeals, District of Columbia Circuit; 1968, U.S. Supreme Court. *Education:* Harvard University (A.B., 1955; LL.B., 1961). Member, Board of Editors, 1959-1961 and President, 1960-1961, Harvard Law Review. Law Clerk to Hon. J. Edward Lumbard, Chief Judge, U.S. Court of Appeals, Second Circuit, 1961-1962. Assistant Legal Adviser (Economic Affairs), Department of State, 1967-1968. Deputy Solicitor General of the United States, 1968-1971. *Member:* The District of Columbia Bar; American Bar Association. ***PRACTICE AREAS:*** Antitrust Law; Appellate Practice; Federal Practice. ***Email:*** SpringerJ@dsmo.com

PAUL R. TASKIER, born Brooklyn, New York, June 5, 1955; admitted to bar, 1983, District of Columbia; 1984, U.S. Tax Court, U.S. District Court, District of Columbia and U.S. Court of Appeals, District of Columbia Circuit; 1987, U.S. Supreme Court; 1988, U.S. Court of Appeals, Eleventh Circuit; 1991, New York and U.S. District Court, Southern and Eastern Districts of New York; 1994, U.S. Court of Appeals, Fourth and Second Circuits; 1996, U.S. District Court, District of Maryland; 2000, U.S. Court of Appeals, First Circuit. *Education:* Tufts University (B.A., cum laude, 1978); Georgetown University (J.D., 1982). Lead Articles Editor, The Tax Lawyer, 1981-1982. Law Clerk: Hon. Sidney M. Aronovitz, U.S. District Court, Southern District of Florida, 1982-1983; Hon. Randolph F. Caldwell, Jr., Special Trial Judge, U.S. Tax Court,

(This Listing Continued)

1982. *Member:* The District of Columbia Bar; American Bar Association (Member, Sections on: Litigation; Tort and Insurance Practice). ***PRACTICE AREAS:*** Insurance Coverage Litigation; Commercial Litigation; Civil Litigation. ***Email:*** TaskierP@dsmo.com

EDWARD TESSLER, born New York, N.Y.. October 25, 1949; admitted to bar, 1980, New York and U.S. District Court, Southern and Eastern Districts of New York; 1981, Florida; 1985, U.S. Court of Appeals, Second Circuit; 1992, New Jersey and U.S. District Court, District of New Jersey. *Education:* Union College (B.S. and B.A., 1971); State University of New York at Stony Brook (M.S., 1973); Brooklyn Law School (J.D., 1979). Member: Moot Court Honor Society; Brooklyn Law Review, 1978-1979. *Member:* The Florida Bar; American Bar Association (Member, Litigation Section). (Resident, New York, N.Y. Office). ***Email:*** TesslerE@dsmo.com

MARK J. THRONSON, born Roundup, Montana, July 16, 1959; admitted to bar, 1989, District of Columbia; 1994, U.S. Court of Appeals, Federal Circuit; registered to practice before U.S. Patent and Trademark Office. *Education:* University of Wisconsin-Platteville (B.S. Civil Eng., with honors, 1982); George Washington University (J.D., with honors, 1988). Co-Author: "Intellectual Property Legal Opinions," (Aspen Law and Business); "In Opinions to Clients, Intellectual Property Lawyers Face Risks," The National Law Journal, 1993; "Standard of Care in Intellectual Property Law Opinions," European Intellectual Property Review, 1993; "Design Patents and Computer-Generated Icons," The Computer Lawyer, 1996; "Legal Ethics and Intellectual Property Opinions," Insight Press, 1997. Author: "Times Have Changed: General Practice Firms Provide Full Service For Clients," The Law Works, 1995; "It's Purely a Matter of Opinion," Legal Times, 1996; "Responses to Auditor Inquiries," Insight Press, 1999. Adjunct Professor, Johns Hopkins University, 1994-2000. Examiner, U.S. Patent and Trademark Office, 1982-1988. *Member:* American Bar Association (Chairman, Subcommittee on Intellectual Property Third Party Opinions, 1994-1996), American Intellectual Property Law Association; The Patent and Trademark Office Society. ***PRACTICE AREAS:*** Intellectual Property; Patent Law. ***Email:*** ThronsonM@dsmo.com

STEPHANIE KAREN WADE, born Greensboro, North Carolina, August 1, 1955; admitted to bar, 1981, District of Columbia. *Education:* University of North Carolina (B.A., 1977); University of Georgia (J.D., cum laude, 1981). ***PRACTICE AREAS:*** Intellectual Property.

BETH L. WEBB, born Washington, D.C., April 13, 1958; admitted to bar, 1985, Maryland; 1986, District of Columbia. *Education:* University of North Carolina-Chapel Hill (B.A., 1979); Creighton University (J.D., summa cum laude, 1984). Phi Beta Kappa. Staff Member, Creighton Law Review, 1982-1983. *Member:* The District of Columbia Bar; Maryland State Bar Association. ***PRACTICE AREAS:*** Energy Law. ***Email:*** WebbB@dsmo.com

STEPHAN G. WEIL, born Paris, France, January 27, 1949; admitted to bar, 1982, District of Columbia; 1984, Temporary Emergency Court of Appeals of the United States. *Education:* Grinnell College (B.S., 1969); University of Chicago (J.D., 1981). Member, 1979-1980 and Associate Editor, 1980-1981, University of Chicago Law Review. Winner, Karl Llewellyn Moot Court Cup, 1981. Author: "Spreading the Costs: Insurance Coverage and the Year 2000 Problem," Year/2000 Journal, Vol. 1, No. 2, 1997. *Member:* Third, Sixth, Eighth and District of Columbia Court of Appeals of the United States Bars; District of Columbia Bar; Supreme Court of the United States Bar. ***PRACTICE AREAS:*** Insurance Litigation; Commercial Litigation. ***Email:*** WeilS@dsmo.com

KENT T. WITHYCOMBE, born Portland, Oregon, July 29, 1961; admitted to bar, 1989, New York; 1998, District of Columbia. *Education:* Columbia University (B.A., magna cum laude, 1984); New York University (J.D., 1988). Phi Beta Kappa. Member, Review of Law and Social Change, 1985-1986. *Member:* District of Columbia Bar; New York State and American Bar Associations. ***PRACTICE AREAS:*** General Litigation; Insurance Litigation. ***Email:*** WithycombeK@dsmo.com

REBECCA WRIGHT, born Winston-Salem, North Carolina, October 6, 1948; admitted to bar, 1979, District of Columbia. *Education:* Vassar College (B.A., with honors, 1970); Johns Hopkins University School of Advanced International Studies (M.A., 1972); Georgetown University (J.D., cum laude, 1979). Member, 1977-1978 and Editor, 1978-1979, Georgetown Law Journal. Economist, Office of the Assistant Secretary for Energy and Minerals, U.S. Department of the Interior, 1972-1977. *Member:* The District of Columbia Bar; American Bar Association. ***PRACTICE AREAS:*** Corporate Law; Finance Law; Securities Law; Project Finance Law. ***Email:*** WrightR@dsmo.com

L. ANDREW ZAUSNER, born Plainfield, New Jersey, May 1, 1949; admitted to bar, 1975, Pennsylvania; 1978, U.S. Supreme Court; 1979, District of Columbia. *Education:* Boston University (B.A., 1971); University of Pennsylvania (M.B.A., J.D., 1975). Phi Beta Kappa. Special Assistant to General Counsel, 1977-1978 and Executive Assistant to Deputy Secretary, 1978-1979, U.S. Department of Energy. Director, Government Relations, 1979-1981, Vice President, 1981-1985, Pennzoil Company. Member, Board of Directors, Dauphin Deposit Corporation, 1990 and Chairman, Trust and Investment Committee,

(This Listing Continued)

Dauphin Deposit Bank and Trust Company, 1995-1997. *Member:* The District of Columbia Bar; Pennsylvania Bar Association. ***PRACTICE AREAS:*** Government; Legislative; Energy Law. ***Email:*** ZausnerA@dsmo.com

SENIOR COUNSEL

SIDNEY DICKSTEIN, born Brooklyn, New York, May 13, 1925; admitted to bar, 1949, New York; 1950, U.S. District Court, Southern District of New York; 1959, District of Columbia; 1960, U.S. Claims Court; 1961, U.S. Supreme Court; 1967, U.S. District Court, District of Maryland. *Education:* Franklin & Marshall College (A.B., 1947); Pennsylvania State College; Columbia University (J.D., 1949). Member, Board of Trustees, Franklin & Marshall College, 1981—. Member, Board of Governors, American Jewish Committee. *Member:* The District of Columbia Bar; Bar Association of the District of Columbia; American Bar Association. ***PRACTICE AREAS:*** Antitrust Law; Corporate Law; Mergers and Acquisitions Law; Securities Litigation. ***Email:*** DicksteinS@dsmo.com

SEYMOUR GLANZER, born New York, N.Y., May 22, 1926; admitted to bar, 1961, New York; 1965, District of Columbia; 1967, U.S. Supreme Court; U.S. District Court for the District of Columbia; U.S. Court of Appeals for the District of Columbia Circuit; U.S. District Court, Southern and Eastern Districts of New York; U.S. District Court, District of Maryland; U.S. Court of Appeals, Fourth Circuit; U.S. Court of Appeals, Sixth Circuit. *Education:* Juilliard (B.S., 1955); New York University; New York Law School (LL.B., 1960). Author of a number of articles relating to the use of the Fifth Amendment on SEC Investigations, responding to Grand Jury Subpoenas, Attorney-Client Privilege regarding Grand Jury proceedings, and RICO forfeiture provisions, among others. Lecturer, Department of Justice, Advocacy Institute, 1974-1975. Adjunct Professor of Law, Georgetown University Law Center, 1974-1975. Adjunct Professor, Columbus School of Law, The Catholic University of America, 1978-1979. Special Master, U.S. District Court, District of Columbia, 1991. Attorney, Securities & Exchange Commission, 1962-1965. Assistant U.S. Attorney, 1966-1974. Chief, Fraud Section, U.S. Attorney's Office, District of Columbia, 1967-1974. Member, The American Law Institute, 1978—. Member: Judicial Conference, District of Columbia Circuit, 1974—; Judicial Conference for the District of Columbia, 1979-1984. Member, Bureau of National Affairs, Advisory Board Securities Regulations and Law Section, 1977-1980. *Member:* The District of Columbia Bar (Member, Criminal Practice Institute, 1979); American Bar Association (Member, Sections on: Litigation; Criminal Justice; Member, Committee on Grand Jury, 1975-1978; Chairman, Committee on Prosecution and Defense of SEC Cases, 1979-1980; Council Member of the Criminal Justice Section, 1980-1981; Member, Civil and Criminal Tax Penalties Committee, 1983-1985; Member, Securities Subcommittee of Committee on Complex Crimes Litigation, 1990—). ***PRACTICE AREAS:*** Litigation; White Collar Criminal Defense; Complex Civil Litigation; Grand Jury Practice; Federal Regulatory Law; Regulatory Agency Practice; Regulatory Investigations. ***Email:*** GlanzerD@dsmo.com

SALLIE H. HELM, born Crowville, Louisiana, August 7, 1931; admitted to bar, 1975, District of Columbia; 1991, U.S. Court of Appeals for the District of Columbia Circuit; 1992, Maryland. *Education:* Northwestern State University (B.S., 1952); Louisiana State University (M.S., 1955); Georgetown University (J.D., 1974). Adjunct Professor, Appellate Advocacy, Georgetown University Law Center, 1975-1976. Assistant United States Attorney for the District of Columbia, 1975-1978. *Member:* The District of Columbia Bar; Maryland State, Federal and American Bar Associations; Women's Bar Association of District of Columbia. ***PRACTICE AREAS:*** Commercial Litigation; Intellectual Property; Insurance Litigation; Antitrust and Trade Regulation; Unfair Competition. ***Email:*** HelmS@dsmo.com

CHARLES H. MORIN, born Waltham, Massachusetts, August 18, 1922; admitted to bar, 1948, Massachusetts; 1961, District of Columbia; 1962, U.S. Supreme Court. *Education:* Harvard University (B.S., 1943); Boston University (LL.B., 1948). Chairman, Commission on the Review of the National Policy Toward Gambling, 1972-1976. Founder, Morin Center for Banking and Financial Law, Boston University School of Law. *Member:* The District of Columbia Bar; Boston Bar Association. ***PRACTICE AREAS:*** Casinos and Gambling; Client Counseling; Banking; Legal Ethics and Professional Responsibility; Money Management. ***Email:*** MorinC@dsmo.com

DAVID I. SHAPIRO, born Brooklyn, New York, June 17, 1928; admitted to bar, 1949, New York; 1955, U.S. Supreme Court; 1958, District of Columbia and U.S. Court of Appeals, District of Columbia Circuit; 1961, U.S. Court of Appeals, Ninth Circuit. *Education:* University of Wisconsin; Brooklyn College; Brooklyn Law School (LL.B., 1949). *Member:* The District of Columbia Bar; Bar Association of the District of Columbia; The Association of the Bar of the City of New York; American Bar Association. ***PRACTICE AREAS:*** Alternative Dispute Resolution.

JOSEPH D. TYDINGS, born Asheville, North Carolina, May 4, 1928; admitted to bar, 1952, Maryland; 1962, U.S. Supreme Court; 1971, District of Columbia. *Education:* University of Maryland (B.A., 1951; LL.B., 1953). Delta Theta Phi; Omicron Delta Kappa; Phi Kappa Phi; Phi Eta Sigma. Member,

(This Listing Continued)

DICKSTEIN SHAPIRO MORIN & OSHINSKY LLP, Washington—Continued

Board of Editors, Maryland Law Review, 1952-1953. Author: "Improving the Federal Judicial System," American Criminal Law Quarterly, Winter, 1966; "Modernizing the Federal Judiciary," Journal of Missouri Bar, November, 1966; "A Fresh Approach to Judicial Administration," Journal of American Judicature Society, August-September, 1966; "Modernizing the Administration of Justice," Judicature, April, 1967; "Management Consultants can Break Logjams in Nation's Courts," American Trial Lawyers, March, 1967; "A National Program for Reform in Judicial Administration," Trial Judges Journal, January, 1967; "Court of the Future," St. Louis University Law Journal, 1969; "Air Crash Litigation: A Judicial Problem-A Congressional Solution," American University Law Review, March, 1969; "Fair Play for Consumers," Trial, March, 1970; "D.C. Court Reform and Criminal Procedure Act of 1970: An Overview," D.C. Bar Journal, August-December, 1970; "Improving Archaic Judicial Machinery," ABA Journal, February, 1971; "Born to Starve," Wm. & Co. 1970. Member, Maryland House of Delegates, 1955-1961. U.S. Attorney, District of Maryland, 1961-1963. U.S. Senator, Maryland, 1965-1971. Senior Consultant, United Nations Fund For Population Activities, 1971-1988. Member, 1974-1984, Vice Chairman, 1980-1982 and Chairman, 1982-1984, Board of Regents, University of Maryland. Member, Board of Regents University System of Maryland, 2000. Chairman, U.S. Circuit and District Courts Nominating Commission for the District of Columbia, 1977-1979. Co-Chairman, Population Action International, 1975-2000. Chairman Council, Population Action International, 2000—. Special Consultant to Steering Committee, World Conference of Parliamentarians Concerned With Population and Development. SRI LANKA, 1979. Founding Trustee and President, Global Committee of Parliamentarians Concerned with Population and Development, 1982-1985. Trustee, U.S. Japan Foundation, 1983-1992. Trustee, University of Maryland Foundation, 1984—. *Member:* District of Columbia Bar; Maryland State Bar Association. **Email:** TydingsJ@dsmo.com

OF COUNSEL

ROBERT F. ALDRICH, born Minneapolis, Minnesota, August 18, 1952; admitted to bar, 1979, District of Columbia. *Education:* Yale University (B.A., 1973); University of Virginia (J.D., 1977). ***PRACTICE AREAS:*** Telecommunication Law. ***Email:*** AldrichR@dsmo.com

LAURA HAMILTON CALALUCA, born Lynchburg, Virginia, September 17, 1954; admitted to bar, 1987, Virginia, U.S. District Court, Eastern and Western Districts of Virginia and U.S. Court of Appeals, Fourth Circuit; 1999, District of Columbia. *Education:* Lynchburg College (B.A., cum laude, 1976); University of Georgia (M.A., 1982); University of Virginia (J.D., 1986). Law Clerk to Hon. John D. Butzner, Jr., U.S. Court of Appeals, Fourth Circuit, 1986-1987. *Member:* American, Virginia State and Virginia Bar Associations. ***LANGUAGES:*** Norwegian. ***PRACTICE AREAS:*** Commercial Litigation; Insurance Litigation; ERISA Litigation. ***Email:*** CalalucaL@dsmo.com

MICHAEL D. COX, born Tulsa, Oklahoma, July 12, 1948; admitted to bar, 1973, California; 1997, District of Columbia and U.S. Supreme Court. *Education:* University of Oklahoma (B.A., 1970); University of Virginia (J.D., 1973). Author: "The Indian Gaming Regulatory Act: An Overview," 7 St. Thomas Law Review 769, 1995. *Member:* State Bar of California; District of Columbia Bar. ***SPECIAL AGENCIES:*** Minority Counsel, Senate Indian Affairs Committee, 1976-1980. General Counsel, National Indian Gaming Commission, 1990-1996. ***PRACTICE AREAS:*** Indian Law; Gaming Law; Government Law; Legislative Practice. ***Email:*** CoxM@dsmo.com

JOAN M. DARBY, born Washington, D.C., January 10, 1953; admitted to bar, 1979, District of Columbia and Wisconsin. *Education:* Wellesley College (B.A., 1975); George Washington University (J.D., 1978). *Member:* State Bar of Wisconsin; The District of Columbia Bar; Women's Bar Association of District of Columbia. ***PRACTICE AREAS:*** Energy. ***Email:*** DarbyJ@dsmo.com

MICHAEL I. GILMAN, born New York, N.Y., July 15, 1962; admitted to bar, 1991, Pennsylvania; 1993, District of Columbia. *Education:* University of Virginia (B.A., with highest distinction, 1985; J.D., 1989). Phi Beta Kappa; Order of the Coif. Articles Editor, Virginia Law Review, 1988-1989. Author: "More Light on Set-Asides," New Perspectives, p. 12, Summer 1986; "Tax Traps and Other Problems for Y2K Expenses," Mondaq Business Briefing, Aug. 25, 1998. Contributor: *Bank Investment Products Deskbook*, Warren, Gorman and Lamont, 1995. Law Clerk to Judge Walter K. Stapleton, U.S. Court of Appeals, Third Circuit, 1989-1990. ***PRACTICE AREAS:*** Tax. ***Email:*** GilmanM@dsmo.com

DOUGLAS N. JACOBSON, born Kansas City, Missouri, July 3, 1961; admitted to bar, 1990, Maryland, U.S. Court of International Trade and U.S. Court of Appeals, Federal Circuit (Not admitted in District of Columbia). *Education:* University of Texas (B.A., 1983); Washington University (D.M.D., 1987); American University (J.D., 1990). Phi Delta Phi. Articles Editor, American University Law Review, 1989-1990. Author, "After Cipollone v. Liggett Group, Inc.: How Wide Will the Floodgates of Cigarette Litigation Open?" 38 Am. U.L. Rev. 1921, 1989. *Member:* Bar Association of the District of Columbia; Maryland State and American Bar Associations. ***PRACTICE AREAS:*** International Trade; Aviation Law. ***Email:*** JacobsonD@dsmo.com

GEORGE E. JOHNSON, born Port Washington, New York, August 6, 1942; admitted to bar, 1968, New York; 1970, District of Columbia; 1983, Maryland. *Education:* Cornell University (B.A., 1964); Columbia University (J.D., cum laude, 1967). Harlan Fiske Stone Scholar. Barney Jaffin Prize. Revision Editor, Columbia Journal of Law and Social Problems. Attorney Advisor, Office of General Counsel, International Affairs, U.S. Treasury Department, 1969-1971. Associate Solicitor, Office of Special Counsel for Compliance, U.S. Department of Energy, 1977-1981. Senior Litigation Attorney, Office of the General Counsel, U.S. Nuclear Regulatory Commission, 1981-1988. Associate, Swidler & Berlin, Ltd., 1988-1995. Attorney Advisor, Common Carrier Bureau, Federal Communications Commission, 1995. *Member:* District of Columbia Bar. [Captain, U.S. Army, 1967-1969]. ***PRACTICE AREAS:*** Electric Utility Regulation; Regulatory Litigation; Nuclear Energy. ***Email:*** JohnsonG@dsmo.com

ROBERT MANGAS, born Toledo, Ohio, March 25, 1960; admitted to bar, 1986, Virginia; 1999, District of Columbia. *Education:* University of Kentucky (B.A., 1983); Columbia University School of Law (J.D., 1986). ***Email:*** MangasR@dsmo.com

AMY MARMER NICE, born Washington, D.C., March 24, 1962; admitted to bar, 1987, Virginia; 1988, District of Columbia and U.S. District Court, District of Maryland. *Education:* Tulane University (B.A., cum laude, 1984); George Washington University (J.D., 1987). Phi Beta Kappa. Author: "Analysis: Multinational Companies and the Immigration Act of 1990," International Company & Corporate Law Review (UK) Vol. 2, No. 3, 1991. *Member:* The District of Columbia; Virginia State and American Bar Associations; American Immigration Lawyers Association. ***PRACTICE AREAS:*** Immigration Law. ***Email:*** NiceA@dsmo.com

STANFORD E. PARRIS, born 1929; admitted to bar, 1958, Virginia; 1980, District of Columbia. *Education:* University of Illinois (B.S., 1950); George Washington University (J.D., 1958). Virginia Secretary of State, 1978-1979. Member, U.S. Congress, 1973-1975 and 1981-1991. ***PRACTICE AREAS:*** Government; Legislative Law. ***Email:*** ParrisS@dsmo.com

RICHARD P. PERRIN, born Youngstown, Ohio, September 26, 1946; admitted to bar, 1974, District of Columbia. *Education:* Harvard University; Bowling Green State University (B.S., 1968); New York Law School (J.D., cum laude, 1973). *Member:* District of Columbia Bar; American Bar Associations. ***Email:*** PerrinR@dsmo.com

MARK L. PERLIS, born Lafayette, Indiana, November 4, 1952; admitted to bar, 1978, District of Columbia. *Education:* Yale College (B.A., magna cum laude, 1974); Harvard University (J.D., cum laude, 1977). Member, Harvard Law Review, 1975-1977. Law Clerk to Honorable Francis L. Van Dusen, U.S. Court of Appeals, Third Circuit, 1977-1978. Attorney-Advisor, Tax Legislative Counsel's Office, U.S. Treasury Department, 1983-1987. Member, Board of Directors and Vice President, Emissions Marketing Association. *Member:* American Bar Association (Member: Energy and Natural Resources and Taxation Sections; Vice Chair, ABA Special Committee on Climate Change and Sustainable Development). ***PRACTICE AREAS:*** Energy; Taxation. ***Email:*** PerlisM@dsmo.com

STEVEN JOHN ROMAN, born Baltimore, Maryland, January 20, 1956; admitted to bar, 1980, California and U.S. District Court, Central District of California; 1985, District of Columbia. *Education:* University of Virginia (B.A., 1977); Yale University (J.D., 1980). Phi Beta Kappa; Omicron Delta Kappa. Honor Award Scholar. Assistant U.S. Attorney, District of Columbia, 1985-1999; Chief, Narcotics Section, U.S. Attorney's Office, 1994-1999. ***PRACTICE AREAS:*** Commercial Litigation; Complex Civil Litigation; Criminal Law. ***Email:*** RomanS@dsmo.com

MICHAEL J. RUSTUM, born Buffalo, New York, January 16, 1964; admitted to bar, 1989, Maryland; 1991, District of Columbia. *Education:* State University of New York at Stony Brook (B.A., 1986); Syracuse University (J.D., cum laude, 1989; M.P.A., 1989). Member, Justinian Law Society. ***PRACTICE AREAS:*** Energy Law. ***Email:*** RustumM@dsmo.com

LAURA J. V. SZABO, born Bridgeport, Connecticut, February 8, 1964; admitted to bar, 1991, New York and Connecticut; 1992, District of Columbia. *Education:* Sacred Heart University (B.S., summa cum laude, 1986); George Washington University (J.D., 1990). Law Clerk to Hon. Colleen Kollar-Kotelly, District of Columbia Superior Court, 1990-1991. *Member:* District of Columbia Bar; Bar Association of the District of Columbia; American Bar Association; Federal Energy Regulatory Bar Association. ***PRACTICE AREAS:*** Energy Law; Domestic and International Energy Project Development. ***Email:*** SzaboL@dsmo.com

COUNSEL

GEOFFREY BESTOR, born New York, N.Y., May 20, 1955; admitted to bar, 1982, New York and U.S. District Court, Eastern and Southern Districts of

(This Listing Continued)

New York; 1983, District of Columbia. *Education:* American College, Paris, France (B.A., magna cum laude, 1976); University of Michigan (J.D., cum laude, 1981). Order of the Coif. Editor, University of Michigan Law Review, 1980-1981. Assistant U.S. Attorney, District of Columbia, 1989-1997; Attorney-Advisor, Office of Legal Counsel, U.S. Department of Justice, 1997; Deputy Assistant Attorney General, Office of Policy Development, U.S. Department of Justice, 1997-1999. *Member:* The District of Columbia Bar; American Bar Association (Member, Sections on: Litigation; Courts, Lawyers and the Administrative Justice). ***LANGUAGES:*** French. ***PRACTICE AREAS:*** Energy; Y2K; Litigation. ***Email:*** BestorG@dsmo.com

JOHN J. CARR, born Brooklyn, New York, September 30, 1941; admitted to bar, 1965, New York; 1973, New Jersey. *Education:* St. John's University (B.B.A., 1962; LL.B., 1965); New York University (LL.M., 1971). *Member:* The Association of the Bar of the City of New York; New York State (Member, Real Estate Law Section), New Jersey State and American (Member, Section of Real Property, Probate and Trust Law) Bar Associations. (Resident, New York, N.Y. Office). ***PRACTICE AREAS:*** Commercial Real Estate; Trusts and Estates; General Practice. ***Email:*** jcarr@rsklaw.com

LINDA J. CHASE, born Brooklyn, New York, July 1, 1948; admitted to bar, 1983, New York and U.S. District Court, Southern and Eastern Districts of New York; 1985, Illinois, U.S. District Court, Northern District of Illinois and U.S. Court of Appeals, Seventh Circuit; 1987, U.S. District Court, Northern District of Ohio and U.S. Court of Appeals, Sixth Circuit; 1989, U.S. Supreme Court; 1996, District of Columbia and U.S. District Court, Eastern District of Texas. *Education:* State University of New York (B.A., 1969); Fordham University School of Law (J.D., 1982). Editor, Moot Court Board. Recipient, United States Law Award, 1982. Author: "The Pollution Exclusion: Has the Worm Turned?" Inside Litigation, Vol. 2., No. 7, May 1988. ***PRACTICE AREAS:*** Civil Litigation; Insurance Coverage. ***Email:*** ChaseL@dsmo.com

ANDREW C. COOPER, born New London, Connecticut, May 30, 1964; admitted to bar, 1991, Connecticut; 1992, New York and District of Columbia. *Education:* Yale University (B.A., 1986); University of Pennsylvania (J.D., 1991). Senior Editor, University of Pennsylvania Journal of International Business Law. Primary Author, "EPA Issues Revised Policy on Supplemental Environmental Projects," (lead article in both EPA Administrative Law Reporter - June 1998 and Chemical Waste Litigation Reporter - July 1998). Author: "New Protections From Environmental Liability" (The Practical Lawyer - February 1997); "New Lender and Fiduciary Liability Protection Under Superfund" (New York State Banking Journal - 1996). Co-Author: "Liability for Hazardous Waste" (chapter 30) in B. Dunaway, The Law of Distressed Real Estate (Clark Boardman Callaghan 1985-1997); "In the Recently Passed Appropriations Bill, Congress Clarified When Lenders and Fiduciaries Are Liable Under CERCLA ..." (National Law Journal - November 11, 1996); "Teaming up With Consultants" (Legal Times - April 17, 1995, The Recorder - Autumn 1995); "Even You May Need An Environmental Consultant," (Barrister - Summer 1994). *Member:* American Bar Association (Chair, Young Lawyers Division, Natural Resources & Environmental Law, 1995-1997). ***REPORTED CASES:*** Nat'l. Tel. Cooperative Ass'n. v. Exxon Corp. 38 F. Supp 2d 1 (D.D.C. 1998); Foster v. United States, 922 F. Supp. 642, 922 F. Supp.663, 926 F. Supp. 199 (D.D.C. 1996); Northwestern Mutual Likfe Ins. Co. v. Atlantic Research Corp. 847 F. Supp. 389 (E.D. Va. 1994). ***PRACTICE AREAS:*** Environmental.

MICHAEL J. DeCARLO, born Birmingham, Alabama, March 1, 1956; admitted to bar, 1989, District of Columbia. *Education:* Auburn University (B.A., 1979); Cumberland School of Law of Samford University (J.D., 1987). Phi Alpha Delta. Editor-in-Chief, American Journal of Trial Advocacy. *Member:* American Bar Association; National Health Lawyers Association. ***PRACTICE AREAS:*** Health Care. ***Email:*** DeCarloM@dsmo.com

MICHAEL R. ENGLEMAN, born Louisville, Kentucky, March 11, 1961; admitted to bar, 1988, Kentucky and U.S. District Court, Western District of Kentucky; 1989, U.S. District Court, Eastern District of Kentucky; 1991, U.S. Court of Appeals, Sixth and Seventh Circuits (Not admitted in District of Columbia). *Education:* University of Louisville (B.S., 1984; J.D., cum laude, 1988). Member, Brandeis Society. *Member:* Louisville, Kentucky and American Bar Associations; American Bankruptcy Institute. ***REPORTED CASES:*** Westmoreland - LG&E Partners v. Virginia Electric and Power Co., 486 S.E.2d 289 (Va. 1997); Daniels v. Louisville Gas & Electric Co., 933 S.W.2d 821 (Ky. 1996); Pleasant Pointe Apartments, Ltd. et al v. Kentucky Housing Corp., 139 B.R. 828 (W.D. Ky. 1992). Commissioners of the Sinking Fund of the City of Louisville v. South Central Bell Telephone, 809 S.W.2d 380 (Ky. 1991);. ***PRACTICE AREAS:*** Energy Law; Litigation. ***Email:*** EnglemanM@dsmo.com

ROBERT C. FALLON, born 1956; admitted to bar, 1986, Kentucky; 1997, District of Columbia. *Education:* University of Louisville (B.A., 1978; J.D., 1986). Author: "Antitrust Growing Concern on Gas Industry," Natural Gas, November 1999; "Commission Stays Firm on Capacity Turnback, Reverses Contested Settlements," Natural Gas, October 1999. ***PRACTICE AREAS:*** Energy. ***Email:*** FallonR@dsmo.com

(This Listing Continued)

JOSEPH FRANCIS FIELDS, born Brooklyn, New York, January 1, 1962; admitted to bar, 1986, Connecticut; 1987, New York; 1990, U.S. District Court, Southern and Eastern Districts of New York. *Education:* Manhattanville College (B.A., 1984); New York Law School (J.D., 1986). *Member:* Association of the Bar of the City of New York; New York State and American Bar Associations; New York New Media Association. (Resident, New York, N.Y. Office). ***PRACTICE AREAS:*** Litigation; Commercial Transactions; Internet Law. ***Email:*** jfields@rsklaw.com

JOEL A. FISCHMAN, born Pittsburgh, Pennsylvania, December 20, 1962; admitted to bar, 1988, Pennsylvania and U.S. Court of Appeals, Fourth Circuit; 1990, District of Columbia; 1992, U.S. Court of Appeals, Ninth Circuit; 1995, U.S. Court of Federal Claims. *Education:* University of Michigan (A.B., with distinction, 1984); University of North Carolina, Chapel Hill (J.D., with honors, 1987). Order of the Coif. Editor, North Carolina Law Review, 1986-1987. Author: "In Re Truesdell: North Carolina Adopts Two New and Conflicting Standards for Sterilization of Mentally Retarded Persons," 64 North Carolina L. Rev. 1196, 1986. Law Clerk to Hon. James M. Sprouse, U.S. Court of Appeals, Fourth Circuit, 1987-1988. *Member:* District of Columbia Bar; Pennsylvania (Member, Criminal Defense Section) and American (Member, Sections on: Civil Litigation; Criminal Justice) Bar Associations. ***REPORTED CASES:*** Kofa v. INS slip op No.—(4th Cir. 1995) (INBanc); Westfarm Associates LP v. International Fabricare Institute Slip of No.—(4th Cir. 1995). ***PRACTICE AREAS:*** Civil Litigation; Complex Commercial Litigation.

ALLAN C. HUBBARD, born Miami Beach, Florida, February 26, 1943; admitted to bar, 1972, Virginia; 1973, District of Columbia. *Education:* Washington and Lee University (B.A., 1965); University of Virginia (J.D., 1972). *Member:* Federal Communications Bar Association. [Captain, U.S. Naval Reserve, 1965-1995]. ***PRACTICE AREAS:*** Telecommunications. ***Email:*** HubbardA@dsmo.com

ANDREW S. KERSTING, born Albuquerque, New Mexico, March 6, 1962; admitted to bar, 1987, Colorado and U.S. Court of Appeals for the District of Columbia Circuit; 1990, District of Columbia; 1998, Virginia. *Education:* University of Southern California (B.A., 1984); University of Colorado (J.D., 1987). *Member:* Colorado and Virginia Bar Associations; Federal Communications Bar Association (Member: Judicial Practice Committee, 1993-1995; Mass Media Practice Committee, 1993-2000; Transactional Practice Committee, 1994-1997). ***PRACTICE AREAS:*** Communications Law. ***Email:*** kerstinga@dsmo.com

MARK KOTLARSKY, born Kiev, USSR., May 1, 1952; admitted to bar, 1985, Pennsylvania; 1986, District of Columbia. *Education:* Moscow State University, Moscow, USSR; The Johns Hopkins University (Ph.D., 1980); University of Maryland (J.D., with honors, 1985); Georgetown University (LL.M., Taxation, with distinction, 1991). Research Editor, University of Maryland Law Review, 1984-1985. Author: "Dependent Care Assistance Plans in 1989," 67 Taxes 324, 1989; "Capital Gains and Tax Policy," 41 Tax Notes, 819, 1988; "Stepping up Basis: Asset or Stock Purchase," 39 Tax Notes 1101, 1988; The Art of M&A (principal author of the tax section), Dow Jones Irvin, 1988; "The Reverse Loan Theory of Debt Discharge," 6 The American Journal of Tax Policy 51, 1987; Note, "Caspary v. Louisiana Land & Exploration Co.-The Common Law Right to Inspect Corporate Records for Proper Purpose," 43 Maryland Law Review 572, 1984. ***LANGUAGES:*** Russian and Ukrainian. ***PRACTICE AREAS:*** Tax Law. ***Email:*** KotlarskyM@dsmo.com

HAROLD K. McCOMBS, JR., born Pittsburgh, Pennsylvania, December 30, 1950; admitted to bar, 1975, District of Columbia; 1979, U.S. Supreme Court; 1981, Maryland. *Education:* University of Michigan; University of Texas (B.A., with honors, 1972; B.J., with honors, 1972); George Washington University (J.D., with honors, 1975). *Member:* The District of Columbia Bar; Federal Communications Bar Association. ***PRACTICE AREAS:*** Communications Law. ***Email:*** McCombsH@dsmo.com

EDWARD G. MODELL, born Brooklyn, New York, May 18, 1946; admitted to bar, 1974, Virginia; 1975, District of Columbia; 1979, U.S. Supreme Court. *Education:* Yale University (B.A., 1968); University of Virginia (J.D., 1974). Finalist, Lile Moot Court Competition. Co-Author: "The Subcarrier Question-The Rural Advantage," Telocator March, 1983. Law Clerk to Hon. Robert R. Merhige, Jr., U.S. District Court, Eastern District of Virginia, 1974-1975. *Member:* Virginia State Bar; American Bar Association. [Contracting Officer, USAF, 1969-1972]. ***PRACTICE AREAS:*** Administrative Law; Litigation; State and Federal Grants Law. ***Email:*** ModellE@dsmo.com

JAMES RICHARD O'NEILL, born Washington, D.C., March 20, 1950; admitted to bar, 1975, District of Columbia; 1976, U.S. Tax Court. *Education:* Southern Methodist University (B.B.A., high honors, 1972; J.D., cum laude, 1975). Certified Public Accountant, Texas, 1975; Maryland, 1977. *Member:* Bar Association of the District of Columbia; Federal (Taxation and Housing Law Committees) and American (Taxation Section) Bar Associations; Texas Society of Certified Public Accountants; Maryland Association of Certified Public Accountants; American Institute of Certified Public Accountants. ***PRACTICE AREAS:*** Taxation; Trusts and Estates; Probate; Real Estate; Corporate Law.

(This Listing Continued)

DICKSTEIN SHAPIRO MORIN & OSHINSKY LLP, Washington—Continued

JOHN P. PIERCE, born Lafayette, Indiana, February 27, 1958; admitted to bar, 1985, California; 1986, Illinois; 1999, Virginia (Not admitted in District of Columbia). *Education:* Purdue University (B.S., Econ., 1980); University of Texas (J.D., 1984). Instructor, Legal Research, Writing and Oral Advocacy, University of Texas School of Law, 1983-1984. Assistant U.S. Attorney, 1987-2000 (San Diego, California, 1987-1995; Washington, D.C., 1995-1997; Alexandria, Virginia, 1997-2000). Coordinator, Health Care Fraud, Eastern District of Virginia, 1997-2000. *Member:* Los Angeles County and Illinois State Bar Associations; State Bar of California; The Association of Trial Lawyers of America; California Trial Lawyers Association. ***PRACTICE AREAS:*** Litigation. ***Email:*** piercej@dsmo.com

CHARLOTTE ROTHENBERG ROSEN, born Washington, D.C., May 28, 1960; admitted to bar, 1986, Maryland; 1988, District of Columbia; 1997, U.S. District Court, District of Maryland. *Education:* George Washington University School of Public and International Affairs (B.A., 1982); George Washington University (J.D., 1985). Phi Beta Kappa. Assistant Counsel, U.S. Navy Office of the General Counsel, 1987-1988. Editor, Federal Bar News and Journal, 1987-1993. Speaker, National Contract Management Association. *Member:* American Bar Association (Member, Bid Protest Committee, Public Contracts Section, 1989-1999). ***PRACTICE AREAS:*** Government Contracts; Technology Transactions. ***Email:*** RosenC@dsmo.com

LAWRENCE P. SANDOR, born New York, N.Y., April 18, 1962; admitted to bar, 1987, California; 1990, Georgia; 1995, New York; 1998, District of Columbia. *Education:* Boston University (B.S., 1983); Emory University School of Law (J.D., 1986). ***PRACTICE AREAS:*** Securities Compliance and Enforcement; Securities; Securities Arbitration; Securities Mediation; Broker Dealer. ***Email:*** SandorL@dsmo.com

EDWARD STILL, born Augusta, Georgia, February 22, 1946; admitted to bar, 1971, Alabama; 1994, District of Columbia; U.S. Supreme Court; U.S. Court of Appeals, District of Columbia Circuit; U.S. Court of Appeals, Fourth, Fifth, Sixth and Eleventh Circuits; U.S. District Court, District of Columbia; U.S. District Court, Norhtern, Middle and Southern Disticts of Alabama. *Education:* University of Alabama (B.A., 1968; J.D., 1971). Phi Beta Kappa. Member, Bench and Legal Honor Society. Adjunct Professor: University of Alabama, 1996-1997; American University, 1999-2000. Member, American Political Science Association. Co-Author: "The Nature of the American Constitution: Is There a Constitutional Right to Vote and Be Represented?" Amer. U. L. Rev., Vol. 48, Issue Number 3 (1999) (edited transcript of conference session); with R. Richie "Alternative Electoral Systems as Voting Rights Remedies," FEC Journal of Election Administration, Vol. 18, Issue 1 (1997); with R.L. Engstrom, J.R. Kirskey, "One Person, Seven Votes: The Cumulative Voting Experience in Chilton County, Alabama," Affirmative Action and Representation: Shaw v. Reno and the Future of Voting Rights, Anthony A. Peacock, ed. Carolina Academic Press (1997); with J.R. Kirskey and R.L. Engstrom, "Alternative Voting: How it Works," Voting Rights Review (Spring 1995); with P. Karlan, "Cumulative Voting as a Remedy in Voting Rights Cases," National Civic Review, Volume 84, Issue 4 (1995); with P. McCrary, J. Gary and H. Perry, "Alabama," in The Quiet Revolution: The Impact of the Voting Rights Act in the South, 1965-1990, Chandler Davidson and Bernard Grofman, eds., Princeton University Press (1994). Author, "Symposium: The Supreme Court, Racial Politics, and the Right to Vote: Shaw v. Reno and the Future of the Voting Rights Act," Amer. U.L. Rev., Vol. 44, Issue 1 (1994) (edited transcript of conference); "Cumulative and Limited Voting in Alabama," in United States Electoral Systems: Their Impact on Minorities and Women, Wilma Rule and Joseph F. Zimmerman, eds., Greenwood Press (1992); "The Hunting of the Gerrymanders," (review of Political Gerrymandering and the Courts, edited by Bernard Grofman), UCLA Law Review, Volume 38, Issue 4 (1991); "Voluntary Constituencies: Modified At-Large Voting As A Remedy For Minority Vote Dilution In Judicial Elections," Yale Law & Policy Review, Volume 9, Issue 2 (1991); "Alternatives to Single-Member Districts," in Minority Vote Dilution, Chandler Davidson, ed., Howard University Press, 1984. *Member:* American Bar Association; The Association of Trial Lawyers of America; George Washington American Inn of Court; American Political Science Association: Southern Political Science Association; International Political Science Association. (Director, Voting Rights). ***REPORTED CASES:*** Holt Civic Club v. City of Tuscaloosa, 439 US 60 (1978); Hunter v. Underwood, 471 U.S. 222 (1985); Presley v. Etowah County Commission, 502 U.S. 491 (1992); Presley v. Etowah County Commission, 502 U.S. 491 (1992); Baker v. Glover, 776 f. Supp. 1511 (M.D. Ala. 1991); Ex parte Graddick, 495 So.2d 1367 (Ala. 1986); Lynch v. Baxley, 386 F.Supp. 378 (M.D. Ala. 1974) (three judge court). ***PRACTICE AREAS:*** Voting Rights; Elections; Redistricting. ***Email:*** stille@dsmo.org

LAURA A. VIKANDER, born St. Louis, Missouri, December 21, 1956; admitted to bar, 1983, District of Columbia; 1984, U.S. District Court, District of Columbia; 1985, Virginia. *Education:* Duke University (B.A., magna cum laude, 1978); University of Virginia (J.D., 1983). *Member:* The District of Columbia Bar; Virginia Bar Association; Virginia State Bar. ***PRACTICE AREAS:*** Civil Litigation; Alternative Dispute Resolution; Insurance Litigation. ***Email:*** VikanderL@dsmo.com

CARLA PERANTONI WALSH, born Somerville, New Jersey, January 8, 1954; admitted to bar, 1985, Virginia; 1986, District of Columbia. *Education:* Georgetown University (B.A., 1976); Columbus School of Law, Catholic University of America (J.D., 1985). *Member:* The District of Columbia Bar; Virginia State Bar. ***PRACTICE AREAS:*** Labor and Employment Law. ***Email:*** WalshC@dsmo.com

ALEXANDER D. WIDELL, born New York, N.Y., September 26, 1962; admitted to bar, 1991, New York; 1993, U.S. District Court, Southern and Eastern Districts of New York; 1996, U.S. Court of Appeals, First Circuit; 1997, U.S. Court of Appeals, Federal Circuit. *Education:* State University of New York at Albany (B.A., 1984); New York Law School (J.D., cum laude, 1990). Recipient: New York State Trial Lawyers Sidney Tolmage Memorial Scholarship Award; American Jurisprudence Awards: Excellence, Federal Courts and Federal Systems; Excellence, Trial Advocacy. Co-Author: with Nancy E. Barton: "Securities Litigation: Joint and Several Liability and Contribution," Practising Law Institute, PLI Order No. H4-5196 October 1994 (509 PLI/LIT 599); with N. Barlia, "Defending Claims Following Bankruptcy Dismissal," New York Law Journal, May 9, 2000. Adjunct Professor of Law, New York Law School, 1994-1995. *Member:* New York State and American Bar Associations; New York County Trial Lawyers' Association. (Resident, New York, N.Y. Office). ***REPORTED CASES:*** Kunica v. St. Jean Financial, Inc., 223 B.R. 46 (S.D.N.Y. 1999); Bibara v. Locke, 99 F.3d 1233 (1st Cir. 1996); SEC v. Posner, 16 F.3d 520 (2nd Cir. 1994). ***TRANSACTIONS:*** Represented Tyco Toys, Inc. in connection with its 1998 merger with Mattel, Inc. ***PRACTICE AREAS:*** Commercial Litigation; Business Litigation; Appellate Practice. ***Email:*** widella@dsmo.com

NICHOLAS J. ZOOGMAN, born New York, N.Y., April 2, 1947; admitted to bar, 1974, New York and U.S. District Court, Southern and Eastern Districts of New York; 1975, U.S. Court of Appeals, Second Circuit; 1979, U.S. Supreme Court; 1988, U.S. District Court, Eastern District of Michigan; 1989, U.S. Court of Appeals, District of Columbia Circuit; 1993, U.S. Court of Appeals, Sixth Circuit; 1997, U.S. Court of Appeals, Fifth Circuit. *Education:* New York University (B.A., 1967); Harvard University (M.A., 1969; J.D., 1973). Phi Beta Kappa; Pi Sigma Alpha. Author: "If Lawyers Practice in MDP's," New York Law Journal, (January 8, 2001); "Policyholders Advisory: Year 2000 Information Readiness Disclosure Act," Manufacturing Risk Management and Insurance Newsletter (April 1999); "Year 2000 Bug Insurance Coverage Considerations," The Environmental Corporate Counsel Report (February 1999); "Year 2000 Liability and Insurance Coverage Issues for Banks and Other Financial Institutions," The Banking Law Journal (July/August 1998); "Year 2000 Computer Bug: Liability and Insurance Coverage Issues," Mealey's Insurance Law Weekly (June 22, 1998); "The Year 2000 Computer Crisis Is Upon Us Now," Bank Security Report (May 1998); "Year 2000 Computer Bug: Liability and Insurance Coverage Issues," Managing Risk (July 1998); "Year 2000 Computer Bug: Liability and Insurance Coverage Issues," Policyholder Advisor (June 1998); "Not Even a Prison Door Bars Insurer's Duty to Defend," Trials Digest (March 23, 1998); "Liability and Insurance Coverage Issues for the Year 2000 Computer Crisis," U.S. Insurance Report (Summer 1997); "Protecting You and Your Company From Health Insurance Overbilling," Policyholder Advisor (August 1996); "What Every Corporate Lawyer Should Know About Insurance Coverage," The Corporate Analyst (February 1996). *Member:* The Association of the Bar of the City of New York; New York State and American Bar Associations. (Resident, New York, N.Y. Office). ***Email:*** ZoogmanN@dsmo.com

ASSOCIATES

PETER J. ANDREWS, born New York, N.Y., May 20, 1969; admitted to bar, 1993, New York; 1994, U.S. District Court, Southern and Eastern Districts of New York; 2000, U.S. Supreme Court. *Education:* Hunter College of the City University of New York (B.A., summa cum laude, 1989); Columbia University (J.D., 1992). Harlan Fiske Stone Scholar. Author: "Insurance Coverage For Employee Theft Losses," 29 U. of Mem. L. Rev. 363, Winter, 1999. Guest Lecturer, Vytautas Magnus University, Kaunas, Lithuania, July, 1997. *Member:* New York State and American Bar Associations. (Resident, New York, N.Y. Office). ***REPORTED CASES:*** Weyerhaeuser v. Aetna Cas. & Sur. Co., 123 Wash. 2d 891, 874 P.2d 142 (1994); Olds-Olympic v. Commercial Union, 129 Wash. 2d 464, 918 P.2d 923 (1996); American Mutual Fire Ins. v. B&L Trucking, 134 Wash. 2d 413, 951 P.2d 250 (1998); In Re: Payroll Express (Pereira v. Aetna Cos. & Sun. Co.), 186 F.3d 196 (2d Cir. 1999). ***PRACTICE AREAS:*** Insurance Coverage Litigation; General Litigation. ***Email:*** AndrewsP@dsmo.com

CONSTANCE ELAINE ARABATZIS, born Dania, Florida, January 23, 1961; admitted to bar, 1990, Connecticut; 1991, New York and District of Columbia; 1993, Florida. *Education:* Lehman College of the City University of New York (B.S., summa cum laude, 1986); New York University (J.D., 1989).

(This Listing Continued)

Phi Alpha Delta. *Member:* The District of Columbia Bar; The Florida Bar. (Resident, New York, N.Y. Office). ***PRACTICE AREAS:*** Commercial Litigation. ***Email:*** arabatzise@dsmo.com

ELIZABETH ARENSON, born Boston, Massachusetts, October 19, 1973; admitted to bar, 2000, California and U.S. District Court, Central District of California (Not admitted in District of Columbia). *Education:* Duke University (A.B., 1996); American University (J.D., 2000). ***PRACTICE AREAS:*** Civil Litigation. ***Email:*** ArensonE@dsmo.com

GABRIEL ASSAAD, born Rochester, New York, August 17, 1973; (admission pending). *Education:* University of Florida (B.S.M.E., 1996); Vanderbilt University (J.D., 2001). ***Email:*** assaadg@dsmo.com

RUXANDRA BARBULESCU, born Bucharest, Romania, December 26, 1971; admitted to bar, 1999, New York; 2000, District of Columbia. *Education:* Boston University (B.A., magna cum laude, 1994); Cornell University (J.D., 1998). ***LANGUAGES:*** Romanian and Spanish. ***PRACTICE AREAS:*** Energy Project Finance; Energy Regulatory. ***Email:*** BarbulescuS@dsmo.com

ROBYN R. BENDER, born Milwaukee, Wisconsin, November 25, 1969; admitted to bar, 1997, Ohio; 2000, District of Columbia. *Education:* Duke University (A.B., 1992); Georgetown University Law Center (J.D., 1997). Author: "Implementation of the Family Cap: Models for Integrating Family Planning Services," Georgetown Journal on Fighting Poverty, Vol. IV, No. 2, Spring 1997. *Member:* The District of Columbia Bar. ***PRACTICE AREAS:*** Litigation. ***Email:*** BenderR@dsmo.com

ERIC A. BENSKY, born Madison, Wisconsin, February 13, 1971; admitted to bar, 1997, New York; 1998, District of Columbia and U.S. Court of Appeals, Third Circuit; 2000, U.S. Court of Appels, Eleventh Circuit. *Education:* University of Michigan (B.A., with high honors and high distinction, 1993); University of Chicago (J.D., with honors, 1996). ***PRACTICE AREAS:*** Securities Litigation; Criminal Defense. ***Email:*** BenskyE@dsmo.com

JASON S. BROWN, born Arlington, Virginia, July 6, 1971; admitted to bar, 1996, Virginia; 2001, District of Columbia. *Education:* University of Virginia (B.A., 1993); Marshall-Wythe School of Law, College of William & Mary (J.D., 1996). National Merit Scholar. R.M. Hughes Sr. Scholarship. *Member:* Virginia State Bar. ***PRACTICE AREAS:*** Insurance Litigation; Antitrust Litigation. ***Email:*** BrownJ@dsmo.com

JASON M. BRUNO, born Boston, Massachusetts, February 20, 1972; admitted to bar, 2000, North Carolina; 2001, District of Columbia. *Education:* University of North Carolina at Wilmington (B.A., cum laude, 1995); University of North Carolina at Chapel Hill (J.D., with honors, 2000). Member, 1998-1999 and Editor, 1999-2000, University of North Carolina Law Review. ***PRACTICE AREAS:*** Complex Dispute Resolution. ***Email:*** BrunoJ@dsmo.com

PHILIP BUSMAN, born Washington, D.C., February 4, 1975; admitted to bar, 2000, Virginia (Not admitted in District of Columbia). *Education:* University of Michigan (B.A., 1997); American University (J.D., cum laude, 2000). ***PRACTICE AREAS:*** Insurance Litigation; Bankruptcy; Creditors Rights. ***Email:*** busmanp@dsmo.com

DEBORAH ANN CARPENTIER, born La Plata, Maryland, June 21, 1966; admitted to bar, 1992, Maryland; 1993, District of Columbia. *Education:* University of Maryland (B.A., 1988); George Washington University (J.D., 1992). Executive Managing Editor, George Washington Journal of International Law and Economics, 1991-1992. Contributor: "Government Guidelines for Comparative Collaborations to Clarify Future Gas Ventures," Natural Gas (January 2000); Antitrust: "Growing Concern in Gas Industry," Natural Gas (November 1999). Co-author: "Commission Stays Firm on Capacity Turnback, Reverses Contested Settlements," Natural Gas (October 1999); "The Case for Reasonable Incentives to Promote Independent Transmission Companies," The Electricity Journal (August/September 1999); "Many Questions about Approval of Settlements under Free Market," Natural gas (March 1999); "Commission Battles Capacity Turnback in Recent Case," Natural gas (October 1998). *Member:* District of Columbia Bar; American and Federal Energy Bar Associations. ***PRACTICE AREAS:*** Energy Law. ***Email:*** CarpentierD@dsmo.com

CHRISTOPHER S. CHOW, admitted to bar, 1993, New Jersey; 1994, New York; registered to practice before U.S. Patent and Trademark Office (Not admitted in District of Columbia). *Education:* Cornell University (B.S., 1988); Albany Law School of Union University (J.D., 1993). ***PRACTICE AREAS:*** Intellectual Property. ***Email:*** ChowC@dsmo.com

NICOLE M. COBER, born Oakland, California, July 1, 1971; admitted to bar, 1996, California; 1999, District of Columbia. *Education:* University of California, Berkeley (B.A., 1993); Howard University (J.D., 1996). Member, National Moot Court. Member Law Journal. Recipient, American Jurisprudence Award in Legal Writing. Law Clerk, Chief Judge Wagner, D.C. Court of Appeals for the District of Columbia, 1996-1998. *Member:* American Bar Association. ***PRACTICE AREAS:*** Employment Litigation; Antitrust Litigation. ***Email:*** CoberN@dsmo.com

ANDRES COLON, born Rochester, New York, March 10, 1970; admitted to bar, 1995, New York; 2000, District of Columbia. *Education:* State University of New York at Brockport (B.A., 1991); State University of New York at Buffalo (J.D., 1994). ***LANGUAGES:*** Spanish. ***PRACTICE AREAS:*** General Litigation. ***Email:*** ColonA@dsmo.com

GABRIELA I. COMAN, born Tulcea, Romania, June 25, 1968; admitted to bar, 2000, New York; 2001, District of Columbia. *Education:* Bernard M. Baruch College of the City University of New York (B.S., Biology, summa cum laude, 1996);Brooklyn Law School (J.D., 1999). Recipient, Excellence Award in Natural Sciences. Member, Baruch College Alumni Association in Liberal Arts and Sciences. Notes and Comments Editor, Brooklyn Law Review. ***LANGUAGES:*** Romanian, French and Italian. ***PRACTICE AREAS:*** Intellectual Property. ***Email:*** ComanG@dsmo.com

SANDRINE COUSQUER, born Lyon Gęarrdt, Rhône, France, December 15, 1976; (admission pending). *Education:* University of Paris, France (DEUG, 1996); Cornell University (J.D., 2000); University of Pantheon-Sorbonne (Maitrise En Droit, 2000). Member, Moot Court Board. Member, Cornell Journal of Law and Public Policy, 1997-1999. Legal Intern, New York State Department of Environmental Conservation, 1996. *Member:* New York State and American Bar Associations. ***LANGUAGES:*** French. ***PRACTICE AREAS:*** Energy; Contract Law. ***Email:*** CousquerS@dsmo.com

JEREMY A. CUBERT, born Philadelphia, Pennsylvania, April 14, 1966; admitted to bar, 1995, Maryland; 1998, District of Columbia. *Education:* Rutgers College (B.A., 1987); University of Medicine and Dentistry, New Jersey (M.S., 1989); George Mason University (J.D., 1995). Author: "U.S. Patent and Biotechnology: Growing Pains on the Cutting Edge," 7 JPTOS 155, 1995. Speaker, "Intellectual Property Issues on the Internet," Association of Federal Technology Transfer Executives Meeting, San Francisco, February 1997. Speaker, "Antitrust Limitations on Intellectual Property Rights," National Cancer Institute, May 2000. *Member:* The District of Columbia Bar; Maryland State and American Bar Associations. ***PRACTICE AREAS:*** Patent; Licensing; Technology Transfer; Antitrust. ***Email:*** CubertJ@dsmo.com

ELI CURI, JR., born Orange, New Jersey, April 21, 1967; admitted to bar, 1997, New York, New Jersey and U.S. District Court, District of New Jersey. *Education:* The University of Chicago (A.B., 1992); Fordham University School of Law (J.D., 1996). (Resident, New York, N.Y. Office). ***LANGUAGES:*** Spanish.

ESTELINA L. DALLETT, born Newport, Rhode Island, October 17, 1964; admitted to bar, 1994, Massachusetts; 1995, District of Columbia. *Education:* Harvard University (A.B., magna cum laude, 1987; J.D., cum laude, 1993). Phi Beta Kappa. Law Clerk to Chief Judge Frank W. Bullock, Jr., U.S. District Court for the Middle District of North Carolina, 1993-1994. *Member:* Bar Association of the District of Columbia; American Bar Association; Society of Professionals in Dispute Resolution. ***PRACTICE AREAS:*** Alternative Dispute Resolution; Mass Tort Settlements; Insurance. ***Email:*** DallettE@dsmo.com

WILLIAM C. DENNIS, born Burlington, Vermont, March 20, 1968; admitted to bar, 1995, New York. *Education:* Binghamton University (B.A., with outstanding academic performance, 1991); Boston University School of Law (J.D., 1994). Case and Note Editor, American Journal of Law and Medicine. *Member:* The Association of the Bar of the City of New York. (Resident, New York, N.Y. Office). ***Email:*** wdennis@rsklaw.com

LYNNE CELANDER DeSARBO, born Mount Kisco, New York, May 5, 1971; (admission pending). *Education:* University of Michigan (B.A., with distinction, 1992; M.S.W., 1993); University of Pennsylvania (J.D., 1999). Golden Key Honor Society; Psi Chi Honor Society. Recipient, James J. Mandenino Award, Philadelphia Trial Lawyers Association for Excellence in Trial Advocacy. Member, National Association of Social Workers. ***PRACTICE AREAS:*** Civil Litigation; Health Care; Legislative; Regulatory. ***Email:*** DeSarboL@dsmo.com

KIRSTEN LEA DOOLITTLE, born Jackson, Mississippi, July 4, 1974; admitted to bar, 2000, Virginia (Not admitted in District of Columbia). *Education:* Dartmouth College (B.A., 1996); University of Southern California (J.D., 2000). Author, "Don't Ask, You May Not Want to Know: Custody Preferences of Children of Lesbian and Gay Parents," 73 S. Cal. L. Rev. 677 (March 2000). Instructor, Lawyering Skills, USC Law School, 1998-2000. Member, Lawyers Guild, 1997—. ***PRACTICE AREAS:*** Litigation; Labor. ***Email:*** doolittlek@dsmo.com

JENNIFER M. ECK, born Levittown, Pennsylvania, September 18, 1965; admitted to bar, 1995, Maryland; 1996, District of Columbia. *Education:* Pennsylvania State University (B.S., in Accounting, with highest distinction, 1987); University of North Carolina at Chapel Hill (J.D., with honors, 1995). Order of the Coif. Editor-in-Chief, North Carolina Journal of International Law and Commercial Regulation. *Member:* District of Columbia Bar; Maryland State and American Bar Associations; American Institute of Certified Public Accountants. ***PRACTICE AREAS:*** Mergers and Acquisitions; Corporate; Securities. ***Email:*** EckJ@dsmo.com

CHARLES ERNEST EDGAR, IV, born Mobile, Alabama, August 9, 1965; admitted to bar, 1994, Virginia; 1995, District of Columbia and U.S.

(This Listing Continued)

DICKSTEIN SHAPIRO MORIN & OSHINSKY LLP, Washington—Continued

District Court, Eastern District of Virginia; 1996, U.S. District Court for the District of Columbia; 1997, U.S. Court of Federal Claims; 2000, U.S. Court of Appeals, Fourth, District of Columbia and Federal Circuits. *Education:* Virginia Military Institute (B.S.C.E., 1987); University of Virginia (J.D., 1994). Tau Beta Pi. Editor, Virginia Environmental law Journal. Professional Engineer, Virginia, 1994. Member: Society of American Military Engineers; American Society of Civil Engineers. Author: "United States Use of Armed Force Under The UN," 10 J. L. Pol. 299 (1994). Co-Author: "An Imperfect Shield: How Private Parties Can Attack and Defeat the Executive Privilege for Deliberative Process in Government Procurement Litigation," 28 Pub. Cont. L.J. 127 (1999); "Partnering, Innovative Response to Conflict Prevention Can Streamline Both Contracting for and Performing Environmental Remediation," Eighth Annual Environment Virginia Symposium, 1997; "Environmental Cleanup Contracting: Challenges and Opportunities," Fifth Annual Construction Leadership Conference, 1995. *Member:* Virginia State Bar; American Bar Association; Court of Federal Claims Bar Association. [Capt., U.S. Army, 1987-1991, USAR, 1991—]. ***PRACTICE AREAS:*** Government Contracts; Environmental; Construction. ***Email:*** EdgarE@dsmo.com

CARMELA N. EDMUNDS, born Norfolk, Virginia, September 6, 1963; admitted to bar, 1992, Virginia; 1993, District of Columbia. *Education:* Hampton Institute (B.A., highest honors, 1985); Duke University (J.D., 1992). Adjunct Professor, George Mason University, Winter 1996. *Member:* The District of Columbia Bar; Virginia State Bar; American Bar Association; National Bar Association (Member, Women's Lawyer Division). ***PRACTICE AREAS:*** Litigation. ***Email:*** EdmundsC@dsmo.com

STEVEN R. EICHEL, born Brooklyn, New York, October 4, 1971; admitted to bar, 1997, New York. *Education:* Binghamton University (B.A., 1993); Fordham University School of Law (J.D., 1996). Symposium Editor, "Emerging Issues in Civil Rights Law Enforcement," 23 Fordham Urban Law Journal 4, 1996. (Resident, New York, N.Y. Office). ***PRACTICE AREAS:*** Corporate and Finance.

JASON R. EIG, born Silver Spring, Maryland, February 7, 1972; admitted to bar, 1999, Maryland; 2000, District of Columbia. *Education:* Georgetown University (B.A.S., 1994); Georgetown University Law Center (J.D., 1999). *Member:* The District of Columbia Bar; Maryland State and American Bar Associations. ***PRACTICE AREAS:*** Corporate; Mergers and Acquisitions; Securities. ***Email:*** EigJ@dsmo.com

JODY M. ENDRES, born Hastings, Michigan, March 12, 1970; (admission pending). *Education:* University of South Dakota (B.A., 1992); University of Illinois (J.D., cum laude, 2000). Member, Elder Law Journal, 1998-2000. Author: "Reconciling EC-US Organic Food Laws to Facilitate Transatlantic Trade," San Joaquin Agricultural Law Journal, Fall, 2000. *Member:* American Agricultural Law Association. ***LANGUAGES:*** German. ***PRACTICE AREAS:*** Litigation; Insurance; Environmental. ***Email:*** EndresJ@dsmo.com

JACOB S. FARBER, born Philadelphia, Pennsylvania, January 15, 1969; admitted to bar, 1994, Maryland; 1997, District of Columbia. *Education:* University of Michigan (B.A., 1991); George Washington University (J.D., 1994). Member, George Washington Journal of International Law and Economics. *Member:* Federal Communications Bar Association. ***PRACTICE AREAS:*** Communications. ***Email:*** FarberJ@dsmo.com

MARIA FARINELLA, born Paterson, New Jersey, July 29, 1970; admitted to bar, 1995, Maryland and New Jersey; 1999, District of Columbia. *Education:* Smith College (B.A., 1992), Phi Beta Kappa; Washington College of Law, American University (J.D., 1995). Judicial Law Clerk, Judge Graydon S. McKee, III, Seventh Judicial Circuit of Maryland. *Member:* District of Columbia Bar; Energy and American Bar Associations. ***PRACTICE AREAS:*** Energy. ***Email:*** FarinellaM@dsmo.com

LAURA BETH FEIGIN, born New York, N.Y., December 20, 1959; admitted to bar, 1990, New York and District of Columbia; 1996, U.S. Supreme Court. *Education:* Brown University (A.B., magna cum laude, 1981); Columbia University (M.A., 1984); Stanford University (J.D., 1987). Notes Editor, Stanford Law Review, 1986-1987. Co-Author: "The Deprivation of 'Intangible Rights' Under the Mail Fraud Statute: Some Key Considerations," 1994 ABA Section of Litigation Complex Crimes Journal. *Member:* District of Columbia Bar; Bar Association of the District of Columbia; American Bar Association; Women's Bar Association of the District of Columbia. ***PRACTICE AREAS:*** Criminal and Civil Litigation. ***Email:*** FeiginL@dsmo.com

ROBERT N. FELGAR, born Montreal, Quebec, April 4, 1970; admitted to bar, 1998, Maryland; 2000, District of Columbia. *Education:* McGill University (B.A., 1992); George Washington University (J.D., 1997). *Member:* Federal Communications Bar Association. ***LANGUAGES:*** French. ***PRACTICE AREAS:*** Telecommunications Law; Broadcasting Law. ***Email:*** FelgarR@dsmo.com

(This Listing Continued)

LAURENCE E. FISHER, born Washington, D.C., October 13, 1951; admitted to bar, 1989, Maryland; 1992, District of Columbia; registered to practice before U.S. Patent and Trademark Office. *Education:* University of Maryland (B.S., 1979); Drexel University (M.B.A., 1984); Georgetown University (J.D., 1989). Associate Articles Editor, Journal of Legal Ethics, 1989. Registered Professional Engineer, Pennsylvania, 1983. ***PRACTICE AREAS:*** Intellectual Property. ***Email:*** FisherL@dsmo.com

RYAN H. FLAX, born Silver Spring, Maryland, October 25, 1973; admitted to bar, 1999, Maryland (Not admitted in District of Columbia). *Education:* Wake Forest University (B.S., 1995); Southern Methodist University (J.D., cum laude, 1999). Phi Delta Phi; Phi Alpha Delta. Symposium Editor, Member, Southern Methodist Law Review. Author: "NAFTA and the Patent Systems of its Members: Is There Potential for Unification of the North American Patent Systems?" 5 NAFTA L. and Bus. Rev. Am. 461 (Summer 1999). ***PRACTICE AREAS:*** Intellectual Property Litigation and Prosecution. ***Email:*** FlaxR@dsmo.com

KENNETH H. FRENCHMAN, born New York, N.Y., October 28, 1971; admitted to bar, 2000, New York. *Education:* University of Colorado (B.S., Business Administration, 1993); Tulane University School of Law; New York University School of Law (J.D., 1999). (Resident, New York, N.Y. Office). ***PRACTICE AREAS:*** Litigation. ***Email:*** kfrenchman@rsklaw.com

ROBERT FRIEDMAN, born Brooklyn, New York, April 16, 1973; admitted to bar, 1999, New York. *Education:* Cornell University (B.S., 1995); Harvard University (J.D., 1998). Law Clerk, Honorable Naomi Reice Buchwald, Southern District of N.Y., 1998-1999. (Resident, New York, N.Y. Office). ***PRACTICE AREAS:*** Insurance Law. ***Email:*** FriedmanR@dsmo.com

VALERIE M. FURMAN, born Los Angeles, California, May 6, 1968; admitted to bar, 1995, District of Columbia and Connecticut. *Education:* Brandeis University (B.A., 1990); American University Washington College of Law (J.D., 1993). Phi Alpha Delta. *Member:* Federal Communications and American Bar Associations. ***PRACTICE AREAS:*** Communications Law; Administrative Law; Corporate Law. ***Email:*** FurmanV@dsmo.com

KEISHA A. GARY, born Savannah, Georgia, March 13, 1970; admitted to bar, 1995, Maryland; 1997, District of Columbia. *Education:* Radcliffe College, Harvard University (A.B., cum laude, 1992); Georgetown University Law Center (J.D., 1995). Member, 1993-1994 and Editor in Chief, 1994-1995, Georgetown Immigration Law Journal. Author: Note, "Congressional Proposals to Revive Guilt By Association: An Ineffective Plan to Stop Terrorism," 8 Geo. Immigr. L. J. 227, 1994; "International Developments," 7 Geo. Immigr. L. J. 891, 1993. *Member:* District of Columbia Bar; Maryland State, National (Greater Washington Area Chapter; Women Lawyers Division) and American Bar Associations. ***PRACTICE AREAS:*** Civil Litigation; Insurance Litigation. ***Email:*** GaryK@dsmo.com

DAVID S. GASPEROW, born Washington, D.C., April 29, 1974; (admission pending). *Education:* Washington University (B.S.B.A., 1996); Columbia University (J.D., 2001). Harlan Fiske Stone Scholar. Certified Public Accountant, Missouri, 1996. ***PRACTICE AREAS:*** Mergers and Acquisitions; Securities; Corporate Law. ***Email:*** gasperowd@dsmo.com

JOHN A. GIBBONS, born Silver Spring, Maryland, August 27, 1973; admitted to bar, 1998, Maryland (Not admitted in District of Columbia). *Education:* University of Maryland (B.A., 1995); Catholic University of America (J.D., magna cum laude, 1998). Editor-in-Chief, Journal of Contemporary Health Law and Policy. Author: "Who's Your Daddy: A Constitutional Analysis of Post-Mortem Insemination," Vol. 14, Iss. 1 Journal of Contemporary Health Law and Policy. Law Clerk to The Hon. Ann O'Regan Keary, Associate Judge of the Superior Court of District of Columbia, 1998-1999. ***PRACTICE AREAS:*** Litigation. ***Email:*** GibbonsJ@dsmo.com

ANDREW GILMAN, born Tarrytown, New York, June 7, 1975; admitted to bar, 2000, New York and New Jersey. *Education:* Haverford College (B.A., 1997); New York University (J.D., 2000). Phi Beta Kappa. (Resident, New York, N.Y. Office). ***PRACTICE AREAS:*** Litigation; Corporate Law.

JONATHAN M. GOODMAN, born Washington, D.C., October 25, 1969; admitted to bar, 1995, Maryland; 1998, District of Columbia. *Education:* Cornell University (B.S., 1991); University of Maryland School of Law (J.D., with honors, 1995). Articles Editor, University of Maryland Law Review. Law Clerk to the Hon. James P. Salmon, Court of Special Appeals of Maryland, 1995-1996. Author: "Clarifying the Scope of Maryland's Implied Warranties," 53 Univ. of Md. L.Rev. 986 (1994). (Resident, New York, N.Y. Office). ***PRACTICE AREAS:*** Commercial Litigation; Insurance Coverage Litigation. ***Email:*** GoodmanJ@dsmo.com

DAVID H. GREENBERG, born Silver Spring, Maryland, April 1, 1975; admitted to bar, 2000, Maryland; 2001, District of Columbia. *Education:* Syracuse University (B.A., 1997); American University (J.D., magna cum laude, 2000). Recipient, Administrative Law Review, Book Award winner in Antitrust, Wills Trusts and Estates, and Civil Practice. ***PRACTICE AREAS:*** Complex Civil Litigation; Insurance Coverage. ***Email:*** GreenbergD@dsmo.com

(This Listing Continued)

MARI C. GREENE, born San Francisco, California, November 4, 1974; (admission pending). *Education:* Stanford University (B.A., 1996); University of Chicago (J.D., 2000). President, Black Law Students Association, 1998-1999. ***Email:*** GreeneM@dsmo.com

JENNIFER DUNCAN HACKETT, born Tuba City, Arizona, August 21, 1973; (admission pending). *Education:* Lewis and Clark College (B.A., 1995); New York University (J.D., 2001). ***Email:*** hackettj@dsmo.com

EDWARD S. HAMMERMAN, born Washington, D.C., March 21, 1969; admitted to bar, 1994, Pennsylvania; 1998, District of Columbia and Florida. *Education:* Emory University (B.A., 1991); Catholic University of America (J.D., 1994; Post Graduate Certificate Law Studies, 1994). Executive Editor, CommLaw Conspectus, Journal of Communications Law and Policy, 1993-1994. Regular Contributor: "Tower Times," (National Association of Tower Erectors, April 1999); "Industry expert:" Office.com, Telecommunications web page (May 2000-March 2001). Editor, "Broadcasting and the Law," (Matthew L. Leibowitz, pub., Edward S. Hammerman, ed., April 1996-January 1998) Monthly Newsletter, April 1996-January 1998. Author: Edward S. Hammerman for Samuel A. Simon, "Telecommunication Regulation in Regulation & Consumer Protection: Politics, Bureaucracy & Economics,," (Kenneth Meier & E. Thomas Garman eds., November 1994); U.S. Congress, Office of Technology Assessment, "Protecting Privacy in Computerized Medical Information," OTA-TCT-576 (Washington, D.C.; U.S. Government Printing Office, September 1993). Speeches, "A Summary of the Telecommunications Act of 1996," Address Before Lexis/Nexis Account Managers of Communications Law Firms (February 28, 1996); "Becoming a Communications Lawyer: One Year Out," Address Before First-Year Law School Students Enrolled in the Institute for Communications Law Studies (September 10, 1994). Listed in Who's Who in American Law, Eleventh Edition (Marquis 1999-2000; 2001-2002); Who's Who in America (Marquis 2000); Who's Who Among American Law Students 12th Edition.. *Member:* Federal Communications Bar Association.. ***SPECIAL AGENCIES:*** Federal Communications Commission; Office of Copyright; Library of Congress. ***PRACTICE AREAS:*** Communications; Transactional; Intellectual Property. ***Email:*** HammermanT@dsmo.com

WALKER G. HARMAN, JR., born Norman, Oklahoma, September 5, 1970; admitted to bar, 2000, New York. *Education:* Marymount-Manhattan College (B.F.A., 1993); Fordham University (J.D., 1999). (Resident, New York, N.Y. Office). ***PRACTICE AREAS:*** Litigation; Insurance Coverage Litigation. ***Email:*** HarmanW@dsmo.com

TERESA L. HARVEY, born Oakland, Maryland, March 17, 1965; admitted to bar, 1993, Pennsylvania; 1998, District of Columbia. *Education:* Alleghany Community College (A.A., 1985); Angelo State University (B.S., 1987); Southern Methodist University (J.D., 1993). Order of the Coif. John Marshall Constitutional Award, 1993. Leading Articles Editor, Southern Methodist University Law Review, 1992-1993. Author: "The Killing Words? How the New Quality-of-Life Ethic Affects People with Severe Disabilities," 46 SMU Law Review, 805, 1992. ***PRACTICE AREAS:*** Civil Litigation; Insurance Coverage Litigation; Employment Law; Constitutional Law. ***Email:*** HarveyT@dsmo.com

ELIZABETH B. HAYWOOD, born Concord, North Carolina, May 27, 1969; admitted to bar, 1994, North Carolina; 1999, District of Columbia. *Education:* University of North Carolina at Chapel Hill (A.B., with distinction and highest honors, 1991; J.D., 1994). Phi Beta Kappa. ***PRACTICE AREAS:*** Legislative Practice; Regulatory Law; Health Care. ***Email:*** HaywoodE@dsmo.com

BRIDGET M. HEALY, born Abilene, Texas, November 6, 1972; admitted to bar, 1999, New York. *Education:* St. Lawrence University (B.A., 1994); Fordham University (J.D., 1998). (Resident, New York, N.Y. Office). ***PRACTICE AREAS:*** Bankruptcy.

MARIA COLSEY HEARD, born Philadelphia, Pennsylvania, May 2, 1968; admitted to bar, 1994, New Jersey and Pennsylvania; 1996, District of Columbia. *Education:* LaSalle University (B.A., maxima cum laude, 1990); George Washington University (J.D., with honors, 1993). Judicial Clerk to The Honorable Steffen W. Graae, District of Columbia Superior Court, 1993-1995. ***PRACTICE AREAS:*** Public Sector Litigation; Civil Litigation; Alternative Dispute Resolution. ***Email:*** HeardM@dsmo.com

JENNIFER TARA GETER HOLUBAR, born New York, N.Y., January 10, 1969; admitted to bar, 1995, New York; 1996, District of Columbia. *Education:* University of Maryland, European Division (B.S., 1990); Georgetown University Law Center (J.D., 1994). *Member:* The District of Columbia Bar; New York State and American Bar Associations. ***PRACTICE AREAS:*** Civil Litigation; Securities Litigation; Insurance Litigation. ***Email:*** HolubarJ@dsmo.com

SAMUEL L. JEFFERSON, JR., born Washington, D.C., May 7, 1968; admitted to bar, 1994, Pennsylvania; 1996, District of Columbia; 1999, U.S. Supreme Court; 2000, U.S. Federal Bar. *Education:* Georgetown University (A.B., 1990; J.D., 1994). Associate Editor, Georgetown Journal of Fighting Poverty, 1992-1994. Judicial Law Clerk, Magistrate Judge Deborah Robinson, U.S. District Court for the District of Columbia, 1994-1995. *Member:* American and National Bar Associations. ***PRACTICE AREAS:*** Insurance Litigation; Civil Litigation; Sports Law. ***Email:*** JeffersonS@dsmo.com

ADAM S. KAPLAN, born Great Neck, New York, October 17, 1974; (admission pending). *Education:* Polytechnic University (B.S., Computer Science, 1997); Boston University (J.D., 2000). ***Email:*** KaplanA@dsmo.com

PATRICK J. KEALY, born Providence, Rhode Island, March 5, 1970; admitted to bar, 2000, Maryland (Not admitted in District of Columbia). *Education:* American University (B.A., 1992); Washington College of Law of American University (J.D., 1999). *Member:* American Bar Association; Energy Bar Association. ***PRACTICE AREAS:*** Electric Power; Energy; Corporate Law. ***Email:*** kealyp@dsmo.com

MICHAEL S. KIMBERLING, born Ceiba, Puerto Rico, May 6, 1968; admitted to bar, 1996, Maryland; 1998, District of Columbia. *Education:* Bucknell University (B.A., 1990); Catholic University of America (J.D., 1995). Staff Member, Commlaw Conspectus. ***PRACTICE AREAS:*** Civil Litigation. ***Email:*** KimberlingM@dsmo.com

J. BRIAN KING, born Easley, South Carolina, March 8, 1975; admitted to bar, 2000, Georgia; 2001, District of Columbia, U.S. District Court, Northern District of Georgia, U.S. District Court, Eastern District of Texas and U.S. Court of Appeals, District of Columbia Circuit. *Education:* Clemson University (B.A., Political Science, 1997); Emory University School of Law (J.D., 2000). Law Clerk to Chief Judge Richard A. Schell, U.S. District Court, Eastern District of Texas, 2000-2001. Author: "The State Political Processes Theory of the Eleventh Amendment," The Review of Litigation, University of Texas School of Law, 19 Rev. Litig. 355 (2000); "Jurisprudential Analysis of Justiciability Under Article III," 10 Kan. J.L. & Pub. Pol'y 217 (2000). *Member:* The District of Columbia Bar; State Bar of Georgia; American Bar Association. ***PRACTICE AREAS:*** Securities Litigation; Antitrust. ***Email:*** kingb@dsmo.com

JEREMY M. KING, born Charlottesville, Virginia, July 24, 1976; (admission pending). *Education:* University of Richmond (B.A., Philosophy, 1998); Fordham University (J.D., 2001). (Resident, New York, N.Y. Office). ***PRACTICE AREAS:*** Civil Litigation. ***Email:*** kingj@dsmo.com

PAUL W. KISSLINGER, born Cleveland, Ohio, January 13, 1968; admitted to bar, 1993, Pennsylvania; 1995, New Jersey, U.S. District Court, District of New Jersey and U.S. District Court, Eastern and Middle Districts of Pennsylvania; 2000, District of Columbia. *Education:* University of Pennsylvania (B.A., cum laude, 1989); University of Pittsburgh (J.D., cum laude, 1992). Associate Editor, Journal of Law and Commerce. Recipient: Esther F. Teplitz Memorial Award; George M. Bloom Memorial Scholarship. Law Clerk to Hon. Edwin M. Kosik, U.S. District Court, Middle District of Pennsylvania. Author: "Without a Trace: The Harmful Consequences of the Insurance Industry's Document Destruction," New Jersey Law Journal, 154 N.J.L.J. 773, November 30, 1998. Co-Author, "Coverage Exists for Public Lawsuits Against Targeted Products: Damages Sought Are 'Because of' Bodily Injury," Journal of Insurance Coverage, Spring 2001. *Member:* The District of Columbia Bar; Pennsylvania and American Bar Associations. ***PRACTICE AREAS:*** Commercial Litigation; Employment Counseling and Litigation; Insurance Coverage Litigation. ***Email:*** KisslingerP@dsmo.com

JORGE KOTELANSKI, born Washington, D.C., March 20, 1968; admitted to bar, 1996, New York and District of Columbia. *Education:* Duke University (A.B., 1990); New York University (J.D., 1994). Law Clerk to Judge Marcel Livaudais, Jr., U.S. District Court, Eastern District of Louisiana, 1994-1995. ***PRACTICE AREAS:*** Litigation; Employment Law. ***Email:*** KotelanskiJ@dsmo.com

MALATHI KRISHNAMACHARI, born Thanjavur Tamilnadu, India, October 14, 1974; admitted to bar, 2000, New York. *Education:* Fordham University (B.S., 1996); University of Pennsylvania (J.D., 2000). Beta Gamma Sigma; Alpha Sigma Nu. *Member:* The Association of the Bar of the City of New York; New York State and American Bar Associations. (Resident, New York, N.Y Office). ***LANGUAGES:*** Tamil and Spanish. ***PRACTICE AREAS:*** Litigation. ***Email:*** KrishnamachariM@dsmo.com

VICTORIA A. KUMMER, born Baltimore, Maryland, February 8, 1958; admitted to bar, 1993, New York and U.S. District Court, Southern and Eastern Districts of New York; 1996, U.S. District Court, Northern District of New York and U.S. Court of Appeals, Second Circuit; 1997, U.S. Supreme Court. *Education:* Cornell University (B.A., 1980); Benjamin N. Cardozo School of Law, Yeshiva University (J.D., magna cum laude, 1992). Notes Editor, Cardozo School of Law Law Review, 1991-1992. Author: "How a Dispute Becomes a Case," Chapter in "Elements of Law," Anderson, 1994; "The Successor Corporation's Continuing Duty to Warn," BMA Product Safety & Liability Reporter, Vol. 23, No. 36, 1995. Adjunct Professor of Law, Benjamin N. Cardozo School of Law, 1998—. Certified Arbitrator, Securities Customers and Employment Disputes, National Associaton of Securities Dealers. *Member:* The Association of the Bar of the City of New York (Secretary, Committee on Sex and Law, 1995-1998; Committee on Gays and Lesbians, 2000—). (Resident, New York, N.Y. Office). ***LANGUAGES:*** French. ***REPORTED CASES:*** Malkent-

(This Listing Continued)

DICKSTEIN SHAPIRO MORIN & OSHINSKY LLP, Washington—Continued

zos v. DeBuono, 923 F.Supp. 505 (SDNY 1996), rev'd on other grounds, 102 F.3d 50 (2nd Cir. 1996); In re Jacob/Dana, 86 N.Y.2d 651 (N.Y. 1995). ***PRACTICE AREAS:*** Commercial Litigation. ***Email:*** kummerv@dsmo.com

GREGORY D. KWAN, born May 9, 1972; admitted to bar, 2000, Maryland (Not admitted in District of Columbia). *Education:* University of Maryland (B.A., 1994); University of Virginia (J.D., 1999); Georgetown University Law Center (LL.M., Telecommunications, 2001). ***Email:*** kwang@dsmo.com

JACK MING YANG LEE, (admission pending). *Education:* University of California at San Diego (B.A., 1996); Georgetown University (J.D., 2000). Phi Alpha Delta (President, 1995). ***LANGUAGES:*** Taiwanese. ***PRACTICE AREAS:*** Insurance Coverage; General Litigation.

CHRISTOPHER LEONARDO, born N.Y., N.Y., September 4, 1971; admitted to bar, 1998, New York (Not admitted in District of Columbia). *Education:* Gettysburg College (B.A., 1993); American University (J.D., 1997). ***PRACTICE AREAS:*** Antitrust; Insurance. ***Email:*** leonardoc@dsmo.com

SELENA J. LINDE, born Glendale, California, May 12, 1969; admitted to bar, 1997, Maryland; 1998, District of Columbia. *Education:* George Mason University (B.A., with highest distinction, 1994); University of Virginia (J.D., 1997). Recipient, Stephen T. Early, Jr. Award in Government and Politics, 1993-1994. Member: Moot Court Board; Jessup International Moot Court World Rounds, 1995. 1997. Author: "Insurance for Cyberspace: A Safe Harbor for Policy Holders," Mealey's Energy Insurance Disputes, Vol. 2, No. 11, June 5, 1997. *Member:* Bar Association of the District of Columbia; American Bar Association; Womens Bar Association. ***PRACTICE AREAS:*** Insurance Coverage Litigation; Civil Litigation. ***Email:*** LindeS@dsmo.com

SUSAN A. LITTELL, born Washington, D.C., September 12, 1968; admitted to bar, 1996, New York; 1998, District of Columbia. *Education:* University of Maryland (B.S., 1991); New York Law School (J.D., 1995). Executive Editor, New York Law School Journal of Human Rights. ***PRACTICE AREAS:*** Litigation. ***Email:*** LittellS@dsmo.com

DARREN E. LONG, born Washington, D.C., February 7, 1969; admitted to bar, 2000, Virginia (Not admitted in District of Columbia). *Education:* University of North Carolina, Asheville (B.A., 1993); University of Pittsburgh (J.D., cum laude, 2000). Member, Editorial Board, University of Pittsburgh Law Review. *Member:* American Society of Naval Engineers. ***PRACTICE AREAS:*** Litigation. ***Email:*** LongD@dsmo.com

PAUL R. LUCEY, born Washington, D.C., January 17, 1960; admitted to bar, 1991, Massachusetts; 1993, New Hampshire; 1995, District of Columbia. *Education:* Harvard University (A.B., 1981); Cornell University (J.D., 1991). Associate and Editorial Board Member, Cornell Law Review, 1989-1991. ***PRACTICE AREAS:*** Insurance Litigation; Commercial Litigation. ***Email:*** LuceyP@dsmo.com

RYAN SHAWN LUFT, born Brooklyn, New York, July 11, 1974; (admission pending). *Education:* State University of New York at Binghamton (B.A., 1996); Boston University (J.D., Intellectual Property, with honors, 2001). Author, Legal Update, "Attention Wal-Mart Shoppers: Supreme Court Requires Showing of Secondary Meaning for Product Design," 7 B.U. J. Sci. & Tech. Law 168 (2001). (Resident, New York, N.Y. Office). ***PRACTICE AREAS:*** Civil Litigation. ***Email:*** luftr@dsmo.com

MARILYN T. LYNCH, born Salisbury, Maryland, May 15, 1970; admitted to bar, 1996, Maryland; 1997, U.S. District Court, District of Maryland (Not admitted in District of Columbia). *Education:* University of Maryland (B.A., 1992); University of San Diego (J.D., 1995). Phi Beta Kappa; Phi Alpha Delta. American Inn of Court, Montgomery County. Law Clerk to the Hon. Martha G. Kavanaugh, Circuit Court for Montgomery County, Maryland, 1995-1997. *Member:* Montgomery County, Maryland State and American Bar Associations; National Association of Women Lawyers. ***PRACTICE AREAS:*** Complex Commercial Litigation; Antitrust; Alternative Dispute Resolution; Insurance Coverage Litigation. ***Email:*** LynchM@dsmo.com

JOSEPH R. MAGNAS, born Syracuse, New York, May 10, 1970; admitted to bar, 2000, New York. *Education:* University of Maryland, College Park (B.A., 1996); University of Pennsylvania (J.D., 1999). (Resident, New York, N.Y. Office). ***LANGUAGES:*** Hebrew. ***Email:*** jmagnas@rsklaw.com

SHIBANI MALHOTRA, born New Delhi, India, October 12, 1974; admitted to bar, 2000, Maryland; 2001, District of Columbia. *Education:* McGill University (B.A., 1996); Washington College of Law of American University (J.D., 2000). ***LANGUAGES:*** Hindi. ***PRACTICE AREAS:*** Antitrust Civil Litigation; International Trade Remedies. ***Email:*** MalhotraS@dsmo.com

CARLA M. MARCOLIN, born Sault Ste. Marie, Ontario, August 25, 1961; admitted to bar, 1988, Maryland; 1990, District of Columbia. *Education:* Syracuse University (B.S., 1983); Catholic University (J.D., 1988). Author: "Rousey v. Rousey: The District of Columbia Joins the National Trend Toward Abolition of Parental Immunity," Vol. 37, Cath. Univ. L. Rev., 767-789, Spring

(This Listing Continued)

1988. Co-author: "Survey: Developments in District of Columbia Case Law," Vol. 37, No. 3, Cath. Univ. L. Rev., 677-703, Spring 1988. Law Clerk to Hon. Colleen Kollar-Kotelly, Superior Court, District of Columbia, 1988-1989. *Member:* The District of Columbia Bar; Maryland State Bar Association. ***PRACTICE AREAS:*** Civil Litigation; Labor and Employment. ***Email:*** MarcolinC@dsmo.com

KEITH A. MARKEL, born New York, N.Y., January 21, 1971; admitted to bar, 1999, New York; 2000, U.S. District Court, Southern and Eastern Districts of New York. *Education:* University of Michigan (B.A., with distinction, 1993); Fordham University (J.D., 1998). Author: "Circuit Court Holds Altai Test Applicable to Case of Non-Literal Copying of Software," 3 U.S. Intellectual Law Advisor, David A. Einhorn ed., Winter 1997-1998. *Member:* The Association of the Bar of the City of New York; New York State and American Bar Associations. (Resident, New York, N.Y. Office). ***PRACTICE AREAS:*** Litigation. ***Email:*** markelk@dsmo.com

JAMES ROBERTSON MARTIN, born Burbank, California, November 2, 1963; admitted to bar, 1994, California and U.S. District Court, Central District of California; 1999, District of Columbia. *Education:* University of Massachusetts, Amherst (B.A., 1987); Loyola University of Los Angeles (J.D., 1994). Order of the Coif. Recipient: American Jurisprudence Awards: Legal Process, Civil Procedure, Constitutional Law I, Commercial Law, Sales and Payments. Member, 1992-1993; Articles Editor, 1993-1994, International and Comparative Law Journal. *Member:* State Bar of California; Association of Business Trial Lawyers; Consumer Attorneys Association of Los Angeles (Member, Real Property Litigation Section); Inns of Court. ***PRACTICE AREAS:*** Civil Litigation; Antitrust. ***Email:*** MartinJ@dsmo.com

ANDREW J. McFARLAND, born West Lafayette, Indiana, May 7, 1971; admitted to bar, 1998, Virginia; 2001, District of Columbia. *Education:* American University (B.A., 1993); Catholic University of America (J.D., 1998). Author: Note, "Lewis v. United States: A Requiem for Aggregation," 46 Cath. U. L.Rev. 1057 (1997). [USMCR, 1989-1997, Sgt.]. ***PRACTICE AREAS:*** Insurance Litigation. ***Email:*** McFarlandA@dsmo.com

CHARLES V. MEHLER, III, born Neptune, New Jersey, November 9, 1969; admitted to bar, 1996, Virginia; 1997, Maryland and New Jersey (Not admitted in District of Columbia). *Education:* Rutgers University, Rutgers College (B.A., 1992); Washington & Lee University (J.D., cum laude, 1996). Staff Writer, Washington & Lee Law Review. Recipient, American Jurisprudence Award for Criminal Law. ***PRACTICE AREAS:*** Litigation. ***Email:*** MehlerC@dsmo.com

CHARLES L. MILLER, JR., born Bellefonte, Pennsylvania, December 25, 1952; admitted to bar, 1987, California; 1989, District of Columbia. *Education:* Wesleyan University (B.A., cum laude, 1975); University of Rochester (Ph.D., 1982); University of California at Berkeley (J.D., 1987). Phi Beta Kappa. Articles Editor, Ecology Law Quarterly, 1986-1987. *Member:* The District of Columbia Bar; State Bar of California. ***PRACTICE AREAS:*** Civil and Environmental Litigation. ***Email:*** MillerC@dsmo.com

FRANCES J. MILLER, born Newark, New Jersey, March 29, 1950; admitted to bar, 1996, Virginia; 1997, District of Columbia. *Education:* New York University (B.A., 1972); University of Houston (M.B.A., 1979); George Mason University School of Law (J.D., 1996). Clerk, 19th Circuit Court of Virginia, 1996-1997. *Member:* The District of Columbia Bar; Virginia State Bar; American Bar Association; Virginia Women Attorneys Bar Association; Women's Bar Association of the District of Columbia. ***PRACTICE AREAS:*** Complex Dispute Resolution; Real Estate; Finance. ***Email:*** MillerF@dsmo.com

LISA M. R. MILLER, born Plattsburgh, New York, July 13, 1966; admitted to bar, 1997, Maryland; 1998, U.S. District Court, District of Maryland; 1999, District of Columbia; U.S. District Court for the District of Columbia; U.S. District Court, Southern District of Mississippi. *Education:* Vassar College (B.A., 1988); Columbus School of Law of Catholic University of America (J.D., cum laude, 1997). *Member:* The District of Columbia Bar; Maryland State and American Bar Associations; Women's Bar Association of District of Columbia. ***PRACTICE AREAS:*** Civil Litigation. ***Email:*** MillerL@dsmo.com

STEVEN L. MILLER, born Reading, Pennsylvania, March 5, 1964; admitted to bar, 1990, Pennsylvania; 1998, Maryland (Not admitted in District of Columbia). *Education:* Pennsylvania State University (B.A., 1986); American University, Washington College of Law (J.D., 1990). *Member:* Pennsylvania, Maryland State and Energy Bar Associations. [U.S. Navy Judge Advocate General's Corps, 12990-1999; LCDR (D-4)]. ***PRACTICE AREAS:*** Energy. ***Email:*** millersteven@dsmo.com

JULIE M. MINDER, born Camden, New Jersey, March 23, 1976; (admission pending). *Education:* University of Pennsylvania (B.A., 1998); Catholic University of America (J.D., 2001). Delta Theta Phi. ***Email:*** minderj@dsmo.com

GIANNI MINUTOLI, born Oceanside, New York, December 1, 1966; admitted to bar, 1998, New York, District of Columbia U.S. District Court for the District of Columbia and U.S. Court of Appeals for the Federal Circuit. *Education:* State University of New York at Stony Brook (B.E.E.E., 1988); St.

(This Listing Continued)

John's University (J.D., cum laude, 1997). *Member:* New York State, Federal Circuit and American Bar Associations; American Intellectual Property Law Association. ***LANGUAGES:*** Italian. ***PRACTICE AREAS:*** Intellectual Property. ***Email:*** MinutoliG@dsmo.com

CHRISTOPHER A. MONSEY, born Oklahoma City, August 7, 1966; admitted to bar, 1997, Maryland and Oklahoma (Not admitted in District of Columbia). *Education:* Park College (B.S., Business Mgt., 1992; B.S., Computer Science, magna cum laude, 2000); Oklahoma City University School of Law (J.D., magna cum laude, 1995). *Member:* Maryland State and Oklahoma Bar Associations; Experimental Aircraft Association; American Intellectual Property Law Association. [JAG, U.S. Air Force; Capt., U.S. Air Force, 1986-2001]. ***PRACTICE AREAS:*** Intellectual Property. ***Email:*** monseyc@dsmo.com

ROBERT JAMES MOSS, born Ann Arbor, Michigan, August 16, 1969; admitted to bar, 1994, Maryland; 1997, District of Columbia; U.S. Court of Federal Claims. *Education:* University of Michigan (B.A., 1991); George Washington University National Law Center (J.D., with honors, 1994). *Member:* Maryland State Bar Association; Bar Association of the District of Columbia; American Bar Association. ***PRACTICE AREAS:*** Government Contracts Litigation; Information Technology Contracts. ***Email:*** MossR@dsmo.com

SABRINA A. NELSON, born Okinawa, Japan, January 12, 1971; admitted to bar, 1996, New York; 1999, District of Columbia. *Education:* Dartmouth College (B.A., 1992); Cornell Law School (J.D., 1996). ***PRACTICE AREAS:*** Civil Litigation. ***Email:*** NelsonS@dsmo.com

TARA L. NEWMYER, born Summit, New Jersey, April 21, 1970; admitted to bar, 1998, New Jersey; 1999, New York and District of Columbia. *Education:* Rutgers University (B.S., with high honors, 1993); Eagleton Institute of Politics - Rutgers University (M.A., Public Policy, 1994); University of Virginia (J.D., 1998). Senior Editorial Board, *Journal of Law and Politics.* ***PRACTICE AREAS:*** Litigation; Government Contracts. ***Email:*** MehrbachT@dsmo.com

STEPHEN L. NICHOLS, born Warsaw, New York, March 11, 1976; (admission pending). *Education:* Rensselaer Polytechnic Institute (B.S., 1998); Columbia University School of Law (J.D., 2000). Harlan Fiske Stone Scholar. (Resident, New York, N.Y. Office). ***PRACTICE AREAS:*** Corporate Law. ***Email:*** snichols@rsklaw.com

JONATHAN C. ODELL, born Alexandria, Virginia, July 22, 1964; admitted to bar, 1995, Florida; 1996, District of Columbia. *Education:* Cornell College (B.S.S., 1986); University of Miami (J.D., cum laude, 1994). Dean's Honor Scholarship; Order of the Coif. Associate Editor, Inter-American Law Review. *Member:* The Florida Bar; Bar Association of the District of Columbia. ***PRACTICE AREAS:*** Mergers and Acquisitions; Corporate; Venture Capital; Securities. ***Email:*** OdellJ@dsmo.com

BENJAMIN R. OGLETREE, born Atlanta, Georgia, November 17, 1971; admitted to bar, 1999, Maryland (Not admitted in District of Columbia). *Education:* College of Charleston (B.A., 1994); Catholic University of America (J.D., magna cum laude, 1998). Author: Antiterrorism and Effective Death Penalty Act of 1996 Chapter 154: The Key to the Courthouse Door or Slaughterhouse Justice?" 47 Catholic University Law Review 603, 1998. ***PRACTICE AREAS:*** Securities Litigation. ***Email:*** OgletreeB@dsmo.com

EDWIN OH, born Seoul, South Korea, 1972; admitted to bar, 1999, New York; registered to practice before U.S. Patent and Trademark Office (Not admitted in District of Columbia). *Education:* State University of New York at Binghamton (B.S., 1994); Albany Law School of Union College (J.D., cum laude, 1997). Associate Editor, Journal of Science and Technology. Patent Examiner/Trademark Attorney, U.S. Patent and Trademark Office, 1998-1999. (Resident, New York, N.Y. Office). ***PRACTICE AREAS:*** Intellectual Property. ***Email:*** OhE@dsmo.com

CHRISTOPHER C. O'HARA, born New York, N.Y., August 13, 1967; admitted to bar, 1993, Maryland; 1994, Pennsylvania and U.S. District Court, District of Maryland; 1996, District of Columbia. *Education:* University of Pennsylvania (B.A., 1989); University of Maryland (J.D., with Honor, 1993). Assistant Editor, Maryland Law Review, 1992-1993. Law Clerk to the Hon. H. Chester Goudy, Jr., Circuit Court of Anne Arundel County, 1995. Author, "Marr v. Langhoff: Fiduciary Duty and Professional Service Corporations," 51 Md. Law Rev. 597 (1992). *Member:* Maryland State Bar Association. ***PRACTICE AREAS:*** Administrative; Energy; Litigation. ***Email:*** OharaC@dsmo.com

C. TODD PICZAK, born Ft. Belvoir, Virginia, February 22, 1971; admitted to bar, 2001, Virginia (Not admitted in District of Columbia). *Education:* University of Virginia (B.A., 1993); University of Pittsburgh (M.P.A. in Public and International Affairs, J.D., 2000). Member, University of Pittsburgh Law Review. Recipient, Scribes Award. Author, "The Helms Burton Act: U.S. Foreign Policy Towards Cuba, The National Security Exception to the GATT and the Political Question Doctrine," University of Pittsburgh Law Review, Vol. 61, 1999. ***PRACTICE AREAS:*** Energy. ***Email:*** piczakt@dsmo.com

EDEN M. POLATNICK, born Hartford, Connecticut, February 8, 1972; admitted to bar, 1998, New Jersey; 1999, New York (Not admitted in District of Columbia). *Education:* Connecticut College (B.A., 1995); American University (J.D., 1998). ***PRACTICE AREAS:*** Legislative and Governmental Affairs. ***Email:*** PolatnickE@dsmo.com

R. EDWARD POOLE, born Wilmington, Delaware, September 4, 1969; admitted to bar, 1995, Illinois; 1997, District of Columbia. *Education:* University of Chicago (A.B., 1991); Washington College of Law of American University (J.D., 1995). *Member:* Illinois State and American Bar Associations. ***PRACTICE AREAS:*** Insurance Litigation. ***Email:*** PooleR@dsmo.com

WILLIAM E. POWELL III, born Rochester, New York, June 9, 1959; admitted to bar, 1993, Virginia and U.S. Court of Appeals, Fourth Circuit; 1994, District of Columbia; registered to practice before U.S. Patent and Trademark Office. *Education:* Texas A & M University (B.A., 1981; B.S., 1985); Boston University (J.D., cum laude, 1993). Member, Society of Petroleum Engineers, 1982-1985. *Member:* Virginia State and American Bar Associations; Bar Association of the District of Columbia; American Intellectual Property Law Association. ***PRACTICE AREAS:*** Intellectual Property; Patent Prosecution; Trademark Prosecution; Copyright Prosecution; Copyright Litigation; Technology Licensing; Technology Transfers. ***Email:*** PowellW@dsmo.com

DEBRA H. REDNIK, born New Brunswick, New Jersey, March 7, 1973; admitted to bar, 1998, Maryland; 2001, District of Columbia. *Education:* Washington University (A.B., 1995); George Washington University (J.D., 1998). Author: "FERC Gambles on Transmission," Legal Times, April 24, 2000. *Member:* Federal Energy Bar Association. ***PRACTICE AREAS:*** Energy Law. ***Email:*** RednikD@dsmo.com

TINA D. REYNOLDS, born Woonsocket, Rhode Island, October 5, 1970; admitted to bar, 1995, North Carolina; 1998, District of Columbia. *Education:* American University (B.A., with high honors, 1992); University of North Carolina at Chapel Hill (J.D., with honors, 1995). Member, Invitational Team, Moot Court, 1995. Member, North Carolina Journal of International Law and Commercial Regulation. *Member:* North Carolina and American Bar Associations. ***PRACTICE AREAS:*** Government Contracts; Litigation; Regulatory Law; White Collar Crime. ***Email:*** ReynoldsT@dsmo.com

JEFFREY RHODES, born Meriden, Connecticut, June 20, 1967; admitted to bar, 1995, Maryland; 1997, District of Columbia. *Education:* The American University (B.A., 1989); Washington College of Law, The American University (J.D., cum laude, 1995). Articles Editor, The American University Law Review, 1993-1994. Law Clerk, Hon. Duncan W. Keir, U.S. Bankruptcy Judge, District of Maryland, 1995-1997. ***PRACTICE AREAS:*** Bankruptcy; Creditors Rights; Commercial Litigation. ***Email:*** RhodesJ@dsmo.com

CARA ROMANZO, born Albany, New York, July 30, 1970; admitted to bar, 1998, Virginia; 2000, District of Columbia; U.S. District Court, District of Columbia and U.S. Court of Appeals, District of Columbia Circuit; U.S. Court of Appeals, Ninth Circuit. *Education:* University of Rochester (B.A., German, B.A., Russian, B.A., Pol. Sc., 1992); Georgetown University Law Center (J.D., 1996). Author: "Makah Whaling: A Stepping Stone to Undermining the Global Moratorium on Commercial Whaling?" Colorado Journal of International Environmental Law & Policy (January 1998). *Member:* Virginia State Bar; The District of Columbia Bar; American and Energy Bar Associations; Women's Bar Association. ***LANGUAGES:*** German, Russian. ***PRACTICE AREAS:*** Energy; Environmental; Administrative; Family Law; Corporate. ***Email:*** RomanzoC@dsmo.com

MEREDITH J. ROSS, born Boston, Massachusetts, May 20, 1971; admitted to bar, 1998, Massachusetts (Not admitted in District of Columbia). *Education:* Tufts University (B.A., cum laude, 1993); Boston College (J.D., 1998). ***PRACTICE AREAS:*** Corporate Law. ***Email:*** RossM@rsmo.com

CARRIE M. SAFFORD, born Pittsburgh, Pennsylvania, July 7, 1972; admitted to bar, 1999, New York; 2001, District of Columbia. *Education:* University of Rochester (B.S., 1994); Pace University (J.D., 1998). Phi Alpha Delta. *Member:* New York State and Energy Bar Associations; Women's Bar Association of the District of Columbia. ***PRACTICE AREAS:*** Energy Law. ***Email:*** SaffordC@dsmo.com

ANDRA E. SCHNABOLK, born New York, N.Y., April 15, 1974; admitted to bar, 2001, New York (Not admitted in District of Columbia). *Education:* Cornell University (B.S., 1997); Georgetown University (J.D., 2000). *Member:* Women's Bar Association. ***PRACTICE AREAS:*** Energy and Regulatory. ***Email:*** SchnabolkA@dsmo.com

DAVID T. SCHUR, born White Plains, New York, February 23, 1974; admitted to bar, 2000, New York (Not admitted in District of Columbia). *Education:* Tufts University (B.A., cum laude, 1996); Boston University (J.D., magna cum laude, 2000). ***PRACTICE AREAS:*** Securities Litigation. ***Email:*** SchurD@dsmo.com

JULIE P. SEAMON, born Springfield, Illinois, March 5, 1974; admitted to bar, 1999, Maryland; 2000, District of Columbia. *Education:* College of William & Mary (B.A., cum laude, 1996); American University Washington College of Law (J.D., cum laude, 1999). Executive Editor, American University Inter-

(This Listing Continued)

DICKSTEIN SHAPIRO MORIN & OSHINSKY LLP, Washington—Continued

national Law Review. *Member:* Maryland State and American Bar Associations; The District of Columbia Bar. ***PRACTICE AREAS:*** Corporate. ***Email:*** SeamonJ@dsmo.com

EDWARD E. SHARKEY, born Baltimore, Maryland, June 3, 1968; admitted to bar, 1993, Maryland and Pennsylvania; 1994, U.S. District Court, District of Maryland; 1997, U.S. Court of Appeals, Fourth Circuit; 2000, District of Columbia. *Education:* Yale University (B.A., Economics, 1990); University of Virginia (J.D., 1993). *Member:* American Bar Association. ***PRACTICE AREAS:*** Commercial Litigation; Securities Litigation. ***Email:*** SharkeyE@dsmo.com

MICHAEL T. SHARKEY, born Washington, D.C., January 26, 1969; admitted to bar, 1994, Maryland; 1995, U.S. District Court, District of Maryland; 1997, District of Columbia. *Education:* Yale University (B.A., summa cum laude, 1991; J.D., 1994). *Member:* Maryland State, Federal and American Bar Associations. ***PRACTICE AREAS:*** General Litigation; Insurance Litigation. ***Email:*** SharkeyM@dsmo.com

BERNARD F. SHEEHAN, JR., born Santa Barbara, California, October 28, 1966; admitted to bar, 2000, Virginia; 2001, District of Columbia. *Education:* Cornell University (B.A., 1988); University of Southern California (M.A., Physics, 1991; M.S., Education, 1992); Georgetown University (J.D., magna cum laude, 2000). ***LANGUAGES:*** French and Spanish. ***PRACTICE AREAS:*** Litigation. ***Email:*** SheehanB@dsmo.com

APRIL EVERETTE SHELTON, born Kinston, North Carolina; admitted to bar, 1997, Georgia; 1998, District of Columbia. *Education:* University of North Carolina at Chapel Hill (B.A., 1993; J.D., with honors, 1997). Staff Member, 1995-1996 and Note Editor, 1996-1997, North Carolina Law Review. Author: Note, "United States Fidelity and Guaranty Co. v. A&S Manufacturing Co.: Realignment of Parties in Diversity Jurisdiction Cases," 74 N.C. L. Rev. 1979, 1996. ***PRACTICE AREAS:*** Corporate; Mergers and Acquisitions; Securities. ***Email:*** SheltonA@dsmo.com

NANCI SHIP, born Montreal, Quebec, December 8, 1974; (admission pending). *Education:* McGill University (B.A., 1996; L.B., 2000; B.C.L., 2000). Recipient, Rosa B. Gualtieri Prize; Guérin Provincial Trial Advocacy Cup. Finalist, Sopinka National Trial Advocacy. (Resident, New York, N.Y. Office). ***LANGUAGES:*** French. ***PRACTICE AREAS:*** Corporate Law; Litigation. ***Email:*** nship@rsklaw.com

KRISTI SINGLETON, born Newport News, Virginia, June 21, 1974; admitted to bar, 1999, Virginia and District of Columbia. *Education:* George Mason University (B.A., 1996); University of Virginia (J.D., 1999). ***PRACTICE AREAS:*** Contracts; Labor and Employment. ***Email:*** SingletonK@dsmo.com

PATRICK T. SKACEL, born Natrona Heights, Pennsylvania, January 21, 1965; admitted to bar, 2000, New York; registered to practice before U.S. Patent and Trademark Office (Not admitted in District of Columbia). *Education:* Albright College (B.S., 1987); Fordham University (J.D., 1999). Notes and Articles Editor, Fordham International Law Journal, 1998-1999. ***PRACTICE AREAS:*** Intellectual Property. ***Email:*** skacelp@dsmo.com

MICHAEL J. SLATTERY, born Bronx, New York, October 17, 1967; admitted to bar, 1999, New York; 2000, District of Columbia. *Education:* Catholic University of America (B.M.E., 1989); George Mason University (M.A., 1992); George Washington University (J.D., with honors, 1998). ***PRACTICE AREAS:*** Government Contracts. ***Email:*** SlatteryM@dsmo.com

JOHN CHARLES SNODGRASS, born Key West, Florida, November 28, 1968; admitted to bar, 1998, New York (Not admitted in District of Columbia). *Education:* University of Virginia (B.A., 1991); College of William & Mary (J.D., 1997); University of London (LL.M., 1998). Member, William & Mary University Law Review, 1995-1997. *Member:* American Bar Association; American Intellectual Property Law Association; International Trademark Association. ***PRACTICE AREAS:*** Intellectual Property. ***Email:*** snodgrassj@dsmo.com

PAUL SPACKMAN, born Shreveport, Louisiana, December 17, 1970; admitted to bar, 1999, Virginia; 2000, U.S. District Court, Eastern District of Virginia (Not admitted in District of Columbia). *Education:* American University (B.A., 1992); Washington College of Law, American University (J.D., cum laude, 1999). ***PRACTICE AREAS:*** Insurance Coverage Litigation. ***Email:*** spackmanp@dsmo.com

TIMOTHY D. SPARAPANI, born Fort Wayne, Indiana, October 14, 1974; (admission pending). *Education:* Georgetown University (B.A., cum laude, 1996); University of Michigan (J.D., 2000). ***PRACTICE AREAS:*** Complex Litigation. ***Email:*** sparapanit@dsmo.com

LESLIE H. SPIEGEL, born Cincinnati, Ohio, June 19, 1971; admitted to bar, 2000, Maryland (Not admitted in District of Columbia). *Education:* University of Virginia (B.A., 1993); University of Maryland (J.D., with honors,

(This Listing Continued)

2000). Order of the Coif. Articles Editor, Maryland Law Review. Author: Note, "Judicial Discretion and Problems of Perception," 58 Md. L. Rev. 892, 1999. ***PRACTICE AREAS:*** Complex Dispute Resolution. ***Email:*** SpiegelL@dsmo.com

SALVATORE P. TAMBURO, born Brooklyn, New York, February 9, 1968; admitted to bar, 1999, New York; 2000, District of Columbia; registered to practice before the U.S. Patent and Trademark Office. *Education:* Polytechnic Institute (B.S.E.E., 1989); St. John's University School of Law (J.D., 1998). *Member:* New York State, Federal Circuit and American Bar Associations; Institute of Electrical and Electronics Engineers; American Intellectual Property Law Association; Glen S. Rich Inn of Court. ***PRACTICE AREAS:*** Intellectual Property. ***Email:*** TamburoS@dsmo.com

CHRISTOPHER MARK TANNER, born Bay City, Michigan; admitted to bar, 1998, Florida; 2000, District of Columbia and U.S. Court of Appeals, District of Columbia Circuit; 2001, U.S. Court of Appeals, Federal Circuit; registered to practice before the U.S. Patent and Trademark Office. *Education:* Florida Atlantic University (B.S.E.E., with honors, 1989); University of Florida (J.D., 1997). Tau Beta Phi; Phi Kappa Phi. Patent Examiner, U.S. Patent and Trademark Office, 1998. *Member:* The Florida Bar; American Bar Association; Federalist Society.

KATE TAPLEY, born New York, N.Y.; admitted to bar, 1997, New York; 1999, District of Columbia. *Education:* Wellesley College (B.A., 1980); Columbia University (J.D., 1996). Harlan Fiske Stone Scholar. ***Email:*** TapleyK@dsmo.com

JEFFREY H. TIGNOR, born New Haven, Connecticut, February 9, 1974; admitted to bar, 1999, Maryland; 2000, District of Columbia; registered to practice before U.S. Patent and Trademark Office. *Education:* Harvard University (A.B., cum laude, 1996); Duke University School of Law (J.D., 1999). *Member:* Maryland State and American Bar Associations. ***PRACTICE AREAS:*** Telecommunications. ***Email:*** TignorJ@dsmo.com

KENNETH B. TROTTER, born Melbourne, Florida, September 6, 1966; admitted to bar, 1993, Alabama and U.S. District Court, Middle District of Alabama; 1996, District of Columbia; 2000, Florida and U.S Supreme Court. *Education:* Brigham Young University (B.A., 1990); Vanderbilt University School of Law (J.D., 1993). Instructor, Business Law, Troy State University, 1994. *Member:* Alabama State Bar; District of Columbia Bar; The Florida Bar. ***LANGUAGES:*** Portuguese. ***PRACTICE AREAS:*** Civil Litigation; Insurance Coverage. ***Email:*** TrotterK@dsmo.com

JODI TRULOVE, born West Point, Mississippi, June 22, 1971; admitted to bar, 1996, Maryland; 1997, Massachusetts; 1997, District of Columbia. *Education:* Georgetown University (B.S.B.A., magna cum laude, 1993; J.D., magna cum laude, 1996). Editor, Survey of White Collar Crime, American Criminal Law Review. *Member:* Maryland State, Massachusetts and American Bar Associations; National Association of Criminal Defense Lawyers; Edward Bennett Williams American Inn of Court. ***PRACTICE AREAS:*** White Collar Criminal Defense; Civil Litigation. ***Email:*** TruloveJ@dsmo.com

BRIAN D. UNROE, born Gallipolis, Ohio, February 2, 1974; admitted to bar, 2000, New York. *Education:* Vanderbilt University (B.E., magna cum laude, 1996); University of Virginia (J.D., 1999). Tau Beta Pi. (Resident, New York, N.Y. Office). ***Email:*** bunroe@rsklaw.com

GABRIEL B. VALLE, born Madrid, Spain, January 4, 1970; admitted to bar, 1998, New York (Not admitted in District of Columbia). *Education:* Hofstra University (B.S., 1991); American University Law School (J.D., cum laude, 1998). Associate, American University International Law Review. ***LANGUAGES:*** Spanish. ***PRACTICE AREAS:*** Corporate. ***Email:*** ValleG@dsmo.com

ADAM VANN, born Washington, D.C., July 5, 1973; admitted to bar, 1998, Maryland; 1999, District of Columbia. *Education:* Yale University (B.A., 1995); University of North Carolina (J.D., 1998). *Member:* Maryland State Bar Association. ***PRACTICE AREAS:*** Energy Law. ***Email:*** VannA@dsmo.com

GARY L. VERON, born Brooklyn, New York, June 19, 1968; admitted to bar, 1994, Maryland; 1995, District of Columbia; registered to practice before U.S. Patent and Trademark Office. *Education:* Virginia Polytechnic Institute and State University (B.S., cum laude, 1990); University of Virginia (J.D., 1993). Editor, Virginia Environmental Law Journal, 1992-1993. *Member:* District of Columbia Bar; American Intellectual Property Law Association. ***PRACTICE AREAS:*** Intellectual Property. ***Email:*** verong@dsmo.com

PETER A. VEYTSMAN, born Kishinev, Moldova, April 30, 1968; admitted to bar, 2000, Virginia and New Jersey; 2001, District of Columbia; registered to practice before U.S. Patent and Trademark Office. *Education:* Rutgers University (B.S.M.E., 1991); Temple University (J.D., 2000). Associate Research Editor, Temple Law Review. Professional Engineer, Pennsylvania, 1996. Author: "Drug Testing Student Athletes and Fourth Amendment Privacy," 73 Temp. L. Rev. 295. *Member:* American Intellectual Property Law Association. ***LANGUAGES:*** Russian. ***PRACTICE AREAS:*** Intellectual Property. ***Email:*** VeytsmanP@dsmo.com

(This Listing Continued)

NICOLE M. VORRASI, born Rochester, New York, May 29, 1972; admitted to bar, 1998, New York and U.S. District Court, Western District of New York; 1999, U.S. District Court, Northern District of New York (Not admitted in District of Columbia). *Education:* William Smith College (B.A., 1994); Columbus School of Law of The Catholic University of America (J.D., cum laude, 1997); Georgetown University (LL.M., Taxation, 2001). ***LANGUAGES:*** Spanish. ***PRACTICE AREAS:*** Taxation. ***Email:*** vorrasin@dsmo.com

STEVEN WALTER, born New York, N.Y., October 9, 1975; admitted to bar, 2000, Maryland; 2001, District of Columbia. *Education:* Cornell University (B.S., with distinction, 1997); George Washington University (J.D., with honors, 2000). ***PRACTICE AREAS:*** Corporate; Finance. ***Email:*** WalterS@dsmo.com

KATHERINE A. WALTHER, born Chicago, Illinois, May 17, 1970; admitted to bar, 1999, New York and U.S. District Court, Southern and Eastern Districts of New York; 2000, District of Columbia. *Education:* Washington and Lee University (B.A., 1992); University of Virginia (J.D., 1998). ***PRACTICE AREAS:*** Securities Litigation; Products Liability; Antitrust. ***Email:*** WaltherK@dsmo.com

ANDREW M. WEINER, born Baltimore, Maryland, December 3, 1974; admitted to bar, 1999, Maryland; 2000, District of Columbia. *Education:* University of Maryland (B.A., cum laude, 1996); University of Virginia (J.D., 1999). ***PRACTICE AREAS:*** Litigation; Insurance. ***Email:*** WeinerA@dsmo.com

STEVEN M. WEINSTEIN, born Manhasset, New York, May 20, 1967; admitted to bar, 1993, New York; 1994, District of Columbia. *Education:* Cornell University (B.S., with honors, 1989); Columbia University (J.D., 1992). Harlan Fiske Stone Scholar. *Member:* District of Columbia Bar; New York State and American Bar Associations. ***PRACTICE AREAS:*** Corporate Law; Mergers, Acquisitions, Divestitures; Corporate Finance. ***Email:*** WeinsteinS@dsmo.com

MICHAEL J WENTWORTH, born Hoyt Lakes, Minnesota; admitted to bar, 1987, Minnesota (Not admitted in District of Columbia). *Education:* Concordia College (B.A., 1984); University of Minnesota (J.D., 1987). [Judge Advocate, U.S. Navy General's Corps; LCDR, U.S. Navy, 1985-2001]. ***PRACTICE AREAS:*** Energy; Military Justice. ***Email:*** wentworthm@dsmo.com

MIALEEKA C. WILLIAMS-BIBBS, born Gardena, California, March 9, 1973; admitted to bar, 1999, Virginia and Maryland; registered to practice before the U.S. Patent and Trademark Office (Not admitted in District of Columbia). *Education:* Howard University (B.S., Chemical Engineering, 1995); George Washington University (J.D., 1999). Patent Examiner, Chemical Arts, U.S. Patent and Trademark Office. *Member:* Virginia State and Maryland State Bar Associations; The Association of Trial Lawyers of America. ***PRACTICE AREAS:*** Patents; Trademarks; Licensing; Copyright. ***Email:*** williamsm@dsmo.com

BRADLEY D. WINE, born Cleveland, Ohio, July 29, 1970; admitted to bar, 1995, Maryland; 1996, District of Columbia. *Education:* American University (B.A., 1992); Vermont Law School (J.D., magna cum laude, 1995). Editor-in-Chief, Vermont Law Review, 1994-1995. Author, "Can You Get to Kings County From I-85? A Reevaluation of United Jewish Organizations v. Carey in Light of Shaw v. Reno," 19 Vt. L.Rev. 843. *Member:* Maryland State and American Bar Associations; The District of Columbia Bar. ***PRACTICE AREAS:*** Government Contracts Litigation; Regulatory Law. ***Email:*** WineB@dsmo.com

JAMES M. WINES, born Alexandria, Virginia, September 25, 1970; admitted to bar, 1997, New York; 1998, District of Columbia. *Education:* University of North Carolina, Greensboro (B.A., 1992); University of North Carolina, Chapel Hill (J.D., with honors, 1995). Order of the Coif. Note and Comment Editor, North Carolina Journal of International Law and Commercial Regulations. ***PRACTICE AREAS:*** Securities Litigation; Business Crimes. ***Email:*** WinesJ@dsmo.com

JOHN P. WINSBRO, born Oak Ridge, Tennessee, April 28, 1958; admitted to bar, 1988, New York. *Education:* New York University (B.A., 1980); Emory University (J.D., 1987). Executive Notes and Comments Editor, Emory Law Journal, 1987. Author: "Misrepresentation In Political Advertising: The Role Of Legal Sanctions," 36 Emory Law Journal 853 (1987). Co-author: with Eugene R. Anderson and Catherine M. Ward, "Environmental Insurance Coverage in New Jersey: A Tale of Two Stories," 24 Rutgers Law Journal 83 (1992). (Resident, New York, N.Y. Office). ***PRACTICE AREAS:*** Insurance Litigation. ***Email:*** winsbroj@dsmo.com

BECKI L. YOUNG, born Pullman, Washington, April 24, 1971; admitted to bar, 1999, Maryland; 2000, District of Columbia. *Education:* University of Pennsylvania (B.A., 1993); Georgetown University (J.D., 1999). Author: "Trafficking of Humans Across U.S. Borders: How U.S. Laws Can be Used to Punish Traffickers and Protect Victims," Georgetown Immigration Law Journal, Vol. 13 No. 1, Fall 1998. ***LANGUAGES:*** Japanese. ***PRACTICE AREAS:*** Immigration. ***Email:*** YoungB@dsmo.com

ADAM S. ZIFFER, born Killeen, Texas, May 31, 1970; admitted to bar, 1996, New York and U.S. District Court, Southern and Eastern Districts of New

(This Listing Continued)

York; 1998, U.S. Court of Appeals, Second Circuit. *Education:* University of Florida (B.S., 1992); Fordham University (J.D., 1995). Editor, Moot Court Board. (Resident, New York, N.Y. Office). ***PRACTICE AREAS:*** Commercial Litigation; Insurance. ***Email:*** ZifferA@dsmo.com

JEAN E. ZIMMERMAN, born Holyoke, Massachusetts, February 25, 1960; admitted to bar, 1989, New York; 1990, U.S. District Court, Southern and Eastern Districts of New York. *Education:* University of Massachusetts at Amherst/University of Manchester, England (B.A./B.S., summa cum laude, 1984); New York University (J.D., 1988). Member, New York University Journal of International Law and Politics, 1986-1987. *Member:* The Association of the Bar of the City of New York. (Resident, New York, N.Y. Office). ***PRACTICE AREAS:*** Insurance Coverage Litigation; Civil Litigation. ***Email:*** ZimmermanJ@dsmo.com

DILLINGHAM & MURPHY, LLP

Established in 1982

1155 CONNECTICUT AVE., N.W., SUITE 1120
WASHINGTON, D.C. 20036-3419
Telephone: 202-835-9880
Cable Address: "Paladin"
Fax: 202-835-9885
Email: DM@wirepaladin.com
URL: http://www.wirepaladin.com

San Francisco, California Office: 225 Bush Street, Sixth Floor, 94104-4207. Telephone: 415-397-2700. Fax: 415-397-3300.

General Civil Trial Practice, Business Planning, Litigation, Commercial Law, Intellectual Property, Internet Law, Technology and Science, Employment Law, Products Liability, Environmental Law, Toxic Torts, Real Estate Law, Insurance Law, Labor and Employment, Contracts, Business Law, Corporate Law, Investments, Probate, Trust and Estate, Securities, Civil Rights, Construction Law, Personal Injury and Torts, International Law, Admiralty and Maritime, Creditors Rights, Bankruptcy, Landlord and Tenant Law.

FIRM PROFILE: Dillingham & Murphy specializes in civil litigation and business transactions.

Dillingham & Murphy was founded in 1982 by two colleagues from Pillsbury Madison & Sutro. Its clients include AT&T, Barnes & Nobles, Costco, DuPont, Federated Department Stores, Inc., The Gap, Home Depot, Lucent Technologies, Qantas, Safeway, Commercial Union Insurance Companies and the California Department of Corrections.

The firm was selected by DuPont in 1992 as one of its thirty-eight legal partners nationwide. This selection led to the Forbes Magazine Technology Supplement describing Dillingham & Murphy as a model for the future, referring to its advanced use of technology in serving its clients.

Clients work directly with partners and senior attorneys who recognize the clients' individual needs. We conserve our clients' resources.

ALBERT A. FOSTER, JR., born New York, NY, March 23, 1957; admitted to bar, 1984, New York; 1986, U.S. District Court, Southern and Eastern Districts of New York; 1999, District of Columbia; 2000, U.S. District Court, District of Maryland, U.S. District Court, District of Columbia and U.S. Court of Appeals, District of Columbia Circuit. *Education:* State University of New York at Stony Brook (B.S., 1977); State University of New York at Buffalo (J.D., 1983). Member, Congressional Black Caucus Foundation's Scholarship Committee, 1999-2000. *Member:* Association of the Bar of the City of New York; American Bar Association. ***REPORTED CASES:*** Federal Ins. Co. v. Cablevision Systems Development Co., 836 F.2d 54, C.A.2 (N.Y.) (1987); Royal Ins. Co. of America v. Cathy Daniels, Ltd., 684 F.Supp. 786, S.D.N.Y. (1988); Retirement Fund of Fur Mfg. Industry by Foner v. Republic Ins. Co., 755 F.Supp. 625, S.D.N.Y. (1991). ***PRACTICE AREAS:*** Employment Law; Toxic Torts; Civil Rights; Insurance Defense. ***Email:*** aaf@dillingham-murphy.com

LAURIE A. ERDMAN, born San Diego, California, July 3, 1967; admitted to bar, 1994, California; 1999, Oregon; 2000, Maryland; 2001, District of Columbia. *Education:* University of California at Davis (B.S., 1989); McGeorge School of Law (J.D., 1994). Order of the Coif. Member, Traynor Society. Author: "Gantt v. Sentry Insurance: When Can An Employee Be Discharged?" 25 Pac. L.J. 107. *Member:* Bar Association of San Francisco; Bar Association of the District of Columbia; Women Lawyers of the District of Columbia. ***REPORTED CASES:*** Bd. of Educ. v. Superior Court, 61 Cal.App 4th 411; Cortez v. Vogt 52 Cal.App 4th 917. ***PRACTICE AREAS:*** Labor and Employment; Civil Rights; Litigation. ***Email:*** lae@dillingham-murphy.com

OF COUNSEL

JOHN J. LYNCH, born New York, N.Y., September 7, 1959; admitted to bar, 1984, New York; 1988, U.S. District Court, Southern and Eastern Districts

(This Listing Continued)

DILLINGHAM & MURPHY, LLP, Washington—Continued

of New York; 1990, U.S. Court of Appeals, Second Circuit; 2001, Maryland (Not admitted in District of Columbia). *Education:* St. John's University (B.A., 1980; J.D., 1983). Associate Editor, St. John's Law Review, 1982-1983. Author: Survey: "Misapplication of Bank Funds Under N.Y. Banking Law § 633," 56 St. John's Law Review 179 (1982); "Notice of Intrafamily Claims Under N.Y. Insurance Law § 167 (1)," 56 St. John's Law Review 750 (1982); "Contractural Limitation on Liability Enforced Asbent Intent to Harm: Now York's High Court Interprets Provisions of Software Agreement," Computer Law Strategist, P. 1, November, 1994. Law Clerk to the Judges of the New York State Court of Appeals, 1983-1985. Principal Law Clerk to Hon. Fritz W. Alexander, III, New York State Court of Appeals, 1985-1986. *Member:* The Association of the Bar of the City of New York (Member, Litigation Committee, 1993-1997); New York State Bar Association. ***PRACTICE AREAS:*** Information Technology; Intellectual Property; Business Law; Employment Law; Civil Litigation. ***Email:*** jjl@wirepaladin.com

ASSOCIATE

GRACE M. LEE, born Erie, Pennsylvania, October 31, 1967; admitted to bar, 1999, Virginia (Not admitted in District of Columbia). *Education:* University of Virginia (B.A., 1989); George Mason University School of Law (J.D., 1999). Member, Journal of International Legal Studies, 1997-1999. President, Sports, Entertainment and Art Law Society, 1998-1999. Attorney, 19th Judicial Circuit of Virginia, 1999-2000. Member: DC Board of Trade, 2000—; Northern Virginia Technology Council, 2000—. *Member:* Fairfax County (Member, Board of Directors, Young Lawyers Division, 2000—), Virginia and American Bar Associations; Womens' Law Association (Treasurer, 1997-1998); Virginia Women Attorneys Association. ***LANGUAGES:*** French and Korean. ***PRACTICE AREAS:*** Intellectual Property; Internet Law; E-Commerce; Corporate Law; Labor and Employment; Insurance Coverage; Civil Litigation; Commercial Litigation. ***Email:*** gml@dillingham-murphy.com

REPRESENTATIVE CLIENTS: AT&T Corp.; California Department of Corrections; California Public Utilities Commission; Circle-K Stores, Inc.; CGU; Conoco, Inc.; Crescent Communications of California, L.P.; E.I. Du Pont de Nemours & Co., Inc.; Gould's Pumps, Inc.; Heftel Broadcasting; Home Depot U.S.A., Inc.; Lucent Technologies, Inc.; Oregon Steel Mills, Inc.; Pycon, Inc.; Pernod Ricard; Safeway, Inc.; Safety Mutual; Utica Mutual Insurance Co.

(For Complete Biographical Data on all Personnel, see Professional Biographies at San Francisco, California)

DILWORTH PAXSON PLLC

1200 NINETEENTH AVENUE, N.W.
WASHINGTON, D.C. 20036
Telephone: 202-452-0900
Fax: 202-452-0930
Email: lawyers@dilworthlaw.com
URL: http://www.dilworthlaw.com

Cherry Hill, New Jersey Office: Liberty View Suite 700, 457 Haddonfield Road, 08002. Telephone: 856-663-8877. Fax: 856-663-8855.

Harrisburg, Pennsylvania Office: 305 N. Front Street, Suite 403, 17101-1236. Telephone: 717-236-4812. Fax: 717-236-7811.

Newtown Square, Pennsylvania Office: 11 Campus Boulevard, Suite 150, 19073. Telephone: 610-325-3200. Fax: 610-325-3293.

Philadelphia, Pennsylvania Office: 3200 Mellon Bank Center, 1735 Market Street, 19103-7595. Telephone: 215-575-7000. Fax: 215-575-7200.

Turnersville, New Jersey Office: P.O. Box 762, University Executive Campus Suite 201, 151 Fries Mill Road, 08012. Telephone: 856-227-6100. Fax: 856-227-7373.

Wilmington, Delaware Office: First Federal Plaza, Suite 500, 19801. Telephone: 302-571-9800. Fax: 302-571-8875.

General Practice in all Courts, Corporate, Litigation, Bankruptcy and Insolvency, Criminal and Regulatory Investigations, E-Commerce, Employment and Management Labor Relations, Entertainment, Environmental, Healthcare, Insurance Regulation, Intellectual Property, International, Public Finance, Real Estate Securities, Tax, Trust and Estates.

JOEL F. BRENNER, admitted to bar, 1975, Virginia; 1976, District of Columbia; 1980, U.S. Supreme Court; 1988, New York. *Education:* University of Wisconsin (B.A., 1969); University of London, London, England, L.S.E. (Ph.D., 1973); Harvard University (J.D., 1975). Marshall Scholar. Author: "Exon-Florio Provision: Presidential Authority to Prohibit Acquisitions, Mergers, or Takeovers by Foreign Persons," Westlaw, 1990. Trial Lawyer, Antitrust Division of the U.S. Department of Justice, 1978-1982. Member, Legal Counsels' Forum, American Consulting Engineers Council. Co-Counsel and Staff Director, Special Committee on Governance, Philadelphia Stock Exchange, 1997. Arbitration Counsel, SEC v. Prudential Securities, Inc., 1993—. *Member:* National Association of Securities Dealers (Member, Board of Arbitrators, 1990—). ***LANGUAGES:*** French. ***Email:*** JBrenner@dilworthlaw.com

(This Listing Continued)

MICHAEL J. DIXON, admitted to bar, 1993, Maryland; 1994, Virginia and District of Columbia. *Education:* College of William & Mary (B.A., 1975); University of Virginia (M.A., 1979); George Washington University (J.D., 1993). ***Email:*** MDixon@dilworthlaw.com

REBECCA A. DONNELLAN, admitted to bar, 1975, Massachusetts; 1977, District of Columbia; 1979, U.S. Court of Appeals for the District of Columbia Circuit; 1982, U.S. Claims Court; 1983, U.S. Court of Appeals, Federal and Tenth Circuits. *Education:* Massachusetts Institute of Technology (S.B., 1972); Harvard Law School (J.D., 1975). Postdoctoral Fellow, Marine Policy and Ocean Management, Woods Hole Oceangraphic Institution, 1975-1976. Member, Board of Trustees, M.I.T. Corporation, 1972-1977. Special Assistant: Assistant Administrator for Policy and Planning NOAA (1977-1978); Trial Lawyer, Environment and Natural Resources Division of the U.S. Department of Justice (1978-1991). Consultant, Environmental Law Institute, 1991-1992. ***PRACTICE AREAS:*** Environmental; Corporate Litigation; Personal Injury Litigation; Securities Litigation; Litigation; Native American; Minority Business Law. ***Email:*** RDonnellan@dilworthlaw.com

GEORGE R. A. DOUMAR, admitted to bar, 1986, Virginia; 1988, District of Columbia, U.S. District Court, Eastern District of Virginia, U.S. District Court, District of Columbia and U.S. Court of Appeals, Fourth and District of Columbia Circuits. *Education:* Georgetown University (B.S.F.S., magna cum laude, 1983); University of Virginia (J.D., 1986). Phi Beta Kappa; Order of the Coif. Member, Editorial Board, Virginia Law Review, 1985-1986. ***Email:*** GDoumar@dilworthlaw.com

RICHARD S. KRAUT, admitted to bar, 1967, New York; 1971, District of Columbia. *Education:* Colgate University (B.A., 1963); Columbia University (LL.B., 1966). Author: "Going Public," Progressive Rentals, Association of Progressive Rental Organizations, 1986; "The 'Poison Pill' and the Business Judgment Rule," Director's Monthly, National Association of Corporate Directors, January, 1986; International Aspects of the Federal Securities Laws: Foreign Investment in the United States and in the European Community," International Institute on Tax and Business Planning, NYU School of Continuing Education in Law and Taxation, Matthew Bender, 1978. Co-Author: "Accountants' Malpractice," The Cambridge Institute, 1988; "Another Regulator is Waiting in the Wings," Savings Institutions, February 1984. Senior Counsel, Institutional Investors Study, 1969-1971 and Assistant Director, Division of Enforcement, 1973-1978, U.S. Securities and Exchange Commission. Senior Vice President and General Counsel, National Corp. for Housing Partnerships, 1984-1985. *Member:* The District of Columbia Bar (Vice Chairman, 1982, Acting Chairman, 1983 and Member, Steering Committee, 1981-1982, Corporation, Finance and Securities Division). ***Email:*** RKraut@dilworthlaw.com

RALPH DRURY MARTIN, admitted to bar, 1972, Louisiana; 1976, U.S. Supreme Court; 1981, District of Columbia; 1992, California. *Education:* Tulane University (B.A., 1969); University of Madrid, Spain; Washington University (J.D., 1972). Order of the Coif. Tulane Scholar. Editor, Washington University Law Quarterly, 1971-1972. Law Clerk for Chief U.S. District Judge Frederick J.R. Heebe, Eastern District of Louisiana, 1972-1974. Adjunct Professor, Washington College of Law of American University, 1990-1991. Task Force Member, Attorney General's Advocacy Institute, 1980-1981. Special Counsel, U.S. Department of State, 1990-1991. Senior Prosecutor, Public Integrity Section, U.S. Department of Justice, 1982-1990. Legal Adviser to U.S. Delegation to U.N. General Assembly, 1981. Associate Representative of U.S. Before International Court of Justice, 1980. Trial Attorney, Civil Rights Division, U.S. Department of Justice, 1975-1980. Special Assistant U.S. Attorney, 1974-1975. ***LANGUAGES:*** Spanish and Portuguese. ***PRACTICE AREAS:*** Securities Law; Litigation; International. ***Email:*** RMartin@dilworthlaw.com

JON S. NICHOLAS, admitted to bar, 1989, Kansas; 1991, District of Columbia. *Education:* Washburn University of Topeka (B.B.A., magna cum laude, 1986); University of Chicago (J.D., 1989). ***Email:*** JNicholas@dilworthlaw.com

ALLEN H. ORENBERG, admitted to bar, 1982, Pennsylvania, U.S. Court of Federal Claims; 1983, U.S. Tax Court; 1985, District of Columbia; 1986, U.S. District Court, District of Columbia; 1994, Maryland; U.S. Court of Military Appeals; U.S. District Court, District of Maryland, U.S. Court of Appeals, District of Columbia Circuit; U.S. Court of Appeals, Third, Fourth, Eleventh and Federal Circuits; U.S. Supreme Court. *Education:* Hebrew Union College (1974-1975); University of Maryland (B.A., 1977); South Texas College of Law (J.D., 1980). Co-Author: "Protection of Intellectual Property in the People's Republic of China," International Business and Trade Reporter, Nov., 1985. Member, Criminal Practitioner's Advisory Group to the U.S. Sentencing Guidelines Commission, 1995-1997. *Member:* District of Columbia Association of Criminal Defense Lawyers (President, 1996-1998). ***LANGUAGES:*** Hebrew. ***PRACTICE AREAS:*** Criminal Law; Corporate Litigation; Securities. ***Email:*** AOrenberg@dilworthlaw.com

IRVING M. POLLACK, admitted to bar, 1942, New York; 1979, District of Columbia. *Education:* Brooklyn College (B.A., cum laude, 1938); Brooklyn Law School (LL.B., magna cum laude, 1942). Co-Editor: The Handbook on Fixed Income Securities (Dow Jones Irwin, 1983, 1986, 1991); The Municipal

(This Listing Continued)

Bond Handbook (Dow Jones Irwin, 1983, 1987). Commissioner, Securities and Exchange Commission, 1974-1980. Assistant General Counsel, Director Trading and Markets and Enforcement Divisions, 1946-1974. ***Email:*** IPollack@dilworthlaw.com

MAX RIEDERER VON PAAR, admitted to bar, 1998, New York; 1999, Virginia; 2000, Germany (Munich) (Not admitted in District of Columbia). *Education:* Freie Universitat, Berlin, Germany (First State Exam, 1992; Second State Exam, 1995); George Washington University (LL.M., 1996). (Resident, Arlington, Virginia Office). ***LANGUAGES:*** German. ***PRACTICE AREAS:*** International Estate Planning; Computer Law; Internet Law; International Business Law; Corporate Law; International Law. ***Email:*** MRiederer@dilworthlaw.com

LAURENCE STORCH, admitted to bar, 1974, Massachusetts; 1975, District of Columbia; 1981, New York; 1982, U.S. Court of International Trade. *Education:* Massachusetts Institute of Technology (S.B., 1971; S.M., 1971); Harvard Law School (J.D., 1974). Member, Board of Trustees, MIT Corporation, 1971-1972, 1973-1978. Executive Assistant to the Special Counsel for Compliance, U.S. Department of Energy, 1977-1978. Deputy Assistant Legal Advisor for Politico Military Affairs, U.S. Department of State, 1978-1981. Member, Army Science Board, Department of the Army, 1983-1990. Member, Advisory Panel on Government-Industry Relations, Department of Defense, 1989-1990. ***Email:*** Storch@dilworthlaw.com

JOHN A. WHITNEY, admitted to bar, 1956, Ohio; 1960, District of Columbia; 1965, Maryland. *Education:* Williams College (B.A., 1953); Harvard University (LL.B., 1956). Phi Beta Kappa. Member, Maryland House of Delegates, 1967-1969. Assistant General Counsel for Procurement Matters, NASA, 1969-1973. ***PRACTICE AREAS:*** Government Contract Law; Surety Law; Construction Law; Probate Law. ***Email:*** JWhitney@dilworthlaw.com

NON-ATTORNEY MEMBER

DWIGHT N. MASON. *Education:* Brown University (A.B., cum laude, high honors in History, 1961); University of California (M.A., 1962). American Political Science Association, Congressional Fellow. Fellow, Woodrow Wilson School, Princeton University, 1972. Member, Foreign Service of the United States, 1962-1991. Deputy Chief of Mission and Minister, U.S. Embassy Ottawa, 1986-1990. Service in Morocco, Columbia, Ecuador, Canada, U.S. Arms Control and Disarmament Agency and the Department of State. Member: Atlantic Council of the United States; Canadian Institute of Strategic Studies; Canadian-American Business Council; Canada West Foundation; Association for Diplomatic Studies and Training; Appointed by the President to be U.S. Chairman of the Permanent Joint Board of Defense, Canada-U.S., July 1994. ***Email:*** DMason@dilworthlaw.com

C. L. DIMOS

WASHINGTON, D.C.

(See Middleburg, Virginia)

Trusts and Estates, Nonprofit and Charitable Organizations.

DKW LAW GROUP, PC

Established in 1988

1620 L STREET, N.W., SUITE 1210

WASHINGTON, D.C. 20036

Telephone: 202-955-5080
Telecopier: 202-955-6070
Email: dkwlaw@dkwlaw.com
URL: http://www.dkwlaw.com

Pittsburgh, Pennsylvania Office: 58th Floor, USX Tower, 600 Grant Street. Telephone: 412-355-2600. Fax: 412-355-2609.

Southfield, Michigan Office: 4000 Town Center, Suite 1500. Telephone: 248-358-2090. Fax: 248-358-3599.

Cleveland, Ohio Office: 26th Floor, BP Tower, 200 Public Square. Telephone: 216-875-4800. Fax: 216-875-4809.

Harrisburg, Pennsylvania Office: 4th Floor, Locust Court, 212 Locust Street. Telephone: 717-232-9500. Fax: 717-232-3524.

FIRM PROFILE: DKW Law Group, PC is a business law firm with offices in Cleveland, Detroit, Harrisburg, Pittsburgh and Washington, D.C. Established in 1988, the Firm is a leader in the development of ancillary practices to serve clients' legal and business needs. Through the Firm's ancillary services groups-DKW Capital Markets, Renaissance Partners, FiCap Strategic Partners and Concord Health Partners- -clients receive the legal, investment banking and business consulting services they need to position their businesses for the future. The Firm's practice spans the full range of commercial matters, including corporate mergers and acquisitions, corporate and governmental finance and securities, banking,

(This Listing Continued)

intellectual property, complex civil litigation, labor and employment relations, tax and succession planning, environmental law, government relations, real estate, franchising and creditors' rights and bankruptcy.

JEFFREY W. LETWIN

MICHAEL A. WEISS (Not admitted in District of Columbia).

LEO A. KEEVICAN, JR. (Not admitted in District of Columbia).

CLYDE H. SLEASE, III, born Pittsburgh, Pennsylvania, May 2, 1944; admitted to bar, 1969, Pennsylvania and U.S. District Court, Western District of Pennsylvania; 1972, U.S. District Court, District of Columbia. *Education:* Duke University (A.B., 1966); University of Pittsburgh School of Law (J.D., 1969). Member, Federal Judicial Nominating Commission for Pennsylvania, 1977—. ***Email:*** cslease@dkwlaw.com

OF COUNSEL

JOHN J. McGOVERN, JR., born Washington, D.C., December 22, 1955; admitted to bar, 1985, District of Columbia. *Education:* Vanderbilt University; University of Maryland (B.S., 1979); Georgetown University (J.D., 1984). Legislative Assistant to Senator Richard Lugar, 1978-1983. Professional Staff to Section Chairman John Shad, 1983-1985. (Also Member, Higgins, McGovern & Smith, L.L.C.) (Resident). ***Email:*** mcgovern@dkwlaw.com

DOBIN & SENATORE, P.C.

Established in 1958

1025 CONNECTICUT AVENUE, N.W., SUITE 515

WASHINGTON, D.C. 20036

Telephone: 202-659-3232
Facsimile: 202-296-1064
URL: http://www.dobinlaw.com
Email: info@dobinlaw.com
URL: http://www.lawyers.com/dobinlaw

Silver Spring, Maryland Office: 8701 Georgia Avenue. Suite 750. Telephone: 301-585-6677.

Elder Law, Estate Planning, Estates, Trusts, Probate Law, Estate and Gift Taxation, Wealth Preservation, Family Business Succession, Disability and Retirement Planning, Will Contests, Medicaid, Small Business Law, Corporate Law, Business Planning, Nonprofit Law, Real Estate.

FIRM PROFILE: The law firm of Dobin & Senatore, P.C. is the successor to Ebert, Dobin and Green and Ebert and Bowytz founded by Eugene Ebert in 1958. The firm represents clients throughout the Washington, D.C. Metropolitan Region and Suburban Maryland.

MEMBERS OF FIRM

PHYLLIS J. DOBIN, born Washington, D.C., February 14, 1952; admitted to bar, 1976, Maryland; 1977, District of Columbia; U.S. Court of Appeals, Fourth Circuit. *Education:* Washington University (B.A., 1972); University of Strasbourg School of Law, Strasbourg, France and University of Maryland (J.D., with honor, 1976). Phi Beta Kappa. Book Review Editor, 1974-1975 and Notes and Comments Editor, 1975-1976, The International Trade Law Journal. Author: "A Study in Trade: Franco-Chinese Relations, 1949-1976," Issues and Studies, Taiwan, August, 1977. Member, Washington Metropolitan Bioethics Network. *Member:* District of Columbia Bar; The Bar Association of the District of Columbia; Maryland State, Federal and American Bar Associations; National Academy of Elder Law Attorneys. ***LANGUAGES:*** French. ***PRACTICE AREAS:*** Elder Law; Estate Planning; Estates; Trusts; Probate; Estate and Gift Taxation; Wealth Preservation; Family Business Successions; Disabilities; Retirement Planning; Will Contests; Medicaid; Small Business Law; Corporate Law; Business Planning; Nonprofit Law. ***Email:*** pdobin@dobinlaw.com

E. TAYLOR SENATORE, born Long Island, New York, May 20, 1972; admitted to bar, 1999, Maryland (Not admitted in District of Columbia). *Education:* University of Miami (B.BA., 1994); Catholic University of America (J.D., 1999). *Member:* Maryland State and American Bar Associations. ***PRACTICE AREAS:*** Elder Law; Estate Planning; Estates; Trusts; Probate; Estate and Gift Taxation; Wealth Preservation; Family Business Successions; Disabilities; Retirement Planning; Will Contests; Medicaid; Small Business Law; Corporate Law; Business Planning. ***Email:*** esenatore@dobinlaw.com

REPRESENTATIVE CLIENTS: Dodge Color, Inc.; Reed Electric Co.; East European Jewish Heritage Project (USA), Ltd.
REFERENCE: SunTrust Bank, Connecticut and L Street Branch, Washington D.C.

DOCTER, DOCTER & LYNN, P.C.

666 ELEVENTH STREET, N.W., SUITE 1010
WASHINGTON, D.C. 20001-4542
Telephone: 202-628-6800
Telefax: 202-628-5445
Email: ddl@bankruptcy-docter.com
URL: http://www.lawyers.com/docterdocter&lynn

Bankruptcy, Reorganization, Creditors Rights, Insolvency Matters, Commercial Law. Corporation Law.

CHARLES A. DOCTER, born Hamburg, Germany, August 5, 1931; admitted to bar, 1956, Ohio; 1959, District of Columbia and U.S. Supreme Court; 1960, U.S. Court of Appeals, Fourth Circuit; 1962, Maryland and U.S. District Court, District of Maryland. *Education:* Kenyon College (B.A., magna cum laude, 1953); University of Chicago (J.D., 1956). Member, Maryland House of Delegates, 1967-1979. Former Member, Trustee in Bankruptcy Panel for D.C. and Maryland. Presidential Appointee, Board of Directors of Pennsylvania Avenue Development Corporation. Director, Downtown Business Improvement District. *Member:* District of Columbia Bar; Bar Association of the District of Columbia (Chairman, Bankruptcy Committee, 1985-1988); Maryland State Bar Association; Walter Chandler American Inn of court (Master Emeritus); American Bankruptcy Institute. Fellow, American College of Bankruptcy. ***LANGUAGES:*** German, Russian. ***REPORTED CASES:*** Nova Real Estate Investment Trust, 30 B.R. 347 (Bankr. E.D. Va. 1983); Sherwood Square Associates, 87 B.R. 388 (Bankr. D. Md. 1988); In Re Inslaw, Inc., 88 B.R. 484 Bkrptcy. D. Dist. Col. 1987); In re AOV Industries, Inc., 31 B.R., 1005 (D.C. Cir. 1983). ***PRACTICE AREAS:*** Reorganization Law; Bankruptcy Law; Insolvency Law. ***Email:*** cad@bankruptcy-docter.com

MARCIA K. DOCTER, born Philadelphia, Pennsylvania, September 19, 1933; admitted to bar, 1957, District of Columbia; 1958, Pennsylvania; 1962, Maryland. *Education:* University of Pennsylvania (B.S., 1954; LL.B., 1957). Former Member, Trustee in Bankruptcy Panel for Maryland. *Member:* The District of Columbia Bar; Montgomery County and Maryland State Bar Associations; Maryland State Women's Bar Association. ***PRACTICE AREAS:*** Reorganization Law; Creditors Rights Law; Commercial Litigation. ***Email:*** mkd@bankruptcy-docter.com

DAVID E. LYNN, born Washington, D.C., May 9, 1953; admitted to bar, 1982, District of Columbia; 1983, U.S. District Court for the District of Columbia; 1984, U.S. District Court, District of Maryland; 1986, U.S. Supreme Court; 1998, U.S. Court of Appeals, Fourth Circuit. *Education:* Brown University (A.B., 1975); Georgetown University (J.D., 1981). Member, Local Rules Committee for the United States Bankruptcy Court for the District of Columbia, 1988—. *Member:* District of Columbia Bar; Bar Association of the District of Columbia (Chair, Bankruptcy Committee, 1990-1992); American Bar Association; Walter Chandler American Inn of Court (Barrister); American Bankruptcy Institute. (Certified Specialist, Business Bankruptcy Law, American Bankruptcy Board of Certification). ***PRACTICE AREAS:*** Bankruptcy Law; Commercial Law; Reorganization Law. ***Email:*** dlynn@bankruptcy-docter.com

---

HENRY DAVID WILL DOCTER, born Washington, D.C., November 23, 1960; admitted to bar, 1996, Maryland (Not admitted in District of Columbia). *Education:* Carleton College (B.A., with Distinction in History, cum laude, 1983); New York University (J.D., 1988). ***LANGUAGES:*** Spanish. ***PRACTICE AREAS:*** Elder Law; Probate; Consumer Law. ***Email:*** Henry@bankruptcy-docter.com

DOHERTY, SHERIDAN & PERSIAN, L.L.P.

1050 17TH STREET NW SUITE 1250
WASHINGTON, D.C. 20036
Email: ds.law@erols.com

Fairfax, Virginia Office: Suite 200, 8408 Arlington Boulevard, 22031. Telephone: 703-698-7700. Facsimile: 703-641-9645.
Bethesda, Maryland Office: 4701 Sangamore Road, Suite S-225, 20816.
Vero Beach, Florida Office: 1701 Highway AIA, Suite 220, 32963.

General Civil and Trial Practice. Probate, Insurance, Corporation, Creditors Rights, Negligence.

MEMBERS OF FIRM

CORNELIUS H. DOHERTY, JR., born Washington, D.C., August 15, 1935; admitted to bar, 1959, Virginia; 1960, District of Columbia and U.S. Court of Appeals, District of Columbia Circuit; 1975, U.S. Supreme Court; 1997, Florida. *Education:* Georgetown University (B.S., S.S., 1957; J.D., 1959). Assistant Commonwealth Attorney, Arlington, Virginia, 1960-1961. *Member:* Fairfax, Arlington County, Virginia and American Bar Associations; District of Columbia Bar; Virginia State Bar; The Florida Bar; District of Columbia Defense Lawyers Association. ***PRACTICE AREAS:*** Probate; Corporate Law; Estate Planning. ***Email:*** ds.law@erols.com

EDWIN A. SHERIDAN, born Washington, D.C., June 29, 1935; admitted to bar, 1964, Virginia; 1965, District of Columbia and U.S. Supreme Court. *Education:* West Virginia University (B.S., Bus. Admin., 1958); American University (J.D., 1964). Phi Alpha Delta. *Member:* Fairfax and American Bar Associations; District of Columbia Bar; Bar Association of the District of Columbia; Virginia State Bar; Northern Virginia Defense Lawyers Association; District of Columbia Defense Lawyers Association; The Association of Trial Lawyers of America. ***PRACTICE AREAS:*** Civil Practice; Personal Injury Litigation. ***Email:*** ds.law@erols.com

ERIC M. PERSIAN, born Washington, D.C., April 3, 1959; admitted to bar, 1984, Virginia; 1985, District of Columbia; 1997, Maryland, U.S. District Court, Eastern District of Virginia and U.S. Court of Appeals, Fourth Circuit. *Education:* University of Maryland (B.A., 1981); George Mason University School of Law (J.D., 1984). Delta Theta Phi; Alpha Phi Sigma. *Member:* Fairfax Bar Association; District of Columbia Bar; Virginia State Bar; District of Columbia Defense Lawyers Association; Northern Virginia Defense Lawyers Association; Virginia Trial Lawyers Association. ***PRACTICE AREAS:*** Civil Litigation; Criminal Law; Traffic Law. ***Email:*** ds.law@erols.com

REPRESENTATIVE CLIENTS: Hartford Accident & Indemnity Co.; John Deere Insurance Co.; Ranger Insurance Co.; State Auto; Erie Insurance Exchange; Ryder Truck Rental, Inc.; Superior Insurance Co.; No. Carolina Farm Bureau Insurance Co.; State Capitol Insurance Co.; Independent Fire Insurance Co.; Ohio Casualty Insurance Co.; Burlington Insurance Co.; First Financial Insurance; Great West Casualty Co.; Armed Forces Insurance Exchange; CGU/Commercial Union Ins. Co.; Canal Insurance Co.; Claims Control, Inc.; Travelers Property Casualty Co.; Middlesex Mutual Assurance Co.; UML Insurance Programs; Cardinal Freight Carriers, Inc.; Enterprise Leasing; Markel Insurance; Southern Insurance Company; Kemper Insurance; Golden Eagle Insurance Corp.; Old Republic Insurance of Canada; Overnight Transportation Services; Infinity Insurance Company; Andover Insurance.

THE DONAHUE LAW FIRM

SUITE 930
1120 G. STREET, N.W.
WASHINGTON, D.C. 20005
Telephone: 202-371-1080
URL: http://www.thedonahuelawfirm.com
URL: http://www.lawyers.com/thedonahuelawfirm

Annapolis, Maryland Office: 18 West Street. 21401. Telephone: 410-280-2023. Fax: 410-280-0905.

Wrongful Death, Products Liability, Medical Malpractice, Major Personal Injury, Banking Law, Bank Transactions, Family Law, Business Law and Litigation, Criminal, Probate and Estate Planning.

(For biographical data on all personnel, see Professional Biographies at Annapolis, Maryland)

DORN & KLAMP, P.C.

1625 MASSACHUSETTS AVENUE, N.W., SUITE 450
WASHINGTON, D.C. 20036
Telephone: 202-986-3300
Fax: 202-986-0823
Email: DORNKLMP@EROLS.COM
URL: http://www.DK-Law.com

Non-Profit Association Law.

FIRM PROFILE: The firm has a national practice acting as general counsel to non-profit associations in matters involving governance, taxation, antitrust, employee relations, disciplinary matters and contract review. We believe that proactive, preventative legal counseling best serves our clients' needs. The firm is designed to meet the specialized needs of small and medium-sized nonprofit clients including charities, membership societies, certification organizations, professional associations, international non-governmental organizations, and private foundations and other philanthropies.

SUSAN E. DORN, born Duluth, Minnesota, September 29, 1956; admitted to bar, 1985, Pennsylvania; 1986, District of Columbia; 1996, Maryland. *Education:* The College of William & Mary (B.A., 1981); Antioch School of Law (J.D., 1985). Co-author: *The Licensure and Certification Mission*, Professional Examination Service, 2000; *The Nonprofit Board's Guide to Bylaws*, National Center for Nonprofit Boards, 1996; "Answers to Your Certification Legal Questions," ASAE *Association Educator,* 1993. Author: "Certification and the Law," Association Management, May 2000; "Test Score Reporting: What is Your Discretion?" CLEAR *Exam Review,* 1992; Speaker: "Private Credentialing Organizations," ASAE Legal Symposium, 1999; "Fostering a Healthy Relationship with the Membership Association," National Association for Competency

(This Listing Continued)

Assurance, 1997; "Intermediate Sanctions," Finance and Administration Roundtable, ASAE, 1996; "Hotel Contracts," ASAE Annual Meeting, 1993; "Board-Staff Relations: Helping the Board Meet Its Fiduciary Obligations," National Organization for Competency Assurance, 1997. Discussion Leader, "Bylaws," National Center for Nonprofit Boards, 1997. *Member:* The District of Columbia Bar (Member, Taxation Section); Pennsylvania (Member, Taxation Section) and American Bar Associations. ***Email:*** sdorn@dk-law.com

CAROLYN KLAMP, born Ann Arbor, Michigan, August 24, 1959; admitted to bar, 1986, Maryland; 1989, District of Columbia. *Education:* University of Virginia (B.A., 1982); Harvard University (J.D., 1985). *Member:* The District of Columbia Bar (Member, Taxation Section); American Bar Association (Member, Taxation Section). ***Email:*** cklamp@dk-law.com

---

MICHELLE A. HANSON, born Crookston, Minnesota; admitted to bar, 1998, Minnesota (Not admitted in District of Columbia). *Education:* Bemidji State University (B.A., 1994); University of North Dakota (J.D., 1997). *Member:* Minnesota State Bar Association. ***PRACTICE AREAS:*** Nonprofit Organizations Law. ***Email:*** mhanson@dk-law.com

---

DORSEY & WHITNEY LLP

1001 PENNSYLVANIA AVENUE, N.W., SUITE 300 SOUTH
WASHINGTON, D.C. 20004
Telephone: 202-824-8800
Facsimile: 202-824-8990
URL: http://www.dorseylaw.com

Minneapolis, Minnesota Office: Suite 1500, 50 South Sixth Street, 55402-1498. Telephone: 612-340-2600.

Seattle, Washington Office: U.S. Bank Building Centre, 1420 Fifth Avenue, Suite 3400, 98101. Telephone: 206-903-8800.

New York, New York Office: 250 Park Avenue, 10177. Telephone: 212-415-9200.

Denver, Colorado Office: 370 Seventeenth Street, Republic Plaza Building, Suite 4700, 80202-5647. Telephone: 303-629-3400.

London, England Office: 21 Wilson Street, EC2M 2TD. Telephone: 011-44-207-588-0800.

Brussels, Belgium Office: 35 Square De Meeûs 1000. Telephone: 011-32-2-504-4611.

Hong Kong Office: Suite 3008, One Pacific Place, 88 Queensway. Hong Kong. Telephone: 011-852-252-65000. Fax: 011-852-252-43000.

Tokyo, Japan Office: Shiroyama JT Mori Building 16F, 4-3-1 Toranomon Minato-Ku, 105-6016. Telephone: 81 3 5403 4876. Fax: 81 3 5403 4877.

Shanghai, China Office: Suite 6211-12, Plaza 66, No. 1266 Nanjing Xi Lu, Shanghai, 200040. Telephone: 86-21-6288-2323. Fax: 86-21-6288-3222.

Toronto, Ontario Office: BCE Place, 161 Bay Street, Suite 4310. M5J 2S1. Telephone: 416-367-7370. Fax: 416-367-7371.

Vancouver, British Columbia Office: 666 Burrard Street, Suite 500, V6C 3P6. Telephone: 604-687-5151.

Anchorage, Alaska Office: 1031 West 4th Avenue, Suite 600, 99501. Telephone: 907-276-4557.

Des Moines, Iowa Office: 801 Grand, Suite 3900, 50309. Telephone: 515-283-1000.

Salt Lake City, Utah Office: Wells Fargo Plaza, 170 South Main Street, Suite 900, 84101. Telephone: 801-933-7360.

Orange County, California Office: Center Tower, 650 Town Center Drive, Suite 1850, P.O. Box 5066, Costa Mesa, 92626. Telephone: 714-662-7300.

Billings, Montana Office: 1200 First Interstate Center, 401 North 31st Street, P.O. Box 7188, 59103. Telephone: 406-252-3800.

Fargo, North Dakota Office: Dakota Center, 51 North Broadway, Suite 402, P.O. Box 1344, 58107-1344. Telephone: 701-235-6000.

Great Falls, Montana Office: 507 Davidson Building, 8 Third Street North, P.O. Box 1566, 59401. Telephone: 406-727-3632.

Rochester, Minnesota Office: 201 First Avenue, S.W., Suite 340, 55902. Telephone: 507-288-3156.

Missoula, Montana Office: 125 Bank Street, Suite 600, 59802. Telephone: 406-721-6025.

Paramus, New Jersey Office: East 80, Route 4, 07652. Telephone: 201-291-8904. Fax: 201-712-9444.

International Trade, International Transactions, Intellectual Property, Energy, Environmental and Natural Resources, Federal Indian, Administrative and Legislative Law, Litigation, Project Finance, Agricultural, Cooperatives, Telecommunications.

MEMBERS OF FIRM

PHILIP BAKER-SHENK, born 1957; admitted to bar, 1984, Pennsylvania; 1985 District of Columbia; 1998, U.S. Supreme Court. *Education:* Eastern Mennonite College (B.S., 1979); Catholic University (J.D. 1984). *Member:* The District of Columbia Bar Association; American Bar Association. ***PRACTICE AREAS:*** Native American Law; Federal Indian Law; Federal Civil Practice;

(This Listing Continued)

Government Relations; Indian Gaming Law; Administrative Adjudications; Legislative Practice; Public Policy; Litigation Practice; Entertainment and Music Industry Practice. ***Email:*** bakershenk.philip@dorseylaw.com

ALAN I. BARON, born 1942; admitted to bar, 1966, Maryland; 1967, U.S. District Court, District of Maryland and U.S. Court of Appeals, Fourth Circuit; 1980, U.S. Supreme Court; 1981, District of Columbia; 1982, U.S. Court of Appeals, District of Columbia Circuit. *Education:* Princeton University (B.A., 1963); Harvard Law School (LL.B., 1966). Law Clerk to Chief, U.S. District Court for Maryland, 1966-1967. Assistant U.S. Attorney for Maryland, 1967-1970. Special Impeachment Counsel, United States House of Representatives, 1987-1990. Special Counsel, Select Commission to Investigate Failure of Privately Insured Financial Institutions in Rhode Island, 1991-1992. Special Counsel, Anne Arundel County Board of Education investigation into sexual abuse of students by faculty, 1994; Minority Chief Counsel, U.S. Senate Governmental Affairs Committee Special Investigation into Campaign Finance Abuses, 1997. Legal Analyst for NBC News. Member, Judicial Conference Fourth Circuit Court of Appeals. Author: "The Federal Rules of Appellate Procedure: An Overview," Maryland Appellate Practice Handbook, 1977; "Federal Sentencing Law and Practice," West Publishing, 1989, Advisory Panel; "Watergate Procedures for All?" 36 Md. Law Review 35 (1976); "Construction Bid Rigging," (Co-Author), Federal Publications, Inc., 1984; "Surreptitious Recording of Conversations in Maryland: A Trap for the Uninformed," (Co-Author), Maryland Bar Journal, 1986; "Justice for Judges and the National Inquest," (Co-Author with Congressman Jack Brooks (D.Tex.) and John Bryant (D.Tex.)), Legal Times, May 6, 1991; "The Curious Case of Alcee Hastings," 19 Nova L. Rev. 873 (1995). ***PRACTICE AREAS:*** White Collar Criminal Defense; Complex Civil Litigation. ***Email:*** baron.alan@dorseylaw.com

DAVID A. BIEGING, born 1949; admitted to bar, 1976, Minnesota; 1978, District of Columbia. *Education:* Harvard University (B.A., 1971); William Mitchell College of Law (J.D., 1976). ***PRACTICE AREAS:*** Legislation and Federal Regulatory Practice. ***Email:*** bieging.dave@dorseylaw.com

VIRGINIA WALKER BOYLAN, born 1941; admitted to bar, 1979, Virginia; 1996, District of Columbia. *Education:* American University (B.A., 1965); Catholic University (J.D., 1979). ***PRACTICE AREAS:*** Indians and Native Populations; Government Law; Casinos and Gambling; Legislative. ***Email:*** boylan.virginia@dorseylaw.com

PHILIPPE M. BRUNO, born 1955; admitted to bar, 1980, France; 1987, Virginia; 1998, District of Columbia. *Education:* University of Grenoble, (J.D., 1977; LL.M., 1978; Doctorate, 1982); Georgetown University (LL.M., 1984). ***LANGUAGES:*** French. ***PRACTICE AREAS:*** International Law. ***Email:*** bruno.philippe@dorseylaw.com

PAMELA M. DEESE, born 1958; admitted to bar, 1984, Pennsylvania; 1986, U.S. Court of Appeals for the Federal Circuit and U.S. Court of International Trade; 1990, District of Columbia; 1992, U.S. Court of Appeals, Fourth Circuit; 1995, U.S. Supreme Court; U.S. Court of Appeals for the District of Columbia Circuit. *Education:* American University (B.S., 1980; J.D., 1983). Assistant Director, U.S. Generalized System of Preferences, U.S. Trade Representatives Office, 1978-1983. Author: "Negotiating and Structuring a Character License Agreement that Successfully Defines the Business Relationship," The Licensing Journal, June 1999. *Member:* The District of Columbia Bar; Pennsylvania and American Bar Associations; International Trade Commission Trial Lawyers Association; American Intellectual Property Lawyers Association; International Licensing Industry Merchandising Association; Licensing Executives Society. ***PRACTICE AREAS:*** Intellectual Property; Advertising Law; Litigation. ***Email:*** deese.pamela@dorseylaw.com

FREDERICK S. FREI, born 1945; admitted to bar, 1974, District of Columbia; 1985, Texas; 1989, Massachusetts; registered to practice before U.S. Patent and Trademark Office. *Education:* Cornell University (B.S., Chem. Engr., 1968); Georgetown University (J.D., 1973). Law Clerk to the Honorable Chief Judge, Harry Phillips, U.S. Court of Appeals, Sixth Circuit, 1973-1974. *Member:* American Bar Association (Member, Sections on: Intellectual Property; Antitrust; Litigation); American Intellectual Property Law Association. ***PRACTICE AREAS:*** Patent; Intellectual Property; Antitrust; Litigation. ***Email:*** frei.fred@dorseylaw.com

MARK L. HOGGE, born 1953; admitted to bar, 1984, Virginia; 1986, District of Columbia; registered to practice before U.S. Patent and Trademark Office. *Education:* George Mason University (B.A., cum laude, 1975); George Mason University School of Law (J.D., 1984). Registered Medical Technologist, 1979. *Member:* American Bar Association (Member, Patent and Antitrust Sections); Federal Circuit Bar Association; American Intellectual Property Law Association; Federal American Inn of Court (Master of the Bench). ***PRACTICE AREAS:*** Unfair Competition Litigation; Patent Infringement; Antitrust; Trademark Infringement; Trade Dress; Trade Name Infringement; Trade Secret Misappropriation; False Advertising; Common Law Unfair Competition; Fraud; Tortious Contract Interference; Tortious Prospective Economic Benefit Interference; Injurious Falsehood. ***Email:*** hogge.mark@dorseylaw.com

(This Listing Continued)

DORSEY & WHITNEY LLP, Washington—Continued

CREIGHTON R. MAGID, born 1961; admitted to bar, 1987, Iowa and Minnesota; 1988, Montana (Not admitted in District of Columbia). *Education:* Princeton University (A.B., 1984); University of Michigan (J.D., 1987). ***PRACTICE AREAS:*** Litigation. ***Email:*** magid.chip@dorseylaw.com

J. GARY McDAVID, born 1947; admitted to bar, 1973, District of Columbia; 1980, U.S. Supreme Court. *Education:* Ohio State University (B.A., 1970); University of Bonn, Germany (1968-1969); Georgetown University Law Center (J.D., 1973). Note Editor, Law and Policy in International Business, 1973. Law Clerk, Chief Judge Wilson Cowen, U.S. Court of Claims, 1973-1975. Adjunct Professor, Georgetown University Law Center, 1982-1985. *Member:* The District of Columbia Bar; American Bar Association. ***PRACTICE AREAS:*** Cooperatives; Corporate Law.

ALDO NOTO, born 1964; admitted to bar, 1990, Virginia; 1991, District of Columbia; registered to practice before U.S. Patent and Trademark Office. *Education:* Coast Guard Academy (B.S.E.E., 1985); State University of New York at Albany (B.S., Math., 1985); George Washington University (J.D., 1990; LL.M., Intellectual Property Law, 1993). ***PRACTICE AREAS:*** Patent Law, Other Intellectual Property Law; Computer Law; Litigation; Patent Licensing; Electronic Patents; Computer and Software Patents; International Trade Law. ***Email:*** noto.aldo@dorseylaw.com

RICHARD E. POWERS, JR., born 1952; admitted to bar, 1977, Texas; 1979, District of Columbia; 1988, U.S. Supreme Court; 1980, U.S. Court of Appeals for the District of Columbia Circuit and U.S. District Court, District of Columbia; 1987, U.S. Court of Appeals, Fifth Circuit; 1989, U.S. Court of International Trade; 1992, U.S. Court of Federal Claims. *Education:* Gonzaga University (B.S., 1974); University of Notre Dame (J.D., 1977). Alpha Sigma Nu; Pi Mu Epsilon. *Member:* The District of Columbia Bar; American Bar Association; State Bar of Texas. ***PRACTICE AREAS:*** Energy; Administrative; Public Utility; Legislative Practice; International; Customs. ***Email:*** powers.richard@dorseylaw.com

DELBERT D. SMITH, born 1940; admitted to bar, 1969, Wisconsin; 1982, District of Columbia. *Education:* University of Wisconsin (B.S., 1963; M.S., 1965; J.D., 1969); Cambridge Univ., England (Ph.D., International Law, 1968); Hague Academy of International Law, The Netherlands (Diploma). Trustee, Space Shuttle Children's Fund. *Member:* International Astronautical Federation, International Institute of Space Law; American Institute of Aeronautics and Astronautics; International Institute of Communications, London; Royal Television Society, London. ***PRACTICE AREAS:*** Telecommunications Law; International Law; Space Law; Satellite Law. ***Email:*** smith.delbert@dorseylaw.com

GEORGE Y. SUGIYAMA, born 1949; admitted to bar, 1976, Maryland; 1989, District of Columbia. *Education:* Drake University (B.A., 1970); University of Maryland (J.D., 1976). ***PRACTICE AREAS:*** Environmental Law; Regulatory Agency Practice; Federal Administrative Law. ***Email:*** sugiyama.george@dorseylaw.com

RALPH A. TAYLOR, JR., born 1948; admitted to bar, 1975, Virginia; 1976, District of Columbia; 1989, Maryland. *Education:* Princeton University (B.S.E., Electrical Engineering, with honors, 1970); University of Virginia (J.D., 1975). Order of the Coif. Notes Editor, Virginia Law Review, 1974-1975. Author: Comment, "Equal Protection and Exclusionary Zoning: Boraas v. Village of Belle Terre," 60 Virginia Law Review 163, 1974. Co-Author: Note, "Review of EPA's Significant Deterioration Regulations: An Example of the Agency-Court Partnership in Environmental Law," 61 Virginia Law Review 1115, 1975. Contributing Author, *International Technology Transfers* (H. Ruben, ed., 1995). Engineer, U.S. Environmental Protection Agency, Boston, Massachusetts, 1970-1972. Associate Editor, 1985— and Executive Editor, 1999—, ABA Litigation News. Listed in: Who's Who in America; Who's Who in American Law. Head of Technology and Intellectual Property Litigation Group. *Member:* American Bar Association (Sections of Litigation, Dispute Resolution, Science and Technology and Intellectual Property Law). ***PRACTICE AREAS:*** Intellectual Property; Commercial Litigation. ***Email:*** taylor.ralph@dorseylaw.com

RAYMOND VAN DYKE, born 1957; admitted to bar, 1990, New Jersey; 1991, New York; 1997, Texas; U.S. Supreme Court; U.S. Court of Appeals, Third, Fifth and Federal Circuits; U.S. District Court, Southern and Eastern Districts of New York, Northern District of Texas and District of New Jersey; Court of International Trade; Federal Court of Claims; registered to practice before U.S. Patent and Trademark Office (Not admitted in District of Columbia). *Education:* Wilbur Wright (A.A., highest honors, 1980); University of North Carolina (B.S. in Computer Science, with honors, summa cum laude, 1985; M.S. in Computer Science, 1989; J.D., 1990). Author: "E Wars, Episode One: The Patent Menace," Conference Proceedings of the 17th Annual Pacific Rim Computer Law Institute, June 2, 2000; "Software Patents Offer Opportunities and Obstacles," National Law Journal, May 24, 1999; "Drawing the Line Between Legal Tying and Patent Misuse," Journal of the Patent and Trademark Office Society, 1993 (R. Van Dyke et al.). Adjunct Professor, Southern Methodist University, Computer Science and Engineering Department, 2001. *Member:* New York, New Jersey and Dallas/Fort Worth Intellectual Property Associations; American Intellectual Property Law Association (acting Chair, Latin America Committee); Licensing Executives Society (Chapter President); German-American Law Association; Computer Law Association; Association for Computing Machinery; Optics Society; Institute of Electrical and Electronics Engineers; Institute of Electrical and Electronics Engineers Computer Society. ***PRACTICE AREAS:*** Intellectual Property; Intellectual Property Litigation; Licensing; Opinion; E-Commerce Law; Computer Law; Internet Law; Technology Law; Software; Electronic Patents; Business Methods Patents. ***Email:*** vandyke.raymond@dorseylaw.com

LANCE L. VIETZKE, born 1965; admitted to bar, 1994, Minnesota; 1996, District of Columbia; registered to practice before the U.S. Patent and Trademark Office. *Education:* University of Minnesota (B.S.E.E., with distinction, 1988); William Mitchell College of Law (J.D., cum laude, 1994). *Member:* American Bar Association; American Intellectual Property Law Association. ***PRACTICE AREAS:*** Intellectual Property. ***Email:*** vietzke.lance@dorseylaw.com

KEVIN J. WADZINSKI, born 1966; admitted to bar, 1993, Wisconsin and Minnesota; 1996, District of Columbia. *Education:* University of Wisconsin (B.A., 1988; J.D., cum laude, 1993). ***PRACTICE AREAS:*** Federal Indian Law; Employment Law; Tribal Law; State-Tribal Relations; Tribal Taxation; Indian Gaming Law; Government Relations. ***Email:*** wadzinski.kevin@dorseylaw.com

OF COUNSEL

DANIEL E. FISHER, born 1947; admitted to bar, 1978, Maryland and U.S. District Court, District of Maryland; 1983, U.S. Tax Court; 1991, District of Columbia; 1999, U.S. Supreme Court. *Education:* Johns Hopkins University (B.S.E., with honors, 1979); University of Maryland (M.B.A., 1973); George Washington University (J.D., 1978). Delta Theta Phi. Registered Professional Engineer, Maryland, 1973. Principal Engineer, Westinghouse Electric Corporation, Electronic Systems Group, 1965-1990. *Member:* Maryland State Bar Association, Inc.; Bar Association of the District of Columbia; (Member, Section on Patent, Trademark and Copyright Law); American Bar Association (Member, Section of Science and Technology); American Intellectual Property Law Association; Maryland Patent Law Association; Institute of Electrical and Electronics Engineers (Member and Past Chairman, Intellectual Property Committee; Member, Committee on Communication and Information Policy); Engineering Management Society. ***PRACTICE AREAS:*** Intellectual Property Law; Patents; Intellectual Property Licensing; Electrical Intellectual Property; Computer and Software Patents. ***Email:*** fisher.daniel@dorseylaw.com

MUNFORD PAGE HALL, II, born 1948; admitted to bar, 1980, District of Columbia; 1988, U.S. Supreme Court; 1992, Virginia. *Education:* Duke University (B.A., 1970); American University (M.A., 1980; J.D., magna cum laude, 1980). ***PRACTICE AREAS:*** International Trade Law; Customs Law; Civil Litigation. ***Email:*** hall.page@dorseylaw.com

MARTHA K. LANDESBERG, born 1950; admitted to bar, 1989, Ohio (Not admitted in District of Columbia). *Education:* Yale College (B.A., 1971); University of Cincinnati (J.D., 1989). ***PRACTICE AREAS:*** Civil Trial; Criminal Law. ***Email:*** landesberg.martha@dorseylaw.com

STEFAN M. LOPATKIEWICZ, born 1948; admitted to bar, 1973, Pennsylvania; 1975, District of Columbia; 1978, U.S. Supreme Court. *Education:* University of Virginia (B.A., 1970); Harvard University (J.D., 1973). *Member:* Society of Satellite Professionals International; Federal Communications Bar Association. ***PRACTICE AREAS:*** Telecommunications; International Corporate Law; Nonprofit Organizations; Satellite Law. ***Email:*** lopatkiewicz.stefan@dorseylaw.com

ASSOCIATES

Steven A. Adducci
Bryneé Kyonne Baylor (Not admitted in DC)
Kevin B. Bedell
Patricia Russell Brown
Chris Casieri (Not admitted in DC)
Kevin L. Chapple
W. Robinson H. Clark
Kathryn L. Clune
Brian Gunn
Tania W. Hanna
John K. Harrop
Rosa S. Jeong (Not admitted in DC)
Julia A. Jones (Not admitted in DC)
Christopher A. Karns
Kelly T. Lee (admission pending)
Robin P. Levine
Victor Mroczka
Trystan Phifer O'Leary
Linda B. Popejoy
Rebecca Roby (Not admitted in DC)
Ami P. Shah (Not admitted in DC)
Bruce K. Trauben
Sean Wooden

(This Listing Continued)

(This Listing Continued)

RETIRED MEMBER

DAVID BUSBY, born 1926; admitted to bar, 1950, Oklahoma; 1959, New York, District of Columbia and U.S. Supreme Court. *Education:* Yale University (B.A., 1948); University of Oklahoma (LL.B., 1951).

JOHN B. REHM, born 1930; admitted to bar, 1955, New York; 1969, District of Columbia; 1988, U.S. Supreme Court. *Education:* Harvard University (A.B., 1952); Columbia University (LL.B., 1955); Wesley Theological Seminary (M.T.S., 1990).

(For personnel and biographical data on Dorsey & Whitney's other offices, see that specific city and state listing)

DOW, LOHNES & ALBERTSON, PLLC

Established in 1918

1200 NEW HAMPSHIRE AVENUE, N.W.
SUITE 800
WASHINGTON, D.C. 20036-6802
Telephone: 202-776-2000
Facsimile: 202-776-2222
Email: info@dlalaw.com
URL: http://www.dlalaw.com

Atlanta, Georgia Office: One Ravinia Drive, Suite 1600. Telephone: 770-901-8800. Telecopier: 770-901-8874.

General Civil and Administrative Practice including Antitrust, Aviation, Cable Television, Commercial TV and Radio Broadcasting, Communications, Compensation and Benefits, Corporate, Employee Relations/Benefits, Environmental, Estate Planning and Administration, Financial Institutions, Government Contracts, Government Relations, Health Care, Intellectual Property, Media and Information Technology, Labor, Legislation, Litigation, Mergers and Acquisitions, Non-Profit Institutions, Public Broadcasting and Telecommunications, Real Estate, Satellite Communications, Securities, Telecommunications and Telephones and Tax.

MEMBERS OF THE FIRM

CORINNE M. ANTLEY, born Chamblee, Georgia, October 25, 1955; admitted to bar, 1981, District of Columbia. *Education:* Indiana University of Pennsylvania (B.A., summa cum laude, 1977); University of Virginia (J.D., 1981). ***Email:*** cantley@dlalaw.com

MICHAEL D. BASILE, born Brooklyn, New York, April 21, 1958; admitted to bar, 1983, District of Columbia. *Education:* Lafayette College (B.A., 1980); Washington College of Law (J.D., 1983). ***Email:*** mdbasile@dlalaw.com

LEONARD J. BAXT, born Lebanon, Pennsylvania, 1948; admitted to bar, 1973, District of Columbia. *Education:* University of Pittsburgh (B.A., 1969); University of Michigan (J.D., cum laude, 1972). Assistant Editor, Michigan Law Review, 1970-1971. (Chairman, Board of Directors). ***Email:*** lbaxt@dlalaw.com

RAYMOND G. BENDER, JR., born Hoboken, New Jersey, 1947; admitted to bar, 1973, District of Columbia; 1974, U.S. Claims Court. *Education:* Georgetown University (B.S.F.S., 1969; J.D., 1973; M.L.T., 1985). Law Clerk to Hon. James R. Durfee, U.S. Court of Claims, 1973-1975. ***Email:*** rbender@dlalaw.com

RICHARD L. BRAUNSTEIN, born New York, N.Y., 1933; admitted to bar, 1958, New York; 1959, District of Columbia. *Education:* New York University (A.B., magna cum laude, 1954); Harvard University (LL.B., 1957).

LISA C. BUREAU, born Framingham, Massachusetts, November 1, 1960; admitted to bar, 1986, Virginia; 1988, District of Columbia. *Education:* Colby College (A.B., magna cum laude, 1982); Georgetown University Law Center (J.D., 1986). Phi Beta Kappa. Member of Staff, 1984-1985 and Lead Article Editor, 1985-1986, Law and Policy in International Business. ***Email:*** lbureau@dlalaw.com

JAMES M. BURGER, born New York, N.Y., February 22, 1946; admitted to bar, 1972, New York and District of Columbia; 1975, U.S. Supreme Court; 1986, Texas. *Education:* New York University (B.A., with honors, 1967; M.A., 1968; J.D., cum laude, 1971). Order of the Coif. Editor, New York University Law Review, 1970-1971. Adjunct Professor, University of Virginia School of Law, 1973-1982. *Member:* The District of Columbia Bar; Bar Association of the District of Columbia; American Bar Association (Member, Administrative Law Section); Federal Communications Bar Association. ***Email:*** jburger@dlalaw.com

BLAIN B. BUTNER, born Winston Salem, North Carolina, October 15, 1953; admitted to bar, 1980, District of Columbia; 1981, North Carolina; 1987, U.S. Supreme Court. *Education:* Davidson College (A.B., cum laude, 1975); Duke University (J.D., 1980). Phi Beta Kappa; Omicron Delta Kappa. Charles A. Dana Scholar; B.S. Womble Scholar. Managing Editor, Duke Law Journal, 1979-1980. Board of Directors, 1984-1987 and Treasurer, 1987, Younger Lawyers Division, Federal Bar Association; National Association of College and University Attorneys. ***Email:*** bbutner@dlalaw.com

(This Listing Continued)

JOHN T. BYRNES, JR., born Jersey City, New Jersey, July 16, 1952; admitted to bar, 1977, New Jersey; 1981, District of Columbia. *Education:* Georgetown University (B.S.B.A., magna cum laude, 1974); University of Pennsylvania (J.D., 1977). Law Secretary, Associate Justice, New Jersey Supreme Court, 1977-1978. ***Email:*** jbyrnes@dlalaw.com

PETER C. CANFIELD, born Bryn Mawr, Pennsylvania, March 6, 1954; admitted to bar, 1980, California; 1982, Alabama; 1985, Wisconsin; 1987, Georgia. *Education:* Amherst College (B.A., 1976); Yale University (J.D., 1979). Phi Beta Kappa. Editor, Yale Law Journal, 1978-1979. Law Clerk to Hon. Frank M. Johnson, Jr., U.S. Court of Appeals, Fifth Circuit, 1979-1980; Hon. Myron H. Thompson, U.S. District Court, Middle District of Alabama, 1980-1981. Attorney, Civil Rights Division, U.S. Department of Justice, Washington, D.C., 1981-1983. Special Assistant U.S. Attorney, Washington, D. C., 1982-1983. Deputy District Attorney, Montgomery, Alabama, 1983-1984. *Member:* State Bar of Georgia; The Association of Trial Lawyers of America. (Resident, Atlanta, Georgia Office). ***Email:*** pcanfield@dlalaw.com

PETER C. CASSAT, born Katonah, New York, February 8, 1963; admitted to bar, 1989, Wisconsin and District of Columbia. *Education:* Bates College (B.A., cum laude, 1985, Phi Beta Kappa); University of Wisconsin (J.D., cum laude, 1989). Senior Editor and Comment Editor, Wisconsin Law Review. *Member:* American Bar Association. ***Email:*** pcassat@dlalaw.com

THOMAS M. CLYDE, born New York, N.Y., February 26, 1966; admitted to bar, 1992, Georgia. *Education:* Princeton University (A.B., 1988); Duke University (J.D., with honors, 1992). Editorial Board, Duke Law Journal, 1991-1992. *Member:* State Bar of Georgia. (Resident, Atlanta, Georgia Office). ***Email:*** tclyde@dlalaw.com

JAMES A. DEMETRY, born Detroit, Michigan, January 27, 1960; admitted to bar, 1985, Georgia. *Education:* University of Michigan (B.A., in Economics, 1982); Ohio State University (J.D., 1985). Articles Editor, Ohio State Law Journal, 1984-1985. Co-Editor in Chief, Ohio State Journal on Dispute Resolution, 1984-1985. *Member:* State Bar of Georgia. (Resident, Atlanta, Georgia Office). ***Email:*** jdemetry@dlalaw.com

WILLIAM S. DUDZINSKY JR., born Stuttgart, Germany, April 17, 1962; admitted to bar, 1988, New York; 1997, District of Columbia. *Education:* Georgetown University (B.S.F.S., 1984); University of Pennsylvania (J.D., 1987). ***Email:*** wdudzinsky@dlalaw.com

PETER H. FEINBERG, born Kew Gardens, New York, March 16, 1946; admitted to bar, 1973, New York; 1975, District of Columbia. *Education:* New York University (B.A., 1968); George Washington University (J.D., with honors, 1972). *Member:* The District of Columbia Bar; American Bar Association; Federal Communications Bar Association. ***Email:*** pfeinberg@dlalaw.com

JOHN R. FEORE, JR., born New Britain, Connecticut, 1946; admitted to bar, 1975, District of Columbia. *Education:* Boston College (B.A., magna cum laude, 1968); University of Wisconsin-Madison (M.A., magna cum laude, 1969); Georgetown University (J.D., 1974). Member, Board of Editors, Georgetown University Law Journal, 1973-1974. ***Email:*** jfeore@dlalaw.com

PATRICIA A. FRANCIS, born Amory, Mississippi, 1963; admitted to bar, 1989, New York; 1994, District of Columbia. *Education:* Mississippi State University (B.A., summa cum laude, 1984); University of Virginia (J.D., 1988). Phi Delta Phi. Dillard Fellow. *Member:* District of Columbia Bar. ***Email:*** pfrancis@dlalaw.com

LINDA A. FRITTS, born Batavia, New York, May 19, 1954; admitted to bar, 1979, Connecticut; 1981, District of Columbia. *Education:* Elmira College (B.A., 1976); University of Virginia (J.D., 1979); Georgetown University (M.L.T., 1984). Phi Beta Kappa. ***Email:*** lfritts@dlalaw.com

JONATHON C. GLASS, born Pittsburgh, Pennsylvania, September 27, 1953; admitted to bar, 1991, District of Columbia; 1992, Maryland. *Education:* Carleton College (B.A., cum laude, 1975); Pacific School of Religion (M.Div., 1979); Georgetown Law School (J.D., cum laude, 1991). ***Email:*** jglass@dlalaw.com

MICHAEL B. GOLDSTEIN, born New York, N.Y., 1943; admitted to bar, 1967, New York; 1974, Illinois; 1978, District of Columbia. *Education:* Cornell University (A.B., 1964); New York University (J.D., 1967). Director, New York City Urban Corps., 1967-1970. Director of University of Relations and Assistant City Administrator, Office of the Mayor, New York City, 1970-1972. Adjunct Assistant Professor, John Jay College of Criminal Justice, 1969-1972. Associate Vice Chancellor and Associate Professor, University of Illinois (Chicago), 1972-1977. Chair, Education Law Committee, Administrative Law Section, American Bar Association, 1991—. Chair, Education Law Committee, Federal Bar Association, 1985-1986, 1990—. National Office Committee, National Association of College and University Attorneys, 1986—. Loeb Fellow in Advanced Urban and Environmental Studies, Harvard University, 1970. Chair, Committee on Public Policy, American Council on Education Commission on Higher Education and the Adult Learner. Trustee, Mount Vernon College, Fielding Institute, Greater Washington Research Center, Washington Center. ***Email:*** mgoldstein@dlalaw.com

(This Listing Continued)

DOW, LOHNES & ALBERTSON, PLLC, Washington—Continued

TODD D. GRAY, born Chicago, Illinois, 1954; admitted to bar, 1979, District of Columbia. *Education:* Wheaton College (B.A., with highest honors, 1976); Harvard Law School (J.D., magna cum laude, 1979). Member, Board of Editors, Harvard Journal of Legislation, 1978-1979. ***Email:*** tgray@dlalaw.com

JOYCE TRIMBLE GWADZ, born Marlboro, Massachusetts, 1949; admitted to bar, 1976, Connecticut; 1977, District of Columbia. *Education:* Smith College (A.B., 1970); University of Michigan (J.D., magna cum laude, 1976). *Member:* Connecticut and American Bar Associations. ***Email:*** jgwadz@dlalaw.com

RALPH W. HARDY, JR., born Ogden, Utah, 1941; admitted to bar, 1969, California and District of Columbia. *Education:* Brigham Young University and University of Utah (B.S., cum laude, 1965); Boalt Hall School of Law, University of California at Berkeley (J.D., 1968). ***Email:*** rhardy@dlalaw.com

J.G. HARRINGTON, born Red Bank, New Jersey, February 23, 1960; admitted to bar, 1987, New York; 1991, District of Columbia and U.S. Court of Appeals for the District of Columbia Circuit. *Education:* Cook College of Rutgers University (B.S., 1983); Massachusetts Institute of Technology; New York University (J.D., 1986). George H. Cook Scholar. Semi-Finalist, National Moot Court Competition. Member, The Order of Barristers. *Member:* Federal Communications Bar Association; National Forensic Association; Speech Communication Association. ***Email:*** jharringto@dlalaw.com

JONATHAN D. HART, born Philadelphia, Pennsylvania, July 21, 1956; admitted to bar, 1985, U.S. Virgin Islands; 1986, District of Columbia. *Education:* Middlebury College (B.A., magna cum laude, 1978); Stanford Law School (J.D., 1983). Phi Beta Kappa. Faculty, Stanford Professional Publishing Course, 1994—. Law Clerk to: Hon. Almeric L. Christian, Chief Judge, District Court of the Virgin Islands, 1983-1985; Hon. Jerome Farris, U.S. Court of Appeals, Ninth Circuit, 1985-1986. *Member:* District of Columbia Bar; Virgin Islands Bar Association. ***Email:*** jhart@dlalaw.com

MICHAEL D. HAYS, born Oklahoma City, Oklahoma, April 7, 1948; admitted to bar, 1977, District of Columbia. *Education:* Princeton University (B.A., cum laude, 1970); Georgetown University (J.D., 1976). Editor, Georgetown Law Journal, 1975-1976. Law Clerk to Judge Lloyd MacMahon, U.S. District Judge, Southern District of New York, 1976-1977. Assistant U.S. Attorney for the District of Columbia, 1979-1984. Recipient, U.S. Department of Justice Special Achievement, 1983. Faculty: National Institutes of Trial Advocacy, Georgetown University; Appellate Advocacy Course (2000), co-sponsored by the United States Court of Appeals for the District of Columbia Circuit and the D.C. Bar. Member, Executive Committee and Board of Directors, Council for Court Excellence. ***Email:*** mhays@dlalaw.com

MICHAEL A. HEPBURN, born Nürnberg, Germany, August 13, 1963; admitted to bar, 1988, Maryland; 1990, District of Columbia. *Education:* Western Maryland College (B.A., 1985); George Washington University (J.D., with honors, 1988). ***Email:*** mhepburn@dlalaw.com

JONATHAN B. HILL, born Boston, Massachusetts, 1944; admitted to bar, 1969, Massachusetts; 1972, District of Columbia; 1977, U.S. Supreme Court. *Education:* Colby College (A.B., 1966); Boston University (J.D., 1969). Attorney, Federal Aviation Administration, 1969-1972. Partner, Markham & Hill, 1972-1979. ***Email:*** jhill@dlalaw.com

J. MICHAEL HINES, born Lenoir, North Carolina, 1945; admitted to bar, 1971, District of Columbia. *Education:* University of North Carolina (B.A., with highest honors, 1967); Harvard University (J.D., 1970). Phi Eta Sigma; Phi Beta Kappa. [Judge Advocate General's Department, U.S. Air Force, 1971-1974]. ***Email:*** mhines@dlalaw.com

R. DALE HUGHES, born Charleston, South Carolina, May 13, 1961; admitted to bar, 1986, Georgia. *Education:* Emory University (B.B.A., with distinction, 1983); University of Georgia (J.D., cum laude, 1986). Welborn E. Cody Scholar. Recent Developments Editor, Georgia Journal of International and Comparative Law, 1985-1986. *Member:* State Bar of Georgia. (Resident, Atlanta, Georgia Office). ***Email:*** rhughes@dlalaw.com

JOHN C. JOST, born Fort Benning, Georgia, 1953; admitted to bar, 1978, District of Columbia. *Education:* School of Foreign Service of Georgetown University (B.S.F.S., cum laude, 1975); University of Virginia (J.D., 1978). Member, Editorial Board, Virginia Journal of International Law, 1976-1977. Articles Editor, Virginia Journal of International Law, 1977-1978. Co-Author, "Foreign Investment in United States Communications" in Manual of Foreign Investment in the United States. ***Email:*** jjost@dlalaw.com

TIMOTHY J. KELLEY, born Cleveland, Ohio, June 19, 1952; admitted to bar, 1979, Ohio; 1986, District of Columbia. *Education:* Dartmouth College (B.A., magna cum laude, Phi Beta Kappa, 1974); Johns Hopkins University (M.A., 1976); Case Western Reserve University (J.D., 1979). Order of the Coif. ***Email:*** tkelley@dlalaw.com

(This Listing Continued)

KEVIN J. KUZAS, born Smithtown, New York, October 5, 1966; admitted to bar, 1992, Virginia; 1994, District of Columbia. *Education:* University of Southern California (B.A., cum laude, 1989); University of Virginia School of Law (J.D., 1992). Law Clerk, U.S. District Judge Samuel Conti, U.S. District Court, Northern District of California, 1992-1993. *Member:* Virginia State Bar; The District of Columbia Bar. ***Email:*** kkuzas@dlalaw.com

PAUL R. LANG, born Hackensack, New Jersey, December 5, 1957; admitted to bar, 1983, District of Columbia. *Education:* University of Colorado (B.A., with distinction, 1979; B.S., magna cum laude, 1979); George Washington University (J.D., with high honors, 1983). Order of the Coif. ***Email:*** plang@dlalaw.com

JOHN S. LOGAN, born Hattiesburg, Mississippi, January 1, 1953; admitted to bar, 1979, District of Columbia. *Education:* Vanderbilt University (B.A., summa cum laude, 1974); University of Virginia (J.D., 1977). Phi Beta Kappa; Order of the Coif. Notes Editor, Virginia Law Review. Law Clerk, Hon. Charles Clark, Judge, U.S. Court of Appeals, Fifth Circuit, 1977-1978. ***Email:*** jlogan@dlalaw.com

BERNARD J. LONG, JR., born Washington, D.C., 1940; admitted to bar, 1965, District of Columbia; 1978, Maryland; 1989, New York. *Education:* College of the Holy Cross (A.B., cum laude, 1962); University of Virginia (LL.B., 1965). Member, Order of the Coif. Member, Editorial Board, University of Virginia Law Review, 1963-1965. Law Clerk to Judge John J. Sirica, U.S. District Court for D.C., 1965-1966. ***Email:*** blong@dlalaw.com

STEPHANIE M. LOUGHLIN, born Windham, Connecticut, November 11, 1964; admitted to bar, 1988, District of Columbia. *Education:* Catholic University of America (B.A., summa cum laude, 1985); University of Virginia (J.D., 1988). Phi Beta Kappa. *Member:* The District of Columbia Bar. ***Email:*** sloughlin@dlalaw.com

JUDITH A. MATHER, born Akron, Ohio, January 2, 1952; admitted to bar, 1977, Maryland; 1979, District of Columbia. *Education:* Niagara University (B.A., magna cum laude, 1973); Georgetown University (J.D., 1977). Delta Epsilon Sigma. Editor, Georgetown University, Law and Policy in International Business, 1976-1977. Law Clerk to the Hon. Herbert F. Murray, U.S. District Court Judge for the District of Maryland, 1977-1978. Attorney-Advisory and Senior Trial Attorney, U.S. Department of Energy, Office of General Counsel (Superior Performance Award), 1978-1982. Deputy Assistant General Counsel for Regulatory Litigation, U.S. Department of Energy, 1982-1984. ***Email:*** jmather@dlalaw.com

ELIZABETH ANNE McGEARY, born Springfield, Massachusetts, July 8, 1964; admitted to bar, 1991, Virginia and U.S. Court of Appeals, Fourth Circuit; 1993, District of Columbia. *Education:* Trinity College (B.A., 1986); University of Virginia (J.D., 1991). Phi Beta Kappa. *Member:* Federal Communications and American Bar Associations. ***Email:*** emcgeary@dlalaw.com

RICHARD P. McHUGH, born Wilmington, Delaware, October 22, 1955; admitted to bar, 1980, Ohio; 1981, U.S. Tax Court; 1985, District of Columbia. *Education:* Georgetown University (A.B., cum laude, 1977); Georgetown University Law Center (J.D., 1980). Alpha Sigma Nu. Member, Southern Employee Benefit Conference. Member, ESOP Association. *Member:* District of Columbia Bar (Member, Employee Benefits Committee); American Bar Association (Member, Employee Benefits Committee, Tax Section). ***Email:*** rmchugh@dlalaw.com

JOHN W. McNAMARA, born East Orange, New Jersey, May 22, 1959; admitted to bar, 1987, Maryland; 1988, District of Columbia; 1999, Georgia. *Education:* University of Delaware (B.S., cum laude, 1981); Duke University (J.D., cum laude, 1986). Note and Comment Editor, Duke Law Journal, 1985-1986. *Member:* State Bar of Georgia; Maryland State Bar Association; The District of Columbia Bar. (Resident, Atlanta, Georgia Office). ***Email:*** jmcnamara@dlalaw.com

MARGARET L. MILLER, born Jefferson City, Missouri, August 8, 1964; admitted to bar, 1990, Missouri; 1991, District of Columbia. *Education:* Washington University (B.S., 1986); University of Utah (J.D., 1989). Omicron Delta Kappa. Note Editor, University of Utah Law Review, 1988-1989. *Member:* The District of Columbia Bar; The Missouri Bar; Federal Communications Bar Association. ***Email:*** mmiller@dlalaw.com

DAVID E. MILLS, born Rochester, New York, September 18, 1960; admitted to bar, 1986, Maryland, District of Columbia and U.S. Court of Appeals, Fourth Circuit; 1987, U.S. District Court, District of Columbia; 1988, U.S. Court of Appeals, District of Columbia Circuit; 1989, U.S. Tax Court; 1992, U.S. Court of Federal Claims; 1993, U.S. Supreme Court. *Education:* Brandeis University (B.A., with honors, 1982); Duke University (J.D., with honors, 1985). Recipient, Duke Law Merit Scholarship. Articles Editor, Alaska Law Review. Assistant U.S. Attorney, Washington, D.C., 1989-1992. Recipient, Special Achievement Award. ***Email:*** dmills@dlalaw.com

EDWARD J. O'CONNELL, born Hartford, Connecticut, February 3, 1956; admitted to bar, 1983, District of Columbia. *Education:* Yale University (B.A., 1977); Georgetown University (J.D., cum laude, 1983). *Member:* Ameri-

(This Listing Continued)

can Bar Association (Member, Sections on: Business Law; Taxation Law; Member, Forum Committee on the Entertainment and Sports Industries); Federal Communications Bar Association. ***Email:*** eoconnell@dlalaw.com

TIMOTHY J. O'ROURKE, born Baltimore, Maryland, October 24, 1956; admitted to bar, 1981, District of Columbia; 1982, U.S. District Court, District of Columbia, U.S. Court of Appeals for the District of Columbia Circuit and U.S. Supreme Court. *Education:* University of Virginia (B.A., with highest distinction, 1978; J.D., 1981). Phi Beta Kappa. Recipient: C.S. Ashby Henry Prize; Stephen Pierre Traynor Appellate Advocacy Award. Member, Moot Court Board. Winner, Lile Moot Court Competition. Deputy Assistant Attorney General, Counselor to the Assistant Attorney General, U.S. Department of Justice, Civil Division, 1992-1993. *Member:* American Bar Association (Member, Sections on: Litigation; Antitrust Law; Communications Law). ***Email:*** torourke@dlalaw.com

B. DWIGHT PERRY, born Oklahoma City, Oklahoma, 1933; admitted to bar, 1964, District of Columbia. *Education:* University of Oklahoma (B.A., 1955); Georgetown University (J.D., 1963). Note Editor, Georgetown Law Journal, 1962-1963. Law Clerk, Senior Judge E. Barrett Prettyman, U.S. Court of Appeals for D.C. Circuit, 1963-1964. (Chair, Management Committee). ***Email:*** bperry@dlalaw.com

THOMAS J. PETERS IV, born Eustis, Florida, August 1, 1960; admitted to bar, 1988, Georgia. *Education:* Duke University (B.A., 1982); University of North Carolina at Chapel Hill (J.D., 1988). *Member:* State Bar of Georgia. (Resident, Atlanta, Georgia Office). ***Email:*** jpeters@dlalaw.com

LAURA HATHAWAY PHILLIPS, born Niagara Falls, New York, June 15, 1958; admitted to bar, 1986, District of Columbia; 1987, U.S. District Court for the District of Columbia and U.S. Court of Appeals for the District of Columbia. *Education:* Trinity College (B.A., with honors in Economics, 1980); Washington College of Law of American University (J.D., 1986). *Member:* The District of Columbia Bar; American Bar Association; Federal Communications Bar Association. ***Email:*** lphillips@dlalaw.com

JOHN H. POMEROY, born Macon, Georgia, 1948; admitted to bar, 1979, District of Columbia. *Education:* United States Air Force Academy (B.S., with distinction, 1970); University of Arkansas (M.A., 1976); Harvard Law School (J.D., cum laude, 1979). *Member:* The District of Columbia Bar. [Capt. U.S. Air Force, 1970-1976]. ***Email:*** jpomeroy@dlalaw.com

MARY K. QUALIANA, born Rochester, New York, June 1, 1959; admitted to bar, 1985, Maryland; 1987, District of Columbia. *Education:* Michigan State University (B.A., 1981); George Washington University (J.D., with honors, 1984). Phi Beta Kappa; Phi Alpha Delta. Member, National Moot Court Team. Trial Attorney, Office of the Chief Counsel, Federal Railroad Administration, 1984-1987. *Member:* District of Columbia Bar; American Bar Association; Womens Bar Association of the District of Columbia. ***Email:*** mqualiana@dlalaw.com

J. CHRISTOPHER REDDING, born Washington, D.C., July 16, 1952; admitted to bar, 1979, Oklahoma; 1981, District of Columbia. *Education:* Duke University (B.A., 1974); University of Tulsa (J.D., with highest honors, 1979). Order of the Curule Chair. Member, Moot Court Board, 1977-1979. Staff Member, 1977-1978 and Notes and Comments Editor, 1978-1979, Tulsa Law Journal. Law Clerk to the Honorable William J. Holloway, Jr., U.S. Circuit Judge, U.S. Court of Appeals, Tenth Circuit, 1979-1981. ***Email:*** credding@dlalaw.com

KEVIN F. REED, born Washington, D.C., 1948; admitted to bar, 1973, District of Columbia. *Education:* College of the Holy Cross (B.A., 1970); Georgetown Law Center (J.D., 1973). Case and Note Editor, Georgetown Law Journal, 1972-1973. Law Clerk to Judge Charles Fahy, U.S. Court of Appeals, District of Columbia Circuit, 1973-1974. ***Email:*** kreed@dlalaw.com

CURTIS A. RITTER, born Philadelphia, Pennsylvania, February 1, 1947; admitted to bar, 1976, Virginia; 1977, District of Columbia; 1982, Maryland. *Education:* University of Maryland (B.S., Engineering, with high honors, 1973); George Washington University (J.D., with high honors, 1976). Order of the Coif; Tau Beta Pi; Pi Tau Sigma. Assistant Counsel to the White House Conference on Balanced National Growth and Economic Development, 1978. ***Email:*** critter@dlalaw.com

KENNETH D. SALOMON, born Bridgeport, Connecticut, February 25, 1945; admitted to bar, 1970, District of Columbia; 1974, U.S. Supreme Court; 1976, Maryland. *Education:* Tufts University (B.A., cum laude, 1967); George Washington University (J.D., with honors, 1970). Member, George Washington University Law Review, 1968-1970. Adjunct Professor of Law, American University, 1978-1979. Attorney, Federal Communications Commission, 1970-1972, 1975-1978. Deputy Chief Counsel, National Telecommunications and Information Administration, U.S. Department of Commerce, 1978-1980. ***Email:*** ksalomon@dlalaw.com

JAMES R. SAXENIAN, born Syracuse, New York, July 26, 1965; admitted to bar, 1990, Connecticut; 1991, New York and District of Columbia. *Education:* State University of New York, Albany (B.S., Accounting, summa cum laude, 1987); George Washington University (J.D., with honors, 1990); Georgetown University (LL.M. in Taxation, with distinction, 1997). Beta Gamma Sigma; Phi Alpha Delta. Member, George Washington Law Review. Recipient, Thomas B. Chetwood Award for Most Distinguished Academic Performance in Tax Law, 1997. *Member:* New York State Bar Association; The District of Columbia Bar. ***Email:*** jsaxenian@dlalaw.com

STUART A. SHELDON, born Elmira, New York, 1948; admitted to bar, 1974, Georgia; 1976, District of Columbia. *Education:* Johns Hopkins University (B.A., 1971; M.A., 1971); University of Pennsylvania (J.D., 1974). Member, Order of the Coif. Article & Book Review Editor, University of Pennsylvania Law Review, 1973-1974. ***Email:*** ssheldon@dlalaw.com

SEAN R. SMITH, born Oklahoma City, Oklahoma, April 13, 1962; admitted to bar, 1988, Georgia. *Education:* Harvard University (A.B., magna cum laude, 1985); University of Chicago (J.D., with honors, 1988). Order of the Coif. Member, Chicago Law Review, 1986-1988. *Member:* State Bar of Georgia. (Resident, Atlanta, Georgia Office). ***Email:*** ssmith@dlalaw.com

MITCHELL H. STABBE, born Brooklyn, New York, October 12, 1955; admitted to bar, 1980, District of Columbia; 1982, Maryland; 1993, Florida. *Education:* University of Rochester (B.A., magna cum laude, 1977); University of Chicago (J.D., 1980). Phi Beta Kappa; Phi Delta Phi. *Member:* District of Columbia Bar; The Florida Bar; Maryland State, Federal and American Bar Associations. ***Email:*** mstabbe@dlalaw.com

M. ANNE SWANSON, born Washington, D.C., 1954; admitted to bar, 1981, District of Columbia. *Education:* West Virginia University (B.S.J., magna cum laude, 1974); Princeton University (M.P.A., 1979); Yale University (J.D., 1979). Law Clerk to Honorable C. B. Renfrew, Northern District of California, 1979-1980 and Honorable Richard D. Cudahy, U.S. Court of Appeals, Seventh Circuit, 1980. *Member:* District of Columbia Bar; American Bar Association; Federal Communications Bar Association. ***Email:*** aswanson@dlalaw.com

THOMAS D. TWEDT, born San Francisco, California, October 21, 1963; admitted to bar, 1992, Texas; 1996, District of Columbia. *Education:* University of North Texas (B.B.A., 1989); University of Houston (J.D., 1992). Member, Securities and Exchange Commission. *Member:* State Bar of Texas; The District of Columbia Bar. ***Email:*** ttwedt@dlalaw.com

JOHN D. WARD, born Allentown, Pennsylvania, 1952; admitted to bar, 1977, Massachusetts; 1979, District of Columbia. *Education:* Dartmouth College (A.B., 1974); Columbia University (J.D., 1977). ***Email:*** jward@dlalaw.com

LESLIE H. WIESENFELDER, born New York, N.Y., 1945; admitted to bar, 1971, New York; 1972, District of Columbia. *Education:* Cornell University (B.A., 1967); Syracuse University (J.D., 1971). Member, Order of the Coif. Articles Editor, Syracuse Law Review, 1970-1971. Attorney, U.S. Department of Justice, 1972-1976. ***Email:*** lwiesen@dlalaw.com

DAVID DANIEL WILD, born Washington, D.C., January 6, 1955; admitted to bar, 1981, District of Columbia. *Education:* American University; University of Maryland (B.A., magna cum laude, 1977); Boalt Hall School of Law, University of California (J.D., 1981). Articles Editor, Ecology Law Quarterly, 1980-1981. ***Email:*** dwild@dlalaw.com

RICHARD A. WILHELM, born Cincinnati, Ohio, November 13, 1952; admitted to bar, 1982, Georgia. *Education:* University of Cincinnati (B.A., 1976; M.A., 1978); University of Braunschweig (1978-1979); University of Georgia (J.D., 1982). Phi Beta Kappa; Order of the Coif. Executive Research Editor, Georgia Law Review, 1981-1982. *Member:* State Bar of Georgia. (Resident, Atlanta, Georgia Office). ***LANGUAGES:*** German. ***Email:*** rwilhelm@dlalaw.com

DAVID J. WITTENSTEIN, born Atlanta, Georgia, July 24, 1956; admitted to bar, 1981, District of Columbia; 1982, Georgia. *Education:* Haverford College (B.A., magna cum laude, 1978); Duke University (J.D., 1981). Member, Editorial Board, Duke Law Journal, 1980-1981. ***Email:*** dwittens@dlalaw.com

---

BRUCE S. ANTLEY, born Clarksville, Arkansas, December 30, 1967; admitted to bar, 1999, Virginia; 2000, District of Columbia. *Education:* Indiana University of Pennsylvania (B.A., 1989); University of Virginia (J.D., 1999). ***Email:*** bantley@dlalaw.com

CHESTER H. ARTER, III, born Miami, Florida, October 5, 1970; admitted to bar, 1998, Georgia. *Education:* Franklin and Marshall College (B.A., 1995); University of Miami (J.D., magna cum laude, 1998). Order of the Coif. *Member:* State Bar of Georgia. (Resident, Atlanta, Georgia Office). ***Email:*** carter@dlalaw.com

ETHAN ATTICKS, born Hartford, Connecticut, September 14, 1974; admitted to bar, 1999, Virginia; 2000, District of Columbia. *Education:* College of William and Mary (B.A., 1995); University of Virginia (J.D., 1999). ***Email:*** eatticks@dlalaw.com

ADISA P. BAKARI, born Washington, D.C., February 28, 1973; admitted to bar, 1998, Wisconsin and Maryland; 1999, District of Columbia. *Education:*

(This Listing Continued)

DOW, LOHNES & ALBERTSON, PLLC, Washington—Continued

Delaware State University (B.A., 1995); University of Wisconsin (J.D., 1998). Summer Intern, White House, 1994. *Member:* American and National Bar Associations. ***Email:*** abakari@dlalaw.com

TRACY BENJAMIN, born Brooklyn, New York, June 15, 1966; admitted to bar, 2000, Maryland; 2001, District of Columbia. *Education:* Grambling State University (B.S., 1987); George Washington University (J.D., 2000). ***Email:*** tbenjamin@dlalaw.com

REBECCA S. BJORK, born Minneapolis, Minnesota, January 1, 1961; (admission pending). *Education:* University of Minnesota (B.A., 1983); University of Southern California (Ph.D., 1989); Georgetown University (J.D., 2001). *Member:* American Forensic Association. ***Email:*** rbjork@dlalaw.com

MATTHEW A. BLOCK, born Detroit, Michigan, February 22, 1969; admitted to bar, 1994, Georgia. *Education:* University of Michigan (B.A., with distinction, 1991; J.D., cum laude, 1994). *Member:* State Bar of Georgia. (Resident, Atlanta, Georgia Office). ***Email:*** mblock@dlalaw.com

STEVEN E. BLUMENTHAL, born Los Angeles, California, January 18, 1970; admitted to bar, 1995, Tennessee; 1999, Georgia. *Education:* Tulane University (B.A., 1992); University of Virginia (J.D., 1995). Phi Beta Kappa. (Resident, Atlanta, Georgia Office). ***PRACTICE AREAS:*** Corporate. ***Email:*** sblumenthal@dowlohnes.com

KEVIN P. BRANDON, born Queens, New York, March 7, 1967; admitted to bar, 1993, New York; 1995, District of Columbia. *Education:* Catholic University of America (B.A., summa cum laude, 1989); New York University (J.D., 1992; LL.M., 1993). Phi Beta Kappa. *Member:* New York State Bar Association. ***Email:*** kbrandon@dlalaw.com

DOUGLAS E. BRAUNSTEIN, born Washington, D.C., April 12, 1967; admitted to bar, 1993, Maryland; 2000, District of Columbia. *Education:* Ithaca College (B.S., 1989); Vanderbilt University (J.D., 1992). *Member:* Maryland State Bar Association. ***Email:*** dbraunstein@dlalaw.com

CHRISTOPHER J. BROOKHART, born Provo, Utah, July 8, 1969; admitted to bar, 1999, Utah; 2000, District of Columbia. *Education:* Brigham Young University (B.A., 1996; J.D., 1999). Phi Delta Phi. ***Email:*** cbrookhart@dlalaw.com

DENICE SAYERS BURCH, born Lakeland, Florida, October 30, 1968; admitted to bar, 1995, Georgia. *Education:* Oglethorpe University (B.A., with honors, 1991); University of Georgia (J.D., cum laude, 1995). Notes Editor, Georgia Journal of International and Comparative Law, 1994-1995. *Member:* State Bar of Georgia. (Resident, Atlanta, Georgia Office). ***Email:*** dburch@dlalaw.com

CHRISTINA HOSP BURROW, born Bryn Mawr, Pennsylvania, December 20, 1963; admitted to bar, 1993, Virginia; 1994, District of Columbia. *Education:* University of Virginia (B.S., Commerce, 1985); George Mason University (J.D., with distinction, 1993). Associate Justice, Moot Court Board, 1991-1993. Regional Quarterfinalist, National Trial Advocacy Competition, 1993. Member, 1991-1992 and Production Editor, 1992-1993, George Mason University Law Review. *Member:* Federal Communications Bar Association. ***Email:*** cburrow@dlalaw.com

LAURENT M. CAMPO, born New York, N.Y., January 6, 1970; admitted to bar, 1996, New York; 1997, District of Columbia. *Education:* Cornell University (B.A., with distinction, 1992); Duke Law School (J.D., 1995). Phi Beta Kappa. Member, 1993-1994 and Editor-in-Chief, 1994-1995, Duke Journal of Comparative and International Law. Co-Author: with Jonathan Ocko, Special Focus, "Forward: The Corporatization Process in China," 5 Duke J. Comp. & Int'l. L. 150, 1995; with Jens Rosenkvist, Current Developments, "Recent Legal Developments of the European Community," 4 Duke J. Comp. & Int'l. L. 189, 1994. *Member:* District of Columbia Bar. ***LANGUAGES:*** French. ***Email:*** lcampo@dlalaw.com

ADAM CHARLES CHASE, born Silver Spring, Maryland, September 26, 1974; admitted to bar, 1999, Maryland; 2000, District of Columbia. *Education:* Cornell University (B.A., 1996); University of Virginia (J.D., 1999). ***LANGUAGES:*** Spanish. ***Email:*** achase@dlalaw.com

JILL C. COAN, born West Point, New York, May 25, 1971; admitted to bar, 1996, Georgia. *Education:* Emory University (B.A., 1993); University of Georgia (J.D., magna cum laude, 1996). Phi Beta Kappa; Order of the Coif. Member, Georgia Law Review, 1994-1995. *Member:* State Bar of Georgia. (Resident, Atlanta, Georgia Office). ***Email:*** jcoan@dlalaw.com

PETER D. COFFMAN, born Plainfield, New Jersey, January 4, 1965; admitted to bar, 1990, Georgia; 1996, District of Columbia. *Education:* Princeton University (A.B., magna cum laude, 1987); University of Michigan (J.D., cum laude, 1990); Cambridge University (LL.M., 1996). Law Clerk to Hon. Orinda D. Evans, U.S. District Court, Northern District of Georgia, 1990-1991.

(This Listing Continued)

Member: State Bar of Georgia; The District of Columbia Bar. (Resident, Atlanta, Georgia Office). ***LANGUAGES:*** French. ***Email:*** pcoffman@dlalaw.com

SCOTT D. DAILARD, born San Diego, California, June 16, 1968; admitted to bar, 1994, California; 1995, District of Columbia. *Education:* Harvard College (B.A., 1990); Boalt Hall School of Law, University of California at Berkeley (J.D., 1993). Judicial Law Clerk, Hon. Samuel Conti, U.S. District Court, Northern District of California, San Francisco. *Member:* State Bar of California; The District of Columbia Bar. ***Email:*** sdailard@dlalaw.com

RICHARD S. DENNING, born Brooklyn, New York, August 29, 1966; admitted to bar, 1991, Pennsylvania; 1993, District of Columbia; 2000, Georgia. *Education:* Messiah College (B.S., 1987); George Washington University National Law Center (J.D., 1991). Order of the Coif. Member, George Washington Law Review, 1990-1991. *Member:* Pennsylvania Bar Association; The District of Columbia Bar; State Bar of Georgia. (Resident, Atlanta, Georgia Office). ***Email:*** rdenning@dlalaw.com

WHITING G. DIMOCK, born Stoughton, Massachusetts, September 24, 1971; admitted to bar, 1996, Colorado; 1998, District of Columbia. *Education:* Williams College (B.A., 1992); University of Colorado (J.D., 1996). *Member:* The District of Columbia Bar; American Bar Association. ***Email:*** wdimock@dlalaw.com

DAVID DOHERTY, born White Plains, December 5, 1973; admitted to bar, 2001, New York (Not admitted in District of Columbia). *Education:* University of Notre Dame (B.A., 1996; J.D., 2000). ***Email:*** ddoherty@dlalaw.com

MARY TERESA ANASTASIA DOUD, born Baltimore, Maryland, July 13, 1970; admitted to bar, 1997, Maryland; 1998, District of Columbia. *Education:* Haverford College (B.A., 1992); Bryn Mawr College (M.A., 1992); University of Pennsylvania Law School (J.D., 1997). *Member:* The District of Columbia Bar; American Bar Association; American Intellectual Property Lawyers Association. ***LANGUAGES:*** French and Italian. ***Email:*** tdoud@dlalaw.com

JAMES D. DOUGLAS, born New York, New York, January 23, 1973; admitted to bar, 1998, New York and U.S. District Court, Northern District of New York (Not admitted in District of Columbia). *Education:* University of Florida (B.A., 1994); Albany Law School of Union College (J.D., cum laude, 1997). Justinian Society. Member, Albany Law School Law Review. Author: "Cash Balance Plans," Tax Management Memorandum, 2/14/00 Volume 41 Number 4. ***Email:*** jdouglas@dlalaw.com

MARCI J. FINKELSTEIN, born Detroit, Michigan, January 9, 1970; admitted to bar, 2000, Virginia; 2001, District of Columbia. *Education:* Michigan State University (B.A., 1992); University of Michigan at Ann Arbor (J.D., 2000). ***Email:*** mfinkelstein@dlalaw.com

JASON E. FRIEDRICH, admitted to bar, 1999, New Jersey; 2000, District of Columbia. *Education:* George Washington University (B.A., 1996); Catholic University of America (J.D., 1999). *Member:* The District of Columbia Bar; Federal Communications Bar Association. ***Email:*** jfriedrich@dlalaw.com

DANIEL FULKERSON, born Dubois, Pennsylvania, December 18, 1974; (admission pending). *Education:* University of North Carolina at Chapel Hill (B.A., 1997); University of Wisconsin-Madison (J.D., with honors, 2001). ***Email:*** dfulkerson@dowlohnes.com

KATHLEEN E. FULLER, born Washington, D.C., September 14, 1967; (admission pending). *Education:* Trinity College, Hartford (B.A., 1989); University of North Carolina at Chapel Hill (M.A., in Communications, with honors, 1992); Duke University (J.D., cum laude, 2001). Executive Editor, Duke Law and Technology Review, 1999-2001. ***Email:*** kfuller@dlalaw.com

SUZANNE R. GARMENT, born Buffalo, New York, March 2, 1946; admitted to bar, 2000, Maryland (Not admitted in District of Columbia). *Education:* Radcliffe College (B.A., 1967); Georgetown University Law Center (J.D., 2000). Member, American Society for Public Administration, 1997. ***Email:*** sgarment@dlalaw.com

JEFFREY J. GEE, born Ft. Monmouth, New Jersey; admitted to bar, 1999, District of Columbia. *Education:* Syracuse University (B.A., 1995); Georgetown University Law Center (J.D., 1998). *Member:* The District of Columbia Bar. ***Email:*** jgee@dlalaw.com

BARBARA A. GOFFMAN, born Freeport, New York, February 25, 1969; admitted to bar, 1999, Maryland; 2000, District of Columbia. *Education:* University of Michigan (B.A., summa cum laude, 1991); Northwestern University (M.S.J., 1993); Duke University (J.D., 1999). Special Projects and Note Editor, Law & Contemporary Problems, Duke Law Journal, 1998-1999. ***Email:*** bgoffman@dlalaw.com

WILLIAM GOLDBERG, born Bay Shore, New York; (admission pending). *Education:* Wesleyan University (B.A., 1994); University of Wisconsin-Madison (J.D., cum laude, 2001). ***LANGUAGES:*** Spanish. ***Email:*** wgoldberg@dlalaw.com

(This Listing Continued)

LARS GOLUMBIC, born Washington, D.C., December 27, 1967; admitted to bar, 1998, Virginia; 2000, District of Columbia. *Education:* Northwestern University (B.A., 1990); University of Pennsylvania (J.D., 1998). *Member:* Virginia State Bar. ***Email:*** lgolumbic@dlalaw.com

LISA A. GOMEZ, born Toronto, Canada, September 13, 1971; admitted to bar, 1996, Illinois (Not admitted in District of Columbia). *Education:* University of Michigan (B.A., 1993); Boston University (J.D., 1996). ***Email:*** lgomez@dlalaw.com

GREG ERIC GORDON, born Norfolk, Virginia, May 12, 1975; (admission pending). *Education:* University of Virginia (B.A., 1997); Syracuse University (J.D., magna cum laude, 2001). Phi Alpha Delta. Member, Syracuse Law Review, 1999-2001. ***Email:*** ggordon@dlalaw.com

LESLI NICOLE GREEN, born Columbus, Indiana, January 10, 1976; (admission pending). *Education:* Purdue University (B.A., 1997); Vanderbilt University (J.D., 2001). ***Email:*** lgreen@dowlohnes.com

CAROLYN R. GREER, born Washington, D.C., December 5, 1967; admitted to bar, 2000, Maryland (Not admitted in District of Columbia). *Education:* George Washington University (B.B.A., 1989); Georgetown University (J.D., 1995). ***Email:*** cgreer@dlalaw.com

HAROLD HANCOCK, born Madison, Wisconsin, March 11, 1971; admitted to bar, 2000, Virginia; 2001, Wisconsin (Not admitted in District of Columbia). *Education:* University of California at Santa Cruz (B.A., 1993); University of Wisconsin-Madison (J.D., 2000). *Member:* State Bar of Wisconsin. ***Email:*** hhancock@dlalaw.com

MICHAEL R. HEATH, born Olympia, Washington, January 30, 1975; admitted to bar, 2000, Virginia; 2001, District of Columbia. *Education:* Whitman College (B.A., 1997); Duke University School of Law (J.D., cum laude, 2000). *Member:* Virginia State Bar; The District of Columbia Bar. ***Email:*** mheath@dlalaw.com

SHANNAN E. HIGGINS, born Providence, Rhode Island, January 20, 1974; admitted to bar, 1999, Virginia; 2000, District of Columbia. *Education:* Brown University (B.A., 1996); Georgetown University (J.D., 1999). *Member:* Virginia State Bar. ***Email:*** shiggins@dlalaw.com

MICHAEL C. HOCHMAN, born New York, New York, October 8, 1969; admitted to bar, 1996, New York; 1997, District of Columbia. *Education:* University of Pennsylvania (B.A., 1990); Boston College Law School (J.D., 1995). Supervising Editor, Uniform Commercial Code Reporter-Digest, 1994-1995. Law Clerk, Vice Chancellor Myron T. Steele, Delaware Court of Chancery, 1995-1996. *Member:* The District of Columbia Bar; New York State and American (Member, Sections on: Intellectual Property; Litigation) Bar Associations; International Trademark Association (Member, Remedies and Penalties Subcommittee, Anti-Counterfeiting and Enforcement Committee); Federal American Inn of Court. ***LANGUAGES:*** Spanish and French. ***Email:*** mhochman@dlalaw.com

JOHN B. HOOVER, born Harrisonburg, Virginia, September 14, 1960; admitted to bar, 1985, Georgia; 1986, Virginia; 1998, District of Columbia. *Education:* University of Virginia (B.S., 1982); University of Georgia (M.B.A., 1985; J.D., 1985); Georgetown University Law Center (LL.M., Taxation, with distinction, 1994). *Member:* State Bar of Georgia; Virginia State Bar; The District of Columbia Bar. ***Email:*** jhoover@dlalaw.com

KEVIN A. HUGHES, born Cleveland, Ohio, August 9, 1974; (admission pending). *Education:* Boston College, Chestnut Hill (B.A., cum laude, 1996); Columbus School of Law of the Catholic University of America, Washington (J.D., 2001). ***Email:*** khughes@dlalaw.com

LAWRENCE T. HUMPHREY, born Bryn Mawr, Pennsylvania, January 5, 1962; admitted to bar, 1997, Georgia. *Education:* Duke University (B.S., 1983); University of South Carolina (M.B.A., 1988); University of Georgia (J.D., magna cum laude, 1997). Order of the Coif. Articles Editor, Georgia Law Review, 1996-1997. *Member:* State Bar of Georgia. (Resident, Atlanta, Georgia Office). ***Email:*** lhumphrey@dlalaw.com

JEFF JANICKE, born Port Angeles, Washington, January 19, 1973; (admission pending). *Education:* University of Washington (B.A., 1995); George Washington University (J.D., 2001). ***Email:*** jjanicke@dlalaw.com

AARON KANTER, born New York, N.Y., January 21, 1972; admitted to bar, 1998, Virginia; 2000, District of Columbia. *Education:* University of Michigan (B.A., 1994); University of Virginia (J.D., 1998). Editor, Virginia Law Review, Journal of Law and Politics. *Member:* Virginia State Bar; The District of Columbia Bar. ***Email:*** akanter@dlalaw.com

NAM EUN KIM, born May 7, 1971; admitted to bar, 1999, Virginia; 2000, District of Columbia. *Education:* Columbia University (B.A., 1993); Georgetown University (J.D., 1999). *Member:* Virginia State Bar. ***Email:*** nkim@dlalaw.com

TODD B. KLESSMAN, born Silver Spring, Maryland, November 3, 1974; admitted to bar, 1999, Maryland; 2000, District of Columbia. *Education:* University of Michigan (B.B.A., with highest distinction, 1996; J.D., 1999). *Member:* The District of Columbia Bar. ***Email:*** tklessman@dlalaw.com

(This Listing Continued)

JASON PAUL LANGLEY, born Searcy, Arkansas, December 6, 1973; admitted to bar, 2000, Maryland; 2001, District of Columbia. *Education:* Arkansas State University (B.A., 1996); Georgetown University (J.D., 2000).

KEVIN P. LATEK, born Park Ridge, Illinois, July 31, 1970; admitted to bar, 1996, California; 1997, District of Columbia. *Education:* Georgetown University (B.S.B.A., summa cum laude, 1992); University of Virginia (J.D., 1996). *Member:* State Bar of California; The District of Columbia Bar. ***Email:*** klatek@dlalaw.com

CLARK L. LeBLANC, (admission pending). *Education:* Hampden-Sydney College (B.A., 1989); American University, Washington (J.D., cum laude, 2001). Legislative Assistant, U.S. Senate Olympia J. Snowe, 1995-1997. Professional Staff Member, U.S. Senate Committee on Commerce, Science and Transportation, 1997-1999. ***Email:*** cleblanc@dlalaw.com

JOHN M. LEE, born Columbus, Georgia, February 28, 1971; admitted to bar, 1996, Georgia and Alabama. *Education:* Tulane University of Louisiana (B.A., 1993); University of Georgia (J.D., magna cum laude, 1996). Order of the Coif. Member, Georgia Law Review, 1994-1995. *Member:* Alabama State Bar; State Bar of Georgia. (Resident, Atlanta, Georgia Office). ***Email:*** jlee@dlalaw.com

MARK E. LINIADO, born Atlanta, Georgia, December 16, 1968; admitted to bar, 1999, Tennessee; 2000, District of Columbia. *Education:* Wesleyan University (B.A., 1991); Vanderbilt University (J.D., 1999). ***Email:*** mliniado@dlalaw.com

KARA D. LITTLE, born Atlanta, Georgia, October 12, 1973; admitted to bar, 1998, Maryland; 1999, District of Columbia. *Education:* University of Virginia (B.A., with distinction, 1995); Georgetown University (J.D., cum laude, 1998). *The District of Columbia Bar; Maryland State and American Bar Associations.* ***Email:*** klittle@dlalaw.com

REBECCA A. LITTLETON, born Lake Charles, Louisiana, December 3, 1962; admitted to bar, 1998, Georgia. *Education:* Georgia State University (B.B.A., 1985; M.S., 1989; J.D., cum laude, 1998). *Member:* State Bar of Georgia. (Resident, Atlanta, Georgia Office). ***Email:*** blittleton@dlalaw.com

TRACY ANDERSON LOCKLIN, born Washington, D.C., October 27, 1969; admitted to bar, 1998, Virginia; 1999, District of Columbia. *Education:* University of Virginia (B.A., 1992; J.D., 1998); College of William & Mary (M.P.P., 1999). Member, Editorial Board, Virginia Law Review. *Member:* Virginia State Bar; The District of Columbia Bar. ***Email:*** tlocklin@dlalaw.com

STEPHEN E. LOPEZ, born Ramsey, New Jersey, January 7, 1967; admitted to bar, 1992, New Mexico; 1996, District of Columbia. *Education:* University of Texas, Austin (B.B.A., with high honors, 1989; J.D., with honors, 1992); New York University (LL.M., Taxation, 1996). *Member:* State Bar of New Mexico; The District of Columbia Bar; American Bar Association. ***Email:*** slopez@dlalaw.com

GARY S. LUTZKER, born Nürnberg, Germany, August 12, 1952; admitted to bar, 1994, New York; 1997, District of Columbia. *Education:* Berklee College of Music (B.Mus., Composition, 1975); Fordham University; Benjamin N. Cardozo School of Law (J.D., 1993). Editor-in-Chief, Cardozo Arts & Entertainment Law Journal. *Member:* New York State Bar Association (Intellectual Property Law Section); The District of Columbia Bar; Federal Communications Bar Association; Copyright Society of the U.S.A. ***Email:*** glutzker@dlalaw.com

MELISSA APRIL MARSHALL, born Washington, D.C., November 16, 1975; (admission pending). *Education:* Cornell University (B.A., 1998); Georgetown University (J.D., 2001). Phi Beta Kappa. ***Email:*** marshallm@dlalaw.com

JASON S. McCARTER, born Knoxville, Tennessee, August 8, 1974; admitted to bar, 1999, Georgia. *Education:* University of Tennessee (B.A., summa cum laude, 1996); University of Virginia (J.D., 1999). Phi Beta Kappa. Editorial Board, Virginia Journal of International Law, 1997-1998. *Member:* State Bar of Georgia. (Resident, Atlanta, Georgia Office). ***Email:*** jmccarter@dlalaw.com

ROGELYN D. McLEAN, born Raleigh, North Carolina, July 28, 1974; admitted to bar, 2000, North Carolina (Not admitted in District of Columbia). *Education:* University of North Carolina at Chapel Hill (B.A., 1996); North Carolina Central University School of Law (J.D., 2000). *Member:* North Carolina State Bar. ***Email:*** rmclean@dlalaw.com

CHRISTOPHER LEE MEAZELL, born Atlanta, Georgia, September 9, 1967; (admission pending). *Education:* Florida State University (B.A., 1989); University of Georgia (J.D., 2001). Editor in Chief, Georgia Law Review, 2000-2001. (Resident, Atlanta, Georgia Office). ***Email:*** cmeazell@dowlohnes.com

AMY MIELKE, born Alexandria, Virginia, May 31, 1973; (admission pending). *Education:* Oberlin College (B.A., 1995); Vanderbilt University (J.D., 2001). ***Email:*** amielke@dlalaw.com

BARBARA K. MILLER, born Austin, Texas, August 14, 1972; admitted to bar, 1997, New York; 2000, Georgia. *Education:* Washington University (B.A., magna cum laude, 1994); University of Texas, Austin (J.D., with honors, 1997). Associate Editor, Texas Law Review, 1996-1997. *Member:* New York State Bar Association. (Resident, Atlanta, Georgia Office). ***Email:*** bmiller@dlalaw.com

(This Listing Continued)

DOW, LOHNES & ALBERTSON, PLLC, Washington—Continued

J. KEVIN MILLS, born Richmond, Virginia, November 23, 1966; admitted to bar, 1993, California; 1996, District of Columbia. *Education:* Harvard University (A.B., Government, cum laude, 1989); University of Chicago (J.D., cum laude, 1993). Comment Editor, University of Chicago Legal Forum, 1992-1993. *Member:* Los Angeles County Bar Association; State Bar of California; The District of Columbia Bar. ***Email:*** jmills@dlalaw.com

FRANCESCA MURATORI, born Charlotte, North Carolina, February 14, 1957; admitted to bar, 2000, Maryland (Not admitted in District of Columbia). *Education:* University of Miami (B.A., cum laude, 1982); Georgetown University Law Center (J.D., 2000). Andrew Hull Baker Scholar, Georgetown Law, 1998-1999. Recipient, 2000 Securities Law Writing Competition Award. Associate Editor, Georgetown Law Journal, 1998-2000. Author: "Criminal Procedure- Identifications and Custodial Interrogation," Georgetown Law Journal, May 1999. Appellate Board Member, State of Vermont Department of Development and Community Affairs, 1986-1992. *Member:* American Bar Association (Member, Business Law Section). ***Email:*** fmuratori@dlalaw.com

CARLOS M. NALDA, admitted to bar, 1993, Pennsylvania and U.S. Court of Federal Claims; 1994, U.S. Court of Appeals for the Federal Circuit; 1995, District of Columbia and U.S. Court of International Trade. *Education:* American University School of International Service (B.A., 1987); George Washington University Law School (J.D., magna cum laude, 1993). Order of the Coif. Prettyman-Leventhal American Inn of Court, 1992-1994. Recipient, Imogene Williford Constitutional Law Prize. Staff Writer, Journal of International Law and Economics. Law Clerk to Hon. Lawrence S. Margolis, U.S. Court of Federal Claims, 1993-1994. *Member:* The District of Columbia Bar. ***Email:*** cnalda@dlalaw.com

EDWARD JOHN PALMIERI, born New Britain, Connecticut, May 10, 1976; (admission pending). *Education:* College of the Holy Cross (B.A., 1998); Catholic University of America, Washington (J.D., 2001). ***Email:*** epalmieri@dlalaw.com

HARRY S. PANGAS, born Plainview, New York, February 18, 1971; admitted to bar, 1997, New York and Massachusetts (Not admitted in District of Columbia). *Education:* Syracuse University (B.S., 1993); Tulane University (J.D., 1996). ***LANGUAGES:*** French. ***Email:*** hpangas@dlalaw.com

SCOTT S. PATRICK, born Knoxville, Tennessee, November 14, 1963; admitted to bar, 1996, Maryland; 1997, District of Columbia. *Education:* Tennessee Technological University (B.S.E.E., 1987); University of Maryland (M.S.E.E., 1990); University of Virginia (J.D., 1996). *Member:* The District of Columbia Bar; Institute of Electrical and Electronics Engineers. ***Email:*** spatrick@dlalaw.com

BARRY PERSH, born Silver Spring, Maryland, September 13, 1974; admitted to bar, 1999, Maryland; 2000, District of Columbia. *Education:* Duke University (A.B., 1996); University of Virginia (J.D., 1999). ***Email:*** bpersh@dlalaw.com

DANIEL D. PRICHARD, born Arlington, Virginia, July 14, 1974; admitted to bar, 2000, Virginia (Not admitted in District of Columbia). *Education:* Emory University (B.S., 1995); University of Virginia (J.D., 2000). *Member:* Virginia State Bar. ***Email:*** dprichard@dlalaw.com

JASON E. RADEMACHER, born Orlando, Florida, July 17, 1972; admitted to bar, 2000, Wisconsin and District of Columbia. *Education:* University of Pittsburgh (B.A., 1995); University of Wisconsin (J.D., 2000). *Member:* State Bar of Wisconsin. ***Email:*** jrademacher@dlalaw.com

THEODORE L. RADWAY, born Framingham, Massachusetts, March 24, 1971; admitted to bar, 1999, Massachusetts; 2000, U.S. District Court, District of Massachusetts; 2001, District of Columbia. *Education:* Brandeis University (B.A., 1995); Georgetown University Law Center (J.D., 1999). *Member:* Massachusetts and American Bar Associations. ***Email:*** tradway@dlalaw.com

MAUREEN M. RICHARDSON, born Albany, New York, June 11, 1974; admitted to bar, 2000, New York (Not admitted in District of Columbia). *Education:* Cornell University (B.S., 1996); Georgetown University (J.D., 1999). Order of the Coif. ***Email:*** mrichardson@dlalaw.com

CHRISTOPHER D. ROMAINE, born New York, New York, January 5, 1972; admitted to bar, 1998, Delaware; 1999, New York; 2001, District of Columbia. *Education:* Brown University (A.B., magna cum laude, 1994); University of Pennsylvania (J.D., 1997). ***Email:*** cromaine@dlalaw.com

ELISA P. ROSEN, born Princeton, New Jersey, March 5, 1968; admitted to bar, 1993, New Jersey; 1995, District of Columbia. *Education:* University of Pennsylvania (B.A., 1990); George Washington University (J.D., with honors, 1993). *Member:* The District of Columbia Bar. ***Email:*** erosen@dlalaw.com

MICHAEL D. ROTHBERG, born Miami, Florida, August 23, 1969; admitted to bar, 1994, Maryland; 1996, District of Columbia. *Education:* Washington University (B.A., 1991); Harvard Law School (J.D., cum laude, 1994).

(This Listing Continued)

Phi Beta Kappa; Omicron Delta Kappa. *Member:* Maryland State and American Bar Associations; The District of Columbia Bar. ***Email:*** mrothber@dlalaw.com

DAVID M. RUDIN, born Los Angeles, California, December 13, 1971; admitted to bar, 1998, Massachusetts; 2001, District of Columbia. *Education:* University of California at Santa Barbara (B.A., 1994); Boston University (J.D., 1998). *Member:* The District of Columbia Bar. ***Email:*** drudin@dlalaw.com

HEATHER BERNER SACHS, born Brooklyn, New York, December 16, 1974; admitted to bar, 1999, California; 2001, District of Columbia. *Education:* University of Pennsylvania (B.A., magna cum laude, 1996); Columbia University School of Law (J.D., 1999). Harlan Fiske Stone Scholar. Editor, Columbia Journal of Law and the Arts. *Member:* State Bar of California; The District of Columbia Bar; American Bar Association. ***Email:*** hsachs@dlalaw.com

BRIAN M. SALB, born Washington, D.C., July 28, 1975; admitted to bar, 2000, California (Not admitted in District of Columbia). *Education:* Boston College (B.A., 1997); Duke University (J.D., 2000). ***Email:*** bsalb@dlalaw.com

ELIZABETH M. R. SALGADO, born Lynchburg, Virginia, July 19, 1966; admitted to bar, 1998, Virginia; 1999, District of Columbia. *Education:* Indiana University (B.A., Phi Beta Kappa, 1988); University of Virginia (M.Ed., 1991; J.D., 1998). Member, Editorial Board, 1996-1997 and Tax Cite Editor, 1997-1998, Virginia Tax Review. *Member:* Virginia State Bar; The District of Columbia Bar. ***Email:*** esalgado@dlalaw.com

CAROLYN SCHAFER, born Philadelphia, Pennsylvania, June 25, 1968; admitted to bar, 1996, Massachusetts and District of Columbia. *Education:* Villanova University (B.A., 1990); Catholic University (J.D., 1995). *Member:* The District of Columbia Bar. ***Email:*** cschafer@dlalaw.com

CHRISTOPHER A. SCHWAB, born Honolulu, Hawaii, February 5, 1975; admitted to bar, 1999, Georgia. *Education:* University of Georgia (B.B.A., 1996); University of Tennessee at Knoxville (J.D., summa cum laude, 1999). Order of the Coif. Articles Editor, Tennessee Law Review, 1998-1999. *Member:* State Bar of Georgia. (Resident, Atlanta, Georgia Office). ***Email:*** cschwab@dlalaw.com

NINA SHAFRAN, born Trenton, New Jersey; admitted to bar, 1991, Pennsylvania and District of Columbia. *Education:* Bryn Mawr College (B.A., 1975); Georgetown University (M.A., 1978); George Washington University (J.D., with honors, 1990). Senior Articles Editor, George Washington Journal of International Law and Economics, 1990-1991. *Member:* The District of Columbia Bar; American Bar Association (Member, International Law and Practice Section); Federal Communications Bar Association. ***Email:*** nshafran@dlalaw.com

RANDALL R. SMITH, born Stark, Florida, January 10, 1960; admitted to bar, 1994, Georgia. *Education:* Bob Jones University (B.A., 1982; M.A., 1983); University of Virginia (J.D., 1994). *Member:* State Bar of Georgia. (Resident, Atlanta, Georgia Office). ***Email:*** rsmith@dlalaw.com

MARCIA BULL STADEKER, born Kingston, Jamaica, September 20, 1968; admitted to bar, 1995, Alabama; 1996, New York; 2000, Georgia. *Education:* Harvard University (B.A., cum laude, 1989; J.D., 1994). *Member:* New York State Bar Association; Alabama State Bar; State Bar of Georgia. (Resident, Atlanta, Georgia Office). ***PRACTICE AREAS:*** Labor and Employment; First Amendment Law; Litigation. ***Email:*** mstadeker@dlalaw.com

MICHAEL J. STAWASZ, born Holyoke, Massachusetts, March 6, 1971; admitted to bar, 1997, Massachusetts (Not admitted in District of Columbia). *Education:* Dartmouth College (A.B., 1993); Georgetown University (J.D., 1997). ***Email:*** mstawasz@dlalaw.com

PHILIP R. STRZALKA, born Chicago, Illinois, May 14, 1971; admitted to bar, 1998, Illinois; 2000, Virginia (Not admitted in District of Columbia). *Education:* University of Illinois (B.S., with honors, 1992); Chicago-Kent College of Law, Illinois Institute of Technology (J.D., cum laude, 1998). *Member:* American Bar Association. ***Email:*** pstrzalka@dlalaw.com

DEBREA M. TERWILLINGER, born Norfolk, Virginia, December 11, 1974; (admission pending). *Education:* Indiana University, Bloomington (B.A., Journalism and Political Science, 1996); Columbus School of Law of The Catholic University of America (J.D., magna cum laude, 2001). Production Editor, CommLaw Conspectus, 2000-2001. *Member:* Federal Communications Bar Association. ***Email:*** dterwillinger@dlalaw.com

BRIANA E. THIBEAU, born Caribou, Maine; (admission pending). *Education:* Colby College (B.A., 1996); Boston College, Newton Centre (J.D., 2001). ***Email:*** bthibeau@dlalaw.com

KATHLEEN M. TOMCHO, born Detroit, Michigan, October 9, 1972; admitted to bar, 1997, California; 2000, Georgia. *Education:* California State University, Long Beach (B.S., cum laude, 1994); University of Southern California (J.D., 1997). Managing Editor, Southern California Law Review, 1996-1997. *Member:* State Bar of California; State Bar of Georgia. (Resident, Atlanta, Georgia Office). ***Email:*** ktomcho@dlalaw.com

SUZANNE M. UNDERWALD, born Summit, New Jersey, March 15, 1970; admitted to bar, 1995, Maryland; 1996, District of Columbia. *Education:*

(This Listing Continued)

Rutgers College (B.A., with highest honors, 1992); Georgetown University (J.D., magna cum laude, 1995). Phi Beta Kappa; Order of the Coif. *Member:* The District of Columbia Bar. ***Email:*** sunderwald@dlalaw.com

E. ADAM WEBB, born Lexington, Kentucky, February 25, 1971; admitted to bar, 1996, Georgia. *Education:* Harvard University (B.A., cum laude, 1993); University of Georgia (J.D., cum laude, 1996). Member, Georgia Law Review, 1994-1995. *Member:* State Bar of Georgia. (Resident, Atlanta, Georgia Office). ***Email:*** awebb@dlalaw.com

BETH D. WILKINSON, born Newark, New Jersey, October 25, 1963; admitted to bar, 1989, New York; 1991, District of Columbia; 1998, North Carolina. *Education:* Johns Hopkins University (B.A., 1985); Duke University (J.D., 1988). *Member:* New York State Bar Association; North Carolina State Bar; The District of Columbia Bar. (Resident, Atlanta, Georgia Office). ***Email:*** bwilkinson@dlalaw.com

BRIAN J. WINTERFELDT, born Cincinnati, Ohio, September 7, 1972; admitted to bar, 2000, New York; 2001, District of Columbia. *Education:* Emory University (B.A., 1993); Georgetown University Law Center (J.D., 1999). Member, International Trademark Association, 2000. *Member:* The District of Columbia Bar. ***Email:*** bwinterfeldt@dlalaw.com

JILL M. WOOD, born Arlington, Texas, May 9, 1965; admitted to bar, 1992, Georgia. *Education:* University of Georgia (A.B.J., magna cum laude, 1987); Georgia State University (J.D., cum laude, 1992). Member, Georgia State Law Review, 1990-1992. *Member:* State Bar of Georgia. (Resident, Atlanta, Georgia Office). ***Email:*** jwood@dlalaw.com

MATTHEW F. WOOD, born Pittsburgh, Pennsylvania, April 23, 1972; (admission pending). *Education:* Columbia University (B.A., 1994); Harvard University (J.D., 2001). Phi Beta Kappa. Radio Operator, FCC License, U.S., 1989. ***LANGUAGES:*** Limited Proficiency in Spanish and French. ***Email:*** mwood@dlalaw.com

LAWRENCE K. WORKMAN, JR., born Okinawa, Japan, May 21, 1969; admitted to bar, 2000, New York; 2001, District of Columbia. *Education:* The Citadel (B.S.E.E., 1991); University of Virginia (J.D., 1999). Tau Beta Pi. *Member:* Institute of Electric and Electronic Engineers. [U.S. Navy, (Nuclear), 1989-1996; Active Lt. 1996—, inactive]. ***Email:*** kworkman@dlalaw.com

NICOLE WYNN, born Baltimore, Maryland, December 23, 1969; admitted to bar, 1997, Maryland; 1998, District of Columbia. *Education:* Yale University (B.A., 1991); University of Chicago Law School (J.D., 1996). *Member:* Maryland State and American Bar Associations; The District of Columbia Bar. ***LANGUAGES:*** French, German and Spanish. ***Email:*** nwynn@dlalaw.com

SENIOR COUNSEL

CHRISTINA S. WADYKA, born Stockholm, Sweden, October 19, 1962; admitted to bar, 1987, District of Columbia. *Education:* Smith College (B.A., 1984); Emory University (J.D., 1987). Order of the Coif. Notes and Comments Editor, Emory Law Journal, 1986-1987. Recipient, American Jurisprudence Award in Civil Procedure and Antitrust Law. *Member:* The District of Columbia Bar. ***LANGUAGES:*** Swedish, French. ***Email:*** cwadyka@dlalaw.com

TO-QUYEN TRUONG, born Saigon, Vietnam, September 6, 1965; admitted to bar, 1989, Virginia; 1991, District of Columbia. *Education:* Yale University (B.A., summa cum laude, 1986; J.D., 1989). Associate Cable Bureau Chief, Federal Communications Commission, 1999-2000. *Member:* Virginia State Bar; The District of Columbia Bar. ***Email:*** ttruong@dlalaw.com

OF COUNSEL

FAYETTE B. DOW (1881-1962).

GAYLEN D. KEMP, born Stamford, Connecticut, October 3, 1952; admitted to bar, 1977, Massachusetts; 1979, Georgia. *Education:* University of Colorado (B.A., magna cum laude, 1974); Boston University (J.D., 1977). Symposium Editor, Boston University Law Review, 1976-1977. *Member:* State Bar of Georgia (Chairperson, Corporate & Banking Law Section, 1993-1994); Massachusetts Bar Association. (Resident, Atlanta, Georgia Office). ***Email:*** gkemp@dlalaw.com

HORACE L. LOHNES (1897-1954).

FRED W. ALBERTSON, born Fairgrove, Michigan, 1908; admitted to bar, 1934, Michigan; 1935, District of Columbia. *Education:* University of Michigan (A.B., 1931); University of Michigan Law School (J.D., 1934). Chairman, Washington Section, Institute of Electrical and Electronics Engineers (Institute of Radio Engineers), 1946-47. Member, House of Delegates, American Bar Association, 1953-54. Chairman, Standing Committee on Communications, American Bar Association, 1957-58. President, Federal Communications Bar Association, 1953-54. Life Fellow, American Bar Foundation.

CONSULTANT

JAMES SEARS BRYANT, born Enid, Oklahoma, May 11, 1953; admitted to bar, 1978, Oklahoma; 1984, U.S. Supreme Court; 1985, District of Columbia; 1988, Texas. *Education:* Phillips University (B.S., 1975); Southern Methodist University (J.D., 1978); Harvard University; Brandeis University (M.A., 1980). Phi Delta Phi. Adjunct Professor, Political Science, American Judiciary, Phillips University, 1984 and 1986. Assistant District Attorney, 1979-1980, Special District Judge, 1981, Associate District Judge, 1982-1984, and District Judge, 1984-1985. Member, Board of Trustees, Phillips University, 1986—. General Counsel, Philips Theological Seminary. *Member:* Oklahoma Bar Association; The District of Columbia Bar; State Bar of Texas; American Historical Association; Organization of American Historians. ***LANGUAGES:*** French.

(This Listing Continued)

DOWELL & DOWELL, P.C.

WASHINGTON, D.C.

(See Arlington, Virginia)

Patents, Trademarks, Copyrights, Unfair Competition and Intellectual Property.

DRENNAN & ASSOCIATES

Established in 1992

1216 SIXTEENTH STREET, N.W.
WASHINGTON, D.C. 20036
Telephone: 202-835-2600
Facsimile: 202-835-0452
Email: jdrennan@drennanassoc.com
URL: http://www.lawyers.com/janedrennanlaw

Energy, Transportation, Environmental Law and related Regulatory Matters.

D. JANE DRENNAN, born Champaign, Illinois, March 4, 1944; admitted to bar, 1969, Indiana; 1976, U.S. Supreme Court; 1980, District of Columbia. *Education:* Connecticut College; Indiana University (B.A., 1965); Indiana University (J.D., 1969); Georgetown University (LL.M., 1975). Attorney, Federal Energy Regulatory Commission, 1976-1979. Special Assistant, Federal Power Commission, 1974-1976. General Counsel for Policy, Federal Property Council, Executive Office of the President, 1973-1974. *Member:* Federal Energy Bar Association; American Bar Association (Member, Public Utility, Natural Resources and Administrative Law Sections; Member, Presidential Private Sector Task Force Study, 1982). ***Email:*** jdrennan@drennanassoc.com

DRINKER BIDDLE & REATH LLP

A Pennsylvania Limited Liability Partnership

1500 K STREET, N.W., SUITE 1100
WASHINGTON, D.C. 20005-1208
Telephone: 202-842-8800
Fax: 202-842-8465.
Cable Address: "Debemac"
URL: http://www.dbr.com

Philadelphia, Pennsylvania Office: One Logan Square, 18th & Cherry Streets. Telephone: 215-988-2700. Telefax: 215-988-2757. Cable Address: "Debemac."

Florham Park, New Jersey Office: Drinker Biddle & Shanley LLP, 500 Campus Drive, Telephone: 973-360-1100. Fax: 973-285-1625.

Princeton, New Jersey Office: Drinker Biddle & Shanley LLP, Suite 300, 105 College Road East. Telephone: 609-716-6500. Telefax: 609-799-7000.

Berwyn, Pennsylvania Office: Suite 300, 1000 Westlakes Drive. Telephone: 610-993-2200. Telefax: 610-993-8585.

Federal Administrative, Legislative and Litigation Practice including: Communications, common carrier, satellite, telephony, emerging technologies, broadcast and cable; Antitrust, including merger approval, treble damage litigation, and practice before the Federal Trade Commission; Insurance including directors' and officers' liability, fidelity bond, environmental and other forms of business insurance; Intellectual Property; Education Law; Legislative Advocacy and Commercial Litigation.

RESIDENT PARTNERS

JOE D. EDGE, born Birmingham, Alabama, October 28, 1948; admitted to bar, 1973, Alabama; 1975, District of Columbia. *Education:* Auburn University (B.S., 1970); University of Alabama (J.D., 1973); George Washington University (LL.M., 1976). ***PRACTICE AREAS:*** Telecommunications Law; Regulatory Law; Antitrust Law. ***Email:*** edgejd@dbr.com

MICHAEL L. GASSMANN, born Lincoln, Nebraska, October 9, 1952; admitted to bar, 1978, Virginia; 1980, District of Columbia. *Education:* University of Virginia (B.A., 1975); Harvard University (J.D., 1978). ***PRACTICE AREAS:*** Directors & Officers Liability and Insurance Law; Professional Liability Insurance Law. ***Email:*** gassmaml@dbr.com

(This Listing Continued)

DRINKER BIDDLE & REATH LLP, Washington—Continued

JOHN C. HOCKENBURY, born Somerville, New Jersey, December 7, 1951; admitted to bar, 1987, Maryland; 1989, District of Columbia. *Education:* Moravian College (B.A., 1973); Drew University (M.A., 1979); George Washington University (J.D., 1986). ***PRACTICE AREAS:*** Directors and Officers Liability Insurance. ***Email:*** hockenjc@dbr.com

ALAN J. JOAQUIN, born Fall River, Massachusetts, May 2, 1960; admitted to bar, 1986, New York; 1992, Massachusetts; 1995, District of Columbia. *Education:* Providence College (B.A., 1982); Catholic University of America (J.D, 1985). ***PRACTICE AREAS:*** Commercial Litigation. ***Email:*** joaquiaj@dbr.com

JOSEPH F. JOHNSTON, JR., born Birmingham, Alabama, October 8, 1933; admitted to bar, 1961, New York; 1970, District of Columbia; 1981, Pennsylvania. *Education:* Princeton University (A.B., 1954); Harvard University (M.A., 1956; LL.B., 1960). ***PRACTICE AREAS:*** Directors & Officers Liability and Insurance Law; Professional Liability Insurance Law. ***Email:*** johnstjf@dbr.com

DOUGLAS M. MANGEL, born Elizabeth, New Jersey, April 30, 1960; admitted to bar, 1985, Maryland; 1987, District of Columbia. *Education:* Emory University (B.A., 1982; Georgetown University (J.D., 1985). ***Email:*** mangeldm@dbr.com

JOAQUIN A. MARQUEZ, born Humacao, Puerto Rico, August 1, 1942; admitted to bar, 1967, Puerto Rico; 1972, District of Columbia. *Education:* Wharton School of University of Pennsylvania (B.S. in Economics, 1964); University of Puerto Rico, San Juan, Puerto Rico (LL.B., 1967); Georgetown University (LL.M. in Taxation, 1974). ***LANGUAGES:*** Spanish and French. ***PRACTICE AREAS:*** Corporate and Securities Law; Banking Law; Legislation Law. ***Email:*** marqueja@dbr.com

PHILIP J. MAUSE, born Brooklyn, New York, September 26, 1944; admitted to bar, 1968, Iowa; 1969, California; 1973, District of Columbia. *Education:* Georgetown University (A.B., 1965); Harvard University (J.D., 1968; M.P.P., 1975). ***PRACTICE AREAS:*** Energy; Litigation; International Trade; Telecommunications Law. ***Email:*** mausepj@dbr.com

MICHAEL J. McMANUS, born Fort Sill, Oklahoma, February 20, 1950; admitted to bar, 1976, Virginia; 1979, District of Columbia. *Education:* University of Notre Dame (B.A., 1972); Tulane University of Louisiana (J.D., 1975). ***PRACTICE AREAS:*** Litigation; Insurance Coverage Litigation. ***Email:*** mcmanumj@dbr.com

M. HOWARD MORSE, born Louisville, Kentucky, May 30, 1959; admitted to bar, 1984, District of Columbia. *Education:* Dartmouth College (A.B., 1981); Harvard University (J.D., 1984). ***PRACTICE AREAS:*** Antitrust Law. ***Email:*** morsemh@dbr.com

MARK L. PELESH, born New York, N.Y., November 7, 1953; admitted to bar, 1978, District of Columbia. *Education:* Stanford University (A.B., 1975); Yale University (J.D., 1978). ***SPECIAL AGENCIES:*** U.S. Department of Education; Postal Rate Commission; Federal Communications Commission. ***PRACTICE AREAS:*** Litigation; Education; Administrative Law. ***Email:*** peleshml@dbr.com

MICHAEL J. REMINGTON, born Baraboo, Wisconsin, June 5, 1945; admitted to bar, 1973, Wisconsin; 1981, District of Columbia. *Education:* University of Wisconsin-Madison (B.S., 1967; J.D., 1973). ***PRACTICE AREAS:*** Intellectual Property; General Lobbying. ***Email:*** remingmj@dbr.com

RICHARD M. SINGER, born Mt. Vernon, New York, September 3, 1946; admitted to bar, 1972, District of Columbia and New York. *Education:* University of Pennsylvania (B.A., 1968; J.D., 1971). ***PRACTICE AREAS:*** Telecommunications Law; Regulatory Law. ***Email:*** singerrm@dbr.com

ROBERT A. SKITOL, born Albany, New York, 1946; admitted to bar, 1970, District of Columbia. *Education:* Hobart College (B.A., 1967); New York University (J.D., 1970). ***PRACTICE AREAS:*** Antitrust; Litigation. ***Email:*** skitolra@dbr.com

NORM D. ST. LANDAU, born New Brunswick, New Jersey, March 2, 1956; admitted to bar, 1980, New Mexico; 1983, District of Columbia. *Education:* Occidental College (A.B., 1977); Antioch School of Law (J.D., 1979). ***PRACTICE AREAS:*** Intellectual Property Law; Advertising Law; Entertainment Law. ***Email:*** stlandnd@dbr.com

COUNSEL

STEPHEN G. JANOSKI, born New York, N.Y., December 20, 1962; admitted to bar, 1989, Pennsylvania; 1990, District of Columbia; 1991, New York. *Education:* University of Pennsylvania (B.A., 1985); University of Baltimore (J.D., 1989). ***Email:*** janosksg@dbr.com

JOHN R. PRZYPYSZNY, born Chicago, Illinois, April 1, 1965; admitted to bar, 1990, Illinois; 1991, District of Columbia. *Education:* Georgetown University (A.B., 1987); Georgetown University Law Center (J.D., 1990). ***SPECIAL AGENCIES:*** Federal Communications Commission; U.S. Department of Education. ***Email:*** przypyjr@dbr.com

OF COUNSEL

ROBERT N. COOK, born Frankfurt, Germany, October 12, 1957; admitted to bar, 1990, District of Columbia; 1993, Virginia. *Education:* Johns Hopkins University (B.A., 1979); George Mason University School of Law (J.D., 1990). ***PRACTICE AREAS:*** Antitrust; Trade Regulation; Administrative Law. ***Email:*** cookrn@dbr.com

HENRY W. LEEDS, born Atlantic City, New Jersey, April 25, 1931; admitted to bar, 1956, Michigan and District of Columbia. *Education:* Wharton School of Commerce and Finance, University of Pennsylvania (B.S. in Ec., 1953); University of Michigan (J.D., 1956). ***PRACTICE AREAS:*** Trademark Law; Copyright Law. ***Email:*** leedshw@dbr.com

KENNETH E. RYAN, born Mystic, Connecticut, February 27, 1963; admitted to bar, 1988, Massachusetts; 1989, District of Columbia. *Education:* Boston College (B.A., 1985); George Washington University (J.D., 1988). ***PRACTICE AREAS:*** Insurance Law; Civil Litigation. ***Email:*** ryanke@dbr.com

RESIDENT ASSOCIATES

ADAM L. BAREA, born New York, New York, July 24, 1973; admitted to bar, 2000, New York and Maryland (Not admitted in District of Columbia). *Education:* Columbia University (B.A., 1996; J.D., 1999). Harlan Fiske Stone Scholar. Law Clerk to the Hon. Alexander Harvey, II. ***LANGUAGES:*** Spanish. ***Email:*** bareaal@dbr.com

JENNIFER L. BLUM, born New York, N.Y., April 12, 1966; admitted to bar, 1995, Maryland; 1997, District of Columbia. *Education:* Trinity College (B.A., 1988); The Columbus School of Law, Catholic University of America (J.D., 1995).

AMY E. CARROLL, born Norman, Oklahoma, December 14, 1968; admitted to bar, 1996, Maryland; 1998, District of Columbia. *Education:* University of California, San Diego (B.A., 1992); American University, Washington College of Law (J.D., 1996). ***Email:*** carrolae@dbr.com

BRIAN A. COLEMAN, born Red Bank, New Jersey, January 21, 1972; admitted to bar, 1997, Virginia; 1998, Maryland and District of Columbia. *Education:* Bucknell University (B.A., 1994); George Washington University (J.D., 1997). ***Email:*** colemaba@dbr.com

JENNIFER L. DEAN, born Pittsburgh, Pennsylvania, October 30, 1971; admitted to bar, 1997, Maryland; 1998, District of Columbia. *Education:* Western Maryland College (B.A., 1993); Boston University School of Law (J.D., 1997). ***Email:*** deanjl@dbr.com

MARK F. DEVER, born Boston, Massachusetts, September 16, 1968; admitted to bar, 1993, Maryland; 1995, District of Columbia. *Education:* Boston College (B.A., 1990); Duke University (J.D., 1993). ***Email:*** devermf@dbr.com

ALISA M. EVERTS, born Hahn, Germany, June 7, 1966; admitted to bar, 1996, Virginia; 2000, District of Columbia. *Education:* University of Maryland (B.A., 1989); Vanderbilt University (J.D., 1995). ***Email:*** evertsam@dbr.com

JANET FRIES, born Scranton, Pennsylvania, May 2, 1949; admitted to bar, 1995, New York; 1996, District of Columbia. *Education:* Smith College (B.A., 1971); San Francisco State University (M.A., 1976); George Washington University (J.D., 1994). ***Email:*** friesj@dbr.com

LAURA S. GALLAGHER, born Bayport, New York, January 14, 1968; admitted to bar, 1994, Maryland; 1996, District of Columbia. *Education:* Boston College (B.A., 1990); Washington College of Law (J.D., 1994). ***Email:*** gallagls@dbr.com

DINA M. GOLD, born Far Rockaway, New York, December 11, 1967; admitted to bar, 1994, New York and District of Columbia; 1995, Maryland. *Education:* Cornell University (B.S., 1989); George Washington University (J.D., 1993). ***Email:*** golddm@dbr.com

TIMOTHY R. HUGHES, born Colorado Springs, Colorado, March 3, 1972; admitted to bar, 1997, Maryland (Not admitted in District of Columbia). *Education:* Georgetown University (B.S.F.S., cum laude, 1994); College of William & Mary (J.D., 1997). ***LANGUAGES:*** French. ***Email:*** hughestr@dbr.com

JEFFREY J. LOPEZ, born Mountain View, California, November 29, 1966; admitted to bar, 1996, California and District of Columbia. *Education:* Santa Clara University (B.A., 1992); Georgetown University (J.D., 1995). ***Email:*** lopezjj@dbr.com

ELIZABETH A. MARSHALL, born Wilmington, Delaware, March 18, 1963; admitted to bar, 1990, Virginia; 1991, District of Columbia. *Education:* Duke University (A.B., 1984); University of Virginia (J.D., 1990). ***Email:*** marshaea@dbr.com

(This Listing Continued)

JANET R. McFADDEN, born Philadelphia, Pennsylvania, September 29, 1952; admitted to bar, 1998, Maryland; 1999, District of Columbia. *Education:* Boston College (B.A., 1989); University of Texas at Austin (J.D., 1998). ***Email:*** mcfaddjr@dbr.com

KATHLEEN S. O'NEILL, born Bryn Mawr, Pennsylvania, March 31, 1971; admitted to bar, 1998, Pennsylvania (Not admitted in District of Columbia). *Education:* University of Pennsylvania (B.A., with distinction in English, 1994); Tulane Law School (J.D., cum laude, 1998). Member, Moot Court Interschool Appellate Team. Senior Managing Editor, Tulane Environmental Law Journal. ***Email:*** oneillks@dbr.com

TINA M. PIDGEON, born Schenectady, New York, September 18, 1968; admitted to bar, 1994, Virginia; 1995, District of Columbia. *Education:* University of Notre Dame (B.A., 1990); University of Virginia (J.D., 1994). ***Email:*** pidgeotm@dbr.com

JENNIFER G. SMITH, born Santa Clara, California, December 27, 1972; admitted to bar, 1998, New York (Not admitted in District of Columbia). *Education:* Florida State University (B.A., 1994); Fordham University (J.D., 1997). ***Email:*** smithjg@dbr.com

PATRICIA N. VERCELLI, born November 15, 1963; admitted to bar, 1998, Maryland (Not admitted in District of Columbia). *Education:* George Mason University (B.A., 1990); American University (J.D., 1997). ***LANGUAGES:*** Spanish and Italian. ***Email:*** vercelpn@dbr.com

MARY PATRICIA WEYBACK, born New Orleans, Louisiana, June 7, 1961; admitted to bar, 1989, Virginia; 1990, District of Columbia. *Education:* University of Virginia (B.A., 1983); Georgetown University (J.D., 1989). ***Email:*** weybacmp@dbr.com

LEGAL SUPPORT PERSONNEL
SPECIALIST (NON-LAWYER)

SHARON H. BOB, born Buffalo, New York, April 4, 1949. *Education:* State University of New York at Buffalo (B.A., 1991); University of Maryland (Ph.D., 1976). (Higher Education Specialist on Policy and Regulation). ***PRACTICE AREAS:*** Federal Higher Education Student Assistance; Compliance with Department of Education Regulations. ***Email:*** bobsh@dbr.com

(For Biographical data on all Personnel, see Professional Biographies at Philadelphia, Pennsylvania).

DRISCOLL & DRAUDE

SECOND FLOOR
1230 THIRTY-FIRST STREET, N.W.
WASHINGTON, D.C. 20007
Telephone: 202-333-0330
Cable Address: "Driscoll"
Telecopier: 202-298-6699

General Corporate, Government Contracts, Construction, Computer Law and Licensing, Environmental Law, Real Property Law and Land Use Regulation, Civil Litigation in Federal and State Courts.

MEMBERS OF FIRM

BRIAN G. DRISCOLL, born Winthrop, Massachusetts, July 18, 1948; admitted to bar, 1973, District of Columbia; 1974, U.S. District Court for the District of Columbia and U.S. Court of Appeals for the District of Columbia Circuit; 1981, U.S. Supreme Court; 1984, U.S. Claims Court; 1987, Maryland. *Education:* Amherst College (B.A., cum laude, 1970); Columbia University (J.D., 1973). *Member:* The District of Columbia Bar (Member, Government Contracts Division); Bar Association of the District of Columbia; American Bar Association (Member: Public Contract Law Section; Science and Technology Section; Construction Industry Forum Committee, 1983—); Computer Law Association. ***PRACTICE AREAS:*** Commercial Law; Construction Law; Computer Law.

JAMES T. DRAUDE, born Lancaster, Pennsylvania, February 11, 1947; admitted to bar, 1973, District of Columbia; 1974, U.S. District Court for the District of Columbia, U.S. Court of Appeals for the District of Columbia Circuit and U.S. Court of Appeals, Fourth Circuit; 1978, U.S. Claims Court; 1980, U.S. Supreme Court; 1982, U.S. Court of Appeals for the Federal Circuit; 1990, Maryland; 1993, Virginia. *Education:* Georgetown University (B.A., magna cum laude, 1969); Harvard Law School (J.D., cum laude, 1973). Trial Attorney, Land and Natural Resources Division, U.S. Department of Justice, 1978-1989. *Member:* The District of Columbia Bar (Member, Real Estate, Housing and Land Use Section); American Bar Association (Member: Business Law Section; Litigation Section; Real Property, Probate and Trust Section). ***PRACTICE AREAS:*** Civil Litigation; Land Use Regulation; Environmental Law.

DUANE, MORRIS & HECKSCHER LLP

1667 K STREET, N.W., SUITE 700
WASHINGTON, D.C. 20006-1608
Telephone: 202-776-7800
Fax: 202-776-7801
URL: http://www.duanemorris.com

Philadelphia, Pennsylvania Office: Suite 4200, One Liberty Place. Telephone: 215-979-1000. Fax: 215-979-1020.
New York, New York Office: 380 Lexington Avenue. Telephone: 212-692-1000. Fax: 212-692-1020.
London, England Office: 4 Chiswell Street, 5th Floor, EC1Y 4UP. Telephone: +44 20 7786 2100. Fax: +44 20 7786 2101.
Chicago, Illinois Office: 227 West Monroe Street, Suite 3400. Telephone: 312-499-6700. Fax: 312-499-6701.
San Francisco, California Office: 100 Spear Street, Suite 1500. Telephone: 415-371-2200. Fax: 415-371-2201.
Boston, Massachusetts Office: 470 Atlantic Avenue, Suite 500. Telephone: 617-289-9200. Fax: 617-289-9201.
Atlanta, Georgia Office: 945 East Paces Ferry Road, Suite 2440. Telephone: 404-495-4900. Fax: 404-495-4901.
Miami, Florida Office: 200 South Biscayne Boulevard, Suite 3410. Telephone: 305-960-2200. Fax: 305-960-2201.
Wilmington, Delaware Office: 1100 North Market Street, Suite 1200. Telephone: 302-657-4900. Fax: 302-657-4901.
Harrisburg, Pennsylvania Office: 305 North Front Street, 5th Floor, P.O. Box 1003. Telephone: 717-237-5500. Fax: 717-232-4015.
Malvern, Pennsylvania Office: 200 Chesterfield Parkway, Suite 100. Telephone: 610-251-6900. Fax: 610-251-6901.
Cherry Hill, New Jersey Office: 51 Haddonfield Road, Suite 340. Telephone: 856-488-7300. Fax: 856-488-7021.
Newark, New Jersey Office: One Riverfront Plaza, 2nd Floor. Telephone: 973-424-2000. Fax: 973-424-2001.
Palm Beach, Florida Office: 249 Royal Palm Way, Suite 403. Telephone: 561-366-5400. Fax: 561-366-5401.
Allentown, Pennsylvania Office: 968 Postal Road, Suite 200, P.O. Box 90400. Telephone: 610-266-3650. Fax: 610-266-3651.
Houston, Texas Office: One Greenway Plaza, Suite 500. Telephone: 713-552-9900. Fax: 713-552-0109.
Bangor, Maine Office: 88 Hammond Street, Suite 500. Telephone: 207-262-5400. Fax: 207-262-5401.
Princeton, New Jersey Office: 100 College Road West, Suite 100. Telephone: 609-919-4400. Fax: 609-919-4401.
Westchester County, New York Office: 555 Pleasantville Road, Suite 200 North Building, Briarcliff Manor, New York. Telephone: 914-749-3700. Fax: 914-749-3701.

Alternative Dispute Resolution, Bankruptcy, Commercial Law, Corporate Law, Energy, Environmental Law, Estates and Asset Planning, Franchise Law, Health Care Law, Immigration Law, Intellectual Property, International Law, Labor and Employment, Litigation, Product Liability, Real Estate, Regulatory Compliance, Reorganization and Finance, Securities Taxation and Telecommunications.

FIRM PROFILE: Duane Morris is a full-service law firm. Founded in 1904, the firm has 19 offices in the United States. In 2000, the firm established itself in the United Kingdom with the formation of Duane, Morris & Heckscher, a law firm of solicitors and registered foreign lawyers, located in London and regulated by the Law Society in the conduct of investment business.

The firm's practice is varied and sophisticated, serving clients on local, national and international levels. A versatile and committed group of lawyers employing leading edge technologies and a strong administrative infrastructure enable Duane Morris to function cohesively and effectively in today's business climate. The firm is a member of several international networks, including Multilaw and TerraLex, to enhance client service and to support a growing international practice.

PARTNERS

VIKKI A. ADAMS, admitted to bar, 1986, Pennsylvania; 1996, District of Columbia. *Education:* University of Arkansas (B.A., 1972); Stanford University; Golden Gate University (J.D., 1985). *Member:* The District of Columbia Bar. ***PRACTICE AREAS:*** International, Business and Trade; Intellectual Property; Immigration Law. ***Email:*** vaadams@duanemorris.com

BRIAN D. ALPRIN, born Providence, Rhode Island, August 3, 1954; admitted to bar, 1979, Rhode Island; 1980, District of Columbia. *Education:* Yale University (B.A., 1976); The George Washington University (J.D., 1979). Judicial Clerk to Honorable Joseph R. Weisberger of Rhode Island Supreme Court, 1979-1980. ***PRACTICE AREAS:*** Financial Institutions Law; Antitrust Law; Corporate Law. ***Email:*** bdalprin@duanemorris.com

STEPHEN M. AZIA, admitted to bar, 1989, District of Columbia and Connecticut. *Education:* Colgate University (B.A., 1986); University of Con-

(This Listing Continued)

DUANE, MORRIS & HECKSCHER LLP, Washington—Continued

necticut School of Law (J.D., 1989). ***PRACTICE AREAS:*** Healthcare Law; Managed Care; Medicare and Medicaid Reimbursement and Coverage; Fraud and Abuse; Legislative and Regulatory Advocacy. ***Email:*** smazia@duanemorris.com

GARY L. BOHLKE, born Yakima, Washington, March 9, 1941; admitted to bar, 1967, District of Columbia; 1996, Maryland. *Education:* University of Washington (B.A., 1963); The American University, Washington College of Law (J.D., 1966); University of London, School of Economics and Political Science (LL.M., 1967); London Institute of World Affairs, International and Comparative Air and Space Law (Diploma, 1967). Assistant Solicitor and Senior Attorney, Office of the Solicitor, U.S. Department of the Interior, 1974-1988. Attorney Advisor, Office of the General Counsel, U.S. Army Corps of Engineers, Washington, D.C., 1972-1974. ***PRACTICE AREAS:*** International Law; Environmental Law; Corporate Law. ***Email:*** glbohlke@duanemorris.com

ALAN C. BROWN, born Milwaukee, Wisconsin, May 19, 1952; admitted to bar, 1977, Virginia; 1980, District of Columbia. *Education:* University of Notre Dame (B.A., 1974); George Washington University (J.D., high honors, 1977). Trial Attorney, Civil Division, Frauds Section and Commercial Litigation Branch, U.S. Department of Justice, 1977-1981. Vice Chair, Technology Committee of the Health Law Section of the American Bar Association. ***PRACTICE AREAS:*** Information and Privacy; Security; Healthcare; Government Contracts. ***Email:*** acbrown@duanemorris.com

CHRISTOPHER L. CROSSWHITE, born Garden Grove, California, March 5, 1958; admitted to bar, 1983, Texas; 1996, District of Columbia. *Education:* Rice University (B.A., 1980); University of Texas (J.D., 1983). ***PRACTICE AREAS:*** Health Care Law; Medicare and Medicaid; Corporate Compliance Matters; Medicare Reimbursement Controversies and Appeals; Healthcare Fraud; Abuse Provisions. ***Email:*** clcrosswhite@duanemorris.com

VALERIE J. EASTWOOD, born Miami, Florida, December 14, 1955; admitted to bar, 1987, Florida (Not admitted in District of Columbia). *Education:* Florida International University (B.F.A., 1980); University of Miami (J.D., 1987); Georgetown University (LL.M., in Taxation, 1994). Judicial Law Clerk, Honorable Nicholas Laezza and the Honorable Giles McCarthy, U.S. Department of Labor. Office of Hearings and Appeals, Social Security Administration: Attorney/Advisor, Office of the Chief Administrative Law Judge, Division of Medicare Part B, Washington, D.C., 1995; Attorney/Advisor, U.S. Department of Health and Human Services, Washington, D.C., 1989-1995. Attorney/Advisory, Office of Administrative Law Judges, U.S. Department of Labor, Washington, D.C., 1987-1989. ***PRACTICE AREAS:*** Healthcare Law; Fraud and Abuse; Medicare and Medicaid Reimbursement; Compliance Reviews and Guidance. ***Email:*** vjeastwood@duanemorris.com

KEITH H. ELLIS, born Northampton, Pennsylvania, 1950; admitted to bar, 1976, Virginia; 1977, District of Columbia; 1993, Delaware. *Education:* The George Washington University (B.A., 1972); Washington College of Law of American University (J.D., 1976). State Bar Commissioner, Dover, State of Delaware, 1988-1994. Legislative Counsel/Director of Federal Legislation, 1980-1988. Counsel, U.S. House of Representatives, Committee Banking Finance and Urban Affairs, Washington, D.C., 1979-1980. ***PRACTICE AREAS:*** Financial Institutions; Administrative Law; Corporate Law. ***Email:*** khellis@duanemorris.com

JOHN W. GRIFFIN, born Boston, Massachusetts, July 13, 1946; admitted to bar, 1973, District of Columbia. *Education:* Trinity College (B.A., 1969); Georgetown University (J.D., 1973). Attorney Advisor, Office of the Chief Counsel, Division of Corporation Finance, 1973; Staff Member, Division of Trading and Markets and Division of Corporation Finance, 1969-1973, Securities and Exchange Commission. *Member:* The District of Columbia Bar. ***PRACTICE AREAS:*** Corporate and Securities Law; Litigation; Transactional Matters; Securities; Exchange Commission Enforcement Matters. ***Email:*** jwgriffin@duanemorris.com

SHEILA SLOCUM HOLLIS, born Denver, Colorado, July 15, 1948; admitted to bar, 1974, Colorado; 1975, District of Columbia. *Education:* University of Colorado (B.S., 1971); University of Denver (J.D., 1973). Partner-in-Charge, Washington, D.C. Office, Duane, Morris & Heckscher LLP. Director, Office of Enforcement of the Federal Energy Regulatory Commission, Washington, D.C., 1977-1980. Trial Attorney, Federal Power Commission, Washington, D.C., 1974-1975. President, Women's Council on energy and Environment, 1997—. Chair, 2000-2001, Representative to the House of Delegates, 1995— and Chair, Standing Committee on Environmental, 1997—, Section of Environment, Energy and Resources, American Bar Association. ***LANGUAGES:*** Spanish. ***PRACTICE AREAS:*** Energy Transactions; Energy Regulatory Law; International Law; Administrative Law. ***Email:*** sshollis@duanemorris.com

BRAD C. JOHNSON, born Mankato, Minnesota, February 10, 1949; admitted to bar, 1975, District of Columbia. *Education:* Mankato State University, formerly Minnesota State Teachers College (B.S., 1971); Georgetown University (J.D., 1975). Washington Counsel to Governor Mario M. Cuomo, 1976-1993. Director, New York State Office of Federal Affairs, 1978-1985. Legislative Counsel, New York State Office of Federal Affairs, 1975-1977. ***PRACTICE AREAS:*** International Project Development and Finance; Governmental Relations. ***Email:*** bcjohnson@duanemorris.com

LAURENCE S. LESE, born Philadelphia, Pennsylvania, May 8, 1945; admitted to bar, 1970, Maryland; 1982, Colorado; 1983, District of Columbia. *Education:* Cornell University (B.A., 1967; J.D., 1970). Special Counsel, 19800-1981 and Attorney-Adviser, 1970-1980, Securities and Exchange Commission, Division of Corporation Finance, Washington, D.C. ***PRACTICE AREAS:*** Federal and State Securities; Mergers and Acquisitions; Corporate Law; Partnership Law. ***Email:*** lese@duanemorris.com

CHRISTOPHER W. MAHONEY, born Buffalo, New York, April 20, 1959; admitted to bar, 1985, District of Columbia. *Education:* Union College (B.A., summa cum laude, 1981); London School of Economics, London, England; Georgetown University (J.D., 1985). Phi Beta Kappa. Staff Member, 1983-1984 and Associate Editor, 1984-1985, The Tax Lawyer. Co-Author: "Water Contamination Suits Likely to Hit N.Y.: Vexing Issues Seen Arising in Claims Over MTBE," *The Metropolitan Corporate Counsel*, December 1999 at 6. Author: "Anatomy of a Winning Defense," *Inside Litigation*, Vol. 12, No. 7, July 1998 at 6. ***PRACTICE AREAS:*** Complex Civil Litigation; Environmental; Toxic Tort; Mass Torts; Commercial And Business Tort Matters; Product Liability. ***Email:*** cmahoney@duanemorris.com

WILLIAM R. MAPES, JR., born Cleveland, Ohio, November 29, 1952; admitted to bar, 1978, District of Columbia. *Education:* Miami University (B.S., 1974); American University (J.D., 1977). ***PRACTICE AREAS:*** Energy Law; Litigation; Appellate Practice. ***Email:*** wrmapes@duanemorris.com

ANDREW E. MISHKIN, born New York, N.Y., November 14, 1947; admitted to bar, 1975, District of Columbia. *Education:* Yale University (A.B., 1968); Georgetown University (J.D., 1975). ***PRACTICE AREAS:*** Environmental Law; Real Estate Law; Regulatory Law; Commercial Law; Transactional Matters. ***Email:*** aemishkin@duanemorris.com

MARK F. PRETZAT, born New York, New York, March 16, 1956; admitted to bar, 1982, District of Columbia and New York. *Education:* Georgetown University (A.B., 1978); St. John's University (J.D., 1981). Chairman, Financial Institutions Subcommittee, Corporation, Finance and Securities Law Section, District of Columbia Bar, 2001-2002. Senior Attorney, 1984-1987 and Attorney, 1981-1984, Federal Deposit Insurance Corporation, Legal Division, Washington, D.C. ***PRACTICE AREAS:*** Financial Institutions Law; Corporate Law. ***Email:*** pretzat@duanemorris.com

TERRY F. QUILL, born Detroit, Michigan, July 8, 1954; admitted to bar, 1988, Michigan; 1991, District of Columbia. *Education:* Wayne State University (B.S., 1976; M.S., Biology, 1977); University of Michigan (M.S., in Toxicology, 1983); University of Michigan Law School (J.D., 1988). *Member:* American Bar Association (Chair, Special Committee on Science and Technology, Section of Environment, Energy and Resources). ***PRACTICE AREAS:*** Environmental Law; Toxic Substances. ***Email:*** tfquill@duanemorris.com

DAVID H. ROBBINS, born Lancaster, Pennsylvania, November 1, 1953; admitted to bar, 1993, Maryland; 1995, District of Columbia. *Education:* Temple University (B.B.A., 1975; M.B.A., 1977); George Washington University (J.D., 1993). ***PRACTICE AREAS:*** Health Care Fraud; Health Care Litigation; Regulation; Medicare Reimbursement Appeals; "Stark" Rules; Health Care Law. ***Email:*** dhrobbins@duanemorris.com

DENYSE SABAGH, born Washington, D.C., September 27, 1948; admitted to bar, 1977, Virginia; 1982, District of Columbia. *Education:* University of Maryland (B.A., 1970); George Mason University (J.D., 1977). ***PRACTICE AREAS:*** Immigration and Nationality Law; Immigration Litigation. ***Email:*** dsabagh@duanemorris.com

STEPHEN L. TEICHLER, born Charleston, West Virginia, January 30, 1952; admitted to bar, 1977, Virginia; 1979, District of Columbia. *Education:* University of Virginia (B.A., 1974; J.D., 1977). ***PRACTICE AREAS:*** Energy Law and Litigation. ***Email:*** slteichler@duanemorris.com

DANIEL P. WEITZEL, born Detroit, Michigan, September 23, 1956; admitted to bar, 1981, District of Columbia. *Education:* John Carroll University (B.S., 1978); Georgetown University Law Center (J.D., 1981). ***PRACTICE AREAS:*** Banking Law; Corporate Law; Securities; Executive Compensation; Employee Benefits. ***Email:*** dpweitzel@duanemorris.com

DOUGLAS WOLOSHIN, born Queens, New York, February 19, 1948; admitted to bar, 1973, District of Columbia. *Education:* Villanova University (B.A., 1970); Georgetown University (J.D., 1973). ***LANGUAGES:*** French. ***PRACTICE AREAS:*** Corporate Law; Taxation. ***Email:*** dwoloshin@duanemorris.com

ASSOCIATE

GREGG K. STEPAN, born Salt Lake City, Utah, November 20, 1971; admitted to bar, 1999, Utah; 2000, District of Columbia. *Education:* Brigham

(This Listing Continued)

Committee on Energy and Environment, National Governors' Association, 1983-1985. *Member:* The District of Columbia Bar; Energy and American Bar Associations. ***PRACTICE AREAS:*** Energy; Legislative Law; Environmental Law. ***Email:*** jcg@dwgp.com

THOMAS L. RUDEBUSCH, born Milwaukee, Wisconsin, January 17, 1956; admitted to bar, 1986, Wisconsin; 1993, District of Columbia. *Education:* University of Wisconsin-Milwaukee (B.A., with honors, 1977); Washington University (A.M., 1979); University of Wisconsin (J.D., 1986). Attorney-Advisor, Office of Administrative Law Judges, Federal Energy Regulatory Commission, 1986-1987. *Member:* State Bar of Wisconsin; The District of Columbia Bar; Energy and American Bar Associations. ***PRACTICE AREAS:*** Energy; Administrative Law. ***Email:*** tlr@dwgp.com

MICHAEL R. POSTAR, born Providence, Rhode Island, January 8, 1954; admitted to bar, 1979, Rhode Island and Massachusetts; 1981, District of Columbia. *Education:* George Washington University (B.A., 1976); Washington University (J.D., 1979). Co-Author, "Warren's Cable Regulation Manual," Warren Publishing, Inc., 1993. *Member:* Rhode Island, Massachusetts, Federal and American Bar Associations; The District of Columbia Bar. ***PRACTICE AREAS:*** Energy; Communications Law. ***Email:*** mrp@dwgp.com

TATJANA M. SHONKWILER, born Zagreb, Croatia, March 9, 1964; admitted to bar, 1990, Massachusetts; 1991, District of Columbia. *Education:* University of Toronto, Toronto, Ontario, Canada (B.A., 1985); Harvard University (J.D., 1988). Co-Author, "Warren's Cable Regulation Manual," Warren Publishing, Inc., 1993. *Member:* The District of Columbia Bar; American Bar Association. ***PRACTICE AREAS:*** Public Utility Law; Communications Law; Environmental Law. ***Email:*** tms@dwgp.com

ELI D. EILBOTT, born Hewlett, New York, November 10, 1961; admitted to bar, 1987, New York; 1988, District of Columbia; U.S. Supreme Court; U.S. Court of Appeals, Federal, D.C. and Fifth Circuits; U.S. District Court, District of Columbia; registered to practice before U.S. Patent and Trademark Office. *Education:* University of Pennsylvania (B.A., 1983); American University, Washington College of Law (J.D., 1986). Deputy General Counsel, Environmental Technology Council, 1991-1996. *Member:* The District of Columbia Bar; American Bar Association; International Trademark Association. ***PRACTICE AREAS:*** Intellectual Property; Patents; Trademarks; Energy; Public Utility Law; Environmental Law. ***Email:*** EDE@dwgp.com

---

LISA S. GAST, born New Brunswick, New Jersey, October 14, 1970; admitted to bar, 1997, Maryland; 1998, U.S District Court, District of Columbia; 1999, District of Columbia. *Education:* Pennsylvania State University (B.S., 1992); Rutgers University Law School (J.D., 1997). Editor, Rutgers Law Journal. Author, "Developments in State Constitutional Law: 1995," Judicial and Legislative Branch, Rutgers Law Journal, Summer 1996. *Member:* Energy and American Bar Associations. ***PRACTICE AREAS:*** Energy. ***Email:*** lsg@dwgp.com

SEAN M. NEAL, born San Diego, California, April 2, 1974; admitted to bar, 1999, Maryland; 2000, District of Columbia. *Education:* Stanford University (B.A., 1996); Georgetown University Law Center (J.D., 1999). Phi Beta Kappa. Recipient, The International Academy of Trial Lawyers Advocacy Award. Managing Editor, Georgetown International Environmental Law Review, 1998-1999. Author: "Bringing Developing Nations on Board the Climate Change Protocol: Using Debt-for-Nature Swaps To Implement the Clean Development Mechanism," Georgetown International Environmental Law Review, Vol. XI Issue I (Fall 1999). *Member:* Energy Bar Association. ***LANGUAGES:*** German. ***PRACTICE AREAS:*** Energy Law; Environmental Law. ***Email:*** smn@dwgp.com

JOSEPH C. HALL, born Niantic, Connecticut, July 31, 1973; admitted to bar, 2000, Maryland (Not admitted in District of Columbia). *Education:* Vanderbilt University (B.S., 1996); Tulane University of Louisiana, School of Law (J.D., 2000). Senior Justice, Moot Court Board, 1999-2000. Member, Philip Jessup International Law Appellate Team. Senior Notes and Comments Editor, The Tulane Environmental Law Journal, 1999-2000. *Member:* American Bar Association. ***PRACTICE AREAS:*** Energy Law; Telecommunications. ***Email:*** jch@dwgp.com

OF COUNSEL

FREDERICK L. MILLER, JR., born Jersey City, New Jersey, June 24, 1943; admitted to bar, 1968, District of Columbia; 1974, U.S. Supreme Court. *Education:* Yale University (B.A., 1965); Georgetown University (J.D., 1968); George Washington University (LL.M., Natural Resources, 1975). Professorial Lecturer in Law, George Washington University Law School, 1975-1981. Assistant General Counsel, National Capital Planning Commission, 1968-1970. Trial Attorney, Land and Natural Resources Division, U.S. Department of Justice, 1970-1974. Special Assistant Attorney General: State of North Dakota, 1977-1987; State of South Dakota, 1982-1986. Special Deputy Attorney General, State of Nevada, 1982-1987. *Member:* The District of Columbia Bar; American Bar Association. ***PRACTICE AREAS:*** Natural Resources; Energy; Civil Litigation.

(This Listing Continued)

BARRY F. McCARTHY, born Chicago, Illinois, September 20, 1948; admitted to bar, 1975, California. *Education:* Marquette University; University of Santa Clara (B.A., 1970; J.D., cum laude, 1975). Assistant City Attorney, City of Santa Clara, 1977-1984. *Member:* State Bar of California. (Resident, San Jose, CA Office; also practicing individually, San Jose, CA). ***PRACTICE AREAS:*** Energy; Municipal Law; Communications Law. ***Email:*** bmcc@mccarthylaw.com

THOMAS J. LYNCH, born Syracuse, New York, April 17, 1946; admitted to bar, 1973, New York; 1975, U.S. District Court, Northern District of New York. *Education:* Canisius College (B.S., 1968); State University of New York at Buffalo (J.D., 1972). Town Justice, 1986-1987. Village Attorney, Village of Solvay, 1991—. *Member:* New York State and American Bar Associations. [U.S. Army Infantry Reserve, 1970-1976]. (Resident, Syracuse, NY Office; also practicing individually, Syracuse, NY). ***Email:*** lynchlaw@aiusa.com

TERRY E. SINGER, born New York, N.Y., May 8, 1954; admitted to bar, 1994, Pennsylvania; 1996, District of Columbia. *Education:* Bryn Mawr College (A.B., cum laude, 1975); Yale University (M.B.A., 1981); George Washington University (J.D., 1994). Executive Director, National Association of Energy Service Companies, 1986—. *Member:* The District of Columbia Bar. ***PRACTICE AREAS:*** Energy. ***Email:*** tes@dwgp.com

JAMES F. FLUG, born Brooklyn, New York, January 17, 1939; admitted to bar, 1963, New York; 1975, District of Columbia; U.S. Supreme Court. *Education:* Harvard University (A.B., magna cum laude, 1960; LL.B., magna cum laude, 1963). Phi Beta Kappa. Member, Harvard Law Review, 1961-1963. Law Clerk to Chief Judge David Bazelon, D.C. Circuit, 1963-1964. Legal Assistant to the Assistant Attorney General, Tax Division, 1964-1965. Confidential Assistant to the Attorney General of the United States, 1965-1967. Legislative Assistant, U.S. Senator Edward M. Kennedy, 1967-1969. Chief Counsel, Subcommittee on Administrative Practice and Procedure, U.S. Senate Committee on the Judiciary, 1969-1973. Executive Director, National Legal Aid and Defender Association, 1973-1975. Director and Counsel, Energy Action, 1975-1979. Partner, Lobel, Novins & Lamont; Lobel, Novins, Lamont & Flug, 1980-1994. Member, Administrative Conference of the United States, 1974-1980. Chair, Harvard Law School Association Public Interest Committee. *Member:* The District of Columbia Bar; American Bar Association. ***PRACTICE AREAS:*** Energy; Administrative Law; Federal Litigation; State Representation. ***Email:*** jff@dwgp.com

PAULA N. DINERSTEIN, born New York, N.Y., June 10, 1949; admitted to bar, 1980, District of Columbia; 1996, U.S. Court of Appeals, Federal Circuit; 1999, U.S. Court of Appeals, Tenth Circuit. *Education:* University of Maryland (B.S., 1973); George Washington University (J.D., 1980). Law Clerk to Judge Joyce Hens Green, U.S. District Court, District of Columbia, 1980-1982. *Member:* The District of Columbia Bar. ***Email:*** pnd@dwgp.com

KATHLEEN L. MAZURE, born Bad Axe, Michigan, February 22, 1961; admitted to bar, 1985, Maryland; 1989, Virginia and District of Columbia; U.S. Court of Appeals, District of Columbia Circuit; 1992, U.S. Court of Appeals, Eleventh Circuit and U.S. Supreme Court. *Education:* University of Michigan (B.A., 1981); College of William and Mary, Marshall Wytle School of Law (J.D., 1985). Attorney Advisor to the Federal Energy Regulatory Commission Administrative Law Judges, 1986-1988. Assistant People's Counsel, District of Columbia, 1988-1990. *Member:* Federal Energy Bar Association. ***PRACTICE AREAS:*** Energy Law; Public Utility Law. ***Email:*** KLM@DWGP.com

A List of Representative Clients will be furnished upon request.
REFERENCE: NationsBank, N.A.

LAW OFFICES OF
MICHAEL C. DURNEY

1072 THOMAS JEFFERSON STREET, N.W.
WASHINGTON, D.C. 20007
Telephone: 202-965-7744
Fax: 202-965-7745
Email: mcd@mdurney.com

Civil and Criminal Tax Controversy, Federal Fraud Practice in Federal Courts and Before Federal Departments and Agencies, Mediation and Arbitration, International Tax Controversies.

MICHAEL C. DURNEY, born Piedmont, California, May 20, 1943; admitted to bar, 1969, California; 1972, District of Columbia and U.S. Supreme Court. *Education:* University of California at Berkeley (A.B., 1965); Hastings College of Law, University of California (J.D., 1968). Phi Delta Phi. Member, Editorial Board, Hastings Law Journal, 1967-1968. Trial Attorney, Tax Division, Department of Justice, 1968-1972. Deputy Assistant and Acting Assistant Attorney General, Tax Division, Department of Justice, 1986-1988. Co-Author:

(This Listing Continued)

LAW OFFICES OF MICHAEL C. DURNEY, Washington—Continued

"Criminal Tax Procedure," Tax Management Portfolio No. 162-2nd. Member, U.S. Court of Federal Claims Advisory Council, 1993—. *Member:* The District of Columbia Bar; State Bar of California; Federal (Chairman: Court and Tax Procedure Committee, 1977-1982; Section of Taxation, 1982-1984; Senior Advisory Committee, 1984—) and American (Member, Sections of: Taxation; Criminal Justice; Litigation) Bar Associations. (Also Of Counsel to Moore & Bruce, Washington, D.C.).

DYER ELLIS & JOSEPH

A PROFESSIONAL CORPORATION

WATERGATE - ELEVENTH FLOOR
600 NEW HAMPSHIRE AVENUE, N.W.
WASHINGTON, D.C. 20037
Telephone: 202-944-3000
Telecopier: 202-944-3068
URL: http://www.dyerellis.com
Email: info@dejlaw.com
URL: http://www.dejlaw.com

Practice before Federal Courts and Agencies, Legislative Practice, Shipping, Government Contracts, Healthcare, Antitrust, International Transactions, General Corporate, Securities Regulation, Tax, Environmental, White Collar Crime, Litigation, Trademark and Copyright.

THOMAS M. DYER, born Orange, New Jersey, October 19, 1945; admitted to bar, 1973, District of Columbia. *Education:* Georgetown University (B.A., 1967); George Washington University (J.D., with highest honors, 1973). Order of the Coif. Member, George Washington Law Review, 1971-1973. [Lt., U.S. Navy, 1967-1969]. ***PRACTICE AREAS:*** Maritime Law; Transactions; Ship Finance. ***Email:*** tmd@dejlaw.com

JAMES B. ELLIS II, born Washington, D.C., October 5, 1944; admitted to bar, 1973, District of Columbia. *Education:* United States Coast Guard Academy (B.S., with highest honors, 1966); Massachusetts Institute of Technology (M.S., Management, 1980); George Washington University (J.D., with highest honors, 1973). Order of the Coif. Member, George Washington University Law Review, 1971-1973. Special Assistant to the Secretary of Transportation and Alternate U.S. Representative to the Third United Nations Conference on the Law of the Sea, 1980-1982. [Comdr., U.S. Coast Guard, 1966-1982]. ***PRACTICE AREAS:*** Maritime Law; Maritime Finance; Corporate Finance. ***Email:*** jbe@dejlaw.com

MICHAEL JOSEPH, born Reading, Pennsylvania, May 22, 1936; admitted to bar, 1961, District of Columbia. *Education:* Cornell University (A.B., 1958); University of Pennsylvania (LL.B., 1961). Attorney, Office of the General Counsel, Securities and Exchange Commission, 1961-1966. ***PRACTICE AREAS:*** Litigation; Securities; Mergers, Acquisitions and Divestitures; Capital Formation; Entrepreneurial Business Law. ***Email:*** mj@dejlaw.com

BRIAN A. BANNON, born Brooklyn, New York, September 27, 1951; admitted to bar, 1981, District of Columbia. *Education:* Brooklyn College of the City University of New York (B.A., cum laude, 1973); George Washington University (J.D., with honors, 1981). Deputy Chief of Contracts, U.S. Arms Control and Disarmament Agency, Washington, D.C., 1977-1982. ***PRACTICE AREAS:*** Government Contracts; Intellectual Property; Proprietary Rights; Copyrights. ***Email:*** bab@dejlaw.com

EDWARD M. BARBERIC, born Cleveland, Ohio, March 10, 1949; admitted to bar, 1988, New York; 1995, District of Columbia. *Education:* Case Western Reserve University (B.A., 1971; M.A., 1973); University of Pennsylvania (M.A., 1975; Ph.D., 1979; J.D., 1987). Editor, University of Pennsylvania Journal of International Business Law, 1985-1987. *Member:* American Bar Association (Taxation Section). ***PRACTICE AREAS:*** Tax Law; International Trade and Transactions; Mergers and Acquisitions. ***Email:*** emb@dejlaw.com

JANE F. BARRETT, born Monterey, California, September 13, 1952; admitted to bar, 1976, Maryland; 1979, District of Columbia. *Education:* Loyola College (B.A., 1973); University of Maryland (J.D., 1976). Assistant U.S. Attorney, District of Maryland. ***PRACTICE AREAS:*** Litigation; White Collar Criminal Defense; Environmental Criminal Defense; Environmental Law; Environmental Compliance. ***Email:*** jfb@dejlaw.com

ALEX BLANTON, born Lake City, Florida, February 13, 1944; admitted to bar, 1973, District of Columbia; 1985, Texas. *Education:* United States Coast Guard Academy (B.S., 1966); Catholic University of America (J.D., 1972). Editor-in-Chief, Catholic University Law Review, 1971-1972. [Comdr., U.S. Coast Guard, 1966-1986]. ***PRACTICE AREAS:*** Litigation; Maritime Law; Administrative Litigation; Shipbuilding and Repair; Appellate Practice. ***Email:*** eab@dejlaw.com

(This Listing Continued)

PATRICK O. CAVANAUGH, born Glendive, Montana, June 25, 1958; admitted to bar, 1983, Virginia; 1986, District of Columbia. *Education:* George Mason University (B.S., with distinction, 1980; J.D., 1983). Phi Delta Phi. Editor-in-Chief, GMU Law Review. Trial Attorney, Torts Branch, Civil Division, U.S. Department of Justice, 1983-1986. ***PRACTICE AREAS:*** Litigation; Product Liability; Environmental Law; Business Planning. ***Email:*** poc@dejlaw.com

JOSEPH O. CLICK, born Columbus, Ohio, February 23, 1954; admitted to bar, 1986, California; 1989, District of Columbia. *Education:* San Diego State University (A.B., cum laude, 1981); University of California at Davis (J.D., 1986). Order of the Coif. Recipient, American Jurisprudence Award for Civil Procedure, Evidence, Constitutional Law, Trust Wills and Estates. Law Clerk, U.S. Court of Appeals, Ninth Circuit, 1986-1988. Staff Attorney, Office of the General Counsel, Securities and Exchange Commission, 1988-1990. ***PRACTICE AREAS:*** Litigation; Bankruptcy; Securities Fraud. ***Email:*** joc@dejlaw.com

THOMAS M. DiBIAGIO, born Baltimore, Maryland, June 6, 1960; admitted to bar, 1985, Maryland; 1986, District of Columbia. *Education:* Dickinson College (B.A., 1982); University of Richmond (J.D., 1985). Adjunct Professor, University of Baltimore. ***PRACTICE AREAS:*** White Collar Crime; Environmental Law; Commercial Litigation. ***Email:*** tdb@dejlaw.com

JAMES S. W. DREWRY, born Alexandria, Virginia, April 9, 1944; admitted to bar, 1969, Virginia; 2000, District of Columbia. *Education:* Randolph-Macon College (B.A., 1966); University of Virginia (LL.B., 1969); London School of Economics (LL.M., 1975). Lieutenant, Judge Advocate General's Corps, U.S. Navy, 1969-1974. Attorney, Office of General Counsel, National Oceanic and Atmospheric Administration, 1975-1980. Democratic General Counsel, Committee on Commerce, Science, and Transportation, U.S. Senate, 1980-1999. [Lt. Comdr., U.S. Naval Reserve, 1969-1978]. ***PRACTICE AREAS:*** Legislative Practice; Lobbying; Technology and Science. ***Email:*** jsd@dejlaw.com

BRETT M. ESBER, born Cleveland, Ohio, December 28, 1958; admitted to bar, 1984, Virginia; 1985, District of Columbia. *Education:* The Ohio State University (B.S., summa cum laude, 1981); Georgetown University Law Center (J.D., 1984). ***PRACTICE AREAS:*** Maritime Law; Commercial Law; Corporate Law; Finance. ***Email:*** bme@dejlaw.com

JEANNE MARIE GRASSO, born Camden, New Jersey, January 18, 1961; admitted to bar, 1994, Maryland; 1995, District of Columbia. *Education:* University of Notre Dame (B.S., 1983); University of Southern California (M.M.A., 1985); University of Maryland (J.D., with honors, 1994). Order of the Coif. ***PRACTICE AREAS:*** Environmental Law; Maritime Law; Environmental Compliance; Federal Regulatory Law. ***Email:*** jmg@dejlaw.com

JOHN E. GRAYKOWSKI, born Colorado Springs, Colorado, August 17, 1953; admitted to bar, 1989, District of Columbia. *Education:* State University of New York-Brockport (B.Sc., magna cum laude, 1975); George Washington University (M.A., 1980); Catholic University (J.D., 1989). Staff Counsel, U.S. Senate Commerce Committee, 1989. Professional Staff, U.S. House of Representatives and U.S. Senate, 1975-1988. Deputy Maritime Administrator, U.S. Maritime Administration. ***PRACTICE AREAS:*** Maritime Finance; Maritime Law; Transportation; Legislative; Government. ***Email:*** jeg@dejlaw.com

JOHN G. HENDERSON, born New York, N.Y., April 6, 1962; admitted to bar, 1990, Virginia (Not admitted in District of Columbia). *Education:* Lake Forest College (B.A., 1983); American University (J.D., 1989). Former Assistant General Counsel, Export-Import Bank of the United States, 1990-1998. ***PRACTICE AREAS:*** Structured Finance; Aircraft Finance and Leasing; Project Finance; Financial Restructuring; Debtor and Creditor Workouts. ***Email:*** jgh@dejlaw.com

PAUL M. HONIGBERG, born Northampton, Massachusetts, November 16, 1955; admitted to bar, 1980, District of Columbia. *Education:* Duke University (A.B., History, cum laude, 1977); Vanderbilt University (J.D., 1980). Associate Editor, Vanderbilt Journal of Transnational Law. Trial Attorney, Torts Branch, Civil Division, U.S. Department of Justice, 1980-1984, 1991-1996, 1999. Trial Attorney, Commercial Litigation Branch, Civil Division, U.S. Department of Justice, 1996-1999. Deputy Director, Tobacco Litigation Team, Torts Branch, Civil Division, U.S. Department of Justice, 2000-2001. *Member:* The District of Columbia Bar; American Bar Association (Member, Section on Litigation). ***PRACTICE AREAS:*** Litigation; Environmental Law; Toxic Torts; Products Liability; Government Contracts. ***Email:*** phonigberg@dejlaw.com

JOHN F. KEARNEY, born Washington, D.C., November 24, 1958; admitted to bar, 1991, Maryland; 1993, District of Columbia. *Education:* University of Maryland (B.A., 1981; M.B.A., 1984); George Washington University (J.D., with honors, 1991). Staff Member, 1984-1992, Branch Chief, 1989-1992, Division of Corporation Finance, U.S. Securities and Exchange Commission. ***PRACTICE AREAS:*** Securities; Mergers and Acquisitions; Capital Formation. ***Email:*** jfk@dejlaw.com

WAYNE A. KEUP, born Aberdeen, South Dakota, June 3, 1947; admitted to bar, 1976, Virginia; 1991, District of Columbia. *Education:* University of

(This Listing Continued)

Southern California (B.A., 1969); Catholic University of America (J.D., cum laude, 1976). Member, Catholic University Law Review, 1975-1976. Senior Trial Attorney, Office of the General Counsel, Department of the Navy, 1976-1982. [Lt., U.S. Navy, 1969-1976]. ***PRACTICE AREAS:*** Government Contracts; Litigation. ***Email:*** wak@dejlaw.com

RICHARD A. KIRBY, born Paris, France, November 30, 1949; admitted to bar, 1974, Maryland; 1978, District of Columbia. *Education:* Lehigh University (B.S., 1971); Catholic University of America (J.D., 1974). Senior Litigation Counsel 1989-1991 and Assistant General Counsel 1984-1989. Adjunct Professor, George Washington University; Office of General Counsel, Securities and Exchange Commission, 1978-1991. [Capt. U.S. Army (JAGC), 1975-1978]. ***PRACTICE AREAS:*** Litigation; Alternative Dispute Resolution; Bankruptcy; Securities. ***Email:*** rak@dejlaw.com

BARBARA D. LINNEY, born Winnipeg, Manitoba, September 23, 1955; admitted to bar, 1982, Saskatchewan; 1984, Alberta; 1993, New York; 1999, District of Columbia. *Education:* University of Manitoba (B.Comm., with honors, 1978); University of Saskatchewan (LL.B., with distinction, 1981); Georgetown University (LL.M., 1991). ***PRACTICE AREAS:*** Securities; Mergers and Acquisitions; International Trade; Import and Export Law; Executive Employment Law. ***Email:*** bdl@dejlaw.com

EDWARD L. LUBLIN, born New York, New York, November 14, 1940; admitted to bar, 1966, New York; 1976, California and District of Columbia; 1979, Maryland. *Education:* University Of Michigan (B.B.A., 1962; M.B.A., 1965; J.D., 1965). Attorney-Advisor, Office of the General Counsel, Securities and Exchange Commission, 1965-1968. Deputy Assistant General Counsel for Coal Regulations, Department of Energy, 1979-1982. *Member:* State Bar of California; Maryland State and American Bar Associations. ***PRACTICE AREAS:*** Corporate Law; Securities; Mergers and Acquisitions. ***Email:*** ell@dejlaw.com

WILLIAM R. MARTIN, born Pittsburgh, Pennsylvania, 1949; admitted to bar, 1976, Ohio and U.S. District Court, Southern District of Ohio; 1982, U.S. Court of Appeals, Ninth Circuit; 2000, District of Columbia. *Education:* Howard University (B.A., 1973); University of Cincinnati (J.D., 1976). United States Department of Justice, 1978-1990. Executive Assistant and Trial Assistant, U.S. Attorney, Washington, D.C., 1984-1990. Senior Trial Attorney, San Francisco Strike Force, Northern District of California, 1980-1984. Attorney in Chart, U.S. Attorney's Office, Southern District of Ohio, Dayton Office, 1978-1980. Assistant City Attorney, Cincinnati, Ohio, 1976-1978. Lead Attorney for Critical Witness, Office of Independent Counsel (Starr) investigation of President William Jefferson Clinton. ***PRACTICE AREAS:*** Litigation; White Collar Defense; Criminal Litigation; Sports and Entertainment Law; Commercial Litigation. ***Email:*** wrm@dejlaw.com

R. ANTHONY SALGADO, born Washington, D.C., May 22, 1962; admitted to bar, 1987, Virginia; 1988, District of Columbia. *Education:* University of Virginia (B.A., with distinction, 1984; J.D., 1987). Member: Senior Editorial Board, 1987; Editorial Board, 1986-1987; Virginia Journal of International Law. Law Clerk, Hon. Randy J. Holland, Supreme Court of Delaware, 1987-1988. ***PRACTICE AREAS:*** Corporate Law; International Business Law; Maritime Law; Ship Finance; Charter Parties. ***Email:*** ras@dejlaw.com

LAWRENCE S. SHER, born Newark, New Jersey, October 7, 1964; admitted to bar, 1990, New York; 1991, District of Columbia; 1993, Colorado; 1996, U.S. District Court, District of Maryland. *Education:* University of Massachusetts (B.A., cum laude, 1986), Phi Beta Kappa; Washington College of Law, American University (J.D., cum laude, 1989). *Member:* The District of Columbia Bar (Computer & Telecommunications Law Section); Inter-American Bar Association (Committees on: Business Law; Telecom & Technology). ***LANGUAGES:*** Spanish. ***PRACTICE AREAS:*** Corporate Law; Securities; Litigation. ***Email:*** lss@dejlaw.com

DUNCAN C. SMITH III, born Dover, New Jersey, August 12, 1947; admitted to bar, 1976, Virginia and District of Columbia. *Education:* Drew University (B.A., 1969); College of William & Mary (J.D., 1976). Law Specialist, Office of Chief Counsel, U.S. Coast Guard, 1976-1978. Attorney, Office of General Counsel, Department of the Treasury, 1978-1980. Chief Minority Counsel, Merchant Marine and Fisheries Committee, U.S. House of Representatives, 1980-1990. *Member:* Federal Bar Association (Chairman, Young Lawyers Division, 1978-1979); Maritime Law Association of the United States. [Capt. U.S. Coast Guard Reserve, 1970—]. ***PRACTICE AREAS:*** Legislative Practice; Lobbying; Regulatory Law. ***Email:*** dcs@dejlaw.com

JONATHAN K. WALDRON, born Washington, D.C., February 11, 1949; admitted to bar, 1981, Florida; 1990, District of Columbia. *Education:* United States Coast Guard Academy (B.S., 1971); University of Miami (J.D., with honors, 1981). Agency Law of the Sea Attorney, 1986-1990. [Comm., U.S. Coast Guard, 1971-1991]. ***PRACTICE AREAS:*** Environmental Law; Maritime Law; International Law; Pollution. ***Email:*** jkw@dejlaw.com

MARCUS R. WYLER, born Albuquerque, New Mexico, 1961; admitted to bar, 1991, Pennsylvania; 1999, District of Columbia. *Education:* Cornell University (B.A., 1983); University of Lausanne, Switzerland (Licence en droit,

(This Listing Continued)

1986); University of Pittsburgh (J.D., 1990). ***PRACTICE AREAS:*** Corporate Law; Intellectual Property; International Investments; Joint Ventures; International Business Law. ***Email:*** mrw@dejlaw.com

PAT MUNROE WOODWARD, JR., born Atlanta, Georgia, February 20, 1962; admitted to bar, 1991, Virginia and Florida; 1993, District of Columbia. *Education:* Davidson College (B.A. in History, 1984); George Mason University School of Law (J.D., 1990). Assistant to U.S. Attorney General Dick Thornburgh, 1989-1991. Assistant U.S. Attorney, District of Columbia, 1992-2001. Bush-Cheney Justice Transition Team, 2001. ***PRACTICE AREAS:*** White Collar Criminal Defense; Corporate Investigations; Corporate Compliance; Civil Litigation; Appellate Litigation. ***Email:*** PWoodward@dejlaw.com

OF COUNSEL

JOAN M. BONDAREFF, born Utica, New York, January 7, 1944; admitted to bar, 1975, Maryland; 1978, District of Columbia. *Education:* George Washington University (B.A., 1965); Washington College of Law of American University (J.D., magna cum laude, 1975). Senior Counsel, National Earth Satellite Service, 1980-1982, Assistant General Counsel for Administration, 1981-1982 and Assistant General Counsel for Ocean Services, 1982-1987, National Oceanic and Atmospheric Administration (NOAA), U.S. Dept. of Commerce. Senior Counsel, Committee on Merchant Marine and Fisheries, U.S. House of Representatives, Washington, D.C., 1987-1994. Chief Counsel, Maritime Administration, 1994-1998 and Acting Deputy Maritime Administrator, Maritime Administration, 1997-1998, U.S. Dept. of Transportation, Washington, D.C. *Member:* American Bar Association (Vice-Chair, Marine Resources Committee, National Resources and Environmental Law Section). ***PRACTICE AREAS:*** Maritime Law; Environmental Law; Administrative Law. ***Email:*** jbondareff@erols.com

GEOFFREY P. GITNER, born Chicago, Illinois, July 23, 1944; admitted to bar, 1970, Illinois and U.S. Court of Appeals, Seventh Circuit; 1972, District of Columbia and U.S. Court of Appeals, District of Columbia Circuit; 1980, U.S. Supreme Court; 1985, Virginia and U.S. Court of Appeals, Fourth Circuit; 1996, Maryland; U.S. District Court, District of Maryland. *Education:* University of Illinois (B.S., cum laude, 1966); Georgetown University (J.D., 1970). Editor, Georgetown Law Journal, 1968-1970. Author: "Prisoners' Rights under the Civil Rights Act-1983," 57 Georgetown Law Journal 1271. Northwestern University Criminal Defense Program and Ford Foundation Fellowship, 1970-1971. District of Columbia Public Defender, 1972-1974. Trial Counsel, United States Nuclear Regulatory Commission, 1975-1978. *Member:* Bar Association of the District of Columbia; The District of Columbia Bar; Virginia State Bar; Illinois State Bar Association; The Association of Trial Lawyers of America. ***PRACTICE AREAS:*** Business Litigation; Professional Malpractice; Securities Litigation; Real Estate Litigation; Arbitration; Alternative Dispute Resolution. ***Email:*** gpg@dejlaw.com

NATHALIA S. A. HARDY, born Beaufort, South Carolina, December 16, 1963; admitted to bar, 1991, Michigan and U.S. District Court, Eastern District of Michigan; 1997, Colorado (Not admitted in District of Columbia). *Education:* George Mason University (B.A., 1986); Case Western Reserve University (J.D., 1991). ***PRACTICE AREAS:*** Environmental; White Collar Crime; Litigation. ***Email:*** nsh@dejlaw.com

DEBRA M. ROBBINS, born Jackson, Mississippi, August 4, 1959; admitted to bar, 1984, Mississippi; 1991, District of Columbia. *Education:* Mississippi State University (B.S., 1980); Mississippi College School of Law (J.D., 1984). Associate Editor, Mississippi College Law Review, 1983-1984.

LINDA K. ROSENTHAL, born Oswego, New York, March 28, 1961; admitted to bar, 1987, New York; 1989, District of Columbia. *Education:* University of Virginia (B.A., 1983; J.D., 1986). Phi Beta Kappa. Executive Editor, Virginia Journal of Natural Resources Law. ***PRACTICE AREAS:*** Securities; Mergers, Acquisitions and Divestitures; Corporate Law. ***Email:*** lkr@dejlaw.com

WILLIAM L. SCHACHTE, JR., born Charleston, South Carolina, May 1, 1940; admitted to bar, 1973, South Carolina; 1977, District of Columbia. *Education:* Clemson University (B.A., 1963); University of South Carolina (J.D., 1973); George Washington University (LL.M., with highest honors, 1989). Acting Judge Advocate General of the Navy, 1992-1993. Commander, Naval Legal Service Command, 1991-1993. Member, Chairman of the Sea Subcommittee of International Law, American Bar Association, 1991-1992. DOD Representative for Ocean Policy Affairs, 1990-1993. Deputy Judge Advocate General of the Navy, 1991-1993. Commander, Naval Investigative Service Command, 1989-1990. Assistant Judge Advocate General of the Navy, 1988-1989. Certified Mediator, State and Federal Courts. Member, American Arbitration Association, National Panel of Arbitrators. [Rear Adm. (retd), U.S. Navy, 1963-1993]. ***PRACTICE AREAS:*** Government Contracts; Defense Contracts; Government. ***Email:*** bshach@aol.com

TODD D. SNYDER, born State College, Pennsylvania, December 26, 1963; admitted to bar, 1994, District of Columbia and Maryland; 1995, U.S. Tax Court. *Education:* University of Maryland (B.A., 1985; B.S., 1989; J.D., with honors, 1993). Certified Public Accountant, Maryland, 1990. ***PRACTICE***

(This Listing Continued)

DYER ELLIS & JOSEPH, A PROFESSIONAL CORPORATION, Washington—Continued

AREAS: Corporate Law; Finance; Securities; Mergers, Acquisitions and Divestitures; International Commercial Finance. ***Email:*** TSnyder@dejlaw.com

SIDNEY A. WALLACE, born Alcoa, Tennessee, 1927; admitted to bar, 1969, District of Columbia. *Education:* U.S. Coast Guard Academy (B.S., 1949); George Washington University (J.D., with honors, 1968); Auburn University (M.P.S., 1969). Counsel, Committee on Merchant Marine and Fisheries, U.S. House of Representatives, 1979-1981. Maritime Policy Advisor to Secretary of Transportation, 1977-1978. Chairman, Marine Environment Protection Committee, International Maritime Organization, 1989-1992. Chairman, Marine Board, National Academy of Sciences and National Academy of Engineering, 1988-1990. [Rear Adm. (retd), U.S. Coast Guard, 1945-1978]. ***PRACTICE AREAS:*** Maritime Law; Maritime Regulation; Marine Environmental Law; International Law; United Nations Law. ***Email:*** saw@dejlaw.com

---

THOMAS Z. CHEPLO, born Washington, D.C., October 30, 1972; admitted to bar, 1999, Maryland; 2000, District of Columbia. *Education:* University of Maryland (B.A., Economics and Spanish, 1995; M.B.A., 1999; J.D., with honors, 1999). ***Email:*** tzc@dejlaw.com

CAROLYN COFFEY, born Evanston, Illinois, April 21, 1962; admitted to bar, 1998, Maryland; 1999, District of Columbia. *Education:* University of Maryland (B.S., 1984); Catholic University of America (J.D., magna cum laude, 1998). Senior Lead Articles Editor, Journal of Contemporary Health Law and Policy, 1997-1998. Law Clerk, Hon. Howard Chasanow, Maryland Court of Appeals, 1998-1999. ***Email:*** ckc@dejlaw.com

KATIA I. FANO, born Lima, Peru, September 29, 1967; admitted to bar, 2000, Maryland (Not admitted in District of Columbia). *Education:* University of Maryland, College Park (B.S., 1995); American University (J.D., magna cum laude, 2000). ***Email:*** kif@dejlaw.com

ALAN M. FREEMAN, born Silver Spring, Maryland, August 26, 1971; admitted to bar, 1996, Maryland; 1997, District of Columbia. *Education:* Columbia University (B.A., 1993); George Washington University (J.D., 1996). Law Clerk, Hon. John Terry, District of Columbia Court of Appeals, 1996-1997. ***PRACTICE AREAS:*** Commercial Litigation; Alternative Dispute Resolution. ***Email:*** amf@dejlaw.com

CHRISTOPHER T. FURLOW, admitted to bar, 2000, Maryland (Not admitted in District of Columbia). *Education:* The University of Virginia (B.A., with distinction, 1997); The University of Virginia School of Law (J.D., 2000). Phi Beta Kappa. Dillard Fellow, 1998-1999. Senior Dillard Fellow, 1999-2000. ***LANGUAGES:*** German, French. ***Email:*** ctf@dejlaw.com

NATALIA W. GEREN, born Madrid, Spain, April 16, 1973; admitted to bar, 1999, Texas; 2000, District of Columbia. *Education:* University of Houston (B.B.A., 1995); South Texas College of Law (J.D., 1999). ***PRACTICE AREAS:*** International Trade and Transactions. ***Email:*** nwg@dejlaw.com

PETER R. JOHNSON, admitted to bar, 1999, Maryland (Not admitted in District of Columbia). *Education:* University of Maryland (B.S., 1993; J.D., 1999). Order of Barristers; International Moot Court Board, National Trial Team. Law Clerk to the Honorable Robert M. Bell, Chief Judge, Court of Appeals of Maryland, 1999-2000. ***Email:*** prj@dejlaw.com

LARA BERNSTEIN MATHEWS, born Malden, Massachusetts, February 22, 1969; admitted to bar, 1995, Maryland; 2000, District of Columbia. *Education:* University of California, Los Angeles (B.A., 1991); George Washington University; Santa Clara University (J.D., 1995). Editor, Santa Clara Law Review. ***PRACTICE AREAS:*** Legislative Practice; Maritime Law; Environmental Law; Transportation. ***Email:*** lbm@dejlaw.com

J. CHRISTOPHER NAFTZGER, born Kettering, Ohio, March 5, 1967; admitted to bar, 1995, Maryland; 1997, District of Columbia. *Education:* Hampden-Sydney College (B.A., 1989); Willamette University (J.D., 1994). Managing Editor, Willamette Law Review. ***PRACTICE AREAS:*** Administrative Law; Corporate Finance; Corporate Reorganization. ***Email:*** jcn@dejlaw.com

SHAILA LAKHANI OHRI, born Mombasa, Kenya, August 23, 1972; admitted to bar, 1997, Maryland; 1998, District of Columbia. *Education:* American University (B.A., 1994); George Washington University (J.D., 1997). Articles Editor, The George Washington Journal of International Law & Economics, 1996-1997. Law Clerk, Hon. Herbert B. Dixon, Jr., District of Columbia Superior Court, 1997-1998. ***PRACTICE AREAS:*** Corporate Law; International Business Law. ***Email:*** slo@dejlaw.com

KRISTINE L. SENDEK, born Detroit, Michigan, October 29, 1968; admitted to bar, 1997, Maryland; 1998, District of Columbia. *Education:* University of Michigan (B.A., 1990); Catholic University of America (J.D., magna cum laude, 1997). ***PRACTICE AREAS:*** Complex Litigation; Civil Litigation; Commercial Litigation. ***Email:*** kls@dejlaw.com

(This Listing Continued)

STEVEN P. STEINBERG, born Brooklyn, New York, July 29, 1968; admitted to bar, 1993, Maryland; 1994, Pennsylvania; 2000, District of Columbia. *Education:* Cornell University (B.S., 1990); George Washington University (J.D., 1993). ***PRACTICE AREAS:*** Employment Law; Litigation. ***Email:*** sps@dejlaw.com

LUIS VERNAZA, born Guayaquil, Ecuador, March 31, 1969; admitted to bar, 1995, Ecuador; 1999, New York (Not admitted in District of Columbia). *Education:* Catholic University of Guayaquil, Ecuador (B.A., 1991; J.D., 1995); George Washington University (LL.M. in International and Comparative Law, 1996). ***PRACTICE AREAS:*** International Law; International Maritime Law; International Trade. ***Email:*** lav@dejlaw.com

SUSAN L. WATSON, admitted to bar, 2000, Texas (Not admitted in District of Columbia). *Education:* Austin College (B.A., 1987); LBJ School of Public Affairs (M.P.Aff., 1993); University of Texas-Austin (J.D., 2000). ***LANGUAGES:*** Spanish. ***Email:*** slw@dejlaw.com

SHAWN M. WRIGHT, born Jackson, Mississippi, January 13, 1968; admitted to bar, 1995, Maryland; 1998, District of Columbia. *Education:* Howard University (B.A., 1992); Santa Clara University (J.D., 1995). ***PRACTICE AREAS:*** White Collar Criminal Defense; Civil Litigation; Administrative Law; Criminal Law. ***Email:*** smw@dejlaw.com

---

DYKEMA GOSSETT PLLC

FRANKLIN SQUARE, SUITE 300 WEST
1300 I STREET, N.W.
WASHINGTON, D.C. 20005-3353
Telephone: 202-906-8600
Fax: 202-906-8669
Email: mstarrs@dykema.com
URL: http://www.dykema.com

Ann Arbor, Michigan Office: 315 East Eisenhower Parkway, Suite 100, 48108-3336. Telephone: 734-214-7660. Fax: 734-214-7696.
Bloomfield Hills, Michigan Office: 39577 Woodward Avenue, Suite 300, 48304-2820. Telephone: 248-203-0700. Fax: 248-203-0763.
Chicago, Illinois Office: 55 East Monroe Street, Suite 3050, 60603-5709. Telephone: 312-551-4900. Fax: 312-551-4919.
Detroit, Michigan Office: 400 Renaissance Center, 48243-1668. Telephone: 313-568-6800. Fax: 313-568-6545.
Grand Rapids, Michigan Office: Suite 700, 300 Ottawa Avenue, N.W., 49503-2306. Telephone: 616-776-7500. Fax: 616-776-7573.
Lansing, Michigan Office: 800 Michigan National Tower, 48933-1742. Telephone: 517-374-9100. Fax: 517-374-9191.

General Practice. Antitrust and Trade Regulation, Commercial Litigation, Intellectual Property, Trademark Law, Trade Associations, Energy Law, Transportation Law, Government Contracts, Health Care Law, White Collar Crime, Regulatory Law and Legislative Practice.

FIRM PROFILE: Founded in 1926, Dykema Gossett PLLC is one the oldest and largest law firms in the United States. We represent a wide variety of clients, including Fortune 500 multinational corporations, financial institutions and health care organizations, manufacturers, retailers and distributors, government unites and trade associations, nonprofit entities and family businesses. All members of the firm participate in continuing legal education seminars, professional association activities and civic affairs. Dykema Gossett has also been recognized for outstanding contributions in pro bono legal work.

RESIDENT MEMBERS

HILARY STEPHEN CAIRNIE, born Orrville, Ohio, March 29, 1956; admitted to bar, 1989, Virginia, U.S. Court of Appeals, Fourth Circuit and U.S. District Court, Eastern and Western Districts of Virginia; 1990, U.S. Court of Appeals, Federal Circuit; 1996, U.S. Court of Federal Claims; 1997, District of Columbia; registered to practice before U.S. Patent and Trademark Office. *Education:* Purdue University (B.S.M.S.E., 1978); Massachusetts Institute of Technology (S.M., 1981), Sigma Xi; Catholic University of America (J.D., with honors, 1989). *Member:* Virginia, Federal (Member, Automatic Data Processing Procurement Committee) and American Bar Associations; Virginia State Bar; The District of Columbia Bar. ***PRACTICE AREAS:*** Government Contracts; Intellectual Property; Technology and Science. ***Email:*** hilary@dykema.com

STEVEN A. DIAZ, born New York, N.Y., May 2, 1948; admitted to bar, 1974, California, U.S. District Court, Northern and Southern Districts of California, U.S. District Court, Eastern District of Wisconsin; U.S. District Court, Northern District of Illinois; U.S. Court of Appeals, Seventh and Ninth Circuits; 1978, U.S. Supreme Court; 1994, District of Columbia. *Education:* San Francisco State University (B.A., 1970); University of Santa Clara (J.D., 1973). Faculty, College of Trial Advocacy, Hastings College of Law, University of California (1982-1986). Chief Counsel, Federal Transit Administration (1989-1993); Member, Access Board, U.S. Architectural and Transportation Barriers

(This Listing Continued)

Compliance Board (1985-1988); San Francisco State Building Authority (1985-1989); Deputy City Attorney, City and County of San Francisco, California (1974-1985). Chairman, Passenger Transportation Committee, Association for Transportation Law, Logistics and Policy (1998); Chairman, Transit and International Transportation Law Committee, Transportation Research Board, National Academies of Science (1992-1998); Quarterly Chairman, Commonwealth Club of California (1978). *Member:* Federal (President, San Francisco, CA Chapter, 1987-1988) and American (Member, 1974-1989, 1993—; Standing Committee on Law and the Electoral Process, 1984-1989) Bar Associations. ***PRACTICE AREAS:*** Transportation; Infrastructure Development; Government Contracts. ***Email:*** sdiaz@dykema.com

JOHN P. DELUCA, born New York, N.Y., March 17, 1944; admitted to bar, 1969, New York; 1972, District of Columbia; 1976, New Jersey; registered to practice before U.S. Patent and Trademark Office. *Education:* Manhattan College (B.E.E., 1965); St. John's University (J.D., 1968). Phi Alpha Delta. *Member:* The District of Columbia Bar; American Intellectual Property Law Association; Institute of Electrical and Electronics Engineers. ***PRACTICE AREAS:*** Electrical Patent; Mechanical Patent; Computer Science Patent; Trademarks; Copyrights. ***Email:*** jdeluca@dykema.com

EDWARD A. GROOBERT, born Colchester, Connecticut, October 27, 1935; admitted to bar, 1960, Connecticut; 1964, District of Columbia; 1965, U.S. Supreme Court. *Education:* Columbia University (A.B., 1957); Columbia University Law School (LL.B., 1960). Member, Board of Editors, Columbia Law Review, 1959-1960. Attorney: Appellate Section, Civil Division, U.S. Department of Justice, 1961-1963; Perlman, Lyons and Emmerglick, 1963-1965. *Member:* The District of Columbia Bar; Bar Association of the District of Columbia; Federal and American Bar Associations. ***PRACTICE AREAS:*** Trade and Professional Associations; Equipment Leasing. ***Email:*** egroobert@dykema.com

DONALD N. HUFF, born Livonia, New York, February 7, 1945; admitted to bar, 1973, District of Columbia and Virginia; registered to practice before U.S. Patent and Trademark Office. *Education:* Alfred University (B.S., Ceram. Eng., 1967; M.S., 1969); Georgetown University (J.D., 1972). Blue Key. *Member:* The District of Columbia Bar; Virginia State Bar. ***PRACTICE AREAS:*** Trademarks; Copyrights; Unfair Competition; Patents. ***Email:*** dhuff@dykema.com

D. BIARD MACGUINEAS, born Washington, D.C., April 19, 1940; admitted to bar, 1966, District of Columbia; 1973, U.S. Supreme Court. *Education:* Harvard University (A.B., 1962); Harvard Law School (LL.B., 1965). Attorney, Office of the General Counsel, Federal Communications Commission, 1965-1970. *Member:* The District of Columbia Bar; Bar Association of the District of Columbia; Federal and Federal Energy Bar Associations. ***PRACTICE AREAS:*** Trade Regulation Law; Energy Law. ***Email:*** bmacguineas@dykema.com

HOWARD E. O'LEARY, JR., born Grosse Pointe Farms, Michigan, March 22, 1938; admitted to bar, 1964, Michigan; 1973, District of Columbia. *Education:* University of Michigan (B.A., 1960; J.D., 1963). Assistant U.S. Attorney, Eastern District of Michigan, 1965-1969. Chief Counsel and Staff Director, U.S. Senate Committee on the Judiciary, Subcommittee on Antitrust and Monopoly, 1969-1977. *Member:* The District of Columbia Bar; State Bar of Michigan; American Bar Association. ***PRACTICE AREAS:*** Litigation; Business Crimes Law. ***Email:*** holeary@dykema.com

LAWRENCE R. RADANOVIC, born Harrisburg, Pennsylvania, February 15, 1938; admitted to bar, 1967, District of Columbia, U.S. Supreme Court, U.S. Court of Appeals for the Federal Circuit, registered to practice before the U.S. Patent and Trademark Office. *Education:* Catholic University of America (B.C.E., 1959; LL.B., 1963). Phi Alpha Delta. *Member:* The District of Columbia Bar; International Association for the Protection of Industrial Property; International Federation of Industrial Property; American Intellectual Property Law Association; International Trademark Association. ***PRACTICE AREAS:*** Mechanical Patents; Patent Law; Trademarks; Licensing; Litigation. ***Email:*** lradanovic@dykema.com

RICHARD H. TUSHIN, born Washington, D.C., September 19, 1946; admitted to bar, 1973, Virginia; 1976, U.S. Court of Customs and Patent Appeals; 1977, District of Columbia; registered to practice before U.S. Patent and Trademark Office. *Education:* Cornell University (B.S., 1968); Georgetown University (J.D., 1972). *Member:* The District of Columbia Bar; Virginia State Bar; American Intellectual Property Law Association. ***PRACTICE AREAS:*** Intellectual Property; Chemical Intellectual Property; Mechanical Intellectual Property. ***Email:*** rtushin@dykema.com

FRED L. WOODWORTH, born Detroit, Michigan, November 12, 1940; admitted to bar, 1966, Michigan; 1970, District of Columbia. *Education:* Amherst College (A.B., 1962); University of Michigan (J.D., with distinction, 1965). Trial Attorney, Antitrust Division, U.S. Department of Justice, 1969-1970. Assistant Director, Office of Policy Planning and Evaluation, Federal Trade Commission, 1970-1972. *Member:* Detroit Metropolitan (President, 1983-1984; Member, Board of Directors, 1979-1984) and American (Member, House of Delegates, 1991-1994) Bar Associations; State Bar of Michigan

(This Listing Continued)

(President, 1991-1992; Commissioner, 1985-1992; Chairman, Antitrust Law Section, 1976-1977). (Member in Charge of Washington, D.C. Office). ***PRACTICE AREAS:*** Antitrust Law; Trade Regulation Law. ***Email:*** fwoodworth@dykema.com

STEPHEN H. ZIMMERMAN, born Fremont, Ohio, February 4, 1947; admitted to bar, 1972, Ohio; 1977, Michigan (Not admitted in District of Columbia). *Education:* Thiel College (B.A., 1969); Ohio State University (J.D., 1972). *Member:* Ingham County and American Bar Associations; State Bar of Michigan. ***PRACTICE AREAS:*** Legislative Practice; Insurance Law. ***Email:*** szimmerman@dykema.com

OF COUNSEL

WILLIAM H. CARROLL, born Providence, Rhode Island, August 21, 1938; admitted to bar, 1971, District of Columbia. *Education:* Providence College (B.A., 1963); Catholic University of America (J.D., 1968). General Counsel, Ballistic Missile Defense Organization, 1985-1994. Special Assistant for Contracting Integrity, Defense Logistics Agency, 1985. Associate Counsel, Contracts, Defense Logistics Agency, 1976-1984. Assistant Counsel, Department of Navy, 1971-1975. Adjunct Professor of Law and Lecturer: American University, 1996—; Catholic University of America, 1993-1996. *Member:* American Bar Association. ***PRACTICE AREAS:*** Government Contracts; Administrative Law. ***Email:*** wcarroll@dykema.com

SANFORD B. RING, born Flint, Michigan, June 26, 1961; admitted to bar, 1990, Michigan; 1991, District of Columbia. *Education:* Michigan State University (B.A., 1983); Catholic University of America (J.D., 1989). ***PRACTICE AREAS:*** Government; International Trade. ***Email:*** sring@dykema.com

RESIDENT ASSOCIATES

WILLIAM A. BONK, III, born Detroit, Michigan, July 28, 1964; admitted to bar, 1995, Michigan; registered to practice before U.S. Patent and Trademark Office (Not admitted in District of Columbia). *Education:* University of Michigan (B.S.M.E., 1986); Detroit College of Law at Michigan State University (J.D., cum laude, 1994). *Member:* State Bar of Michigan. ***PRACTICE AREAS:*** Intellectual Property. ***Email:*** wbonk@dykema.com

JUDY PARKER JENKINS, born Detroit, Michigan, October 30, 1956; admitted to bar, 1985, Maryland; 1986, District of Columbia. *Education:* Michigan State University (B.A., 1978); American University (J.D., 1984). *Member:* The District of Columbia Bar; Maryland State and American Bar Associations. ***Email:*** jjenkins@dykema.com

SANDRA SNAPP, born Pueblo, Colorado, May 14, 1965; admitted to bar, 1995, Wyoming; 1996, Colorado; 1997, District of Columbia. *Education:* University of Wyoming (B.S., 1989); Thomas M. Cooley Law School (J.D., 1993). *Member:* Wyoming State Bar; The District of Columbia Bar; American Intellectual Property Law Association. ***SPECIAL AGENCIES:*** Examiner, U.S. Patent and Trademark Office, 1993-1997. ***Email:*** ssnapp@dykema.com

EATON & McCLELLAN

1111 14TH STREET, N.W., SUITE 777
WASHINGTON, D.C. 20005
Telephone: 202-789-0088
Fax: 202-789-1377
Email: apeem@earthlink.net

Philadelphia, Pennsylvania Office: 230 South Broad Street, Third Floor, 19102. Telephone: 215-875-0600. Fax: 215-875-0617.

Civil Litigation. Professional Liability, Medical Malpractice, Auto Torts, Aviation Law, Products Liability, Insurance, Wrongful Death, Commercial Employment and Labor Law, Toxic Torts Insurance Law, General Practice.

MEMBERS OF FIRM

ALLEN T. EATON, born Laurel, Mississippi, January 12, 1935; admitted to bar, 1970, Virginia; 1971, District of Columbia and U.S. District Court for the District of Columbia. *Education:* West Virginia State College (B.S., 1956); George Washington University Law School (J.D., with honors, 1970). Author: "Strict Liability For Prescription Drug Injuries: The Improper Marketing Theory," 26 St. Louis U.L.J.#1 (1981); "Explosion In Mass Tort Litigation-Handling And Maintaining Mass Tort Cases," Volume 2, Number 2, National Bar Association Magazine, 1988. Adjunct Professor of Law, Washington College of Law, American University, Washington, D.C., 1989-1993. Citizen Member, Commonwealth of Virginia Consolidated Laboratory Services Advisory Board, 1990-1995. *Member:* National Bar Association; Trial Lawyers Association of Metropolitan Washington, D.C. (Member, Board of Governors, 1988-1992); Trial Lawyers for Public Justice (Founding Member); Washington, D.C. Lawyers Committee for Civil Rights Under Law (Member, Board of Directors, 1988-1995). [Major, Artillery, U.S. Army, 1957-1967]. ***REPORTED CASES:*** Reese v. Batesville Casket Company; Stanton v. Astra Pharmaceuticals, Inc. 718

(This Listing Continued)

EATON & McCLELLAN, Washington—Continued

F.2d 553 (3d Cir 1983); Washington v. Washington Hospital Center, 579 A.2d 177 (D.C. App. 1990); McDaniel v. Merck, Sharpe & Dohme 533 A.2d 436 (Pa. Sup. 1987). ***PRACTICE AREAS:*** Professional Negligence (Medical, Dental, Legal); Directors and Officers Liability Claims; Products Liability. ***Email:*** ateem@earthlink.net

FRANK M. McCLELLAN, born Marion, South Carolina, February 5, 1945; admitted to bar, 1971, Pennsylvania and District of Columbia. *Education:* Rutgers University (A.B., 1967); Duquesne University Law School (J.D., with honors, 1971); Yale University (LL.M., 1974). Member, Duquesne University Law Review, 1966-1968. Recipient: Merit Award for Academic Excellence, Duquesne; Felix S. Cohen Prize in Jurisprudence, Yale. Law Clerk to the Hon. William H. Hastie, former Chief Judge, U.S. Court of Appeals, Third Circuit. Author: Publications: Contingent Fees, Ethical, Legal and Economic Considerations, National Bar Association Magazine, Vol. 2 No. 3 (July 1988); The Law of Medical Malpractice; An overview, Ch. 1 in Bundy, *Radiology and the Law* (1988); Making Health Care Decisions for Handicapped Infants, Temple Esquire (alumni magazine) (Spring 1985); Informed Consent to Medical Therapy and Experimentation: The Case for Invoking Punitive Damages to Deter Impingement of Individual Autonomy, 3 The Journal of Legal Medicine 81 (March 1982); Strict Liability for Drug-Induced Injuries: An Excursion Through the Maze of Products Liability, Negligence and Absolute Liability, 25 Wayne Law Review 1 (1978), reprinted in Specialty Law Digest: Health Care (August 1979). Co-Author: Publications: (with T. Tate and A. Eaton), Liability for Prescription Drug Injuries: The Improper Marketing Theory, 26 St. Louis U.L.J. 1 (1981). Book: (with Phillips, Terry & Maraist), Torts: Cases, Materials & Problems (Michie Co. 1991). Medical Malpractice (Temple University 1994). Professor of Law: Duquesne University School of Law; 1972-1980; Temple University School of Law, 1981—. Adjunct Professor, Temple University School of Medicine, 1984—. Recipient, Lindback Award, Temple University, 1986. President, Board of Directors, Pennsylvania Legal Services Center. *Member:* American Bar Association; National Bar Association; The Association of Trial Lawyers of America. (Resident, Philadelphia Office). ***REPORTED CASES:*** Wiltshire v. Government of V.I., 893 F.2d 629 (3d Cir. 1990); McDaniel v. Merck, Sharp & Dohme, 367 Pa Sup. 660, 533 A.2d 436 (1987); Stanton v. Astra Pharmaceuticals, Inc., 718 F.2d 553, (3d Cir. 1983). ***PRACTICE AREAS:*** Medical Malpractice; Commercial Litigation; Products Liability. ***Email:*** eatonmcc@aol.com

ASSOCIATES

LA' VERN D. WILEY, born Natchez, Mississippi, March 16, 1958; admitted to bar, 1983, Louisiana; 1990, District of Columbia; 1991, Maryland; 1992, U.S. District Court, District of Maryland; 1994, U.S. District Court, District of Columbia; 1997, U.S. Supreme Court. *Education:* Jackson State University (B.A., cum laude, 1978); Southern University (J.D., with honors, 1982); George Washington University. Editor-In-Chief, Southern University Law Review, 1981-1982. Author: "A Change of Custody: Determining the Best Interests of the Child," 6 So. Univ. L. Rev. 279, 1980. *Member:* Trial Lawyers Association of Metropolitan Washington, D.C.; The Association of Trial Lawyers of America. ***REPORTED CASES:*** Washington Metropolitan Area Transit Authority v. Johnson, 726 A.2d 172 (D.C. App. 1999); Tandra S. v. Tyrone W.; Baltimore City Office of Child Support Enforcement of the State of Maryland, Department of Human Resources v. John S., Jr., 336 Md 303, 648 A.2d 439 (1994); Washington Metropolitan Area Transit Authority v. Johnson, 699 A.2d 404 (D.C. App. 1997). ***PRACTICE AREAS:*** Personal Injury; Medical Malpractice; Products Liability. ***Email:*** yleem@earthlink.net

EMMANUEL O. IHEUKWUMERE, born Kafanchan, Kaduna State, Nigeria, December 14, 1962; admitted to bar, 1995, Pennsylvania (Not admitted in District of Columbia). *Education:* Clarion University of Pennsylvania (B.A., 1990); Temple University (J.D., 1995). Recipient: Bertram K. Wolf Prize, Temple University School of Law, 1995; Distinguished Class Performances in: Civil Rights Remedies; Constitutional Law; Constitutional Law and Foreign Policy; Employment Law; Trusts and Estates. Law Clerk to the Hon. Ricardo C. Jackson, Philadelphia Court of Common Pleas. Author: "HIV Positive Medical Practitioners: Legal and Ethical Obligations to Disclose," 71 St. John's L. Rev. 715, Fall 1997; "Punitive Damages in Pennsylvania: Is Gross Negligence Enough?" 69 Pa. B.A.Q. 180, October 1998; "Prescription Drugs Liability: Is Strict Liability Dead?" 70 Pa. B.A.Q. 135, July 1999; "Not Enough Progress (on Minority Hiring, Promotion, and Retention)," 21-AUG Pa. Law. 38, Pennsylvania Lawyer, July 1999; "Reality of Discrimination, Necessity of Affirmative Action," Philadelphia Lawyer Magazine, Vol. 62, No. 3, Fall 1999. Co-Author, with C. L. Thorpe, "Admissibility of Scientific Evidence Under Pennsylvania Law: An Excursion Through the Frye Test," Pa. B.A.Q., July 2000. *Member:* Philadelphia and Pennsylvania Bar Associations; The Association of Trial Lawyers of America. ***PRACTICE AREAS:*** Medical Malpractice; Products Liability; Personal Injury.

CAROL E. BELL, born Pittsburgh, Pennsylvania, July 28, 1959; admitted to bar, 1999, Pennsylvania; New Jersey (Not admitted in District of Columbia). *Education:* Cornell University (B.S., 1986); Temple University (J.D., 1999). *Member:* Philadelphia, Pennsylvania (Member, Minority Bar Committee), National and American Bar Associations. ***PRACTICE AREAS:*** Medical Malpractice; Products Liability.

ECCLESTON AND WOLF

A PROFESSIONAL CORPORATION

1750 K STREET, N.W., SUITE 450

WASHINGTON, D.C. 20006-2300

Telephone: 202-857-1696

Fax: 202-857-0762

Baltimore, Maryland Office: 729 E. Pratt Street - 7th Floor, Scarlett Place. Telephone: 410-752-7474. Fax: 410-752-0611.

Fairfax, Virginia Office: 10875 Main Street, Suite 201. Telephone: 703-218-5330.

General Trial and Appellate Practice in all Courts with concentration in Insurance Defense Litigation including Legal Malpractice, Medical Malpractice, Claims against Architects, Engineers, Accountants, Realtors, School Boards and other Professionals and Products Liability, Pharmaceutical Manufacturer's Liability, Automobile Tort, Workers Compensation and General Aviation. Additional areas of concentration: Insurance Coverage, Corporate, Contract, Commercial Law, Labor and Employment Law.

AARON L. HANDLEMAN, born Bridgeport, Connecticut, March 31, 1946; admitted to bar, 1971, District of Columbia; 1972, Maryland and U.S. District Court, District of Columbia Circuit; 1978, U.S. Supreme Court; 1984, U.S. Court of Appeals for the Federal Circuit and U.S. Court of Appeals, Fourth Circuit; 1988, U.S. District Court, District of Maryland. *Education:* Marietta College (B.A., cum laude, 1968); George Washington University (J.D., with honors, 1971). Phi Beta Kappa. Member, Board of Trustees, Marietta College, Marietta, Ohio, 1985-1990; 1992-1994. Author: Co-Contributor, American Insurance Attorneys, "Insurance & Tort Desk Reference - D.C. Section," Fall 1990. *Member:* The District of Columbia Bar; Maryland State and American (Member, Sections on: Litigation; Tort and Insurance Practice; General Practice) Bar Associations. ***PRACTICE AREAS:*** Insurance Defense Law; Professional Malpractice Law; Legal Malpractice Law; Insurance Coverage; Complex Litigation. ***Email:*** handleman@ewdc.com

RONALD W. FUCHS, born Baltimore, Maryland, November 27, 1944; admitted to bar, 1974, Maryland, U.S. District Court, District of Maryland and U.S. Court of Appeals, Fourth Circuit; 1996, District of Columbia; 1997, U.S. District Court for the District of Columbia. *Education:* University of Virginia (B.S., 1967); University of Baltimore (J.D., magna cum laude, 1974). Member, Heuisler Honor Society. *Member:* The Bar Association of Baltimore City; Maryland State and American Bar Associations. [Lt., USNR, 1967-1971]. ***PRACTICE AREAS:*** Insurance Defense Law; Professional Malpractice Law; Accounting Malpractice Law; Legal Malpractice Law; Architectural Malpractice Law; Aviation Law; Construction Defect Litigation; Complex Litigation; Real Estate Errors and Omissions. ***Email:*** fuchs@ewdc.com

JEFFREY J. HINES, born Decatur, Alabama, November 29, 1959; admitted to bar, 1985, Maryland; 1986, District of Columbia; 1987, U.S. District Court, District of Maryland; 1988, U.S. District Court, District of Columbia; 1998, U.S. Court of Appeals for the District of Columbia Circuit; 1999, Virginia. *Education:* University of Maryland (B.A., 1981; J.D., with honor, 1985). Recipient, American Jurisprudence Award, Domestic Relations. Co-Author: "The Erosion of Secondary Liability for Attorneys Under The Federal Securities Laws," ABA Section of Litigation, Professional Litigation News-Letter, Summer 1994. *Member:* The District of Columbia Bar; Virginia State Bar; District of Columbia Defense Lawyers Association; Defense Research Institute. ***PRACTICE AREAS:*** Insurance Defense Law; Professional Malpractice Law; Securities Litigation; Legal Malpractice Law; Appellate Practice; Real Estate Errors and Omissions; Psychotherapy Law. ***Email:*** hines@ewdc.com

Richard W. Driscoll
Craig Stephen Brodsky
Heather Shanan O'Connor (Not admitted in DC)
Matthew William Lee
Juli Z. Simonyi
Theresa M. Hummel
George S. Mahaffey, Jr. (Not admitted in DC)

REPRESENTATIVE CLIENTS: American National Lawyers Insurance Reciprocal; CNA Insurance Companies; Coregis Group; Design Professionals Insurance Company; Environmental Claims Administration, Inc.; Executive Risk Management Services, Inc.; First Colony Life Insurance Company; Frontier Insurance Company; Gate Pharmaceuticals; Gerling American Insurance Company; Insurance Company of North American (CIGNA); Lawyers Title Insurance Company; Legal Mutual Insurance Society of Maryland, Inc.; Life of Virginia Insurance Company; Metropolitan Property and Liability Insurance Company; Montgomery Mutual Insurance; Motors Insurance Corporation (MIC); National Union Fire Insurance Company of Pittsburgh, P.A. (American International Group); Nationwide Insurance Company; Philadelphia Insurance Companies; Premo Pharmaceutical Laboratories, Inc.; Pro-

(This Listing Continued)

fessional Risk Management Services, Inc.; Providian Insurance Company; Reliance National Insurance Companies; Risk Enterprise Management Limited (REM); St. Paul Fire & Marine Insurance Companies; T.I.G. Insurance Company; Tamarack American; Teva Pharmaceuticals, U.S.A., Inc.; United States Aircraft Insurance Group; Vanliner Insurance Company; Zurich American Insurance Group.

(For Complete Biographical Data on all Personnel, see Professional Biographies at Baltimore, Maryland)

THE ECK LAW FIRM

1101 30TH STREET, N.W., SUITE 500
WASHINGTON, D.C. 20007
Telephone: 202-625-4342
Fax:202-318-1136
Email: teck@ecklawfirm.com
URL: http://www.ecklawfirm.com

San Francisco, California Office: 50 California Street, Suite 1500, 94111. Telephone: 415-399-9797. Fax: 415-276-2870.

Business Litigation, Emerging Business Law, Electronic Commerce Law, Internet Law, Complex Litigation, Small Business Law, Financial Planning, Commercial Transactions, Uniform Commercial Code.

FIRM PROFILE: Mr. Eck is a versatile business litigation and commercial transaction attorney. He has offices on both the east and the west coast of the United states and regularly represents a variety of small to large business nationwide. His clients include dot.com companies, high-tech and bio-tech business, mortgage banks, manufacturers and many other types of small business and international corporations.

F. THOMAS ECK, IV, born Los Angeles, California, November 6, 1964; admitted to bar, 1989, California and U.S. District Court, Central District of California; 1991, Nevada and U.S. District Court, District of Nevada; 1998, District of Columbia. *Education:* University of Southern California (B.A., magna cum laude, 1986; J.D., 1989). Phi Beta Kappa. Chair, Hale Moot Court Honors Program, 1988-1989. Instructor, Legal Assistantship Program, University of California-Irvine. *Member:* The District of Columbia Bar; State Bar of California; State Bar of Nevada. ***Email:*** teck@ecklawfirm.com

ECKERT SEAMANS CHERIN & MELLOTT, LLC

Established in 1958
SUITE 700
1250 24TH STREET, N.W.
WASHINGTON, D.C. 20037
Telephone: 202-659-6600
Facsimile: 202-659-6699
Email: escm@escm.com
URL: http://www.escm.com

Pittsburgh, Pennsylvania Office: 44th Floor, 600 Grant Street. Telephone: 412-566-6000. Facsimile: 412-566-6099.
Harrisburg, Pennsylvania Office: 213 Market Street, Eighth Floor. Telephone: 717-237-6000. Facsimile: 717-237-6019.
Philadelphia, Pennsylvania Office: 1515 Market Street, Ninth Floor. Telephone: 215-851-8400. Facsimile: 215-851-8383.
Boston, Massachusetts Office: One International Place, 18th Floor. Telephone: 617-342-6800. Facsimile: 617-342-6899.
Haddonfield, New Jersey Office: 36 Tanner Street, Second Floor. Telephone: 856-427-6240. Facsimile: 856-427-0611.
Morgantown, West Virginia Office: 2400 Cranberry Square. Telephone: 304-594-1000. Facsimile: 304-594-1181.

General Practice including Alternative Dispute Resolution, Antitrust and Trade Regulations, Appellate, Bankruptcy, Construction, Corporate and Finance, Creditors' Rights, E-Commerce and Information Technology, Education, Employee Benefits/ERISA, Energy, Environmental, Estate Planning and Administration, Government Contracts, Government Relations, Health Care, Immigration, Insurance, Intellectual Property, including Patents, Trademarks, Trade Secrets, Licensing and Copyrights, Intellectual Property Litigation, International Business and Trade, Labor and Employment, Land Use, Litigation, Municipal Law and Municipal Finance, Product Liability, Public Utilities Law, Real Estate, Religious Organizations, Securities, Sports and Entertainment, Taxation, Toxic Tort Litigation, Transportation, Trusts and White Collar Criminal Defense Law.

MEMBERS OF FIRM

EDWARD J. LONGOSZ, II, born 1955; admitted to bar, 1983, District of Columbia, U.S. District Court for the District of Columbia and U.S. Court of Appeals for the District of Columbia Circuit; 1987, U.S. Claims Court, U.S. Court of Appeals for the Federal Circuit; 1990, U.S. District Court, District of

(This Listing Continued)

Maryland; 1992, U.S. Court of Appeals, Fourth Circuit; 1995, U.S. Supreme Court; 1996, Virginia and U.S. District Court, Eastern District of Virginia. *Education:* St. Francis College (B.A., 1977); London School of Economics; Ohio Northern Univ. (J.D., 1981). ***PRACTICE AREAS:*** Product Liability; Medical Malpractice Liability; Professional Liability; Fraud, Insurance and Commercial Litigation. ***Email:*** edward.longosz@escm.com

EDWARD R. NOONAN, born 1951; admitted to bar, 1980, District of Columbia; 1976, Rhode Island; 1989, Pennsylvania; U.S. District Court, Western District of Pennsylvania; U.S. Court of Appeals, Third Circuit; U.S. District Court, District of Maryland. *Education:* Brown University (A.B., 1973); George Washington University (J.D., with honors, 1976). ***PRACTICE AREAS:*** Labor and Employment Law. ***Email:*** ern@escm.com

GEORGE J. WALLACE, born 1942; admitted to bar, 1967, Connecticut; 1975, Iowa; 1981, Pennsylvania; 1983, New Jersey; 1994, District of Columbia and U.S. District Court, District of Maryland. *Education:* Yale University (B.A., cum laude, 1964); University of Virginia (LL.B., 1967). ***PRACTICE AREAS:*** Real Estate Law; Bankruptcy; Consumer Regulatory Agencies. ***Email:*** gjw@escm.com

MICHAEL A. WIEGARD, born 1948; admitted to bar, 1980, District of Columbia. *Education:* George Washington University (B.A., 1970); Georgetown University (J.D., magna cum laude, 1980). ***PRACTICE AREAS:*** Environmental Law; Product Safety Regulation Litigation. ***Email:*** mzw@escm.com

ASSOCIATE

EMILY A. NACK, born 1966; admitted to bar, 1992, Virginia; 1994, Maryland; 1996, District of Columbia. *Education:* Mary Washington College (B.A., 1988); Columbus School of Law of The Catholic University of America (J.D., 1992). *Member:* Virginia State Bar; Maryland State and American Bar Associations. ***PRACTICE AREAS:*** Litigation. ***Email:*** emily.nack@escm.com

(For Biographical Data of other Firm Personnel, see Professional Biographies at Pittsburgh, Harrisburg, and Philadelphia, Pennsylvania, Boston, Massachusetts, Morgantown, West Virginia and Haddonfield, New Jersey)

EGAN & ASSOCIATES, PLLC

WASHINGTON, D.C.

(See McLean, Virginia)

Science and Technology Law and Litigation, Nuclear Law, Energy and Environmental Law, Public Utilities Law, Energy Department Counseling, International Matters, Independent Power, Antitrust, Whistleblower Law.

MICHAEL J. EIG AND ASSOCIATES, P.C.

WASHINGTON, D.C.

(See Chevy Chase, Maryland)

Special Education Law, Education Law, School District Liability, Educational Testing, Children's Disability.

ELIAS, MATZ, TIERNAN & HERRICK L.L.P.

Established in 1972
12TH FLOOR THE WALKER BUILDING
734 15TH STREET, N.W.
WASHINGTON, D.C. 20005
Telephone: 202-347-0300
Fax: 202-347-2172
URL: http://www.emth.com

Banking, Thrift Institution, Securities, Corporate, Taxation Law. Administrative Practice before Federal Agencies.

MEMBERS OF FIRM

TIMOTHY B. MATZ, born Pittsburgh, Pennsylvania, May 18, 1944; admitted to bar, 1970, Missouri; 1972, District of Columbia. *Education:* University of Virginia (B.A., 1966); George Washington University (J.D., 1969); Georgetown University (LL.M., 1975). *Member:* District of Columbia Bar; American Bar Association. ***Email:*** tmatz@emth.com

STEPHEN M. EGE, born New Orleans, Louisiana, August 21, 1943; admitted to bar, 1973, District of Columbia. *Education:* University of Chicago (A.B., cum laude, 1965; J.D., 1968). Editor, University of Chicago Law Review, 1967-1968. Instructor, University of Virginia School of Law, 1968-1969. Assistant Professor of Law, University of Georgia School of Law, 1969-1971. Assistant to the Chairman, Federal Home Loan Bank Board, 1977-1979. Chairman, National Law Journal Annual Financial Institution Conference, 1984—. *Member:* District of Columbia Bar. ***Email:*** sege@emth.com

(This Listing Continued)

ELIAS, MATZ, TIERNAN & HERRICK L.L.P., Washington—Continued

RAYMOND A. TIERNAN, born Providence, Rhode Island, October 18, 1950; admitted to bar, 1976, Rhode Island; 1980, District of Columbia. *Education:* Brown University (A.B., 1973); Catholic University Law School (J.D., 1976). Staff Attorney, Office of General Counsel, Federal Home Loan Bank Board, 1976-1979. *Member:* District of Columbia Bar; Rhode Island and American (Member, Section of Corporation, Banking and Business Law) Bar Associations. ***Email:*** rtier@emth.com

GERARD L. HAWKINS, born Norwood, Massachusetts, December 23, 1953; admitted to bar, 1978, District of Columbia. *Education:* Boston College (A.B., summa cum laude, 1975); Georgetown University Law Center (J.D., magna cum laude, 1978). Phi Beta Kappa. Editor, Georgetown University Law Journal, 1977-1978. Co-author: "Shark Repellents and Golden Parachutes: A Handbook for the Practitioner," Law & Business, Inc./Harcourt Brace Jovanovich, 1983. Adjunct Professor of Law, Georgetown University Law Center, 1982-1983. *Member:* District of Columbia Bar; American Bar Association. ***Email:*** ghawk@emth.com

JOHN P. SOUKENIK, JR., born Warren, Ohio, October 5, 1951; admitted to bar, 1976, Ohio (Not admitted in District of Columbia). *Education:* Kent State University (B.A., cum laude, 1973); Catholic University (J.D., 1976). Member, Catholic University Law Review, 1975-1976. Staff Attorney, 1976-1981 and Associate General Counsel, Director of Corporate and Regulatory Structure, Federal Home Loan Bank Board, 1982-1983. *Member:* Ohio State Bar Association. ***Email:*** jsouk@emth.com

GERALD F. HEUPEL, JR., born Trenton, New Jersey, June 4, 1956; admitted to bar, 1980, District of Columbia. *Education:* Widener College (B.A.,B.S., summa cum laude, 1977); Boston University (J.D., cum laude, 1980). Member, Boston University Law Review, 1979-1980. Author: "Plea Bargains vs. Confessions," Boston University Law Review, March 1980. Senior Branch Attorney-Adviser, Division of Corporation Finance, U.S. Securities and Exchange Commission, 1980-1983. *Member:* District of Columbia Bar. ***Email:*** gheup@emth.com

JEFFREY A. KOEPPEL, born Washington, D.C., July 31, 1953; admitted to bar, 1978, Maryland; 1984, New York; 1985, District of Columbia. *Education:* University of Maryland (B.A., 1975); Loyola College (M.F., 1983); University of Baltimore (J.D., 1978). Phi Alpha Theta. Member, John Marshall Law Society. Author: "Warding Off Hostile Takeovers," Best's Review, June 1989; "Side Stepping the Deal Stoppers," Best's Review, April 1991; "Demutualization: Charting a Course," Best's Review, July 1992; "Mutual Holding Companies: Crafting a New Structure," Best's Review, February 1998. The State of Demutualization, 1991 & 1996. Senior Branch Attorney-Adviser, Division of Corporation Finance, U.S. Securities and Exchange Commission, 1981-1983. *Member:* District of Columbia Bar; Maryland State, New York State and American Bar Associations. ***PRACTICE AREAS:*** Corporate; Securities; Mergers and Acquisitions. ***Email:*** jkoep@emth.com

PHILIP R. BEVAN, born Atlanta, Georgia, September 28, 1954; admitted to bar, 1979, North Carolina; 1984, District of Columbia. *Education:* Franklin & Marshall College (A.B., 1976); Duke University (J.D., 1979). *Member:* District of Columbia Bar; North Carolina State Bar; American Bar Association. [Lt., JAGC, U.S. Navy, 1979-1983]. ***Email:*** rbeva@emth.com

HUGH T. WILKINSON, born Washington, D.C., June 7, 1956; admitted to bar, 1981, Maryland; 1986, District of Columbia. *Education:* Georgetown University (A.B., cum laude, 1978; J.D., 1981; M.L.S.R., 1984). Editor, The American Criminal Law Review, 1980-1981. Author: "The Affirmative Duty To Disclose After Chiarella and Dirks," The Journal of Corporation Law, Spring, 1985. Attorney-Adviser, Division of Market Regulation, 1982-1983 and Division of Corporation Finance, 1983-1985, U.S. Securities and Exchange Commission. *Member:* District of Columbia Bar; Maryland State Bar Association. ***Email:*** hwilk@emth.com

KEVIN M. HOULIHAN, born Bethesda, Maryland, July 13, 1961; admitted to bar, 1986, Maryland; 1989, District of Columbia. *Education:* Villanova University (B.A., 1983); Georgetown University (J.D., 1986). *Member:* District of Columbia Bar; Maryland State and American (Member, Section of Corporation, Banking and Business Law) Bar Associations. ***Email:*** khoul@emth.com

KENNETH B. TABACH, born New York, N.Y., July 18, 1957; admitted to bar, 1982, Virginia and Maryland; 1983, District of Columbia. *Education:* University of Maryland (B.S., 1979); T.C. Williams University of Richmond (J.D., 1982). Delta Theta Phi. Attorney-Advisor, Division of Corporation Finance, U.S. Securities and Exchange Commission, 1985-1988. *Member:* District of Columbia Bar; Maryland State and American (Member, Section of Corporation, Banking and Business Law) Bar Associations; Virginia State Bar. ***Email:*** ktaba@emth.com

---

PATRICIA J. WOHL, born Arlington, Virginia, February 2, 1959; admitted to bar, 1990, Virginia and U.S. Court of Appeals for the Fourth Circuit; 1991, U.S. District Court, Eastern District of Virginia; 1996, District of Columbia. *Education:* Duke University (A.B., cum laude, 1980); Vanderbilt University (M.B.A., 1982); Washington & Lee University (J.D., 1990). Phi Alpha Delta (Treasurer, Staples Chapter, 1989-1990). *Member:* District of Columbia Bar; Virginia State Bar; American Bar Association (Member, Corporation, Banking and Business Law Section). ***Email:*** pwohl@emth.com

DAVID TEEPLES, born Canyon, Texas, February 15, 1969; admitted to bar, 1997, Georgia; 1998, District of Columbia. *Education:* University of Oklahoma (B.A., 1991; M.A., Economics, 1994); University of North Carolina at Chapel Hill (J.D., with honors, 1997). Phi Beta Kappa. Note and Comment Editor, North Carolina Journal of International Law & Commercial Regulation. Author: "Young v. Mangans: Just When You Thought It Was Safe To Get In The Water," North Carolina Journal of International Law and Commercial Regulation, Summer, 1996. *Member:* District of Columbia Bar; American Bar Association. ***Email:*** dteep@emth.com

ERIC M. MARION, born Dover, New Hampshire, September 3, 1972; admitted to bar, 1998, Virginia; 1999, District of Columbia. *Education:* Franklin & Marshall College (B.A. with honors, 1994); William & Mary School of Law (J.D., 1998). Phi Delta Phi. Board Editor, William & Mary Law Review, 1997-1998. ***Email:*** emari@emth.com

SPECIAL COUNSEL

W. MICHAEL HERRICK, born Elizabeth City, Virginia, April 26, 1943; admitted to bar, 1977, District of Columbia. *Education:* University of Delaware (B.S., Business, 1971); Washington College of Law of American University (J.D., 1977). Examiner, Financial Analyst, Attorney, Federal Home Loan Bank Board, 1971-1978. Assistant Director, Securities and Corporate Practices Law Department, Office of the Comptroller of Currency, 1979-1980. *Member:* District of Columbia Bar; American Bar Association. ***Email:*** wherr@emth.com

OF COUNSEL

ALLIN P. BAXTER, born Sanitary Springs, New York, May 1, 1929; admitted to bar, 1957, District of Columbia; 1965, U.S. Court of Appeals for the District of Columbia Circuit; 1976, U.S. District Court, District of Maryland; 1981, U.S. District Court, Southern District of Texas. *Education:* University of Virginia (B.A., 1952); George Washington University (LL.B., 1957). Phi Delta Phi. Attorney, Securities and Exchange Commission, 1957-1961. *Member:* District of Columbia Bar; Federal and American (Member: Committee on Partnerships and Unincorporated Business, 1981-1994; Committee on Developments in Investment Services, 1982-1994; Committee on Savings Institutions, 1983-1994) Bar Associations. ***Email:*** abaxter@mail.cvn.net

JACK I. ELIAS, born Brooklyn, New York, March 12, 1918; admitted to bar, 1950, District of Columbia. *Education:* Bernard M. Baruch College of the City University of New York (B.B.A., 1941); George Washington University (LL.B., 1949). Co-Author: "Savings & Loan Conversions-An Overview," 1973; "Federal Home Loan Bank Board Rules and Regulations—Mutual-to-Stock Conversions," 1976. Member of Staff, Securities and Exchange Commission, 1938-1958. Director, Holding Company Section of Federal Home Loan Bank Board, 1968-1972. *Member:* District of Columbia Bar; Federal and American Bar Associations.

SHERYL JONES ALU, born Allentown, Pennsylvania, January 7, 1953; admitted to bar, 1981, District of Columbia; 1990, Maryland. *Education:* Franklin and Marshall College (B.A., Government, 1973); George Washington University (Certification, Legal Research, 1974); Emory University (J.D., 1981). Senior Vice President and General Counsel, Perpetual Financial Corporation and Perpetual Savings Bank, F.S.B., McLean, Virginia, 1991-1992. *Member:* District of Columbia Bar (Member, Corporation, Finance and Securities Law Section); Calvert County (Maryland), Maryland State (Member, Real Property and Business Sections) and American (Member, Corporation, Banking and Business Law Sections) Bar Associations. ***Email:*** salu@emth.com

(This Listing Continued)

EMORD & ASSOCIATES, P.C.

Established in 1993

1050 SEVENTEENTH STREET, N.W.
SUITE 600
WASHINGTON, D.C. 20036
Telephone: 202-466-6937
Fax: 202-466-6938
URL: http://www.emord.com
Email: emordall@erols.com
URL: http://www.lawyers.com/emordlaw

Burke, Virginia Office: Burke Professional Center, 5282 Lyngate Court. Telephone: 202-466-6937.

Constitutional Law, Food and Drug Law, False Advertising Law, General Civil Litigation, First Amendment Law, Libel Law, Administrative Law, Communications Law, and Corporate Law.

(This Listing Continued)

EPSTEIN BECKER & GREEN, P.C., Washington—Continued

SENIOR COUNSEL

WILLIAM G. KOPIT, born New York, N.Y., April 7, 1940; admitted to bar, 1965, New York; 1972, District of Columbia; 2000, Maryland. *Education:* Bucknell University (B.A., 1961); Columbia University (J.D., cum laude, 1964). Recipient, William Gritzinger Award, highest average in Economics, 1961. Harlan Fiske Stone Scholar. Author: "Rethinking the Significance of Merging Hospitals' Non-Profit Status Under the Sherman and Clayton Acts," February 18, 1998; "Antitrust Remedies for Managed Care: Attacking Barriers to Free Markets," Managed Healthcare Handbook, 4th Edition, 1999. ***PRACTICE AREAS:*** Antitrust Law; Health Law. ***Email:*** wkopit@ebglaw.com

HELEN E. QUICK, born Cardiff, Wales, United Kingdom, June 9, 1967; admitted to bar, 1991, Maryland; 1992, District of Columbia. *Education:* University of Virginia (B.A., 1988; J.D., 1991). Editor, Virginia Tax Review. *Member:* District of Columbia Bar; Maryland State Bar Association. ***PRACTICE AREAS:*** Corporate Law. ***Email:*** hquick@ebglaw.com

OF COUNSEL

CATHIE A. SHATTUCK, admitted to bar, 1970, Nebraska; 1971, Colorado; 1975, U.S. Supreme Court; 1977, U.S. Court of Appeals, 10th Circuit; 1984, District of Columbia. *Education:* University of Nebraska (J.D., 1970). Vice Chairman, U.S. Equal Employment Opportunity Commission, 1982-1984. *Member:* American Bar Association (Management Co-Chair, Immigration Law Committee, 1987-1990; Management Co-Chair, Federal Legislative Developments Committee, 1990-1994; Member, Board of Editors, The Practical Litigator, 1989—; Member, Labor and Employment Law Section, 1987—). Fellow, College of Labor and Employment Lawyers, 1997—. ***Email:*** cshattuck@ebglaw.com

KATHLEEN M. WILLIAMS, admitted to bar, 1980, District of Columbia. *Education:* University of Pennsylvania (B.A., cum laude, 1974); George Washington University (J.D., 1980). *Member:* The District of Columbia Bar; American Bar Association. ***PRACTICE AREAS:*** Labor Law; Employment Law. ***Email:*** kwilliams@ebglaw.com

SPECIAL COUNSEL

CARA C. BACHENHEIMER, born New York, N.Y., October 20, 1961; admitted to bar, 1987, District of Columbia and Maryland. *Education:* Trinity College of Connecticut (B.A., 1983); Georgetown University (J.D., 1986). Published in: Home Health Care Dealer/Provider; Caring Magazine; Home and Community Care International; Home Care Magazine. Speaker: 1992-2000 Medtrade; Southwest Regional Home Health Meeting (LA, NM, OK, TX), August 31, 1999; Home Health Line's "State of the Industry" Conference, January 25, 1999; National Association for Home Care Annual Meeting and Convention, Boston, MA, October 18, 1997. *Member:* American Bar Association; Women in Government Relations. ***PRACTICE AREAS:*** Health; Government Relations. ***Email:*** cbachenheimer@ebglaw.com

LEE CALLIGARO, born Passaic, New Jersey, July 9, 1942; admitted to bar, 1967, New Jersey; 1973, District of Columbia; 1968, U.S. Court of Military Appeals; 1975, U.S. Supreme Court. *Education:* Middlebury College (B.A., 1964); Rutgers University (J.D., 1967). Articles Editor, Rutgers Law Review, 1966-1967. Law Clerk, Hon. Haydn Proctor, New Jersey Supreme Court, 1967-1968. *Member:* The District of Columbia Bar (Member, Health Law Section); American Bar Association (Member, Antitrust Law Section); American Health Lawyers Association. [JAGC, U.S. Army, 1968-1972]. ***PRACTICE AREAS:*** Litigation; Health Law; Corporate Law. ***Email:*** lcalligaro@ebglaw.com

SENIOR ASSOCIATE

BRIAN W. STEINBACH, admitted to bar, 1978, District of Columbia; 1984, Illinois. *Education:* Wesleyan University (B.A., cum laude, 1975); University of Virginia (J.D., 1978). Order of the Coif. Adjunct Professor, Chicago-Kent School of Law, 1988-1994. *Member:* American Bar Association (Member, Labor and Employment Law Section). ***PRACTICE AREAS:*** Labor and Employment Law. ***Email:*** bsteinbach@ebglaw.com

ASSOCIATES

KIRSTEN BACKSTROM, admitted to bar, 1997, Virginia; 2000, District of Columbia. *Education:* George Washington University (B.A., cum laude, 1994; M.A. and J.D., 1997). *Member:* The District of Columbia Bar; Virginia State Bar; American Bar Association; American Health Lawyers Association. ***PRACTICE AREAS:*** Health Law. ***Email:*** kbackstrom@ebglaw.com

JANINE SCHOLLNICK BENTON, admitted to bar, 1995, Virginia; 1998, District of Columbia. *Education:* State University of New York at Binghamton (B.A., 1991); George Mason University School of Law (J.D., 1995). Dean's Scholar. Member and Associate Business Editor, George Mason University Law Review, 1992-1995. *Member:* District of Columbia Bar; Virginia State Bar; American Bar Association (Member, Section on Intellectual Property); Washington Area Lawyers for the Arts. ***PRACTICE AREAS:*** Commercial Litigation; Government Contracts Law; Technology Law. ***Email:*** jbenton@ebglaw.com

MICHAEL R. BISSEGGER, admitted to bar, 1992, Maryland; 2001, District of Columbia. *Education:* Brigham Young University (B.A., 1989); Cornell University (J.D., 1992). *Member:* American Health Lawyers Association. ***PRACTICE AREAS:*** Antitrust Law. ***Email:*** mbissegger@ebglaw.com

GEORGE B. BREEN, admitted to bar, 1989, Virginia and U.S. Court of Appeals, Fourth Circuit; 1991, District of Columbia; 1997, Maryland. *Education:* Connecticut College (B.A., 1986); Catholic University of America (J.D., 1989). Recipient, American Jurisprudence Award for Trial Practice, 1989. Law Clerk to the Honorable Bruce S. Mencher, Superior Court of the District of Columbia, 1990-1991. ***PRACTICE AREAS:*** Litigation; Professional Liability Defense; Health Law. ***Email:*** gbreen@ebglaw.com

WILLIAM C. BURGESS, admitted to bar, 2000, Maryland (Not admitted in District of Columbia). *Education:* Catholic University of America (B.A., magna cum laude, 1995); George Washington University (J.D., with high honors, 2000; M.P.H., 2000). Phi Beta Kappa; Order of the Coif. Member, The George Washington Law Review. *Member:* American Health Lawyers Association. ***PRACTICE AREAS:*** Health. ***Email:*** wburgess@ebglaw.com

ANDREA R. CALEM, admitted to bar, 1987, California and U.S. District Court, Central District of California; 1992, District of Columbia and U.S. District Court, District of Columbia and Maryland. *Education:* Brown University (B.A., 1980); University of Virginia (J.D., 1986). ***PRACTICE AREAS:*** Labor and Employment Law. ***Email:*** acalem@ebglaw.com

REBECCA CYR, (admission pending). *Education:* Boston College (B.S., 1996); Boston University School of Public Health (M.P.H., 1998); George Washington University (J.D., 2001). ***Email:*** rcyr@ebglaw.com

JOHN WESLEY ERIKSEN, II., (admission pending). *Education:* University of Wisconsin at Madison (B.A., 1989); University of Maryland (J.D., 2001); University of Minnesota (M.P.H.). ***PRACTICE AREAS:*** Litigation. ***Email:*** jeriksen@ebglaw.com

RYAN M. FADEN, admitted to bar, 2000, New Jersey; 2001, New York (Not admitted in District of Columbia). *Education:* University of California, Los Angeles (B.A., History, 1993); University of California, Los Angeles, School of Public Health (M.P.H., 1995); Seton Hall University School of Law (J.D., Health Law, 2000). *Member:* American Health Lawyers Association. ***PRACTICE AREAS:*** Health. ***Email:*** rfaden@ebglaw.com

ROBERT B. FOX, admitted to bar, 1995, Maryland; 1997, District of Columbia. *Education:* Villanova University (B.A., cum laude, 1992); George Washington University National Law Center (J.D., 1995). Member, Journal of International Law and Economics. *Member:* American Health Lawyers Association. ***PRACTICE AREAS:*** Corporate Law; Health Law. ***Email:*** rfox@ebglaw.com

KAREN RUSSELL GALLY, admitted to bar, 1997, New York and Maryland; 1998, District of Columbia. *Education:* Dartmouth College (B.A., 1988); University of Maryland (J.D., 1996). *Member:* American Bar Association; American Health Lawyers Association. ***PRACTICE AREAS:*** Health Law; Government Investigations; Health Care Fraud and Abuse. ***Email:*** kgally@ebglaw.com

ALICIA M. HAWKINS, admitted to bar, 1991, Pennsylvania (Not admitted in District of Columbia). *Education:* California State University, Northridge (B.A., 1986); University of Pittsburgh (J.D., cum laude, 1991). Managing Editor, University of Pittsburgh Law Review, 1991. *Member:* Allegheny County Bar Association (Member, Health Law Section); American Health Lawyers Association. ***PRACTICE AREAS:*** Managed Care Law. ***Email:*** ahawkins@ebglaw.com

TINA BATRA HERSHEY, born September 21, 1974; admitted to bar, 1999, Pennsylvania; 2000, District of Columbia. *Education:* Villanova University (B.A., cum laude, 1996); The George Washington University School of Public Health and Health Services (M.P.H., 1999); The George Washington University Law School (J.D., with honors, 1999). *Member:* The District of Columbia Bar; American Bar Association; American Health Lawyers Association. ***PRACTICE AREAS:*** Health Law. ***Email:*** tbhershey@ebglaw.com

TAMMY HOPKINS, admitted to bar, 1997, Maryland; 1998, District of Columbia. *Education:* Westminster College (B.S., summa cum laude, 1988); College of William & Mary Marshall-Wythe Law School (J.D., 1997). Member, Order of the Coif. ***PRACTICE AREAS:*** Government Contracts. ***Email:*** thopkins@ebglaw.com

ROBERT J. HUDOCK, born June 14, 1973; admitted to bar, 2000, New York (Not admitted in District of Columbia). *Education:* St. Lawrence University (1996); Cornell University (J.D., cum laude, 2000). *Member:* American Health Lawyers Association. ***PRACTICE AREAS:*** Health; Litigation; Antitrust. ***Email:*** rhudock@ebglaw.com

(This Listing Continued)

MARCIA S. HANDLER, admitted to bar, 1989, New Jersey; 1990, Pennsylvania and Illinois; 1996, District of Columbia. *Education:* Franklin & Marshall College (B.A., 1986); George Washington University National Law Center (J.D., 1989); Loyola University of Chicago School of Law (LL.M., Health Law, 1991). *Member:* American Health Lawyers Association. ***PRACTICE AREAS:*** Health Law. ***Email:*** mhandler@ebglaw.com

DOUGLAS A. HASTINGS, born Oak Park, Illinois, July 28, 1949; admitted to bar, 1981, District of Columbia; 1982, U.S. District Court, District of Columbia and U.S. Court of Appeals, District of Columbia Circuit. *Education:* Duke University (A.B., magna cum laude, 1971); University of Virginia (J.D., 1981). Phi Beta Kappa. Member, Order of the Coif. Listed in: Best Lawyers in America; Who's Who in American Law. Member, Advisory Board, BNA Health Law Reporter. *Member:* The District of Columbia Bar; American Bar Association; American Health Lawyers Association (Member, Board of Directors, 1991—; President, 2001-2002); American Society of Law, Medicine & Ethics; Washington Council of Lawyers; National Committee for Quality Health Care (Member, Board of Directors, 2001—); George Washington University Medical Faculty Associates (Member, Board of Directors). ***PRACTICE AREAS:*** Managed Care; Integrated Delivery Systems; Health Law; Hospital Law. ***Email:*** dhastings@ebglaw.com

JEAN MARIE JONES, born Washington, D.C., 1950; admitted to bar, 1983, Maryland; 1992, District of Columbia. *Education:* University of Maryland (B.S., 1972); Catholic University of America (M.S.N., 1979); University of Maryland (J.D., 1983). *Member:* American Bar Association; Maryland Association of Defense Trial Lawyers; American and Maryland Societies of Healthcare Risk Managers; American Association of Nurse Attorneys. ***PRACTICE AREAS:*** Medical Malpractice; Litigation; Health Care Defense. ***Email:*** jjones@ebglaw.com

ANN LEOPOLD KAPLAN, born Harrisburg, Pennsylvania, September 19, 1962; admitted to bar, 1987, Pennsylvania; 1989, District of Columbia. *Education:* University of Pittsburgh (B.A., magna cum laude, 1984); University of Pennsylvania (J.D., 1987). Phi Beta Kappa; Chancellor's Scholar. *Member:* The District of Columbia Bar (Member, Health Law Section); American Health Lawyers Association. ***PRACTICE AREAS:*** Health Law; Managed Care Law; E-Health. ***Email:*** akaplan@ebglaw.com

MARK E. LUTES, born Morristown, New Jersey, March 22, 1956; admitted to bar, 1984, Maryland and District of Columbia. *Education:* Georgetown University School of Foreign Service (B.S.F.S., cum laude, 1978); Eagleton Institute of Politics, Rutgers University (M.A., 1979); Georgetown University Law Center (J.D., cum laude, 1983). Legislative Advisor, U.S. Federal Trade Commission, 1979-1984. Published in: Healthcare Financial Management Magazine; Group Practice Journal; 1992 and 1994 Health Law handbook; Physician Executive Magazine; The Managed Health Care Handbook; BEST's Review. *Member:* The District of Columbia Bar (Member, Health Law Section); Maryland State Bar Association, Inc. (Member, Health Law Section); American Bar Association (Member, Antitrust Law Section); American Health Lawyers Association. ***PRACTICE AREAS:*** Health Law; Corporate Law; Insurance Law; Antitrust Law. ***Email:*** mlutes@ebglaw.com

DAVID E. MANOOGIAN, born Arlington, Virginia, 1944; admitted to bar, 1969, District of Columbia; 1970, Maryland, U.S. Supreme Court, U.S. Court of Appeals, Fourth, Sixth, Seventh and Ninth Circuits, U.S. District Court for the District of Columbia, U.S. District Court, District of Maryland, U.S. District Court, Eastern District of Michigan, U.S. District Court, District of Nevada and U.S. District Court, District of Utah. *Education:* Dickinson College (B.A., 1966); George Washington University (J.D., 1969). Author: Book Chapter, "Risk Management in Managed Care Organizations," Two-part Series, "The Role of the HMO Risk Manager in Medical Malpractice Cases," Journal for Healthcare Quality. Co-Author: "Medical Malpractice Law of Maryland," (2d. Ed.); "Medical Malpractice and Managed Care Law of Maryland," (3rd. Ed.). Book Chapter, "The Legal Environment for PPOs," published by the American Accreditation Healthcare Commission/URAC; Mr. Manoogian has also written for or been quoted in: The National Law Journal; Managed Care Week; Business Insurance; Best's Insurance Review. *Member:* Maryland Association of Defense Trial Counsel (Former Chairman, Professional Malpractice Section); American Society of Healthcare Risk Managers (ASHRM); Maryland Society of Healthcare Risk Managers. ***PRACTICE AREAS:*** Litigation; Medical Malpractice; Health Litigation. ***Email:*** dmanoogian@ebglaw.com

DAVID A. MATYAS, admitted to bar, 1993, New York and New Jersey; 1994, District of Columbia. *Education:* University of Pennsylvania (B.A., 1990); University of Texas (J.D., 1992). Adjunct Faculty, Washington College of Law, American University, 1999—. Author, "Legal Issues in Health Care Fraud and Abuse Navigating the Uncertainties". *Member:* The District of Columbia Bar (Member, Health Law Section); New York State (Member, Health Law Section) and American (Member, Health Law Section) Bar Associations; American Health Lawyers Association. ***PRACTICE AREAS:*** Health Law; Health Care Fraud; Medicare and Medicaid Reimbursement. ***Email:*** dmatyas@ebglaw.com

(This Listing Continued)

FRANK C. MORRIS, JR., admitted to bar, 1973, Pennsylvania; 1975, District of Columbia; 1976, U.S. Supreme Court. *Education:* Northwestern University (B.S., with distinction, 1970); University of Virginia (J.D., 1973). Recipient, Social Security Admin. Commissioner's Commendation For Collective Bargaining. Adjunct Professor, George Washington University Law School, 1984—. Speaker, Judicial Conferences for Federal, Third, Fourth, Fifth, Sixth, Seventh, Eighth and Eleventh Circuits on disability and discrimination law. Co-Chair: ALI-ABA Current Developments in Employment Law, 1994—; ALI-ABA "How to Present and Challenge Experts in Employment Cases: Persuading the Jury." Attorney, Appellate Court Branch, National Labor Relations Board, 1973-1976. ***PRACTICE AREAS:*** Litigation; Labor Law; Employment Law. ***Email:*** fmorris@ebglaw.com

JOHN M. MURDOCK, admitted to bar, 1986, Virginia; 1989, District of Columbia; 1991, Connecticut. *Education:* Williams College (B.A., 1981); Vanderbilt University (J.D., 1985). Adjunct Professor of Law, American University, Washington College of Law, 2000—. ***PRACTICE AREAS:*** Litigation. ***Email:*** jmurdock@ebglaw.com

ROBERT D. REIF, born Philadelphia, Pennsylvania, November 4, 1952; admitted to bar, 1977, Virginia and District of Columbia; 1979, U.S. Tax Court; 1982, California (inactive); 1988, New York. *Education:* Lehigh University and University of Delaware (B.A., magna cum laude, 1974); Columbus School of Law, Catholic University of America (J.D., 1977). *Member:* American Bar Association (Member, Corporate Law Division); American Health Lawyers Association. ***PRACTICE AREAS:*** Health Law; Corporate Law. ***Email:*** rreif@ebglaw.com

LYNN SHAPIRO SNYDER, admitted to bar, 1979, District of Columbia; 1981, Florida. *Education:* Franklin & Marshall College (B.A., magna cum laude, 1976); George Washington University (J.D., 1979). Phi Beta Kappa; Pi Gamma Mu. Chair, Third Party Payment Practice Group. Co-Chair, Health Care Fraud Practice Group. *Member:* The District of Columbia Bar; The Florida Bar;American Bar Association (Member, Health Law Section); American Health Lawyers Association; Academy for International Health Studies; National Academy of Social Insurance. ***PRACTICE AREAS:*** Health Law; Hospital Law; Health Care Fraud; Medicare and Medicaid Reimbursement; Pharmaceutical Health Regulatory Law; International Health Law. ***Email:*** lsnyder@ebglaw.com

DAVID B. TATGE, born Schenectady, N.Y., April 29, 1956; admitted to bar, 1986, Virginia; 1987, District of Columbia; 1989, U.S. District Court, District of Maryland. *Education:* College of William & Mary (B.B.A., 1978); American University (M.S., Taxation, 1982); George Washington University (J.D., with honors, 1986). Certified Public Accountant, Maryland, 1979. Author: Tatge, et al, The Chapter 7 Bankruptcy Trustee's Manual, J. Wiley & Sons, 1993. Adjunct Professor of Law: George Mason University School of Law, 1996 and 1998; George Washington University Law School, 1997 and 1999. *Member:* The District of Columbia Bar; Virginia State Bar; American Bar Association (Member, Sections on: Litigation; Business Law; Taxation; Real Property, Probate and Trust Law; Health Law); American Bankruptcy Institute; Walter Chandler American Inn of Court (Master of the Bench); J. Edgar Murdoch American Inn of Court. (Also at Alexandria, Virginia Office). ***PRACTICE AREAS:*** Creditors' Rights Law; Bankruptcy Law; Commercial Litigation; Business Transactions; Health Law. ***Email:*** dtatge@ebglaw.com

DALY D. E. TEMCHINE, admitted to bar, 1969, New Jersey; 1973, Maryland; 1975, District of Columbia. *Education:* Columbia College (A.B., 1965); Rutgers University Law School (J.D., 1969). Member, Editorial Board, The Rutgers Law Review, 1968-1969. Author: "Eroding ERISA: The Legal Assault on Managed Health Care," Washington Legal Foundation, No. 31, June, 1999. Law Clerk, Hon. Melvin P. Antell, 1969-1970. Deputy Attorney General, New Jersey, 1970-1973. Deputy Associate Solicitor for Special Litigation, Office of the Solicitor of Labor, 1986-1988. Senior Trial Attorney, Plan Benefits Security Division, Office of the Solicitor of Labor, 1988-1989. *Member:* Maryland State Bar Association, Inc.; New Jersey State Bar Association; The District of Columbia Bar. ***PRACTICE AREAS:*** Health Care Litigation; ERISA Litigation; Fraud and Abuse. ***Email:*** dtemchine@ebglaw.com

CARRIE VALIANT, born Brooklyn, New York, 1956; admitted to bar, 1983, District of Columbia. *Education:* State University of New York at Buffalo (B.A., magna cum laude, 1977); The National Law Center, George Washington University (J.D., with honors, 1983). Phi Beta Kappa. Author: "Legal Issues in Health Care Fraud and Abuse: Navigating the Uncertainties." *Member:* The District of Columbia Bar (Member, Health Law Section); American Health Lawyers Association. ***PRACTICE AREAS:*** Health; Health Care Fraud; Medicare-Medicaid Reimbursement. ***Email:*** cvaliant@ebglaw.com

KENNETH B. WECKSTEIN, born August 28, 1952; admitted to bar, 1976, Virginia; 1977, District of Columbia; 1979, U.S. Tax Court; 1980, U.S. Supreme Court; 1982, U.S. Court of Federal Claims; 1987, Maryland; 1988, New York. *Education:* American University (B.A., cum laude, 1973); George Washington University (J.D., with honors, 1976; LL.M., in Taxation, 1979). ***PRACTICE AREAS:*** Government Contracts Law; Litigation; Construction Law; Trade Secrets Law. ***Email:*** kweckstein@ebglaw.com

(This Listing Continued)

TERESA L. JAKUBOWSKI, admitted to bar, 1993, Pennsylvania; 1996, District of Columbia. *Education:* Drake University (B.A., summa cum laude, 1989); Georgetown University Law Center (J.D., cum laude, 1993). ***PRACTICE AREAS:*** Labor and Employment Law; Disability Law. ***Email:*** tjakubowski@ebglaw.com

SAREENA JERATH, (admission pending). *Education:* College of William & Mary (B.S., Biology and Linguistics, 1991; M.A., Biology, 1995); Boston College (J.D., 2001). ***Email:*** sjerath@ebglaw.com

JoANNA JESPERSON, admitted to bar, 1984, California; 1995, District of Columbia; 1996, Maryland. *Education:* University of Michigan (B.M., magna cum laude, 1972; M.M., maximum cum laude, 1973); University of West Los Angeles School of Law (J.D., 1984). ***PRACTICE AREAS:*** Medical Malpractice; Litigation; Health Insurance Defense Law. ***Email:*** jjesperson@ebglaw.com

SHLOMO D. KATZ, admitted to bar, 1990, Maryland; 1993, District of Columbia. *Education:* University of Maryland at College Park, School of Architecture (B.S., 1986); George Washington University (J.D., 1990). ***PRACTICE AREAS:*** Government Contracts Law; Wage and Hour Law. ***Email:*** skatz@ebglaw.com

KIMBERLY S. KEITH, born December 11, 1970; admitted to bar, 1997, Maryland (Not admitted in District of Columbia). *Education:* Virginia Polytechnic Institute and State University (B.S., 1993); George Mason University School of Law (J.D., 1996). *Member:* Maryland State Bar Association. ***PRACTICE AREAS:*** Corporate; Secured Transactions; Bankruptcy. ***Email:*** kkeith@ebglaw.com

TIFFANY NATASHA KITHCART, admitted to bar, 2001, Texas (Not admitted in District of Columbia). *Education:* University of Texas at Austin (B.A., 1994); George Washington University (M.H.S.A., 1998); University of Houston (J.D., 2001). ***Email:*** tkithcart@ebglaw.com

MICHAEL B. LEHRHOFF, born September 9, 1953; admitted to bar, 1992, Pennsylvania; 1998, District of Columbia. *Education:* Wesleyan University (B.A., cum laude, 1975); Georgetown University Law Center (J.D., 1981). *Member:* American Bar Association (Member, Labor and Employment Law Section). (Disability Practice Group; ADA/FMLA). ***PRACTICE AREAS:*** Labor and Employment Law. ***Email:*** mlehrhoff@ebglaw.com

MICHAEL D. MALONEY, admitted to bar, 1988, Maryland; 1989, District of Columbia. *Education:* University of Richmond (B.A., 1984); George Washington University (J.D., 1988). *Member:* Bar Association of the District of Columbia. ***PRACTICE AREAS:*** Government Contracts; Litigation. ***Email:*** mmaloney@ebglaw.com

MARY R. MARTA, admitted to bar, 1999, Maryland; 2001, District of Columbia. *Education:* Temple University (B.A., cum laude, 1991); Yale University School of Nursing (M.S., Nursing, 1986); University of Maryland (J.D., with honors, 1999). Recipient, 2000 Award for Writing Excellence - ASHRM. Editor, Journal for Healthcare Quality, 1994-1996. Member, Editorial Staff, Journal for Healthcare Policy and Research, 1997-1999. *Member:* Maryland Society for Healthcare Risk Management; American Society for Healthcare Risk Management (CEO/CFO Task Force, 2001); American Health Lawyers Association. ***PRACTICE AREAS:*** Health Law. ***Email:*** mmarta@ebglaw.com

CORI FISHER McRAE, admitted to bar, 1995, New Jersey (Not admitted in District of Columbia). *Education:* Harvard University (A.B., 1988); Duke University (M.P.P., 1995); Fordham University (J.D., 1995). Member, Healthcare Compliance Association. *Member:* New Jersey State Bar Association (Member, Section on Health and Hospital Law). ***PRACTICE AREAS:*** Health Law. ***Email:*** cmcrae@ebglaw.com

JOHN B. MORIARTY, JR., admitted to bar, 1994, Virginia; 2000, District of Columbia. *Education:* University of Virginia (B.A., with distinction, 1989); University of Georgia (J.D., cum laude, 1994). Director, Medicaid Fraud Control Unit/Investigative and Enforcement Section, Virginia Office of the Attorney General, 1997-1999. Special Assistant U.S. Attorney, U.S. Department of Justice, Eastern and Western Districts of Virginia, 1997-1999. *Member:* American Health Lawyers Association. ***PRACTICE AREAS:*** Health Law; Government Investigations; Fraud and Abuse; Health Litigation. ***Email:*** jmoriarty@ebglaw.com

ELIZABETH KONDONIJAKOS MURPHY, admitted to bar, 1997, Pennsylvania and Maryland; 1998, District of Columbia. *Education:* Beaver College (B.A., Valedictorian, summa cum laude, 1992); Temple University School of Law (J.D., cum laude, 1996). *Member:* The District of Columbia Bar; American Bar Association; American Health Lawyers Association. ***PRACTICE AREAS:*** Health Law. ***Email:*** emurphy@ebglaw.com

NICHOLAS A. NARDI, admitted to bar, 1998, Oregon; 2001, District of Columbia. *Education:* Tufts University (B.A., cum laude, 1994); Northwestern School of Law, Lewis and Clark College (J.D., 1998). ***PRACTICE AREAS:*** Government Contracts and Technology; Health. ***Email:*** nnardi@ebglaw.com

CLAYTON J. NIX, admitted to bar, 1994, Ohio; 1995, Maine; 1997, District of Columbia. *Education:* University of Texas at Austin (B.A., 1991); Case Western Reserve University (J.D., 1994). *Member:* American Bar Association (Member, Health Law Section); American Health Lawyers Association. ***PRACTICE AREAS:*** Health Law. ***Email:*** cnix@ebglaw.com

LESLIE V. NORWALK, admitted to bar, 1996, Illinois; 2001, District of Columbia. *Education:* Wellesley College (B.S., cum laude, 1988); George Mason University School of Law (J.D., 1996). Associate Business Editor, George Mason Law Review. Dean's Scholar. *Member:* American Health Lawyers Association. ***PRACTICE AREAS:*** Health Law. ***Email:*** lnorwalk@ebglaw.com

KENYA PARRISH-DIXON, admitted to bar, 1996, Virginia; 1997, District of Columbia and U.S. District Court, Eastern District of Virginia; 1998, U.S. District Court, Western District of Virginia. *Education:* Norfolk State University (B.A., summa cum laude, 1993); College of William & Mary (J.D., 1996). Member, Moot Court Team, 1995-1996. *Member:* American Health Lawyers Association. ***PRACTICE AREAS:*** Health Care Litigation; Government Contract and Technology Litigation. ***Email:*** kdixon@ebglaw.com

COREY M. PERMAN, born Skokie, Illinois, July 10, 1973; admitted to bar, 1999, Maryland; 2001, District of Columbia. *Education:* Northwestern University (B.S., with honors, 1995); Washington University (J.D., 1998). Author: "Diagnosing The Truth: Determining Physician Liability In Cases Involving Munchaugen Syndrome By Proxy," 54 Wash. U.J. Urb. and Contemp. L. 267-2990, 1998. Trial Attorney, Office of the Solicitor, U.S. Department of Labor, 1998-2001. *Member:* Maryland State Bar Association; Bar Association of the District of Columbia; American Health Lawyers Association. ***PRACTICE AREAS:*** Health Law; Litigation. ***Email:*** cperman@ebglaw.com

KATHLEEN A. PETERSON, admitted to bar, 2000, Maryland; 2001, District of Columbia. *Education:* State University of New York College at Geneseo (B.A., 1997); Boston University School of Law (J.D., Health Concentration, with honors, 2000). Omicron Delta Epsilon; Pi Sigma Alpha. Managing Editor, American Journal of Law and Medicine, 1999-2000. *Member:* American Bar Association; American Health Lawyers Association. ***PRACTICE AREAS:*** Health Law. ***Email:*** kpeterson@ebglaw.com

MICHAEL S. PORTNOY, admitted to bar, 1998, Massachusetts; 2000, District of Columbia; 2001, New York. *Education:* Brown University (B.A., 1994); Boston University (J.D., 1998). Editor, American Journal of Law and Medicine. *Member:* The District of Columbia Bar; American Bar Association; American Health Lawyers Association. ***PRACTICE AREAS:*** Health Law. ***Email:*** mportnoy@ebglaw.com

KATHY POTTER, admitted to bar, 1995, District of Columbia. *Education:* Georgetown University (B.A., 1991); George Mason University School of Law (J.D., 1995). *Member:* American Health Lawyers Association. ***PRACTICE AREAS:*** Health Law; Litigation; ERISA Litigation. ***Email:*** kpotter@ebglaw.com

JOHN S. RAH, admitted to bar, 1993, Maryland; 1994, Florida (Not admitted in District of Columbia). *Education:* New York University (B.A., with honors, 1990); Georgetown University Law Center (J.D., 1993). *Member:* American Health Lawyers Association. ***PRACTICE AREAS:*** Health Law. ***Email:*** jrah@ebglaw.com

LENA ROBINS, born Washington, D.C., October 29, 1969; admitted to bar, 1995, Maryland; 1998, District of Columbia. *Education:* Colgate University (B.A., magna cum laude, 1992) Phi Beta Kappa; University of Maryland School of Law (J.D., with honors, 1995). *Member:* American Bar Association; American Health Lawyers Association. ***PRACTICE AREAS:*** Health Law. ***Email:*** lerobins@ebglaw.com

JAYSON SLOTAIK, (admission pending). *Education:* University of Rochester (B.A., 1992); George Washington University (M.P.H., 1998); University of Maryland (J.D., 2001). ***PRACTICE AREAS:*** Health Law. ***Email:*** jslotaik@ebglaw.com

LESLIE BURRIS THORPE, admitted to bar, 1999, Missouri; 2000, District of Columbia. *Education:* Emory University (B.A., 1995); St. Louis University (J.D., 1999). ***PRACTICE AREAS:*** Health. ***Email:*** lthorpe@ebglaw.com

TANYA B. VANDERBILT, admitted to bar, 1991, Pennsylvania and New Jersey; 1993, District of Columbia. *Education:* Swarthmore College (B.A., with distinction, 1988); University of Pennsylvania (J.D., 1991). ***PRACTICE AREAS:*** Antitrust Law; Health Law. ***Email:*** tvanderbilt@ebglaw.com

PATRICIA M. WAGNER, admitted to bar, 2000, Missouri; 2001, District of Columbia. *Education:* University of Kansas (B.A., 1984; Ph.D., 1990); St. Louis University School of Law (J.D., cum laude, 2000). ***PRACTICE AREAS:*** Health Care. ***Email:*** pwagner@ebglaw.com

JONATHAN D. WEINBERG, admitted to bar, 1992, Maryland; 1994, District of Columbia. *Education:* University of Wisconsin, Madison (B.A., 1989); Catholic University of America (J.D., 1992). *Member:* American Health Lawyers Association. ***PRACTICE AREAS:*** Health Law. ***Email:*** jweinberg@ebglaw.com

CONSTANCE A. WILKINSON, born Washington, D.C., March 17, 1960; admitted to bar, 1985, District of Columbia. *Education:* Catholic University

(This Listing Continued)

EPSTEIN BECKER & GREEN, P.C., Washington—Continued

(B.A., magna cum laude, 1980); George Washington University (J.D., 1984). ***PRACTICE AREAS:*** Government Contracts Law; Health Law. ***Email:*** cwilkinson@ebglaw.com

BRIAN J. WISE, born November 3, 1974; admitted to bar, 2000, Virginia (Not admitted in District of Columbia). *Education:* Duke University (B.A., History, with honors, Political Science, 1997); University of Virginia (J.D., 2000). Recipient, Rankin Prize for American Constitutional Law, Duke University. Member, 1998-1999 and Board Member, 1999-2000, Moot Court. ***Email:*** bwise@ebglaw.com

HOWARD A. WOLF-RODDA, admitted to bar, 1994, Maryland, U.S. District Court, District of Maryland and U.S. Court of Appeals, Fourth Circuit; 1996, District of Columbia. *Education:* American University, Washington, D.C. (B.A., cum laude, 1985); University of Maryland (J.D., with honors, 1993). Order of the Coif. *Member:* American Bar Association. ***PRACTICE AREAS:*** Government Contracts; Commercial Litigation; Insurance Coverage Law. ***Email:*** hwolf-rodda@ebglaw.com

(For other Personnel and Biographical Data, see Professional Biographies at Los Angeles and San Francisco, California, Stamford, Connecticut, Miami, Florida, Chicago, Illinois, Boston, Massachusetts, Newark, New Jersey, New York, N.Y. and Dallas, Texas Offices)

EPSTEIN, EDELL, SHAPIRO, FINNAN & LYTLE, LLC

WASHINGTON, D.C.

(See Rockville, Maryland)

Patent, Trademark and Copyright Practice.

LAW OFFICES OF PAMELA B. FAIRCHILD

WASHINGTON, D.C.

(See Alexandria, Virginia)

Commercial and Residential Real Estate Law Practice.

THE FALK LAW FIRM PLLC

A Professional Limited Liability Corporation

Established in 1978

SUITE 260
ONE WESTIN CENTER
2445 M STREET, N.W.
WASHINGTON, D.C. 20037
Telephone: 202-833-8700
Telecopier: 202-872-1725
Email: falklaw@falklawfirm.com

General Civil and Criminal Practice in all Federal, State and Local Courts in the District of Columbia, Virginia, Maryland, Pennsylvania and West Virginia.

FIRM PROFILE: The Firm, founded in 1978, serves a broad range of business to business and business to government clients throughout the United States, Canada and Europe in the traditional legal fields as well as emerging fields of law which have become more significant in recent years including alternative dispute resolution, internal investigations, product liability, and technology law.

JAMES H. FALK, SR., born Tucson, Arizona, August 17, 1938; admitted to bar, 1965, Arizona; 1968, U.S. District Court, District of Arizona; 1971, District of Columbia; U.S. District Court, District of Maryland; 1972, U.S. Court of Appeals, District of Columbia, Fourth, Sixth, Ninth and Federal Circuits; U.S. Court of Appeals for the District of Columbia Circuit; U.S. Supreme Court; 1995, U.S. Tax Court. *Education:* University of Arizona (B.S.B.A., 1960; LL.B., 1965). Assistant City Attorney and City Prosecutor, Tucson, Arizona, 1966-1967. Staff Assistant to the President, 1971-1974 and Associate Director, Domestic Council, 1974-1976, the White House, Washington, D.C. President's Representative on matters pertaining to State and Local Government, 1974-1975. Appointed by the Board of Governors to Successive three year terms on the District of Columbia Bar Judicial Evaluation Committee 1992-1995 and 1995-1998. Representative of U.S. President to People's Republic of China, 1974. Listed in: Who's Who in America and Who's Who in American Law. *Member:* District of Columbia Bar (Member, Litigation Section); State Bar of Arizona; American Bar Association. ***REPORTED CASES:*** Derecktor v. Goldschmidt, 516 F.Supp 1085; Prieto v. U.S., 655 F.Supp. 1187; Nicol v. ImageMatrix, 767 F.Supp. 744; Power v. Arlington Hospital, 800 F.Supp. 1384.

(This Listing Continued)

PRACTICE AREAS: Civil Trials; Government Contract Law; Intellectual Property; Insurance; Labor and Employment; Estate and Trust Law. ***Email:*** jhfsr@falklawfirm.com

JAMES H. FALK, JR., born Pasadena, California, December 4, 1960; admitted to bar, 1987, West Virginia, Pennsylvania, U.S. Supreme Court, U.S. District Court, Northern and Southern Districts of West Virginia and U.S. District Court, Western District of Pennsylvania; 1988, U.S. Court of International Trade, U.S. Claims Court and U.S. Court of Appeals, Third Circuit; 1989, District of Columbia, U.S. Court of Appeals for the District of Columbia Circuit and U.S. District Court, District of Columbia. *Education:* Washington & Lee University (B.A., cum laude, 1983); West Virginia College of Law (J.D., 1987). Managing Editor, West Virginia Law Review, 1986-1987. Lecturer, Public Contract Law, National Institute of Federal Procurement, 1990—. Adjunct Professor, Trial Practice, George Washington University National Law Center, 1994—. Co-Director, College of Trial Advocacy, George Washington University, 1992—. Instructor and Advisor, Consortia of Colleges and Universities, 1992—. Instructor, Washington D.C. Metro Transit Police, 1992—. *Member:* West Virginia, Pennsylvania and American Bar Associations; The District of Columbia Bar (Chairman, Litigation Section, 1991-1993; Section Member, 1989—; Member, Government Contract Section; Co-Director, College of Trial Advocacy, 1992—); National Association of Bond Lawyers. ***REPORTED CASES:*** Nicol v. ImageMatrix, 767 F.Supp. 744; Power v. Arlington Hospital, 800 F.Supp. 1384. ***PRACTICE AREAS:*** Business Transactions; Civil Trials; Labor and Employment; Commercial Contracts; Government Contracts; Insurance; Public Utility. ***Email:*** jfj@falklawfirm.com

JOHN M. FALK, born Tucson, Arizona, May 6, 1964; admitted to bar, 1991, Virginia, U.S. District Court, Eastern District of Virginia and U.S. Court of Appeals, Fourth Circuit; 1993, District of Columbia, U.S. District Court for the District of Columbia, U.S. Court of Appeals for the District of Columbia Circuit, U.S. Court of Federal Claims; 1996, U.S. Tax Court; 1997, U.S. Supreme Court. *Education:* Washington & Lee University (B.A., cum laude, 1986; J.D., 1990). Member: National Congressional Award Board and Foundation, 1990—; Board of Directors, D.C. Alumni Chapter of Washington & Lee University. *Member:* Virginia and American (Member, Public Contract Law Section; Administrative Law Section) Bar Associations; Virginia State Bar; The District of Columbia Bar. ***PRACTICE AREAS:*** Civil Trials; Government Contracts; International Trade; High Technology; Law Enforcement; Intellectual Property. ***Email:*** jms@falklawfirm.com

MEREDITH N. LONG, born Newport, Rhode Island, December 21, 1973; admitted to bar, 1998, Virginia (Not admitted in District of Columbia). *Education:* Washington and Lee University (B.A., cum laude 1995); College of William and Mary (J.D., 1998). Phi Eta Sigma. Omicron Delta Epsilon. Pi Sigma Alpha. Member, Moot Court Bar. Law Clerk, Virginia Court of Appeals, 1998-2000. *Member:* Virginia State Bar. ***PRACTICE AREAS:*** Civil Trials; Civil Appeals; Commercial Contracts; Government Contracts; Estate Administration; Probate. ***Email:*** MLong@falklawfirm.com

NICOLE S. BIDDLE, born Dayton, Ohio, April 22, 1972; admitted to bar, 2000, Kentucky (Not admitted in District of Columbia). *Education:* Denison University (B.A., 1994); Michigan State University (J.D., cum laude, 1999); Georgetown University (LL.M., 2000). *Member:* American Bar Association. ***PRACTICE AREAS:*** Securities; Commercial Contracts; Government Contracts; Corporate Law; Labor and Employment. ***Email:*** nsbiddle@falklawfirm.com

REPRESENTATIVE CLIENTS: AIG Claim Services, Inc.; American Shipyard Corporation; Alco Power, Inc.; Avon Marine (UK); British Airways (UK); Burke & Herbert Bank & Trust Company; Chubb Insurance Group; East Coast Hockey League; FN Herstal (BEL); FNMI (US); GEC Alsthom (UK); Liberty Mutual Insurance; Lloyds of London (UK); Maguire Group; Man B&W Diesel Inc.; Verify Medical; WesTest Engineering, Inc.; National Capital Group.

JAMES J. FARIS

Established in 1974

SUITE 350
3201 NEW MEXICO AVENUE, N.W.
WASHINGTON, D.C. 20016-2756
Telephone: 202-895-1372
Fax: 301-292-0720
URL: http://www.lawyers.com/jamesjfaris

Estate Planning and Administration, Probate, Wills, Trusts and Taxation Law.

JAMES J. FARIS, born Muncie, Indiana, June 13, 1938; admitted to bar, 1966, Virginia; 1967, District of Columbia, U.S. District Court, Eastern and Western Districts of Virginia, U.S. District Court for the District of Columbia, U.S. Claims Court, U.S. Tax Court and U.S. Court of Military Appeals; 1969, U.S. Supreme Court. *Education:* Duke University (B.A., 1960; LL.B., 1966). Counsel, Antitrust Subcommittee of the House Judiciary Committee, U.S.

(This Listing Continued)

House of Representatives, 1969-1971. Counsel, Surface Transportation Subcommittee, Senate Commerce Committee (Penn Central Investigation), 1971-1972. *Member:* The District of Columbia Bar; Virginia State Bar.

FARR & TARANTO

Established in 1981

SUITE 800

1220 19TH STREET, N.W.

WASHINGTON, D.C. 20036-2435

Telephone: 202-775-0184

Telecopier: 202-223-8679

Supreme Court and Appellate Practice in all substantive areas, including Constitutional Law, Telecommunications Law.

MEMBERS OF FIRM

H. BARTOW FARR, III, born New York, N.Y., November 11, 1944; admitted to bar, 1974, Arizona; 1977, U.S. Supreme Court; 1980, District of Columbia. *Education:* Princeton University (A.B., 1966); Arizona State University (J.D., summa cum laude, 1973). Editor-in-Chief, Arizona State University Law Review, 1972-1973. Law Clerk to Justice William H. Rehnquist, U.S. Supreme Court, 1973-1974. Assistant to the Solicitor General, U.S. Department of Justice, 1976-1978. *Member:* District of Columbia Bar; State Bar of Arizona; American Bar Association (Member, Communications Law Section). ***PRACTICE AREAS:*** Appellate Practice.

RICHARD G. TARANTO, born New York, N.Y., May 6, 1957; admitted to bar, 1982, New York; 1984, District of Columbia; 1985, U.S. Supreme Court. *Education:* Pomona College (B.A., summa cum laude, 1977); Yale University (J.D., 1981). Phi Beta Kappa. Article & Book Review Editor, Yale Law Journal, 1980-1981. Law Clerk to: Judge Abraham D. Sofaer, U.S. District Court, Southern District of New York, 1981-1982; Judge Robert H. Bork, U.S. Court of Appeals, D.C. Circuit. 1982-1983; Justice Sandra Day O'Connor, U.S. Supreme Court, 1983-1984. Assistant to the Solicitor General, 1986-1989. Adjunct Professor, Supreme Court Practice, Federal Courts, Georgetown Law School. *Member:* District of Columbia Bar; New York State Bar Association. ***PRACTICE AREAS:*** Appellate Practice; Telecommunications; Antitrust.

JOHN M. FEDDERS

1742 N STREET, N.W.

WASHINGTON, D.C. 20036

Telephone: 202-659-2424

Facsimile: 202-785-2210

URL: http://www.fedderssecuritieslaw.com

Email: JFedders@erols.com

URL: http://www.lawyers.com/johnfedderslaw

Federal Court Practice and before the Securities and Exchange Commission and Commodity Futures Trading Commission. Corporate, Securities, Commodities and Finance Practice. Litigation, Arbitration and Reparations.

JOHN M. FEDDERS, born Covington, Kentucky, October 21, 1941; admitted to bar, 1967, District of Columbia and New York; U.S. Supreme Court. *Education:* Marquette University (B.A., 1963); The Catholic University of America (LL.B., 1966). Phi Alpha Delta; Sigma Delta Chi. Business Editor, The Catholic University of America Law Review, 1965-1966. Associate, Cadwalader, Wickersham & Taft, New York, N.Y., 1966-1971. Executive Vice-President, Gulf Life Holding Company, Dallas, Texas, 1971-1973. Associate/Partner, Arnold & Porter, Washington, D.C., 1973-1981. Director, Division of Enforcement, Securities and Exchange Commission, 1981-1985. Partner, Miller, Cassidy, Larroca & Lewin, Washington, D.C., 1985-1987. Recipient: Marquette University Alumni Service Award, 1977; The Catholic University of America Alumni Achievement Award--Government and Law, 1982; Securities and Exchange Commission, Chairman's Award for Excellence, 1982, Supervisory Excellence Award, 1983. *Member:* District of Columbia Bar (Member, 1979-1981 and Chairman, 1980-1981, Corporation, Finance and Securities Law Divisions Steering Committee); The Association of the Bar of the City of New York; American Bar Association (Governmental Representative, Section of Litigation, 1981-1985; Member: Subcommittee of the Federal Regulation of Securities Committee, Section of Corporation, Banking and Business Law, 1982-1985; White Collar Crime Committee, Section of Criminal Justice, 1981-1984). ***PRACTICE AREAS:*** Securities Law; Commodities Law; Business Crimes; Corporate Law; Business Litigation.

FEDER, SEMO, CLARK & BARD, P.C.

Established in 1974

SUITE 600, 1350 CONNECTICUT AVENUE, N.W.

WASHINGTON, D.C. 20036-1712

Telephone: 202-955-8305

Facsimile: 202-955-8311; 202-466-5109

URL: http://www.lawyers.com/federsemoclarkbard

Employee Benefits, Labor Law, Health Care, Civil Litigation, Appellate Litigation, Administrative and Legislative Practice.

FIRM PROFILE: The firm's regular clients are dozens of national, regional, and local collectively bargained multiemployer pension, and health and welfare plans. The firm also represents plans, individual trustees, plan participants, and plan service providers, in federal court litigation, under the Employee Retirement Income Security Act of 1974 (ERISA).

GERALD M. FEDER, born New York, N.Y., November 24, 1936; admitted to bar, 1966, New York; 1967, U.S. Supreme Court; 1975, District of Columbia, U.S. Court of Appeals for the District of Columbia Circuit and U.S. District Court, District of Columbia; 1976, U.S. Court of Appeals, Seventh, and Ninth Circuits; 1983, U.S. Court of Appeals, Fourth, Fifth and Eleventh Circuits and U.S. District Court, Northern District of California. *Education:* Bates College (B.A., 1961); Columbia University (LL.B., cum laude, 1965). Author: "Highlights of the New Wage and Hour Law," BNA, 1974; "Multiemployer Plans—Special Rules," Tax Management, 1982; "Handbook on Job Creating Investments," BCTD, AFL-CIO, 1985. Chief Counsel, U.S. Senate Subcommittee on Labor, 1969-1974. Chairman, U.S. Minimum Wage Study Commission, 1978-1979. Member, U.S. Department of Labor ERISA Advisory Council, 1978-1985. *Member:* The District of Columbia Bar; American Bar Association (Co-Chairman, Subcommittee on Fiduciary Standards, Employee Benefits Committee, Labor Law Section, 1978-1988). ***PRACTICE AREAS:*** Employee Benefits. ***Email:*** gmfeder@federlaw.com

JOSEPH SEMO, born Pittsburgh, Pennsylvania, June 6, 1951; admitted to bar, 1976, Virginia and District of Columbia; 1985, Maryland; 1995, Wisconsin. *Education:* University of Pennsylvania (B.S., 1973); George Washington University (J.D., 1976). Author: "ERISA Preemption, A Comparison of Wayne Chemical, Inc. vs. Columbus Agency Services Corp. and Dawson vs. Wheland," 3 Journal of Pension Planning and Compliance 368, 1977; "Salary Reduction SEP, Can Be a Low-Cost Employee Benefit," 49 Taxation For Accountants, August, 1992; "Benefits Legislation in the New Congress," Milliman & Robertson Perspectives, March, 1995; "Salary Reduction SEPs Can be a Low-Cost Employee Benefit," Tax Ideas, March, 1995. Co-Author: "The Multiemployer Pension Plan Amendments Act of 1980: Explanation, Analysis, Recommendations, and Suggested Amendments to Multiemployer Plans," 362 BNA Pension Reporter, October 5, 1981. Chairman, Membership Committee, 1982-1984, and President, 1987-1989, Wharton School Club of Washington. Chairman, Administrative Committee of the City of Annapolis Police and Firemen's Retirement Pension Fund, 1983—. Associate Member, No-Load Mutual Fund Association, 1986-1988. Associate Member, Montgomery County High Technology Council, Inc., 1987-1989. Director, National Employee Benefits Institute, 1991—. *Member:* Maryland State Bar Association, Inc.; Virginia State Bar; The District of Columbia Bar; State Bar of Wisconsin; American Bar Association (Member: Labor and Employment Section; Employee Benefits Committee; Co-Chair, Legislative and Administrative Oversight Sub-Committee, 1998—; Co-Chair, MEWA Sub-Committee, 1993-1998). ***PRACTICE AREAS:*** Multi-Employer Benefits; Executive Compensation; Pension Plans; Health Care; Fiduciary Defense Litigation. ***Email:*** jsemo@federlaw.com

DENISE M. CLARK, born Indianapolis, Indiana, January 3, 1961; admitted to bar, 1987, Indiana, Illinois and U.S. District Court, Northern and Southern Districts of Indiana; 1989, District of Columbia and U.S. District Court for the District of Columbia, U.S. Court of Appeals for the Federal Circuit, U.S. Tax Court and U.S. Court of Appeals for the District of Columbia Circuit; 1991, New York and U.S. District Court, Eastern and Southern Districts of New York. *Education:* Marquette University (B.A., 1983); North Carolina Central University (J.D., 1986); Georgetown University (M.L.L., M.L.T., 1990). Phi Alpha Delta. Member and Staff Member, North Carolina Central Law Review. *Member:* District of Columbia Bar (Section on: Labor and Employment Law; Chair, Employee Benefits Committee); American Bar Association (Member, Section on: Labor and Employment Law; Member, Committee on Employee Benefits, 1987—; Co-Chair, Subcommittee on Preemption; Tort and Insurance Practice (Vice Chair, Committee on Employee Benefits Law, 1996—). ***Email:*** dmclark@federlaw.com

HOWARD M. BARD, born Baltimore, Maryland, October 11, 1963; admitted to bar, 1988, Maryland (Not admitted in District of Columbia). *Education:* George Washington University (B.B.A., 1985; J.D., 1988). Phi Alpha Delta. U.S. Department of Labor, Pension and Welfare Benefits Administration, Office of Enforcement, 1988-1993. *Member:* Maryland State Bar Association,

(This Listing Continued)

FEDER, SEMO, CLARK & BARD, P.C., Washington—Continued

Inc.; American Bar Association; American Health Lawyers Association. ***PRACTICE AREAS:*** Fiduciary Counseling; ERISA; Health Care. ***Email:*** hmbard@federlaw.com

MARK C. NIELSEN, born Buffalo, New York, June 7, 1971; admitted to bar, 1997, New York (Not admitted in District of Columbia). *Education:* Indiana University (B.A., 1992); State University of New York at Buffalo (J.D., 1996); Georgetown University Law Center (LL.M., Labor and Employment Law, 1997). Phi Beta Kappa. Investigator, United States Department of Labor, Pension and Welfare Benefits Administration, 1997-1998. *Member:* New York State and American (Member, Sections on: Antitrust; Labor and Employment) Bar Associations. ***PRACTICE AREAS:*** Employee Benefits; ERISA; Health Care; Antitrust. ***Email:*** mcnielsen@federlaw.com

OF COUNSEL

TERENCE G. CRAIG, born Chicago, Illinois, March 16, 1946; admitted to bar, 1979, California; 1986, District of Columbia; 1987, Illinois. *Education:* United States Military Academy (B.S., 1969); Boalt Hall School of Law, University of California (J.D., 1979). *Member:* State Bar of California; District of Columbia Bar; American Bar Association (Member, Employee Benefits Committee, Labor Section; Co-Chair, Subcommittee). ***PRACTICE AREAS:*** ERISA; Litigation.

THE FEINBERG GROUP, LLP

Established in 1993

1120 20TH STREET, N.W.
SUITE 740 SOUTH
WASHINGTON, D.C. 20036-3437
Telephone: 202-371-1110
Fax: 202-962-9290
Email: kfeinberg@thefeinberggroup.com
URL: http://www.thefeinberggroup.com

New York, N.Y. Office: 780 3rd Avenue, Suite 2202. Telephone: 212-527-9600. Fax: 212-527-9611. Email: kfeinberg@thefeinberggroup.com.

Mediation and Arbitration, Products Liability.

FIRM PROFILE: Established in 1993, the firm specializes in mediation, arbitration, negotiation and other forms of alternative dispute resolution. Members of the firm have been appointed by various federal and state courts to act as Special Settlement Masters in various products liability, employment discrimination and other complex litigations.

PARTNERS

KENNETH R. FEINBERG, admitted to bar, 1971, New York; 1977, District of Columbia; 1980, Massachusetts. *Education:* University of Massachusetts (B.A., cum laude, 1967); New York University School of Law (J.D., 1970). Articles Editor, New York University Law Review, 1969-1970. Law Clerk to Chief Judge Stanley H. Fuld, New York State Court of Appeals, 1970-1972. Recipient, Charles A. Fahy Annual Award for Best Adjunct Professor of Law, Georgetown University Law Center, 1988-1989. Listed in: "Profiles in Power: The 100 Most Influential Lawyers in America," National Law Journal, March 25, 1991; June 12, 2000. "The Next Establishment: Twenty-Seven Future Leaders of America's Major Firms," The American Lawyer, March 1986; "125 Alumni to Watch," University of Massachusetts, October 25, 1988. Adjunct Professor of Law: Georgetown University Law Center, 1979—; University of Pennsylvania Law School, 1999; NYU School of Law, 2000; University of Virginia Law School, 2000; The Graduate School of Political Management, 1988-1990. Assistant U.S. Attorney, Southern District of New York, 1972-1975. Special Counsel, United States Committee on the Judiciary, 1975-1980. Administrative Assistant to Senator Edward M. Kennedy, 1977-1979. Partner, Kaye, Scholer, Fierman, Hays & Handler, 1980-1992. Special Settlement Master: In re: Agent Orange Product Liability Litigation, 1984-1993; In re: Eagle-Picher Industries, Inc. (national asbestos personal injury/wrongful death class action); In re: Joint Eastern and Southern District Asbestos Litigation (federal and state asbestos personal injury/wrongful death Litigation arising out of exposures at the Brooklyn Navy Yard); County of Suffolk, et al. vs. Long Island Lighting Co., et al. (Shorham Nuclear Faculty class action); In re: Asbestos Personal Injury Litigation (asbestos personal injury/wrongful death litigation pending in the Maryland State Courts); In re: Joint Eastern and Southern District Asbestos Litigation (federal asbestos personal injury/wrongful death litigation arising out of exposure at various New York utilities); In re: DES litigation (federal and state DES personal injury litigation); Andrew Herman, et al v. Westinghouse Elec. Corp. (Maryland employment discrimination litigation); McCain v. Koch, et al (homeless persons, State litigation against the City of New York); Brown et al v. Giuliani, et (federal welfare class action against the City of New York). Trustee, Dalkon Shield Claimants' Trust, 1988-1990. Member, Presidential Advisory committee on Human Radiation Experiments, 1997—. Member, Presidential Commission on Catastrophic Nuclear Accidents, 1989-1990. Member, Carnegie Commission Task Force on Science and Technology in Judicial and Regulatory Decisionmaking, 1989-1993. Member, National Panel, Center for Public Resources. Member, Panel of Arbitrators, American Arbitration Association. Chairman, New York State Committee on Sentencing Guidelines, 1985-1986. Court-Appointed Special Settlement Master. *Member:* The District of Columbia Bar; The Association of the Bar of the City of New York (Member, Committee on Federal Courts, 1983-1985); Massachusetts and American (Vice-Chair, Committee on Alternative Dispute Resolution, 1991-1993) Bar Associations. ***PRACTICE AREAS:*** Arbitration and Mediation; Products Liability. ***Email:*** kfeinberg@thefeinberggroup.com

(This Listing Continued)

DEBORAH E. GREENSPAN, admitted to bar, 1981, Michigan; 1985, District of Columbia. *Education:* University of Michigan (B.S., with highest distinction, 1976; J.D., magna cum laude, 1981). Order of the Coif. Senior Editor, Michigan Law Review, 1980-1981. Law Clerk to: The Hon. Edward A. Tamm, U.S. Court of Appeals for the District of Columbia Circuit, 1983-1984; The Hon. Horace W. Gilmore, U.S. District Court, Eastern District of Michigan, 1981-1983; Court Appointed Special Master, In Re Agent Orange Products Liability Litigation, 1993—; Reported, AAA Task Force on Alternative Dispute Resolution and Mass Torts - Recommendations, March 1997. *Member:* American Bar Association; The District of Columbia Bar; State Bar of Michigan. ***PRACTICE AREAS:*** Alternative Dispute Resolution; Products Liability. ***Email:*** dgreenspan@thefeinberggroup.com

MICHAEL K. ROZEN, born 1964; admitted to bar, 1989, New Jersey; 1990, New York. *Education:* Tufts University (B.A., 1986); Georgetown University (J.D., 1989). Special Settlement Master, In re Joint Eastern and Southern District Asbestos Litigation, 1994—; Special Settlement/Discovery Master/Referee, In re New York City Asbestos Litigation, 1994—; Special Settlement/Discovery Master, In re Informix Corporation Securities Litigation, 1998—; Court-Appointed Mediator, Rapid American v. Allstate Insurance Co. et al., 1998-1999; Special Settlement Master, Herman v. Westinghouse Electric Company, 1996-1997; Special Settlement Master, Cook v. Georgia Pacific Corp., et al., 1997; Court-Appointed Mediator, Maxicare Health Plans, Inc. v. Pennsylvania Dept. of Public Welfare, et al., 1997; Special Settlement Master, In re Eastern District Asbestos Litigation, 1998. *Member:* The Association of the Bar of the City of New York (Member, Special Committee on Alternative Dispute Resolution, 1995-1998); New York State, New Jersey State and American (Member, Tort and Insurance Practice Section, 1997—) Bar Associations; New York County Lawyers' Association (Chair, Subcommittee on Alternative Dispute Resolution, 1995). (Resident, New York Office). ***PRACTICE AREAS:*** Alternative Dispute Resolution; Products Liability; Insurance Coverage. ***Email:*** mkrozen@feinberggroup.com

PETER H. WOODIN, born August 27, 1949; admitted to bar, 1989, New York. *Education:* Wesleyan University (B.A., 1971); Columbia University (J.D., 1988). Stone Scholar. Member and Senior Editor, Columbia Law Review, 1986-1988. Moot Court Best First Year Brief Prize. Law Clerk to Hon. Jack B. Weinstein, U.S. District Court, Eastern District of New York, 1988-1989. Consultant, Presidential Commission on Catastrophic Nuclear Accidents, 1990. Court appointed Special Master, "Agent Orange" Litigation, 1989-1993; Court appointed Special Master, DES Products Liability Litigation, 1993—. *Member:* New York State and American Bar Associations; The Association of the Bar of the City of New York (Committee on Product Liability). (Resident, New York Office). ***PRACTICE AREAS:*** Alternative Dispute Resolution; Products Liability; Insurance Coverage. ***Email:*** pwoodin@feinberggroup.com

ASSOCIATE

FREDRIC M. BROOKS, born New York, N.Y., March 25, 1967; admitted to bar, 1993, New York and U.S. District Court, Southern District of New York; 2000, District of Columbia. *Education:* Yale University (B.A., cum laude, 1989); Columbia University (J.D., 1992). Harlan Fiske Stone Scholar. ***Email:*** rbrooks@thefeinberggroup.com

SENIOR COUNSEL

JACQUELINE E. ZINS, born Newark, New Jersey, August 19, 1953; admitted to bar, 1978, New York; 1980, District of Columbia. *Education:* Princeton University (B.A., summa cum laude, 1975); Yale University (J.D., 1978). Phi Beta Kappa. Law Clerk to Judge Whitman Knapp, U.S. District Court, Southern District of New York, 1978-1980. *Member:* The District of Columbia Bar; New York State Bar Association. ***PRACTICE AREAS:*** Mediation. ***Email:*** jzins@thefeinberggroup.com

FELDESMAN, TUCKER, LEIFER, FIDELL & BANK LLP

2001 L STREET, N.W., 2ND FLOOR
WASHINGTON, D.C. 20036
Telephone: 202-466-8960
Telefax: 202-293-8103
Email: info@feldesmantucker.com
URL: http://www.feldesmantucker.com

Rockville, Maryland Office: One Church Street, Suite 800. Telephone: 301-279-6770.

Falls Church, Virginia Office: 5661 Columbia Pike, Suite 200. Telephone: 703-671-5800. Fax: 703-671-5805.

Family Law, Matrimonial Law and Domestic Relations, Health Care Law, Business, Corporate, Complex Commercial Litigation, Special Education Law and Disability Rights, Trial and Appellate Practice before Federal and State Courts, Court Martial and Administrative Agencies, Estate Planning, Trusts, Wills, Probate.

FIRM PROFILE: Feldesman, Tucker, Leifer, Fidell & Bank was founded in 1970. Since then, we have grown to more than 30 lawyers, practicing out of offices in the District of Columbia, Maryland and Virginia. Our clients range from major corporations and nationally known nonprofit organizations to small businesses, families and individuals. We are committed to maintaining the highest standards of the bar with respect to public service and improvement of the legal system. Lawyers in our firm have long been involved not only as leaders of the bar, but also in public interest organizations, teaching and professional writing.

MEMBERS OF FIRM

JAMES L. FELDESMAN, born New York, New York, October 4, 1939; admitted to bar, 1966, District of Columbia, Maryland, U.S. Court of Appeals, Federal Circuit and U.S. Supreme Court. *Education:* University of Pennsylvania (B.S., 1961); Georgetown University (J.D., 1965). Author: *The Federal Grants Management Handbook,* Thompson Publishing Co., 1983; *The Federal Audit Information Service,* National Association of College and University Business Officers, 1992. Staff Attorney, Office of Solicitor, U.S. Labor Department, 1965-1968. General Counsel, President's Council on Youth Opportunity, 1969-1970. *Member:* District of Columbia Bar; Maryland State Bar Association. ***REPORTED CASES:*** National Family Planning v. Sullivan, 979 F.2d 227 (D.C. Cir. 1992); Comm. of Mass. v. Secretary of Health and Human Services, 899 F.2d 53 (1st Cir. 1990); exrt. gr. & vacated sub nom. Sullivan v. Massachusetts, 111 S.Ct 2252 (1991); West Va. Assn. of Comm. Health Cntr., Inc. v. Sullivan, 737 F.Supp. 929 (S.D. W.Va. 1990); Action, Inc. v. Donovan, 789 F.2d 1453 (10th Cir. 1986). ***PRACTICE AREAS:*** Administrative Law; Health Care Law; Federal Grant and Contract Matters; Federal Inspector General Problems. ***Email:*** jfeldesman@feldesmantucker.com

MARNA S. TUCKER, born Philadelphia, Pennsylvania, March 5, 1941; admitted to bar, 1966, District of Columbia; 1969, California; 1970, U.S. Supreme Court. *Education:* University of Texas (B.S., 1962); Georgetown University (LL.B., 1965); University of District of Columbia (J.D., Honorary, 1995). Recipient: Women Lawyer of the Year (Women's Bar Association of the District of Columbia), 1985; Alumni Achievement Award (Georgetown Law Center), 1998; Annual Alumni Achievement Award (Georgetown Alumni Club), 1986; Exceptional Achievement Award (NAACP Legal Defense and Educational Fund, Inc., Washington Committee), 1985; national Legal Aid and Defender Association Annual Award, 1993. Special Assistant to Congressman Allard K. Lowenstein, 1969-1970. Deputy Director, Legal Services Program, Western Region, Office of Economic Opportunity, 1967-1969. Adjunct Professor of Law, Georgetown University Law Center, 1972. Lecturer of Law, Catholic University, Columbus School of Law, 1972-1974. Member, Board of Professional Responsibility, appointed by D.C. Court of Appeals, 1977-1983. Commissioner, U.S. Commission on Child and Family Welfare (Senate Appointment, 1994). Member, Board of the Federal Judicial Center Foundation, 1997-2000 (appointed by Chief Justice); Member: United States Circuit Court Committee on Admissions and Grievances, 1979-1988; United States Judicial Nominating Commission for the District of Columbia, 1977-1980; Board of Regents, Georgetown University, 1986-1989; Board of Visitors, Georgetown University Law Center, 1994-2000; Board of Trustees, Center for Law and Social Policy, 1977-1999; Board of Trustees, Public Defender Service of the District of Columbia, 1986-1992; Board of Trustees, National Women's Law Center, 1981—. Chair, Mayor's Commission on Violence Against Women, 1996—. *Member:* District of Columbia Bar (President, 1984-1985; Delegate to ABA House of Delegates, 1974-1980, 1988—; American Bar Association (Chairperson, Section of Individual Rights and Responsibilities, 1982-1983; Chair, Commission on Public Understanding About the Law, 1979-1982; Chairperson, Standing Committee on Professional Discipline, 1987-1990; Co-Chair, Commission on Domestic Violence, 1995-1997); American Academy of Matrimonial Lawyers; Fellows of the

(This Listing Continued)

American Bar Foundation (Chair, 1995). Fellow, American College of Trial Lawyers. ***PRACTICE AREAS:*** Family Law; Domestic Relations; Trial Practice. ***Email:*** mtucker@feldesmantucker.com

JACQUELINE C. LEIFER, born Flushing, New York, February 28, 1952; admitted to bar, 1977, District of Columbia. *Education:* Cornell University (B.A., 1974; J.D., 1977). Co-Author: *A Guidance for Providers of Mental Health and Addictive Disorder Services in Managed Care Contracting,* The Center for Health Policy Research, 1997; *A Guidance for Certified Nurse-Midwives in Managed Care Contacting,* The Center for Health Policy Research, 1997; *Negotiating Managed Care Contracts:* A Guide for Health Centers, 1994; United Cerebral Palsy Associations Affiliate Support Newsletter, 1992-1994; *Basic Information:* Community and Migrant Health Centers, 1992; *The Legal Obligations of Nonprofit Boards:* A Guidebook for Board Members, 1998; *The Legal Obligations of Nonprofit Boards,* National Center for Nonprofit Boards; *Federal Auditing Information Service for Higher Education,* National Association of College and University Business Officers (1992). Author: United Cerebral Palsy Affiliate Newsletter (1992); *Federal Disability Discrimination Law:* A Compliance Guidebook for Community and Migrant Health Centers (1992). Author: *Implementation of the Federal Debt Collection Act of 1986,* A Report to the Administrative Conference of the United States, 1984; *An Update on Federal Agency Recognition of Grantee Due Process Rights,* 59 Washington University Law Review 1139, 1982. Co-Author: *Federal Grant Disputes -- A Report for the Administrative Conference of the United States,* Matthew Bender, 1982. Attorney Advisor, Office of General Counsel, U. S. Department of Health and Human Services, 1977-1980. *Member:* District of Columbia Bar. ***PRACTICE AREAS:*** Health Care; Corporate Litigation. ***Email:*** jleifer@feldesmantucker.com

EUGENE R. FIDELL, born New York, New York, March 31, 1945; admitted to bar, 1968, New York; 1972, District of Columbia, Massachusetts and U.S. Supreme Court; 1987, Maryland. *Education:* Queens College of the City University of New York (B.A., cum laude, 1965); Harvard University (LL.B., 1968). Phi Beta Kappa. Author: *Federal Protection of Private Sector Health and Safety Whistleblowers,* 2 Ad. L.J. 1 (1988); *Guide to the Rules of Practice and Procedure for the U.S. Court of Appeals for the Armed Forces,* 9th ed. 2000. Visiting Lecturer in Law, Yale Law School, 1993, 1998. Consultant: Food and Agriculture Organization of the United Nations, 1978-1989; Administrative Conference of the United States, 1986-1987. Founder and President, National Institute of Military Justice, 1991—. Chairman, Advisory Committee on Pro Se Litigation (D.D.C.), 1998—. Chairman, Board of Directors, National Veterans Legal Services Program, 1986-1995. Member: Advisory Board on the Investigative Capability of the Department of Defense, 1994; Advisory Committee on Law of the Sea, U.S. Department of State, 1979-1982; Rules Advisory Committee, U.S. Court of Appeals for the Armed Forces, 1981-1996. Member, Editorial Board, Journal of Maritime Law and Commerce, 1978-1990. *Member:* District of Columbia Bar (Chairman, Committee on Military and Veterans Rights, 1980-1984, 1991-1994); American Law Institute. [Lt. Comdr., U.S. Coast Guard Reserve (ret); Active Duty, 1969-1972]. ***PRACTICE AREAS:*** Civil Litigation; Administrative Litigation; Military Litigation. ***Email:*** efidell@feldesmantucker.com

RITA M. BANK, born New York, New York, April 3, 1946; admitted to bar, 1978, District of Columbia; 1985, Maryland. *Education:* Hunter College of the City University of New York (B.A., 1967); Catholic University (J.D., 1978). Author: *Divorce in the Washington Metropolitan Area,* Women's Legal Defense Fund, 1985. Co-Author: *Legal Remedies for Domestic Relations Crises in the District of Columbia,* Women's Legal Defense Fund, 1980. Associate Professor, Catholic University Law School, 1979-1981. Law Clerk to Hon. Gladys Kessler, Superior Court, District of Columbia, 1978-1979. Past President, Women's Legal Defense Fund, 1985, 1986, 1987. Board of Visitors, Catholic University Law School, 1998—. *Member:* District of Columbia Bar (Co-Chairman, Task Force on Family Law Representation, 1991—; General Counsel, 1996-1998); Maryland State Bar Association; American Academy of Matrimonial Lawyers (Past President, D.C. Chapter). ***PRACTICE AREAS:*** Family Law; Business Law; Investments. ***Email:*** rbank@feldesmantucker.com

MARY S. PENCE, born Atlanta, Georgia, March 28, 1945; admitted to bar, 1984, Maryland and District of Columbia. *Education:* University of Michigan (B.S., 1967; M.S., 1972); George Washington University (J.D., with honors, 1984). Phi Beta Kappa. Trustee, Ann Arbor Board of Education, 1977-1978. *Member:* District of Columbia Bar; Montgomery County, Maryland State and American Bar Associations. ***PRACTICE AREAS:*** Family Law; Matrimonial Law. ***Email:*** mpence@feldesmantucker.com

JONATHAN M. DANA, born Boston, Massachusetts, June 22, 1955; admitted to bar, 1984, District of Columbia; 1995, Maryland. *Education:* University of Wisconsin (B.A., 1977); Antioch Law School (J.D., 1984). Law Clerk, Hon. Rufus King, III, Superior Court of the District of Columbia, 1984-1986. Voting Delegate to the Annual Judicial Conference of the District of Columbia, 1989-1995. Participant, Charles Fahy American Inn of Court, 1990. *Member:* District of Columbia Bar (Member, Family Law Division, 1984—; Treasurer, 1988-1990, 1993-1995; Co-Chair, 1995-1996, Steering Committee). ***PRACTICE AREAS:*** Family Law. ***Email:*** jdana@feldesmantucker.com

(This Listing Continued)

FELDESMAN, TUCKER, LEIFER, FIDELL & BANK LLP, Washington—Continued

EDWARD T. WATERS, born Inglewood, California, April 17, 1961; admitted to bar, 1988, Virginia; 1990, District of Columbia. *Education:* Washington University (B.A., 1983); University of Virginia (J.D., 1988). Law Clerk, Department of Energy Board of Contract Appeals, 1988-1989. *Member:* District of Columbia Bar; Virginia State Bar; Federal and American (Member, Section on Public Contract Law) Bar Associations; National Contract Management Association. ***PRACTICE AREAS:*** Federal Grants; Federal Contracts; Health Care Law; Corporate Litigation. ***Email:*** ewaters@feldesmantucker.com

ROGER A. SCHWARTZ, born Meriden, Connecticut, July 16, 1944; admitted to bar, 1970, Connecticut; 1973, U.S. Supreme Court; 1979, District of Columbia; 1982, Virginia. *Education:* University of Connecticut (B.A., 1966); Georgetown University Law Center (J.D., 1969). Phi Beta Kappa. Author: *An Advocates' Guide to the Medicaid Program,* National Clearinghouse for Legal Services, Inc., 1985; *The Omnibus Budget Reconciliation Act of 1987:* Legislative Changes in Medicaid, Clearinghouse Review, Vol. 21, No. 11, April, 1988; *Changes in Medicaid:* Recent Legislative Development, Health Advocate, No 158, Fall, 1988. MCH Related Federal Programs: *Legal Handbooks for Program Planners-Medicaid,* 1990; *A Guidance for Providers of Mental Health and Addictive Disorder Services in Managed Care Contracting,* 1997. Programs Adjunct Professor, Georgetown University Law Center, Spring Semester, 1986, 1987, 1988 and 1989. ***PRACTICE AREAS:*** Health Care Law. ***Email:*** rschwartz@feldesmantucker.com

MICHAEL B. GLOMB, born Pittsburg, Pennsylvania, September 8, 1944; admitted to bar, 1970, West Virginia; 1971, District of Columbia; 1974, Pennsylvania; 1990, Virginia. *Education:* Georgetown University (A.B., 1966; J.D., 1969). Phi Alpha Delta. Author: *The Disability Insurance Benefits Program and Low Income Claimants in Appalachia,* 73 West Virginia Law Review 109, 1971; *Legal Issues in Pediatric HIV Practice: A Handbook for Health Care Providers,* National Pediatric HIV Resource Center, 1993. Co-Author: *Federal Disability Discrimination Law: A Compliance Handbook for Community and Migrant Health Centers,* National Association of Community Health Centers, 1991; *Federal Auditing Information Service,* National Association of College and University Business Officers, 1992—; "The Legal Obligations of Nonprofit Boards, 1992; *Confidentiality and Medical Records: The Legal Obligations of Health Centers,* National Association of Community Health Centers, 1992. *Member:* District of Columbia Bar (Member, Sections on: Taxation-Exempt Organizations, 1992—); Arlington County Bar Association; Virginia State Bar (Member, Section on: Health Law, 1992—); National Center for Nonprofit Boards (Council of Editorial Advisors, 1999—). ***PRACTICE AREAS:*** Health Care Law; Nonprofit Organizations; Business Law; Commercial Law. ***Email:*** mglomb@feldesmantucker.com

TANYA A. HARVEY, born Rochester, New York, March 14, 1957; admitted to bar, 1983, New York; 1990, Virginia; 1991, Maryland and District of Columbia; 1993, U.S. District Court, District of Maryland; 1994, U.S. District Court, District of D.C. *Education:* New York State University at Alfred (A.S., summa cum laude, 1977); New York State University at Albany (B.S., magna cum laude, 1979); New York State University of Buffalo (J.D., 1982). Phi Alpha Delta (Vice Justice, 1981-1982). Member, Moot Court Board, 1979-1982. Best Brief, Niagara Cup Moot Court Competition, 1981. *Member:* Virginia Bar Association. [Maj., U.S. Army Judge Advocate General's Corps, Reserve; Active Duty, 1983-1987]. ***PRACTICE AREAS:*** Estate Planning; Special Education; Disability Rights. ***Email:*** tharvey@feldesmantucker.com

RICHARD C. SHADYAC, JR., born Washington, D.C., April 4, 1957; admitted to bar, 1982, Virginia; 1983, District of Columbia. *Education:* Marquette University (B.A., magna cum laude, 1979); Loyola University of Illinois (J.D., 1982). Phi Beta Kappa; Alpha Sigma Nu. *Member:* District of Columbia Bar; Arlington, Fairfax County and American Bar Associations; Virginia State Bar; Virginia Trial Lawyers Association. ***PRACTICE AREAS:*** Domestic Relations; Litigation; Civil; Criminal; Personal Injury; Commercial; Business Litigation; Criminal Law. ***Email:*** RShadyac@feldesmantucker.com

BRUCE F. HOFFMEISTER, born Vandalia, Illinois, January 31, 1961; admitted to bar, 1986, Missouri; 1987, Illinois; 1988, District of Columbia and U.S. Tax Court. *Education:* University of Illinois, Urbana (B.S., 1983); Washington University, St. Louis (J.D., 1986). Member, Illinois Certified Public Accountant Society, 1983. *Member:* The District of Columbia Bar; The Missouri Bar; American Bar Association (Member, Sections on Taxation and Real Property, Probate and Trust Law); American Institute of Certified Public Accountants. ***PRACTICE AREAS:*** Estate Planning; Probate; Individual and Corporate Tax; Tax-Exempt Organizations. ***Email:*** bhoffmeister@feldesmantucker.com

JEFFREY L. CRAIG, born Philadelphia, Pennsylvania, January 25, 1962; admitted to bar, 1990, Pennsylvania; 2000, District of Columbia. *Education:* Indiana University (B.S., 1983); Temple University (J.D., 1990). Legal Teachings, Shippensburg University (1997-1998). Chief Deputy Attorney General

(This Listing Continued)

(1997-1998). *Member:* Pennsylvania and District of Columbia Bars; American Bar Association; Healthcare Compliance Association. ***PRACTICE AREAS:*** Health Care Law; Criminal Law; Corporate Law.

ASSOCIATES

JENNIFER B. PENNINGTON, born Morristown, New Jersey, February 3, 1966; admitted to bar, 1993, Virginia; 1995, District of Columbia. *Education:* American University (B.A., 1988); University of Richmond (J.D., 1992). Order of the Barristers. Member, Moot Court Board. *Member:* The District of Columbia Bar; Virginia State Bar; Women' s Bar Association. ***PRACTICE AREAS:*** Federal Grants Law; Special Education Law; Disability Rights. ***Email:*** jpennington@feldesmantucker.com

MARCIE H. ZAKHEIM, born Massapequa, New York, 1961; admitted to bar, 1998, District of Columbia and California. *Education:* State University of New York at Albany (B.S., 1983); George Washington University Law School (J.D., 1996). Co-Author: *An Evaluation of Agreements Between Managed Care Organizations and Community-Based Mental Health and Addictive Disorder Treatment and Prevention Providers* (2000); *Negotiating The New Health Care System: A Nationwide Study of Medicaid Managed Care Contracts,* first, second and third editions, published by the Center for Health Services Research and Policy at the George Washington University Medical School (February, 1997, February 1998 and Summer 1999); *Guidance for Certified Nurse-Midwives in Managed Care Contracting* (1997); *A Guide for Providers of Mental Health and Addictive Disorder Services in Managed Care Contracting* (1998). *Member:* The District of Columbia Bar (Member, Health Law Section); American Health Lawyers Association. ***PRACTICE AREAS:*** Health Care Law; Corporate Law; Nonprofit Organizations Law. ***Email:*** mzakheim@feldesmantucker.com

KATHY S. GHILADI, born Baltimore, Maryland, August 16, 1967; admitted to bar, 1991, Maryland; 1992, District of Columbia; 1995, U.S. District Court, District of Columbia; 1996, U.S. Court of Federal Claims and U.S. District Court, District of Maryland; 1997, U.S. Court of Appeals, District of Columbia Circuit. *Education:* American University (B.A., cum laude, 1988); University of Maryland (J.D., 1991). ***LANGUAGES:*** French and Farsi. ***PRACTICE AREAS:*** Government Contracts; Federal Grants; Health Care Law; Litigation; Employment Law. ***Email:*** kghiladi@feldesmantucker.com

DANIEL L. GRAY, born Arlington, Virginia, November 19, 1970; admitted to bar, 1997, Virginia; 1998, District of Columbia and Maryland. *Education:* University of Virginia (B.A., 1993); George Mason University School of Law (J.D., 1996). Law Clerk to the Honorable J. Howe Brown, Fairfax County Circuit Court, 1996-1997. *Member:* Fairfax County, Arlington County and Montgomery County Bar Associations; Virginia State Bar (Chairman, YLC Membership Involvement Committee; YLC Circuit Representative, 17th Circuit); Virginia Trial Lawyers Association. ***PRACTICE AREAS:*** Domestic Relations; Litigation. ***Email:*** Dgray@feldesmantucker.com

JENNIFER DZIEDIC-LEONARD, born Buffalo, New York, April 14, 1972; admitted to bar, 1999, District of Columbia. *Education:* State University of New York at Buffalo (B.A., cum laude, 1995); George Washington University (J.D., 1998; MPH, 1998). *Member:* The District of Columbia Bar; American Bar Association (Member, Sections on: Health; Employment Law); Women's Bar Association. ***LANGUAGES:*** French. ***PRACTICE AREAS:*** Health Care; Federal Grants; Corporate Litigation. ***Email:*** jleonard@feldesmantucker.com

MICHAEL D. GOLDE, born Costa Rica, November 16, 1970; admitted to bar, 1998, District of Columbia and California. *Education:* University of California at Berkeley (B.A., 1994); George Washington University (J.D., M.P.H., 1998). *Member:* The District of Columbia Bar; American Health Lawyers Association. ***PRACTICE AREAS:*** Health Care; Corporate Law; Nonprofit Organizations Law. ***Email:*** mgolde@feldesmantucker.com

DANELL PALLADINE DEAN, born Willingboro, New Jersey, October 1, 1963; admitted to bar, 1988, Delaware; 1989, Pennsylvania; 1995, District of Columbia; 1996, Maryland, Virginia, U.S. District Court, Eastern District of Pennsylvania, U.S. District Court, District of Delaware, U.S. District Court for the District of Columbia, U.S. District Courts, Eastern and Western Districts of Virginia and U.S. Court of Appeals, Fourth Circuit. *Education:* University of Pennsylvania (B.A., 1985); Tulane University School of Law; Delaware Law School of Widener University (J.D., cum laude, 1988). Phi Delta Phi. Member, Delaware Journal of Corporate Law, 1987-1988. Member, Board of Editors, The Journal of the Delaware Bar Association, 1990-1994. *Member:* Fairfax, Maryland State, Virginia and American Bar Associations; The District of Columbia Bar; Virginia Trial Lawyers Association. ***PRACTICE AREAS:*** Family Law; Commercial Litigation; Construction Litigation. ***Email:*** ddean@feldesmantucker.com

HOLLY A. WHITTIER, born Warwick, Rhode Island, June 2, 1972; admitted to bar, 1999, Maryland; 2000, U.S. District Court, District of Maryland; 2001, District of Columbia. *Education:* Towson State University (B.S., 1994); University of Baltimore School of Law (J.D., 1999). Law Clerk to the Hon. Louise G. Scrivener, Circuit Court for Montgomery County, Maryland, 1999-2000. Author, "Recent Development, Baker v. General Motors Corp.: Injunction Granted in One State Barring Employee From Testifying Against Former Em-

(This Listing Continued)

ployer Does Not Bar Testimony in Another State When Given Pursuant to Court Order," 28.2 U.Balt. L.F. 17 (1998). *Member:* Montgomery County and Maryland State Bar Associations. ***PRACTICE AREAS:*** Domestic Relations. ***Email:*** hwhittier@feldesmantucker.com

JESSICA S. WALTON, born Washington, D.C., March 14, 1962; admitted to bar, 1993, Maryland; 1995, District of Columbia and U.S. District Court, District of Maryland. *Education:* Randolph-Macon Woman's College (B.A., cum laude, 1985); Columbus School of Law, Catholic University of America (J.D., 1993). Phi Beta Kappa. Production Editor, Catholic University Law Review, 1992-1993. Author: Comment, "*Air Transport Association of America v. Department of Transportation:* Excess Baggage for Rules of Agency Procedure," 42 Cath. U. L. Rev. 313 (Winter 1993). *Member:* District of Columbia Bar; Maryland State and American Bar Associations; The Women's Bar Association of the District of Columbia. ***LANGUAGES:*** German. ***PRACTICE AREAS:*** Health Care Law. ***Email:*** jwalton@feldesmantucker.com

STEVEN H. WISHOD, born Huntington, New York, November 11, 1965; admitted to bar, 2000, Maryland, U.S. Court of Appeals, Fourth and Federal Circuits, U.S. Court of Appeals for the Armed Forces and U.S. Court of Federal Claims; 2001, District of Columbia. *Education:* Hobart and William Smith Colleges (B.A., cum laude, 1987); George Washington University (J.D., 2000). Phi Beta Kappa. Contributing Editor, "Federal Auditing Information Service," National Association of College and University Business Officers, 1992—. Researcher and Writer, "Administration of Government Contracts," George Washington University Government Contracts Program, 1995. *Member:* Maryland State, Federal Circuit and American (Member, Sections on: Public Contract Law; Litigation) Bar Associations. ***LANGUAGES:*** Russian. ***PRACTICE AREAS:*** Federal Grants; Government Contracts; Military Law; Civil Litigation. ***Email:*** swishod@feldesmantucker.com

ALANE A. PERAGALLO, born Waterloo, Iowa, December 30, 1962; admitted to bar, 1996, Virginia; 1997, Maryland; 1998, District of Columbia. *Education:* Wofford College (B.A., 1985); American University (J.D., 1996). Phi Beta Kappa. ***PRACTICE AREAS:*** Family Law; Civil Litigation; Criminal Law. ***Email:*** AP4@MC1.HHLAW.COM

JORDANA J. HUGHES, born Surrey, England, July 26, 1971; admitted to bar, 2000, Virginia (Not admitted in District of Columbia). *Education:* University of Maryland (B.A., 1993); George Washington University School of Law (J.D., 2000). Member, Moot Court Board. Member, International Law Review. Author: "The Trend Toward Liberal Enforcement of Repatriation Claims in Cultural Property Disputes," George Washington International Law Review. *Member:* Virginia Bar Association. ***LANGUAGES:*** Spanish. ***PRACTICE AREAS:*** Domestic Relations.

KAREN L. HECKER, born Waco, Texas, March 19, 1965; admitted to bar, 1993, Colorado (Not admitted in District of Columbia). *Education:* Cornell University (B.S., 1987); University of Colorado at Boulder (J.D., 1993). [U.S. Air Force, 1993-2000]. ***PRACTICE AREAS:*** Military Law; Litigation. ***Email:*** khecker@feldesmantucker.com

NANCY LEE FELDMAN

WASHINGTON, D.C.

(See Arlington, Virginia)

Wealth Preservation, Estate Planning, Trusts and Estates, Wills, Probate, Family Wealth Transfer, Trust and Estate Taxation, Family Business Law, Small Business Law, Business Formation, Business Successions, Tax Planning, Family Law, Divorce, Premarital Agreements, Postnuptial Agreements, Cohabitation Agreements, Separation Agreements.

FENWICK & WEST LLP

Established in 1972

1920 N STREET, N.W., SUITE 650
WASHINGTON, D.C. 20036
Telephone: 202-261-0400
Fax: 202-463-6520; 202-887-5143
URL: http://www.fenwick.com

Palo Alto, California Office: Two Palo Alto Square. Telephone: 650-494-0600. Fax: 650-494-1417.
San Francisco, California Office: 275 Battery Street, Suite 1500. Telephone: 415-875-2358. Fax: 415-281-1350.
Boise, Idaho Office: 877 West main Street, suite 706, 83702. Telephone: 208-331-0700. Fax: 208-331-7723.

General Practice. Corporate, Securities, Mergers and Acquisitions, Executive Compensation and Employee Benefits, Intellectual Property, Including Patent, Trademark and Copyright, Licensing and Online Commerce, Computer and High Technology Law, Government Contracts and Procurement, Litigation and Alternative Dispute Resolution, Antitrust and Trade Regulation, Trade Secrets, Employment and Labor Law and Domestic and International Taxation.

(This Listing Continued)

FIRM PROFILE: Established in 1972, we have grown to over 200 lawyers serving clients of national and international standing. Fenwick & West's national offices, its diverse clientele, its international correspondent relationships, and its size and breadth of experience enable it to offer both a full-service national and international practice and an entrepreneurial, aggressive approach to counseling and problem solving. Our full-service practice represents companies ranging from start-ups to major domestic and international companies. We specialize in the legal issues facing companies in the high-technology arena, particularly in the computer software and hardware, electronics and Internet industries. We have substantial experience in venture capital transactions and public offerings, intellectual property protection, counseling and litigation, business dispute resolution and antitrust, employment, tax, and securities litigation and domestic and international taxation.

ROGER M. GOLDEN, born New Brunswick, New Jersey, June 14, 1942; admitted to bar, 1967, New Jersey; 1968, District of Columbia; 1971, U.S. Supreme Court; 1982, U.S. Court of International Trade. *Education:* Princeton University (A.B., cum laude, 1964); University of Michigan Law School (J.D., 1967). ***PRACTICE AREAS:*** International Business; Trade; Customs Law; Export Control; Internet Law; Privacy Law; Information Security.

GARRY S. GROSSMAN, born Cleveland, Ohio, August 13, 1950; admitted to bar, 1982, District of Columbia. *Education:* University of Michigan (A.B., with honors, 1973); University of Toronto (M.Sc., 1977); George Washington University (J.D., with high honors, 1982). ***PRACTICE AREAS:*** Government Contracts; Technology Transfers; Computer Law; Privacy Law; Information Security.

BRIAN S. KELLY, born Raleigh, North Carolina, August 19, 1968; admitted to bar, 1993, North Carolina; 1997, California (Not admitted in District of Columbia). *Education:* University of Georgia (B.B.A., summa cum laude, 1990); Duke University (J.D., LL.M., 1993). ***PRACTICE AREAS:*** Licensing and Online Commerce; Complex Transactions; Copyright Protection; Trade Secret Protection.

C. KEVIN KELSO, born Indianapolis, Indiana, August 14, 1954; admitted to bar, 1980, California (Not admitted in District of Columbia). *Education:* University of Illinois (B.A., 1975); Harvard University (J.D., 1978). Law Clerk to Justice Anthony M. Kennedy, U.S. Court of Appeals, Ninth Circuit, 1978-1980. ***PRACTICE AREAS:*** Corporate Securities; Mergers and Acquisitions.

ASSOCIATES

PHYLLIS E. ANDES, born Commack, New York, September 15, 1961; admitted to bar, 1993, Virginia; 1996, District of Columbia; U.S. Court of International Trade; U.S. District Court, Eastern District of Virginia and District of Columbia; U.S. Court of Appeals, Fourth Circuit. *Education:* State University of New York at Stony Brook (B.A., 1983); George Washington University (J.D., with honors, 1993). ***PRACTICE AREAS:*** Corporate Trade; International Trade.

MARC S. BERGER, born Suffern, New York, September 27, 1971; admitted to bar, 1999, New York and The District of Columbia. *Education:* Pennsylvania State University (B.S., 1994); University of Miami (J.D./M.B.A., 1998). Author: "Keeping Pace with the Expanding Internet: Can the Courts Keep Up?" 9 Alb. L.J. Sci & Tech 52 (1998). ***PRACTICE AREAS:*** Licensing and Online Commerce; Entertainment/New Media; Commercial Encryption Applications.

CHRISTOPHER M. TOBIN, born Yonkers, New York, 1964; admitted to bar, 1993, Pennsylvania; 1996, California (Not admitted in District of Columbia). *Education:* Villanova University (B.S. Electrical Engineering, 1986; J.D., 1992). ***PRACTICE AREAS:*** Patent Law; Intellectual Property.

(For complete biographical data on all personnel, see Professional Biographies at Palo Alto, California)

DANIEL R. FERRY & ASSOCIATES

600 14TH STREET, N.W.
SUITE 600
WASHINGTON, D.C. 20005-2004
Telephone: 202-659-0146
Fax: 202-659-0148
Email: ftasinc@aol.com
URL: http://www.lawyers.com/danielrferrylaw

International Private Law, International Commercial Transactions, International Personal Injury Law, Corporate and Business Law.

DANIEL R. FERRY, born Nevada, Missouri, July 7, 1941; admitted to bar, 1965, Missouri; 1974, District of Columbia. *Education:* Central Methodist College (B.A., 1962); University of Missouri (J.D., 1965); George Washington University (LL.M., 1974). Phi Gamma Mu; Phi Delta Phi (Province President, 1969-1971 and Member, 1969-1985, Board of Directors). Contributing Editor, Will and Testamentary Trust Forms, Young Lawyers Section, Bar Association of

(This Listing Continued)

DANIEL R. FERRY & ASSOCIATES, Washington—Continued

the District of Columbia, 1974. Prosecuting Attorney, Vernon County, Missouri, 1967-1969. Assistant Prosecuting Attorney, Vernon County, Missouri, 1965-1967. *Member:* Vernon County (President, 1966-1969) and American (Member, Sections of: Corporation, Business and Banking; International; International Law Committee, 1965—; Secretary, 1973-1976) Bar Associations; District of Columbia Bar; The Missouri Bar; Inter-American Bar Association.

FILLER & WELLER, P.C.

WASHINGTON, D.C.

(See Alexandria, Virginia)

Aviation, Administrative Law, Litigation and Legislation.

JOEL M. FINKELSTEIN

Established in 1969

1742 N STREET, N.W.

WASHINGTON, D.C. 20036

Telephone: 202-659-3322

FAX: 202-785-2210

Email: attorneydc@aol.com

URL: http://www.lawyers.com/joelfinkelstein

General Negligence, Trials and Appeals. Medical Malpractice, Personal Injury, Automobile Accidents, Legal Malpractice, Professional Malpractice, Premises Liability, Wrongful Death, Products Liability Law.

FIRM PROFILE: Mr. Finkelstein represents individuals and families from all over the metropolitan Washington, D.C. region including suburban and Maryland and Virginia. His practice has included trials and courtroom appearances on behalf of his clients for more than 35 years.

JOEL M. FINKELSTEIN, born New York, N.Y., August 6, 1939; admitted to bar, 1964, New York; 1967, District of Columbia; 1968, U.S. Supreme Court; 1969, U.S. Claims Court. *Education:* Tulane University of Louisiana (B.B.A., 1960); Cornell University (LL.B., 1964). Lecturer: American University Law School and Washington College of Law, 1969-1970. Trial Attorney, Civil Rights Division, Department of Justice, 1964-1966. Deputy Chief of Appellate Section, U.S. Attorney's Office for the District of Columbia, 1967-1968. Assistant U.S. Attorney for the District of Columbia, 1966-1969. President, Assistant U.S. Attorneys Association of District of Columbia, 1969-1971. *Member:* The District of Columbia Bar; The Bar Association of the District of Columbia; The Association of Trial Lawyers of America. (Also of Counsel to Karp, Frosh, Lapidus & Wigodsky, P.A.).

NATHAN I. FINKELSTEIN

WASHINGTON, D.C.

(See Bethesda, Maryland)

Civil Trial Practice in Maryland and The District of Columbia. Auto Negligence, Medical/Dental Malpractice and Product Liability, Real Estate, Trust and Estates, Small Business Law, Commercial Litigation.

FINNEGAN, HENDERSON, FARABOW, GARRETT & DUNNER, L.L.P.

Established in 1965

1300 I STREET, N.W., SUITE 700

WASHINGTON, D.C. 20005

Telephone: 202-408-4000

Facsimile: 202-408-4400

Email: info@finnegan.com

URL: http://www.finnegan.com

Atlanta, Georgia Office: 3200 SunTrust Plaza, 303 Peachtree Street, N.E., 30308. Telephone: 404-653-6400. Facsimile: 404-653-6444.

Cambridge, Massachusetts Office: 55 Cambridge Parkway, 02142: Telephone: 617-444-8508. Facsimile: 617-444-8608.

Palo Alto, California Office: 700 Hansen Way, 94304. Telephone: 650-849-6600. Facsimile: 650-849-6666.

Brussels, Belgium Office: Avenue Louise 326, Box 37, B-1050. Telephone: 011-322-646-0353. Facsimile: 011-322-646-2135.

Tokyo, Japan Office: Toranomon No. 45 Mori Building, Third Floor, 1-5, Toranomon 5-Chome Minato-Ku, 105-0001. Telephone: 011-813-3431-6943. Facsimile: 011-813-3431-6945.

(This Listing Continued)

Patents, Trademarks, Copyrights, Trade Secrets, Chemical IP, Electrical IP, IP Infringement, IP Licensing, IP Litigation, IP Portfolio Management, IP Procurement, IP Rights, International IP, Mechanical IP, Pharmaceutical IP, Biotechnology IP, Information Technology Licensing.

FIRM PROFILE: Finnegan Henderson is the largest intellectual property boutique in the U.S. with more than 265 lawyers. The firm's full service IP practice has extensive expertise in virtually every scientific and technical field. The firm practices patent, trademark, copyright, and trade secret law and related litigation, licensing, international trade, asset management, Internet, government contract, antitrust, and unfair competition law.

MEMBERS OF FIRM

MARCUS B. FINNEGAN (1927-1979).

DOUGLAS B. HENDERSON, born Pittsburgh, Pennsylvania, September 21, 1935; admitted to bar, 1962, Virginia; 1963, District of Columbia; 1965, U.S. Supreme Court; registered to practice before U.S. Patent and Trademark Office. *Education:* Pennsylvania State University (B.S.I.E., 1957); The George Washington University National Law Center (J.D., with honors, 1963). Law Clerk to the Honorable Donald E. Lane, U.S. Court of Claims, 1962-1963. Author: "Third Party Practice in the United States Court of Claims or Two's Company, Three's a Crowd," Journal of the Patent Office Society, June 1976; "Developments in United States Licensing Law," International Business Lawyer, September 1983. Co-Author: "Prefiling Considerations and Initiating Suits," Litigation Institute of American Intellectual Property Law Association, January, 1978; "Motions, Discovery, and Pretrial Practicing in United States Claims Court," *Handbook on Trial Practice Before the United States Claims Court and United States Court of Appeals for the Federal Circuit,* September, 1986. Member: House of Delegates of the American Bar Association, 1999—; Fellow, American Bar Foundation, 2000—; Advisory Council, United States Court of Federal Claims, 1982—; Board of Advisors, George Washington University Law School, 1991-1997; Legal Advisory Board, Martindale-Hubbell, LEXIS/NEXIS, 1997—. *Member:* The District of Columbia Bar; Bar Association of the District of Columbia (Member, Board of Directors, 1975-1976; Trustee, Research Foundation, 1980-1981; Chairman, 1974-1975, Patent Trademark and Copyright Law Section; Chairman: Court of Claims Committee, 1973-1974; U.S. Court of Appeals for The Federal Circuit Committee, Chairman, 1982-1983); Virginia, Federal, American (Chairman, Patent Division, 1980-1981 and Member of Council, 1981-1985, Section on Patent, Trademark and Copyright Law) and International Bar Associations; Virginia State Bar; ITC Trial Lawyers Bar Association (Founder, 1984); Federal Circuit Bar Association (Founder and Member of Board of Directors, 1985-1986; 1996-1999; Judicial Selection Committee, 1990—); U.S. Court of Federal Claims Bar Association (Founder and Member of Board of Directors, 1987-1990); American Intellectual Property Law Association; U.S. Chamber of Commerce (Chairman, Patent, Trademark and Copyright Council, 1980-1982); International Trademark Association; Intellectual Property Owners Association; Supreme Court Historical Society; American Arbitration Association. ***PRACTICE AREAS:*** Intellectual Property Litigation; Patents; Technology Licensing; Trade Secrets; Trademarks. ***Email:*** douglas.henderson@finnegan.com

FORD F. FARABOW JR., born Charlotte, North Carolina, January 6, 1938; admitted to bar, 1963, South Carolina; 1965, District of Columbia; 1981, U.S. Supreme Court; 1982, U.S. Court of Appeals for the Federal Circuit; registered to practice before U.S. Patent and Trademark Office. *Education:* Clemson University (B.S.Ch.E., 1959); The George Washington University National Law Center (J.D., with honors, 1963). Order of the Coif; Phi Eta Sigma; Delta Theta Phi. *Member:* The District of Columbia Bar; Bar Association of the District of Columbia; South Carolina Bar; American Bar Association (Member, Sections on: Litigation; Antitrust Law; Patent, Trademark and Copyright Law); Federal Circuit Bar Association; American Intellectual Property Law Association (Member, Committee on Federal Practice and Procedure, 1982—); American Judicature Society; Giles S. Rich American Inn of Court. ***PRACTICE AREAS:*** Chemical Intellectual Property; Intellectual Property Arbitration; Intellectual Property Infringement; Intellectual Property Litigation; Pharmaceutical Intellectual Property. ***Email:*** ford.farabow@finnegan.com

ARTHUR S. GARRETT, born Drexel Hill, Pennsylvania, January 19, 1938; admitted to bar, 1964, District of Columbia; 1965, Pennsylvania; registered to practice before U.S. Patent and Trademark Office. *Education:* Rensselaer Polytechnic Institute (B.S.Ch.E., 1959); The George Washington University National Law Center (LL.B., 1963). Delta Theta Phi. *Member:* The District of Columbia Bar; Bar Association of the District of Columbia; Federal Circuit and American (Member, Sections on: Patent, Trademark and Copyright Law; Economics of Law Practice) Bar Associations; American Intellectual Property Law Association; International Association for the Protection of Industrial Property; International Federation of Industrial Property Attorneys. ***PRACTICE AREAS:*** International Patent Prosecution; International Licensing; Trademark Registration. ***Email:*** arthur.garrett@finnegan.com

(This Listing Continued)

DONALD R. DUNNER, born Brooklyn, New York, May 12, 1931; admitted to bar, 1958, District of Columbia; 1958-1982, U.S. Court of Customs and Patent Appeals; 1963, U.S. Supreme Court; 1982, U.S. Court of Appeals for the Federal Circuit; registered to practice before U.S. Patent and Trademark Office. *Education:* Purdue University (B.S.Ch.E., 1953); Georgetown University Law Center (J.D., 1958). Recipient, Purdue University Distinguished Engineering Alumnus Award, 2001. Member, Board of Editors, Georgetown University Law Review, 1957-1958. Law Clerk to the Honorable Noble J. Johnson, Chief Judge, U.S. Court of Customs and Patent Appeals, 1956-1958. Co-Author: *Court Review of Patent Office Decisions,* 1969, 1973. Co-Author: *Patent Law Perspectives,* 1970-1988; Co-Author: Court of Appeals for the Federal Circuit Practice and Procedure, 1985. Recipient, Joseph Rossman Memorial Award, 1979, and Patent Resources Group Patent Prize, 1980. Lecturer: John Marshall Law School Symposium, 1964, 1973, 1979, 1986, 1995, 1996, 1999; Practising Law Institute, 1967, 1968, 1978, 1981, 1983, 1985, 1986, 1993; Southwestern Legal Foundation, 1972, 1978. Professorial Lecturer in Law, The George Washington University National Law Center, 1969-1982. Adjunct Professor, Washington College of Law, American University, 1992—. Chairman, Advisory Committee of the Court of Appeals for the Federal Circuit, 1982-1992. President's Advisory Committee on Industrial Innovation, 1978-1979. Advisory Commission on Patent Law Reform, 1991-1992. *Member:* The District of Columbia Bar (Chair, Patent, Trademark and Copyright Division, 1976-1977); Bar Association of the District of Columbia (Chairman, 1964-1965, Patent, Trademark and Copyright Law Section; Member, Board of Directors, 1965-1966); American Bar Association (Chair, Section of Intellectual Property Law, 1995-1996); American Intellectual Property Law Association (President, 1979-1980); National Council of Patent Law Associations (Secretary, 1963-1966); Federal Circuit Bar Association (Board of Directors, 1999-2002). Fellow, American College of Trial Lawyers. [U.S. Army, 1953-1955]. ***PRACTICE AREAS:*** Intellectual Property Litigation; Intellectual Property Appeals. ***Email:*** don.dunner@finnegan.com

BRIAN G. BRUNSVOLD, born Mason City, Iowa, April 10, 1938; admitted to bar, 1967, Virginia and District of Columbia; 1982, U.S. Court of Appeals for the Federal Circuit; 1993, U.S. Supreme Court; registered to practice before U.S. Patent and Trademark Office. *Education:* Iowa State University (B.S.Ch.E., 1960); The George Washington University National Law Center (J.D., with honors, 1967). Order of the Coif; Tau Beta Pi. Law Clerk, U.S. Court of Claims, 1966-1967. Author: "Recent Developments in the Law Relating to Licensing," Journal of the Licensing Executives Society, 1979—. Co-Author: "Patent and Copyright Practice Before the International Trade Commission," Patent Resources Institute, 1989; "Drafting Patent License Agreements," BNA Books, 1984, 1991, 1998—. Editor-in-Chief, Licensing Law and Business Report, 1979-1982. Professorial Lecturer in Law, George Washington University National Law Center, 1975-1996. *Member:* The District of Columbia Bar; Virginia State Bar; American Bar Association; American Intellectual Property Law Association; ITC Trial Lawyers Association (President, 1985-1986). ***PRACTICE AREAS:*** Antitrust and Trade Regulation; Chemical Intellectual Property; Intellectual Property Licensing; Intellectual Property Litigation; Pharmaceutical Intellectual Property. ***Email:*** brian.brunsvold@finnegan.com

JERRY D. VOIGHT (Resident Partner, Palo Alto, California Office).

LAURENCE R. HEFTER, born New York, New York, October 13, 1935; admitted to bar, 1964, Virginia; 1967, New York; 1973, District of Columbia; registered to practice before U.S. Patent and Trademark Office. *Education:* Rensselaer Polytechnic Institute (B.M.E., 1957; M.S.M.E., 1960); The George Washington University National Law Center (J.D., with honors, 1964). Order of the Coif. Professorial Lecturer of Law (Trademarks), The George Washington University National Law Center, 1981-1990. Listed in "Best Lawyers in America" and "Guide to the World's Leading Experts in Trademark Law" and "Guide to the World's Leading Experts in Patent Law". Member, Advisory Committee for Patents and Trademarks, U.S. Patent and Trademark Office, 1988-1990. Panelist on the CPR Institute for Dispute Resolution and INTA Trademark and Unfair Competition Panel of Neutrals. *Member:* The District of Columbia Bar; New York State, American (Governing Committee Forum on Franchising, 1994—) and International (Chairman, Committees on: Patents, 1985-1986; Trademarks, 1987-1990) Bar Associations; Virginia State Bar (Member, Board of Governors, Section on Patent, Trademark and Copyright Law, 1976-1979); American Intellectual Property Law Association (Member, Board of Directors, 1981-1984); International Trademark Association (Member, Board of Directors, 1982-1984; Member, Trademark Review Commission). ***PRACTICE AREAS:*** Trademarks; Trademark Litigation; Unfair Competition; Intellectual Property Litigation; Alternative Dispute Resolution.

HERBERT H. MINTZ, born Brooklyn, New York, April 24, 1946; admitted to bar, 1972, District of Columbia and U.S. Court of Federal Claims; 1972-1982, U.S. Court of Customs and Patent Appeals; 1981, U.S. Supreme Court; 1982, U.S. Court of Appeals for the Federal Circuit; registered to practice before U.S. Patent and Trademark Office. *Education:* Cooper Union School of Engineering and Science (B.Ch.E., 1966); The George Washington University National Law Center (J.D., with honors, 1971). Associate Editor, The George Washington Law Review, 1970-1971. Technical Advisor and Law Clerk to the Honorable Donald E. Lane, Judge, U.S. Court of Customs and Patent Appeals,

(This Listing Continued)

1971-1973. *Member:* The District of Columbia Bar (Chairman, Patent, Trademark, and Copyright Division, 1978); American Bar Association (IPL Section, CLE Committee Vice-Chair, 1994-1995); Federal Circuit Bar Association (Member or Officer, Board of Directors, 1986-1994; President, 1992-1993); Supreme Court Bar Association; American Intellectual Property Law Association (Member, Board of Directors, 1986-1988). ***PRACTICE AREAS:*** Patent Interference Practice; Patent Litigation. ***Email:*** herbert.mintz@finnegan.com

C. LARRY O'ROURKE (Resident Partner, Palo Alto, California Office).

ALBERT J. SANTORELLI, born New York, New York, October 17, 1938; admitted to bar, 1964, District of Columbia; 1968, U.S. Supreme Court and U.S. Court of Appeals for the Federal Circuit; registered to practice before U.S. Patent and Trademark Office. *Education:* Rensselaer Polytechnic Institute (B.S.E.E., 1961); Georgetown University Law Center (LL.B., 1964). Member, Georgetown Law Journal, 1962-1964. Author: "Presenting Direct Evidence From the Accused Infringer's Point of View," AIPLA Fourth Annual Institute Patent Jury Litigation, Jan. 1981. *Member:* The District of Columbia Bar; Federal and American Bar Associations; American Intellectual Property Law Association. ***PRACTICE AREAS:*** Patent Litigation; Patents; Patent Interference Practice; Patent Infringement. ***Email:*** albert.santorelli@finnegan.com

MICHAEL C. ELMER (Resident Partner, Palo Alto, California Office).

RICHARD H. SMITH, born Wyandotte, Michigan, September 12, 1937; admitted to bar, 1965, Minnesota; 1968, Massachusetts; 1976, District of Columbia; 1982, U.S. Court of Appeals for the Federal Circuit; registered to practice before U.S. Patent and Trademark Office. *Education:* Lehigh University (B.S.I.E., 1959); The George Washington University National Law Center (LL.B., 1964). *Member:* The District of Columbia Bar; Bar Association of the District of Columbia (Member, Section on Patent, Trademark and Copyright Law); Federal and American (Member, Sections on: Patent, Trademark and Copyright Law; Science and Technology) Bar Associations; American Intellectual Property Law Association (Chairman, Programmable Machines and Processes Committee, 1982-1984). ***PRACTICE AREAS:*** Patent Prosecution; Patent Litigation; Patent Licensing; Computer and Software Patents. ***Email:*** richard.smith@finnegan.com

STEPHEN L. PETERSON, born Oakland, California, September 15, 1944; admitted to bar, 1974, Ohio; 1975, District of Columbia; 1981, U.S. Supreme Court; 1983, U.S. Court of Appeals for the Federal Circuit; registered to practice before U.S. Patent and Trademark Office. *Education:* California State University at San Jose (B.S., Material Science, 1967); Capital University Law School (J.D., 1974). *Member:* The District of Columbia Bar; Bar Association of the District of Columbia (Member, Section on Patent, Trademark and Copyright Law; Council, 1982-1985, 1992-1993; Chairman, 1986-1987; Board of Directors, 1987-1988); American Bar Association; Federal Circuit Bar Association (Board of Directors, 1994-1997); ITC Trial Lawyers Association; American Intellectual Property Law Association. [United States Marine Corps, 1969-1975]. ***PRACTICE AREAS:*** Patent Prosecution; Patent Litigation; Trade Secrets. ***Email:*** stephen.peterson@finnegan.com

JOHN M. ROMARY, born Paterson, New Jersey, August 7, 1947; admitted to bar, 1973, District of Columbia; registered to practice before U.S. Patent and Trademark Office. *Education:* Lehigh University (B.S.E.E., with honors, 1969); Georgetown University Law Center (J.D., 1973). Tau Beta Pi; Eta Kappa Nu; Phi Eta Sigma. Editor-at-Large, Law & Policy in International Business, 1972-1973. Law Clerk to the Honorable James L. Latchum, Chief Judge, U.S. District Court, District of Delaware, 1973-1975. *Member:* The District of Columbia Bar; Bar Association of the District of Columbia; Federal and American Bar Associations; American Intellectual Property Law Association; Licensing Executives Society. ***PRACTICE AREAS:*** Patent Litigation; Patent Prosecution; Patent Licensing. ***Email:*** john.romary@finnegan.com

BRUCE C. ZOTTER, born New Britain, Connecticut, September 18, 1942; admitted to bar, 1975, Virginia; 1976, District of Columbia; 1982, U.S. Court of Appeals for the Federal Circuit; registered to practice before U.S. Patent and Trademark Office. *Education:* Massachusetts Institute of Technology (B.S.M.E., 1965; M.S.M.E., 1966); The George Washington University National Law Center (J.D., with honors, 1975). Pi Tau Sigma; Sigma Xi. Engineer, Knolls Atomic Power Laboratory, Schenectady, New York. Professional Engineer, New York, 1970. *Member:* The District of Columbia Bar; Bar Association of the District of Columbia; Virginia State Bar; American Bar Association; American Intellectual Property Law Association. ***PRACTICE AREAS:*** Patent Litigation. ***Email:*** bruce.zotter@finnegan.com

D. PATRICK O'REILLEY, born Corpus Christi, Texas, December 4, 1943; admitted to bar, 1975, District of Columbia; 1975-1982, U.S. Court of Customs and Patent Appeals; 1982, U.S. Court of Appeals for the Federal Circuit; registered to practice before U.S. Patent and Trademark Office. *Education:* United States Naval Academy (B.S., 1966); The George Washington University National Law Center (J.D., 1975). Member, George Washington Law Review, 1973-1975. Co-Author: "Drafting Patent License Agreements," 4th ed. (BNA 1998). Adjunct Professor, George Mason University Law School. *Member:* The District of Columbia Bar; Bar Association of the District of Columbia; American Bar Association; American Intellectual Property Law Association;

(This Listing Continued)

FINNEGAN, HENDERSON, FARABOW, GARRETT & DUNNER, L.L.P., Washington—Continued

Licensing Executives Society. [Lt., U.S. Navy, 1966-1972]. ***PRACTICE AREAS:*** Intellectual Property Infringement; Intellectual Property Licensing; Intellectual Property Litigation; International Licensing; Mechanical Intellectual Property. ***Email:*** pat.oreilley@finnegan.com

ALLEN M. SOKAL, born Philadelphia, Pennsylvania, December 17, 1946; admitted to bar, 1973, Virginia; 1974, District of Columbia; U.S. Court of Appeals for the Federal Circuit; U.S. Supreme Court; registered to practice before U.S. Patent and Trademark Office. *Education:* University of Pennsylvania (B.S.Ch.E., cum laude, 1968); Georgetown University Law Center (J.D., 1972). Tau Beta Pi; Phi Lambda Upsilon. Patent Examiner, 1968-1973. Member, Georgetown Law Journal, 1971-1972. Technical Advisor and Law Clerk to the Honorable Jack R. Miller, Judge, U.S. Court of Customs and Patent Appeals, 1974-1976. Author: "Impact of Decisions of the Court of Appeals for the Federal Circuit on the Duty of Disclosure," 66 JPOS 29, 1984. Co-author: *Chemical Patent Law,* Patent Resources Group, 1996. Contributing Writer: *Patent Law Perspectives,* Matthew Bender & Co., 1988. Member, Intellectual Property Advisory Committee to U.S. District Court for the District of Delaware, 1992-1994. Lecturer: "Chemical Patent Practice," Patent Resources Group, Inc., 1996—. *Member:* The District of Columbia Bar (Member, Patent, Trademark and Copyright Law Steering Committee, 1983-1985; Chairman, 1984-1985); American Bar Association (Member, Section on Patent, Trademark and Copyright Law; Chairman, Subcommittee on Review of PTO Rule Changes, 1988); American Intellectual Property Law Association (Chairman, Current Court Cases Subcommittee, Chemical Practice Committee, 1979-1981); Federal Circuit Bar Association (Amicus Committee, 1995—); Giles S. Rich American Inn of Court. ***PRACTICE AREAS:*** Intellectual Property Rights; Chemical Patents; Patent Litigation; Patent Prosecution; Pharmaceutical Patents. ***Email:*** allen.sokal@finnegan.com

ROBERT D. BAJEFSKY, born New York, New York, February 3, 1943; admitted to bar, 1970, District of Columbia; 1974, U.S. Supreme Court; 1982, U.S. Court of Appeals for the Federal Circuit; registered to practice before U.S. Patent and Trademark Office. *Education:* Virginia Polytechnic Institute (B.S.Ch.E., 1964); Georgetown University Law Center (J.D., 1970). Tau Beta Pi; Phi Lambda Upsilon. Co-author: "Can the Attorney Who Prepares and Infringement or Validity Opinion Serve as Litigator in a Later Patent Case?" Legal Times, IP Supplement, March 1996; revised and published in *IP Litigator,* November/December, 1997; "Hilton Davis: The Impact on Biotech," National Law Journal, June 16, 1997. *Member:* The District of Columbia Bar; Bar Association of the District of Columbia; Federal Circuit and American Bar Associations; American Intellectual Property Law Association. ***PRACTICE AREAS:*** Biotechnology Patents; Chemical Patents; Medical Patents; Patent Litigation; Pharmaceutical Patents. ***Email:*** robert.bajefsky@finnegan.com

RICHARD LEE STROUP, born Shelby, Ohio, May 17, 1948; admitted to bar, 1976, Virginia; 1977, District of Columbia and U.S. Court of Federal Claims; 1982, U.S. Court of Appeals for the Federal Circuit; registered to practice before U.S. Patent and Trademark Office. *Education:* Ohio Northern University (B.S., Mechanical Engineering, 1970); University of Virginia School of Law (J.D., 1976). Tau Beta Pi; Phi Kappa Phi. Law Clerk to the Honorable Francis C. Browne, Trial Judge, U.S. Court of Claims, 1976-1977. *Member:* The District of Columbia Bar; Bar Association of the District of Columbia; Virginia State Bar; American Bar Association; American Intellectual Property Law Association; International Trademark Association. [U.S. Army, 1970-1972]. ***PRACTICE AREAS:*** Intellectual Property Litigation; Mechanical Intellectual Property; Civil Litigation; Technology Licensing; Trademarks; Trade Secrets; Unfair Competition. ***Email:*** richard.stroup@finnegan.com

DAVID W. HILL, born Taunton, Massachusetts, May 27, 1946; admitted to bar, 1977, District of Columbia; 1978, U.S. District Court for the District of Columbia and U.S. Court of Appeals for the District of Columbia Circuit; 1981, U.S. Supreme Court; 1982, U.S. Court of Appeals for the Federal Circuit and U.S. Court of Federal Claims; registered to practice before U.S. Patent and Trademark Office. *Education:* University of Massachusetts and United States Military Academy (B.S., 1969); Boston University (M.S., Business Administration, with honors, 1974); The George Washington University National Law Center (J.D., 1977; LL.M., with highest honors, Patent and Trade Regulation Law, 1981). Technical Advisor, U.S. Court of Customs and Patent Appeals, 1976-1977. Member, U.S. Bar/Japanese Patent Office Liaison Council (Vice Chairman, 1992-1993; Chairman, 1994-1995). *Member:* District of Columbia Bar (Member, Intellectual Property Law Section, Steering Committee, 1985-1986, 1991-1997; Co-Chairman, 1992-1994); American Intellectual Property Law Association (IP Practice in Japan Committee, 1990—; Co-Chairman, 1995-1997; Vice Chairman, International and Foreign Law Committee, 2000—; Alternative Dispute Resolution Committee); Licensing Executives Society; International Trademark Association; Brand Names Education Foundation (Chairman, Board of Governors Nominating Committee, 1999—). [Active Duty, U.S. Army Corps of Engineers, 1969-1974; Major, U.S. Army Reserve, Retired]. ***PRACTICE AREAS:*** Alternative Dispute Resolution; Intellectual Property; Patents; Trademarks; Unfair Competition. ***Email:*** david.hill@finnegan.com

THOMAS L. IRVING, born Salt Lake City, Utah, April 29, 1951; admitted to bar, 1977, District of Columbia; 1982, U.S. Court of Appeals for the Federal Circuit; registered to practice before U.S. Patent and Trademark Office. *Education:* University of Utah (B.A.Chem., magna cum laude, 1974); Duke University School of Law (J.D., 1977). Phi Beta Kappa; Phi Kappa Phi. Recipient, American Jurisprudence Book Award in Evidence, Duke University School of Law, 1976. Co-Author: "Chemical Patent Law," Patent Resources Group, 1996-2001; "Patents Under GATT's Uruguay Round Agreements Act," Patent Resources Group, 1995; "Crafting and Drafting Winning Patents," Patent Resources Group, 2000-2001. Adjunct Professor of Patent Law, Washington College of Law, American University, 1988-1993. *Member:* American Bar Association (Member, Patent, Trademark and Copyright Law Section; Chairman: Chemical Practice Committee; Subcommittees on CAFC; District Court, 1985-1987; CLE, 1988-1989; Program Chairman, 1985-1986; Chairman, 1987; Chairman, Nominations and Elections, 1988); American Intellectual Property Law Association (Board of Directors, 1991-1994; Chairman, Chemical Practice Committee, 1989-1991); American Chemical Society (Chairman, Division of Chemistry and the Law). ***LANGUAGES:*** Spanish. ***PRACTICE AREAS:*** Chemical Intellectual Property; Chemical Patent Prosecution; Chemical Patents; Patent Interference Practice. ***Email:*** irvingt@finnegan.com

CHARLES E. LIPSEY, born Pensacola, Florida, November 27, 1950; admitted to bar, 1977, Virginia; 1979, District of Columbia; U.S. Court of Appeals for the Federal Circuit; registered to practice before U.S. Patent and Trademark Office. *Education:* Georgia Institute of Technology (B.S.Ch.E., 1972); The George Washington University National Law Center (J.D., with high honors, 1977; LL.M., Patent and Trade Regulation Law, with highest honors, 1981). Order of the Coif; Tau Beta Pi. Technical Advisor to the Honorable Giles S. Rich, Associate Judge, U.S. Court of Customs and Patent Appeals, 1976-1978. Professional Lecturer in Law, George Washington University National Law Center, 1984-1989. Co-Author: "Patent Law Perspectives," Matthew Bender & Co., 1982-1988. *Member:* The District of Columbia Bar; Bar Association of the District of Columbia; Virginia State Bar; American Bar Association; American Intellectual Property Law Association. ***PRACTICE AREAS:*** Intellectual Property Litigation; Patent Infringement. ***Email:*** charles.lipsey@finnegan.com

THOMAS W. WINLAND, born Lancaster, Ohio, March 18, 1949; admitted to bar, 1974, Ohio; 1980-1982, U.S. Court of Customs and Patent Appeals; 1981, District of Columbia; 1982, U.S. Court of Appeals for the Federal Circuit; U.S. Court of Federal Claims; registered to practice before U.S. Patent and Trademark Office. *Education:* Ohio State University (B.S., 1971); Duke University School of Law (J.D., 1974). *Member:* The District of Columbia Bar; Bar Association of the District of Columbia; Ohio State and American (Member, Sections on: Patent, Trademark and Copyright Law; Public Contract Law) Bar Associations; American Intellectual Property Law Association (Member, Government Intellectual Property Policy Committee, 1975—, Chairman, 1992—); Licensing Executives Society. ***PRACTICE AREAS:*** Intellectual Property Litigation; Intellectual Property Arbitration; Intellectual Property Licensing; Proprietary Rights. ***Email:*** tom.winland@finnegan.com

BASIL J. LEWRIS, born Manhattan, New York, February 26, 1949; admitted to bar, 1977, Virginia; 1978, U.S. Court of Federal Claims; 1979, District of Columbia; 1981, U.S. Supreme Court; 1982, U.S. Court of Appeals for the Federal Circuit; registered to practice before U.S. Patent and Trademark Office. *Education:* City College of the City University of New York (B.S.Ch.E., cum laude, 1972); The George Washington University National Law Center (J.D., with high honors, 1977; LL.M., Patent and Trade Regulation Law, 1980). Order of the Coif; Delta Theta Phi; Tau Beta Pi; Omega Chi Epsilon. Law Clerk to the Honorable Donald E. Lane, Associate Judge, U.S. Court of Customs and Patent Appeals, 1977-1979. Lecturer, Patent Resources Group, Inc., 1982-1991. Co-Author: "Federal Circuit Patent Law Update," Patent Resources Group, Inc., 1983; "Federal Circuit Patent Law," Patent Resources Group, Inc., 1984; "Federal Circuit Patents and Statutory Changes, 1984-1985;" *Patent Law Perspectives,* Matthew Bender & Co., 1984-1988; "Federal Circuit Patent Law, 1985-1986," Patent Resources Group, Inc., 1985; "Federal Circuit Patent Law, 1985-1987," Patent Resources Institute, Inc., 1986; "Federal Circuit Patent Law, 1986-1988," Patent Resources Institute, Inc., 1987; "Securing Evidence in Patent Litigation in the United States," International Bar Association, 1987; "Federal Circuit Patent Law, 1987-1989," Patent Resources Institute, Inc., 1988; "Federal Circuit Patent Law, 1988-1990," Patent Resources Institute, Inc.; "A Comprehensive Guide to Patent Litigation in the United States, Maximizing Recovery ... Minimizing Loss," EuroForum (1996). *Member:* The District of Columbia Bar; Virginia State Bar; American Bar Association; American Intellectual Property Law Association; The Association of Trial Lawyers of America. ***PRACTICE AREAS:*** Civil Appeals; Chemical Intellectual Property; Intellectual Property Litigation; Pharmaceutical Intellectual Property; Biotechnology. ***Email:*** bill.lewris@finnegan.com

MARTIN I. FUCHS, born Newark, New Jersey, November 2, 1952; admitted to bar, 1978, District of Columbia, New Jersey, U.S. District Court, District of New Jersey; 1979, U.S. District Court for the District of Columbia; 1982,

(This Listing Continued)

U.S. Court of Appeals for the Federal Circuit; registered to practice before U.S. Patent and Trademark Office. *Education:* Rutgers College (B.A., 1974); The George Washington University National Law Center (J.D., 1978). Law Clerk and Technical Advisor to the Honorable Donald E. Lane, Associate Judge, U.S. Court of Customs and Patent Appeals, 1978-1980. Member, Permanent Lawyers Advisory Committee for the U.S. District Court, District of Delaware, Subcommittee on Uniform Jury Instructions for Patent Cases, 1992-1994. ***PRACTICE AREAS:*** Patent Infringement. ***Email:*** martin.fuchs@finnegan.com

E. ROBERT YOCHES, born Denver, Colorado, January 23, 1953; admitted to bar, 1980, District of Columbia; 1982, U.S. Court of Appeals for the Federal Circuit; 1993, U.S. Supreme Court; registered to practice before U.S. Patent and Trademark Office. *Education:* University of Colorado (B.S.E.E. & C.S., with highest honors, 1974); University of Pennsylvania Law School (J.D., 1980). Editorial Board, The Computer Law Reporter, 1992—; Internet Newsletter, 1996—. *Member:* The District of Columbia Bar (Vice-Chairman, Steering Committee, Computer Law Division, 1985-1986; Chairman, 1986-1987); Bar Association of the District of Columbia; D.C. Computer Law Forum (Board of Directors, 1992-1993); Licensing Executive Society (Vice Chair, Computer Industry Committee, 1993-1995, Chairman, Telecommunications Industry Committee, 1996-1998; Chair, Information Technologies and Electronics Industries Section, 1998-2000); Advanced Computer Law Institute (Co-Chair, 1992—). ***PRACTICE AREAS:*** Information Technology Licensing; Software Copyright; Software Licensing; Software Protection; Intellectual Property Litigation. ***Email:*** bob.yoches@finnegan.com

BARRY W. GRAHAM, born Rome, Georgia, July 7, 1947; admitted to bar, 1977, Georgia; 1979, District of Columbia; 1982, U.S. Court of Appeals for the Federal Circuit; 1983, U.S. Supreme Court; 1987, U.S. Court of Federal Claims; registered to practice before U.S. Patent and Trademark Office. *Education:* University of Virginia (B.S.E.E., 1970); University of Georgia School of Law (J.D., with honors, 1977); The George Washington University National Law Center (LL.M., Patent and Trade Regulation Law, 1983). Omicron Delta Kappa. Technical Advisor to the Honorable Phillip B. Baldwin, Associate Judge, U.S. Court of Customs and Patent Appeals, 1980-1982. *Member:* State Bar of Georgia; The District of Columbia Bar; Bar Association of the District of Columbia; American Bar Association; American Intellectual Property Law Association; Federation Internationale des Conseils en Propriete Industrielle (Member, U.S. Section). [Lt. (jg), U.S. Navy, 1971-1974]. ***PRACTICE AREAS:*** Electronic Intellectual Property; Intellectual Property Infringement; Intellectual Property Litigation; Computer and Software Patents; Technology Protection. ***Email:*** barry.graham@finnegan.com

SUSAN HABERMAN GRIFFEN, born Milwaukee, Wisconsin, March 23, 1956; admitted to bar, 1982, District of Columbia; 1984, U.S. District Court, District of Columbia; 1985, U.S. Court of Appeals for the Federal Circuit; registered to practice before the U.S. Patent and Trademark Office. *Education:* Iowa State University (B.S., Bacteriology, with honors, 1978); University of Iowa College of Law (J.D., with honors, 1982). Co-Recipient, Iowa Academy of Trial Lawyers Award. Adjunct Faculty, George Washington University National Law Center, 1991-1997. *Member:* The District of Columbia Bar Association; American Bar Association; Women's Bar Association of the District of Columbia; American Intellectual Property Law Association; Licensing Executives Society. ***PRACTICE AREAS:*** Biotechnology Patents. ***Email:*** susan.griffen@finnegan.com

RICHARD B. RACINE, born Cleveland, Ohio, March 20, 1956; admitted to bar, 1981, Ohio; 1984, District of Columbia; registered to practice before U.S. Patent and Trademark Office. *Education:* Georgetown University (B.S., 1978); Case Western Reserve University School of Law (J.D., 1981). Co-Author: "Third-Party Opinions: Traps and Pitfalls," Fed. Cir. Bar J., Vol. 4, 46, Winter 1994; "The Battle Over Science in the Courtroom," Fed. Law., Vol. 42, 37, February 1995; "Willful Infringement: A Real Concern," Fed. Cir. Bar J., Vol. 3, 409, Winter 1993; "To Sue or Not To Sue," Chemtech, 53, March 1994. Lecturer, Patent Law Institute, Southwestern Legal Foundation, 1993-1994. *Member:* The District of Columbia Bar; Bar Association of the District of Columbia; Federal Circuit and American (Subcommittee Chair, Attorney Opinions Committee, 1993-1994) Bar Associations; American Intellectual Property Law Association; American Chemical Society (Division of Chemistry and the Law Program Chair, 1991-1993; Division Chair-Elect, 1993; Division Chair, 1994). ***PRACTICE AREAS:*** Patent Litigation; Pharmaceutical Patents; Chemical Patents. ***Email:*** rich.racine@finnegan.com

THOMAS H. JENKINS III, born Washington, D.C., October 25, 1951; admitted to bar, 1980, New York; 1984, District of Columbia; registered to practice before U.S. Patent and Trademark Office. *Education:* Davidson College (B.S., 1974); Pennsylvania State University (M.S., 1976); University of Virginia School of Law (J.D., 1979). *Member:* The District of Columbia Bar; Bar Association of the District of Columbia. ***PRACTICE AREAS:*** Patent Litigation; Patent Prosecution. ***Email:*** thomas.jenkins@finnegan.com

ROBERT E. CONVERSE JR., born Buffalo, New York, May 6, 1945; admitted to bar, 1977, Pennsylvania; 1982, U.S. Court of Appeals for the Federal Circuit; 1984, District of Columbia; registered to practice before U.S. Patent and Trademark Office. *Education:* Northwestern University (B.S.E.E.,

(This Listing Continued)

1968); Duquesne University School of Law (J.D., 1973). *Member:* The District of Columbia Bar; Bar Association of the District of Columbia; American Bar Association. ***PRACTICE AREAS:*** Patent Prosecution; Patent Litigation. ***Email:*** converse@finnegan.com

CLAIR X. MULLEN JR., born Pittsburgh, Pennsylvania, March 11, 1933; admitted to bar, 1960, Pennsylvania; 1964, U.S. District Court, Western District of Pennsylvania; 1985, District of Columbia; registered to practice before U.S. Patent and Trademark Office. *Education:* Saint Vincent College (B.S. Chemistry, 1955); University of Pittsburgh School of Law (LL.B., 1958). *Member:* The District of Columbia Bar; American Intellectual Property Law Association; Patent Law Association of Pittsburgh; Licensing Executives Society. ***PRACTICE AREAS:*** International Patent Prosecution; Metallurgical Patents; Patent Licensing; Patent Prosecution. ***Email:*** clair.mullen@finnegan.com

CHRISTOPHER P. FOLEY, born Washington, D.C., November 25, 1953; admitted to bar, 1983, District of Columbia and U.S. Court of Appeals for the Federal Circuit; registered to practice before U.S. Patent and Trademark Office. *Education:* United States Naval Academy (B.S., 1975); Georgetown University Law Center (J.D., 1983). *Member:* The District of Columbia Bar; Bar Association of the District of Columbia; American Bar Association; American Intellectual Property Law Association. [Lt., U.S. Navy, 1971-1980]. ***PRACTICE AREAS:*** Trademark Registration; Trademark Litigation; Patent Litigation; Patent Prosecution. ***Email:*** christopher.foley@finnegan.com

JOHN C. PAUL, born Norwalk, Connecticut, March 3, 1954; admitted to bar, 1979, Ohio; 1981, District of Columbia and U.S. Court of Appeals for the District of Columbia Circuit; 1982, U.S. District Court for the District of Columbia and U.S. Court of Appeals for the Federal Circuit; 1983, U.S. Supreme Court; registered to practice before U.S. Patent and Trademark Office. *Education:* Brown University (A.B., 1976); Case Western Reserve University School of Law (J.D., 1979). Author: "Recent Developments in the Law Relating to Licensing," Les Nouvelles, 1991—; "Licensing to South Korea," Les Nouvelles, September 1995; "Licensing to Korea: 1997," Les Nouvelles, June 1998. Adjunct Faculty Member: The Catholic University of America, 1997—. Lecturer: U.S. Department of Justice Legal Education Institute Course on Patent, Trademark and Copyright Law, 1984-1988. *Member:* Bar Association of the District of Columbia (Member: Amicus Brief Subcommittee of the CAFC Committee, 1982-1984; Board of Directors, Young Lawyers Division, 1982-1986; Executive Council, Young Lawyers Section, 1987-1990); Federal Circuit (Member, Board of Directors, Young Lawyers Division, 1982-1986) and American (Chairman, District of Columbia Young Lawyers Division Membership, 1983-1990; Vice-Chairman, Young Lawyers Division, Patent, Trademark and Copyright Law Committee, 1989-1990) Bar Associations; American Intellectual Property Law Association (Subcommittee Chairman, Foreign and International Law Committee, 1994-1995); Licensing Executives Society (Chairman, Washington Chapter, 1994—; Co-Chair: Education and Professional Development Committee, 2000—; Publications Committee, 2000—); American Society of Mechanical Engineers (Member: Industry/Laboratory Technology Transfers Committee; Chairman, Technology and Law Committee, 1996-1998; Chairman, Technology and Society Division, 1998-2000); American Chamber of Commerce in Italy (Intellectual Property Law Committee); Washington Area Lawyers for the Arts (Board of Directors, 1997—). ***PRACTICE AREAS:*** Intellectual Property Portfolio Management; Intellectual Property Licensing; Patent Litigation; Patent Prosecution. ***Email:*** john.paul@finnegan.com

ROGER D. TAYLOR (Resident Partner, Atlanta, Georgia Office).

GRIFFITH B. PRICE JR., born Lawrence, Kansas, August 15, 1942; admitted to bar, 1967, New York; 1991, District of Columbia. *Education:* Harvard University (A.B., cum laude, 1964); New York University (LL.B., 1967). Root-Tilden Scholar. Managing Editor, Annual Survey of American Law, 1966-1967. Author: "The Federal Circuit Courts of Appeals Standards For Likelihood of Confusion" (AIPLA, 1993); "Recent Developments Under Section 43(a) of the Lanham Act Relevant To The Computer Industry" in *Protection of Computer Software Products Under Principles Of Copyright And Trademark Law* (D.C. Bar Computer Law Section, 1992); "Maximize the Benefits of the New Trademark Law: Intent To Use Applications; Expansion of Lanham Act Section 43(a) Liability; Protection of Trade Dress and Product Configuration," 5th Annual Advanced Computer Law Institute (Georgetown University, 1992); "False Advertising and Related Claims in the Computer Industry Under Section 43(a) of the Lanham Act As Amended by the Trademark Law Revision Act of 1988," 4th Annual Advanced Computer Law Institute (Georgetown University, 1991); "New Ways to Violate the Federal Trademark Laws," in *The Licensing Book* (March, 1991); "False Advertising and Related Claims Under Section 43(a) of The Lanham Act as Amended by the Trademark Law Revision Act of 1988" in *Domestic Protection and Enforcement Issues in Intellectual Property* (Georgetown University, 1990); "Impending Issues To Be Confronted By The PTO And Courts Under The Trademark Law Revision Act" in *Intellectual Property Law - Agency, Licensing, Litigation and Corporate Practice* (ABA PTC Section Meeting, 1990); "Current Developments In Trademark Law And Issues Relevant To The Computer Industry," 3d Annual Advanced Computer Law Institute (Georgetown University, 1990); "Remedies When Planning Fails: Trademark Infringement, Lanham Act Section 43(a), Anti-Counterfeiting Act

(This Listing Continued)

FINNEGAN, HENDERSON, FARABOW, GARRETT & DUNNER, L.L.P., Washington—Continued

Of 1984, Customs Service Remedies, And ITC Proceedings" in *The Commerce Department Speaks* (PLI, 1987); "Counterfeiting of Computer Goods and Trademarks: Strategy and Tactics With Customs on Infringement" in *Computer Software and Chips* (PLI, 1986); "Import Controls And Copyright Enforcement," 6th Annual Computer Law Institute (Law & Business, 1985); "Counterfeiting Of Computer Goods And Trademarks: Strategy And Tactics With Customs On Infringement" in *Computer Software and Chips* (PLI, 1985); "Other Legal Forms Of Protection Against Piracy, Counterfeiting and Infringement: Trademark; Lanham Act Section 43(a); Customs Remedies; Pending Anti-Counterfeiting Legislation" in *Software Protection and Marketing* (PLI, 1983). Co-Author: Sections on "Trade Regulation Pertinent To Technology And Trademark Licensing" in *Milgrim on Trade Secrets* (Matthew Bender & Co., 1987). Adjunct Lecturer and Professor, George Washington University National Law Center, 1989-1993. *Member:* Federal Circuit and American (Member, Sections on: Antitrust; Litigation; Intellectual Property Law) Bar Associations; American Intellectual Property Law Association (Member, Board of Directors, 2001—; Founding Chair, Trademark Law Practice Group, 1998-1999; Chair, Trademark Law Committee, 1997-1998); International Trademark Association (Chairman, Committees on: Federal Legislation, 1981-1983; Commercial Counterfeiting, 1983-1985); Licensing Executives Society. ***PRACTICE AREAS:*** Trade Secrets; Domain Name Infringement; Internet Trademark Law; Intellectual Property Litigation; Patent Litigation. ***Email:*** griff.price@finnegan.com

JOHN F. HORNICK, born Baltimore, Maryland, August 18, 1956; admitted to bar, 1984, District of Columbia. *Education:* North Carolina School of Arts; Temple University (B.A., Philosophy, cum laude, 1979); Columbus School of Law, Catholic University of America (J.D., 1984). Author: "Software Licensing," Monthly Column in The Licensing Journal; "Computer Program Copyrights: Look and Feel No Evil," 5 Software Law Journal, 355, 1992; "Copyright Law for Business People: A Revised Guide for the Unwary," CCH Business Strategies, Sept. 1990; Co-Author: "How to Prepare and Try a Software Infringement Case," 9 AIPLA Selected Legal Papers 13, 1992; Co-editor: Country Guides, Basic Information on Trademark Registration Worldwide; Editor and Co-Author: U.S. Section of International Intellectual Property Litigation Treatise. *Member:* The District of Columbia Bar (Chair, Copyright Committee, Intellectual Property Section, 1993-1996; Chair, Trademark Committee, 1996-1997; Steering Committee, 1997-1998; Chair, Trade Secret Committee, 1998-1999); Bar Association of the District of Columbia; American Bar Association; Copyright Society of the U.S.A.; American Intellectual Property Law Association; International Trademark Association; Cosmos Club. ***PRACTICE AREAS:*** Intellectual Property Litigation; Software Protection; Software Licensing; Copyright Litigation; Trade Secrets. ***Email:*** john.hornick@finnegan.com

ROBERT D. LITOWITZ, born Trenton, New Jersey, January 28, 1956; admitted to bar, 1981, District of Columbia. *Education:* Dickinson College (B.A., magna cum laude, 1978); The George Washington University National Law Center (J.D., with honors, 1981). Phi Beta Kappa; Omicron Delta Kappa. Author: "EEC Regulation 2641/84-A New Challenge to Section 337 Jurisdiction," International Business and Law Reporter, Vol. 1, Issue 6 Jan./Feb. 1986. Co-Author: "The Song Remains the Same—But Not Necessarily the Name," 39 The American University Law Review 4, Summer, 1990. *Member:* The District of Columbia Bar (Member, Section on Patent, Trademark and Copyright Law); Federal Circuit Bar Association; International Trademark Association; ITC Trial Lawyers Association. ***PRACTICE AREAS:*** Trademark Litigation. ***Email:*** rob.litowitz@finnegan.com

DAVID M. KELLY, born Mount Pleasant, Pennsylvania, October 18, 1957; admitted to bar, 1983, Pennsylvania (nonresident active status); 1985, Louisiana; 1987, District of Columbia; registered to practice before U.S. Patent and Trademark Office. *Education:* University of Pittsburgh (B.S., 1979; M.S., 1980); Duquesne University School of Law (J.D., 1983). Chi Epsilon. Member, Duquesne Law Review, 1981-1983. Author: "Trademarks: Protection of Merchandising Properties in Professional Sports," Duquesne Law Review 927, 1983; "Protection of Merchandising Properties in Professional Sports," 3 The Merchandising Reporter 11, 1984; "Broadening Trademark Protection in Louisiana: Enactment of the Louisiana Anti-Dilution Statute," 33 Louisiana Bar Journal 224, 1985; "Developments in American Unfair Competition Law—Implications for the Computer Industry," EIPR, April 10, 1995; "Certification Marks: A Trap for the Unwary," Association Law & Policy, Oct. 15, 1994; "The Politics of Color as a Trademark," Association Trends, April 21, 1995; "A Rainbow of Ideas to Trademark Color," Advertising Age, April 24, 1995; "*Qualitex* Makes Visible The Strategic Spectrum: Corporate 'Color Warriors' Have Numerous Tactics at Their Disposal," The National Law Journal, May 8, 1995; "Trademark Liability of Bulletin Board Operators," Association Law and Policy, July 1995. Professorial Lecturer of Trademarks and Patents, Loyola University School of Law, 1985-1986. *Member:* The District of Columbia Bar; Pennsylvania, Louisiana State and American Bar Associations; American Intellectual Property Law Association; International Trademark Association. ***PRACTICE AREAS:*** Trademark Litigation; Trademark Prosecution; Domain Names; Trade Dress. ***Email:*** david.kelly@finnegan.com

KENNETH JOHN MEYERS, born Chicago, Illinois, February 29, 1940; admitted to bar, 1971, Virginia; 1972, District of Columbia; 1976, U.S. Supreme Court; 1982, U.S. Court of Appeals for the Federal Circuit; registered to practice before U.S. Patent and Trademark Office. *Education:* Michigan Technological University (B.S.C.E., 1962); Northwestern University (M.B.A., 1967); Georgetown University Law Center (J.D., 1971). Tau Beta Pi; Phi Lambda Upsilon; Blue Key. *Member:* The District of Columbia Bar (Member, Steering Committee, 1990-1991); Bar Association of the District of Columbia; Virginia State Bar; American Bar Association; American Intellectual Property Law Association; Patent Lawyers Club of Washington, D.C. (President, 1980-1981). ***PRACTICE AREAS:*** Pharmaceutical Patents; Biotechnology Patents. ***Email:*** kenneth.meyers@finnegan.com

CAROL P. EINAUDI, born Boston, Massachusetts, March 2, 1937; admitted to bar, 1985, Maryland, District of Columbia and U.S. Court of Appeals for the Federal Circuit; registered to practice before the U.S. Patent and Trademark Office. *Education:* Simmons College (B.S., 1958); The George Washington University National Law Center (J.D., 1985). Past-President, Maryland Patent Law Association. *Member:* The District of Columbia Bar; Maryland State and American Bar Associations; Women's Bar Association of the District of Columbia; American Intellectual Property Law Association. ***PRACTICE AREAS:*** Patent Prosecution. ***Email:*** carol.einaudi@finnegan.com

WALTER Y. BOYD JR., born Burlington, North Carolina, February 14, 1956; admitted to bar, 1984, North Carolina, U.S. Court of Appeals for the Federal Circuit; 1985, District of Columbia and U.S. Claims Court; 1988, U.S. Supreme Court; registered to practice before the U.S. Patent and Trademark Office. *Education:* Elon College (B.A., cum laude, 1976); University of North Carolina (M.A., 1980); North Carolina Central University School of Law (J.D., cum laude, 1983); The George Washington University National Law Center (LL.M., 1985). Member, North Carolina Central University Law Review, 1982-1983. Law Clerk to the Honorable Edward S. Smith and the Honorable Marion T. Bennett, Circuit Judges, U.S. Court of Appeals for the Federal Circuit, 1985-1986. Co-Author: "The Federal Circuit and Chemical Practice, 1987-1988: A Look at Significant Decisions Affecting Chemical Practice, Apr. 1987-Apr. 1988," AIPLA Selected Legal Papers, Vol. VI, No. 1, 1988; "35 U.S.C.: 112 and Chemical Patent Practice," AIPLA Basic Chemical and Biotechnology Practice, 1988; "The Significant Federal Circuit Cases Interpreting Section 112," 41 The American University Law Review 621, 1992. Chairman, Patent Committee, D.C. Bar, 1992-1993. *Member:* American Intellectual Property Association. ***PRACTICE AREAS:*** Patent Prosecution; Patent Licensing. ***Email:*** walter.boyd@finnegan.com

STEVEN M. ANZALONE, born Brooklyn, New York, May 15, 1957; admitted to bar, 1984, New York; 1988, District of Columbia; registered to practice before the U.S. Patent and Trademark Office. *Education:* Princeton University (B.S.E., 1979); University of North Carolina School of Law (J.D., summa cum laude, 1983). Order of the Coif. Recipient: First Prize, Senior Debate for the Lynde Prize, Princeton University, 1979; Walter Clark Award, American Jurisprudence Book Awards in Antitrust, Contracts, Corporations, Corporate Taxation, Criminal Law, Criminal Procedure, Legal Ethics, Securities Regulation and Torts, University of North Carolina, 1981-1983. Member of Staff, 1981-1982, and Research Editor, 1982-1983, University of North Carolina Law Review. Author: "What's a Jury To Do?" Legal Times (May 15, 1995); "Infringement Under the Doctrine of Equivalents in Hilton Davis," Patent World (October 1995); "Infringement Under the Doctrine of Equivalents: The Search for Certainty," Patent World (September 1996). *Member:* American Bar Association; American Intellectual Property Law Association. ***PRACTICE AREAS:*** Patent Infringement. ***Email:*** steven.anzalone@finnegan.com

DARREL C. KARL, born Evanston, Illinois, August 13, 1960; admitted to bar, 1985, Maryland; 1989, U.S. Court of Appeals for the Federal Circuit; 1998, District of Columbia. *Education:* Loyola College (B.S., cum laude, 1981); Columbus School of Law, Catholic University of America (J.D., 1984). Sigma Pi Sigma; Omicron Delta Epsilon. Member, Catholic University Law Review, 1982-1984. Law Clerk to the Honorable Pauline Newman, Circuit Judge, U.S. Court of Appeals for the Federal Circuit, 1984-1986. Author: Martindale-Hubbell Patent Law Digest, 2000—; "'Look-Alike' Capsules, Generic Drug Substitution and the Lanham Act: The Elusive Contributory Infringement Standard of Inwood Laboratories, Inc. v. Ives Laboratories, Inc.," 32 Catholic University Law Review 345 (1982). Columnist, "Federal Circuit Update," The IP Litigator, 1995-2000. Lecturer: "Federal Circuit Patent Law," Patent Resources Group, Inc., 1996-1999. *Member:* Maryland State and American (Member, Patent, Trademark and Copyright Law Section) Bar Associations; Federal Circuit Bar Association; American Intellectual Property Law Association; Giles S. Rich American Inn of Court (Barrister). ***PRACTICE AREAS:*** Intellectual Property Litigation; Mechanical Patents; Metallurgical Patents; Patent Litigation. ***Email:*** darrel.karl@finnegan.com

JEAN BURKE FORDIS (Resident Partner, Palo Alto, California Office).

(This Listing Continued)

BARBARA CLARKE McCURDY, born New York, New York, February 19, 1960; admitted to bar, 1986, Massachusetts; 1988, District of Columbia; 1993, U.S. Supreme Court; registered to practice before U.S. Patent and Trademark Office. *Education:* Duke University (B.S.M.E., 1982); Suffolk University Law School (J.D., cum laude, 1985). *Member:* Bar Association of the District of Columbia; Massachusetts, Federal Circuit and American Bar Associations; American Intellectual Property Law Association; Women's Bar Association of the District of Columbia. ***PRACTICE AREAS:*** Intellectual Property Infringement; Intellectual Property Litigation; Mechanical Intellectual Property; Medical Intellectual Property; Technology Protection. **Email:** barbara.mccurdy@finnegan.com

JAMES K. HAMMOND, born Kingsport, Tennessee, 1952; admitted to bar, 1978, Virginia; 1980, New York; 1987, Connecticut; 1993, District of Columbia; registered to practice before U.S. Patent and Trademark Office. *Education:* University of Virginia (B.S.E.E., 1975; J.D., 1978). Law Clerk, U.S. District Court, Western District of Virginia, 1978-1979. ***PRACTICE AREAS:*** Patent Prosecution; Patent Litigation. **Email:** james.hammond@finnegan.com

RICHARD V. BURGUJIAN, born New York, New York, August 11, 1949; admitted to bar, 1985, New Jersey and U.S. District Court, District of New Jersey; 1987, New York; 1989, District of Columbia; registered to practice before U.S. Patent and Trademark Office. *Education:* Stevens Institute of Technology (B.E., 1971); Rensselaer Polytechnic Institute (M.E., 1972); Fairleigh Dickinson University (M.S., 1975); Rutgers University School of Law (J.D., 1984). Licensed Professional Engineer, New Jersey. *Member:* The District of Columbia Bar; New York State Bar Association; American Bar Association; Institute of Electrical and Electronic Engineers; American Intellectual Property Law Association. ***PRACTICE AREAS:*** Electronic Patents; Patent Infringement; Patent Prosecution. **Email:** rich.burgujian@finnegan.com

JOHN MICHAEL JAKES, born Waukegan, Illinois, May 28, 1957; admitted to bar, 1986, Virginia; 1988, District of Columbia, U.S. Court of Appeals for the Federal Circuit; 1993, U.S. Supreme Court, U.S. District Court, Eastern District of Virginia; registered to practice before U.S. Patent and Trademark Office. *Education:* Duke University (B.S.E.E., summa cum laude, 1979); Johns Hopkins University (M.S., 1983); Georgetown University Law Center (J.D., magna cum laude, 1986). Order of the Coif; Tau Beta Pi; Eta Kappa Nu. Editor, Georgetown Law Journal, 1985-1986. Law Clerk to the Honorable Giles S. Rich, U.S. Court of Appeals for the Federal Circuit, 1986-1988. Co-author: *Court of Appeals for the Federal Circuit: Practice & Procedure,* Matthew Bender & Co. (1993—). Lecturer on Patent Law, Catholic University of America, The Columbus School of Law, 1993-1996. *Member:* The District of Columbia Bar; Virginia State Bar; Federal Circuit and American Bar Associations; American Intellectual Property Law Association. ***PRACTICE AREAS:*** Intellectual Property Litigation; Appellate Practice; Electrical Intellectual Property; Computer and Software Patents; Medical Patents. **Email:** mike.jakes@finnegan.com

JOHN C. LOWE, born Allentown, Pennsylvania, December 3, 1936; admitted to bar, 1967, Virginia and U.S. District Court, Fourth Circuit; 1972, U.S. Supreme Court; 1976, U.S. Court of Appeals, Eighth Circuit; 1979, U.S. Court of Appeals, Ninth Circuit; 1988, North Carolina; 1991, Maryland and District of Columbia; 1993, U.S. Court of Appeals, Federal Circuit; 1996, U.S. Court of Appeals, District of Columbia Circuit. *Education:* Lehigh University (B.S., Chemistry, 1957); University of Virginia School of Law (J.D., 1967). ***PRACTICE AREAS:*** Patent Litigation; Trademark Litigation; Copyright Litigation; Trade Secrets Litigation. **Email:** john.lowe@finnegan.com

THOMAS W. BANKS (Resident Partner, Cambridge, Massachusetts Office).

CHRISTOPHER P. ISAAC, born Pittsburgh, Pennsylvania, March 28, 1959; admitted to bar, 1987, Virginia; 1989, District of Columbia; registered to practice before U.S. Patent and Trademark Office. *Education:* University of Pittsburgh (B.S.M.E., 1981); The George Washington University National Law Center (J.D., with honors, 1987). *Member:* The District of Columbia Bar; Virginia State Bar; American Intellectual Property Law Association. ***PRACTICE AREAS:*** Patent Prosecution. **Email:** chris.isaac@finnegan.com

BRYAN C. DINER (Resident Partner, Brussels, Belgium Office).

M. PAUL BARKER (Resident Partner, Palo Alto, California Office).

ANDREW CHANHO SONU, born Seoul, Korea, June 6, 1946; admitted to bar, 1987, Pennsylvania and New Jersey; 1988, District of Columbia; registered to practice before U.S. Patent and Trademark Office. *Education:* University of California (B.S.E.E., 1970); Ohio State University (M.S.E.E., 1972); Northwestern University (M.B.A., 1977); Widener University Delaware Law School (J.D., 1987). *Member:* American Bar Association; American Intellectual Property Law Association; Licensing Executives Society. ***LANGUAGES:*** Korean (Native Tongue). ***PRACTICE AREAS:*** Intellectual Property Litigation; Intellectual Property Licensing; Intellectual Property Arbitration; Technology Transfer; Patent Prosecution. **Email:** andy.sonu@finnegan.com

MARK SOMMERS, born Chicago, Illinois, March 29, 1956; admitted to bar, 1982, Illinois; 1985, New York and Massachusetts; 1989, District of Columbia. *Education:* Ohio Wesleyan University (B.A., 1978); Northern Illinois University College of Law (J.D., 1982); University of London, England (LL.M., 1983). ***PRACTICE AREAS:*** Domain Name Infringement; Internet Trademark Law; Trade Dress; Trademark Infringement; Trademark Litigation. **Email:** mark.sommers@finnegan.com

KENNETH M. FRANKEL, born New York, New York, April 22, 1948; admitted to bar, 1973, Virginia; 1979, U.S. Supreme Court; 1981, District of Columbia; 1982, U.S. Court of Appeals for the Federal Circuit; 1995, U.S. District Court, Eastern District of Virginia. *Education:* University of Pennsylvania (B.S.M.E., 1970); The George Washington University National Law Center (J.D., with honors, 1973). Law Clerk, U.S. Court of Claims, 1973-1974. Trial Attorney, Antitrust Division (Intellectual Property and Litigation II Sections), U.S. Department of Justice, 1974-1990. Member, BNA Electronic Commerce & Law Report, Advisory Board Member, 1996-1999. *Member:* The District of Columbia Bar (Member, Computer Law Section: Former Chair, Steering Committee, Trade Regulation Committee); Virginia State Bar; American Bar Association (Member, Sections on: Litigation; Antitrust Law; Patent, Trademark and Copyright Law); District of Columbia Computer Law Forum (Former President and Member, Board of Directors); American Intellectual Property Law Association (Vice-Chair, Trade Secret Committee; Chair, Antitrust Committee, 1994-1995). ***PRACTICE AREAS:*** Antitrust and Trade Regulation; Intellectual Property Litigation. **Email:** kenneth.frankel@finnegan.com

WILLIAM H. PRATT, born Plainfield, New Jersey, July 31, 1954; admitted to bar, 1988, Maryland; 1989, District of Columbia. *Education:* Southern Connecticut State University (B.S., 1976); The George Washington University (M.P.A., 1982); Washington College of Law, American University (J.D., 1988). Author: "Business Methods Patents in the United States," Journal of the Customs Intellectual Property Information Center (Japan), No. 111, April 2000; "The 'Deemed Export' Rule: Foreign Nationals in U.S. Companies," Journal of the Customs Intellectual Property Information Center (Japan), No. 89, June 1999; "Going International: Fundamentals of International Business: Intellectual Property Rights--What Are They and How Does a Company Secure Them?" International Trade for the Nonspecialist, 2nd Edition 1997; "Arbitrating Patent Disputes," Managing Intellectual Property, March 1994. *Member:* The District of Columbia Bar; Federal Circuit and American Bar Associations; The Washington International Trade Association; American Intellectual Property Law Association; International Trade Commission Trial Lawyers Association; Licensing Executives Society (Chairman of Committee on Government Regulation of Technology Exports); United States Council for International Business. ***PRACTICE AREAS:*** Intellectual Property Arbitration; Intellectual Property Licensing; International Intellectual Property; International Licensing; Technology Licensing. **Email:** bill.pratt@finnegan.com

DAVID S. FORMAN, born Detroit, Michigan, December 10, 1942; admitted to bar, 1987, District of Columbia; 1989, U.S. Court of Appeals for the Federal Circuit; 1991, U.S. Court of Veterans Appeals; 1993, U.S. District Court for the District of Columbia and U.S. Supreme Court; registered to practice before U.S. Patent and Trademark Office. *Education:* Harvard University (B.A., summa cum laude, 1964); Cambridge University; Rockefeller University (Ph.D., 1971); The George Washington University National Law Center (J.D., with highest honors, 1987). Order of the Coif. Law Clerk to the Honorable Oscar H. Davis, Circuit Judge, U.S. Court of Appeals for the Federal Circuit, 1987-1988. Lecturer, Catholic University Law School. Adjunct Associate Professor, Uniformed Services University of the Health Sciences, 1991-1996. *Member:* Federal Circuit Bar Association; American Bar Association (Chairman, Subcommittee on International Patent Practice of Biotechnology Committee, 1990-1993); American Intellectual Property Law Association; American Society for Cell Biology; Society for Neuroscience; American Association for the Advancement of Science. ***PRACTICE AREAS:*** Patent Law. **Email:** david.forman@finnegan.com

VINCENT P. KOVALICK, born Endicott, New York, May 22, 1961; admitted to bar, 1988, Virginia; Supreme Court of Virginia; 1995, District of Columbia; registered to practice before U.S. Patent and Trademark Office. *Education:* Pennsylvania State University (B.S.E.E., 1983); The George Mason University Law School (J.D., 1988). *Member:* Bar Association of the District of Columbia; Virginia and American (Member, Section on Intellectual Property Law) Bar Associations; American Intellectual Property Law Association; Federal Circuit Bar Association; Computer Law Association. ***PRACTICE AREAS:*** Patent Litigation; Patent Prosecution; Patent Licensing. **Email:** vincent.kovalick@finnegan.com

DON O. BURLEY, born Philadelphia, Pennsylvania, August 5, 1949; admitted to bar, 1976, Pennsylvania; 1993, District of Columbia. *Education:* University of Pennsylvania (B.A., 1971); Villanova University School of Law (J.D., cum laude, 1976). Department of Justice, Antitrust and Civil Divisions, 1976-1992. Author: "Long-Arm Wrestling with Pennsylvania's Jurisdiction Over Nonresident Individuals," 21 Villanova Law Review, 410 (1976). Member, Writing Committee, Food & Drug Law Institute, 1984-1992; Editorial Board, Food & Drug Law Journal, 1989-1993. ***PRACTICE AREAS:*** Intellectual Property Litigation; Intellectual Property Licensing. **Email:** don.burley@finnegan.com

(This Listing Continued)

FINNEGAN, HENDERSON, FARABOW, GARRETT & DUNNER, L.L.P., Washington—Continued

GERSON S. PANITCH, born Altoona, Pennsylvania, January 16, 1963; admitted to bar, 1988, Wisconsin and District of Columbia; registered to practice before U.S. Patent and Trademark Office. *Education:* University of Wisconsin (B.S.I.E., 1985; J.D., 1988). Member, Board of Editors, Patent Strategy & Management, 2000—. Instructor, Patent Resources Institute, 1992-1999. Author: "Maximizing Patent Protection Ex Post Festo," Patent Strategy & Management, February 2001; "When Acquiring Patent Rights, How Much Diligence is Due?" Patent Strategy & Management, October 2000; "Sailing on a Notion - Vital Patent Planning for Start-Ups and Records from Discovery," The Intellectual Property Strategist, Vol. 6, No. 9, June 2000; "Patent Law: Strategic Due Diligence," National Law Journal, May 15, 2000; "Market-Driven Method Preserves Patents' Value," National Law Journal, February 14, 2000; "New Trial Strategies in View of Markman: The Risk of a Narrow Focus," Patent World, Issue 95, September 1997. *Member:* The District of Columbia Bar (Member, Patent, Trademark and Copyright Section); State Bar of Wisconsin (Member, Patent Law Section); American Bar Association (Member, Patent, Copyright and Trademark Section); American Intellectual Property Law Association; Federal Circuit Bar Association. ***PRACTICE AREAS:*** Intellectual Property Portfolio Management; Medical Patents; Patent Litigation; Patent Protection. ***Email:*** gerson.panitch@finnegan.com

JAMES W. EDMONDSON, born Cleveland, Ohio, May 26, 1957; admitted to bar, 1988, Virginia and U.S. Court of Appeals, Fourth Circuit; 1989, District of Columbia; 1993, U.S. Court of Federal Claims; 1996, U.S. Court of Appeals for the Federal Circuit; registered to practice before U.S. Patent and Trademark Office. *Education:* United States Naval Academy (B.S., 1979); Georgetown University Law Center (J.D., 1988). Member, National Rifle Association. *Member:* Virginia State Bar; The District of Columbia Bar; U.S. Court of Federal Claims Bar Association; American Intellectual Property Law Association; Federation Internationale des Conseils en Propriete Industrielle (FICPI). [Lt., U.S. Navy, 1975-1984]. ***PRACTICE AREAS:*** Intellectual Property Infringement; Intellectual Property Licensing; Intellectual Property Litigation; Mechanical Intellectual Property; Proprietary Rights; Patent Prosecution. ***Email:*** james.edmondson@finnegan.com

MICHAEL R. McGURK, born Abington, Pennsylvania, February 11, 1960; admitted to bar, 1988, Pennsylvania and New Jersey; 1990, District of Columbia and U.S. Court of Appeals for the Federal Circuit; 1993, U.S. Supreme Court; registered to practice before U.S. Patent and Trademark Office. *Education:* University of Delaware (B.S.Ch.E., 1983); The George Washington University National Law Center (J.D., 1988). *Member:* The District of Columbia Bar (Member: Section on Patent, Trademark and Copyright Law); Pennsylvania, Federal Circuit and American (Member, Sections on: Litigation; Patent, Trademark and Copyright Law) Bar Associations; American Intellectual Property Law Association. ***PRACTICE AREAS:*** Intellectual Property Litigation; Patent Interference Practice; Patent Licensing; Patent Prosecution. ***Email:*** michael.mcgurk@finnegan.com

CHERI M. TAYLOR, born Urbana, Illinois, August 31, 1948; admitted to bar, 1986, Virginia; 1988, District of Columbia and U.S. Court of Appeals for the District of Columbia Circuit; 1993, U.S. Supreme Court; 1994, U.S. District Court, District of Columbia; registered to practice before U.S. Patent and Trademark Office. *Education:* Auburn University (B.S., 1970); Georgia State University (M.S., Genetics, 1974; Ph.D., 1979); George Mason University School of Law (J.D., 1986). Member, George Mason University Law Review, 1985-1986. Recipient, American Jurisprudence Book Award in Civil Procedure. Listed in *Who's Who.* Co-author, *Alternative Uses of Section 337,* with George C. Summerfield, 722 PLI/Comm 485, *499 and 77 J. Pat & Trademark Office Society 259, *270; *Antitrust at the ITC?,* with George C. Summerfield, The Antitrust News, AIPLA Comm. on Antitrust Law, Vol. IV, No. 3, April 1995. *Member:* The District of Columbia Bar (Member, Section of Patent, Trademark and Copyright Law); American Bar Association (Member, Intellectual Property Section, Chair, IPL Committee 603-International Trade Commission, 1998-1999, 1999-2000; Chair, Chemical Patent Practice, 2000-2001); Federal Circuit Bar Association; ITC Trial Lawyers Association; Women's Bar Association. ***PRACTICE AREAS:*** Biotechnology; Pharmaceuticals; Chemical Patents; Cosmetics; International Trade; International Trade Regulation. ***Email:*** cheri.taylor@finnegan.com

JOANN M. NETH, born Fairfield, Connecticut, October 5, 1959; admitted to bar, 1989, District of Columbia; 1990, U.S. Court of Appeals for the Federal Circuit; 1993, U.S. Supreme Court and U.S. District Court for the District of Columbia; registered to practice before U.S. Patent and Trademark Office. *Education:* Bryn Mawr College (A.B., 1981); Brown University (Ph.D., Physical Organic Chemistry, 1987); University of Virginia School of Law (J.D., 1989). Member, Virginia Journal of Environmental Law, 1987-1989. *Member:* The District of Columbia Bar; American and Federal Circuit Bar Associations; American Intellectual Property Law Association; American Chemical Society;

(This Listing Continued)

Women's Bar Association of the District of Columbia. ***PRACTICE AREAS:*** Chemical Intellectual Property; Chemical Patents; Patent Infringement; Patent Licensing; Patent Litigation. ***Email:*** joann.neth@finnegan.com

LINDA A. WADLER, born Chicago, Illinois, September 1, 1963; admitted to bar, 1988, New York and U.S. District Court, Eastern and Southern Districts of New York; 1990, District of Columbia and U.S. Court of Appeals for the Federal Circuit; registered to practice before U.S. Patent and Trademark Office. *Education:* University of Illinois (B.S., 1984); University of Michigan Law School (J.D., 1987). ***PRACTICE AREAS:*** Patent Litigation; Patent Prosecution. ***Email:*** linda.wadler@finnegan.com

LIAM O'GRADY, born Newark, New Jersey, September 24, 1950; admitted to bar, 1977, Virginia; 1978, U.S. District Court, Eastern District of Virginia; 1980, U.S. Court of Appeals, Fourth Circuit (Not admitted in District of Columbia). *Education:* Franklin & Marshall College (B.A., 1973); George Mason University Law School (J.D., 1977). Associate Professor: George Washington University, Forensic Science Graduate School, 1988—; U.S. Attorney General's Advocacy Institute, 1989-1992. Assistant U.S. Attorney, Eastern District of Virginia, 1986-1992. Assistant Commonwealth Attorney, Arlington, Virginia, 1983-1986. *Member:* Arlington and American Bar Associations; Virginia State Bar (Member, Criminal Law Section, 1978—); American Intellectual Property Law Association. ***PRACTICE AREAS:*** Patent Infringement; Trademark Infringement. ***Email:*** liam.ogrady@finnegan.com

CHARLES E. VAN HORN, born Philadelphia, Pennsylvania, January 30, 1942; admitted to bar, 1968, Virginia; 1998, District of Columbia; registered to practice before U.S. Patent and Trademark Office. *Education:* Lehigh University (B.S.Ch.E., 1963); American University (J.D., 1968); The George Washington University (M.B.A., 1973). Author, "Effects of GATT and NAFTA on PTO Practice," Journal of Patent and Trademark Office Society, pp. 231-45 (March, 1995). *Member:* Patent and Trademark Office Society; American Intellectual Property Law Association. ***PRACTICE AREAS:*** Patents. ***Email:*** charles.vanhorn@finnegan.com

JEFFREY A. BERKOWITZ, born Norwich, Connecticut, April 19, 1963; admitted to bar, 1988, New Jersey; 1989, New York; 1990, U.S. Court of Federal Claims; 1995, District of Columbia; registered to practice before U.S Patent and Trademark Office. *Education:* Rutgers University (B.A., Computer Science, 1985); Jacob D. Fuchsberg Law Center, Touro College (J.D., cum laude, 1988). Member, 1986-1988 and Managing Editor, 1987-1988, Touro College Law Review. Recipient: First Prize (Touro) Nathan Burkan Memorial Competition; American Jurisprudence Awards in Legal Research and Writing, Civil Procedure, Judicial Clerkship, and Jurisprudence. Law Clerk to the Honorable Marian Blank Horn, Judge, U.S. Claims Court, 1988-1989. Author: "Computer Software Copyright Infringement: The Second Generation," 4 Touro Law Rev. 97, 1987; "A Look At Significant Decisions Affecting Patent Practice," April 1989-Oct. 1990, Selected Legal Papers, American Intellectual Property Law Association, Vol. VIII, Nos. 1 & 2, Feb. 1991; "Recent Developments in Patent Protection for Computer-Related Inventions," Computer Law Reporter, Vol. 18, No. 4, Dec. 1993; "The Patent Office Takes Another Look at a Controversial Patent," Computer Law Reporter, Vol. 18, No. 5, Jan. 1994; "IBM Tops the Patent Charts in 1993," Computer Law Reporter, Vol. 18, No. 6, Feb. 1994; "Software Patents You Can Take to the Bank," Computer Law Reporter, Vol. 19, No. 1, Mar. 1994; "In re Donaldson: Federal Circuit Gets the Last Word on Section 112, Paragraph 6," Computer Law Reporter, Vol. 19, No. 3, May 1994; "Welcome to the Brave New World of Software Patents: A Road Map for the Corporate Legal Department," The Law Works, Vol. 1, Nos. 5 and 6, May and June 1994; "A Cautionary Approach to the Internet," The Greater Washington Board of Trade News, Vol. 50, No. 4, July/August 1995. Co-author of bimonthly column "Federal Circuit Report," The IP Litigator, 1995—; Editorial Advisory Board, Obtaining Patents by Thomas A. Turano, James Publishing, 1997. *Member:* The District of Columbia Bar (Chairman, IP Committee of Computer and Telecommunications Section, 1996-1997); New Jersey State, New York State and American (Chairman, Subcommittee D-Intellectual Property Law Section) Bar Associations; U.S. Court of Federal Claims Bar Association (Co-Chairman, Intellectual Property Section, 1994); Computer Law Association; American Intellectual Property Law Association (Recording Secretary, Emerging Technologies Committee, 1996-1997); District of Columbia Computer Law Forum. ***PRACTICE AREAS:*** Patent Prosecution; Computer and Software Patents; Software Copyright. ***Email:*** jeffrey.berkowitz@finnegan.com

MICHAEL R. KELLY (Resident Partner, Tokyo, Japan Office).

JAMES B. MONROE, born Tulsa, Oklahoma, December 16, 1963; admitted to bar, 1991, Virginia; 1994, U.S. Court of Appeals, Federal Circuit; 1996, District of Columbia; registered to practice before U.S. Patent and Trademark Office. *Education:* Washington University (B.S., Chem.Eng., 1986); The George Washington University National Law Center (J.D., 1991). Deans Honorary Scholar, Washington University, 1982-1986. Law Clerk to Hon. Judge Giles Sutherland Rich, U.S. Court of Appeals for the Federal Circuit, 1992-1994. Formerly with U.S. Patent and Trademark Office, 1986-1989. *Member:* The District of Columbia Bar (Member, Sections on: Litigation; Intellectual Property); Virginia (Member, Sections on: Litigation; Intellectual Property), Federal Circuit and American (Member, Sections on: Litigation; Intellectual

(This Listing Continued)

Property) Bar Associations; Giles S. Rich American Inns of Court; American Institute of Chemical Engineers; American Intellectual Property Law Association (Past Vice-Chair, Young Lawyers Committee; Past Chair, Awards Committee). ***PRACTICE AREAS:*** Chemical Intellectual Property; Intellectual Property Litigation; Intellectual Property Portfolio Management; Pharmaceutical Intellectual Property; Patent Litigation. ***Email:*** james.monroe@finnegan.com

DORIS JOHNSON HINES, born Queens, New York, June 13, 1964; admitted to bar, 1991, Virginia; 1994, District of Columbia; registered to practice before U.S. Patent and Trademark Office. *Education:* Rensselaer Polytechnic Institute (B.S.E.E., 1986); The George Washington University National Law Center (J.D., 1991). Law Clerk to the Honorable Giles S. Rich, U.S. Court of Appeals for the Federal Circuit. Coauthor: "Growing Pains: Software Patents Come of Age," Advanced Computer Law Institute, March 1996. *Member:* Bar Association of the District of Columbia; Virginia, Federal Circuit and American Bar Associations; American Intellectual Property Law Association. ***PRACTICE AREAS:*** Patent Litigation; Electrical Patent Prosecution. ***Email:*** dori.hines@finnegan.com

DAVID AVRUM MANSPEIZER, born New York, New York, December 19, 1963; admitted to bar, 1991, New Jersey; 1992, U.S. Court of Appeals for the Federal Circuit; 1993, District of Columbia; registered to practice before U.S. Patent and Trademark Office. *Education:* University of Pennsylvania (B.A. Biology, 1986); Rutgers School of Law (J.D., 1991). Managing Editor, Rutgers Law Review. Author: "The Cheshire Cat, the March Hare, and the Harvard Mouse: Animal Patents Open Up a New Genetically Engineered Wonderland," 43 Rutgers Law Review, Winter, 1991; "The Many Roles of Patent Attorneys: A Lawyer May Prepare a Patent Validity of Infringement Opinion and Litigate a Later Related Case," Legal Times, April 8, 1996; "Can the Attorney Who Prepares a Validity/Infringement Opinion Act as Trial Counsel in a Later Case," 3IP Litigator, November/December, 1997; "Hilton Davis Now," Patent World, March 1998. *Member:* Federal Circuit and American Bar Associations; District of Columbia Bar; American Intellectual Property Law Association. ***PRACTICE AREAS:*** Intellectual Property Litigation; Pharmaceutical Intellectual Property; Federal Litigation; Biotechnology Patent Prosecution; Biotechnology Patents. ***Email:*** david.manspeizer@finnegan.com

LORI-ANN JOHNSON (Resident Associate, Atlanta, Georgia Office).

LISA PELLER LONDON, born Woodmere, New York, January 6, 1964; admitted to bar, 1989, Pennsylvania; 1990, District of Columbia. *Education:* Cornell University (B.S., 1986); The George Washington University National Law Center (J.D., with honors, 1989). ***PRACTICE AREAS:*** International Trademarks; Trademark Protection; Trademark Prosecution; Trademark Litigation. ***Email:*** lisa.london@finnegan.com

JOHN R. ALISON, born Los Angeles, California, October 14, 1956; admitted to bar, 1986, District of Columbia and U.S. Court of Appeals for the Federal and Fourth Circuits. *Education:* Swarthmore College (B.A., with distinction, 1979); University of Chicago (M.A., 1980); Georgetown University (J.D., 1984). Member, American Criminal Law Review, 1983-1984. Law Clerk to Chief Judge Howard T. Markey, United States Court of Appeals for the Federal Circuit, 1984-1986. Advanced Federal Circuit Patent Law, Patent Resources Group, 1994-2001. *Member:* The Bar Association of the District of Columbia; Federal Circuit, Fourth Circuit and American Bar Associations; American Intellectual Property Law Association. ***PRACTICE AREAS:*** Patent Litigation; Trade Secrets. ***Email:*** john.alison@finnegan.com

ALLEN R. JENSEN, born Tremonton, Utah, September 13, 1950; admitted to bar, 1977, Utah; 1980, District of Columbia; registered to practice before U.S. Patent and Trademark Office. *Education:* Utah State University (B.S., magna cum laude, 1974); The George Washington University National Law Center (J.D., with honors, 1977). Co-Author: "Chemical Patent Law," Patent Resources Group, 1998-2001; "Crafting & Drafting Winning Patents," Patent Resources Group, 1999-2000; "Patent Prosecution After Festo: In Search of Literal Infringement," Colorado Bar, PTC Section, 2001; "Why Festo Will Change Your Patenting Strategy," Managing Intellectual Property, April 2001; "The Real 'Killer App' - What Are the Lessons of Festo for Those Drafting Patent Applications?" Legal Times, May 7, 2001; "U.S. Claim Drafting," 1BC-UK Conferences, 2001. Adjunct Professor of Law, J. Reuben Clark Law School, Brigham Young University, 1985-1994. Law Clerk, U.S. Court of Customs and Patent Appeals. *Member:* American (Intellectual Property Law Section) and Federal Circuit Bar Associations; American Intellectual Property Law Association; National Counsel of Intellectual Property Law Associations (Former Chairman); National Inventors Hall of Fame (Former President). ***PRACTICE AREAS:*** Chemical Patent Prosecution; Intellectual Property Portfolio Management; Pharmaceutical Patent Prosecution. ***Email:*** allen.jensen@finnegan.com

SCOTT R. MOSKO (Resident Partner, Palo Alto, California Office).

RONALD A. BLEEKER, born New York, N.Y., June 1, 1949; admitted to bar, 1974, New York and U.S. District Court, Southern and Eastern Districts of New York; 2001, District of Columbia; registered to practice before U.S. Patent and Trademark Office. *Education:* Columbia University (B.S., 1970; J.D., 1973). Author, "Foreign Patent Agents and U.S. Corporations," Del. J. of Corporate Law, 1977. Former General Intellectual Property Counsel, Mobil Oil Corp. Associate General Counsel, Allied Signal, 1993-1995. Chief Patent Counsel, W.R. Grace & Co., 1987-1991. Senior Patent Counsel, W.R. Grace & Co., 1980-1987. Associate, Pennie & Edmonds, 1973-1980. Director: Intellectual Property Owners, 1993-1994, 1996; New York Intellectual Property Law Association, 1995-1996. *Member:* American Intellectual Property Law Association; Association of Corporate Patent Counsel; Licensing Executive Society. ***PRACTICE AREAS:*** Intellectual Property Litigation. ***Email:*** ronald.bleeker@finnegan.com

JOHN A. RISSMAN (Not admitted in District of Columbia; Resident Partner, Cambridge, Massachusetts Office).

GERALD F. IVEY, born Rocky Mount, North Carolina, July 26, 1957; admitted to bar, 1982, District of Columbia. *Education:* University of Virginia (B.A., with distinction, 1979; J.D., 1982). Adjunct Professor, George Washington University Law School, 1993—. Seminar Instructor: GWU Law School/D.C. Bar Association College of Trial Advocacy, 1993-1994; University of Virginia Law School Trial Advocacy Institute, 1995—. *Member:* The District of Columbia Bar; Bar Association of the District of Columbia; American Bar Association; Washington Council of Lawyers; The Association of Trial Lawyers of America. ***PRACTICE AREAS:*** Biotechnology Patents; Medical Intellectual Property; Mechanical Patents; Intellectual Property Litigation. ***Email:*** gerald.ivey@finnegan.com

JAMES H. JOHNSON, JR. (Resident Partner, Atlanta, Georgia Office).

R. BRUCE BOWER (Resident Partner, Atlanta, Georgia Office).

JULIA ANNE MATHESON, born Summit, New Jersey, July 27, 1966; admitted to bar, 1990, Pennsylvania and New Jersey; 1997, District of Columbia; 2001, California. *Education:* Oxford University; Johns Hopkins University (B.A., 1990); Columbia Law School (J.D., 1990). Adjunct Professor, The George Washington University Law School, Trademarks and Unfair Competition, 1998-2000. Author: "Can a Phase Out Phase Out Trademark Rights," Legal Times, August 3, 1998. Co-Author: "A Review of Recent Trademark Decisions of the United States Court of Appeals for the Federal Circuit," 47 Am. U.L. Rev.-1491. *Member:* Bar Association of the District of Columbia; Philadelphia and American Bar Associations; State Bar of California; International Trademark Association. (Resident Partner, Palo Alto, California Office). ***Email:*** julia.matheson@finnegan.com

YITAI HU, born Taipei, Taiwan, January 13, 1965; admitted to bar, 1994, Maryland; 1997, District of Columbia, U.S. District Court for the District of Columbia; U.S. Court of Appeals, Federal Circuit; registered to practice before U.S. Patent and Trademark Office. *Education:* University of Kansas (B.A., Physics, 1991); University of Maryland School of Law (J.D., 1994). Author: "Trade Secrets Act of the ROC (Taiwan)," IP Asia, March, 1996; "Counter Balance Between U.S. Patent Law and Antitrust Laws, (Chinese)," Industrial Property and Standards Journal, September, 1996. *Member:* American Bar Association; American Intellectual Property Law Association; Licensing Executives Society. ***LANGUAGES:*** Chinese, Taiwanese. ***PRACTICE AREAS:*** Intellectual Property Litigation; Intellectual Property Licensing; International Intellectual Property; International Licensing. ***Email:*** yitai.hu@finnegan.com

VIRGINIA L. CARRON (Resident Partner, Atlanta, Georgia Office).

MARTIN F. MAJESTIC (Resident Partner, Palo Alto, California Office).

THERESE A. HENDRICKS (Resident Partner, Cambridge, Massachusetts Office).

M. LAWRENCE OLIVERIO (Resident Partner, Cambridge, Massachusetts Office).

KENNETH W. CURTIS, born Buffalo, New York, June 26, 1942; admitted to bar, 1973, Virginia; 1979, U.S. District Court, Eastern District of Virginia; 1981, District of Columbia and U.S. Court of Appeals for the District of Columbia Circuit; 1982, U.S. District Court, District of Columbia; 1993, U.S. Court of Appeals, Fourth Circuit; 1995, Maryland; 1996, U.S. District Court, District of Maryland. *Education:* University of Buffalo (B.S., in Chemistry, 1964); Seton Hall University (M.S., in Analytical Chemistry, 1968); George Washington University (J.D., 1972). Adjunct Professor of Law: International School of Law and George Mason University School of Law, 1979-1989. Instructor, Criminal Law and Procedure, Northern Virginia Criminal Justice Academy, 1981-1983. Lecturer: "Preparing and Using Evidence Before and During Trial," Virginia Trial Lawyers Association, September 1982; "Expert Testimony - Evidence at Trial," National Education Network, May 1983; "Virginia Objections at Trial - Similarities and Differences - Virginia Interpretations and the Federal Rules of Evidence," and "Objections at Trial and How to Deal with the Difficult Lawyer," National Practice Institute, February 1994; "Opinions and Evidence in the Courtroom," Regional Judicial Conference Continuing Judicial Education, Virginia Supreme Court, September 1994; "Expert Witnesses," State Judicial Conference Continuing Legal Education, May 1995; "Evidence for Trial Lawyers," Virginia Trial Lawyers Association, 1997. Seminar: Chair, Annual Medical-Legal Seminar, "Personal Injury Medicine: What You Must Know to Win Your Case," Virginia Trial Lawyers Association, 1996. Assistant Commonwealth's Attorney, Arlington County, Virginia, 1975-1979. Member, Virginia Medical Malpractice Review Panel, 1984—. Neutral Case

(This Listing Continued)

(This Listing Continued)

FINNEGAN, HENDERSON, FARABOW, GARRETT & DUNNER, L.L.P., Washington—Continued

Evaluator, 1995—; Conciliator, 1996—, Circuit Court of Fairfax County, Virginia. *Member:* Fairfax and American Bar Associations; The District of Columbia Bar; Bar Association of the District of Columbia; Virginia State Bar (Member, 10th District Grievance Committee, 1985-1989); Virginia Trial Lawyers Association (Member, Continuing Legal Education Committee, 1995—); The Association of Trial Lawyers of America; Defense Research Institute; George Mason Inn of Court (Founding Member, 1989—; Master of the Bench and Executive Committee, 1989—; Chair and Co-Chair, Continuing Legal Education Committee, 1989—); Virginia Etheridge Society. ***PRACTICE AREAS:*** Civil Litigation; Intellectual Property Litigation; Federal Litigation; Trial Practice.

SENIOR COUNSEL

TIPTON D. JENNINGS IV, born Charleston, South Carolina, October 13, 1932; admitted to bar, 1960, Florida; 1963, Virginia; 1972, District of Columbia; 1974, U.S. Supreme Court; 1982, U.S. Court of Appeals for the Federal Circuit; registered to practice before U.S. Patent and Trademark Office. *Education:* University of Miami (B.S.E.E., 1954); The George Washington University National Law Center (J.D., with honors, 1959). Tau Beta Pi; Omicron Delta Kappa; Phi Eta Sigma; Pi Mu Epsilon; Phi Delta Phi. Co-Author: "Antitrust Risks in Settling Patent Disputes Through Licensing," Licensing Law and Business Report, May-June, 1982; "Aspects of Patent Misuse and Patent Licensing," Licensing Law and Business Report, Jan.-Feb., 1984. Adjunct Professor of Law, George Mason University Law School, 1991-1993. *Member:* The District of Columbia Bar; Virginia State Bar (Chairman, 1975-1976, Section on Patent, Trademark and Copyright Law); Virginia and American (Chairman, Patent Committee, Administrative Law Section, 1978-1980) Bar Associations; The Florida Bar; American Intellectual Property Law Association (Chairman, Dinners and Meetings Committee, 1968-1970; Chairman, Unfair Competition Committee, 1976-1977); Licensing Executives Society (Chairman, Software Transfer Committee, 1984-1986); Federation Internationale des Conseils en Propriete Industrielle, U.S. Section (Member of Council, 1991-1994; Secretary-Treasurer, 1995-1997; President, 1997—). [1st Lieutenant, USAF, 1954-1956]. ***PRACTICE AREAS:*** Patent Prosecution; Trademarks; Intellectual Property Licensing; Intellectual Property Litigation; International Intellectual Property. ***Email:*** tipton.jennings@finnegan.com

KENNETH E. PAYNE, born Kansas City, Kansas, January 12, 1936; admitted to bar, 1965, Missouri; 1966, District of Columbia; registered to practice before U.S. Patent and Trademark Office. *Education:* University of Kansas School of Engineering (B.S., 1959); Washington College of Law, American University (J.D., 1965). Assistant General Counsel, U.S. Department of Commerce, 1971-1973. U.S. Department of State Delegate, Inter-American Commission on Science and Technology Transfer, 1974-1975. Consultant of the United Nations Industrial Development Organization, Vienna, Austria, 1979. Author: "Trade Secret Licensing - Definition, Duration and Disposition," Licensing Law and Business Report, 1979; "Effects of Restrictive Clauses," Les Nouvelles, June 1981; "Licensing v. Litigation-Cost Comparisons: USA," Les Nouvelles, Dec., 1983. Co-Author: "Creative Patent and Know-How Licensing," Patent Resources Group, 1977; "United States Copyright Law: Visions of the Future," Annual of Industrial Property Law, 1977 and Licensing Law and Business Institute, 1979; "U.S. Antitrust Aspects of the International Transfer of Technology," North Carolina Journal of International Law & Commercial Regulations, Vol. 5, No. 1, Winter, 1980; "Five Independent Clauses: A Practical Guide," Licensing Law and Business Institute, 1983. *Member:* The District of Columbia Bar; Bar Association of the District of Columbia; American (Member, Sections on: Patent, Trademark and Copyright Law; Antitrust Law; Litigation) and International Bar Associations; American Intellectual Property Law Association; Licensing Executives Society (International-U.S. Delegate, 1976-1985; Treasurer, 1985-1987; President-Elect, 1987-1988; President, 1989. U.S.A.-Canada, Secretary, 1978-1980; Vice President International, 1981-1983; President-Elect, 1983-1984; President, 1984-1985); The Association of Trial Lawyers of America. ***PRACTICE AREAS:*** Intellectual Property Litigation; Patent Infringement; Technology Transfers; International Intellectual Property; Mechanical Intellectual Property. ***Email:*** ken.payne@finnegan.com

OF COUNSEL

SMITH RUFUS BRITTINGHAM IV, born Newark, New Jersey, August 11, 1962; admitted to bar, 1987, Ohio; 2001, District of Columbia. *Education:* Oberlin College (B.A., 1984); Ohio State College of Law (J.D., with honors, 1987). Judicial clerk to the Honorable Richard M. Markus, Ohio Court of Appeals for the Eighth District, 1987-1988. *Member:* American Bar Association; American Intellectual Property Law Association; International Trade Commission Trial Lawyers Association. ***PRACTICE AREAS:*** Intellectual Property Litigation; Patent Litigation. ***Email:*** smith.brittingham@finnegan.com

(This Listing Continued)

ERNEST F. CHAPMAN, born Lake Ariel, Pennsylvania, September 2, 1935; admitted to bar, 1972, New York; 1975, U.S. District Court, Western District of New York; 1979, U.S. Supreme Court; 1980, U.S. Tax Court and U.S. Court of Federal Claims; 1982, U.S. Court of Appeals for the Federal Circuit; 1996, District of Columbia; registered to practice before U.S. Patent and Trademark Office. *Education:* University of Scranton (B.S., 1957); Temple University School of Law (J.D., 1969). *Member:* New York State Bar Association; American Intellectual Property Law Association; Research Scientific Society of America. [U.S. Army]. ***PRACTICE AREAS:*** Patents; Chemical Patent Prosecution; Chemical Patents.

WILLIAM B. DYER, III (Resident Counsel, Atlanta, Georgia Office).

ROBERT J. EICHELBURG, born New York, New York, November 11, 1935; admitted to bar, 1963, Virginia; 1964, District of Columbia; 1968, New York; 1969, U.S. District Court, Southern and Eastern Districts of New York; 1969-1984, U.S. Court of Customs and Patent Appeals; 1984, U.S. Court of Appeals for the Federal Circuit; registered to practice before U.S. Patent and Trademark Office. *Education:* Fordham University (B.S., 1956); The George Washington University National Law Center (J.D., 1963). Instructor, Moot Court Practice, Pace University School of Law, 1980-1982. Judge, Town of Pound Ridge, New York, 1970-1984. *Member:* New York State Bar Association; The District of Columbia Bar. ***PRACTICE AREAS:*** Chemical Patent Prosecution; Coatings Technology; Inorganic Chemistry; Organic Chemistry; Polymers. ***Email:*** robert.eichelburg@finnegan.com

C. EDWARD GOOD, born Atlanta, Georgia, January 17, 1945; admitted to bar, 1971, Virginia (Not admitted in District of Columbia). *Education:* University of North Carolina at Chapel Hill (A.B., 1967); University of Virginia (J.D., 1971). Counsel and Writer-in-Residence, Finnegan Henderson, 1993—. Columnist, "IP Dialogue," monthly column for *Corporate Legal Times,* 1999-2000; "Writing Wrongs," monthly column on effective legal writing for *U.S. Business Litigation,* 1996-1997. Author: Books: *Mightier than the Sword* (Reword, Inc., Charlottesville, Va., 1989); *Citing & Typing the Law* (Reword, Inc., Charlottesville, Va., 1991); *Legal Research ... Without Losing Your Mind* (Reword, Inc., Charlottesville, Va., 1993). Articles: "The 'Writer-in-Residence': A New Solution to an Old Problem," 74 Mich. B.J. 568 (1995); "'To Be' or Not 'To Be': An Easy Way to Improve Legal Writing," Trial Magazine (May 1995); "Winning with Plain Language," Trial Magazine (Oct. 1995). Director of Legal Research and Writing, University of Virginia School of Law, 1975-1977, 1978-1980. Adjunct Professor, Georgetown University Legal Assistant Program, 1978-1980. Trainer, courses on effective legal writing for corporate legal departments, federal agencies, and law firms, 1980—. Judicial Fellow, Supreme Court of the United States, 1977-1978. ***Email:*** ed.good@finnegan.com

WAYNE W. HERRINGTON, born San Francisco, California, November 24, 1945; admitted to bar, 1971, District of Columbia; 1975, U.S. Supreme Court; 1982, U.S. Court of Appeals for the Federal Circuit; registered to practice before U.S. Patent and Trademark Office. *Education:* University of Mississippi (B.A., with distinction, 1967); Columbia University School of Law (J.D., 1970); The George Washington University National Law Center (LL.M., 1978). Phi Kappa Phi; Omicron Delta Kappa. Law Clerk and Technical Advisor to the Honorable Giles S. Rich, Associate Judge, U.S. Court of Customs and Patent Appeals, 1975-1977. Attorney-Advisor, 1982-1987, Senior Attorney, 1987-1989, Senior Counsellor and Special Advisor, Intellectual Property and Technology, 1989-1992, U.S. International Trade Commission. Editor and Co-Author: "International Trade Commission Patent Practice," Patent Resources Group, 1979; "Federal Circuit Patent Law, 1985-1987," Patent Resources Group, 1987; "Patent and Copyright Practice Before the International Trade Commission," Patent Resources Group, 1986; "Federal Circuit Patent Law, 1986-1988," Patent Resources Group, 1988; "Patent and Copyright Practice Before the International Trade Commission After the New Trade Act," Patent Resources Group, 1989; "Issues at the Interface of International Trade and Intellectual Property," Brooklyn Journal of International Law (Vol. XVIII, No. 3, 1992); "Patent Import Restrictions," International Intellectual Property Law and Policy (Vol. 1, 1996). Member: Chartered Institute of Arbitrators (Associate); American Intellectual Property Law Association; American Chemical Society; American Bar Association. ***PRACTICE AREAS:*** Intellectual Property Litigation; Patent Litigation; Patent Protection; International Intellectual Property. ***Email:*** wayne.herrington@finnegan.com

GEORGE E. HUTCHINSON, born Washington, D.C., August 31, 1923; admitted to bar, 1955, District of Columbia and U.S. Court of Appeals for the District of Columbia Circuit; 1961, U.S. Supreme Court; 1982, U.S. Court of Appeals for the Federal Circuit. *Education:* Ball State Teachers College; The George Washington University (A.B., 1951; LL.B., 1954). Phi Delta Phi. Page, Assistant Librarian and Assistant Marshal, Supreme Court of the United States, 1938-1962. Marshal, U.S. Court of Customs and Patent Appeals, 1962-1964. Clerk, U.S. Court of Customs and Patent Appeals, 1964-1982. Clerk, U.S. Court of Appeals for the Federal Circuit, 1982-1985. *Member:* The District of Columbia Bar; Federal and American Bar Associations; Federal Circuit Bar Association; American Intellectual Property Law Association; Court of Federal Claims Bar Association; Court of International Trade Bar Association. [Ser-

(This Listing Continued)

geant, United States Army, 405th Infantry, 102nd Infantry Division, 1943-1946]. ***PRACTICE AREAS:*** Federal Civil Litigation; Appellate Practice. ***Email:*** george.hutchinson@finnegan.com

THOMAS L. JARVIS, born Raleigh, North Carolina, March 28, 1956; admitted to bar, 1986, New York; 1987, New Jersey; 2000, District of Columbia; registered to practice before U.S. Patent and Trademark Office. *Education:* University of North Carolina (B.A., 1978; J.D., 1985). Senior Investigative Attorney, 1989-1999 and Co-Chair, ABA Committee 603, U.S. International Trade Commission. *Member:* International Trade Commission Trial Lawyers Association. ***PRACTICE AREAS:*** Patent Litigation; Electrical Intellectual Property; Computer and Software Patents; Semiconductor Technology. ***Email:*** tom.jarvis@finnegan.com

MARY C. KENNEDY, born Red Bank, New Jersey, March 5, 1958; admitted to bar, 1984, New York; 1985, District of Columbia and U.S. District Court, District of Columbia; 1992, U.S. Supreme Court. *Education:* Swarthmore College (B.A., cum laude, 1980); New York University (J.D., 1983); Georgetown University (LL.M, 1986). Instructor: Trial Advocacy, George Washington University Law School, 1994—; Trial Skills, Prettyman Program, Georgetown University Law School. 1997—. *Member:* The District of Columbia Bar (Member, Criminal Law and Individual Rights Section); American Bar Association (Member, Criminal Justice Section); National Association of Criminal Defense Lawyers; National Legal Aid and Defender Association; District of Columbia Association of Criminal Defense Lawyers; New York County Lawyers Association. ***PRACTICE AREAS:*** Trial Advocacy; Criminal Defense. ***Email:*** mary.kennedy@finnegan.com

ARTHUR J. LEVINE, born Bridgeport, Connecticut, July 6, 1936; admitted to bar, 1964, District of Columbia, U.S. Supreme Court, U.S. Court of Appeals for the District of Columbia and Maryland. *Education:* Wesleyan University (B.A., 1958); Columbia University School of Law (LL.B., 1962). Assistant Chief, Examining Division, U.S. Copyright Office, 1966-1971. Co-Author: "Notice, Deposit and Registration: The Importance of Being Formal," 24, UCLA Law Review 1232; "Piracy And The New Technologies," Justice For A Generation, 1985; "The Information Executive's Guide to Intellectual Property Rights," Information Industry Association, 1985. Adjunct Professor of Law, Georgetown University Law Center, 1975-1988. Executive Director, National Commission on New Technological Uses of Copyrighted Works (CONTU), 1975-1978. Consultant to World Intellectual Property Organization and UNESCO Working Group on Copyright Problems Arising From the Use of Computers, Geneva, 1979. Member, Advisory Board, Bureau of National Affairs, Patent, Trademark and Copyright Journal, 1984—. *Member:* The District of Columbia Bar (Member, Patent, Trademark and Copyright Law Section; Chairman, Committees on: Copyright Office Affairs, 1972-1973; Copyright Law Revision, 1973-1974; Copyright and New Technology, 1978-1980; Copyright Legislation, 1982-1984; Copyright Division, 1984-1985; Authors, 1985-1987); American Intellectual Property Law Association (Chairman, Copyright Matters Committee, 1984-1986); Copyright Society of the U.S.A. (Trustee, 1976-1978). ***PRACTICE AREAS:*** International Copyright Law; Software Copyright; Copyright Protection. ***Email:*** arthur.levine@finnegan.com

LAURA P. MASUROVSKY, born New York, New York, March 4, 1957; admitted to bar, 1984, New York; 1985, District of Columbia; 1991, Virginia and Maryland. *Education:* Tufts University (B.A., summa cum laude, 1977); Harvard University (J.D., cum laude, 1983). Women's Professional Association Fellow, 1982. New York Stock Exchange Registered Representative, 1978. U.S. Department of State, 1983-1985. U.S. Attorney's Office, Washington, D.C., 1985-1986. Member, Washington Area Lawyers for the Arts. *Member:* The District of Columbia Bar; New York State and Maryland State Bar Associations; Virginia State Bar; District of Columbia Woman's Bar Association. ***LANGUAGES:*** French. ***PRACTICE AREAS:*** Intellectual Property Litigation. ***Email:*** laura.masurovsky@finnegan.com

ROBERT F. McCAULEY, III (Resident Counsel, Palo Alto, California Office).

WILLIAM T. McCLAIN, born Louisville, Kentucky, June 4, 1926; admitted to bar, 1958, Louisiana; 1960, Illinois; 1964, Oklahoma; 1982, U.S. Court of Appeals for the Federal Circuit; 1989, District of Columbia; registered to practice before U.S. Patent and Trademark Office. *Education:* University of Kentucky (B.S.Met.E., 1948); Loyola University School of Law (J.D., 1958). Member: Intellectual Property Owners, Inc., 1981-1986; Board of Directors, National Inventors Hall of Fame, 1983-1985; Board of Governors, Pacific Industrial Property Association, 1985-1986. *Member:* The District of Columbia Bar; American Bar Association (Member, Section on Patent, Trademark and Copyright Law; Chairman, Committees on: Trade Secrets, 1979; Amicus Briefs, 1989-1990; Inventors, 1991-1992; Government Relations, 1993-1994; Ross Essay Contest, 1995—); American Intellectual Property Law Association (Chairman, Committees on: Licensing, 1982-1983; Interference, 1984-1985; Member, Board of Directors, 1986-1987; Treasurer, 1989); Patent Law Association of Chicago (Chairman, Antitrust Committee, 1972; Member, Board of Directors, 1979-1981; President, 1982); Licensing Executives Society. [U.S. Navy, 1944-1946]. ***PRACTICE AREAS:*** Chemical Intellectual Property; Intellectual Property Infringement; Intellectual Property Licensing; International Licensing; Mechanical Intellectual Property. ***Email:*** william.mcclain@finnegan.com

LESLIE A. McDONELL (Resident Counsel, Boston, Massachusetts Office).

STEVEN H. MORRISSETT (Resident Counsel, Palo Alto, California Office).

ROBERT F. ROTELLA, born New York, New York, March 16, 1941; admitted to bar, 1968, Virginia; 1969, District of Columbia; registered to practice before U.S. Patent and Trademark Office. *Education:* New York University (B.E.E., 1962); George Washington University (J.D., 1966). *Member:* District of Columbia Bar; Virginia State Bar; American Bar Association; Licensing Executives Society; American Intellectual Property Law Association. ***PRACTICE AREAS:*** Intellectual Property. ***Email:*** robert.rotella@finnegan.com

RUSSELL L. SANDIDGE (Resident Counsel, Atlanta, Georgia Office).

ROBERT F. ZIEMS, born Lake Linden, Michigan, April 29, 1929; admitted to bar, 1958, District of Columbia; 1961, U.S. Supreme Court; 1970, Virginia; U.S. Court of Appeals for the Federal Circuit; registered to practice before U.S. Patent and Trademark Office. *Education:* Michigan College of Mining & Technology (B.S., 1951); The George Washington University National Law Center (LL.B., 1958). *Member:* The District of Columbia Bar; The Bar Association of the District of Columbia; American Intellectual Property Law Association. ***PRACTICE AREAS:*** Mechanical Patents; Mechanical Intellectual Property. ***Email:*** robert.ziems@finnegan.com

ASSOCIATES

JENNIFER R. ADAMS DRAFFEN, born Atlanta, Georgia, February 26, 1973; admitted to bar, 1999, New York. *Education:* Mississippi State University (B.A., magna cum laude, 1994); Duke University School of Law (J.D., 1998). *Member:* New York State and American Bar Associations; New York Women's Bar Association. (Resident Associate, Palo Alto, California Office). ***Email:*** jennifer.adamsdraffen@finnegan.com

ERIC WILLIAM ADCOCK, born Washington, D.C., December 13, 1971; admitted to bar, 2000, Virginia; 2001, District of Columbia; registered to practice before U.S. Patent and Trademark Office. *Education:* University of Maryland (B.S., 1994); George Washington University Law School (J.D., 2000). Member, Moot Court Board. *Member:* Virginia and American Bar Associations; Virginia State Bar; American Intellectual Property Law Association; American Institute of Chemical Engineers. ***PRACTICE AREAS:*** Intellectual Property Litigation; Chemical Patents; Patent Litigation; Patent Prosecution; Pharmaceutical Patents. ***Email:*** eric.adcock@finnegan.com

ANDREA ANDERSON, born Arkadelphia, Arkansas, October 1, 1966; admitted to bar, 1997, Washington; 1999, District of Columbia. *Education:* University of Virginia (B.A., 1988); University of Washington (M.A., Middle East Studies, 1994); The George Washington University Law School (J.D., with highest honors, 1997). Order of the Coif. Member, George Washington Law Review. Law Clerk to the Honorable Raymond C. Clevenger, III, United States, 1997-1998. Author: "Limitations on the Automatic Stay Provision," 64 Geo. Wash. L. Rev. 876. *Member:* Bar Association of the District of Columbia; Federal Circuit and American Bar Associations; International Trademark Association; American Intellectual Property Law Association. ***PRACTICE AREAS:*** International Trademarks; Trademark Litigation; Trademark Prosecution; Trademark Infringement; Trademark Protection. ***Email:*** andrea.anderson@finnegan.com

ERIKA HARMON ARNER, born Charlottesville, Virginia, September 23, 1971; admitted to bar, 1999, Virginia; 2000, District of Columbia. *Education:* College of William & Mary (B.S., Computer Science, 1993); Washington & Lee University School of Law (J.D., cum laude, 1999). Burks Scholar, Washington & Lee University School of Law, 1998-1999. Article Editor, Environmental Law Digest, Virginia State Bar Environmental Law Section, 1997-1998. *Member:* American Intellectual Property Law Association. ***PRACTICE AREAS:*** Computer and Software Patents; Intellectual Property Portfolio Management; Patent Prosecution; Computer Architecture Patents. ***Email:*** erika.arner@finnegan.com

ADAM AVRUNIN (Resident Associate, Atlanta, Georgia Office).

EYAL HANAN BARASH, born Lafayette, Indiana, June 5, 1969; admitted to bar, 1997, Illinois; 1998, District of Columbia; registered to practice before U.S. Patent and Trademark Office. *Education:* Indiana University (B.S., B.A., 1991); University of California at Berkeley (M.S., 1994); Northwestern University (J.D., 1997). First Prize, Lowden-Wigmore Moot Court Competition. Articles Editor, Law Review, 1997. Author: "Experimental Uses, Patents, and Scientific Progress," Northwestern University Law Review, Winter 1997. *Member:* American Chemical Society. ***PRACTICE AREAS:*** Chemical Intellectual Property; Pharmaceutical Intellectual Property. ***Email:*** eyal.barash@finnegan.com

(This Listing Continued)

(This Listing Continued)

FINNEGAN, HENDERSON, FARABOW, GARRETT & DUNNER, L.L.P., Washington—Continued

JAMES R. BARNEY, born Corpus Christi, Texas, October 13, 1968; admitted to bar, 2000, Virginia; registered to practice U.S. Patent and Trademark Office (Not admitted in District of Columbia). *Education:* United States Naval Academy (B.S., with honors, 1990), Yale University Law School (J.D., 1999). *Member:* Federal Circuit Bar Association. [With U.S Navy, 1990-1996]. ***PRACTICE AREAS:*** Patent Litigation; Chemical Intellectual Property; Pharmaceutical Intellectual Property. ***Email:*** james.barney@finnegan.com

KENNETH D. BASSINGER (Resident Associate, Atlanta, Georgia Office).

F. LESLIE BESSENGER III (Resident Associate, Atlanta, Georgia Office).

BARRY D. BIDDLE (Resident Associate, Atlanta, Georgia Office).

DANIEL BRIAN BINSTOCK, born Silver Spring, Maryland, April 20, 1973; admitted to bar, 2000, Maryland; 2001, New Jersey and District of Columbia. *Education:* University of Maryland (B.A., 1995); American University - Washington College of Law (J.D., magna cum laude, 2000). Business and Development Editor, American University International Law Review, 1998-2000. Co-author, "Virtual Contempt: Trademark Injunctions on the Internet," IP Worldwide (March 2001 issue); "Domain Name Cases Decided Under the U.S. Anti-Cybersquatting Consumer Protection Act," Trademark World (April 2001 Domain Name Supplement). ***PRACTICE AREAS:*** Domain Name Infringement; Internet Trademark Law; Trademark Prosecution; Trademark Litigation. ***Email:*** daniel.binstock@finnegan.com

LESLIE I. BOOKOFF, born Baltimore, Maryland, June 18, 1968; admitted to bar, 1993, Maryland; 1994, District of Columbia; registered to practice before U.S. Patent and Trademark Office. *Education:* University of Maryland (B.S., summa cum laude, 1990); University of Pennsylvania (J.D., cum laude, 1993). Member, University of Pennsylvania Law Review. ***REPORTED CASES:*** 120 F. Supp. 2d 864. ***PRACTICE AREAS:*** Intellectual Property Portfolio Management; Intellectual Property Litigation; Mechanical Intellectual Property; Medical Intellectual Property; Patent Prosecution. ***Email:*** les.bookoff@finnegan.com

MICHELE C. BOSCH, born Washington, D.C., April 29, 1968; admitted to bar, 1993, Virginia; 1997, District of Columbia; registered to practice before U.S. Patent and Trademark Office. *Education:* University of Virginia (B.A., 1990); College of William & Mary (J.D., 1993). Co-Author: "Willful Infringement: A Real Concern," Federal Circuit Bar Journal; "Third Party Opinions-Traps and Pitfalls and How to Avoid Them," Federal Circuit Bar Journal; "Being Prepared for U.S. Litigation Can Make All the Difference," Patent World. *Member:* Virginia, Federal Circuit and American Bar Associations; The District of Columbia Bar; American Intellectual Property Law Association; American Chemical Society. ***LANGUAGES:*** French. ***PRACTICE AREAS:*** Pharmaceutical Patents; Chemical Patents; Biochemical Patents; Patent Interference Practice; Patent Prosecution; Patent Protection. ***Email:*** michele.bosch@finnegan.com

JAMES J. BOYLE, born October 26, 1964; admitted to bar, 1999, Virginia; 2000, District of Columbia; registered to practice before U.S. Patent and Trademark Office. *Education:* University of Wisconsin-Parkside (B.S., 1986); University of Virginia (Ph.D., Physics, 1992; J.D., 1999). Editor-in-Chief, Virginia Journal of Law & Technology. Consulting Editor, American Heritage Dictionary, Fourth Edition, 2000. *Member:* American Physical Society. ***PRACTICE AREAS:*** Patent Prosecution; Patent Protection; Electronics; Fiber Optics; Physics. ***Email:*** james.boyle@finnegan.com

WILLIAM J. BROGAN, admitted to bar, 1999, Virginia; 2000, District of Columbia; registered to practice before U.S. Patent and Trademark Office. *Education:* Boston University (B.S., Computer Engineering, 1984); George Washington University Law School (J.D., with honors, 1999). Member, The George Washington Law Review, 1998-1999. *Member:* American Intellectual Property Law Association. ***PRACTICE AREAS:*** Computer and Software Patents; Intellectual Property Litigation; Software Protection; Patent Prosecution. ***Email:*** william.brogan@finnegan.com

WALTER W. BROWN (Resident Associate, Atlanta, Georgia Office).

PAUL W. BROWNING, born Summit, New Jersey, October 2, 1968; admitted to bar, 1999, Massachusetts; 2000, District of Columbia; 2001, U.S. Court of Appeals for the Federal Circuit. *Education:* Brown University (B.S., magna cum laude, 1991); University of Chicago (M.S., 1993; Ph.D., 1996); Harvard University (J.D., cum laude, 1999). *Member:* American Bar Association; American Intellectual Property Law Association. ***PRACTICE AREAS:*** Chemical Intellectual Property; Chemical Patent Prosecution; Pharmaceutical Patents. ***Email:*** paul.browning@finnegan.com

JASON R. BURATTI, born Johnson City, New York, January 22, 1972; admitted to bar, 2000, Virginia (Not admitted in District of Columbia). *Education:* University of Virginia (B.A., 1994); University of North Carolina at Wilmington (Master of Science-Biology, 1996); George Mason University School of Law (J.D., cum laude, 2000). ***PRACTICE AREAS:*** Genetics; Biotechnology Patents; Chemical Patents; Patent Litigation; Pharmaceutical Patents. ***Email:*** jason.buratti@finnegan.com

ELIZABETH MARIE BURKE, admitted to bar, 2000 ,Virginia; registered to practice before U.S. Patent and Trademark Office (Not admitted in District of Columbia). *Education:* Catholic University of America (B.S., 1990); Clemson University (M.S., 1996); Columbus School of Law of The Catholic University of America (J.D., magna cum laude, 2000). ***PRACTICE AREAS:*** Patent Prosecution. ***Email:*** elizabeth.burke@finnegan.com

BRIAN BURN, born Marietta, Georgia, July 5, 1968; admitted to bar, 2001, Virginia; registered to practice before U.S. Patent and Trademark Office (Not admitted in District of Columbia). *Education:* King College (B.S., 1990); George Mason University (J.D., 2000). *Member:* Federal Circuit and American Bar Associations. ***PRACTICE AREAS:*** Chemical Intellectual Property; Pharmaceutical Intellectual Property; Chemical Patent Prosecution; Chemical Patents; Patent Litigation. ***Email:*** brian.burn@finnegan.com

ROBERT L. BURNS, born Indianapolis, February 17, 1968; admitted to bar, 1995, Illinois; 1996, U.S. Court of Appeals for the Federal and Fourth Circuits; 1997, District of Columbia; registered to practice before U.S. Patent and Trademark Office. *Education:* Purdue University (B.S.A. & A.E., 1990); The John Marshall Law School (J.D., cum laude, 1995). Phi Kappa Phi. Editor-in-Chief, Journal of Computer & Information Law, 1994-1995. *Member:* American Institute of Aeronautics and Astronautics; American Society of Mechanical Engineers; American Intellectual Property Law Association; Computer Law Association. ***PRACTICE AREAS:*** Mechanical Intellectual Property; Aerospace Law; Technology Law. ***Email:*** robert.burns@finnegan.com

L. SCOTT BURWELL, born Cleveland, Ohio, April 15, 1969; admitted to bar, 1993, Virginia; 1995, District of Columbia; registered to practice before U.S. Patent and Trademark Office. *Education:* Amherst College (A.B., 1990); Harvard University (J.D., 1993). *Member:* American Bar Association; American Intellectual Property Law Association. ***PRACTICE AREAS:*** Intellectual Property Litigation; Pharmaceutical Intellectual Property; Biotechnology Patents; Patent Litigation. ***Email:*** scott.burwell@finnegan.com

KELLY A. CASEY (Resident Associate, Atlanta, Georgia Office).

CHARLES W. CHESNEY, born Norristown, Pennsylvania, November 30, 1968; admitted to bar, 1998, District of Columbia and Virginia. *Education:* The Pennsylvania State University (B.S.E.E., 1991); The George Washington University (M.S.E.E., 1995); University of Virginia (J.D., 1998). ***PRACTICE AREAS:*** Software Protection; Electronic Intellectual Property; Electrical Patent Prosecution; Patent Litigation; Patent Protection. ***Email:*** charles.chesney@finnegan.com

GREGORY A. CHOPSKIE, born Greensboro, North Carolina, January 14, 1970; admitted to bar, 1999, Virginia; 2000, District of Columbia; registered to practice before U.S. Patent and Trademark Office. *Education:* Georgetown University (B.S., 1992); George Mason University School of Law (J.D., with honors, 1999). *Member:* American Intellectual Property Law Association. ***PRACTICE AREAS:*** Pharmaceutical Patents; Pharmaceutical Intellectual Property; Patent Litigation; Patent Prosecution. ***Email:*** greg.chopskie@finnegan.com

KIMANI CLARK, born New York, New York, May 9, 1972; admitted to bar, 1997, Maryland; 1998, District of Columbia. *Education:* Massachusetts Institute of Technology (B.S., 1994); Stanford Law School (J.D., 1997). Coauthor: "Current Issues Affecting Patent Prosecution for Software-Related Inventions," Corporate Counsel Magazine, September 1995. *Member:* Maryland State and American Bar Associations; The District of Columbia Bar; American Intellectual Property Law Association. ***PRACTICE AREAS:*** Computer and Software Patents; Patent Prosecution; Patent Protection; Intellectual Property Rights; Intellectual Property Portfolio Management. ***Email:*** kimani.clark@finnegan.com

CAROL L. COLE, born Wilmington, Delaware, November 24, 1972; admitted to bar, 2000, Virginia; registered to practice before U.S. Patent and Trademark Office (Not admitted in District of Columbia). *Education:* University of Maryland (B.S., 1994); Washington College of Law of American University (J.D., 2000). *Member:* Virginia Bar Association; American Intellectual Property Law Association. ***PRACTICE AREAS:*** Biotechnology Patent Prosecution; Chemical Patent Prosecution; Patent Infringement; Patent Prosecution. ***Email:*** carol.cole@finnegan.com

VANESSA J. COOPER, born New Rochelle, New York, June 28, 1969; admitted to bar, 1997, New York; 2001, District of Columbia. *Education:* Howard University (B.A., 1992); Catholic University of America (M.A., 1996); Columbus School of Law, Catholic University of America (J.D., 1996). ***PRACTICE AREAS:*** Trademark Prosecution; International Intellectual Property. ***Email:*** vanessa.cooper@finnegan.com

CHRISTOPHER L. CRUMBLEY (Resident Associate, Atlanta, Georgia Office).

(This Listing Continued)

KATHLEEN ALICE DALEY, born Rochester, New York, March 27, 1966; admitted to bar, 1993, Virginia; 1995, District of Columbia; registered to practice before U.S. Patent and Trademark Office. *Education:* Cornell University (B.S., 1988); The George Washington University National Law Center (J.D., with honors, 1993). Law Clerk to the Honorable Glenn L. Archer, Jr., Chief Judge, U.S. Court of Appeals for the Federal Circuit, 1995-1997. Law Clerk to the Honorable Wilkes C. Robinson, U.S. Court of Federal Claims, 1993-1995. ***PRACTICE AREAS:*** Intellectual Property Licensing; Intellectual Property Litigation; Mechanical Intellectual Property; Biomedical Technology. ***Email:*** kathleen.daley@finnegan.com

CHRISTOPHER WILLIAM DAY, born Madison, Wisconsin, March 23, 1969; admitted to bar, 2000, Maryland; registered to practice before U.S. Patent and Trademark Office (Not admitted in District of Columbia). *Education:* North Carolina State University (B.S., 1994); Columbus School of Law of the Catholic University of America (J.D., cum laude, 2000). Author, "Kiowa Tribe v. Manufacturing Technologies, Inc.: Doing the Right Thing for All the Wrong Reasons," 49 Cath. U. L. Rev. 279 (1999). ***PRACTICE AREAS:*** Intellectual Property Infringement; Intellectual Property Litigation; International Intellectual Property; Mechanical Intellectual Property; Computer and Software Patents. ***Email:*** christopher.day@finnegan.com

FRANK A. DECOSTA III, born Baltimore, Maryland, 1963; admitted to bar, 1996, Maryland; 1997, District of Columbia; registered to practice before U.S. Patent and Trademark Office. *Education:* Cornell University (B.S., 1985; M.Eng., Electrical Engineering, 1986); Howard University (Ph.D., Electrical Engineering, 1992); Georgetown University (J.D., cum laude, 1996). *Member:* American Intellectual Property Law Association; Institute of Electronic and Electrical Engineers. ***LANGUAGES:*** French. ***PRACTICE AREAS:*** Intellectual Property; Computers and Software; Litigation; Patent Licensing; Patent Prosecution. ***Email:*** frank.decosta@finnegan.com

MATTHEW DELGIORNO, born Bethesda, Maryland, September 8, 1971; admitted to bar, 1996, Maryland; 1997, District of Columbia. *Education:* Virginia Polytechnic Institute & State University (B.S.E.E., summa cum laude, 1993; M.S.E.E., 1997); University of Virginia Law School (J.D., 1996). Editorial Review Board (Articles Review Board), Virginia Journal of International Law. Cofounder, Student Intellectual Property Law Association. Law Clerk to the Honorable Randall R. Rader, U.S. Court of Appeals for the Federal Circuit, 1997-1999. *Member:* American Intellectual Property Law Association. ***PRACTICE AREAS:*** Patent Litigation; Electrical Intellectual Property; Patent Infringement. ***Email:*** matthew.delgiorno@finnegan.com

TIMOTHY B. DONALDSON, born Anchorage, Alaska, April 10, 1970; admitted to bar, 2000, Virginia; registered to practice before U.S. Patent and Trademark Office (Not admitted in District of Columbia). *Education:* Wake Forest University (B.S., magna cum laude, 1992; M.S., 1994); George Mason University School of Law (J.D., magna cum laude, 1999). Phi Beta Kappa. *Member:* American Bar Association; American Intellectual Property Law Association. ***PRACTICE AREAS:*** Biotechnology Patent Prosecution; Biotechnology Patents; Chemical Patent Prosecution; Molecular Biology Patents; Patent Interference Practice. ***Email:*** timothy.donaldson@finnegan.com

ANTHONY DREUX, born Washington, D.C., 1964; admitted to bar, 1996, Maryland; 1998, District of Columbia. *Education:* Howard University (B.S., Electrical Engineering, 1988); The John Marshall Law School, 1993-1994. The George Washington University Law School (J.D., 1996). *Member:* Federal Circuit and American Bar Associations; American Intellectual Property Law Association. ***PRACTICE AREAS:*** Patent Litigation; Computer Architecture Patents; Electrical Patent Prosecution; Computer and Software Patents. ***Email:*** anthony.dreux@finnegan.com

JOSÉ A. DUTHIL (Resident Associate, Atlanta, Georgia Office).

HOUTAN KHALILI ESFAHANI, born Tehran, Iran, August 2, 1964; admitted to bar, 1995, New York; 1997, District of Columbia and U.S. Court of Appeals for the Federal Circuit; registered to practice before the U.S. Patent and Trademark Office. *Education:* Columbia University (B.S.E.E., with honors, 1986; M.S.E.E., with honors, 1987); Rutgers University Law School (J.D., 1994). Eta Kappa Nu; Tau Beta Pi. *Member:* American Bar Association; Institute of Electrical and Electronics Engineers. ***LANGUAGES:*** Persian. ***PRACTICE AREAS:*** Intellectual Property; Patents. ***Email:*** houtan.esfahani@finnegan.com

MARGARET A. ESQUENET, born Warsaw, Poland, June 10, 1973; admitted to bar, 1999, Maryland; 2000, District of Columbia; 2001, U.S. District Court, District of Columbia. *Education:* University of California, Berkeley (B.A., 1995); American University, Washington College of Law (J.D., 1999). Author: "First Court Test of 'Veggie Libel': Laws Pits Texas Cattleman Against Oprah Winfrey," *The First Amendment and the Media, 103 (Richard T. Kaplar ed., 1998); "Focus on Newsgathering," Quill Magazine, Dec. 1998 at 5. Co-Author, "Putting an End to the Trade Secret Plaintiff's Game of Bait and Switch," IP Litigator, May 2001. Member:* American Bar Association; American Intellectual Property Law Association; International Trademark Association. ***PRACTICE AREAS:*** Software Licensing; Intellectual Property Litigation; Trademark Prosecution. ***Email:*** margaret.esquenet@finnegan.com

(This Listing Continued)

YORK MOODY FAULKNER, born San Francisco, California, April 24, 1965; admitted to bar, 1992, Utah; 1997, District of Columbia. *Education:* Brigham Young University (B.S., cum laude, 1989; J.D., magna cum laude, 1992). Trial Attorney, U.S. Department of Justice, Tax Division, Criminal Enforcement Section, 1992-1996. Author: "Pulling the Threads from Blanket Protective Orders: Courts Move Carefully Scrutinize Litigants' Requests for Secrecy," IP Litigator, February 2000; "New Challenges When Using Employment Contract to Protect Trade Secrets, Confidential Information, and Competitive Advantage," IP Litigator, April 2001. Co-Author: "Putting an End to the Trade Secret Plaintiff's Game of Bait and Switch," IP Litigator, June 2001; "Judicial Review of State Regulation that Impacts Foreign Trade: A Second Look at South Central Timber Development v. Wunnicke," B.Y.U. Law Review, 1991; "A Market Analysis of Anticompetition Agreements in Labor Contracts," B.Y.U. Law Review, 1992; "A Negative Incentive Based Proposal for Campaign Finance Reform: A Lesson from Nottingham," B.Y.U. Law Review, 1992. Chairman, Trade Secrets Committee, Intellectual Property Section, District of Columbia Bar, 2000-2001. ***LANGUAGES:*** Japanese. ***PRACTICE AREAS:*** Intellectual Property Infringement; Intellectual Property Litigation; Patent Litigation; Trade Secrets.

MICHAEL J. FLIBBERT, born Methuen, Massachusetts, July 11, 1964; admitted to bar, 1994, Virginia; 1996, District of Columbia; registered to practice before U.S. Patent and Trademark Office. *Education:* Georgetown University (B.S., 1986); The George Washington University National Law Center (J.D., with honors, 1994). Order of the Coif. Law Clerk to the Honorable Alan D. Lourie, Circuit Judge, U.S. Court of Appeals for the Federal Circuit, 1994-1996. ***PRACTICE AREAS:*** Chemical Intellectual Property; Chemical Patents; Patent Litigation; Pharmaceutical Patents. ***Email:*** michael.flibbert@finnegan.com

DAVID PENN FRAZIER, born December 19, 1966; admitted to bar, 2000, Maryland; 2001, District of Columbia; registered to practice before U.S. Patent and Trademark Office. *Education:* Pennsylvania State University (B.S., with distinction, 1988); Harvard University (Ph.D., 1996); Georgetown University (J.D., magna cum laude, 2000). Order of the Coif. *Member:* American Bar Association; Giles S. Rich American Inn of Court; American Association for the Advancement of Science. ***PRACTICE AREAS:*** Intellectual Property Portfolio Management; Pharmaceutical Intellectual Property; Biotechnology Patents; Patent Litigation; Pharmaceutical Patents. ***Email:*** david.frazier@finnegan.com

SUSAN M. FREEDMAN, born New York, N.Y., May 22, 1962; admitted to bar, 1992, Connecticut; 1993, New York and District of Columbia. *Education:* Hamilton College (B.A., magna cum laude, 1984); University of Tuebingen (Fulbright Grant, 1984-1985); The George Washington University National Law Center (J.D., 1992). Moot Court Board, George Washington University, 1989-1992. Author: "Counterfeits in the Internet Age," IP Litigator, April 2001; "Internet Auction Sites: Is Immunity from Infringement Going... Going... Gone!" IP Litigator, June-July 2001. *Member:* District of Columbia Bar (Intellectual Property Law Section); American Bar Association (Intellectual Property Law Section; Litigation Section); International Trademark Association. ***LANGUAGES:*** German. ***PRACTICE AREAS:*** Trademark Infringement; Trademark Litigation; Trademark Prosecution; Trademark Protection; Trademark Registration. ***Email:*** susan.freedman@finnegan.com

LAWRENCE FRANCIS GALVIN, born East Saint Louis, Illinois, September 19, 1955; admitted to bar, 1998, Maryland; 1999, District of Columbia; registered to practice before U.S. Patent and Trademark Office. *Education:* U.S. Naval Academy (B.S., Mathematics, with distinction, 1978); Massachusetts Institute of Technology, Woods Hole Oceanographic Institution (M.S., Ocean Engineering, 1991); Georgetown University Law Center (J.D., 1998). Phi Kappa Phi. [Commander, U.S. Navy, 1974-1998]. ***PRACTICE AREAS:*** Mechanical Intellectual Property; Design Patents; Electrical Patent Prosecution; Mechanical Patents; Patent Prosecution. ***Email:*** larry.galvin@finnegan.com

STEPHANIE S. CONIS GAUTHIER (Resident Associate, Atlanta, Georgia Office).

JONATHAN M. GELCHINSKY, born Brooklyn, New York, May 3, 1973; admitted to bar, 2000, New York and District of Columbia. *Education:* Brandeis University (B.A., cum laude, 1995); American University, Washington College of Law (J.D., summa cum laude, 1999). Projects Editor, American University Law Review, 1998-1999. Co-Author: "Evolving Internet Intellectual Property Issues," Trademark World, December 1998-January 1999; "No Fair! Stop Using My Marks," Intellectual Property Today, July 1999; "Trademarks on the Internet: How Does Fair Use Fare?" Trademark World, February 1999; "Evolving Internet Intellectual Property Issues," Wiley Intellectual Property Law Update, 2000. *Member:* American Bar Association (Intellectual Property Law Section); American Intellectual Property Law Association. ***PRACTICE AREAS:*** Domain Name Infringement; Internet Trademark Law; Trademark Infringement; Trademark Prosecution; Trademark Protection. ***Email:*** jon.gelchinsky@finnegan.com

JASON E. GORDEN, born Milwaukee, Wisconsin, December 28, 1971; admitted to bar, 2000, California; registered to practice before U.S. Patent and

(This Listing Continued)

FINNEGAN, HENDERSON, FARABOW, GARRETT & DUNNER, L.L.P., Washington—Continued

Trademark Office. *Education:* University of Missouri (B.S., 1994); University of Missouri Law School (J.D., 2000). (Resident Associate, Palo Alto, California Office). ***Email:*** jason.gorden@finnegan.com

PAUL C. GOULET, born Miami, Florida, June 1, 1972; admitted to bar, 1997, Maryland; 2000, District of Columbia. *Education:* University of Pennsylvania (B.A., 1994; J.D., 1997). *Member:* American Bar Association; American Intellectual Property Law Association; International Trade Commission Trial Lawyers Association. ***PRACTICE AREAS:*** Patent Litigation; Patent Infringement; International Intellectual Property. ***Email:*** paul.goulet@finnegan.com

TROY EDWIN GRABOW, born New Hartford, New York, May 22, 1971; admitted to bar, 2001, Virginia and District of Columbia. *Education:* Union College (B.S., Mechanical Engineering, 1993); George Washington University (J.D., with high honors, 2000). Member, Giles S. Rich American Inn of Court. Law Clerk to the Honorable Timothy B. Dyk, Circuit Judge, U.S. Court of Appeals for the Federal Circuit, 2000-2001. Patent Examiner, U.S. Patent and Trademark Office, 1994-1998. *Member:* American Bar Association; American Intellectual Property Law Association. ***PRACTICE AREAS:*** Intellectual Property Litigation; Electro-Mechanical Patents; Patent Infringement; Patent Litigation; Patent Prosecution. ***Email:*** troy.grabow@finnegan.com

C. GREGORY GRAMENOPOULOS (Resident Associate, Brussels, Belgium Office).

ANTHONY M. GUTOWSKI, born Pontiac, Michigan, July 20, 1967; admitted to bar, 1994, Virginia; 1996, District of Columbia; registered to practice before U.S. Patent and Trademark Office. *Education:* Villanova University (B.M.E., 1989); The George Washington University National Law Center (J.D., with honors, 1994). Tau Beta Pi; Pi Tau Sigma. Patent Examiner, U.S. Patent Office, 1989-1994. *Member:* American Intellectual Property Law Association. ***PRACTICE AREAS:*** Mechanical Patents; Electro-Mechanical Patents; Medical Patents; Patent Protection; Patent Prosecution. ***Email:*** gutowski@finnegan.com

ANTHONY A. HARTMANN, born Milwaukee, Wisconsin, June 20, 1966; admitted to bar, 1996, Illinois and U.S. District Court, Northern District of Illinois; 1999, District of Columbia; registered to practice before U.S. Patent and Trademark Office. *Education:* University of Virginia (B.S., with distinction, 1988); University of Notre Dame (J.D., 1996). Phi Alpha Delta; Tau Beta Pi. Managing Editor, Journal of College and University Law. Licensed Professional Engineer, New York, 1993. *Member:* District of Columbia Bar; Chicago, Illinois State and American Bar Associations; American Intellectual Property Law Association; American Institute of Chemical Engineers; National Society of Professional Engineers. ***PRACTICE AREAS:*** Intellectual Property Litigation; Chemical Intellectual Property. ***Email:*** anthony.hartmann@finnegan.com

KRISTEN M. HEALEY, born Brockton, Massachusetts, June 6, 1969; admitted to bar, 1999, Georgia; 2000, District of Columbia. *Education:* Brown University (B.A., Physics, 1991; B.A., English and American Literature, 1991); American University, Washington College of Law (J.D., 1999). Author: "The Scope of Eleventh Amendment Immunity From Suits Arising Under Patent Law After Seminole Tribe v. Florida," 47 Am. U. L.Rev. 1735 (1998). ***PRACTICE AREAS:*** Intellectual Property; Patents; Patent Litigation. ***Email:*** kristen.healey@finnegan.com

B. BRETT HEAVNER, born Kansas City, Missouri, November 29, 1966; admitted to bar, 1992, Virginia; 1993, District of Columbia. *Education:* St. John's College (B.A., Liberal Arts, 1989); Duke University School of Law (J.D., with honors, 1992; LL.M., 1992). Duke Journal of International and Comparative Law, 1991-1992. Co-Author: "E.C. Registration Offers Advantages to Owner," National Law Journal, May 20, 1996. Speaker, Patent and Trademark Institute of Canada, The Canadian Institute. *Member:* International Trademark Association; American Intellectual Property Law Association (Subcommittee Chairman, Annual Trademark Case Report, Trademark Committee, 1998; Editor, Trademark Practice Committee Newsletter, 1999; Vice Chair, Trademark Litigation Committee). ***PRACTICE AREAS:*** Trademark Litigation; Trademark Prosecution; Copyright Infringement; International Trademarks; Trademark Infringement. ***Email:*** brett.heavner@finnegan.com

CHRISTIE BATY HEINZE (Resident Associate, Atlanta, Georgia Office).

SCOTT A. HERBST (Resident Associate, Palo Alto, California Office).

REBECCA D. HESS, born Honolulu, Hawaii, December 6, 1972; admitted to bar, 1999, Minnesota (Not admitted in District of Columbia). *Education:* Middlebury College (B.A., 1995); University of Minnesota (J.D., 1999). Coauthor: "Different Inventive Entities Under 35 U.S.C. 102(e) and Affidavit Practice Under 37 C.F.R. 1.132," *Journal of the Patent and Trademark Office Society,* January 1999, Vol. 81, No. 1, pgs 33-41. ***PRACTICE AREAS:*** Patent Prosecution; Pharmaceutical Patents; Biotechnology Patents; Patent Litigation. ***Email:*** rebecca.hess@finnegan.com

(This Listing Continued)

CHRISTINA J. HIEBER, born New York, N.Y., 1972; admitted to bar, 1999, New York; 2001, District of Columbia. *Education:* Dartmouth College (B.A., cum laude, 1994); George Washington University Law School (J.D., 1998). Author, "New Law Gives Trademark Owners Weapon to Combat Cybersquatting," The Cyberspace Lawyer, Vol. 4, No. 10 (January 2000). Co-Author: "Is Liability Just a Click Away?" Internet Law & Business (March 2001); "Confusion, Dilution Still the Focus of Linking Cases in Ruling on Trademark Claims Over Third-Party Sites," National Law Journal (February 5, 2001); "Taking Aim at Cybersquatters: A New Weapon for U.S. Trademark Owners," Trademark World (March 2000); "How to Use and Attack Consumer Surveys in Trademark Infringement and False Advertising Cases," Trademark World (March 1999); "Untangling a Web of Minimum Contracts; The Internet and Personal Jurisdiction in Trademark and Unfair Competition Cases," 87 Trademark Reporter 526 (1997); "Wired for Jurisdiction: Is Plugging In Enough?" Trademark World (May 1997). *Member:* New York State and American Bar Associations; American Intellectual Property Law Association. ***PRACTICE AREAS:*** Trademarks; Internet Law; Unfair Competition. ***Email:*** christina.hieber@finnegan.com

TIMOTHY M. HSIEH, born Baltimore, Maryland, August 25, 1961; admitted to bar, 1998, Maryland; 1999, District of Columbia; registered to practice before U.S. Patent and Trademark Office. *Education:* Johns Hopkins University (B.E.S., 1983; M.E.S., 1985; Ph.D., 1989); University of Virginia (J.D., 1998). Sigma Xi; Phi Delta Phi. Founding & Executive Editor, Virginia Journal of Law & Technology, 1996-1998. *Member:* American Bar Association; American Intellectual Property Law Association; Maryland Patent Law Association; ASM International; American Society for Nondestructive Testing; Society for Advanced Materials and Process Engineering. ***PRACTICE AREAS:*** Patent Litigation; Patent Prosecution; Fiber Optics; Semiconductor Technology. ***Email:*** timothy.hsieh@finnegan.com

JOHN A. HUDALLA (Resident Associate, Atlanta, Georgia Office).

LYNN M. JORDAN, born Scranton, Pennsylvania, June 5, 1970; admitted to bar, 1995, Virginia; 1996, U.S. Court of Appeals, Fourth Circuit and U.S. District Court, Eastern District of Virginia; 1997, District of Columbia. *Education:* Pennsylvania State University (B.S., with highest distinction, 1992); University of Tulsa (J.D., with highest honors, 1995). Phi Delta Phi. Magister, Rogers Inn, 1993-1995. Balfour Scholar. Member: Order of the Curule; Jessup International Moot Court Team. Note and Comment Editor, Energy Law Journal, 1994-1995. Judicial Clerk to the Honorable Herman A. Whisenant, Jr., 31st Judicial Circuit Court, Virginia. Author: "Naming a Drug in Just One Color - Trademark Protection for Organoleptic Properties of Pharmaceuticals," 135 Trademark World 28 (March 2001); "Name Tag—Domain Name Trademark Liability," Cyber Esq., Spring 1999. Co-Author: "Qualitex Co. v. Jacobson Products Co., The Unanswered Question—Can Color Ever Be Inherently Distinctive?" 85 Trademark Reporter 371, 1995. *Member:* American Bar Association (Co-Chair, Young Lawyers Division, Intellectual Property Law Section, 1996-1999); International Trademark Association (Member, Public Relations Committee, 1998—). ***PRACTICE AREAS:*** Trademarks. ***Email:*** lynn.jordan@finnegan.com

D. BRIAN KACEDON, born Livingston, New Jersey, September 8, 1975; admitted to bar, 2000, Maryland; registered to practice before U.S. Patent and Trademark Office (Not admitted in District of Columbia). *Education:* Duke University (B.S.E., cum laude with distinction, 1997); New York University (J.D., 2000). *Member:* Maryland State Bar Association; American Intellectual Property Law Association. ***PRACTICE AREAS:*** Mechanical Patents; Patent Licensing; Patent Litigation; Patent Prosecution. ***Email:*** brian.kacedon@finnegan.com

VAMSI K. KAKARLA, born Harrisburg, Pennsylvania, July 11, 1974; admitted to bar, 2001, New York (Not admitted in District of Columbia). *Education:* Pennsylvania State University (B.S., Electrical Engineering, 1996); Yeshiva University, Benjamin N. Cardozo School of Law (J.D., 2000). *Member:* New York State Bar Association. ***PRACTICE AREAS:*** Electrical Patent Prosecution; Electronic Patents; Patent Infringement; Patent Litigation; Patent Prosecution.

LARA CHAPMAN KELLEY, born Columbia, South Carolina, May 30, 1969; admitted to bar, 1999, Virginia; 2000, District of Columbia; registered to practice before U.S. Patent and Trademark Office. *Education:* Wake Forest University (B.S., Biology, magna cum laude, 1991); Georgetown University Law Center (J.D., cum laude, 1999). Patent Examiner, U.S. Patent and Trademark Office, 1993-1997. *Member:* American Intellectual Property Law Association. ***PRACTICE AREAS:*** Biotechnology Patent Law; Chemical Patent Law. ***Email:*** lara.kelley@finnegan.com

SANG HUI MICHAEL KIM (Resident Associate, Palo Alto, California Office).

PAUL ALAN LARSON, born Torrance, California, May 25, 1971; admitted to bar, 2000, Virginia (Not admitted in District of Columbia). *Education:* Brigham Young University (B.S., 1997); George Washington University (J.D.,

(This Listing Continued)

2000). *Member:* American Bar Association; American Society of Mechanical Engineers. ***PRACTICE AREAS:*** Mechanical Patents; Medical Patents; Patent Prosecution. ***Email:*** alan.larson@finnegan.com

LIONEL M. LAVENUE, born Jackson, Tennessee, May 31, 1966; admitted to bar, 1992, Florida; 1993, U.S. Court of Federal Claims; 1994, District of Columbia; 1995, U.S. Court of Appeals for the Federal Circuit. *Education:* Vanderbilt University (B.A., magna cum laude, 1988); Washington College of Law, American University (J.D., 1992); The George Washington University National Law Center (LL.M., 1994); George Mason University (M.S., 1997). Phi Beta Kappa. Law Clerk to the Honorable Glenn L. Archer, Jr., U.S. Court of Appeals for the Federal Circuit, 1994-1996. Law Clerk to the Honorable Robert J. Yock, U.S. Court of Federal Claims, 1992-1994. Editor, American University Journal of International Law & Policy. Recipient, The International Law Journal Award for Best Student Work. Author: "Survey of Government Contract Cases in the United States Court of Appeals for the Federal Circuit: 1997 in Review," 47 Am. U. L.Rev. 1393 (1998); "Database Rights and Technical Data Rights: The Expansion of Intellectual Property for the Protection of Databases," 38 Santa Clara L.Rev. 1 (1997); "Technical Data Rights in Government Procurement and Database Rights: Intellectual Property Protection for Computer Software and the Indicia of Information Systems and Technology," 32 U. San Francisco L.Rev. 1 (1997). Co-Author, Survey, "1996 Patent Law Decisions of the Federal Circuit," 47 Am. U. L.Rev. 1675 (1997); "Patent Infringement by the United States and Government Contractors Under 28 U.S.C.§1498 in the United States Court of Federal Claims," 2 J. Intell. Prop. L. 389 (1995). *Member:* American Bar Association; The Federalist Society; American Intellectual Property Law Association; Lawyer-Pilots Bar Association; German American Law Association. ***LANGUAGES:*** German. ***PRACTICE AREAS:*** Software Protection; Intellectual Property Litigation; Intellectual Property Portfolio Management; Computer and Software Patents; Patent Litigation. ***Email:*** lionel.lavenue@finnegan.com

CHRISTINE E. LEHMAN, born North Tarrytown, New York, January 27, 1970; admitted to bar, 1994, New York and District of Columbia; 1995, U.S. Court of Appeals for the Federal Circuit, U.S. Court of Federal Claims, U.S. District Court, District of Columbia, U.S. District Court, Northern District of California; registered to practice before U.S. Patent and Trademark Office. *Education:* Swarthmore College (B.S., 1990); New York University (J.D., 1993). Investigative Attorney, U.S. International Trade Commission, 1996-1999. *Member:* American Intellectual Property Law Association; ITC Trial Lawyers Association. ***PRACTICE AREAS:*** Patent Litigation; Intellectual Property Litigation. ***Email:*** christine.lehman@finnegan.com

KENNETH M. LESCH, born Staten Island, New York, March 29, 1970; admitted to bar, 1998, Massachusetts (Not admitted in District of Columbia). *Education:* University of Pennsylvania (B.S.E.E., cum laude, 1992; M.S.E.E., 1995); The George Washington University Law School (J.D., with honors, 1998). Pi Mu Epsilon. Recipient, Corpus Juris Secundum Award for Scholastic Excellence in Property. Author: Case Note, "Aggressive Application of Federal Jurisdiction: The Younger Abstention Doctrine in *Bridges v. Kelly,*" 65 Geo. Wash. L. Rev. (1997). *Member:* American Bar Association; Institute of Electrical and Electronics Engineers; Giles S. Rich American Inn of Court. ***PRACTICE AREAS:*** Electrical Patent Prosecution. ***Email:*** kenneth.lesch@finnegan.com

HOWARD WARREN LEVINE, born New York, New York, December 15, 1967; admitted to bar, 1993, New York; 1994, Pennsylvania, District of Columbia; U.S. Supreme Court; U.S. Court of Appeals for the Federal Circuit, U.S. District Court for the District of Columbia. *Education:* Duke University (B.A., cum laude, 1990); Georgetown University Law Center (J.D., cum laude, 1993). Recipient, American Jurisprudence Award for Torts. Member: Georgetown International Environmental Law Review. ***PRACTICE AREAS:*** Intellectual Property Litigation; Biotechnology. ***Email:*** howard.levine@finnegan.com

LOUIS J. LEVY, born Jersey City, New Jersey, January 21, 1956; admitted to bar, 1996, Maryland; 1997, District of Columbia. *Education:* Northwestern University (B.A., Slavic Languages and Literature, 1978); University of Toronto (M.A., Slavic Languages and Literature, 1979); Columbia University (M.A., International Affairs, 1986); American University, Washington College of Law (J.D., 1995). Co-Author: "To Catch a Thief: Laws Evolve to Combat Cyberpiracy," IP Litigator, May 2001; "U.S. Reinforces Defence Against Grey Goods," Managing Intellectual Property, April 2000; "Recent IP Developments in Japan," IP Asia, May 1999; "The 'Deemed Export' Rule: Foreign Nationals in U.S. Companies," CIPIC (Journal of the Customs Intellectual Property Information Center, Japan), June 1999; "U.S. Customs Service Amends Gray Market Import Rule," Trademark Rule, May 1999; "The Impact of the Economic Espionage Act of 1996," I.P.R. (Intellectual Property News Report, Japan), August 1998; "Tokyo High Court Rules Texas Instruments' 'Kilby' Patent Not Infringed by Fujitsu," IP Asia, December 1997; "Proposed Revisions to Japan's Design Law," IP Asia, October 1997; "Japan Revises Trademark Law," Trademark World, February 1997. Migration Specialist, accredited to represent refugees before U.S. Immigration and Naturalization Service, HIAS, Inc., 1979-1984. Soviet/East European Policy Analyst, Committee for National Security, 1987-1988. Telecommunications Regulatory and Policy Analyst/Russian-Soviet

(This Listing Continued)

Policy Analyst, Booz, Allen & Hamilton, Inc., 1988-1995. Adjunct Professor, Temple University (Japan), January 1997-May 1997. *Member:* District of Columbia Bar; Maryland State Bar Association; American Intellectual Property Law Association; International Trademark Association. ***LANGUAGES:*** Russian. ***PRACTICE AREAS:*** Trademarks; Copyrights; Unfair Competition. ***Email:*** louis.levy@finnegan.com

ESTHER H. LIM, born Pusan, Korea; admitted to bar, 1995, Maryland; 1996, District of Columbia; 1999, U.S. Court of Appeals, Federal Circuit; registered to practice before U.S. Patent and Trademark Office. *Education:* Towson University (B.A., summa cum laude, 1992); University of Maryland School of Law (J.D., 1995). Senior Managing Editor, 1994-1995 and Associate Editor, 1993-1994, Maryland Journal of International Trade. Co-Author: "Let Seller Beware: Indemnification Can Cost Big," The National Law Journal, C18 (June 22, 1998); "Liability Issues Change With Economic Shift," Les Nouvelles, Vol. XXXII, No. 4 (December 1997); "Enforcing Intellectual Property Licences in Korea," IP Asia, Vol. 10, No. 9 (November 1997); "The Current State of Patent Protection for Software-Related Inventions in the United States," AIPPI Korea Journal, Vol. 1, No. 5 (May 1997). *Member:* Maryland State, Federal Circuit and American Bar Associations; American Intellectual Property Law Association; Asian Pacific American Bar Association (President, 2001-2002; President-Elect, 2000-2001; Treasurer, 1999-2000); Maryland Patent Law Association; D.C. Computer Law Forum. ***LANGUAGES:*** Korean and Spanish. ***PRACTICE AREAS:*** Intellectual Property Litigation; Computer and Software Patents; Technology Licensing; International Intellectual Property; Software Protection. ***Email:*** esther.lim@finnegan.com

KURT ALBERT LUTHER, born Phoenix, Arizona, June 5, 1968; admitted to bar, 1997, Virginia; 1998, District of Columbia; registered to practice before the U.S. Patent and Trademark Office. *Education:* University of Arizona (B.S.M.E., 1990); Arizona State University (J.D., cum laude, 1997). Author: "The School Improvement Act," 27 Ariz. St. L.J. 389 (1995). ***PRACTICE AREAS:*** Patent Prosecution; Patent Litigation; Mechanical Patents; Computer and Software Patents; Electro-Mechanical Patents. ***Email:*** kurt.luther@finnegan.com

KEITH DOUGLAS MACMILLAN, born Cumberland, Maryland, November 13, 1962; admitted to bar, 2000, Virginia; 2001, District of Columbia; registered to practice before U.S. Patent and Trademark Office. *Education:* University of Delaware (B.A., 1987); George Washington University (J.D., 2000). Dean's Scholar. *Member:* American Intellectual Property Law Association. ***PRACTICE AREAS:*** Chemical Patent Prosecution; Patent Infringement. ***Email:*** keith.macmillan@finnegan.com

ELIZABETH MCGOOGAN MAGNUSON, born Saratoga Springs, New York, September 11, 1970; admitted to bar, 1995, Illinois; 2001, District of Columbia. *Education:* Indiana University (B.A., 1992); Duke University (J.D., 1995). *Member:* Illinois State and American Bar Associations; International Trademark Association. ***PRACTICE AREAS:*** Trademark Litigation; Trademark Prosecution; Copyright Litigation; Internet Trademark Law. ***Email:*** elizabeth.magnuson@finnegan.com

PHIL N. MAKROGIANNIS (Resident Associate, Palo Alto, California Office).

ROBERT W. MANN (Resident Associate, Palo Alto, California Office).

GEOFFREY COLBOURNE MASON, born Chicago, Illinois, December 28, 1971; admitted to bar, 1997, Maryland; 1998, District of Columbia; registered to practice before U.S. Patent and Trademark Office. *Education:* Harvard College (A.B., magna cum laude, 1994); Georgetown University Law Center (J.D., cum laude, 1997). Honors: Corpus Juris Secundum Award for Highest Exam in Contracts; Corpus Juris Secundum Award for Highest Exam in Torts. Associate Editor, Georgetown Law Journal. *Member:* American Intellectual Property Law Association; Federal Circuit Bar Association. ***PRACTICE AREAS:*** Pharmaceutical Intellectual Property; Civil Litigation; Biotechnology Patent Prosecution. ***Email:*** geoff.mason@finnegan.com

MATTHEW JERALD MASON, born Mount View, California, September 13, 1970; admitted to bar, 2000, Texas; 2001, District of Columbia; registered to practice before U.S. Patent and Trademark Office. *Education:* Brigham Young University (B.S.Ch.E., cum laude, 1997); University of Texas at Austin (J.D., with honors, 2000). ***PRACTICE AREAS:*** Chemical Patents; Pharmaceutical Patents. ***Email:*** matthew.mason@finnegan.com

ROBERT A. MATTHEWS, JR., born Lake Success, New York, October 29, 1963; admitted to bar, 1992, North Carolina; 1996, Pennsylvania; 1999, District of Columbia; registered to practice before U.S. Patent and Trademark Office. *Education:* Virginia Polytechnic Institute & State University (B.S.M.E., 1985); State University of New York at Stony Brook (M.S., 1987); University of Virginia School of Law (J.D., 1992). Registered Professional Engineer: Virginia, 1989; North Carolina, 1992. American Society of Mechanical Engineers, 1981-1989. *Member:* American Intellectual Property Law Association. ***PRACTICE AREAS:*** Electro-Mechanical Patents; Patent Infringement; Patent Litigation. ***Email:*** robert.matthews@finnegan.com

(This Listing Continued)

FINNEGAN, HENDERSON, FARABOW, GARRETT & DUNNER, L.L.P., Washington—Continued

TIMOTHY JAMES MAY, born Buffalo, New York, November 7, 1968; admitted to bar, 1998, Virginia; registered to practice before U.S. Patent and Trademark Office (Not admitted in District of Columbia). *Education:* University of Wisconsin (B.S.E.E., 1992); George Mason School of Law (J.D., with honors, 1998). Member, George Mason University Law Review, 1995-1998. Former Patent Examiner, U.S. Patent and Trademark Office, 1992-1996. *Member:* Virginia Bar Association; American Intellectual Property Law Association. ***PRACTICE AREAS:*** Intellectual Property Litigation; Patent Prosecution. ***Email:*** timothy.may@finnegan.com

ROLAND GEORGE McANDREWS, JR., born Philadelphia, Pennsylvania, April 24, 1968; admitted to bar, 1998, Pennsylvania; 1999, District of Columbia; registered to practice before U.S. Patent and Trademark Office. *Education:* Villanova University (B.M.E., 1990); Catholic University, Columbus School of Law (J.D., 1998). *Member:* American Intellectual Property Law Association. ***PRACTICE AREAS:*** Mechanical Patents. ***Email:*** roland.mcandrews@finnegan.com

KEVIN WILLIAM McCABE, born New York, New York, February 5, 1970; admitted to bar, 1999, Virginia; 2000, District of Columbia; U.S. District Court, Eastern District of Virginia; registered to practice before U.S. Patent and Trademark Office. *Education:* University of Richmond (B.S., 1992); University of Maryland (M.S., 1994); The George Washington University Law School (J.D., with honors, 1998). Student Intellectual Property Law Association (President, 1997-1998; Vice President, 1996-1997). Member, Public Contract Law Journal, 1997-1998. Author: "Implications of the Cellpro Determination on Inventions Made with Federal Assistance: Will the Government Ever Exercise Its March-In Right?" 27 Pub. Contract L.J. 645 (1998); "The January 1999 Review of Article 27 of the TRIPS Agreement: Diverging Views of Developed and Developing Countries Toward the Patentability of Biotechnology," 6 J. Prop. L.41 (1998). Co-Author, "Snakes & Snails and DNA Details," Legal Times, October 16, 2000 at S-72. *Member:* Virginia, Federal Circuit and American Bar Associations; American Intellectual Property Law Association; American Association for the Advancement of Science; Giles Sutherland Rich American Inn of Court. ***PRACTICE AREAS:*** Patent Litigation; Biotechnology Patent Prosecution. ***Email:*** kevin.mccabe@finnegan.com

MICHAEL J. McCABE II (Resident Associate, Atlanta, Georgia Office).

ELLEN KATHLEEN McDONNELL, born Abilene, Texas, December 7, 1970; admitted to bar, 1997, Virginia; 1998, District of Columbia. *Education:* George Mason University (B.A., cum laude, 1993); University of San Francisco Law School (J.D., 1996). *Member:* Virginia and American Bar Associations; District of Columbia Bar; American Intellectual Property Association. ***PRACTICE AREAS:*** Trademark Prosecution; Trademark Litigation; Copyright Prosecution; Copyright Litigation; International Trademarks. ***Email:*** ellen.mcdonnell@finnegan.com

REBECCA McNEILL, born N. Tarrytown, New York, November 19, 1970; admitted to bar, 1997, New Jersey; 1998, District of Columbia; registered to practice before U.S. Patent and Trademark Office. *Education:* Oberlin College (B.A., 1991); Duke University (M.S., 1993); Georgetown University Law Center (J.D., cum laude, 1997). The Georgetown Journal of Legal Ethics. Co-Author: "Alternative Dispute Resolution in Commercial Intellectual Property Disputes," 47 Am. U. L.Rev. 1709 (1998). Author: "Hey Circuit, Listen to Your PTO," Legal Times, August 16, 1999, at 31. Co-Chair, Intellectual Property Law Forum, The Women's Bar Association of D.C., 2001-2002. ***PRACTICE AREAS:*** Biotechnology Patent Prosecution; International Intellectual Property. ***Email:*** rebecca.mcneill@finnegan.com

COURTNEY BETH MEEKER, born Pontiac, Michigan, January 22, 1975; admitted to bar, 2000, District of Columbia. *Education:* University of Virginia (B.S., 1997); George Washington University (J.D., 2000). ***Email:*** courtney.meeker@finnegan.com

ARIE M. MICHELSOHN, born New York, N.Y., January 17, 1962; admitted to bar, 1999, New York and U.S. Court of Appeals for the Federal Circuit; registered to practice before U.S. Patent and Trademark Office (Not admitted in District of Columbia). *Education:* Columbia University (B.A., 1982); California Institute of Technology (Ph.D. in Biology, 1992); George Washington University Law School (J.D., with high honors, 1998). Phi Lambda Upsilon; Order of the Coif. Patent Examiner, U.S. Patent and Trademark Office, 1994-1995. Law Clerk to the Honorable Raymond C. Clevenger, III, Circuit Judge, U.S. Court of Appeals for the Federal Circuit, 1998-1999. Co-Author: "Claim Interpretation After *Markman:* How the Federal Circuit Interprets Claims," 46 Am. L.Rev. 1887-1933 (1997). *Member:* Federal Circuit and American Bar Associations; American Intellectual Property Law Association. ***LANGUAGES:*** Hebrew. ***PRACTICE AREAS:*** Intellectual Property Litigation; Intellectual Property Portfolio Management; Biotechnology Patents; Chemistry; Life Sciences. ***Email:*** arie.michelsohn@finnegan.com

(This Listing Continued)

MICHAEL A. MORIN, born Cleveland, Ohio, October 23, 1970; admitted to bar, 1995, Illinois; 1996, U.S. Court of Appeals for the Federal Circuit; 1997, District of Columbia Court of Appeals; registered to practice before U.S. Patent and Trademark Office. *Education:* Purdue University (B.S.I.E., 1992); The George Washington University National Law Center (J.D., with honors, 1995). Order of the Coif. Co-author, "An Overlooked Weapon in Antisubmarine Warfare," 75, 76, Patent World, 1995; Co-Author, "Troubles for Most-Favored Licenses," Les Nouvelles, March 1998. *Member:* Illinois State, Federal Circuit and American Bar Associations; District of Columbia Bar; American Intellectual Property Law Association; Licensing Executives Society. ***PRACTICE AREAS:*** Intellectual Property Litigation; Technology Licensing; Civil Appeals. ***Email:*** michael.morin@finnegan.com

CAROLYN E. MORRIS, born Massachusetts, 1973; admitted to bar, 1998, Massachusetts; 1999, District of Columbia. *Education:* Brown University (A.B., 1995); University of Virginia School of Law (J.D., 1998). ***PRACTICE AREAS:*** Trademark Prosecution; Trademark Litigation. ***Email:*** carolyn.morris@finnegan.com

ALLEN J. MOSS, born Boston, Massachusetts, August 31, 1964; admitted to bar, 1997, Arizona; registered to practice before U.S. Patent and Trademark Office (Not admitted in District of Columbia). *Education:* United States Naval Academy (B.S., with honors, 1987); Arizona State University (J.D., 1997). *Member:* American Bar Association; American Intellectual Property Law Association. [Officer, U.S. Navy, 1987-1992]. ***PRACTICE AREAS:*** Patent Litigation; Electrical Patent Prosecution; Software Patent Prosecution; Mechanical Patent Prosecution. ***Email:*** aj.moss@finnegan.com

SEAN CHRISTOPHER MYERS-PAYNE, born Cincinnati, Ohio, October 29, 1967; admitted to bar, 2001, Virginia; registered to practice before the U.S. Patent and Trademark Office (Not admitted in District of Columbia). *Education:* Ohio Wesleyan University (B.A., Biology, 1990); University of Cincinnati (Ph.D., Pharmacology, 1995); George Mason University School of Law (J.D., cum laude, 2001). ***PRACTICE AREAS:*** Patent Prosecution; Biochemical Patents; Pharmaceutical Patents; Biotechnology Patents; Chemical Patents. ***Email:*** sean.myerspayne@finnegan.com

WILLIAM NAKHLEH, admitted to bar, 1999, Virginia; registered to practice before U.S. Patent and Trademark Office (Not admitted in District of Columbia). *Education:* American University (B.S., Chemistry, 1989); George Mason University (M.S., Chemistry, 1998) Georgetown University (J.D., 1999). Article Selection Editor, American Criminal Law Review, 1998. Co-Author: "Intellectual Property, Project, Twelfth Survey of White Collar Crime," 34 Am Crim. L.Rev. 741 (1997). ***PRACTICE AREAS:*** Chemical Intellectual Property; Pharmaceutical Intellectual Property. ***Email:*** william.nakleh@finnegan.com

CHARLES D. NIEBYLSKI, born Detroit, Michigan, January 8, 1960; admitted to bar, 2000, Maryland; registered to practice before U.S. Patent and Trademark Office (Not admitted in District of Columbia). *Education:* University of Notre Dame (B.S., 1982); Wayne State University (M.S., 1987; Ph.D., 1990); Catholic University of America (J.D., 2000). ***PRACTICE AREAS:*** Chemical Patent Prosecution; Pharmaceutical Intellectual Property; Intellectual Property Portfolio Management. ***Email:*** charles.niebylski@finnegan.com

ELIZABETH ANN NIEMEYER, born Minneapolis, Minnesota, April 4, 1972; admitted to bar, 2000, Virginia (Not admitted in District of Columbia). *Education:* Bryn Mawr College (A.B., 1994); University of Texas at Austin (J.D., 2000). ***PRACTICE AREAS:*** Patent Litigation; Patent Prosecution; Electrical Patent Prosecution; Semiconductor Technology. ***Email:*** elizabeth.niemeyer@finnegan.com

KARNA JEAN NISEWANER (Resident Associate, Palo Alto, California Office).

MICHELLE O'BRIEN, born Toledo, Ohio, July 27, 1970; admitted to bar, 1999, Maryland (Not admitted in District of Columbia). *Education:* University of Toledo (B.A., Chemistry, 1996); Georgetown University (J.D., 1999). *Member:* American Bar Association; American Intellectual Property Law Association. ***PRACTICE AREAS:*** Chemical Intellectual Property. ***Email:*** michelle.obrien@finnegan.com

STEVEN P. O'CONNOR, born Biloxi, Mississippi, May 13, 1960; admitted to bar, 1996, Georgia and District of Columbia; registered to practice before U.S. Patent and Trademark Office. *Education:* Rutgers University (B.A., 1982); University of Minnesota (Ph.D., 1987); University of Virginia School of Law (J.D., 1996). ***PRACTICE AREAS:*** Pharmaceutical Intellectual Property; Biomedical Technology; Microbiology; Biochemical Patents; Biotechnology Patents. ***Email:*** steven.oconnor@finnegan.com

KRISTEN RAE JAKOBSEN OSENGA, born DeKalb, Illinois, June 20, 1972; admitted to bar, 2000, Virginia; 2001, District of Columbia; registered to practice before U.S. Patent and Trademark Office. *Education:* University of Iowa (B.S.E., 1994); University of Illinois (J.D., magna cum laude, 2000); Southern Illinois University (M.S., 2001). Order of the Coif. Author: "Space-Age Medicine, Stone-Age Government: How Medicare Reimbursement of Telemedicine Services is Depriving the Elderly of Quality Medical Treatment," 8

(This Listing Continued)

Elder Law Journal 151, Spring 2000. *Member:* Virginia State Bar; American Intellectual Property Law Association. ***Email:*** kristen.osenga@finnegan.com

STEVEN L. PARK (Resident Associate, Atlanta, Georgia Office).

ROBERT A. POLLOCK, born Pittsburgh, Pennsylvania, May 3, 1962; admitted to bar, 1999, Virginia; 2000, District of Columbia; registered to practice before U.S. Patent and Trademark Office. *Education:* University of Pittsburgh (B.S., Biochemistry and Biophysics, cum laude, 1984); Yale University (Ph.D., Human Genetics, 1990); The George Washington University School of Law (J.D., with honors, 1999). ***PRACTICE AREAS:*** Genetics; Immunology; Biotechnology Patent Prosecution; Biotechnology Patents; Molecular Biology Patents. ***Email:*** robert.pollock@finnegan.com

SCOTT J. POPMA, born Grand Rapids, Michigan, 1973; admitted to bar, 1999, California; 2000, District of Columbia. *Education:* University of Michigan (B.S., Biology, 1995; J.D., 1998). Phi Delta Phi (President, Kent Inn, 1996-1998). Michigan Telecommunications and Technology Law Review, Associate Editor, 1997-1998 and Note Editor, 1998. ***PRACTICE AREAS:*** Genetics; Immunology; Biotechnology Patent Prosecution; Patent Litigation; Pharmaceutical Patents. ***Email:*** scott.popma@finnegan.com

MONTIA GIVENS PRESSEY, born Newport News, Virginia, November 24, 1966; admitted to bar, 1992, Virginia; 1999, District of Columbia. *Education:* University of Virginia (B.A., 1989); Georgetown University Law Center (J.D., 1992). ***PRACTICE AREAS:*** Trademarks. ***Email:*** montia.pressey@finnegan.com

ERIK R. PUKNYS (Resident Associate, Palo Alto, California Office).

ERIC P. RACITI, born Oklahoma City, Oklahoma, May 1, 1966; admitted to bar, 1995, Massachusetts; 1997 District of Columbia; registered to practice before U.S. Patent and Trademark office. *Education:* Virginia Polytechnic Institute and State University (B.S., cum laude, 1989); Catholic University of America (J.D., 1994); Katholieke Universiteit Leuven, Belgium (LL.M., magna cum laude, 1995). Author: "The Incompletion of the European Common Market: Problems in Extending Pharmaceutical Patent Protection," in "Innovation and the Intellectual Property System, ed. Andrew Webster and Kathryn Packer, London: Kluwer Law International, 1996); "The Harmonizing of Trademarks in the European Community," 78 Journal of the Patent and Trademark Office Society, January 1996, reviewed 86 Trademark Report 632 (September-October 1996). *Member:* American Bar Association; American Intellectual Property Law Association; Boston Patent Law Association. ***PRACTICE AREAS:*** Intellectual Property Procurement; International Intellectual Property; Electro-Mechanical Patents; Medical Patents; Patent Litigation.

RICHARD L. RAINEY (Resident Associate, Atlanta, Georgia Office).

AARON M. RAPHAEL, born Huntington, New York, December 9, 1973; admitted to bar, 1999, Georgia; 2000, District of Columbia; registered to practice before U.S. Patent and Trademark Office. *Education:* University of Michigan (B.S., Chemistry, 1996); Emory University School of Law (J.D., 1999). ***PRACTICE AREAS:*** Patent Law. ***Email:*** aaron.raphael@finnegan.com

EVAN A. RAYNES, born Highland Park, Michigan, September 3, 1959; admitted to bar, 1993, California; 1994, District of Columbia. *Education:* University of Michigan (B.G.S., 1981; M.A., 1983); George Washington University Law School (J.D., 1993). *Member:* Bar Association of the District of Columbia; District of Columbia Bar (Member, Intellectual Property Law Section); State Bar of California; American Bar Association (Member, Intellectual Property Law Section); International Trademark Association. ***PRACTICE AREAS:*** Trademarks; Copyrights; Unfair Competition; Intellectual Property Litigation. ***Email:*** evan.raynes@finnegan.com

DOUGLAS A. RETTEW, born Teaneck, New Jersey, June 30, 1970; admitted to bar, 1995, Maryland and New Jersey; 1997, District of Columbia. *Education:* The University of Michigan (B.A., 1992); The George Washington University National Law Center (J.D., 1995). Adjunct Professor, The George Washington University School of Law, Trademarks and Unfair Competition. Co-Author: "A Review of Recent Trademark Decisions of the United States Court of Appeals for the Federal Circuit," 47 Am. U.L. Rev.-1491; "New Federal Trademark Dilution Act Has Implications Both Offensive and Defensive for In-House Counsel," 11 BNA's Corporate Counsel Weekly 8, 1996; "Dilution on the Information Superhighway," Corporate Counsel Magazine, June 1996; "What is 'Dilution' Under the New U.S. Federal Trademark Dilution Act?" European Intellectual Property Report, Vol. 18 Issue 11, November 1996; "Cleansing and Clarifying the Mark," Legal Times, December 1996; "Courts Order Internet 'Pirate' to Walk the Plank," Intellectual Property Counselor, Issue 6, June 1997. *Member:* Bar Association of the District of Columbia; American Bar Association; International Trademark Association; American Intellectual Property Law Association; Federal Circuit Bar Association. ***PRACTICE AREAS:*** Trademark Litigation; Copyright Protection; Trademark Licensing; Trademark Protection; International Intellectual Property. ***Email:*** douglas.rettew@finnegan.com

MONICA ANNE RIVA, born Arlington, Virginia, September 27, 1966; admitted to bar, 1997, Virginia; 1998, District of Columbia. *Education:* University of Richmond (B.S.B.A., 1988); George Mason University School of

(This Listing Continued)

Law (J.D., 1997). Dean's Scholar, 1996-1997; Moot Court Board, 1994-1996. *Member:* American Intellectual Property Law Association; International Trademark Association. ***PRACTICE AREAS:*** Trademark Infringement; Trademark Litigation; Trademark Prosecution; Trademark Protection; Trademark Registration. ***Email:*** monica.riva@finnegan.com

RAFAEL E. ROSADO (Resident Associate, Cambridge, Massachusetts Office).

BARBARA R. RUDOLPH, born Syracuse, New York, April 8, 1959; admitted to bar, 1994, Pennsylvania; 1996, District of Columbia. *Education:* Syracuse University (B.S., cum laude, 1981); University of California at Davis (Ph.D., Chemistry, 1986); The George Washington University National Law Center (J.D., with highest honors, 1993). Order of the Coif. Moot Court Board. Student Intellectual Property Law Association. Recipient: Scholarships: Willian Brinks Olds Hofer Gilson & Lione Scholarship for Excellence in Intellectual Property Law; Jacob Burns Scholarship; Awards: The John Bell Larner Award, for Attaining the Highest Cumulative Average Grade in the entire course for degree of Juris Doctor; The Willard Waddington Catchell Prize, for Academic Achievement during the entire course for the degree of Juris Doctor; The Jennie Hassler Walburn Prize, for Excellence in Civil Procedure; The Kappa Beta Pi Prize, for Attaining the Highest Cumulative Average Grade in the first year; The Anne Wells Branscomb Prize, for Attaining the Highest Cumulative Average Grade in the Evening Division. Author: Ph.D. Dissertation: Empirical Energy Calculations on Intercalator-DNA Complexes; Note, Subjective Evaluations of Technology as a Basis for Rule 10b-5 Securities Violations: Liability for Scientific Consultants," 61 Geo. Wash. L. Rev. 1856 (1993). Law Clerk for the Honorable Randall R. Rader, United States Court of Appeals for the Federal Circuit, 1993-1994. *Member:* Pennsylvania Bar Association; District of Columbia Bar. ***PRACTICE AREAS:*** Intellectual Property Litigation; Pharmaceutical Patents; Patent Infringement; Patent Prosecution. ***Email:*** barbara.rudolph@finnegan.com

CHRISTOPHER S. SCHULTZ (Resident Associate, Cambridge, Massachusetts Office).

STEVEN J. SCOTT, born Wooster, Ohio, October 24, 1970; admitted to bar, 1997, Ohio; 1998, District of Columbia; registered to practice before U.S. Patent and Trademark Office. *Education:* University of Cincinnati (B.S., Chemistry, 1994); The George Washington University Law School (J.D., 1997). *Member:* Ohio State Bar Association; American Institute of Chemical Engineers. (Resident Associate, Brussels, Belgium Office). ***Email:*** steven.scott@finnegan.com

JULIE M. SEAMAN, born Coraopolis, Pennsylvania, December 7, 1971; admitted to bar, 1999, New York, U.S. District Court, Eastern and Southern Districts of New York and U.S. Court of Appeals, Federal Circuit; 2001, U.S. District Court, District of Colorado (Not admitted in District of Columbia). *Education:* Mount Holyoke College (A.B., 1993); Harvard University (A.M., 1994); Notre Dame University (J.D., 1998). Sigma Xi. *Member:* American Bar Association. ***PRACTICE AREAS:*** Intellectual Property Procurement; Chemical Patents. ***Email:*** julie.seaman@finnegan.com

ROBERT FREDERIC SHAFFER, born Washington, DC, June 11, 1970; admitted to bar, 2000, Virginia; 2001, District of Columbia. *Education:* Georgetown University (B.A., 1992); Medical College of Virginia (M.S., 1996); George Mason University School of Law (J.D., magna cum laude, 2000). *Member:* Federal Circuit and American Bar Associations; Virginia State Bar (Member, Intellectual Property Section); Giles S. Rich American Inn of Court; American Intellectual Property Law Association; Intellectual Property Owners Association (Member, Committee on IP Insurance). ***PRACTICE AREAS:*** Biochemical Technology; Intellectual Property Arbitration; Intellectual Property Infringement; Intellectual Property Portfolio Management; Patent Litigation. ***Email:*** robert.shaffer@finnegan.com

PARMANAND "ANAND" K. SHARMA, born Georgetown, Guyana, August 23, 1971; admitted to bar, 1998, New York and New Jersey; 1999, District of Columbia; registered to practice before U.S. Patent and Trademark Office. *Education:* University of Maryland (B.S.M.E., 1994); New York Law School (J.D., 1997). *Member:* New York State and Federal Circuit Bar Associations; American Intellectual Property Law Association. ***PRACTICE AREAS:*** Intellectual Property Litigation; Patent Prosecution; Intellectual Property Portfolio Management. ***Email:*** anand.sharma@finnegan.com

PATRICIA ANN SHATYNSKI, born Elizabeth, New Jersey, December 21, 1962; admitted to bar, 1999, New Jersey; 2000, District of Columbia; registered to practice before U.S. Patent and Trademark Office. *Education:* New Jersey Institute of Technology (B.S.Ch.E., cum laude, 1984; M.S.Ch.E, 1986); Widener University School of Law (J.D., 1998). ***PRACTICE AREAS:*** Chemical Patent Prosecution; Pharmaceutical Patent Prosecution; Chemicals; Organic Chemistry; Semiconductor Technology. ***Email:*** patricia.shatynski@finnegan.com

MICHAEL T. SIEKMAN, born Bethlehem, Pennsylvania, September 14, 1967; admitted to bar, 1995, Massachusetts; 1996, District of Columbia; registered to practice before U.S. Patent and Trademark Office. *Education:* Bates College (B.S., 1990); Boston University (J.D., Intellectual Property, with hon-

(This Listing Continued)

FINNEGAN, HENDERSON, FARABOW, GARRETT & DUNNER, L.L.P., Washington—Continued

ors, 1995). Paul J. Liacos Scholar. Regional Semifinalist, Giles Sutherland Rich Moot Court. Founder and Articles Editor, Boston University Journal of Science & Technology Law. Author: "The Expanded Hypothetical Claim Test: A Better Test for Infringement of Biotechnology Patents Under the Doctrine of Equivalents," Boston University Journal of Science & Technology Law 6 (1996). *Member:* American Intellectual Property Law Association; Boston Patent Law Association. ***PRACTICE AREAS:*** Pharmaceutical Patent Prosecution; Patent Litigation; Intellectual Property Portfolio Management; Patent Interference Practice. ***Email:*** michael.siekman@finnegan.com

RANJEEV SINGH, admitted to bar, 1999, Texas; 2001, District of Columbia. *Education:* S.G.S. Institute of Technology and Science, University of Indore, India (B.S., Electronics and Communications Engineering, in first class and with distinction, 1989); University of Maryland at College Park (M.S., Electrical Engineering, 1992); University of Texas School of Law (J.D., with honors, 1999). *Member:* American Bar Association; American Intellectual Property Law Association; Institute of Electrical and Electronics Engineers. ***LANGUAGES:*** Hindi. ***PRACTICE AREAS:*** Intellectual Property Portfolio Management; Computer and Software Patents; Electrical Patent Prosecution; Electronic Patents; Patent Litigation. ***Email:*** ranjeev.singh@finnegan.com

LEONARD SMITH, JR., born Trenton, New Jersey, April 15, 1961; admitted to bar, 1995, Colorado; 1998, District of Columbia; registered to practice before U.S. Patent and Trademark Office. *Education:* U.S. Naval Academy (B.S., 1983); Claremont Graduate University (M.S., 1985); Georgetown University Law Center (J.D., 1994). *Member:* District of Columbia Bar; American Bar Association (Intellectual Property Law Section). [United States Air Force (May 1983-November 1991)]. ***PRACTICE AREAS:*** Computer and Software Patents; Computer Architecture Patents; Biotechnology Patent Prosecution; Biotechnology Patents; Patent Litigation. ***Email:*** leonard.smith@finnegan.com

JEMY SOEGENG, born Surabaya, Indonesia, September 30, 1968; admitted to bar, 1998, Maryland; 1999, District of Columbia; registered to practice before U.S. Patent and Trademark Office. *Education:* California State Polytechnic University (B.S., cum laude, 1993); University of Oregon (J.D., 1997). *Member:* Maryland State Bar Association; Federal Circuit Bar Association; American Intellectual Property Law Association. ***LANGUAGES:*** Bahasa Indonesia. ***PRACTICE AREAS:*** Intellectual Property Portfolio Management; Mechanical Patents; Medical Patents; International Patent Prosecution. ***Email:*** jemy.soegeng@finnegan.com

JAY A. STELACONE, born Wilkes-Barre, Pennsylvania, July 20, 1964; admitted to bar, 1993, Pennsylvania; 1996, District of Columbia; registered to practice before U.S. Patent and Trademark Office. *Education:* Pennsylvania State University (B.S.A.E., 1986); University of Nebraska at Lincoln (J.D., with distinction, 1993). Patent Examiner, U.S. Patent and Trademark Office, 1994-1997. ***PRACTICE AREAS:*** Patent Litigation; Patent Infringement; Patent Interference Practice. ***Email:*** jay.stelacone@finnegan.com

DANIEL KENT STIER (Resident Associate, Atlanta, Georgia Office).

KARA FARNANDEZ STOLL, born Wilmington, Delaware, November 15, 1968; admitted to bar, 1997, Virginia and U.S. Court of Appeals for the Fourth Circuit; 1998, U.S. Court of Appeals for the Federal Circuit; 2001, District of Columbia; registered to practice before U.S. Patent and Trademark Office. *Education:* Michigan State University (B.S.E.E., cum laude, 1991); Georgetown University Law Center (J.D., cum laude, 1997). Law Clerk to the Honorable Alvin A. Schall, U.S. Court of Appeals for the Federal Circuit, 1997-1998. Co-Author: "Means for Functioning in a Vacuum?" 76 J. Pat. Off. Soc'y 229, 239-43 (1994). *Member:* American Intellectual Property Law Association; Edward Coke Appellate Inn of Court. ***PRACTICE AREAS:*** Intellectual Property Litigation; Electrical Patent Prosecution. ***Email:*** kara.stoll@finnegan.com

WILLIAM L. STRAUSS, born New York, New York, April 5, 1951; admitted to bar, 1998, Maryland; 1999, District of Columbia. *Education:* Colgate University (B.A., 1973); State University of New York at Buffalo (Ph.D., 1980); University of Pennsylvania (J.D., 1998). *Member:* American Bar Association; Society for Neuroscience. ***PRACTICE AREAS:*** Intellectual Property Litigation. ***Email:*** william.strauss@finnegan.com

PEDRO F. SUAREZ, born Rochester, New York, August 7, 1964; admitted to bar, 2000, California; registered to practice before the U.S. Patent and Trademark Office (Not admitted in District of Columbia). *Education:* United States Air Force Academy (B.S.E.E., 1986); Air Force Institute of Technology (M.S.E.E., 1991); George Washington University (J.D., with honors, 2000). *Member:* American Intellectual Property Law Association; Institute of Electrical and Electronics Engineers. [U.S. Air Force]. ***PRACTICE AREAS:*** Software Protection; Intellectual Property Infringement; Intellectual Property Litigation; Electrical Patent Prosecution; Electronic Patents. ***Email:*** pedro.suarez@finnegan.com

(This Listing Continued)

SANYA SUKDUANG, born Dover, New Hampshire, October 16, 1973; admitted to bar, 1999, Maryland; 2000, District of Columbia; registered to practice before U.S. Patent and Trademark Office. *Education:* Boston College (B.S., Biology, 1996); American University, Washington College of Law (J.D., cum laude, 1999). *Member:* American Intellectual Property Law Association; Asian Pacific American Bar Association (Member, Board of Directors, Educational Fund). ***PRACTICE AREAS:*** Patent Litigation; Patent Interference Practice; Chemical Patent Prosecution; Biotechnology Patent Prosecution. ***Email:*** sanya.sukduang@finnegan.com

JENNIFER S. SWAN, born Reading, Pennsylvania; admitted to bar, 2001, Virginia and New Jersey; registered to practice before U.S. Patent and Trademark Office (Not admitted in District of Columbia). *Education:* University of Pittsburgh (B.A., 1992; J.D., 2000). ***PRACTICE AREAS:*** Biochemical Technology; Intellectual Property Litigation; Pharmaceutical Intellectual Property. ***Email:*** jennifer.swan@finnegan.com

MARK D. SWEET, born Washington, D.C., June 19, 1966; admitted to bar, 1999, District of Columbia; registered to practice before U.S. Patent and Trademark Office. *Education:* The College of William & Mary (B.S., Chemistry, 1988); The Catholic University, Columbus School of Law (J.D., 1998). Patent Examiner, 1988-1994 and Primary Patent Examiner, 1994-1997, U.S. Patent and Trademark Office. ***PRACTICE AREAS:*** Chemical Intellectual Property; Patent Prosecution. ***Email:*** mark.sweet@finnegan.com

JEANNE M. TANNER, born Ayer, Massachusetts, October 31, 1958; admitted to bar, 1997, Virginia; 1998, District of Columbia; registered to practice before the U.S. Patent and Trademark Office. *Education:* Massachusetts Institute of Technology (B.S.M.E., 1982; M.S.M.E., 1982); George Mason University School of Law (J.D., 1997). Law Review Articles Editor, 1997. CA Licensed Professional Engineer. *Member:* American Intellectual Property Law Association; Women's Bar Association of the District of Columbia; Giles S. Rich American Inn of Court. ***PRACTICE AREAS:*** Intellectual Property Litigation; Mechanical Intellectual Property; Mechanical Patents. ***Email:*** jeanne.tanner@finnegan.com

LINDA JEAN THAYER (Resident Associate, Palo Alto, California Office).

SUSANNE C. TINKER, born Silver Spring, Maryland, August 13, 1970; admitted to bar, 2001, Virginia; registered to practice before U.S. Patent and Trademark Office (Not admitted in District of Columbia). *Education:* University of Maryland (B.S.M.E., magna cum laude, 1992; M.S., Mechanical Engineering, 1994); Georgetown University (J.D., magna cum laude, 2001). *Member:* American Society of Mechanical Engineers (Vice Chair, Technology and Society Division, 2000). ***PRACTICE AREAS:*** Mechanical Patents; Medical Patents; Patent Prosecution; Medical Technology. ***Email:*** susanne.tinker@finnegan.com

RACHEL H. TOWNSEND, born Washington, D.C., April 25, 1969; admitted to bar, 2000, Massachusetts and District of Columbia; 2001, U.S. Court of Appeals, Federal Circuit; registered to practice before U. S. Patent and Trademark Office. *Education:* Tufts University (B.S., Biology and Chemical Engineering, 1992); Georgetown University (J.D., 1999). Law Clerk to the Honorable Richard Linn, 2000-2001. Patent Examiner, 1992-1997. *Member:* American Bar Association; American Intellectual Property Law Association. ***Email:*** rachel.townsend@finnegan.com

ANTHONY C. TRIDICO (Not admitted in District of Columbia; Resident Associate, Brussels, Belgium Office).

LOUIS M. TROILO, born Philadelphia, Pennsylvania, April 1, 1967; admitted to bar, 1998, Pennsylvania; 1999, District of Columbia. *Education:* Pennsylvania State University (B.S., 1990; M.S., 1991); Catholic University Law School (J.D., 1998). *Member:* American Bar Association. ***PRACTICE AREAS:*** Chemical Patents; Medical Patents; Metallurgical Patents; Patent Litigation; Patent Prosecution. ***Email:*** lou.troilo@finnegan.com

ANDREW JOSEPH VANCE, born Detroit, Michigan, June 14, 1972; admitted to bar, 1998, Michigan; 1999, District of Columbia and U.S. Court of Appeals for the Federal Circuit. *Education:* University of Michigan (B.S.E., magna cum laude, 1994; M.S.E., 1995; J.D., 1998). Pi Tau Sigma. *Member:* American Bar Association; American Intellectual Property Law Association. ***PRACTICE AREAS:*** Intellectual Property Rights. ***Email:*** andrew.vance@finnegan.com

THALIA V. WARNEMENT, born Wilmington, Delaware, August 3, 1967; admitted to bar, 1993, Virginia; 1994, District of Columbia. *Education:* University of Virginia (B.A., 1989); College of William & Mary (J.D., 1993). *Member:* District of Columbia Bar; Virginia State Bar; American Bar Association; American Intellectual Property Law Association; American Chemical Society. ***LANGUAGES:*** Greek. ***PRACTICE AREAS:*** Chemical Patent Prosecution; Patent Infringement; Patent Interference Practice. ***Email:*** thalia.warnement@finnegan.com

DOUGLAS SCOTT WEINSTEIN (Resident Associate, Atlanta, Georgia Office).

(This Listing Continued)

CHARLENA L. WILLIAMS (Resident Associate, Atlanta, Georgia Office).

JAMES T. WILSON, born Albion, Michigan, April 9, 1968; admitted to bar, 1999, Virginia; registered to practice before U.S. Patent and Trademark Office (Not admitted in District of Columbia). *Education:* Pennsylvania State University (B.S.E.E., 1990); Washington College of Law of American University (J.D., 1999). ***PRACTICE AREAS:*** Patent Prosecution; Patent Litigation; Patent Infringement; Intellectual Property Portfolio Management. ***Email:*** james.wilson@finnegan.com

BART W. WISE, born Springfield, Ohio, July 27, 1964; admitted to bar, 2000, California. *Education:* University of Kansas (B.S., 1987); Carnegie Mellon University (Ph.D., 1995); University of California, Berkeley Law School (J.D., 2000). Sterling Winthrop Undergraduate Research Fellowship; University of Kansas College Honors Program Undergraduate Research Award; Kansas Endowment Association Scholarship; National Science Foundation Undergraduate Research Program Award; Alpha Chi Sigma Honorary Chemistry Society. NIH Training Program Predoctoral Awardee. Article Editor and Web Editor, Berkeley Technology Law Journal. Author: Chavez v. Arte Publico Press, 14(1) Berkeley Technology Law Journal 3 (1999); "The Future Direction of the Internet and the Practice of E-Commerce Law," in The internet Guide for California Lawyers, 2000; Publisher: Continuing Education of the Bar, California (1999). Member, Berkeley Technology Law Journal. *Member:* American Bar Association; Healthcare Law Society; American Association for the Advancement of Science. (Resident Associate, Palo Alto, California Office). ***Email:*** bart.wise@finnegan.com

NAOKI YOSHIDA, born Japan, March 3, 1968; admitted to bar, 1998, New York and District of Columbia. *Education:* Rutgers University (B.S.M.E., 1992); Syracuse University College of Law (J.D., 1997); Johns Hopkins University (M.S.E.E., 2001). *Member:* New York State and American Bar Association; American Intellectual Property Law Association. ***LANGUAGES:*** Japanese. ***PRACTICE AREAS:*** Intellectual Property; Litigation; Patents; Intellectual Property Portfolio Management. ***Email:*** naoki.yashida@finnegan.com

REFERENCE: Crestar Bank, N.A., Washington, D.C.

FISH & RICHARDSON P.C.

601 13TH STREET N.W.
WASHINGTON, D.C. 20005
Telephone: 202-783-5070
Fax: 202-783-2331
Email: info@fr.com
URL: http://www.fr.com

Boston, Massachusetts Office: 225 Franklin Street. Telephone: 617-542-5070. Fax: 617-542-8906.

Redwood City, California Office: 500 Aguello Street, Suite 500. Telephone: 650-322-5070. Fax: 650-854-0875.

Minneapolis, Minnesota Office: Fish & Richardson, P.C., P.A., 60 South Sixth Street, 3300 Dain Rauscher Plaza. Telephone: 612-335-5070. Fax: 612-288-9696.

San Diego, California Office: 4350 La Jolla Village Drive, Suite 500. Telephone: 858-678-5070. Fax: 858-678-5099.

New York, N.Y. Office: 45 Rockefeller Plaza, Suite 2800. Telephone: 212-765-5070. Fax: 212-258-2291.

Wilmington, Delaware Office: 919 North Market Street, Suite 1000, P.O. Box 1114. Telephone: 302-652-5070. Fax: 302-652-0607.

Dallas, Texas Office: 5000 Bank One Center, 1717 Main Street. Telephone: 214-747-5070. Fax: 214-747-2091

Intellectual Property, Complex Litigation, Technology Law: Patents, Trademarks, Copyrights, Trade Secrets, Intellectual Property Litigation, Business Litigation, Technology Regulations, Antitrust Law, Corporate and Securities, White Collar Crime.

FIRM PROFILE: Fish & Richardson is one of the largest firms in the United States that focuses on intellectual property, complex litigation, and technology law. Fish & Richardson has a regulatory group that advises clients who seek to market products subject to FCC and FDA regulation. The firm's Corporate and Securities Section helps clients with capital structuring and financing, public equity and debt offerings and a wide range of corporate transactions.

Founded in 1878, Fish & Richardson has long represented great innovators and business entrepreneurs. The firm served pioneering inventors such as Alexander Graham Bell, Thomas Edison, and the Wright brothers. Today, the firm has over 250 attorneys and technology specialists in eight offices across the nation.

A significant component of the firm's work is litigation. Our litigation victories have appeared on the National Law Journal's biggest winners list for four straight years. In a survey published in May 2001, IP Worldwide found that in the year 2000 Fish & Richardson handled more patent litigation than any other firm. In addition to intellectual property litigation, the firm handles a wide variety of complex high-stakes, high-tech business litigation, including white collar criminal defense work.

In 2000 the firm obtained over 1,300 issued patents and filed almost 4,000 new patent applications, ranking it among the most active law firms in the United States. On the trademark side, in 2000, the firm obtained over 300 registered trademarks and filed almost 900 new trademark applications. The firm also provides advice on copyrights and copyright registration and licensing.

Fish, Richardson & Neave .... (1916-1969)

FREDERICK P. FISH (1855-1930).

W. K. RICHARDSON (1859-1951).

KEITH A. BARRITT, admitted to bar, 1989, Virginia; 1991, District of Columbia. *Education:* University of Virginia (B.A., Foreign Affairs and Philosophy, cum laude, 1983; J.D., 1989). ***PRACTICE AREAS:*** Communications Law; Regulatory Affairs; Trademarks. ***Email:*** barritt@fr.com

RUFFIN B. CORDELL, admitted to bar, 1989, Texas; 1993, Virginia; 1995, District of Columbia; registered to practice before U.S. Patent and Trademark Office. *Education:* Louisiana State University (B.S.E.E., 1985); Georgetown University (J.D., magna cum laude, 1989). ***PRACTICE AREAS:*** Litigation; Intellectual Property Law; International Trade Commission Proceedings. ***Email:*** cordell@fr.com

JILL B. DEAL, admitted to bar, 1979, District of Columbia. *Education:* University of California, Berkeley (B.S., 1964); Catholic University of America (J.D., 1979). ***PRACTICE AREAS:*** Food and Drug Regulation; European Union Law; Drug and Medical Device Litigation. ***Email:*** deal@fr.com

ALEXANDER J. HADJIS, born Wheeling, West Virginia, January 19, 1967; admitted to bar, 1995, Virginia; 1996, District of Columbia; registered to practice before U.S. Patent and Trademark Office. *Education:* The Ohio State University (B.S.E.E., 1990); University of Pittsburgh (J.D., 1993); George Washington University (LL.M., 1996). Law Clerk to The Honorable Wilson Cowen, U.S. Court of Appeals for the Federal Circuit, 1996-1997. *Member:* Virginia State Bar; The District of Columbia Bar; American Bar Association; Federal Circuit Bar; American Intellectual Property Law Association. ***PRACTICE AREAS:*** Intellectual Property Law. ***Email:*** hadjis@fr.com

JOHN F. HAYDEN, admitted to bar, 1992, Massachusetts; 1994, District of Columbia; registered to practice before U.S. Patent and Trademark Office. *Education:* University of Cincinnati (B.S., summa cum laude, 1989); Harvard Law School (J.D., cum laude, 1992). ***PRACTICE AREAS:*** Intellectual Property; Patents. ***Email:*** hayden@fr.com

LINDA LIU KORDZIEL, admitted to bar, 1993, Maryland; 1995, District of Columbia; registered to practice before U.S. Patent and Trademark Office. *Education:* Duke University (B.S., Biomedical Engineering, Electrical Engineering, magna cum laude, 1990; J.D., 1993). ***PRACTICE AREAS:*** Intellectual Property; Patents; Litigation. ***Email:*** kordziel@fr.com

TERRY G. MAHN, admitted to bar, 1975, Virginia; 1976, District of Columbia. *Education:* University of Michigan (B.S.S.E., 1970); Catholic University of America (J.D., 1975). ***SPECIAL AGENCIES:*** FCC and FDA. ***PRACTICE AREAS:*** Intellectual Property; FCC Regulation; Software Copyright; Software Licensing. ***Email:*** mahn@fr.com

MICHAEL J. McKEON, born New London, Connecticut, September 21, 1968; admitted to bar, 1997, New York; 1998, District of Columbia; 1999, Virginia; registered to practice before U.S. Patent and Trademark Office. *Education:* University of Connecticut (B.S., magna cum laude, 1990); George Washington University (J.D., with highest honors, 1996). Member, Order of the Coif, The George Washington University Law School. Co-Author: "Lotus v. Borland: Copyright Protection of Computer Software in a State of Transition," 53 Copyright World 16, September 1995; "The Patent Marking and Notice Stature: A Question of 'Fact' or 'Act'?" 9 Harvard Journal of Law & Technology 421, Summer 1996. Patent Examiner, United States Patent and Trademark Office. Previous Employment: Baker & McKenzie. *Member:* The District of Columbia Bar. ***PRACTICE AREAS:*** Intellectual Property Litigation. ***Email:*** mckeon@fr.com

RALPH A. MITTELBERGER, admitted to bar, 1975, Virginia; 1976, District of Columbia; 1983, Maryland; registered to practice before U.S. Patent and Trademark Office. *Education:* Massachusetts Institute of Technology (B.S., 1968; M.S., 1970); Georgetown University (J.D., 1975). ***PRACTICE AREAS:*** Intellectual Property; Litigation; International Trade Commission. ***Email:*** mittelberger@fr.com

OF COUNSEL

JAMES E. MROSE, admitted to bar, 1989, Massachusetts; 2000, District of Columbia; registered to practice before U.S. Patent and Trademark Office.

(This Listing Continued)

FISH & RICHARDSON P.C., Washington—Continued

Education: Harvard University (S.B.E.E., 1986); Boston University (J.D., 1989). ***PRACTICE AREAS:*** Intellectual Property; Patents. ***Email:*** mrose@fr.com

RENE D. TEGTMEYER, admitted to bar, 1963, Virginia and District of Columbia; registered to practice before U.S. Patent and Trademark Office. *Education:* Washington University, St. Louis (B.S.M.E., 1956); George Washington University (J.D., 1963). Former Assistant Commissioner, Patents, U.S. Patent and Trademark Office. ***PRACTICE AREAS:*** Intellectual Property; Patents; Litigation. ***Email:*** tegtmeyer@fr.com

ROBERT J. UNGAR, born Brooklyn, New York, September 25, 1942; admitted to bar, 1967, District of Columbia. *Education:* St. John's College (B.A., 1964); Georgetown University (J.D., 1967). Former Legal Advisor to the Chief Engineer, Federal Communications Commission. *Member:* The District of Columbia Bar. ***PRACTICE AREAS:*** Telecommunications; FCC Regulation. ***Email:*** ungar@fr.com

ASSOCIATES

Scott R. Boalick
Andrew F. Bodendorf (Not admitted in DC)
Joseph V. Colaianni, Jr.
Lauren A. Degnan
Benjamin D. Driscoll (Not admitted in DC)
Harold H. Fox
Richard G. Green
William D. Hare
Joseph Franklin Key
Andrew Kopsidas (Not admitted in DC)
Phyllis Kristal (Not admitted in DC)
Kevin J. McNeely
Heather Morin
Brian R. Nester (Not admitted in DC)
Brian T. Racilla (Not admitted in DC)
Robert V. Racunas (Not admitted in DC)
W. Karl Renner (Not admitted in DC)
Gary Savitt
Mark Edward Wadrzyk (Not admitted in DC)
Gregory A. Walters
R. Whitney Winston

(For biographical data on personnel at Boston, Massachusetts, Dallas, Texas, Menlo Park, California, Minneapolis, Minnesota, San Diego, California, New York, New York and Wilmington, Delaware, see Professional Biographies at those locations)

FISHER, CHRISTEN & SABOL

Established in 1923

SUITE 1401
1725 K STREET, N.W.
WASHINGTON, D.C. 20006
Telephone: 202-659-2000
Fax: 202-659-2015
Email: FCSabol@aol.com
URL: http://www.lawyers.com/fisherchristen&sabol

Patent, Trademark, Copyright, Unfair Competition and related Litigation. Mechanical Patents, Chemical Patents, Biotechnology Patents.

FIRM PROFILE: Established in 1914, the firm's practice includes preparation and prosecution of U.S. and foreign patent and trademark applications, patentability and trademark searches, patent and trademark litigation, patent validity/invalidity opinions, patent and trademark infringement opinions, patent interferences, trademark oppositions, license drafting and counseling, and monitoring competitors' patents.

MARTIN T. FISHER (1890-1964).

ARNOLD B. CHRISTEN (1915-1980).

EUGENE SABOL (1928-1993).

VIRGIL H. MARSH, born Phoenix, Arizona, March 26, 1935; admitted to bar, 1964, Maryland; 1967, New York and U.S. Supreme Court; 1968, District of Columbia; 1982, U.S. Court of Appeals for the Federal Circuit. *Education:* University of Maryland (B.S.Ch.E., 1959); Georgetown University (J.D., 1963); New York University (LL.M., 1966). Phi Alpha Delta. *Member:* District of Columbia Bar; Federal and American Bar Associations; New York Patent Law Association; American Intellectual Property Law Association; American Institute of Chemical Engineers; International Trademark Association. ***PRACTICE AREAS:*** Patent, Trademark, Copyright; Unfair Competition and related Litigation. ***Email:*** marshvh@aol.com

KARA M. ARMSTRONG, born Summit, New Jersey, April 9, 1966; admitted to bar, 1991, New Hampshire; 1992, District of Columbia and U.S. Court of Appeals for the Federal Circuit; 1993, Maryland. *Education:* Mount Holyoke College (A.B., 1988); Vanderbilt University School of Law (J.D., 1991); John Hopkins University (M.S., Biotechnology, 2000). Boston University School of Law (Visiting Student, 1990-1991). Phi Alpha Delta. *Member:* District of Columbia Bar (Member, Intellectual Property Section); Maryland Patent Law Association; International Trademark Association. ***PRACTICE AREAS:*** Patent; Trademark; Copyright; Unfair Competition and related Litigation. ***Email:*** kmarmstron@aol.com

(This Listing Continued)

THE FISHER LAW GROUP, PLLC

WASHINGTON, D.C.

(See Upper Marlboro, Maryland)

Foreclosure/Creditors Bankruptcy, Chapter 11 Bankruptcy. Real Estate Litigation, Title Insurance Litigation, Probate, General Civil Litigation.

FITCH, EVEN, TABIN & FLANNERY

1801 K STREET, N.W., SUITE 401L
WASHINGTON, D.C. 20006-1201
Telephone: 202-419-7000
Fax: 202-419-7007
Email: email@fitcheven.com
URL: http://www.fitcheven.com

Chicago, Illinois Office: 120 South La Salle, Suite 1600. 60603. Telephone: 312-577-7000. Fax: 312-577-7007.

San Diego, California Office: 4250 Executive Square, Suite 510. Telephone: 858-552-1311. Telecopier: 858-552-0095.

Intellectual Property and Technology-Related Law including United States and International Patents, Trademarks, Trade Secret, Copyrights and Unfair Competition, Antitrust and International Trade Commission Causes and Related Litigation.

EDWARD W. GRAY, JR., born Gary, Indiana, March 15, 1946; admitted to bar, 1970, Illinois and U.S. District Court, Northern District of Illinois; 1976, California; 1984, District of Columbia, U.S. District Court, District of Columbia and U.S. Supreme Court. *Education:* University of Chicago (B.A., 1967); Columbia University (J.D., 1970); Parker School of Foreign & Comparative Law (Certificate, 1980). Chair-Elect, National Bar Association Intellectual Property Law Section, 2001. Co-Chairman, Diversity Subcommittee International Trademark Association, 2001. *Member:* District of Columbia Bar; National and American Bar Associations. ***PRACTICE AREAS:*** Trademarks; Trademark Licensing; Litigation; Copyrights; Taxation; Unfair Competition; International Intellectual Property; Technology Licensing; Patent Licensing; Government Contracts. ***Email:*** ewgray@fitcheven.com

SHERRI N. BLOUNT, born Durham, North Carolina, November 4, 1955; admitted to bar, 1980, District of Columbia; 1981, U.S. District Court, District of Columbia and U.S. Court of Appeals for the District of Columbia Circuit; 1986, U.S. Supreme Court. *Education:* University of North Carolina (B.A., 1977); Howard University (J.D., 1980). Associate Editor, Howard University Law Review, 1978-1980. Adjunct Professor, Howard University, Communications Law, 1992-1999. ***PRACTICE AREAS:*** Trademarks; Copyrights; Entertainment Law; New Media Law; Intellectual Property Licensing; Advertising Law. ***Email:*** sblount@fitcheven.com

KENDREW H. COLTON, born St. Charles, Missouri, September 27, 1955; admitted to bar, 1980, District of Columbia; 1990, U.S. Supreme Court; registered to practice before U.S. Patent and Trademark Office. *Education:* Colby College (B.A., 1977); Case Western Reserve University (J.D., 1980). Member, Robert F. Wagner National Labor Law Moot Court Team; Moot Court Executive Board. Author: "Patent Pitfalls In Government Contracting," 25 ABA Public Contract Newsletter 5 (1990); "Generic Animal Drug Patent Team Extension Act of 1988--An Overview," Patent World, January, 1990; "New Judicial Interpretation of Product-By-Process Claims," Intellectual Property Business Briefing, July/August, 1991; "Experimental Use As An Exception or Defense In A Patent Infringement Action in the United Kingdom and Canada (II)," 37 Journal Japanese Group of AIPPI 28 (Jan. 1992). Co-Author: "Patent Law Developments In The United States Court of Appeals for the Federal Circuit During 1992," 42 Am. Univ. L. Rev. 909 (1993). *Member:* Bar Association of the District of Columbia; American Bar Association (Member: Patent, Trademark and Copyright Law Section; Administrative Law Section; Public Contract Law Section; Litigation Section; Standing Committees on: Environmental Law, 1982; Amicus Curiae Briefs, 1982-1984; Member, Inequitable Conduct and Antitrust Matters, Patent, Trademark and Copyright Law Section, 1983-1984); The Federal Circuit Bar Association; Patent Trademark Institute of Canada; American Intellectual Property Law Association; American Chemical Society; Society of Plastic Engineers. ***PRACTICE AREAS:*** Intellectual Property Law; Patents; Biotechnology; Chemicals; Trade Secrets; Technology and Science; Litigation. ***Email:*** kcolton@fitcheven.com

CHARLES W. PETERSON, JR., born St. Louis, Missouri, March 2, 1950; admitted to bar, 1991, New York; 1992, Missouri; 1998, Virginia; registered to practice before U.S. Patent and Trademark Office (Not admitted in

(This Listing Continued)

District of Columbia). *Education:* Washington University (B.S.E.E., 1977; M.S., 1978); George Washington University (J.D., 1990). Tau Beta Pi. *Member:* New York State and American Bar Associations; The Missouri Bar; Virginia State Bar; American Intellectual Property Law Association. [U.S. Coast Guard, 1971-1975 ST2]. **Email:** cpeterson@fitcheven.com

---

CHRISTOPHER E. GEORGE, born Washington, D.C., September 24, 1967; admitted to bar, 1993, Virginia; 1996, District of Columbia. *Education:* University of Virginia (B.A., 1989); Emory University Law School (J.D., 1993). Member: Moot Court Society; Lamar Inn of Court. *Member:* American Bar Association. ***PRACTICE AREAS:*** Trademark; Intellectual Property; Litigation; Corporate Law; Environmental Law. **Email:** cgeorge@fitcheven.com

RAMON R. HOCH, born Emporia, Kansas, November 20, 1959; admitted to bar, 1991, Virginia; 1994, Minnesota; registered to practice before U.S. Patent and Trademark Office (Not admitted in District of Columbia). *Education:* University of Kansas (B.S.Ch.E., 1983); George Mason University (J.D., 1991). Primary Patent Examiner, U.S. Patent & Trademark Office, 1983-1990. *Member:* Virginia State Bar; Minnesota State Bar Association. (Also at Chicago, Illinois Office). ***PRACTICE AREAS:*** Intellectual Property. **Email:** rhoch@fitcheven.com

PATENT AGENT

JONATHAN HALL BACKENSTOSE, born Harrisburg, Pennsylvania, December 10, 1962. *Education:* Lehigh University (M.S.M.E., 1992). (Patent Agent). ***PRACTICE AREAS:*** Intellectual Property. **Email:** jhbackenstose@fitcheven.com

(For Complete Personnel and Biographical Data, see Professional Biographies at Chicago, Illinois)

HENRY ST. JOHN FITZGERALD

WASHINGTON, D.C.

(See Arlington, Virginia)

Commercial Law, Commercial Litigation, Troubled Loans, Real Estate, Appellate Practice.

FITZPATRICK & ASSOCIATES

Established in 1972

UNIVERSAL BUILDING NORTH

1875 CONNECTICUT AVENUE, N.W.

SUITE 1140

WASHINGTON, D.C. 20009-5728

Telephone: 202-588-5300

Facsimile: 202-588-5023

Email: fitzlaw@erols.com

URL: http://www.lawyers.com/fitzpatricklaw

Labor, Employment and International Employment Law.

FIRM PROFILE: Robert Brian Fitzpatrick is the principal in the law firm of Fitzpatrick & Associates in Washington, D.C. where he represents clients in employment law and employee benefits matters. Mr. Fitzpatrick has concentrated his practice in employment law disputes for over thirty years and has been described by the National Law Journal as being among the top employment lawyers in the country and by Washingtonian Magazine as "tops in employment law" in the Washington, D.C. area.

ROBERT B. FITZPATRICK, born Washington, D.C., June 6, 1941; admitted to bar, 1968, District of Columbia, U.S. District Court, District of Columbia and U.S. District Court, Northern District of Mississippi; 1971, U.S. Court of Appeals, Sixth and District of Columbia Circuits; 1972, U.S. Court of Appeals, Fourth Circuit and U.S. Supreme Court; 1982, U.S. Court of Appeals, Federal Circuit; 1985, U.S. District Court, District of Maryland including Trial Bar. *Education:* George Washington University (B.A., 1964; LL.B., with honors, 1967). Delta Theta Phi; Order of the Coif. Co-Author: *Litigating Wrongful Discharge Claims,* published by Callaghan & Sons, 1987; "The Law of Wrongful Discharge in Virginia," George Mason University Law Review, Fall 1987; "A Damages Questionnaire for Wrongful Termination Cases," Practical Lawyer, March 1993; "Alcoholism as a Handicap," 22 The Lawyer's Brief, November 30, 1992; "Americans With Disabilities Act and AIDS," 8 The Labor Lawyer, 249-269, Summer 1992; "Damages and Other Remedies for Illegal Discharge," Chapter 10 of 1993 Wiley Employment Law Update; "Applying the Americans with Disabilities Act to AIDS," 16 ALI-ABA CMJ 79, April 1992; "Privacy Issues in the Electronic Monitoring and Surveillance of Employees," 1 Employment Testing 37, April 1992; "Reasonable Accommodation and Undue Hardship Under the ADA," Federal Bar News & Journal, January 1992; "Privacy Issues in the Workplace: Drug Testing, Employment Screening, Intelligence Test, and the Like," 59 UMKC Law Rev. 961, Summer 1991; "Americans With Disabilities Act of 1990," 11 Journal of the National Association of Administrative Judges, 13-24 Spring 1991; "Alcoholism as a Handicap Under Federal and State Employment Discrimination Laws," 7 The Labor Lawyer 395-430, Spring 1991. District of Columbia Human Rights Commission, 1978-1979. *Member:* District of Columbia Bar (Member, Steering Committee, Labor Relations Section, 1978-1979, 1988—; Co-Chair, Committee on Individual Employee Rights & Responsibilities in the Workplace, Labor Relations Section, 1985-1990); Federal (Co-Chair, Committee on Equal Employment Opportunity, 1986—) and American (Member: Employee Rights and Responsibilities in the Work Place Committee, 1984— and Equal Employment Opportunity Committee, Labor and Employment Law Section; Employer-Employee Committee and Long Range Planning Committee, Torts and Insurance Practice Section; Sections on: Labor and Employment Law; Torts and Insurance Practice; Administrative Law; Individual Rights and Responsibilities; International Law and Practice; Committee on Pro Se Litigation, U.S. District Court, District of Columbia; Co-Chair, Individual Employee Rights and Responsibilities Committee, 1988-1992; Trustee, Dalkor Shield Other Claimants Trust). ***PRACTICE AREAS:*** Employment Law; International Employment Law; Labor Law. **Email:** fitzlaw@erols.com

(This Listing Continued)

FITZPATRICK, CELLA, HARPER & SCINTO

1900 K STREET, N.W.

WASHINGTON, D.C. 20006-1110

Telephone: 202-530-1010

Facsimile: 202-530-1055

URL: http://www.fitzpatrickcella.com

New York, N.Y. Office: 30 Rockefeller Plaza. Telephone: 212-218-2100. Facsimile: 212-218-2200.

Orange County, California Office: 650 Town Center Drive, Suite 1600, Costa Mesa. Telephone: 714-540-8700. Facsimile: 714-540-9823.

Intellectual Property Practice. Patent, Trademark, Copyright, Trade Secret, Unfair Competition, Computer, Licensing, Antitrust and International Trade Law. Trials and Appeals in Federal and State Courts and Administrative Agencies.

FIRM PROFILE: Founded in 1971, Fitzpatrick, Cella, Harper & Scinto has grown to over 150 attorneys specializing in intellectual property law. The firm has offices in New York, Washington, D.C., and Orange County, California. Each of our lawyers practices exclusively in the intellectual property field, and most have extensive experience in various fields of technology including electronics, chemistry, physics, biotechnology, pharmaceuticals, software, and computers. The firm's clients include some of the world's largest multinational corporations as well as smaller corporations and universities in the United States, Asia, Europe, Australia and South America. Counseling of clients includes advice for both domestic and global intellectual property strategies. The firm is involved in all aspects of litigation with respect to patents, trademarks, counterfeiting, trade secrets, unfair competition, international trade, and copyrights, including trials and appeals, and proceedings before the International Trade Commission. The firm has an extensive practice in the prosecution of patent and trademark applications in the United States and abroad, and handles patent interferences, trademark oppositions and cancellations, due diligence studies, patent and trademark opinions, technology transfers and licensing.

RESIDENT PARTNERS

JOHN W. BEHRINGER, born Leetonia, Ohio, January 29, 1938; admitted to bar, 1968, District of Columbia; registered to practice before U.S. Patent and Trademark Office. *Education:* University of Dayton (B.S., Chem., 1959); George Washington University (J.D., cum laude, 1968). Order of the Coif. *Member:* The District of Columbia Bar (Chair, Council on Sections, 1996-1997; Co-Chair, Intellectual Property Law Section, 1994-1995); American Bar Association (Chairman: Patents and Copyrights Committee, Section of Administrative Law, 1980-1982; Committee on Reception of Scientific Evidence, Section of Science and Technology, 1984-1988); International Trademark Association (Member, Board of Editors, The Trademark Reporter, 2000—); American Intellectual Property Law Association. **Email:** jbehringer@fchs.com

LAWRENCE A. STAHL, born Washington, D.C., November 8, 1954; admitted to bar, 1979, District of Columbia; 1982, New York; registered to practice before U.S. Patent and Trademark Office. *Education:* Boston University (A.B., Mathematics, 1976); George Washington University (J.D., with honors, 1979). Law Clerk to Honorable Joseph V. Colaianni, U.S. Court of Claims, 1979-1980. *Member:* The District of Columbia Bar (Co-Chair, Steering Committee, Intellectual Property Law Section, 1998—; Chair, Patent Committee, Intellectual Property Section, 1995-1998; Co-Chairman, Intellectual Property

(This Listing Continued)

FITZPATRICK, CELLA, HARPER & SCINTO, Washington—Continued

Committee, Computer Law Section, 1990-1991); ITC Trial Lawyers Association; American Bar Association; American Intellectual Property Law Association. ***Email:*** lstahl@fchsdc.com

WILLIAM M. WANNISKY, born Pottsville, Pennsylvania, April 25, 1948; admitted to bar, 1975, Virginia; 1978, District of Columbia; registered to practice before U.S. Patent and Trademark Office. *Education:* Pennsylvania State University (B.S.E.E., 1970); Georgetown University (J.D., 1975). Eta Kappa Nu; Tau Beta Pi. *Member:* The District of Columbia Bar; Virginia State Bar; Federal Circuit Bar Association; Virginia Bar Association; American Bar Associations; American Intellectual Property Law Association; Patent Lawyers Club of Washington (President, 1992-1993). ***Email:*** wwannisky@fchs.com

WARREN E. OLSEN, born Brooklyn, New York, December 18, 1946; admitted to bar, 1975, District of Columbia; registered to practice before U.S. Patent and Trademark Office. *Education:* City College of the City University of New York (B.E. Mech., 1969); Georgetown University (J.D., 1975). Editor, Georgetown Law Journal, 1973-75. Pi Tau Sigma. *Member:* The District of Columbia Bar; American Bar Association; American Intellectual Property Law Association; International Trademark Association (Associate Member; Chairman, Trademark Usage Committee, 1995-1996). ***Email:*** wolsen@fchs.com

SCOTT D. MALPEDE, born Pittsburgh, Pennsylvania, January 21, 1961; admitted to bar, 1988, Pennsylvania; 1998, District of Columbia; registered to practice before U.S. Patent and Trademark Office. *Education:* Pennsylvania State University (B.S.M.E., 1983); George Washington University (J.D., 1987). *Member:* Pennsylvania and American Bar Associations; American Intellectual Property Law Association. ***Email:*** smalpede@fchs.com

THOMAS J. O'CONNELL, born Boston, Massachusetts, December 25, 1948; admitted to bar, 1986, Pennsylvania; 1987, Maryland; 1988, District of Columbia; registered to practice before U.S. Patent and Trademark Office. *Education:* University of Massachusetts (B.S., Chemistry, 1970; M.B.A., 1974); American University (J.D., 1986). *Member:* The District of Columbia Bar; Maryland State, Pennsylvania and Federal Circuit Bar Associations; American Intellectual Property Law Association; ITC Trial Lawyers Association. ***Email:*** to'connell@fchs.com

STEVEN E. WARNER, born Binghamton, New York, August 26, 1959; admitted to bar, 1988, Virginia; 1989, District of Columbia; registered to practice before U.S. Patent and Trademark Office. *Education:* Rochester Institute of Technology (B.S.M.E., 1982) Tau Beta Pi, Pi Tau Sigma; George Washington University (J.D., 1988). *Member:* The District of Columbia Bar (Member, Board of Elections, 1998-2001, Chair, Patent Committee, Intellectual Property Section, 2000—); Virginia State Bar; Federal Circuit and American Bar Associations; American Intellectual Property Law Association; International Trademark Association (Member, Trademark Reporter Editorial Board); ITC Trial Lawyers Association. ***Email:*** swarner@fchs.com

MARK A. WILLIAMSON, born Havertown, Pennsylvania, September 23, 1962; admitted to bar, 1990, Pennsylvania; 1991, District of Columbia; registered to practice before U.S. Patent and Trademark Office. *Education:* Drexel University (B.S.M.E., 1985); Georgetown University (J.D., 1990). *Member:* Bar Association of the District of Columbia (Member, Patent, Trademark and Copyright Section); American Intellectual Property Law Association. ***Email:*** mwilliamson@fchs.com

ANNE M. MAHER, born Wilkes-Barre, Pennsylvania, August 14, 1961; admitted to bar, 1991, New York; 1999, District of Columbia; registered to practice before U.S. Patent and Trademark Office. *Education:* Bucknell University (B.A., Biology/B.S.E.E., 1984); Georgetown University (J.D., 1990). End Notes Editor, Journal of Law and Technology, 1989-1990. Law Clerk to Honorable H. Robert Mayer, U.S. Court of Appeals for the Federal Circuit, 1990-1991. *Member:* Federal Circuit and American Bar Associations; American Intellectual Property Law Association (Chair, Public Information Committee, 1999-2000). ***Email:*** amaher@fchs.com

DANIEL S. GLUECK, born Boston, Massachusetts, February 6, 1966; admitted to bar, 1993, California; 1994, District of Columbia; registered to practice before U.S. Patent and Trademark Office. *Education:* Harvard University (A.B., Chemistry and Physics, magna cum laude, 1988; J.D., cum laude, 1993). ***Email:*** dglueck@fchs.com

BRIAN L. KLOCK, born Bethesda, Maryland, June 5, 1967; admitted to bar, 1994, Virginia; 1997, District of Columbia; registered to practice before U.S. Patent and Trademark Office. *Education:* Virginia Tech (B.S.E.E., cum laude, 1988; M.S.E.E., 1990); George Washington University (J.D., with high honors, 1994). Tau Beta Pi, Eta Kappa Nu. *Member:* American Bar Association; American Intellectual Property Law Association. ***Email:*** bklock@fchs.com

COUNSEL

ROBERT C. KLINE, born Palmerton, Pennsylvania, May 27, 1927; admitted to bar, 1955, District of Columbia; registered to practice before U.S. Patent and Trademark Office. *Education:* Pennsylvania State University (B.S., Chemistry, 1951); George Washington University Law School (J.D., 1955). *Member:* Federal Circuit and American Bar Associations; American Intellectual Property Law Association (President, 1986-1987); Philadelphia Intellectual Property Law Association. ***Email:*** rkline@fchs.com

RESIDENT ASSOCIATES

CHRISTOPHER PHILIP WRIST, born Chillicothe, Ohio, May 28, 1958; admitted to bar, 1985, Colorado; 1990, New York; 1991, District of Columbia; registered to practice before U.S. Patent and Trademark Office. *Education:* University of Colorado (B.S., Engineering Physics/Bioengineering, 1981); University of Denver (J.D., 1984). *Member:* The District of Columbia Bar (Intellectual Property Law Section; Chair, Patent Committee, 1998—; Steering Committee, 1999—); The Colorado, New York State, Federal Circuit and American Bar Associations; American Intellectual Property Law Association; ITC Trial Lawyers Association; Giles S. Rich American Inn of Court (Programs Chair, 1999-2000; Counselor, 2000-2001). ***Email:*** cwrist@fchs.com

GARY M. JACOBS, born New York, N.Y., October 12, 1951; admitted to bar, 1976, Texas; 1978, District of Columbia; registered to practice before U.S. Patent and Trademark Office. *Education:* University of Texas (B.A., Physics, with high honors, 1973; J.D., 1975). Phi Beta Kappa; Sigma Pi Sigma. *Member:* The District of Columbia Bar; State Bar of Texas; American Intellectual Property Law Association. ***Email:*** gjacobs@fchs.com

JACK S. CUBERT, born Brooklyn, New York, July 19, 1931; admitted to bar, 1967, New Jersey; registered to practice before U.S. Patent and Trademark Office (Not admitted in District of Columbia). *Education:* City College of New York (B.E.E., Electrical Engineering, 1952); New York University (M.E.E., 1955); Temple University (J.D., 1967). ***Email:*** jcubert@fchs.com

JEAN K. DUDEK, born Orange, Massachusetts, October 24, 1957; admitted to bar, 1985, New York; 1992, District of Columbia; registered to practice before U.S. Patent and Trademark Office. *Education:* Smith College (A.B., Biological Sciences, cum laude, 1979); New York University (J.D., 1984). *Member:* The District of Columbia Bar; American Bar Association; New York Intellectual Property Law Association; American Intellectual Property Law Association; Patent Lawyers Club of Washington (Treasurer). ***Email:*** jdudek@fchs.com

NATALIE M. DERZKO, born Toronto, Ontario, Canada, September 30, 1970; admitted to bar, 1995, Massachusetts; 1996, New York and Ontario, Canada; 2001, District of Columbia. *Education:* Trinity College; University of Toronto (B.Sc. in Human Biology, 1991); Osgoode Hall; York University (LL.B., 1993); Harvard Law School (LL.M., 1995); Johns Hopkins University (M.S. in Biotechnology, 2001). Fulbright Scholar. Senior Editor, Osgoode Hall Law Journal, 1992-1993. Line Editor, Harvard Environmental Law Review, 1994-1995. Law Clerk to the late Honorable Justice John Sopinka, Supreme Court of Canada, 1993-1994. *Member:* Boston, New York State and American Bar Associations; Intellectual Property Institute of Canada; American Intellectual Property Law Association. ***Email:*** nderzko@fchs.com

SHAWN W. FRASER, born Richmond, Virginia, August 14, 1968; admitted to bar, 1994, Pennsylvania; 1999, District of Columbia. *Education:* Massachusetts Institute of Technology (B.S., Electrical Engineering, 1990); University of California, Los Angeles (J.D., 1993). Editor, University of California, Los Angeles Law Review, 1992-1993. *Member:* Pennsylvania and American Bar Associations; The District of Columbia Bar; American Intellectual Property Law Association. ***Email:*** sfraser@fchs.com

EDMUND J. HAUGHEY, III, born Westmont, New Jersey, December 27, 1972; admitted to bar, 1998, Virginia; 2000, District of Columbia; registered to practice before U.S. Patent and Trademark Office. *Education:* University of Pennsylvania (B.S.E., Mechanical Engineering, magna cum laude, 1995); William & Mary School of Law (J.D., 1998). Tau Beta Pi. Order of the Coif. William & Mary Law Review. *Member:* Virginia State Bar; Virginia and American Bar Associations; American Intellectual Property Law Association. ***Email:*** ehaughey@fchs.com

JUSTIN J. OLIVER, born Norristown, Pennsylvania, June 18, 1972; admitted to bar, 1997, Virginia; registered to practice before U.S. Patent and Trademark Office (Not admitted in District of Columbia). *Education:* Trinity College (B.S. in Neuroscience, 1994); Washington College of Law, American University (J.D., magna cum laude, 1997). Order of the Barristers. Executive Editor, Journal of International Law & Policy, 1996-1997. *Member:* Virginia State Bar; American Intellectual Property Law Association. ***Email:*** joliver@fchs.com

STEPHEN E. BELISLE, born St. Albans, Vermont, October 8, 1970; admitted to bar, 2000, Virginia (Not admitted in District of Columbia). *Education:* Clarkson University (B.S., Mechanical Engineering, with great distinction, 1992; M.B.A., 1997); The George Washington University Law School (J.D., 2000). *Member:* Virginia State Bar; American Bar Association; American Intellectual Property Law Association. [Former Captain, U.S. Army Corps of Engineers (Ranger, Airborne)]. ***Email:*** sbelisle@fchs.com

(This Listing Continued)

SIMON D. ROBERTS, born Coventry, United Kingdom, June 29, 1968; admitted to bar, 1991, England and Wales; 1995, New York; registered to practice before the U.S. Patent and Trademark Office (Not admitted in District of Columbia). *Education:* Exeter University, Exeter, United Kingdom (B.Sc., with honors, Chemistry and Law, 1989; B.A., Law, with honors, 1990); Inns of Court School of Law (Barrister at Law, 1991). *Member:* New York State Bar Association; Honorable Society of Gray's Inn; Licensing Executives Society. **Email:** sroberts@fchs.com

(For Biographical data on all Personnel, see Professional Biographies at New York, New York)

LAW OFFICE OF SUSAN FINDLING FLEIG

1025 CONNECTICUT AVENUE NW, SUITE 1012
WASHINGTON, D.C. 20036
Telephone: 202-857-9707
Fax: 301-656-8646
URL: http://www.estatehelp.com
Email: sffleig@erols.com
URL: http://www.fleiglaw

Trusts and Estates, Wills, Taxation, Charitable Giving, Probate, Wealth Preservation, Estate and Gift Taxation.

FIRM PROFILE: Ms. Fleig's practice is devoted exclusively to estate planning including the following trusts: marital, education, special needs, charitable, premarital and insurance. Her firm has a special interest in blended families and serves clients from her two office locations in Washington, D.C. and Chevy Chase, MD.

SUSAN FINDLING FLEIG, admitted to bar, 1991, Maryland; 1997, District of Columbia and U.S. Court of Appeals, 4th, 5th and 10th Circuits. *Education:* University of Maryland (B.A., magna cum laude, 1970); Georgetown University (J.D., 1990). Member, *The Tax Lawyer,* 1988-1990. Law Clerk, Honorable Jonathan R. Steinberg, U.S. Court of Veterans Appeals, 1990-1991. *Member:* Montgomery County (Member, Trusts and Estates Section) and American (Member, Sections on: Taxation, Real Property; Trusts and Estates, Law Practice Management) Bar Associations; District of Columbia Bar (Member, Section on: Probate, Trusts and Estates, Taxation, Law Practice Management); Maryland State Bar Association, Inc.; Virginia Estate Planning Council; Bethesda-Chevy Chase Chamber of Commerce; Women of Washington; Hospice Caring; Planned Giving Study Group; Bethesda Friends Meeting; Washington Area Lawyers for the Arts; Washington Area Bicyclist Association. ***PRACTICE AREAS:*** Estate Planning; Estate and Gift Taxation; Generation Skipping Tax; Charitable Trusts and Foundations; Estate Administration; Family Limited Partnerships; Living Wills; Living Trusts; Premarital and Postnuptial Agreements.

WALTER H. FLEISCHER

WASHINGTON, D.C.

(See McLean)

Appellate Practice, Litigation, Government Contracts.

FLEISCHMAN AND WALSH, L.L.P.

1400 SIXTEENTH STREET, N.W.
WASHINGTON, D.C. 20036
Telephone: 202-939-7900
Facsimile: 202-745-0916
Email: fw@fw-law.com

General Practice before Federal and State Administrative Agencies and Courts. Communications, Utilities, Legislative, Litigation, Transportation, Corporate and Securities Practice.

PARTNERS

AARON I. FLEISCHMAN, born Chicago, Illinois, January 8, 1939; admitted to bar, 1965, District of Columbia. *Education:* Trinity College, Connecticut (B.A., with honors, 1960); Harvard Law School (LL.B., 1963). Phi Beta Kappa; Pi Gamma Mu. *Member:* District of Columbia Bar; Federal Communications Bar Association.

CHARLES S. WALSH, born Washington, D.C., April 16, 1942; admitted to bar, 1968, District of Columbia. *Education:* University of Maryland (B.A., with honors, 1964); George Washington University (J.D., with honors, 1967). Beta Gamma Sigma; Order of the Coif. *Member:* District of Columbia Bar; Federal Communications Bar Association.

ARTHUR H. HARDING, born Olympia, Washington, April 25, 1950; admitted to bar, 1975, Washington; 1978, District of Columbia. *Education:* Washington State University (B.A., 1972); University of Washington (J.D., 1975). *Member:* District of Columbia Bar; Washington State Bar Association; Federal Communications Bar Association.

STUART F. FELDSTEIN, born Fort Wayne, Indiana, March 18, 1938; admitted to bar, 1964, District of Columbia; 1968, U.S. Supreme Court; 1979, U.S. Court of Federal Claims. *Education:* University of Michigan (B.B.Ad., 1960; J.D., 1963). *Member:* District of Columbia Bar; Federal Bar Association; Federal Communications Bar Association.

JEFFRY L. HARDIN, born McCook, Nebraska, January 20, 1954; admitted to bar, 1979, Texas; 1985, District of Columbia. *Education:* University of Wisconsin (B.A., 1976); Columbia University (J.D., 1979). Phi Beta Kappa; Phi Delta Phi; Phi Kappa Phi. *Member:* District of Columbia Bar; American Bar Association.

STEPHEN A. BOUCHARD, born Austin, Texas, January 3, 1958; admitted to bar, 1982, District of Columbia. *Education:* University of Texas (B.B.A., with highest honors, 1979; J.D., with honors, 1982). Phi Delta Phi; Phi Kappa Phi; Beta Alpha Psi. Certified Public Accountant, Texas, 1981. *Member:* District of Columbia Bar; American Bar Association.

R. BRUCE BECKNER, born Charleston, South Carolina, April 15, 1949; admitted to bar, 1978, District of Columbia. *Education:* Princeton University (A.B., 1971); Johns Hopkins University (M.A., 1972); University of Virginia (J.D., 1978). *Member:* District of Columbia Bar; American Bar Association (Associate Editor, Litigation Magazine, 1987—); U.S. Supreme Court Bar.

CHRISTOPHER G. WOOD, born Bronxville, New York, October 7, 1959; admitted to bar, 1985, Pennsylvania; 1986, District of Columbia. *Education:* University of Virginia (B.A., with distinction, 1981); Georgetown University (J.D., cum laude, 1985). *Member:* District of Columbia Bar; Pennsylvania and American Bar Associations; Federal Communications Bar Association.

SETH A. DAVIDSON, born Washington, D.C., February 17, 1953; admitted to bar, 1978, District of Columbia. *Education:* University of Virginia (B.A., 1975); Columbia University (J.D., 1978). Phi Beta Kappa. Member, Board of Editors, Columbia Law Review. Harlan Fiske Stone Scholar. *Member:* District of Columbia Bar; Federal Communications Bar Association.

JAMES F. MORIARTY, born Newark, New Jersey, December 24, 1957; admitted to bar, 1982, District of Columbia; 1987, U.S. Supreme Court; 1988, U.S. Court of Federal Claims. *Education:* Rutgers University (B.A., 1979); Catholic University of America (J.D., 1982); Georgetown University Law Center (LL.M., 1989). *Member:* District of Columbia Bar; U.S. Supreme Court Bar; Federal Energy Bar Association; Association for Transportation Law, Logistics and Policy.

MATTHEW D. EMMER, born New York, New York, April 24, 1962; admitted to bar, 1988, Pennsylvania; 1989, District of Columbia. *Education:* Emory University (B.A., 1984); Boston University (J.D., 1987). *Member:* District of Columbia Bar; Pennsylvania Bar Association; Federal Communications Bar Association.

LOUIS H. DUPART, born Monterey, California, October 20, 1950; admitted to bar, 1985, Virginia (Not admitted in District of Columbia). *Education:* Wagner College (B.A., 1972); American University, Washington College of Law (J.D., 1984). Chief Counsel/Staff Director, Senate Judiciary Committee, Subcommittee on Antitrust, 1997-1998. Chief Counsel, House Permanent Select Committee on Intelligence, 1988-1997. *Member:* Virginia State Bar.

SHARON O'MALLEY MONAHAN, born Springfield, Massachusetts, May 5, 1957; admitted to bar, 1983, Massachusetts (Not admitted in District of Columbia). *Education:* Vassar College (B.A., 1979); Western New England College (J.D., 1983). *Member:* Massachusetts Bar Association; Federal Communications Bar Association.

LAWRENCE R. FREEDMAN, born Santa Monica, California, September 9, 1956; admitted to bar, 1985, Maryland; 1996, District of Columbia. *Education:* Pomona College (B.S., 1978); American University, Washington College of Law (J.D., 1983). *Member:* District of Columbia Bar; Maryland State Bar Association; Federal Communications Bar Association.

ERIC E. BREISACH, born Kalamazoo, Michigan, December 28, 1957; admitted to bar, 1989, Michigan; 1997, Illinois (Not admitted in District of Columbia). *Education:* Western Michigan University (B.B.A., summa cum laude, 1978; M.B.A., summa cum laude, 1984); Thomas M. Cooley Law School (J.D., magna cum laude, 1989). *Member:* Kalamazoo County and American (Member, Sections on: Business Law; Tax Law; Committee on Communications Law) Bar Associations; State Bar of Michigan; American Institute of Certified Public Accountants.

JOEL D. BONFIGLIO, born Toledo, Ohio, February 7, 1958; admitted to bar, 1986, California; 1994, District of Columbia. *Education:* Defiance College (B.S., cum laude, 1980); Schiller International University, Paris, France (M.A., magna cum laude, 1981); Pepperdine University (J.D., with distinction, 1986);

(This Listing Continued)

FLEISCHMAN AND WALSH, L.L.P., Washington—Continued

Georgetown University (LL.M., 1999). *Member:* The District of Columbia Bar; Northern Virginia Technology Council; International Trade Association of Northern Virginia.

ASSOCIATES

JILL KLEPPE McCLELLAND, born Bismarck, North Dakota, March 18, 1963; admitted to bar, 1991, Maryland; 1992, District of Columbia. *Education:* University of Colorado (B.A., with distinction, 1984); Georgetown University (J.D., 1991). Phi Beta Kappa. *Member:* District of Columbia Bar; American Bar Association; Federal Communications Bar Association.

REGINA FAMIGLIETTI PACE, born Washington, D.C., March 20, 1970; admitted to bar, 1994, District of Columbia. *Education:* University of Virginia (B.A., with distinction, 1991; J.D., 1994). Phi Beta Kappa. *Member:* District of Columbia Bar; Federal Communications Bar Association.

CRAIG A. GILLEY, born Harvey, Illinois, April 3, 1969; admitted to bar, 1995, District of Columbia. *Education:* Brown University (A.B., 1992); Georgetown University (J.D., 1995). *Member:* District of Columbia Bar; Federal Communications Bar Association.

SUSAN A. MORT, born Rochester, New York, July 8, 1971; admitted to bar, 1997, New York and District of Columbia. *Education:* Cornell University (B.A., cum laude, 1993); Syracuse University (J.D., magna cum laude, 1996); Georgetown University (LL.M., 1998). Order of the Coif. *Member:* New York State Bar Association; District of Columbia Bar; Federal Communications Bar Association.

MARK D. PIHLSTROM, born Minneapolis, Minnesota, May 26, 1970; admitted to bar, 1997, New York and Massachusetts; 1999, District of Columbia. *Education:* Carleton College (B.A., 1992); American University, Washington College of Law (J.D., 1996). *Member:* New York State and Massachusetts Bar Associations; The District of Columbia Bar.

BRIAN C. MALADY, born Rochester, New York, February 15, 1968; admitted to bar, 1996, New York; 1998, District of Columbia. *Education:* Syracuse University (B.A., magna cum laude, 1990); Boston University (J.D., cum laude, 1996). *Member:* District of Columbia Bar.

THOMAS E. KNIGHT, born Syracuse, New York, December 25, 1970; admitted to bar, 1996, Massachusetts; 1997, New York; 1998, District of Columbia. *Education:* Johns Hopkins University (B.A., 1993); American University, Washington College of Law (J.D., cum laude, 1996). *Member:* New York State Bar Association; Commonwealth of Massachusetts Bar; The District of Columbia Bar.

SETH M. WARNER, born Oceanport, New Jersey, February 2, 1968; admitted to bar, 1994, Maryland; 1995, District of Columbia. *Education:* Tufts University (B.A., 1990); American University, Washington College of Law (J.D., 1994). *Member:* District of Columbia Bar; Maryland State Bar Association, Inc.

MARK B. DENBO, born Wauwatosa, Wisconsin, May 21, 1970; admitted to bar, 1998, Maryland; 2000, District of Columbia. *Education:* University of Pennsylvania (B.A., 1992); American University, Washington College of Law (J.D., 1997). *Member:* Maryland State Bar Association, Inc.; Federal Communications Bar Association.

CARA E. SHEPPARD, born Kings Park, New York, February 1, 1971; admitted to bar, 1998, Connecticut and Maryland; 1999, District of Columbia. *Education:* State University of New York at Geneseo (B.A., 1993); Columbus School of Law, Catholic University (J.D., 1997). *Member:* District of Columbia Bar; Maryland State and Connecticut Bar Associations; Federal Communications Bar Association.

STEVEN J. HAMRICK, born Baltimore, Maryland, June 15, 1965; admitted to bar, 1994, Pennsylvania; 1996, District of Columbia. *Education:* The American University (B.A., 1987); American University, Washington College of Law (J.D., 1993). *Member:* District of Columbia Bar; Federal Communications Bar Association.

KEVIN C. BRENNAN, born Stamford, Connecticut, December 2, 1972; admitted to bar, 1998, California; 1999, District of Columbia. *Education:* University of North Carolina at Chapel Hill (B.A., 1994); Georgetown University (J.D., 1997). *Member:* District of Columbia Bar; State Bar of California.

RICHARD L. DAVIS, born Portland, Oregon, August 11, 1971; admitted to bar, 1997, Maryland; 1998, District of Columbia. *Education:* Abilene Christian University (B.B.A., summa cum laude, 1993); George Washington University (J.D., with high honors, 1997). *Member:* Maryland State Bar Association; The District of Columbia Bar.

SHARI L. WILKOZEK, born Elmhurst, Illinois, March 25, 1971; admitted to bar, 1998, Illinois (Not admitted in District of Columbia). *Education:* Elmhurst College (B.A., 1994); Chicago-Kent College of Law, Illinois Institute of Technology (J.D., 1998). Member, Women in Cable and Telecommunications Association. *Member:* Chicago and American Bar Associations; Federal Communications Bar Association.

LISA CHANDLER CORDELL, born New York, N.Y., February 24, 1970; admitted to bar, 1996, Illinois; 1997, District of Columbia. *Education:* Indiana University (B.A., 1992); De Paul University (J.D., 1996). Member, Women in Cable and Telecommunications. *Member:* The District of Columbia Bar; Federal Communications Bar Association.

DAVID J. LAVAN, born Alexandria, Virginia, September 16, 1962; admitted to bar, 1997, New York (Not admitted in District of Columbia). *Education:* University of Virginia (B.A., 1982); California Western School of Law (J.D., 1995).

AIMEE E. KNAPP, born Washington, D.C., November 21, 1974; admitted to bar, 2000, Maryland and Massachusetts; 2001, District of Columbia. *Education:* James Madison University (B.S., 1996); Columbus School of Law of The Catholic University of America (J.D., 1999); Institute for Communications Law Studies (Post-Graduate Certificate, 1999). *Member:* Massachusetts Bar Association; Federal Communications Bar Association.

PETER B. SANCHEZ, born Brooklyn, New York, January 29, 1971; admitted to bar, 2000, New York (Not admitted in District of Columbia). *Education:* Brooklyn College of the City University of New York (B.A., cum laude, 1996); Southern Illinois University (J.D., magna cum laude, 1999); Georgetown University Law Center (L.L.M., Securities and Financial Regulation, 2000).

(This Listing Continued)

FLETCHER, HEALD & HILDRETH, P.L.C.

Established in 1936

2000 L STREET, NW, SUITE 200
WASHINGTON, D.C. 20036
Telephone: 202-828-5700
Email: office@fhhlaw.com
URL: http://www.fhhlaw.com

Arlington, Virginia Office: 1300 North 17th Street, 11th Floor. Telephone: 703-812-0400. Fax: 703-812-0486.

Practice before Federal and State Courts and Federal and State Administrative Agencies primarily in the fields of Domestic and International Communications Law, including radio and television broadcasting, satellites, telephone, commercial wireless communications, cable television, private land mobile, microwave, maritime, aeronautical radio, new technology and equipment authorizations. Practice also in the fields of Antitrust, Energy Law, Public Utility Law, Trademark, Copyright, Trade Associations, EEO, Privacy, Computer, Entertainment, Transactional and Emerging Technology Law, as well as Bankruptcy, Estate Planning, Business Law and Civil Litigation.

(For complete biographical data on all personnel, see professional biographies at Arlington, VA)

FOLEY & FOLEY

Established in 1914

624 BOWEN BUILDING
815 15TH STREET, N.W.
WASHINGTON, D.C. 20005
Telephone: 202-737-8055

General and Administrative Practice. Energy, Trusts, Probate, Labor, Tax and Commercial Law.

JOHN R. FOLEY (1890-1953).

JOHN R. FOLEY, JR., born Wabasha, Minnesota, October 16, 1917; admitted to bar, 1947, District of Columbia; 1953, Maryland. *Education:* College of St. Thomas (B.A., 1940); Georgetown University (LL.B., 1947); Catholic University of America (LL.M., 1950). Phi Alpha Delta. Instructor on Administrative Law, Catholic University of America Law School, 1953-1957. Judge of Probate, Montgomery County Orphans' Court, Maryland, 1954-1958. Member of Congress from Maryland's Sixth District, 86th Congress, 1959-1960. *Member:* The District of Columbia Bar; The Bar Association of the District of Columbia; Maryland State Bar Association.

FOLEY, HOAG & ELIOT LLP

1747 PENNSYLVANIA AVENUE, N.W.
WASHINGTON, D.C. 20006
Telephone: 202-223-1200
Telecopier: 202-785-6687
URL: http://www.foleyhoag.com

Boston, Massachusetts Office: One Post Office Square. Telephone: 617-832-1000. Telecopier: 617-832-7000.

(This Listing Continued)

General and Administrative Practice, International; International Arbitration; Government Affairs; Tax and Commercial Law, Real Estate, Corporate, Trust and Estate Planning.

MEMBERS OF FIRM

JANIS H. BRENNAN, admitted to bar, 1987, District of Columbia. *Education:* University of Georgia (B.A., magna cum laude, 1974); Georgetown University Law Center (J.D., 1987). ***LANGUAGES:*** French. ***PRACTICE AREAS:*** International Commercial Law; International Investment; Litigation; International Commercial Arbitration; Immigration. ***Email:*** jhbrenna@foleyhoag.com

JOHN L. BURKE, JR., admitted to bar, 1972, Maryland and District of Columbia. *Education:* Fairfield University (B.A., cum laude, 1967); Georgetown University (J.D., 1971). ***PRACTICE AREAS:*** Electronic Commerce; Corporate; Taxation; Trade Association; Law Firm Counselling. ***Email:*** jburke@foleyhoag.com

GARY S. GUZY, admitted to bar, 1983, New York and U.S. Court of Appeals, Eleventh Circuit; 1984, District of Columbia. *Education:* Cornell University (B.A., magna cum laude, 1979; J.D., cum laude, 1982). ***PRACTICE AREAS:*** Environmental Law; Government; Strategic Alliances. ***Email:*** gguzy@foleyhoag.com

JAMES T. MONTGOMERY, JR., admitted to bar, 1981, Alabama; 1982, Georgia; 1984, District of Columbia. *Education:* Morehouse College (A.B., summa cum laude, 1977) Phi Beta Kappa; Georgetown University (J.D., with honors, 1981; LL.M. in Taxation, with highest honors, 1983). ***PRACTICE AREAS:*** Taxation. ***Email:*** jmontgom@foleyhoag.com

PAUL S. REICHLER, admitted to bar, 1973, District of Columbia. *Education:* Tufts University (B.A., magna cum laude, 1969); Harvard University (J.D., magna cum laude, 1973). ***LANGUAGES:*** Spanish. ***PRACTICE AREAS:*** International Arbitration; Litigation; International Business Law; Government Affairs; Lobbying. ***Email:*** preichler@foleyhoag.com

COUNSEL

STEPHANIE CUTLER, admitted to bar, 1984, Texas; 1986, District of Columbia. *Education:* Cornell University (B.A., with distinction, 1981); Georgetown University (J.D., 1984). ***PRACTICE AREAS:*** Business; Real Estate. ***Email:*** scutler@foleyhoag.com

TRACI DUVALL HUMES, admitted to bar, 1990, Virginia and U.S. Court of Appeals, Fourth Circuit; 1991, District of Columbia; 1992, U.S. Court of Appeals for the District of Columbia Circuit; District Court for the District of Columbia. *Education:* Georgetown University (B.A., 1985; J.D., 1990). ***PRACTICE AREAS:*** Securities; Corporate Law; International Trade. ***Email:*** thumes@foleyhoag.com

ALIMA JONED, admitted to bar, 1986, West Malaysia; 1989, New York; 1995, District of Columbia. *Education:* University of Malaya (LL.B., Hons., 1977); London University (LL.M., 1978); Yale University (LL.M, 1988; J.S.D., 1990). ***LANGUAGES:*** Bahasa; Malaysia (Malay); Indonesian. ***PRACTICE AREAS:*** International. ***Email:*** ajoned@foleyhoag.com

GARE A. SMITH, admitted to bar, 1985, Maryland; 1986, District of Columbia. *Education:* Johns Hopkins University (B.A., 1979); University of Michigan (J.D., 1983). ***LANGUAGES:*** Spanish. ***PRACTICE AREAS:*** International; Corporate Social Responsibility; Legislative. ***Email:*** gsmith@foleyhoag.com

ASSOCIATES

LAWRENCE H. MARTIN, admitted to bar, 1998, Massachusetts (Not admitted in District of Columbia). *Education:* Bowdoin College (B.A., summa cum laude, 1988); Harvard Law School (J.D., magna cum laude, 1997). ***PRACTICE AREAS:*** Litigation. ***Email:*** lmartin@foleyhoag.com

MARIANA PRIETO, admitted to bar, 1991, Buenos Aires, Argentina; 1996, New York (Not admitted in District of Columbia). *Education:* University of Buenos Aires School of Law, Buenos Aires, Argentina (Lawyer, 1990). ***LANGUAGES:*** French and Spanish. ***PRACTICE AREAS:*** International Business Transactions; Securities Regulation. ***Email:*** mprieto@foleyhoag.com

(For complete biographical data on all personnel, see Professional Biographies at Boston, Massachusetts)

FOLEY & LARDNER

Established in 1842

WASHINGTON HARBOUR, SUITE 500
3000 K STREET, N.W.
WASHINGTON, D.C. 20007-5109
Telephone: 202-672-5300
Facsimile: 202-672-5399
Email: webmaster@foleylaw.com
URL: http://www.foleylardner.com

Other Washington, D.C. Office: 888 Sixteenth Street, N.W. Telephone: 202-835-8000. Fax: 202-835-8136.
Los Angeles, California Office: 2029 Century Park East, 35th Floor. Telephone: 310-277-2223. Fax: 310-557-8475.
Sacramento, California Office: 300 Capitol Mall, Suite 1125. Telephone: 916-443-8005. Fax: 916-443-2240.
San Diego, California Office: 402 West Broadway, 23rd Floor. Telephone: 619-234-6655. Fax: 619-234-3510.
San Diego/North County, California Office: 11250 El Camino Real, Suite 200. Telephone: 858-847-6700. Facsimile: 858-792-6773.
San Francisco, California Office: One Maritime Plaza, Sixth Floor. Telephone: 415-434-4484. Fax: 415-434-4507.
Denver, Colorado Office: 1999 Broadway, Suite 2560. Telephone: 303-297-0260. Fax: 303-297-0266.
Jacksonville, Florida Office: The Greenleaf Building, 200 Laura Street. P.O. Box 240. Telephone: 904-359-2000. Facsimile: 904-359-8700.
Orlando, Florida Office: Suite 1800, 111 North Orange Avenue, P.O. Box 2193. Telephone: 407-423-7656. Facsimile: 407-648-1743.
Tallahassee, Florida Office: 106 East College Avenue, Highpoint Center, Suite 900, P.O. Box 1819. Telephone: 850-222-6100. Facsimile: 850-561-6475.
Tampa, Florida Offices: Suite 2700, 100 N. Tampa Street, P.O. Box 3391. Telephones: 813-229-2300; Pinellas County: 813-442-3296. Facsimile: 813-221-4210.
West Palm Beach, Florida Office: 777 South Flagler Drive, Suite 901, West Tower. Telephone: 561-655-5050. Facsimile: 561-655-6925.
Chicago, Illinois Office: One IBM Plaza, 330 N. Wabash Avenue, Suite 3300. Telephone: 312-755-1900. Facsimile: 312-755-1925.
Other Chicago, Illinois Office: Three First National Plaza, 70 West Madison, Suite 4100. Telephone: 312-558-6600. Fax: 312-558-6676.
Annapolis, Maryland Office: Suite 102, 175 Admiral Cochrane Drive. Telephone: 410-266-8077. Facsimile: 410-266-8664.
Detroit, Michigan Office: 150 West Jefferson, Suite 1000. Telephone: 313-963-6200. Fax: 313-963-9308.
Madison, Wisconsin Office: Verex Plaza, 150 East Gilman Street, P.O. Box 1497. Telephone: 608-257-5035. Facsimile: 608-258-4258.
Milwaukee, Wisconsin Office: Firstar Center, 777 East Wisconsin Avenue. Telephone: 414-271-2400. Facsimile: 414-297-4900.
Brussels, Belgium Office: Avenue Louise, 283. Telephone: 32-2-646-2777. Facsimile: 32-2-646-7574.

General Practice, International and Domestic Patent, Trademark and Copyright, Biotechnology and related Intellectual Property Law, Health Law, Litigation, including Intellectual Property Litigation, Insurance, Telecommunications, International Trade.

PARTNERS

M. PETER ADLER, admitted to bar, 1984, Minnesota; U.S. District Court, District of Minnesota; 1989, District of Columbia. *Education:* Ohio University (B.S., cum laude, 1977); William Mitchell College of Law (J.D., 1983); Georgetown University (LL.M., with distinction, International, 1993). Author: "Critical Infrastructure Protection Begins at Home: Regulated or De Facto Security Standards at the Organizational Level," Third Annual Conference on Online Liability, American Conference Institute, New York, February 14, 2000; "Avoid Another Last-Minute Rush--Start HIPAA Compliance Process Now," Washington G-2 Compliance Report, Vol. ii, No. 3, March 2000; "Opportunity in Disguise," Decisions in Imaging Economics, Vol. 13, No. 2, March/April 2000. Lecturer: "Best Industry Practices for Assessing, Implementing and Monitoring Network and Cyberspace Security," Third Annual Conference on Online Liability, American Conference Institute, New York, February 14, 2000; "HIPAA Privacy, Security and e-Health Standards," 2000 Federal Health Care Acquisition Conference, Orlando, Florida, June 6, 2000; "HIPAA: Using Health Information in Marketing, Disease Management and Community Outreach-Walking the Thin Line between Criminal and Exemplary Activity," HFMA's 2000 Corporate Compliance Conference, Washington, DC, August 25, 2000. *Member:* New York Electronic Crimes Task Force; American Health Lawyers Association. (Washington Harbor Office). ***PRACTICE AREAS:*** E-health; HIPAA Compliance; E-Commerce; Information Security; Privacy; Technology Transfers.

STEPHEN A. BENT, admitted to bar, 1981, District of Columbia; registered to practice before U.S. Patent and Trademark Office. *Education:* Earlham

(This Listing Continued)

FOLEY & LARDNER, Washington—Continued

College (B.S., 1973); University of Connecticut (M.A., 1976); George Washington University (J.D., with high honors, 1981). Phi Beta Kappa. Author: "Living Matter Found to Be Patentable: In re Chakrabarty," Connecticut Law Review 11(2), Winter, 1979; "Patent Protection for DNA Molecules," J.Off. 64 (2), February 1982; "Export Controls and U.S. Biotechnology," B.L.R. 2(1), January 1983; "Production of Plant Material Under the General Patent Statute: A Sensible Policy at the PTO?" B.L.R. 4, March 1985; "Biotechnology Products Liability and the Public Interest," World Biotech Report, 1985, Vol 1: Europe (Online Publ., London); "Stan Allen's Invention - The World His Oyster," CIPA, November 1987 at 30-37. Co-Author: *Intellectual Property Rights in Biotechnology Worldwide,* (Macmillan 1987); "Animal Patents: Issues and Prospects in the United States," *Animal Patents: The Legal, Economic and Social Issues* (Macmillan, 1989). Technical Assistant to Phillip B. Baldwin, Circuit Judge, U.S. Court of Appeals for the Federal Circuit, 1981-1983. Adjunct Professor, BioTechnology Patent Law, George Mason School of Law, 1989—. Advisory Panel, "Biotechnology in a Global Economy: Options for U.S. Strategy," Office of Technology Assessment. *Member:* The District of Columbia Bar; American Bar Association; American Intellectual Property Law Association; American Association for the Advancement of Science. (Washington Harbor Office). ***PRACTICE AREAS:*** Biotechnology; Pharmaceutical; Intellectual Property.

JAMES N. BIERMAN, admitted to bar, 1970, District of Columbia; 1973, U.S. Supreme Court. *Education:* Washington University (A.B., magna cum laude, 1967); Harvard University (J.D., 1970). Phi Beta Kappa; Pi Sigma Alpha; Omicron Delta Kappa; Phi Eta Sigma. Managing Editor, Harvard Journal on Legislation, 1969-1970. Assistant Dean, Harvard Law School, 1973-1975. Member, Civil Rights Reviewing Authority, Department of Health, Education and Welfare, 1979-1980. Board of Directors, Washington Lawyers' Committee for Civil Rights and Urban Affairs. *Member:* The District of Columbia Bar; Federal and American Bar Associations. (Washington Harbor Office). ***PRACTICE AREAS:*** Federal Regulatory Law (75%); International Trade Law (25%). ***Email:*** jbierman@foleylaw.com

ARTHUR H. BILL, admitted to bar, 1970, District of Columbia and Maryland. *Education:* Rutgers University (B.A., 1963); Boston University (J.D., 1969). Author: "Positioning a Company for a Future Initial Public Offering," Business Law Today, Jan./Feb., 1993; "Securities Offerings by Foreign Companies in the United States," Bowne and Company, 1993. Attorney, Securities and Exchange Commission, 1969-1972. *Member:* The District of Columbia Bar; Bar Association of the District of Columbia; Maryland State, Federal and American Bar Associations (Member, Committee on Securities Regulation, Business Law Section). (Washington Harbor Office). ***PRACTICE AREAS:*** Securities Law; Corporate Law. ***Email:*** abill@flks.com

DAVID A. BLUMENTHAL, admitted to bar, 1974, Virginia; 1974-1982, U.S. Court of Customs and Patent Appeals; 1975, U.S. District Court, Eastern District of Virginia; 1978, U.S. Claims Court; 1979, District of Columbia; 1980, U.S. Supreme Court; 1982, U.S. Court of Appeals for the Federal Circuit; 1996, California and U.S. District Court, Central District of California; registered to practice before U.S. Patent and Trademark Office. *Education:* College of William and Mary (B.S., 1966); University of Pennsylvania (Ph.D., 1970); George Washington University (J.D., with honors, 1974). Phi Beta Kappa; Phi Delta Phi; Sigma Pi Sigma. Recipient, Joseph Rossman Memorial Award, 1980-1981. Author: "The Status of Programmable Inventions in the United States," Gewerblicher Rechtsschutz and Urheberrecht International Teil, 1980; "Statutory or Non-Statutory?: An Analysis of the Patentability of Computer Related Inventions," Journal of the Patent Office Society, Vol. 62, No. 8, Aug., 1980; "Supreme Court Sets Guidelines for Patentability of Computer Related Inventions," Journal of the Patent Office Society, February, 1981; "Computer Programs: Recent Developments in U.S. Patent, Copyright and Trade Secret Law," AIPPI Journal, June, 1982; "Software Protection in the United States," NIKKEI Computer, September, 1982; "Lifeforms, Computer Programs, and the Pursuit of a Patent," Technology Review, Feb./March 1983. Lecturer and Chairman, Electronics and Computer Patent and Copyright Practice, Patent Resources Group, Florida and Washington, D.C., 1986-1998. Adjunct Professor of Law, George Mason University, 1990-1996. *Member:* Virginia State Bar; District of Columbia Bar; State Bar of California; American Bar Association (Member, Patent, Trademark and Copyright Law Section); American Intellectual Property Law Association. (Washington Harbor Office) (Also at Foley & Lardner Los Angeles, California Office). ***PRACTICE AREAS:*** Intellectual Property. ***Email:*** dblumenthal@foleylaw.com

THEODORE H. BORNSTEIN, admitted to bar, 1978, Illinois; 1980, District of Columbia. *Education:* Washington University (B.A., cum laude, 1971); IIT/Chicago-Kent College of Law (J.D., 1977). Director, Department of Defense Reinvestment Task Force, 1993. Chief of Staff, U.S. Senator Herb Kohl, 1993-1997. Chief of Staff, U.S. Representative Les Aspin, 1987-1993. Chief of Staff, U.S. Representative Cecil Heftel, 1984-1986. Director, State of Missouri Washington Office, 1978-1984. (Washington Harbor Office). ***PRACTICE AREAS:*** Legislative Practice; Regulatory Law; Public Affairs. ***Email:*** tbornstein@foleylaw.com

(This Listing Continued)

SHARIE A. BROWN, admitted to bar, 1982, Pennsylvania; 1984, District of Columbia. *Education:* University of Pennsylvania (B.A., M.A., 1979); Georgetown University (J.D., 1982). Clark Scholar; Mayor's Scholar. Law Clerk to the Honorable Richard M. Bilby, U.s. District Court, Tucson, AZ, 1982-1983. Associate, Peabody, Lambert & Meyers, Washington, DC, 1983-1984. Assistant U.S. Attorney, Eastern District of Pennsylvania, 1984-1988. *Member:* District of Columbia Bar. (Washington Harbor Office). ***LANGUAGES:*** Spanish. ***PRACTICE AREAS:*** Environmental Litigation; General Commercial Litigation; Corporate.

ROBERT A. BURKA, admitted to bar, 1971, New York; 1975, District of Columbia. *Education:* Dartmouth College (A.B., summa cum laude, 1966); London School of Economics and Political Science, London, England (M.Sc. Econ., 1967); Harvard University (J.D., cum laude, 1970). Phi Beta Kappa. Fulbright Scholar. Law Clerk to Hon. Milton Pollack, Southern District of New York, 1971. Co- Author, with William J. Isaacson, "A Fresh Look at the Labor Injunction," (Pts. 1-2), 43 N.Y. St. B.J. 243, 323 1971. Member, Board of Student Advisers, Harvard Law School, 1968-1970. Visiting Lecturer, Economics, The American University, 1968. Deputy Assistant Director, 1979-1982 and Acting Assistant Director, 1981-1982, Bureau of Competition, Federal Trade Commission. *Member:* Federal and American (Member, Section on Antitrust Law) Bar Associations. (Washington Harbor Office). ***REPORTED CASES:*** Ethyl Corp., 101 F.T.C. 425 (1983); Burka v. Dept. of Health & Human Services, 87 F.3d 508 (D.C. Cir. 1996); Railway Labor Executives' Assn. v. Consolidated Rail Corp., 666 F. Supp. 1573 (Sp. Ct., R.R.R.A. 1987 Three Judge Court); Zolfaghari v. Sheikholeslami, 943 F.2d 451 (4th Cir. 1991); Northeastern Ed. TV v. Educational TV Assn., 758 F.Supp. 1568 (N.D. Ohio 1998); Flat Iron Mac Associates v. Foley, 90 Md.App. 281, 600 A.2d 1156 (1992). ***PRACTICE AREAS:*** Antitrust and Trade Regulation Law; Administrative Law; Litigation. ***Email:*** rburka@foleylaw.com

BETH A. BURROUS, admitted to bar, 1993, District of Columbia; registered to practice before U.S. Patent and Trademark Office. *Education:* Cornell University (B.S., Nutritional Biochemistry, with honors, 1982); Massachusetts Institute of Technology (Ph.D., Nutritional Biochemistry, 1987); Georgetown University Law Center (J.D., 1992). Omicron Nu; Sigma Chi. Law Clerk to the Honorable Pauline Newman, U.S. Court of Appeals for the Federal Circuit, 1993-1995. Practice Group Leader, Biotechnology and Pharmaceutical Practice Group. (Washington Harbor Office). ***LANGUAGES:*** French. ***PRACTICE AREAS:*** Biotechnology; Strategic Business Planning; Patent Validity and Infringement Opinions. ***Email:*** bburrous@foleylaw.com

RACHEL DANISH CAMPBELL, admitted to bar, 1991, New York and U.S. District Court, Southern District of New York; 1993, District of Columbia; 1994, U.S. District Court, District of Columbia and Federal Court of Claims. *Education:* Manhattanville College (B.A., 1987); Georgetown University (J.D., 1990). *Member:* The District of Columbia Bar (Member, Litigation Section). (888 Sixteenth Street Office). ***PRACTICE AREAS:*** Litigation. ***Email:*** rcampbell@foleylaw.com

ALAN I. CANTOR, admitted to bar, 1975, Virginia; 1975-1982, U.S. Court of Customs and Patent Appeals; 1977, District of Columbia; 1982, U.S. Court of Appeals for the Federal Circuit; 1990, U.S. Supreme Court; registered to practiced before U.S. Patent and Trademark Office. *Education:* Cooper Union (B.E., 1969); University of Baltimore (J.D., 1975). Patent Examiner, U.S. Patent and Trademark Office, 1970-1976. Patent Attorney, U.S. Army Material Development and Readiness Command, 1976-1977. *Member:* District of Columbia Bar; Virginia State Bar; American Bar Association; American Intellectual Property Law Association. (Washington Harbor Office). ***PRACTICE AREAS:*** Intellectual Property.

STEVEN B. CHAMEIDES, admitted to bar, 1971, New York; 1976, District of Columbia. *Education:* University of Michigan (B.S.E., Naval Architecture and Marine Engineering; B.S.E., Mathematics, 1967; J.D., cum laude, 1970). Research Editor, Journal of Law Reform, 1969-1970. *Member:* American and International Bar Associations; Maritime Law Association of the United States; Society of Naval Architects. [JAGC, U.S. Navy, 1971-1974]. (Washington Harbor Office). ***PRACTICE AREAS:*** Corporate Law; Transactional Law; International Business Law; Maritime Law; Commercial Litigation. ***Email:*** schameides@foleylaw.com

RICHARD T. CHOI, admitted to bar, 1987, Virginia; 1988, District of Columbia, U.S. Court of Appeals, Fourth Circuit and U.S. District Court, Eastern District of Virginia. *Education:* University of Chicago (B.A., honors, 1984); University of Virginia (J.D., 1987). Articles Development Editor, Journal of Law and Politics, 1986-1987. *Member:* Virginia State Bar; The District of Columbia Bar. (Washington Harbor Office). ***PRACTICE AREAS:*** Securities Law. ***Email:*** rchoi@flks.com

GARY O. COHEN, admitted to bar, 1964, District of Columbia. *Education:* Vanderbilt University (A.B., magna cum laude, 1959); Harvard University (J.D., 1963). Phi Beta Kappa; Omicron Delta Kappa. Co-Author, "The Insurance-Security Identity Crisis," 46 George Washington Law Review 790, 1978. Guest Lecturer, Georgetown University Law Center, Financial Institutions—Investment Management, 1982-1990. Speaker: FBA-ICI Mutual Funds and Invest-

(This Listing Continued)

ment Management Conference, 1981, 1992, 1996; ALI-ABA Life Insurance Company Products Conference, 1983-1987, 1989-1999; PLI '40 Act Institute, 1998-2000; Hartford Institute of Insurance Taxation, 1998; SEC/ICI Procedures Conference, 1983; SEC Staff Training Program, 1988. Assistant Chief Counsel, 1968 and Attorney, 1963-1968, Division of Investment Management, U.S. Securities and Exchange Commission. Member, Editorial Board, "The Investment Lawyer." *Member:* American Bar Association (Member, Subcommittee on Securities Activities of Insurance Companies, Federal Securities Law Committee); Bar Association of the District of Columbia; National Association for Variable Annuities, Inc. (Member, Regulatory Affairs Committee). (Washington Harbor Office). ***PRACTICE AREAS:*** Securities Law. ***Email:*** gcohen@flks.com

PAUL E. COONEY, admitted to bar, 1977, District of Columbia. *Education:* Franklin and Marshall College (A.B., magna cum laude, 1974); George Washington University (J.D., with honors, 1977). Phi Beta Kappa. Member, George Washington Law Review, 1975-1977. Adjunct Professor, George Washington University Law School, 1998—. Chancellor, Episcopal Diocese of Washington, 1992-1996. *Member:* The District of Columbia Bar; American Bar Association; American Health Lawyers Association; National Association of Bond Lawyers. (Washington Harbor Office). ***PRACTICE AREAS:*** Corporate Law; Health Law.

JOHN G. DeGOOYER, admitted to bar, 1968, District of Columbia. *Education:* Duke University (A.B., 1964); American University (J.D., 1967). Phi Delta Phi. Law Clerk to Judge Alexander Holtzoff, U.S. District Court for the District of Columbia, 1967-1968. *Member:* The District of Columbia Bar; The Bar Association of the District of Columbia; Federal and American Bar Associations. (888 Sixteenth Street Office). ***PRACTICE AREAS:*** Litigation; Government Contracts Law. ***Email:*** jdegooyer@foleylaw.com

THOMAS R. DEVINE, admitted to bar, 1979, California; 1998, District of Columbia. *Education:* Stanford University (A.B., with distinction, 1976; J.D., 1979). Phi Beta Kappa. Attorney, Legislative Staff, Office of Chief Counsel, Federal Aviation Administration, 1979-1985. Vice President, Legal and Environmental Affairs, Airports Council International-North America (ACI-NA), 1989-1991. General Counsel, National Commission to Ensure a Strong Competitive Airline Industry, May-Aug. 1993. Co-author (with Michael Schneiderman), ACI-NA Airport Environmental Management Handbook, 1993. *Member:* District of Columbia Bar. (888 Sixteenth Street Office). ***PRACTICE AREAS:*** Airport Law (Regulatory, Environmental, Financing). ***Email:*** tdevine@foleylaw.com

MARC B. DORFMAN, admitted to bar, 1976, District of Columbia; 1989, Maryland. *Education:* Yale University (A.B., magna cum laude, 1973); Harvard University (J.D., cum laude, 1976). Editor, Harvard International Law Journal, 1975-1976. Trial Attorney and Special Counsel, U.S. Securities and Exchange Commission, Division of Enforcement, 1978-1981. *Member:* The District of Columbia Bar; American Bar Association (Member: Committee on Federal Regulation of Securities; Securities Litigation Committee); Association of Trial Lawyers of America. (Washington Harbor Office). ***PRACTICE AREAS:*** Litigation; Securities Law. ***Email:*** mdorfman@flks.com

MURRAY DRABKIN, admitted to bar, 1953, District of Columbia; 1966, New York. *Education:* Hamilton College (A.B., 1950); Harvard University (LL.B., 1953). Phi Beta Kappa; Delta Sigma Rho. Counsel, Committee on the Judiciary, U.S. House of Representatives, 1957-1965. Chief Counsel, Special Subcommittee on State Taxation, 1961-1965. Special Consultant on Tax Policy and Special Assistant to Mayor of New York City, 1966-1968. Director, Connecticut Revenue Task Force, 1969-1971. Consultant, Blue Ribbon Defense Panel, 1969-1970. Member, National Bankruptcy Conference, 1969—(Chairman, Committee on Railroad Organization, 1984—). Member, Advisory Panel, Board of Governors, Federal Reserve System, 1970-1971. Member, District of Columbia Tax Revision Commission, 1976-1977. *Member:* The District of Columbia Bar; New York State Bar Association. Fellow, American College of Bankruptcy. (888 Sixteenth Street Office). ***PRACTICE AREAS:*** Bankruptcy; Bankruptcy Reorganization; State and Local Taxation. ***Email:*** mdrabkin@foleylaw.com

JOSEPH D. EDMONDSON, JR., admitted to bar, 1991, Maryland; 1992, District of Columbia and U.S. District Court, District of Maryland; 1993, U.S. District Court, District of Columbia; 1994, U.S. Court of Appeals, Fourth and District of Columbia Circuits; 1995, U.S. Supreme Court. *Education:* George Washington University (B.A., magna cum laude, 1988; J.D., with honors, 1991). Phi Beta Kappa. Member, 1989-1991 and Associate Editor, 1990-1991, George Washington Journal of International Law and Economics. Author: "Supreme Court Ruling Allows State Product Liability Claims Regarding Medical Devices," Inside Health Law, October 1996; "D.C. Circuit Overturns SEC Sanctions as Punitive," National Law Journal, February 10, 1997. *Member:* Maryland State (Litigation Section) and American (Litigation Section) Bar Associations. (Washington Harbor Office). ***PRACTICE AREAS:*** General Commercial and Securities Litigation; Regulatory Law; Food and Drug Law. ***Email:*** jedmondson@foleylaw.com

WILLIAM T. ELLIS, admitted to bar, 1975, Virginia; 1979, District of Columbia; 1987, New York; registered to practice before U.S. Patent and Trademark Office. *Education:* University of Illinois (B.S.E.E., 1971); Catholic University of America (J.D., 1975). Author: "The Chip Protection Act," in Intellectual Property Counseling and Litigation (Matthew Bender, 1988). Papers: "E.U. Failure to Protect Computer Programs by Patent," Intellectual Property Rights in the Framework of the Joint EU-US Action Plan, Rome, Italy, May 28-29, 1996; "The Role of Patents in the Development of the Software Industry," Intellectual Property Conference of the Americas, Los Angeles, California, July 14-17, 1996; "Patent and Copyright Protection for Software in the Post TRIPs World," Council on Foreign Relations (1996); "The Global Treatment of Statutory Subject Matter in the Year 2000," AIPLA (1996); "New World of Software Patents," ABA (1995); "Survey of EU Intellectual Property Legislation," (1994) and "North American Free Trade Agreement," (1993), Pacific Intellectual Property Association; "Standards and Intellectual Property," Harvard/NIST (1994); "Copyright Protection for Computer Programs," International Copyright Institute (1993); "Software Protection in Eastern Europe and the USSR," and "Copyright Protection for Computer Software," Prentice-Hall Law and Business (1990). Seminar: "Intellectual Property Protection," Beijing, China (1993). Member, Industry Functional Advisory Committee on Standards for Trade Policy Matters (IFAC-2 Government Trade Advisory Committee), 1994; Member, Industry Functional Advisory Committee on Intellectual Property Rights for Trade Policy Matters (IFAC-3 Government Trade Advisory Committee), 1995-1996. *Member:* American Bar Association (Chair, Computer Programs Committee, 1992-1994; Chair, Information Retrieval Committee, 1994-1995; Chair, Division 7-Information, 1995-1996); American Intellectual Property Law Association; Computer Law Association. (Washington Harbor Office). ***PRACTICE AREAS:*** Electronics; Patents; Computer Law; E-commerce; Contracts; Licensing; International Intellectual Property. ***Email:*** wtellis@foleylaw.com

JOHN J. FELDHAUS, admitted to bar, 1980, Virginia; 1985, U.S. District Court, Eastern District of Virginia; 1988, U.S. Court of Appeals for the Federal and Ninth Circuits; registered to practice before U.S. Patent and Trademark Office (Not admitted in District of Columbia). *Education:* Rensselaer Polytechnic Institute (B.S., 1970); George Mason University (J.D., with distinction, 1980). Co-Author: *Electronics and Computer Patent Practice* Patent Resources Group, Washington, D. C., 1985, 1986. Co-Author: *Electronics and Computer Patent and Copyright Practice,* Patent Resources Group, Washington, D.C., 1987, 1988, 1990, 1993. Lecturer Patent Resources Group, 1985-1994. *Member:* Virginia State Bar; American Bar Association; American Intellectual Property Law Association (Member, Programmable Machines and Processes Committee, 1983-1985). (Washington Harbor Office). ***PRACTICE AREAS:*** Electrical and Mechanical Intellectual Property Procurement; Litigation.

HOWARD W. FOGT, JR., admitted to bar, 1967, Ohio; 1970, District of Columbia. *Education:* Princeton University (A.B., magna cum laude, 1964); University of Virginia (J.D., 1967); Certificat Pratique de Français Commercial de la Chambre de Commerce et de l'Industrie de Paris. Law Clerk to the Honorable C. William O'Neill, Supreme Court of Ohio, 1967-1968. Adjunct Professor, European Community Law, Georgetown University Law Center. Associate Counsel, Committee on the Judiciary, U.S. House of Representatives, 1968-1970. *Member:* The District of Columbia Bar; Bar Association of the District of Columbia; American Bar Association (Chairman, Subcommittee on Unfair International Competition, Committee on International Trade, Antitrust Section, 1982-1984; Vice-Chairman, Committee on International Aspects of Antitrust Law, Section on International Law and Practice, 1984-1988). (Washington Harbor Office) (Also at Brussels, Belgium Office). ***LANGUAGES:*** French, Italian. ***PRACTICE AREAS:*** Antitrust Law; European Community Law; International Trade Law.

JAY W. FREEDMAN, admitted to bar, 1968, District of Columbia; 1973, U.S. Supreme Court. *Education:* Williams College (B.A., 1964); Yale University (J.D., 1967). Phi Delta Phi. Member, Executive Committee, Yale Law School Association, 1999-2001. *Member:* The District of Columbia Bar; Bar Association of the District of Columbia; Federal and American Bar Associations; The Economic Club of Washington. (Washington Harbor Office). ***PRACTICE AREAS:*** Corporate Law; Securities Law; Probate; Estate Planning Law. ***Email:*** jfreedman@flks.com

THOMAS E. HARTMAN, admitted to bar, 1991, Illinois and Wisconsin; 2001, District of Columbia. *Education:* University of Michigan (B.S.E., 1984); University of Wisconsin (J.D., cum laude, 1991). Order of the Coif. [Lieutenant, United States Navy, 1984-1988]. ***PRACTICE AREAS:*** Securities; Mergers & Acquisitions; General Corporate. ***Email:*** thartman@foleylaw.com

DONALD M. ITZKOFF, admitted to bar, 1987, New York; 1988, District of Columbia and Pennsylvania. *Education:* Brown University (A.B., magna cum laude, 1983); University of Michigan (J.D., 1986). Contributing Editor, Railway Age, 1990-1991. Author: "Off the Track," Greenwood Press, 1985. Deputy Administrator, Federal Railroad Administration, 1994-1999; Senior Counsel and Staff Counsel, Senate Committee on Commerce, Science and Transportation, 1991-1994. Associate Attorney, Reed Smith Shaw & McClay, 1986-1991. (888 Sixteenth Street Office). ***PRACTICE AREAS:*** Transportation; Legislative; Regulatory. ***Email:*** dmitzkoff@foleylaw.com

(This Listing Continued)

FOLEY & LARDNER, Washington—Continued

THOMAS L. JAMES, admitted to bar, 1985, District of Columbia. *Education:* University of Maryland (B.S., in Bus., 1980); Georgetown University (J.D., 1985). Phi Delta Phi. Member, Gate & Key National Honorary Society. *Member:* The District of Columbia Bar; American Bar Association. (Washington Harbor Office). ***PRACTICE AREAS:*** Securities Law; Corporate Law. ***Email:*** tjames@flks.com

MARY CYNTHIA ATCHLEY JESTER, admitted to bar, 1989, Virginia; 1991, District of Columbia; 1996, U.S. Supreme Court. *Education:* University of Oklahoma; Oklahoma State University (B.A., 1968); George Washington University (J.D., 1989). Editor, The George Washington Journal of International Law and Economics, 1988-1989. *Member:* Virginia State Bar; Fairfax County and American Bar Associations; American Intellectual Property Law Association; Intellectual Property Owners Association; Northern Virginia Building Industry Association; National Association of Home Builders. (Washington Harbor Office). ***PRACTICE AREAS:*** General Corporate Litigation; Health Law; Intellectual Property Litigation.

MICHAEL D. KAMINSKI, admitted to bar, 1987, Illinois; 1988, District of Columbia; U.S. District Court, Northern District of Illinois; U.S. Court of Appeals for the Federal Circuit; U.S. Court of Appeals, Sixth Circuit; U.S. District Court, Northern District of Texas; U.S. Supreme Court; U.S. District Court, District of Nebraska; U.S. District Court, District of Connecticut; registered to practice before U.S. Patent and Trademark Office. *Education:* University of Michigan (B.S.Ch.E., magna cum laude, 1982; B.S., Chemistry; A.B., Communications, with high honors, 1982); University of Michigan Law School (J.D., cum laude, 1986). Kappa Tau Alpha; Alpha Chi Sigma. Member, 1985-1986 and Executive Editor, 1986-1987, Michigan Yearbook of International Legal Studies. Co-Author: "Conducting U.S. Patent Prosecution With a View Toward Potential Litigation," 74 Patent World 36 (1995); "Being Prepared for U.S. Litigation Can Make All the Difference," 75 Patent World 32 (1995); "New Boundaries and Burdens for a Patentee Attempting to Claim Certain Lost Profits Infringement Damages," 76 Patent World 17 (1995); "Hilton Davis: What Does It Mean?" AIPLA Coursebook (1996); "The Doctrine of Equivalents Heats Up," International Legal Strategies, Vol. V-7 (1996); "Conducting Patent Prosecution With a View Toward Litigation," Selected Legal Papers, Vol XV, No. 1 (1997); "The Future of the Doctrine of Equivalents," (Ohio Institute); "When A Licensee Can Stop Paying Royalties," Patent World (1997); "The 1997 Year in Review: United States Patent Law," Patent World (1998); "Conducting Prosecution With a View Toward Litigation," AIPLA Coursebook; "Nobelpharma-Antitrust Level Patent Fraud," Patent World (1998). Editorial Boards: IP World, 1997—; Patent World, 1995—; AIPLA Quarterly Journal, 1994—. Legal Writing Instructor, University of Michigan Law School, 1986. Adjunct Instructor, John Marshall Law School, 1988-1990. Legal Writing Instructor, Illinois Institute of Continuing Legal Education, 1989. Adjunct Professor of Patent Law, Washington College of Law, American University, 1991—; George Mason University, 1997—. *Member:* American Bar Association; The District of Columbia Bar; Bar Association of the District of Columbia; American Chemical Society (Chair, Division of Chemistry and the Law, 1999); American Intellectual Property Law Association (Member, Board of Directors, 1999—; Chemical Practice Chair, 1997-1999 and Vice Chair, 1995-1997; Education Committee Chair, 1993-1995). (Washington Harbor Office). ***PRACTICE AREAS:*** Patent Litigation; Patent Licensing. ***Email:*** mkaminski@foleylaw.com

LYLE KIMMS, admitted to bar, 1990, Virginia, Virginia Supreme Court and U.S. Court of Appeals, 4th Circuit; 1992, District of Columbia; registered to practice before U.S. Patent and Trademark Office. *Education:* Manhattan College (B.E.M.E., 1984); Georgetown University (J.D., 1990). *Member:* The District of Columbia Bar. (Washington Harbor Office). ***PRACTICE AREAS:*** Intellectual Property. ***Email:*** lkimms@foleylaw.com

KENNETH E. KROSIN, admitted to bar, 1972, District of Columbia, U.S. Court of Appeals, District of Columbia Circuit and U.S. District Court, District of Columbia; 1975, U.S. Supreme Court; 1982, U.S. Court of Appeals for the Federal Circuit; 1990, Virginia Supreme Court and U.S. Court of Appeals, Fourth Circuit; registered to practice before U.S. Patent and Trademark Office. *Education:* Princeton University (B.S.E.E., cum laude, 1966); University of Michigan (M.S.E.E., 1967); George Washington University (J.D., 1971). Member, George Washington University, Law Review. Law Clerk, U.S. Court of Claims, 1971-1972. Speeches: "Trial of a Patent Infringement Case," Patent Resources Group, April 29-30, 1999 (Orlando, FL), April 21-25 (Naples, FL) April 28-30, 1997 (Hilton Head, SC); Roundtable Discussion: "The Markman-Hilton-Davis Aftermath: From the Perspective of the PTO, Patent Practitioners, and the Judiciary," 15th Annual Judicial Conference of the U.S. Court of Appeals for the Federal Circuit, June 12, 1997. Publications: "Current Developments In The Patent/Antitrust Interface And Patent Misuse Doctrine," Practicing Law Institute's "Patent Litigation 1999," New York, New York, November 15-16, 1999; "Current Developments in the Patent/Antitrust Interface and Patent Misuse Doctrine," Practising Law Institute's Seminar "Patent Litigation 1998," New York, N.Y.; "En Banc Decisions Of The Federal Circuit," Practicing

(This Listing Continued)

Law Institute Seminar "Patent Litigation," November 16-17, 1995; "Strategies for Enforcing Patents on Software Inventions," The Georgetown University Law Center Sixth Annual Advanced Computer Law Institute, March 1993; "The Expanding Law of Patent Damages," Practising Law Institute Seminar "Patent Litigation," October 1-2, 1990. Editor, "Federal Circuit Patent Law Decisions," AIPLA, 1985-1994. Member, Advisory Board, BNA Patent, Trademark & Copyright Journal, 1991—. Member, Advisory Board, BNA Patent, Trademark & Copyright Journal, 1991—. *Member:* The District of Columbia Bar (Chairman, Trade Regulation Committee, Computer Law Section, 1989-1990); Virginia State Bar; American Bar Association; American Intellectual Property Law Association (Member, Fellows of the American Intellectual Property Law Association, 2000—; Chairman, Management of IP Assets Committee, October 1999—; Board of Directors, 1991-1994; Treasurer, 1990-1991, Chairman, Federal Litigation Committee, 1987-1989); D.C. Computer Law Forum (Member, Board of Directors, 1987). (Washington Harbor Office). ***PRACTICE AREAS:*** Intellectual Property Litigation. ***Email:*** kkrosin@foleylaw.com

JOHNNY A. KUMAR, admitted to bar, 1993, District of Columbia; registered to practice before U.S. Patent and Trademark Office. *Education:* University of Texas (B.S.E.E., with highest honors, 1983); George Mason University School of Law (J.D., with honors, 1993). *Member:* American Bar Association; American Intellectual Property Law Association; Licensing Executives Society; Institute of Electrical and Electronic Engineers. (Washington Harbor Office). ***PRACTICE AREAS:*** Intellectual Property Law; Electrical and Computer Patent Law. ***Email:*** jkumar@foleylaw.com

JACK L. LAHR, admitted to bar, 1963, Virginia and District of Columbia; registered to practice before U.S. Patent and Trademark Office. *Education:* University of Toledo (B.S.M.E., 1956); George Washington University (J.D., with honors, 1963). Order of the Coif. Recent Cases Editor, George Washington Law Review, 1961-1962. Author: "Bias and Prejudice Against Foreign Corporations in Patent and Other Technology Jury Trials," Federal Circuit Bar Journal (Winter 1992). Co-Author: *An Intellectual Property Law Primer,* Macmillan, 1975; Clark-Boardman, 1982. Adjunct Professor of International Licensing, Georgetown University Law Center, 1980-1983. Arbitration and Mediation Neutral for the World Intellectual Property Organization, Geneva, Switzerland, 1998—. *Member:* The District of Columbia Bar; American Bar Association (Council Member, Administrative Law Section, 1971-1974; Chairman, Administrative Law Judges Committee, 1974-1978). (Washington Harbor Office). ***PRACTICE AREAS:*** Litigation; Intellectual Property Law; Antitrust Law; Administrative Law. ***Email:*** jlahr@foleylaw.com

STEVEN C. LAMBERT, admitted to bar, 1975, District of Columbia. *Education:* Duke University (B.A., 1969); Georgetown University (J.D., 1974). Executive Editor, Georgetown Law Journal, 1973-1974. Co-author: "A Practical View of the Eleventh Amendment-Lower Court Interpretations and the Supreme Court's Reaction," 61 Georgetown Law Journal 1473, 1973; "Tax Ideas Desk Book," Prentice-Hall, Inc., 1980. Law Clerk to Chief Judge Wilson Cowen, U.S. Court of Claims, 1974-1975. Member, Panel of Arbitrators, American Arbitration Association. *Member:* The District of Columbia Bar; Bar Association of the District of Columbia (Member, Board of Directors, 1981-1983; Chairman, U.S. Court of Claims Committee, 1980-1981); Federal Circuit (Member, Board of Directors, 1985-1988); U.S. Claims Court (Member, Board of Directors, 1987-1989; President-Elect, 1989-1990; President, 1990-1991) and American (Member, Sections on: Natural Resources; Litigation) Bar Associations. Fellow: American Bar Foundation. (888 Sixteenth Street Office). ***PRACTICE AREAS:*** Litigation; Valuation Law; Government Contracts. ***Email:*** slambert@foleylaw.com

THOMAS C. LAUERMAN, admitted to bar, 1975, New York; 1978, Georgia; 1981, District of Columbia. *Education:* Yale University (B.A., cum laude, 1970); University of Virginia (J.D., 1973). Attorney-Advisor, Division of Investment Management, U.S. Securities and Exchange Commission, 1975-1977. *Member:* The District of Columbia Bar; State Bar of Georgia; New York State and American Bar Associations (Member, Committee on Securities Regulation Business Law Section). (Washington Harbor Office). ***PRACTICE AREAS:*** Securities Law; Corporate Law. ***Email:*** tlauerman@flks.com

GLENN LAW, admitted to bar, 1992, Virginia; 1994, District of Columbia; registered to practice before U.S. Patent and Trademark Office. *Education:* Cornell University (B.S.E.E., 1983); George Washington University (J.D, with high honors, 1992). Tau Beta Pi; Order of the Coif; Licensed Professional Engineer, Virginia. Member, The George Washington Law Review, 1990-1992. Author, "Liability Under the Process Patent Amendments Act of 1988 for the Use of a Patented Process Outside the United States," 60 The George Washington Law Review, 245, 1991. [Lt. U.S. Navy, 1983-1988]. (Washington Harbor Office). ***PRACTICE AREAS:*** Patent Law and Litigation; Intellectual Property. ***Email:*** glaw@foleylaw.com

JERRIS LEONARD, admitted to bar, 1955, Wisconsin; 1973, District of Columbia, U.S. Supreme Court. *Education:* Marquette University (B.S., in B.A., 1952; J.D., 1955). Delta Sigma Pi; Sigma Nu Phi; Alpha Sigma Nu. Member: Wisconsin State Assembly, 1957-1961; Wisconsin State Senate, 1967-1969. Majority Leader, Wisconsin State Senate, 1961-1969. Assistant Attorney General, U.S. Department of Justice, 1969-1971. Administrator, Law Enforce-

(This Listing Continued)

ment Assistance Administration, U.S. Department of Justice, 1971-1973. *Member:* The District of Columbia Bar; State Bar of Wisconsin; American Bar Association. (888 Sixteenth Street Office). ***REPORTED CASES:*** Connor vs. Finch, 431 U.S. 407, 1977; Davis vs. Board of Commissioners of Mobile County, 402 U.S. 33, 1971; Phillips vs. Martin Marietta, 400 U.S. 542, 1971; Daniel vs. Paul, 395 U.S. 298, 1969. ***PRACTICE AREAS:*** Government Contract Law; Lobbying; State and Federal Legislative Practice; Financial Organization; Litigation. ***Email:*** jleonard@foleylaw.com

MELINDA F. LEVITT, admitted to bar, 1989, Maryland; 1991, District of Columbia. *Education:* Brandeis University (B.A., cum laude, 1980); The Johns Hopkins University School of Advanced International Studies (M.A., 1982); George Washington University (J.D., with honors, 1989). (Washington Harbor Office). ***LANGUAGES:*** French and Italian. ***PRACTICE AREAS:*** Litigation; International Trade. ***Email:*** mlevitt@foleylaw.com

PETER G. MACK, admitted to bar, 1973, Virginia and U.S. District Court, Eastern District of Virginia; 1973, U.S. Claims Court; 1973-1982, U.S. Court of Customs and Patent Appeals; 1980, U.S. Supreme Court; 1982, U.S. Court of Appeals for the Federal Circuit and U.S. Court of Appeals, Eleventh Circuit; 1984, U.S. District Court, District of Maryland; 1985, U.S. Court of Appeals, Fourth Circuit; 1993, District of Columbia; 1995, U.S. District Court, Eastern District of Michigan; registered to practice before U.S. Patent and Trademark Office. *Education:* Marquette University (B.M.E., 1968); George Washington University (J.D., 1972). *Member:* Virginia State Bar (Member, Board of Governors, Patent Section, 1981-1984); American Bar Association (Member, Intellectual Property Law and Litigation Sections); American Intellectual Property Law Association. (Washington Harbor Office). ***PRACTICE AREAS:*** Intellectual Property Litigation.

STEPHEN B. MAEBIUS, admitted to bar, 1994, Virginia; 1996, District of Columbia; registered to practice before U.S. Patent and Trademark Office. *Education:* Cornell University (B.A., 1989); Tokyo University (Comparative Law Program, 1991); George Washington University (J.D., 1994). Author: "Extending Process Claims from Intermediate to Final Product: Avoiding the Trap of Eli Lilly," JPTOS (1998). Lecturer: Practicing Law Institute on IP Due Diligence in High Tech Mergers and Acquisitions. Visiting Associate Professor of Intellectual Property Law, Tokyo University, 1999. (Washington Harbor Office). ***LANGUAGES:*** Spanish. ***PRACTICE AREAS:*** Intellectual Property. ***Email:*** smaebius@foleylaw.com

LISA S. MANKOFSKY, admitted to bar, 1986, Maryland; 1987, District of Columbia and U.S. District Court, District of Maryland; 1989, U.S. District Court, District of Connecticut; 1990, U.S. District Court, District of Columbia; 1991, U.S. District Court, Central District of Illinois; 1995, U.S. Court of Appeals for the Federal Circuit. *Education:* State University of New York at Binghamton (B.A., 1983); University of Michigan Law School (J.D., 1986). Phi Beta Kappa. *Member:* The District of Columbia Bar; Maryland State and American Bar Associations; American Intellectual Property Law Association; Federal Circuit Bar Association. (Washington Harbor Office). ***PRACTICE AREAS:*** Intellectual Property Litigation; Manufacturer and Distributor Relations. ***Email:*** lmankofsky@foleylaw.com

LAWRENCE G. McBRIDE, admitted to bar, 1974, California; 1986, U.S. Court of Federal Claims, 1989, District of Columbia. *Education:* Stanford University (A.B., 1970); Boalt Hall School of Law, University of California, Berkeley (J.D., 1973). Co-Author, Coal Chapter in *Sustainable Environmental Law,* West, 1993. Author: "Inverse Condemnation Issues in Revising the Mining Law," 38 Rocky Mtn. Min'l Inst., ch. 7 (1992). Adjunct Professor, George Washington University National Law Center, 1983-1990. Assistant Section Chief, U.S. Department of Justice, Land and Natural Resources Division, 1986-1988; U.S. Department of the Interior, 1973-1985. *Member:* The District of Columbia Bar; State Bar of California. (Washington Harbor Office). ***PRACTICE AREAS:*** Natural Resources Law; Regulatory Law. ***Email:*** lmcbride@flks.com

FRANCIS O. McDERMOTT, admitted to bar, 1960, District of Columbia; 1961, U.S. Tax Court; 1964, U.S. Supreme Court; 1968, U.S. Court of Claims; 1982, U.S. Claims Court. *Education:* Creighton University; George Washington University; American University (LL.B., 1960). *Member:* The District of Columbia Bar; Federal (Member, National Counsel, 1968-1970) and American (Member, Section of Taxation, 1981—) Bar Associations. (888 Sixteenth Street Office). ***PRACTICE AREAS:*** Tax (Administrative) Law; Legislative Law. ***Email:*** fmcdermott@foleylaw.com

BRIAN J. McNAMARA, admitted to bar, 1986, Maryland; 1989, District of Columbia; registered to practice before U.S. Patent and Trademark Office. *Education:* Manhattan College (B.E.E., 1973); Johns Hopkins University (M.S.E.E., 1976; M.A.S., 1980); University of Maryland (J.D., with honors, 1986). Member, Moot Court Board. Adjunct Professor, George Mason University, 1996—. Lecturer, Electronics and Computer Patent and Copyright Practice, Patent Resources Group, 1995 and 1996. Author and Instructor: Patent Law for the Business Practitioner, MICPEL, 1991; Purchase and Sale of Closely Held Business, MICPEL, 1994, 1996, 1998. Author: "What Every Lawyer Must Know About Trademarks," Anne Arundel County Barrister, 1990; "An Artificial

(This Listing Continued)

Intelligence Approach to High Speed Mux Bus Control—Layered Reservation Access," Proceedings, AIAA Sixth Digital Avionics Systems Conference, 1984; "The Arinc Research Signal Evaluation For Emitter Recognition (SEER) Model," Proceedings South West Old Crows Technical Symposium, 1985; "Decision Support (AI) Technologies For The Attack Warning/Attack Assessment System," Proceedings, Armed Forces Communications & Electronics Assn., Space Technologies Symposium, 1986. *Member:* Anne Arundel County, Maryland State and American Bar Associations; The District of Columbia Bar; Federal Circuit Bar Association; Institute of Electrical and Electronics Engineers; American Intellectual Property Law Association; Anne Arundel County High Technology Council (Director). (Washington Harbour Office). ***PRACTICE AREAS:*** Electronics; Intellectual Property. ***Email:*** bmcnamara@foleylaw.com

ROBERT J. MEYER, admitted to bar, 1985, Pennsylvania; 1986, District of Columbia. *Education:* Boston University (B.A., 1982; M.A., 1982); University of Virginia (J.D., 1985). Member, Editorial Board, 1983-1984 and Notes Editor, 1984-1985, Virginia Law Review. Law Clerk, Judge George E. MacKinnon, U.S. Court of Appeals, District of Columbia Circuit, 1985-1986. Assistant United States Attorney, District of Columbia, 1989-1992. Associate Independent Counsel, Office of Independent Counsel Arlin M. Adams, 1992-1994. Trial Attorney, Public Integrity Section, Criminal Division, United States Department of Justice, 1994-2000. *Member:* The District of Columbia Bar; Pennsylvania and American Bar Associations. (Washington Harbor Office). ***PRACTICE AREAS:*** White Collar Criminal Defense; Government Enforcement; Compliance. ***Email:*** rmeyer@foleylaw.com

CLETA DEATHERAGE MITCHELL MITCHELL, admitted to bar, 1976, Oklahoma; U.S. District Court, Western District of Oklahoma; 1988, U.S. Supreme Court; 1989, U.S. District Court, Northern District of Oklahoma and U.S Court of Appeals, Tenth Circuit; 1992, District of Columbia and U.S. District Court for the District of Columbia; 1994, U.S. Court of Appeals, District of Columbia Circuit and U.S. Court of Appeals, Ninth Circuit. *Education:* University of Oklahoma (B.A., with high honors, 1973; J.D., 1975). Phi Beta Kappa. Lecturer: Administrative Law Seminar, University of Oklahoma CLE, 1988; Administrative Law Seminar, Oklahoma Bar Association CLE, 1989. Member, Oklahoma House of Representatives, 1976-1984. Chairman, Appropriations and Budget Committee, Oklahoma House of Representatives, 1980-1983. Member, Professional Responsibility Tribunal by Oklahoma Supreme Court, 1989—. Fellow, Institute of Politics, Harvard University, 1981. Shapiro Fellow, George Washington University Law School of Media and Public Affairs, 2000. President and General Counsel, Term Limits Legal Institute, 1991-1998. *Member:* Cleveland, Oklahoma County and Oklahoma Bar Associations; The District of Columbia Bar. ***PRACTICE AREAS:*** Public Affairs; Constitutional Law; Election, Campaign and Political Law. ***Email:*** cmitchell@foleylaw.com

PAUL R. MONSEES, admitted to bar, 1982, District of Columbia; 1983, Maryland. *Education:* Lafayette College (B.A., 1978); Catholic University (J.D., 1982). Member, 1980-1981 and Associate Editor, 1981-1982, Catholic University Law Review. Law Clerk, The Honorable Donald S. Smith, Superior Court of The District of Columbia, 1982-1983. Master, Thurgood Marshall American Inn of Court. *Member:* The District of Columbia Bar; Maryland State and American Bar Associations. (Washington Harbor Office). ***PRACTICE AREAS:*** Commercial Litigation; Employment. ***Email:*** pmonsees@foleylaw.com

PHILIP A. NACKE, admitted to bar, 1973, District of Columbia. *Education:* University of Tennessee (A.B., 1969); Georgetown University (J.D., 1972). Phi Beta Kappa. Managing Editor, Georgetown Law Journal 276, 1971-1972. *Member:* The District of Columbia Bar; U.S. Court of Federal Claims (President-Elect, 1997; President, 1998) and American (Member, Sections on: Litigation; Natural Resources) Bar Associations. (888 Sixteenth Street Office). ***PRACTICE AREAS:*** Litigation; Valuation Law; Natural Resources Law; Government Contracts Law. ***Email:*** pnacke@foleylaw.com

RICHARD C. PEET, admitted to bar, 1994, Pennsylvania; 1996, District of Columbia; registered to practice before U.S. Patent and Trademark Office. *Education:* Haverford College (B.S., 1976); University of California, Berkeley (Ph.D., 1985); Catholic University of America (J.D., cum laude, 1994). Former Primary Examiner, U.S. Patent and Trademark Office. *Member:* American Bar Association; American Intellectual Property Law Association; American Association Advancement Sciences; American Chemical Society; American Society of Plant Physiology. (Washington Harbor Office). ***LANGUAGES:*** Dutch; Spanish. ***PRACTICE AREAS:*** Patents; Trademarks; Licensing; Litigation. ***Email:*** rcpeet@foleylaw.com

GEORGE E. QUILLIN, admitted to bar, 1984, South Carolina; 1988, U.S. Supreme Court; registered to practice before the U.S. Patent and Trademark Office (Not admitted in District of Columbia). *Education:* United States Military Academy (B.S., 1973); University of South Carolina (J.D., 1984). Law Clerk to Honorable Jean Galloway Bissell, Circuit Judge, U.S. Court of Appeals for the Federal Circuit, 1984-1986. Adjunct Professor, George Mason University Law School, 1993-2000. Co-Editor of textbook "Patent Office Practice" (1996). Lecturer, Japan Intellectual Property Association, 1994—. Claim Draft-

(This Listing Continued)

FOLEY & LARDNER, Washington—Continued

ing Instructor, Patent Resources Group, 1993-1999. *Member:* South Carolina Bar; Federal Circuit and American (Member, Section on: Intellectual Property Law) Bar Associations; Christian Legal Society. (Washington Harbor Office). ***PRACTICE AREAS:*** Intellectual Property Law. ***Email:*** gquillin@foleylaw.com

DAVID T. RALSTON, JR., admitted to bar, 1980, New York; 1985, District of Columbia; 1987, Virginia. *Education:* Georgetown University (B.S.F.S., 1976; J.D., cum laude, 1979). Phi Alpha Delta. Author: "The New Government Contracts Bid Protest Law," 15 Pub. Cont. L.J. 177, 1985. Board Member, Washington Metropolitan Airports Authority, 1994—; Chairman, 1997—. Member, Virginia Debt Capacity Advisory Committee. Trial Attorney, Attorney-Advisor and Appellate Attorney, JAGC, U.S. Army, 1980-1984, awarded Meritorious Service Medal. Trial Judge (IMA), U.S. Army Reserve, 1984-1994. Executive Committee, Federal City Council, 1998—; Executive Committee, Greater Washington Board of Trade, 1998—; Member, Economic Club of Washington; Advisory Committee on Management of Privatized Industries, George Washington University, D.C., 1998—. *Member:* Fairfax and Virginia Bar Associations; The District of Columbia Bar; Virginia State Bar. (888 Sixteenth Street Office). ***PRACTICE AREAS:*** Civil Practice; White Collar; Criminal Litigation; Government Contract Law; Airport Regulation. ***Email:*** dralston@foleylaw.com

ANDREW E. RAWLINS, admitted to bar, 1992, Virginia; 1995, District of Columbia. *Education:* Pennsylvania State University (B.S.I.E., 1987); American University (J.D., magna cum laude, 1992). Alpha Pi Mu. Patent Examiner, U.S. Patent and Trademark Office, 1987-1990. *Member:* Federal Circuit and American (Member, Section on Patent, Trademark and Copyright Law) Bar Associations; Bar Association of the District of Columbia; American Intellectual Property Law Association. (Washington Harbor Office). ***PRACTICE AREAS:*** Intellectual Property. ***Email:*** arawlins@foleylaw.com

JAMIE PALTER RENNERT, admitted to bar, 1992, Maryland; 1993, District of Columbia; U.S. Court of Federal Claims; U.S. Court of Appeals for the Federal, District of Columbia and Sixth Circuits. *Education:* University of Michigan (A.B., 1989) London School of Economics; University of Pennsylvania (J.D., 1992). Clerk to the Hon. Judge Moody Tidwell, III, U.S. Court of Federal Claims, 1992-1993. *Member:* District of Columbia Bar. (888 Sixteenth Street Office). ***PRACTICE AREAS:*** Transportation; Administrative Law. ***Email:*** jrennert@foleylaw.com

RICHARD F. RILEY, JR., admitted to bar, 1983, District of Columbia; 1987, U.S. Supreme Court. *Education:* Yale University (B.A., magna cum laude, 1980); Duke University (J.D., with honors, 1983). Co-author: "Criminal Tax Procedure," BNA Tax Management Portfolio, 1987. Member, Editorial Advisory Board, *The Tax Adviser,* 1994—. Director, Riley Memorial Hospital, Meridian, Miss., 1989-1998. Director, Riley Family Foundation, Meridian, Miss., 1998—. *Member:* The District of Columbia Bar (Member, Tax Section); Federal (Member, Tax Section) and American (Member, Section on Taxation) Bar Associations; J. Edgar Murdock American Inn of Court. (888 Sixteenth Street Office). ***PRACTICE AREAS:*** Taxation Law; Transportation Law. ***Email:*** rriley@foleylaw.com

DAVID A. SACKS, admitted to bar, 1967, Maryland; 1968, District of Columbia. *Education:* University of Baltimore (B.S., 1961); Georgetown University (J.D., 1967). Certified Public Accountant, Maryland, 1963. Law Clerk to Honorable Collins J. Seitz, U.S. Court of Appeals, Third Circuit, 1967-1968. *Member:* District of Columbia Bar; Maryland State Bar. (Washington Harbor Office). ***PRACTICE AREAS:*** Federal Taxation Law; Corporate Law. ***Email:*** dsacks@foleylaw.com

JACQUELINE MARIE SAUE, admitted to bar, 1975, District of Columbia; 1976, U.S. District Court, District of Columbia and U.S. Court of Appeals, District of Columbia Circuit; 1980, U.S. Supreme Court; 1981, U.S. Court of Appeals, Fourth Circuit; 1984, Maryland and U.S. District Court, District of Maryland. *Education:* Mount Holyoke College (B.A., magna cum laude, 1972); Georgetown University (J.D., 1975). Phi Beta Kappa. Editor, Law and Policy in International Business, 1974-1975. *Member:* The District of Columbia Bar; State Bar Association of Maryland; American Bar Association; American Association of Health Plans; American Health Lawyers Association. (Washington Harbor Office). ***PRACTICE AREAS:*** Health Law; Antitrust Law; Corporate Law; Litigation. ***Email:*** jsaue@foleylaw.com

BERNHARD D. SAXE, admitted to bar, 1981, Virginia; 1982, U.S. Court of Appeals for the Federal Circuit; 1998, District of Columbia; registered to practice before the U.S. Patent and Trademark Office. *Education:* Johns Hopkins University (B.A., with honors, 1960); Columbia University (M.A., 1961; Ph.D., 1966); George Washington University (J.D., with honors, 1981). Phi Beta Kappa; Sigma Xi. Woodrow Wilson Graduate Fellowship, 1960-1961. NIH Postdoctoral Fellowship, Strasbourg, France, 1966-1967. Assistant/Associate Professor of Chemistry, Beloit College, Beloit, Wisconsin, 1967-1976. Vice President, Patent Affairs, Immunomedics, Inc., New Jersey, 1984-1988. *Member:* Virginia State Bar; The District of Columbia Bar; American Bar Association; American Intellectual Property Law Association; American Chemical Society. (Washington Harbor Office). ***LANGUAGES:*** French, German. ***PRACTICE AREAS:*** U.S. and Foreign Chemical, Pharmaceutical; Biotechnological Patent, Licensing and Litigation; Trademarks; Technology Transfers. ***Email:*** bsaxe@foleylaw.com

CHARLES F. SCHILL, admitted to bar, 1973, Ohio; 1976, District of Columbia; 1978, U.S. Supreme Court; 1982, U.S. Court of Appeals for the Federal Circuit; 1985, U.S. Court of International Trade; registered to practice before U.S. Patent and Trademark Office. *Education:* LeMoyne College (B.S., 1968); Capital University College of Law (J.D., 1973). Member, Order of the Curia. Author: "Injury Determinations in Section 337 Inv.," Northwestern Journal of International Law and Business, Vol. 4, No. 1, 1982; "Protection of Intellectual Property Rights," A Practical Approach to Patents, Trademarks and Copyrights, Vol. 2 (4), 1982; "The New Amendments to Section 337," Computer Law Reporter, Vol. 8, No. 4, 1988; Protection of Intellectual Property Rights at the U.S. International Trade Commission: Section 337 Practice and Recent Developments," Computer Law Reporter, Vol. 13, Nos. 2 & 3, April/May 1991; "Computer-Related Intellectual Property Actions at the International Trade Commission-Experience Under the Trade Act of 1988," American Intellectual Property Law Association, The Law of Computer Related Technology, Vol. II, January, 1992. Senior Investigative Attorney, U.S. International Trade Commission, 1975-1979. *Member:* The District of Columbia Bar; Federal Circuit Bar Association (Chair, ITC/CIT Committee, 1994-1999; Member, Board of Directors, 1999—); American Intellectual Property Law Association (Member: International Trade Commission Committee, 1989-1991; Inventor Relations Committee, 1993-1995; Chair, Communication Law Committee, 1996-1998); International Trade Commission Trial Lawyers Association (Executive Committee). (Washington Harbor Office). ***PRACTICE AREAS:*** International Trade Regulation; Intellectual Property; Litigation; Patents; Trademarks. ***Email:*** cschill@foleylaw.com

RICHARD L. SCHWAAB, admitted to bar, 1971, Virginia; 1980, U.S. Supreme Court; 1982, U.S. Court of Appeals for the Federal Circuit; 1999, District of Columbia; registered to practice before U.S. Patent and Trademark Office. *Education:* University of Wisconsin (B.S.Ch.E., with honors, 1967); George Washington University (J.D., cum laude, 1971; LL.M., International Law, with highest honors, 1979). Phi Kappa Phi; Tau Beta Pi. Member, George Washington University Law Review, 1970-1971. Max Planck Institute Fellowship, Munich, Germany, 1971-1972. Author: "Enforcement of Biotechnology Patents," Biotechnology Patent Practice, Patent Resources Institute, 1986. Co-Author: "Patent Practice," Patent Resources Institute, 1976-1999; "Intellectual Property Rights," Biotechnology Worldwide, Stockton Press, 1987. Professorial Lecturer of Law, George Washington University, 1978, 1984, 1986, 1988, 1998. Adjunct Professor of Law, George Mason University, 1990-1999. (Washington Harbor Office). ***LANGUAGES:*** German. ***PRACTICE AREAS:*** Intellectual Property Law. ***Email:*** rschwaab@foleylaw.com

LARRY L. SHATZER II, admitted to bar, 1987, Tennessee; 1989, District of Columbia; 1990, U.S. Court of Appeals for the Federal Circuit, U.S. Court of International Trade, U.S. District Court of the District of Columbia and U.S. Court of Appeals, Ninth Circuit; 1992, U.S. Supreme Court; 1994, U.S. Court of Appeals, Eleventh Circuit; 1995, U.S. Court of Appeals, Fourth Circuit; 1996, U.S. Court of Federal Claims, U.S. Court of Appeals for the D.C. Circuit. *Education:* David Lipscomb College (B.A., magna cum laude, 1984); Georgetown University (J.D., cum laude, 1987). Author (with Charles Schill): "Computer-Related Intellectual Property Actions at the International Trade Commission-Experience Under the Trade Act of 1988," American Intellectual Property Law Association, The Law of Computer-Related Technology, Vol. II, January, 1992; "Cardinal v. Morton: Supreme Court Rejects Vieau Vacatur Policy," 3 Fed. Cir. B.J. 181 (1993). *Member:* International Trade Commission Trial Lawyers Association (Executive Committee, 1995—; Vice-President, 1999-2000); American Intellectual Property Law Association. (Washington Harbor Office). ***PRACTICE AREAS:*** Intellectual Property Litigation; International Trade; Trademarks; Antidumping. ***Email:*** lshatzer@foleylaw.com

MICHELE M. SIMKIN, admitted to bar, 1993, District of Columbia. *Education:* University of Wisconsin - Madison (B.S., 1988); George Washington University Law Center (J.D., 1993). (Washington Harbor Office). ***PRACTICE AREAS:*** Intellectual Property; Biotechnology; Pharmaceutical. ***Email:*** msimkin@foleylaw.com

SAMUEL B. STERRETT, JR., admitted to bar, 1988, New York and District of Columbia. *Education:* Amherst College (B.A., 1982); London School of Economics (1980); University of Virginia (J.D., 1987). Law Clerk to Hon. James S. Halpern, U.S. Tax Court (1990-1992). Allens Arthur Robinson, Melbourne & Sydney, Australia, 1987-1988. Member, Managing Board, Virginia Journal of Natural Resources Law, 1986-1987. Author: "Advantages of Putting IP Rights Into a Limited Liability Corp.," The Intellectual Property Strategist (July 1999); "Directors Need to Get Involved in Solutions for Y2K, "Washington Business Journal (May 28, 1999); "Taxing the Mind," Legal Times (May 2, 1994); "Taking a Tax Bite From Tax-Exempt Groups," Legal Times (March 14, 1994); "Bankruptcy, Hazardous Waste and Product Liability," 6 Va. J. Nat. Resources Law 179 (1986). *Member:* The District of Columbia

(This Listing Continued)

Bar; New York State and American Bar Associations. (Washington Harbor Office). ***PRACTICE AREAS:*** Federal and State Tax Law; Corporate; Technology Licensing; Technology Transactions.

RICHARD G. STOLL, admitted to bar, 1971, District of Columbia. *Education:* Westminster College (B.A., magna cum laude, 1968); Georgetown University (J.D., 1971). Recipient, Distinguished Alumni Award, 1998. Staff Member, Georgetown Law Journal, 1970-1971. Instructor, Environmental Law and Policy, University of Virginia-Charlottesville, 1981-1990. Attorney, 1973-1981 and Assistant General Counsel, 1978-1981, Office of General Counsel, U.S. Environmental Protection Agency. Deputy General Counsel, Chemical Manufacturers Association, Washington, D.C., 1981-1984. *Member:* The District of Columbia Bar; American Bar Association (Chairman, Section of Natural Resources, Energy, and Environmental Law, 1990-1991; Council Member, 1985-1988; Chairman, Committee on Solid and Hazardous Waste, 1983-1985 and Committee on Water Quality, 1980-1982). [Capt., U.S. Army Signal Corps, active duty, 1972]. (Washington Harbor Office). ***PRACTICE AREAS:*** Environmental Law. ***Email:*** rstoll@flks.com

PAUL E. SULLIVAN, admitted to bar, 1979, California and U.S. District Court, Northern District of California; 1981, U.S. District Court, Eastern District of California; 1994, U.S. Supreme Court (Not admitted in District of Columbia). *Education:* University of Santa Clara (B.S., 1974); Pepperdine University (J.D., 1979). Executive Assistant to Commissioner, Federal Election Commission, 1982-1985. Assistant Legal Counsel, National Republican Congressional Committee, 1981-1982. *Member:* The California State Bar; Federalist Society. ***PRACTICE AREAS:*** Public Affairs. ***Email:*** psullivan@foleylaw.com

CHARLES MICHAEL TOBIN, admitted to bar, 1968, Massachusetts; 1970, Maryland and District of Columbia; 1972, U.S. Supreme Court. *Education:* Boston College and Boston Univ. (A.B., 1963); Catholic Univ. of America (J.D., cum laude, 1968); Georgetown Univ. (LL.M. in Taxation, 1978). Delta Theta Phi. Comment Editor, Catholic University Law Review, 1967-1968. Contributor: Emerging Problems Under the Federal Rules of Evidence, ABA, Section of Litigation, 1983. *Member:* District of Columbia Bar; Montgomery County (Member, Executive Committee, 1984-1986; Chairman, Litigation Section, 1980-1982), Maryland State (Chairman, Section on Litigation, 1982-1983; Member, Litigation Section Counsel, 1979—; Liaison to Federal Courts, 1979-1984; Chairman, Litigation Rules Committee, 1979-1984; Consultant, Court of Appeals, Rules Subcommittee on Evidence, 1990-1991) and American (Chairman, Committee on Trial Evidence, Section of Litigation, 1983-1986; Member, Committee on Civil and Criminal Penalties, Section of Taxation, 1977-1988) Bar Associations. ***PRACTICE AREAS:*** Litigation; Commercial Law; Trade Regulation. ***Email:*** ctobin@foleylaw.com

SHELDON L. TRUBATCH, admitted to bar, 1978, New York; U.S. Court of Appeals, District of Columbia Circuit and U.S. Court of Appeals, Tenth Circuit; 1991, District of Columbia. *Education:* Polytechnic University Brooklyn (B.S., magna cum laude, 1962); Brandeis University (Ph.D. in Physics, 1968); Columbia University (J.D., 1977). Harlan Fiske Stone Scholar. Professional Articles Editor, Columbia Journal of Environmental Law, 1976-1977. Author: "Informed Judicial Decisionmaking: A Suggestion for a Judicial Office for Understanding Science and Technology," Columbia Journal of Environmental Law, 1985; "Legal Criteria for Establishing de minimis Levels for Exposure to Radiation from Low-Level Radioactive Waste and Uranium Mill Tailings," Geotechnical & Geohydrological Aspects of Waste Management, 1986. Member, Board of Directors, Columbia Journal of Environmental Law. Associate Professor of Physics, California State University, Long Beach, 1967-1974. Acting Solicitor, 1981 and Special Assistant General Counsel for Technical Matters, 1983-1985, U.S. Nuclear Regulatory Commission. *Member:* The District of Columbia Bar; American Bar Association; American Association for Artificial Intelligence; American Nuclear Society; American Physical Society. (888 Sixteenth Street Office). ***PRACTICE AREAS:*** Nuclear Law; Administrative Law. ***Email:*** strubatch@foleylaw.com

JAY N. VARON, admitted to bar, 1975, California; 1976, District of Columbia; 1985, Maryland. *Education:* University of Pennsylvania (B.S. in Economics, 1972); Stanford University (J.D., 1975). Order of the Coif; Beta Gamma Sigma. Articles Editor, Stanford Law Review, 1974-1975. Author: Note, "A Re-examination of the Law Enforcement Assistance Administration," 27 Stanford Law Review 1303 (1975); "Promoting Settlements and Limiting Litigation Costs by Means of the Offer of Judgment, Some Suggestions for Using and Revising Rule 68," 33 American University Law Review, 813 (1984). Law Clerk to Honorable Robert F. Peckham, Chief Judge of the U.S. District Court, Northern District of California, 1975-1976. *Member:* The District of Columbia Bar; State Bar of California; Maryland State and American Bar Associations. (Washington Harbor Office). ***PRACTICE AREAS:*** Litigation; Antitrust Law; RESPA.

ROBERT P. VOM EIGEN, admitted to bar, 1971, Connecticut; 1978, District of Columbia. *Education:* Wesleyan University (B.A., 1967); Boalt Hall School of Law, University of California (J.D., 1970). *Member:* The District of Columbia Bar; Association of Transportation Law, Logistics and Policy. (888 Sixteenth Street Office). ***PRACTICE AREAS:*** Transportation Law; Administrative; Legislative Advocacy. ***Email:*** rvomeigen@foleylaw.com

J. MARK WAXMAN, admitted to bar, 1973, California; 1974, U.S. District Court, Central, Southern, Eastern and Northern Districts of California and U.S. Court of Appeals, Ninth Circuit; 1980, U.S. Court of Appeals, Eighth Circuit; 1981, U.S. Supreme Court; 1986, U.S. Claims Court (Not admitted in District of Columbia). *Education:* University of California at San Diego (B.A., summa cum laude, 1970); Boalt Hall School of Law, University of California at Berkeley (J.D., 1973). Articles and Book Review Editor, Ecology Law Quarterly, 1972-1973. Assistant U.S. Attorney, Central District of California, 1974-1977. Legal Counsel, California Association of Health Facilities. *Member:* National Health Lawyers Association (Member, Board of Directors, 1986-1992; Chairman, First and Second Symposium on Preferred Provider Organizations, 1983-1984); American Academy of Healthcare Attorneys; American Hospital Association (Member, Adjunct Task Force on Antitrust). (Washington Harbor Office) (Also at Los Angeles, California Office). ***REPORTED CASES:*** Summit Health Ltd. v. Pinhas, 111 S.Ct. 1842 (1991). ***PRACTICE AREAS:*** Commercial Litigation; Health Care; Administrative Law; Antitrust and Trade Regulation.

HAROLD C. WEGNER, admitted to bar, 1969, Virginia (inactive); 1971, District of Columbia; 1978, U.S. Supreme Court; 1982, U.S. Court of Appeals for the Federal Circuit; registered to practice before U.S. Patent and Trademark Office. *Education:* Northwestern University (B.A., 1965); Georgetown University Law Center (J.D., 1969). Author: *Patent Law in Biotechnology, Chemistry and Pharmaceuticals,* 1992, 1994; *Patent Harmonization,* 1993. Co-Author: *Business and Commercial Litigation in Federal Courts,* Patents Chapter, West, 1998; *Patents,* West, 1998; *Japanese Patent Law,* 1986; *Japanese Patent Practice,* 1989. Research Fellow, Max Planck Institute for Foreign and International Patent, Copyright and Competition Law, Munich, Germany, 1974-1976. Kenshuin, Kyoto University Law Faculty, Kyoto, Japan, 1977. Adjunct Professor of Law, Georgetown University Law Center, 1983-1989, 1999. Professor of Law and Director of the Intellectual Property Law Program, George Washington University Law School, 1981-1998. Visiting Professor, Tokyo University, 1999. Patent Examiner, United States Department of Commerce, 1965-1969. Director, Dean Dinwoodey Center for Intellectual Property Studies, 1992-1998. Distinguished Scholar in Residence, George Washington University Law School, 1999—. Member, United Nations Committee of Experts on Patent Harmonization, World Intellectual Property Organization, 1985-1989. *Member:* Bar Association of the District of Columbia (Member, Board of Governors, 1999-2000; Chairman, Patent Trademark Copyright Law Section, 1998-1999); Virginia State Bar (Chairman, Patent Trademark Copyright Section, 1980-1981); American Intellectual Property Law Association (Member, Amicus Committee, 1987—; Board of Directors, 1985-1987). (Washington Harbor Office). ***PRACTICE AREAS:*** Intellectual Property; Intellectual Property Asset Management. ***Email:*** hwegner@foleylaw.com

MARTIN J. WEINSTEIN, admitted to bar, 1985, Maryland and District of Columbia; 1990, Georgia. *Education:* Dartmouth College (B.A., honors Govt., 1981); University of Virginia (J.D., 1984). Recipient: John Marshall Award, 1995; Federal Law Enforcement Officers' Association Prosecution Award, 1995. Author: "Designing And Implementing An Effective Corporate Compliance Program," Antitrust Review Of The Americas 2000, Global Competition Review, 1999. Expert Witness, Foreign Corrupt Practices Act. Chair, Compliance Counseling And Government Enforcement Group, Foley & Lardner, 1998—. Co-Chair, Prosecution Function Committee, Criminal Justice Section, American Bar Association, 1995-1996. U.S. Attorney General's Advocacy Institute, 1992-1993. Assistant U.S. Attorney, Atlanta, Northern District of Georgia, 1989-1996. Tax Division Trial Attorney, U.S. Department of Justice, 1988-1989. *Member:* The District of Columbia Bar; Maryland State Bar Association; State Bar of Georgia. (Washington Harbor Office). ***LANGUAGES:*** French and Romanian. ***PRACTICE AREAS:*** International Business Law; Foreign Corrupt Practices Act; Criminal Law; Government Investigations. ***Email:*** mweinstein@foleylaw.com

KENNETH B. WINER, admitted to bar, 1981, District of Columbia. *Education:* University of Pennsylvania (B.S., summa cum laude, 1978); Harvard University (J.D., cum laude, 1981). Author: "Securities Firms and the Foreign Corrupt Practices Act," Securities and Commodities Regulation, March 28, 2000; "Corporate Internal Investigations," BNA/ACCA Compliance Manual (BNA 1999); *Responding to an Inquiry from the SEC Division of Enforcement* (BNA 1998); "Defending the Insider Trading Probe," 41 The Practical Lawyer 63 (September 1995); "When the SEC Comes Calling: A Step-by-Step Guide by Former Enforcers," 3 Business Law Today 13 (ABA July/August 1994), Branch Chief, 1986-1988; Senior counsel, 1985-1986; Staff Attorney, 1984-1985, U.S. Securities and Exchange Commission, Division of Enforcement. Co-Chair: Task Force on Rule 102(e) of the Subcommittee on Civil Litigation and SEC Enforcement Matters of the ABA Section of Business Law. Chair, Committee on Broker-Dealer Regulation and SEC Enforcement of the D.C. Bar. (Washington Harbor Office). ***PRACTICE AREAS:*** SEC Enforcement; Securities Litigation; Internal Investigations; FCPA Compliance.

(This Listing Continued)

FOLEY & LARDNER, Washington—Continued

SAMUEL J. WINER, admitted to bar, 1974, Massachusetts; 1975, District of Columbia. *Education:* Wesleyan University (B.A., cum laude, 1971); Boston University (J.D., 1974). Editor, Boston University Law Review, 1973-1974. Author: "New Limitations on the Scope of Discretion of the Commissioner of Internal Revenue," 54 Boston University Law Review 425, 1974. Co-author: "Corporate Disclosure: When and How Do the Securities Laws Require Public Companies to Announce Merger Negotiations," Legal Times, Vol. IX, No. 43, 1987; "Liability of Accountants for Audits of Savings and Loan Associations," 7 The Review of Banking and Financial Services 199 (Standard & Poors, December 7, 1991); "Anticipating and Responding to an Inquiry by the SEC Enforcement Division's Working Group on Insurance Companies," 14 Insurance Litigation Reporter 581 (Shepard's, December 1992); "Prompt Action Taken in Response to SEC Investigation May Ease Impact of Potentially Long, Burdensome Process," 9 BNA's Corporate Counsel Weekly 8 (February 2, 1994); "When the SEC Comes Calling: A Step-by-Step Guide by Former Enforcers," 3 Business Law Today 13 (ABA July/August 1994), reprinted in Bowne Digest, Vol. 8, No. 10, p.5 (October 1994); "Ex Parte Contacts with Officers and Employees in SEC Investigations," 8 Insights: The Corporate and Securities Law Advisor 13 (Prentice Hall Law and Business, November 1994); "Reducing the Liability Exposure of Derivatives Dealers," *The Review of Securities and Commodities Regulation,* Vol. 27, No. 22 (Standard & Poor's Dec. 21, 1994); "Defending The Insider Trading Probe," *The Practical Lawyer,* Sept. 1995; *Responding to an Inquiry from the SEC Division of Enforcement,* BNA Corporate Practice Series, No. 72 (1998). Law Clerk to Chief Justice Thomas H. Roberts, Supreme Court of Rhode Island, 1974-1975 term. Staff Attorney, 1977-1979 and Special Counsel, 1979-1981, Division of Enforcement, U.S. Securities and Exchange Commission. Member: Public Securities Association; Market Regulation and Civil Litigation and SEC Enforcement Matters Subcommittees of the ABA Committee on Federal Regulation of Securities; Broker-Dealer Subcommittee of the ABA Securities Litigation Committee; Securities Industry Association, Legal and Compliance Section. (Washington Harbor Office). ***PRACTICE AREAS:*** Business Law; Broker-Dealer.

MICHAEL D. WOLK, admitted to bar, 1984, Michigan (Not admitted in District of Columbia). *Education:* University of Maryland (B.A., Political Science, 1980); Thomas M. Cooley Law School (J.D., summa cum laude, 1984). ***PRACTICE AREAS:*** Business Law; SEC Compliance. ***Email:*** mwolk@foleylaw.com

JEFF ZIMMERMAN, admitted to bar, 1973, District of Columbia; 1977, U.S. Supreme Court. *Education:* Amherst College (A.B., 1970); George Washington University (J.D., magna cum laude, 1973). Senior Trial Attorney, Land and Natural Resources Division, U.S. Department of Justice, 1973-1979. Senior Counsel, American Mining Congress, 1979-1980. Manager, Environmental Regulatory and Legislative Affairs, ARCO Chemical Company, 1980-1981. Senior Counsel and Director of Environmental Health and Safety Regulation and Compliance, Occidental Petroleum Corporation, 1981-1989. *Member:* Federal and American (Vice-Chairman, Water Quality Committee, 1982-1986; Member: Natural Resources, Energy and Environmental Law Section; Litigation Section, Environmental Litigation Committee; Co-Chair, Environmental Enforcement Conference, 1991-1994; 1998) Bar Associations; The District of Columbia Bar. (Washington Harbor Office). ***PRACTICE AREAS:*** Regulatory Law; Environmental Law; OSHA; Environmental Litigation; Real Estate. ***Email:*** jzimmerman@foleylaw.com

GARY M. ZINKGRAF, admitted to bar, 1988, Wisconsin; 1989, Maryland; 1990, District of Columbia, U.S. District Court, District of Maryland, District of Columbia and Eastern District of Wisconsin, U.S. Court of Appeals, Fourth and Seventh Circuits. *Education:* University of Wisconsin (B.A., 1985; J.D., 1988). Order of the Coif. Associate Editor, Wisconsin Law Review, 1987-1988. Law Clerk, Honorable John W. Reynolds, U.S. District Court, Eastern District of Wisconsin, 1988-1990. Member, Wisconsin Law Review. *Member:* State Bar of Wisconsin; American Bar Association. (Washington Harbor Office). ***PRACTICE AREAS:*** Litigation; Patent Litigation; Transportation. ***Email:*** gzinkgraf@foleylaw.com

RETIRED PARTNERS

EDWIN JASON DRYER, admitted to bar, 1940, New York; 1946, Utah; 1951, Oregon and U.S. Supreme Court; 1953, U.S. Court of Military Appeals; 1954, District of Columbia. *Education:* Yale University (B.A., 1937); Yale Law School (LL.B., 1940). Phi Beta Kappa. Co-Author, "Water Resources Law," Vol. III of Report of President's Water Resources Policy Commission, 1950. Attorney, Securities & Exchange Commission, 1940-1941. Assistant General Counsel, Bonneville Power Administration, Portland, Oregon, 1948-1950. Deputy Administrator and General Counsel, Defense Electric Power Administration, Washington, D.C., 1951-1953. *Member:* The District of Columbia Bar; Bar Association of the District of Columbia; Federal and American (Member, Sections on: Antitrust and Administrative Law) Bar Associations; Utah State Bar; American Law Institute. [Col., U.S. Army Transportation Corps, active duty, 1941-1946; Reserve, 1938-1968]. ***PRACTICE AREAS:*** Energy (Oil and Gas and Electric Power); Antitrust Law.

DONALD D. JEFFERY, admitted to bar, 1961, Ohio; 1967, U.S. District Court for the District of Columbia Circuit; 1967, U.S. Court of Customs and Patent Appeals; 1968, District of Columbia; 1970, U.S. Claims Court; 1971, U.S. Supreme Court; 1977, Court of Appeals of Maryland; 1979, Virginia; 1982, U.S. Court of Appeals for the Federal Circuit; registered to practice before U.S. Patent and Trademark Office. *Education:* University of Wisconsin (B.S.Min.E., 1958); George Washington University (LL.B., 1961). Author: "The Patentability and Infringement of Sport Varieties," Journal of the Patent Office Society, pp. 645-658, October, 1977. Co-Author: "Section 101 Plant Patents—Panacea or Pitfall?" American Patent Law Association, Selected Legal Papers, Volume 1 Number 2, 1984; "Patent Protection for Plants," Genetic Engineering News, Volume 4 No. 3, March-April 1984. Co-Author: "Intellectual Property Rights in Biotechnology Worldwide," Stockton Press, 1987. Patent Examiner, U.S. Patent Office, 1957-1960. *Member:* The District of Columbia Bar; Maryland State and American Bar Associations; American Intellectual Property Law Association; Virginia State Bar; Maryland Patent Law Association; CIOPORA (International Community of Breeders of Asexually Reproduced Ornamentals).

ARTHUR SCHWARTZ, admitted to bar, 1963, Virginia, District of Columbia and Nebraska; 1963-1982, U.S. Court of Customs and Patent Appeals; 1965, U.S. Court of Appeals for District of Columbia Circuit; 1968, U.S. Supreme Court; 1971, Maryland; 1982, U.S. Court of Appeals for the Federal Circuit; registered to practice before U.S. and Canadian Patent and Trademark Offices. *Education:* Iowa State University (B.S.I.E., 1958); George Washington University (J.D., 1963). Phi Alpha Delta; Alpha Pi Mu. Author: "The Foreign Trademark Owner Living With American Products Liability Law," The North Carolina Journal of International Law and Commercial Regulation, Vol. 12, Issue 3, 1987; "La Révision de la Loi Americaine Sur Les Marques," APRAM meeting, Paris, France, January, 1989 and BMM Meeting, Antwerp, Belgium, April, 1989; "Foreign Registration in the U.S.: Use or Lose," Trademark World, Sept. 1990; "Warning to Trademark Applicants: Be Prepared to Prove Intent to Use," National Law Journal, 16 May 1994; "New Mark on the Map: Community Trade Marks," Legal Times, 1996; "Dilution Comes of Age: The United States, Europe and South Africa," The Trademark Reporter, Vol. 87, 1-33, 1997. Adjunct Professor, Trademark Law, The Columbus School of Law, The Catholic University of America, 1988-1998. Lecturer: Co-Chair, "Trademark Basics," (U.S.T.A.), Arlington, Va., Sept. 1991; "Trademark Litigation," (I N.T.A.), Tokyo, Japan, Oct. 1993; Co-Chair, "Community Trademark/Madrid Protocol Forum" (INTA), New York, NY, Feb. 1996. Patent Examiner (Electronics), U.S. Patent Office, 1960-1963. *Member:* The District of Columbia Bar ; Nebraska State, Maryland State and American Bar Associations; Virginia State Bar; American Intellectual Property Law Association; Patent and Trademark Institute of Canada; International Trademark Association; Association Francaise des Praticians du Droit des Marques et des Modèles; Association Benelux des Conseils en Marques et Modēles; European Community Trade Mark Practitioners Association. ***LANGUAGES:*** French. ***REPORTED CASES:*** Sunrise Jewelry Mfg. Corp. v. Fred S.A., 175 F3d 1322 (Fed. Cir. 1999). ***PRACTICE AREAS:*** Intellectual Property Law. ***Email:*** aschwartz@foleylaw.com

OF COUNSEL

JOHN H. CHETTLE, admitted to bar, 1966, Transvaal, South Africa; 1984, District of Columbia. *Education:* University of Natal, Pietermaritzburg, South Africa (B.A., 1959); Oxford University, Oxford, England (M.A., 1962); University of Witwatersrand, Johannesburg, South Africa (LL.B., 1966); Georgetown University (LL.M., 1983). University of Natal Scholar; Rhodes Scholar; John Higden Scholar, Magdalen College, Oxford; Senior Scholar, St. Antony's College, Oxford. Author: "The Law and Policy of Divestment of South African Stock," in Law and Policy in International Business The International Law Journal of Georgetown University Law Center, Vol. 15, No. II, 1983; "The Politicization of the International Monetary Fund," South Africa International, Vol. 14, No. 2, 1983. Council Member, South African Institute of International Affairs, 1974-1975. *Member:* The District of Columbia Bar; American Bar Association. (Washington Harbor Office). ***PRACTICE AREAS:*** International Trade Law; Immigration Law; Charitable Law. ***Email:*** jchettle@flks.com

WALTER FREEDMAN, admitted to bar, 1937, Missouri; 1940, U.S. Supreme Court; 1946, District of Columbia. *Education:* Washington University (A.B., 1937; J.D., 1937); Harvard University (LL.M., cum laude, 1938). Order of the Coif; Phi Beta Kappa; Omicron Delta Kappa. Recipient, Washington University School of Law Distinguished Alumni Award, 1995. Editor-in-Chief, Washington University Law Quarterly, 1936-1937. Attorney, Securities and Exchange Commission, 1938-1941. Attorney, Bituminous Coal Division, 1941-1942. Chief Counsel, Office of Export Control, 1942-1943. Deputy Director and later Director, Export Control, Foreign Economic Administration, 1943-1945. Decorated Chevalier de l' Order de la Couronne (Belgium) 1950. *Member:* The District of Columbia Bar; Bar Association of the District of Columbia; Federal and American Bar Associations; American Law Institute. (Also Mem-

(This Listing Continued)

ber, Freedman, Levy, Kroll & Simonds, Washington, D.C.) (Washington Harbor Office). ***PRACTICE AREAS:*** Securities Law; Corporate Law; Probate Law; Estate Planning Law. ***Email:*** wfreedman@flks.com

MARY GAYLE HOLDEN, admitted to bar, 1980, Virginia; 1981, U.S. District Court, Eastern District of Virginia; 1994, U.S. Court of Appeals, Fourth Circuit; 1998, District of Columbia. *Education:* Roanoke College (B.A., cum laude, 1970); University of Virginia (J.D., 1980). Cardinal Key. Phi Alpha Delta. Affirmative Action Committee Loudoun County, Virginia. Member, Committee for Dulles, 1984— (Board of Directors, 1998—). Board of Directors, American Cancer Society (Loudoun County), 1997—; Board of Directors, Women in Technology, 1999—; Board of Directors, Loudoun County Transportation Association. Listed in: Who's Who in American Law; Who's Who of American Women; Who's Who in America; Outstanding People of the Twentieth Century. *Member:* District of Columbia Bar; Virginia Bar Association. (Washington Harbour Office). ***PRACTICE AREAS:*** Corporate Law; Business Law; Trusts and Estates; Real Estate Law. ***Email:*** mholden@foleylaw.com

PETER C. LINZMEYER, admitted to bar, 1968, Wisconsin; 1981, District of Columbia and U.S. Supreme Court. *Education:* Georgetown University (B.S., 1964; J.D., 1967); Sorbonne University of Paris, Paris, France; University of Frankfurt am Main, Frankfurt, Germany. International Legal Exchange Program, Germany, 1975. *Member:* District of Columbia Bar; American Bar Association; State Bar of Wisconsin; American Society of International Law. (Washington Harbor Office). ***LANGUAGES:*** German and French. ***PRACTICE AREAS:*** Joint Ventures; Licensing; Business Acquisitions; Distribution; Strategic Alliances; Project Finance; Telecommunications; Biotechnology; High Technology; Corporate Law. ***Email:*** pclinzmeyer@foleylaw.com

BARBARA ANN McDOWELL, admitted to bar, 1987, Virginia; registered to practice before the U.S. Patent and Trademark Office (Not admitted in District of Columbia). *Education:* Westminster College (B.S., Biology, magna cum laude, 1975); University of Pittsburgh (B.S.Chem.E., magna cum laude, 1981); George Washington University (J.D., with honors, 1987). *Member:* Virginia State Bar. (Washington Harbor Office). ***PRACTICE AREAS:*** Chemistry; Biotechnology; Patent Prosecution.

PETER E. PANARITES, admitted to bar, 1959, District of Columbia. *Education:* Cornell University (B.S., 1954); Georgetown University (J.D., 1959). Phi Delta Phi. Attorney, Securities and Exchange Commission, 1959-1961. Visiting Associate Professor, "Federal Securities Laws and the Hospitality Industry," Cornell University, 1978-1986. *Member:* The District of Columbia Bar; American Bar Association. (Washington Harbor Office). ***PRACTICE AREAS:*** Securities Law; Corporate Law. ***Email:*** ppanarites@flks.com

SPECIAL COUNSEL

NORMAN C. BENSLEY, admitted to bar, 1969, New York; 1979, U.S. District Court, Southern and Eastern Districts of New York (Not admitted in District of Columbia). *Education:* Princeton University (A.B., 1965); London School of Economics (M.Sc., 1966); Columbia University (J.D., 1969); New York University (LL.M., Taxation, 1972). Author: "Untangling the Tax Code, How the New Code Ties Up Your Insurance Clients," The Brief, Winter, 1987. Co-Author: Life Insurance and Annuity Products 1988 Development in Securities and Tax Law, Tort & Insurance Law Journal, Winter, 1989; Life insurance Tax Legislation: The Current Agenda, Tax Analysts, The Insurance Tax Review, Vol. 2, No. 3, January-February, 1988; Reconciling Yourself to the 1993 Tax Act, The Brief, Winter, 1994. Speaker ALI-ABA Program on Life Insurance Company Products, 1985 and 1986. Vice President, New York Life Insurance Company, 1973-1986. *Member:* The Association of the Bar of the City of New York (Member, Committee on International Human Rights, 1980-1984); New York State (Member: Section on Taxation, Committees on Employee Benefits, Insurance and Financial Institutions; Co-Chair, Committee on Insurance Companies, Tax Section, 1988-1989) and American (Chair, Committee on Taxation of Insurance Companies, 1985-1987; Member: Section on Tort and Insurance Practice; Committee on Employee Benefits, 1988-1989; Section Council. Continuing Legal Education Board, 1992-1994; Financial Officer, 1995-1999) Bar Associations. (Washington Harbor Office). ***PRACTICE AREAS:*** Taxation Law; Insurance Law; Corporate Law; Securities. ***Email:*** nbensley@flks.com

KAREN M. GRANE, admitted to bar, 1988, Virginia; 1990, District of Columbia; U.S. District Court, Eastern District of Virginia; U.S. District Court, District of Maryland; U.S. District Court for the District of Columbia. *Education:* Ohio Northern University (B.A., 1977); George Mason University School of Law (J.D., 1988). Co-Author: "Most Dangerous Violations," ABA Bank Compliance Magazine, Fall & Winter, 1984. Associate National Bank Examiner, Office of the Comptroller of the Currency, 1977-1981, Management Consultant for financial institutions, 1983-1985. *Member:* American Bar Association. (888 Sixteenth Street Office). ***PRACTICE AREAS:*** Civil Practice; Banking Law. ***Email:*** kgrane@foleylaw.com

JAYME A. HULEATT, admitted to bar, 1988, Virginia; 1995, Texas; 1998, District of Columbia; registered to practice before U.S. Patent and Trademark Office. *Education:* West Chester State College (B.A. in biology, with honors, 1970); Rutgers University Graduate School (M.S., in microbiology, 1973); Rutgers University School of Business Administration (M.B.A., 1980); Catholic University of America (J.D., 1986). *Member:* Virginia State Bar; State Bar of Texas; The District of Columbia Bar; American Bar Association (Member, Science and Technology Section); American Intellectual Property Lawyers Association (Member, Biotechnology Committee); Patent Office Society. (Washington Harbor Office). ***PRACTICE AREAS:*** Patents; Trademarks; Copyrights; Intellectual Property.

NINA M. OSSEIRAN, admitted to bar, 2000, California (Not admitted in District of Columbia). *Education:* American University (B.A., International Relations, 1990); Santa Clara University (J.D., 2000). *Member:* State Bar of California. ***LANGUAGES:*** German. ***PRACTICE AREAS:*** Intellectual Property; Patents; Trademarks. ***Email:*** nosseiran@foleylaw.com

SENIOR COUNSEL

ALICIA J. BATTS, admitted to bar, 1991, New York; 1993, District of Columbia. *Education:* Harvard University (A.B., 1987); Columbia University (J.D., 1990). Member, 1988-1990 and Managing Editor, 1989-1990, Columbia Business Law Review. Lecturer, Hot Topics Panel, American Bar Association, Spring Meeting. Co-Editor, Clayton Act Newsletter. Attorney Advisor, FTC Commissioner Mozelle Thompson. *Member:* The District of Columbia Bar; American Bar Association (Member, Antitrust Section; Member, Clayton Act Committee). (Washington Harbor Office). ***PRACTICE AREAS:*** Antitrust Litigation. ***Email:*** abatts@foleylaw.com

GEORGE C. BECK, admitted to bar, 1993, Virginia; 1994, District of Columbia and U.S. Court of Appeals for the Federal Circuit; registered to practice before U.S. Patent and Trademark Office. *Education:* Georgetown University (B.S., 1989; J.D., 1993). Phi Beta Kappa; Alpha Sigma Nu. *Member:* American Bar Association; American Intellectual Property Law Association. (Washington Harbor Office). ***PRACTICE AREAS:*** Intellectual Property. ***Email:*** gbeck@foleylaw.com

TODD J. BURNS, admitted to bar, 1995, Virginia; 1997, Minnesota; 1999, District of Columbia; registered to practice before U.S. Patent and Trademark Office. *Education:* State University of New York at Buffalo (B.S.Ch.E., magna cum laude, 1989); George Washington University (J.D., with honors, 1995). Tau Beta Pi. *Member:* American Intellectual Property Law Association. (Washington Harbor Office). ***PRACTICE AREAS:*** Intellectual Property; Chemical Patent; Pharmaceutical Patent Law. ***Email:*** tburns@foleylaw.com

SIMON E. DANCE, admitted to bar, 1991, Pennsylvania; 1993, District of Columbia. *Education:* Imperial College of Science & Technology (B.Sc., 1976); Notre Dame Law School (J.D., 1991). Phi Delta Phi. Editor-in-Chief, Journal of Legislation, 1990-1991. Society of Petroleum Engineers, 1973-1988. BP Petroleum Development Ltd., 1975-1978. Manager, Sohio Petroleum Co., 1978-1984. Senior Manager, BP America (1984-1988). *Member:* Pennsylvania and American (Member: Litigation Section; SONREEL; Intellectual Property Section) Bar Associations; District of Columbia Bar. (Washington Harbor Office). ***PRACTICE AREAS:*** Litigation; Intellectual Property Litigation; Environmental Law. ***Email:*** sdance@foleylaw.com

ALLISON C. GEORGE, admitted to bar, 1993, Maryland; 1994, District of Columbia, U.S. District Court, District of Columbia; 1996, Connecticut. *Education:* Yale University (B.A., 1990); Duke University (J.D., 1993). Member, Duke Law Journal. *Member:* District of Columbia Bar; State Bar Association of Maryland; American Bar Association. (Washington Harbor Office). ***LANGUAGES:*** French. ***PRACTICE AREAS:*** International Business Law (40%); White Collar Crime (40%); Commercial Litigation (20%).

BRYAN B. HOUSE, admitted to bar, 1993, Wisconsin; 1997, Virginia; 1999, District of Columbia. *Education:* Indiana University (B.A., with distinction, 1990) Phi Beta Kappa; University of Minnesota (J.D., cum laude, 1993). Primary Editor, Journal of Law and Inequality. (Washington Harbor Office). ***REPORTED CASES:*** Westowne Shoes, Inc. v. Brown Group, Inc., 104 F.3d 994 (7th Cir. 1997); Badger III Limited Partnership v. Howard, Needles, Tammen & Bergendoff, 539 N.W. 2d 904 (Wis. Ct. App. 1995); M & I First National Bank v. Episcopal Homes Management, Inc., 536 N.W. 2d 175 (Wis. Ct. App. 1995); Roeder v. ChemRex, Inc. and UNUM Life Insurance Company, 863 F.Supp. 817 (E.D. Wis. 1994); Securities and Exchange Commission v. Rauscher Pierce Refsnes, Inc., 17 F. Supp. 2d 985 (D. Ariz. 1998). ***PRACTICE AREAS:*** Litigation; Securities Litigation; Securities Enforcement; White Collar Crime.

PATRICK J. KEARNEY, admitted to bar, 1983, Maryland; 1984, District of Columbia; 1987, U.S. Supreme Court; 1991, Virginia. *Education:* University of Illinois (A.B., 1980); Washington College of Law, American University (J.D., 1983). *Member:* Montgomery County, Maryland State and Virginia Bar Associations; Maryland Bankruptcy and Northern Virginia Bankruptcy Bar Associations. (Washington Harbor Office). ***PRACTICE AREAS:*** Litigation; Debtor and Creditor Rights. ***Email:*** pkearney@flks.com

MARY MICHELLE KILE, admitted to bar, 1995, California; 1996, District of Columbia and U.S. Court of Appeals for the Federal Circuit; registered to practice before U.S. Patent and Trademark Office. *Education:* Duke Univer-

(This Listing Continued)

(This Listing Continued)

FOLEY & LARDNER, Washington—Continued

sity (B.S.E., cum laude, 1990) Tau Beta Pi; University of Virginia (J.D., 1994). Law Clerk to Judge Randall R. Rader, U.S. Court of Appeals for the Federal Circuit, 1994-1995. *Member:* Federal Circuit Bar Association; American Bar Association. (Washington Harbor Office). ***PRACTICE AREAS:*** Intellectual Property.

JEFFREY G. MICKLOS, admitted to bar, 1994, Pennsylvania and Maryland (Not admitted in District of Columbia). *Education:* Villanova University (B.A., 1989); Catholic University of America (J.D., 1993). Author: "Developing Provider-Sponsored Organization Solvency Standards Through Negotiated Rulemaking," 51 Admin. L. Rev. 261, 1999. Staff Attorney, Office of General Counsel, Health Care Financing Division, U.S. Department of Health and Human Services. (Washington Harbor Office). ***REPORTED CASES:*** Appalachian Reg. HealthCare v. Shalala, 131 F.3d 1050 (D.C.Cir. 1997); Foothill Presbyterian Hosp. v. Stalala, 152 F.2d 1132 (9th Cir. 1998). ***PRACTICE AREAS:*** Health Care; Litigation. ***Email:*** jmicklos@foleylaw.com

JEFFREY S. NEWMAN, admitted to bar, 1994, Pennsylvania; 2000, District of Columbia. *Education:* University of Rochester (B.A. in Political Science, cum laude, 1991); Case Western Reserve University School of Law (J.D., 1994; M.A. in Political Science, with honors, 1994). Editor-in-Chief, 1993-1994 and Associate Editor, 1992-1993, Case Western Reserve University Journal of International Law. Harmon S. Potter Scholar, University of Rochester, 1989-1991. Co-Author, "Leveraging Technical Data and Computer Software In Major Defense Acquisition Programs Under the New DFARS Final Rule," Contract Management, March, 1996. (888 Sixteenth Street Office). ***PRACTICE AREAS:*** Government Contracts; Litigation. ***Email:*** jnewman@foleylaw.com

LEO F. ORENSTEIN, admitted to bar, 1980, California; 1984, U.S. Supreme Court; 1993, District of Columbia. *Education:* Yale University (B.A., magna cum laude, 1977); Harvard Law School (J.D., 1980). Wasserstein Fellow, Harvard Law School, Fall, 1994. Professorial Lecturer in Law, George Washington University, 1989-1990. Attorney (1985-1989), Branch Chief (1987-1991) and Assistant Chief Litigation Counsel (1991-1999), U.S. Securities and Exchange Commission, Division of Enforcement. *Member:* American Bar Association (Member, Sections on: Business Law and Litigation). (Washington Harbor Office). ***REPORTED CASES:*** SEC v. Drexel Burnham Lambert Inc., 837 F.Supp. 587 (S.D.N.Y. 1993). aff'd 16 F.3d 520 (2d Cir. 1994); SEC v. Drexel Burnham Lambert Inc., 956 F.Supp. 503 (S.D.N.Y.), aff'd, 133 F.3d 170 (2d Cir. 1997); SEC v. First City Financial Corp., 688 F.Supp. 705 (D.D.C. 1988), aff'd, 890 F.2d 1215 (D.C. Cir. 1989); SEC v. Life Partners, Inc., 898 F.Supp. 14 (D.D.C. 1995); 912 F.Supp. 4 (D.D.C. 1996); rev'd 87 F.3d 536 (D.C.Cir.); SEC v. Feminella, 947 F.Supp. 722 (S.D.N.Y. 1996); SEC v. Rana Research, Inc.; Fed. Sec. L. Rep. (CCH) 95,750 (C.D. Cal. 1990), aff'd, 8 F3d 1358 (9th Cir. 1993); Moreno v. City and County of San Francisco, 567 F. Supp. 458 (N.D. Cal. 1983). ***PRACTICE AREAS:*** Litigation; Securities Regulation; SEC and SRO Enforcement. ***Email:*** lorenstein@flks.com

PATRICK W. REILLY, admitted to bar, 1986, Pennsylvania; 1989, District of Columbia. *Education:* Boston College (B.A., Economics, magna cum laude, 1983); University of Virginia School of Law (J.D., 1986). ***PRACTICE AREAS:*** Regulatory; Surface Transportation.

ALAN D. RUTENBERG, admitted to bar, 1994, Virginia; 1996, District of Columbia. *Education:* Transylvania University (B.A., summa cum laude, 1991); Harvard University (J.D., cum laude, 1994). Harvard Ames Moot Court First Place Team; Delta Sigma Phi; Omicron Delta Kappa. (Washington Harbor Office). ***PRACTICE AREAS:*** Antitrust; Regulatory; Commercial Litigation. ***Email:*** arutenberg@foleylaw.com

RESIDENT ASSOCIATES

PAVAN KUMAR AGARWAL, admitted to bar, 1996, Virginia and District of Columbia. *Education:* University of Maryland at College Park (B.S.E.E., First in Class, with highest honors, 1993); George Washington Law School (J.D., with highest honors, 1996). Order of the Coif; Eta Kappa Nu. Law Review. Recipient, Jacob Burns Scholarship. Judicial Clerk, U.S. Court of Appeals for the Federal Circuit. *Member:* American Bar Association; American Intellectual Property Law Association. (Washington Harbor Office). ***PRACTICE AREAS:*** Electronics. ***Email:*** pagarwal@foleylaw.com

PHILLIP JOHN ARTICOLA, admitted to bar, 1994, Maryland and District of Columbia; registered to practice before U.S. Patent and Trademark Office. *Education:* University of Maryland (B.S.E.E., cum laude, 1981; M.S.E.E., 1984; J.D., with honors, 1994). Tau Beta Pi; Eta Kappa Nu; Phi Kappa Phi. Author: "Intervening Rights for Reissues and Reexaminations," Mealey's Litigation Reports-Intellectual Property, March 18, 1996; Primer: "How to Speed Up the Patent Application Process," The Intellectual Property Strategist, June, 1997; "In Re McGrew," Intellectual Property Today, January, 1998. *Member:* American Bar Association; American Intellectual Property Law

(This Listing Continued)

Association. (Washington Harbor Office). ***PRACTICE AREAS:*** Intellectual Property; Computer Law; Communications Law; Semiconductor Technology. ***Email:*** particola@foleylaw.com

SANDY M. BALLOU, admitted to bar, 1996, Wisconsin (Not admitted in District of Columbia). *Education:* Cornell College (B.A., 1993); University of Michigan (J.D., 1996). Phi Delta Phi. *Member:* State Bar of Wisconsin. (Washington Harbour Office). ***PRACTICE AREAS:*** Health Law. ***Email:*** sballou@foleylaw.com

VINEETA BATHIA, (admission pending). *Education:* Duke University (B.A., 1998); Washington University School of Law (J.D., 2001). ***PRACTICE AREAS:*** Business Law. ***Email:*** vbathia@foleylaw.com

GEORGE C. BEST, admitted to bar, 1997, Illinois; registered to practice before U.S. Patent and Trademark Office (Not admitted in District of Columbia). *Education:* University of Chicago (S.B., 1989; J.D., 1997); California Institute of Technology (Ph.D., 1995). Clerk, U.S. Court of Appeals for the Federal Circuit. (Washington Harbor Office). ***PRACTICE AREAS:*** Intellectual Property. ***Email:*** gbest@foleylaw.com

DR. THOMAS BILODEAU, (admission pending). *Education:* University of Vermont (B.S., Physics, 1982); Rensselaer Polytechnic Institute (Ph.D., Physics, 1990); George Mason University School of Law (J.D., 1999). ***PRACTICE AREAS:*** Intellectual Property; Electronics. ***Email:*** tbilodeau@foleylaw.com

RACHEL D. BORAK, admitted to bar, 1999, Illinois (Not admitted in District of Columbia). *Education:* University of Illinois (B.A., 1996); George Washington University (J.D., with honors, 1999). Associate, George Washington Law Review. (888 Sixteenth Street, N.W. Office). ***PRACTICE AREAS:*** Financial Services; Bankruptcy. ***Email:*** rborak@foleylaw.com

RANDY ELIZABETH BRENNER, born November 19, 1967; admitted to bar, 1998, District of Columbia; 2000, U.S. Court of Appeals for the Federal Circuit. *Education:* Smith College (A.B., cum laude, 1989); University of Illinois (J.D., 1998). Editor, Elder Law Journal. Law Clerk to Honorable Judge Alan D. Lourie, U.S. Court of Appeals for the Federal Circuit, Washington, D.C., 1998-2000. Member, Giles Rich American Inn of Court, 1998—. (Washington Harbor Office). ***PRACTICE AREAS:*** Intellectual Property; Litigation. ***Email:*** rbrenner@foleylaw.com

AARON C. CHATTERJEE, admitted to bar, 1998, Virginia; 1999, District of Columbia and U.S. District Court, Eastern District of Virginia; registered to practice before U.S. Patent and Trademark Office. *Education:* Indian Institute of Technology, New Delhi, India (B.S., Eng., 1984); Drexel University (M.S., Computer Science, 1990); George Mason Law School (J.D., with honors, 1997). Upsilon Pi Epsilon. Member, Law Review, 1996-1997. *Member:* American Bar Association; American Intellectual Property Law Association; Federal Circuit Bar Association. (Washington Harbor Office). ***LANGUAGES:*** Hindu and Bengali. ***PRACTICE AREAS:*** Intellectual Property. ***Email:*** achatterjee@foleylaw.com

JI-LI CHUNG, (admission pending). *Education:* National Taiwan University (B.S., Chemical Engineering, 1993; M.B.A., 1995); University of California at Los Angeles School of Law (J.D., 2001). ***LANGUAGES:*** Mandarin Chinese and Taiwanese. ***PRACTICE AREAS:*** Biotechnology; Pharmaceutical; Chemical; Intellectual Property.

MARTIN COSENZA, (admission pending). *Education:* Syracuse University (B.S., Aerospace Engineering, 1993); Eastern College (M.A., Education, 1994); Drexel University (M.S., Mechanical Engineering, 1997); Georgetown University Law Center (J.D., 2001). ***PRACTICE AREAS:*** Intellectual Property; Consumer and Industrial Products.

CHRISTIAN B. DINNEEN-LONG, admitted to bar, 1995, Illinois and U.S. District Court, Northern District of Illinois; 1996, Wisconsin; 2000, Missouri (Not admitted in District of Columbia). *Education:* University of Wisconsin-Madison (B.B.A., 1992); Chicago-Kent College of Law, Illinois Institute of Technology (J.D., 1995). Member, Chicago-Kent Law Review, 1994-1995. Executive Board Vice President, Chicago-Kent Moot Court Honor Society, 1994-1995. *Member:* Chicago Bar Association. (Washington Harbor Office). ***PRACTICE AREAS:*** Business Law. ***Email:*** cdinneen-long@foleylaw.com

ADAM J. EISNER, (admission pending). *Education:* University of Pennsylvania (B.A., cum laude, 1998); George Washington University Law School (J.D., with honors, 2001). ***PRACTICE AREAS:*** Securities Litigation. ***Email:*** aeisner@foleylaw.com

ROBERT M. HANSEN, admitted to bar, 1999, Virginia; registered to practice before U.S. Patent and Trademark Office (Not admitted in District of Columbia). *Education:* University of Florida (M.S., 1978); George Mason University School of Law (J.D., 1999). [with U.S. Navy, 1978-1985]. (Washington Harbour Office). ***PRACTICE AREAS:*** Intellectual Property Law. ***Email:*** rhansen@foleylaw.com

JULIET DAWN HIZNAY, admitted to bar, 1997, Virginia; 1999, U.S. District Court, Eastern District of Virginia and U.S. Court of Federal Claims (Not admitted in District of Columbia). *Education:* Boston College (B.A., cum laude, 1991); George Mason University (J.D., with honors, 1997). Phi Alpha

(This Listing Continued)

Delta (Justice, Mason Chapter, 1996-1997; Marshal, National Capital Area Alumni Chapter, 1997—). *Member:* Arlington County Bar Association; Virginia State Bar. ***LANGUAGES:*** Spanish and Portuguese. ***PRACTICE AREAS:*** Litigation; Commercial Law; Business Law; Misdemeanors; Theft. ***Email:*** jhiznay@foleylaw.com

PARVIN HUDA, born St. Louis, Missouri, June 9, 1970; admitted to bar, 1999, Illinois (Not admitted in District of Columbia). *Education:* Georgetown University (B.A., 1992; J.D., 1999). (Washington Harbor Office). ***LANGUAGES:*** French. ***PRACTICE AREAS:*** Communications Law; Regulatory law; International Trade. ***Email:*** phuda@foleylaw.com

KRISTEN GRIM HUGHES, admitted to bar, 1998, Virginia; 1999, District of Columbia, Maryland and U.S. District Court, Eastern District of Virginia. *Education:* University of California (B.A., with honors, 1970; M.A., 1972); Georgetown University (J.D., 1998). *Member:* District of Columbia Bar; Maryland State, Federal and American Bar Associations; Virginia State Bar; The Association of Trial Lawyers of America. William B. Bryant American Inn of Court (Program Chair, 1999—). (888 Sixteenth Street Office). ***PRACTICE AREAS:*** Litigation. ***Email:*** khughes@foleylaw.com

JOO-MEE KIM, admitted to bar, 1991, Korea as Patent and Trademark Attorney (Not admitted in District of Columbia). *Education:* College of Pharmacy, Seoul National University (B. Pharm., 1989); George Washington University Law School (J.D., 1999). ***LANGUAGES:*** Korean and Japanese. ***PRACTICE AREAS:*** Intellectual Property; Biotechnology; Pharmaceutical; Chemical. ***Email:*** jmkim@foleylaw.com

SUSAN M. C. KOVAROVICS, admitted to bar, 1996, Virginia; 1997, District of Columbia. *Education:* Drew University (B.A., summa cum laude, 1993); Georgetown University Law Center (J.D., cum laude, 1996). Phi Beta Kappa. (Washington Harbor Office). ***PRACTICE AREAS:*** International Law; Corporate Law.

MARVIN C. LUNDE, III, admitted to bar, 1998, Texas; 1999, District of Columbia. *Education:* University of North Carolina at Chapel Hill (B.A., 1993); University of Texas (J.D., 1998). (Washington Harbor Office). ***PRACTICE AREAS:*** Securities Law.

THOMAS W. MAC ALLISTER, admitted to bar, 1999, Virginia; 2000, District of Columbia. *Education:* James Madison University (B.S., with honors, 1987); Duke University (Ph.D., 1991); George Washington University (J.D., 1998). (Washington Harbor Office). ***PRACTICE AREAS:*** Intellectual Property. ***Email:*** tmacallister@foleylaw.com

GEOFFREY M. McNUTT, admitted to bar, 1995, Virginia (Not admitted in District of Columbia). *Education:* College of William & Mary (B.A., 1992); George Mason University School of Law (J.D., 1995). Member, 1993-1995 and Assistant Articles Editor, 1994-1995, George Mason Law Review. U.S. Patent and Trademark Office, 1996-2000. (Washington Harbor Office). ***PRACTICE AREAS:*** Trademark Law; Copyright. ***Email:*** gmcnutt@foleylaw.com

AMY WILSEY MILLER, admitted to bar, 1999, Virginia; 2000, District of Columbia. *Education:* Oklahoma State University (B.A., cum laude, 1991); Georgetown University (J.D., cum laude, 1999). Charles Fahy Inns of Court. (Washington Harbor Office). ***PRACTICE AREAS:*** Litigation. ***Email:*** amiller@foleylaw.com

NALINI K. PANDE, admitted to bar, 1997, Maryland; 1998, District of Columbia. *Education:* Princeton University (A.B., magna cum laude, 1993); Harvard Law School (J.D., cum laude, 1997). Executive Editor, Harvard International Law Journal, 1996-1997. Author: "The Fine Line Between Innocent Mistake and Reckless Disregard," Journal of Health Care Compliance," Vol. 2, No. 3, May/June 2000. *Member:* Maryland State Bar Association; The District of Columbia Bar. (Washington Harbor Office). ***PRACTICE AREAS:*** Health Law; Regulatory Law. ***Email:*** npande@foleylaw.com

ARDEN T. PHILLIPS, admitted to bar, 1998, Maryland; 2000, District of Columbia. *Education:* Columbia University (B.A., 1993); Duke University (J.D., 1998). *Member:* American and National Bar Associations. ***PRACTICE AREAS:*** Business Law; Mergers and Acquisitions. ***Email:*** aphillips@foleylaw.com

JOHN C. PISA-RELLI, admitted to bar, 1993, Pennsylvania; 1996, District of Columbia and U.S. Court of International Trade. *Education:* LaSalle University (B.A., 1988); Widener University Law School (J.D., 1991). Phi Delta Phi. Harrington Inn Honor Chapter, 1989—. Consulting Attorney, Gardner, Carton & Douglas; Graham & James, 1995-1996. With: U.S. Department of Commerce, Bureau of Export Administration, 1991-1994; U.S. Department of State, Office of Defense Trade Controls, 1994-1995; U.S. Department of the Treasury, Office of Foreign Assets Control, 1996-1999. *Member:* American Bar Association (Section of International Law and Practice); Society for International Affairs. (Washington Harbour Office). ***PRACTICE AREAS:*** International Trade; Foreign Asset Control; International Trade Regulation; International Corporate Law; Antiboycott Compliance; Export Compliance. ***Email:*** jpisarelli@foleylaw.com

LEON RADOMSKY, born January 4, 1969; admitted to bar, 1999, Virginia; 2000, District of Columbia. *Education:* Columbia University (B.S., magna cum laude, 1991); George Mason University School of Law (J.D., 1999). Member, Materials Research Society, 1991-1994. Author: "Intellectual Property Today," Journal of the Patent & Trademark Office Society, August 2000. *Member:* American Intellectual Property Lawyers Association (Vice-Chair, Committee on: Young Lawyers, 2000—). (Washington Harbor Office). ***PRACTICE AREAS:*** Patent Law; Intellectual Property. ***Email:*** lradomsky@foleylaw.com

IRWIN PERRY RAIJ, admitted to bar, 1995, Florida and District of Columbia. *Education:* University of Miami (B.B.A., 1992); Washington University, St. Louis (J.D., 1995). ***PRACTICE AREAS:*** Public Affairs; Regulatory Law.

NORMAN J. RICH, admitted to bar, 1992, Pennsylvania (Not admitted in District of Columbia). *Education:* American University (B.A., 1988); Temple University School of Law (J.D., 1992). Associate Editor, Temple International and Comparative Law Journal, 1990-1992. Author: "United States Participation in the Madrid Protocol: What is the Price of Admission?" Temple International and Comparative Law Journal, Volume 5, Number 1, 1991. Former Attorney-Advisor, U.S. Patent and Trademark Office, 1993-1997. Member, U.S. Patent and Trademark Office Society, 1993-1997. *Member:* American Bar Association; International Trademark Association. (Washington Harbor Office). ***PRACTICE AREAS:*** Intellectual Property; Trademarks; Copyrights. ***Email:*** nrich@foleylaw.com

GARTH D. RICHMOND, admitted to bar, 1997, South Carolina; 1997, District of Columbia. *Education:* Central Florida Community College (A.S., 1985); University of Iowa (B.S., 1993; J.D., 1997). Member: Health Physics Society, 1990—; National Registry of Radiation Protection Technologists, 1985—. (888 Sixteenth Street Office). ***PRACTICE AREAS:*** Energy Law; Nuclear Energy. ***Email:*** grichmond@foleylaw.com

GREGG H. ROSENBLATT, admitted to bar, 1999, Maryland (Not admitted in District of Columbia). *Education:* Wake Forest University (B.S., magna cum laude, 1986; M.S., Physics, 1987); George Mason University School of Law (J.D., 1999). Member, Optical Society of America, 1988-1997. (Washington Harbor Office). ***PRACTICE AREAS:*** Patent Prosecution; Patent Applications; Patent Litigation; Licensing; Intellectual Property Agreements. ***Email:*** grosenblatt@foleylaw.com

HEIDI ELISABETH ROSENBERG, admitted to bar, 1999, Illinois; 2000, District of Columbia. *Education:* Harvard University (A.B., 1996; J.D., 1999). (Washington Harbor Office). ***LANGUAGES:*** French. ***PRACTICE AREAS:*** Intellectual Property Litigation. ***Email:*** hrosenberg@foleylaw.com

GARY S. ROVNER, admitted to bar, 1995, Illinois; 1997, District of Columbia. *Education:* Dartmouth College (B.A., 1992); George Washington University (J.D., 1995). (Washington Harbor Office). ***PRACTICE AREAS:*** Environmental Law; Patent Litigation; Trademark Litigation. ***Email:*** grovner@foleylaw.com

DAVID SETH SANDERS, admitted to bar, 1996, Maryland, District of Columbia, U.S. District Court, District of Maryland, and U.S. Court of Appeals, Fourth Circuit; 1997, Virginia, U.S. Court of Appeals for the District of Columbia Circuit and U.S. District Court for the District of Columbia; U.S. District Court, Eastern District of Virginia; U.S. Bankruptcy Court. *Education:* University of Michigan (B.A., 1992); Georgetown University Law Center (J.D., 1995). Co-Author, "Asset Protection and Affordable Housing Projects Involving Exempt Organizations," Journal of Asset Protection, May/June 1998. Contributing Author: "Sanders Michael I., Partnership and Joint Ventures Involving Tax Exempt Organizations," John Wiley & Son. *Member:* Montgomery County and Virginia Bar Associations; Maryland State Bar Association, Inc.; District of Columbia Bar. (Washington Harbor Office). ***PRACTICE AREAS:*** Corporate Law; Mergers and Acquisitions; Securities. ***Email:*** dsanders@flks.com

ANKUR D. SHAH, admitted to bar, 1997, Virginia; 1999, District of Columbia; registered to practice before U.S. Patent and Trademark Office. *Education:* The Pennsylvania State University (B.S., with honors, Electrical Engineering, 1992); George Washington University (J.D., 1997). Tau Beta Pi; Eta Kappa Nu. Author: "The Burden of Patent Prosecution in Light of Hilton Davis and its Progeny," Patent World, Issue 122, May 2000. *Member:* Asian Pacific American Bar Association; American Intellectual Property Law Association. (Washington Harbor Office). ***PRACTICE AREAS:*** Intellectual Property. ***Email:*** ashah@foleylaw.com

MORGAN WAYNE SHELTON, admitted to bar, 1999, Georgia (Not admitted in District of Columbia). *Education:* Radford University (B.S., 1995); Mercer University (J.D., cum laude, 1999). Member, Mercer University Law Review Board. (Washington Harbor Office). ***PRACTICE AREAS:*** Electronic Business; Information Technology. ***Email:*** mshelton@foleylaw.com

DR. CHRISTAL A. SHEPPARD, (admission pending). *Education:* University of Delaware (B.A., Biological Sciences, 1990); University of Michigan (Ph.D. and M.S. in Cellular and Molecular Biology, 1998); Cornell University (J.D., 2001). ***PRACTICE AREAS:*** Intellectual Property; Biotechnology. ***Email:*** csheppard@foleylaw.com

HOWARD N. SHIPLEY, admitted to bar, 1996, Virginia; 1998, District of Columbia; registered to practice before U.S. Patent and Trademark Office.

(This Listing Continued)

FOLEY & LARDNER, Washington—Continued

Education: Virginia Polytechnic Institute and State University (B.S., 1987); George Mason University (J.D., 1996). Law Clerk to the Hon. Claude M. Hilton, U.S. District Court, Eastern District of Virginia, Alexandria Division, 1996-1997. Patent Examiner, 1994-1995. *Member:* American Bar Association; American Intellectual Property Law Association; Giles Rich American Inn of Court. [U.S. Navy, Nuclear Submarine Officer, 1987-1994]. (Washington Harbor Office). ***PRACTICE AREAS:*** Intellectual Property. ***Email:*** hshipley@foleylaw.com

JAMES M. SILBERMANN, admitted to bar, 1996, Virginia and U.S. Court of Appeals, Fourth Circuit; 1997, District of Columbia; 1998, U.S. Court of Appeals for the Federal Circuit and U.S. District Court for the District of Columbia; registered to practice before U.S. Patent and Trademark Office. *Education:* University of Maryland (B.S.Ch.E., 1989); Catholic University of America (J.D., magna cum laude, 1996). Author: "The North American Free Trade Agreement's Effect on Pharmaceutical Patents: A Bitter Pill to Swallow or A Therapeutic Solution," 12 J. Contemp. Health L. & Pol'y 607, 1996. *Member:* American Bar Association; American Intellectual Property Law Association; Giles Sutherland Rich American Inn of Court. (Washington Harbor Office). ***PRACTICE AREAS:*** Intellectual Property; Patent Law. ***Email:*** jsilbermann@foleylaw.com

ANTHONY H. SON, admitted to bar, 1997, California; 1999, District of Columbia; registered to practice before U.S. Patent and Trademark Office. *Education:* University of Maryland, Baltimore County (B.S., Biochemistry and Molecular Biology, 1994); Benjamin N. Cardozo School of Law (J.D., 1997). ***PRACTICE AREAS:*** Intellectual Property; Litigation. ***Email:*** ason@foleylaw.com

TODD N. SPALDING, admitted to bar, 2001, Virginia (Not admitted in District of Columbia). *Education:* Brigham Young University (B.S., Zoology, 1991); John Hopkins University (M.S., Biotechnology, 1998); College of William & Mary (J.D., 2001). Order of the Coif. ***PRACTICE AREAS:*** Intellectual Property; Biotechnology. ***Email:*** tspalding@foleylaw.com

FREDERIC T. TENNEY, admitted to bar, 2000, Virginia (Not admitted in District of Columbia). *Education:* Duke University (B.S.E., 1997; J.D., 2000). (Washington Harbor Office). ***PRACTICE AREAS:*** Patent Prosecution; Patent Litigation. ***Email:*** ftenney@foleylaw.com

CYNTHIA E. TIDLER, admitted to bar, 1997, Maryland; 2001, District of Columbia and U.S. District Court, Federal District of District of Columbia. *Education:* University of Maryland (B.A., Government and Politics, high honors, 1993); Harvard University Law School (J.D., 1997). ***LANGUAGES:*** Spanish and German. ***PRACTICE AREAS:*** Litigation; Compliance; Counseling; Government Enforcement. ***Email:*** ctidler@foleylaw.com

C. ANTHONY TRAMBLEY, admitted to bar, 1995, Maryland, U.S. Court of Federal Claims and U.S. Court of Appeals for the Federal Circuit; 1996, District of Columbia; 1997, U.S. District Court, District of Maryland. *Education:* University of California, Davis (B.A., 1989); Junior Year Abroad, University of Bath, England; Vermont Law School (J.D., cum laude, 1994). Law Clerk, The Honorable Christine Odell Cook Miller, U.S. Court of Federal Claims, 1994-1995. (Washington Harbor Office). ***PRACTICE AREAS:*** Litigation. ***Email:*** ctrambley@foleylaw.com

HEATHER M. TREW, admitted to bar, 2001, New York and District of Columbia. *Education:* Stanford University (B.A., English, 1997); University of Michigan School of Law (J.D., 2000). ***PRACTICE AREAS:*** Litigation. ***Email:*** htrew@foleylaw.com

MARC K. WEINSTEIN, admitted to bar, 1999, Virginia; registered to practice before U.S. Patent and Trademark Office (Not admitted in District of Columbia). *Education:* Pennsylvania State University (B.S.E.E., 1993); Georgetown University (J.D., 1999). Notes Editor, Law & Policy in International Business, 1997-1998. Examiner, U.S. Patent and Trademark Office, 1994-1996. *Member:* Federal Circuit Bar Association. (Washington Harbor Office). ***PRACTICE AREAS:*** Intellectual Property; Software Patents; Computer and Software Patents; Electronic Patents. ***Email:*** mkweinstein@foleylaw.com

RODERICK B. WILLIAMS, admitted to bar, 1992, Virginia, U.S. District Court, Eastern District of Virginia and U.S. Court of Appeals, Fourth Circuit; 1993, District of Columbia, Maryland, U.S. District Court for the District of Columbia and U.S. Court of Appeals for the District of Columbia Circuit; 1994, U.S. District Court, District of Maryland, U.S. Bankruptcy Court, Eastern District of Virginia and U.S. Court of Federal Claims. *Education:* Colgate University (B.A. in Political Science, cum laude, 1989); George Washington University (J.D., 1992). *Member:* Alexandria, Fairfax, Maryland State and American Bar Associations; District of Columbia Bar; Virginia State Bar. (888 Sixteenth

(This Listing Continued)

Street Office). ***REPORTED CASES:*** Helmick v. Town of Warrenton, 254 Va. 225, 492 S.E.2d 113 (1997). ***PRACTICE AREAS:*** Civil Litigation; Government Contract Law; Bankruptcy. ***Email:*** rbwilliams@foleylaw.com

(See Foley & Lardner Listings at Milwaukee and Madison, Wisconsin, Chicago, Illinois, Annapolis, Maryland, Jacksonville, Orlando, Tallahassee, Tampa and West Palm Beach, Florida, Los Angeles, Sacramento, San Diego and San Francisco, California, Denver, Colorado and Detroit, Michigan for professional biographies on attorneys resident in those offices)

FORD & HARRISON LLP

1300 19TH STREET, N.W., SUITE 700
WASHINGTON, D.C. 20036
Telephone: 202-719-2000
Fax: 202-719-2077
Email: firm@fordharrison.com
URL: http://www.fordharrison.com

Atlanta, Georgia Office: 600 Peachtree at the Circle Building, 1275 Peachtree Street, N.E., 30309. Telephone: 404-888-3800. Fax: 404-888-3863.

Denver, Colorado Office: 1675 Broadway, Suite 2150, 80202. Telephone: 303-592-8860. Fax: 303-592-8861.

Los Angeles, California Office: 333 South Grand Avenue, Suite 3680, 90071. Telephone: 213-680-3410. Fax: 213-680-4161.

Memphis, Tennessee Office: 6750 Poplar Avenue, Suite 600, 38138. Telephone: 901-291-1500. Fax: 901-291-1501.

Miami, Florida Office: 516 Ingraham Building, 25 S.E. 2nd Avenue, 33131. Telephone: 305-379-3811. Fax: 305-358-5933.

Orlando, Florida Office: 300 South Orange Avenue, Suite 1300, 32801. Telephone: 407-418-2300. Fax: 407-418-2327.

Tampa, Florida Office: 101 E. Kennedy Boulevard, Suite 900, 33602. Telephone: 813-261-7800. Fax: 813-261-7899.

Jacksonville, Florida Office: 121 West Forsyth Street, Suite 1000, P.O. Box 41566, 32203. Telephone: 904-356-8073. Fax: 404-358-2319.

Birmingham, Alabama Office: 505 North 20th Street, Suite 1201, 35203. Telephone: 205-254-9480. Fax: 205-254-9848.

Labor and Employment Law representing Employers, including Employment Litigation, Discrimination, Harassment, Class Action Litigation, Affirmative Action, Wrongful Termination, Wage and Hour Law, ADA/FMLA, Airline Labor Law, Labor Union Organizing, Collective Bargaining, Arbitration, Layoffs and Plant Closings, Mergers and Acquisitions (Labor), Employment Contracts, Alternative Dispute Resolution, Business Immigration, Employee Benefits, Workplace Safety and Environmental Law.

FIRM PROFILE: Since its founding in 1978, the firm has grown to over 130 lawyers with offices in Atlanta, Birmingham, Denver, Jacksonville, Los Angeles, Memphis, Miami, Orlando, Tampa and Washington, D.C. Nonetheless, the firm remains committed to meeting the individual needs of each client in a practical and economical fashion.

MEMBERS OF FIRM

RONALD C. HENSON, born Clayton, Georgia, October 8, 1942; admitted to bar, 1973, Georgia and U.S. District Court, Northern District of Georgia; 1980, U.S. Court of Appeals, Sixth Circuit; 1981, U.S. Court of Appeals, Fifth and Eleventh Circuits; 1985, U.S. Court of Appeals, Seventh Circuit; 1996, District of Columbia. *Education:* University of North Carolina (B.A., 1967); Emory University (J.D., with distinction, 1972). *Member:* State Bar of Georgia; The District of Columbia Bar; American Bar Association. ***PRACTICE AREAS:*** Management Labor Law; Contracts; Collective Bargaining; Arbitration. ***Email:*** rhenson@fordharrison.com

JOSHUA M. JAVITS, born New York, N.Y., January 2, 1950; admitted to bar, 1979, District of Columbia; 1983, California. *Education:* Yale University (B.A., 1972); Georgetown University (J.D., 1978). Author: "High Court to Revisit Issue of Mandatory Arbitration," National Law Journal," October 5, 1998; "Mediation's On-Grab a Spoon," HR Magazine, April 2000; "Mandatory Arbitration and Labor Not an Ideal Mix," National Law Journal, June 26, 2000; "Airline Collective Bargaining in a Global Environment," 62 Journal of Transportation Law, Logistics and Policy 187, 1995; "Emergency Board Procedures Under the Railway Labor Act" and "Grievance Procedures," ALI-ABA Course on Airline Labor and Employment Law, 1994-1998; "The International Trade Commission," October, 1976 to September, 1977, 10 Law and Policy Int'l. Bus. 26, 1978. Adjunct Faculty, Labor Law, Georgetown University Law Center, 1990-1999. Chairman and Member, National Mediation Board, 1988-1993. *Member:* The District of Columbia Bar (Member, Steering Committee, Labor Law Section); State Bar of California; Industrial Relations Research Association. ***PRACTICE AREAS:*** Arbitration; Collective Bargaining; Labor Relations. ***Email:*** jjavits@fordharrison.com

PETER J. PETESCH, born Evanston, Illinois, January 25, 1960; admitted to bar, 1985, Maryland; 1986, District of Columbia, U.S. District Court, District

(This Listing Continued)

of Maryland, U.S. District Court for the District of Columbia and U.S. Court of Appeals, Third, Fourth and Ninth Circuits; U.S. Supreme Court. *Education:* University of Michigan (A.B., with high honors, magna cum laude, 1982); Georgetown University (J.D., 1985). Author: "Legal Trends" Column, for HR Magazine. *Member:* District of Columbia Bar; Maryland State Bar Association, Inc.; American Bar Association; Society for Human Resource Management. ***LANGUAGES:*** Spanish. ***PRACTICE AREAS:*** Discrimination; Employment Termination; Executive Employment Law; Labor Relations; Disability and Workplace Harassment Law. ***Email:*** ppetesch@fordharrison.com

DAVID A. ROSENBERG, born Linden, New Jersey, January 5, 1958; admitted to bar, 1986, Maryland; 1992, District of Columbia. *Education:* Ithaca College (B.A., cum laude, 1979); University of Maryland (M.A., 1981); University of Baltimore (J.D., with honors, 1985). Member, Montgomery County Chamber of Commerce. Member, University of Baltimore, Student Mentoring Program. *Member:* Montgomery County Bar Association (Member, Labor Law Section); The District of Columbia Bar (Member, Labor Law Section); Maryland Defense Trial Bar. ***PRACTICE AREAS:*** Employment Litigation; Employment Termination; Discrimination; Sexual Harassment Law; Commercial Litigation; Insurance Coverage. ***Email:*** drosenberg@fordharrison.com

RESIDENT SENIOR COUNSEL

DANNIE B. FOGLEMAN, born Stuttgart, West Germany, October 26, 1948; admitted to bar, 1975, South Carolina; 1984, North Carolina; 1988, District of Columbia. *Education:* University of North Carolina (B.A., 1970); University of South Carolina (J.D., cum laude, 1974); Georgetown University (LL.M., 1981). Wig and Robe Honor Society. Adjunct Professor of Law, Georgetown University Law Center, 1991-1993. *Member:* South Carolina Bar; District of Columbia Bar; North Carolina State Bar; American Bar Association (Member, Employee Rights and Responsibilities Committee, Labor and Employment Law Section). [Lt. Jg., U.S.N.R., 1970-1972]. ***PRACTICE AREAS:*** Litigation; Management Labor Law; Discrimination. ***Email:*** dfogleman@ fordharrison.com

RESIDENT ASSOCIATES

KEVIN M. KRAHAM, born Albany, New York, August 15, 1970; admitted to bar, 1998, District of Columbia. *Education:* Boston University (B.A., 1992); Washington College of Law of American University (J.D., 1996). *Member:* The District of Columbia Bar. ***LANGUAGES:*** Spanish. ***PRACTICE AREAS:*** Labor and Employment Law; Mediation. ***Email:*** kkraham@fordharrison.com

DARLENE H. SMITH, born Washington, D.C., September 15, 1970; admitted to bar, 1997, Maryland (Not admitted in District of Columbia). *Education:* University of Virginia (B.A., 1992); Syracuse University (J.D., 1996). *Member:* Maryland State and American Bar Associations; Charlotte E. Ray Inn of Court. ***PRACTICE AREAS:*** Employment Law; Employment Litigation; Labor Law. ***Email:*** dhsmith@fordharrison.com

RANDY C. SPARKS, JR., born Portsmouth, Virginia, July 12, 1971; admitted to bar, 1996, Virginia (Not admitted in District of Columbia). *Education:* University of Virginia (B.A., 1993); Marshall-Wythe School of Law, College of William & Mary (J.D., 1996). *Member:* Virginia State Bar. ***PRACTICE AREAS:*** Labor and Employment Law; Insurance Coverage. ***Email:*** rsparks@ fordharrison.com

MARK WISE, born Brooklyn, New York, January 5, 1956; admitted to bar, 1984, New York; 1986, Virginia; 1989, South Carolina (Not admitted in District of Columbia). *Education:* Rensselaer Polytechnic Institute (B.S., 1978); Pace University (J.D., 1983). *Member:* South Carolina Bar. ***PRACTICE AREAS:*** Labor and Employment. ***Email:*** mwise@fordharrison.com

REPRESENTATIVE CLIENTS: ABX Air, Inc.; Argyle Communications, Inc.; Athlete's Foot Group, Inc.; Atlantic Southeast Airlines; Automobile Dealers Educational Assistance Foundation, Inc. (Cleveland, Ohio ADA); Behavioral Healthcare Corporation; Champion Enterprises, Inc.; Coats North America; COMAIR, Inc.; Corrections Corporation of America; Darden Resturants, Inc.; Delta Air Lines, Inc.; DHL Airways, Inc.; Federal Express Corp.; Gategourmet International; General Shale Products Corp.; HCA-The Healthcare Company; Hendrick Automotive Group; Holiday Inns, Inc.; Hunter Fan Co.; Kay-Bee Toy Stores; Kellogg Company; Kliklok Corp.; The Knight Publishing Co. (Charlotte, Observer); LIN Television Corp.; Lockheed Martin Corporation; The Mead Corporation; Nestle USA, Inc.; Nike, Inc.; Northern Telecom, Inc.; Qwest Communications; Regional Airline Assn.; Saturn Retail Enterprises, Inc.; Schering-Plough, Inc.; Solvay Automotive, Inc.; Southwest Airlines Co.; Spherion Workforce Architects; The Weather Channel; WorldSpan; Wyle Laboratories, Inc.

(For Complete Biographical Data on all Personnel, see Professional Biographies at Atlanta, Georgia)

J. GORDON FORESTER, JR.

1742 N STREET, N.W.
WASHINGTON, D.C. 20036
Telephone: 202-293-3353
Facsimile: 202-785-2210
Email: jgfcadence@earthlink.net

Civil and Criminal Litigation, General and Appellate Practice, Trusts and Estates.

(This Listing Continued)

J. GORDON FORESTER, JR., born Wilkesboro, North Carolina, January 14, 1933; admitted to bar, 1962, District of Columbia; 1965, U.S. Court of Appeals for the District of Columbia Circuit; 1968, U.S. Supreme Court; 1988, U.S. Court of Appeals, Fourth Circuit; 1993, Maryland. *Education:* University of North Carolina (B.S., 1955); George Washington University (LL.B., 1962). Phi Delta Phi. Author: "Protracted Litigation in Airline Seniority Disputes," Labor Law Journal, March, 1979; "Return the 12-man Jury," Litigation, Summer, 1984; "The Language of the Law," Litigation Summer, 1998. Law Clerk to Leonard P. Walsh, U.S. District Court for the District of Columbia, 1963-1964. Member: Judicial Conference District of Columbia Circuit, 1981, 1982, 1992; District of Columbia Judicial Conference, 1993; The Civil Justice Reform Act Advisory Group, 1990-1993. Executive Committee, Council for Court Excellence, 1988—. Chairman, Special Committee for Lawyer Malpractice, District of Columbia Bar, 1987. *Member:* District of Columbia Bar (President-elect, 2000); Bar Association of the District of Columbia; Maryland State and American (Member, Litigation Section) Bar Associations; The Counsellors (President, 1984-1985). [Lt. Cmdr., U.S. Navy, 1955-1958]. ***REPORTED CASES:*** Carey v. Hume 492 F.2d 631 (D.C. Cir. 1974); D.C. v. Colston 468 A. 2d 954 (D.C. 1983); Hoai v. Sun Refining and Marketing Co. 935 F.2d 308 (D.C. Cir. 1991); Propert v. D.C. 948 F.2d 1327 (D.C. Cir. 1991).

ELIZABETH FORGOTSON, P.C.

WASHINGTON, D.C.

(See Rockville, Maryland)

Government Contracts, Federal Contracts, Local Government Contracts, Arbitration, Bid Protests, Debtor and Creditor Law, Commercial Collections, Small Business Law, Freedom of Information, Professional Immigration, Zoning, Homeowners' Association Law.

JACQUELINE FOX

5746 MACARTHUR BOULEVARD, N.W.
WASHINGTON, D.C. 20016-5303
Telephone: 202-966-5610
Fax: 202-966-5476
URL: http://www.lawyers.com/jacquelinefox
Email: jfox@jacquelinefox.com
URL: http://www.jacquelinefox.com

Managed Care - Patient Advocate - Elder Law.

FIRM PROFILE: Jacqueline Fox represents patients and doctors in appeals with their managed care organizations, health insurance companies and HMOs. Also works as an expert witness in cases brought by other attorneys.

JACQUELINE FOX, born Manhasset, N.Y., September 27, 1966; admitted to bar, 1991, Maryland; 1993, District of Columbia; 1994, U.S. District Court, District of Columbia. *Education:* Sarah Lawrence College (B.A., 1988); Georgetown University (J.D., cum laude, 1991; LL.M., 1995). *Member:* The District of Columbia Bar. ***PRACTICE AREAS:*** Managed Care; Health Insurance Coverage; Health Maintenance Organizations; Patients Rights; Health Care Reimbursement; Elder Law.

RENEE ISLA FOX

Established in 1982
1725 K STREET N.W.
12TH FLOOR, SUITE 1202
WASHINGTON, D.C. 20006
Telephone: 202-429-0444
Fax: 202-429-9340
Email: rif@reneefox.com
URL: http://www.lawyers.com/reneeislafoxlaw

Estate Planning, Estate Administration and Litigation. Conservatorship and Guardianship Law, Elder Law, Wills and Trusts, Probate.

RENEE ISLA FOX, born 1936; admitted to bar, 1979, District of Columbia. *Education:* Brandeis University (A.B., 1957); Catholic University of America (J.D., 1979). Newsletter Editor, Estates, Trusts and Probate Section, District of Columbia Bar, 1998-2000. Member, Probate Rules Advisory Committee, D.C. Superior Court, 1989-1994. Lecturer: Women's Bar Association; District of Columbia Bar; Legal Counsel for the Elderly on topics including estate planning, Elderlaw, conservatorships and disability planning, 1994—. *Member:* District of Columbia Bar (Vice Chair, Steering Committee Estates, Trusts and Probate Law Section, 1992-1994; Chair, Elder Law and Disability Planning Committee, 1994-1997 and 2000-2001); National Association of Elder Law Attorneys; District of Columbia Estate Planning Council. ***LANGUAGES:*** Spanish.

FOXKISER

Established in 1986

750 SEVENTEENTH STREET, N.W.
SUITE 1100
WASHINGTON, D.C. 20006
Telephone: 202-778-2300
Telecopier: 202-778-2330

General Civil Practice, Administrative Law, Civil Litigation and Legislative Practice at the Federal, State and International Levels, with emphasis on Biomedical Research, Environmental Compliance, Food, Drug and Cosmetic Regulation, Health Care Reimbursement, Medical Publishing and Communications Issues.

ALLAN M. FOX, born Philadelphia, Pennsylvania, January 6, 1948; admitted to bar, 1972, Pennsylvania; 1980, District of Columbia. *Education:* Temple University (A.B., 1969; J.D., 1972); Yale University (LL.M., 1975). Co-Author, with Alan R. Bennett, "Legislative History of the Drug Price Competition and Patent Term Restoration Act of 1984," Food and Drug Institute, 1987. Assistant District Attorney, Frauds Division, City of Philadelphia, 1972. Assistant Attorney General, Department of Justice, Commonwealth of Pennsylvania, 1972-1974. General Counsel, Governor's Council on Drug and Alcohol Abuse, Commonwealth of Pennsylvania, 1972-1974. Special Counsel, Commissioner of Health, Department of Health, Commonwealth of Pennsylvania, 1974. Fellow in Law, Science and Medicine, Yale Law School, 1974-1975. General Counsel, Health and Scientific Research Subcommittee, Committee on Labor and Public Welfare, U.S. Senate, 1975-1977. Chief of Staff and Chief Legislative Assistant to Senator Jacob K. Javits, U.S. Senate, 1977-1979. *Member:* The District of Columbia Bar; Pennsylvania, Federal and American Bar Associations; National Health Lawyers Association; American Society of Law and Medicine. ***Email:*** afox@foxkiser.com

JOHN DANIEL KISER, born Bowman, South Carolina, August 10, 1946; admitted to bar, 1974, Georgia; 1985, District of Columbia. *Education:* Furman University (B.A., magna cum laude, 1968); Yale University (M.M.A., 1971); Emory University (J.D., 1974). Book Review Editor, Emory Law Journal, 1973-1974. Law Clerk to the Hon. Frank A. Hooper, U.S. District Judge, Northern District of Georgia, 1974-1975. Assistant Regional Attorney, 1976-1980, Senior Attorney/Litigation, Public Health Division, 1980-1983 and Special Assistant to the Deputy General Counsel, 1983-1985, U.S. Department of Health and Human Services. *Member:* The District of Columbia Bar; State Bar of Georgia; National Health Lawyers Association.

MICHAEL B. WAITZKIN, born Coral Gables, Florida, November 24, 1949; admitted to bar, 1974, California; 1975, District of Columbia; 1981, U.S. Supreme Court. *Education:* University of Virginia (B.A., 1971); Stanford University (J.D., 1974); Yale University (LL.M., 1975). Phi Beta Kappa, Echols Scholar. Member, Stanford Law Review. Fellow, Law, Science and Medicine, Yale Law School. Trial Attorney, Public Defender Service, District of Columbia, 1975-1979. Staff Member, Senator Edward M. Kennedy, 1979-1980. Faculty Member, National Institute for Trial Advocacy, 1984-1995. Special Counsel to the President and Liaison to the Vice President's Counsel, White House Counsel's Office, 1997-1998. *Member:* The District of Columbia Bar; State Bar of California. ***Email:*** mwaitzkin@foxkiser.com

JOHN M. ENGEL, born Boulder, Colorado, May 26, 1963; admitted to bar, 1992, Virginia and U.S. Court of Appeals, Fourth Circuit; 1994, District of Columbia. *Education:* Catholic University of America (B.A., magna cum laude, 1985); Georgetown University (J.D., magna cum laude, 1992). Order of the Coif. Winner/Best Advocate, Georgetown University Law Center Leahy Prize Moot Court Competition, 1990. Member, National Moot Court Team, Georgetown University Law Center, 1990-1991. Listed in: Who's Who Among American Law Students; Georgetown University Roll of Best Advocates. Senior Staff and Member, The Tax Lawyer, 1989-1992. Member, Legislative and Professional Staff, U.S. Senator Steve Symms, 1983-1986. *Member:* The District of Columbia Bar; Virginia State Bar; American Bar Association. ***PRACTICE AREAS:*** Biotechnology; Food and Drug Regulation; Intellectual Property. ***Email:*** jengel@foxkiser.com

MATTHEW D. PETERSON, born Munich, Bavaria, Germany, July 23, 1968; admitted to bar, 1994, Pennsylvania; 1995, U.S. Court of Appeals, Third Circuit; 1996, District of Columbia and U.S. Court of Appeals, District of Columbia; U.S. Court of Appeals, Federal Circuit. *Education:* American University (B.A., 1990); New York University (J.D., 1994); University of Paris (Law, 1994). *Member:* The District of Columbia Bar. ***LANGUAGES:*** French and Spanish. ***PRACTICE AREAS:*** Food and Drug Regulation; Health Law; Litigation. ***Email:*** mpeterson@foxkiser.com

DIANE E. ROBERTSON, PH.D., born New Brunswick, New Jersey, September 16, 1963; admitted to bar, 1999, Maryland; 2000, District of Columbia. *Education:* Mount Holyoke College (B.A., cum laude, 1986); Boston College (Ph.D., Chemistry, 1991); Georgetown University (J.D., cum laude, 1998). Sigma Xi. Executive Editor, Georgetown Journal of Legal Ethics, 1996-1997. Scientist, Food and Drug Administration, 1992-1997. Health Policy Fellow to Senate Labor and Human Resources Committee, 1997-1998. *Member:* American Chemical Society. ***PRACTICE AREAS:*** Food and Drug Regulation; Legislation. ***Email:*** drobertson@foxkiser.com

ASSOCIATES

WILLIAM E. HOLTZ, born Erie, Pennsylvania, August 17, 1972; admitted to bar, 2001, Maryland and District of Columbia. *Education:* University of Pittsburgh (B.S., Pharmacy, 1995); Georgetown University Law Center (J.D., 2000). Registered Pharmacist, Virginia, 1995; Maryland, 1997. Author: "Consumer Directed Prescription Drug Advertising: Effects on Public Health," Journal of Law and Health, Vol. 13 Issue 2, 1998-1999. *Member:* The District of Columbia Bar. ***PRACTICE AREAS:*** Food and Drug Regulation; Health Law. ***Email:*** wholtz@foxkiser.com

ANITA D. NOVITT, born Newark, New Jersey, January 6, 1957; admitted to bar, 2000, New Jersey (Not admitted in District of Columbia). *Education:* Rutgers University, Newark (M.S., 1982); Seton Hall University, Newark (J.D., 1998). ***Email:*** anovitt@foxkiser.com

GENINE C. SWANZEY, born New York, N.Y., October 16, 1973; admitted to bar, 2000, Maryland and New Jersey; 2001, District of Columbia. *Education:* College of the Holy Cross (B.A., magna cum laude, 1995); Georgetown University Law Center (J.D., 1999). Phi Beta Kappa; Psi Chi. Author: "Using Class Actions to Litigate Mass Torts: Is There Justice for the Individual?" Georgetown Journal of Legal Ethics, 1998. Formerly with Wilkinson, Barker, Knauer, LLP. *Member:* American Bar Association. ***PRACTICE AREAS:*** Food and Drug Regulation; Health Law. ***Email:*** gswanzey@foxkiser.com

OF COUNSEL

ANDREW C. FISH, born Princeton, New Jersey, May 17, 1967; admitted to bar, 1995, Virginia; 1996, District of Columbia. *Education:* Yale University (B.A., 1989); Stanford University (J.D., 1995). *Member:* American Bar Association. ***PRACTICE AREAS:*** Biotechnology; Life Sciences; Regulatory Law; Government Affairs.

DAVID E. MEADE, born Philadelphia, Pennsylvania, August 23, 1934; admitted to bar, 1962, District of Columbia and Virginia. *Education:* Williams College (B.A., 1956); University of Virginia (LL.B., 1962). [Sgt., U.S. Army, 1956-1959]. ***Email:*** dmeade@foxkiser

GRAYDON J. FORRER, born Flint, Michigan, December 29, 1958; admitted to bar, 1986, Michigan; 2001, District of Columbia. *Education:* Duke University (B.A., magna cum laude, 1981); Washington University School of Law (J.D., 1985). Presidential Appointment, Director of Consumer Affairs, Food and Nutrition Service, U.S. Department of Agriculture, 1994-1998. *Member:* Genesee County Bar Association; State Bar of Michigan. ***PRACTICE AREAS:*** Food and Drug Regulation; Health Care. ***Email:*** gforrer@foxkiser.com

(This Listing Continued)

FRAGOMEN, DEL REY, BERNSEN & LOEWY, P.C.

1212 NEW YORK AVENUE, N.W., SUITE 850
WASHINGTON, D.C. 20005
Telephone: 202-223-5515
Facsimile: 202-371-2898
URL: http://www.fragomen.com

New York, New York Office: 515 Madison Avenue. Telephone: 212-688-8555. Facsimile: 212-758-7215; 212-319-5236.

Buffalo, New York Office: 50 Fountain Plaza, Suite 1320. Telephone: 716-856-5444. Facsimile: 716-856-5151.

Coral Gables, Florida Office: 241 Sevilla Avenue, Suite 802. Telephone: 305-774-5800. Facsimile: 305-774-6666.

Chicago, Illinois Office: 150 North Wacker Drive, Suite 1120. Telephone: 312-263-6101. Facsimile: 312-346-1970.

San Francisco, California Office: 100 Pine Street, Suite 1575. Telephone: 415-986-1446. Facsimile: 415-986-7964.

Los Angeles, California Office: 12121 Wilshire Boulevard, Suite 1001. Telephone: 310-820-3322. Facsimile: 310-820-2702.

Santa Clara, California Office: 2804 Mission College Boulevard, 2nd Floor. Telephone: 408-919-0600. Facsimile: 408-919-0615.

Irvine, California Office: 18401 Von Karman Avenue, Suite 255. Telephone: 949-261-0209. Facsimile: 949-261-2821.

Sacramento, California Office: 2399 Gateway Oaks Drive, Suite 200. Telephone: 916-564-6900. Facsimile: 916-564-5015.

Oakland, California Office: 1999 Harrison Street, Suite 1400. Telephone: 510-444-4208. Facsimile: 510-444-4873.

San Diego, California Office: 11512 El Camino Real, Suite 300. Telephone: 858-847-9060. Facsimile: 858-847-9119.

Stamford, Connecticut Office: One Atlantic Street. Telephone: 203-352-1871. Facsimile: 203-352-1874.

(This Listing Continued)

Iselin, New Jersey Office: Fragomen, Del Rey, Bernsen & Loewy, 99 Wood Avenue South. Telephone: 732-906-1230. Facsimile: 732-906-9190.

Troy, Michigan Office: Fragomen, Del Rey, Bernsen and Loewy, P.L.L.C., 2301 West Big Beaver Road, Suite 225. Telephone: 248-649-5404. Facsimile: 248-649-5121.

Atlanta, Georgia Office: 1175 Peachtree Street, N.E., 100 Colony Square, Suite 700. Telephone: 404-249-9300. Facsimile: 404-249-9291.

Dallas, Texas Office: 5000 Quorum Drive, Suite 215. Telephone: 972-233-6646. Facsimile: 972-233-3134.

Phoenix, Arizona Office: 3101 North Central Avenue, Suite 1470. Telephone: 602-631-9200. Facsimile: 602-631-9300.

Vienna, Virginia Office: 1595 Spring Hill Road, Suite 320. Telephone: 703-748-2380. Facsimile: 703-748-2387.

Brussels, Belgium Office: Vossendreef 6-B.I-Dreve Des Renards, 1180 Brussels, Belgium. Telephone: 011-322-374-7-37. Facsimile: 011-322-374-90-45.

U.S. and Foreign Immigration and Nationality Law.

SCOTT J. FITZGERALD, born Needham, Massachusetts, July 16, 1967; admitted to bar, 1992, Connecticut; 1993, New York (Not admitted in District of Columbia). *Education:* The Johns Hopkins University (B.A., 1989); Fordham University (J.D., 1992). Business Editor, Fordham Urban Law Journal. *Member:* Association of the Bar of the City of New York (Member, Sports Law Committee, 1994-1997); Federal and American Bar Associations; United States Chamber of Commerce (Labor Relations Committee); American Immigration Lawyers Association; Council for Emerging National Securities Affairs (Board Member and Treasurer). ***Email:*** sfitzgerald@fragomen.com

---

LUCRECIA M. BLAIR, born Honduras, December 22, 1973; admitted to bar, 1999, Virginia; 2000, District of Columbia. *Education:* Rollins College (B.A., 1995); Syracuse University (J.D., 1999). Business Editor, The Digest Law Journal, 1998-1999. *Member:* Virginia State Bar; The District of Columbia Bar. ***PRACTICE AREAS:*** Immigration Law. ***Email:*** lblair@fragomen.com

RANDALL K. HULME, born Philadelphia, Pennsylvania, November 14, 1956; admitted to bar, 1990, District of Columbia. *Education:* American University (B.A., 1983); Columbus School of Law, Catholic University of America (J.D., 1990). Pi Sigma Alpha. Member, Mortar Board. Associate Moot Court. Recipient, American Jurisprudence Award, Corporations. *Member:* District of Columbia Bar; American Bar Association; American Immigration Lawyers Association. ***Email:*** rhulme@fragomen.com

STACY SHORE, born Pennsylvania, August 11, 1971; admitted to bar, 1999 Pennsylvania (Not admitted in District of Columbia). *Education:* Brandeis University (B.A., 1993); Temple University (J.D., 1999). *Member:* American Immigration Lawyers Association; National Lawyers Guild. ***Email:*** sshore@fragomen.com

OF COUNSEL

SAM BERNSEN, born New York, N.Y., July 13, 1919; admitted to bar, 1950, New York; 1977, District of Columbia. *Education:* City College of the City of New York; Brooklyn Law School (LL.B., cum laude, 1949). Distinguished Lecturer, Catholic University Law School, 1979-1985. Adjunct Professor of Law, American University, Washington, D.C., 1983—. District Director, New Orleans, 1955-1958; Assistant Commissioner, Adjudications, 1965-1974; General Counsel, 1974-1977, Immigration and Naturalization Service. Director of Legal Research, Select Commission on Immigration and Refugee Law, 1981-1982.

GARY N. MERSON, born Lewiston, Maine, July 20, 1972; admitted to bar, 1998, Massachusetts (Not admitted in District of Columbia). *Education:* Vanderbilt University (B.A., 1994); Tulane Law School (J.D., cum laude, 1998). Advocacy Associate, American Immigration Lawyers Association. *Member:* American Immigration Lawyers Association. ***LANGUAGES:*** Spanish. ***Email:*** gmerson@fragomen.com

(For complete biographical data on Personnel at New York, New York and Buffalo, New York, Coral Gables, Florida, Chicago, Illinois, San Francisco, Los Angeles, Santa Clara, Irvine, Sacramento, Oakland and San Diego, California, Stamford, Connecticut, Iselin, New Jersey, Troy, Michigan, Atlanta, Georgia, Dallas, Texas, Phoenix, Arizona, Vienna, Virginia and Brussels, Belgium, see Professional Biographies at those locations)

FRANCH, JARASHOW, BURGMEIER & SMITH, P.A.

SUITE 514
2600 VIRGINIA AVENUE, N.W.
WASHINGTON, D.C. 20036
Telephone: 202-337-3080
Fax: 202-337-1185
Email: fjhlaw@erols.com
URL: http://www.FJBSlaw.com

Annapolis, Maryland Office: 111 Cathedral Street. P.O. Box 827. Telephone: 410-268-5600; 410-269-0463; 301-261-1332. Fax: 410-269-1446.

Baltimore, Maryland Office: Suite 900, 210 N. Charles Street. Telephone: 410-269-0463.

Affiliated With: Coston & Lichtman, New York, Los Angeles, San Francisco, South Florida and Boston.

General Civil and Trial Practice in all State and Federal Courts. Family Law, Divorce, Custody, Negligence, Personal Injury, Equipment Leasing, Corporation, Business Law, Bankruptcy, Insurance Law. Insurance Defense, Employment Law.

(For Biographical data on Personnel, see Professional Biographies at Annapolis, Maryland)

FREDRIKSON & BYRON, P.A.

Established in 1948
1825 I STREET N.W.
SUITE 400
WASHINGTON, D.C. 20006
Telephone: 202-828-6280
Fax: 202-429-2727
Email: smurphy@fredlaw.com
URL: http://www.fredlaw.com

Minneapolis, Minnesota Office: 1100 International Centre, 900 Second Avenue South, 55402-3397. Telephone: 612-347-7000. Telecopier: 612-347-7077.

London, England Office: 16 Bedford Street, Covent Garden, WC2 9HF. Telephone: 011-44-207-395-3030. Fax: 011-44-207-836-9966.

General Practice including: Advertising, Alternative Dispute Resolution, Aviation, Banking and Commercial,, Business Litigation, Business Risk Management and Compliance, Business and Tax Planning, Business Technology, Commercial Litigation, Commercial Transactions, Communications and Entertainment, Condemnation, Corporate Acquisitions and Securities, Creditor Remedies and Bankruptcy, Directors and Officers Services, Emerging Business, Eminent Domain, Employee Benefits, Employment and Labor, Environmental, Estate Planning, Probate and Trusts, Executive and Professional Compensation, Family Business, Family Law, Finance, Franchise Law, Health Care and Hospitals, High Technology and Communications, Immigration, Insurance, Intellectual Property, International Law, Litigation, Local Government and Education, Medicare Fraud and Compliance, Mergers and Acquisitions, Non-Profit Organizations, Partnerships, Property Tax, Shareholder Rights, Software Licensing, Syndications and Tax Shelters, Professional Corporations, Real Estate, Regulatory Defense, Sports Law, Travel, White Collar.

OF COUNSEL

JOHN E. MULLEN, born Appleton, Wisconsin, September 30, 1938; admitted to bar, 1964, Illinois; 1976, U.S. Supreme Court; 1977, District of Columbia. *Education:* University of Wisconsin at Madison (B.S., 1960); Harvard University (J.D., 1963); University of Chicago (M.Comp.L., 1967). Awarded, Foreign Law Fellow, University of Chicago. Author: "Export Promotion: Legal and Structural Limitation on a Broad U.S. Commitment," Law & Policy in International Business, Georgetown University Law Center, 1975. *Member:* The District of Columbia Bar; American Bar Association (Advisory Board, Central and East European Law Initiative). (Resident). ***PRACTICE AREAS:*** International Finance; International Law; Federal Administrative Law. ***Email:*** jmullen@fredlaw.com

REPRESENTATIVE CLIENTS: BSI Corporation; Campbell-Mithun-Esty Advertising Agency; Dahlberg, Inc.; Fairview Riverside Medical Center; Food Engineering Corporation; John G. Kinnard & Company; Marigold Foods Inc.; Medtronic, Inc.; Minnesota Epilepsy Group; North Memorial Health Care; Richfield Bank and Trust Co.; Pasteur Sanofi Diagnostics, S.A.; The Pillsbury Company.

(For Complete Personnel and Biographical Data, see Professional Biographies at Minneapolis, Minnesota).

FREIDEMAN, IRELAN, WARD & LAMBERTON, P.C.

1000 POTOMAC STREET, N.W., SUITE 400
WASHINGTON, D.C. 20007-3551
Telephone: 202-625-1800
Fax: 202-625-1616
Email: r.freideman@fiwllaw.com
URL: http://www.fiwllaw.com

Charities, Non-Profit Associations Law, Employment Law, Education Law, Trusts and Estate Planning and Administration, Taxation, Corporate Law, International Business and Commercial Law. Civil Litigation including Commercial Trial Work, Fiduciary and Discrimination Litigation.

FIRM PROFILE: The firm's clients include individuals, charities and non-profit organizations, educational associations and institutions, private foundations, trade associations, and public and private corporations. The firm serves a broad base of both national and international clients including individuals seeking advice as to estates and trust planning, administration and contested matters, employment law, higher education, litigation of matters in federal and local court and representation before the Foreign Service Grievance Board.

ROBERT S. FREIDEMAN, born San Mateo, California, November 9, 1949; admitted to bar, 1975, District of Columbia; 1979, Maryland; 1980, U.S. Court of Appeals, Fourth Circuit; 1981, U.S. District Court for the District of Columbia, U.S. Court of Appeals for the District of Columbia Circuit, U.S. District Court, District of Maryland and U.S. Tax Court. *Education:* Yale University (B.A., cum laude, 1971); Georgetown University (J.D., 1975; LL.M. in Taxation, 1978). *Member:* District of Columbia Bar; Bar Association of the District of Columbia; Maryland State Bar Association. ***PRACTICE AREAS:*** Taxation Law; Estate Planning and Probate; Non-Profit Organizations Law. ***Email:*** r.freideman@fiwllaw.com

WILLIAM T. IRELAN, born Dayton, Ohio, June 4, 1940; admitted to bar, 1966, Ohio; 1970, New York; 1983, Virginia and District of Columbia; 1989, U.S. District Court, Eastern District of Virginia; U.S. District Court, Western District of Virginia; 1992, U.S. District Court, District of Maryland; 1994, U.S. District Court for the District of Columbia and U.S. Court of Appeals for the District of Columbia Circuit. *Education:* Monmouth College-Illinois (A.B., 1962); University of Geneva, Switzerland (1961); University of Virginia (J.D., 1965). Member, Editorial Staff, Virginia Law Weekly, 1964-1965. Member, Editorial Staff, Virginia Journal of International Law, 1964-1965. Author: "Tunisia's New Investment Code," Middle East Executive Reporter, Vol. 11, No. 4, p.9, 1988. Co-author: "Law and Economics in the Evolution of Contemporary Egypt," Middle Eastern Studies, Vol. 25, No. 2, p. 163, 1989, Frank Cass and Company Limited, London, England. Member, United Nations Development Programme, 1965-1966. Member, The Ford Foundation, 1967-1977. *Member:* District of Columbia Bar; Bar Association of the District of Columbia; Virginia State Bar; Ohio State and New York State Bar Associations; National Association of College and University Attorneys. ***LANGUAGES:*** French. ***PRACTICE AREAS:*** Corporate Law; Non-Profit Organizations Law; Litigation; Employer-Employee Relations Law. ***Email:*** w.irelan@fiwllaw.com

NICHOLAS D. WARD, born New York, N.Y., July 30, 1941; admitted to bar, 1967, District of Columbia; 1977, U.S. Supreme Court. *Education:* Columbia University (B.A., 1963); Georgetown University (LL.B., 1966). Phi Delta Phi. Recipient, Samuel Green Award, 1991. Author: "Diagnosing an Employment Civil Rights Claim," 6 Journal of College and University Law, 279, 1980; "Copyright In Museum Collections," 7 Journal of College and University Law 297, 1981; "Can the Common Law Accommodate the Problems of Title in the Art World," 8 Journal of College and University Law 533, 1982; "The Charitable Fiduciary Liability Question," 17 Real Property, Probate and Trust Law Journal 700, 1982; "What is a Reasonable Estimate of the Fair Market Value of a Wrong Note," The Exempt Organization Tax Review, Vol. 2, No. 2, April-May, 1989; "A Practitioner's Handbook—Wills, Trusts & Estates," 1993. Adjunct Instructor, The Catholic University of America, School of Law, 1986-1988. Member, Superior Court of the District of Columbia Advisory Committee on Fiduciary and Probate Rules, 1975—. Member, Judicial Conference of the District of Columbia Circuit, 1981, 1984 and 1985. Consultant Register of Wills, District of Columbia, 1987-1988. *Member:* The District of Columbia Bar (Trustee, 1981-1990 and Chair, 1983-1990, Clients' Security Fund; Chair, Estates, Trusts and Probate Section, 1984-1986); Bar Association of the District of Columbia (Member, Board of Directors, 1979-1981 and 1993-1995; Treasurer, 1982-1985; Research Foundation Trustee, 1990-1993 and President, 1992-1993); American Bar Association (Chairman, Committee on Charitable Institutions Tax and other problems of Real Property, Probate and Trust Section, 1985-1989; Chairman, Committee on Estate Planning and Drafting, Charitable Giving, 1990-1992); American Counsel Association (Secretary-Treasurer, 1987-1989); Selden Society. Fellow: National Association of College and University Attorneys (Secretary-Treasurer, 1979-1986); American College of Trust

(This Listing Continued)

and Estate Counsel (State Chairman, 1987-1992). ***PRACTICE AREAS:*** Estate Planning Law; Estate Administration; Trusts Law; Fiduciary Law; Bankruptcy. ***Email:*** n.ward@firllaw.com

BENJAMIN P. LAMBERTON, born Washington, D.C., March 8, 1940; admitted to bar, 1966, District of Columbia; 1970, U.S. Supreme Court; 1973, U.S. Court of Appeals for the District of Columbia; 1983, U.S. Court of Appeals, Fourth, Fifth and Eleventh Circuits. *Education:* St. Andrews University, Scotland; Union College (B.A., 1962); University of Virginia (LL.B., 1965). Phi Beta Kappa. Notes Editor, Virginia Journal of International Law, 1964-1965. Author, "The Case for Co-ops," The Washington Lawyer, Vol. 12, No. 4, March/April 1998. Law Clerk to the Hon. Richmond B. Keech, U.S. District Court for the District of Columbia, 1965-1966. Professorial Lecturer, Trial Practice, The American University. President, Board of Directors, University Legal Services, 1976-1979. President, Washington Center for Law and Education, 1997—. *Member:* District of Columbia Bar. ***REPORTED CASES:*** The American University v. D.C. Commission on Human Rights, 598 A.2d 416; Morgan v. The American University, 534 A.2d 323; Granfield v. Catholic University of America, 530 F.2d 1035, cert. denied, 429 U.S. 821; Marjorie Webster Jr. College v. Middle States Association of Colleges and Secondary Schools, 432 F.2d 650, cert. denied, 400 U.S. 965. ***PRACTICE AREAS:*** Litigation; Employment Law; Higher Education Law. ***Email:*** b.lamberton@fiwllaw.com

FREILICHER & HOFFMAN, P.C.

Established in 1988

SUITE 200, 1925 K STREET, N.W.
WASHINGTON, D.C. 20006
Telephone: 202-331-9450
Telecopier: 202-466-8151
URL: http://www.lawyers.com/freilicher&hoffmanpc

Immigration and Nationality Law Specialist practicing before all agencies involved in Immigration for U.S. and International Corporations, Law Firms, Universities and Research Institutions, International Organizations and Individuals.

MIRIAM S. FREILICHER, born Rockaway Beach, New York, January 29, 1941; admitted to bar, 1980, District of Columbia. *Education:* University of Maryland (B.A., with honors, 1963); Cornell University (M.I.L.R., 1970); George Washington University (J.D., 1979). *Member:* District of Columbia Bar (Chair, Clients Security Fund, 1995-2000; Vice Chair, Clients' Security Fund, 1992-1993); American Bar Association; American Immigration Lawyers Association. ***PRACTICE AREAS:*** Immigration and Nationality Law. ***Email:*** MSF@FHIMMLAW.COM

LINDA M. HOFFMAN, born Chicago, Illinois, December 4, 1953; admitted to bar, 1985, Virginia; 1986, District of Columbia. *Education:* Northwestern University (B.A., 1975); University of Wisconsin at Madison (Ph.D., 1983); George Mason University (J.D., 1985). Author: "Immigration Through Family Relationships," Immigration and Nationality Law, Vol. I, American Immigration Lawyers Association, Annual Conference (June 1990); "United States Immigration Law As a Foreign Policy Tool: The Beijing Crises and the United States Response," Georgetown Immigration Law Journal, Vol. 3, No. 3 (Fall 1989); "Preparing the Labor Certification Application (ETA 750)," Federal Bar Association, 11th Annual Seminar (April 17-18, 1990). *Member:* District of Columbia Bar (Vice Chair, Committee on Unauthorized Practice, 1993-1994); Virginia State Bar; American Immigration Lawyers Association (President, D.C. Chapter, 1988-1990; Secretary, D.C. Chapter, 1987-1988). ***PRACTICE AREAS:*** Immigration and Nationality Law. ***Email:*** LMH@FHIMMLAW.COM

FRESHFIELDS BRUCKHAUS DERINGER LLP

1300 I STREET, NW, 12TH FLOOR EAST
WASHINGTON, D.C. 20005-3314
Telephone: 202-969-4500; 202-777-4500
Fax: 202-969-4555; 202-777-4555
Email: email@freshfields.com
URL: http://www.freshfields.com

Freshfields Bruckhaus Deringer offices in: Amsterdam, Bangkok, Barcelona, Beijing, Berlin, Bratislava, Brussels, Budapest, Cologne, Düsseldorf, Frankfurt, Hamburg, Hanoi, Ho Chi Minh City, Hong Kong, London, Madrid, Milan, Moscow, Munich, New York, Paris, Prague, Rome, ★Shanghai, Singapore, Tokyo, Vienna, Washington.

★associate office.

Competition and Trade; Corporate; Dispute Resolution; Employment, Pensions and Benefits; Finance; Intellectual Property; Real Estate; Tax.

PARTNERS

ELLEN L. HAYES, born Toronto, Ontario, January 23, 1963; admitted to bar, 1987, Ontario (Barrister and Solicitor); 1998, England and Wales (Solici-

(This Listing Continued)

tor) (Not admitted in the United States). *Education:* Osgoode Hall Law School, York University (LL.B., 1985); University of Sydney (LL.M., 1992). ***PRACTICE AREAS:*** Project Finance; Finance; Corporate Finance; Debt Restructuring; Banking; Insolvency. ***Email:*** ehayes@freshfields.com

THOMAS P. HECHL, born Vienna, Austria, November 8, 1958; admitted to bar, 1987, California (Not admitted in District of Columbia). *Education:* University of Vienna Law School (J.D., 1984); University of San Diego School of Law (M.C.L., 1985). Senior Counsel, International Finance Corporation, 1993-1995. *Member:* American and International Bar Associations; State Bar of California. ***LANGUAGES:*** German and French. ***Email:*** thechl@freshfields.com

GREGORY EVERS MAY, born Harrisonburg, Virginia, September 17, 1953; admitted to bar, 1978, Virginia; 1985, District of Columbia; 1987, New York; 1994, England and Wales as Registered Foreign Lawyer. *Education:* College of William & Mary (A.B., 1975); Harvard Law School (J.D., magna cum laude, 1978). Law Clerk to: Judge John D. Butzner, U.S. Court of Appeals, 4th Circuit, 1978-1979; Justice Powell, U.S. Supreme Court, 1979-1980. *Member:* The District of Columbia, Virginia State, New York State and American Bar Associations; International Fiscal Association. ***PRACTICE AREAS:*** International Taxation; Corporate Taxation. ***Email:*** gmay@freshfields.com

CLAUDE B. STANSBURY, born Berkeley, California, March 31, 1965; admitted to bar, 1991, California; 1993, District of Columbia. *Education:* London School of Economics and Political Science, London, U.K.; Georgetown University (B.S.F.S., cum laude, 1987); Boalt Hall School of Law, University of California, Berkeley (J.D., 1991). Recipient, Landegger International Business Diplomacy Certificate, Georgetown University. Member, International Tax and Finance Forum. *Member:* District of Columbia Bar; State Bar of California; American Bar Association (Member, Section of Taxation, Corporate Tax Committee ; Chair, Task Force on Section 304, 1998—; Tax Accounting Committee; Co-Chair, Task Force on Environmental Remediation, 1993-1995). ***PRACTICE AREAS:*** Tax. ***Email:*** claude.stansbury@freshfields.com

FRIED, FRANK, HARRIS, SHRIVER & JACOBSON

A Partnership including Professional Corporations

SUITE 800, 1001 PENNSYLVANIA AVENUE, N.W.
WASHINGTON, D.C. 20004-2505
Telephone: 202-639-7000
Telecopy: 202-639-7008
Email: info@ffhsj.com

New York, New York Office: One New York Plaza. Telephone: 212-859-8000. Cable Address: "Steric New York." W.U. Intl. Telex: 662119. W.U. Domestic: 128173. Telecopier: 212-859-4000 (Dex 6200).
Los Angeles, California Office: 350 South Grand Avenue, 32nd Floor. Telephone: 213-473-2000.
London, England Office: 99 City Road, London EC1Y 1AX. Telephone: 011-44-171-972-9600. Fax: 011-44-171-972-9602.
Paris, France Office: 7, Rue Royale, 75008. Telephone: (011 331) 40-17-04-04. Fax: (011 331) 40-17-08-30.

General Practice.

WASHINGTON, D.C. PARTNERS

RICHARD I. ANSBACHER, born Jacksonville, Florida, September 17, 1958; admitted to bar, 1984, Florida (inactive); 1985, District of Columbia. *Education:* University of Florida (B.S. in Accounting, cum laude, 1979; J.D., cum laude, 1983); New York University (LL.M., 1984). Beta Alpha Psi; Omicron Delta Kappa; Order of the Coif. Chief Tax Editor and Articles Editor, University of Florida Law Review, 1983. ***PRACTICE AREAS:*** Corporate Law. ***Email:*** richard_ansbacher@ffhsj.com

DAVID L. ANSELL, born New York, N.Y., April 2, 1954; admitted to bar, 1979, Pennsylvania; 1984, U.S. Supreme Court; 1985, District of Columbia. *Education:* University of Pennsylvania, Wharton School (B.S., cum laude, 1976); Temple University (J.D., 1979); ABA International Legal Exchange Program, London, England, 1983. Temple Law Quarterly, 1978-1979. *Member:* The District of Columbia Bar; American Bar Association. ***Email:*** david_ansell@ffhsj.com

LAWRENCE R. BARD, born Queens, New York, October 28, 1965; admitted to bar, 1993, Pennsylvania; 1995, District of Columbia. *Education:* University of Delaware (B.S., Accounting, 1988); George Washington University (J.D., with high honors, 1993). Treasurer, Moot Court Board. Notes Editor, George Washington University Law Review. Certified Public Accountant, Pennsylvania, 1990. Author: "Securities," National Law Journal (March 9, 1998) (with Stephen I. Glover); "Beyond the Blue Horizon," Los Angeles Lawyer (Sept. 1996) (with Harvey L. Pitt, Mark J. Dorsey & Edward B. Whittemore); "More Than 'Classical GAAS': Audits and Corporate Illegality Under the Litigation Reform Act," 8 Corporate Analyst 1 (Aug. 1996) (with Harvey L. Pitt and David B. Hardison); "Disclosure of Restructuring Charges," 9 Insights No. 6 (June 1995) (with Richard A. Steinwurtzel and Vasiliki B. Tsaganos); Note, "A Distinct Responsibility Approach to Accountants' Liability Under Rule 10b-5," 61 Geo. Wash. L.Rev. 193 (1992). Law Clerk to the Honorable Carolyn Berger, Delaware Court of Chancery and Delaware Supreme Court, 1993-1994. ***PRACTICE AREAS:*** Corporate Law; Securities. ***Email:*** lawrence_bard@ffhsj.com

(This Listing Continued)

DOUGLAS W. BARUCH, born New Brunswick, New Jersey, April 17, 1962; admitted to bar, 1987, Maryland; 1988, District of Columbia and U.S. Court of Appeals, Fourth Circuit; 1990, U.S. District Court for the District of Columbia; 1993, U.S. Supreme Court; 1995, U.S. Court of Appeals, District of Columbia and Federal Circuits and U.S. District Court, District of Maryland; 1996, U.S. Court of Appeals, Ninth Circuit. *Education:* John's Hopkins University (B.A., 1984); Georgetown University (J.D., 1987). Articles Editor, The Tax Lawyer, 1986-1987. Author: "AIDS in the Courts: Tort Liability for the Sexual Transmission of Acquired Immune Deficiency Syndrome," 22 Tort and Insurance Law Journal 165, 1987; "Equal Protection and State Taxation of Foreign Insurers: Metropolitan Life Insurance Co. v. Ward," 40 The Tax Lawyer 447, 1987. *Member:* The District of Columbia Bar; Maryland State and American Bar Associations. ***PRACTICE AREAS:*** Civil and Criminal Fraud Litigation; Business Litigation; International Arbitration. ***Email:*** douglas.baruch@ffhsj.com

DAVID E. BIRENBAUM, born Waterbury, Connecticut, November 30, 1937; admitted to bar, 1962, Connecticut; 1964, District of Columbia; 1985, U.S. Court of Appeals for the Federal Circuit. *Education:* Brown University (B.A., 1959); Harvard University (LL.B., cum laude, 1962). Phi Beta Kappa. Author: "Business Ventures in Eastern Europe and the Soviet Union: The Emerging Legal Framework for Foreign Investment," Prentice Hall Law & Business (2 volumes) June 1991, updated 1994. Lecturer of International Trade Law, University of Pennsylvania Law School, 1987-1990. Adjunct Professor, Georgetown University Law Center, Laws of Eastern Europe and the Soviet Union, 1991. Law Clerk, Honorable M. Joseph Blumenfeld, U.S. District Court, Hartford, Connecticut, 1962-1963. Assistant General Counsel, National Advisory Commission on Civil Disorders, 1967-1968. General Counsel and Member, Board of Directors, Handgun Control, Inc., 1982-1994, 1996 and Center to Prevent Handgun Violence, 1979-1994, 1996. Public Member, U.S. Delegation to the U.N. Conference on Human Rights, Geneva, 1993. Panelist: Bi-National Panel pursuant to the Canada-United States Free Trade Agreement, 1992-1994 and 1997—; World Trade Organization, 1997—. Ambassador of the United States to the United Nations for U.N. Management and Reform, 1994-1996. Chairman of the Board of Directors of the Emergency Coalition for U.S. Financial Support of the United Nations, 1997—. Member, Board of Directors, Americans for Peace Now, 1999. Member, Council on Foreign Relations, 1997. Committee Member, ABA Standing on World Order Under Law, 1997—. *Member:* The District of Columbia Bar; Bar Association of the District of Columbia; American (Co-Chairman, Ad Hoc Task Force on the Extraterritorial Application of U.S. Law, International Law Section) and International Bar Associations; American Law Institute. ***Email:*** birenda@ffhsj.com

JOHN T. BOESE, born St. Louis, Missouri, January 8, 1947; admitted to bar, 1973, District of Columbia; 1977, U.S. Supreme Court. *Education:* Washington University (B.S., 1969); St. Louis University (J.D., magna cum laude, 1972). Alpha Sigma Nu; Delta Theta Phi. Associate Editor, St. Louis University Law Review, 1971-1972. Author: "Civil False Claims and *Qui Tam* Actions," Aspen Law & Business (2d ed., 2001); Lead Editor and Contributor for "Best Practices Handbook in Advising Clients on Fraud & Abuse Issues" (AHLA June 1999), *Healthcare Exclusions: A Comprehensive Guide* (ABA 1997) and the Second Edition of *The Practitioner's Guide to Suspension and Debarment* (ABA 1996). Journal Articles include "Why *Thompson* Is Wrong: Misuse of the False Claims Act to Enforce the Anti-Kickback Act," *Alabama Law Review,* Vol. 51, No. 1 (Fall 1999); "When Angry Patients Become Angry Prosecutors: Medical Necessity Determinations, Quality of Care and the *Qui Tam* Law," *Saint Louis University Law Journal,* Vol. 43, No. 1 (Spring 1999); "Private Enforcement of State Fraud Laws: A Comparative Analysis of State *Qui Tam* Provisions," *Journal of Health and Hospital Law,* Volume 31, No. 1 (Winter 1998); "The Dark Side of *Qui Tam* Enforcement," *Health Law Litigation,* Issue No. 4 (Summer 1996). Co-Chair, ABA National Institute on the Civil False Claims Act and *Qui Tam* Enforcement, 1998 and 2000. Lecturer, Department of Justice Civil Enforcement Conference, Summer 1994. Faculty, ABA National Institute on White Collar Crime, 1992-1995, 1998-2001. Chair, "*Qui Tam:* Beyond Government Contracts," Practising Law Institute 1993. Trial Attorney, U.S. Department of Justice, Civil Division, 1972-1977. *Member:* The District of Columbia Bar (Co-Chair, Committee on Court Rules, 1983-1985; Chair, Section on Courts, Lawyers and Administration of Justice, 1986-1987); American Bar Association (Member, Sections on Criminal Justice; Litigation; Public Contracts; Co-Chair of *Qui Tam* Subcommittee of the ABA White Collar Crime Committee; Vice-Chair, Committee on Suspension and Debarment); American Health Lawyers Association (Chair, Best Practices Task Force, 1999). ***Email:*** john_boese@ffhsj.com

(This Listing Continued)

FRIED, FRANK, HARRIS, SHRIVER & JACOBSON, Washington—Continued

MICHAEL R. BROMWICH, born Los Angeles, California, December 19, 1953; admitted to bar, 1980, District of Columbia; 1984, U.S. Court of Appeals, Second Circuit; 1989, U.S. District Court, District of Columbia and U.S. Court of Appeals, District of Columbia Circuit; 1991, U.S. District Court, District of Maryland. *Education:* Harvard College (A.B., summa cum laude, 1976); Harvard University, John F. Kennedy School of Government (M.P.P., 1980); Harvard Law School (J.D., 1980). Phi Beta Kappa. Author: Book Review, "Law & Policy in International Business," Vol. 14:3337, 1983; "Symposium Issue on the Selection and Function of the Modern Jury," The American University Law Review, Vol. 40, No. 2, Winter 1991; "Iraqgate: The Making of an Investigation," Harper's, January 1993; "IG Gate - Investigating Major Scandals: Climate That Leads to IG Handling," The Journal of Public Inquiry, Summer 1997; "Running Special Investigations: The Inspector General Model," The Georgetown Law Journal, Vol. 86, No. 6, July 1998; "The Regulation and Ethical Responsibilities of Federal Prosecutors," Fordham Urban Law Journal, Vol. XXVI, No. 3, March 1999; "An Eye on the FBI," The Washington Post, September 5, 1999; "I Sat on a Jury That Followed the Evidence," Legal Times, September 6, 1999; "The LAPD Must Open Its Doors to Oversight," Los Angeles Times, November 3, 1999; "Put a Stop to Savage Sentencing," The Washington Post, November 22, 1999; "Miranda Reconsidered," in *The New York Times,* December 7, 1999; "Politics Colors Pursuit of Wen Ho Lee," in *Los Angeles Times,* December 17, 1999; "Police Have Good Reasons to Support Miranda Warning," in *The Boston Globe,* February 7, 2000. Co-Author: with Andrew L. Frey, Esq., "Sentencing of Organizations," in Phylis Skloot Bamberger, ed., *Practice Under the New Federal Sentencing Guidelines,* Prentice-Hall Law & Business, 1992, 1999; with Dorann Banks, Esq., "Today is the Day to Implement Compliance Programs," New York Law Journal, July 26, 1993; with Glenn A. Fine, Esq., "IG Gate - Investigating Major Scandals: Part II: The Nuts and Bolts," The Journal of Public Inquiry, Fall 1997; "The FBI Needs a Manager," The New York Times, May 24, 2001. Assistant U.S. Attorney, Southern District of New York, 1983-1987. Deputy Chief, 1985-1986; Chief, 1986-1987, Narcotics Unit. Associate Counsel, 1987-1989 and Special Counsel, 1989, 1990, 1991, Office of Independent Counsel (Iran/Contra). Inspector General, Department of Justice, 1994-1999. *Member:* The District of Columbia Bar (Member, Sections on: Criminal Law; Litigation); American Bar Association (Member, Sections on: Litigation; Criminal Justice). (Also at New York, N.Y. Office). ***PRACTICE AREAS:*** Investigations, Monitoring and Oversight; White Collar Criminal Defense; Corporate Compliance. ***Email:*** michael_bromwich@ffhsj.com

TIMOTHY D. CASEY, born Los Angeles, California, June 26, 1961; admitted to bar, 1988, California; 1996, District of Columbia. *Education:* University of Nevada (B.S.E., 1984); Santa Clara University (J.D., 1988). Author: "ISP Liability Survival Guide: Strategies for Managing Copyright, Spam, Cache and Privacy Regulation," John Wiley & Sons, 2000; "A Hybrid Model of Self-Regulation & Government Regulation of Ecommerce;" "Making Intellectual Property a Business Priority," Hidden Value: Profiting from the Intellectual Property Economy, 1999; "On The Other Hand, IP Rights May Not Be The Best Defense," Legal Times, May 7, 2001. Adjunct Professor, Law, Santa Clara University. Chairman: Intellectual Property Committee, Information Technology Association of America; Advisory Board, BNA's Electronic Commerce & Law Report; National Academy of Sciences, Computer Sciences and Technology Board's Internet Navigation and the Domain Name System Committee. *Member:* The District of Columbia Bar; American Bar Association. ***PRACTICE AREAS:*** Intellectual Property; Technology Transactions; Litigation; Corporate Transactions. ***Email:*** caseyti@ffhsj.com

JOHN W. CHIERICHELLA, born New York, N.Y., March 26, 1947; admitted to bar, 1973, New York; 1975, District of Columbia; 1976, U.S. District Court, District of Columbia; 1976, U.S. Claims Court; 1980, U.S. Supreme Court; 1997, California and U.S. District Court, Northern, Southern, Central and Eastern Districts of California. *Education:* Cornell University (A.B., 1969); Columbia University (J.D., 1972). Phi Eta Sigma. James Kent Scholar; Harlan Fiske Stone Scholar. Member, Columbia University Law Review, 1971-1972. Attorney Advisor to the Secretary, U.S. Air Force General Counsel's Office, 1973-1975. Member, Board of Governors, Board of Contract Appeals Bar Association, 1993-1996. Member, Advisory Board, Federal Contracts Report, 1987-1993. Member, Advisory Board, The Government Contractor, 1993—; Commentary to the Criminal Division Chapter of Prentice Hall's Annotated Edition of Department of Justice Manual. Author: The Buy American Act and the Use of Foreign Sources in Federal Procurements-An Issues Analysis," 9 *Public Contract Law Journal* 73 (December 1977); "New Interim DOD Rules Ease Security-Related Restrictions on Foreign Ownership of U.S. Contractors," *Contract Management* (December 1983) (Co-Author with Lisa A. Everhart); "Financing Government Contracts," *The Government Contractor Briefing Papers,* No. 86-7 (1986) (Co-Author with Lisa A. Everhart, Jeffrey M. Villet and Dale H. Oliver); "Antitrust Considerations Affecting Teaming Agreements," 57 *Antitrust Law Journal* 555 (1988); "Foreign Investment in Defense-Related Companies," 51 *Federal Contracts Report* 837 (BNA, May 8, 1989), reprinted in *Foreign Investments in the U.S. News & Analysis* (London, June 1989) (Co-Author with Douglas E. Perry); "IR&D vs. Contract Effort," *Government Contract Cost, Pricing & Accounting Report,* Issue 90-2 (February 1990); "Foreign Selling Costs Under the Cost Principles," *Government Contract Cost, Pricing & Accounting Report,* Issue 90-12 (December 1990) (Co-Author with Rosemary Maxwell); "Negotiated Teaming Agreements," *Acquisition Issues,* Volume 1 (June 1991) (Co-Author with Douglas E. Perry); "Improving Business Opportunities Through Teaming," *Federal Acquisition Report,* Volume VIII, No. 4 (April, 1991) (Co-Author with Douglas E. Perry); "Comparative Bid Protest Procedures in International Contracting," *International Quarterly,* Vol. 4, No. 4 (October 1992) (Co-Author with Rosemary Maxwell); "Government Procurement Under the North American Free Trade Agreement," 58 *Federal Contracts Report* (BNA, October 26, 1992) (Co-Author with Rosemary Maxwell); "IR&D Redux," *Government Contract Cost, Pricing & Accounting Report,* Issue 93-2 (February 1993) (Co-Author with Lynda T. O'Sullivan and Douglas E. Perry); "Mergers and Acquisitions of Government Contractors: Special Considerations and Due Diligence Concerns," *American Bar Association Public Contract Law Journal,* Vol. 23, No. 4, 1994 (Co-Author with Douglas E. Perry); "Complying With the New Limits on Personal Compensation Under FY 1995 DOD Contracts," *Government Contract Costs, Pricing & Accounting Report,* Issue 95-1, Jan. 1995 (Co-Author with James M. Weitzel, Jr); "Commissions & Fees Paid to Overseas Agents: Cost Recovered & Related Rules," Government Contract Costs, Pricing & Accounting Reports, Issue 98-8 Aug. 1998 (Co-Author with Douglas E. Perry and Michael L. Waldman); "Disputing a Commercial KO," *Legal Times,* April 26, 1999; "A Qui Tam Conundrum," *Legal Times,* February 28, 2000; "The Buy American Act/FAR Part 25 Rewrite--A Law of Unintended Consequences," *The Government Contractor,* August 16, 2000; "The Civil False Claims Act: More Relevant Than You May Think," *Director's Monthly,* October 2000; "The Government's Assault of FOIA Exemption 4: Do You Know Where Your Data Are?," *Off The Shelf,* October 2000; "When is Information Confidential? The Government and Courts' Ongoing Tug-of-War Over FOIA's Exemption 4 Leaves Contracts Professionals in a Bind," *Contract Management,* November 2000; *Domestic & Foreign Product Preferences,* Briefing Papers, Second Series, December 2000; Developments in Administrative Law and Regulatory Practice 1999-2000, *ABA Section of Administrative Law and Regulatory Practice,* (Public Contracts and Procurement), February 2001; "Unwary Rabbits Beware: IDIQ Means Never Having to Say You're Sorry," *Government Contract Audit Report,* February 2001. *Member:* American Bar Association (Co-Chair, Public Contracts Committee, Section on Administrative Law and Regulatory Practice, 2000-2001); National Contract Management Association. (Also at Los Angeles, California Office). ***SPECIAL AGENCIES:*** Top Secret Security Clearance. ***PRACTICE AREAS:*** Government Contracts; Litigation. ***Email:*** chierjo@ffhsj.com

MARK J. DORSEY, born Cincinnati, Ohio, September 1, 1953; admitted to bar, 1984, New York, New Jersey, U.S. District Court, District of New Jersey and U.S. District Court, Southern District of New York; 1988, District of Columbia. *Education:* Northern Kentucky University (B.A., 1977); New York Law School (J.D., cum laude, 1983). Articles Editor, New York Law School Law Review, 1982-1983. Co-Author: "Disciplinary Proceedings Before Self-Regulatory Organizations in Broker Dealers: New Legal, Business and Compliance Developments," Corporate Law and Practice Handbook Series, No. 461, PLI, 1984; "Manipulation, Broker-Dealer Retail Fraud and Compliance," in United States Securities and Investments Regulation Handbook (1992); "Beyond the Blue Horizon," Los Angeles Lawyer (Sept. 1996); "Protecting the Online Investor and the Markets: SEC and SRO Activities," In Securities in the Electronic Age (2000). Special Counsel, Division of Enforcement, Securities and Exchange Commission, 1984-1986. *Member:* The District of Columbia Bar. ***Email:*** mark_dorsey@ffhsj.com

PAUL H. FALON, born Brooklyn, New York, April 29, 1951; admitted to bar, 1983, District of Columbia; 2001, New York. *Education:* University of Michigan (B.A., with high distinction, 1972; J.D., 1983). Phi Beta Kappa. Co-Author: "Insurer Insolvencies: Interstate Cooperation," Law and Practice of Insurance Company Insolvency 119 (A.B.A. Nat'l Inst.). Member, Editorial Review Board, Journal of Insurance Regulation. ***PRACTICE AREAS:*** Insurance. ***Email:*** falonpa@ffhsj.com

DEBORAH A. GARZA, born Chicago, Illinois, November 19, 1956; admitted to bar, 1982, District of Columbia. *Education:* Northern Illinois University (B.A., magna cum laude, 1978); University of Chicago (J.D., 1981). Special Assistant to the Assistant Attorney General for Antitrust, United States Department of Justice, 1983-1984. Counsel and Chief of Staff to Assistant Attorney General for Antitrust, United States Department of Justice, 1987-1989. Incoming Editorial Chair, *Antitrust* magazine. ***PRACTICE AREAS:*** Antitrust; Litigation. ***Email:*** deborah.garza@ffhsj.com

JACK B. GORDON, born Brooklyn, New York, October 26, 1955; admitted to bar, 1980, New York and District of Columbia. *Education:* State University of New York at Albany (B.A., magna cum laude, 1976); The National Law Center, George Washington University (J.D., with high honors, 1979). Order of the

(This Listing Continued)

Coif. Senior Associate, George Washington Law Review, 1978-1979. Co-Author: Case Note, "Singer v. Magnavox," 46 George Washington Law Review 877, 1978. **Email:** jack_gordon@ffhsj.com

KARL A. GROSKAUFMANIS, born Timmins, Ontario, August 6, 1961; admitted to bar, 1988, Massachusetts; 1989, District of Columbia. *Education:* Cornell University (B.S., with honors, 1984); University of Toronto (LL.B., 1987); University of Pennsylvania (J.D., 1988). Author: "What Films We May Watch: Videotape Distribution and the First Amendment," 136 University of Pennsylvania Law Review 1263, 1988. Co-Author: with Harvey L. Pitt: "Promises Made, Promises Kept: The Practical Implications of the Private Securities Litigation Reform Act of 1995," San Diego Law Review 845 (1996); "When Bad Things Happen to Good Companies: A Crisis Management Primer," 15 Cardozo Law Review 951 (1994); "A Tale of Two Instruments: Insider Trading in Non-Equity Securities," 49 Business Lawyer 187 (1993); "Mischief AFoot: The Need for Incentives to Control Corporate Criminal Conduct," 71 Boston University Law Review 447 (1991); "Minimizing Corporate Civil and Criminal Liability: A Second Look at Corporate Codes of Conduct," 78 Georgetown Law Journal 1559 (1990). **Email:** karl_groskaufmanis@ffhsj.com

DAVID B. HARDISON, born Havre de Grace, Maryland, July 20, 1959; admitted to bar, 1984, District of Columbia. *Education:* Princeton University (A.B., cum laude, 1981); Columbia University (J.D., 1984). Phi Beta Kappa. Harlan Fiske Stone Scholar. Writing and Research Editor, Columbia Journal of Law and Social Problems, 1983-1984. Co-author with Harvey L. Pitt: "Promises Made, Promises Kept: The Practical Implications of the Private Securities Litigation Reform Act of 1955," 33 San Diego L. Rev. 845, Summer 1996; "More Than 'Classical GAAS': Audits and Corporate Illegality Under the Litigation Reform Act," The Corporate Board, May/June 1996; "Games Without Frontiers: Trends in the International Response to Insider Trading," 55 Law and Contemporary Problems 1991 Autumn 1992; "Eagle on the Spreadsheet: The SEC's New Accounting Activism," Director's Monthly, August 1992; "Problems of Enforcement in the Multinational Securities Market," 9:3 University of Pennsylvania Journal of International Business Law, Summer, 1987. *Member:* The District of Columbia Bar; American Bar Association (Member, Section of Business Law Task Force on Rule 102(e) Proceedings). ***LANGUAGES:*** French. **Email:** david_hardison@ffhsj.com

LANAE HOLBROOK, born Washington, D.C., August 3, 1965; admitted to bar, 1993, Florida; 1994, District of Columbia. *Education:* Worcester State College (B.S., magna cum laude, 1988); University of Miami (J.D., summa cum laude, 1992). Order of the Coif. Executive Editor, University of Miami Law Review, 1991-1992. Law Clerk to Honorable James M. Sprouse, U.S. Court of Appeals for the Fourth Circuit, Lewisburg, West Virginia, 1992-1993. ***PRACTICE AREAS:*** Corporate; Securities. **Email:** lanae_holbrook@ffhsj.com

DIXIE LYNN JOHNSON, born Omaha, Nebraska, May 23, 1957; admitted to bar, 1986, New Mexico; 1987, District of Columbia. *Education:* Oklahoma Baptist University (B.A., 1977); New Mexico Highlands University (M.B.A., 1983); University of New Mexico (J.D., 1986). Order of the Coif. Case Note Editor, New Mexico Law Review, 1985-1986. Editor, The Securities Reporter, a publication of the ABA Federal Regulation of Securities Committee Since 1995. Columnist on Enforcement and Litigation Developments for the Investment Lawyer. Trustee and Executive Committee Member, SEC Historical Society. *Member:* The District of Columbia Bar; State Bar of New Mexico; Federal (Member, Executive Council of Securities Law Committee) and American (Member, Subcommittee on Civil Litigation and SEC Enforcement of the Business Law Section's Committee on Federal Securities Regulation; Vice-Chair, Committee on Federal Regulation of Securities, Business Law Section) Bar Associations. **Email:** dixie_johnson@ffhsj.com

ALAN S. KADEN, born New York, N.Y., March 12, 1956; admitted to bar, 1982, New York and District of Columbia. *Education:* University of Pennsylvania (B.S., magna cum laude, 1978); Columbia University (J.D., 1981). Member, Columbia Law Review, 1980-1981. Author: "The Savings and Loan Tax Shelter," Tax Notes, May, 1989. Co-author: "Installment Method Asset Sales By S Corporations," The American University Law Review, Vol. 39, Summer 1990, No. 4, at 915; "Spin-offs, Split-offs and Split-ups: A Detailed Analysis of Section 355," Tax Notes, July, 1989; "Judicial Review of Executive Action in Domestic Affairs," 80 Columbia Law Review 1535. Adjunct Professor of Law, Georgetown University Law Center, 1989-1991, 1993-1997. *Member:* The District of Columbia Bar; New York State and American (Member, Section on Taxation) Bar Associations. **Email:** alan.kaden@ffhsj.com

KEVIN M. KEYES, born Cleveland, Ohio, March 15, 1956; admitted to bar, 1983, Ohio; 1989, District of Columbia. *Education:* Bowling Green State University (B.S., 1979); Case Western Reserve University (J.D., 1983). Order of the Coif. Certified Public Accountant, Ohio, 1986. Author: *Federal Taxation of Financial Instruments and Transactions* (Warren Gorham Lamont, 1997). Adjunct Professor of Law, Georgetown University Law Center, Business Planning and Income Tax Accounting. Editor, Corporations, Shareholders Department, The Journal of Taxation. Former Chairman, American Bar Association Section on Taxation, Committee on Corporate Tax, Subcommittee on Bankruptcy Tax Problems; Former Co-Chairman, Financial Transactions Committee, Subcommittee on Interest Rate Agreements. ***PRACTICE AREAS:*** Taxation Law.

(This Listing Continued)

JAY R. KRAEMER, born St. Louis, Missouri, September 7, 1948; admitted to bar, 1973, Maryland; 1974, District of Columbia. *Education:* George Washington University (B.A., with distinction, 1970; J.D., with highest honors, 1973). Co-Author with M. Rowden: "Nuclear Export Control," Callagham & Co. Energy Law Service, August 1978. Law Clerk to The Honorable James R. Miller, Jr., U.S. District Court for The District of Maryland, 1973-1974. Adjunct Professor, Georgetown University Law Center, 1997—. *Member:* Maryland State and American Bar Associations; The District of Columbia Bar; International Nuclear Law Association. **Email:** jay_kraemer@ffhsj.com

ROBERT H. LEDIG, born Bronx, New York, August 4, 1958; admitted to bar, 1983, District of Columbia and New Jersey. *Education:* State University of New York at Binghamton (B.A., with honors, 1979); George Washington University (J.D., with honors, 1982). Co-Author with T. Vartanian and A. Conover: "A Survey of Selected Federal Regulatory and Legal Developments in Electronic Financial Services," The Business Lawyer, Nov. 1997. Co-Author with T. Vartanian, E. Whittemore and J. Baetzhold: "Georgia Internet Law Raises Jurisdictional Questions for Electronic Commerce," Electronic Banking Law and Commerce Report, Feb. 1997. Co-Author with T. Vartanian and E. Whittemore: "Integrion Financial Network: A New Stage for Electronic Banking," Electronic Banking Law and Commerce Report, Oct. 1996. Co-Author with T. Vartanian and Y. Demianczuk: "Echoes of the Past With Implications For The Future: The Stomp Payments Act of 1862 and Electronic Commerce," BNA's Banking Report, Sept. 23, 1996. Co-Author with T. Vartanian: "The Business of Banking in the Age of the Internet: Fortress or Prison?" Banking Policy Report, Mar. 4-18, 1996. Co-Author with T. Vartanian and A. Babitz: "Disporate Impact Discrimination: Fair Lending At A Crossroads," Consumer Finance Law Quarterly Report, Winter 1995. Co-Author with T. Vartanian and L. Bruneau: "21st Century Money, Banking & Commerce," 1998. Co-Author: "The Management of Risks Created by Internet-Initiated Value Transfers," National Automated Clearing House Association, 1998. Co-Author with T. Vartanian and A. Babitz: "The Fair Lending Guide," Glosser Legal Works, 1995. Co-Author with J. McCullough and T. Vartanian: "Contracting with the RTC and FDIC," Prentice Hall Law and Business, 1991. Lecturer in Law, George Mason University Law School, 1995—. Co-Chair, Y2K Joint Task Force, Cyberspace Law and Business Litigation Committees, Business Law Section, American Bar Association. Member, Stored-Value Cards Task Force, American Bar Association. *Member:* The District of Columbia Bar; American Bar Association (Member, Business Law Section). **Email:** robert_ledig@ffhsj.com

DANIEL E. LOEB, born Madison, Wisconsin, September 13, 1953; admitted to bar, 1982, Colorado; 1985, District of Columbia; 1988, U.S. District Court for the District of Columbia and U.S. Court of Appeals for the District of Columbia Circuit. *Education:* Boston University; Colorado State University (B.S., 1979); University of Colorado (J.D., 1982). Order of the Coif. Law Clerk to Hon. Sherman G. Fincsilver, Chief Judge, U.S. District Court for the District of Colorado, 1982-1984. Trial Attorney, U.S. Department of Justice, Civil Division, Commercial Litigation Branch, 1984-1987. *Member:* The District of Columbia Bar; American Bar Association (Member, Sections on: Litigation; Business Law). **Email:** loebda@ffhsj.com

JAMES J. McCULLOUGH, born Philadelphia, Pennsylvania, July 25, 1947; admitted to bar, 1976, Virginia; 1977, U.S. Claims Court; 1979, District of Columbia; 1980, U.S. Supreme Court. *Education:* Villanova University (B.A., cum laude, 1969); University of Virginia (J.D., 1976). Trial Attorney and Assistant to the General Counsel, Office of The General Counsel of the Navy, 1977-1979. Co-Author with T. Vartanian and R. Ledig, "Contracting With the RTC and FDIC," Prentice Hall Law and Business, 1991. *Member:* The District of Columbia Bar; Federal and American (Member, Public Contract Law and Litigation Sections) Bar Associations; National Contract Management Association; National Security Industrial Association. [Lt., U.S. Navy, 1969-1973]. ***PRACTICE AREAS:*** Government Contracts; Litigation. **Email:** james_mccullough@ffhsj.com

DENEEN J. MELANDER, born Tacoma, Washington, December 15, 1960; admitted to bar, 1987, Virginia; 1988, District of Columbia. *Education:* Cornell University (B.S.E.E., 1981); George Washington University (J.D., highest honors, 1987). Order of the Coif. *Member:* The District of Columbia Bar; Virginia State Bar; American Bar Association. **Email:** deneen_melander@ffhsj.com

MATT T. MORLEY, born Johnson City, New York, May 22, 1956; admitted to bar, 1983, District of Columbia; 2000, New York. *Education:* Colgate University (B.A., magna cum laude, 1978); Yale University (J.D., 1983). Author: *Combatting Bribery,* National Law Journal (March 27, 2000); *Corporate Compliance Programs: Effective Programs May Protect Corporate Directors From Personal Liability,* White Collar Crime Reporter (Jan. 1997) (with John T. Boese); *De-Greasing the Wheels of Commerce: U.S. Anti-Bribery Initiatives Signal Stiffening FCPA Enforcement,* Insights (April 1997) (with Yan Liu); *An Overview of the U.S. Foreign Corrupt Practices Act,* China Futures Weekly, Oct. 23, 1995 (with Yan Liu). *Member:* The District of Columbia Bar; American Bar Association. **Email:** morlema@ffhsj.com

BERNARD A. NIGRO, JR., born Buffalo, New York, March 4, 1960; admitted to bar, 1986, Maryland; 1987, District of Columbia; 1993, U.S. Supreme Court. *Education:* St. Lawrence University; Georgetown University

(This Listing Continued)

FRIED, FRANK, HARRIS, SHRIVER & JACOBSON, Washington—Continued

(A.B., 1982); George Washington University (J.D., 1986). Member and Associate, George Washington Law Review, 1984-1986. Author: "The Role of Antitrust in Deregulating Telecommunications Markets," Antitrust Report (January 1999) (co-authored with Richard C. Park); "New Technologies in Telecommunications, The Telecommunications Industry--Effects of the 1996 Act," ABA Section of Antitrust Law and Public Utility Law (September 18-19, 1997); "The Exclusionary Rule in Administrative Law Proceedings," 54 George Washington Law Review 564, 1986; "Are You Charging a Franchise Fee Without Knowing It?" 2 Franchise Legal Digest 6, 1988. Co-Author: "Membership, Antitrust of Trade Associations," ABA Section of Antitrust Law (1996) (co-authored with Patricia M. Vaughan); "New Department of Justice Intellectual Property Guidelines Remarkable for Lack of Change, Computer Industry," ABA Section of Antitrust Law 5 (1994) (co-authored with Joseph J. Simons). Law Clerk to the Honorable Charles R. Richey, U.S. District Court for the District of Columbia, 1986-1987. *Member:* The District of Columbia Bar (Member, Steering Committee, Antitrust, Trade Regulation, and Consumer Affairs Section); Maryland State, Federal (Member, Antitrust Committee) and American (Member, Antitrust Section and Chair, Communications Industry Committee) Bar Associations. ***SPECIAL AGENCIES:*** Department of Justice and Federal Trade Commission. ***PRACTICE AREAS:*** Antitrust and Trade Regulation; Criminal Defense; Franchising and Distribution Law. ***Email:*** barry.nigro@friedfrank.com

DOUGLAS E. PERRY, born Cincinnati, Ohio, September 1, 1962; admitted to bar, 1988, Pennsylvania; 1989, District of Columbia. *Education:* Kenyon College (A.B., with honors, 1985); Cornell University (J.D., 1988). Editor, Cornell Law Review, 1987-1988. Recipient, American Jurisprudence Award, American Legal Theory. Author: "Article Two Warranties in Commercial Transactions: An Update," 72 Cornell Law Review 1159 (September 1987). Co-Author: with John W. Chierichella, "Foreign Investment in Defense-Related Companies," 51 Federal Contracts Report 837 (BNA, May 8, 1989) reprinted in Foreign Investment in The U.S. News and Analysis (London, June 1989); with John W. Chierichella, "Negotiating Teaming Agreements," 1 Acquisition Issues (June 1991); with John W. Chierichella and Lynda Troutman O'Sullivan, "IR&D Redux," 92-2 CP&A Report 3-13 (February 1993); with James J. McCullough and Abram J. Pafford, "Federal Agency/Contractor Strategic Alliances: Recent Developments & Emerging Issues," *Briefing Papers* (Second Series), February 2001; "Mergers and Acquisitions of Government Contractors-Special Considerations and Due Diligence Concerns," 23 Public Contract Law Journal 471 (Summer 1994); Feature Comment, "The Need for Reviewing IR&D Charging Practices After Mayman v. Martin Marietta," 37 The Government Contractor ¶532 (Oct. 18, 1995); "The New Commercial Item Acquisition Rules: What Contractors Need to Know," 5 Acquisition Issues, No. 617 (December 1995). Feature Comment: "Untangling the FY 1997 Limitations on Allowable Individual Compensation Costs," 38 The Government Contractor 498 (Oct. 23, 1996); with John W. Chienchella & Michael L. Waldman, "Commissions & Fees Paid to Overseas Agents: Cost Recovery & Related Rules," 98-8 CP&A Report, 3-21 (Aug. 1998); with Lynda Troutman O'Sullivan, "Commercial Item Acquisitions," 97-5 Briefing Papers (April 1997); with Ambassador David E. Birebaum and Douglas R.M. King, "Selling to the United Nations," 5 Acquisition Issues No. 11 (1996); with Richard C. Park, "New DOJ/FTC Antitrust Guidelines Set Forth Framework for Evaluating Exclusive Teaming Arrangements and Other Competitor Collaborations," 42 *The Government Contractor* 193 (May 17, 2000); with Richard C. Park, "Exclusive Teaming Arrangements: Impact on Antitrust Guidelines," 00-6 *Briefing Papers* (Second Series) (May 2000); with James J. McCullough and Abram J. Pafford, "Ally to the State: New Cooperative Agreements With the Government Have Benefits and Risks," *Legal Times* (March 5, 2001) at 29. ***LANGUAGES:*** French, Spanish. ***PRACTICE AREAS:*** Government Contracts; Litigation; Export Compliance. ***Email:*** douglas_perry@ffhsj.com

ELLIOT E. POLEBAUM, born Lowell, Massachusetts, September 8, 1950; admitted to bar, 1978, New York and Massachusetts; 1981, District of Columbia. *Education:* Middlebury College (A.B., magna cum laude, 1972, Phi Beta Kappa); Harvard University (M.P.A., 1975); New York University School of Law (J.D., cum laude, 1977). Order of the Coif. Managing Editor, New York University Law Review, 1976-1977. Law Clerk to: Judge James L. Oakes, U.S. Court of Appeals for the Second Circuit, 1977-1978; Associate Justice William J. Brennan, Jr., Supreme Court of the United States, 1980-1981. Author: "Discovery in the U.S. in Aid of Foreign Litigation Under Section 1782," International Business Lawyer (October, 1996); "U.S. Courts' Position on Judicial Assistance to Foreign Tribunals," International Business Lawyer (December 1991); "Proper Venue In Which to Petition to Vacate a Foreign Arbitration Award," International Business Lawyer (April 1991); "U.S. Foreign Sovereign Immunities Act and the Kingdom of Swaziland Case," International Legal Practitioner (December 1990); "Effect of Proposed Amendments to the Federal Rules of Civil Procedure on Litigation Involving Foreign Parties," International Business Lawyer (June 1990); Case Note, "Hague Convention," International Business Lawyer (March 1990). Contributing Author, Internet and Online Law,

(This Listing Continued)

Law Journal Seminars Press (1996 and 1997, 1998, 1999 and 2000 updates). *Member:* American and International Bar Associations. ***LANGUAGES:*** French. ***PRACTICE AREAS:*** International Arbitration; Commercial Litigation; Intellectual Property Litigation. ***Email:*** elliot_polebaum@ffhsj.com

MICHAEL J. RIVERA, born New York, N.Y., April 30, 1966; admitted to bar, 1992, New York; 1993, District of Columbia. *Education:* St. John's University (B.S., magna cum laude, 1988); University of Pennsylvania (J.D., 1991). Co-Author: "The Rhyme of Securities Litigation: 1993 Judicial Update," *Insights* (1994); "SEC Suspensions and Bars," *Investment Lawyer* (1995); "The Smallest Trade Can Wreak Havoc," *Counsel Connect* (1996); "Between Consenting Adults: Second Circuit Upholds The Right To Contract," *SecMail* (1996); "Ex-NBA Player's Fraud Allegations 'Foul Out' of Seventh Circuit," *SecMail* (1996); "To Tell Or Not To Tell: Reassessing Disclosure Of Uncharged Misconduct," *Insights* (1999); "SEC Explains How Internet Offshore Securities Activities Can Avoid U.S. Registration," *Canadian-U.S. Securities Regulation, Infonex Conference* (1999). *Member:* The District of Columbia Bar (Member, Corporation, Finance and Securities Law Section); American Bar Association (Member, Business Law Section). ***PRACTICE AREAS:*** Securities Regulation and Compliance; Securities Enforcement; Corporate. ***Email:*** michael.rivera@ffhsj.com

CHARLES F. (RICK) RULE, born Nashville, Tennessee, April 28, 1955; admitted to bar, 1983, District of Columbia. *Education:* Vanderbilt University (B.A., summa cum laude, 1978); University of Chicago (J.D., 1981). Distinguished Adjunct Professor, Washington College of Law, American University. Assistant Attorney General, Antitrust Division, U.S. Department of Justice, 1986-1989; Deputy Assistant Attorney General, Antitrust Division, 1984-1986; Special Assistant to the Assistant Attorney General, Antitrust Division, 1982-1984. Partner, Covington & Burling, 1989-2001. Member, Bureau of National Affairs Antitrust Rules and Regulations Advisory Board; Member, Advisory Boards of the Washington Legal Foundation and Landmark Legal Foundation; Member, Visiting Committee of the University of Chicago Law School. Chair, Corporations, Securities, and Antitrust Practice Group, Federalist Society, 1997-2000; Chair, Economics Committee of the American Bar Association Antitrust Section, 1989-1991. Chairman of the Antitrust Department, Fried, Frank, Harris, Shriver & Jacobson. ***PRACTICE AREAS:*** Antitrust; Competition Law; International Antitrust. ***Email:*** ruleri@ffhsj.com

RICHARD A. SAUBER, born Philadelphia, Pennsylvania, March 7, 1950; admitted to bar, 1977, Rhode Island; 1985, District of Columbia. *Education:* Yale University (B.A., 1972); Oxford University, England (M.Litt., 1975); New York University (J.D., 1977). Prosecutor, Criminal Fraud Section, 1977-1982 and Chief, Defense Procurement Fraud Unit, 1982-1984, U.S. Justice Department. *Member:* The District of Columbia Bar; Rhode Island and American (Member, Section on Public Contract Law) Bar Associations. ***Email:*** sauberi@ffhsj.com

JAMES H. SCHROPP, born Lebanon, Pennsylvania, June 20, 1943; admitted to bar, 1973, District of Columbia. *Education:* University of Richmond (B.A., 1965); Georgetown University (J.D., 1973). Adjunct Professor of Securities Law, Georgetown University, 1983-1987. Assistant General Counsel, Securities and Exchange Commission, 1973-1979. *Member:* The District of Columbia Bar; Federal and American (Member: Section on Corporation, Banking and Business Law; Litigation Committee on Takeover Litigation and Discovery, 1984-1986; Task Force on Broker-Dealer Supervision and Compliance, 1988-1989) Bar Associations. ***Email:*** james_schropp@ffhsj.com

RICHARD A. STEINWURTZEL, born Newark, New Jersey, January 1, 1950; admitted to bar, 1975, District of Columbia; 1982, New York. *Education:* Union College (B.A., cum laude, 1972); National Law Center, George Washington University (J.D., with honors, 1975). Member, Legal and Compliance Division, Securities Industry Association, 1985—. Author: Rethinking Disclosure Policies and Practices in the Wake of the SEC's New Selection Disclosure Rules To Our Clients, September 15, 2000; "The SEC Adopts IOSCO Disclosure Standards for Foreign Private Issuers," *To Our Clients,* October 5, 1999; "SEC Amends Performance Fee Rule," *To Our Clients,* July 29, 1998; "SEC Amends Regulation S and Imposes Additional Burdens on Offshore Offerings of Domestic U.S. Reporting Issuers' Equity Securities," *To Our Clients,* March 4, 1998; "SEC Adopts Significant Amendments to Reporting Regime for 5% Shareholders and Announces Interpretive Relief," *To Our Clients,* January 28, 1998; "New Qualified Purchaser Funds," *To Our Clients,* April 14, 1997; "Amendments to Rule 144 and Regulation S," *SecMail No. 97-02-21,* February 21, 1997; "Regulation M: A New Era of Trading Practices Regulation," *To Our Clients,* January 9, 1997; "Capsule Summary of Proposed Regulation M," *To Our Clients,* January 9, 1997; "Exhibit A: Summary of Defined Terms Used in the Capsule Summary," *To Our Clients,* January 9, 1997; "New Section 16 Rules," *To Our Clients,* June 1, 1996; "Proposed Amendments to the Trading Practices Rules," *SecMail No. 96-4-9,* April 23, 1996; "Proposed Amendments to the Trading Practices Rules," *To Our Clients,* April 19, 1996; "Continuing Education Program for Securities Industry Professionals," May 5, 1995; "Disclosure of Restructuring Charges," March 24, 1995; "United States Supreme Court Eliminates Rescission Remedy for Secondary Market Purchasers," March 1995; SIA Annual Compliance & Legal Program, "Avoiding Legal

(This Listing Continued)

Landmines in Special Transactions," May 2, 1995; "Proposed Revisions to Section 16 Rules," *To Our Clients,* August 15, 1994; Executive Compensation Workshop, "Compensation Committees and Executive Pay," December 1993; American Stock Exchange Regional CEO Program, "The New Rules: Executive Compensation, Proxy Reform and Accounting for Stock Options," October 1993; American Stock Exchange Regional CEO Program, "The New Rules: Executive Compensation Proxy Reform and Accounting for Stock Options," June 1993; Articles, SIA Compliance & Legal Seminar, "Avoiding Legal Landmines in Special Transactions," March, 1993; SEC Executive Pay Rule Seminar, January 13, 1993, Prentice Hall; Executive Compensation: SEC and State Law Aspects - Slide Presentation, December 1992; "The New Proxy and Executive Compensation Rules," Fried, Frank, Harris, Shriver & Jacobson Seminar, December 2, 1992; "Proxy Reform and Executive Compensation Reporting Requirements: A New Era of SEC Activism," October 29, 1992; "The SEC's New Preference for Prophecy," *Legal Times,* July 6, 1992; SIA Seminar, "Avoiding Legal Landmines in Special Transactions," April 1992; "MD&A Through The Eyes Of Management: A Closer Look At The SEC's Caterpillar Decision," *To Our Clients,* April 23, 1992; *A Practical Guide to Section 16: Reporting and Compliance,* (Chapter 11: Merger and Acquisition Implications) September 1991 and February 1992 (Contributor); "Section 16 - New Rule Changes," American Society of Corporate Secretaries, October 1991; "The SEC's Roll-Up Initiatives," July 1991; "Proxy Rule Reform Begins," June 1991; "Gollust v. Mendell: Section 16(b) Claim Survives Merger," June 1991; "New Section 16 Rules," March 1991; "SEC Adopts Section 16 Rule Proposals," *To Our Clients,* January 14, 1991; "Recession Heightens Financial Institution Proxy Contest and Shareholder Proposal Possibilities," *To Our Clients,* January 14, 1991; "SEC Financial Institutions Task Force Update: Bank of New England Corporation Enters into Consent Agreement Regarding Loan Loss Provisions," *To Our Clients,* January 11, 1991; "SEC Revises Form S-8 Registration Requirements," September 1990; "SEC Topics of Current Interest," American Society of Corporate Secretaries, September 1990; "Event Risk Update: Credit Sensitive Securities," March 1990; "Super Poison Puts as a Protection Against Event Risks," October 1989; "SEC Staff Reviews Poison Puts," October 1989; "Legal Issues in the International Securities Markets - Rights Issues, Tender Offers and Merger and Acquisition Law," December 1987; "Past, Present & Future International Investing," November 1987; "An Overview of Issues in Restructuring," September 1987; SIA Workshop - "Money Managers," March 1987; "Liability for Insider Trading," January 1987; "Developments of Merger Negotiations: Heublin/Carnation Release," December 1986; "The Evolving Business Judgment Rule," November 1986; "Cutting the Deal - Dynamics of a Mortgage Banking Deal," November 1986; "A Review of Broker-Dealer Litigation Involving Options," October 1985; SIA Seminar, "Soft Dollar Payments," April 1985; "Self-Regulatory Enforcement Action," April 1983. *Member:* The District of Columbia Bar; New York State and American (Member, Section on Corporation, Banking and Business Law) Bar Associations. ***Email:*** richard_steinwurtzel@ffhsj.com

VASILIKI B. TSAGANOS, born Chicago, Illinois, September 2, 1965; admitted to bar, 1990, Illinois; 1992, District of Columbia. *Education:* The American University (B.A., 1987); Northwestern University (J.D., 1990). Member, Journal of International Law and Business. Former Vice President, General Counsel and Assistant Secretary of Fresh Fields Markets, Inc. ***LANGUAGES:*** Greek, French. ***PRACTICE AREAS:*** Corporate; Securities. ***Email:*** tsagava@ffhsj.com

ANDREW P. VARNEY, born Glens Falls, New York, May 30, 1962; admitted to bar, 1987, Massachusetts; 1988, Virginia; 1989, District of Columbia. *Education:* Middlebury College (A.B., summa cum laude, 1984); Harvard University (J.D., cum laude, 1987). Phi Beta Kappa. *Member:* The District of Columbia Bar; Virginia State Bar; American Bar Association. ***Email:*** andrew.varney@ffhsj.com

THOMAS P. VARTANIAN, born Forest Hills, New York, November 16, 1949; admitted to bar, 1977, New York; 1979, District of Columbia; 1983, U.S. Supreme Court. *Education:* Cathedral College (B.A., cum laude, 1971); Brooklyn Law School (J.D., cum laude, 1976). Special Assistant to the Chief Counsel and Senior Trial Attorney, Office of the Comptroller of the Currency, 1976-1981. General Counsel, Federal Home Loan Bank Board and the Federal Savings and Loan Insurance Corporation, 1981-1983. Adjunct Professor, Graduate Law Program, Georgetown University Law Center (1996—), Boston University Law School, Morin School of Banking (1999-2000) and George Washington University School of Law (2000—). Chairman, Committee on Cyberspace Law (1998—). Member: Digital Signature Technical Advisory Committee, Virginia Legislature's Joint Commission on Technology and Science; Information Security Exploratory Committee, National Information Infrastructure ("NII") Task Force, President's National Security Telecommunications Advisory Committee ("NTSAC"); Board of Advisors, Electronic Banking Law and Commerce Report. Co-Authored, books: *21st Century Money, Banking & Commerce,* May 1998 (Nacha Payments Publications); *The Management of Risks Created by Internet-Initiated Value Transfers,* January 1998 (Nacha Payments Publications); *The Fair Lending Guide,* 1995 (Glasser LegalWorks); *Contracting with the RTC and FDIC,* 1991 (Prentice Hall). Articles: "Multiple Legal Setups Imperil Electronic Commerce," *American Banker* (July 9, 1997); "Digital Certification:

(This Listing Continued)

New Wrinkles in Managing Risk," *American Banker* (July 1, 1997); "Doing Business on the Net Sure to Change Risk Profiles," *American Banker Future Banking* (Feb. 18, 1997); "Stored Value Cards and Electronic Payment Systems," *The Review of Banking & Financial Services* (Nov. 20, 1996); "Key Questions for Emerging Systems: Where is the Money?" *American Banker Future Banking* (June 17, 1996); "Mondex's Swindon Test Points to Future of Electronic Cash," *American Banker Future Banking* (Apr. 15, 1996); "Bank Takeovers: Where Shareholder Expectations Meet Investor Impatience," *Banking Policy Report* (June 5, 1995); "Echoes of the Past With Implications for the Future: The Stamp Payments Act of 1862 and Electronic Commerce," *BNA's Banking Report,* Vil. 67 (Sept. 23, 1996); "Line of Business Joint Venture Opportunities," *SNL Securities Compliance Fax* (Mar. 18, 1996; "The Challenge of Cultural Consolidation: SEC-OCC Joint Fund Examinations Agreement," *NSCP Currents* (Oct. 1995); "The Chevy Chase Case: Setting a New Direction for Federal Fair Lending Efforts," *Banking Policy Report* (Sept. 19, 1994). "When Tech Marries Money," *Legal Times* (March 1, 1999), p. S36; "A US Perspective on The Global Jurisdictional Checkpoints in Cyberspace," *Pike & Fischer Internet Law and Regulation* (May 1999); "It's a Question of Jurisdiction; Irreconcilable Differences in Cyberspace," *Business Law Today* (July/August 1999), pages 22-26; "If You Build It, They Will Come," *American Banker* (September 10, 1999), pages 8-9. Co-Author: with R.H. Ledig and A.C. Conover, "A Survey of Selected Federal Regulatory and Legal Developments in Electronic Financial Services," *The Business Lawyer* (November 1997), Vol. 53, No. 1; with Harvey L. Pitt, "Knocking on Boardroom Doors," *Legal Times* (February 14, 2000), pages 45-46; "Cookies, Telephones & Spleens: The Evolving Theology of Data Control," *Electronic Banking Law and Commerce Report* (March 2001). Member, Advisory Board, *Electronic Banking Law and Commerce Report. Member:* The District of Columbia Bar; New York State, Federal and American (Member, Section on Business Law) Bar Associations. ***Email:*** vartath@ffhsj.com

MICHAEL L. WALDMAN, born New York, N.Y., March 3, 1960; admitted to bar, 1987, Massachusetts and U.S. Court of Appeals, Eleventh Circuit; 1988, District of Columbia; 1990, U.S. Supreme Court. *Education:* Harvard University (B.A., magna cum laude, 1982; J.D., cum laude, 1986). Phi Beta Kappa. Author: "Beyond Upjohn: The Attorney-Client Privilege in the Corporate Context," William & Mary Law Review, Vol. 28, 1987; "1986 Amendments to the False Claims Act: Retroactive or Perspective?" Public Contract Law Journal, June, 1989; "Time to Blow The Whistle: Weighing the Value of Whistleblower Law," National Law Journal, March 25, 1991; "Damage Control: A Defendant's Approach to the Damage and Penalty Provisions of the Civil False Claims Act," Public Contract Law Journal, Winter, 1992; "Employee-Employer Relations in a Qui Tam World," The Corporate Analyst, May, 1992; "What's Wrong With the False Claims Act: A Case in Point," Contract Management, March, 1995. Co-Author: with Richard Sauber, "Government Wiretaps: Opportunities for Defense Counsel," White-Collar Crime Reporter, May, 1990; "Unlimited Power: Rule 29(A) and the Unreviewability of Directed Judgments of Acquittal," 44 American University Law Review 433, December, 1994; "Recent Summary Judgment for Aerojet Has Significant Implications for Defending FCA Cases," Government Contract Litigation Reporter, July 4, 1996; with Gejaa Gobena, "Hands Across The Water: U.S. Prosecutors Are Going Overseas to Gather Evidence," Legal Times, September 20, 1999; with John Chierichella and Douglas Perry, "Commissions and Fees Paid To Overseas Agents: Cost Recovery and Related Rules," Government Contract Costs, Pricing and Accounting Report, August, 1998. Law Clerk to Judge Robert S. Vance, U.S. Court of Appeals for the Eleventh Circuit, 1986-1987. *Member:* The District of Columbia Bar. ***Email:*** michael_waldman@ffhsj.com

OF COUNSEL

MILTON EISENBERG, (P.C.), born Brooklyn, New York, August 7, 1928; admitted to bar, 1950, New York; 1951, District of Columbia; 1958, U.S. Supreme Court. *Education:* Cornell University (B.A., 1948; J.D., 1950). Adjunct Professor of Law, Georgetown Law School, 1962-1966. Trial Attorney, National Labor Relations Board, 1952-1953. Law Clerk to Hon. John A. Danaher, U.S. Circuit Court, 1953-1955. Assistant U.S. Attorney, 1955-1957. Minority Counsel, House Judiciary Committee, 1957-1958. Administrative Assistant and Counsel to Senator Kenneth B. Keating, 1959-1964. President, Edward Bennett Williams American Inn of Court, 1989-1990. Editor of the "Lawyer's Desk Book on White Collar Crime," published by National Legal Center for the Public Interest, 1991. *Member:* The District of Columbia Bar; Bar Association of the District of Columbia; American Bar Association (Chair, Corporate Criminal Liability Subcommittee, White Collar Crime Committee, 1992-1994). Fellow, American College of Trial Lawyers. Emeritus. ***Email:*** milton_eisenberg@ffhsj.com

JOEL R. FEIDELMAN, (P.C.), born Hazleton, Pennsylvania, February 11, 1934; admitted to bar, 1958, District of Columbia; 1962, U.S. Supreme Court. *Education:* Syracuse University (B.A., magna cum laude, 1955); Yale University (LL.B., 1958). Phi Beta Kappa. Lecturer on Government Contract Law, School of Logistics, Ohio State University, 1960-1965. Lecturer, The Government Contracts Program, The George Washington University Law School,

(This Listing Continued)

FRIED, FRANK, HARRIS, SHRIVER & JACOBSON, Washington—Continued

1965-1968. Government Contracts Consulting Editor, "Legal Times of Washington," 1978-1986. Member, Advisory Board, Federal Contracts Report, 1973-1987. Member, National Board of Advisors, National Contract Management Association, 1987—. *Member:* The District of Columbia Bar; Federal and American Bar Associations. [Lt. and Capt., U.S.A.F., J.A.G., 1958-1961]. ***Email:*** joel_feidelman@ffhsj.com

MARTIN D. GINSBURG, (P.C.), born New York City, N.Y., June 10, 1932; admitted to bar, 1959, New York; 1980, District of Columbia. *Education:* Cornell University (A.B., 1953); Harvard University (J.D., magna cum laude, 1958); Awarded LL.D. (Hon.) by Northwestern School of Law, Lewis and Clark College, 1992; Wheaton College, 1997. Recipient: Marshall-Wythe Medallion, College of William & Mary School of Law 1996; Georgetown University Vicennail Medal 2000. Co-author: with J.S. Levin, "Mergers, Acquisitions, and Buyouts," 3 vols. (revised and republished semi-annually), 2001. Professor of Law: Georgetown University Law Center, 1980—. Charles Keller Beekman Professor of Law, Columbia Law School, 1979-1980. Adjunct Professor of Law, Graduate Program in Taxation, New York University School of Law, 1967-1979. Visiting Professor of Law: New York University School of Law, 1993; University of Chicago Law School, 1990; Harvard Law School, 1986; Stanford University Law School, 1978. Lecturer, Salzburg Seminar (Austria), 1984; Leiden University (Holland), 1982. Member, Tax Division Advisory Committee, Department of Justice, 1980-1981. Member, Advisory Group to the Commissioner of Internal Revenue, 1978-1980. Member, Advisory Board, University of California Securities Regulation Institute, 1973-1991. Chairman, CCH Tax Advisory Board, 1984-1994. Chairman, Little, Brown Tax Advisory Board, 1994-1996. Member, Board of Directors, Tax Analysts, 1988-1991. Member, 1983-1988 and Co-Chairman, 1986-1988, Board of Advisors, New York University Internal Revenue Service Continuing Professional Education Program. Member, Board of Editors, The Journal of Corporate Taxation, 1974—. Member, Subcouncil on Capital Allocation and Co-Chairman, Taxation Expert Group, Competitiveness Policy Council, 1993-1995. Member, Visiting Committee, Harvard Law School, 1994-1998. Honoree: Martin D. Ginsburg Chair in Taxation, Georgetown University Law Center, established 1986. *Member:* The Association of the Bar of the City of New York (Member, Committee on Taxation, 1975-1979; Chairman, 1977-1979; Member, Audit Committee, 1980-1982), New York State (Chairman, 1975 and Member, Executive Committee, 1969—, Tax Section; Member, House of Delegates, 1976-1977) and American (Chairman, Committee on Simplification, 1979-1981 and Member of Council, 1984-1987, Section of Taxation) Bar Associations; American Law Institute (Consultant, ALI Federal Income Tax Project, Subchapters C & K, and Corporate-Shareholder Integration, 1974-1993). Fellow: American College of Tax Counsel; American Bar Foundation (Member, Board of Directors, 2000—). ***Email:*** ginsbma@ffhsj.com

MAX M. KAMPELMAN, born New York, N.Y., November 7, 1920; admitted to bar, 1947, New York; 1950, District of Columbia; 1951, U.S. Supreme Court; 1956, Maryland. *Education:* New York University (A.B., 1940; J.D., 1945); University of Minnesota (M.A., 1946; Ph.D., 1951). Doctor of Philosophy, Honoris Causa, Hebrew University of Jerusalem, 1982; Doctor of Humane Letters, Honoris Causa: Hebrew Union College, 1984; Georgetown University, 1984; University of Minnesota, 1987. Doctor of Law, Honoris Causa: Bates, 1986; Bar-Ilan University, 1987; Doctor of Humane Letters, Honoris Causa, University of Minnesota, 1987; The Jewish Theological Seminary of America, 1988; New York University, 1988; Doctor of Humane Letters, Yeshiva, University, 1990; Doctor of Laws Honorary Degree, Adelphi, 1992; Doctor of Philosophy, Honoris Causa, 1992; Doctor of Laws, Ben Gurion University of the Negev, 1992; Doctor of Humane Letters, Honoris Causa, Florida International University, 1993; Doctor of Laws, Brandeis University, 1993 . Author: *Entering New Worlds: The Memoirs of a Private Man in Public Life,* published by Harper Collins in 1991. *The Communist Party vs. The C.I.O.: A Study in Power Politics,* published by Praeger in 1957.Co-author: with Kirkpatrick, *The Strategy of Deception,* published by Farrar, Straus, 1963; *Three Years at the East-West Divide,* Freedom House, 1983; *Negotiating with the Soviets in Madrid,* World Affairs, 1982; "Congress, The Media and The President," Proceedings of the Academy of Political Science, Vol. 32, No. 1, 1975; Chapter in *Congress Against the President,* edited by Harvey Mansfield, Praeger, 1976; "The Power of the Press: A Problem for our Democracy," Policy Review, Fall, 1978. Recipient: Spirit of Democracy Award, American Jewish Congress, 1993; Eleanor Roosevelt Award, United Nations Association, 1993; Freedom Award, Freedom House, 1993; Presidents Award, Glassboro State College, 1992; Cosmos Club Award, 1991; George P. Kennan Award, Citizens Exchange Council, 1989; George Washington Honor Medal, Freedoms Foundation at Valley Forge, 1989; Philip M. Klutznick Award for Public Service, B'nai B'rith, November 8, 1989; Albert Einstein Award, American Society for Technion, September 21, 1989; Henrietta Szold Award for Distinguished Humanitarian Service, Hadassah, July 18, 1989; Distinguished Public Service Award, American Jewish Committee, May 18, 1989; The Freedom Award, Jamestown Foundation, May 2, 1989; The

(This Listing Continued)

Presidential Citizens Medal, January 18, 1989; Pi Sigma Alpha Award, National Capital Area, APSA, 1989; Trainor Award for Distinction in the Conduct of Diplomacy, Georgetown University, 1988; The Secretary of State's Distinguished Service Award, July, 1988; Henry M. Jackson Award, JINSA, November, 1987; Hubert H. Humphrey Award, APSA, 1987; Judge Learned Hand Award, Institute of Human Relations, 1985; Knight Commander's Cross (Badge and Star) of the Order of Merit of the Federal Republic of Germany, 1984; Masaryk Award, Czechoslovak National Council of America, 1983; Isaiah Award, AJC, 1983. Visiting Professor, Claremont College, 1963. Visiting Professorial Lecturer, Department of Government, Howard University, 1954-1956. Instructor, Political Science, University of Minnesota, 1946-1948. Of Counsel, Fried, Frank Harris, Shriver & Jacobson (Partner, 1955-1985, 1989-1991). Faculty: Political Economy, Bennington College, 1948-1950; School for Workers, University of Wisconsin, 1947-1948. Counselor of the U.S. Department of State, 1987-1989. Ambassador and Head of U.S. Delegation to the Negotiations on Nuclear and Space Arms, Geneva, 1985-1989. Ambassador and Head of U.S. Delegation Conference on Security and Cooperation in Europe, Madrid, 1980-1983, Copenhagen, June 1990, Geneva, July, 1991 and Moscow, September, 1991. Vice Chairman, United States Institute of Peace, 1992—. Member, Executive Board, American Bar Association Central and East European Law Institute, 1990—. Member, Board of Trustees, 1979-1990, Chairman, 1979-1981, Woodrow Wilson International Center for Scholars. Chairman, Freedom House, New York, 1983-1985, 1989-1993. Chairman, Board of Governors, United Nations Association of the United States of America, 1989-1993 . Chairman, The Jerusalem Foundation, 1989-1993. Chairman, Advisory Committee, Jewish Institute for National Security Affairs, 1989-1993. Member: Advisory Council, Institute for International Studies, Stanford University, 1989—; Advisory Board, Center for Strategic and International Studies, 1989—; Board of Directors, American Academy of Diplomacy, 1989—; Chairman, Ethics and Public Policy Center, 1990—; Board of Directors, Jerusalem Center for Public Affairs, 1989—; Chairman, Institute for the Study of Diplomacy, Georgetown University, 1992—. Adjunct Fellow, American Enterprise Institute, 1993. Vice Chairman, U.S. Institute of Peace, 1992—. Chairman, National Advisory Council, American Jewish Committee, 1993—. ***Email:*** max_kampelman@ffhsj.com

MARCUS A. ROWDEN, born Detroit, Michigan, March 13, 1928; admitted to bar, 1953, Michigan; 1978, District of Columbia. *Education:* University of Michigan (A.B., 1950; J.D., 1953). Order of the Coif. Editor, Michigan Law Review, 1952-1953. General Counsel, Atomic Energy Commission, 1973-1975. Chairman and Commissioner, Nuclear Regulatory Commission, 1975-1977. Awarded, Officer of the Order of the Legion of Honor of the Republic of France, 1983. *Member:* Federal and American Bar Associations; International Nuclear Law Association. ***Email:*** marcus_rowden@ffhsj.com

SARGENT SHRIVER, born Westminster, Maryland, November 9, 1915; admitted to bar, 1941, New York; 1959, Illinois; 1966, U.S. Supreme Court; 1971, District of Columbia. *Education:* Yale University (B.A., with honors, 1938); Yale Law School (LL.B., 1941). Honorary degrees conferred by: University of Notre Dame, 1961, Brandeis University, Kansas State and Fordham University, 1962, Yale University, New York University, Georgetown University, Wesleyan University, Chulalongkorn University, Thailand and University of Liberia, 1963 and Jewish Theological Seminary of America, 1965, University of South Carolina, 1965 and Wheeling College, 1978; Doctor of Public Service, George Washington University, 1982; St. Thomas University, Miami, 1986; College of the Holy Cross, 1986—. Recipient: Chicago Medal of Merit, 1957; Yale Medal, 1957; James J. Hoey Award (Catholic Interracial Council of New York), 1958; Golden Heart Presidential Award (Philippines), 1964; Notre Dame Patriotism Award, 1965; Philip Murray-William Green Award, 1966; Pacem in Terris Peace and Freedom Award, 1966; National Brotherhood Award, 1966; Laetare Medal (Notre Dame), 1968; St. Louis University Medical Center Award for Leadership in Medical Ethics, 1981. President, Board of Education, City of Chicago, 1955-1960. Director, Peace Corps, 1961-1966. Director, Office of Economic Opportunity, VISTA, Headstart, Foster Grandparents, Job Corps, Green Thumb, Upward Bound, Legal Services, Neighborhood Health Centers, Migrant Opportunities, Community Action, Neighborhood Youth Corps, Indian Opportunities and Work Experience, 1964-1968. Special Assistant to President Johnson, 1964-1968. United States Ambassador to France, 1968-1970. Chairman: Congressional Leadership for the Future, 1970-1971; International Advisory Board, Kennedy Institute of Ethics, Georgetown University, 1971—; International Patrons of the Israel Museum, 1972-1975. Member: Council on Foreign Relations, 1971—; American Committee East-West Accord, 1978—; Americans for SALT, 1979—. Honorary National Chairman, National Inter-Religious Task Force on Soviet Jewry, 1977-1978. Co-Chairman, Friends of VISTA, 1980—. Chairman & CEO, Special Olympics International, 1990-1996. Chairman of the Board of Special Olympics International, 1996—. Member, Board of Directors, American Arms Control Association, 1983—. Presidential Medal of Freedom, 1994. Franklin D. Roosevelt "Freedom From Want Award" 1994.

DANIEL M. SINGER, born Brooklyn, New York, October 10, 1930; admitted to bar, 1956, New York; 1957, District of Columbia; 1959, U.S. Supreme Court. *Education:* Swarthmore College (B.A. with honors, 1951); Yale University (LL.B., 1954). Member, Editorial Board, Yale Law Journal, 1953-1954.

(This Listing Continued)

Law Clerk, U.S. Court of Appeals, District of Columbia Circuit, 1956-1958. Member, National Panel of Arbitrators, American Arbitration Association. Mediator, U.S. District Court. Member, Board of Managers, Swarthmore College, 1988-1991. Special Assistant Corporation Counsel, D.C., 1995-2000. *Member:* The District of Columbia Bar; American Bar Association. [U.S. Army, Signal Corps., 1954-1956]. ***Email:*** daniel.singer@ffhsj.com

MICHAEL A. VATIS, born New York, N.Y., October 14, 1963; admitted to bar, 1989, New York; 1990, District of Columbia. *Education:* Princeton University (A.B., magna cum laude, 1985); Harvard University (J.D., magna cum laude, 1988). Phi Beta Kappa. Supervising Editor, Harvard Law Review, 1987-1988. Law Clerk to Judge Ruth Ginsburg, U.S. Court of Appeals for the DC Circuit, 1988-1989; Law Clerk, Justice Thurgood Marshall, U.S. Supreme Court, 1989-1990. Attorney, Mayer, Brown & Platt, Washington, D.C., 1990-1993. Department of Defense, Office of General Counsel, 1993-1994; Associate Deputy Attorney General and Deputy Director, Executive Office for National Security, Department of Justice, 1994-1998; Director, National Infrastructure Protection Center, FBI, 1998-2001; Director, Institute for Security Technology Studies, Dartmouth College, 2001—. ***PRACTICE AREAS:*** Internet Law; E-Commerce; Privacy Law; Litigation. ***Email:*** michael.vatis@ffhsj.com

LOUIS D. VICTORINO, born Lemoore, California, May 27, 1945; admitted to bar, 1971, California; 1978, District of Columbia. *Education:* Stanford University (B.A., 1967); University of California at Los Angeles (J.D., 1970). Member, Board of Editors, UCLA Law Review, 1969-1970. Author: "Government Failure to Disclose," Government Contract Briefing Papers, No. 92-10, Sept. 1992; "Anti-trust Implications of Defense Industry Combinations," Government Contract Briefing Papers, No. 93-7, June 1993; "Multiple Award Task & Delivery Order Contracts, Government Contract Briefing Papers, No. 96-10, Sept. 1996. Member, Legal Remedies Staff, Commission on Government Procurement 1971. Member: Advisory Board, *The Government Contractor,* 1991-1998; Board of Editors, The Public Contract Law Journal, 1991-1995. *Member:* Federal and American (Member, Public Contract Law Section, 1971—) Bar Associations. (Also at Los Angeles, California Office). ***Email:*** louis_victorino@ffhsj.com

SPECIAL COUNSEL

MARK FAJFAR, born St. Louis, Missouri, October 11, 1966; admitted to bar, 1992, Maryland; 1994, District of Columbia and U.S. Court of International Trade. *Education:* Washington University (B.A., 1988); Georgetown University (M.S.F.S., 1992; J.D., magna cum laude, 1992). Phi Beta Kappa; Order of the Coif. Author: "An Economic Analysis of Informed Consent to Medical Care," 80 Geo. L.J. 1941 (1992). Co-Author: "Tougher Standards for Audit Committees: The Report of the 'Blue Ribbon' Committee," Corp. Counsel's Quarterly (October 1999); "Start-Up Kits," Tech Counsel (August 2000). *Member:* The District of Columbia Bar. ***LANGUAGES:*** French. ***Email:*** mark.fajfar@ffhsj.com

DAVID L. FENIMORE, born Elmira, New York, May 12, 1947; admitted to bar, 1989, Pennsylvania (Inactive); 1990, District of Columbia. *Education:* Bowdoin College (B.A., 1969); Southern Illinois University (M.A., Government, 1977); Columbus School of Law of the Catholic University of America (J.D., 1988). Lecturer, Securities Regulation & Enforcement, Columbus School of Law, Catholic University, 1996-1997. ***PRACTICE AREAS:*** Securities Law Enforcement; Broker-Dealer Compliance; Corporate. ***Email:*** david.fenimore@ffhsj.com

ROBERT M. FISHER, born Washington, D.C., September 9, 1954; admitted to bar, 1991, Maryland; 1993, District of Columbia. *Education:* Duke University (A.B., 1976; A.M., 1977; Ph.D., 1982); Harvard Law School (J.D., magna cum laude, 1991). *Member:* The District of Columbia Bar. ***PRACTICE AREAS:*** Securities Law; Banking; Antitrust. ***Email:*** fishero@ffhsj.com

KAREN T. GRISEZ, born Washington, D.C., November 20, 1955; admitted to bar, 1990, Maryland; 1992, District of Columbia. *Education:* University of Maryland (B.A., summa cum laude, 1987); Catholic University of America (J.D., 1990). Public Service Counsel. *Member:* The District of Columbia Bar; Maryland State, Federal and American Bar Associations; American Immigration Lawyers Association; Maryland Women's Bar Association; District of Columbia Women's Bar Association. ***Email:*** karen_grisez@ffhsj.com

JONATHAN M. JACOBS, born Baltimore, Maryland, May 31, 1962; admitted to bar, 1988, Maryland; 1989, U.S. District Court, District of Maryland and U.S. Court of Appeals, Fourth Circuit; 1990, District of Columbia. *Education:* Duke University (A.B., magna cum laude, 1984), Phi Eta Sigma; University of Pennsylvania (J.D., 1988). Associate and Special Projects Editor, University of Pennsylvania Law Review, 1986-1988. Law Clerk to: Judge Paul V. Niemeyer, U.S. District Court for the District of Maryland, 1988-1989. ***PRACTICE AREAS:*** Civil Litigation. ***Email:*** jonathan.jacobs@ffhsj.com

DEBORAH MILLER, born Baltimore, Maryland, October 2, 1965; admitted to bar, 1992, Maryland; 1993, District of Columbia; registered to practice before U.S. Patent and Trademark Office. *Education:* University of Maryland (B.S., 1987); University of Virginia (J.D., 1992). ***PRACTICE AREAS:*** Patents; Licensing; Intellectual Property; Corporate Law. ***Email:*** debbie.miller@ffhsj.com

ANNE B. PERRY, born Allentown, Pennsylvania, July 9, 1964; admitted to bar, 1989, Pennsylvania; 1995, District of Columbia. *Education:* Dickinson College (B.A., 1986); George Washington University (J.D., with honors, 1989). Omicron Delta Kappa. *Member:* The District of Columbia Bar; Pennsylvania and American (Public Contract Law Section) Bar Associations. ***PRACTICE AREAS:*** Government Contracts Litigation; Civil Litigation. ***Email:*** anne_perry@ffhsj.com

CATHERINE EVANS POLLACK, born Harvey, Illinois, November 23, 1961; admitted to bar, 1991, Pennsylvania; 1995, U.S. Court of Appeals for the Federal Circuit; 1997, District of Columbia; 1998, U.S. Court of Federal Claims. *Education:* College of William and Mary (B.A., 1983); George Mason University (J.D., 1990). Attorney-Advisor, U.S. General Accounting Office, Procurement Law Division, 1991-1994. *Member:* American Bar Association (Member, Section on Public Contracts, Bid Protest Committee). ***PRACTICE AREAS:*** Government Contracts; Litigation. ***Email:*** pollaca@ffhsj.com

PAUL M. ROTHSTEIN, born Brooklyn, New York; admitted to bar, 1990, California; 1992, District of Columbia. *Education:* Yale University (B.A., 1987); Stanford University (J.D., 1990). *Member:* State Bar of California; The District of Columbia Bar. ***PRACTICE AREAS:*** Technology Transactions; Internet Transactions; Intellectual Property. ***Email:*** rothspa@ffhsj.com

ASSOCIATES

STEVEN A. ALERDING, born Boston, Massachusetts, December 16, 1966; admitted to bar, 1997, Virginia; 1999, District of Columbia. *Education:* University of Massachusetts at Amherst (B.A., magna cum laude, 1988); University of Michigan (J.D., cum laude, 1997). [Lt., USNR, 1988-1994]. ***PRACTICE AREAS:*** Litigation; Government Contracts. ***Email:*** alerdst@ffhsj.com

MICHAEL J. ALTER, born New York, New York, October 26, 1971; admitted to bar, 1997, Massachusetts; 1998, District of Columbia. *Education:* Union College (B.A., magna cum laude, 1993); George Washington University (J.D., with honors, 1997). ***LANGUAGES:*** Hebrew. ***PRACTICE AREAS:*** Taxation. ***Email:*** michael_alter@ffhsj.com

MICHAEL J. ANSTETT, born Big Spring, Texas, October 23, 1973; admitted to bar, 2000, New York; 2001, District of Columbia. *Education:* University of Portland (B.A., maxima cum laude, 1996); Duke University (J.D., 1999). Law Clerk, Kenneth F. Ripple, U.S. Court of Appeals, Seventh Circuit, 1999-2000. ***Email:*** michael.anstett@ffhsj.com

JONATHAN S. ARONIE, born Boston, Massachusetts, May 13, 1968; admitted to bar, 1993, Maryland; 1994, District of Columbia and U.S. District Court, District of Columbia; 1995, U.S. District Court, District of Maryland; 1997, U.S. Court of Federal Claims. *Education:* Brandeis University (B.A., cum laude, with honors in Political Science, 1993); Duke University (J.D., 1993). Member: Moot Court Board; Alaska Law Review, 1992-1993. Law Clerk to the Honorable Patricia Wynn, District of Columbia Superior Court, 1993-1994. Author: "Assessing Alaska's (Medical Malpractice) Expert Advisory Panel," 10 Alaska L. Rev. 401 (Dec. 1992); "Solid Footing for D.C. Real Estate," The Washington Lawyers, page 36 (Nov./Dec. 1997); "Ethics/Compliance Programs for Government Contractors: An Idea of Biblical Proportions," Coalition for Government Procurement Newsletter (December 1998); "GSA IG Audit — You Can't Afford To Be Unprepared," Coalition for Government Procurement Newsletter (August 1998); GSA's MAS Program: Look Before You Leap," Federal Computer Week (August 10, 1998); GSA's Revised MAS IT Solicitation — It's Not Quite Commercial," National Contract Management Association On-Line Journal (May 15, 1998); "Open Market, Insert Foot," *Federal Computer Week* (August 30, 1999); "Multiple-Award Schedule Contracts: The Good, the Bad, the Ugly," *Washington Technology* (August 30, 1999); "The Dark Side Revisited--A Few Thoughts on GEIA's Petition of the OFPP," *Off the Shelf* (official magazine of the Coalition for Government Procurement) (July 1999). Co-Author: with James J. McCullough, "Check or Checkmate? OFPP's Recent Decision Affirming the Legality of GSA's Post-Award Audit Clause," *Contract Management* (December 1999); with John W. Chierichella, "Disputing a Commercial KO," *Legal Times* (April 26, 1999); with James McCullough, "Access Board Issues Draft Regulations Implementing Section 508," *Government Contracts Alert,* (April 30, 2000); with William H. Taft, IV, "Understanding DSCA's New FMF Guidelines," *The Government Contractor* (August 30, 2000); with James J. McCullough and John W. Chierichella, "The Government's Assault of FOIA Exemption 4: Do You Know Where Your Data Are?," *Off The Shelf,* October 2000; with James J. McCullough and John W. Chierichella, "When is Information Confidential? *Contract Management,* November 2000; with Andrew Skowronek and John W. Chierichella, "Domestic & Foreign Product Preferences," *Briefing Papers, Second Series,* December 2000; with John W. Chierichella and Jonathan S. Aronie, "Developments in Administrative Law and Regulatory Practice 1999-2000," *ABA Section of Administrative Law and Regulatory Practice,* (Public Contracts and Procurement), February 2001; with John W. Chierichella, "Unwary Rabbits Beware: IDIQ Means Never Having to Say

(This Listing Continued)

(This Listing Continued)

FRIED, FRANK, HARRIS, SHRIVER & JACOBSON, Washington—Continued

You're Sorry," *Government Contract Audit Report,* February 2001; Featured Article: with James J. McCullough, "Final FAR Rules Governing EIT Accessibility Answer Some Questions, Raise Others," *Fried Frank Government Contracts Alert,* (April 30, 2001). *Member:* The District of Columbia Bar; Maryland State, Federal and American Bar Associations; Board of Contract Appeals Bar Association. ***PRACTICE AREAS:*** Government Contracts; Litigation; Internal Investigations, Compliance and Monitoring; Qui Tam Defense. ***Email:*** aronijo@ffhsj.com

STEPHEN R. BAUER, born Summit, New Jersey, October 19, 1970; admitted to bar, 1996, New Jersey, New York and District of Columbia. *Education:* Princeton University (A.B., magna cum laude, 1992); Harvard Law School (J.D., magna cum laude, 1995). Phi Beta Kappa. Previous Employment: Shaw Pittman. *Member:* The District of Columbia Bar; New Jersey State and New York State Bar Associations. ***PRACTICE AREAS:*** Corporate Law; Securities; Private Equity. ***Email:*** stephen_bauer@ffhsj.com

TOMMY P. BEAUDREAU, born Wheatridge, Colorado, August 19, 1972; admitted to bar, 1997, Virginia; 2001, District of Columbia and U.S. District Court, Eastern District of Virginia. *Education:* Yale University (B.A., with distinction, 1994); Georgetown University Law Center (J.D., cum laude, 1997). Law Clerk to the Hon. Jerome B. Friedman, U.S. District Court, Eastern District of Virginia, 2000-2001. ***PRACTICE AREAS:*** Litigation; Civil Fraud; White Collar Crime. ***Email:*** beaudto@ffhsj.com

NOAH A. BERLIN, born Atlanta, Georgia, October 12, 1973; admitted to bar, 2000, New Jersey, New York and District of Columbia. *Education:* Sarah Lawrence College (B.A., 1995); University of Pennsylvania (J.D., 1999). Recipient, Fred J. Leebron Award in Constitutional Law. Author: "Constitutional Conflict With The Japanese Imperial Role: Accession, Yasukuni Shrine, and Obligatory Reformation," 1 U. PA. J. Const. L. 383 (1998). ***LANGUAGES:*** Japanese. ***PRACTICE AREAS:*** Securities. ***Email:*** berlino@ffhsj.com

MAYA A. BERNSTEIN, born North Tarrytown, New York, April 13, 1963; admitted to bar, 2000, California; 2001, District of Columbia. *Education:* University of Michigan, Ann Arbor (A.B., with honors, 1987); Massachusetts Institute of Technology; American University (J.D., cum laude, 1999). Law Clerk, Honorable Vanessa Ruiz, District of Columbia Court of Appeals, 1999-2000. Policy Analyst, U.S. Office of Management and Budget, 1990-1999. ***PRACTICE AREAS:*** E-Commerce; Technology Transactions; Corporate Law. ***Email:*** maya.bernstein@ffhsj.com

JENNIFER JEWELL BLACK, admitted to bar, 1999, California; 2000, District of Columbia. *Education:* University of California, Berkeley (B.A., with honors, 1992); University of Virginia (J.D., 1999). *Member:* American Bar Association. ***LANGUAGES:*** Spanish. ***PRACTICE AREAS:*** Taxation. ***Email:*** blackje@ffhsj.com

ANDREA J. BOYACK, born Madison, Wisconsin, August 24, 1968; admitted to bar, 1997, New York; 1998, District of Columbia. *Education:* Brigham Young University (B.A., 1991); University of Virginia Law School (J.D., 1995); The Fletcher School of Law and Diplomacy, Tufts University (M.A.L.D., 1995). Law Clerk, Honorable John Gleese, U.S. District Court, Eastern District of New York, 1995-1996. Author, "Independence and Group Rights in the Baltics: A Double Minority Problem," 35 Va. J. Int'l. Law 485 (1995). ***LANGUAGES:*** Russian. ***PRACTICE AREAS:*** Finance. ***Email:*** andrea_boyack@ffhsj.com

NOEL P. BROCK, born Beckley, West Virginia, June 13, 1967; admitted to bar, 1996, West Virginia; 1997, U.S. Court of Appeals, Fifth Circuit; 1998, District of Columbia. *Education:* Concord College (B.S.B.A., summa cum laude, 1989); West Virginia University (M.P.A., 1990; J.D., 1996). Order of the Coif. Editor-in-Chief, West Virginia Law Review, 1995-1996. Certified Public Accountant, West Virginia, 1991. Lecturer, Columbus School of Law, The Catholic University of America. *Member:* District of Columbia Bar (Member, Taxation Section); American Bar Association (Member, Taxation Section; Corporate Tax Committee and Partnership Tax Committee). ***PRACTICE AREAS:*** Federal Income Tax. ***Email:*** brockno@ffhsj.com

JUSTIN J. BROOKMAN, born August 4, 1974; admitted to bar, 2000, New York; 2001, District of Columbia. *Education:* University of Virginia (B.A., 1995); New York University (J.D., 1998). ***Email:*** justin.brookman@ffhsj.com

CRISTINA BURBACH, born Washington, D.C., May 9, 1974; admitted to bar, 2000, Maryland; 2001, District of Columbia. *Education:* Georgetown University (B.A., magna cum laude,1996) Phi Beta Kappa; Harvard University (J.D., 2000). ***Email:*** cristina_burbach@ffhsj.com

KAMI NICOLE CHAVIS, born Raleigh, North Carolina, March 14, 1974; admitted to bar, 2000, Maryland; 2001, District of Columbia and U.S. District Court for the District of Columbia. *Education:* University of North Carolina at Chapel Hill (B.A., 1996); Harvard University (J.D., 1999). Phi Beta Kappa. ***LANGUAGES:*** Spanish. ***PRACTICE AREAS:*** Litigation. ***Email:*** chavika@ffhsj.com

(This Listing Continued)

BETH HILLIARD COLLEYE, born Cleveland, Ohio, April 11, 1966; admitted to bar, 1997, New York; 1998, District of Columbia. *Education:* Columbia University (B.A., 1989); University of Chicago (J.D., 1996). Robbins Memorial Scholar. Previous Employment: Legislative Assistant to Congressman Howard L. Berman. *Member:* The District of Columbia Bar; American Bar Association. ***LANGUAGES:*** French, Spanish. ***PRACTICE AREAS:*** Corporate Law; Securities. ***Email:*** beth_colleye@ffhsj.com

MICHELLE L. COLMAN, born Philadelphia, Pennsylvania, April 26, 1974; admitted to bar, 1999, Virgina; 2000, District of Columbia. *Education:* Duke University (B.A., 1996); University of Notre Dame (J.D., cum laude, 1999). Law Clerk, Honorable Sherne L. Kranser, 7th Judicial Circuit of Maryland, 1999-2000. ***PRACTICE AREAS:*** Securities; Corporate Law. ***Email:*** michelle.colman@ffhsj.com

TASHA L. COOPER, admitted to bar, 1999, Georgia; 2000, District of Columbia. *Education:* Hampton University (B.A., 1996); Columbia University (J.D., 1999). Harlan Fiske Stone Scholar. Co-Author: "The Internet and the Online Investor: SEC Educational Efforts and Enforcement Activities," Securities in the Electronic Age: A Practical Guide to the Law and Regulation, Grasser Legal Works, 2000. *Member:* State Bar of Georgia; American and National Bar Associations. ***PRACTICE AREAS:*** Corporate Law. ***Email:*** tasha_cooper@ffhsj.com

URVI M. DOSHI, born Buffalo, New York; admitted to bar, 1999, New York and District of Columbia. *Education:* University of Michigan (B.A., summa cum laude, 1994); New York University School of Law (J.D., 1998). Phi Beta Kappa. Author: Note, "The Protection of an Employer's Privacy Rights in Public Carrier Supported Corporate E-Mail," Ann. Surv. Am. L. 4, 1998. Member, Annual Survey of American Law, New York University School of Law. Previous Employment: Donaldson, Lufkin & Jenrette, New York, New York. *Member:* New York State Bar Association (Member, Tax Section); The District of Columbia Bar (Member, Tax Section); Women's Bar Association; South Asian Bar Association. ***LANGUAGES:*** French. ***PRACTICE AREAS:*** Taxation. ***Email:*** urvi_doshi@ffhsj.com

JACK C. EASTON, born Arlington, Virginia, May 15, 1973; admitted to bar, 1999, Virginia; 2000, District of Columbia. *Education:* Johns Hopkins University (B.A., 1995); University of Virginia (J.D., 1999). ***PRACTICE AREAS:*** Corporate. ***Email:*** eastoja@ffhsj.com

THOMAS M. FALLAS, born Niskayuna, New York, October 29, 1973; admitted to bar, 2000, New York and District of Columbia. *Education:* Rutgers University (B.A., 1995); Georgetown University (J.D., 1999). *Member:* New York State Bar Association; The District of Columbia Bar. ***PRACTICE AREAS:*** Corporate Law. ***Email:*** fallath@ffhsj.com

DAWN E. FARIS, born Bloomington, Indiana, July 9, 1966; admitted to bar, 1996, New York and District of Columbia. *Education:* Indiana University (B.A., 1988); Columbia University (J.D., 1995; Ph.D., 1995). Phi Beta Kappa. *Member:* New York State and American Bar Associations; The District of Columbia Bar. ***PRACTICE AREAS:*** Corporate. ***Email:*** dawn_faris@ffhsj.com

WENDY P. FEINER, born Hollywood, Florida, December 23, 1973; admitted to bar, 1999, Florida; 2000, District of Columbia. *Education:* University of Florida (B.A., 1994); George Washington University (J.D., with high honors, 1998). Order of the Coif. Member, Moot Court Board. Dean's Fellow, 1997-1998. Articles Editor, The Environmental Lawyer, 1997-1998. Author: Note, "Just When You Thought It Was Safe to Go Back in the Water: A Guide to Complying with the 1996 Amendments to the Safe Drinking Water Act," 4 The Environmental Lawyer 193, Sept., 1997. ***PRACTICE AREAS:*** Litigation. ***Email:*** wendy.feiner@ffhsj.com

SHELLEY FINGER, born New Haven, Connecticut, November 11, 1974; admitted to bar, 2000, Maryland; 2001, District of Columbia. *Education:* American University (B.A., 1996); Washington College of Law (J.D., with honors, 2000). Author: "Jones v. SEC: Upholding the SEC's Ability to Impose Sanctions in Addition to those of the NASD," Administrative Law Review, Vol. 51, No. 3, 1999. ***PRACTICE AREAS:*** Corporate. ***Email:*** shelley.finger@ffhsj.com

DAVID B. FISHBERG, born New York, N.Y., January 16, 1975; admitted to bar, 2000, New York and District of Columbia. *Education:* Colgate University (B.A., cum laude, 1996); George Washington University (J.D., with honors, 1999). ***PRACTICE AREAS:*** Litigation. ***Email:*** fishbeda@ffhsj.com

REX Y. FUJICHAKU, born Honolulu, Hawaii, April 15, 1969; admitted to bar, 1998, Hawaii (Not admitted in District of Columbia). *Education:* Occidental College (A.B., 1991); University of Hawaii at Manoa (J.D., 1996); Fletcher School of Law and Diplomacy, Tufts University (M.A.L.D., 1998). Casenote Editor, University of Hawaii Law Review. Trial Attorney, Antitrust Division, U.S. Department of Justice, 1998-2001. *Member:* American Bar Association; American Society of International Law. ***PRACTICE AREAS:*** Antitrust. ***Email:*** fujicre@ffhsj.com

DAVID S. GALLAGHER, born Salt Lake City, Utah, February 11, 1972; admitted to bar, 2001, Virginia (Not admitted in District of Columbia). *Educa-*

(This Listing Continued)

tion: University of Utah (B.A., 1997); American University (J.D., 2001). ***PRACTICE AREAS:*** Litigation; Government Contracts; False Claims Act. ***Email:*** david_gallagher@ffhsj.com

JANET G. GAMER, born New Haven, Connecticut, June 24, 1938; admitted to bar, 1965, District of Columbia. *Education:* Smith College (A.B., 1960); New York University (LL.B., 1964). Co-Author: "Monitoring the Dance: An Assessment of the Regulation 13D-G Amendments," 12 Insights (April 1998); "Beneficial Ownership Under Section 16 of the Securities Exchange Act," 71 Western Reserve Law Review 1054, 1966. Member, U.S. Securities and Exchange Commission, 1964-1969; Office of Chief Counsel, Division of Corporation Finance, 1964-1966. Associate, Ginsburg, Feldman & Bress, 1969-1971. ***Email:*** janet_gamer@ffhsj.com

JOSHUA J. GESSLER, born Benson, Arizona, June 25, 1969; admitted to bar, 2000, Pennsylvania (Not admitted in District of Columbia). *Education:* American University (B.A., 1995); George Mason University School of Law (J.D., magna cum laude, 2000). ***Email:*** gessljo@ffhsj.com

GEJAA TEMESGIEN GOBENA, born Alexandria, Virginia, December 31, 1974; admitted to bar, 1999, New York and District of Columbia. *Education:* University of Virginia (B.A., with high distinction, 1995); Columbia Law School (J.D., 1998). Phi Beta Kappa. *Member:* New York State and American Bar Associations; The District of Columbia Bar. ***LANGUAGES:*** French and Amharic. ***PRACTICE AREAS:*** Litigation. ***Email:*** gobenge@ffhsj.com

MICHELLE BERK GOLD, born New York, New York, October 12, 1971; admitted to bar, 1997, Virginia; 1998, District of Columbia. *Education:* Brandeis University (B.A., 1993); Georgetown University Law Center (J.D./M.B.A., 1997). Beta Gamma Sigma; Order of the Coif. *Member:* The District of Columbia Bar (Member, Tax Section); American Bar Association (Member, Tax Section). ***PRACTICE AREAS:*** Tax. ***Email:*** michelle_gold@ffhsj.com

KEVIN J. HARNISCH, born Atlanta, Georgia, November 10, 1969; admitted to bar, 1995, Washington; 2000, District of Columbia. *Education:* University of Notre Dame (B.B.A., magna cum laude, 1992); Seattle University (J.D., magna cum laude, 1995). Member, Seattle University Law Review, 1994-1995. Staff Attorney, Senior Counsel and Branch Chief, Securities and Exchange Commission, Division of Enforcement, 1995-1999. *Member:* American Bar Association (Member: Sections on: Business; Litigation). ***PRACTICE AREAS:*** Securities Enforcement and Regulation; Securities Litigation; Corporate Internal Investigations. ***Email:*** kevin_harnisch@ffhsj.com

TAYLOR YOUNG HONG, born December 3, 1969; admitted to bar, 2000, New York; 2001, District of Columbia. *Education:* Bennington College (B.A., 1992); Columbia University (J.D., 1999). ***PRACTICE AREAS:*** Corporate Law; Securities. ***Email:*** taylor_hong@ffhsj.com

JOHN R. INGRASSIA, born New York, N.Y., October 2, 1967; admitted to bar, 1996, New York and New Jersey; 1997, District of Columbia. *Education:* Pace University (B.A., 1989); Hofstra University (J.D., 1995). *Member:* American Bar Association (Member: Antitrust Law Section; Clayton Act Committee). ***PRACTICE AREAS:*** Antitrust. ***Email:*** john_ingrassia@ffhsj.com

DAVID WILSON JOLLY, born Clearwater, Florida, October 31, 1972; admitted to bar, 2001, Virginia (Not admitted in District of Columbia). *Education:* Emory University (B.A., 1994); George Mason University School of Law (J.D., cum laude, 2001). Member, George Mason Law Review. Author: "Knowing Possession vs. Actual Use: Due Process and Social Costs in Civil Insider Trading Actions," 8 George Mason Law Review 223, 1999. Member, Congressional Staff, U.S. House of Representatives, 1995-2001. *Member:* Virginia State Bar. ***Email:*** jollyda@ffhsj.com

JONATHAN S. KANTER, born New York, July 30, 1973; admitted to bar, 1999, New York; 2001, District of Columbia. *Education:* State University of New York at Albany (B.A., 1995); Washington University (J.D., 1998). ***PRACTICE AREAS:*** Antitrust. ***Email:*** jonathan—kanter@ffhsj.com

RACHEL S. KATZ, born New Brunswick, New Jersey, April 2, 1974; admitted to bar, 2000, New York; 2001, District of Columbia. *Education:* Union College (B.A., 1996); American University (J.D., 1999). ***PRACTICE AREAS:*** Corporate Law. ***Email:*** katzra@ffhsj.com

WALID A. KHURI, born New York, N.Y., February 28, 1968; admitted to bar, 1997, New York; 1998, District of Columbia. *Education:* Brown University (B.A., 1991); George Washington University (J.D., 1996). ***PRACTICE AREAS:*** Corporate Law. ***Email:*** khuriwa@ffhsj.com

MELISSA E. LAMB, born New Brunswick, New Jersey, October 26, 1973; admitted to bar, 1998, Maryland; 1999, District of Columbia and U.S. District Court, District of Maryland. *Education:* Cornell University (B.A., with distinction, 1995); Harvard University (J.D., cum laude, 1998). Phi Beta Kappa. ***PRACTICE AREAS:*** White Collar Criminal Defense; Civil Litigation. ***Email:*** melissa.lamb@ffhsj.com

JoELLEN LOTVEDT LEGG, born Wolf Point, Montana, October 9, 1961; admitted to bar, 1998, Virginia; 1999, District of Columbia. *Education:* Eastern Washington University (B.A., summa cum laude, 1989); George Washington University (M.A., 1994); Columbus School of Law, Catholic University (J.D., magna cum laude, 1998). ***PRACTICE AREAS:*** Corporate Law; Securities. ***Email:*** leggjo@ffhsj.com

RON LEVINER, born New York, N.Y.; admitted to bar, 2000, New York (Not admitted in District of Columbia). *Education:* University of Pennsylvania (B.A., cum laude, 1996); Columbia University (J.D., 1999). Harlan Fiske Stone Scholar. ***PRACTICE AREAS:*** Corporate Law; Mergers and Acquisitions. ***Email:*** levinro@ffhsj.com

RUSSELL LIGHT, born New York, N.Y.; admitted to bar, 2001, Illinois (Not admitted in District of Columbia). *Education:* Massachusetts Institute of Technology (B.S., B.S., M.Eng., 1998); University of Chicago (J.D., high honors, 2001). Order of the Coif. Managing Editor, University of Chicago Law Review. Editor, Chicago Journal of International Law. ***PRACTICE AREAS:*** Tax. ***Email:*** lightru@ffhsj.com

CHARLES W. LOCKYER, JR., born Philadelphia, Pennsylvania, April 6, 1944; admitted to bar, 1996, Maryland; 1997, District of Columbia. *Education:* Fordham University (A.B., cum laude, 1966); Phi Beta Kappa; Princeton University (M.A., 1968; Ph.D., 1971); Georgetown University (J.D., 1995). Member: American Hotel and Motel Association; Industry Real Estate Finance Advisory Committee, 1985-1989; Robert Morris Associates, 1972-1979; 1984-1990. Contributing Author: "Partnerships," The District of Columbia Practice Manual, Seventh Edition, Volume I, 1998. Instructor: Accounting Concepts for Lawyers, Georgetown University Law Center, 1996; Accounting and Law, George Washington National Law Center, 1996. ***PRACTICE AREAS:*** Corporate; Banking Regulation; E-Commerce. ***Email:*** charles_lockyer@ffhsj.com

BRADFORD LUCAS, born September 19, 1975; admitted to bar, 2001, Virginia (Not admitted in District of Columbia). *Education:* University of Virginia (B.A., Economics/Philosophy, 1997); George Mason University School of Law (J.D., magna cum laude, 2000). Managing Editor, George Mason University, 1999-2000). ***PRACTICE AREAS:*** Corporate; Securities. ***Email:*** brad_lucas@ffhsj.com

NATASHA R. LUDDINGTON, born Indianapolis, Indiana, December 14, 1974; admitted to bar, 1999, Texas; 2001, District of Columbia. *Education:* Indiana University (B.S., 1996); George Washington University (J.D., with honors, 1999). Managing Editor, Environmental Lawyer. *Member:* American (Member, Business Law Section) Bar Association. ***PRACTICE AREAS:*** Corporate Finance; Corporate Law. ***Email:*** luddina@ffhsj.com

JEFF L. MAGENAU, born Concord, New Hampshire, April 28, 1963; admitted to bar, 1996, Maryland; 2001, District of Columbia. *Education:* Boston University (B.A., 1985); American University (J.D., 1996). ***PRACTICE AREAS:*** Intellectual Property; Information Technology; Internet Law; E-Commerce. ***Email:*** jeff.magenau@ffhsj.com

JAY D. MAJORS, born Torrejon USAFB, Spain, February 6, 1968; admitted to bar, 1993, Virginia and U.S. Court of Appeals, Fourth Circuit; 1995, District of Columbia. *Education:* Harvard University (A.B., 1989); University of Virginia (J.D., 1992). Order of the Coif. Law Clerk to the Honorable Albert V. Bryan, Jr., U.S. District Court, Eastern District of Virginia, 1992-1993. ***PRACTICE AREAS:*** Civil Litigation. ***Email:*** jay_majors@ffhsj.com

BETH C. McCLAIN, born Riverside, New Jersey, January 22, 1961; admitted to bar, 1992, New Jersey and Pennsylvania (Not admitted in District of Columbia). *Education:* Boston College (B.S.N., magna cum laude, 1983); Stanford University (J.D., with distinction, 1992). Author: With John T. Boese, "Why Thompson is Wrong: Misuse of the False Claims Act to Enforce the Anti-Kickback Act, 51 Ala. L. Rev. 1 (1999). ***PRACTICE AREAS:*** Civil False Claims Act; Health Care. ***Email:*** beth.mcclain@ffhsj.com

JULIA A. McDONOUGH, born Glendale, California, August 5, 1960; admitted to bar, 1997, Virginia; 1998, District of Columbia. *Education:* Loyola Marymount University (B.A., summa cum laude, 1982); University of Virginia (M.A., History, 1984; Ph.D., History, 1993; J.D., 1997). ***PRACTICE AREAS:*** Securities Law; Corporate. ***Email:*** julia_mcdonough@ffhsj.com

DAVID MYERS, born Iowa City, Iowa, December 20, 1965; admitted to bar, 1991, Minnesota; 2000, Victoria, Australia (Not admitted in District of Columbia). *Education:* Iowa State University (B.S., 1988); University of Iowa (J.D., 1991; M.A., 1991). Author: "Refusals to Deal in Telecommunications Markets: Is the Commission Reading Purpose into the Effects Test?" Trade Practices L.J., Vol. 8, No. 4, Dec. 2000; "Indonesia's New Competition Law: What Will the Latest Reform Effort Mean for Businesses Operating in Indonesia?" Australian Business L.Rev., Vol. 28, No. 4, Aug. 2000. ***PRACTICE AREAS:*** Antitrust. ***Email:*** myersda@ffhsj.com

JOHN S. NARGISO, born January 31, 1974; admitted to bar, 2000, New York; 2001, District of Columbia. *Education:* Rutgers University (B.A., 1996); George Washington University (J.D., 1999). Henry Rutgers Honor Scholar. ***PRACTICE AREAS:*** Corporate Finance; Real Estate. ***Email:*** john.nargiso@ffhsj.com

DAVID A. NEUMAN, born St. Louis, Missouri, July 9, 1973; admitted to bar, 1999, Missouri; 2000, District of Columbia. *Education:* University of Michigan (B.A., 1995); George Washington University (J.D., highest honors,

(This Listing Continued)

FRIED, FRANK, HARRIS, SHRIVER & JACOBSON, Washington—Continued

1999). Order of the Coif. Student Attorney, D.C. Law Students in Court, 1998-1999. Member, Journal of International Law & Economics. Law Clerk, Honorable Ronnie L. White, Munoun Supreme Court, 1999-2000. *Member:* American Bar Association (Member, Business Law Section). ***LANGUAGES:*** Hebrew. ***PRACTICE AREAS:*** Corporate Securities. ***Email:*** david.neuman@ffhsj.com

ABRAM J. PAFFORD, born Perth Amboy, New Jersey, December 27, 1972; admitted to bar, 2000, New York; 2001, District of Columbia. *Education:* Liberty University (B.S., 1996); George Washington University (J.D., 1999). ***PRACTICE AREAS:*** White Collar Crime; Commercial Litigation; Government Contracts. ***Email:*** paffoab@ffhsj.com

JULIE J. PANIGRAHI, born South Bend, Indiana, June 9, 1972; admitted to bar, 2000, New York (Not admitted in District of Columbia). *Education:* Johns Hopkins University (B.A., 1994); University of Pennsylvania (J.D., 1999). ***PRACTICE AREAS:*** Corporate Law.

GEORGE B. PARIZEK, born Bellefonte, Pennsylvania, August 28, 1968; admitted to bar, 1994, Pennsylvania; 2000, District of Columbia. *Education:* Pennsylvania State University (B.A., 1991); Golden Gate University (J.D., 1994). Member, 1994-1999, Staff Attorney, 1994-1997 and Senior Counsel, 1998-1999, U.S. Securities and Exchange Commission, Division of Enforcement. *Member:* Amercian Bar Association (Member, Business Law Section). ***PRACTICE AREAS:*** Corporate Law; Securities. ***Email:*** george_parizek@ffhsj.com

RICHARD C. PARK, born Cleveland, Ohio, May 5, 1970; admitted to bar, 1997, New York; 1998, District of Columbia. *Education:* Cornell University (B.A., 1992); Northeastern University (J.D., 1995); Georgetown University (LL.M., 1997). *Member:* American Bar Association (Member: Antitrust Section; Telecommunications Section). ***PRACTICE AREAS:*** Antitrust; Telecommunications. ***Email:*** richard.park@ffhsj.com

STEVEN C. PARKER, born Clinton, Iowa, July 2, 1959; admitted to bar, 1995, New York; 1996, District of Columbia. *Education:* George Mason University (B.A., 1991); Yale University (J.D., 1995). ***PRACTICE AREAS:*** Litigation. ***Email:*** steven_parker@ffhsj.com

PAUL H. PASHKOFF, born Silver Spring, Maryland; August 10, 1972; admitted to bar, 1997, Maryland; 1998, District of Columbia. *Education:* University of Michigan (B.A., 1994); George Washington University (J.D., with high honors, 1997). Order of the Coif. Member, The George Washington Law Review, 1996-1997. Author: "The Boundaries of Judicial Power Under The Tunney Act," 64 Geo. Wash. L. Rev. 824 (1996). ***PRACTICE AREAS:*** Securities Law. ***Email:*** pashkpa@ffhsj.com

STACY L. PAXSON, born Atlantic City, New Jersey, June 7, 1967; admitted to bar, 1994, New Jersey; 1995, Pennsylvania and Maryland; 1996, District of Columbia. *Education:* University of Delaware (B.S.B.A., 1989); Catholic University of America (J.D., 1994); Georgetown University Law Center (LL.M., with distinction, Securities and Financial Regulation, 1998). Member, SEC Historical Society. Co-Author: with Harvey L. Pitt and Dixie L. Johnson, "SEC Collateral Bars and Suspensions: Barred By The Court," Insights (April 2000). Previous Employment: NASD Regulation, Inc.; Michael Goldfarb Associates, Inc. (MGA); Office of U.S. Senator Bill Bradley. *Member:* Bar Association of the District of Columbia; American Bar Association; SEC Historical Society. ***PRACTICE AREAS:*** SEC Enforcement; Broker-Dealer Regulation. ***Email:*** paxsost@ffhsj.com

DUCCHI T. QUAN, born Saigon, Vietnam, November 28, 1974; admitted to bar, 1999, Illinois; 2001, District of Columbia. *Education:* State University of New York at Stony Brook (B.A., 1994); Northwestern University (J.D., 1999). Associate Articles Editor, Northwestern University Law Review, 1998-1999. ***LANGUAGES:*** Vietnamese. ***PRACTICE AREAS:*** Corporate Law. ***Email:*** ducchi.quan@ffhsj.com

LOUIS RAMOS, born New York, N.Y., January 28, 1973; admitted to bar, 1998, New York; 2001, District of Columbia. *Education:* Cornell University (B.A., 1994); University of Pennsylvania (J.D., 1997). ***LANGUAGES:*** Spanish. ***PRACTICE AREAS:*** Litigation. ***Email:*** louis.ramos@ffhsj.com

DONYALE Y. HOOPER REAVIS, born Philadelphia, Pennsylvania, August 20, 1970; admitted to bar, 2001, New Jersey (Not admitted in District of Columbia). *Education:* Boston University (B.A., 1992); University of Pennsylvania (J.D., 1999; M.G.A., 1999). Member: Women in Technology, 2000—; Washington Area Lawyers For the Arts, 2001—. ***LANGUAGES:*** French, Spanish. ***PRACTICE AREAS:*** Intellectual Property; E-Commerce; Corporate Law. ***Email:*** donyale.reavis@ffhsj.com

JAMES E. RHILINGER, born Attleboro, Massachusetts, October 11, 1970; admitted to bar, 1997, Massachusetts; 2001, District of Columbia. *Education:* Bryant College (B.S., 1992); Catholic University of America (J.D., magna cum laude, 1996). ***PRACTICE AREAS:*** Antitrust. ***Email:*** james.rhilinger@ffhsj.com

RENÉ L. ROCQUE, born New Orleans, Louisiana, October 25, 1975; admitted to bar, 2000, Texas and District of Columbia. *Education:* Harvard University (A.B., 1997; J.D., 2000). *Member:* State Bar of Texas; American Bar Association. ***PRACTICE AREAS:*** General Litigation. ***Email:*** rene.rocque@ffhsj.com

ERIC P. RUBENFELD, born Los Angeles, California, September 17, 1970; admitted to bar, 1996, New York; 2001, District of Columbia. *Education:* University of California, Los Angeles (B.A., magna cum laude, 1991); Harvard University (J.D., cum laude, 1995). Phi Beta Kappa. ***PRACTICE AREAS:*** Structured Finance. ***Email:*** eric.rubenfeld@ffhsj.com

CHRISTOPHER M. SALTER, born Cleveland, Ohio, March 8, 1967; admitted to bar, 1995, Virginia; 2000, District of Columbia. *Education:* James Madison University (B.B.A., cum laude, 1989); George Mason University School of Law (J.D., 1995). Beta Gamma Sigma. Beta Alpha Psi. Member, Golden Key. Certified Public Accountant, Virginia, 1989. Previous Employment: U.S. Securities and Exchange Commission; U.S. General Accounting Office; KPMG Peat Marwick. *Member:* American Bar Association (Member, Business Law Section). ***PRACTICE AREAS:*** Securities Regulation; Securities Enforcement. ***Email:*** saltech@ffhsj.com

JONATHAN P. SCOTT, born London, England, August 14, 1969; admitted to bar, 1995, Maryland; 1998, District of Columbia. *Education:* Boston University (B.S. in Journalism, 1991); Washington College of Law at American University (J.D., summa cum laude, 1995). Law Clerk: Judge Harriett Taylor, District of Columbia Superior Court, 1995-1996; Judge Stanley Sporkin, U.S. District Court, District of Columbia, 1996-1997. *Member:* The District of Columbia Bar; American Bar Association. ***PRACTICE AREAS:*** SEC Enforcement; Securities Regulation; Securities Litigation. ***Email:*** scottjo@ffhsj.com

MATTHEW L. SKIDMORE, born Salt Lake City, Utah, February 13, 1971; admitted to bar, 2000, Utah; 2001, District of Columbia. *Education:* University of Utah (B.A., cum laude, 1996); University of Pennsylvania (J.D., 2000). *Member:* Utah State Bar. ***LANGUAGES:*** Spanish. ***PRACTICE AREAS:*** Corporate Law. ***Email:*** matthew.skidmore@ffhsj.com

ANDREW DIETER SKOWRONEK, born 1971; admitted to bar, 1998, District of Columbia; 2000, Virginia. *Education:* Williams College (B.A., 1993); George Washington Law School (J.D., magna cum laude, 1998). Member, Order of the Coif. ***PRACTICE AREAS:*** Civil Fraud; Commercial Litigation. ***Email:*** andrew_skowronek@ffhsj.com

THOMAS PETER SMITH, JR., born New York, New York, May 12, 1966; admitted to bar, 1998, Virginia; 1999, District of Columbia. *Education:* United States Naval Academy (B.S.M.E., 1988); Georgetown University Law Center (J.D., 1998). [Lt., U.S. Navy, 1988-1995; Lt. Commander, U.S. Naval Reserve, 1995—]. ***PRACTICE AREAS:*** Corporate Law. ***Email:*** smithth@ffhsj.com

JACQUELINE STEPHENS, admitted to bar, 1998, California; 1999, Tennessee and U.S. District Court, Eastern District of Tennessee; 2000, District of Columbia. *Education:* University of Southern California (B.S., 1994); University of Virginia (J.D., 1997). Technical Editor, Journal of Social Policy and the Law. Law Clerk, U.S. District Court Judge Curtis L. Collier. ***PRACTICE AREAS:*** Litigation; Internal Investigations. ***Email:*** stephja@ffhsj.com

TRICIA CHWENCHII SU, born 1972; admitted to bar, 1999, New York; 2000, District of Columbia. *Education:* University of Illinois, Urbana (B.S.; M.S., 1994); New York University (J.D., 1998). Senior Notes Editor, New York University Environmental Law Journal. ***PRACTICE AREAS:*** Tax; Corporate. ***Email:*** tricia.su@ffhsj.com

SHARAN K. SURI, born Mt. Holly, New Jersey, August 5, 1973; admitted to bar, 1998, Michigan; 1999, District of Columbia. *Education:* University of Michigan (B.A., 1995); University of Michigan Law School (J.D., 1998). *Member:* American Bar Association. ***PRACTICE AREAS:*** Litigation. ***Email:*** surish@ffhsj.com

LARISA AVNER TRAINOR, born Kiev, Ukraine, July 30, 1970; admitted to bar, 1998, Virginia; 1999, District of Columbia. *Education:* State University of New York at Albany (B.S., 1992); The George Washington University Law School (J.D., 1998). Certified Public Accountant, New York, September 1995. ***LANGUAGES:*** Russian. ***PRACTICE AREAS:*** Corporate Law; Securities. ***Email:*** larisa_trainor@ffhsj.com

MICHAEL ARTHUR UMAYAM, born Quezon City, Philippines, January 28, 1974; admitted to bar, 2001, Virginia (Not admitted in District of Columbia). *Education:* College of William & Mary (B.A., Government, 1996); Catholic University of America (J.D., magna cum laude, 2001). ***PRACTICE AREAS:*** Litigation. ***Email:*** umayami@ffhsj.com

C. TUCKER WALDRUFF, born Camp Lejune, North Carolina, September 6, 1972; admitted to bar, 2001, Virginia (Not admitted in District of Co-

(This Listing Continued)

lumbia). *Education:* University of Virginia (B.A., with high distinction, 1994); Harvard University (J.D., 2001). Phi Beta Kappa. *Member:* Virginia State Bar. ***PRACTICE AREAS:*** Corporate. ***Email:*** tucker.waldruff@ffhsj.com

KARIN E. WEINER, born New Jersey; admitted to bar, 1998, Connecticut; 1999, New York; 2000, District of Columbia. *Education:* Yale University (B.A., 1993); Northwestern University (J.D., 1998). ***PRACTICE AREAS:*** Corporate Law. ***Email:*** weineka@ffhsj.com

PYONG W. YOON, admitted to bar, 1999, New Jersey; 2000, District of Columbia; registered to practice before U.S. Patent and Trademark Office. *Education:* Drexel University (B.S.M.E., 1989); Temple University School of Law (J.D., 1999). ***LANGUAGES:*** Korean. ***PRACTICE AREAS:*** Intellectual Property; Patents; Corporate Law. ***Email:*** pyong.yoon@ffhsj.com

(For Biographical Data of New York, New York, Personnel, see Professional Biographies at New York, New York).
(For Biographical Data of Los Angeles, California Personnel, see Professional Biographies at Los Angeles, California).
(For Biographical Data of London Personnel, see Professional Biographies at London, England).
(For Biographical Data of Paris Personnel, see Professional Biographies at Paris, France).

FRIEDLANDER & FRIEDLANDER, P.C.

WASHINGTON, D.C.

(See McLean, Virginia)

Civil Trial Practice, Virginia and District of Columbia. Business Law, Business Formation, Corporate, Construction, Mechanic's Liens, Zoning & Land Use, Landlord-Tenant Law, Estate Planning, Trusts & Estates, Wills & Probate, Franchising, Real Estate, Contracts, Personal Injury, and Products Liability.

FRIEDLANDER, MISLER, SLOAN, KLETZKIN & OCHSMAN, PLLC

Established in 1964

1101 SEVENTEENTH STREET, N.W., SUITE 700
WASHINGTON, D.C. 20036-4704
Telephone: 202-872-0800
Cable Address: "FMSHLAW"
Telex: 64273
Facsimile: 202-857-8343
URL: http://www.dclawfirm.com

Real Estate, Corporate, Creditors' Rights and Bankruptcy Law, Estate Planning. General Civil Practice, including Trial, Administrative and Appellate, Insurance Law, Tax, Probate and Worker's Compensation.

FIRM PROFILE: Friedlander, Misler, Friedlander, Sloan & Herz, PLLC was founded in 1964 by Jack L. Friedlander and Stephen H. Friedlander. Starting with a local general practice, this firm has grown to provide representation in the metropolitan Washington, D.C. area and the mid-Atlantic region. The firm specializes in real estate matters, banking and creditors' rights, taxation, estate planning and administration of estates, business associations, insurance and guaranty fund issues, workers' compensation cases, insurance defense and general civil litigation including trial and appellate representation in state and federal courts.

MEMBERS OF FIRM

STEPHEN H. FRIEDLANDER, born Washington, D.C., December 28, 1937; admitted to bar, 1962, District of Columbia. *Education:* Washington & Lee University (B.A., 1959); Georgetown University (J.D., 1962). *Member:* District of Columbia Bar; American Bar Association. ***PRACTICE AREAS:*** Commercial Real Estate; Commercial Leasing; Business Associations Law. ***Email:*** sfriedlander@dclawfirm.com

LEONARD A. SLOAN, born Washington, D.C., December 30, 1940; admitted to bar, 1968, Virginia; 1970, District of Columbia. *Education:* American University (B.S.B.A., 1962); George Washington University (J.D., 1968). Certified Public Accountant, Maryland, 1964. General Counsel, FWB Bank. President, FWB Bancorporation, 1985-1993. *Member:* District of Columbia Bar; The Virginia and American Bar Associations. ***PRACTICE AREAS:*** Banking; Real Estate; Commercial Law; Corporate Law. ***Email:*** lsloan@dclawfirm.com

MORRIS KLETZKIN, born New York, N.Y., November 9, 1946; admitted to bar, 1972, District of Columbia, U.S. Court of Appeals for the District of Columbia Circuit and U.S. Court of Military Appeals; 1976, U.S. Supreme Court; 1977, Maryland; 1980, U.S. Court of Appeals, Fourth Circuit. *Education:* University of Hartford (B.A., 1968); American University (J.D., 1971). *Member:* District of Columbia Bar; Bar Association of the District of Columbia; Montgomery County, Maryland State and American Bar Associations. ***REPORTED CASES:*** Riso vs. Marshall, 500 F.Supp. 351, 1981; also at 100 F.R.D. 395, 1983; Carol Mason vs. Bernado Rostad, 476 A.2d 662, 1984; Helen Bernstein vs. Dean Kapneck, 290 Md. 452, 430 A.2d 602, 1981; 46 Md. App. 231, 417 A.2d 456, 1980; Graham, et al vs. O Street Ltd. Ptnrshp., D.C.; Hollestelle v. Metropolitan Washington Airports Authority, 145 F.3d 1324 (4th Cir. 1998) (unpublished); Laughlin v. Metropolitan Washington Airports Authority, 149 F.3d 253 (4th Cir. 1998); Malik v. District of Columbia, 703 A.2d 1250 (D.C. 1998). ***PRACTICE AREAS:*** General Civil Litigation; Employment Litigation; Rental Vehicles Litigation; Insurance; Guaranty Fund Law; Business Torts; Bank Litigation; Foreign Labor Litigation. ***Email:*** mkletzkin@dclawfirm.com

JEFFREY W. OCHSMAN, born Washington, D.C., September 10, 1952; admitted to bar, 1977, District of Columbia; 1978, U.S. District Court for the District of Columbia, U.S. Court of Appeals for the District of Columbia Circuit and U.S. Court of Military Appeals; 1980, Maryland; 1981, U.S. Court of Appeals, Fourth Circuit and U.S. Supreme Court. *Education:* College of William and Mary (B.A., 1974); The American University (J.D., cum laude, 1977). *Member:* District of Columbia Bar; Maryland State and American Bar Associations. ***REPORTED CASES:*** Byrd v. Nationwide Mutual Ins. Co., 415 A.2d 807 (D.C. App. 1980); Pfister v. Dir., Office of Workers' Comp. Programs, U.S. Dept of Labor, 675 F.2d 1314 (D.C. Cir. 1982); Madison Hotel v. District of Columbia, 512 A.2d 303 (D.C. App. 1986); Southernly v. Perfect Auto Radiator Co., Inc., 101 Md. App. 113, 643 A.2 501 (1994); Evans Financial v. Director, Office of Workers' Compensation Programs, 161 F.3d 30 (C.A.D.C. 1998). ***PRACTICE AREAS:*** Workers Compensation Law; Personal Injury Law; Insurance Defense Law. ***Email:*** jochsman@dclawfirm.com

JEROME OSTROV, born Boston, Massachusetts, December 2, 1942; admitted to bar, 1967, New York; 1970, District of Columbia and U.S. Tax Court; 1991, Maryland. *Education:* Boston University (B.S. in Business Administration, cum laude, 1964); Albany Law School of Union University (J.D., 1967); New York University (LL.M. in Taxation, 1968); John F. Kennedy School of Government, Harvard University (M.P.A., 1980). Beta Gamma Sigma. Law Clerk to Judge Leo H. Irwin, U.S. Tax Court, 1969-1971. Assistant to the Editor, The Tax Lawyer, 1971-1973. Author: *Tax Planning with Real Estate*, PLI Press, 2001. Deputy Associate General Counsel, United States Environmental Protection Agency, 1977-1979. Public Administration Fellow, John F. Kennedy School of Government, Harvard University, 1979-1980. Legislative Fellow/Counsel, House of Representatives Committee on Science and Technology, Investigations and Oversight Subcommittee, 1982-1983. *Member:* District of Columbia Bar; Maryland State Bar Association, Inc. ***PRACTICE AREAS:*** Tax; Estate Planning; Commercial Law; Appellate Practice. ***Email:*** jostrov@dclawfirm.com

JANA KAY GUGGENHEIM, born Milwaukee, Wisconsin, September 27, 1958; admitted to bar, 1987, Virginia; 1988, Maryland, U.S. District Court, Eastern District of Virginia, U.S. Court of Appeals, 4th Circuit, District of Columbia and U.S. District Court, District of Maryland. *Education:* University of Wisconsin at Milwaukee (B.A., 1977); American University, Washington College of Law (J.D., 1987). *Member:* District of Columbia Bar; Maryland State, Virginia and American Bar Associations; Virginia Trial Lawyers Association. ***LANGUAGES:*** French. ***PRACTICE AREAS:*** Commercial Real Estate; Banking; Commercial Law; Business Associations; Creditors' Rights. ***Email:*** jguggenheim@dclawfirm.com

ALAN DEAN SUNDBURG, born Northampton, Massachusetts, August 9, 1961; admitted to bar, 1987, Pennsylvania (inactive); 1989, District of Columbia; 1991, Virginia and U.S. Court of Appeals, 4th Circuit; 1998, U.S. Court of Appeals for the District of Columbia Circuit. *Education:* Hamilton College (A.B., 1983); Marshall-Wythe School of Law (J.D., 1986). *Member:* The District of Columbia Bar; Virginia State Bar. ***PRACTICE AREAS:*** Workers Compensation Law; Insurance Defense Law. ***Email:*** asundburg@dclawfirm.com

MARK D. CRAWFORD, born Binghamton, New York, October 12, 1964; admitted to bar, 1993, Virginia; U.S. Court of Appeals, Fourth Circuit; 1994, U.S. District Court, Eastern District of Virginia; 1996, District of Columbia; 1998, U.S. Court of Appeals for the District of Columbia Circuit; 1999, U.S. District Court, District of Columbia. *Education:* Cornell University (B.S., 1986); George Mason University (J.D., with distinction, 1993). Associate Editor, George Mason Independent Law Review. *Member:* American Bar Association. ***PRACTICE AREAS:*** Civil Litigation; Insurance Defense; Labor and Employment. ***Email:*** mcrawford@dclawfirm.com

ASSOCIATES

PHILIPPA T. GASNIER, born Berkeley, California, August 27, 1961; admitted to bar, 1988, Maryland; 1990, District of Columbia. *Education:* University of Maryland (B.A., cum laude, 1983); Georgetown University (J.D., 1988). Phi Beta Kappa. *Member:* District of Columbia Bar; Maryland State and American Bar Associations. ***PRACTICE AREAS:*** Banking; Commercial Law; Business Associations Law; Creditors' Rights. ***Email:*** pgasnier@dclawfirm.com

TODD S. SAPIRO, born New Brunswick, New Jersey, October 7, 1967; admitted to bar, 1992, Maryland and New Jersey; 1993, District of Columbia. *Education:* University of Michigan (B.A., 1989); American University (J.D.,

(This Listing Continued)

FRIEDLANDER, MISLER, SLOAN, KLETZKIN & OCHSMAN, PLLC, Washington—Continued

1992). **PRACTICE AREAS:** Workers Compensation; Personal Injury; Products Liability; Insurance Defense; Civil Litigation. **Email:** tsapiro@dclawfirm.com

JOAN M. LURIA, born Silver Spring, Maryland, October 25, 1966; admitted to bar, 1992, Maryland (Not admitted in District of Columbia). *Education:* University of Maryland at College Park (B.A., 1988); Syracuse University (J.D., 1992). Dean Robert W. Miller Scholar, 1989-1990. Associate Editor, Syracuse Law Review, 1991-1992. *Member:* American Bar Association. **PRACTICE AREAS:** Commercial Finance; Commercial Real Estate; Commercial Leasing; Business Law. **Email:** jluria@dclawfirm.com

THOMAS FRANCIS MURPHY, born Newport, Rhode Island, February 22, 1971; admitted to bar, 1996, Georgia; 1997, Maryland; 1999, District of Columbia, Virginia, U.S. District Court, Eastern District of Virginia and U.S. Court of Federal Claims; 2001, U.S Bankruptcy Court, Eastern District of Virginia. *Education:* James Madison University (B.S., cum laude, 1993); University of Georgia (J.D., 1996). **PRACTICE AREAS:** Civil Litigation; Commercial Leasing; Business Law. **Email:** tfmurphy@dclawfirm.com

DENISE E. JACKSON, born Rochester, New York, March 22, 1960; admitted to bar, 1994, Maryland; 1995, District of Columbia. *Education:* American University (B.S., 1982); University of Maryland (J.D., 1994). Recipient, American Jurisprudence Award, Criminal Procedure. Co-Chair, Moot Court Board, 1993-1994. *Member:* Maryland State, American and National Bar Associations (Greater Washington Area Chapter, Women Lawyers Division); District of Columbia Bar. (Attorney). **PRACTICE AREAS:** Commercial Real Estate; Commercial Finance; Commercial Leasing. **Email:** djackson@dclawfirm.com

BARBARA J. PRASSE, born Fredericksburg, Virginia, September 24, 1972; admitted to bar, 2000, Virginia, U.S. District Court, Eastern District of Virginia and U.S. Court of Appeals, Fourth Circuit; 2001, Maryland (Not admitted in District of Columbia). *Education:* Virginia Commonwealth University (B.S., 1995); George Mason University School of Law (J.D., cum laude, 2000). *Member:* Virginia State Bar; American Bar Association. **PRACTICE AREAS:** Civil Litigation; Insurance Defense; Workers Compensation. **Email:** bprasse@dclawfirm.com

OF COUNSEL

ROBERT E. GREENBERG, born New York, N.Y., January 8, 1949; admitted to bar, 1972, Florida; 1973, District of Columbia; 1978, Maryland. *Education:* Herbert H. Lehman College of the City University of New York (A.B., 1970); University of Florida (J.D., 1972); Georgetown University (LL.M., 1975). Attorney-Advisor: Interstate Commerce Commission, Office of Proceedings, 1972-1973. Legislative Assistant, Honorable Jonathan B. Bingham, 1973-1975. Assistant General Counsel, Metropolitan Police Department, Washington, D.C., 1975-1978. *Member:* The District of Columbia Bar; Maryland State Bar Association; The Florida Bar. **PRACTICE AREAS:** Commercial Law; Real Estate; Litigation; Commercial Leasing; Creditors Rights Law. **Email:** rgreenberg@dclawfirm.com

DAVID M. ASTROVE, born New York, N.Y., March 6, 1957; admitted to bar, 1982, District of Columbia. *Education:* University of Pennsylvania (B.A., 1979); Columbia University (J.D., 1982). Harlan Fiske Stone Scholar, 1981-1982. Associate Editor, Human Rights Law Review, 1981-1982. *Member:* The District of Columbia Bar; American Bar Association. **PRACTICE AREAS:** Commercial Finance; Commercial Real Estate; Commercial Leasing; Business Law. **Email:** dastrove@dclawfirm.com

DEBORAH G. SEGAL, born Philadelphia, Pennsylvania, October 3, 1957; admitted to bar, 1983, California; 1991, District of Columbia. *Education:* Tufts University (B.A., magna cum laude, 1979); Boston University (J.D., 1983). Phi Beta Kappa. *Member:* The District of Columbia Bar; American Bar Association. **PRACTICE AREAS:** Commercial Finance; Commercial Real Estate; Commercial Leasing; Business Law. **Email:** dsegal@dclawfirm.com

LOIS J. VERMILLION, born Washington, D.C., October 19, 1945; admitted to bar, 1977, Virginia; 1978, District of Columbia. *Education:* American University (B.A., 1973); George Mason University School of Law (J.D., magna cum laude, 1977). Member and Editor, George Mason University Law Review, 1976-1977. *Member:* The District of Columbia Bar (Co-Chairperson, Real Estate, Housing & Land Use Division, 1985-1986; Member, Steering Committee, 1984-1986; Chair, Standing Committee on Rental Housing, 1988-1990); Bar Association of the District of Columbia; Virginia State Bar; American Bar Association. **PRACTICE AREAS:** Commercial Transactional Real Estate; Leasing. **Email:** lvermillion@dclawfirm.com

REFERENCES: American Security Bank; Grand Bank; Franklin National Bank of Washington.

ALVIN FRIEDMAN

700 NEW HAMPSHIRE AVENUE, N.W.
WASHINGTON, D.C. 20037
Telephone: 202-255-8383
Fax: 202-333-6328
Email: afwins@aol.com

Litigation and Counseling in Domestic and International Corporate and Commercial Transactions including Acquisitions, Dispositions and Financing of Aircraft.

ALVIN FRIEDMAN, born Brooklyn, New York, June 19, 1931; admitted to bar, 1957, Texas; 1958, District of Columbia. *Education:* Cornell University (B.A., 1952); Yale University (LL.B., 1957). Order of the Coif. Note Editor, Yale Law Journal, 1956-1957. Deputy Assistant Secretary of Defense for International Security Affairs, Department of Defense, 1964-1966. *Member:* District of Columbia Bar; State Bar of Texas. [With US Air Force, 1952-1954]

FRIEDMAN LAW OFFICES P.L.L.C.

Established in 1993

1735 NEW YORK AVENUE, N.W., SUITE 500
WASHINGTON, D.C. 20006
Telephone: 202-661-3925
Fax: 202-331-1024
Email: friedman@consumerlawhelp.com
URL: http://www.consumerlawhelp.com

Civil Litigation, Election Law and Consumer Class Actions.

MEMBER OF THE FIRM

PHILIP S. FRIEDMAN, born Sacramento, California, February 1, 1960; admitted to bar, 1987, California; 1989, District of Columbia; 1994, Maryland. *Education:* University of California at Berkeley (B.A., with high honors, 1982); Stanford University (J.D., 1987). Phi Beta Kappa. Associate Editor, Stanford Law Review, 1986-1987. Author, "Delegate Committees in Presidential Elections: Just Another Loophole in the Campaign Act?," 39 Stanford Law Review 981, 1987; "The Democrats' Quota System," The Wall Street Journal, April 19, 1995; "Abdicating Community Interests, "Does the NJDC truly represent Jews?" Washington Jewish Week, June 15, 1995. Deputy General Counsel, Clinton for President, 1991-1992. General Counsel and Member, American Israel Public Affairs Committee. Board of Directors, B'Nai Tzedek Congregation. *Member:* State Bar of California; State Bar of Maryland; The District of Columbia Bar; American Bar Association; Democratic National Committee National Lawyers Council; American Trial Lawyers Association; National Association of Consumer Advocates; Trial Lawyers for Public Justice; National Association of Consumer Advocates; Trial Lawyers for Public Justice. **REPORTED CASES:** United Cable Television of Baltimore v. Burch, 354 Md. 768, 732 A2d 887 (1999); FEC v. Akins, 524 U.S. 11 (1998). **PRACTICE AREAS:** Civil Litigation; Election Law; Consumer Class Actions.

FRANK W. FRISK, JR., P.C.

Established in 1977

SUITE 125, CANAL SQUARE
1054 THIRTY-FIRST STREET, N.W.
WASHINGTON, D.C. 20007
Telephone: 202-333-8433
Fax: 202-333-8431
Email: ffrisk@gslink.com

Energy, Environmental, Natural Resources, Municipal, Administrative and Legislative Law. Hydroelectric Regulation and Licensing, Cogeneration and Electric Utility Rates. General Practice before all Courts and Government Agencies.

FIRM PROFILE: For over 25 years, Mr. Frisk has advised and counselled electric utilities, independent energy developers, municipalities, public utility districts, energy companies and electric power associations.

FRANK W. FRISK, JR., born Seattle, Washington, November 25, 1939; admitted to bar, 1970, Virginia; 1973, U.S. Supreme Court; 1976, District of Columbia. *Education:* University of Washington (B.A., 1962; J.D., 1965). Phi Delta Phi. *Member:* The District of Columbia Bar; Virginia State Bar; Federal Energy and American (Member, Sections on: Public Utility Law; Antitrust Law; Natural Resources Law) Bar Associations.

FULBRIGHT & JAWORSKI L.L.P.

Established in 1919

801 PENNSYLVANIA AVENUE, N.W.
WASHINGTON, D.C. 20004-2604
Telephone: 202-662-0200
Fax: 202-662-4643
Email: info@fulbright.com
URL: http://www.fulbright.com

Houston, Texas Office: 1301 McKinney, Suite 5100, 77010. Telephone: 713-651-5151. Fax: 713-651-5246.
Austin, Texas Office: 600 Congress Avenue, Suite 2400, 78701. Telephone: 512-474-5201. Fax: 512-536-4598.
San Antonio, Texas Office: 300 Convent Street, Suite 2200, 78205. Telephone: 210-224-5575. Fax: 210-270-7205.
Dallas, Texas Office: 2200 Ross Avenue, Suite 2800, 75201. Telephone: 214-855-8000. Fax: 214-855-8200.
New York, New York Office: 666 Fifth Avenue, 31st Floor. 10103. Telephone: 212-318-3000. Fax: 212-318-3400.
Los Angeles, California Office: 865 South Figueroa Street, 29th Floor, 90017. Telephone: 213-892-9200. Fax: 213-680-4518.
Minneapolis, Minnesota Office: 225 South Sixth Street, Suite 4850, 55402. Telephone: 612-321-2800. Fax: 612-321-9600.
London, England Office: 2 St. James's Place, SW1A 1NP Telephone: 011-4420-7629-1207. Fax: 011-4420-7493-8259.
Hong Kong Office: The Hong Kong Club Building, Nineteenth Floor, 3A Chater Road, Central. Telephone: 011-852-2523-3200. Fax: 011-852-2523-3255.

General Civil Practice. Trial and Appellate Practice before Federal and State Courts, Departments and Agencies. Administrative and Legislative, Antitrust and Trade Regulations, Banking, Corporate and Securities, Customs, Education and Intercollegiate Sports Law, Energy, Environmental, Health Care, Immigration and Export Law, International, Labor and Employment, Patent, Project Finance, Trademark and Copyright, Taxation, Transportation, White Collar Criminal Law.

FIRM PROFILE: Founded in 1919, Fulbright & Jaworski L.L.P. offers comprehensive legal services to its domestic and international clients. With over 700 attorneys, the firm is one of the largest in the United States. The firm represents individuals, public sector entities, charitable organizations and business entities of every description. By virtue of its size, its presence in major business, financial and governmental centers, and its experience, the firm is able to be responsive to the varied legal needs of its clients.

PARTNERS

R. C. FULBRIGHT (1881-1940).

RICHARD W. BECKLER, admitted to bar, 1968, New York; 1972, Connecticut; 1979, District of Columbia. *Education:* Williams College (B.A., 1961); Fordham University (J.D., 1968). Assistant District Attorney, New York County, 1968-1972. Member, U.S. Department of Justice, 1973-1979. Deputy Chief, 1976-1978 and Acting Chief, 1979, Fraud Section, Criminal Division. Master, Edward Bennett Williams Inn of Court, 1989—. *Member:* The District of Columbia Bar; New York State. Connecticut and American Bar Associations. Fellow, American College of Trial Lawyers. ***PRACTICE AREAS:*** Antitrust; Class Action Defense; Foreign Corrupt Practices Act; Complex Litigation; White Collar Crime. ***Email:*** rbeckler@fulbright.com

ROBERT ANTHONY BURGOYNE, admitted to bar, 1982, District of Columbia; 1996, Pennsylvania. *Education:* Ohio Wesleyan University (B.A., 1978); University of North Carolina (J.D., 1982). *Member:* National Association of College and University Attorneys. ***PRACTICE AREAS:*** Complex Business Litigation; Energy Contracts; International Arbitration; Federal Administrative Law; College and University Law; Copyright Litigation. ***Email:*** rburgoyne@fulbright.com

IRWIN COHEN, admitted to bar, 1970, Maryland; 1986, District of Columbia. *Education:* University of Michigan (B.B.A., 1963); University of Baltimore (J.D., 1970). *Member:* National Health Lawyers Association (Director, 1984-1990); American Health Lawyers Association. ***PRACTICE AREAS:*** Health Care. ***Email:*** icohen@fulbright.com

THOMAS E. DOWDELL, admitted to bar, 1987, Texas; 1989, District of Columbia. *Education:* University of Pennsylvania (B.A., 1982); George Washington University (J.D., 1987). Memberships: Vice Chair of American Bar Association Health Section, Payment and Reimbursement Interest Group; District of Columbia Bar's Health Law Section; State Bar of Texas' Health Law Section; American Health Lawyers Association. ***PRACTICE AREAS:*** Health Care. ***Email:*** tdowdell@fulbright.com

STEPHEN M. FELDHAUS, admitted to bar, 1973, Texas; 1984, District of Columbia. *Education:* University of Notre Dame (A.B., 1967); Stanford University (J.D., 1973). *Member:* International Bar Association. ***PRACTICE AREAS:*** International Law; Taxation; Corporate Law. ***Email:*** sfeldhaus@fulbright.com

DAVID M. FOSTER, admitted to bar, 1981, Virginia; 1981, District of Columbia; 1989, U.S. Supreme Court. *Education:* University of Virginia (B.A., 1975; J.D., 1981). Member, Arlington County, Virginia School Board. *Member:* The District of Columbia Bar; Virginia State Bar. ***PRACTICE AREAS:*** Antitrust and Trade Regulation; Litigation. ***Email:*** dfoster@fulbright.com

LARRY G. FRANCESKI, admitted to bar, 1980, Texas; 1985, District of Columbia. *Education:* Louisiana State University (B.A., 1977); Harvard University (J.D., 1980). Phi Beta Kappa. *Member:* State Bar of Texas; The District of Columbia Bar; American Bar Association; American Bankruptcy Institute. ***PRACTICE AREAS:*** International Law; Bankruptcy; Corporate Law. ***Email:*** lfranceski@fulbright.com

JEFFREY H. GOODMAN, admitted to bar, 1979, District of Columbia. *Education:* Amherst College (B.A., 1974); University of Michigan (J.D., 1979). *Member:* The District of Columbia Bar; American Bar Association (Former Co-Chair, Committee on International Investment and Development; Former Chairman, Subcommittee on Land Use in Privatization). ***PRACTICE AREAS:*** Project Finance; International Law; Real Estate; Corporate Law. ***Email:*** jgoodman@fulbright.com

JOHN F. HARRINGTON, admitted to bar, 1969, Massachusetts; 1971, U.S. Court of Appeals, Fifth Circuit; 1972, District of Columbia and U.S. Court of Appeals, District of Columbia Circuit; 1981, U.S. Court of Appeals, Eleventh Circuit; 1986, U.S. Court of Appeals, Third Circuit; 1987, U.S. Court of Appeals, Fourth Circuit. *Education:* Colby College (A.B., 1966); Boston University (J.D., 1969). Attorney, Federal Power Commission, 1969-1971. *Member:* American and Federal Energy Bar Associations. ***PRACTICE AREAS:*** Administrative Law; Energy; Natural Resources. ***Email:*** jharrington@fulbright.com

GREGG W. HARRIS, admitted to bar, 1984, Illinois; 1985, District of Columbia. *Education:* Williams College (B.A., 1981); Northwestern University (J.D., 1984). ***PRACTICE AREAS:*** Project Finance; Real Estate. ***Email:*** gharris@fulbright.com

PETER F. HEALEY, JR., admitted to bar, 1967, Rhode Island; 1968, District of Columbia; 1971, U.S. Supreme Court; 1994, Maryland. *Education:* Brown University (B.A., 1964); Georgetown University Law Center (J.D., 1967). Phi Delta Phi. The Barristers (President, 1990). Fellow, The College of Labor and Employment Lawyers. ***PRACTICE AREAS:*** Labor and Employment; Litigation. ***Email:*** phealey@fulbright.com

ROBERT J. KOCH, admitted to bar, 1973, Virginia; registered to practice before U.S. Patent and Trademark Office (Not admitted in District of Columbia). *Education:* University of Detroit (B.S., 1968); Catholic University of America (J.D., 1973). Research Fellow, Max-Planck Institute for Foreign and International Copyright and Competition Law, 1973-1975. Examiner, U.S. Patent and Trademark Office, 1969-1971. *Member:* Washington Patent Lawyers Club; American Society of International Law; Federation International Des Conseils En Propriete Industrielle, Chartered Institute of Patent Agents. ***LANGUAGES:*** German. ***PRACTICE AREAS:*** Intellectual Property; Technology and Science; Technology Transfers. ***Email:*** rkoch@fulbright.com

L. POE LEGGETTE, admitted to bar, 1978, Ohio; 1991, District of Columbia. *Education:* Tufts University (B.A., 1974); University of Virginia (J.D., 1977). ***PRACTICE AREAS:*** Oil and Gas Law; Litigation; Administrative Law; Public Land Law. ***Email:*** pleggette@fulbright.com

ALAN B. LEVENSON, admitted to bar, 1962, New York; 1964, District of Columbia. *Education:* Dartmouth College (A.B., 1956); Oxford University (B.A., 1958; M.A., 1962); Yale University (LL.B., 1961). Phi Alpha Delta. Director, Division of Corporation Finance, Securities and Exchange Commission, 1970-1976. Public Director, Board of Directors, American Institute of Certified Public Accountants, 1983-1990. Governor-At-Large, National Association of Securities Dealers, 1984-1987, Member of Executive Committee, 1987, Chairman, Legal Advisory Board, 1988-1993. Member, Consultants Panel to Comptroller General of the U.S. 1989-2000. Member, Audit Advisory Committee of GAO, 1992—. Chairman, 1984-1987, Chairman Emeritus, 1987—, Annual Securities Regulation Institute (San Diego). Member of Board of Trustees of SEC Historical Society, and Chair of its Audit Committee and its Oral Histories Committee, 2000—. Member of Board of Directors of Transparency International USA, 1999—. Adjunct Professor, Georgetown University Law Center, 1964, 1981-1983. Lecturer, Catholic University Law School, 1964-1968 and Columbia University School of Law, 1973. *Member:* Federal Bar Association (Emeritus Member, Executive Council, Securities Law Committee); American Law Institute. ***PRACTICE AREAS:*** Securities; Corporate Law. ***Email:*** alevenson@fulbright.com

KERRY B. LONG, admitted to bar, 1981, New York and U.S. District Court, Southern and Eastern Districts of New York; 1985, District of Columbia. *Education:* Colgate University (A.B., 1972); Cornell University (J.D., magna cum laude, 1980). Order of the Coif. [Lt., U.S. Navy, 1972-1977]. ***PRACTICE AREAS:*** Corporate Finance; Aircraft Finance and Leasing.

(This Listing Continued)

FULBRIGHT & JAWORSKI L.L.P., Washington—Continued

JOHN E. LYNCH, admitted to bar, 1964, New York; 2000, District of Columbia; registered to practice before U.S. Patent and Trademark Office. *Education:* Fordham University (B.S., in Chem., 1960); Georgetown University (J.D., 1963). Adjunct Professor of Law, Georgetown University Law Center, 1997 and University of San Francisco School of Law. *Member:* Federal Circuit Bar Association; New York Patent, Trademark and Copyright Law Association; American Intellectual Property Law Association; International Association for the Protection of Industrial Property; International Federation of Industrial Property Attorneys; Society of University Patent Administrators; Licensing Executives Society; Georgetown National Law Alumni Board. ***PRACTICE AREAS:*** Intellectual Property. ***Email:*** jlynch@fulbright.com

MICHAEL J. MANNING, admitted to bar, 1969, Kansas; 1970, District of Columbia; U.S. Court of Appeals, Fifth, Tenth, Eleventh and District of Columbia Circuits. *Education:* University of Kansas (A.B., 1966); Washburn University (J.D., 1969). Attorney Advisor to Vice Chairman, Federal Power Commission, 1969-1971. Trial and Appellate Counsel, Federal Energy Regulatory Commission, 1972-1973. *Member:* Kansas, Federal Energy Bar Association (Board of Directors, 1993-1996). ***PRACTICE AREAS:*** Energy; Oil and Gas Law; Natural Resources; Administrative Law; Litigation. ***Email:*** mmanning@fulbright.com

STEPHEN M. McNABB, admitted to bar, 1982, District of Columbia. *Education:* Harvard College (A.B., 1978); Georgetown University (J.D., 1982). ***PRACTICE AREAS:*** White Collar Crime; Civil Practice Litigation; Appellate Practice. ***Email:*** smcnabb@fulbright.com

MARILYN MOONEY, admitted to bar, 1977, Massachusetts; 1985, District of Columbia; 1990, Pennsylvania. *Education:* University of Pennsylvania (B.A., 1973; J.D., 1976). Attorney, E.I. du Pont de Nemours and Company 1976-1985. Member: Securities Law Committee, American Society of Corporate Secretaries; Section on Business Law, International Bar Association; Federal Regulation of Securities Committee, American Bar Association. ***PRACTICE AREAS:*** Mergers and Acquisitions; Joint Ventures; Business Divestitures; Securities Offerings; Securities Regulation; Corporate Governance. ***Email:*** mmooney@fulbright.com

DAN M. PETERSON, admitted to bar, 1978, Iowa; 1979, Texas; 1989, District of Columbia and Virginia. *Education:* University of Iowa (B.A., 1972); Harvard University (J.D., 1977). Phi Beta Kappa. Instructor in Medical Jurisprudence, Baylor College of Medicine, 1980-1982. Adjunct Professor of Law, George Mason University Law School, 1987-1988. ***PRACTICE AREAS:*** Health Care; Litigation. ***Email:*** dpeterson@fulbright.com

STEVEN B. PFEIFFER, admitted to bar, 1976, New Jersey; 1978, District of Columbia. *Education:* Wesleyan University (B.A., 1969); Oxford University, England (B.A., 1971; M.A., 1983); University of London, England (M.A., 1973) Rhodes Scholar; Yale University (J.D., 1976). *Member:* International Bar Association. ***PRACTICE AREAS:*** Corporate Law; Commercial Law; International Law; Energy Law. ***Email:*** spfeiffer@fulbright.com

CRAIG T. REDINGER, admitted to bar, 1977, Virginia, U.S. District Court, Western and Eastern, Districts of Virginia, U.S. Bankruptcy Court, Western and Eastern Districts of Virginia and U.S. Court of Appeals, Fourth Circuit; 1982, U.S. Supreme Court; 1994, District of Columbia. *Education:* University of Virginia (B.A., high honors, 1973); University of Heidelberg, Heidelberg, Germany. Dupont Fellow, Echols Scholar. Lecturer: University of Richmond School of Law, Internationales Fachinstitut für Steuer- und Wirtschafts-Recht, Frankfurt, Germany, 1988. *Member:* International Bar Association; The Association of Trial Lawyers of America; Virginia Trial Lawyers Association. ***LANGUAGES:*** German. ***PRACTICE AREAS:*** International Law; Corporate Law; Mergers, Acquisitions and Divestitures. ***Email:*** credinger@fulbright.com

FREDERICK ROBINSON, admitted to bar, 1982, District of Columbia; 1992, Maryland. *Education:* Duke University (A.B., 1979; J.D., 1982). *Member:* American Bar Association; American Health Lawyers Association; National Association of College and University Attorneys; American Compliance Institute. ***PRACTICE AREAS:*** Federal Criminal Law; False Claims Act; Business Crimes; Government Investigations; Health Care Fraud; Health Care Compliance. ***Email:*** frobinson@fulbright.com

LANCE L. SHEA, admitted to bar, 1989, Texas; 1993 Arizona (Not admitted in District of Columbia). *Education:* University of Arizona (B.S., with distinction, 1982); Arizona State University (M.S., 1986); University of San Diego (J.D., magna cum laude, 1989). ***PRACTICE AREAS:*** Toxic Torts; Environmental Law. ***Email:*** lshea@fulbright.com

JOHN M. SIMPSON, admitted to bar, 1979, District of Columbia; 1988, North Carolina. *Education:* Harvard University (A.B., 1972); Columbia University (J.D., 1978). Civic Boards: Member, Board of Visitors, Columbia University School of Law, Vice President and Director, Columbia Law School Association of Washington, D.C. *Member:* North Carolina State Bar. ***PRACTICE AREAS:*** Federal Administrative Law; Arbitration; Commercial Litigation; College and University Law; Employment Litigation; Complex Litigation. ***Email:*** jsimpson@fulbright.com

JOSEPH T. SMALL, JR., admitted to bar, 1975, Virginia; 1977, District of Columbia. *Education:* Washington and Lee University (B.A., 1969); University of Virginia (J.D., 1975). Phi Beta Kappa. [U.S. Navy, 1969-1971]. ***LANGUAGES:*** Chinese/Mandarin. ***PRACTICE AREAS:*** White Collar Crime; General Litigation; Export Regulation; Administrative Law. ***Email:*** jsmall@fulbright.com

JULIE A. TASSI, admitted to bar, 1989, Virginia; 1990, Maryland; 1991, District of Columbia. *Education:* American University (B.A., 1980); Georgetown University (J.D., 1989). ***PRACTICE AREAS:*** Real Estate. ***Email:*** jtassi@fulbright.com

MICHAEL D. TRAGER, admitted to bar, 1985, Massachusetts; 1986, Connecticut; 1988, Florida; 1989, District of Columbia. *Education:* Wesleyan University (B.A., 1981); Boston University (J.D., 1985). Attorney, Division of Enforcement, U.S. Securities and Exchange Commission, Washington, D.C., 1985-1987. ***PRACTICE AREAS:*** Securities Regulation; Securities Litigation; Corporate Law. ***Email:*** mtrager@fulbright.com

PETER V.B. UNGER, admitted to bar, 1984, Ohio; 1985, District of Columbia; 1991, U.S. Supreme Court. *Education:* Miami University (B.A., 1980); University of Cincinnati (J.D., 1983); Georgetown University (LL.M., 1987). ***PRACTICE AREAS:*** Corporate Law; Litigation. ***Email:*** punger@fulbright.com

MARK E. UNGERMAN, admitted to bar, 1988, California; 1990, District of Columbia; registered to practice before U.S. Patent and Trademark Office. *Education:* State University of New York at Buffalo (B.S.E.E., 1981); George Washington University (J.D., 1986). ***PRACTICE AREAS:*** Intellectual Property; Technology and Science Transfers; Patents; Trademarks; Computer and Software Patents; Information Technology. ***Email:*** mungerman@fulbright.com

CARL W. VOGT, admitted to bar, 1965, Texas; 1972, District of Columbia; 1980, U.S. Supreme Court. *Education:* Boalt Hall School of Law, University of California; University of Texas (LL.B., 1965). Chairman and Member, National Transportation Safety Board, June, 1992-Nov., 1994. President (interim), Williams College, 1999-2000. *Member:* Federal (Co-Chairman, Committee on Equal Employment Opportunity, 1976-1977, Member, 1974—) and American (Member, Administrative Law Section; Chairman: Equal Employment Opportunity Committee, 1973—; Labor Law Committee, 1978, Council Member, 1977-1978; Member, Section of Labor Law, 1973—; Member, Litigation Section, 1981—; Director and Chair, Forum on Air and Space Law, 1996—) Bar Associations; National Association of College and University Attorneys; American Society of Hospital Attorneys (Member, Advisory Committee on Labor Law to General Counsel); American Hospital Association; National Association of Manufacturers (Chairman, Legal Advisory Committee of Employment Law, 1979-1981). ***PRACTICE AREAS:*** Alternative Dispute Resolution; Administrative Law. ***Email:*** cvogt@fulbright.com

DANIEL L. WELLINGTON, admitted to bar, 1979, District of Columbia. *Education:* Catholic University of America (B.A., 1967; M.A., 1968); George Washington University (J.D., with honors, 1979). ***PRACTICE AREAS:*** Antitrust and Trade Regulation. ***Email:*** dwellington@fulbright.com

CHARLES R. WENNER, admitted to bar, 1974, Connecticut; 1978, District of Columbia. *Education:* College of Charleston (B.A., 1969); University of Connecticut (J.D., 1973). Attorney, 1974-1976 and Special Counsel to the Chairman, 1976-1977, Securities and Exchange Commission. ***PRACTICE AREAS:*** Securities. ***Email:*** cwenner@fulbright.com

WILLIAM A. WILLIAMS, admitted to bar, 1977, Virginia; 1980, District of Columbia. *Education:* George Mason University (B.S., 1974); University of Virginia (J.D., 1977). Attorney, Federal Energy Regulatory Commission, 1977-1980. *Member:* Federal Energy Bar Association. [USMC, 1967-1970]. ***PRACTICE AREAS:*** Energy. ***Email:*** wwilliams@fulbright.com

RETIRED PARTNER

Warren Belmar.

SENIOR COUNSEL

ANTHONY E. DiRESTA, admitted to bar, 1984, Georgia, U.S. District Court, Northern District of Georgia and U.S. Court of Appeals, Eleventh Circuit; 1989, Florida and U.S. District Court, Middle District of Florida; 1991, U.S. Supreme Court; 2000, District of Columbia. *Education:* Rollins College (B.A., 1977); Harvard University (M.Ed., Philosophy, 1978); Florida State University (J.D., 1982). Articles and Notes Editor, Florida State University Law Review, 1981-1982. Law Clerk, Honorable J. Owen Forrester, U.S. District Judge, Atlanta, 1982-1984. *Member:* State Bar of Georgia; The Florida Bar; American Bar Association (Section on Litigation, Associate Editor, Litigation News; ALI-ABA Committee on Continuing Legal Education); American Law

(This Listing Continued)

Institute; American Judicature Society. ***PRACTICE AREAS:*** Antitrust; Business Litigation; Securities; Communications and Media Law. ***Email:*** adiresta@fulbright.com

ALLEN K. HALPERIN, admitted to bar, 1968, Virginia; 1972, District of Columbia. *Education:* University of Virginia (B.S., 1964; LL.B., 1967); New York University (LL.M., Taxation, 1972). ***PRACTICE AREAS:*** Taxation; Aircraft Finance and Leasing; Equipment Finance and Leasing. ***Email:*** ahalperin@fulbright.com

JAMES P. WHITE, admitted to bar, 1985, District of Columbia; 1986, U.S. Court of Appeals, Fifth, Tenth and District of Columbia Circuits; 1993, U.S. Court of Appeals, Fourth and Eleventh Circuits. *Education:* Georgetown University (B.S., 1980); American University (J .D., 1985). ***PRACTICE AREAS:*** Energy; Administrative Law. ***Email:*** jwhite@fulbright.com

COUNSEL

Andrew E. Falk; Thomas S. Hahn; Arthur A. Impastato; Maha S. Jadallah (Not admitted in DC); ***Amy Kertgate*** (Not admitted in DC); ***John C. Letteri; Karen M. Moran; Janet S. Nolan; Brenda J. Oliver; Michael J. Strauss.***

SENIOR ASSOCIATES

Glenn S. Benson; Nancy E. Burton; Yeages Cowan; Cynthia C. Henderson (Not admitted in DC); ***Lisa Zeiler Joiner; Sean J. Klein; Robert Jeffrey Layne; Seth H. Lundy; Laura S. Morton*** (Not admitted in DC); ***Nancy L. Pell; Mary Anne Schofield*** (Not admitted in DC).

ASSOCIATES

Neely B. Agin; Lori-Ann S. Bellan; William E. Bradley; Wendy Butler Curtis (Not admitted in DC); ***Elizabeth Fritze; Gabriele Haist Fuqua; Joseph E. Hartman; Jeremy Ambler Hushon; Chantal E. Jean-Baptiste*** (admission pending); ***Erica D. Jones; Matthew H. Kirtland; Ben Konop*** (Not admitted in DC); ***Michael LaClare*** (admission pending); ***Kerry Elizabeth Larsen; Joshua R. Martin; Kristin McGovern*** (Not admitted in DC); ***Letitia W. McKoy; Kristina G. McNeff*** (admission pending); ***Caroline Marie Mew; Michelle Ciszak Pardo; Lara E. Parkin*** (admission pending); ***René Y. Quashie; Einar Stole*** (Not admitted in DC); ***Bret A. Sumner; Yan Wang*** (Not admitted in DC); ***Steven War*** (Not admitted in DC); ***Carol I. Wicks*** (Not admitted in DC).

STAFF ATTORNEYS

Katherine M. DuBray (Not admitted in DC); ***A. Scott English*** (Not admitted in DC); ***Christopher M. Gerlach*** (Not admitted in DC); ***Dimitri Seletzky.***

SCIENTIFIC ADVISOR

MARK E. FLANIGAN, born Augusta, Georgia, June 4, 1970; (admission pending). *Education:* Virginia Tech (B.S., 1992); University of Houston. ***PRACTICE AREAS:*** Intellectual Property.

(For Biographies of Houston, Texas Personnel, see Houston, Texas Professional Biographies).
(For Biographies of Austin, Texas Personnel, see Austin, Texas Professional Biographies).
(For Biographies of San Antonio, Texas Personnel, see San Antonio, Texas Professional Biographies).
(For Biographies of Dallas, Texas Personnel, see Dallas, Texas Professional Biographies).
(For Biographies of London, England Personnel, see London, England Professional Biographies).
(For Biographies of New York, New York Personnel, see New York, New York Professional Biographies).
(For Biographies of Los Angeles, California Personnel, see Los Angeles, California Professional Biographies).
(For Biographies of the Hong Kong Personnel, see Hong Kong Professional Biographies).
(For Biographies of Minneapolis, Minnesota Personnel, see Minneapolis, Minnesota Professional Biographies).

FULLERTON & WISE

WASHINGTON, D.C.

(See Fairfax)

General Civil and Trial Practice, Construction Law, Public Contract Law, Payment & Performance Bonds, Mechanic's Liens and Commercial Litigation.

FUREY, DOOLAN & ABELL, L.L.P.

WASHINGTON, D.C.

(See Chevy Chase, Maryland)

Real Estate, Condominium, Cooperative, Homeowners' Associations, Land Use, Corporate, Partnership, Estate Planning, Commercial, Probate, Early Childhood Education and Day Care Centers, Family Law, Taxation Law and Related Litigation. State and Local Legislative, Regulatory, Administrative Practice, Litigation in State and Federal Courts. Estate and Trust Litigation. Hospital Law, Nonprofit Organization Law, Employment Law.

THOMAS J. GAGLIARDO

WASHINGTON, D.C.

(See Silver Spring, Maryland)

Employment Law, Wrongful Termination, Employment Discrimination, Executive Employment Law, Executive Severance Contracts, Federal Employment Law, Academic Employment Law, Wage and Hour Law, Personnel Policies, Personnel Training, Small Business Employment, Employee Discipline, Hiring Practices, Employee Handbook Drafting, Employment Mediation.

GALLAGHER, BOLAND AND MEIBURGER

Established in 1940

1023 15TH STREET, N.W., SUITE 900
WASHINGTON, D.C. 20005-2602
Telephone: 202-289-7200
Fax: 202-289-7698
URL: http://www.GBMDC.com

Federal Energy Regulation, Natural Gas, Natural Gas Pipelines, Electric Utility Regulation, Gas Utilities, Hydroelectricity Licensing, Alternative Energy, Independent Power.

FIRM PROFILE: The firm has expertise in all aspects of the regulation of utilities. The firm's attorneys appear and practice before the Federal Energy Regulatory Commission (FERC), the Department of Energy, state utility regulatory agencies, Federal appellate courts and the National Energy Board of Canada representing the interests of natural gas pipelines, electric utility companies, local gas distribution companies, producers and marketers. The firm's founding partner, in the regulatory field, was formerly the General Counsel of the Federal Power Commission, the predecessor of the FERC. All of the firm's attorneys are members of the Energy Bar Association. Two have been president of the Association. Four have previously served as attorneys on the Staff of the FERC or legal advisors to FERC Commissioners or to Administrative Law Judges at the FERC.

MEMBERS OF FIRM

RICHARD J. CONNOR (1901-1984).

WALTER E. GALLAGHER (1910-1996).

JAMES M. BROADSTONE, born San Diego, California, April 25, 1945; admitted to bar, 1972, Ohio; 1974, District of Columbia. *Education:* The Ohio State University (B.A., 1968; J.D., 1972). Attorney, Federal Power Commission, 1972-1973. General Counsel, Gas Research Institute, 1981-1992. *Member:* The District of Columbia Bar; Ohio State Bar Association; Energy Bar Association. ***PRACTICE AREAS:*** Alternative Energy; Energy; Gas Utilities; Public Utility Rates. ***Email:*** jamesbroad@earthlink.net

FRANK X. KELLY, born Jersey City, New Jersey, April 29, 1948; admitted to bar, 1975, District of Columbia; 1978, U.S. Supreme Court. *Education:* Georgetown University (A.B., cum laude, 1970); Georgetown University Law Center (J.D., 1974). *Member:* The District of Columbia Bar; American Bar Association; Federal Energy Bar Association. ***PRACTICE AREAS:*** Energy Regulation; Natural Gas; Natural Gas Pipelines; Gas Utilities; Public Utility Rates; Regulatory Agency Practice. ***Email:*** fkelly@gbmdc.com

PETER C. LESCH, born Lafayette, Indiana, June 12, 1948; admitted to bar, 1973, Michigan; 1980, District of Columbia; 1981, U.S. Supreme Court. *Education:* Oberlin College (B.A., magna cum laude, 1970); University of Michigan (J.D., 1973). Attorney: Federal Power Commission, 1973-1977; Energy Regulatory Commission, 1977-1979. *Member:* The District of Columbia Bar; State Bar of Michigan; American Bar Association; Energy Bar Association. ***PRACTICE AREAS:*** Electric Utility Regulation; Natural Gas Regulation; Independent Power; Hydroelectricity Licensing; Regulatory Agency Practice. ***Email:*** plesch@gbmdc.com

STEVE STOJIC, born Detroit, Michigan, February 25, 1956; admitted to bar, 1980, District of Columbia; 1989, U.S. Supreme Court. *Education:* University of Michigan (B.A., with high distinction, 1977; J.D., 1980). Attorney, Federal Energy Regulatory Commission, 1980-1982. *Member:* The District of

(This Listing Continued)

GALLAGHER, BOLAND AND MEIBURGER, Washington—Continued

Columbia Bar; American Bar Association; Energy Bar Association. ***PRACTICE AREAS:*** Federal Energy Regulation; Natural Gas; Natural Gas Pipelines; Gas Utilities; Public Utility Rates; Regulatory Agency Practice. ***Email:*** sstojic@gbmdc.com

SENIOR COUNSEL

CHRISTOPHER T. BOLAND, born Scranton, Pennsylvania, 1915; admitted to bar, 1941, Pennsylvania; 1948, District of Columbia. *Education:* Valley Forge Military Academy, Wayne, Pennsylvania; Georgetown University (B.S., cum laude, 1937); Harvard Law School (LL.B., 1940). Staff Director, United States Senate Committee on Atomic Energy; Counsel—Staff Director, Joint Congressional Committee on Atomic Energy, 1945-47. *Member:* The District of Columbia Bar; American Bar Association; Energy Bar Association (President, 1970-1971). [Lieut.-Colonel, U.S. Army, 1941-45]. ***PRACTICE AREAS:*** Administrative Law; Energy; Utility Law. ***Email:*** cboland@gbmdc.com

GEORGE J. MEIBURGER, born Argyle, Missouri, August 14, 1921; admitted to bar, 1952, Missouri; 1953, District of Columbia; 1959, Oklahoma. *Education:* St. Louis University; Georgetown University (J.D., 1952). *Member:* The District of Columbia Bar; American Bar Association; Energy Bar Association (President, 1987-1988). ***PRACTICE AREAS:*** Energy; Utility Contracts. ***Email:*** gmeib@gbmdc.com

---

GALLAND, KHARASCH, GREENBERG, FELLMAN & SWIRSKY, P.C.

CANAL SQUARE
1054 THIRTY-FIRST STREET, N.W.
WASHINGTON, D.C. 20007-4492
Telephone: 202-342-5200
Telecopier: 202-342-5219
Email: gkglaw@gkglaw.com
URL: http://www.gkglaw.com

Baltimore, Maryland Office: 9199 Reisterstown Road, Suite 200B, 21117. Telephone: 443-394-6310. Fax: 443-394-6320.

Advertising, Alternative Dispute Resolution, Antitrust, Aviation, Commercial, Corporate, Employment Law, Energy, Food and Drug, Gaming, Government Contracts, Information Technology, Intellectual Property, International Trade, Legislative Affairs, Litigation, Maritime, Real Estate, Securities, Surface Transportation, Taxation, Tax Controversy, representation before IRS and State Taxing Authorities, Telecommunications, Trade and Professional Associations, and Wildlife.

FIRM PROFILE: Galland, Kharasch is a Washington, D.C. firm with a regional, national and international practice. Since its founding in 1955, Galland, Kharasch has assembled a team of talented attorneys and dedicated legal support personnel committed to serving the needs of clients promptly, efficiently, and effectively. Common sense counsel, attention to detail and pride in workmanship are legacies of the Firm's founders and continuing hallmarks of its practice. Galland, Kharasch takes pride in providing quality legal services at competitive billing levels in an environment of cooperation and collegiality.

GEORGE F. GALLAND (1910-1985).

EDWARD D. GREENBERG, born Philadelphia, Pennsylvania, September 1, 1942; admitted to bar, 1968, District of Columbia; 1977, U.S. Supreme Court; 1985, Maryland. *Education:* Johns Hopkins University (B.A., 1964); Catholic University of America (J.D., 1968). Regional Counsel, Interstate Commerce Commission, 1973-1976. Special Counsel for Pipelines, Interstate Commerce Commission, 1977. Director and Chief Counsel, Trans Alaska Pipeline System Project, Federal Energy Regulatory Commission, 1978. *Member:* District of Columbia Bar; Association of Transportation Practitioners (Former Chairman, District of Columbia Chapter); Maritime Lawyers Association; Maritime Administrative Bar Association; Transportation Lawyers Association; Johns Hopkins University Alumni Association (Member, Executive Committee); Counsel, National Customs Brokers and Forwarders Association of America. ***Email:*** egreenbe@gkglaw.com

DAVID K. MONROE, born Dunkirk, New York, June 22, 1950; admitted to bar, 1981, District of Columbia; 1984, California. *Education:* University of Chicago; State University of New York at Stony Brook (B.S., 1972); Harvard University (J.D., 1981). *Member:* State Bar of California; District of Columbia Bar. ***Email:*** dmonroe@gkglaw.com

DAVID P. STREET, born Evansville, Indiana, August 12, 1945; admitted to bar, 1976, District of Columbia; 1987, California. *Education:* Duke University (B.A., 1967); George Washington University (M.A., 1972); Georgetown University (J.D., 1976). Author: "The Break-Up of the Soviet Monolith in

(This Listing Continued)

Eastern Europe," The Journal of International and Comparative Studies, Washington 1971; "Intermediaries: NVOCC's Forwards and Shippers' Associations," Survey of Maritime Administrative Law, Washington, July 1998; "The Ocean Shipping Reform Act of 1998: Impacts on Intermediaries," Survey of Maritime Administrative Law, August, 1999. Member, Georgetown Law Journal, 1974-1975. *Member:* District of Columbia Bar; State Bar of California (inactive); Maritime Law Association of the United States; Maritime Administration Bar Association. ***LANGUAGES:*** French. ***Email:*** dstreet@gkglaw.com

STEVEN JOHN FELLMAN, born New York, N.Y., June 26, 1938; admitted to bar, 1962, New York; 1965, District of Columbia; 1966, U.S. Supreme Court. *Education:* Williams College (A.B., 1959); New York University (LL.B., 1962). Author: "Pre-complaint Practice Before the Federal Trade Commission," A.B.A. Law Notes, 1968; "How The Commission Can Get The Most Out Of A Trade Association," XVII Antitrust Bulletin 427, 1972; "What Services Must a Trade Association Render to Non-Members," XVIII Antitrust Bulletin 167, 1973. Contributing Author, "Associations and the Law," Book IV, Book V and VII, U.S. Chamber of Commerce, 1971-1976. Co-Author: "Antitrust Joint Counsel Considerations," Mercer Law Review, 1975; "Compliance and Counseling in the New Antitrust Era," ABA, 1988. Co-Author, Antitrust Advisor, 4th Ed., 1999. Co-Author, "Antitrust and Trade Associations," ABA, 1996. Trial Attorney, Federal Trade Commission, 1962-1964. Recipient, Federal Trade Commission Superior Service Award, 1964. Chair, Legal Section, American Society of Association Executives, 1996-1997. *Member:* District of Columbia Bar; Bar Association of the District of Columbia (Co-Chair, Association and Antitrust Law Committee, 2000—); American Bar Association (Member, Antitrust Section; Council, 1992-1995; Chair, Trade Association Committee, 1986-1991). Lifefellow, American Bar Foundation. ***PRACTICE AREAS:*** Antitrust; Trade Association Law; ADA; FDA. ***Email:*** sfellman@gkglaw.com

KEITH G. SWIRSKY, born Riverside, California, September 18, 1959; admitted to bar, 1984, Virginia; 1986, District of Columbia. *Education:* Cornell University (B.S., with distinction, 1981); Georgetown University (J.D., 1984; LL.M. in Taxation, 1988). Author: "Use of S Corporations Post 1986 TRA," BNA, Tax Management, Inc., 1988; "Purchase Price Allocations in Taxable Asset Acquisitions," CCH and Prentice-Hall, 1989; "Planning Corporate Separations Under Section 355," WG v L, 1990; "Multiple Recognition Rules Complicate Partner-Partnership Transactions," WG v L, 1993. Fairfax and D.C. Bar Associations and Society of Virginia C.P.A.s (Corporate Acquisitions - NOL Carryovers and Purchase Price Allocations) 1988, (Corporate Divisions under Section 355), 1989, (Business and Tax Considerations in Structuring Taxable and Tax-Free Acquisitions), 1990; National Business Institute (S Corporations - Issues in Acquisition Transactions), 1994; National Business Aircraft Association; National Aircraft Resale Association and National Aircraft Finance Association (Fractional Ownership Programs for Business Jet Aircraft; Tax-Free Exchanges of Aircraft Under Section 1031; Federal and State Taxation of Aircraft Acquisitions and Operations; IRS enforcement in Aviation Excise Tax Audits; current Tax Issues Affecting Aircraft Leasing and Financing) 1994-2000. Co-Chairman, North American Section of Taxation of Interlaw, 1995-1997; Tax Committee Appointment - National Business Aircraft Association, 1995-2000; Former Chairman, Section of Taxation, Fairfax County, Virginia Bar Association, 1991. ***PRACTICE AREAS:*** Aviation Law; Federal and State Tax and FAA Planning; Aircraft Acquisitions, Sales and Operations; Aircraft Tax-Free Exchanges. ***Email:*** kswirsky@gkglaw.com

MARTIN JACOBS, born Brooklyn, New York, February 16, 1940; admitted to bar, 1964, New York; 1967, District of Columbia and U.S. Supreme Court; 1994, Maryland. *Education:* Baruch School of Business, College of the City of New York (B.B.A., 1960); New York University (LL.B., 1963). Ginsburg, Feldman and Bress, Chartered, Member, 1971-1994, Associate, 1967-1971. Executive Vice President, 1989-1994, General Counsel, 1984—, The Maryland Jockey Club. Member, Maryland Transportation Commission, 1995-1998 (Chairman, 1997-1998). Trial Attorney, U.S. Department of Justice, Attorney General's Program for Honor Law Graduates, 1963-1967. *Member:* District of Columbia Bar; Maryland State and American Bar Associations. ***PRACTICE AREAS:*** Business and Corporate; Gaming; Real Estate. ***Email:*** mjacobs@gkglaw.com

RICHARD B. BAR, born New York, N.Y., May 9, 1961; admitted to bar, 1986, Maryland; 1987, Pennsylvania and District of Columbia. *Education:* Skidmore College (B.A., magna cum laude, 1983); George Washington University (J.D., 1986). Phi Beta Kappa. Moot Court Board. Articles Editor, National Law Center, Consumer Protection Reporting Service, 1985-1986. *Faculty:* Goucher College Center for Continuing Studies. Member, Board of Directors, Montgomery County Public School Education Foundation. *Member:* Maryland State Bar Association, Inc.; American Bar Association; District of Columbia Bar. ***PRACTICE AREAS:*** Corporate; Real Estate; Business; Trade Association; Commercial Leasing; Workouts; Sports. ***Email:*** rbar@gkglaw.com

WILLIAM F. KREBS, born Pittsburgh, Pennsylvania, May 5, 1952; admitted to bar, 1977, Virginia and U.S. Court of Appeals, 4th Circuit; 1978, District of Columbia, U.S. Court of Appeals for the District of Columbia Circuit, U.S. District Court for the District of Columbia and Eastern and Western Districts of Virginia; 1980, U.S. Court of Appeals, 8th and 9th Circuits; 1981,

(This Listing Continued)

U.S. Court of Appeals, 7th Circuit; 1988, U.S. Tax Court; 1992, U.S. District Court for the District of Maryland; 1995, U.S. Court of Federal Claims; 1996, U.S. Court for International Trade; 2000, U.S. Court of Appeals, 2nd Circuit. *Education:* Pennsylvania State University (B.A., with high distinction, 1974); Georgetown University (J.D., 1977). Phi Beta Kappa; Phi Kappa Phi; Phi Alpha Theta. President, Pi Sigma Alpha, Beta Pi Chapter, 1973-1974. Editor, Law and Policy in International Business, 1976-1977. Instructor, Washington College of Law, American University, 1981. *Member:* The District of Columbia Bar; Fairfax Bar Association; Virginia State Bar; Virginia Trial Lawyers Association. ***PRACTICE AREAS:*** Civil and White Collar Criminal Litigation; Appellate Litigation; Commercial Law; Admiralty Law. ***Email:*** wkrebs@gkglaw.com

STUART M. SCHABES, born Washington, Pennsylvania, 1959; admitted to bar, 1984, Ohio; 1985, U.S. Tax Court; 1987, Maryland (Not admitted in District of Columbia). *Education:* Duquesne University (B.S., magna cum laude, 1981); Hofstra University (J.D., 1984); Georgetown University (M.L.T., 1986). Notes and Comment Editor, Hofstra Law Review, 1983-1984. Author: Case Comment, "Roemer v. Commissioner," 12 Hofstra Law Review 211, 1984. Attorney-Advisor, U.S. Tax Court, 1984-1986. Guest Lecturer: Maryland Association of C.P.A.'s (numerous programs on IRS Tax Controversy Offer-in-Compromise Collections (Intricacies of tax liens and levies) and Business Law Topics 1993-present); Air Transportation Association (Federal Exercise Tax Related Matters, 1997-1998; Hotel Tax Executive Committee Meeting Presentations, 1997, 1998 and 1999, Chesapeake Tax Conference Presentations on IRS Topics, 2000 and 2001). *Member:* Maryland State and American Bar Associations. (Resident, Baltimore, Maryland Office). ***PRACTICE AREAS:*** Corporate Law; Tax Controversy-representation before IRS and State Taxing Authorities; Aviation Tax Law; Frequent Flyer; Tax Law. ***Email:*** sschabes@gkglaw.com

---

KATHARINE V. FOSTER, born Watertown, New York, October 17, 1970; admitted to bar, 1998, New York; New Jersey; 1999, District of Columbia. *Education:* Colgate University (B.A., 1993); American University (J.D., 1998). ***PRACTICE AREAS:*** Corporate Law; Association; Transportation. ***Email:*** kfoster@gkglaw.com

MICHAEL P. COYLE, born Evanston, Illinois, March 27, 1968; admitted to bar, 1994, Maryland; 1996, District of Columbia. *Education:* Franklin & Marshall College (B.A., 1990); American University (J.D., magna cum laude, 1994). Member, American University Law Review.

CYNTHIA J. HURWITZ, born Portland, Oregon, December 26, 1972; admitted to bar, 2000, Virginia. *Education:* Bryn Mawr College (B.A., 1995); University of Denver (J.D., 2000); American University (M.P.P., 1997). Author, Comment: "Viability of a Sustainable and Feasible National Transportation System," 26 Transp. L.J. 133 (Fall 1998). *Member:* American Bar Association; Transportation Lawyers Association; Association for Transportation Law, Logistics & Policy. ***PRACTICE AREAS:*** Transportation; Maritime Law; Customs. ***Email:*** churwitz@gkglaw.com

OF COUNSEL

ROBERT N. KHARASCH, born Washington, D.C., December 13, 1926; admitted to bar, 1952, District of Columbia. *Education:* University of Chicago (Ph.B., 1946; B.S., 1948; J.D., 1951). Phi Beta Kappa; Order of the Coif. Consultant to Department of Transportation, 1967-1968. Maritime Transportation Research Board, National Academy of Sciences, 1975-1979. *Member:* District of Columbia Bar. ***Email:*** rkharasc@gkglaw.com

REX E. REESE, born Erwin, Tennessee, April 22, 1959; admitted to bar, 1985, Pennsylvania; 1987, Virginia; 1988, U.S. Tax Court; 1991,U.S. Court of Federal Claims; 1992, U.S. District Court, Northern District of Virginia (Not admitted in District of Columbia). *Education:* University of Tennessee; Florida Southern College (B.S., 1981); University of Tulsa (J.D., 1985); Georgetown University (LL.M. in Taxation, 1989). Co-author: "Temporary Regulations on Passive Activity Losses Provide Tests for Material Participation," Journal of Taxation of S Corporations, 1990; "The Employee/Independent Contractor Dilemma: When Misclassification Becomes a Crime," Corporate Controller 1990, Corporate Taxation, 1989; "Preserving an S Election in a Reorganization," Journal of Corporate Taxation, 1989; "Key Estate Planning Considerations for S Corporation Shareholders," Journal of Taxation of S Corporations, 1989. Associate, Verner, Liipfert, Bernhard, McPherson & Hand, 1985-1987. Law Intern, Hon. Moody R. Tidwell, III, U.S. Court of Federal Claims, 1985. *Member:* Pennsylvania Bar Association; Virginia State Bar. ***PRACTICE AREAS:*** Asset-based and Project Finance; Aerospace and Aviation; Domestic and International Taxation; Corporate Transactions; Commercial Transactions. ***Email:*** rreese@gkglaw.com

GARDNER, CARTON & DOUGLAS

SUITE 900, EAST TOWER
1301 K STREET, N.W.
WASHINGTON, D.C. 20005-3317
Telephone: 202-408-7100
Facsimile: 202-289-1504
URL: http://www.gcd.com

Chicago, Illinois Office: Quaker Tower, Suite 3400, 321 North Clark Street, 60610-4795. Telephone: 312-644-3000.

Administrative Law, Affirmative Action, Alternative Dispute Resolution, Antitrust and Trade Regulation, Appellate Practice, Bankruptcy, Banks and Banking, Broadcasting Law, Broadcasting Television, Broker-Dealer Arbitration, Broker-Dealer Regulation, Business Dispute Resolution, Business Law, Business Reorganization, Business Successions, Cable TV, Civil Litigation, Clean Water Act, Closely Held Business Law, Coastal Environmental Law, COBRA, Collective Bargaining, Commercial Banking, Commercial Law, Commodities, Communications and Media, Complex Litigation, Computer Law, Computers and Software, Constitutional Law, Consumer Law, Contested Trusts and Estate, Contracts, Cooperate Fiduciary Law, Copyright Protection, Copyrights, Corporate Commercial Law, Corporate Contracts, Corporate Governance, Corporate Law, Corporate Tax Planning, Criminal Antitrust, Criminal Law, Custom Law, Debtor and Creditor, Deferred Compensation, Drug and Medical Device, Educational Law, Employee Benefits Trusts, Employee Benefits, Employee Compensation, Employee Stock Ownership Plans, Employment Civil Rights, Employment Discrimination, Employment Litigation, Energy, Entertainment and the Arts, Environmental Auditing, Environmental Cleanup, Environmental Compliance, Environmental Cost Recovery, Environmental Insurance, Environmental Law, Environmental Litigation, Environmental Permitting, Equal Employment Opportunity Law, Equipment Finance and Leasing, ERISA Compliance, ERISA, Estate and Gift Taxation, Estate Planning, Executive Compensation, Executive Employment, Export Regulation, False Claims Act, Family Wealth Transfer, FCC Regulation, Federal Civil Litigation, Federal Energy Regulation, Federal Income Tax, Finance, Foreign Corrupt Practices Act, Foreign Investment, Government, Health Benefits, Health Care Finance, Health Care Mergers and Acquisitions, Health Care Regulation, Health Care Reimbursement, Health Care Taxation, Health Care, Health Insurance, Health Law Fraud, Health Law, Indians and Native Populations, Information Technology, Infringement Intellectual Property Litigation, Initial Public Offerings, Insurance Defense, Insurance, Integrated Health Care Delivery Systems, Intellectual Property Litigation, Intellectual Property, Intellectual Technology Contracts, International Corporate Finance, International Corporate Law, International Dispute Resolution, International Energy Law, International Environmental Law, International Law, International Mergers and Acquisitions, International Telecommunication Law, International Trade, Internet Law, Investment Management, Investment Partnerships, Investments, Labor and Employment, Labor Relations, Land Acquisitions, Land Sales, Leases and Leasing, Legal Ethic and Professional Responsibility, Literary Property, Litigation, Loans, Long Term Care, Managed Care, Management Labor Law, Mass Media Law, Media Antitrust, Medicare and Medicaid, Mental Health Law, Mergers and Acquisitions, Mergers, Acquisitions and Divestitures, Municipal Law, Music Law, Mutual Funds, National Environmental Law, New Media Law, Non-Qualified Benefits, Nonprofit and Charitable Organizations, Nonprofit Corporations, Partnership Law, Pension and Profit Sharing Plan, Personnel Policies, Physicians Contracts, Planning and Land Use, Private Placement, Probate, Products Liability, Professional Liability, Public Finance, Public Offerings, Qualified Retirement Plans, Qui Tam Litigation, Radio Common Carrier, Real Estate Acquisitions, Real Estate Brokerage Law, Real Estate Development, Real Estate Finance, Real Estate Leasing, Real Estate Sales, Real Estate Secured Lending, Real Estate Zoning, Real Estate, Regulatory Law, Religious Institutions, Resource Conservation and Recovery Act, Retirement Benefit Plans, Secured Lending, Securities Arbitration, Securities Fraud Arbitration, Securities Fraud Class Actions, Securities Litigation, Securities Offerings, Securities, Sports Law, State Taxation, Tax Controversies, Tax Exempt Finance, Tax Law, Tax Planning, Taxation, Technology and Science, Technology Licensing, Telecommunications Contracts, Telecommunications Law, Telecommunications Licensing, Telecommunications Regulation, Telephone Utility Regulation, Title VII Discrimination, Toxic Torts, Trademark Infringement, Trademarks, Tribal Taxation, Trust and Estates, Underground Storage Tanks, University Finance, Utility Acquisitions Utility Finance, Utility Law, Venture Capital, White Collar Criminal Defense Litigation, Wills, Wireless Communications, Wrongful Termination Defense, Zoning, Planning and Land Use.

MEMBERS OF FIRM

FRANCIS E. FLETCHER, JR., born Brooklyn, New York, November 2, 1943; admitted to bar, 1968, Virginia; 1971, District of Columbia; 1976, U.S. Supreme Court. *Education:* College of William & Mary (A.B., 1965; J.D., 1968). Phi Alpha Delta. *Member:* The District of Columbia Bar; Virginia State Bar; Federal Communications Bar Association. (Resident). ***PRACTICE AREAS:*** Communications and Technology; International Telecommunications Law; Telecommunications and Technology Contracts; Telecommunications Law; Telecommunications Licensing. ***Email:*** ffletcher@gcd.com

(This Listing Continued)

GARDNER, CARTON & DOUGLAS, Washington—Continued

ARTHUR G. HOUSE, born New York, N.Y., May 1, 1947; admitted to bar, 1972, Virginia; 1973, District of Columbia, Maryland and U.S. Court of Appeals for the District of Columbia Circuit; 1977, U.S. District Court, District of Maryland; 1978, U.S. Court of Appeals, Fourth Circuit; 1980, U.S. Supreme Court. *Education:* Tufts University (B.A., cum laude, 1969); University of Virginia (J.D., 1972). Co-author: "Proposed Changes in Statutory Regulation of Obscenity," 57 Virginia Law Review 1636, 1971. Member, Baltimore Washington Venture Group. *Member:* Montgomery County (Past and current committee memberships, Judicial Selections Committee, Section on Technology and Law; Chairman, 1991-1992; Administration of Justice), Maryland State and American (Member, Sections on: Litigation; Tort and Insurance Law; Patent, Trademark and Copyright Law) Bar Associations; The District of Columbia Bar (Member, Appeals Advisory Panel, 1976-1979); Virginia State Bar; The Association of Trial Lawyers of America (sustaining member). ***LANGUAGES:*** French, Spanish and Italian. ***Email:*** ahouse@gcd.com

M. SCOTT JOHNSON, born St. Louis, Missouri, December 15, 1944; admitted to bar, 1969, Alabama; 1970, District of Columbia; 1976, U.S. Supreme Court. *Education:* Birmingham Southern College (B.A., 1966); Duke University (J.D., 1969). Omicron Delta Kappa; Phi Delta Phi. *Member:* The District of Columbia Bar; Alabama State Bar; American Bar Association; Federal Communications Bar Association. (Resident). ***PRACTICE AREAS:*** Communications and Media; Communications Law; FCC Regulation; Mass Media Law; Telecommunications Law; Equipment Finance and Leasing. ***Email:*** msjohnson@gcd.com

W. N. HARRELL SMITH IV, born Berkeley, California, December 29, 1938; admitted to bar, 1966, District of Columbia. *Education:* Williams College (B.A., magna cum laude, Phi Beta Kappa, 1960); Oxford University, Oxford, England (B.A./M.A., 1962); Harvard University (LL.B., 1965). Marshall Scholar. Co-Author: With G.C. Hufbauer and F.G. Vukmanic, "Bilateral Trade Relations," Mexico-United States Relations, 34 Proceedings of the Academy of Political Science 136 (1981). *Member:* The District of Columbia Bar; American Bar Association; American Society of International Law. ***PRACTICE AREAS:*** Administrative Law; International Trade; International Dispute Resolution; Regulatory Law. ***Email:*** hsmith@gcd.com

PATRICK C. ROCK, born Omaha, Nebraska, May 12, 1959; admitted to bar, 1984, Pennsylvania and Nebraska; 1986, U.S. Court of Appeals for the District of Columbia Circuit; 1989, U.S. Court of Appeals, Seventh Circuit; 1991, District of Columbia. *Education:* University of Notre Dame (B.A., 1981); Catholic University (J.D., 1984). *Member:* Federal Energy and American Bar Associations. ***PRACTICE AREAS:*** Energy; Federal Energy Regulation; International Energy Law; Environmental Law; International Drug Regulatory Affairs; International Environmental Law. ***Email:*** prock@gcd.com

RODNEY H. GLOVER, born Mount Vernon, Virginia, October 2, 1951; admitted to bar, 1978, Virginia; 1985, District of Columbia. *Education:* University of Maryland (B.A., 1973); University of Richmond (J.D., 1978). Author: "Defining an Applicant: Maintaining Records in the Electronic Age," Legal Report, SHRM, Summer 1996; "'Employee' Defined," The National Law Journal, August 16, 1999; "Employment in Cyberspace: The Final Frontier," CyberStrategies, Spring 2000; "Technology-Driven Issues in the Workplace," 2001 Annual Conference, SHRM. Member: Joint Commission on Technology and Science, Virginia General Assembly; Executive Board of Advisors, George Mason University School of Law; National Center for Technology and Law. President, High Tech Net Board of Governors, Society for Human Resource Management. *Member:* The District of Columbia Bar; Virginia State Bar. (Managing Partner, D.C. Office). ***PRACTICE AREAS:*** Intellectual Property Litigation; Employment Litigation; Privacy Law. ***Email:*** rglover@gcd.com

BALLARD JAMIESON, JR., born Washington, D.C., October 7, 1946; admitted to bar, 1972, California; 1973, U.S. District Court, Northern District of California; 1975, U.S. Court of Appeals, Ninth Circuit; 1980, District of Columbia. *Education:* Princeton University (B.A., 1968); Yale University (J.D., 1971). Editor, Yale Law Journal, 1970-1971. Author: "The Resource Conservation and Recovery Act," Chapter 4, Guide to Federal Environmental Law, Practicing Law Institute, 1981; "U.S. Bares Teeth, Snaps at Environmental Law Violators," Legal Times of Washington, April 21, 1980 at 47. Co-Author: "Environmental Impairment Liability Policies," Environmental Regulation Analyst, August, 1981. Board of Governors, Yale Legislative Services. Attorney, Office of General Counsel, Council on Environmental Quality, Executive Office of the President, 1976-1979. *Member:* The District of Columbia Bar; State Bar of California. ***PRACTICE AREAS:*** Environmental Law; International Environmental Law. ***Email:*** jjamieson@gcd.com

JAMES M. JORLING, born Lawton, Oklahoma, November 21, 1958; admitted to bar, 1984, Ohio and U.S. District Court, Southern District of Ohio; 1994, District of Columbia. *Education:* Miami University (A.B., 1981); University of Cincinnati (J.D., 1984). Co-Authored: "A World That Won't Stand Still: Enterprise Liability by Private Contract," 1994 De Paul Law Review 1007 (Summer, 1994). *Member:* American Bar Association; American Health Lawyers Association. ***PRACTICE AREAS:*** Health Law; Health Care Contracts; Health Care Corporate Law; Managed Care; Disease Management. ***Email:*** jjorling@gcd.com

LAURA C. MOW, born Monterey, California, September 9, 1957; admitted to bar, 1982, District of Columbia; 1983, U.S. Court of Appeals for the District of Columbia Circuit and U.S. District Court for the District of Columbia. *Education:* Wellesley College (B.A., 1979, Wellesley Scholar); Case Western Reserve University School of Law (J.D., 1982). Editor, Case Western Reserve University Law Review, 1981-1982. Author: *The Spectrum Regulation Handbook,* Thompson Publishing Group, 1994. *Member:* The District of Columbia Bar; Federal Communications Bar Association. ***PRACTICE AREAS:*** Communications and Media; FCC Regulation; Radio Common Carrier; Telecommunications Contracts; Wireless Communications. ***Email:*** lmow@gcd.com

THOMAS J. DOUGHERTY, JR., born Washington, D.C., August 6, 1953; admitted to bar, 1981, District of Columbia; 1982, U.S. District Court for the District of Columbia and U.S. Court of Appeals for the District of Columbia Circuit; 1993, Virginia. *Education:* Denison University (B.A., 1975); Catholic University of America (J.D., 1981). Associate Editor, Catholic University Law Review, 1981. Author: Note, "The Use of Section 214 of the Communications Act of 1934 to Control Shifts in Corporate Control Over Common Carriers," 19 Catholic University Law Review 891, 1980. *Member:* The District of Columbia Bar; American Bar Association (Member, Section of Corporation, Banking and Business Law); Federal Communications Bar Association. ***PRACTICE AREAS:*** Communications and Media; Telecommunications Contracts; Telecommunications Licensing; Utility Law; Telephone Utility Regulation. ***Email:*** tdougherty@gcd.com

KATHLEEN M. NILLES, born Fargo, North Dakota, May 27, 1951; admitted to bar, 1985, District of Columbia. *Education:* University of Santa Clara (B.A., magna cum laude, 1973); Yale Divinity School (M.A.R., 1976); University of Virginia (J.D., 1985); Georgetown University (LL.M. in Taxation, with distinction, 1992). Author: "Congress Preserves Offshore Tax Advantage For Hospital and University Captives," The Insurance Tax Review, pp. 177-190, February, 1997. Co-Author: "The Risk in Bearing Risk: Insurance and Tax Regulators Confront Health Care Providers' New Arrangements," with James M. Jacobson, The Insurance Tax Review, pp. 909-924, November, 1996; "Tax-Exempt Status of Health Care Organizations," with Bernadette M. Broccolo, BNA's Health Law and Business Series, June, 1996. Tax Counsel, Committee on Ways and Means, U.S. House of Representatives, 1990-1994. ***PRACTICE AREAS:*** Taxation; Nonprofit and Charitable Organization; Health Care; Health Care Taxation; Indian and Native Populations; Tribal Taxation; Insurance. ***Email:*** knilles@gcd.com

T. J. SULLIVAN, born Greenwich, Connecticut, November 30, 1953; admitted to bar, 1985, District of Columbia. *Education:* Salem College (B.A., 1977); West Virginia University (M.P.A., 1979); George Washington University (J.D., with honors, 1985); Georgetown University Law Center (LL.M. in Taxation, with distinction, 1991). Technical Assistant, (Health Care Industries) Internal Revenue Service, Office of Associate Chief Counsel (Employee Benefits and Exempt Organizations), 1989-1994. Special Assistant (Health Care), Office of Assistant Commissioner (Employee Plans and Exempt Organizations), Internal Revenue Service, 1994-1996. General Counsel, Coalition for Nonprofit Health Care, 1997—. *Member:* The District of Columbia Bar; American Bar Association (Member: Taxation Section; Exempt Organization Committee, 1985—); American Health Lawyers Association (Member, Board of Directors, 1995—). ***PRACTICE AREAS:*** Health Care; Taxation. ***Email:*** tsullivan@gcd.com

ATTISON L. BARNES III, born Easton, Maryland, August 7, 1964; admitted to bar, 1989, Virginia; 1991, District of Columbia; U.S. Court of Appeals, Fourth, Tenth and District of Columbia Circuits; U.S. District Court, Eastern District of Virginia and District of Columbia. *Education:* University of Virginia (B.A., 1986); Cambridge University, Emmanuel College, Cambridge, England; T.C. Williams School of Law (J.D., 1989). Co-author: "Ownership of Design Plans," *Civil Engineering* (March 2000); "When Trade Secrets Take Flight: Protecting Valuable Assets From Your Competitors," *Legal Report* (Sept. 1999); ; "Qui Tam Decision Upset Precedent," 20 (25) National Law B11 (Feb., 1998); "Application of the Economic Loss Rule," 43 (7) Va. Lawyer 21 (Feb., 1995); "Arbitrating Employment Disputes," 18 (2) Legal Times §27 (May, 1995). Law Clerk to the Honorable W. Curtis Sewell, Eastern District of Virginia, 1989-1990. *Member:* Alexandria, Virginia (Executive Council, Young Lawyers Division; Chairman, Model Judiciary Program) and American Bar Associations. ***PRACTICE AREAS:*** Commercial Law; Technology; Intellectual Property Litigation. ***Email:*** abarnes@gcd.com

GEORGE N. GRAMMAS, born Minneapolis, Minnesota, March 4, 1964; admitted to bar, 1989, Minnesota; 1990, District of Columbia and U.S. Court of International Trade; 1991, U.S. Court of Appeals for the Federal Circuit. *Education:* Lawrence University (B.A., cum laude, 1984); William Mitchell College of Law (J.D., 1988). Associate Editor, William Mitchell Law Review, 1987-1988. Author: Note, "The Test for Proving Copyright Infringement of Computer Software: Structure, Sequence, and Organization and 'Look and Feel' Cases," 14 William Mitchell Law Review 105, 1988; "Multilateral Responses to the

(This Listing Continued)

Iraqi Invasion of Kuwait: Economic Sanctions and Emerging Proliferation Controls," 15 Md. J. Intl. L. & Trade, 1991; "An Overview of the New Export Administration Regulations," 25 A.B.A. Int'l Law News 1, 1996; "Traveling with a Laptop May Land You in Trouble," National Law Journal, 1998. *Member:* The District of Columbia Bar. ***PRACTICE AREAS:*** Corporate Law; Export Regulation; International Trade; Customs Law; Technology and Science; Technology Licensing. ***Email:*** ggrammas@gcd.com

PHILIP G. HAMPTON, II, born Washington, D.C., July 1, 1954; admitted to bar, 1981, New York; 1985, U.S. Court of Appeals for the Federal Circuit; 1991, U.S. Claims Court; registered to practice before U.S. Patent and Trademark Office (Not admitted in District of Columbia). *Education:* Massachusetts Institute of Technology (S.B., S.M., 1977); University of Chicago (J.D., 1980). Assistant Commissioner for Trademarks, U.S. Patent and Trademark Office, 1994-1998. *Member:* National Bar Association (Chair, IP Section, 1989-1991; Member, Executive Committee, 1990-1993); International Trademark Association (Member, Parallel Imports, Exhaustion Subcommittee); American Intellectual Property Association (Member, Minorities in The Profession Committee, 1998-2000). ***PRACTICE AREAS:*** Intellectual Property. ***Email:*** phampton@gcd.com

CARIN J. SIGEL, born Miami, Florida, September 18, 1959; admitted to bar, 1986, Pennsylvania and District of Columbia. *Education:* University of Pennsylvania (B.A., cum laude, 1981); Boston University (J.D., 1985). ***PRACTICE AREAS:*** Medicare; Health Care. ***Email:*** csigel@gcd.com

ANITA J. CICERO, born Pittsburgh, Pennsylvania, September 8, 1965; admitted to bar, 1991, Pennsylvania; 1996, District of Columbia. *Education:* Oberlin College (B.S., 1988); Yale Law School (J.D., 1991). Phi Beta Kappa. Recipient, Harry S. Truman Scholarship. *Member:* American Bar Association (Member, Section of Natural Resources, Energy and Environment, 1998—). ***PRACTICE AREAS:*** International Treaty Law; Pharmaceutical Policy and Regulation. ***Email:*** acicero@gcd.com

MARK R. FITZGERALD, born Hartford, Connecticut, November 10, 1957; admitted to bar, 1982, District of Columbia; 1983, Maryland. *Education:* Fairfield University (B.A., 1979); Catholic University of America (J.D., 1982). Note Editor, Catholic University Law Review, 1981-1982. Author: "Stark II Regulations," Academic Clinical Practice, Vol. 11, No. 1, Winter 1998; "New Safe Harbors Rule Poses Questions," American Academy of Orthopaedic Surgeons Bulletin, Vol. 48, No. 1, Feb. 2000. *Member:* The District of Columbia Bar; Maryland State Bar Association; American Health Lawyers Association. ***PRACTICE AREAS:*** Health Care Law; Corporate Law. ***Email:*** mfitzgerald@gcd.com

TROY M. CALKINS, born Oak Park, Illinois, June 10, 1966; admitted to bar, 1991, Illinois; 2001, District of Columbia. *Education:* Michigan State University (B.A., with honors, 1988); University of Michigan (J.D., 1991). *Member:* American Bar Association (Member, Federal Regulation of Securities Committee). ***PRACTICE AREAS:*** Securities; Mergers and Acquisitions; Corporate. ***Email:*** tcalkins@gcd.com

ASSOCIATES

Lynne D. Anderson (Not admitted in DC); ***Mary E. Devlin Capizzi; Joseph S. Carlin; Maureen E. Donahue; Jessica L. Eisenhaure; Sandra Jill Farrington; Laurie A. Holmes; Anne Kurtz Flam; Demetrios Kouzoukas*** (Not admitted in DC); ***Holley Thames Lutz; Neela A. Paykel; Lee G. Petro; Jason Schlosberg*** (Not admitted in DC); ***Corey A. Stewart.***

THE GARDNER LAW FIRM, P.C.

601 PENNSYLVANIA AVENUE NW, SUITE 900

WASHINGTON, D.C. 20004

Telephone: 202-271-0552; 301-249-8820

Fax: 301-249-6234

Email: beegard@aol.com

Taxation, IRS Controversies, Estate & Gift Taxation, Tax Appeals, Tax Audits, Tax Fraud, Tax Planning, Non-Profit Tax Law, Charitable Giving, Tax Exempt Organizations, Estates & Trusts, Wills, Probate, Power of Attorney, Wealth Preservation, Business Successions, Family Wealth Transfer, Financial Planning, Contracts, Negotiations and Review, Small Business Law, Criminal Tax Law.

FIRM PROFILE: Mr. Gardner is a former trial Attorney, Administrator and revenue agent for the IRS. As a state and federal tax law specialist, Mr. Gardner brings a unique perspective and over 20 years of experience to his National Tax, Estate and Business Law practice. Clients served by his law firm include individuals, families, retireers, small businesses, corporations, executives, family run companies, professional associations, Non-Profit & Charitable organizations and people controlled with IRS controversies.

BRUCE E. GARDNER, born New York, N.Y., January 28, 1953; admitted to bar, 1981, Illinois; 1988, Texas; 1990, District of Columbia. *Education:* University of California-Los Angeles (B.A., Accounting/Economics, 1975);

(This Listing Continued)

Syracuse University (J.D., 1978); Georgetown University (LL.M., Taxation, 1987). Adjunct Professor, Strayer University, 1997-1998. Attorney Advisor, District of Columbia Department of Finance & Revenue, 1995-1996 and Assistant General Counsel, Office of the Chief Financial Officer, District of Columbia Government, 1995-1997. General Attorney, Department of Treasury, IRS Office of Chief Counsel, Sacramento, California, 1991-1994. Senior Attorney, IRS Director of Practice Office, Washington, D.C., 1987-1991. Appeals Officer, IRS Office of the Commissioner, Houston, Texas, 1986-1987. Tax Law Specialist, Washington, D.C., 1984-1986. Internal Revenue Agent, Houston, Texas, 1982-1984. Estate Tax Law Clerk, Chicago, Illinois, 1979-1980. Hearing Officer, Sales Tax Division, Illinois Department of Revenue, Chicago, Illinois, 1981-1982. Assistant General Counsel, United Negro College Fund, 2000—. *Member:* American, Federal and National Bar Associations. ***PRACTICE AREAS:*** Taxation; Labor Law; Bankruptcy Law.

GARDNER, MIDDLEBROOKS, FLEMING, GIBBONS & KITTRELL, P.C.

1919 S STREET NW

WASHINGTON, D.C. 20009

Telephone: 202-667-8278

Birmingham, Alabama Office: Suite 450, 2013 1st Avenue, North. Telephone: 205-250-7776.

Mobile, Alabama Office: 1119 Government Street. Telephone: 334-433-8100. Fax: 334-433-8181.

General Civil Trial Practice. Labor, Personal Injury, Toxic Torts, Admiralty, F.E.L.A., Insurance, Workers' Compensation, Longshore and Harbor Worker's Compensation Act, Employee Benefits.

SAMUEL H. HELDMAN, born Birmingham, Alabama, April 17, 1965; admitted to bar, 1990, Alabama and U.S. District Court, Northern District of Alabama; 1991, U.S. District Court, Middle and Southern Districts of Alabama and U.S. Court of Appeals, First, Fifth and Eleventh Circuits; 1993, U.S. Court of Appeals, Fourth and Sixth Circuits; 1999, District of Columbia. *Education:* Harvard University (B.A., cum laude, 1986; J.D., magna cum laude, 1989). Member, Harvard Law Review, 1988-1989. Law Clerk to Judge Sam C. Pointer, Jr., U.S. District Court, Northern District of Alabama. *Member:* Alabama State Bar; American Bar Association. ***Email:*** SHeldman@GMlegal.com

HILARY E. BALL, born Miami, Florida, June 11, 1964; admitted to bar, 1991, Alabama; U.S. District Court, Northern District of Alabama and District of Puerto Rico; U.S. Court of Appeals, Third and Eleventh Circuits; 1999, District of Columbia. *Education:* Trinity University (B.A., 1986); Edinburgh University; Cumberland School of Law of Samford University (J.D., magna cum laude, 1991); Georgetown University Law Center. Curia Honoris. Arbitrator: S.E.C. v. Prudential Securities Incorporated; Trained Mediator. *Member:* Alabama State Bar; American Bar Association. ***LANGUAGES:*** Spanish and French. ***Email:*** HBall@GMlegal.com

REPRESENTATIVE CLIENTS: Alabama AFL-CIO; Southwest Alabama Labor Council, AFL-CIO; Greater Mobile Port Council, AFL-CIO; Mobile/Pensacola; Building Trades Council, AFL-CIO; Paper Allied-Industrial Chemical Energy Workers International Union, AFL-CIO; International Organization of Masters, Mates & Pilots, AFL-CIO; International Brotherhood of Boilermakers, AFL-CIO; International Alliance of Theatrical Stage Employees & Moving Picture Machine Operators, AFL-CIO; International Longshoremen's Association, AFL-CIO; United Union of Roofers, Waterproofers and Allied Workers, AFL-CIO; United Transportation Union; International Brotherhood of Firemen & Oilers, AFL-CIO; Alabama Education Assn.; International Union of Bricklayers & Allied Workers, AFL-CIO; International Longshoremen's Association, Locals 1985, 1459, 1410-1, 1988, 1516, 1986, 1984, 1995; National Roofing Industry Pension Plan; International Organization of Masters, Mates & Pilots Pension Plan & Health & Benefit Plan; MSA-ILA Pension, Welfare & Vacation Plans; MSA-ILA Maintenance Pension Plan; MSA-ILA Supplemental Benefit Plan; Office & Professional Employees International Union, AFL-CIO; Amalgamated Transit Workers Union; Millwright & Machinery Erectors Union, Local 2734; International Association of Bridge, Structural & Ornamental Iron Workers, AFL-CIO, Local 798; UA, Local 119; Boilermakers Locals, 112, 109; IBEW, Locals 505 and 1315; IBEW-NECA Welfare and Pension Funds; CNA Insurance Cos.; Lyon Properties, Inc.; Bay Equipment Co.; Safeway Insurance Company of Alabama; Southside Storage; UAW Local 1639; Laborer's Local 70; International Union of Police Associations, Local 80; Teamsters Local Union 991.

(For complete biographical data on all personnel, see Professional Biographies at Mobile, Alabama).

LAW OFFICES OF GARFINKLE & ASSOCIATES

Established in 1990

1150 CONNECTICUT AVENUE, N.W., SUITE 505

WASHINGTON, D.C. 20036

Telephone: 202-457-0200

Facsimile: 202-857-0550

Email: agarfinkle@garfinklelaw-com

URL: http://www.lawyers.com/washingtonartlaw

Art Law, Intellectual Property, Entertainment and the Arts, Wills, Trusts and Estates, Probate, Family Law, Real Estate, General Practice.

FIRM PROFILE: Garfinkle & Associates is a general Practice law firm providing Art and Entertainment legal services, including contracts, copyright and trademark, licensing agreements and all matter of representation for individuals and for profit and non-profit businesses. Trusts & Estates and Probate, including wills, trusts and probate in general with an expertise in the same for artists and collectors of all artistic expression. Family Law, including prenuptial agreements, separation agreements and divorce. Real Estate Law representing small and community based developers and individuals.

ANN M. GARFINKLE, born New York, N.Y., July 11, 1942; admitted to bar, 1968, New York; 1970, U.S. District Court, Southern District of New York; 1973, District of Columbia; 1977, U.S. District Court for the District of Columbia. *Education:* University of Wisconsin (B.S., 1964); Brooklyn Law School (J.D., 1968). Co-Author: "Estate Planning for Artists and Collectors," Washington Area Lawyers for the Arts, 1996; "Art Conservation and the Legal Obligation to Preserve Artistic Intent," Journal of the American Institute for Conservation, Volume 36, No. 2, Summer 1997. Board of Trustees, Maryland Institute College of Art. Member, Washington, D.C. Estate Planning Council and ArtTable. *Member:* The District of Columbia Bar; New York State and American Bar Associations; Washington Area Lawyers for the Arts. ***PRACTICE AREAS:*** Art Law; Intellectual Property; Family Law; Wills; Trusts and Estates; Probate; Real Estate. ***Email:*** agarfinkle@garfinklelaw.com

OF COUNSEL

ROBERT JOSEPH FREDA, born Newark, New Jersey, 1952; admitted to bar, 1977, New Jersey; 1978, District of Columbia; 1985, Maryland; 1993, Virginia. *Education:* Georgetown University (B.S.B.A., magna cum laude, 1974; J.D., 1977). Member, Georgetown Law Journal, 1975. Adjunct Faculty, Georgetown University, 1978-1980, 1986-1992. Certified Public Accountant, Maryland, 1978. *Member:* Board of Governors, District of Columbia Institute of Certified Public Accountants (Chairman: Employee Benefits Committee, 1986-1992; Estate and Gift Tax Committee, 1993-1995). (Also Practicing Individually, McLean, Virginia).

ALLIE JOHNSON SHEFFIELD, born Wilmington, North Carolina, November 24, 1950; admitted to bar, 1976, North Carolina; 1977, District of Columbia. *Education:* University of North Carolina, Chapel Hill (A.B., 1970); Antioch School of Law (J.D., 1976). Public Defender Service of the District of Columbia, 1979-1999. Law Clerk to the Honorable Andrew Hood, Senior Judge, District of Columbia Court of Appeals, 1977-1978. Law Clerk to the Honorable Charles W. Halleck, Judge, Superior Court of the District of Columbia, 1976-1977.

GARVEY, SCHUBERT & BARER

Established in 1966

FIFTH FLOOR, 1000 POTOMAC STREET, N.W.

WASHINGTON, D.C. 20007

Telephone: 202-965-7880

Telecopier: 202-965-1729

URL: http://www.GSBlaw.com

Seattle, Washington Office: 1191 Second Avenue, 18th Floor, 98101. Telephone: 206-464-3939. Telecopier: 206-464-0125.

Portland, Oregon Office: Eleventh Floor, 121 S.W. Morrison Street, 97204. Telephone: 503-228-3939. Telecopier: 503-226-0259.

New York, N.Y. Office: Eighth Floor, 599 Broadway, 10012. Telephone: 212-431-8700. Telecopier: 212-334-1278.

Administrative Process, Legislative Process, Government Relations, Bankruptcy and Creditors' Rights, Business, and Litigation. Admiralty, Antitrust, Commercial Transactions, Communications, Customs, E-Commerce and Emerging Technologies, Employee Benefit Plans, Environmental Law, Estate Planning and Probate, Ethics/Scientific Misconduct, Federal Election Law, Fisheries, Government Contracts, Health and Safety Regulation, Health Care, Housing, Immigration, Insurance Coverage and Defense, Intellectual Property and Information Regulation,

(This Listing Continued)

International Trade and Business, Maritime, Mergers and Acquisitions, Natural Resources, Securities, Federal Taxation, State and Local Taxation, Technology and Transportation.

FIRM PROFILE: Garvey, Schubert & Barer offers a sophisticated business practice, complemented by zealous but pragmatic litigators and highly skilled practitioners in many niche areas of the law. We serve as outside general counsel to established market leaders and recently launched enterprises. On behalf of Fortune 500 companies, among many other clients, we handle such varied matters as customs disputes, software licensing, employment litigation, property tax appeals and federal government relations. Our diverse client base includes tennis stars and trade associations, paper mills and public radio stations, as well as foreign governments, "dot com" companies, and high tech manufacturers.

This listing provides information about our attorneys' educational backgrounds, bar admissions and practice areas. For more detailed biographical information, please consult our Web site at www.GSBlaw.com.

MEMBERS OF FIRM

HAROLD G. BAILEY, JR., born September 14, 1959; admitted to bar, 1984, District of Columbia. *Education:* Williams College (B.A., magna cum laude, 1981); Georgetown University (J.D., 1984). ***LANGUAGES:*** Spanish. ***PRACTICE AREAS:*** Environmental Law; Legislative Process; Government Contracts; International Trade and Transactions. ***Email:*** bbailey@gsblaw.com

ROBERT A. W. BORAKS, born March 27, 1943; admitted to bar, 1968, District of Columbia; 1969, U.S. Court of Appeals for the District of Columbia Circuit; 1972, U.S. Supreme Court; 1985, U.S. Court of Appeals, 4th Circuit. *Education:* University of Pennsylvania (B.S., 1965); George Washington University (J.D., with honors, 1968). Assistant U.S. Attorney for the District of Columbia, 1969-1972. Assistant Legal Director, National Capital Area Civil Liberties Union, 1972-1973. Staff Attorney, D.C. Public Defender Service, 1973-1977. Special Trial Counsel, Commodity Futures Trading Commission, 1977-1978. ***PRACTICE AREAS:*** Criminal Law; Securities Law; Commodities Law; Malpractice; Negligence Law; Commercial Litigation. ***Email:*** bboraks@gsblaw.com

RICHARD D. GLUCK, born March 13, 1950; admitted to bar, 1978, District of Columbia; 1979, Pennsylvania. *Education:* University of Chicago (A.B., with honors, 1972); Georgetown University Law Center (J.D., 1978). ***PRACTICE AREAS:*** Government Contracts Law; Transportation Law; Maritime Law; International Trade; E-Commerce. ***Email:*** rgluck@gsblaw.com

ELDON V. C. GREENBERG, born July 26, 1944; admitted to bar, 1970, New York; 1972, District of Columbia. *Education:* Harvard College (B.A., magna cum laude, 1965); Harvard Law School (J.D., cum laude, 1969). Deputy General Counsel, U.S. Agency for International Development, 1977. General Counsel, National Oceanic and Atmospheric Administration, U.S. Department of Commerce, 1978-1981. ***PRACTICE AREAS:*** Litigation; Administrative Law; Environmental Law; Natural Resources Law; Ethics/Scientific Misconduct. ***Email:*** egreenberg@gsblaw.com

PAUL S. HOFF, born October 6, 1942; admitted to bar, 1968, District of Columbia. *Education:* Harvard University (B.A., cum laude, 1964); Yale University (LL.B., 1967). Member, Yale Law Journal, 1967. Associate Chief Counsel, Senate Governmental Affairs Committee, 1975-1981. ***PRACTICE AREAS:*** International Trade; Export Regulation; Administrative Law; Legislative Process. ***Email:*** phoff@gsblaw.com

MATTHEW R. SCHNEIDER, born November 7, 1948; admitted to bar, 1976, District of Columbia; 1994, U.S. District Court, District of Columbia. *Education:* College of Arts and Sciences, Cornell University (B.A., 1970); Catholic University of America (J.D., 1974). Chief of Staff, U.S. Senator Jeff Bingaman, 1983-1985. Senior Counsel, Division of Corporation Finance, U.S. Securities Commission, 1982. Director, Office of Legislative Affairs, U.S. Securities and Exchange Commission, 1979-1981. Special Assistant Office of the Secretary of Defense, 1977-1979. Counsel, U.S. Senate Committee on Government Affairs, 1974-1977. Staff Member, U.S. Senate Judiciary Subcommittee, 1973-1974. ***PRACTICE AREAS:*** Administrative Law; FIFRA; Trade Association Law; Environmental Law; Consumer Product Regulation; Federal Election Law; Foreign Asset Control; Information Law; Financial Services Regulation; Legislative Process. ***Email:*** mschneider@gsblaw.com

RICHARD A. WEGMAN, born November 17, 1938; admitted to bar, 1965, New York; 1981, District of Columbia. *Education:* Brown University (A.B., 1960); New York University (M.S. in Mathematics, 1962); Harvard University (J.D., 1965). Adjunct Professor of Law, Georgetown University Law Center, 1979-1982. Appellate Attorney, Antitrust Division, U.S. Department of Justice, 1965-1968. Legislative Assistant to U.S. Senator William Proxmire, 1968-1973. Chief Counsel and Staff Director: U.S. Senate Committee on Governmental Affairs, 1975-1981. Chief Counsel and Staff Director, U.S. Senate Subcommittee on Executive Reorganization, 1974-1975. ***PRACTICE AREAS:*** Administrative Law; Environmental Law; Legislative Process. ***Email:*** dwegman@gsblaw.com

(This Listing Continued)

OF COUNSEL

MICHAEL H. BADER, born August 28, 1929; admitted to bar, 1954, District of Columbia; 1993, Virginia. *Education:* George Washington University; National Law Center of George Washington University (LL.B., 1952); Georgetown University (M.A., 1980); Marymount University (Doctor of Humane Letters, causa honoris, 1997). ***PRACTICE AREAS:*** Communications Law; Media Law; Telecommunications Law; Cable Law; Technology Law; Science Law; Business Law; Corporate Law. ***Email:*** mbader@gsblaw.com

JOHN CRIGLER, born August 6, 1947; admitted to bar, 1981, District of Columbia; 1993, Virginia. *Education:* Wesleyan University (B.A., magna cum laude, 1969); Yale University (Ph.D., 1976); Georgetown University (J.D., 1981). ***PRACTICE AREAS:*** Communications Law; Television Law; First Amendment Law; Non-Profit Organizations; Radio Law; Copyright Law; Trademark Law; Internet Law. ***Email:*** jcrigler@gsblaw.com

JAMES E. DUNSTAN, born June 23, 1958; admitted to bar, 1983, District of Columbia; 1993, Virginia. *Education:* Arizona State University; Claremont Men's College (B.A., cum laude, 1980); Georgetown University (J.D., 1983). ***PRACTICE AREAS:*** Television Law; Cable Law; Space Law; Computer Law; Copyrights; Trade Secrets. ***Email:*** jdunstan@gsblaw.com

JOHN WELLS KING, born July 22, 1946; admitted to bar, 1972, Nebraska and District of Columbia; 1992, Virginia. *Education:* University of Nebraska (B.A., 1969; J.D., with distinction, 1972). Editor-in-Chief, Federal Communications Bar Journal, 1974-1977. ***PRACTICE AREAS:*** Administrative Law; Communications Law; Media Law; Regulatory Law; Trademark Law. ***Email:*** jking@gsblaw.com

BENJAMIN J. LAMBIOTTE, born January 1, 1960; admitted to bar, 1989, District of Columbia; 1992, Virginia; 1995, Maryland. *Education:* University of Hawaii; The American University (B.A., 1983); Catholic University, Columbus School of Law (J.D., Valedictorian, 1989). ***PRACTICE AREAS:*** Commercial Law; Litigation; Intellectual Property. ***Email:*** blambiotte@gsblaw.com

JOHN M. PELKEY, born August 1, 1950; admitted to bar, 1975, District of Columbia; 1993, Virginia. *Education:* Georgetown University (B.S.F.S., 1972; J.D., 1975). ***PRACTICE AREAS:*** Communications Law; First Amendment Law; Radio Law; Telecommunications Law; Telephone, Paging and Cellular Law. ***Email:*** jpelkey@gsblaw.com

WILLIAM E. PERRY, admitted to bar, 1978, District of Columbia; 1980, Massachusetts; 1987, U.S. Court of International Trade and U.S. Court of Appeals for the Federal Circuit. *Education:* Ohio University (B.A., summa cum laude, 1972); Columbia University (J.D., 1978). Attorney-Adviser, Office of General Counsel, U.S. International Trade Commission, 1980-1985. Attorney, Office of Chief Counsel, Office of Antidumping Investigations, U.S. Department of Commerce, Jan. 1986 to May 1987. ***LANGUAGES:*** Japanese, Marshallese. ***PRACTICE AREAS:*** International Trade and Investment Law; Customs and Antidumping Law; Intellectual Property Law. ***Email:*** wperry@gsblaw.com

HENRY A. SOLOMON, born June 4, 1939; admitted to bar, 1963, New York; 1965, District of Columbia; 1992, Virginia. *Education:* University of Michigan (B.A., 1960; LL.B., 1963). Attorney with the Federal Communications Commission, 1963-1966. ***LANGUAGES:*** Spanish. ***PRACTICE AREAS:*** Communications and Media; Business Law; Administrative Law; Corporate Law; Mergers and Acquisitions. ***Email:*** hsolomon@gsblaw.com

MELODIE A. VIRTUE, born February 27, 1957; admitted to bar, 1982, District of Columbia; 1992, Virginia. *Education:* George Washington University (B.A., with distinction, 1979); Washington College of Law of The American University (J.D., 1982). ***PRACTICE AREAS:*** Radio Law; Television Law; Communications Law; Telecommunications Law; Entertainment Law. ***Email:*** mvirtue@gsblaw.com

ASSOCIATES

MICHAEL IAN GOULDING, born November 22, 1964; admitted to bar, 1997, Maryland; 1998, District of Columbia. *Education:* University of Zagreb, Former Yugoslavia; Free University, Former West Berlin; Oberlin College (B.A., 1987); The Catholic University of America, Columbus School of Law (J.D., 1996). Legislative Assistant: U.S. Representative Paul E. Kanjorski, 1987-1988; U.S. Representative Nick J. Rahall, II, 1989-1990. ***PRACTICE AREAS:*** Maritime; Environmental; Legislative Practice. ***Email:*** mgoulding@gsblaw.com

JOHN C. KALITKA, born March 21, 1964; admitted to bar, 1990, Virginia; 1998, District of Columbia. *Education:* Washington & Lee University (B.A., Politics/Journalism, cum laude, 1987); T.C. Williams School of Law, University of Richmond (J.D., 1990); George Mason University (M.A., International Commerce & Policy, 1998). Attorney-Advisor, Commissioner Carol T. Crawford, U.S. International Trade Commission, 1999-2000. ***PRACTICE AREAS:*** International Trade; Litigation. ***Email:*** jkalitka@gsblaw.com

(This Listing Continued)

AMY B. LEVENSON, born August 29, 1969; admitted to bar, 1997, Pennsylvania; 1998, Maryland and District of Columbia. *Education:* University of Maryland (B.A., 1991); George Washington University (J.D., 1997). ***PRACTICE AREAS:*** Litigation. ***Email:*** alevenson@gsblaw.com

LISA M. PATERA STERLING, born June 11, 1967; admitted to bar, 1998, Virginia; 2000, District of Columbia. *Education:* University of Nebraska (B.A., 1989); Catholic University of America, Columbus School of Law (J.D., 1997). ***PRACTICE AREAS:*** Communications Law; Media Law; Administrative Law; Trademark and Copyright Law; Internet Law. ***Email:*** lpatera@gsblaw.com

CAROLYN A. PRINCE, admitted to bar, 1997, California; 1998, Virginia; 1999, District of Columbia; U.S. Court of Federal Claims. *Education:* L'Universite de Provence, Aix-Marseille III, 1988-1989; California State University, Long Beach (B.A., French, 1991); The American University (M.A., International Affairs, 1994); The American University, Washington College of Law (J.D., cum laude, 1997). ***PRACTICE AREAS:*** Litigation; Government Contracts; Corporate Law. ***Email:*** cprince@gsblaw.com

Languages: English, French, German, Japanese, Korean, Italian, Mandarin Chinese, Marshallese and Spanish.

REPRESENTATIVE CLIENTS: At-sea Processors Association; Bioganic Safety Brands, Inc.; Boston Transit Group; Children's Healthcare Research Group; China Ocean Shipping (Group) Company; Covance Inc.; East Coast Tuna Association; Embassy of Canada; Foss Maritime Company; GOTO.com; Government of Bermuda; Harry Winston Research Foundation; Heaven Hill Distilleries; Innovative Fragrance Solutions; iSkyCom, Inc.; International Association of Antarctica Tour Operators; International Federation of Freight Forwarders Associations (FIATA); Interocean Ugland Management Corp.; Japan Fisheries Assn.; National Association of Independent Fee Appraisers; National Fisheries Institute; Primavera Laboratories, Inc.; Prudential Securities, Inc.; Safe Solutions, Inc.; Samson Tug & Barge Co., Inc.; The Prudential Group; Totem Ocean Trailer Express, Inc.; USX Corporation; WebPutty, Inc.

(For other data on firm personnel see Seattle, Washington, New York, New York and Portland Oregon)

LAW OFFICES OF PAUL G. GASTON

1120 NINETEENTH STREET, N.W., SUITE 750
WASHINGTON, D.C. 20036
Telephone: 202-296-5856
Fax: 202-296-4154
Email: pgaston@attglobal.net

Complex Commercial Litigation emphasizing International Trade, Copyright, Trademark, Banking, Contracts and Antitrust.

FIRM PROFILE: The Law Offices of Paul G. Gaston is engaged in all phases of civil litigation. The firm's founder and principal, Paul G. Gaston, represents a broad spectrum of clients, including corporate and individual clients involved in technology, health care, publishing, and banking, and domestic and foreign clients involved in international trade issues, including Customs matters.

PAUL G. GASTON, born Budapest, Hungary, February 16, 1953; admitted to bar, 1979, District of Columbia; 1983, U.S. Court of International Trade; 1985, U.S. Court of Appeals, District of Columbia Circuit; 1987, U.S. Court of Appeals, Third Circuit; 1988, U.S. Court of Appeals, First and Ninth Circuits; 1989, U.S. Court of Appeals, Second and Federal Circuits and U.S. Claims Court; 1990, U.S. District Court, District of Columbia and U.S. District Court, District of Maryland; 1992, U.S. Court of Appeals, Fourth Circuit; 1997, U.S. Supreme Court. *Education:* Yale University (B.A., magna cum laude, 1974; J.D., 1979); Trinity College, Cambridge, England (B.A., Honors, 1976). Co-Author: "OTS Argument that FIRREA Relieves Regulators of Binding Contractual Commitments Is Bad Policy," 55 Banking Report 861, 1990; "What Is a 'Domestic Industry' for Purposes of Application of the United States Trade Laws," Chapter 13 of International Trade Policy: The Lawyer's Perspective, American Bar Association, 1985; "Contract Claims Arising from FIRREA'S Goodwill Provisions," 7 Banking and Financial Services, No. 22, 1991. Author: "Contract Rights Are Property, Too," Legal Times, March 23, 1992; "New Laws Don't Cancel Old Deals," National Law Journal," July 13, 1992; Comment, "Zealous Rulemaking Imperils S&L Industry," American Banker, June 4, 1992. *Member:* District of Columbia Bar; American Bar Association (Member, Sections on: Litigation; International Law). (Also Of Counsel, Marzouk & Parry, Washington, D.C.).

GEBHARDT & ASSOCIATES, LLP

1101 17TH STREET N.W., SUITE 607
WASHINGTON, D.C. 20036
Telephone: 202-496-0400
Fax: 202-496-0404
Email: cday@pressroom.com
URL: http://www.lawyers.com/gebhardt

Employment Law in the District of Columbia and Maryland (Representing Institutions, Corporations, Managers, Employees including Federal and Private Employees and Unions), Discrimination Law, Civil Rights and Women's Rights. General Civil Litigation in all Courts. Matters before the Equal Employment Opportunity Commission, the Merit Systems Protection Board and Local Human Rights Agencies.

JOSEPH D. GEBHARDT, born New York, N.Y., July 14, 1946; admitted to bar, 1972, District of Columbia and U.S. District Court, District of Columbia; 1976, U.S. Court of Appeals for the District of Columbia Circuit; 1977, U.S. Supreme Court; 1978, U.S. Court of Appeals, Third Circuit; 1981, Maryland; 1982, U.S. Court of Appeals for the Federal Circuit; 1984, U.S. Court of Appeals, Ninth Circuit; 1985, U.S. District Court, District of Maryland; 1996, U.S. Court of Appeals, Fourth Circuit. *Education:* Cornell College (B.A., magna cum laude, 1968, Phi Beta Kappa); Harvard Law School (J.D., 1971). Chairman, Advisory Council, Center for the Study of Race and Ethnic Relations, George Mason University, 1988-1990. Member, Interstate Commission on the Potomac River Basin (Chairman, 1982-1983; Federal Commissioner, 1978-1983). Staff Attorney with the Center on Corporate Responsibility (1973), the Democratic National Committee (1972), and the Center for Political Reform (1971-1972). Member, Metropolitan Washington Employment Lawyers Association. *Member:* District of Columbia Bar; American Bar Association. ***PRACTICE AREAS:*** Employment Law; Employment Discrimination; Civil Rights; Federal Civil Practice; Civil Litigation.

CHARLES WILLIAMSON DAY, JR., born Washington, D.C., July 4, 1965; admitted to bar, 1998, New York, Maryland and District of Columbia; 1999, U.S. District Court for the District of Columbia and U.S. District Court, District of Maryland. *Education:* Yale University (B.A., 1987); University of Chicago (M.A., 1993); George Washington University (J.D., 1997). Member, Metropolitan Washington Employment Lawyers Association. *Member:* District of Columbia Bar; Maryland State, New York State and American Bar Associations. ***PRACTICE AREAS:*** Employment Law; Employment Discrimination; Civil Rights; Federal Civil Practice; Civil Litigation. ***Email:*** cday@pressroom.com

LORI N. NACHT, born Staten Island, New York, May 21, 1974; admitted to bar, 1999, Maryland; 2000, District of Columbia and U.S. District Court, District of Maryland. *Education:* George Washington University (B.A., cum laude, 1996); Emory University (J.D., 1999). Intern: Atlanta Legal Aid Society, 1998-1999; U.S. Equal Employment Opportunity Commission, 1998. ***PRACTICE AREAS:*** Employment Law; Employment Discrimination; Disability Retirement; Civil Rights; Federal Civil Practice; Civil Litigation.

ELAINE L. FITCH, born 1966; admitted to bar, 1996, California (Not admitted in District of Columbia). *Education:* University of California at Berkeley (B.S., 1989); Hastings College of the Law, University of California (J.D., 1996).

OF COUNSEL

SUSAN C. LEE, born Houston, Texas, January 2, 1954; admitted to bar, 1982, California; 1983, District of Columbia. *Education:* University of Maryland (B.A., 1976; M.P.A., 1978); University of San Francisco School of Law (J.D., 1982). Attorney, U.S. Patent & Trademark Office, Department of Commerce, 1988-1993. Executive Director, National Democratic Council of Asian and Pacific Americans, 1986-1988. Attorney, U.S. Commission on Civil Rights, 1983-1986. Law Clerk Richard Figone, San Francisco Superior Court. *Member:* Women's Bar Association for the District of Columbia; Asian-Pacific American Bar Association. ***LANGUAGES:*** Japanese and Spanish. ***PRACTICE AREAS:*** Intellectual Property; Administrative Law.

GELB & GELB, P.C.

Established in 1954

1120 CONNECTICUT AVENUE, N.W., SUITE 421
WASHINGTON, D.C. 20036
Telephone: 202-331-7227
Fax: 202-452-1855
Email: lawyers@gelbandgelb.com
URL: http://www.lawyers.com/gelbandgelb

Personal Injury, Medical Malpractice Law, Automobile Accidents, Truck Accidents, Motorcycle Accidents, Bus Accidents, Surgeons Liability.

(This Listing Continued)

FIRM PROFILE: Gelb & Gelb, P.C. takes pride in the fact that our firm has handled negligence claims for over 45 years. That experience in addition to the quality of our staff enables our office to provide the very best representation in the negligence field of law. Our philosophy is that we will base our reputation on the quality of service we have provided in the past and count on former clients and referring counsel for our new cases and clients.

JOSEPH D. GELB, born Wilkes-Barre, Pennsylvania, December 13, 1923; admitted to bar, 1954, District of Columbia; 1963, Maryland; 1972, U.S. Supreme Court. *Education:* University of Scranton (B.S., 1950); George Washington University (J.D., 1952). Who's Who in American Law. *Member:* The District of Columbia Bar; Bar Association of the District of Columbia; Maryland State and American Bar Associations; Trial Lawyers Association of Metropolitan Washington, D.C.; The Association of Trial Lawyers of America (ATLA). ***REPORTED CASES:*** roth v. Speck, 126 A.2d 153; McGettigan v. National Bank of Washington, 320 F.2d 703. ***PRACTICE AREAS:*** Personal Injury; Medical Malpractice; Trials.

ROGER K. GELB, born Washington, D.C., November 21, 1965; admitted to bar, 1992, Pennsylvania; 1993, District of Columbia; 1994, U.S. District Court, District of Columbia; 1995, U.S. Court of Appeals, District of Columbia Circuit; 1996, U.S. Supreme Court. *Education:* University of South Carolina (B.A., 1987); Nova Southeastern University (J.D., 1991). Phi Alpha Delta. Listed in Who's Who in American Law. *Member:* The District of Columbia Bar; American Bar Association; The Association of Trial Lawyers of America; Association of Jewish Lawyers and Jurists; District of Columbia Trial Lawyers Association; The Million Dollar Advocates Forum; The Trial Lawyers Association of Washington, D.C. ***PRACTICE AREAS:*** Personal Injury; Medical Malpractice; Automobile Accidents; Dental Malpractice; Wrongful Death; Civil Litigation.

STEPHEN N. GELL, P.C.

1101 30TH STREET, N.W., SUITE 500
WASHINGTON, D.C. 20007
Telephone: 202-625-8311
Fax: 703-522-5503
Email: sgell@his.com

Land Use, Zoning, Boundary Disputes, Building Permits, Street and Alley Closings, Real Estate Tax Appeals, Alcoholic Beverage Commission Licenses, Property Issues.

FIRM PROFILE: Mr. Gell has resolved land use and zoning problems both in D.C. government (from 1980-1989, Chief of Land Use, Office of Corporation Counsel) and in private practice representing small and large developers, private property owners and neighborhood associations.

STEPHEN N. GELL, born Boston, Massachusetts, November 25, 1938; admitted to bar, 1963, Massachusetts; 1964, District of Columbia. *Education:* Dartmouth College (A.B., 1960); University of Pennsylvania (LL.B., 1963); George Washington University (LL.M., 1966). Author: *Real Estate Practice in the District of Columbia, Maryland and Virginia,* Chapters on D.C. Zoning and Real Property Tax Appeals. *Member:* Bar Association of the District of Columbia (Chair, Real Property Law Committee, 1994-2001); The District of Columbia Bar (Member, Sections on: Real Estate; Tax Appeals; Land Use); D.C. Building Industry Association (Past Co-Chair, Economic Development Committee).

THOMAS G. GHERARDI, P.C.

Established in 1978

1229 NINETEENTH STREET, N.W.
WASHINGTON, D.C. 20036
Telephone: 202-223-1535
FAX: 202-429-4912
Email: tomg@counsellor.com
URL: http://www.lawyers.com/thomasgherardi

General Practice including Negotiation of Complex Transactions; Television, Music and Multi Media Acquisition, Production and Distribution; Communications Law; and Licensing of Copyrights, Trademarks and Intellectual Properties.

THOMAS G. GHERARDI, born Jersey City, New Jersey, March 7, 1942; admitted to bar, 1966, New York; 1970, U.S. Supreme Court; 1972, District of Columbia. *Education:* Fordham University (A.B., 1963); New York University (J.D., 1966). John Ben Snow Scholar, 1963-1964. Elihu Root-Samuel J. Tilden Scholar, 1964-1966. Attorney, Office of the General Counsel, U.S. Atomic Energy Commission, 1966-1967. Deputy Counsel, Subcommittee on Improvements in Judicial Machinery, U.S. Senate Committee on the Judiciary, 1967-1968. Assistant to the Assistant Secretary for Legislation, U.S. Department of Health, Education and Welfare, 1969. Counsel to Hon. Ralph T. Smith, U.S.

(This Listing Continued)

Senator from Illinois, 1969-1970. Director of Congressional Affairs, U.S. General Services Administration, 1970-1972. Senior Vice President, General Counsel and Secretary, The Corporation for Public Broadcasting, 1972-1978. Partner, Deane, Snowdon & Gherardi, 1978-1989. *Member:* District of Columbia Bar; Federal and American Bar Associations; Federal Communications Bar Association; Institute of Judicial Administration. (Also of Counsel to Goldberg, Godles, Wiener and Wright). ***Email:*** tomg@counsellor.com

GIBSON, DUNN & CRUTCHER LLP

Established in 1890

1050 CONNECTICUT AVENUE, N.W.

WASHINGTON, D.C. 20036-5306

Telephone: 202-955-8500

Telecopier: 202-467-0539

URL: http://www.gibsondunn.com

Los Angeles, California Office: 333 South Grand Avenue. Telephone: 213-229-7000. Telecopier: 213-229-7520; 213-229-7268.

General Civil Trial and Appellate Practice, State and Federal Courts. Antitrust Law. Specialized Criminal Defense. General Corporation, Securities, Administrative, Labor and Employment, Employee Benefits, Taxation, Estate Planning, Probate and Trust, International Business, Entertainment, Real Estate Development and Financing, Banking, Commercial, Insolvency, Bankruptcy and Reorganization, Natural Resources, Oil and Gas, Environmental, Energy, Municipal and Public Utility Law.

FIRM PROFILE: Gibson, Dunn & Crutcher LLP, originating in Los Angeles, has been providing legal services to clients since 1890. Today, the firm has grown to one of the largest law firms in the world with approximately 750 active attorneys in 11 offices situated in most of the world's important business centers. The firm has experts in virtually every area of the law, particularly those which relate to commercial transactions and disputes, and has more effective geographical coverage in the United States than any other major firm. The firm's lawyers and staff are dedicated to providing quality service on a timely and cost effective basis.

Gibson, Dunn & Crutcher's Washington, D.C. office has been serving national, local and international clients since 1977. Approximately 120 lawyers provide a full range of legal services, including general commercial representation and the representation of clients before key federal agencies and federal and state courts.

Many of the practice areas in the Washington, D.C. office are led by lawyers who have previously served at the highest levels of government, including in the Justice Department, State Department, Treasury Department, Labor Department, Securities and Exchange Commission, Overseas Private Investment Corporation, Occupational Safety and Health Administration, Environmental Protection Agency, Comptroller of the Currency and the U.S. House of Representatives.

Some of the more important activities of the Washington, D.C. office practice groups are as follows:

Supreme Court and Appellate Litigation: Representing Clients before federal and state appellate courts across the country, including numerous cases in the Supreme Court of the United States involving a wide range of issues.

Antitrust and Competition Law: Counseling domestic and international clients on United States and international laws regarding competition; representing plaintiffs and defendants in investigations and litigation; advising as to Hart-Scott-Rodino compliance.

Media Law: Representation of major newspapers, magazines, broadcasters, book publishers and other media entities in First Amendment matters and virtually all areas of free speech and press including defamation, invasion of privacy, access to government, prior restraint, and subpoenas on reporters.

White Collar Crime and Special Investigations: Representing corporate and individual clients targeted by criminal and civil governmental investigations and representing special committees and acting as special counsel, in all types of corporate internal investigations.

General Commercial and Class Action Litigation: Representing clients in all types of commercial litigation, including securities and tort class action cases and patent, trademark and copyright cases brought in federal and state courts throughout the country.

General Corporate, Securities, Bankruptcy and M & A Advice: Representing national and local clients in corporate transactions and SEC regulatory matters including initial public offerings, all types of financings, mergers and acquisitions, and executive compensation matters.

(This Listing Continued)

Securities Law Enforcement: Representing corporations and individuals before the S.E.C. and related agencies, in processing transactions, obtaining regulatory determinations and defending clients that are subject to enforcement investigations.

Financial Institutions Regulatory Practice: Advising banks, thrifts, insurance companies, and securities firms in matters related to federal, state and international regulation and transactions.

International Trade and Customs Law: Providing advice regarding international trade and investment issues and transactions, including application of the Foreign Corrupt Practices Act, U.S. foreign sanctions, export controls and the anti-boycott laws; advising importers and domestic industries, and representing them before government agencies in anti-dumping, countervailing duties, Section 337 and other trade proceedings, and in matters involving the World Trade Organization, advice and representation in foreign sovereign claims litigation.

Federal, State and International Tax: Advising national, local and international clients with respect to corporate, cross border and related tax matters including tax litigation.

Labor, Employment, and Employee Benefits Law: Counseling, litigation, and legislative representation on the full range of labor and employment matters, including discrimination laws, labor-management relations, occupational safety and health, wage and hour regulation, grievance arbitration, and employee benefits planning and litigation.

Environmental Law: Providing advice and representing national and local clients before federal and state courts and agencies with respect to environmental matters, including toxic torts and air and water quality issues.

Governmental Contracts Law: Providing advice and representing national and local clients before federal and state courts and agencies with respect to contracts with government entities.

Intellectual Property Law: Counseling and handling litigation for clients in the information technology industry and other industries in copyright, patent, trade secret, and other intellectual property matters.

Administrative Law and Regulation: Representing clients in the regulatory proceedings, enforcement actions, and rulemaking challenges involving numerous federal and state agencies.

Legislative Advocacy: Ongoing retainer arrangements and specific representations for major clients and trade associations.

PARTNERS

JOHN F. OLSON, born 1939; admitted to bar, 1965, California; 1977, District of Columbia. *Education:* University of California at Berkeley (A.B., with highest honors, 1961); Harvard University (LL.B., cum laude, 1964). Phi Beta Kappa. Co-Author: "Director and Officer Liability: Indemnification and Insurance," West Publishing, 1990 (rev'd 2001). Co-Editor: "A Practical Guide to SEC Proxy and Compensation Rules," Aspen Law & Business, 1996, 2d ed. 1996 (rev'd 2001); "Securities in the Electronic Age: A Practical Guide," Aspen Law & Business, 2ed. 2000 (rev'd 2001); Co-Editor-in-Chief, "wallstreetlawyer.com". Contributing Editor, Legal Times, 1978-1986. Member, Editorial Board: "Insights: The Corporate & Securities Law Advisor," 1987—; "The Corporate Governance Advisor"; Advisory Boards, "Securities Regulation & Law Report," Bureau of National Affairs, 1989—, San Diego Securities Law Conference, 1990—; Practising Law Institute Annual Securities Regulation Institute, 1995—. Member, Legal Advisory Board, National Association of Securities Dealers, Inc., 1990-1995. Trustee, American College of Investment Counsel, 1981-1985. Member: Legal Advisory Committee, New York Stock Exchange, Inc., 1990-1997, 1999—; National Association of Corporate Directors' Blue Ribbon Commissions on CEO Succession (1997—) Audit Committees (1998-1999) and Role of the Board in Strategic Planning (2000). *Member:* The District of Columbia Bar (General Counsel, Board of Governors, 1983-1985); Federal (Member, Executive Council, Securities Law Committee, 1985—) and American (Chairman, Foreign Claims Committee, 1983-1986; Section Representative, Coordinating Group on Regulatory Reform, 1980-1985; Chairman, Special Task Force on Insider Trading Regulation, 1984-1988; Chairman, Subcommittee on Civil Liabilities and Litigation, 1985-1987. Vice Chairman, 1987-1991 and Chairman, 1991-1995, Committee on Federal Regulation of Securities; Chairman, Task Force on Delivery of Business Law Services, 1995-1996; Member, Committee on Corporate Laws, 1995—, Member, Council of the Business Law Section, 1998—; Chairman, Committee on Corporate Governance, 2000—) Bar Associations; American Law Institute. Senior Partner and coordinator for the Corporate and Business Practices Department, 1991-1998; Member, Executive Committee, 1990—, Gibson, Dunn & Crutcher. ***LANGUAGES:*** French. ***SPECIAL AGENCIES:*** Securities and Exchange

(This Listing Continued)

GIBSON, DUNN & CRUTCHER LLP, Washington—Continued

Commission. ***PRACTICE AREAS:*** Securities Law and Litigation; Mergers and Acquisitions; General Corporate Law; Administrative Law. ***Email:*** jolson@gibsondunn.com

ROBERT C. BONNER, born January 29, 1942; admitted to bar, 1966, District of Columbia; 1967, California. *Education:* Maryland University (B.A., magna cum laude, 1963); Georgetown University (J.D., 1966). Law Clerk to the Honorable Albert Lee Stephens, U.S. District Court for the Central District of California, 1966-1967. Assistant U.S. Attorney, Central District of California, 1971-1975. U.S. Attorney, Central District of California, 1984-1989. U.S. District Judge, Central District of California, 1989-1990. Administrator of the United States Drug Enforcement Administration, 1990-1993. Chair, California Commission on Judicial Performance, 1996-1999. Fellow, American College of Trial Lawyers. President, Federal Bar Association, Los Angeles Chapter, 1982-1983. *Member:* The District of Columbia Bar; State Bar of California; American Bar Association (Co-Chair, Subcommittee on Criminal Antitrust, 1994—). [Lt., JAG Corps, U.S. Navy, 1967-1971]. (Washington, D.C. and Los Angeles, California Offices). ***PRACTICE AREAS:*** White Collar Crime; Complex Business Litigation; Appellate Practice; Antitrust and Trade Regulation; Intellectual Property. ***Email:*** rbonner@gibsondunn.com

WILLIAM J. KILBERG, born June 12, 1946; admitted to bar, 1970, New York; 1972, District of Columbia. *Education:* Cornell University (B.S., 1966); Harvard University (J.D., 1969). Recipient: Father Wm. J. Kelley, O.M.I. Scholarship; New York State Scholarship; Arthur S. Flemming Award, 1975; Judge Wm. B. Groat Alumni Award, Cornell University, 1977. White House Fellow, Special Assistant to the U.S. Secretary of Labor, 1969-1970. General Counsel, Federal Mediation and Conciliation Service, 1970-1971. Associate Solicitor of the U.S. Department of Labor, 1971-1973. Solicitor of the U.S. Department of Labor, 1973-1977. Deputy Team Leader, Labor Department Transition Team, Reagan-Bush Transition, 1980-1981. Charter Fellow: College of Labor and Employment Lawyers, 1996—. Charter Fellow: College of Employee Benefits Lawyers, 2000—; Advisory Board, American Employment Law Council, 1997—; Public Member, Administrative Conference of the United States, 1990-1995; General Accounting Office Legal Affairs Advisory Committee, 1991-1996; Council on Foreign Relations, 1973-1978; Advisory Council, School of Industrial and Labor Relations, Cornell University, 1976-1981; Council of Advisors, Graduate Center for Industrial Relations, New York Institute of Technology, 1978-1985; Advisory Board, Bureau of National Affairs, Pension Reporter, 1978-1985; President's Commission on White House Fellowships, 1982-1983. Member, Board of Directors: Jewish Community Center, 1984-1985; Palmer National Bank, 1984-1997; Presidential Trust, 1988-1992; National Jewish Coalition, 1988—. Editor-in-Chief, Employee Relations Law Journal, 1985—. Co-Author: "Employers' Rights and Responsibilities," National Legal Center for the Public Interest, 1988; "Pitfalls for Japanese Employers in the United States," Nikkei, 1993. Successfully represented United Parcel Service in the United States Supreme Court in Murphy v. UPS, 119 S.Ct. 2133 (1999). Counsel to Petitioner in Egelhoff vs. Egelhoff, No. 99-1529, United States Supreme Court, argued November 8, 2000. *Member:* American Bar Association. ***PRACTICE AREAS:*** Labor; Pension Plans and Employee Benefits. ***Email:*** wkilberg@gibsondunn.com

PETER L. BAUMBUSCH, born August 5, 1944; admitted to bar, 1972, California; 1978, District of Columbia. *Education:* Dartmouth College (A.B., cum laude, 1965); Harvard University (J.D., magna cum laude, 1972). Phi Beta Kappa. Staff Member, Harvard Board of Student Advisors and Harvard Law Review, 1971-1972. *Member:* Los Angeles County (Chair, Committee on Fair Political Practices, 1976-1978; Member, Board of Directors of Human Rights Section, 1974-1977) and American (Chair, Committee on Foreign Activities of U.S. Taxpayers, Tax Section, 1992-1994) Bar Associations; State Bar of California. ***PRACTICE AREAS:*** Corporate Taxation; Mergers and Acquisitions; Foreign Investment in the United States; Section 482 Intercompany Pricing; Executive Compensation. ***Email:*** pbaumbusch@gibsondunn.com

JOSEPH H. PRICE, born January 31, 1939; admitted to bar, 1964, Alabama; 1968, District of Columbia. *Education:* University of Alabama (A.B., 1961); Harvard University (LL.B., cum laude, 1964); The London School of Economics (Research Student in International Law). Phi Beta Kappa. Awarded, Knox Memorial Fellowship by Harvard University for Legal Research in England, 1964-1965. Law Clerk to Justice Hugo L. Black, U.S. Supreme Court, 1967-1968. Vice President for Insurance, Overseas Private Investment Corporation, 1971-1973. *Member:* The District of Columbia Bar; Alabama State Bar; American Bar Association; American Society of International Law. [Captain, U.S. Army Intelligence, Vietnam (1966-1967), Awarded Bronze Star]. ***PRACTICE AREAS:*** International Trade; International Business Transactions; International Arbitrations; Customs and Administrative Law. ***Email:*** jprice@gibsondunn.com

CANTWELL FAULKNER MUCKENFUSS III, born April 25, 1945; admitted to bar, 1973, New York; 1976, District of Columbia. *Education:* Vanderbilt University (B.A., with honors, 1967); Yale Law School (J.D., 1971). Phi Beta Kappa. Law Clerk, Hon. William E. Miller, U.S. Court of Appeals for the Sixth Circuit, 1971-1972. Attorney and Project Developer, Bedford Stuyvesant D and S Corporation, Brooklyn, New York, 1972-1973. Special Assistant to the Director, 1974-1977 and Counsel to the Chairman, 1977-1978, Federal Deposit Insurance Corporation, Washington, D.C. Member, Administrative Conference of the United States, 1977-1978. Member, Editorial Advisory Board, "Issues in Bank Regulation," 1977-1991. Member, Board of Advisors, "Review of Banking and Financial Services," 1985—. Member, Editorial Advisory Board, "Electronic Banking Law and Commerce Report," 1997—. Senior Deputy Comptroller for Policy, Office of the Comptroller of the Currency, Washington, D.C., 1978-1981. Member, Board of Directors, Fair Tax Education Fund, 1987-1989. Member, Federal Savings and Loan Advisory Council, 1988-1989. *Member:* The District of Columbia Bar; Federal and American Bar Associations. ***PRACTICE AREAS:*** Financial Institutions Law and Regulation; Legislative and Public Policy Matters; Mergers and Acquisitions. ***Email:*** cmuckenfuss@gibsondunn.com

CHRISTOPHER H. BUCKLEY JR., born July 16, 1940; admitted to bar, 1968, District of Columbia; 1979, U.S. Supreme Court. *Education:* University of Notre Dame (B.A., 1962); Harvard Law School (LL.B., 1967). *Member:* The District of Columbia Bar; Federal and American Bar Associations. Chair, Environment and Natural Resources Practice Group, Gibson, Dunn & Crutcher. ***PRACTICE AREAS:*** Litigation; Environmental Law; Toxic Torts; Class Actions; Construction Law. ***Email:*** cbuckley@gibsondunn.com

DAVID R. JOHNSON, born September 12, 1946; admitted to bar, 1971, Texas; 1977, District of Columbia. *Education:* Tulane University (B.A., cum laude, 1968); University of Virginia (J.D., 1971). Phi Beta Kappa; Order of the Coif. Editor-in-Chief, Virginia Law Review, 1970-1971. Associate Editor, Public Contract Law Journal, 1989-1994. *Member:* The District of Columbia Bar. Chair, Government and Commercial Contracts Practice Group, Gibson, Dunn & Crutcher. [Attorney, Office of the General Counsel, U.S. Air Force, 1972-1974]. ***PRACTICE AREAS:*** Government Contracts Law; Contracts; Computers and Software; White Collar Crime; Administrative Law. ***Email:*** djohnson@gibsondunn.com

DONALD HARRISON, born March 2, 1946; admitted to bar, 1972, District of Columbia. *Education:* Harvard University (B.A., magna cum laude, 1967; J.D., magna cum laude, 1971). Member, Board of Editors, Harvard Law Review, 1969-1971. Law Clerk to Hon. Francis L. Van Dusen, U.S. Court of Appeals, Third Circuit, 1971-1972. *Member:* American Bar Association. ***PRACTICE AREAS:*** International Trade Law; Customs Law. ***Email:*** dharrison@gibsondunn.com

WAYNE A. SCHRADER, born July 14, 1950; admitted to bar, 1975, California; 1982, District of Columbia. *Education:* University of Southern California (B.A., 1972); University of California School of Law at Los Angeles (J.D., 1975). Order of the Coif. Managing Editor, University of California at Los Angeles Law Review, 1974-1975. ***PRACTICE AREAS:*** Insurance Coverage; Bad Faith/Insurer Conduct; Employment; Litigation. ***Email:*** wschrader@gibsondunn.com

PETER H. TURZA, born August 18, 1949; admitted to bar, 1975, District of Columbia. *Education:* Yale University (B.A., cum laude, 1971); Georgetown University (J.D., 1974). Management Co-Chair, Employee Benefits Committee of the American Bar Association Section on Labor and Employment Law, 1997-2000. Member, Joint Committee on Employee Benefits of the American Bar Association, 1997-2000. Member of the Board of Governors and Charter Fellow of the American College of Employee Benefits Counsel, 2000—. Co-Chair, Employee Benefits and Executive Compensation Practice Group of Gibson, Dunn & Crutcher, 1999—. Chair, Health Care Work Group of the U.S. Department of Labor's Advisory Council on Employee Welfare and Pension Benefit Plans, 1994. Special Council for Pension and Welfare Plan Laws, U.S. Congressional Joint Economic Committee, 1979-1981. Associate Minority Counsel, U.S. Senate Subcommittee on Labor of the Committee on Human Resources, 1977-1979. Member, Board of Editors, *Benefits Law Journal*. ***PRACTICE AREAS:*** Employee Benefits; Labor; Tax; Health Services. ***Email:*** pturza@gibsondunn.com

MICHAEL L. DENGER, born September 8, 1945; admitted to bar, 1970, District of Columbia. *Education:* Northwestern University (B.S., with highest distinction, 1967); Harvard Law School (J.D., cum laude, 1970). Chair, 1992-1993, Chair-Elect, 1991-1992, Secretary, 1988-1991, Vice Chairman, 1985-1986, Council Member, 1982-1985 and Chair, Editorial Board, Federal and State Price Discrimination Law, 1991, Co-Editor-in-Chief, State Antitrust Practice and Statutes, 1990, and Vice-Chairman, Editorial Board, Antitrust Law Developments (Second) 1984, Section of Antitrust Law, American Bar Association. ***PRACTICE AREAS:*** Antitrust and Trade Regulation Law; False Advertising Law; Administrative Law; Litigation. ***Email:*** mdenger@gibsondunn.com

F. JOSEPH WARIN, born May 25, 1950; admitted to bar, 1975, Nebraska; 1976, District of Columbia. *Education:* Creighton University (B.A., cum laude, 1972); Georgetown University Law Center (J.D., 1975). Editor, Law and Policy

(This Listing Continued)

in International Business, 1974-1975. Professor, Washington Center, 1979-1984. Law Clerk, The Honorable J. Calvitt Clarke, United States District Court for the Eastern District of Virginia, 1975-1976. Assistant United States Attorney, United States Attorney's Office for District of Columbia, 1976-1983. U.S. Department of Justice, Special Achievement Award, 1983. Hearing Committee Member, District of Columbia Board of Professional Responsibility, 1983-1986. Special Prosecutor, D.C. Superior Court, 1988-1990. Edward B. Williams' Inn of Court, 1989—. Settlement Mediator, D.C. Superior Court, 1988-1994. Lecturer, District of Columbia Criminal Practice Institute, 1985-1990. *Member:* Bar Association of the District of Columbia (Member, Executive Council, Young Lawyers Section, 1980-1983); American Bar Association (Member, Criminal Justice Section, White Collar Crime Committee, 1989—). ***PRACTICE AREAS:*** Antitrust; Securities and White Collar Crime Litigation. ***Email:*** jwarin@gibsondunn.com

DANIEL J. PLAINE, born August 23, 1943; admitted to bar, 1970, District of Columbia; U.S. Supreme Court. *Education:* Williams College (B.A., magna cum laude, 1965); Cambridge University, England (Marshall Scholar, LL.B. in International Law, 1967); Yale University (J.D., 1970). Phi Beta Kappa. Chair, International Business Law Committee, Business Law Section, American Bar Association. Co-Chair, International Trade Practice Group and Co-Partner in Charge of the Washington, D.C. Office, Gibson, Dunn & Crutcher. *Member:* American Bar Association; American Society of International Law; Washington Institute of Foreign Affairs. ***SPECIAL AGENCIES:*** International Trade Commission. ***PRACTICE AREAS:*** International Trade; International Law; Antitrust and Trade Regulations; International Transactions. ***Email:*** dplaine@gibsondunn.com

JAMES R. LOFTIS, III, born February 7, 1943; admitted to bar, 1968, District of Columbia. *Education:* Washington & Lee University (A.B., 1965); George Washington University (J.D., with honors, 1968). Order of the Coif. Member of Staff, 1966-1967 and Editor-in-Chief, 1967-1968, The George Washington Law Review. Editorial Board Chairman, "ABA Antitrust Section, Antitrust Law Developments," American Bar Association, 2d. ed., 1984. Author: "The New Efficiencies Guidelines: Transparency or Peek-a-Boo," (FTC Watch, 1997). Member FTC/DOJ Working Group on Criminal Antitrust Enforcement, 1998. Program Chair, Advanced Criminal Antitrust Workshop (Toronto) 1998. Round Table Discussion Leader, Pacific Economic Cooperation Council Conference on Trade and Competition Policy (1997 Montreal). Author and Program Chair, ABA Criminal Antitrust Law and Procedure Workshop, 1995. Author: ABA, Antitrust Section Annual Review of 1992 Antitrust Law Developments (1993); "Dual Distribution," PLI 1990, 1991; "Non-Horizontal Mergers," Law and Policy (ABA 1988); "How to Analyze Dual Distribution Systems," Von Kalinowski, Antitrust Counseling and Trial Techniques, Matthew Bender, 1986; "A Counselors' Guide To Analyzing Price and Pricing Practices," Von Kalinowski, Antitrust Counseling and Trial Techniques, Matthew Bender, 1987; "Benchmarking The Dark Side," 1996 ABA Trade Associations and Antitrust; "Compliance Programs For Antitrust," ABA, 1996 Distribution Counseling The Tough Problems; "Monopoly," Massachusetts Continuing Legal Education, Inc., 1986. Law Clerk to Judge Oliver Gasch, United States District Court for the District of Columbia, 1968-1969. *Member:* The District of Columbia Bar; American Bar Association (Immediate Past Chair, 1997-1998; Chair, 1996-1997, Chair-Elect, 1995-1996 and Secretary, 1993-1995, Antitrust Law Section; Chairman, Antitrust Law Developments Committee, Antitrust Law Section, 1975-1984; Council Member, Antitrust Law Section, 1982-1985, 1990-1993; Vice Chairman, Antitrust Law Section, 1985-1986; Chairman, Monograph Committee, 1986-1989; Chairman, Sports and Entertainment Committee, Antitrust Section, 1990-1993; Antitrust Section Liaison to the Canadian Bar Association, 1997-1998; 1999-2001, Chairman, Antitrust Section Task Force on Fundamental Theory). ***PRACTICE AREAS:*** Antitrust. ***Email:*** jloftis@gibsondunn.com

HOWARD B. ADLER, born April 29, 1951; admitted to bar, 1976, New York; 1979, District of Columbia. *Education:* The Johns Hopkins University (B.A., 1972); New York University (J.D., 1975). Omicron Delta Kappa. Note and Comment Editor, New York University Law Review, 1974-1975. *Member:* The District of Columbia Bar (Chair, Task Force on Lawyers for the Redevelopment of the District of Columbia; Treasurer, 1996-1997; Member: Budget Committee, 1996-1997; Investment Committee, 1996-1997; Treasurer and Member, Development Committee, Public Service Activities Corporation, 1996-1997; Member, Steering Committee, Corporation, Finance and Securities Law Section, 1991-1995; Chairman, 1994-1995; Vice Chairman, 1993-1994); Federal (Member, Executive Council, Banking Law Committee, 1993-1998) and American (Member, Banking Law Committee) Bar Associations; Archdiocesan Legal Network of Washington, D.C. (Member, Advisory Board); Knight of Malta. ***PRACTICE AREAS:*** Securities; Mergers, Acquisitions and Divestitures; Corporate Law; Banks and Banking; Finance. ***Email:*** hadler@gibsondunn.com

LARRY L. SIMMS, born March 12, 1944; admitted to bar, 1974, Vermont and Massachusetts; 1976, District of Columbia. *Education:* Dartmouth College (A.B., 1966); Boston University (J.D., cum laude, 1973). Editor-in-Chief, Boston University Law Review, 1972-1973. Law Clerk to: Honorable James L. Oakes, U.S. Circuit Judge, Second Circuit, 1973-1974; Honorable Byron R. White, Associate Justice, Supreme Court of the United States, 1974-1975. Adjunct Professor of Law, Georgetown University Law Center, 1976-1985. Deputy Assistant Attorney General, Office of Legal Counsel, U.S. Department of Justice, 1979-1985. Counsel, US-China Business Council, 1999—. *Member:* American Bar Association (Co-Chair, China Law Committee, 1997-2000). [LT. USN, 1966-1970]. ***PRACTICE AREAS:*** Appellate Litigation; Constitutional Litigation; Insurance Law (International and Domestic); Chinese Law; International Arbitration. ***Email:*** lsimms@gibsondunn.com

(This Listing Continued)

JOHN H. STURC, born June 15, 1950; admitted to bar, 1975, District of Columbia. *Education:* Cornell University (A.B., summa cum laude, 1972); Harvard Law School (J.D., cum laude, 1975). Phi Beta Kappa. Law Clerk to U.S. District Judge C. Stanley Blair, District of Maryland, 1975-1976. Associate Director, 1984-1990, Deputy Chief Litigation Counsel, 1982-1984 and Assistant Chief Trial Attorney, 1982-1983, Division of Enforcement, U.S. Securities and Exchange Commission. Assistant U.S. Attorney, District of Columbia, 1976-1981. Co-Author: *Civil RICO Litigation* (Prentice-Hall, 1992). Editor, *Securities Lawyer,* Newsletter of the American Bar Association Committee on Federal Regulation of Securities. Member, Board of Advisors, The SEC Institute, Inc. *Member:* American Bar Association (Member, Sections on: Business Law; Litigation; Criminal Justice). ***PRACTICE AREAS:*** Securities; Civil and Criminal Litigation. ***Email:*** jsturc@gibsondunn.com

JOSEPH KATTAN, born August 24, 1952; admitted to bar, 1976, Illinois (inactive); 1980, District of Columbia. *Education:* Case Western Reserve University (A.B., 1978); Northwestern University (J.D., 1976); University of Chicago (A.M., 1978). Listed in: Chambers Global, The World's Leading Lawyers; An International Who's Who of Competition Lawyers; Euromoney Guide to the World's Leading Competition and Antitrust Lawyers; Mondaq's Guide to leading Competition Attorneys. Adjunct Professor of Law, Washington and Lee University, 1999—. Member, Board of Advisors, Antitrust Counselor, 1994—. Published more than 40 articles on antitrust issues. ***LANGUAGES:*** Hebrew. ***SPECIAL AGENCIES:*** Federal Trade Commission; Antitrust Division, US Department of Justice; European Commission. ***PRACTICE AREAS:*** Antitrust; Consumer Protection. ***Email:*** jkattan@gibsondunn.com

ROBERT C. EAGER, born September 25, 1946; admitted to bar, 1981, District of Columbia. *Education:* Vanderbilt University (B.A., magna cum laude, 1967); Stanford University (M.A., 1969; Ph.D., 1977); Georgetown University (J.D., magna cum laude, 1981). Phi Beta Kappa. Articles Editor, Georgetown Law Journal, 1980-1981. Co-Author: *Federal Deposit Insurance Corporation Improvement Act of 1991* (Sheshunoff, 1991); Optional Federal Chartering and Regulation of Insurance Companies (AEI, 2000). ***PRACTICE AREAS:*** Gram-Leach-Bliley and Financial Institutions Law; Financial Institutions Law; Bank and Savings Association Regulation; Legislation; Transactional Matters for Banks and Thrift Law; Federal-State Insurance Banking Relationships; Preemption Law. ***Email:*** reager@gibsondunn.com

STEPHEN I. GLOVER, born May 26, 1955; admitted to bar, 1982, District of Columbia. *Education:* Amherst College (B.A., summa cum laude, 1977); Harvard Law School (J.D., 1980). Managing Editor, Harvard Law Review, 1979-1980. Law Clerk to: Judge J. Skelly Wright, U.S. Court of Appeals, District of Columbia Circuit, 1980-1981; Justice Thurgood Marshall, U.S. Supreme Court, 1981-1982. Adjunct Professor, Georgetown Law School. Member, Advisory Board, Merger & Acquisition Law Report. Member, Board of Editors, Start -Up and Emerging Companies Strategist. Member, Board of Editors, M&A Lawyer. Member (1996—) and Co-Chair (1999-2000), Steering Committee, Corporation, Finance and Securities Law Section of the District of Columbia. New York Tri Bar Opinion Committee, 1998. Chair, Subcommittee on Governmental Regulation of Venture Capital, Venture Capital Committee, Business Law Section, American Bar Association. *Member:* The District of Columbia Bar; American Bar Association. (Also at Los Angeles, CA). ***PRACTICE AREAS:*** Corporate Law; Securities; Mergers, Acquisitions and Divestitures. ***Email:*** siglover@gibsondunn.com

BARUCH A. FELLNER, born March 23, 1944; admitted to bar, 1969, District of Columbia. *Education:* George Washington University (A.B., magna cum laude, 1965) Phi Beta Kappa; Harvard University (J.D., 1968). Associate General Counsel, Pension Benefit Guaranty Corporation, 1980-1986. Counsel for Regional Litigation, Department of Labor Solicitor's Office, Occupational Safety and Health Division, 1972-1980. Member, Appellate Court Branch, National Labor Relations Board, 1968-1972. Co-Author: "Occupational Safety and Health Law and Practice," PLI, 1975. *Member:* American Bar Association. ***LANGUAGES:*** Hebrew. ***PRACTICE AREAS:*** Labor Relations Law; Employee Benefits Law; Occupational Safety and Health Law; Litigation. ***Email:*** bfellner@gibsondunn.com

ARTHUR DAVID PASTERNAK, born January 22, 1958; admitted to bar, 1983, District of Columbia. *Education:* Brown University (B.A., magna cum laude, 1979); Boalt Hall School of Law, University of California; Yale University (J.D., 1983). ***Email:*** apasternak@gibsondunn.com

TERENCE P. ROSS, born December 30, 1958; admitted to bar, 1983, District of Columbia; 1985, New York; 1986, Virginia. *Education:* Stanford

(This Listing Continued)

GIBSON, DUNN & CRUTCHER LLP, Washington—Continued

University (A.B., B.S., 1980); University of Virginia (J.D., 1983). Research Editor, Virginia Law Review, 1981-1983. Law Clerk to The Honorable Roger Robb, U.S. Court of Appeals, for the District of Columbia Circuit, 1983-1984. Author: *Intellectual Property Law:* Damages and Remedies. Co-Chair, ABA Subcommittee on Copyright Litigation, 1998—. ***PRACTICE AREAS:*** Technical Litigation; Intellectual Property Litigation; Communications and Media Law; Computers and Software Law. ***Email:*** tross@gibsondunn.com

JOHN C. MILLIAN, born January 30, 1958; admitted to bar, 1984, Washington; 1987, California; 1988, District of Columbia. *Education:* University of California at Berkeley (B.A., with great distinction, 1980); Yale Law School (J.D., 1983). Phi Beta Kappa. Law Clerk to the Hon. Gerhard A. Gesell, U.S. District Judge, District of Columbia, 1983-1984. ***PRACTICE AREAS:*** Complex and Multi-District Litigation; Class Actions; Securities; Banking. ***Email:*** jmillian@gibsondunn.com

RAYMOND B. LUDWISZEWSKI, born May 20, 1958; admitted to bar, 1985, Massachusetts; 1988, District of Columbia. *Education:* Northeastern University (B.S., 1981); Harvard University (J.D., 1984). Articles Editor, Harvard Law Review, 1983-1984. Author: "Improving Trade and Protecting the Environment," 10 Envir. F. 34 (1993); "Superfund Liability at Issue," 15 Nat. L.J. 29 (June 14, 1993); "Pollution Prevention Plays Enforcement Role," 23 Poll. Eng. 13 (1991). Teaching Fellow, Harvard Law School, 1983-1984. General Counsel, U.S. EPA, 1991-1993. Assistant Administrator for Enforcement, U.S. EPA, 1990-1991. Associate Deputy Attorney General, Department of Justice, 1988-1989. Law Clerk to Judge Henry J. Friendly, U.S. Court of Appeals for the 2nd Circuit, 1984-1985. Vice Chair, ABA Special Committee on Environmental Crimes and Enforcement, 1991-1993. Chair, Environment and Natural Resources Section, Claims Court Bar Association, 1990-1991. ***SPECIAL AGENCIES:*** EPA. ***PRACTICE AREAS:*** Environmental Law. ***Email:*** rludwiszewski@gibsondunn.com

AMY G. RUDNICK, born April 21, 1954; admitted to bar, 1980, Connecticut (inactive); 1982, District of Columbia. *Education:* Stanford University (B.A., 1976); George Washington University (J.D., with honors, 1980). Law Clerk to Judge Ellen Bree Burns, U.S. District Court, Connecticut, 1980-1981. Trial Attorney, U.S. Department of Justice, Criminal Division, Honors Program, 1981-1984. Director, Office of Financial Enforcement, U.S. Department of the Treasury, 1987-1990. Member, Bank Secrecy Act, Advisory Group, Department of the Treasury, 1994—. *Member:* The District of Columbia Bar; Connecticut and American (Member, Criminal Justice Section, 1981—; Vice Chair, Criminal Justice Section, White Collar Crime Committee, 1993-1994; Co-Chair, Criminal Justice Section, White Collar Crime, Money Laundering Subcommittee, 1991-1994) Bar Associations; District of Columbia Women's Bar Association. ***PRACTICE AREAS:*** White Collar Crime; Financial Institutions. ***Email:*** arudnick@gibsondunn.com

BRIAN J. LANE, born July 29, 1958; admitted to bar, 1983, Maryland (Not admitted in District of Columbia). *Education:* Washburn University (B.A., magna cum laude, 1980); American University (J.D., 1983). Phi Kappa Phi. Author: Insights Articles, "Is it Time to Redefine 'Investment Company' in the Age of Internet," The Corporate and Securities Law Advisor, Vol. 14, Number 5, May 2000. Adjunct Professor of Law, Georgetown University Law School, 1993-1995. Member, ASCS, 2000. Member, U.S. Securities & Exchange Commission. Director, Division of Corporations Finance, 1996-1999. Counsel to the Chairman, 1995-1996. Counsel to Commission Richard Y. Roberts, 1992-1995. Special Counsel, Division of Corporate Finance, 1986-1992. Staff Attorney, Division of Market Regulation, 1983-1986. *Member:* Maryland State Bar Association. ***PRACTICE AREAS:*** Securities; Mergers, Acquisitions and Divestitures; Corporate Law. ***Email:*** blane@gibsondunn.com

JULIA A. DAHLBERG, born December 11, 1960; admitted to bar, 1987, California; 1993, District of Columbia. *Education:* Cambridge University, England; University of California at Los Angeles (B.A., cum laude, 1982); University of California, Hastings College of the Law (J.D., magna cum laude, 1986). Order of the Coif. Thurston Honor Society. Senior Note and Comment Editor, Hastings Law Journal, 1985-1986. Judicial Clerk, Judge Harold H. Greene, U.S. District Court, District of Columbia, 1986-1987. Extern Law Clerk, Judge Cecil F. Poole, United States Court of Appeals for the Ninth Circuit, 1985. ***PRACTICE AREAS:*** Litigation; Securities; Labor and Employment; Communications. ***Email:*** jdahlberg@gibsondunn.com

THEODORE J. BOUTROUS, JR., born September 23, 1960; admitted to bar, 1987, California; 1989, District of Columbia. *Education:* Arizona State University (B.S., 1984); University of North Dakota; University of San Diego School of Law (J.D., summa cum laude, 1987) Valedictorian. Co-Chair, Appellate and Constitutional Law Practice Group and Media Law Practice Group, Gibson, Dunn & Crutcher. Editor-in-Chief, San Diego Law Review, 1986-1987. (Los Angeles, California and Washington, D.C. Offices). ***PRACTICE AREAS:*** Appellate Litigation; Media Law; Constitutional Law; Libel, Slander and Defamation; Legal Ethics and Professional Responsibility. ***Email:*** tboutrous@gibsondunn.com

(This Listing Continued)

JUDITH A. LEE, born October 20, 1962; admitted to bar, 1987, Virginia; 1988, District of Columbia. *Education:* Tunghai University, Taichung, Taiwan; Mt. Holyoke College (B.A., 1984); College of William & Mary (J.D., 1987). Order of the Coif. Practice Group Co-Chair, Customs and International Trade Practice Group, Gibson, Dunn & Crutcher. Co-Chair, Customs Committee, Business Regulation Division, Section of International Law and Practice, American Bar Association. Board of Directors, Customs and International Trade Bar Association. *Member:* District of Columbia Bar Association; Virginia State Bar. ***LANGUAGES:*** Mandarin Chinese. ***PRACTICE AREAS:*** Customs Law; International Trade Law; Export Controls; Foreign Corrupt Practices Act; Economic Sanctions and Embargoes; International Privacy. ***Email:*** jalee@gibsondunn.com

RONALD O. MUELLER, born March 27, 1960; admitted to bar, 1987, New York; 1989, District of Columbia. *Education:* Vanderbilt University (B.A., 1982); Columbia University (J.D., 1986). Phi Beta Kappa. James Kent Scholar. Writing and Research Editor, Columbia/VLA Journal of Law & the Arts, 1985-1986. Counsel to Commissioner, U.S. Securities and Exchange Commission, 1989-1991. ***PRACTICE AREAS:*** Securities; Corporate Disclosure and Proxy Regulation; Executive Compensation. ***Email:*** rmueller@gibsondunn.com

DOUGLAS R. COX, born August 25, 1956; admitted to bar, 1982, New York; 1998, District of Columbia. *Education:* Princeton University (A.B., 1977); Harvard Law School (J.D., 1980). Editor-in-Chief, Harvard Journal of Law and Public Policy, 1979-1980; Pembroke College, Oxford University, 1980-1981. Deputy Assistant Attorney General, 1990-1992 and Principal Deputy Assistant Attorney General, 1992-1993, Office of Legal Counsel, Department of Justice. ***PRACTICE AREAS:*** Litigation; Constitutional; Government; Regulatory Law. ***Email:*** dcox@gibsondunn.com

THOMAS G. HUNGAR, born January 16, 1962; admitted to bar, 1989, California; 1995, District of Columbia. *Education:* Willamette University (B.S., 1984); Yale Law School (J.D., 1987). Senior Editor, Yale Law & Policy Review. Assistant to the Solicitor General of the United States, 1992-1994. Law Clerk to: Justice Anthony M. Kennedy, U.S. Supreme Court, 1988-1989; Judge Alex Kozinski, U.S. Court of Appeals, Ninth Circuit, 1987-1988. Co-chair, Appellate and Constitutional Law Practice Group. ***PRACTICE AREAS:*** Appellate Practice; Constitutional Law; Litigation. ***Email:*** thungar@gibsondunn.com

MICHAEL F. FLANAGAN, born July 18, 1964; admitted to bar, 1991, New York; 1993, District of Columbia. *Education:* Cornell University (A.B., 1986); University of Michigan (J.D., 1990). ***PRACTICE AREAS:*** Litigation; Securities. ***Email:*** mflanagan@gibsondunn.com

STEPHANIE TSACOUMIS, born August 31, 1956; admitted to bar, 1981, District of Columbia; 1982, Maryland. *Education:* College of William & Mary (B.A., 1978); University of Virginia (J.D., 1981). Phi Beta Kappa. Lile Moot Court Finalist. Senior Editor, Virginia Journal of International Law. Contributing Author: *Securities in the Electronic Age,* Glasser LegalWorks 2001. Adjunct Faculty, Georgetown University Law Center, Securities Disclosure, 2001. *Member:* District of Columbia Bar; Maryland State and American Bar Associations. ***SPECIAL AGENCIES:*** Securities and Exchange Commission. ***PRACTICE AREAS:*** Securities; Corporations; Mergers, Acquisitions and Divestitures; Venture Capital; Financial Services Law. ***Email:*** stsacoumis@gibsondunn.com

MIGUEL A. ESTRADA, born September 25, 1961; admitted to bar, 1987, New York (Not admitted in District of Columbia). *Education:* Columbia College (A.B., magna cum laude, 1983); Harvard Law School (J.D., magna cum laude, 1986). Phi Beta Kappa. Editor, Harvard Law Review, 1984-1986. Law Clerk to: The Honorable Anthony M. Kennedy, U.S. Supreme Court, 1988-1989; The Honorable Amalya L. Kearse, U.S. Court of Appeals for the Second Circuit, New York, N.Y., 1986-1987. ***LANGUAGES:*** Spanish. ***SPECIAL AGENCIES:*** Office of the Solicitor General, Assistant to the Solicitor General, United States Department of Justice, Washington, D.C., 1992-1997; United States Attorney's Office for the Southern District of New York, N.Y., Deputy Chief, Appellate Section, 1992 and Assistant United States Attorney, 1990-1992. ***PRACTICE AREAS:*** Appellate Practice; White Collar Crime. ***Email:*** mestrada@gibsondunn.com

CHRISTOPHER J. BELLINI, born October 17, 1961; admitted to bar, 1989, Massachusetts; 1990, District of Columbia. *Education:* University of Massachusetts (B.B.A., 1983); Georgetown University (J.D., 1989). Order of the Coif. Co-Chair, Financial Institutions Practice Group. Certified Public Accountant. *Member:* American Bar Association. ***SPECIAL AGENCIES:*** Federal Reserve Board, Office of the Comptroller of the Currency; Federal Deposit Insurance Corporation, Office of Thrift Supervision. ***PRACTICE AREAS:*** Banking; Privacy Law. ***Email:*** cbellini@gibsondunn.com

PETER P. MURPHY, born March 25, 1965; admitted to bar, 1990, California; 1997, Maryland; 1998, District of Columbia. *Education:* Georgetown University (B.S.F.S., 1987); University of Michigan (J.D., 1990). Phi Beta Kappa. Assistant to General Counsel, Department of Army. ***LANGUAGES:*** French. ***PRACTICE AREAS:*** Environmental. ***Email:*** ppmurphy@gibsondunn.com

(This Listing Continued)

ADVISORY COUNSEL

STEPHEN E. TALLENT, born August 10, 1937; admitted to bar, 1963, California; 1981, District of Columbia; 1984, New York. *Education:* Stanford University (A.B., 1959); University of Chicago (J.D., 1962); Lincoln University (LL.D., with honors., 1990). Order of the Coif. Associate Editor, University of Chicago Law Review, 1961-1962. President, Southern California Chapter, Industrial Relations Research Association, 1975-1976. Co-Chairman, ABA Committee on Equal Employment Opportunity Law, Labor and Employment Law Section, 1977-1980. Chairman, Employment Law Committee, Defense Research Institute, 1982-1985. Chairman, NAM Labor Law Advisory Committee, 1986-1987. Co-Chairman, Membership and Finance Committee, 1985-1987 and Member of the Council, ABA Labor and Employment Section, 1987—. Chair-Elect, ABA Labor and Employment Law Section, 1997. Chair, ABA Labor and Employment Law Section, 1998-1999. Founding Director, American Employment Law Council, 1993—. Founding Fellow and President, 1995-1997 and Governor, 1995—, The College of Labor and Employment Lawyers, Inc. ***PRACTICE AREAS:*** Labor; Employee Benefits; Employment and Discrimination Litigation; International Labor Law. ***Email:*** stallent@gibsondunn.com

THEODORE B. OLSON, born Chicago, Illinois, September 11, 1940; admitted to bar, 1966, California; 1982, District of Columbia. *Education:* University of the Pacific (B.A., cum laude, 1962); University of California, Boalt Hall School of Law (LL.B., 1965). Order of the Coif. Staff Member, California Law Review, 1964-1965. Member, California Commission on Uniform State Laws, 1972-1974. Assistant Attorney General, Office of Legal Counsel, U.S. Department of Justice, 1981-1984. *Member:* American Bar Association (Member of Council, Administrative Law Section, 1991-1994; Delegate to the House of Delegates, 1996-2000). Fellow: American Academy of Appellate Lawyers; American College of Trial Lawyers. (Co-Chair, Appellate and Constitutional Law Practice Group, Gibson, Dunn & Crutcher) (Washington, D.C. and Los Angeles, California Offices). ***PRACTICE AREAS:*** Constitutional Law; Appellate Litigation; Commercial Law; Administrative Law; First Amendment Litigation. ***Email:*** tolson@gibsondunn.com

PETER J. WALLISON, born June 6, 1941; admitted to bar, 1967, New York; 1977, District of Columbia. *Education:* Harvard University (B.A., 1963; LL.B., 1966). Counsel to the Vice President of the United States, 1974-1977. General Counsel of the Treasury, 1981-1985. Counsel to the President of the United States, 1986-1987. Member, Shadow Financial Regulatory Committee. *Member:* Association of the Bar of the City of New York; The District of Columbia Bar. ***PRACTICE AREAS:*** Banking Law and Regulation; Corporate Transactions; Securities and Financial Services Law. ***Email:*** pwallison@gibsondunn.com

AULANA L. PETERS, born November 30, 1941; admitted to bar, 1974, California (Not admitted in District of Columbia). *Education:* College of New Rochelle (B.A., 1963); University of Southern California (J.D., 1973). Co-Chair, Moot Court Honors Program, 1973. Commissioner, U.S. Securities and Exchange Commission, 1984-1988. Member, Legal Advising Committee, National Association of Security Dealers. Member Board of Directors: New York Stock Exchange, 1989-1995; American Institute of Certified Public Accountants, 1991-1994. (Los Angeles, California and Washington, D.C. Offices). ***LANGUAGES:*** French; Italian. ***SPECIAL AGENCIES:*** Securities and Exchange Commission. ***PRACTICE AREAS:*** Securities Litigation; Securities Law; SEC Regulatory Matters; Accountant's Liability; Commercial Litigation. ***Email:*** apeters@gibsondunn.com

OF COUNSELS

GRACIA M. BERG, born April 26, 1945; admitted to bar, 1980, District of Columbia. *Education:* Augsburg College (B.A., 1967); University of Notre Dame (J.D., 1980). Chair, International Trade Regulation Committee, American Bar Association Section of Ad Law and Regulatory Practice. ***PRACTICE AREAS:*** International Trade. ***Email:*** gberg@gibsondunn.com

PAUL BLANKENSTEIN, born December 2, 1946; admitted to bar, 1974, New York; 1980, District of Columbia. *Education:* City College of New York (B.S., 1969); Brooklyn Law School (J.D., cum laude, 1973). Member, 1971-1972 and Second Circuit-Note Editor, 1972-1973, Brooklyn Law Review. Staff Attorney, Appellate Section, 1973-1978, Assistant Branch Director, Federal Programs Branch, 1978-1984 and Appellate Litigation Counsel, 1984-1985, Civil Division, Department of Justice. ***PRACTICE AREAS:*** Litigation of Complex Commercial Cases. ***Email:*** pblankenstein@gibsondunn.com

ANDREA F. DYNES, born August 21, 1960; admitted to bar, 1989, District of Columbia. *Education:* Indiana University (B.A., 1981); American University, Washington College of Law (J.D., cum laude, 1988). ***LANGUAGES:*** German. ***PRACTICE AREAS:*** International Trade. ***Email:*** adynes@gibsondunn.com

AMY L. GOODMAN, born August 17, 1951; admitted to bar, 1975, Massachusetts; 1999, District of Columbia. *Education:* Boston University (A.B., 1973; J.D., cum laude, 1975); Georgetown University Law Center (LL.M., 1983). ***PRACTICE AREAS:*** Securities; Corporate Law. ***Email:*** agoodman@gibsondunn.com

(This Listing Continued)

LINDA NOONAN, born March 22, 1951; admitted to bar, 1977, California; 1980, District of Columbia. *Education:* American University (B.A., 1973); American University, Washington College of Law (J.D., 1977). ***PRACTICE AREAS:*** Money Laundering. ***Email:*** lnoonan@gibsondunn.com

MALCOLM R. PFUNDER, born April 29, 1944; admitted to bar, 1971, District of Columbia. *Education:* Harvard University (A.B., magna cum laude, 1965); Yale University (J.D., 1971). ***PRACTICE AREAS:*** Antitrust and Trade Regulation; Mergers, Acquisitions and Divestitures; Hart-Scott-Rodino Act. ***Email:*** mpfunder@gibsondunn.com

DIANA GALE RICHARD, born November 3, 1953; admitted to bar, 1988, Maryland; 1990, District of Columbia. *Education:* University of Montevallo (B.S., 1975); University of Maryland (J.D., 1988). Order of the Coif. ***PRACTICE AREAS:*** Government Contracts; Computers and Software. ***Email:*** dgrichard@gibsondunn.com

VICTORIA P. ROSTOW, born September 29, 1956; admitted to bar, 1985, New York and District of Columbia. *Education:* Yale University (B.A., 1978); Cambridge University (M.A., 1980); Yale Law School (J.D., 1983). Senior Editor, Yale Law Journal. Law Clerk to the Honorable Stephen Reinhardt, U.S. Court of Appeals for the 9th Circuit, 1983-1984. ***PRACTICE AREAS:*** Banks and Banking; Government. ***Email:*** vrostow@gibsondunn.com

RICHARD A. ZIMMER, born August 16, 1944; admitted to bar, 1971, New York; 1975, New Jersey (Not admitted in District of Columbia). *Education:* Yale University (B.A., with honors, 1966; LL.B., 1969). Board of Editors, Yale Law Journal. New Jersey Assembly, 1982-1987; New Jersey Senate, 1987-1991; United States House of Representatives, 1991-1997. ***PRACTICE AREAS:*** Government; Corporate Law. ***Email:*** rzimmer@gibsondunn.com

SPECIAL COUNSEL

DERRY DEAN SPARLIN JR., born April 13, 1957; admitted to bar, 1986, Virginia; 1987, District of Columbia. *Education:* George Washington University; Catholic University of America (B.A., 1980); College of William & Mary (J.D., 1986). Order of the Coif. Managing Editor, William & Mary Law Review, 1985-1986. ***PRACTICE AREAS:*** Labor and Employment; Employee Benefits. ***Email:*** dsparlin@gibsondunn.com

ASSOCIATES

ELISE C. KEEGAN, born October 6, 1967; admitted to bar, 1993, New York; 2000, District of Columbia. *Education:* University of Virginia (B.A., 1989; J.D., 1992). Phi Beta Kappa. Order of the Coif. Managing Editor, Virginia Law Review, 1991-1992. ***PRACTICE AREAS:*** Corporate Law; Securities. ***Email:*** ekeegan@gibsondunn.com

DANIEL W. NELSON, born July 11, 1968; admitted to bar, 1994, New York; 1996, District of Columbia. *Education:* Colgate University (B.A., magna cum laude, 1990); University of Michigan (J.D., cum laude, 1993). Phi Beta Kappa. ***PRACTICE AREAS:*** Litigation; General Litigation; Appellate Practice. ***Email:*** dnelson@gibsondunn.com

PETER E. SELEY, born July 13, 1968; admitted to bar, 1993, Pennsylvania (inactive); 1995, District of Columbia. *Education:* Princeton University (A.B., 1990); Cornell Law School (J.D., cum laude, 1993). Associate Editor, Cornell Law Review, 1991-1992. ***PRACTICE AREAS:*** Environmental; Toxic Tort. ***Email:*** pseley@gibsondunn.com

D. JARRETT ARP, born September 9, 1966; admitted to bar, 1991, Virginia; 1994, District of Columbia. *Education:* Wheaton College (B.A., 1988); Marshall-Wythe School of Law, College of William & Mary (J.D., 1991). Executive Editor, Professional Articles, William & Mary Law Review, 1990-1991. ***PRACTICE AREAS:*** Litigation; Antitrust and Trade Regulation. ***Email:*** jarp@gibsondunn.com

JONATHAN K. TYCKO, born February 11, 1968; admitted to bar, 1993, New York; 1995, District of Columbia. *Education:* Johns Hopkins University (B.A., 1989); Columbia University (J.D., 1992). Harlan Fiske Stone Scholar. Notes Editor, Columbia-VLA Journal of Law and the Arts, 1991-1992. Law Clerk, Hon. Alexander Harvey, II, United States District Court for the District of Maryland, 1992-1994. ***PRACTICE AREAS:*** Litigation; Media Law. ***Email:*** jtycko@gibsondunn.com

ALICE W. DETWILER, admitted to bar, 1995, California (Not admitted in District of Columbia). *Education:* Princeton University (A.B., cum laude, 1991); Harvard Law School (J.D., magna cum laude, 1994). Clerk, Hon. Charles E. Wiggins, Ninth Circuit Court of Appeals, 1994-1995. Deputy Legal Affairs Secretary, Office of Governor Wilson, 1995-1997. ***PRACTICE AREAS:*** Litigation; Securities; Appellate Practice. ***Email:*** adetwiler@gibsondunn.com

DAVID W.T. DANIELS, born March 24, 1967; admitted to bar, 1994, California; 1998, District of Columbia. *Education:* Princeton University (A.B., 1989); University of Chicago (J.D., 1994). Staff Member, University of Chicago Law Review. ***PRACTICE AREAS:*** Securities Litigation; Intellectual Property Litigation; Complex Commercial Litigation. ***Email:*** ddaniels@gibsondunn.com

(This Listing Continued)

GIBSON, DUNN & CRUTCHER LLP, Washington—Continued

DELWEN A. JONES, born October 3, 1968; admitted to bar, 1994, Washington (Not admitted in District of Columbia). *Education:* University of Washington (B.A., magna cum laude, 1990); Georgetown Law Center (J.D., 1993). ***PRACTICE AREAS:*** General Litigation; Antitrust. ***Email:*** dajones@gibsondunn.com

TODD D. KANTORCZYK, born September 20, 1970; admitted to bar, 1996, New York; 1997, District of Columbia. *Education:* Cornell University (B.A., 1992); University of California School of Law at Los Angeles (J.D., 1995). Comments Editor, 1994-1995 and Staff Member, 1993-1994, UCLA Law Review. ***PRACTICE AREAS:*** Environmental Law; Toxic Torts. ***Email:*** tkantorczyk@gibsondunn.com

HASSAN A. ZAVAREEI, born March 12, 1969; admitted to bar, 1996, California; 1997, District of Columbia. *Education:* Duke University (B.A., cum laude, 1990); University of California, Boalt Hall School of Law (J.D., 1995). Order of the Coif. ***LANGUAGES:*** Russian. ***PRACTICE AREAS:*** Commercial Litigation; Litigation; International Law. ***Email:*** hzavareei@gibsondunn.com

GAVIN A. BESKE, born January 7, 1967; admitted to bar, 1996, California (Not admitted in District of Columbia). *Education:* Princeton University (A.B., 1989); Columbia University (J.D., 1995). Harlan Fiske Stone Scholar. Managing Editor, 1994-1995 and Staff Member, 1993-1994, Columbia Law Review. ***PRACTICE AREAS:*** Corporate Law; Mergers, Acquisitions and Divestitures. ***Email:*** gbeske@gibsondunn.com

ANTOINETTE DeCAMP, born November 18, 1972; admitted to bar, 1996, New York; 1998, California (Not admitted in District of Columbia). *Education:* Harvard University (B.A., magna cum laude, 1992); Columbia Law School (J.D., 1995). Harlan Fiske Stone Scholar. Staff Member and Co-Head Notes Editor, Columbia Journal of Transnational Law, 1993-1995. ***PRACTICE AREAS:*** General Litigation; Securities Litigation. ***Email:*** adecamp@gibsondunn.com

HILL B. WELLFORD, III, born March 23, 1970; admitted to bar, 1995, Virginia; 1999, District of Columbia. *Education:* Dartmouth College (B.A., magna cum laude, 1992); University of Virginia (J.D., 1995). Member, Editorial Board, Virginia Environmental Law Journal, 1993-1995. Law Clerk to Judge Richard L. Williams, U.S. District Court, Eastern District of Virginia, 1995-1996. ***PRACTICE AREAS:*** Intellectual Property; Litigation. ***Email:*** hwellford@gibsondunn.com

PAUL DeCAMP, born 1971; admitted to bar, 1995, Ohio (inactive); 1998, California (Not admitted in District of Columbia). *Education:* Harvard University (A.B., magna cum laude, 1992); Columbia University (J.D., 1995). Harlan Fiske Stone Scholar. Notes Editor, Columbia Law Review. Law Clerk to the Honorable Alan E. Norris, U.S. Court of Appeals, Sixth Circuit, 1995-1996. ***PRACTICE AREAS:*** Appellate Practice; Labor and Employment. ***Email:*** pdecamp@gibsondunn.com

MICHAEL J. COLLINS, born February 27, 1969; admitted to bar, 1995, Virginia (Not admitted in District of Columbia). *Education:* University of Notre Dame (B.B.A., 1991; J.D., summa cum laude, 1995). Member, Notre Dame Law Review, 1993-1995. ***PRACTICE AREAS:*** Employee Benefits; Taxation. ***Email:*** mcollins@gibsondunn.com

ALISA BABITZ, born September 12, 1968; admitted to bar, 1995, New York; 1996, District of Columbia. *Education:* Columbia University (B.A., magna cum laude, 1990); Harvard Law School (J.D., cum laude, 1993). ***PRACTICE AREAS:*** Corporate. ***Email:*** ababitz@gibsondunn.com

ROBERT C. BLUME, born March 1, 1967; admitted to bar, 1993, Massachusetts; 2001, District of Columbia. *Education:* Brown University (B.A., 1989); Georgetown University (J.D., 1992). Associate Editor, Georgetown Law Journal, 1991-1992. Law Clerk to the Honorable Judge Edward Rafeedie, U.S. District Court, Central District of California, 1992-1993. Organized Crime and Racketeering Section, Criminal Division, Department of Justice, 1993-1997. U.S. Attorney's Office, District of Columbia, 1997-2000. ***PRACTICE AREAS:*** White Collar Crime; Litigation. ***Email:*** rblume@gibsondunn.com

DEBORAH J. KATZ, born August 31, 1972; admitted to bar, 1997, New York; 2001, District of Columbia. *Education:* Duke University (A.B., 1993); Vanderbilt University (J.D., 1996). Student Writing Editor, Vanderbilt Law Review. Moot Court Board. ***PRACTICE AREAS:*** Antitrust and Trade Regulation; Litigation. ***Email:*** dkatz@gibsondunn.com

JACQUELINE E. COLEMAN, born August 20, 1970; admitted to bar, 1996, Pennsylvania; 1998, District of Columbia. *Education:* Harvard University (B.A., 1992); University of Michigan (J.D., 1996). Recipient, Jason L. Honigman Award 1996. Associate Editor, 1994-1995 and Executive Editor, 1995-1996, Michigan Law Review. Law Clerk to the Hon. Theodore A. McKee, United States Court of Appeals for the Third Circuit, 1996-1997. ***PRACTICE AREAS:*** General Litigation; Litigation; Securities Litigation; Antitrust. ***Email:*** jcoleman@gibsondunn.com

DAVID B. SALMONS, born January 10, 1968; admitted to bar, 1998, Georgia (Not admitted in District of Columbia). *Education:* Brigham Young University (B.A., 1993); University of Chicago (J.D., 1996). Order of the Coif. Editor-in-Chief, University of Chicago Law Review, 1995-1996. Law Clerk, Hon. W. Eugene Davis, Fifth Circuit Court of Appeals, 1996-1997. ***PRACTICE AREAS:*** Appellate Practice; Litigation. ***Email:*** dsalmons@gibsondunn.com

LISA A. MURRAY, born November 6, 1967; admitted to bar, 1997, New York; 1998, District of Columbia. *Education:* Oberlin College (B.A., Honors, 1988); University of Michigan (M.A., 1996); Michigan Law School (J.D., cum laude, 1996). Judicial Clerk, Hon. Dominick L. Carlo, U.S. Court of International Trade, 1996-1998. Executive Editor, Michigan Journal of International Law, 1995-1996. ***PRACTICE AREAS:*** International Trade; Litigation. ***Email:*** lmurray@gibsondunn.com

ANDREW S. TULUMELLO, born June 22, 1970; admitted to bar, 1998, California; 2001, District of Columbia. *Education:* Harvard College (A.B., 1991); Harvard Law School (J.D., 1996). Law Clerk, The Honorable Pamela A. Rymer, U.S. Court of Appeals for the Ninth Circuit, 1996-1997. ***PRACTICE AREAS:*** Litigation. ***Email:*** atulumello@gibsondunn.com

CHRISTOPHER E. HUMBER, born August 18, 1969; admitted to bar, 1996, Illinois; 1999, District of Columbia. *Education:* University of Chicago (B.A., with honors, 1992); Harvard Law School (J.D., cum laude, 1996). Phi Beta Kappa. Law Clerk to the Honorable George W. Lindberg, U.S. District Court, Northern District of Illinois, 1996-1998. ***PRACTICE AREAS:*** Labor and Employment; Litigation. ***Email:*** chumber@gibsondunn.com

CORINNE A. LAMMERS, born November 15, 1970; admitted to bar, 1996, Maryland; 1998, District of Columbia; 1999, Pennsylvania. *Education:* The American University (B.A., magna cum laude, 1993); Duke Law School (J.D., cum laude, 1996). Articles Editor, Law & Contemporary Problems. Moot Court Board. ***PRACTICE AREAS:*** International Trade. ***Email:*** clammers@gibsondunn.com

JAMES D. SLEAR, born March 23, 1957; admitted to bar, 1992, Nevada; 2001, District of Columbia. *Education:* University of Evansville (B.A., 1979); Oregon State University (M.S., 1987); Georgetown University (J.D., 1992); U.S. Army Judge Advocate General School (LL.M., 1998). Order of the Coif. Associate Editor, Georgetown Law Journal, 1991-1992. [USAF, 1984-2000]. ***PRACTICE AREAS:*** Litigation; Government Contracts; Antitrust. ***Email:*** jslear@gibsondunn.com

MONTGOMERY N. KOSMA, born October 14, 1967; admitted to bar, 1998, Virginia; 2000, District of Columbia. *Education:* Harvey Mudd College (B.S., with honors, 1988); University of Chicago (J.D., with high honors, 1997). Order of the Coif. University of Chicago Law Review (1995-1997). Founder and Executive Editor, The Green Bag: An Entertaining Journal of Law, (1997—). Law Clerk, Judge David B. Sentelle, U.S. Court of Appeals for the D.C. Circuit, (1997-1998). ***PRACTICE AREAS:*** Antitrust and Trade Regulation; Computers and Software. ***Email:*** mkosma@gibsondunn.com

THOMAS H. DUPREE, JR., born June 14, 1970; admitted to bar, 1998, Massachusetts; 2000, District of Columbia. *Education:* Williams College (B.A., 1992); University of Chicago (J.D., 1997). Recipient, Beale Prize for Legal Research and Writing. Staff Member, 1995-1996 and Member, Managing Board, 1996-1997, University of Chicago Law Review. Clerk, The Hon. Jerry E. Smith, U.S. Court of Appeals, for the Fifth Circuit, 1997-1998. ***Email:*** tdupree@gibsondunn.com

JOHN CHRISTOPHER WOOD, born February 10, 1968; admitted to bar, 1998, Texas (Not admitted in District of Columbia). *Education:* Rice University (B.S., B.A., 1989); Stanford University (M.A., 1991); University of Texas at Austin (J.D., 1997). Chancellor's List. Articles Editor, Texas Law Review, 1996-1997. Judicial Clerk to the Hon. William C. Bryson, U.S. Court of Appeals for the Federal Circuit, 1997-1998. ***LANGUAGES:*** Japanese. ***PRACTICE AREAS:*** International Trade; Intellectual Property; Antitrust. ***Email:*** cwood@gibsondunn.com

MEGAN A. BARNETT, admitted to bar, 1998, South Carolina; 1999, District of Columbia. *Education:* University of Virginia (B.A., 1993); Yale Law School (J.D., 1997). Senior Editor, Yale Law Journal. Judicial Clerkship, Hon. R. Lanier Anderson, U.S. Court of Appeals for the Eleventh Circuit, 1997-1998. ***PRACTICE AREAS:*** Intellectual Property. ***Email:*** mbarnett@gibsondunn.com

MICHAEL J. SCANLON, born October 2, 1970; admitted to bar, 1997, Maryland; 1999, District of Columbia. *Education:* Middlebury College (B.A., 1992); Georgetown University (J.D., cum laude, 1997). The Tax Lawyer, 1994-1996. Law Clerk, Judge Richard N. Goldberg, U.S. Court of International Trade, 1997-1999. *Member:* Maryland State Bar Association. ***Email:*** mscanlon@gibsondunn.com

(This Listing Continued)

(This Listing Continued)

GILLIAN McPHEE, born March 3, 1972; admitted to bar, 1997, Maryland; 1998, District of Columbia. *Education:* Yale University (B.A., magna cum laude, 1993); University of Texas (J.D., with honors, 1997). Book Review Editor, Texas International Law Journal, 1996-1997. ***LANGUAGES:*** French. ***PRACTICE AREAS:*** Corporate Law; Securities. ***Email:*** gmcphee@gibsondunn.com

SCOTT E. SILVERSTEIN, born November 7, 1972; admitted to bar, 1998, New York; 1999, District of Columbia. *Education:* Cornell University (B.S., 1994); New York University (J.D., 1997). Staff Editor, NYU Review of Law and Social Change, 1995. ***Email:*** ssilverstein@gibsondunn.com

JASON C. SCHWARTZ, admitted to bar, 1999, Virginia; 2000, District of Columbia. *Education:* The George Washington University (B.A., cum laude, 1994); Georgetown University Law Center (J.D., magna cum laude, 1999). Order of the Coif. ***PRACTICE AREAS:*** Labor and Employment; Litigation. ***Email:*** jschwartz@gibsondunn.com

ALBERT Y. KIM, born June 19, 1971; admitted to bar, 1999, New York; 2000, District of Columbia. *Education:* Swarthmore College (B.A., 1993); University of Chicago (J.D., 1998). University of Chicago Law Review, 1997-1998. Law Clerk, Hon. Ellsworth van Graafeiland, U.S. Court of Appeals, Second Circuit, 1998-1999. ***PRACTICE AREAS:*** Litigation; Antitrust; Mergers and Acquisitions. ***Email:*** akim@gibsondunn.com

MARK E. PAPADOPOULOS, born July 10, 1973; admitted to bar, 1999, Connecticut; 2000, District of Columbia. *Education:* Haverford College (B.A., 1995); Cornell Law School (J.D., 1998). Order of the Coif. Cornell Law Review. Law Clerk to The Honorable J.L. Edmondson, Eleventh Circuit Court of Appeals, 1998-1999. ***PRACTICE AREAS:*** Litigation; Appellate Practice; Constitutional Law. ***Email:*** mpapadopoulos@gibsondunn.com

CURTIS E. GANNON, born October 7, 1973; admitted to bar, 1998, Virginia; 2001, District of Columbia. *Education:* Harvard University (A.B., magna cum laude, 1994); University of London, Institute of United States Studies (M.A., with distinction, 1995); University of Chicago (J.D., with honors, 1998). Member, The University of Chicago Law Review, 1996-1998. Law Clerk to Hon. Edith H. Jones, U.S. Court of Appeals, Fifth Circuit, 1998-1999. ***PRACTICE AREAS:*** Appellate Practice. ***Email:*** cgannon@gibsondunn.com

RACHEL A. CLARK, admitted to bar, 2000, California; 2001, District of Columbia. *Education:* Wellesley College (B.A., magna cum laude, 1991); Harvard Law School (J.D., cum laude, 1998). Notes Editor, Harvard Law Review. Winning Team, Harvard Law School Ames Moot Court Competition. Law Clerk, Hon. John T. Noonan, U.S. Court of Appeals, Ninth Circuit. ***PRACTICE AREAS:*** Litigation. ***Email:*** raclark@gibsondunn.com

SCOTT L. CRADDOCK, born August 1, 1972; admitted to bar, 1999, Tennessee; 2001, District of Columbia. *Education:* University of Kentucky (B.A., with high distinction, 1994); Columbia University (J.D., 1998). Harlan Fiske Stone Scholar. Recipient, Thomas Clark Award. *Member:* Nashville, Tennessee and American Bar Associations. ***Email:*** scraddock@gibsondunn.com

JEFFREY W. GLADSTONE, born July 6, 1973; admitted to bar, 1999, New York; 2001, District of Columbia. *Education:* University of Pennsylvania, Wharton School (B.S., 1995); Georgetown University Law Center (J.D., 1998). ***PRACTICE AREAS:*** Corporate Law; Securities. ***Email:*** jgladstone@gibsondunn.com

GREGORY C. GERDES, born April 14, 1972; admitted to bar, 1998, Michigan; 2001, District of Columbia. *Education:* Michigan State University (B.A., 1994); University of Michigan (J.D., cum laude, 1997). Phi Beta Kappa Honor Society. Law Clerk to Judge Evan J. Wallach, U.S. Court of International Trade, New York, N.Y., 1998-2000. ***PRACTICE AREAS:*** International Trade. ***Email:*** ggerdes@gibsondunn.com

HARRY M. GRUBER, born September 18, 1973; admitted to bar, 1999, Maryland; 2001, District of Columbia. *Education:* University of Michigan (B.B.A., 1995); George Washington University Law School (J.D., 1998). Order of the Coif. George Washington Law Review, 1996-1998. Law Clerk: Hon. Roger J. Miner, U.S. Court of Appeals, Second Circuit, 1999-2000; Hon. Thomas A. Flannery, U.S. District Court for the District of Columbia, 1998-1999. ***PRACTICE AREAS:*** Litigation; Appellate Practice. ***Email:*** hgruber@gibsondunn.com

COLIN L. BLACK, born April 10, 1974; admitted to bar, 1999, New York; 2001, District of Columbia. *Education:* Tulane University (B.A., 1996; J.D., 1998). Order of the Coif. Member, 1996-1997, Editor-in-Chief, 1997-1998, Tulane Law Review. Law Clerk: Hon. Juan R. Torruella, U.S. Court of Appeals, First Circuit, 1999-2000; Hon. Royce C. Lamberth, U.S. District Court for the District of Columbia, 1998-1999. ***LANGUAGES:*** Spanish. ***PRACTICE AREAS:*** Appellate Practice; Constitutional Law. ***Email:*** cblack@gibsondunn.com

JOSHUA LIPTON, born May 19, 1972; admitted to bar, 1999, District of Columbia. *Education:* Amherst College (B.A., cum laude, 1994); University of Michigan (J.D., magna cum laude, 1998). Associate Editor, 1996-1997 and Contributing Editor, 1997-1998, Michigan Law Review,. ***PRACTICE AREAS:*** Antitrust. ***Email:*** jlipton@gibsondunn.com

(This Listing Continued)

MICHAEL K. MURPHY, born February 11, 1971; admitted to bar, 1999, Virginia; 2000, District of Columbia. *Education:* Georgetown University (B.S., 1993); University of Edinburgh (M.Sc., 1994); University of Virginia (J.D., 1999). Editor, Virginia Journal of International Law. ***PRACTICE AREAS:*** Government Contracts; Environmental Law. ***Email:*** mmurphy@gibsondunn.com

DANIEL A. CANTU, born October 18, 1961; admitted to bar, 1999, Virginia; 2000, District of Columbia. *Education:* University of California at Berkeley (B.A., 1983); Princeton University (M.P.A., 1986); University of Chicago (J.D., 1999). Law Clerk, Hon. Vanessa Ruiz, District of Columbia Court of Appeals. ***LANGUAGES:*** Spanish. ***PRACTICE AREAS:*** Litigation. ***Email:*** dcantu@gibsondunn.com

LAUREN S. GOODMAN, born June 30, 1975; admitted to bar, 1999, Virginia; 2000, District of Columbia. *Education:* Cornell University (B.S., 1996); Harvard University (J.D., 1999). ***Email:*** lgoodman@gibsondunn.com

BRIAN J. ROHAL, born April 18, 1974; admitted to bar, 1999, Maryland; 2000, District of Columbia. *Education:* University of Notre Dame (B.A., 1996); Duke University (J.D., LL.M., 1999). Articles Editor, Law and Contemporary Problems. ***PRACTICE AREAS:*** International Trade. ***Email:*** brohal@gibsondunn.com

MARK K. MOLLER, born December 19, 1971; admitted to bar, 1999, Virginia (Not admitted in District of Columbia). *Education:* Duke University (B.A., magna cum laude, 1994); University of Chicago (J.D., 1999); University of Cambridge (LL.M., 2000). Staff Member, The University of Chicago Law Review. ***Email:*** mmoller@gibsondunn.com

ANNE H. LEE, born December 12, 1972; admitted to bar, 2000, New York; 2001, District of Columbia. *Education:* University of Michigan (B.A., 1995); University of Pennsylvania Law School (J.D., 1999). ***Email:*** alee@gibsondunn.com

KATHLEEN M. KEDIAN, admitted to bar, 2000, New York; 2001, District of Columbia. *Education:* James Madison University (B.A., 1990); The American University (M.A., 1992); William and Mary School of Law (J.D., 1999). Order of the Coif. Editor-in-Chief, William and Mary Law Review, 1998-1999. Law Clerk to the Honorable David M. Ebel, U.S. Court of Appeals, Tenth Circuit, 1999-2000. ***Email:*** kkedian@gibsondunn.com

NICOLLE SCIARA, born November 27, 1974; admitted to bar, 1999, Texas (Not admitted in District of Columbia). *Education:* University of Texas at Austin (B.A., 1995); University of Pennsylvania (J.D., 1999). Member, University of Pennsylvania Law Review, 1997-1999. Law Clerk to Honorable Jorge Solis, U.S. District Court, Northern District of Texas, 1999-2000. ***Email:*** nsciara@gibsondunn.com

JEFFREY A. WADSWORTH, born November 8, 1972; admitted to bar, 1999, Virginia; 2001, District of Columbia. *Education:* College of William & Mary (B.A., 1995); George Washington University (J.D., 1999). Order of the Coif. Judicial Clerk to the Honorable Judge Karen J. Williams, U.S. Court of Appeals, Fourth Circuit, 1999-2000. Editor-in-Chief, The George Washington Law Review, 1998-1999. ***PRACTICE AREAS:*** Appellate Practice; General Litigation. ***Email:*** jwadsworth@gibsondunn.com

JENNIFER G. LOY, born November 12, 1974; admitted to bar, 2000, Georgia; 2001, Virginia (Not admitted in District of Columbia). *Education:* Yale University (B.A., 1996); Columbia University (J.D., 1999). Kent Scholar, 1998-1999. Executive Editor, Columbia Law Review, 1998-1999. Law Clerk: Hon. Laurence H. Silberman, U.S. Court of Appeals, District of Columbia Circuit, 2000-2001; Hon. J.L. Edmondson, U.S. Court of Appeals, Eleventh Circuit, 1999-2000. ***PRACTICE AREAS:*** Litigation. ***Email:*** jloy@gibsondunn.com

LAUREN ELIZABETH SCHMIDT, born August 13, 1975; admitted to bar, 2001, California (Not admitted in District of Columbia). *Education:* College of William & Mary (B.A., cum laude, 1997); University of Michigan (J.D., 1999). ***PRACTICE AREAS:*** Environmental Law; Litigation. ***Email:*** lschmidt@gibsondunn.com

JASON M. ANTHONY, born October 5, 1970; admitted to bar, 2000, California and District of Columbia. *Education:* University of Maryland (B.A., 1993); University of Southern California (M.P.P., 1997); Georgetown University (J.D., magna cum laude, 2000). ***Email:*** janthony@gibsondunn.com

ELIZABETH A. ISING, born April 27, 1970; admitted to bar, 2000, North Carolina; 2001, District of Columbia. *Education:* James Madison University (B.S., 1992); University of North Carolina at Chapel Hill (J.D., 2000). Order of the Coif. Staff Member, North Carolina Journal of International Law and Commercial Regulation, 1998-2000. ***Email:*** eising@gibsondunn.com

BENJAMIN H. RIPPEON, born November 28, 1974; admitted to bar, 2000, Maryland; 2001, District of Columbia. *Education:* Washington & Lee University (B.S., 1997); Georgetown University Law Center (J.D., cum laude, 2000). ***Email:*** brippeon@gibsondunn.com

(This Listing Continued)

GIBSON, DUNN & CRUTCHER LLP, Washington—Continued

KEVIN M. ST. JOHN, born November 13, 1974; admitted to bar, 2000, Virginia (Not admitted in District of Columbia). *Education:* University of Wisconsin-Madison (B.S., 1997); University of Chicago (J.D., with honors, 2000). ***Email:*** kstjohn@gibsondunn.com

BENJAMIN C. ADAMS, born March 22, 1971; admitted to bar, 2000, Virginia; 2001, District of Columbia. *Education:* George Washington University (B.A., 1994); Georgetown University Law Center (J.D., 2000). Order of the Coif. Georgetown International Environmental Law Review, 1998-2000. ***Email:*** badams@gibsondunn.com

TANYA AXENSON MACALLAIR, born April 15, 1975; admitted to bar, 2001, New York, Massachusetts and District of Columbia. *Education:* Cornell University (B.S., 1997); Harvard University (J.D., 2000). Hewlett Foundation Law and Negotiation Research Fellowship, 1999-2000. Harvard Negotiation Law Review. Law Clerk, Honorable Frederick J. Scullin, Jr., Chief Judge Northern District of New York, 2000-2001. ***Email:*** tmacallair@gibsondunn.com

DAWN FIGUEIRAS, born August 2, 1966; admitted to bar, 2000, Virginia (Not admitted in District of Columbia). *Education:* Virginia Polytechnic Institute (B.A.Ed., 1987); College of William & Mary (J.D., 2000). Order of the Coif. Notes Editor, William & Mary Law Review, 1998-2000. Judicial Clerk, Honorable James T. Turner, U.S. Court of Federal Claims, 2000-2001. ***Email:*** dfigueiras@gibsondunn.com

CORY J. SKOLNICK, born June 6, 1975; admitted to bar, 2000, Virginia (Not admitted in District of Columbia). *Education:* Princeton University (A.B., 1997); Duke University (J.D. and LLM, 2000). Moot Court Board. Member, Duke Law Journal, 1998-2000. Law Clerk, Hon. Eugene E. Siler, Jr. U.S. Court of Appeals, Sixth Circuit, 2000-2001. ***Email:*** cskolnick@gibsondunn.com

STAFF ATTORNEYS

ANDREW A. CLINE, born November 24, 1967; admitted to bar, 1994, New Jersey; 1996, New York; 1999, District of Columbia. *Education:* Columbia University (B.S., 1990); George Washington University (J.D., 1994). ***PRACTICE AREAS:*** Antitrust and Trade Regulation. ***Email:*** acline@gibsondunn.com

DANIELLE K. MOSKOWITZ, born February 17, 1968; admitted to bar, 1995, New York; 1996, District of Columbia. *Education:* McGill University (B.Sc., 1990); University of Pittsburgh at Pittsburgh (J.D., 1994). ***PRACTICE AREAS:*** Antitrust and Trade Regulation. ***Email:*** dmoskowitz@gibsondunn.com

SYDNEY M. SMITH, born January 1, 1952; admitted to bar, 1987, District of Columbia. *Education:* University of California at San Diego (B.A., 1974); George Washington University Law Center (J.D., 1987). ***PRACTICE AREAS:*** Antitrust. ***Email:*** ssmith@gibsondunn.com

(For information on firm personnel, address and telephone information regarding the firm's offices located in Century City, Irvine, Palo Alto and San Francisco, California; Denver, Colorado; New York, N.Y.; Dallas, Texas; Paris, France; London, England, see professional biographies at Los Angeles, California)

GILBERT HEINTZ & RANDOLPH LLP

1350 I STREET, NW
SUITE 200
WASHINGTON, D.C. 20005-3324
Telephone: 202-772-2200
Facsimile: 202-772-3333
URL: http://www.ghrdc.com

Insurance Coverage, Commercial Litigation, Alternative Dispute Resolution.

FIRM PROFILE: Gilbert Heintz & Randolph LLP was formed in January 2001 to provide innovative legal services in complex dispute resolution, insurance coverage negotiation and litigation, strategic corporate risk management and strategic risk management.

MEMBERS OF FIRM

SCOTT D. GILBERT, born New York, N.Y., June 19, 1953; admitted to bar, 1979, District of Columbia; 1980, U.S. Court of Appeals for the District of Columbia Circuit and U.S. District Court for the District of Columbia; 1984, U.S. Court of International Trade; 1987, U.S. Supreme Court. *Education:* Northwestern University (B.A., 1975) Phi Beta Kappa; University of Chicago (J.D., 1979). Recipient, Center for Public Resources Special Award for Excellence and Innovation in Alternative Dispute Resolution, 1985. Founder and Editor, Chicago Forum, 1978-1979. Negotiator and Drafter, The Wellington Agreement. Member, Board of Directors: Asbestos Claims Facility, 1985-1987; District of Columbia Associates of Ben-Gurion University of the Negev, 1996—. Guest Lecturer, University of Michigan Law School and University of Virginia Law School. Expert Witness, in foreign reinsurance disputes re U.S. insurance law. Mediator and Arbitrator in commercial and insurance disputes. *Member:* District of Columbia Bar; American Bar Association (Member, Sections on: Dispute Resolution; Tort and Insurance Practice). ***PRACTICE AREAS:*** Arbitration; Alternative Dispute Resolution; Mediation; Insurance; Products Liability.

JOHN E. HEINTZ, born Bronxville, New York, December 12, 1948; admitted to bar, 1977, District of Columbia; 1978, U.S. District Court, District of Columbia; 1979, U.S. Court of Appeals, D.C. Circuit and U.S. Court of Appeals, 4th Circuit; 1982, U.S. Court of Appeals, Third Circuit and U.S. Court of Appeals, Ninth Circuit; 1997, U.S. Court of Appeals, Second Circuit. *Education:* Cornell University (B.A., 1970); Princeton University - Woodrow Wilson School (M.P.A., 1974); New York University (J.D., 1977). Co-Author: with M. Gallozzi and T. Gillis, "Interpreting the Scope of Coverage for Unexpected Results," 2 Environmental Claims Journal 377 (Spring, 1990); "Strategies for Settling Environmental, Toxic Tort and Other Complex Insurance Coverage Cases," Legal Times, June, 1995. *Member:* The District of Columbia Bar. ***PRACTICE AREAS:*** Insurance Coverage; Commercial Litigation; Torts; Mediation and Arbitration.

DAVID B. KILLALEA, born Alexandria, Virginia, April 1, 1963; admitted to bar, 1988, Virginia; 1989, District of Columbia, U.S. District Court, Eastern District of Virginia and U.S. Court of Appeals, Fourth Circuit; 1992, U.S. District Court, District of Maryland; 1993, U.S. Supreme Court. *Education:* Virginia Tech (B.A., cum laude, 1985); University of Virginia (J.D., 1988). Executive Editor, Journal of Law and Politics, 1987-1988. Lecturer, Business Law, Certified Benefits Specialist Program, 1989-1991. *Member:* District of Columbia Bar. ***PRACTICE AREAS:*** Alternative Dispute Resolution; Commercial Litigation; Insurance Coverage Litigation.

RACHEL S. KRONOWITZ, born Savannah, Georgia, July 8, 1960; admitted to bar, 1988, New York and District of Columbia. *Education:* Smith College (B.A., cum laude, 1982); Columbia University (M.A., 1984); Harvard University (J.D., cum laude, 1987). Comments Editor, Harvard Civil Rights-Civil Liberties Law Review, 1987-1988. *Member:* District of Columbia Bar. ***PRACTICE AREAS:*** Alternative Dispute Resolution; Insurance Coverage Law.

CRAIG J. LITHERLAND, born Beaumont, Texas, March 13, 1959; admitted to bar, 1983, Texas, (Not admitted in District of Columbia). *Education:* Rice University (B.A., 1980); University of Texas (J.D., 1983). *Member:* State Bar of Texas; American Bar Association (Member, Section of Litigation and Business Law; Current Chair, Bankruptcy Subcommittee of the Commercial and Banking Committee, Litigation Section). (Resident, Austin Office). ***PRACTICE AREAS:*** Bankruptcy Law; Insolvency; Complex Commercial Litigation.

RICHARD D. MILONE, JR., born New York, N.Y., September 5, 1965; admitted to bar, 1992, New York; 1993, District of Columbia. *Education:* University of Notre Dame (B.A., 1987); Georgetown University (J.D., cum laude, 1990). Staff Member, 1988-1989 and Writing Program Director, 1989-1990, Journal of Law & Policy in International Business. Law Clerk, Hon. John T. Nixon, U.S. District Court, Nashville, Tennessee, 1990-1991. *Member:* New York State Bar Association; District of Columbia Bar. ***PRACTICE AREAS:*** Insurance Coverage; Antitrust; Commercial Litigation.

BETTE M. ORR, born Deadwood, South Dakota, October 17, 1943; admitted to bar, 1989, District of Columbia. *Education:* Dunbarton College (B.A., 1974); Yale University (J.D., 1989). Articles Editor, Yale Law and Policy Review, 1988-1989. *Member:* District of Columbia Bar. ***PRACTICE AREAS:*** Alternative Dispute Resolution; Insurance.

MARK A. PACKMAN, born Washington, D.C., November 30, 1955; admitted to bar, 1980, District of Columbia. *Education:* Princeton University (A.B., cum laude, 1977); Georgetown University (J.D., 1980). Editor, Georgetown Law Journal, 1979-1980. Author: "That's Some Catch, That Catch-22: Resolving the Conflict Between the Voting Rights Act and the Equal Protection Clause," *Census 2000: Considerations and Strategies for State and Local Government,* American Bar Association, 2000. Co-Author: "Amended Section of the Voting Rights Act: What Is the Intent of the Results Test?" 36 Emory L.J. 1 (1987); "Settlement of Securities Litigation Through the Issuance of Securities Without Registration," 50 Fordham Law Review 533 (1982). *Member:* The District of Columbia Bar; American Bar Association (Vice Chair, Government Operation Committee, 1990-1992, Section of Urban, State and Local Government Law). ***PRACTICE AREAS:*** Election Law; Litigation; RICO; Securities Law; White Collar Criminal Defense; Insurance Coverage.

JEROME C. RANDOLPH, born Cincinnati, Ohio, March 21, 1948; admitted to bar, 1974, U.S. Court of Appeals, Seventh Circuit; 1978, Ohio and U.S. Supreme Court; 1983, U.S. District Court, Southern District of Ohio and Eastern District of Kentucky; 1985, U.S. Court of Appeals, Sixth Circuit (Not admitted in District of Columbia). *Education:* Xavier University (B.A., 1970); University of Chicago (J.D., 1973). Member, U.S. Attorney's Office, Chicago, Illinois, 1974-1978. *Member:* Cincinnati, Ohio State and American Bar Associations. ***PRACTICE AREAS:*** Litigation; Insurance Coverage.

(This Listing Continued)

RICHARD D. SHORE, born San Francisco, California, January 23, 1961; admitted to bar, 1988, New York; 1989, District of Columbia. *Education:* University of Maryland (B.A., Phi Beta Kappa, 1984); Columbia University (J.D., Harlan Fiske Stone Scholar, 1987); Keio University, Tokyo (Monbusho Scholar, 1987-1988). Co-Author: "The Trigger of Coverage Under CGL Policies," Insurance Coverage Litigation '93: Critical Issues and Strategy. *Member:* District of Columbia Bar. ***PRACTICE AREAS:*** Insurance Coverage; Alternative Dispute Resolution; Election Law; International Trade.

GARY THOMPSON, born Cheverly, Maryland, July 2, 1965; admitted to bar, 1991, New York; 1992, District of Columbia; 1993, U.S. District Court, District of Columbia and U.S. Court of Appeals, District of Columbia Circuit. *Education:* Georgetown University (B.A., cum laude, 1987); Rutgers University Law School (J.D., 1990). Senior Articles Editor, Rutgers University Law Review, 1989-1990. Author: "The Rooker-Feldman Doctrine and The Subject Matter Jurisdiction of Federal District Courts," 42 Rutgers Law Review 859 (1990). *Member:* District of Columbia Bar; American Bar Association. ***PRACTICE AREAS:*** Commercial Litigation; Insurance Coverage; Antitrust.

ASSOCIATES

JENNIFER A. BRENNAN, born Minneapolis, Minnesota, December 11, 1971; admitted to bar, 1999, Maryland (Not admitted in District of Columbia). *Education:* Carleton College (B.A., cum laude, 1994); American University (J.D., summa cum laude, 1999). Member, 1997-1998, Associate Managing Editor, 1998-1999, American University Law Review. *Member:* Maryland State and American Bar Associations. ***PRACTICE AREAS:*** Complex Dispute Resolution; Insurance Coverage.

BARRY I. BUCHMAN, born New York, N. Y., September 6, 1971; admitted to bar, 1997, Maryland; 1998, District of Columbia; 1999, Virginia. *Education:* Indiana University (B.A. with Distinction, 1994); Washington College of Law at American University (J.D., summa cum laude, 1997). Author: "Case Note: Northeast Erectors Association v Secretary of Labor," 49 Admn. L. Review 199. *Member:* Maryland State Bar Association; Association of Trial Lawyers of America; Trial Lawyers Association of Metropolitan Washington, D.C. (Chairman, Young Lawyers Division). ***PRACTICE AREAS:*** Insurance Coverage; Personal Injury; Automobile Negligence; Premises Liability; Litigation.

JONATHAN M. COHEN, born Park Ridge, Illinois, March 21, 1968; admitted to bar, 1997, Maryland and District of Columbia; U.S. Supreme Court; U.S. Court of Appeals, Fourth and Ninth Circuit. *Education:* University of Chicago (B.A./M.A., 1989; Ph.D., 1997); Boalt Hall School of Law, University of California, Berkeley (J.D., 1995). Editor-in-Chief, International Tax and Business Lawyer, 1994-1995. Law Clerk, Judge F. Fernandez, U.S. Court of Appeals, Ninth Circuit, 195-1996. *Member:* District of Columbia Bar. ***PRACTICE AREAS:*** Complex Dispute Resolution.

ELIZABETH H. FEINBERG, born Middletown, New York, July 27, 1971; admitted to bar, 1998, New York and Maryland; 2000, District of Columbia. *Education:* State University of New York at Albany (B.A., B.S., 1993); American University Law School (J.D., 1997). *Member:* District of Columbia Bar. ***PRACTICE AREAS:*** General Litigation; Insurance.

TED J. FELDMAN, born New Hyde Park, New York, April 12, 1966; admitted to bar, 1993, New York and U.S. District Court, Southern and Eastern Districts of New York; 1999, District of Columbia. *Education:* State University of New York at Binghamton (B.A., 1988); Hofstra University (J.D., 1992). Associate Editor, Hofstra Law Review, 1991-1992. Author: "An Examination of the Right to Jury Trial Where Copyright Statutory Damages are Elected," 21 Hofstra Law Review 261, 1002. *Member:* District of Columbia Bar; American Bar Association. ***PRACTICE AREAS:*** Complex Dispute Resolution.

ERIN ELIZABETH JOHNSON, born Dallas, Texas, March 11, 1975; admitted to bar, 1999, Texas (Not admitted in District of Columbia). *Education:* University of Georgia (B.A., cum laude, 1996); Georgetown University Law Center (J.D., cum laude, 1999). Student Attorney, Georgetown Criminal Justice Clinic, 1998-1999. *Member:* State Bar of Texas. ***PRACTICE AREAS:*** Commercial Litigation; Insurance Coverage.

AARON R. LANCASTER, born Champaign, Illinois, October 8, 1973; (admission pending). *Education:* George Washington University (B.A., 1995); University of Illinois (J.D., magna cum laude, 2000). ***PRACTICE AREAS:*** Insurance Coverage.

RICHARD D. MARTINDALE, born Aberdeen, Maryland, June 26, 1970; admitted to bar, 1995, Texas; 1998, Virginia, U.S. District Court, Northern District of Texas and U.S. District Court, Eastern District of Virginia; 1999, U.S. Court of Appeals, Fifth Circuit (Not admitted in District of Columbia). *Education:* Vanderbilt University (B.A., 1992); Washington University in St. Louis (J.D., 1995). Phi Delta Phi. Regional Champion, National Mock Trial Competition, 1995; National Quarterfinalist, National Mock Trial Competition, 1995. Recipient: Lewis F. Powell, Jr. Medal for Excellence in Advocacy, American College of Trial Lawyers, 1995; William Pomerantz Trial Prize for Excellence in Advocacy, 1995. Assistant District Attorney, Harris County, Texas, 1995-1998.

(This Listing Continued)

Member: Federal and American Bar Associations; State Bar of Texas; Virginia State Bar. ***PRACTICE AREAS:*** Complex Dispute Resolution; Commercial Litigation; Insurance Litigation.

KAMI QUINN, born Platteville, Wisconsin, June 18, 1975; (admission pending). *Education:* Drake University (B.A., 1996); University of Chicago (J.D., 2000). ***PRACTICE AREAS:*** Insurance Coverage; Insurance Insolvency.

JAY R. RAMAN, born Oak Ridge, Tennessee, November 18, 1975; (admission pending). *Education:* University of Tennessee at Knoxville (B.A., 1997); Harvard University (J.D., 2000). ***PRACTICE AREAS:*** Insurance Coverage; Litigation.

GLENN SCHLACTUS, born Brooklyn, New York, August 15, 1968; admitted to bar, 2000, California (Not admitted in District of Columbia). *Education:* Goergetown University (A.B., 1990; J.D., cum laude, 1998). Law Clerk for Judge Patricia Wald, U.S. Court of Appeals for the District of Columbia Circuit. ***PRACTICE AREAS:*** Litigation; Insurance Coverage.

LARA HOPE SCHWARTZ, born Rockville Centre, New York, December 24, 1971; admitted to bar, 1999, Maryland; 2000, District of Columbia. *Education:* Brown University (A.B., 1993); Harvard University (J.D., 1998). Phi Betta Kappa. Law Clerk, Judge Ronald Lee Gilman, U.S. Court of Appeals, Sixth Circuit, 1998-1999. *Member:* District of Coulmbia Bar. ***PRACTICE AREAS:*** Litigation; Insurance Coverage.

DIVONNE SMOYER, born Dugway, Utah, March 13, 1970; admitted to bar, 1996, New York; 1997, District of Columbia. *Education:* Smith College (A.B., summa cum laude, Phi Beta Kappa, 1992); Harvard University (J.D., cum laude, 1995). Phi Beta Kappa. Adjunct Professor: Negotiation and Alternative Dispute Resolution, Georgetown University Law Center, 1998; George Washington University Law School, 1998-2000. *Member:* District of Columbia Bar. ***PRACTICE AREAS:*** Alternative Dispute Resolution; Litigation; Insurance.

JASON D. WALLACH, born Dayton, Ohio, May 12, 1968; admitted to bar, 1996, Maryland; 1997, District of Columbia. *Education:* Hiram College (B.A., cum laude, 1990); George Washington University (J.D., with high honors, 1996). Order of the Coif. *Member:* District of Columbia Bar. ***PRACTICE AREAS:*** Litigation; Insurance.

GILMAN & ASSOCIATES

Established in 1980

600 PENNSYLVANIA AVENUE S.E., SUITE 410

WASHINGTON, D.C. 20003

Telephone: 202-547-9080

Fax: 202-547-8944

Email: ndgilman@aol.com

URL: http://www.lawyers.com/gilmanairlaw

McLean, Virginia Office: Suite 1070, 8180 Greensboro Drive. Telephone: 703-356-5070. Fax: 703-356-5085.

Aviation Law, Airplane Crash Litigation, Aviation Accidents, Automobile, Maritime, Railroad and other Transportation Litigation. Medical Malpractice, Product Liability, Negligence, Insurance and International Law. Civil, Criminal and Administrative Trials and Appeals in all Courts, including Multi-national and Multi-District Tort Disasters, U.S. and Foreign Personal Injuries and Wrongful Deaths.

FIRM PROFILE: Since 1980 Gilman & Associates and its predecessors have handled aviation trials and appeals with an emphasis on negligence and products liability in foreign and domestic aviation accidents. The firm routinely handles other litigation including foreign and domestic auto, rail, and maritime/admiralty as well as general negligence, toxic tort, and products liability matters.

MEMBERS OF FIRM

NICHOLAS GILMAN, born Elizabeth, New Jersey, June 8, 1938; admitted to bar, 1972, Pennsylvania; 1973, District of Columbia; 1982, Maryland; U.S. Supreme Court, U.S. Court of Appeals, 2nd, 3rd, 4th, 5th, 7th, 10th, Federal and District of Columbia Circuits and U.S. Claims Court;. *Education:* Stanford University (B.A., 1960); Sorbonne, Paris, France; Columbia University (M.A., 1968); University of Madrid, Spain; George Washington University (J.D., with honors, 1971). Sigma Delta Pi. Commercial Pilot Certificate, Single, Multi-engine Land and Instrument Ratings, 1965. Author: "Significant Recent Legislative Developments for the Air Law Practitioner," 46 Journal of Air Law and Commerce 877, 1981; "F.O.I.A. as a Discovery Tool in Aviation Product Liability Litigation," The Law of Aviation Symposium, Federal Aviation Administration, 1981; "Problems Relating to Jurisdiction and Forum Non Conveniens," 28 Trial Lawyer's Guide 150, 1984; "Preparation of an Aviation Damages Trial," Litigating the Aviation Case, ABA (TIPS) 1987; "What is Sufficient Proof of Wilful Misconduct for Air Carrier Liability Under the Warsaw Convention in a Terrorist Case," 3 ALB. L.J.S.&T. 217 (1993). Law Clerk, Judge John Biggs, Jr., Circuit Judge, U.S. Court of Appeals, Third Circuit, 1971-1972. Assistant U.S. Attorney, District of Columbia, 1972-1976. Aviation Trial Attorney, U.S. Department of Justice, 1976-1979. *Member:* Maryland State, Federal

(This Listing Continued)

GILMAN & ASSOCIATES, Washington—Continued

and American Bar Associations (Sections on: Air and Space; Tort and Insurance Practice; Litigation); Lawyer-Pilots Bar Association; The Association of Trial Lawyers of America; National Transportation Safety Board Bar Association; Washington Trial Lawyers Association. [Flight Duty With U.S. Air Force, 1961-1965; 1968-1969; Capt., New Jersey and District of Columbia Air National Guards, 1965-1968]. ***LANGUAGES:*** French; Spanish. ***PRACTICE AREAS:*** Aviation Law; Aviation Accidents; Airplane Crash Litigation; Aviation Disasters; Aviation Torts; International Aviation; Negligence Law; Products Liability and Medical Malpractice; Multi-District Litigation. ***Email:*** ndgilman@aol.com

JOHN J. CARLINO (1946-1987).

ASSOCIATE

JOHN M. GREEN, born Fresno, California, September 5, 1948; admitted to bar, 1999, Maryland; U.S. District Court, District of Columbia; 2000, U.S District Court, District of Maryland (Not admitted in District of Columbia). *Education:* California State University, Fresno (B.S., 1973); University of Southern California (M.S., 1985); George Washington University (J.D., 1998). Licensed Airline Transport Pilot. *Member:* Montgomery County, Prince Georges County, Maryland State and American Bar Associations. [Captain, U.S. Air Force, 1974-1985]. ***PRACTICE AREAS:*** Aviation Law; Aviation Accidents; Personal Injury; Family Law; Negligence; Product Liability. ***Email:*** jmgreen48@yahoo.com

OF COUNSEL

WILLIAM J. OLSON (Also practicing individually Washington, D.C. and McLean Virginia).

GINGELL & JENKINS, P.C.

WASHINGTON, D.C.

(See Silver Spring, Maryland)

General Trial, Administrative, Appellate Practice. Probate, Estate Planning, Wills, Estate and Gift Taxation, Family Wealth Transfer, Living Trusts, Elder Law, Family Business Successions, Real Estate Litigation, Real Estate Settlements, Construction, Negligence and Personal Injury Law. Automobile Accidents and Injuries, Traffic Law, Corporate, Bankruptcy, Aviation Law, Criminal, Family Law.

GINS & GREENFELD, P.C.

Established in 1980

5028 WISCONSIN AVENUE, N.W., SUITE 300

WASHINGTON, D.C. 20016

Telephone: 202-537-7050

Fax: 202-364-5165

URL: http://www.ginsandgreenfeld.lawoffice.com

Gaithersburg, Maryland Office: Fourth Floor, 806 West Diamond Avenue, 20878 Telephone: 301-258-9777. Fax: 301-670-9026.

Bankruptcy, Reorganization and Commercial Law.

FIRM PROFILE: The attorneys at Gins & Greenfeld, P.C. have been representing debtors and creditors before the Bankruptcy Courts of the District of Columbia, Maryland and Virginia for close to thirty years. The firm is unique in the sense that it is small, but maintains a large presence in the bankruptcy and insolvency community.

The firm's size also allows it to foster long-lasting relationships with its clients, and as a result, the firm continues to provide legal assistance to its clients for many years in other areas of the law and in other State and Federal Courts, including, collection matters, negotiations with taxing authorities, reorganizations, corporate affairs, and general commercial litigation.

RICHARD H. GINS, born Charlotte, North Carolina, July 2, 1942; admitted to bar, 1968, District of Columbia; 1971, Maryland; 1979, U.S. Court of Appeals, Fourth Circuit. *Education:* University of North Carolina (A.B., 1964); George Washington University (J.D., 1967; LL.M., 1969). Phi Delta Phi. Co-Author: "Maryland Mortgage Foreclosures," Professional Education Systems, Inc., 1983. Trial Attorney, Federal Trade Commission, 1967-1968. Assistant Corporation Counsel, Office of the Corporation Counsel, District of Columbia Government, 1968-1972. *Member:* District of Columbia Bar; Bar Association of the District of Columbia (Member: Domestic Relations Committee, 1976-1980; Montgomery County (Chairman, Bankruptcy Section, 1983-1984), Maryland State (Member, Committee on Bankruptcy, 1978—) and American Bar Associations; Bankruptcy Bar Association for the District of Maryland; The Walter Chandler American Inn of Court. ***PRACTICE AREAS:*** Bankruptcy Law; Insolvency Law; General Commercial Law. ***Email:*** rgins@ginsandgreenfeld.lawoffice.com

(This Listing Continued)

STEVEN H. GREENFELD, born Altus AFB, Oklahoma, June 7, 1962; admitted to bar, 1989, Virginia and U.S. District Court, District of Maryland; 1990, Maryland, District of Columbia and U.S. District Court, Eastern District of Virginia. *Education:* Tulane University (B.S.M., 1984); George Mason University (J.D., 1989). Phi Delta Phi. Certified Public Accountant, Maryland, 1987. Author: "Preferential Transfer and Basic Letter of Credit Concepts in U.S. Bankruptcy Cases," Letter of Credit Update, Oct. 1989 and Nov. 1989. Standing Chapter 7 Trustee (Greenbelt, MD). Member, Board of Directors, Bid4Assests, Inc. *Member:* Virginia State Bar; District of Columbia Bar (Chairman, Pro Bono Bankruptcy Clinic); American Bar Association; Montgomery County Chapter (LXI) American Inns of Court; National Association of Bankruptcy Trustees. ***PRACTICE AREAS:*** Bankruptcy Law; Insolvency Law; General Commercial Litigation. ***Email:*** sgreenfeld@ginsandgreenfeld.lawoffice.com

---

MELINDA M. BOLLING, born Asheville, North Carolina, July 13, 1964; admitted to bar, 1998, New Jersey and Maryland; 2000, District of Columbia. *Education:* Georgia Institute of Technology (B.S., 1987); Catholic University (J.D., 1998); University of District of Columbia (M.B.A., 1990). *Member:* National Bar Association; Womens Bar Association; Charlotte E. Ray American Inn of Court; Walter E. Chandler American Inn of Court. ***PRACTICE AREAS:*** Bankruptcy Law; Insolvency Law; Commercial Litigation.

PETER R. GINSBERG, P.C.

Established in 1998

SUITE 600

1201 CONNECTICUT AVENUE, N.W.

WASHINGTON, D.C. 20036

Telephone: 202-293-1410

Fax: 202-293-1484

URL: http://www.lawyers.com/pginsberglaw

White Collar Criminal Defense, Complex Commercial Litigation, Sports Law, Appellate Practice, Business Fraud.

PETER R. GINSBERG, born Cleveland, Ohio, June 24, 1953; admitted to bar, 1981, Vermont, New York and U.S. District Court, Eastern and Southern Districts of New York; 1986, U.S. Court of Appeals, Second Circuit; 1996, District of Columbia; 1997, U.S. District Court for the District of Columbia; 1999, U.S. Court of Appeals, Fifth and District of Columbia Circuits; 2000, U.S. District Court, Western District of New York; and U.S. Court of Appeals, Third Circuit. *Education:* University of Pennsylvania (B.A., 1976); London School of Economics and Political Science (M.S.C., 1977); Columbia University (J.D., 1980). Thouron Fellow. Recipient, U.S. Attorney General's John Marshall Award, 1992. Assistant U.S. Attorney, Eastern District of New York, 1985-1992. Of Counsel to Moskowitz & Book, New York, New York. ***PRACTICE AREAS:*** White Collar Criminal Defense; Securities; Commercial Litigation; Sports Law. ***Email:*** prginsberg@erols.com

---

MICHELE Y. SIMS, born Mt Vernon, New York, January 12, 1970; (admission pending). *Education:* Wellesley College (B.A., 1996); University of Iowa, College of Law (J.D., 1999).

GKRSE

Established in 1993

1500 K STREET, N.W., SUITE 330

WASHINGTON, D.C. 20005

Telephone: 202-408-5400

Telecopier: 202-408-5406

Email: gkrse@gkrse-law.com

URL: http://www.gkrse-law.com

Energy, Administrative, Litigation, Environmental Law. General Practice before Administrative Agencies, Government Departments and Federal Appellate Courts and Congress.

MEMBERS OF FIRM

ELISA J. GRAMMER, born Dover, New Jersey, February 5, 1952; admitted to bar, 1976, Virginia and District of Columbia; 1983, U.S. Supreme Court and U.S. Court of Appeals, District of Columbia and Fifth Circuits. *Education:* Lafayette College (A.B., summa cum laude, 1973); College of William and Mary (J.D., 1976); George Washington University (LL.M., Energy and Environmental Law, with highest honors, 1980). Phi Beta Kappa; Phi Alpha Theta.

(This Listing Continued)

Author: "Back to Basics in Natural Gas & Electric: Who Should Be Regulated and Why?" CCH Power & Telecom Law, Sep/Oct., 1998; "The Legal Edge," Petroleum Management, monthly column, 1987-1991; "Water Wars-Federal and State Roles in Hydroelectric Licensing and Relicensing," Hydro Review, June 1989; "Environmental Issues in Gas Distribution and Transmission," Natural Gas Lawyer's Journal, 1989; "State Regulation of Gas Purchasing: Back to the Future or New Horizons," Petroleum Management, Nov./Dec., 1988." Attorney, Economic Regulatory Administration, U.S. Department of Energy, 1980; Office of Executive Legal Director, U.S. Nuclear Regulatory Commission, 1978-1980; Office of General Counsel, U.S. General Accounting Office, 1976-1978. *Member:* District of Columbia Bar; Virginia, Federal and American Bar Associations; Energy Bar Association. ***PRACTICE AREAS:*** Administrative Law; Environmental Law; Oil and Gas; Natural Gas. ***Email:*** ejgrammer@gkrse-law.com

PETER C. KISSEL, born Watertown, New York, September 29, 1947; admitted to bar, 1973, District of Columbia; 1976, U.S. Claims Court; 1978, U.S. Supreme Court; 1979, U.S. District Court, District of Columbia and U.S. Court of Appeals, Ninth Circuit; 1983, U.S. Court of Appeals, District of Columbia Circuit; 1986, U.S. Court of Appeals, Third Circuit; 1988, U.S. Court of Appeals, Fifth Circuit. *Education:* Syracuse University (B.A., 1969); American University (J.D., 1972). Author: "Electric and Magnetic Fields: Responding to the Real Issues", Hydro Review, Vol. XVl, No. 7, December, 1997; "Reinforcing the Soundness of FERC'S Hydro Licensing Process," Hydro Review, Vol. XI, No. 2, April 1992; "New Licensing Rules Emphasize Pre-Filling Responsibilities," Hydro Review, Vol. VIII, No. 4, Aug. 1989; "The New Environmental Requirements of ECPA," Alternative Sources of Energy Magazine, January, 1988; "Relicensing and Project Renewal: Environmental Issues Are Key," Hydro Review Vol. IV, No. 1, Spring 1985; "Availability and Use of Discovery at the Federal Energy Regulatory Commission: The Need for Modernization," 2 Energy Law Journal 79, 1981. Business Manager, Energy Law Journal, 1989-1992. Trial Attorney, Office of the General Counsel, Federal Power Commission, 1973-1977. *Member:* District of Columbia Bar; Federal Energy Bar Association; Electric Cooperative Bar Association. ***PRACTICE AREAS:*** Utility Regulation; Hydroelectricity; Natural Gas Regulation; Administrative Law; Appellate Practice; Legislative. ***Email:*** pckissel@gkrse-law.com

ALAN I. ROBBINS, born New York, New York, February 4, 1953; admitted to bar, 1978, District of Columbia; 1985, U.S. Supreme Court; 1986, New York. *Education:* State University of New York at Albany (B.A., magna cum laude, 1975); George Washington University (J.D., with honors, 1978). Phi Beta Kappa. Co-Author: "Legal Implications of Electric Utility Restructuring and Deregulation for Local Governments," Municipal Lawyer, Vol. 40, No. 1, Jan/Feb. 1999; "Municipalities May Now Regulate Cable Television Rates," Cities & Villages, Vol. XXXXI, No. 4, Apr. 1993; "Overcoming Anti-Hydro Policies in the Ohio River Basin," Hydro Review, Vol. X, No. 1, February 1991; "Federal Electric Preference Power Marketing in the 1980's: Developing Legal Trends," 4 Energy Law Journal 1, 1983. *Member:* New York State (non resident) and American Bar Associations; Energy Bar Association; American Public Power Association. ***PRACTICE AREAS:*** Electric Utilities; Electric Power; Municipal Law; Utilities; Electric Utility Regulation. ***Email:*** airobbins@gkrse-law.com

NANCY J. SKANCKE, born Gary, Indiana, March 24, 1950; admitted to bar, 1975, Virginia and District of Columbia; 1988, U.S. Supreme Court, U.S. Court of Appeals for the District of Columbia, Fifth and Eleventh Circuits and U.S. Court of Federal Claims. *Education:* Purdue University (B.S., with honors, 1972); George Washington University (J.D., with honors, 1975). Author: "Electric and Gas Municipal Franchises: In An Age of Industry Restructuring," Municipal Lawyer, March/April 1996; "Federal Regulatory Actions Affecting Royalties," Buying and Selling Gas: A Practical Guide for Operators and Royalty Owners, Exec. Enter., 1990. Fellow, American Bar Foundation, 1993—. Master of the Bench, The Prettyman-Leventhal American Inn of Court (President, 1992-1993). Chair, DC Metro Council, American Inns of Court, 1993-1996. *Member:* District of Columbia Bar; Virginia State Bar; American Bar Association (Member, Sections on: Administrative and Regulatory Practice; Natural Resources, Energy and Environmental Law; Vice-Chair, Ad Hoc Comm. on Review of Recruitment of ALJ's); Energy Bar Association (Member: Board of Directors, 1985-1988; Board of Directors of Foundation of the Energy Law Journal, 1986-1989, 1998-2001; Chair, Various Committees). ***PRACTICE AREAS:*** Energy Law; Commercial Law; Natural Gas Regulations; Hydroelectric Licensing; Public Utilities Regulation; Administrative Law. ***Email:*** njskancke@gkrse-law.com

KATHERINE B. EDWARDS, born Washington, D.C., April 18, 1947; admitted to bar, 1981, District of Columbia. *Education:* Randolph-Macon Woman's College (B.A., with honors, 1969); Memphis State University (M.A., with highest honors, 1972); University of Texas (J.D., 1980). Member, Texas Law Review, 1978-1980. Author: "Judicial Review of Federal Environmental Decisionmaking: NRC Regulation of Nuclear Waste Management & Disposal," Texas Law Review, February 1980; "Annual Natural Gas Report," American Bar Association, 1992-1996; "Negotiated Recourse Rate Alternative-A Giant Step Backward," Natural Gas, May 1996; "Natural Gas Forum Interview," Public Utilities Fortnightly, October 15, 1996; "Negotiated Terms and Conditions of Service-A Proposal in Search of a Justification," Infrastructure, Winter 1999. Fellow, American Bar Foundation, 2000. *Member:* District of Columbia Bar; American Bar Association (Chair, Natural Gas Committee, 1993-1996; Chair of Section of Public Utility, Communication and Transportation Law, 1999-2000); Energy Bar Association (Co-Chair, Program Committee, 1997-1998). ***PRACTICE AREAS:*** Energy Law; Natural Gas Pipelines; Public Utilities Regulation; Administrative Law. ***Email:*** kbedwards@gkrse-law.com

DONALD H. CLARKE, born Everett, Washington, May 13, 1949; admitted to bar, 1975, New York; 1977, District of Columbia. *Education:* Stanford University (A.B., 1971); University of Hamburg; Cornell University (J.D., 1974). Author: "The Hydropower Development Boom: A Legal Perspective," Federal Bar News & Journal, 1982; "FERC Licensing: Taking Steps in the Right Direction," Hydro Review, June, 1990; "Hydropower into the Mainstream: A View from the Potomac," Hydro Review, April, 1992; "Relicensing Hydropower: The Many Faces of Competition," Natural Resources & Environment, Vol. 11, No. 2, Fall, 1996. Senior Legal Advisor to the Chairman, Federal Energy Regulation Commission, 1988-1989. Legal Advisor to Commissioner Naeve, FERC, 1986-1988. Deputy Assistant General Counsel, FERC, 1983-1985. Washington D.C. Representative for Northwest Hydroelectric Association; General Counsel, National Hydropower Association. Executive Director, U.S. Hydropower Council for International Development. *Member:* The District of Columbia Bar; New York State and American Bar Associations. ***LANGUAGES:*** German and French. ***PRACTICE AREAS:*** Energy; Natural Resources; International; Environmental. ***Email:*** dhclarke@gkrse-law.com

ASSOCIATES

ELIZABETH TEUWEN, born Waltham, Massachusetts, November 5, 1971; admitted to bar, 1999, Massachusetts (Not admitted in District of Columbia). *Education:* College of the Holy Cross (B.A., 1993); Georgetown University (J.D., 1999). Notes and Articles Editor, Law and Policy in International Business Law, Georgetown University Law Review, 1998-1999. ***PRACTICE AREAS:*** Energy; Administrative Law. ***Email:*** ebteuwen@gkrse-law.com

JOHN P. FLOOM, born Mission Viejo, California, August 10, 1974; admitted to bar, 1999, Virginia (Not admitted in District of Columbia). *Education:* University of North Carolina at Chapel Hill (B.A., 1996); Boston University (J.D., 1999). Managing Editor, Boston University Public Interest Law Journal, 1998-1999. *Member:* Energy Bar Association. ***LANGUAGES:*** French. ***PRACTICE AREAS:*** Energy. ***Email:*** jpfloom@gkrse-law.com

GLASSMAN & BULLOCK

1111 19TH STREET, N.W.
SUITE 1200
WASHINGTON, D.C. 20036-3603
Telephone: 202-452-0000
Fax: 202-835-9846
Email: gblawdc@erols.com
URL: http://www.lawyers.com/glassman&bullock

Vienna, Virginia Office: 1950 Old Gallows Road, Suite 700, Tysons Corner. Telephone: 703-902-9500. Fax: 703-902-9501. Email: gblaw@erols.com

Laytonsville, Maryland Office: 5515 Riggs Road. Telephone: 301-670-9200. Fax: 301-670-9246. Email: gblaw@erols.com

Elder Law, Commercial Transactions and Litigation; Civil Trial Law. Military Law. Veterinary and Equine Law; Family Law (including Military Divorce and International Custody Law). Probate, Estate Planning and Administration; Legal and Medical Malpractice; Tax Controversies, Employment Law; General Counsel Services.

MEMBERS OF FIRM

STEPHEN C. GLASSMAN, born New York, N.Y., July 20, 1942; admitted to bar, 1967, Virginia and U.S. Court of Appeals, Seventh Circuit; 1970, District of Columbia and U.S. Court of Military Appeals; 1972, U.S. Court of Appeals, Fourth Circuit; 1978, Maryland; 1980, U.S. Court of Appeals for the District of Columbia; 1983, New York; 1989, U.S. Court of Appeals, Ninth Circuit. *Education:* American University (B.A., 1964); Georgetown University (J.D., 1967); George Washington University. Phi Alpha Delta. Author: "The Tangled International Divorce Web," Family Advocate, Spring, 1987; "From Civil Servants to Soldiers," Family Advocate, Fall, 1990; "Legal Assistance," MacMillan: International Military and Defense Encyclopedia, 1992. Professorial Lecturer, American University, 1971-1972. Partner, Bonner & O'Connell, 1985-1994. Of Counsel, Lane and Edson, P.C., 1974-1976. Attorney, Department of Justice, Lands and Natural Resources Division, 1967-1968. *Member:* The District of Columbia Bar (Member, Military Law Committee, 1976—); Bar Association of the District of Columbia (Vice Chairman, Military Law Committee, 1977—); Fairfax, Maryland State, American and Federal Bar Associations; Virginia State Bar (Founder and Former Chairman, Military Law Committee, 1981-1992).

(This Listing Continued)

GLASSMAN & BULLOCK, Washington—Continued

[CAPT, United States Navy Reserves (RST), JAGC, 1967—; Reserve Military Law Judge, 1990-1995]. (Also at Vienna, Virginia and Laytonsville, Maryland Offices). ***PRACTICE AREAS:*** Military Law. ***Email:*** gblaw@erols.com

ROBERT S. BULLOCK, born Brookline, Massachusetts, August 27, 1946; admitted to bar, 1972, District of Columbia; 1976, Virginia. *Education:* Lafayette College (B.A., with honors, 1968); University of Pennsylvania (J.D., 1971). Recipient: ARC-Riggs Bank Educational Leadership Award (1998). Student Intern, Center for Law and Social Policy, Washington, D.C., 1970-1971. Staff Attorney, Center for Auto Safety, Washington, D.C., 1971-1972. Managing Attorney, Courts Office, Neighborhood Legal Services Program, Washington, D.C., 1973-1975. Associate, Law Offices of Stanley B. Frosh, 1975-1977. Associate, Goldstein, Ahalt, Glassman & Bennett, 1978-1979. Managing Partner, Heller, Temple, Boraks & Bullock, 1989-1992. Member: Alexandria Advisory Committee on Special Education, 1981-1993 (Chairperson, 1986-1987 and 1990-1992); Citizens Regional Planning Advisory Committee, 1988-1989; Alexandria Baseball, Inc., 1996-1999, (Director and Vice President, 1996-1999); Gonzaga Baseball Boosters (President, 2001). *Member:* The District of Columbia Bar; Virginia State Bar; National Academy of Elder Law Attorneys. ***PRACTICE AREAS:*** Elder Law; Estate Planning; Administrative Law. ***Email:*** gblawdc@erols.com

GLEASON, FLYNN, EMIG & FOGLEMAN

CHARTERED

WASHINGTON, D.C.

(See Rockville, Maryland)

Plaintiff and Defense Litigation, Medical Malpractice, Products Liability, Employment Law, Workers Compensation, Auto Tort, Insurance Defense, Construction Litigation, Criminal Law, Health Care Law, Banking, Commercial Litigation, Collections and Foreclosures.

THE GOLD GROUP

CHARTERED

1319 F STREET, N.W.

SUITE 1000

WASHINGTON, D.C. 20004

Telephone: 202-347-5542; 301-963-1148

Telefax: 202-628-1258; 301-963-1168

Antitrust, Trade Regulations, General Legislative and Merchant Banking Services.

FIRM PROFILE: The Gold Group provides experienced counselling in the areas of Legislative, Regulatory and Antitrust Law. The firm also provides Merchant Banking Service, Representing major investment banks and Hedge funds both nationally and internationally.

PETER F. GOLD, born New York, N.Y., November 10, 1945; admitted to bar, 1972, New York; 1973, U.S. District Court, Southern and Eastern Districts of New York; 1988, District of Columbia. *Education:* Cornell University (A.B., 1967); London School of Economics, England (M.Sc. Economics, 1968); New York University (J.D., 1971). Editor in Chief, Review of Law and Social Change, 1968-1969. Legislative Director, U.S. Senator Gary Hart, 1975-1981. Director of Policy, Hart for President Campaign, 1984. Clinton-Gore Transition Team Member, 1992-1993. Partner and Co-Founder, Washington Office, Winthrop, Stimson, Putnam and Roberts, 1984-1994. President, C.B. Sloan & Co. Auctioneers. Co-Founder and Chairman, First Book. Director, Share Our Strength. Senior Advisor, Pace Financial Network. *Member:* The District of Columbia Bar; The Association of the Bar of the City of New York; Federal Bar Association. ***Email:*** pfg2000@aol.com

GOLD MORRISON & LAUGHLIN PC

Established in 1984

1200 G STREET, N.W., SUITE 800

WASHINGTON, D.C. 20003

Telephone: 703-836-7004

Email: info@goldmorrison.com

URL: http://www.goldmorrison.com

Tysons Corner, Virginia Office: 1660 International Drive, Suite 450, Telephone: 703-836-7004. Facsimile: 703-548-9430.

Alexandria, Virginia Office: 1800 Diagonal Road, Suite 600. 22314-2808.

Restructures, Insolvency, Bankruptcy, Creditors' Rights, Foreclosures, Banking Law, Federal Court Litigation.

(This Listing Continued)

FIRM PROFILE: Gold Morrison & Laughlin PC, is one of the leading independent creditors' rights and bankruptcy, restructure and insolvency law, practices in the Washington, D.C. Metropolitan area. The firm primarily represents clients on various sides of complex financial restructures, bankruptcy and reorganization proceedings, credit recovery litigation, foreclosures and the purchase and sale of distressed companies and assets. In its areas of practice the firm has resources and capabilities matched only by the largest of area firms.

(For Complete Biographical Data on all Personnel, see Professional Biographies at Tysons Corner, Virginia)

JOEL J. GOLDBERG

1050 17TH STREET, N.W.

SUITE 1200

WASHINGTON, D.C. 20036

Telephone: 202-822-4668

Fax: 202-822-4676

Email: jgoldlaw@worldnet.att.net

URL: http://www.lawyers.com/joelgoldberglaw

Commercial Real Estate, Real Estate Finance, Leasing, Landlord and Tenant Law, Commercial Transactions, Corporate Law, Commercial Law.

FIRM PROFILE: Offering over 15 years experience, the firm represents developers, lenders, investors, tenants, entrepreneurs, institutions, buyers and sellers in the negotiating and structuring of a wide variety of real estate and others commercial business transactions.

JOEL J. GOLDBERG, born Philadelphia, Pennsylvania, September 22, 1953; admitted to bar, 1983, Pennsylvania; 1987, District of Columbia; 1994, Virginia; 1995, Maryland. *Education:* Rutgers University (B.A., high honors and distinction in Pol. Sc., 1975); University of Michigan (M.P.P., 1977; J.D., 1982). Research and Development Editor, University of Michigan Journal of Law Reform, 1982-1983. Co-Author: "The Ten Major Mistakes Most Often Made By Tenants in the Negotiation of Office Leases," The Commercial Real Estate Tenant's Handbook, 1987. Primary Contributor and Co-Editor: "Commercial Tenant's Transactions Guide (Forms and Strategies)," 1991. Co-Author: "Work Letter," Construction Renovation Formbook, Wiley Law Publications, 1991; "Opinion Letters in Real Estate Transactions," Negotiating and Structuring Real Estate Transactions, 2nd ed., 1993; "Lease Term Extension Options and Expansion Options," American Conference Institute, November, 1996; "Percentage Rent," November, 1995; "Subordination," November, 1995; "Declarations of Covenants, Conditions and Restrictions," ABA Section of Real Property, Probate and Trust Law 8th Annual Spring CLE and Committee Meeting, 1997. *Member:* Philadelphia, Pennsylvania, Maryland State, Virginia State, and American Bar Associations; District of Columbia Bar.

GOLDBERG & FINNEGAN, LLC

WASHINGTON, D.C.

(See Silver Spring, Maryland)

Personal Injury, Product Liability, Automobile Accidents, Internet Law, Contracts, Trademarks. Criminal Defense. Discrimination, Sexual Harassment, Race Discrimination, and ADA cases.

GOLDBERG, GODLES, WIENER & WRIGHT

Established in 1983

1229 NINETEENTH STREET, N.W.

WASHINGTON, D.C. 20036

Telephone: 202-429-4900

Telecopier: 202-429-4912

Email: general@G2W2.com

URL: http://www.2w2.com

Communications and Media, Broadcasting Law, FCC Regulation, International Telecommunications Law, Mass Media Law, Satelite Communications, Telecommunications Contracts, Telecommunications Law, Telecommunications Licensing, Wireless Communications.

MEMBERS OF FIRM

HENRY GOLDBERG, born Boston, Massachusetts, December 28, 1939; admitted to bar, 1965, New York; 1967, District of Columbia. *Education:* Boston University (A.B., 1961); Columbia University (LL.B., cum laude, 1964). Harlan Fiske Stone Scholar. Editor and Business Manager, Columbia Law Review, 1963-1964. Author: "A U.S. Observer's View of the Green Paper," 5 Telematics No. 5, 1988; "120 Years of International Communications," 37 Federal Communications Law Journal 131, 1985; "Cable Television, Government Regulation and the First Amendment," 3 Comm/Ent 577, 1981 (Co-author);

(This Listing Continued)

"Peculiar Characteristics: An Analysis of the First Amendment Implications of Broadcast Regulation," 31 Federal Communications Law Journal 1, 1978; "A Proposal to Deregulate Broadcast Programing," 42 George Washington Law Review 73, 1973; Note, "The Second Circuit: Federal Judicial Administration in Microcosm," 63 Columbia Law Review 874, 1963; Comment, "Absolute Privilege as Applied to Investigators for Congressional Committees," 63 Columbia Law Review 326, 1963. *Member:* District of Columbia Bar; Federal, American (Member: Committee on Agency Rule Making, 1966—; Special Committee on Communications, 1967-1980; Chairman, Committee on Communications, Section of Science and Technology, 1975-1980) and International (Vice-Chairman, Committee L, 1988-1993; Co-Chairman, Committee CM, 1993-1998) Bar Associations; Federal Communications Bar Association (Co-Chairman, Engineering and Technical Practice Committee). ***PRACTICE AREAS:*** Communications and Media. ***Email:*** general@G2W2.com

JOSEPH A. GODLES, born Brooklyn, New York, October 28, 1955; admitted to bar, 1980, District of Columbia; 1981, California. *Education:* Cornell University (B.S., 1976); University of Pennsylvania (J.D., cum laude, 1979). Member, University of Pennsylvania Law Review, 1977-1979. Co-Author, "Broadcast Clues: Legal Issues in Acquisitions of Television Stations," Atlanta Lawyer, Vol. 37, No. 3, 1991. Law Clerk to Justice Sidney M. Schreiber, New Jersey Supreme Court, 1979-1980. *Member:* District of Columbia Bar; State Bar of California; Federal Communications Bar Association (Member, Committees on: Mass Media Practice; International Practice). ***PRACTICE AREAS:*** Communications and Media. ***Email:*** general@G2W2.com

JONATHAN L. WIENER, born Washington, D.C., May 26, 1955; admitted to bar, 1980, District of Columbia. *Education:* Connecticut College (B.A., summa cum laude, 1977); Harvard University (J.D., magna cum laude, 1980). Phi Beta Kappa. Editor, Harvard Law Review, 1979-1980. Law Clerk to Judge John L. Ferren, District of Columbia Court of Appeals, 1980-1981. *Member:* District of Columbia Bar; American Bar Association; Federal Communications Bar Association. ***PRACTICE AREAS:*** Communications and Media. ***Email:*** general@G2W2.com

ASSOCIATES

SHERYL J. LINCOLN, born Atlanta, Georgia, April 17, 1952; admitted to bar, 1995, Maryland; 1996, District of Columbia. *Education:* Washington University (B.A., magna cum laude, 1974; M.A., 1975); Georgetown University Law Center (J.D., 1995). Associate Editor, Law & Policy in International Business, 1994-1995. Law Clerk, Hon. Warren R. King, District of Columbia Court of Appeals, 1995-1996. *Member:* District of Columbia Bar; Federal Communications Bar Association. ***PRACTICE AREAS:*** Communications and Media; Internet Law. ***Email:*** general@g2w2.com

MICHAEL A. McCOIN, born Grand Rapids, Michigan; admitted to bar, 1995, Michigan (Not admitted in District of Columbia). *Education:* University of Michigan (B.A., 1978; M.A., 1980); University of Detroit (J.D., 1994). Attorney, Federal Communications Commission, 1994-2001. Telecommunications Professor, University of Detroit, 1987-1994. *Member:* State Bar of Michigan; Federal Communications Bar Association (Co-Chairman, Continuing Legal Education Committee); American Bar Association. ***PRACTICE AREAS:*** Communications; Media. ***Email:*** general@g2w2.com

ERIC J. SCHWALB, born Belleville, Illinois, November 14, 1975; admitted to bar, 2001, Illinois (Not admitted in District of Columbia). *Education:* Saint Louis University (B.A., summa cum laude, 1998); Georgetown University Law Center (J.D., 2001). ***PRACTICE AREAS:*** Communications; Media; Internet. ***Email:*** general@g2w2.com

COUNSEL

HENRIETTA WRIGHT, born Austin, Texas, March 28, 1957; admitted to bar, 1986, District of Columbia. *Education:* Yale University (B.A., cum laude, 1978; J.D., 1984). Editor, Yale Law Journal, 1983-1984. Law Clerk to Judge Clement F. Haynsworth, Jr., United States Court of Appeals for the Fourth Circuit, 1984-1985. Member, White House Staff, 1979-1981. *Member:* District of Columbia Bar; Federal Communications Bar Association (Member: Engineering and Technical Practice Committee; American Law Network Subcommittee); The American Law Institute. ***PRACTICE AREAS:*** Communications and Media. ***Email:*** general@G2W2.com

THOMAS G. GHERARDI, P.C., born Jersey City, New Jersey, March 7, 1942; admitted to bar, 1966, New York; 1970, U.S. Supreme Court; 1972, District of Columbia. *Education:* Fordham University (A.B., 1963); New York University (J.D., 1966). John Ben Snow Scholar, 1963-1964 and Elihu Root-Samuel J. Tilden Scholar, 1964-1966, New York University Law School. Attorney, Office of the General Counsel, U.S. Atomic Energy Commission, 1966-1967. Deputy Counsel, Subcommittee on Improvements in Judicial Machinery, U.S. Senate Committee on the Judiciary, 1967-1968. Assistant to the Assistant Secretary for Legislation, U.S. Department of Health, Education and Welfare, 1969. Counsel to Hon. Ralph T. Smith, United States Senator from Illinois, 1969-1970. Director of Congressional Affairs, U.S. General Services Administration, 1970-1972. General Counsel, The Corporation for Public Broadcasting, 1972-1978. Partner, Deane, Snowdon & Gherardi, 1978-1989. *Member:* District of Columbia Bar; Federal and American Bar Associations; Federal Communications Bar Association; Institute of Judicial Administration. (Also Practicing Individually, Washington, D.C.). ***PRACTICE AREAS:*** Entertainment and the Arts. ***Email:*** general@G2W2.com

(This Listing Continued)

GOLDEN & NELSON, PLLC

1420 K STREET N.W.
SUITE 500
WASHINGTON, D.C. 20005
Telephone: 202-842-0456
Fax: 703-751-4583
URL: http://www.lawyers.com/golden&nelsonlaw

Maryland, Millersville Office: 8285 Highglade Court, 21108. Telephone: 410-729-4285. Fax: 410-729-2246.

Corporate Law, Business Law, International Business Law, Securities, Taxation, Commercial Law, Contracts, Mergers, Acquisitions and Divestitures, Finance, Commercial Leasing.

FIRM PROFILE: Golden & Nelson, PLLC provides creative solutions to business problems and goals with an emphasis on personal service. The firm's attorneys have combined many years of experience with an appreciation of each client's financial and business needs and objectives. The firm represents established and start-up domestic and international businesses in a wide range of corporate, securities, business and financial transactions and strategic planning.

MICHAEL D. GOLDEN, born Herkimer, New York, 1940; admitted to bar, 1965, New York; 1972, District of Columbia. *Education:* Cornell University (B.A., 1962); New York University (J.D., 1965); Georgetown University (LL.M. in Taxation, 1972). Comment Editor, New York University Law Review, 1964-1965. Attorney, Securities and Exchange Commission, 1969-1971. Professorial Lecturer in Securities Regulation and Business Planning, American University Law School, 1973-1979. *Member:* The District of Columbia Bar; New York State Bar Association. ***PRACTICE AREAS:*** Corporate Law; Business Law; Mergers, Acquisitions and Divestitures; Securities Law; Education Law. ***Email:*** MDG333333@aol.com

HEDY L. NELSON, born Queens, New York, October 14, 1959; admitted to bar, 1985, Maryland; 1989, District of Columbia. *Education:* State University of New York at Binghamton (B.S., 1981); George Washington University National Law Center (J.D., 1984). *Member:* The District of Columbia Bar; Maryland State Bar Association. ***PRACTICE AREAS:*** Corporate Law; Business Law; Commercial Law; Finance; Contracts. ***Email:*** golnel2@cablespeed.com

THE GOLDSMITH LAW FIRM

1900 L STREET, N.W., SUITE 614
WASHINGTON, D.C. 20036
Telephone: 202-775-0040
Fax: 202-775-0005
Email: lgoldsmith@goldsmithfirm.com

Labor and Employment, Litigation, Discrimination, Sexual Harassment, Contracts, Torts, Unpaid Wages, Overtime, Federal Civil Service, Wrongful Termination, Torts, Civil Rights.

FIRM PROFILE: Since 1992, The Goldsmith Firm has represented clients in employment matters arising in both the private and public sectors. These matters often involve employment contracts, severance, wage and hour violations and discrimination. The Goldsmith Firm's services include litigation before the federal and local courts, as well as various administrative agencies including the Equal Employment Opportunity Commission and the Merit Systems Protection Board.

LEIZER Z. GOLDSMITH, born Halifax, Nova Scotia, Canada, June 22, 1962; admitted to bar, 1988, Massachusetts; 1989, District of Columbia; 1992, Maryland, U.S. Court of Appeals, 4th, 5th and District of Columbia Circuits; 1995, U.S Supreme Court. *Education:* University of Michigan (B.A., 1985); Boston College (J.D., 1988). Litigator, Appellate Litigation Branch, National Labor Relations Board. Former Associate, Connerton, Ray & Simon. *Member:* The District of Columbia Bar; National Employment Lawyers Association; Metropolitan Washington Employment Lawyers Association (Executive). ***Email:*** lgoldsmith@goldsmithfirm.com

ASSOCIATE

JULIE GLASS MARTIN, born Raleigh, North Carolina, June 11, 1961; admitted to bar, 1993, Maryland; 1995, District of Columbia. *Education:* University of Maryland (B.S., Computer Science, 1982); Catholic University of America (J.D., 1993). *Member:* Montgomery County and Maryland State Bar Associations. ***PRACTICE AREAS:*** General Practice.

GOLDSTEIN & ASSOCIATES, P.C.

Established in 1988

1757 P STREET, N.W.

WASHINGTON, D.C. 20036

Telephone: 202-872-8740

Telecopier: 202-872-8744

Energy, Environmental, Administrative and International Law. Civil Litigation.

MELVIN GOLDSTEIN, born New York, N.Y., August 31, 1940; admitted to bar, 1966, New York; 1969, District of Columbia; 1970, U.S. Supreme Court. *Education:* University of Pennsylvania (B.A., 1962); Institute of International Studies of the University of Geneva; Harvard University (J.D., cum laude, 1965). Assistant to the Director, Federal Trade Commission, Bureau of Competition, 1974. Director: Office of Exceptions and Appeals, Federal Energy Administration, 1974-1978; Office of Hearings and Appeals, Department of Energy, 1978-1980. *Member:* District of Columbia Bar; New York State Bar Association. ***PRACTICE AREAS:*** Energy Law; Environmental Law; Litigation. ***Email:*** mgoldstein@goldstein-law.com

---

WILLIAM L. MILLER, born Isfahan, Iran, August 6, 1960; admitted to bar, 1992, Massachusetts; 1994, District of Columbia and U.S. District Court for the District of Columbia; 2000, U.S. Supreme Court. *Education:* Williams College (B.A., 1982); Northeastern University (J.D., 1990). Staff Attorney, ACLU Information Technology Projection, 1990-1992. *Member:* District of Columbia Bar; American Bar Association. ***PRACTICE AREAS:*** Energy; Environmental Law; Litigation. ***Email:*** wmiller@goldstein-law.com

GOLDSTEIN HANDLER & LEVINE, P.C.

WASHINGTON, D.C.

(See Bethesda, Maryland)

General and Appellate Civil Litigation in all area Courts, Estate Planning, Probate, Probate Litigation, Family Business Succession, Employment, Wrongful Termination, Disability and Discrimination, Family Law (Divorce, Separation and Custody), Corporate (including LLC's and Non-profits), Commercial, Real Estate, Personal Injury, Negligence and Construction Law (including Mechanic's Liens).

GOLDSTEIN & LOOTS, PC

1700 K STREET, N.W., SUITE 801

WASHINGTON, D.C. 20006

Telephone: 202-223-1983

Facsimile: 202-223-2002

Email: info@goldlootslaw.com

URL: http://www.goldlootslaw.com

Union, New Jersey Office: 2042 Morris Avenue. Telephone: 908-688-7281. Fax: 908-688-7284.

Franchise Law, Franchise Litigation, Dealership Law, Franchise Arbitration, Franchise Termination, Hotel Franchise Law, Franchise Distribution and Licensing, Small Business Law, Commercial Leasing, Corporate Law, Emerging Business Law, Commercial Litigation, Employment Law, Employment Dispute Resolution, Executive Compensation, Employment Policy Review and Development, Wrongful Termination.

FIRM PROFILE: Goldstein & Loots, P.C. is best known nationally for its franchise litigation and employment law practices. The firm has represented many franchisees and hotel owners in their disputes with franchisors. Attorneys for the firm also represent employees, employers, small businesses, executives and corporations in a variety of employment and business law matters.

MEMBERS

JAMES M. LOOTS, born Iowa City, Iowa, May 24, 1958; admitted to bar, 1984, District of Columbia; 1985, U.S. District Court, District of Columbia; 1986, U.S. Court of Appeals for the District of Columbia Circuit; 1989, U.S. Tax Court; 1992, U.S. District Court, District of Maryland; 1997, U.S. Court of Federal Claims; 2000, U.S. Court of Appeals, Fourth Circuit. *Education:* Northwestern University (B.S., 1980); University of Michigan (J.D., cum laude, 1984). Editorial Board, Michigan Law Review. Adjunct Instructor, American University Washington College of Law. Associate: Skadden, Arps, Slate, Meagher & Flom, 1984-1989; Jones, Day, Reavis & Pogue, 1989-1992. Partner, Barrymore & Loots, 1993-1995; Levi, Perry, Simmons and Loots, 1995-1998. Member, 1988-1994, and Treasurer, 1993-1994, Board of Directors, District of Columbia Legal Counsel for the Elderly. Member, 1993— and Chairman, 1993-1997, District of Columbia Human Rights Commission. *Member:* District of Columbia Bar (Pro Bono Lawyer of the Year, 1988); Bar Association of the

(This Listing Continued)

District of Columbia (Member, Litigation Committee). ***PRACTICE AREAS:*** Employment Law; Litigation; Small Business Law; Association Law; Franchise Law. ***Email:*** jloots@goldlootslaw.com

JEFFREY M. GOLDSTEIN, born Peekskill, New York, March 10, 1957; admitted to bar, 1983, District of Columbia and Massachusetts; 1994, Pennsylvania; 1999, New York. *Education:* Bucknell University (B.A. magna cum laude, 1979); Boston University (M.A., 1983; J.D., 1983). Recipient, Paul J. Liacos Scholarship. Adjunct Professor, George Washington University, 1983-1986. Assistant to Deputy Director, Federal Trade Commission. Morgan Lewis & Bockius, 1986-1988; Skadden Arps Slate Meagher & Flom, 1986-1991; Assistant Corporation Counsel, District of Columbia, 1991-1993; Member, Spector Gadon & Rosen, 1993-1998. Editor, "Franchise Trends" 1998—. Member: American Franchise Association; American Association of Franchisees and Dealers. *Member:* The District of Columbia Bar. ***PRACTICE AREAS:*** Franchise Law; Complex Litigation; Antitrust; Securities. ***Email:*** jgoldstein@goldlootslaw.com

OF COUNSEL

STEPHEN D. CHACE, born Newport News, Virginia, April 10, 1957; admitted to bar, 1989, Virginia (Not admitted in District of Columbia). *Education:* Virginia Military Institute (B.A., with distinction, honors in History, 1980); T.C. Williams School of Law, University of Richmond (J.D., 1989). *Member:* Alexandria Bar Association; Virginia State Bar. [Major, U.S. Marine Corps, Retired]. ***PRACTICE AREAS:*** Trial Litigation; Appellate Litigation; Commercial Litigation; Banking Litigation; Casualty Defense Litigation; Wills and Trusts Litigation; Military Justice (Criminal Defense) Litigation.

ASSOCIATES

MATTHEW J. KREUTZER, born Denver, Colorado, December 1, 1973; admitted to bar, 1998, Maryland (Not admitted in District of Columbia). *Education:* American University (B.S., 1995); George Washington University (J.D., 1998). Golden Key. *Member:* Maryland State and American Bar Associations. ***Email:*** mkreutzer@goldlootslaw.com

BRIAN A. LOFFREDO, born New York, N.Y., January 31, 1974; admitted to bar, 1999, Maryland (Not admitted in District of Columbia). *Education:* University of Maryland (B.A., cum laude, 1996); Catholic University of America (J.D., 1999). *Member:* Maryland Bar Association. ***PRACTICE AREAS:*** Employment Law; Family Law. ***Email:*** bloffredo@goldlootslaw.com

DAVID G. ROSS, born Morristown, New Jersey, November 4, 1971; admitted to bar, 1997, New Jersey and U.S. District Court, District of New Jersey; 2000, Maryland (Not admitted in District of Columbia). *Education:* Lafayette College (B.A., 1994); American University, Washington College of Law (J.D., 1997). *Member:* Warren County and New Jersey State Bar Associations. ***PRACTICE AREAS:*** Franchise Law. ***Email:*** dross@goldlootslaw.com

GOODWIN PROCTER LLP

A Partnership including Professional Corporations

1717 PENNSYLVANIA AVENUE, N.W.

WASHINGTON, D.C. 20006

Telephone: 202-974-1000

Telecopier: 202-331-9330

URL: http://www.goodwinprocter.com

Boston, Massachusetts Office: Exchange Place, Telephone: 617-570-1000. Telecopier: 617-523-1231.

New York, N.Y. Offices: 599 Lexington Avenue. Telephone: 212-813-8800. Telecopier: 212-355-3333; 1285 Avenue of the Americas. Telephone: 212-956-1500. Telecopier: 212-956-3252.

Roseland, New Jersey Office: Seven Becker Farm Road. Telephone: 973-992-1990. Fax: 973-992-4643.

Alternative Dispute Resolution, Antitrust and Trade Regulation, Banking, Bankruptcy, Corporate, Corporate Finance, Corporate Governance, Securities, Litigation and Mergers and Acquisitions, ERISA/Employee Benefits, Energy, Environmental and Environmental Litigation, Estate Planning, Consumer Financial Services, Financial Services, Housing, Finance and Economic Development, Insurance, Intellectual Property/Technology, Labor and Employment, Intellectual Property Litigation, Litigation, Private Equity/Emerging Companies, Patent and Trademarks, Real Estate Development, Real Estate Investment Management, Real Estate Securities and Capital Markets, Regulatory Compliance, Securities, Tax, Electronic Commerce, Legislative and Economic Development.

MEMBERS OF FIRM

JEREMIAH S. BUCKLEY, admitted to bar, 1969, Connecticut; 1972, District of Columbia; 1980, U.S. Supreme Court. *Education:* Fairfield University (B.A., cum laude, 1966); University of Virginia (J.D., 1969). ***PRACTICE AREAS:*** Banking; Mortgage Finance; Consumer Finance; Regulatory; Real Estate; Legislative Practice. ***Email:*** jbuckley@goodwinprocter.com

(This Listing Continued)

JOSEPH M. KOLAR, admitted to bar, 1985, Maryland and District of Columbia; 1989, Virginia. *Education:* University of Iowa (B.B.A., 1982); Georgetown University (J.D., cum laude, 1985). ***PRACTICE AREAS:*** Mortgage and Consumer Finance Regulation; Real Estate; Banking. ***Email:*** jkolar@goodwinprocter.com

KEITH D. SHUGARMAN, admitted to bar, 1988, District of Columbia. *Education:* Skidmore College (B.A., 1985); Cornell University (J.D., 1988). ***PRACTICE AREAS:*** Antitrust; Trade Regulation. ***Email:*** kshugarman@goodwinprocter.com

THOMAS M. HEFFERON, admitted to bar, 1986, Massachusetts; 1999, District of Columbia, U.S. District Court, Districts of Massachusetts, District of Columbia, Western District of Michigan and U.S. Supreme Court, U.S. Court of Appeals for the District of Columbia Circuit, First, Sixth and Eleventh Circuits. *Education:* Trinity College (B.A., 1982); University of Chicago (J.D., 1986). ***PRACTICE AREAS:*** Civil Litigation; Consumer Finance; Class Actions; Insurance. ***Email:*** thefferon@goodwinprocter.com

JEFFREY P. NAIMON, admitted to bar, 1991, District of Columbia and New York. *Education:* Yale University (B.A., magna cum laude, 1985); University of Virginia (J.D., 1990). ***PRACTICE AREAS:*** Mortgages; Consumer Finance; Regulatory Law; Legislative Practice. ***Email:*** jnaimon@goodwinprocter.com

ANDREA LEE NEGRONI, admitted to bar, 1982, District of Columbia; 1983, Florida. *Education:* Emory University (B.A., 1975); Columbia University School of Law (J.D., 1982). ***PRACTICE AREAS:*** Regulatory Law; Administrative Law; Mortgage Banking Law; Real Estate. ***Email:*** alnegroni@goodwinprocter.com

JOHN P. KROMER, admitted to bar, 1993, Virginia; 1999, District of Columbia. *Education:* University of Notre Dame (B.A., 1988); University of Virginia School of Law (J.D., 1993). ***PRACTICE AREAS:*** Consumer Financial Services. ***Email:*** jkromer@goodwinprocter.com

MARGO H.K. TANK, admitted to bar, 1992, Maryland; 1995, District of Columbia. *Education:* University of Vermont (B.A., 1985); Drake University Law School (J.D., 1992). ***PRACTICE AREAS:*** Consumer Financial Services. ***Email:*** mtank@goodwinprocter.com

DAVID L. PERMUT, admitted to bar, 1993, Massachusetts; 1994, U.S. District Court, District of Massachusetts; 1998, U.S. District Court, District of Columbia and U.S. Court of Appeals for the District of Columbia Circuit; 1999, District of Columbia. *Education:* Dartmouth College (A.B., cum laude, 1990); University of Virginia (J.D., 1993). ***PRACTICE AREAS:*** Mortgage Banking Law; Antitrust; Class Action Defense. ***Email:*** dpermut@goodwinprocter.com

GORDON & BARNETT

Established in 1983

SUITE 450, TWO LAFAYETTE CENTRE
1133 21ST STREET, N.W.
WASHINGTON, D.C. 20036
Telephone: 202-833-3400
Telecopier: 202-223-0120

Trial and Appellate Practice in all Courts. Labor and Employee Benefits Law including Commercial Law, Government Contracts, Insurance Law, Health Law, Criminal Law.

FIRM PROFILE: The firm has a national practice representing insurance companies, associations, employee organizations and general business clients including individuals and corporations.

MEMBERS OF FIRM

DENIS F. GORDON, born Scranton, Pennsylvania, June 21, 1939; admitted to bar, 1968, District of Columbia; 1973, U.S. Supreme Court. *Education:* Lafayette College (A.B., 1961); University of Pennsylvania (J.D., 1967). Trial Attorney and Deputy Section Chief, Civil Rights Division, United States Department of Justice, 1967-1975. *Member:* District of Columbia Bar; American Bar Association. ***PRACTICE AREAS:*** Trial and Appellate Practice; Corporate Law; Labor Law; Employee Benefits. ***Email:*** dgordon@gordon-barnett.com

JAMES R. BARNETT, born Middletown, Ohio, October 9, 1947; admitted to bar, 1972, Wisconsin; 1973, U.S. Court of Military Appeals; 1975, U.S. Supreme Court; 1979, District of Columbia. *Education:* University of Wisconsin (B.A., cum laude, 1969; J.D., cum laude, 1972). Order of the Coif. Member, University of Wisconsin Law Review, 1970-1971. *Member:* District of Columbia Bar; American Bar Association; American Health Lawyers Association. [Lt., JAGC, USNR, 1972-1975]. ***PRACTICE AREAS:*** Government Contracts; Trial and Appellate Practice; Health Law; Employee Benefits Law; Insurance Law; Labor and Employment Law. ***Email:*** jbarnett@gordon-barnett.com

FRANK PETRAMALO, JR., born Rochester, New York, December 29, 1943; admitted to bar, 1969, Maryland; 1973, District of Columbia. *Education:* University of Notre Dame (A.B., cum laude, 1965); Georgetown University (J.D., 1969). Editor, Georgetown Law Journal, 1968-1969. Adjunct Professor, Georgetown University Law Center, 1983-1985. Trial Attorney, Civil Rights Division, Employment Section, U.S. Department of Justice, 1969-1973. Trial Attorney, Public Defender Service for the District of Columbia, 1973-1974. *Member:* District of Columbia Bar; American Bar Association; The Association of Trial Lawyers of America. AFL-CIO Lawyers Coordinating Committee. ***PRACTICE AREAS:*** Labor and Employment; Trial Practice; Appellate Practice. ***Email:*** fpetramalo@gordon-barnett.com

JOHN F. CONROY, born New York, N.Y., July 26, 1942; admitted to bar, 1966, New York; 1978, District of Columbia and U.S. District Court for the District of Columbia; 1979, U.S. Court of Appeals for the District of Columbia Circuit; 1987, U.S. District Court, District of Maryland, including Trial Bar. *Education:* Hamilton College (B.A., 1963); Fordham University (J.D., 1966). Trial Attorney, Civil Rights Division, 1970-1975; Deputy Chief, Criminal Section, 1975-1978, U.S. Department of Justice. *Member:* District of Columbia Bar; American Bar Association (Member, Committees on: White Collar Crime; Health Fraud; Member, Sections on: Criminal Justice; Litigation). [Lt., USNR, 1966-1969]. ***PRACTICE AREAS:*** Criminal Law; Trial Practice. ***Email:*** jconroy@gordon-barnett.com

DAVID M. ERMER, born New Haven, Connecticut, December 22, 1954; admitted to bar, 1979, District of Columbia. *Education:* University of Connecticut (B.A., summa cum laude, 1976); George Washington University (J.D., with high honors, 1979). Order of the Coif. Member, George Washington University Law Review, 1977-1979. Author: "ERISA," 15 The Complete Lawyer 32, July/August 1998; "Employer Liability in the Managed Care Setting," 18 Employee Benefits Journal 19, June, 1993. BNA Compensation and Benefits Guide Advisory Board. *Member:* District of Columbia Bar; American Bar Association; American Health Lawyers Association. ***PRACTICE AREAS:*** Trial and Appellate Practice; Government Contract Law; Health Law; Employee Benefits Law; Insurance Law. ***Email:*** dermer@gordon-barnett.com

BRAD W. SPENCER, born New York, N.Y., March 27, 1957; admitted to bar, 1983, District of Columbia; 1988, U.S. Supreme Court. *Education:* Cornell University (B.S., 1979); Duke University (J.D., 1982). Staff, International Comparative Law Institute, "Law and Contemporary Problems," 1981-1982. General Counsel, The Merallis Company, 1995—. *Member:* District of Columbia Bar; American Bar Association (Member, Sections on: Labor and Employment Law; Litigation); William B. Bryant American Inn of Court. ***PRACTICE AREAS:*** Labor Law; Employee Benefits; Health Law; Commercial Law; Insurance; Trial Practice; Appellate Practice; Government Contracts; Corporate Law. ***Email:*** spencer@gordon-barnett.com

SCOTT R. JAMISON, born Winston-Salem, North Carolina, December 21, 1960; admitted to bar, 1987, Maryland; 1999, District of Columbia. *Education:* University of the South (B.A., 1983); University of Maryland (J.D., 1987). Notes and Comments Editor, Maryland Journal of International Law and Trade, 1987. *Member:* Maryland State and American Bar Associations. ***PRACTICE AREAS:*** Government Contracts; Employee Benefits Law; Health Law; Insurance Law; Trial and Appellate Practice. ***Email:*** sjamison@gordon-barnett.com

ASSOCIATES

MARY M. SIFFERMANN, born Davenport, Iowa, June 12, 1965; admitted to bar, 1994, Illinois; 1996, Virginia; 1997, District of Columbia. *Education:* St. Norbert College (B.A., 1987); Chicago-Kent College of Law (J.D., 1994). *Member:* The District of Columbia Bar; Virginia State Bar; Illinois State Bar Association. ***PRACTICE AREAS:*** Employment Law; Employee Benefits Law; Health Law; Insurance Law; Trial and Appellate Practice. ***Email:*** msiffermann@gordon-barnett.com

ROBERT G. IADICICCO, born Bronx, New York, August 8, 1963; admitted to bar, 1996, New Jersey; 1997, New York; 1998, District of Columbia. *Education:* State University of New York at Albany (B.A., 1985); University of Georgia (M.P.A., 1988); George Mason University School of Law (J.D., 1996). *Member:* District of Columbia Bar; New York State and American Bar Associations; American Health Lawyers Association. ***PRACTICE AREAS:*** Employee Benefits; Health Law; Government Contracts; Insurance. ***Email:*** riadicicco@gordon-barnett.com

(This Listing Continued)

GORDON & BRYANT

Established in 1988

CURTIS HOUSE
1742 S STREET, N.W.
WASHINGTON, D.C. 20009-6145
Telephone: 202-833-8011
Fax: 202-833-0352
Email: albryant@clark.net
URL: http://www.lawyers.com/gordon&bryantlaw

Immigration and Nationality Law. Business Immigration.

(This Listing Continued)

GORDON & BRYANT, Washington—Continued

FIRM PROFILE: Gordon & Bryant is a boutique law firm specializing exclusively in immigration and nationality matters. The firm routinely handles immigrant applications which rely either on corporate sponsorships or family relationships or are the consequences of political turmoil. Ms. Bryant places special emphasis on the representation of businesses and individuals facing complex immigration problems.

CHARLES GORDON (1905-1999).

ANN LAKE BRYANT, born Springfield, Ohio, June 7, 1949; admitted to bar, 1983, District of Columbia. *Education:* Colby College (B.A., 1971); Clark University, Worcester, Ma.; Institute of European Studies, Rome, Italy; Catholic University (J.D., 1983). Contributing Author: Gordon and Mailman, "Immigration Law and Procedure," Matthew Bender, 1985, 1989, 1991, 1992. Occasional Lecturer in Immigration Law, Georgetown University Law Center, 1985-1991. Adjunct Professor of Law, Georgetown University, 1993—. Member, Board of Directors, 1983-1992 and President, 1988, AYUDA, Inc. *Member:* District of Columbia Bar; American Immigration Lawyers Association. ***LANGUAGES:*** Spanish, French, Italian, Portuguese. ***PRACTICE AREAS:*** Immigration Law; International adoptions; Citizenship; International Business Personnel Transfers. ***Email:*** albryant@clark.net

GORDON, SILBERMAN, WIGGINS & CHILDS, P.C.

1621 CONNECTICUT AVENUE, N.W., SUITE 400
WASHINGTON, D.C. 20009
Telephone: 202-238-0690
Facsimilie: 202-238-0968
URL: http://www.gswc.com

Birmingham, Alabama Office: 1400 South Trust Tower, 420 North 20th Street, 35203. Telephone: 205-328-0640. Facsimile: 205-254-1500.

General Civil Trial and Appellate Practice in all State and Federal Courts. Class Action Litigation, Corporate/Business, Acquisitions and Mergers, Corporate Finance, Banking, Real Estate, Taxation, Securities, Administrative, Estate Planning, Labor, Employment Discrimination, Sex Harassment, ERISA, Wage and Hour, Employee Benefits, Disability, Discrimination, Special Education Law.

RESIDENT ASSOCIATES

DAVID W. SANFORD, born Newark, New Jersey, February 10, 1957; admitted to bar, 1997, Maryland, District of Columbia and U.S. District Court, District of Maryland. *Education:* Vassar College (A.B., 1980); University of North Carolina (M.A., 1984); Stanford University (J.D., 1995). Law Clerk Judge Gladys Kessler, U.S. District Court for the District of Columbia, 1995-1996; Member, William B. Bryant Inn of Court, 1996—. *Member:* Maryland State Bar Association, Inc.; The District of Columbia Bar. ***LANGUAGES:*** German. ***PRACTICE AREAS:*** Civil Rights; Employment Litigation; Appellate Practice. ***Email:*** dsanford@gswc.com

TIMOTHY B. FLEMING, born Plymouth, Indiana, January 24, 1955; admitted to bar, 1980, Texas; 1981, District of Columbia. *Education:* University of Texas (B.A., magna cum laude, with honors, special honors in government, 1977; J.D., with honors, 1980). *Member:* The District of Columbia Bar; State Bar of Texas. ***PRACTICE AREAS:*** Civil Rights Litigation; Employment Discrimination. ***Email:*** tfleming@gswc.com

LORI B. KISCH, born New York, N.Y., April 6, 1970; admitted to bar, 1997, Maryland (Not admitted in District of Columbia). *Education:* State University of New York at Albany (B.A., 1992); Northeastern University School of Law (J.D., 1997). *Member:* Maryland State Bar Association. ***PRACTICE AREAS:*** Civil Rights Litigation; Employment Discrimination. ***Email:*** lkisch@gswc.com

S. NICOLE NARDONE, born Wilkes-Barre, Pennsylvania, December 10, 1970; admitted to bar, 1997, California (Not admitted in District of Columbia). *Education:* Kings College (B.A., 1992); University of San Francisco School of Law (J.D., 1996). ***PRACTICE AREAS:*** Civil Rights Litigation; Employment Discrimination. ***Email:*** nnardone@gswc.com

(For complete biographical data on Birmingham, Alabama personnel, see Professional Biographies at Birmingham, Alabama)

PHILIP A. GORELICK

WASHINGTON, D.C.

(See McLean, Virginia)

General Practice, Commercial Real Estate Transactions, Mortgage Finance, Buying and Selling of Businesses, Employment Contracts, Employment Claims, Negotiation of Commercial Disputes.

GORMAN & WILLIAMS

WASHINGTON, D.C.

(See Baltimore, Maryland)

Corporate and Commercial Law; Litigation, Arbitration, and Mediation; Insurance; Patents, Copyrights, and Trademarks Licensing and Infringement; Maritime and Marine Financing; Bankruptcy and Creditor's Rights; Construction Law; International Trade Law.

GOTTESDIENER LAW FIRM

3901 YUMA STREET, N.W.
WASHINGTON, D.C. 20016
Telephone: 202-243-1000
Fax: 202-537-1989
Email: egottesdiener@gottesdienerlaw.com
URL: http://www.gottesdienerlaw.com

Civil and Criminal Litigation in Federal and State Court. Class Action, ERISA, White Collar, Criminal Defense, Consumer Fraud, Business Fraud, Professional Malpractice, Complex Civil.

FIRM PROFILE: Gottesdiener Law Firm and its principal, Eli Gottesdiener, specialize in complex civil and criminal litigation on behalf of plaintiffs and defendants, including individuals, classes and businesses, in federal and state courts.

ELI GOTTESDIENER, born New London, Connecticut, September 21, 1961; admitted to bar, 1987, Pennsylvania; 1989, District of Columbia. *Education:* Bates College (1979-1981, Dana Scholar); American University (B.A., 1983, Presidential Scholar); Université de Paris-Sorbonne (M.A., with honors, 1984); Georgetown University Law Center (J.D., cum laude, 1987). Associate Editor, Georgetown Law Review. Co-Author, "Grand Jury Investigations: Benefiting from Witness' Right to a Transcript of Testimony," *Business Crimes Bulletin*, Vol. 5, No. 4, May 1998; "For Parties-in-Interest, the Party's Over: Harris Trust and its Aftermath," Vol. I, ABA-CLE ERISA Basics (2001). Featured Speaker, 13th Annual ERISA Litigation Conference, September 2000. Presenter, Secretary of Labor's ERISA Advisory Council, September 2000. Partner, Sprenger & Lang, 1999-2000. Senior Associate, Weil, Gotshal & Manges, 1997-1999. Staff Attorney, Public Defender Service for the District of Columbia, 1990-1997. Associate, Patton, Boggs, 1987-1990. ***LANGUAGES:*** French. ***PRACTICE AREAS:*** Class Actions; Complex Litigation; ERISA.

GOULSTON & STORRS

A PROFESSIONAL CORPORATION

Counsellors at Law

1717 PENNSYLVANIA AVENUE
WASHINGTON, D.C. 20006
Telephone: 202-721-0011
Fax: 202-721-1111
Email: info@goulstonstorrs.com
URL: http://www.goulstonstorrs.com

Boston, Massachusetts Office: 400 Atlantic Avenue. Telephone: 617-482-1776. Fax: 617-574-4112.

Affordable Housing, Commercial Law, Commercial Lending, Bankruptcy. Corporate, Business Formation, E-Commerce, Securities Law, Mergers and Acquisitions, Equity and Debt Financing, Closely-Held Businesses, Investment Funds, Intellectual Property, Emerging Technologies, Retail Businesses, Manufacturing Businesses, Employment Law, Non-Profit Organizations. Health Care, Assisted Living, Telemedicine, Hospitals/Health Centers, Professional Associations, Long Term Care, Corporate Compliance, Healthcare Practitioners, Managed Care, Home Health Providers. International, Joint Ventures, Tax Planning, Acquisitions/Financing, Latin American Group. Litigation, Land Use/Environmental, Intellectual Property, Employment Law, ADR, Construction, Regulatory Compliance, Tax Abatement, Insurance, Business and Commercial. Philanthropic Advisors. Real Estate/ Environmental, Retail/Shopping Centers, Office, Real Estate Finance, Leasing, REIT/Securities, Development/Permitting, Environmental, Hospitality/Recreation, Affordable Housing, Multi-Family. Tax, Business Transactions, Real Estate Transactions, International Planning, Individual Tax Planning, Wealth Transfer, Tax-Exempt Entities, Tax Incentive Programs, Executive Compensation, ERISA/Employee Benefits. Trusts and Estates, Estate Planning, Fiduciary Administration, Charitable Planning.

CYNTHIA LANGELIER PAINE, admitted to bar, 1999, Virginia (Not admitted in District of Columbia). *Education:* Northeastern University (B.S., 1985); Georgetown University (J.D., 1999). ***PRACTICE AREAS:*** Corporate; Real Estate. ***Email:*** cpaine@goulstonstorrs.com

(This Listing Continued)

COUNSEL

N. LINDA GOLDSTEIN, admitted to bar, 1979, Pennsylvania; 1980, District of Columbia, U.S. District Court for the District of Columbia and U.S. Court of Appeals for the District of Columbia Circuit. *Education:* American University (B.A., 1975); Franklin Pierce Law Center (J.D., 1978). Attorney, Office of the General Counsel, U.S. Department of Housing and Urban Development, 1978-1984. Author: "HUD Rules for Multifamily Sales," *Mortgage Banking,* September, 1983; "The Conversion and Resyndication of Non-Profit HUD-Insured Projects," *Mortgage Banking,* April, 1984; "Recreational Use Statutes: Time for Reform," Property and Probate, July/August 1989; "The Challenge of Affordable Housing," *Property and Probate,* March/April 1992; "An Attitude Change at HUD," Urban, State and Local Law, Spring, 1993; "Anacostia Washington, D.C. Bold Revitalization Plans Unfold," *CRA Bulletin,* September 1994. Co-Author: *CRA/Fair Lending Handbook,* Warren, Gorham and Lamont, 1996; "HUD: Reclaim the Mission," Journal of Affordable Housing & Community Development, Fall 1997; "Linking our Troubled Communities to the New Economy: A Role for the ABA?", Journal of Affordable Housing & Community Development, Winter 1998; "Forum Symposium Indifference or Ignorance?" Summer, 1998; "Broadband Deployment - A City-Wide Objective," Pipeling, May/June 2000; "Building the Dream in Southeast," Legal Times, August 14, 2000. Member, Advisory Committee, Community Empowerment Initiative, The Martin Luther King Center, Atlanta, Georgia, 1993-1997. Honorary Trustee, National Institute for Community Empowerment, Atlanta, Georgia, 1997—. Director, District of Columbia Building Industry Association, Washington, 1998—. *Member:* The District of Columbia Bar (Member, Real Estate Section); American Bar Association (Member, Real Property Section; Chair, Special Committee on Affordable Housing, 1991-1993; Chair, Affordable Housing and Community Development Committees, 1993-1996; Member, Governing Committee, ABA Forum on Affordable Housing and Community Development Law, 1993-1997; Chair, Forum on Affordable Housing and Community Development Law, 1997-1998). ***PRACTICE AREAS:*** Real Estate Law; Housing Law; Affordable Housing. ***Email:*** lgoldstein@goulstonstorrs.com

DAVID I. GRANGER

1800 MASSACHUSETTS AVENUE, N.W., SUITE 600
WASHINGTON, D.C. 20036
Telephone: 202-785-1274
Fax: 202-785-1631
Email: grangerdi@aol.com

General Practice.

DAVID I. GRANGER, born Washington, D.C., September 4, 1932; admitted to bar, 1959, District of Columbia. *Education:* Princeton University (A.B., 1954); Harvard University (LL.B., 1959). Attorney, Tax Division, U.S. Department of Justice, 1961-1965. *Member:* The District of Columbia Bar; Bar Association of the District of Columbia; American Bar Association.

CAROL LYNN GREEN

WASHINGTON, D.C.

(See Bethesda, Maryland)

Environmental Law, Clean Air Act, Clean Water Act, Hazardous Waste, Superfund; Oil Pollution, Habitat Conservation; Toxic Substances, Underground Storage Tanks, Environmental Liability, Due Diligence, Environmental Compliance, Permitting Risk Management, Regulation Mediation, Environmental Business Law, Real Estate.

GREEN AND FOUSHEE

Established in 1988

1130 SEVENTEENTH STREET, N.W., SUITE 210
WASHINGTON, D.C. 20036
Telephone: 202-785-1171
Fax: 202-785-8108
Email: iriseagain@aol.com
URL: http://www.lawyers.com/greenandfoushee

Civil Trial Practice including Personal Injury (Medical Malpractice), Probate, Family, Appellate and Educational Law. Civil Rights and Constitutional Law including Women's Rights Issues and Sexual Harassment. Complex Commercial and Business Litigation. Telecommunications Law including Cable Regulatory Issues. Employment Law, Wrongful Termination, Race Discrimination.

FIRM PROFILE: Founded in 1988 by sisters Iris McCollum Green and Trudi McCollum Foushee, the firm represents a varied clientele of individuals and corporations in a national legal counseling and litigation practice.

(This Listing Continued)

IRIS M. GREEN, born Clinton, North Carolina, 1954; admitted to bar, 1977, District of Columbia; U.S. District Court for the District of Columbia and District of Maryland; U.S. Court of Appeals for the District of Columbia, Fourth and Ninth Circuits; U.S. Supreme Court. *Education:* American University (B.A., cum laude, 1972); George Washington University (J.D., 1976). Attorney General's Advocacy Institute, 1978; Attorney General's Appellate Advocacy Institute, 1985. Senior Trial Attorney, Civil Rights Division, U.S. Department of Justice, 1977-1988. Program Specialist, U.S. Office of Education, 1973. Equal Employment Opportunity Officer, U.S. General Services Administration, 1970-1971. Staff Assistant, U.S. Representative Adam Clayton Powell, 1969-1970. Administrative Assistant, District of Columbia Office of Community Renewal, 1963-1969. Board of Directors, George Washington University, National Law Center Alumni Association, 1988-1992. Member, Executive Committee, African American Women and the Law Conference, 1994. *Member:* National Bar Association (Executive Committee and Board Member; Chairperson, Civil Rights Law Section); Trial Lawyers of the District of Columbia; Association of Trial Lawyers of America. ***REPORTED CASES:*** Randall v. United States, 30 F.3d 518 (4th Cir. 1995), cert. den. May 15, 1995; Seattle School Dist No. 1 of King County v. City of Washington, 473 F. Supp. 996 (W.D. Wash. 1979).

TRUDI McCOLLUM FOUSHEE, born Clinton, North Carolina, July 18, 1956; admitted to bar, 1982, District of Columbia; 1986, Missouri; 1989, U.S. District Court, Eastern District of Missouri. *Education:* North Central University (B.A., cum laude, 1978); Georgetown University (J.D., 1981). Vice President and Senior Counsel, Western Division Charter Communications. *Member:* Mound City (Chair, Membership Committee, 1990-1991; 1991-1992) and National Bar Associations. (Also Vice President and Senior Counsel of Charter Communications, Inc., St. Louis, Missouri). ***PRACTICE AREAS:*** Corporate Law; Human Resources; Employment; Communications Law.

GREENBERG & LIEBERMAN

WASHINGTON, D.C.

(See Takoma Park, Maryland)

Intellectual Property, Patents, Trademarks, Copyright, Bio Medical Patent, Business Method Patents, Chemical Patent, Software Patents, Complex Methods, Computer, Mechanical, Electrical Patent, Trademarks, General Practice, Computer Law, Licensing, Mediation and Civil Litigation.

GREENBLUM & BERNSTEIN, P.L.C.

WASHINGTON, D.C.

(See Reston, Virginia)

Patent, Trademark and Copyright Law.

GREENSTEIN DeLORME & LUCHS, P.C.

Established in 1989

1620 L STREET, N.W., SUITE 900
WASHINGTON, D.C. 20036-5605
Telephone: 202-452-1400
Facsimile: 202-452-1410

General and Business Practice including Civil Litigation, Real Estate, Banking and Savings and Loan, Creditors Rights, Financial Institutions, Development Law, Housing and Urban Development, Condominiums and Cooperatives, Local Government, Securities, Taxation, Trade Organizations, Zoning, Land Use, Real Property Assessment Appeals, Municipal Government and Public Finance Law.

WILLIAM H. HARRIS, JR., born New Orleans, Louisiana, September 8, 1942; admitted to bar, 1969, District of Columbia and U.S. Court of Appeals, District of Columbia Circuit; 1983, U.S. Supreme Court. *Education:* Xavier University, Louisiana (B.A., 1965); Howard University (J.D., 1968). Phi Alpha Delta. General Counsel's Office, Department of Housing and Urban Development, 1968-1969. Member, D.C. Commission on Housing Production, 1985-1989. *Member:* District of Columbia Bar (Member, Section on Real Estate, Housing and Land Use); American (Member, Real Estate Property, Probate and Trust Law, Section) and National Bar Associations. ***Email:*** WHH@GDLLAW.COM

RICHARD G. WISE, born Alameda, California, March 6, 1944; admitted to bar, 1970, District of Columbia, U.S. Court of Appeals, District of Columbia Circuit and U.S. Court of Military Appeals; 1975, U.S. Supreme Court; 1976, California; 1983, Maryland; 1994, U.S. District Court, Northern District of California; 1995, U.S. Court of Appeals, Ninth Circuit. *Education:* San Diego State College (B.A., cum laude, 1965); University of California at Los Angeles (J.D., 1968). Trial Attorney, D.C. Office of the Corporation Counsel, 1972-1980. *Member:* District of Columbia Bar (Member, Section on Real Estate, Housing and Land Use); State Bar of California; Maryland State and American (Mem-

(This Listing Continued)

GREENSTEIN DeLORME & LUCHS, P.C., Washington—Continued

ber, Litigation Section) Bar Associations; Maryland Bankruptcy Bar Association; Congressman Walter Chandler American Inn of Court. [Col., U.S. Marine Corps Reserve (Ret.)]. ***Email:*** RGW@GDLLAW.COM

ABRAHAM J. GREENSTEIN, born New York, N.Y., September 23, 1945; admitted to bar, 1968, District of Columbia and U.S. Court of Appeals for the District of Columbia Circuit. *Education:* New York University (B.A., 1965); George Washington University (J.D., 1968). Phi Alpha Delta. Recipient, Distinguished Service Award from Legal Aid Bureau, 1968. Author: "Federally Assisted Code Enforcement-Problems and Approaches," 4 Urban Lawyer, 629, American Bar Association Quarterly on Local Government Law, 1971. Member, Mayor's Advisory Committee on Consumer Affairs, 1974-1976. Chairman, D.C. Board for Condemnation of Insanitary Buildings, 1979. Member, District of Columbia Real Estate Commission, 1984-1987, Reappointed, 1988-1990. Member, National Association of Housing and Redevelopment Officials, 1970-1980. Member, Board of Directors, 1982-1992; Counsel, 1994—; Chairman, Legislative Committee, 1982-1984, District of Columbia Building Industry Association. Vice Chairman, Condominium and Cooperative Committee, 1981. Member, Board of Directors, 1984 and General Counsel, 1984—, Washington, D.C. Association of Realtors. General Counsel, Greater Washington Commercial Association of Realtors, 1990—. Member: Steering Committee of Legislative/Fiscal Bureau, Greater Washington Board of Trade, 1982-1991; Editorial Advisory Board, D.C. Real Estate Reporter, 1981—; Board of Directors, Neighborhood Housing Services, Inc., 1983-1984. Member, D.C. Commission on Housing Production, 1985-1989. Member, Mayor's Rent Control Study Advisory Group, 1986-1989. Member, Board of Directors, 1993-1995, Executive Committee, 1995—and Chairman, 1990-1996, Tax Policy Committee, Apartment and Office Building Association. Member, Editorial Advisory Board, Institute of Real Estate Management Journal of Property Management, 1992-1993. *Member:* District of Columbia Bar (Member, Sections on: Real Estate, Housing and Land Use and District of Columbia Affairs); American Bar Association. ***Email:*** AJG@GDLLAW.COM

GILBERT E. DeLORME, JR., born Atlanta, Georgia, January 2, 1945; admitted to bar, 1968, District of Columbia. *Education:* Brown University (A.B., in Economics, 1965); University of Pennsylvania (LL.B., 1968). Hogan & Hartson, Associate, 1968-1969. Special Assistant to Assistant Secretary and Deputy Area Director, U.S. Department of Housing and Urban Development, 1969-1972. General Counsel, National Center for Housing Management, 1972-1979. General Counsel, Perpetual American Bank, F.S.B., 1979-1983. Member, Fannie Mae Advisory Committee, 1990-1991. Chairman, District of Columbia Political Action Committee, Greater Washington Board of Trade, 1993-1998. Trustee, and Executive Committee Member, Federal City Council. Board of Trustees, National Building Museum. Board of Trustees, Marriott Employee Trust. *Member:* District of Columbia Bar; American Bar Association (Member, Section on Corporation, Banking and Business Law); American Bar Foundation; National Bar Association. ***Email:*** GED@GDLLAW.COM

VINCENT MARK J. POLICY, born Warren, Ohio, March 29, 1948; admitted to bar, 1974, New York; 1975, District of Columbia; 1977, U.S. Supreme Court. *Education:* University of Maryland (B.A., with high honors, 1970); Georgetown University (J.D., 1973). Omicron Delta Kappa; Phi Beta Kappa. Member, Georgetown Law Journal, 1972-1973. Member: Mayor's Tenant-Housing Provider Advisory Committee to the District of Columbia Rent Control Study, 1986-1989; Washington, D.C. Association of Realtors, 1988—; District of Columbia Building Industry Association Legislative/Government Affairs Committee, 1986. Greater Washington Board of Trade Economic Growth Committee, 1991-1993; Initiative, Referendum and Recall Task Force, 1986—. Instructor, Graduate Realtor Institute, 1988—. *Member:* District of Columbia Bar (Member, Section on Real Estate Housing and Land Use; Member, Standing Committee on Rental Housing, 1986—; Chairperson, Standing Committee on Rental Housing, 1986-1988); American Bar Association (Member, Commercial Leasing Committee). ***Email:*** VMP@GDLLAW.COM

RICHARD W. LUCHS, born Washington, D.C., February 12, 1951; admitted to bar, 1976, District of Columbia; 1977, U.S. Court of Appeals for the District of Columbia Circuit; 1980, U.S. Supreme Court; 1983, Maryland; 1988, U.S. Court of Appeals, Fourth Circuit. *Education:* Oberlin College (A.B., with high honors, 1973); George Washington University (J.D., with honors, 1976). Instructor, Graduate Realtor Institute, 1988-1994. Member, Apartment and Office Building of Metropolitan Washington Tax Policy Committee, 1992. Chair, Apartment and Office Building of Metropolitan Washington Maryland Legislative Committee, 1996—. Chair, Montgomery County, MD, Task Force on Tenant Rights of First Refusal Regulations, 2000-2001. Co-Presenter of Videotape: "Fair Housing Do's & Don'ts for the New Millennium." *Member:* District of Columbia Bar (Member: Section on Real Estate, Housing and Land Use; Standing Committee on Rental Housing, 1988—; Landlord/Tenant Task Force, 1995—; Council for Court Excellence, 1995—); Bar Association of the District of Columbia; American Bar Association. ***Email:*** RWL@GDLLAW.COM

(This Listing Continued)

JUDITH R. GOLDMAN, born Washington, D.C., October 2, 1951; admitted to bar, 1982, District of Columbia, U.S. District Court, District of Columbia and Maryland. *Education:* American University (B.S., 1972); University of Maryland (M.Ed., 1973); George Washington University (J.D., with honors, 1982). Member, District of Columbia Building Industry Association. Member, Commercial Real Estate Women. *Member:* District of Columbia Bar (Member, Section on Real Estate, Housing and Land Use); Maryland State and American Bar Associations. ***Email:*** JRG@GDLLAW.COM

JACQUES B. DePUY, born Easton, Pennsylvania, November 18, 1943; admitted to bar, 1975, District of Columbia. *Education:* Harvard University and American University (B.A., 1965); University of Wisconsin-Madison (M.A., 1967); Georgetown University (J.D., 1974). Co-Author: "Bringing Democracy to the Nation's Last Colony: The District of Columbia Self-Government and Governmental Reorganization Act," The American University Law Review, Vol. 24, Spring, 1975. Author: "The District of Columbia Land Use Maze," The Realtor, 1976. Instructor: Graduate Realtor Institute, 1991-1994. Legislative Assistant to Hon. Brock Adams, U.S. House of Representatives, 1969-1973. Subcommittee Counsel, District of Columbia Committee, U.S. House of Representatives, 1973-1974. Legislative Assistant to Hon. Abner Mikva, U.S. House of Representatives, 1975. Member, Apartment and Office Building Association. Member, District of Columbia Building Industry Association. *Member:* District of Columbia Bar; Bar Association of the District of Columbia (Co-chair, Real Property Law Committee, 1995-1997). ***Email:*** JBD@GDLLAW.COM

JEFFREY H. GELMAN, born New Haven, Connecticut, October 14, 1959; admitted to bar, 1984, Connecticut; 1985, District of Columbia, Massachusetts and Pennsylvania; 1986, Maryland, U.S. District Court for the District of Columbia and U.S. District Court for the District of Connecticut; 1988, U.S. Supreme Court. *Education:* Clark University (B.A., magna cum laude, 1981); George Washington University (J.D., 1984). Phi Beta Kappa. Member, Society of Federal Labor Relations Professionals, 1982-1985. Member, District of Columbia Building Industry Association (Member, Board of Directors; Chair, Housing Committee). *Member:* District of Columbia Bar (Member, Sections on: Real Estate, Housing and Land Use; Corporation, Finance and Securities Law); Connecticut, Massachusetts, Pennsylvania, Maryland State and American (Member, Sections on: Real Property, Probate and Trust Law; Business Law; Forum on Affordable Housing and Community Development Law) Bar Associations; Mortgage Bankers Association of America. ***Email:*** JHG@GDLLAW.COM

ALAN S. WEITZ, born Washington, D.C., June 30, 1945; admitted to bar, 1971, District of Columbia; 1974, U.S. Supreme Court. *Education:* University of Pennsylvania (B.S., summa cum laude, 1967); Harvard University (J.D., magna cum laude, 1970). Editor, Harvard Law Review, 1968-1970. Sheldon Fellow, Harvard Law School, 1970-1971. Assistant Counsel, Senate Watergate Committee, 1973-1974. Author: "Meeting the Challenge and Maximizing Opportunities for Employees with Disabilities," The Curve, 2000; "Making Diversity Work," Chain Store Age Executive, 1995; "Effect of ADA on Facility and Store Design," World Coffee & Tea, 1992; "Effect of ADA on Convenience Store Design," Petroleum Marketer, 1992. Counsel, Food Marketing Institute Task Forces on Racial and Gender Diversity in Management and on Americans with Disabilities Act. *Member:* District of Columbia Bar (Member, Labor Section, Ethics Education Committee); American Bar Association (Member, Sections: Alternative Dispute Resolution; Labor Law). Fellow, American Bar Foundation. ***PRACTICE AREAS:*** Employment Law; Mediation; Litigation. ***Email:*** ASW@GDLLAW.COM

WILLIAM C. CASANO, born Bridgeport, Connecticut, July 3, 1953; admitted to bar, 1978, Pennsylvania; 1981, District of Columbia; 1995, Maryland. *Education:* Fairfield University (B.A., 1975); University of Pittsburgh (J.D., 1978). Law Clerk: Hon. Gwilym A. Price, Jr., Associate Judge, Pennsylvania Superior Court, 1978-1980; Hon. Julia Cooper Mack, Associate Judge, District of Columbia Court of Appeals, 1980-1981. *Member:* District of Columbia Bar; Pennsylvania and Maryland State Bar Associations. ***PRACTICE AREAS:*** Civil Litigation; Employment Law; Administrative Law; Corporate Law; Trade Regulation. ***Email:*** WCC@GDLLAW.COM

STEPHEN H. ABRAHAM, born Washington, D.C., February 10, 1958; admitted to bar, 1984, Maryland; 1985, District of Columbia, Virginia and U.S. District Court for the District of Columbia; 1987, U.S. District Court, Eastern District of Virginia; 1988, U.S. Court of Appeals, Fourth and District of Columbia Circuits and U.S. District Court, District of Maryland; U.S. Bankruptcy Court, Eastern District of Virginia; 1994, U.S. Supreme Court; 1996, Colorado. *Education:* Washington & Lee University (B.A., cum laude, 1980); University of Alabama; Washington & Lee University (J.D., 1983). Omicron Delta Kappa; Pi Sigma Alpha; Phi Delta Phi. Instructor: Graduate Realtor Institute, 1993—; Bom: Institute Property Manager's Course on Commercial Law, 1999—; Realtor Fair, 1999. Member, Judicial Conference of the District of Columbia, 1999. *Member:* District of Columbia Bar (Member, Litigation Section); Virginia State Bar (Member, Litigation Section); Maryland State (Member, Litigation Section) and American (Member, Litigation Section) Bar Associations. ***Email:*** SHA@GDLLAW.COM

(This Listing Continued)

LEWIS F. MORSE, born Albany, New York, August 5, 1948; admitted to bar, 1975, District of Columbia and Maryland; 1979, U.S. Tax Court. *Education:* Cornell University (B.S., 1970); George Washington University (J.D., with honors, 1974); Georgetown University (LL.M. in Taxation, 1980). *Member:* The District of Columbia Bar (Member, Taxation Section); Maryland State and American (Member, Sections on: Taxation; Real Property, Probate and Trust Law) Bar Associations. ***Email:*** LFM@GDLLAW.COM

JOHN PATRICK BROWN, JR., born New York, N.Y., June 13, 1960; admitted to bar, 1988, Maryland; 1989, District of Columbia. *Education:* Boston College (B.A., Political Science, 1983); George Washington Universit y (J.D. 1987). *Member:* Maryland State Bar Association; The District of Columbia Bar (Member, Sections on: Real Estate; Housing and Land Use; District of Columbia Affairs). [JAGC, U.S. Army Reserve, 1988-2000]. ***PRACTICE AREAS:*** Real Estate Development; Zoning Law; Land Use; Historic Preservation; Municipal Law. ***Email:*** JPB@GDLLAW.COM

LYLE M. BLANCHARD, born Philadelphia, Pennsylvania, September 4, 1958; admitted to bar, 1999, Maryland; 2000, District of Columbia. *Education:* Marlboro College (B.A., 1984); Antioch School of Law (M.A., Legal Studies, 1985); Catholic University of America, Columbus School of Law (J.D., 1998). Legislative Analyst, 1988-1991, and Legislative Advisor, 1991-1992, Office of the Director, District of Columbia Department of Consumer and Regulatory Affairs. Committee Clerk to the Honorable James Nathanson, D.C. Council Committee on Governmental Operations, 1992-1993. Legislative Assistant to the Honorable James Nathanson, D.C. Council Committee on the Judiciary, 1993-1994. Committee Clerk to the Honorable Jack Evans, D.C. Counsel Committee on Public Services and Regional Authorities, 1995-1996. Member, Committee on the Judiciary, 1997-1998, and Committee on Finance and Revenue, 1999-2000. Member, New York Avenue Development Task Force, 1996. Member, Washington Convention Center Advisory Committee, 1997. Member, District of Columbia Chamber of Commerce. *Member:* District of Columbia Bar (Member, Real Estate, Housing and Land Use, and District of Columbia Affairs Sections), Maryland State (Member, Real Property, Planning and Zoning Section) and American (Member, Real Property, State and Local Government Sections) Bar Associations; Japan Commerce Association; George Washington American Inn of Court. ***PRACTICE AREAS:*** Land Use; Estate Planning; Zoning Law; Historic Preservation; Municipal Law; Alcoholic Beverage Control; Legislative Practice. ***Email:*** lmb@gdllaw.com

DONALD F. HOLMES, JR., born Scranton, Pennsylvania, July 6, 1966; admitted to bar, 1994, Pennsylvania and U.S. District Court, Middle District of Pennsylvania; 1996, District of Columbia; 1997, New York. *Education:* Temple University (B.B.A., 1988); Catholic University of America, Columbus School of Law (J.D., 1993). Moot Court Associate. Lead Articles Editor, Journal of Contemporary Health Law and Policy, Volume, 9. *Member:* American Bar Association. ***Email:*** DFH@GDLLAW.COM

MIRIAM HELLEN JONES, born Portsmouth, New Hampshire, June 14, 1949; admitted to bar, 1982, District of Columbia. *Education:* Kalamazoo College and Federal City College (B.S., cum laude, 1971); Catholic University of America, Columbus School of Law (J.D., 1979). Chief, Condominium and Cooperative Conversion and Sales Branch, Department of Housing and Community Development, District of Columbia, 1979-1983. Superintendent of Corporations for the District of Columbia, 1983-1991. Enforcement Officer, District of Columbia Department of Consumer and Regulatory Affairs, 1991-1994. Chief of the Office of Compliance, District of Columbia Department of Consumer and Regulatory Affairs, 1994-1997. Member: District of Columbia Real Estate Commission, 1984-1991; District of Columbia Chamber of Commerce. Hearing Officer, Mayor's Agent for Historic Preservation, 1995-1997. I Member: The District of Columbia Bar (Member, Sections on: Corporation, Finance and Securities Law; District of Columbia Affairs; Real Estate, Housing and Land Use; Arts, Entertainment and Sports Law); District of Columbia Building Industry Association. ***PRACTICE AREAS:*** Commercial Real Estate; Real Estate Development; Land Use; Historic Preservation; Administrative Law; Regulatory Practice. ***Email:*** MHJ@GDLLAW.COM

SARAE T. LEUCKEL, born Allentown, Pennsylvania, December 1, 1968; admitted to bar, 1993, Pennsylvania; 1994, Florida; 1996, Virginia; 1998, District of Columbia. *Education:* University of Maryland (B.A., Government and Politics, 1989); University of Puget Sound School of Law (J.D., 1993). *Member:* American (Member, Administrative Law and Regulatory Practice and Natural Resources, Energy and Environmental Law Sections) and Inter-American Bar Associations; The Florida Bar; Virginia State Bar; The District of Columbia Bar. ***LANGUAGES:*** Spanish. ***PRACTICE AREAS:*** Real Estate; Land Use; International Law. ***Email:*** STL@GDLLAW.COM

ISABEL P. RUIZ DE GAMBOA, born Santiago, Chile, March 9, 1972; admitted to bar, 1997, Virginia (Not admitted in District of Columbia). *Education:* Virginia Polytechnic Institute and State University (B.S., 1994); George Washington University Law School (J.D., 1997). *Member:* American Bar Association (Member, Real Property, Probate and Trust Law Section). ***LANGUAGES:*** Spanish. ***PRACTICE AREAS:*** Commercial Real Estate; Real Estate Finance; Commercial Leasing; Financial Institutions Law. ***Email:*** IPR@GDLLAW.COM

JAMES D. SADOWSKI, born Trenton, Michigan, June 7, 1965; admitted to bar, 1992, Maryland; 1996, District of Columbia, Virginia, U.S. Court of Appeals, Fourth Circuit, U.S. District Court, Eastern District of Virginia and U.S. District Court, District of Maryland; 1998, U.S. District Court for the District of Columbia; 2000, U.S. Bankruptcy Court, Eastern District of Virginia. *Education:* George Washington University (B.A., 1989); Catholic University of America (J.D., 1992). Recipient, American Jurisprudence Award in Contracts. Member and Editorial Assistant, The Catholic University Law Review, 1990-1992. Law Clerk to Honorable Brook Hedge, District of Columbia Superior Court, 1992-1994. Member, Judicial Conference of the District of Columbia, 1995-1997, 1999-2000. *Member:* Virginia State Bar; The District of Columbia Bar; Maryland State Bar Association. ***Email:*** JDS@GDLLAW.COM

GRIFFIN, FARMER, TARBY & MURPHY, LLP

Established in 1976

1912 SUNDERLAND PLACE, N.W.

WASHINGTON, D.C. 20036-1608

Telephone: 202-429-9000

Telefax: 202-232-7365

Email: gglaw1912@aol.com

URL: http://www.washlaw.com

Fairfax, Virginia Office: 10476 Armstrong Street, 22030. Telephone: 703-591-4300. Fax: 703-591-4323.

Commercial Transactions, Corporate Law, Commercial and Residential Real Estate, Land Use and Zoning, Federal and State Taxation, Estate Planning and Probate, Civil and Administrative Litigation before all Courts, Departments and Agencies, General Practice.

FIRM PROFILE: Griffin, Farmer, Tarby & Murphy, LLP represents a diverse, entrepreneurial, domestic and international clientele in the practice areas of Business Formation and Counseling, Real Estate, Land Use and Zoning, Federal and State Taxation, Estate Planning, and Civil Litigation in the Washington-Suburban Maryland-Northern Virginia region. The firm provides a broad range of counseling services to individuals, enterprises, and institutions in areas including commercial and residential real estate acquisitions, sales, and leasing, structured and/or syndicated transactions, financing, taxation, and zoning and land use issues, as well as in the formation, operation, and transformation of business entities. The firm also provides comprehensive estate planning and probate services for individuals and families.

MARK G. GRIFFIN, born Port Chester, New York, March 30, 1947; admitted to bar, 1973, Maryland; 1974, District of Columbia. *Education:* Georgetown University (A.B., 1969; J.D., 1973). Chairman, Maryland State Board of Maritime Pilots, 1994-2201. Assistant Attorney, Village of Chevy Chase, Maryland, 1974-1979. Law Member, District of Columbia Real Estate Commission, 1976-1979. Legal Counsel, 1980-1984 and President, 1984-1988, The Historical Society of Washington, D.C. Member, Board of Regents, Georgetown University, 1989-1994. *Member:* The District of Columbia Bar; Bar Association of the District of Columbia; Maryland State and American Bar Associations. ***PRACTICE AREAS:*** Real Estate; Estate Planning; Probate; Business Law; Corporate Law; Civil Litigation. ***Email:*** gglaw1912@aol.com

JONATHAN L. FARMER, born Washington, D.C., October 26, 1952; admitted to bar, 1977, Michigan; 1978, District of Columbia. *Education:* Brown University (A.B., 1974); University of Michigan (J.D., 1977). ***PRACTICE AREAS:*** Zoning, Planning and Land Use; Municipal Law; Environmental Law. ***Email:*** jfarmer@washlaw.com

BRIAN P. MURPHY, born Providence, Rhode Island, June 29, 1943; admitted to bar, 1969, District of Columbia; 1976, Maryland. *Education:* Georgetown University (A.B., 1965); Catholic University of America (J.D., 1968); City of London College (International Law Program, 1968). *Member:* The District of Columbia Bar. ***PRACTICE AREAS:*** Corporate Law; Civil Practice; Real Estate; International Law; Business Law. ***Email:*** BMurphy470@aol.com

ALEXANDER DJORDJEVICH, born Paris, France, January 15, 1966; admitted to bar, 1992, Maryland; 1995, District of Columbia; 1996, U.S. District Court, District of Maryland. *Education:* University of California at Berkeley (A.B., 1988); Washington College of Law of American University (J.D., 1992). Member, Moot Court Board. Law Clerk to the Honorable Christine Odell Cook Miller, Judge, U.S. Court of Federal Claims. *Member:* The District of Columbia Bar (Member, Sections on: Estates & Trusts; Real Estate and Land Use). ***LANGUAGES:*** French. ***PRACTICE AREAS:*** Business Transactions (35%); Real Estate (20%); Litigation (20%); Wills (20%); Trust Law; Probate. ***Email:*** alexd@washlaw.com

(This Listing Continued)

GRIFFIN, FARMER, TARBY & MURPHY, LLP, Washington—Continued

ASSOCIATES

DAVID K. McRAE, born Winchester, Massachusetts, June 4, 1962; admitted to bar, 1994, Maryland; 1999, District of Columbia. *Education:* Cornell University (A.B., 1984); University of Maryland (J.D., 1994). *Member:* The District of Columbia Bar. ***PRACTICE AREAS:*** Corporate Law; Civil Practice; Real Estate; Administrative Law. ***Email:*** dmcrae@washlaw.com

JAMES T. HEISE, born Baltimore, Maryland, September 6, 1971; admitted to bar, 1999, Maryland; 2000, U.S. District Court, District of Maryland (Not admitted in District of Columbia). *Education:* University of Baltimore (B.S., cum laude, 1995; J.D., cum laude, 1999). Phi Delta Phi. Author: "University of Baltimore Journal of Environmental Law," Fall, 1997. Member, Maryland Bar Association, 1999-2000. ***PRACTICE AREAS:*** Real Property; Business Law; Trusts and Estates. ***Email:*** jheise@washlaw.com

OF COUNSEL

DALE L. JERNBERG, born Clayton, New Mexico, January 15, 1924; admitted to bar, 1950, District of Columbia; 19 54, Maryland. *Education:* George Washington University (A.A., 1947; J.D., 1949). *Member:* District of Columbia Bar; Bar Association of the District of Columbia; American Bar Association; Estate Planning Council of the District of Columbia. (Also practicing individually in Greenbelt, Maryland). ***PRACTICE AREAS:*** Trusts and Estates; Estate Planning; Wills; Real Estate; Elder Law. ***Email:*** daleatty@aol.com

---

GRIGGS & ADLER

Established in 1992

1225 EYE STREET, N.W., SUITE 500
WASHINGTON, D.C. 20005
Telephone: 202-682-4766; 888-317-0853
Fax: 703-716-2865
Email: GRIGGSLAW@AOL.COM
URL: http://www.lawyers.com/griggs&adlerlaw

Reston, Virginia Office: Griggs & Adler, P.C., 1801 Robert Fulton Drive, Suite 400. Telephone: 703-758-6701.

Energy Regulation, Administrative Agency Practice, Natural Resources, Commercial Leasing.

FIRM PROFILE: Founded in 1992, Griggs and Adler offers personalized service tailored to meet the client's specialized needs in selected practice areas.

JOHN WYETH GRIGGS, born West Palm Beach, Florida, March 27, 1947; admitted to bar, 1973, District of Columbia; 1977, Florida; 1980, U.S. Supreme Court; 1985, Alaska; U.S. Court of Appeals, District of Columbia, 4th, 5th, 9th, 10th and 11th Circuits. *Education:* Colgate University (B.A., 1969); Columbia University (J.D., 1973). Administrative Editor, Columbia Human Rights Law Review, 1972-1973. Member, Solicitor's Honors Program, U.S. Department of the Interior, 1973-1974. Author: "Competitive Bidding and Independent Power Producers: Is Deregulation Coming to the Electric Utility Industry?" 9 Energy L.J. 415, 1988; "Restructuring the Natural Gas Industry: Order No. 436 and Other Regulatory Initiatives," 7 Energy L.J. 71, 1986. Attorney, Office of the General Counsel, Nuclear Regulatory Commission, 1976-1978. Partner, Birch, Horton, Bittner & Cherot, 1989-1992. *Member:* District of Columbia Bar; The Florida Bar; Alaska and Federal Energy Bar Associations. ***PRACTICE AREAS:*** Energy Regulation; Civil Litigation; Commercial Real Estate; Natural Resources.

DEBRA B. ADLER, born Brooklyn, New York, February 11, 1960; admitted to bar, 1988, Virginia; 1989, District of Columbia, U.S. District Court, District of Columbia, U.S. District Court, Eastern District of Virginia and U.S. Court of Appeals, Fourth Circuit. *Education:* University of Massachusetts (B.A., 1982); George Washington University (J.D., with honors, 1988). Phi Beta Kappa. *Member:* Virginia State Bar; District of Columbia Bar. ***PRACTICE AREAS:*** Corporate Law; Civil Litigation; Energy Regulation; Employment Law; Mediation.

REPRESENTATIVE CLIENTS: Cap Rock Electric Cooperative, Inc.; Conoco Inc.; Live Oak Realty, Inc.; OXY USA Inc.; NewCorp Resources, Inc.; Secure Engineering Services, Inc.; Tycon One, Inc.; Union Oil Company of California.

GROOM LAW GROUP

CHARTERED

Established in 1975

SUITE 1200
1701 PENNSYLVANIA AVENUE, N.W.
WASHINGTON, D.C. 20006-5893
Telephone: 202-857-0620
Telecopier: 202-659-4503
Email: info@groom.com
URL: http://www.groom.com

Employee Benefits, Health, Litigation, Tax and Legislation.

FIRM PROFILE: Groom Law Group, Chartered, was founded in 1975. With nearly 40 lawyers and other professionals specializing in employee benefits, health, insurance, securities and tax law, the firm's clients include some of the world's largest domestic and multinational corporations, financial institutions, private and public employee welfare benefit plans, trade associations and tax-exempt organizations. The Groom Law Group provides a full range of legal services, including planning, advice, litigation and representation in legislative and administrative proceedings, as well as in regulatory controversies before government agencies.

THEODORE R. GROOM, born Wichita, Kansas, June 14, 1934; admitted to bar, 1960, Virginia; 1961, District of Columbia. *Education:* Bucknell University (A.B., 1956); Harvard University (LL.B., cum laude, 1960). ***PRACTICE AREAS:*** ERISA; Tax Law; Employee Benefits; Pension and Profit Sharing; Health Care. ***Email:*** trg@groom.com

LOUIS T. MAZAWEY, born Weehawken, New Jersey, June 8, 1949; admitted to bar, 1975, District of Columbia. *Education:* New York University (B.A., cum laude, 1971); Georgetown University Law Center (J.D., 1974). Phi Beta Kappa. Editor, Georgetown Law Journal, 1973-1974. ***PRACTICE AREAS:*** Employee Benefits; Labor and Employment; Pension and Profit Sharing; Tax Law; ERISA. ***Email:*** ltm@groom.com

GARY M. FORD, born Lawton, Oklahoma, April 18, 1950; admitted to bar, 1977, Massachusetts; 1978, District of Columbia. *Education:* Harvard University (A.B., magna cum laude, 1972); Boston University (J.D., 1977). Staff Attorney, 1977-1979 and Special Counsel, 1979, Pension Benefit Guaranty Corporation. Labor Counsel, Committee on Labor and Human Resources, United States Senate, 1980-1981. General Counsel, Pension Benefit Guaranty Corporation, 1987-1989. ***PRACTICE AREAS:*** Employee Benefits Law; Insurance Litigation; Pension and Profit Sharing; Mergers and Acquisitions; Labor and Employment; ERISA. ***Email:*** gmf@groom.com

ROBERT P. GALLAGHER, born Bryn Mawr, Pennsylvania, September 16, 1945; admitted to bar, 1971, Pennsylvania; 1973, District of Columbia; 1974, Trust Territory of Pacific Islands. *Education:* George Washington University (B.A., 1968; J.D., with honors, 1971). Articles Editor, Journal of International Law & Economics, 1970-1971. Trial Attorney, U.S. Department of Justice, 1971-1974. Counsel for Litigation, Plan Benefits Security Division, Office of the Solicitor, U.S. Department of Labor, 1976-1982. ***PRACTICE AREAS:*** Health Care; Employee Benefits; Pension and Profit Sharing; ERISA. ***Email:*** rpg@groom.com

STEPHEN M. SAXON, born Washington, D.C., January 11, 1951; admitted to bar, 1979, District of Columbia. *Education:* Colgate University (A.B., 1973); Georgetown University (J.D., 1979). ***PRACTICE AREAS:*** Business Law; Employee Benefits; Health Care; Tax; Labor and Employment; ERISA. ***Email:*** sms@groom.com

DOUGLAS W. ELL, born Manchester, Connecticut, August 3, 1949; admitted to bar, 1979, District of Columbia. *Education:* Massachusetts Institute of Technology (B.A., 1971); University of Maryland (M.A., 1973); University of Connecticut (J.D., magna cum laude, 1979). Executive Editor, University of Connecticut Law Review, 1978-1979. ***PRACTICE AREAS:*** Labor and Employment; Insurance Defense; Mergers and Acquisitions; Tax; Employee Benefits; ERISA. ***Email:*** dwe@groom.com

CHARLES W. SHERMAN, JR., born Miami Beach, Florida, June 21, 1945; admitted to bar, 1983, District of Columbia. *Education:* Yale University; Florida State University (B.A., 1968; M.S., 1971); Hastings College of Law, University of California; Boalt Hall School of Law, University of California (J.D., 1983). Editor-in-Chief, California Law Review, 1982-1983. ***PRACTICE AREAS:*** Employee Benefits; Pension and Profit Sharing; Tax Law; ERISA. ***Email:*** cws@groom.com

THOMAS F. FITZGERALD, born Norfolk, Virginia, November 3, 1953; admitted to bar, 1981, District of Columbia. *Education:* St. Joseph's University (B.A., 1976); Loyola College (M.B.A., 1978); Georgetown University (J.D., 1981). *Member:* District of Columbia Bar; Maryland State Bar Association. ***PRACTICE AREAS:*** Employee Benefits Law; Health Care Law; ERISA; Civil Litigation. ***Email:*** tff@groom.com

(This Listing Continued)

IAN D. LANOFF, born Chicago, Illinois, September 23, 1942; admitted to bar, 1967, Illinois; 1971, U.S. Court of Appeals, Sixth Circuit; 1973, District of Columbia, U.S. Court of Appeals for the District of Columbia Circuit and U.S. Supreme Court. *Education:* University of Michigan (B.A., 1964; J.D., 1967); Georgetown University (LL.M., 1969). Phi Beta Kappa. Co-author with Florian Bartosic: "Escalating the Struggle Against Taft-Hartley Contemnors," University of Chicago Law Review, Vol. 39, No. 2, 1972. Author: "Reporting and Disclosure and Prudence in Investment Under ERISA," Labor Law Journal, Vol. 29, No. 6, 1978. Administrator, Pension and Welfare Benefits Program, U.S. Department of Labor, 1977-1981. *Member:* District of Columbia Bar; American Bar Association (Member, Sections on: Corporation, Banking and Business Law; Labor and Employment Law). ***PRACTICE AREAS:*** Employee Benefits; Labor and Employment; Pension and Profit Sharing; Health Care Law; ERISA. ***Email:*** idl@groom.com

LONIE HASSEL, born Pittsburgh, Pennsylvania, July 31, 1955; admitted to bar, 1980, District of Columbia; 1981, U.S. District Court for the District of Columbia; 1987, U.S. Court of Appeals, Second, Fourth, Fifth and District Circuits. *Education:* Catholic University of America (B.A., summa cum laude, 1977); University of Virginia (J.D., 1980). Phi Beta Kappa. Attorney and Assistant General Counsel, Pension Benefit Guaranty Corporation, 1980-1988. ***LANGUAGES:*** French. ***PRACTICE AREAS:*** Mergers and Acquisitions; Pension and Profit Sharing; Insurance Litigation; Employee Benefits; ERISA. ***Email:*** lah@groom.com

THOMAS S. GIGOT, born Milwaukee, Wisconsin, November 19, 1958; admitted to bar, 1984, District of Columbia; 1985, U.S. District Court for the District of Columbia, U.S. Court of Appeals, Second, Third, Fourth, Sixth, Seventh, Eighth, Eleventh and District of Columbia Circuits. *Education:* Marquette University (B.S., magna cum laude, 1980); Georgetown University (J.D., cum laude, 1984). Phi Beta Kappa. ***PRACTICE AREAS:*** Employee Benefits; Labor and Employment; Pension and Profit Sharing; Insurance Defense; ERISA. ***Email:*** tsg@groom.com

WILLIAM M. EVANS, born Rexburg, Idaho, 1959; admitted to bar, 1986, North Carolina; 1996, District of Columbia. *Education:* Ricks College (A.A., highest honors, 1981); Brigham Young University (B.A., summa cum laude, 1983); University of Virginia (J.D., 1986). Phi Kappa Phi. *Member:* North Carolina and American Bar Associations; North Carolina State Bar. ***PRACTICE AREAS:*** Employee Benefits; Labor and Employment; Pension and Profit Sharing; Tax Law; ERISA. ***Email:*** wme@groom.com

ANDRÉE M. ST. MARTIN, born LaPlace, Louisiana, March 27, 1958; admitted to bar, 1983, District of Columbia; 1986, U.S. District Court, District of Columbia and U.S. Court of Appeals, Fourth and Sixth Circuits. *Education:* Spring Hill College (B.A., summa cum laude, 1980); Harvard Law School (J.D., cum laude, 1983). Attorney, U.S. Department of Labor, Solicitor's Office, Plan Benefits Security Division, 1983-1985. ***PRACTICE AREAS:*** Employee Benefits; Pension and Profit Sharing; ERISA.

JON W. BREYFOGLE, born Homestead, Florida, June 23, 1960; admitted to bar, 1995, Maryland; 1997, District of Columbia. *Education:* University of Cincinnati (B.A., with honors in Political Science, 1982); Indiana University (M.P.A., 1985); George Mason Law School (J.D., with distinction, 1995). Member, Pi Alpha Alpha Honorary Society, 1985. Member, George Mason University Law Review, 1992-1994. Fellow: Lilly Community, 1984-1985; School of Public and Environmental Affairs, 1982-1983. Governor's Fellow, Office of the Governor, State of Illinois, 1983-1984. Member, Presidential Management Internship Program, Office of Management and Budget, Executive Office of the President, Washington, D.C., 1985-1987. Special Assistant to the Executive Director for Congressional Affairs, U.S. Pension Benefit Guaranty Corporation, 1987-1989. Senior Legislative Officer, Office of the Secretary of Labor, U.S. Department of Labor, Washington, D.C., 1989-1992. *Member:* Maryland State Bar Association. ***PRACTICE AREAS:*** Health Care; Employee Benefits; Pension and Profit Sharing; Legislative, Regulatory and Judicial Representations; ERISA. ***Email:*** jwb@groom.com

DAVID W. POWELL, born Galveston, Texas, 1957; admitted to bar, 1982, Louisiana; 1983, Texas; 1986, District of Columbia; 1988, New York. *Education:* Southern Methodist University (B.B.A., cum laude, 1979); University of Texas (J.D., 1982). Certified Public Accountant, Louisiana, 1983. ***PRACTICE AREAS:*** Employee Benefits Law; Tax Law; ERISA. ***Email:*** dwp@groom.com

ROBERTA J. UFFORD, born Madison, Wisconsin, June 25, 1960; admitted to bar, 1994, District of Columbia. *Education:* Goucher College (B.A., with honors, honors in Int. Rel., 1982); George Washington University (J.D., high honors, 1992). Member, Order of the Coif. Member, Journal of International Law & Economics. *Member:* District of Columbia Bar (Member, Corporate and Securities Law Section); American Bar Association. [Capt., U.S. Army, 1982-1987]. ***PRACTICE AREAS:*** Employee Benefits; ERISA; Securities; Pension and Profit Sharing. ***Email:*** rju@groom.com

MARK L. LOFGREN, born Washington, D.C., January 25, 1962; admitted to bar, 1992, Minnesota; 1998, District of Columbia. *Education:* University of Maryland (B.S., 1984); College of William & Mary (J.D., 1992). Order of the

(This Listing Continued)

Coif. Managing Editor, Administrative Law Review. Certified Public Accountant, Maryland, 1986. ***PRACTICE AREAS:*** Pension and Profit Sharing; Employee Benefits; ERISA. ***Email:*** mll@groom.com

EDWARD A. SCALLET, born St. Louis, Missouri, July 22, 1950; admitted to bar, 1975, Missouri; 1982, U.S. Court of Appeals, Fifth and Eighth Circuits; 1983, District of Columbia, U.S. Court of Appeals for the District of Columbia Circuit and U.S. Supreme Court; 1991, U.S. District Court, District of Maryland and U.S. District Court for the District of Columbia; 1993, U.S. District Court, Eastern District of Michigan and U.S. Tax Court; 1996, U.S. Court of Appeals, Fourth Circuit; 1997, U.S. Court of Appeals, Eleventh Circuit; 1998, U.S. Court of Appeals, Ninth Circuit; 2000, U.S. Court of Appeals, Sixth Circuit. *Education:* Harvard University (A.B., magna cum laude, 1972); Washington University (J.D., 1975). Order of the Coif. Author: "A Critical Guide to ERISA Preemption in the Courts," Benefits Law Journal, Autumn, 1988; "A New Approach to Service-Provider Liability," Benefits Law Journal, Autumn, 1989. ***PRACTICE AREAS:*** Employee Benefits; Litigation. ***Email:*** eas@groom.com

RICHARD K. MATTA, born Wilkinsburg, Pennsylvania, February 3, 1957; admitted to bar, 1982, Pennsylvania and U.S. District Court, Western District of Pennsylvania; 1985, District of Columbia. *Education:* University of Pittsburgh (B.A., summa cum laude, 1979); Georgetown University (J.D., 1982). Phi Beta Kappa. Recipient, Constitutional Law Book Award. Member, National Moot Court Competition. Author: "ERISA Section 408(b)(8): Can an Old Dog Learn New Tricks?" American Bankers Association Trusts & Investments, Jan./Feb., 2001; "ERISA PTE 77-3 and 77-4: The Hot Issue Cools," ABA Trusts & Investments, Jul./Aug., 1999; "Daily Valuation of 401(k) Plans: Fiduciary Considerations," The Investment Lawyer, Aspen Law & Business, March, 1997; "Special Credit Risks of Bank Loans to Private Employee Benefit Plans in the United States," 7 Journal of International Banking Law 304, July, 1995; "Acquisition and Performance Fees from ERISA Accounts: AEW Steps Ahead," Institutional Read Estate Newsletter, July, 1993; "[Fidelity Mutual Life] Implications for Real Estate Managers and Advisers," Institutional Real Estate Newsletter, December, 1992; "Fiduciary Liability of Corporate Officers Under ERISA - New Decision Adds to Uncertainty," Institutional Real Estate Newsletter, June, 1992. Co-Author: "ERISA PTE 77-3 and 77-4: The Next Generation of Issues," ABA Trusts & Investments, Dec., 1997; " Insuring the Lives of Borrowers: The New Trend in Bank-Owned Life Insurance," ABA Banking Journal, 1997; Bank Investment Products Deskbook, B. Smith ed., Warren, Gorham & Lamont, 1995; A501(c)(25) Corporation is Vehicle of Choice for Many Commingled Real Estate Investment Funds," Institutional Real Estate Newsletter, May, 1995; "Carrots and Sticks: The New IRS Voluntary Compliance Resolution Program and Increased Audits for Plan Operational Defects," reprinted in Tax Analysts' Highlights and Documents, Doc. 93-672, Jan. 14, 1993. *Member:* The District of Columbia Bar (Member, Taxation Division); American Bar Association. ***PRACTICE AREAS:*** ERISA; Securities; Tax; Corporate Law. ***Email:*** rkm@groom.com

OF COUNSEL

WILLIAM F. HANRAHAN, born Los Angeles, California, February 1, 1948; admitted to bar, 1973, California; 1982, District of Columbia. *Education:* University of California at Los Angeles (B.A., cum laude, 1970); University of California at Berkeley (J.D., 1973). Law Clerk for Chief Judge Richard H. Chambers, U.S. Court of Appeals, Ninth Circuit, 1973-1975. Trial Attorney, Pension Benefit Guaranty Corporation, 1975-1979. General Counsel, UMWA Health and Retirement Funds, 1982-1986. ***PRACTICE AREAS:*** Employee Benefits Law; Civil Trial Practice; Pension and Profit Sharing; Appellate Practice; ERISA. ***Email:*** wfh@groom.com

JOHN P. McALLISTER, born Washington, D.C., April 7, 1951; admitted to bar, 1977, Connecticut; 1982, U.S. Claims Court and U.S. Tax Court; 1983, District of Columbia. *Education:* Yale University (B.A., summa cum laude, 1973); Georgetown University (J.D., 1977). Phi Beta Kappa. Trial Attorney, Tax Division, United States Department of Justice, 1979-1982. ***PRACTICE AREAS:*** Employee Benefit Taxation; Employee Benefits Law; Tax Law; Civil Trial Practice; Appellate Practice; ERISA. ***Email:*** jpm@groom.com

MICHAEL A. THRASHER, born Norfolk, Virginia, February 15, 1945; admitted to bar, 1970, North Carolina; 1998, District of Columbia. *Education:* Duke University (B.A., 1967); University of North Carolina (J.D., 1970); Georgetown University (LL.M., Taxation, 1975). Adjunct Professor, Georgetown University Law Center, 1989—. Chief Counsel's Office, Internal Revenue Service, 1970-1996; Assistant Chief Counsel, Employee Benefits and Exempt Organizations, 1990-1996. *Member:* District of Columbia Bar; American Bar Association (Member, Section of Taxation, Employee Benefits Committee, 1983—). ***PRACTICE AREAS:*** Employee Benefits; Exempt Organizations; ERISA. ***Email:*** mat@groom.com

ROBERT D. VALER, born New Rockford, North Dakota, May 31, 1950; admitted to bar, 1986, Maryland and California; 1988, Colorado; 1991, District of Columbia. *Education:* Minot State College (B.S., 1971); Boston University (Ed.M., 1979); Georgetown University (J.D., 1985; LL.M. in Taxation, 1995).

(This Listing Continued)

GROOM LAW GROUP, CHARTERED, Washington—Continued

Member: The District of Columbia Bar; American Bar Association. ***PRACTICE AREAS:*** Employee Benefits; ERISA; Tax Law. ***Email:*** rdv@groom.com

ALVARO I. ANILLO, born Washington, D.C., April 12, 1967; admitted to bar, 1992, Tennessee; 1994, District of Columbia. *Education:* Duke University (B.A., cum laude, 1989); Vanderbilt University (J.D., 1992). Managing Editor, Vanderbilt Law Review. Law Clerk, The Honorable Judge Juan Torruella, U.S. Court of Appeals for the First Circuit. *Member:* The District of Columbia Bar. ***LANGUAGES:*** Spanish. ***Email:*** aia@groom.com

KENDALL W. DAINES, born Denver, Colorado, February 3, 1956; admitted to bar, 1987, Virginia; 1992, District of Columbia; 1995, Illinois. *Education:* Williams College (B.A. in History, 1978); University of North Carolina at Chapel Hill (B.S.N., 1981); University of Michigan (J.D., cum laude, 1987). Order of the Coif. *Member:* The District of Columbia Bar. ***PRACTICE AREAS:*** Employee Benefits. ***Email:*** kwd@groom.com

---

MICHAEL J. PRAME, born Batavia, New York, 1968; admitted to bar, 1994, New York and Maryland; 1996, District of Columbia. *Education:* Le Moyne College (B.S., summa cum laude, 1990); Georgetown University (J.D., 1993).

ELIZABETH THOMAS DOLD, born Danbury, Connecticut, January 27, 1969; admitted to bar, 1994, New Jersey; 1995, Pennsylvania (Not admitted in District of Columbia). *Education:* Pennsylvania State University (B.S., Accounting, Minor in Business Law, with highest distinction, 1991); Dickinson School of Law (J.D., magna cum laude, 1994); New York University (LL.M., Taxation, 1996). Woolsack Honor Society. Listed in Who's Who Among American Law Students, 1992-1994. Recipient: Edward N. Polisher Federal Estate & Gift Tax Award; Trusts and Estates/Estate Planning Award; West Publishing Company Law Student Award. Member, Dickinson Law Review, 1992-1994. Coordinator, Volunteer Income Tax Assistance Program (VITA), 1992-1994. *Member:* Pennsylvania, New Jersey State and American Bar Associations. ***PRACTICE AREAS:*** Taxation Law; Employee Benefits; Pension and Profit Sharing; ERISA. ***Email:*** etd@groom.com

DANIEL LEE HOGANS, born Baltimore, Maryland, September 6, 1967; admitted to bar, 1993, Virginia; 1999, District of Columbia. *Education:* George Mason University (B.S., 1989); University of Virginia (M.S., 1990); College of William & Mary (J.D., 1993). Beta Gamma Sigma. ***PRACTICE AREAS:*** Retirement Benefit Plans; Executive Compensation; Securities. ***Email:*** dhogans@groom.com

STEPHANIE L. NAPIER, born Kansas City, Missouri, November 18, 1971; admitted to bar, 1997, Maryland; 1999, District of Columbia. *Education:* University of Michigan (B.A., with distinction, 1993); Georgetown University Law Center (J.D., cum laude, 1997). Articles Editor, The Tax Lawyer, 1996-1997. ***PRACTICE AREAS:*** Employee Benefits; ERISA; Health Care Law. ***Email:*** sln@groom.com

DAVID N. LEVINE, admitted to bar, 1998, New York; 1999, District of Columbia. *Education:* Johns Hopkins University (B.A., 1994); University of Pennsylvania (J.D., 1997). Jessup International Moot Court Competition. ***REPORTED CASES:*** Andrews v. Gorby, 237 Conn. 12, 675 A.2d 449 (1996). ***PRACTICE AREAS:*** Employee Benefits; Tax. ***Email:*** dnl@groom.com

CHRISTY A. TINNES, born Port Arthur, Texas, November 14, 1969; admitted to bar, 1998, South Carolina (Not admitted in District of Columbia). *Education:* University of South Carolina (B.S., 1992; MACC, 1993; J.D., 1998). Member, University of South Carolina Law Review. Wig and Robe. ***PRACTICE AREAS:*** Employee Benefits. ***Email:*** cat@groom.com

JENNIFER E. ELLER, born Santo Domingo, Dominican Republic, March 21, 1971; admitted to bar, 2000, Maryland (Not admitted in District of Columbia). *Education:* Georgetown University (J.D., 2000). ***PRACTICE AREAS:*** Employee Benefits. ***Email:*** jee@groom.com

ELENA C. BARONE, born Pittsburgh, Pennsylvania, July 19, 1974; admitted to bar, 1999, Virginia; 2000, District of Columbia. *Education:* Duke University (B.A., with distinction, 1996); George Washington University (J.D., with honors, 1999). Articles Editor, The Environmental Lawyer, 1998-1999. *Member:* Virginia State Bar; The District of Columbia Bar; American Bar Association (Member, Tax Section). ***PRACTICE AREAS:*** ERISA; Tax Law. ***Email:*** ebarone@groom.com

C. DUNCAN MACRAE, born St. Louis, Missouri, April 14, 1940; admitted to bar, 1994, Virginia; 1996, District of Columbia. *Education:* Harvard University (A.B., 1962); George Mason University School of Law (J.D., 1994); Cambridge University (Ph.D., Economics, 1996). National Merit Scholar. University Research Scholar. Adelaide Stoll Scholar. Certified Public Accountant, District of Columbia, 1983. Adjunct Professor, George Mason University School of Law, 1997-1998. *Member:* American Bar Association. ***PRACTICE AREAS:*** Employee Benefits. ***Email:*** dmacrae@groom.com

JASON O. KEENE, born Washington, D.C.; admitted to bar, 2000, New York (Not admitted in District of Columbia). *Education:* University of Maryland at College Park (B.A., Journalism, 1995); New York University (J.D., 1999). Golden Key. Member, New York University Review of Law and Social Change, 1998-1999. ***PRACTICE AREAS:*** Employee Benefits; Executive Compensation. ***Email:*** jkeene@groom.com

JONATHAN J. BOYLES, born Richmond, Virginia, June 22, 1973; admitted to bar, 2001, New York (Not admitted in District of Columbia). *Education:* University of Virginia (B.A., 1995); Georgetown University (J.D., 2000). Managing Editor, Georgetown Journal of Gender and the Law, First Annual Review of Gender and Sexuality Law, 1999-2000. Author: "Employer - Sponsored Domestic Partner Benefits," Georgetown Journal of Gender and the Law. ***LANGUAGES:*** French. ***PRACTICE AREAS:*** Employee Benefits. ***Email:*** jboyles@groom.com

(This Listing Continued)

CYNTHIA A. GROOMES, P.C.

WASHINGTON, D.C.

(See Bethesda, Maryland)

Immigration Law, Business Immigration, Employment Visas, Employment Authorizations, Labor Certification, Investor Visas, Permanent Residency Visas, Political Asylum, H-1B, J-1 Waivers.

GROSSBERG, YOCHELSON, FOX & BEYDA, LLP

Established in 1930

2000 L STREET, N.W., SUITE 675

WASHINGTON, D.C. 20036-4907

Telephone: 202-296-9696

Telecopier: 202-296-7777

URL: http://www.GYFB.com

Commercial Real Estate, Real Estate Finance, Real Estate Tax, Corporate Taxation, Probate and Estate Planning, Health Care Law.

MEMBERS OF FIRM

SOLOMON GROSSBERG (1905-1994).

IRVING B. YOCHELSON (1906-1983).

ISADORE BRILL (1905-1964).

C. RICHARD BEYDA, born Washington, D.C., February 6, 1937; admitted to bar, 1962, District of Columbia; 1963, U.S. Tax Court. *Education:* George Washington University (B.A., 1959; J.D., 1962). *Member:* District of Columbia Bar; Bar Association of the District of Columbia; American Bar Association. ***Email:*** Beyda@GYFB.com

LAWRENCE A. MILLER, born Pittsburgh, Pennsylvania, February 25, 1936; admitted to bar, 1960, District of Columbia; 1968, U.S. Supreme Court; 1984, Maryland. *Education:* University of Pittsburgh (A.B., 1957; LL.B., 1960). Order of the Coif. *Member:* District of Columbia Bar; Bar Association of the District of Columbia; Maryland State Bar Association, Inc.; American Bar Association; American Academy of Hospital Attorneys. ***Email:*** Miller@GYFB.com

GERALD P. GROSSBERG, born Washington, D.C., October 27, 1940; admitted to bar, 1966, District of Columbia. *Education:* Pennsylvania State University (B.A., 1962); George Washington University (LL.B., 1965). Phi Delta Phi. *Member:* District of Columbia Bar; Bar Association of the District of Columbia; American Bar Association. ***Email:*** Grossberg@GYFB.com

STEVEN G. FRIEDMAN, born Brooklyn, New York, December 5, 1948; admitted to bar, 1975, District of Columbia; 1984, Maryland. *Education:* Wharton School of Finance, University of Pennsylvania (B.S.E., 1970); George Washington University (J.D., with honors, 1974). *Member:* District of Columbia Bar; Maryland State Bar Association, Inc. ***Email:*** Friedman@GYFB.com

RICHARD F. LEVIN, born New Orleans, Louisiana, March 23, 1953; admitted to bar, 1979, District of Columbia; 1980, U.S. Claims Court. *Education:* Pennsylvania State University (B.S., with high distinction, 1975); George Washington University (J.D., with honors, 1979). Beta Gamma Sigma. *Member:* District of Columbia Bar. ***Email:*** Levin@GYFB.com

LINTON W. HENGERER, born Buffalo, New York, October 14, 1954; admitted to bar, 1980, District of Columbia; 1981, U.S. Court of Appeals for the District of Columbia Circuit. *Education:* Boston University (B.S.B.A., magna cum laude, 1977); George Washington University (M.B.A., 1984; J.D., with honors, 1980). Beta Gamma Sigma. *Member:* District of Columbia Bar. ***Email:*** Hengerer@GYFB.com

BRETT D. ORLOVE, born Silver Spring, Maryland, January 29, 1966; admitted to bar, 1991, Maryland; 1992, District of Columbia. *Education:* Uni-

(This Listing Continued)

versity of Pennsylvania (B.A., 1988); George Washington University (J.D., with honors, 1991). *Member:* District of Columbia Bar; Maryland State Bar Association, Inc.; American Bar Association. ***Email:*** Orlove@GYFB.com

ASSOCIATES

BRUCE C. JOHNSON, born Chicago, Illinois, August 28, 1957; admitted to bar, 1986, Maryland (Not admitted in District of Columbia). *Education:* St. Ambrose University (B.A., 1981); University of Iowa (M.A.P.A., 1984); Catholic University (J.D., 1986); Georgetown University Law School (LL.M., 1994). *Member:* Maryland State Bar Association (Member, Tax Section Council); Washington Estate Planning Council. ***PRACTICE AREAS:*** Estate Planning; Probate; Real Estate; Tax. ***Email:*** johnson@gyfb.com

MICHAEL D. RAVITCH, born Rio de Janeiro, Brazil, December 2, 1967; admitted to bar, 1995, Maryland; 1996, District of Columbia. *Education:* Pennsylvania State University (B.S., Accounting, 1989); George Washington University (J.D., with honors, 1995). Beta Gamma Sigma; Beta Alpha Psi. Order of the Coif. Member, George Washington University Law Review, 1993-1995. Certified Public Accountant, Pennsylvania, 1990. *Member:* The District of Columbia Bar; Maryland State Bar Association, Inc. ***Email:*** Ravitch@GYFB.com

MARY SCHNEIDER CHYUN, born New York, N.Y., January 3, 1943; admitted to bar, 1975, District of Columbia; 1991, Maryland. *Education:* University of Rochester (B.S., 1971); Columbus School of Law, Catholic University of America (J.D., 1974). *Member:* The District of Columbia Bar; Maryland State Bar Association, Inc. ***PRACTICE AREAS:*** Estate Planning; Trust Planning. ***Email:*** Chyun@GYFB.com

SIDNEY JEROME ROSENBAUM IV, born Roanoke, Virginia, August 29, 1972; admitted to bar, 1998, Virginia; 2000, District of Columbia. *Education:* Virginia Polytechnic Institute (B.S., Finance, 1994); Cambridge University, Cambridge, England (International Law Program, 1995); University of Richmond (J.D., cum laude, 1998; M.B.A., 1998). Member, Moot Court Board, 1996-1998. Member, University of Richmond Law Review. Law Clerk, the Honorable Jackson L. Kiser, U.S. District Court, Western District of Virginia, 1998-1999. *Member:* District of Columbia Bar; Virginia State Bar; Virginia and American Bar Associations. ***PRACTICE AREAS:*** Construction; Government Contracts; Real Estate; International; Commercial Litigation; Contracts; Corporate. ***Email:*** rosenbaum@gyfb.com

RETIRED

JULIUS I. FOX, born Philadelphia, Pennsylvania, October 3, 1928; admitted to bar, 1957, District of Columbia, Maryland and U.S. Tax Court; 1962, U.S. Supreme Court; 1975, Israel. *Education:* Lowell Technological Institute (B.S., 1950); Southeastern University (B.C.S., 1952; M.C.S., 1953); Washington College of Law, American University (J.D., 1957). *Member:* District of Columbia Bar; Bar Association of the District of Columbia; Maryland State Bar Association, Inc.; Israel Chamber of Advocates.

ANDREW GROSSO

2121 K STREET, N.W., SUITE 800
WASHINGTON, D.C. 20037
Telephone: 202-261-3593
Fax: 202-261-3595
Email: agrosso@acm.org

Civil and Criminal Litigation, including Health Care and Defense Procurement Fraud, and Qui Tam and Corporate Compliance Matters. Electronic Commerce, including Computer and Information Security, Internet Law, Digital Copyrights, Trademarks, Domain Name Registration, and Financial, Medical and Electronic Privacy.

ANDREW GROSSO, born Brooklyn, New York, October 20, 1953; admitted to bar, 1981, New York and District of Columbia; 1994, Florida; 1995, U.S. Supreme Court. *Education:* Rensselaer Polytechnic Institute (B.S., 1975; M.S., Physics, 1977; M.S., Computer Science, 1979); University of Notre Dame (J.D., 1980). National Moot Court Team. London Law Centre, 1978-1979. Columnist: "Legally Speaking," Communications of the ACM, 1999—. Member, Editorial Board, The Pastin Report on Health Care Compliance Programs, 2000—. Author: "Computer Crime," Criminal Defense Techniques, Matthew Bender and Co., Inc., 1996; "Essentials for the Prosecution and Defense of Government Program Fraud," Criminal Defense Techniques, Matthew Bender and Co., Inc., 1994; "The National Information Infrastructure: Implications for Commerce, Security, and Law Enforcement," Federal Bar News and Journal, 1994; "Medical Necessity and the Medicare and Medicaid Anti-Kickback Statute," Federal Bar News and Journal, 1993; "Prosecuting Health Care Fraud: Tools of the Trade," Federal Bar News and Journal, 1993; "Legislation for the Patenting of Living Organisms: Specificity, Public Safety and Ethical Considerations," Journal of Legislation, 1980. Co-author: "The Geostationary Orbit: Legal, Technical and Political Issues Surrounding Its Use in World Telecommunications," Case Western Reserve Journal of International Law, 1983. Assistant U.S. Attorney: Middle District of Florida, 1983-1990; District of Massachusetts, 1990-1994 (Health Care Fraud Working Group, U.S. Department of Justice). *Member:* American Bar Association (Criminal Justice Section: Council Member, 1998-1999; Chair, Committee on Science & Technology, 1996-1998); Association for Computer Machinery (Chair, Committee on Law and Computer Technology, 1999—; Member, U.S. Policy Committee, 1995—); American Physical Society.

(This Listing Continued)

GROVE, JASKIEWICZ AND COBERT

Established in 1964
SUITE 400, 1730 M STREET, N.W.
WASHINGTON, D.C. 20036
Telephone: 202-296-2900
Telecopier: 202-296-1370
Email: rcobert@gjcobert.com
URL: http://www.gjcobert.com

Baltimore, Maryland Office: Suite 407, 2400 Boston Street, 21224. Telephone: 410-522-3200.

General Practice and Administrative Law, including Practice before United States Trial and Appellate Courts, Government Departments, Federal and State Agencies. Antitrust, Trade Regulation, Corporate, Copyright, Customs, Health Care, International Trade, Labor, Legislative, Litigation, Patent, Pension, Tax, Trademark, and Transportation Law.

FIRM PROFILE: Grove, Jaskiewicz and Cobert, founded in 1964, has a well-established practice and represents clients located in the United States and Canada, as well as certain other foreign countries. Clients range from "Fortune 100" corporations to small companies and include trade associations, cooperatives, partnerships and individuals.

The firm's broad general practice evolved as a complement to its expertise in transportation and litigation services provided to a variety of clients nationwide over the past 30 years.

MEMBERS OF FIRM

WILLIAM J. GROVE (1914-1988).

RONALD N. COBERT, born New York, New York, November 15, 1935; admitted to bar, 1960, District of Columbia; 1965, U.S. Supreme Court. *Education:* College of the Holy Cross (A.B., 1957); Georgetown University (J.D., 1960). ***PRACTICE AREAS:*** Business Law; Transportation; International Trade; Health Care. ***Email:*** rcobert@gjcobert.com

EDWARD J. KILEY, born Jersey City, New Jersey, September 9, 1948; admitted to bar, 1973, District of Columbia. *Education:* Villanova University (A.B., 1970); George Washington University (J.D., with honors, 1973). ***PRACTICE AREAS:*** Transportation Safety; Cargo Claims; Hazardous Materials Transportation; Intellectual Property. ***Email:*** ekiley@gjcobert.com

ROBERT L. COPE, born St. Louis, Missouri, September 22, 1947; admitted to bar, 1973, Missouri; 1975, District of Columbia; 1977, U.S. Supreme Court; 1978, Maryland. *Education:* Southern Illinois University (B.A., 1970); University of Missouri (J.D., 1973). ***PRACTICE AREAS:*** Transportation; Litigation; General Corporate. ***Email:*** rcope@gjcobert.com

ANDREW M. DANAS, born Redwood City, California, April 25, 1955; admitted to bar, 1982, District of Columbia. *Education:* University of Connecticut (B.A., 1977); George Washington University (J.D., 1982). ***PRACTICE AREAS:*** Maritime; Transportation; Antitrust; Litigation; International Law; International Trade. ***Email:*** adanas@gjcobert.com

OF COUNSEL

LEONARD A. JASKIEWICZ, born Norwich, Connecticut, August 25, 1927; admitted to bar, 1954, District of Columbia and U.S. Court of Appeals for the District of Columbia Circuit. *Education:* University of Connecticut (B.A., 1949); Syracuse University (M.A., 1950); George Washington University (J.D., 1954). Delta Theta Phi.

JAMES F. FLINT, born Washington, D.C., March 16, 1943; admitted to bar, 1973, District of Columbia. *Education:* University of Notre Dame (B.A., 1965); Harvard University (M.A., 1967); Georgetown University (J.D., 1973). ***PRACTICE AREAS:*** Administrative Law; Litigation; Railroads; Transportation; Children Law.

LAWRENCE E. DUBÉ, JR., born Chicago, Illinois, September 25, 1948; admitted to bar, 1973, Illinois; 1982, Pennsylvania and Maryland; 1983, District of Columbia. *Education:* Knox College (B.A., cum laude, 1970); University of Iowa (J.D., with distinction, 1973). ***PRACTICE AREAS:*** Employment Litigation; Employment Discrimination; Collective Bargaining; Labor Relations; Wage and Hour Law.

JAMES K. JEANBLANC, born Tuscaloosa, Alabama, July 10, 1941; admitted to bar, 1966, Illinois; 1967, U.S. Court of Federal Claims and U.S. Tax

(This Listing Continued)

GROVE, JASKIEWICZ AND COBERT, Washington—Continued

Court; 1969, U.S. Supreme Court; 1970, District of Columbia. *Education:* University of Illinois (B.S., with high honors, 1963; J.D., 1966); George Washington University (LL.M. in Taxation, 1967). Certified Public Accountant, Illinois, 1964. ***PRACTICE AREAS:*** Business Law; Corporate Law; Tax Law; Trusts and Estates.

EDMUND M. JASKIEWICZ, born Norwich, Connecticut, July 5, 1923; admitted to bar, 1953, District of Columbia and U.S. Supreme Court; registered to practice before U.S. Patent and Trademark Office. *Education:* University of Connecticut (B.S.E., 1947); George Washington University (J.D., 1952). ***PRACTICE AREAS:*** International Intellectual Property; Patent Licensing; Patent Prosecution; Trademark Licensing; Trademark Prosecution.

ROBIN W. GROVER

1747 PENNSYLVANIA AVENUE N.W.
SUITE 1000
WASHINGTON, D.C. 20006-4693
Telephone: 202-302-1653
Email: RGrover716@aol.com
URL: http://www.lawyers.com/robingrover

All aspects of international trade including export licensing issues (BXA and ODTC); OFAC regulations and licensing; Customs import requirements (country of origin, classification, marking, FTA, tariff preference and policy issues); CFIUS, foreign investment reporting and sectoral limitations. The full range of issues involving trade association law, including those of organization, governance, membership, codes and standards. Practice before federal, state and local regulatory agencies.

ROBIN W. GROVER, born Princeton, New Jersey, June 30, 1953; admitted to bar, 1982, District of Columbia; 1983, U.S. District Court, District of Columbia and U.S. Court of International Trade. *Education:* Dickinson College (B.A., summa cum laude, 1975); University of Virginia (J.D., 1982). Phi Beta Kappa. Formerly with Keck, Mahin & Cate, 1982-1997. Member, Legal Section Council of American Society of Association Executives, 1994-1996. ***PRACTICE AREAS:*** International Trade and Investment Law; Trade Associations Law; Administrative Law.

GRUNFELD, DESIDERIO, LEBOWITZ, SILVERMAN & KLESTADT LLP

A Partnership
SUITE 975, 1500 K STREET, N.W.
WASHINGTON, D.C. 20005
Telephone: 202-783-6881
Telecopy: 202-783-0405
URL: http://www.GDLSK.com

New York, N.Y. Office: 245 Park Avenue, 33rd Floor. Telephone: 212-557-4000. Fax: 212-557-4415.
Boston, Massachusetts Office: Grunfeld, Desiderio, Lebowitz, Silverman, Klestadt & Wright, LLP, Old City Hall, 45 School Street, 2nd Floor. Telephone: 617-742-8550. Telecopy: 617-523-9429.
Los Angeles, California Office: 707 Wilshire Boulevard, Suite 4900. Telephone: 213-624-1970. Telecopy: 213-624-1678.

Customs Law, International Trade Law, Trade Regulations and Administrative Law. Trials and Appeals.

PARTNERS

HAROLD M. GRUNFELD, born New York, N.Y., December 15, 1947; admitted to bar, 1974, New York and U.S. District Court, Southern and Eastern Districts of New York; 1982, U.S. Court of International Trade and U.S. Court of Appeals for the Federal Circuit. *Education:* City College of the City University of New York (B.A., 1969); Boston University; New York University (J.D., 1973). *Member:* New York State and American Bar Associations; Customs and International Trade Bar Association (Member, Section on International Law and Practice). (Resident Partner, New York, N.Y. Office). ***PRACTICE AREAS:*** Customs Law; Import and Export Law; International Trade Regulations. ***Email:*** hgrunfeld@GDLSK.com

FRANK J. DESIDERIO, born New York, N.Y., October 7, 1947; admitted to bar, 1973, New York; 1975, U.S. District Court, Eastern and Southern Districts of New York; 1976, U.S. Court of Federal Claims; 1982, U.S. Court of International Trade and U.S. Court of Appeals for the Federal Circuit. *Education:* St. John's University (B.S., 1969; J.D., 1972). Author: "Increasing Profits by Lowering Custom Duties," Trade with Italy, May/June, 1983; "General Export Concerns," Trade with Italy, November, 1987; "GATT, Textiles, MFN & Vietnam," Vietnam Today, April, 1994; "U.S. Customs' Concerns About Origin," The Strategist, November/December, 1994; "Trading Without MFN," The Vietnam Business Journal, January/February, 1995; "Transfer Pricing and U.S. Customs," Italy Today Fall issue 1999; "New US Marking Rules for Certain Silk Products," Italy Today, Millenium issue 1999. Instructor: Customs Law, World Trade Institute (New York and New Jersey Port Authority), 1977-1980, 1995-1997; Harmonized Tariff System Workshop: World Trade Institute (Pace University 1998-2000); Customs Law, International Business Machines, 1992 and 1993; South African Professional Development Program, 1995. U.S. Customs Valuation and the Interplay with Transfer Pricing, Executive Enterprises: 1994; Importing for Exporters: An Overview, 1996. Trial Attorney, U.S. Department of Justice, Civil Division, Customs Section, 1972-1976. Director, Thai-American Chamber of Commerce (Vice President, 1992-1995); Vietnam-American Chamber of Commerce (Secretary/Treasurer, 1992-1995; President, 1995-1996). Director, Italy-America Chamber of Commerce, 2000-2003; Customs & Trade Advisor, 2000—; Member, British America Chamber of Commerce, 1996—. Member, Hong Kong Association of New York. *Member:* New York State (Member, Committee on International Trade) and American Bar Associations; Customs and International Trade Bar Association. (Resident Partner, New York, N.Y. Office). ***PRACTICE AREAS:*** Customs Law; Foreign Trade Sanctions; International Trade Regulations. ***Email:*** fdesiderio@GDLSK.com

ALAN G. LEBOWITZ, born New York, N.Y., March 14, 1951; admitted to bar, 1979, New York and U.S. District Court, Southern and Eastern Districts of New York; 1982, U.S. Court of International Trade and U.S. Court of Appeals for the Federal Circuit; 1993, U.S. District Court, Northern District of New York. *Education:* Cornell University (B.S., 1972); New York University (J.D., 1978). Author: "Maximizing Profits by Reducing Customs Duties on International Sales," International Bar Association 2000 Conference, Sept., 2000. Instructor: Customs Law, World Trade Institute (New York and New Jersey Port Authority), 1982-1984; Fordham University School of Law Continuing Legal Education, 1993. Lecturer/Panelist: International Bar Association, 1999-2000. *Member:* New York State, American and International (Member, Trade and Customs Law Subcommittee) Bar Associations; New York County Lawyers Association; Customs and International Trade Bar Association. (Resident Partner, New York, N.Y. Office). ***PRACTICE AREAS:*** Customs Law; Trade Legislation; Product Licensing/Admissibility; Export Sanctions; International Trade Regulations. ***Email:*** alebowitz@GDLSK.com

ROBERT B. SILVERMAN, born New York, N.Y., July 15, 1947; admitted to bar, 1973, New York; 1974, U.S. District Court, Eastern District of New York; 1976, U.S. District Court, Southern District of New York; 1982, U.S. Court of International Trade and U.S. Court of Appeals for the Federal Circuit. *Education:* Brooklyn College of the City University of New York (B.S. in Accounting, 1969); Brooklyn Law School (J.D., cum laude, 1972). Member, Brooklyn Law Review, 1971-1972. Trial Attorney, U.S. Department of Justice, Civil Division, Customs Section, 1972-1976. *Member:* New York State and American Bar Associations; Customs and International Trade Bar Association. (Resident Partner, New York, N.Y. Office). ***PRACTICE AREAS:*** Customs Law; Customs Litigation, Valuation, Classification; International Trade Regulations. ***Email:*** rsilverman@GDLSK.com

PETER W. KLESTADT, born Queens, New York, July 4, 1959; admitted to bar, 1984, New York; 1988, U.S. Court of International Trade; 1989, U.S. Court of Appeals for the Federal Circuit. *Education:* New York University (B.A., 1980); Brooklyn Law School (J.D., 1983). Department of the Treasury, U.S. Customs Service Customhouse Broker's License No. 7484, 1982. Instructor, New York University: Customhouse Brokerage for License Applicants, 1985; Customs Law Survey, 1986; Minimizing Customs Duties, 1987; Customs Law Survey: Making the Law Work for You, 1988. Instructor, Food and Drug Law Institute: Advanced Food Law Workshop, Imports of Foods, 1992. Instructor, World Trade Institute: Harmonized Tariff System Workshop, 1996-2000. *Member:* Westchester County and New York State Bar Associations; Customs and International Trade Bar Association; Transportation Lawyers Association; New York County Lawyers Association. Consulegis. (Resident Partner, New York, N.Y. Office). ***PRACTICE AREAS:*** Customs Law; International Trade Regulation; Food, Drug and Cosmetic Law. ***Email:*** pklestadt@GDLSK.com

STEVEN P. FLORSHEIM, born New York, N.Y., October 18, 1941; admitted to bar, 1969, New York; 1970, U.S. Court of International Trade, U.S. Court of Appeals for the Federal Circuit and U.S. District Court, Southern and Eastern Districts of New York. *Education:* State University of New York at Farmingdale (AAS, 1961); Michigan State University (B.S., 1964); New York Law School (J.D., 1969). Peace Corps. Volunteer, Colombia, 1964-1966. Trial Attorney, U.S. Department of Justice, Civil Division, Customs Section, 1970-1977. *Member:* Association of the Bar of the City of New York; American Bar Association; Customs and International Trade Bar Association. (Resident Partner, New York, N.Y. Office). ***PRACTICE AREAS:*** Customs Law; Litigation. ***Email:*** sflorsheim@GDLSK.com

BRUCE M. MITCHELL, born New York, N.Y., March 22, 1950; admitted to bar, 1976, New York; 1978, U.S. District Court, Southern District of New

(This Listing Continued)

York; 1982, U.S. Court of International Trade and U.S. Court of Appeals for the Federal Circuit; 1992, District of Columbia. *Education:* New York University (B.A., 1971); New York Law School (J.D., 1975). Member, Coat of Arms Society. Trial Attorney, U.S. Department of Justice, Civil Division, Commercial Litigation Branch, International Trade Field Office, 1975-1978. *Member:* New York State and American (Chairman, Subcommittee on International Law and Foreign Trade, 1979-1985) Bar Associations; The District of Columbia Bar; Customs and International Trade Bar Association; U.S.-Mexico Law Institute. (Resident Partner, New York, N.Y. Office). ***PRACTICE AREAS:*** Antidumping; Unfair Trade; International Trade Law. ***Email:*** bmitchell@GDLSK.com

MAX F. SCHUTZMAN, born New York, N.Y., December 6, 1946; admitted to bar, 1974, New York and U.S. Court of International Trade; 1974-1982, U.S. Court of Customs and Patent Appeals; 1975, New Jersey, U.S. Court of Appeals, Second Circuit, U.S. District Court, Southern and Eastern Districts of New York and U.S. District Court, District of New Jersey; 1982, U.S. Court of Appeals for the Federal Circuit; 1985, U.S. Supreme Court; 1995, U.S. Court of Appeals, Fourth Circuit. *Education:* Queens College of the City University of New York (B.A., 1968); Brooklyn Law School (J.D., 1973). Recipient, American Jurisprudence Awards for Conflict of Laws and Creditors' Rights. Trial Attorney, U.S. Department of Justice, Customs Section, Civil Division, 1973-1976. *Member:* New York State Bar Association. (Resident Partner, New York, N.Y. Office). ***PRACTICE AREAS:*** Antidumping; Unfair Trade; International Trade Law; Intellectual Property. ***Email:*** mschutzman@GDLSK.com

ALAN R. KLESTADT, born Queens, New York, May 25, 1958; admitted to bar, 1984, New York; 1988, U.S. Court of International Trade; 1989, U.S. Court of Appeals for the Federal Circuit. *Education:* New York University (B.A., 1980); Hofstra University (J.D., 1983). Staff Member, International Property Investment Journal, 1982-1983. Department of the Treasury, U.S. Customs Service Customhouse Broker's License No. 3847, 1981. Instructor, New York University: Customhouse Brokerage for License Applicants, 1985; Customs Law Survey, 1986; Minimizing Customs Duties, 1987; Customs Law Survey: "Making The Law Work For You," 1988. *Member:* New York State and American Bar Associations; Customs and International Trade Bar Association. (Resident Partner, New York, N.Y. Office). ***PRACTICE AREAS:*** Customs Law; North American Free Trade Agreement; International Trade Regulation. ***Email:*** aklestadt@GDLSK.com

BARRY E. POWELL, born Glendale, California, March 1, 1948; admitted to bar, 1987, California; 1990, U.S. District Court, Central District of California. *Education:* California State University, Northridge (B.A., magna cum laude, 1970); U.S. Customs Service Academy (Advanced Import Specialist Training Certificate, 1986); Loyola Law School (J.D., cum laude, 1987). Senior Import Specialist, U.S. Customs Service, 1973-1987. Licensed Customs Broker, 1993. *Member:* Los Angeles County (Chairman, Customs Committee, 1990-1992; Member, Executive Committee, International Law Section, 1993-1999) and American Bar Associations; State Bar of California; Foreign Trade Association of Southern California (Member and Officer, Board of Directors). (Resident Partner, Los Angeles, California Office). ***PRACTICE AREAS:*** Customs Law; International Trade Regulation. ***Email:*** bpowell@GDLSK.com

MARY ELIZABETH WRIGHT, born Boston, Massachusetts, May 13, 1949; admitted to bar, 1979, Massachusetts, U.S. District Court, District of Massachusetts and U.S. Court of Appeals, First Circuit; 1980, U.S. Court of International Trade and U.S. Tax Court; 1982, U.S. Court of Appeals for the Federal Circuit. *Education:* Colby College (B.A., 1971); Suffolk University (J.D., 1979). Instructor, Grunfeld, Desiderio, Lebowitz, Silverman, Klestadt & Wright LLP Customs Broker License Examination Preparatory Course, 1982—. Import Specialist, U.S. Customs Service, Boston, Massachusetts, 1974-1980. Import Specialist, U.S. Customs Service, St. Albans, Vermont, 1971-1974. Chairman, Import Committee, 1981-1990, Assistant Secretary, 1984-1986, Secretary, 1986-1990, Vice President, 1987-1990, Director, 1984-1994, International Business Center of New England, Inc. Department of Treasury, U.S. Customs Service Customs Broker License No. 9027, 1984. *Member:* Boston, Massachusetts and American Bar Associations. (Resident Partner, Boston, Massachusetts Office). ***PRACTICE AREAS:*** Customs Law; International Trade Regulation. ***Email:*** mwright@GDLSK.com

RICHARD M. WORTMAN, born Far Rockaway, New York, December 23, 1959; admitted to bar, 1988, New York; 2001, California, U.S. Court of International Trade and U.S. Court of Appeals for the Federal Circuit. *Education:* Boston University (B.A. in Psychology, cum laude, 1980); Case Western Reserve (J.D., 1987). *Member:* The Association of the Bar of the City of New York; Los Angeles, New York State and American Bar Associations; Customs and International Trade Bar Association; New York County Lawyers Association. (Resident Partner, Los Angeles, California Office). ***PRACTICE AREAS:*** Customs Law. ***Email:*** rwortman@GDLSK.com

ANDREW B. SCHROTH, born Philadelphia, Pennsylvania, November 29, 1961; admitted to bar, 1989, Massachusetts; 1990, U.S. Court of Appeals for the Federal Circuit and U.S. Court of International Trade; 1991, District of Columbia. *Education:* Tulane University (B.A., 1984); University of Sussex, Brighton, England (M.A., 1985); Vanderbilt University (J.D., 1988); London School of Economics, London, England. President, Vanderbilt International Law Society,

(This Listing Continued)

1987. *Member:* Association of the Bar of the City of New York; Massachusetts, American (Member, International Law Section) and International Bar Associations; The District of Columbia Bar; Customs and International Trade Bar Association. (Resident Partner, New York, N.Y. Office). ***PRACTICE AREAS:*** International Trade Law; International Trade Regulation; Antidumping; Countervailing Duties; Unfair Trade Practices; Trade Litigation. ***Email:*** aschroth@GDLSK.com

DAVID M. MURPHY, born Stamford, Connecticut, April 24, 1961; admitted to bar, 1986, New York and New Jersey; 1987, Connecticut; 1990, District of Columbia; U.S. District Court, Southern and Eastern Districts of New York; U.S. District Court, District of New Jersey; U.S. Court of International Trade; U.S. Court of Appeals for the Federal Circuit. *Education:* Fordham University (B.A., 1983); Brooklyn Law School (J.D., 1986). U.S. Customs Service Customhouse Broker's License No. 13334, 1992. Co-Author: "Import Quotas," "Country of Origin Marking," Import Handbook (1997); "Internal Audits & Compliance Programs," ATTN: Apparel Trade & Transportation News (Sept./Oct. 1993); "Surviving Search and Seizure, " Journal of Commerce (Oct. 31, 1991); "8 Ways to Save on Foreign Customs," Export Today, Vol. 7y, No. 9 (Dec. 1991). Instructor, U.S. Customs Broker Examination Preparation Course, 1995—. Vice-President, Board Member, New York Chapter of SAR. Citizen of U.S. and Ireland. *Member:* American Bar Association; Customs and International Trade Bar Association; Republican National Lawyers Association; National Association of Foreign Trade Zones; Ireland Chamber of Commerce in the United States; United States China Chamber of Commerce; Manhattan Chamber of Commerce; Irish Business Organization; St. Andrew's Society. ***PRACTICE AREAS:*** Customs; International Business Transactions; Trade Regulation; Foreign Trade Zones; International Sanctions Programs (OFAC); Export Regulations. ***Email:*** dmurphy@GDLSK.com

EDWARD B. ACKERMAN, born New York, N.Y., July 14, 1951; admitted to bar, 1977, New York; 1979, U.S. Court of International Trade; 1982, U.S. Court of Appeals for the Federal Circuit. *Education:* State University of New York at Binghamton (B.A., 1973); Hofstra University (J.D., 1976). Attorney, U.S. Customs Service, 1977-1979. *Member:* New York County Lawyers Association; Customs and International Trade Bar Association (Member, Special Committee on Trade Agreements, 1990-1991; Chairman, Publications Committee, 1992-1995; Member, Board of Directors, 1992-1995). (Resident Partner, New York, N.Y. Office). ***PRACTICE AREAS:*** Customs Law; International Trade Law. ***Email:*** eackerman@GDLSK.com

ASSOCIATES

JEFFREY S. GRIMSON, born Evanston, Illinois, March 30, 1967; admitted to bar, 1992, Connecticut, U.S. Court of Appeals for the Federal Circuit and U.S. Court of International Trade; 1993, New York; 1994, District of Columbia. *Education:* University of Illinois (B.A., 1989); The Washington College of Law, American University (J.D., 1992). *Member:* Federal Circuit and American (Member, International Law and Practice Section) Bar Associations; The District of Columbia Bar; Customs and International Trade Bar Association; U.S.-Mexico Law Institute. (Resident). ***Email:*** jgrimson@GDLSK.com

ERIK D. SMITHWEISS, born Livingston, New Jersey, December 27, 1965; admitted to bar, 1992, New Jersey and U.S. District Court, District of New Jersey; 1993, U.S. Court of International Trade; 1995, New York; 1996, U.S. Court of Appeals for the Federal Circuit; U.S. Supreme Court; U.S. Court of Federal Claims. *Education:* Hamilton College (B.A., 1987); Rutgers University (J.D., 1992). *Member:* New Jersey State and American (Section on International Law) Bar Associations; Customs and International Trade Bar Association; National Bonded Warehouse and Cargo Association of the IWLA; International Commerce Club of New Jersey; Spain-U.S. Chamber of Commerce; National Association of Export Companies. (Resident Associate, New York, N.Y. Office). ***PRACTICE AREAS:*** Customs Law; International Trade Regulation. ***Email:*** esmithweiss@GDLSK.com

DAVID J. EVAN, born New York, N.Y., August 18, 1967; admitted to bar, 1994, New York, U.S. Court of International Trade and U.S. Court of Appeals for the Federal Circuit. *Education:* State University of New York at Binghamton (B.A., 1989); New York Law School (J.D., 1993). *Member:* The Association of the Bar of the City of New York; New York State and American Bar Associations; Customs and International Trade Bar Association. (Resident Associate, New York, N.Y. Office). ***Email:*** devan@GDLSK.com

MARK E. PARDO, born New York, N.Y., March 8, 1966; admitted to bar, 1994, New York (Not admitted in District of Columbia). *Education:* Duke University (B.A., cum laude, 1988); Vanderbilt University (J.D., 1993). Executive Articles Editor, 1992-1993 and Staff Member, 1991-1992, Vanderbilt Journal of Transnational Law. (Resident). ***Email:*** mpardo@GDLSK.com

BRETT IAN HARRIS, born Flushing, New York, November 22, 1968; admitted to bar, 1994, New York and U.S. Court of International Trade. *Education:* Cornell University (B.A., with distinction, 1990); New York University (J.D., 1993). Assistant, Binational Panel - U.S.-Canada Free Trade Agreement, 1993. *Member:* New York State Bar Association; Customs and International

(This Listing Continued)

GRUNFELD, DESIDERIO, LEBOWITZ, SILVERMAN & KLESTADT LLP, Washington—Continued

Trade Bar Association. (Resident Associate, New York, N.Y. Office). ***PRACTICE AREAS:*** Customs Law; International Trade Law. ***Email:*** bharris@GDLSK.com

LAURENCE M. FRIEDMAN, born Mount Kisco, New York, February 24, 1960; admitted to bar, 1987, New York; 1989, U.S. Court of International Trade and U.S. Court of Appeals for the Federal Circuit; 1995, U.S. District Court, Southern and Northern Districts of New York; 1997, U.S. Supreme Court and U.S. Court of Federal Claims; 1999, U.S. District Court, Eastern District of New York. *Education:* Bard College (B.A., 1982); Brooklyn Law School (J.D., 1986). Staff Member, 1984-1985, Notes Editor, 1985-1986, Brooklyn Journal of International Law. President, Brooklyn Law School Entertainment Law Society, 1984-1986. *Member:* Association of the Bar of the City of New York; New York State Bar Association; Customs and International Trade Bar Association (Chairman: Committee on Continuing Legal Education and Professional Responsibilities, 1996-1998; Committee on Membership, 1998-2000). (Resident Associate, New York, N.Y. Office). ***PRACTICE AREAS:*** Customs and International Trade Law; Domestic and Foreign Administrative Law; International Business; Federal Practice Litigation. ***Email:*** lfriedman@GDLSK.com

MICHAEL T. CONE, born East Grand Rapids, Michigan, July 27, 1964; admitted to bar, 1994, Michigan; 1998, New York. *Education:* University of Michigan (B.A., 1991); Wayne State University (J.D., 1994); Washington College of Law, American University (LL.M., 1995). Law Clerk to Hon. R. Kenton Musgrave, U.S. Court of International Trade, 1995-1997. *Member:* New York State Bar Association; State Bar of Michigan. (Resident Associate, New York, N.Y. Office). ***LANGUAGES:*** French. ***PRACTICE AREAS:*** Customs; International Trade; Litigation. ***Email:*** mcone@GDLSK.com

ELLEN A. DILAPI, born Petygorsk, Russia, January 17, 1972; admitted to bar, 1999, New York, U.S. District Court, Southern and Eastern Districts of New York and U.S. Court of International Trade. *Education:* State University of New York at Binghamton (B.A., magna cum laude, 1994); Benjamin N. Cardozo School of Law (J.D., 1997). Staff Member, Cardozo Arts & Entertainment Law Journal. Vice President, International Law Society. *Member:* New York State and American Bar Associations; New York County Lawyers Association. (Resident Associate, New York, N.Y. Office). ***LANGUAGES:*** Russian and German. ***PRACTICE AREAS:*** Customs; International Trade Regulation; Foreign Trade Zones; European Union Law. ***Email:*** edilapi@GDLSK.com

STEPHANIE A. GOLDFISCHER, born New York, N.Y., August 6, 1969; admitted to bar, 1996, New York; 1997, U.S. District Court, Southern and Eastern Districts of New York and U.S. Court of International Trade. *Education:* University of Rochester (B.A., with distinction in Philosophy, magna cum laude, 1991) Phi Beta Kappa; Benjamin N. Cardozo School of Law (J.D., 1995). National Member, Order of the Barristers. Recipient, Jacob Burns Medal for Distinguished Achievement in Moot Court Competition. Co-Author: " U.S. Customs Modifies Compliance Audit Standards," The Metropolitan Corporate Counsel, October, 2000. *Member:* New York State and American Bar Associations; New York County Lawyer's Association; Women in International Trade; Customs and International Trade Bar Association; National Association of Foreign Trade Zones; American Association of Exporters and Importers. (Resident Associate, New York, N.Y. Office). ***PRACTICE AREAS:*** Customs and International Trade Law; Foreign Trade Zones; European Community Law; Federal Practice Litigation. ***Email:*** sgoldfischer@GDLSK.com

ANTHONY A. TONUCCI, born Buffalo, New York, May 23, 1963; admitted to bar, 1990, District of Columbia. *Education:* Canisius College (B.A., 1985); Catholic University of America (J.D., 1988). Customs Attorney, Office of Regulations and Rulings, U.S. Customs Service Headquarters: Penalties Branch, 1988-1991; Valuation and Marking Branch, 1991-1994; Special Classification and Marking Branch, 1994-1996. (Resident Associate, New York, N.Y. Office). ***PRACTICE AREAS:*** International Trade; Customs Law. ***Email:*** atonucci@GDLSK.com

STACY L. WEINBERG, born Detroit, Michigan, April 13, 1974; admitted to bar, 2000, New York, District of Columbia, U.S. District Court, Southern and Eastern Districts of New York, U.S. Court of Appeals for the Federal Circuit and U.S. Court of International Trade. *Education:* University of Michigan (B.A., 1996); Brooklyn Law School (J.D., 1999). *Member:* New York County Lawyers Association; New York State Bar Association; Women in International Trade. (Resident Associate, New York, N.Y. Office). ***PRACTICE AREAS:*** Customs Law; International Trade. ***Email:*** sweinberg@GDLSK.com

ADAM M. DAMBROV, born Hartford, Connecticut, August 25, 1968; admitted to bar, 2000, New York; U.S. Court of International Trade; U.S. Court of Appeals for the Federal Circuit (Not admitted in District of Columbia). *Education:* Syracuse University (B.A., 1990); New York Law School (J.D., 1999). *Member:* New York State and American Bar Associations; Asia Society; Japan Society. (Resident Associate, New York, N.Y. Office). ***PRACTICE AREAS:*** Antidumping; Countervailing Duties; Customs Law. ***Email:*** adambrov@GDLSK.com

(This Listing Continued)

OF COUNSEL

HAROLD I. LORING, born New York, N.Y., February 2, 1950; admitted to bar, 1978, New York; 1979, District of Columbia. *Education:* New York University (B.A., 1971); Brooklyn Law School (J.D., 1977). Customs Attorney, Office of Regulations and Rulings, U.S. Customs Service Headquarters: Classification Branch, 1977-1978; Regulations Branch, 1978-1980; Penalties Branch, 1980-1984; Entry-Marking Branch, 1984-1985. *Member:* The District of Columbia Bar. (Resident Of Counsel, New York, N.Y. Office). ***PRACTICE AREAS:*** Customs Law. ***Email:*** hloring@GDLSK.com

PRINCIPAL

BARRY HIPSHMAN, born New York, N.Y., March 25, 1949; admitted to bar, 1979, New York. *Education:* City College of the City University of New York (B.B.A., 1972); New York Law School (J.D., 1979). Author: Numerous articles in tax journals pertaining to topics such as International Bank Taxation, International Banking Facilities in New York State, Handling Contributions to Tort Settlement Funds, Accounting and Tax Issues for Tort Settlement Claims Funds. Senior International Tax Partner, KPMG Peat Marwick, retired 1991. Editor, "Corporate Taxation" (Faulkner & Gray) magazine, 1988-1990. (Resident, New York, N.Y. Office). ***PRACTICE AREAS:*** Taxation. ***Email:*** bhipshman@GDLSK.com

(For complete biographical data on all personnel, see Professional Biographies at New York, New York)

GUERRIERI, EDMOND & CLAYMAN, P.C.

Established in 1985

1625 MASSACHUSETTS AVENUE, N.W., SUITE 700

WASHINGTON, D.C. 20036-2243

Telephone: 202-624-7400

Facsimile: 202-624-7420

Litigation, Labor, Tort, Bankruptcy and Employee Benefits Law.

JOSEPH GUERRIERI, JR., born Detroit, Michigan, June 11, 1947; admitted to bar, 1973, District of Columbia, U.S. Court of Appeals for the District of Columbia Circuit and U.S. Court of Appeals, Second, Third, Fourth, Fifth, Seventh and Eighth Circuits; 1977, U.S. Supreme Court. *Education:* University of Michigan (B.A., 1969); George Washington University (J.D., with honors, 1972). Phi Delta Phi. Law Clerk to the Honorable Nicholas S. Nunzio, Associate Judge, Superior Court of the District of Columbia, 1972-1973. Assistant United States Attorney for the District of Columbia, 1973-1977. *Member:* District of Columbia Bar; Federal and American (Co-Chairman of the Railway and Airline Labor Committee, Labor and Employment Law Section, 1982-1985; Co-Chairman of the Union Administration and Procedure Committee, Labor and Employment Law Section, 1988-1992) Bar Associations. ***Email:*** jguerrieri@geclaw.com

JOHN A. EDMOND, born Washington, D.C., May 7, 1956; admitted to bar, 1981, District of Columbia, U.S. Court of Appeals for the District of Columbia Circuit and U.S. Court of Appeals, Second, Fourth, Fifth, Seventh and Eighth Circuits; 1987, U.S. Supreme Court. *Education:* University of Michigan (B.A., 1978); George Washington University (J.D., 1981). Associate Counsel, UMWA Health and Retirement Funds, 1982-1984. *Member:* District of Columbia Bar; American Bar Association. ***PRACTICE AREAS:*** Litigation. ***Email:*** jedmond@geclaw.com

ROBERT S. CLAYMAN, born Perth Amboy, New Jersey, May 20, 1953; admitted to bar, 1978, Georgia and U.S. District Court, Northern District of Georgia; 1989, District of Columbia; U.S. Court of Appeals for the District of Columbia Circuit. *Education:* Tufts University (B.A., 1975); Emory University (J.D., 1978). *Member:* District of Columbia Bar. ***Email:*** rclayman@geclaw.com

JEFFREY A. BARTOS, born Lancaster, Ohio, May 25, 1965; admitted to bar, 1990, Illinois; U.S. Court of Appeals, Fourth Circuit; 1993, District of Columbia; 1994, U.S. Court of Appeals, Sixth Circuit. *Education:* Columbia University (B.A., 1987): Yale University (J.D., 1990); Georgetown University (LL.M., Advocacy, 1992). ***Email:*** jbartos@geclaw.com

---

JONATHAN P. ROLFE, born Duluth, Minnesota, July 6, 1972; admitted to bar, 1998, Maryland (Not admitted in District of Columbia). *Education:* University of Minnesota (B.A., 1994; J.D., 1998). ***Email:*** jrolfe@geclaw.com

SOYE KIM, born Liverpool, England, May 12, 1955; admitted to bar, 1999, Maryland; 2001, District of Columbia. *Education:* Juilliard School (B.M., 1976, M.M., 1977); University of Virginia School of Law (J.D., 1998). Law Clerk to the Honorable Steffen W. Grace, Deputy Presiding Judge, Civil Division, Superior Court of the District of Columbia, 1998-2000. *Member:* Maryland State Bar Association. ***LANGUAGES:*** French. ***PRACTICE AREAS:*** Litigation; Labor and Employment. ***Email:*** skim@geclaw.com

(This Listing Continued)

ELEANORE A. IRWIN, born Baltimore, Maryland, December 9, 1973; admitted to bar, 1998, Illinois; 2001, District of Columbia. *Education:* Binghamton University (B.A., with honors, 1995); Howard University School of Law (J.D., with honors, 1998). Recipient, Merit Scholarship. Member, Howard Law Journal. Law Clerk to the Honorable Joe B. McDade, Chief Judge, United States District Court for the Central District of Illinois, 1998-2000. *Member:* Illinois Bar Association, 1998-1999. ***Email:*** eirwin@geclaw.com

LAW OFFICES OF PAUL S. HAAR

1150 CONNECTICUT AVENUE, N.W., NINTH FLOOR
WASHINGTON, D.C. 20036
Telephone: 202-862-4328
Fax: 202-862-4397
Email: paulhaar@aol.com
URL: http://www.lawyers.com/haarlaw

Immigration and Nationality Law, Immigration Litigation, Business Immigration, Employment Visa, International Corporate, Transnational Litigation, Arbitration.

PAUL S. HAAR, born Detroit, Michigan, April 11, 1953; admitted to bar, 1983, District of Columbia; 1986, Maryland; 1990, New York; 1998, Florida. *Education:* University of Michigan (B.A., magna cum laude, 1977); University of Aix-Marseille, Aix-en-Provence, France; The Hague Academy of International Law; American University, Washington College of Law (J.D., 1981); Institut d'Etudes Europeennes, Universite Libre de Bruxelles, Licence Speciale en Droit Europeen avec grande distinction, Brussels, Belgium, (LL.M., magna cum laude, 1981). Phi Beta Kappa. Fulbright Scholar (Brussels, Belgium). Listed in: Who's Who in American Law; Outstanding Young Men of America. Faculty, Immigration Law, District of Columbia Bar PSAC Program. Arbitrator, American Arbitration Association. Mentor, Central American Refugee Center. *Member:* District of Columbia Bar (Past Chairman, International Law Section); American Immigration Lawyers Association; Washington Foreign Law Society (Past President);. ***LANGUAGES:*** French, Spanish, German, Portuguese and Chinese.

HAAS & ANDERSON, P.C.

WASHINGTON, D.C.
(See McLean, Virginia)

General Business and Civil Practice, Real Estate, Zoning and Land Use, , Condominium, Corporate, Banking, International, Construction, Mortgage Banking and Bankruptcy.

LAW OFFICE OF FORREST A. HAINLINE III

Established in 1989
SUITE 440
5335 WISCONSIN AVENUE, N.W.
WASHINGTON, D.C. 20015
Telephone: 202-966-1962
Fax: 202-966-1891
Email: aikidoLaw@aol.com
URL: http://www.lawyers.com/hainline

FIRM PROFILE: Mr. Hainline represents major corporations and firms in large stakes litigation throughout the country. Mr. Hainline will assemble a support team from local and/or specialized firms, and he will then serve as principal trial lawyer. Mr. Hainline has tried jury cases in over 20 states in both Federal and State courts in diverse areas of commercial law, including agriculture (grower disputes), antitrust, construction claims, contract and fraud claims, distributor disputes, environmental law, employment issues (including ERISA), intellectual property (advertising, patent, trademark and trade secret cases), partnership disputes, professional (attorney and accountant) malpractice, and securities law. Mr. Hainline also regularly serves as a party arbitrator.

FORREST A. HAINLINE III, born Washington, D.C., May 23, 1946; admitted to bar, 1974, Michigan; 1975, California; 1983, U.S. Supreme Court; 1984, District of Columbia. *Education:* University of Notre Dame (B.A., 1968); State University of New York at Buffalo (M.A., 1970); University of Michigan (J.D., 1974). Phi Beta Kappa. Teaching Fellow, State University of New York at Buffalo, 1968-1971. Instructor, Legal Writing and Research, University of Michigan Law School, 1973-1974. Adjunct Professor, Antitrust Law, Golden Gate University, San Francisco, 1978-1979. *Member:* District of Columbia; State Bar of California; State Bar of Michigan; American Bar Association (Member, Litigation Section).

(This Listing Continued)

REPRESENTATIVE CORPORATE CLIENTS: Campbell Soup Company; The Gillette Company; Vlasic Foods International.

HALE AND DORR LLP

A Partnership including Professional Corporations
1455 PENNSYLVANIA AVENUE, N.W.
WASHINGTON, D.C. 20004
Telephone: 202-942-8400
Cable Address: "Hafis Wsh"
Telecopier: 202-942-8484
URL: http://www.haledorr.com

Boston, Massachusetts Office: 60 State Street. Telephone: 617-526-6000. Cable Address: "Hafis." Telex: 94-0472. Telecopier: Domestic 617-526-5000; 617-742-9108.
Waltham, Massachusetts Office: Bay Colony Corporate Center, 1100 Winter Street, Suite 4650. Telephone: 781-966-2000. Telecopier: 781-966-2100.
Princeton, New Jersey Office: 650 College Road East. Telephone: 609-750-7600. Telecopier: 609-750-7700.
New York, N.Y. Office: 300 Park Avenue. Telephone: 212-937-7200. Fax: 212-937-7300.
Reston, Virginia Office: One Freedom Square, 11951 Freedom Drive, Suite 1400. Telephone: 703-654-7000. Fax: 703-654-7100.

General Practice. Corporate, Securities, Trusts, Real Estate, Taxation, Probate, Estate Planning, Pension, Bankruptcy, Reorganization and Creditors Rights, Antitrust and Trade Negotiation, Government Contracts and Legislative, International, State and Federal Trial and Appellate Practice including Complex Commercial Transactions, Antitrust, Securities Regulation, Unfair Competition and Trade Secrets, Product Liability, Environmental Claims, Other Civil and Criminal Litigation, Biotechnology, Family Business, Finance, Emerging Companies, Publicly Traded Companies, Telecommunication and Software, Venture Capital, Initial Public Offerings, Intellectual Property, Trademarks, Investment Management, Labor and Employment, Employee Benefits, ERISA and Real Estate Capital Management.

FIRM PROFILE: Hale and Dorr LLP has a strategic relationship with Hutchison & Mason, PLLC.

RESIDENT MEMBERS

JOHN C. CHRISTIE, JR., born 1936; admitted to bar, 1963, Illinois; 1973, District of Columbia; 1978, U.S. Supreme Court. *Education:* Brown University (A.B., magna cum laude, 1959) Phi Beta Kappa; Harvard Law School (J.D., 1962). ***PRACTICE AREAS:*** Litigation. ***Email:*** john.christie@haledorr.com

JEFFREY J. DAVIDSON, born 1950; admitted to bar, 1977, District of Columbia; 1988, U.S. Supreme Court. *Education:* Duke University (A.B., 1973; M.A., 1977; J.D., 1977). ***PRACTICE AREAS:*** Environmental Law. ***Email:*** jeffrey.davidson@haledorr.com

IRAH H. DONNER, born 1962; admitted to bar, 1991, New Jersey; 1992, New York and District of Columbia; registered to practice before U.S. Patent and Trademark Office. *Education:* Case Western Reserve University (B.S., high honors, 1985; M.S., 1987); Case Western Reserve University (J.D., magna cum laude, 1991). ***PRACTICE AREAS:*** Intellectual Property. ***Email:*** irah.donner@haledorr.com

MICHAEL D. ESCH, born 1954; admitted to bar, 1980, District of Columbia. *Education:* Harvard University (A.B., magna cum laude, 1976; J.D., cum laude, 1979). ***PRACTICE AREAS:*** International Trade Law. ***Email:*** michael.esch@haledorr.com

ALLEN H. FOX, born 1951; admitted to bar, 1976, Virginia; 1977, District of Columbia; 1982, Maryland. *Education:* Washington University (B.A., cum laude, 1973); George Washington University (J.D., with honors, 1976). Phi Beta Kappa. ***PRACTICE AREAS:*** Real Estate Law. ***Email:*** allen.fox@haledorr.com

MARK A. HELLER, born 1947; admitted to bar, 1973, Wisconsin; 1981, District of Columbia. *Education:* University of Wisconsin at Madison (B.A., 1970; J.D., 1973). ***PRACTICE AREAS:*** Drug and Medical Device Regulation. ***Email:*** mark.heller@haledorr.com

LOUISE NICHOLSON HOWE, born 1961; admitted to bar, 1987, New York; 1989, District of Columbia. *Education:* Princeton University (A.B., cum laude, 1983); University of Virginia (J.D., 1986). ***PRACTICE AREAS:*** Government; Regulatory Law. ***Email:*** louise.howe@haledorr.com

GILBERT B. KAPLAN, born 1951; admitted to bar, 1977, Massachusetts; 1989, District of Columbia. *Education:* Harvard College (A.B., magna cum laude, 1974); Harvard Law School (J.D., cum laude, 1977). ***Email:*** gilbert.kaplan@haledorr.com

MICHAEL J. LEVITIN, born 1960; admitted to bar, 1987, New York; 1988, District of Columbia. *Education:* Harvard University (A.B., magna cum

(This Listing Continued)

HALE AND DORR LLP, Washington—Continued

laude, 1982; J.D., 1986); Fletcher School of Law and Diplomacy (M.A.L.D., 1990). ***PRACTICE AREAS:*** Corporate Law. ***Email:*** michael.levitin@haledorr.com

MEGHAN H. MAGRUDER, born 1958; admitted to bar, 1983, Georgia; 1985, Massachusetts; 1999, District of Columbia. *Education:* Emory University (B.A., 1980); Emory University School of Law (J.D., 1983). ***PRACTICE AREAS:*** Environmental Law. ***Email:*** meghan.magruder@haledorr.com

WILLIAM G. McELWAIN, born 1955; admitted to bar, 1982, Massachusetts; 1986, District of Columbia; 1989, Virginia. *Education:* Yale University (B.A., cum laude, 1978); Harvard Law School (J.D., magna cum laude, 1982). ***Email:*** william.mcelwain@haledorr.com

KENNETH R. MEADE, born 1961; admitted to bar, 1985, Maryland; 1989, District of Columbia; 1997, Massachusetts. *Education:* University of Michigan (B.A., 1982); George Washington University (J.D., with honors, 1985). ***PRACTICE AREAS:*** Environmental Law. ***Email:*** ken.meade@haledorr.com

JAMES L. QUARLES III, born 1946; admitted to bar, 1974, Massachusetts; 1981, District of Columbia; 1985, Maryland; 2000, Virginia. *Education:* Denison University (B.S., cum laude, 1968); Harvard Law School (J.D., cum laude, 1972). Phi Beta Kappa. ***PRACTICE AREAS:*** Litigation. ***Email:*** james.quarles@haledorr.com

KENNETH H. SLADE, born 1955; admitted to bar, 1979, District of Columbia; 1984, New York; 1985, California; 1994, Massachusetts. *Education:* Princeton University (A.B., magna cum laude, 1977); Columbia University (J.D., 1979). Phi Beta Kappa. ***PRACTICE AREAS:*** Corporate Law. ***Email:*** kenneth.slade@haledorr.com

STEVEN S. SNIDER, born 1956; admitted to bar, 1980, District of Columbia. *Education:* Cornell University (A.B., summa cum laude, 1977); University of Chicago (J.D., 1980). Phi Beta Kappa. ***PRACTICE AREAS:*** Corporate Law. ***Email:*** steven.snider@haledorr.com

JAY P. URWITZ, born 1949; admitted to bar, 1976, District of Columbia. *Education:* Harpur College, The State University of New York at Binghamton (B.A., cum laude, 1970); Harvard University (M.P.P., 1974; J.D., cum laude, 1974). ***PRACTICE AREAS:*** Government Relations Law. ***Email:*** jay.urwitz@haledorr.com

PAUL G. WALLACH, born 1947; admitted to bar, 1973, New York; 1975, District of Columbia; 1978, U.S. Supreme Court; 1984, Massachusetts. *Education:* Rutgers University (B.A., 1969); University of Virginia (J.D., 1972). ***PRACTICE AREAS:*** Environmental Law. ***Email:*** paul.wallach@haledorr.com

KATHLEEN M. WEINSTEIN, born 1960; admitted to bar, 1990, Maryland; 1991, District of Columbia. *Education:* Lynchburg College (B.A., summa cum laude, 1981); The Washington College of Law of American University (J.D., summa cum laude, 1990). ***PRACTICE AREAS:*** Real Estate. ***Email:*** kathleen.weinstein@haledorr.com

DAVID A. WILSON, born 1957; admitted to bar, 1988, Massachusetts; 1991, District of Columbia; 1994, Maryland. *Education:* Harvard University (A.B., cum laude, 1980); Georgetown University (J.D., cum laude, 1988). ***PRACTICE AREAS:*** Litigation. ***Email:*** david.wilson@haledorr.com

HENRY N. WIXON, born 1954; admitted to bar, 1986, Maryland; 1989, District of Columbia; 1990, U.S. Supreme Court; registered to practice before U.S. Patent and Trademark Office. *Education:* University of Maryland (B.S., 1976; M.S., 1980); George Washington University (J.D., with honors, 1986). ***PRACTICE AREAS:*** Intellectual Property Law. ***Email:*** henry.wixon@haledorr.com

COUNSEL

MIRIAM R. GAMSON, born 1959; admitted to bar, 1984, Texas; 1989, District of Columbia. *Education:* University of California, Los Angeles (B.A., magna cum laude, 1981); Tulane University (J.D., 1984). Phi Beta Kappa. ***PRACTICE AREAS:*** Real Estate. ***Email:*** miriam.gamson@haledorr.com

PAUL W. JAMESON, born 1951; admitted to bar, 1979, District of Columbia. *Education:* University of Pittsburgh (B.A., cum laude, 1973; M.A., 1976); Georgetown University (J.D., 1979). ***PRACTICE AREAS:*** International Trade Law. ***Email:*** paul.jameson@haledorr.com

CRIS R. REVAZ, born 1959; admitted to bar, 1988, District of Columbia. *Education:* Connecticut College (B.A., 1981); Catholic University of America (J.D., 1988). ***PRACTICE AREAS:*** International Trade. ***Email:*** cris.revaz@haledorr.com

(This Listing Continued)

WENDY ANDERSON TERRY, born 1967; admitted to bar, 1992, Virginia; 1993, District of Columbia. *Education:* Smith College (B.A., magna cum laude, 1989) Phi Beta Kappa; University of Virginia (J.D., 1992). ***PRACTICE AREAS:*** Litigation. ***Email:*** wendy.terry@haledorr.com

(For complete biographical data on all personnel, see Professional Biographies at Boston, Massachusetts)

HALL, ESTILL, HARDWICK, GABLE, GOLDEN & NELSON

A PROFESSIONAL CORPORATION

SUITE 700, NORTH BUILDING
1120 20TH STREET, N.W.
WASHINGTON, D.C. 20036-3406
Telephone: 202-973-1200
Facsimile: 202-973-1212
Email: attorney_name@HallEstill.Com
URL: http://www.HallEstill.Com

Tulsa, Oklahoma Office: 320 South Boston Avenue, Suite 400, 74103. Telephone: 918-594-0400. Facsimile: 918-594-0505.
Oklahoma City, Oklahoma Office: Bank One Center, Suite 2900, 100 North Broadway, 73102-8827. Telephone: 405-553-2828. Facsimile: 405-553-2855.
Fayetteville, Arkansas Office: One East Center Street, Suite 315, 72701. Telephone: 501-973-5200. Facsimile: 501-973-0520.

General and Administrative Practice before all Courts and Administrative Agencies. Energy Regulatory and Natural Resources Law. Indian Law and Water Law. Government Relations.

FIRM PROFILE: Hall, Estill, Hardwick, Gable, Golden & Nelson, P.C. is listed in Martindale Hubbell's Bar Register of Preeminent Lawyers.

JOHN B. RUDOLPH, born Buffalo, New York, July 18, 1948; admitted to bar, 1974, Oklahoma; 1975, District of Columbia; U.S. Court of Appeals, Fifth, Eighth, Tenth and District of Columbia Circuits; U. S. District Court, District of Columbia; U.S. Supreme Court and U.S. Claims Court. *Education:* University of Virginia (B.A., 1970); University of Oklahoma (J.D., 1973). Phi Delta Phi. *Member:* District of Columbia Bar; Oklahoma, Federal Energy and American Bar Associations. ***Email:*** JRUDOLPH@HallEstill.Com

JOSEPH R. MEMBRINO, JR., born Waterbury, Connecticut, September 14, 1946; admitted to bar, 1972, Connecticut; 1979, District of Columbia. *Education:* Georgetown University (A.B., 1968); Boston College (J.D., 1971). *Member:* District of Columbia Bar; Connecticut Bar Association. ***PRACTICE AREAS:*** Administrative Law; Indians and Native Populations; Natural Resources. ***Email:*** JMEMBRINO@HallEstill.Com

DONALD R. DINAN, born Nashua, New Hampshire, August 28, 1949; admitted to bar, 1975, Massachusetts; 1976, District of Columbia; 1981, New York. *Education:* University of Pennsylvania (B.S., 1971); Georgetown University (J.D., 1974); London School of Economics, London, England (LL.M., 1975). Adjunct Professor of International Law, Georgetown University Law Center, 1988—. Director, Unfair Import Investigations Division, U.S. International Trade Commission, 1981-1982. General Counsel, D.C. Democratic State Committee, 1988-1992, 1994—. *Member:* Federal and American Bar Associations; ITC Trial Lawyers Association; American Intellectual Property Law Association (Chair, Committee on International Trade Commission, 1986-1989; Chair, Committee on Export Controls, 1984-1993, 1994-1996). ***PRACTICE AREAS:*** International Trade; Litigation; Trademarks; Copyrights. ***Email:*** DDINAN@HallEstill.Com

JOHN J. McDERMOTT, born Knoxville, Tennessee, 1951; admitted to bar, 1976, Virginia and District of Columbia; 1977, U.S. Supreme Court, U.S. Court of Appeals for the District of Columbia, Fourth, Fifth and Sixth Circuits; U.S. District Court for the District of Columbia, Eastern and Western Districts of Virginia. *Education:* Georgetown University (B.A., 1973; J.D., 1976). Trial Attorney, U.S. Department of Justice Antitrust Division, 1976-1977. Assistant U.S. Attorney for District of Columbia, 1977-1982. Co-chairman, District of Columbia Criminal Practice Institute, 1980-1981. Author: "How to Design a Compliance Program," BNA/ACCA Compliance Manual Prevention of Corporate Liability, 1993. Instructor, Trial Practice, Washington Center, 1980-1982. Instructor, D.C. Bar/G.W.U. Trial Skills Series, 1995-1998. *Member:* District of Columbia Bar; Virginia State Bar; American Bar Association (Subcommittee on White Collar Crime). ***PRACTICE AREAS:*** Litigation; White Collar Criminal Defense; Trade Association Law. ***Email:*** JMCDERMOTT@HallEstill.Com

JAMES B. WILCOX, JR., born Boston, Massachusetts, March 13, 1949; admitted to bar, 1974, Colorado; 1976, District of Columbia. *Education:* University of Pennsylvania (B.A., with honors, 1971); Georgetown University (J.D., 1974). *Member:* The District of Columbia Bar (Computer and Telecommuni-

(This Listing Continued)

cations Law Section); Federal Energy Bar Association. **LANGUAGES:** French. **PRACTICE AREAS:** Civil Litigation; Complex Litigation; Energy. **Email:** JWILCOX@HallEstill.Com

CRAIG A. KOENIGS, born Fond du Lac, Wisconsin, December 31, 1963; admitted to bar, 1990, District of Columbia. *Education:* University of Wisconsin at Madison (B.A., with distinction, 1986); Georgetown University (J.D., 1989). Delta Theta Phi. *Member:* District of Columbia Bar (Member, Sections on: International Trade; Intellectual Property). **Email:** CKOENIGS@HallEstill.Com

JOHN J. CALLAHAN, born Boston, Massachusetts, March 1, 1962; admitted to bar, 1994, Pennsylvania; 1995, District of Columbia and U.S. Court of Appeals, District of Columbia Circuit. *Education:* Boston College (B.A., 1984); Catholic University of America (J.D., 1993). **PRACTICE AREAS:** Litigation. **Email:** JCALLAHAN@HallEstill.Com

SANDEEP KATHURIA, born Denville, New Jersey, August 18, 1974; admitted to bar, 1999, Pennsylvania and New Jersey; 2000, District of Columbia. *Education:* George Washington University (B.A., 1996); Villanova University (J.D., 1999). Phi Delta Phi. Virginia Alumni Scholar. **PRACTICE AREAS:** Corporate Litigation; Oil and Gas Contracts; Business Torts; International Trade. **Email:** SKATHURIA@HallEstill.Com

OF COUNSEL

DAVID L. HILL, born Gadsden, Alabama, 1941; admitted to bar, 1969, District of Columbia and U.S. Court of Appeals for the District of Columbia Circuit; 1972, U.S. Supreme Court. *Education:* University of Alabama (B.S., 1964); George Washington University (J.D., 1968). Delta Theta Phi. *Member:* The District of Columbia Bar; American Bar Association; Federal Communications Bar Association; National Lawyers Club. (Also Of Counsel, O'Connor & Hannan, L.L.P.). **Email:** DHILL@HallEstill.Com

AUDREY P. RASMUSSEN, born Muskegon, Michigan, 1946; admitted to bar, 1983, District of Columbia. *Education:* Hope College (B.A., 1966); American University (M.A., 1976); George Mason School of Law (J.D., 1983). Member, Moot Court Board. *Member:* The District of Columbia Bar; American Bar Association; Federal Communications Bar Association. **Email:** ARASMUSSEN@HallEstill.Com

---

HALL & EVANS, L.L.C.

Established in 1932

SUITE 610
1341 G. STREET, N.W.
WASHINGTON, D.C. 20005
Telephone: 202-638-4633
Fax: 202-408-5146
Email: hallevans@hallevans.com
URL: http://www.hallevans.com

Denver, Colorado Office: Suite 1700, 1200 Seventeenth Street, 80202. Telephone: 303-628-3300. Fax: 303-628-3368.
Colorado Springs, Colorado Office: Suite 600, 102 South Tejon Street, 80903-2264. Telephone: 719-578-5600. Fax: 719-635-7458.

General Civil and Trial Practice in all State and Federal Courts, including Administrative Law; Alternative Dispute Resolution; Complex and Multi-District Litigation; Environmental Law; Government Contracts; Litigation; Regulatory Law.

FIRM PROFILE: Hall & Evans, L.L.C., has provided legal services in the Rocky Mountain Region for over 65 years. Our commitment and responsiveness to our clients' needs have resulted in diversified services with representation on local, regional, and national levels, and we handle a broad range of litigation and transactional work for both business and individual clients. For matters ranging from routine to the complex, Hall & Evans is committed to delivering innovative solutions, prompt dispute resolution, and multidimensional legal strategies in a practical, timely, and cost-effective manner. Member of Bar Register of Preeminent Lawyers.

MEMBER

F. GREGORY McKENNA, born Chicago, Illinois, October 4, 1952; admitted to bar, 1978, District of Columbia; 1981, Maryland; 1986, Nevada; 1993, Colorado. *Education:* Holy Cross College (B.A., cum laude, 1974); Georgetown University (J.D., 1978). *Member:* American Bar Association (Member, Section on: Public Contract Law). (Also at Denver, Colorado Office). **PRACTICE AREAS:** Government Contracts; Environmental Law. **Email:** mckenng@hallevans.com

(For Complete Biographical data on other Personnel, see Professional Biographies at Denver, Colorado)

HALL, PRIDDY, MYERS & VANDE SANDE

WASHINGTON, D.C.

(See Potomac, Maryland)

Patents, Trademarks, Copyrights, Unfair Competition, Intellectual Property.

HALLORAN & SAGE LLP

Established in 1935

1627 I STREET, N.W., SUITE 610
WASHINGTON, D.C. 20006
Telephone: 202-496-9270
Fax: 202-496-9279
URL: http://www.halloran-sage.com

Hartford, Connecticut Office: One Goodwin Square, 225 Asylum Street, 06103. Telephone: 860-522-6103. Fax: 860-548-0006.
Middletown, Connecticut Office: 300 Plaza Middlesex, 06457. Telephone: 860-346-8641. Fax: 860-344-1641.
Westport, Connecticut Office: 315 Post Road West, 06880-4739. Telephone: 203-227-2855. Fax: 203-227-6992.

Administrative Law, Arbitration, Commercial Litigation, Construction Law, Employment Law, Government Contracts, Insurance, International Trade and Reinsurance Law.

MEMBERS OF FIRM

JAMES C. STEARNS, born Minneapolis, Minnesota, February 11, 1950; admitted to bar, 1977, District of Columbia. *Education:* Dartmouth College (A.B., cum laude, 1972); University of Manchester (M.A., 1974); Georgetown University (J.D., 1976). Member, National Moot Court Team. Editor, Law and Policy in International Business, 1975-1976. Author: "Renewal of the Export Administration Act of 1979: An Overview," Middle East Executive Reports, April, 1983. Counsel, Georgetown University, Health Policy Center, 1976-1977. Special Assistant to the Commissioner, Public Buildings Service, GSA, 1977-1978. Chief Counsel, GSA Board of Contract Appeals, 1978-1980. Deputy Assistant Secretary, Department of Education, 1980-1981. Legislative Counsel, Department of Commerce, 1981-1984. Acting Chief Counsel, Minority Business Development Agency, 1984. Member, Chamber of Commerce Council on Small Business, 1984-1987. Trustee, The Holderness School, 1985-1994. President, United Cerebral Palsy Association, Inc., 1993-1995; Vice Chairman, United Cerebral Palsy Association, Inc., 1995-1997. *Member:* The District of Columbia Bar. **PRACTICE AREAS:** Administrative; Government Contracts; International Trade. **Email:** stearns@halloran-sage.com

THERESA W. HAJOST, born Kansas City, Missouri, December 19, 1954; admitted to bar, 1985, Maryland; 1988, District of Columbia. *Education:* University of Dallas (B.A., cum laude, 1977); University of Toledo (M.A., 1981); George Washington University (J.D., cum laude, 1984). Winner, Van Vleck Moot Court First Year Competition. Member, Office of the General Counsel, U.S. Nuclear Regulatory Commission, Honor Law Graduate, 1984-1986. *Member:* The District of Columbia Bar; Defense Research Institute. **PRACTICE AREAS:** Litigation; Insurance; Reinsurance; Commercial Litigation. **Email:** hajost@halloran-sage.com

OF COUNSEL

GINA L. SCHAECHER, born Omaha, Nebraska, June 30, 1965; admitted to bar, 1994, Nebraska and U.S. District Court, District of Nebraska; 2000, U.S. Court of Appeals, Sixth Circuit; 2001, District of Columbia and U.S. Court of Federal Claims. *Education:* University of Nebraska at Omaha (B.S.B.A., magna cum laude, 1990); University of Nebraska at Lincoln (J.D., with distinction, 1993). Recipient, Legal Excellence Award in Law and Global Economy. Senior Member, Allen Moot Court Board. Judicial Clerkship, Honorable D. Nick Caporale, Nebraska Supreme Court, 1994-1996. Member: Washington Building Congress; Associated General Contracts. *Member:* The District of Columbia Bar; American Bar Association; National Association of Women in Construction. **REPORTED CASES:** Willers v. Willers, 255 Neb. 769, 587 N.W.2d 390 (1998). **PRACTICE AREAS:** Commercial Litigation; Construction Law; Government Contracts. **Email:** schaecher@halloran-sage.com

(For Complete Biographical data on all personnel, see Professional Biographies at Hartford, Connecticut)

HALPRIN, TEMPLE, GOODMAN & MAHER

950 NORTH
555 12TH STREET, N.W.
WASHINGTON, D.C. 20004
Telephone: 202-371-9100
Fax: 202-371-1497
Email: htgm@htgm.com
URL: http://www.htgm.com

Domestic and International Telecommunications Law, Communication Legislative Advocacy, Wireless, Cellular, Satellite, PCS, Administrative Legal Practice.

FIRM PROFILE: The firm serves as a specialized telecommunications counsel for clients from all parts of the world. The firm represents clients before the Federal Communications Commission, the Executive Branch, the Congress and Federal and State Courts as well as before various international fora dealing with communications issues. The firm is recognized internationally for its talents in transforming telecommunication systems from national monopolies to competitive companies. This includes technology development, strategic business planning and legislative advocacy in complex governmental policy issues.

MEMBERS OF FIRM

ALBERT HALPRIN, born New York, N.Y., October 18, 1947; admitted to bar, 1975, Massachusetts and U.S. District Court, District of Massachusetts; 1990, District of Columbia; 1992, U.S. District Court, District of C olumbia and Massachusetts and U.S. Court of Appeals, District of Columbia Circuit. *Education:* Western Washington University (B.A., with distinction, 1971); Harvard University (J.D., 1974). Policy and Program Planning Division, Common Carrier Bureau, Federal Communications Commission, 1982-1984. Chief, Common Carrier Bureau, Federal Communications Commission, 1984-1987. *Member:* The District of Columbia Bar; Massachusetts Bar Association. ***PRACTICE AREAS:*** Communications Law; International Communications Law; Internet Litigation. ***Email:*** Bert@htgm.com

RILEY K. TEMPLE, born Richmond, Virginia; admitted to bar, 1975, Virginia; 1978, District of Columbia and U.S. Court of Appeals for the District of Columbia Circuit. *Education:* Lafayette College (A.B., 1971); Georgetown University (J.D., 1974). Assistant General Counsel, Corporation for Public Broadcasting, 1974-1977. Legislative Assistant, Senator Charles McC. Mathias, Jr., 1977-1978. Senior Counsel, R.C.A. Global Communications, Inc., 1978-1981. Communications Counsel, U.S. Senate Committee on Commerce, Science and Transportation, 1981-1983. Assistant Vice President for Telecommunications Policy Bell Communications Research, Inc., 1983-1985. *Member:* The District of Columbia Bar; Virginia State Bar; Federal Communications Bar Association. ***PRACTICE AREAS:*** Legislative Law; Telecommunications Law. ***Email:*** rkt@htgm.com

STEPHEN L. GOODMAN, born Miami, Florida, October 3, 1956; admitted to bar, 1980, Florida; 1981, District of Columbia; 1992, District of Columbia and U.S. Court of Appeals, District of Columbia Circuit. *Education:* Rensselaer Polytechnic Institute (B.S., cum laude, 1977); Cornell University (J.D., cum laude, 1980). Editor, Cornell Law Review, 1979-1980. Law Clerk to Judge William P. Gray, U.S. District Court, Central District of California, 1980-1981 term. Deputy Chief, Industry Analysis Division, Federal Communications Commission, 1984-1988. *Member:* The District of Columbia Bar; The Florida Bar; Federal Communications Bar Association. ***PRACTICE AREAS:*** Telecommunications Law; Antitrust Law. ***Email:*** slg@htgm.com

WILLIAM F. MAHER, JR., born Pittsburgh, Pennsylvania, January 20, 1957; admitted to bar, 1984, Pennsylvania; 1995, District of Columbia. *Education:* University of Notre Dame (B.S., 1978); Massachusetts Institute of Technology (M.S., 1980); Harvard University (J.D., 1984). Tau Beta Pi; Eta Kappa Nu. Member, Technical Staff, Bell Labs, 1980-1981. Attorney-Advisor and Special Counsel, Competitive Issues, Common Carrier Bureau, Federal Communications Commission, 1985-1989. Associate Administrator, National Telecommunications and Information Administration, U.S. Department of Commerce, 1989-1994. *Member:* The District of Columbia Bar; U.S. Supreme Court Bar; Federal Communications Bar Association. ***PRACTICE AREAS:*** Telecommunications Law; Computer Law. ***Email:*** wfm@htgm.com

JOEL H. BERNSTEIN, born Cleveland, Ohio, October 21, 1963; admitted to bar, 1988, California; 1989, District of Columbia. *Education:* Colgate University (B.A., cum laude, 1985); University of California at Los Angeles (J.D., 1988). Business Editor, Federal Communications Law Journal, 1986-1988. Intern, Office of Commissioner Mimi Weyforth Dawson, Federal Communications Commission, 1987. Legislative Counsel, Office of Rep. Don Ritter, 1990-1992. *Member:* American and Federal Communications Bar Associations. ***PRACTICE AREAS:*** Telecommunications Law; Legislative Law. ***Email:*** jb@htgm.com

OF COUNSEL

JANICE I. OBUCHOWSKI, born 1951; admitted to bar, 1976, District of Columbia. *Education:* Wellesley College (B.A., 1973); Georgetown University Law Center (J.D., 1976). Editor, Georgetown Law Journal. Assistant Secretary, National Telecommunications and Information Administration, 1989-1992. Senior Advisor to Chairman, Federal Communications Commissions, 1985-1987. ***PRACTICE AREAS:*** Communications Law; International Law. ***Email:*** jo@htgm.com

(This Listing Continued)

HAMILTON AND HAMILTON, LLP

Established in 1876

SUITE 1100
1775 PENNSYLVANIA AVENUE, N.W.
WASHINGTON, D.C. 20006
Telephone: 202-463-8282
Telecopier: 202-463-7282; 202-659-8285
Email: mailbox@hamiltonlaw.com
URL: http://www.hamiltonlaw.com

Civil Litigation, Complex Multi-District Litigation, Business Law, Corporate Law, Education Law, Employment Law, Estate Planning, Trusts, Wills, Probate, Tax Exempt Organizations, Insurance Coverage Disputes, Municipal Law, Personal Injury, Professional Malpractice, Real Estate Law, Real Estate Tax, Taxation, Land Use and Zoning, Transportation.

FIRM PROFILE: In practice continuously since 1876, Hamilton and Hamilton, LLP is the District of Columbia's oldest law firm. It represents both individuals and corporations in a variety of areas. By choice, Hamilton and Hamilton, LLP has remained a small-to-medium sized firm in order to maintain close personal client relationships, some of which have endured for over a century. The firm is committed to high-quality representation of its clients, by the delivery of legal services at reasonable rates and the use of modern technology to achieve maximum efficiency.

SOUTH TRIMBLE, III (1925-2000).

PARTNERS

MICHAEL A. CAIN, born Washington, D.C., May 29, 1945; admitted to bar, 1970, District of Columbia and U.S. District Court for the District of Columbia; 1971, U.S. Court of Appeals for the District of Columbia Circuit; 1974, U.S. Supreme Court; 1992, Maryland. *Education:* Catholic University of America (B.A., 1967; J.D., 1970). Attorney Adviser, LEAA General Counsel, U.S. Department of Justice, 1970-1971. Law Clerk, Hon. E.T. Daly, Superior Court of the District of Columbia, 1971-1972. Assistant Corporation Counsel, District of Columbia, 1972-1979. Member, Tax Division Rules Advisory Committee, Superior Court of the District of Columbia, 1994—. *Member:* Montgomery County Bar Association; The District of Columbia Bar (Chair, Council on Sections, 1987-1988; Co-Chair, Steering Committee, Real Estate, Housing and Land Use Section, 1984-1988). ***PRACTICE AREAS:*** Land Use; Civil Litigation; Real Estate Tax; Municipal Law. ***Email:*** mac@hamiltonlaw.com

RICHARD E. JORDAN, born New York, N.Y., May 15, 1952; admitted to bar, 1977, Maryland; 1981, District of Columbia; 1985, Virginia; 1992, U.S. Supreme Court. *Education:* Georgetown University (B.A., 1974); Catholic University (J.D., 1977). Staff Member, 1975-1976 and Production Editor, 1976-1977, Catholic University Law Review. Assistant States Attorney, Montgomery County, Maryland, 1978-1984. Law Clerk to the Honorable Joseph M. Mathias, Judge, Circuit Court for Montgomery County, Maryland, 1977-1978. ***PRACTICE AREAS:*** Civil Litigation; Personal Injury; Business Litigation; Employment Litigation; Professional Malpractice. ***Email:*** rej@hamiltonlaw.com

PATRICK KAVANAUGH, born Washington, D.C., September 22, 1947; admitted to bar, 1974, District of Columbia; 1988, U.S. Supreme Court; 1994, Maryland. *Education:* University of Notre Dame (B.A., 1970); George Washington University (J.D., with honors, 1974). Assistant Corporation Counsel for the District of Columbia, 1974-1981. Arbitrator and Mediator, Superior Court of the District of Columbia, 1991—. *Member:* The District of Columbia Bar; Bar Association of the District of Columbia; Defense Research Institute; District of Columbia Defense Lawyers Association (President, 1992-1993). ***PRACTICE AREAS:*** Civil Litigation; Personal Injury; Insurance Litigation. ***Email:*** pk@hamiltonlaw.com

GEORGE T. MASSON, JR., born Evanston, Illinois, June 28, 1942; admitted to bar, 1968, California; 1971, Illinois and District of Columbia; 1972, U.S. Supreme Court; 1980, Maryland. *Education:* Carleton College (B.A., 1964); University of Michigan (J.D., 1967). Assistant Corporation Counsel for the District of Columbia, 1971-1979. Arbitrator, Superior Court of the District of Columbia, 1991—. *Member:* The District of Columbia Bar; State Bar of California; Maryland State Bar Association; District of Columbia Defense Lawyers Association; The Counsellors. [With U.S. Army; Instructor, U.S. Army Intelligence School, 1968-1970]. ***PRACTICE AREAS:*** Civil Litigation; Personal Injury; Employment Law. ***Email:*** gtm@hamiltonlaw.com

STEPHEN W. NEALON, born Washington, D.C., October 13, 1946; admitted to bar, 1974, Maryland; 1975, District of Columbia. *Education:* Lehigh University (B.A., 1968); University of Texas (J.D., 1973). Law Clerk, District of

(This Listing Continued)

Columbia Court of Appeals, 1973-1974. *Member:* The District of Columbia Bar (Member, Steering Committee, Estates, Trust and Probate Law Section, 1989-1991); Montgomery County, Maryland State and American Bar Associations; Washington, D.C. Estate Planning Council; The Supreme Court Historical Society (Trustee). [U.S. Army, Military Intelligence, 1968-1971]. ***PRACTICE AREAS:*** Estate Planning; Probate; Real Estate; Business Law. ***Email:*** swn@hamiltonlaw.com

JAMES B. SARSFIELD, born Washington, D.C., January 21, 1949; admitted to bar, 1974, Maryland; 1975, District of Columbia. *Education:* Georgetown University (A.B., 1971); Catholic University of America (J.D., 1974). Law Clerk to Judge Joseph M. Hannon, Superior Court of the District of Columbia, 1975-1976. Mediator, Superior Court for the District of Columbia Courts, 1982-1990. *Member:* The District of Columbia Bar; National Association of Railroad Trial Counsel (Member, Executive Committee, 1991—); National Association of College and University Attorneys; National Diocesan Attorneys Association; District of Columbia Defense Lawyers Association (President, 2000-2001); The Counsellors (President 1995-1996). ***PRACTICE AREAS:*** Civil Litigation; Personal Injury; Employment Law; Education Law. ***Email:*** jbs@hamiltonlaw.com

E. TILLMAN STIRLING, born Washington, D.C., November 5, 1927; admitted to bar, 1954, District of Columbia; 1958, U.S. Supreme Court; 1960, Maryland. *Education:* George Washington University (B.S., 1951); George Washington University Law School (J.D., 1953). Law clerk to Judge Wilbur K. Miller, U.S. Court of Appeals for the District of Columbia Circuit, 1954-1955. Assistant U.S. Attorney, District of Columbia, 1955-1958. *Member:* The District of Columbia Bar; Maryland State and American Bar Associations. Fellow, American College of Trust and Estate Counsel. ***PRACTICE AREAS:*** Estate Planning; Probate; Trusts. ***Email:*** ets@hamiltonlaw.com

PHILIP J. SWEENEY, III, born Braddock, Pennsylvania, January 4, 1944; admitted to bar, 1969, Virginia; 1972, District of Columbia; 1979, U.S. Tax Court. *Education:* College of William and Mary (A.B., 1966); American University (J.D., 1969); George Washington University (LL.M., 1974). Phi Alpha Delta. Author: "Income Exclusion for Disabled Employees— How to Preserve Favorable Lump-Sum Distribution Rights," Prentice-Hall, Inc., 1980. Attorney, Interpretative Division, Office of the Chief Counsel, Internal Revenue Service, 1972-1978. Northern Virginia Estate Planning Council. *Member:* District of Columbia Bar; Virginia State Bar; American Bar Association. ***PRACTICE AREAS:*** Taxation; Exempt Organizations; Estate Planning; Corporate; Business Law. ***Email:*** pjs@hamiltonlaw.com

ASSOCIATE

DIANE P. PRITCHETT, born Kansas City, Missouri, August 31, 1967; admitted to bar, 1994, Missouri; 1995, Illinois; 1997, District of Columbia. *Education:* University of Kansas; University of Missouri-Columbia (B.S., 1991; J.D., 1994). *Member:* District of Columbia Bar; Missouri State Bar; Illinois State Bar; American Bar Association. ***PRACTICE AREAS:*** Civil Litigation; Employment Law; Education Law; Corporate Law. ***Email:*** dpp@hamiltonlaw.com

SPECIAL COUNSEL

THOMAS D. QUINN, JR., born Washington, D.C., May 10, 1930; admitted to bar, 1956, District of Columbia and U.S. Court of Appeals for the District of Columbia Circuit; 1967, U.S. Supreme Court. *Education:* University of Maryland; George Washington University (J.D., 1956). Attorney, Office of the General Counsel, U.S. Post Office Department, 1956-1957. Law Clerk to Judge Edward M. Curran, U.S. District Court for the District of Columbia, 1957-1959. Assistant U.S. Attorney for the District of Columbia, 1959-1962. *Member:* The District of Columbia Bar; National Association of College and University Attorneys. ***PRACTICE AREAS:*** Civil Litigation; Education Law; Employment Law. ***Email:*** tdq@hamiltonlaw.com

STEPHEN A. TRIMBLE, born Washington, D.C., July 25, 1933; admitted to bar, 1961, District of Columbia; 1965, U.S. Supreme Court; U.S. Court of Federal Claims. *Education:* University of North Carolina (A.B., 1955); Georgetown University (LL.B., 1961). Law Clerk to Judge Richmond B. Keech, U.S. District Court for the District of Columbia, 1959-1961. Assistant Corporation Counsel for the District of Columbia, 1962. Committee Member, 1977-1983, Vice Chairman, 1978-1979 and Chairman, 1979-1983, Committee on Grievances, U.S. District Court for the District of Columbia. Chairman, Rule 711 Counseling Panel, U.S. District Court for the District of Columbia, 1990-1995. *Member:* The District of Columbia Bar (Member, Board of Governors, 1978-1981); Bar Association of the District of Columbia (President, 1976-1977); American Bar Association (Member, House of Delegates, 1976-1977); National Association of Railroad Trial Counsel (President, 1977-1978; Distinguished Service Award, 1995); National Association of College and University Attorneys; Defense Research Institute, Inc.; National Conference of Bar Presidents. Fellow: American College of Trial Lawyers (State Chairman, District of Columbia, 1980-1982); American Bar Foundation. [With U.S. Marine Corps., 1st Lt., 1955-1958]. ***PRACTICE AREAS:*** Appellate Practice; Civil Litigation; Personal Injury. ***Email:*** sat@hamiltonlaw.com

OF COUNSEL

ALLEN JONES, JR., born Washington, D.C., May 24, 1930; admitted to bar, 1957, District of Columbia; 1961, U.S. Supreme Court; 1962, Maryland. *Education:* Michigan State University (B.A., 1952); Georgetown University (J.D., 1957). Phi Alpha Delta. Member, Board of Editors, Georgetown Law Journal, 1956-1957. Who's Who in American Law. Member: Judicial Conference of the District of Columbia, 1977-1998; Judicial Conference of the District of Columbia Circuit, 1986-1988; Superior Court Civil Delay Reduction Task Force, 1988-1991; Board and Executive Committee, Council for Court Excellence (Treasurer, 1996-1998). President, Research Foundation, 1985. Superior Court Mediator, 1987—. *Member:* The District of Columbia Bar; Bar Association of the District of Columbia (President, 1986; Member, Board of Directors, 1977-1980); Maryland State and American (Member, House of Delegates, 1986-1987) Bar Associations; The Barristers (President, 1982); The Counsellors; The Lawyers Club. ***Email:*** aj@hamiltonlaw.com

HARRY J. JORDAN, born Gettysburg, Pennsylvania, February 8, 1934; admitted to bar, 1960, District of Columbia; 1996, U.S. Supreme Court. *Education:* Mount St. Mary's College (B.S., 1955); University of Pittsburgh (LL.B., 1958). Motor Carrier Editor, Interstate Commerce Commission Practitioners' Journal, 1966-1968. General Attorney, American Trucking Associations, Inc., 1962-1968. General Counsel, Interstate Truckload Carrier Conference, 1978-1979. *Member:* The District of Columbia Bar; American Bar Association; Transportation Lawyers Association. ***PRACTICE AREAS:*** Civil Litigation; Administrative Law; Transportation; Corporate; Employment Law; Labor Law. ***Email:*** hjj@hamiltonlaw.com

EDWARD R. KUMP, born Bridgeport, Connecticut, February 28, 1953; admitted to bar, 1978, Connecticut; 1984, District of Columbia and U.S. Supreme Court. *Education:* Catholic University of America (B.A., magna cum laude, 1974; J.D., 1977). Phi Beta Kappa. *Member:* The District of Columbia Bar; American Bar Association; Federal Communications Bar Association. ***PRACTICE AREAS:*** Communications Law; Corporate Law; Business Law. ***Email:*** erk@hamiltonlaw.com

REPRESENTATIVE CLIENTS: The Archdiocese for Military Services, USA; Bradford White Corporation; The Catholic University of America; Consolidated Rail Corp.; Crawford and Co.; Frank Parsons Paper Company; The George Washington University; Hospital for Sick Children; KFC National Management Co.; Norfolk Southern Corporation; North American Van Lines, Inc.; Owens Corning; Penn National Insurance Company; Resources for the Future; Superfresh Food Markets of Maryland, Inc.; Tricon Global Restaurants, Inc.; Washington Area New Automobile Dealers Association.

PAUL W. HAMMACK, JR.

WASHINGTON, D.C.

(See Fairfax, Virginia)

General Practice. Litigation, Negligence, Contracts, Family, Divorce, Child Custody, Child Support, Business Law, Wills, Probate Law, Elder Law, Guardianships, Trusts and Estate Planning, Estate Administration, Personal Injury, Automobile Accidents. Trials in State and Federal Courts.

PATRICK T. HAND

3201 NEW MEXICO AVENUE, N.W.,
SUITE 350
WASHINGTON, D.C. 20016
Telephone: 202-895-1332
Fax: 202-537-1200
Email: patrickhand@aol.com

Wills, Estates, Trusts, Probate, Powers of Attorney, Contested Wills, Conservatorships, Guardianships, Estate and Gift Taxation, Estate Litigation, Retirement Planning, Family Business Succession Planning.

FIRM PROFILE: Mr. Patrick T. Hand is a well known and trusted Estate Planning and Administration attorney with over 17 years of probate litigation experience. His practice frequently involves the sensitive handling of private civil commitment proceedings where the mental health of a family member is a serious concern. The firm carefully represents a wide array of professionals and retirees from suburban Maryland and Washington, D.C.

PATRICK T. HAND, born Jacksonville, North Carolina, May 3, 1958; admitted to bar, 1984, New York, District of Columbia and U.S. District Court for the District of Columbia; 1985, U.S. Court of Appeals for the District of Columbia Circuit; 1991, Maryland; 1992, U.S. Supreme Court. *Education:* Catholic University of America (B.A., 1980); Fordham University (J.D., 1983). Commentary Editor, Volume XI, Fordham Urban Law Journal, 1982-1983.

(This Listing Continued)

PATRICK T. HAND, Washington—Continued

Co-Author, "The Probate Process from Start to Finish in Washington, D.C." (2000). *Member:* The District of Columbia Bar; The Bar Association of the District of Columbia; New York State Bar Association; The George Washington American Inn of Court (President, 2001-2002; Vice President, 1999-2000). ***PRACTICE AREAS:*** Trusts and Estates; Mental Health Law.

HANSON & MOLLOY

Established in 1932

1250 EYE STREET, N.W., SUITE 701

WASHINGTON, D.C. 20005-3922

Telephone: 202-842-1116

Facsimile: 202-842-1597

Email: hanson-molloy.com

URL: http://www.lawyers.com/h&mlaw

General counsel to both profit and non-profit corporations. Internet litigation and governance, civil litigation with substantive concentration in insurance and reinsurance, labor and employment, antitrust, media, First Amendment, tax, government, commercial contracts, real estate, trusts and estates.

FIRM PROFILE: Founded in 1932, the Hanson firm has represented leading professional and trade associations, charities and foundations. From 1962-1989, the firm was led by Arthur B. "Tim" Hanson (Maj. Gen. USMCR) who acted as general counsel to numerous national non-profit organizations. Mr. Hanson also founded several insurance companies in Bermuda which continue to insure risks for members of U.S. trade associations and for U.S. corporations.

ARTHUR B. HANSON (1916-1989).

JAMES DENNIS MOLLOY, born Brooklyn, New York, July 16, 1943; admitted to bar, 1983, District of Columbia; 1985, Virginia; U.S. District Court for the District of Columbia; U.S. Court of Appeals for the District of Columbia; U.S. District Court, Eastern District of Virginia; U.S. Court of Appeals, Fourth Circuit. *Education:* Mount Saint Mary's College (B.S., 1965); Antioch School of Law (J.D., 1983). Phi Delta Phi. Tang Inn of Court. Director, Vice President Labor Relations, Metropolitan Hospital Center, New York, New York, 1970-1977. Vice President, Labor Divisions, Printing Industries of America, 1977-1985; Senior Vice President and Association Counsel, 1985-1989. U.S. General Counsel: United Insurance Company Limited, 1989—; Print Management Limited, 1989—; American Registry for Internet Numbers, Inc.; United States Capitol Historical Society. *Member:* Virginia State Bar; District of Columbia Bar. [U.S. Army, 1967-1973]. ***PRACTICE AREAS:*** Corporate Law; Commercial Law; Insurance and Reinsurance; Antitrust; Trusts; Exempt Organizations; Employment and Labor Law. ***Email:*** dmolloy@hanson-molloy.com

ARTHUR D. McKEY, born Washington, D.C., 1949; admitted to bar, 1978, Idaho and U.S. District Court, District of Idaho; 1979, District of Columbia and U.S. District Court for the District of Columbia; 1983, U.S. Supreme Court; 1985, U.S. District Court, Western District of Michigan and U.S. Court of Appeals, Sixth Circuit; 1992, U.S. District Court, Northern District of California and Northern District of Texas. *Education:* Boston College (B.A., 1970; M.A. with distinction, 1973); University of Maryland (M.A., 1975); University of Idaho (J.D., 1978). Lead Articles Editor, Idaho Law Review, 1977-1978. General Counsel, The Childrens Inn at NIH, 1988—; Creative Internet Applications, Inc., 1997—. Member, Advisory Board, Media Law Reporter, 1989—. Special Appointment, Communications and Finance Section/Civil Task Force, Antitrust Division, U.S. Department of Justice, 1993-1995. ***PRACTICE AREAS:*** Litigation; Antitrust; Internet Law; Media/First Amendment Law; Non-Profit Organizations; Trademark; Insurance Law. ***Email:*** amckey@hanson-molloy.com

MICHAEL B. McGOVERN, born New York, N.Y., March 6, 1947; admitted to bar, 1973, District of Columbia; 1978, Maryland. *Education:* Georgetown University (A.B., 1969; J.D., 1972); George Washington University (LL.M. in Taxation, 1987). *Member:* District of Columbia Bar; Maryland State Bar Association. ***PRACTICE AREAS:*** Real Estate; Estate Planning; Trust Law; Litigation. ***Email:*** mmcgovern@hanson-molloy.com

OF COUNSEL

RON L. DURST, born Gallipolis, Ohio, 1953; admitted to bar, 1987, Virginia; U.S. District Court, Eastern District of Virginia (Not admitted in District of Columbia). *Education:* West Virginia University (B.S., Economics, 1975; J.D., 1980); Georgetown University (M.L.T., Tax, 1987). *Member:* Virginia State Bar. ***PRACTICE AREAS:*** Federal Taxation; Corporate Taxation; Estate and Trusts; Exempt Organizations. ***Email:*** rdurst@hanson-molloy.com

SPECIAL LEGAL CONSULTANT

BALA NADARAJAH, born Sri Lanka, February 28, 1935; admitted to bar, 1960, Sri Lanka; 1986, Bermuda (Not admitted in the United States). *Education:* University of Ceylon, GAQ (1956); Ceylon Law College (J.D., 1959); Georgetown University (Master of Comparative Law Degree, 1979). Law Chambers, Sri Lanka, practicing before original, appellate courts and the Privy Council in London 1960-1976. Attorney General's Chambers, Bermuda, 1979-1986. Legal Advisor: Bermuda Ministry of Finance, Registrar of Companies, Bermuda Monetary Authority and Insurance Advisory Committee. Of Counsel: Law Office of Hanson, O'Brien, Birney & Butler, Washington D.C. 1986-1989; Milligan-Whyte & Smith, 1993—. ***LANGUAGES:*** Tamil and Sinhalese. ***PRACTICE AREAS:*** Corporate; Insurance; Reinsurance; International Commercial Law.

(This Listing Continued)

HARKINS CUNNINGHAM

Established in 1992

SUITE 600, 801 PENNSYLVANIA AVENUE, N.W.

WASHINGTON, D.C. 20004-2615

Telephone: 202-973-7600

Facsimile: 202-973-7610

Email: dhirsh@harkinscunningham.com

URL: http://www.harkinscunningham.com

Philadelphia, Pennsylvania Office: 2800 One Commerce Square, 2005 Market Street, 19103-7042. Telephone: 215-851-6700. Facsimile: 215-851-6710.

New York, New York Office: 10 Rockefeller Plaza, Suite 1250, 10020. Telephone: 212-218-1990. Facsimile: 212-218-1999.

Complex and Multi-District Litigation, Economic Regulation, Legislative Policy, Antitrust and Trade Regulation, Biotechnology, Corporate Governance, Corporate and Securities Transactions, Business Law, Energy, Administrative Law, Taxation, Transportation, Utility Law and Alternative Dispute Resolution.

FIRM PROFILE: Harkins Cunningham lawyers have many years of experience working together on complex litigation and on competition and other economic regulatory matters involving network industries. The firm represents business entities, public bodies and industry coalitions in: resolving controversies through court or agency litigation or through appropriate alternative dispute resolution means; devising and implementing regulatory, legislative or other initiatives to redefine or resolve controversies and to create benefits and opportunities; advising on corporate strategy and governance issues; shaping and handling financing, intellectual property and other types of transactions; and counseling on taxation matters.

MEMBERS OF FIRM

PAUL A. CUNNINGHAM, born Everett, WA, 1946; admitted to bar, 1972, Washington; 1979, District of Columbia. *Education:* Whitman College (B.A., 1969); University of Washington (J.D., 1972). Staff Counsel, U.S. Senate Committee on Commerce, 1972-1976. *Member:* District of Columbia Bar; Washington State Bar Association. ***Email:*** pac@harkinscunningham.com

DAVID A. BONO, born Savannah, Georgia, 1960; admitted to bar, 1987, Pennsylvania; 1988, District of Columbia. *Education:* Duke University (B.A., magna cum laude, 1982); Harvard Law School (J.D., magna cum laude, 1986). Editor, 1984-1986 and Notes Office Co-Chairman, 1985-1986, Harvard Law Review. Law Clerk, Judge Edward R. Becker, U.S. Court of Appeals, Third Circuit, 1986-1987. Trial Attorney, U.S. Department of Justice, 1996-1999. *Member:* The District of Columbia Bar; Pennsylvania and American Bar Associations. ***PRACTICE AREAS:*** Litigation; Administrative Law; Regulated Industries. ***Email:*** dbono@harkinscunningham.com

RICHARD B. HERZOG, born New York, N.Y., 1939; admitted to bar, 1965, District of Columbia. *Education:* Williams College (B.A., cum laude,, with highest honors, 1960); Harvard University (LL.B., 1963). Phi Beta Kappa. Deputy Assistant Director for General Litigation, 1972-1973 and Assistant Director for National Advertising, 1973-1977, Bureau of Consumer Protection, Federal Trade Commission. Assistant Administrator for Enforcement, 1977-1978 and Deputy Administrator for Policy, 1978-1979, Economic Regulatory Administration, Department of Energy. *Member:* District of Columbia Bar. ***PRACTICE AREAS:*** Regulated Industries; Administrative Law; Appellate Litigation; Antitrust Law; Advertising; Energy; Transportation. ***Email:*** rherzog@harkinscunningham.com

DAVID A. HIRSH, born Boston, Massachusetts, 1959; admitted to bar, 1983, District of Columbia. *Education:* Brandeis University (B.A., cum laude, 1980); Georgetown University Law Center (J.D., cum laude, 1983). *Member:* The District of Columbia Bar; American Bar Association. ***PRACTICE AREAS:*** Transportation Law; Regulated Industries; Administrative Law; Commercial Contracts; Appellate Litigation. ***Email:*** dhirsh@harkinscunningham.com

A. CARL KASEMAN, III, born Toledo, Ohio, 1941; admitted to bar, 1971, Pennsylvania; 1980, District of Columbia; 1989, U.S. Tax Court. *Education:* Ohio State University (B.A., with honors and distinction, 1968); University of Pennsylvania (J.D., 1971). Phi Beta Kappa. Editor, University of Pennsylvania

(This Listing Continued)

Law Review, 1969-1971. *Member:* District of Columbia Bar; American Bar Association (Former Chair, Capital Recovery and Leasing Committee, Tax Section). ***PRACTICE AREAS:*** Tax Law; Business Law; Regulated Industries. ***Email:*** ack@harkinscunningham.com

GERALD P. NORTON, born West Roxbury, Massachusetts, 1940; admitted to bar, 1964, New York; 1966, District of Columbia. *Education:* Princeton University (A.B., magna cum laude, 1961); Columbia University (LL.B., magna cum laude, 1964). Managing and Research Editor, Columbia Law Review, 1963-1964. Winner of Government-Wide Arthur E. Flemming Award. Law Clerk to Hon. Leonard P. Moore, U.S. Court of Appeals, Second Circuit, 1964-1965. Assistant to the Solicitor General, U.S. Department of Justice, 1973-1975. Deputy General Counsel, Federal Trade Commission, 1975-1979. Mediator, U.S. District Court for the District of Columbia. Member: D.C. Circuit Committee on Admissions and Grievances, 1988-1994; D.C. Circuit Advisory Committee on Procedure, 1999—; District of Columbia Bar Rules of Professional Conduct Review Committee, 1995—; D.C. Bar Legal Ethics Committee, 1989-1995; D.C. Bar Special Committee on Application of Rules of Professional Conduct to Government Lawyers 1998; Supreme Court Moot Court Panel; National Association of Attorneys General. ***PRACTICE AREAS:*** Litigation; Appellate Practice; Administrative Law; Antitrust; Employment Law; Regulated Industries; Legal Ethics. ***Email:*** gnorton@harkinscunningham.com

JAMES G. RAFFERTY, born Boston, Massachusetts, 1951; admitted to bar, 1985, Maryland and District of Columbia. *Education:* Brown University (A.B., 1974); Princeton University (M.A., 1980); Georgetown University (J.D., cum laude, 1984). Brown University Club of Boston Scholar, 1969-1970. *Member:* District of Columbia Bar; American Bar Association (Former Chair, Affiliated and Related Corporations Committee, Tax Section). ***PRACTICE AREAS:*** Tax Law; Business Law; Economic Regulation. ***Email:*** jrafferty@harkinscunningham.com

OF COUNSEL

JAMES M. GUINIVAN, born Bethesda, Maryland, 1954; admitted to bar, 1988, Virginia; 1990, District of Columbia. *Education:* University of Virginia (B.A., 1976; J.D., 1988). Omicron Delta Kappa. Recipient, American Jurisprudence Award in Property. *Member:* District of Columbia Bar; Virginia State Bar. ***LANGUAGES:*** Spanish. ***PRACTICE AREAS:*** Regulated Industries; Administrative Law; Litigation. ***Email:*** jguinivan@harkinscunningham.com

JULIE A. WADDELL, born Grand Rapids, Michigan, 1959; admitted to bar, 1984, Pennsylvania; 1992, District of Columbia. *Education:* Kalamazoo College (B.A., summa cum laude, 1981); University of Michigan (J.D., 1984). Phi Beta Kappa. *Member:* American Bar Association; The District of Columbia Bar. ***PRACTICE AREAS:*** Regulated Industries; Administrative Law; Antitrust; Litigation. ***Email:*** jwaddell@harkinscunningham.com

ASSOCIATES

ROBERT A. WIMBISH, born Inglewood, California, 1968; admitted to bar, 1993, Virginia; 1995, District of Columbia. *Education:* Georgetown University (B.A., magna cum laude, 1990; J.D., 1993). Phi Beta Kappa. Recipient, American Jurisprudence Award in Administrative Law and in Bankruptcy and Creditor's Rights. *Member:* District of Columbia Bar; American Bar Association; Association of Transportation Practitioners. ***PRACTICE AREAS:*** Administrative Law; Interstate Commerce; Transportation; Railroads. ***Email:*** rwimbish@harkinscunningham.com

HARMON, WILMOT & BROWN, L.L.P.

Established in 1977

SUITE 810
1010 VERMONT AVENUE, N.W.
WASHINGTON, D.C. 20005
Telephone: 202-783-9100
Facsimile: 202-783-9103

Legislative Advocacy, Corporate, Commercial and Municipal Government and Litigation, Environmental, Energy, Government Contracts, Risk Management.

HERBERT N. HARMON, born Columbus, Ohio, November 15, 1944; admitted to bar, 1973, District of Columbia, U.S. District Court, District of Columbia, U.S. Court of Appeals for the District of Columbia Circuit, U.S. Court of Military Appeals, U.S. Court of Appeals for the Federal Circuit, U.S. Supreme Court and U.S. Tax Court. *Education:* University of Detroit (B.A., 1966); Georgetown University (J.D., 1973). Phi Alpha Delta; Blue Key. Member, University of Detroit Law Journal, 1966-1967. Instructor, Business Law, University of Virginia, 1982; 1984. President, Marine Corps Reserve Officers Association, 1986-1987. National Judge Advocate General, Marine Corps Aviation Association, 1988-1998. Mediator, Evaluator, Arbitrator, D.C. Superior Court, 1988—. President, Exchange Club of Capital Hill, 1989-1990. President, Reserve Officers Association, 1997-1998. *Member:* District of Columbia Bar; Bar Association of the District of Columbia (President, 1990-1991). [Col., USMCR, Ret.]. ***PRACTICE AREAS:*** Personal Injury; General Corporate Law; Business Law; Commercial Litigation; Civil Practice. ***Email:*** herbharmon@msn.com

DAVID W. WILMOT, born Panama Canal, April 26, 1944; admitted to bar, 1973, District of Columbia, Pennsylvania, U.S. District Court, District of Columbia and U.S. Court of Appeals for the District of Columbia Circuit and U.S. Supreme Court. *Education:* University of Arkansas (B.A., 1970); Georgetown University (J.D., 1973). Recipient: Jeffrey Crandall Award; Washington Law Reporter Prize. Martin Luther King, Jr. Fellow. Robert D. L'Heureaux Scholar. Author: *Street Law,* West Publishing Company, 1974. Dean of Admissions, Georgetown University Law Center, 1973-1991. General Counsel, Hotel Association of Washington. Chairman, District of Columbia Public Employee Relations Board. *Member:* District of Columbia Bar; Bar Association of the District of Columbia (Director, 1990-1991); American Bar Association; National Bar Association; National Conference of Black Lawyers; Association of American Law Schools. [With USAF, 1963-1967]. ***LANGUAGES:*** Spanish. ***PRACTICE AREAS:*** Lobbying; General Corporate Law. ***Email:*** DWWDC@aol.com

OMER F. BROWN, II, born Somerville, New Jersey, March 4, 1947; admitted to bar, 1972, New Jersey; 1974, District of Columbia; 1976, U.S. Supreme Court. *Education:* Rutgers University (A.B., 1969); Cornell University (J.D., 1972). Deputy Attorney General of New Jersey, 1972-1975. Senior Trial Attorney, U.S. Department of Energy, 1979-1983. Member, OECD Contact Group on Liability of Nuclear Safety Assistance Programmes for Eastern Europe, 1994—. Member, Ukrainian/G-7 Joint Task Force on Ukrainian Nuclear Legislation, 1996—. *Member:* Federal, American (Member, Coordinating Group on Energy Law, 1995-1999; Council, Tort and Insurance Practice Section, 1993-1996; Chair, 1984-1985, Senior Vice Chair, 1987-1993, Energy Resources Law Committee; Chair, Punitive Damages Task Force, 1985-1987; Chair, Governmental Liability Committee, 1987-1988; Chair, Professionalism Committee, 1994-1995) and International Bar Associations; Bar Association of the District of Columbia (Chair, Energy Committee, 1989-1992); International Nuclear Law Association. [Capt. U.S. Army Reserve, 1969-1975]. ***PRACTICE AREAS:*** Environmental; Energy; Risk Management; Government Contracts; International. ***Email:*** omerb@aol.com

ASSOCIATE

ANDREA MERRITT BAGWELL, born Sharon, Connecticut, May 29, 1961; admitted to bar, 1992, District of Columbia. *Education:* Hampton Institute (B.A., 1983); Georgetown University (J.D., 1987). Board Member, National Not-For-Project, Research Analysis Development Action, Inc. Assistant Counsel, District of Columbia Association of Health Maintenance Organizations. ***PRACTICE AREAS:*** Lobbying; Corporate Law; Administrative Law. ***Email:*** attbagwell@aol.com

HARNESS, DICKEY & PIERCE, P.L.C.

888 SIXTEENTH STREET, N.W.
WASHINGTON, D.C. 20006
Telephone: 202-835-7480
Email: info@hdp.com
URL: http://www.hdp.com

Troy, Michigan Office: 5445 Corporate Drive, Suite 400. Telephone: 248-641-1600. Telefacsimile: 248-641-0270.

St. Louis, Missouri Office: 7700 Bonhomme, Suite 400. Telephone: 314-726-7500. Fax: 314-726-7501.

Patent, Trademark, Copyright, Unfair Competition, Computer Law, Trade Secrets, Trade Regulation. Trial and Appellate Practice in State and Federal Courts.

FIRM PROFILE: Harness, Dickey & Pierce is one of the nation's largest intellectual property law firms, and is internationally known, operating globally since the 1920s in representing client intellectual property interests in the U.S. and all major foreign markets. The firm is now the oldest and largest intellectual property law firm in its headquarters state of Michigan. The firm has intellectual property attorneys with engineering or science degrees. Their technical disciplines range from mechanical engineering, electrical engineering and chemical engineering to the computer sciences and genetics, as well as materials and metallurgical engineering, chemistry, physics, biochemistry and agricultural engineering.

W. R. DUKE TAYLOR, born Akron, Ohio, September 2, 1958; admitted to bar, 1984, Ohio; 1985, Michigan; 1995, District of Columbia; registered to practice before U.S. Patent and Trademark Office. *Education:* University of Akron (B.S.M.E., 1981; B.S., 1981; J.D., 1984). Delta Theta Phi. *Member:* State Bar of Michigan; Ohio State and American Bar Associations; American Society of Mechanical Engineers. ***PRACTICE AREAS:*** Patent, Trademark and Intellectual Property. ***Email:*** wrtaylor@hdp.com

(This Listing Continued)

HARNESS, DICKEY & PIERCE, P.L.C., Washington—Continued

REPRESENTATIVE CLIENTS: BASF Corporation; Biomet, Inc.; The Black & Decker Manufacturing Co.; The Budd Co.; DaimlerChrysler Corp.; Denso Co. Ltd.; Emerson Electric Co.; Emthome-OMI Corp.; Flint Ink Corporation; Ford Motor Co.; General Motors Corp.; Johnson Controls; Kelly Services, Inc.; Kmart Corp.; La-Z-Boy Incorporated; Matsushita Electric; Michigan Consolidated Gas Co.; Michigan State University; Monroe Auto Equipment Co.; New Venture Gear; Nike, Inc.; Ross Operating Valve; Seiko Epson Co.; Standard Products Co.; Sun Microsystems Laboratories Inc.; Tenneco Automotive; Thetford Corp.; TRW Space & Defense; University of Michigan.

(For Complete Biographical Data on all Personnel, see Professional Biographies at Troy, Michigan)

HARRIS BEACH LLP

SUITE 300
1776 K STREET, N.W.
WASHINGTON, D.C. 20006
Telephone: 202-861-0001
Fax: 202-861-0011
URL: http://www.harrisbeach.com

Rochester, New York Office: Granite Building, 130 East Main Street. Telephone: 716-419-8800. Fax: 716-419-8801.
Pittsford, New York Office: 99 Garnsey Road. Telephone: 716-419-8800. Fax: 716-419-8801.
Plattsburgh, New York Office: One Cumberland Avenue. Telephone: 518-561-4400. Fax: 518-561-4848.
Ithaca, New York Office: 119 East Seneca Street. Telephone: 607-273-6444.
Albany, New York Office: 20 Corporate Woods Boulevard. Telephone: 518-427-9700. Fax: 518-427-0235.
Hamburg, New York Office: One Grimsby Drive. Telephone: 716-646-5050. Fax: 716-648-8201.
Syracuse, New York Office: Suite 400, One Park Place, 300 South State Street. Telephone: 315-423-7100. Fax: 315-422-9331.
New York, N.Y. Office: 500 Fifth Avenue, 5th Floor. Telephone: 212-687-0100. Fax: 212-687-0659.
Newark, New Jersey Office: 2 Gateway Center, 12th Floor. Telephone: 973-848-1244. Fax: 973-848-1594.

General Practice.

OF COUNSEL

JAMES R. COOKE, admitted to bar, 1968, Virginia; 1969, District of Columbia. *Education:* Indiana University (B.S., 1964); University of Michigan (J.D., 1967). ***PRACTICE AREAS:*** Telecommunications Law; Corporate Law; Legislation; Government Law. **Email:** jcooke@harrisbeach.com

(For complete biographical data on all personnel, see Professional Biographies at Rochester, New York)

HARRIS ELLSWORTH & LEVIN

THE WATERGATE
2600 VIRGINIA AVENUE, N.W., SUITE 1113
WASHINGTON, D.C. 20037
Telephone: 202-337-8338
Facsimile: 202-337-6685
Email: hel@idt.net
URL: http://www.internationaltrade-law.com

Customs, International Trade Regulation, Unfair Competition and Antitrust Law. Legislative Practice.

MEMBERS OF FIRM

HERBERT E. HARRIS II, born Kansas City, Missouri, April 14, 1926; admitted to bar, 1952, District of Columbia; 1953, U.S. Court of Appeals, District of Columbia Circuit; 1981, U.S. Court of International Trade; 1984, U.S. Court of Appeals for the Federal Circuit. *Education:* Missouri Valley College; University of Notre Dame; Rockhurst College (A.B., 1948); Georgetown University (J.D., 1951). Delta Theta Phi. President, Fairfax County Federation of Citizens Association, 1960-1961. Trustee, Fairfax Hospital Association, 1968-1974. U.S. Congressman, Virginia, 1975-1981. Vice Chairman: Washington Metropolitan Area Transit Authority, 1970-1974; Fairfax County Board of Supervisors, 1968-1974. Commissioner, Northern Virginia Transportation Commission, 1968-1974. *Member:* District of Columbia Bar; The Missouri Bar. [Lt., U.S. Navy, 1944-1947]. ***PRACTICE AREAS:*** Customs Law; International Trade Regulation; Unfair Competition; Antitrust Law; Legislative Practice. **Email:** heh@internationaltrade-law.com

CHERYL ELLSWORTH, born Oneonta, New York, November 25, 1955; admitted to bar, 1981, District of Columbia; 1982, U.S. Court of International Trade; 1983, U.S. Court of Appeals for the Federal Circuit. *Education:* Elmira College (B.A., magna cum laude, 1977); Universidad Iberoamericana, Mexico City, Mexico; State University of New York at Buffalo (J.D., 1981). Phi Beta Kappa. *Member:* District of Columbia Bar (Member, International Law Section), American (Member, Sections on: International Law and Practice; Law Practice Management) and Inter-American Bar Association. ***LANGUAGES:*** Spanish. ***PRACTICE AREAS:*** Customs Law; International Trade Regulation; Unfair Competition; Antitrust Law; Legislative Practice. **Email:** cne@internationaltrade-law.com

JEFFREY S. LEVIN, born Brooklyn, New York, November 27, 1962; admitted to bar, 1988, Maryland; 1989, U.S. Court of International Trade and U.S. Court of Appeals for the Federal Circuit; 1991, District of Columbia. *Education:* State University of New York at Binghamton (B.A., with high honors, 1984); Washington College of Law, American University (J.D., 1987). *Member:* District of Columbia Bar; Maryland State and American (Member, Section on International Law and Practice) Bar Associations. ***PRACTICE AREAS:*** Customs Law; International Trade Regulation; Unfair Competition; Antitrust Law; Legislative Practice. **Email:** jsl@internationaltrade-law.com

---

JOHN BURT TOTARO, JR., born Harrisburg, Pennsylvania, August 2, 1968; admitted to bar, 1994, Virginia; 2000, District of Columbia and U.S. Court of International Trade. *Education:* Kenyon College (A.B., 1990); T.C. Williams School of Law (J.D., 1993); University of Amsterdam (LL.M., 1994). *Member:* Virginia State Bar (Member, International Practice Section). ***PRACTICE AREAS:*** International Trade Regulation; Customs Law. **Email:** jbt@internationaltrade-law.com

JENNIFER DE LAURENTIIS, born Livonia, Michigan, June 4, 1966; admitted to bar, 1992, Virginia; 1993, District of Columbia, U.S. Court of International Trade and U.S. Court of Appeals for the Federal Circuit. *Education:* Albion College (B.A., cum laude, 1988); Washington College of Law of American University (J.D., 1992). Alpha Lambda Delta (President); Joseph Irwin Society; Webster Scholarship. *Member:* District of Columbia Bar; Virginia State Bar (Associate Member). ***LANGUAGES:*** Spanish and Italian. ***PRACTICE AREAS:*** Customs Law; International Trade Regulation; Unfair Competition; Antitrust Law; Legislative Practice. **Email:** jdl@internationaltrade-law.com

HARRIS, WILTSHIRE & GRANNIS LLP

1200 EIGHTEENTH STREET, N.W.
SUITE 1200
WASHINGTON, D.C. 20036
Telephone: 202-730-1300
Fax: 202-730-1301
Email: info@harriswiltshire.com
URL: http://www.harriswiltshire.com

Communications, Intellectual Property, International, Corporate, Commercial Transactions, Litigation, Appellate.

MEMBERS OF FIRM

SCOTT BLAKE HARRIS, born June 18, 1951; admitted to bar, 1977, District of Columbia. *Education:* Brown University (A.B., magna cum laude, 1973); Harvard University (J.D., magna cum laude, 1976). Phi Beta Kappa. Law Clerk to the Hon. Gerhard A. Gesell, U.S. District Court for the District of Columbia. 1976. Chief Counsel, Bureau of Export Administration, Department of Commerce, 1993-1994. Chief, International Bureau, FCC, 1994-1996. Federal Communications Bar Association (Co-Chair: International Practice Committee, 1996-1998; Online Communications Committee, 2000-2001). Chair, FCC Advisory Committee on 1997 World Radio Conference, 1996-1997. Chair, Study Group, Info Technology and Foreign Policy, Council on Foreign Relations, 1996. Adjunct Professor, Georgetown University Law Center, 1997-1998, 2001. Trustee, FCBA Foundation, 1997-1998. Co-Chair, ABA Committee on Int'l Communications, 2000-2001. Member, Advisory Board, Telecommunications Reports International, 2000-2001. Member, Editorial Advisory Board, Satellite Communications Magazine, 1996-1998. Member, Advisory Board, Center for Wireless Telecommunications, Virginia Tech University, 1996-1998. ***PRACTICE AREAS:*** Communications; International; Intellectual Property; Commercial; Telecommunications. **Email:** sharris@harriswiltshire.com

JOHN T. NAKAHATA, born San Francisco, California, August 16, 1961; admitted to bar, 1986, California; 1988, District of Columbia. *Education:* Wesleyan University (B.A., 1983); Harvard University (J.D., cum laude, 1986). Law Clerk, Hon. John H. Pratt, U.S. District Court for the District of Columbia, 1986-1987. Legislative Assistant to Senator Joe Lieberman, 1989-1995. Staff Director, U.S. Senate Subcommittee on Regulation and Government Informa-

(This Listing Continued)

tion, 1993-1994. Legal Advisor, 1995 and Senior Legal Advisor, 1996, to Federal Communications Commission Chairman Reed Hundt. Chief, Competition Division Office of General Counsel, Federal Communications Commission, 1997. Acting Deputy Chief, Common Carrier Bureau, Federal Communications Commission, 1997. Chief of Staff, Federal Communications Commission, 1997-1998. *Member:* State Bar of California; American Bar Association. ***PRACTICE AREAS:*** Communications Law; Antitrust; Legislative Practice. ***Email:*** JNakahata@harriswiltshire.com

WILLIAM M. WILTSHIRE, born January 30, 1962; admitted to bar, 1988, Virginia; 1989, District of Columbia. *Education:* Princeton University (A.B., summa cum laude, 1984); University of Virginia (J.D., 1988). Order of the Coif. Editorial Board Member, Virginia Law Review, 1987-1988. Senior Legal Advisor, International Bureau and Special Counsel, Mass Media Bureau, Federal Communications Commission, 1994-1996. *Member:* Federal Communications Bar Association. ***PRACTICE AREAS:*** Communications; Media Law; Litigation; Commercial Law. ***Email:*** wwiltshire@harriswiltshire.com

THOMAS G. CONNOLLY, born Omaha, Nebraska, November 27, 1961; admitted to bar, 1988, Virginia and District of Columbia. *Education:* Northwestern University (B.S., 1984); College of William and Mary (J.D., 1987). Member, Edward Bennett Williams Inn of Court, 1990-1991. *Member:* Virginia and American Bar Associations. ***PRACTICE AREAS:*** White Collar Criminal Defense; Civil Litigation. ***Email:*** tconnolly@harriswiltshire.com

MARK A. GRANNIS, born June 26, 1963; admitted to bar, 1989, California; 1991, District of Columbia. *Education:* Georgetown University (A.B., cum laude, 1985); University of Michigan (J.D., cum laude, 1988). Associate Editor, 1986-1987 and Note Editor, 1987-1988, Michigan Law Review. Law Clerk to the Hon. Stephen Reinhardt, U.S. Court of Appeals for the Ninth Circuit, 1989-1990. Senior Legal Advisor, Federal Communications Commission, International Bureau, 1994-1996. ***PRACTICE AREAS:*** Communications. ***Email:*** mgrannis@harriswiltshire.com

KENT D. BRESSIE, born Portland, Oregon, September 26, 1969; admitted to bar, 1994, Illinois; 1996, District of Columbia. *Education:* Stanford University (A.B., with distinction, 1991); Oxford University (1990); University of Chicago (J.D., 1994). Associate Editor, 1993-1994 and Staff Member, 1992-1993, University of Chicago Legal Forum. *Member:* American (Co-Chair, Young Lawyers Forum, Section of International Law and Practice, 1999-2000) and Federal Communications (Co-Chair, Global Telecommunications Development Committee, 2000-2001) Bar Associations. ***LANGUAGES:*** French. ***PRACTICE AREAS:*** Telecommunications Law; International Law. ***Email:*** kbressie@harriswiltshire.com

JONATHAN B. MIRSKY, born September 17, 1968; admitted to bar, 1995, Maryland; 1996, District of Columbia. *Education:* London School of Economics (1988-1989); Union College (B.A., summa cum laude, 1990); Yale Law School (J.D., 1994). Articles Editor, Yale Journal on Regulation. Law Clerk to the Hon. Ralph K. Winter, U.S. Court of Appeals for the Second Circuit, 1994-1995. ***PRACTICE AREAS:*** Communications. ***Email:*** jmirsky@harriswiltshire.com

KAREN LYNN GULICK, born Houston, Texas, March 18, 1966; admitted to bar, 1993, California; 1995, District of Columbia. *Education:* Stanford University (B.A., with honors, 1988); Yale University (J.D., 1993). Phi Beta Kappa. Law Clerk to the Hon. Jane R. Roth, U.S. Court of Appeals, Third Circuit. Author: "Creative Control, Attribution, and the Need for Disclosure: A Study of Incentives in the Motion Picture Industry," 22 Connecticut Law Review, pgs. 53-117, 1994. Legal Advisor to Federal Communications Commission Commissioner, Gloria Tristani, 1997-1999. Assistant Chief, Wireless Bureau, Federal Communications Commission, 1996-1997. *Member:* The District of Columbia Bar; Federal Communications Bar Association. ***LANGUAGES:*** Italian and Spanish. ***PRACTICE AREAS:*** Telecommunications Law; Administrative Law; Appellate Practice. ***Email:*** kgulick@harriswiltshire.com

CHRISTOPHER J. WRIGHT, born Detroit, Michigan, July 7, 1952; admitted to bar, 1982, District of Columbia. *Education:* Harvard University (A.B., 1974); University of California at Berkeley (M.A., 1975); Stanford University (J.D., 1980). Phi Beta Kappa; Order of the Coif. Senior Note Editor, Stanford Law Review, 1979-1980. Law Clerk: Judge Joseph T. Sneed, U.S. Court of Appeals, Ninth Circuit, 1980-1981; Chief Justice Warren E. Burger, U.S. Supreme Court, 1981-1982. General Counsel, Federal Communications Commission, 1997-2000. Deputy General Counsel, Federal Communications Commission, 1994-1997. Assistant to the Solicitor General, U.S. Department of Justice, 198601994. *Member:* The District of Columbia Bar. ***PRACTICE AREAS:*** Appellate Practice; Telecommunications; Administrative. ***Email:*** cwright@harriswiltshire.com

ASSOCIATES

TIMOTHY J. SIMEONE, born New York, N.Y., April 17, 1968; admitted to bar, 1995, Pennsylvania and District of Columbia. *Education:* Harvard University (A.B., cum laude, 1990); Middlebury College (M.A., 1991); University of Chicago (J.D., with high honors, 1994). Order of the Coif. Judicial Clerk, Justice David Souter, U.S. Supreme Court, 1996-1997. Judicial Clerk, Judge Patricia Wald, U.S. Court of Appeals for the District of Columbia Circuit, 1994-1995. Author: "Remanding to Congress: The Supreme Court's New 'On The Record' Review of Federal Statutes," 86 Cornell Law Review 328 (2001). Visiting Assistant Professor, Villanova Law School, 2000-2001. ***PRACTICE AREAS:*** Appellate Practice; Administrative Law; Telecommunications Law; Litigation. ***Email:*** tsimeone@harriswiltshire.com

KELLY SWEENEY McGINN, born Torrington, Connecticut, July 2, 1969; admitted to bar, 1996, Maryland; 1997, District of Columbia. *Education:* Georgetown University (B.S.F.S., summa cum laude, 1991); University of Virginia (J.D., 1996). Phi Beta Kappa. *Member:* Federal Communications Bar Association. ***PRACTICE AREAS:*** Telecommunications. ***Email:*** kmcginn@harriswiltshire.com

MICHAEL G. GRABLE, born Dallas, Texas, June 16, 1970; admitted to bar, 1997, Texas; 1998, District of Columbia. *Education:* Duke University (A.B., 1992); College of William and Mary (J.D., with honors, 1997). Omicron Delta Kappa. Member, Order of Barristers. Topics and Research Editor, William and Mary Law Review, 1996-1997. Law Clerk to Justice Enoch, Supreme Court of Texas, 1997-1998. ***PRACTICE AREAS:*** Telecommunications Law; Litigation. ***Email:*** mgrable@harriswiltshire.com

PATRICK O'DONNELL, born Washington, D.C., March 8, 1967; admitted to bar, 1997, Virginia; 1998, District of Columbia. *Education:* University of Pennsylvania (B.A., 1989); Georgetown University (J.D., magna cum laude, 1997). Order of the Coif. Recipient, International Association of Trial Lawyers Award. Special Assistant to the Chief of Staff, U.S. Treasury Department, 1993-1994. Aide to U.S. Senators Lloyd Bentsen and Bob Krueger, 1990-1993. ***PRACTICE AREAS:*** Criminal Law; Litigation; Civil Litigation.

FRED B. CAMPBELL, JR, born Council Bluffs, Iowa, July 18, 1971; admitted to bar, 1997, Nebraska; 2000, District of Columbia. *Education:* University of the State of New York (B.A., 1993); University of Nebraska College of Law (J.D., with Distinction, 1997). Order of the Coif. Delta Theta Phi. Tribune, 1996-1997. Executive Editor, Nebraska Law Review. Law Clerk, Nebraska Supreme Court, 1997-1999. Adjunct Faculty, University of Nebraska College of Law, Legal Research & Writing, 1999-2000. ***LANGUAGES:*** Arabic. ***PRACTICE AREAS:*** Telecommunications Law; Corporate Law. ***Email:*** fcampbell@harriswiltshire.com

LEGAL SUPPORT PERSONNEL

DAMON C. LADSON, born Indianapolis, Indiana, April 5, 1960. *Education:* Cornell University (B.S.E.E., 1982). Vice-Chair, U.S. Delegation to World Radiocommunication Conference 2000. Deputy Chief, Planning and Negotiations Division, International Bureau, FCC. *Member:* Institute of Electrical and Electronic Engineers.

OF COUNSEL

NANCY A. BARD, born New York, N.Y., July 29, 1956; admitted to bar, 1986, New York; 1990, District of Columbia. *Education:* Brown University (A.B., 1978); New York University (J.D., 1985). Member, New York University Law Review, 1983-1984. Law Clerk to the Hon. Raymond J. Dearie, U.S. District Court, Eastern District of New York, 1986. ***PRACTICE AREAS:*** Corporate. ***Email:*** nbard@harriswiltshire.com

(This Listing Continued)

ALLEN H. HARRISON, JR.

WASHINGTON, D.C.

(See Arlington, Virginia)

Railroad Equipment Financing, Trademarks, and Transactions Involving All Types of Intellectual Property Used as Loan Collateral.

HAWKINS, DELAFIELD & WOOD

601 13TH STREET, N.W.
SUITE 800 SOUTH
WASHINGTON, D.C. 20005
Telephone: 202-682-1480
Fax: 202-682-1497

New York, N.Y. Office: 67 Wall Street. Telephone: 212-820-9300. Fax: 212-514-8425.

Hartford, Connecticut Office: City Place, 185 Asylum Street. Telephone: 860-275-6260. Fax: 860-527-5786.

Newark, New Jersey Office: One Gateway Center. Telephone: 973-642-8584. Fax: 973-642-6773.

Los Angeles, California Office: 633 West Fifth Street, Suite 3550. Telephone: 213-236-9050. Fax: 213-236-9060.

San Francisco, California Office: One Embarcadero, Suite 1040. Telephone: 415-486-4200. Fax: 415-397-1513.

(This Listing Continued)

HAWKINS, DELAFIELD & WOOD, Washington—Continued

General Practice. Law of State, Municipal and Public Financing, Federal Securities, Tax, Litigation, Domestic and International Corporate and Banking, Real Estate, Probate.

RESIDENT MEMBERS

JOHN M. McNALLY, born Philadelphia, Pennsylvania, July 19, 1951; admitted to bar, 1976, Pennsylvania; 1979, District of Columbia. *Education:* University of Pennsylvania (A.B., cum laude, 1972); Georgetown University (J.D., 1976). *Member:* District of Columbia Bar. ***Email:*** jmmcnally@hdw.com

JOHN J. CROSS, III, born Louisville, Kentucky, February 2, 1956; admitted to bar, 1981, Georgia; 1988, U.S. Tax Court; 1997, District of Columbia; 1998, Maryland. *Education:* Brown University (B.A., 1978); Vanderbilt University (J.D., 1981); Georgetown University Law Center (LL.M. in Taxation, 1988). Member, Vanderbilt Law Review, 1979-1981. Author: Final Private Activity Bond Regulations," Municipal Finance Journal, Summer 1997; "Overview of Final Private Activity Bond Tax Regulations," GFOA Government Finance Review, August 1997; "Working Capital Financings: Special Arbitrage Considerations," Public Finance Advisor, January 1997; "Final Contingent Debt Rules," Public Finance Advisor, October 1996; "Final Debt Reissuance Rules," Public Finance Advisor, August 1996; "Tax-exempt Bond Audit Program Notes," Public Finance Advisor, July 1996; "Forward and Option Refundings of Tax-exempt Bonds," Public Finance Advisor, April 1996; "Purchase Price Allocations and Amortization of Intangibles," BNA Tax Management Portfolio Number 209, 1991; "The ABC's of Tax-free Like-Kind Exchanges," 3 The Practical Lawyer 39, 1989; "Taxpayer Bill of Rights," 75 American Bar Association Journal, June, 1989; "Taxation of Intellectual Property in International Transactions," 8 University of Virginia Tax Review 553, 1989; "The Continuing Evolution of the Installment Method of Tax Accounting," 66 TAXES 421, 1988; "Ethical Issues Facing Lawyer-Spouses and Their Employers," 34 Vanderbilt Law Review 1435, 1981. Member, Editorial Board, Municipal Finance Journal. Counsel to Assistant Chief Counsel (Financial Institutions and Products), Internal Revenue Service, 1990-1993. *Member:* American Bar Association (Member and Chair of Tax Reform and Simplification Task Force, 1999-2001, Tax-Exempt Financing Committee, Section of Taxation); National Association of Bond Lawyers (Chair of Financial Products Task Force, 1999-2000; Chair of General Tax Committee, 1995-1998). ***Email:*** jjcross3@hdw.com

FLORENCE A. WOOD, born Chicago, Illinois, January 5, 1948; admitted to bar, 1973, Massachusetts; 1976, District of Columbia. *Education:* Boston University (B.A., 1969); Boston College (J.D., 1972). *Member:* The District of Columbia Bar; Massachusetts Bar Association; National Association of Bond Lawyers. ***Email:*** fawood@hdw.com

ANTHONY S. FREEDMAN, born New York, N.Y., May 24, 1945; admitted to bar, 1968, New York; 1991, District of Columbia. *Education:* City College of the City University of New York (B.S., 1965); Stanford Law School (LL.B., 1968). Deputy Director, Legislation, U.S. Environmental Protection Agency, 1977-1978. Deputy Assistant Secretary, Housing Policy and Budget, U.S. Department of Housing and Urban Development, 1979-1981. Counsel, National Housing Task Force, 1987-1988. Author: *The Essential Guide to Housing Credit Compliance. Member:* American Bar Association; National Association of Bond Lawyers; National Housing Conference; National Council of State Housing Agencies. ***PRACTICE AREAS:*** Public Finance; Low-Income Housing Tax Credits; Multifamily Housing Finance and Development; Military Housing; Low Income Housing. ***Email:*** asfreedman@hdw.com

ASSOCIATES

JILL CHESSEN CORK, born Minneapolis, Minnesota, December 24, 1966; admitted to bar, 1992, California; 1994, Pennsylvania; 1995, District of Columbia. *Education:* Northwestern University (B.S., 1989); University of Pennsylvania (J.D., 1992). Alpha Lambda Delta. *Member:* American Bar Association; State Bar of California; District of Columbia Bar; Women In Housing and Finance. ***PRACTICE AREAS:*** Multifamily Housing Finance and Development; Low Income Housing. ***Email:*** jccork@hdw.com

AVIVA M. ROTH, born New York, New York, February 3, 1974; admitted to bar, 1998, New Jersey and New York (Not admitted in District of Columbia). *Education:* Queens College (B.A., 1994); Benjamin N. Cardova School of Law (J.D., 1997); New York University (LL.M. 1999). ***Email:*** aroth@hdw.com

HAYNES AND BOONE, LLP

555 ELEVENTH STREET, N.W.
SUITE 650
WASHINGTON, D.C. 20004
Telephone: 202-654-4500
Telecopy: 202-654-4501
URL: http://www.haynesboone.com

Austin, Texas Office: 600 Congress Avenue, Suite 1600. Telephone: 512-867-8400. Telecopy: 512-867-8470.

(This Listing Continued)

Other Austin, Texas Office: 7501 North Capital of Texas Highway, Building A, Suite 130, 78731. Telephone: 512-692-8300. Fax: 512-692-8370.
Dallas, Texas Office: 901 Main Street, Suite 3100. Telephone: 214-651-5000. Telecopy: 214-651-5940. Telex: 73-0187.
Fort Worth, Texas Office: 201 Main Street, Suite 2200. Telephone: 817-347-6600. Telecopy: 817-347-6650.
Houston, Texas Office: 1000 Louisiana Street, Suite 4300. Telephone: 713-547-2000. Telecopy: 713-547-2600.
Richardson, Texas Office: 2505 North Plano Road, Suite 400. Telephone: 972-739-6900. Telecopy: 972-680-7551.
San Antonio, Texas Office: 112 East Pecan Street, Suite 1600. Telephone: 210-978-7000. Telecopy: 210-978-7450.
Mexico City, Mexico Office: Haynes and Boone, S.C., Blvd. Manuel Avila Camacho, No. 40, Despacho 1801 Lomas de Chapultepec. Telephone: (525) 540-5558. Telecopy: (525) 540-0630.

Antitrust, Appellate, Business Litigation, Business Reorganization and Bankruptcy, Commercial Litigation, Corporate/Securities, Employee Benefits/ERISA, Energy, Environmental, Finance, Government Contracts, Government Investigations, Health Care, Insurance Litigation, International, Labor and Employment, Mergers and Acquisitions, Real Estate, Securities Litigation, Tax, Technology/Intellectual Property, White Collar Criminal Defense.

MEMBERS OF FIRM

ELLEN GIBSON McGINNIS, born Morristown, New Jersey, June 21, 1960; admitted to bar, 1986, New York and New Jersey; 1990, Texas; 1996, District of Columbia. *Education:* Yale University (B.A., cum laude, 1982); New York University (J.D., 1985). *Member:* Dallas, New York State and American Bar Associations; State Bar of Texas. ***Email:*** mcginnie@haynesboone.com

KENNETH B. REISENFELD, born Shaker Heights, Ohio, April 1, 1953; admitted to bar, 1979, Ohio; 1981, District of Columbia; 1986, U.S. Court of International Trade; 1991, U.S. Court of Appeals for the Federal Circuit. *Education:* Oberlin College (B.A., with honors, 1975); Harvard University (J.D., 1978). Author: "Service of United States Process Abroad: A Practical Guide to Service Under the Hague Service Convention and the Federal Rules of Civil Procedure," 24 International Lawyer 55, Spring 1990. Speaker: "The Selection of Arbitrators in International Arbitrations," IBA Conference, Barcelona, Spain, 1999; "Extraterritorial Application of U.S. Economic Sanctions," 11th Annual Advanced International Law Institute, Dallas, Texas, 1999; "WTO Dispute Resolution System," IBA 1998 Conference, Vancouver, B.C., 1998; "The Art of Selecting Arbitrators in International Arbitrations," ABA Spring Meeting, New York, 1998; "Exporting U.S. Trade Policy," ABA Spring Meeting, New York, 1997. Co-Editor, The World Trade Organization Dispute Settlement System, Oxford University Press, 2000. Law Clerk, Chief Judge Frank J. Battisti, U.S. District Court, Northern District of Ohio, 1978-1979. Counsel, Attorney General's Office, U.S. Department of Justice, 1979-1981. Panelist: U.S.- Canada Free Trade Agreement Binational Panel; NAFTA Chapter 19 Dispute Panels. International Arbitrator, American Arbitration Association. *Member:* American (Vice-Chair, Section on International Law and Practice; former Chair, International Trade Committee; Chair, International Arbitration Committee) and International (ABA Liaison) Bar Associations. ***PRACTICE AREAS:*** International Trade; Customs; International Arbitration. ***Email:*** reisenfk@haynesboone.com

ASSOCIATE

HALE E. SHEPPARD, born St. Louis, Missouri, December 2, 1970; admitted to bar, 1999, Florida; 2000, Texas (Not admitted in District of Columbia). *Education:* University of Kansas (B.S., Journalism, with distinction, 1993; J.D., 1997; M.A., Latin American Studies, with honors, 1999); University of Chile School of Law, South America (Magister in International Law, with highest distinction, 1999). Phi Beta Delta International Honors Society; Kappa Tau Alpha National Journalism Honors Society; Spanish National Honors Society. Recipient, Tinker Foundation Scholarship, 1998. Senator James B. Pearson Fellow, 1994-1995. Recipient, Harry S. Truman Foundation Scholarship. Fellow, National Security Education Program (NSEP), U.S. Department of Defense, 1997-1998. Publications: "Overcoming Apathetic Internationalism to Generate Hemispheric Benefits: Analysis of and Arguments for Recent Secured Transactions Law in Mexico," Florida State Journal of Transnational Law & Policy, Spring 2001; "The New Insolvency Law in Mexico: Imperative Legal Modernization and Policy Justifications for US Assistance," UCLA Journal of International Law and Foreign Affairs, Vol. 6(1), 2001; "La Internacionalidad de los mercados, la responsabilidad objetiva y la comercializacion de productos defectuosos provenientes de Chile," Revista del Derecho, Universidad de Concepción, Chile No. 206, 2000; "Dollarization of Ecuador: Sound Policy Dictates US Assistance to This Guinea Pig of Latin America," Indiana International & Comparative Law Review, Vol. 11, 2000; "El uso sustentable del bosque chileno: los defectos de la Ley de Bases y los acuerdos internacionales," Revista Chilena de Derecho, Chile, Vol. 27(1), 2000; "Timber Certification: An Alternative to the Destruction of the Chilean Forests," Journal of Environmental Law and Litigation (JELL), Vol. 14(2), 1999; "The Lome Convention in the Next Millennium: Modification of the Trade/Aid Package," Kansas Journal of Law &

(This Listing Continued)

Public Policy, University of Kansas School of Law, Vol. 7(3), 1998. *Member:* State Bar of Texas (Member, International Law Section); The Florida Bar (Member, International Law Section); American Bar Association. ***LANGUAGES:*** Spanish. ***PRACTICE AREAS:*** International Law; Trade Regulation; Customs Law. ***Email:*** shepparh@haynesboone.com

Languages: English, French, German, Hebrew, Italian, Korean, Spanish, Japanese, Vietnamese, Chinese (Mandarin, Cantonese, Shanghainese).

REPRESENTATIVE CLIENTS: Exxon-Mobil; Blockbuster Entertainment; Commercial Metals; Burlington Northern Santa Fe; RadioShack Corporation; Tenet Healthcare Corp.; Bank of America; Hillenbrand Industries; Cellstar Corp.; Sabre, Inc.; Input/Output, Inc.; Panda Energy Interna; Trilogy Software, Inc.; Dell U.S.A.; Archon Group, L.P.; AMR Corp.; Radiologix, Inc.; Huntsman Petrochemic; Engles Urso Follmer; Dresser Industries; El Paso Energy; Credit Lyonnais; Triton Energy Corp.; Trinity Industries, Inc.; Bank One; pcOrder.com, Inc.; JMB Realty Corp.; IMCO; LaQuinta Inns; USAA; Valero Energy Corporation; Ultramar Diamond Shamrock Corporation.

(For Biographical Data of other Firm Personnel, See Professional Biographies at Dallas, Austin, Fort Worth, Houston, Richardson and San Antonio, Texas and Mexico City)

HEENAN, ALTHEN & ROLES, LLP

1110 VERMONT AVENUE, N.W., SUITE 400
WASHINGTON, D.C. 20005
Telephone: 202-887-0800
Fax: 202-775-8518
Email: info@harlaw.com
URL: http://www.harlaw.com

Charleston, West Virginia Office: BB&T Square, 300 Summers Street. Telephone: 304-342-8960. Fax: 304-342-5761.

General Litigation and Administrative Practice before Federal Courts, Departments and Agencies. Corporate, Labor Relations and Employment, Mining, Trade Association, Pension and Employee Benefits (ERISA), Taxation, Real Estate, Safety and Environmental Law.

FIRM PROFILE: Heenan, Althen & Roles, LLP maintains a diversified human resources practice. Firm representation includes all aspects of employee relations and labor issues through secondary boycott litigation, compliance with safety and health statutes, and mediation of disputes. The Firm serves clients through advice, training, audits, programs and administrative and judicial litigation.

MEMBERS OF FIRM

MICHAEL T. HEENAN, born Pittsburgh, Pennsylvania, January 28, 1942; admitted to bar, 1967, Pennsylvania; 1972, District of Columbia. *Education:* Mount St. Mary's College (B.S., 1964); University of Pittsburgh (J.D., 1967). Author: *Understanding MSHA,* McGraw Hill, 1981; *Safety and Health at Mines, A Manual for Operators and Contractors,* Advanstar, 1999. Co-Author: *Workplace Safety and Health,* Clark Boardman Callahan, 1995; *Occupational Safety and Health Law Handbook,* Government Issues, 2001; *Concepts and Processes in Mine Safety and Health Management,* SME 2001. Legal Editor, *Pit and Quarry,* Advanstar, 1996—. Member, Board of Trustees: Energy & Mineral Law Foundation; Council of Counsel, National Stone Sand and Gravel Association. *Member:* The District of Columbia Bar; Pennsylvania and American Bar Associations. [Lt. USNR, active duty, 1967-1971]. ***PRACTICE AREAS:*** Mine Safety and Health; Occupational Safety and Health; Regulatory Agency Practice; Government Inspections and Investigations. ***Email:*** mheenan@harlaw.com

WILLIAM I. ALTHEN, born Denver, Colorado, December 26, 1946; admitted to bar, 1971, District of Columbia. *Education:* Georgetown University (A.B., 1968; J.D., 1971). Executive Editor, Georgetown Law Journal, 1970-1971. Law Clerk for Judge George R. Gallagher, District of Columbia Court of Appeals, 1971-1972. *Member:* District of Columbia Bar. ***Email:*** walthen@harlaw.com

FORREST H. ROLES, born Baltimore, Maryland, August 19, 1942; admitted to bar, 1967, West Virginia. *Education:* Davidson College (A.B., 1964); West Virginia University (J.D., 1967). Member, Board of Editors, West Virginia Law Review, 1966-1967. *Member:* West Virginia State Bar; American Bar Association. (Resident, Charleston, West Virginia Office). ***PRACTICE AREAS:*** Labor Law; Employment Law; Litigation. ***Email:*** froles@harlaw.com

RONALD E. MEISBURG, born Bowling Green, Kentucky, July 28, 1947; admitted to bar, 1974, Kentucky; 1980, District of Columbia. *Education:* Carson-Newman College (B.A., 1969); University of Louisville (J.D., 1974). Blue Key. Adjunct Professor: Robert H. Smith School of Business, University of Maryland, 2001—. Appellate Counsel, Division of Mine Safety and Health, U.S. Department of Labor, 1978-1980. Secretary of Labor's Distinguished Achievement Award, 1978. President, Energy and Mineral Law Foundation, 1944-1995. Member: Employment Lawyers Advisory Council, National Association of Manufacturers, 1996-1998; Industrial Relations Committee, U.S. Council for International Business, 1993-1998. *Member:* District of Columbia

(This Listing Continued)

Bar; Kentucky and American Bar Associations. ***PRACTICE AREAS:*** Labor and Employment Law; Labor Arbitration; Employment Dispute Resolution; Litigation; International Labor Law. ***Email:*** meisburg@harlaw.com

JOHN R. WOODRUM, born Cabin Creek, West Virginia, July 15, 1947; admitted to bar, 1974, California; 1976, District of Columbia. *Education:* Harvard University (B.A., 1969); University of Southern California (J.D., 1974). Co-author: "Proposals For Funding United Mine Workers of America Retiree Health Benefits: The Constitutional Dimensions," 93 W. Va. L. Rev. 633, 1991; "Analysis of the Coal Industry Retiree Health Benefit Act of 1992," 19 BNA Pension Reporter 2402, December 21, 1992; "Allocating Responsibility for Unknown Liabilities in Stock and Asset Transactions," 17 Energy Min. L. Inst., ch. 3, 1997. Field Solicitor, Division of Surface Mining, Region I, U.S. Department of the Interior, 1979-1983. *Member:* District of Columbia Bar; State Bar of California; American Bar Association. ***PRACTICE AREAS:*** Coal Law; ERISA; Labor Law. ***Email:*** jwoodrum@harlaw.com

ANNA MARIE DAILEY, born Waukegan, Illinois, May 25, 1954; admitted to bar, 1979, West Virginia. *Education:* Vanderbilt University (B.A., 1975); West Virginia University (J.D., 1979). *Member:* District of Columbia Bar; West Virginia and American (Member, Committees on: Employment Law; Alternative Dispute Resolution; Litigation) Bar Associations. (Resident, Charleston, West Virginia Office). ***PRACTICE AREAS:*** Labor and Employment Law; Civil Litigation; Environmental Law; Mediation. ***Email:*** adailey@harlaw.com

MARK A. CARTER, born Berrien Springs, Michigan, October 13, 1960; admitted to bar, 1986, West Virginia. *Education:* Western Michigan University; University of Michigan, Ann Arbor (B.A., 1982); Loyola University; West Virginia University (J.D., 1986). Author: "Using RICO To Take the Wind Out of a Corporate Campaign," Labor Policy Association, 1998. Co-Author: "Union Violence: The Record and the Response by Courts, Legislatures and the NLRB," George Mason University, 1999. *Member:* American Bar Association (Co-Chair: Annual Meetings Subcommittee, Section of Labor and Employment Law, 1998—; Antitrust, RICO and Labor Law Committee, 1995-1998). (Resident, Charleston, West Virginia Office). ***PRACTICE AREAS:*** RICO; Labor Law; Employment Law; Litigation. ***Email:*** mcarter@harlaw.com

WILLIAM K. DORAN, born Hartford, Connecticut, March 30, 1963; admitted to bar, 1989, Virginia and District of Columbia. *Education:* University of Virginia (B.A., 1985); Catholic University (J.D., 1988). Member, Catholic University Law Review, 1986-1988. Author: "Vicarious Liability For Mine Safety and Health Violations," 11 J. Nat. Resources and Environmental Law 99, 1996. Co-Author: *Inspections and Investigations,* Workplace Safety and Health, Clark Boardman Callahan, 1995; "OSHA Compliance Update in Virginia," National Business Institute, 1998. *Member:* District of Columbia Bar; Virginia State Bar; American Bar Association. ***PRACTICE AREAS:*** Occupational Safety and Health; Employment Law; Litigation. ***Email:*** wdoran@harlaw.com

DONNA COLBERG KELLY, born Lansing, Michigan, December 18, 1964; admitted to bar, 1990, West Virginia. *Education:* West Virginia University (B.S., 1986); Wake Forest University (J.D., 1990). *Member:* West Virginia State Bar; District of Columbia Bar; West Virginia and American Bar Associations. (Resident, Charleston, West Virginia Office). ***PRACTICE AREAS:*** Mine Safety Law; Occupational Safety and Health Law; Labor Law. ***Email:*** dkelly@harlaw.com

MARK E. HEATH, born Smyrna, Tennessee, March 18, 1961; admitted to bar, 1986, Kentucky. *Education:* Western Kentucky University (B.A., cum laude, 1983); University of Kentucky (J.D., 1986). Trustee, Energy and Mineral Law Foundation, 2000-2001. *Member:* West Virginia State Bar; Kentucky and American (Member, Litigation Section) Bar Associations. [Capt., U.S. Army, JAGC, 1987-1990]. (Resident, Charleston, West Virginia Office). ***PRACTICE AREAS:*** OSHA and MSHA; Labor and Employment Law; WARN Act; FMLA; Wage and Hour Law; Environmental Law. ***Email:*** mheath@harlaw.com

DAVID J. HARDY, born Charleston, West Virginia, April 21, 1958; admitted to bar, 1983, West Virginia. *Education:* West Virginia Institute of Technology (B.S.B.A., 1980); University of Tennessee at Knoxville (J.D., 1983). Member, City Council, Charleston, West Virginia, 1995-2000. Commissioner, Kawanha County, 2001—. *Member:* West Virginia State Bar. (Resident, Charleston, West Virginia Office). ***PRACTICE AREAS:*** Mine Safety; Occupational Safety and Health. ***Email:*** dhardy@harlaw.com

ASSOCIATES

MARGARET S. LOPEZ, born Washington, D.C., February 7, 1962; admitted to bar, 1996, Maryland; 1997, District of Columbia. *Education:* University of Virginia (B.A., with distinction, 1984); Georgetown University (M.A., 1989); George Washington University (J.D., with honors, 1996). Book Review Editor, The George Washington Journal of International Law and Economics, 1994-1995. Author: "Application of the Audit Privilege to Occupational Safety and Health Audits: Lesson Learned from Environmental Audits," 12 J. Nat. Resources and Envtl. Law 211, 1996-1997. Co-author: " Occupational Safety and Health Law Handbook, Government Institutes, 2001. *Member:* Maryland

(This Listing Continued)

HEENAN, ALTHEN & ROLES, LLP, Washington—Continued

State Bar Association; District of Columbia Bar; American Bar Association. ***PRACTICE AREAS:*** Employment Law; Occupational Safety and Health Law; ERISA; Labor Law. ***Email:*** mlopez@harlaw.com

W. GREGORY MOTT, born Pittsburgh, Pennsylvania, November 17, 1962; admitted to bar, 1992, Pennsylvania; 1993, District of Columbia. *Education:* Georgetown University (B.S.S.F.S., 1985; J.D., 1991). Co-author: "Allocating Responsibility for Unknown Liabilities in Stock and Asset Transactions," 17 Energy Min. L. Inst., ch. 3, 1997. *Member:* District of Columbia Bar. ***PRACTICE AREAS:*** Labor Law; Coal Mining; Health Benefits; Administrative Hearings and Appeals; Federal Civil Litigation. ***Email:*** gmott@harlaw.com

ALLISON S. WILLIAMS, born Orange, California, May 8, 1973; admitted to bar, 1998, Tennessee; 2000, West Virginia. *Education:* University of Mississippi (B.B.A., 1995); Washington & Lee University (J.D., 1998). Burks Scholar. Law Clerk to the Hon. David A. Faber, U.S. District Judge, Southern District of West Virginia. *Member:* Kanawah County, West Virginia and American Bar Associations. (Resident, Charleston, West Virginia Office). ***PRACTICE AREAS:*** Labor and Employment. ***Email:*** williams@harlaw.com

MEIKKA A. CUTLIP, born Ames, Iowa, October 24, 1966; admitted to bar, 1992, West Virginia; 2001, District of Columbia. *Education:* University of Iowa (B.A., with honors, 1989); George Washington University, National Law Center (J.D., 1992). *Member:* West Virginia State Bar; District of Columbia Bar; American Bar Association; District of Columbia Women's Bar Association. ***LANGUAGES:*** French. ***PRACTICE AREAS:*** Labor and Employment; Trade Association Law; Litigation. ***Email:*** mcutlip@harlaw.com

COUNSEL

TIMOTHY B. McBRIDE, born Paterson, New Jersey, April 13, 1946; admitted to bar, 1975, Virginia and New Jersey; 1977, District of Columbia. *Education:* University of Santa Clara (B.A., 1967); Georgetown University (J.D., 1975; M.L.T., 1980). Administrative Editor, The Tax Lawyer, 1973-1975. Law Clerk, U.S. District Court, Newark, New Jersey, 1975-1976. Trial Attorney, Tax Division, Department of Justice, Attorney General's Honors Program, 1976-1979. Member: Board of Regents, Georgetown University, 1996—; Georgetown University Planned Giving Advisory Committee, 1994—. Director, Keystone Property Trust, 1997-1999. *Member:* District of Columbia Bar (Chair, Taxation Division, 1983-1984); Virginia State Bar; New Jersey State and American Bar Associations. [Capt., USAF, 1967-1972]. ***PRACTICE AREAS:*** Closely Held Business; Real Estate; Taxation; Estate and Trust Planning; Wealth Management and Transfers. ***Email:*** mcbride@harlaw.com

(For complete biographical data on other personnel, see Professional Biographies at Charleston, West Virginia)

HEGGESTAD & WEISS, P.C.

Established in 1977

SUITE 600
1320 19TH STREET, N.W.
WASHINGTON, D.C. 20036
Telephone: 202-289-8333
Fax: 202-289-8307
Email: heggestad@radix.net

Federal and State Civil Trial and Appellate Practice including Administrative, Contracts, Corporate, Trade Regulation, Insurance, International, Construction, Insurance Coverage, Environmental, Medical Malpractice, Professional Malpractice, Corporation.

FIRM PROFILE: For over 20 years Heggestad & Weiss, P.C. has successfully and efficiently represented its clients in a national practice centered primarily around insurance coverage issues. The firm is best known for its ability to effectively handle complex- multijurisdictional litigation.

ROBERT E. HEGGESTAD, born Fergus Falls, Minnesota, July 28, 1946; admitted to bar, 1972, Iowa; 1978, District of Columbia; U.S. Supreme Court; U.S. Court of Appeals, District of Columbia, Fourth, Fifth, Ninth and Eleventh Circuits; U.S. District Court, District of Columbia, Western District of Virginia and Northern District of California. *Education:* University of Iowa (B.B.A., 1969; M.A., 1973; J.D., 1972). *Member:* District of Columbia Bar; Iowa State and American Bar Associations. ***PRACTICE AREAS:*** Personal Injury; Professional Liability; Insurance Coverage. ***Email:*** heggestad@radix.net

ALEXANDER WILSON WHITAKER, born Washington, D.C., February 23, 1940; admitted to bar, 1973, District of Columbia. *Education:* United States Military Academy (B.S., 1963); George Washington University (J.D., with honors, 1972). Phi Delta Phi. *Member:* The District of Columbia Bar; Bar Association of the District of Columbia; Federal and American Bar Associations; D.C. Defense Lawyers Association. [Capt. USMC, 1963-1969; Retired, Lt. Col. USMCR, 1969-1989]

(This Listing Continued)

OF COUNSEL

CHRISTOPHER A. HANSEN, born Yakima, Washington, December 10, 1934; admitted to bar, 1963, Maryland; 1973, U.S. Supreme Court; 1978, U.S. Court of Appeals, Fourth Circuit and District of Columbia. *Education:* Cornell University (B.S., 1957); University of Maryland (J.D., 1963). Phi Alpha Delta. Law Clerk, Circuit Court for Baltimore County, 1960-1963. *Member:* District of Columbia Bar; The Bar Association of Baltimore City; Baltimore County, Maryland State and American Bar Associations; Association of Defense Trial Counsel. (Also Practicing Individually, Towson, Maryland). ***PRACTICE AREAS:*** Civil Litigation; Insurance Law; Products Liability Law.

MARY ANN HAMMETT, born Helena, Arkansas, January 2, 1945; admitted to bar, 1979, Tennessee, District of Columbia, and U.S. Court of Appeals for the District of Columbia and Federal Circuits. *Education:* University of Mississippi (B.A., English, 1967); Memphis State University (J.D., 1978). *Member:* The District of Columbia Bar; American Bar Association. ***PRACTICE AREAS:*** Insurance Coverage; Civil Litigation; Contracts; Torts; Administrative.

APPROVED COUNSEL FOR: TIG (Transamerica Insurance Co.); Freemont Insurance Co.; Commercial Underwriters Insurance Co.

THE HEIDEMAN LAW GROUP, P.C.

Established in 1973

1714 N STREET, N.W.
WASHINGTON, D.C. 20036-2907
Telephone: 202-462-8990
Fax: 202-462-8995
Email: attorneys@heidemanlaw.com
URL: http://www.Heidemanlaw.com

Criminal Defense and Civil Trial Practice. Personal Injury, Wrongful Death, Corporate Law, Real Property, Civil Rights, Military, Sports, Health Care. Ethics, Government Relations, International Trade and International Corporate Transactions.

RICHARD D. HEIDEMAN, born Detroit, Michigan, April 4, 1947. admitted to bar, 1972, Maryland, Kentucky and U.S. District Court, Western District of Kentucky; 1974, U.S. Court of Appeals, Sixth Circuit; 1979, Indiana and Wyoming; 1982, U.S. Supreme Court; U.S. Court of Military Appeals; U.S. District Court, Southern District of Indiana and U.S. District Court, Eastern District of Kentucky; 1984, District of Columbia and U.S Court of Appeals, District of Columbia Circuit; 1989, U.S. District Court, District of Maryland; 1990, U.S. District Court, District of Columbia and Court of International Trade; 1992, U.S. Court of Claims; U.S. Court of Appeals, Fourth Circuit; 1994, U.S. District Court, Western District of Wisconsin; U.S. Court of Appeals, Seventh Circuit. *Education:* University of Michigan (B.A., 1969); Attended, Law & Policy Institute, American/Hebrew University, Jerusalem Israel; George Washington University (J.D., 1972). Author: "Pretrial Motions in Criminal Cases: An Alternative Approach to Plea Bargaining," Criminal Defense Magazine; "Legal Assistants in the Criminal Practice," ABA Manual on Legal Assistants. Recipient, B'nai B'rith International Young Leadership Award, 1983. Mayor, Spring Valley, Kentucky, 1984. International Vice President, B'nai B'rith International, Washington, D.C., 1988-1992; Senior International Vice President B'nai B'rith, Washington, D.C., 1992-1996; International Chairman, B'nai B'rith Center for Public Policy, 1996-1998. Elected, International President, B'nai B'rith International, Washington, D.C., Jerusalem Convention,, August 1998 for 1998-2000 term; reelected August 2000 for 2000-2002 term. President, The Heideman International Group, Inc. President, American-Israel Chamber of Commerce of Washington, D.C., Inc. *Member:* Bar Association of the District of Columbia Bar (Chair, Criminal Law Committee); District of Columbia Bar (Member, Steering Committee, Criminal Law and Individual Rights); Louisville, Kentucky, Indiana State, Maryland State, Federal and American Bar Associations; Wyoming State Bar; The Association of Trial Lawyers of America; Wyoming Trial Lawyers Association; District of Columbia Association of Criminal Defense Lawyers; National Association of Criminal Defense Lawyers (Vice Chair, Legislative Committee). ***LANGUAGES:*** Hebrew. ***PRACTICE AREAS:*** Criminal Defense; Civil Trial; Personal Injury; Wrongful Death; International Trade; Corporate Transactions. ***Email:*** rdheideman@heidemanlaw.com

NOEL J. NUDELMAN, born Englewood, New Jersey, January 5, 1967; admitted to bar, 1993, New Jersey; 1994, New York and U.S. District Court, District of New Jersey and Western District of Wisconsin; 1996, District of Columbia. *Education:* Boston University (B.A., 1989); Brooklyn Law School (J.D., 1993). Member: B'nai B'rith International; American Israel Chamber of Commerce. *Member:* The District of Columbia Bar; New York State, New Jersey State and American Bar Associations. ***PRACTICE AREAS:*** Civil Litigation; Criminal Defense; Corporate; International Trade; Corporate Transactions. ***Email:*** njnudelman@heidemanlaw.com

(This Listing Continued)

TRACY REICHMAN KALIK, born St. Louis, Missouri, December 24, 1969; admitted to bar, 1996, Maryland; 1997, U.S. District Court, District of Maryland, Missouri and U.S. District Court, Eastern District of Missouri; 1999, District of Columbia; 2001, U.S. District Court, District of Columbia Circuit. *Education:* Emory University (B.A., 1993); The George Washington University (J.D., 1996). Member, Journal of International Law and Economics, 1994-1996. *Member:* Maryland and American Bar Associations; The Missouri Bar; District of Columbia Bar. **PRACTICE AREAS:** Civil Litigation; Criminal Defense. **Email:** trkalik@heidemanlaw.com

OF COUNSEL

SANFORD R. CARDIN, born Baltimore, Maryland, May 22, 1957; admitted to bar, 1981, Maryland; 1985, District of Columbia and Florida; U.S. District Court, District of Maryland; U.S. Supreme Court. *Education:* Harvard University (B.A., magna cum laude, 1978); University of Maryland (J.D., 1981). Order of the Coif. *Member:* District of Columbia Bar; The Bar Association of Baltimore City; Maryland State Bar Association. **PRACTICE AREAS:** Corporate Law; Real Property; Professional Conduct; International Corporate Law. **Email:** attorneys@heidemanlaw.com

SPECIAL COUNSEL

AVIGDOR WARSHA, born Poland, June 11, 1929; admitted to bar, Israel. *Education:* School of Law and Economics, Israel (LL.B., 1954). **PRACTICE AREAS:** Corporate Law. **Email:** attorneys@heidemanlaw.com

THE HELEIN LAW GROUP, P.C.

WASHINGTON, D.C.

(See McLean, Virginia)

Telecommunications, International Telecommunications and Trade, Internet, Corporate, Litigation, Government Relations, E-Commerce, Regulatory Compliance, Administrative Law, Trademark and Copyright.

MILTON HELLER & ASSOCIATES

927 15TH STREET, N.W.
WASHINGTON, D.C. 20005
Telephone: 202-737-4300
Fax: 202-628-4608
Email: mheller@erols.com
URL: http://www.lawyers.com/miltonhellerlaw

General Civil Trial Practice before all Courts of the District of Columbia and Maryland. Malpractice, Products Liability and Negligence Law, Family Law.

MILTON HELLER, born Washington, D.C., August 11, 1929; admitted to bar, 1958, District of Columbia; 1962, U.S. Supreme Court; 1965, Maryland. *Education:* George Washington University (B.S., 1950; J.D., 1957). Member, Scribes. Member, George Washington University Law Review, 1956-1957. Author: "Remittiturs of Civil Jury Verdicts," District of Columbia Bar Journal, March, 1963; "Recent Trends in the Field of Products Liability," Trial Magazine, September-October, 1972 and District of Columbia Bar Journal, October-February, 1973; "Medical and Legal Malpractice: Are 'Ceilings' and 'Panels' Constructive?" The Journal of Legal Medicine, Vol. 4, No. 10, November/December, 1976. Member: U.S. Judicial Conference for the District of Columbia Circuit, 1972-1978; Judicial Conference for the District of Columbia, 1979—. Consultant, Food and Drug Administration, Bureau of Medical Devices and Diagnostic Products, 1976-1980. *Member:* District of Columbia Bar (Chairman, Steering Committee, Personal Injuries Section, 1982-1985); The Bar Association of the District of Columbia (Member, Board of Directors, 1969-1970; Chairman: Negligence Committee, 1973-1974; Superior Court Committee, 1979-1981; Chairman, District Court Committee, 1986-1987; Director, Research Foundation, 1987-1989); Maryland State and American (State Chairman, Membership Committee, 1975) Bar Associations; Trial Lawyers Association of Metropolitan Washington, D.C. (President, 1966-1967; Plaintiff's Lawyer of the Year, 1973); Maryland Trial Lawyers Association; The Association of Trial Lawyers of America (Member, Board of Governors, 1968-1973, 1989-1994); American College of Legal Medicine; American Academy of Forensic Sciences; American Board of Professional Liability Attorneys (Diplomate); American Board of Trial Advocates (Advocate). [Captain, US Army Reserve, Ret., active duty, 1961]. **PRACTICE AREAS:** Product Liability; Medical Malpractice; Personal Injury; Civil Litigation.

ASSOCIATE

BARBARA MOIR CONDOS, born Fort Bragg, North Carolina, January 3, 1944; admitted to bar, 1977, District of Columbia; 1986, Maryland. *Education:*

(This Listing Continued)

Lakeland College (B.A., 1968); George Washington University (J.D., 1975). *Member:* The District of Columbia Bar; Bar Association of the District of Columbia; American Bar Association; Women's Bar Association of the District of Columbia; Trial Lawyers Association of Metropolitan Washington, D.C. (Treasurer, 1987-1990); Maryland Trial Lawyers Association. **PRACTICE AREAS:** Personal Injury; Divorce; Family Law.

REFERENCE: First Union National Bank.

HELLER EHRMAN WHITE & McAULIFFE LLP

A Partnership of Professional Corporations
Established in 1890
1666 K STREET, NW, SUITE 300
WASHINGTON, D.C. 20006-1228
Telephone: 202-912-2000
Facsimile: 202-912-2020
URL: http://www.hewm.com

Gaithersburg, Maryland Office: 101 Orchard Ridge Drive. Telephone: 301-721-6100. Facsimile: 301-721-6299.
San Francisco, California Office: 333 Bush Street. Telephone: 415-772-6000. Facsimile: 415-772-6268. Cable Address: "Helpow". Telex: 340-895; 184-996.
Anchorage, Alaska Office: 550 West 7th Avenue, Suite 1900. Telephone: 907-277-1900. Facsimile: 907-277-1920.
Los Angeles, California Office: 601 S. Figueroa Street. Telephone: 213-689-0200. Facsimile: 213-614-1868.
Menlo Park, California Office: 275 Middlefield Road. Telephone: 650-324-7000. Facsimile: 650-324-0638.
San Diego, California Office: 4350 La Jolla Village Drive, Suite 700. Telephone: 858-450-8400. Facsimile: 858-450-8499.
Madison, Wisconsin Office: One East Main Street, Suite 201. Telephone: 608-663-7460. Facsimile: 608-663-7499.
New York, New York Office: 120 West 45th Street, 21st Floor. Telephone: 212-832-8300. Facsimile: 212-763-7600.
Portland, Oregon Office: 200 S.W. Market Street, Suite 1750. Telephone: 503-227-7400. Facsimile: 503-241-0950.
Seattle, Washington Office: 701 Fifth Avenue, Suite 6100. Telephone: 206-447-0900. Facsimile: 206-447-0849.
Hong Kong Office: 6308-09 The Center, 99 Queens Road Central, Hong Kong. Telephone: (011) 852-2526-6381. Facsimile: (011) 852-2810-6242.
Singapore Office: 50 Raffles Place, 17-04 Singapore Land Tower. Telephone: (011) 65 538-1756. Facsimile: (011) 65 538-1537.
Affiliated Carnelutti Office: Cabinet Carnelutti, 6, Avenue George V, Paris, France 75008. Telephone: (1) 4723-3181. Fax: (1) 4720-2509.
Affiliated Carnelutti Office: Studio Legale associato con Carnelutti, Via Parigi, 11, Rome, Italy 00185. Telephone: (06)473-901. Fax: (06) 481-9833. Email: CARNELUTTIROME@FLASH.NET.it.
Affiliated Carnelutti Office: Studio Legale associato Carnelutti, Corso Matteotti, Via Principe Amedeo, 3, 20121 Milan, Italy. Telephone: (011) 3902-655851. Fax: (011) 3902-6558-5585. Email: CARNELUTTI@carnelutti.com

General Practice.

SHAREHOLDERS

††MARY L. AZCUENAGA, born Council, Idaho, July 25, 1945; admitted to bar, 1973, District of Columbia and U.S. Court of Appeals, District of Columbia Circuit; 1974, U.S. District Court, District of Columbia; 1977, California and U.S. District Court, Southern District of California; 1997, U.S. Supreme Court. *Education:* Stanford University (A.B., 1967); University of Chicago School of Law (J.D., 1973). Chairman, Hinton Moot Court. Author: *Essential Facilities and Regulation: Court or Agency Jurisdiction?* 58 Antitrust L.J. 879 (1989); *The Tariff Is Still the Mother of Trust*, 29 Washburn L.J. 359 (1990); *Market Power as a Screen in Evaluating Horizontal Restraints*, 60 Antitrust L.J. 935 (1991); *The Evolution of International Competition Policy: A Federal Trade Commission Perspective*, 1992 Fordham Corp. L. Inst. 1 (B. Hawk ed. 1993); *Price Surveys, Benchmarking and Information Exchanges: Antitrust Risks for Associations*, before the 8th Annual American Soc'y of Ass'n Executives Legal Symposium (Nov. 8, 1994)(parts 1-2), *reprinted in* 8 A.S.A.E. Ass'n Law & Policy-4,at 5 (1994); *Developments in Consumer Protection at the Federal Trade Commission: Achieving Customer Satisfaction in a Government Law Enforcement Agency*, before the Promotion Marketing Ass'n of America (PMAA) Promotion Law/Marketing Conference (Nov. 20, 1996), *reprinted in* 36 Ill. St. B. A. Antitrust & Unfair Competion Law 1 (1997); *Panel Discussion on Technological Innovation, International Trade and Competition Policy*, before the Japan Fair Trade Commission, 50th Anniversary Symposium (Dec. 1, 1997), *reprinted in* 569 Kosei Torihiki [Fair Trade Institute, Tokyo] 13 (1998). Commissioner, Federal Trade Commission, 1984-1998. *Member:* The District

(This Listing Continued)

HELLER EHRMAN WHITE & McAULIFFE LLP, Washington—Continued

of Columbia Bar; State Bar of California; American Bar Association (Member, Antitrust Section). ***PRACTICE AREAS:*** Antitrust; Advertising; Federal Trade Commission. ***Email:*** mazcuenaga@hewm.com

††***KENNETH L. CHERNOF,*** born Los Angeles, California, July 29, 1967; admitted to bar, 1991, California; 1992, District of Columbia. *Education:* Harvard University (A.B., cum laude, 1988); Georgetown University (J.D., magna cum laude, 1991). Deputy Associate Attorney General and Chief of Staff to the Associate Attorney General. ***PRACTICE AREAS:*** Litigation; Financial Institutions Law; Antitrust; Alternative Dispute Resolution.

JAMES NICHOLAS CZABAN, born Fairfax, Virginia, May 2, 1966; admitted to bar, 1992, Virginia; 1995, New York; 1998, District of Columbia; U.S. Supreme Court, U.S. District Court for the District of Columbia, U.S. District Court, Southern and Eastern Districts of New York, U.S. District Court, District of Maryland, U.S. Court of Appeals, Second, Fourth and Eleventh Circuits, U.S. Court of Appeals for the District of Columbia Circuit and U.S. Court of Appeals for the Federal Circuit. *Education:* University of California, Berkeley (B.A., 1988); University of Virginia (J.D., 1992). Member, Journal of Law and Politics; Managing Board, Virginia Law Weekly; President, Federalist Society (1991-1992). Co-Author: "Human Drug Regulation," in 2 Fundamentals of Law and Regulations; An In-Depth Look at Therapeutic Products, (Food and Drug Law Institute, 1997); Articles, FDA's New DTC Broadcast Guidance: Get Ready For The Marketing Revolution," (Food and Drug Law Institute Update, Issue 4, 1997); "The Invisible Hand, Or An Iron Fist?" Internet Commerce Can Flourish On Its Own, But Will Government Resist The Temptation To Interfere?" Net Profits, Vol. 1, No. 1 (Nov./Dec., 1997); "New Bottles, Old Whine: On The Internet, The Product and The Message, Not The Medium, Are Still The Key to Avoiding Government Regulation," Electronic Retailing, Vol. 4, No. 4 (July/Aug., 1997); "More Than Just a Touch of Gray: FDA Regulation of Prescription Drug Marketing on the Internet," Electronic Retailing Vol. 4, No. 3 (May/June, 1997); "GMPs for Dietary Supplements? The Devil is in The Details," HSR's Supplement Industry Insider, Vol. 2, No. 4 (February, 1997); "Internet Promotion of Dietary Supplements: FTC Compliance and Emerging Issues," HSR's Supplement Industry Insider, Vol. 1, No. 7 (May, 1996): *Member:* Virginia and New York State Bar Associations; Food and Drug Law Institute. ***REPORTED CASES:*** Teva Pharmaceuticals v. FDA 182 F.3d 1003 (D.C. Circuit, 1999). ***PRACTICE AREAS:*** Food, Drug and Cosmetics; Advertising; Litigation; Intellectual Property Litigation. ***Email:*** jczaban@hewm.com

††***PATRICIA D. GRANADOS,*** admitted to bar, 1987, Maryland and Pennsylvania; 1991, District of Columbia; registered to practice before U.S. Patent and Trademark Office. *Education:* Boston University (B.A., cum laude, 1975); Johns Hopkins University (M.A.S., 1979); University of Maryland (J.D., 1987). Member, Moot Court Board. Recipient: Bridgewater M. Arnold Prize; American Jurisprudence Prize for Sales and Secured Transactions. Law Clerk, Hon. Philip B. Baldwin, U.S. Court of Appeals, Federal Circuit. ***PRACTICE AREAS:*** Biotechnology and Pharmaceutical Patent Law. ***Email:*** pgranados@hewm.com

††***DAVID HARTH,*** admitted to bar, 1979, Wisconsin; 2001, District of Columbia. *Education:* University of Wisconsin-Madison (B.A., 1976; J.D., 1979). Order of the Coif. Articles Editor, Wisconsin Law Review, 1978-1979. Law Clerk, Chief Judge W. Reynolds, U.S. District Judge for the Eastern District of Wisconsin, 1979-1980. *Member:* Seventh Circuit Bar Association; Federal Circuit Bar Association. ***PRACTICE AREAS:*** Intellectual Property and Commercial Litigation. ***Email:*** dharth@hewm.com

††***JOHN P. ISACSON, JR.,*** admitted to bar, 1988, Maryland; 1989, Illinois, District of Columbia, U.S. Supreme Court and U.S. Court of Appeals for the Federal Circuit; registered to practice before the U.S. Patent and Trademark Office. *Education:* University of Maryland (B.A., 1984; M.S., 1985); George Washington University (J.D., with honors, 1988). Sigma Alpha Omicron Microbiological Honor Society. Associate Editor, George Washington Journal of International Law and Economics, 1987-1988. Law Clerk to the Honorable Daniel J. Davidson, Chief Administrative Law Judge, U.S. Food and Drug Administration, 1988-1989. Lecturer before the Biotechnology Industry Organization and the Food and Drug Law Institute. *Member:* American Intellectual Property Law Association (Member, Biotechnology Committee; Interference Committee); Licensing Executives Society. ***PRACTICE AREAS:*** U.S. and Foreign Patent Law; Regulatory Law. ***Email:*** jisacson@hewm.com

††***BRUCE F. MACKLER,*** born Philadelphia, Pennsylvania, March 11, 1941; admitted to bar, 1979, District of Columbia. *Education:* Temple University (B.A., 1964); Pennsylvania State University (M.S., 1965); University of Oregon Medical School (Ph.D. 1970); South Texas College of Law (J.D., magna cum laude, 1979). ***PRACTICE AREAS:*** Food and Drug Regulation Law; Environmental Law; Agriculture Law. ***Email:*** bmackler@hewm.com

††***MONICA P. MEDINA,*** born Montgomery, Alabama, February 7, 1962; admitted to bar, 1986, Georgia; 1988, District of Columbia. *Education:* Georgetown University (B.A., cum laude, 1983); Columbia Law School (J.D., 1986); Harvard Law School. Stone Scholar. General Counsel, National Oceanic Atmospheric Administration. Deputy Associate Attorney General, Department of Justice, 1996-1997. [Captain, U.S. Army, Army General Counsel's Office, 1986-1990]. (Also at Gaithersburg, Maryland Office). ***PRACTICE AREAS:*** Environmental; Government Affairs; Litigation.

††***KIT A. PIERSON,*** born Eugene, Oregon, December 30, 1957; admitted to bar, 1986, Michigan and District of Columbia; 1990, Maryland; 1996, Oregon. *Education:* Macalester College (B.A., magna cum laude, 1979); University of Michigan (J.D., magna cum laude, 1983). Order of the Coif. Note Editor, Michigan Law Review, 1982-1983. Law Clerk to: Hon. Harry T. Edwards, U.S. Court of Appeals, District of Columbia Circuit, 1983-1984; Hon. John Feikens, U.S. District Court, Eastern District of Michigan, 1984-1985. *Member:* State Bar of Michigan; The District of Columbia Bar; Oregon State Bar. ***PRACTICE AREAS:*** Media Law; Association Law; Civil Litigation. ***Email:*** kpierson@hewm.com

††***BRENT N. RUSHFORTH,*** born Salt Lake City, Utah, February 18, 1941; admitted to bar, 1970, California; 1981, District of Columbia. *Education:* Stanford University (B.A., with distinction, 1964; M.A., 1966); University of California, Boalt Hall School of Law (J.D., 1969). Member, Board of Editors, California Law Review, 1968-1969. Co-founder, Center for Law in the Public Interest, 1973. Deputy General Counsel, U.S. Department of Defense, 1978-1980. *Member:* State Bar of California; The District of Columbia Bar. ***LANGUAGES:*** German. ***PRACTICE AREAS:*** Civil Litigation; Antitrust Law; Cable Television and Telecommunications Law. ***Email:*** brushforth@hewm.com

COLIN G. SANDERCOCK, admitted to bar, 1984, Pennsylvania; 1985, District of Columbia; 1990, U.S. Supreme Court and U.S. Court of Appeals for the Federal Circuit; registered to practice before the U.S. Patent and Trademark Office. *Education:* Moravian College (B.S., in Chem., 1978); University of Pennsylvania (M.S.E., in Chemical and Biochemical Engineering, 1980); Catholic University (J.D., 1984). Recipient, Ashton Fellowship, University of Pennsylvania, 1979, 1980. Co-Author: "The Federal Circuit and Chemical Patent Practice, 1988-1989," AIPLA Selected Legal Papers, Vol. 7, No. 1, p. 1-55, July, 1989. Co-Author and Co-Editor: "Federal Circuit Patent Practice, 1989-1990," AIPLA Selected Legal Papers, Vol. 8, Nos. 1, 2, pp 127-280. Co-Author: "Tools for Coping with Biotechnology Patent Disputes," PRG, 1991-1994. *Member:* American and Pennsylvania Bar Associations; The District of Columbia Bar; American Intellectual Property Law Association (Chairman, Electronic Records Subcommittee); Federal Circuit Bar Association. ***PRACTICE AREAS:*** Intellectual Property Law; Patent Law. ***Email:*** csandercock@hewm.com

JOHN S. SKILTON, admitted to bar, 1969, Wisconsin; 2001, District of Columbia. *Education:* University of Wisconsin (B.A., 1966; J.D., 1969). Articles Editor, Wisconsin Law Review, 1968-1969. Awards: President's Award of Excellence (1989); Gordon Sinykin Award of Excellence (1996); L.A.W.'s "Beyond The Call" Award. Law Clerk to Hon. Thomas E. Fairchild, U.S. Court of Appeals, Seventh Circuit, 1969-1970. Chairman, Board of Visitors, University of Wisconsin Law School, 1988-1989. President, Equal Justice Coalition (1997-2000); President, State Bar of Wisconsin (1995-1996); President (Elect), Wisconsin Law Foundation (2000-2002); Trustee, American Inns of Court Foundation, 1995-1998. President, Wisconsin Law Alumni Association, 1993-1995. Chairman, ABA Standing Committee on the Delivery of Legal Services (1997-2000). Chairman, ABA Consortium on Legal Services and The Public (2000). Member: Eastern District Rules Committee, 1980-1982; Western District Rules Committee, 1989-1990. Chairman, Seventh Circuit Advisory Committee on Circuit Rules, 1994-2000. Chairman, Western District Advisory Group, Civil Justice Reform Act of 1990, 1991-1995. President, Western District of Wisconsin Bar Association, 1992-1993. Member and Counsellor, James E. Doyle Inn of Court. Member, Governor's Task Force on the Creation of a Wisconsin Business Court, 1994. Chairman, Federal Judicial Nominating Commission (Wisconsin), 1994. *Member:* Dane County Bar Association; Seventh Circuit Bar Association (Member, Board of Governor's, 1980-1995; President, 1985-1986); American Law Institute; American Academy of Appellate Lawyers. Fellow: American College of Trial Lawyers; International Academy of Trial Lawyers; American Bar Foundation. ***PRACTICE AREAS:*** Commercial and Intellectual Property Litigation. ***Email:*** jskilton@hewm.com

††***MICHAEL A. STOSSER,*** born Tel Aviv, Israel, April 27, 1952; admitted to bar, 1979, California; 1980, District of Columbia. *Education:* California State University (B.A., cum laude, 1974); Southwestern University (J.D., cum laude, 1978). Associate Staff Member, 1976-1977 and Member, Editorial Board, 1977-1978, Southwestern Law Review. Staff Attorney, 1979-1986 and Assistant General Counsel, 1986-1988, Federal Energy Regulatory Commission. *Member:* State Bar of California; The District of Columbia Bar; American Bar Association; Energy Bar Association. ***LANGUAGES:*** Hebrew, French. ***PRACTICE AREAS:*** Energy Law. ***Email:*** mstosser@hewm.com

SPECIAL COUNSEL

PAUL M. BOOTH, born Goole, England, October 22, 1959; admitted to bar, 1996, Maryland; 1998, District of Columbia; registered to practice before

(This Listing Continued)

U.S. Patent and Trademark Office. *Education:* Imperial College of Science, Technology and Medicine, London, England, (B.Sc., Chemistry, First Class Honours, 1981; Ph.D., Organic Chemistry, 1984); Georgetown University (J.D., magna cum laude, 1996). Order of the Coif. Recipient: Entrance Scholarship, Imperial College, 1978; Imperial College Scholarship, 1979-1981; Edmund White Prize for Organic Chemistry, Imperial College, 1981; ETH (Zurich) Exchange Scholarship, 1981; First Prize, H. Thomas Austern Writing Competition, Food and Drug Law Institute, 1996. Author, "FDA Implementation of Standards Developed by the International Conference on Harmonisation," Food and Drug Law Journal, 52, 203-223, 1997. Co-Author, with Stephen A. Bent: "ICH Sets Standards for Drug Developers," National Law Journal, 18 (15), 1996; "Genomics Race Raises Ownership Boundary Issue," National Law Journal, 20 (22), 1998. *Member:* American Bar Association; American Association for the Advancement of Science; American Chemical Society; American Intellectual Property Law Association. (Also at Gaithersburg, Maryland Office). **Email:** pbooth@hewm.com

ADELIA S. BORRASCA, born Dothan, Alabama, November 2, 1948; admitted to bar, 1983, District of Columbia; 1984, Alabama. *Education:* University of Alabama (B.A., 1970); Georgetown University (J.D., 1983). Phi Beta Kappa. Office of General Counsel, Federal Regulatory Commission, 1985-1987. *Member:* Alabama State Bar; The District of Columbia Bar; Federal Energy Bar Association. ***PRACTICE AREAS:*** Energy; Legislative. **Email:** aborrasca@hewm.com

JOAN L. HEIM, born Louisville, Kentucky; admitted to bar, 1968, Minnesota; 1999, District of Columbia. *Education:* Wellesley College (A.B., 1964); University of Minnesota (J.D., magna cum laude, 1968). Order of the Coif. Editor, Minnesota Law Review. ***SPECIAL AGENCIES:*** Federal Trade Commission, 1979-1999. ***PRACTICE AREAS:*** Antitrust. **Email:** jheim@hewm.com

PAUL B. MOHLER, born Cedar City, Utah; admitted to bar, 1993, Virginia (Not admitted in District of Columbia). *Education:* San Diego State University (A.B., Economics, with high honors, 1979); George Washington University (M.A., Economics, 1986); George Mason University School of Law (J.D., 1993). *Member:* American and Energy Bar Associations; International Association for Energy Economics. [With U.S. Navy, 1970-1976]. **Email:** pmohler@hewm.com

DAVID F. SMUTNY, born Rochester, Minnesota, November 6, 1965; admitted to bar, 1990, Illinois; 1992, District of Columbia. *Education:* University of Wisconsin at LaCrosse (B.A., summa cum laude, 1987); University of Chicago (J.D., 1990). Bradley Fellowship for Criminal Justice, 1989. Trial Attorney: U.S. Department of Justice, Antitrust Division, Communications and Finance Section (Honor's Program), 1990-1992; U.S. Department of Justice, Antitrust Division, Telecommunications Task Force, 1995-2001. Special Assistant United States Attorney, District of Columbia, 1996. **Email:** dsmutny@hewm.com

JANE E. STELCK, born Des Moines, Iowa, August 16, 1946; admitted to bar, 1978, District of Columbia. *Education:* University of Illinois (B.A., with honors, 1972; M.A., 1973); American University School of Law (J.D., 1978). *Member:* The District of Columbia Bar; Federal Energy Bar Association. ***PRACTICE AREAS:*** Energy Law. **Email:** jstelck@hewm.com

ASSOCIATES

JOSEPH H. FAGAN, born Trenton, New Jersey, October 2, 1966; admitted to bar, 1993, Connecticut; 1996, District of Columbia. *Education:* Wesleyan University (B.A., with honors, 1988); George Washington University (J.D., 1993). Phi Delta Phi. Winner, Essay Competition, National Energy Law and Policy Institute Energy Law, 1993. Author: "From Regulation to Deregulation: The Declining Role of the Small Consumer in the Natural Gas Industry," 29 Tulsa Law Journal 707, Spring and Summer, 1994. *Member:* Energy Bar Association (Member: Young Lawyer's Committee; Judicial Review Committee; Natural Gas Committee; Web Site Committee). **Email:** jfagan@hewm.com

JOHN A. JURATA, JR., born Phoenixville, Pennsylvania, April 22, 1970; admitted to bar, 2001, Virginia (Not admitted in District of Columbia). *Education:* Villanova University (B.A., 1992); University of San Diego (J.D., summa cum laude, 2000). Order of the Coif. Recipient, Student Advocacy Award, International Academy of Trial Lawyers. Editor-in-Chief, San Diego Law Review, 1999-2000. Author, "The Tort That Refuses to Go Away: The Subtle Re-emergence of Public Disclosure of Private Facts," 36 San Diego Law Review 489 (1999). *Member:* Virginia State Bar; American Bar Association. [Lieutenant, U.S. Navy, 1992-1999]. **Email:** jjurata@hewm.com

HYUN SUN KIM, admitted to bar, 1992, New Jersey; 1993, New York (Not admitted in District of Columbia). *Education:* Barnard College (B.A., 1987); University of Pittsburgh (J.D., 1992). **Email:** hkim@hewm.com

NATASHA V. LESKOVSEK, born Silver Spring, Maryland, May 2, 1967; admitted to bar, 1996, Maryland; 1998, District of Columbia. *Education:* University of Maryland (B.S.N., 1989; M.B.A., 1991; M.P.M., 1991); Georgetown

(This Listing Continued)

University (J.D., 1996). Registered Nurse, Maryland, 1989. *Member:* American Health Lawyers Association; Food and Drug Law Institute. **Email:** nleskovsek@hewm.com

MIREYA A.R. LLAURADO, born Milwaukee, Wisconsin, May 5, 1972; admitted to bar, 1998, California and Maryland; 1999, District of Columbia. *Education:* University of California at Riverside (B.A., with high honors, 1994); Georgetown University Law Center (J.D., 1997). ***LANGUAGES:*** Spanish. **Email:** mllaurado@hewm.com

MARTINA M. STEWART, born Chicago, Illinois, August 8, 1972; admitted to bar, 1997, California (Not admitted in District of Columbia). *Education:* Yale University (B.A., cum laude, 1994); Harvard University (J.D., cum laude, 1997). Member, 1995-1996, and Co-Lead Articles Editor, 1996-1997, Harvard Civil Rights-Civil Liberties Law Review. Ames Fellow, Harvard Law School, 1998-1999. Law Clerk to: Hon. Carlos R. Mereno, U.S. District Court, Central District of California, 1999-2000; Hon. Judith W. Rogers, U.S. Court of Appeals, District of Columbia Circuit, 2000-2001. **Email:** mstewart@hewm.com

JOHN P. WUNDERLI, born Salt Lake City, Utah, January 25, 1967; admitted to bar, 1995, Utah; 1996, District of Columbia. *Education:* University of Utah (B.A., magna cum laude, 1991); Harvard Law School (J.D., cum laude, 1994). Phi Beta Kappa; Omicron Delta Epsilon. Author: "Squeeze Play: The Game of Owners, Cities, Leagues, and Congress," 5 Marquette Sports Law Journal 83 (Fall 1994). Law Clerk, Judge Michael Wilkins, Utah Court of Appeals, 1994-1995. *Member:* Utah State Bar; The District of Columbia Bar; American Bar Association. ***LANGUAGES:*** Afrikaans. **Email:** jwunderli@hewm.com

†† Lawyer who is a stockholder and an employee of a professional corporation which is a member of the firm

(For complete biographical data on San Francisco, California, Anchorage, Alaska, Los Angeles, California, Menlo Park, California, San Diego, California, Portland, Oregon, New York, New York, Seattle, Washington, Madison, Wisconsin, Gaithersburg, Maryland, Hong Kong and Singapore office personnel, see Professional Biographies at each of those cities)

HENDERSON & STURM LLP

1301 PENNSYLVANIA AVENUE, N.W.
SUITE 1020
WASHINGTON, D.C. 20004-1707
Telephone: 202-296-3854
Fax: 202-223-9606
URL: http://www.hsllp.com

Other Offices: Des Moines, Iowa; Davenport, Iowa; Omaha, Nebraska.

Patent, Trademark, Copyright and Unfair Competition Law and Federal Trial Practice Exclusively, Intellectual Property.

FIRM PROFILE: Henderson & Sturm was founded in 1962 by H. Robert Henderson and serves a wide spectrum of U.S. and International Clients. The firm's attorneys have a broad and diverse range of educational backgrounds, experience and expertise enabling them to effectively communicate and serve clients in all areas of technology.

The Firm's Washington, D.C. office serves as the firm's international patent and trademark department, handling the filing and prosecution of patent and trademark applications with the United States Patent and Trademark Office received from its international clients. The firm's Washington, D.C. office is also particularly attractive to many clients for providing invaluable assistance in conducting patent and trademark searches and conducting personal interviews with examiners of the United States Patent and Trademark Office.

MEMBERS OF FIRM

WILLIAM H. WRIGHT, born 1943; admitted to bar, 1970, Virginia; 1972, District of Columbia; 1972, registered to practice before U.S. Patent and Trademark Office. *Education:* Catholic University of America (B.S.M.E., 1965; J.D., 1969). Examiner, U.S. Patent and Trademark Office, 1966-1971. **Email:** Wright@hsllp.com

MICHAEL O. STURM, born 1943; admitted to bar, 1973, Virginia; 1974, Iowa; 1982, Nebraska; 1974, registered to practice before U.S. Patent and Trademark Office (Not admitted in District of Columbia). *Education:* Iowa State University (B.S., Engr., 1966); Catholic University of America (J.D., 1973). Examiner, U.S. Patent and Trademark Office, 1966-1971. **Email:** Sturm@hsllp.com

(For complete biographical data on all personnel, see Professional Biographies at Des Moines, Iowa).

HENRICHSEN SIEGEL, P.L.L.C.

1850 M STREET N.W., SUITE 250
WASHINGTON, D.C. 20036
Telephone: 202-293-7766
Facsimile: 202-293-7778
Email: administrator@hslawyers.com
URL: http://www.hslawyers.com

Jacksonville, Florida Office: 200 East Forsyth Street, 32202. Telephone: 904-355-2233. Fax: 904-596-5705.

Construction and Surety Law, Government Contracts, Employment and Labor Law, Civil Rights, Creditors Rights, Commercial Torts, General Civil Litigation, Environmental Litigation, Products Liability, Class Action, Litigation.

NEIL L. HENRICHSEN, born New York, N.Y., January 20, 1963; admitted to bar, 1989, New Jersey and District of Columbia; 1990, U.S. District Court, District of Maryland and U.S. Court of Federal Claims; 1991, Virginia; 1997, Florida and U.S. Supreme Court. *Education:* Hunter College (B.A., cum laude, 1984); American University (M.A., Law and International Affairs, 1988); Washington College of Law of American University (J.D., 1988). Recipient, New York State Assembly Legislative Fellowship, 1984. Contributor to The Most Important Questions a Surety Can Ask About Performance Bonds, ABA, TIPS Section, 1997. *Member:* The District of Columbia Bar; Virginia State Bar; The Florida Bar; American Bar Association (Member: Forum on the Construction Industry, 1991; Fidelity and Surety Law Committee, Torts and Insurance Practice Section; Litigation Section); The Association of Trial Lawyers of America; Metropolitan Washington Employment Lawyers Association (Member, Board of Directors, 1993-1999); National Employment Lawyers Association. ***PRACTICE AREAS:*** Construction and Surety Law; Commercial Torts; Employment Law; Civil Rights; Civil Litigation; Creditors Rights; Products Liability. ***Email:*** nhenrichsen@hslawyers.com

ERIC L. SIEGEL, born Washington, D.C., September 21, 1964; admitted to bar, 1990, New York; 1991, District of Columbia and U.S. Court of Veterans Appeals; 1994, U.S. Supreme Court; 1995, Maryland; U.S. Court of Appeals, District of Columbia Circuit and U.S. District Court, District of Columbia and District of Maryland; U.S. Court of Appeals, Fourth Circuit. *Education:* Tufts University (B.A., magna cum laude, 1986); University of California at Los Angeles School of Law (J.D., 1989). Comments Editor, Federal Communications Law Journal, 1988-1989. Judicial Extern, Hon. David V. Kenyon, U.S. District Court, Central District of California, 1988. *Member:* District of Columbia and American (Member, Sections on: Labor and Employment; Law Practice Management) Bar Associations; District of Columbia Bar (Co-Chair, 1997-1999 and Member, Steering Committee, 1995—, Labor and Employment Law Section; Co-Chair, 1994-1996 and Member, Steering Committee, 1994-1998, Law Practice Management Section); National Employment Lawyers Association (Co-Chair, 1998— Title VII Committee); Metropolitan Washington Employment Lawyers Association (Governing Board, 1995—). ***PRACTICE AREAS:*** Civil Rights; Disability Rights; Constitutional Law; Commercial Torts; Litigation. ***Email:*** esiegel@hslawyers.com

DAWN C. STEWART, born Brooklyn, New York, September 5, 1963; admitted to bar, 1987, Virginia; 1998, Maryland; 1999, District of Columbia; U.S. District Court, Eastern and Western Districts of Virginia and U.S. Court of Appeals, Fourth and Federal Circuits. *Education:* Washington College (B.A., 1984); Washington & Lee University (J.D., 1987). Burks Scholar (Legal Writing and Oral Advocacy Instructor, 1986-1987). Law Clerk to the Hon. Ross W. Krumm, Judge, U.S. Bankruptcy Court, 1987-1988. *Member:* Virginia State Bar; Maryland State Bar; District of Columbia Bar; American Bar Association (Member, Torts and Insurance Practice Section). ***PRACTICE AREAS:*** Insurance Law; Civil Litigation; Construction Law; Surety Law; Creditors Rights. ***Email:*** dstewart@hslawyers.com

AARON NISENSON, born Washington, D.C., December 30, 1963; admitted to bar, 1990, Maryland; 1992, District of Columbia; 1996, Virginia. *Education:* State University of New York at Albany (B.A., cum laude, 1986); Boston College (J.D., 1990). Member, Arlington County Parks and Recreation Commission, 1996-2001. *Member:* Arlington County and Virginia State Bar Associations; District of Columbia Bar; National Employment Lawyers Association; Metropolitan Washington Employment Lawyers Association (Chair, High-Tech Employment Committee, D.C. Bar Labor and Employment Law Section, 2001—). ***REPORTED CASES:*** Thomson v. Dept. of Treasury, 165 F.3d 1378 (Fed. Cir. 1999); Anderson v. I.T.T. Industries, 92 F.Supp.2d 516 (F.D.Va. 2000). ***PRACTICE AREAS:*** Employment Law; Labor Law; Products Liability; Class Actions; Litigation. ***Email:*** anisenson@hslawyers.com

WILLIAM J. MOORE, III, born Jacksonville, Florida, May 20, 1966; admitted to bar, 1993, Florida. *Education:* University of Florida (B.A., 1989); University of South Carolina (J.D., 1 992). Member, Environmental Law Journal, Phi Delta Phi. Law Clerk to the Hon. Donald S. Russell, U.S. Court of Appeals, Fourth Circuit, 1992. U.S. Department of Justice, Environmental Enforcement Section, Washington, D.C., 1993-1998. *Member:* Jacksonville and American Bar Associations; The Florida Bar (Environmental and Land Use Section); The American Trial Lawyers Association (Section on Toxic, Environmental and Pharmaceutical Tort Litigation). (Resident, Jacksonville, Florida Office). ***PRACTICE AREAS:*** Environmental Litigation; Toxic Tort Litigation; Surety Law. ***Email:*** wmoore@hslawyers.com

ASSOCIATES

HELEN H. ALBEE, born Clark Air Force Base, Philippines, February 19, 1967; admitted to bar, 1993, Florida; 1994, U.S. District Court, Middle District of Florida; 2000, U.S. District Court, Northern and Southern Districts of Florida. *Education:* University of Florida (B.S.B.A., Finance, with honors, 1989; J.D., with honors, 1993). Member, Council of Ten, University of Florida, 1992-1993. Recipient, Book Award, Water, Wetlands, Wildlife, University of Florida, Fall 1992. Author, "A Comparison of EEC Treaty Article 85(3) and the U.S. Supreme Court's Rule of Reason Analysis Under the Sherman Act," Int'l Law Q., Sept. 1992. *Member:* Jacksonville Bar Association; The Florida Bar; Jacksonville Women Lawyers Association (Treasurer, 2000—). (Resident, Jacksonville, Florida Office). ***PRACTICE AREAS:*** Surety Law; Labor and Employment; Environmental Law; Criminal Law. ***Email:*** halbee@hslawyers.com

COLLEEN M. LEYRER, born Plattsburgh, New York, August 12, 1965; admitted to bar, 1999, Virginia and Maryland; 2000 District of Columbia. *Education:* Douglass College of Rutgers University (B.A., 1987); Columbia University (M.A., 1989); University of Maryland (J.D., with honors, 1998). *Member:* Maryland State Bar Association; Virginia State Bar; The District of Columbia Bar (Member, Labor and Employment Section); Metropolitan Washington Employment Lawyers Association. ***PRACTICE AREAS:*** Employment Law; Civil Rights; Litigation. ***Email:*** cleyrer@hslawyers.com

JOEL M. LONG, born Longmont, Colorado, October 10, 1971; admitted to bar, 1998, Maryland; 2000, District of Columbia. *Education:* University of Colorado at Boulder (B.A., Economics, with distinction, 1994), Phi Beta Kappa; George Washington University (J.D., 1998). *Member:* Maryland State Bar Association. ***PRACTICE AREAS:*** Construction Law; Surety Law; Commercial Law; Civil Litigation. ***Email:*** jlong@hslawyers.com

OF COUNSEL

LORRAINE M. MAGEE, born New York, N.Y., March 13, 1964; admitted to bar, 1990, Virginia; 1999, District of Columbia. *Education:* St. Thomas Aquinas College (B.S., magna cum laude, 1986) Alpha Chi; Georgetown University (J.D., 1989). Senior Editor, Georgetown Journal of Legal Ethics, 1988-1989. Law Fellow, Georgetown University Law Center, 1987-1988. *Member:* Virginia State Bar; The District of Columbia Bar. ***PRACTICE AREAS:*** Civil Litigation; Construction Law; Surety Law; Insurance. ***Email:*** lmagee@hslawyers.com

JOANNA R. ONORATO, born Long Beach, New York, August 10, 1971; admitted to bar, 1998, Maryland; 1999, District of Columbia and U.S. District Court, District of Maryland; 2000, U.S. District Court, District of Columbia; U.S. Court of Appeals, Fourth Circuit. *Education:* Trinity College (B.A., 1993); Washington College of Law of American University (J.D., 1998). *Member:* Maryland State and American (Member, Torts and Insurance Practice Section) Bar Associations. ***PRACTICE AREAS:*** Construction Law; Surety Law; Employment Law; Civil Litigation. ***Email:*** jonorato@hslawyers.com

JOANNE RONEY HEPWORTH

305 H STREET, N.W.
WASHINGTON, D.C. 20001
Telephone: 202-789-0037
Fax: 202-408-1606
Email: jrhepworth@erols.com
URL: http://www.lawyers.com/jrhepworthlaw

Civil Rights and Constitutional Tort Civil Litigation, Personal Injury, Premises Liability, Auto Negligence, Criminal Defense, Drug Crimes, White Collar Criminal Defense, Alternatives to Criminal Prosecution, Domestic Relations, Divorce, Separation, Custody Issues, Auto Accidents, Drunk Driving.

FIRM PROFILE: The firm represents both individuals and business entities primarily in matters requiring litigation expertise in Metropolitan Washington, D.C. and Central and Southern Maryland.

JOANNE RONEY HEPWORTH, born Washington, D.C., June 24, 1948; admitted to bar, 1980, District of Columbia and U.S. Court of Appeals, District of Columbia Circuit; 1987, U.S. District Court for the District of Columbia; 1991, Maryland; 1995, U.S. Supreme Court. *Education:* Catholic University of America (B.A., magna cum laude, 1977; J.D., 1980). Phi Beta Kappa. Member, Board of Directors: Christ Child Society, 1990—; Clean and Sober Streets, 1993—. *Member:* The District of Columbia Bar (Member, Law Office and Management Section); The Association of Trial Lawyers of America; National Association of Criminal Defense Attorneys. ***PRACTICE AREAS:*** Criminal Law; Civil Rights; Personal Injury; Family Law.

(This Listing Continued)

LEGAL SUPPORT PERSONNEL

CHARLES ROACH, JR.

LAW OFFICE OF DOUGLAS C. HERBERT

Established in 1990

1000 CONNECTICUT AVENUE, N.W., SUITE 301
WASHINGTON, D.C. 20036
Telephone: 202-659-1400
Telecopier: 202-659-2435
Email: dougherbert@mindspring.com
URL: http://www.lawyers.com/herbertlaw

Employment Law, Civil Litigation.

DOUGLAS C. HERBERT, born Bethesda, Maryland, May 25, 1953; admitted to bar, 1979, District of Columbia; 1984, Virginia; 1992, Maryland; 1996, U.S. Supreme Court. *Education:* Mississippi State University (B.A., with highest distinction, 1975); University of Chicago (J.D., cum laude, 1978). Phi Kappa Phi; Order of the Coif. Member, 1976-1977 and Executive Editor, 1977-1978, University of Chicago Law Review. Co-Author: "A Pragmatic Argument Against Applying the Disparate Impact Doctrine in Age Discrimination Cases," 37 South Texas Law Review 625 (1996) (with Lani S. Shelton). Author: "Discrimination Claims Against Drug Testing," 3 Employee Testing and the Law 1, Jan. 1988. Law Clerk to Hon. John C. Godbold, U.S. Court of Appeals, Fifth Circuit, 1978-1979.

HERGE, SPARKS & CHRISTOPHER, LLP

WASHINGTON, D.C.

(See McLean, Virginia)

General Practice in Virginia and the District of Columbia including Civil Litigation and Appellate Practice before all Federal and State Courts and Administrative Agencies. Agency and Advertising Law, Commercial and Corporation Law, Federal Election Campaign Law, Elder Law, Real Estate, Tax Exempt Organizations, Taxation, Trademark and Copyright Law, Trust Administration, Estate Planning and Probate Law.

MARIO L. HERMAN

Established in 1983

5335 WISCONSIN AVENUE, N.W., SUITE 440
WASHINGTON, D.C. 20015-2003
Telephone: 202-686-2886
Fax: 301-874-1585
URL: http://www.franchise-law.com
Email: mherman@franchise-law.com
URL: http://www.lawyers.com/franchiselaw

Franchise Law, Franchise Litigation, Franchise Arbitration, Franchise Mediation, Franchise Termination.

MARIO L. HERMAN, born Lima, Peru, March 13, 1958; admitted to bar, 1983, District of Columbia. *Education:* American University, School of International Service (B.A., cum laude, 1979); Georgetown University (J.D., 1983). Member, Iberoamerican Chamber of Commerce. *Member:* District of Columbia Bar; American Bar Association; Inter-American Bar Association; American Association of Franchises and Dealers (Supporting Member of the Year, 1998—). ***LANGUAGES:*** Spanish.

HERTZ & McELWAINE, P.A.

WASHINGTON, D.C.

(See Greenbelt, Maryland)

Personal Injury, Automobile Accidents, Slip & Fall, Dog Bites, Medical Malpractice and Workers Compensation, Family Law, Child Custody, Child Support, Divorce, Adoptions, Real Estate Litigation, Real Estate Settlements, Social Security, Criminal Defense, DWI & Traffic Violations.

HESSEL AND ALUISE, P.C.

1050 SEVENTEENTH STREET, N.W., SUITE 900
WASHINGTON, D.C. 20036
Telephone: 202-466-5300
Telecopier: 202-466-5508
Email: firm@hapc.com
URL: http://www.lawyers.com/hesselandaluise

Housing and Urban Development Law, Real Estate and Real Estate Finance including Residential, Commercial and Health Care Facilities. Partnership and Business Association Matters, Legislative Services, Construction Law, Administrative Enforcement and Fair Housing Matters, Dispute Resolution and Litigation.

ARTHUR R. HESSEL, born St. Louis, Missouri, 1942; admitted to bar, 1967, Missouri; 1972, District of Columbia. *Education:* Harvard University (B.A., magna cum laude, 1964); Yale University (LL.B., 1967); Washington University HUD Urban Studies Fellow, Washington University Law School. Special Assistant to Assistant Secretary, H.U.D., 1969-1972. *Member:* District of Columbia Bar; American Bar Association. ***Email:*** ahessel@hapc.com

TIMOTHY J. ALUISE, born 1956; admitted to bar, 1980, District of Columbia. *Education:* Georgetown University (B.A., cum laude, 1977); University of Notre Dame (J.D., 1980); Notre Dame London Law Centre, England. Phi Alpha Theta. Editor, 1978-1979 and Editor-in-Chief, 1979-1980, Journal of Legislation. Assistant Clerk, U.S. Supreme Court, 1979. Director, National Housing Conference. *Member:* District of Columbia Bar (Member, Real Estate Section); American Bar Association (Member, Forum Committee on Affordable Housing; Chair, Federal Assistance Programs Practice Division). ***Email:*** taluise@hapc.com

OF COUNSEL

MORTON W. SCHOMER, born New York, N.Y., August 2, 1928; admitted to bar, 1953, New York; 1968, District of Columbia. *Education:* New York University (B.A., 1948; LL.B., 1951). Contributing Editor on Housing and Real Estate, Legal Times, 1978-1986. Attorney Advisor, Office of General Counsel, Federal Housing Administration, 1955-1962. Chief Counsel, 1962-1967; Assistant Commissioner, 1967-1970, Multifamily Housing, Federal Housing Administration, U.S. Department of Housing and Urban Development. Partner, Brownstein, Zeidman and Schomer, 1970-1992. Director, National Housing Conference. Member, National Panel of Arbitrators for the Construction Industry, American Arbitration Association. *Member:* District of Columbia Bar; New York State, Federal and American Bar Associations.

KRISTIN M. NEUN, born Baltimore, Maryland, November 29, 1963; admitted to bar, 1993, Maryland; 1996, District of Columbia. *Education:* Dickinson College (B.A., 1985); The Washington College of Law, The American University (J.D., cum laude, 1993). *Member:* District of Columbia Bar; Maryland State and American Bar Associations. ***Email:*** kneun@hapc.com

MARY E. ANDREWS, born Kansas City, Kansas, May 6, 1958; admitted to bar, 1992, Maryland (Not admitted in District of Columbia). *Education:* West Virginia University (B.A., 1982); Washington and Lee University (J.D., 1992). ***Email:*** mandrews@hapc.com

MARIO GRESZES, born Hovellanos, Matanzas, Cuba, March 19, 1957; admitted to bar, 1986, District of Columbia. *Education:* Emory University (B.A., 1978; M.A., 1979); George Washington University National Law Center (J.D., 1985). Phi Beta Kappa; Phi Sigma Alpha. *Member:* The District of Columbia Bar. ***LANGUAGES:*** Spanish. ***PRACTICE AREAS:*** HUD Administrative Proceedings; Real Estate Litigation; Bankruptcy; Multi-Family Housing. ***Email:*** mgreszes@hapc.com

ERIC M. KEIFER, born Westfield, Massachusetts, December 9, 1971; admitted to bar, 1999, New York (Not admitted in District of Columbia). *Education:* Bob Jones University (B.A., 1994); Western New England College School of Law (J.D., 1997). ***Email:*** ekeifer@hapc.com

CHRISTOPHER W. HORNIG, admitted to bar, 1979, District of Columbia; 1981, U.S. District Court for the District of Columbia; 1987, U.S. Court of Appeals for the District of Columbia Circuit; 1989, Maryland; 1990, U.S. District Court, District of Maryland and U.S. Supreme Court. *Education:* Harvard University (B.A., cum laude, 1976); Stanford University (J.D., 1979). Order of the Coif. Author: "Public Housing Authorities and HOPE 1: May HUD Give Away What it Doesn't Own?" The Urban Lawyer, Winter 1993. Deputy Assistant Secretary, U.S. HUD, 1996-1997. *Member:* The District of Columbia Bar; American Bar Association (ABA Forum on Affordable Housing and Community Development Law, 1992-1999). ***PRACTICE AREAS:*** Affordable Housing; Real Estate. ***Email:*** chornig@hapc.com

LEGAL SUPPORT PERSONNEL

NANCY LIBSON, born Pittsburgh, Pennsylvania, February 15, 1947. *Education:* Cornell University (B.A., 1968); University of Pittsburgh, Graduate

(This Listing Continued)

HESSEL AND ALUISE, P.C., Washington—Continued

School of Public and International Affairs (M.P.A., 1970). Member, Women in Housing and Finance. National Capital Housing Authority, 1970-1972. National Center for Housing Management, 1972-1978. Vice President, The Bernstein Group, 1978-1980. Housing Director, Appalachian Regional Commission, 1980-1990. Professional Staff and Staff Director, House Committee on Banking, Subcommittee on Housing, 1990-1998. Senior Advisor for Legislative Initiatives, HUD, 1998-1999. ***PRACTICE AREAS:*** Federal Legislative Practice; State Legislative Practice; Housing Law. ***Email:*** nlibson@hapc.com

HIGHSAW, MAHONEY & CLARKE, P.C.

Established in 1970

SUITE 590

1050 SEVENTEENTH STREET, N.W.

WASHINGTON, D.C. 20036

Telephone: 202-296-8500

Fax: 202-296-7143

Email: hmcjobc@worldnet.att.net

URL: http://www.lawyers.com/highsawmahoneyclarke

General Practice before all Federal Courts, Departments and Agencies. Interstate Commerce, Labor Law, Aviation Law, Employee Benefits, Pension Plans, ERISA, Employment Discrimination, Complex Litigation.

FIRM PROFILE: Highsaw, Mahoney & Clarke, P.C. was founded in 1970 as Highsaw & Mahoney by James L. Highsaw, Jr. and William G. Mahoney who first met in 1955 when employed by another law firm. They were joined in 1974 by John O'B. Clarke, Jr. Since 1970 the firm has represented its clients, principally railroad and airline labor unions, before federal courts, including the Supreme Court, and state courts throughout the country, administrative agencies, arbitrations and in testimony before committees of the Congress in support of or in opposition to specific proposed legislation. Members of the firm are frequent lecturers at the AFL-CIO George Meany Studies Center and ALI-ABA seminars and are active in the ABA section activities.

JAMES L. HIGHSAW (1970-1992).

JOHN O'B. CLARKE, JR., born Brooklyn, New York, August 23, 1943; admitted to bar, 1968, Illinois; 1969, New York and District of Columbia; 1973, U.S. Supreme Court; 1979, Virginia. *Education:* Mt. St. Mary's College (B.S. in Acct., 1965); Georgetown University (J.D., 1968); Northwestern University (LL.M., 1975). Editor, Georgetown Law Journal, 1967-1968. Assistant State's Attorney, Cook County, Illinois, 1968-1969. Assistant U.S. Attorney, Washington, D.C., 1969-1974. Special Assistant U.S. Attorney, Washington, D.C., 1974-1975. *Member:* District of Columbia Bar; Federal and American Bar Associations; Virginia State Bar; The Barristers. ***SPECIAL AGENCIES:*** Surface Transportation Board. ***REPORTED CASES:*** LeBlanc v. Cahill 153 Fed. 3rd 134, 4th App. Cir., 1998; Burlington Northern R.R. v. BMWE, 481 U.S. 429 (1987); Pittsburgh & Lake Erie R.R. v. RLEA, 491 U.S. 490 (1989). ***TRANSACTIONS:*** Interstate Commerce Commission, National Mediation Board. ***PRACTICE AREAS:*** Federal Court Trial and Appellate Practice; Supreme Court Practice; Railway Labor Act; Transportation; Bankruptcy; Administrative Law. ***Email:*** hmcjobc@worldnet.att.net

OF COUNSEL

WILLIAM G. MAHONEY, born Washington, D.C., October 5, 1925; admitted to bar, 1950 District of Columbia; 1961, U.S. Supreme Court. *Education:* University of Notre Dame (J.D., cum laude, 1950). Secretary, Notre Dame Lawyer, 1949-1950. Chairman, Committee on Professional Ethics and Grievances, Association of Interstate Commerce Commission Practitioners, 1967-1968. *Member:* District of Columbia Bar; Bar Association of the District of Columbia; Federal and American Bar Associations; The Barristers. ***SPECIAL AGENCIES:*** Department of Labor; Department of Transportation; National Mediation Board; Surface Transportation Board. ***TRANSACTIONS:*** Amtrak Enabling Legislation; Conrail Privatization. ***PRACTICE AREAS:*** Appellate Court Practice; Supreme Court Practice; Railway Labor Act; Contract and Legislative Negotiations; Interstate Commerce Act; Federal Labor Legislation.

HILLS & STERN

1200 NINETEENTH STREET, N.W.

WASHINGTON, D.C. 20036

Telephone: 202-822-1600

Fax: 202-822-1622

International Finance, International Trade, Corporate Finance.

(This Listing Continued)

RODERICK M. HILLS, born Seattle, Washington, March 9, 1931; admitted to bar, 1957, California; 1960, U.S. Supreme Court; 1979, District of Columbia; U.S. Court of Appeals, Ninth Circuit. *Education:* Stanford University (B.A., 1952; LL.B., 1955). Order of the Coif. Comment Editor, Stanford Law Review, 1953-1955. Law Clerk to Justice Stanley F. Reed, Supreme Court of the United States, 1955-1957. Visiting Lecturer in Law, Stanford University School of Law, 1960-1970. Professor, Harvard University Schools of Law and Business, 1969-1970. Distinguished Faculty Member and Lecturer, International Finance, Yale University School of Organization and Management, 1985-1988. Counsel to the President of the United States, 1975. Chairman, Securities and Exchange Commission, 1975-1977. Vice-Chairman, Trustees of Claremont College, 1970-1975. Vice-Chairman, U.S.-ASEAN Council for Business and Technology, 1985—. Chairman, Research Committee, 1965-1969, and Fellow, 1989—, American Bar Foundation. Trustee, Committee for Economic Development, 1978—. *Member:* Los Angeles County and American Bar Associations; District of Columbia Bar; State Bar of California; Bar Association of the District of Columbia; U.S. Supreme Court Bar; Chancery Club; Bretton Woods Committee.

CARLA ANDERSON HILLS, born Los Angeles, California, January 3, 1934; admitted to bar, 1959, California; 1965, U.S. Supreme Court; 1974, U.S. Court of Federal Claims; 1977, District of Columbia. *Education:* St. Hilda's College, Oxford University, England; Stanford University (A.B., cum laude, 1955); Yale University (LL.B., 1958). Editor and Co-Author, "Antitrust Adviser," published by McGraw-Hill, 1971, 3rd ed., 1985. Adjunct Professor, Antitrust Law, University of California School of Law, 1972. Assistant Attorney General, Civil Division, Department of Justice, 1974-1975. Secretary, Department of Housing and Urban Development, 1975-1977. U.S. Trade Representative, 1989-1993. Member, Board of Trustees, Urban Institute, 1977-1989; Chair, Urban Institute, 1983-1989; Member, Executive Committee, Institute for International Economics, 1993—; Vice Chair, U.S. - China Business Council, 1993—; and Member, National Committee, U.S. - China Relations, 1993—; Brookings Institution, 1977-1981; Federal Accounting Standards Advisory Council, 1978-1980. *Member:* Los Angeles County, Federal (President, Los Angeles Chapter, 1963) and American (Member: Antitrust Law Section; Council, 1974, 1977-1989; Chairman, 1982; Chairman, 1983 Conference of Section Chairmen) Bar Associations; District of Columbia Bar; State Bar of California; Womens' Bar Association (President, 1964); U.S. Supreme Court Bar; American Law Institute. Fellow, American Bar Foundation.

SAMUEL A. STERN, born Philadelphia, Pennsylvania, January 21, 1929; admitted to bar, 1952, Massachusetts; 1957, District of Columbia. *Education:* University of Pennsylvania (A.B., 1949); Harvard University (LL.B., 1952). Law Clerk to: Chief Judge Calvert Magruder, U.S. Court of Appeals for the First Circuit, 1955; Earl Warren, Chief Justice of the United States, 1956. Partner, Wilmer, Cutler & Pickering, 1962-1988. Visiting Professor from Practice, Harvard Law School, 1976. Adjunct Professor of Law, Georgetown University Law Center, 1978-1992. Assistant Counsel, Warren Commission, 1964. *Member:* District of Columbia Bar; American and International Bar Associations; American Law Institute. ***PRACTICE AREAS:*** Project Finance; Investment and Trade with Emerging and Transitional Economies; International Commercial Arbitration.

OF COUNSEL

IRINA PALIASHVILI, born Moscow, Russia, March 1, 1961; admitted to bar, 1983, U.S.S.R.; 1992, Ukraine; 1995, Russia (Not admitted in the United States). Licensed to Practice Russian and Ukrainian Law in the District of Columbia as a Special Legal Consultant, 1995. *Education:* Kiev State University School of International Law (with honors, 1983; Ph.D., International Law, 1987); George Washington University (LL.M., 1993). Law Professor, Kiev State University, School of International Law, Kiev Business Management School, 1989-1992. General Counsel: Kiev Electronmash, 1987-1990; Microprocessor, Kiev, Ukraine, 1990-1992. Advisor, Ukrainian Chamber of Commerce and Industry, 1992. President, Russian-Ukrainian Legal Group, P.A., 1996—. Member: Russian International Law Association, 1982—; Foreign Lawyers Forum, Washington D.C., 1993—; Board of Governors, Washington Foreign Law Society, 1994—. *Member:* Kiev Bar. (Also Counsel to Russian-Ukrainian Legal Group, Washington, DC and Member, Russin & Vecchi L.L.P., Washington, DC). ***LANGUAGES:*** Russian, Ukrainian, Georgian, Spanish. ***PRACTICE AREAS:*** Corporate Law; International Business Law; Foreign Investment; Oil and Gas Law.

REFERENCE: First Chicago Corp.

DEBORAH K. HINES

1700 K STREET, N.W.
WASHINGTON, D.C. 20036
Telephone: 202-824-8124
Facsimile: 202-628-7220
Email: dkhines@aol.com
URL: http://www.lawyers.com/lawyerhines

Automobile Accidents, Motorcycle Accidents, Slip and Fall, Premises Liability, Wrongful Death, Product Liability, Lead Paint Poisoning, Asbestos, Inadequate Security Liability, Criminal Defense, Domestic Abuse, Personal Injury, Medical Malpractice.

FIRM PROFILE: Over the past 20 years, Attorney Hines has tried many personal injury cases, with individual verdicts up to six million dollars. Ms. Hines serves on the Board of Governors of the D.C. Trial Lawyers Association and is a frequent lecturer throughout the U.S. and Canada to other trial lawyers. She has lectured and published articles on representing women and the law. Her accomplishments have been featured in USA Today, the Wall Street Journal, the National Law Journal, the Washington Times, and the Baltimore Sun. As a former Baltimore City prosecutor, Deborah K. Hines also has a background in criminal law.

DEBORAH K. HINES, born Baltimore, Maryland, July 2, 1954; admitted to bar, 1978, Pennsylvania; 1979, Maryland and U.S. District Court, District of Maryland; 1992, District of Columbia, U.S. District Court for the District of Columbia and and U.S. Supreme Court. *Education:* University of Pennsylvania (B.A., 1975); George Washington University (J.D., 1978). Author: "Products Liability Litigation - Case Evaluation- Appendix 9A - What Does it Mean When Your Client is a Woman?", West Group Publication, 1998. Speaker: Minority Caucus Program, Direct Examination of a Plaintiff, ATLA Convention, Chicago, Illinois, 1994; Managing Complex Litigation, ATLA Seminar, Chicago, Illinois, 1995; Women's Caucus Litigation - What Does it Mean When Your Client is a Woman?, ATLA Convention, San Diego, California, 1997; Proving Landlord's Liability for Lead Paint Poisoning, ATLA Convention, Washington, D.C., 1998. Assistant State's Attorney, Office of the State's Attorney Trial Division, Baltimore, Maryland, 1983-1987. Assistant Attorney General, Office of the Attorney General Consumer Protection Division, Baltimore, Maryland, 1979-1983. *Member:* District of Columbia Bar (Member Personal Injury and Property Sections); District of Columbia Trial Lawyers Association (Member, Board of Governors); The Association of Trial Lawyers of America (Member, Key Persons Committee, 1998). ***REPORTED CASES:*** Sealover v. Carey Canada, et. al. 996 F.2d, 42 (3rd Cir. 1993); see also 791 F.Supp. 1059 (M.D. Pa. 1992) and 793 F.Supp. 569 (M.D. Pa. 1992). ***PRACTICE AREAS:*** Personal Injury; Medical Malpractice; Premises Liability; Products Liability; Wrongful Death.

FREDERICK S. HIRD, JR.

1850 M STREET, N.W., SUITE 280
WASHINGTON, D.C. 20036
Telephone: 202-778-0878
Fax: 202-778-0688

Federal Administrative and Regulatory Law; General Practice.

FREDERICK S. HIRD, JR., born Des Moines, Iowa, 1935; admitted to bar, 1960, District of Columbia. *Education:* Harvard University (A.B., 1957); Harvard Law School (LL.B., 1960). *Member:* District of Columbia Bar; Bar Association of the District of Columbia (Chairman, Legislation Committee and Member, Board of Directors, 1973-1975); American Bar Association.

THE LAW OFFICES OF JANE HO

WASHINGTON, D.C.

(See North Potomac)

Immigration Law, Business Immigration, Employment Visas, Deportation, Political Asylum, Refugee Law, Religious Visas, Consular Law, Immigration Discrimination, Small Business Law, International Corporate Law, International Joint Venture, Business Litigation, Mergers, Acquisitions and Divestitures, Business Planning Development, Business Formation, Incorporation Franchise Law, Shareholder Agreements, Small Business, General Counselling, Estate Planning, Wills, Family Law, Personal Injury, Wrongful Death, Slip and Fall, Automobile Accidents and Injuries.

HODES, ULMAN, PESSIN & KATZ, P.A.

1025 THOMAS JEFFERSON STREET NW
WASHINGTON, D.C. 20007
Telephone: 202-338-2172
Email: Hupk@Hupk.com
URL: http://www.HUPK.com

Towson, Maryland Office: 901 Dulaney Valley Road, Suite 400, 21204. Telephone: 410-938-8800. FAX: 410-938-8806.
Columbia, Maryland Office: 10500 Little Patuxent Parkway, Suite 650. Telephone: 410-740-2000; D.C. Direct: 301-596-1717. FAX: 410-740-2005.
Havre de Grace, Maryland Office: 131 South Union Avenue, Second Floor, 21078. Telephone: 410-938-8800.
Bethesda, Maryland Office: 3 Bethesda Metro Center, 7th Floor, 20814. Telephone: 301-596-1717.
Bel Air, Maryland Office: 112 South Main Street, Suite 102, 21014-3818. Telephone: 410-893-2333.
Cambridge, Maryland Office: 317 Crusader Road, 21613. Telephone: 410-228-1040.

Estates and Trusts, Elder Law, Probate, Taxation, Corporate, Environmental, Health Law, Franchise Law, Litigation, Family Law, White Collar Criminal Defense, Intellectual Property, E-Commerce, Executive Compensation, Banking and Commercial Transactions, Real Estate, Construction and Land Use/Zoning, Associated Civil Trial and Appellate Practice Before all State and Federal Courts and Administrative Agencies. Labor and Employment, Bankruptcy and Creditors Rights.

FIRM PROFILE: Headquartered in Towson, with offices in Columbia, Havre de Grace, Bethesda, Bel Air, Washington, D.C. and Cambridge, Maryland, Hodes, Ulman, Pessin & Katz, P.A. is a 47-attorney law firm that concentrates its practice in the areas of general, civil and business litigation, white collar criminal defense, commercial, corporate, employment law, health, environmental law, taxation, executive compensation, trusts, estates and elder law, intellectual property and e-commerce, franchise and distributorship, construction, land use and zoning, real estate, domestic relations.

(For Complete Biographical Data on all Personnel, see Professional Biographies at Towson, Maryland)

HOFFMAN, WASSON & GITLER, P.C.

WASHINGTON, D.C.

(See Arlington, Virginia)

Patent, Trademark, Copyright and Unfair Competition Law.

HOGAN & HARTSON L.L.P.

555 13TH STREET, N.W.
WASHINGTON, D.C. 20004-1109
Telephone: 202-637-5600
Telex: 89-2757
Cable Address: "Hogander Washington"
Fax: 202-637-5910
URL: http://www.hhlaw.com

Berlin, Germany Office: Potsdamer Platz 1, 10785. Telephone: 49-30 726 115-0. Fax: 49-30 726 115-100.
Brussels, Belgium Office: Avenue des Arts 41, 1040. Telephone: (32.2) 505.09.11. Fax: (32.2) 505.09.96.
Budapest, Hungary Office: Nagy & Pintér, Hogan & Hartson Law Office, Budapest V., Szabadság tér 7-9, 1054. Telephone: (36-1) 302-9050. Fax: (36-1) 302-9060.
London, England Office: One Angel Court, EC2R 7HJ. Telephone: +(44) 207-367-0200. Fax: +(44) 207-367-0220.
Moscow, Russia Office: 14, Prechistenskiy Pereulok, 119034. Telephone: 7 (095) 797-9900. Fax: 7 (095) 797-9961.
Paris, France Office: Cariddi, Mee, Rué, Avocats Associés à la Cour de Paris, 12, rue de la Paix, 75002. Telephone: (33-1) 42.61.57.71. Fax: (33-1) 42.61.79.21.
Prague, Czech Republic Office: Hogan & Hartson, advokátní kanceláře, Tržiště 13, 118 00. Telephone: (420-2) 2211-7111. Fax: (420-2) 2211-7222.
Tokyo, Japan Office: Shinjuku Center Building, 46th Floor, 25-1 Nishi-Shinjuku 1-Chome, Shinjuku-ku, 163-0646. Telephone: 813-5908-4070. Fax: 813-5908-4071.
Warsaw, Poland Office: Kancelaria Prawna Hogan & Hartson M. Jamka, A. Galos i Wspólnicy Spólka Ko., Al. Jana Pawla II 25, 00-854. Telephone: (48-22) 653-4200. Fax: (48-22) 653-4250.
Baltimore, Maryland Office: 111 South Calvert Street. Telephone: 410-659-2700. Fax: 410-539-6981.

(This Listing Continued)

HOGAN & HARTSON L.L.P., Washington—Continued

Boulder, Colorado Office: 1800 Broadway. Telephone: 720-406-5300. Fax: 720-406-5301.
Colorado Springs, Colorado Office: Two North Cascade Avenue. Telephone: 719-448-5900. Fax: 719-448-5922.
Denver, Colorado Office: 1200 Seventeenth Street. Telephone: 303-899-7300. Fax: 303-899-7333.
Irvine, California Office: 3 Park Plaza. Telephone: 949-250-4550. Fax: 949-833-0976.
Los Angeles, California Office: 500 S. Grand Avenue. Telephone: 213-337-6700. Fax: 213-337-6701.
McLean, Virginia Office: 8300 Greensboro Drive. Telephone: 703-610-6100. Fax: 703-610-6200.
Miami, Florida Office: 1111 Brickell Avenue. Telephone: 305-459-6500. Fax: 305-459-6550.
New York, New York Office: 885 Third Avenue. Telephone: 212-409-9800. Fax: 212-409-9801.
Other New York, New York Office: 875 Third Avenue. Telephone: 212-918-3000. Fax: 212-918-3100.
Philadelphia, Pennsylvania Office: 1515 Market Street. Telephone: 215-864-8087. Fax: 215-569-4963

Antitrust and Trade Regulation, Appellate and Supreme Court Practice, Arbitration, Mediation and Alternative Dispute Resolution, Communications, Corporate and Securities, Education, Election Law, Energy and Natural Resources, Environmental, Estate Planning and Administration, Financial Institutions and Transactions, Food, Drug and Medical Devices, Franchise Law, Government Contracts, Health, Immigration, International Trade, Internet Law, Labor and Employment, Legislation, Litigation, Privatization, Private Equity, Project Finance, Public Finance, Real Estate, Sports Law, Sports Facilities Law, Tax, Technology Licensing and Intellectual Property (Copyright, Trademark and Patent Law), Transportation, and Venture Capital.

MEMBERS OF FIRM

FRANK J. HOGAN (1877-1944).

NELSON T. HARTSON (1887-1976).

JONATHAN L. ABRAM, born April 1, 1956; admitted to bar, 1981, Florida (inactive); 1982, U.S. District Court, Middle District of Florida; 1984, U.S. Court of Appeals, Fifth Circuit; 1985, District of Columbia and U.S. Court of Federal Claims; 1987, U.S. District Court, District of Columbia; 1990, U.S. Court of Appeals for the Federal Circuit and U.S. District Court, District of Maryland; 1991, U.S. Supreme Court, U.S. Court of Appeals for the District of Columbia Circuit and U.S. Court of Appeals, Fourth and Sixth Circuits. *Education:* University of Florida (B.A., with high honors, 1978); Duke University (J.D., with distinction, 1981). Phi Beta Kappa; Order of the Coif. Note and Comment Editor, Duke Law Journal, 1980-1981. Law Clerk: Hon. Ben Krentzman, U.S. District Court, Middle District of Florida, 1981-1983; Hon. Thomas M. Reavley, Fifth Circuit Court of Appeals, 1983-1984. *Member:* The District of Columbia Bar; The Florida Bar. ***PRACTICE AREAS:*** Complex Commercial Litigation; Constitutional Litigation; Technical Litigation; Oil and Gas Litigation; Contract Litigation; Administrative Litigation; Arbitration; Mediation. ***Email:*** jlabram@hhlaw.com

GIL A. ABRAMSON (Resident, Baltimore, Maryland Office).

DONNA LADY ALPI, born Washington, D.C., June 9, 1965; admitted to bar, 1990, Pennsylvania; 1991, District of Columbia. *Education:* Pennsylvania State University (B.A., with distinction, 1987); University of Pennsylvania (J.D., 1990); Georgetown University Law Center (LL.M., 1993). Phi Beta Kappa. *Member:* The District of Columbia Bar; Bar Association of the District of Columbia; American Bar Association (Member, Tax Section; Assistant to the Vice-Chair, Committee Operations, 1995-1998; Secretary, Committee on S Corporations, 1998-1999); Women's Bar Association of the District of Columbia. ***PRACTICE AREAS:*** Corporate Taxation; Partnership Taxation; Real Estate Investment Taxation; Real Estate Taxation; Federal Income Tax. ***Email:*** dlalpi@hhlaw.com

PATRICIA RILEY AMBROSE, born Utica, New York, July 30, 1951; admitted to bar, 1978, District of Columbia and Virginia; 1979, U.S. Court of Appeals for the District of Columbia Circuit; 1980, U.S. Court of Appeals, 5th Circuit; 1983, U.S. Court of Appeals, 4th Circuit. *Education:* LeMoyne College (B.A., 1973); Georgetown University (J.D., 1978). Editor, Georgetown Law Journal, 1976-1978. Law Clerk, Honorable Edward A. Tamm, U.S. Court of Appeals for District of Columbia Circuit, 1978-1979. *Member:* The District of Columbia Bar (Member, Section of Labor Relations); American Bar Association (Member, Section of Labor and Employment Law). ***PRACTICE AREAS:*** Labor and Employment; Equal Employment Opportunity Law; Employment Contracts; Personnel Training; Personnel Policies; Employment Mediation. ***Email:*** prambrose@hhlaw.com

(This Listing Continued)

AUDREY J. ANDERSON, born Des Plaines, Illinois, August 21, 1963; admitted to bar, 1990, Illinois; 1993, District of Columbia. *Education:* Northwestern University (B.S., 1985); University of Michigan (J.D., magna cum laude, 1990). Order of the Coif. Note Editor, Michigan Law Review, 1989-1990. Author: Note, "Corporate Life After Death: CERCLA Preemption of State Corporate Dissolution Law," 88 Mich. L. Rev. 131 (1989). Law Clerk: Hon. William H. Rehnquist, Chief Justice U.S. Supreme Court, 1991-1992; Hon. Harold H. Greene, U.S. District Court for the District of Columbia, 1990-1991. *Member:* The District of Columbia Bar; American Bar Association. ***PRACTICE AREAS:*** Education Litigation; Appellate Litigation; Supreme Court Litigation; Litigation. ***Email:*** ajanderson@hhlaw.com

JEANNE S. ARCHIBALD, born Copiague, New York, January 30, 1951; admitted to bar, 1977, District of Columbia. *Education:* State University of New York at Stoney Brook (B.A., 1973); Georgetown University Law Center (J.D., 1977). Professional Staff, Subcommittee on Trade, Ways and Means Committee, U.S. House of Representatives, 1975-1980. Associate General Counsel, USTR, 1980-1986. Deputy Assistant General Counsel, International Affairs, Department of Treasury, 1986-1988. Deputy General Counsel, Department of Treasury, 1988-1990. General Counsel, Department of Treasury, 1990-1993. *Member:* The District of Columbia Bar (Member, International Section). ***PRACTICE AREAS:*** International Trade Law; Financial Institution Regulation. ***Email:*** jsarchibald@hhlaw.com

EDWIN P. ARO (Resident, Denver, Colorado Office).

DEBORAH TAYLOR ASHFORD, born Athens, Alabama, February 22, 1950; admitted to bar, 1982, District of Columbia. *Education:* University of Alabama (B.A., 1972; M.A., 1974); Yale University (J.D., 1981). Phi Beta Kappa. Assistant in Instruction, Yale Law School, Fall 1980. *Member:* The District of Columbia Bar; Bar Association of the District of Columbia; American Bar Association; American Society of Association Executives. ***PRACTICE AREAS:*** Corporate Law; Nonprofit and Charitable Organizations. ***Email:*** dtashford@hhlaw.com

HELEN CLARK ATKESON (Resident, Denver, Colorado Office).

MATTHEW T. BAILEY, born December 16, 1963; admitted to bar, 1989, Virginia; 1991, District of Columbia; registered to practice before U.S. Patent and Trademark Office. *Education:* Rensselaer Polytechnic Institute (B.S.E.E., 1986); Catholic University of America (J.D., 1989). ***PRACTICE AREAS:*** Intellectual Property Law; Patent Law. ***Email:*** mtbailey@hhlaw.com

STEVEN E. BALLEW, born Greenwood, South Carolina, June 17, 1945; admitted to bar, 1978, California; 1981, District of Columbia. *Education:* Duke University (A.B., 1967); Indiana University (Ph.D., 1974); University of Southern California (J.D., 1978). Order of the Coif. Author: "Joint Ventures in Poland," Corporate Finance, 1992; "Assignment of Rights, Franchises and Obligations of the Disappearing Corporation in a Merger," The Business Lawyer, 1982. Resident: Berlin, Germany Office, 2001—; Warsaw, Poland Office, 1992-1998. *Member:* The District of Columbia Bar; State Bar of California; American Bar Association. ***PRACTICE AREAS:*** Corporate and Public Finance; Securities Law; International Transactions; General Commercial. ***Email:*** seballew@hhlaw.com

JAMES T. BANKS, born Manhattan, Kansas, January 9, 1949; admitted to bar, 1976, Michigan; 1979, District of Columbia. *Education:* University of Kansas (B.S.C.E., with distinction, 1972); University of Michigan (J.D., 1975). Senior Attorney, Natural Resources Defense Council, 1976-1985. Vice President and General Counsel, Chemical Waste Management, Inc., 1990-1993. Director of Government Affairs, WMX Technologies, Inc., 1985-1989, 1994-1995. Author: "EPA's New Enforcement Policy: At Last a Reliable Roadmap to Civil Penalty Mitigation for Self-Disclosed Violations," The Environmental Law Reporter, 1996; "Substantial Penalty Mitigation for Environmental Crimes: A 'Gold Standard' Proposal Worth Considering," Federal Sentencing Reporter, 1996. Adjunct Professor, George Washington University Law School, 1981-1982. Teacher: University of Georgia, Course of Study on Environmental Law, 1977-1979; George Washington University, Environmental Law for Engineers and Administrators, 1978-1979. Vice-Chair, ABA Water Quality Committee, Section on Natural Resources, 1977-1981. ***PRACTICE AREAS:*** Environmental; Regulation; Legislative; Litigation. ***Email:*** jtbanks@hhlaw.com

SUZANNE A. BARR, born Los Angeles, California, October 14, 1966; admitted to bar, 1992, California; 1993, U.S. District Court, Northern District of California and U.S. Court of Appeals, Ninth Circuit; 1998, District of Columbia. *Education:* Harvard University (A.B., 1988; J.D., 1991). *Member:* The District of Columbia Bar; State Bar of California (Inactive); American Bar Association. ***PRACTICE AREAS:*** Emerging Growth Companies; Corporate Formation; Corporate Governance; Public Corporations; Initial Public Offerings; Insider Trading; Private Placement; Public Offerings; Securities Disclosure; Securities Offerings; Securities Registration; Securities Regulation. ***Email:*** sabarr@hhlaw.com

GEORGE P. BARSNESS, born Portland, Maine, September 29, 1955; admitted to bar, 1985, District of Columbia. *Education:* University of Texas

(This Listing Continued)

(B.A., 1976); Brown University (M.A., 1979); University of Texas (J.D., 1981). Phi Beta Kappa. *Member:* The District of Columbia Bar. ***PRACTICE AREAS:*** Corporate Law; Securities. ***Email:*** gpbarsness@hhlaw.com

RAYMOND J. BATLA, JR., born Cameron, Texas, September 1, 1947; admitted to bar, 1973, Texas and District of Columbia. *Education:* Texas Tech University and University of Texas (B.S.C.E., with highest honors, 1970); University of Texas (J.D., with honors, 1973). Tau Beta Pi; Chi Epsilon; Phi Delta Phi; Order of the Coif. Research Scholar, Texas Law Review, 1972-1973. Member, International Observer Delegation to Czechoslovak National Elections, 1990. Columnist and Editorial Advisory Board, "Natural Gas," The Journal for Producers, Pipelines, Distributors and End Users, 1984-1991; Secretary, Council on Alternate Fuels, Washington, D.C., 1987-1997. *Member:* The District of Columbia Bar; Bar Association of the District of Columbia; Federal, American (Member, Sections on: International Law; Corporation, Banking and Business Law), Federal Energy (Chairman, Committee on International Energy Transactions, 1993-1994) and International Bar Associations; State Bar of Texas. (Also at London, England Office). ***LANGUAGES:*** Czech. ***PRACTICE AREAS:*** Corporate Finance; Project Finance; Mergers and Acquisitions; Technology. ***Email:*** rjbatla@hhlaw.com

GEORGE BEALL (Resident, Baltimore, Maryland Office).

RICHARD K.A. BECKER (Resident, McLean, Virginia Office).

DAVID W. BEIER, born Albany, New York, August 27, 1948; admitted to bar, 1974, New York (Not admitted in District of Columbia). *Education:* Colgate University (B.A., 1970); Albany Law School - Union University (J.D., 1973). Co-Author: (with Robert Benson) *Biotechnology Patent Protection Act,* 68 University of Denver Law Review 173 (1991); (with Robert W. Kastenmeier) *International Trade and Intellectual Property: Promise Risks and Reality,* 22 Vanderbilt Journal of Transnational Law 285 (1989); (with Robert W. Kastenmeier and Deborah Leavy) *Electronic Communications Privacy Act,* Wisconsin Law Review 715 (1989); (with Robert W. Kastenmeier) *Protection of United States Process Patents,* 5 Industrial Property 228 (1986)(published by World Intellectual Property Organization, Geneva, Switzerland); (with Robert W. Kastenmeier and Deborah Leavy) *Communications Privacy,* 5 Communication Lawyer 1 (1987); (with Robert W. Kastenmeier) *Bail Reform Revisited,* 32 Federal Bar Journal 82 (1985); (with Robert F. Drinan and Michael E. Ward) *The Federal Criminal Code: The Houses are Divided,* 18 American Criminal Law Review 509 (1981); *Crime and Punishment in New York: An Inquiry into Sentencing and the Criminal Justice System (1979). Senior Fellow, Wharton School, University of Pennsylvania, 2001. White House, Chief Domestic Policy Advisor, 1998-2001.* ***PRACTICE AREAS:*** Health Law; Internet Law; Telecommunications Law; Trade; Legislative. ***Email:*** dbeier@hhlaw.com

JOSEPH C. BELL, born Louisville, Kentucky, November 11, 1940; admitted to bar, 1968, Massachusetts; 1977, District of Columbia. *Education:* University of Colorado (B.A., summa cum laude, 1962); Harvard University (A.M., Economics, 1965); Yale University (LL.B., 1968); University of California at Berkeley. Phi Beta Kappa. Editor, Yale Law Journal, 1967-1968. Attorney: Cabinet Task Force on Oil Import Controls, 1969; Antitrust Division, Department of Justice, 1970-1972. Assistant Professor, Duke Law School and Institute of Policy Studies, 1972-1974. Assistant General Counsel for International and Special Programs, Federal Energy Administration, 1974-1977. Advisor, Polish Ministry of Finance, 1989-1991. Resident, Warsaw, Poland Office, 1991-1993. Director, Project on Economic Reform in Ukraine, 1990-1995. U.S. Representative to International Energy Agency Dispute Resolution Center, Paris, 1995—. Member, Wilson Council, Woodrow Wilson International Center, 1998—. Founding Director, Polish American Freedom Foundation, 1999—. *Member:* The District of Columbia Bar; Federal Energy and American (Member, Sections on: Administrative Law; International Law; Natural Resource Law) Bar Associations. (Also at Warsaw, Poland Office). ***PRACTICE AREAS:*** Project Finance; Energy Regulation; Mergers and Acquisitions; International Law. ***Email:*** jcbell@hhlaw.com

BARBARA BENNETT, born Columbia, South Carolina, June 18, 1952; admitted to bar, 1984, Louisiana (inactive); 1986, Tennessee; 1998, District of Columbia. *Education:* Vanderbilt University (B.S., magna cum laude, 1973; J.D., 1983). Order of the Coif. Articles Editor, Vanderbilt Law Review, 1982-1983. Law Clerk to the Honorable Thomas A. Wisemann, Jr., Judge, Federal District Court, Middle District of Tennessee, 1983-1984. General Counsel and Corporate Secretary, TriPoint Health Group, 1995-1997. Associate General Counsel, Vanderbilt University, 1986-1995. Private Practice, 1984-1986. Appointed to and served on the Tennessee Supreme Court Commission on Alternative Dispute Resolution and the Civil Justice Reform Act Advisory Committee for the U.S. District Court for the Middle District of Tennessee. *Member:* The District of Columbia Bar; American Bar Association; American Health Lawyers Association; National Association of College and University Attorneys. ***PRACTICE AREAS:*** Health Care; Internet; Commercial Transactions; Corporate; Higher Education. ***Email:*** bbennett@hhlaw.com

DOUGLAS L. BERESFORD, born Washington, D.C., June 1, 1956; admitted to bar, 1982, District of Columbia. *Education:* Harvard University (A.B., cum laude, 1978); Georgetown University (J.D., 1982). Editor, American Crimi-

(This Listing Continued)

nal Law Review, 1981-1982. *Member:* American and Energy Bar Associations. ***PRACTICE AREAS:*** Energy; Public Utility Law; Electric Cooperatives Law; Administrative Law; Appellate Practice. ***Email:*** dlberesford@hhlaw.com

LEE E. BERNER (Resident, McLean, Virginia Office).

LAURA BESVINICK (Resident, Miami, Florida Office).

PETER R. BISIO, born Plainfield, New Jersey, November 8, 1963; admitted to bar, 1992, Minnesota; 1993, New Jersey; 1998, District of Columbia. *Education:* New School for Social Research (B.A., 1984); Columbia University (J.D., 1992). James Kent Scholar; Harlan Fiske Stone Scholar. Editor, Columbia Law Review. *Member:* The District of Columbia Bar. ***PRACTICE AREAS:*** Litigation. ***Email:*** prbisio@hhlaw.com

LISA BONANNO, born Washington, D.C., February 2, 1958; admitted to bar, 1983, District of Columbia. *Education:* Georgetown University (B.S.F.S., summa cum laude, 1980); Yale University (J.D., 1983). Recipient, Thurman Arnold Award, 1983. Law Clerk, Hon. Richard L. Williams, U.S. District Judge, Eastern District of Virginia, 1983-1984. *Member:* The District of Columbia Bar (Member, Litigation Section); American Bar Association. ***LANGUAGES:*** Spanish and Italian. ***PRACTICE AREAS:*** Civil Litigation; Complex Litigation; Defense Litigation; Federal Civil Litigation; Federal Litigation. ***Email:*** lrbonanno@hhlaw.com

DAVID W. BONSER, born Dallas, Texas, April 30, 1962; admitted to bar, 1987, Texas; 1988, District of Columbia. *Education:* Duke University (B.S., cum laude, 1984); University of Texas (J.D., with honors, 1987). Order of the Coif. Chancellors. Associate Editor, Texas Law Review, 1986-1987. *Member:* The District of Columbia Bar; State Bar of Texas; American Bar Association (Member, Section of Corporation, Banking and Business Law); National Association of Real Estate Investment Trusts. ***PRACTICE AREAS:*** Corporate Law; Securities Law. ***Email:*** dwbonser@hhlaw.com

JOHN W. BORKOWSKI, born Nelsonville, Ohio, May 29, 1962; admitted to bar, 1988, District of Columbia; 1991, Louisiana; U.S. Court of Appeals, Fourth, Fifth, Eighth, Eleventh and District of Columbia Circuits; U.S. Supreme Court. *Education:* University of Notre Dame (B.A., summa cum laude, 1984); Northwestern University (J.D., cum laude, 1987). Phi Beta Kappa. Order of the Coif. Wigmore Scholar. Jessup International Law Moot Court Team. Articles Editor, Northwestern Law Review. Adjunct Professor, Law and Education, Loyola University School of Law, New Orleans. Law Clerk to Chief Judge Patricia Wald, U.S. Court of Appeals for the District of Columbia Circuit, 1987-1988. *Member:* Louisiana State Bar Association; The District of Columbia Bar. (Also practicing in New Orleans, Louisiana). ***LANGUAGES:*** French. ***PRACTICE AREAS:*** Education Law; Civil Litigation; Commercial Litigation; Appellate Litigation. ***Email:*** jwborkowski@hhlaw.com

DONNA A. BOSWELL, born Anna, Illinois, April 8, 1950; admitted to bar, 1989, Pennsylvania; 1990, Maryland; 1990, District of Columbia. *Education:* Wake Forest University (B.A., cum laude with honors in psychology, 1972; M.A., 1974); Pennsylvania State University (Ph.D., 1977); University of Pennsylvania (J.D., 1989). Executive Editor, University of Pennsylvania Law Review, 1988-1989. *Member:* Sigma Xi, The Scientific Research Society of North America; American Health Lawyers Association. ***PRACTICE AREAS:*** Health Law; Health Care Legislation; Medical Records Confidentiality; Health Care Reimbursement; Patients Rights. ***Email:*** daboswell@hhlaw.com

CHRISTINE BOUGIS (Resident, Paris, France Office).

WILLIAM J. BOWMAN, born Willard, Ohio, December 11, 1951; admitted to bar, 1976, District of Columbia; 1977, U.S. District Court for the District of Columbia; 1978, U.S. Court of Appeals for the District of Columbia Circuit; 1980, U.S. Supreme Court; 1985, U.S. District Court, District of Maryland; 1989, U.S. Court of Appeals, Fifth Circuit and U.S. District Court, Eastern District of Michigan. *Education:* Harvard College (A.B., cum laude, 1973); Georgetown University (J.D., 1976). Author: "Reapportionment— Legislation Consideration of Race," 63 Geo. L. J. 1321 (1975). Law Clerk, Hon. Thomas A. Flannery, U.S. District Court for the District of Columbia, 1976-1977. Assistant U.S. Attorney for the District of Columbia, 1977-1983. Chief, Career Criminal Unit, 1981-1983. Chief Counsel, U.S. Senate Committee on the Judiciary, Subcommittee on Juvenile Justice, 1983-1984. *Member:* The District of Columbia Bar; American Bar Association. ***PRACTICE AREAS:*** Litigation. ***Email:*** wjbowman@hhlaw.com

MARC H. BOZEMAN (Resident, Los Angeles, California Office).

ROBERT P. BRADY, born Omaha, Nebraska, April 3, 1947; admitted to bar, 1972, Maryland; 1980, District of Columbia. *Education:* University of Rochester (A.B., 1969); George Washington University (J.D., with honors, 1972). Law Clerk to the Honorable: Jerrold V. Powers, Maryland Court of Special Appeals, 1972-1973; James L. Wray, Fifth Judicial Circuit of Maryland, 1973-1974. Associate Chief Counsel, Bureau of Biologics, Associate Chief Counsel for Enforcement, 1976-1980. Associate Chief Counsel, Bureau of Foods, 1980-1981, Office of the Chief Counsel, United States Food and Drug Administration. Executive Assistant to the Commissioner of Food and Drugs, United States Food and Drug Administration, 1981-1983. FDA Award of Merit, 1982. Vice-President and General Counsel, Cosmetic, Toiletry and Fragrance

(This Listing Continued)

HOGAN & HARTSON L.L.P., Washington—Continued

Association, 1984-1986. Executive Vice President, Cosmetic, Toiletry and Fragrance Association, 1986-1988. Editorial Board, Food Drug Cosmetic Law Journal, 1988-1994. *Member:* The District of Columbia Bar. ***PRACTICE AREAS:*** Pharmaceutical; Biotechnology; Food Law. ***Email:*** rpbrady@hhlaw.com

DR. MAX BRAEUER (Resident, Berlin, Germany Office).

PATRICIA A. BRANNAN, born Milwaukee, Wisconsin, November 20, 1953; admitted to bar, 1980, District of Columbia; 1996, Maryland. *Education:* Marquette University (B.A., summa cum laude, 1975); Harvard University (J.D., cum laude, 1979). Phi Beta Kappa; Alpha Sigma Nu. Co-Author: "Adverse Impact on Educational Opportunity in Cases Challenging State School Financing Schemes," 65 West Educ. Law Reporter 279 (1991); "Critical Details: Amending the United States Constitution," 16 Harvard Journal on Legislation 763 (1979). Author: "The Implications of *Missouri v. Jenkins* for Municipal and School District Finance," 12 Municipal Finance Journal (1991). Clerk to Hon. John M. Ferren, District of Columbia Court of Appeals, 1979-1980. Member, Board of Editors, West's Education Law Reporter, 1989—. Member, District of Columbia Board on Professional Responsibility, 1994-2001 (Chair, 1998-2001). *Member:* The District of Columbia Bar; Maryland State Bar Association. ***PRACTICE AREAS:*** Education Law; Civil Rights; Federal Civil Practice. ***Email:*** pabrannan@hhlaw.com

DR. ECKHARD BREMER (Resident, Berlin, Germany Office).

REBECCA B. BRONSON, born Fort Worth, Texas, August 16, 1947; admitted to bar, 1980, Texas (Not admitted in District of Columbia). *Education:* Tulane University of Louisiana (B.A., 1969); University of Texas (M.A., 1977; J.D., 1980). *Member:* State Bar of Texas; American and International Bar Associations; National Association of Bond Lawyers. (Also at Moscow, Russia Office). ***PRACTICE AREAS:*** International Corporate and Financial Transactions; Project and Infrastructure Finance; Corporate Investments; Corporate Privatization Transactions. ***Email:*** rbbronson@hhlaw.com

STANLEY J. BROWN (Resident, McLean, Virginia Office).

ANDREA M. BRUCE, born Mount Vernon, New York, November 15, 1965; admitted to bar, 1993, California; 1995, District of Columbia. *Education:* Johns Hopkins University (B.A., 1987); University of California, Boalt Hall School of Law (J.D., 1992). Phi Beta Kappa. Order of the Coif. Judicial Clerk, U.S. District Court for the Western District of Tennessee, 1992-1993. *Member:* State Bar of California; The District of Columbia Bar. ***PRACTICE AREAS:*** Food, Drug and Cosmetic Law; Food and Agriculture; Food Labeling and Inspection; Advertising and Labeling. ***Email:*** ambruce@hhlaw.com

THOMAS N. BULLEIT, JR., born Washington, D.C., February 11, 1957; admitted to bar, 1987, Maryland; 1988, District of Columbia, U.S. District Court, District of Maryland and U.S. Claims Court; 1991, U.S. Supreme Court. *Education:* Yale University (A.B., cum laude, 1979); University of Michigan (J.D., 1985). Recipient, Louis Honigman Award. Author: "Public-Private Partnerships in Biomedical Research: Resolving Conflicts of Interest Arising Under the Federal Technology Transfer Act of 1986," 4. J.L. & Health 1, 1990. Co-Author: "Kickbacks, Courtesies or Cost Effectiveness?: Application of the Medicare Antikickback Law to the Marketing and Promotional Practices of Drug and Medical Device Manufacturers," 54 Food & Drug Law Journal 279, 1999; "Technology Transfer: Trends in the Federalization of Biomedical Research," 71 Academic Medicine 709, 1996; "Federal Oversight of the Commercialization of New Biomedical Technologies," 1996 Clark Boardman Health Law Handbook; "Pitfalls in Medicaid Reimbursement of Physical Therapy for Nursing Home Patients," Physical Therapy Today, Winter, 1990; "The Ethics in Patient Referrals Act of 1989," Resources, Spring, 1989; "Effects of Sibling Relationships on Preschoolers' Behavior at Home and at School," 21 Developmental Psychology 761, 1985. Editor, Symposium: "The Family, the State and the Law," 18 U. Mich. J.L. Ref. 799, 1985. Law Clerk, Honorable Bailey Brown, U.S. Court of Appeals, Sixth Circuit, 1985-1986. *Member:* The District of Columbia Bar (Council on Sections, 1994-1997; Chair, 1997-1998; Steering Committee Health Law Section, 1992-1998; Chair, 1994-1997); Maryland State and American Bar Associations; American Health Lawyers Association. ***PRACTICE AREAS:*** Health Care Corporate Law; Health Care Mergers and Acquisitions; Medicare Fraud and Abuse; Medical Technology; Medicare and Medicaid Reimbursement. ***Email:*** tnbulleit@hhlaw.com

DAVID W. BURGETT, born Lansing, Michigan, June 10, 1955; admitted to bar, 1981, District of Columbia; 1983, U.S. District Court of the District of Columbia, U.S. Court of Federal Claims, U.S. Supreme Court and U.S. Court of Appeals for the Federal and District of Columbia Circuits. *Education:* Université de Provence, Aix-en-Provence, France; University of Michigan (B.A., summa cum laude, 1977); Harvard University (J.D., cum laude, 1981); J.F. Kennedy School of Government, Harvard University (M.P.P., 1981). Phi Beta Kappa. Angell Scholar. Law Clerk to Hon. Theodore Newman, Jr., D.C. Court of Appeals. Author: "Substantive Due Process Limits on the Duration of Civil Commitment for the Treatment of Mental Illness," Harvard Civil Rights-Civil Liberties Law Review, Vol. 16, No. 1; "Government Rights in Software &

(This Listing Continued)

Technical Data," Briefing Papers No. 88-3 (Fed. Pubs. 1988); "Government Rights in Software & Technical Data-Update," 8 Briefing Papers Collection (Fed. Pubs. 1990); "ADP & Telecommunications Procurements: Recurring Issues," Briefing Papers No. 92-3 (Federal Pubs. 1992); "Protectionism and Internationalization in Defense Procurement," 40 FBA News & J. 448, 1993; "Domestic Preference Provisions," Briefing Papers No. 94-3 (Fed. Pubs. 1994); "Government Rights in Data and Software/Edition II," Briefing Papers No. 95-11 (Fed. Pubs. 1995), Briefing Papers No. (Fed. Pubs. 2000). *Member:* The District of Columbia Bar; Federal (Chair, Government Contract Section), American (Member, Public Contract Law Section; Chair, Pro Bono Committee) and International Bar Associations; Judicial Conference of the District of Columbia; Washington Council of Lawyers. ***LANGUAGES:*** German and French. ***PRACTICE AREAS:*** Government Contracts Law; Technology and Licensing Law; International Transactions. ***Email:*** dwburgett@hhlaw.com

CAROL W. BURTON (Resident, Denver, Colorado Office).

RAYMOND S. CALAMARO, born Cairo, Egypt, May 28, 1944; admitted to bar, 1970, New York; 1975, U.S. Supreme Court; 1976, District of Columbia. *Education:* Cornell University (A.B., 1966); New York University (J.D., 1969). Associate Editor, New York University Journal of International Law and Politics, 1968-1969. Legislative Director for U.S. Senator Gaylord Nelson, 1973-1975. Deputy Assistant U.S. Attorney General, 1977-1979. Clinton-Gore Transition Team Leader, 1992-1993. U.S. Vice-Chair, U.S.-Korea Committee on Business Cooperation, 1997-1999. *Member:* The District of Columbia Bar. ***PRACTICE AREAS:*** International Trade Law; Legislative and Regulatory Law. ***Email:*** rscalamaro@hhlaw.com

ALAN F. CARIDDI (Resident, Paris, France).

GEORGE U. CARNEAL, born New York, N.Y., May 31, 1935; admitted to bar, 1961, Virginia; 1962, District of Columbia. *Education:* Princeton University (A.B., 1957); University of Virginia (LL.B., 1961). Order of the Coif; Phi Alpha Delta. Member, Raven Society. Member, Editorial Board, 1959-1960 and Decisions Editor, 1960-1961, Virginia Law Review. Lecturer, Georgetown Law Center, 1965-1968. Law Clerk to Judge E. Barrett Prettyman, U.S. Court of Appeals, D.C. Circuit, 1961-1962. Special Assistant, Secretary of Transportation, 1969-1970. General Counsel, Federal Aviation Administration, 1970-1972. *Member:* Virginia State Bar; The District of Columbia Bar (Chairman, Trustees of D.C. Bar Clients' Security Fund, 1973-1978); Federal and American (Member, Standing Committee on Aeronautical Law, 1971-1979, 1982-1983; Chairman, Aviation Advisory Committee, 1980-1982) Bar Associations. ***PRACTICE AREAS:*** Aviation Law; Transportation Law; Trade Association Law; Foreign Governments. ***Email:*** gucarneal@hhlaw.com

ROBERT B. CAVE, born Washington, D.C., October 2, 1948; admitted to bar, 1977, Virginia; 1979, District of Columbia; 1984, U.S. Supreme Court. *Education:* University of Virginia (B.A., with distinction, 1970; J.D., 1977). Managing Editor, Virginia Law Review, 1976-1977. Law Clerk to Hon. William B. Jones, U.S. District Court for the District of Columbia, 1977-1978. *Member:* The District of Columbia Bar; Virginia State Bar. [Capt., Naval Flight Officer, USMC, 1970-1974]. ***PRACTICE AREAS:*** Litigation. ***Email:*** rbcave@hhlaw.com

MICHAEL L. CHEROUTES (Not admitted in District of Columbia; Resident, Denver, Colorado Office).

ALPHONSO A. CHRISTIAN, II, born St. Thomas, Virgin Islands, November 26, 1945; admitted to bar, 1968, New York; 1969, Virgin Islands and U.S. Court of Military Appeals; 1970, District of Columbia; 1976, U.S. Supreme Court. *Education:* University of Notre Dame (B.A., cum laude, 1965); Harvard University (J.D., 1968). *Member:* The District of Columbia Bar; American Bar Association; Washington Bar Association; National Bar Association. ***PRACTICE AREAS:*** Corporate Law; Administrative Law. ***Email:*** aachristian@hhlaw.com

CLAUDETTE M. CHRISTIAN, born St. Thomas, U.S. Virgin Islands, June 1, 1954; admitted to bar, 1980, District of Columbia. *Education:* University of Pennsylvania (B.A., magna cum laude, 1976); Harvard Law School (J.D., 1979). Phi Beta Kappa. Counsel, Export-Import Bank of The United States, 1979-1984. *Member:* The District of Columbia Bar; American Bar Association. ***PRACTICE AREAS:*** Project Finance; International Commercial Transactions. ***Email:*** cmchristian@hhlaw.com

JACQUELINE P. CLEARY, born Groton, Massachusetts, September 17, 1963; admitted to bar, 1991, Pennsylvania; 1993, District of Columbia. *Education:* Oberlin College (B.A., 1984); Catholic University of America (J.D., 1991). *Member:* The District of Columbia Bar. ***Email:*** jpcleary@hhlaw.com

NANCY ANDREAS CLODFELTER (Resident, Denver, Colorado Office).

TY COBB, born Great Bend, Kansas, August 25, 1950; admitted to bar, 1979, District of Columbia; 1980, U.S. Court of International Trade; 1986, U.S. Supreme Court; 1987, Maryland. *Education:* Harvard University (A.B., 1972); Georgetown University (J.D., 1978). Author: "Responding Strategically to a Criminal Investigation in the United States-An Antitrust Model," International Bar Association, distributed by Section on Business Law (2000); "Criminal

(This Listing Continued)

Liability for Export Sales Transactions," 1991 ABA Complex Crimes Journal; "Criminal Enforcement of Environmental Statutes: Strict Criminal Liability for Reporting Violations," 1989 ABA Complex Crimes Journal. Co-author: "Congress Moves Promptly In Response to McNally," 1989 ABA Complex Crimes Journal. Law Clerk, The Honorable Herbert F. Murray, United States District Court for the District of Maryland, 1978-1979. Press Secretary, U.S. Representative Larry Winn (R-Kansas), 1974. Legislative Assistant, U.S. Representative Larry Pressler (R-S.D.), 1975. Assistant U.S. Attorney, 1981-1986. Chief of Criminal Cases, Office of the United States Attorney for the District of Maryland, 1984-1986. Mid-Atlantic Regional Coordinator, President's Organized Crime and Drug Enforcement Task Force, 1985-1986. Special Trial Counsel, Office of Independent Counsel (HUD), 1994-1995. *Member:* American College of Trial Lawyers; Fourth Circuit Judicial Conference; Colorado, Maryland State, American (Member, Sections on: Litigation; Criminal Justice; Judicial Administration Division) and International Bar Associations; District of Columbia Bar. (Also at Denver, Colorado Office). ***PRACTICE AREAS:*** White Collar Criminal Defense; Congressional Investigations; Complex Litigation. ***Email:*** tcobb@hhlaw.com

VINCENT H. COHEN, born Brooklyn, New York, April 7, 1936; admitted to bar, 1960, New York; 1966, U.S. Supreme Court; 1967, Ohio; 1968, District of Columbia. *Education:* Syracuse University (A.B., cum laude, 1957); Syracuse University College of Law (LL.B., cum laude, 1960). Order of the Coif (Honorary Member). Member, Justinian Law Society. Recent Decisions Editor, 1958-1959 and Associate Editor, 1959-1960, Syracuse Law Review. Trial Attorney, Consolidated Edison Company of New York, Inc., 1960-1962. Trial Attorney, U.S. Department of Justice, 1962-1967. Corporate Attorney, Ohio Bell Telephone Company, 1967. *Member:* The District of Columbia Bar; New York State, American and National Bar Associations; American College of Trial Lawyers. ***PRACTICE AREAS:*** Litigation. ***Email:*** vhcohen@hhlaw.com

MICHAEL D. COLGLAZIER (Resident, Baltimore, Maryland Office).

JOSEPH G. CONNOLLY, JR., born Queens, New York, January 3, 1949; admitted to bar, 1974, New York; 1981, District of Columbia. *Education:* Manhattan College (B.A., cum laude, 1970); Georgetown University (J.D., 1973). Epsilon Sigma Phi; Phi Alpha Theta. Editorial Assistant, The Tax Lawyer, 1972-1973. Adjunct Professor, Washington School of Law of the American University, 1982—Attorney, U.S. Securities and Exchange Commission, 1973-1986 (Chief, Office of Tender Offers, 1980-1986). *Member:* The District of Columbia Bar; New York State Bar Association. ***PRACTICE AREAS:*** Corporate Law; Securities. ***Email:*** jgconnolly@hhlaw.com

JONATHAN A. CONSTINE, born Richmond, Virginia, January 25, 1961; admitted to bar, 1986, Virginia; 1988, District of Columbia. *Education:* Harvard University (A.B., 1983); University of Virginia (J.D., 1986). Order of the Coif. Quarter Finalist, Lile Moot Court Competition. Law Clerk to Hon. Robert G. Doumar, U.S. District Court for the Eastern District of Virginia, 1986-1987. *Member:* The District of Columbia Bar; Virginia State Bar. ***PRACTICE AREAS:*** Civil Litigation; Insurance Litigation; Commercial Insurance. ***Email:*** jaconstine@hhlaw.com

JOHN W. COOK (Resident, Colorado Springs, Colorado Office).

ROBERT L. CORN-REVERE, born Mattoon, Illinois, October 15, 1954; admitted to bar, 1983, District of Columbia. *Education:* Eastern Illinois University (B.A., 1977); University of Massachusetts (M.A., 1980); Catholic University (J.D., 1983). Recipient, American Jurisprudence Award, Constitutional Law, 1981. Lead Articles Editor, Catholic University Law Review, 1983. Adjunct Faculty, Catholic University School of Law, 1987-1990; 1992-2001. Legal Advisor, FCC Commissioner James H. Quello, 1990-1994. Chief Counsel to Interim Chairman Quello, 1993. *Member:* The District of Columbia Bar; Federal Communications Bar Association. ***PRACTICE AREAS:*** First Amendment Law; Internet Law; Communications Law. ***Email:*** cornrevere@hhlaw.com

MARYANNE COURTNEY, born Brooklyn, New York, September 25, 1963; admitted to bar, 1988, District of Columbia and New Jersey. *Education:* The Johns Hopkins University (B.A., 1985); State University of New York at Buffalo (J.D., cum laude, 1988). *Member:* The District of Columbia Bar. ***PRACTICE AREAS:*** Commercial Law; International; Project Finance. ***Email:*** mcourtney@hhlaw.com

MICHELE C. COYLE (Resident, Los Angeles, California Office).

COLIN W. CRAIK (Prague, Czech Republic and London, England Offices).

CELINE JIMENEZ CROWSON, born Washington, D.C., May 4, 1965; admitted to bar, 1990, Maryland; 1991, U.S. Court of Appeals, Third Circuit, U.S. Court of Appeals, Second Circuit and U.S. Court of Appeals for the Federal Circuit; 1992, District of Columbia; 1994, U.S. Supreme Court; registered to practice before U.S. Patent and Trademark Office. *Education:* Duke University (B.S.E.E., cum laude, 1987); Georgetown University (J.D., 1990). Eta Kappa Nu Honor Society. Lecturer: "Patent and Licensing Issues: Law of the Internet Conference," Washington, D.C., 1995 and 1998; "Internet Litigation Issues," American Intellectual Property Law Association Conference, 1998. Co-Author:

(This Listing Continued)

Internet and the Law: Legal Fundamentals for the Internet User, 1996; "Whose Mind is it Anyway? Intellectual Property is a Key to Corporate Success," Washington Business Forward, 1999. *Member:* District of Columbia Bar; American Bar Association (Member, Patent, Trademark and Copyright and Litigation Section); Federal Circuit Bar Association; American Intellectual Property Law Association; International Trademark Association (INTA); Institute of Electrical and Electronics Engineers (IEEE). ***PRACTICE AREAS:*** Intellectual Property. ***Email:*** cjcrowson@hhlaw.com

DANIEL M. DAVIDSON, born Lynbrook, New York, July 9, 1950; admitted to bar, 1975, District of Columbia; 1977, California; 1979, U.S. Tax Court; 1992, U.S. Supreme Court. *Education:* Williams College (B.A., summa cum laude, 1972); Harvard University (J.D., magna cum laude, 1975). Phi Beta Kappa. Expert Advisor, U.S. Competitiveness Policy Council. Law Clerk to Hon. Robert Braucher, Massachusetts Supreme Judicial Court, 1975-1976. *Member:* The District of Columbia Bar (Member, Sections on: Tax; Business Law); State Bar of California; American Bar Association (Member, Sections on: Taxation; Business Law). ***PRACTICE AREAS:*** Taxation Law; Business Law. ***Email:*** dmdavidson@hhlaw.com

W. SIDNEY DAVIS, JR. (Resident at 100 Park Avenue, New York, New York Office).

MARGARET A. DE LISSER, born Kingston, Jamaica, West Indies, 1961; admitted to bar, 1988, Pennsylvania; 1992, California; 2000, District of Columbia. *Education:* University of Pennsylvania (B.A., 1984; J.D.,1988). ***PRACTICE AREAS:*** Executive Compensation; Equity Incentives; Employee Benefits. ***Email:*** mdelisser@hhlaw.com

EDWARD S. DESMARAIS, JR., born Worcester, Massachusetts, February 11, 1964; admitted to bar, 1989, Florida; 1991, District of Columbia. *Education:* University of Florida (B.A., 1985; J.D., with high honors, 1988). Order of the Coif; Phi Beta Kappa; Phi Kappa Phi. Member, University of Florida Law Review. Fellowship Instructor, Legal Research and Writing, University of Florida College of Law, 1987-1988. *Member:* The District of Columbia Bar; The Florida Bar; American Bar Association. ***PRACTICE AREAS:*** Federal Estate and Gift Taxation; Fiduciary Income Tax; Generation Skipping Tax; Trusts and Estates Taxation. ***Email:*** esdesnarais@hhlaw.com

SARA-ANN DETERMAN, born Palmerton, Pennsylvania, August 17, 1938; admitted to bar, 1968, District of Columbia. *Education:* Connecticut College, Stanford University and University of Delaware (A.B., with Honors and Distinction, 1960); George Washington Law School (LL.B., with Honors, 1967). Phi Beta Kappa; Order of the Coif. Editor-in-Chief, George Washington Law Review, 1966-1967. Law Clerk to Senior Circuit Judge Henry W. Edgerton, U.S. Court of Appeals for the District of Columbia, 1967-1968. Co-Chair, Washington Lawyers Committee for Civil Rights and Urban Affairs, 1995-1997. *Member:* The District of Columbia Bar (President, 1990-1991); Bar Association of the District of Columbia; American Bar Association (Chair, Committee on Delivery of Legal Services, 1992-1994; Chair, Section of Individual Rights and Responsibilities, 1986-1987; Assembly Delegate, 1991-1994); Women's Bar Association of District of Columbia. ***PRACTICE AREAS:*** Wills; Trusts and Estates; Estate and Gift Taxation; Non-profit and Charitable Organizations; Estate Planning. ***Email:*** sdeterman@hhlaw.com

JOHN F. DIENELT, born Alexandria, Virginia, November 24, 1943; admitted to bar, 1970, District of Columbia; 1983, New York. *Education:* University of Virginia (B.A., 1965); Fletcher School of Law & Diplomacy (M.A., 1966); Yale University (LL.B., 1969). Phi Beta Kappa. Order of the Coif. Managing Editor, Yale Law Journal, 1968-1969. Law Clerk, Hon. G.A. Gesell, U.S. District Court for the District of Columbia, 1969-1970. Assistant to the Solicitor General, U.S. Department of Justice, 1970-1972. *Member:* The District of Columbia Bar; American Bar Association Forum on Franchising (Chair, 1999-2001; Governing Committee, 1996-1999). ***PRACTICE AREAS:*** Complex Commercial Litigation; Class Actions; Franchise and Distribution Litigation; Antitrust; Trade Regulation Litigation; Trademark; Unfair Competition Litigation; Arbitration; Mediation. ***Email:*** jfdienelt@hhlaw.com

EDWARD C. DOLAN, born New York, N.Y., September 25, 1953; admitted to bar, 1978, Maryland; 1979, District of Columbia; 1980, U.S. District Court, District of Maryland and U.S. District Court for the District of Columbia; 1983, U.S. Supreme Court; 1995, U.S. Court of Appeals, Fourth Circuit; 1997, U.S. District Court, District of Colorado. *Education:* Columbia University (B.A., 1975); Georgetown University (J.D., 1978). Phi Alpha Delta. Author: "Treating Environmental Claims in Bankruptcy," The Maryland Bar Journal, Volume XXVII, Number 5, Sept./Oct. 1994. Co-Author: "Commercial Claims," Practice Manual for the Maryland Lawyer, Maryland State Bar Association, Inc., 1981. Contributing Author: *The Law of Distressed Real Estate,* Clark Boardman & Company, 1988; *Environmental Aspects of Real Estate Transactions*, American Bar Association, 1995. Member, Standing Committee on Local Rules of the U.S. Bankruptcy Court for the District of Maryland (Chair, 1996—). Vice President, 1988-1989, President, 1989-1990, Bankruptcy Bar Association for the District of Maryland, Inc. *Member:* The District of Columbia Bar (Chair, Business Bankruptcy Committee, 1995—); Prince George's County (Member and Chairman, 1981-1983, Bankruptcy Committee; Member,

(This Listing Continued)

HOGAN & HARTSON L.L.P., Washington—Continued

Ethics Committee, 1982-1983; Member and Vice Chairman, Federal Court Liaison Committee, 1986-1987; Member, Co-Operative Guidance Program in Bankruptcy; Member, Special Committee on Professionalism, 1988-1992), Montgomery County (Member, Bankruptcy Section, Ethics Committee), Maryland State (Member, Corporations, Banking and Business Section) and American (Member, Corporation, Banking and Business Law Section) Bar Associations. Walter Chandler Bankruptcy Inn of Court (Master). ***PRACTICE AREAS:*** Bankruptcy; Commercial Law; Finance; Real Estate. ***Email:*** ecdolan@hhlaw.com

AGNES PEK DOVER, born Cleveland, Ohio, December 27, 1953; admitted to bar, 1981, District of Columbia; 1988, Arizona. *Education:* Baldwin-Wallace College (B.A., magna cum laude, 1976); Catholic University of America (J.D., 1981). Member, Catholic University Law Review, 1980-1981. *Member:* The District of Columbia Bar; State Bar of Arizona (Inactive). ***PRACTICE AREAS:*** Government Contracts; Energy; Intellectual Property. ***Email:*** apdover@hhlaw.com

EDWARD C. DUCKERS, born Salina, Kansas, November 18, 1957; admitted to bar, 1985, District of Columbia. *Education:* University of Kansas (B.S., 1981); Georgetown University (J.D., 1985). Editor, Georgetown Law Journal, 1983-1985. Legislative Assistant, Office of Senator Robert J. Dole, 1981-1985. *Member:* The District of Columbia Bar. ***PRACTICE AREAS:*** Antitrust Law; Litigation. ***Email:*** ecduckers@hhlaw.com

ROBERT B. DUNCAN, born Ithaca, New York, February 8, 1956; admitted to bar, 1987, Virginia; 1988, District of Columbia. *Education:* University of Pennsylvania (B.A., 1977); Catholic University of America (M.A., 1984); University of Virginia (J.D., 1987). Head of Community Services Department. *Member:* Virginia State Bar; The District of Columbia Bar. (Also at McLean, Virginia Office). ***PRACTICE AREAS:*** Commercial Litigation; Intellectual Property Litigation; Technology Litigation; Employment Litigation; Real Estate Litigation. ***Email:*** rbduncan@hhlaw.com

DAVID DUNN (Resident at 100 Park Avenue, New York, New York Office).

ISABEL P. DUNST, born New York, February 21, 1947; admitted to bar, 1971, New York; 1973, District of Columbia. *Education:* University of Wisconsin (B.S., with honors, 1967); New York University (J.D., cum laude, 1971); Harvard School of Public Health (M.P.H., 1979). Member, New York University Law Review, 1970-1971. Attorney, 1971-1979, Associate General Counsel, 1977-1987 and Deputy General Counsel, 1987-1990, Department of Health and Human Services. *Member:* The District of Columbia Bar; American Bar Association (Member: Section on Administrative Law; Forum Committee on Health Law); American Health Lawyers Association; Women's Bar Association. ***PRACTICE AREAS:*** Medicare and Medicaid; Health Care; Regulatory Law; Government. ***Email:*** ipdunst@hhlaw.com

ALAN L. DYE, born Augusta, Georgia, November 21, 1953; admitted to bar, 1978, Georgia; 1980, New York; 1984, District of Columbia. *Education:* Emory University (B.A., with high honors, 1975); University of Georgia (J.D., magna cum laude, 1978). Omicron Delta Kappa; Phi Kappa Phi. Order of the Coif. Editor-in-Chief, Georgia Law Review, 1977-1978. Author: "Scienter and Injunctive Relief Under Rule 10b-5," 11 Georgia Law Review 879, 1977. Co-Author: "Section 16 Treatise and Reporting Guide," Executive Press, Inc., 1994; "Section 16 Forms and Filings Handbook," Executive Press, Inc., 2000; "Comprehensive Section 16 Outline," (Executive Press, Inc. 2000); "Section 16 Reporting Guide," Executive Press, Inc., 1989; "The SEC's New Insider Trading Rules," 34 Rev. Sec. and Commodities Reg. 1, 2001; Developments Under Section 16, 33 Rev. Sec. and Commodities Reg.155, (Part I) and 171, (Part II), 2000; Managing the Risk of Section 16 Liability, 4 The M&A Lawyer 1, Dec. 2000; "The New Section 16 Regulatory Scheme," 24 Rev. Sec. & Commodities Reg. 105, 1991; "The New Reporting System," 5 Insights 3, 1991; "Reforming Section 16," 22 Rev. Sec. & Commodities Reg. 23, 1989; "Recent Decision, Connally v. State," 11 Georgia Law Review 200, 1976. Member, Editorial Advisory Board, Executive Compensation, The Service, Prentice Hall Law & Business. Member, Advisory Board, National Association of Stock Plan Professionals. Chairman/Co-Chairman, Securities, Commodities and Exchanges Committee of ABA Section of Administrative Law, 1995—. Adjunct Professor, Georgetown University Law Center, 1991-1996. Special Counsel to Chairman, U.S. Securities and Exchange Commission, 1984-1986. Attorney, SEC Division of Corporation Finance, 1982-1984. Clerk, Hon. Ellsworth A. Van Graafeiland, U.S. Court of Appeals, 2nd Circuit, 1978-1979. *Member:* The District of Columbia Bar; State Bar of Georgia; New York State and American Bar Associations. ***PRACTICE AREAS:*** Corporate Law; Securities. ***Email:*** aldye@hhlaw.com

STEVEN M. EDWARDS (Resident at 100 Park Avenue, New York, New York Office).

BIJAN-EMMANUEL EGHBAL (Resident, Paris France Office).

CLAUD v. S. ELEY, born Lexington, Virginia, May 31, 1957; admitted to bar, 1982, Virginia; 1995, Brussels; 2001, District of Columbia. *Education:* College of William & Mary (B.A., 1979); Emory University (J.D., 1982). (Also at Brussels, Belgium Office). ***PRACTICE AREAS:*** Commercial Law; Contracts; Corporate Law; International Corporate Law; International Law; Joint Ventures; Mergers, Acquisitions and Divestitures; International Mergers and Acquisitions. ***Email:*** cveley@hhlaw.com

E. TAZEWELL ELLETT, born Richmond, Virginia, June 9, 1952; admitted to bar, 1977, Virginia; 1978, District of Columbia. *Education:* Davidson College (B.A., 1974); University of Virginia (J.D., 1977). Member, Editorial Board, Virginia Law Review, 1976-1977. Author: "The National Air Transportation System: Design by City Hall?" 53 J. Air L. & Commerce, 1987; Case Comment, "United States v. Mazzei: Hobbs Act Extortion Under Color of Official Right," 62 Va. L. Rev. 439, 1976. Special Assistant to Member Donald D. Engen, National Transportation Safety Board, 1982-1984. Special Counsel to the Administrator, Federal Aviation Administration, 1984. Chief Counsel, Federal Aviation Administration, 1985-1988. *Member:* The District of Columbia Bar (Member, Sections of: Administrative Law; International Law); Virginia State Bar (Member, Sections of: Business Law; International Law); Virginia (Member, Business Law Section, 1981—; Member, Young Lawyers Section Membership Committee, 1982-1988; Chairman, Young Lawyers Section Membership Committee, 1984; Member, Young Lawyers Section Executive Committee, 1985-1988; Member, Transportation Law Section, 1993—; Chairman, Transportation Law Section, 1993-1995; Member, Executive Committee, 2000—), Federal (Member, D.C. Chapter Agency Representative for the Private Bar, 1980-1982; Member, Air and Space Law Committee, 1983—; Advisory Board of Transportation Law Section, 1987; Chairman, Steering Committee of Transportation Law Section, 1988-1990; Vice Chairman, Transportation Law Section, 1991-1992; Chairman, Transportation Law Section, 1992-1993), American (Member: Aviation Law Committee of Tort and Insurance Law Section, 1986—; Forum Committee on Air and Space Law, 1983—; Annual Law Forum Program Committee, 1986-1989; Sections of: International Law; Corporate, Business and Banking; Administrative Law) and International Bar Associations; Lawyer-Pilots Bar Association; National Transportation Safety Board Bar Association (Member, Board of Directors, 1983). ***PRACTICE AREAS:*** Aeronautical Regulation; Aerospace Law; Airline Regulation; Airport Law; Airport Privatization; Aviation Accidents; Aviation Law; Aviation Regulation; Business Aviation Regulation; Federal Aviation Licenses; International Aviation Law. ***Email:*** etellett@hhlaw.com

KEVIN D. EVANS (Resident, Denver, Colorado Office).

FRANK J. FAHRENKOPF, JR., born Brooklyn, New York, August 28, 1939; admitted to bar, 1965, Nevada; 1983, U.S. Supreme Court; 1984, District of Columbia and U.S. Court of Appeals for the District of Columbia Circuit. *Education:* University of Nevada (B.A., 1962); Boalt Hall School of Law, University of California (J.D., 1965). Member, Boalt Hall Moot Court Board, 1964-1965. Author: "The Value and Use of Motions in Limine," Nevada State Bar Journal, January, 1967; "The Trap for the Unwary or Article 9 of the Nevada Commercial Code," Nevada State Bar Journal, July, 1968; April, 1969; August, 1970; "Will Self-Help Help You," Nevada State Bar Journal, January, 1974. Criminal Law Instructor, University of Nevada, 1967-1982. Member of the Board of Trustees, 1994-2000; and Chairman of the Council, 1989-1994, For the Future of the National Judicial College. Panelist-Reporter, Citizens Conference on Nevada Courts, 1968. Chairman, Board of Directors, Nevada Cancer Society, 1978-1983. Vice President, Barristers Club of Nevada, 1969-1975. Member, Nevada State Board of Bar Examiners, 1971-1985. Reno Municipal Judge Pro tem, 1973-1982. Member, Panel of Arbitrators, American Arbitration Association, 1997-1998;. Member, Administrative Conference of the United States, 1986-1990. *Member:* Washoe County (President, 1973-1974) and American (Chairman, Gaming Law Committee, 1983-1984; Member, Governing Council, General Practice Section, 1986-1990) Bar Associations; The District of Columbia Bar; State Bar of Nevada; Nevada Trial Lawyers Association (Chairman, Commercial Law Committee, 1980-1982); Northern Nevada Trial Lawyers Association (Vice President, 1969); American Judicature Society; Commercial Law League of America; National Association of Gaming Attorneys (Founding Trustee and President, 1982-1983). ***PRACTICE AREAS:*** International Law; Legislative Law; Corporate Law. ***Email:*** fjfahrenkopf@hhlaw.com

MICHELE C. FARQUHAR, born De Ridder, Louisiana, May 29, 1957; admitted to bar, 1984, California; 1985, District of Columbia. *Education:* Duke University (B.A., magna cum laude, 1979); University of Virginia (J.D., 1984). Past President, Duke University Alumni Association, 1997-1998. Member, Board of Trustees, Duke University, 1997-1999. *Member:* State Bar of California; The District of Columbia Bar; American Bar Association; Federal Communications Bar Association (Member, Executive Committee; Chair, FCBA Foundation, 1996-1997). ***PRACTICE AREAS:*** Communications. ***Email:*** mcfarquhar@hhlaw.com

PRENTISS E. FEAGLES, born Somerville, New Jersey, April 10, 1951; admitted to bar, 1976, Ohio; 1980, District of Columbia. *Education:* Cornell University (B.A., with distinction, 1973); Duke University (J.D., with distinction, 1976). Order of the Coif. Member, Editorial Board, Duke Law Journal, 1974-1976. Assistant to the General Counsel, Department of the Army, 1976-

(This Listing Continued)

1980. *Member:* The District of Columbia Bar; American Bar Association (Member, Section on Taxation). [Capt., JAGC, U.S. Army, 1976-1980]. ***PRACTICE AREAS:*** Taxation Law; Real Estate Investment Trusts; Partnership Taxation; Corporate Taxation. ***Email:*** pefeagles@hhlaw.com

IRA M FEINBERG (Resident at 100 Park Avenue, New York, New York Office).

DOUGLAS A. FELLMAN, born New York, N.Y., June 19, 1962; admitted to bar, 1987, Virginia; 1988, District of Columbia and Maryland. *Education:* Johns Hopkins University (B.A., 1984); Cornell University (J.D., 1987). Phi Beta Kappa. Note and Comment Editor, Cornell International Law Journal, 1986-1987. Recipient: Alexander K. Barton Cup; Royal Society of Arts Silver Medal; John J. Kelly Prize. Law Clerk to Hon. James A. Belson, District of Columbia Court of Appeals. *Member:* The District of Columbia Bar; Bar Association of the District of Columbia; Virginia State Bar; Maryland State and Virginia Bar Associations. ***PRACTICE AREAS:*** Complex Civil Litigation; White Collar Criminal Defense; Professional Liability; Attorney Malpractice. ***Email:*** dafellman@hhlaw.com

MIRIAM L. FISHER, born Baltimore, Maryland, June 25, 1960; admitted to bar, 1985, Maryland; 1992, District of Columbia. *Education:* Loyola College (B.A., summa cum laude, 1982); University of Maryland (J.D., with honors, 1985). Special Assistant to Assistant Attorney General, Tax Division, U.S. Department of Justice, 1989-1991. *Member:* District of Columbia Bar (Member, Steering Committee, Tax Section; Former Chair, Tax Audits and Litigation); American Bar Association (Member, Tax Section; Vice-Chair Elect, Civil and Criminal Penalties). ***PRACTICE AREAS:*** Tax Controversies; Tax Litigation; Tax Fraud. ***Email:*** mfisher@hhlaw.com

ARI Q. FITZGERALD, born South Hill, Virginia, December 13, 1962; admitted to bar, 1991, Connecticut; 1992, New York; 1994, District of Columbia. *Education:* Harvard College (A.B., Social Studies, cum laude, 1984); Yale Law School (J.D., 1990). *Member:* Federal Communications Bar Association. ***PRACTICE AREAS:*** Communications Law; Project Finance.

HOWARD I. FLACK, born Syracuse, N.Y., April 1, 1951; admitted to bar, 1977, New York; 1980, District of Columbia. *Education:* Rutgers University (A.B., 1973); University of Warwick, England; New York Law School (J.D., cum laude, 1976). *Member:* The District of Columbia Bar; American Bar Association. ***PRACTICE AREAS:*** Mergers, Acquisitions and Divestitures; Business Law; Corporate Law; Securities; Financial Institutions; Health Care. ***Email:*** hiflack@hhlaw.com

WILLIAM P. FLANAGAN (Resident, McLean, Virginia Office).

DAVID M. FOX, born East Northport, New York, July 17, 1964; admitted to bar, 1990, New York; 1992, California (Not admitted in District of Columbia). *Education:* College of William and Mary (B.A., 1985) Phi Beta Kappa; New York University (J.D., 1989). Recipient, New York State Bar Association Award in Legal Ethics, 1989. Member, 1987-1988 and Articles Editor, 1988-1989, New York University Law Review. Assistant Chief Counsel for Enforcement, U.S. Food and Drug Administration, 1994-1995; Associate Chief Counsel for Drugs, U.S. Food and Drug Administration, 1995-2000. ***PRACTICE AREAS:*** Food and Drug Law. ***Email:*** dmfox@hhlaw.com

JONATHAN S. FRANKLIN, born Washington, D.C., May 4, 1964; admitted to bar, 1990, Pennsylvania; 1991, District of Columbia. *Education:* Harvard College (A.B., 1986); Yale Law School (J.D., 1990). *Member:* The District of Columbia Bar. Barrister Member, Edward Coke American Inn of Court. Barrister Member, Edward Coke American Appellate Inn of Court. ***PRACTICE AREAS:*** Litigation; U.S. Supreme Court Litigation; Appellate Practice. ***Email:*** jsfranklin@hhlaw.com

AMY BOWERMAN FREED (Resident, Baltimore, Maryland Office).

SEAN R. GALLAGHER (Resident, Denver, Colorado Office).

ALEKSANDER GALOS (Resident, Warsaw, Poland Office).

JOHN M. GARDNER (Resident, Denver, Colorado Office).

MARK D. GATELY (Resident, Baltimore, Maryland Office).

JAMES A. GEDE, JR. (Resident, Baltimore, Maryland Office).

JEFFREY S. GEORGE (Resident, Colorado Springs, Colorado Office).

JAY E. GERBER (Resident at 100 Park Avenue, New York, New York Office).

JAMES R. GHISELLI (Resident, Boulder, Colorado Office).

GERALD E. GILBERT (Resident, McLean, Virginia Office).

BRUCE W. GILCHRIST, born Bangor, Maine, August 8, 1951; admitted to bar, 1981, District of Columbia; 1999, New York. *Education:* Columbia University (B.A., cum laude, 1972; M.A., 1974; J.D., 1980). James Kent Scholar; Harlan Fiske Stone Scholar. Notes and Comments Editor, Columbia Law Review, 1979-1980. Law Clerk to Hon. Morris Pashman, Supreme Court of New Jersey, 1980-1981. *Member:* The District of Columbia Bar; New York State and American (Member, Section of Business Law) Bar Associations.

(This Listing Continued)

PRACTICE AREAS: Corporate Finance; Securities Offerings; Mergers and Acquisitions; Real Estate Investment Trusts; Bankruptcy Reorganization. ***Email:*** bwgilchrist@hhlaw.com

GARDNER F. GILLESPIE, born Pittsburgh, Pennsylvania, July 16, 1945; admitted to bar, 1973, Virginia; 1975, District of Columbia. *Education:* Williams College (B.A., cum laude, 1967); University of Virginia (J.D., 1973). Order of the Coif. Executive Editor, Virginia Law Review, 1972-1973. Law Clerk to Judge John Minor Wisdom, U.S. Court of Appeals for the 5th Circuit, 1973-1974. Visiting Lecturer, Communications Law, University of Virginia Law School, 1980-1983. Lecturer, Communications Law, Washington College of Law, American University, 1985. *Member:* The District of Columbia Bar; Virginia and American Bar Associations. ***PRACTICE AREAS:*** Communications and Media; Cable TV; Cable Franchising; Telecommunications Law; Civil Litigation. ***Email:*** gfgillespie@hhlaw.com

C. MICHAEL GILLILAND, born Albertville, Alabama, February 8, 1952; admitted to bar, 1980, Alabama; 1990, District of Columbia. *Education:* University of Alabama (B.S., 1976); Cumberland School of Law of Samford University (J.D., cum laude, 1980); Georgetown University (M.L.T., 1983). Member, Order of Barristers. Member, International Moot Court Team, 1980. Legislative Director, Office of U.S. Senator Howell Heflin, 1981-1986. Staff Attorney, U.S. Senate Subcommittee on Courts, 1980-1981. Tax and Legislative Counsel, American Insurance Association, 1986-1987. *Member:* Alabama State Bar; The District of Columbia Bar; American Bar Association (Member, Taxation Section). ***PRACTICE AREAS:*** Election Campaign and Political Law; Lobbying; Government Relations; Legislative Practice; Public Policy. ***Email:*** cmgilliland@hhlaw.com

J. WARREN GORRELL, JR., born Lexington, Kentucky, February 7, 1954; admitted to bar, 1979, District of Columbia; 1995, New York. *Education:* Princeton University (A.B., magna cum laude, 1976); University of Virginia (J.D., 1979). *Member:* The District of Columbia Bar; New York State Bar Association. (Also at Third Avenue New York, N.Y. Office). ***PRACTICE AREAS:*** Corporate Finance; Securities Offerings; Mergers and Acquisitions; Real Estate Investment Trusts. ***Email:*** jwgorrell@hhlaw.com

KEVIN G. GRALLEY (Resident, Baltimore, Maryland Office).

DARREL J. GRINSTEAD, born 1940; admitted to bar, 1969, District of Columbia. *Education:* Duke University (B.A.); University of Michigan (J.D.). Chief Counsel, Health Care Financing Administration, 1988-1997. *Member:* The District of Columbia Bar; American Bar Association; American Health Lawyers Association. ***PRACTICE AREAS:*** Health Law; Medicare and Medicaid. ***Email:*** djgrinstead@hhlaw.com

CHRISTOPHER J. HAGAN, born Lansing, Michigan, April 3, 1961; admitted to bar, 1986, Texas; 1989, District of Columbia. *Education:* Albion College (B.A., magna cum laude, 1983); Duke University (J.D., 1986). *Member:* State Bar of Texas; The District of Columbia Bar; American Bar Association. ***PRACTICE AREAS:*** Corporate Law; Securities Law; Mergers and Acquisitions; Venture Capital Transactions. ***Email:*** cjhagan@hhlaw.com

MARTIN J. HAHN, born Sandusky, Ohio, November 12, 1963; admitted to bar, 1989, Ohio (Inactive); 1990, Pennsylvania (Inactive); 1991, District of Columbia. *Education:* The Ohio State University (B.S., cum laude with distinction, 1986); Northwestern University (J.D., 1989). *Member:* The District of Columbia Bar; American Bar Association. ***PRACTICE AREAS:*** Food, Drug and Cosmetic Law; Food and Drug Regulation; Food and Agriculture; Food Labeling and Inspection; Food Processing. ***Email:*** mjhahn@hhlaw.com

WILLIAM F. HAIGNEY (Resident at 100 Park Avenue Office).

BENTON R. HAMMOND, born Kenosha, Wisconsin, June 6, 1950; admitted to bar, 1975, District of Columbia; 1985, Maryland. *Education:* University of Wisconsin (B.A., with honors, 1972); Columbia University (J.D., 1975). Phi Kappa Phi. Harlan Fiske Stone Scholar of Law, 1973-1974 and 1974-1975. *Member:* The District of Columbia Bar; Maryland State and American Bar Associations. ***PRACTICE AREAS:*** Banking Law; Commercial Real Estate Law; Commercial Law. ***Email:*** brhammond@hhlaw.com

KAREN M. HARDWICK, born Washington, D.C., April 29, 1963; admitted to bar, 1989, Maryland; 1990, District of Columbia; U.S. Court of Appeals for the District of Columbia Circuit; U.S. Court of Appeals, Fourth Circuit; U.S. District Court, District of Maryland; U.S. District Court, District of Columbia. *Education:* University of Virginia (B.S.E., 1985); Harvard University (J.D., 1988). *Member:* The District of Columbia Bar (Co-Chairperson, District of Columbia Affairs Section; Member, Legal Aid Society Board of Directors); Maryland State and National Bar Associations. ***PRACTICE AREAS:*** Commercial Litigation. ***Email:*** kmhardwick@hhlaw.com

MICHELE SASSE HARRINGTON (Resident, McLean, Virginia Office).

JOSEPH M. HASSETT, born Buffalo, New York, May 1, 1943; admitted to bar, 1967, New York; 1970, District of Columbia. *Education:* Canisius College (A.B., summa cum laude, 1964); Harvard University (LL.B., cum laude, 1967); University College, Dublin, Ireland (M.A., 1st cl. hon., 1981; Ph.D., 1985).

(This Listing Continued)

HOGAN & HARTSON L.L.P., Washington—Continued

Member: The District of Columbia; New York State and American Bar Associations. ***PRACTICE AREAS:*** Litigation; Securities Litigation. ***Email:*** jmhassett@hhlaw.com

CATRIONA HATTON (Resident, Brussels, Belgium Office).

KENNETH J. HAUTMAN (Resident, McLean, Virginia Office).

ELIZABETH BLOSSOM HEFFERNAN, born Cleveland, Ohio, January 12, 1952; admitted to bar, 1980, District of Columbia; 1983, Florida. *Education:* Radcliffe College (B.A., summa cum laude, 1975); Georgetown University (J.D., magna cum laude, 1980). Phi Beta Kappa. Articles Editor, Georgetown Law Journal, 1979-1980. Law Clerk, Honorable John M. Ferren, District of Columbia Court of Appeals, 1980-1981. *Member:* The District of Columbia Bar; The Florida Bar; Federal and American Bar Associations; National Association of College and University Attorneys. ***PRACTICE AREAS:*** Education Law; Government Contracts Law. ***Email:*** ebheffernan@hhlaw.com

DR. JAN HEGEMANN (Resident, Berlin, Germany Office).

DAVID J. HENSLER, born Alexandria, Virginia, June 9, 1943; admitted to bar, 1967, Missouri; 1969, District of Columbia; 1971, U.S. Supreme Court. *Education:* St. Louis University (A.B., cum laude, 1965; J.D., cum laude, 1967). Notes and Comments Editor, St. Louis University Law Journal, 1966-1967. Attorney, General Counsel's Office, Securities and Exchange Commission, 1967-1968. Adjunct Professor, Georgetown University Law Center, 1978-1986. Member, Executive Committee, Council for Court Excellence, 1986-1990. *Member:* The District of Columbia Bar; Federal and American (Member, Litigation Section) Bar Associations. Fellow, American College of Trial Lawyers. ***PRACTICE AREAS:*** Civil Litigation; Commercial Litigation; Complex Litigation; Corporate Litigation; Insurance Coverage Litigation. ***Email:*** djhensler@hhlaw.com

PATRICK F. HOFER, born Las Cruces, New Mexico, August 30, 1961; admitted to bar, 1986, Virginia; 1988, District of Columbia. *Education:* University of Virginia (B.A., cum laude, 1983; J.D., 1986). Omicron Delta Kappa. Raven Society. Co-Author: "The Fallacy of Personal Injury Liability Insurance for Environmental Claims," 12 Va. Environmental L.J. 393 (1993). Law Clerk to Honorable Frank W. Bullock, Jr., U.S. District Judge for the Middle District of North Carolina, Greensboro, 1986-1987. Member, John Carroll Society, 1991—. *Member:* Virginia State Bar; The District of Columbia Bar. ***LANGUAGES:*** German and Spanish. ***PRACTICE AREAS:*** Insurance; Insurance Coverage Litigation; Litigation. ***Email:*** pfhofer@hhlaw.com

STEVEN P. HOLLMAN, born Washington, D.C., February 20, 1958; admitted to bar, 1983, District of Columbia, U.S. District Court for the District of Columbia and U.S. Court of Appeals for the District of Columbia Circuit; 1984, Maryland; 1985, U.S. District Court, District of Maryland; U.S. Court of Appeals, Fourth Circuit; 1987, U.S. Supreme Court; 1996, U.S. Court of Appeals for the Federal Circuit; 1997, U.S. Court of Federal Claims. *Education:* Harvard University (B.A., magna cum laude, 1980); University of Virginia (J.D., 1983). Phi Beta Kappa. Member, Virginia Law Review, 1982-1983. *Member:* The District of Columbia Bar; Montgomery County, Maryland State and American Bar Associations; American Intellectual Property Law Association; International Trademark Association. ***LANGUAGES:*** French. ***PRACTICE AREAS:*** Civil Litigation; Commercial Litigation; Patent Litigation; Trademark Litigation; Trade Secret Litigation; Copyright Litigation; Condemnations; Landlord-Tenant; Real Estate Litigation. ***Email:*** sphollman@hhlaw.com

WHITNEY A. HOLMES (Resident, Denver, Colorado Office).

HOWARD M. HOLSTEIN, born New York, N.Y., December 12, 1946; admitted to bar, 1973, District of Columbia and U.S. District Court for the District of Columbia and U.S. Court of Appeals for the District of Columbia Circuit; 1976, U.S. Supreme Court. *Education:* University of Rhode Island (B.S., 1968); Georgetown University (J.D., 1972). Business Editor, AM-Criminal Law Review, 1971-1972. Member, Editorial Board: Barristers Council, 1970-1971; Food, Drug & Cosmetic Law Journal, 1983-1987. *Member:* The District of Columbia Bar; Federal Bar Association. ***PRACTICE AREAS:*** Regulatory Law; Medical Device Regulation; Food and Drug Regulation; Food, Drug and Cosmetic Law. ***Email:*** hmholstein@hhlaw.com

JANET PITTERLE HOLT, born Eau Claire, Wisconsin, March 5, 1955; admitted to bar, 1981, District of Columbia; 1988, Virginia; 1997, Maryland. *Education:* Georgetown University (B.S.B.A., summa cum laude, 1977); University of Virginia (J.D., 1981). Law Clerk: Hon. Stanley S. Harris, District of Columbia Court of Appeals, 1981-1982; Hon. James A. Belson, District of Columbia Court of Appeals, 1982. *Member:* The District of Columbia Bar (Member, Litigation Section); Maryland State Bar Association; Virginia State Bar. ***PRACTICE AREAS:*** Commercial Litigation; Insurance Law; Employment Litigation; Securities Litigation; Special Education; University Tenure. ***Email:*** jpholt@hhlaw.com

CRAIG A. HOOVER, born Inglewood, California, August 28, 1956; admitted to bar, 1984, California; 1985, District of Columbia; 1987, Virginia. *Education:* University of Redlands (B.A., magna cum laude, 1978); Duke University (J.D., 1983). Note and Comment Editor, Duke Law Journal, 1982-1983. Law Clerk, Hon. Robert J. Kelleher, U.S. District Court, Central District of California, 1983-1984. *Member:* The District of Columbia Bar; State Bar of California; Virginia State Bar; American Bar Association. ***LANGUAGES:*** French. ***PRACTICE AREAS:*** Civil Litigation; Commercial Litigation; Health Care Litigation. ***Email:*** cahoover@hhlaw.com

RICHARD T. HORAN, JR. (Resident, McLean, Virginia Office).

JAMES A. HOURIHAN, born Elizabeth, New Jersey, September 30, 1936; admitted to bar, 1961, District of Columbia. *Education:* Lafayette College (A.B., 1958); University of Michigan (J.D., 1961). Order of the Coif. Assistant Editor, Michigan Law Review, 1960-1961. Member, Committee on Admissions, District of Columbia Court of Appeals, 1971-1979. *Member:* The District of Columbia Bar; Bar Association of The District of Columbia (Member, Board of Directors, 1980-1984); American Bar Association (Chairman, Environmental Law Committee, Litigation Section, 1976-1981; Chairman, Toxic and Hazardous Substance and Environmental Law Committee, 1985-1986; Member, Product Liability Advisory Counsel, 1990—); The Counsellors (President, 1976-1977); International Association of Defense Counsel (Member, Executive Committee, 1981-1984); Defense Research Institute (State Chairman, 1979-1999). Fellow: American College of Trial Lawyers; International Society of Barristers; International Academy of Trial Lawyers. ***PRACTICE AREAS:*** Civil Litigation; Commercial Litigation; Environmental Law; Product Liability. ***Email:*** jahourihan@hhlaw.com

WILLIAM MIKE HOUSE, born Birmingham, Alabama, December 19, 1945; admitted to bar, 1971, Alabama; 1993, District of Columbia. *Education:* Auburn University (B.A., 1968); University of Alabama (J.D., 1971). Phi Alpha Delta (President, 1970). Bench and Bar Honor Society. Legislative Assistant to James M. Collins of Texas, 1971-1972. Administrative Assistant to Chief Justice Howell Heflin, 1973-1975. Director, Citizens Conference on Alabama State Courts, 1973-1976. Chief of Staff, U.S. Senator Howell Heflin of Alabama, 1979-1986. Co-Chairman, of the Potomac Group, 1986-1994. Selected for Society of International Business Fellows, 1987; Vice President, 1995. Listed in: Who's Who in American Politics; Who's Who in America; Who's Who in American Law; International Who's Who in Community Service; Men & Women of Distinction. *Member:* Alabama State Bar (President, Young Lawyers Section, 1976-1977); The District of Columbia Bar. ***PRACTICE AREAS:*** Legislation and Government Regulation. ***Email:*** wmhouse@hhlaw.com

EVE N. HOWARD, born Baltimore, Maryland, November 17, 1962; admitted to bar, 1988, New York; 1989, District of Columbia. *Education:* Dartmouth College (A.B., 1984); Duke University (J.D., 1987). Member, Duke Law Journal, 1985-1987. *Member:* The District of Columbia Bar; American Bar Association. ***PRACTICE AREAS:*** Corporate Law; Securities Law. ***Email:*** enhoward@hhlaw.com

GEORGE F. HRITZ (Resident at 100 Park Avenue, New York, New York Office).

JAMES A. HUTCHINSON, born Washington, D.C., April 27, 1966; admitted to bar, 1993, Maryland; 1994, District of Columbia. *Education:* University of Pennsylvania (B.A., 1988); Georgetown University Law Center (J.D., cum laude, 1993). *Member:* The District of Columbia Bar. ***PRACTICE AREAS:*** Corporate Mergers and Acquisitions; Corporate Finance; Corporate Securities. ***Email:*** jahutchinson@hhlaw.com

STEPHEN J. IMMELT (Resident, Baltimore, Maryland Office).

MACIEJ JAMKA (Resident, Warsaw, Poland Office).

HARRY T. JONES, JR., born Misawa, Japan, November 20, 1953; admitted to bar, 1977, District of Columbia; 1984, U.S. Supreme Court; 1997, Maryland; U.S. District Court for the District of Columbia and District of Maryland and U.S. Court of Appeals for the District of Columbia Circuit; U.S. Court of Appeals, Fourth Circuit. *Education:* Harvard University (A.B., cum laude, 1974; J.D., 1977). *Member:* The District of Columbia Bar; Bar Association of the District of Columbia; Washington, American and National Bar Associations. ***PRACTICE AREAS:*** Civil Litigation; Employment Litigation; Business Litigation. ***Email:*** htjones@hhlaw.com

JONATHAN S. KAHAN, born New York, N.Y., April 5, 1948; admitted to bar, 1973, District of Columbia. *Education:* George Washington University (B.A., 1970; J.D., 1973). Phi Beta Kappa; Phi Eta Sigma; Order of the Coif. Member, George Washington Law Review, 1971-1973. Contributing Editor: Medical Device and Diagnostic Industry Magazine, 1984—; Clinica Magazine, 1987—. Member, Editorial Advisory Board, Food Drug Cosmetic Law Journal, 1988-1992. Law Clerk to Judge Oliver Gasch, U.S. District Court for the District of Columbia, 1973-1974. Author: "Medical Device Development: A Regulatory Overview," (Parexel 2000); "Medical Devices: Obtaining FDA Market Clearance," (Parexel 1995); "The New Enforcement Provisions of the Safe Medical Devices Act of 1990," 46 Food Drug Cosmetic Law Journal 177 (1991); "Legal Implications of Software Validation in Pharmaceutical Manufacturing," 21 Drug Information Journal 481, 1987; "Regulation of Computer Hardware and Software as Medical Devices," 4 Canadian Computer Law Reporter 50, 1987; "Medical Device Reclassification: The Evolution of FDA

(This Listing Continued)

Policy," 42 Food Drug Cosmetic Law Journal 288, 1987; "The Evolution of FDA Regulation of New Medical Device Technology and Product Applications," 41 Food, Drug, Cosmetic Law Journal 207, 1986; "Premarket Approval Versus Premarket Notification: Different Routes to the Same Market," 39 Food, Drug, Cosmetic Law Journal, 1984; "The Effect of Proposed Food Safety Legislation on Colors," 39 Food Drug, Cosmetic Law Journal, 1984; "Reporting of Substantial Product Hazards Under Section 15 of the Consumer Product Safety Act," 30 Administrative Law Review 289, 1978; "Reporting Substantial Risks Under Section 8(e) of the Toxic Substances Control Act," 19 Boston College Law Review 859, 1978; "Criminal Liability Under the Federal Food, Drug and Cosmetic Act - the Large Corporation Perspective," 36 Food, Drug, Cosmetic Law Journal 314, 1981; "Laser and Electronic Medical Devices - An Overview of Food and Drug Administration Regulation," 38 Food, Drug, Cosmetic Law Journal 220, 1983. Co-Author: "Expedited Availability of New Drugs," 45 Food Drug Cosmetic Law Journal 81, 1990; "Federal Regulation of Food and Food Additive Biotechnology," 38 Administrative Law Review 1, 1986; "The Impact on Medical Malpractice Cases of Food and Drug Administration Regulation," 20 The Forum 418, 1985; "Recent Developments Regarding Look-Alike Drugs," 35 Food, Drug, Cosmetic Law Journal 4, 1980. *Member:* The District of Columbia Bar; Bar Association of the District of Columbia (Co-Chairman, Steering Committee, Section on Administrative Law and Agency Practice, 1987-1992); Federal (Chairman, Health and Human Services Section, 1983-1989) and American (Member, Sections on: Antitrust Law; Administrative Law; Business Law; Member, Food, Drug and Cosmetic Law Committee, 1982-1992) Bar Associations. ***PRACTICE AREAS:*** Food and Drug Regulation; Food, Drug and Cosmetic Law; Drug and Medical Device Regulation. ***Email:*** jskahan@hhlaw.com

HENRY D. KAHN (Resident, Baltimore, Maryland Office).

ROBERT H. KAPP, born Chicago, Illinois, March 9, 1934; admitted to bar, 1958, Illinois; 1961, District of Columbia. *Education:* University of Pennsylvania (B.S., 1955); University of Michigan (S.J.D., 1958). Phi Alpha Delta. Associate Editor, Michigan Law Review, 1957-1958. Trial Attorney, Tax Division, Department of Justice, 1958-1961. Professorial Lecturer in Law, The National Law Center, George Washington University, 1970-1975. *Member:* The District of Columbia Bar; American Bar Association. ***PRACTICE AREAS:*** Taxation Law; Arbitration; Mediation. ***Email:*** rhkapp@hhlaw.com

MARK A. KASS, born Boston, Massachusetts, June 20, 1960; admitted to bar, 1986, New York, U.S. District Court, District of Maryland, U.S. Court of Appeals for the District of Columbia Circuit and U.S. Court of Appeals, Fourth Circuit; 1987, District of Columbia; 1996, Israel. *Education:* Yale University (B.A., cum laude, with distinction in History, 1982); Columbia University (J.D., 1985). Stone Scholar. Articles Editor, Columbia Journal of Law & Social Problems, 1984-1985. Law Clerk to Hon. Edward S. Northrop, U.S. District Court, District of Maryland, 1985-1986. Author: "Due Diligence in Israel: Special Considerations," Israel Hi-Tech Investor, Issue Number 5, 1999-2000; "Acquisitions of Israeli Companies: The Legal and Regulatory Framework," International Quarterly, Volume 12, Number 1, 2000, reprinted in April 2000, Supplement to International Trade Law. Associate, Arnold & Porter, Washington, D.C., 1986-1993. Special Counsel, Arnold & Porter, Washington, D.C., 1994-1995. Associate, Yigal Arnon & Co., Tel Aviv, Israel, 1996-1999. *Member:* The District of Columbia Bar; Israel Bar Association. ***LANGUAGES:*** Hebrew. ***PRACTICE AREAS:*** Technology Business Startups; Telecommunications; Israeli-Related Transactions; Corporate Contracts. ***Email:*** mkass@hhlaw.com

STEVEN M. KAUFMAN, born New York, N.Y., April 15, 1959; admitted to bar, 1985, Massachusetts and District of Columbia. *Education:* Yale University (B.A., summa cum laude, 1981); Harvard University (J.D., cum laude, 1984). Phi Beta Kappa. *Member:* The District of Columbia Bar (Member, Sections on: Corporate, Finance and Securities Law); Massachusetts Bar Association. ***PRACTICE AREAS:*** Corporate Law; Securities Law. ***Email:*** smkaufman@hhlaw.com

JOHN C. KEENEY, JR., born Washington, D.C., August 29, 1951; admitted to bar, 1976, Maryland; 1977, District of Columbia; 1980, U.S. Supreme Court. *Education:* University of Notre Dame (A.B., summa cum laude, 1973); Harvard University (J.D., cum laude, 1976). Phi Beta Kappa. Law Clerk, Hon. Alexander Harvey, II, U.S. District Judge, District of Maryland, 1976-1978. Co-Author: Civil and Criminal Remedies for Racially and Religiously Motivated Violence (published by Washington Lawyers' Committee for Civil Rights Under Law in 1983). Member: Board of Governors (Executive Committee); District of Columbia Bar; Board of Directors, Washington Lawyers' Committee for Civil Rights and Urban Affairs. Counsel, Credentials Committee, Democratic National Committee 1989-1992. Hearing Officer, Standing Committee on Credentials, Democratic National Convention, 1992; 1996. Professional Lecturer in Legal Ethics, Washington College of Law, American University. *Member:* The District of Columbia Bar; Maryland State and American (Co-Chair, Adjudication Committee, Administrative Law Section; Advisory Board, Election Law Committee) Bar Associations. ***PRACTICE AREAS:*** Civil Litigation; Federal Litigation; Professional Liability; Civil Rights; Election, Campaign and Political Law. ***Email:*** jckeeney@hhlaw.com

(This Listing Continued)

NEVIN J. KELLY, born Doylestown, Pennsylvania, February 24, 1959; admitted to bar, 1984, Pennsylvania; 1985, District of Columbia. *Education:* Princeton University (A.B., 1981, Phi Beta Kappa); Stanford University (J.D., 1984). Associate Editor, Stanford Law Review, 1983-1984. *Member:* The District of Columbia Bar. (Also at Warsaw, Poland Office). ***PRACTICE AREAS:*** Commercial Lending; Commercial Real Estate; International Real Estate; International Project Finance; Polish Commercial Transactions. ***Email:*** njkelly@hhlaw.com

J. HOVEY KEMP, born Denver, Colorado, December 24, 1953; admitted to bar, 1980, Colorado; 1989, District of Columbia. *Education:* Harvard University (A.B., magna cum laude, 1976); Georgetown University (J.D., 1980). *Member:* The District of Columbia Bar; American Bar Association. ***PRACTICE AREAS:*** Corporate Law; Mergers and Acquisitions; Venture Capital Transactions. ***Email:*** jhkemp@hhlaw.com

ROBERT J. KENNEY, JR., born Boston, Massachusetts, January 16, 1948; admitted to bar, 1972, Massachusetts; 1973, District of Columbia; 1977, U.S. Supreme Court; 1985, U.S. Court of Appeals for the Federal Circuit and U.S. Claims Court. *Education:* Harvard University (A.B., 1969; J.D., 1972). Author: Article, *Perspectives on Multiple Award Schedule Pricing*, Government Contract Audit Report, Vol. 2, No. 9 (Nov. 1997); Article, *The Lobbying Disclosure Act of 1995 and its Impact on Federal Contractors*, Vol. 38, No. 3 (Jan. 24, 1996); Article, *GSA's New Recommended Year 2000 Warranty Clauses Balance Competing Interests*, The Government Contractor, Vol. 38, No. 35 (Sept. 18, 1996). Co-Author: Briefing Papers for Federal Publications on: "*Most Favored Customer*" *Provisions*, 86-3 (Feb. 1986); *Domestic Preference Provisions*, 89-3 (Feb. 1989); *Gratuities*, No. 90-3 (Feb. 1990); *Best Value Procurement*, No. 93-4 (March 1993); *Domestic Preference Provisions — Edition II*, No. 94-3 (Feb. 1994); *The Lobbying Disclosure Act of 1995*, No. 96-5 (April 1996); *The "Year 2000" Problem in Federal Procurement*, No. 98-3 (Feb. 1998). *Member:* The District of Columbia Bar; Massachusetts, Federal (Chairman, Government Contracts Section, 1992-1994; Deputy Chairperson, Government Contracts Section, 1987-1989; Chairman, ADP Procurement Committee, 1990-1992; Chairman, Government Contracts Committee, 1986-1987) and American (Member, Section on Public Contract Law) Bar Associations; Computer Law Association. [With U.S. Navy, JAGC, 1972-1976]. ***PRACTICE AREAS:*** Computer Software Law; Information Technology Contracts; Federal Grants; Government Contract Fraud; Government Procurement. ***Email:*** rjkenney@hhlaw.com

MICHAEL L. KIDNEY, born Milan, Italy, October 18, 1963; admitted to bar, 1990, Pennsylvania and U.S. Court of Appeals, Tenth Circuit; 1991, District of Columbia and U.S. District Court for the District of Columbia; 1996, U.S. Court of Appeals for the District of Columbia Circuit and U.S. District Court, District of Maryland. *Education:* Yale University (B.A., cum laude, 1986); University of Michigan (J.D., cum laude, 1989). Article Editor, University of Michigan Journal of Law Reform, 1988-1989. Law Clerk to the Hon. Deanell Reece Tacha, U.S. Court of Appeals, Tenth Circuit, 1989-1990. *Member:* The District of Columbia Bar; American Bar Association. ***PRACTICE AREAS:*** Civil Litigation; Complex Litigation; Defense Litigation; Federal Civil Litigation; Federal Litigation; Products Liability; Automotive Products Liability; Drug and Medical Device Litigation; Products Liability Defense. ***Email:*** mlkidney@hhlaw.com

DAVID A. KIKEL, born Bedford, Ohio, December 9, 1946; admitted to bar, 1978, District of Columbia; 1980, California; 1995, Maryland. *Education:* Kansas University (A.B., B.S.E.E., with distinction, 1969); University of California at Berkeley (M.C.P., 1978; J.D., 1978). Order of the Coif. *Member:* The District of Columbia Bar; State Bar of California; Maryland State and American (Member, Sections on: Litigation; Intellectual Property Law) Bar Associations; AIPLA; Defense Research Institute. [Lt., USN, 1969-1973]. ***PRACTICE AREAS:*** Intellectual Property Litigation; Products Liability Defense; Drug and Medical Device Defense; Complex Civil Litigation. ***Email:*** dakikel@hhlaw.com

CAROL WELD KING, born Roanoke, Virginia, June 11, 1961; admitted to bar, 1986, Virginia; 1988, District of Columbia. *Education:* University of Virginia (B.A., 1983; J.D., 1986). *Member:* Virginia State Bar; The District of Columbia Bar; American Bar Association. ***PRACTICE AREAS:*** Commercial Real Estate Law. ***Email:*** cwking@hhlaw.com

DAVID P. KING (Resident, Baltimore, Maryland Office).

SANDRA FOLSOM KINSEY, born Fort Lauderdale, Florida, June 30, 1950; admitted to bar, 1980, Georgia and District of Columbia; 2000, Florida. *Education:* Emory University (B.A., cum laude, 1972); University of Georgia (J.D., cum laude, 1980). Comments Editor, Georgia Law Review, 1979-1980. Attorney Fellow (1990-1992), Senior Attorney (1992-1998) and Senior International Counsel (1998-2000), Office of International Corporate Finance, Securities and Exchange Commission. *Member:* The District of Columbia Bar; State Bar of Georgia; The Florida Bar; American Bar Association. (Also at Miami, Florida Office). ***PRACTICE AREAS:*** Securities; Corporate Law; International Capital Markets; Foreign Investment in the United States. ***Email:*** sfkinsey@hhlaw.com

(This Listing Continued)

HOGAN & HARTSON L.L.P., Washington—Continued

DUNCAN S. KLINEDINST (Resident, McLean, Virginia Office).

EDWARD L. KORWEK, born Erie, Pennsylvania, December 5, 1946; admitted to bar, 1979, District of Columbia; 1980, U.S. Court of Appeals for the District of Columbia Circuit; 1983, U.S. Supreme Court. *Education:* Gannon University (B.S., Pre Medicine, 1969); University of Pittsburgh (Ph.D., Biochemistry, 1974); Duquesne University (J.D., cum laude, 1979). Member, Duquesne Law Review, 1977-1978. Author: "Labeling Biotech Foods: Opening Pandora's Box?" 54 Food Technology 38, 2000; Food Biotech Labeling: Trials & Triumphs," 121 Seed Trade News 20, 2000; "Drug User Fees and Beyond: The New Food and Drug Administration Modernization Act of 1997," 4 Journal of Biotechnology in Healthcare 300 (1998); 1997 U.S. Biotechnology Regulations Handbook, Food and Drug Law Institute; "Human Biological Drug Regulation: Past, Present, and Beyond the Year 2000," Food and Drug Journal 123 (1995) (Special Issue Celebrating the Journal's 50th Anniversary); "Orphan Drug Trials and Tribulations: Profitability, Patient Ceiling, Market Exclusivity, AIDS, and Biotechnology," 3 Regulatory Affairs 133 (1991); "Food Biotechnology Regulation: Overview and Selected Issues," 44 Food Technology 76, 1990; "Releases of Organisms into the Environment: Options to Trigger, Exempt Products From Oversight," 13 Chemical Regulation Reporter 1454, 1990; "Brave New World: Oversight of Biotechnology into the 21st Century," The Bureau of National Affairs, Inc., Special Report Series on Biotechnology, 1989. Co-Author: Biologics Update, 2 Update Food and Drug Law, Regulation, and Education 4, Food and Drug Law Institute, March/April, 2001; The FDA's regulation of Internet promotion and sales of prescription products, 7 Journal of Commercial Biotechnology 122, 2001 (Special Issue on the Impact of the Internet on the Bioscience Industry); "Boon or Threat to International Trade in Biotechnology?" 17 Nature Biotechnology 513, 1999; "Food Biotechnology - A Scientific Status Summary," 42 Food Technology 133, 1988. Member: United States Department of Agriculture, Advisory Committee on Agriculture Biotechnology; Advisory Board, Biotechnology Law Report; Board of Directors, Food and Drug Law Institute; Chair, Publications Committee, Food and Drug Law Institute; Biotechnology; Regulatory Law; Food and Drug Law; Agricultural Law; Environmental Law; Technology and Science; Food and Drug Law Journal, 1993-1996; Journal of Biotechnology in Healthcare; NIH Recombinant DNA Advisory Committee, 1985-1988; U.S. Congress, Office of Technology Assessment Advisory Committee, New Developments in Biotechnology, 1986-1988, Agriculture Biotechnology Research Advisory Committee, 1988-1991; National Academy of Sciences/National Research Council, Committee on Scientific Principles Underlying Environmental Release Decisions Involving Biotechnology, 1989; National Research Council, Committee on Biotechnology, 1990-1995; National Research Council, Commission on Physical Sciences, Mathematics, and Applications, Space Studies Board, Task Group on Issues in Sample Return; NASA Advisory Council, Planetary Protection Task Force of the Space Science Advisory Committee. *Member:* The District of Columbia Bar; American Bar Association; American Association for the Advancement of Science; American Chemical Society. ***PRACTICE AREAS:*** Biotechnology Law; Food and Drug Regulation; Technology and Science; Environmental Law. ***Email:*** elkorwek@hhlaw.com

JOSEPH G. KRAUSS, born Wilmington, Delaware, April 27, 1956; admitted to bar, 1984, Delaware, Pennsylvania (inactive), U.S. District Court, District of Delaware and U.S. Court of Appeals, Third Circuit; 1999, District of Columbia. *Education:* University of Delaware (B.S., 1978); Delaware Law School of Widener University (J.D., 1983). Federal Trade Commission: Recipient, Distinguished Service Award, 1999; Assistant Director, Premerger Notification Office, 1997-1999; Acting Assistant Director, Mergers II, 1997-1998; Deputy Assistant Director, Mergers II, 1994-1997; Attorney Advisor, Commissioner Dennis Yao, 1993-1994; Recipient, Superior Service Award, 1992; Attorney Advisor, Commissioner Roscoe B. Starek, III, 1991-1992; Senior Staff Attorney, Bureau of Competition, 1988-1991. Associate Herlihy & Weir, Wilmington, Delaware, 1983-1987. Author: "Antitrust Review of New Economy Acquisitions," with Ilene Knable Gotts, Antitrust Magazine Vol. 15, No.1, (Fall 2000); "Update: Divestiture Policy for New Economy Transaction," with Ilene Knable Gotts, Antitrust Magazine, Vol.15, No.2, (Spring 2001); "Second Request Reform: Are Recent Proposal Changes Enough to Address the Problems," with Andrea T. Cummings, Clayton Act Newsletter, Vol. 1, No. 1, (Summer 2000). Prepared Remarks, "New Developments in the Premerger Notification Program," before the District of Columbia Bar Association, Antitrust, Trade Regulation and Consumer Affairs Section, Washington, D.C., October 7, 1998; Speech, "Mergers, Acquisitions and Joint Ventures: Overcoming the Hart-Scott-Rodino Hurdle," Business Development Associates, Inc. and Corporate Counsel Institute, San Francisco, California, March 2, 1998; Speech, "The Life of an HSR Filing," before the District of Columbia Bar Association, Antitrust, Trade Regulation and Consumer Affairs Section, Washington, D.C., December 3, 1997; Prepared Remarks, "Fundamentals of Mergers and Acquisitions," before the Antitrust Section Spring Meeting, American Bar Association, March 27, 1996; Paper on "Prospects for Harmonization of U.S. and E.U. Antitrust Laws Concerning International Strategic Alliances," with Dennis A. Yao, presented at the Symposium on International Harmonization of Competition Laws, Taipei, Taiwan,

(This Listing Continued)

March 12-14, 1994. Co-Chair, Clayton Act Committee of Antitrust Section of the American Bar Association. *Member:* The District of Columbia Bar; American Bar Association. ***PRACTICE AREAS:*** Antitrust Counseling; Mergers and Acquisitions; Joint Ventures; Trade Associations; Civil Investigations; Litigation. ***Email:*** jgkrauss@hhlaw.com

WILLIAM J. KUBIDA (Resident, Colorado Springs, Colorado Office).

DR. WOLFGANG KUHLA (Resident, Berlin, Germany Office).

S. GREGG KUNZI, born Augusta, Georgia, June 21, 1954; admitted to bar, 1986, Minnesota; 1996, District of Columbia. *Education:* Texas Christian University (B.S., 1976); University of Minnesota (J.D., magna cum laude, 1986); The U.S. Army Judge Advocate General's School (LL.M., distinguished graduate, 1991). Order of the Coif. Articles Editor, Minnesota Law Review. Kaplan Scholar. Recipient, Ernest Brannon Award for Government Contract Law. Author: National Drug Formularies-Implications for Pharmaceutical Executive (April, 1999); Government Shutdown Claims, Contract Management (May, 1996); Losing Sight of Christian Values: The Evolution and (Disturbing) Implications of The Christian Doctrine, The Army Lawyer, January 1992, at 11. *Member:* Minnesota State, Federal and American Bar Associations; The District of Columbia Bar; National Contract Management Association. [U.S. Army JAG Corps, 1987-1994, Major]. ***PRACTICE AREAS:*** Government Contracts; Health Care Contracting; Federal Grants; Federal Tort Claims; Bid Protests; Federal Contracts. ***Email:*** sgkunzi@hhlaw.com

RAYMOND A. KURZ, born New York, N.Y., August 6, 1957; admitted to bar, 1981, District of Columbia; 1982, U.S. District Court, District of Columbia; 1985, U.S. Court of Appeals for the District of Columbia Circuit; 1986, U.S. Court of Appeals for the Federal Circuit; 1989, U.S. Supreme Court. *Education:* State University of New York at Albany (B.A., magna cum laude, 1978); George Washington University (J.D., 1981). Lecturer, Trademark Issues, American Seed Trade Association Legal Seminar, St. Louis, Missouri, 1994. Program Chairman and Lecturer: Law of the Internet Conference: Compliance in Cyberspace, 1995. Lecturer: Internet for the Environmental Professional: Legal Issues for Internet Users, Boston, MA, 1996; Patent Trademarks and Copyright Planning Issues, District of Columbia Bar Conference, "The In-House Counsel's Bird's Eye View to the Year End and the Year Ahead," 1997; Co-Chair and Lecturer, Internet and the Law Conference, Washington, D.C., 1998. Principal Author/Editor: Internet and the Law: Fundamentals for the Internet User, 1996; "Changes in the law regarding copyright notice in the United States," I.R.D.I. Intellectuele Rechten Droits Intellectuels, 1996-2000; "Copyright and the Internet", EMIS Tech, Vol. 1, No. 3 (November 1997). *Member:* The District of Columbia Bar (Member, Patent, Trademark and Copyright Law Section); American Bar Association (Member, Intellectual Property Law Section); International Trademark Association; American Intellectual Property Law Association; Intellectual Property Owners Association. ***PRACTICE AREAS:*** Intellectual Property. ***Email:*** rakurz@hhlaw.com

GARY JAY KUSHNER, born Bronx, New York, March 17, 1950; admitted to bar, 1975, Maryland; 1976, District of Columbia; 1978, U.S. District Court for the District of Columbia; 1978, U.S. Court of Appeals for the District of Columbia Circuit; 1984, U.S. Supreme Court; 1991, U.S. Court of Appeals for the Federal Circuit; 1992, U.S. Court of Appeals for the Fifth Circuit; 1994, U.S. Court of Appeals for the Ninth Circuit. *Education:* University of Michigan (A.B., with distinction, 1972); Georgetown University Law Center (J.D., 1975). Law Clerk to the Honorable John R. Hess, Superior Court of the District of Columbia, 1975-1976. Staff Counsel, Scientific Affairs, Grocery Manufacturers of America, Inc., 1976-1978. Associate: Leighton, Conklin, Lemov and Jacobs, 1978-1980; Collier, Shannon, Rill and Scott, 1980-1982. Vice President and General Counsel, American Meat Institute, 1982-1985. Co-Author: *A Guide to Federal Food Labeling Requirements* prepared for the U.S. Department of Agriculture and the U.S. Department of Health and Human Services, Government Printing Office, Washington, D.C., 1990; HACCP Management Manual: A Guide to Food Regulatory Compliance, Food Chemical News, Washington, D.C., 1996. Contributing Columnist for Meat Marketing & Technology magazine, Poultry magazine, and Food Processing magazine. Adjunct Fellow, Georgetown University Center for Food and Nutrition Policy. Member, USDA Graduate School Advisory Board. Member, U.S. Delegation to Codex Alimentarius (Committee on Import and Export Food Inspection and Certification System). Member, U.S. Chamber of Commerce (Food and Agriculture Committee, 1996-1999). Member, Board of Directors, Advocates for Better Children's Diets. *Member:* The District of Columbia Bar; Maryland State, Federal (Chairman: Food and Drug Committee, 1978-1980; Council on Health and Human Services, 1980-1982) and American Bar Associations; American Agricultural Law Association; Institute of Food Technologists (Laws and Regulations Committee); American Society of Association Executives (Chairman, Legal Section Council, 1999-2000). ***PRACTICE AREAS:*** Food and Drug Law; Agricultural Law; Regulatory Law; Trade Association Law. ***Email:*** gjkushner@hhlaw.com

ROBERT D. KYLE, born Evanston, Illinois, March 20, 1955; admitted to bar, 1982, District of Columbia. *Education:* Cornell University (B.A., magna cum laude, 1977); Harvard Law School (J.D., with honors, 1982). Associate Director for National Security and International Affairs, 1998-2001. President

(This Listing Continued)

Clinton's Special Assistant for International Trade and Finance, 1993-1998. Chief International Trade Counsel to the U.S. Senate Committee on Finance, 1989-1993. ***PRACTICE AREAS:*** International Trade; Legislative. ***Email:*** rdkyle@hhlaw.com

STUART M. LANGBEIN, born New Rochelle, New York, December 3, 1965; admitted to bar, 1991, Pennsylvania; 1992, District of Columbia. *Education:* Tufts University (B.A., magna cum laude, 1987); University of Pennsylvania (J.D., 1991). Psi Chi. *Member:* The District of Columbia Bar; American Bar Association (Member, Health Law Section). ***PRACTICE AREAS:*** Health Care. ***Email:*** smlangbein@hhlaw.com

KEVIN J. LANIGAN, born Oceanside, California, August 25, 1957; admitted to bar, 1982, Arizona; 1983, District of Columbia; 1997, Maryland. *Education:* University of Kansas (B.A., with distinction, 1979); University of Virginia (J.D., 1982). Phi Beta Kappa; Phi Kappa Phi; Pi Sigma Alpha; Order of the Coif. Editor, Virginia Journal of International Law, 1980-1982. Assistant Attorney General, Arizona Attorney General's Office, 1982-1983. Executive Director, Arizona Center for Law in The Public Interest, 1988-1990. *Member:* The District of Columbia Bar; State Bar of Arizona. ***PRACTICE AREAS:*** Litigation; Administrative Law; Civil Rights; Education Law; Government. ***Email:*** kjlanigan@hhlaw.com

PHILIP C. LARSON, born Clarinda, Iowa, June 14, 1946; admitted to bar, 1971, District of Columbia; 1975, U.S. Supreme Court. *Education:* Iowa State University (B.S., 1968); Duke University (J.D., with honors, 1971). Order of the Coif. Article Editor, Duke Law Journal, 1970-1971. Author: "The Local Government Antitrust Act of 1984," 67 Public Management 17 (March 1985); "Supreme Court Extends Antitrust Protection for Local Governments," 67 Public Management 19 (July, 1985); "Relationships with Competitors - Joint Economic Activities," ABA Section of Antitrust Law, Course Materials for Nov. 1988 National Institute on Compliance and Counseling. Co-Author: with W. Monts and R. Johnson, "Federal Trade Commission - Advertising Regulation," Course Materials for FDLI Basic Food Law Workshop (Oct. 1989); with Timothy Leary and Janet Mc David, "How to Avoid Negotiations on Second Requests," 13 Antitrust 41 (Summer 1999). *Member:* The District of Columbia Bar; American Bar Association (Member, Sections on: Antitrust Law; Litigation). ***PRACTICE AREAS:*** Antitrust and Trade Regulation; Business Torts; Litigation; Advertising and Marketing. ***Email:*** pclarson@hhlaw.com

C. STEPHEN LAWRENCE (Resident, Irvine, California Office).

MITCHELL J. LAZRIS, born Englewood, New Jersey, February 18, 1966; admitted to bar, 1992, Virginia; 1994, District of Columbia. *Education:* Princeton University (A.B., magna cum laude, 1988); Harvard Law School (J.D., cum laude, 1992). Phi Beta Kappa. Trial Attorney, United States Department of Justice, Civil Fraud Section, 1992-1996. *Member:* The District of Columbia Bar. ***PRACTICE AREAS:*** Litigation; Health Law. ***Email:*** mjlazris@hhlaw.com

DIRK LEERMAKERS (Resident, Brussels, Belgium Office).

ROBERT F. LEIBENLUFT, born Brooklyn, New York, July 5, 1952; admitted to bar, 1980, District of Columbia. *Education:* Yale University (B.A., magna cum laude, 1973); University of California, Boalt Hall School of Law (J.D., 1980). Order of the Coif. Assistant Director for Health Care, Bureau of Competition, Federal Trade Commission, 1996-1998. *Member:* The District of Columbia Bar; American Bar Association (Member: Antitrust Section; Health Law Committee, Vice Chair, 1996-1998, 1999—); American Health Lawyers Association (Member, Board of Directors, 1989-1998; Vice President, 1992-1994). ***PRACTICE AREAS:*** Antitrust; Health Law. ***Email:*** rfleibenluft@hhlaw.com

LEWIS E. LEIBOWITZ, born Baltimore, Maryland, December 3, 1947; admitted to bar, 1975, Maryland; 1976, District of Columbia; 1979, U.S. Supreme Court. *Education:* University of Maryland (B.A., 1970; J.D., with honors, 1975). Order of the Coif. Recipient, William Strobel Thomas Prize. Member, 1973-1974 and Notes and Comments Editor, 1974-1975, Maryland Law Review. Law Clerk, Hon. Roszel C. Thomsen, Senior U.S. District Judge, District of Maryland, 1975-1976. Adjunct Professor, University of Maryland School of Law, 1995-1997. *Member:* The District of Columbia Bar; American Bar Association; National Foreign Trade Council; National Association of Foreign Trade Zones; German American Business Council. ***PRACTICE AREAS:*** International Trade Law; Antidumping; Countervailing Duties; Safeguards; Customs Law; U.S. Foreign Trade Zones; International Trade Legislation; World Trade Organization; International Intellectual Property. ***Email:*** leleibowitz@hhlaw.com

CRAIG A. LEWIS, born New York, N.Y., March 8, 1962; admitted to bar, 1991, Pennsylvania; 1993, U.S. Court of International Trade and U.S. Court of Appeals for the Federal Circuit; 1995, District of Columbia. *Education:* University of Pennsylvania (B.A., 1984); Columbia University School of International and Public Affairs (M.A., 1986); Georgetown University Law Center (J.D., cum laude, 1991). Editor, Law & Policy in International Business, 1990-1991. Author: "Waiting for the Big One: Principle, Policy, and the Restriction of Imports Under Section 232," 22 L. & Pol'y Int'l Bus. 357 (1991). *Member:* The District of Columbia Bar; American Bar Association (Member, Sections on:

(This Listing Continued)

Administrative Law; International Law). ***LANGUAGES:*** German and Spanish. ***PRACTICE AREAS:*** International Trade; Litigation. ***Email:*** calewis@hhlaw.com

SCOTT R. LILIENTHAL, born Duluth, Minnesota, January 5, 1961; admitted to bar, 1987, Maryland; 1989, U.S. Tax Court; 1994, District of Columbia. *Education:* University of Colorado (B.A., 1983); University of Maryland School of Law (J.D., with honors, 1987). Order of the Coif. Notes and Comments Editor, Maryland Law Review, 1986-1987. Attorney Advisor, Office of Assistant and Chief Counsel (Financial Institutions and Products), Internal Revenue Service, 1990-1993. *Member:* Maryland State and American (Member, Taxation Section) Bar Associations; The District of Columbia Bar; National Association of Bond Lawyers. ***PRACTICE AREAS:*** Federal Taxation; Public Finance. ***Email:*** srlilienthal@hhlaw.com

JOHN R. LILYESTROM, born Worcester, Massachusetts, April 26, 1962; admitted to bar, 1989, Maryland; 1998, District of Columbia. *Education:* Harvard University (B.A., 1985); University of Maryland (J.D., 1989). *Member:* The District of Columbia Bar; Maryland State, Federal Energy and American Bar Associations. ***PRACTICE AREAS:*** Electric Power; Energy Contracts; Electric Utility Regulation; Public Utility Law. ***Email:*** jrlilyestrom@hhlaw.com

KEVIN J. LIPSON, born Fall River, Massachusetts, July 31, 1955; admitted to bar, 1980, District of Columbia. *Education:* George Washington University (B.A., with distinction, 1977); Washington University (J.D., 1980). Phi Beta Kappa; Omicron Delta Epsilon; Pi Sigma Alpha. Articles Editor, Washington University Law Quarterly, 1979-1980. Member, Board of Directors, Foundation of the Energy Law Journal. *Member:* The District of Columbia Bar. ***PRACTICE AREAS:*** Energy. ***Email:*** kjlipson@hhlaw.com

TIMOTHY A. LLOYD, born Youngstown, Ohio, January 6, 1957; admitted to bar, 1982, Wisconsin, Illinois and U.S. District Court, Northern District of Illinois; 1985, District of Columbia. *Education:* Miami University (B.A., cum laude with Departmental honors, 1979); University of Wisconsin (J.D., cum laude, 1982). *Member:* The District of Columbia Bar; State Bar of Wisconsin; American Bar Association (Member, Section of Taxation, Partnerships Committee). ***PRACTICE AREAS:*** Taxation; Corporate Law; Partnership Law; Estate Planning. ***Email:*** talloyd@hhlaw.com

LAURA E. LOEB, born Lawrenceville, Illinois, October 27, 1959; admitted to bar, 1984, California; 1985, District of Columbia. *Education:* University of Illinois (B.S., 1981); Stanford University (J.D., 1984). Certified Public Accountant, Illinois, 1981. *Member:* The District of Columbia Bar; American Bar Association; American Health Lawyers Association; National Association of College and University Attorneys. ***PRACTICE AREAS:*** Medicare and Medicaid; Regulatory Law. ***Email:*** leloeb@hhlaw.com

WALTER G. LOHR, JR. (Resident, Baltimore, Maryland Office).

MILAN LOVÍŠEK (Resident, Prague, Czech Republic Office).

JEFFREY ALAN LOWE, born Mineola, New York, January 17, 1965; admitted to bar, 1990, New York and U.S. District Court, Southern District of New York; 1992, District of Columbia. *Education:* Cornell University (B.S., 1986); Marshall-Wythe School of Law; College of William & Mary (J.D., 1989). Order of the Coif. Board of Editors, William & Mary Law Review. With Mori Sogo Law Offices, Tokyo, Japan, 1994-1995. *Member:* District of Columbia Bar; American Bar Association. ***PRACTICE AREAS:*** Corporate Law; Mergers and Acquisitions. ***Email:*** jalowe@hhlaw.com

DAVID L. LUBITZ (Resident, Los Angeles, California and Tokyo, Japan Offices).

STUART LUBITZ (Resident, Los Angeles, California Office).

DANIEL H. MACCOBY (Resident, London, England Office).

PAUL D. MANCA, born Fremont, California, June 14, 1968; admitted to bar, 1993, Virginia; 1994, District of Columbia. *Education:* Santa Clara University (B.S., 1990); Georgetown University Law Center (J.D., cum laude, 1993). Author: "Deductibility of Takeover and Non-Takeover Expenses in the Wake of Indopco," 45 Tax Law. 815 (1992). *Member:* Virginia and American Bar Associations; The District of Columbia Bar. ***PRACTICE AREAS:*** Commercial Law; Corporate Law; Mergers and Acquisitions; Divestitures; Securities. ***Email:*** pdmanca@hhlaw.com

THENE M. MARTIN (Resident, Baltimore, Maryland Office).

WARREN H. MARUYAMA, born San Francisco, California, February 21, 1955; admitted to bar, 1980, Minnesota; 1982, District of Columbia. *Education:* Carleton College (B.A., cum laude, 1976); Cornell Law School (J.D., cum laude, 1980). Member, Cornell Legal Aid Clinic. Author: "A NAFTA for Europe," (co-author with Ambassador Clayton K. Yeutter) Wall Street Journal (May 19, 1995); "A New Pillar of the WTO: Sound Science," The International Lawyer (1998); "Section 301 and the Appearance of Unilateralism," Michigan Journal of International Law (1990); "The Evolution of the Escape Clause," Brigham Young Univ. Law Review (1989). Associate Director, International Economic Policy, Office of the Policy Development, The White House, 1992. Deputy Associate Director, Office of Policy Development, The White House, 1989-1991. Associate General Counsel, Office of the U.S. Trade Representative,

(This Listing Continued)

HOGAN & HARTSON L.L.P., Washington—Continued

1983-1989. Attorney-Advisor, U.S. International Trade Commission, 1980-1983. Member, Board of Governors, Japanese-American National Museum. *Member:* The District of Columbia Bar. ***PRACTICE AREAS:*** International Trade Law. ***Email:*** whmaruyama@hhlaw.com

MARY ANNE MASON, born Baltimore, Maryland, 1949; admitted to bar, 1983, District of Columbia. *Education:* College of William & Mary (B.A., 1970); Georgetown University (J.D., cum laude, 1983). Member, Board of Editors, Journal of Law and Policy in International Business, 1981-1983. Executive Director, U.S. Delegation to the Third United Nations Conference on the Law of the Sea and Deputy Director, Office of Oceans Law and Policy, Department of State, 1981-1982. *Member:* The District of Columbia Bar; American Bar Association (Chair, Fuel and Energy Committee, Antitrust Section, 1999-2001). ***PRACTICE AREAS:*** Antitrust and Trade Regulation; Energy Regulation; Mergers and Acquisitions. ***Email:*** mamason@hhlaw.com

GEORGE W. MAYO, JR., born Waycross, Georgia, December 23, 1946; admitted to bar, 1973, Virginia; 1974, District of Columbia. *Education:* Emory University (A.B., 1967); University of Virginia (J.D., 1973). Phi Alpha Delta; Order of the Coif. Member, Editorial Board, Virginia Law Review, 1968-1969 and 1972-1973. *Member:* The District of Columbia Bar; Virginia State Bar; American Bar Association (Member, Sections on: Litigation; Administrative Law). [Lt., U.S. Army, 1969-1971]. ***PRACTICE AREAS:*** Insurance Coverage; Transportation; Litigation; Administrative Law. ***Email:*** gwmayo@hhlaw.com

MARK E. MAZO, born Philadelphia, Pennsylvania, January 12, 1950; admitted to bar, 1975, District of Columbia; 1977, U.S. Court of Appeals for the District of Columbia Circuit; 1989, U.S. Supreme Court. *Education:* Princeton University (A.B., magna cum laude, 1971); Harvard University (J.D., cum laude, 1974). Phi Beta Kappa. (Also at Paris, France Office). ***PRACTICE AREAS:*** International Mergers and Acquisitions; International Business Law; International Joint Ventures; Foreign Investment in the U.S.; Buying and Selling of Businesses. ***Email:*** memazo@hhlaw.com

SCOTT D. McCLURE, born St. Louis, Missouri, December 25, 1965; admitted to bar, 1991, Maryland; 1992, District of Columbia. *Education:* Southern College (B.B.A., summa cum laude, Acct., 1988); Duke University (J.D., with high honors, 1991). Order of the Coif. Author: "Religious Preferences in Employment Decisions: How Far May Religious Organizations Go?" 1990 Duke Law Journal. *Member:* The District of Columbia Bar. ***PRACTICE AREAS:*** Tax. ***Email:*** sdmcclure@hhlaw.com

MARK S. McCONNELL, born East Chicago, Indiana, June 15, 1953; admitted to bar, 1979, District of Columbia. *Education:* Johns Hopkins University (B.A., 1975); Stanford University (M.B.A., 1979; J.D., 1979). Associate Editor, Stanford Law Review, 1978-1979. Member, Board of Editors, Trade Law Topics, 1987-1988. Recipient, Silver Medal, Royal Society of Arts, Manufactures and Commerce, Great Britain, 1975. Author: "Implementation of the Canada-U.S. Free Trade Agreement in the U.S. Congress," Trade Law Topics, 1988; "The Softwood Lumber Case: A U.S. Perspective," Trade Law Topics, 1987; "Outlook for U.S. Trade Legislation in 1986," Nihon Keizai, Shimbun, 1986; "U.S. Trade Remedies," Trade Law Topics, 1986; "U.S.-Canada Trade Talks," Trade Law Topics, 1985; ' "Limitations Imposed by the Constitution and Treaties of the United States on the Regulation of Foreign Investment," ' Chapter 1 of Manual of Foreign Investment in the United States, McGraw Hill, 1984; Note, "Accelerated Depreciation and Ratemaking: An Economic Perspective on the Shareholders' and Ratepayers' Interests," 31 Stanford Law Review 303, 1979. *Member:* The District of Columbia Bar; Federal (Chairman, Private International Law Committee, 1986-1988) and American Bar Associations. ***PRACTICE AREAS:*** International Law; International Trade Law. ***Email:*** msmcconnell@hhlaw.com

JANET L. McDAVID, born Minneapolis, Minnesota, January 24, 1950; admitted to bar, 1975, District of Columbia, U.S. Supreme and U.S. Claims Court. *Education:* Northwestern University (B.A., with honors, 1971); Georgetown University (J.D., 1974). Editor, Georgetown Law Journal, 1973-1974. Co-Editor and Principal Author: ABA Antitrust Law Section, "Antitrust Evidence Handbook," 1991. Author: "Failing Companies and the Antitrust Laws," 14 University of Michigan J. L. Ref. 229, 1981; "Litigation Support Systems: A Non-Technical Primer for Lawyers," 6 District Lawyer 26, 1982; "Pillsbury v. Conboy: Decision Will Have Major Impact on Depositions in Civil Litigation," Vol. 5, No. 27, Nat. L. J., 1983; "The Court's Welcome Demise of the 'Bathtub' Conspiracy Doctrine," Vol. 6, No. 46, Nat. L.J., 1984; "The California Experience: The Hole in the Illinois Brick Wall?" 1 Antitrust 16, 1987; Using Alternative Dispute Resolution in Antitrust Cases, 4 Antitrust 25, 1990; "Report of the Task Force on Competition Policy of the ABA Section of Antitrust Law," 61 Antitrust L.J. 977 (1993); "The 1992 Horizontal Merger Guidelines: A Practitioner's View of Key Issues," 61 Antitrust L.J. 459 (1993); "Kodak Decision Revitalizes Tying Claims," 12 Franchise L.J. 3 (1992); "Distribution Methods," 8 Corp. Couns. Q. 74 (Oct. 1992); "Antitrust Issues in Health Care Reform," 43 DePaul L. Rev. (1994); "Globalization of Premerger Notification and Review: Practical Problems and Solutions," Fordham Corporate Law Institute, 2000.

(This Listing Continued)

Co-Author: Mergers and Acquisitions, 2000; Antitrust and Health Care, 1999; Antitrust and Trade Associations Practice Guide, 1996; "How to Avoid Negotiations on Second Requests," Antitrust Vol. 13, No. 3 at 41, (Summer, 1999); "The Defense of Mergers in the Defense Industry," 7 Antitrust 4, Summer 1993; "Report of the American Bar Association Section of Antitrust Law Task Force to Review the Supreme Court's Decision in California v. ARC America," 59 Antitrust L.J. 273 (1990); "Antitrust Consent Decrees: Ten Years of Experience Under the Tunney Act," 53 Antitrust Law Journal, 1981; A.B.A. Antitrust Discovery Handbook, 1982; "Oligopolies, Cereal and Section Five of the Federal Trade Commission Act," 61 Geo. L. J. 1145, 1973. Member: Advisory Team for FTC Transition Team for Bush Administration, 2001; Clinton Administration Federal Trade Commission Transition Team, December, 1992; Department of Defense Task Force on Antitrust Aspects of Defense Industry Consolidations, 1993-1994; Department of Defense Task Force on Vertical Integration and Supplier Decisions, 1997-1999; Antitrust Council, U.S. Chamber of Commerce. Co-Chair, ABA Antitrust Section Task Force providing antitrust advice to Clinton Administration. *Member:* The District of Columbia Bar; Bar Association of the District of Columbia; American Bar Association (Member, Sections on: Antitrust Law; Litigation; Program Officer, Antitrust Law Section, 1994-1997; Member of Council, 1991-1994, Program Officer, 1994-1997, Vice Chair, Antitrust, 1997-1998 and Chair-Elect, 1998-1999; Chair, Antitrust Law Section; Chair: Franchising Committee, Antitrust Law Section, 1990-1991; Vice Chairman: Section 2 Committee, Antitrust Law Section, 1989-1990; Civil Practice and Procedure Committee, 1985-1989, Antitrust Law Section; Liaison, ABA Commission on the Status of Women in the Profession; Member, Forum on Franchising - Governing Committee, 1991-1997). ***PRACTICE AREAS:*** Antitrust Law. ***Email:*** jlmcdavid@hhlaw.com

THOMAS L. McGOVERN III, born Travis A.F.B., California, September 27, 1957; admitted to bar, 1988, California; 1988, District of Columbia; 1989, U.S. District Court for the District of Columbia. *Education:* United States Air Force Academy (B.S., 1979); Babson College (M.B.A., with distinction, 1982); Stanford University (J.D., with distinction, 1987). Associate Editor, Stanford Law Review. *Member:* The District of Columbia Bar (Member, Government Contracts and Litigation Section); American (Member, Section on: Public Contract Law) and Federal Bar Associations. [U.S. Air Force, 1979-1984, Captain; U.S. Air Force Reserve, Lt. Col., 1984—]. ***PRACTICE AREAS:*** Government; Government Contracts. ***Email:*** tlmcgovern@hhlaw.com

JAMES G. McMILLAN, born Montreal, Quebec, Canada, September 2, 1959; admitted to bar, 1985, Maryland and District of Columbia. *Education:* University of Virginia (B.A., 1981); Harvard Law School (J.D., 1984). Phi Beta Kappa. Raven Society. Notes Editor, Harvard Journal on Legislation. Counsel to U.S. Senate Republican Leader, Sen. Robert J. Dole, 1990-1993. *Member:* The District of Columbia Bar. ***PRACTICE AREAS:*** Corporate Commercial Law; Securities Regulation; Federal Legislative Practice. ***Email:*** jgmcmillan@hhlaw.com

DAVID MEDINE, born New York, N.Y., July 15, 1953; admitted to bar, 1978, District of Columbia; 1986, Indiana. *Education:* Hampshire College (B.A., 1975); University of Chicago (J.D., 1978). Author: "Alternative Financial Delivery Systems," Proceedings of the 36th Annual Conference on Bank Structure and Competition, Federal Reserve Bank of Chicago (2000); "Regulatory Issues in Internet Privacy: The FTC's Role," Electronic Banking Law and Commerce Report, Vol. 3, No. 6, pp. 7-12 (1998); "The Implications of Emerging Electronic Payment Systems on Electronic Privacy," Electronic Banking Law and Commerce Report, Vol. 2, No. 6, pp. 6-12 (1997); "Law and Kurosawa's *Rashomon*," Literature/Film Quarterly, Vol. 20, No. 1, pp. 55-60 (1992); "The Constitutional Right to Expert Assistance for Indigents in Civil Cases," Hastings Law Journal, Vol. 41, pp. 281-349 (1990); "The Adverse Testimony Privilege: Time to Dispose of a 'Sentimental Relic'," Oregon Law Review, Vol. 67, pp. 519-560 (1988); "The Noise Control Act Legislative and Administrative Problems of Implementation," Environmental Law, Vol. 9, pp. 313-345 (1979). Co-Author, "Consumer Protection," chapter, The District of Columbia Practice Manual, 1987. Clinical Instructor, George Washington University National Law Center, 1983-1986. Associate Professor, Indiana University School of Law, 1986-1989. Senior Advisor, National Economic Council, The White House. ***PRACTICE AREAS:*** Privacy Law; Financial Services Law; Consumer Protection; Advertising Law; Internet Law. ***Email:*** dmedine@hhlaw.com

BRUCE C. MEE (Resident, Paris, France).

DR. GERNOD MEINEL (Resident, Berlin, Germany Office).

GEORGE H. MERNICK, III, born Providence, Rhode Island, February 29, 1952; admitted to bar, 1979, District of Columbia; 1989, Maryland. *Education:* University of Rochester (A.B., 1973); Georgetown University (J.D., magna cum laude, 1979). Author: Note, "Search and Seizure, The United States Courts of Appeals: 1976-1977 Term Criminal Law and Procedure," 66 Georgetown Law Journal 269-88, 351-60, 1977. Clerk to Hon. Murray M. Schwartz, U.S. District Court, District of Delaware, 1979-1980. *Member:* The District of Columbia Bar; Maryland State Bar Association. ***PRACTICE AREAS:*** Federal Litigation; Trial Practice; Securities Litigation; Corporate Litigation. ***Email:*** ghmernick@hhlaw.com

(This Listing Continued)

MARTIN MICHAELSON, born Boston, Massachusetts, April 12, 1943; admitted to bar, 1968, New York; 1973, District of Columbia and U.S. Supreme Court; 1983, Massachusetts. *Education:* University of Chicago (B.A., 1965); Boston College (J.D., 1968). *Member:* The District of Columbia Bar; Boston, Massachusetts, Federal and American Bar Associations. ***PRACTICE AREAS:*** Administrative Law; Business Law; Education Law; Government; Labor and Employment. ***Email:*** mmichaelson@hhlaw.com

GEORG MIGGEL (Resident, Berlin, Germany Office).

EVAN MILLER, born 1956; admitted to bar, 1982, New York; 1983, District of Columbia. *Education:* Columbia University (B.A., 1978); Georgetown University (J.D., 1981). Law Clerk, Hon. Anthony A. Alaimo, Chief Judge, U.S. District Court for the Southern District of Georgia, 1981-1982. *Member:* The District of Columbia Bar; New York State Bar Association. ***PRACTICE AREAS:*** Employee Benefits. ***Email:*** emiller@hhlaw.com

GEORGE W. MILLER, born Schenectady, New York, July 12, 1941; admitted to bar, 1966, New York; 1968, District of Columbia; 1978, Virginia. *Education:* Princeton University (B.A., magna cum laude, 1963); Harvard University (LL.B., 1966); George Washington University (LL.M. in Taxation 1968). Phi Beta Kappa. Law Clerk to Judge Bruce M. Forrester, Tax Court of the United States, 1966-1967. Member, 1985-1991, Vice-Chairman, 1988-1989 and Chairman 1989-1991, District of Columbia Court of Appeals' Board on Professional Responsibility. Member, Task Force on Racial and Ethnic Bias in the District of Columbia Courts, 1990-1993. Member, Advisory Council, U.S. Court of Federal Claims, 1994—. *Member:* The District of Columbia Bar; Bar Association of the District of Columbia; Federal and American (Member, Sections on: Litigation; Environment, Energy and Resources; Public Contract Law) Bar Associations; Virginia State Bar; U.S. Court of Federal Claims Bar Association; Federal Circuit Bar Association. [Lt., U.S. Navy, JAGC, 1967-1970]. ***PRACTICE AREAS:*** Litigation; Appellate Practice; Natural Resources; Environmental Law; Government Contracts. ***Email:*** gwmiller@hhlaw.com

H. TODD MILLER, born Buffalo, New York, September 19, 1947; admitted to bar, 1971, North Carolina; 1973, District of Columbia. *Education:* State University of New York at Buffalo (B.A., 1969); Duke University (J.D., 1971). Phi Beta Kappa; Phi Alpha Delta; Order of the Coif. Notes Editor, Duke Law Journal, 1970-1971. Law Clerk to Judge Charles R. Simpson, U.S. Tax Court, 1971-1973. *Member:* The District of Columbia Bar; American Bar Association (Member, Section of Taxation). ***PRACTICE AREAS:*** Federal Income Tax; International Income Tax; Tax Controversies; Corporate Taxation. ***Email:*** htmiller@hhlaw.com

BARBARA F. MISHKIN, born Philadelphia, Pennsylvania, February 19, 1936; admitted to bar, 1982, District of Columbia; 1989, U.S. Supreme Court; 1995, U.S. Court of Appeals, Fourth Circuit. *Education:* Mt. Holyoke College (A.B., cum laude, 1957); Yale University (M.A., 1958); American University (J.D., cum laude, 1981). Member, Ethics Committee, National Hospice Organization, 1983-1987. Contributing Editor, AAAS Professional Ethics Report, 1988-2000. Member, Board of Managers, Bon Secours Health System, 1983-1991. Member, Executive Committee, Legal Counsel for the Elderly, 1985-1988. Trustee, Mount Holyoke College, 1985-1990. Fellow, American Association for the Advancement of Science (AAAS), 1990—. Member, Committee on Scientific Freedom and Responsibility, American Association for the Advancement of Science, 1986-1992. Member: Advisory Board, Center for Humanizing Healthcare, Medlantic Healthcare Group, 1986-1988; National Advisory Board, Foundation for Critical Care, 1985—. Member, Board of Directors, Hebrew Home of Greater Washington, 1987-1991. Pro Bono Attorney of the Year, D.C. Bar, 1987-1988. Member, AAA S/ABA National Conference of Lawyers and Scientists, 1992-1997. *Member:* The District of Columbia Bar; American Bar Association (ABA Co-Chair, National Conference of Lawyers and Scientists, 1993-1997; Member, Section on Science and Technology, 1992—; Chair, Committee on Regulating Research, 1996-1998; Co-Chair, 1986-1987, Chair, 1988-1992, Subcommittee on Health and the Environment); American Health Lawyers Association. ***PRACTICE AREAS:*** Administrative Agency Practice; Administrative Hearings and Appeals; Federal Administrative Law; False Claims Act; Federal Grants; Public Policy; Qui Tam Litigation; Fraud; Bioethics; Patients Rights; Right of Privacy; Professional Conduct; Federal Regulatory Law; Regulatory Investigations; Life Sciences; Medical Technology. ***Email:*** bfmishkin@hhlaw.com

AUSTIN S. MITTLER, born Far Rockaway, New York, April 2, 1939; admitted to bar, 1963, New York; 1968, District of Columbia. *Education:* Dartmouth College (B.A., 1960); New York University School of Law (LL.B., 1963). Attorney, Criminal Division, U.S. Department of Justice, 1963-1966. Law Secretary to Justice James J. Crisona, Supreme Court, Queens County, New York, 1966. Special Attorney, Staff Assistant to Assistant Attorney General, U.S. Department of Justice, 1967-1968. *Member:* The District of Columbia Bar; New York State Bar Association. ***PRACTICE AREAS:*** Civil Litigation; White Collar Criminal Defense; Equine Law. ***Email:*** asmittler@hhlaw.com

WILLIAM L. MONTS, III, born Columbia, South Carolina, July 14, 1961; admitted to bar, 1989, Virginia; 1991, District of Columbia. *Education:* Yale University (B.A., cum laude, 1984); University of South Carolina (J.D., cum

(This Listing Continued)

laude, 1989). Order of the Coif; Wig and Robe. Associate Editor-in-Chief, University of South Carolina Law Review, 1988-1989. Author: "Allied Tube & Conduit Corp. v. Indian Head, Inc.: An Emerging Conceptual Framework for Claims of Noerr Immunity," 41 South Carolina Law Review 633 (1990). *Member:* The District of Columbia Bar; Virginia State Bar; American Bar Association. ***PRACTICE AREAS:*** Antitrust; Litigation. ***Email:*** wlmonts@hhlaw.com

JEAN S. MOORE, born Akron, Ohio, December 18, 1947; admitted to bar, 1972, Ohio; 1975, District of Columbia. *Education:* The Ohio State University (B.A., 1969; J.D., summa cum laude, 1972). Order of the Coif. Articles Editor, The Ohio State University Law Review, 1971-1972. Attorney: U.S. Department of Justice Honors Program, 1972-1973; Office of Special Counsel, The White House, 1974. Editor, Matthew Bender Federal Evidence Practice Guide Reporter, 1989—. Member, Committee on Admissions, District of Columbia Court of Appeals, 1991-1994. Mediator, United States Court of Appeals for the District of Columbia. *Member:* The District of Columbia Bar; Ohio State Bar; Bar Association of District of Columbia; American Bar Association. ***PRACTICE AREAS:*** Litigation; Arbitration; Financial Fraud; Securities Fraud; Civil Litigation; Complex Litigation. ***Email:*** jsmoore@hhlaw.com

DENNIS K. MOYER (Resident, McLean, Virginia Office).

JEFFREY W. MUNK, born New York, N.Y., June 6, 1961; admitted to bar, 1988, District of Columbia. *Education:* DePauw University (B.M., 1983); Syracuse University College of Law (J.D., cum laude, 1987); Georgetown University Law College (LL.M., Taxation, 1994). Law Clerk to Special Trial Judge John J. Pajak, U.S. Tax Court, 1987-1988. Legislative Counsel to U.S. Senator Kay Bailey Hutchison, 1993-1996. *Member:* The District of Columbia Bar. ***PRACTICE AREAS:*** Tax Legislative Practice; Energy Legislative Practice; Transportation Legislative Practice; Appropriations; Legislative Practice. ***Email:*** jwmunk@hhlaw.com

KORNELIA NAGY-KOPPANY, born Budapest, Hungary, March 29, 1955; admitted to bar, 1981, Hungary (Not admitted in United States). *Education:* Loránd Eötvös University School of Law, Budapest, Hungary (J.D., summa cum laude, 1978); Faculté Internationale de Droit Comparé, Strasbourg, France (Master of International Comparative Law, 1978); New York University School of Law (LL.M., 1989). *Member:* Budapest Bar Association; International Bar Association. Special Legal Consultant, District of Columbia Bar. (Also at Budapest, Hungary Office). ***LANGUAGES:*** Hungarian, French and English. ***PRACTICE AREAS:*** Insolvency; Advertising Law; Corporate Formation; Real Estate Sales. ***Email:*** knagykoppany@hhlaw.com

HELEN A. NASTASIA (Resident, McLean, Virginia Office).

WILLIAM L. NEFF, born Macon, Missouri, June 5, 1947; admitted to bar, 1975, District of Columbia; 1976, Virgin Islands and Colorado. *Education:* University of Missouri (A.B., 1969); Harvard University (J.D., magna cum laude, 1974); Georgetown University Law Center (N.L.T., 1982). Phi Beta Kappa. Law Clerk to Judge Young, U.S. District Court for the Virgin Islands, 1974-1975. *Member:* The District of Columbia Bar. ***PRACTICE AREAS:*** Employee Benefits; Taxation; Tax Law; Deferred Compensation; Public Employee Retirement. ***Email:*** wlneff@hhlaw.com

J. PATRICK NEVINS, born Silver Spring, Maryland, May 27, 1967; admitted to bar, 1992, Maryland; 1997, District of Columbia. *Education:* University of Virginia (B.A., with distinction, 1989); Georgetown University Law Center (J.D., magna cum laude, 1992). Order of the Coif. John M. Olin Fellow in Law & Economics. Recipient, American Jurisprudence Awards in Torts, Corporations and Jurisprudence. Lead Articles Editor, The Tax Lawyer. *Member:* Maryland State and American Bar Associations; The District of Columbia Bar; Federal Energy Bar Association. ***PRACTICE AREAS:*** Energy Law; Natural Resources; Utility Law. ***Email:*** jpnevins@hhlaw.com

KAROL LYN NEWMAN, born Monterey, California, December 24, 1949; admitted to bar, 1973, Maryland; 1974, District of Columbia. *Education:* University of Maryland (B.A., with honors, 1971); University of Maryland School of Law (J.D., with honors, 1973). Order of the Coif. Articles Editor, University of Maryland Law Review, 1972-1973. Law Clerk, Honorable William J. McWilliams, Maryland Court of Appeals, 1973-1974. *Member:* The District of Columbia Bar; American Bar Association. ***PRACTICE AREAS:*** Energy. ***Email:*** klnewman@hhlaw.com

DAVID NEWMANN, born Boston, Massachusetts, December 16, 1967; admitted to bar, 1993, Illinois; 1995, District of Columbia; 1998, Pennsylvania. *Education:* Indiana University (B.A., with distinction, 1989); University of Michigan (J.D., magna cum laude, 1992). Phi Beta Kappa; Order of the Coif. Law Clerk, U.S. District Judge John W. Reynolds, Eastern District of Wisconsin, 1992-1994. *Member:* The District of Columbia Bar; Illinois State, Pennsylvania and American Bar Associations. (Also at Philadelphia, Pennsylvania, Office). ***PRACTICE AREAS:*** Civil Litigation. ***Email:*** dnewman@hhlaw.com

WILLIAM D. NUSSBAUM, born Bronx, New York, March 17, 1953; admitted to bar, 1977, District of Columbia; 1978, U.S. District Court for the District of Columbia, U.S. Court of Appeals for the District of Columbia Circuit; 1984, U.S. District Court for the District of Maryland; 1985, Maryland; 1986, U.S. Court of Appeals, Fourth Circuit. *Education:* Boston University

(This Listing Continued)

HOGAN & HARTSON L.L.P., Washington—Continued

(B.S., cum laude, 1974); American University (J.D., summa cum laude, 1977). Note and Comment Editor, American University Law Review, 1976-1977. Member, American University Law School National Moot Court Team, 1976-1977. Instructor, American University Law School, 1979-1981. Law Clerk to Judge J. Walter Yeagley, District of Columbia Court of Appeals, 1977-1978. Assistant U.S. Attorney for the District of Columbia, 1978-1984. Recipient, U.S. Department of Justice Special Achievement Award, 1982, 1983. Instructor, National Institute for Trial Advocacy. *Member:* The District of Columbia Bar; Maryland State and American Bar Associations. ***PRACTICE AREAS:*** Civil Litigation; White Collar Criminal Litigation; Civil Rights Defense; College and University Law; School Tenure. ***Email:*** wdnussbaum@hhlaw.com

GERALD E. OBERST, JR. (Resident, Brussels, Belgium Office).

MAUREEN O'BRYON, born Marshalltown, Iowa, April 3, 1946; admitted to bar, 1975, District of Columbia; 1976, U.S. Court of Appeals for the District of Columbia Circuit and U.S. District Court for the District of Columbia; 1977, U.S. Court of Appeals, Fifth Circuit; 1980, U.S. Supreme Court; 1982, Temporary Emergency Court of Appeals; 1984, U.S. Court of Appeals, Ninth Circuit. *Education:* University of Iowa (B.A., magna cum laude, 1968); Georgetown University (J.D., 1975). Phi Beta Kappa. Member, Board of Trustees (Formerly Executive Committee), Washington Lawyers Committee for Civil Rights Under Law, 1978—. *Member:* The District of Columbia Bar; American Bar Association. ***PRACTICE AREAS:*** Antitrust and Trade Regulation; Complex Litigation and Multi-District Litigation; Antitrust Class Actions; Litigation. ***Email:*** mobryon@hhlaw.com

BOB GLEN ODLE, born McKinney, Texas, November 4, 1937; admitted to bar, 1966, Texas; 1967, District of Columbia. *Education:* University of Texas (B.A., 1960; LL.B., 1966). Phi Beta Kappa. Associate Editor, Texas Law Review, 1965-1966. *Member:* The District of Columbia Bar; State Bar of Texas; American Bar Association. ***PRACTICE AREAS:*** Commercial Law; Corporate Law. ***Email:*** bgodle@hhlaw.com

LINDA L. OLIVER, born Rome, Italy, August 7, 1953; admitted to bar, 1980, District of Columbia. *Education:* Yale University (B.A., 1976); Georgetown University Law Center (J.D., 1980). Legal Advisor to FCC Commissioner Ervin S. Duggan, 1990-1994. Trial Attorney, Litigation Division, FCC Office of General Counsel, 1982-1990. Attorney, Administrative Law Division, FCC Office of General Counsel, 1980-1982. *Member:* The District of Columbia Bar; Federal Communications Bar Association. ***LANGUAGES:*** Spanish. ***PRACTICE AREAS:*** Telecommunications Law; Cable TV; FCC and State Regulation; Wireless Communications. ***Email:*** lloliver@hhlaw.com

NANCY DOERR O'NEIL, born Somerville, New Jersey, March 5, 1957; admitted to bar, 1982, Maryland; 2001, District of Columbia. *Education:* University of Virginia (B.S., 1979); Georgetown University (J.D., cum laude, 1982). Editor, The Tax Lawyer, 1980-1982. Author: "Tax Court Restricts CFC Branch Rule," 1 *International Tax Journal* No. 6, 364 (1991); "Helping US Debt Survive an Audit," *International Financial Law Review* Vol. IX, No. 12 (1990); ALI-ABA Continuing Legal Education, "Treatment of Property Owned by Partnerships with Both Tax-Exempt and Taxpaying Entities as Partners" (1986); "Supreme Court Decisions in Taxation: 1980 Term, *Commissioner v. Portland Cement Co.*," 35 *Tax Lawyer* 443,533 (1982). *Member:* Maryland State (Member, Taxation Section) and American (Member, Sections on: Taxation; Business Law) Bar Associations; District of Columbia Bar. (Also at Baltimore, Maryland Office). ***PRACTICE AREAS:*** Taxation. ***Email:*** ndoneil@hhlaw.com

CHRISTOPHER D. OZEROFF (Resident, Boulder, Colorado Office).

CHRISTINE M. PALLARES (Resident, Third Avenue New York, N.Y. Office).

JEFFREY D. PARISER, born New York, N.Y., March 18, 1965; admitted to bar, 1993, New Jersey and U.S. District Court, District of New Jersey; 1994, New York; 1995, U.S. District Court, Southern and Eastern Districts of New York; 1999, District of Columbia. *Education:* University of Virginia (B.A., 1987); New York University (J.D., magna cum laude, 1993). Order of the Coif. Adjunct Legal Writing Instructor, Brooklyn Law School, August, 1997-April, 1998. *Member:* The District of Columbia Bar. ***PRACTICE AREAS:*** Litigation. ***Email:*** jdpariser@hhlaw.com

BRUCE E. PARMLEY, born Buffalo, New York, May 14, 1948; admitted to bar, 1976, District of Columbia; 1981, Maine. *Education:* Ohio University (B.S.C., 1970); Catholic University of America (J.D., 1976). Law Clerk to Chief Judge Harold H. Greene, Superior Court of the District of Columbia, 1976-1977. Co-Chairman, Real Estate Division, District of Columbia Bar, 1980-1981. *Member:* The District of Columbia Bar; American Bar Association. ***PRACTICE AREAS:*** Commercial Real Estate Law; Commercial Law; Business Law; Leases and Leasing; Real Estate. ***Email:*** beparmley@hhlaw.com

RICHARD J. PARRINO (Resident, McLean, Virginia Office).

BERT R. PEÑA, born McAllen, Texas, August 18, 1949; admitted to bar, 1974, Texas; 1978, District of Columbia. *Education:* University of Texas at Edinburg (B.A., 1971); St. Mary's Law School (J.D., 1974). Assistant District Attorney, Bexar County, 1974-1977. Subcommittee Counsel, U.S. House Committee on Agriculture, 1977-1980. Legislative Counsel, Bristol-Myers, 1980-1988. Staff Director, U.S. House Committee on Agriculture, 1988-1990. *Member:* The District of Columbia Bar; State Bar of Texas. ***PRACTICE AREAS:*** Legislative; Regulatory Law; International Trade; Agriculture; Tax; Health; Environmental; Franchise Issues; Mexico and Latin America. ***Email:*** hrpena@hhlaw.com

ROBERT B. PENDER, JR., born Utica, New York, 1953; admitted to bar, 1983, New York; 1985, District of Columbia. *Education:* Middlebury College (B.A., 1976); Georgetown University (J.D., 1982). *Member:* New York State Bar Association; The District of Columbia Bar. ***PRACTICE AREAS:*** Corporate Finance; Project Finance; International Transactions; Mergers and Acquisitions. ***Email:*** rbpender@hhlaw.com

PATRICK K. PERRIN (Resident, Boulder, Colorado Office).

M. ELIZABETH PETERS, born Philadelphia, Pennsylvania, July 9, 1965; admitted to bar, 1991, New York; 1992, District of Columbia. *Education:* Duke University (B.A., magna cum laude, 1987); Columbia University (J.D., 1990). Phi Beta Kappa; Phi Eta Sigma; Pi Sigma Alpha. Harlan Fiske Stone Scholar. Notes Editor, Columbia Journal of Transnational Law, 1989-1990. Author: Note, "Free Trade Area Agreements as the Economic and Legal Solution to Bilateral Trade Relationships: The Case of Japan," 28 Columbia Journal of Transnational Law, pp. 499-530, 1990. *Member:* Bar Association of the District of Columbia; American Bar Association; American Immigration Lawyers Association. ***PRACTICE AREAS:*** International Trade; Immigration Law. ***Email:*** mepeters@hhlaw.com

PETER J. PETTIBONE (Resident at Moscow, Russia and Third Avenue, New York, N.Y. Offices).

JOHN E. PORTER, born Evanston, Illinois, June 1, 1935; admitted to bar, 1961, Illinois (Not admitted in District of Columbia). *Education:* Massachusetts Institute of Technology and Northwestern University (B.S.B.A., 1957); University of Michigan (J.D., with distinction, 1961). Michigan Law Review. Honor Law Graduate Attorney, U.S. Department of Justice Civil Division, Appellate Section, 1961-1963. State Representative, Illinois General Assembly, 1973-1979. U.S. Representative, U.S. House of Representatives, 1980-2001. Chairman, House Appropriations Subcommittee on Labor, Health and Human Services, and Education Vice-Chairman, House Appropriations Subcommittee on Foreign Operations. [Enlisted U.S. Army (Reserve), 1958-1964]. ***PRACTICE AREAS:*** Health Law; Legislative; Education Law. ***Email:*** jeporter@hhlaw.com

PHILIP D. PORTER (Resident, McLean, Virginia Office).

JOHN M. POTTER (Resident, Los Angeles, California Office).

SHARIS ARNOLD POZEN, born Jefferson City, Missouri, January 31, 1964; admitted to bar, 1989, Missouri; 1995, District of Columbia. *Education:* Connecticut College (B.A., with distinction, 1986); Washington University (J.D., 1989). *Member:* The Missouri Bar; The District of Columbia Bar; American Bar Association (Member, Antitrust Section). ***PRACTICE AREAS:*** Antitrust and Trade Regulation; Litigation. ***Email:*** sapozen@hhlaw.com

E. BARRETT PRETTYMAN, JR., born Washington, D.C., June 1, 1925; admitted to bar, 1954, District of Columbia. *Education:* Yale University (B.A., 1949); University of Virginia (LL.B., 1953). Phi Delta Phi. Winner, Moot Court Competition, Best Law Review Note, 1953. Recipient: 2000 Justice Potter Stewart Award, Council for Court Excellence; 1999 Lawyer of the Year, D.C. Bar Association; Common Cause Public Service Achievement Award, 1999; D.C. Governments Distinguished Public Service Award, 1999. Decisions Editor, Virginia Law Review, 1952-1953. Co-Editor, Justice Jackson's The Supreme Court in the American System of Government, 1955. Author: *Death and The Supreme Court,* Harcourt, Brace and World, Inc., 1961. Winner, Mystery Writers of America and Scribes Awards. Law Clerk to Justice Jackson, 1953-1954, Justice Frankfurter, 1954-1955 and Justice Harlan, 1955, U.S. Supreme Court. Associate Hogan & Hartson, 1955-1963; Partner, 1964-1998, 1999—. Inspector General of District of Columbia, 1998-1999. Special Assistant to the Attorney General of the United States, 1963 and to the White House, 1963-1964. Member, Board of Trustees, Executive Committee: American University, 1972-1987, Trustee Emeritus, 1987—. Chairman, Committee to Write Bicentennial History of D.C. Circuit, 1976. Member, Board of Governors, St. Albans School, 1957-1963, 1965-1971, Chairman, 1965-1967. Member, Advisory Board: Media Law Reporter, 1976-1985; Institute for Communications Law Studies of Columbus School of Law, Catholic University, 1982-1990. Special Counsel to House Committee on Standards of Official Conduct, 1980-1982. Outside Counsel to Subcommittee on Oversight and Investigations, House Committee on Interstate and Foreign Commerce, 1978. Special Consultant to Subcommittee to Investigate Problems Connected with Refugees and Escapees, Senate Judiciary Committee, 1967-1968. Trustee and Member, Executive Committee, 1982— and Vice President and Chairman, Publications Committee, 1997—, Supreme Court Historical Society. Member, International Advisory Group, Toshiba Corp., 1993-1997. Member, Executive Committee and Board of Trustees, Washington Journalism Center, 1974-1993. Member, National Advisory Committee, National Institute for Citizen Education in the Law, 1985-1991. Member, PEN/

(This Listing Continued)

(This Listing Continued)

Faulkner Foundation Board, President, 1990-1993. President, American Academy of Appellate Lawyers, 1992-1993. President, Lawyers Club, 1996-1997. Co-Chair, Bicentennial Celebration of the D.C. Federal Courts, 1999-2000. *Member:* The District of Columbia Bar (President, 1972-1973; Member, Board of Governors, 1973-1974); Bar Association of the District of Columbia (Member, Board of Directors, 1965-1967); American Judicature Society (Vice-President; Member, Executive Committee, Board of Trustees, 1989-1994). Fellow: District of Columbia Bar Foundation (Successively President, Vice-President and Treasurer); American Bar Foundation; American College of Trial Lawyers. ***PRACTICE AREAS:*** Administrative Law; Appellate Practice; Civil Appeals. ***Email:*** ebprettyman@hhlaw.com

MICHAEL A. PROETT (Resident, London, England Office).

GERARD J. PRUD'HOMME, born Baltimore, Maryland, September 25, 1949; admitted to bar, 1986, Maryland; 1987, U.S. District Court, District of Maryland; 1994, District of Columbia. *Education:* Johns Hopkins University (B.A., 1971; M.A., 1973); University of Maryland (J.D., with honors, 1986). Member, American Statistical Association, 1976-1986. Co-Author: "Designing Clinical Trials," Med. Device & Diag. Indus., 18:2, 1996; "Tort Claims Against U.S. Govt.-Perils, Pitfalls & Practical Problems," MD Bar Journal, 21:4, 1988; "Risk Management Implications and Ethical Concerns in Withholding Life Sustaining Treatment," Perspectives in Healthcare Risk Mgt., 10:1, 1990; "Quality Assurance and Monitoring in the Hypertension Prevention Trial," *Controlled Clinical Trials* 10: 3:84-94, Sept., 1989; "Factors influencing the development of visual loss in advanced diabetic retinopathy: DRS Report #10," *Investigative Ophthal.* 26: 7:983-991, 1985; "Influence of adherence to treatment and response of cholesterol on mortality in the Coronary Drug Project," *New Eng. J Med* 303: 1038-1041, 1980. *Member:* Maryland State, Federal and American Bar Associations; The District of Columbia Bar. ***PRACTICE AREAS:*** Regulatory Law; Food, Drug and Cosmetic Law; Drug and Medical Device Regulation; Food and Drug Regulation. ***Email:*** gjprudhomme@hhlaw.com

PATRICK M. RAHER, born Kalamazoo, Michigan, June 15, 1947; admitted to bar, 1972, Virginia; 1973, District of Columbia. *Education:* University of Notre Dame (B.B.A., 1969); Georgetown University Law Center (J.D., 1972). Professor, Legal Research and Creditors Rights, International School of Law, Washington, D.C., 1972-1975. Law Clerk to Hon. Roger Robb, U.S. Circuit Judge for the District of Columbia Circuit, 1972-1973. Vice-Chair, District of Columbia Judicial Disabilities and Tenure Commission, 1986-1992. Member, EPA Clean Air Act Advisory Committee. Co-Chair, EPA Newsource Review Committee. Co-Chair, EPA Ozone Coordination Advisory Committee. *Member:* The District of Columbia Bar; Virginia and American Bar Associations. ***PRACTICE AREAS:*** Clean Air Act; Environmental Compliance; Environmental Criminal Defense; Environmental Dispute Resolution; Environmental Due Diligence; National Environmental Policy Act (NEPA); Federal Insecticide, Fungicide and Rodenticide Act (FIFRA); Water Pollution. ***Email:*** pmraher@hhlaw.com

PROF. DR. PETER RAUE (Resident, Berlin, Germany Office).

JOHN A. REDMON (Resident at 100 Park Avenue, New York, New York Office).

JONATHAN T. REES, born Lawrence, Massachusetts, January 17, 1963; admitted to bar, 1991, Maryland; 1994, District of Columbia. *Education:* Brown University (A.B., 1985); University of Virginia (J.D., 1991). Member: Virginia Law Review; Virginia Journal of International Law. Law Clerk to the Hon. John M. Steadman, District of Columbia Court of Appeals, 1991-1992. *Member:* The District of Columbia Bar. ***PRACTICE AREAS:*** Labor and Employment; Litigation. ***Email:*** jtrees@hhlaw.com

SCOTT H. REISCH (Resident, Denver, Colorado Office).

TERRI STEINHAUS REISKIN, born Buffalo, N.Y., November 12, 1959; admitted to bar, 1984, District of Columbia; 1985, U.S. District Court for the District of Columbia; 1987, U.S. Court of Appeals for the District of Columbia Circuit; 1988, U.S. District Court, District of Maryland; 1991, U.S. Court of Appeals, Third Circuit; 1992, U.S. District Court, Western District of New York; 1994, U.S. Court of Appeals, Eleventh Circuit; 1995, Maryland; 1999, U.S. Court of Appeals, Fourth Circuit. *Education:* Princeton University (A.B., magna cum laude, 1981); Harvard University (J.D., cum laude, 1984). Phi Beta Kappa. Judicial Clerk, Hon. Thomas P. Jackson, U.S. District Court for the District of Columbia, 1984-1985. *Member:* The District of Columbia Bar; American Bar Association (Member: Litigation Section; Products Liability Committee); Defense Research Institute. ***PRACTICE AREAS:*** Automotive Products Liability; Drug and Medical Device Defense; Products Liability Defense; Complex Litigation; Class Action Defense. ***Email:*** tsreiskin@hhlaw.com

THOMAS E. REPKE (Resident, Baltimore, Maryland Office).

MARISSA G. REPP, born Brooklyn, New York, June 19, 1956; admitted to bar, 1984, District of Columbia; 1991, U.S. Court of Appeals for the District of Columbia Circuit. *Education:* State University of New York at Stony Brook (B.A., with honors, 1977); Georgetown University (J.D., magna cum laude, 1984). Phi Beta Kappa. Member, Georgetown Law Journal, 1982-1984. Law

(This Listing Continued)

Clerk to the Hon. James A. Belson, Associate Judge, District of Columbia Court of Appeals, 1984-1985. *Member:* The District of Columbia Bar; Federal Communications Bar Association. ***PRACTICE AREAS:*** Communications Law; Commercial Transactions; FCC Regulation; Broadcast Regulations; Broadcast Station Transfers; FCC Licensing; Public Broadcasting; Telecommunications Law; Telephone Utility Regulation. ***Email:*** mgrepp@hhlaw.com

JAI H. RHO (Resident, Los Angeles, California Office).

LESLIE S. RITTS, born Boston, Massachusetts, March 20, 1955; admitted to bar, 1980, Virginia; 1985, District of Columbia. *Education:* Princeton University (A.B., cum laude, 1977); College of William and Mary (J.D., 1980). Appointed, EPA New Source Review Committee, 1993-1997; EPA Operating Permit Workgroup, 1994-1997; Chair, Air and Waste Management Association Government Affairs Committee, 1993-1996. Author: "Compensation for Environmental Injuries: An Examination of Virginia Law," 2 Virginia J. Nat. Res. L. 233, 1982; "The Regulation of Toxic and Oxidant Air Pollution in North America," CCH, 1986. *Member:* The District of Columbia Bar; Virginia State Bar; American Bar Association. ***PRACTICE AREAS:*** Clean Air Act; Environmental Compliance; Environmental Litigation; Environmental Regulation; Wetlands Regulation. ***Email:*** lsritts@hhlaw.com

JOHN G. ROBERTS, JR., born Buffalo, New York, January 27, 1955; admitted to bar, 1981, District of Columbia; 1982, U.S. Claims Court and U.S. Court of Appeals for the Federal Circuit; 1987, U.S. Supreme Court; 1988, U.S. Court of Appeals for the District of Columbia, Fifth and Ninth Circuits; 1995, U.S. Court of Appeals, Third and Eleventh Circuits; 1996, U.S. Court of Appeals, Seventh and Tenth Circuits; 1998, U.S. Court of Appeals, Fourth and Sixth Circuits; 1999, U.S. Court of Appeals, Eighth Circuit. *Education:* Harvard College (A.B., summa cum laude, 1976); Harvard Law School (J.D., magna cum laude, 1979). Phi Beta Kappa. National Merit Scholar. Member, 1977-1979 and Managing Editor, 1978-1979, Harvard Law Review. Law Clerk to: Judge Henry J. Friendly, U.S. Court of Appeals for the Second Circuit, 1979-1980; Justice William H. Rehnquist, U.S. Supreme Court, 1980-1981. Special Assistant to U.S. Attorney General William French Smith, 1981-1982. Associate Counsel to the President, 1982-1986. Principal Deputy Solicitor General of the United States, 1989-1993. *Member:* The District of Columbia Bar; American Law Institute; American Academy of Appellate Lawyers. ***PRACTICE AREAS:*** U.S. Supreme Court Litigation; Appellate Practice; Federal Litigation. ***Email:*** jgroberts@hhlaw.com

WILLIAM R. ROBERTS (Resident, Boulder, Colorado Office).

STEVEN N. ROBINSON, born Portland, Maine, October 7, 1950; admitted to bar, 1984, Virginia; 1985, District of Columbia. *Education:* Brown University (A.B., Economics, 1972); Columbus School of Law (J.D., 1984). [Active Duty, U.S. Naval Officer, 1972-1984; Capt., U.S. Naval Reserves, 1984-1993]. ***PRACTICE AREAS:*** Corporate Law; Securities. ***Email:*** snrobinson@hhlaw.com

RICHARD S. RODIN, born New York, N.Y., August 23, 1938; admitted to bar, 1963, New York; 1969, District of Columbia. *Education:* Columbia College (B.A., 1960); Columbia University (LL.B., 1963). Staff Attorney, National Labor Relations Board, 1964-1969. *Member:* The District of Columbia Bar; American Bar Association; Federal Communications Bar Association. ***PRACTICE AREAS:*** Communications and Media; Broadcast Radio; Broadcast Regulation; Broadcast Television; FCC Regulation. ***Email:*** rsrodin@hhlaw.com

PAUL G. ROGERS, born Ocilla, Georgia, June 4, 1921; admitted to bar, 1948, Florida; 1953, U.S. Supreme Court; 1978, District of Columbia. *Education:* University of Florida (B.A., 1942); George Washington University and University of Florida (J.D., 1948). Phi Delta Phi. Member, Florida Blue Key. Recipient: Academy of Sciences Public Welfare Medal, 1982; Albert Lasker Award for Public Service, 1993; The 1994 Allied Signal Achievement Award in Aging; 1994 Distinguished Leadership Award from the University of Florida Health Sciences Center; 1995 National Osteoporosis Foundation Leadership Award; The 1996 Maxwell Finland Award; The 1997 American Cancer Society Distinguished Service Award; The National Community Pharmacists Association 1998 Distinguished American Award; The 1999 IONA's Outstanding Citizen Award. By Act of Congress (December 21, 2000) the Main Plaza at the National Institute of Health was designated as the "Paul G. Rogers Plaza" on June 12, 2001. Member of Congress, 1955-1979. Chairman, Subcommittee on Health and the Environment, U.S. Congress, 1971-1979. Member, Advisory Committee on Civil Rules of the Judicial Conference of the U.S., 1979-1984. Dean's Council: Harvard School of Public Health; The Scripps Research Institute. Chair: National Council on Patient Information and Education (N.C.P.I.E.), 1985—; National Osteoporosis Foundation (N.O.F.), 1986—; Friends of National Library of Medicine, 1990—; National Foundation for Infectious Diseases, 1995; Research! America, 1996. Co-Chair, National Coalition for Health Care (N.L.C.H.),1989—. *Member:* The District of Columbia Bar; Bar Association of the District of Columbia; The Florida Bar; American Bar Association; National Academy of Sciences (Institute of Medicine). [Major, U.S. Army, active duty, 1942-1946]. ***PRACTICE AREAS:*** Corporate Law; Health Law; Environmental Law; Legislative Law. ***Email:*** pgrogers@hhlaw.com

(This Listing Continued)

HOGAN & HARTSON L.L.P., Washington—Continued

PETER A. ROHRBACH, born Hartford, Connecticut, April 11, 1953; admitted to bar, 1979, District of Columbia; 1980, U.S. District Court, District of Columbia. *Education:* Yale University (B.A., magna cum laude, 1975); Stanford University (J.D., 1979). Senior Note Editor, Stanford Law Review, 1978-1979. *Member:* The District of Columbia Bar; Federal Communications Bar Association. ***PRACTICE AREAS:*** Telecommunications Law; Satellite Communications; Broadcasting Law; International Communications Law; Internet Law. ***Email:*** parohrbach@hhlaw.com

PETER J. ROMEO, born Darby, Pennsylvania, August 1, 1942; admitted to bar, 1968, Virginia; 1969, District of Columbia, U.S. District Court for the District of Columbia and U.S. Court of Appeals for the District of Columbia Circuit; 1972, U.S. Supreme Court. *Education:* Georgetown University (B.S.B.A., 1964); George Washington University (J.D., 1967; LL.M., 1969). Certified Public Accountant, District of Columbia, 1969. Author: "The Registration Process," CPR 7A of Sowards, Federal Securities Act, updated 2001; numerous articles on various securities law topics. Co-Author: "Section 16 Treatise and Reporting Guide," Executive Press, Inc. (1994); "Section 16 Forms and Filings Handbook," Executive Press, Inc. (4th ed. 2000); "Comprehensive Section 16 Outline," Executive Press, Inc. (2000, updated annually); "Section 16 Updates," Executive Press, Inc., issued quarterly since January 1991. Attorney, U.S. Securities & Exchange Commission, 1969-1984; Chief Counsel, Division of Corporation Finance, 1980-1984. *Member:* The District of Columbia Bar; Virginia State Bar; American Bar Association. ***PRACTICE AREAS:*** Securities. ***Email:*** pjromeo@hhlaw.com

JAMES J. ROSENHAUER, born Chicago, Illinois, May 25, 1942; admitted to bar, 1968, District of Columbia. *Education:* Catholic University of America (A.B., magna cum laude, 1964); Yale Law School (LL.B., 1967). Phi Beta Kappa. Member, Tri Bar Opinion Committee. *Member:* The District of Columbia Bar; Bar Association of the District of Columbia; American (Member, Business Law Opinion Committee), International and Inter-American Bar Associations. ***PRACTICE AREAS:*** International Finance; Mergers, Acquisitions and Divestitures; Project Finance; Corporate Law; Commercial Real Estate. ***Email:*** jjrosenhauer@hhlaw.com

MACE J. ROSENSTEIN, born Chicago, Illinois, February 27, 1953; admitted to bar, 1984, District of Columbia. *Education:* Harvard College (B.A., cum laude, 1975); University of Chicago (J.D., 1984). *Member:* The District of Columbia Bar; Federal Communications Bar Association. ***PRACTICE AREAS:*** Communications and Media; Broadcast Regulation; Broadcast Station Transfers; Public Broadcasting; Telecommunications Regulation. ***Email:*** mjrosenstein@hhlaw.com

HOWARD J. ROSENSTOCK, born Washington, D.C., February 9, 1954; admitted to bar, 1980, Pennsylvania; 1982, District of Columbia. *Education:* University of Maryland (B.A., summa cum laude, 1975); Georgetown University (J.D., magna cum laude, 1979). Phi Beta Kappa; Pi Sigma Alpha. Member, John Marshall Society. Author: "Don't Be Burned by Fire-Proper Allocation of Risk Between Landlord and Tenant," CLLS, September, 1988. Member, Advisory Board, Chicago Title Insurance Company, 1988—. ***PRACTICE AREAS:*** Real Estate; Finance. ***Email:*** hjrosenstock@hhlaw.com

STEVEN J. ROUTH, born Urbana, Illinois, July 28, 1957; admitted to bar, 1983, District of Columbia. *Education:* University of Pennsylvania (B.A., magna cum laude, 1979); University of London, London, England (M.A., 1980); Harvard University (J.D., magna cum laude, 1983). Law Clerk, Hon. John M. Ferren, District of Columbia Court of Appeals, 1983-1984. *Member:* The District of Columbia Bar. ***PRACTICE AREAS:*** Litigation; Complex Litigation; Intellectual Property Litigation; Trial Practice; Education Law; College and University Law; Educational Testing. ***Email:*** sjrouth@hhlaw.com

FABRICE RUÉ (Resident, Paris, France).

JAMES P. RUGGERI, born Syracuse, New York, January 8, 1965; admitted to bar, 1991, New York and District of Columbia. *Education:* Colgate University (B.A., 1987); Vanderbilt University (J.D., 1990). Articles Editor, Vanderbilt Law Review, 1988-1990. Law Clerk, United States District Judge Rebecca Beach Smith, Eastern District of Virginia, Norfolk, Virginia, 1990-1991. *Member:* The District of Columbia Bar; New York State and American Bar Associations. ***Email:*** jpruggeri@hhlaw.com

GEORGE A. SALTER (Resident at 100 Park Avenue, New York, New York Office).

DAVID J. SAYLOR, born Johnstown, Pennsylvania, September 12, 1945; admitted to bar, 1971, Hawaii; 1972, District of Columbia; 1973, U.S. Court of Appeals for the District of Columbia Circuit; 1974, U.S. Supreme Court; 1980, U.S. Court of Appeals, 2nd Circuit; 1987, U.S. Court of Appeals, 3rd Circuit; 1988, U.S. Court of Appeals, 11th Circuit. *Education:* Williams College (A.B., 1967); Harvard University (J.D., 1970). Member, Board of Editors, Harvard Law Review, 1969-1970. Law Clerk, Chief Judge, U.S. District Court, Honolulu, Hawaii, 1970-1971. Deputy General Counsel, Federal Communications Commission, 1978-1981. Assistant Director, Bureau of Competition, Federal Trade Commission, 1975-1978. *Member:* The District of Columbia Bar. ***PRACTICE AREAS:*** Communications and Media; Antitrust and Trade Regulation. ***Email:*** djsaylor@hhlaw.com

TODD D. SCHAFER, born Pittsburgh, Pennsylvania, February 17, 1962; admitted to bar, 1990, New York; 1991, District of Columbia; 1992, U.S. Court of Appeals, District of Columbia Circuit. *Education:* Vassar College (B.A., 1984); Oxford University, Oxford, England (M.Ph., 1986); Harvard University (J.D., 1989). *Member:* The District of Columbia Bar; New York State Bar Association. (Also at Moscow, Russia Office). ***LANGUAGES:*** Russian, Spanish. ***PRACTICE AREAS:*** International Corporate Law; International Financial Transactions and Restructurings; International Regulatory Law; International Arbitration. ***Email:*** tdschafer@hhlaw.com

WILLIAM C. SCHMIDT, born Alexandria, Virginia, April 7, 1948; admitted to bar, 1974, Virginia; 1975, District of Columbia; 1979, Illinois and U.S. Tax Court. *Education:* University of Virginia (B.S., with distinction, 1971; J.D., 1974). Sigma Gamma Tau; Order of the Coif. Member, Editorial Board, Virginia Law Review, 1972-1974. *Member:* The District of Columbia Bar; Virginia State Bar; Virginia, Illinois State and American (Member, Taxation Section) Bar Associations. ***PRACTICE AREAS:*** Employee Benefits; Taxation; Federal Income Tax; Executive Compensation; Tax Exempt Organizations. ***Email:*** wcschmidt@hhlaw.com

JEFFREY G. SCHNEIDER (Resident, Third Avenue New York, N.Y. Office).

FRIEDRICH TOBIAS SCHÖNE (Resident, Berlin, Germany Office).

DR. CARL-STEPHAN SCHWEER (Resident, Berlin, Germany Office).

DAVID J. SCOTT (Resident, Denver, Colorado Office).

LAWRENCE R. SEIDMAN (Resident, Baltimore, Maryland Office).

DR. HANS M. SEILER (Resident, Berlin, Germany Office).

JEFFREY N. SHANE, born New York, N.Y., March 27, 1941; admitted to bar, 1967, District of Columbia. *Education:* Princeton University (A.B., 1962); Columbia University (LL.B., 1965). Articles Editor, Columbia Journal of Law and Social Problems. Chairman, Commission on Air Transport, International Chamber of Commerce, 1994—; Chairman, Military Airlift Committee, National Defense Transportation Association, 1994—. Member, Study Group of Experts on Future Regulatory Arrangements, International Civil Aviation Organization, 1993-1994. Member, Architectural and Transportation Barriers Compliance Board, 1989-1993 (Vice-Chairman, 1992). Vice Chairman, Advisory Commission on Conferences in Ocean Shipping, 1992. Board of Directors, International Institute of Air and Space Law, University of Leiden, 1993-1995. Adjunct Professor of Law (International Transportation Law), Georgetown University, 1985-1989. Assistant Secretary for Policy and International Affairs, Department of Transportation, 1989-1993. Deputy Assistant Secretary for Transportation Affairs, Department of State, 1985-1989. Deputy Assistant Secretary for Policy and International Affairs, Department of Transportation, 1983-1985. *Member:* District of Columbia Bar and American Bar Association (Chair-Elect, Forum on Air and Space Law, 2000-2001). ***PRACTICE AREAS:*** Aviation; Commercial Space Transportation; Administrative Law. ***Email:*** jnshane@hhlaw.com

JEFFREY K. SHAPIRO, born New York, N.Y., January 11, 1961; admitted to bar, 1986, California; 1990, Pennsylvania; 1991, District of Columbia. *Education:* Brown University (A.B., magna cum laude, 1983); Harvard Law School (J.D., cum laude, 1986). Phi Beta Kappa. Department of Justice, Office of Legal Counsel, 1991-1994. *Member:* The District of Columbia Bar; State Bar of California; Pennsylvania Bar Association. ***PRACTICE AREAS:*** Food, Drug and Cosmetic Law; Drug and Medical Device Regulation. ***Email:*** jkshapiro@hhlaw.com

JAMES E. SHOWEN, born Charleston, West Virginia, November 26, 1953; admitted to bar, 1979, District of Columbia and West Virginia. *Education:* Duke University (A.B., magna cum laude, 1975); West Virginia University (J.D., 1979). Member, 1977-78 and Lead Articles Editor, 1978-79, West Virginia Law Review. Order of the Coif. *Member:* The District of Columbia Bar. ***PRACTICE AREAS:*** Partnership Law; Securities Law; Corporate Law. ***Email:*** jeshowen@hhlaw.com

DAVID L. SIERADZKI, born Oakland, California, June 17, 1962; admitted to bar, 1989, California; 1990, District of Columbia. *Education:* University of California, Berkeley (B.A., with high distinction, 1984, Phi Beta Kappa; M.P.P., 1988); Yale Law School (J.D., 1989). Attorney-Advisor, Common Carrier Bureau, Federal Communications Commission, 1991-1996. Chief, Legal Branch, Competitive Pricing Division, Common Carrier Bureau, Federal Communications Commission, 1996. *Member:* State Bar of California; The District of Columbia Bar. ***PRACTICE AREAS:*** Communications. ***Email:*** dlsieradzki@hhlaw.com

HOWARD S. SILVER, born New York, N.Y., May 27, 1959; admitted to bar, 1985, New York and District of Columbia. *Education:* Wharton School of Finance, University of Pennsylvania (B.S. in Economics, magna cum laude, 1981); Georgetown University (J.D., magna cum laude, 1984). Associate Editor,

(This Listing Continued)

Georgetown Law Journal, 1983-1984. Author: "Joinder and Severance," Thirteenth Annual Review of Criminal Procedure 72 Geo. L.J. 413, 1983. Research Assistant to former U.S. Supreme Court Justice Arthur J. Goldberg, 1983-1984. *Member:* The District of Columbia Bar; New York State and American Bar Associations. ***PRACTICE AREAS:*** Nonprofit and Charitable Organizations; Tax-Exempt Organizations; Nonprofit Tax Law; Public Charities; Private Foundations; Trade Associations. ***Email:*** hssilver@hhlaw.com

MICHAEL J. SILVER (Resident, Baltimore, Maryland Office).

RICHARD S. SILVERMAN, born Salina, Kansas, November 4, 1943; admitted to bar, 1968, New Jersey; 1972, District of Columbia; 1973, U.S. Supreme Court; 1978, North Carolina. *Education:* Rutgers University (B.A., 1965; J.D., 1968). Senior Editor, Rutgers Law Review, 1967-1968. Harkavy Scholar, 1967-1968 Author: *How to Get Your Food Additive Product Approved* in How to Work with the FDA 37, (Wayne L. Pines, ed., Food and Drug Law Institute, 2000); "Legal Implications of Risk Assessments in Food Processing Operations," Food Technology Magazine, December 1996; "State Regulation of the Legal Profession— Lay Intermediary and Unauthorized Practice of Law," 21 Rutgers Law Review 577, 1967; "Living Without the Regulators: Alternatives to Governmental Regulatory Action," 38 Food Drug Comm. L.J. 77, 1983. Co-Author: "A Guide to Federal Food Labeling Requirements," prepared for the U.S. Department of Agriculture and the U.S. Department of Health and Human Services, Government Printing Office, Washington, D.C., 1990. Editor, *Fundamentals of Law and Regulation, Volume I: An In-depth look at Foods, Veterinary Medicines and Cosmetics* (1997 Edition) published by the Food and Drug Law Institute, Washington, D.C. Associate Chief Counsel for Enforcement, U.S. Food and Drug Administration, 1970-1975. Secretary and General Counsel, RJR Foods, Inc., 1975-1979. Associate General Counsel, R.J. Reynolds Industries, Inc., Winston-Salem, North Carolina, 1978-1979. Chairman, National Juice Products Association Lawyers Advisory Committee, 1976-1979. Chairman, American Frozen Foods Institute Committee of Attorneys, 1976-1979. Legal Advisor, Laws and Regulations Committee of the Association of Food and Drug Officials, 1976—. Member, Food and Agriculture Committee, U.S. Chamber of Commerce, 1983-1993. Chairman, Food Integrity Subcommittee, 1988-1993. Member, Council I, Laws and Regulations for the Conference for Food Protection, 1988—. Member: Board of Governors, Food Update, 1990-1995 (Chairman of the Board, 1993-1994); Institute of Food Technologists, 1975—. *Member:* The District of Columbia Bar; New Jersey State and North Carolina Bar Associations. ***PRACTICE AREAS:*** Agricultural Law; Food, Drug and Cosmetic Law; Food Labeling and Inspection; Food Processing; Food and Drug Regulation. ***Email:*** rssilverman@hhlaw.com

PAUL C. SKELLY, born New York, N.Y., December 31, 1953; admitted to bar, 1979, District of Columbia; 1981, Virginia. *Education:* University of Virginia (B.A., 1976; J.D., 1979). Omicron Delta Kappa. Member, Raven Society. Winner, William Minor Lile Moot Court Competition, 1979. *Member:* The District of Columbia Bar; Virginia and American Bar Associations. ***PRACTICE AREAS:*** Employment Law; Litigation. ***Email:*** pcskelly@hhlaw.com

EDWARD C. SLEDGE (Resident, Baltimore, Maryland Office).

DAVID W. SMAIL, born St. Paul, Minnesota, May 30, 1965; admitted to bar, 1991, Minnesota; 1992, District of Columbia; 1996, Paris. *Education:* Macalester College (B.A., summa cum laude, 1987); Harvard Law School (J.D., cum laude, 1991). Phi Beta Kappa. Co-Author: "Privatisations: Ouverture du marché Américain?" *Banque* n'543, Dec. 1993, p. 30. *Member:* The District of Columbia Bar; Minnesota State Bar Association. ***LANGUAGES:*** English and French. ***PRACTICE AREAS:*** Commercial Law. ***Email:*** dwsmail@hhlaw.com

MAREE F. SNEED, born Holdenville, Oklahoma, April 4, 1948; admitted to bar, 1983, Illinois and U.S. District Court, Northern District of Illinois including Trial Bar; 1986, Maryland; 1987, District of Columbia. *Education:* University of Oklahoma (B.A., 1970; M.Ed., 1972); George Washington University (Ed.D., 1979); University of Chicago; Georgetown Law Center (J.D., 1983). Lecturer, Graduate School of Education, Harvard University. Member: Council of School Attorneys; Board of Directors, Council of School Attorneys (1990-1996). *Member:* The District of Columbia Bar; American Bar Association. ***PRACTICE AREAS:*** Education Law; Civil Litigation; Appellate Litigation. ***Email:*** mfsneed@hhlaw.com

LORRAINE SOSTOWSKI, born Scranton, Pennsylvania, November 11, 1953; admitted to bar, 1977, Massachusetts; 1986, District of Columbia. *Education:* Tufts University (A.B., magna cum laude, 1974); Harvard Law School (J.D., 1977). *Member:* The District of Columbia Bar; American Bar Association (Member, Sections on: Business Law; International Law). ***LANGUAGES:*** French. ***PRACTICE AREAS:*** Electronic Intellectual Property; Emerging Companies; Corporate Contracts; Corporate Finance; Mergers and Acquisitions; Securities Offerings; Corporate Governance; Venture Capital Finance. ***Email:*** lsostowski@hhlaw.com

PETER S. SPIVACK, born Menlo Park, California, April 4, 1963; admitted to bar, 1988, California and U.S. District Court, Central District of California; 1989, U.S. Court of Appeals, Ninth Circuit; 1997, District of Columbia; 1998, U.S. Court of Appeals, District of Columbia Circuit. *Education:* Stanford University (B.A., 1984); University of California School of Law, Los Angeles (J.D.,

(This Listing Continued)

1988). Order of the Coif. Member, 1985-1988 and Board of Editors, 1988, UCLA Law Review. Author: "Does Form Follow Function: The Idea-Expression Dichotomy in Copyright Protection of Computer Software," 35 UCLA L. Rev. 732 (1988). Clerk, Honorable William D. Keller, U.S. District Court for the Central District of California, 1988-1989. Clerk, Honorable Arthur Alarcon, U.S. Court of Appeals for the Ninth Circuit, 1989-1990. U.S. Attorney's Office, Central District of California, 1990-1997 (Recipient, Director's Award, 1994). *Member:* State Bar of California; The District of Columbia Bar. ***PRACTICE AREAS:*** White Collar Criminal; False Claims Act; Civil Litigation. ***Email:*** psspivack@hhlaw.com

TIMOTHY CHARLES STANCEU, born Canton, Ohio, July 31, 1951; admitted to bar, 1980, District of Columbia. *Education:* Colgate University (A.B., 1973); Georgetown University (J.D., 1979). Phi Beta Kappa. Deputy Director, Office of Trade and Tariff Affairs, U.S. Treasury Department, 1985-1989. Member, Board of Directors, National Association of Foreign Trade Zones, 1993—. *Member:* The District of Columbia Bar. ***PRACTICE AREAS:*** Customs Law; Foreign Trade Sanctions; International Trade Regulation; North American Free Trade Agreement; U.S. Foreign Trade Zones. ***Email:*** tcstanceu@hhlaw.com

JOHN S. STANTON, born Park Forest, Illinois, September 6, 1954; admitted to bar, 1979, California; 1980, District of Columbia and U.S. District Court, Central District of District of Columbia; 1985, U.S. Tax Court. *Education:* University of California at Berkeley (A.B., with great distinction, 1976); Harvard University (J.D., cum laude, 1979). Phi Beta Kappa. Co-Author: "BNA Tax Management Portfolio on Research and Development Expenditures," Bureau of National Affairs, 1987. Law Clerk to Hon. Robert J. Kelleher, U.S. District Court, Central District of California, 1979-1980. Member, Professional Staff, House Banking Committee, U.S. Congress, 1974. *Member:* The District of Columbia Bar; State Bar of California. ***PRACTICE AREAS:*** Legislative Practice; Taxation; Public Pension Plans. ***Email:*** jsstanton@hhlaw.com

STUART G. STEIN, born Norfolk, Virginia, April 16, 1960; admitted to bar, 1985, Virginia; 1988, District of Columbia. *Education:* George Washington University (B.B.A., Acct.; with distinction, 1982); University of Virginia (J.D., 1985). Beta Alpha Psi; Beta Gamma Sigma. Member, Editorial Board, Virginia Tax Review, 1983-1985. Research and Articles Development Editor, 1984-1985. Certified Public Accountant, Virginia, 1986. *Member:* The District of Columbia Bar; Virginia State Bar; Federal and American Bar Associations; American Institute of Certified Public Accountants. ***PRACTICE AREAS:*** Bank Holding Company Law; Bank Mergers and Acquisitions; Electronic Banking; Thrift Institutions Law; Corporate Law; Securities Law. ***Email:*** sgstein@hhlaw.com

STEVEN B. STEINBORN, born Alpena, Michigan, April 28, 1962; admitted to bar, 1987, Michigan; 1990, District of Columbia. *Education:* Michigan State University (B.A., with honors, 1984); University of Michigan (J.D., 1987). Co-Author: "A Guide to Federal Food Labeling Requirements," prepared for the U.S. Department of Agriculture and U.S. Department of Health and Human Services, Government Printing Office, Wash. D.C., 1990. *Member:* The District of Columbia Bar; State Bar of Michigan. ***PRACTICE AREAS:*** Food and Agriculture; Food and Drug Regulation; Trade Regulation Law. ***Email:*** sbsteinborn@hhlaw.com

MARK A. STERLING, born New York, N.Y., 1954; admitted to bar, 1979, District of Columbia; 1999, Florida. *Education:* University of Michigan (B.A., with high distinction, 1976; M.P.P., 1978; J.D., cum laude, 1979). Phi Beta Kappa. Managing Editor, Michigan Law Review, 1978-1979. General Counsel and Secretary (1993-1996) and Senior Vice President, Strategic Development and Special Counsel for Regulatory Affairs (1997-1999), Vitas Healthcare Corporation. President, Board of Directors, Hospice Care of the District of Columbia, 1990-1993. Member, Board of Directors, Comprehensive Care Management Corporation, Bronx, New York, 1994—. Member, Editorial Board, The Health Lawyer, 1989-1991. *Member:* The Florida Bar; The District of Columbia Bar; American Judicature Society; American Health Lawyers Association. (Also at Miami, Florida Office). ***PRACTICE AREAS:*** Health Care; Mergers and Acquisitions; Government Regulation; Corporate. ***Email:*** masterling@hhlaw.com

JOHN T. STOUGH, JR., born Houston, Texas, December 18, 1944; admitted to bar, 1974, Texas; 1978, District of Columbia. *Education:* Harvard University (B.A., 1967); University of Texas (J.D., with honors, 1974). Trial Attorney, Office of General Counsel, Federal Power Commission, 1974-1977. *Member:* Energy Bar Association (Chairman: Natural Gas Act Rate and Accounting Committee, 1982-1983; Tax Developments Committee, 1984-1985; Non-Utility Generating Committee, 1993-1994). [Capt., USMCR, 1967-1971]. ***PRACTICE AREAS:*** Administrative Law; Energy; Regulatory Law; Utility Law. ***Email:*** jtstough@hhlaw.com

CLIFFORD D. STROMBERG, born New York, N.Y., June 1, 1949; admitted to bar, 1975, New York, District of Columbia, U.S. District Court, Eastern and Southern Districts of New York, U.S. Court of Appeals, Second Circuit and U.S. Court of Appeals for the District of Columbia Circuit; 1980, U.S. Supreme Court. *Education:* Yale University (B.A., summa cum laude, 1971);

(This Listing Continued)

HOGAN & HARTSON L.L.P., Washington—Continued

Harvard University (J.D., 1974). Phi Beta Kappa. Member, Board of Editors, Harvard Law Review, 1973-1974. Teaching Fellow in Government, Harvard University, 1973-1974. Editor-in-Chief, "HealthSpan: The Report of Health Business and Law," 1984-1987. Board of Editors, "Managed Care Law Strategist, 1999—. Co-Author and Editor: Book, *Entrepreneurial Healthcare: How to Structure Successful New Ventures,* Harcourt Brace Jovanovich, 1985; Book, *Alternatives to the Hospital: Ambulatory Surgery Centers and Emergicenters,* Harcourt Brace Jovanovich, 1984. Co-Author: Book, *The Psychologists Legal Handbook,* Council for the National Register, 1988; Book, *Mental Health and Law: A System in Transition*, Jason Aronson Inc., 1975; "Health Care Credentialing: Implications for Academic Health Centers," *Human Resources for Health: Defining the Future,* AAHC 1992; *A Model State Law on Civil Commitment of the Mentally Ill,* 20 HARV. J. On LEGIS. 276, 1983. Author: "Health Care Provider Networks: Antitrust Issues and Practical Suggestions," in Developments in Antitrust Health Care Law, 1990; "Key Issues In Professional Ethics," Reflections on Ethics, ASHA, 1990; "Access to Hospital Information: Problems and Strategies," 4 Frontiers of Health Services Mgt. 3, 1987; "Health Law Comes of Age: Economics and Ethics in a Changing Industry," 92 YALE L. J. 203, 1983. Adjunct Associate Professor, George Washington University School of Medicine and Health Sciences, 1991-1998. Advisor to the National Conference of Commissioners on Uniform State Laws, 1982-1985. Deputy Executive Secretary, U.S. Department of Health and Human Services, 1978-1979. Consultant to the Federal Trade Commission, 1979-1980. Law Clerk to Hon. Orrin Judd, U.S. District Judge, Eastern District of New York, 1974-1975. Member, Board of Directors, National Children's Eye Care Foundation, 1986-1988. *Member:* The District of Columbia Bar; American Bar Association (Chair, Working Group on Health Care Reform, 1992-1997; Chairperson, 1988-1989; Executive Council Member, 1980-1990; Section of Individual Rights and Responsibilities; Member: Standing Committee on Legal Aid and Indigent Defendants, 1981-1987; Member, Governing Board, Forum Committee on Health Law, 1987-1990; Antitrust Law Section; Litigation Section; State Membership Chairman for the District of Columbia, 1984-1986); American Health Lawyers Association; National Association of College and University Attorneys; American Society of Association Executives. Fellow, American Bar Foundation. ***PRACTICE AREAS:*** Health Care; Corporate Law; Mergers, Acquisitions and Divestitures; Antitrust and Trade Regulation; Trade Association Law. ***Email:*** cdstromberg@hhlaw.com

MARY ANNE SULLIVAN, born Albany, New York, April 13, 1951; admitted to bar, 1976, District of Columbia; 1980, U.S. Supreme Court. *Education:* Fordham University (B.A., 1973); Yale Law School (J.D., 1976). Phi Beta Kappa. General Counsel, U.S. Department of Energy, 1998-2001. Deputy General Counsel, Environmental and Nuclear Programs, U.S. Department of Energy, 1994-1998. Law Clerk, Honorable Walter K. Stapleton, U.S. District Court, District of Delaware, 1976-1977. U.S. Attorney General's Council on ADR, 1999-2001. *Member:* District of Columbia Bar (Environment, Energy and Natural Resources). ***PRACTICE AREAS:*** Energy; Nuclear Energy; Federal Lands; Environmental Law; Global Climate Change; Energy Litigation. ***Email:*** masullivan@hhlaw.com

THOMAS J. SWEENEY, III (Resident at 100 Park Avenue, New York, New York Office).

JAN TANZER (Resident, Prague, Czech Republic Office).

DENNIS H. TRACEY, III (Resident at 100 Park Avenue, New York, New York Office).

LYNDON M. TRETTER (Resident at 100 Park Avenue, New York, New York Office).

HELEN R. TRILLING, born Boston, Massachusetts, May 13, 1950; admitted to bar, 1977, Massachusetts; 1978, U.S. District Court, District of Massachusetts; 1980, U.S. Supreme Court; 1984, District of Columbia and U.S. Court of Appeals, 10th Circuit. *Education:* Radcliffe College (A.B., magna cum laude, 1973); Harvard University (J.D., 1976). Phi Beta Kappa. Assistant General Counsel, Blue Cross & Blue Shield of Massachusetts, 1976-1979. Special Assistant to the General Counsel, U.S. Department of Health and Human Services, 1979-1983. *Member:* The District of Columbia Bar; American Bar Association (Member: Forum Committee on Health Law; White Collar Crime Health Care Fraud and Abuse subcommittee); National Health Lawyers Association. ***PRACTICE AREAS:*** Health Law; Health Care Compliance; Health Care Regulation; Health Care Reimbursement; Medicare and Medicaid Reimbursement; Medicare Fraud and Abuse. ***Email:*** hrtrilling@hhlaw.com

ANDREW J. TRUBIN (Resident, Third Avenue New York, N.Y. Office).

SHAWNA R. TUNNELL, born Wichita, Kansas, December 29, 1965; admitted to bar, 1992, Connecticut and New York; 1998, District of Columbia. *Education:* University of Kansas (B.A., magna cum laude, 1988); New York University (J.D., 1991; LL.M., 1994). Phi Beta Kappa; Phi Kappa Phi. Member, Review of Law and Social Change. *Member:* The District of Columbia Bar; New York State and American Bar Associations. ***PRACTICE AREAS:*** Transactional Tax. ***Email:*** srtunnell@hhlaw.com

(This Listing Continued)

ALBERT W. TURNBULL, born Charlottesville, Virginia, May 13, 1963; admitted to bar, 1988, Virginia; 1989, District of Columbia, U.S. Court of Appeals, Fourth and Ninth Circuits and U.S. District Court, Eastern District of Virginia; 1990, U.S. District Court for the District of Columbia and U.S. Court of Appeals for the District of Columbia Circuit; 1991, U.S. District Court, District of Maryland; 1992, U.S. Supreme Court; 1996, U.S. Court of Appeals, Fifth Circuit; 1997, U.S. Tax Court; 1998, U.S. Court of Appeals, Eighth Circuit. *Education:* Hamilton College (A.B., 1985); University of Virginia (J.D., 1988). Phi Beta Kappa; Order of the Coif. *Member:* The District of Columbia Bar; Virginia State Bar; American Bar Association. ***PRACTICE AREAS:*** Corporate Litigation; Securities Litigation; Securities Class Actions; Shareholder Derivative Actions; Legal Ethics. ***Email:*** awturnbull@hhlaw.com

NIKI FRANGOS TUTTLE (Resident, Denver, Colorado Office).

RALPH S. TYLER (Resident, Baltimore, Maryland Office).

CRAIG H. ULMAN, born Washington, D.C., September 11, 1951; admitted to bar, 1977, District of Columbia. *Education:* Harvard University (B.A., 1973; J.D., 1977); Magdalen College, Oxford, England. Phi Beta Kappa. Recipient: LeBaron Russell Briggs Prize; Knox Fellowship. *Member:* The District of Columbia Bar. ***PRACTICE AREAS:*** Bankruptcy; ATM Networks; Uniform Commercial Code; Creditors Rights; Structured Finance. ***Email:*** chulman@hhlaw.com

CRAIG A. UMBAUGH (Resident, Denver, Colorado Office).

CHRISTINE A. VARNEY, born Washington, D.C., December 17, 1955; admitted to bar, 1986, New York; 1987, District of Columbia. *Education:* State University of New York at Albany (B.A., magna cum laude, 1977); Syracuse University (M.P.A., magna cum laude, 1979); Georgetown University (J.D., 1986). General Counsel, Democratic National Committee, 1989-1991. Chief Counsel, Clinton/Gore '92 Committee, 1992. General Counsel, 1993 Presidential Inaugural Committee. Secretary to the Cabinet, 1993-1994. Federal Trade Commissioner, 1994-1997. *Member:* The District of Columbia Bar; American Bar Association. ***PRACTICE AREAS:*** Internet Law; Antitrust Law; Consumer Protection. ***Email:*** cvarney@hhlaw.com

ANN MORGAN VICKERY, born Anderson, South Carolina, June 25, 1944; admitted to bar, 1978, District of Columbia. *Education:* Mary Baldwin College (A.B., 1965); Georgetown University (J.D., 1978). Editor, Georgetown Law Journal, 1977-1978. *Member:* The District of Columbia Bar. ***PRACTICE AREAS:*** Health Care Legislation; Health Care Reform; Health Care Regulation; Medicare and Medicaid. ***Email:*** amvickery@hhlaw.com

CHRISTIAN VON HAMMERSTEIN (Resident, Berlin, Germany Office).

ERIC VON SALZEN, born New York, N.Y., March 1, 1943; admitted to bar, 1968, District of Columbia; 1980, U.S. Court of Appeals, District of Columbia Circuit; 1992, U.S. Court of Appeals, Fourth Circuit; 1993, Maryland. *Education:* Harvard University (B.A., cum laude, 1965); Columbia Law School (LL.B., cum laude, 1968). Editor, Columbia Law Review, 1967-1968. *Member:* The District of Columbia Bar; Bar Association of the District of Columbia; Maryland State and American Bar Associations. ***PRACTICE AREAS:*** Appellate Practice; Eminent Domain; Litigation; Real Estate; Transportation. ***Email:*** eavonsalzen@hhlaw.com

DR. CHRISTOPH WAGNER (Resident, Berlin, Germany Office).

MORRIS WAISBROT (Resident, 100 Park Avenue, New York, N.Y. Office).

ROBERT J. WALDMAN, born Bronx, New York, August 22, 1947; admitted to bar, 1972, New York; 1974, District of Columbia; 1989, Maryland. *Education:* Duke University (A.B., magna cum laude, 1968); Harvard University (J.D., magna cum laude, 1971). Phi Beta Kappa. Member, Board of Editors, Harvard Law Review, 1970-1971. Assistant to the General Counsel, Department of the Army, 1971-1974. *Member:* The District of Columbia Bar; New York State and American Bar Associations. ***PRACTICE AREAS:*** Business Law; Corporate Finance; Corporate Law; Securities Law; International Law. ***Email:*** rjwaldman@hhlaw.com

DONIS G. WALKER (Denver and Colorado Springs, Colorado Offices).

NICOLA S. WALKER (Resident, London, England Office).

CHRISTOPHER J. WALSH (Resident, Denver, Colorado Office).

PHYLLIS V. WAN (Resident, Denver, Colorado Office).

HOWARD S. WEBER (Resident at 100 Park Avenue, New York, New York Office).

RICHARD L.A. WEINER, born White Plains, New York, June 30, 1959; admitted to bar, 1987, California; 1988, District of Columbia. *Education:* Harvard University (A.B., magna cum laude, 1981); University of Cambridge (M.Phil., 1982); Columbia University (J.D., 1985). Expert Consultant, Commission of the European Communities, Directorate-General for External Relations, 1991-1992. *Member:* State Bar of California; The District of Columbia Bar. (Also at Brussels, Belgium Office). ***LANGUAGES:*** English, French and Spanish. ***PRACTICE AREAS:*** European Union Law; International Trade Law; International Arbitration; Aviation Law. ***Email:*** rlweiner@hhlaw.com

(This Listing Continued)

DAVID F. WERTHEIMER (Resident at 100 Park Avenue, New York, New York Office).

T. CLARK WEYMOUTH, born Fort Smith, Arkansas, July 4, 1957; admitted to bar, 1984, Illinois; 1985, District of Columbia. *Education:* Dartmouth College (A.B., with high distinction, 1979); Northwestern University (J.D., 1984). Editor, Northwestern Law Review, 1983-1984. *Member:* The District of Columbia Bar; Illinois State and American Bar Associations; American Immigration Lawyers Association. ***LANGUAGES:*** Spanish, Italian and French. ***PRACTICE AREAS:*** International Trade; Immigration. ***Email:*** tcweymouth@hhlaw.com

DOUGLAS P. WHEELER, born Brooklyn, New York, January 10, 1942; admitted to bar, 1966, North Carolina; 1999, District of Columbia. *Education:* Hamilton College (A.B., with honors, 1963); Duke University (LL.B., 1966). Contributor, *Land Use in America*, Island Press (1996). Deputy Assistant Secretary of the Interior, 1972-1977. California Resources Secretary, 1991-1999. Listed in Who's Who in America. *Member:* North Carolina State Bar; The District of Columbia Bar. [U.S. Naval Reserve, JAG (Lt.) 1969-1973]. ***PRACTICE AREAS:*** Natural Resources; Land Use; Environmental Regulation. ***Email:*** dpwheeler@hhlaw.com

ZDZISLAW W. WIECKOWSKI (Resident, Warsaw, Poland Office).

MARCY J. WILDER, born New York, June 22, 1963; admitted to bar, 1989, California; 1990, District of Columbia; 1992, U.S. Supreme Court. *Education:* Union College (B.A., Political Science, magna cum laude, 1985); Stanford University (J.D., 1988). Phi Beta Kappa. Deputy General Counsel, U.S. Department of Health and Human Services, 1997-2001. *Member:* American Bar Association. ***PRACTICE AREAS:*** Health Privacy; Federal Regulatory Law; Medical Research. ***Email:*** mwilder@hhlaw.com

MICHAEL CUNNINGHAM WILLIAMS, born Washington, D.C., April 8, 1959; admitted to bar, 1984, Virginia; 1985, District of Columbia. *Education:* University of Virginia (B.A., with distinction, 1981; J.D., 1984); University of Cambridge (LL.M., 1985). Omicron Delta Kappa. Raven Society. Editor-in-Chief, Virginia Journal of International Law, 1983-1984. *Member:* The District of Columbia Bar; Virginia State Bar; American Bar Association. ***PRACTICE AREAS:*** Corporate Law; Securities Law; Life Sciences Law. ***Email:*** mcwilliams@hhlaw.com

EDWARD C. WILSON, JR., born St. Louis, Missouri, April 7, 1965; admitted to bar, 1990, Virginia; 1991, District of Columbia. *Education:* Davidson College (A.B., cum laude, with honors in French, 1987); University of Virginia (J.D., 1990). Phi Beta Kappa. Recipient, Charles J. Frankel Award in Health Law. *Member:* Virginia State Bar; The District of Columbia Bar. ***LANGUAGES:*** French. ***PRACTICE AREAS:*** Drug and Medical Device Regulation. ***Email:*** ecwilson@hhlaw.com

RONALD J. WILTSIE, II, born Nice, France, October 26, 1958; admitted to bar, 1989, Virginia; 1992, District of Columbia. *Education:* University of Virginia (B.S., with distinction, 1980; J.D., 1989). Order of the Coif. Managing Editor, Virginia Law Review, 1988-1989. *Member:* Virginia State Bar; The District of Columbia Bar; Virginia Bar Association. ***PRACTICE AREAS:*** Civil Litigation. ***Email:*** rjwiltsie@hhlaw.com

JOEL S. WINNIK, born Milwaukee, Wisconsin, October 10, 1949; admitted to bar, 1974, Illinois; 1979, U.S. Court of Appeals, District of Columbia Circuit and District of Columbia. *Education:* University of Wisconsin (B.A., 1971); University of Notre Dame, London, England and Washington University (J.D., 1974). Attorney: Federal Communications Commission, Appellate Litigation Division, 1978-1979; Common Carrier Bureau, Office of the General Counsel, 1974-1978. *Member:* The District of Columbia Bar; Illinois State, Federal and American (Member, Public Utility Law Section) Bar Associations. ***PRACTICE AREAS:*** Telecommunications Law; International Trade Law. ***Email:*** jswinnik@hhlaw.com

DAVID A. WINTER, born Boston, Massachusetts, May 15, 1967; admitted to bar, 1993, Maryland; 1996, District of Columbia. *Education:* Columbia College (B.A., cum laude, 1989); University of Michigan (J.D., cum laude, 1993). *Member:* Maryland State and American Bar Associations; The District of Columbia Bar. ***PRACTICE AREAS:*** Taxation. ***Email:*** dawinter@hhlaw.com

PAMELA G. WINTHROP, born Fort Worth, Texas, June 6, 1956; admitted to bar, 1982, New York and U.S. District Court, Western District of New York; 1983, U.S. District Court, Southern District of New York; 1984, District of Columbia. *Education:* Wellesley College (B.A., 1977); Amherst College; George Washington University (J.D., with honors, 1981). Staff Member, 1979-1980 and Articles Editor, 1981, Journal of International Law and Economics. *Member:* The District of Columbia Bar; New York State and American Bar Associations. ***PRACTICE AREAS:*** Corporate Finance; Project Finance. ***Email:*** pgwinthrop@hhlaw.com

MARCIA A. WISS, born 1947; admitted to bar, 1973, District of Columbia. *Education:* Georgetown University (B.S.F.S., 1969; J.D., 1972). Editor, Georgetown Journal of Law and Policy in International Business, 1971-1972. Adjunct Faculty Member: "International Project Finance and Investment," Georgetown University Law Center, 1984—; "International Investment Law," Johns Hopkins School of Advanced International Studies, 2001. Attorney, Office of General Counsel, Overseas Private Investment Corporation, 1973-1978. General Counsel, Society for International Development, Washington Chapter, 1979-2001. General Counsel, Association for Women in Development, 1982—. General Counsel, International Policy Council on Agriculture, Food and Trade, 1990—. *Member:* The District of Columbia Bar (Member, International Steering Committee, 1985-1988); American Bar Association (Member, Section of International Law and Practice; Co-Chair, ILEX, 1989-1994; Member, Nominating Committee, 1994); American Society of International Law (Member, Executive Council, 1987-1990; Vice President, 1992-1994); Washington Foreign Law Society (President, 1983); Women's Bar Association of The District of Columbia. ***PRACTICE AREAS:*** International Project Finance; International Business Law; Aircraft Finance and Leasing; Corporate Law. ***Email:*** mawiss@hhlaw.com

WILLIAM H. WRIGHT (Resident, Los Angeles, California Office).

ERIK B. WULFF, born May 24, 1952; admitted to bar, 1976, Illinois; 1992, District of Columbia. *Education:* Indiana University (B.S., with distinction, 1973; J.D., cum laude, 1976). Beta Gamma Sigma. Member, Indiana Law Journal, 1975-1976. Editor-In-Chief, Leader's Franchising Business and Law Alert. *Member:* The District of Columbia; American Bar Association (Member, Governing Committee, ABA Forum on Franchising, 1988-1991). ***PRACTICE AREAS:*** Franchise Law. ***Email:*** ewulff@hhlaw.com

MICHAEL K. WYATT, born Charleston, West Virginia, January 13, 1945; admitted to bar, 1973, District of Columbia; 1996, Maryland. *Education:* Princeton University (A.B., cum laude, 1967); Oxford University (M.A., 1969); Harvard Law School (J.D., 1972). Phi Beta Kappa. Keasbey Scholar to Oxford. Author: "Small Business Compliance Advisor," Thompson, 1993. Adjunct Professor, Cornell ILR School, 1990-1994. General Counsel, United States Small Business Administration, 1991-1993. Associate Deputy Secretary of Labor, 1989-1991. *Member:* The District of Columbia Bar; Maryland State and American Bar Associations. ***LANGUAGES:*** French, Spanish. ***PRACTICE AREAS:*** Small Business Investment Companies; Private Equity; Labor and Employment. ***Email:*** mkwyatt@hhlaw.com

EMILY M. YINGER (Resident, McLean, Virginia Office).

JOSEPH H. YOUNG (Resident, Baltimore, Maryland Office).

COUNSEL

MERRY C. ANDERSON, born Rio de Janeiro, Brazil, December 31, 1962; admitted to bar, 1988, Maryland and District of Columbia. *Education:* Harvard University (A.B., cum laude, 1984); Stanford University (J.D., 1987). Member, Stanford Law Review, 1985-1987. *Member:* The District of Columbia Bar; Maryland State and American Bar Associations. ***LANGUAGES:*** Spanish. ***PRACTICE AREAS:*** Banking Law; Mergers and Acquisitions; Corporate Law; Securities Law. ***Email:*** mcanderson@hhlaw.com

STEVEN F. BARLEY, born Leonardtown, Maryland, 1963; admitted to bar, 1990, Maryland; 1991, U.S. District Court, District of Maryland; 1992, U.S. Court of Appeals, Fourth Circuit. *Education:* Univ. of Virginia (B.A., 1985); Univ. of Maryland (J.D., with honors, 1990); College for Financial Planning, 1988. Order of the Coif. Recipient: John S. Strayhorn Memorial Prize; American Jurisprudence Awards for Trial Planning and Advocacy, Evidence, Legal Writing and Civil Procedure and Conflicts of Laws. *Member:* Bar Assn. of Baltimore City; Maryland State and American Bar Assns.; Maryland Assn. of Defense Trial Counsel. (Resident, Baltimore, Maryland Office). ***PRACTICE AREAS:*** General Litigation; Commercial Litigation; Title Insurance and Real Estate Litigation; Securities Litigation. ***Email:*** sfbarley@hhlaw.com

DALE E. BONNER (Resident, Los Angeles, California Office).

PAVEL BRADAC (Resident, Prague, Czech Republic Office).

LANCE D. BULTENA, born Lennox, South Dakota, May 18, 1963; admitted to bar, 1991, Pennsylvania; 1993, South Dakota and District of Columbia. *Education:* University of South Dakota (B.S., summa cum laude, 1985); Oxford University, Oxford, England (M.Phil., 1987; D.Phil., 1990); Harvard Law School (J.D., 1991). Phi Beta Kappa; Omicron Delta Kappa. Counsel, Senate Committee on Commerce Science and Transportation, Subcommittee on Consumer Affairs, Foreign Commerce and Tourism, 1995-1999. *Member:* State Bar of South Dakota; The District of Columbia Bar. ***PRACTICE AREAS:*** Legislation; Federal Regulatory Law; Legal Reform; Internet Law; Communications; Antitrust and Consumer Law. ***Email:*** ldbultena@hhlaw.com

BROOKE BUMPERS, born Charleston, Arkansas, April 10, 1962; admitted to bar, 1992, California; 1994, District of Columbia; 1999, U.S. District Court, District of Columbia. *Education:* Vassar College (A.B., 1984); Georgetown University (J.D., cum laude, 1992). *Member:* State Bar of California; The District of Columbia Bar (Member, Health Law Section); American Bar Association; American Health Lawyers Association. ***PRACTICE AREAS:*** Medicare and Medicaid Reimbursement; Health Care Regulation; Health Law; Managed Care; Health Care Licensing; Internet Health Business. ***Email:*** mbbumpers@hhlaw.com

(This Listing Continued)

HOGAN & HARTSON L.L.P., Washington—Continued

JAMES C. CHEN, born Buffalo, New York, December 3, 1965; admitted to bar, 1992, New York and District of Columbia. *Education:* State University of New York at Buffalo (B.A., 1988); Case Western Reserve University (J.D., cum laude, 1991). Phi Delta Phi. *Member:* The District of Columbia Bar; American Bar Association. ***PRACTICE AREAS:*** Environmental; OSHA; Transportation Law; Government Regulatory. ***Email:*** jcchen@hhlaw.com

LAURIE A. CLARKE, born Milford, Massachusetts, August 13, 1963; admitted to bar, 1991, Massachusetts and District of Columbia. *Education:* Smith College (A.B., cum laude, 1985); Harvard University, John F. Kennedy School of Government (M.P.P., 1987); Stanford Law School (J.D., 1990). *Member:* The District of Columbia Bar; Massachusetts Bar Association. ***PRACTICE AREAS:*** Regulatory Law; Drug and Medical Device Regulation; Food and Drug Regulation; Food, Drug and Cosmetic Law. ***Email:*** laclarke@hhlaw.com

DONALD B. DILLPORT (Resident at 100 Park Avenue, New York, New York Office).

KEVIN M. DOWNEY, born Austin, Texas, May 10, 1965; admitted to bar, 1990, Pennsylvania; 1992, District of Columbia. *Education:* Texas Christian University; Colorado State University (B.A., 1986); Dickinson School of Law (J.D., 1990). Phi Beta Kappa; Phi Kappa Phi; Phi Alpha Delta. Comments Editor, Dickinson Law Review, 1989-1990. ***PRACTICE AREAS:*** Energy; Utility Law. ***Email:*** kmdowney@hhlaw.com

CYNTHIA A. FEIGIN (Resident at 100 Park Avenue, New York, New York Office).

KATHRYN L. GOETZ (Resident at 100 Park Avenue, New York, N.Y. Office).

JACQUELYN E. GRILLON, admitted to bar, 1985, Maryland and District of Columbia. *Education:* University of Massachusetts (B.S., magna cum laude, 1976); Catholic University of America (J.D., 1984). Member, 1982-1983 and Editor-in-Chief, 1983-1984, Catholic University Law Review. *Member:* The District of Columbia Bar; Maryland State and American Bar Associations. ***PRACTICE AREAS:*** Corporate Law; Commercial Law; Communications Law. ***Email:*** jegrillon@hhlaw.com

JAMES C. HANSEN (Resident at 100 Park Avenue, New York, New York Office).

KARIS A. HASTINGS, born Van Nuys, California, November 1, 1962; admitted to bar, 1988, Maryland; 1989, District of Columbia. *Education:* University of Michigan (B.A., 1983); Duke University (J.D., with high honors, 1987). Order of the Coif. *Member:* The District of Columbia Bar. ***PRACTICE AREAS:*** Communications Law; Satellite Communications; Telecommunications Law; Telecommunications Licensing; Telecommunications Regulation. ***Email:*** kahastings@hhlaw.com

STEN A. JENSEN, born New Orleans, Louisiana, April 6, 1964; admitted to bar, 1993, Pennsylvania; 1994, District of Columbia; 1995, Virginia. *Education:* Duke University (B.A., cum laude, 1986); University of Virginia (J.D., 1992). Law Clerk, Honorable Roderick McKelvie, U.S. District Court for the District of Delaware, 1992-1993. *Member:* The District of Columbia Bar; Virginia State Bar; American Bar Association. ***PRACTICE AREAS:*** Litigation. ***Email:*** sajensen@hhlaw.com

LYNN G. KAMARCK, born Madison, Wisconsin, May 4, 1953; admitted to bar, 1977, District of Columbia. *Education:* Grinnell College (B.A., 1977); Columbia University (J.D., 1977). Phi Beta Kappa. Harlan Fiske Stone Scholar. Managing Editor, Columbia Journal of Law and Social Problems. Member, Board of Directors, 1987-1993, and Vice-President, 1988-1989, Washington International Trade Association. Author: "U.S. Department of Commerce Issues New Antidumping Duty Regulations," *Canadian International Lawyer*, Vol. 2, No. 4 pp.238-239 (1997); "Uruguay Round Agreement Makes Substantial Changes to Antidumping Codes," *East Asian Executive Reports*, Vol. 16, No. 3, pp. 6 & 15-18 (1994); "Update on Upstream Subsidies," PLI, The Commerce Department Speaks, 1990, Supp. to Vol. 2, pp. 1-24 (1990). Co-Author: G. Kaplan, L. Kamarck, and M. Parker, "Cost Analysis Under the Antidumping Law," George Washington Journal of International Law and Economics, Vol. 21, No. 3, pp. 357-418 (1988); L. Kamarck and T. Harr, "Current Issues Relating to the Scope of Antidumping and Countervailing Duty Orders," PLI, The Commerce Department Speaks, 1987, Vol. 2, pp. 13-77 (1987); G. Kaplan, L. Kamarck, and M. Parker, "Cost of Production and Constructed Value Analysis: A Legal and Policy View," PLI, U.S. Trade Law and Policy, pp. 31-170 (1987). Author: "Foreign Industrial Targeting Practices and their Relationship to International Agreements and U.S. Trade Laws," ABA, International Trade Policy: The Lawyer's Perspective, pp. 15-1-15-40 (1985). Co-Author: C. Levy and L. Kamarck, "Practical and Legal Considerations of Countertrade Transactions," 1 Asian Pacific Commercial Lawyer, 62-65 (1984). Executive Editor, ABA, International Trade Policy: The Lawyer's Perspective (1985). Senior Counsel, Antidumping/Countervailing Duty Proceedings, U.S. Department of Commerce, 1986-1991. Attorney-Advisor, Office of Chief Counsel for International Trade, U.S. Department of Commerce, 1984-1986. *Member:* The District of Columbia Bar. ***PRACTICE AREAS:*** International Trade; Countervailing Duties; Antidumping; Import and Export Law; Asia Trade. ***Email:*** lgkamarck@hhlaw.com

MICHELE A. KULERMAN, born Brooklyn, New York, February 6, 1952; admitted to bar, 1985, District of Columbia. *Education:* Stanford University (B.A., 1974); Stanford University Graduate-at-Large Program (1975); Southwestern University School of Law (J.D., 1979). Recipient, American Jurisprudence Book Award, 1978. *Member:* The District of Columbia Bar; American Bar Association (D.C. Liaison for ABA State Regulation of Securities Committee and Co-Chair of Subcommittee on Liaison with Securities Administrators and NASD; Subcommittees on: Developments in State Securities Regulation; Investment Companies; Broker-Dealers and Investment Advisors; Committee on Federal Securities Regulation, Subcommittee on Investment Companies and Investment Advisers); Women's Bar Association. ***PRACTICE AREAS:*** Blue Sky Law; Corporate Law; Securities. ***Email:*** makulerman@hhlaw.com

GERALD J.S. LAPORTE, born Windsor, Ontario, Canada, October 16, 1946; admitted to bar, 1976, Michigan; 1977, District of Columbia; 1980, U.S. Supreme Court. *Education:* Sacred Heart Seminary College, Detroit (B.A., 1968); St. Paul University, Ottawa, Ontario (S.T.B., cum laude, 1971); University of Ottawa (B.Th., cum laude, 1971); Georgetown University (M.A., 1974); George Washington University (J.D., with honors, 1976). Pi Sigma Alpha. Managing Editor, George Washington Law Review, 1975-1976. Legislative Assistant to U.S. Congressman Wm. J. Randall, 1971-1975. Law Clerk to U.S. District Court Judge John H. Pratt, District of D.C., 1976-1977. Senior Special Counsel for Legislation and Investment Management, SEC Office of General Counsel, 1982-1985. Counsel to SEC Commissioner J.A. Grundfest, 1985-1987. *Member:* State Bar of Michigan; The District of Columbia Bar (Chairman, Corporation, Finance and Securities Law Section, 1997-1998); American Bar Association (Member, Business Law Section, Federal Regulation of Securities Committee, Subcommittee on SEC Administration, Budget and Legislation); National Association of Bond Lawyers (Vice Chairman, Securities Law and Disclosure Committee, 1994-1996). ***PRACTICE AREAS:*** Securities; Debt and Equity Finance; Investment Partnerships; Public Offerings; Emerging Growth Companies. ***Email:*** gjlaporte@hhlaw.com

MELVIN E. LEFKOWITZ, admitted to bar, 1973, District of Columbia; U.S. Court of Federal Claims; U.S. Court of Appeals, Third and Ninth Circuits. *Education:* University of Maryland (B.A., 1966); George Washington University (J.D., 1972); New York University (LL.M., Taxation, 1973). Member, District Counsel of the IRS, 1996. *Member:* Bar Association of the District of Columbia; American Bar Association (Member, Tax Section). ***PRACTICE AREAS:*** Tax; Business; Finance.

NORMA B. LEVY (Resident at 100 Park Avenue, New York, New York Office).

TIMOTHY J. LOCKHART (Resident, McLean, Virginia Office).

HELEN P. McCLURE, born Washington, D.C., May 22, 1955; admitted to bar, 1985, Maryland; 1986, District of Columbia. *Education:* Northwestern University (B.S., 1977); George Washington University (J.D., with high honors, 1985). Order of the Coif. Associate, George Washington Law Review, 1983-1985. Author: Note, "Liability of Administrative Officials," The George Washington Law Review, Vol. 53, Nos. 1 & 2, Nov. 1984 - Jan. 1985. *Member:* The District of Columbia Bar; Maryland State and American (Member, Section of Corporation, Finance and Securities Law) Bar Associations. ***PRACTICE AREAS:*** Business Law; Commercial Law; Telecommunications Contracts; Fiber Optics; Technology Contracts; Technology Joint Ventures; Technology Transfers; Computer and Software; Commercial Contracts; International Contracts; Mergers, Acquisitions and Divestitures. ***Email:*** hpmcclure@hhlaw.com

GORDON L. MILLER, born Kansas City, Missouri, January 17, 1953; admitted to bar, 1980, Texas; 1982, Oklahoma (Not admitted in District of Columbia). *Education:* Stanford University (A.B., 1975); The Law School of the University of Chicago (J.D., 1980). Member, State Bar of Texas, 1980-1992, inactive, 1992—. Counsel, Board of Governors of Federal Reserve System, 1992-2001. *Member:* Oklahoma and American Bar Associations. ***PRACTICE AREAS:*** Banking Regulation; Mergers and Acquisitions; Electronic Commerce. ***Email:*** glmiller@hhlaw.com

DOUGLAS R. M. NAZARIAN (Resident, Baltimore, Maryland Office).

STEPHEN B. PARKER (Resident, McLean, Virginia Office).

STEVEN C. PETERSEN (Resident, Boulder, Colorado Office).

AUREL PINTER (Resident, Budapest, Hungary Office).

JOHN HOUSTON POPE (Resident at 100 Park Avenue, New York, New York Office).

ROBERT N. RABECS, born Scranton, Pennsylvania, March 19, 1964; admitted to bar, 1990, Pennsylvania; 1992, District of Columbia. *Education:* University of Scranton (B.A., summa cum laude, 1986); Georgetown University Law Center (J.D., cum laude, 1990). Alpha Sigma Nu. Fulbright Scholar, Philippines, 1986-1987. Author: "Kickbacks as False Claims: The Use of the Civil

(This Listing Continued)

False Claims Act to Prosecute Violations of the Federal Health Care Programs Antikickback Statue," 2001 L.Rev. M.S.U.-D.C.L. 1; "Agrarian Reform in the Philippines and its Effect on the Multinationals," 21 Law and Policy in International Business 441 (1990). *Member:* The District of Columbia Bar; American Bar Association; American Health Lawyers Association. ***PRACTICE AREAS:*** Health Care. ***Email:*** rnrabecs@hhlaw.com

BETH L. ROBERTS, born Ravenna, Ohio, July 8, 1966; admitted to bar, 1994, Pennsylvania; 1996, District of Columbia. *Education:* University of Pennsylvania, Wharton School (B.S., magna cum laude, 1988); University of Texas at Austin (J.D., with honors, 1993). Order of the Coif. Administrative Editor, 1992-1993 and Member, 1991-1992, Texas Int'l Law Journal. Author: "The Impact of the Maastricht Summit on European Community Social Policy: A Breakthrough for Worker Participation or the Creation of a Two-Speed Europe?" 28(2) Texas Int'l L. J. (Spring 1993). Law Clerk, Hon. John Ferren, District of Columbia Court of Appeals, 1993-1994. *Member:* The District of Columbia Bar; Pennsylvania and American Bar Associations; American Health Lawyers Association. ***PRACTICE AREAS:*** Health Care. ***Email:*** blroberts@hhlaw.com

MARGARET E. ROGGENSACK, born Lancaster, Wisconsin, November 11, 1954; admitted to bar, 1984, District of Columbia; 1985, U.S. Tax Court and U.S. Court of International Trade; 1986, U.S. District Court for the District of Columbia. *Education:* Carleton College (B.A., magna cum laude, 1976); George Washington University (J.D., with honors, 1984). Mortar Board. Recipient, Second Century Award. Thomas J. Watson Fellow. Articles Editor, George Washington Journal of International Law & Economics, 1983-1984. President Emeritus, Washington Foreign Law Society. Co-Author: with John D. Hushon, "Strategic Issues in the Decision to Operate a National Resources Project in Latin America," 38 Rocky Mt. Min. L. Inst. 3-1 (1992). Author: "U.S. Countervailing Duty Law As Applied to Mexico: The Need for a Material Injury Test," (NOTE), 18 G.W. J. Intl. L. & Econ. 183 (1984). *Member:* The District of Columbia Bar; American Bar Association; Inter-American Bar Association; Women's Bar Association; CIT Bar Association; American Society of International Law. ***LANGUAGES:*** Spanish. ***PRACTICE AREAS:*** International Government Relations; Legislative Practice; International Trade Regulation; Latin America Trade; Customs Law. ***Email:*** meroggensack@hhlaw.com

ROBERT C. SATROM (Resident, Moscow, Russia Office).

ELLEN SIEGLER, born Mt. Vernon, New York; admitted to bar, 1975, District of Columbia. *Education:* University of Wisconsin (B.A., 1967); University of Connecticut (J.D., with honors, 1974). *Member:* The District of Columbia Bar. ***PRACTICE AREAS:*** Clean Air Act; Clean Water Act. ***Email:*** esiegler@hhlaw.com

FRANK T. SPANO (Resident at 100 Park Avenue, New York, New York Office).

ROBERT L. SPENCER, born York, Pennsylvania, September 11, 1937; admitted to bar, 1991, Maryland; 1992, District of Columbia. *Education:* Towson State University (B.S., 1963); University of Maryland (J.D., with honors, 1991). *Member:* Maryland State and American Bar Associations; The District of Columbia Bar. ***PRACTICE AREAS:*** Drug and Medical Device Regulation. ***Email:*** rlspencer@hhlaw.com

JOLANTA STERBENZ, born Szczecin, Poland, January 20, 1961; admitted to bar, 1993, Virginia; 1995, District of Columbia. *Education:* Adam Mickiewicz University, Poznan, Poland (M.A., with honors, 1985); University of Pennsylvania (J.D., 1993). Articles Editor, Comparative Labor Law Journal. *Member:* Virginia State Bar; The District of Columbia Bar. ***LANGUAGES:*** Polish, Russian, German. ***PRACTICE AREAS:*** Energy Regulation; Natural Gas; Electric Power. ***Email:*** jsterbenz@hhlaw.com

LOWELL R. STERN, born Boston, Massachusetts, November 21, 1963; admitted to bar, 1991, Virginia; 1994, District of Columbia. *Education:* Wesleyan University (B.A., 1985); University of Virginia (J.D., 1991). Staff Assistant to Senator Christopher J. Dodd, 1985-1988. *Member:* Virginia State Bar; The District of Columbia Bar. ***PRACTICE AREAS:*** Antitrust and Trade Litigation; Civil Litigation; Franchise Litigation. ***Email:*** lrstern@hhlaw.com

CHRISTOPHER S. STOKES, born Arizona, January 28, 1961; admitted to bar, 1989, New York; 1990, District of Columbia. *Education:* Washington & Lee University (B.S., 1983); Georgetown University (J.D., 1988). Phi Beta Kappa. ***LANGUAGES:*** Portuguese and French. ***PRACTICE AREAS:*** International Trade. ***Email:*** csstokes@hhlaw.com

J. MICHAEL THESZ, JR., admitted to bar, 1974, Virginia; 1975, District of Columbia. *Education:* University of Notre Dame (B.S.E.E., 1965); Georgetown University Law Center (J.D., 1973). Patent Examiner, U.S. Patent and Trademark Office, 1968-1982; Senior Legal Advisor, U.S. Patent and Trademark Office, 1982-1996; Editor, Manual of Patent Examining Procedure, U.S. Patent and Trademark Office, 1991-1996. *Member:* State Bar of Virginia; The District of Columbia Bar; American Intellectual Property Law Association. ***PRACTICE AREAS:*** Computer and Software Patents; Electrical Patent Prosecution; Electrical Patents; Electro-Mechanical Patents; Electronic Patents; Patent Applications; Patent Infringement; Patent Prosecution; Patent Protection. ***Email:*** jmthesz@hhlaw.com

(This Listing Continued)

STEPHEN G. VASKOV, born Pittsburgh, Pennsylvania, October 11, 1958; admitted to bar, 1985, Pennsylvania and U.S. District Court, Western District of Pennsylvania; 1988, District of Columbia; 1989, U.S. District Court, District of Columbia; 1990, U.S. Court of Appeals for the District of Columbia Circuit. *Education:* University of Pennsylvania (B.A., 1980); Washington College of Law, American University (J.D., magna cum laude, 1985). Author: "Judicial Review of Dismissals of Civil Service Employees for Off-Duty Misconduct: The Approach of the Federal Circuit," 34 American University Law Review 939, 1985. Law Clerk for the Honorable Alan N. Bloch, U.S. District Court, Western District of Pennsylvania, 1985-1987. *Member:* The District of Columbia Bar; American Bar Association. ***PRACTICE AREAS:*** Federal Civil Practice; International Arbitration; Complex Litigation; Antitrust Litigation; Contract Litigation; Products Liability Defense; Civil Appeals. ***Email:*** sgvaskov@hhlaw.com

PAUL W. VIRTUE, born 1955; admitted to bar, 1982, Maryland and West Virginia (inactive); 1999, District of Columbia. *Education:* West Virginia University (B.S., 1978); West Virginia University College of Law (J.D., 1982). U.S. Immigration and Naturalization Service: General Counsel, 1998-1999; Executive Associate Commissioner, Office of Programs, 1997-1998; Deputy General Counsel, 1988-1997; Associate General Counsel, 1983-1988. *Member:* Federal Bar Association; American Immigration Lawyers Association. ***PRACTICE AREAS:*** Immigration. ***Email:*** pwvirture@hhlaw.com

MITCHELL E. ZAMOFF, born New York, N.Y., May 25, 1967; admitted to bar, 1992, Virginia; 1993, District of Columbia, U.S. Court of Appeals, 4th Circuit and U.S. District Court, Eastern District of Virginia; 1995, U.S. District Court, District of Columbia. *Education:* University of Virginia (B.A., American Government, 1989; J.D., 1992). Phi Beta Kappa. Order of the Coif. Member, Editorial Board, Virginia Law Review. Executive Editor, The Cavalier Daily. Champion, William Lile Minor Moot Court Competition. Law Clerk, The Hon. Richard L. Williams, U.S. District Court Judge for the Eastern District of Virginia, Richmond, Virginia, 1992-1993. Experience: Assistant United States Attorney for the Eastern District of Pennsylvania, 1997-2000, Deputy Chief, 2000. *Member:* Virginia State Bar; District of Columbia Bar; American Bar Association. ***PRACTICE AREAS:*** Civil Litigation; Complex Litigation; Federal Criminal Law; Grand Jury Practice; Insurance Coverage; Insurance Bad Faith; Employment Discrimination; Employment Claims. ***Email:*** mezamoff@hhlaw.com

STEPHEN J. ZEMPOLICH, born Washington, D.C., November 6, 1963; admitted to bar, 1992, Virginia and U.S. Court of Appeals, Fourth Circuit; 1993, District of Columbia. *Education:* Duke University (A.B., magna cum laude, 1985); Georgetown University Law Center (J.D., magna cum laude, 1992). Order of the Coif. Topics Editor, Law & Policy in International Business, 1991-1992. *Member:* Virginia State Bar; The District of Columbia Bar; American Bar Association; National Health Lawyers Association. [U.S. Army, 1985-1989, Lieutenant; U.S. Army Reserves, 1989—, Major]. ***PRACTICE AREAS:*** Corporate Law; Commercial Law; Health Care Law. ***Email:*** sjzempolich@hhlaw.com

EUROPEAN COUNSEL

VUONG VAN BAC (Resident, Paris, France Office).

OF COUNSEL

JOHN P. ARNESS, born Yankton, South Dakota, February 8, 1927; admitted to bar, 1952, District of Columbia; 1958, Maryland; 1965, U.S. Supreme Court. *Education:* Harvard University (A.B., 1949); Georgetown University (J.D., 1951). Author: "Architects and Engineers: A Consideration of Basic Liability Principles and Legal Trends in Foundation Engineering," Insurance Counsel Journal, July 1967; "The Appropriateness of Class Action Certification in the Litigation of Private Claims Arising from Nuclear and Chemical Pollution," Environmental Law Symposium, Tort and Insurance Practice Section of the American Bar Association, 1982; "Insurance Coverage for 'Property Damage' in Asbestos and Other Toxic Tort Cases," Virginia Law Review, Vol. 72, No. 5, August 1986; "Preventing Successor Liability for Defective Products: Safeguards for Acquiring Corporations," Washington University Law Quarterly, Spring 1989. Law Clerk to Chief Judge, U.S. Court of Appeals for District of Columbia Circuit, 1951-1952. Lecturer, Trial Practice, Columbus School of Law, Catholic University, 1969-1971. Trustee, 1979-1995 and Chairman, 1988-1990, National Institute for Trial Advocacy. *Member:* The District of Columbia Bar; Bar Association of the District of Columbia (President, 1977-1978); Maryland State and American (Member, House of Delegates, 1976-1978) Bar Associations; Federation of Insurance Counsel; International Association of Defense Counsel; D.C. Defense Lawyers Association; National Conference of Bar Presidents. Fellow: American College of Trial Lawyers (Regent, 1984-1988); American Bar Foundation; International Academy of Trial Lawyers; International Society of Barristers (Member, Board of Governors, 1994-2000). ***PRACTICE***

(This Listing Continued)

HOGAN & HARTSON L.L.P., Washington—Continued

AREAS: Commercial Litigation; Construction Litigation; Excess Coverage; Extra Contractual Insurance Claims; Reinsurance. ***Email:*** jparness@hhlaw.com

KATHRYN WEBB BRADLEY (Resident, Denver, Colorado Office).

DEAN W. CROWELL, born Ogden, Utah, September 7, 1949; admitted to bar, 1975, Colorado; 1989, District of Columbia. *Education:* University of Colorado (B.A., 1971); University of California, Hastings College of the Law (J.D., 1974). *Member:* The District of Columbia Bar; American Bar Association. ***PRACTICE AREAS:*** International Commercial Transactions. ***Email:*** dwcrowell@hhlaw.com

MARVIN J. DIAMOND, born New York, N.Y., January 21, 1941; admitted to bar, 1968, District of Columbia; 1979, U.S. Supreme Court. *Education:* Princeton University (A.B., cum laude, 1962); Yale Law School (LL.B., 1968). *Member:* The District of Columbia Bar. ***PRACTICE AREAS:*** Communications Law. ***Email:*** mjdiamond@hhlaw.com

ROBERT J. ELLIOTT, born Bayonne, New Jersey, January 1, 1934; admitted to bar, 1961, District of Columbia; 1984, Maryland; U.S. Supreme Court. *Education:* St. Mary's College (A.B., 1957); Georgetown University (J.D., 1961). Alpha Sigma Nu; Phi Alpha Delta. Editor-in-Chief, Georgetown Law Journal, 1960-1961. Adjunct Professor Secured Transactions, 1968; Commercial Paper, 1971, Georgetown University Law Center. General Counsel, Metropolitan Washington Board of Trade, 1991, 1992. *Member:* The District of Columbia Bar; The Bar Association of the District of Columbia; Maryland State Bar Association. ***PRACTICE AREAS:*** Real Estate; Business Law. ***Email:*** rjelliott@hhlaw.com

ANDREW J. KILCARR, born New York, N.Y., January 28, 1932; admitted to bar, 1960, District of Columbia; 1964, U.S. Supreme Court. *Education:* Manhattan College (B.S., 1953); Georgetown University (J.D., 1959). Trial Attorney, Antitrust Division, U.S. Department of Justice, 1959-1964. Serves as Early Neutral Evaluator for U.S. District Court for the District of Columbia. *Member:* The District of Columbia Bar; Bar Association of the District of Columbia; American Bar Association. Fellow, American College of Trial Lawyers. ***PRACTICE AREAS:*** Antitrust Law; Litigation. ***Email:*** ajkilcarr@hhlaw.com

BOGUDAR KORDASIEWICZ (Resident, Warsaw, Poland Office).

DENNIS J. LEHR, born New York, N.Y., February 7, 1932; admitted to bar, 1959, New York; 1967, District of Columbia. *Education:* New York University (B.A., 1954; LL.M., 1961); Yale University (LL.B., 1957). Phi Beta Kappa; Phi Alpha Delta. Associate Chief Counsel, Office of the Comptroller of the Currency, 1964-1967. Legal Editor, The National Banking Review, 1965-1967. Adjunct Professor, Federal Control of Financial Institutions, Georgetown University Law School, 1966-1970. Member, Panel of Commercial Arbitrators, American Arbitration Association. Advisory Counsel to U.S. Senate Small Business Committee, 1968-1969. Member of: Legal Advisory Committee, National Center on Financial Services, 1984—; Advisory Board, Banking Law Institute, Southern Methodist University, Graduate School of Banking, 1984—. Public Member of the Administrative Conference of the United States, 1987-1994. *Member:* The Association of the Bar of The City of New York; The District of Columbia Bar; Bar Association of the District of Columbia; Federal (Member: Executive Council and Chairman of Banking Law Committee, 1972—; Executive Council of Securities Law Committee, 1972—) and American (Member: Banking Law Committee, 1981—; Chairman, 1986-1990; Committee on Developments in Investment Services, 1981—; Chairman, 1990-1994; Member: Committee on Long Range Issues Affecting Business Law Practice; Council Business Law Section, 1994—; Standing Committee on Gavel Awards, 1997—) Bar Associations. ***PRACTICE AREAS:*** Financial Law; Banking Law; Bank Securities; Administrative Agency Practice. ***Email:*** djlehr@hhlaw.com

LEE LOEVINGER, born St. Paul, Minnesota, April 24, 1913; admitted to bar, 1936, Minnesota; 1966, District of Columbia. *Education:* University of Minnesota (B.A. summa cum laude, 1933; J.D., 1936). Phi Beta Kappa; Sigma Xi; Delta Sigma Rho. Author: "Science as Evidence," 35 Jurimetrics J. 153 (1995); "Defending Antitrust Lawsuits," 24 American Jurisprudence Trials 1, 1977; and numerous articles in legal and science journals. Visiting Professor and Lecturer, University of Minnesota, 1953-1961. Associate Justice, Minnesota Supreme Court, 1960-1961. Assistant Attorney General in charge of Antitrust Division, U.S. Department of Justice, 1961-1963. Commissioner, Federal Communications Commission, 1963-1968. *Member:* The District of Columbia Bar; Bar Association of the District of Columbia; Hennepin County, Minnesota State and American (Member, House of Delegates, 1974-1980; Chairman, Science and Technology Section, 1982-1983) Bar Associations; American Academy of Appellate Lawyers; National Conference of Lawyers and Scientists. ***PRACTICE AREAS:*** Antitrust and Trade Regulation; Business Combinations; Appellate Practice. ***Email:*** lloevinger@hhlaw.com

SHERWIN J. MARKMAN, born Des Moines, Iowa, January 19, 1929; admitted to bar, 1952, Iowa; 1968, District of Columbia. *Education:* University of Iowa (A.B., magna cum laude, 1949); Yale University (LL.B., 1952; winner, Munson Prize, 1951). Phi Beta Kappa; Omicron Delta Kappa; Delta Sigma Rho; Phi Alpha Delta. Author: *The Election,* Random House, Inc., 1970; USSR, 1988. Assistant to the President of the United States, 1966-1968. *Member:* The District of Columbia Bar; American Bar Association. ***PRACTICE AREAS:*** Litigation (Civil, Criminal, Commercial, Appellate).

SEYMOUR S. MINTZ, born Newark, New Jersey, March 7, 1912; admitted to bar, 1936, District of Columbia. *Education:* George Washington University (A.B., 1933; J.D., 1936). Order of the Coif. Attorney, Office of UnderSecretary of Treasury, 1937-38; Special Attorney, Internal Revenue Service, 1938-45 (leave of absence for war service, 1942-1945). Member, Advisory Group to the Commissioner of Internal Revenue, 1961. Adjunct Professor, Georgetown University Law School, 1952-55. *Member:* The District of Columbia Bar; Bar Association of the District of Columbia; American Bar Association (Member, Council Taxation Section, 1959-1962); American Law Institute; American College of Tax Counsel. ***PRACTICE AREAS:*** Taxation Law.

WILLIAM S. REYNER, JR., born Greenville, South Carolina, October 11, 1945; admitted to bar, 1970, District of Columbia; 1978, U.S. Supreme Court; 1992, U.S. Court of Appeals, Seventh Circuit. *Education:* Yale University (B.A., 1967; LL.B., 1970). *Member:* The District of Columbia Bar; Federal Communications Bar Association. ***PRACTICE AREAS:*** Communications Law; Commercial Transactions; Sports and Entertainment Law. ***Email:*** wsreyner@hhlaw.com

JOHN J. ROSS, born Kings County, New York, April 6, 1929; admitted to bar, 1956, District of Columbia. *Education:* Virginia Military Institute (B.S., distinguished, 1951); Georgetown University (LL.B., 1956). *Member:* The District of Columbia Bar; Bar Association of the District of Columbia; Federal and American Bar Associations; American Judicature Society; American Academy of Hospital Attorneys. Fellow, American Bar Foundation. ***PRACTICE AREAS:*** Labor Law.

DAVID E. SKAGGS, born Cincinnati, Ohio, February 22, 1943; admitted to bar, 1968, New York; 1971, Colorado; 1999, District of Columbia. *Education:* Wesleyan University (B.A., 1964); Yale University (LL.B., 1967). Member: Colorado House of Representatives, 1981-1986; U.S. House of Representatives, 1987-1999. *Member:* Boulder County and Colorado Bar Associations; The District of Columbia Bar. [U.S. Marine Corps, Active Duty, 1968-1971, Captain; U.S. Marine Corps Reserves, 1971-1979, Major]. (Also at Denver, Colorado Office). ***PRACTICE AREAS:*** Legislative; Government Relations; Nonprofit and Charitable Organizations. ***Email:*** deskaggs@hhlaw.com

JAC K. SPERLING (Resident, Denver, Colorado Office).

PETER W. TREDICK, born Washington, D.C., July 26, 1940; admitted to bar, 1965, New Jersey; 1969, District of Columbia. *Education:* Princeton University (B.A., 1962); Harvard University (J.D., 1965). Counsel, Special Subcommittee on Labor, U.S. House of Representatives, 1967-1969. *Member:* The District of Columbia Bar; Bar Association of the District of Columbia. (Also at Los Angeles, California Office). ***PRACTICE AREAS:*** Equal Employment Opportunity Law; Management Labor Law; Employment Litigation. ***Email:*** pwtredick@hhlaw.com

BRUCE S. WOLFF, born New York, N.Y., June 11, 1943; admitted to bar, 1969, New York; 1979, District of Columbia. *Education:* Amherst College (B.A., magna cum laude, 1965); Harvard Law School (LL.B., magna cum laude, 1968). Special Assistant to Secretary and Deputy Assistant Secretary for Legislation, U.S. Department of Health, Education and Welfare, 1977-1979. Vice President and Senior Counsel for Health Operations, Aetna Life and Casualty, 1992-1996. Chairman, Committee on Medicine and Law, The Association of the Bar of the City of New York, 1982-1984. Member, National Board of Directors, Muscular Dystrophy Association, 1992-1996. *Member:* The District of Columbia Bar. (Also at Third Avenue, New York, N.Y. Office). ***PRACTICE AREAS:*** Health Care Mergers and Acquisitions; Managed Care; Health Care Contracts; Health Care Reform; Nonprofit Organizations Law; International Health. ***Email:*** bswolff@hhlaw.com

CLAYTON K. YEUTTER, born Eustis, Nebraska, December 10, 1930; admitted to bar, 1963, Nebraska; 1977, District of Columbia. *Education:* University of Nebraska (B.S., with high distinction, 1952; J.D., cum laude, 1963; Ph.D., 1966). Alpha Zeta; Gamma Sigma Delta; Phi Alpha Delta. Order of the Coif. Editor, Nebraska Law Review. Assistant Secretary for Marketing and Consumer Services, U.S.D.A., 1973-1974. Assistant Secretary (now Undersecretary) for International Affairs and Commodity Programs, U.S.D.A., 1974-1975. Deputy Special Trade Representative, Executive Office of the President, 1975-1977. U.S. Trade Representative, Executive Office of the President, 1985-1989. Secretary of Agriculture, 1989-1991. Counselor to the President, 1992. Director, University of Nebraska Mission to Colombia (South America), 1968-1970. Chairman, Republican National Committee, 1991-1992. President and CEO, Chicago Mercantile Exchange, 1978-1985. *Member:* Nebraska State Bar Association; The District of Columbia Bar. ***PRACTICE AREAS:*** International Trade; Business Law. ***Email:*** cyeutter@hhlaw.com

(This Listing Continued)

RESIDENT ASSOCIATES

KIM M. ALLEN, born Albany, New York, June 25, 1969; admitted to bar, 2000, Virginia; 2001, District of Columbia. *Education:* St. Lawrence University (B.A., cum laude, with honors in History, 1991); The University of Chicago (J.D., 2000). Phi Beta Kappa. ***Email:*** kmallen@hhlaw.com

NALINI P. ANAND, born Yonkers, New York, January 16, 1969; admitted to bar, 1996, Maryland; 1998, District of Columbia. *Education:* Cornell University (B.A., 1991); Stanford Law School (J.D., 1996). *Member:* The District of Columbia Bar. ***Email:*** npanand@hhlaw.com

ANA CRISTINA ARUMI, born Durham, North Carolina, April 16, 1970; admitted to bar, 1996, Maryland; 1997, District of Columbia. *Education:* University of North Carolina (A.B., 1992); Duke Law School (J.D., 1995); Georgetown Law School (LL.M., 1996). *Member:* The District of Columbia Bar. ***LANGUAGES:*** Spanish. ***Email:*** acarumi@hhlaw.com

ROSE MARIE L. AUDETTE, born Providence, Rhode Island, April 5, 1959; admitted to bar, 1993, Maryland; 1994, District of Columbia; U.S. Court of Appeals for the Fourth and District of Columbia Circuits. *Education:* Georgetown University (B.A., magna cum laude, 1981); Georgetown University Law Center (J.D., magna cum laude, 1993). Phi Beta Kappa. Order of the Coif. Member, Georgetown Law Journal. *Member:* U.S. District Courts for Maryland and the District of Columbia; The District of Columbia Bar; Maryland State and American Bar Associations. ***PRACTICE AREAS:*** Litigation; Education Law. ***Email:*** rmlaudette@hhlaw.com

FRANK BACELLI, born Buffalo, New York, March 6, 1972; admitted to bar, 1999, Maryland; 2000, District of Columbia. *Education:* State University of New York at Buffalo (B.A., cum laude, 1995); Catholic University of America (J.D., magna cum laude, 1999). Author: U.S. v. Thomas: When the Preservation of Juror Secrecy Outweighs the Ability to Dismiss a Juror for Nullification," 48 Cath. Univ. L. Rev. 125, (1998). ***Email:*** fabacelli@hhlaw.com

ELIZABETH V. BALTZAN, born Saskatoon, Saskatchewan, Canada, September 21, 1970; admitted to bar, 1997, California; 1999, District of Columbia. *Education:* Stanford University (B.A., International Relations, with honor, 1991); Georgetown University (J.D., 1996). Co-Author: with Abigale Tate, "Harley-Davidson and Adjusting to the Costs of Free Trade," Pew Case Studies, 1995; with Frank R. Samelos, "U.S. Trade Preferences for Developing Countries," in United States Regulation of International Trade, Occana Publications, 1996. ***LANGUAGES:*** French, German. ***PRACTICE AREAS:*** International Trade. ***Email:*** evbaltzan@hhlaw.com

BARTLEY L. BAREFOOT, born Raleigh, North Carolina, May 12, 1973; admitted to bar, 1999, North Carolina; 2000, District of Columbia. *Education:* Duke University (A.B., cum laude, 1995); University of North Carolina at Chapel Hill (J.D., magna cum laude, 1999). Order of the Coif. Executive Articles Editor, North Carolina Law Review. Author: "Enacting a Health Information Confidentiality Law: Can Congress Beat the Deadline?" 77 N.C. L. Rev. 283 (1998). ***PRACTICE AREAS:*** Health Law; Health Care Regulation. ***Email:*** bbarefoot@hhlaw.com

SONIA GUPTA BARROS, born Dayton, Ohio, September 17, 1970; admitted to bar, 1997, Illinois (Not admitted in District of Columbia). *Education:* Wright State University (B.S., summa cum laude, 1992); University of Chicago Law School (J.D., 1997). Editor-in-Chief, 1996-1997 and Staff, 1995-1996, University of Chicago Legal Forum. Author: "Bulletin Board Systems and Personal Jurisdiction: What Comports with Fair Play and Substantial Justice?" University of Chicago Legal Forum, Vol. 1996; "Commercial Loan Decisions: The Japanese Way," Bankers Magazine 177.1 (Jan/Feb. 1994): 56-59. *Member:* American Bar Association. ***PRACTICE AREAS:*** Corporate; Mergers and Acquisitions; Securities. ***Email:*** sgbarros@hhlaw.com

OLESYA VLADIMIROVNA BARSUKOVA-SPANDAU, born St. Petersburg, Russia; admitted to bar, 2000, Georgia; 2001, District of Columbia. *Education:* Russia's State A.I. Herzen Pedagogical University (1990-1994); University of Georgia (B.B.A., summa cum laude, 1996; J.D., cum laude, 2000). *Member:* State Bar of Georgia; District of Columbia Bar; American Bar Association; American Society of International Law. ***Email:*** obspandau@hhlaw.com

LYNNE M. BAUM, admitted to bar, 2000, New York; 2001, Puerto Rico (Not admitted in District of Columbia). *Education:* University of Wisconsin - Madison (B.A., 1994); Georgetown University Law Center (J.D., magna cum laude, 1999). Phi Beta Kappa; Order of the Coif. Author: Wisconsin International Law Review - 19 Wisconsin International Law Review 197, 2001; American Criminal Law Review - 35 American Criminal Law Review 823, 1998; El Otro Derecho - 8 El Otro Derecho 139, 1998. Formerly with The Honorable Jaime Pieras, Jr., U.S. District Court, District of Puerto Rico. *Member:* Federal and American Bar Associations. ***LANGUAGES:*** Spanish. ***Email:*** lmbaum@hhlaw.com

JOHN B. BECKMAN, born Baltimore, Maryland, March 8, 1971; admitted to bar, 1997, Maryland; 2001, District of Columbia. *Education:* Towson University (B.S., 1994); University of Baltimore (J.D., magna cum laude, 1997). Member, Heuisler Honor Society. Staff Member, 1995-1996 and Articles Editor, 1996-1997, University of Baltimore Law Review. *Member:* Maryland State and American (Member, Business Law Section) Bar Associations. ***PRACTICE AREAS:*** Corporate Finance; Securities; Mergers and Acquisitions. ***Email:*** jbbeckman@hhlaw.com

KEITH J. BENES, born Lincoln, Nebraska, March 28, 1972; admitted to bar, 2000, Maryland (Not admitted in District of Columbia). *Education:* University of Nebraska - Lincoln (B.A., 1995); Georgetown University Law Center (J.D., magna cum laude, 1999). Order of the Coif. ***Email:*** beneskj@hhlaw.com

LESLIE ANNE BENTON, born Atlanta, Georgia, March 31, 1963; admitted to bar, 1989, California; 1990, Georgia; 1998, District of Columbia. *Education:* University of Tennessee (B.A., 1985); Emory University (J.D., 1988); Harvard Law School (LL.M., 1996). Harvard Law School Ames Fellow, 1996-1997. Phi Beta Kappa. Order of the Coif. Co-Author: with Carol R. Berry, "Negligent Infliction of Emotional Distress Attendant to Economic Injury: A Reassessment," 35 Ariz. L. Rev. 4 1995; with Glenn T. Ware, "Haiti: A Case Study of the International Response and the Efficacy of Non-Governmental Organizations in Crisis," 12 Emory International Law Journal (Spring 1998). Professor, California Western School of Law, 1992-1995. *Member:* State Bar of California; State Bar of Georgia; The District of Columbia Bar. ***PRACTICE AREAS:*** Civil Litigation; Antitrust; Antitrust Class Actions; Federal Civil Practice; Complex Litigation; Multi District Litigation; Insurance Coverage Defense. ***Email:*** labenton@hhlaw.com

BEVERLY L. BLANK, born Washington, D.C., November 27, 1972; admitted to bar, 1997, California; 1998, District of Columbia. *Education:* University of Virginia (B.A., 1994); University of Michigan (J.D., 1997). Associate Editor, Journal of Law Reform, 1995-1996. ***PRACTICE AREAS:*** Corporate Law; Securities; Private Equity. ***Email:*** blblank@hhlaw.com

ROBERT M. BLUE, born Charlottesville, Virginia, September 3, 1967; admitted to bar, 1994, Virginia; 1997, District of Columbia. *Education:* University of Virginia (B.A., with honors, 1989); Yale Law School (J.D., 1994). Phi Beta Kappa. Law Clerk, Honorable Richard L. Williams, Senior District Judge, U.S. District Court for the Eastern District of Virginia, 1994-1995. *Member:* Virginia State Bar; The District of Columbia Bar. ***PRACTICE AREAS:*** Civil Litigation; Insurance Litigation. ***Email:*** rmblue@hhlaw.com

PAMELA MORRIS BLUMENTHAL, admitted to bar, 1995, District of Columbia. *Education:* Cornell University (B.A., cum laude); University of Michigan Law School (J.D., cum laude). Author: "A Dress Rehearsal for the Consumer, not the Bank," ABA Bank Compliance, Sept. 1996. Director, Young Lawyers Section, Maine State Bar Association, 1993. Staff Attorney, Division of Consumer and Community Affairs, Federal Reserve Board, 1997-1999. *Member:* The District of Columbia Bar. ***PRACTICE AREAS:*** Corporate and Securities; Commercial Practice. ***Email:*** pmblumenthal.com

DEBORAH L. BOARDMAN, born Silver Spring, Maryland, May 21, 1974; admitted to bar, 2000, Virginia (Not admitted in District of Columbia). *Education:* Villanova University (B.A., 1996); University of Virginia (J.D., 2000). Virginia Law Review. ***Email:*** dlboardman@hhlaw.com

ANN M. BOECKMAN, born Silver Spring, Maryland, May 7, 1969; admitted to bar, 1998, Maryland; 1999, District of Columbia. *Education:* Oklahoma State University (B.S., Nutrition and Dietetics, 1991); Catholic University of America (J.D., cum laude, 1997). Editor-in-Chief, Catholic University Law Review, 1996-1997, Volume 46. Registered Dietitian, 1993. Author: "An Exercise in Administrative Creativity: The FDA's Assertion of Jurisdiction over Tobacco," 46 Catholic University Law Review 991, 1996. ***PRACTICE AREAS:*** Food Law; Administrative Law. ***Email:*** amboeckman@hhlaw.com

RONALD P. BROWER, born 1972; admitted to bar, 1996, Maryland; 1998, District of Columbia. *Education:* Prince George's Community College (A.A.S., with honors, 1990); George Washington University (B.A., summa cum laude, 1992; J.D., with honors, 1996). Phi Beta Kappa; Omicron Delta Epsilon; Phi Theta Kappa. *Member:* Maryland State and American Bar Associations; The District of Columbia Bar. ***PRACTICE AREAS:*** Aviation and Aerospace; Transportation Law; Administrative Law. ***Email:*** rpbrower@hhlaw.com

CATHERINE T. BROWN, admitted to bar, 1999, District of Columbia and New York. *Education:* Southern Methodist University (B.B.A., 1987); American University, Washington College of Law (J.D., summa cum laude, 1998). ***PRACTICE AREAS:*** Corporate Law; Securities; Real Estate Securities. ***Email:*** ctbrown@hhlaw.com

RENÉ E. BROWNE, born June 23, 1971; admitted to bar, 1998, Virginia; 1999, District of Columbia. *Education:* Duke University (A.B., 1993); Georgetown University Law Center (J.D., 1998). *Member:* Virginia State Bar; The District of Columbia Bar. ***Email:*** rbrowne@hhlaw.com

ELLEN DUNHAM BRYANT, born Wellsboro, Pennsylvania, April 11, 1970; admitted to bar, 1998, Massachusetts and Pennsylvania; 2000, District of Columbia. *Education:* Allegheny College (B.A., magna cum laude, 1992); Duke University School of Law (J.D., cum laude, 1998). Phi Beta Kappa. Duke Law Journal. ***PRACTICE AREAS:*** Labor and Employment. ***Email:*** edbryant@hhlaw.com

(This Listing Continued)

HOGAN & HARTSON L.L.P., Washington—Continued

TAYLOR L. BURKE, born Washington, D.C., August 25, 1973; admitted to bar, 1999, Maryland; 2000, District of Columbia and U.S. District Court, District of Maryland. *Education:* Washington & Lee University (B.A., 1995); Washington College of Law of American University (J.D, magna cum laude, 1999). ***Email:*** tlburke@hhlaw.com

PAUL A. BURKETT, born Austin, Texas, September 29, 1965; admitted to bar, 1995, Illinois and U.S. District Court, Northern District of Illinois; 1997, District of Columbia. *Education:* United States Naval Academy (B.S., 1987); University of Virginia (J.D., 1995). *Member:* The District of Columbia Bar; American Bar Association. [U.S. Navy, 1987-1992]. ***PRACTICE AREAS:*** Tax; Corporate Law; Securities. ***Email:*** paburkett@hhlaw.com

MARY ELLEN CALLAHAN, born Syracuse, New York, November 16, 1968; admitted to bar, 1998, New York; 1999, District of Columbia. *Education:* University of Pittsburgh (B.Phil., magna cum laude, 1990); University of Chicago (J.D., 1997). Chancellor's Scholar; Truman Scholar. *Member:* The District of Columbia Bar; American Bar Association. ***LANGUAGES:*** Russian, French. ***PRACTICE AREAS:*** Litigation; Antitrust; Consumer Protection. ***Email:*** mecallahan@hhlaw.com

BRUCE D. CAMPBELL JR., born Pittsburgh, Pennsylvania, March 1, 1972; admitted to bar, 1998, Pennsylvania; 1999, District of Columbia. *Education:* University of Pittsburgh (B.A., summa cum laude, 1994); George Washington Law School (J.D., with honors, 1998). *Member:* The District of Columbia Bar. ***Email:*** bdcampbell@hhlaw.com

GARY J. CAMPBELL, born Cambridge, Massachusetts, November 22, 1968; admitted to bar, 1999, Massachusetts; 2000, District of Columbia. *Education:* Boston College (B.S., 1990); University of Richmond (M.B.A., 1995); George Mason University School of Law (J.D., with high honors, 1998). ***PRACTICE AREAS:*** Government Contracts. ***Email:*** gjcampbell@hhlaw.com

CHRISTOPHER P. CARDACI, born Washington, D.C., June 5, 1969; admitted to bar, 1997, Maryland; 1998, District of Columbia and U.S. District Court, District of Puerto Rico; 2000, U.S. District Court, District of Columbia. *Education:* Lehigh University (B.A., 1993; B.S., 1993); Georgetown University Law Center (J.D., magna cum laude, 1996). Order of the Coif. Law Clerk to Hon. Jamie Pieras, U.S. District Court for Puerto Rico. *Member:* The District of Columbia Bar; Maryland State Bar Association, Inc. ***PRACTICE AREAS:*** Litigation; Insurance Coverage. ***Email:*** ccardaci@hhlaw.com

ALISON B. CERA, born Rochester, New York, March 2, 1964; admitted to bar, 1999, Virginia; 2000, District of Columbia. *Education:* Cornell University (B.S.I.L.R., 1987); Georgetown University (J.D., 1998). ***PRACTICE AREAS:*** Employee Benefits. ***Email:*** abcera@hhlaw.com

CAROL B. CHESLEY, born New York, N.Y., April 9, 1971; admitted to bar, 1996, Wisconsin; 1998, New York; 1999, District of Columbia. *Education:* Colgate University (B.A., magna cum laude, 1993); University of Pennsylvania (J.D., 1996). Phi Beta Kappa. ***PRACTICE AREAS:*** Real Estate. ***Email:*** cbchesley@hhlaw.com

EUN AH CHOI, born Seoul, Korea, May 2, 1973; admitted to bar, 2000, Virginia (Not admitted in District of Columbia). *Education:* University of Oxford (Visiting Student, 1994); Georgetown University (B.F.S.F., magna cum laude, 1995; J.D., magna cum laude, 2000);. Phi Beta Kappa; Order of the Coif. ***LANGUAGES:*** Korean. ***Email:*** eachoi@hhlaw.com

KAIJA M. CLARK, admitted to bar, 1999, Virginia; 2000, District of Columbia. *Education:* University of Notre Dame (B.S., 1994); George Washington University (J.D., with highest honors, 1998). Editor, George Washington University Law Review. Law Clerk to Hon. James C. Cacheris of the Eastern District of Virginia. ***PRACTICE AREAS:*** Litigation. ***Email:*** kmclark@hhlaw.com

KAREN RENFREE CLARK, admitted to bar, 1989, California; 1991, District of Columbia. *Education:* University of Santa Clara (B.A., 1985); George Washington Law School (J.D., with honors, 1989). *Member:* State Bar of California; The District of Columbia Bar. ***PRACTICE AREAS:*** Corporate. ***Email:*** krclark@hhlaw.com

JOHN CLASBY, admitted to bar, 1999, Maryland; 2000, District of Columbia and U.S. District Court, District of Maryland. *Education:* St. John's College, Annapolis (B.A., 1995); University of Virginia (J.D., 1998). Law Clerk, Honorable Howell Cobb, U.S. District Court, Eastern District of Texas, 1998-1999. *Member:* Maryland State Bar; The District of Columbia Bar; The U.S. District Court for the District of Columbia Bar. ***Email:*** jclasby@hhlaw.com

TRACY-ELIZABETH CLAY, admitted to bar, 1997, Illinois; 1998, District of Columbia. *Education:* Stanford University (B.A., 1993); Harvard Law School (J.D., magna cum laude, 1997). Editor and Co-Chair, Reviews and Commentaries, Harvard Law Review, 1995-1997. Harvard Human Rights Fellow. John Gardner Public Service Fellow. Law Clerk, Chief Judge Anne E. Thompson, U.S. District Court for the District of New Jersey, 1997-1998. *Member:* The District of Columbia Bar. ***PRACTICE AREAS:*** Antitrust; Litigation; Health Care; Government Regulation. ***Email:*** teclay@hhlaw.com

KEVIN C. CLAYTON, born Lafayette, Indiana, December 15, 1970; admitted to bar, 1998, Virginia; 1999, District of Columbia. *Education:* University of Virginia (B.A., 1992; J.D., 1998). Articles Review Editor, Virginia Journal of International Law, 1997-1998. ***PRACTICE AREAS:*** Corporate Law; Finance; Investments; Mergers, Acquisitions and Divestitures; Securities; Technology and Science. ***Email:*** kcclayton@hhlaw.com

HELENE F. COMBE, born Perigueux, France, August 31, 1972; admitted to bar, 1999, Paris Courts of Appeal, France (Not admitted in the United States). *Education:* University of Bordeaux, 1993; University of Paris II, Panthéon-Assas, 1995; Law University of Paris, Paris II Panthéon-Assas (D.E.A., Tax Law/Public Finances, Valedictorian, with high honors, 1996; D.E.S.S., International Taxation, with honors, 1997); University of Virginia (LL.M., 2001). ***LANGUAGES:*** French, Spanish. ***PRACTICE AREAS:*** Corporate Securities; International Business Transactions; Tax Law. ***Email:*** hfcombe@hhlaw.com

SUSAN M. COOK, admitted to bar, 1998, Maryland; 1999, District of Columbia. *Education:* Yale University (B.A., cum laude, 1995); Harvard Law School (J.D., cum laude, 1998). Harvard Law School Board of Student Advisors. *Member:* The District of Columbia Bar. ***Email:*** smcook@hhlaw.com

CRAIG T. CRONHEIM, born Belleville, New Jersey, August 21, 1976; admitted to bar, 2001, Virginia (Not admitted in District of Columbia). *Education:* University of Richmond (B.A., 1998); Harvard Law School (J.D., 2001). ***Email:*** ctcronheim@hhlaw.com

EDWARD C. CROOKE, admitted to bar, 1999, Maryland; 2001, District of Columbia. *Education:* Haverford College (B.A., with honors, 1994); University of Virginia (J.D., 1999). ***Email:*** ecrooke@hhlaw.com

ANDREA T. CUMMINGS, admitted to bar, 1998, Virginia (Not admitted in District of Columbia). *Education:* University of Virginia (B.A., 1994; J.D., 1998). Staff Member, Virginia Law Review. *Member:* Virginia State Bar. ***Email:*** atcummings@hhlaw.com

ALICE T. VALDER CURRAN, born Arlington, Virginia, October 28, 1967; admitted to bar, 1993, Pennsylvania; 1998, District of Columbia. *Education:* Pomona College (B.A., cum laude, 1989); Columbia University (J.D., 1992). Law Clerk to the Honorable Royce C. Lamberth, United States Court for the District of Columbia. Notes and Comments Editor, 1991-1992, and Staff Member, 1990-1991, Columbia Law Review. ***PRACTICE AREAS:*** False Claims Act; Qui Tam Litigation; Government Investigations; Civil Fraud; Health Care Fraud; Medicare Fraud and Abuse; Health Care Compliance; Federal Grants; Government Contract Fraud; Fraud; Federal Civil Litigation; Trial Practice. ***Email:*** avcurran@hhlaw.com

WILLIAM J. CURTIN, III, born Washington, D.C., May 8, 1969; admitted to bar, 1996, Maryland; 1997, District of Columbia. *Education:* Duke University (A.B., cum laude, 1992); University of Virginia School of Law (J.D., 1996). Co-Author: "Commentary on the Constitution of Malawi," January, 1995 (University of Virginia Project on Constitution and Democracy). Visiting Professor: Université de Paris XI, Faculté Jean Monnet, Paris, France, 1992-1993; L'Institut d'Etudes Politiques, Paris, France, 1992-1993. Member, The Vergennes Institute. *Member:* The District of Columbia Bar. ***LANGUAGES:*** French. ***PRACTICE AREAS:*** International Business Transactions; Corporate and Securities Law. ***Email:*** wjcurtin@hhlaw.com

DAVID F. CUTTER, born Wiesbaden, Germany, November 6, 1967; admitted to bar, 1995, Maryland; 1997, District of Columbia. *Education:* University of Michigan (B.G.S., 1989); Catholic University of America, Columbus School of Law (J.D., magna cum laude, 1995). Law Clerk to the Honorable Aubrey E. Robinson, Jr., United States District Court for the District of Columbia. Executive Editor, 1994-1995 and Staff Member, 1993-1994, Catholic University Law Review. Faculty Award Winner. *Member:* The District of Columbia Bar. ***PRACTICE AREAS:*** Litigation. ***Email:*** dfcutter@hhlaw.com

RICHARD L. DAVIS, born Springfield, Missouri, January 23, 1972; admitted to bar, 2000, Maryland; 2001, District of Columbia. *Education:* Truman State University (B.S., 1994); University of Maryland (J.D., with honors, 1999). Order of the Coif. ***Email:*** rldavis@hhlaw.com

BRAD DEUTSCH, born New York, N.Y., October 21, 1965; admitted to bar, 1995, New York; 1996, Maryland; 2000, District of Columbia. *Education:* Brown University (A.B., 1987); Fordham University (J.D., 1994). ***PRACTICE AREAS:*** Communications Law; FCC Regulation; Television Law; Radio Law. ***Email:*** bcdeutsch@hhlaw.com

M. COLETTE DEVINE, born Washington, D.C., June 9, 1965; admitted to bar, 1997, Maryland; 1998, District of Columbia. *Education:* Georgetown University (B.A., with distinction, 1987); Harvard University (M.A., East Asian Studies, 1992); University of Virginia School of Law (J.D., 1997). Rotary International Graduate Fellow. *Member:* The District of Columbia Bar. ***LANGUAGES:*** Japanese and French. ***Email:*** mcdevine@hhlaw.com

(This Listing Continued)

MARGARET E. DiPENTIMA, born Baltimore, Maryland, June 19, 1973; admitted to bar, 1999, Maryland; 2000, District of Columbia. *Education:* Princeton University (A.B., magna cum laude, 1995); University of Virginia (J.D., 1999). ***Email:*** medipentima@hhlaw.com

KRISTEN A. DONOGHUE, born Teaneck, New Jersey, May 9, 1968; admitted to bar, 1996, Maryland; 1997, District of Columbia. *Education:* Georgetown University (B.A., magna cum laude, 1990); University of Michigan (J.D., cum laude, 1995). Co-Author: "Cumulative Voting in the United States," 1995 U. Chi. Legal F. 241 (1995). Judicial Clerk, The Honorable Fred I. Parker, United States Court of Appeals for the Second Circuit, 1995-1996. ***Email:*** kadonoghue@hhlaw.com

YARON DORI, born Santa Monica, California, August 24, 1970; admitted to bar, 1996, California; 1998, District of Columbia. *Education:* Brandeis University (B.A., summa cum laude, 1992); Boston College Law School (J.D., 1996). Phi Beta Kappa. *Member:* State Bar of California; The District of Columbia Bar; American Bar Association; Federal Communications Bar Association. ***LANGUAGES:*** Hebrew. ***PRACTICE AREAS:*** Communications. ***Email:*** ydori@hhlaw.com

ALEXANDER E. DREIER, born New York, N.Y., May 11, 1966; admitted to bar, 1997, Maryland; 1998, District of Columbia. *Education:* Harvard University (A.B., magna cum laude, 1988); Oxford University (A.B., 1990; M.A., 1996); Yale Law School (J.D., 1995). Rhodes Scholar. Phi Beta Kappa. Adjunct Professor, University of Oklahoma College of Law, 1995-1996. Judicial Clerk, The Honorable Robert H. Henry, United States Court of Appeals for the Tenth Circuit, 1996. Co-Author: "The 1996-1997 Supreme Court Term and Its Impact on Public Schools," 122 Ed. Law Rep. 361 (1998); "The 1997-1998 Supreme Court Term and Its Impact on Public Schools," 129 Ed. Law Rep. 887 (1998); "Board of Education of the Township of Piscataway v. Sharon Taxman," 24 J. Coll. & Univ. L. 671 (1998); "The 1998-1999 Term of the Supreme Court and Its Impact on Public Schools," 138 Ed. Law Rep. 1 (1999); "Katuria E. Smith, et al., v. The University of Washington Law School , et al., Brief of Amici Curiae," 26 J. Coll. & Univ. L. 467 (2000); The 1999-2000 Term of the Supreme Court and Its Impact on Public Schools," 148 Ed. Law Rep.1 (2000). *Member:* The District of Columbia Bar; State Bar of Maryland, Inc.; American Bar Association; National Association of College and University Attorneys; National Association of College and University Business Officers. ***PRACTICE AREAS:*** Education Law; College and University Law; Public School Law; Special Education; Litigation; Civil Litigation; Federal Litigation. ***Email:*** aedreier@hhlaw.com

ALEKSANDAR DUKIC, born Belgrade, Serbia, Yugoslavia, December 1, 1970; admitted to bar, 1999, Virginia; 2000, District of Columbia. *Education:* University of Belgrade Law School (1990-1993); Stockton State College (B.A., 1996); George Washington University (J.D., 1999). Order of the Coif. Salutatorian, Stockton State College. *Member:* American Bar Association. ***LANGUAGES:*** Serbian, Croatian, Slovenian, Macedonian and Russian. ***Email:*** adukic@hhlaw.com

ALISON H. EATON, admitted to bar, 1997, Georgia; 1999, District of Columbia. *Education:* College of William & Mary (B.A., 1993); Emory University School of Law (J.D., 1996). ***Email:*** aheaton@hhlaw.com

WILLIAM L. ELDER, born Columbus, Ohio, September 23, 1958; admitted to bar, 1997, Maryland; 1998, District of Columbia. *Education:* United States Naval Academy (B.S., with honors, 1980); Georgetown University Law Center (J.D., cum laude, 1997). Airline Transport Pilot Certificate: Multiengine Land, L-188; Commercial Privileges, SEL, 1990. Certified Flight Instructor: SEL, 1988; MEL, 1992; Instrument Airplane, 1988. Author: Comment, "Free Flight: Legal Implications of Air Transportation Entering the Twenty-First Century," Journal of Air Law and Commerce, volume 62:3. *Member:* The District of Columbia Bar; National Transportation Safety Board Bar Association; Lawyer-Pilots Bar Association; Aero Club of Washington; Aircraft Owners and Pilots Association; Airline Pilots Association (Active Member, 1989-1991; Inactive Participant, 1991—); Association of Naval Aviation; Experimental Aircraft Association; National Association of Flight Instructors. [U.S. Navy, 1980-1989; U.S. Naval Reserve, 1989-1997; Naval Aviator and Commander, U.S.N.R., Ret.]. ***PRACTICE AREAS:*** Administrative Agency Practice; Aviation Law; Aviation Regulation; Hazardous Materials Transportation. ***Email:*** wlelder@hhlaw.com

EVAN R. FARBER, born Long Island, New York, September 6, 1972; admitted to bar, 1998, New York (Not admitted in District of Columbia). *Education:* State University of New York at Binghamton (B.A., 1994); George Washington University (J.D., 1997). Phi Beta Kappa. Editor-in-Chief, Public Contract Law Journal, 1996-1997. Author: Note, "The Allowability of Costs Incurred in the Preparation of REAs After Reflectone," Public Contract Law Journal. ***PRACTICE AREAS:*** Corporate Law; Securities; Mergers and Acquisitions; Private Equity; Public Offerings. ***Email:*** erfarber@hhlaw.com

TERESA MAUREA PANTOJA DA COSTA FARIA, born Rio de Janeiro, Brazil, October 26, 1974; admitted to bar, 1997, Rio de Janeiro, Brazil; 2001, New York (Not admitted in District of Columbia). *Education:* Pontificia Universidade Catolica (Law Degree, 1996); Georgetown University Law Center (LL.M., 2000). *Member:* American Bar Association. ***LANGUAGES:*** Portuguese, Spanish. ***PRACTICE AREAS:*** Business Law; Finance; Project Finance. ***Email:*** tmfaria@hhlaw.com

ADAM S. FEUERSTEIN, born New York, N.Y., March 21, 1971; admitted to bar, 1997, New York; 1998, Maryland and District of Columbia. *Education:* Cornell University (B.S., with honors, 1993); Harvard University (J.D., cum laude, 1997; M.P.P., 1997). Phi Kappa Phi. Member, Golden Key. Contributing Editor, New York Forms, Limited Liability Companies, Lawyer Cooperative Publishing, 1996. *Member:* Montgomery County and New York State Bar Associations; District of Columbia Bar; Maryland State Bar Association, Inc. ***PRACTICE AREAS:*** Tax; Corporate. ***Email:*** asfeuerstein@hhlaw.com

MARSHALL FITZ, born Baltimore, Maryland, July 27, 1968; admitted to bar, 1999, Massachusetts; 2000, District of Columbia. *Education:* University of Virginia (B.A., 1991; J.D., 1998). Member, University of Virginia Law Review, 1996-1998. Clerkship, U.S. Court of Appeals, First Circuit, Judge Selya. ***LANGUAGES:*** Spanish. ***PRACTICE AREAS:*** Immigration Law. ***Email:*** mdfitz@hhlaw.com

UTE FOSHAG, born Stuttgart, Germany, August 31, 1967; admitted to bar, 1997, Germany (Not admitted in the United States). *Education:* Kiel, Germany (1. State Exam, 1994); Georgetown University (LL.M., Securities and Financial Regulation, 2001). ***LANGUAGES:*** German. ***Email:*** ufoshag@hhlaw.com

JODY M. FOSTER, born Austin, Texas, May 27, 1958; admitted to bar, 1993, Maryland; 1995, District of Columbia. *Education:* University of Oklahoma (B.A., 1979; M.A., 1983); University of California, Boalt Hall School of Law (J.D., 1993). Phi Beta Kappa. Member, University of California Law Review. *Member:* The District of Columbia Bar. ***PRACTICE AREAS:*** Environmental Regulation; Clean Air Act; Clean Water Act; National Environmental Policy Act (NEPA); Endangered Species; Federal Administrative Law; Environmental Administrative Law; Federal Energy Regulation. ***Email:*** jmfoster@hhlaw.com

BRIAN D. FOWLER, admitted to bar, 1999, Virginia; 2001, District of Columbia. *Education:* Virginia Polytechnic Institute and State University (B.A., 1996); Duke University (J.D., 1999). Phi Beta Kappa. *Member:* American Bar Association (Labor and Employment Section). ***Email:*** bdfowler@hhlaw.com

SHINOBU K. GARRIGUES, admitted to bar, 1998, Minnesota; 2000, District of Columbia. *Education:* University of Colorado at Boulder (B.A., International Affairs, magna cum laude, 1992); University of Minnesota (J.D., cum laude, 1998). Law Clerk, Honorable Edward Toussaint, Minnesota Court of Appeals, 1999. ***Email:*** skgarrigues@hhlaw.com

JOHN F. GAUL, born Cleveland, Ohio, January 19, 1968; admitted to bar, 1994, Maryland; 1997, District of Columbia. *Education:* Georgetown University (B.S., cum laude, 1990); Georgetown University Law Center (J.D., magna cum laude, 1994). Order of the Coif. Member, *The Tax Lawyer*. *Member:* Maryland State and American Bar Associations; The District of Columbia Bar. ***PRACTICE AREAS:*** Corporate; Securities. ***Email:*** jfgaul@hhlaw.com

ROBERT A. GECKLE, JR., born Stamford, Connecticut, November 20, 1970; admitted to bar, 1996, Connecticut; 1997, New York; 1998, District of Columbia. *Education:* Middlebury College (B.A., cum laude, 1993); Boston College (J.D., cum laude, 1996). *Member:* Connecticut and American Bar Associations. ***LANGUAGES:*** French. ***PRACTICE AREAS:*** Corporate Law; Securities Law. ***Email:*** rageckle@hhlaw.com

ANGELA ELIZABETH GIANCARLO, born Buffalo, New York, December 9, 1963; admitted to bar, 1996, Virginia and U.S. District Court, Eastern District of Virginia; 1997, U.S. Court of Appeals, Fourth Circuit; 2000, U.S. Court of Appeals for the District of Columbia Circuit and U.S. Court of Federal Claims (Not admitted in District of Columbia). *Education:* Trinity College, Washington, D.C. (B.A., 1986); Catholic University of America (J.D., 1996). Former Law Clerk, Federal Communications Commission. Author: Angela E. Giancarlo, "Wireless Web Presents Challenge to Privacy." TR Wireless News, May 14, 2001; Michele C. Farquhar and Angela E. Giancarlo, "FCC Targets Development of Software-Defined Radios, " TR Wireless News, January 4, 2001; Michele C. Farquhar and Angela E. Giancarlo, "Consumer Issues Keys to Wireless Industry," TR Wireless News, November 23, 2000. Member, Board of Directors, Alumnae Association of Trinity College, 1996-1998. Counsel and Director, Federal Regulatory Affairs, Personal Communications Industry Association, 1997-2000. *Member:* Virginia State Bar; Federal Communications Bar Association. ***SPECIAL AGENCIES:*** Federal Communications Commission. ***PRACTICE AREAS:*** Telecommunications; Wireless; Common Carrier. ***Email:*** aegiancarlo@hhlaw.com

JOSEPH E. GILLIGAN, admitted to bar, 1997, Maryland; 1999, District of Columbia. *Education:* Loyola College (B.B.A., 1989; M.B.A., Finance, 1994); Georgetown University Law Center (J.D., 1997). Dean's List. Certified Public Accountant, 1993. *Member:* The District of Columbia Bar. [U.S. Army, Lieutenant, 1989-1993]. ***PRACTICE AREAS:*** Corporate Law; Securities; Mergers and Acquisitions; Corporate Finance. ***Email:*** jegilligan@hhlaw.com

VICTORIA W. GIRARD, born San Antonio, Texas, November 8, 1962; admitted to bar, 1988, Maryland; 1989, District of Columbia. *Education:* Drew

(This Listing Continued)

HOGAN & HARTSON L.L.P., Washington—Continued

University (B.A., cum laude, 1984); Georgetown University (J.D., magna cum laude, 1987). Order of the Coif. *Member:* The District of Columbia Bar; Maryland State Bar Association. ***PRACTICE AREAS:*** Food and Drug Regulation; Food, Drug and Cosmetic Law. ***Email:*** vwgirard@hhlaw.com

STEPHANIE J. GOLD, born Lompoc, California, July 28, 1969; admitted to bar, 1998, Massachusetts, New York and District of Columbia. *Education:* Brown University (A.B., 1991); University of Michigan Law School (J.D., cum laude, 1996). *Member:* The District of Columbia Bar; National Association of College and University Attorneys. ***PRACTICE AREAS:*** Education Law; College and University Law; School Law; Student Loans. ***Email:*** sjgold@hhlaw.com

F. JOSEPH GORMLEY, born Nashua, New Hampshire, July 9, 1968; admitted to bar, 1993, Maryland; 1994, U.S. District Court, District of Maryland; 1995, Massachusetts and U.S. Court of Appeals, Fourth Circuit; 1999, District of Columbia. *Education:* University of New Hampshire (B.A., 1990); University of Maryland (J.D., 1993). Order of the Coif. *Member:* Federal Bar Association (Assistant Chair for Policy and Planning, Antitrust and Trade Regulation, 1997-1998); American Bar Association (Member, Section on: Antitrust Law; Vice Chair, Committee on: Treatises and Publications, 1999-2000). ***PRACTICE AREAS:*** Antitrust. ***Email:*** fjgormley@hhlaw.com

CHARLES S. GREENE, III, admitted to bar, 1997, California (Not admitted in District of Columbia). *Education:* Duke University (B.A., 1989); University of California at Berkeley, Boalt Hall School of Law (J.D., 1997). Formerly with U.S. Department of Justice. [Army, 1990-1994; Army Reserve, 1994-1998; Captain]. ***PRACTICE AREAS:*** Litigation.

JONATHAN M. GROSSMAN, born Dearborn, Michigan, September 27, 1970; admitted to bar, 2000, New York and District of Columbia. *Education:* University of Michigan (B.A., 1992); Harvard University (J.D., 2000); Harvard University - John F. Kennedy School of Government (M.P.P., 2000). ***Email:*** jgrossman@hhlaw.com

MICHAEL GRYNBERG, born Boston, Massachusetts, January 12, 1971; admitted to bar, 2000, District of Columbia. *Education:* Carleton College (B.A., 1993); University of Virginia (J.D., 1999). Order of the Coif. Articles Editor, Virginia Law Review, 1998-1999. Law Clerk to the Honorable Edward R. Becker, U.S. Court of Appeals, Third Circuit.

CATHERINE R. GUTTMAN-McCABE, born New York, N.Y., May 10, 1968; admitted to bar, 1995, Maryland; 1997, District of Columbia. *Education:* Swarthmore College (B.A., with distinction, 1990); Harvard University (J.D., cum laude, 1995). Author: "Listen to the Children: The Decision to Transfer Juveniles to Adult Court," 30 Harvard CR-CL, Summer 1995. *Member:* Maryland State and American Bar Associations; The District of Columbia Bar; National Association of College and University Attorneys. ***PRACTICE AREAS:*** Education Law; College and University Law; School Law; Employment Discrimination; Employment Law. ***Email:*** crguttmanmccabe@hhlaw.com

WILLIAM S. HAFT, born New York, N.Y., July 30, 1964; admitted to bar, 1999, Colorado; 2000, District of Columbia and U.S. Court of Appeals for the District of Columbia Circuit. *Education:* Carleton College (B.A., magna cum laude, 1986); Harvard University (J.D., cum laude, 1998). Author: Charter Schools & the 19th Century Corporation," 30 Ariz. St. L.J. 1023 (1999). ***LANGUAGES:*** French. ***PRACTICE AREAS:*** Education Law; School Law; Legislative Practice; Litigation. ***Email:*** whaft@hhlaw.com

CHRISTOPHER R. HALL, born Cherry Point, North Carolina, March 17, 1970; admitted to bar, 1998, Texas; 2000, District of Columbia. *Education:* Baylor University (B.A., 1992); University of Texas School of Law (J.D., 1998). Notes Editor, Texas Law Review, 1997-1998. Law Clerk, Hon. Samuel B.. Kent, United States District Court for the Southern District of Texas. *Member:* Texas State Bar; District of Columbia Bar. ***PRACTICE AREAS:*** Litigation. ***Email:*** chall@hhlaw.com

CHRISTOPHER TODD HANDMAN, born Santa Monica, California, January 13, 1972; admitted to bar, 1998, Maryland; 2000, U.S. Court of Appeals for the District of Columbia Circuit; 2001, District of Columbia and U.S. District Court for the District of Columbia. *Education:* American University (B.A., summa cum laude, 1993); Yale University (J.D., 1997). Law Clerk, Hon. Patricia M. Wald, U.S. Court of Appeals for the District of Columbia Circuit, 1999; Law Clerk, Hon. Collen Kollar-Kotelly, U.S. District Court for the District of Columbia, 1997-1999. Author: "The Doctrine of Political Accountability and Supreme Court Jurisdiction: Applying a New External Constraint to Congress's Exceptions Clause Power," 106 Yale L.J. 197 (1996). Adjunct Professor, Washington College of Law, 1999-2000. *Member:* American Bar Association. ***PRACTICE AREAS:*** Appellate Litigation; Litigation. ***Email:*** cthandman@hhlaw.com

LISA A. HARIG, born Bethesda, Maryland, May 28, 1968; admitted to bar, 1993, Virginia and U.S. Court of Appeals, Fourth Circuit; 1995, District of Columbia. *Education:* Pennsylvania State University (B.A., with honors, 1990); Duke University (J.D., 1993). Member, Duke Law Journal. Author: "Ignorance

(This Listing Continued)

is Not Bliss: Responsible Corporate Officers Convicted of Environmental Crimes and the Federal Sentencing Guidelines," 42 Duke L.J. 145 (1992). *Member:* Virginia State Bar; The District of Columbia Bar. ***PRACTICE AREAS:*** Corporate Law; Securities Law; Aviation Law. ***Email:*** laharig@hhlaw.com

LORANE F. HEBERT, born Pomona, California, July 18, 1964; admitted to bar, 1995, California; 1999, District of Columbia. *Education:* San Francisco State University (B.A., cum laude, 1988); Stanford Law School (J.D., 1994). Associate Editor, Stanford Law Review, 1992-1994. Law Clerk: The Hon. W. Eugene Davis, United States Court of Appeals for the Fifth Circuit; The Hon. Roderick R. McKelvie, United States District Court for the District of Delaware. *Member:* State Bar of California; The District of Columbia Bar. ***PRACTICE AREAS:*** Litigation. ***Email:*** lfhebert@hhlaw.com

GEORGE F. HOBDAY, JR., born Towson, Maryland, February 8, 1967; admitted to bar, 1994, Maryland; 1995, District of Columbia. *Education:* Dartmouth College (A.B., magna cum laude, 1989); Georgetown University Law Center (J.D., magna cum laude, 1994). Phi Beta Kappa. Order of the Coif. Member, The Georgetown Law Journal. ***Email:*** ghobday@hhlaw.com

E. DESMOND HOGAN, born Alliance, Ohio, June 23, 1968; admitted to bar, 1996, Pennsylvania; 1998, District of Columbia; 1999, Court of International Trade; 2000, U.S. Court of Appeals for the District of Columbia. *Education:* Allegheny College (B.A., 1991); Howard University (J.D., summa cum laude, 1996). Valedictorian. Associate Editor, Howard Law Journal. Author: "Remembered Hero, Forgotten Contribution: Charles Hamilton Houston, Legal Realism, and Labor Law," 14 Harvard Black Letter Law Journal 1 (1998); "A Consistent Interpretation for 801 (d)(1)(B) Prior Consistent Statements," 39 Howard Law Journal 819 (1996). Law Clerk to The Honorable Wiley Y. Daniel, U.S. District Court, District of Colorado, 1996-1997. *Member:* The District of Columbia Bar. ***PRACTICE AREAS:*** Litigation; Civil Rights. ***Email:*** edhogan@hhlaw.com

JANICE MARCHIAFAVA HOGAN, born Bryn Mawr, Pennsylvania, September 14, 1966; admitted to bar, 1995, Maryland; 1997, District of Columbia; 1998, Pennsylvania. *Education:* Massachusetts Institute of Technology (B.S., 1988); Georgetown Law Center (J.D., magna cum laude, 1995). Order of the Coif. Editor in Chief, Law & Policy in International Business. Law Clerk, Hon. Irma S. Raker, Maryland Court of Appeals, 1995-1996. *Member:* Maryland State and American Bar Associations; The District of Columbia Bar; American Health Lawyers Association. (Also at Philadelphia, Pennsylvania, Office). ***PRACTICE AREAS:*** Biotechnology. ***Email:*** JH9@DC2.HHLAW.COM

BRIAN H. HOOK, born Philadelphia, Pennsylvania, June 4, 1968; admitted to bar, 2000, Iowa and District of Columbia. *Education:* College of St. Thomas (B.A., 1990); Boston College (M.A., Philosophy, 1996); University of Iowa (J.D., with distinction, 1999). Member, Iowa Law Review. ***Email:*** bhhook@hhlaw.com

ALEX HORTIS, born Minneapolis, Minnesota, November 24, 1972; admitted to bar, 2001, Maryland (Not admitted in District of Columbia). *Education:* Macalester College (B.A., 1995); New York University School of Law (J.D., 1999). New York University Law Review.

THERESA M. HOWALD, admitted to bar, 1998, California; 1999, District of Columbia. *Education:* University of California, Los Angeles (B.S., 1993); John Hopkins University (M.P.H., 1997); Georgetown University (J.D., 1997). ***PRACTICE AREAS:*** Health Law; White Collar Crime; Litigation. ***Email:*** tmhowald@hhlaw.com

DEBORAH JAMES, born Boston, Massachusetts, June 24, 1959; admitted to bar, 1990, Florida; 1991, New York (Not admitted in District of Columbia). *Education:* Barnard College, Columbia University (B.A., magna cum laude, 1981); Yale Law School (J.D., 1987). Member, Board of Editors, Yale Law Journal. Member, Board of Directors, Moot Court Board. Author, "Voter Registration and the Fundamental Right to Vote," Yale Law Journal, 1987. ***LANGUAGES:*** Spanish, Portuguese, French, Italian. ***PRACTICE AREAS:*** International Business Transactions; Corporate Law; Securities; Energy; Government Contracts. ***Email:*** dsjames@hhlaw.com

LASHAWN M. JOHNSON, born Newbern, Alabama, December 21, 1972; admitted to bar, 1999, Maryland (Not admitted in District of Columbia). *Education:* Howard University (B.A., summa cum laude, 1994); University of Michigan (M.P.P., 1996); University of California, Berkeley, Boalt Hall School of Law (J.D., 1999). Phi Beta Kappa. Member, Moot Court Board. Member, California Law Review. Law Clerk , Hon. Chief Judge U.W. Clemon, U.S. District Court for the Northern District of Alabama, 1999-2000. *Member:* Maryland State and American Bar Associations. ***Email:*** lmjohnson@hhlaw.com

MARY L. JOHNSON, born Washington, D.C., February 25, 1969; admitted to bar, 1997, District of Columbia. *Education:* Princeton University (A.B., 1991); Duke University School of Law (M.A., and J.D., 1996). ***PRACTICE AREAS:*** Pharmaceutical Regulation. ***Email:*** mljohnson@hhlaw.com

(This Listing Continued)

KATHLEEN MARIE JOYCE, born Brooklyn, New York, March 17, 1953; admitted to bar, 1997, Maryland; 1998, District of Columbia. *Education:* John Carroll University (B.S., 1975); Columbus School of Law of The Catholic University of America (J.D., 1997). Staff Member, *Catholic University Law Review*. ***PRACTICE AREAS:*** Food and Drug Law. ***Email:*** kmjoyce@hhlaw.com

WILLIAM P. KAHN, born Antwerp, Belgium, April 27, 1973; admitted to bar, 2001, New York and District of Columbia. *Education:* (University of Brussels School of Law (J.D., 1996); University of Paris I - Sorbonne (D.E.S.S., 1997); Duke University School of Law (J.D., 2000). ***LANGUAGES:*** French. ***PRACTICE AREAS:*** International Business Transactions; Corporate Law; Securities. ***Email:*** wpkahn@hhlaw.com

JONATHAN S. KALLMER, born Seattle, Washington, June 20, 1972; admitted to bar, 1999, California; 2000, District of Columbia. *Education:* Stanford University (A.B., Public Policy and History, with honors, 1994); Georgetown University (J.D., cum laude, 1999). Legal Extern, Honorable Phyllis Hamilton, U.S. District Court, Northern District of California; Legal Extern, Central and Eastern European Law Initiative, American Bar Association. Editor, Law and Policy in International Business. ***LANGUAGES:*** German. ***Email:*** jskallmer@hhlaw.com

H. DEEN KAPLAN, admitted to bar, 1997, Virginia; 1998, District of Columbia. *Education:* Duke University (B.A., magna cum laude, 1982); Georgetown University Law Center (J.D., magna cum laude, 1997). Order of the Coif. Articles Editor, Georgetown Law Journal. *Member:* Virginia State Bar; The District of Columbia Bar; American Bar Association. ***PRACTICE AREAS:*** International Trade. ***Email:*** hdkaplan@hhlaw.com

DAVID P. KASSEBAUM, born January 22, 1972; admitted to bar, 2001, New York and District of Columbia. *Education:* University of California at Berkeley (B.A., with honors, 1994); Columbia University, School of Law (J.D., 2000). Stone Scholar, 1998-2000. Editor-in-Chief, Columbia Journal of International Law. Author, "A Question of Facts — The Legal Use of Private Security Firms in Bosnia," Columbia Journal of Transnational Law 38:3, pp. 581-602. *Member:* New York State and American Bar Associations. ***Email:*** dpkassebaum@hhlaw.com

ELIZABETH L. KATKIN, born Buffalo, New York, March 28, 1968; admitted to bar, 1995, California; 1996, District of Columbia. *Education:* Yale University (B.A., 1989); Columbia School of International and Public Affairs (M.I.A., 1992); Columbia University (J.D., 1995). Senior Editor and Treasurer, Columbia Law Review. *Member:* The District of Columbia Bar; The State Bar of California. ***PRACTICE AREAS:*** Corporate Law; Securities; International Transactions; Private Equity. ***Email:*** elkatkin@hhlaw.com

R. DANIEL KEATING, born Ann Arbor, Michigan, July 10, 1970; admitted to bar, 1998, New York; 1999, District of Columbia. *Education:* Michigan State University (B.S., 1992); Georgetown Law Center (J.D., 1996). ***Email:*** rdkeating@hhlaw.com

ELLEN SWENNES KENNEDY, born Winston-Salem, North Carolina, September 4, 1972; admitted to bar, 1997, Virginia; 1999, District of Columbia. *Education:* Duke University (B.A., 1994); University of Virginia (J.D., 1997). Phi Beta Kappa. Order of the Coif. Law Clerk, Honorable Stanley S. Harris, United State District Court for the District of Columbia, 1997-1998. *Member:* Virginia State Bar; The District of Columbia Bar. ***PRACTICE AREAS:*** Litigation. ***Email:*** eskennedy@hhlaw.com

BEHNAZ L. KIBRIA, born Dhaka, Bangladesh, February 18, 1975; admitted to bar, 1999, California; 2000, District of Columbia, U.S. Court of International Trade and U.S. Court of Appeals for the Federal Circuit. *Education:* Wesleyan University (B.A., with high honors, 1996); George Washington University (J.D., with high honors, 1999). Order of the Coif. Moot Court Board. Senior Notes Editor, The George Washington Law Review, 1998-1999. Law Clerk, Hogan & Hartson. Author: "Linking an Employer's Refusal to Bargain with the Subsequent Loss of Majority Support for a Union," 66 Geo. Wash. L. Rev. 1015 (1998). *Member:* California and American Bar Associations. ***Email:*** blkibria@hhlaw.com

CHRISTOPHER L. KILLION, born Wichita, Kansas, July 15, 1959; admitted to bar, 1984, Kansas; 1987, District of Columbia. *Education:* Emporia State University (B.A., 1981); University of Kansas (J.D., 1984). Staff Member, Kansas Law Review. *Member:* The District of Columbia Bar. ***PRACTICE AREAS:*** Litigation; Franchise and Distribution; Antitrust. ***Email:*** clkillion@hhlaw.com

ALETHIA N. KING, born Brooklyn, New York, September 12, 1968; admitted to bar, 1997, Wisconsin and Virginia; 1998, District of Columbia. *Education:* University of Maryland (B.A., 1990; M.Ed., 1992); University of Wisconsin-Madison (J.D., 1997). Member, University of Wisconsin Moot Court Team, 1996. Associate Editor, Wisconsin Law Review, 1996-1997. *Member:* State Bar of Wisconsin; Virginia State Bar; The District of Columbia Bar. ***PRACTICE AREAS:*** Corporate; Securities; Public Finance. ***Email:*** anking@hhlaw.com

(This Listing Continued)

JOSH KLATZKIN, born New Haven, November 30, 1974; admitted to bar, 1999, Connecticut; 2001, District of Columbia. *Education:* Franklin & Marshall College (B.A., cum laude, with Government Department honors, 1996); University of Virginia School of Law (J.D., 1999). *Member:* New Haven, Connecticut and American Bar Associations. ***Email:*** jnklatzkin@hhlaw.com

AUDREY E. KLEIN, born Philadelphia, Pennsylvania, January 31, 1959; admitted to bar, 1991, New York; 1996, California; 2001, District of Columbia; registered to practice before U.S. Patent and Trademark Office. *Education:* Temple University School of Pharmacy (B.S., Pharmacy, magna cum laude, 1984); Georgetown University Law Center (J.D., cum laude, 1990). Rho Chi. Licensed Pharmacist: Pennsylvania, 1984; California, 1993. ***PRACTICE AREAS:*** Intellectual Property. ***Email:*** aeklein@hhlaw.com

DOUGLAS A. KLEIN, born Albany, New York, May 10, 1970; admitted to bar, 1996, New York; 1998, District of Columbia. *Education:* State University of New York at Binghamton (B.A., 1992); George Washington University (J.D., with high honors, 1995). Member, Moot Court Board. Senior Managing Editor, The George Washington Law Review. *Member:* The District of Columbia Bar; New York State, American and Federal Communications Bar Associations. ***PRACTICE AREAS:*** Telecommunications Regulation; International Telecommunications Law. ***Email:*** daklein@hhlaw.com

MAYA RENATA KOBERSY, born 1975; admitted to bar, 1999, Michigan; 2000, District of Columbia. *Education:* University of Michigan (B.A., French and Honors History, magna cum laude, 1996); Harvard Law School (J.D., 1999). Finalist and Oralist, Ames Moot Court Competition, 1999. Executive Editor, Harvard Law Review, 1997-1999. Author: Note, "Maintaining Confidence in Confidentiality: The Applicability of the Attorney-Client Privilege to Government Counsel," 112 Harv. L. Rev. 1995 (1999). *Member:* The District of Columbia Bar; State Bar of Michigan. ***Email:*** mrkobersy@hhlaw.com

AJAY KUNTAMUKKALA, born India, March 3, 1973; admitted to bar, 2000, Maryland; 2001, District of Columbia. *Education:* Boston College (B.A., summa cum laude, 1995); John F. Kennedy School of Government, Harvard University (M.P.P., 1998); Georgetown University Law Center (J.D., 2000). *Member:* American Bar Association (Member, International Section). ***Email:*** akuntamukkala@hhlaw.com

ANNA J. KURIAN, born Kerala, India, July 18, 1974; admitted to bar, 1999, District of Columbia. *Education:* Duke University (B.A., 1996); Georgetown University Law Center (J.D., 1999). Member, Georgetown Immigration Law Journal. *Member:* District of Columbia Bar (Member, Intellectual Property Law Section). ***Email:*** ajkurian@hhlaw.com

KEITH D. LARSON, born Summit, New Jersey, July 13, 1971; admitted to bar, 1996, New Jersey; 1998, New York; 2001, District of Columbia. *Education:* Lafayette College (A.B., 1993); Syracuse University (M.A., International Relations, 1996); Syracuse University College of Law (J.D., cum laude, 1996). Executive Editor, Syracuse Law Review. *Member:* American Bar Association (Member, International Law and Practice Section). ***PRACTICE AREAS:*** Project Finance; Eurobonds. ***Email:*** kdlarson@hhlaw.com

MARK D. LEARN, born Seattle, Washington, December 17, 1960; admitted to bar, 1998, Maryland; 1999, District of Columbia. *Education:* University of Maryland (B.S., 1983); Temple University (J.D., magna cum laude, 1998). Member and Note/Comment Editor, Temple Law Review, 1995-1997. Author: "Same Product, New Uses: FDA Encourages Manufacturers to Increase Indications in Product Labeling," Managed Healthcare News, 16 (Sep. 1997); "Applying Medicare and Medicaid Anti-Kickback Laws to Disease Management Programs: Ramifications for the Pharmaceutical Industry and a Regulatory Proposal," 69 Temple Law Review 245 (1996). *Member:* The District of Columbia Bar. ***Email:*** mdlearn@hhlaw.com

F. WILLIAM LEBEAU, born Silver Spring, Maryland, May 7, 1970; admitted to bar, 1995, Virginia; 1997, District of Columbia. *Education:* University of Virginia (B.S., summa cum laude, 1992); Harvard Law School (J.D., cum laude, 1995). Tau Beta Pi; Sigma Gamma Tau; Omicron Delta Kappa. Rodman Scholar. Member, Harvard Law Review. Author: "Custodial Engineering: Cleaning Up The Scope of *Miranda* Custody During Coercive *Terry* Stops," 108 Harv. L. Rev. 665 (1995). Law Clerk, Judge Sentelle, U.S. Court of Appeals, D.C. Circuit, 1995-1996. *Member:* Virginia State Bar; The District of Columbia Bar. ***PRACTICE AREAS:*** FCC Licensing; FCC Regulation; Mass Media Law; Broadcast Applications; Broadcast Licensing; Broadcast Radio; Broadcast Regulation; Broadcast Station Transfers; Broadcast Television; Broadcasting Law. ***Email:*** fwlebeau@hhlaw.com

KATHERINE R. LEIBOWITZ, born Boston, Massachusetts, April 27, 1967; admitted to bar, 1994, Virginia; 1995, District of Columbia (Inactive); 2000, Pennsylvania. *Education:* Princeton University (A.B., cum laude, 1989); University of Pennsylvania (J.D., 1994). Author: "Tied Aid Credits and The New OECD Agreement," University of Pennsylvania Journal of International Business Law, Vol. 114 No. 3 Fall 1993. *Member:* Virginia State Bar; The District of Columbia Bar. (Also at Philadelphia, Pennsylvania, Office). ***LANGUAGES:*** French, Italian, Spanish. ***PRACTICE AREAS:*** Intellectual Property Licensing; Internet Law; Computer and Software Law; Privacy Law; Technology Law; Computer Law; E-Commerce Transactions. ***Email:*** krleibowitz@hhlaw.com

(This Listing Continued)

HOGAN & HARTSON L.L.P., Washington—Continued

ADAM K. LEVIN, born Manhasset, New York, August 3, 1972; admitted to bar, 1997, Florida; 1998, District of Columbia. *Education:* University of Pennsylvania (B.A., summa cum laude, 1994); New York University School of Law (J.D., magna cum laude, 1997). Phi Beta Kappa. Order of the Coif. Order of the Barristers. Law Clerk to The Honorable Marjorie O. Rendell, U.S. Court of Appeals for the Third Circuit, 1997-1998. *Member:* The Florida Bar; The District of Columbia Bar (Member, Section on Litigation; District of Columbia Affairs); American Bar Association (Member, Litigation Section). ***PRACTICE AREAS:*** Civil Litigation; Complex Litigation; Federal Litigation; Trial Practice; Federal Civil Litigation. ***Email:*** aklevin@hhlaw.com

MELISSA B. LEVINE, born Silver Spring, Maryland, September 4, 1973; admitted to bar, 1998, Maryland; 1999, District of Columbia. *Education:* American University (B.A., magna cum laude, 1995); Georgetown University (J.D., cum laude, 1998). Phi Beta Kappa; Psi Chi. Author: "Section 7430 Awards in Pro Bono Cases," 50 Tax Lawyer 671, Spring 1997. *Member:* District of Columbia Bar (Member, Health Law Section); American Health Lawyers Association. ***PRACTICE AREAS:*** Health Law; Health Care Fraud; Medicare Fraud and Abuse; Health Care Regulation; Privacy Law. ***Email:*** mblevine@hhlaw.com

ERIK J. LICHTER, born Brooklyn, New York, April 27, 1972; admitted to bar, 1997, Maryland; 2000, District of Columbia. *Education:* Emory University (B.A., 1994); University of Maryland (J.D., 1997). Order of the Coif; Notes and Comments Editor, Maryland Journal of Contemporary Legal Issues, 1996-1997. *Member:* Maryland State Bar Association, Inc.; American Bar Association (Member, Section on: Business Law). ***PRACTICE AREAS:*** Securities Law; Corporate Law. ***Email:*** ejlichter@hhlaw.com

RONALD G. LONDON, born Flushing, New York, October 5, 1968; admitted to bar, 1995, Maryland; 1996, District of Columbia. *Education:* University of Florida (B.S., summa cum laude, 1990); Georgetown University Law Center (J.D., cum laude, 1995). Kappa Tau Alpha. Recipient, Respess Award for Outstanding Advertising Scholar. Administrative Editor, Georgetown Journal on Law & Policy in International Business. *Member:* Maryland State and American Bar Associations; The District of Columbia Bar. ***PRACTICE AREAS:*** Communications; Telecommunications; Internet; Trademark. ***Email:*** rglondon@hhlaw.com

HARRIETTE H. LOPP, born Durham, North Carolina, April 5, 1971; admitted to bar, 1996, Texas; 2000, District of Columbia. *Education:* Davidson College (B.A., with honors, 1993); Duke University School of Law (J.D., 1996; LL.M., 1996). *Member:* State Bar of Texas; American Bar Association; The District of Columbia Bar. ***PRACTICE AREAS:*** Corporate Law; Securities. ***Email:*** hhlopp@hhlaw.com

ROBERT MAHINI, born New York, N.Y., December 26, 1975; admitted to bar, 2001, Virginia and District of Columbia. *Education:* University of Virginia (B.A., 1997); Vanderbilt Law School (J.D., 2001). Order of the Coif; Phi Delta Phi. Author, "There's No Place Like Home: The Availability of Judicial Review Over Certification Decisions Invoking Federal Jurisdiction under the Juvenile Justice and Delinquency Prevention Act," 53 Vanderbilt Law Review 1311. ***Email:*** rbmahini@hhlaw.com

ROBERT G. MALKIN, born Plattsburgh, New York, July 6, 1970; admitted to bar, 1997, Missouri; 2001, District of Columbia. *Education:* Princeton University (B.A., 1992); Washington University (M.H.A., 1997; J.D., 1997). *Member:* American Bar Association (Member, Health Law Section); American Health Lawyers Association. ***PRACTICE AREAS:*** Health Law; Health Care Fraud; Health Care Compliance; Health Care Reimbursement. ***Email:*** rgmalkin@hhlaw.com

TIMOTHY C. MAPLES, born Colorado Springs, Colorado, May 26, 1969; admitted to bar, 1996, Ohio; 2000, District of Columbia. *Education:* Northwestern University (B.A., 1991); Northwestern University School of Law (J.D., 1996). *Member:* American Bar Association. ***PRACTICE AREAS:*** Corporate Law; Mergers and Acquisitions; Securities. ***Email:*** tcmaples@hhlaw.com

LYNDA K. MARSHALL, born Wilmington, Delaware, June 10, 1968; admitted to bar, 1995, Virginia and U.S. District Court, Eastern District of Virginia; 1996, District of Columbia; 1997, U.S. Court of Appeals for the District of Columbia Circuit; 1998, U.S. District Court, District of Columbia. *Education:* University of Notre Dame (B.A., 1990); University of Virginia (J.D., 1995). *Member:* Virginia State Bar; The District of Columbia Bar; American Bar Association (Member, Antitrust Law Section). ***LANGUAGES:*** French. ***PRACTICE AREAS:*** Antitrust. ***Email:*** lkmarshall@hhlaw.com

DAVID L. MARTIN, born Shreveport, Louisiana, April 5, 1966; admitted to bar, 1998, Virginia; 1999, District of Columbia. *Education:* Texas Christian University (B.A., magna cum laude, 1988); University of Virginia (J.D., 1998). Executive Editor, *Virginia Journal of International Law.* ***LANGUAGES:*** French. ***Email:*** dmartin@hhlaw.com

MICHAEL F. MASON, born Bellmawr, New Jersey, June 3, 1968; admitted to bar, 1996, Maryland; 1998, District of Columbia. *Education:* Ursinus College (B.A., 1991); George Washington University (J.D., with honors, 1996). Phi Delta Phi; Omicron Delta Epsilon. Recipient, Juris Corpus Secundum Award for Contracts. W.W. Smith Scholar. Moot Court Board. Senior Notes Editor, Public Contract Law Journal, 1995-1996. Co-Author: "Section 508 of the Rehabilitation Act: An Overview and Analysis of the Government's Duty to Purchase Accessible Electronics and Information Technology Goods and Services," Federal Contracts Report (Bureau of National Affairs, Inc., 2000); "Year 2000 Federal Procurement Disputes: An Examination of Selected Issues," The Government Contractor, Vol. 41, No. 48 (Federal Publications 1999); "Federal Government Outsourcing Under OMB Circular A-76—One Year After the FAIR Act," The Government Contractor, Vol. 41, No. 38, (Federal Publications 1999); "The 'Year 2000' Problem in Federal Procurement," Briefing Papers, No. 98-3 (Federal Publications 1998); Author: "Bid Protests and the U.S. District Courts: Why Congress Should Not Allow the Sun to Set on This Effective Relationship," 26 Public Contract Law Journal 567 (1997). Member, Editorial Board, Public Contract Law Journal, 1998—. *Member:* The District of Columbia Bar; Maryland State and American (Member, Public Contract Law Section; Vice Chair, Section of Public Contract Law Committee on Outsourcing and Privatization) Bar Associations; National Contract Management Association. ***Email:*** mfmason@hhlaw.com

BRIAN E. MAZUREK, born Muskegon, Michigan, March 4, 1966; admitted to bar, 1991, Ohio; 1993, U.S. District Court, Southern District of Ohio; 1994, Maryland; 1995, District of Columbia and U.S. District Court, District of Maryland. *Education:* Albion College (A.B., summa cum laude, 1987); University of Michigan (J.D., cum Laude, 1990). Phi Beta Kappa. Mortar Board. Associate and Contributing Editor, Michigan Law Review, 1989-1990. Law Clerk to Judge Joseph P. Kinneary, U.S. District Court, Southern District of Ohio, 1991-1993. Adjunct, Research and Writing Program, Ohio State University College of Law, 1991-1993. *Member:* Maryland State and American Bar Associations; The District of Columbia Bar. ***PRACTICE AREAS:*** Litigation; Labor and Employment. ***Email:*** bemazurek@hhlaw.com

SUSAN ROTATORI McAULIFFE, born Hartford, Connecticut, November 7, 1960; admitted to bar, 1988, Connecticut; 1989, District of Columbia. *Education:* Connecticut College (B.A., magna cum laude, 1982); Columbia University (J.D., 1988). Phi Beta Kappa. *Member:* Connecticut and American Bar Associations; District of Columbia Bar. ***PRACTICE AREAS:*** Clean Water Act; Environmental Compliance; Environmental Health and Safety; Environmental Regulation; Resource Conservation and Recovery Act (RCRA); Superfund. ***Email:*** srmcauliffe@hhlaw.com

JOHN E. McCARRICK, admitted to bar, 1994, Maryland; 1997, District of Columbia; 1999, New York. *Education:* Georgetown University (B.S., 1990); Georgetown University Law Center (J.D., 1994). *Member:* The District of Columbia Bar. ***PRACTICE AREAS:*** Corporate; Private Equity. ***Email:*** jemccarrick@hhlaw.com

S. TOVAN McDANIEL, born St. Louis, Missouri, July 9, 1972; admitted to bar, 1997, North Carolina; 1998, District of Columbia. *Education:* Washington University (B.A., summa cum laude, 1994); Duke University (J.D., 1997; LL.M., 1997). Phi Beta Kappa. National Security Education Program (NSEP) Fellowship. *Member:* The District of Columbia Bar; American Bar Association. ***LANGUAGES:*** Spanish and Portuguese. ***PRACTICE AREAS:*** Corporate Law; Commercial Law; Project Finance; Mergers, Acquisitions and Divestitures; Aircraft Finance and Leasing; International Project Finance. ***Email:*** stmcdaniel@hhlaw.com

JOHN J. McDONALD, born Bayshore, New York, November 30, 1971; admitted to bar, 1999, New York; 2000, District of Columbia. *Education:* State University of New York at Stony Brook (B.S., magna cum laude, 1994); Georgetown University Law Center (J.D., cum laude, 1998). Phi Beta Kappa. Lead Articles Editor, The Tax Lawyer, 1997-1998. Author: "All Events Test is Satisfied by Execution Rather Than Settlement of Securities Trades: Charles Schwab Corp. v. Commissioner," 51 Tax Law. 177, 1997. *Member:* The District of Columbia Bar; New York State Bar Association. ***PRACTICE AREAS:*** Corporate Law; Private Equity; Mergers and Acquisitions. ***Email:*** jjmcdonald@hhlaw.com

SHELLY LYNN McGEE, admitted to bar, 1996, Ohio; 1997, U.S. District Court, Southern District of Ohio; 1999, North Carolina; 2000, District of Columbia. *Education:* University of Kentucky (B.A., 1992); University of Cincinnati (J.D., 1996). ***PRACTICE AREAS:*** Trademark; Copyright; Unfair Competition. ***Email:*** slmcgee@hhlaw.com

SCOTT A. McINTOSH, born Temple City, California, October 6, 1971; admitted to bar, 1998, Virginia; 1999, District of Columbia. *Education:* University of California at Los Angeles (B.A., magna cum laude, 1993);Georgetown University (M.S.F.S., 1998); Georgetown University Law Center (J.D., cum laude, 1998). Phi Beta Kappa; Regents Scholar; Alumni Scholar; Presidential Scholar. Articles Editor, Georgetown International Environmental Law Review, 1996-1997. Author: "Fair Criticism, Cyberlibel, and Unlawful coordinated Action over the Internet," Fran.L.J.181, Spring, 2001. *Member:* Virginia Bar Association; The District of Columbia Bar; American Bar Association (Member, Forum on Franchising). ***LANGUAGES:*** Spanish. ***PRACTICE***

(This Listing Continued)

(This Listing Continued)

AREAS: Franchise Arbitration; Franchise Law; Franchise Licensing; Franchise Litigation; Franchise Termination; Civil Litigation. ***Email:*** samcintosh@hhlaw.com

CYNTHIA M. McKNIGHT, born Toledo, Ohio, January 14, 1967; admitted to bar, 1997, District of Columbia. *Education:* Miami University (B.S., magna cum laude, 1989); Georgetown University Law Center (J.D., magna cum laude, 1995). Order of the Coif. Staff Member, Georgetown University Law Journal. Law Clerk, The Honorable David B. Sentelle, U.S. Court of Appeals for the District of Columbia Circuit, 1995-1996. *Member:* The District of Columbia Bar. ***PRACTICE AREAS:*** Corporate Law. ***Email:*** cmmcknight@hhlaw.com

MARGARET E.K. MIDDLETON, born Boston, Massachusetts, July 31, 1967; admitted to bar, 1993, Massachusetts; 1995, District of Columbia. *Education:* Boston College (B.A., 1989; J.D., 1993). *Member:* American Bar Association. ***PRACTICE AREAS:*** Civil Litigation; Franchises and Franchising. ***Email:*** mekmiddleton@hhlaw.com

KATHY MARLO MILJANIC, born Brooklyn, New York, June 16, 1962; admitted to bar, 1992, Virginia; 1993, District of Columbia. *Education:* State University of New York at Binghamton (B.A., with honors, 1983); University of Virginia (M.A., 1986); University of Pennsylvania (J.D., 1992). Editor, University of Pennsylvania Law Review, 1991-1992. *Member:* Virginia State Bar; The District of Columbia Bar; Federal and American Bar Associations; District of Columbia Bar; Aero Club of Washington; Women's Bar Association of the District of Columbia. ***PRACTICE AREAS:*** Aviation and Aerospace; Aviation Regulation; Airport Regulation; Aeronautical Regulation; Airport Law; Aviation Accidents; Federal Aviation Licenses; International Aviation Law; Air Cargo; Airline Regulation; Aviation Law. ***Email:*** kmmiljanic@hhlaw.com

EMILY A. MILLER, born New York, N.Y., October 4, 1971; admitted to bar, 1997, New York; 1999, District of Columbia. *Education:* University of Michigan (B.A., 1993); George Washington University (J.D., with honors, 1996). Articles Editor, The George Washington Journal of International Law and Economics. Law Clerk to the Hon. S. Martin Teel, Jr., U.S. Bankruptcy Judge. *Member:* American Bar Association; Walter Chandler Inn of Court; Women in Housing and Finance. ***LANGUAGES:*** French. ***PRACTICE AREAS:*** Financial Institutions Law. ***Email:*** eamiller@hhlaw.com

ERICA S. MINTZER, born Philadelphia, Pennsylvania, August 8, 1968; admitted to bar, 1993, Pennsylvania (inactive); 1994, New York (inactive); 1996, District of Columbia. *Education:* Tufts University (B.A., magna cum laude, 1990); University of Pennsylvania (J.D., 1993); California Institute of Technology (M.S., Economics and Political Theory, 1996). Phi Beta Kappa. *Member:* The District of Columbia Bar; American Bar Association. ***PRACTICE AREAS:*** Antitrust. ***Email:*** esmintzer@hhlaw.com

ANTHONY L. MIRANDA, born Coral Gables, Florida, January 7, 1974; admitted to bar, 2000, Maryland; 2001, District of Columbia and U.S. Court of Federal Claims. *Education:* University of Washington (B.A., English, 1997); Boston University School of Law (J.D., cum laude, 2000). *Member:* Hispanic Bar Association of D.C. ***Email:*** almiranda@hhlaw.com

ARTHUR C. MOK, born Tokyo, Japan, December 30, 1971; admitted to bar, 1997, California and U.S. District Court, Northern District of California; 1998, District of Columbia. *Education:* Columbia University (A.B., 1994); George Washington University (J.D., 1997). *Member:* American Bar Association; National Asian Pacific American Bar Association. ***LANGUAGES:*** Mandarin Chinese. ***PRACTICE AREAS:*** Corporate; Securities; Private Equity; Emerging Company Transactions. ***Email:*** acmok@hhlaw.com

R. LATANE MONTAGUE, IV, born Alexandria, Virginia, March 15, 1970; admitted to bar, 1998, Virginia; 1999, District of Columbia. *Education:* University of Virginia (B.A., 1992; J.D., 1997). Editorial Board, Virginia Law Review. Order of the Coif. Law Clerk, The Honorable Sam C. Pointer, Chief U.S. District Court Judge, Northern District of Alabama. *Member:* Virginia State Bar; The District of Columbia Bar. ***PRACTICE AREAS:*** Environmental; Transportation. ***Email:*** rlmontague@hhlaw.com

JEREMY TODD MONTHY, admitted to bar, 2000, New York and District of Columbia. *Education:* Yale University (B.A., Ethics, Politics and Economics, 1995); University of Texas (J.D., 1999); Lyndon B. Johnson School of Public Affairs (M.P.Aff, 1999). Executive Editor, Texas International Law Journal. Intern, United States Department of State, Embassy of the United States, Beijing, PRC, 1997; Clerk, Texas Defender Service, Houston, Texas, 1996. Author: "The Foreign Sovereign Immunities Act and Chinese Enterprise Reform; Defining 'Agencies and Instrumentalities ' in an Era of Zhengqi Fenkai," Edie and Lew Wasserman Public Affairs Library, 1999; "Internal Perspectives on Chinese Human Rights Reform: The Death Penalty in the PRC," 33 Tex. Int'l L.J. 189 (1998). ***PRACTICE AREAS:*** Litigation. ***Email:*** jtmonthy@hhlaw.com

AUDREY ELAINE MOOG, born Washington, D.C., December 21, 1966; admitted to bar, 2000, New York and District of Columbia. *Education:* New York University (B.A., 1990); Columbus School of Law of The Catholic University of America (J.D., 1999). Author: "California Penal Code Section 645:

(This Listing Continued)

Legislators Practice Medicine on Child Molesters," 15 Journal of Contemporary Health Law and Policy 711 (1999). *Member:* New York State and American Bar Associations. ***Email:*** amoog@hhlaw.com

THOMAS C. MOREY, born Chevy Chase, Maryland, May 22, 1971; admitted to bar, 1997, Texas; 1998, District of Columbia. *Education:* Princeton University (A.B., 1993); Duke University School of Law (J.D., 1996). Member, Duke Law Journal, 1994-1996. President, Duke Bar Association, 1993-1995. *Member:* State Bar of Texas; The District of Columbia Bar. ***Email:*** tcmorey@hhlaw.com

NATASHA T. MUHAMMAD, born Brockton, Massachusetts, August 10, 1974; admitted to bar, 1999, Massachusetts; 2000, District of Columbia. *Education:* Howard University (B.A., 1996); Harvard University (J.D., 1999). ***PRACTICE AREAS:*** Health Law. ***Email:*** ntmuhammad@hhlaw.com

THERESA K. NABORS, admitted to bar, 1996, Maryland; 1999, District of Columbia. *Education:* University of Notre Dame (B.A., 1993); University of North Carolina at Chapel Hill (J.D., 1996). Order of the Coif. Member, North Carolina Law Review, 1994-1996. ***PRACTICE AREAS:*** Tax Controversies; Litigation. ***Email:*** tknabors@hhlaw.com

JAMES NAMIKI, born Oklahoma City, Oklahoma, May 26, 1958; admitted to bar, 2000, Virginia; 2001, District of Columbia. *Education:* University of Washington (B.S., Chemical Engineering, 1980); University of Hawaii (M.B.A., Business, 1993); Syracuse University (M.S., Electrical Engineering, 2000; J.D., cum laude, 2000). *Member:* American Intellectual Property Law Association; Institute of Electrical and Electronics Engineers. ***LANGUAGES:*** Japanese. ***PRACTICE AREAS:*** Patent Prosecution; Patent Litigation; Trademarks. ***Email:*** jjnamiki@hhlaw.com

DAVID D. NELSON, born Saigon, Vietnam, October 8, 1971; admitted to bar, 1997, New York; 2001, California; registered to practice before U.S. Patent and Trademark Office (Not admitted in District of Columbia). *Education:* University of Virginia (B.A., 1993); Cornell University (J.D., 1996); George Mason University (M.S., Electrical Engineering, 1998). *Member:* State Bar of California. ***LANGUAGES:*** Vietnamese. ***PRACTICE AREAS:*** Patents. ***Email:*** ddnelson@hhlaw.com

JEFFREY C. NELSON, born St. Joseph, Michigan, September 21, 1972; admitted to bar, 1997, Maryland; 1999, District of Columbia; U.S. Court of Appeals for the District of Columbia Circuit. *Education:* University of Michigan (B.S., 1994; J.D., 1997); Georgetown University (LL.M., 1999). ***PRACTICE AREAS:*** Environmental Law. ***Email:*** jcnelson@hhlaw.com

WILLIAM F. NIXON, born 1966; admitted to bar, 1998, District of Columbia; 1999, Court of Appeals for the Federal Circuit; registered to practice before U.S. Patent and Trademark Office. *Education:* Virginia Military Institute (B.S., with distinction, 1988); University of Dayton School of Engineering (M.S., 1993); University of Dayton School of Law (J.D., cum laude, 1997). Phi Theta Phi, Eta Kappa Nu, Tau Beta Pi. Articles Editor, University of Dayton Law Review. *Member:* American Bar Association, AIPLA. [Caption, U.S. Air Force, 1988-1994]. ***PRACTICE AREAS:*** Intellectual Property. ***Email:*** wfnixon@hhlaw.com

JEFFREY S. O'DWYER, born Rochester, New York; admitted to bar, 1993, Illinois; 1994, New York; 2001, District of Columbia. *Education:* Princeton University (A.B., English Literature, 1989); Oxford University (Special Diploma in Social Studies, 1990); Cornell Law School (J.D., 1993). *Member:* American Health Lawyer's Association.

BENJAMIN K. OLSON, born Bethesda, Maryland, April 12, 1974; admitted to bar, 2001, Virginia (Not admitted in District of Columbia). *Education:* Tulane University (B.A., cum laude, 1993); Georgetown University (J.D., magna cum laude, 2001). Order of the Coif. Author, "The Transportation Act for the Twenty-First Century: The Failure of Metropolitan Planning Organizations to Reform Federal Transportation Policy in Metropolitan Areas," 28 Transportation Law Journal 147 (2000). ***Email:*** bkolson@hhlaw.com

GREGORY F. PARISI, admitted to bar, 2000, District of Columbia. *Education:* University of Richmond (B.A., Leadership Studies, 1995); Georgetown University (J.D., cum laude, 1999). Executive Editor, The Georgetown Law Journal. ***Email:*** gfparisi@hhlaw.com

ALEXANDER J. PARK, born Seoul, South Korea, October 17, 1971; admitted to bar, 1996, Maryland; 1998, District of Columbia. *Education:* George Washington University (B.A.A., magna cum laude, 1993); George Washington Law School (J.D., 1996). Beta Gamma Sigma; Beta Alpha Psi; National Golden Key. Recipient, FEI Award. Member, Board of Directors, AEF, 1997-1998. *Member:* Maryland State Bar Association; The District of Columbia Bar. ***LANGUAGES:*** Korean. ***PRACTICE AREAS:*** Capital Markets; Private Equity; Mergers and Acquisitions; General Corporate Law; Securities. ***Email:*** ajpark@hhlaw.com

EDWARD B. PARKS, II, admitted to bar, 1995, Virginia; 1997, District of Columbia. *Education:* Marymount University (B.A., summa cum laude, 1991); University of Virginia School of Law (J.D., 1995). Order of the Coif. Member,

(This Listing Continued)

HOGAN & HARTSON L.L.P., Washington—Continued

Virginia Law Review. Assistant U.S. Attorney, District of Columbia, 1998-2001. ***PRACTICE AREAS:*** Insurance Coverage Litigation; Bankruptcy Litigation. ***Email:*** ebparks@hhlaw.com

AARTI J. PATEL, born Bradford, England, August 11, 1974; admitted to bar, 1998, Pennsylvania; 2001, District of Columbia. *Education:* Stetson University (B.B.A., summa cum laude, 1995); Emory University (J.D., 1998). Managing Editor, Emory Law Journal. *Member:* District of Columbia Bar; Pennsylvania and American Bar Associations; American Institute of Certified Public Accountants. ***LANGUAGES:*** Gujarati. ***PRACTICE AREAS:*** Securities; Mergers, Acquisitions and Divestitures; Corporate Law. ***Email:*** ajpatel@hhlaw.com

MARK PAULDING, born Washington, D.C., November 30, 1972; admitted to bar, 1998, Maryland; 1999, District of Columbia. *Education:* Princeton University (A.B., 1994); Harvard Law School (J.D., 1998). *Member:* Maryland State Bar Association; The District of Columbia Bar. ***PRACTICE AREAS:*** Antitrust; Litigation. ***Email:*** mdpaulding@hhlaw.com

SCOTT D. PETERMAN, born Williamsport, Pennsylvania, October 13, 1951; admitted to bar, 1997, New York; 1998, District of Columbia. *Education:* Bloomsburg University (B.A., cum laude, 1973); The Ohio State University (M.A., 1974); Vanderbilt University (M.A., 1975); Stanford University (Ph.D., 1986); Georgetown University Law Center (J.D., cum laude, 1996). Pi Kappa Delta. Listed in Who's Who Among American University and College Students, 1973. *Member:* The District of Columbia Bar. ***LANGUAGES:*** Mandarin Chinese and Japanese. ***PRACTICE AREAS:*** Private Equity; Telecoms and High-Tech Transactions; Securities. ***Email:*** sdpeterman@hhlaw.com

G. LAURENCE PLAISTED, born Iowa City, Iowa, June 18, 1971; admitted to bar, 1996, Kansas; 1998, District of Columbia. *Education:* University of Kansas (B.S., 1993); University of Kansas School of Law (J.D., 1996); Georgetown University Law Center (LL.M., 1997). Omicron Delta Kappa. Golden Key. Publications Editor, Kansas Journal of Law & Public Policy. *Member:* The District of Columbia Bar; American Bar Association. ***PRACTICE AREAS:*** Business Law; Corporate Law; Securities. ***Email:*** glplaisted@hhlaw.com

MARTIN A. PRICE, born Boston, Massachusetts, December 27, 1971; admitted to bar, 1998, Massachusetts; 2000, California; 2001, New York and District of Columbia. *Education:* George Washington University (B.A., 1994); Duke University (M.A., 1995); George Washington University Law School (J.D., 1998). Moot Court. Law Review. Law Clerk to Hon. W. Curtis Sewell, U.S. District Court, Eastern District of Virginia. ***PRACTICE AREAS:*** Commercial Litigation; White Collar Crime. ***Email:*** maprice@hhlaw.com

STEPHEN F. PROPST, born Atlanta, Georgia, May 11, 1970; admitted to bar, 1998, Maryland; 1999, District of Columbia. *Education:* Princeton University (B.A., 1992); University of Virginia (J.D., 1998). Raven Society. Member, Articles Review Board, Virginia Law Review, 1997-1998. Graduate Fellow, John M. Olin Program in Law and Economics, 1997-1998. *Member:* The District of Columbia Bar. ***Email:*** sfpropst@hhlaw.com

JENNIFER A. PURVIS, born Boulder, Colorado, May 29, 1968; admitted to bar, 1995, Maryland; 1997, District of Columbia and Colorado. *Education:* Tufts University (B.A., magna cum laude, 1990); Georgetown University Law Center (J.D., cum laude, 1995); Georgetown University School of Foreign Service (M.S.F.S., 1995). Phi Beta Kappa. Recipient, Award for Academic Excellence. Author: "The Long Arm of the Law? Extraterritorial Application of U.S. Environmental Legislation to Human Activity in Outer Space," 6 Geo. Int'l Envtl. L. Rev. 455 (1994). Articles Editor, Georgetown International Environmental Law Review, 1994-1995. *Member:* Maryland State, Colorado and American Bar Associations; District of Columbia Bar; Federal Communications Bar Association. ***LANGUAGES:*** Spanish. ***PRACTICE AREAS:*** Communications. ***Email:*** jpurvis@hhlaw.com

JOHN M. RAFFERTY, born Washington, D.C., September 8, 1972; admitted to bar, 1997, Virginia; 1998, District of Columbia. *Education:* Arizona State University (B.A., magna cum laude, 1994); New York University (J.D., 1997). Phi Beta Kappa. Moot Court Board, New York University, 1996-1997. *Member:* Virginia State Bar; The District of Columbia Bar. ***PRACTICE AREAS:*** Corporate Law; Securities. ***Email:*** jmrafferty@hhlaw.com

OMYRA M. RAMSINGH, born Bronx, New York, March 29, 1970; admitted to bar, 1996, Pennsylvania; 1998, District of Columbia; 1999, Florida. *Education:* University of Florida (B.S., cum laude, 1991; M.A., 1993); Catholic University (J.D., cum laude, 1996). Author: "Disciplining Children With Disabilities Under the Individuals with Disabilities Education Act," Journal of Contemporary Health Law & Policy, Volume 12, p. 155, 1995. *Member:* District of Columbia Bar; The Florida Bar. ***PRACTICE AREAS:*** Corporate; Securities; Private Equity. ***Email:*** omramsingh@hhlaw.com

SIOBHAN C. RAUSCH, born New Orleans, Louisiana, July 8, 1970; admitted to bar, 1997, Maryland; 1999, District of Columbia. *Education:* Catholic University of America (B.A., summa cum laude, 1992; J.D., magna cum laude, 1997). Phi Beta Kappa. Executive Editor, 1996-1997 and Staff Member, 1995-1996, Catholic University Law Review. Co-Author: "Tax Simplification Versus the Legislative Process," Trusts & Estates, March 1, 1994. *Member:* Maryland State and American Bar Associations. ***PRACTICE AREAS:*** Tax. ***Email:*** scrausch@hhlaw.com

MARCOS RIOS, born Santiago, Chile, October 14, 1967; admitted to bar, 1996, Chile (Not admitted in the United States). *Education:* Universidad de Chile School of Law (J.D. equivalent, 1994); Georgetown University Law Center (LL.M., with distinction, 2001). Lecturer, Washington College of Law and Instituto de Estudias Internacionales. Semi-Finalist, Phillip C. Jessup International Law Moot Court Competition. International Associate, Simpson Thacher & Bartlett, 1999-2000. Associate, Carey y Cia. Ltde., 1996-1999. ***LANGUAGES:*** Spanish and English. ***PRACTICE AREAS:*** Corporate; Securities; Private Equity; Project Finance. ***Email:*** mrios@hhlaw.com

MARGARET RHINELANDER RIZZI, born New York, N.Y., March 23, 1965; admitted to bar, 1994, Virginia and U.S. Court of Appeals, Fourth Circuit; 1996, District of Columbia. *Education:* Stanford University (A.B., with distinction, 1988; A.M., 1989); University of Virginia (J.D., 1993). Law Clerk, Hon. Albert V. Bryan, Jr., Senior U.S. District Judge, U.S. District Court for the Eastern District of Virginia, 1993-1994. *Member:* Virginia State Bar; The District of Columbia Bar; American Bar Association. ***Email:*** mrrizzi@hhlaw.com

MARK J. ROBERTSON, born Washington, D.C., August 15, 1971; admitted to bar, 1999, New York; 2001, District of Columbia. *Education:* Hampden-Sydney College (B.A., Political Science and German, 1993); University of Virginia School of Law (J.D., 1998). Omicron Delta Kappa. Virginia Tax Review. ***LANGUAGES:*** German. ***PRACTICE AREAS:*** Corporate Law; Securities. ***Email:*** mjrobertson@hhlaw.com

DEAN A. ROMHILT, admitted to bar, 1999, Virginia; 2000, District of Columbia. *Education:* Duke University (B.A., with distinction, magna cum laude, 1995); University of Virginia (J.D., 1999). ***Email:*** daromhilt@hhlaw.com

EVAN L. ROSENFELD, born New Haven, Connecticut, November 12, 1966; admitted to bar, 1991, Illinois; 1992, District of Columbia; registered to practice before U.S. Patent and Trademark Office. *Education:* Harvard College (A.B., 1988); University of Pennsylvania Law School (J.D., 1991); Medical College of Virginia/Virginia Commonwealth University (M.D., 2000). John Harvard Scholarship, 1987-1988. Chairman, Moot Court Board, 1990-1991. Co-Author, with K. A. Buck "Foreign Investment in the U.S.: Threat to National Security or Boost to Our Industrial Base?" *National Security Law Report* November 1991; 13(11): 3-6. Author, "The Strict Products Liability Crisis and Beyond: Is There Hope for an AIDS Vaccine?" *Jurimetrics Journal* 1991; 31(2): 1987-203. Numerous scientific articles, abstracts, and presentations. ***PRACTICE AREAS:*** Food and Drug Regulation; Drug and Medical Device Regulation. ***Email:*** elrosenfeld@hhlaw.com

COREY W. ROUSH, born Freeport, Illinois, May 2, 1972; admitted to bar, 1997, Ohio; 1999, U.S. Court of Appeals for the Federal Circuit; 2000, District of Columbia. *Education:* Vanderbilt University (B.A., magna cum laude, 1994); Georgetown University Law Center (J.D., cum laude, 1997). Senior Articles and Notes Editor, American Criminal Law Review, 1996-1997. Author: "Warrantless Public Housing Searches: Individual Violations or Community Solutions," 34 Am. Crim. L. Rev. 261 (1996). Co-Author: "What's the FTC up to?" National Law Journal, April 2000; "Electronic Media," National Law Journal, June 2000. *Member:* District of Columbia Bar; American Bar Association (Member, Antitrust Section). ***PRACTICE AREAS:*** Antitrust and Trade Regulation; Consumer Law; Privacy Law; Internet Law; Unfair Competition. ***Email:*** cwroush@hhlaw.com

ANDREW M. ROWELL, born Hattiesburg, Mississippi, August 23, 1973; admitted to bar, 1999, Georgia; 2000, U.S. Court of Federal Claims; 2001, District of Columbia. *Education:* Duke University (B.A., magna cum laude, 1995); University of Virginia (J.D., 1999). Articles Editor, University of Virginia Journal of Law and Social Policy, 1998-1999. Law Clerk, Hon. Francis M. Allegra, United States Court of Federal Claims, 1999-2000. ***PRACTICE AREAS:*** Estate Planning; Corporate Tax. ***Email:*** amrowell@hhlaw.com

MARTHA L. RUSSO, born Galesburg, Illinois, September 12, 1972; admitted to bar, 2000, Texas (Not admitted in District of Columbia). *Education:* Tulane University (B.A., 1992); University of Texas at Austin (J.D., 2000). Chancellor. Notes Editor, Texas Law Review. ***PRACTICE AREAS:*** Litigation. ***Email:*** mlrusso@hhlaw.com

AMIT SALUJA, admitted to bar, 1997, Maryland; 1998, District of Columbia. *Education:* George Washington University (B.S., magna cum laude, 1994; J.D., 1997). Administrative Editor, The Environmental Lawyer, 1996-1997. ***PRACTICE AREAS:*** Corporate Law; Securities; Mergers and Acquisitions; Finance. ***Email:*** asaluja@hhlaw.com

SHERRI A. BRADEN SAMPSON, born Cleveland, Ohio, January 20, 1969; admitted to bar, 1995, Washington; 1997, Maryland; 1998, District of Columbia. *Education:* Duke University (B.A., with distinction, 1991); University of Washington (J.D., 1995). *Member:* Washington State (Member, Young Lawyers Division), Maryland State, American and National Bar Associations; The District of Columbia Bar; Women's Bar Association of the District of

(This Listing Continued)

Columbia (Member, Greater Washington Chapter, Women Lawyers Division). ***LANGUAGES:*** Japanese, French. ***PRACTICE AREAS:*** Corporate; Securities.

DAVID R. SAN MARTIN, born Santiago, Chile; admitted to bar, 1997, Oklahoma; 1998, District of Columbia and Minnesota. *Education:* Oklahoma Baptist University (B.S., 1980); University of Oklahoma College of Law (J.D., 1997). President, Oklahoma International Law Society, 1996-1997. Supreme Justice, University of Oklahoma Student Association, 1995-1997. ***LANGUAGES:*** Spanish, Italian, Portuguese. ***PRACTICE AREAS:*** Intellectual Property; Bioscience Transactions; International High Technology; Entertainment. ***Email:*** drsanmartin@hhlaw.com

ATUL SARAN, born Dallas, Texas, July 5, 1973; admitted to bar, 1999, California; 2000, District of Columbia. *Education:* Stanford University (B.S., 1994); University of Illinois (J.D., summa cum laude, 1998). Order of the Coif. Articles Editor, University of Illinois Law Review, 1995-1998. ***LANGUAGES:*** Hindi and Spanish. ***PRACTICE AREAS:*** Business Law; Corporate Law; Computers and Software; Biotechnology; Investments. ***Email:*** asaran@hhlaw.com

NATHAN H. SAUNDERS, born Sanford, Maine, February 10, 1972; admitted to bar, 2000, Virginia; 2001, District of Columbia. *Education:* Dartmouth College (A.B., 1994); Duke University (J.D., 2000). Staff Editor, 1998-1999 and Articles Editor, 1999-2000, Duke Law Journal. ***Email:*** nhsaunders@hhlaw.com

CATHERINE SCHENKER, born New Haven, Connecticut, December 30, 1971; admitted to bar, 1999, New York; 2000, District of Columbia. *Education:* Yale University (B.A., 1994); New York University (J.D., 1998). ***LANGUAGES:*** Polish, French and Italian. ***Email:*** cischenker@hhlaw.com

CHRISTOPHER A. SCHINDLER, born Lexington, Kentucky, December 28, 1965; admitted to bar, 1994, Virginia; 1996, District of Columbia. *Education:* Vanderbilt University (B.A., cum laude, 1988); George Washington University (M.A., International Affairs, 1991; J.D., with honors, 1994). Member, George Washington Law Review, 1992-1994. Member, Moot Court Board, 1993-1994. *Member:* Virginia State Bar; The District of Columbia Bar; Federal Energy and American Bar Associations. ***Email:*** caschindler@hhlaw.com

JODI K. SCOTT, born Seoul, Korea, September 28, 1972; admitted to bar, 1998, Colorado; 1999, District of Columbia. *Education:* Drake University College of Pharmacy (B.S., 1995); Catholic University Columbus School of Law (J.D., cum laude, 1998). Registered Pharmacist, Virginia, 1995. Author: "Umbilical Cord Blood Stem Cells; My Body Makes Them, But Do I get to Keep Them? Analysis of the FDA Proposed Regulations and the Impact on Constitutional Property Rights," 14 J Contemp. H. Law. & Pol'y 477 (1998); "He's All Heart...And a Little Pig Too: A Look at the FDA Draft Xenotransplant Guideline," 52 Food & Drug Law J. 429 (1997). *Member:* Colorado Bar Association; The District of Columbia Bar; American Society for Pharmacy Law. ***PRACTICE AREAS:*** Federal Food and Drug Law. ***Email:*** jkfredrickson@hhlaw.com

KELLEEN McGINNIS SCOTT, born Washington, D.C., December 13, 1970; admitted to bar, 1998, Maryland; 1999, District of Columbia. *Education:* Georgetown University (B.A., cum laude, 1993); George Washington University Law School (J.D., with high honors, 1997). Order of the Coif. Author: "Federal Rule of Civil Procedure 68: Exploring the Possibility of Revoking Rule 68 Offer of Judgment," 64 Geo. Wash. L. Rev. 884 (1996). Judicial Clerk, The Honorable Henry Coke Morgan, Jr., U.S. District Court Judge for the Eastern District of Virginia. *Member:* The District of Columbia Bar; Maryland State Bar Association, Inc.; American Bar Association. ***PRACTICE AREAS:*** Federal Election Law; Securities Fraud; Securities Litigation; Corporate Litigation. ***Email:*** kmscott@hhlaw.com

SUMEET SEAM, born 1974; admitted to bar, 1999, Maryland; 2000, District of Columbia. *Education:* George Washington University (B.A., 1996); Columbia University (J.D., 1999). ***Email:*** sseam@hhlaw.com

LORI J. SEARCY, admitted to bar, 2000, Virginia and District of Columbia. *Education:* University of Maryland (B.S., 1991); Georgetown University (J.D., cum laude, 1999). Associate Editor, Georgetown Law Journal, 1996-1998. Department of Justice, 1994-1999. ***Email:*** ljsearcy@hhlaw.com

CATHERINE S. SEERY, born Cincinnati, Ohio, December 2, 1965; admitted to bar, 1996, Illinois; 1998, District of Columbia. *Education:* Georgetown University (B.A., magna cum laude, 1987); Washington College of Law, American University (J.D., summa cum laude, 1996). Phi Beta Kappa. *Member:* The District of Columbia Bar; American Bar Association (Member, Health Law Section); American Health Lawyers Association. ***PRACTICE AREAS:*** Health Care Corporate Law; Health Law. ***Email:*** csseery@hhlaw.com

SCOTT A. SHAIL, born Poughkeepsie, New York, December 28, 1971; admitted to bar, 1999, Maryland; 2000, District of Columbia, U.S. District Court, District of Maryland, U.S. District Court for the District of Columbia and U.S. Court of Appeals, 4th Circuit. *Education:* Appalachian State University (B.S., cum laude, 1993); University of Baltimore (J.D., magna cum laude, 1999). Staff Member, 1997-1998 and Comments Editor, 1998-1999, University of Baltimore Law Review. Judicial Clerk, The Honorable Paul Mannes, Chief Judge of the United States Bankruptcy Court for District of Maryland, 1999-2000. Author: Note, "Reno v. ACLU: The First Congressional Attempts to Regulate Pornography on the Internet Fails First Amendment Scrutiny," 28.1 U. Balt. L. Rev. 273 (Fall 1998). ***Email:*** sashail@hhlaw.com

TAMAR SHAPIRO, admitted to bar, 2000, Pennsylvania (Not admitted in District of Columbia). *Education:* Harvard College (A.B., 1993); Harvard Law School (J.D., 1999).

KEVIN G. SHAW, born Pequannock, New Jersey, January 17, 1974; admitted to bar, 1999, California; 2001, District of Columbia; registered to practice before the U.S. Patent and Trademark Office. *Education:* University of Pennsylvania (B.S.E., 1996); George Washington University (J.D., 1999). *Member:* American Bar Association; American Intellectual Property Lawyers Association; American Institute of Chemical Engineers. ***PRACTICE AREAS:*** Intellectual Property; Patents; Computer and Software Patents. ***Email:*** kgshaw@hhlaw.com

BRIAN L. SHIKER, born Lansing, Michigan, July 14, 1973; admitted to bar, 1998, Texas; 2001, District of Columbia. *Education:* University of Chicago (B.A., with honors, 1995); Vanderbilt University (J.D., 1998). Phi Alpha Delta. *Member:* State Bar of Texas; American Bar Association. ***PRACTICE AREAS:*** Employee Benefits; ERISA. ***Email:*** blshiker@hhlaw.com

CHARLES E. SIEVING, born Cincinnati, Ohio, July 20, 1972; admitted to bar, 1999, District of Columbia. *Education:* Denison University (B.A., 1994); University of Cincinnati (J.D., 1997). Publications Editor, University of Cincinnati Law Review. *Member:* District of Columbia; American Bar Association. ***Email:*** cesieving@hhlaw.com

KERRI R. SIKORSKI, born Washington, D.C., July 19, 1974; admitted to bar, 2000, New York and District of Columbia. *Education:* Villanova University (B.S., summa cum laude, 1996); Harvard Law School (J.D., 1999). *Member:* District of Columbia; American Bar Association; Womens Bar Association. ***Email:*** krsikorski@hhlaw.com

ELIZABETH J. SILVA, born Albany, New York, September 10, 1968; admitted to bar, 2000, New York and District of Columbia. *Education:* Trinity College (B.A., 1990); Georgetown University (J.D., magna cum laude, 1999). Member: Georgetown Law Journal. ***PRACTICE AREAS:*** Corporate Law. ***Email:*** ejsilva@hhlaw.com

MELANIE A. SIMMONS, born Enterprise, Alabama, February 11, 1967; admitted to bar, 1998, Virginia; 1999, District of Columbia. *Education:* Troy State University (B.S., summa cum laude, 1989); The George Washington University Law School (J.D., with honors, 1998). Member, Public Contract Law Journal. Certified Public Accountant, Commonwealth of Virginia, 1994. Federal Law Enforcement Training Center, Honor Graduate, September 1989. Cost Accountant, Atlanta, Georgia, 1989-1991, Assets Manager, Washington, D.C., 1991-1993 and Financial Program Specialist, 1993-1998, U.S. Department of Justice, Federal Prison Industries, Inc., UNICOR. ***PRACTICE AREAS:*** Corporate Law; Securities. ***Email:*** masimmons@hhlaw.com

PAULA PRIMOST SKALABAN, born Long Branch, New Jersey, September 4, 1972; admitted to bar, 1997, Maryland; 1998, District of Columbia. *Education:* University of Pennsylvania (B.A., magna cum laude, 1993); Harvard University (J.D., cum laude, 1997). ***PRACTICE AREAS:*** Insurance Coverage Litigation; Litigation.

JAMES O. SMITH, born Miami, Florida, October 26, 1969; admitted to bar, 1997, Florida; 1998, District of Columbia. *Education:* Duke University (A.B., 1991; J.D., 1997); University of Georgia (M.A., 1993). *Member:* American Bar Association. ***PRACTICE AREAS:*** Corporate. ***Email:*** josmith@hhlaw.com

MELINDA A. SOSSAMON, born Ponca City, Oklahoma, September 19, 1970; admitted to bar, 2000, District of Columbia. *Education:* University of Oklahoma (B.A., magna cum laude, 1992); Georgetown University (J.D., 1999). Competitor, National Moot Court Team; Jessup International Moot Court Team; U.S. National Champion. Member, Georgetown Immigration Law Journal. Law Clerk, Hogan & Hartson L.L.P., 1998-1999. Law Clerk, Miller, Cassidy, Larroca & Lewin, 1997-1998. Senior Legislative Aide, Arter and Hadden, 1995-1997. Legislative Assistant, U.S. Senator David L. Boren, 1992-1994. Student Body President, University of Oklahoma, 1991-1992. ***Email:*** masossamon@hhlaw.com

GINA M. SPADE, born Pratt, Kansas, February 25, 1969; admitted to bar, 1996, Massachusetts; 1998, District of Columbia. *Education:* Wichita State University (B.A., 1990); Georgetown University Law Center (J.D., 1996). *Member:* The District of Columbia Bar; Commonwealth of Massachusetts Bar; Federal Communications Bar Association. ***PRACTICE AREAS:*** Communications and Media; Telecommunications; Internet; Regulatory Law; Corporate Law. ***Email:*** gmspade@hhlaw.com

KIMBERLY J. STAHLMAN, born Atlanta, Georgia, August, 1968; admitted to bar, 1998, Georgia; 1999, District of Columbia. *Education:* American University (B.S.B.A., magna cum laude, 1990); Harvard University (J.D., cum

(This Listing Continued)

HOGAN & HARTSON L.L.P., Washington—Continued

laude, 1998). *Member:* State Bar of Georgia; The District of Columbia Bar (Member, Tax Section); American Bar Association. ***PRACTICE AREAS:*** Employee Benefits; Taxation. ***Email:*** kjstahlman@hhlaw.com

DEBORAH KIM STAUDINGER, born Philadelphia, Pennsylvania, November 7, 1955; admitted to bar, 1998, Connecticut and Maryland; 1999, District of Columbia. *Education:* Ursinus College (B.A., 1977); Georgia Institute of Technology (B.C.E., 1978); University of Tulsa (J.D., with honors, 1997). Phi Delta Phi. Editor-in-Chief, Energy Law Journal. *Member:* The District of Columbia Bar; American Bar Association. ***PRACTICE AREAS:*** Energy; Commercial. ***Email:*** dkstaudinger@hhlaw.com

GABRIEL STEPHEN STERLING, III, born Hollywood, Florida, November 2, 1972; admitted to bar, 1998, Texas; 1999, District of Columbia. *Education:* Harvard University (A.B., with general honors, 1995); Georgetown University (J.D., cum laude, 1998). Executive Editor, The Tax Lawyer, 1997-1998. ***PRACTICE AREAS:*** Energy. ***Email:*** gsterling@hhlaw.com

CATHERINE E. STETSON, born Albany, New York, August 6, 1969; admitted to bar, 1994, Virginia; 1996, District of Columbia. *Education:* Duke University (A.B., cum laude, 1991); University of Virginia School of Law (J.D., 1994). Order of the Coif. Law Clerk: The Honorable Stanley S. Harris, U.S. District Court for the District of Columbia, 1994-1996; The Honorable David S. Tatel, U.S. Court of Appeals for the District of Columbia Circuit, 1996-1997. *Member:* Virginia State Bar; The District of Columbia Bar; American Bar Association. ***PRACTICE AREAS:*** Litigation. ***Email:*** cestetson@hhlaw.com

JOY E. STURM, born Flushing, New York, December 1, 1967; admitted to bar, 1995, New York; 1996, District of Columbia. *Education:* University of Pennsylvania (B.A., cum laude, with distinction, 1989); George Washington University Law School (J.D., 1994). Member, Moot Court Board. *Member:* American Bar Association (Member, Public Contract Law Section); Federal Circuit Bar Association; U.S. Court of Federal Claims Bar Association; International Association of Jewish Lawyers & Jurists (President, D.C. Chapter). ***LANGUAGES:*** Hebrew. ***PRACTICE AREAS:*** Government Contracts; Health Care Contracting; International Contracts. ***Email:*** jesturm@hhlaw.com

MARTA I. TANENHAUS, born Binghamton, New York, April 11, 1956; admitted to bar, 1991, Maryland; 1992, U.S. District Court, District of Maryland; 1993, District of Columbia. *Education:* State University of New York at Albany (B.A., summa cum laude, 1977); Georgetown University (M.S., 1985); University of California, Boalt Hall School of Law at Berkeley (J.D., 1991). Phi Beta Kappa. Member, California Law Review. *Member:* Maryland State and American Bar Associations; The District of Columbia Bar. ***LANGUAGES:*** Spanish. ***PRACTICE AREAS:*** Civil Litigation; Transportation. ***Email:*** mitanenhaus@hhlaw.com

ADAM B. TANKEL, born Fairfax, Virginia, August 19, 1965; admitted to bar, 1997, New York; 1998, District of Columbia. *Education:* University of Pennsylvania (B.A., B.S., cum laude, 1987); University of Virginia (J.D., M.B.A., 1996). [Lieutenant, United States Navy, 1987-1991.]. ***PRACTICE AREAS:*** Corporate Law; Private Equity. ***Email:*** atankel@hhlaw.com

SHARON L. TASMAN, born Plainview, New York, December 12, 1965; admitted to bar, 1992, Maryland; 1993, U.S. District Court, District of Maryland; 1994, U.S. Court of Appeals for the District of Columbia, U.S. Court of Appeals, Fourth Circuit; 1995, District of Columbia; 1996, Virginia. *Education:* Rensselaer Polytechnic Institute; University of Maryland (B.S., summa cum laude, 1989; J.D., with honors, 1992); Tulane Institute of European Legal Studies, Paris, France (Certificate in European Legal Studies, 1990). Phi Kappa Phi. Member, 1990-1991 and Assistant Editor, 1991-1992, Maryland Law Review. Co-Author: "Government Regulation of Multimedia Telecommunication Regulation," Chapter 27 A.02, *Multimedia: Law & Practice*. *Member:* Maryland State, Virginia and American Bar Associations; The District of Columbia Bar. ***LANGUAGES:*** French. ***PRACTICE AREAS:*** Computer and Software Law; Internet Law; E-Commerce Law; Technology Licensing; Intellectual Property; Biotechnology Licensing. ***Email:*** sltasman@hhlaw.com

FARINAZ S. TEHRANI, born Tehran, Iran, May 11, 1966; admitted to bar, 1991, New York and District of Columbia. *Education:* Tufts University (B.A., cum laude, 1987); Georgetown University Law Center (J.D., 1990). Phi Beta Kappa. Associate Editor, The American Criminal Law Review, 1989-1990. *Member:* New York State and American Bar Associations; The District of Columbia Bar. ***LANGUAGES:*** Farsi, French, Spanish. ***PRACTICE AREAS:*** Corporate Law; Securities. ***Email:*** fstehrani@hhlaw.com

C. JEFFREY TIBBELS, born Abington, Pennsylvania, June 14, 1971; admitted to bar, 1999, Pennsylvania; 2001, District of Columbia. *Education:* Wesleyan University (B.A., Phi Beta Kappa, 1993); School of International Service at American University (M.A., 1999); Washington College of Law at American University (J.D., cum laude, 1999). First Place, Suffolk University Academic Convocation, 1999. Author: "Delineating the Foreign Affairs Function in the Age of Globalization," 23 Suffolk Transnat'l L. Rev. 389 (1999). Note and Comment Editor, American Bar Association's Administrative Law Review, 1998-1999. Awarded, Washington College of Law Service to Community Award, 1999. *Member:* Pennsylvania and American Bar Associations; The District of Columbia Bar; Federal Communications Bar Association. ***LANGUAGES:*** Czech, Russian. ***Email:*** cjtibbels@hhlaw.com

PATRICK D. TRAYLOR, born Hammond, Louisiana, December 21, 1969; admitted to bar, 1994, Texas; 1996, District of Columbia. *Education:* Texas A & M University (B.A., 1991); South Texas College of Law (J.D., 1994); George Washington University Law School (LL.M. in Environmental Law, 1998). Co-Author: with Robert Fuhrman, "Explaining the Controversy Surrounding United States v. Smithfield Foods, Inc.," 23 William & Mary Environmental Law & Policy Review 479 (1999). Author: "Presumptive MACT as a Regulatory Tool to Streamline the Development of National Emission Standards for Hazardous Air Pollutants," 4 Envir. Lawyer 393 (1998); "Liability of Past Owners: Does CERCLA Incorporate a Causation-Based Standard?" 35 So. Tex. L.R. 535 (1994). *Member:* State Bar of Texas (Member, Environmental Law Section); The District of Columbia Bar (Member, Environmental Law Section). ***PRACTICE AREAS:*** Environmental. ***Email:*** pdtraylor@hhlaw.com

ROBERT TYLER, admitted to bar, 1999, New York; 2000, District of Columbia. *Education:* University of California at Berkeley (B.A., 1994); New York University School of Law (J.D., 1997). Phi Beta Kappa. ***PRACTICE AREAS:*** Private Equity. ***Email:*** rtyler@hhlaw.com

NATALIE S. TYNAN, admitted to bar, 1999, Pennsylvania; 2000, District of Columbia. *Education:* Lafayette College (B.A., cum laude, 1995); The Catholic University of America, Columbus School of Law (J.D., magna cum laude, 1999). Note and Comment Editor, Catholic University Law Review, 1998-1999. Legal Intern, The National Women's Law Center. Law Clerk, The Law Offices of Joseph Bianculli. Author: "Genetic Information and Third Party Access to Information: New Jersey's Pioneering Legislation as a Model for Federal Privacy Protection of Genetic Information," 47 Cath. U. L. Rev. 1105 (1998). ***Email:*** ntynan@hhlaw.com

ANN M. UNGVARSKY, born Elgin, Illinois, April 15, 1974; admitted to bar, 2000, Maryland; 2001, District of Columbia. *Education:* University of Illinois (B.S. in Economics, 1996); University of Virginia (J.D., 2000). ***Email:*** amungvarsky@hhlaw.com

MICHAEL J. VERNICK, born Washington, D.C., August 28, 1969; admitted to bar, 1997, Maryland; 1998, District of Columbia. *Education:* Tufts University (B.A., cum laude, 1991); George Mason University School of Law (J.D., with high honors, 1997). Member, Board of Editors, George Mason Law Review. Law Clerk, Honorable Christine O.C. Miller, U.S. Court of Federal Claims, 1997-1998. ***Email:*** mjvernick@hhlaw.com

KATHARINE T. VESTAL, born Tampa, Florida, October 13, 1972; admitted to bar, 1997, Virginia; 1998, District of Columbia. *Education:* University of Mississippi (B.A., magna cum laude, 1994); American University, Washington College of Law (J.D., magna cum laude, 1997). Phi Alpha Delta. *Member:* Virginia State Bar; The District of Columbia Bar. ***Email:*** ktvestal@hhlaw.com

EMILY C. VITAN, born Martinsville, Virginia, April 2, 1975; admitted to bar, 2000, Virginia (Not admitted in District of Columbia). *Education:* University of Virginia (B.A., with distinction, 1997; J.D., 2000). ***Email:*** ecvitan@hhlaw.com

NAOMI ABE VOEGTLI, born Nishio-shi, Aichi-ken, Japan, January 16, 1964; admitted to bar, 1998, California; 1999, New York; 2000, District of Columbia; registered to practice before U.S. Patent and Trademark Office. *Education:* University of Texas at Austin (B.S., with highest honors, 1986); University of Illinois at Urbana-Champaign (M.S., 1987; M.S., 1991); Harvard Law School (J.D., magna cum laude, 1997). Law Clerk, Hon. John S. Martin, Jr., U.S. District Court, Southern District of New York, 1997-1998. Author: "Rethinking Derivative Rights," 63 Brook L. Rev. 1213 (1997); "Recent Developments in U.S. Laws Regarding Grey Market Goods and Parallel Imports," Int'l Legal Strategy, Vol. VIII-11 (1999). *Member:* American Bar Association; American Intellectual Property Law Association; Association of Computing Machinery. ***LANGUAGES:*** Japanese. ***PRACTICE AREAS:*** Patent Litigation; Patent Prosecution; Patent Licensing; Computer Software Patents; Computer Architecture Patents; Computer Law; Software Licensing; Software Protection. ***Email:*** navoegtli@hhlaw.com

KEVIN L. VOLD, born St. Louis Park, Minnesota, February 7, 1971; admitted to bar, 1996, Illinois; 1998, District of Columbia. *Education:* Stanford University (A.B., with distinction, 1993); Northwestern University School of Law (J.D., 1996). *Member:* The District of Columbia Bar. ***Email:*** klvold@hhlaw.com

PEGGY YU PING WANG, born Taipei, Taiwan, September 30, 1972; admitted to bar, 2000, New York; 2001, District of Columbia. *Education:* The University of Michigan (B.A., 1994); Duke University School of Law (J.D., 1998; LL.M., 1998). ***LANGUAGES:*** Mandarin. ***PRACTICE AREAS:*** Corporate Law. ***Email:*** pywang@hhlaw.com

TE MIKA S. WARNER, born Brooklyn, New York, January 25, 1977; admitted to bar, 2001, New York (Not admitted in District of Columbia). *Education:* St. John's University (B.A., 1997); Harvard Law School (J.D., 2000). *Member:* New York State and American Bar Associations.

(This Listing Continued)

SHAUNDRA L. WATSON, born Palm Beach Gardens, Florida, June 6, 1974; admitted to bar, 1999, Florida; 2000, District of Columbia. *Education:* Howard University (B.A., 1996); University of Virginia (J.D., 1999). Phi Beta Kappa. Golden Key National Honor Society. *Member:* The Florida Bar; The District of Columbia Bar; American Bar Association; American Society of International Law. ***Email:*** slwatson@hhlaw.com

STEVEN P. WILLMORE, born Washington, D.C., June 24, 1966; admitted to bar, 2000, New York (Not admitted in District of Columbia). *Education:* Virginia Polytechnic Institute (B.S.E.E., 1988); William and Mary (J.D., 1999; M.B.A., 1999). Eta Kappa Nu. Order of the Barristers. ***PRACTICE AREAS:*** Intellectual Property. ***Email:*** spwillmore@hhlaw.com

GORDON C. WILSON, born New York, N.Y., October 2, 1968; admitted to bar, 1996, New York; 1998, District of Columbia. *Education:* College of William & Mary (B.A., 1990); Yale University (M.A., 1993); University of Virginia (J.D., 1995). Phi Beta Kappa. ***PRACTICE AREAS:*** Secured Finance; International Finance; Asset Sales. ***Email:*** gcwilson@hhlaw.com

KEVIN J. WOLFF, born Detroit, Michigan, May 5, 1953; admitted to bar, 1978, District of Columbia. *Education:* Denison University (B.A., high honors, 1975); Vanderbilt University (J.D., 1978). Order of the Coif. Editor in Chief, Vanderbilt Law Review, 1977-1978. *Member:* District of Columbia Bar.

GRACE SING-FEIN YEH, born Taiwan, Taiwan, Republic of China, March 27, 1971; admitted to bar, 1997, New York; 2000, District of Columbia. *Education:* Harvard University (A.B., cum laude, 1993; J.D., 1996). ***LANGUAGES:*** Mandarin, Taiwanese. ***PRACTICE AREAS:*** Securities Law; Mergers and Acquisitions; Corporate Law. ***Email:*** gsyeh@hhlaw.com

JENNY WU YEH, born Oakland, California, February 20, 1974; admitted to bar, 1999, California; 2000, District of Columbia. *Education:* University of California at Los Angeles (B.A., 1995; J.D., Moot Court honors program, 1999). Counsel to Commissioner Norman S. Johnson, U.S. Securities and Exchange Commission, 1999-2000. Senior Counsel, SEC Office of General Counsel, 1998-1999. ***LANGUAGES:*** Mandarin Chinese. ***PRACTICE AREAS:*** Corporate; Real Estate. ***Email:*** jwyeh@hhlaw.com

LUCINDA T. YEH, born West Chester, Pennsylvania, April 15, 1971; admitted to bar, 1998, Maryland (Not admitted in District of Columbia). *Education:* Yale University (B.A., 1993); University of Virginia (J.D., 1998). ***LANGUAGES:*** Mandarin (Chinese) and Taiwanese. ***Email:*** yehlt@hhlaw.com

LEE F. HOLDMANN

CHARTERED

WASHINGTON, D.C.

(See Bethesda, Maryland)

Trust and Estate Planning, Revocable Trusts, Real Estate, Corporations, U.S. and International Tax Planning. Mediation and Arbitration.

HOLLAND & KNIGHT LLP

2099 PENNSYLVANIA AVENUE, N.W.
SUITE 100
WASHINGTON, D.C. 20006
Telephone: 202-955-3000
Fax: 202-955-5564
URL: http://www.hklaw.com

Annapolis, Maryland Office: State Circle Building, 47 State Circle, Suite 400, 21401. Telephone: 410-263-7800. Fax: 410-263-3768.

Atlanta, Georgia Office: One Atlantic Center, 1201 West Peachtree Street, N.E., Suite 2000, 30309. Telephone: 404-817-8500. Fax: 404-881-0470.

Bethesda, Maryland Office: 3 Bethesda Metro Center, Suite 800, 20814. Telephone: 301-654-7800. Fax: 301-656-3978.

Boston, Massachusetts Office: 10 St. James Avenue, 02116. Telephone: 617-523-2700. Fax: 617-523-6850.

Bradenton, Florida Office: 1001 3rd Avenue West, Suite 600, 34205. Telephone: 941- 748-7076. Fax: 941-747-9774.

Chicago, Illinois Office: 55 West Monroe Street, Suite 800, 60603. Telephone: 312-263-3600. Fax: 312-578-6666.

Fort Lauderdale, Florida Office: One East Broward Boulevard, Suite 1300, 33301. Telephone: 954-525-1000. Fax: 954-463-2030.

Helsinki, Finland Office: Holland & Knight Oy, Pohjoisesplanadi 33, FIN-00100. Telephone: 358-9-684-1520. Fax: 358-9-6841-5252.

Jacksonville, Florida Office: 50 North Laura Street, Suite 3900, 32202. Telephone: 904-353-2000. Fax: 904-358-1872.

Lakeland, Florida Office: 92 Lake Wire Drive, 33815. Telephone: 863-682-1161. Fax: 863-688-1186.

Los Angeles, California Office: 633 West Fifth Street, 21st Floor, 90071. Telephone: 213-896-2400. Fax: 213-896-2450.

(This Listing Continued)

Melbourne, Florida Office: 1499 South Harbor City Boulevard, Suite 201, 32901. Telephone: 321-951-1776. Fax: 321-951-1849.

Mexico City, Mexico Office: Paseo de los Tamarindos 400-B, Piso 2, Delegación Cuajimalpa, Bosques de las Lomas, 05120, Mexico, D.F. Telephone: 011-525-261-1866. Fax: 011-525-261-1867.

Miami, Florida Office: 701 Brickell Avenue, Suite 3000, 33131. Telephone: 305-374-8500. Fax: 305-789-7799.

New York, New York Office: 195 Broadway, 10007. Telephone: 212-513-3200. Fax: 212-385-9010.

Northern Virginia: 1600 Tyson Boulevard, Suite 700, McLean, Virginia, 22102. Telephone: 703-720-8600. Fax: 703-720-8610.

Orlando, Florida Office: 200 South Orange Avenue, Sun Trust Building, Suite 2600, 32801. Telephone: 407-425-8500. Fax: 407-244-5288.

Portland, Oregon Office: 2300 U.S. Bancorp Tower, 111 Southwest Fifth Avenue, 97204. Telephone: 503-243-2300. Fax: 503-241-8014.

Providence, Rhode Island Office: One Financial Plaza, Suite 1800, 02903. Telephone: 401-751-8500. Fax: 401-553-6850.

Rio de Janeiro, Brazil Office: Rua de Assembléia, 58-10th Floor, 20011-000. Telephone: 011-55-21-2509-5050. Fax: 011-55-21-2221-9035.

San Antonio, Texas Office: Weston Centre, 112 East Pecan Street, Suite 2700, 78205. Telephone: 210-229-3000. Fax: 210-229-1194.

San Francisco, California Office: 50 California Street, Suite 2800, 94111. Telephone: 415-743-6900. Fax: 415-743-6910.

São Paulo, Brazil Office: Rua Pedroso Alvarenga, 1,284 - 10th Floor, Suite 102, 04531-000. Telephone: 011-55-11-3079-2300. Fax: 011-55-11-3079-2004.

Seattle, Washington Office: 2600 Pike Tower, 520 Pike Street, 98101. Telephone: 206-340-1825. Telecopier: 206-623-4363.

St. Petersburg, Florida Office: 200 Central Avenue, Suite 1600, 33701. Telephone: 727-896-7171. Fax: 727-822-8048.

Tallahassee, Florida Office: 315 South Calhoun Street, Suite 600, 32301. Telephone: 850-224-7000. Fax: 850-224-8832.

Tampa, Florida Office: 400 North Ashley Drive, Suite 2300, 33602. Telephone: 813-227-8500. Fax: 813-229-0134.

Tokyo, Japan Office: Suite 613, New Otemachi Building, 2-2-1 Otemachi, Chiyoda-ku, 100-0004. Telephone: 011-81-3-3-242-1289. Fax: 011-81-3-3-242-1290.

West Palm Beach, Florida Office: 625 North Flagler Drive, Suite 700, 33401. Telephone: 561-833-2000. Fax: 561-650-8399.

Representative Offices:

Caracas, Venezuela Office: Tinoco, Travieso, Planchart & Núñez, Avenida Francisco De Miranda, Torre Country Club, Piso 1 y 2, Chacaito, 1050. Telephone: 011-582-12-952-9033 (Master). Fax: 011-582-12-953-1053/8365/7583. Email: ttpn@ttpn.com.ve.

Tel Aviv, Israel Office: 23 Derech Petach-Tikva, 18th Floor, 66184. Telephone: 011-972-3-566-7666. Fax: 011-972-3-566-7667.

General Practice including: Administrative and Rulemaking, Agriculture, Aircraft Finance and Leasing, Alternative Dispute Resolution, American Continental Group Strategic Affiliation, Antitrust, Trade Regulation and Competition, Appropriations, Asia Practice, Automotive and Automotive Finance, Aviation, Bankruptcy and Creditors' Rights and Workouts, Beverage Alcohol, Bond Financing, Brownfields, Cash Flow and Asset-Based Lending, Charitable Giving, Civil Rights, Computer Law, Construction and Design, Consumer Fraud, Contests and Sweepstakes, Corporate and Securities, Corporate Compliance, Corporate Finance, Corporate Relocation and Expansion, Corporate Trust, Customs and International Trade, Development of Regional Impact, Directors' and Officers' Liability, Diversity Counseling, Drug & Medical Devices, E-Commerce, Education, Elder Law, Elections-State, Eminent Domain and Condemnation, Energy, Entertainment, Environmental, Equipment Financing & Leasing, ERISA, Employee Benefits and Executive Compensation, Financial Institutions, Franchise, Gaming, Government (GSA) Real Estate Contracting, Government - Illinois State & Local, Government - State and Local, Government Contracts, Grants and Infrastructure, Growth Management, Concurrency and Land Use, GSA Holdovers and Condemnation Disputes, Health Care, Hospitality, Hotel, Timeshare and Resort Development, Housing, Immigration, Nationality and Consular Law, Indian Law, Individual and Private Business, Insurance, Intellectual Property, Intellectual Property - Copyright, Intellectual Property - Patent, Intellectual Property - Trademark, International, International Procurement, Internet Resource Team, Investment Funds and Asset Management, Israel Practice, Labor and Employment Relations, Legislation - Federal, Legislation - State, Litigation - Airline Accident, Litigation - Appellate, Litigation - Class Action, Litigation - Commercial, Litigation - Criminal Defense, Litigation - Environmental, Litigation - International, Litigation - Securities, Marital and Family Law, Maritime and Shipping, Media & Communications, Mergers and Acquisitions, Mexico Practice, Mining, Minority Initiative, Money Laundering, Mortgage Banking, Natural Gas, OSHA, Personal Injury and Wrongful Death, Power Plant and Transmission Line Siting, Privatization, Product Liability, Project Finance, Public Finance, Public Law, Public Utilities, Rapid Response Team, Real Estate Investment Trusts (REITs), Real Estate Environmental and Land Use, Retail Development, Retail Real Estate, Securitization of Financial Assets, Space Law, Sports - Amateur, Sports - Collegiate Administration and Compliance, Sports Practice, Syndication and Partnership, Taxation - Federal, Taxation - State and Local,

(This Listing Continued)

HOLLAND & KNIGHT LLP, Washington—Continued

Taxation - Tax-Exempt Organizations, Technology, Technology Transfers & Licensing, Telecommunications, Transportation, Trusts and Estates, U.S. Export Compliance, Venture Capital, Water/Wastewater Practice, White Collar Crime.

FIRM PROFILE: Holland & Knight LLP is one of the 20 largest law firms in the world, with more than 1,300 lawyers in 32 cities.

Holland & Knight counsels clients whose business interests range from local to international. Clients include: financial institutions; utility companies; insurance companies; domestic and foreign governments; a variety of media enterprises; passenger cruise lines; several foreign aircraft companies and carriers; land developers; phosphate mining and manufacturing companies; citrus producers and other agricultural enterprises; trade associations; and many other companies, institutions and individuals.

The firm conducts numerous charitable activities through the Holland & Knight Charitable Foundation. "Opening Doors for Children" and "The Holocaust Remembrance Project" are two of the Foundation's outreach programs.

August 2000, the San Antonio, Texas, law firm of Sessions & Sessions combined its practice with Holland Knight.

January 2001, as part of the firm's continued expansion throughout Latin America, Holland & Knight LLP forged a formal association with the law firm of Evaldo Ramos-Advogados Associados and created a presence in São Paulo and Rio de Janeiro, Brazil.

February 2001, McGovern Noel & Benik, Incorporated, a Providence, Rhode Island-based law firm, combined its practice with Holland & Knight.

February 2001, 12 partners and five associates from Wilkes Artis joined the Washington, D.C. office. The team includes the land use, zoning and real estate transaction practice, and members of the corporate and public law departments. The addition of these lawyers made Holland & Knight the dominant real estate law firm in the Washington area.

April 2001, six labor and employment law partners from Fox and Grove joined the Chicago office, bringing significant traditional labor experience and clients. The addition of these lawyers made the national Labor and Employment group nearly 100 strong.

June 2001, Gilbert, Segall and Young, a New York City-based law firm, with an affiliate office in Helsinki, combined its 28-lawyer practice with Holland & Knight.

October 2001, Weiss Jensen Ellis & Howard, a law firm with offices in Portland, Oregon and Seattle, Washington combined its 22-lawyer practice with Holland & Knight.

WASHINGTON, D.C. MEMBERS AND ASSOCIATES

R. GREGORY BAILEY, born Salisbury, Maryland, August 11, 1961; admitted to bar, 1987, Virginia; 1995, Florida; 1998, District of Columbia. *Education:* Wake Forest University (B.A., 1983; J.D., 1986). Legislation Counsel, U.S. Congress Joint Committee on Taxation, April, 1999-June, 2001. *Member:* American Bar Association (Member, Tax Section, 2001—). ***PRACTICE AREAS:*** ERISA and Employee Benefits; Executive Compensation; Federal Tax Legislation. ***Email:*** gbailey@hklaw.com

MARKHAM BALL, born March 24, 1934; admitted to bar, 1961, District of Columbia; 1968, U.S. Supreme Court. *Education:* Amherst College (B.A., 1956); Oxford University, England (B.A., 1958; M.A., 1973); Harvard University (LL.B., 1960). Law Clerk to Chief Justice Earl Warren, Justice Stanley Reed and Justice Harold Burton, U.S. Supreme Court, 1960-1961. Assistant General Counsel, U.S. Office of Economic Opportunity and General Counsel, VISTA, 1964-1966. Staff Director, Peace Corps, 1966-1967. General Counsel, U.S. Agency for International Development, 1977-1979. Lecturer on International Commercial Arbitration, University of Virginia Law School, 1991—. Fellow: American Bar Foundation. ***PRACTICE AREAS:*** International Arbitration; International Contracts. ***Email:*** mball@hklaw.com

TIMOTHY J. BLOOMFIELD, born New Rochelle, New York, October 30, 1939; admitted to bar, 1967, Maryland; 1968, District of Columbia; 1970, U.S. Supreme Court. *Education:* Wesleyan University (B.A., 1961); University of Virginia (LL.B., 1967). Order of the Coif; Phi Delta Phi. Member, Raven Society. Notes Editor, University of Virginia Law Review, 1966-1967. Law Clerk to Hon. Albert V. Bryan, U.S. Court of Appeals, Fourth Circuit, 1967-1968. Member, National and Construction Panels of Arbitrators, American Arbitration Association. Member of D.C. Board of Professional Responsibility. *Member:* The District of Columbia Bar; The Bar Association of the District of Columbia; American Bar Association. [Lt., USNR, 1961-1964]. ***PRACTICE AREAS:*** Commercial Litigation; Construction Law; Antitrust and Trade Regulation. ***Email:*** tbloomfi@hklaw.com

(This Listing Continued)

STEPHEN A. BOGORAD, born Brooklyn, New York, March 16, 1959; admitted to bar, 1983, District of Columbia and U.S. District Court for the District of Columbia, U.S. Court of Appeals for the District of Columbia Circuit; 1990, U.S. Claims Court; 1991, Maryland and U.S. District Court, District of Maryland; 1994, U.S. Court of Appeals, Fourth Circuit. *Education:* State University of New York at Buffalo (B.A., magna cum laude, 1980); Georgetown University (J.D., magna cum laude, 1983). Phi Beta Kappa. Staff Member, 1981-1982 and Editor, 1982-1983, American Criminal Law Review. *Member:* The District of Columbia Bar (Member: Section on Litigation; Business Bankruptcy Committee); American Bar Association (Member, Section on Litigation). ***PRACTICE AREAS:*** Commercial Litigation; Bankruptcy Law. ***Email:*** sbogorad@hklaw.com

JEFFREY F. BOOTHE, born July 30, 1955; admitted to bar, 1987, Virginia; 1988, District of Columbia. *Education:* Stanford University (B.A., 1977); George Mason University School of Law (J.D., 1987). Recipient, American Jurisprudence Award in Business Finance. Professional Staff Member, U.S. Senate Appropriations Committee, 1982-1987. Legislative Assistant, Senator Mark O. Hatfield, 1978-1982. Employed by: Oppenheimer, Wolff & Donnelly LLP, 1995-2000; Schwabe, Williamson & Wyatt LLP, 1987-1995. Member, Virginia State Bar (inactive). *Member:* The District of Columbia Bar. ***PRACTICE AREAS:*** Health Care; Legislative Practice; Transportation; Federal Regulatory Law. ***Email:*** jboothe@hklaw.com

LEIGH A. BRADLEY, born Indianapolis, Indiana, December 15, 1956; admitted to bar, 1982, Alabama; 2000, District of Columbia; U.S. Court of Federal Claims; U.S. Court of Veteran Appeals; U.S. Court of the Armed Forces. *Education:* University of Alabama (B.A., magna cum laude, 1978; J.D., 1981). Phi Beta Kapa. Recipient: Department of Defense Medal for Distinguished Public Service, 1998; Department of Veterans Affairs Exceptional Service Award, 2000. Co-Author: "A Privatization Alternative: The Department of Veteran Affairs' Enhanced-Use Leasing Program," 30 Public Contract Law Journal, 2001. General Counsel, U.S. Department of Veterans Affairs, 1998-2001. Principal Deputy General Counsel, Department of the Navy, 1994-1998. *Member:* American Bar Association. [Judge Advocate, U.S. Air Force, 1982-1987; Air Force Reserve, 1987-1992 (O-4)]. ***PRACTICE AREAS:*** Federal Government Contracts; Litigation; Privatization. ***Email:*** labradley@hklaw.com

DAVID W. BRIGGS, born Taunton, Massachusetts, March 20, 1946; admitted to bar, 1975, Virginia; 1980, District of Columbia. *Education:* University of Massachusetts (B.A., 1968); University of South Florida; George Washington University (J.D., 1975). Co-Chair, Legislative and Governmental Affairs Committee, District of Columbia Building Industry Association. First Vice President, Rosslyn Renaissance Arlington, Virginia. Former Chairman, Arlington County, Virginia Commission for the Arts. [United States Air Force, 1969-1972]. ***PRACTICE AREAS:*** Commercial Real Estate Acquisitions; Commercial Real Estate Sales; Commercial Real Estate Leasing; Land Use; Zoning Law. ***Email:*** dbriggs@hklaw.com

THOMAS WILLCOX BROOKE, born Clinton, Iowa, February 4, 1960; admitted to bar, 1991, Virginia and District of Columbia; U.S. Supreme Court; U.S. Court of Appeals, Fourth Circuit; U.S. Court of Appeals, Federal Circuit; U.S. District Court, Eastern District of Virginia; U.S. District Court for the District of Columbia. *Education:* College of William and Mary (B.A., 1982); Marshall Wythe School Law, College of William and Mary (J.D., 1990). Speaker, American Bar Association Section of Intellectual Property Law, Practical Tips on Trademark Litigation Seminar, 2001. Faculty Member, International Trademark Association Spring Forum, 1997. Staff Assistant, Congressman Frank Wolf, 1983. Legislative Assistant, Senator John McCain, 1983-1987. *Member:* The District of Columbia Bar; Virginia State Bar; American Bar Association (Member, Intellectual Property Law Section; Chair, Division VII Information, 2001—; Chair - Division IX Publication and Publica Education, 2000-2001; Chair, Committee on Internet Use, 1999-2000; Chair, Subcommittee on Patent-Trade Dress, 1996-2000); International Trademark Association (Chairman, U.S. Legislation Subcommittee, 1998—; Chairman, INTA-PAC, 1999—). ***REPORTED CASES:*** Conopco v. May Department Stores Co., 46 F.3d 1556 (Fed. Cir. 1994); L.A. Gold Clothing Co., Inc. v. L.A. Gear, Inc., 954 F.Supp. 1068 (W.D. Pa. 1996). ***PRACTICE AREAS:*** Intellectual Property Litigation; Intellectual Property Counseling; Trademark Prosecution; Copyright Prosecution; Technology Transfers; Technology Licensing. ***Email:*** tbrooke@hklaw.com

HENRY J. BROTHERS II, born New Orleans, Louisiana, September 17, 1957; admitted to bar, 1984, Virginia; 1988, District of Columbia. *Education:* Tulane University (B.A., 1979); George Washington University (J.D., 1984). Omicron Delta Kappa; Phi Alpha Delta. Member, Moot Court Honor Board. *Member:* The District of Columbia Bar (Steering Committee, Real Estate Housing and Land Use Section-Chair, 1999-2000 and 2000-2001; Member, D.C. Affairs Section); Virginia State Bar; American Bar Association (Member, Real Property, Probate and Trust Law Section; Affordable Housing Forum). ***PRACTICE AREAS:*** Commercial Real Estate Development Law; Multifamily Housing; Finance Law; Housing Development; Community Development. ***Email:*** hbrother@hklaw.com

(This Listing Continued)

JOHN M. BRYSON, II, born Columbus, Ohio, March 21, 1949; admitted to bar, 1977, Virginia; 1978, District of Columbia; 1982, U.S. Supreme Court, U.S. Court of Appeals, Third, Fourth, Fifth, Sixth, Seventh, Eighth, Ninth, Tenth, Eleventh, Federal and the District of Columbia Circuit, U.S. District Court, Eastern District of Virginia, U.S. District Court, District of Maryland and U.S. District Court for the District of Columbia. *Education:* University of Virginia (B.S.N.E., with high distinction, 1971; J.D., 1977). Tau Beta Pi. Member, Virginia Medical Malpractice Review Panel. *Member:* The District of Columbia Bar; Virginia State Bar; American Bar Association (Member, Section of Litigation). ***PRACTICE AREAS:*** Litigation; Employment; Corporate Law. ***Email:*** jbryson@hklaw.com

HAROLD R. BUCHOLTZ, born Newark, New Jersey, January 24, 1952; admitted to bar, 1976, Virginia; 1980, District of Columbia, U.S. Tax Court and U.S. Supreme Court. *Education:* Rutgers University (B.A., 1973); University of Virginia (J.D., 1976); Georgetown University (LL.M. in Taxation, 1980). Attorney, Interpretative Division, Office of Chief Counsel, Internal Revenue Service, 1976-1981. Author: "Using Restrictive Sales Agreements to Fix A Low Estate Tax Value for A Business Interest," Estate Planning, May, 1981; "Consent Dividends May Allow A Step-Up in Basis or Increase the Foreign Tax Credit," Journal of Taxation, March, 1982. Co-Author: "Despite Restrictions, Foreign Trusts Can Be Effective Tax Planning Devices," Estate Planning, March, 1985; "Tax-Exempt Redevelopment Financing in Florida," XX-3 Stetson Law Review 667, 1991. *Member:* American Law Institute. ***PRACTICE AREAS:*** Tax Exempt Financing Law; Tax Exempt Organizations; Taxation (Local, State and Federal). ***Email:*** hbucholt@hklaw.com

KEVIN A. BUFORD, born Royal Oak, Michigan, July 13, 1957; admitted to bar, 1986, California; 1987, Texas; 1988, Colorado; 2001, District of Columbia; U.S. Court of Appeals, Fifth, Ninth and Federal Circuits; U.S. District Court, Eastern District of Texas; U.S. District Court, Central District of California; registered to practice before U.S. Patent and Trademark Office. *Education:* U.S. Coast Guard Academy (B.S., with honors, 1979); University of Texas at Austin (J.D., 1986). Member, Texas International Law Journal, 1985-1986. *Member:* American Bar Association; American Intellectual Property Law Association. ***PRACTICE AREAS:*** Technology Law; Commercial Law; Intellectual Property Law; Patents; Copyrights, Trademarks and Trade Secrets. ***Email:*** kbuford@hklaw.com

TANJA H. CASTRO, born Madison, Wisconsin, February 27, 1959; admitted to bar, 1986, Pennsylvania; 1987, District of Columbia; 1988, Virginia. *Education:* Vassar College (A.B., 1981); American University (J.D., 1985). Member, Executive Committee, 1994— and President, 1999-2000, Commercial Real Estate Women (CREW). Member, Board of Directors, District of Columbia Building Association (DCBIA), 1996—. Member: Advisory Committee on the Rules and Procedure of the Tax Division of Superior Court; D.C. Office of Tax and Revenue Advisory Group. Member, Leadership Washington, Class of 2001. *Member:* The District of Columbia Bar; Virginia State Bar; American Bar Association. ***PRACTICE AREAS:*** Real Estate Tax Assessment; Eminent Domain; Condemnation; Guardianships and Conservatorships; Estate Planning; Administration. ***Email:*** tcastro@hklaw.com

J. MICHAEL CAVANAUGH, born Columbus, Ohio, 1949; admitted to bar, 1974, Ohio; 1977, District of Columbia. *Education:* Ohio State University (B.A., 1971); Stanford University (J.D., 1974). Phi Beta Kappa. Author: "Prospects for Privatization of Nuclear Generation Facilities," International Privatization Review 2001-2002; "Steering Off Course - Section 12106(e) Lease Finance Transactions," Euromoney Shipping Finance Annual 2001-2002; "Privatization of Marine Port Facilities," Juras Vestas (Latvia), June 1998; "Privatization of State-Owned Ocean Carriers," Juras Vestas (Latvia), January 1998; "Ending Shipbuilding Protectionism in the United States-The Mills of the Gods Grind Slowly," presented at Austrade Shipbuilding Forum, May 1996; "U.S. Product Liability Laws-Impact on the Software Industry," presented at Australian National University, October 1995; "United States Coastwise Law Restrictions on Vessel Construction-Coping with the Existing Regime and Prospects for Change," Baird's Shipbuilding (Australia), August 1995; "Eastern Promise: Opportunities for Western Law Firms in the Asia Pacific Region," Lawyers in Europe, November 1993; "An Overview of U.S. Warranty Law," Kaigai Shijo. Adjunct Professor, George Mason University School of Law, 1997—. Attorney-Advisor, Office of the General Counsel, Maritime Administration, U.S. Department of Commerce, 1974-1977. Chairman, Water Transportation Law Committee, Federal Bar Association, 1979-1980. ***REPORTED CASES:*** Autolog v. Regan, 731 F.2d 25 (D.C. Cir. 1984); American Association of Cruise Passengers v. Carnival Cruise Lines, 911 F.2d 786 (D.C. Cir. 1990). ***PRACTICE AREAS:*** International Commercial Law; Mergers and Acquisitions; Transportation Law. ***Email:*** mcavanau@hklaw.com

ROBERT M. CHASNOW, born Baltimore, Maryland, December 21, 1948; admitted to bar, 1974, New Jersey; 1976, District of Columbia; 1982, Florida and U.S. Supreme Court. *Education:* Wharton School University of Pennsylvania (B.S., 1971); George Washington University (J.D., 1974). Executive Editor, Land Development Law Reporter, 1974-1992. Author: "Hotels and Time Sharing," Property Writes Newsletters; "Trends in Florida Timeshare Law," University of Miami School of Law Institute on Condominium Developments. Co-

(This Listing Continued)

author: "Federal Interstate Land Sales Act An Overview," ABA Probate and Property Journal, July, 1988; "Vacation Ownership and Your Hotel," American Hotel and Motel Magazine, 1989; Hocking v. Dubois-Condominium Securities, ARDA Developments, 1990; "Recent Interstate Land Sales Enforcement ARDA Developments, 1993; "Legal Issues in Off-Site Timeshare Marketing," ARDA Developments, 1993; "Federal Telemarketing Law," ARDA, 1996; "Legal Issues of Timeshare Resales," ARDA, 1996. *Member:* The District of Columbia Bar; The Florida Bar; New Jersey State and American Bar Associations. ***SPECIAL AGENCIES:*** U.S. Department of HUD; State Timeshare and Land Sales Registration Agencies. ***TRANSACTIONS:*** RTC legal advisor selling $31 million in timeshare receivables and units, 1991; Securitization of $200 million in timeshare receivables, 1996-1999. ***PRACTICE AREAS:*** Timeshare; Resort Community Development Law; Land Sales Law. ***Email:*** rchasnow@hklaw.com

MICHAEL W. CLANCY, born Lowell, Massachusetts, January 25, 1957; admitted to bar, 1982, District of Columbia, U.S. District Court for the District of Columbia, U.S. Court of Federal Claims and U.S. Court of Appeals for the Federal Circuit. *Education:* University of Notre Dame (B.A., with high honors, 1979); George Washington University (J.D., with honors, 1982). Department of the Navy Office of General Counsel (1982-1986). Contributing Editor, Contracts, Federal Circuit Bar Journal, 1996-1997. Virginia Joint Commission on Technology and Science (Economic Development and Law & Technology Advisory Committees)(1999). Co-Chair, Government Contractors Committee, Fairfax County Chamber of Commerce (2000). *Member:* The District of Columbia Bar (Member, 1996-1999 and Co-Chair, 1997-1999, Steering Committee, Government Contracts and Litigation Section); Federal Bar Association; U.S. Court of Federal Claims Bar Association; Information Technology Association of America (Member: Procurement Policy Committee and Federal Outsourcing Task Group). ***PRACTICE AREAS:*** Government Contracts; Government Investigations; FOIA Litigation; Commercial Litigation. ***Email:*** mclancy@hklaw.com

LOUISE B. COBBS, born Miami, Florida, December 7, 1947; admitted to bar, 1978, New York; 1984, District of Columbia; U.S. Supreme Court, U.S. Circuit Courts for the District of Columbia Circuit, Third, Fourth, Fifth, Seventh and Ninth Circuits and U.S. District Court for the District of Columbia. *Education:* Smith College (A.B., 1969). Study of Law in a law office, New York, 1974-1978. Author: "The Shifting Meaning of 'Accident' Under Article 17 of the Warsaw Convention: What did the Airline Know and What Did It Do About It?," KLUWER Air and Space Law Journal, 1999. *Member:* The District of Columbia Bar; Federal (Transportation Section Leadership, 1992—) and American Bar Associations. ***LANGUAGES:*** French and Spanish. ***PRACTICE AREAS:*** Aviation Law; Aerospace Casualty Litigation; Products Liability; International Law. ***Email:*** lcobbs@hklaw.com

JERALD S. COHN, born Washington, D.C., September 8, 1959; admitted to bar, 1985, Maryland; 1987, District of Columbia; U.S. District Court, District of Maryland; U.S. District Court, District of Columbia. *Education:* Syracuse University (B.A., cum laude with honors in History, 1981); Georgetown University Law Center (J.D., 1985). Recipient, Newcomen Award in Business History, 1981. Clerk to the Honorable Lawrence F. Rodowsky, Court of Appeals of Maryland, 1985-1986. *Member:* The District of Columbia Bar; Maryland State Bar Association. ***PRACTICE AREAS:*** Commercial Real Estate Acquisitions and Sales; Real Estate Finance; Loan Workouts; Foreclosure; Secured Creditor Bankruptcy Representation. ***Email:*** jcohn@hklaw.com

MARK D. COLLEY, born Alexandria, Virginia, August 6, 1955; admitted to bar, 1980, Virginia; 1981, District of Columbia, U.S. Courts of Appeals for the District of Columbia Circuit and U.S. Court of Appeals, Fourth Circuit; 1988, U.S. Court of Appeals for the Federal Circuit; 1989, U.S. Court of Appeals, Eleventh Circuit; 1991, U.S. Court of Federal Claims. *Education:* College of William & Mary (B.A., with high honors, 1977); University of Virginia (J.D., 1980). Editor, "Post-Award Bid Protests at the U.S. Court of Federal Claims," ABA, Nov. 1997. Author: "GAO's Proposed Bid Protest Rules: On the Road to an Improved Process," *Federal Contracts Report* (April 3, 1995); GAO Protest Costs: New Rule Provides Little Benefit To Service Contractors When Agencies Take Corrective Action," *Contract Management* 39 (July, 1993). *Member:* Federal and American (Member, Sections on: Public Contract Law; Chair, Bid Protest Committee; Litigation) Bar Associations; Federal Circuit Bar Association; Boards of Contract Appeals Bar Association; National Contract Management Association. ***PRACTICE AREAS:*** Government Contracts Law; Litigation. ***Email:*** mcolley@hklaw.com

CHRISTOPHER H. COLLINS, born Staten Island, N.Y., July 13, 1953; admitted to bar, 1979, District of Columbia; 1980, Maryland; 1982, U.S. Supreme Court. *Education:* Boston College (A.B., magna cum laude, 1975); Catholic University of America (J.D., 1978). Catholic University Law Review, 1977-1978. Board of Directors, Metropolitan Washington Builders' Council, 1993—. Board of Directors, District of Columbia Building Industry Association, 1986—; Board of Directors, DCBIA Community Services Corporation, 1996—. Board of Trustees, Meridian International Center, 2001—. *Member:* The District of Columbia Bar; Maryland State Bar Association; DC Building Industry Association; DC Chapter, American Institute of Architects; Urban

(This Listing Continued)

HOLLAND & KNIGHT LLP, Washington—Continued

Land Institute. ***PRACTICE AREAS:*** Land Use and Zoning Law; Real Estate; Municipal Law; Historic Preservation; Foreign Missions; Environmental Law. ***Email:*** ccollins@hklaw.com

PETER M. CONNOLLY, born Boston, Massachusetts, August 2, 1951; admitted to bar, 1977, New York; 1978, District of Columbia. *Education:* Yale University (B.A., magna cum laude, with honors in History, 1973); Columbia University (J.D., 1976). Legislative Counsel, U.S. Senator Gaylord Nelson, 1978-1980. *Member:* The District of Columbia Bar; American Bar Association; Federal Communications Bar Association. ***PRACTICE AREAS:*** Telecommunications Law. ***Email:*** pconnoll@hklaw.com

STEPHEN J. CRIMMINS, born Brooklyn, New York, March 22, 1949; admitted to bar, 1974, New York; 1985, Massachusetts and District of Columbia. *Education:* Fordham University (B.A., 1970); Columbia University (J.D., 1973). Articles Editor, Columbia Journal of Law & Social Problems, 1972-1973. Publication: "SEC Resolves Long-Standing Questions About Its Cease-and-Desist Remedy," Securities Regulation & Law Report (BNA), Vol. 33, No. 29 (July 23, 2001). Deputy Chief Litigation Counsel, Division of Enforcement, Securities and Exchange Commission, 1993-2001; Trial Attorney, SEC Division of Enforcement, 1987-93; litigation practice with firms in Boston, 1985-87, and New York, 1973-85. ***PRACTICE AREAS:*** SEC Enforcement; Securities Litigation; Commercial Litigation. ***Email:*** scrimmin@hklaw.com

CAROL DiBATTISTE, born Philadelphia, Pennsylvania, December 28, 1951; admitted to bar, 1982, Pennsylvania and U.S. Court of the Armed Forces; 1985. U.S. Supreme Court; 1989, New York, District of Columbia and U.S. Court of Appeals for the District of Columbia; 1990, Florida; 1991, U.S. District Court, Southern District of Florida and U.S. Court of Appeals, Eleventh Circuit. *Education:* LaSalle College (B.A., magna cum laude, 1976); Temple University (J.D., 1981); Columbia University School of Law (LL.M., 1986). Author: "Air Force Espionage, Recurring Issues," Air Force Law Review, Vol. 32, p. 377 (1990); "Federal and Military Rape Shield Rules: Are They Serving Their Purpose?" Naval Law Review, Vol. 37, p. 123 (Winter 1988); "The Prosecution Sentencing Case," Air Force Law Review, Vol. 27, No. 2, p. 203 (1987); Editor, The Reporter. Faculty: University of Miami School of Law, Trial Skills Program, Miami, Fl., 1998-1999; Team Leader, National Institute for Trial Advocacy, 1986-1992 (Regional Programs, New Orleans, La., Berkeley, Ca., Philadelphia, Pa. and New York, N.Y.; Advanced Trial Advocacy Program, Berkeley, Ca.); Air Force Judge Advocate General School, Maxwell Air Force Base, Montgomery, Al., 1986-1989 (Instructor, Basic Law Course in Criminal Law, Criminal Procedure, Trial Advocacy and Advanced Trial Advocacy for New Lawyers and Air Force Reserve Attorneys). Prior positions: Under Secretary, U.S. Air Force, 1999-2001. Deputy U.S. Attorney, Southern District of Florida, Miami, Fl., 1997-1999. Director, Executive Office for U.S. Attorneys, Department of Justice, Washington, D.C., 1994-1997. Principal Deputy General Counsel, U.S. Navy and Marine Corps, Washington, D.C., 1993-1994. Director, Office of Legal Education, Department of Justice, Washington, D.C., 1992-1993. Assistant U.S. Attorney, Southern District of Florida, Miami, Fl., 1991-1992. Member: Board of Directors, Holland & Knight Consulting, Inc., 2001—; Peer Review Committee, Southern District of Florida, 1998-1999; U.S. Magistrate Selection Committee, Southern District of Florida, 1998-1999; Board of Visitors, Temple University School of Law, 1996-1999; The Retired Officers' Association, 1991—; Air Force Association, 1976—. Trustee, Air Force Judge Advocate General School Foundation, 1993-1996. *Member:* American Bar Association (Member, Public Contract Law Section, and Employment Law Section, 2001—; Member, Government and Public Sector Lawyers Division, 1994-2000; Chair, Standing Committee on Military Law, 1989-1991; Member, Criminal Justice Section Rules of Criminal Procedure and Evidence Committee, 1987-1991; Member, General Practice Section Litigation Committee, 1987-1988; Standing Committee on Military Law, 1986-1989; Vice Chair, General Practice Professional Competence Committee, 1985-1987); Federal Bar Association; National Institute for Trial Advocacy. [Major, United States Air Force, 1971-1991, Retired.]. ***REPORTED CASES:*** United States v. Mansfield, 33 M.J. 972 (A.F.C.M.R. 1991). ***PRACTICE AREAS:*** Corporate Diversity; Counseling; Government Relations; Government Contracts; Criminal Litigation; Civil Litigation. ***Email:*** cdibattiste@hklaw.com

G. RICHARD DUNNELLS, born Port Washington, New York, April 28, 1937; admitted to bar, 1967, District of Columbia. *Education:* Dartmouth College (B.A., 1959); University of Virginia (LL.B., 1967). Holland & Knight Firm-Wide Hiring Partner. Deputy Assistant Secretary for Urban Renewal and Housing and Deputy Assistant Secretary for Housing Management, U.S. Department of Housing and Urban Development, 1969-1973. Member, The President's Commission on Housing, 1981-1982. *Member:* The District of Columbia Bar. [U.S. Marine Corps, 1957-1959; LTJG, U.S. Navy Aviation, 1959-1963]. ***PRACTICE AREAS:*** Housing Development and Financing; Commercial Real Estate Transactions; Housing and Urban Development; Federal Housing Law; Affordable Housing Finance. ***Email:*** rdunnell@hklaw.com

STUART S. DYE, born Ogden, Utah, 1939; admitted to bar, 1967, Virginia and District of Columbia. *Education:* University of Utah (B.S., cum laude,

(This Listing Continued)

1961); University of Virginia (LL.B., 1967). Phi Alpha Delta. Member, Editorial Board, Virginia Journal of International Law, 1966-1967. Contributing Editor, Oil and Gas Regulations Analyst, 1976-1982. Secretary of the Navy Staff, Deep Submergence Systems Review Group, Office of Legislative Affairs, 1963-1964. Special Assistant on Law of the Sea Matters, International Law Division, Office of the Judge Advocate General, 1965 and 1966. Member, Board of Directors, 1988—and Chairman, 1999—, U.S.- Mexico Chamber of Commerce. Member, National Advisory Council, University of Utah, 2001—. *Member:* American Bar Association (Member, Sections on: Natural Resources Law; Administrative Law); Maritime Law Association of the United States; Maritime Administrative Bar Association. [Lt. Cmdr., USNR]. ***PRACTICE AREAS:*** International Transactions; International Finance; Transportation Law; Energy Law. ***Email:*** sdye@hklaw.com

AMY L. EDWARDS, born Northampton, Massachusetts, April 2, 1953; admitted to bar, 1978, District of Columbia; 1989, Virginia; 1990, Maryland. *Education:* Smith College (A.B., cum laude with honors in Govt., 1975); George Washington University (J.D., 1978). Attorney-Advisor, Federal Energy Regulatory Commission, Office of Administrative Law Judges, 1978-1979. Women in Government Relations Distinguished Member, 1991. Author: "Long Term Enforcement and Stewardship of Institutional Controls," BNA's *Environmental Due Diligence Reporter; Chapter on:* "Institutional Controls," in the American Bar Association's *Environmental Aspects of Real Estate Transactions, Second Edition, 1999 and in the American Bar Association's Brownfields, Second Edition, 2001; "Raising the Stakes:* EPA Region V's Challenge Regarding the Long Term Viability and Enforceability of Institutional Controls at Brownfields Sites," The Metropolitan Corporate Counsel, April, 2000; "Restoring Private Property Values in the World of CERCLA's Emerging Alternatives," *Environmental Law and Practice,* May/June, 1996. *Member:* The District of Columbia Bar; Virginia State Bar; Maryland State Bar Association, Inc.; American Bar Association; The Women's Bar Association of The District of Columbia. ***REPORTED CASES:*** W.C. and A.N. Miller Companies v. United States, 963 F. Supp. 1231 (D.D.C. 1997) and 173 F.R.D. 1 (1997). ***PRACTICE AREAS:*** Environmental. ***Email:*** aedwards@hklaw.com

PHILIP TUCKER EVANS, born Glen Ridge, New Jersey, March 11, 1960; admitted to bar, 1993, Maryland; 1994, District of Columbia. *Education:* Williams College (B.A., with honors, 1982); Georgetown University (J.D., cum laude, 1993). ***PRACTICE AREAS:*** Civil Litigation; Commercial Litigation; Bankruptcy; Creditor's Rights; E-Commerce; Technology Law. ***Email:*** pevans@hklaw.com

ERIC FISHMAN, born 1949; admitted to bar, 1977, New York; 1983, District of Columbia; 1997, Virginia. *Education:* University of Chicago (A.B., 1970); Columbia University (J.D., 1976; Ph.D., 1980). Attorney-Adviser, Federal Communications Commission, 1978-1983. *Member:* The District of Columbia Bar; Federal Communications Bar Association. ***LANGUAGES:*** Hebrew. ***SPECIAL AGENCIES:*** Federal Communications Commission, State Public Service Commissions, International Telecommunication Union. ***PRACTICE AREAS:*** Telecommunications; Corporate. ***Email:*** efishman@hklaw.com

TILLIE K. FOWLER, born Atlanta, Georgia, December 23, 1942; admitted to bar, 1967, Georgia; 2001, District of Columbia. *Education:* Emory University (A.B., 1964; J.D., 1967). U.S. Representative, Florida 4th District, 1992-2001. Member: President's Commission on the Future of the Aerospace Industry, 2001-2002; Defense Policy Board, 2001. (Also at Jacksonville, Florida Office). ***PRACTICE AREAS:*** Public Law; Federal Appropiations. ***Email:*** tfowler@hklaw.com

MICHAEL M. GABA, born Brooklyn, N.Y., November 21, 1961; admitted to bar, 1987, Maryland and U.S. District Court, District of Maryland; 1988, District of Columbia. *Education:* Franklin & Marshall College (B.A., 1983); George Washington University (J.D., 1986). *Member:* District of Columbia Bar (Member, Health Law Section); Maryland State Bar Association (Member, Health Law Section); American Health Lawyers Association. ***PRACTICE AREAS:*** Government Relations; Health Care. ***Email:*** mgaba@hklaw.com

NORMAN M. GLASGOW, SR., born Washington, D.C., August 14, 1922; admitted to bar, 1949, District of Columbia; 1956, U.S. Supreme Court; 1960, Maryland. *Education:* University of Maryland (B.S., 1943); George Washington University (LL.B., 1949; J.D., 1949). Lambda Alpha (President, 1987); Who's Who in America; Who's Who in American Law. Recipient: Award For Distinguished Professional Service from George Washington University; 1992 Member of the Year Award from Lambda Alpha International. Member: Metropolitan Washington Board of Trade, Board of Directors & Executive Committee, Legislative Steering Committee, General Counsel, 1986, 1987, 1988; Maryland PAC, Chairman, 1983-1993; Citizen's Advisory Committee for the rewriting of the D.C. Zoning Regulations; Subcommittee of Chapters 1 and 6 for the drafting of the D.C. Building Regulations (Chairman); Maryland State Convention Authority, 1990-1992; Governor's Compensation Committee; Governor's Special Committee on Vehicle Emissions Inspection Program; Governor's Advisory Committee on Redistricting of Congressional and State Legislative Districts; Governor's State Task Force for State-Wide Building Performance Standard (Chairman); State of Maryland Economic Growth Task Force (Chairman);

(This Listing Continued)

Maryland Economic Growth, Resource Protection and Planning Commission; Maryland Stadium Authority, 1994-1997; American Planning Association; Washington Building Congress, Board of Governors, 1988-1989; Urban Land Institute, 1962—; Greater Washington Research Center. *Member:* The District of Columbia Bar; Bar Association of the District of Columbia; Maryland State and American Bar Associations; The Barristers. ***PRACTICE AREAS:*** Real Estate; Zoning, Planning and Land Use; Municipal Law; Government Relations; Legislative Affairs. ***Email:*** nmglasgo@hklaw.com

NORMAN M. GLASGOW, JR., born Bethesda, Maryland, August 29, 1952; admitted to bar, 1977, Maryland; 1978, District of Columbia. *Education:* Georgetown University (B.A., 1974; J.D., 1977). Metropolitan Washington Airports Authority, Vice Chairman, Board of Directors, Chairman, Planning Committee. Member: Federal City Council, Washington Metropolitan Board of Trade, 1978; Washington Building Congress, 1982; Urban Land Institute, Full Member; D.C. Builders Association, 1983; Advisory Committee, Jubilee Support Foundation; President, Lambda Alpha - Land Economics Fraternity, George Washington Chapter. Board of Directors, National Center for Children & Families. *Member:* The District of Columbia Bar (Member, Zoning and Land Use Section); Maryland State Bar Association. ***PRACTICE AREAS:*** Real Estate; Zoning, Planning and Land Use; Municipal Law; Historic Preservation. ***Email:*** nglasgow@hklaw.com

RICHARD M. GOLD, born Jackson Heights, New York, January 13, 1964; admitted to bar, 1988, Virginia; 1989, District of Columbia. *Education:* University of Vermont (B.S., 1985); George Washington University (J.D., with honors, 1988). Special Assistant to Senator Lloyd Bentsen, 1991-1992. Special Assistant to EPA Administrator Carol M. Browner, 1993-1994. Practice Area Leader for Holland & Knight's Federal Practice Group. *Member:* The Virginia Bar; The District of Columbia Bar; American Bar Association (Member, Sections on: Natural Resources and Energy and Environmental Law). ***PRACTICE AREAS:*** Environmental Law; Federal Practice; Federal Litigation; Legislative Law; Administrative Law. ***Email:*** rgold@hklaw.com

ARTHUR B. GOODKIND, born New York, N.Y., August 17, 1935; admitted to bar, 1960, District of Columbia. *Education:* Wesleyan University (B.A., 1956); Harvard University (LL.B., 1960). Attorney, 1960-1966 and Assistant to Chairman, 1965-1966, Federal Communications Commission. *Member:* District of Columbia Bar; American Bar Association; Federal Communications Bar Association. ***PRACTICE AREAS:*** Telecommunications Law. ***Email:*** agoodkin@hklaw.com

STEVEN D. GORDON, born Detroit, Michigan, November 14, 1949; admitted to bar, 1975, Oklahoma and District of Columbia; 1980, U.S. Supreme Court. *Education:* Swarthmore College (B.A., with high honors, 1971); Harvard University (J.D., cum laude, 1974). Phi Beta Kappa. Law Clerk to Hon. William J. Holloway, Jr., U.S. Court of Appeals for the Tenth Circuit, 1974-1975. Assistant U.S. Attorney, District of Columbia, 1975-1986. *Member:* The District of Columbia Bar. ***PRACTICE AREAS:*** White Collar Criminal Litigation; Civil Litigation; Administrative Procedure Act Litigation. ***Email:*** sgordon@hklaw.com

ROBERT L. GORHAM, born Akron, Ohio, November 6, 1942; admitted to bar, 1974, District of Columbia; 1980, Maryland. *Education:* Miami University (B.A., 1964); George Washington University (M.B.A., 1971); National Law Center, George Washington University (J.D., with honors, 1974). Omicron Delta Kappa; Pi Sigma Alpha. Assistant to the Associate Director for Fiscal Matters, Division of Naval Reactors, U.S. Atomic Energy Commission, 1968-1972. *Member:* The District of Columbia Bar; Bar Association of the District of Columbia; Montgomery County, Maryland State and American (Member, Section of Real Property, Probate and Trust Law) Bar Associations; American College of Real Estate Lawyers; Mortgage Bankers Association of Metropolitan Washington, Inc. (Income Property Committee, 1988-1993); Washington, D.C. Association of Realtors, Inc.; D.C. Building Industry Association (Legislative Governmental Affairs Committee, 1988); National Association of Industrial and Office Parks; American Land Title Association. [Lt. Comdr., U.S. Navy, 1964-1972]. ***PRACTICE AREAS:*** Commercial Transactional Real Estate; Commercial Real Estate Acquisitions and Sales; Finance; Leasing; Loan Workouts; Foreclosure; Secured Creditor Bankruptcy Representation. ***Email:*** rgorham@hklaw.com

T. WAYNE GRAY, born Roanoke, Virginia, July 21, 1944; admitted to bar, 1969, Virginia; 1980, District of Columbia. *Education:* Virginia Military Institute (B.A., 1966); University of Virginia (LL.B., 1969). Co-Editor: Quarterly Report on International Construction Disputes Decisions, International Bar Association, 1985—. Author: "New Approaches To Solving Major Problems in International Construction Contracting," Euro Conferences, 1985. Co-Author: "Resolving International Construction Claims," Crown Eagle Communications, Ltd., 1984. Saudi Arabia District Counsel, U.S. Army Corps of Engineers, 1975-1978. Trial and Claims Attorney, U.S. Army, (Vietnam, Germany and Italy), 1969-1974. *Member:* Virginia State Bar; District of Columbia Bar; Federal, American (Vice Chair, 1997-1998, Co-Chair, 1998—, Middle Eastern Law Committee, International Law Section) and International Bar Associations.

(This Listing Continued)

[Capt. JAGC, U.S. Army, 1969-1975]. ***LANGUAGES:*** German, French and Italian. ***PRACTICE AREAS:*** Project Finance; Construction; Government Contracts; International Law. ***Email:*** twgray@hklaw.com

CHRISTOPHER B. HANBACK, born Washington, D.C., March 13, 1950; admitted to bar, 1975, Illinois; 1976, District of Columbia. *Education:* Duke University (A.B., cum laude, 1972); Northwestern University (J.D., cum laude, 1975). Order of the Coif. Member, Editorial Board, Northwestern University Law Review, 1975. Author: "Right of Reply Statutes: Unconstitutional Abridgement of the Freedom of the Printed Press," 69 Northwestern University Law Review 143, 1974; "Apartment Owners' Rights and Cable Television," Journal of Property Management (May/June, 1993); "Fair Housing and Seniors - What's Legal?" Multifamily Executive Magazine, Dec., 1998; "Building Wiring Agreements-It's All About Negotiations," Multifamily Executive Magazine, April 2001. Law Clerk to United States District Judge Richard W. McLaren, Northern District of Illinois, 1975-1976. Senior Vice President and General Counsel, National Corporation for Housing Partnerships, 1990. Program Chairman, Washington Metropolitan Area Corporate Counsel Association, 1988-1990. Member, American Society of Association Executives. *Member:* The District of Columbia Bar (Co-Chair, Corporate Counsel Committee Section 3, 1984-1988); American Bar Association (Chair, Residential Landlord and Tenant/Property Management Committee, 1993-1997; Member, Membership Committee, 1998-2002; Books and Media, Acquisition Editor, 2000-2002; Section of Real Property, Probate and Trust Law); American Seniors Housing Association (Member, Board of Directors, 2000-2002); National Multi Housing Council (Chair, Lawyers Forum, 2000-2001). ***PRACTICE AREAS:*** Real Estate; Fair Housing; Americans with Disabilities Act; Telecommunications; Senior Citizen Housing; Trade Associations. ***Email:*** chanback@hklaw.com

MICHAEL R. HATCHER, born Gloucester, Massachusetts, July 3, 1962; admitted to bar, 1987, Massachusetts; 1989, District of Columbia; 1994, Maryland. *Education:* Dartmouth College (A.B., cum laude, 1984); Georgetown University (J.D., cum laude, 1987). ***Email:*** mhatcher@hklaw.com

ROBIN BELTON HAYES, born Winston-Salem, North Carolina, November 21, 1959; admitted to bar, 1986, Florida; 1988, District of Columbia. *Education:* University of North Carolina at Chapel Hill (B.A., 1981); University of Florida (J.D., with honors, 1986). *Member:* The District of Columbia Bar (Member, Section on Real Estate, Housing and Land Use; Chair, Zoning and Land Use Committee, 1992-1993); The Florida Bar; District of Columbia Building Industry Association (Vice Chair, Legislative Government Affairs Committee, 1995-1996). ***PRACTICE AREAS:*** Commercial Leasing; Zoning; Land Use; Commercial Leasing. ***Email:*** rbhayes@hklaw.com

ERIC B. HOLMBERG, born Cleveland, Ohio, October 25, 1960; admitted to bar, 1989, Virginia; 1991, District of Columbia. *Education:* Pennsylvania State University (B.S.B.A., 1983); George Mason University (J.D., 1989). *Member:* Virginia Bar Association; The District of Columbia Bar. ***Email:*** eholmber@hklaw.com

DENNIS M. HORN, born Elmira, New York, April 10, 1950; admitted to bar, 1976, District of Columbia; 1978, Florida. *Education:* University of Rochester (B.A., magna cum laude, 1972); London School of Economics (M.S., 1973); University of Pennsylvania (J.D., 1976). Phi Beta Kappa. Author: Project Manager, "Mapping the Steps Towards Economic Revitalization," Policy Papers for D.C. Commerce Board, 1998; "Developing and Financing Retirement Center Housing," Real Estate Finance, 1985; "Negotiating a Commercial Real Estate Acquisition Contract," *Negotiating Real Estate Transactions,* John Wiley & Sons, 1988-1993. Associate Editor, Real Property of Probate Magazine, 1993-1995; "Drafting For Partner Liability in Law Firm Leases," The Practical Real Estate Lawyer, May 1994. *Member:* The District of Columbia Bar; The Florida Bar; American Bar Association (Member, Sections on: Real Property; Probate and Trust Law; Leasing Publications Committee (Chair); Managing Editor, ABA *Commercial Leasing Symposium,* 1994-1996). ***PRACTICE AREAS:*** Commercial Real Estate Development; Finance Law; Commercial Leasing; Business and Financial Restructuring. ***Email:*** dhorn@hklaw.com

EDWARD W. HUMMERS, JR., born New York, N.Y., May 31, 1936; admitted to bar, 1964, Maryland, District of Columbia and U.S. Court of Appeals for the District of Columbia Circuit; 1967, U.S. Supreme Court; 1993, Virginia. *Education:* Lehigh University (B.S., 1958); George Washington University (J.D., 1964). *Member:* The District of Columbia Bar; Bar Association of the District of Columbia; Virginia State Bar; American Bar Association; The Barristers; Federal Communications Bar Association (President, 1979-1980). ***PRACTICE AREAS:*** Telecommunications. ***Email:*** ehummers@hklaw.com

MARGOT SMILEY HUMPHREY, born Washington, D.C., November 9, 1944; admitted to bar, 1969, District of Columbia. *Education:* Wellesley College (B.A., 1966); Harvard University (J.D., cum laude, 1969). Wellesley Scholar. *Member:* The District of Columbia Bar; Federal Communications Bar Association; American Bar Association. ***PRACTICE AREAS:*** Telecommunication Law. ***Email:*** mhumphre@hklaw.com

THOMAS J. HUTTON, born King City, California, May 17, 1956; admitted to bar, 1981, District of Columbia. *Education:* Georgetown University

(This Listing Continued)

HOLLAND & KNIGHT LLP, Washington—Continued

(B.S.F.S., 1978); Boalt Hall School of Law, University of California (J.D., 1981). Associate Editor, California Law Review, 1980-1981. ***PRACTICE AREAS:*** Communications. ***Email:*** thutton@hklaw.com

DAVID S. KAHN, born New York, N.Y., 1951; admitted to bar, 1976, Virginia and District of Columbia; 1981, Pennsylvania. *Education:* Cornell University (A.B., with distinction, 1973); George Washington University (J.D., with highest honors, 1976). Member, Order of the Coif. Law Clerk to Judge John F. Doyle, Superior Court of the District of Columbia, 1976-1977. Member, Editorial Advisory Board: District of Columbia Real Estate Reporter, 1987—; The Corridor Real Estate Journal, 1993—. ***PRACTICE AREAS:*** Commercial Real Estate Finance; Acquisitions and Dispositions; Loan Workouts; Commercial Leasing. ***Email:*** dkahn@hklaw.com

SAMUEL P. KASTNER, born Rochester, New York, January 12, 1954; admitted to bar, 1978, District of Columbia and U.S. Tax Court. *Education:* State University of New York at Binghamton (B.S., magna cum laude, 1975); Georgetown University Law Center (J.D., 1978; M.L.T., 1982). Author: "Family Limited Partnerships in the District of Columbia," National Business Institute, Inc. Seminar, April 1995; "How Should Your Business Be Organized?" Info-Text, The Interactive Telephone Magazine, December 1991; "Fiduciary Responsibilities and Prohibited Transactions under ERISA," AICPA National Conference on Tax-Advantaged Compensation Planning, November, 1985 and September, 1986; "Permissible Uses of Plan Assets," ALI-ABA/AICPA Course Incorporating the Law or CPA Firm, May 1982 and January 1983. *Member:* District of Columbia Bar; American Bar Association (Member, Sections on: Taxation; Corporation, Banking and Business Law). ***PRACTICE AREAS:*** Business Planning; Corporate Law; Taxation Law; Estates. ***Email:*** skastner@hklaw.com

PAUL J. KIERNAN, born Teaneck, New Jersey, April 4, 1958; admitted to bar, 1983, New Jersey; 1985, District of Columbia; 1990, Maryland; U.S. Supreme Court; U.S. Court of Appeals for the District of Columbia; U.S. Court of Appeals, Third and Fourth Circuits; U.S. District Court for the District of Columbia and U.S. Bankruptcy Court; U.S. District Court, District of Maryland and U.S. Bankruptcy Court. *Education:* Rutgers University (B.A., magna cum laude, 1980); Harvard University (J.D., cum laude, 1983). Law Clerk to Justice Daniel J. O'Hern, New Jersey Supreme Court, 1983-1984. Associate and Partner, Dunnells, Duvall, Bennett & Porter, 1984-1993. Partner, Holland & Knight, 1994-1997. Partner, Wilkes, Artis, Hedrick & Lane, 1997-2000. ***REPORTED CASES:*** National Cathedral Neighborhood Ass'n v. D.C. Board of Zoning Adjustment, 753 A.2d 984 (D.C. 2000); Hotel Tabard Inn v. D.C. Department of Consumer & Regulatory Affairs, 747 A.2d 1168 (D.C. 2000); Cathedral Park Condominium Committee v. D.C. Zoning Commission, 743 A.2d 1231 (D.C. 2000); Board of Supervisors of Fairfax County v. Washington, D.C. SMSA L.P., 258 Va. 558, 522 S.E.2d 876 (1999); Chevy Chase Land Co. v. U.S., 355 Md. 110, 733 A.2d 1055 (1999); Burka v. Aetna Life Ins. Co., 312 U.S.App.D.C. 439, 56 F.3d 1509 (1995), on remand, 894 F.Supp. 28 (D.D.C. 1995), aff'd, 318 U.S.App.D.C. 244, 87 F.3d 478 (1996); District of Columbia v. Group Insurance Admin., 633 A.2d 2 (D.C.1993). ***PRACTICE AREAS:*** Commercial Litigation; Real Property Litigation; Land Use Disputes; Eminent Domain; Landlord and Tenant Law; Development Litigation; Administrative Litigation; Appellate Practice; Federal Civil Practice. ***Email:*** pkiernan@hklaw.com

PAUL F. KILMER, born Iowa Falls, Iowa, July 26, 1953; admitted to bar, 1980, District of Columbia; 1984, U.S. Court of Appeals for the Federal Circuit; 1995, U.S. Supreme Court. *Education:* University of Northern Iowa (B.A., cum laude, 1975); Washington College of Law of American University (J.D., 1980). Author of Works on Intellectual Property Law appearing in the Trademark Reporter, Intellectual Property Review of the PTIC, Advertising Age and elsewhere. Lecturer on Intellectual Property Issues: Hong Kong, 1988; Thailand, 1988; Republic of China, 1989; United States Trademark Association, 1991 and 1992; D.C. Bar Seminars, 1994 and 1995; International Trademark Association, 1995; Mass. Continuing Legal Education Internet Forum, 1996; U.S. Department of State, 1996; ABA, Third Annual Federal Procurement Institute, 1997; Society of Civil Engineers, 1998, U.S/India Chamber of Commerce, 1999; American Federation of Teachers Lawyers' Conference, 1999. D.C. Bar Committee Chair and Steering Council Member, 1993-1999. Chair, International Trademark Association Committee and Subcommittee Chair, 1990—. Delegate of the International Trademark Association to Paraguay Intellectual Property Rights Mission of the U.S. Department of State, 1997. ***PRACTICE AREAS:*** Copyrights; Trademarks; Unfair Competition; Transactional and Internet Law Issues. ***Email:*** pkilmer@hklaw.com

BERNARD KOTEEN, born Paterson, New Jersey, November 8, 1915; admitted to bar, 1940, District of Columbia. *Education:* Oberlin College and University of Wisconsin (B.A., 1937); Harvard University (LL.B., 1940). Chief, Review Section, Federal Communications Commission, 1946-1948. *Member:* The District of Columbia Bar; American Bar Association; Federal Communications Bar Association. [Lieut. Commander, U.S.N.R., 1942-1945]. ***PRACTICE AREAS:*** Telecommunications Law. ***Email:*** bkoteen@hklaw.com

(This Listing Continued)

DEBORAH L. KRAMM, admitted to bar, 1977, Massachusetts and U.S. Court of Appeals for the Federal Circuit; 1978, District of Columbia; 1979, Illinois; 1982, New York. *Education:* Trinity College; Bradley University (B.S., 1974); New England School of Law (J.D., 1977). Phi Alpha Theta; Phi Alpha Delta. Member, Board of Trustees, The Martha Graham Dance Company, 1989—. Member, New York Board, National Foundation for Advancement in the Arts, 1988-1991. Member, Board of Directors, International Trademark Association, 1985-1989. *Member:* The District of Columbia Bar; American Bar Association. ***PRACTICE AREAS:*** Trademarks; Licensing; Copyrights. ***Email:*** dkramm@hklaw.com

WELDON H. LATHAM, born Brooklyn, New York, January 2, 1947; admitted to bar, 1972, District of Columbia; 1975 U.S. Supreme Court; 1982, Virginia. *Education:* Howard University (B.A., 1968); Georgetown University (J.D., 1971). Practice Area Leader, Holland & Knight, LLP, 2001-present; Senior Partner, Shaw, Pittman, Potts, & Trowbridge, 1992-2000; Managing Partner, Virginia Office, Reed, Smith, Shaw, & McClay, LLP, 1986-1992. Guest Professor, University of Virginia Law School, 1976-1991. Adjunct Professor, Howard University School of Law, 1972-1982. *Career Highlights:* Executive Assistant and Counsel to the Chairman and CEO, Planning Research Corporation, 1983-1986. Vice President and General Counsel, Sterling Systems Incorporated, 1981-1983. General Deputy Assistant Secretary, U.S. Department of Housing and Urban Development, 1979-1981. Assistant General Counsel, Executive Office of the President, The White House, Office of Management and Budget, 1974-1976. Office of the Secretary of the Air Force, General Counsel's Honors Program, The Pentagon, 1973-1974. *Awards/Honors:* Honorary Vice Chair, Clinton/Gore Campaign, 1996. Advocate of the Year, Minority Business Development Agency, U.S. Department of Commerce, 1996. Memberships/Activities: TeleCommunication Systems, Inc., 1999-; Board of Trustees, American University 1999-; Member: Economic Club of Washington, D.C., 1998-2000; Metropolitan Washington Airports Authority, 1997—; Board of Governors, Joint Center for Political and Economic Studies, 1997—Board of Advisors, First Union National Bank, 1995-1999; U.S. Small Business Administrator's National Advisory Council, 1994-1999. General Counsel, National Coalition of Minority Businesses, 1994—. Columnist *Minority Business Entrepreneur* Magazine, 1991—. Member: Board of Directors, Washington Hospital Center Foundation, 1996-1999; Burger King Corporation Diversity Action Council, 1996-1997; Maryland Economic Development Commission, 1996-1997. Chairman, District of Columbia Mayor's Business Advisory Council, 1994-1995. Civilian Aide to the Secretary of the Army, 1994-1998. Member, Maryland Governor's Transition Team, 1994. Member, Board of Directors, Chairman Regional Affairs Committee and Corporate Secretary, Greater Washington Board of Trade, 1991-1995. Member: U.S. Department of Defense Advisory Committee on Technical Data Rights, 1991-1992; Board of Visitors, George Mason University, 1990-1994; American Bar Association Section on Public Contract Law, Vice Chair Socio-Economic Policies and Regulations Committee, 1990-1993; Board of Directors, Washington Urban League, 1986-1990; Board of Visitors, Virginia Commonwealth University, 1985-1989; Editorial Advisory Board, *Washington Business Journal,* 1985-1988; Virginia Governor's Regulatory Reform Advisory Board, 1982-1984; Washington Steering Committee NAACP Legal Defense & Education Fund, 1976-1996. ***PRACTICE AREAS:*** Corporate Diversity Counseling; Government Contracts; Corporate; Government Relations; Corporate Law; Employment Law; Legislation. ***Email:*** wlatham@hklaw.com

RICHARD E. LEAR, born Keene, New Hampshire, March 10, 1958; admitted to bar, 1983, New Hampshire; 1985, Virginia, U.S. Court of Appeals, Fourth Circuit and U.S. Bankruptcy Court, Eastern District of Virginia; 1986, District of Columbia, U.S. District Court, District of Columbia and U.S. Bankruptcy Court, District of Columbia; 1987, U.S. District Court, District of Maryland and U.S. Bankruptcy Court, District of Maryland; 1992, U.S. District Court, Eastern and Western Districts of Virginia and U.S. Bankruptcy Court, Western District of Virginia. *Education:* University of New Hampshire (B.A., magna cum laude, 1980); Washington & Lee University School of Law (J.D., 1983). Phi Beta Kappa; Pi Sigma Alpha; Pi Gamma Mu. Member, Washington & Lee Law Review, 1982-1983. Law Clerk to the Honorable Martin V. B. Bostetter, Jr., Chief Bankruptcy Judge, Eastern District of Virginia, 1983-1985. Lecturer on Bankruptcy and Creditors' Rights, Virginia Continuing Legal Education, 1990-1994; District of Columbia Bar Continuing Legal Education, 1998—. *Member:* District of Columbia Bar; New Hampshire, Virginia and American Bar Associations; Virginia State Bar; American Bankruptcy Institute (Member, Subcommittee on Secured Creditors); Northern Virginia Bankruptcy Bar Association; Bankruptcy Mediation Panel, Eastern District of Virginia, Alexandria Division. ***REPORTED CASES:*** Robbins v. Chase Manhatten Bank, N.A., 1994 WL 149597 (W.D. Va. 1994); Robbins v. Chase Manhatten Bank, N.A., 1993 WL 310632 (W.D. Va. 1993); Consolidated Rail Corp. v. Dicello, 121 B.R. 406 (Sp.Ct.R.R.R.A. 1990); In re Fay Assocs. L.P., 225 B.R. 1 (Bankr. D. D.C. 1998); In re 1560 Wilson Blvd. L.P., 206 B.R. 819 (Bankr. E.D. Va. 1996); In re 1550 Wilson Blvd. L.P., 206 B.R. 812 (Bankr. E.D. Va. 1996); In re Monica Rd. Assocs., 147 B.R. 385 (Bankr. E.D. Va. 1992); In re

(This Listing Continued)

Walt Robbins, Inc., 129 B.R. 452 (Bankr. E.D. Va. 1991). ***PRACTICE AREAS:*** Bankruptcy; Litigation; Workouts; Creditor Rights; Commercial Law; Transactional Matters. ***Email:*** rlear@hklaw.com

LAWRENCE R. LIEBESMAN, born Long Branch, New Jersey, 1947; admitted to bar, 1974, District of Columbia; 1975, U.S. District Court for the District of Columbia; 1976, U.S. Court of Appeals for the District of Columbia Circuit; 1980, Maryland, U.S. Claims Court and U.S. Supreme Court. *Education:* Rutgers University (B.A., magna cum laude, 1969); George Washington University (J.D., with honors, 1973). Phi Beta Kappa. Author: "Developer's Guide to Federal Wetlands Regulation," National Association of Homebuilders, 1990 and "The Water Supplier's Guide to Wetlands Regulation and Management," American Water Works Association, 1996. U.S. Environmental Protection Agency, 1974-1976. Senior Trial Attorney, Environment and Natural Resources Division, U.S. Department of Justice, 1977-1987. Special Detail to President's Council on Environmental Quality, 1978-1980. *Member:* American Bar Association (Member, Section on Natural Resources, Energy and Environmental Law). ***PRACTICE AREAS:*** Natural Resources Law; Administrative Law; Environmental Law. ***Email:*** lliebesm@hklaw.com

GEORGE T. MAGEE, born Philadelphia, Pennsylvania, October 24, 1960; admitted to bar, 1985, Maryland; 1987, District of Columbia. *Education:* La Salle College (B.A., magna cum laude, 1982); American University (J.D., 1985). *Member:* The District of Columbia Bar; Maryland State and American Bar Associations. ***PRACTICE AREAS:*** Real Estate Development Law; Finance Law. ***Email:*** gmagee@hklaw.com

KENNETH L. MARCUS, born Sharon, Massachusetts, October 7, 1966; admitted to bar, 1992, Pennsylvania; 1993, District of Columbia; 1995, U.S. District Court for the District of Columbia and U.S. Court of Appeals, Eleventh Circuit; 1996, U.S. Court of Federal Claims; 1998, U.S. Court of Appeals, Ninth and Federal Circuits; 1999, U.S. Supreme Court. *Education:* Williams College (B.A., magna cum laude, 1988); University of California, Boalt Hall School of Law (J.D., 1991). Phi Beta Kappa. ***PRACTICE AREAS:*** Trial and Appellate Litigation; Financial Services Litigation; Constitutional Litigation. ***Email:*** kmarcus@hklaw.com

CAROL L. B. MATTHEWS, born Detroit, Michigan, April 17, 1945; admitted to bar, 1971, District of Columbia; 1982, U.S. Court of Customs and Patent Appeals; 1972, U.S. Court of Appeals for the District of Columbia Circuit; 1982, U.S. Court of Appeals for the Federal Circuit. *Education:* University of Michigan (B.A., 1965); University of North Carolina (LL.B., 1970). *Member:* The District of Columbia Bar; American Bar Association; American Intellectual Property Law Association (AIPLA); International Association for the Protection of Industrial Property (AIPPI), (Member, Trademark and Tradename Section). ***PRACTICE AREAS:*** Trademark Law; Copyright Law. ***Email:*** cmatthews@hklaw.com

DONALD H. MEIERS, born 1958; admitted to bar, 1987, New York; 1989, District of Columbia. *Education:* Dickinson College (B.A., Economics, summa cum laude, 1980); Cornell University Johnson Graduate School of Management (M.B.A., Finance, 1985); Cornell University (J.D., Business Law, 1986). Phi Beta Kappa. Author of "The DOs and DON'Ts: Best Practices for 'Fair Disclosure' Following the SEC's Adoption of Regulation FD" (2000); "Rule 10b5-1 Trading Plans: A Win-Win Situation" (2001). Staff Attorney, U.S. Securities and Exchange Commission, Division of Corporate Finance, 1994-1996. *Member:* The District of Columbia Bar (Member, Corporation, Finance and Securities Section); New York State and American Bar Associations. ***SPECIAL AGENCIES:*** U.S. Securities and Exchange Commission. ***PRACTICE AREAS:*** Securities Law; Mergers and Acquisitions; General Corporate Law. ***Email:*** dmeiers@hklaw.com

PETER T. MESZOLY, born Budapest, Hungary, May, 18, 1943; admitted to bar, 1971, District of Columbia; 1984, Maryland. *Education:* Lehigh University (A.B., cum laude, 1965); Duke University (J.D., with distinction, 1971). Attorney, Chief Counsel for Civil Rights, General Services Administration, 1971-1973. Assistant Director and General Counsel, U.S. Pennsylvania Avenue Development Corporation, 1973-1982. *Member:* The District of Columbia Bar; Maryland State Bar Association, Inc. [1st Lt., U.S. Army Reserve, Two years active duty in Germany and France, 1965-1967.]. ***LANGUAGES:*** Hungarian and German. ***PRACTICE AREAS:*** Commercial Real Estate; Multi-Family Housing. ***Email:*** pmeszoly@hklaw.com

DAVID P. METZGER, born Milwaukee, Wisconsin, April 25, 1948; admitted to bar, 1974, Wisconsin; 1982, District of Columbia; 1983, Virginia. *Education:* University of Wisconsin (B.A., with Honors, 1970; J.D., 1974). Former President, Board of Contract Appeals Bar Association. Past Chairman, Bid Protest Working Group, Professional Services Council. Member, Federal Contracts Report Advisory Board, 1991—. Author, Publications: A Privatization Alternative: The Department of Veteran's Affairs' Enhanced-Use Leasing Program, (co-authored), ABA Public Contract Law Journal, Summer, 2001; Regulations, Risk & Opportunities, Department of Defense/National Science Foundation High Technology Conference, Washington, DC, Spring, 2000; The DIVAD Decision: Another Scanwell Sea Change or Merely A Torncello Ripple? (co-authored), Federal Contracts Report, Bureau of National Affairs, July 22,

(This Listing Continued)

1996; GAO's Proposed Bid Protest Rules: On the Road to an Improved Process (co-authored), Federal Contracts Report, Bureau of National Affairs, April 3, 1995; Government Contractor Teaming Arrangements and The Antitrust Laws -- A Brief Comment on United States v. Alliant Techsystems and Aerojet-General Corporation (co-authored), Federal Contracts Report, Bureau of National Affairs, March 28, 1994; Emerging Trends in Research and Technology, a speech presented at The Consortium for Plant Biotechnology Research Symposium (Chicago) (1993). Co-Instructor, Advanced Issues Procurement Workshop, Educational Services Institute. ***PRACTICE AREAS:*** Government Contracts Law; Litigation. ***Email:*** dmetzger@hklaw.com

NELSON F. MIGDAL, born Bronx, New York, May 4, 1953; admitted to bar, 1979, New York and U.S. District Court, Northern District of New York; 1988, District of Columbia. *Education:* Hofstra University (B.A., cum laude, 1975); Albany Law School of Union University (J.D., cum laude, 1978). Phi Sigma Alpha. Member, Albany Law Review, 1977-1978. Member, The Justinian Society. Adjunct Faculty, Broome Community College, 1985-1988. Author: "The Model Agreement" for Telecommunications Building Access; "Building Access Made Easy," A Continuing Legal Education Program. Contributing Author, Corridor Real Estate Journal, Legal Times & Washington Business Journal. Instructor: Real Estate Training Institute, 1986; Graduate Realtor Institute, 1991-1995; Real Estate Education Foundation, 1992-1994; National Education Network, 1992-1995; Commercial Property News, 1998-2000. Featured Speaker: Commercial Property News, 1999—; BOMA Broadband Conferences, 2000-2001; IRR Building Access Conferences, 2000-2001; The Lodging Conference, 1999-2001. Member: District of Columbia Building Industry Association Executive Council; Editor, Property Writes, 1997-2000. Co-Chair, Hospitality Industry Practice Group. *Member:* American Bar Association; District of Columbia Bar. ***Email:*** nmigdal@hklaw.com

WILLIAM J. MUTRYN, born Schenectady, New York, June 7, 1948; admitted to bar, 1975, Maryland and District of Columbia. *Education:* Case Western Reserve University (B.S., 1970); George Washington University (J.D., cum laude, 1975). Order of the Coif. Member, George Washington Law Review, 1973-1975. *Member:* The District of Columbia Bar; Maryland State Bar Association, Inc.; American Bar Association. ***PRACTICE AREAS:*** Corporate Law; Securities; Mergers and Acquisitions; Health Care Law; Finance Law. ***Email:*** wmutryn@hklaw.com

CHRISTOPHER A. MYERS, born Mt. Vernon, New York, December 9, 1949; admitted to bar, 1977, Virginia; 1979, District of Columbia and U.S. Court of Appeals for the District of Columbia Circuit; 1983, U.S. District Court for the District of Columbia; 1984, U.S. District Court, Eastern District of Virginia; 1985, U.S. Court of Appeals, Fourth Circuit and U.S. District Court, Western District of Virginia; 1989, U.S. Supreme Court; 1992, U.S. District Court, District of Maryland and U.S.Court of Appeals, Federal Circuit; 2000, Maryland. *Education:* Kenyon College (B.A. cum laude, 1971); Catholic University of America (J.D., 1977). Assistant U.S. Attorney for the District of Columbia, 1979-1984. Law Clerk to Hon. W. Byron Sorrell, Superior Court of the District of Columbia, 1977-1979. Member, Litigation Section, American Bar Association, 1984—. Faculty Member, National Institute for Trial Advocacy, 1987—. Associate Professorial Lecturer-in-Law, The George Washington University, 1989-1992. Co-author: "Looking Closely at Doctors' Bills," Legal Times, March 4, 1996. Co-Author "Investigations in the Health Care Industry," in Corporate Fraud Investigations and Compliance Programs, (Oceana Publications, Inc. 2000); author of "Practical Solutions to High Cost, Complexity of Corporate Compliance Programs," Health Care Fraud Report, Vol. 4, No. 22 (BNA 11/15/2000); "Corporate Compliance Programs: The Benefits Extend Far Beyond the Criminal Prosecution Context," Vol. 7, No. 6 (The Metropolitan Corporate Counsel 6/1999). *Member:* American Bar Association (Member, Section of Litigation; Criminal Justice Section; Health Law Section); American Health Lawyers Association. ***PRACTICE AREAS:*** Complex Civil and Criminal Litigation; White Collar Criminal Defense and Compliance Programs; Health Care. ***Email:*** cmyers@hklaw.com

ALAN Y. NAFTALIN, born Minneapolis, Minnesota, May 1, 1926; admitted to bar, 1952, District of Columbia; 1954, U.S. Court of Appeals for the District of Columbia; 1965, U.S. Supreme Court; 1967, U.S. Court of Appeals, Sixth Circuit; 1975, U.S. Court of Federal Claims and U.S. Court of Appeals, Tenth Circuit; 1996, U.S. Court of Appeals, Third and Fifth Circuits. *Education:* Yale University (B.A., 1949; LL.B., 1952). Order of the Coif. Member, Editorial Board, Yale Law Journal, 1951-1952. Attorney, Federal Communications Commission, 1952-1953. Associate, 1953-1960 and Partner, 1960-2000, Koteen & Naftalin, Washington, D.C. *Member:* The District of Columbia Bar; American Bar Association; Federal Communications Bar Association. [United States Army, 1943-1946]. ***PRACTICE AREAS:*** Telecommunication Law. ***Email:*** anaftali@hklaw.com

CHARLES R. NAFTALIN, born Washington, D.C., September 20, 1958; admitted to bar, 1985, District of Columbia. *Education:* Oberlin College (A.B., 1979); Seattle University School of Law (J.D., cum laude, 1985). *Member:* The District of Columbia Bar; American Bar Association; Federal Communications Bar Association. ***PRACTICE AREAS:*** Telecommunications Law. ***Email:*** cnaftali@hklaw.com

(This Listing Continued)

HOLLAND & KNIGHT LLP, Washington—Continued

LA FONTE NESBITT, born Spartanburg, South Carolina, November 16, 1958; admitted to bar, 1988, Virginia; 1989, District of Columbia; 1991, U.S. District Court, Eastern District of Virginia. *Education:* James Madison University (B.S., cum laude, 1980); University of Virginia (J.D., 1988). Pi Gamma Mu; Omicron Delta Kappa. *Member:* Virginia State Bar; District of Columbia Bar (Member, Real Estate, Housing and Land Use Section); American Bar Association (Member: Real Property, Probate and Trust Law; Forum on Affordable Housing and Community Development Law). ***PRACTICE AREAS:*** Multi-family Housing Finance and Development; Commercial Real Estate Finance and Development; Community Development; Military Housing; Privatization. ***Email:*** lnesbitt@hklaw.com

STEPHEN D. NILES, born Oceanside, New York, December 14, 1961; admitted to bar, 1987, Virginia; 1988, District of Columbia. *Education:* Franklin & Marshall College (B.A., 1984); American University (J.D., 1987). Senior Staff, The Administrative Law Journal of The American University, 1986-1987. *Member:* The District of Columbia Bar; Virginia State Bar; American Bar Association. ***PRACTICE AREAS:*** Housing Development; Housing Finance; Mortgage Banking; Commercial Real Estate. ***Email:*** sniles@hklaw.com

RONALD A. OLEYNIK, born Shelton, Connecticut, April 4, 1960; admitted to bar, 1990, District of Columbia; 1991, U.S. Court of International Trade and U.S. Court of Appeals for the Federal Circuit. *Education:* University of Connecticut (B.A., 1982); George Washington University (M.A., 1984; J.D., 1990). Author: "Paying for Sales Commissions," Legal Times, p.S31, September 9, 1996; "Information Security: New Encryption Rules Give U.S. Companies Opportunity to Compete," Metropolitan Corporate Counsel (May 2000) (co-authored with Jonathan Epstein). Co-Author: with Jonathan Epstein, "Information Security: New Encryption Rules Give U.S. Companies Opportunity to Compete," Metropolitan Corporate Counsel, May 2000. *Member:* The District of Columbia Bar; American Bar Association; Customs and International Trade Bar Association (Member, Committee on Customs and Tariffs); American Society of International Law. ***PRACTICE AREAS:*** International Trade; Customs; Export Controls. ***Email:*** roleynik@hklaw.com

TIMOTHY P. O'SHEA, born Brooklyn, New York, January 28, 1963; admitted to bar, 1995, New York (Not admitted in District of Columbia). *Education:* Yale University (B.A., 1985); New York University Leonard N. Stern School of Business (M.B.A., 1989); Fordham University (J.D., 1992). ***PRACTICE AREAS:*** Corporate; Finance. ***Email:*** toshea@hklaw.com

MARK J. PALCHICK, born Columbus, Ohio, June 13, 1950; admitted to bar, 1975, Pennsylvania; 1978, District of Columbia. *Education:* Miami University (B.A., 1971; M.A., 1972); Dickinson School of Law (J.D., 1975). Adjunct Professor: University of Colorado, 1980-1981; Dickinson School of Law, 1994—. *Member:* Pennsylvania and American Bar Associations; District of Columbia Bar; Federal Communications Bar Association; Washington Metropolitan Cable Association. ***PRACTICE AREAS:*** Communications and Media; Cable Communications Law. ***Email:*** mpalchick@hklaw.com

ALAN K. PALMER, born Bradford, Pennsylvania, February 9, 1941; admitted to bar, 1970, District of Columbia. *Education:* Dartmouth College (A.B., summa cum laude, 1963); Magdalen College, Oxford; Harvard University (J.D., magna cum laude, 1967). Law Clerk to: Hon. Stanley Barnes, U.S. Court of Appeals, Ninth Circuit, 1967-1968; Associate Justice Potter Stewart, U.S. Supreme Court, 1968-1969. ***PRACTICE AREAS:*** Litigation; Antitrust; Consumer Protection; Federal Indian Law. ***Email:*** apalmer@hklaw.com

FRANK K. PETERSON, born Erie, Pennsylvania, October 25, 1943; admitted to bar, 1981, District of Columbia; 1982, Maryland. *Education:* United States Naval Academy (B.S., 1965); United States Naval Postgraduate School (M.S., 1970); Georgetown University (J.D., magna cum laude, 1981). Editor, Georgetown Law Journal. Co-Chair, Information Systems Committee. *Member:* American Bar Association (Member, Public Contracts Law Section). [U.S. Marine Corps, 1965-1974; Marine Corps Reserves, 1974-1991]. ***PRACTICE AREAS:*** Government Contracts; Telecommunications; Information Technology. ***Email:*** fpeterso@hklaw.com

WHAYNE S. QUIN, born Louisville, Kentucky; admitted to bar, 1964, Tennessee; 1965, District of Columbia; 1997, Montana. *Education:* Vanderbilt University (B.A., 1959); University of Virginia (LL.B., 1964). Law Clerk to U.S. District Court Judges Joseph C. McGarraghy and David A. Pine, 1964-1966. ***PRACTICE AREAS:*** Real Estate; Zoning, Planning and Land Use; Municipal Law; Historic Preservation; Environmental Law. ***Email:*** wquin@hklaw.com

ROBERT L. RHODES, JR., born North East, Pennsylvania, May 5, 1947; admitted to bar, 1972, Florida; 1993, District of Columbia. *Education:* Emory University (B.A., with high honors, 1969); University of Virginia (J.D., 1972). Phi Beta Kappa; Order of the Coif. Selected Best Lawyers in America, 1999-2000. Member, Editorial Board, Virginia Law Review, 1971-1972. Chair, National Advisory Council for Environmental Policy and Technology, 1995—. Author: "Federal Resource Conservation and Recovery Act," Florida Environmental and Land Use Law, 1986 and 1988 Supplement. Author, "The Contract with America and Environmental Regulation: Some Unintended Consequences for Corporate America," *BNA Daily Environmental Report* (3/10/96); "Where Do We Go From Here? Reforming Our Environmental Laws in the 104th Congress," *BNA Environmental Reporter* (9/29/95). *Member:* The Florida Bar; American Bar Association (Member, 1998-2001, Chair, 2000-2001, Standing Committee on Environmental Law). [U.S. Air Force, 1972-1976]. ***PRACTICE AREAS:*** Environmental Law. ***Email:*** rrhodes@hklaw.com

MARVIN ROSENBERG, born Erie, Pennsylvania, April 4, 1936; admitted to bar, 1961, District of Columbia; 1968, U.S. Supreme Court; 1993, Virginia. *Education:* Gannon College (B.S. in B.A., cum laude, 1958); Georgetown University (J.D., 1961; LL.M. in Taxation, 1967). Staff Member, Georgetown Law Journal, 1959-1961. *Member:* The District of Columbia Bar; Bar Association of the District of Columbia; Virginia State Bar; American Bar Association; Federal Communications Bar Association. ***PRACTICE AREAS:*** Communications Law. ***Email:*** mrosenb@hklaw.com

STEVEN S. ROSENTHAL, born Cleveland, Ohio, May 22, 1949; admitted to bar, 1974, Florida; 1975, District of Columbia; 1983, California. *Education:* Dartmouth College (A.B., magna cum laude, 1971); Harvard Law School (J.D., magna cum laude, 1974). Phi Beta Kappa. Law Clerk to Judge Malcolm Richard Wilkey, U.S. Court of Appeals, District of Columbia Circuit, 1974-1975. President, 1986-1988, Vice President, 1981-1983 and Member, Board of Trustees, 1978-1983, 1985—, Family and Child Services of Washington, D.C. *Member:* American Law Institute. ***REPORTED CASES:*** Succesfully argued in the U.S. Supreme Court NationsBank v. VALIC, 513 U.S. 251 (1995); United States v. Hatter, 121 S.Ct. 1782 (2001). Counsel in over 40 reported cases. ***PRACTICE AREAS:*** Trial and Appellate Litigation; Administrative Law; Financial Institutions. ***Email:*** srosenth@hklaw.com

MICHAEL J. RUANE, born Scranton, Pennsylvania, 1946; admitted to bar, 1973, Maryland; 1974, District of Columbia. *Education:* University of Scranton (B.A., 1968); George Washington University (J.D., 1973). Order of the Coif. Notes Editor, George Washington Law Review, 1972-1973. Law Clerk to Judge John H. Pratt, U.S. District Court, District of Columbia, 1973-1974. *Member:* Maryland State and American Bar Associations. ***PRACTICE AREAS:*** Commercial Real Estate Financing; Commercial Real Estate Sales; Leasing; Hotel Management; Hotel Development; Partnerships; Joint Ventures; Lender Liability. ***Email:*** mruane@hklaw.com

ALBAN SALAMAN, born Philadelphia, Pennsylvania, 1949; admitted to bar, 1974, Pennsylvania; 1977, U.S. Tax Court; 1978, District of Columbia. *Education:* University of Pennsylvania (B.A., 1971); Temple University Law School (J.D., 1974); New York University Law School (LL.M., 1975); The American College (C.L.U., 1978). Attorney and Assistant Branch Chief, Interpretative Division Office of Chief Counsel, Internal Revenue Service, 1977-1983. Member: District of Columbia Estate Planning Council. ***PRACTICE AREAS:*** Estate Planning; Estate Administration; Employee Benefits; Tax. ***Email:*** asalaman@hklaw.com

TARA A. SCANLON, born Poughkeepsie, New York, May 13, 1966; admitted to bar, 1991, Connecticut; 1995, Virginia; 1996, District of Columbia. *Education:* Hamilton College (B.A., cum laude, with honors, Philosophy, 1988); University of Pennsylvania (J.D., 1991). *Member:* The District of Columbia Bar; Virginia State (Business Section) and American Bar Associations. ***PRACTICE AREAS:*** Commercial Real Estate; Business Law. ***Email:*** tscanlon@hklaw.com

JANIS B. SCHIFF, born Bridgeport, Connecticut, July 6, 1958; admitted to bar, 1983, Maryland; 1984, District of Columbia; 1985, U.S. District Court, District of Columbia and District of Maryland. *Education:* Brandeis University (B.S., 1980); Suffolk University (J.D., cum laude, 1983). Comment Editor, Suffolk Transnational Law Journal, 1982-1983. Author: "Case Comment - Presidential Powers - The Iranian Hostage Claims and Settlement Act - A Valid Exercise of Presidential Powers, Dames and Moore v. Regan, 101 S. Ct. 2972, 1981," Suffolk Transnational Law Journal 210, Vol. 6, No. 1, 1982. Law Clerk to the Honorable Alan Wilner, Maryland Court of Special Appeals, 1983-1984. Member, National Network of Commercial Real Estate Women. Member, Women in Retail Real Estate. Director, International Council of Shopping Centers, Maryland, District of Columbia, Northern Virginia, 1996-1999. *Member:* Montgomery County, Maryland State and American Bar Associations; The District of Columbia Bar; Women's Bar Association. ***LANGUAGES:*** Spanish. ***PRACTICE AREAS:*** Real Estate; Leasing; Commercial Law. ***Email:*** jschiff@hklaw.com

CHRISTOPHER "KIP" SCHWARTZ, born New York, N.Y., 1953; admitted to bar, 1980, New York; 1991, U.S. District Court, Southern and Eastern Districts of New York; 1994, District of Columbia and U.S. District Court for the District of Columbia; 1997, U.S. District Court, District of Maryland. *Education:* Hamilton College (B.A., 1975); New York Law School (J.D., 1980). Author, "A Copy is a Copy is a Copy;" April 1997 Legal Times Special Report on Intellectual Property. Staff Member, U.S. Congress House Committee on Interstate Commerce, 1975-1977. Senior Trial Attorney, Federal Trade Commission, 1980-1987. General Counsel, Barr Laboratories, Inc., 1988-1991. Partner, Graham & James, 1991-1996 and Chair, D.C. Litigation Practice Group for

(This Listing Continued)

(This Listing Continued)

Graham & James, 1994-1996. Partner, Holland & Knight, 1997—. *Member:* American Bar Association (Member, Section on Litigation). ***REPORTED CASES:*** ACS, etal. v. MAI Systems Corp., 845 F, Supp. 356 (1994). ***PRACTICE AREAS:*** Litigation; Intellectual Property; Employment Law. ***Email:*** cschwart@hklaw.com

STEPHEN BRETT SHAPIRO, born Minneapolis, Minnesota, August 23, 1962; admitted to bar, 1987, Virginia; 1988, District of Columbia. *Education:* University of Maryland (B.A., 1984); George Washington University (J.D., 1987). Co-Author: "Construction Claims Deskbook," Wiley Law, 1996; "Notice Provisions in Construction Contracts, Construction Briefing," Federal Publications, Inc., February 1993; "Cost Principles & Accounting in Federal Government Contracts, Construction Briefings," Federal Publications, Inc., October, 1991. Author: "Quantum Meruit Recovery, Construction Briefings," Federal Publications, Inc., July 1988. Member, Forum on the Construction Industry. *Member:* The District of Columbia Bar; Virginia and American Bar Associations; National Contract Management Association. ***PRACTICE AREAS:*** Government Contracts; Construction Law; Litigation. ***Email:*** sshapiro@hklaw.com

STEVEN E. SHER, born Brooklyn, New York, May 9, 1948; (admission pending). *Education:* Brooklyn College (B.A., 1969); Cornell University (M.R.P., 1971). Executive Director, District of Columbia Zoning Secretariat, 1977-1985. Member, Mayor's Commission on Downtown Housing, District of Columbia, 1988-1989. Member, Metropolitan Council of Governments, Metropolitan Development Policy Committee, Community Advisory Committee, 1997—. Member: Lambda Alpha (Honorary Land Economics Society); American Planning Association. ***PRACTICE AREAS:*** Real Estate; Zoning, Planning and Land Use; Municipal Law. ***Email:*** ssher@wilkesartis.com

GERALD E. SIKORSKI, born Breckenridge, Minnesota, April 26, 1948; admitted to bar, 1974, Minnesota; 1997, District of Columbia. *Education:* University of Minnesota (B.A., summa cum laude, 1970; J.D., magna cum laude, 1973). Member: Minnesota State Senate, 1976-1982; U.S. House of Representatives, Minnesota Sixth District, 1983-1993 (Vice Chair, House Health and Environment Subcommittee). *Member:* The District of Columbia Bar; American Bar Association. ***PRACTICE AREAS:*** Public Law; Intellectual Property; Indian Law. ***Email:*** gsikorsk@hklaw.com

RICHARD P. SILLS, born Philadelphia, Pennsylvania, September 6, 1945; admitted to bar, 1970, Pennsylvania; 1971, District of Columbia; 1977, U.S. Supreme Court, U.S. Tax Court and U.S. Claims Court. *Education:* University of Pennsylvania (B.A., 1966; LL.B., 1969); George Washington University (LL.M. in Taxation, with highest honors, 1974). Author: "The Dealer-Investor Problem," Jour. of Real Estate Taxation, Fall, 1974; "The Dealer-Investor Problem Revisited," Jour. of Real Estate Taxation, Fall, 1976; "Incorporating a Law Practice," District Lawyer, Jan/Feb., 1982; "Professional Corporations: Is There Life After TEFRA?" District Lawyer, Sept., 1982. Co-Author: "Preparing an Effective IRS Protest: How to Win the Tax Case Without Going to Court," Taxation for Accts, Oct., 1986; "The Internal Revenue Code of 1986: The Tax Law Reborn," The Washington Lawyer, Nov/Dec., 1986. Lecturer: George Washington University National Law Ctr., Taxation of Partnerships and Subchapter S Corporations, 1977-1983; Georgetown University Law Ctr., Federal Tax Treatment of Charities and Nonprofit Orgs., 1977-1983; Albany (N.Y.) Law School, Estate Planning and Subchapter S Corporations, 1977-1980; D.C. Bar Continuing Legal Education Program, Taxation for the General Practitioner, 1979-1997; Practicing before the U.S. Tax Court, 1988. Attorney-Adviser to Judge Charles R. Simpson, U.S. Tax Court, 1969-1971. Attorney-Adviser, 1971-1973; Asst. Branch Chief, 1973-1974, Legislation and Regulations Division, Office of the Chief Counsel, IRS. *Member:* The District of Columbia Bar (Chairman, Steering Committee, Tax Div., 1984-1985); Pennsylvania and American Bar Associations. ***PRACTICE AREAS:*** Trusts and Estates; Tax Law; Business Law; Exempt Organizations. ***Email:*** rsills@hklaw.com

THEODORE S. SILVA, JR., born Meunchweiller, Germany, 1958; admitted to bar, 1986, Virginia; 1988, District of Columbia. *Education:* University of Notre Dame (B.A., 1981); George Mason University (J.D., 1985). *Member:* The District of Columbia Bar; Virginia State Bar; Virginia and American Bar Associations. ***PRACTICE AREAS:*** Commercial Real Estate Law; Corporation Law. ***Email:*** tsilva@hklaw.com

DAVID C. SILVER, born Allentown, Pennsylvania, April 3, 1959; admitted to bar, 1988, Georgia; 1990, District of Columbia. *Education:* Lehigh University (B.S., 1981); Georgetown University (J.D., 1988). Certified Public Accountant, Maryland. Adjunct Professor, George Washington University Law Center, 1991-1992. Director, Jubilee Support Alliance, 1995—. Member, Board of Directors, Anti-Defamation League. *Member:* The District of Columbia Bar; State Bar of Georgia. ***PRACTICE AREAS:*** Commercial Transactions; Real Estate Law; Corporate Law. ***Email:*** dsilver@hklaw.com

ANDREW W. STEPHENSON, born Abington, Pennsylvania, February 12, 1950; admitted to bar, 1976, Pennsylvania; 1977, Louisiana; 1979, District of Columbia; 1982, Virginia; 1989, U.S. Court of Federal Claims and U.S. Court of Appeals for the Federal Circuit; 1999, U.S. Supreme Court. *Education:* Indiana University of Pennsylvania (B.A., 1972); Georgetown University (J.D., 1976). Special Projects Editor, Law and Policy in International Business, 1974-1976.

(This Listing Continued)

Author: "The Deepwater Port Act of 1974," Law and Policy in International Business, Vol. 7, No. 4, 1975. Co-Author: "Construction Strikes and Picketing," Construction Briefings, #86-8, July 1986; "Recovering From Construction Lenders," Construction Briefings, #89-3, August 1989; Chapter on Labor Relations, "Construction Contracting," George Washington University Publication, 1991. Author/Lecturer: Labor Law in the Construction Industry, Federal Publications, Inc., 1981—; Labor Relations, George Washington University Government Contracts Program On Construction Contracting, 1986—; Engineering News Record Construction Education Management Corporation, 1988—; CEMC Construction Leadership Conference, 1996; The Construction Super Conference and DCBIA. *Member:* The District of Columbia Bar; Pennsylvania State, Louisiana State, Virginia State and American (Steering Committee, ABA Construction Forum, Division 6, Employment Law and Labor Relations) Bar Associations. [2nd Lt., USAR, 1972-1978]. ***PRACTICE AREAS:*** Construction Law; Government Contracts; Labor Law. ***Email:*** astephen@hklaw.com

SCOTT ANDREW STERLING, born Los Angeles, California, July 16, 1955; admitted to bar, 1981, District of Columbia. *Education:* Washington University (A.B., magna cum laude, 1977); George Washington University (J.D., with honors, 1981). *Member:* The District of Columbia Bar; American Bar Association (Member: Forum on Affordable Housing and Community Development Law). ***PRACTICE AREAS:*** Commercial Real Estate Acquisition, Development and Finance; Affordable Multifamily Housing. ***Email:*** ssterling@hklaw.com

JEFFREY B. STERN, born New York, N.Y., May 15, 1950; admitted to bar, 1976, New York and District of Columbia. *Education:* Trinity College (B.A., 1972); George Washington University (J.D., 1975). Chairman: Urban Land Institute "Real Estate Workouts, Strategies and Solutions," 1991; The Banking Law Institute, "Real Estate Loan Workouts," 1989. Author: "Workout Decision Making and Documentation," in "The New Workout Game," Executive Enterprises Publications Co., Inc., 1991; "Understanding Environmental Risks and Liability for Commercial Lenders," "The Liability Game," Executive Enterprises Publications Co., Inc., 1988; "The Sale of Timeshare Portfolios by the RTC and FDIC," Vacation Industry Review, 1994; "The New Timeshare: Shaking a Negative Image, Vacation Industry Redefines Itself," Legal Times, 1997. *Member:* The District of Columbia Bar; New York State Bar Association. ***PRACTICE AREAS:*** Real Estate Law; Financial Institutions Law; Resort Timeshares; Hotel and Resort Development; Hotel and Resort Law; Finance Law. ***Email:*** jstern@hklaw.com

JANET R. STUDLEY, born New York, N.Y., May 9, 1950; admitted to bar, 1976, Florida; 1980, District of Columbia. *Education:* Emmanuel College (B.A., with honors, 1972); University of Florida (J.D., with honors, 1976). Law Clerk, U.S. Court of Appeals, Fifth Circuit, 1976-1977. Chief Counsel, Subcommittee on Federal Spending Practices and Open Government, U.S. Senate Committee on Governmental Affairs, 1977-1981. *Member:* The District of Columbia Bar; The Florida Bar; American Bar Association (Member: Section of Individual Rights and Responsibilities Executive Council; Chair 1992-1993, Officer 1987-1994; Standing Committee on Legal Aid and Indigent Defendants 2000 - present); Federal Communications Bar Association. Fellow, American Bar Foundation and Florida Bar Foundation. ***PRACTICE AREAS:*** Federal Legislative Practice; Administrative Law. ***Email:*** jstudley@hklaw.com

JOHN E. THEBERGE, born Methuen, Massachusetts, October 31, 1944; admitted to bar, 1983, District of Columbia. *Education:* St. Michaels College (B.A., cum laude, 1966); Georgetown University (J.D., 1972). *Member:* The District of Columbia Bar; American Bar Association; National Association of Bond Lawyers. [U.S. Army, 1969-1972]. ***PRACTICE AREAS:*** Federal Taxation; Public Finance. ***Email:*** jtheberge@hklaw.com

PAUL M. THOMAS, born New York, N.Y., November 5, 1948; admitted to bar, 1975, Massachusetts; 1980, District of Columbia. *Education:* Lake Forest College (A.B., 1970); Harvard University (J.D., 1975). *Member:* American Bar Association. ***PRACTICE AREAS:*** Employment Law; Corporate Diversity Counseling; Litigation. ***Email:*** pthomas@hklaw.com

CHARLES D. TOBIN, born New York, New York, July 11, 1962; admitted to bar, 1989, Florida and U.S. District Court, Middle District of Florida; 1991, U.S. District Court, Northern District of Florida; 1997, District of Columbia. *Education:* University of Florida (B.S., Journalism, with high honors, 1984; J.D., with honors, 1989). Phi Delta Phi. Editor-in-Chief, Journal of Law and Public Policy, 1988-1989. Adjunct Professor, Media Law, University of North Florida, 1992-1993; Research and Writing Instructor, University of Florida College of Law, 1988-1989; Graduate Teaching Assistant, University of Florida College of Journalism and Communications, 1987-1988. Bureau Chief, Fort Myers News-Press, 1984-1986. Member, Gabel, Taylor & Dees, P.A., Jacksonville, FL, 1990-1993. Assistant General Counsel, Gannett Co., Inc., Arlington, Virginia, 1993-2001. *Member:* The Florida Bar (Vice-Chair, Torts and Insurance Practice Section, Media and Defamation Torts Committee); American Bar Association (Associate Editor, Litigation Magazine); The District of Columbia Bar. ***LANGUAGES:*** Spanish. ***REPORTED CASES:*** Lopez v. The Sun, 27 Med.L.Rptr. 1088 (Cal. Super. Ct. 1998); Reilly v. North Hills News Record, 27 Med.L.Rptr. 1569 (W.D. Pa. 1998); Wilson v. Gannett Co., 26 Med.L.Rptr. 1703

(This Listing Continued)

HOLLAND & KNIGHT LLP, Washington—Continued

(Fla. Cir. Ct. 1998) and 28 Med.L.Rptr. 1694 (Fla. Cir. Ct. 2000); Cross v. Carnes, 26 Med.L.Rptr. 1191 (Ohio Ct. Comm, Pls. 1997); Fancher v. Lee County Humane Society, 25 Med.L.Rptr. 2565 (Fla.Cir.Ct. 1997); Raycraft Printing Co. v. Gannett Satellite Information Network, Inc., 25 Med.L.Rptr. 1318 (N.J. Super. Ct. 1996); WorldNet Software Co. v. Gannett Co., 25 Med.L. Rptr. 2331 (Oh. Ct. App. 1997), 25 Med.L.Rptr. 1089 (Ohio Ct. Cm. Pleas 1996); Allison v. Barrett, 25 Med.L.Rptr. 1275 (N.D. Ga. 1996); LeFever v. Great Falls Tribune, 24 Med.L.Rptr. 2086 (Mont. Dist. Ct. 1995); Gold v. Harrison, 24 Med.L.Rptr. 1383 (Hi.Cir.Ct.1995) and 26 Med.L.Rptr. 2313 (HI 1998); Posato v. Oken, 24 Med.L.Rptr. 1285 (N.Y.Sup.Ct. 1995); Mortensen v. Gannett Co., Inc., 26 Med.L.Rptr. 1415 (Nev. Sup. Ct. 1997), 24 Med.L.Rptr. 1190 (Nev. Dist. Ct. 1995); Rogers v. Jackson Sun, 23 Med.L.Rptr. 1670 (Tenn.Cir.Ct.1995); Jefferson v. Winnebago County, 23 Med.L.Rptr. 1641 (N.D.Ill. 1995); Madarassy v. Gannett Satellite Information Network, Inc., 23 Med.L.Rptr. 1363 (N.Y.Sup.Ct.1995); Graziano v. The Sun Co. of San Bernardino, 23 Med.L.Rptr. 1028 (Cal.Super. Ct. 1995); Pravda v. Gannett Satellite Information Network, Inc., 22 Med.L.Rptr. 2413 (N.Y.Supr.Ct.1994) and 24 Med.L.Rptr. 1633, 637 N.Y.S.2d 508 (App. Div. 1996); Stem v. Gannett Satellite Information Network, Inc., 866 F.Supp. 355 (W.D. Tenn. 1994); Parrish v. Gannett River States Publishing Corp., 22 Med.L.Rptr. 1413 (S.D.Miss. 1994); Friedrich v. Salinas Newspapers, Inc., 22 Med.L.Rptr. 1478 (Cal.Super.Ct. 1993); Georgescu v. Times Herald, 22 Med.L.Rptr. 2062 (Mich. Cir. Ct. 1994); Richards v. Gannett Satellite Information Network, Inc., 21 Med.L.Rptr. 2288 (Ill.Cir.Ct. 1993); Benedict v. Exec. Risk Consultants, 616 So.2d 525 (Fla.Dist.Ct.App. 1993); Schwab v. Television 12 of Jacksonville, Inc., 21 Med.L.Rptr. 1157 (Fla.Cir.Ct. 1993); Fla. Pub. Co. v. Shorstein, 20 Med.L.Rptr. 2102 (Fla.Dist.Ct.App. 1992); Fla. v. Rolling, 20 Med.L.Rptr. 1127 and 20 Med.L.Rptr. 1991 (Fla.Cir.Ct. 1992); In Re Brown, 18 Med.L.Rptr. 1460 (Fla.Cir.Ct. 1990); Hatch v. Marsh, 134 F.R.D. 300 (M.D. Fla. 1990). ***Email:*** ctobin@hklaw.com

JEFFERY A. TOMASEVICH, born South Holland, Illinois, June 24, 1963; admitted to bar, 1989, New York; 1990, District of Columbia. *Education:* Cornell University (B.S., with distinction, 1985); New York University School of Law (J.D., 1988). Managing Editor, Annual Survey of American Law. Author, Due Process for the Indigent and Rendering Effective Assistance of Counsel to a Perjurious Client, 1987 Ann. Surv. Am. L. 223. Law Clerk to Hon. Jane R. Roth, U.S. District Judge, District of Delaware, 1988-1989. Assistant Attorney General, Republic of Palau, 1995-1996. Legal Counsel to the President, Republic of Palau, 1996-1997. ***PRACTICE AREAS:*** Litigation; Administrative Law; Administrative Litigation; Airport Law. ***Email:*** jtomasev@hklaw.com

CHARLES WELCH TIEDEMANN, born Bronxville, New York, January 30, 1956; admitted to bar, 1981, District of Columbia. *Education:* University of Notre Dame (A.B., 1978); Catholic University of America (J.D., 1981). *Member:* The District of Columbia Bar; American Bar Association. ***PRACTICE AREAS:*** Commercial Real Estate Law; Commercial Finance; Workouts. ***Email:*** ctiedema@hklaw.com

ALAN P. VOLLMANN, born March 27, 1948; admitted to bar, 1980, District of Columbia; 1987, Maryland; 1996, Virginia. *Education:* University of California at Irvine (B.A., 1970); San Francisco State University (M.A., 1974); Catholic University of America (J.D., 1980). Editor-in-Chief, 1979-1980, Catholic University Law Review. Visiting Lecturer, Land Transactions and Finance, Catholic University School of Law, Washington, D.C., 1991-1993. Author: "Environmental Costs: Making Lenders Liable," 1 Review of European Community and International Environmental Law 422 (1992); "Double Jeopardy: Lender Liability Under Superfund," 16 Real Estate L.J. 3 (1987). Adjunct Professor, Allan L. Berman Real Estate Institute at The Johns Hopkins University. ***PRACTICE AREAS:*** Commercial Real Estate; Finance. ***Email:*** avollmann@hklaw.com

SUSAN LEE VOSS, born Los Angeles, California, August 29, 1932; admitted to bar, 1984, Virginia and U.S. Court of Appeals, Fourth Circuit; 1985, District of Columbia; 1991, U.S. District Court, Eastern District of Virginia. *Education:* George Mason University (B.A., 1980); Georgetown University (J.D., cum laude, 1984). Member: Georgetown University Law Review, 1983-1984. Author: "Regulation of Advertising on the Internet" (Vacation Industry Review, Jan/Feb. 1997); "The ADA's Enactment Creates More Questions Than Answers," (Developments, March 1996); "Retirement Communities," (Insights, 1995). ADA Employment Provisions Cover More Businesses (Developments, July 1994); "The Improved Lot Exemption and the Interstate Land Sales Full Disclosure Act," (Probate and Property, Sept./Oct., 1992); "FTC Privacy (Developments, June 2000). *Member:* District of Columbia Bar; Virginia State Bar; American Bar Association (Chairman, Legal Aspects of the Marketing of Real Estate Committee, 1997-2000); American Resort Development Association (Chairman, Regulation of the Internet Subcommittee); National Land Council; Community Associations Institute. ***PRACTICE AREAS:*** Real Estate Law; Financial Institutions Law; Timesharing; Resort Development; Golf Clubs. ***Email:*** svoss@hklaw.com

FREDERICK P. WAITE, born Troy, New York, November 17, 1945; admitted to bar, 1972, New York and U.S. District Court, Northern District of New York; 1974, U.S. Supreme Court; 1975, District of Columbia; 1984, U.S. Court of International Trade and U.S. Court of Appeals, Federal Circuit. *Education:* Princeton University (A.B., cum laude, 1967); Australian National University, Australia; Harvard University (J.D., cum laude, 1971). Phi Beta Kappa. Co-Author: "Responsible Controls or 'Nets to Catch the Wind'? The Commerce Departments New U.S. Controls or Exports of Chemical Precursors," 22 California Western International Law Journal 193, 1991-1992; "National Security Review of Foreign Investments in the United States," 6 Florida Journal of International Law 191, 1991; "Customs Service Seeks to Improve Trade Compliance Through Nationwide Prototype Test," 7 The Metropolitan Corporate Counsel 15, 1999. [U.S. Air Force (Captain, Office of the Judge Advocate General, 1972-1976)]. ***REPORTED CASES:*** Gerald Metals, Inc. v. United States, 132 F.3d 716 (Fed. Cir. 1997). ***PRACTICE AREAS:*** International Trade Law; Customs Law; International Transactions. ***Email:*** fwaite@hklaw.com

MEL S. WEINBERGER, born New York, N.Y., March 29, 1956; admitted to bar, 1981, District of Columbia. *Education:* University of Rochester (B.A., cum laude, with high distinction, 1978); Georgetown University Law Center (J.D., cum laude, 1981). Law Fellow, Georgetown University, 1979-1980. Staff Member, 1979-1980 and Editor, 1980-1981, American Criminal Law Review. Contributing Editor, Resort Development Law Reporter. Author: "Timesharing for the Next Century," The Complete Lawyer, April/May 1999; "Can the U.S. 'Trust' the Europeans?," Developments, September 1999; "Sharing Time in the City," Property Writes, Fourth Quarter, 1997; "Sharing Time in Vacation Ownership," Urban Land, August 1997; "Model Legislation Sets Industry Parameters-An Overview of the Vacation Club Model Act," Developments, September 1995. Co-Chairman, "New Accountability Standards Under FIRREA: Directors, Officers, and Third Party Professionals and Contractors," The Banking Law Institute, 1989-1990; principal drafter of ARDA's Vacation Club Model Act. Full Member: The Urban Land Institute. *Member:* American Bar Association. ***PRACTICE AREAS:*** Resort Timeshares; Hotel Development; Community Development; Finance; Real Estate Law. ***Email:*** mwein@hklaw.com

STEPHEN J. WEISS, born New York, N.Y., September 12, 1938; admitted to bar, 1963, New York; 1966, District of Columbia. *Education:* Queens College (B.S., 1959); Cornell University (LL.B., 1962); Georgetown University (LL.M., 1966). Author: Navigating the D&O Maze; A Handbook for Purchasers of Directors' and Officers' Liability Insurance (Bowne 1997); Navigating the EPLI Maze; A Handbook for Purchasers of Employment Practices Liability Insurance (Bowne, 1998); Regulation D and Section 4 (6) Under the Securities Act-A Practical Guide (1994); Doing D&O Insurance Right, 4 Business Law Today 50 (1994); Getting the Best D&O Coverage, 18 Directors & Boards 4 (1994); The Best D&O Coverage, Revisited, 20 Directors & Boards 28 (1996); Filling the Gaps in D&O Insurance, 6 Business Law Today 77 (1997); "Your Worst Nightmare: How You Can Protect Yourself Against Abrupt Rescission of Your D&O; Policy," 24 Directors & Boards 3 (2000); "Think Dual Coverage: For Directors and Officers, A D&O Policy is Often Not Enough," 24 Directors & Boards 4 (2000); "How to Get Your Due From Your D&O Insurer," 25 Directors & Boards 3 (2001); "Contesting Erosion of Your D&O Coverage," 25 Directors & Boards 4 (2001); "Why Your Directors and Officers May Need Employment Practices Liability Insurance," Metropolitan Corporate Counsel (April 2001). Insurance Columnist, Director & Boards Magazine. Attorney, Division of Corporation Finance, Securities and Exchange Commission, 1962-65. Member, Advisory Board, Securities Regulation & Law Report, Bureau of National Affairs, 1980—. Member, Executive Committee, Cornell Law Association, 1981-84. President, Cornell Law School Association of Washington, 1970-1979. *Member:* Federal (Chairman, 1968-70 and Executive Council, 1971—, Securities Law Committee; Chairman, 1971-73 and Deputy Chairman, 1970-71, Council on Financing and Taxation; Member, National Council, 1972-81; Chairman, Publications Board, 1977-78; Leadership Commendation, 1973; Distinguished Service Award, 1970) and American (Member, 1971—, and Chairman, Subcommittee on Rule 10b-5, 1976-78; Chairman, Subcommittee on Civil Liabilities, 1978-81, Federal Regulation of Securities Committee; Chairman, Ad Hoc Committee on Foreign Corrupt Practices Act Legislation, 1976-77) Bar Associations; American Law Institute (Life Member). ***PRACTICE AREAS:*** Corporate Law; Securities Law; Insurance Law. ***Email:*** sweiss@hklaw.com

GEORGE Y. WHEELER, III, born Washington, D.C., July 30, 1941; admitted to bar, 1967, District of Columbia. *Education:* Princeton University (A.B., 1963); University of Michigan (LL.B., 1966). Phi Delta Phi. General Attorney, Office of General Counsel, Federal Communications Commission, 1966-1969. *Member:* The District of Columbia Bar; American Bar Association; Federal Communications Bar Association. [Fighter Pilot, Va. Air Natl. Guard, 1967-1973]. ***PRACTICE AREAS:*** Telecommunication Law. ***Email:*** gwheeler@hklaw.com

JOSEPH B. WHITEBREAD, JR., born Washington, D.C.; admitted to bar, 1977, Florida; 1978, U.S. Tax Court; 1980, District of Columbia. *Education:* George Washington University (B.A., 1973); University of Virginia (J.D., 1977); Georgetown University (LL.M., in Taxation, 1982). Author: "Tax Incentives for the Preservation of Historic Properties," 60 Taxes 446, 1982; "Historic Preservation Tax Incentives - The Impact of Recent Legislation," 61 Taxes 243, 1983;

(This Listing Continued)

"Partnerships and Charitable Partners," Tax Management Real Estate Journal, July 1986. *Member:* The District of Columbia Bar (Member, Real Estate Section and Tax Section); The Florida Bar; American Bar Association (Member, Tax Section). ***PRACTICE AREAS:*** Business Planning; Corporate; Tax Law; Estates; Partnership and Limited Liability Company Law. ***Email:*** jwhitebread@hklaw.com

DAVID L. WINSTEAD, born Baltimore, Maryland, August 23, 1947; admitted to bar, 1987, Pennsylvania; 1990, U.S. District Court, District of Maryland; 1992, District of Columbia. *Education:* Denison University (B.A., 1969); Columbia University (M.B.A., 1972); Columbus School of Law, Catholic University of America (J.D., 1984). Legislative Assistant, U.S. Senate. Executive Director, Washington/Baltimore Regional Association. President, Challenger Center for Space Science Education. Secretary, Maryland Department of Transportation. Chairman, Maryland Transportation Commission, 1991-1995. Chairman, Maryland Port Commission, 1995-1999. President, American Association of State Highway and Transportation Officials - AASHTO, 1998. Member, Urban Land Institute. Past Trustee, Transportation Research Board. Legal Counsel, National Association of Industrial and Office Parks (NAIOP - District of Columbia and Suburban Maryland). Partner, Wilkes Artis LLC. *Member:* The District of Columbia Bar; Pennsylvania Bar Association; American Association of State Highway & Transportation Officials (President, 1998). [Member, District of Columbia Air National Guard, Discharged, 1975]. ***PRACTICE AREAS:*** Land Use; Municipal Law; Transportation; Public Law; Legislative Practice. ***Email:*** dwinstea@hklaw.com

LAWRENCE J. WOLK, born New York, N.Y., May 14, 1949; admitted to bar, 1975, New York; 1995, District of Columbia. *Education:* Johns Hopkins University (B.A., 1971); New York University (J.D., 1974). Member and Editor, New York University Review of Law and Social Change, 1973-1974. Assistant General Counsel for Real Estate-Resolution Trust Corporation, 1994-1995. Assistant General Counsel, Assets and Special Issues, Federal Deposit Insurance Corporation, 1996. *Member:* New York State and American (Chair, Public-Private Partnerships Subcommittee and Securitized Mortgage Lending Committee) Bar Associations; American College of Real Estate Lawyers. ***PRACTICE AREAS:*** Commercial Real Estate Financing; Disposition; Leasing; Loan Workouts; Multi-Asset Sales; Privatization. ***Email:*** lwolk@hklaw.com

ROBERT T. WRAY, born Evanston, Illinois, October 23, 1935; admitted to bar, 1960, District of Columbia and Illinois; 1962, U.S. Tax Court; 1980, U.S. Court of International Trade; 1982, U.S. Court of Appeals for the Federal Circuit. *Education:* Loyola University (B.S. with highest honors, 1957); University of Michigan (J.D., 1960). Alpha Sigma Nu. Member, Barristers Society. Author: "Airport Global Finance- New Approaches," Euromoney Airport Finance, 1999. General Counsel, Agency for International Development, Department of State, 1970-1971. Senior Counsel, Export-Import Bank of U.S., 1974-1979. *Member:* District of Columbia Bar; Federal (Member, International Trade and Customs Law Section) and American (Member, Sections on: Corporation, Banking and Business Law; International Law; Air and Space Law) Bar Associations; American Society of International Law; International Law Association (American Branch; Member, Bretton Woods Committee). [LT (jg), USNR, 1961, Lt., USNR, 1962]. ***PRACTICE AREAS:*** International Business Law; Aircraft Finance and Leasing; Project Finance; Transportation; Infrastructure; Privatization. ***Email:*** rwray@hklaw.com

XIAOHUA ZHAO, born Beijing, China, February 24, 1956; admitted to bar, 1992, Indiana; 2000, District of Columbia. *Education:* Beijing Language Institute (B.A., 1983); Indiana University (M.A., 1989); Valparaiso University (J.D., 1992). Recipient: First Place for Future Writing, Society of Professional Journalists, Sigma Delta Chi Mark of Excellence Contest, 1987. Member, Midwest Environmental Law Caucus, 1990-1992. Author: "Chinese Maintain Control Over Internet Access," Doing Business in China, 1998; "China Foreign Investment Guidelines Revised," Legal Times, 1998; "The Ministry of Post and Telecommunications of China Experiments with New Legal Structure," Telecommunications Reports International, 1997. *Member:* American (Member, International Law Section) and International (Member, Business Law Section) Bar Associations; Federal Communications Bar Association. ***LANGUAGES:*** Chinese. ***PRACTICE AREAS:*** International Commercial Transactions; Corporate; Joint Ventures; Project Finance; Telecommunications; Intellectual Property. ***Email:*** xzhao@hklaw.com

SENIOR COUNSEL

ROBERT H. BRADNER, born Chicago, Illinois, July 2, 1962; admitted to bar, 1992, Illinois; 1995, District of Columbia. *Education:* Yale University (B.A., 1984); Georgetown University (J.D., cum laude, 1992). Author: "The Jackson - Vanik Amendment to the Trade Act of 1974," 4 Gco Immig. L.J. 639 (1990); "ILLINOIS JURISPRUDENCE: MUNICIPAL LAW," Chapter 16: Public Improvements, Lawyers Coop. Pub. (1994). Chief of Staff and Counsel to the Hon. John Edward Porter, M.C., 1990-1993; 1995-2000. *Member:* The District of Columbia Bar. ***PRACTICE AREAS:*** Legislative; Health Law; Education Law; Employment Law; Environmental Law. ***Email:*** rbradner@hklaw.com

(This Listing Continued)

DENNIS L. BRYANT, born Lebanon, Oregon, October 31, 1946; admitted to bar, 1976, Tennessee and District of Columbia; 1979, California. *Education:* United States Coast Guard Academy (B.S., 1968); Vanderbilt University (J.D., 1975). Author: "The Maritime Compliance Program: Foghorn Protection for the Ship Owner," 24 Tulane Mar. L. J. 591 (2000). Contributing Author: 'Environmental Criminal Prosecutions in the Maritime Industry' in "Corporate Fraud Investigations and Compliance Programs" by Eugene Propper (Oceana Publications, 2000). Co-Author: 'Maritime Financing' in "Commercial Finance Guide" (Matthew Bender, 1999). Chair: Navigation, Coast Guard and Government Regulation Committee, MLA; Vice-President, MABA. *Member:* American Bar Association; Maritime Law Association; Maritime Administrative Bar Association. [U.S. Coast Guard, 1968-1995; Capt. USCG (Ret.)]. ***PRACTICE AREAS:*** Government Relations; Shipping Regulation; Admiralty; Regulatory; Legislative; Environmental. ***Email:*** dbryant@hklaw.com

BRIAN E. BURKE, born Cambridge, Massachusetts, April 10, 1959; admitted to bar, 1989, Massachusetts and District of Columbia. *Education:* Brown University (A.B., 1983); Georgetown University (J.D., 1988). ***PRACTICE AREAS:*** Public Law; Environmental Law; Regulatory; Corporate Diversity; Municipal. ***Email:*** beburke@hklaw.com

JOHN M. BURKMAN, born Pittsburgh, Pennsylvania, February 24, 1966; admitted to bar, 1992, Pennsylvania; 1999, District of Columbia. *Education:* University of Pittsburgh (B.A., 1988); Georgetown University (J.D., 1992; M.S.F.S., 1992). ***LANGUAGES:*** French. ***PRACTICE AREAS:*** Federal Legislative; Federal Administrative Law. ***Email:*** jburkman@hklaw.com

REBECCA F. DUKE, born Chapel Hill, North Carolina, 1964; admitted to bar, 1990, Florida; 2001, District of Columbia. *Education:* Rhodes College (B.A., 1987); George Washington University (J.D., with honors, 1990). Member, George Washington Journal of International Law and Economics, 1988-1990. *Member:* The Florida Bar; The District of Columbia Bar; American Bar Association; Federal Communications Bar Association. ***PRACTICE AREAS:*** Telecommunications; Government; Municipal Law; Land Use. ***Email:*** rhduke@hklaw.com

STEPHANIE A. LIPINSKI GALLAND, born Norfolk, Virginia; admitted to bar, 1989, Virginia (Not admitted in District of Columbia). *Education:* Christopher Newport College (B.A., 1986); College of William & Mary (J.D., 1989). State Tax Regional Editor, State and Local Tax Lawyer, American Bar Association. Member, State and Local Tax Advisory Board, Georgetown Law Center, 1999—. Member, State Tax Advisory Board, BNA Tax Management, 2001. Member, CCH, Electronic State and Local Advisory Board, 1999—. *Member:* American Bar Association (Member, Executive Committee, State and Local Tax Comittee). ***PRACTICE AREAS:*** State Tax; Local Tax; Electronic Commerce Taxation; Canadian Goods and Service Tax. ***Email:*** slgallan@hklaw.com

ALVIN J. GESKE, born Whitefish, Montana, April 17, 1942; admitted to bar, 1967, Texas; 1972, District of Columbia; 1982, U.S. Tax Court; 1984, U.S. Court of Appeals, Fourth Circuit; 1992, U.S. Court of Federal Claims. *Education:* Southern Methodist University (B.A., with highest honors, 1964); University of Chicago (J.D., with honors, 1967); George Washington University (LL.M., Taxation, with highest honors, 1974). Phi Beta Kappa; Order of the Coif; Phi Delta Phi. Attorney, Legislation and Regulation Division Office of Chief Counsel, Internal Revenue Service, 1970-1972; Assistant Branch Chief, 1972-1974; Legislation Attorney, Joint Committee on Taxation, U.S. Congress, 1975-1977; Assistant Legislation Counsel, 1978-1981. *Member:* The District of Columbia Bar; State Bar of Texas; American Bar Association (Chairman, Committee on Agriculture, Section of Taxation, 1986-1987). ***PRACTICE AREAS:*** Federal Income; Estate Law; Excise Tax Law. ***Email:*** ageske@hklaw.com

DIRK HAIRE, born Jeffersonville, Indiana, October 24, 1967; admitted to bar, 1994, Indiana; 1995, Minnesota; 1998, District of Columbia; 1999, Maryland. *Education:* Ball State University (B.S., cum laude, 1990); George Washington University (J.D., 1993). ***PRACTICE AREAS:*** Construction. ***Email:*** ddhaire@hklaw.com

JEFFREY P. HILDEBRANT, born Schenectady, New York, February 4, 1953; admitted to bar, 1987, Maryland; 1988, District of Columbia. *Education:* Fordham University (B.S., 1975); Loyola University (M.B.A.; J.D., 1987). Author, Publications: "SBA - HUB Zone Empowerment Contracting Program," Holland & Knight Government Contracts Newsletter, September, 2001; "New SBA Industry Codes: What Do They Mean for Small Businesses?" Holland & Knight Government Contracts Newsletter, June 2001; "E-Commerce and the Internet for Government Contractors," Federal Contracts Report, July 26, 1999; "Accounting for Capitalized Costs of Internet Use Computer Software under AICPA SOP 98-1," Contractor Management, January 1999; "Recent Developments in the Law on Terminations for Convenience," Costs, Pricing and Accounting Report, April 1998; "Recovering Patent-Related Costs Under Government Contracts," Costs, Pricing and Accounting Report, April 1997. Co-Author: "Giving Orders - Taking Advantage of the President's Executive Order for Small and Minority Businesses," Minority Business Entrepreneur, Nov/Dec 2000; "Gould and the Adjustment of Pension Costs After the Sale of a Segment: Where Do We Go From Here?" 70 Federal Contracts Report, November 9,

(This Listing Continued)

HOLLAND & KNIGHT LLP, Washington—Continued

1998. *Member:* American Bar Association; National Defense Industrial Association; National Contract Management Association. **Email:** jhildebrant@hklaw.com

LLOYD J. JORDAN, born Chicago, Illinois, July 25, 1955; admitted to bar, 1981, Missouri; 1982, Illinois; U.S. Supreme Court; U.S. Court of Appeals, Eighth Circuit; U.S. District, Eastern District of Missouri (Not admitted in District of Columbia). *Education:* Washington University (B.S., 1977); St. Louis University (J.D., 1981). Harvard University, Kennedy School of Government, Certification from Senior Executive Program. Director, Regulatory Affairs in Washington, D.C., 1998-2000. Chief Administrative Officer, St. Louis, Missouri 1993-1996. *Member:* Mound City, St. Louis Illinois State and American and National Bar Associations; The Missouri Bar. ***PRACTICE AREAS:*** Public Law; Government; Business Transactions; Regulatory; Litigation. **Email:** ljjordan@hklaw.com

KEITH D. LIND, born New Haven, Connecticut, August 3, 1947; admitted to bar, 1985, Massachusetts; 1987, District of Columbia. *Education:* University of Michigan (B.S.N., 1974); Harvard School of Public Health (M.S., 1980); University of Michigan (J.D., 1984). Registered Nurse: Michigan, 1974 and Massachusetts, 1978. Special Assistant to the Chief of Staff, U.S. Department of Health and Human Services, 1988-1989. Member Professional Democratic Staff, U.S. Senate, Finance Committee, 1995-1996. *Member:* The District of Columbia Bar (Member, Health Law Section); American Bar Association (Member, Health Law Section). ***PRACTICE AREAS:*** Health Law; Medicare and Medicaid Law; Legislative Practice; Regulatory Law; Business Law; Corporate Law. **Email:** klind@hklaw.com

JIM J. MARQUEZ, born Los Lunas, New Mexico, March 10, 1941; admitted to bar, 1973, Kansas and U.S. District Court, District of Kansas; 1981, U.S. Court of Appeals, Tenth Circuit; 1987, District of Columbia, U.S. District Court for the District of Columbia, U.S. Supreme Court and U.S. Court of Military Appeals; 1990, U.S. Court of Appeals, for the District of Columbia Circuit. *Education:* University of New Mexico (B.A., 1965); Washburn University (J.D., 1972). United States Attorney, Kansas, 1981-1983. General Counsel, U.S. Department of Transportation, 1984-1986. *Member:* Kansas and Federal Bar Associations; The District of Columbia Bar. ***LANGUAGES:*** Spanish. ***PRACTICE AREAS:*** Transportation Law; Aviation; Motor Carrier Regulation; International Transactions. **Email:** jmarquez@hklaw.com

MADONNA A. McGWIN, born Providence, Rhode Island, July 18, 1956; admitted to bar, 1979, District of Columbia; 1981, U.S. District Court for the District of Columbia; 1982, U.S. Court of Appeals for the District of Columbia Circuit; 1992, U.S. District Court, District of Maryland; 1997, U.S. Supreme Court. *Education:* University of Rhode Island (B.A., highest distinction, 1976); Georgetown University (J.D., 1979). Phi Kappa Phi; Phi Sigma Alpha. Recipient, International Trial Lawyer's Award for Excellence in the Art and Science of Advocacy, 1979. Trial Attorney, Commodity Futures Trading Commission, 1980-1986. *Member:* The District of Columbia Bar; Society for Human Resource Management; Women in Technology. ***PRACTICE AREAS:*** Employment Law; Mediation; Litigation; Professional Practices. **Email:** mamcgwin@hklaw.com

DOUGLAS J. PATTON, born Dundee, Iowa, December 21, 1940; admitted to bar, 1970, Iowa; 1976, District of Columbia; 1993, Colorado. *Education:* Marquette University (1961); University of Iowa (B.A., Political Science, 1963; J.D., 1970). Phi Delta Phi; Phi Delta Theta. Author: "The Effect of the Federal Election Campaign Act Contribution and Expenditure Limitations on the Political Party Committees—A Prospect for Party Discipline," 57 N.D.L. Rev. 3, 1981. Member, Board of Directors and Co-Founder, Century National Bank, Washington, D.C., 1982-1986. Member, YMCA Partners for Youth Campaign, Major Gifts Committee, Washington, D.C., 1982-1988. Member, Board of Directors: Potomac Cable Service Company, 1988; Columbia National Bank, Washington, D.C., 1989-1991; Young Audiences, 1991-1995; First National Bank of Maryland, Washington, D.C., 1991-1996. Member, D.C. Lottery Commission, 1989-1990. Member, District of Columbia Board of Zoning Adjustment, 1980-1985. Chairman, Business Regulatory Reform Commission, 1996-1997. Deputy Mayor, District of Columbia, 1999. Ex-Officio Member, Federal Election Commission, 1976-1995. *Member:* The District of Columbia Bar; Colorado and Iowa State Bar Associations. ***PRACTICE AREAS:*** Legislative; Land Use; Securitization; Elections. **Email:** dpatton@hklaw.com

SUNG PARK REYNOLDS, born Pusan, Korea, January 1, 1952; admitted to bar, 1979, District of Columbia; 1980, U.S. District Court for the District of Columbia and U.S. Court of Appeals for the District of Columbia Circuit. *Education:* Duke University (B.S., cum laude, 1975); Georgetown University (J.D., 1978). *Member:* The District of Columbia Bar. ***PRACTICE AREAS:*** Land Sales Regulation; Real Estate Law; Resort Timeshares. **Email:** sreynold@hklaw.com

MIGUEL EUGENIO RUBIO, born Havana, Cuba, February 4, 1962; admitted to bar, 1989, Maryland and District of Columbia; 1994, Florida. *Education:* Georgetown University (B.S.F.S., 1984; M.S.F.S., 1988; J.D., 1988). Pi Sigma Alpha. Recipient, Ernst H. Feilchenfeld Award in International Law, 1984. Senior Counsel, Export-Import Bank of the U.S., 1989-1999. ***LANGUAGES:*** Spanish. ***TRANSACTIONS:*** Samalayuca II Power Project Finance, Mexico, 1996; Avantel Long-Distance Network Finance, 1997; Pemopro/Madero Refinery Rehabilitation Finance, Mexico, 1999. ***PRACTICE AREAS:*** Project Finance; Privatization; International Finance; International Business Transactions. **Email:** mrubio@hklaw.com

STEVEN A. SADEL, born Washington, D.C., May 21, 1952; admitted to bar, 1977, Florida; 1978, District of Columbia; 1987, Maryland. *Education:* Emory University (B.A., 1974); University of Miami (J.D., 1977); New York University School of Law (LL.M., 1978). Phi Beta Kappa. *Member:* The Florida Bar; The District of Columbia Bar; American Bar Association (Member, Sections on: Corporation, Banking and Business Law; Real Property, Probate and Trust Law; Taxation). ***PRACTICE AREAS:*** Retail Real Estate; Real Estate. **Email:** sasadel@hklaw.com

KEVIN J. SMITH, born Bronxville, New York, November 6, 1954; admitted to bar, 1982, Missouri; 1986, District of Columbia; 1998, Arizona. *Education:* St. Louis University (A.B., 1976; M.A., 1982; J.D., 1982). ***PRACTICE AREAS:*** Real Estate; Commercial Leasing; Commercial Finance; Real Estate Development. **Email:** ksmith@hklaw.com

RODERIC L. WOODSON, born Philadelphia, Pennsylvania, August 23, 1947; admitted to bar, 1973, Pennsylvania and U.S. District Court, Eastern District of Pennsylvania; 1974, Georgia; 1979, District of Columbia. *Education:* Pennsylvania State University (B.A., 1969); Howard University (J.D., 1973). Delta Theta Phi. Recipient: Outstanding Alumni Award, George E.C. Hayes Senate; Outstanding Service Award, Howard University Law Alumni, 1980; Frederick B. Abramson Award (MCLE Committee), District of Columbia Bar, 1995; Committee of the Year Award (CLE Sub-Committee on New Admittees), District of Columbia Bar, 1995. Author: "Reflections on Utility Pricing Theory and Business Decision-Making," NBA Law Journal, 1982; "Designed for Investors - D.C. Investment Advisor Act of 1992," Washington Lawyer (May/June 1993). Lecturer on Securities Regulation, Howard University School of Law, 1975-1979. Chairman and Moderator, Securities Regulation Seminar, National Bar Association Annual Convention, 1975-1979. Attorney-Adviser for Corporation Finance, U.S. Securities and Exchange Commission, 1973-1975. FOIA Officer and Special Counsel, U.S. Securities and Exchange Commission, 1976-1979. Secretary and Member, Board of Directors, Washington Bar Association, 1977-1983. President, Howard University Law Alumni Association of Greater Washington Area, 1978-1979. Member: National Council, Federal Bar Association, 1979-1980; District of Columbia Legal Services Corporation Advisory Board, 1983-1984; Legal Task Force, National Council of State Housing Agencies, 1988-1991. Expert Witness before Georgia State Assembly, 1984. General Counsel, District of Columbia Housing Finance Agency, 1987-1991. Member, District of Columbia Insurance Advisory Council, 1996—. Member, District of Columbia Securities Advisory Committee, 1998—. Chairman, District of Columbia Alcoholic Beverage Control Board, 1999—. Director: Progressive Life Center, Inc., 1987—; D.C. Appleseed Center for Law and Justice, 1995—; Penn State Alumni Association, 1997—; Abramson Foundation, 1998—; Shuker Foundation, 1998—. *Member:* The District of Columbia Bar (Member, Steering Committee, D.C. Affairs Section, 1988-1994; Co-Chairman, 1991-1994; Member: Task Force on Mandatory Continuing Legal Education, 1992-1995; Continuing Legal Education Committee, 1993—; Member, Mandatory Course for New Admittees Committee, 1993-1995 and Follow-Up Committee, 1997-1998; Judicial Evaluation Committee, 1996—; Chairman, 1997—); State Bar of Georgia; Pennsylvania Bar Association; National Association of Bond Lawyers. [Army National Guard]. ***REPORTED CASES:*** Boyhin v. District of Columbia 484 A.2d 560 (1984). ***TRANSACTIONS:*** First collateralized single family mortgage bond financing for DC Housing Finance Agency. ***PRACTICE AREAS:*** Legislative Practice (40%); Administrative Law (30%); Public Finance (5%); Corporate Finance (5%); Public Utility Regulation (20%). **Email:** rwoodson@hklaw.com

---

ETHAN ARENSON, born Baltimore, Maryland, March 27, 1975; admitted to bar, 2000, Virginia; 2001 District of Columbia. *Education:* American University (B.A., 1997); George Washington University (J.D., with honors, 2000). ***PRACTICE AREAS:*** Commercial Litigation. **Email:** earenson@hklaw.com

LYNN ESTES CALKINS, born Topeka, Kansas, September 23, 1968; admitted to bar, 1993, Maryland, Pennsylvania and U.S. District Court, District of Maryland; 1995, District of Columbia and U.S. Court of Appeals, Fourth Circuit; 1996, U.S. District Court for the District of Columbia and U.S. Court of Appeals for the District of Columbia Circuit. *Education:* University of Delaware (B.A., magna cum laude, 1990); American University (J.D., magna cum laude, 1993). Law Clerk to Honorable Deborah K. Chasanow, U.S. District Court, District of Maryland, 1995. ***PRACTICE AREAS:*** Commercial Litigation; Real Estate Litigation. **Email:** lcalkins@hklaw.com

CHRISTOPHER L. CAMARRA, born Chelsea, Massachusetts, February 27, 1972; admitted to bar, 1998, Connecticut; 2000, District of Columbia.

(This Listing Continued)

Education: Boston College (B.A., magna cum laude, 1994); University of Connecticut (J.D., with honors, 1998). *Member:* The District of Columbia Bar; American Bar Association. ***PRACTICE AREAS:*** Real Property Law. ***Email:*** ccamarra@hklaw.com

KARA L. DANIELS, born Baltimore, Maryland, May 6, 1973; admitted to bar, 1998, Maryland; 2000, District of Columbia and U.S. District Court, District of Maryland; 2001, U.S. Court of Appeals, Fourth Circuit and U.S. District Court, Eastern District of Michigan. *Education:* Haverford College (B.A., 1995); George Washington University (J.D., with honors, 1998). *Member:* Maryland State Bar Association, Inc.; The District of Columbia Bar; American Bar Association. ***PRACTICE AREAS:*** Commercial Litigation; Trade Secrets Litigation; Media Law. ***Email:*** kdaniels@hklaw.com

OLGA L. DEL RIO, born Kharkov, Ukraine, July 4, 1967; admitted to bar, 1995, Florida; 1998, District of Columbia; 2000, England and Wales. *Education:* Surrey University, Department of Linguistic and International Studies, Great Britain (Certificate, 1988); Moscow State Pedagogical University (Bachelors, with highest honors, 1990); University of Miami School of Law (J.D., cum laude, 1995; Master of Laws in Taxation, Certificate of Specialization in International Tax, 1997). *Member:* The Florida Bar; The District of Columbia Bar; The Law Society of England and Wales; American Bar Association. ***LANGUAGES:*** Russian. ***PRACTICE AREAS:*** Corporate; International; Transactional. ***Email:*** odelrio@hklaw.com

STEVEN L. DUBE, born Nashua, New Hampshire, March 30, 1966; admitted to bar, 1998, Massachusetts (Not admitted in District of Columbia). *Education:* College of the Holy Cross (B.A., 1988); New York University (J.D., 1998). Root Tilden Snow Scholarship. ***LANGUAGES:*** French and Spanish. ***PRACTICE AREAS:*** Real Estate Development and Finance; Zoning Law; Land Use. ***Email:*** sldube@hklaw.com

ELIZABETH M. DUNNE, born Kansas City, Missouri, July 3, 1977; admitted to bar, 2001, Georgia (Not admitted in District of Columbia). *Education:* Rockhurst College (B.A., 1997); Emory University (J.D., 2000). Judicial Clerkship, Judge B. Avant Edenfield, U.S. District Court, Southern District of Georgia, August 2000 - August 2001. ***PRACTICE AREAS:*** Litigation. ***Email:*** emdunne@hklaw.com

JONATHAN M. EPSTEIN, born St. Louis, Missouri, May 26, 1963; admitted to bar, 1995, Virginia; 1996, Maryland and District of Columbia. *Education:* Hamilton College (B.A., magna cum laude, 1985); Georgetown University (J.D., cum laude, 1995). Co-Chair, Commercial Space Division of A.B.A. Forum on Air and Space Law. Editor-in-Chief, Georgetown Journal of Legal Ethics. Recipient, American Jurisprudence Award, Constitutional Law. Author: "The In-House Ethics Advisor: Practical Benefits for the Modern Law Firm," 7 Geo. J. Legal Ethics 1011, 1994; "Global Positioning System (GPS): Defining the Legal Issues of its Expanding Civil Use," 61 J. Air. L. & Com. 243, 1995; "The Role of the Global Positioning System in the Environment," 6 N.Y.U. Env. L.J. 72, 1997; "The American Decision: Federal Court Recognized Aviation Safety Data Privilege", Aviation Litigation Newsletter (May/June 1997)(Co-authored with Louise Cobbs); "Information Security: New Encryption Rules Give U.S. Companies Opportunity to Compete", Metropolitan Corporate Counsel (May 2000)(co-authored with Ron Oleynik). [With U.S. Navy, 1986-1990, Lcdr., U.S.N.R.]. ***PRACTICE AREAS:*** Telecommunications Law; Space Law; International Law; Export Compliance. ***Email:*** jepstein@hklaw.com

ANDREA M. EWART, born Jamaica, West Indies, November 16, 1957; admitted to bar, 2000, Florida; 2001, District of Columbia. *Education:* Patrice Lumumba University (B.A., 1983); University of Miami (M.A., 1989; J.D., 2000). *Member:* American Bar Association; National Bar Association. ***LANGUAGES:*** Russian. ***PRACTICE AREAS:*** International Trade and Customs; Administrative; Regulatory; Legislative. ***Email:*** aewart@hklaw.com

JENNIFER A. GOODRICH, born Warwick, Rhode Island, May 29, 1969; admitted to bar, 1995, New York; 1997, Ohio; 1998, District of Columbia. *Education:* Georgetown University (B.A., cum laude, 1991); Georgetown University Law Center (J.D., 1994). Member, The Tax Lawyer. Author: "I'd Like to Buy Six Hotels on the Boardwalk: Ruling that Monopoly is Unlikely in Lodging Industry Has Helped Spark Boom in Acquisition," Legal Times, October 20, 1994; "Cover Your Assets: Environmental Cleanup Liability," Office & Industrial Properties, June 1998. (Also at New York, N.Y. Office). ***PRACTICE AREAS:*** Real Estate; Commercial Leasing. ***Email:*** jgoodric@hklaw.com

MARGARET A. HACKBARTH, born Meriden, Connecticut, February 16, 1966; admitted to bar, 1992, Virginia; 1993, Maryland; 1995, District of Columbia. *Education:* Bucknell University (B.A., 1988); University of Pittsburgh (J.D., 1992). ***Email:*** mhackbar@hklaw.com

JOANNA HAN, born Seoul, Korea, June 30, 1973; admitted to bar, 1998, Pennsylvania, New Jersey, District of Columbia, U.S. District Court, District of New Jersey and U.S. District Court, Eastern District of Pennsylvania; U.S. Court of Appeals, Third Circuit. *Education:* Yale College (B.A., 1995); George Washington University Law School (J.D., 1998). Member, Moot Court. Editor, George Washington Journal of International Law & Economics. *Member:* Pennsylvania and New Jersey State Bar Associations; The District of Columbia Bar. ***LANGUAGES:*** French. ***PRACTICE AREAS:*** Labor and Employment; Corporate Diversity Counseling. ***Email:*** jshan@hklaw.com

(This Listing Continued)

JOHN A. HENRY, JR., born Norristown, Pennsylvania, January 31, 1972; admitted to bar, 1998, Virginia; 2000, District of Columbia. *Education:* Bucknell University (B.A., 1995); Washington & Lee University (J.D., 1998). Author: Race & Ethnic Ancestry Law Journal, Note, "Hopwood v. Texas," 3 Race & Ethnic Ancestry L. Dig. 97 (1997) *Member:* Virginia and American Bar Associations; The District of Columbia Bar. ***PRACTICE AREAS:*** Real Estate Transactions; Development and Finance; Leasing; Affordable Housing. ***Email:*** jahenry@hklaw.com

MICHELLE D. HERTZ, born Manhasset, New York, May 17, 1967; admitted to bar, 1998, Virginia; 1999, District of Columbia. *Education:* St. Lawrence University (B.A., 1988); George Mason University (J.D., 1997). *Member:* National Contract Management Association (NCMA); Women in Defense (WID); Board of Contract Appeals Bar Association (BCABA). ***PRACTICE AREAS:*** Government Contracts; Litigation. ***Email:*** mhertz@hklaw.com

CRAIG A. HOLMAN, born Washington, D.C., November 11, 1968; admitted to bar, 1993, Maryland; 1994, U.S. District Court, District of Maryland and U.S. Court of Federal Claims; 1995, District of Columbia; 1998, U.S. Court of Appeals, Fourth Circuit and U.S. Court of Appeals for the Federal Circuit; 1999, U.S. District Court for the District of Columbia and U.S. District Court, District of Colorado. *Education:* Boston College (B.A., 1990); George Washington University National Law Center (J.D., cum laude, 1993). Co-Author: "How To File A Monetary Claim Under The Contract Disputes Act," 4 Acquisition Issues 1 (1994); "The Eichleay Formula: A Resilient Means For Recovering Unabsorbed Overhead," 24 Public Contract Law Journal 2 (1995); "Is This The End of Federal Minority Contracting?" 42 Federal Lawyer 2 (1995); "Affirmative Action After Adarand," 95 Construction Briefings 10 (1995). ***PRACTICE AREAS:*** Government Contracts; Litigation. ***Email:*** caholman@hklaw.com

DENNIS R. HUGHES, born Knoxville, Tennessee, 1969; admitted to bar, 1995, Virginia; 1999, District of Columbia. *Education:* Vanderbilt University (B.A., 1991); Tulane University School of Law (J.D., cum laude, Certificate of Specialization in Environmental Law, 1995); University of Virginia School of Architecture (M.Arch.Hist., Historic Preservation, 1999). *Member:* Virginia State Bar; District of Columbia Bar; National Trust for Historic Preservation; American Institute of Architects-Allied Member; Society of Architectural Historians. ***PRACTICE AREAS:*** Real Estate; Zoning, Planning and Land Use; Municipal Law; Historic Preservation. ***Email:*** drhughes@hklaw.com

KARLYN J. HUNTER, born Montgomery, Alabama, February 21, 1974; admitted to bar, 1999, Maryland (Not admitted in District of Columbia). *Education:* Hampton University (B.S., summa cum laude, 1996); Columbia University Law School (J.D., 1999). Tony Patiño Fellow. Recipient, Hampton University President's Award. Federal Law Clerk, Hon. William B. Bryant, U.S. District Court, District of Columbia, 1999-2001. *Member:* Maryland Bar Association, Inc. (Member, Young Lawyers Division); American Bar Association. ***PRACTICE AREAS:*** Litigation. ***Email:*** kjhunter@hklaw.com

KRISTEN SCHMEELCKE ITTIG, born Williamsburg, Virginia, September 1, 1968; admitted to bar, 1997, Maryland; 1998, District of Columbia. *Education:* The American University (B.A., 1990); Vanderbilt University (J.D., 1996). ***PRACTICE AREAS:*** Litigation. ***Email:*** kittig@hklaw.com

LISA L. JACKSON, born Washington, D.C., June 18, 1966; admitted to bar, 1993, Maryland; 2001, District of Columbia. *Education:* University of Virginia (B.A., 1988); University of Maryland (J.D., 1993). Member, 1991-1993 and Technical Editor, 1992-1993, Maryland Journal of Contemporary Legal Issues. *Member:* Prince George's County and Maryland State Bar Associations; J. Franklyn Bourne Bar Association. ***PRACTICE AREAS:*** Real Estate; Land Use; Environmental. ***Email:*** lljackso@hklaw.com

STEPHEN J. JEFFRIES, born Houston, Texas, February 4, 1963; admitted to bar, 1989, Maryland; 1990, District of Columbia. *Education:* Wake Forest University (B.A., 1986; J.D., 1989). *Member:* Bar Association of the District of Columbia (Member, Intellectual Property Law Section). ***PRACTICE AREAS:*** Trademarks; Copyrights; Unfair Competition. ***Email:*** sjeffries@hklaw.com

JOHN G. KELLY, born Baltimore, Maryland, October 7, 1969; admitted to bar, 1995, Maryland; 2000, District of Columbia. *Education:* Virginia Polytechnic Institute and State University (B.S., 1992); University of Maryland (J.D., 1995); University of Miami (LL.M., 1999). ***PRACTICE AREAS:*** Real Estate; Real Estate Development; Real Estate Finance; Commercial Leasing. ***Email:*** jgkelly@hklaw.com

JOSEPH L. KITTO, born St. Louis, Missouri, May 15, 1966; admitted to bar, 1999, Virginia; 2000, District of Columbia and Creek Nation. *Education:* University of Oklahoma (B.A., 1994; M.P.A., 1996); Cornell University (J.D., 1999). [Corporal, USMC, 1984-1988; U.S.N. Reserves, 1992-1994; U.S. Army Reserves, 1994-1996]. ***PRACTICE AREAS:*** Indian Law; Public Law; Litigation. ***Email:*** jkitto@hklaw.com

EILEEN C. LEE, born Sacramento, California, January 6, 1972; admitted to bar, 1997, Maryland; 1998, District of Columbia and U.S. District Court,

(This Listing Continued)

HOLLAND & KNIGHT LLP, Washington—Continued

District of Maryland. *Education:* University of California, Berkeley (B.A., 1993); Washington College of Law, American University (J.D., cum laude, 1997). ***PRACTICE AREAS:*** Commercial Real Estate. ***Email:*** elee@hklaw.com

MICHAEL L. LEFKOWITZ, born Silver Spring, Maryland, March 10, 1969; admitted to bar, 1994, Maryland; 1995, Virginia and U.S. District Court, District of Maryland; 1996, District of Columbia and U.S. District Court, Eastern District of Virginia; 1997, U.S. District Court for the District of Columbia. *Education:* Muhlenberg College (B.A., magna cum laude, 1991); University of Baltimore (J.D., cum laude, 1994). ***PRACTICE AREAS:*** Commercial Real Estate (100%). ***Email:*** mlefkowitz@hklaw.com

THOMAS D. LELAND, born Middletown, New York, June 3, 1969; admitted to bar, 1998, Virginia; 1999, District of Columbia. *Education:* University of Colorado at Boulder (B.A., 1994); George Mason University (J.D., with honors, 1998). *Member:* Virginia and Federal Bar Associations. ***PRACTICE AREAS:*** Civil Litigation; Commercial Litigation; International Litigation; Aviation. ***Email:*** tleland@hklaw.com

KELLY LODDE, born Kokomo,, Indiana, January 19, 1971; admitted to bar, 2000, Indiana (Not admitted in District of Columbia). *Education:* Indiana University School of Law (J.D., 2000). ***PRACTICE AREAS:*** Timeshare; Resort Development.

CHRISTOPHER G. MARGAND, born Bay Shore, New York, December 20, 1960; admitted to bar, 1991, Virginia; 1992, District of Columbia. *Education:* Georgetown University (B.S., 1982; J.D., cum laude, 1991). ***PRACTICE AREAS:*** Litigation. ***Email:*** cmargand@hklaw.com

ANTHONY R. MASIELLO, born Everett, Massachusetts, 1956; admitted to bar, 1987, New York; 1989, Massachusetts; 1999, District of Columbia. *Education:* Harvard University (A.B., magna cum laude, 1978; J.D., 1985). ***PRACTICE AREAS:*** Trademarks; Unfair Competition; Copyrights. ***Email:*** amasiello@hklaw.com

SELWA MASRI, born Louisville, Kentucky, November 19, 1967; admitted to bar, 1998, Maryland (Not admitted in District of Columbia). *Education:* Georgetown University (B.S., 1989); Boston University (M.S., 1993); American University (J.D., 1997). ***PRACTICE AREAS:*** Content Licensing; Software Distribution Contracts; Drafting Negotiations. ***Email:*** smasri@hklaw.com

GERALDINE R.S. MATAKA, born San Fernando, Pampanga, Philippines, August 30, 1970; admitted to bar, 2000, District of Columbia. *Education:* University of Virginia (B.A., 1993); George Mason University School of Law (J.D., 1999). ***PRACTICE AREAS:*** Aircraft Finance and Leasing; Project Finance; Corporate. ***Email:*** gmataka@hklaw.com

DAVID M. MATUSZEWSKI, born Detroit, Michigan, September 7, 1961; admitted to bar, 1986, Texas; 1993, Virginia and District of Columbia. *Education:* University of Michigan (B.B.A., 1983; J.D., 1986). Law Clerk to Chief Judge Bostetter, U.S. Bankruptcy Court, Eastern District of Virginia, 1991-1992. ***Email:*** dmatusze@hklaw.com

LESLIE S. McADOO-BROBSON, born Port Huron, Michigan, June 13, 1968; admitted to bar, 1996, Maryland; 1997, District of Columbia, Virginia, U.S. District Court, District of Maryland, U.S. District Court Eastern and Western Districts of Virginia and U.S. Court of Appeals, Fourth Circuit; 2000, U.S. Supreme Court; 2001, U.S. District Court, District of Columbia. *Education:* Towson State University (B.A., summa cum laude, 1989); Georgetown University Law Center (J.D., cum laude, 1996). Recipient: Joseph Cox Award; Merit Scholarship Award; Vincent G. Panati Memorial Award; Michael Feldman Advocacy Award; American Jurisprudence Award, Legal Research and Writing. Law Clerk, Honorable Ellen L. Hollander, Maryland Court of Special Appeals, 1996-1997. Author: "Tax Treatment of Minimum Tax Preference Carryovers: DuPont v. Commissioner," 48 Tax Lawyer 897 (Spring, 1995). *Member:* Maryland State and American Bar Associations; Maryland Criminal Defense Attorneys Association; National Association of Criminal Defense Lawyers. ***LANGUAGES:*** French. ***PRACTICE AREAS:*** White Collar Crime; Civil Litigation; Corporate Compliance. ***Email:*** lmcadoo@hklaw.com

MARC E. MILLER, born Washington, D.C., June 21, 1969; admitted to bar, 1995, Virginia; 1996, District of Columbia. *Education:* Yale University (B.A., 1991); George Washington University (J.D., 1995). ***PRACTICE AREAS:*** Civil Litigation; Commercial Litigation; Real Estate Litigation. ***Email:*** memiller@hklaw.com

DAVID A. O'CONNOR, born St. Petersburg, Florida, August 29, 1969; admitted to bar, 1998, New York; 1999, District of Columbia. *Education:* Florida State University (B.A., cum laude, 1992); Brooklyn Law School (J.D., cum laude, 1997); Georgetown University (LL.M., with distinction, International and Comparative Law, 1998). Managing Editor, Brooklyn Journal of International Law. Author, Note, "Public Morality Exceptions to Free Movement in Europe: Ireland's Role in a Changing European Union," 22 Brook J. Int'l. L. 693 (1997). ***PRACTICE AREAS:*** Telecommunications; International; Administrative. ***Email:*** doconnor@hklaw.com

(This Listing Continued)

RAFE PETERSEN, born Smithtown, NY, August 23, 1970; admitted to bar, 1997, Virginia; 1998, Maryland; 1999, District of Columbia. *Education:* Hobart College (B.A., cum laude, with high honors, 1992) Phi Beta Kappa; Fulbright Scholar, University of the Philippines (1992-1993); George Washington University Law School (J.D., with honors, 1997). Member, Moot Court Board. Book and Database Review Editor, The Environmental Lawyer, George Washington University Law School; Intern, U.S. Senate Committee on Environment and Public Works, 1997. *Member:* Virginia State Bar; Maryland State Bar Association; The District of Columbia Bar. ***PRACTICE AREAS:*** Environmental. ***Email:*** rapeters@hklaw.com

BRYAN R. PHILLIPS, born Bethesda, Maryland, December 5, 1962; admitted to bar, 1999, Virginia (Not admitted in District of Columbia). *Education:* Catholic University of America (B.S., Architecture, 1984); University of Texas at Arlington (M.Arch., 1986); George Mason University School of Law (J.D., 1998). Licensed Architect, Florida 1988. ***PRACTICE AREAS:*** Construction Litigation; Government Contracts; Construction Law. ***Email:*** bphillip@hklaw.com

SCOTT M. PRITCHETT, born Nashville, Tennessee, June 19, 1957; admitted to bar, 1993, North Carolina; 1996, District of Columbia. *Education:* University of Connecticut (B.S., summa cum laude, 1989); Duke University (J.D., 1992). Chairman, Moot Court Board. Siegel Scholar. *Member:* American Bar Association (Member, Health and Corporate Law Sections); American Health Lawyers Association; Health Care Compliance Association. ***PRACTICE AREAS:*** Health Care; Regulatory and Civil/Criminal Fraud Defense; Corporate. ***Email:*** spritche@hklaw.com

CHRISTOPHER S. REYNOLDS, born Washington, D.C., February 25, 1974; admitted to bar, 1999, Maryland (Not admitted in District of Columbia). *Education:* Georgetown University (B.A., 1996; J.D., 1999). Phi Beta Kappa. ***PRACTICE AREAS:*** Real Estate Finance; Commercial Leasing; Real Estate Acquisitions. ***Email:*** creynolds@hklaw.com

FEMI S. RICHARDS, born Pontiac, Michigan, August 29, 1971; admitted to bar, 1997, Connecticut (Not admitted in District of Columbia). *Education:* University of Massachusetts, Amherst (B.A., 1994); University of Connecticut, Hartford (J.D., 1997); John F. Kennedy School of Government at Harvard University (M.P.P., 1999). *Member:* Connecticut and American Bar Associations. ***PRACTICE AREAS:*** Corporate Diversity Counseling; Government Relations. ***Email:*** fsrichar@hklaw.com

LEO G. RYDZEWSKI, born Athens, Greece, August 4, 1968; admitted to bar, 1997, Florida and U.S. District Court, Southern District of Florida; 1998, U.S. District Court, Eastern District of Wisconsin; 1999, District of Columbia; 2000, U.S. District Court, District of Maryland; 2001, U.S. District Court for the District of Columbia and U.S. Supreme Court. *Education:* Georgetown University (B.A., 1990); Florida State University (J.D., summa cum laude, 1996). Order of the Coif. Law Clerk, Hon. Federico A. Moreno, U.S. District Court, Southern District of Florida, 1997. ***PRACTICE AREAS:*** Litigation. ***Email:*** lrydzews@hklaw.com

CURTIS L. SANO, born Torrance, California, September 19, 1966; admitted to bar, 1993, California; 1994, Hawaii; 1999, District of Columbia. *Education:* Yale University (B.A., 1988); University of California at Berkeley (M.P.P., 1993); Boalt Hall School of Law, University of California (J.D., 1993). *Member:* Hawaii State and American Bar Associations; State Bar of California (Member, Real Property Section); The District of Columbia Bar. ***PRACTICE AREAS:*** Real Estate Purchase and Sale; Real Estate Finance; Retail Development and Leasing; Office Development and Leasing; Affordable Housing. ***Email:*** csano@hklaw.com

AMEE A. SHAH, born New York, N.Y., June 3, 1972; admitted to bar, 1999, Maryland; 2000, District of Columbia. *Education:* Webb Institute (B.S., 1994); Georgetown University (J.D., 1999). Author: "Parent-Child Testimonial Privilege-Has the Time for it Finally Arrived," 47 Clev. St. L. Rev. 41. *Member:* South Asian Bar Association (Member, Board of Directors, 2000—). ***PRACTICE AREAS:*** Employment; Commercial Litigation. ***Email:*** ashah@hklaw.com

CHRISTINE MOSELEY SHIKER, born Dallas, Texas, April 27, 1972; admitted to bar, 1997, Texas and U.S. District Court, Northern District of Texas (Not admitted in District of Columbia). *Education:* College of William & Mary (B.A., 1993; M.P.P., 1997; J.D., 1997). Omicron Delta Kappa; Moot Court Team; Moot Court Board. Dean's Certificate. Recipient, American Jurisprudence Book Award for Civil Procedure. *Member:* Dallas and American Bar Associations; State Bar of Texas; Dallas Association of Young Lawyers; American Planning Association. ***PRACTICE AREAS:*** Zoning; Land Use. ***Email:*** cmshiker@hklaw.com

C. KRISTOPHER SIMPSON, born Washington, D.C., January 31, 1972; admitted to bar, 1997, Maryland; 1999, District of Columbia. *Education:* University of Maryland, College Park (B.S., 1994); George Washington University (J.D., 1997). *Member:* The Maryland Bar; American Bar Association; American Health Lawyers Association; National Association of Health Service Executives (Associate Member). ***PRACTICE AREAS:*** Corporate Law; Health Care Law. ***Email:*** ksimpson@hklaw.com

(This Listing Continued)

DOROTHY C. SLOVAK, born Philadelphia, Pennsylvania, September 17, 1958; admitted to bar, 2000, Maryland and U.S. Court of Federal Claims; 2001, District of Columbia and U.S. District Court for the District of Columbia. *Education:* LaSalle University (B.S., magna cum laude, 1992); Villanova University (M.S., 1994); Catholic University of America (J.D., 1999). Alpha Sigma Lambda. *Member:* The District of Columbia Bar; Maryland State Bar Association; American Bar Association; National Contract Management Association. ***PRACTICE AREAS:*** Litigation; Government Contracts. ***Email:*** dslovak@hklaw.com

BERNARD L. SMITH, born Syracuse, New York, April 21, 1969; admitted to bar, 1994, Virginia; 1996, District of Columbia. *Education:* Syracuse University (B.S.CE., magna cum laude, first in Civil Engineering Class, 1991); George Washington University (J.D., 1994). *Member:* The District of Columbia Bar; Virginia State Bar; American Bar Association. ***PRACTICE AREAS:*** Commercial Real Estate Development; Hotel and Resort Development; Condominium Development; Timeshare Development; Finance; International Finance; Mergers and Acquisitions. ***Email:*** blsmith@hklaw.com

C. DENNIS SOUTHARD IV, born Kansas City, Missouri, December 22, 1961; admitted to bar, 1989, Pennsylvania, New Jersey, U.S. District Court, Eastern District of Pennsylvania and U.S. District Court, District of New Jersey; 1990, U.S. Court of Appeals, Third Circuit; 1995, District of Columbia and U.S. District Court for the District of Columbia; 1996, U.S. Court of Appeals for the District of Columbia Circuit and U.S. Court of Federal Claims; 1999, U.S. District Court, District of Colorado; 2001, U.S. Court of Appeals, Fourth Circuit and U.S. District Court, District of Maryland. *Education:* University of Michigan (B.A., 1984); Syracuse University (J.D., cum laude, 1989). *Member:* American Bar Association (Member, Litigation Section). ***PRACTICE AREAS:*** Civil Litigation. ***Email:*** dsouthard@hklaw.com

LESLIE S. SPITALNEY, born Baltimore, Maryland, August 29, 1967; admitted to bar, 1992, Florida; 1996, Virginia; 1997, District of Columbia. *Education:* University of Virginia (B.A., intermediate honors, 1989); George Washington University (J.D., with honors, 1992). ***PRACTICE AREAS:*** Intellectual Property; Litigation. ***Email:*** lspitaln@hklaw.com

DAMIEN G. STEWART, born Washington, D.C., July 14, 1970; admitted to bar, 1997, Florida; 1999, District of Columbia; U.S. District Court, Southern District of Florida; U.S. District Court, District of Maryland; U.S. District Court, District of Columbia. *Education:* George Washington University (B.A., cum laude, 1992); University of Virginia (J.D., 1995). Law Clerk to the Honorable Donald L. Graham, U.S. District Court, Southern District of Florida, 1995-1997. ***PRACTICE AREAS:*** Employment and Labor Law (100%). ***Email:*** dgstewart@hklaw.com

SARAH E. TIPPET, born Norwalk, Connecticut, August 2, 1974; admitted to bar, 1998, Connecticut; 1999, New York; 2001, District of Columbia. *Education:* University of Virginia (B.A., 1995); University of Connecticut School of Law (J.D., 1998). ***PRACTICE AREAS:*** Real Estate Law. ***Email:*** stippet@hklaw.com

DOUGLAS A. TUCKER, born Boston, Massachusetts, June 6, 1966; admitted to bar, 1996, Virginia; 1997, District of Columbia. *Education:* United States Naval Academy (B.S., with distinction, 1988); University of Virginia (J.D., 1996). Armor Scholar, University of Virginia. *Member:* Virginia State Bar; The District of Columbia Bar. [Lt., U.S.N., 1988-1992]. ***PRACTICE AREAS:*** Trial and Appellate Litigation. ***Email:*** datucker@hklaw.com

MARIA A. WHITEHORN, born Winchester, Massachusetts, May 17, 1972; admitted to bar, 1999, Virginia (Not admitted in District of Columbia). *Education:* Williams College (B.A., 1994); University of Virginia (J.D., 1999). Law Clerk to the Honorable Theresa Carroll Buchanan, U.S. District Court, Eastern District of Virginia, Alexandria Division, 1999-2000. ***PRACTICE AREAS:*** Litigation; Antitrust; Employment. ***Email:*** mwhitehorn@hklaw.com

DAVID C. WHITESTONE, born Falls Church, Virginia, May 11, 1969; admitted to bar, 1999, Virginia (Not admitted in District of Columbia). *Education:* George Mason University (B.A., 1991); George Mason University School of Law (J.D., 1998). ***PRACTICE AREAS:*** Transportation; Public Infrastructure; Government Relations. ***Email:*** dwhitestone@hklaw.com

KIMBERLY YOUNG, born Gassaway, West Virginia, October 23, 1966; admitted to bar, 1993, Pennsylvania; 1997, Maryland, U.S. Court of International Trade and U.S. Court of Appeals for the Federal Circuit; 1998, District of Columbia. *Education:* West Virginia University (B.A., summa cum laude, 1988); University of Virginia (J.D., 1993). Phi Beta Kappa. ***REPORTED CASES:*** Gerald Metals, Inc. v. United States, 132 F.3d 716 (Fed. Cir., 1997). ***PRACTICE AREAS:*** International Trade; Customs Law. ***Email:*** kyoung@hklaw.com

OF COUNSEL

STUART MARSHALL BLOCH, born 1942; admitted to bar, 1968, Michigan; 1969, District of Columbia. *Education:* University of Miami (A.B., 1964); Harvard University (LL.B., 1967). Editor: The Real Estate Workout Game, 1986-1991; A Practical Guide to FIRREA, 1989; the Lender Liability Game, 1988. Co-Editor: "Land Development Law Reporter," "Digest of State Land Sales Regulations," 1975; "Time Sharing: An Analysis of Multiple Ownership and Use Techniques," Urban Land Institute, 1977, 1982. *Member:* The District of Columbia Bar; State Bar of Michigan; American Bar Association. (Also Member, Ingersoll and Bloch, Washington, D.C.). ***PRACTICE AREAS:*** Financial Institutions Law; Real Estate Law; Interstate Land Sales; Timesharing. ***Email:*** smbloch@hklaw.com

DAVID M. BOND, born Washington, D.C., June 25, 1937; admitted to bar, 1966, District of Columbia; 1971, U.S. Supreme Court. *Education:* University of Maryland (B.S. with high honors, 1962); George Washington University (LL.B., 1965). Beta Alpha Psi; Beta Gamma Sigma. Certified Public Accountant, Maryland, 1962. *Member:* The District of Columbia Bar; American Bar Association. ***PRACTICE AREAS:*** Commercial Transactional Real Estate; Leasing; Condominium Law; Real Estate Sales. ***Email:*** dbond@hklaw.com

PHILIP N. HOGEN, born Kadoka, South Dakota, November 15, 1944; admitted to bar, 1970, South Dakota, U.S. District Court, District of South Dakota, Oglala Sioux Tribal Court (Not admitted in District of Columbia). *Education:* Augustana College (B.S., 1967); University of South Dakota (J.D., 1970). Member and Vice Chairman, National Indian Gaming Commission, Washington, D.C., 1995-1999. Director, Office of The American Indian Trust, Dept. of the Interior, Washington, D.C., 1992-1993; United States Attorney of the District of South Dakota, Sioux Falls, S.D., 1981-1991. Jackson County States Attorney, Kadoka, S.D., 1975-1981. *Member:* State Bar of South Dakota; Chairman, Indian Affairs Subcommittee, Attorney General's Advisory Committee of the U.S. Attorneys, 1986-1991; President, South Dakota States Attorneys Association, 1979-1980. ***PRACTICE AREAS:*** Indian Law; Gaming Law; Administrative Law. ***Email:*** phogen@hklaw.com

WILLIAM B. INGERSOLL, born Washington, D.C., 1938; admitted to bar, 1968, Virginia; 1969, District of Columbia; 1972, U.S. Supreme Court. *Education:* Brigham Young University (B.S., 1964); Catholic University of America (J.D., 1968). General Counsel, American Resort Development Association (1970—). Co-Editor: "Land Development Law Reporter," "Resort Law Reporter," and "Digest of State Resort Development Regulations," 1975—. Author: "Interstate Land Sales: How to Deal with HUD's New Regulations," New York Law Journal; "Consumer Protection in Interstate Land Sales," Practising Law Institute; "Land Sales Regulatory Crackdowns," New York Law Journal; "A Guide for Salesmen," (8th Edition); "Time Sharing: An Analysis of Multiple Ownership and Use Techniques," Urban Land Institute. *Member:* District of Columbia Bar; Virginia and American (Member, Real Property Law Section) Bar Associations. (Also Member, Ingersoll and Bloch, Washington, D.C.). ***Email:*** wingerso@hklaw.com

MARC LEVY, born Brooklyn, New York, November 17, 1961; admitted to bar, 1986, Maryland; 1987, District of Columbia. *Education:* Brandeis University (B.A., magna cum laude, 1983); George Washington University (J.D., with honors, 1986). Author: "Financial Statements and Loan Loss Revenues," Journal of Banking and Financial Services, October 2, 1991. *Member:* Maryland State and American (Member, Business Section) Bar Associations; The District of Columbia Bar. ***PRACTICE AREAS:*** Securities; Corporate; Financial Services Law. ***Email:*** mplevy@hklaw.com

THOMAS F. RAILSBACK, born Moline, Illinois, 1932; admitted to bar, 1957, Illinois; 1978, District of Columbia. *Education:* Grinnell College (B.A., 1954); Northwestern University (J.D., 1957). Recipient: Alumni Award for Distinguished Service, Grinnell College, 1973; Flandrau Award for the National Council on Crime and Delinquency, 1974. Member: U.S. House of Representatives, 1966-1982; Illinois General Assembly, 1962-1966. *Member:* District of Columbia Bar (Vice Chair, General Practice Section, 1985-1986); American Bar Association (Vice Chair: Legislative Action Committee, General Practice Section, 1985-1987; Member: Patent, Trademark and Copyright Committee, 1985-1987; Advisory Committee on Governmental Affairs, 1986-1987; Judiciary Committee, General Practice Section, 1987-1988). [With U.S. Army, 1957-1959]. ***PRACTICE AREAS:*** Federal Legislative; Patent; Copyright; Trademark; Telecommunications. ***Email:*** trailsback@aol.com

RICHARD S. WEINSTEIN, born New York, N.Y., 1925; admitted to bar, 1949, Florida and Connecticut (Not admitted in District of Columbia). *Education:* University of Florida (J.D., with honors, 1949). Phi Eta Sigma; Phi Kappa Phi. Member, Florida Law Review, 1949. Chairman, Fairfield County National Bank (Conn.), 1964-1976. Founder and Trustee, Land Preservation Trust of Palm Beach County, 1990—; Chairman, Board of Governors, The Nature Conservancy, 1990-1992; Chairman, Anti-Defamation League, Palm Beach Regional Board Member, 1992-1996, National Commissioner, 1994—. *Member:* The Florida Bar; Connecticut and American Bar Associations. Fellow, American Bar Foundation; Trustee, Darwin Scientific Foundation; Director, Florida Atlantic University Foundation, 1997—; Vice-Chairman, John D. MacArthur State Park Board; Director, Community Foundation, Palm Beach and Martin County, 1997—. (Also in West Palm Beach, Florida Office). ***PRACTICE AREAS:*** Alternative Dispute Resolution; Probate; Estate Planning; Business Law. ***Email:*** rweinste@hklaw.com

(For Biographical Data of other firm Personnel, see Professional Biographies at other offices indicated in the heading of this card).

(This Listing Continued)

HOLLANDER LAW FIRM, P.L.C.

WASHINGTON, D.C.

(See Fairfax, Virginia)

Intellectual Property, Patent Trademarks and Copyrights, Unfair Competition and Related Litigation.

HOLMAN & STERN

CHARTERED, PLLC

WASHINGTON, D.C.

(See Jacobson, Holman, PLLC)

HOLMES, SCHWARTZ & GORDON

WASHINGTON, D.C.

(See Rockville, Maryland)

Government Contract Law, Bid Protests, Complex Commercial Litigation, Uniform Commercial Code, Contract Litigation, Breach of Contract, Defense Contracts, Defense Contract Fraud, Government Constuction Contracts, Government Procurement, Local Government Contracts, Small Business Law, Commercial Law, Property Tax Abatement.

HOLTZ & FORET, LLC

WASHINGTON, D.C.

(See Chevy Chase, Maryland)

Products Liability, Medical Malpractice, Personal Injury and Premises Liability.

HOOVER PARTNERS

1101 CONNECTICUT AVENUE, N.W., SUITE 1000
WASHINGTON, D.C. 20036
Telephone: 202-828-2428
Fax: 202-318-2657
URL: http://www.hooverpartners.com
Email: kim@hooverpartners.com
URL: http://www.lawyers.com/hoover

Banks and Banking, International Financial Institutions, Federal Regulatory Privacy, Information Security.

KIMBERLY HILL HOOVER, born Fort Worth, Texas, January 22, 1958; admitted to bar, 1984, Texas; 1985, District of Columbia. *Education:* Baylor University (B.A., magna cum laude, 1980); Duke University (J.D., 1983). Latty Scholar. Executive Editor, Duke Law Journal, 1982-1983. Author: Note, "Foreign Government—Owned Corporations, The Foreign Sovereign Immunities Act and the Right to Jury Trial," 1982 Duke Law Journal 1071. Adjunct Faculty, Washington College of Law, American University, 1990—. Director, Treasury Bank, Ltd., 1990-1992. *Member:* The District of Columbia Bar; State Bar of Texas; American Bar Association; Women's Bar Association; Washington Area Lawyers for the Arts. ***PRACTICE AREAS:*** Financial Institutions Law; Financial Infrastructures; Banking Law; International Finance; Information and Privacy. ***Email:*** kim@hooverpartners.com

---

THE LAW OFFICES OF HOPP & ASSOCIATES, P.L.L.C

Established in 1995
1250 24TH STREET, N.W.
SUITE 300
WASHINGTON, D.C. 20037
Telephone: 202-467-8339
Fax: 202-467-8340
URL: http://www.ecolaw.com
Email: hopp&associates@ecolaw.com
URL: http://www.ecolaw.com

Domestic and International Environmental, Natural Resources and Related Business Law, Including:: Air Pollution, Water Pollution (TMDL's, Criteria), Climate Change/Joint Implementation, Ozone Depletion, Endangered Species, Compliance Counseling, Enforcement, Contractor Debarment, Litigation, Sustainable Development Finance, Environmental Commodity Transactions and Permits (Effluent Trading, Acid Rain Allowances, International Greenhouse Gas Offsets), Conservation Easements, Renewable Energy, Environmental Due Diligence, Regulatory Flexibility.

(This Listing Continued)

FIRM PROFILE: The Law Offices of Hopp and Associates, P.L.L.C,. in Washington D.C., is dedicated exclusively to the practice of environment, natural resources and related business law matters. Our professionals include former U.S. Environmental Protection Agency (USEPA), The Department of State and Agency for International Development officials and employees, experienced environmental litigators, regulatory and legislative experts, and bi-lingual experts in international environmental law negotiations and transactions. Recognized for our unparalleled achieyements in designing low-cost, flexible solutions to our clients' environmental concerns, we advise and represent businesses and individuals, government and municipal agencies, other law firms and international organizations on a range of complex matters.

RACHEL M. HOPP, born Washington, D.C., February 16, 1952; admitted to bar, 1979, District of Columbia; 1980, U.S. Court of Appeals for the District of Columbia Circuit; 1985, U.S. Supreme Court. *Education:* University of Zulia, Venezuela (1973); University of Maryland (B.A., with honors, 1974); Catholic University of America, Columbus School of Law (J.D., with honors, 1979). Sigma Delta Phi Spanish Honor Society. Recipient: Corpus Juris Secundum Award, 1979; American Judicature Society Award, 1979; Certificate of Participation in 1st Round U.S. Initiative on Joint Implementation (JSIJI), 1996; U.S. Environmental Protection Agency Gold Medal for Exceptional Service, 1990 Clean Air Act (CAA) Amendments; Silver Medal for Superior Service, Acid Rain Program, 1991; Bronze Medal for Commendable Service, Asbestos Air Pollution Enforcement Initiative, 1989; Special Act Awards, 1985-1990. Co-Author: "Politics, Pollution and TMDLs: New Directions in Point and Nonpoint Source Liability For Watershed Restoration, J.Envtl.Reg. & Permitting, Summer 2000, with E. Napoli. Author: "The Kyoto Protocol to the United Nations Framework Convention on Climate Change-Part I: The Unfinished Agenda; Part II: Emissions Trading-The Emerging Responsibilities & Opportunities," J.Envtl.Reg. & Permitting, Summer 1998 and Fall 1998; "Settling with P2, P2 Rev. Legacy and the Browner Reorganization, Part II-EPA's New Office of Enforcement and Compliance Assurance," EPA Admin.L.Rep. Sep. and Oct. 1993. Former Chief, Acid Rain Permits and Technologies Section, U.S. Environmental Protection Agency. Enforcement Attorney, U.S. Environmental Protection Agency, 1984-1993. Member, Board of Editorial Advisors: Environmental Manager; The Journal of Environmental Regulation and Permitting. Principal, Council for Excellence in Government. Member: Emissions Management Association; Waste Management Association; Environmental Law Institute Association of Metropolitan Sewerage Agencies. Lead Counsel: Western Carolina Regional Sewer Authority v. South Carolina Department of Health and Environmental Control, Docket Nos. 98-ALJ-07-0267-CC, 98-ALJ-0585-CC , 1999 SC ENV LEXIS (S.C ALJ Div., September 22, 1999) (Clean Water Act Total Maximum Daily Load, Phosphorus, Nutrient Criteria). First Chair, Rio Bravo U.S. IJIP Project, Belize, 1994-1995. Noel Kempff Mercado USIJP Project, Bolivia, 1996. *Member:* The District of Columbia Bar (Member, Sections on: International Law; Energy Environment; National Resources); American Bar Association (Member, Sections on: International Law; Natural Resources; Energy and Environment Law; Member, Air Quality Committee; Member, Special Section on Global Change); Inter-American Bar Association (Member, Environmental Law Section). ***LANGUAGES:*** Spanish, French, Italian, Portuguese. ***PRACTICE AREAS:*** Environmental Law; Environmental Compliance; Environmental Litigation; Conservation Law; Land Trusts; Commodities; Regulation; Plan Variety Protection. ***Email:*** rhopp@ecolaw.com

---

ERIC LOUIS NAPOLI, admitted to bar, 1999, New York (Not admitted in District of Columbia). *Education:* Washington College of Law, American University (J.D., 1999). Former Project Attorney, U.S. Agency for International Development (Strategies for National Councils of Sustainable Development in Latin America). ***LANGUAGES:*** Spanish. ***PRACTICE AREAS:*** International Law; Environmental Law; Environmental Regulation. ***Email:*** cnapoli@ecolaw.com

---

HOPPEL, MAYER & COLEMAN

Established in 1953
1000 CONNECTICUT AVENUE, N.W., SUITE 400
WASHINGTON, D.C. 20036
Telephone: 202-296-5460
Telecopier: 202-296-5463
Email: hmc@hmc-law.com
URL: http://www.lawyers.com/hmc-law

Maritime Administrative Law, Maritime Commercial Law, Transportation Regulations, Administrative Law, Transportation Arbitration.

FIRM PROFILE: For over 34 years we have advised, counseled and represented ocean common carriers, shippers, non-vessel-operating common carriers, freight forwarders, marine terminal operators, and public port authorities, in connection

(This Listing Continued)

with corporate, business, and commercial issues, as well as statutory and regulatory matters arising under maritime, surface transportation and related statutes.

MEMBERS OF FIRM

NEAL MICHAEL MAYER, born New York, N.Y., December 4, 1941; admitted to bar, 1967, District of Columbia, U.S. Court of Appeals for the District of Columbia Circuit and U.S. Customs Court; 1970, U.S. Supreme Court; 1975, U.S. Court of Appeals, Fifth Circuit. *Education:* Kenyon College (B.A., with honors, 1963); Georgetown University (J.D., 1966). Phi Alpha Delta. President, Kenyon College Alumni Association, 1993-1994. Trustee, Kenyon College, 1995—. *Member:* The District of Columbia Bar; American Bar Association (Member, Sections on: Administrative Law; Antitrust Law); Maritime Administrative Bar Association (President, 1978-1979). ***PRACTICE AREAS:*** Maritime Administrative Law; Transportation; International Maritime Law; Shipping Regulations. ***Email:*** nmayer@hmc-law.com

PAUL D. COLEMAN, born Alexandria, Virginia, September 28, 1947; admitted to bar, 1973, Maryland; 1974, District of Columbia; 1975, U.S. Court of Appeals for the District of Columbia Circuit and U.S. District Court for the District of Maryland including Trial Bar; 1983, U.S. Supreme Court. *Education:* University of North Carolina (B.S., 1969); Georgetown University (J.D., 1973). Editor, Survey of Maritime Administrative Law, Vol. 7, July 1998. *Member:* The District of Columbia Bar; Maryland State and American (Member, Administrative Law Section) Bar Associations; Maritime Administrative Bar Association (President, 1998-1999). ***PRACTICE AREAS:*** Maritime Administrative Law; Shipping Regulations; Transportation; Energy Law. ***Email:*** pcoleman@hmc-law.com

HOULON & BERMAN, LLC

WASHINGTON, D.C.

(See New Carrollton)

General Civil Practice. Real Estate, Settlements, Mortgages, Foreclosures, Corporate, Business Law, Negligence, Personal Injury, Automobile Accidents, Product Liability, Criminal Law, Traffic, Bankruptcy, Family, Divorce, Child Custody, Adoptions, Juvenile Law, Guardianship, Wrongful Death, Driving While Intoxicated.

HOWE, ANDERSON & STEYER, P.C.

815 CONNECTICUT AVENUE, N.W., SUITE 620
WASHINGTON, D.C. 20006
Telephone: 202-296-5680
Facsimile: 202-331-8049
Email: info@haspc.com
URL: http://www.haspc.com

Administrative, Association, Labor and Employment, Legislative, Civil and Criminal Litigation, Antitrust and Trade Regulation, Nonprofit Taxation, Trademark and Pension Law.

WILLIAM H. HOWE, born Washington, D.C., May 15, 1944; admitted to bar, 1970, District of Columbia and U.S. Court of Appeals for the District of Columbia Circuit; 1973, U.S. Court of Appeals, Third Circuit; 1974, U.S. Supreme Court; 1976, U.S. Court of Appeals, Fourth Circuit; 1981, U.S. Court of Appeals, Eleventh Circuit. *Education:* Dartmouth College (A.B., 1966); University of Virginia (LL.B., 1969). *Member:* District of Columbia Bar; American Bar Association. ***PRACTICE AREAS:*** Labor Law; Legislative Law; Employment Law; Association Law. ***Email:*** whowe@haspc.com

JAMES E. ANDERSON, born Oklahoma City, Oklahoma, April 11, 1942; admitted to bar, 1967, Iowa; 1976, District of Columbia. *Education:* College of St. Thomas (B.A., 1964); State University of Iowa (J.D., 1967). Phi Alpha Delta (Vice Justice, 1966-1967). Special Agent, Federal Bureau of Investigation, 1967-1970. Assistant U.S. Attorney, District of Maryland, 1970-1976. *Member:* District of Columbia Bar; Iowa State and American Bar Associations. ***PRACTICE AREAS:*** Antitrust Law; Trade Regulation Law; Association Law; Civil and Criminal Litigation. ***Email:*** janderson@haspc.com

RICHARD ALAN STEYER, born New York, N.Y., May 1, 1951; admitted to bar, 1977, New York; 1978, District of Columbia; 1994, Maryland. *Education:* Washington University (A.B., 1973); George Washington University (J.D., with honors, 1976). Attorney, National Labor Relations Board, 1976-1979. *Member:* District of Columbia Bar; American Bar Association (Member, Labor and Employment Law Section). ***PRACTICE AREAS:*** Labor and Employment Law; Nonprofit Associations; Trade Regulation; Legislative. ***Email:*** rsteyer@haspc.com

MARY LOU SMITH, born Trafford, Pennsylvania, April 5, 1956; admitted to bar, 1981, Pennsylvania; 1985, District of Columbia; 1986, U.S. Court of Appeals, Fourth Circuit; 1987, U.S. Court of Appeals, Sixth Circuit; 1992, U.S. Court of Appeals for the District of Columbia Circuit and U.S. Supreme Court. *Education:* Michigan State University (B.A., 1978); University of Pennsylvania (J.D., 1981). *Member:* District of Columbia Bar (Member, Section of Labor Relations). ***Email:*** mlsmith@haspc.com

(This Listing Continued)

ROBERT J. WEIL, born Bethlehem, Pennsylvania, June 16, 1954; admitted to bar, 1980, Florida; 1983, Connecticut; 1994, Virginia, District of Columbia and Maryland. *Education:* St. Joseph's University (B.A., 1976); Catholic University of America (J.D., 1979). *Member:* The Florida Bar; Connecticut Bar Association; The District of Columbia Bar; Virginia State Bar; Maryland State Bar Association, Inc. ***PRACTICE AREAS:*** Civil Litigation; Insurance Law; Legislative Practice; Association Law. ***Email:*** rweil@haspc.com

HOWE & HUTTON, LTD.

Established in 1985

1054 THIRTY-FIRST STREET, N.W., SUITE 200
WASHINGTON, D.C. 20007
Telephone: 202-466-7252
Fax: 202-466-5829
Email: hh@howehutton.com
URL: http://www.howehutton.com

Chicago, Illinois Office: 20 North Wacker Drive, Suite 4200, 60606-9833. Telephone: 312-263-3001. Fax: 312-372-6685.

Ballwin (St. Louis), Missouri Office: 1421 Buckhurst Court, 63021. Telephone: 636-256-3351. Fax: 636-256-3727.

General Representation of Not for Profit Organizations, Associations and Related Entities, Antitrust, Corporate, Employment, Contract, Administrative, Tax, Travel, Transportation, Meetings, Expositions and Hospitality Industry, Intellectual Property Law, Arbitration, Alternative Dispute Resolution, Trial and Appellate Practice.

JONATHAN T. HOWE, born Evanston, Illinois, December 16, 1940; admitted to bar, 1966, Illinois; 1967, U.S. Court of Appeals, 7th Circuit and U.S. Tax Court; 1970, U.S. Supreme Court; 1976, District of Columbia; 1980, U.S. Court of Appeals, 9th Circuit; 1984, U.S. Court of Appeals, 5th, 6th and 11th Circuits; 1990, U.S. Claims Court; 1992, U.S. District Court, Northern District of Texas. *Education:* Northwestern University (B.A., with honors, 1963); Duke University (J.D., with highest distinction, 1966). Order of the Coif; Phi Alpha Delta. Recipient, Phi Alpha Delta Outstanding Scholastic Achievement Award. ***PRACTICE AREAS:*** Not For Profit Corporations; Travel, Tourism, Hotel and Meetings Liability; Arbitration; Alternative Dispute Resolution; Trial and Appellate. ***Email:*** jth@howehutton.com

LELAND J. BADGER, born Evanston, Illinois, May 15, 1948; admitted to bar, 1973, Illinois and U.S. District Court, Northern District of Illinois; 1975, U.S. Court of Claims, and U.S. Court of Appeals, District of Columbia Circuit; 1976, District of Columbia and U.S. Court of Appeals, Seventh Circuit; 1977, U.S. Supreme Court; 1983, U.S. District Court for the District of Columbia; 1982, U.S. Court of Appeals for the Federal Circuit. *Education:* Dartmouth College (A.B., summa cum laude with highest distinction, 1970); Harvard Law School (J.D., 1973). Phi Beta Kappa. Member, Harvard Journal on Legislation, 1971-1972. Attorney Advisor to the Assistant General Counsel to the Secretary of the Air Force for International Matters and Civil Aviation (Attorney, Honors Program, Office of Air Force General Counsel, The Pentagon, 1973-1975). National Institute of Trial Advocacy: Graduate, 1977; Assistant Teaching Team Leader, 1979. Assistant Lecturer in Trial Practice, Northwestern University Law School, 1978. *Member:* The District of Columbia Bar; Chicago, Illinois State (Member, Sections of: Civil Practice and Procedure; Tort Law; Antitrust Law; Health Law; Corporation Law), Federal (Member, Sections of: Antitrust; Government Contracts) and American (Member, Sections of: Litigation; Antitrust Law; Health Forum; Business Law) Bar Associations. [Capt., U.S. Air Force, 1973-1975]. ***PRACTICE AREAS:*** Not for Profit Corporations; Association Law; Health Care Law; Litigation; Antitrust Law; Government Contracts Law. ***Email:*** ljb@howehutton.com

(For Complete Biographical Data on all Personnel, see Professional Biographies at Chicago, Illinois)

HOWES & KINNANE, P.C.

WASHINGTON, D.C.

(See Annapolis, Maryland)

Personal Injury, Automobile Accidents, Criminal Law, Driving While Intoxicated, Traffic Violations, Employment Discrimination, Family Law, Divorce, Custody, Support, Adoptions, Business Law, Civil Practice, Energy and Utility Law.

IRENE E. HOWIE

WASHINGTON, D.C.

(See Annapolis, Maryland)

Aviation Law, International Law, Administrative Law.

HOWREY SIMON ARNOLD & WHITE, LLP

1299 PENNSYLVANIA AVENUE, N.W.
WASHINGTON, D.C. 20004-2402
Telephone: 202-783-0800
Fax: 202-383-6610
URL: http://www.howrey.com

Century City, California Office: 1925 Century Park East, Suite 2100, 90067-2512. Telephone: 310-712-1000. Fax: 310-712-1099.

Los Angeles, California Office: Suite 1400, 550 South Hope Street, 90071-2604. Telephone: 213-892-1800. Fax: 213-892-2300.

Menlo Park, California Office: 301 Ravenswood Avenue, 94025. Telephone: 650-463-8100. Fax: 650-463-8400.

Houston, Texas Office: 750 Bering Drive, 77057-2198. Telephone: 713-787-1400. Fax: 713-787-1440.

Minneapolis, Minnesota Office: 4850 U.S. Bank Place, 601 Second Avenue South, 55402-4320.

Irvine, California Office: 2020 Main Street, Suite 1000. Telephone: 949-721-6900.

Chicago, Illinois Office: 321 North Clark Street, Suite 800, 60610. Telephone: 312-595-1239. Fax: 312-595-2250.

London Office: City Point, One Ropemaker Street, EC2Y 9HS. Telephone: 011 44 207 6283303. Fax: 011 44 207 065 6650.

General and Trial Practice including Antitrust, Commercial Litigation, Corporate and Transactional, Environmental, Government Contracts, Insurance Coverage, Intellectual Property, International Trade, Products Liability, Securities Litigation, Supreme Court and Appellate and White Collar Criminal Defense.

FIRM PROFILE: Howrey Simon Arnold & White, LLP is a world leader in intellectual property, antitrust/competition, and complex business litigation. Founded in 1956, Howrey Simon Arnold & White, LLP employs more than 500 attorneys, as well as over 50 economic, financial, environmental consultants, and economic research analysts in offices in Washington, D.C., Houston, Los Angeles, Menlo Park, Irvine, Chicago and London. Howrey is the second most-frequently mentioned firm in the National Law Journal's 2000 survey "Who Represents Corporate America," a listing of law firms preferred by Fortune 250 non-financial companies and ranked first in IP Worldwide's 1999 survey of "Who Represents the World's Most Valuable IP Rights?". Howrey is also the leading antitrust firm in the world according to the Global Competition Review (2000) and its attorneys include many former FTC and DOJ officials and current and former ABA officers, council members, and committee chairs. Unrivaled in our plaintiff and defense work in high-stakes cases, the firm has litigated in the federal courts of 49 states and represented clients in over 1,500 federal and state court cases since 1995 and handled 444 Supreme Court and appellate matters over the past 6 years. The firm is ranked in the top 25 firms nationally for its pro bono efforts.

WILLIAM SIMON, born Chicago, Illinois, 1912; admitted to bar, 1935, Illinois; 1953, District of Columbia. *Education:* Crane College; Chicago-Kent College of Law (LL.B., 1935). General Counsel, Trade Policies Sub-committee, Senate Interstate and Foreign Commerce Committee, 1948-1949. General Counsel of Petroleum Administration for Defense, 1952-1953. General Counsel, Advisory Committee on Foreign Trade to Senate Banking and Currency Committee, 1953-1954. General Counsel, FHA Investigation, Senate Banking and Currency Committee, 1954. Member, Attorney General's National Committee to Study the Antitrust Laws, 1953-1955. *Member:* The District of Columbia Bar; American Bar Association (Chairman, Antitrust Section, 1954-1955). Fellow: American College of Trial Lawyers.

DAVID C. MURCHISON, born New York, N.Y., 1923; admitted to bar, 1949, District of Columbia. *Education:* University of North Carolina and George Washington University; George Washington University Law School (J.D., with honors, 1949). Order of the Coif; Phi Delta Phi. Legal Assistant to Under Secretary of the Army, 1949-1951. Associate General Counsel, Small Defense Plants Administration, 1952-1953. Legal Adviser and Assistant to the Chairman, Federal Trade Commission, 1953-1955. Legal Adviser to United States Delegation to United Nations Economic and Social Council, 1955. Chairman, Southern Africa Wildlife Trust, 1991—. *Member:* The District of Columbia Bar; Bar Association of the District of Columbia; New York State, American and Federal Bar Associations; American Society of International Law. ***Email:*** murchisond@howrey.com

HAROLD F. BAKER, born Moriah, New York, 1921; admitted to bar, 1949, District of Columbia. *Education:* Asbury College and George Washington University (J.D., with honors, 1949). Order of the Coif; Phi Delta Phi. *Member:* The District of Columbia Bar; American Bar Association. Fellow: American College of Trial Lawyers.

COUNSEL

VICTOR L. COHEN, born Washington, D.C., January 5, 1945; admitted to bar, 1971, Maryland, District of Columbia, U.S. District Court, District of Washington and U.S. Court of Appeals, District of Columbia Circuit. *Education:* University of Maryland (B.S., 1966; J.D., 1971). Beta Alpha Psi. Contributing Author: "Premerger Notification Practice Manual," ABA Section of Antitrust, 1991. *Member:* American Bar Association (Member, Antitrust Law Section, 1998-1999). ***PRACTICE AREAS:*** Antitrust Law. ***Email:*** cohenvictor@howrey.com

TERRENCE C. SHEEHY, born Garden City, Kansas, October 24, 1937; admitted to bar, 1963, Virginia and District of Columbia. *Education:* Regis College (B.S., 1959); Georgetown University (LL.B., 1962). *Member:* The District of Columbia Bar; Virginia State Bar; American Bar Association. ***PRACTICE AREAS:*** Antitrust; Litigation. ***Email:*** sheehyt@howrey.com

MEMBERS OF FIRM

ROBERT G. ABRAMS, born Paterson, New Jersey, July 6, 1946; admitted to bar, 1972, Colorado; 1975, District of Columbia. *Education:* Colgate University (A.B., 1968); George Washington University (J.D., with honors, 1972). Member, 1970-1971 and Managing Editor, 1971-1972, George Washington University Law Review. Law Clerk, Hon William E. Doyle, U.S. Court of Appeals for the Tenth Circuit, 1972-1973. *Member:* The District of Columbia Bar; Colorado and American Bar Associations. ***PRACTICE AREAS:*** Antitrust; Intellectual Property; Appellate Practice; Commercial Litigation. ***Email:*** abramsr@howrey.com

SCOTT ARNOLD, born Brooklyn, New York, May 22, 1957; admitted to bar, 1982, District of Columbia; 1983, U.S. District Court for the District of Columbia; 1985, U.S. Court of Federal Claims. *Education:* State University of New York at Albany (B.A., magna cum laude, 1979); George Washington University (J.D., with honors, 1982). Attorney Advisor, Department of Transportation Contract Appeals Board, 1982-1984. Assistant Counsel, Naval Facilities Engineering Command, Department of the Navy, 1984-1985. *Member:* The District of Columbia Bar; American Bar Association (Member, Section on Public Contract Law). ***PRACTICE AREAS:*** Government Contracts; Litigation. ***Email:*** arnolds@howrey.com

RICHARD E. AYRES, born Salem, New Jersey, February 2, 1942; admitted to bar, 1972, New York and U.S. Court of Appeals, 1st and 5th Circuits; 1973, U.S. Court of Appeals, 2nd, 5th, 8th, 9th and 10th Circuits; 1975, District of Columbia and U.S. Court of Appeals, 6th Circuit; 1976, U.S. Supreme Court. *Education:* Woodrow Wilson School of Public and International Affairs; Princeton University (A.B., with honors, 1964); Yale Graduate School of Political Science (M.A., 1969); Yale Law School (LL.B., 1969). Projects Editor, Yale Law Journal, 1968-1969. Recipient, Peres Prize. Yale Law School Association of Washington for Outstanding Service to the Public Interest, 1988; Yale Law School Environmental Law Association for Role in Creating Environmental Law, 1989. Author: "Interrogations in New Haven: The Impact of Miranda," 76 Yale Law Journal, 1519 (1967); "Environmental Pollution Control on Stationary Sources Under The Clean Air Act Amendments of 1970," 4 Ecol. L.Q. 441 (1975); "New Source Standard for Power Plants II: Consider the Law," 3 Harv. E.L. Rev. 63 (1979); "The Proposed WEPCo Rule: Making the Problem Fit the Solution," 22 Environmental Reporter 10201 (1992); "Developing a Market in Emission Credits Incrementally: An 'Open Market' Paradigm For Market-Based Pollution Control," 25 BNA Environment Reporter No. 31 (Dec. 2, 1994); "Clean Air Permitting Manual" (1995) (with James T. O'Reilly, Professor William V. Luneberg, Kim Burke and James Witt). Commissioner, National Commission on Air Quality, 1978-1981; Carnegie Commission on Science, Technology and Government, Task Force on Science and Technology in Judicial and Regulatory Decisionmaking, 1991-1994; Center for Strategic and International Studies, Enterprise for the Environment, 1995-1998; The Keystone Center, 1998—; Vermont Law School Advisory Committee, 1992—. *Member:* The District of Columbia Bar. ***PRACTICE AREAS:*** Environmental Law. ***Email:*** ayresr@howrey.com

GREGORY L. BAKER, born Baytown, Texas, December 7, 1954; admitted to bar, 1979, Texas and District of Columbia. *Education:* University of Virginia (B.A., with distinction, 1976); University of Texas (J.D., with honors, 1978); Wharton School, University of Pennsylvania (M.B.A., 1999). Comments Editor, Urban Law Review, 1977-1978. *Member:* The District of Columbia Bar; State Bar of Texas; American Bar Association (Member, Sections on Antitrust, Litigation, and Science and Technology); American Intellectual Property Law Association. ***PRACTICE AREAS:*** Litigation; Antitrust Law; Intellectual Property. ***Email:*** bakerg@howrey.com

J. DOUGLAS BALDRIDGE, born 1962; admitted to bar, 1987, Florida; 1992, Virginia; 1993, District of Columbia and Maryland; U.S. Supreme Court; U.S. Court of Appeals for the District of Columbia, Fourth, Eleventh and

(This Listing Continued)

Federal Circuits; U.S. District Court for the District of Columbia, Eastern District of Virginia, District of Maryland and Middle District of Florida; U.S. Claims Court. *Education:* Florida State University (B.A., magna cum laude, 1984); George Washington University (J.D., with honors, 1987). Phi Beta Kappa; Omicron Delta Kappa; Phi Delta Phi. Member, Mortar Board. ***PRACTICE AREAS:*** Litigation. ***Email:*** baldridged@howrey.com

MICHAEL J. BELL, born Scranton, Pennsylvania, July 6, 1959; admitted to bar, 1989, Virginia; 1990, District of Columbia; registered to practice before U.S. Patent and Trademark Office. *Education:* University of Notre Dame (B.S.M.E., 1982); Georgetown University Law Center (J.D., 1989). Member, Journal of Legal Ethics, 1987-1989. *Member:* The District of Columbia Bar (Member, Intellectual Property Section); Virginia State Bar (Member, Intellectual Property Law Section); American Bar Association (Member, Section on Patent, Trademark and Copyright Law; Special Committee 351 Hague Agreement, Industrial Designs); American Intellectual Property Law Association (Member, Industrial Design Section); Maryland Patent Bar. ***PRACTICE AREAS:*** Intellectual Property. ***Email:*** bellm@howrey.com

DARREN B. BERNHARD, born Yonkers, New York, February 8, 1961; admitted to bar, 1986, Pennsylvania; 1988, District of Columbia. *Education:* Franklin & Marshall College (B.A., 1983); American University (M.A., 1986; J.D., 1986). American University Law Review, 1984-1986. ***PRACTICE AREAS:*** Antitrust; Intellectual Property. ***Email:*** bernhardd@howrey.com

JOHN BODNER, JR., born Lake Hopatcong, New Jersey, 1927; admitted to bar, 1953, District of Columbia; 1954, Illinois. *Education:* Cornell University; Northwestern University (J.D., 1953); Johns Hopkins University (M.L.A., 1969). Bigelow Teaching Fellow, University of Chicago Law School, 1953-1954. Member, Antitrust Division, Department of Justice, 1954-1956. Visiting Howrey Professor of Trial Advocacy, George Washington University Law School, 1986-1987. Lecturer in Law: George Washington University, 1960-1961, 1978-1987; University of Virginia, 1966-1980. *Member:* The District of Columbia Bar; Bar Association of the District of Columbia; Federal and American Bar Associations. ***PRACTICE AREAS:*** Antitrust; Complex Litigation; Appellate Practice. ***Email:*** bodnerj@howrey.com

SEAN F. X. BOLAND, born Washington, D.C., February 11, 1953; admitted to bar, 1978, District of Columbia. *Education:* Duke University; Georgetown University (A.B., magna cum laude, 1975; J.D., 1978). Phi Beta Kappa. *Member:* The District of Columbia Bar; American Bar Association (Member, Section of Antitrust). ***PRACTICE AREAS:*** Antitrust. ***Email:*** bolands@howrey.com

RAY S. BOLZE, born Carlisle, Pennsylvania; admitted to bar, 1966, District of Columbia; U.S. Supreme Court; U.S. Court of Appeals, District of Columbia, Second, Third, Fourth, Eighth and Ninth Circuits; U.S. Court of Appeals for the Federal Circuit. *Education:* Pennsylvania State University (B.A., 1957); George Washington University (J.D., with honors, 1965). Co-Author: Public Utility, Communications and Transportation Law Annual Report (author of Antitrust Chapter), 1992-2001; "Utility Restructuring Against the Backdrop of Regulation: Antitrust Issues," Practicing Law Institute 1998-2001; "Antitrust Law Regulation: A New Focus for a Competitive Energy Industry," Industry," Energy Law Journal Vol., 21, 2000; "Reconciliation of the Sherman Act with Federal Health Planning," The Antitrust Bulletin, Vol. 29, 1984. *Member:* The District of Columbia Bar (Member, Hearing Committee, Board of Professional Responsibility, 2001-2004); Federal Energy (Chairman, Antitrust Committee, 1989-1990) and American (Chairman, Antitrust Committee, Section on Public Utility, Communications and Transportation Law, 1992-2001; Section Program Chair, 1997-1998; Section Vice Chair, 2000-2001) Bar Associations. ***PRACTICE AREAS:*** Antitrust; Complex Litigation; Energy. ***Email:*** bolzer@howrey.com

TIMOTHY E. BOYLE, born Cleveland, Ohio, March 11, 1961; admitted to bar, 1986, Maryland; 1989, District of Columbia; U.S. District Court for the District of Columbia; U.S. Court of Appeals for the District of Columbia. *Education:* Denison University (B.A., with highest honors, 1983); Duke University (J.D., with honors, 1986). *Member:* The District of Columbia Bar; Maryland State and American Bar Associations. ***PRACTICE AREAS:*** Antitrust; Commercial and Intellectual Property Litigation; Products Liability Law. ***Email:*** boylet@howrey.com

JEFFREY W. BRENNAN, born Troy, New York, September 10, 1959; admitted to bar, 1986, New York; 1991, U.S. Court of Appeals, Federal Circuit and U.S. Court of International Trade; 1995, District of Columbia. *Education:* Holy Cross College (A.B., 1981); Georgetown University (J.D., 1985). Editor, American Criminal Law Review, 1984-1985. Contributor, "White Collar Crime: Third Annual Survey of Law," 22 American Criminal Law Review 388, 1985. Trial Attorney, Bureau of Competition, Federal Trade Commission, 1985-1990. *Member:* Bar Association of the District of Columbia; New York State and American Bar Associations. ***PRACTICE AREAS:*** Antitrust; Trade Regulation; Civil Litigation. ***Email:*** brennanj@howrey.com

JOHN DeQ. BRIGGS, III, born Concord, Massachusetts, 1943; admitted to bar, 1973, District of Columbia. *Education:* Harvard University (A.B., 1965); Georgetown University (J.D., 1972). Executive Editor, Law and Policy in International Business, 1971-1972. Chairman, Editorial Board, Antitrust Law Developments, Second, 1984-1988. Author/Co-author: "Waiting for Godot: Antitrust 1988-1989," Antitrust, Summer 1989; "An Overview of Current Law and Policy Relating to Mergers and Acquisitions," 56 Antitrust L.J. 657, 1988; "Antitrust 1986-1987: Power and Access (Part 1)," 32 Antitrust Bull. 275, 1987; "Antitrust 1986-1987: Power and Access (Part II)," 32 Antitrust Bull. 699, 1988; "The Antitrust Sand Dune," Antitrust, June 1986. Law Clerk to Hon. Frank J. Murray, U.S. District Court for the District of Massachusetts, 1972-1973. *Member:* District of Columbia Bar; Bar Association of the District of Columbia; American Bar Association (Chair, 1995-1996, Chair-Elect, 1994-1995, Program Officer, 1993-1994 and Secretary, 1991-1993, Section of Antitrust Law). [Lieutenant, U.S. Navy, 1966-1969]. ***PRACTICE AREAS:*** Antitrust; Intellectual Property Counseling and Litigation; Commercial and Civil Litigation; Products Liability Law; Appellate Practice. ***Email:*** briggsj@howrey.com

ROBERT J. BROOKHISER, JR., born Rochester, New York, August 30, 1949; admitted to bar, 1975, District of Columbia; U.S. Supreme Court; U.S. Court of Appeals, Second, Third, Fourth, Fifth, Ninth, Eleventh, District of Columbia and Federal Circuits. *Education:* Yale University (B.A., 1971); Harvard University (J.D., 1974). *Member:* The District of Columbia Bar; American Bar Association. ***PRACTICE AREAS:*** Antitrust; Complex Litigation. ***Email:*** brookhiserb@howrey.com

JOHN F. BRUCE, born Washington, D.C., August 19, 1940; admitted to bar, 1966, District of Columbia and U.S. Court of Appeals for the District of Columbia Circuit; 1968, U.S. Supreme Court; 1970, U.S. Court of Military Appeals; 1982, U.S. Court of International Trade; 1986, U.S. Court of Appeals for the Federal Circuit. *Education:* George Washington University (B.A., 1962); University of Virginia (LL.B., 1965); George Washington University Graduate School of Public Law (LL.M., 1966). Phi Alpha Delta. Teaching Fellow, George Washington University Graduate School of Public Law, 1965-1966. Law Clerk to Hon. Walter M. Bastian, U.S. Court of Appeals for the District of Columbia Circuit, 1966-1967. *Member:* The District of Columbia Bar; The Bar Association of the District of Columbia; American Bar Association (Member, Sections on: Antitrust, Litigation, Business and International Law); International Bar Association. ***PRACTICE AREAS:*** Antitrust; Complex Litigation; International Trade Law; Commercial Litigation. ***Email:*** brucej@howrey.com

BARBARA O. BRUCKMANN, born Port Hueneme, California, September 29, 1945; admitted to bar, 1986, Virginia; 1998, District of Columbia. *Education:* Wellesley College (B.A., 1967); Washington & Lee University (J.D., summa cum laude, 1986). Order of the Coif. Recipient, American Jurisprudence Award in Business Organization and Corporate Law. Executive Editor, Washington & Lee Law Review, 1985-1986. Author: "Bidding in the Private Sector: Practical Advice for Avoiding Robinson-Patman Pitfalls," 59 Antitrust L.J. 901 (1991); "Discounts, Discrimination, and Exclusive Dealing: Issues Under the Robinson-Patman Act," 68 Antitrust L.J. 253 (2000). Co-Author, with Irving Scher, "Antitrust Adviser," 4th ed., West Group (1998). Program Chair, "Pricing and Marketing Arrangements for Distribution and Franchising," Section of Antitrust Law, American Bar Association, May 1-2, 1997. *Member:* American Bar Association (Chair, Robinson-Patman Act Committee, 1993-1996, Council Member, 1996-1999 and Officer, 1999—, Antitrust Law Section). ***PRACTICE AREAS:*** Antitrust.

ROBERT M. BRUSKIN, born New York, N.Y., August 3, 1946; admitted to bar, 1973, District of Columbia. *Education:* City College of the City University of New York (B.Ch.E., 1968); Georgetown University (J.D., 1972). Editor, Georgetown Law Journal, 1970-1972. Law Clerk to Hon. Tim Murphy, Superior Court for The District of Columbia, 1972-1973. *Member:* The District of Columbia Bar; American Bar Association. ***PRACTICE AREAS:*** Intellectual Property; Antitrust Law; Complex Litigation. ***Email:*** bruskinr@howrey.com

PATRICIA G. BUTLER, born Bronx, N.Y., June 17, 1958; admitted to bar, 1984, District of Columbia; 1985, U.S. Court of Appeals for the District of Columbia Circuit; 1987, U.S. District Court, Northern District of Texas; 1996, U.S. District Court, District of Maryland; U.S. District Court for the District of Columbia. *Education:* Harvard University (A.B., cum laude, 1980); University of Pennsylvania Law School (J.D., 1984); Wharton Graduate School of Business, University of Pennsylvania (M.B.A., 1984). Publications: with Alexander Berger, "Online Consumer Fraud Regulations," Internet Newsletter, October 1998; with Alexander Berger, "Policing Copyright, Trademark Violations Online," Internet Newsletter, December 1998; "Directors and Officer Insurance and Bond Claims, Possession and Title of Receivers, and Rights and Obligations of Receivers," *Bank and Thrift Regulatory Enforcement and Receivership,* Matthew Bender Company, Inc., 1991. *Member:* The District of Columbia Bar; American Bar Association. ***PRACTICE AREAS:*** Commercial Litigation; Antitrust. ***Email:*** butlert@howrey.com

CARLA C. CALCAGNO, born Buffalo, New York, March 10, 1957; admitted to bar, 1982, District of Columbia; not registered to practice before U.S. Patent and Trademark Office. *Education:* Georgetown University (B.A., 1978; J.D., 1981). Attorney-Examiner, Trademark Trial and Appeal Board, 1986-1991. *Member:* American Bar Association; American Intellectual Property Law As-

(This Listing Continued)

HOWREY SIMON ARNOLD & WHITE, LLP, Washington—Continued

sociation. ***LANGUAGES:*** French. ***PRACTICE AREAS:*** Trademarks; International Trademarks; Trademark Litigation; Trademark Prosecution; Trademark Protection. ***Email:*** ccalcagno@howrey.com

JOHN G. CALENDER, born Watertown, New York, August 31, 1951; admitted to bar, 1977, District of Columbia. *Education:* Union University (B.A., 1973); George Washington University (J.D., 1977). Associate, 1977-1984; Partner, 1985-1991, Clifford & Warnke, Washington, D.C. *Member:* The District of Columbia Bar; American Bar Association. ***PRACTICE AREAS:*** Antitrust; Commercial Litigation; Complex Litigation. ***Email:*** calenderj@howrey.com

CELINE T. CALLAHAN, born Pittsburgh, Pennsylvania, June 14, 1963; admitted to bar, 1991, Virginia and District of Columbia; 1993, U.S. Court of Appeals, Federal Circuit; 1998, U.S. District Court, Eastern District of Virginia; 1999, U.S. District Court, District of Columbia; registered to practice before U.S. Patent and Trademark Office. *Education:* Catholic University of America (B.Ch.E., 1985); George Washington University (J.D., with honors, 1990). Law Clerk, Hon. Glenn L. Archer, Jr., former Chief Judge, U.S. Court of Appeals for the Federal Circuit, 1991-1993. Patent Examiner, U.S. Patent and Trademark Office, 1987-1990. *Member:* District of Columbia Bar; Virginia, American and Federal Circuit Bar Associations; American Intellectual Property Law Association. ***PRACTICE AREAS:*** Intellectual Property Law; Patent and Trademark Litigation; Counseling and Procurement. ***Email:*** callahanc@howrey.com

MICHAEL N. CLARK, born Wilmington, Delaware, February 15, 1967; admitted to bar, 1993, Connecticut; 1994, Maryland; 1997, U.S. District Court, District of Maryland; 2000, District of Columbia. *Education:* Towson State University (B.S., 1989); Georgetown University Law Center (J.D., 1992). ***PRACTICE AREAS:*** Commercial Litigation; Antitrust. ***Email:*** clarkm@howrey.com

KELLY A. CLEMENT, born Cincinnati, Ohio, January 13, 1965; admitted to bar, 1993, Pennsylvania; 1995, District of Columbia; 1997, U.S. Court of Appeals for the Federal Circuit; 1999, U.S. District Court for the District of Columbia; 2000, U.S. Court of Appeals, Third Circuit. *Education:* Syracuse University (B.A., 1987); University of Pennsylvania (J.D., 1993). *Member:* The District of Columbia Bar; American Bar Association. ***PRACTICE AREAS:*** Antitrust Law; Commercial Litigation; Intellectual Property Law. ***Email:*** clementk@howrey.com

MICHAEL PAUL AUSTERN COHEN, born Monterey, California, October 12, 1965; admitted to bar, 1990, Virginia; 1992, District of Columbia, U.S. District Court, Eastern District of Virginia and U.S. Court of Appeals, Fourth Circuit; 1994, U.S. District Court for the District of Columbia; 1998, U.S. Supreme Court; 2001, U.S. Court of International Trade. *Education:* Virginia Polytechnic Institute and State University (B.A., 1987); Washington & Lee University (J.D., magna cum laude, 1990). Phi Alpha Theta; Sigma Pi Alpha; Order of the Coif. Associate Lead Articles Editor, Washington & Lee University Law Review, 1989-1990. Author: "The Constitutional Infirmity of RICO Forfeiture," 46 Wash. & Lee L. Rev. 937 1989. *Member:* The District of Columbia Bar; Virginia and American Bar Associations. ***PRACTICE AREAS:*** Antitrust Law; Appellate Practice; Commercial Law; Complex Litigation; Products Liability Law. ***Email:*** cohenm@howrey.com

RICHARD T. COLMAN, born Boston, Massachusetts, September 22, 1935; admitted to bar, 1962, Massachusetts; 1966, District of Columbia. *Education:* University of Notre Dame (A.B., magna cum laude, 1957); Boston College (LL.B., cum laude, 1962). Trial Attorney, Antitrust Division, Department of Justice, 1962-1966. *Member:* The District of Columbia Bar; Federal and American Bar Associations; International Bar Association. ***PRACTICE AREAS:*** Antitrust Law; Commercial Law; Litigation. ***Email:*** colmanr@howrey.com

GREGORY J. COMMINS, JR., born Mineola, New York, July 28, 1965; admitted to bar, 1991, New York; 1992, District of Columbia; U.S. Court of Appeals for the District of Columbia Circuit. *Education:* Cornell University (B.A., 1987); Georgetown University (J.D., magna cum laude, 1990). Phi Alpha Delta; Order of the Coif. Executive Editor, Georgetown Journal of Legal Ethics. *Member:* The District of Columbia Bar; American Bar Association. ***PRACTICE AREAS:*** Antitrust; Commercial Law; Insurance Coverage. ***Email:*** comminsg@howrey.com

MICHAEL G. COWIE, born Rockville Centre, New York, July 4, 1964; admitted to bar, 1992, District of Columbia. *Education:* Hobart College (B.A., magna cum laude, 1986) Phi Beta Kappa; Georgetown University (J.D., cum laude, 1989). Associate Editor, The Georgetown Law Journal, 1989. ***Email:*** cowiem@howrey.com

BASIL C. CULYBA, born North Charleroi, Pennsylvania, February 11, 1949; admitted to bar, 1978, District of Columbia; 1980, U.S. District Court, District of Columbia; 1987, Ohio. *Education:* Washington & Jefferson College (B.A., cum laude, 1971); Rutgers University (J.D., with high honors, 1978). Member, Rutgers University Law Review, 1977-1978. Recipient, American

(This Listing Continued)

Jurisprudence Award. *Member:* The District of Columbia Bar; American Bar Association (Member, Sections on: Antitrust; Litigation). [Lt. jg., U.S.N.R., 1971-1974]. ***PRACTICE AREAS:*** Antitrust Law; Appellate Practice; Commercial Law; Complex Litigation; Government Regulation; Litigation. ***Email:*** culybab@howrey.com

MARTIN F. CUNNIFF, born Washington, D.C., June 23, 1961; admitted to bar, 1990, District of Columbia; 1992, U.S. District Court, District of Columbia. *Education:* Loyola University (B.B.A., 1983); University of Florida (J.D., 1989). Member, University of Florida Law Review, 1988-1989. *Member:* The District of Columbia Bar; American Bar Association. ***Email:*** cunniffm@howrey.com

JAMES F. DAVIS, born Fort Wayne, Indiana, August 11, 1934; admitted to bar, 1964, District of Columbia and Illinois. *Education:* University of Illinois (B.S.Ch.E., cum laude, 1957); Georgetown University (J.D., 1963). Phi Alpha Delta. Technical Advisor to Hon. Giles S. Rich, U.S. Court of Customs and Patent Appeals, 1963-1964. Adjunct Professor of Law, Georgetown University, 1967-1968, 1995-1999. Trial Judge, U.S. Court of Claims, 1966-1972. Member, Panel of Arbitrators, American Arbitration Association. *Member:* The District of Columbia Bar; Bar Association of the District of Columbia; American Bar Association; American Intellectual Property Law Association. ***PRACTICE AREAS:*** Intellectual Property; Patent Law; Patent, Trademark and Copyright Law. ***Email:*** davisj@howrey.com

MINDY G. DAVIS, born Pittsburgh, Pennsylvania, February 23, 1962; admitted to bar, 1987, Pennsylvania; 1988, District of Columbia. *Education:* University of Pittsburgh (B.A., 1984; J.D., 1987). Omicron Delta Kappa. Executive Editor, University of Pittsburgh Law School Journal of Law and Commerce, 1986-1987. Member, Order of the Barristers. *Member:* District of Columbia Bar; Pennsylvania and American Bar Associations. ***PRACTICE AREAS:*** Commercial Litigation; Insurance Coverage. ***Email:*** davism@howrey.com

THOMAS M. DUNHAM, born Binghamton, New York, December 22, 1963; admitted to bar, 1995, District of Columbia; registered to practice before U.S. Patent and Trademark Office. *Education:* State University of New York, Binghamton (B.S., 1987); Villanova University (J.D., 1995); George Washington University National Law Center (Visiting Student, 1994-1995). Sigma Pi Sigma; Phi Theta Kappa. Member Villanova University Law Review. *Member:* American Bar Association; American Intellectual Property Law Association. ***PRACTICE AREAS:*** Intellectual Property Law. ***Email:*** dunhamt@howrey.com

W. NEIL EGGLESTON, born Evansville, Indiana, July 5, 1953; admitted to bar, 1979, Virginia; 1986, New York; 1987, District of Columbia. *Education:* Duke University (A.B., 1975); Northwestern University (J.D., 1978). Law Clerk: Hon. James Hunter III, U.S. Court of Appeals, Third Circuit, 1978-1979; Hon. Warren E. Burger, Chief Justice, U.S. Supreme Court, 1979-1980. Assistant U.S. Attorney, Southern District of New York, 1981-1987. Chief Appellate Attorney, Office of the U.S. Attorney, Southern District of New York, 1986-1987. Deputy Chief Counsel, U.S. House of Representatives Select Committee to Investigate Covert Arms Transactions with Iran, 1987-1988. Associate Counsel to the President, The White House, 1993-1994. *Member:* District of Columbia Bar; Virginia State Bar; New York State and American (Member, White Collar Crime Committee, Criminal Section) Bar Associations. ***Email:*** egglestonn@howrey.com

CHARLES J. (TIM) ENGEL, III, born Syracuse, New York, January 2, 1955; admitted to bar, 1981, District of Columbia; U.S. Court of Federal Claims; U.S. Court of Appeals, District of Columbia, Third, Fourth and Fifth Circuits; U.S. Supreme Court. *Education:* Georgetown University (B.A., 1978); Syracuse University (J.D., magna cum laude, 1981). Order of the Coif. Recipient, American Jurisprudence Award. Associate Editor, Syracuse University Law Review, 1980-1981. *Member:* The District of Columbia Bar; American Bar Association; Federal Energy Bar Association. ***PRACTICE AREAS:*** Antitrust; Complex Litigation; Energy. ***Email:*** engelt@howrey.com

LISA J. FALES, born Indianapolis, Indiana, April 3, 1962; admitted to bar, 1990, Maryland and U.S. District Court, District of Maryland; 1992, District of Columbia. *Education:* University of Maryland (B.A., 1984); University of Baltimore School of Law (J.D., 1990). Articles Editor, University of Baltimore Law Review, 1989-1990. Chair, Consumer Affairs Committee, 1994-1996; Member, Steering Committee, 1996-1997, Antitrust, Trade Regulation and Consumer Affairs Section, The District of Columbia Bar. Member, Board of Directors, Women's Law Center, 1984-1986, 1991-1992. *Member:* District of Columbia Bar; Maryland State and American (Member, Antitrust Section) Bar Associations; D.C. Women's Bar Association. ***PRACTICE AREAS:*** Antitrust; Trade Regulation. ***Email:*** falesl@howrey.com

THOMAS D. FINA, born Bologna, Italy, December 2, 1960; admitted to bar, 1989, District of Columbia. *Education:* Harvard University (A.B., cum laude, 1982); University of Virginia (J.D., 1989). Order of the Coif. *Member:* District of Columbia Bar; American Bar Association (Member, Antitrust Section). ***LANGUAGES:*** Italian. ***PRACTICE AREAS:*** Antitrust. ***Email:*** finat@howrey.com

(This Listing Continued)

ALAN M. FISCH, born Minneapolis, Minnesota, June 29, 1966; admitted to bar, 1995, Pennsylvania; 1996, District of Columbia and U.S. Court of Appeals for the Federal Circuit. *Education:* University of Texas at Austin (B.A., 1988); Tulane University (J.D., cum laude, 1994). Alpha Lambda Delta; Phi Eta Sigma. Senior Editor, Tulane Environmental Law Journal, 1993-1994. First Place, Tulane University, Nathan Burkan Memorial Competition, 1994. Author: "Addressing Copyright and Patent as Software's Legal Aegis: A Review of Software and Intellectual Property Protection," 5 Cornell Journal of Law and Public Policy 119, 1996; "Compulsory Licensing of Professional Team Sporting Event Telecasts (PTSETs): Using Copyright Law to Mitigate Monopolistic Behavior," 32 Harvard Journal on Legislation 403, 1995; "Seeking the Intersection of Two Legal Sets: A Review of The Commercial Law of Intellectual Property," 19 Columbia-VLA Journal of Law and the Arts 301, 1995; "Compulsory Licensing of Pharmaceutical Patents: An Unreasonable Solution to an Unfortunate Problem," 34 Jurimetrics Journal 295, 1994; "Citizens Against Burlington v. Busey: Defining Reasonable Alternatives to be Examined in as NEPA-Required Environmental Impact Statement," 22 Real Estate Law Journal 32, 1993; "Arkansas v. Oklahoma: Formalizing EPA Authority to Mandate Compliance with an Affected State's Water Quality Standards," 6 Tulane Environmental Law Journal 439, 1993. *Member:* American Bar Association; American Intellectual Property Law Association. ***PRACTICE AREAS:*** Litigation; Intellectual Property. ***Email:*** fischa@howrey.com

SCOTT E. FLICK, born Nurnberg, Germany, January 15, 1952; admitted to bar, 1976, District of Columbia. *Education:* University of Michigan (A.B., with high honors, 1973); Northwestern University (J.D., cum laude, 1976). Adjunct Professor of Law, Georgetown University Law Center, 2000—. *Member:* The District of Columbia Bar; American Bar Association. ***PRACTICE AREAS:*** Antitrust Law; Complex Litigation. ***Email:*** flicks@howrey.com

JOHN G. FROEMMING, born Milwaukee, Wisconsin, November 18, 1959; admitted to bar, 1985, Virginia; 1986, District of Columbia; 1989, U.S. District Court, Eastern District of Virginia; 1991, U.S. District Court, District of Columbia and U.S. Court of Appeals, District of Columbia Circuit. *Education:* Dartmouth College (A.B., cum laude, 1982); Northwestern University (J.D., 1985). Member, Jessup International Law Moot Court Team, 1983-1985. Chairman, Judicial Council, Northwestern University School of Law, 1984-1985. *Member:* The District of Columbia Bar; Virginia and American Bar Associations; German American Law Association (President, Capital Area Chapter, 1996—). ***LANGUAGES:*** German. ***PRACTICE AREAS:*** Complex Litigation; Antitrust Law; Intellectual Property Litigation. ***Email:*** froemmingj@howrey.com

JERROLD J. GANZFRIED, born New York, N.Y., December 8, 1948; admitted to bar, 1975, New York, U.S. District Court, Southern and Eastern Districts of New York and U.S. Court of Appeals, Second Circuit; 1977, U.S. Tax Court; 1979, U.S. Supreme Court; 1988, U.S. Court of Appeals, Fourth and Eleventh Circuits; 1989, District of Columbia and U.S. Court of Appeals, Sixth Circuit; 1991, U.S. Court of Appeals, District of Columbia and Seventh Circuits and U.S. District Court, District of Columbia; 1992, U.S. Court of Appeals, Third and Ninth Circuits; 1993, U.S. Court of Appeals, Federal Circuit; 1994, U.S. Court of Appeals, Fifth Circuit; 1996, U.S. Court of Appeals, Tenth Circuit. *Education:* Yale University (B.A., cum laude, 1970); Stanford University (J.D., 1973). President, Stanford Law Review, 1972-1973. Recipient, Kilborne Fellowship. Author: "Bringing Business Judgment to Business Litigation: Mediation and Settlement in the Federal Courts of Appeals," 65 George Washington Law Review 531, 1997; "Government, Courts and Regulators in Washington, D.C.," Global Law & Business, October 1995 at 28; "Double Jeopardy and the Waiver of Jurisdiction in California's Juvenile Courts," 24 Stanford Law Review 874, 1972. Law Clerk to Chief Judge Irving R. Kaufman, Second Circuit, 1973-1974. Assistant to the Solicitor General of the United States, 1981-1987. Member, Board of Directors, Yale Alumni Fund. Charter Member of Executive Committee, Council of Appellate Lawyers, ABA Judicial Division Appellate Judges Conference. Former Member, Board of Directors, BCC Baseball, Inc. *Member:* The District of Columbia Bar; American Bar Association (Member, Sections of: Antitrust Law; Litigation, Committee on Appellate Practice; International Law). ***PRACTICE AREAS:*** Supreme Court and Appellate Litigation; Complex Litigation; Antitrust; Intellectual Property. ***Email:*** ganzfriedj@howrey.com

CECILIA H. GONZALEZ, born Caracas, Venezuela, September 18, 1955; admitted to bar, 1980, District of Columbia. *Education:* McGill University (B.A., with honors, 1976); Georgetown University (J.D., 1979). *Member:* The District of Columbia Bar; American Bar Association; International Trade Commission Trial Lawyers Association. ***PRACTICE AREAS:*** International Trade; Intellectual Property; Litigation. ***Email:*** gonzalezc@howrey.com

ALLEN B. GREEN, born Lakeland, Florida, October 12, 1947; admitted to bar, 1975, Virginia and District of Columbia. *Education:* University of Virginia (B.A., 1969; J.D., 1975). Member, Managing Board, Virginia Journal of International Law, 1974-1975. General Counsel, American League for Exports and Security Assistance, 1986—. ***PRACTICE AREAS:*** International Arbitration and Litigation; International Law; Government Contracts. ***Email:*** greena@howrey.com

(This Listing Continued)

ROBERT L. GREEN, JR., born East Lansing, Michigan, May 4, 1951; admitted to bar, 1976, Maryland; 1977, District of Columbia. *Education:* University of Pennsylvania (B.S., 1973); University of Maryland (J.D., 1976). Managing Editor, Maryland Law Review, 1975-1976. Law Clerk to the Hon. C. Stanley Blair, U.S. District Judge, District of Maryland, 1976-1977. *Member:* The District of Columbia Bar; Maryland State and American Bar Associations. ***PRACTICE AREAS:*** Antitrust; Complex Litigation; Litigation. ***Email:*** greenr@howrey.com

ALAN M. GRIMALDI, born New York, N.Y., April 23, 1944; admitted to bar, 1972, Maryland and District of Columbia; U.S. Supreme Court; registered to practice before U.S. Patent and Trademark Office. *Education:* City College of the City University of New York (B.Ch.E., 1966); Catholic University of America (J.D., 1971). Editor, Catholic University Law Review, 1971. Law Clerk to Hon. Barrington D. Parker, U.S. District Court for the District of Columbia, 1971-1972. *Member:* The District of Columbia Bar; Maryland State and American Bar Associations; AIPLA. ***PRACTICE AREAS:*** Antitrust; Commercial Law; Intellectual Property; Arbitration; Insurance Coverage; Complex Litigation. ***Email:*** grimaldia@howrey.com

EDWARD HAN, born New York, N.Y., July 28, 1958; admitted to bar, 1985, District of Columbia; 1987, New York. *Education:* Johns Hopkins University (B.A., with honors, 1979); Georgetown University (J.D., cum laude, 1985). Author: Note, "Protection From Commercial Counterfeiters in Taiwan for U.S. Firms," 16 Law & Policy in International Business 641, 1984. ***PRACTICE AREAS:*** Antitrust; Intellectual Property; Insurance Coverage; Complex Litigation. ***Email:*** hane@howrey.com

STUART H. HARRIS, born New York, N.Y., March 23, 1950; admitted to bar, 1975, District of Columbia; 1976, U.S. District Court, District of Columbia and U.S. Court of Appeals, District of Columbia Circuit; 1978, U.S. Court of Appeals, Fourth and Fifth Circuits; 1979, U.S. Supreme Court; 1985, U.S. Court of International Trade; 1986, U.S. Court of Appeals, Eleventh Circuit; 1988, U.S. Court of Appeals, Federal Circuit; 1991, U.S. Court of Appeals, Third Circuit; 1998, U.S. District Court, District of Maryland. *Education:* Tufts University (B.A., magna cum laude, 1972); George Washington University (J.D., with honors, 1975). Adjunct Faculty Member, George Washington University National Law Center, 1989-1991. *Member:* The District of Columbia Bar; American Bar Association. ***PRACTICE AREAS:*** Antitrust Law; Complex Litigation; Franchise Law. ***Email:*** harriss@howrey.com

EDWARD P. HENNEBERRY, born Harrisburg, Pennsylvania, July 31, 1945; admitted to bar, 1970, Massachusetts; 1976, District of Columbia; 1979, U.S. District Court for the District of Columbia and U.S. Supreme Court; 1983, U.S. Court of Appeals, 3rd and 9th Circuits; 1985, U.S. Court of Appeals, 11th Circuit; 1987, U.S. District Court, District of Maryland; 1988, U.S. Court of Appeals, 4th Circuit; 1997, U.S. Court of Appeals, 7th Circuit. *Education:* Boston College (B.A., 1967; J.D., 1970). Trial Attorney, Honors Program, U.S. Department of Justice, Antitrust Division, 1970-1975. *Member:* The District of Columbia Bar; American Bar Association. ***PRACTICE AREAS:*** Antitrust; Commercial Litigation; Products Liability Law. ***Email:*** henneberrye@howrey.com

ROXANN E. HENRY, born Westover Air Force Base, Massachusetts, June 24, 1953; admitted to bar, 1979, Pennsylvania; 1980, New Jersey; 1981, District of Columbia; 1984, U.S. Supreme Court. *Education:* Vassar College (A.B., 1975); Rutgers University (J.D., cum laude, 1978). Articles Editor Rutgers Law Journal, 1977-1978. Law Clerk to the Hon. Floyd R. Gibson, U.S. Court of Appeals, Eighth Circuit, 1978-1980. Editor: Antitrust Section, Criminal Practice and Procedure Committee Newsletter, American Bar Association, 1996—; Merger Process-United States: The Hart-Scott-Rodino Antitrust Review Process, Washington, D.C., Howrey & Simon, 1998. *Member:* The District of Columbia Bar; New Jersey State, Pennsylvania and American (Vice Chair, 1997-1999 and Chair, 1999—, Antitrust Section, Criminal Practice and Procedure Committee) Bar Associations. ***PRACTICE AREAS:*** Antitrust; Complex Litigation; White Collar Criminal Defense. ***Email:*** henryr@howrey.com

WILLIAM A. HENRY, born Detroit, Michigan, August 9, 1956; admitted to bar, 1984, District of Columbia. *Education:* Harvard University (A.B., cum laude, 1979); Columbia University (J.D., 1984). Recipient, Charles Joseph Bonaparte Prize. Harvard National Scholar. Editorial Staff, 1982-1983, Casenote and Comment Editor, 1983-1984, Columbia Journal of Transnational Law; Harlan Fiske Stone Scholar. Legislative Director, Rep. Bill Gradison, 1979-1981. *Member:* The District of Columbia Bar; American Bar Association (Member, Section on: Antitrust). ***PRACTICE AREAS:*** Antitrust; Trade Regulation.. ***Email:*** henrywilliam@howrey.com

THOMAS N. HEYER, born Poughkeepsie, New York, April 21, 1956; admitted to bar, 1981, District of Columbia; 1990, U.S. Supreme Court. *Education:* Union College (B.A., summa cum laude, 1978); Cornell Law School (J.D., 1981). Phi Beta Kappa. Member, Moot Court Board. *Member:* The District of Columbia Bar; American Bar Association. ***PRACTICE AREAS:*** Antitrust; Complex Litigation; Intellectual Property. ***Email:*** heyert@howrey.com

THOMAS A. ISAACSON, born Lewiston, Maine, April 25, 1958; admitted to bar, 1984, District of Columbia. *Education:* Dartmouth College (A.B., cum

(This Listing Continued)

HOWREY SIMON ARNOLD & WHITE, LLP, Washington—Continued

laude, 1980); University of Pennsylvania (J.D., 1983). Winner, Edwin R. Keedy Moot Court Competition, 1982-1983. Law Clerk to Chief Justice Vincent L. McKusick, Supreme Judicial Court of Maine, 1983-1984. *Member:* The District of Columbia Bar. ***PRACTICE AREAS:*** Antitrust; Complex Litigation; Environmental Law. ***Email:*** isaacsont@howrey.com

MARCIA PRESS KAPLAN, born Hartford, Connecticut, November 6, 1954; admitted to bar, 1979, District of Columbia. *Education:* University of Connecticut (B.A., summa cum laude, 1976); Rutgers University (J.D., with honors, 1979). Phi Beta Kappa. Member, Rutgers Law Review, 1978-1979. *Member:* The District of Columbia Bar; American Bar Association. ***PRACTICE AREAS:*** Antitrust; Complex Litigation. ***Email:*** kaplanm@howrey.com

ROGER A. KLEIN, born Oak Ridge, Tennessee, January 1, 1950; admitted to bar, 1975, District of Columbia; 1978, U.S. Tax Court and U.S. Supreme Court; 1980, Maryland. *Education:* Washington University (B.A., 1971); Georgetown University (J.D., 1974). Omicron Delta Kappa. Author: "Political Expenditures," 231 2nd Tax Management Portfolio (BNA), 1982. Lecturer, Estate and Gift Tax, Catholic University, 1978-1980. *Member:* The District of Columbia Bar; American Bar Association. ***PRACTICE AREAS:*** Corporate Law; Real Estate Law; Commercial Law. ***Email:*** kleinr@howrey.com

JAMES G. KRESS, born Washington, D.C., November 5, 1965; admitted to bar, 1990, Maryland; 1992, District of Columbia. *Education:* University of Maryland (B.S., cum laude, 1987); Georgetown University (J.D., magna cum laude, 1990). Associate Editor, 1989-1990 and Staff, 1988-1989, Georgetown Law Journal. Order of the Coif; American Inns of Court. *Member:* American Bar Association (Member, Sections on: Litigation and Antitrust). ***PRACTICE AREAS:*** Litigation; Antitrust. ***Email:*** kressj@howrey.com

JOSEPH P. LAVELLE, born Scranton, Pennsylvania, September 7, 1957; admitted to bar, 1982, District of Columbia; registered to practice before U.S. Patent and Trademark Office. *Education:* Wilkes College (B.S., Physics, 1979); University of Pittsburgh (J.D., summa cum laude, 1982). Member, Order of the Coif. Managing Editor, University of Pittsburgh Law Review, 1981-1982. Adjunct Professor of Law, Georgetown University Law Center, 1996—. *Member:* The District of Columbia Bar; American Bar Association; American Association for Advancement of Science; The American Physical Society. ***PRACTICE AREAS:*** Intellectual Property; Antitrust; Complex Litigation. ***Email:*** lavellej@howrey.com

EZRA C. LEVINE, born New York, N.Y., April 8, 1944; admitted to bar, 1969, New York and District of Columbia. *Education:* Antioch College (B.A., 1965); Rutgers University (J.D., 1968). Editor, Rutgers Law Review, 1967-1968. Attorney, Office of Opinions and Review, Federal Communications Commission, 1968-1969. Senior Litigation Attorney, Federal Energy Office, Executive Office of the President, 1974. Deputy Assistant General Counsel, Compliance, Federal Energy Administration, 1975-1977. Assistant General Counsel, Interpretations and Rulings, Department of Energy and Federal Energy Administration, 1977-1978. Member, Model Legislation Committee, Money Transmitter Regulators Association. Member, U.S. Treasury Bank Secrecy Act Advisory Group. *Member:* The District of Columbia Bar; American Bar Association. ***PRACTICE AREAS:*** Antitrust; Insurance Coverage; Environmental; Litigation; Government Regulation; Bank Secrecy Act; Non-Bank Funds Transmission. ***Email:*** levinee@howrey.com

MARK I. LEVY, born Chicago, Illinois, June 28, 1949; admitted to bar, 1976, District of Columbia; 1977, U.S. District Court, District of Columbia; 1980, U.S. Supreme Court; 1987, Illinois; 1990, U.S. Court of Appeals, District of Columbia, Sixth, Seventh and Eighth Circuits and U.S. Tax Court; 1993, U.S. Court of Appeals, Ninth Circuit; 1994, U.S. Court of Appeals, Second, Fourth and Tenth Circuit; 1996, U.S. Court of Appeals, Third, Fifth and Eleventh Circuits and U.S. Court of Appeals for the Federal Circuit; 2000, U.S. Court of Appeals, First Circuit. *Education:* Yale University (B.A., summa cum laude, 1971; J.D., 1975). Phi Beta Kappa. Recipient, Israel H. Peres Prize, Yale Law School, 1975. Executive Editor, Yale Law Journal, 1974-1975. Author: "High Court Takes Care of Business," 18 National Law Journal C8, July 29, 1996; "Amicus Briefs in the Supreme Court: The Need for a Corporate Amicus Program," 8 ACCA Docket 18, American Corporate Counsel Association, Winter 1990, reprinted in 12 Business Counsel 3, U.S. Chamber of Commerce, Spring 1990; "There is a Studied Way to Practice Preventive Law in the Supreme Court," 8 Preventive Law Reporter 6, September 1989; Note, "The Function of the Preliminary Hearing in Federal Pretrial Procedure," 83 Yale L.J. 771, 1974. Co-Author: "The Supreme Court's Rules for the '90s," 76 ABA J. 70, April 1990; "The Constitutionality of Punitive Damages," 73 ABA J. 88, 1987. Adjunct Faculty, Member, University of Virginia School of Law, Appellate Practice Seminar, Spring 1999. Lecturer: "Supreme Court Media Briefing," U.S. Chamber of Commerce, September 1998 and September 1997; "Supreme Court Review," Washington Legal Foundation's Media Briefing, June 1998 and February 1996; "Supreme Court and Appellate Advocacy," Yale Law School, December 1997, November 1999 and February 1990; "Supreme Court Review," American Trucking Associations' Forum for Motor Carrier General Counsel, June 1995; Presentations on "Appellate Brief Writing" and "Oral Argument," Fifth Circuit Bar Conference on Appellate Practice and Advocacy, March 1994; "Appellate Advocacy in the 1990's," ABA Section of Litigation, October 1991; "How to Prepare for an Oral Argument in the '90s," ABA Section of Litigation, August 1991; "Amicus Curiae Briefs in Preemption and Products Liability Cases," Product Liability Advisory Council, April 1991; "Punitive Damages," Young Presidents' Organizations of South Bend, Indiana, March 1991; "Containing Runaway Legal Costs," Illinois Manufacturers' Association Program, September 1990; "Amicus Curiae Briefs," ABA Section of Litigation, Products Liability Committee, April 1990; "Amicus Briefs in the Supreme Court," presented to the Conference on Preventive Law held by the American Corporate Counsel Association and the University of Denver College of Law's National Center for Preventive Law, July 1989. Law Clerk to Hon. Gerhard A. Gesell, U.S. District Court, District of Columbia, 1975-1976. Deputy Assistant Attorney General (Appellate), Civil Division, U.S. Department of Justice, 1993-1995. Assistant to the Solicitor General, U.S. Department of Justice, 1979-1981, 1983-1986. Adjunct Faculty, University of Virginia School of Law (appellate seminar), 1998-1999 (spring term), 2000-2001 (spring term). Former Member and Treasurer and Member, Executive Committee, Yale Law School Alumni Association, 1987-1990. *Member:* The American Academy of Appellate Lawyers; D.C. Circuit Advisory Committee on Procedures; The Lawyers Club of Chicago. ***PRACTICE AREAS:*** Appellate and Supreme Court Litigation. ***Email:*** levym@howrey.com

KAREN M. LOCKWOOD, born Plainfield, New Jersey, June 15, 1950; admitted to bar, 1978, District of Columbia; 1979, U.S. District Court for the District of Columbia and U.S. Court of Appeals for the District of Columbia Circuit; 1988, U.S. Court of Appeals, Second Circuit; 1989, U.S. Court of Appeals, Fourth Circuit and U.S. Supreme Court; 1991, U.S. Court of Appeals, Third and Eleventh Circuits and U.S. Court of International Trade; 1995, U.S. District Court, District of Maryland; 1996, U.S. Court of Claims and U.S. Court of Appeals, Sixth and Ninth Circuits; 1999, U.S. Court of Appeals, Federal Circuit. *Education:* College of Wooster (B.A., with honors, 1972); Washington College of Law, American University (J.D., cum laude, 1978). Senior Articles Editor, American University Law Review, 1977-1978. Faculty, NITA Trial Advocacy, 2000—. Author: Comment, 27 American University Law Review 488, 1978. Instructor, Legal Research and Writing, Washington College of Law, American University, 1980-1981, 1982-1983. *Member:* The District of Columbia Bar; Bar Association of the District of Columbia; Federal, American and International Bar Associations; American Arbitration Association. ***PRACTICE AREAS:*** Litigation; Arbitration; Antitrust. ***Email:*** LockwoodK@howrey.com

CHARLES A. LOUGHLIN, born Holyoke, Massachusetts, May 21, 1967; admitted to bar, 1994, Massachusetts; 1995, District of Columbia. *Education:* University of New Hampshire (B.A., summa cum laude, 1989); Georgetown University (J.D., cum laude, 1993). *Member:* American Bar Association (Member, Antitrust Section). ***PRACTICE AREAS:*** Antitrust; Commercial Litigation. ***Email:*** loughlinc@howrey.com

KAREN LOUISE MANOS, born Alexandria, Virginia, November 1, 1959; admitted to bar, 1986, North Carolina; 1987, District of Columbia. *Education:* United States Air Force Academy (B.S., distinguished graduate, 1981); Duke University (J.D., with highest honors, 1986). Note Editor, Duke Law Journal. Author: "A Critical Analysis of the FAR Council's New Rule on Labor Relations Costs and Costs Relating to Legal and Other Proceedings," *Federal Contracts Report (Jan. 2, 2001); "Heads We Win, Tails You Lose:* The CAS Board's Remarkable New Proposal on Accounting for the Costs of PRB Plans," *The Government Contractor (Oct. 25, 2000); "Affirmative Action Plans & The 'Equal Pay Initiative'," Briefing Papers* (July, 2000); with Alan M. Grimald, "Pretrial Motions Under the False Claims Act," ABA Pub. Cont. L.J., 2000; with J. Roger Holbrook, "A Critical Analysis of the CAS Board's Proposed Rule on Cost Accounting Practice Changes," 41-36 & 41-37 The Government Contractor (Sep. 1999). Author: "Government Claims to Surplus Pension Assets," Catholic Univ. Law Rev., Summer 1999; "The Statute of Frauds in Cyberspace: Purchasing Today," April 1999; "Allowability of ESOP Interest Costs: DCAA's Misguided Audit Guidance," 98-6 Costs, Pricing and Accounting Report, June 1998; "Allowability of Executive Compensation Costs," Briefing Papers, Dec. 1997. Co-Author: with M. A. Worthington and W. A. Roberts, "Executive Compensation: A Critical Examination of the Proposed Contract Costs Act of 1997," 97-3 Costs, Pricing, and Accounting Rep., March 1997; with Joel Giskin, "Special Allocations Under the Cost Accounting Standards," 96-10 Costs, Pricing and Accounting Rep., October 1996; with R. David Carlton, "Voluntary Accounting Changes: A Windfall for the Government?" 25 ABA Pub. Cont. L.J. 3, Spring 1996. Author: "Novation Agreements in Restructuring: The Government's Contractual Stealth Weapon," 26 ABA Pub. Cont. L.J. 3, Spring, 1997; "Protecting Proprietary Information," Briefing Papers, Dec., 1994; "The Antideficiency Act Without an "M" Account: Reasserting Constitutional Control," 23 ABA Pub. Cont. L.J. 3, Spring, 1994; "Recovery of Environmental Costs, A Government Perspective," 92-7 Costs, Pricing & Acct. Rep. Aug, 1992. Instructor, U.C.L.A. Extension, Government Contract Management Program, 1992-1994. *Member:* American Bar Association (Member, Public Contract Law Section, 1994—; Co-Chair, Accounting, Cost and Pricing

(This Listing Continued)

Committee, 2000) ; National Contract Management Association. [Maj., USAF, 1981-1995]. ***PRACTICE AREAS:*** Government Contracts; Commercial Litigation. ***Email:*** manosk@howrey.com

CHRISTOPHER J. MACAVOY, born Corning, New York, April 28, 1957; admitted to bar, 1982, District of Columbia; 1989, U.S. Supreme Court; U.S. Court of Appeals, Third, Fourth, Fifth, Sixth and Ninth Circuits. *Education:* Harvard University (B.A., cum laude, 1979); Georgetown University (J.D., 1982). *Member:* The District of Columbia Bar; American Bar Association (Member, Sections on: Antitrust Law; Litigation). ***PRACTICE AREAS:*** Antitrust; Trade Regulation. ***Email:*** macavoyc@howrey.com

ELIZABETH B. MCCALLUM, born Hamilton, Ohio, September 5, 1964; admitted to bar, 1991, Tennessee; 1996, District of Columbia. *Education:* University of Virginia (B.A., with distinction, 1986); Vanderbilt University (J.D., 1990). Order of the Coif. Senior Student Writing Editor, Vanderbilt Law Review, 1989-1990. Author: "The Constitutionality of an Off-Duty Smoking Ban for Public Employees," 43 Vanderbilt Law Review 491, 1990. Law Clerk to the Honorable Chief Judge Gerald B. Tjoflat, U.S. Court of Appeals, Eleventh Circuit, 1990-1991. Adjunct Instructor, Legal Writing, Vanderbilt Law School, 1993. *Member:* Tennessee and American (Member, Antitrust Section) Bar Associations; District of Columbia Bar. ***PRACTICE AREAS:*** Antitrust; Commercial Litigation. ***Email:*** mccallumb@howrey.com

ROSEMARY H. MCENERY, born Lubbock, Texas, October 8, 1957; admitted to bar, 1983, Texas; 1985, District of Columbia. *Education:* Texas Christian University (B.A., magna cum laude, 1979); University of Texas (J.D., 1983). Phi Beta Kappa. Law Clerk, Hon. Halbert O. Woodward, Chief Judge, U.S. District Court, Northern District of Texas, 1983-1984. *Member:* The District of Columbia Bar; State Bar of Texas; American Bar Association. ***PRACTICE AREAS:*** Antitrust; Commercial Litigation. ***Email:*** mceneryr@howrey.com

VIRGINIA R. METALLO, born Ft. Rucker, Alabama, November 26, 1957; admitted to bar, 1988, Pennsylvania; 1989, District of Columbia. *Education:* Dickinson College (B.A., 1979); Catholic University of America (J.D., 1988). Miller Cup Finalist, Spring 1988. Senior Staff Member, The Catholic University Law Review, 1986-1988. Co-Author: "Globalization of Competition: The Case for Convergence," 24 Int'l Merger Law, August 24, 1992; "Competition Policy: A Force to Open Markets," 61 Antitrust Law J. 637 (1993); "The Next Step: Convergence of Procedure and Enforcement," Fordham University School of Law; "Convergence of Premerger Notification and Review: A Case Study," Wake Forest Law Review. *Member:* Pennsylvania Bar Association; The District of Columbia Bar; American Bar Association (Member, Antitrust Section). ***SPECIAL AGENCIES:*** Department of Justice and Federal Trade Commission. ***PRACTICE AREAS:*** Antitrust; Trade Regulation. ***Email:*** metallovr@howrey.com

HELEN KATHERINE MICHAEL, born Atlanta, Georgia, August 14, 1959; admitted to bar, 1988, Maryland; 1990, District of Columbia. *Education:* Hampshire College (B.A., 1981); University of Sussex, Great Britain, 1979-1980; University of North Carolina-Chapel Hill (J.D., with honors, 1986); George Washington University (LL.M., with highest honors, 1989). Staff Member, 1984-1985 and Articles Editor, 1985-1986, North Carolina Journal of International Law and Commercial Regulation. Author: "The Role of Natural Law in Early American Constitutionalism," 69 N.C.L. Rev. 421, (1991); "Covert Involvement in Essentially Internal Conflicts: United States Assistance to the Contras Under International Law," 23 Vanderbilt J. Transnatl. L. 539, (1990). *Member:* The District of Columbia Bar; Maryland State Bar and American (Member, Sections on: Antitrust; Litigation) Bar Associations. ***PRACTICE AREAS:*** Antitrust Law; Complex Litigation; Class Action Litigation; Insurance Coverage Litigation; Products Liability. ***Email:*** michaelh@howrey.com

VICTOR J. MILLER, born Queens, New York, March 15, 1966; admitted to bar, 1993, Maryland; 1995, District of Columbia. *Education:* Yale University (B.A., 1988); College of William & Mary (J.D., 1993). Member: National Moot Court Team; College of William & Mary Law Review. Author: "An End Run Around the Exclusionary Rule: The Use of Illegally Seized Evidence Under the Federal Sentencing Guidelines," 34 William & Mary Law Review, 1992. Law Clerk, The Honorable Michael Farrell, U.S. Court of Appeals for the District of Columbia Circuit, 1993-1994. ***PRACTICE AREAS:*** Antitrust; Commercial Litigation; Products Liability. ***Email:*** millerv@howrey.com

PETER E. MOLL, born Jersey City, New Jersey, February 6, 1949; admitted to bar, 1975, Massachusetts; 1976, District of Columbia; 1989, New Jersey. *Education:* Boston College (B.A., summa cum laude, 1971; J.D., summa cum laude, 1975). Phi Beta Kappa; Order of the Coif. Editor, Boston College Industrial & Commercial Law Review, 1974-1975. *Member:* The District of Columbia Bar; Massachusetts, New Jersey State and American Bar Associations. ***PRACTICE AREAS:*** Antitrust; Complex Litigation; Litigation. ***Email:*** mollp@howrey.com

P. TODD MULLINS, born Heidelberg, German Federal Republic, April 18, 1964; admitted to bar, 1989, Maryland; 1991, District of Columbia. *Education:* West Virginia University (B.S., 1986); George Washington University (J.D., magna cum laude, 1989). Member, George Washington Law Review, 1987-1989. Author: "The Militia Clauses, The National Guard and Federalism: A Constitutional Tug of War," 57 Geo. Wash. L. Rev. 328 (1989). ***PRACTICE AREAS:*** Commercial Litigation; Antitrust. ***Email:*** mullinst@howrey.com

REED W. NEUMAN, born New Rochelle, New York, September 26, 1952; admitted to bar, 1977, Illinois; 1988, District of Columbia. *Education:* Denison University (B.A., 1974); Case Western Reserve University (J.D., 1977). Member, Case Western Reserve University Law Review, 1975-1976. Assistant Attorney General, State of Illinois, Environmental Control Division, 1977-1983; Chief, Environmental Control Division, Southern Region, State of Illinois, 1982-1983. Senior Trial Attorney, Environmental Enforcement Section, Land and Natural Resources Division, U.S. Department of Justice, 1983-1986. *Member:* The District of Columbia Bar; American Bar Association. ***PRACTICE AREAS:*** Environmental; Complex Litigation; Administrative. ***Email:*** neumanr@howrey.com

JOHN W. NIELDS, JR., born New York, N.Y., September 24, 1942; admitted to bar, 1969, New York; 1980, District of Columbia. *Education:* Yale University (B.A., 1964); University of Pennsylvania (LL.B., 1967). Assistant United States Attorney, Southern District of New York, 1969-1974. Chief, Civil Division, 1973-1974. Chief Appellate Attorney, 1972-1973. Senior Law Clerk to Mr. Justice White, Associate Justice, United States Supreme Court, 1974-1977. Chief Counsel, Committee on Standards of Official Conduct, Korea Influence Investigation, United States House of Representatives, 1977-1978. Special Counsel, U.S. Department of Justice, 1979-1980. Chief Council, House Select Committee to Investigate Covert Arms Transactions with Iran, 1987. Special Counsel, RISDIC Commission, 1991-1992. *Member:* The District of Columbia Bar (President, 2000-2001); American Bar Association. ***PRACTICE AREAS:*** White Collar Criminal Defense; Intellectual Property. ***Email:*** nieldsj@howrey.com

WILLIAM R. O'BRIEN, born Providence, Rhode Island, August 31, 1944; admitted to bar, 1969, District of Columbia. *Education:* College of the Holy Cross (A.B., 1966); Georgetown University Law Center (J.D., 1969). Law Clerk to Hon. John J. Sirica, U.S. District Court for the District of Columbia, 1969-1970. *Member:* The District of Columbia Bar; American Bar Association. ***PRACTICE AREAS:*** Antitrust; Complex Litigation; Insurance Coverage. ***Email:*** o'brienb@howrey.com

JAMES W. OLSON, born Hollywood, California, September 21, 1947; admitted to bar, 1973, California; 1976, District of Columbia; 1980, U.S. Court of Appeals, Fourth and Tenth Circuits and U.S. Supreme Court; 1984, Michigan; 1987, Pennsylvania. *Education:* Edinburgh University and University of California at Berkeley (A.B., with great distinction, 1969); Yale University (J.D., 1972). Phi Beta Kappa. Author or Co-Author: with Lionel Kestenbaum, "Federal Amicus Intervention in Private Antitrust Litigation Raising Issues of Extraterritoriality: A Modest Proposal," International Lawyer 16, Fall 1982; with Lawrence J. Spiwack, "Can Short-Term Limits on Strategic Vertical Restraints Improve Long-Term Cable Industry Market Performance?" Cardozo Arts & Entertainment Law Journal 13, Spring 1995:283-315; "Competition to the Local Cable Monopoly: Time to Enhance the Program Access Regime?" National Law Journal, October 20, 1997; "Promoting Competition in the Multichannel Video Programming Distribution Market," Antitrust Report, October 1997; with Gregory F. Intoccia: "Regulation of the Internet: Round One at the FCC," CCH Power & Telecom Law, July/August 1998; CCH Power and Telecom Law, July-August 1998, "A Thin Red Line," Telephony, June 7, 1999: 254, "Internet-Telecom Mergers Raise Antitrust Scrutiny," Los Angeles Daily Journal, April 19, 1999 5, :6, "Telecommunications," National Law Journal, July 13, 1999; "FCC's LMDS Victory Shows Value of Reasoned Decision-Making," Radio Communications Report, February 23, 1998: 51; "An Interview with Reed E. Hundt, FCC Chairman," CCH Power & Telecom Law November/December 1997. Editor-in-Chief, CCH Power and Telecom Law, 1997-1999. Trial Attorney, 1972-1975 and Assistant to the Director, Bureau of Competition, 1975-1976, Federal Trade Commission. Chief, Competition Division, Federal Communications Commission, 1993-1997. *Member:* American Bar Association (Member, Section of Antitrust Law); Federal Communications Bar Association (Co-Chair, Ad Hoc Committee on Telecommunications Competition Issues, 1997—). ***PRACTICE AREAS:*** Antitrust; Telecommunications; Computer Law. ***Email:*** olsonj@howrey.com

JOSEPH A. OSTOYICH, born Kingston, New York, August 5, 1966; admitted to bar, 1992, New York; 1993, District of Columbia and U.S. Court of Appeals, Fourth Circuit. *Education:* Cornell University (B.A., with distinction, 1988); University of Chicago (J.D., 1991). Phi Beta Kappa; Phi Kappa Phi. *Member:* New York State (Member, Antitrust Section) and American (Member, Antitrust Section) Bar Associations. ***PRACTICE AREAS:*** Antitrust Law; Commercial Litigation. ***Email:*** ostoyichj@howrey.com

JOHN C. PEIRCE, born Arlington, Virginia, March 26, 1953; admitted to bar, 1980, District of Columbia; 1984, U.S. Supreme Court; U.S. Court of Appeals, Fourth and Ninth Circuits; U.S. Court of Appeals for the District of Columbia Circuit; U.S. Court of Appeals for the Federal Circuit; U.S. District Court, District of Columbia; U.S. Court of International Trade. *Education:* Yale University (B.A., 1975); Cornell University (J.D., cum laude, 1980). Co-Author: "Driving Defensively on the Information Superhighway: An Antitrust Primer

(This Listing Continued)

HOWREY SIMON ARNOLD & WHITE, LLP, Washington—Continued

for Utilities, Pipelines and Other Right-of-Way Companies," Utilities Telecommunications Council, April, 1995. *Member:* District of Columbia Bar; American Bar Association (Chair, Fuel and Energy Committee, Antitrust Section); Federal Energy Bar Association. ***PRACTICE AREAS:*** Antitrust; Complex Litigation; Insurance Coverage; Electric Utilities; International Trade Law. **Email:** peircej@howrey.com

KEITH E. PUGH, JR., born Los Angeles, California, March 17, 1937; admitted to bar, 1962, California; 1969, District of Columbia; U.S. District Court, Northern, Central, Eastern and Southern Districts of California, District of Maryland, District of Columbia and Southern District of Alabama; U.S. Court of Appeals Third, Fourth, Fifth, Ninth, Federal and District of Columbia Circuits; U.S. Supreme Court; U.S. Court of International Trade. *Education:* Principia College; University of Southern California (J.D., 1962). Phi Delta Phi. Listed in Marquis Who's Who in the World, North America and American Law. Deputy Attorney General, Antitrust Section, State of California Department of Justice, 1962-1965. *Member:* The District of Columbia Bar; The State Bar of California; American Bar Association. ***PRACTICE AREAS:*** Antitrust; Complex Commercial Litigation. **Email:** pughk@howrey.com

BERT C. REISER, born Chicago, Illinois, November 22, 1963; admitted to bar, 1990, Virginia; 1996, District of Columbia. *Education:* Central College (B.A., 1985); American University (J.D., 1990). Attorney Advisor to Hon. Paul J. Luekern, U.S. International Trade Commission, 1991-1995. ***LANGUAGES:*** Spanish. ***PRACTICE AREAS:*** International Trade; Section 337. **Email:** reiserb@howrey.com

WILLIAM BRADFORD REYNOLDS, born Bridgeport, Connecticut, June 21, 1942; admitted to bar, 1968, New York; 1971, District of Columbia; 1973, U.S. Supreme Court. *Education:* Yale University (B.A., 1964); Vanderbilt University (LL.B. and S.J.D., 1967). Order of the Coif. Assistant to U.S. Solicitor General, 1970-1973. Distinguished Fellow, National Legal Center for Public Interest, 1988-1989. Distinguished Scholar, Free Congress Foundation for Law and Public Policy, 1988-1989. Assistant Attorney General, Civil Rights Division, U.S. Department of Justice, 1981-1988. Counselor to U.S. Attorney General, 1987-1988. Chairman, Architectural Barriers & Compliance Board, 1982-1983. *Member:* The District of Columbia Bar; New York State, Federal and American Bar Associations. ***PRACTICE AREAS:*** Antitrust Litigation (Trial Court); Commercial Litigation (Trial Court); Federal Appellate Practice. **Email:** reynoldsw@howrey.com

JAMES F. RILL, born Evanston, Illinois, March 4, 1933; admitted to bar, 1959, District of Columbia and U.S. Court of Appeals for the District of Columbia Circuit; 1965, U.S. Supreme Court. *Education:* Dartmouth College (A.B., 1954); Harvard University (LL.B., 1959). Member: Editorial Board, Antitrust Bulletin; Advisory Board, Bureau of National Affairs, Antitrust and Trade Regulation Report; Board of Editors, Antitrust Report (Matthew Bender & Co.). Assistant Attorney General, Antitrust Division, U.S. Department of Justice, 1989-1992. Co-Chair, U.S. Department of Justice International Competition Advisory Committee, 1997-2000. Public Member, Administrative Conference of the United States, 1992-1994. Member, Department of State Advisory Committee on International Investment, 1992-1993. Member, Advisory Panel on Office of Technology Assessment of Multinational Firms and the U.S. Technology Base, 1992-1995. Council Principal, The Council for Excellence in Government. *Member:* The District of Columbia Bar; Bar Association of the District of Columbia; American Bar Association (Co-Chairman, Antitrust and Global Economy Task Force, 1995-1999; Member, Tri-National NAFTA Task Force; Chairman, 1987-1988; Chairman-Elect, 1986-1987; Finance Officer, 1984-1986; Council Member, 1981-1984 and Chairman, Robinson-Patman Committee, 1978-1981, Antitrust Section); Organization for Economic Cooperation and Development (Vice Chair, Business and Industry Advisory Committee (BIAC), OECD Competition Law and Policy Committee, 1992—). Fellow, American Bar Foundation. ***PRACTICE AREAS:*** Antitrust; Trade Regulation. **Email:** rillj@howrey.com

RICHARD A. RIPLEY, born Castro Valley, California, March 21, 1960; admitted to bar, 1986, Pennsylvania and U.S. District Court, Eastern District of Pennsylvania; 1988, District of Columbia and U.S. Court of Appeals, Eleventh Circuit; 1992, U.S. Court of Appeals, Third Circuit. *Education:* Ohio State University (B.A., 1983; Phi Beta Kappa); George Washington University National Law Center (J.D., with honors, 1986). Delta Theta Phi; Dean, Wilson Senate, 1986. Member, 1984-1986 and Articles Editor, 1986, George Washington Law Review. *Member:* The District of Columbia Bar; Pennsylvania and American Bar Associations. ***PRACTICE AREAS:*** Antitrust; Complex Litigation; White Collar Criminal Defense. **Email:** ripleyr@howrey.com

HOWARD T. ROSENBLATT, born Miami, Florida, May 22, 1961; admitted to bar, 1986, New York; 1987, District of Columbia; 1991, U.S. Supreme Court. *Education:* Vanderbilt University (B.A., magna cum laude, 1983); Duke University (M.A., 1986; J.D., 1986). Phi Beta Kappa. Recipient, American Jurisprudence Award in Constitutional Law. Member, Dean's Advisory Council.

(This Listing Continued)

Moot Court Finalist and Board Vice Chairman. *Member:* The District of Columbia Bar; American Bar Association. ***PRACTICE AREAS:*** Antitrust; Commercial Litigation. **Email:** rosenblatth@howrey.com

JOHN J. ROSENTHAL, born Baltimore, Maryland, March 16, 1962; admitted to bar, 1989, Maryland and U.S. District Court District of Maryland; 1990, District of Columbia and U.S. District Court, Northern District of California; 1996, U.S. District Court for the District of Columbia. *Education:* The Johns Hopkins University (B.A., 1985); University of Virginia (J.D., 1988). Pi Sigma Alpha; Omicron Delta Kappa. *Member:* Maryland State and American Bar Associations; District of Columbia Bar. ***PRACTICE AREAS:*** Antitrust Law; Complex Commercial Litigation; Franchise Litigation. **Email:** rosenthalj@howrey.com

ROBERT F. RUYAK, born Columbus, Ohio, July 9, 1949; admitted to bar, 1974, Pennsylvania; 1976, District of Columbia; U.S. District Court for the District of Columbia; U.S. Court of Appeals, Third, Fourth, Fifth, Federal and District of Columbia Circuits; U.S. Supreme Court. *Education:* Gannon University (B.A., 1971); Georgetown University Law Center (J.D., 1974). Law Clerk to Hon. John J. Sirica, U.S. District Court for the District of Columbia, 1974-1976. *Member:* The District of Columbia Bar; Federal and American Bar Associations. ***PRACTICE AREAS:*** Antitrust; Patent Litigation; Trademark Litigation; Trade Secrets; Copyright Litigation; International Trade Litigation; Complex Commercial Litigation; Litigation. **Email:** ruyakr@howrey.com

LISA J. SAKS, born Harvey, Illinois, December 13, 1956; admitted to bar, 1985, Maryland and District of Columbia. *Education:* Oberlin College (B.A., with highest honors, 1978); George Washington University (J.D., with honors, 1984). Phi Beta Kappa; Sigma Xi; Order of the Coif. Editor, George Washington Journal of International Law and Economics, 1983-1984. *Member:* The District of Columbia Bar; Maryland State and American Bar Associations. ***PRACTICE AREAS:*** Antitrust; Complex Litigation. **Email:** saksl@howrey.com

RICHARD H. SALTSMAN, born Washington, D.C., January 29, 1948; admitted to bar, 1973, District of Columbia; 1980, U.S. Supreme Court. *Education:* Princeton University (B.A., cum laude, 1970); George Washington University (J.D., with honors, 1973). Assistant United States Attorney for the District of Columbia, 1974-1979. Adjunct Professor of Law, Georgetown University, 1983-1987. *Member:* District of Columbia Bar; American Bar Association. ***PRACTICE AREAS:*** Commercial Litigation; White Collar Criminal Defense.

RALPH J. SAVARESE, born New York, N.Y., September 4, 1936; admitted to bar, 1962, New York; 1963, District of Columbia. *Education:* Iona College (B.B.A., 1958); Fordham University (LL.B., 1961); University of Michigan (graduate law study fellowship, 1961-1963). ***PRACTICE AREAS:*** Antitrust Law; Complex Commercial Litigation. **Email:** savareser@howrey.com

MARK C. SCHECHTER, born Pittsburgh, Pennsylvania, September 3, 1951; admitted to bar, 1978, Pennsylvania and U.S. District Court, Eastern District of Pennsylvania; 1987, U.S. Supreme Court; 1995, District of Columbia. *Education:* Pennsylvania State University (B.A., 1973; M.A., Economics, 1975); Antioch School of Law (J.D., 1978); Europa Institute, Netherlands (D.E.I., 1993). Phi Kappa Phi; Omicron Delta Epsilon. Recipient: Antitrust Division Award of Distinction, 1988; John Marshall Award for Outstanding Legal Achievement, presented by the Attorney General, 1994. Co-Author: with Scott E. Flick, "Competition by Collaboration: U.S. Joint Venture Analysis in a Competitive World," United States Antitrust Review, Special Report by the Global Competition Review, 1998; as a Member of Working Group, "Comments of The Section of Antitrust Law of The American Bar Association on the European Commission's 'White Papter on Modernization of the The Rules Implementing Articles 85 and 86 of the EC Treaty,'" American Bar Association, 1999; with Joseph P. Lavelle and Eva Almirantearena, "Microsoft: What Remedy is Appropriate?," Corporate Counsel Magazine, 1999; with Howard T. Rosenblatt, "Trends in U.S. Government Antitrust Enforcement," Global Competition Review Special Report: The Antitrust Review of the Americas 2000, 1999; Mark C. Schechter and Howard T. Rosenblatt, "Trends in the U.S. Government Antitrust Enforcement," *Global Competitive Review Special Report: The Antitrust Review of the Americas 2001* (Fall 2000); Mark C. Schechter and Howard T. Rosenblatt, "Beware of the Competition Regulators: The Recently Issued Covisint Case Shows that U.S. Anti-trust Authorities are Taking a Close Look at the Internet B2B Market," *International Internet Law Review* 9 (November 2000); Mark C. Schecthter and Howard T. Rosenblatt, "Federal Antitrust Enforcement — Year 2000 and Beyond," *National Law Journal* (October, 1999). Reviewer for the National Research Council of "Entry and Competition in The U.S. Airline Industry," Special Report No. 255, Transportation Research Board, 1999. Author: "The Rule of Reason in European Competition Law," Legal Issues of European Integration 1, 1983/2; "The Legal Cost of Dying Rich," 20 Am. Econ. 69, 1976. Co-Author: with Robert Latham, "The Price Structure of the Legal Service Industry: Minimum Fee Schedules and Price Discrimination," 24 Antitrust Bull. 43, 1979; with James B. Herendeen, "Alternative Models of the Corporate Enterprise: Growth Maximization and Value Maximization, An Empirical Test," 43 S. Econ. J. 1505, 1977 and 15 J. Econ. Lit. 1254, 1977; with Benjamin Henszey, "A Rational Approach to the Maximization of Lifetime Gifts," 53 Taxes 687, 1975. U.S. Department of Justice,

(This Listing Continued)

Antitrust Division: Deputy Director of Operations in Charge of Civil Enforcement, 1993-1995; Chief, Transportation, Energy and Agriculture Section, 1988-1993; Assistant Chief, Litigation II and Intellectual Property Sections, 1985-1988; Trial Attorney, 1978-1984. ***PRACTICE AREAS:*** Antitrust. ***Email:*** schechterm@howrey.com

MARC G. SCHILDKRAUT, born New York, N.Y., May 8, 1951; admitted to bar, 1977, New York; 1978, District of Columbia; U.S. District Court for the District of Columbia; U.S. Court of Appeals for the Federal and District of Columbia Circuits. *Education:* Columbia University (B.A., magna cum laude, 1973; J.D., 1976). Phi Beta Kappa; Harlan Fiske Stone Scholar; Charles Evan Hughes Fellow. Editor and Chief, Columbia Journal of Law and Social Problems. Author: "Areas of Primary Responsibility, Passovers and Other Territorial Restraints in Channels of Distribution under the Antitrust Laws," 11 Colum. J. of Law & Soc. Prob. 509, 1975; "FTC Consent Orders in Merger Matters," Corporate Counsel's Guide to Merger Analysis, 1995. Adjunct Professor of Law, Advanced Antitrust Course, Georgetown University Law Center, 1986. Trial Attorney, 1976-1980, Deputy Assistant Director, 1980-1988, Assistant Director, 1988-1993, Bureau of Competition, Federal Trade Commission. *Member:* American Bar Association (Chairman, Federal Trade Commission Committee, Antitrust Section). ***PRACTICE AREAS:*** Antitrust Law. ***Email:*** schildkrautm@howrey.com

EDWARD B. SCHWARTZ, born Huntington, New York, 1957; admitted to bar, 1985, New York; 1991, District of Columbia. *Education:* Hamilton College (B.A., 1979); Boston College (J.D., cum laude, 1984). Editor-in-Chief, Boston College Environmental Affairs Law Review. Legislative Assistant, Congressman M. Caldwell Butler, 1979-1981. District of Columbia Advisory Neighborhood Commissioner, 1993-1995. ***PRACTICE AREAS:*** Antitrust Litigation; Commercial Litigation. ***Email:*** schwartze@howrey.com

FREDERICK F. SHAHEEN, born Utica, New York, July 10, 1953; admitted to bar, 1993, Virginia; 1994, District of Columbia. *Education:* Syracuse University (A.B., 1976); U.S. Naval Postgraduate School (M.A., 1985); George Washington University National Law Center (J.D., 1993). Author: "The New Brokering Regulations of the Department of State: More Than Meets the Eye," National Contract Management Association Journal, Volume 29, No. 1, 1998. Special Assistant to the Advisor to the President and the Secretary of State, 1985-1987. Special Assistant, Office of the Secretary of Defense, 1989-1990. Deputy Chief, Office of Strategic and Nuclear Affairs, U.S. Arms Control and Disarmament Agency/U.S. Department of State, 1991-1993. Chairman, U.S. Soviet Standing Consultative Commission Interagency Group, 1991-1992. [Lt. Commander, U.S. Navy, 1977-1990]. ***PRACTICE AREAS:*** International Commercial Law; Foreign Military Sales; Export Regulation. ***Email:*** shaheenf@howrey.com

HARVEY G. SHERZER, born Philadelphia, Pennsylvania, May 19, 1944; admitted to bar, 1970, District of Columbia, U.S. Court of Federal Claims and U.S. Court of Appeals for the Federal Circuit; 1974, U.S. Supreme Court. *Education:* Temple University (B.A., 1965); George Washington University (J.D., with honors, 1968). Phi Sigma Alpha; Phi Delta Phi. Member, George Washington Law Review, 1967-1968. Author: "A Complete Guide to the Department of Defense Voluntary Disclosure Program," 1996; "Foreign Military Sales," Federal Publications, Inc. 1997; "Export Control of Equipment and Technology," Federal Publications Inc., 1992; "Law and Policy Framework," International Government Contracting, Federal Publications Inc., 1985; "Government Requirements," Subcontracting, Federal Publications Inc., 1985; "Export Controls Over Direct Commercial Sales of Military and Strategic Goods and Technologies: Who's In Charge?" 7 B.C. Int'l. & Comp. L. Rev. 303, 1984; "Manual for Practice Before Boards of Contract Appeals," Federal Bar Association, 1981; "Foreign Military Sales: A Guide to the United States Bureaucracy," 13 J. Int'l. L. & Econ. 545, 1979; "Contract Cases-General and Wunderlich Act," Manual for Practice in the United States Court of Claims, 1976, 1979 rev.; Note, "Certification of Out-of-State Attorneys Before the Federal District Courts: A Plea for National Standards," 36 Geo. Wash. L. Rev. 204, 1967. Law Clerk to: Hon. Wilson Cowen, Chief Judge, U.S. Court of Claims, 1969-1970 and to Trial Judges, U.S. Court of Claims, 1968-1969. *Member:* The District of Columbia Bar; Bar Association of the District of Columbia; Federal and American Bar Associations. ***PRACTICE AREAS:*** Government Contracts Law. ***Email:*** sherzerh@howrey.com

LAURA S. SHORES, born Birmingham, Alabama, January 22, 1964; admitted to bar, 1988, Alabama and U.S. Court of Appeals, Eleventh Circuit; 1989, U.S. District Court, Northern District of Alabama; 1990, District of Columbia; 1991, U.S. Court of Appeals, District of Columbia Circuit; 1992, U.S. Court of Appeals, Fourth Circuit. *Education:* Smith College (A.B., cum laude, 1985); University of Chicago (J.D., 1988). Clerk, Hon. Robert S. Vance, United States Court of Appeals for the Eleventh Circuit, 1988-1989. *Member:* The District of Columbia Bar; American Bar Association. ***LANGUAGES:*** French. ***PRACTICE AREAS:*** White Collar Criminal Defense; Litigation. ***Email:*** shoresl@howrey.com

ROBERT H. SHULMAN, born Ithaca, New York, May 16, 1953; admitted to bar, 1980, District of Columbia and Louisiana; U.S. Court of Appeals for the District of Columbia Circuit; U.S. Court of Appeals, Fourth Circuit; U.S. Court of Appeals, Third Circuit. *Education:* Cornell University (B.A., 1975); Tulane University of Louisiana (J.D., cum laude, 1979). Co-author: "Trigger and Scope of Coverage Under Comprehensive General Liability Insurance Policies in Toxic Substance Cases," 3 Legal Notes and Viewpoints 95, 1982; "Bausch & Lomb: The Death of Armco and MRAZ," The Report, June 22, 1993; "Strategies for Settling Environmental, Toxic Tort and Other Complex Insurance Coverage Case," Legal Times, June 1995; "Alternative Dispute Resolution: Managing Complex Insurance Disputes," Legal Times, January 1996; "ADR Aids Resolution of Insurance Coverage Cases," The National Law Journal, April 1996; "Pursuing A Comprehensive Strategy For Defending Class Actions and Other Mass Tort and Consumer Claims In a Hostile Jurisdiction Throughout Litigation And Alternative Dispute Resolution," The Metropolitan Corporate Counsel, Vol. 5, No. 9, September 1997; "Companies Can Get Coverage for Attorneys Fees They Paid in Class Action Settlements," The Recorder, October 1997. Clerk to Hon. George Arceneaux, Jr., U.S. District Court, Eastern District of Louisiana, 1979-1981. *Member:* District of Columbia Bar; Louisiana State Bar Association. ***PRACTICE AREAS:*** Insurance Coverage; Complex Litigation; Litigation. ***Email:*** shulmanr@howrey.com

TRACY A. HEINZMAN SMITH, born Rochester, New York, February 3, 1964; admitted to bar, 1992, Virginia; 1998, District of Columbia. *Education:* State University of New York at Geneseo (B.A., cum laude, 1985); University of Virginia (J.D., 1992). *Member:* District of Columbia Bar; Virginia Bar; American Bar Association. ***PRACTICE AREAS:*** Environmental. ***Email:*** heinzmansmitht@howrey.com

KOOROSH TALIEH, born Tehran, Iran, October 9, 1960; admitted to bar, 1988, Pennsylvania; 1994, District of Columbia. *Education:* Amherst College (B.A., 1983); Georgetown University (J.D., 1988). *Member:* District of Columbia Bar; Pennsylvania and American Bar Associations. ***LANGUAGES:*** French and Farsi. ***PRACTICE AREAS:*** General Litigation; Insurance Litigation. ***Email:*** kooroshtalieh@howrey.com

PETER L. TRACEY, born New London, Connecticut, June 4, 1960; admitted to bar, 1989, Delaware; 1990, Pennsylvania, U.S. District Court, District of Delaware and U.S. Court of Appeals, Third Circuit; 1997, U.S. Supreme Court; 2000, District of Columbia. *Education:* Yale University (B.A., cum laude, 1986); Dickinson School of Law (J.D., 1989). Member, Irving R. Kaufman Securities Law Moot Court Team. Member: Dickinson Law Review and Dickinson Journal of International Law. Co-Author: Contributor to D. J. Wolfe, Jr., and M. A. Pittenger, "Procedures in Equity: Corporate and Commercial Practice in the Delaware Court of Chancery," Lexis Law Publishing, 1998; with S. R. Fallon, "Insurance Coverage Law in Delaware," National Business Institute, 1996; with C. S. Crompton, Jr., "Further Reflection On the Owned Property Exclusion," Environmental Claims J., Spring 1998. Author: Comment, "International Advertising: Regulatory Pitfalls for the Unwary Marketer," 7 Dick. J. Int'l. L. 229, 1989; Comment, "The Delaware Debate on Takeover Legislation: No Small Wonder," 93 Dick. L. Rev. 339, 1989. *Member:* Delaware and American Bar Associations. ***LANGUAGES:*** French and Spanish. ***PRACTICE AREAS:*** Insurance Coverage Litigation; Commercial Litigation. ***Email:*** traceyp@howrey.com

WILLIAM L. WEBBER, born Fort Wayne, Indiana, December 10, 1953; admitted to bar, 1981, District of Columbia and California. *Education:* Yale University (B.A., cum laude with distinction in Economics, 1976); London School of Economics (G.C., 1975); Duke University (J.D., 1980). Editorial Assistant, Law & Contemporary Problems, 1979-1980. Associate Editor, "Regulation and Innovation," 43 Law & Contemporary Problems 1 (1979). Co-Author: "Antitrust and Hospital Privileges: Testing the Conventional Wisdom," 70 California Law Review 595 (1982). Assistant U.S. Attorney, Criminal Division, 1981-1984 and Deputy Chief, Criminal Complaints, 1984, Central District of California. Trial Attorney, Antitrust Division, U.S. Department of Justice, 1980-1981. *Member:* The District of Columbia Bar; State Bar of California; American Bar Association (Member, Antitrust, Litigation and Criminal Law Sections). ***PRACTICE AREAS:*** Advertising; Antitrust; Appellate Practice; Litigation; White Collar Criminal Defense. ***Email:*** webberb@howrey.com

MARK D. WEGENER, born Cedar Rapids, Iowa, November 1, 1948; admitted to bar, 1974, District of Columbia. *Education:* Central College (B.A., cum laude, 1970); Rutgers Law School (J.D., 1973). *Member:* The District of Columbia Bar; Bar Association of the District of Columbia; American Bar Association. ***PRACTICE AREAS:*** Antitrust; Commercial Law; Complex Litigation; Government Regulation; Litigation. ***Email:*** wegenerm@howrey.com

DAVID B. WEINBERG, born Newark, New Jersey, May 25, 1948; admitted to bar, 1973, District of Columbia. *Education:* Yale University (A.B., 1970); University of Pennsylvania (J.D., cum laude, 1973); Georgetown University (LL.M., 1974). Author/Co-Author: "The Freedom of Information Act," 63 Georgetown University Law Journal 49 (1974); "Recent Trends in Antitrust Civil Action Damage Determinations," 1976 Duke Law Journal 485 (1975); "Hazardous Waste Regulation Handbook," 1985; "Environmental Audit Handbook," 1981, 1983. Senior Assistant to the Director, Office of Presidential Personnel. The White House, 1979-1980. Member, Committee on Environment, U.S. Chamber of Commerce (Chair of the Ad Hoc Superfund Task Force); Advisory Boards, Chemical Waste Litigation Reporter, EPA Administrative

(This Listing Continued)

HOWREY SIMON ARNOLD & WHITE, LLP, Washington—Continued

Law Reporter, ELI Environmental Forum; National Advisory Board, Center for National Policy. *Member:* The District of Columbia Bar (Member, Steering Committee, 1974-1975 and Chairperson, 1975-1976, Division of Environment, Energy and Natural Resources); American Bar Association. ***Email:*** weinbergd@howrey.com

WILLIAM K. WEST, JR., born Wilmington, Ohio, February 21, 1937; admitted to bar, 1962, District of Columbia; registered to practice before U.S. Patent and Trademark Office. *Education:* Duke University (B.S.M.E., 1959; LL.B., 1962). Phi Delta Phi. Co-author: "The Law of 'Public Use' and 'On Sale': Past, Present and Future," 72 JPTOS 114, 1990. Member, BNA Patent, Trademark, Copyright Journal Advisory Board, 1983—. *Member:* The District of Columbia Bar; Bar Association of the District of Columbia; American Bar Association; American Intellectual Property Law Association. ***PRACTICE AREAS:*** Patent; Trade-dress; Antitrust; Complex Litigation. ***Email:*** westw@howrey.com

J. PAUL WILLIAMSON, born Hornell, New York, June 6, 1948; admitted to bar, 1973, Illinois; 1976, Virginia; 1979, Texas; 1986, District of Columbia. *Education:* Purdue University (B.S.A.E., 1970); University of Illinois (J.D., 1973). Phi Eta Sigma. Trademark Attorney, 1973-1976 and Trademark Petitions Attorney, 1976-1979, U.S. Patent and Trademark Office. Member, International Committee, International Trademark Association, 1990-1995. *Member:* Houston, Federal Circuit, Illinois State, Virginia and American Bar Associations; Virginia State Bar; State Bar of Texas; The District of Columbia Bar; American Intellectual Property Law Association. ***PRACTICE AREAS:*** Trademarks; International Trademarks; Trademark Litigation; Trademark Prosecution; Trademark Protection. ***Email:*** williamsonp@howrey.com

A. DUNCAN WHITAKER, born Fort Wayne, Indiana, 1932; admitted to bar, 1957, Michigan; 1959, District of Columbia; 1961, U.S. Supreme Court. *Education:* Yale University (B.A., 1954); University of Michigan (J.D., 1957). Order of the Coif; Phi Beta Kappa; Phi Alpha Delta. Editor, Michigan Law Review, 1955-1957. Trial Attorney, Antitrust Division, Department of Justice, 1957-1959. Lecturer on Law, George Washington University, 1960. Adjunct Professor, George Mason University School of Law, 1985-1986. *Member:* The District of Columbia Bar; Federal and American Bar Associations. ***PRACTICE AREAS:*** Antitrust Law; Complex Litigation; Commercial Law. ***Email:*** whitakerd@howrey.com

ALAN M. WISEMAN, born Long Branch, New Jersey, July 6, 1944; admitted to bar, 1968, Maryland; 1970, Illinois; 1973, U.S. Supreme Court; 1974, District of Columbia. *Education:* Johns Hopkins University (B.A, 1965); Georgetown University Law Center (J.D., 1968). Editor, Georgetown Law Journal, 1967-1968. Law Clerk to Judge William J. McWilliams, Maryland Court of Appeals, 1968-1969. Member, Council on Antitrust Policy, U.S. Chamber of Commerce, 1983—. *Member:* The District of Columbia Bar. ***PRACTICE AREAS:*** Antitrust; Appellate Practice; Commercial Law; Complex Litigation; Litigation. ***Email:*** wisemana@howrey.com

CARMINE R. ZARLENGA, born Youngstown, Ohio, July 1, 1959; admitted to bar, 1984, Ohio; 1985, District of Columbia; 1987, U.S. District Court for the District of Columbia. *Education:* Youngstown State University; The Ohio State University (B.A., cum laude, 1981); University of Cincinnati (J.D., 1984). Student Articles Editor, University of Cincinnati Law Review, 1982-1983. Member, Editorial Board, Franchise Law Bibliography 2d, 1991-1993. *Member:* The District of Columbia Bar; Ohio State and American (Member, Sections of: Antitrust Law; Litigation; Forum Committee on Franchising; Member, Task Force for UCC Article 2 Revision, 1996) Bar Associations. ***PRACTICE AREAS:*** Antitrust; Commercial Litigation; Franchise Law. ***Email:*** zarlengac@howrey.com

MARGARET M. ZWISLER, born Evanston, Illinois, January 24, 1949; admitted to bar, 1976, District of Columbia; U.S. District Court, District of Maryland; U.S. District Court for the District of Columbia; U.S. Court of Appeals, Second, Third, Fourth, Eleventh, District of Columbia and Federal Circuits. *Education:* Saint Mary's College (B.A., cum laude, 1971); George Washington University (J.D., with high honors, 1976). Order of the Coif. *Member:* The District of Columbia Bar; American Bar Association (Member, Section of Litigation; Vice-Chair, Robinson-Patman Act Committee, Section of Antitrust Law); International Trademark Association. ***PRACTICE AREAS:*** Antitrust; Complex Litigation; Government Regulation. ***Email:*** zwislerm@howrey.com

OF COUNSEL

GREGORY F. INTOCCIA, born Memphis, Tennessee, August 24, 1956; admitted to bar, 1985, Colorado; 1992, Pennsylvania; 1994, New York; 1997, District of Columbia. *Education:* United States Air Force Academy (B.S., 1978); Wichita State University (M.A., 1981); University of Denver (J.D., 1985); University of Missouri, St. Louis (Ph.D., 1998). Phi Sigma Alpha; Phi Kappa Phi. Editorial Staff, Denver Journal of International Law and Policy, 1984-1985. Co-author: "Federal Communications Commission and Regulation of the Internet," CCH Power & Telecommunications, 1998. Author: "Governing Telecommunications: A New Regime in Public Law and Public Policy", 10 Glendale Law Review 1, 1991. *Member:* Federal Communications Bar Association. [Active duty, U.S. Air Force, 1978-1992; JAGC, 1985-1992; Lt. Col., U.S. Air Force Reserve, 1992—]. ***PRACTICE AREAS:*** Telecommunications. ***Email:*** intocciag@howrey.com

HILLARY L. SNYDER, born Denver, Colorado, September 6, 1959; admitted to bar, 1987, New York; 1988, District of Columbia. *Education:* University of Pennsylvania (B.A., magna cum laude, 1981); New York University (J.D., 1986). U.S. Department of Justice, Antitrust Division: Consultant, 1996-1999; Special Assistant, Office of Operations, 1992-1994; Trial Attorney, 1990-1992, 1994-1996; Special Assistant U.S. Attorney, E.D. VA, 1994. Member, American Bar Association, Antitrust Section; Women's Bar Association. ***Email:*** snyderh@howrey.com

JAMES R. WAGNER, born Bangor, Maine, January 11, 1966; admitted to bar, 1992, New York; 1993, District of Columbia; U.S. District Court, District of Columbia; U.S. District Court, Southern District of New York; U.S. Court of Appeals, Sixth Circuit. *Education:* Boston University (B.A., magna cum laude, 1988); Georgetown University (J.D., 1991). Editor, Georgetown International Environmental Law Review. *Member:* District of Columbia Bar; New York State and American Bar Associations. ***LANGUAGES:*** French. ***PRACTICE AREAS:*** Insurance; Commercial Disputes.

MARK L. WHITAKER, born Rochester, New York, July 27, 1958; admitted to bar, 1990, Pennsylvania; 1992, District of Columbia; 1995, U.S. District Court, District of Columbia; 1996, U.S. Court of Federal Claims; 1997, U.S. District Court, District of Maryland; 2000, U.S. Court of Appeals for the Federal Circuit. *Education:* Northeastern University (B.S., Public Administration, Political Science, magna cum laude, Pi Sigma Alpha, 1981); Georgetown University Law Center (J.D., 1990). Lecturer, Old Dominion Bar Association Annual Meeting, Arlington, Virginia, 2000. Instructor, Blacks In Government Annual Convention, Washington, D.C., 1997 and 1998. Investigator/Intern, U.S. Equal Employment Opportunity Commission, 1977-1982. Member, Legislative Affairs Committee, Fairfax County Chamber of Commerce. Senior Associate, ShawPittman, Washington, D.C., 1994-2000. *Member:* American (Member, Litigation Section) and National Bar Associations; District of Columbia Bar (Member, Sections on: Litigation; Intellectual Property); George Mason American Inns of Court; Greater Washington Urban League; American Intellectual Property Law Association. [U.S. Navy (Surface Warfare), 1983-1990; Lt., U.S. Navy, 1983-1994; J.A.G.C., U.S. Navy, 1990-1994]. ***PRACTICE AREAS:*** Litigation.

SPECIAL COUNSEL

JULIANA M. COFRANCESCO, born Vienna, Austria, February 23, 1958; admitted to bar, 1987, Massachusetts; 1988, District of Columbia; U.S. Court of International Trade; U.S. Court of Appeals for the Federal Circuit; U.S. Supreme Court. *Education:* Hunter College; State University of New York at Albany (B.A., magna cum laude, 1979); Georgetown University (J.D., cum laude, 1987). Phi Alpha Delta (Treasurer, 1984-1985). Lead Articles Editor, Law and Policy in International Business, 1986-1987. *Member:* The District of Columbia Bar; Massachusetts and American Bar Associations; Customs and International Trade Bar Association. ***LANGUAGES:*** Hungarian. ***PRACTICE AREAS:*** International Trade Law; Import and Export Law. ***Email:*** cofrancescoj@howrey.com

GILBERT S. KETELTAS, born Frankfurt, Germany, August 22, 1964; admitted to bar, 1989, District of Columbia. *Education:* Cornell University (B.S. in Labor Relations, 1986); Georgetown University (J.D., 1989). Law Fellow, Business Editor, Georgetown International Environmental Law Review, 1988-1989. Member, Mortar Board Honor Society. ***Email:*** keteltasg@howrey.com

JEFFREY M. LENSER, born La Crosse, Wisconsin, September, 11, 1965; admitted to bar, 1991, District of Columbia. *Education:* College of William and Mary (B.A., 1988); University of Texas (J.D. with honors, 1991). Delta Theta Phi (Exchequer, 1989-1991). *Member:* The District of Columbia; Bar Association of the District of Columbia; American Bar Association (Member, Section on Litigation). ***PRACTICE AREAS:*** Insurance Coverage; Litigation. ***Email:*** lenserj@howrey.com

RACHEL LISA STRONG, born Loch Haven, Pennsylvania, April 25, 1969; admitted to bar, 1994, Maryland; 1996, District of Columbia. *Education:* University of Maryland (B.A., summa cum laude, 1991); George Washington University (J.D., cum laude, 1994). Member, The George Washington Law Review. ***PRACTICE AREAS:*** Public Service Counsel. ***Email:*** strongr@howrey.com

ASSOCIATES

BRENT H. ALLEN, born Florissant, Missouri, March 15, 1969; admitted to bar, 1995, Pennsylvania and New Jersey; 1999, District of Columbia. *Educa-*

(This Listing Continued)

tion: University of Pennsylvania (B.A., 1991); Vanderbilt University (J.D., 1994). Vanderbilt Law Review. Author: "The First Amendment: The Need for an Expanded Interpretation," 47 Vand. L. Rev. 1073 (1994); "Who Takes Out the Garbage? Double Jeopardy and Environmental Crimes Under United States v. Halper," 1 Vand. Crim. L. Update 34 (1995). Clerk to the Honorable Joseph D. O'Keefe, Court of Common Pleas, Philadelphia County, 1994-1995. *Member:* The District of Columbia Bar; American Bar Association. ***PRACTICE AREAS:*** Commercial Litigation. ***Email:*** allenbrent@howrey.com

TIMOTHY K. ARMSTRONG, born Spokane, Washington, January 19, 1968; admitted to bar, 1993, Texas; 1994, District of Columbia. *Education:* University of Texas (B.A., 1989; M.P.Aff., 1993; J.D., 1993). Phi Delta Phi (Historian, 1991); Order of the Coif; Chancellors. Managing Editor, 1992-1993, Articles and Notes Editor, 1991-1992, Texas International Law Journal. Author: Note, "Transnational Production Joint Ventures and United States Antitrust Law: Evaluating the Proposed National Cooperative Production Amendments," 28 Tex. Int'l L.J. 119, 1993. Co-Author: with W. Neil Eggleston, "Attorney-Client Privilege When the Client is a Public Official: Litigating the Opening Act of the Impeachment Drama," ABA Center for Continuing Legal Education and Criminal Justice, White Collar Crime, at A-1, 1999. Law Clerk to Hon. John Minor Wisdom, U.S. Court of Appeals, Fifth Circuit, 1993-1994. *Member:* State Bar of Texas; District of Columbia Bar; American Bar Association. ***PRACTICE AREAS:*** Appellate Practice; Commercial Litigation. ***Email:*** armstrongt@howrey.com

JOHN T. BATTAGLIA, born Newport, Rhode Island, November 16, 1969; admitted to bar, 1997, Massachusetts; 2000, District of Columbia. *Education:* Boston College (B.A., cum laude, 1992; J.D., cum laude, 1997). Phi Delta Phi; Omicron Delta Epsilon; Golden Key Honor Society. Law Clerk to Hon. William T. Prince, U.S. District Court, Eastern District of Virginia, 1998-1999. Trial Attorney, Department of Justice Honors Program, 1997-1998. *Member:* American Bar Association (Member, Litigation Section). ***PRACTICE AREAS:*** Commercial Litigation; Intellectual Property Litigation; Antitrust Litigation. ***Email:*** battagliaj@howrey.com

CANDACE N. BECK, born Geneva, Alabama, April 11, 1973; admitted to bar, 1999, Texas (Not admitted in District of Columbia). *Education:* Auburn University (B.A., magna cum laude, 1973); University of Alabama (M.A., 1996); American University (J.D., cum laude, 1999). Co-Editor-in-Chief, 1998-1999 American University Journal of Gender, Social Policy and the Law. Law Clerk to Hon. Paul D. Stickney, U.S. District Court, Northern District of Texas, 1999-2000. *Member:* American Bar Association (Member, International Law Section, Criminal Justice Section). ***PRACTICE AREAS:*** Commercial Litigation; Antitrust; White Collar Crime. ***Email:*** beckcandace@howrey.com

ALEXANDER B. BERGER, born Bayshore, New York, October 24, 1971; admitted to bar, 1997, Texas; 1998, District of Columbia. *Education:* University of Virginia (B.A., 1993); University of Texas (J.D., 1997). Articles Editor, Texas Journal of Business Law, 1996-1997. *Member:* American Bar Association. ***PRACTICE AREAS:*** Commercial Litigation; Antitrust; Trademark Litigation. ***Email:*** bergera@howrey.com

ERIK BERTIN, born Washington, D.C., March 25, 1971; admitted to bar, 1997, California and District of Columbia. *Education:* The Johns Hopkins University (B.A., with honors, 1993); University of Pennsylvania (J.D., 1996). Associate Editor, 1994-1995 and Articles Editor, 1995-1996, University of Pennsylvania Law Review. ***PRACTICE AREAS:*** Commercial Litigation; Insurance Coverage; Trademark Litigation. ***Email:*** bertine@howrey.com

DIANE E. BIERI, born Johnstown, Pennsylvania, April 11, 1970; admitted to bar, 1995, Pennsylvania; 1997, District of Columbia. *Education:* University of Pittsburgh (B.A., summa cum laude, 1992); Georgetown University (J.D., cum laude, 1995). Primary Editor, Criminal Procedure Project, Georgetown Law Journal. *Member:* American Bar Association. ***PRACTICE AREAS:*** Antitrust; Commercial Litigation. ***Email:*** bierid@howrey.com

JOSHUA BIRENBAUM, born San Jose, California, June 9, 1974; admitted to bar, 2000, Virginia (Not admitted in District of Columbia). *Education:* Bard College (B.A., 1996); University of Virginia (J.D., 2000).

JAMES B. BOLES, born Toledo, Ohio, September 10, 1969; admitted to bar, 2000, Maryland (Not admitted in District of Columbia). *Education:* University of Chicago (B.A., 1991); Georgetown University (J.D., 2000). *Member:* Energy and American Bar Associations. ***PRACTICE AREAS:*** Commercial Litigation; Environmental Law. ***Email:*** bolesj@howrey.com

DEANA L. CAIRO, born New York, New York, March 17, 1973; admitted to bar, 1999, Maryland; 2000, District of Columbia. *Education:* University of Maryland (B.S., in Biology, with honors, 1995); George Washington University (J.D., with honors, 1999). Phi Beta Kappa. Member, Moot Court Board, 1997-1999. Articles Editor, The George Washington Journal of International Law and Economics. Finalist, Van Vleck Constitutional Law Moot Court Competition, 1999. ***PRACTICE AREAS:*** Antitrust; Litigation. ***Email:*** cairod@howrey.com

DYLAN M. CARSON, born Montague, Massachusetts, October 28, 1972; admitted to bar, 1997, Massachusetts; 1999, New York and U.S. District Court, District of Massachusetts; 2000, District of Columbia. Lead Articles Editor and Staff Member, Suffolk University Law Review. Law Clerk to the Honorable Frank Freedman, U.S. District Court, District of Massachusetts. Author: "The Browning of Sports Law: Defining the Non-Statutory Exemption to Antitrust Scrutiny in Professional Sports," 30 Suffolk Univ. L. Rev. 1143 (1997). *Member:* American Bar Association. ***LANGUAGES:*** French. ***PRACTICE AREAS:*** Antitrust; Commercial Litigation. ***Email:*** carsond@howrey.com

ELIZABETH J. CHANDLER, born Buffalo, New York, April 20, 1965; admitted to bar, 1994, California; 1996, District of Columbia. *Education:* Georgetown University (B.S.B.A., 1983); George Mason University School of Law (J.D., 1994). Member, Moot Court Board. President, Business Law Society. Production Editor, George Mason Independent Law Review. ***PRACTICE AREAS:*** Antitrust; Commercial Litigation. ***Email:*** chandlere@howrey.com

JENNY W. CHEN, born Taipei, Taiwan, Republic of China, December 1, 1973; admitted to bar, 1999, California; 2000, U.S. District Court, Northern and Central District of California; registered to practice before U.S. Patent and Trademark Office (Not admitted in District of Columbia). *Education:* Northwestern University (B.S.E.E., 1996); Case Western Reserve University (J.D., 1999). Recipient, CALI's Award in International Business Transactions. *Member:* American Bar Association (Member, Sections on: Asian-Pacific; Intellectual Property; Young Property); American Intellectual Property Law Association. ***LANGUAGES:*** Mandarin, Taiwanese and Japanese. ***PRACTICE AREAS:*** Intellectual Property; International Trade; Patent Law. ***Email:*** chenj@howrey.com

VINA CHIN, born Phnom Penh, Cambodia, March 14, 1970; admitted to bar, 1997, California; U.S. District Court, Central District of California (Not admitted in District of Columbia). *Education:* University of California, Berkeley (B.A.,in history and french, with high distinction, 1992); Boalt Hall School of Law, University of California (J.D., 1996). Phi Beta Kappa. *Member:* American Bar Association. ***LANGUAGES:*** French. ***PRACTICE AREAS:*** Commercial Litigation; Insurance Coverage Litigation.

ALEXANDER R. COLLINS, born Washington, D.C., April 6, 1972; admitted to bar, 2000, Massachusetts (Not admitted in District of Columbia). *Education:* Brown University (B.A., 1995); Boston College (J.D., 2000). ***PRACTICE AREAS:*** Antitrust.

STEPHEN R. COOK, born California, 1971; admitted to bar, 1999, California; 2000, District of Columbia. *Education:* Brigham Young University (B.A., 1995); American University (J.D., cum laude, 1999). Managing Editor, American University Law Review. Author: "Management Reform Under the DC Financial Responsibility and Management Assistance Act," American University Law Review, 1998. *Member:* American Bar Association. ***LANGUAGES:*** Arabic. ***PRACTICE AREAS:*** Commercial Litigation; Antitrust. ***Email:*** cookstephen@howrey.com

MICHELLE COTTER, born Mount Kisco, New York, December 12, 1975; (admission pending). *Education:* Fordham University (B.A., American Studies, 1998); George Washington University (J.D., cum laude, 2001). Former Law Clerk, Government Contracts & Compliance Group, Morgan Lewis & Bockius. ***PRACTICE AREAS:*** Litigation. ***Email:*** cotterm@howrey.com

ROBERT H. COX, born Alexandria, Virginia, February 17, 1965; admitted to bar, 1991, Virginia; 1992, District of Columbia. *Education:* Duke University (A.B., 1987); University of Virginia (M.B.A., 1991; J.D., 1991). Pi Sigma Alpha. *Member:* District of Columbia Bar; Virginia State Bar; American Bar Association (Member, Litigation Section, 1999—; Antitrust Section). ***PRACTICE AREAS:*** Commercial Litigation; Antitrust. ***Email:*** coxr@howrey.com

PAUL C. CUOMO, born Syosset, New York, August 3, 1970; admitted to bar, 1995, Maryland; 1998, District of Columbia. *Education:* Villanova University (B.A., 1992); American University (J.D., cum laude, 1995). *Member:* Maryland State and American Bar Associations. ***PRACTICE AREAS:*** Antitrust. ***Email:*** cuomop@howrey.com

JEFFERY S. DAVIDSON, born Havre de Grace, Maryland, May 19, 1967; admitted to bar, 1998, Pennsylvania; 1999, U.S. District Court, Eastern District of Pennsylvania; 2000, District of Columbia. *Education:* York College of Pennsylvania (B.S., 1993); Temple University (J.D., cum laude, 1997). Executive Editor, Temple Political, Civil Rights Law Review. Law Clerk to the Hon. Louis C. Bechtle, U.S. District Court, Eastern District of Pennsylvania. *Member:* The District of Columbia; American Bar Association. ***PRACTICE AREAS:*** Antitrust and Trade Regulation; Commercial Litigation; Copyright Litigation. ***Email:*** davidsonjeff@howrey.com

SARAH E. DAVIS, born Atlanta, Georgia, August 11, 1971; admitted to bar, 1997, Florida; 1998, District of Columbia. *Education:* Dartmouth College (A.B., 1993); University of Miami (J.D., cum laude, 1997). Phi Delta Phi. Member, 1995-1997 and Articles and Comments Editor, 1996-1997, University of Miami Inter-American Law Review. *Member:* American Bar Association. ***PRACTICE AREAS:*** Commercial Litigation. ***Email:*** davissarah@howrey.com

LARA A. DEGENHART, born Ashtabula, Ohio, April 21, 1967; admitted to bar, 1992, South Carolina; 1995, District of Columbia. *Education:* Université de Dijon (Diplome d'Etudes Françaises, 1988); Southwestern University

(This Listing Continued)

HOWREY SIMON ARNOLD & WHITE, LLP, Washington—Continued

(B.S.S.S., cum laude, 1989); University of South Carolina (J.D., 1992). Order of the Wig and Robe; Phi Delta Phi; Cardinal Key. Member, South Carolina Law Review. *Member:* South Carolina Bar; District of Columbia Bar; American Bar Association. ***LANGUAGES:*** French. ***PRACTICE AREAS:*** Commercial Litigation; Insurance Coverage. ***Email:*** degenhartl@howrey.com

CHRISTOPHER J. DELLICARPINI, born Rockville Centre, New York, May 22, 1971; admitted to bar, 1997, New York; 1999, District of Columbia and U.S. Court of Appeals, Federal Circuit; 2000, U.S. District Court, District of Columbia. *Education:* University of Notre Dame (B.A., magna cum laude, 1993); Columbia University (J.D., 1996). Senior Notes Editor, Columbia Business Law Review. *Member:* The District of Columbia Bar; New York State and American Bar Associations. ***PRACTICE AREAS:*** Litigation; Antitrust.

LATIF DOMAN, born Philadelphia, Pennsylvania, July 7, 1970; admitted to bar, 1998, Pennsylvania (Not admitted in District of Columbia). *Education:* Morehouse College (B.A., 1992); University of Pennsylvania (J.D., 1995). Member, University of Pennsylvania Law Review. Law Clerk to Chief Judge John Garrett Penn, U.S. District Court, District of Columbia. ***PRACTICE AREAS:*** Intellectual Property Litigation. ***Email:*** domanl@howrey.com

KENNETH W. DONNELLY, born Frankfurt, Germany, October 5, 1968; admitted to bar, 1993, Florida; 1994, U.S. Court of Appeals, Eleventh Circuit, U.S. District Court, Northern and Middle Districts of Florida; 1996, U.S. District Court, Southern District of Florida; 1999, District of Columbia. *Education:* University of Miami (B.S., cum laude, 1990); Florida State University (J.D., with high honors, 1993). Order of the Coif; Phi Delta Phi. Executive Editor, 1992-1993, Associate Editor, 1991-1992, Journal of Land Use and Environmental Law and Associate Editor, Florida Style Manual, 1991, Florida State University Law Review. *Member:* The Florida Bar; American Bar Association. ***PRACTICE AREAS:*** Antitrust; Complex Commercial Litigation. ***Email:*** donnellyk@howrey.com

DONNA DRAKE, born California, May 29, 1965; admitted to bar, 1993, California; 1999, District of Columbia. *Education:* California State University at Long Beach (B.S., with honors, 1989); Loyola Law School, Los Angeles (J.D., 1993). Phi Beta Kappa. *Member:* The District of Columbia Bar. ***PRACTICE AREAS:*** Commercial Litigation; Insurance Coverage. ***Email:*** draked@howrey.com

DAWN A. ELLISON, born Skokie Valley, Illinois, March 21, 1971; admitted to bar, 1998, North Carolina (Not admitted in District of Columbia). *Education:* Pennsylvania State University (B.A., with highest distinction, 1993); University of North Carolina at Chapel Hill (J.D., 1998); Georgetown University Law Center. Phi Beta Kappa; Phi Kappa Phi; Golden Key; Order of the Coif. Member, Mortar Board. Staff Member, University of North Carolina Law Review. Author: Comment, "Sexual Harassment in Education: A Review of Standards for Institutional Liability Under Title IX," Vol 75, Issue 6, University of North Carolina Law Review. ***PRACTICE AREAS:*** Commercial Law; Insurance Coverage. ***Email:*** ellisond@howrey.com

EDWARD L. FERGUSON, JR., born Holyoke, Massachusetts, February 24, 1960; admitted to bar, 1992, Pennsylvania; 1995, District of Columbia. *Education:* St. Lawrence University (B.S., Geology, 1983); Columbus School of Law, Catholic University of America (J.D., 1992). Former Aide to Congressman Silvio Conte, Republican, Massachusetts. *Member:* District of Columbia Bar (Member, Environmental, Energy and Natural Resources Section); American Bar Association; Environmental Law Institute. ***PRACTICE AREAS:*** Environmental Law; Regulatory; Litigation; Legislative Practice. ***Email:*** fergusone@howrey.com

TIMOTHY T. FINLEY, born Seoul, South Korea, July 27, 1970; admitted to bar, 1995, Wisconsin and U.S. Court of Appeals, Seventh Circuit; 1997, Illinois; 2001, District of Columbia. *Education:* University of Arizona (B.A., cum laude, 1992); Northwestern University School of Law (J.D., 1995). Associate Articles Editor, Journal of Criminal Law & Criminology. Author: "Retroactivity of Postconviction Rulings in Federal Habeas Corpus," 84 Journal of Criminal Law & Criminology 975, 1994. Law Clerk to Honorable Myran L. Gordon, Senior District Judge, U.S. District Court, Eastern District of Wisconsin.

MERYL S. FISHMAN, born New York, N.Y., December 13, 1939; admitted to bar, 1985, New York; 1998, District of Columbia. *Education:* Pace University (B.P.S., with distinction, 1980); New York Law School (J.D., cum laude, 1984). *Member:* New York State Bar Association; District of Columbia Bar. ***Email:*** fishmanm@howrey.com

AMY R. FITZPATRICK, born Washington, D.C., February 6, 1970; admitted to bar, 1996, Virginia; 1998, District of Columbia. *Education:* Brown University (B.A., 1992); Marshall-Whythe School of Law, College of William & Mary (J.D., 1996). Student Notes Mentor, William & Mary Law Review. Law Clerk to the Honorable Thomas F. Hogan, U.S. District Court for the District of Columbia; 1996-1997. *Member:* District of Columbia Bar; Virginia and American Bar Associations. ***PRACTICE AREAS:*** Commercial Litigation; Patent Litigation; Antitrust Litigation. ***Email:*** fitzpatricka@howrey.com

COLIN FOLEY, born New York, N.Y., January 27, 1971; admitted to bar, 1999, Massachusetts, New York and District of Columbia. *Education:* University of Pennsylvania (B.A., 1993); Boston College (J.D., 1998). *Member:* The District of Columbia Bar. ***PRACTICE AREAS:*** Trademarks; Copyrights; Commercial Litigation. ***Email:*** foleyc@howrey.com

JAMES J. FOURNIER, born Santa Rosa, California, March 9, 1970; admitted to bar, 1997, New York; 1998, New Jersey; 1999, District of Columbia. *Education:* University of California, Berkeley (B.A., 1991); Fordham University Law School (J.D., 1996). Co-Author: "Fighting Insurance Company Fraud With RICO and the McCarran-Ferguson Act," Am. J. Trial Advoc., Summer 1998; "Renewal Policies Cannot Reduce Insurance Coverage Without Proper Notice To The Policyholder," Envtl. Claims J., Summer 1998; "The Ethics of Policyholders' Defense Counsel: Who Is The Client, Who Is The Boss?" Coverage, July/August 1998; "Why Courts Enforce Insurance Policyholders' Objectively Reasonable Expectations of Insurance Coverage," Conn. Ins. L.J., Summer 1998; "The Reasonable Expectations Doctrine: Understanding The Law and The Lore Behind Upholding The Reasonable Expectations of Insurance Policyholders," Risk Mgmt. and Ins. Rev., Winter 1998; "When Insurance Companies Buy Legal Decisions—and Then Lie to Courts and Policyholders About It," The Advocate, September/October 1997. ***PRACTICE AREAS:*** Insurance Coverage; Commercial Litigation. ***Email:*** fournierj@howrey.com

SARAH H. GARB, born Fargo, North Dakota, May 15, 1970; admitted to bar, 1996, Minnesota; 1997, U.S. District Court, District of Minnesota 1999, District of Columbia. *Education:* Oberlin College; University of Wisconsin (B.A., magna cum laude, 1993); University of Minnesota (J.D., cum laude, 1996). Staff Member, 1994-1995, Managing Editor, 1995-1996, Law and Inequality: A Journal of Theory and Practice. Law Clerk to Judge Kyle, U.S. District Court, District of Minnesota, 1996-1997. Author, "Sex For Money is Sex For Money: The Illegality of Pornographic Film is Prostitution," 13.1 Law and Inequality: A Journal of Theory and Practice. Member, Board of Visitors, University of Minnesota Law School, 1999—. *Member:* American (Member, Antitrust Section) and Federal Bar Associations; Minnesota Women Lawyers. ***PRACTICE AREAS:*** Antitrust; Litigation. ***Email:*** garbs@howrey.com

GRACE GRAHAM, born Alabaster, Alabama, April 23, 1973; admitted to bar, 2000, Alabama (Not admitted in District of Columbia). *Education:* Birmingham-Southern College (B.A., summa cum laude, 1995); Boston College (J.D., magna cum laude, 2000). Phi Beta Kappa. ***PRACTICE AREAS:*** Commercial Litigation. ***Email:*** grahamg@howrey.com

GURBIR SINGH GREWAL, born Jersey City, New Jersey, June 23, 1973; admitted to bar, 1999, New Jersey; 2000, New York (Not admitted in District of Columbia). *Education:* Bates College; Georgetown University (B.S.F.S., 1995); College of William & Mary (J.D., 1999). Phi Delta Phi. ***LANGUAGES:*** Punjab, Hindi and Urdu. ***PRACTICE AREAS:*** Commercial Litigation; Antitrust and Trade Regulation. ***Email:*** grewalg@howrey.com

JACQUELINE I. GRISE, born Providence, Rhode Island, August 5, 1970; admitted to bar, 1995, Rhode Island; 1996, Maryland; 1998, District of Columbia. *Education:* Bryant College (B.S., cum laude, 1992); New England School of Law (J.D., 1995). Recipient, American Jurisprudence Award, Business Organizations. ***PRACTICE AREAS:*** Antitrust; Mergers and Acquisitions; Commercial Litigation. ***Email:*** grisej@howrey.com

MELISSA GUNTHNER, born Rockhill, South Carolina, November 9, 1975; (admission pending). *Education:* Duke University (B.A., 1997); George Washington University (J.D., with honors, 2000). ***PRACTICE AREAS:*** Antitrust.

DANIELLE D. HALLCOM, born Los Angeles, California; admitted to bar, 1999, New York; 2000, District of Columbia. *Education:* Columbia College (B.A., 1993); Columbia Law School (J.D., 1998). Law Clerk to the Honorable Eugene R. Sullivan, U.S. Court of Appeals for the Armed Forces, 1998-1999. ***LANGUAGES:*** Spanish. ***PRACTICE AREAS:*** Commercial Litigation; Environmental; Insurance Coverage. ***Email:*** hallcomd@howrey.com

GENE HEALY, born Rahway, New Jersey, November 16, 1970; admitted to bar, 1999, Virginia; 2000, District of Columbia. *Education:* Georgetown University (B.A., cum laude, 1993); University of Chicago (J.D., 1999). ***PRACTICE AREAS:*** Commercial Litigation. ***Email:*** healyg@howrey.com

KENNETH N. HICKOX, JR., born Atlanta, Georgia, August 18, 1960; admitted to bar, 1995, West Virginia; 1998, District of Columbia; U.S. District Court, Northern and Southern Districts of West Virginia and District of Columbia and U.S. Court of Appeals, Fourth and Eleventh Circuits. *Education:* Georgetown University (B.S.F.S., cum laude, 1982), Phi Alpha Theta; College of William & Mary (J.D., 1995). Phi Delta Phi. *Member:* American Bar Associations; The Association of Trial Lawyers of America. [With U.S. Army Reserve, 1984—]. ***LANGUAGES:*** Spanish. ***PRACTICE AREAS:*** Commercial Litigation; Insurance Coverage; Employment Discrimination; Civil Rights. ***Email:*** hickoxk@howrey.com

(This Listing Continued)

(This Listing Continued)

JASON FOSTER HOFFMAN, born Silver Spring, Maryland; admitted to bar, 1997, Maryland; 2000, District of Columbia. *Education:* Brandeis University (B.A., magna cum laude, 1994); University of Pennsylvania (J.D., cum laude, 1997). Phi Beta Kappa. Managing Editor, Comparative Labor Law Journal, 1996-1997. Law Clerk to the Honorable James M. Rosenbaum, U.S. District Court, District of Minnesota, 1997-1998. ***PRACTICE AREAS:*** Intellectual Property; Commercial Litigation. ***Email:*** hoffmanjason@howrey.com

BRIAN A. HOWIE, born Orange, New Jersey, May 12, 1971; admitted to bar, 1996, Virginia; 1997, U.S. Court of Appeals, Fifth Circuit; 1998, District of Columbia. *Education:* Middlebury College (B.A., magna cum laude, 1993); Washington & Lee University (J.D., summa cum laude, 1996). Phi Beta Kappa; Order of the Coif. Senior Articles Editor, Washington & Lee Law Review. Law Clerk to the Honorable Rhesa H. Barksdale, U.S. Court of Appeals for the Fifth Circuit, 1996-1997. Author: "A Remedy Without A Wrong: J.E.B. and The Extension of Batson to Sex-Based Peremptory Challenges," 52 Washington & Lee Law Review 1725, 1996. ***PRACTICE AREAS:*** Antitrust; Commercial Litigation. ***Email:*** howieb@howrey.com

ROBERT P. JACOBS, born New York, N.Y., March 3, 1963; admitted to bar, 1988, Florida; 1989, District of Columbia. *Education:* University of Florida (B.S., with high honors, 1985); Georgetown University Law Center (J.D., 1988). Member, Executive Board, Law and Policy in International Business, 1987-1988. *Member:* The Florida Bar (Member, International Law Section); District of Columbia Bar; American Bar Association. ***PRACTICE AREAS:*** Insurance Coverage Litigation; Commercial Litigation. ***Email:*** jacobsr@howrey.com

JAMES K. KALEIGH, born Syracuse, NY, July 28, 1972; admitted to bar, 2000, New York and District of Columbia. *Education:* Colby College (B.A., 1994); American University (J.D., cum laude, 1999). Developments Editor, ABA Administrative Law Review. *Member:* New York State and American Bar Association. ***PRACTICE AREAS:*** Antitrust. ***Email:*** kaleighj@howrey.com

PAMELA S. KANE, born Englewood, New Jersey, January 20, 1968; admitted to bar, 1994, Texas; 1996, District of Columbia. *Education:* Connecticut College (B.A., 1989); Tulane University of Louisiana (J.D., cum laude, 1994). Recipient: American Jurisprudence Awards: Professional Responsibility, Contract Law and Community Property; Robert G. Pollack Award; David L. Herman Award. Notes and Comments Editor, Tulane Law Review. Author: "Why Have You Singled Me Out? The Use of Prosecutorial Discretion for Selective Prosecution," 67 Tul. L. Rev. 2293, 1993. *Member:* American Bar Association. ***PRACTICE AREAS:*** Antitrust; Commercial Litigation; Copyrights; Trademarks. ***Email:*** kanep@howrey.com

MELISSA B. KIMMEL, born Queens, New York, August 18, 1971; admitted to bar, 1998, New York; 1999, District of Columbia. *Education:* University of Vermont (B.A., 1993); George Washington University (J.D., 1997). Member, Moot Court. *Member:* The District of Columbia Bar. ***PRACTICE AREAS:*** Antitrust; Commercial Litigation. ***Email:*** kimmelm@howrey.com

DONNA D. KING, born Fairfield, Alabama, April 9, 1968; admitted to bar, 1999, Georgia; 2000, District of Columbia; registered to practice before U.S. Patent and Trademark Office. *Education:* Vanderbilt University (B.E., 1990; J.D., 1998); George Washington University (LL.M., Patent and Intellectual Property Law, 1999). Member, Vanderbilt Journal of Transnational Law, 1997-1999. *Member:* State Bar of Georgia; District of Columbia Bar (Member, Intellectual Property Section); American Intellectual Property Law Association; Society of Women Engineers.

STACEY H. KING, born Philadelphia, Pennsylvania, October 10, 1971; admitted to bar, 2001, District of Columbia. *Education:* Hampshire College (B.A., 1993); American University (J.D., 2000). Editor-in-Chief, Administrative Law Review. Recipient, Brinks, Hofer, Gilson and Lione Award of Excellence in Intellectual Property. Author, "The 'Law That It Deems Applicable': ICANN, Dispute Resolution and the Problem of Cybersquatting," 22 Hastings Comm. & Ent. L.J. 453 (2000); "Are We Ready to Answer the Question?: *Baker v. Selden,* the Post-*Feist* Era, and Database Protections," 41 IDEA 65 (2001). *Member:* The District of Columbia Bar; American Bar Association; Women's Bar Association of the District of Columbia; International Trademark Association; Copyright Society of the USA.

MARK ANDREW KLAPOW, born Manhasset, New York, January 31, 1974; admitted to bar, 1999, Connecticut; 2000, New York (Not admitted in District of Columbia). *Education:* Washington University (B.A., 1996); Syracuse University College of Law (J.D., cum laude, 1999). Lead Articles Editor, Syracuse Law Review. ***PRACTICE AREAS:*** Commercial; Antitrust. ***Email:*** klapowm@howrey.com

ERIK T. KOONS, born Sayre, Pennsylvania, June 18, 1973; admitted to bar, 1998, New Jersey and U.S. District Court, District of New Jersey; 1999, New York and U.S. District Court, Northern District of New York; 2000, District of Columbia. *Education:* Rutgers University (B.A., cum laude, 1995); Villanova University (J.D., 1998). Production Editor, Villanova University School of Law Environmental Law Journal. Judicial Clerk to the Honorable Norman A. Mordue, U.S. District Court, Northern District of New York, 1999-2000. Author, "Without a Clue and Still Without a Master Plan: Municipalities Left Uncertain How to Manage Waste Disposal Crisis in Wake of Third Circuit Decision in *Harvey & Harvey, Inc. v. County of Chester*, 9 Vill, Envtl, L.J. (1997). Co-Chair, Law, Youth & Citizenship Committee, Onondaga County Bar Association, 1999-2000. ***PRACTICE AREAS:*** Antitrust; Commercial Litigation. ***Email:*** koonse@howrey.com

(This Listing Continued)

SUZANNAH LAND, born Brantford, Ontario, Canada; (admission pending). *Education:* University of Pittsburgh (B.A., 1997); George Washington University (J.D., 2000). Member, International Law Review. ***PRACTICE AREAS:*** Antitrust.

AARON M. LEVINE, born New Castle, Pennsylvania, June 29, 1973; admitted to bar, 1999, New York (Not admitted in District of Columbia). *Education:* Cornell University (B.S., in Engineer, with distinction, 1995); New York University (J.D., 1998). *Member:* New York Intellectual Property Law Association. ***PRACTICE AREAS:*** Patent Litigation. ***Email:*** levinea@howrey.com

MARGARET D. MACDONALD, born Philadelphia, Pennsylvania, June 21, 1969; admitted to bar, 1995, Maryland; 1996, District of Columbia. *Education:* Trinity College (B.A., 1991); Washington College of Law, American University (M.A., 1994; J.D., 1994). Phi Beta Kappa; Order of the Barristers. ***PRACTICE AREAS:*** Intellectual Property. ***Email:*** macdonaldm@howrey.com

JAMES A. MAYSONETT, born Hackensack, New Jersey, April 15, 1972; admitted to bar, 1998, New York; 1999, District of Columbia. *Education:* Princeton University (A.B., cum laude, 1994); New York University School of Law (J.D., magna cum laude, 1997). Order of the Coif. *Member:* New York State and American Bar Associations. ***PRACTICE AREAS:*** Environmental. ***Email:*** maysonettj@howrey.com

ERIC J. McCARTHY, born Bellmore, New York, July 15, 1971; admitted to bar, 1996, Maryland and New Jersey; 1997, Colorado and District of Columbia; U.S. District Court for the District of Columbia; U.S. District Court, District of New Jersey; U.S. Court of Appeals for the District of Columbia Circuit. *Education:* Dartmouth College (A.B., cum laude, 1993); Lady Margaret Hall, Oxford, England; University of Pennsylvania (J.D., 1996). Comments Editor, University of Pennsylvania Journal of International Economics Law, 1995-1996. Chairman, Moot Court Board, 1995-1996. Author: "Networking in Cyberspace: Electronic Defamation and the Potential for International Forum Shopping," 16 Univ. of Penn. J. Intl. Business L. 527 (1995). *Member:* District of Columbia Bar; American Bar Association. ***PRACTICE AREAS:*** Antitrust; Commercial Litigation; Products Liability. ***Email:*** mccarthye@howrey.com

JENNIFER K. McDANNELL, born December 10, 1971; admitted to bar, 1997, Illinois; 1998, District of Columbia. *Education:* Tulane University (B.S., summa cum laude, 1994); Duke University (J.D., cum laude, 1997). Phi Beta Kappa. Siegel Fellow. Moot Court Executive Board. Editor-in-Chief, Alaska Law Review. Author: "Assignability of Legal Malpractice Claims," 14 Alaska L. Rev. 141, June 1997. ***PRACTICE AREAS:*** Commercial Litigation; Patent Litigation; Products Liability. ***Email:*** mcdannellj@howrey.com

LAURA C. MILLER, born Heidelberg, Germany, March 27, 1972; admitted to bar, 2000, Utah (Not admitted in District of Columbia). *Education:* University of Virginia (B.A., 1994); Louisiana State University (M.S., 1995); George Mason University (J.D., 1999). ***PRACTICE AREAS:*** Intellectual Property. ***Email:*** millerlaura@howrey.com

POLLY A. MYERS, born Wright-Patterson A.F.B., Ohio, February 27, 1962; admitted to bar, 1988, Virginia; 1989, District of Columbia. *Education:* Ohio State University (B.A., 1984); Georgetown University Law Center (J.D., 1988). Clerk, Hon. Spottswood W. Robinson III, U.S. Court of Appeals for the District of Columbia Circuit, 1988-1989. Member, Society of Professionals in Dispute Resolution, 1997—. ***PRACTICE AREAS:*** Litigation; Antitrust. ***Email:*** myersp@howrey.com

MATTHEW J. MOORE, born Syracuse, New York, November 9, 1968; admitted to bar, 1996, New York; 1997, District of Columbia and U.S. Court of Appeals for the Federal Circuit; 2000, U.S. Supreme Court; registered to practice before U.S. Patent and Trademark Office. *Education:* Syracuse University (B.S., Electrical Engineering, 1991; J.D., 1995); University of Pennsylvania (M.S., Systems Engineering, 1993); George Washington, University (LL.M., in Intellectual Property, 2000). ***PRACTICE AREAS:*** Patent Litigation; Patent Prosecution; Copyright; Trademark; Licensing. ***Email:*** moorem@howrey.com

DANIELLE R. ODDO, born Hauppauge, New York, November 21, 1973; admitted to bar, 1999, New York and District of Columbia. *Education:* Boston College (B.A., summa cum laude, 1995; J.D., 1998). Phi Beta Kappa. Author: Note, "Removing Confidentiality Protections and the 'Get Tough' Rhetoric: What has Gone Wrong with the Juvenile Justice System?" Boston College Third World Law Journal, vol. 28, 1998. *Member:* Bar Association of the District of Columbia; New York State and American Bar Associations. ***PRACTICE AREAS:*** Commercial Litigation; Antitrust Litigation. ***Email:*** oddod@howrey.com

DOUGLAS S. ONLEY, born Durham, North Carolina, October 9, 1964; admitted to bar, 1996, Virginia; 1998, District of Columbia. *Education:* University of Virginia (B.A., 1986); College of William & Mary (J.D., 1996). Editor, William & Mary Law Review. Author: "Treading on Sacred Ground:

(This Listing Continued)

HOWREY SIMON ARNOLD & WHITE, LLP, Washington—Continued

Congress's Power to Subject White House Advisers to Senate Confirmation," William & Mary Law Review, Vol. 37, Spring 1996. Clerk to the Hon. Bernice B. Donald, U.S. District Court, Western District of Tennessee, 1996-1997. Legal Affairs Reporter, Education Daily, 1990-1993. *Member:* Virginia and American Bar Associations. ***PRACTICE AREAS:*** Antitrust Litigation; Commercial Litigation. ***Email:*** onleyd@howrey.com

HAE-CHAN PARK, born Jinju, Korea, June 28, 1962; admitted to bar, 1985, Korea; 1992, New York (Not admitted in District of Columbia). *Education:* Seoul National University (LL.B., 1984); University of Pennsylvania Law School (LL.M., 1991); George Washington University (M.S., in computer science, 19 94). *Member:* New York State and American (Member, Sections on: Intellectual Property; International Law) Bar Associations; Korean Bar Association; American Intellectual Property Lawyer's Association. ***LANGUAGES:*** Korean. ***PRACTICE AREAS:*** Intellectual Property Law; International Trade Law. ***Email:*** parkh@howrey.com

EDWARD I. RICHARDS, born Wilmington, Delaware, January 24, 1972; admitted to bar, 2000, District of Columbia. *Education:* Bowdoin College (B.A., 1994); University of Maryland (J.D., 1999). Notes and Comments Editor, Journal of Healthcare Law & Policy. ***PRACTICE AREAS:*** Antitrust. ***Email:*** richardse@howrey.com

JASON C. RAOFIELD, born Cincinnati, Ohio, May 22, 1971; admitted to bar, 1998, Massachusetts; 1999, District of Columbia and U.S. District Court, District of Massachusetts. *Education:* Syracuse University (B.A., summa cum laude, 1995); Boston College (J.D., cum laude, 1998). Phi Beta Kappa. Member, J. Braxton Craven National Moot Court Championship Team, 1998. *Member:* American Bar Association. [Staff Sgt., U.S. Marine Corps Reserve, 1989-1995]. ***PRACTICE AREAS:*** Antitrust; Commercial Litigation. ***Email:*** raofieldj@howrey.com

BRIAN ROSENTHAL, born Ottawa, Ontario, Canada, July 16, 1978; admitted to bar, 2001, New York (Not admitted in District of Columbia). *Education:* University of Western Ontario (B.Sc., with honors, 1997); Cornell Law School (J.D., magna cum laude, 2000).

SCOTT D. RUSSELL, born San Francisco, California, August 2, 1971; admitted to bar, 1999, Virginia; 2001, District of Columbia. *Education:* College of William & Mary (B.A., Quantitative Economics and Government, 1994; M.P.P., Economics, 2000); George Mason University School of Law (J.D., cum laude, 1998). Recipient: Best Brief Honors, George Mason University School of Law. Thomas Jefferson Fellowship for Graduate Study. Law Clerk to: Office of General Counsel, U.S. Department of Education, 1995; Computers and Finance Section, Antitrust Division, U.S. Department of Justice, 1997. Attorney Advisor and Law Clerk to the Hon. Bruce C. Levine, Commodity Futures Trading Commission, 1999—. Summer Research Associate, Employee Benefit Research Institute, 1996. *Member:* Virginia State Bar; The District of Columbia Bar; American Bar Association (Member, Sections on: Antitrust, 1999—; Public Utilities and Telecommunications, 1999—). ***PRACTICE AREAS:*** Antitrust. ***Email:*** russells@howrey.com

CHRISTINA GUEROLA SARCHIO, born New York, New York, August 11, 1969; admitted to bar, 1995, New Jersey and U.S. District Court, District of New Jersey; 1996, New York; 1997, District of Columbia; 1999, U.S. District Court, District of Columbia. *Education:* Cornell University (B.A., 1991); George Washington University (J.D., 1995). Author: "The Degradable Ring Rule," The Environmental Lawyer, Vol. 1 Issue 1, Fall 1994. Adjunct Professor, George Washington University Law School, 1999-2001. Member: Board of Directors, District of Columbia Hispanic Bar Association. Member, New York District Attorney's Office, 1995-1998. *Member:* The District of Columbia Bar; American Bar Association; Hispanic Bar Association (Vice-President, 1999-2001). ***LANGUAGES:*** Spanish. ***REPORTED CASES:*** Tangires vs. The John Hopkins Hospital, 79 F. Supp. 2d 587 (D. MD. 2000). ***PRACTICE AREAS:*** Commercial Litigation; White Collar. ***Email:*** sarchiochristina@howrey.com

JON SCHIFFRIN, born Miami, Florida, June 2, 1971; admitted to bar, 1996, Florida; 1999, District of Columbia. *Education:* University of Florida (B.S., 1992); University of Miami (J.D., 1996). ***Email:*** schiffrinj@howrey.com

BRADLEY J. SCHLOZMAN, born Kansas City, Missouri, February 6, 1971; admitted to bar, 1996, Kansas; 1997, Missouri; 1999, District of Columbia. *Education:* University of Pennsylvania (B.A., magna cum laude, with distinction, 1993); George Washington University (J.D., with honors, 1996). Law Clerk to Chief U.S. District Judge G.T. Van Bebber, District of Kansas, 1996-1998; Law Clerk to U.S. Circuit Judge Mary Beck Briscoe, U.S. Court of Appeals, Tenth Circuit, 1998-1999. ***PRACTICE AREAS:*** Litigation; Appellate Litigation. ***Email:*** schlozmanb@howrey.com

GREGORY S. SEADOR, born Camp Hill, Pennsylvania, December 18, 1973; (admission pending). *Education:* Eastern Kentucky University (B.S., 1996); Syracuse University College of Law (J.D., summa cum laude, 2001). Author: Note, "A Search for the Truth or a Game of Strategy? The Circuit Split

(This Listing Continued)

Over the Prosecution's Obligation to Disclose Inadmissible Exculpatory Information to the Accused," 51 Syracuse Law Review 140, 2001. ***PRACTICE AREAS:*** International Litigation. ***Email:*** seadorg@howrey.com

BRIAN SHERWOOD SEAL, born Richmond, Virginia, January 23, 1969; admitted to bar, 2001, District of Columbia. *Education:* University of Virginia (B.A., Foreign Affairs, 1991); University of Alabama (J.D., 2000). Law Clerk to the Hon. Edward S. Smith, Senior Circuit Judge, U.S. Court of Appeals, Federal Circuit, 2000-2001. *Member:* The District of Columbia Bar; Federal Circuit and American Bar Associations. ***PRACTICE AREAS:*** Intellectual Property Litigation. ***Email:*** sealb@howrey.com

JASON D. SMITH, born Smithtown, New York, April 20, 1972; admitted to bar, 1998, New York; 1999, District of Columbia. *Education:* State University of New York at Binghamton (B.A., cum laude, 1994); George Washington University (J.D., with high honors, 1997). Order of the Coif. Member, Moot Court Board. Editor-in-Chief, The George Washington Journal of International Law and Economics. Law Clerk, The Honorable Robert E. Payne, U.S. District Judge, Eastern District of Virginia, 1997-1998. ***PRACTICE AREAS:*** Antitrust; Commercial Litigation. ***Email:*** smithjason@howrey.com

TIMOTHY MARTIN SMITH, born Morristown, New Jersey, July 21, 1971; admitted to bar, 1998, New York and New Jersey; practice limited to matters and proceedings before federal courts and agencies (Not admitted in District of Columbia). *Education:* University of Michigan (B.A., with high honors, 1992); London School of Economics (M.Sc., Econ, 1994); Tulane Law School (J.D., cum laude, 1997). Senior Articles Editor, 1996-1997 and Managing Editor, 1995-1996, Tulane Journal of International and Comparative Law. ***LANGUAGES:*** German and Spanish. ***PRACTICE AREAS:*** Antitrust.

JOHN F. STANTON, born Van Nuys, California, May 17, 1971; admitted to bar, 1997, Maryland; 1999, District of Columbia and U.S. Court of Appeals, Sixth Circuit. *Education:* Dartmouth College (B.A., 1993); Georgetown University Law Center (J.D., cum laude, 1997). Senior Notes and Comments Editor, Georgetown Immigration Law Journal. Author: Note, "The Immigration Laws From a Disability Perspective: Where We Were, Where We Are, Where We Should Be," 10 Geo. Immigr. L. J. 441, 1996. Law Clerk, Honorable Nathaniel R. Jones, U.S. Court of Appeals, Sixth Circuit, 1998-1999. ***LANGUAGES:*** American Sign Language. ***PRACTICE AREAS:*** Commercial Litigation; Appellate Advocacy; Insurance Coverage. ***Email:*** stantonj@howrey.com

COKE MORGAN STEWART, born Norfolk, Virginia, January 1, 1972; admitted to bar, 1997, Virginia; 1998, U.S. District Court, Eastern District of Virginia; 1999, District of Columbia. *Education:* Duke University (B.A., cum laude, 1994); University of Virginia (J.D., 1997). Executive Editor, Virginia Tax Review. Clerk, U.S. Court of Federal Claims. ***PRACTICE AREAS:*** Commercial Litigation. ***Email:*** stewartcoke@howrey.com

TERRY L. SULLIVAN, born Melbourne, Florida, October 14, 1961; admitted to bar, 1995, Virginia; 1997, District of Columbia. *Education:* University of Washington (B.A., 1983); George Washington University (J.D., 1995); Florida Institute of Technology (M.B.A., 1987). Member, George Washington Journal of International Law and Economics. Author: Note, "The Future of State Unitary Taxation of Foreign Owned U.S. Subsidiaries After Barclays Bank PLC v. Franchise Tax Board," August 1996. ***PRACTICE AREAS:*** Antitrust Litigation; Commercial Litigation. ***Email:*** sullivant@howrey.com

STEVEN A. SUSSWEIN, born New York, N.Y., July 11, 1969; admitted to bar, 1996, Michigan (Not admitted in District of Columbia). *Education:* University of Michigan (B.A., with distinction, 1991); George Washington University (J.D., with honors, 1996). *Member:* State Bar of Michigan; American Bar Association. ***PRACTICE AREAS:*** Commercial Litigation. ***Email:*** sussweins@howrey.com

ALAN B.T. SUTTON, born Houston, Texas, June 16, 1970; admitted to bar, 1996, Texas (Not admitted in District of Columbia). *Education:* University of Texas at Austin (B.S., cum laude, 1992; B.A., cum laude, 1992); University of Houston (J.D., cum laude, 1996). Order of the Barons. *Member:* Houston and American Bar Associations; State Bar of Texas; Texas and Houston Young Lawyers Associations. ***PRACTICE AREAS:*** Government Contracts; Export Regulation.

JENNIFER A. TUNICK, born New York, New York, August 25, 1971; admitted to bar, 1999, New York and District of Columbia. *Education:* Georgetown University (B.A., cum laude, 1993); American University (J.D., 1998). *Member:* New York State and American Bar Associations. ***PRACTICE AREAS:*** Antitrust. ***Email:*** tunickj@howrey.com

JENNIFER M. VASTA, born Bellingham, Washington, May 16, 1973; admitted to bar, 1998, California; 1999, District of Columbia. *Education:* University of California, Berkeley (B.A., 1994); George Washington University (J.D., with honors, 1998). *Member:* State Bar of California; The District of Columbia Bar; American Bar Association. ***PRACTICE AREAS:*** Antitrust.

MARGARET M. VIERBUCHEN, born Washington, D.C., December 27, 1967; admitted to bar, 1997, Maryland; 1998, District of Columbia and U.S. District Court, District of Maryland. *Education:* Michigan State University (B.A., with high honors, 1990); Georgetown University Law Center (J.D., ma-

(This Listing Continued)

gna cum laude, 1997). Order of the Coif. Staff, Georgetown Law Journal, 1994-1995. Editor, Criminal Procedure Project, Georgetown Law Journal, 1995-1996. ***PRACTICE AREAS:*** Commercial Litigation; Antitrust. ***Email:*** vierbuchennm@howrey.com

TARA M. VOLD, born New York, N.Y., October 10, 1971; admitted to bar, 1996, Illinois; 1998, District of Columbia and Virginia. *Education:* Dartmouth College (B.A., cum laude, 1993); Northwestern University (J.D., 1996). ***PRACTICE AREAS:*** Trademarks; Litigation. ***Email:*** voldt@howrey.com

JONATHAN MICHAEL WEINRIEB, born Silver Spring, Maryland, January 4, 1972; admitted to bar, 1999, Maryland; 2001, District of Columbia. *Education:* Washington University (B.A., 1994); George Washington University (J.D., with honors, 1999). Psi Chi; Order of Omega. *Member:* The District of Columbia Bar; American Bar Association; American Intellectual Property Law Association. ***PRACTICE AREAS:*** Insurance Coverage; Products Liability. ***Email:*** weinriebj@howrey.com

STEPHEN WEISSMAN, born New York, New York, January 14, 1969; admitted to bar, 1994, Maryland; 1995, U.S. District Court, District of Maryland; 1996, District of Columbia, Virginia, US. District Court, Eastern District of Virginia and U.S. District Court, District of Columbia; 1997, U.S. Court of Appeals, Fourth Circuit. *Education:* Tufts University (B.A., 1991); University of Pennsylvania (J.D., 1994). Member, Penn Law Society, 1994—. *Member:* Maryland State, Virginia and American (Member, Antitrust Section) Bar Associations. ***REPORTED CASES:*** FTC v. Cardinal Health, Inc. and McKesson Corp., 12 F. Supp. 2d 34 (D.D.C., 1998). ***PRACTICE AREAS:*** Antitrust; Litigation. ***Email:*** weissmas@howrey.com

EVAN JEFFREY WERBEL, born Norfolk, Virginia, March 16, 1965; admitted to bar, 1994, Georgia; 1995, U.S. Court of Appeals, Third Circuit; 1996, District of Columbia. *Education:* Tulane University of Louisiana (B.A., cum laude, 1987); Georgetown University (J.D., magna cum laude, 1994). Order of the Coif. ***PRACTICE AREAS:*** Antitrust; Commercial Litigation; White Collar Criminal Defense. ***Email:*** werbele@howrey.com

RAMSEY J. WILSON, born Lansing, Michigan, April 10, 1972; admitted to bar, 1998, Maryland; 1999, District of Columbia. *Education:* University of Michigan (B.B.A., with distinction, 1995; M.Acc., with distinction, 1995); Georgetown University (J.D., cum laude, 1998). Beta Gamma Sigma. Co-Author: with Smith, "How Best to Guide the Development of Electronic Currency Law," 46 Am.U.L. 1105, 1997. *Member:* The District of Columbia Bar; American Bar Association (Member, Sections on: Antitrust Law and Intellectual Property Law). ***PRACTICE AREAS:*** Antitrust; Competition.

MATTHEW M. WOLF, born Ithaca, New York, May 5, 1968; admitted to bar, 1994, Maryland, U.S. District Court, District of Maryland and U.S. Court of Appeals, Fourth Circuit; 1997, District of Columbia. *Education:* Yale University (B.A., cum laude, 1990); University of Virginia (J.D., 1994). Law Clerk to Senior District Judge Joseph H. Young, U.S. District Court, District of Maryland, 1994-1995. *Member:* Maryland State and American Bar Associations. ***PRACTICE AREAS:*** Corporate Litigation; Intellectual Property. ***Email:*** wolfm@howrey.com

JOHN H. ZACHARIA, born Beirut, Lebanon; admitted to bar, 1995, Florida; 1996, U.S. District Court, Middle District of Florida; 1997, District of Columbia and U.S. Court of Appeals, Eleventh Circuit. *Education:* University of Virginia (B.A., with distinction, 1992; J.D., 1995). Phi Beta Kappa. Managing Editor, Virginia Journal of International Law. Technical Editor, Virginia Journal of Social Policy and the Law. Co-Author: with Jerry Orten, "Allocation of Damages for Tort Liability in Common Interest Communities," 31 Real Prop. Prob. & Tr. J. 647, Winter 1997; with Mark D. Wegener and Allen B. Green, "The New Rules of Engagement: Looking at International Intellectual Property Arbitration," Supplement to *Corporate Legal Times,* December 2000. *Member:* The Florida Bar; District of Columbia Bar; American Bar Association. ***LANGUAGES:*** French and Arabic. ***PRACTICE AREAS:*** Complex Litigation; International Arbitration and Litigation; Insurance Coverage; Antitrust; Intellectual Property. ***Email:*** zachariaj@howrey.com

JENNIFER A. ZENKER, born Baltimore, Maryland, August 2, 1971; admitted to bar, 1999, Massachusetts; 2000, District of Columbia. *Education:* University of Madison (B.A., 1993); George Washington University (J.D., 1999). ***PRACTICE AREAS:*** Commercial Litigation; Antitrust Litigation. ***Email:*** zenkerj@howrey.com

STAFF ATTORNEY

PHILIP M. INGENERI, born 1973; admitted to bar, 1999, New York (Not admitted in District of Columbia). *Education:* Sarah Lawrence College (B.A., 1995); Boston University (J.D., 1998). ***PRACTICE AREAS:*** Antitrust; Intellectual Property; International Trade. ***Email:*** ingenerim@howrey.com

HUBER LAWRENCE & ABELL

1001 G STREET, N.W., TWELFTH FLOOR
WASHINGTON, D.C. 20001
Telephone: 202-737-3880

New York, N.Y. Office: 605 Third Avenue, 27th Floor. Telephone: 212-682-6200.

General Practice, Corporate, Securities, Litigation, Public Utility, Energy, Communications, Taxation, Corporate Finance and Environmental Law.

MEMBERS OF FIRM

BARBARA S. JOST, born Brooklyn, New York, November 19, 1951; admitted to bar, 1978, District of Columbia. *Education:* State University of New York at Buffalo (B.A., 1973); University of Virginia (M.A., 1974); Georgetown University Law Center (J.D., 1978). Phi Beta Kappa. Editor, Law and Policy in International Business, 1977-1978. Co-Author: "Who Will Regulate Utility-Owned Fiber-Optic Networks? The States or The FCC?" Public Utility Fortnightly, 1988. Author: "FERC's First-in-Time Rule: An Impediment to Hydropower Development," Energy Law Journal, 1984; "Leveling the Playing Field—Can Retail Reciprocity Work?" Natural Resources and Environment, 1997. *Member:* The District of Columbia Bar; Federal Energy and American Bar Associations; National Hydropower Association. ***PRACTICE AREAS:*** Energy Law; Public Utility Law; Natural Resources Law. ***Email:*** bjost@huberlaw.com

RICHARD M. LORENZO, born New York, N.Y., April 13, 1951; admitted to bar, 1975, Ohio and U.S. District Court Northern District of Ohio; 1979, New York; 1980, U.S. District Court, Southern and Eastern Districts of New York; 1993, U.S. Court of Federal Claims; U.S. Supreme Court; U.S. Court of Appeals, Second Circuit; U.S. Court of Appeals for the District of Columbia Circuit (Not admitted in District of Columbia). *Education:* State University of New York at Albany (B.S., 1972); Case Western Reserve University (J.D., 1975); Columbia University (LL.M., 1981). Editor, Case Western Reserve Journal of International Law, 1973-1975. Fellow, Center for Law and Economic Studies, Columbia University, 1980-1981. Clerk, Honorable Leo A. Jackson, Chief Judge, Court of Appeals of Ohio, 1975-1977. Author: Note, "The Judicial System of Japan," 6 C.W.R.U. Journal of International Law, 294 (1974); Chapter on Natural Gas Transportation, "Energy Law and Transactions" (1995) Matthew Bender; "FERC Fails To Resolve Aspects of Rolled-in Versus Incremental Debate," Natural Gas (August 1995). Associate in Law, Columbia University School of Law, 1979-1980. *Member:* New York State, Federal Energy and American Bar Associations. ***PRACTICE AREAS:*** Litigation; Antitrust Law; Energy Law; Public Utility Law; Securities. ***Email:*** rlorenzo@huberlaw.com

JONATHAN D. SCHNEIDER, born New York, N.Y., September 27, 1956; admitted to bar, 1982, New York, U.S. Court of Appeals for the District of Columbia Circuit and U.S. Court of Appeals, 1st, 3rd, 4th and 10th Circuits (Not admitted in District of Columbia). *Education:* Colgate University (B.A., with honors, 1978); Albany Law School of Union University (J.D., 1982). Omicron Delta Epsilon. Author: "The Discounted Rate Puzzle," The Natural Gas Journal, July 1999; "What Me Worry?, FERC Looks at a Wave of Pipeline Proposals," CCH Power and Telecom Reports, January 1998; "FERC Stumbles in Incremental/Rolled-in Policy Statement," The Natural Gas Journal, April 1995; "Regulatory Reform Critical Under Order No. 636," Natural Gas Journal, April 1993. Co-Author: Chapter on Natural Gas Transportation, "Energy Law and Transactions," Matthew Bender, 2000. *Member:* New York State and Federal Energy Bar Associations; The District of Columbia Bar. (Resident). ***PRACTICE AREAS:*** Administrative Law; Energy Law; Communications Law; Public Utility Law. ***Email:*** jschneider@huberlaw.com

ASSOCIATES

ADAM H. BARTSCH, born Flemington, New Jersey, October 20, 1964; admitted to bar, 1999, New York and Massachusetts (Not admitted in District of Columbia). *Education:* University of Massachusetts (B.A., 1989); Northwestern University (M.S., 1991); George Washington University (J.D., 1998). *Member:* Federal Energy Bar Association; New York County Lawyer's Association. (Resident). ***PRACTICE AREAS:*** Energy Law; Public Utility Law. ***Email:*** abartsch@huberlaw.com

JOHN R. MATSON, III, born Haverhill, Massachusetts, March 14, 1969; admitted to bar, 1994, Maryland; 1995, District of Columbia, U.S. District Court for the District of Columbia, U.S. District Court, District of Maryland, U.S. Court of Appeals for the District of Columbia Circuit and U.S. Court of Appeals, Fourth Circuit. *Education:* Dartmouth College (B.A., 1991); George Washington University (J.D., 1994). Adjunct Professor, George Washington University Law School, 1996-2000. *Member:* District of Columbia Bar; American Bar Association; Federal Energy Bar Association (Chair, Committee on: Young Lawyers, 1999-2000). (Resident. ***PRACTICE AREAS:*** Energy Law; Public Utility Law. ***Email:*** jmatson@huberlaw.com

(This Listing Continued)

HUBER LAWRENCE & ABELL, Washington—Continued

COUNSEL

HEIDI MARIE WERNTZ, born Madison, Wisconsin; admitted to bar, 1993, Virginia; 1995, District of Columbia. *Education:* Brown University (A.B., 1985); Yale University (M.A., 1989); Columbus School of Law of the Catholic University of America (J.D., 1992). *Member:* Virginia State Bar; The District of Columbia Bar; Federal Energy Bar Association. (Resident). ***LANGUAGES:*** Chinese, Japanese and French. ***PRACTICE AREAS:*** Energy Law; Public Utility Law. ***Email:*** hwerntz@huberlaw.com

(For Complete Data on all Personnel see Professional Biographies at New York, New York)

HUDDLES & JONES, P.C.

WASHINGTON, D.C.

(See Columbia, Maryland)

Government and Construction Contract Law. Practice before State and Federal Courts, Administrative Appeal Boards, Arbitration and Mediation Tribunals.

EDWIN E. HUDDLESON, III

316 F STREET, N.E.
WASHINGTON, D.C. 20002
Telephone: 202-543-2233
Fax: 202-543-2257
Email: huddlesone@aol.com
URL: http://www.lawyers.com/huddleson

General Civil Practice.

EDWIN E. HUDDLESON, III, born Washington, D.C., October 20, 1945; admitted to bar, 1970, California; 1977, District of Columbia; 1978, U.S. Supreme Court; 2001, Maryland. *Education:* Stanford University (B.S., 1967); University of Chicago Law School (J.D., 1970). Member, 1968-1970 and Comment Editor, 1969-1970, University of Chicago Law Review. Author: "Waiver of Miranda Rights," 36 University of Chicago L.Rev. 413; "Confidentiality for the Editorial Process," Washington Post, November 1978; "Old Wine in New Bottles: UCC Article 2A-Leases," in symposium, 39 Alabama L.Rev. 615; Treatise on Article 2A Leases of Goods, in UCC Transaction Guide, West 1988—; New Developments: Leasing, 1993 Commercial Law Annual 115; "Preserving Your Record for Appeal," ALI-ABA Practical Litigator, March, 1991; "Toward a New Consensus: Expanding Protections for Lenders in Environmental Law," 41 Federal Bar News & Journal 114, February 1994. Law Clerk to Judge Charles M. Merrill, U.S. Court of Appeals, Ninth Circuit, 1970-1971. Attorney, Civil Division, U.S. Department of Justice, 1971-1977. *Member:* The District of Columbia Bar (Co-chair, Steering Committee, Administrative Law & Agency Practice Section, 1996-1997; originator: Harold Leventhal talks (http://www.dcbar.org/sections/adm/leventhal.html); Chair, Court Rules & Legislation Committee, 2001—); State Bar of California; American Bar Association (Vice Chair, Subcommittee on Leasing of UCC Committee, 1998—); Fellow, American Bar Foundation; Master, Charles Fahy Inn of Court (1993-2000); American Law Institute. ***PRACTICE AREAS:*** Trial and Appellate Practice in State and Federal Courts; Administrative Law; Corporate and Business Law; Employment; Equipment Leasing; Government Contracts; Intellectual Property; Legislative and Government Relations; Public Utilities; Trade Associations.

HUDGINS LAW FIRM

WASHINGTON, D.C.

(See Alexandria)

General Civil Trial Practice, Insurance Defense, Insurance Law, Appellate Litigation.

LAW OFFICES OF
DARYL J. HUDSON III

Established in 1987

1042 31ST STREET, NW
WASHINGTON, D.C. 20007
Telephone: 202-342-1700
Fax: 202-342-7234
Email: dhudson@starpower.net
URL: http://www.lawyers.com/djhudsonlaw

Litigation, S.E.C. Enforcement, Corporate and Partnership Law, International Litigation, Corporate Transactions, Investments.

(This Listing Continued)

DARYL J. HUDSON, III, born Dallas, Texas, 1952; admitted to bar, 1979, District of Columbia. *Education:* University of Oklahoma (B.A., 1974); University of Texas (M.A., 1975); Georgetown University (J.D., 1979). Phi Beta Kappa; Phi Alpha Theta. Attorney and Senior Counsel, Securities and Exchange Commission, Division of Enforcement, 1982-1985. *Member:* The District of Columbia Bar. ***PRACTICE AREAS:*** Transactions; Litigation; Securities.

ASSOCIATE

THOMAS F. STOLLMAN, born Medicine Hat, Alberta, Canada, March 18, 1965; admitted to bar, 1996, Minnesota; 1998, District of Columbia. *Education:* Carleton University (B.A., 1988); London School of Economics, London, England (M.SC., 1990); William Mitchell College of Law (J.D., 1994). Formerly with Department of Justice, Ottawa, Canada, 1994-1999. ***PRACTICE AREAS:*** Securities Law; Corporate Law; Litigation.

BYRON L. HUFFMAN, P.C.

WASHINGTON, D.C.

(See Columbia, Maryland)

Civil Practice. Real Estate, Probate, Trusts, Corporate, Creditors Rights and Bankruptcy Law.

HUGHES HUBBARD & REED LLP

1775 I STREET, N.W.
WASHINGTON, D.C. 20006-2401
Telephone: 202-721-4600
Telex: 89-2674
Telecopier: 202-721-4646
Email: info@hugheshubbard.com
URL: http://www.hugheshubbard.com

New York, New York Office: One Battery Park Plaza, 10004. Telephone: 212-837-6000. Telex: 427120. Telecopier: 212-422-4726.
Los Angeles, California Office: 350 S. Grand Avenue, Suite 3600, 90071-3442. Telephone: 213-613-2800. Telecopier: 213-613-2950.
Miami, Florida Office: 201 South Biscayne Boulevard, Suite 2500, 33131-4332. Telephone: 305-358-1666. Fax: 305-371-8759. Telex: 518785.
Paris, France Office: 47, Avenue Georges Mandel, 75116. Telephone: 33 1 44 05 80 00. Telex: 645440. Telecopier: 33 1 45 53 15 04.

General Practice.

RESIDENT PARTNERS

LAWRENCE F. BATES, born June 1, 1954; admitted to bar, 1981, Georgia; 1993, District of Columbia. *Education:* Indiana University; Denison University (B.A., 1976); Emory Law School (J.D., 1980). ***PRACTICE AREAS:*** Banking; Bankruptcy. ***Email:*** bates@hugheshubbard.com

CATHERINE CURTISS, born July 29, 1950; admitted to bar, 1980, District of Columbia; 1982, California. *Education:* University of Michigan (B.A., 1972; M.A., cum laude, 1973); Georgetown University Law Center (J.D., cum laude, 1980). ***PRACTICE AREAS:*** International Trade and Investment Law; Federal Litigation; Customs Law. ***Email:*** curtiss@hugheshubbard.com

THOMAS A. FERRIGNO, born April 3, 1949; admitted to bar, 1975, District of Columbia. *Education:* Georgetown University (A.B., 1971) Georgetown University Law Center (J.D., 1974). ***PRACTICE AREAS:*** Securities Regulation and Enforcement; Litigation. ***Email:*** ferrigno@hugheshubbard.com

DENNIS S. KLEIN, born August 26, 1954; admitted to bar, 1981, District of Columbia; 1982, Virginia. *Education:* Muhlenberg College (B.A., magna cum laude, 1976); University of Virginia (M.A., 1978; J.D., 1981). ***PRACTICE AREAS:*** Litigation; Financial Institutions. ***Email:*** klein@hugheshubbard.com

ROBERT P. REZNICK, born September 8, 1954; admitted to bar, 1979, District of Columbia. *Education:* Harvey Mudd College (B.S., with honors and distinction, 1976); Harvard University (J.D., cum laude, 1979). ***PRACTICE AREAS:*** Litigation; Antitrust; Government Contracts. ***Email:*** reznick@hugheshubbard.com

KATHLEEN M. RUSSO, born September 15, 1954; admitted to bar, 1979, District of Columbia. *Education:* American University (B.S., cum laude, 1976); Georgetown University (J.D., magna cum laude, 1979). ***PRACTICE AREAS:*** Corporate; Securities; Financial Services. ***Email:*** russo@hugheshubbard.com

WILLIAM R. STEIN, born March 23, 1952; admitted to bar, 1978, New York; 1980, District of Columbia. *Education:* Columbia University (A.B., magna cum laude, 1974; J.D., 1977). ***LANGUAGES:*** Spanish. ***PRACTICE AREAS:*** Appeals; Litigation; Regulatory and Legislative Matters. ***Email:*** stein@hugheshubbard.com

JOHN M. TOWNSEND, born March 21, 1947; admitted to bar, 1972, New York; 1974-1975, Conseil Juridique, Paris, France; 1990, District of Columbia.

(This Listing Continued)

Education: Yale University (B.A., cum laude, 1968; J.D., 1971). ***PRACTICE AREAS:*** Litigation; Antitrust; Arbitration. ***Email:*** townsend@hugheshubbard.com

SPECIAL COUNSEL

ROBERT B. FUNKHOUSER, born January 3, 1959; admitted to bar, 1988, New York; 1993, District of Columbia; 1996, Maryland. *Education:* Harvard University (A.B., magna cum laude, 1981); Fordham University (J.D., 1987). ***PRACTICE AREAS:*** Banking Litigation; Insurance Coverage; Antitrust. ***Email:*** funkhous@hugheshubbard.com

JOSEPH M. FUREY, born Pittsfield, Massachusetts, October 16, 1955; admitted to bar, 1984, Maryland; 1994, District of Columbia. *Education:* Boston College (A.B., 1977); University of Baltimore (J.D., 1984); Georgetown University (LL.M. in Securities Regulation, 1990). Member and Associate Editor, University of Baltimore Law Review, 1981-1984. Assistant Director, Division of Market Regulation, Securities and Exchange Commission, 1989-1994. Deputy Chief Hearing Officer, National Association of Securities Dealers Regulation, 1996-1999. ***LANGUAGES:*** Russian. ***PRACTICE AREAS:*** Securities Litigation; Securities Regulation Law; Insurance; Litigation; Corporate Law. ***Email:*** furey@hugheshubbard.com

ALAN G. KASHDAN, born November 24, 1953; admitted to bar, 1980, District of Columbia. *Education:* Princeton University (B.A., magna cum laude, 1975); Harvard University (J.D., cum laude, 1980). ***LANGUAGES:*** Russian and Mandarin Chinese. ***PRACTICE AREAS:*** International Trade. ***Email:*** kashdan@hugheshubbard.com

J. DAVID HUGHES & ASSOCIATES, PLLC

1815 PENNSYLVANIA AVENUE N.W.
SUITE 550
WASHINGTON, D.C. 20006
Telephone: 202-347-3100
Fax: 202-331-8893; 703-370-1760
Email: jdavehughes@home.com

Arbitration, Mediation, Civil Litigation, Federal Energy Regulation, Immigration.

FIRM PROFILE: Active participant in civil litigation and arbitration. Mediator for the past nine years with the Superior Court, District of Columbia. Defense of U.S. Customs seizure and forfeiture proceedings.

J.D. HUGHES & ASSOCIATES, PLLC, born Lubbock, Texas, April 24, 1935; admitted to bar, 1964, Texas; 1965, U.S. District Court, Northern District of Texas; 1973, U.S. Court of Appeals, Fifth Circuit; and U.S. Supreme Court; 1985, U.S. Court of Appeals for the District of Columbia Circuit and District of Columbia. *Education:* University of Texas (B.B.A., 1958); American University (J.D., 1961). Recipient: Secretary of Energy Meritorious Service Award, FERC Chairman's Medal for Exemplary Service, 1984 and Multi-Door Distinguished Service Medal Award, Superior Court, D.C., 2000. Commissioner, FERC, 1980-1984. Advisory Counsel, Gas Research Institute. Distinguished Alumnus, American University, 1984. *Member:* District of Columbia Bar; State Bar of Texas.

HULL McGUIRE PC

1155 CONNECTICUT AVENUE, N.W.
SUITE 300
WASHINGTON, D.C. 20036-4306
Telephone: 202-429-6520
Fax: 202-429-0977
Email: info@hullmcguire.com
URL: http://www.hullmcguire.com

Pittsburgh, Pennsylvania Office: 32nd Floor, USX Tower, 600 Grant Street, 15219-2702. Telephone: 412-261-2600. Fax: 412-261-2627.

Corporate Law, Taxation, International Law, Intellectual Property, Complex Business Litigation and Arbitrations, Employment Law, Environmental Law and Natural Resources, Federal Courts, Federal Legislative Practice.

FIRM PROFILE: Hull McGuire PC focuses on corporate planning and transactions, taxation and business litigation in the U.S. and abroad. The firm serves as both business counselors and litigators to a variety of Fortune 500, medium-sized and start-up companies headquartered in California, Illinois, Maryland, Michigan, Missouri, Ohio, Pennsylvania, Tennessee, Texas, Virginia and Washington, D.C. The practice ranges from planning and prevention to litigation and appellate work before regulatory agencies and courts, and complex arbitrations domestically and abroad. The Firm is an active member of the International Business Law Consortium based in Salzburg, Austria.

(This Listing Continued)

JOHN DANIEL HULL, IV, born Washington, D.C., February 27, 1953; admitted to bar, 1980, District of Columbia; 1983, U.S. District Court for the District of Columbia; 1984, U.S. Court of Appeals for the District of Columbia Circuit; 1985, U.S. Court of Appeals, Tenth Circuit; 1989, Pennsylvania, Maryland and U.S. Supreme Court. *Education:* Duke University (B.A., cum laude, 1975); University of Cincinnati (J.D., 1978). Member, 1976-1977 and Student Articles Editor, 1977-1978, University of Cincinnati Law Review. Author, Casenotes: 45 U. Cin. L. Rev. 684, 1976; 46 U. Cin. L. Rev. 611, 1977; Note, 47 U. Cin. L. Rev. 64, 1978. Legislative Assistant, 95th and 96th U.S. Congresses, 1978-1980. *Member:* The District of Columbia Bar; Maryland, Pennsylvania and American Bar Associations (Member, Sections on: Litigation, Natural Resources, Energy and Environmental Law). ***LANGUAGES:*** Spanish. ***REPORTED CASES:*** NRDC v. Thomas, 838 F. 2d 1224 (DC Cir. 1988) cert. denied 488 U.S. 888 (1988); State of New York v. EPA, 852 F. 2d 574 (DC Cir. 1988) cert. denied 489 U.S. 1065 (1989); Pennsylvania v. Union Gas Co., 491 U.S. 1 (1989); UMC Petroleum Corp. v. J&J Enterprises, Inc., 758 F. Supp. 1069 (W.D. Pa. 1991). ***PRACTICE AREAS:*** Complex Business Litigation; Environmental Law; Natural Resources; Intellectual Property; Federal Legislative Practice.

JULIE E. McGUIRE, born Pittsburgh, Pennsylvania, August 23, 1958; admitted to bar, 1985, Pennsylvania and U.S. District Court, Western District of Pennsylvania; 1992, U.S Tax Court; 1996, U.S. Court of Appeals, Third Circuit (Not admitted in District of Columbia). *Education:* Carnegie-Mellon University (B.S., 1980, Graduated First in Class); Duquesne University (J.D., magna cum laude, 1985, Graduated First in Class). Recent Decisions Editor, Duquesne Law Review, 1984-1985. Clerk, Commonwealth Court, Judge David Craig, 1984. Recipient: American Jurisprudence Awards for Excellent Achievement in the Study of: Corporations, 1983-1984; Estate Planning, 1984-1985; West Company Book Award; Awards for Academic Excellence, 1983-1984, 1984-1985; Duquesne University Law School Scholarship, 1984-1985; Allegheny County Bar Association Award, 1985. Certified Public Accountant, Pennsylvania, 1982. Author: Comment: 23 Duq. L. Rev. 659, 1985; Casenote: 22 Duq. L. Rev. 1185, 1984. Member: Board of Directors, Pittsburgh Airport Area Chamber of Commerce, 1994-1997; Pittsburgh High Technology Council; American Institute of CPAs (Tax Section); Pennsylvania Institute of CPAs. Member, 1992—and Chairperson, 1994—, World Trade Development Committee, Pittsburgh Airport Area Chamber of Commerce. Allegheny Tax Society (Program Chairperson, 1994-1995). *Member:* Allegheny County (Member, Tax Section), Pennsylvania and American Bar Associations. ***PRACTICE AREAS:*** Corporate Law; Business Planning; Mergers, Acquisitions and Divestitures; Taxation; International Taxation. ***Email:*** jmcguire@hullmcguire.com

(For complete Biographical Data on all personnel see Pittsburgh, Pennsylvania)

HUNTON & WILLIAMS

1900 K STREET, N.W.
WASHINGTON, D.C. 20006-1109
Telephone: 202-955-1500
Telex: 350 362 H&W WASH UD
FAX: 202-778-2201 (Rapicom); 202-778-2202 (Ricoh230)
URL: http://www.hunton.com

Miami, Florida Office: Barclays Financial Center, 1111 Brickell Avenue, Suite 2500, 33131. Telephone: 305-810-2500. Fax: 305-810-2460.

Atlanta, Georgia Office: Bank of America Plaza, 600 Peachtree Street, N.E., Suite 4100, 30308-2216. Telephone: 404-888-4000. Fax: 404-888-4190 and Georgia-Hill Office: Southside Legal Center, 250 Georgia Avenue, S.E., Suite 211, 30312. Telephone: 404-688-5512; 404-688-5513.

New York, New York Office: 200 Park Avenue, 43rd Floor, 10166-0136. Telephone: 212-309-1000. Cable Addresses: "Huntwand, New York" and "Dialboard." Telex: 424 549 HUNT UI. Fax: 212-309-1100.

Charlotte, North Carolina Office: Bank of America Plaza, 101 South Tryon Street, Suite 3500, 28280. Telephone: 704-3778-4700. Telecopier: 704-378-4890.

Raleigh, North Carolina Office: One Hannover Square, 421 Fayetteville Street Mall, Suite 1400, 27601. Telephone: 919-899-3000. Fax: 919-833-6352.

Knoxville, Tennessee Office: 2000 Riverview Tower, 900 South Gay Street, Suite 2000, 37902. Telephone: 865-549-7700. Fax: 865-549-7704.

McLean, Virginia Office: 1751 Pinnacle Drive, Suite 1700, Tysons Corner, 22102. Telephone: 703-714-7400. Fax: 703-714-7410.

Norfolk, Virginia Office: SunTrust Center, Suite 1000, 500 East Main Street, 23510-3889. Telephone: 757-640-5300. FAX: 757-625-7720.

Richmond, Virginia Office: Riverfront Plaza, East Tower, 951 East Byrd Street, 23219-4074. Telephone: 804-788-8200. Cable Address: "Huntwand". Telex: 804-684-4251. Fax: 804-788-8218. TWX: 710-956-0061 and Church Hill Office: 2300 East Marshall Street, 23223. Telephone: 804-775-2248.

Brussels, Belgium Office: Ave Louise 326, B6, 1050 Brussels, Belgium. Telephone: 32(0)-2-643-5800. Fax: 32(0)-2-643-5822.

Hong Kong, Office: 23/F CITIC Tower, 1 Tim Mei Avenue, Central, Hong Kong. Telephone: (852) 2841-9100. Fax: (852) 2841-9191.

(This Listing Continued)

HUNTON & WILLIAMS, Washington—Continued

Bangkok, Thailand Office: Hunton & Williams (Thailand) Limited, 34/F Abdulrahim Place, 990 Rama IV Road, Bangkok, Thailand, 1050. Telephone: 011 (662) 636-2366. Fax: 011 (662) 636-2377.

Warsaw, Poland Office: Warsaw Stock Exchange Building, Ksi ążęca 4, 00-498 Warsaw, Poland. Telephone: 011 (48-22) 690 61 00. Telecopier: 011 (48-22) 690 62 22.

London, England Office: Fleetway House, 25 Farringdon Street, London EC4A 4AB, England. Telephone: 44 (0)20 7246 5700. Fax: 44 (0)20 7246 5772.

General Practice.

SENIOR COUNSEL

JOHN J. ADAMS, born Toledo, Ohio, November 12, 1934; admitted to bar, 1959, Virginia; 1968, District of Columbia. *Education:* Denison University (B.A., 1956); University of Virginia (LL.B., 1959). Phi Alpha Delta; Omicron Delta Kappa. Member: Raven Society; Board of Editors, Virginia Law Review, 1958-1959. Member, Natural Resources Law Section, American Bar Association. ***PRACTICE AREAS:*** Corporate; Environmental Law. ***Email:*** jadams@hunton.com

GEORGE CLEMON FREEMAN, JR., born Birmingham, Alabama, January 3, 1929; admitted to bar, 1956, Alabama; 1958, Virginia; 1974, District of Columbia. *Education:* Vanderbilt University (B.A., magna cum laude, 1950); Yale Law School (LL.B., 1956). Phi Beta Kappa; Phi Delta Phi; Omicron Delta Kappa. Law Clerk to Justice Hugo L. Black, U. S. Supreme Court, 1956-1957. Member, Congressional Study Group under section 301(e) of the Superfund Act, 1980-1982. Chairman: Advisory Council of the Energy Policy Studies Center of the University of Virginia, 1981-1985; Chairman, Legal Advisory Committee, Virginia Commission on Transportation in the 21st Century, 1986-1987. Member, Virginia Governor's Commission to Study Historic Preservation, 1987-1989. Councillor, The Atlantic Council of The United States, 1985-1992. Member: The Virginia Board of Historic Resources, 1989-1995, Chairman, 1989-1991. American Bar Association: Chairman, Committee on Facilities of the Law Library of Congress, 1967-1973. Member: Coordinating Group on Regulatory Reform, 1979-1985; Chairman, Coordinating Group on Civil Justice Reform, 1990-1993; Section of Business Law: Chair, 1990-1991. *Member:* American Law Institute (Member of Council, 1980—; Advisor to the Council on Reporters' Study on Enterprise Responsibility for Personal Injury, 1986-1991; Advisor, Restatement of the Law Third, Torts: Liability for Physical Harm, Basic Principles, 2000—; Advisor, Restatement Third of Torts, Apportionment, 1994-1999, General Principles, 1998—). Fellow, American Bar Foundation. (Also at Richmond, Virginia Office). ***Email:*** gjfreeman@hunton.com

WILLIAM A. PUSEY, born Richmond, Virginia, March 17, 1936; admitted to bar, 1963, California; 1964, Virginia; 1987, District of Columbia. *Education:* Princeton University (A.B., 1958); University of Virginia (J.D., 1962). Phi Beta Kappa; Omicron Delta Kappa; Order of the Coif. Member, Raven Society. Articles Editor, Virginia Law Review, 1960-1961; Trustee, 1981—, Member, Executive Committee, 1983-1989 and President, 1987-1988, Eastern Mineral Law Foundation. *Member:* American Law Institute. ***LANGUAGES:*** French. ***PRACTICE AREAS:*** Corporate; Securities. ***Email:*** wpusey@hunton.com

MEMBERS OF FIRM

STANISLAUS AKSMAN, born June 9, 1950; admitted to bar, 1980, Virginia; 1990, U.S. Court of Appeals for the Federal Circuit; 1995, U.S. District Court, Eastern District of Virginia; 1999, District of Columbia; registered to practice before U.S. Patent and Trademark Office. *Education:* Cornell University (B.S., 1974); George Washington University (J.D., 1979). Senior Patent Attorney, Mobil Oil Corporation, 1980-1990. *Member:* Virginia State Bar (Former Chair, Intellectual Property Law Section); American Bar Assn.; American Intellectual Property Law Assn.; Licensing Executives Society (Former Co-Chair, Trade Secrets Licensing Committee; Member, Central Europe Committee); Patent Lawyers Club of Washington. ***LANGUAGES:*** Polish and Russian. ***PRACTICE AREAS:*** Intellectual Property Law.

JENNIFER A. ALBERT, born Pittsburgh, Pennsylvania, July 15, 1960; admitted to bar, 1985, South Carolina; 1986, District of Columbia; registered to practice before the U.S. Patent and Trademark Office. *Education:* Purdue University (B.S.E.E., 1982); University of South Carolina (J.D., cum laude, 1985). Order of the Coif; Order of the Wig and Robe. Editorial Staff, *South Carolina Law Review*, 1983-85. Survey Staff, South Carolina Law Review, 1984. *Member:* American Intellectual Property Law Association; Licensing Executives Society (U.S./Canada and International Chapters; Commerce and Information Technology Law Committee). ***PRACTICE AREAS:*** Information Technology; Electronic Commerce; Intellectual Property; Patents; Trademarks; Copyrights; Trade Secrets; Computer Law; Antitrust. ***Email:*** jalbert@hunton.com

VIRGINIA S. ALBRECHT, born Chicago, Illinois, December 11, 1942; admitted to bar, 1981, District of Columbia. *Education:* University of Wisconsin (B.S., 1964); University of Pennsylvania (M.A., 1970); Vanderbilt University (J.D., 1981). Articles Editor, Vanderbilt Law Review, 1980-1981. Law Clerk to Honorable John P. Wiese, U.S. Court of Claims, Trial Division, 1981-1982. ***PRACTICE AREAS:*** Environmental Law; Administrative Law. ***Email:*** valbrecht@hunton.com

IAN P. BAND, born Washington, D.C., April 27, 1962; admitted to bar, 1987, Maryland; 1988, District of Columbia. *Education:* University of Maryland (B.A., 1984); American University, Washington College of Law (J.D., 1987). *Member:* American Immigration Lawyers Association. ***PRACTICE AREAS:*** Immigration. ***Email:*** iband@hunton.com

A. NEAL BARKUS, born Charleston, West Virginia, July 17, 1947; admitted to bar, 1974, West Virginia; 1976, Virginia; 1982, District of Columbia; 1994, U.S. Supreme Court. *Education:* University of Virginia (B.A., 1969); Washington & Lee University (J.D., 1974). Order of the Coif. Executive Editor, Washington & Lee Law Review, 1973-1974. Attorney, Criminal Division, U. S. Department of Justice, 1974-1975. Member, Labor and Employment Law Section, American Bar Association. *Member:* American Immigration Lawyers Association. ***PRACTICE AREAS:*** Labor; Employment; Business Immigration. ***Email:*** nbarkus@hunton.com

MICHAEL B. BARR, born Freeport, New York, July 24, 1948; admitted to bar, 1973, District of Columbia. *Education:* Georgetown University (B.S., 1970); George Washington University (J.D., 1973). *Member:* American Bar Association (Member, Sections on: Business Law; International Law). ***PRACTICE AREAS:*** International; Investments; Energy; Finance. ***Email:*** mbarr@hunton.com

PHILIP M. BATTLES, III, born Lowell, Massachusetts, April 10, 1944; admitted to bar, 1973, Virginia; 1974, District of Columbia. *Education:* Syracuse University (B.A., cum laude, 1967); University of Arkansas and Georgetown University (J.D., 1973). Pi Sigma Alpha; Phi Alpha Delta. Recipient, The Lawyers Cooperative Publishing Company Book Award. ***PRACTICE AREAS:*** Project Finance; Leveraged Leasing; Real Estate; Finance; International; Investments. ***Email:*** pbattles@hunton.com

MARK B. BIERBOWER, born Washington, D.C., May 26, 1951; admitted to bar, 1980, District of Columbia; 1983, Virginia; 1986, Maryland; 1988, U. S. Supreme Court. *Education:* Northwestern University (B.A., 1976); Georgetown University Law Center (J.D., 1979). President, Bar Association of the District of Columbia, 1993-1994 (President-elect, 1992-1993; Treasurer, 1989-1992; Chair, Young Lawyers Section, 1986-1987). Trustee, Foundation of Bar Association of D.C. Member: District of Columbia Bar; Maryland State and Virginia Bar Associations. Member, American Bar Association Sections of Litigation, Committees on Commercial and Banking, Product Liability Litigation, and Business Law; Federal Communications Bar Association; ABA House of Delegates, 1990-1994; Governing Committee, ABA Forum Committee on Entertainment and Sports Industries, 1983-1989; National Conference of Lawyers and Certified Public Accountants, 1989-1993. Legislative Assistant: U. S. Senate (1974-1976). Fellow, American Bar Foundation. ***PRACTICE AREAS:*** Litigation. ***Email:*** mbierbower@hunton.com

F. WILLIAM BROWNELL, born Ashland, Wisconsin, July 18, 1952; admitted to bar, 1978, District of Columbia; 1979, U. S. Court of Appeals for the District of Columbia; 1983, U. S. Supreme Court; 1987, U. S. Court of Appeals 11th Circuit; 1988, U. S. Court of Appeals, 2nd and 7th Circuits. *Education:* Georgetown University (B.S., 1974; M.S., 1978; J.D., 1978). Phi Beta Kappa. Member, Sections on: Administrative Law; International Law; Energy and Environmental Law, American Bar Association. Member, Administrative Law Section, The District of Columbia Bar. ***LANGUAGES:*** French. ***PRACTICE AREAS:*** Environmental; Administrative Law; Appellate Practice; International Law. ***Email:*** bbrownell@hunton.com

KRISTY A. NIEHAUS BULLEIT, born St. Louis, Missouri, July 20, 1957; admitted to bar, 1982, Virginia; 1986, District of Columbia. *Education:* University of Detroit (B.A., summa cum laude, 1979); Boston University (J.D., cum laude, 1982). Alpha Sigma Nu. Member, American Bar Association, Section of Administrative Law; Section of Natural Resources, Energy and Environmental Law, Chair, Water Quality Committee, 1988-1990 and Vice-chair, 1986-1987, Council Member, 1990-1992, Continuing Legal Education Officer, 1992-1994, Vice-chair, Scope and Correlation Committee 1993-1994, Vice-chair, Publications Coordination and Marketing Committee 1993-1994, Chair, Section Annual Meeting Site-Selection Committee 1994-1995. Chair, ABA Annual Meeting Committee, 1995-1996; Chair, *The Environmental Lawyer*, 1996-1999; Liaison to ABA Commission on Women in the Profession, 1999-2000. Section of Public Utility, Communications and Transportation Law, Vice-chair, Environmental Committee, 1995-2000. ***PRACTICE AREAS:*** Environmental; Administrative Law. ***Email:*** kbulleit@hunton.com

ELLIS M. BUTLER, born Richmond, Virginia, September 21, 1967; admitted to bar, 1993, Virginia; 1996, District of Columbia. *Education:* University of Virginia (B.A., with distinction, 1989); Kennedy School of Government, Harvard University (M.P.P., 1993); Harvard Law School (J.D., cum laude, 1993). Phi Beta Kappa. *Member:* American Bar Association (Member, Sections

(This Listing Continued)

on: Business Law; International Law). ***PRACTICE AREAS:*** Project Finance; Independent Power Development; Asset Finance; Leasing. ***Email:*** ebutler@hunton.com

KEVIN L. FAST, born Ann Arbor, Michigan, January 23, 1960; admitted to bar, 1986, Virginia; 1988, District of Columbia. *Education:* University of Maryland (B.A., summa cum laude, 1981); University of Virginia (J.D., 1986). Order of the Coif. *Member:* Virginia Bar Association; Bar Association of the District of Columbia. ***PRACTICE AREAS:*** Environmental. ***Email:*** kfast@hunton.com

NORMAN W. FICHTHORN, born Nelsonville, Ohio, September 26, 1958; admitted to bar, 1985, Virginia; 1986, District of Columbia. *Education:* Bowling Green State University (B.A., summa cum laude, 1980); Stanford University (J.D., 1985). Phi Kappa Phi. *Member:* American Bar Association (Vice Chair, Air Quality Committee, Natural Resources, Energy and Environmental Law Section, 1989-1997). ***PRACTICE AREAS:*** Environmental; Administrative. ***Email:*** nfichthorn@hunton.com

ANDREA BEAR FIELD, born New London, Connecticut, November 30, 1949; admitted to bar, 1974, Virginia; 1977, District of Columbia. *Education:* Wellesley College; Yale University (B.A., 1971); University of Virginia (J.D., 1974). American Bar Association Section of Natural Resources, Energy and Environmental Law, Section Chair, 1989-1990, Chair Elect, 1988-1989, Section Vice Chairman, 1987-1988, Vice-Chair, Section Teleconference Committee, Council Member, 1984-1987, 1990-1991, Chairman, Air Quality Committee, 1982-1984 and Vice Chairman, 1980-1982. Vice Chair, Teleconference Committee, 1990—, American Bar Association Section on Business Law, Chair, Environment Controls Committee, 1990-1991. American Bar Association Representative on the National Conference of Lawyers and Scientists, 1990-1993. American Bar Association Science and Technology Section, Council Member, 1991-1992. American Bar Association Real Property, Probate and Trust Law Section, Vice Chair, Environmental Law Committee, 1990-1991. Member, Conference of Section Chairs Ad Hoc Committee on National Institutes, 1989. Chair, ABA's Standing Committee on National Conference Groups, 1993-1994. Chairman of the Virginia Bar Association's Environmental Committee, 1979-1980. ***PRACTICE AREAS:*** Environmental. ***Email:*** afield@hunton.com

LAUREN E. FREEMAN, born Seattle, Washington, June 15, 1962; admitted to bar, 1990, Virginia; 1992, District of Columbia; U.S. Court of Appeals for the District of Columbia Circuit and Fourth Circuit; U.S. Supreme Court. *Education:* Bowdoin College (A.B., 1984); College of William & Mary (J.D., 1990). Order of the Coif. ***PRACTICE AREAS:*** Environmental; Administrative Law. ***Email:*** lfreeman@hunton.com

DAVID F. GENESON, born New York, New York, August 29, 1947; admitted to bar, 1974, Florida; 1975, U. S. District Court, Southern District of Florida and U.S. Court of Appeals, 5th Circuit; 1979, District of Columbia, U. S. Court of Appeals for the District of Columbia Circuit and U.S. Supreme Court; 1994, Virginia and U. S. District Court, Western District of Virginia; 1996, U.S. District Court, Eastern District of Virginia and U.S. Court of Appeals, 4th Circuit; 1998, U.S. District Court, Middle District of Florida, U.S. District Court, Southern District of Texas and U.S. Court of Appeals, 11th Circuit; 2001, U.S. District Court, Western District of Texas. *Education:* Rensselaer Polytechnic Institute (B.S., 1969); University of Miami School of Law (J.D., 1973). Member, Barrister Journal, 1972-1973. Editor, Computer Related Criminal Law, U.S. Department of Justice, 1988. Regional and Masters Team Leader, National Institute for Trial Advocacy. Member Sections on: Criminal Defense; Litigation and Business Law. Master, American Inns of Court. ***PRACTICE AREAS:*** Litigation. ***Email:*** dgeneson@hunton.com

PATTI L. GRANT-WILKINSON, born Washington, D.C., November 9, 1963; admitted to bar, 1988, Maryland; 1990, District of Columbia. *Education:* Georgetown University (B.A., 1985; J.D., 1988). Board Member: Mentors, Inc.; HomeCare Partners. Advisory Board Member, Metropolitan Access. *Member:* District of Columbia Bar; Bar Association of the District of Columbia; Maryland State and National Bar Associations; National Association of Bond Lawyers. ***PRACTICE AREAS:*** Municipal Finance; Real Estate. ***Email:*** pwilkinson@hunton.com

RAY V. HARTWELL III, born Anniston, Alabama, June 19, 1947; admitted to bar, 1975, Virginia; 1980, District of Columbia. *Education:* Washington & Lee University (B.A., 1969; J.D., summa cum laude, 1975). Omicron Delta Kappa; Order of the Coif; Delta Theta Phi. Winner, John W. Davis Prize, 1975. Editor-in-Chief, Washington & Lee Law Review, 1974-1975. Listed in, International Who's Who of Competition Lawyers, 1997, 2000. Member, Editorial Advisory Boards, The Antitrust Bulletin and The Journal of Reprints for Antitrust Law and Economics, 1978—. Chair, 1998-2001, Member, Steering Committee, Antitrust, Trade Regulation and Consumer Affairs Section, District of Columbia Bar, 1997—. Member, American Bar Association Antitrust Sentencing Guidelines Task Force, 1995-1997; American Bar Association Task Force on NAFTA Competition and Trade Law Issues, 1993-1994; Council Member, 1992-1995; Chair, Consumer Protection Committee, 1989-1992, Vice-Chair, Criminal Practice and Procedure Committee, 1987-1989, American Bar Association Section of Antitrust Law. Chairman, 1979-1980 and Member, Board of

(This Listing Continued)

Governors, 1977-1981, Antitrust Franchising and Trade Regulation Section, Virginia State Bar. Member: International Bar Association; ABA Sections of Science and Technology, Intellectual Property Law; Steering Committee, Antitrust, Trade Regulation and Consumer Affairs Section, District of Columbia Bar, 1997—. [Lt.(Jg.), U.S. Navy, 1969-1972]. (Also in Richmond, Virginia Office). ***LANGUAGES:*** French. ***PRACTICE AREAS:*** Antitrust; Intellectual Property. ***Email:*** rhartwell@hunton.com

ROBERT W. HAWKINS, born Regensburg, West Germany, September 24, 1949; admitted to bar, 1976, Virginia and District of Columbia. *Education:* Amherst College (B.A., cum laude, 1971); Cambridge University, Cambridge, England (LL.B., 1973); University of Virginia (J.D., 1976). ***PRACTICE AREAS:*** Litigation; International Commercial Arbitration. ***Email:*** rhawkins@hunton.com

JUAN C. ITURREGUI, born San Juan, Puerto Rico, June 14, 1965; admitted to bar, 1990, Pennsylvania; 1991, District of Columbia. *Education:* University of Massachusetts, Amherst (B.A., Political Science, 1986); Catholic University of America (J.D., 1990). *Member:* American Bar Association; Hispanic National Bar Association. (Director of Governmental Affairs). ***LANGUAGES:*** Spanish. ***PRACTICE AREAS:*** Government Affairs; Legislative Practice; Trade and Commerce Issues; Project Development. ***Email:*** jiturregui@hunton.com

THOMAS F. KAUFMAN, born Buffalo, New York, September 10, 1949; admitted to bar, 1976, Virginia; 1977, District of Columbia; 1996, Maryland; registered to practice before U.S. Patent and Trademark Office. *Education:* State University of New York at Buffalo (B.S.E.E., cum laude, 1971); Georgetown University Law Center (J.D., 1976); The Wharton School, University of Pennsylvania (M.B.A., with honors, 2001). Adjunct Professor, Georgetown University Law Center, 1986—. Law Clerk to Chief Judge Harry Phillips, U. S. Court of Appeals, 6th Circuit, 1976-1977. *Member:* American College of Real Estate Lawyers. ***PRACTICE AREAS:*** Finance; Real Estate; Technology; Corporate. ***Email:*** tkaufman@hunton.com

DARRYL S. LEW, born Cleveland, Ohio, March 15, 1964; admitted to bar, 1990, New York; 1992, District of Columbia; 1994, Virginia. *Education:* King's College (B.A., summa cum laude, 1985); College of Europe (A.E.S., 1986); Columbia University (J.D., 1989). Fulbright Scholar; Harlan Fiske Stone Scholar. Articles Editor, Columbia Journal of Transnational Law, 1987-1989. Law Clerk to the Honorable Frank X. Altimari, U.S. Court of Appeals, Second Circuit, 1991-1992; Law Clerk to the Honorable Robert E. Payne, U.S. District Court, Eastern District of Virginia, 1992-1993. ***LANGUAGES:*** French. ***PRACTICE AREAS:*** Commercial Litigation; International Arbitration. ***Email:*** dlew@hunton.com

C. KING MALLORY, III, born Norfolk, Virginia, November 16, 1936; admitted to bar, 1961, Louisiana; 1965, California; 1972, District of Columbia. *Education:* Yale University (B.A., 1958); Tulane University (LL.B., 1961). Member, Board of Editors, 1960-1961 and Assistant Editor, 1961, Tulane Law Review. Acting Executive Director, U. S. Securities and Exchange Commission, 1972-1973. Deputy Assistant Secretary of Interior, Resources and Regulation, 1973-1974. Acting Assistant Secretary of Interior, Energy and Minerals, 1974. Member: Reagan-Bush Energy Transition Team, 1980-1981; President's Private Sector Survey on Cost Control in Federal Government (Grace Commission) 1982. *Member:* Louisiana State and Energy Bar Associations; The State Bar of California; National Association of Bond Lawyers. [Lt., USNR, 1961-1964]. ***PRACTICE AREAS:*** Energy; Finance. ***Email:*** kmallory@hunton.com

JEFFREY N. MARTIN, born St. Paul, Minnesota, June 26, 1952; admitted to bar, 1978, District of Columbia. *Education:* Lawrence University (B.A., summa cum laude, 1974); Harvard University (J.D., 1978). Phi Beta Kappa. Thomas J. Watson Foundation Post Graduate Fellow. Foreign Developments Editor, Harvard Environmental Law Review, 1977-1978. Law Clerk to the Hon. John H. Pratt, U. S. District Court for the District of Columbia, 1978-1979. ***PRACTICE AREAS:*** Environmental. ***Email:*** jmartin@hunton.com

RICHARD EDWARD MAY, born Austin, Texas, February 5, 1946; admitted to bar, 1973, District of Columbia; 1974, U. S. Tax Court and U. S. Claims Court; 1976, U. S. Supreme Court; 1982, Texas; 1984, Virginia. *Education:* University of Maryland (A.B., cum laude, 1967); Georgetown University (J.D., 1973). Phi Kappa Phi; Omicron Delta Kappa. Executive Editor, Georgetown Law Journal, 1972-1973. Adjunct Professor, Georgetown University Law Center, 1978-1980, 1989-1990. Member, Committee on Closely Held Corporations, 1974-1988, Member, Corporate-Shareholder Relations, 1978—, Vice Chair, 1983-1985, Chair, 1985-1987, Member, Committee on Committees, 1987, Assistant Secretary, 1988-1989, Secretary, 1989-1991; Council Director, 1991-1993, Vice-Chair, Government Relations, 1993-1995; Taxation Section, American Bar Association. Special Assistant to the Chief Counsel, Internal Revenue Service, 1979-1981. Fellow, American College of Tax Counsel. [Lt., USN, 1968-1971]. ***PRACTICE AREAS:*** Taxation. ***Email:*** rmay@hunton.com

JAMES FORREST MILLER, born Sioux City, Iowa, January 28, 1952; admitted to bar, 1978, District of Columbia. *Education:* Dartmouth College (A.B., magna cum laude, 1974); Columbia Law School (J.D., 1977). Stone Scholar. Associate Tax Legislative Counsel, U.S. Treasuty Department. *Mem-*

(This Listing Continued)

HUNTON & WILLIAMS, Washington—Continued

ber: The District of Columbia Bar; American (Member: Tax Section; Government Affairs Committee) Bar Association. ***PRACTICE AREAS:*** Governmental Affairs. ***Email:*** millerj@gtlaw.com

JACK A. MOLENKAMP, born Grand Rapids, Michigan, October 1, 1952; admitted to bar, 1979, Virginia; 1999, District of Columbia. *Education:* Michigan State University (B.A., 1974); University of Michigan (J.D., 1979). Phi Beta Kappa; Phi Eta Sigma; Order of Coif. Member, Michigan Law Review, 1977-1979. *Member:* Virginia State Bar (Past Chair, Board of Governors, Business Law Section); American Bar Association (Past Chair, Partnership Committee's Subcommittee on REITs, REMICs and Financing Trusts). ***PRACTICE AREAS:*** Corporate Law; Securities; Project Finance. ***Email:*** jmolenkamp@hunton.com

ERIC J. MURDOCK, born Hartford, Connecticut, March 2, 1960; admitted to bar, 1985, Connecticut; 1989, U.S. Court of Appeals for the Federal Circuit; 1990, U.S. Court of International Trade and U.S. Court of Appeals for the District of Columbia Circuit; 1994, District of Columbia; 1996, U.S. Court of Appeals, 4th Circuit. *Education:* Princeton University (A.B., cum laude, 1982); Duke University School of Law (J.D., with honors, 1985). Member, Editorial Board, Duke Law Journal, 1984-1985. Author: "A Decade of Superfund Caselaw, 1981-1991, Envir. L. Rep. (1991); "Finally, Government Ethics as if People Mattered," 58 G. Wash. L. Rev. 502 (1990); Note, "The Due-on-Sale Controversy," Duke L. J. 121 (1984). Assistant General Counsel of the Army, 1985-1989. Assistant Special Counsel to the Secretary of Defense, 1989. ***PRACTICE AREAS:*** Environmental Law; Litigation. ***Email:*** emurdock@hunton.com

KIMBERLY A. NEWMAN, born Newport News, Virginia, November 8, 1961; admitted to bar, 1989, Virginia; 1991, District of Columbia. *Education:* University of Virgina (B.A., highest distinction, 1984; J.D., 1989); University of California at Los Angeles (M.A., 1985). Echols Scholar; Phi Beta Kappa; Phi Delta Phi; Raven Society. Law Clerk to the Hon. Albert V. Bryan, Jr., Chief Judge Eastern District of Virginia, 1989-1990. ***PRACTICE AREAS:*** Antitrust; Telecommunications; Litigation. ***Email:*** knewman@hunton.com

HENRY V. NICKEL, born Chicago, Illinois, August 8, 1943; admitted to bar, 1968, District of Columbia. *Education:* University of Virginia (A.B., 1965); George Washington University (J.D., 1968). Order of the Coif. Research Editor, George Washington Law Review, 1967-1968. ***PRACTICE AREAS:*** Environmental. ***Email:*** hnickel@hunton.com

BRUCE D. PETERSON, born Chicago, Illinois, November 14, 1956; admitted to bar, 1982, Virginia; 1990, District of Columbia; 2001, New York. *Education:* North Park College (B.A., cum laude, 1978); Notre Dame Law School (J.D., 1982). Administrative Editor and Member, Notre Dame Lawyer, 1980-1982. Foreign Service Officer, Copenhagen, Denmark, Budapest, Hungary and Washington, D.C., U. S. Department of State, 1982-1988. ***LANGUAGES:*** Danish. ***PRACTICE AREAS:*** Project Finance. ***Email:*** bpeterson@hunton.com

ARNOLD H. QUINT, born Boston, Massachusetts, January 3, 1942; admitted to bar, 1967, District of Columbia. *Education:* Haverford College (B.A., 1963); Yale University (LL.B., 1966). Attorney, Office of the General Counsel, Federal Power Commission, 1966-1970. Vice-Chairman and Chairman, Committee on Regulation under Part I of the Federal Power Act, 1976-1978, 1979-1980, Vice Chairman, Programs and Meetings Committee, 1982-1983, Member, Board of Directors, 1989-1992, Federal Energy Bar Association. ***PRACTICE AREAS:*** Energy. ***Email:*** aquint@hunton.com

JOHN JAY RANGE, born Kansas City, Missouri, March 28, 1955; admitted to bar, 1980, Virginia; 1983, District of Columbia; 1993, Maryland. *Education:* University of Michigan (A.B., 1977); University of North Carolina (J.D., 1980). Phi Beta Kappa. Note and Comment Editor, North Carolina Journal of International Law and Commercial Regulation, 1979-1980. Co-Author: "Rethinking the Fiduciary Exception to the Attorney-Client Privilege in Light of *Varity Corporation v. Howe*," 10 Benefits Law Journal 25 (Winter 1997). Vice Chairman, Committee on Pre-Trial Practice and Discovery, Litigation Section, American Bar Association, 1987-1991. ***PRACTICE AREAS:*** Litigation. ***Email:*** jrange@hunton.com

JOHN M. RATINO, born Washington, D.C., December 17, 1956; admitted to bar, 1985, District of Columbia and Maryland. *Education:* University of Maryland (B.S., 1978); Catholic University of America (J.D., 1984). Associate Editor, Catholic University Law Review, 1983-1984. ***PRACTICE AREAS:*** Corporate Finance; Real Estate. ***Email:*** jratino@hunton.com

SCOTT L. ROBERTSON, born Perth Amboy, New Jersey, July 21, 1957; admitted to bar, 1987, Massachusetts; 1989, U.S. District Court, District of Massachusetts; 1993, U.S. District Court, Northern District of California; 1997, District of Columbia and U.S. Court of Appeals, First and Federal Circuit; 1998, U.S. District Court, District of Columbia, U.S. Court of Appeals, District of Columbia Circuit and U.S. Supreme Court. *Education:* Brown University (B.A., 1980); Boston University (J.D., magna cum laude, 1987). G. Joseph Tauro and Edward F. Hennessey Distinguished Scholar. Note and Case Editor, Boston University Law Review, 1986-1987. Recipient, American Jurisprudence Awards in Trial Advocacy, English Legal History, Torts, Labor Law, Land Use and Constitutional Takings. Law Clerk to Hon. Ernest C. Torres, U.S. District Court, District of Rhode Island, 1987-1988. Member: Intellectual Property, Antitrust and Litigation Sections, American Bar Association. *Member:* District of Columbia Bar Association; Federal Circuit Bar Association. ***PRACTICE AREAS:*** Intellectual Property; Patent; Antitrust; Commercial Litigation. ***Email:*** srobertson@hunton.com

PAULINE A. SCHNEIDER, born Bridgeton, New Jersey, May 25, 1943; admitted to bar, 1978, District of Columbia. *Education:* Glassboro State College (B.A., 1965); Syracuse University; Howard University (M.U.S., 1972); Yale University Law School (J.D., 1977). Staff Assistant, White House Office of Intergovernmental Affairs, 1978-1981 and Director, Office of Intergovernmental Relations, District of Columbia Government, 1983-1985. Secretary, 1986-1987, Board of Governors, 1988-1993, President-Elect, 1993-1994, President, 1994-1995, District of Columbia Bar. Council, Section on Legal Education and Admission to the Bar, 1999—, Accreditation Committee, 1989-1995, Chair, Election Law Committee, 1995-1997, Nominating Committee, 1998—, American Bar Association. Board of Directors, Economic Club of Washington, Access Group Inc. Chair, Federal City Council; Lab School of Washington; Joint Center for Political and Economic Studies; MedStar Health (formerly Medlantic Healthcare Group), Vice-Chair; National Partnership for Women & Families; Women's Legal Defense Fund Vice Chair. *Member:* National Association of Bond Lawyers; National Association of Securities Professionals; American Law Institute; American Bar Foundation. ***PRACTICE AREAS:*** Public Finance; Government Relations. ***Email:*** pschneider@hunton.com

ROBERT M. SCHULMAN, born Newark, New Jersey, May 6, 1958; admitted to bar, 1983, District of Columbia; registered to practice before U.S. Patent and Trademark Office. *Education:* Rutgers University (B.S., with honors in Biochemical Engineering, 1980); American University (J.D., 1983). Phi Alpha Delta. Author: "Genetic Screening and the Law," Medical Trial Technique Quarterly, Winter, 1984. *Member:* The District of Columbia Bar; American Bar Association; American Intellectual Property Law Association; Federation Internationale des Conseils en Propriété Intellectuelle (FICPI); American Institute of Chemical Engineers. ***LANGUAGES:*** French.

THOMAS J. SCOTT, JR., born Montgomery, Alabama, December 30, 1943; admitted to bar, 1974, Virginia; 1975, District of Columbia; 1980, New York, 1981, U.S. Tax Court; 1982, U.S. Claims Court and U.S. Court of Appeals for the Federal Circuit; 1984, U.S. Supreme Court; 1986, U.S. District Court for the District of Columbia; registered to practice before U.S. Patent and Trademark Office. *Education:* Yale University (B.E., Electrical Engineering, 1966; B.A., Economics, 1967); Vanderbilt University (J.D., with honors, 1974). Member, Moot Court Board. Co-Author, Publications: with John R. Alison, "Emerging Patent Infringement Problems for Government Contractors: Where Does the Buck Stop?" 3 Journal of Proprietary Rights 16, 1991; with Tyler S. Brown, "Inventions Abroad Warrant Careful Contracting," The National Law Journal, May 18, 1998; with Kevin J. Dunleavy and Tyler S. Brown, "Ownership of Patent Rights to Employee/Consultant Inventions or Other Technical Developments—A Growing Business Concern and a Trap for the Unwary," Hunton & Williams, July, 1999; with Kevin T. Duncan, "Buyer Beware: A Cross-Licence May Still Be Lurking," The National Law Journal, July 24, 2000. Author, Publication: *Guide to the Protection of Computer Software in the United States*, Hunton & Williams, March 1998, updated version issued September 2000. Trial Attorney, Patent Section, 1974-1978, Senior Trial Attorney, Intellectual Property Staff, Commercial Litigation Branch, 1980-1984, Senior Trial Counsel, Intellectual Property Staff, Commercial Litigation Branch, 1984-1985, Civil Division, Department of Justice. Partner, Pennie & Edmonds, Washington, D.C., 1985-1990. Partner, Howrey & Simon, Washington, D.C., 1990-1997. *Member:* The District of Columbia Bar; Virginia State Bar (Member, Patent, Trademark and Copyright Section); Federal and American Bar Associations; American Intellectual Property Law Association; New York Patent, Trademark and Copyright Law Association. [Capt., U.S.N.R. active duty, 1966-1971]. ***PRACTICE AREAS:*** Intellectual Property; Patent. ***Email:*** tscott@hunton.com

WILLIAM SILVERMAN, born Philadelphia, Pennsylvania, March 1, 1945; admitted to bar, 1969, Illinois; 1974, District of Columbia; 1980, U.S. Court of International Trade; 1982, U.S. Court of Appeals for the Federal Circuit. *Education:* University of Pennsylvania (B.A., 1966); University of Chicago (J.D., 1969). ***PRACTICE AREAS:*** International Trade. ***Email:*** wsilverman@hunton.com

LAURENCE E. SKINNER, born Fort Sill, Oklahoma, March 23, 1956; admitted to bar, 1984, Virginia (Not admitted in District of Columbia). *Education:* College of William & Mary (B.B.A., 1977); T. C. Williams School of Law, University of Richmond (J.D., magna cum laude, 1984). Phi Delta Phi. Member: McNeill Law Society; University of Richmond Law Review, 1983-1984. Certified Public Accountant, Virginia, 1981. ***PRACTICE AREAS:*** Energy; Project Finance and Development. ***Email:*** lskinner@hunton.com

(This Listing Continued)

TURNER T. SMITH, JR., born Washington, D.C., December 16, 1940; admitted to bar, 1968, Virginia; 1977, District of Columbia. *Education:* Princeton University (B.A., magna cum laude, 1962); Harvard Law School (LL.B., cum laude, 1968). Co-Author: European Community Desk Book, 1992. Co-Editor, Understanding U.S. and European Environmental Law -- A Practitioner's Guide, 1989. Associate Editor, Oxford Journal of Environmental Law, 1989—. Instructor: Environmental Law, College of William & Mary, 1979-1980; Washington & Lee Law School, 1978. Chairman: Environmental Controls Committee, Corporation, Banking and Business Law Section, American Bar Association, 1973-1980; Chairman, Standing Committee on Environmental Law, American Bar Association, 1983-1986; Chairman, 1997-1998, Secretary/Treasurer, 1992-1995 and Member, Board of Directors, Environmental Law Institute, 1989—. *Member:* International Bar Association. ***LANGUAGES:*** English and French. ***PRACTICE AREAS:*** Environmental; International Criminal Law. ***Email:*** tsmith@hunton.com

MICHAEL L. TEAGUE, born Alexandria, Virginia, October 3, 1948; admitted to bar, 1976, Virginia; 1977, District of Columbia. *Education:* University of Virginia (B.S.N.E., 1970; M.S.N.E., 1972; J.D., 1976). Phi Eta Sigma; Tau Beta Pi. Member, Board of Editors, Virginia Law Review, 1974-1976. ***PRACTICE AREAS:*** Environmental. ***Email:*** mteague@hunton.com

MARK G. WEISSHAAR, born Elgin, Illinois, April 1, 1950; admitted to bar, 1978, California; 1980, District of Columbia. *Education:* Yale University (B.A., 1972); George Washington University (J.D., 1977). Order of the Coif. Executive Editor, George Washington Law Review, 1976-1977. Law Clerk to the Hon. John Grady, U. S. District Court, Northern District of Illinois, 1977-1978. Associate Editor, Natural Resources & Environment, 1984-1986. ***PRACTICE AREAS:*** Environmental; Government Contracts. ***Email:*** mweisshaar@hunton.com

WILLIAM F. YOUNG, born New York, N.Y., January 6, 1948; admitted to bar, 1977, Virginia; 1988, District of Columbia. *Education:* University of Virginia (B.A., 1970); Harvard Law School (J.D., 1977). Phi Beta Kappa. Member, Raven Society. Member: Virginia District Export Council, 1983-1994; Boards of Governors, Antitrust Section, 1985-1989 and International Practice Section, 1985-1993 and Chairman, International Practice Section, Virginia State Bar, 1989-1990. Member: Antitrust Law and International Law and Practice Sections, American Bar Association; Energy Bar Association. ***PRACTICE AREAS:*** Antitrust; Energy. ***Email:*** byoung@hunton.com

LEE B. ZEUGIN, born Leavenworth, Kansas, December 30, 1952; admitted to bar, 1980, Virginia; 1994, District of Columbia. *Education:* University of Kansas (B.S.Ch.E., 1974); University of Michigan (J.D., 1979). Tau Beta Pi. ***PRACTICE AREAS:*** Environmental. ***Email:*** lzeugin@hunton.com

COUNSEL

RICHARD L. AGUGLIA, born Rochester, New York, July 11, 1945; admitted to bar, 1971, District of Columbia; 1978 Maryland. *Education:* St. Michael's College, University of Toronto (B.A., 1967); Catholic University (J.D., 1970). Delta Theta Phi. Author: "Legislative Limitations on Ad Valorem Taxation: Wheel of Fortune or Temple of Doom?" American Bar Association, Real Estate Journal; "Real Property Tax Assessments," The District of Columbia Bar Practice Manual, Revised, January 1989. Law Clerk to the Hon. W. Byron Sorrell, Superior Court, D.C., 1971-1972. Assistant Corporation Counsel, D.C. Tax Section, 1972-1979; Chief Finance Section, D.C. Office of Corporation Counsel, 1979-1986. Deputy Corporation Counsel, D.C., Community Development Division, 1986-1990. Chair, Land Use and Zoning Section, The District of Columbia Bar, 1994-1996. Member: D.C. Building Industry Association; Institute for Professionals in Taxation; Greater Washington Board of Trade. ***PRACTICE AREAS:*** Real Estate; Property Tax Appeals; Land Use; Zoning Law; Historic Preservation; State Taxation; Local Taxation; Administrative Law. ***Email:*** raguglia@hunton.com

THOMAS E. ANDERSON, born Binghamton, New York, December 27, 1962; admitted to bar, 1996, New York, Massachusetts, U.S. District Court, District of Massachusetts, U.S. Court of Appeals, First Circuit and U.S. Court of Appeals for the Federal Circuit; 1997, District of Columbia; registered to practice before U.S. Patent and Trademark Office. *Education:* Rochester Institute of Technology (B.S.E.E., 1986); Syracuse University (M.S.E.E., 1989); Seton Hall University School of Law (J.D., 1995). *Member:* The District of Columbia Bar; Massachusetts, New York State and American Bar Associations; American Intellectual Property Law Association; Boston Patent Law Association; Institute of Electrical and Electronic Engineers; Northern Virginia Technology Council. ***PRACTICE AREAS:*** Patents; Trademarks; Copyrights; Electronic Commerce; Intellectual Property Licensing.

KENNETH A. BARRY, born Fort Lauderdale, Florida, October 2, 1948; admitted to bar, 1974, New York; 1978, Virginia (Not admitted in District of Columbia). *Education:* University of Virginia (B.A., magna cum laude, 1970; M.A., 1971; J.D., 1974). Phi Beta Kappa. *Member:* Virginia State Bar (Member, Administrative Law Section); Energy Bar Association (Member, Electronic Commerce Subcommittee). ***LANGUAGES:*** French. ***PRACTICE AREAS:*** Energy Regulation; Energy Litigation; Energy Contracts; Electric Power; Natural Gas; Oil and Gas Law. ***Email:*** kbarry@hunton.com

FRED H. CATE, born McRae, Georgia, May 20, 1963; admitted to bar, 1987, California; 1988, District of Columbia; 1998, Indiana; registered to practice before U.S. Patent and Trademark Office. *Education:* Stanford University (A.B., 1984; J.D., 1987). Phi Beta Kappa. Author: "Privacy in the Information Age," Brookings, 1997; "The Internet and the First Amendment," Phi Delta Kappa, 1998; "Privacy in Perspective," AEI Press, 2001. Professor of Law, Indiana University School of Law, Bloomington, 1990—. *Member:* Indiana State and American Bar Associations; The District of Columbia Bar; State Bar of California; Federal Communications Bar Association. ***PRACTICE AREAS:*** Information and Privacy; Intellectual Property; Communications Law.

JENNIFER HINKEBEIN CULOTTA, born Louisville, Kentucky, November, 19, 1962; admitted to bar, 1988, Louisiana; 1994, U.S. District Court, Western District of Louisiana (Not admitted in District of Columbia). *Education:* University of Louisville, (B.A., cum laude, 1984, J.D., 1987). Phi Kappa Pi. Omicron Delta Kappa. Mortar Board. American Jurisprudence Book Award in Domestic Relations. Listed in Who's Who and Outstanding Young Women in America. Instructor, National Academy, Federal Law Enforcement Training Center, 1996—. *Member:* Baton Rouge and Louisiana State Bar Associations. ***PRACTICE AREAS:*** Litigation.

CRAIG S. HARRISON, born Santa Monica, California, May 22, 1948; admitted to bar, 1984, Hawaii; 1989, District of Columbia. *Education:* University of California at Berkeley (B.A., great distinction, 1970); Humboldt State University (M.A., 1974); University of Hawaii (J.D., 1984). Phi Beta Kappa. Author: "Midkiff v. Tom: The Constitutionality of Hawaii's Land Reform Act," 6 Hawaii Law Review 561, 1984; "A Marine Sanctuary in the Northwestern Hawaiian Island: An Idea Whose Time Has Come," 25 Natural Resources Journal 317, 1985. ***PRACTICE AREAS:*** Environmental. ***Email:*** charrison@hunton.com

DOUGLAS J. HEFFNER, born Detroit, Michigan, June 20, 1957; admitted to bar, 1983, Michigan; 1985, District of Columbia. *Education:* Albion College (B.A., 1979); University of Detroit-Mercy (J.D., 1983) Franco-American Graduate Fellowship; Georgetown University (LL.M., 1985). Franco-American Fellowship. Editor, University of Detroit-Mercy Law Review. *Member:* State Bar of Michigan; The District of Columbia Bar. ***PRACTICE AREAS:*** International Law. ***Email:*** dheffner@hunton.com

LUCINDA MINTON LANGWORTHY, born Paris, France, January 3, 1956; admitted to bar, 1981, District of Columbia. *Education:* Bucknell University (B.A., cum laude, 1978); George Washington University (J.D., with honors, 1981). Staff Member, George Washington Law Review, 1979-1981. Law Clerk to the Atomic Safety & Licensing Board Panel, U. S. Nuclear Regulatory Commission, 1981-1983. Member, Sections on: Natural Resources Energy and Environmental Law; Administrative Law, American Bar Association. *Member:* Prettyman-Leventhal American Inn of Court; Air & Waste Management Association. ***PRACTICE AREAS:*** Environmental. ***Email:*** clangworthy@hunton.com

MAIDA ORINGHER LERNER, born New York, N.Y., December 15, 1952; admitted to bar, 1977, New York and U.S. District Court, Eastern and Southern Districts of New York; 1982, U.S. Court of Appeals, 2nd Circuit and U.S. Supreme Court; 1984, District of Columbia. *Education:* State University of New York at Albany (B.A., summa cum laude, 1973); Boston University School of Law (J.D., 1976). Recipient, American Jurisprudence Award in Bankruptcy. ***PRACTICE AREAS:*** Environmental. ***Email:*** mlerner@hunton.com

JOHN J. RHODES, born Council Grove, Kansas, September 18, 1916; admitted to bar, 1942, Kansas; 1945, Arizona; 1962, District of Columbia. *Education:* Kansas State University (B.S., 1938); Harvard University (LL.B., 1941). Blue Key. Author: "Labor Court," University of Arizona Law Review, 1971; "The Futile System," EPM Publications, Inc., 1976; "The Far Side of the Hill," Foreign Affairs, December, 1982. Member, U. S. House of Representatives, 1953-1983. House Minority Leader, 1973-1981. International President, Beta Theta Pi Fraternity, 1984-1987. President, U. S. Association of Former Members of Congress, 1990. Permanent Chairman, Republican National Conventions, 1976 and 1980, American Bar. *Member:* Kansas Bar Association; State Bar of Arizona; District of Columbia Bar. [USAF, 1941-1946; USAR, 1947-1965]. ***PRACTICE AREAS:*** Energy. ***Email:*** jjrhodes@hunton.com

JOHN J. RHODES, III, admitted to bar, 1968, Arizona; 1995, District of Columbia. *Education:* Yale University (B.A., 1965); University of Arizona (J.D., 1968). Member, U.S. House of Representative, First District, Arizona, 1987-1993. Member: Interior and Insular Affairs Energy and Environment Subcommittee, 1987-1993; Ranking Republican, 1991-1993; Water and Power Resources Subcommittee, 1987-1993; National Parks and Public Lands Subcommittee, 1987-1993; Science, Space and Technology Committee, 1990-1993; Space Subcommittee, Small Business Committee, 1987-1990; Republican Policy Committee, 1987-1993; Ad Hoc Task Forces on Campaign Reform, Health Care; House Rules Reform. Chairman, Republican Task Force on Indian Affairs. Representative, Central Arizona Water Conservation District. Repre-

(This Listing Continued)

HUNTON & WILLIAMS, Washington—Continued

sentative, San Carlos (Arizona) Irrigation and Drainage District. Representative, Imperial Irrigation California District. [with U.S. Army, 1968-1970]. ***PRACTICE AREAS:*** Environmental; Natural Resources; Federal Legislative Practice. ***Email:*** jrhodes@hunton.com

LINDA L. WALSH, born New Haven, Connecticut, December 21, 1960; admitted to bar, 1987, Connecticut; 1988, New York; 1992, District of Columbia. *Education:* University of Connecticut (B.A., 1982); University of Hartford (M.A., 1984); Syracuse University (J.D., cum laude, 1987). Author: "Stranded Costs: The Evidentiary Burden of Showing Reasonable Expectation," CCH Power and Telecom Law, July/Aug. 1998. Co-Author: "Antitrust Law Regulation: A New Focus for a Competitive Energy Industry," Energy Law Journal, Spring 2000. *Member:* Energy Bar Association (Member, Board of Directors, 2001—; Co-Chair, Program Committee, 2000-2001). ***PRACTICE AREAS:*** Public Utility Regulation; Electric Industry Restructuring. ***Email:*** lwalsh@hunton.com

O. JULIA WELLER, born Montreal, Quebec, September 21, 1949; admitted to bar, 1979, District of Columbia. *Education:* McGill University (B.A., 1970; LL.B., Second Class Honors, 1978); Carleton University (B.J., honors, 1971); Georgetown University (LL.M., 1979). *Member:* American Bar Association; Energy Bar Association; Women's Council on Energy and the Environment. ***LANGUAGES:*** French, German. ***PRACTICE AREAS:*** Energy; International; Regulatory Reform; Privatization; Project Finance. ***Email:*** jweller@hunton.com

SUSAN FRIER WILTSIE, born Cleveland, Ohio, July 5, 1962; admitted to bar, 1989, Virginia; 1991, District of Columbia; U.S. Court of Appeals, Fourth Circuit; U.S. Court of Appeals for the District of Columbia Circuit; U.S. District Court for the District of Columbia; U.S. District Court, District of Maryland; U.S. District Court, Eastern and Western Districts of Virginia. *Education:* College of William & Mary (B.A., 1984); Wake Forest University (J.D., cum laude, 1989). Faculty Law Scholar. Articles Editor, Wake Forest Law Review, 1988-1989. *Member:* Virginia and American (Member, Sections on: Labor and Employment; Occupation Safety and Health) Bar Associations; Women's Bar Association. ***PRACTICE AREAS:*** Labor and Employment. ***Email:*** swiltsie@hunton.com

ASSOCIATES

REL S. AMBROZY, born Jersey City, New Jersey, March 10, 1961; admitted to bar, 1995, Maryland; 1996, District of Columbia. *Education:* Wake Forest University (B.S., Biology-Mathematics, 1983); University of Miami (M.S., Biomedical Engineering, 1989); Catholic University (J.D., 1995). Beta Beta Beta. Co-Author: "Copyright Antitrust and Misuse in the Wake of MAI Systems and Virtual Maintenance," 18 Computer Law Reporter 746, December, 1993. *Member:* The District of Columbia Bar; Federal Circuit and American (Chair, Committee 105, Government Relations To Patents, 1999; Chair, Committee 104, Patents Other Than Patent Contracts, 1998) Bar Associations; American Intellectual Property Law Association; Licensing Executives Society. ***PRACTICE AREAS:*** Litigation; Licensing; Electronic Commerce.

SCOTT D. BALDERSTON, born Trenton, New Jersey, December 10, 1963; admitted to bar, 1989, Pennsylvania and New Jersey; registered to practice before U.S. Patent and Trademark Office (Not admitted in District of Columbia). *Education:* Villanova University (B.E.E., summa cum laude, 1986); University of Pennsylvania (J.D., cum laude, 1989). Phi Kappa Phi. National Merit Scholar. Recipient, Dean's Award for Academic Achievement. ***PRACTICE AREAS:*** Intellectual Property.

PAUL A. BALLONOFF, born Cleveland, Ohio, April 3, 1943; admitted to bar, 1992, California (Not admitted in District of Columbia). *Education:* University of California at Los Angeles (B.A., 1964, Ph.D., 1970); California State University at Sacramento (J.D., 1991). *Member:* State Bar of California. ***LANGUAGES:*** Spanish. ***PRACTICE AREAS:*** Energy; General.

CARL LYNFORD BENSON, born West Chester, Pennsylvania, December 20, 1966; admitted to bar, 1999, Maryland; registered to practice before the U.S. Patent and Trademark Office (Not admitted in District of Columbia). *Education:* Webb Institute of Naval Architecture; University of Michigan (B.S.E., 1990) Georgetown University (J.D., cum laude, 1999). *Member:* Maryland State Bar Association; American Intellectual Property Law Association. ***PRACTICE AREAS:*** Intellectual Property; Patent Prosecution; Counseling.

BETHANY M. BURNS, born Fort Lauderdale, Florida, March 26, 1969; admitted to bar, 1997, Maryland; 1998, District of Columbia. *Education:* Virginia Polytechnic Institute and State University (B.A., 1991); Columbus School of Law at Catholic University (J.D., cum laude, 1997). Author, "Reforming the Newspaper Industry: Achieving First Amendment Goals of Diversity through Structural Regulation," Issue 1, CommLaw Conspectus: Journal of Communications Law and Policy.

BRIAN MARK BUROKER, born Bellefontaine, Ohio, August 5, 1969; admitted to bar, 1996, Virginia and U.S. Court of Appeals, Fourth Circuit; 1997,

(This Listing Continued)

District of Columbia, U.S. Court of Appeals, Federal Circuit and U.S. Court of Federal Claims. *Education:* North Carolina State University (B.S.E.E., cum laude, 1992; B.S., Comp.E., cum laude, 1992); Georgetown University (J.D., magna cum laude, 1996).

GABRIEL CALVO, born Buenos Aires, Argentina, March 10, 1969; admitted to bar, 1999, Virginia; 2000, District of Columbia. *Education:* Duke University (A.B., 1991; M.E.M., 1995); Georgetown University (J.D., 1999). Contributions Editor, Duke Environmental Law and Policy Forum, 1994-1995. Lead Articles Editor, The Tax Lawyer, 1996. ***LANGUAGES:*** Spanish. ***PRACTICE AREAS:*** Environmental Law.

KENNETH C. CESTARI, born Oceanside, New York, September 20, 1963; admitted to bar, 1994, Virginia; 1998, District of Columbia. *Education:* Bucknell University (B.A., 1986); University of Richmond (J.D., cum laude, 1994). McNeil Law Society. *Member:* Virginia State Bar; Virginia and American Bar Associations. [1st Lt., U. S. Army, 1986-1990, Capt., U. S. Army Reserves, 1990-2001]. ***PRACTICE AREAS:*** Real Estate; Project Development; Project Finance; Corporate. ***Email:*** kcastari@hunton.com

PETER M. CLEVELAND, born Boston, Massachusetts, May 15, 1965; admitted to bar, 2000, District of Columbia. *Education:* Columbia University (B.A., 1987); Georgetown University (J.D., 1997). *Member:* The District of Columbia Bar. ***PRACTICE AREAS:*** Project Development; Finance and Leasing.

WILLIAM WOODHOUSE DAVIS, born Fullerton, California, August 2, 1969; admitted to bar, 2000, Virginia (Not admitted in District of Columbia). *Education:* Washington & Lee University (B.A., Economics, 1992); Wake Forest University (J.D., 2000; M.B.A., 2000). ***PRACTICE AREAS:*** International Project Finance; Domestic Project Finance; Leveraged Lease Financing.

DEIDRE G. DUNCAN, born Bloomington, Indiana, February 1, 1971; admitted to bar, 1996, Ohio; 1999, District of Columbia. *Education:* Duke University (A.B., cum laude, 1993); University of Cincinnati (J.D., 1996). Order of the Coif. Articles Editor, University of Cincinnati Law Review. [Capt., U.S. Army, 1996-2000]. ***PRACTICE AREAS:*** Environmental Law; Land Use.

DOUGLAS DZIAK, born Sheffield Village, Ohio, 1970; admitted to bar, 1999, Maryland; 2000, District of Columbia and U.S. District Court, District of Maryland. *Education:* Ohio University (A.B., summa cum laude, 1993; M.A., 1995); College of William & Mary School of Law (J.D., 1999). Articles Editor, College of William & Mary, Environmental Law & Policy Review. *Member:* Maryland State and American (Member, Antitrust Division) Bar Associations; The District of Columbia Bar. ***PRACTICE AREAS:*** Antitrust; International Trade; Regulatory Litigation.

DAVID D'ZURILLA, born Trenton, New Jersey, November, 27, 1959; admitted to bar, 1991, Virginia and U.S. Court of Appeals for the Fourth Circuit; 1992, District of Columbia and U.S. Court of Appeals for the Federal Circuit; 1997, U.S. Court of Veterans Appeals; registered to practice before U.S. Patent and Trademark Office. *Education:* Pennsylvania State University (B.S., Food Science, 1982); Trenton State College (B.S., Computer Science, 1985); American University (J.D., 1991). Member, Giles S. Rich American Inn of Court. *Member:* Bar Association of the District of Columbia (Programs and Meetings Chair, Patent, Trademark and Copyright Section, 1996-1998; Treasurer, 1998; Chair-Elect, 1999; Chair, 2000); Federal Circuit Bar Association; American Intellectual Property Law Association; Institute of Food Technologists (Food Law and Regulations, Product Development and Biotechnology Divisions). ***Email:*** dd'zurilla@hunton.com

ROBERT H. EDWARDS, JR., born Brooklyn, New York, April 18, 1961; admitted to bar, 1991, New York; 1994, District of Columbia. *Education:* Harvard University (A.B., magna cum laude, 1983); Stanford Graduate School of Business (M.B.A., 1990); Stanford University (J.D., 1990). Recipient, Hilmer Oehlmann, Jr., Award for Excellence in Legal Research and Writing. Associate Managing Editor, Stanford Journal of International Law. Co-Author: "International Legal Developments in Review 2000- Business Regulation Division," The International Lawyer, forthcoming; "International Legal Developments in Review, 1998- Business Regulation Division," The International Lawyers, Vol. 33, No. 2, Summer, 1999; "Towards a More Comprehensive World Trade Organization Agreement on Trade Related Investment Measures," Stanford Journal of International Law, Vol.33, No.2, Summer, 1997. *Member:* New York State and American (Co-Chair and Assistant Budget Office, International Investment and Development Committee, International Law and Practice Section) Bar Associations; District of Columbia Bar. ***LANGUAGES:*** French. ***PRACTICE AREAS:*** Project Finance; Energy Acquisitions; Divestitures.

JAMES D. ELLIOTT, born Philadelphia, Pennsylvania, November 30, 1967; admitted to bar, 1996, West Virginia, U.S. District Court, Southern District of West Virginia and West Virginia Supreme Court of Appeals; 2000, District of Columbia. *Education:* Bucknell University (B.A., 1990); Pace University School of Law (J.D., 1996). Editor-in-Chief, Environmental Law Review, 1995-1996. Member, Environmental Moot Court Board. Author: "Electric Utility Regulation Reform in New York: Economic Competitiveness at the

(This Listing Continued)

Expense of the Environment," 13.1 Pace Envtl. L. Rev. 281 (1995). *Member:* Kanawha County Bar Association; West Virginia State Bar; The District of Columbia Bar. ***PRACTICE AREAS:*** Environmental; Litigation; Energy.

H. MALLOY EVANS, III, born Cheraw, South Carolina, June 23, 1973; admitted to bar, 2001, Virginia (Not admitted in District of Columbia). *Education:* Davidson College (B.S., 1995); Washington & Lee University (J.D., cum laude, 2001).

OZZIE A. FARRES, born Miami Beach, Florida, June 28, 1969; admitted to bar, 1998, Florida; 1999, U.S. Court of Appeals, Eleventh and Federal Circuits and U.S. District Court, Southern District of Florida; registered to practice before U.S. Patent and Trademark Office (Not admitted in District of Columbia). *Education:* Florida State University (B.S., 1994); Franklin Pierce Law Center (Certificate, Intellectual Property Summer Institute, 1996); Florida International University (B.S.E.E., 1998); University of Miami (J.D., cum laude, 1998). Omicron Delta Epsilon. Member, University of Miami Business Law Journal, 1996-1998. *Member:* American Intellectual Property Law Association. ***LANGUAGES:*** Spanish. ***PRACTICE AREAS:*** Intellectual Property Litigation.

RICHARD P. FERRIN, born Bartlesville, Oklahoma, October 31, 1961; admitted to bar, 1997, New York and U.S. Court of International Trade; 1998, District of Columbia. *Education:* Northwestern University (B.A., 1985); American University (J.D., 1996). Staff Member, 1994-1995 and Federal Circuit Editor, 1995-1996, American University Law Review. *Member:* The District of Columbia Bar. ***PRACTICE AREAS:*** International Trade Regulation (100%). ***Email:*** rferrin@hunton.com

THOMAS M. FINAN, born Laguna Beach, California, February 24, 1970; admitted to bar, 1996, New Jersey and U.S. District Court, District of New Jersey; 1997, District of Columbia. *Education:* University of Virginia (B.A., with high distinction, 1992); University of Minnesota (J.D., cum laude, 1996). Phi Beta Kappa; Member, National Moot Court Competition Team; Echols Scholar. Law Clerk to The Honorable James A Kennedy, New Jersey Superior Court, 1996-1997. *Member:* Bar Association of the District of Columbia; American Bar Association. ***PRACTICE AREAS:*** Telecommunications Litigation. ***Email:*** tfinan@hunton.com

FRANCINE E. FRIEDMAN, born Washington, D.C., May 13, 1973; admitted to bar, 1999, Virginia and Maryland; 2000, District of Columbia. *Education:* Georgetown University (B.A., 1995); College of William & Mary (J.D., 1999). ***PRACTICE AREAS:*** Commercial Litigation. ***Email:*** ffriedman@hunton.com

DARRIN LEWIS GLYMPH, born Brooklyn, New York, May 29, 1964; admitted to bar, 1994, Virginia; 1999, District of Columbia. *Education:* Williams College (B.A., 1985); Tulane University of Louisiana (J.D., 1993). Director, Industrial Development Authority of the City of Richmond, Virginia, 1997-1998. ***PRACTICE AREAS:*** Public Finance; Real Estate.

MATTHEW FALK GOLDBERG, born Evanston, Illinois, July 4, 1972; admitted to bar, 1997, Maryland (Not admitted in District of Columbia). *Education:* Haverford College (B.A., 1994); Northwestern University (J.D., 1997). ***PRACTICE AREAS:*** Environmental; Administrative.

GLORIA J. HALSTEAD, born High Point, North Carolina, November 17; admitted to bar, 2001, District of Columbia. *Education:* Wake Forest University (B.A., cum laude, 1969); Duke University; American University (J.D.). Phi Sigma Iota; Phi Alpha Theta. George Foster Hankins Scholar. Recipient: Forrest Clonts Award for Excellence in History; Duke Scholarship; Natural Resources Award. *Member:* The District of Columbia Bar (Member, Sections on: Energy and Environment; Litigation; Energy Bar Association (Member, Committees on: Alternative Dispute Resolution; Electric Utilities Committees); Women's Council on Energy and the Environment.

JEFFREY B. HARDIE, born Williamsburg, Virginia, November 26, 1962; admitted to bar, 1994, Virginia; 1995, U. S. District Court, Eastern District of Virginia; 1996, District of Columbia. *Education:* Virginia Polytechnic Institute and State University (B.A., 1985); Tulane University of Louisiana (J.D., 1994).

DAVID STUART HARLOW, born Richmond Virginia, March 1, 1960; admitted to bar, 1986, Virginia; 1997, District of Columbia. *Education:* College of William & Mary (B.A., 1982); University of Virginia School of Law (J.D., 1986). Co-Author, "Complying with the CFC Prohibitions of the Clean Air Act: A Guide for HVAC Compliance," Government Institutes, 1994.

SCOT A. HINSHAW, born Tucson, Arizona, May 10, 1974; admitted to bar, 1999, Maryland; 2000, District of Columbia. *Education:* University of Maryland (B.A., 1996); Georgetown University (J.D., 1999). Member, Georgetown Barristers, 1998-1999. Member, American Criminal Law Review, 1997-1999. Instructor, Trial Advocacy, Georgetown University Law Center, 2000 . ***PRACTICE AREAS:*** Labor and Employment; Litigation.

THOMAS M. HUGHES, admitted to bar, 1996, Massachusetts; 1998, District of Columbia. *Education:* Bryant College (B.A., 1987); Suffolk University (J.D., magna cum laude, 1996). Member, Suffolk University Law Review, 1994-1995. [1st Lt. U.S. Army, 1987-1990]

(This Listing Continued)

MAKRAM JABER, born Beirut, Lebanon, January 1, 1963; admitted to bar, 1996, Georgia; 1998, District of Columbia; 1999, U.S. Court of Appeals for the District of Columbia Circuit. *Education:* American University of Beirut (B.E., 1984); Emory University, School of Law (J.D., first honor, 1996); University of California, Berkeley (M.S., 1985; Ph.D., 1989). Order of the Coif. Recipient of 7 Amjur Awards. Law Clerk to Hon. Stanley F. Birch, Jr., U.S. Court of Appeals, Eleventh Circuit, 1996-1997. Executive Articles Editor, Emory University Law Review, 1995-1996. Licensed Professional Engineer, Georgia, 1992; Maryland, 1992. Author: "Unfunded Mandates: An Issue of Federalism or a 'Brilliant Sound Bite'?," 45 Emory L.J. 281 (1996). American Society of Civil Engineers, 1985—. *Member:* District of Columbia Bar; State Bar of Georgia. ***LANGUAGES:*** Arabic and French. ***PRACTICE AREAS:*** Environmental Law. ***Email:*** mjaber@hunton.com

HERBERT V. KERNER, born Fort Sill, Oklahoma, January 1, 1969; admitted to bar, 1994, North Carolina; 1999, District of Columbia; registered to practice before U.S. Patent and Trademark Office. *Education:* Campbell University (B.A., 1991); Loyola University (J.D., 1994); Tulane University (B.S., 1995). ***PRACTICE AREAS:*** Patent Prosecution; Licensing; Litigation.

RYAN T. KETCHUM, born 1973; admitted to bar, 1998, Virginia; 2000, District of Columbia. *Education:* College of William & Mary (J.D., 1998). Law Clerk to the Hon. Henry H. Whiting, Supreme Court of Virginia, 1998-1999. ***PRACTICE AREAS:*** Project Development; Finance; Leasing. ***Email:*** rketchum@hunton.com

GREGORY L. KINZELMAN, born Columbus, Ohio; admitted to bar, 1995, New York; 1996, District of Columbia. *Education:* University of Notre Dame (B.A., 1989); University of Virginia (J.D., 1993); University of Oxford (M.A., 1997). ***PRACTICE AREAS:*** Antitrust; Competition Law; International Trade; Litigation; Election Law.

RAYMOND KRNCEVIC, born Cleveland, Ohio, December 17, 1973; admitted to bar, 1998, Ohio and U.S. District Court, Northern District of Ohio; 2001, District of Columbia. *Education:* Northwestern University (B.A., 1995); University of Virginia (J.D., 1998). *Member:* Bar Association of the District of Columbia; Ohio State and American Bar Associations. ***LANGUAGES:*** German.

LEWIS E. LAMB III, born Winston-Salem, North Carolina, April 18, 1962; admitted to bar, 1993, North Carolina; 1994, U.S. District Court, Eastern, Middle and Western Districts of North Carolina; 1995, District of Columbia; 1997, Georgia. *Education:* Georgetown University (B.A., 1988); Cambridge University, Cambridge, England (M.Phil., 1989); University of North Carolina (J.D., 1993). Member, 1991-1992 and Articles Editor, 1992-1993, North Carolina Journal of International Law and Commercial Regulation. Author: "Cruz v. Chesapeake Shipping, Inc.: Statutory Interpretation or Non-Statutory Choice of Laws - What is the Proper Juristic Standard When International Political Objectives and Federal Law Intersect?" 17 North Carolina Journal of International Law and Commercial Regulation, 341, 1992; "Information and Enhanced Services: A Retrospective of Regulated and Unregulated Services and an Examination of Their Treatment and Policy," Ablex Publishing Corporation, 1998 (Co-Author). *Member:* International Trademark Association (INTA); Federal Communications Bar Association (FCBA). ***LANGUAGES:*** French and Russian. ***PRACTICE AREAS:*** Trademarks; Copyrights; Internet Law; Unfair Competition.

BRADLEY T. LENNIE, born Middletown, Ohio, 1968; admitted to bar, 1995, Maryland; 1998, District of Columbia. *Education:* University of Wisconsin-Madison (B.A., with distinction, 1991); American University (J.D., 1995). ***PRACTICE AREAS:*** Litigation; Intellectual Property. ***Email:*** blennie@hunton.com

R. ANDREW LIEN, born Oakland, California, October 15, 1969; admitted to bar, 1999, California; 2000, District of Columbia. *Education:* University of California at Santa Cruz (B.A., with honors, 1992); Boston University (J.D., 1998; M.A., 1999). Managing Editor, Boston University International Law Journal, 1997-1998. Author, "Still Thirsting: Prospects for a Multilateral Treaty on the Tigris and Euphrates Rivers Following the Adoption of the United Nations Convention on International Watercourses," 16 BU Int'l L.J. 273 (1998). ***LANGUAGES:*** French. ***PRACTICE AREAS:*** Project Finance; Leasing. ***Email:*** alien@hunton.com

JONATHAN LINK, born Owosso, Michigan, 1972; admitted to bar, 1998, Virginia; 1999, District of Columbia; registered to practice before the U.S. Patent and Trademark Office. *Education:* University of Illinois (B.S.E.E., 1994); George Mason University School of Law (J.D., 1998). ***PRACTICE AREAS:*** Intellectual Property Litigation; Prosecuting; Licensing. ***Email:*** jlink@hunton.com

PETER J. LOUGHLIN, born Kingston, New York, July 28, 1968; admitted to bar, 1998, New York; 2000, California (Not admitted in District of Columbia). *Education:* St. Alphonsus College (B.A., summa cum laude, 1990); University of Notre Dame (J.D., magna cum laude, 1997). [U.S. Navy JAGC, 1997-2001; Lieut.]. ***PRACTICE AREAS:*** Litigation; Intellectual Property; Antitrust. ***Email:*** ploughlin@hunton.com

(This Listing Continued)

HUNTON & WILLIAMS, Washington—Continued

AUDREY C. LOUISON, born Taunton, Massachusetts, May 2, 1958; admitted to bar, 1994, Virginia and Massachusetts (Not admitted in District of Columbia). *Education:* Georgetown University; Boston College (J.D., cum laude, 1994). (Also at Richmond, Virginia Office). ***Email:*** alouison@hunton.com

TYLER MADDRY, born Ann Arbor, Michigan, January 12, 1966; admitted to bar, 1995, Virginia; 1997, New York; registered to practice before U.S. Patent and Trademark Office (Not admitted in District of Columbia). *Education:* Harvard University (A.B., cum laude, 1988); George Washington University (J.D., with honors, 1995). Burns Doane Swecker & Mathis, Alexandria, Virginia, 1994-1996. Patent Attorney, General Electric Co., Schenectady, New York, 1997—. *Member:* New York State Bar Association (Member, Intellectual Property Section, 1998—); American Intellectual Property Law Association. ***PRACTICE AREAS:*** Patent and Technology Licensing; Patent Prosecution; Patent Litigation.

DAVID T. McINDOE, born Boston, Massachusetts, February 12, 1972; admitted to bar, 1998, Virginia (Not admitted in District of Columbia). *Education:* Dartmouth College (B.A., 1994); Washington & Lee University (J.D., 1998). ***Email:*** dmcindoe@hunton.com

DAVID H. MILLIGAN, born Washington, D.C., February 16, 1974; admitted to bar, 1999, Virginia; registered to practice before U.S. Patent and Trademark Office (Not admitted in District of Columbia). *Education:* University of Nebraska (B.S., Biological Systems Engineering, 1996); George Washington University (J.D., 1999). ***PRACTICE AREAS:*** Patent Prosecution. ***Email:*** dmilligan@hunton.com

DEVIN S. MORGAN, born Rochester, New York, April 19, 1974; admitted to bar, 1999, Virginia; 2000, District of Columbia; registered to practice before U.S. Patent and Trademark Office. *Education:* Dartmouth College (B.A., 1996); Franklin Pierce Law Center (J.D., 1999; M.I.P., 1999). ***PRACTICE AREAS:*** Intellectual Property. ***Email:*** dmorgan@hunton.com

TED J. MURPHY, born Rockville Centre, New York, October 9, 1971; admitted to bar, 1996, New York; 1998, District of Columbia. *Education:* State University of New York, Albany (B.A., 1992); University of Virginia (J.D., 1995). ***PRACTICE AREAS:*** Energy Regulation. ***Email:*** tmurphy@hunton.com

ANDREW H. MURRAY, born Erie, Pennsylvania, June 28, 1974; admitted to bar, 1999, California; 2000, District of Columbia. *Education:* George Washington University (B.A., cum laude, 1996); Georgetown University Law School (J.D., 1999). ***PRACTICE AREAS:*** Project Finance; Lease Finance.

KERRY H. OWENS, born Washington, D.C., May 16, 1963; admitted to bar, 1994, Maryland; registered to practice before U.S. Patent and Trademark Office (Not admitted in District of Columbia). *Education:* University of Wisconsin-Madison (B.S., 1985); B.S.E.M., 1989); George Washington University (J.D., 1994). *Member:* American Intellectual Property Law Association. ***LANGUAGES:*** German. ***PRACTICE AREAS:*** Patents; Trademarks; Trade Secrets; Copyrights. ***Email:*** kowen@hunton.com

BETH H. REGAS, born Silver Spring, Maryland, May 20, 1965; admitted to bar, 1995, Massachusetts and Colorado; 1997, District of Columbia and U.S. District Court, District of Colorado. *Education:* University of Vermont (B.A., 1987); Vermont Law School (J.D., cum laude, 1994).

RICHARD A. RICE, JR., born Atlanta, Georgia, December 4, 1968; admitted to bar, 1994, Virginia; 1997, U.S. Court of Appeals for the Armed Forces; 1998, U.S. Supreme Court; 1999, District of Columbia and U.S. District Court, Eastern District of Virginia. *Education:* University of Georgia (B.A., 1990); University of Notre Dame (J.D., 1994). White Scholar. Managing Editor, Journal of Law, Ethics & Public Policy. [Lt., U.S. Navy, 1994-1998]. ***PRACTICE AREAS:*** White Collar Criminal Defense; Commercial Litigation; Products Liability.

ADAM J. ROSSER, born Newton, Massachusetts, December 6, 1971; admitted to bar, 2001, District of Columbia. *Education:* Franklin Pierce College; Boston College (B.A., 1995); Georgetown University Law Center (J.D., cum laude, 1999). *Member:* District of Columbia Bar. ***PRACTICE AREAS:*** Immigration; Nationality. ***Email:*** arosser@hunton.com

STEPHEN T. SCHREINER, born Ford Ord, California, June 5, 1964; admitted to bar, 1997, Virginia; registered to practice before U.S. Patent and Trademark Office (Not admitted in District of Columbia). *Education:* Virginia Polytechnic Institute and State University (B.S.E.E., cum laude, 1987); Georgetown University (J.D., magna cum laude, 1997). Order of the Coif. Recipient, Marshall Hahn Engineering Scholarship. *Member:* American Bar Association; American Intellectual Property Lawyers Association. ***PRACTICE AREAS:*** Patent; Trade Secret; Copyright.

ELIZABETH (NENA) C. SHAW, born Madrid, Spain, May 5, 1970; admitted to bar, 1999, Florida; 2000, District of Columbia. *Education:* University of Michigan (B.S., 1992); Duke University (J.D., 1999). ***PRACTICE AREAS:*** Environmental Law. ***Email:*** nshaw@hunton.com

(This Listing Continued)

JAMES R. SIMOES, born Providence, Rhode Island, October 28, 1972; admitted to bar, 1998, Virginia (Not admitted in District of Columbia). *Education:* Boston University (B.S., 1994); George Washington University (J.D., 1998).

YISUN SONG, born Seoul, Korea, March 6, 1972; admitted to bar, 2000, Virginia; 2001, District of Columbia; registered to practice before U.S. Patent and Trademark Office. *Education:* University of Maryland (B.S.E.E., cum laude, 1994); George Washington University (J.D., with honors, 2000). Tau Beta Pi. ***PRACTICE AREAS:*** Patents.

LINDA C. TREES, born Washington, D.C., April 2, 1962; admitted to bar, 1992, Virginia; 1994, District of Columbia and U.S. Court of Appeals for the District of Columbia Circuit. *Education:* Smith College (A.B., cum laude, 1984); University of Wisconsin (M.A., 1989); College of William & Mary (J.D., 1992). Order of the Coif. Law Clerk to the Hon. Sam W. Coleman, III, Court of Appeals of Virginia, 1992-1993. Member, Section of Natural Resources, Energy and Environmental Law, American Bar Association. ***LANGUAGES:*** Russian; German. ***Email:*** ltrees@hunton.com

ANDREW J. TURNER, born Spokane, Washington, November 9, 1966; admitted to bar, 1992, Pennsylvania; 1998, U.S. Supreme Court; 2000, U.S. Court of Appeals for the District of Columbia; 2001, District of Columbia and U.S. District Court for the District of Columbia. *Education:* Florida Atlantic University (B.B.A., 1988); West Virginia University (J.D., 1992); George Washington University (LL.M., 2000). Treasurer, West Virginia University College of Law Environmental Law Society, 1990-1992. Member, West Virginia Law Review. *Member:* American Bar Association. [Captain, U.S. Air Force, 1993-1999]. ***PRACTICE AREAS:*** Environmental Law; Administrative Law; Litigation.

SAMSON VERMONT, born Santa Fe, New Mexico, September 11, 1968; admitted to bar, 1994, Georgia; registered to practice before U.S. Patent and Trademark Office (Not admitted in District of Columbia). *Education:* Rhodes College (B.A., 1990); University of Georgia (J.D., 1994); Georgia State University (1997). Faculty Scholar, Chemistry, Georgia State University. Founder and Editor (Formerly Chief Editor), "Patent Strategy & Management". Columnist and Advisor, "The Patent Journal". Lawyer, Children's Hospital, 2000—. *Member:* State Bar of Georgia (Member, Intellectual Property Law Section, 1996-1998, 2001); American Intellectual Property Law Association; Patent & Trademark Office Society. ***PRACTICE AREAS:*** Patents.

STEPHEN J. WENDEROTH, born Jamaica, New York, August 24, 1960; admitted to bar, 1989, Connecticut; 1991, District of Columbia; 2000, U.S. Supreme Court. *Education:* Franklin & Marshall College (B.A., 1982); Pace University (J.D., cum laude, 1989). Managing Editor, Pace Law Review, 1988-1989. *Member:* District of Columbia Bar; American Bar Association. ***PRACTICE AREAS:*** Environmental Law; Government Contracts. ***Email:*** swenderoth@hunton.com

MICHELLE R. WILDSTEIN, born Atlanta, Georgia, September 4, 1971; admitted to bar, 1999, Georgia (Not admitted in District of Columbia). *Education:* Johns Hopkins University (B.A., 1993); Catholic University of America (J.D., 1998). ***LANGUAGES:*** French. ***Email:*** mwildstein@hunton.com

BLAKE H. WINBURNE, born Austin, Texas, June 12, 1967; admitted to bar, 1996, Virginia; 1998, District of Columbia. *Education:* University of Texas at Austin (B.B.A., 1991); George Mason University (J.D., 1995); Georgetown University (LL.M., with honors, 1997). ***PRACTICE AREAS:*** Project Finance; Leasing. ***Email:*** bwinburne@hunton.com

ALLISON D. WOOD, born Burbank, California, September 26, 1967; admitted to bar, 1998, Virginia; 2000, District of Columbia. *Education:* California State University, Northridge (B.S., Accounting, 1993); George Washington University (J.D., with honors, 1998). Editor-in-Chief, The Environmental Lawyer, 1997-1998. Publications Chair, Moot Court Board, 1997-1998. ***PRACTICE AREAS:*** Environmental Law. ***Email:*** awood@hunton.com

RUSSELL G. WOOD, JR., born Alexandria, Virginia, November 22, 1968; admitted to bar, 1999, District of Columbia. *Education:* James Madison University (B.A., cum laude, 1990); George Washington University (J.D., cum laude, 1999). Dean' Fellow, George Washington University Law School, 1998-1999. Member, Moot Court Board, 1996-1999. Notes Editor, George Washington Journal of International Law and Economics, 1997-1999. *Member:* American Bar Association; Energy Bar Association. ***PRACTICE AREAS:*** Project Finance; Corporate Law; Energy Law. ***Email:*** rwood@hunton.com

SCOTT F. YARNELL, born Merion, Pennsylvania, April 7, 1969; admitted to bar, 1997, Maryland; registered to practice before U.S. Patent and Trademark Office (Not admitted in District of Columbia). *Education:* Drexel University (B.S., cum laude, 1994); George Washington University (J.D., 1997). *Member:* Maryland State Bar Association. ***PRACTICE AREAS:*** Patents.

Most Lawyers listed are Members of the American Bar Association and/or the Virginia State Bar or The District of Columbia Bar.

(For complete biographical data on other personnel, see Professional Biographies at other locations)

HUSTON & ANGUS

WASHINGTON, D.C.

(See Arlington, Virginia)

General Civil and Trial Practice. Business, Contract Litigation, Commercial, Banking, Creditors Rights, Collections.

BARBARA B. HUTCHINSON

WASHINGTON, D.C.

(See New Carrollton, Maryland)

Employment Law, Union Labor Law, Union Contract Negotiations, Employment Discrimination, Unemployment Compensation, Wrongful Termination, Wage and Hour Law, Employee Rights, Employment Mediation.

HYMAN, PHELPS & McNAMARA, P.C.

Established in 1980

700 THIRTEENTH STREET, N.W., SUITE 1200
WASHINGTON, D.C. 20005
Telephone: 202-737-5600
Fax: 202-737-9329
URL: http://www.hpm.com

Irvine, California Office: Hyman, Phelps & McNamara. 2603 Main Street, Suite 760. Telephone: 949-553-7400. Fax: 949-553-7433.

Durham, North Carolina Office: Hyman, Phelps & McNamara., P.C. 4819 Emperor Boulevard, Suite 400. Telephone: 919-313-4750. Fax: 919-313-4751.

Practice before all Courts, Government Agencies and International Regulatory Authorities involving Foods, Drugs, Cosmetics, Medical Devices, Biologics, Pesticides, Controlled Substances and Consumer Products.

FIRM PROFILE: Hyman, Phelps & McNamara, P.C. is a law firm that advises and represents a broad range of clients on legal issues concerning food, drug, medical device and cosmetic law and regulation. In 1980, three former U.S. Food and Drug Administration (FDA) lawyers opened the firm in Washington, D.C. to concentrate in this area of the law. In 1989, the firm formed a partnership in California to serve clients on the West Coast more effectively. The firm opened an office in Durham, North Carolina, in 2001. Hyman, Phelps & McNamara, P.C. now has one of the most extensive food and drug practices in the United States.

ROBERT T. ANGAROLA (1945-1996).

JAMES R. PHELPS, born East Bernstadt, Kentucky, December 1, 1938; admitted to bar, 1962, Ohio; 1965, Kentucky; 1967, District of Columbia and U.S. Supreme Court; 1970, Illinois. *Education:* University of Cincinnati (A.B., with honors, 1960; LL.B., 1962). Trial Attorney, Food and Drug Administration, 1965-1967. Assistant U.S. Attorney, Washington, D.C., 1967-1969. Vice President and General Counsel, G.D. Searle & Co., 1977-1979. Regulatory Professional of the Year, Regulatory Affairs Professional Society, 1990. *Member:* The District of Columbia Bar. ***Email:*** jrp@hpm.com

PAUL M. HYMAN, born Atlantic City, New Jersey, January 10, 1940; admitted to bar, 1966, District of Columbia; 1975, U.S. Supreme Court. *Education:* University of Chicago (B.A., 1961); Yale University (LL.B., 1965). Trial Attorney, Food and Drug Administration, 1966-1968. *Member:* District of Columbia Bar; Federal and American Bar Associations. ***Email:*** pmh@hpm.com

ROBERT A. DORMER, born New York, N.Y., October 7, 1945; admitted to bar, 1972, Virginia; 1979, District of Columbia. *Education:* Dartmouth College (A.B., 1967); University of Virginia (J.D., 1972). Phi Delta Phi. Assistant and Associate Chief Counsel for Enforcement and Radiological Health, Food and Drug Administration, 1976-1979. Treasurer, Regulatory Affairs Professionals Society, International Section, 1987-1988. *Member:* Virginia State Bar; District of Columbia Bar; Federal and American Bar Associations. ***Email:*** rad@hpm.com

STEPHEN H. McNAMARA, born New York, N.Y., April 12, 1943; admitted to bar, 1967, Virginia; 1981, District of Columbia. *Education:* University of Virginia (B.A., 1964; J.D., 1967). Phi Beta Kappa. National Merit Scholar. Recipient: American Jurisprudence Prize in Criminal Law; FDA Award of Merit, 1974, 1978; Federal Bar Association Younger Federal Lawyer Award, 1976. Member, 1982-1992 and Chair, 1991-1992, Editorial Advisory Board, Food Drug Cosmetic Law Journal. Annual Lecturer, Institute of Food Technologists, 1987-1996. Trial Attorney, 1970-1972, Senior Trial Attorney, 1972-1974, Associate Chief Counsel for Food, 1974-1978 and Acting Chief Counsel, 1977, U.S. Food and Drug Administration. Vice President for Legal Affairs and General Counsel, 1978-1980 and Senior Vice President and General Counsel, 1980-1983, Cosmetic, Toiletry and Fragrance Association, Washington, D.C. Member: Board of Governors, Annual Food Update Program of Food and Drug Law Institute, 1988-1994; Editorial Advisory Board, Trends in Food Science and Technology, Cambridge, U.K., 1990—; Board of Trustees, International Life Sciences Institute (ILSI) of North America, 1993-2000. *Member:* District of Columbia Bar; Virginia State Bar; American Bar Association (Chairman, Committee on Food, Drug and Cosmetic Law, Corporation, Banking and Business Law Section, 1983-1986). ***Email:*** shm@hpm.com

ROGER C. THIES, born Libertyville, Illinois, August 29, 1944; admitted to bar, 1969, Illinois; 1988, District of Columbia. *Education:* Wabash College (A.B., 1966); University of Chicago (J.D., 1969). Attorney, 1970-1981, Associate General Counsel, Litigation and Administrative Law, 1981-1985 and Vice President and General Counsel, 1985-1987, G.D. Searle & Co. *Member:* District of Columbia Bar; Illinois State Bar Association. ***Email:*** rct@hpm.com

THOMAS SCARLETT, born Charlottesville, Virginia, July 20, 1943; admitted to bar, 1969, New York; 1973, District of Columbia. *Education:* Columbia University (B.A., summa cum laude, 1966); Yale University (J.D., 1969). Phi Beta Kappa; Order of the Coif. Member, Yale Law Journal, 1966-1969. Chief Counsel, U.S. Food and Drug Administration, 1981-1989. *Member:* New York State Bar Association; District of Columbia Bar. ***Email:*** tom@hpm.com

JEFFREY N. GIBBS, born Newark, New Jersey, April 27, 1953; admitted to bar, 1978, New Jersey; 1981, New York; 1984, District of Columbia. *Education:* Princeton University (B.A., summa cum laude, 1975); New York University (J.D., cum laude, 1978). Order of the Coif. Projects Editor, New York University Law Review, 1977-1978. Law Clerk to the Honorable Frederick B. Lacey, District Court of New Jersey, 1978-1980. Associate Chief Counsel for Enforcement, Food and Drug Administration, 1980-1984. *Member:* District of Columbia Bar; American Bar Association; The Association of Clinical Research Professionals (Member, Board of Trustees, 1993-1995). ***Email:*** jng@hpm.com

BRIAN J. DONATO, born New York, N.Y., August 23, 1940; admitted to bar, 1971, Virginia; 1988, Florida; 1989, District of Columbia; 1991, California. *Education:* Manhattan College (B.A., 1963); University of Virginia (J.D., 1970). Judge, General District Court for Albemarle County, Virginia, 1976-1980. Chief Judge, General District Courts for 16th Judicial District, 1978-1979. Faculty Member, University of Virginia Law School Annual Trial Advocacy Institute, 1982—. Lecturer, University of Virginia, 1978-1988. *Member:* Orange County (California) and Virginia Bar Associations; State Bar of California; Virginia State Bar; The Florida Bar; District of Columbia Bar. (Resident, Irvine, California Office). ***Email:*** bjd@hpm.com

FRANK J. SASINOWSKI, born Schenectady, New York, January 14, 1953; admitted to bar, 1982, District of Columbia. *Education:* Cornell University (B.S., 1975); University of California at Berkeley (M.P.H., 1977; M.S., 1978); Georgetown University (J.D., 1982). Regents Fellow; Kaiser Fellow. Lecturer, Health Law, Washington College of Law, American University, 1987. Member, Board of Directors of the National Organization for Rare Disorders (NORD), 2000-2001. *Member:* District of Columbia Bar; American Public Health Association (Chairman, Food and Nutrition Section, 1989-1991). ***Email:*** fjs@hpm.com

DIANE BARBER McCOLL, born Charleston, South Carolina, March 13, 1954; admitted to bar, 1984, Texas; 1985, District of Columbia. *Education:* University of South Carolina (B.S., cum laude, 1976; J.D., 1984). Order of the Wig and Robe. Associate Editor-in-Chief, South Carolina Law Review, 1983-1984. Licensed Pharmacist: Tennessee, 1976; South Carolina, 1977. Member: Society for Biomaterials; International Society of Regulatory Toxicology and Pharmacology. *Member:* District of Columbia Bar; State Bar of Texas; American Bar Association; European Food Law Association; American Pharmaceutical Association; American Society for Pharmacy Law. ***Email:*** dbm@hpm.com

A. WES SIEGNER, JR., born Buffalo, New York, June 14, 1952; admitted to bar, 1987, District of Columbia. *Education:* Brown University (B.A., Biology, 1974); University of Minnesota (M.A., Biology, 1984); Cornell University (J.D., 1986). *Member:* District of Columbia Bar. ***Email:*** aws@hpm.com

ALAN M. KIRSCHENBAUM, born Buffalo, New York, December 26, 1948; admitted to bar, 1986, Maryland; 1988, District of Columbia. *Education:* University of Pennsylvania (B.A., cum laude, 1970); Harvard University (J.D., cum laude, 1986). Member, Food and Drug Law Institute, 1995—. *Member:* District of Columbia Bar (Member, 1994-1998 and Chair, 1996-1997, Programs and Education Committee, Health Law Section; Member, Steering Committee, Health Law Section); American Health Lawyers Association. ***Email:*** amk@hpm.com

DOUGLAS B. FARQUHAR, born Washington, D.C., April 9, 1954; admitted to bar, 1983, Maryland; 1984, U.S. District Court, District of Maryland and U.S. Court of Appeals, Fourth Circuit; 1985, District of Columbia and U.S. District Court, District of Columbia; 1998, U.S. Court of Appeals for the District of Columbia Circuit; 2000, U.S. Court of Appeals, Seventh Circuit; 2001, U.S. Court of Appeals, Federal Ciruit. *Education:* Boston University (B.S., magna cum laude, 1975); Yale University (J.D., 1983). Law Clerk to the Hon. Joseph H. Young, U.S. District Court, District of Maryland, 1983-1984. Assistant U.S. Attorney, Maryland, 1990-1997. Member, Fourth Circuit Judicial Conference. *Member:* District of Columbia Bar; Maryland State Bar Association. ***Email:*** dbf@hpm.com

(This Listing Continued)

HYMAN, PHELPS & McNAMARA, P.C., Washington—Continued

JOHN A. GILBERT, JR., born Boston, Massachusetts, September 30, 1957; admitted to bar, 1992, Virginia; 1995, District of Columbia. *Education:* Westfield State College (B.A., 1979); Catholic University (J.D., 1992). Associate Editor, Catholic University Law Review, 1992. Law Clerk, Office of Administrative Law Judges, Drug Enforcement Administration, 1992-1993. Attorney Advisor, Office of Chief Counsel, Drug Enforcement Administration, 1993-1995. *Member:* The District of Columbia Bar; Virginia and American Bar Associations. ***SPECIAL AGENCIES:*** Drug Enforcement Administration - Office of Chief Counsel; Office of Administrative Law Judges. ***Email:*** jag@hpm.com

JOHN R. FLEDER, born White Plains, New York, January 26, 1947; admitted to bar, 1973, District of Columbia. *Education:* Franklin & Marshall College (B.A., 1969); New York University (J.D., 1972). Author: "A Voluntary Disclosure Program for FDA - The Time Has Come," 54 Food and Drug Law Journal 389-399, 1999; "The History, Provisions, and Implementation of the Generic Drug Enforcement Act of 1992," 49 Food Drug Cosmetic Law Journal 89-107, 1994; "The Role of the Department of Justice in Enforcement Matters Relating to the Food and Drug Administration," 46 Food Drug Cosmetic Law Journal 781-192, November, 1991; Administrative Inspections by the Food and Drug Administration: The Role of the Department of Justice," 44 Food Drug Cosmetic Law Journal 297-314, July, 1989. Co-Author: "Use of the Grand Jury - The Beech-Nut Case," with Assistant Attorney General John R. Bolton, 4 The Investigators Journal 8-10, Fall, 1988. Member, Editorial Advisory Board, Food Drug Law Journal, 1990-1994. Director, Office of Consumer Litigation, U.S. Department of Justice, 1985-1992. Special Assistant U.S. Attorney, Baltimore, Maryland, 1992-1993. *Member:* The District of Columbia Bar. ***SPECIAL AGENCIES:*** Food and Drug Administration; Department of Justice; Federal Trade Commission; Consumer Product Safety Commission. ***PRACTICE AREAS:*** Litigation; Food, Drug and Cosmetic Law; White Collar Crime; Administrative Law. ***Email:*** jrf@hpm.com

---

MARC H. SHAPIRO, born Richmond, Virginia, June 27, 1950; admitted to bar, 1975, Virginia; 1976, District of Columbia; 1985, North Carolina. *Education:* University of North Carolina (A.B., 1972); University of Virginia (J.D., 1975). Phi Beta Kappa. Senior Lecturing Fellow, Duke University School of Law, 2000-2001. *Member:* District of Columbia Bar; Virginia State Bar; North Carolina State Bar; American Bar Association. (Resident, Durham, North Carolina Office). ***PRACTICE AREAS:*** Food and Drug Law. ***Email:*** mhs@hpm.com

JENNIFER B. DAVIS, born New York, N.Y., May 31, 1968; admitted to bar, 1994, Georgia; 1995, District of Columbia. *Education:* Duke University (B.A., 1990); Emory University (J.D., 1994). Member, Emory International Law Review. Dean's Fellow Teaching Assistant, Reading, Writing and Advocacy Course, Emory University, 1993-1994. *Member:* State Bar of Georgia; District of Columbia Bar; American Bar Association. ***Email:*** jbd@hpm.com

FRANCES K. WU, born Buffalo, New York, January 15, 1970; admitted to bar, 1996, California; 1997, District of Columbia. *Education:* University of California at Berkeley (B.A., 1991); Boston University (J.D., 1995). Articles Editor, Boston University Public Interest Law Journal. *Member:* State Bar of California; The District of Columbia Bar; American Bar Association. ***Email:*** fkw@hpm.com

DAVID B. CLISSOLD, born Arcadia, California, February 17, 1958; admitted to bar, 1996, Maryland; 1998, District of Columbia. *Education:* University of California at Los Angeles (B.S., 1981); Indiana University (M.A., 1988); University of Maryland (J.D., 1996). First Place, H. Thomas Austern Memorial Writing Competition, 1994. Author, "Prescription for the Orphan Drug Act: The Impact of FDA's 1992 Regulations and the Latest Congressional Proposals for Reform," 50 Food and Drug Law Journal 125, 1995. *Member:* Maryland State and American Bar Associations; The District of Columbia Bar. ***PRACTICE AREAS:*** Food and Drug Regulation. ***Email:*** dbc@hpm.com

CASSANDRA A. SOLTIS, born Youngstown, Ohio; admitted to bar, 1995, Ohio; 1999, District of Columbia. *Education:* The Ohio State University (B.A., summa cum laude, 1992; J.D., 1995). *Member:* American Bar Association. ***LANGUAGES:*** French. ***PRACTICE AREAS:*** Food and Drug Regulation. ***Email:*** cas@hpm.com

JOSEPHINE M. TORRENTE, born Trenton, New Jersey, 1966; admitted to bar, 1997, Pennsylvania; 1999, District of Columbia. *Education:* Case Western Reserve University (B.S., with honors, 1988); University of Alabama at Birmingham (M.S., 1991); Temple University School of Law (J.D., summa cum laude, 1997). *Member:* American Bar Association. ***PRACTICE AREAS:*** Food and Drug Law. ***Email:*** jmt@hpm.com

MICHELLE L. BUTLER, born Orange, California, July 26, 1973; admitted to bar, 1998, Maryland; 1999, District of Columbia. *Education:* Stanford University (A.B., 1995); Georgetown University (J.D., 1998). Member, The Tax Lawyer. ***PRACTICE AREAS:*** Food and Drug Regulation. ***Email:*** mlb@hpm.com

PATRICIA ANN ADES VANSTORY, born Charlotte, North Carolina, February 6, 1970; admitted to bar, 1997, Maine; 1998, Massachusetts; 1999, District of Columbia. *Education:* University of North Carolina at Chapel Hill (B.A., 1992); Boston University (J.D., 1997). ***Email:*** pav@hpm.com

THOMAS R. GIBSON, born Washington, D.C., July 12, 1967; admitted to bar, 1997, California; 2000, District of Columbia. *Education:* University of California at Davis (B.A., 1989); Northwestern School of Law of Lewis and Clark College (J.D., cum laude, 1997). Member, Orange County Regulatory Affairs Discussion Group. *Member:* Orange County Bar Association; The District of Columbia Bar; State Bar of California. (Resident, Irvine California Office). ***PRACTICE AREAS:*** Food and Drug Law; Environmental Law; Litigation. ***Email:*** trg@hpm.com

PAUL L. FERRARI, born Detroit, Michigan, January 12, 1960; admitted to bar, 1998, Maryland; 1999, District of Columbia and U.S. District Court, District of Maryland; 2000, U.S. District Court for the District of Columbia. *Education:* University of Michigan (B.A., highest honors, 1982); George Washington University (J.D., 1998). ***PRACTICE AREAS:*** Food and Drug Regulation. ***Email:*** plf@hpm.com

JEFFREY N. WASSERSTEIN, born Brooklyn, New York, April 18, 1971; admitted to bar, 1997, New Jersey and New York; 1998, District of Columbia. *Education:* Columbia University (B.A., 1993; J.D., 1996). James Kent Scholar. Law Clerk: Hon. Allyne Ross (EDNY) 1996-1997; Hon. Samuel Alito USCJ 3rd Circuit, 1997-1998. ***PRACTICE AREAS:*** Food and Drug Regulation; Health Care. ***Email:*** jnw@hpm.com

BRIAN J. MALKIN, born Washington, D.C., March 13, 1966; admitted to bar, 1991, Maryland; 1992, District of Columbia. *Education:* George Washington University (B.A., cum laude, 1988; J.D., 1991). Author: "FDA's Role in Administering the Hatch-Waxman Act," 54 Food and Drug Law Journal 211-214, 1999. *Member:* Maryland State, American and Federal Bar Associations; District of Columbia Bar. ***PRACTICE AREAS:*** Food and Drug Regulation. ***Email:*** bjm@hpm.com

ANNE MARIE MURPHY, born Trenton, New Jersey, November 16, 1961; admitted to bar, 2000, Pennsylvania; 2001, District of Columbia. *Education:* Wesley College (B.S., 1993); Widener University School of Law (J.D., summa cum laude, 2000). Member, Delaware Journal of Corporate Law, 1998-2000. *Member:* District of Columbia Bar; American Bar Association; Supreme Court Historical Society. ***PRACTICE AREAS:*** Food and Drug Law. ***Email:*** amm@hpm.com

MICHAEL D. BERNSTEIN, born Milwaukee, Wisconsin, July 6, 1960; admitted to bar, 1985, Wisconsin; 1997, District of Columbia. *Education:* University of Wisconsin-Madison (B.A., with distinction, 1982; J.D., cum laude, 1985). Recipient, American Jurisprudence Award, Contracts. Associate: Arent Fox Kintner Plotkin & Kahn, PLLC; Buc & Beardsley. U.S. Department of Agriculture, Office of the General Counsel, 1990-1996 (Acting Deputy Assistant General Counsel, 1994, 1996). ***PRACTICE AREAS:*** Food and Drug Regulation; Medical Device Regulation; Advertising Law; Trade Regulation. ***Email:*** mdb@hpm.com

DARA SUSAN KATCHER, born Bronx, New York, October 2, 1973; admitted to bar, 1998, New Jersey; 1999, New York. *Education:* State University of New York at Binghamton (B.A., 1995); Fordham University (J.D., 1998). ***PRACTICE AREAS:*** Food and Drug Regulation. ***Email:*** dsk@hpm.com

LARRY K. HOUCK, born Arlington, Virginia, March 22, 1958; admitted to bar, 1996, Oregon (Not admitted in District of Columbia). *Education:* George Mason University (B.A., 1980; M.A., 1983); Northwestern School of Law (J.D., 1995). Member, Moot Court Mock Trial Team, 1994-1995. ***SPECIAL AGENCIES:*** Drug Enforcement Administration-Office of Diversion Control, from 1986-2001. ***PRACTICE AREAS:*** Pharmaceutical Law; Drug Law; Chemical Law.

OF COUNSEL

MARY KATE WHALEN, born Waltham, Massachusetts, May 27, 1962; admitted to bar, 1991, Massachusetts; 1994, District of Columbia. *Education:* Colby College (B.A., 1984); Suffolk University Law School (J.D., cum laude, 1990). Director, Moot Court Board. Associate Chief Counsel, Drug Enforcement Administration, U.S. Department of Justice. *Member:* American (Member, Administrative Law Section) Bar Association; The District of Columbia Bar; Women's Bar Association of District of Columbia (President, 2000-2001; Administrative Law Agency Section). ***PRACTICE AREAS:*** Food and Drug Regulation; Administrative Law; Litigation. ***Email:*** mkw@hpm.com

(This Listing Continued)

HYNAK & ASSOCIATES, P.C.

WASHINGTON, D.C.

(See Arlington, Virginia)

Trademarks, Copyrights and Patents.

ICE MILLER

Established in 1910

1090 VERMONT AVENUE, N.W.
SUITE 920
WASHINGTON, D.C. 20005
Telephone: 202-824-8600
Fax: 202-824-8601
Email: info@icemiller.com
URL: http://www.icemiller.com

REVISERS OF THE INDIANA LAW DIGEST FOR THIS DIRECTORY

Indianapolis, Indiana Office: One American Square, Box 82001. Telephone: 317-236-2100. Fax: 317-236-2219. Internet E-mail: info@icemiller.com. Web Site Address: http://www.icemiller.com.

Chicago, Illinois Office: 135 South LaSalle Street, Suite 4100. Telephone: 312-726-1567. Fax: 312-641-6263. Internet E-mail: info@icemiller.com. Web Site Address: http://www.icemiller.com.

Granger, Indiana Office: 51323 Pebble Beach Court. Telephone: 219-234-7955. Fax: 219-234-7965. Internet E-mail: info@icemiller.com. Web Site Address: http://www.icemiller.com.

Mission Hills, Kansas Office: 6430 Norwood. Telephone: 913-403-8788. Email: info@icemiller.com. Web Site Address: http://www.icemiller.com.

Administrative Law, Antitrust, Appellate Practice, Architectural Malpractice Law, Banking, Bankruptcy, Broadcasting and Communications, Cable TV, Cable TV Franchising, Civil and Criminal Litigation, Civil Rights, Coal Law, College and University Law, Commercial and Business Litigation, Complex Litigation, Computer Law, Contracting and Litigation, Construction Law, Corporate Law, Corporate Finance, Creditors Rights Law, Drug and Medical Device Litigation, Economic Development and Incentives, Education Law, Employee Benefits Law, Entrepreneurial Services, Environmental Law, Estate Development and Finance, Franchise Law, Gaming Law, Gift and Estate Tax, Governmental Affairs, Governmental Relations, Governmental Services and Lobbying, Government Law, Government (Public) Contract Law, Government Procurement, Guardianship, Health Care Law, Immigration Law, Insurance Law, Intellectual Property and Licensing, International Law, Labor and Employment Law (including Equal Employment Litigation, ERISA Practice and Occupational Safety and Health Matters), Liability Risk Management, Licensing, Management Labor Relations Law, Mergers and Acquisitions, Minerals and Mining, Municipal Finance (Bond) Law, Municipal Finance (Bond), Dispute Resolution and Litigation, Municipal Litigation, Municipal Solid Waste Resource Recovery, Municipal Utility Regulation, Occupational Hazards Law (Black Lung, Asbestosis, etc.), Patent, Trademark and Copyright, Plaintiff's Trial Practice, Probate Law, Product Liability Law, Public Agency, Public Authority Financing Law, Public Contract Law, Public Employment Relations, Public Entity Law, Public Finance, Public Health Law, Public Housing Law, Public Schools, Public Sector Collective Bargaining, Public Utility Law, Public Works, Professional Malpractice Law, Real Estate Law (including Sales, Development and Financing, Mortgage Banking, Secured Transactions, Sale/Leasebacks, Condominiums and Zoning), Regulation, Risk and Claims Management, Securities Regulation Law, Sports Law, Taxation (Federal, State and Local), Tax Exempt Organizations, Tort Law, Toxic Torts, Transportation Law, Utility Law, Venture Capital, Venture Finance Services, Workers' Compensation.

FIRM PROFILE: A full-service law firm that also offers professional business advice, with offices in Indianapolis, South Bend and Chicago, Ice Miller has provided counsel on a local, state and national level since 1910.

The Firm was founded in Indianapolis on April 28, 1910, when three general practitioners formed a partnership under the name of Henley Matson Gates. The Firm experienced continuous growth and acquired a national reputation and a national practice. The Firm presently consists of 220 lawyers and 41 paraprofessionals, and an additional 250 staff employees, making it the largest law firm in Indianapolis.

Ice Miller's core departments are Corporate Law, Litigation, Labor and Employment, Real Estate Development, and Municipal Finance. From these core disciplines, Ice Miller lawyers have developed in-depth experience and knowledge in a variety of highly refined areas of concentration which allows the Firm to put together teams of attorneys to satisfy the increasingly sophisticated and multi-faceted needs of its clients. These areas of concentration are set forth below.

Most notable growth areas include: Advanced Technology Law Banking Law, Construction Law, Drug and Device Law, Employee Benefits Dispute Resolution, Environmental Law, Entrepreneurial Law, Governmental Services, Health Law, Intellectual Property (including Patent Law), International Law, Merger and Acquisition Law, Municipal Law, Occupational Hazards Law, Professional Liability Law, and Sports and Entertainment Law.

Ice Miller also has the largest litigation practice in the state, representing national, regional and locally domiciled clients for which it has obtained numerous "landmark" decisions in areas which include corporate, probate, professional, drug and device, and contractual liability.

LAW FIRM ALLIANCES/ASSOCIATIONS: **UNITED STATES LAW FIRM GROUP:** *United States Law Firm Group (USLFG) - www.uslfg.com.*

EMPLOYMENT LAW ALLIANCE: *Employment Law Alliance (ELA) - www.employmentlawalliance.com.*

MEMBER OF FIRM

G. DANIEL MILLER, born Memphis, Tennessee, August 3, 1949; admitted to bar, 1974, Texas (Not admitted in District of Columbia). *Education:* Vanderbilt University (B.A., 1971; J.D., 1974). Adjunct Professor of Law, Southern Methodist University School of Law, 1984-1986. **PRACTICE AREAS:** Employee Benefits Law; Federal Government Affairs. **Email:** dmiller@icemiller.com

OF COUNSEL

HENRY ROSE, born Olean, New York, 1927; admitted to bar, 1951, New York; 1953, District of Columbia; 1956, U.S. Supreme Court; U.S. Court of Appeals for the District of Columbia, Second, Third, Fourth, Sixth, Ninth and Tenth Circuits; U.S. District Court, Western and Southern Districts of New York; U.S. District Court, Western District of Tennessee. *Education:* University of Buffalo (B.A., cum laude, 1950); University of Buffalo Law School (J.D., cum laude, 1951). Sterling Fellow, Yale University Law School, Associate Professor: University of Toledo College of Law, 1957-1958; Rutgers University Law School, 1958-1962. Associate Solicitor for Legislation and Legal Counsel, U.S. Department of Labor, 1970-1974. General Counsel, Pension Benefit Guaranty Corporation, 1974-1984. Private practice of law, 1985—. **PRACTICE AREAS:** Employee Benefits. **Email:** rose@icemiller.com

ERICA L. SUMMERS, born Buffalo, New York, 1952; admitted to bar, 1977, Pennsylvania; 1979, District of Columbia. *Education:* Yale University (B.A., magna cum laude, 1974); University of Pennsylvania (J.D., cum laude, 1977). Associate Editor, University of Pennsylvania Law Review, 1975-1977. **PRACTICE AREAS:** Employee Benefits Law. **Email:** summerse@icemiller.com

ASSOCIATE

JASON E. LEVINE, born Rochester, New York, September 8, 1970; admitted to bar, 1998, New Jersey; 2001, District of Columbia. *Education:* State University of New York at Albany (B.A., 1993); Rutgers University School of Law (J.D., 1997). Notes and Comments Editor, Women's Rights Law Reporter. **PRACTICE AREAS:** Employee Benefits. **Email:** levine@icemiller.com

REPRESENTATIVE CLIENTS: Aisin U.S.A. Inc. (Aisin Seiki Co., Ltd. & Aisin American, Inc.); Allied Signal; Aluminum Company of America; Amateur Athletic Union of the United States, Inc.; AMAX, Inc.; American United Life Insurance Co.; American Excess Insurance; American Home Products Corp.; Arnett Clinic; Associated Insurance Co.; Associated General Contractors of Indiana, Inc.; Avesta Sheffield; Ball State University; BankOne, Indiana, NA; Baptist Homes of Indiana, Inc.; Baxter Healthcare Corp.; Biomet, Inc.; Bloomington, City of; Butler University; Carpenter Manufacturing, Inc.; Carrier Corporation; Chrysler Corp.; Churchill Downs; CIBA-Giegy Corp.; CID Equity Partners; CID Venture Partners, L.P.; Citizens Gas & Coke Utility; CNA Insurance; Commercial Union; Community Hospital of Indianapolis; Community Hospitals of Indiana, Inc.; Community Hospital of Anderson; Community Action of Greater Indianapolis, Inc.; Cosco, Inc,; Cummins Engine Co.; D.A. INC. (Daiwa Kasei Kogyo); Dana Corporation; Delco Remy America; Diamet Corporation (Mitsubishi Metal America Corporation); Digital Audio Disc Corporation (Sony Corporation); E.T.S., Inc.; ELSA Corporation (Sakamoto Industry Co., Ltd.); Employers Insurance of Warsaw; Evansville, City of; F.A. Wilhelm Construction Co.; Fairbanks Communications; Federal Deposit Insurance Corp.; Ford Motor Company; Fort Harrison Reuse Authority; Fort Wayne Airport Authority; Fuji Component Parts USA, Inc. (Fuji Buhin Kogyo K.K.); GECOM Corporation (Mitsui Mining & Smelting Co., Ltd.); General Seating of America, Inc. (NHK Spring Co., Ltd. & Lear Siegler Seating); General Housewares Corp.; Goshen Rubber Co., Inc.; Haynes International, Inc.; Howard, Needles, Tammen & Bergendoff; ICT Corporation (Isuzu Motors, Ltd.); Indiana Educational Facility Authority; Indiana Housing Finance Authority; Indiana Japanese Language School, Inc.; Indiana Health Facilities Financing Authority; Indiana Insurance Co.; Indiana Chamber of Commerce; Indiana Association of Cities and Towns; Association of Indiana Counties; Indiana Association of Cities and Towns Foundation; Indiana Bankers Association; Indiana University; Indiana, State of; Indiana Development Finance Authority; Indiana Port Commission; Indianapolis Foundation; Indianapolis Airport Authority; Indianapolis, City of ; Indianapolis Motor Speedway Corp.; INTAT Precision, Inc. (Aisin Takaoka Co., Ltd.); Irwin Financial Corporation; Isuzu Motors America, Inc. (Isuzu Motors, Ltd.); Ivy Tech State College; JAYTEC, INC. (F.C.C. CO.,LTD.); Johnson and Johnson; Key Bank; Kmart Corp.; Kobelco Compressors (America), Inc.; Lafayette, City of; Lake Michigan Charters; Liberty Mutual; Lilly Industries, Inc.; Magnequench International, Inc.; Marion General Hospital; McGill Manufacturing Corp.; MMI Co.; Motorola; Mutual Security Life; Navistar International Transportation Corp.; Nucor Steel; Onkyo Manufacturing, Inc. (Onkyo Corporation); Ontario Corporation; Pedcor Investments; Perry County; PHICO Insurance Co.; Precision Tools Service, Inc. (Toyo Corporation, Marubeni Corporation

(This Listing Continued)

ICE MILLER, Washington—Continued

Toyo America, Inc. & Marubeni America Corporation); Procter & Gamble Co.; Public Employees Retirement Fund; Purdue University; Reid Hospital and Health Care Services; Reilly Industries, Inc.; Resort Condominiums International, Inc.; Rexnord, Inc.; Robinson-Nugent, Inc.; Saint Joseph's College; Sexton Companies; Showboar Marina; Sintering Technologies Inc. (Hitachi Powdered Metals Co., Ltd. & Cummins Engine Co.); Sofamor Danek Group, Inc.; Software Artistry; Sony Corporation of America (Sony Corporation); St. Paul Insurance Co.; Steak n Shake, Inc.; Sunshine Promotions, Inc.; Takasago America, Inc. (Takasago Thermal Engineering); Target Stores Division of Dayton-Hudson Corporation; Taylor University; The Buckingham Cos.; The Upjohn Company; The DeMars Corp.; The Coco-Cola Co.; Thomson Consumer Electronics, Inc. (RCA); Toyota Industrial Equipment Mfg., Inc. (Toyota Automatic Loom Works, Ltd.); United Dominion Industries; Wabash Valley Broadcasting Corporation; Warner-Lambert Company; Wavetek; Wyeth-Ayers & Labs.

REVISERS OF THE INDIANA LAW DIGEST FOR THIS DIRECTORY

FREDERICK L. IKENSON, P.C.

Established in 1978

1621 NEW HAMPSHIRE AVENUE, N.W.

WASHINGTON, D.C. 20009

Telephone: 202-483-8900

Facsimile: 202-483-9368

Email: Fikenson@ikenson.com

URL: http://www.lawyers.com/ikensonlaw

Practice before Federal Courts, Government Agencies and Congressional Committees. International Trade and Customs Law.

FREDERICK L. IKENSON, born New York, N.Y., March 27, 1940; admitted to bar, 1968, New York and U.S. Customs Court; 1969, U.S. Court of Customs and Patent Appeals; 1974, District of Columbia; 1975, U.S. District Court for the District of Columbia and U.S. Court of Appeals for the District of Columbia Circuit; 1976, U.S. Supreme Court; 1980, U.S. Court of International Trade; 1982, U.S. Court of Appeals for the Federal Circuit. *Education:* Cornell University (B.A., 1960); New York Law School (J.D., 1968). Trial Attorney, Customs Section, Civil Division, U.S. Department of Justice, 1968-1971. Assistant Chief, Customs Section, Civil Division, Department of Justice, 1971-1973. *Member:* District of Columbia Bar; American Bar Association; Customs and International Trade Bar Association (Director and Chairman, Judicial Selection Committee, 1986-1994). ***PRACTICE AREAS:*** Customs and International Trade Law. ***Email:*** fikenson@ikenson.com

LARRY HAMPEL, born St. Louis, Missouri, July 15, 1951; admitted to bar, 1986, Maryland; 1987, U.S. Court of International Trade and U.S. Court of Appeals for the Federal Circuit; 1988, District of Columbia. *Education:* University of California at Los Angeles (B.A., 1973); University of Baltimore (J.D., 1986). *Member:* The District of Columbia Bar; Maryland State Bar Association. ***PRACTICE AREAS:*** Customs and International Trade Law. ***Email:*** lhampel@ikenson.com

EDWIN T.C. ING

SUITE 800

2121 K STREET, N.W.

WASHINGTON, D.C. 20037

Telephone: 202-457-6630

Telecopier: 202-293-0027

Federal Taxation and Corporate Practice.

EDWIN T.C. ING, born Honolulu, Hawaii, July 9, 1949; admitted to bar, 1975, California; 1976, District of Columbia and U.S. Tax Court; 1980, U.S. Supreme Court. *Education:* Claremont Men's College (B.A., cum laude, 1971); State University of New York at Stony Brook (M.A., 1972); George Washington University (J.D., with honors, 1975; LL.M., 1979). Tax Law Specialist, Internal Revenue Service, National Office, 1975-1977. Legislative Counsel to Hon. Spark M. Matsunaga, U.S. Senate, 1977-1983. *Member:* The District of Columbia Bar; State Bar of California.

INMAN DEMING LLP

HAMILTON SQUARE

600 FOURTEENTH STREET, N.W., SUITE 600

WASHINGTON, D.C. 20005-2004

Telephone: 202-347-6800

Facsimile: 202-347-6013

Email: Inman.Deming@InmanDeming.com

URL: http://www.InmanDeming.com

Kalamazoo, Michigan Office: 229 East Michigan Avenue, Suite 145, 49007-6411. Telephone: 616-382-8080. Facsimile: 616-382-8083. E-Mail: Inman.Deming@InmanDeming.com.

(This Listing Continued)

International Transactions, Investments, Trade and Procurement, Corporate, Securities, Legislative and Administrative Law, Civil, White Collar and International Litigation, International and Domestic Arbitration, Commercial Transactions, Probate and Estates, Admiralty, International Maritime and Maritime Finance Law, and Special Matters Relating to Foreign Corrupt Practices Issues, Economic Sanctions and Visas.

FIRM PROFILE: Inman Deming LLP desires a special quality of service for domestic and international clientele. Toward that end, in addition to providing legal services within the competence of Inman Deming LLP, it shall select and monitor collaborating counsel to assure strong legal support for all aspects of matters entrusted to it. The firm may collaborate on many matters with the law firm of Pepper Hamilton LLP for those engagements acceptable to Pepper Hamilton LLP that come within its expertise and that fulfill client needs. The firm also has similar relationships with Layton Brooks & Hecht of New York City, Damon Key Leong Kupchak Hastert of Honolulu, Hawaii, and Creel, Garcia-Cuellar y Müggenburg, S.C. of Mexico City.

HARRY A. INMAN, admitted to bar, 1952, New York; 1953, District of Columbia. *Education:* Massachusetts Institute of Technology and Harvard University (A.B., 1948); University of Virginia (LL.B., 1951). Co-Author: "Revising the U.N. Trusteeship System — Will It Work?" (Case Study-Somalia), Electronic Journal, http://americandiplomacy.org., Vol. IV, No. 4, Autumn, 1999. Sutherland, Linowitz & Williams, Rochester, New York, 1952. Lord, Day & Lord, Washington office, 1953-1958. Lord, Day & Lord, Washington Representative, 1959-1975. Partner, Patton Boggs LLP, 1969-1995. *Member:* District of Columbia Bar; American (Chairman, Section of International Law, 1971-1972; Representative to the Department of State's Advisory Committee on Private International Law, 1977-1979; Inter-American (Council Member, 1969—) Bar Associations; Pacific Basin Economic Council (Member, Committee on Transparency, 1997—); The Procedural Aspects of International Law Institute, Trustee, 1974—; Washington Institute of Foreign Affairs; American Law Institute. (Also Of Counsel to Damon Key Leong Kupchak Hastert, Honolulu, Hawaii, and International Counsel to Creel, Garcia-Cuellar y Müggenburg, S.C., Mexico, D.F., Mexico). ***PRACTICE AREAS:*** International Business; Business Transactions; Government Relations. ***Email:*** Harry.Inman@InmanDeming.com

STUART H. DEMING, born Kalamazoo, Michigan, December 17, 1951; admitted to bar, 1977, Michigan; 1984, District of Columbia. *Education:* Williams College; University of Michigan (B.A., with high distinction, 1973; J.D., 1977; M.B.A., 1978). Certified Public Accountant, Michigan, 1986. Law Clerk, Honorable Wendell A. Miles, U.S. District Judge, Western District of Michigan, 1979-1980. Assistant U.S. Attorney, Western District of Michigan, 1980-1983. Division of Enforcement, Securities and Exchange Commission, 1983-1985. Trial Attorney, Tax Division, Department of Justice, 1985-1987; Steptoe & Johnson, 1987-1990. Executive Assistant, 1990 Economic Summit of Industrialized Nations, 1990. Special Assistant, U.S. Department of Army, 1991-1992. Special Prosecutor, House Bank Investigation, U.S. Department of Justice, 1992. *Member:* Kalamazoo County and American (Member, Section of International Law and Practice; Council Member, 1997—; Vice Chair, International Transactions Division, 2000—; Co-Chair, Task Force on International Standards for Corrupt Practices, 1994-2000) Bar Associations; State Bar of Michigan (Chair, International Law Section, 1999-2000); District of Columbia Bar (Co-Chair, Committee on Law and National Security, 1987-1992); American Institute of Certified Public Accountants (Member, Responsibilities in Tax Practice Committee, 1989-1992); Pacific Basin Economic Council (Chair, U.S. Committee on Transparency, 1999—). ***PRACTICE AREAS:*** Foreign Corrupt Practices Act; Foreign Asset Control; Corporate Litigation. ***Email:*** Stuart.Deming@InmanDeming.com

OF COUNSEL

ROBERT LAYTON, born New York, New York, February 19, 1931; admitted to bar, 1956, New York (Not admitted in District of Columbia). *Education:* University of Michigan (B.A., with distinction, 1951); Yale University (LL.B., 1954); University of Oxford, England (Institute of International Education Scholarship). Fourth American Recipient, Diploma of the Hague Academy of International Law, 1959. Attorney Advisor, Office of Legal Counsel, U.S. Department of Justice, 1958-1961. Partner, Layton & Sherman (merged with Surrey & Morse), 1973-1984; Partner, Surrey & Morse (merged with Jones, Day, Reavis & Pogue), 1984-1985; Partner (in charge of New York office litigation group), Jones, Day, Reavis & Pogue, 1986-1992. (Also Of Counsel, Sato Law Offices, Tokyo, Japan). ***LANGUAGES:*** Spanish and Hungarian. ***PRACTICE AREAS:*** International and Domestic Litigation; International Arbitration. ***Email:*** Robert.Layton@InmanDeming.com

EDWARD A. DRAGON, born Pawtucket, Rhode Island, October 27, 1928; admitted to bar, 1956, District of Columbia; 1957, Maryland. *Education:* Providence College (B.A., summa cum laude, 1950); Georgetown University (J.D., 1954; LL.M., 1957). U.S. Central Intelligence Agency, 1950-1957. Consultant, Executive Office of the President, 1961-1963. U.S. Agency for International

(This Listing Continued)

Development, (Attorney-Advisor, 1963-1967; Assistant General Counsel for African Affairs, 1974-1982; Regional Legal Advisor to Kenya, Sudan and Tanzania, 1982-1984; Regional Legal Advisor to Senegal, Mali and Mauritania, 1985-1989; Regional Legal Advisor to Jamaica, Haiti and the Dominican Republic, 1990-1993; Legal Advisor for Assistance to the New Haitian Constitutional Government, 1995). ***PRACTICE AREAS:*** International. ***Email:*** Ed.Dragon@InmanDeming.com

JOSEPH P. SMITH III, born Washington, D.C., March 12, 1943; admitted to bar, 1969, Virginia; 1991, District of Columbia. *Education:* Villanova University (B.S., 1965); West Virginia University, 1966; College of William and Mary (J.D., 1969). Federal Bureau of Investigation, 1969-1999, (Legal Counsel, Director, Regional Office, New York City; Supervisor, Special Organized Criminal and White Collar Unit, New York City and Chief, Disclosure Unit, Freedom of Information/Privacy Act Section, Washington, D.C.; Assistant Legal Attaché, U.S. Embassy, Canberra, Australia, 1991; Assistant Legal Attaché, 1992-1998, U.S. Embassy, Brussels, Belgium, for the Benelux Countries, the European Union in Brussels and the International Tribunal for the former Yugoslavia in the Hague.) *Member:* Virginia, Federal, American (Chair, Mutual Legal Assistance Subcommittee; Member, Criminal Law Section) and International Bar Associations. ***LANGUAGES:*** French, Spanish and Dutch. ***PRACTICE AREAS:*** International Criminal Law and Procedures; Legal Due Diligence; Freedom of Information Privacy Act. ***Email:*** Joe.Smith@InmanDeming.com

EMERY W. HARPER, born Hackensack, New Jersey, February 25, 1936; admitted to bar, 1962, New York (Not admitted in District of Columbia). *Education:* Amherst College (B.A., cum laude, 1958); Yale University (LL.B., 1961). Partner, Lord, Day & Lord, 1970-1993. President, Harper Consultants, Inc., 1997—. Advisor, U.S. Delegation, Joint Working Group on Maritime Liens and Mortgages, IMO/UNCTAD, 1986-1989. Private Sector Advisor, U.S. Delegation to IMO/UNCTAD Diplomatic Conference on Maritime Liens and Mortgages, 1993. Co-Founder, Board of Trustees, Admiralty Finance Forum, Inc. President, American Corporations in Coastwise Trade. Liberian Shipowners' Council. Delegate for the International Chamber of Commerce to the Diplomatic Conference on Arrest of Ships, 1999. *Member:* The Association of the Bar of the City of New York (Chairman, Admiralty Committee, 1977-1980); American Bar Association (Chair, Admiralty and Maritime Committee, 20001—; International Law and Practice Section); Maritime Law Association of the United States (Chairman, Committee on Marine Financing, 1979-1987). (Also with Law Offices of Emery W. Harper, New York City, NY). ***PRACTICE AREAS:*** Ship Finance; International Maritime; Maritime Law. ***Email:*** Emery.Harper@InmanDeming.com

GARRY L. WALTON, born Great Lakes, Illinois, December 27, 1954; admitted to bar, 1980, Michigan (Not admitted in District of Columbia). *Education:* University of Michigan (B.A., with high distinction, 1977; J.D., cum laude, 1979). Law Clerk, Honorable Richard A. Enslen, U.S. District Court, Western District of Michigan, 1980-1981. Warner, Norcross & Judd, 1981-1984. Dietrich, Zody, Walton & Lake, P.C., 1984-1989. *Member:* Kalamazoo County Bar Association; State Bar of Michigan (Member, Standing Committee on Character and Fitness, 1997—). (Also with Garry L. Walton, P.C., Kalamazoo, Michigan). ***PRACTICE AREAS:*** Commercial Transactions; Real Estate Acquisitions; Business Formation. ***Email:*** Garry.Walton@InmanDeming.com

IVINS, PHILLIPS & BARKER

CHARTERED

Established in 1936

SUITE 600, 1700 PENNSYLVANIA AVENUE, N.W.

WASHINGTON, D.C. 20006

Telephone: 202-393-7600

Fax: 202-393-7601; 347-4256

Email: IPB@ipbtax.com

URL: http://www.ipbtax.com

Tax Law, Employee Benefits, Estate Planning and Related Litigation.

FIRM PROFILE: Ivins, Phillips & Barker is a firm of approximately 25 lawyers, all of whom practice exclusively in areas relating to federal taxes and employee benefits. The firm was founded in 1936 as the successor firm to the firms of Holmes, Brewster & Ivins and Brewster, Ivins & Phillips. James S.Y. Ivins and Percy W. Phillips were two of the original members of the United States Board of Tax Appeals (now the United State Tax Court) and were appointed to that court by President Calvin Coolidge in 1924.

Since its inception, the firm has been engaged exclusively in a broad practice of tax law with particular emphasis on: (1) corporate acquisitions and reorganizations; (2) pensions, executive compensation, and other employee benefit matters; (3) tax issues of corporate accounting and finance; (4) international tax issues; (5) other tax issues of large corporations; (6) estate and gift tax, closely held business planning, exempt organizations and individual planning; and (7) the handling of controversies and litigation related to these and other areas of tax law.

(This Listing Continued)

JAMES S. Y. IVINS (1885-1960).

PERCY W. PHILLIPS (1892-1969).

RICHARD B. BARKER (1906-1988).

H. STEWART DUNN, JR., born Pittsburgh, Pennsylvania, July 9, 1929; admitted to bar, 1954, District of Columbia. *Education:* Yale University (A.B., 1951); Harvard University (LL.B., magna cum laude, 1954). Member, Board of Editors, Harvard Law Review, 1953-1954. Adjunct Professor, Georgetown University Law Center, 1976-1977. Lecturer on Law, Harvard Law School, Winter Term, 1987. Member, 1977-1979 and Chairman, 1979-1981, United States Committee on the Selection of Federal Judicial Officers. Director, Wilmington Trust Company. *Member:* The District of Columbia Bar; Bar Association of the District of Columbia; American Bar Association (Vice Chairman, Section of Taxation, 1970-1973); American Law Institute; International Fiscal Association. Fellow: American Bar Foundation; American College of Tax Counsel; American College of Trust and Estate Counsel. ***PRACTICE AREAS:*** Federal Tax. ***Email:*** hsdunn@ipbtax.com

CARROLL J. SAVAGE, born Columbia, South Carolina, November 30, 1934; admitted to bar, 1964, District of Columbia. *Education:* University of the South (B.A., with honors, 1956); Fletcher School of Law & Diplomacy (M.A., 1957); Harvard University (J.D., magna cum laude, 1963). Phi Beta Kappa. Member, Board of Editors, Harvard Law Review, 1962-1963. *Member:* The District of Columbia Bar; American Bar Association. ***PRACTICE AREAS:*** Employee Benefits; Employment Taxation; Executive Compensation; ERISA Litigation; ESOPs. ***Email:*** cjsavage@ipbtax.com

ERIC R. FOX, born Jackson Heights, New York, July 4, 1939; admitted to bar, 1964, New York; 1965, District of Columbia. *Education:* Amherst College (A.B., 1961); Harvard University (LL.B., cum laude, 1964). Editor-in-Chief, Journal of International Taxation, 1990-1997. *Member:* The District of Columbia Bar; American Bar Association (Section of Taxation; Vice Chair, 1984-1986 and Chair, 1986-1988, Foreign Activities of U.S. Taxpayers Committee, Vice Chair, 1988-1989 and Chair, 1989-1991, Committee on Government Submissions; Council, 1991-1994; Vice-Chair, Administration, 1996-1998); International Fiscal Association; American College of Tax Counsel. ***PRACTICE AREAS:*** Corporate Taxation; International Taxation; Tax Litigation; Estate and Gift Taxation. ***Email:*** ericfox@ipbtax.com

WILLIAM L. SOLLEE, born Jacksonville, Florida, June 25, 1942; admitted to bar, 1966, Florida; 1967, District of Columbia. *Education:* University of Florida (B.S. in B.A., magna cum laude, 1964; J.D., cum laude, 1966). Order of the Coif. Executive Editor, University of Florida Law Review, 1965. Editor, Compensation Department of the Journal of Taxation, 1985—. *Member:* The District of Columbia Bar; The Florida Bar; American Bar Association (Chairman: Employee Benefits Committee, Section of Taxation, 1982-1984; Joint Committee on Employee Benefits, 1981-1982); American College of Tax Counsel. ***PRACTICE AREAS:*** Employee Benefits; Employment Taxation; Executive Compensation; ERISA Litigation; ESOPs. ***Email:*** billsollee@ipbtax.com

CAROL K. NICKEL, born Boston, Massachusetts, December 17, 1943; admitted to bar, 1968, District of Columbia. *Education:* Wellesley College (B.A., 1965); George Washington Law School (J.D., with honors, 1968). Order of the Coif. Articles and Book Review Editor, George Washington Law Review, 1967-1968. *Member:* The District of Columbia Bar; American Bar Association. ***PRACTICE AREAS:*** Federal Tax; Estate and Gift Taxation; Individual Tax; Tax Exempt Organizations.

ALAN W. GRANWELL, admitted to bar, 1968, Massachusetts; 1970, New York; 1984, District of Columbia. *Education:* Middlebury College (A.B., 1965); Boston University (J.D., 1968; LL.M. in Taxation, 1969); New York University (LL.M., 1976). Adjunct Assistant Professor of Law, New York University School of Law, 1980-1981. International Tax Counsel and Director, Office of International Tax Affairs, U.S. Department of the Treasury, 1981-1984. *Member:* The District of Columbia Bar; New York State (Member, Executive Committee, Tax Section, 1984-1988; Co-Chairman: Committee on Tax Policy, 1987-1988; Co-Chairman, Committee on Foreign Activities of U.S. Taxpayers, 1979, 1986; Committee on U.S. Activities on Foreign Taxpayers, 1980), American (Member, Taxation Section; Articles Editor, The Tax Lawyer, 1978-1980) and International Bar Associations; International Fiscal Association. ***PRACTICE AREAS:*** International Taxation; Federal Income Tax. ***Email:*** awgranwell@ipbtax.com

LESLIE JAY SCHNEIDER, born New York, N.Y., December 27, 1946; admitted to bar, 1971, District of Columbia; 1972, Maryland. *Education:* University of Maryland (B.S., magna cum laude, 1967); Georgetown University (J.D., 1971). Member, Board of Editors, Georgetown Law Journal, 1970-1971. Certified Public Accountant, Maryland, 1971. Author: *"Federal Income Taxation of Inventories,"* Matthew Bender, 1979. Adjunct Professor, Georgetown University Law Center, 1974-1980. Office of Tax Legislative Counsel, U.S. Treasury Department, 1971-1973. Special Assistant to Assistant Secretary for Tax Policy, U.S. Treasury Department, 1973. *Member:* The District of Columbia Bar; American Bar Association; American Institute of Certified Public Accountants. ***PRACTICE AREAS:*** Accounting; Audits; Inventory Taxation. ***Email:*** lschneider@ipbtax.com

(This Listing Continued)

IVINS, PHILLIPS & BARKER, CHARTERED, Washington—Continued

ROBERT H. WELLEN, born Jersey City, New Jersey, August 19, 1946; admitted to bar, 1971, Connecticut; 1972, District of Columbia; 1982, Colorado. *Education:* Yale College (B.A., 1968); Yale University (J.D., 1971); Georgetown University Law Center (LL.M., 1975). Phi Beta Kappa. *Member:* The District of Columbia Bar; Colorado, Connecticut, American (Chair, Committee on Corporate Tax, Section of Taxation, 1991-1992; Supervising Editor, Tax Section Newsletter, 1993-1997; Assistant Secretary, 1997-1998) and Federal Bar Associations. ***PRACTICE AREAS:*** Business Taxation; Corporate Taxation; Federal Tax.

KEVIN P. O'BRIEN, born New York, N.Y., June 27, 1951; admitted to bar, 1976, District of Columbia. *Education:* Georgetown University (A.B., cum laude, with distinction, 1973); Georgetown University Law Center (J.D., 1976; LL.M. in Taxation, 1980). *Member:* The District of Columbia Bar; American Bar Association. ***PRACTICE AREAS:*** Employee Benefits; Employment Taxation; Executive Compensation; ERISA Litigation; ESOPs.

DANIEL B. STONE, born Baltimore, Maryland, February 11, 1955; admitted to bar, 1979, District of Columbia. *Education:* Wesleyan University (B.A., magna cum laude, 1976); Harvard University (J.D., cum laude, 1979). Law Clerk to Hon. Marion T. Bennett, U.S. Court of Claims, 1979-1981. *Member:* The District of Columbia Bar; American Bar Association. ***PRACTICE AREAS:*** Pensions; Employee Benefits; Employment Taxation; ERISA Litigation; ESOPs.

PATRICK J. SMITH, born Devils Lake, North Dakota, November 1, 1951; admitted to bar, 1981, District of Columbia. *Education:* Harvard University (A.B., cum laude, 1973; J.D., magna cum laude, 1981); Florida International University (M.S.M., 1979). Phi Beta Kappa. Member, Board of Editors, Harvard Law Review, 1980-1981. *Member:* The District of Columbia Bar; American Bar Association. ***PRACTICE AREAS:*** Accounting; Inventory Taxation. ***Email:*** psmith@ipbtax.com

MICHAEL R. HUFFSTETLER, born Columbia, South Carolina, July 18, 1954; admitted to bar, 1983, District of Columbia. *Education:* University of South Carolina (B.S. in Accounting, summa cum laude, 1976); University of Michigan (J.D., magna cum laude, 1983). Phi Beta Kappa; Beta Alpha Psi; Phi Eta Sigma; Beta Gamma Sigma. Certified Public Accountant: South Carolina, 1980; Michigan, 1980. Author: "Nonqualified Deferred Compensation," and "Golden Parachutes," Tax Practice Series, Tax Management, Inc., 1989. *Member:* The District of Columbia Bar; American Bar Association. ***PRACTICE AREAS:*** Employee Benefits; Employment Taxation; Executive Compensation; ERISA Litigation; ESOPs. ***Email:*** huffy@ipbtax.com

LAURIE E. KEENAN, born Du Bois, Pennsylvania, August 18, 1952; admitted to bar, 1983, District of Columbia; 1985, California. *Education:* College of William & Mary (A.B., cum laude, 1974); University of Virginia (J.D., 1983). Order of the Coif. Dillard Fellow, University of Virginia, 1981-1983. *Member:* The District of Columbia Bar; State Bar of California; American Bar Association. ***PRACTICE AREAS:*** Employee Benefits; Employment Taxation; Executive Compensation; ERISA Litigation; ESOPs. ***Email:*** lekeenan@mindspring.com

JEFFREY E. MOELLER, born Pittsburgh, Pennsylvania, June 20, 1963; admitted to bar, 1988, Pennsylvania; 1991, District of Columbia. *Education:* Pennsylvania State University (B.A., with high distinction, 1985); Georgetown University (J.D., cum laude, 1988). Phi Beta Kappa. Executive Editor, The Tax Lawyer, 1987-1988. Co-Author: "Foreign Personal Holding Companies," BNA Tax Management Portfolio, 1991. ***PRACTICE AREAS:*** Business Taxation; Corporate Taxation; Federal Tax; Partnerships.

STEVEN H. WITMER, born Abington, Pennsylvania, December 21, 1964; admitted to bar, 1990, Pennsylvania and Massachusetts; 1991, District of Columbia. *Education:* Lebanon Valley College (B.A., summa cum laude, 1987); Harvard University (J.D., cum laude, 1990). *Member:* District of Columbia Bar; American Bar Association. ***PRACTICE AREAS:*** Employee Benefits; Employment Taxation; Executive Compensation; ERISA Litigation; ESOPs. ***Email:*** switmer@ipbtax.com

ROSINA B. BARKER, born Glen Cove, New York, December 21, 1955; admitted to bar, 1990, Maryland; 1992, District of Columbia. *Education:* Harvard University (A.B., cum laude, 1979; M.P.P., 1983); Georgetown University (J.D., magna cum laude, 1990). Order of the Coif. Recipient, Nelson T. Hartson Memorial Award. *Member:* District of Columbia Bar; Maryland State Bar Association, Inc.; American Bar Association. ***PRACTICE AREAS:*** Employee Benefits; Employment Taxation; Executive Compensation; ERISA Litigation; ESOPs. ***Email:*** rosinabarker@ipbtax.com

JODI H. EPSTEIN, born Newton, Massachusetts, May 22, 1966; admitted to bar, 1993, Illinois; 1995, District of Columbia. *Education:* Stanford University (B.A., with distinction, 1988); Harvard University (J.D., cum laude, 1993). Law Clerk, Hon. Suzanne B. Conlon, Federal District Court, Northern District of Illinois, 1993-1994. *Member:* The District of Columbia Bar (Tax Section, 1995-1997 —); American Bar Association (Tax Section, 1994-1997 —). ***PRACTICE AREAS:*** Employee Benefits.

DEAN R. MORLEY, IV, born Atlanta, Georgia, January 13, 1966; admitted to bar, 1991, Georgia; 1997, District of Columbia. *Education:* Duke University (B.A., cum laude, 1988); University of Georgia (J.D., cum laude, 1991); Georgetown University Law Center (LL.M., Taxation, with distinction, 1997). Attorney-advisor, IRS Office of Associate Chief Counsel (Employee Benefits and Exempt Organizations), 1991-1995. *Member:* State Bar of Georgia; The District of Columbia Bar; American Bar Association (Member, Tax Section). ***PRACTICE AREAS:*** Employee Benefits; Pensions; Executive Compensation; Employment Tax. ***Email:*** dmorley@ipbtax.com

DAVID GREGORY COOLIDGE, born Kittery, Maine, December 28, 1965; admitted to bar, 1996, Virginia; 1998, District of Columbia. *Education:* Stanford University (B.A., with distinction, 1988); University of Virginia (J.D., 1996). Recipient, John M. Olin Prize in Law and Economics, University of Virginia School of Law (May 1996). Editor-in-Chief, Virginia Tax Review, 1995-1996. Author: A Square Hole for a Square Peg: Section 165 and Environmental Cleanup Costs, 14 Virginia Tax Review 779 (Spring 1995). *Member:* Virginia and American Bar Associations; Virginia State Bar; Bar Association of the District of Columbia; The District of Columbia Bar. ***PRACTICE AREAS:*** Federal Tax; Employee Benefits; Corporate Taxation. ***Email:*** dcoolidge@ipbtax.com

ERIC D. CHASON, born Brevard, North Carolina, October 19, 1970; admitted to bar, 1996, Virginia (Not admitted in District of Columbia). *Education:* Duke University (B.A., magna cum laude, 1993); University of Virginia (J.D., 1996). Phi Beta Kappa. John M. Olin Law and Economics Fellow; Edwin S. Cohen Tax Prize. Notes Editor and Editorial Board Member, Virginia Law Review, 1994-1996. *Member:* Virginia State Bar; American Bar Association (Member, Section of Taxation). ***PRACTICE AREAS:*** Federal Estate and Gift Taxation; Federal Income Tax.

ROBIN M. SOLOMON, born Boston, Massachusetts, May 28, 1971; admitted to bar, 1997, New York, Maryland (inactive) and District of Columbia. *Education:* Stanford University (A.B., 1993); Harvard University (J.D., 1996). Law Clerk, Hon. Benson E. Legg, U.S. District Court of Maryland, 1996-1997. *Member:* American Bar Association. ***PRACTICE AREAS:*** Tax; Employee Benefits.

LISA M. ROBINSON, born Birmingham, Alabama, April 20, 1969; admitted to bar, 1994, New York; 1999, District of Columbia. *Education:* Harvard University (A.B., magna cum laude, with highest honors, 1992); Harvard Law School (J.D., 1995). *Member:* New York State Bar; The District of Columbia Bar; National Bar Association; American Bar Association (Member, Section of Taxation). ***PRACTICE AREAS:*** Employee Benefits; Executive Compensation; Federal Taxation; Corporate Taxation. ***Email:*** lrobinson@ipbtax.com

COLLEEN L.S. MARKHAM, born Washington, D.C., July 23, 1969; admitted to bar, 1997, Maryland; 1998, District of Columbia. *Education:* Princeton University (A.B., 1991); Georgetown University (J.D., 1997). *Member:* The District of Columbia Bar; Maryland State Bar Association, Inc.; American Bar Association. ***PRACTICE AREAS:*** Trusts and Estates; Federal Taxation; Estate and Gift Taxation; Individual Taxation; Tax Exempt Organizations.

MARLENE ELLEN LARO, born Flint, Michigan, June 11, 1971; admitted to bar, 1998, Maryland; 1998, District of Columbia. *Education:* Georgetown University (B.S.F.S., cum laude, 1993); New York University School Of Law (J.D., 1997; LL.M., Taxation, 1997). Member, National Slavic Honor Society, Georgetown University. Recipient, Dean's List, Georgetown University. ***LANGUAGES:*** Russian. ***PRACTICE AREAS:*** Federal Taxation; International Taxation. ***Email:*** mlaro@ipbtax.com

DAVID D. SHERWOOD, born Los Angeles, California, December 30, 1971; admitted to bar, 1999, California (Not admitted in District of Columbia). *Education:* Columbia college (B.a., summa cum laude, 1993); Harvard University (M.A., Economics, 1996; J.D., cum laude, 1998). Phi Beta Kappa. *Member:* State Bar of California; American Bar Association. ***PRACTICE AREAS:*** Taxation. ***Email:*** dsherwood@ipbtax.com

KAREN SULLIVAN DEAN, born Birmingham, Alabama, May 26, 1972; admitted to bar, 1997, Virginia; 1998, Alabama; 1999, District of Columbia. *Education:* Duke University (A.B., 1994); Washington College of Law of American University (J.D., magna cum laude, 1997). *Member:* Virginia State Bar; Alabama State Bar; The District of Columbia Bar.

OF COUNSEL

JAY W. GLASMANN, born Ogden, Utah, December 1, 1924; admitted to bar, 1950, Utah; 1951, District of Columbia. *Education:* University of Utah, Idaho State College and Harvard University (M.B.A., 1947); Harvard University (LL.B., cum laude, 1950). Assistant General Counsel, Treasury Depart-

(This Listing Continued)

ment, 1959; Assistant to Secretary of the Treasury for Tax Litigation and Head, Legal Advisory Staff, 1959-1961. *Member:* The District of Columbia Bar; Utah State Bar; American Bar Association; American Law Institute.

CLIFTON B. CATES, III, born Norfolk, Virginia, December 17, 1946; admitted to bar, 1975, District of Columbia; 1976, U.S. Tax Court and U.S. Claims Court; 1977, California. *Education:* Yale University (B.A., magna cum laude, 1968); Harvard University (J.D., cum laude, 1975). Phi Beta Kappa. Author: "Venue in Corporate Suits Against Federal Offices and Agencies," 60 Minnesota Law Review 81, 1975; "Pre-Immigration Tax Planning for the U.S. Bound Nonresident Alien," U.S. Taxation of International Operations, Prentice-Hall, 1982; "U.S. Tax Aspects of Foreign Investment in U.S. Real Estate," International Aspects of U.S. Taxation, American Tax Institute in Europe, 1978; "The Foreign Tax Credit: Basic Concepts and Mechanics," World Trade Institute, 1978; "Foreign Investment in the United States," Essentials of International Taxation, State Bar of California, 1979; "Insuring that Special Allocations of Partnership Income and Loss Are Recognized," 9 Taxation for Lawyers 202, 1981; "Making the Most of Special Allocations of Partnership Income and Coping with the Risks," 9 Taxation for Lawyers 302, 1981. *Member:* The State Bar of California (Chair, Section of Taxation, 1982-1983); Los Angeles County and American Bar Associations; The District of Columbia Bar. [Lt., U.S. Navy, 1968-1972]. ***PRACTICE AREAS:*** Taxation Law. ***Email:*** cbcates@mindspring.com

ALAN J. J. SWIRSKI, born Waterbury, Connecticut, December 31, 1963; admitted to bar, 1988, Massachusetts; 1989, District of Columbia. *Education:* Boston College (B.A., magna cum laude, 1985); Georgetown University Law Center (J.D., magna cum laude, 1988). Order of the Coif. Editor, Criminal Procedure Project, Georgetown Law Journal, 1987-1988. Law Clerk to Judge Paul V. Niemeyer, U.S. District Court, District of Maryland, 1988-1989. Trial Attorney, Tax Division, 1995-1997 and Senior Trial Attorney, 1997-1999, United States Department of Justice. *Member:* Bar Association of the District of Columbia; American Bar Association (Member, Tax Section). ***PRACTICE AREAS:*** Corporate Taxation; Tax Litigation. ***Email:*** aswirski@ipbtax.com

JEANNIE LEAHY, born Hartford, Connecticut, January 15, 1959; admitted to bar, 1984, Wisconsin; 1987, Massachusetts and Maine; 1993, California (Not admitted in District of Columbia). *Education:* Brown University (B.A., cum laude, 1980); University of Wisconsin Law School (J.D., cum laude, 1984). Order of the Coif. Previous Employment: Office of the Solicitor, U.S. Department of Labor, Staff Attorney; Pierce Atwood, Portland, Maine, Partner; Northrop Grumman Corporation, Senior Counsel; The Boeing Company, Counsel. *Member:* Maine State and American (Member, Tax Section) Bar Associations; State Bar of California. ***PRACTICE AREAS:*** Pension and Profit Sharing Plans; Employee Benefits.

LEGAL SUPPORT PERSONNEL

JEFFREY T. FREILICH (Librarian).

JACKSON & CAMPBELL, P.C.

ONE LAFAYETTE CENTRE
300 SOUTH TOWER, 1120-20TH STREET, N.W.
WASHINGTON, D.C. 20036
Telephone: 202-457-1600
Telecopier: 202-457-1678
Email: info@jackscamp.com
URL: http://www.jackscamp.com

Rockville, Maryland Office: Suite 225, 200 A Monroe Street. Telephone: 301-340-0450.
Baltimore, Maryland Office: 111 S. Calvert Street, Suite 2700. Telephone: 410-385-5343.
Vienna, Virginia Office: 8300 Boone Boulevard, Suite 500. Telephone: 703-522-1330.

Antitrust and Trade Regulation, Corporate and Securities, Employment, Environmental, Estates and Trusts, Hospitals and Health Care, Insurance Coverage, Intellectual Property, International Telecommunications and International Trade, Litigation, Professional and Medical Malpractice Defense, Property and Asset Management, Tax, Title Insurance, Trade Associations and Charitable Foundations Law. General Practice.

FIRM PROFILE: For more than a century, Jackson & Campbell and its predecessor firms have figured prominently in the Washington legal community. The firm consists of over fifty lawyers based in Washington, D.C. with offices in suburban Virginia, Maryland and in Baltimore. The Firm's size and geographic base have enabled Jackson & Campbell to combine a sophisticated national practice in certain specialized areas of law with a solid local and regional practice representing corporate clients in a wide range of business and commercial legal matters.

(This Listing Continued)

The Firm is a recognized leader nationally in Insurance Coverage, Title Insurance and Property Management law. Internationally, the Firm represents clients engaging in real estate joint ventures, project financing, commercial transactions, mergers and acquisitions and telecommunications.

Jackson & Campbell has built its reputation on a commitment to personal service, responsiveness and individual attention to client needs.

JAMES E. BRAMMER, born Wichita, Kansas, March 21, 1942; admitted to bar, 1970, District of Columbia; U.S. District Court for the District of Columbia; U.S. Court of Appeals for the District of Columbia Circuit; 1980, U.S. Court of Appeals, Fourth Circuit. *Education:* Wichita State University (B.A., 1966); Georgetown University (J.D., 1970). First Vice President and Senior Counsel, GE Capital Asset Management Corporation, 1990-1995; Vice President and Counsel, GE Capital Mortgage Services, Inc., 1993-1995. *Member:* The District of Columbia Bar; Bar Association of the District of Columbia. ***PRACTICE AREAS:*** Property Management; Asset Management; Loan Servicing; Real Estate; Compliance. ***Email:*** jbrammer@jackscamp.com

JOHN J. BRENNAN, III, born New York, N.Y., November 5, 1951; admitted to bar, 1977, District of Columbia; 1978, Virginia; 1985, Maryland. *Education:* Georgetown University (B.A., 1973; J.D., 1977). Member, Board of Directors, Apartment and Office Building Association. Legal Columnist, Multifamily Executive. *Member:* The District of Columbia Bar; Virginia State Bar; Barristers. ***PRACTICE AREAS:*** Property Rights Litigation; Business Litigation; Technology Law; Electronic Commerce; Property Management; Real Estate; Multi-Family Housing Law; Business Law; Employment Law; State Administrative Practice. ***Email:*** jbrennan@jackscamp.com

RICHARD W. BRYAN, born Plainfield, New Jersey, March 28, 1955; admitted to bar, 1980, District of Columbia; 1981, Virginia; 1987, Maryland, U.S. District Courts for the District of Columbia, Eastern District of Virginia and District of Maryland. *Education:* College of William & Mary (B.A., 1977); George Washington University (J.D., with honors, 1980). *Member:* District of Columbia Bar; Virginia State Bar; Maryland State Bar; American Bar Association (Former Co-Chair, Environmental Impairment Liability Subcommittee, Insurance Coverage Committee, TIPS). ***PRACTICE AREAS:*** Automobile Insurance Coverage; Casualty Insurance; Commercial Insurance; Excess Coverage; Insurance Bad Faith; Insurance Coverage; Insurance Litigation; Insurance Mediation; Unfair Insurance Practices; Comercial Insurance Defense; General Liability Defense; Professional Liability Defense; Professional Liability Insurance Coverage. ***Email:*** rbryan@jackscamp.com

ARTHUR D. BURGER, born New York, N.Y., October 17, 1948; admitted to bar, 1973, District of Columbia; 1975, Maryland. *Education:* American University (B.A., 1970); George Washington University (J.D., with honors, 1973). Adjunct Faculty, GWU Law School and frequent Instructor of Ethics and Professional Responsibility at D.C. Bar Mandatory Course for new Admittees and D.C. Bar CLE. Attorney Advisor to the Rules Committee of the Superior Court of the District of Columbia, 1973-1975. Chief, General Litigation Section II of the D.C. Office of Corporation Counsel, 1987-1989. *Member:* American Bar Association (Center for Professional Responsibility); District of Columbia Bar (Vice Chair, Rules of Professional Conduct Review Committee). Chair of Firm's Professional Responsibility Practice Group and Chair of Firm's Ethics Committee. ***PRACTICE AREAS:*** Insurance Coverage; Civil Litigation; Professional Responsibility. ***Email:*** aburger@jackscamp.com

ROBERT CLAYTON COOPER, born San Francisco, California, January 30, 1962; admitted to bar, 1987, Maryland; 1988, U.S. District Court, District of Maryland; 1988, District of Columbia; 1989, U.S. District Court for the District of Columbia. *Education:* Howard University (B.B.A., 1984); George Washington University (J.D., 1987). Elected D.C. Advisory Neighborhood Commissioner, 1990-1994. President, George Washington Law Alumni Association, 1998-2000 Executive Committee (1988-1997). Legal Counsel, D.C. Downtown Jaycees, 1991-1995. Barrister, Charlotte E. Ray, American Inn of Court. *Member:* The District of Columbia Bar; Bar Association of the District of Columbia; Maryland State and American Bar Associations; National Bar Association. ***PRACTICE AREAS:*** Real Estate; Zoning, Planning and Land Use; Trusts and Estates; Corporate Law; Administrative Law; General Civil Litigation. ***Email:*** rcooper@jackscamp.com

DAVID H. COX, born Sendai, Japan, July 11, 1953; admitted to bar, 1978, District of Columbia; 1980, Virginia; 1994, Maryland; U.S. District Court for the District of Columbia, Eastern District of Virginia and Maryland; U.S. Court of Appeals for the District of Columbia Circuit, Fourth Circuit and Federal Circuit. *Education:* The Ohio State University (B.A., cum laude, 1975); Georgetown University (J.D., 1978). Phi Beta Kappa. Member, Kiwanis Club of Washington, D.C. *Member:* The District of Columbia Bar; Bar Association of the District of Columbia; Virginia State Bar; Maryland State and American (Member, Sections on: Real Property, Probate and Trust Law; Litigation; Business Law) Bar Associations; American Land Title Association; Community Associations Institute; The Greater Washington Board of Trade; The Barristers.

(This Listing Continued)

JACKSON & CAMPBELL, P.C., Washington—Continued

PRACTICE AREAS: Business Law; Corporate Law; Real Estate Law; Title Insurance Law; Cooperative Housing Law; General Civil Litigation. ***Email:*** dcox@jackscamp.com

TIMOTHY R. DINGILIAN, born Los Angeles, California, October 22, 1955; admitted to bar, 1983, District of Columbia; 1984, Maryland; U.S. Court of Appeals for the District of Columbia Circuit; U.S. Court of Appeals, Fifth Circuit; U.S. District Court for the District of Columbia. *Education:* University of California at Los Angeles (B.A., 1978); Pepperdine University (J.D., cum laude, 1983). Phi Delta Phi. Staff Member, Pepperdine University Law Review, 1981-1983. *Member:* The District of Columbia Bar; Bar Association of the District of Columbia; Maryland State and American Bar Associations; Barristers. ***PRACTICE AREAS:*** Insurance Coverage Litigation; Medical Malpractice. ***Email:*** tdingilian@jackscamp.com

BENJAMIN W. DULANY, born Washington, D.C., 1919; admitted to bar, 1948, District of Columbia; 1957, Virginia. *Education:* University of Virginia (A.B., 1942); George Washington University (LL.B., 1948). *Member:* The District of Columbia Bar; Bar Association of the District of Columbia; Virginia and American Bar Associations. Fellow, American College of Trial Lawyers. [Capt., U.S. Marine Corps, 1943-1946]. ***PRACTICE AREAS:*** Estate Planning Law; Probate Law; Trust Law. ***Email:*** bdulany@jackscamp.com

ARTHUR C. ELGIN, JR., born Washington, D.C., August 10, 1938; admitted to bar, 1966, Maryland; 1967, District of Columbia; 1970, U.S. Claims Court; 1977, U.S. Supreme Court. *Education:* Princeton University (B.S.E., 1960); George Washington University (J.D., 1966). Delta Theta Phi. *Member:* The District of Columbia Bar; Bar Association of the District of Columbia; Montgomery County (Treasurer, 1985-1986), Maryland State (Member, Ethics Committee, 1988-1992) and American Bar Associations; Montgomery County Bar Foundation (Treasurer, 1986-1987); Maryland Bar Foundation; District of Columbia Estate Planning Council; Estate Planning Council of Suburban Maryland. ***PRACTICE AREAS:*** Business Law; Corporate Law; Civil Litigation; Family Wealth Transfer; Estate Administration; Trust Administration; Estate Planning; Estate and Gift Taxation; Estate Litigation; Trust Litigation; Retirement Planning. ***Email:*** aelgin@jackscamp.com

VERNON W. JOHNSON, III, born Riverdale, Maryland, August 20, 1964; admitted to bar, 1989, Virginia; 1990, District of Columbia; 2000, Maryland. *Education:* Duke University (B.A., 1986); George Washington University (J.D., 1989). *Member:* The District of Columbia Bar; Virginia State Bar Association; Charles S. Fahy American Inn of Court; The Barristers. ***PRACTICE AREAS:*** Civil Litigation; Commercial Litigation; Trial Practice; Real Estate Litigation; Title Insurance Law. ***Email:*** vjohnson@jackscamp.com

ROBERT N. KELLY, born Philadelphia, Pennsylvania, July 18, 1952; admitted to bar, 1977, Florida; 1979, District of Columbia; 1990, Maryland. *Education:* Princeton University (B.S.E., 1974); University of Miami (J.D., 1977). Professional Instructor, Legal Methods Program, Washington College of Law, American University, 1987-1994. Member, Joint Task Force on Environmental Coverage Litigation, American Bar Association. Chair, Maritime Law Committee, Federal Bar Association, 1980-1982. *Member:* American Bar Association (Past Chair, Pollution Sub-Committee, Insurance Coverage Litigation Committee, Tort and Insurance Practice Section); Defense Research Institute (Chair, Intellectual Property Sub-Committee and Past Chair, Emerging Issues Sub-Committee of Insurance Committee); Princeton Club of Washington (Council Member-at-Large). ***Email:*** rkelly@jackscamp.com

RICHARD S. KUHL, born Bay City, Michigan, December 15, 1962; admitted to bar, 1988, Michigan and U.S. District Court, Eastern District of Michigan and U.S. District Court, Western District of Michigan; 1994, District of Columbia; 1996, U.S. Court of Appeals, Fourth Circuit and U.S. District Court, District of Maryland. *Education:* Western Michigan University (B.A., magna cum laude, 1985); University of Michigan (J.D., 1988). Associate Editor, University of Michigan Journal of Law Reform, 1987-1988. Author: Note, "A Proposal to Cap Tort Liability: Avoiding the Pitfalls of Heightened Rationality," 20 U. Mich. J.L. Ref. 1987; "The Concurrent Cause Theory: Inapplicable to Environmental Liability Coverage Disputes," Tort and Insurance Law Journal, Spring, 1995. *Member:* State Bar of Michigan; The District of Columbia Bar; American Bar Association (Member, Section on Tort and Insurance Practice). ***PRACTICE AREAS:*** Insurance Coverage; Civil Litigation. ***Email:*** rkuhl@jackscamp.com

PETER LIPRESTI, born New York, N.Y., 1952; admitted to bar, 1977, District of Columbia; 1991, Virginia. *Education:* State University of New York at Stony Brook (B.A., 1974); Georgetown University (J.D., 1977; M.L.T., 1981). Phi Beta Kappa. Attorney-Advisor, Interpretative Division, Office of Chief Counsel, Internal Revenue Service, Washington, D.C., 1977-1978. *Member:* The District of Columbia Bar; Virginia State and American (Member, Sections of: Taxation and Business Law) Bar Associations. ***PRACTICE AREAS:*** Corporate Law; Health Care; Taxation. ***Email:*** plipresti@jackscamp.com

WARREN C. LUTZ, born Lexington, Kentucky, March 16, 1957; admitted to bar, 1985, Pennsylvania; 1986, Maryland, District of Columbia and U.S. District Court for the District of Columbia; 1989, U.S. Court of Appeals for the District of Columbia Circuit. *Education:* Georgetown University (A.B., cum laude, 1979); George Washington University (J.D., 1985). *Member:* The District of Columbia Bar; Maryland State and American (Member, Sections on: Litigation; Tort and Insurance Law) Bar Associations. ***PRACTICE AREAS:*** Litigation; Products Liability; Construction Litigation; Construction Arbitration; Toxic Torts. ***Email:*** wlutz@jackscamp.com

JOHN J. MATTEO, born New Haven, Connecticut, July 10, 1960; admitted to bar, 1986, New York, District of Columbia and U.S. District Court, District of Columbia; 1987, U.S. District Court, District of Maryland; ; 1992, Maryland and Virginia. *Education:* Fordham University (B.A., 1982); Catholic University of America (J.D., 1985). Pi Sigma Alpha. Member, Jessup Moot Court Team (Chancellor). Instructor, Legal Issues Relevant to Health Care Administration, George Mason College of Nursing and Health Science, 1997—. *Member:* District of Columbia Bar; Virginia State Bar; American Bar Association; American Health Lawyers Association (Business Law Section, Health Law Forum). ***PRACTICE AREAS:*** Corporate Law; Business Law; Business Transactions; Health Law; Real Estate. ***Email:*** jmatteo@jackscamp.com

NICHOLAS S. McCONNELL, born Chicago, Illinois, May 25, 1946; admitted to bar, 1972, Virginia; 1973, District of Columbia; 1978, Maryland. *Education:* Bowdoin College (B.A., 1968); State University of New York at Buffalo and George Washington University (J.D., with honors, 1972). Phi Delta Phi. Member, District of Columbia Circuit Judicial Conference, 1983-1995, 2000. *Member:* The District of Columbia Bar; Bar Association of the District of Columbia; Virginia State Bar; Maryland State and American Bar Associations. ***PRACTICE AREAS:*** Health Law; Hospital Law; Medical Malpractice; General Litigation; Corporate Law; Business Law. ***Email:*** nmcconnell@jackscamp.com

M. ELIZABETH MEDAGLIA, born Suffern, New York, October 13, 1947; admitted to bar, 1972, Virginia; 1974, District of Columbia; 1980, U.S. Supreme Court; 1990, Maryland. *Education:* Sweet Briar College (B.A., 1969); University of Virginia (J.D., 1972). Phi Beta Kappa. Attorney: United States Attorney's Office for D.C., 1974-1979; Federal Labor Relations Authority, 1979-1982. Member, Judicial Conference of The District of Columbia Circuit, 1981—. *Member:* The District of Columbia Bar; American Bar Association (Member, Sections on: Litigation; Tort and Insurance Practice; Chair, TIPS Committee on Insurance Coverage Litigation, 1989-1991); Bar Association of the District of Columbia (Chair, Young Lawyers Section, 1980-1981); Women's Bar Association of D.C. (President, 1982-1983); Charles Fahy American Inn of Court (President, 1990-1992); Federation of Insurance and Corporate Counsel. ***PRACTICE AREAS:*** Civil Litigation; Insurance Coverage Litigation. ***Email:*** lmedaglia@jackscamp.com

JAMES R. MICHAL, born Chicago, Illinois, December 11, 1947; admitted to bar, 1973, District of Columbia; 1981, Maryland. *Education:* Loras College (A.B., 1969); Georgetown University (J.D., 1972). *Member:* The District of Columbia Bar; Bar Association of the District of Columbia; Maryland State and American Bar Associations. ***PRACTICE AREAS:*** Wills; Trust and Probate Law; International Business; Real Estate Law; Zoning, Planning and Land Use; Business Law; Corporate Law. ***Email:*** jmichal@jackscamp.com

ROBERT E. RIDER, JR., born Durham County, North Carolina, April 6, 1963; admitted to bar, 1988, Maryland and U.S. District Court, District of Maryland; 1989, District of Columbia; 1991, Virginia. *Education:* University of Virginia (B.A., 1985; J.D., 1988). Member, Raven Society. Former Member, Charles Fahy American Inn of Court. Vice Chair, TIPS Insurance Coverage Litigation Committee, Newsletter Editor. *Member:* The District of Columbia Bar; Maryland State and American Bar Associations; Virginia State Bar. ***PRACTICE AREAS:*** Insurance Coverage Litigation. ***Email:*** rrider@jackscamp.com

JAMES P. SCHALLER, born Hazleton, Pennsylvania, 1940; admitted to bar, 1969, Virginia and District of Columbia; 1972, U.S. Supreme Court; 1990, Maryland. *Education:* Kings College (B.A., 1965); George Washington University (J.D., 1969). Adjunct Faculty, George Washington University. Secretary and Faculty Member, National Institute for Trial Advocacy. Fellow: American College of Trial Lawyers (D.C. State Chair, 1997-1998; Member, Board of Regents, 1998—). District of Columbia Circuit Judicial Conference; Judicial Conference of D.C.; D.C. Court of Appeals Committee on Unauthorized Practice, 1982-1989. *Member:* The District of Columbia Bar; Bar Association of the District of Columbia; Virginia State Bar; Maryland State Bar Association. ***PRACTICE AREAS:*** Insurance Coverage Litigation; Environmental; Hazardous Waste; Toxic Torts; Professional Liability Litigation; Ethics, Professional Responsibility. ***Email:*** jschaller@jackscamp.com

ALAN R. SWENDIMAN, born Arlington, Virginia, April 5, 1947; admitted to bar, 1973, Maryland; 1974, District of Columbia. *Education:* University of North Carolina (A.B., 1969); Georgetown University (J.D., 1973). Phi Beta Kappa. Law Clerk, Hon. Edward S. Northrop, Chief Judge, U.S. District Court for Maryland, 1973-1974. General Counsel: Federal Labor Relations Authority, 1992-1993. Member, Office of Presidential Personnel, 1988-1989. Member, Board of Directors: Davis Memorial Goodwill Industries; Columbia Lighthouse

(This Listing Continued)

for the Blind (Chairman); Boys Scout of America NCAC; Junior Achievement; Leadership Washington; Point of Light (1999). Member, Greater Washington Board of Trade. Rotary Club of Washington, D.C. *Member:* The District of Columbia Bar; Bar Association of the District of Columbia; Montgomery County and Maryland State Bar Associations; Estate Planning Council of Maryland; Estate Planning Council of District of Columbia. ***PRACTICE AREAS:*** Estate Planning; Estate Administration; Nonprofit Organizations Law; Tax Exempt Organizations; Business Law; Religious Institutions. ***Email:*** aswendiman@jackscamp.com

DONALD L. UTTRICH, born Wilmington, Ohio, June 30, 1963; admitted to bar, 1989, Ohio and U.S. District Court, Southern District of Ohio; 1992, District of Columbia; 1993, U.S. District Court, District of Columbia; 1994, U.S. Court of Appeals, Eleventh Circuit. *Education:* Case Western Reserve University (B.A., magna cum laude, 1985); Georgetown University (M.S., Foreign Service, 1989; J.D., 1989). Phi Beta Kappa. *Member:* The District of Columbia Bar; American Bar Association (Member, Sections on: Tort and Insurance Practice; Vice-Chair, TIPS Excess, Surplus Lines and Reinsurance Committee). ***LANGUAGES:*** French. ***PRACTICE AREAS:*** Insurance Law; Environmental Law; Toxic Substances Law. ***Email:*** duttrich@jackscamp.com

---

RAYMOND P. AUSROTAS, born Boston, Massachusetts, June 15, 1969; admitted to bar, 1998, Massachusetts; 1999, District of Columbia. *Education:* Brown University (A.B., with honors, 1991); George Washington University (J.D., 1998). Member, American Intellectual Property Law Association (AIPLA) Quarterly Journal. *Member:* Massachusetts and American Bar Associations. ***PRACTICE AREAS:*** Litigation; Insurance Coverage. ***Email:*** rausrotas@jackscamp.com

JANET A. BROWN, born Manhasset, New York, April 21, 1973; admitted to bar, 1998, Virginia; 1999, District of Columbia. *Education:* St. John's University (B.A., summa cum laude, 1995); George Washington University (J.D., 1998). Executive Notes Editor, The Environmental Lawyer, Volume 4. *Member:* Virginia State Bar; District of Columbia Bar; Virginia and American Bar Associations; Federal Communications Bar Association. ***PRACTICE AREAS:*** Real Property; Telecommunications Law. ***Email:*** jbrown@jackscamp.com

KRISTAN M. CASSIDY, born Lansing, Michigan, March 11, 1967; admitted to bar, 1993, Illinois; 1999, District of Columbia. *Education:* University of Notre Dame (B.B.A., 1989); DePaul University (J.D., 1992). ***REPORTED CASES:*** Marshall Spiegel v. State Farm Ins. Co. ***PRACTICE AREAS:*** Insurance Coverage Litigation. ***Email:*** kcassidy@jackscamp.com

KENNETH C. CRICKMAN, born Bethesda, Maryland, March 20, 1965; admitted to bar, 1998, Maryland and U.S. District Court, District of Maryland; 1999, District of Columbia. *Education:* Guilford College (B.S., 1987); Widener University (J.D., 1992). ***PRACTICE AREAS:*** Cooperative Housing Law; Quiet Title; Real Estate Contracts; Real Estate Title Insurance; Real Property; Zoning Law; Bankruptcy. ***Email:*** kcrickman@jackscamp.com

NKEISHA J. DUMAS, born Kansas City, Kansas, July 11, 1974; admitted to bar, 2000, Virginia and U.S. Court of Appeals, Fourth Circuit; 2001, District of Columbia. *Education:* Morgan State University (B.S.C.E., 1996); Georgetown University (J.D., 2000). *Member:* American Bar Association. ***PRACTICE AREAS:*** Insurance Coverage; Business Litigation. ***Email:*** ndumas@jackscamp.com

ELISA A. EISENBERG, born Washington, D.C., April 13, 1965; admitted to bar, 1991, Maryland; 1992, District of Columbia; 1993, U.S. District Court, District of Maryland. *Education:* Newcomb College of Tulane University (B.A., 1987); Tulane Law School (J.D., 1991). Senior Fellow. *Member:* District of Columbia Bar; Women's Bar Association of the District of Columbia. ***PRACTICE AREAS:*** Insurance Coverage Litigation; Litigation. ***Email:*** eeisenberg@jackscamp.com

JOHN A. GIANNETTI, JR., born Camp Lejeune, North Carolina, June 9, 1964; admitted to bar, 1995, Maryland (Not admitted in District of Columbia). *Education:* Bucknell University (B.S., 1986); University of Maryland School of Law (J.D., 1994). Member, Maryland General Assembly, Delegate (District 13B). Member, Board of Appeals, Laurel, MD, 1995-1998. *Member:* Prince George's County, Federal and American Bar Associations; Maryland State Bar Association, Inc. ***PRACTICE AREAS:*** Telecommunications Law; Real Property; Litigation. ***Email:*** jgiannetti@jackscamp.com

NGOC H. LAM, born Saigon, Vietnam, February 14, 1970; admitted to bar, 1995, Maryland; 1996, U.S. District Court, District of Maryland; 1999, District of Columbia. *Education:* Pennsylvania State University (B.S., Finance, 1991); The Washington College of Law, American University (J.D., 1994). Member, The American University Law Review. *Member:* Maryland State Bar Association, Inc.; District of Columbia Bar; American Bar Association; Asian Pacific American Bar Association. (Also at Baltimore and Rockville, MD offices). ***LANGUAGES:*** Vietnamese. ***Email:*** nlam@jackscamp.com

DANIEL J. LYNN, born Honolulu, Hawaii, February 1, 1969; admitted to bar, 1997, Maryland; 2000, District of Columbia and U.S. District Court for the

(This Listing Continued)

District of Columbia. *Education:* Providence College (B.A., cum laude, 1991); Blackfriar's College-Oxford University (1989-1990); Columbus School of Law of the Catholic University of America (J.D., 1996). *Member:* District of Columbia Bar; Maryland State and American Bar Associations. ***PRACTICE AREAS:*** Insurance Coverage; Insurance Defense Litigation. ***Email:*** dlynn@jackscamp.com

BARBARA M.R. MARVIN, born Galesburg, Illinois; admitted to bar, 1995, Virginia; 1996, Maryland; 1997, District of Columbia. *Education:* North Park University (B.A., 1976); DePaul University (M.M., 1982); American University (J.D., magna cum laude, 1995). Articles Editor, American University Law Review. Law Clerk to the Honorable Jack B. Stevens, Nineteenth Judicial Circuit of Virginia, 1995-1996. ***PRACTICE AREAS:*** Insurance Coverage. ***Email:*** bmarvin@jackscamp.com

ERIN N. McGONAGLE, born Elizabeth, New Jersey, March 7, 1965; admitted to bar, 1991, California; 1994, District of Columbia; 1997, Maryland. *Education:* University of North Carolina at Chapel Hill (B.A., 1987); Pepperdine University School of Law (J.D., 1991). Note and Comment Editor, Pepperdine Law Review. Author: "California Supreme Court Survey," Pepperdine Law Review, Vol. 18, 1990-1991. Judicial Extern to The Honorable Stephen R. Reinhardt, U.S. Court of Appeals, Ninth Judicial Circuit, 1990. ***Email:*** emcgonagle@jackscamp.com

SYEDA B. NAQVI, born Hyderabad, India, March 11, 1966; admitted to bar, 1997, Maryland; 1999, U.S. District Court, District of Maryland; 2001, District of Columbia. *Education:* Osmania University (B.A., 1986); Catholic University of America (J.D., 1997). Former Law Clerk to: The Honorable Toni E. Clarke, Prince George's County Circuit Court, Maryland; The U.S. Attorney's Office for the District of Maryland, Southern Division; the Honorable John A. Terry, District of Columbia Court of Appeals Intern; the Office of the Inspector General, Corporation for National Service. ***LANGUAGES:*** Urdu and Hindi. ***PRACTICE AREAS:*** Litigation; Commercial Law; Construction Law; Business Law; Zoning, Planning and Land Use; Telecommunications Law. ***Email:*** snaqvi@jackscamp.com

ROBERT NOTIGAN, born Edgewater Park, New Jersey, December 1, 1972; admitted to bar, 1998, Maryland; 2001, District of Columbia. *Education:* Pennsylvania State University (B.A., 1995); George Washington University Law Center (J.D., 1998). *Member:* Virginia Bar Association; Maryland State Bar Association, Inc.; District of Columbia Bar. ***PRACTICE AREAS:*** Corporate Securities; Real Estate; Litigation.

JASON A. PARDO, born Baltimore, Maryland, August 11, 1970; admitted to bar, 1995, Maryland; 1996, District of Columbia; U.S. District Court, District of Columbia. *Education:* Boston College (B.S., 1992); Catholic University of America (J.D., cum laude, 1995). Author: Journal of Contemporary Health Law and Policy, Spring, 1995. ***PRACTICE AREAS:*** Business Litigation; Commercial Litigation; Health Care Litigation. ***Email:*** jpardo@jackscamp.com

SUSAN PHILLIPS, born Columbus, Ohio, December 1, 1968; admitted to bar, 1995, Florida; 1998, District of Columbia; U.S. Court of Appeals for the District of Columbia Circuit; U.S. District Court, Southern and Middle Districts of Florida and District of Columbia. *Education:* Heidelberg College (B.S., cum laude, 1991); University of Miami (J.D., cum laude, 1995). ***PRACTICE AREAS:*** Litigation. ***Email:*** sphillips@jackscamp.com

ANN MARIE TERZAKEN, born Port Jefferson, New York, March 24, 1973; admitted to bar, 1998, Maryland; 1999, District of Columbia. *Education:* American University (B.A., History, cum laude, 1995); George Washington University (J.D., 1998). Member, Moot Court Board. Member, Environmental Lawyer Journal. ***PRACTICE AREAS:*** Health Care Litigation; Hospital Liability Defense; General Litigation; Commercial Litigation. ***Email:*** aterzake@jackscamp.com

OF COUNSEL

JEFFREY L. BERGER, born New York, N.Y., June 28, 1948; admitted to bar, 1974, New York; 1977, District of Columbia; 1992, Maryland. *Education:* SUNY at Buffalo (B.A., 1969); Rutgers University (J.D., 1973); Georgetown University (LL.M. in Tax and Labor Law, 1979). EEOC Mediator, 1999—. Labor Counsel to Computing Technology Industry Assn., 1997—. Member: Board Member: Association for Corporate Growth. Board Advisor: InfoZen, Inc. *Member:* District of Columbia Bar (Elected Member, Law Practice Management Committee, 2000—); American Bar Association (Member, Employment Law Section); High Tech Council of Maryland. (Also practicing individually at same address). ***Email:*** jberger@jackscamp.com

ROY L. KAUFMANN, born Philadelphia, Pennsylvania; admitted to bar, 1978, District of Columbia and U.S. District Court for the District of Columbia. *Education:* State University of New York at Albany (B.A., cum laude, 1975); George Washington University (J.D., 1978). *Member:* District of Columbia Bar; American Arbitration Association. ***PRACTICE AREAS:*** Commercial Business; Real Estate; Title. ***Email:*** rkaufmann@jackscamp.com

MICHAEL PAIGE, born Washington, D.C., May 5, 1941; admitted to bar, 1967, New York; 1981, District of Columbia. *Education:* Harvard University

(This Listing Continued)

JACKSON & CAMPBELL, P.C., Washington—Continued

(B.A., 1963); University of Virginia (LL.B., 1967). Phi Delta Phi. Assistant General Counsel for Petroleum Regulations, Department of Energy, 1977-1979. *Member:* District of Columbia Bar; New York State and American Bar Associations. ***LANGUAGES:*** French. ***PRACTICE AREAS:*** Corporate Law; Securities; International Transactions. ***Email:*** mpaige@jackscamp.com

JACKSON & JESSUP, P.C.

WASHINGTON, D.C.

(See Arlington, Virginia)

Railroad, Motor Carrier, Interstate Commerce, Transportation and related Litigation.

JACKSON & KELLY PLLC

2401 PENNSYLVANIA AVENUE, N.W., SUITE 400

WASHINGTON, D.C. 20037

Telephone: 202-973-0200
Fax: 202-973-0232
Email: info@jacksonkelly.com
URL: http://www.jacksonkelly.com

REVISORS OF THE WEST VIRGINIA LAW DIGEST FOR THIS DIRECTORY

Charleston, West Virginia Office: 1600 Laidley Tower, P.O. Box 553. Telephone: 304-340-1000. Fax: 304-340-1130.

Martinsburg, West Virginia Office: 217 West Burke Street, P.O. Box 1068. Telephone: 304-263-8800. Fax: 304-263-7110.

Morgantown, West Virginia Office: 6000 Hampton Center, P.O. Box 619. Telephone: 304-599-3000. Fax: 304-285-2040.

New Martinsville, West Virginia Office: 256 Russell Avenue, P.O. Box 68. Telephone: 304-455-1751. Fax: 304-455-6314.

Parkersburg, West Virginia Office: 412 Market Street, Suite 202, P.O. Box 1144. Telephone: 304-424-3490. Fax: 304-424-3499.

Fairmont, West Virginia Office: 1000 Technology Drive, Suite 1310. Telephone: 304-368-2000. Fax: 304-368-2020.

Lexington, Kentucky Office: 175 East Main Street, Suite 500, P.O. Box 2150. Telephone: 859-255-9500. Fax: 859-281-6478.

Denver, Colorado Office: Denver Place-Plaza Tower, 1099 Eighteenth Street, Suite 2150. Telephone: 303-390-0003. Fax: 303-390-0177.

Wheeling, West Virginia Office: 1144 Market Street. Telephone: 304-233-4000. Fax: 304-233-4077.

Health, Safety and Environmental, Regulatory and Legislative, Litigation, Corporate, Public Utilities, Coal, Metal and Minerals Development, Construction, Oil and Gas, Natural Resources, Endangered Species and Marine Mammals, Taxation, Municipal Bond, Labor and Employment, Insurance, Estate Planning, Real Estate, Securities, Bankruptcy, Banking, Federal Lands and Royalties, Health Care, Workers Compensation, Federal Black Lung, Admiralty, Government Contracts Law; Intellectual Property.

FIRM PROFILE: Jackson & Kelly PLLC, with 10 offices located in Charleston, Martinsburg, Morgantown, New Martinsville, Fairmont, Wheeling, Parkersburg, West Virginia; Lexington, Kentucky, Washington, D.C. and Denver, Colorado is one of the region's oldest and largest law firms and has provided legal services to clients since the early 1800s. Initially regional in nature, the firm's practice now extends throughout the United States and overseas.

The Firm's practice combines diversity, specialization and a commitment to excellence that have become hallmarks. Jackson & Kelly lawyers are committed to providing each client, whether an individual or a major corporation, with innovative, high-quality legal representation, performed on a timely basis, at a reasonable cost.

LAW FIRM ALLIANCES/ASSOCIATIONS: **LEX MUNDI:** *LEX MUNDI.*

MEMBERS OF FIRM

THAD S. HUFFMAN, born Keyser, West Virginia, June 30, 1952; admitted to bar, 1984, West Virginia; 1990, District of Columbia. *Education:* University of Denver (B.A., 1974; M.B.A., 1977); West Virginia University (J.D., 1984). Senior Manuscript Editor, West Virginia Law Review, 1982-1984. Editorial Board, Journal of College and University Law, 1982-1984. *Member:* Bar Association of the District of Columbia; West Virginia and American (Member, Sections on Natural Resources and Administrative Law) Bar Associations; The District of Columbia Bar; West Virginia State Bar. (Administrative Manager). ***PRACTICE AREAS:*** Natural Resources; Administrative and Commercial Law. ***Email:*** tshuffman@jacksonkelly.com

G. LINDSAY SIMMONS, born New York, N.Y., June 15, 1949; admitted to bar, 1974, Ohio; 1975, District of Columbia; 1985, U.S. Supreme Court; 1980, U.S. Court of Federal Claims. *Education:* Carnegie-Mellon University (B.A., 1971); Case Western Reserve University (J.D., 1974). Attorney, Solicitor's Office, U.S. Department of Labor, Occupational Safety and Health Division, 1975-1978. Assistant Corporation Counsel for The District of Columbia, Civil Division, 1978-1981. In Private Practice since 1981. *Member:* The District of Columbia Bar (Member, Government Contracts and Litigation Sections). ***PRACTICE AREAS:*** Litigation; Government Contracts; Safety and Health. ***Email:*** lsimmons@jacksonkelly.com

JOHN K. McDONALD, born Vinita, Oklahoma, May 29, 1945; admitted to bar, 1973, Oklahoma; 1980, District of Columbia; U.S. Supreme Court; U.S. Court of Appeals, District of Columbia, Fifth, Tenth and Eleventh Circuits; U.S. Court of Appeals for the Federal Circuit; U.S. Court of International Trade; U.S. District Court, District of Columbia; U.S. District Court, Eastern District of Oklahoma. *Education:* University of Oklahoma (B.B.A., 1968; J.D., 1972); Magdalen College, Oxford University, Oxford, England; George Town University Law Center (LL.M., International and Comparative Law, 1999). Phi Delta Phi. Deputy Director, Office of Indian Rights, U.S. Department of Justice, 1973-1976. *Member:* The District of Columbia Bar; Oklahoma, Federal, Federal Energy, American and Inter-American Bar Associations; American Society of International Law. ***PRACTICE AREAS:*** Natural Resources; Administrative. ***Email:*** jmcdonald@jacksonkelly.com

OF COUNSEL

DENNIS J. WHITTLESEY, born Washington, D.C., November 26, 1942; admitted to bar, 1968, Oklahoma and District of Columbia; 1995, U.S. Supreme Court. *Education:* University of Oklahoma (B.A., 1964); Georgetown University Law Center (J.D., 1967; LL.M. in Taxation, 1972). Delta Theta Phi. Trial Attorney, U.S. Department of Justice, Land and Natural Resources Division, 1971-1972. *Member:* The District of Columbia Bar; Oklahoma Bar Association; International Association of Gaming Attorneys. [With U.S. Navy, LTJG, 1968-1969]. ***PRACTICE AREAS:*** Gaming Law; Indian Law; Litigation; Environmental Law. ***Email:*** dwhittlesey@jacksonkelly.com

LEGAL SUPPORT PERSONNEL

TRACEY J. GOEHRIG. *Education:* University of Maryland (B.A.). (Office Manager). ***PRACTICE AREAS:*** Management of all non-legal operations for the Washington, D.C. office. ***Email:*** tgoehrig@jacksonkelly.com

REVISORS OF THE WEST VIRGINIA LAW DIGEST FOR THIS DIRECTORY

(For Complete Biographical Data on all Personnel, See Professional Biographies at Charleston, West Virginia)

JACKSON LEWIS SCHNITZLER & KRUPMAN

1156 FIFTEENTH STREET, N.W.
SUITE 500

WASHINGTON, D.C. 20005

Telephone: 202-347-5200
Facsimile: 202-223-8557
Email: washingtondc@jacksonlewis.com
URL: http://www.jacksonlewis.com

Other offices located in: Atlanta, Georgia; Boston, Massachusetts; Chicago, Illinois; Dallas, Texas; Greenville, South Carolina; Hartford, Connecticut; Long Island, New York; Los Angeles, California; Miami, Florida; Minneapolis, Minnesota; Morristown, New Jersey; New York, New York; Orlando, Florida; Pittsburgh, Pennsylvania; Sacramento, California; San Francisco, California; Seattle, Washington; Stamford, Connecticut; White Plains, New York.

Labor Relations, Employment Discrimination, Wrongful Discharge and Other Employment-Related Litigation, Employee Benefits and Pension Law, Wage and Hour, OSHA, Immigration Law, Public Sector and State Labor Relations Law On Behalf of Management.

MEMBERS OF FIRM

MICHAEL N. PETKOVICH, born Chicago Heights, Illinois, February 1, 1952; admitted to bar, 1979, Illinois; 1981, District of Columbia. *Education:* University of Massachusetts (B.S., cum laude, 1976; M.S., 1981); Valparaiso University (J.D., 1979).

HAROLD R. WEINRICH, born Bronx, N.Y., March 10, 1946; admitted to bar, 1972, New York; 1977, U.S. District Court, Southern District of New York; 1981, District of Columbia; U.S. District Court, District of Columbia; 1988, U.S. Court of Appeals, Second and District of Columbia Circuits; 1995, U.S. District Court, District of Maryland; 1996, U.S. Court of Appeals, Fourth Circuit. *Education:* Hofstra University (B.A., 1967); Brooklyn Law School (J.D., 1971). Trial Attorney, NLRB (1971-1977).

(This Listing Continued)

ASSOCIATE

MONIQUE Y. FORTENBERRY, born Chicago, Illinois, September 1, 1970; admitted to bar, 1997, District of Columbia. *Education:* Northwestern University (B.A., 1992); Georgetown University (J.D., 1995). *Member:* District of Columbia Bar (Chair, Young Lawyers Division, 2000-2001); American Bar Association. ***PRACTICE AREAS:*** Labor and Employment.

DARIA E. NEAL, born Los Angeles, California, September 15, 1974; admitted to bar, 1999, California (Not admitted in District of Columbia). *Education:* Hampton University (B.A., cum laude, 1996); University of California School of Law, Los Angeles (J.D., 1999). *Member:* The District of Columbia Bar (Member, Young Lawyers Division); American and National Bar Associations. ***PRACTICE AREAS:*** Employment Litigation. ***Email:*** neald@jacksonlewis.com

JACOBS & ASSOCIATES

2000 L STREET N.W., SUITE 200
WASHINGTON, D.C. 20036
Telephone: 202-457-0100
Fax: 202-457-0186
URL: http://www.internet-law-firm.com
Email: lawyer@internet-law-firm.com

Rockville, Maryland Office: 50 West Montgomery Avenue, Suite 330, 20850. Telephone: 301-251-5294.

Internet Law, Corporate Law, Intellectual Property, Securities Law.

HARVEY S. JACOBS, born Bradley Beach, New Jersey, December, 1958; admitted to bar, 1984, New York; 1985, District of Columbia; 1995, Maryland. *Education:* George Washington University (B.B.A., 1980); Brooklyn Law School (J.D., 1983). Author: "Netpreneuring," Nautilus Communications Press, 2001. Internet Correspondent, ABC-TV News. ***PRACTICE AREAS:*** Internet Law; Corporate Law; Real Estate Law; Intellectual Property. ***Email:*** jacobs@internet-law-firm.com

OF COUNSEL

DONNA MARIA COLES JOHNSON, born Washington, D.C., December 20, 1962; admitted to bar, 1987, Maryland; 1992, U.S. District Court, District of Maryland (Not admitted in District of Columbia). *Education:* University of South Carolina (B.A., 1983); Catholic University of American (J.D., 1986). . ***PRACTICE AREAS:*** Internet Law; Telecommunications Law; Corporate Law; Real Estate. ***Email:*** johnson@internet-law-firm.com

NEIL I. JACOBS, born New York, N.Y., November 8, 1957; admitted to bar, 1984, New York (Not admitted in District of Columbia). *Education:* State University of New York at Binghamton (B.A., 1980); Hebrew University of Jerusalem; Brooklyn Law School (J.D., 1983). President, North American Conference on Ethiopian Jewry, Inc., 1992-1996. Member, America Israel Chamber of Commerce. *Member:* The Association of the Bar of the City of New York. ***LANGUAGES:*** Hebrew, French. ***PRACTICE AREAS:*** Corporate; Securities; International; Transactional. ***Email:*** lawyer@internet-law-firm.com

JACOBSON, HOLMAN, PLLC

Established in 1969

400 SEVENTH STREET, N.W.
WASHINGTON, D.C. 20004
Telephone: 202-638-6666
Cable Address: "Lawpat"
Telefax: 202-393-5350; 202-393-5351; 202-393-5352
Email: IP@JHIP.COM
URL: http://www.JHIP.COM

Patent, Trademark, Unfair Competition, Copyright, Computer and Antitrust Law. International Patent and Trademark Practice. Practice before all Federal Courts, U.S. Patent and Trademark Office and other Administrative Agencies.

FIRM PROFILE: With a staff of eighty individuals including 22 professionals, the firm represents a range of clients from individual entrepreneurs to Fortune 500 companies in matters involving mechanical, electrical, chemical, biotechnology, high-tech, intellectual property issues, trademarks and copyrights. The firm also represents and co-counsels with other small, medium and large sized international intellectual property firms.

MEMBERS OF FIRM

HARVEY B. JACOBSON, JR., born Chicago, Illinois, November 25, 1936; admitted to bar, 1962, District of Columbia and U.S. Court of Appeals for the District of Columbia Circuit; 1967, U.S. Court of Appeals, Third and Eighth Circuits; 1968, U.S. Court of Appeals, Ninth Circuit; 1971, U.S. Court of Appeals, Fifth and Seventh Circuits; 1973, U.S. Supreme Court; 1979, U.S. Claims Court; 1981, U.S. Court of Appeals, Fourth Circuit; 1983, U.S. Court of Appeals for the Federal Circuit and Sixth Circuit; 1988, U.S. Court of Appeals, Second Circuit; registered to practice before U.S. Patent and Trademark Office. *Education:* Yale University (B.E. in Ch.E., 1958); Harvard University (LL.B., 1961). *Member:* District of Columbia Bar; American Bar Association; American Intellectual Property Law Association; The Association of Trial Lawyers of America. ***PRACTICE AREAS:*** Intellectual Property Litigation; Chemical Patents; Mechanical Patents. ***Email:*** HJACOBSON@JHIP.COM

JOHN CLARKE HOLMAN, born Milwaukee, Wisconsin, April 19, 1938; admitted to bar, 1966, District of Columbia; 1968, U.S. Court of Appeals for the District of Columbia Circuit; 1972, U.S. Supreme Court; 1982, U.S. Court of Appeals for the Federal Circuit; registered to practice before U.S. Patent and Trademark Office. *Education:* University of Wisconsin (B.S., in Met., 1961); Washington College of Law, American University (J.D., 1965); Holborn College of Law, London, England. Delta Theta Phi. Recipient, American Jurisprudence Award, 1964. Staff Editor, American University Law Review, 1964-1965. Author: "United States Patent Law," published 1971 in USSR. U.S. Patent Examiner, 1961-1965. *Member:* District of Columbia Bar; American Bar Association; American Intellectual Property Law Association; International Trademark Association; Patent and Trademark Institute of Canada; The Chartered Institute of Patent Agents (CIPA); The Institute of Trademark Agents (ITMA); International Association for the Protection of Industrial Property (AIPPI); Inter-American Association of Industrial Property (ASIPI); Fédération Internationale Des Conseils en Propriete Industrielle (FICPI); The Association of European Trademark Owners (MARQUES); American Institute of Mining, Metallurgical and Petroleum Engineers; American Society for Metals. ***PRACTICE AREAS:*** Intellectual Property Law; Chemical Patents; Metallurgical Patents; Mechanical Patents; Trademarks. ***Email:*** JHOLMAN@JHIP.COM

SIMOR L. MOSKOWITZ, born Washington, D.C., December 1, 1947; admitted to bar, 1972, Maryland; 1973, District of Columbia and U.S. Court of Appeals, District of Columbia Circuit; 1979, U.S. District Court, District of Maryland; 1981, U.S. Court of Appeals, Second Circuit; 1982, U.S. Court of Appeals for the Federal Circuit; 1996, U.S. Court of Appeals, Tenth Circuit. *Education:* George Washington University (B.A., 1969; J.D., 1972). *Member:* District of Columbia Bar; Maryland State and American Bar Associations; International Trademark Association: European Community Trademark Association. ***PRACTICE AREAS:*** Intellectual Property Law; Trademarks; Copyrights; Trade Regulation. ***Email:*** SMOSKOWITZ@JHIP.COM

ALLEN S. MELSER, born Denver, Colorado, February 5, 1946; admitted to bar, 1972, New Jersey; 1979, District of Columbia; 1982, U.S. Court of Appeals for the Federal Circuit; registered to practice before U.S. Patent and Trademark Office. *Education:* University of Pennsylvania (B.S.E.E., 1968); Boston University School of Public Communications; Georgetown University (J.D., 1971). *Member:* American and New Jersey Bar Associations; District of Columbia Bar; American Intellectual Property Law Association; International Association of the Protection of Industrial Property. ***PRACTICE AREAS:*** Intellectual Property; Electrical Patents; Computer and Software Patents; Multimedia Law. ***Email:*** AMELSER@JHIP.COM

MICHAEL R. SLOBASKY, born Detroit, Michigan, December 24, 1945; admitted to bar, 1972, Virginia and District of Columbia; 1978, U.S. Court of Appeals, Fourth Circuit; 1979, U.S. Claims Court; 1981, U.S. Court of Appeals, District of Columbia Circuit; 1982, U.S. Court of Appeals for the Federal Circuit; 1993, U.S. Supreme Court; registered to practice before U.S. Patent and Trademark Office. *Education:* Wayne State University (B.S.E.E., 1967); Wayne State University and George Washington University (J.D., with honors, 1971). Tau Beta Pi; Eta Kappa Nu; Order of the Coif. Trial Attorney, U.S. Department of Justice Antitrust Division, 1972-1975. *Member:* District of Columbia Bar; Virginia State Bar; American Bar Association; American Intellectual Property Law Association. ***PRACTICE AREAS:*** Intellectual Property Law; Electrical Patents; Mechanical Patents. ***Email:*** MSLOBASKY@JHIP.COM

MARSHA G. GENTNER, born South Bend, Indiana, December 15, 1954; admitted to bar, 1978, District of Columbia and U.S. Court of Appeals for the District of Columbia Circuit; 1984, U.S. Court of Appeals for the Federal Circuit; 1988, U.S. Court of Appeals, Second and Fifth Circuits; 1990, U.S. Court of Appeals, Eleventh Circuit; 1997, U.S. Court of Appeals, Fourth Circuit. *Education:* Indiana University (B.S., summa cum laude, 1975); Georgetown University (J.D., 1978); University of Maryland (B.S. in Computer Science , 1984). American Criminal Law Review, 1976-1978. *Member:* District of Columbia Bar (Member, Sections on: Litigation; Computer, Patent, Copyright and Trademark); Computer Law Association; International Trademark Association. ***PRACTICE AREAS:*** Intellectual Property Law; Information Technology; Computer Law; Trade Regulation; Trademarks; Copyrights. ***Email:*** MGENTNER@JHIP.COM

JONATHAN L. SCHERER, born New York, N.Y., December 6, 1954; admitted to bar, 1982, New York and U.S. Court of Appeals for the Federal Circuit; 1983, District of Columbia; 1995, U.S. Court of Appeals, Fifth Circuit; registered to practice before U.S. Patent and Trademark Office. *Education:* Alfred University (B.S., in Ceramic Engineering, 1976); West Coast University

(This Listing Continued)

JACOBSON, HOLMAN, PLLC, Washington—Continued

(M.S., 1978); Pace University (J.D., 1981). U.S. Patent Examiner, 1981-1983. *Member:* District of Columbia Bar; American Intellectual Property Law Association. ***PRACTICE AREAS:*** Intellectual Property Law; Electrical Patents; Mechanical Patents. ***Email:*** JSCHERER@JHIP.COM

IRWIN M. AISENBERG, born Worcester, Massachusetts, August 8, 1925; admitted to bar, 1958, District of Columbia and U.S. Court of Appeals, District of Columbia Circuit; 1964, U.S. Supreme Court; 1982, U.S. Court of Appeals for the Federal Circuit; registered to practice before U.S. Patent and Trademark Office. *Education:* Carnegie Mellon University (B.S. in Ch.E., 1946); University of Akron; Georgetown University (J.D., 1957). Omicron Delta Kappa. Professional Engineer, Massachusetts, 1952. Patent Examiner, U.S. Patent Office, 1954-1957. Author: "Attorney's Dictionary of Patent Claims," Matthew Bender, 1985; "Patent Law Precedent," Little Brown and Company, 1991, 2nd edition, 1992; "Modern Patent Law Precedent — Dictionary of Key Terms and Concepts," Glasser Legal Works, 1997; "The Status of Co-pending Patents for Precluding Patentability," Journal of the Patent Office Society, Vol. 47, No. 11, November 1965; "A Tale of Two Applicants or How Declaration and Inventorship Requirements Raise the Dickens with Promotion of Progress," Idea, Vol. 21, No. 3, 1980; "A Step Beyond Novelty, Utility and Non-Obviousness," Idea, Vol. 25, No. 3, 1984; "Patents: Their Evolution, Their Posture, Their Procurement and Their Function," INTERCIENCIA, Vol. 6, No. 6, pg. 395, 1981. Member, Editorial Advisory Board, IDEA, The Journal of Law and Technology, 1981-1996. Member, Appeal Board, National Register of Health Services Providers in Psychology, 1987-1989. Member, Board of Editors, Patent Strategy and Management, 2000—. Member, Panel of Arbitrators, American Arbitration Association. *Member:* District of Columbia Bar; American Bar Association (Member, Committee 108, 1965—); American Intellectual Property Law Association (Member, Chemical Practices Committee, 1957—); International Association for the Protection of Industrial Property (AIPPI). ***PRACTICE AREAS:*** Intellectual Property Law; Biotechnology Patents; Chemical Patents. ***Email:*** IAISENBERG@JHIP.COM

GEORGE WILLIAM LEWIS, born Paterson, New Jersey, January 12, 1952; admitted to bar, 1979, New York; 1997, District of Columbia. *Education:* Rutgers College (B.A., 1974); Rutgers Law School-Camden (J.D., 1978). Author, "A Primer On Titles Variety," August 1983. ***LANGUAGES:*** French. ***PRACTICE AREAS:*** Trademark Law; Copyright Law; Internet Law. ***Email:*** glewis@hip.com

WILLIAM E. PLAYER, born Lynn, Massachusetts, September 20, 1951; admitted to bar, 1982, Massachusetts; 1983, U.S. District Court, District of Massachusetts; 1988, District of Columbia; 1993, U.S. Court of Appeals for the Federal Circuit; registered to practice before U.S. Patent and Trademark Office. *Education:* University of Massachusetts (B.S., magna cum laude, 1974); Boston College (J.D., 1982). ***PRACTICE AREAS:*** Intellectual Property Law; Biotechnology Patents; Chemical Patents. ***Email:*** WPLAYER@JHIP.COM

YOON S. HAM, born Pusan, Korea, May 11, 1961; admitted to bar, 1994, Pennsylvania; 1996, District of Columbia; registered to practice before U.S. Patent and Trademark Office. *Education:* Korea University (B.S.E.E., 1984); Franklin Pierce Law Center (J.D., 1994). Author: "GATT Changes Patents," The monthly IP Magazine of Korea, pp.50-54. *Member:* Pennsylvania Bar Association; The District of Columbia Bar; American Intellectual Property Law Association. ***LANGUAGES:*** Korean. ***PRACTICE AREAS:*** Intellectual Property Law; Electrical Patents; Mechanical Patents. ***Email:*** YHAM@JHIP.COM

PHILIP L. O'NEILL, born Cleveland, Ohio, February 26, 1952; admitted to bar, 1977, District of Columbia; 1978, U.S. District Court, District of Columbia; 1989, U.S. Court of Appeals, Fourth Circuit; 1991, U.S. District Court, District of Maryland and U.S. Supreme Court; 1993, U.S. Tax Court; 1998, U.S. Court of Federal Claims; 2000, Maryland; 2001, U.S. District Court, District of Colorado. *Education:* University of Chicago (A.B. with general honors, 1974); Georgetown University Law Center (J.D., 1977). Member, Georgetown Law Journal. General Counsel, National Commission for Certifying Agencies, 1998—. Formerly with: Jackson & Campbell, P.C.; Keck, Mahin & Cate. Member, Legal Section Council, American Society of Association Executives, 1998-2001. *Member:* American Bar Association (Member, Antitrust Section). ***PRACTICE AREAS:*** Trademarks; Copyrights; Antitrust and Trade Regulation; Litigation. ***Email:*** PONEILL@JHIP.COM

ASSOCIATES

LINDA J. SHAPIRO, born Boston, Massachusetts, December 19, 1952; admitted to bar, 1977, Virginia and U.S. Court of Customs and Patent Appeals; 1978, District of Columbia; 1981, U.S. Supreme Court; 1982, U.S. Court of Appeals for the Federal Circuit; registered to practice before U.S. Patent and Trade mark Office. *Education:* Tufts University (B.S., with honors, 1974); George Washington University (J.D., 1977). ***PRACTICE AREAS:*** Intellectual Property Law; Mechanical Patents; Computer and Software Patents. ***Email:*** LSHAPIRO@JHIP.COM

(This Listing Continued)

LEESA N. WEISS, born Washington, D.C., July 30, 1956; admitted to bar, 1987, Pennsylvania; 1988, District of Columbia; 1990, U.S. District Court for the District of Columbia; 1992, U.S. Court of Appeals for the Federal Circuit; 1994, Maryland. *Education:* University of Maryland (B.A., 1978); George Washington University; Catholic University (J.D., 1987). Recipient, First Prize 1987 Nathan Burkan Memorial Competition (A.S.C.A.P.), Catholic University. *Member:* Bar Association of the District of Columbia; Maryland State Bar Association; International Trademark Association. ***PRACTICE AREAS:*** Intellectual Property Law; Trademarks. ***Email:*** LWEISS@JHIP.COM

SUZIN C. BAILEY, born Monterey, California, January 5, 1960; admitted to bar, 1993, Maryland; registered to practice before U.S. Patent and Trademark Office (Not admitted in District of Columbia). *Education:* Brigham Young University (B.S., magna cum laude, 1981); George Washington University (J.D., with honors, 1993). Editor, George Washington Journal of International Law and Economics, 1991-1992. *Member:* Maryland State Bar Association. ***PRACTICE AREAS:*** Patent Prosecution; Litigation; Trademark; Copyright. ***Email:*** SBAILEY@JHIP.COM

MATTHEW J. CUCCIAS, born Monterey, California, September 12, 1966; admitted to bar, 1994, Maryland; 1995, U.S. District Court, District of Maryland; 1998, U.S. District Court, District of Columbia; 1999, District of Columbia. *Education:* University of Virginia (B.S., 1989); George Washington University (J.D., 1994). Co-Author: "How Safe Is the Y2K Harbor for the Good Samaritan?" Mealey's Year 2000 Report, Vol. 1, No. 9 (Oct. 1998) *Member:* Maryland State and American Bar Associations; District of Columbia Bar; American Intellectual Property Law Association (Member, Cyberspace Cases Working Group). ***PRACTICE AREAS:*** Trademarks and Litigation. ***Email:*** MCUCCIAS@JHIP.COM

DANIEL K. DORSEY, born Schenectady, New York, January 25, 1958; admitted to bar, 1990, Pennsylvania; 1991, District of Columbia, U.S. Court of Appeals for the Federal Circuit and U.S. District Court, District of Columbia; 1997, U.S. Supreme Court; 1999, Virginia and U.S. District Court, Eastern District of Virginia; 2000, U.S. Court of Appeals, 4th Circuit; registered to practice before U.S. Patent and Trademark Office. *Education:* United States Military Academy; Western New England College (B.S.E.E., 1982); Antioch School of Law (J.D., 1987). Patent Examiner, U.S. Patent & Trademark Office, 1982-1987. *Member:* American Bar Association; The District of Columbia Bar; Bar Association of the District of Columbia; American Intellectual Property Law Association; . ***PRACTICE AREAS:*** Criminal Law; Intellectual Property Law. ***Email:*** DDORSEY@JHIP.COM

SUZANNAH K. SUNDBY, born Seoul, Korea, March 9, 1972; admitted to bar, 1999, California; registered to practice before the U.S. Patent and Trademark Office (Not admitted in District of Columbia). *Education:* University of Wisconsin (B.S., Biochemistry/Molecular Biology, 1994); Franklin Pierce Law Center (J.D., 1999; M.I.P.). Phi Alpha Delta. Adjunct Professor, Advanced Patent Application Preparation and Prosecution, Franklin Pierce Law Center, Spring 2000-2001. Formerly with: Morrison & Foerster, LLP; Shanks & Herbert. *Member:* American Intellectual Property Law Association; American Chemical Society; American Association for the Advancement of Science; Association of University Technology Managers; Licensing Executives Society. ***PRACTICE AREAS:*** Biotechnology Patents; Chemical Patents; Pharmaceutical Patents; Medical Patents; Patent Applications. ***Email:*** SSUNDBY@JHIP.COM

OF COUNSEL

MARVIN R. STERN, born Philadelphia, Pennsylvania, August 13, 1935; admitted to bar, 1963, Maryland; 1965, District of Columbia; 1966, U.S. Claims Court; 1967, U.S. Supreme Court; 1982, U.S. Court of Appeals for the Federal Circuit; registered to practice before U.S. Patent and Trademark Office. *Education:* Drexel University (B.S., in Ch.E., 1958); George Washington University (J.D., with honors, 1963). Order of the Coif; Phi Alpha Delta (Vice President, 1962); Tau Beta Pi; Phi Kappa Phi; Blue Key. Assistant Patent Editor, George Washington Law Review, 1962-1963. U.S. Patent Examiner, 1959-1961. *Member:* District of Columbia Bar; Maryland State and American Bar Associations; American Intellectual Property Law Association; Licensing Executives Society. ***PRACTICE AREAS:*** Intellectual Property Law; Chemical Patents; Mechanical Patents; Trademarks. ***Email:*** MSTERN@JHIP.COM

NATHANIEL A. HUMPHRIES, born Villa Rica, Georgia, September 10, 1934; admitted to bar, 1965, District of Columbia; 1969, U.S. Court of Appeals, District of Columbia Circuit; 1977, U.S. Supreme Court; 1982, U.S. Court of Appeals for the Federal Circuit; registered to practice before U.S. Patent and Trademark Office. *Education:* University of South Carolina (B.S., 1956); University of Utah (B.S., 1958); George Washington University (J.D., 1964). *Member:* American Intellectual Property Law Association. ***PRACTICE AREAS:*** Intellectual Property; Mechanical Patents. ***Email:*** NHUMPHRIES@JHIP

JAGTIANI & GUTTAG

WASHINGTON, D.C.

(See Fairfax, Virginia)

Patents, Trademarks, Copyrights, Trade Secrets, International Trade, Litigation, Technology Transfer, Mergers and Acquisitions, Intellectual Property.

JAMES & HOFFMAN, P.C.

Established in 1995

1101 17TH STREET, NW

SUITE 510

WASHINGTON, D.C. 20036-4704

Telephone: 202-496-0500

Fax: 202-496-0555

URL: http://www.jamhoff.com

Civil Litigation, Labor Law, Bankruptcy, Tort, Employee Benefits, Employment Discrimination, Insurance, College and University Law and Non-Profit Organization Law.

FIRM PROFILE: James & Hoffman is a litigation and labor law firm located in the District of Columbia. The firm has a nationwide practice representing labor organizations, for profit and nonprofit corporations, and individuals at all levels of the federal and state courts, before administrative agencies and legislative bodies and in alternative dispute resolution proceedings.

EDGAR N. JAMES, born Portland, Oregon, January 7, 1947; admitted to bar, 1980, District of Columbia; 1986, Maryland; U.S. District Court for the District of Columbia; U.S. District Court, District of Maryland; U.S. Court of Federal Claims; U.S. Court of Appeals for the District of Columbia Circuit; U.S. Court of Appeals, Second, Fourth, Fifth, Sixth, Tenth and District of Columbia Circuits; U.S. Supreme Court. *Education:* Portland State University (B.S., 1969); Harvard Law School (J.D., 1979); Harvard School of Public Health (M.P.H., Physiology, 1979). Articles Editor, Harvard Civil Rights and Civil Liberties Law Review, 1978-1979. Author: "Unions and the LMRDA," 13 Harvard Civil Rights and Civil Liberties Law Review 247, 1978. Special Assistant to Secretary of Labor, 1980. *Member:* District of Columbia Bar; Maryland State and American Bar Associations. ***PRACTICE AREAS:*** Litigation; Labor; Nonprofit Organizations Law. ***Email:*** ejames@jamhoff.com

STEVEN K. HOFFMAN, born Philadelphia, Pennsylvania, November 27, 1948; admitted to bar, 1984, District of Columbia; 1985, U.S. Court of Appeals for the District of Columbia Circuit and U.S. District Court for the District of Columbia; 1986, U.S. Court of Appeals, Tenth Circuit; 1987, U.S. Court of Appeals, Fourth Circuit; 1988, U.S. Court of Appeals, Eighth Circuit; 1990, U.S. District Court, District of Maryland; 1992, U.S. Court of Appeals, Eleventh Circuit; 1993, U.S. Court of Appeals, Sixth Circuit; 2000, U.S. Court of Appeals, First Circuit. *Education:* Duke University (B.A., Phi Beta Kappa, 1970; Ph.D., 1976); Yale University (J.D., 1984). *Member:* District of Columbia Bar; American Bar Association. ***PRACTICE AREAS:*** Litigation; Labor and Employment; Insurance; College and University Law. ***Email:*** skhoffman@jamhoff.com

JUDITH A. SCOTT, born Philadelphia, Pennsylvania, March 16, 1949; admitted to bar, 1983, District of Columbia and U.S. Supreme Court; U.S. Court of Appeals for the District of Columbia; U.S. Court of Appeals, Fourth and Sixth Circuits. *Education:* Wellesley College (B.A., 1971); Northeastern University School of Law (J.D., 1974). Author: *Organizing the Law.* Formerly Presidential Appointee, Pension Benefit Guaranty Corporation Advisory Committee, 1994-2000. General Counsel, Service Employees International Union. Assistant General Counsel, United Auto Workers Union, 1978-1981. Legislative Representative, Industrial Union Department, AFL-CIO, 1982-1983. Associate General Counsel. United Mine Workers of America, 1983-1992. Special Counsel, 1992-1993 and General Counsel, 1994-1997, International Brotherhood of Teamsters. Member, Board of Directors, National Partnership for Women and Families. *Member:* District of Columbia Bar. ***PRACTICE AREAS:*** Labor Law; Employment Law. ***Email:*** scottj@seiu.org

KATHY L. KRIEGER, born Detroit, Michigan, May 19, 1953; admitted to bar, 1978, New York; 1985, District of Columbia; U.S. District Court for the District of Columbia; U.S. District Court, District of Colorado; U.S. Court of Appeals for the District of Columbia, Second, Third, Sixth, Seventh, Ninth and Tenth Circuits. *Education:* Yale University (A.B., magna cum laude, 1974); New York University (J.D., cum laude, 1977). Order of the Coif. *Member:* District of Columbia Bar; National Lawyers Guild. ***PRACTICE AREAS:*** Labor Law; Employment Law. ***Email:*** klkrieger@jamhoff.com

DAVID P. DEAN, born Atlanta, Georgia, June 30, 1955; admitted to bar, 1991, New York; 1993, District of Columbia, U.S. Court of Appeals, Second, Fifth and Ninth Circuits and U.S. District Court, District of Arizona. *Education:* University of Chicago (B.A., 1987); Columbia University (J.D., 1990). Recipient, Parker School Recognition with Honors in International and Comparative Law. Harlan Fiske Stone Scholar, 1988-1990. Author: Senior Editor, "Railway Labor Act," American Bar Association/BNA Books, 1995-2001; "What U.S. Laws Hold Private Actors Accountable for Taking Part in Foreign Civil Wars?," Legal Appendix to "Invisible Crimes: U.S. Private Intervention in the War in Mozambique," a publication of the Africa Policy Information Center, 1994. *Member:* District of Columbia Bar; New York State Bar Association; National Lawyers Guild. ***Email:*** dpdean@jamhoff.com

---

MARIE CHOPRA, born Sevenoaks, Kent, United Kingdom, September 20, 1945; admitted to bar, 1995, Maryland; 1996, District of Columbia; U.S. District Court, District of Colorado; U.S. Court of Appeals, Ninth Circuit. *Education:* Oxford University, Oxford, England (B.A., with honors, 1967; M.A., 1971); Georgetown University (J.D., cum laude, 1995). *Member:* District of Columbia Bar; Maryland State and American Bar Associations. ***PRACTICE AREAS:*** Labor Law; Employment Law; Civil Litigation. ***Email:*** mchopra@jamhoff.com

JEFFREY S. VOGT, born Columbus, Ohio, November 10, 1971; admitted to bar, 2000, New York and U.S. District Court, Northern District of New York (Not admitted in District of Columbia). *Education:* Miami University (B.A., 1993); State University of New York at Buffalo (M.A., 1996); Cornell Law School (J.D., 1999; LL.M., International Law, 1999). *Member:* New York State and American Bar Associations; National Lawyers Guild. ***LANGUAGES:*** Swedish. ***PRACTICE AREAS:*** Labor Law; Employment Law; International Law. ***Email:*** jsvogt@jamhoff.com

JESSICA RACHEL ARONS, born Washington, D.C.; admitted to bar, 2000, Virginia (Not admitted in District of Columbia). *Education:* Brown University (B.A., magna cum laude, 1994); College of William & Mary (J.D., 2000). Phi Beta Kappa; Order of the Coif. Recipient, Thurgood Marshall Award for Public Service. *Member:* Virginia and American Bar Associations; Virginia State Bar. ***PRACTICE AREAS:*** Labor and Employment. ***Email:*** jrarons@jamhoff.com

OF COUNSEL

MARY JOYCE CARLSON, born Sparta, Tennessee, October 31, 1947; admitted to bar, 1973, Georgia (Not admitted in District of Columbia). *Education:* Mississippi State University for Women (B.A., 1968); Duke University Law School (J.D., 1971). Author: wrote chapter entitled: "National Labor Relations Board," Relaciones Laborales En El Sigle XXI, Mexico, 2000. Deputy General Counsel, National Labor Relations Board, 1994-2000. *Member:* State Bar of Georgia. ***LANGUAGES:*** Spanish. ***Email:*** mjcarlson@jamhoff.com

MARTHA WALFOORT, born Milwaukee, Wisconsin, October 25, 1949; admitted to bar, 1980, Pennsylvania; 1982, District of Columbia; 1989, U.S. Court of Appeals, Eighth Circuit; 1992, U.S. Court of Appeals, District of Columbia; 1993, U.S. Court of Appeals, Seventh Circuit. *Education:* Reed College (B.A., with commendation, 1972); Bank Street College of Education (M.S., 1980); University of Pennsylvania (J.D., 1980). Arthur Littleton Legal Writing Instructor, University of Pennsylvania Law School, 1979-1980. Law Clerk to Harry Takiff, Philadelphia Court of Common Pleas, 1980-1982. *Member:* District of Columbia Bar; Women's Bar Association of District of Columbia. ***Email:*** mwalfoort@jamhoff.com

CHRISTY HOFFMAN, born New York, N.Y., November 15, 1955; admitted to bar, 1990, Connecticut; 1991, U.S. Court of Appeals, First, Fourth, Sixth and District of Columbia Circuit; 1991, District of Columbia. *Education:* Smith College (B.A., cum laude, 1977); City College of the City University of New York (J.D., cum laude, 1990). Order of the Coif. Root-Tilden-Snow Scholar. Member, International Association of Machinists, 1978-1987; National Hospital and Healthcare Employees, District 1199. Research Consultant, Organization of Economic Cooperation and Development, Paris, France, June-December, 1975, Summer, 1976. Law Clerk, Kirschner, Walters & Willig, Philadelphia, Pennsylvania, Summer, 1988; Cohen, Weiss & Simon, New York, New York, 1988-1990. Associate General Counsel, Service Employees International Union, 1999-2001; International Brotherhood of Teamsters, 1994-1999; United Mineworkers of America, 1990-1994. Staff Attorney, United Mine Workers of America, 1990-1994. *Member:* The District of Columbia Bar. (Counsel). ***LANGUAGES:*** French. ***PRACTICE AREAS:*** Labor Law.

JANIS, SCHUELKE & WECHSLER

Established in 1979

1728 MASSACHUSETTS AVENUE, N.W.

WASHINGTON, D.C. 20036

Telephone: 202-861-0600

Telecopier: 202-223-7230

Email: janisschuelke@msn.com

Litigation. White Collar Criminal and Civil Practice in the United States and Abroad.

(This Listing Continued)

JANIS, SCHUELKE & WECHSLER, Washington—Continued

N. RICHARD JANIS, born Washington, D.C., November 23, 1946; admitted to bar, 1973, District of Columbia, U.S. Court of Appeals for the District of Columbia Circuit and U.S. District Court for the District of Columbia; 1978, U.S. Supreme Court; 1985, U.S. District Court for the District of Maryland. *Education:* University of Wisconsin (B.A., with honors, 1968); Harvard University (J.D., 1972). Phi Eta Sigma. Author: "Incompetency Commitment: The Need for Procedural Safeguards and a Proposed Statutory Scheme," 23 Catholic University Law Review 710, 1974. Lecturer, George Washington University Graduate School of Forensic Sciences, 1977-1983. Assistant U.S. Attorney, District of Columbia, 1972-1976. Hearing Committee, D.C. Bar Board on Professional Responsibility, 1985-1991. *Member:* The District of Columbia Bar; American Bar Association (Member, Sections on: Criminal Justice; Litigation); International Bar Association; National Association of Criminal Defense Lawyers; Edward Bennett Williams Inn of Court (Master). ***PRACTICE AREAS:*** White Collar Criminal Defense; Business Crimes; Federal Grand Jury; Monetary Crimes; Litigation.

HENRY F. SCHUELKE, III, born Newark, New Jersey, November 10, 1942; admitted to bar, 1968, District of Columbia, U.S. District Court for the District of Columbia, U.S. Court of Appeals for the District of Columbia Circuit and U.S. Court of Military Appeals; 1980, U.S. Supreme Court; 1985, U.S. District Court for the District of Maryland. *Education:* St. Peter's College (A.B., 1964); Villanova University (J.D., 1967). Military Judge, U.S. Army Judiciary, 1970-1972. Assistant U.S. Attorney, 1972-1979 and Executive Assistant U.S. Attorney, 1976-1979, District of Columbia. General Counsel, The National Society for Autistic Children, 1980-1990. Special Counsel: District of Columbia Commission on Judicial Disabilities and Tenure, 1982—; U.S. Senate Committee on Foreign Relations, 1980-1981; U.S. Senate Select Committee on Ethics, 1989-1991. Member, Committee on Grievances, U.S. District Court, District of Columbia. *Member:* The District of Columbia Bar; American Bar Association (Member: Judicial Administration Division; Criminal Justice Section); National Association of Criminal Defense Lawyers; American Judicature Society; Fellow, American College of Trial Lawyers. [Capt., JAGC, U.S. Army, 1968-1972]. ***PRACTICE AREAS:*** White Collar Criminal Defense; Business Crimes; International Criminal Law; Federal Grand Jury; Monetary Crimes.

LAWRENCE H. WECHSLER, born Queens, New York, June 14, 1945; admitted to bar, 1971, New York and District of Columbia; 1980, U.S. Supreme Court; 1985, U.S. District Court for the District of Maryland. *Education:* Pennsylvania State University (B.S., 1967); George Washington University (J.D., 1970). Beta Gamma Sigma; Beta Alpha Psi; Order of the Coif. Member, George Washington Law Review, 1969-1970. Author: "The Freedom of Information Act: A Critical Review," 38 George Washington Law Review 150, 1969. Lecturer: George Washington University Graduate School of Forensic Sciences, 1977-1983. Lecturer, American University Law School, 1977-1979. Law Clerk to Judge Joseph C. Waddy, U.S. District Court for the District of Columbia, 1970-1971. Assistant U.S. Attorney, District of Columbia, 1971-1979. President, The Assistant U.S. Attorneys Association, D.C., 1990-1991. *Member:* The District of Columbia Bar; New York State and American (Member, Sections on: Litigation; Corporation, Banking and Business Law) Bar Associations. ***PRACTICE AREAS:*** White Collar Criminal Defense; International Criminal Law.

S. ROBERT SUTTON, born Washington, D.C., February 1, 1955; admitted to bar, 1980, Illinois and U.S. District Court, Northern District of Illinois; 1982, District of Columbia; 1984, U.S. District Court for the District of Columbia and U.S. Court of Appeals for the District of Columbia Circuit. *Education:* Northwestern University (B.A., 1977); Stanford Law School (J.D., 1980). Phi Beta Kappa; Phi Eta Sigma. *Member:* The District of Columbia Bar; Bar Association of the District of Columbia; American Bar Association. ***PRACTICE AREAS:*** White Collar Criminal Defense; Business Crimes.

JOHN W. KERN, born Washington, D.C., October 23, 1957; admitted to bar, 1987, Maryland; 1988, District of Columbia, U.S. District Court, District of Maryland and U.S. District Court, District of Columbia; 1990, U.S. Court of Appeals for the District of Columbia Circuit. *Education:* Princeton University (B.A., magna cum laude, 1980); University of California at Los Angeles (J.D., 1987). Staff Member, 1985-1986, and Editor, 1986-1987, UCLA Law Review. Author, "Price Manipulation in the Commodity Futures Markets: A Reexamination of the Justifications for Simultaneous Causes of Action Under the CEA and the Sherman Act," 34 UCLA Law Review 1305, 1987. Assistant U.S. Attorney, District of Columbia, 1989-1992. *Member:* District of Columbia Bar. ***PRACTICE AREAS:*** White Collar Criminal Defense.

WHITNEY C. ELLERMAN, born Sacramento, California, July 12, 1961; admitted to bar, 1988, Virginia; 1989, District of Columbia. *Education:* University of Virginia (B.A., 1983; J.D., 1988). Member, Editorial Board, 1986-1987 and Special Projects Editor, 1987-1988, Virginia Law Review. ***LANGUAGES:*** Spanish and French. ***PRACTICE AREAS:*** White Collar Criminal Defense.

(This Listing Continued)

OF COUNSEL

WILLIAM B. SHIELDS, born Jackson Heights, New York, January 6, 1949; admitted to bar, 1974, New York and U.S. District Court, Eastern and Southern Districts of New York; 1975, U.S. Court of Appeals, Second Circuit; 1977, U.S. Supreme Court; 1996, District of Columbia. *Education:* Manhattan College (B.A., 1970); New York University (J.D., 1973; LL.M., in Taxation, 1981). Member, Moot Court. Assistant District Attorney to New York County District Attorney, 1973-1977. Special Assistant Attorney General to Deputy Attorney General, State of New York, 1977-1988. *Member:* New York County Lawyers Association. ***PRACTICE AREAS:*** Criminal Defense; Civil Litigation.

JARRARD & RICHARD

WASHINGTON, D.C.

(See Bethesda, Maryland)

General Practice, Commercial Litigation, Construction, Real Estate, Hotel Development and Management, Small Business General Counseling, Emerging Business Law, Leasing, Commercial Landlord and Tenant Law, Shopping Center Leasing, Hotel and Resort Development, Hotel Franchise Law, Franchise Licensing, Closely Held Business Law, Family Business Law, Labor and Employment Law, Employment Discrimination, ERISA, Affirmative Action, Personnel Laws, Workplace Safety Issues.

JENKENS & GILCHRIST

A PROFESSIONAL CORPORATION

Established in 1951

1919 PENNSYLVANIA AVENUE, N.W., SUITE 600

WASHINGTON, D.C. 20006-3404

Telephone: 202-326-1500
Facsimile: 202-326-1555
Email: jenkens@jenkens.com
URL: http://www.jenkens.com

Austin, Texas Office: 2200 One American Center, 600 Congress Avenue. Telephone: 512-499-3800. Facsimile: 512-404-3520.

Dallas, Texas, Office: 1445 Ross Avenue, Suite 3200. Telephone: 214-855-4500. TWX: 910-861-4047. Telex: 73-2595. Facsimile: 214-855-4300. International Facsimile: 214-855-4300.

Los Angeles, California Office: Jenkens & Gilchrist, LLP, 12100 Wilshire Boulevard, 15th Floor. Telephone: 310-820-8800. Facsimile: 310-820-8859.

Chicago, Illinois Office: 225 West Washington, Suite 2600. Telephone: 312-425-3900. Facsimile: 312-425-3909.

Houston, Texas Office: 1100 Louisiana, Suite 1800. Telephone: 713-951-3300. Facsimile: 713-951-3314.

San Antonio, Texas Office: 1400 Frost Bank Tower, 100 West Houston Street. Telephone: 210-246-5000. Facsimile: 210-246-5999.

Great Neck, New York Office: Jenkens & Gilchrist Parker Chapin LLP, 175 Great Neck Road. Telephone: 516-482-4422. Facsimile: 516-482-4469.

Hackensack, New Jersey: Jenkens & Gilchrist Parker Chapin LLP, 190 Moore Street, Suite 307. Telephone: 201-883-6400. Facsimile: 201-883-6404.

New York, New York Office: Jenkens & Gilchrist Parker Chapin LLP, The Chrysler Building, 405 Lexington Avenue. Telephone: 212-704-6327. Facsimile: 212-704-6288.

Administrative Law, Antitrust, Aviation, Bankruptcy, Commercial Lending, Communications, Computer Law, Construction Law, Corporate, Employee Benefits (ERISA); Energy, Environmental Law, Estate Planning, Probate and Trusts, Exempt Organizations, Federal Practice, Financial Institutions, Finance, Franchise and Distribution Law, Governmental Affairs, Health Law, Hospitality (REIT), Immigration, Insurance Defense, Intellectual Property including Patent, Trademark, Tradesecret and Copyright (Prosecution, Litigation and Transactional), International Law, Internet Law, Labor and Employment Law, Land Use, Municipal Law, Litigation (Commercial, Tax and Fiduciary), Mergers and Acquisitions, Product Liability, Real Estate Services, Securities, Tax, Toxic Tort, Trade Regulation, Transportation, Unfair Competition, Venture Capital.

LARRY W. CAUDLE, JR., born Portsmouth, Virginia, January 6, 1959; admitted to bar, 1994, Virginia (Not admitted in District of Columbia). *Education:* James Madison University (B.B.A., 1982); University of Richmond (J.D., 1994). Gamma Gamma. *Member:* Virginia State Bar (Member, Sections on: Young Lawyers and Construction); American Bar Association (Member, Construction Section); Construction Specifications Institute. ***PRACTICE AREAS:*** Construction Law; Insurance Defense; Surety Law; Commercial Litigation. ***Email:*** lcaudle@jenkens.com

MICHAEL H. COOK, born Oshkosh, Wisconsin, June 9, 1947; admitted to bar, 1973, Pennsylvania; 1976, U.S. Supreme Court; 1979, District of Columbia. *Education:* University of Wisconsin; Temple University (B.A., cum laude,

(This Listing Continued)

1969); Villanova University (J.D., 1973). *Member:* The District of Columbia Bar; Pennsylvania and American Bar Associations; National Health Lawyers Association; American Academy of Hospital Attorneys; Healthcare Financial Management Association; National Subacute Care Association; Professional Certification Board; American College of Health Care Administrators; Assisted Living Facility Association of America (Member, Task Force on Managed Care). ***PRACTICE AREAS:*** Health Care Law; Administrative Law. ***Email:*** mcook@jenkens.com

JAN S. GILBERT, born Bronx, New York, August 26, 1965; admitted to bar, 1990, New York; 1991, District of Columbia; 1995, Texas. *Education:* St. Thomas Aquinas College (1981-1983); London School of Economics, London, England (G.C., 1985); McGill University, Montreal, Quebec (B.A., 1986); Boston University (J.D., cum laude, 1989). Edward Hennesey Scholar. Recipient, American Jurisprudence Award-Lawyers Cooperative Publishing Company-Administrative Law. *Member:* The District of Columbia Bar; American Bar Association (Member: Antitrust Section; Forum on Franchising). ***PRACTICE AREAS:*** Franchising; Product Distribution. ***Email:*** jgilbert@jenkens.com

DANIEL J. KRAFTSON, born Petaluma, California, May 15, 1951; admitted to bar, 1977, Virginia; 1978, District of Columbia and U.S. District Court, Eastern District of Virginia; 1979, U.S. Court of Federal Claims; 1980, U.S. Supreme Court; U.S. Court of Appeals for the Fourth and Federal Circuits. *Education:* Wheaton College (B.A., magna cum laude, 1973); College of William & Mary (J.D., 1977). Articles Editor, William & Mary Law Review, 1976-1977. *Member:* District of Columbia Bar; Virginia State Bar. ***PRACTICE AREAS:*** Construction Law; Construction Litigation; Government Contracts.

GARY A. LAX, born Atlantic City, New Jersey, May 17, 1961; admitted to bar, 1986, Pennsylvania; 1988, Arizona; 1990, District of Columbia. *Education:* University of Delaware (B.A., 1983); Delaware Law School of Widener University (J.D., cum laude, 1986); Boston University (LL.M., in Banking Law Studies, 1987). Phi Kappa Phi; Phi Delta Phi. Attorney/Advisor, Legal Advisory Services Division, Office of the Comptroller of the Currency, 1987-1989. *Member:* The District of Columbia Bar; American Bar Association. ***PRACTICE AREAS:*** Financial Institutions; Securities; Corporate Law. ***Email:*** glax@jenkens.com

KEITH W. McGLAMERY, born Stillwater, Oklahoma, January 20, 1947; admitted to bar, 1976, Wisconsin; 1980, Texas (Not admitted in District of Columbia). *Education:* Oklahoma State University (B.A., 1969); University of Wisconsin (J.D., 1975). *Member:* Dallas and American Bar Associations; State Bar of Texas; State Bar of Wisconsin. ***PRACTICE AREAS:*** Real Estate. ***Email:*** kmcglamery@jenkens.com

MICHAEL F. RUGGIO, born New York, N.Y., August 10, 1956; admitted to bar, 1982, Pennsylvania, District of Columbia, U.S. District Court, Eastern District of Pennsylvania and U.S. Tax Court; 1983, Virginia, U.S. District Court, Eastern District of Virginia and U.S. Court of Appeals, Fourth Circuit. *Education:* New York University (B.S., magna cum laude, 1978); University of Pittsburgh (J.D., cum laude, 1982). *Member:* Norfolk and Portsmouth, Philadelphia, Pennsylvania and American Bar Associations; Virginia State Bar; The Association of Trial Lawyers of America. ***PRACTICE AREAS:*** Health Law. ***Email:*** mruggio@jenkens.com

CARL E. ZWISLER III, born Akron, Ohio, August 17, 1948; admitted to bar, 1973, Illinois; 1976, District of Columbia. *Education:* University of Notre Dame (A.B., 1970); DePaul University (J.D., 1973). ***PRACTICE AREAS:*** Franchise Law; Distribution Law; Antitrust Law; Trademark Law; Healthcare Law. ***Email:*** czwisler@jenkens.com

OF COUNSEL

SCOTT R. SCHOENFELD, born Washington, D.C., July 5, 1936; admitted to bar, 1965, District of Columbia, U.S. Court of Appeals, District of Columbia and U.S. District Court, District of Columbia; 1970, U.S. Supreme Court; 1975, U.S. Court of Appeals, 2nd Circuit; 1983, U.S. Court of Appeals, 1st Circuit; 1985, U.S. District Court, Maryland; U.S. Court of International Trade; 1986, U.S. Court of Federal Claims; 1988, U.S. Court of Appeals, Federal Circuit; U.S. District Court, Northern District of Texas. *Education:* Harvard College (A.B., cum laude, 1959); Harvard University (LL.B., 1964). Assistant U.S. Attorney, District of Columbia, 1965-1969. *Member:* The District of Columbia Bar; American Bar Association. ***PRACTICE AREAS:*** Government (Public) Contract Law; Litigation; Regulatory Law. ***Email:*** sschoenfeld@jenkens.com

---

PATRICIA J. ATIENZA, admitted to bar, 1999, Maryland (Not admitted in District of Columbia). *Education:* University of Florida (B.A., with honors, 1995); Washington College of Law of American University (J.D., cum laude, 1998). *Member:* Maryland State Bar Association. ***PRACTICE AREAS:*** Health Law; Medicare Fraud and Abuse. ***Email:*** patienza@jenkens.com

JAMILA BRASWELL, admitted to bar, 1998, Virginia (Not admitted in District of Columbia). *Education:* Harvard University (A.B., cum laude, 1995); University of Virginia (J.D., 1998). *Member:* Virginia State Bar Association. ***PRACTICE AREAS:*** Real Estate; Distribution. ***Email:*** jbraswell@jenkens.com

DAMON BURROWS, II, born Oklahoma City, Oklahoma, July 27, 1970; admitted to bar, 1997, California; 1998, District of Columbia, U.S. District Court for the District of Columbia and U.S. Court of Federal Claims. *Education:* Southwestern College (B.S., 1993); Catholic University of America (J.D., 1997). Phi Delta Phi. *Member:* American Bar Association (Member, White Collar Committee); Association of Trial Lawyers of America; American Health Lawyer's Association. ***PRACTICE AREAS:*** Health Care Fraud; Health Care Litigation; White Collar Fraud. ***Email:*** dburrows@jenkens.com

RACHEL HATFIELD, born Denver, Colorado, May 8, 1974; admitted to bar, 2001, Virginia (Not admitted in District of Columbia). *Education:* University of Colorado at Boulder (B.A., 1996); Washington & Lee University (J.D., 2001). Phi Alpha Delta. Author, Washington & Lee Race & Ethnic Ancestry Law Journal, Volume 6, Issue 1, Spring 2000. Instructor, Legal Research and Writing, Burks Scholar, 2000-2001. *Member:* Virginia State Bar; Virginia (Founder and President, Student Division, 1999-2000) and American (Member, Health Care Section, 2001—) Bar Associations; International Law Society (Treasurer, 1999-2000). ***PRACTICE AREAS:*** Health Law; White Collar Crime. ***Email:*** rhatfield@jenkens.com

JOHN T. KIRSCH, born Laurel, Maryland, October 22, 1964; admitted to bar, 1999, Virginia; 2000, Maryland; 2001, District of Columbia. *Education:* University of Notre Dame (B.A., 1987); St. Mary's University School of Law (J.D., magna cum laude, 1999). *Member:* Virginia State Bar; The District of Columbia Bar. ***PRACTICE AREAS:*** Construction Law; Litigation; Government Contracts. ***Email:*** jkirsch@jenkens.com

IDEN GRANT MARTYN, born Cleveland, Ohio, January 20, 1959; admitted to bar, 1984, Ohio; 1987, U.S. District Court, Northern District of Ohio (Not admitted in District of Columbia). *Education:* Kent State University (B.A., 1980; M.A., 1981); Cleveland Marshall College of Law (J.D., 1984). Phi Beta Kappa. Recipient, Charles Auerbach Award for Outstanding Student in Law of Evidence. *Member:* Cleveland, Ohio State and American Bar Associations; Cleveland Academy of Trial Attorneys; Ohio Academy of Trial Lawyers; The Association of Trial Lawyers of America; American Health Lawyers Association. ***PRACTICE AREAS:*** Health Law; Health Care Fraud; Litigation. ***Email:*** imartyn@jenkens.com

KAREN McMILLAN, born Washington, D.C., May 7, 1975; admitted to bar, 2001, Virginia (Not admitted in District of Columbia). *Education:* Colgate University (B.A., 1997); Georgetown University (J.D., cum laude, 2001). Author, "Strengthening the Legal Framework for Nuclear Energy," Georgetown International Environmental Law Review, Summer 2001. *Member:* Virginia State Bar. ***PRACTICE AREAS:*** Litigation. ***Email:*** kmcmillan@jenkens.com

JOHN BRIAN MORROW, born Wilkinsburg, Pennsylvania, November 4, 1964; admitted to bar, 1997, California (Not admitted in District of Columbia). *Education:* University of California at Davis (B.S., Civil Engineering, 1989); California State University at San Jose (M.S., Civil Engineering, 1994); University of Iowa (J.D., 1996). Phi Delta Phi; Tau Beta Pi; Chi Epsilon. Member, National Engineering Honor Society. Licensed Civil Engineer, California, June 1992. *Member:* Santa Clara County Bar Association; State Bar of California. ***PRACTICE AREAS:*** Construction Law. ***Email:*** bmorrow@jenkens.com

CHERYL L. MULLIN, born Philadelphia, Pennsylvania, July 3, 1967; admitted to bar, 1995, New Jersey and Pennsylvania (Not admitted in District of Columbia). *Education:* Temple University (B.A., 1991); Widener University (J.D., 1995). Co-Author: "The New Jersey Franchise Practices Act: How the Statute and Case Law Construe What Constitutes a Franchisee," New Jersey Law Journal, June 5, 2000; "FTC Notice of Proposed Rule Making Offers Guidance for Electronic Disclosure," Franchise Law Journal, Spring 2000; "The Small Business Franchise Act of 1999: Leveling the Playing Field or Upsetting the Game?" The Franchise Lawyer, Winter 2000; "Restricting Franchisee Purchases: Necessary Control or Illegal Tie?" New Jersey Lawyer, February 2000; "To e or not to e: Using Electronic Communication in Franchise Sales," Franchising World, January/February 2000; "Franchise Laws in an Age of Electronic Communication," Franchise Law Journal, Fall 1999; "NASAA Announces Y2K Disclosure Requirement," The Franchise Lawyer, Spring 1999; "Searching For Tomorrow's Franchises," Franchising World, March/April 1999; "The Use of Franchise Brokers in the Recruitment Process," Franchise Update, 3rd Quarter, 1996. Member, Licensing Executives Society. *Member:* Philadelphia, Pennsylvania (Member, Section on Intellectual Property), New Jersey State (Member, Sections on: Intellectual Property, Corporate and Business Law) and American (Member, Intellectual Property Section, Forum Committee on Franchising) Bar Associations. ***PRACTICE AREAS:*** Franchise Law; Distribution; Intellectual Property; Antitrust; Commercial Law. ***Email:*** cmullin@jenkens.com

MICHAEL ALEXANDER TROY, born Morristown, New Jersey, October 30, 1971; admitted to bar, 1997, Maryland (Not admitted in District of Columbia). *Education:* Boston College (B.A., 1994); Washington College of Law of American University (J.D., cum laude, 1997); Georgetown University (LL.M.,

(This Listing Continued)

(This Listing Continued)

JENKENS & GILCHRIST, A PROFESSIONAL CORPORATION, Washington—Continued

2000). Articles Editor, The American University Law Review. *Member:* Maryland State and American Bar Associations. ***PRACTICE AREAS:*** Securities; Corporate; Financial Institutions. ***Email:*** mtroy@jenkens.com

(For biographical data on other personnel, See Professional Biographies at Dallas, Austin, San Antonio and Houston, Texas, Los Angeles, California, and Chicago, Illinois)

JENNER & BLOCK, LLC

A Partnership including Professional Corporations

601 THIRTEENTH STREET, N.W., TWELFTH FLOOR

WASHINGTON, D.C. 20005

Telephone: 202-639-6000

FAX: 202-639-6066

Cable Address: "Jenblock"

URL: http://www.jenner.com

Chicago, Illinois Office: One IBM Plaza. Telephone: 312-222-9350. FAX: 312-527-0484. Telex: 270469. Cable Address: "Jenblock."

Lake Forest, Illinois Office: One Westminster Place. Telephone: 847-295-9200. FAX: 847-295-7810.

Dallas, Texas Office: 1717 Main Street, Suite 3150. Telephone: 214-746-5700. FAX: 214-746-5757.

General Practice.

RESIDENT PARTNERS

JACQUELINE C. BARES, born Chicago, Illinois, August 14, 1948; admitted to bar, 1990, Illinois; 2001, District of Columbia. *Education:* Marquette University (B.A., 1970); Northwestern University (J.D., cum laude, 1990). Order of the Coif. *Member:* American Bar Association; Bar Association of Circuit Court of Appeals of the District of Columbia. ***PRACTICE AREAS:*** Corporate Law. ***Email:*** jbares@jenner.com

STEVEN N. BERK, born Chicago, Illinois, July 2, 1959; admitted to bar, 1985, Illinois; 1990, District of Columbia. *Education:* Washington University (A.B., with honors, 1981); London School of Economics (M.Sc., International Relations, 1982); Boston College (J.D., cum laude, 1985). Managing Editor, Boston College Law Review, 1984-1985. Trial Attorney, Office of the General Counsel, Security and Exchange Commission, 1989-1990. Assistant U.S. Attorney, District of Columbia, 1990-1994. ***Email:*** sberk@jenner.com

ALAN M. BUIE, born Houston, Texas, January 4, 1966; admitted to bar, 1992, Texas; 1995, District of Columbia. *Education:* University of Texas at Austin (B.A., with highest honors, 1988); Harvard University (J.D., cum laude, 1992). Phi Beta Kappa. Law Clerk to Hon. Emilio M. Garza, U.S. Court of Appeals, Fifth Circuit, 1992-1994. ***Email:*** abuie@jenner.com

JULIA M. CARPENTER, born Hendersonville, North Carolina, September 3, 1961; admitted to bar, 1987, Illinois (inactive); 1989, District of Columbia and Virginia. *Education:* College of William & Mary (B.A., 1983); University of North Carolina (J.D., with honors, 1987). Note and Comment Editor, North Carolina Law Review, 1986-1987. Law Clerk to Hon. Samuel Coleman, Virginia Court of Appeals, 1987-1988. ***PRACTICE AREAS:*** Litigation; Appellate Practice; Supreme Court Practice; Media and First Amendment; Technology Law. ***Email:*** jcarpenter@jenner.com

THERESA CHMARA, born Trenton, New Jersey, December 27, 1963; admitted to bar, 1988, New Jersey and Pennsylvania (inactive); 1990, District of Columbia. *Education:* Boston College (B.A., cum laude, 1985); Georgetown University (J.D., cum laude, 1988). Lead Articles Editor, Georgetown Immigration Law Journal, 1987-1988. ***LANGUAGES:*** Polish. ***PRACTICE AREAS:*** Media and First Amendment; Litigation; Civil Appeals; Advertising Law. ***Email:*** tchmara@jenner.com

DAVID A. CHURCHILL, born Fort Collins, Colorado, May 13, 1952; admitted to bar, 1979, District of Columbia; 1980, U.S. Claims Court and U.S. District Court for the District of Columbia Circuit; 1982, U.S. Court of Appeals for the Federal Circuit. *Education:* University of Colorado (B.A., magna cum laude, 1974); University of Vienna, Austria; Cornell University (J.D., cum laude, 1979). Editor-in-Chief, Cornell International Law Journal, 1978-1979. Law Clerk to the Hon. Louis Spector, Trial Judge, U.S. Court of Claims, 1979-1980. Member, Advisory Council, U.S. Court of Federal Claims, 1993-2001. *Member:* The District of Columbia Bar; Federal Circuit and American (Past Chair, Section of Public Contract Law, 1998-1999) Bar Associations; U.S. Court of Federal Claims Bar Association. ***PRACTICE AREAS:*** Government Contracts Litigation and Counseling; Arbitration; Bid Protests. ***Email:*** dchurchill@jenner.com

PAUL W. "WHIT" COBB, JR., born Durham, North Carolina, November 25, 1964; admitted to bar, 1991, Maryland; 1997, District of Columbia. *Education:* Duke University (A.B., summa cum laude, 1987); Yale University (J.D., 1990). Phi Beta Kappa. Executive Editor, Yale Law Journal, 1989-1990. Author: "Democracy in Search of Utopia: The History, Law and Politics of Relocating the National Capital," 99 Dickenson L. Rev. 527, 1995; Note, "Reviving Mercy in the Structure of Capital Punishment," 99 Yale L.J. 389, 1989. Law Clerk, Hon. Thomas A. Clark, U.S. Court of Appeals, Eleventh Circuit, 1990-1991. Assistant to the General Counsel, Department of the Army, 1991-1995. Judicial Fellow, Administrative Office of the U.S. Courts, 1995-1996. [Capt., U.S. Army, 1991-1995]. ***Email:*** wcobb@jenner.com

JOSEPH P. COVINGTON, born Luxembourg, December 18, 1946; admitted to bar, 1974, Arizona and U.S. District Court, District of Arizona and U.S. Court of Appeals, 9th Circuit; 1978, Supreme Court of Virginia, U.S. District Court, Eastern District of Virginia and U.S. Court of Appeals, 4th Circuit; 1986, District of Columbia. *Education:* University of Virginia (B.A., 1968; J.D., 1973). Assistant U.S. Attorney, Arizona, 1974 and 1982-1985, Litigation Supervisor, Criminal Fraud Division, Department of Justice. Purple Heart, U.S. Army Infantry, Vietnam, 1969. ***LANGUAGES:*** German. ***PRACTICE AREAS:*** Government Contracts; Litigation; Criminal Antitrust; White Collar Criminal Defense; Compliance Counseling; Ethics and Compliance Issues. ***Email:*** jcovington@jenner.com

DAVID W. DeBRUIN, born Hinsdale, Illinois, March 29, 1955; admitted to bar, 1980, District of Columbia. *Education:* Indiana University (B.A., with highest distinction, 1977); University of Michigan (J.D., summa cum laude, 1980). Law Clerk to: Hon. Harry T. Edwards, U.S. Court of Appeals, District of Columbia Circuit, 1980-1981; Justice John Paul Stevens, U.S. Supreme Court, 1981-1982. Staff Attorney, Public Defender Service for the District of Columbia, 1982-1986. Associate Special Counsel, Impeachment of Judge Harry E. Claiborne, Committee on the Judiciary, United States House of Representatives, 1986. ***PRACTICE AREAS:*** Civil, Criminal and Appellate Litigation. ***Email:*** ddebruin@jenner.com

MAUREEN F. DEL DUCA, born Carlisle, Pennsylvania, September 17, 1960; admitted to bar, 1987, Pennsylvania; 1989, District of Columbia. *Education:* Swarthmore College (B.A., 1982); University of California at Berkeley (M.A., 1984); New York University (J.D., 1987); Georgetown University (LL.M., 1990). Senior Articles Editor, New York University Review of Law and Social Change, 1986-1987. Law Clerk to Hon. Leonard I. Garth, U.S. Court of Appeals, Third Circuit, 1990-1991. Instructor, Catholic University, Columbus School of Law, 1987-1988. Supervising Attorney, Appellate Litigation Clinic, Georgetown University Law Center, 1988-1990. ***PRACTICE AREAS:*** Appellate Practice; Regulatory Law; Telecommunications Law; New Media Law; Internet Law; Electronic Commerce. ***Email:*** mdelduca@jenner.com

KEVIN C. DWYER, born Baltimore, Maryland, September 12, 1958; admitted to bar, 1985, District of Columbia; 1987, U.S. Court of Appeals, Fourth Circuit; 1989, U.S. Court of Federal Claims; 1993, U.S. Court of Appeals, Federal Circuit. *Education:* University of Notre Dame (B.A., with honors, 1980); Yale University (M.A., 1981); Duke University (J.D., 1985). Executive Editor, Duke Law Journal, 1984-1985. *Member:* District of Columbia Bar; American Bar Association (Member, Public Contract Law Section). ***PRACTICE AREAS:*** Government Contract Law; Government Contract Cost Accounting; Health Care Contracting. ***Email:*** kdwyer@jenner.com

JEROME L. EPSTEIN, born San Antonio, Texas, December 21, 1961; admitted to bar, 1986, Pennsylvania (inactive); 1988, District of Columbia; 1994, Maryland. *Education:* University of Pennsylvania (B.S., Econ., magna cum laude, 1983; J.D., cum laude, 1986). Comment Editor, University of Pennsylvania Law Review, 1986. Law Clerk to Hon. Thomas Penfield Jackson, U.S. District Court for the District of Columbia, 1986-1987. Trial Attorney, Honors Program, U.S. Department of Justice, Civil Division, 1987-1990. ***PRACTICE AREAS:*** Civil Litigation; Telecommunications Law. ***Email:*** jepstein@jenner.com

IAN HEATH GERSHENGORN, born New York, N.Y., February 21, 1967; admitted to bar, 1994, Massachusetts; 1995, District of Columbia. *Education:* Harvard University (A.B., magna cum laude, 1988; J.D., magna cum laude, 1993). Phi Beta Kappa. Member, Harvard Law Review. Author: "Winship on Rough Waters: The Erosion of the Reasonable Doubt Standard," 106 Harvard Law Review 1093, 1993; "The Fall of the FCC's Personal Attack and Political Editorial Rules," Communications Lawyer, Spring 2001. Co-Author: with Philip B. Heymann, "Pursuing Justice, Respecting the Law: The U.S. Experience with Extraterritorial Statutes," Criminal Law Forum, Autumn 1991; with Philip B. Heymann, "A Comment on United States v. Alvarez-Machain," Criminal Law Forum, Spring 1993. Law Clerk to: Justice John Paul Stevens, U.S. Supreme Court, 1994-1995; Judge Amalya L. Kearse, U.S. Court of Appeals, Second Circuit, 1993-1994. Assistant to Attorney General Janet Reno, 1997 and Special Assistant and Counsel to Deputy Attorney General Jamie S. Gorelick, 1995-1997, U.S. Department of Justice. ***PRACTICE AREAS:*** Civil Litigation; Appellate Practice; Communications. ***Email:*** igershengorn@jenner.com

DAVID A. HANDZO, born Colts Neck, New Jersey, April 20, 1954; admitted to bar, 1980, Illinois; 1984, District of Columbia. *Education:* Princeton University (B.A., magna cum laude, 1976); University of Michigan (J.D., magna

(This Listing Continued)

cum laude, 1980). Order of the Coif. Staff Attorney, Public Defender Service for the District of Columbia, 1984-1988. ***PRACTICE AREAS:*** Civil Law; Criminal Law; Bankruptcy Litigation; Advertising Law. ***Email:*** dhandzo@jenner.com

SAM HIRSCH, born Washington, D.C., December 2, 1962; admitted to bar, 1995, Maryland; 1997, District of Columbia. *Education:* Rice University (B.A., 1984); Harvard University (J.D., 1993). Treasurer and Editor, Harvard Law Review, 1992-1993. ***PRACTICE AREAS:*** Litigation. ***Email:*** shirsch@jenner.com

RICHARD C. JOHNSON, born Knoxville, Tennessee, February 5, 1937; admitted to bar, 1962, Massachusetts; 1968, District of Columbia. *Education:* Harvard University (B.A., magna cum laude, 1958; LL.B., magna cum laude, 1962); University of Cologne, Germany and University of Bonn, Germany. Phi Beta Kappa. Member, Board of Editors, Harvard Law Review, 1960-1962. Member, Office of the General Counsel, Department of the Air Force, 1962-1966. Assistant Executive Director, Federal Power Commission, 1966-1968. ***PRACTICE AREAS:*** Government Contracts Law. ***Email:*** rjohnson@jenner.com

JODIE L. KELLEY, born New Orleans, Louisiana, October 9, 1964; admitted to bar, 1993, Massachusetts; 1995, District of Columbia. *Education:* Pennsylvania State University (B.S.S., 1989); Harvard University (J.D., 1992). Editor, Women's Law Journal. ***PRACTICE AREAS:*** Communications; Media; Civil Litigation; Appellate Practice. ***Email:*** jkelley@jenner.com

LESLIE H. LEPOW, born New York, N.Y., September 16, 1949; admitted to bar, 1975, District of Columbia. *Education:* Columbia University (A.B., 1971); Georgetown University (J.D., 1974). ***PRACTICE AREAS:*** Government Contracts; Minority and Small Business Law; Government Investigations. ***Email:*** llepow@jenner.com

DEANNE E. MAYNARD, born Winston-Salem, North Carolina, March 14, 1965; admitted to bar, 1991, Virginia; 1992, District of Columbia. *Education:* University of Virginia (B.A., with distinction, 1987); Harvard Law School (J.D., magna cum laude, 1991). Editor, Harvard Law Review. Law Clerk to: Justice Stephen G. Breyer, U.S. Supreme Court, 1994-1995; Justice Lewis F. Powell, Jr. (Ret.), U.S. Supreme Court, 1993-1994; Judge Stanley S. Harris, U.S. District Court for the District of Columbia, 1991-1993. ***PRACTICE AREAS:*** Civil Litigation; Appellate Practice; First Amendment Law. ***Email:*** dmaynard@jenner.com

MARK J. McGUIRE, born Middletown, Connecticut, January 10, 1953; admitted to bar, 1981, Michigan; 1985, Illinois; 1995, District of Columbia. *Education:* Southern Connecticut State College (B.A., 1974); St. Louis University (J.D., 1980). *Member:* Federal Energy Bar Association. ***PRACTICE AREAS:*** Energy Law; Public Utility Law; Antitrust. ***Email:*** mmcguire@jenner.com

NORY MILLER, born Chicago, Illinois; admitted to bar, 1989, New York and District of Columbia. *Education:* Swarthmore College (B.A., with honors); Columbia University (J.D., 1988). James Kent Scholar, 1985-1988; John Ordronaux Prize, 1988. Editor-in-Chief, Columbia Law Review. Law Clerk: Hon. Abner Mikva, U.S. Court of Appeals, District of Columbia Circuit, 1988-1989; Justice William J. Brennan, U.S. Supreme Court, 1989-1990. *Member:* District of Columbia Bar; American Bar Association. ***PRACTICE AREAS:*** First Amendment; Intellectual Property; Civil Litigation; Appellate Practice. ***Email:*** nmiller@jenner.com

JOHN B. MORRIS, JR., born Lumberton, North Carolina, May 21, 1958; admitted to bar, 1987, Georgia; 1992, District of Columbia. *Education:* Yale University (B.A., magna cum laude, 1981; J.D., 1986). Managing Editor, Yale Law Journal, 1985-1986. Law Clerk to Hon. Thomas A. Clark, U.S. Court of Appeals, Eleventh Circuit, 1986-1987. ***PRACTICE AREAS:*** Civil and Appellate Litigation; Technology Law; Internet Law; First Amendment Law. ***Email:*** jmorris@jenner.com

CARL S. NADLER, born New Orleans, Louisiana, October 18, 1955; admitted to bar, 1983, Illinois; 1985, District of Columbia. *Education:* Antioch College (B.A., 1978); Washington University (J.D., 1982). Order of the Coif. Notes and Comments Editor, Washington University Law Quarterly, 1981-1982. Law Clerk, Hon. Alvin B. Rubin, U.S. Court of Appeals, 5th Circuit, 1982-1983. ***PRACTICE AREAS:*** Civil Litigation; Antitrust Law; Intellectual Property; Telecommunications Law. ***Email:*** cnadler@jenner.com

THOMAS J. PERRELLI, born Falls Church, Virginia, March 12, 1966; admitted to bar, 1991, Virginia; 1993, District of Columbia. *Education:* Brown University (A.B., magna cum laude, 1988); Harvard University (J.D., magna cum laude, 1991). ***PRACTICE AREAS:*** Litigation; Public Policy. ***Email:*** tperrelli@jenner.com

SUSAN R. PODOLSKY, born Detroit, Michigan, June 18, 1959; admitted to bar, 1987, Virginia; 1988, District of Columbia. *Education:* Dartmouth College (A.B., 1981); University of Virginia (J.D., 1986). Phi Beta Kappa. Law Clerk to Hon. Albert V. Bryan, Jr., U.S. District Court, Eastern District of Virginia, 1986-1988. ***PRACTICE AREAS:*** Civil Litigation; Commercial Litigation. ***Email:*** spodolsky@jenner.com

(This Listing Continued)

ROBERT M. PORTMAN, born Chicago, Illinois, February 28, 1959; admitted to bar, 1986, Illinois and U.S. District Court, Northern District of Illinois; 1991, U.S. Supreme Court; 1995, District of Columbia; 2000, U.S. Court of Appeals, Seventh Circuit. *Education:* Northwestern University (B.A., summa cum laude, 1980), Phi Beta Kappa; Harvard Law School (J.D., magna cum laude, 1985); Kennedy School of Government (M.P.P., 1985). Law Clerk, Judge Mark Wolf, U.S. District Court, Massachusetts, 1985-1986. Special Assistant to the Secretary, U.S. Department of Labor, Jan.-Oct. 1993. Deputy Assistant Secretary, Office of the American Workplace, U.S. Department of Labor, 1993-1995. *Member:* District of Columbia Bar (Member, Health Law Section Steering Committee); American Bar Association (Member, Health Law Section); American Health Lawyers Association; American Society of Medical Association Counsel; American Society of Association Executives. ***PRACTICE AREAS:*** Health Care; Trade Associations. ***Email:*** rportman@jenner.com

MARK D. SCHNEIDER, born New Rochelle, New York, April 4, 1954; admitted to bar, 1984, New York; 1985, District of Columbia; 1995, Maryland. *Education:* Swarthmore College (B.A., with high honors, 1976); Oxford University (M. Phil., 1979); Columbia University (J.D., 1983). Phi Beta Kappa. Leedom Fellow. Stone Scholar. Editor, Columbia Law Review, 1982-1983. Author: "Peaceful Labor Picketing and the First Amendment," 82 Columbia Law Review 1469, 1983. Law Clerk to: Hon. James L. Oakes, Second Circuit, 1983-1984; Hon. Harry A. Blackmun, Associate Justice, U.S. Supreme Court, 1984-1985. *Member:* District of Columbia Bar; American Bar Association. ***PRACTICE AREAS:*** Litigation; Appellate Practice; Supreme Court Practice; Media and First Amendment; Telecommunications Law. ***Email:*** mschneider@jenner.com

PAUL M. SMITH, born Salt Lake City, Utah, March 9, 1955; admitted to bar, 1981, District of Columbia; 1988, Maryland. *Education:* Amherst College (B.A., summa cum laude, 1976); Yale University (J.D., 1979). Phi Beta Kappa. Editor-in-Chief, Yale Law Journal, 1978-1979. Law Clerk to: Judge James L. Oakes, U.S. Court of Appeals, 2nd Circuit, 1979-1980; Justice Lewis F. Powell Jr., U.S. Supreme Court, 1980-1981. *Member:* American Bar Association; Washington Council of Lawyers (President, 1990-1991). ***PRACTICE AREAS:*** Civil and Appellate Litigation; Media and First Amendment Law; Election Law; Antitrust. ***Email:*** psmith@jenner.com

BRUCE SPIVA, born Cleveland, Ohio, February 28, 1966; admitted to bar, 1993, California; 1994, District of Columbia. *Education:* Yale University (B.A., 1988); Harvard Law School (J.D., 1992). Treasurer, Harvard Law Review. Clerk, Hon. Jerome Farris, U.S. Court of Appeals, Ninth Circuit, Seattle, WA. *Member:* District of Columbia Bar; National and American Bar Associations. ***PRACTICE AREAS:*** Litigation; Antitrust; Trade Regulation; Class Action Litigation; Media and First Amendment; Trade Associations. ***Email:*** bspiva@jenner.com

DONALD B. VERRILLI, JR., born New Rochelle, New York, June 29, 1957; admitted to bar, 1987, New York; 1989, District of Columbia. *Education:* Yale University (B.A., cum laude, 1979); Columbia University (J.D., 1983). Editor-in-Chief, Columbia Law Review, 1982-1983. Law Clerk to: Hon. J. Skelly Wright, U.S. Court of Appeals for the District of Columbia Circuit, 1983-1984; Justice William J. Brennan, Jr., U.S. Supreme Court, 1984-1985. Samuel Rubin Research Fellow, Columbia University, 1985-1986. Adjunct Professor of Law, Georgetown University Law Center, 1991-2001. Lecturer, Washington College of Law, American University, 1995. ***PRACTICE AREAS:*** Civil and Appellate Litigation; Telecommunications Law; Media and First Amendment Law; Election Law. ***Email:*** dverrilli@jenner.com

RESIDENT ASSOCIATES

IMAD D. ABYAD, born Damascus, Syria, November 9, 1963; admitted to bar, 1996, Virginia; 1997, Maryland and District of Columbia. *Education:* Illinois Institute of Technology (B.S., 1987); University of Virginia (J.D., 1996). Chi Epsilon. Member, Virginia Law Review. Author: Note, "Commercial Reasonableness in Karl Llewellyn's Uniform Commercial Code Jurisprudence," 83 Virginia Law Review 429, 1997. ***LANGUAGES:*** Arabic. ***PRACTICE AREAS:*** Antitrust; Complex Litigation; Telecommunications. ***Email:*** iabyad@jenner.com

ERIN ALBRITTON, born Palo Alto, California, December 28, 1970; admitted to bar, 1997, Louisiana (Not admitted in District of Columbia). *Education:* Queen's University (B.A., 1992); Tulane University (J.D., magna cum laude, 1997). Order of the Coif. Notes and Comments Editor, Tulane University Law Review. Author: Note, "Hopwood v. Texas: Affirmative Action Encounters A Formidable and Fatal Match in the Fifth Circuit," 71 Tul. L. Rev. 303, 1996. ***PRACTICE AREAS:*** Litigation. ***Email:*** ealbritton@jenner.com

GEOFFREY A. BARROW, born Billings, Montana, January 8, 1971; admitted to bar, 1997, Illinois; 1999, District of Columbia. *Education:* Lawrence University (B.S., cum laude, 1993); George Washington University (J.D., 1996). Law Clerk, Hon. Moody R. Tidwell, U.S. Court of Federal Claims, 1997-1998. ***PRACTICE AREAS:*** Terminations; Litigation; Bid Protests; Export Control. ***Email:*** gbarrow@jenner.com

(This Listing Continued)

JENNER & BLOCK, LLC, Washington—Continued

DAVID C. BELT, born New Haven, Connecticut, October 26, 1970; admitted to bar, 1996, Ohio; 1998, District of Columbia. *Education:* Queen's University (B.A., 1992); Case Western Reserve University (J.D., summa cum laude, 1996). Order of the Coif. Articles Editor, Case Western Reserve Law Review, 1995-1996. Author: Note, "Election of Remedies in Employment Discrimination Law: Doorway Into the Legal Hall of Mirrors," 46 Case W. Res. L. Rev. 145, 1995. Law Clerk to: Hon. Ralph K. Winter, Chief Judge, U.S. Court of Appeals, Second Circuit, 1997-1998; Hon. David F. Hamilton, U.S. District Court, Southern District of Indiana, 1996-1997. *Member:* District of Columbia Bar; American Bar Association. ***PRACTICE AREAS:*** Litigation; Media and First Amendment Law; Appellate Practice. ***Email:*** dbelt@jenner.com

NICOLE G. BERNER, born Woking, United Kingdom, April 3, 1965; admitted to bar, 1997, California; 2001, District of Columbia. *Education:* University of California, Berkeley (B.A., highest honors, 1988); University of California, Boalt Hall School of Law (J.D., 1996). Phi Beta Kappa. Order of the Coif. Law Clerk to: Hon. Betty B. Fletcher, 9th Circuit Court of Appeals, 1996-1997; Hon. Thelton E. Henderson, U.S. District Court, Northern District of California, 1997-1998. ***LANGUAGES:*** Hebrew. ***PRACTICE AREAS:*** Civil Litigation; Civil Rights; E-Commerce Transactions. ***Email:*** nberner@jenner.com

ELIZABETH E. APPEL BLUE, born Greensboro, North Carolina, December 4, 1967; admitted to bar, 1994, Virginia; 1997, District of Columbia. *Education:* Yale University (B.A., summa cum laude, 1990; J.D., 1994). Phi Beta Kappa. Law Clerk to: Judge Francis Murnaghan, U.S. Court of Appeals, Fourth Circuit, 1995-1996; Judge Myron Thompson, U.S. District Court, Middle District of Alabama, 1994-1995. ***Email:*** lblue@jenner.com

ELENA N. BRODER-FELDMAN, born New York, N.Y., January 11, 1972; admitted to bar, 1996, Maryland; 1997, U.S. District Court, District of Maryland and U.S. Court of Appeals, Fourth Circuit; 1998, District of Columbia; 1999, U.S. Court of Appeals, Tenth Circuit. *Education:* Duke University (A.B., magna cum laude, 1993); Yale University (J.D., 1996). Phi Beta Kappa. Notes Development Editor, Yale Law Journal, 1995-1996. Author: "(Net) Workers' Rights: The NLRA and Employee Electronic Communications," 105 Yale L.J., 1639. Law Clerk to the Hon. Paul V. Niemeyer, U.S. Court of Appeals, Fourth Circuit, 1996-1997. *Member:* District of Columbia Bar; American Bar Association. ***LANGUAGES:*** French. ***PRACTICE AREAS:*** Litigation. ***Email:*** ebroder@jenner.com

ELIZABETH A. CAVANAGH, born Brooklyn, N.Y., May 21, 1970; admitted to bar, 1996, Maryland; 1998, District of Columbia. *Education:* Dartmouth College (A.B., summa cum laude, 1992); Yale University (J.D., 1995). Phi Beta Kappa. Executive Editor, Yale Law Journal. Law Clerk to the Honorable Louis F. Oberdorfer, U.S. District Court for the District of Columbia, 1995-1996. Law Clerk to the Honorable John Paul Stevens, U.S. Supreme Court, 1997-1998. *Member:* Maryland State and American Bar Associations. ***PRACTICE AREAS:*** Litigation. ***Email:*** ecavanagh@jenner.com

MICHAEL B. DeSANCTIS, born Los Angeles, California, August 1, 1969; admitted to bar, 1998, New York, New Jersey, District of Columbia, U.S. Court of Appeals, Third Circuit and U.S. District Court, District of New Jersey; U.S. Court of Appeals, Sixth Circuit. *Education:* Boston College (B.A., summa cum laude, 1991); New York University School of Law (J.D., cum laude, 1995). Phi Beta Kappa; Phi Alpha Theta. Editor-in-Chief, NYU School of Law Moot Court Casebook. Clerk: Hon. Dolores K. Sloviter, Chief Judge, U.S. Court of Appeals, Third Circuit, 1997-1998; Hon. Maryanne Trump Barry, U.S. District Court, District of New Jersey, 1995-1997. *Member:* District of Columbia Bar (Member, Section on Communications and Computer Law); Bar Association of the District of Columbia (Member: Appellate Courts Committee; Board of Directors, Young Lawyers Section); American Bar Association (Member: Cyberspace Law Committee; Air and Space Law Forum); Computer Law Association. ***PRACTICE AREAS:*** Litigation. ***Email:*** mdesanctis@jenner.com

KATHERINE A. FALLOW, born Washington, D.C., June 10, 1969; admitted to bar, 1996, Massachusetts; 1999, District of Columbia. *Education:* University of California, Berkeley (B.A., with highest honors, 1991); Harvard University (J.D., magna cum laude, 1996). Phi Beta Kappa. Clerk: Hon. Robert E. Keeton, U.S. District Court, District of Massachusetts, 1996-1997; Hon. Rosemary Barkett, U.S. Court of Appeals, Eleventh Circuit, 1997-1998. ***PRACTICE AREAS:*** Litigation; Appellate Practice. ***Email:*** kfallow@jenner.com

LARA M. FLINT, born Geneva, Switzerland; admitted to bar, 1999, Maryland; 2000, District of Columbia. *Education:* Northwestern University (B.S.J., with highest distinction, 1995); Harvard University (J.D., magna cum laude, 1998). Finalist, Ames Moot Court Competition. Law Clerk, Honorable Milton Shadur, U.S. District Court, Northern District of Illinois, 1998-1999. *Member:* American Bar Association. (Resident, Washington, D.C. Office). ***PRACTICE AREAS:*** Litigation. ***Email:*** lflint@jenner.com

JARED O. FREEDMAN, born Philadelphia, Pennsylvania, November 2, 1969; admitted to bar, 1999, New York; 2000, District of Columbia. *Education:* Harvard University (A.B., magna cum laude, 1991); Yale University (J.D., 1997). Law Clerk: Hon. Dana Fabe, Alaska Supreme Court, 1997-1998; Hon. Michael Ponsor, U.S. District Court, District of Massachusetts, 1998-1999. ***PRACTICE AREAS:*** Litigation. ***Email:*** jfreedman@jenner.com

MARC A. GOLDMAN, born Washington, D.C., May 12, 1966; admitted to bar, 1994, Pennsylvania; 1996, District of Columbia. *Education:* Harvard University (A.B., magna cum laude, 1988; J.D., magna cum laude, 1993). Supervising Editor, Harvard Law Review, 1992-1993. Law Clerk to Hon. Edward Becker, U.S. Court of Appeals, Third Circuit, 1993-1994. Visiting Professor of Constitutional Law, University of Iowa Law School, Spring 1999. ***PRACTICE AREAS:*** Civil Litigation; Appellate Practice; Telecommunications Law. ***Email:*** mgoldman@jenner.com

DANIEL JAMES GREINER, born Columbia, South Carolina, May 10, 1969; admitted to bar, 1997, Virginia; 1998, District of Columbia. *Education:* University of Virginia (B.A., with high honors, 1991); University of Michigan (J.D., magna cum laude, 1995). Phi Beta Kappa. American Inns of Court. Jefferson Scholar; Echols Scholar; Bates Memorial Scholar. Recipient, Stevenson Prize. Campbell Moot Court Winner. Articles Editor, Michigan Law Review. Author, Note: 93 Mich. L. Rev. 301 (1994); Book Notice, 92 Mich. L. Rev. 1962 (1994). ***LANGUAGES:*** Spanish. ***PRACTICE AREAS:*** Agency Law; Constitutional Law; Employment Discrimination; Commercial Litigation; Government Contracts. ***Email:*** jgreiner@jenner.com

MATTHEW HERSH, born Washington, D.C., October 31, 1967; admitted to bar, 1999, District of Columbia. *Education:* Columbia University (B.A., 1990); Georgetown University (J.D., cum laude, 1999). ***PRACTICE AREAS:*** Litigation. ***Email:*** mhersh@jenner.com

WILLIAM A. HOHENGARTEN, born St. Paul, Minnesota, August 27, 1960; admitted to bar, 1995, New York; 1998, District of Columbia. *Education:* Reed College (B.A., 1984); Northwestern University (Ph.D., 1991); Yale University (J.D., 1994). Notes Editor, Yale Law Journal. ***PRACTICE AREAS:*** Litigation. ***Email:*** whohengarten@jenner.com

BOBBY J. HOLLIS, II, born Homestead AFB, Florida, March 24, 1974; admitted to bar, 2000, Illinois; 2001, District of Columbia. *Education:* University of Florida (B.A., 1996); University of Iowa (J.D., 1999). Phi Beta Kappa; Phi Alpha Delta; Golden Key. Corpus Juris Secundum, Contracts. Author: "Lack of Marketability Discounts," Journ. of Corp. Law, Vol. 25, No.1, Fall 1999. ***PRACTICE AREAS:*** Corporate. ***Email:*** bhollis@jenner.com

MARC E. ISSERLES, born Stony Brook, New York, October 21, 1971; admitted to bar, 2001, Maryland (Not admitted in District of Columbia). *Education:* Sarah Lawrence College (B.A., 1993); Harvard Law School (J.D., magna cum laude, 1998). Recipient, Sears Prize, Harvard Law School, 1997. Notes Editor, Harvard Law Review, 1997-1998. Author: "Overcoming Overbreath: Facial Challenges and the Valid Rule Requirement," 48 American University Law Review, 1998. ***PRACTICE AREAS:*** Litigation. ***Email:*** misserles@jenner.com

JANIS C. KESTENBAUM, admitted to bar, 1993, Pennsylvania; 1995, U.S. Court of Appeals, Fifth and Ninth Circuits; 1996, District of Columbia; 1997, U.S. Court of Appeals, Fourth Circuit. *Education:* Duke University (B.A., magna cum laude, 1987); Harvard University (J.D., magna cum laude, 1992). Phi Beta Kappa. Editor, Harvard Law Review. Law Clerk to Hon. Edward R. Becker, U.S. Court of Appeals, Third Circuit, 1992-1993. Trial Attorney, U.S. Department of Justice, Federal Programs Branch, Civil Division, 1993-1997. Recipient, Justice Department Special Achievement Awards, 1995, 1997 and 1998. ***PRACTICE AREAS:*** Litigation; Antitrust; Telecommunications Appellate. ***Email:*** jkestenbaum@jenner.com

JESSIE K. LIU, born Kingsville, Texas, January 2, 1973; admitted to bar, 1998, Texas; 1999, U.S. District Court, Northern District of Illinois and U.S. Court of Appeals, Fifth Circuit; 2000, Illinois; 2001, District of Columbia; U.S. Court of Appeals, Seventh Circuit. *Education:* Harvard University (A.B., 1995); Yale University (J.D., 1998). Phi Beta Kappa. ***PRACTICE AREAS:*** Litigation. ***Email:*** jliu@jenner.com

DANIEL MACH, born Englewood, New Jersey, January 30, 1970; admitted to bar, 1998, New York; 1999, District of Columbia. *Education:* Princeton University (B.A., 1992); New York University (J.D., magna cum laude, 1996). Order of the Coif. Articles Editor, New York University Law Review. Author: "The Bold and the Beautiful: Art, Public Spaces and the First Amendment," 72 N.Y.U. L. Rev. 383, 1997. Law Clerk, The Hon. Barry T. Moskowitz, U.S. District Court, Southern District of California, 1996-1997. ***PRACTICE AREAS:*** Civil Litigation; First Amendment Law; Telecommunications Law; Antitrust Law. ***Email:*** dmach@jenner.com

JENNY S. MARTINEZ, born November 5, 1971; admitted to bar, 1999, Virginia (Not admitted in District of Columbia). *Education:* Yale University (B.A., 1993); Harvard University (J.D., 1997). Recipient, Sears Prize. Member, Harvard Law Review, 1996-1997. *Member:* Hispanic Bar Association of DC (Vice President, Internal Affairs, 2001—). ***PRACTICE AREAS:*** Litigation; First Amendment Law; International Law. ***Email:*** jmartinez@jenner.com

ROBIN M. MERIWEATHER, born Detroit, Michigan, April 17, 1974; admitted to bar, 1998, Illinois (Not admitted in District of Columbia). *Educa-*

(This Listing Continued)

tion: University of Michigan (B.A., 1995); Yale University (J.D., 1998). Phi Beta Kappa. Law Clerk, The Hon. Merrick B. Garland, U.S. Court of Appeals, D.C. Circuit, 1998-1999. *Member:* American Bar Association. ***PRACTICE AREAS:*** Litigation. ***Email:*** rmeriweather@jenner.com

ROBERT STEPHEN NICHOLS, born Tucson, Arizona; admitted to bar, 1994, Arizona; 1996, District of Columbia; 1997, U.S. Court of Appeals, Federal Circuit and U.S. Court of International Trade; 1999, Virgin Islands. *Education:* Northern Arizona University (B.S.B.A., summa cum laude, 1991); Arizona State University (J.D., cum laude, 1996); Georgetown University Law Center (LL.M., with distinction, International and Comparative Law, 1997). Order of the Coif. Law Clerk to Hon. Raymond L. Finch, U.S. District Court, District of U.S. Virgin Islands. Congressional Fellow, U.S. Senate Commerce Committee. Judge Advocate General, Honors Program, U.S. Army Corps of Engineers. *Member:* American Bar Association; American Society of International Law. [Captain, Honors Program, U.S. Army Corps of Engineers, 1994-1998]. ***PRACTICE AREAS:*** Arbitration; Government Contracts Litigation and Counseling; Government Relations. ***Email:*** rnichols@jenner.com

CYNTHIA J. ROBERTSON, born West Lafayette, Indiana, April 27, 1968; admitted to bar, 1998, Illinois and U.S. District Court, Northern District of Illinois (Not admitted in District of Columbia). *Education:* Vanderbilt University (B.A., 1990); University of Illinois (J.D., 1998). Order of the Coif. ***PRACTICE AREAS:*** General Litigation. ***Email:*** crobertson@jenner.com

LAURA M. SCOTT, admitted to bar, 1993, Virginia (Not admitted in District of Columbia). *Education:* George Mason University (B.A., 1990); Howard University (J.D., 1993). ***PRACTICE AREAS:*** Antitrust; Trade Regulation. ***Email:*** lscott@jenner.com

KEVIN M. STACK, born Urbana, Illinois, November 12, 1968; admitted to bar, 2000, Maryland; 2001, District of Columbia. *Education:* Brown University (A.B., magna cum laude, with honors in Philosophy, 1991); University of Oxford, Oxford, England (M.Litt., 1996); Yale Law School (J.D., 1997). Phi Beta Kappa. Coker Fellow. Recipient: Fulbright Scholarship; Felix S. Cohen Prize; Overseas Research Students Award. Member, Yale Law Journal. Articles Editor, Yale Journal of Law and the Humanities. Author: Note, "The Practice of Dissent in the Supreme Court," 105 Yale L.J. 2235, 1996. Law Clerk: Hon. A. Wallace Tashima, U.S. Court of Appeals, Ninth Circuit, 1998-1999; Hon. Kimba M. Wood, U.S. District Court, Southern District of New York, 1997-1998. ***PRACTICE AREAS:*** Litigation. ***Email:*** kstack@jenner.com

OLIVIER SYLVAIN, admitted to bar, 2000, New York; 2001, District of Columbia. *Education:* Williams College (B.A., cum laude, 1995); Georgetown University (J.D., 1999). ***Email:*** osylvain@jenner.com

JAMES A. TRILLING, born Chicago, Illinois, August 11, 1972; admitted to bar, 1999, Maryland; 2000, District of Columbia. *Education:* Indiana University, Bloomington (B.A., summa cum laude, 1994), Phi Beta Kappa; Harvard University (J.D., cum laude, 1998). Author: "The Supreme Court, 1996 Term - The Leading Cases," 111 Harv. L. Rev. 237 (1997); "Developments in the Law - The Civil Jury," 110 Harv. L. Rev. 1489 (1997). *Member:* Maryland State and American Bar Associations. ***PRACTICE AREAS:*** Civil Litigation. ***Email:*** jtrilling@jenner.com

J. ALEX WARD, born Baltimore, Maryland, August 11, 1967; admitted to bar, 1992, Virginia; 1999, District of Columbia. *Education:* Duke University (B.A., magna cum laude, 1989); Harvard University (J.D., cum laude, 1992), Phi Beta Kappa. Law Clerk, Hon. Karen L. Henderson, U.S. Court of Appeals, District of Columbia Circuit, 1996-1997. Assistant to the General Counsel of the Army, 1992-1996. Author: "Copyrighting Context: Law for Plumbing's Sake," 17 Colum.-Vla J. Law & Arts 159, 1993. [Capt., U.S. Army, 1992-1996]. ***PRACTICE AREAS:*** Litigation. ***Email:*** award@jenner.com

KIAL S. YOUNG, born Washington, D.C., March 30, 1969; admitted to bar, 1996, Massachusetts; 1998, District of Columbia. *Education:* Yale University (B.A., summa cum laude, 1991); Stanford University (J.D., 1996). Clerk, Hon. David A. Brock, Chief Justice, New Hampshire Supreme Court, 1996-1997. ***Email:*** kyoung@jenner.com

(For Complete Biographical Data on all Personnel, see Chicago, Illinois Professional Biographies)

BRIAN PAUL JENNY

SUITE 440
5335 WISCONSIN AVENUE, N.W.
WASHINGTON, D.C. 20015-2030
Telephone: 202-362-2165
Facsimile: 703-771-9078
Email: ziik@visuallink.com
URL: http://www.lawyers.com/bpjlaw

Probate, Trusts and Estates, Domestic Relations Law and Criminal Appeals. General Practice.

(This Listing Continued)

BRIAN PAUL JENNY, born Utica, New York, November 17, 1948; admitted to bar, 1976, District of Columbia; 1980, U.S. District Court, District of Columbia; 1984, U.S. Tax Court. *Education:* George Washington University (B.A., 1970; J.D., 1976). *Member:* District of Columbia. ***PRACTICE AREAS:*** Probate Law; Trusts Law; Estates Law; Domestic Relations Law; Criminal Appeals; General Practice.

REFERENCE: NationsBank.

MARK R. JOELSON LAW OFFICE

1776 K STREET, N.W., SUITE 300
WASHINGTON, D.C. 20006
Telephone: 202-785-4155
Fax: 202-785-4157
Email: joelsonmr@msn.com

Trade Regulation, International Trade Law, Arbitration and Mediation.

MARK R. JOELSON, born October 23, 1934; admitted to bar, 1958, District of Columbia; 1963, U.S. Supreme Court. *Education:* Harvard University (B.A., 1955; LL.B., 1958); Oxford University, England (Diploma in Law, 1962). Publication: An International Antitrust Primer, 2001. Adjunct Professor, Georgetown University Law Center. Attorney, Civil Division, U.S. Department of Justice, 1959-1963. *Member:* District of Columbia Bar (Chairman, International Dispute Resolution Committee, International Law Section, 1999-2001); American (Chairman, 1983-1984, International Law and Practice Section), Federal (Chairman, Council on Antitrust and Trade Regulation, 1969-1971; President, District of Columbia Chapter, 1976-1977) and International (American Bar Association Delegate to Council, 1984-1992) Bar Associations; American Arbitration Association (Panel of Arbitrators). ***PRACTICE AREAS:*** Arbitration and Mediation; Antitrust; International Trade Law; Litigation.

JOHN & HENGERER

Established in 1986
SUITE 600
1200 17TH STREET, N.W.
WASHINGTON, D.C. 20036-3013
Telephone: 202-429-8800
Telecopier: 202-429-8805
Email: kquinn@jhenergy.com
URL: http://www.jhenergy.com

Energy Law, Energy Regulation, Administrative Practice and Pipeline Law.

FIRM PROFILE: The firm represents and/or advises a broad spectrum of energy clients, including natural gas producers and processors (U.S., Canadian, Norwegian, and Mexican), gas marketers, intrastate and interstate gas pipelines, gas storage companies, large industrial and municipal end-users of gas, a commodity futures exchange, publicly-owned electric utilities, independent power producers and cogenerators, and power marketers.

MEMBERS OF FIRM

DOUGLAS F. JOHN, born Washington, D.C., January 12, 1948; admitted to bar, 1974, Texas; 1979, District of Columbia. *Education:* Brown University (B.A., 1970); University of Texas (J.D., 1974). Attorney, Federal Power Commission, 1974-1977. *Member:* District of Columbia Bar; State Bar of Texas; Federal Energy Bar Association. ***PRACTICE AREAS:*** Energy Law. ***Email:*** djohn@jhenergy.com

EDWARD W. HENGERER, born Buffalo, New York, October 27, 1945; admitted to bar, 1973, District of Columbia. *Education:* Colgate University (B.A., 1968); George Washington University National Law Center (J.D., with honors, 1973). General Counsel, Office of the Federal Inspector of the Alaska Natural Gas Transportation System, 1979-1983. Attorney, Federal Energy Regulatory Commission, 1974-1978. *Member:* District of Columbia Bar; Federal Energy Bar Association. ***PRACTICE AREAS:*** Energy Law. ***Email:*** ehengerer@jhenergy.com

KEVIN M. SWEENEY, born Washington, D.C., November 20, 1956; admitted to bar, 1982, District of Columbia; 1989, U.S. Supreme Court. *Education:* College of William & Mary (B.A., 1978); George Washington University (J.D., 1981). *Member:* District of Columbia Bar; Federal Energy and American Bar Associations. ***PRACTICE AREAS:*** Energy Law. ***Email:*** ksweeney@jhenergy.com

KIM M. CLARK, born Rochester, New York, 1948; admitted to bar, 1974, New York and District of Columbia. *Education:* Colgate University (A.B., cum laude, 1970); Albany Law School of Union University (J.D., 1973). Member, 1971-1973 and Comments Editor, 1972-1973, Albany Law Review. Trial Attorney, Federal Power Commission, 1973-1977. Legal Advisor to Vice Chairman

(This Listing Continued)

JOHN & HENGERER, Washington—Continued

Don S. Smith, Federal Energy Regulatory Commission, 1977-1979. *Member:* District of Columbia Bar; New York State and Federal Energy Bar Associations. ***PRACTICE AREAS:*** Energy Law. **Email:** kclark@jhenergy.com

GORDON J. SMITH, born Atlanta, Georgia, September 25, 1963; admitted to bar, 1988, Maryland; 1991, District of Columbia. *Education:* Vanderbilt University (B.A., magna cum laude, 1985); George Washington University, National Law Center (J.D., 1988). Phi Beta Kappa. Attorney-Advisor to Administrative Law Judges, Federal Energy Regulatory Commission, 1988-1990. *Member:* District of Columbia Bar; Maryland State and Federal Energy Bar Associations. ***PRACTICE AREAS:*** Energy Law. **Email:** gsmith@jhenergy.com

ASSOCIATES

MATTHEW T. RICK, born St. Petersburg, Florida, January 25, 1974; admitted to bar, 1999, Virginia and Maryland (Not admitted in District of Columbia). *Education:* Michigan State University (B.A., 1996); George Washington University Law School (J.D., 1999). *Member:* Virginia State Bar; Maryland State Bar Association. ***PRACTICE AREAS:*** Energy Law. **Email:** mrick@jhenergy.com

ELIZABETH A. ZEMBRUSKI, born Syosset, New York, March 15, 1975; admitted to bar, 2001, New York (Not admitted in District of Columbia). *Education:* Hofstra University (B.A., 1997); Georgetown University Law Center (J.D., 2000). Phi Beta Kappa. Editor Georgetown International Environmental Law Review, 1999-2000. ***PRACTICE AREAS:*** Energy. **Email:** ezembruski@jhenergy.com

JOHNSON & CLIFTON, LLP

2600 VIRGINIA AVENUE N.W., SUITE 508
WASHINGTON, D.C. 20037-1905
Telephone: 202-337-8400
Telefax: 202-337-3462
Email: rwjohnson@compuserve.com
URL: http://www.lawyers.com/johnson&rogers

Birmingham, Alabama Office: 728 Shades Creek Parkway, Suite 100, 35209. Telephone: 205-870-9588. Fax: 205-870-7288.

International Trade, International Law, Aviation, Customs, Corporate, Legislative and Political Law, Government Relations and Health Law.

ROBERT WINTHROP JOHNSON, born Birmingham, Alabama, September 17, 1946; admitted to bar, 1974, Virginia; 1975, Alabama; 1978, District of Columbia; 1985, U.S. Court of International Trade and U.S. Court of Appeals for the Federal Circuit; 1988, U.S. Tax Court. *Education:* Princeton University (A.B., 1968); Tulane University of Louisiana (J.D., 1974); Georgetown University (LL.M., 1978). Law Clerk, Supreme Court of Alabama, 1975-1976. Attorney, Office of the General Counsel, U.S. Department of Agriculture, 1976-1977. Senior Staff Assistant to Chairman George Mahon, Committee on Appropriations, House of Representatives, 1978-1979. Member, Commodity Policy Advisory Committee, Office of the U.S. Trade Representative, 1984-1986. *Member:* The District of Columbia Bar; Alabama State Bar; Virginia State Bar; Virginia and American (Member, International Law Section) Bar Associations. [Col., USMC, Ret. active duty, 1968-1971]. ***LANGUAGES:*** French, Spanish, Vietnamese. ***PRACTICE AREAS:*** International Trade; International Law; Customs; Corporate; Government Relations Law; Aviation Law. **Email:** rwjohnson@compuserve.com

EDWINA CLIFTON ROGERS, born Montgomery, Alabama, May 27, 1964; admitted to bar, 1991, Pennsylvania; 1992, District of Columbia; 1993, U.S. Court of International Trade and U.S. Court of Appeals for the Federal Circuit; 1995, U.S. Supreme Court. *Education:* University of Alabama (B.S., 1986); Catholic University (J.D., 1991). Special Assistant, International Trade Administration, Department of Commerce, 1989-1991. General Counsel, National Republican Senatorial Committee, 1994. Resident Fellow, John F. Kennedy School of Government, Institute of Politics, Harvard University, 1996. Associate General Counsel, U.S. Senate, 2000. *Member:* The District of Columbia Bar; Pennsylvania and American (Member, Administrative Law and Regulatory Practice Section) Bar Associations. ***PRACTICE AREAS:*** Legislation; Administrative Law; Political Law; International Law. **Email:** edwinarogers@aol.com

JEFFREY JAMES CLIFTON, born Montgomery, Alabama, October 18, 1962; admitted to bar, 1997, Alabama; 1997, U.S. District Court, Middle District of Alabama (Not admitted in District of Columbia). *Education:* Auburn University at Montgomery (B.S., 1988); University of Alabama School of Medicine (M.D., 1992); Marshall Wythe School of Law (J.D., 1997). *Member:* American (Member, Health Law Section) Bar Association; Alabama State Bar; American Medical Association; Medical Association of the State of Alabama;

(This Listing Continued)

American College of Emergency Medicine; Alabama Chapter of American College of Emergency Medicine. Fellow, American College of Legal Medicine. [Capt., USAR]. (Also Of Counsel To Campbell, Waller & Loper in Birmingham, AL). ***PRACTICE AREAS:*** Health Law; Administrative Law; Antitrust; Corporate Law; Business Law. **Email:** jjclifton@msn.com

JOHNSON & ROCHE

WASHINGTON, D.C.

(See McLean, Virginia)

General Litigation in State Federal Courts in Vermont and the District of Columbia. Personal Injury, Medical Malpractice, Products Liability, Corporate Law, Business Law, Family Law, Divorce, Child Custody, Child Support, Estate Planning, Trusts and Estates, Wills and Probate, Criminal Law.

JOHNSON & YANG, P.C.

WASHINGTON, D.C.

(See Wheaton, Maryland)

Immigration and Naturalization Law, Civil Litigation.

JAMES M. JOHNSTONE

Established in 1996
1776 K STREET, THIRD FLOOR
WASHINGTON, D.C. 20006
Telephone: 202-719-7060
Fax: 202-719-7049
Email: jmjatty@dc.infi.net
URL: http://www.lawyers.com/jamesmjohnstone

Federal Practice, Civil Practice, Appellate Practice, Alternative Dispute Resolution, Antitrust and Trade Regulation, Drug and Medical Device Regulation, Advertising Law.

FIRM PROFILE: The firm represents individuals, small to medium-sized corporations, and start-up businesses in varied practice areas throughout Washington D.C. and the East Coast.

JAMES M. JOHNSTONE, born Denver, Colorado, July 24, 1934; admitted to bar, 1960, District of Columbia. *Education:* Yale University (B.A., 1955); Yale Law School (LL.B., 1960). Order of the Coif. Adjunct Professor, Administrative Law, University of Baltimore Law School, 1997—. Attorney: Antitrust Division, Department of Justice, 1960-1962; Kirkland & Ellis, 1962-1983; Wiley, Rein & Fielding, 1983-1996. AAA Commercial Arbitrator, 1983-1999. Arbitrator, NASD Regulation, Inc. Volunteer Mediator, U.S. District Court for the District of Columbia. *Member:* The District of Columbia Bar (Volunteer Arbitrator and Mediator, Attorney Client Arbitration Board); American Bar Association (Chairman, Food, Drug & Cosmetic Law Committee, Section of Corporate, Banking and Business Law, 1981-1983; Vice-Chair, Alternative Dispute Resolution Committee, Senior Lawyers Division, 1996-1999). ***PRACTICE AREAS:*** Administrative Law; Antitrust and Trade Regulation; Advertising and Marketing; Arbitration; Mediation.

AIDAN D. JONES

1818 N STREET, N.W., SUITE 700
WASHINGTON, D.C. 20036
Telephone: 202-293-2386
Facsimile: 202-331-9306
Email: ajones2506@aol.com
URL: http://www.lawyers.com/aidanjones

Business Law, Civil Trials, Appellate Litigation, Estate Planning, Trusts and Estates, Estate and Gift Taxation, Wealth Preservation, Asset Protection, Family Business Succession, Business Formation, Closely Held Business Estate Planning, Probate, E-Commerce Law, Aviation..

AIDAN D. JONES, born Wilmington, Delaware, 1945; admitted to bar, 1975, District of Columbia; 1996, Maryland; U.S. Court of Appeals for the District of Columbia and Ninth Circuits, and U.S. District Court, District of Columbia and District of Maryland; U.S. Supreme Court. *Education:* Wesleyan University (B.A., 1967); Georgetown University (J.D., 1974). Law Clerk to Judge John H. Pratt, U.S. District Court for the District of Columbia, 1974-1975. *Member:* District of Columbia Bar; Maryland State and American (Member, Sections on: Real Property, Probate and Trust Law; Litigation; Tort and Insurance Practice; Vice Chairman, Aviation and Space Law Committee, 1985-1993) Bar Associations. [Lt., USNR (active duty, 1967-1971)]

JONES & BLOUCH L.L.P.

SUITE 410 EAST
1025 THOMAS JEFFERSON STREET, N.W.
WASHINGTON, D.C. 20007-0805
Telephone: 202-223-3500
Telecopier: 202-223-4593
Email: jb@jonesblouch.com
URL: http://www.lawyers.com/jones&blouch

Affiliated Offices: Jorden Burt LLP, Suite 400 East, 1025 Thomas Jefferson Street, Washington, D.C., 20007-0805; Suite 500, 777 Brickell Avenue, Miami, Florida, 33131-2803.

Business Law Practice, Financial Services, Securities Law, Corporate Finance, Corporate Law, Banking Law.

FIRM PROFILE: We represent financial institutions, such as insurance companies, banks, mutual funds and other investment companies, broker-dealers and investment advisers. We have particular expertise with the regulation of variable annuities and variable life insurance contracts and other insurance products under federal securities laws. We also represent public companies and established and start-up closely held corporations, limited liability companies and limited partnerships in connection with general corporate matters, commercial transactions, software licensing and domestic and foreign transactions, including public offerings and private placements of securities, tender offers, mergers, acquisitions and reorganizations.

MEMBERS OF FIRM

J. SUMNER JONES, born Wheeling, West Virginia, February 1, 1940; admitted to bar, 1964, West Virginia; 1965, District of Columbia. *Education:* Yale University (A.B., magna cum laude, 1961); Harvard University (LL.B., 1964). *Member:* District of Columbia Bar; American Bar Association. ***PRACTICE AREAS:*** Securities Law; Corporate Law. ***Email:*** jsjones@jonesblouch.com

JOHN W. BLOUCH, born Terre Haute, Indiana, December 26, 1940; admitted to bar, 1969, District of Columbia. *Education:* Yale University (B.A., 1962); George Washington University (J.D., 1969). *Member:* District of Columbia Bar; American Bar Association. ***PRACTICE AREAS:*** Securities Law; Corporate Law; Banking Law. ***Email:*** jwblouch@jonesblouch.com

ASSOCIATE

ANEAL KRISHNAMURTHY, born Moultrie, Georgia, November 1, 1974; admitted to bar, 1999, New York and District of Columbia. *Education:* Indiana University (B.A., with distinction, 1995); George Washington University (J.D., with honors, 1998); George Washington University-Elliott School (M.A., 1998). Phi Beta Kappa. *Member:* District of Columbia Bar. ***LANGUAGES:*** French and Telugu. ***PRACTICE AREAS:*** Securities Law; Corporate Law.

OF COUNSEL

WILLIAM RANDOLPH THOMPSON, born Oak Hill, West Virginia, September 24, 1946; admitted to bar, 1974, Virginia; 1975, District of Columbia. *Education:* Harvard University (A.B., magna cum laude, 1968); Georgetown University (J.D., 1974). Chief, Office of Insurance Products, 1984-1988, Special Counsel, Office of Investment Company Regulation, 1980-1984, and Attorney, Division of Investment Management, U.S. Securities and Exchange Commission. (Also Member of Jorden Burt Boros Cicchetti Berenson & Johnson LLP). ***PRACTICE AREAS:*** Securities Law. ***Email:*** wrt@wdc.jordenusa.com

BRUCE W. DUNNE, born Orange, New Jersey, March 24, 1949; admitted to bar, 1975, District of Columbia. *Education:* Williams College (B.A., 1971); George Washington University (J.D., 1975). *Member:* District of Columbia Bar. ***PRACTICE AREAS:*** Securities Law; Corporate Law. ***Email:*** bwdunne@jonesblouch.com

JONES, DAY, REAVIS & POGUE

51 LOUISIANA AVENUE, N.W.
WASHINGTON, D.C. 20001-2113
Telephone: 202-879-3939
Telecopier: 202-626-1700
Email: counsel@jonesday.com
URL: http://www.jonesday.com

In Atlanta, Georgia: 3500 SunTrust Plaza, 303 Peachtree Street, N.E. Telephone: 404-521-3939. Telecopier: 404-581-8330.

In Brussels, Belgium: Avenue Louise 480, Louizalaan 480, 1050 Brussels. Telephone: 32-2-645-14-11. Telecopier: 32-2-645-14-45.

(This Listing Continued)

In Chicago, Illinois: 77 West Wacker. Telephone: 312-782-3939. Telecopier: 312-782-8585.

In Cleveland, Ohio: North Point, 901 Lakeside Avenue. Telephone: 216-586-3939. Telecopier: 216-579-0212.

In Columbus, Ohio: 1900 Huntington Center, 41 South High Street. Telephone: 614-469-3939. Telecopier: 614-461-4198.

In Dallas, Texas: 2727 North Harwood Street. Telephone: 214-220-3939. Telecopier: 214-969-5100.

In Frankfurt, Germany: Hochhaus am Park, Grüneburgweg 102, 60323 Frankfurt am Main. Telephone: 49-69-9726-3939. Telecopier: 49-69-9726-3993.

In Hong Kong, China: 31st Floor, Edinburgh Tower, The Landmark, 15 Queen's Road Central. Telephone: 852-2526-6895. Telecopier: 852-2868-5871 or 852-2868-5699.

In Houston, Texas: Chase Tower, 600 Travis Street, Suite 6500. Telephone: 832-239-3939. Telecopier: 832-239-3600.

In Irvine, California: 5 Park Plaza, Suite 1100. Telephone: 949-851-3939. Telecopier: 949-553-7539.

In London, England: Bucklersbury House, 3 Queen Victoria Street. Telephone: 44-20-7236-3939. Telecopier: 44-20-7236-1113.

In Los Angeles, California: 555 West Fifth Street, Suite 4600. Telephone: 213-489-3939. Telecopier: 213-243-2539.

In Madrid, Spain: Velázquez 51. Telephone: 34-91-520-39-39. Telecopier: 34-91-520-39-38.

In New York, New York: 599 Lexington Avenue. Telephone: 212-326-3939. Telecopier: 212-755-7306.

In Palo Alto, California: 1804 Embarcadero Road, Suite 201. Telephone: 650-739-3939. Telecopier: 650-739-3900.

In Paris, France: 120, rue du Faubourg Saint-Honoré. Telephone: 33-1-56-59-39-39. Telecopier: 33-1-56-59-39-38

In Pittsburgh, Pennsylvania: 500 Grant Street, 31st Floor. Telephone: 412-391-3939. Telecopier: 412-394-7959.

In Shanghai, China: 2805 Kerry Centre, 1515 Nanjing Road West. Telephone: 86-21-5298-6568. Telecopier: 86-21-5298-6569.

In Singapore, Singapore: 30 Cecil Street, #29-01 Prudential Tower. Telephone: 65 538 3939. Telecopier: 65 536 3939.

In Sydney, Australia: Governor Phillip Tower, Level 38, 1 Farrer Place. Telephone: 61-2-9210-6921. Telecopier: 61-2-9210-6926.

In Taipei, Taiwan: 8th Floor, 2 Tun Hwa South Road, Section 2. Telephone: (886-2) 2704-6808. Telecopier: (886-2) 2704-6791.

In Tokyo, Japan: Toranomon 45 Mori Building, 3rd Floor, 1-5, Toranomon 5-chome, Minato-ku, Tokyo 105-0001. Telephone: 81-3-3433-3939. Telecopier: 81-3-5401-2725.

Full-Service Civil Practice, Antitrust and Trade Regulation, Business Restructuring and Reorganization, Capital Markets, Corporate Criminal Investigations, Cross-Border Transactions, Employee Benefits, Energy, Environmental, Health and Safety, Finance, General Litigation, General Tax, Government Regulation, Health Care, Issues and Appeals, Intellectual Property, International Securities, Labor and Employment, Lending/Structured Finance, Mergers and Acquisitions, Private Capital, Product Liability and Regulation, Real Estate, Technology Transactions, Trade and Regulatory Law.

MEMBERS OF FIRM IN WASHINGTON, D.C.

JOSEPH S. IANNUCCI, born Brooklyn, New York, December 23, 1931; admitted to bar, 1956, New York; 1964, District of Columbia. *Education:* New York University (B.A., 1953); Harvard University (J.D., 1956); Georgetown University (LL.M., 1962). Tax Specialist, Reorganization Branch, U.S. Internal Revenue Service, 1958-1962. Adjunct Professor of Law, Georgetown University, 1963-1964. ***PRACTICE AREAS:*** Taxation; Corporate Tax Planning; International Taxation; Transfer Pricing. ***Email:*** jsiannucci@jonesday.com

MICHAEL BRADFIELD, born New York, New York, July 24, 1934; admitted to bar, 1961, District of Columbia. *Education:* Union College (B.A., 1956); Columbia University (M. International Affairs, 1960; J.D., 1960). Attorney, 1962-1967, Assistant General Counsel for International Affairs, 1962-1975. U.S. Department of the Treasury. General Counsel, 1981-1989, Federal Reserve System. ***PRACTICE AREAS:*** Banks and Banking; International Banking Law. ***Email:*** mbradfield@jonesday.com

JAMES T. O'HARA, born Hazleton, Pennsylvania, October 11, 1936; admitted to bar, 1962, District of Columbia. *Education:* King's College (B.S., 1958); Catholic University of America (LL.B., 1962); Georgetown University (LL.M., 1967). Fellow, American College of Tax Counsel. Section Chief, Reorganization Branch, U.S. Internal Revenue Service, 1967-1969. Adjunct Professor of Law, Georgetown University, 1976-1996. ***PRACTICE AREAS:*** Taxation; Corporate Tax Planning. ***Email:*** jtohara@jonesday.com

J. LAWRENCE MANNING, JR., born Washington, D.C., April 27, 1943; admitted to bar, 1968, Virginia; 1969, District of Columbia. *Education:* Washington & Lee University (B.S., 1965); University of Virginia (J.D., 1968). Law Clerk to Judge Bryan, U.S. Court of Appeals, Fourth Circuit, 1968-1969. ***PRACTICE AREAS:*** Mergers and Acquisitions; International Securities; Project Finance. ***Email:*** jmanning@jonesday.com

(This Listing Continued)

JONES, DAY, REAVIS & POGUE, Washington—Continued

JONATHAN C. ROSE, born Cleveland, Ohio, June 8, 1941; admitted to bar, 1968, Massachusetts; 1972, District of Columbia; 1978, Ohio. *Education:* Yale University (A.B., 1963); Harvard University (LL.B., 1967). Law Clerk to Justice Cutter, Supreme Judicial Court of Massachusetts, 1967-1968. White House Staff Assistant, 1969-1971. Special Assistant to the President, 1971-1972. General Counsel, Council on International Economic Policy, 1972-1974. Associate Deputy Attorney General and Director, Office of Justice Policy and Planning, 1974-1975. Deputy Assistant Attorney General, Antitrust Division, 1975-1977 and Assistant Attorney General, Office of Legal Policy, 1981-1984, U.S. Department of Justice. ***PRACTICE AREAS:*** International Trade; Federal Legislative Practice. ***Email:*** jcrose@jonesday.com

SIGMUND T. WEINER, born San Antonio, Texas, March 13, 1942; admitted to bar, 1968, Texas; 1988, District of Columbia. *Education:* United States Military Academy (B.S., 1964); University of Texas (LL.B., 1968). Order of the Coif. ***PRACTICE AREAS:*** Real Estate Development; Real Estate Leasing; Real Estate Finance; Real Estate Workouts. ***Email:*** stweiner@jonesday.com

ANDREW M. KRAMER, born New York, New York, November 2, 1944; admitted to bar, 1969, Illinois; 1977, District of Columbia; 1990, Ohio. *Education:* Michigan State University (B.A., 1966); Northwestern University (J.D., 1969). Executive Director, State of Illinois Office of Collective Bargaining, 1973-1974. ***PRACTICE AREAS:*** Labor and Employment; Employment Litigation; Management Labor Law; Collective Bargaining. ***Email:*** akramer@jonesday.com

JAMES A. WILDEROTTER, born Newark, New Jersey, July 25, 1944; admitted to bar, 1969, District of Columbia. *Education:* Georgetown University (A.B., 1966); University of Illinois (J.D., 1969). Order of the Coif. Special Assistant to the Under Secretary, U.S. Department of Commerce, 1971-1973. Executive Assistant to the Secretary, U.S. Department of Housing and Urban Development, 1973-1974. Associate Deputy Attorney General, U.S. Department of Justice, 1974-1975. Associate Counsel to the President, The White House, 1975-1976. General Counsel, U.S. Energy Research and Development Administration, 1976-1977. ***PRACTICE AREAS:*** International Trade; Administrative Law. ***Email:*** jwilderotter@jonesday.com

ROBERT F. McDERMOTT, JR., born Cambridge, Massachusetts, November 3, 1945; admitted to bar, 1970, Connecticut; 1973, Georgia; 1976, Virginia; 1979, District of Columbia. *Education:* Harvard University (A.B., 1967); Yale University (LL.B., 1970). Staff Assistant to the President, 1971-1972. Staff Assistant to Deputy Attorney General, 1974-1975. Associate Deputy Attorney General, 1975, U.S. Department of Justice. Assistant U.S. Attorney for the Eastern District of Virginia, U.S. Attorney's Office, 1976-1979. ***PRACTICE AREAS:*** Litigation; Products Liability; Corporate Criminal Law. ***Email:*** rfmcdermott@jonesday.com

JOE SIMS, born Phoenix, Arizona, September 29, 1944; admitted to bar, 1970, Arizona; 1978, District of Columbia. *Education:* Arizona State University (B.S., 1967; J.D., 1970). Trial Attorney, 1970-1973; Special Assistant to the Assistant Attorney General, 1973-1975; Deputy Assistant Attorney General for Policy Planning and Legislation, 1975-1977; Deputy Assistant Attorney General for Regulated Industries and Foreign Commerce, 1977-1978, Antitrust Division, U.S. Department of Justice. Chairman, Antitrust Committee, Business Law Section, 1988-1990; Chairman, Sherman Act Section 1 Committee, Antitrust Section, 1988-1990; Chairman, Civil Practice and Procedure Committee, Antitrust Section, 1990-1991, American Bar Association. ***PRACTICE AREAS:*** Antitrust and Trade Regulation; Business Combinations; Telecommunications Competition; Internet Law. ***Email:*** jsims@jonesday.com

JAMES J. GRAHAM, born New Brunswick, New Jersey, September 24, 1946; admitted to bar, 1971, Texas; 1988, District of Columbia. *Education:* Boston College (B.A., 1968); University of Texas (J.D., 1971). Trial Attorney, 1971-1976, Chief, Program, Fraud Branch, 1976-1979; Principal Staff Person, Executive Group to Combat Fraud and Waste in Government, 1979-1980, Fraud Section, U.S. Department of Justice. Senior Litigation Counsel, U.S. Attorney's Office, Eastern District of Virginia, 1987. ***PRACTICE AREAS:*** Litigation; White Collar Crime; Corporate Investigations. ***Email:*** jjgraham@jonesday.com

MARK K. SISITSKY, born Springfield, Massachusetts, October 7, 1945; admitted to bar, 1971, New York; 1981, District of Columbia. *Education:* Dartmouth College (B.A., 1967); University of Michigan (J.D., 1970). General Counsel, Municipal Securities Rulemaking Board, 1975-1980. ***PRACTICE AREAS:*** Structured Finance; Derivative Products. ***Email:*** marksisitsky@jonesday.com

JUNIUS C. McELVEEN, JR., born Rogersville, Tennessee, February 17, 1947; admitted to bar, 1972, Virginia; 1975, California; 1978, District of Columbia. *Education:* University of Virginia (B.A., 1969; J.D., 1972). Phi Beta Kappa. ***PRACTICE AREAS:*** Environmental Litigation; OSHA; Toxic Substance Liability. ***Email:*** jcmcelveen@jonesday.com

(This Listing Continued)

PAUL S. RYERSON, born Newark, New Jersey, October 2, 1946; admitted to bar, 1972, New York and District of Columbia. *Education:* Wesleyan University (B.A., 1968); Columbia University (J.D., 1971). Law Clerk to Judge Weinstein, U.S. District Court, Eastern District of New York, 1971-1972. ***PRACTICE AREAS:*** Environmental Law; Environmental Insurance Coverage; Products Liability; Toxic Torts. ***Email:*** psryerson@jonesday.com

TOM D. SMITH, born Denton, Texas, May 24, 1947; admitted to bar, 1972, Virginia; 1975, District of Columbia. *Education:* North Texas State University (B.A., 1969); Georgetown University (J.D., 1972). Law Clerk to Judge Fickling, District of Columbia Court of Appeals, 1972-1973. Trial Attorney, Bureau of Competition, Federal Trade Commission, 1973-1979. ***PRACTICE AREAS:*** Antitrust and Trade Regulation; Premerger Notification; Business Combinations. ***Email:*** tdsmith@jonesday.com

JOSEPH M. DAVID, JR., born Tarrytown, New York, December 8, 1943; admitted to bar, 1973, Missouri; 1982, Pennsylvania; 1998, District of Columbia. *Education:* Susquehanna University (B.S., 1965); Springfield College (M.Ed., 1966); University of Notre Dame (J.D., 1973). ***PRACTICE AREAS:*** Litigation; Products Liability. ***Email:*** jmdavid@jonesday.com

CLARK EVANS DOWNS, born Boston, Massachusetts, July 30, 1946; admitted to bar, 1973, Illinois; 1981, District of Columbia. *Education:* Boston University (A.B., 1968; J.D., 1973). ***PRACTICE AREAS:*** Energy; Energy Regulation; Utility Law. ***Email:*** cedowns@jonesday.com

WILLIS J. GOLDSMITH, born Paris, France, February 21, 1947; admitted to bar, 1973, New York; 1978, District of Columbia. *Education:* Brown University (B.A., 1969); New York University (J.D., 1972). Attorney, Office of the Solicitor, U. S. Department of Labor, 1972-1974. ***PRACTICE AREAS:*** Labor and Employment; Employment Litigation; Management Labor Law; Employee Benefits Litigation. ***Email:*** wgoldsmith@jonesday.com

KENNETH J. KRUPSKY, born Chicago, Illinois, June 30, 1947; admitted to bar, 1973, New York; 1977, Pennsylvania; 1982, District of Columbia. *Education:* Columbia University (B.A., 1969; J.D., 1972). Attorney Adviser, 1979-1981 and Deputy Assistant Secretary, 1997, U.S. Treasury Department. Chair, International Tax Committee, District of Columbia Bar Association, 1993-1996. ***PRACTICE AREAS:*** Taxation; International Taxation; Tax Controversies; Federal Legislative Practice. ***Email:*** kjkrupsky@jonesday.com

PHILLIP A. PROGER, born New York, New York, April 8, 1948; admitted to bar, 1973, Ohio; 1977, District of Columbia. *Education:* University of Maryland (B.A., 1969; J.D., 1973). Chairman, Section 7 Committee, Antitrust Section, 1983-1985. Chairman, Health Care Committee, 1986-1989 and Chair, Antitrust Law Section, 1998-1999, American Bar Association. ***PRACTICE AREAS:*** Antitrust; Antitrust Class Actions; Business Combinations; International Antitrust. ***Email:*** paproger@jonesday.com

THOMAS F. CULLEN, JR., born Scranton, Pennsylvania, March 23, 1949; admitted to bar, 1974, Massachusetts; 1976, District of Columbia. *Education:* Harvard University (A.B., 1971; J.D., 1974). Law Clerk to Judge Winter, U.S. Court of Appeals, Fourth Circuit, 1974-1975. ***PRACTICE AREAS:*** Litigation; Complex Business Litigation; Antitrust. ***Email:*** tfcullen@jonesday.com

ROBERT S. WATERS, born Sikeston, Missouri, March 25, 1945; admitted to bar, 1974, Virginia; 1975, District of Columbia. *Education:* United States Naval Academy (B.S., 1967); University of Virginia (J.D., 1974). ***PRACTICE AREAS:*** Energy; Federal Energy Regulation; Utility Law. ***Email:*** rwaters@jonesday.com

RICHARD D. AVIL, JR., born Philadelphia, Pennsylvania, November 28, 1948; admitted to bar, 1975, New York; 1978, Ohio; 1992, District of Columbia. *Education:* Villanova University (B.E.E., 1970); Cornell University (J.D., 1974). Law Clerk: to Judge Port, U.S. District Court, Northern District of New York, 1974-1976; to Judge Van Graafeiland, U.S. Court of Appeals, Second Circuit, 1976-1977. ***PRACTICE AREAS:*** Energy; Energy Regulation; Energy Contracts; Utility Rates. ***Email:*** rdavil@jonesday.com

DONALD B. AYER, born San Mateo, California, April 30, 1949; admitted to bar, 1975, California; 1978, District of Columbia. *Education:* Stanford University (B.A., 1971); Harvard University (M.A., 1973; J.D., 1975). Phi Beta Kappa. Law Clerk: to Judge Wilkey, U.S. Court of Appeals for the District of Columbia Circuit, 1975-1976; to Justice Rehnquist, U.S. Supreme Court, 1976-1977. Assistant U.S. Attorney, Northern District of California, 1977-1979. U.S. Attorney, Eastern District of California, 1981-1986. Principal Deputy Solicitor General, 1986-1988, Deputy Attorney General, 1989-1990, U.S. Department of Justice. ***PRACTICE AREAS:*** Litigation; Appellate Practice; U.S. Supreme Court Litigation. ***Email:*** dbayer@jonesday.com

MARSHALL B. BABSON, born Boston, Massachusetts, November 27, 1945; admitted to bar, 1975, California; 1978, Connecticut; 1988, District of Columbia; 1989, Maryland and New York. *Education:* University of Pennsylvania (A.B., 1968); Columbia University (J.D., 1975). Order of the Coif. Member, National Labor Relations Board, 1985-1988. Member, Board of Directors, National Chamber Litigation Center, Labor Law Advisory Committee, U.S.

(This Listing Continued)

Chamber of Commerce, 1993—. Fellow, College of Labor and Employment Lawyers. ***PRACTICE AREAS:*** Labor and Employment; Labor Relations; Labor Arbitration; Collective Bargaining. ***Email:*** mbabson@jonesday.com

DAVID C. ROSEMAN, born Winston-Salem, North Carolina, September 29, 1948; admitted to bar, 1975, Virginia; 1976, District of Columbia; 1982, New York. *Education:* Cornell University (B.A., 1970); American University, Washington College of Law (J.D., 1975). ***PRACTICE AREAS:*** Bankruptcy; Creditors Rights; Corporate Trusts; Commercial Transactions; Real Estate Workouts. ***Email:*** dcroseman@jonesday.com

LESTER W. DROLLER, born Washington, D.C., November 8, 1951; admitted to bar, 1976, Virginia; 1977, District of Columbia. *Education:* Northwestern University (B.A., 1973); George Washington University (J.D., 1976); New York University (LL.M., 1978). Phi Beta Kappa. ***PRACTICE AREAS:*** Taxation; Corporate Tax Planning; Mergers and Acquisitions. ***Email:*** lwdroller@jonesday.com

PETER J. ROMATOWSKI, born Quonsett Point, Rhode Island, August 26, 1950; admitted to bar, 1976, New York; 1986, District of Columbia. *Education:* Harvard University (A.B., 1972); Georgetown University (J.D., 1975). Assistant U.S. Attorney, 1979-1986, Chief, Securities and Commodity Frauds Unit, 1984-1986, U.S. Attorney's Office, Southern District of New York. ***PRACTICE AREAS:*** Litigation; White Collar Crime; Government Procurement; SEC Enforcement. ***Email:*** pjromatowski@jonesday.com

RAYMOND J. WIACEK, born Detroit, Michigan, December 5, 1950; admitted to bar, 1976, Michigan; 1977, District of Columbia. *Education:* Yale University (B.A., 1973); Harvard University (J.D., 1976). Phi Beta Kappa. ***PRACTICE AREAS:*** Taxation; International Taxation; International Finance; Transfer Pricing. ***Email:*** rjwiacek@jonesday.com

STEPHEN J. BROGAN, born Manhattan, New York, June 15, 1952; admitted to bar, 1977, District of Columbia. *Education:* Boston College (A.B., 1974); University of Notre Dame (J.D., 1977). Deputy Assistant Attorney General, Office of Legal Policy, U.S. Department of Justice, 1981-1983. ***PRACTICE AREAS:*** Litigation; Complex Business Litigation; Corporate Investigations; Qui Tam Litigation. ***Email:*** sjbrogan@jonesday.com

TIMOTHY J. FINN, born Minneapolis, Minnesota, November 23, 1950; admitted to bar, 1977, Ohio; 1978, District of Columbia. *Education:* Harvard University (A.B., 1973; J.D., 1976). Law Clerk to Chief Judge Battisti, U.S. District Court for the Northern District of Ohio, 1976-1977. Deputy Assistant Attorney General, 1981-1983, Associate Deputy Attorney General, 1983-1984, Office of Legal Policy, U.S. Department of Justice. ***PRACTICE AREAS:*** Litigation; Administrative Litigation. ***Email:*** tjfinn@jonesday.com

ROBERT C. JONES, born Pittsburgh, Pennsylvania, December 28, 1951; admitted to bar, 1977, Virginia; 1980, District of Columbia. *Education:* College of William & Mary (B.A., 1974); University of Richmond (J.D., 1977). Staff Attorney, Bureau of Competition, Federal Trade Commission, 1978-1986. ***PRACTICE AREAS:*** Antitrust and Trade Regulation; Business Combinations. ***Email:*** rcjones@jonesday.com

GREGORY M. LUCE, born Kalamazoo, Michigan, December 19, 1951; admitted to bar, 1977, Virginia; 1981, Maryland; 1986, District of Columbia. *Education:* University of Virginia (B.A., 1974); University of Richmond (J.D., 1977). Assistant Attorney General, Commonwealth of Virginia, 1978-1981. Chairman, Health Law Section, Virginia State Bar Association, 1990-1991. ***PRACTICE AREAS:*** Litigation; Health Care Litigation; Health Care Fraud; False Claims Act. ***Email:*** gmluce@jonesday.com

TOBY G. SINGER, born New York, New York, August 13, 1952; admitted to bar, 1977, District of Columbia. *Education:* Wesleyan University (B.A., 1974); Georgetown University (J.D., 1977). Phi Beta Kappa. Staff Attorney, Office of General Counsel, 1977-1979; Attorney Advisor to Commissioner Robert Pitofsky, 1979-1981. Assistant to the Director, 1981-1982. Senior Staff Attorney, Bureau of Competition (Health Care Division), 1982-1986. Deputy Assistant Director, Bureau of Competition (Health Care Division), 1986-1988, Federal Trade Commission. ***PRACTICE AREAS:*** Antitrust and Trade Regulation; Business Combinations. ***Email:*** tgsinger@jonesday.com

GEOFFREY S. STEWART, born Kansas City, Missouri, October 21, 1951; admitted to bar, 1977, New York; 1980, District of Columbia. *Education:* Brown University (A.B., A.M., 1973); Harvard University (J.D., 1976). Phi Beta Kappa. Deputy Assistant Attorney General, U.S. Office of Legal Policy, 1983. Associate Counsel, Office of Independent Counsel, Iran Arms Sales/Contra Division, 1987-1990. ***PRACTICE AREAS:*** Litigation; Complex Commercial Litigation; White Collar Crime; Internet Law. ***Email:*** gstewart@jonesday.com

TERESA A. BROOKS, born Washington, D.C., October 30, 1946; admitted to bar, 1978, District of Columbia and Michigan. *Education:* Trinity College (A.B., 1968); American University, Washington College of Law (J.D., 1977). ***PRACTICE AREAS:*** Health Care; Health Care Regulation; Health Care Legislation. ***Email:*** tabrooks@jonesday.com

KATHRYN M. FENTON, born Bridgeport, Connecticut, July 24, 1953; admitted to bar, 1978, District of Columbia. *Education:* Fairfield University (B.A., 1975); Georgetown University (J.D., 1978). Law Clerk to Judge Gasch,

(This Listing Continued)

U.S. District Court for the District of Columbia, 1978-1979. Attorney, General Litigation and Planning Office, Bureau of Competition, 1979-1984 and Attorney Adviser to James C. Miller, III, Chairman, Federal Trade Commission, 1983-1984. ***PRACTICE AREAS:*** Antitrust and Trade Regulation; Competition. ***Email:*** kmfenton@jonesday.com

PETER F. GARVIN, III, born Boston, Massachusetts, September 20, 1951; admitted to bar, 1978, District of Columbia. *Education:* Boston College (B.S., 1973); Catholic University of America (J.D., 1978). Chair, Public Contracts and Procurement Committee, Section of Administrative Law and Regulatory Practice, American Bar Association, 1990-1991. ***PRACTICE AREAS:*** Litigation; Contracts; Government Contracts; Construction Contracts. ***Email:*** pgarvin@jonesday.com

KEVIN D. McDONALD, born Cincinnati, Ohio, December 4, 1952; admitted to bar, 1978, Ohio; 1980, District of Columbia. *Education:* Kenyon College (A.B., 1975); Case Western Reserve University (J.D., 1978). Phi Beta Kappa; Order of the Coif. Law Clerk to Judge Kinneary, U.S. District Court for the Southern District of Ohio, 1978-1980. ***PRACTICE AREAS:*** Litigation; Antitrust and Trade Regulation; Medical Antitrust. ***Email:*** kdmcdonald@jonesday.com

JOSEPH F. WINTERSCHEID, born Rock Island, Illinois, February 17, 1953; admitted to bar, 1978, Ohio; 1998, District of Columbia. *Education:* University of Notre Dame (B.A., 1975; J.D., 1978). Phi Beta Kappa. Chairman, Monopolization Subcommittee, 1984-1985; Vice-Chairman, Corporate Counseling Committee, 1985-1989; Chairman, Competition Subcommittee of Federal Trade Commission Committee, 1989-1990; Chairman, Antitrust and Multinational Enterprises Subcommittee of International Antitrust Committee, 1990-1991; Vice-Chairman, 1991-1994 and Chairman, 1994-1996, International Antitrust Committee; Antitrust Section, American Bar Association. Member, Board of Governors, Antitrust Section, Ohio State Bar Association, 1996-2000. ***PRACTICE AREAS:*** Antitrust and Trade Regulation; EU Competition; International Antitrust. ***Email:*** jwinters@jonesday.com

KENNETH J. AYRES, born Plainfield, New Jersey, October 3, 1953; admitted to bar, 1979, District of Columbia. *Education:* Cornell University (B.S., 1975); University of Virginia (J.D., 1978). Order of the Coif. Law Clerk to Judge Campbell, U.S. Court of Appeals, First Circuit, 1978-1979. ***PRACTICE AREAS:*** Mergers and Acquisitions; Securities; Corporate Finance. ***Email:*** kjayres@jonesday.com

ROBERT H. KLONOFF, born Portland, Oregon, March 15, 1955; admitted to bar, 1980, District of Columbia. *Education:* University of California, Berkeley (A.B., 1976); Yale University (J.D., 1979). Phi Beta Kappa. Law Clerk to Judge John Brown, U.S. Court of Appeals, Fifth Circuit, 1979-1980. Assistant U.S. Attorney, U.S. Attorney's Office, District of Columbia, 1983-1986; Assistant to the Solicitor General, U.S. Department of Justice, 1986-1988. Visiting Professor of Law, University of San Diego, 1988-1989. ***PRACTICE AREAS:*** Litigation; Appellate Practice; U.S. Supreme Court Litigation; Class Actions. ***Email:*** rhklonoff@jonesday.com

MARY ELLEN POWERS, born Cleveland, Ohio, February 15, 1955; admitted to bar, 1980, District of Columbia. *Education:* Oberlin College (A.B., 1977); University of Virginia (J.D., 1980). ***PRACTICE AREAS:*** Litigation; Complex Business Litigation; Corporate Investigations; RICO. ***Email:*** mepowers@jonesday.com

STEVEN A. TEITELBAUM, born New York, New York, July 30, 1956; admitted to bar, 1980, District of Columbia; 1983, New York. *Education:* Columbia University (A.B., 1977; J.D., 1980). ***PRACTICE AREAS:*** Commercial Real Estate; Real Estate Finance; Hotel and Resort Development; Leasing. ***Email:*** steitelbaum@jonesday.com

PETER J. BIERSTEKER, born Kaukauna, Wisconsin, July 7, 1955; admitted to bar, 1981, District of Columbia. *Education:* Harvard University (A.B., 1977; J.D., 1981); London School of Economics (M.Sc., 1978). ***PRACTICE AREAS:*** Litigation; Products Liability; Complex Commercial Litigation. ***Email:*** pbiersteker@jonesday.com

CAROLYN Y. THOMPSON, born Montgomery, Alabama, October 3, 1943; admitted to bar, 1981, District of Columbia. *Education:* Vanderbilt University (B.A., 1965); University of Virginia (M.A., 1969; J.D., 1981). Phi Beta Kappa. ***PRACTICE AREAS:*** Energy; Federal Energy Regulation; Utility Rates. ***Email:*** carolynthompson@jonesday.com

MICHAEL A. CARVIN, born Bronxville, New York, September 29, 1956; admitted to bar, 1982, District of Columbia. *Education:* Tulane University of Louisiana (B.A., 1978); George Washington University (J.D., 1982). Special Assistant to the Deputy Assistant Attorney General, 1983-1985; Deputy Assistant Attorney General, 1985-1987, Civil Rights Division; Deputy Assistant Attorney General, Office of Legal Counsel, 1987-1988, U.S. Department of Justice. ***PRACTICE AREAS:*** Litigation; Appellate Practice; U.S. Supreme Court Litigation. ***Email:*** macarvin@jonesday.com

CHRISTOPHER F. DUGAN, born Washington, D.C. November 12, 1948; admitted to bar, 1982, District of Columbia. *Education:* Johns Hopkins University (B.A., 1970); Georgetown University (J.D., 1980). Law Clerk to Judge

(This Listing Continued)

JONES, DAY, REAVIS & POGUE, Washington—Continued

Smith, U.S. District Court for the District of Columbia, 1980-1981. Adjunct Professor of Law, Georgetown University, 1995—. ***PRACTICE AREAS:*** International Trade; International Arbitration; International Litigation. ***Email:*** chrisdugan@jonesday.com

ALISON B. MARSHALL, born Poughkeepsie, New York, August 6, 1959; admitted to bar, 1984, Pennsylvania; 1986, Michigan; 1990, District of Columbia. *Education:* Princeton University (A.B., 1981); University of Pennsylvania (J.D., 1984). Law Clerk to Judge Huyett, U.S. District Court, Eastern District of Pennsylvania, 1984-1986. ***PRACTICE AREAS:*** Labor and Employment; Employment Litigation; Employment Class Actions; Title IX Discrimination. ***Email:*** abmarshall@jonesday.com

GLEN D. NAGER, born Pasadena, Texas, February 20, 1958; admitted to bar, 1985, District of Columbia. *Education:* University of Texas (B.B.A., 1979); Stanford University (J.D., 1982). Order of the Coif. Law Clerk: to Judge Wright, U.S. Court of Appeals for the District of Columbia Circuit, 1982-1983; to Justice O'Connor, U.S. Supreme Court, 1983-1984. Assistant to the Solicitor General, U.S. Department of Justice, 1986-1988. ***PRACTICE AREAS:*** Litigation; Appellate Practice; U.S. Supreme Court Litigation; Employment Litigation. ***Email:*** gdnager@jonesday.com

ADRIAN WAGER-ZITO, born New York, New York, June 8, 1960; admitted to bar, 1985, Maryland; 1988, District of Columbia. *Education:* State University of New York, Albany (B.A., 1981); George Washington University (J.D., 1984). ***PRACTICE AREAS:*** Litigation; Complex Business Litigation; Securities Class Actions. ***Email:*** adrianwagerzito@jonesday.com

JOHN M. MAJORAS, born Lorain, Ohio, May 3, 1961; admitted to bar, 1986, Ohio; 2001, District of Columbia. *Education:* Case Western Reserve University (B.A., 1983; J.D., 1986). Order of the Coif. ***PRACTICE AREAS:*** Litigation; Antitrust; Complex Business Litigation. ***Email:*** jmmajoras@jonesday.com

WILLIAM V. O'REILLY, born Washington, D.C., May 27, 1958; admitted to bar, 1986, Virginia; 1989, District of Columbia. *Education:* University of Virginia (B.A., 1980; J.D., 1986). ***PRACTICE AREAS:*** Litigation; Complex Commercial Litigation; Corporate Investigations; Antitrust. ***Email:*** woreilly@jonesday.com

JAMES D. WAREHAM, born Salt Lake City, Utah, June 5, 1960; admitted to bar, 1986, Illinois; 1987, District of Columbia. *Education:* University of Illinois (B.S., 1981); Northwestern University (J.D., 1986). ***PRACTICE AREAS:*** Litigation; Complex Business Litigation; Corporate Investigations. ***Email:*** jamesdwareham@jonesday.com

MICHAEL P. GURDAK, born Springfield, Vermont, September 29, 1962; admitted to bar, 1987, Maryland; 1990, Pennsylvania; 1991, District of Columbia. *Education:* University of Notre Dame (B.A., 1984; J.D., 1987). ***PRACTICE AREAS:*** Litigation. ***Email:*** mpgurdak@jonesday.com

GREGORY M. SHUMAKER, born Reading, Pennsylvania, July 22, 1962; admitted to bar, 1987, Pennsylvania; 1988, District of Columbia. *Education:* Brown University (Sc.B., 1984); University of Notre Dame (J.D., 1987). ***PRACTICE AREAS:*** Litigation; Complex Business Litigation. ***Email:*** gshumaker@jonesday.com

KEVIN J. McINTYRE, born Dover, Delaware, December 27, 1960; admitted to bar, 1988, Virginia; 1990, District of Columbia. *Education:* San Diego State University (A.B., 1983); Georgetown University (J.D., 1988). ***LANGUAGES:*** French. ***PRACTICE AREAS:*** Energy; Energy Regulation; Utility Mergers. ***Email:*** kjmcintyre@jonesday.com

CANDACE A. RIDGWAY, born Juneau, Alaska, March 24, 1953; admitted to bar, 1988, New York and District of Columbia. *Education:* University of Connecticut (B.A., 1974); Arizona State University (M.B.A., 1984); Cornell University (J.D., 1987). Order of the Coif. ***PRACTICE AREAS:*** Taxation; Corporate Tax Planning; Tax Controversies. ***Email:*** caridgway@jonesday.com

R. CHRISTOPHER COOK, born Atlanta, Georgia, February 4, 1964; admitted to bar, 1989, Georgia; 1997, Illinois (Not admitted in District of Columbia). *Education:* Emory University (B.A., 1986); Harvard University (J.D., 1989). Phi Beta Kappa. Assistant U.S. Attorney, U.S. Attorney's Office, Northern District of Illinois, 1992-1997. ***PRACTICE AREAS:*** Litigation; White Collar Crime; Corporate Investigations; Complex Business Litigation. ***Email:*** christophercook@jonesday.com

JAMES E. GAUCH, born Akron, Ohio, October 12, 1964; admitted to bar, 1989, Ohio; 1995, District of Columbia. *Education:* The Ohio State University (B.A., 1986); University of Chicago (J.D., 1989). Phi Beta Kappa. Law Clerk to: Judge Nelson, U.S. Court of Appeals, 1989-1990; Chief Justice Burger and Justice Thomas, U.S. Supreme Court, 1993-1994. Attorney Advisor, Office of Legal Counsel, U.S. Department of Justice, 1991-1993. ***PRACTICE AREAS:*** Litigation. ***Email:*** jegauch@jonesday.com

DOUGLAS J. WHIPPLE, born Rochester, Pennsylvania, February 4, 1957; admitted to bar, 1989, New York; 2001, District of Columbia. *Education:* New York University (B.A., 1984); Georgetown University (M.S.F.S., 1988; J.D., 1988). Phi Beta Kappa. ***LANGUAGES:*** German. ***PRACTICE AREAS:*** Mergers and Acquisitions; Cross Border Investment; Software Licensing; Technology Contracts. ***Email:*** dwhipple@jonesday.com

EDWARD K.M. BILICH, born Royal Oak, Michigan, January 4, 1964; admitted to bar, 1990, Connecticut; 1992, District of Columbia. *Education:* Wake Forest University (B.A., 1986); Harvard University (J.D., 1990). Phi Beta Kappa. Law Clerk to Judge Lewis, U.S. Court of Appeals, Third Circuit, 1994-1995. ***PRACTICE AREAS:*** Litigation; Class Action Defense; Corporate Investigations. ***Email:*** ekbilich@jonesday.com

GREGORY A. CASTANIAS, born Indianapolis, Indiana, February 22, 1965; admitted to bar, 1990, Indiana; 1993, Virginia; 1994, District of Columbia. *Education:* Wabash College (A.B., 1987); Indiana University (J.D., 1990). Order of the Coif. Law Clerk to Judge Pratt, U.S. Court of Appeals, Second Circuit, 1991-1992. ***PRACTICE AREAS:*** Litigation; Appellate Practice; Intellectual Property; International Arbitration. ***Email:*** gcastanias@jonesday.com

EDWIN L. FOUNTAIN, born Norfolk, Virginia, August 10, 1964; admitted to bar, 1990, Virginia; 1992, District of Columbia. *Education:* University of North Carolina, Chapel Hill (B.A., 1986); London School of Economics (M.Sc., 1987); University of Virginia (J.D., 1990). Phi Beta Kappa. Law Clerk to Judge Doumar, U.S. District Court, Eastern District of Virginia, 1990-1991. ***PRACTICE AREAS:*** Litigation; Antitrust. ***Email:*** elfountain@jonesday.com

DANIEL H. BROMBERG, born Detroit, Michigan, September 24, 1968; admitted to bar, 1991, Pennsylvania; 1993, New York; 1995, District of Columbia. *Education:* Yale University (B.A., 1986); Harvard University (J.D., 1990). Phi Beta Kappa. Law Clerk: to Judge Oberdorfer, U.S. District Court for the District of Columbia, 1990-1991; to Judge Randolph, U.S. Court of Appeals for the District of Columbia Circuit, 1991-1992. ***PRACTICE AREAS:*** Litigation; Appellate Practice. ***Email:*** dhbromberg@jonesday.com

MARTIN V. KIRKWOOD, born Columbus, Ohio, October 9, 1962; admitted to bar, 1991, Maryland; 1993, District of Columbia. *Education:* George Washington University (B.A., 1986); Catholic University of America (J.D., 1991). ***PRACTICE AREAS:*** Energy; Utility Law; Utility Mergers. ***Email:*** mvkirkwood@jonesday.com

JOSEPH A. GOLDMAN, born McKeesport, Pennsylvania, July 27, 1967; admitted to bar, 1992, New York; 1998, District of Columbia. *Education:* Yeshiva University (B.S., 1988); Columbia University (J.D., 1991). ***PRACTICE AREAS:*** Taxation; International Tax; Federal Income Tax; Transfer Pricing. ***Email:*** jagoldman@jonesday.com

BLANEY HARPER, born Pontiac, Michigan, January 20, 1960; admitted to bar, 1992, New York; 1997, District of Columbia; registered to practice before U.S. Patent and Trademark Office. *Education:* University of Michigan (B.S., 1982); University of Vermont (M.S., 1987); Georgetown University (J.D., 1991). Order of the Coif. ***PRACTICE AREAS:*** Intellectual Property; Intellectual Property Litigation. ***Email:*** bharper@jonesday.com

MICHAEL R. SHUMAKER, born Reading, Pennsylvania, September 23, 1966; admitted to bar, 1992, Pennsylvania and District of Columbia. *Education:* Lafayette College (A.B., 1988); University of Notre Dame (J.D., 1991). ***PRACTICE AREAS:*** Litigation; Products Liability; Corporate Investigations. ***Email:*** mrshumaker@jonesday.com

CONSULTANT

HERBERT J. HANSELL, born Pittsburgh, Pennsylvania, November 16, 1925; admitted to bar, 1949, Ohio; 1950, New York (Not admitted in District of Columbia). *Education:* Massachusetts Institute of Technology (B.S., 1946); Yale University (LL.B., 1949). Tau Beta Pi. Legal Adviser, U.S. Department of State, 1977-1979. ***Email:*** hjhansell@jonesday.com

OF COUNSEL

KARL L. KELLAR, born Houston, Texas, December 20, 1954; admitted to bar, 1979, District of Columbia; 1993, Texas. *Education:* University of Houston (B.A., 1976); Harvard University (J.D., 1979). Trial Attorney, Tax Division, U.S. Department of Justice, 1979-1984. Branch Chief/Acting Director, Advance Pricing Agreement Program, Internal Revenue Service, 1996-2000. ***Email:*** klkellar@jonesday.com

KEVYN D. ORR, born Fort Lauderdale, Florida, May 11, 1958; admitted to bar, 1984, Florida (Not admitted in District of Columbia). *Education:* University of Michigan (B.A., 1979; J.D., 1983). Counsel, Federal Deposit Insurance Corporation, 1991. Assistant General Counsel, Resolution Trust Corporation, 1991-1995. Director, U.S. Department of Justice, 1995-2001. ***Email:*** korr@jonesday.com

KENT L. KILLELEA, born Highland Park, Illinois, August 23, 1957; admitted to bar, 1986, New York; 1994, District of Columbia. *Education:* Dartmouth College (A.B., 1979); London School of Economics, England (M.Sc.,

(This Listing Continued)

1981); Harvard University (J.D., 1984). Phi Beta Kappa. Counsel, Joint Committee on Taxation, U.S. Congress, 1996-1998. ***LANGUAGES:*** French. ***Email:*** klkillelea@jonesday.com

JONATHAN M. REDGRAVE, born Asheville, North Carolina, January 16, 1966; admitted to bar, 1991, Minnesota; 2001, District of Columbia. *Education:* University of Notre Dame (B.A., 1988); University of Minnesota (J.D., 1991). Law Clerk to Judge Crippen, Minnesota Court of Appeals, 1991-1992. ***Email:*** jredgrave@jonesday.com

COUNSEL

DAVID A. COPUS, born Porterville, California, February 19, 1942; admitted to bar, 1966, Texas; 1977, District of Columbia. *Education:* Northwestern University (B.A., 1963); Harvard University (LL.B., 1966). Director, Special Investigation and Conciliation Division, Equal Employment Opportunity Commission, Washington, D.C., 1973-1977. ***Email:*** dacopus@jonesday.com

BRIAN J. McMANUS, born Chicago, Illinois, July 15, 1942; admitted to bar, 1969, District of Columbia. *Education:* Georgetown University (A.B., 1964; J.D., 1968). ***Email:*** bjmcmanus@jonesday.com

JEROME J. ZAUCHA, born Uniontown, Pennsylvania, October 27, 1952; admitted to bar, 1977, Pennsylvania; 1978, District of Columbia. *Education:* University of Notre Dame (A.B., 1974); Yale University (J.D., 1977). Phi Beta Kappa. ***Email:*** jjzaucha@jonesday.com

KEVIN B. BYRD, born Washington, D.C., December 27, 1951; admitted to bar, 1978, District of Columbia. *Education:* Princeton University (B.A., 1973); Catholic University of America (J.D., 1978). Law Clerk to Judge McArdle, Superior Court of the District of Columbia, 1978-1979. ***Email:*** kbbyrd@jonesday.com

HEIDI HUGHES BUMPERS, born York, Pennsylvania, October 4, 1957; admitted to bar, 1982, Oregon; 1987, District of Columbia. *Education:* University of California, Santa Barbara (B.A, 1978); Northwestern School of Law of Lewis and Clark College (J.D., 1981). Staff Attorney, Hazardous Waste Enforcement Office, 1981-1984 and Section Chief, Office of Enforcement and Compliance Monitoring, 1984-1986, Environmental Protection Agency. ***Email:*** hhbumpers@jonesday.com

STEPHEN J. GOODMAN, born Cleveland, Ohio, October 25, 1958; admitted to bar, 1985, Ohio; 1992, District of Columbia. *Education:* Harvard University (B.A., 1981); Yale University (J.D., 1985). Phi Beta Kappa. ***Email:*** sjgoodman@jonesday.com

ELIZABETH A. McLAUGHLIN, born Washington, D.C., November 19, 1957; admitted to bar, 1991, Virginia; 1995, Ohio; 1998, District of Columbia. *Education:* College of William & Mary (B.A., 1978); George Mason University (J.D., 1991). ***Email:*** emclaughlin@jonesday.com

ASSOCIATES

CHRISTINE A. BARTLETT, born Wilkinsburg, Pennsylvania, February 20, 1953; admitted to bar, 1980, New York; 1981, District of Columbia; 1995, Maryland. *Education:* San Diego State University (B.S., 1976); Albany Law School of Union University (J.D., 1980). ***Email:*** cbartlett@jonesday.com

MARY L. HALE, born Denver, Colorado, April 21, 1954; admitted to bar, 1985, District of Columbia. *Education:* Georgetown University (B.S., 1976); George Washington University (J.D., 1985). Phi Beta Kappa; Order of the Coif. ***Email:*** mlhale@jonesday.com

JULIA M. BROAS, born Indianapolis, Indiana, December 1, 1960; admitted to bar, 1986, District of Columbia. *Education:* Harvard University (A.B., 1982); Columbia University (J.D., 1985). ***Email:*** jmbroas@jonesday.com

KATHLEEN MARIE McCHESNEY, born Washington, D.C., August 7, 1957; admitted to bar, 1986, Maryland; 1988, District of Columbia. *Education:* University of Maryland (B.A., 1982); Georgetown University (J.D., 1986). ***Email:*** kmcchesney@jonesday.com

JAMES E. ANKLAM, born Ft. Belvoir, Virginia, October 14, 1959; admitted to bar, 1987, Virginia; 1988, District of Columbia. *Education:* University of Virginia (B.A., 1981); Cornell University (J.D., 1987). Order of the Coif. Law Clerk to Judge Buckley, U.S. Court of Appeals for the District of Columbia Circuit, 1987-1988. ***Email:*** jeanklam@jonesday.com

ANTHONY P. LALLA, born Rochester, New York, May 7, 1959; admitted to bar, 1989, Pennsylvania; 1990, District of Columbia. *Education:* St. John Fisher College (B.A., 1981); American University, Washington College of Law (J.D., 1989). ***Email:*** aplalla@jonesday.com

STEVEN J. MINTZ, born Cleveland, Ohio, December 1, 1962; admitted to bar, 1989, Ohio; 1991, District of Columbia. *Education:* Princeton University (A.B., 1985); London School of Economics and Political Science (M.Sc., 1986); Harvard University (J.D., 1989). Phi Beta Kappa. Law Clerk to Judge T. S. Ellis, III, U.S. District Court, Eastern District of Virginia, 1990-1991. ***LANGUAGES:*** French. ***Email:*** sjmintz@jonesday.com

(This Listing Continued)

KIMBERLY A. HARB, born Norwich, Connecticut, March 5, 1966; admitted to bar, 1991, District of Columbia. *Education:* Washington College (B.A., 1988); Syracuse University (J.D., 1991). Attorney Advisor, Office of the Solicitor, 1991-1995, Senior Counselor and Special Assistant to the Director, 1995-2001, Bureau of Land Management, U.S. Department of the Interior. ***Email:*** kharb@jonesday.com

STEPHEN J. JORDEN, born Washington, D.C., January 19, 1966; admitted to bar, 1991, Maryland; 1994, District of Columbia. *Education:* Dickinson College (B.A., 1988); George Washington University (J.D., 1991). ***Email:*** sjjorden@jonesday.com

ROBIN L. JUNI, born New Ulm, Minnesota, March 18, 1966; admitted to bar, 1991, Minnesota; 1994, District of Columbia. *Education:* Hamline University (B.A., 1988); Harvard University (J.D., 1991). Phi Beta Kappa. Trial Attorney, Environment and Natural Resources Division, Environmental Defense Section, U.S. Department of Justice, 1991-1996. Professorial Lecturer in Law, George Washington University, 1995—. ***Email:*** rljuni@jonesday.com

JESSE A. WITTEN, born Baltimore, Maryland, July 2, 1965; admitted to bar, 1991, Ohio; 1992, Illinois; 1994, District of Columbia. *Education:* Princeton University (A.B., 1988); Harvard University (J.D., 1991). Phi Beta Kappa. Law Clerk to Judge Duff, U.S. District Court, Northern District of Illinois, 1991-1992. ***Email:*** jawitten@jonesday.com

GEOFFREY K. BEACH, born Buffalo, New York, June 12, 1962; admitted to bar, 1992, Maryland; 1993, District of Columbia. *Education:* Oberlin College (B.A., 1984); Catholic University of America (J.D., 1992). Law Clerk to Judge Terry, District of Columbia Court of Appeals, 1992-1993. ***Email:*** gkbeach@jonesday.com

THOMAS M. BECK, born Louisville, Kentucky, April 25, 1966; admitted to bar, 1992, Virginia; 1993, District of Columbia. *Education:* University of Virginia (B.A., 1988; J.D., 1992). ***Email:*** tmbeck@jonesday.com

KRISTI D. DREFKE, born Auburn, Nebraska, February 15, 1968; admitted to bar, 1992, Nebraska; 1994, Missouri; 1999, New York; 2000, District of Columbia. *Education:* University of Nebraska (B.S., 1989; J.D., 1992). Law Clerk to Judge Urbom, U.S. District Court, District of Nebraska, 1993. ***Email:*** kdrefke@jonesday.com

LAWRENCE D. ROSENBERG, born Abington, Pennsylvania, May 29, 1967; admitted to bar, 1992, Pennsylvania; 1999, District of Columbia. *Education:* Cornell University (B.A., 1989); University of Pennsylvania (J.D., 1992). Order of the Coif. Law Clerk to Judge Roth, U.S. Court of Appeals, Third Circuit, 1992-1993. Trial Attorney, Civil Division, U.S. Department of Justice, 1993-1998. ***Email:*** ldrosenberg@jonesday.com

PETER J. WANG, born Pittsburgh, Pennsylvania, July 21, 1969; admitted to bar, 1992, California; 1994, District of Columbia. *Education:* Princeton University (A.B., 1989); University of California, Boalt Hall School of Law, Berkeley (J.D., 1992). ***Email:*** pjwang@jonesday.com

JONATHAN BERMAN, born San Francisco, California, November 22, 1968; admitted to bar, 1993, California; 1995, District of Columbia. *Education:* Harvard University (B.A., 1990); Columbia University (J.D., 1993). Law Clerk to Judge McKelvie, U.S. District Court, District of Delaware, 1993-1994. ***Email:*** jberman@jonesday.com

SARAH MACKEY MATHIAS, born Little Rock, Arkansas, January 24, 1967; admitted to bar, 1993, Arkansas; 1995, District of Columbia. *Education:* University of the South (B.A., 1989); University of Arkansas (J.D., 1993). Law Clerk to Judge Arnold, U.S. Court of Appeals, Eighth Circuit, 1993-1995. ***Email:*** smmathias@jonesday.com

MARY-HELEN PERRY, born Washington, D.C., April 6, 1967; admitted to bar, 1993, Maryland; 1996, District of Columbia. *Education:* Wellesley College (B.A., 1988); University of California, Boalt Hall School of Law, Berkeley (J.D., 1993). ***Email:*** mhperry@jonesday.com

PAUL R. REICHERT, born Lackawanna, New York, February 2, 1968; admitted to bar, 1993, Pennsylvania; 1997, District of Columbia. *Education:* Hamilton College (A.B., 1990); George Washington University (J.D., 1993). ***Email:*** preichert@jonesday.com

LYNN A. AIRASIAN, born Framingham, Massachusetts, November 8, 1969; admitted to bar, 1994, Massachusetts; 1997, District of Columbia. *Education:* Boston College (B.A., 1991); Georgetown University (J.D., 1994). ***Email:*** laairasian@jonesday.com

MICHAEL L. KOLIS, born Denville, New Jersey, May 10, 1965; admitted to bar, 1994, Maryland; 1995, District of Columbia. *Education:* Dartmouth College (A.B., 1987); American University, Washington College of Law (J.D., 1994). ***Email:*** mlkolis@jonesday.com

PETER J. LOVE, born Greenwich, Connecticut, August 14, 1968; admitted to bar, 1994, California; 1995, District of Columbia. *Education:* University of California, Berkeley (B.A., 1989); University of Chicago (J.D., 1993). ***Email:*** pjlove@jonesday.com

(This Listing Continued)

JONES, DAY, REAVIS & POGUE, Washington—Continued

KEVIN C. MACLAY, born Washington, D.C., May 19, 1969; admitted to bar, 1994, Maryland; 1996, District of Columbia. *Education:* Bucknell University (B.A., 1991); University of Virginia (J.D., 1994). Phi Beta Kappa. ***Email:*** kmaclay@jonesday.com

SARAH B. McCLURE, born New York, New York, March 24, 1967; admitted to bar, 1994, Maryland; 1995, District of Columbia. *Education:* Bowdoin College (A.B., 1989); Georgetown University (J.D., 1993). ***Email:*** sbmcclure@jonesday.com

ANANT S. NARAYANAN, born Madras, India, February 8, 1959; admitted to bar, 1994, Texas; 2001, District of Columbia; registered to practice before the U.S Patent and Trademark Office. *Education:* Indian Institute of Technology (B.Tech., 1980); Princeton University (M.S.E., 1983); George Washington University (J.D., 1994). ***LANGUAGES:*** Hindi and Tamil. ***Email:*** anarayanan@jonesday.com

PAMELA SAK, born Parma, Ohio, August 28, 1964; admitted to bar, 1994, New York; 1995, District of Columbia. *Education:* Principia College (B.A., 1986); George Washington University (J.D., 1993). ***Email:*** psak@jonesday.com

KENNETH B. DRIVER, born Fairfax, Virginia, September 13, 1967; admitted to bar, 1995, Virginia; 1997, District of Columbia. *Education:* James Madison University (B.S., 1989); Georgetown University (J.D., 1995). ***Email:*** kbdriver@jonesday.com

DAVID H. EVANS, born Chicago, Illinois; admitted to bar, 1995, Ohio; 1997, District of Columbia. *Education:* Northwestern University (B.A., 1991; J.D., 1995). Chair, The Internet Committee, Section of Antitrust Law, American Bar Association, 1999—. ***LANGUAGES:*** French. ***Email:*** dhevans@jonesday.com

JACQUELINE M. HOLMES, born Ft. Lauderdale, Florida, September 7, 1969; admitted to bar, 1995, New York; 1996, District of Columbia. *Education:* California Institute of Technology (B.S., 1991); Loyola Law School, Los Angeles (J.D., 1994). Order of the Coif. ***Email:*** jholmes@jonesday.com

JULIE E. McEVOY, born Washington, D.C., December 7, 1968; admitted to bar, 1995, Virginia; 1997, District of Columbia. *Education:* College of William and Mary (B.A., 1991); University of Notre Dame (J.D., 1995). Law Clerk to Judge Schwelb, District of Columbia Court of Appeals, 1996-1997. ***LANGUAGES:*** Spanish. ***Email:*** jmcevoy@jonesday.com

MICHAEL S. McFALLS, born Cincinnati, Ohio, October 10, 1968; admitted to bar, 1995, Ohio; 2001, District of Columbia. *Education:* University of Michigan (B.A., 1989); University of North Carolina (M.A., 1992); University of Virginia (J.D., 1995). Phi Beta Kappa; Order of the Coif. Staff Attorney, Policy Planning, 1997-1998 and Attorney-Advisor to Chairman Robert Pitofsky, 1998-2000, Federal Trade Commission. ***Email:*** msmcfalls@jonesday.com

BEVIN M.B. NEWMAN, born Pittsburgh, Pennsylvania, September 10, 1970; admitted to bar, 1995, Virginia; 1996, District of Columbia. *Education:* Massachusetts Institute of Technology (S.B., 1992); Columbia University (J.D., 1995). ***Email:*** bmnewman@jonesday.com

HEATHER M. O'SHEA, born Garden City, Michigan, May 20, 1970; admitted to bar, 1995, Texas; 1999, District of Columbia. *Education:* Texas Christian University (B.S., 1992); Loyola University, Chicago (J.D., 1995; LL.M., 1999). ***Email:*** hoshea@jonesday.com

RUSSELL O. PAIGE, born Palos Verdes, California, February 17, 1959; admitted to bar, 1995, Texas; 1998, District of Columbia; registered to practice before U.S. Patent and Trademark Office. *Education:* Rensselaer Polytechnic Institute (B.S.M.E., 1981); University of Texas at Austin (J.D., 1994). ***Email:*** rpaige@jonesday.com

KAREN M. ESPALDON, born Manila, Philippines, April 12, 1964; admitted to bar, 1996, Virginia; 1997, District of Columbia. *Education:* George Mason University (B.S., 1988; J.D., 1995). ***Email:*** kmespaldon@jonesday.com

MICHAEL S. FRIED, born Kansas City, Missouri, January 15, 1970; admitted to bar, 1996, New York; 1998, District of Columbia. *Education:* University of Michigan (B.A., 1991); Columbia University (J.D., 1995). Law Clerk to Judge Mahoney, U.S. Court of Appeals, Second Circuit, 1995-1996. Attorney, Federal Trade Commission, 1998-2000. ***Email:*** msfried@jonesday.com

SUSAN Q. HAINES, born Northampton, Massachusetts, September 28, 1968; admitted to bar, 1996, District of Columbia. *Education:* St. John's College (B.A., 1990); George Washington University (J.D., 1996). Order of the Coif. ***Email:*** sqhaines@jonesday.com

LISA MALLOY NARDINI, born Lubbock, Texas, October 12, 1964; admitted to bar, 1996, Virginia; 1998, District of Columbia. *Education:* University of Virginia (B.A., 1987); American University, Washington College of Law (J.D., 1996). ***Email:*** lmnardini@jonesday.com

(This Listing Continued)

LAURA TUELL PARCHER, born Lawton, Oklahoma, February 20, 1969; admitted to bar, 1996, Virginia; 1997, District of Columbia. *Education:* George Mason University (B.A., 1991); Georgetown University (J.D., 1996). ***Email:*** lparcher@jonesday.com

STEPHEN M. POLOZIE, born Rochester, New York, October 1, 1965; admitted to bar, 1996, Illinois; 1998, District of Columbia. *Education:* McGill University (B.Sc., 1988); Northwestern University (J.D., 1996). ***Email:*** smpolozie@jonesday.com

SHELBY L. PROVENCHER, born Middlebury, Vermont, July 3, 1969; admitted to bar, 1996, Maryland; 1998, District of Columbia. *Education:* University of Vermont (B.A., 1991); Catholic University of America (J.D., 1996). ***Email:*** slprovencher@jonesday.com

DAVID S. RUTKOWSKI, born Royal Oak, Michigan, January 18, 1971; admitted to bar, 1996, Michigan; 1999, District of Columbia. *Education:* Stanford University (A.B., 1993); University of Notre Dame (J.D., 1996). ***Email:*** dsrutkowski@jonesday.com

AARON L. AGENBROAD, born Detroit, Michigan, December 14, 1969; admitted to bar, 1997, Maryland; 1999, District of Columbia. *Education:* University of Washington (B.A., 1992); Georgetown University (J.D., 1997). ***Email:*** alagenbroad@jonesday.com

T. JEFFREY FITZGERALD, born Denver, Colorado, April 30, 1971; admitted to bar, 1997, Colorado; 1998, District of Columbia. *Education:* University of Colorado (B.A., 1993); University of Notre Dame (J.D., 1997). Phi Beta Kappa. ***Email:*** tfitzgerald@jonesday.com

BRIAN K. GRUBE, born Lancaster, Ohio, August 7, 1972; admitted to bar, 1997, Ohio; 1999, District of Columbia. *Education:* Ohio University (B.B.A., 1993); University of Chicago (J.D., 1997). Staff Attorney, Policy Planning, Federal Trade Commission, 1997-1999. ***Email:*** bkgrube@jonesday.com

SHANNON M. KASLEY, born South Haven, Michigan, April 22, 1972; admitted to bar, 1997, New Jersey; 1998, New York; 2000, District of Columbia. *Education:* Mary Washington College (B.A., 1994); Seton Hall University (J.D., 1997). Phi Beta Kappa. Law Clerk to Judge Brown, U.S. District Court, District of New Jersey, 1999-2000. ***Email:*** smkasley@jonesday.com

JOHN B. KENNEDY, born Kuala Lumpur, Malaysia, July 15, 1972; admitted to bar, 1997, Virginia; 1999, District of Columbia. *Education:* Princeton University (A.B., 1994); College of William and Mary (J.D., 1997). Order of the Coif. ***Email:*** jbkennedy@jonesday.com

KATHLEEN M. LAUBENSTEIN, born Pottsville, Pennsylvania, September 16, 1970; admitted to bar, 1997, Pennsylvania and New Jersey; 2001, District of Columbia. *Education:* Barnard College (B.A., 1992); Temple University (J.D., 1996). Law Clerk to Judge Rosenn, U.S. Court of Appeals, Third Circuit, 1996-1997. ***Email:*** kmlaubenstein@jonesday.com

JOSEPH J. MIGAS, born San Mateo, California, March 9, 1966; admitted to bar, 1997, Wisconsin; 1999, District of Columbia. *Education:* University of Wisconsin (B.B.A., 1989); Georgetown University (J.D., 1997). Certified Public Accountant, Maryland, 1992. ***Email:*** jjmigas@jonesday.com

AMY E. MOORHUS, born Chicago, Illinois, January 14, 1967; admitted to bar, 1997, New York; 2001, District of Columbia. *Education:* Rutgers University (B.A., 1989); Fordham University (J.D., 1996). Phi Beta Kappa; Order of the Coif. Attorney-Advisor, U.S. Securities and Exchange Commission, 1999-2000. ***Email:*** aemoorhus@jonesday.com

ELIZABETH REES, born Baltimore, Maryland, October 9, 1972; admitted to bar, 1997, California; 1999, District of Columbia. *Education:* Wake Forest University (B.A., 1994); Emory University (J.D., 1997). Order of the Coif. Law Clerk to: Judge O'Kelley, U.S. District Court, Northern District of Georgia, 1997-1999; Judge Hull, U.S. Court of Appeals, Eleventh Circuit, 2000-2001. Adjunct Professor of Law, Emory University, 1998-1999. ***Email:*** erees@jonesday.com

J. CARTER ANDERSEN, born Gainesville, Florida, June 16, 1969; admitted to bar, 1998, Florida; 1999, District of Columbia. *Education:* University of Florida (B.S., 1991; J.D., 1998). Order of the Coif. ***Email:*** jcandersen@jonesday.com

CYNTHIA L. BAUERLY, born St. Cloud, Minnesota, January 23, 1971; admitted to bar, 1998, Indiana; 2001, District of Columbia. *Education:* Concordia College (B.A., 1993); Indiana University (J.D., 1998; M.P.A., 1998). Law Clerk to: Judge Boehm, Supreme Court of Indiana, 1998-1999; Judge Cooper, U.S. District Court, Central District of California, 1999-2000. ***Email:*** clbauerly@jonesday.com

JACK W. CAMPBELL IV, born Sanford, North Carolina, November 11, 1969; admitted to bar, 1998, North Carolina; 1999, District of Columbia. *Education:* University of North Carolina, Chapel Hill (B.S., 1993); Vanderbilt University (J.D., 1997). Order of the Coif. Law Clerk to Judge Selya, U.S. Court of Appeals, First Circuit, 1997-1998. ***Email:*** jwcampbelliv@jonesday.com

(This Listing Continued)

MIA F. COHEN, born Livingston, New Jersey, March 31, 1972; admitted to bar, 1998, New York; 1999, District of Columbia. *Education:* Brown University (B.A., 1993); University of Michigan (J.D., 1996). ***LANGUAGES:*** French. ***Email:*** mfcohen@jonesday.com

JOSEPH R. DERBIS, born Winchester, Massachusetts, July 25, 1972; admitted to bar, 1998, Maryland; 2000, District of Columbia. *Education:* Washington College, Maryland (B.A., 1995); University of Notre Dame (J.D., 1998). Associate Independent Counsel, Office of Independent Counsel, 1998-2000. ***Email:*** jrderbis@jonesday.com

LOUIS K. FISHER, born New York, New York, December 24, 1971; admitted to bar, 1998, Connecticut; 1999, New York (Not admitted in District of Columbia). *Education:* Yale University (B.A., 1993; J.D., 1997). Phi Beta Kappa. Law Clerk to: Judge Woodlock, U.S. District Court, District of Massachusetts, 1997-1998; Judge Cabranes, U.S. Court of Appeals, Second Circuit, 1999. ***Email:*** lkfisher@jonesday.com

LAURA TALLEY GEYER, born Baltimore, Maryland, August 11, 1968; admitted to bar, 1998, Maryland; 1999, District of Columbia. *Education:* Oberlin College (B.A., 1990); American University, Washington College of Law (J.D., 1998). ***Email:*** ltgeyer@jonesday.com

MARK L. GLASSMAN, born Rochester, New York, September 21, 1967; admitted to bar, 1998, Virginia; 1999, District of Columbia. *Education:* University of Kansas (B.A., 1989); American University, Washington College of Law (J.D., 1998). ***Email:*** mlglassman@jonesday.com

CAREY G.B. KERNEY, born Atlanta, Georgia, May 11, 1969; admitted to bar, 1998, Virginia; 1999, District of Columbia. *Education:* Gettysburg College (B.A., 1991); Catholic University of America (J.D., 1998). ***Email:*** cgbkerney@jonesday.com

BRIAN D. LEFORT, born Woonsocket, Rhode Island, February 11, 1967; admitted to bar, 1998, New York, Connecticut and Massachusetts; 2000, District of Columbia; registered to practice before U.S. Patent and Trademark Office. *Education:* University of Massachusetts (B.S.M.E., 1990); Suffolk University (J.D., 1997). ***Email:*** bdlefort@jonesday.com

STACY R. LINDEN, born Upper Darby, Pennsylvania, November 3, 1973; admitted to bar, 1998, Pennsylvania; 1999, New Jersey; 2000, District of Columbia. *Education:* Catholic University of America (B.A., 1995); American University, Washington College of Law (J.D., 1998). Phi Beta Kappa. Law Clerk to Judge Harrell, Jr., Maryland Court of Special Appeals, 1998-1999. ***Email:*** srlinden@jonesday.com

CHRISTOPHER J. LOVRIEN, born Brainerd, Minnesota, December 21, 1972; admitted to bar, 1998, Virginia; 2000, District of Columbia. *Education:* University of St. Thomas (B.A., 1995); Harvard University (J.D., 1998). Law Clerk to Judge Turner, U.S. District Court, Western District of Tennessee, 1998-1999. ***LANGUAGES:*** French. ***Email:*** cjlovrien@jonesday.com

CHARLES R.A. MORSE, born Winnipeg, Manitoba, Canada, December 14, 1970; admitted to bar, 1998, New York (Not admitted in District of Columbia). *Education:* University of Alberta (B.A., 1992); Harvard University (J.D., 1995). Law Clerk to: Justice Ellen Picard, Alberta Court of Appeals, 1995-1996; Justice Iacabucci, Supreme Court of Canada, 1996-1997. ***LANGUAGES:*** English and French. ***Email:*** crmorse@jonesday.com

J. ANDREW READ, born New York, New York, May 22, 1959; admitted to bar, 1998, Virginia; 1999, District of Columbia. *Education:* University of Virginia (B.S., 1982); American University (M.S., 1984); George Mason University (J.D., 1998). ***Email:*** jaread@jonesday.com

MELISSA D. STEAR, born Warren, Ohio, January 3, 1973; admitted to bar, 1998, Virginia; 2000, District of Columbia. *Education:* Duke University (B.A., 1995); George Washington University (J.D., 1998). Order of the Coif. Law Clerk to Judge Farrell, District of Columbia Court of Appeals, 1998-1999. ***LANGUAGES:*** French. ***Email:*** mdstear@jonesday.com

DAVID S. TORBORG, born Findlay, Ohio, October 15, 1972; admitted to bar, 1998, Ohio (Not admitted in District of Columbia). *Education:* Miami University (B.S., 1995); The Ohio State University (J.D., 1998). Order of the Coif. ***Email:*** dstorborg@jonesday.com

MARK C. CAWLEY, born Camp Hill, Pennsylvania, September 3, 1972; admitted to bar, 1999, Pennsylvania; 2000, District of Columbia. *Education:* University of Notre Dame (B.A., 1994; J.D., 1998). Law Clerk to Chief Judge Robinson, U.S. District Court, District of Delaware, 1998-2000. ***Email:*** mccawley@jonesday.com

MATTHEW S. DUCHESNE, born Concord, New Hampshire, January 21, 1964; admitted to bar, 1999, North Carolina; 2001, District of Columbia. *Education:* Miami University (B.A., 1991); University of North Carolina at Chapel Hill (M.P.A., 1999; J.D., 1999). Order of the Coif. Law Clerk to Judge Nygaard, U.S. Court of Appeals, Third Circuit, 1999-2000. ***Email:*** msduchesne@jonesday.com

(This Listing Continued)

RACHAEL HAMMER, born Washington, D.C., August 1, 1968; admitted to bar, 1999, Maryland; 2000, District of Columbia. *Education:* Jewish Theological Seminary (B.A., 1991); Columbia University (B.A., 1991); Georgetown University (J.D., 1999). ***Email:*** rhammer@jonesday.com

KYMBERLY D. HANKINSON, born Philadelphia, Pennsylvania, August 13, 1966; admitted to bar, 1999, Pennsylvania; 2000, District of Columbia and Maryland. *Education:* Franklin & Marshall College (B.A., 1989); Catholic University of America (J.D., 1999). ***Email:*** kdhankinson@jonesday.com

RENEE M. HOWARD, born Edmonds, Washington, December 27, 1974; admitted to bar, 1999, Michigan; 2001, District of Columbia. *Education:* University of Notre Dame (B.A., 1996; J.D., 1999). ***Email:*** rmhoward@jonesday.com

JENNIFER A. HUNKLER, born Brooklyn, New York, April 23, 1973; admitted to bar, 1999, New Jersey, District of Columbia and New York. *Education:* Rutgers University (B.S., 1995); University of Notre Dame (J.D., 1998). ***Email:*** jahunkler@jonesday.com

TAMARA HARDNEY KASSABIAN, born Yokosuka, Japan, February 13, 1968; admitted to bar, 1999, New York and District of Columbia. *Education:* University of Washington (B.A., 1990); Cornell University (J.D., 1998). ***Email:*** thkassabian@jonesday.com

TASHENA MIDDLETON MOORE, born Yonkers, New York, November 17, 1970; admitted to bar, 1999, Maryland; 2000, District of Columbia. *Education:* Yale University (B.A., 1992); Georgetown University (J.D., 1999). ***Email:*** tmiddletonmoore@jonesday.com

TRACEY L. HALLAM OLEY, born Bethesda, Maryland, December 23, 1974; admitted to bar, 1999, Virginia; 2000, District of Columbia. *Education:* College of William and Mary (A.B., 1995; J.D./M.B.A., 1999). Phi Beta Kappa; Order of the Coif. ***LANGUAGES:*** French and German. ***Email:*** tloley@jonesday.com

JUSTIN J. ROBERTS, born Tulsa, Oklahoma, December 30, 1972; admitted to bar, 1999, New York and District of Columbia. *Education:* University of Texas (B.A., 1995; J.D., 1998). Phi Beta Kappa. ***Email:*** jjroberts@jonesday.com

DEBRA L. SATINOFF, born Suffern, New York, May 27, 1973; admitted to bar, 1999, Maryland; 2000, District of Columbia. *Education:* Washington University (B.A., 1995); American University, Washington College of Law (J.D., 1999). ***Email:*** dlsatinoff@jonesday.com

SHEILA L. SHADMAND, born Norfolk, Virginia, October 31, 1973; admitted to bar, 1999, Virginia; 2000, District of Columbia. *Education:* Mary Washington College (B.A., 1995); University of Virginia (J.D., 1998). ***LANGUAGES:*** Farci. ***Email:*** slshadmand@jonesday.com

JANIE C.I. SHENG, born Taipei, Taiwan, March 3, 1970; admitted to bar, 1999, California and District of Columbia. *Education:* University of Maryland (B.A., 1994); Georgetown University (J.D., 1998). ***Email:*** jcisheng@jonesday.com

STACIE SIMMONS SPERRY, born Oklahoma City, Oklahoma, March 2, 1974; admitted to bar, 1999, Texas; 2000, District of Columbia. *Education:* Oklahoma State University (B.S., 1996); Georgetown University (J.D., 1999). ***Email:*** sssperry@jonesday.com

ROBIN D. STUMPF, born Richmond, Virginia, August 23, 1971; admitted to bar, 1999, Illinois (Not admitted in District of Columbia). *Education:* University of Notre Dame (B.A., 1993); University of Virginia (J.D., 1999). ***Email:*** rstumpf@jonesday.com

VIRGINIA C. THEIS, born Willoughby, Ohio, December 16, 1973; admitted to bar, 1999, Ohio; 2000, District of Columbia. *Education:* University of Virginia (B.A., 1996); George Washington University (J.D., 1999). ***Email:*** vctheis@jonesday.com

HEATHER GUILETTE WALSER, born Morris, Illinois, March 15, 1974; admitted to bar, 1999, Illinois; 2000, District of Columbia. *Education:* University of Notre Dame (B.A., 1996; J.D., 1999). ***Email:*** hguilettewalser@jonesday.com

GEOFFREY T. WRIGHT, born Silver Spring, Maryland, October 25, 1973; admitted to bar, 1999, Florida; 2000, District of Columbia. *Education:* Washington & Lee University (B.A., 1996); University of Miami (J.D., 1999). ***Email:*** gtwright@jonesday.com

JOHN L. CHANEY, born Findlay, Ohio, February 20, 1974; admitted to bar, 2000, Ohio; 2001, District of Columbia. *Education:* The Ohio State University (B.S., 1997; J.D., 2000). Order of the Coif. ***Email:*** jlchaney@jonesday.com

JONATHAN F. CHRISTIAN, born Fairfax, Virginia, February 23, 1970; admitted to bar, 2000, Virginia; 2001, District of Columbia. *Education:* Virginia Polytechnic Institute and State University (B.A., 1992); Washington College of Law of American University (J.D., 2000). ***Email:*** jchristian@jonesday.com

(This Listing Continued)

JONES, DAY, REAVIS & POGUE, Washington—Continued

TIFFANY F. DONOVAN, born Royal Oak, Michigan, January 30, 1969; admitted to bar, 2000, New York and District of Columbia. *Education:* Albion College (B.A., 1991); Oakland University (M.A., 1996); Cornell University (J.D./LL.M., 1999). ***Email:*** tdonovan@jonesday.com

TYLER L. FARMER, born Santa Monica, California, February 11, 1973; admitted to bar, 2000, California (Not admitted in District of Columbia). *Education:* University of Notre Dame (B.A., 1995; J.D., 2000). ***Email:*** tlfarmer@jonesday.com

DOMINICK V. FREDA, born Elizabeth, New Jersey, February 2, 1972; admitted to bar, 2000, Maryland and District of Columbia. *Education:* Rutgers University (B.A., 1994); University of Pennsylvania (J.D., 1998). Law Clerk to Judge Greenberg, U.S. Court of Appeals, Third Circuit, 1998-1999. ***Email:*** dvfreda@jonesday.com

MARK S. HANCOCK, born Norfolk, Virginia, November 2, 1974; admitted to bar, 2000, Massachusetts; 2001, District of Columbia. *Education:* Syracuse University (B.A., 1996; J.D., 1999); Georgetown University (LL.M., 2000). ***Email:*** mhancock@jonesday.com

H. BRIAN HOLLAND, born Williamantic, Connecticut, February 2, 1966; admitted to bar, 2000, New York; 2001, District of Columbia. *Education:* Tufts University (B.A., 1988); Washington College of Law of American University (J.D., 1998). Judicial Clerk, Office of the Staff Attorney, U.S. Court of Appeals, Second Circuit, 1998-2000. ***Email:*** bholland@jonesday.com

MATTHEW J. HOEFLING, born Birmingham, Alabama, November 15, 1974; admitted to bar, 2000, North Carolina (Not admitted in District of Columbia). *Education:* University of Notre Dame (B.A., 1997; J.D., 2000). Law Clerk to Judge Voorhees, U.S. District Court, Western District of North Carolina, 2000-2001. ***Email:*** mjhoefling@jonesday.com

NANCY M. KIM, born Kyungsangdo, South Korea, July 24, 1975; admitted to bar, 2000, Virginia and New Jersey; 2001, District of Columbia. *Education:* Georgetown University (B.S.F.S., 1997; J.D., 2000). ***Email:*** nmkim@jonesday.com

CHRISTOPHER T. KOEGEL, born Pompton Plains, New Jersey, November 15, 1974; admitted to bar, 2000, Pennsylvania; 2001, District of Columbia. *Education:* University of North Carolina at Chapel Hill (B.A., 1997); University of Pennsylvania (J.D., 2000). Phi Beta Kappa. ***Email:*** ctkoegel@jonesday.com

TNI M. LEBLANC, born Santa Barbara, California, August 30, 1973; admitted to bar, 2000, California; 2001, District of Columbia. *Education:* Clark Atlanta University (B.A., 1995); Georgetown University (M.A., J.D., 1999). ***Email:*** tmleblanc@jonesday.com

GREGORY P. LUIB, born Luzern, Switzerland, October 18, 1971; admitted to bar, 2000, New York and District of Columbia. *Education:* University of Virginia (B.A., 1994; J.D., 1999). ***Email:*** gpluib@jonesday.com

ANGELA M. OLSEN, born Iron Mountain, Michigan, December 6, 1968; admitted to bar, 2000, Maryland; 2001, District of Columbia. *Education:* Hamilton College (A.B., 1990); Catholic University of America (M.S., 1993); Washington College of Law of American University (J.D., 2000). ***LANGUAGES:*** French and Spanish. ***Email:*** amolsen@jonesday.com

NOAH D. RUBINS, born Fort Polk, Louisiana, March 7, 1971; admitted to bar, 2000, New York; 2001, Texas (Not admitted in District of Columbia). *Education:* Brown University (A.B., 1993); York University (Certificate in Refugee Law, 1996); Harvard University (J.D., 1999); Fletcher School of Law and Diplomacy (M.A.L.D., 1999). Phi Beta Kappa. ***LANGUAGES:*** French and Russian. ***Email:*** ndrubins@jonesday.com

JENNIFER M. SCHELL, born Rochester, New York, February 23, 1974; admitted to bar, 2000, New York; 2001, District of Columbia. *Education:* University of Notre Dame (B.A., 1996; J.D., 1999). Law Clerk to Judge Ripple, U.S. Court of Appeals, Seventh Circuit, 1999-2000. ***Email:*** jmschell@jonesday.com

RYAN C. THOMAS, born Fairfax, Virginia, September 22, 1975; admitted to bar, 2000, Virginia; 2001, District of Columbia. *Education:* Ohio Wesleyan University (B.A., 1997); University of Virginia (J.D., 2000). ***Email:*** rcthomas@jonesday.com

ANNIE TRAN, born Cholon, Vietnam, September 4, 1972; admitted to bar, 2000, Maryland; 2001, District of Columbia. *Education:* Boston College (B.A., 1994); Catholic University of America (J.D., 2000). ***Email:*** atran@jonesday.com

CAROLINE TSAI, born Sao Paulo, Brazil, April 20, 1969; admitted to bar, 2000, New York and District of Columbia. *Education:* University of Michigan (B.A., 1990); American University, Washington College of Law (J.D., 1999). ***LANGUAGES:*** Chinese. ***Email:*** ctsai@jonesday.com

(This Listing Continued)

GITTE J. WENDELL, born Glostrup, Denmark, March 26, 1974; admitted to bar, 2000, Ohio (Not admitted in District of Columbia). *Education:* Miami University (B.S., 1996); Case Western Reserve University (M.B.A., J.D., 2000). ***LANGUAGES:*** Danish. ***Email:*** gjwendell@jonesday.com

SARA E. YOUNG, born Jackson, Mississippi, July 18, 1973; admitted to bar, 2000, Maryland; 2001, District of Columbia. *Education:* University of Colorado at Boulder (B.A., 1995); Washington College of Law of American University (J.D., 2000). ***Email:*** seyoung@jonesday.com

JODY M. GARDNER, born Groton, Connecticut, June 6, 1975; admitted to bar, 2001, Massachusetts and District of Columbia. *Education:* Southeastern Louisiana University (B.A., 1996); Loyola University, New Orleans (J.D., 2000). ***Email:*** jmgardner@jonesday.com

SANDRA KACZMARCZYK, born Wilmington, Delaware, February 10, 1967; admitted to bar, 2001, Maryland (Not admitted in District of Columbia). *Education:* Harvard University (B.A., 1989); Georgetown University (M.A., 1994; J.D., 2000). ***Email:*** skacmarczyk@jonesday.com

TARA R. KAESEBIER, born Linton, Indiana, March 23, 1973; admitted to bar, 2001, Arizona and District of Columbia. *Education:* Washington University (B.A., 1995); Arizona State University (J.D., 2000); Georgetown University (LL.M., 2001). ***Email:*** trkaesebier@jonesday.com

LAURA J. MERIANOS, born Jersey City, New Jersey, May 5, 1975; admitted to bar, 2001, New York and District of Columbia. *Education:* University of Virginia (B.A., 1997); Washington College of Law of American University (J.D., 2000). ***LANGUAGES:*** Greek and Spanish. ***Email:*** ljmerianos@jonesday.com

MIA C. REYNOLDS, born Boston, Massachusetts, November 19, 1975; admitted to bar, 2001, Massachusetts (Not admitted in District of Columbia). *Education:* Harvard University (B.A., 1997); Washington College of Law of American University (J.D., 2000). ***Email:*** mcreynolds@jonesday.com

SAADEH A. AL-JURF, born Nablus, Jordan, July 7, 1971; (admission pending). *Education:* University of Chicago (B.A., 1993); University of Virginia (J.D., 2001). ***Email:*** sal-jurf@jonesday.com

CAMERON S. ALFORD, born Halifax, Nova Scotia, Canada, February 15, 1976; (admission pending). *Education:* The Ohio State University (B.A., 1998); George Washington University (J.D., 2001). Phi Beta Kappa; Order of the Coif. ***Email:*** csalford@jonesday.com

CATHERINE A. CHESS, born Plantation, Florida, January 21, 1976; (admission pending). *Education:* Georgetown University (B.A., 1998; J.D., 2001). Phi Beta Kappa. ***Email:*** cchess@jonesday.com

SUSAN M. EASTMAN, born Rochester, New York, June 5, 1976; (admission pending). *Education:* Pennsylvania State University (B.S., 1998); Case Western Reserve University (J.D., 2001). Phi Beta Kappa. Order of the Coif. ***Email:*** smeastman@jonesday.com

CHERYL E. FORCHILLI, born Slidell, Louisiana, December 10, 1974; admitted to bar, 2001, Florida (Not admitted in District of Columbia). *Education:* University of Texas (B.A., 1995); University of Florida (J.D., 2001). ***Email:*** ceforchilli@jonesday.com

GEOFFREY P. FORGIONE, born Redwood City, California, March 2, 1975; (admission pending). *Education:* University of Delaware (B.S., 1997); University of Notre Dame (J.D., 2001). ***Email:*** gpforgione@jonesday.com

MAURA K. FRICKEL, born Washington, D.C., January 14, 1976; (admission pending). *Education:* Catholic University of America (B.A., 1997; J.D., 2001). ***LANGUAGES:*** Spanish. ***Email:*** mkfrickel@jonesday.com

CARMEN M. GUERRICAGOITIA, born Ontario, Oregon, September 25, 1976; (admission pending). *Education:* George Fox University (B.S., 1998); Georgetown University (J.D., 2001). ***Email:*** cmguerricagoitia@jonesday.com

FAHAD A. HABIB, born Bombay, India, April 29, 1975; (admission pending). *Education:* University of California, Berkeley (B.A., 1998); Georgetown University (J.D., 2001). ***LANGUAGES:*** Hindi. ***Email:*** fahabib@jonesday.com

THOMAS M. HENRY III, born Terre Haute, Indiana, June 4, 1973; (admission pending). *Education:* University of Maryland (B.A., 1995); University of Notre Dame (J.D., 2001). ***Email:*** tmhenry@jonesday.com

LAUREN B. HOFFER, born Beaumont, Texas, September 9, 1975; (admission pending). *Education:* University of Texas at Austin (B.A., 1998); Georgetown University (J.D., 2001). ***Email:*** lbhoffer@jonesday.com

LILY MAZAHERY, born Tehran, Iran, October 10, 1972; (admission pending). *Education:* George Mason University (B.A., 1994); Washington College of Law of American University, (J.D., 1999). ***Email:*** lmazahery@jonesday.com

PATRICIA E. McDONOUGH, born Boston, Massachusetts, May 8, 1975; (admission pending). *Education:* Princeton University (A.B., 1997); Harvard University (J.D., 2001). ***LANGUAGES:*** German. ***Email:*** pmcdonough@jonesday.com

(This Listing Continued)

LAURA A. POLVINALE, born Ft. Lauderdale, Florida, September 19, 1970; (admission pending). *Education:* Montgomery College (A.A., 1996); Hood College (B.A., 1998); Washington College of Law of American University, (J.D., 2001). ***Email:*** lapolvinale@jonesday.com

ANISH N. SHETH, born Ft. Worth, Texas, June 10, 1978; (admission pending). *Education:* University of Texas at Austin (B.A., 1998); Southern Methodist University (J.D., 2001). ***Email:*** ansheth@jonesday.com

DANIELLE M. TRAYLOR, born Houston, Texas, April 17, 1976; (admission pending). *Education:* University of Texas at Austin (B.A., B.A., 1998; J.D., 2001). Phi Beta Kappa. ***LANGUAGES:*** French. ***Email:*** dmtraylor@jonesday.com

RUSSELL J. UPTON, born Lier, Belgium, January 30, 1976; (admission pending). *Education:* Johns Hopkins University (B.A., 1998); Washington College of Law of American University (J.D., 2001). ***Email:*** rjupton@jonesday.com

VICKI R. WALCOTT-EDIM, born Rockville Center, New York, January 11, 1975; (admission pending). *Education:* College of William & Mary (B.A., 1996); Catholic University of America (J.D., 2001). ***Email:*** vrwalcott@jonesday.com

JENNIFER A. WALKER, born Manhattan, Kansas, June 8, 1974; (admission pending). *Education:* University of Kansas (B.S., 1997); Case Western Reserve University (M.A., J.D., 2001). Order of the Coif. ***Email:*** jawalker@jonesday.com

NOLAN S. YOUNG, born Falls Church, Virginia, August 18, 1974; (admission pending). *Education:* Southwestern University (B.A., 1996); University of Texas at Austin (J.D., 2001). ***Email:*** nsyoung@jonesday.com

SENIOR STAFF ATTORNEYS

JOHN P. McGRANE, JR., born White Plains, New York, February 21, 1951; admitted to bar, 1987, New York; 1989, District of Columbia. *Education:* Georgetown University (B.S., 1973); Catholic University of America (J.D., 1986). ***LANGUAGES:*** French. ***Email:*** jpmcgrane@jonesday.com

PATRICK L. HUBBARD, born Norfolk, Virginia, September 22, 1962; admitted to bar, 1988, Maryland; 1989, District of Columbia. *Education:* University of Dallas (B.A., 1984); Catholic University of America (J.D., 1988). ***Email:*** phubbard@jonesday.com

KERRI S. KUHLMANN, born Bridgeport, Connecticut, January 25, 1961; admitted to bar, 1990, Pennsylvania; 1997, District of Columbia. *Education:* Université de Paris - Sorbonne, Paris, France (Certificat de la Langue Française, 1981); University of Rhode Island (B.A., 1982); Washington College of Law of American University (J.D., 1990). ***LANGUAGES:*** French. ***Email:*** kskuhlmann@jonesday.com

STAFF ATTORNEYS

Anna L. Brown	***Lee A. Friedman***
Dara A. Lutz	***William L. Kearney, Jr.***

Languages: Chinese, Farsi, French, German, Hindi, Greek, Jamaican Patuis, Russian, Spanish, and Tamil.

JONES & LYLES, L.L.C.

WASHINGTON, D.C.

(See Bowie)

Corporate Law, Business Law, Emerging Business, Small Business, Litigation, Business Formation, Government Contracts, Homeowner Association, Condominium, Consumer Law, Civil Litigation, Trusts, Estates, Wills, Probate, Technology Law.

JONES, TULLAR & COOPER, P.C.

WASHINGTON, D.C.

(See Arlington, Virginia)

Patent, Trademark, Unfair Competition and Copyright Practice, Intellectual Property.

JONES, WALDO, HOLBROOK & McDONOUGH

A PROFESSIONAL CORPORATION

Established in 1875

412 FIRST STREET, S.E.

WASHINGTON, D.C. 20003

Telephone: 202-484-4902
Telecopier: 202-484-0109
URL: http://www.joneswaldo.com

Salt Lake City, Utah Office: 1500 Wells Fargo Plaza, 170 South Main Street. Telephone: 801-521-3200. Telecopier: 801-328-0537.
St. George, Utah Office: 301 N. 200 E., Suite 3-A. Telephone: 435-628-1627. Telecopier: 435-628-5225.

General Practice including all Courts, Departments and Agencies on Federal Legislative Matters. Administrative, Regulatory and Communications Law.

OF COUNSEL

ARTHUR H. SILVERMAN, born Perth Amboy, New Jersey, February 14, 1939; admitted to bar, 1963, New Jersey; 1967, District of Columbia; U.S. Court of Appeals, District of Columbia and Third Circuits. *Education:* University of Pennsylvania (B.S., Economics, 1960); Cornell University (J.D., 1967). *Member:* The District of Columbia Bar. ***PRACTICE AREAS:*** Government Relations.

(For complete biographical data on all personnel, see Professional Biographies at Salt Lake City, Utah)

JONES, WALKER, WAECHTER, POITEVENT, CARRÈRE & DENÈGRE, L.L.P.

Established in 1937

499 SOUTH CAPITOL STREET, S.W., SUITE 600

WASHINGTON, D.C. 20003-4013

Telephone: 202-203-1000
Telecopier: 202-203-0000
Email: info@joneswalker.com
URL: http://www.joneswalker.com

Baton Rouge, Louisiana Office: 8555 United Plaza Boulevard. Telephone: 225-248-2000. Telecopier: 225-248-2010.
Lafayette, Louisiana Office: 500 Dover Boulevard, Suite 120. Telephone: 337-406-5610. Telecopier: 337-406-5620.
New Orleans, Louisiana Office: 201 St. Charles Avenue. Telephone: 504-582-8000. Telecopier: 504-582-8583.
Miami, Florida Office: Courvoisier Centre II, Suite 500, 601 Brickell Key Drive. Telephone: 305-679- 5700. Telecopier: 305-679-5710.
The Woodlands, Texas Office: Waterway Plaza Two, Suite 350, 10001 Woodloch Forest Drive. Telephone: 281-296-5900. Telecopier: 281-296-5910.

Admiralty & Maritime; Antitrust & Trade Regulation; Appellate Litigation; Aviation; Banking; Bankruptcy, Restructuring & Creditors-Debtors Rights; Business & Commercial Litigation; Commercial Lending & Finance; Construction; Corporate & Securities; Employee Benefits, ERISA & Executive Compensation; Energy; Environmental & Toxic Torts; ERISA, Life, Health & Disability Insurance Litigation; Gaming; Government Relations; Health Care Litigation, Transactions & Regulation; Intellectual Property & E-Commerce; International; Labor Relations & Employment; Medical Professional & Hospital Liability; Mergers and Acquisitions; Products Liability; Professional Liability; Project Development & Finance; Public Finance; Real Estate: Land Use, Development & Finance; Tax (International, Federal, State & Local); Telecommunications & Utilities; Trusts, Estates & Personal Planning; Venture Capital & Emerging Companies; White Collar Crime.

FIRM PROFILE: Jones, Walker, Founded in 1937, is a full-service law firm with 200 attorneys located in Washington D.C.; New Orleans, Baton Rouge and Lafayette, Louisiana; Coral Gables, Florida and The Woodlands, Texas. The firm handles regional, national and international interests for major multinational, multi state, and private corporations, family-owned businesses, individuals, and international clients doing business in the United States and abroad. The firm is organized administratively into seven sections; four litigation sections (Health Care, General Litigation, Labor and Employment and Maritime) and three transaction sections (Corporate, Estates and Tax, and General Business and Energy). Lawyers from multiple sections frequently combine into practice area groups to satisfy specific client requirements. the firm-wide staff of 455 includes 106 partners, 27 special counsel and 62 associates.

(This Listing Continued)

JONES, WALKER, WAECHTER, POITEVENT, CARRÈRE & DENÈGRE, L.L.P., Washington—Continued

Jones Walker lawyers practice in a wide variety of federal, state and local law matters. The firm's varied areas of practice reflect the diversity of clients and their needs. The firm represents a great number of major enterprises headquartered in Louisiana, as well as many international enterprises, Fortune 500 companies, money center banks, and worldwide insurers doing business in Louisiana. Although the firm is routinely called upon to participate in matters of regional, national and international scope, the representation of individuals and smaller enterprises continues to be an important part of the firm's practice.

RESIDENT PARTNER

R. CHRISTIAN JOHNSEN, born New Orleans, Louisiana, October 16, 1960; admitted to bar, 1985, Louisiana; 1991, District of Columbia and U.S. District Court for the District of Columbia. *Education:* University of Virginia (B.S., 1982); Tulane University (J.D., cum laude, 1985). *Member:* District of Columbia Bar; The Maritime Law Association of the United States. ***PRACTICE AREAS:*** Maritime Law; Government Affairs; Commercial Transactions. ***Email:*** cjohnsen@joneswalker.com

RESIDENT SPECIAL COUNSEL

JOHN J. JASKOT, born Pocatello, Idaho, August 31, 1954; admitted to bar, 1984, District of Columbia; 1995, U.S. Supreme Court. *Education:* U.S. Coast Guard Academy (B.S., with honors, 1976); George Washington University (J.D., with honors, 1984). Member, Maritime Law Association of the United States, 1984— (Fellow, U.S. Senate Transportation Appropriations Subcommittee, 1992; USCG Liaison to U.S. Senate, 1993-1996). [CMDR., U.S. Coast Guard (Ret.), 1976-1996]. ***PRACTICE AREAS:*** Government Affairs; Maritime Law. ***Email:*** jjaskot@joneswalker.com

JAMES D. OGSBURY, born Nogales, Arizona, February 17, 1959; admitted to bar, 1986, Arizona (Not admitted in District of Columbia). *Education:* Harvard University (A.B., 1981); Arizona State University (J.D., 1985). ***PRACTICE AREAS:*** Government Relations. ***Email:*** jogsbury@joneswalker.com

RESIDENT OF COUNSEL

W. RUSSELL KING, born Beaufort, South Carolina, October 17, 1949; admitted to bar, 1974, Georgia; 1975, U.S. District Court, Southern District of Georgia; 1978, District of Columbia. *Education:* University of Georgia (B.B.A., 1971); Hague Academy of International Law, Den Hague Netherlands (1973); University of Georgia School of Law (J.D., 1974). Phi Delta Phi (Vice-President). Board Member, U.S. ASEAN Business Council, 1995—; U.S. Indonesia Society, 2000—; National Mining Association, 2001—. Member, U.S. Department of Commerce, Advisory Committee for Energy, Industrial Section. *Member:* District of Columbia Bar; State Bar of Georgia. ***PRACTICE AREAS:*** Energy; Natural Resources; Environmental; International Law; Agricultural Law. ***Email:*** rking@joneswalker.com

(For Firm and Biographical Data at New Orleans, Louisiana, Baton Rouge, Louisiana, Lafayette, Louisiana, Miami, Florida and The Woodlands, Texas, see Professional Biographies at those locations)

JORDAN COYNE & SAVITS, L.L.P.

1100 CONNECTICUT AVENUE, N.W., SUITE 600

WASHINGTON, D.C. 20036

Telephone: 202-296-4747
Telecopier: 202-496-2800
Email: jocs@idt.net
URL: http://www.jocs-law.com

Rockville, Maryland Office: 33 Wood Lane. Telephone: 301-424-4161.
Baltimore, Maryland Office: 400 E. Pratt Street. Telephone: 410-625-5080.
Fairfax, Virginia Office: 10486 Armstrong Street. Telephone: 703-246-0900. Telecopier: 703-591-3673.

Litigation Defense Practice in Civil and Criminal Cases (State and Federal) including: Appellate Practice, Casualty and Property Insurance, Products Liability, Professional Malpractice, Toxic Torts and Workers Compensation.

MEMBERS OF FIRM

DWIGHT D. MURRAY, born New Orleans, Louisiana, June 20, 1944; admitted to bar, 1976, District of Columbia, U.S. Court of Appeals for the District of Columbia Circuit; 1993, U.S. Court of Federal Claims; 1995, U.S. Court of Appeals for the Fourth Circuit; 1996, U.S. Court of Appeals, Eighth Circuit. *Education:* Xavier University (B.A., 1968); Georgetown University (J.D., 1974). Recipient, Jeffrey Crandell Legal Aid Award, 1974. Adjunct Professor of Law, Catholic University Law School, 1981-1985. Law Clerk to Hon. Tim Murphy, Associate Judge, Superior Court, District of Columbia, 1974-1975. Fellow in the American College of Trial Lawyers. Master, The William Bryant Chapter, American Inns of Court, 1988—. Member, Civil Justice Reform Act Advisory Group for the U.S. District Court for the District of Columbia. Judicial Conference Voting Delegate for the District of Columbia Court of Appeals, 1976-1993. National Conference of Bar Presidents. Member, house of Delegates, American Bar Association (1996-1997). *Member:* The District of Columbia Bar (Member: Committee on Continual Legal Education, 1980—; Judicial Conference Voting Delegate, 1976—; Legal Ethics Committee; Research Foundation Committee); Bar Association of the District of Columbia (Secretary, 1994-1995; Co-Chair, Insurance and Tort Law Committee, 1990-1991; Board of Directors, 1993-1994; President Elect, 1995-1996; President, 1996-1997); Council of Court Excellence; District of Columbia Defense Lawyers Association (Secretary, 1981-1982); The Counsellors (President, 1990-1991); Lawyer's Club. Fellow, American Bar Foundation. [Major, USMCR, 1968-1982]. ***PRACTICE AREAS:*** Litigation; Defense Litigation; U.S. Supreme Court Litigation; Hospital Law; Legal Ethics and Professional Responsibility; Products Liability; Torts. ***Email:*** d.murray@jocs-law.com

JOHN O. EASTON, born Takoma Park, Maryland, November 28, 1943; admitted to bar, 1977, Virginia, U.S. District Court, Eastern and Western Districts of Virginia and U.S. Court of Appeals, Fourth Circuit; 1978, District of Columbia, U.S. District Court, for the District of Columbia, U.S. Court of Appeals, District of Columbia Circuit and U.S. Court of Military Appeals; 1999, West Virginia and U.S. District Court, Southern and Northern Districts of West Virginia. *Education:* Baylor University (B.A., 1966); George Mason University School of Law (J.D., 1977). Member, Virginia Medical Malpractice Review Panel, 1983—. *Member:* The District of Columbia Bar; Bar Association of the District of Columbia; Fairfax County, Prince William County and American Bar Associations; Virginia State Bar; West Virginia State Bar; Northern Virginia Defense Lawyers Association (Treasurer, 1980-1981; Member, Board of Directors, 1981-1984); Virginia Association of Defense Attorneys; The Counsellors. [Col., USMCR (ret.)]. ***PRACTICE AREAS:*** Architects and Engineers Malpractice; Legal Malpractice; Medical Malpractice; Products Liability; Sexual Assault/Abuse. ***Email:*** i.easton@jocs-law.com

DAVID P. DURBIN, born Detroit, Michigan, March 20, 1948; admitted to bar, 1977, District of Columbia; 1978, U.S. District Court for the District of Columbia; 1979, U.S. Court of Appeals, Fourth Circuit; 1980, U.S. Court of Appeals, District of Columbia Circuit; 1983, U.S. District Court, District of Maryland; 1984, U.S. Supreme Court; 2000, Maryland. *Education:* Georgetown University (B.S.F.S., 1970; J.D., 1977). Administrative Assistant to the Director, Federal Judicial Center, 1974-1977. Law Clerk to the Honorable George L. Hart, Jr., U.S. District Court for the District of Columbia, 1977-1978. *Member:* The District of Columbia Bar; Bar Association of the District of Columbia; District of Columbia Defense Lawyers Association; The Counsellors (President, 1993-1994); The Barristers (Secretary, 1992-1993); Lawyers' Club. ***PRACTICE AREAS:*** Professional Liability Defense; Appellate Practice; Defense Litigation; Insurance Defense; Insurance Coverage. ***Email:*** d.durbin@jocs-law.com

CAROL THOMAS STONE, born Columbus, Ohio, June 15, 1954; admitted to bar, 1980, New York; 1981, District of Columbia, Virginia, U.S. District Court, District of Columbia, U.S. District Court, Eastern District of Virginia and U.S. Court of Appeals, District of Columbia and Fourth Circuits; 1983, U.S. District Court, Western District of Virginia and U.S. District Court, Southern and Eastern Districts of New York; 1987, U.S. Bankruptcy Court, Eastern District of Virginia; 1990, U.S. Bankruptcy Court, Western District of Virginia. *Education:* Furman University (B.A., magna cum laude, 1976); George Washington University (J.D., 1979). Phi Beta Kappa. *Member:* Fairfax and New York State Bar Associations; Virginia State Bar; The District of Columbia Bar; Virginia Association of Defense Attorneys; The Counsellors. ***PRACTICE AREAS:*** Legal Malpractice Defense; Accountants Malpractice; Professional Liability Defense; Insurance Coverage; Commercial Litigation; Fair Debt Collection Practices Act Defense. ***Email:*** c.stone@jocs-law.com

JOHN TREMAIN MAY, born Washington, D.C., October 14, 1953; admitted to bar, 1979, District of Columbia; 2000, Maryland. *Education:* Carnegie Mellon University (B.S., 1975; M.S., 1976); Georgetown University (J.D., cum laude, 1979). Author: "Administrative Survey: S.E.C.," 10 Law and Policy International Business 237, 1978. Adjunct Professor, Legal Ethics, Washington College of Law American University. Hearing Committee Chairman, D.C. Board of Professional Responsibility. *Member:* The District of Columbia Bar; Bar Association of the District of Columbia; The William B. Bryant American Inn of Court; The Counsellors; The Barristers. ***PRACTICE AREAS:*** Legal Ethics and Professional Responsibility; NASD Arbitration; Legal Malpractice Defense; Accountants Malpractice; Professional Liability Defense. ***Email:*** j.may@jocs-law.com

D. STEPHENSON SCHWINN, born Salt Lake City, Utah, August 29, 1956; admitted to bar, 1981, District of Columbia; 1983, U.S. District Court for the District of Columbia and U.S. Court of Appeals for the District of Columbia Circuit; 1986, California and Maryland; 1988, U.S. District Court, District of Maryland. *Education:* State University of New York at Stony Brook (B.A.,

(This Listing Continued)

1978); Georgetown University (J.D., 1981). Law Clerk to: Hon. William E. Stewart, Jr., Superior Court of the District of Columbia, 1981-1982; Hon. John R. Hess, Superior Court of the District of Columbia, 1982-1983. *Member:* Bar Association of the District of Columbia (Chair, Continuing Legal Education Committee, 1987-1989; Member: Young Lawyers Section Executive Council, 1987-1989; Governing Board of Directors, 1988-1989). ***PRACTICE AREAS:*** Premises Liability; Personal Injury; Workers Compensation; Environmental Insurance Coverage; Construction Law; Insurance Defense; Products Liability. **Email:** s.schwinn@jocs-law.com

DAVID B. STRATTON, born Pittsfield, Massachusetts, November 10, 1955; admitted to bar, 1980, Massachusetts; 1983, U.S. Court of Military Appeals; 1988, District of Columbia, U.S. Court of Appeals, District of Columbia Circuit, U.S. Court of Appeals, Fourth Circuit; 1990, U.S. District Court, District of Columbia; 1993, Maryland, U.S. District Court, District of Maryland. *Education:* Yale University (B.A., 1977); University of Connecticut (J.D., 1980). Managing Editor, Connecticut Law Review, 1980. Author: Note, "Federal Antitrust Immunity; Exposure of Municipalities to Treble Antitrust Damages Sets Limits for New Federalism," 11 Conn. Law Review 126 (1978). *Member:* The District of Columbia Bar; Maryland State Bar Association, Inc.; Massachusetts and American Bar Associations. [Capt. USMC, 1981-1987]. ***PRACTICE AREAS:*** Appellate Practice; Insurance Defense; Insurance Coverage; Professional Liability Defense; Civil Litigation. **Email:** d.stratton@jocs-law.com

JOHN H. CARSTENS, born Queens, New York, September 19, 1957; admitted to bar, 1983, Virginia; 1984, U.S. District Court, Eastern District of Virginia and U.S. Court of Appeals, Fourth Circuit; 1989, U.S. District Court, Western District of Virginia; 1990, District of Columbia; 1991, U.S. District Court, District of Columbia. *Education:* American University (B.S., cum laude, 1979; J.D., 1983). *Member:* Virginia State Bar; The District of Columbia Bar; Virginia Association of Defense Attorneys; Northern Virginia Defense Lawyers Association (President, 1992; Vice-President, 1990-1991; Treasurer, 1989-1990; Secretary, 1988-1989). ***PRACTICE AREAS:*** Commercial Litigation; Tort Defense; Workers' Compensation; Professional Liability Defense. **Email:** j.carstens@jocs-law.com

DEBORAH MURRELL WHELIHAN, born Philadelphia, Pennsylvania, December 11, 1960; admitted to bar, 1986, Maryland; 1987, U.S. District Court, District of Maryland; 1988, District of Columbia; 1990, U.S. District Court, District of Columbia; 1993, U.S. Court of Appeals, Fourth Circuit. *Education:* Dickinson College (B.A., cum laude, 1983); Washington & Lee University (J.D., 1986). *Member:* Montgomery County, Maryland State and American Bar Associations. ***PRACTICE AREAS:*** Professional Liability Defense; Legal Ethics; Commercial Law; Financial Institutions Law; Lender Liability; Tort Defense; Employment Law; Civil Rights. **Email:** d.whelihan@jocs-law.com

MICHAEL E. REHEUSER, born New York, N.Y., October 10, 1961; admitted to bar, 1986, Pennsylvania; 1989, Illinois and U.S. Court of Military Appeals; 1990, District of Columbia; U.S. District Court, District of Columbia, U.S. Court of Appeals, District of Columbia Circuit; 1993, Virginia, U.S. District Court, Eastern and Western Districts of Virginia. *Education:* Lehigh University (B.S., 1983); Catholic University (J.D., 1986). Chair, Professionalism Committee, Fairfax Bar Association, 1999-2000; Chair, Membership Committee, 1998; Member, Circuit Court Committee, 1998-2001. *Member:* The District of Columbia Bar; Fairfax (Member, Board of Directors, 2000-2001), Virginia, Illinois and Pennsylvania Bar Associations; Defense Research Institute; Virginia Association of Defense Attorneys. [Judge Advocate, U.S. Marine Corps., 1987-1990; Lt. Col., USMCR, 1990—]. ***PRACTICE AREAS:*** Tort Defense; Premises Liability Defense; Construction Law; Military Law; Toxic Tort Defense. **Email:** mer@jocs-law.com

ASSOCIATES

CLINTON R. SHAW, JR., born Washington, D.C., April 17, 1964; admitted to bar, 1994, Virginia. *Education:* Hamilton College (A.B., 1986); Washington & Lee University (J.D., 1993). *Member:* Virginia Bar Association. (Resident, Fairfax, Virginia Office).

SAMANTHA D. VANTERPOOL, born Basseterre, St. Kitts, West Indies, November 11, 1970; admitted to bar, 1997, Virginia. *Education:* George Mason University (B.A., with high distinction, 1992); University of Maryland (J.D., 1996). (Resident, Fairfax, Virginia Office).

GREGORY SAMUEL McKEE, born Silver Spring, Maryland, September 22, 1973; admitted to bar, 1998, Maryland and U.S. District Court, Southern District of Maryland; 1999, District of Columbia and U.S. Court of Appeals, Federal Circuit. *Education:* Randolph-Macon College (B.A., 1995); University of Baltimore (J.D., 1998). Certified Mediator. *Member:* Calvert County and American Bar Associations; Daniel O'Connell Law Society. ***PRACTICE AREAS:*** Litigation; Insurance Defense; Personal Injury Defense; Product Liability; Professional Liability; Workers' Compensation.

CHRITOPHER M. COLEMAN, born Washington, D.C., March 5, 1971; admitted to bar, 1998, Maryland (Not admitted in District of Columbia). *Education:* University of Maryland (B.A., 1994); New England School of Law (J.D., 1998). Lead Articles Editor, New England International and Comparative Law Annual. Law Clerk to the Honorable Annice M. Wagner, Chief Judge, District of Columbia Court of Appeals.

ANNA M. STAFFORD, born Baton Rouge, Louisiana, June 20, 1972; admitted to bar, 1999, Virginia. *Education:* George Washington University (B.A., magna cum laude, 1994); College of William & Mary (J.D., 1999). (Resident, Fairfax, Virginia Office).

MARK A. JOHNSTON, born Camp Hill, Pennsylvania, November 30, 1973; admitted to bar, 1999, District of Columbia; 2000, Maryland. *Education:* Lafayette College (B.A., 1996); Tulane University of Louisiana (J.D., 1999). *Member:* District of Columbia Bar; American Bar Association. ***PRACTICE AREAS:*** Litigation; Insurance Defense; Products Liability.

JUSTIN H. COHEN, born Philadelphia, Pennsylvania, September 25, 1975; admitted to bar, 2000, Pennsylvania and New Jersey (Not admitted in District of Columbia). *Education:* Pennsylvania State University (B.S., 1997); George Washington University (J.D., 2000). Member, Moot Court Board, Washington University. ***PRACTICE AREAS:*** Litigation. **Email:** j.cohen@jocs-law.com

RACHEL H. BOB, born Wilmington, Delaware, April 24, 1974; admitted to bar, 2000, Maryland; 2001, District of Columbia and U.S. District Court, District of Maryland. *Education:* Towson State University (B.S., 1996); University of Baltimore School of Law (J.D., 2000). Law Clerk to: Hon. E. Allen Sheperd, Circuit Court, Prince Georges County, Maryland, 2000-2001; Hon. Paul E. Alpert, Retired Judge, Specially Assigned, Court of Special Appeals, Maryland, 1998. *Member:* Bar Association of Baltimore City; Maryland State and American Bar Associations; The District of Columbia Bar. ***PRACTICE AREAS:*** Litigation; Insurance Defense. **Email:** rbob@jocs-law.com

OF COUNSEL

JAMES F. JORDAN, born Washington, D.C., February 9, 1933; admitted to bar, 1965, District of Columbia; 1969, U.S. Supreme Court. *Education:* Georgetown University (B.S.S., 1955; J.D., 1962). ***PRACTICE AREAS:*** Alternative Dispute Resolution; Construction Law; Dental Malpractice Defense; Insurance Defense.

JOEL M. SAVITS, born New York, N.Y., August 2, 1935; admitted to bar, 1960, District of Columbia and U.S. Court of Military Appeals; 1963, U.S. Supreme Court; 1965, Maryland; 1971, U.S. District Court, District of Maryland. *Education:* Hobart College (B.A., 1956); Georgetown University (J.D., 1959). Pi Gamma Mu; Phi Alpha Delta. ***PRACTICE AREAS:*** Legal Malpractice Defense; Medical Malpractice Defense; Professional Liability Defense; Alternative Dispute Resolution.

REPRESENTATIVE CLIENTS: American International Group; Budget Rent A Car Systems, Inc.; Charles E. Smith Companies; Chubb Group of Insurance Cos.; The Clark Construction Group, Inc.; CNA Insurance Companies; Crawford & Company; Diplomat Parking; Federated Department Stores, Inc.; Frontier Insurance Co.; GAB Robins North America, Inc.; General Conference of Seventh-Day Adventists; Giant Food, Inc.; Goodyear Tire & Rubber Company; Gould Electronics, Inc.; Guaranty National Insurance Co.; The Harleysville Insurance Companies; Hertz Claim Management Corporation; Howard University Hospital; Interstate Insurance Group; ITT Hartford; Kemper Insurance Companies; Lexington Insurance Co.; MAC Risk Management, Inc.; Manville Personal Injury Settlement Trust; Marriott Corp.; May Department Stores; MedStar Health; Metropolitan Property and Casualty Ins. Co.; Minnesota Mining & Manufacturing; National Food Processors Association; Nationwide Insurance Company; OneSource; Podiatry Insurance Company of America; Ridgewell's; Rollins, Inc.; Royal & Sunalliance; Scottsdale Insurance Co.; Sherwin Williams Company; Sibley Memorial Hospital; Travelers Property Casualty; Washington Adventist Hospital; Washington Hospital Center; Westport Insurance Corporation; Zurich American Insurance Group.

(This Listing Continued)

JORDEN BURT LLP

A Partnership including a Professional Association

Established in 1988

SUITE 400 EAST

1025 THOMAS JEFFERSON STREET, N.W.

WASHINGTON, D.C. 20007-0805

Telephone: 202-965-8100

Telecopier: 202-965-8104

URL: http://www.jordenusa.com

Miami, Florida Office: 777 Brickell Avenue, Suite 500. Telephone: 305-371-2600. Telecopier: 305-372-9928.

Washington, D.C. Affiliated Office: Jones & Blouch L.L.P., 1025 Thomas Jefferson Street, N.W., Suite 405 West, Washington D.C. 20007-0805. Telephone: 202-223-3500. Telecopier: 202-223-4593.

San Francisco Affiliated Office: Fleming & Phillips LLP, 1340 Treat Boulevard, Suite 630, Walnut Creek, California 94596. Telephone: 925-296-2600. Telecopier: 925-296-2626.

General Practice.

(This Listing Continued)

JORDEN BURT LLP, Washington—Continued

FIRM PROFILE: Jorden Burt LLP focuses its practice on the representation of the financial services industry, including insurance companies, banks, mutual funds, investment banks and healthcare entities. The firm represents a broad spectrum of national and international clients in these areas. In addition to these financial institutions, its government relations group also represents universities, publishing and media concerns, and state and local governments.

The firm has demonstrated an outstanding track record of success in litigation, including major national and state class actions. It has acted as lead counsel for numerous large financing transactions and for the registration and regulatory counseling (both domestic and international) for numerous insurance companies, investment advisers, mutual funds, and other issuers and distributors, offering the most experienced counseling and representation in the areas in which it practices. The firm's lawyers are active in relevant professional and industry associations, assuring that they acquire the knowledge and maintain the skills necessary to meet the evolving needs of their clients. The firm is an integrated group of more than seventy professionals, with offices in Washington, D.C. and Miami, Florida and affiliated counsel in San Francisco, California.

JEROME V. BOLKCOM, born Minneapolis, Minnesota, 1959; admitted to bar, 1989, Maryland; 1991, District of Columbia; 1992, U.S. Supreme Court. *Education:* Northern Illinois University (B.A., 1984); University of Iowa (J.D., with high distinction, 1989). Order of the Coif. *Member:* Maryland State (Member, Litigation Section) and American (Member, Litigation, Business Law and Health Law Sections; Chairman, ERISA and Pension Litigation Subcommittee, Business and Corporate Litigation Committee, Business Law Section) Bar Associations. ***PRACTICE AREAS:*** Life Insurance Class Actions; ERISA Litigation; Employee Benefits Counseling; Civil Rights Issues. ***Email:*** jvb@wdc.jordenusa.com

JOAN E. BOROS, born New York, N.Y., 1936; admitted to bar, 1980, Maryland and District of Columbia. *Education:* Vassar College; George Washington University (B.A., 1957); University of Maryland (J.D., with honors, 1980). Order of the Coif. Attorney, Office of the Solicitor, Legislation and Legal Counsel Division, U.S. Department of Labor, 1980-1981. Attorney-Advisor, Division of Investment Management, Securities and Exchange Commission, 1981-1983. Private Practice, 1983—. *Member:* The District of Columbia Bar; Maryland State, Federal and American Bar Associations. ***PRACTICE AREAS:*** Securities Law; Financial Services; Mutual Funds; Insurance Products; Corporate. ***Email:*** jeb@wdc.jordenusa.com

FRANKLIN G. BURT, born Detroit, Michigan, 1948; admitted to bar, 1975, Florida; 1999, District of Columbia. *Education:* University of Michigan (A.B., with distinction, 1971); University of Miami (J.D., 1975). Co-author: Florida Section: 50 State Survey, Libel Defense Resource Center. Author: Florida Section: Open Government Manual, Reporters' Committee for Freedom of the Press. ***REPORTED CASES:*** Fender v. City of Miami, 666 So.2d 596; Miami Heart Institute v. Reis, 638 So.2d 530; Dade County v. Matheson, 605 So.2d 469; Futura Realty v. Lone Star, 578 So.2d 368; Miami Herald v. Morejon, 561 So.2d 577; Boehm v. American Bankers, 557 So.2d 91; Feldman v. Glucroft, 522 So.2d 798; Advisory Opinion to the Governor, 509 So.2d 240; Dade County Schools v. Miami Herald, 443 So.2d 268; Jones v. Miami Herald, 416 So.2d 480; Parsons v. Whittemore v. Dade County,429 So.2d 343; State ex rel v. Boca Raton, 353 So.2d 1194; Linder v. Calero, 963 F.2d 332, 747 F. Supp 1452; Cernuda v. Heavey, 720 F.Supp 1544, NCL Corp. v. Lone Star, 144 B.R. 170; Jordan AVCO Financial Services of Georgia, Inc., 117 F.3d 1254; Taylor v. American Bankers, 700 N.Y.S. 2d 458; Edwards v. Your Credit, 148 F 3d 427; Baron v. Best Buy, 79 F. Supp 2d 1350. ***TRANSACTIONS:*** $3.1 billion hostile takeover of American Bankers Insurance Group Inc., $125 million sale of assets from Lone Star Industries, Inc. to Tarmac Florida, Inc., sale and lease of $60 million cement plant, purchase of several concrete companies and associated properties and plants; purchase and sale of media properties, purchase of quarries, sand and aggregate properties. ***PRACTICE AREAS:*** Litigation; Class Action Defense; First Amendment and Environmental Law; Mergers and Acquisitions. ***Email:*** fgb@jordenusa.com

SHEILA J. CARPENTER, born Kyoto, Japan, 1950; admitted to bar, 1975, Maryland; 1977, District of Columbia. *Education:* Purdue University (B.A., with highest distinction, 1972); Yale Law School (J.D., 1975). Phi Beta Kappa. Co-Author: "Excess, Surplus Lines and Reinsurance: Recent Developments," Tort and Insurance Law Journal, XXVIII, No. 2, 232 (Winter 1993) and XXIX, No. 2, 239 (Winter 1994); "Fed Cir. Holds ABE Insurance Program Does Not Constitute Unrelated Business Income," The Journal of Taxation, 63, No. 4, 244 (October 1985); "Do We Need Trial Specialists?" Litigation, 9, No. 1, 3, (Fall 1982); "Discovery of Electronic Documents," The Brief, 29, No. 4 (Summer 2000). Panelist: ABA National Institute, "The State of Insurance Regulation," 1991; ALI-ABA, "Life Insurance Litigation," 1996, 2001; ABA National Program, "Insurance Insolvency Revisited," 1999. Arbitrator, Superior Court of the District of Columbia Multi-Door Division. Arbitrator/Mediator, American Arbitration Association. *Member:* The District of Columbia Bar; Maryland and American (Chair, Excess, Surplus Lines and Reinsurance Committee, Tort and Insurance Practice Section, 1995-1996; Vice Chair, Public Regulation of Insurance Committee, 1996—; Member, Litigation Section) Bar Associations; Defense Research Institute (Web Chair, Life, Health & Disability Insurance Committee, 2000—). ***PRACTICE AREAS:*** Litigation; Arbitration; Insurance. ***Email:*** sjc@wdc.jordenusa.com

(This Listing Continued)

JOSEPHINE CICCHETTI, born Hartford, Connecticut, 1955; admitted to bar, 1980, District of Columbia; 1984, Florida. *Education:* St. Joseph College (B.A., 1977) Trustee Scholar; Georgetown University (J.D., 1980). Associate Editor, The American Criminal Law Review, 1980. (Also at Miami, Florida Office). ***PRACTICE AREAS:*** Corporate; Securities; Insurance Regulatory; Insurance Products; Mergers and Acquisitions. ***Email:*** jc@wdc.jordenusa.com

RAUL A. CUERVO, born Havana, Cuba, 1954; admitted to bar, 1985, Florida; 1986, U.S. District Court, Southern and Middle Districts of Florida and Southern District of Florida Trial Bar; 1987, U.S. Court of Appeals, Eleventh Circuit 1996, U.S. District Court, Northern District of Florida; 1998, U.S. Court of Appeals, Fifth Circuit; 1999, District of Columbia. *Education:* University of Florida (B.A., 1982; J.D., 1985). Editor, University of Florida Law Review, Fall, 1984. Co-Author: "Fundamentals of Bankruptcy Law and Procedure in Florida," published by National Business Institute, Inc., 1997. Author: "The Role of the Judiciary in Class Actions," published by the Life Insurance Law Committee of the American Bar Association, 1998. Co-Author: "Florida Foreclosure and Repossession," published by National Business Institute, Inc., 1999. Panel Member, Florida Foster Care Review Project, 1993-1997. *Member:* Dade County Bar Association; The Florida Bar; South Florida Bankruptcy Bar Association. [With U.S. Army, 1976-1980]. ***LANGUAGES:*** Spanish. ***PRACTICE AREAS:*** Commercial Insurance Litigation; Insurance Regulation; Bankruptcy; Workouts. ***Email:*** rac@jordenusa.com

PAUL A. FISCHER, born Philadelphia, Pennsylvania, 1950; admitted to bar, 1974, Pennsylvania; 1980, District of Columbia. *Education:* University of Pennsylvania (B.S., magna cum laude, 1971; J.D., 1974). Beta Gamma Sigma; Alpha Kappa Psi. Assistant Director, 1980-1986 and Branch Chief, 1978-1980, Division of Enforcement, Securities and Exchange Commission. *Member:* The District of Columbia Bar; Pennsylvania and American (Member, Sections on Litigation; Corporation, Banking and Business Law) Bar Associations; Securities Industry Association (Member, Compliance and Legal Division). ***PRACTICE AREAS:*** SEC, NASD and NYSE Enforcement; Securities; Securities Litigation; Insurance Litigation. ***Email:*** paf@wdc.jordenusa.com

ANN BEGAN FURMAN, born Long Beach, California, 1956; admitted to bar, 1987, California; 1988, District of Columbia; 1991, U.S. Supreme Court. *Education:* University of California, Berkeley (B.S., with honors, 1978); Georgetown University Law Center (J.D., 1987). Member, Journal of Law and Policy in International Business, 1985-1987. Contributor: "ERISA Discrimination Claims and Related Federal Statutory Claims," *Handbook on ERISA Litigation,* Aspen Law & Business, (2d ed. 1997); "Life Insurance and Annuity Developments," *Investment Lawyer,* Aspen Law & Business, 1994—. *Member:* State Bar of California; The District of Columbia Bar; American Bar Association (Member, Sections on Tort and Insurance Practice and Business Law). ***PRACTICE AREAS:*** Securities Law; Mutual Funds; Insurance Products; Investment Management. ***Email:*** abf@wdc.jordenusa.com

STEVE GOLDBERG, born Hartford, Connecticut, 1946; admitted to bar, 1972, Connecticut; 1999, District of Columbia. *Education:* Clark University (B.A., 1969); University of Connecticut School of Law (J.D., with high honors, 1972). Notes Editor, University of Connecticut Law Review, 1971-1972. Vice President and Counsel, Aetna Life & Casualty, 1987-1991. Co-author: "The Case for the Nonapplicaiton of ERISA to Insurer's General Account Assets," XXI Tort and Insurance Law Journal (1984); "Handbook on ERISA Litigation," Prentice Hall Law & Business, January 1993. *Member:* American Bar Association (Member, Sections of: Business Law, Tort and Insurance Practice). ***PRACTICE AREAS:*** Insurance Law; ERISA Litigation; Corporation Law; Securities Law. ***Email:*** shg@wdc.jordenusa.com

ROLAND C. GOSS, born Evanston, Illinois, 1953; admitted to bar, 1978, Florida; 1980, Illinois, U.S. District Court, Middle District of Florida and U.S. District Court, Southern District of Florida including Trial Bar; 1981, U.S. Court of Appeals, Eleventh Circuit; U.S. Court of Appeals, Fourth Circuit; 1984, U.S. Claims Court; 1998, District of Columbia. *Education:* Michigan State University (B.A., with high honors, 1975); Northwestern University (J.D., cum laude, 1978). Phi Kappa Phi; Order of the Coif. *Member:* The Florida Bar; American Bar Association. ***PRACTICE AREAS:*** Class Action Litigation; Insurance Coverage Litigation; Environmental Litigation. ***Email:*** rcg@wdc.jordenusa.com

WAYNE K. JOHNSON, born Logan, Utah, 1945; admitted to bar, 1969, California; 1972, District of Columbia. *Education:* University of California at Berkeley (A.B., 1965; J.D., 1968). *Member:* The District of Columbia Bar; State Bar of California; American Bar Association. ***PRACTICE AREAS:*** Tax; Corporate Securities; ERISA; Insurance. ***Email:*** wkj@wdc.jordenusa.com

(This Listing Continued)

JAMES F. JORDEN, born Sewickley, Pennsylvania, 1941; admitted to bar, 1966, Virginia; 1968, District of Columbia; 1982, Florida. *Education:* Dickinson College (B.A., 1963); George Washington University (LL.B., 1966). Research Editor, George Washington Law Review, 1965-1966. Author: "'Paying Up' For Research: A Regulatory and Legislative Analysis," Duke Law Journal 1103, 1975; "Special Insurance Company Problems in the Marketing and Administration of Pension and Health and Welfare Plans," The Forum, XI, No. 4, 1054, Summer 1976; "Federal Fraud and State Law Fiduciary Duties - A Tour of The Circuits Reveals Continuing Confusion," Idaho Law Review, Spring, 1983. Co-Author: "Section 22 (d) of The Investment Company Act of 1940 - Its Original Purpose and Present Function," Duke Law Journal 975, 1973; "An Appraisal of Disclosure Requirements in Contest For Control Under The Williams Act," 46 George Washington Law Review 817, 1980; "Handbook on ERISA Litigation," Prentice Hall Law & Business, January 1993. Co-Chairman, ALI/ABA Conference on Securities, Tax and ERISA Issues Affecting Insurance Companies, Fall 1983-1999. Chairman, ALI/ABA Conference on Life Insurance Litigation, Spring, 1996-2001. Co-Chairman, Practicing Law Institute Seminar, Insurance Companies and The Federal Securities Laws, 1979. Panelist: Practicing Law Institute Seminars, Representing the Issuer in Venture Capital Financing, 1980-1981; Non-Federal Class Actions, 1999-2001; Investment Company Institute Annual Mutual Funds and Investment Management Conference, 1977, 1979, 1980, 1981, 1982, 1996; Class Action Litigation Panel, Annual Meeting, CCIA, 1996; Developments in ERISA Litigation, Annual Meeting, National Organization of Life and Health Guarantee Association, 1994, 1995; ERISA and Securities Litigation Update, ABA Tips Sect ion, 1995. *Member:* District of Columbia Bar (Chairman, Division of Corporation, Finance and Securities Law, 1974-1978); American Bar Association (Chairman, Committee on Employee Benefits, Tort and Insurance Practice Section, 1978-1980; 1985-1987; Member: Federal Securities Law Committee, 1976—; Chairman, Sub-Committee on Securities Activities of Insurance Companies, 1983—; Member, Business Litigation Committee; Chairman, Sub-Committee on ERISA Litigation); The American Law Institute; American Bar Foundation. ***PRACTICE AREAS:*** Insurance and Securities Industry; Litigation; Corporate and Pension Litigation; Corporate Financing; Securities Law. **Email:** jfj@jordenusa.com

STEPHEN W. KRAUS, born Brooklyn, New York, 1942; admitted to bar, 1968, District of Columbia. *Education:* Brooklyn College (B.S., 1964); George Washington University (J.D., 1967); Georgetown University (LL.M., Taxation). Order of the Coif. George Washington University Law Review. *Member:* The District of Columbia Bar; American Bar Association (Member, Tort and Insurance Law Section, 1968—); Association of Life Insurance Council. ***PRACTICE AREAS:*** Pension Plans; Employee Benefits; Insurance. **Email:** swk@wdc.jordenusa.com

THOMAS F. MORANTE, born New York, N.Y., 1951; admitted to bar, 1977, Virginia; 1979, District of Columbia; 1981, Florida. *Education:* Union College, N.Y. (B.A., magna cum laude, Phi Beta Kappa, 1973); American University, Washington College of Law (J.D., 1977); Georgetown University (LL.M., 1980). Mexican Legal Studies Program, University of Houston Bates College of Law, Mexico, 1976. Assistant Editor: "A Lawyer's Guide to International Business Transactions," Volumes II, III and IV, ALI/ABA, 1978, 1980. Author: "Elimination of Nontariff Barriers to Trade in Services: Recommendations for Future Negotiations," Law & Policy in International Business, Georgetown University Law Center, Spring, 1982. Moderator, Regulatory "Spotlight Reports" Panel, *Latin America Insurance Roundtable,* organized by the International Insurance Council (IIC), New York City, February 1998. Chaired, *Latin American Insurance:* Regional Strategies for Life, P/C & Reinsurance Markets Conference, Miami, March 1998. Delivered a speech at the *International Life Insurance and Pension Symposium,* sponsored by the American Council of Life Insurers (ACLI), October 1998. Participant in "The International Insurance Market" Panel at the *ACLI Annual Meeting* (Legal Section), November 1998. Participant in "Regulatory Development: Life Insurance in Latin America," *Miami Insurance Rendezvous,* sponsored by the IIC, January 1999. Delivered a speech on "Regulatory Developments: Life Insurance and Pensions in Latin America," at the *Latin America Insurance Roundtable,* sponsored by the IIC, February 1999. Delivered a speech on "Recent Regulatory Changes," *Growth Strategies for life, P/C & Reinsurance Markets, Regulatory Developments:* Life Insurance and Pensions in Latin America Conference, Miami, sponsored by the world Research Group, April 1999. Moderated Program on "Mergers and Acquisitions in Latin America," co-sponsored by the Latin American Law Subcommittee, Business Law Section, American Bar Association (ABA), *ABA Annual Meeting,* Atlanta, GA, August 1999. Delivered a speech on "Foreign Regulatory Compliance," at the IBC's 2nd *Offshore Life and Annuities Forum* in Nassau, Bahamas, October 1999. Delivered a speech on "Selling Offshore Life & Annuities to U.S. Citizens and Non-U.S. Citizens -- Understanding the Models and the Methods," at the IIR's *Offshore life Insurance & Annuities Conference,* in New York City, November 1999. Delivered a speech on "Argentina's Proposed Regularization Law with respect to Offshore Insurance," at the ACLI *ICC Meeting,* Washington, D.C., May 2000. Delivered a speech on "Offshore Sales, Opportunities and Risks," at the LIMRA *International Quality Business and Compliance Conference,* San Antonio, Texas, June 2000. Moderated a

(This Listing Continued)

Panel and spoke on "Latin America: Coping with and Evolving Regulatory Environment," at the IBC *International Life & Annuities Forum,* Bermuda, June 2000. Delivered a speech on Financial Services Convergence in Latin America, at a Program presented by the Committee on International Business Law, entitled "Bancassurance: Lessons from Abroad," Annual Meeting, New York, July 2000. Delivered a speech on "Latin American Regulatory Highlights," at the Legal Section Program - International Section at the *ACLI Annual Meeting,* Seattle, Washington, November 2000. Chaired a Program on "Cross Border Finance in Latin America," presented by the Latin American Law Subcommittee, International Business Law Committee, ABA, at the mid-year meeting, Business Law Section, ABA, Philadelphia, March 2001. Chaired the Panel on "Bancassurance," and spoke on "Latin America Pension Reform," at the World Research Group-Latin American Insurance Conference, Miami Beach, FL, March 2001. *Member:* The Florida Bar (Member: International Law Section; Business Law Section; Health Law Section); District of Columbia Bar; Virginia State Bar; American Bar Association (Member: Section of Business Law; Committee on International Business Law; Co-Chairman: Latin American Law Subcommittee; Federal Regulations of Securities Committee); Inter-American Bar Association (Vice President, Committee I, Public and Private International Law). (Also at Miami, Florida Office). ***LANGUAGES:*** Spanish. ***PRACTICE AREAS:*** International Financial Services; Securities; Corporate; Insurance Regulation; Insurance Products; International Finance; Offshore Corporations. **Email:** tfm@jordenusa.com

CHRISTOPHER S. PETITO, born Trenton, New Jersey, 1955; admitted to bar, 1982, New York; 1995, District of Columbia. *Education:* Yale College (B.A., cum laude, 1977); Yale Law School (J.D., 1981). Assistant Regional Administrator, Enforcement, NorthEast Regional Office, Securities and Exchange Commission. *Member:* District of Columbia Bar; American Bar Association. ***PRACTICE AREAS:*** Securities Law; Insurance; Securities Regulation. **Email:** csp@wdc.jordenusa.com

WALDEMAR J. PFLEPSEN, JR., born Buffalo, New York, 1951; admitted to bar, 1977, Michigan; 1979, District of Columbia. *Education:* Michigan State University (B.A., 1973); American University (J.D ., 1976). Law Clerk to the Honorable Patricia J. Boyle, 1978-1979, Honorable Lawrence Gubow, 1977-1978, U.S. District Court, Eastern District of Michigan. Co-Author: "Handbook on ERISA Litigation," Aspen Law and Business (formerly Prentice Hall) (1992 and 1994; 2d ed. 1997). Author: "Market Conduct Annuity Litigation," ALI-ABA (1999); "ERISA Fiduciary Issues for Insurers in the Handling of Employee Benefits Plan Claims," 30 Tort & Insurance Law Journal 895 (Summer 1995); "Recent Developments in ERISA Pension Litigation Against Insurers: Trends in Fiduciary, Non-Fiduciary and Co-Fiduciary Liability," 27 Tort and Insurance Law Journal 65 (Fall 1991). *Member:* The District of Columbia Bar; State Bar of Michigan; American Bar Association (Member: Section of Litigation; Tort and Insurance Practice Section, Task Force on Class Action Litigation, 1998-1999, Corporate Counsel Committee, Chair, 1997-1998, Vice Chair, 1992-1996, Employee Benefits Law, Vice Chair, 1999—; Section of Business Law, Committee on Business and Corporate Litigation). ***PRACTICE AREAS:*** Litigation; Insurance and Securities; ERISA. **Email:** wjp@wdc.jordenusa.com

KEITH J. RUDOLF, born Neenah, Wisconsin, 1951; admitted to bar, 1979, Illinois and U.S. District Court, Northern District of Illinois; practices under the supervision of principals of the firm (Not admitted in District of Columbia). *Education:* Coe College (B.A., with honors, 1974); Northwestern University (M.M., 1979; J.D., summa cum laude, 1979; M.B.A., with distinction, 1979). Omicron Delta Epsilon. Beta Gamma Sigma. Order of the Coif. President, 1992-1994 and Chairman, 1995, Investment Counsel Association of America. Chair, Investment Adviser Committee, Investment Company Institute, 1987-1992. *Member:* American Bar Association (Deputy Chair, 1987-1988 and Chair, 1989, Subcommittee on Investment Companies and Regulation of Securities Committee, Business Law Section). ***PRACTICE AREAS:*** Investment Management; Securities; Corporate. **Email:** kjr@jordenusa.com

PHILLIP E. STANO, born Birmingham, Alabama, 1953; admitted to bar, 1978, Alabama; 1983, U. S. Supreme Court; 1988, District of Columbia. *Education:* University of Alabama at Birmingham (B.A., 1975); University of Alabama (J. D., 1978). Articles Editor, Law and Psychology Review, 1977-1978. Assistant Attorney General and General Counsel, Alabama Insurance Department, 1980-1986. Chief Litigation Counsel, American Council Life Insurers, 1986-1999. Selected Publications: Co-Author, "Class Action Litigation: Are There Any Limits?" Association of Life Insurance Counsel Proceedings (2000). Author: "Recognizing Insurers' Privileged Information (The Rationale and the Results)," 17 J.Ins. Reg. 268 (1999); "Addressing Class Action Vanishing Premium Litigation," Association of Life Insurance Counsel Proceedings (1996); "Confronting a Market Conduct Examination in a Class Action Environment," ABA Tort and Insurance Practices Section Annual Meeting (1996); "Recent Developments in Life and Health Insurance Fraud Legislation in the U.S.," AIDA Colloquium (Prague, The Czech Republic, 1996); "Punitive Damages After *Pacific Mutual Life Ins. Co. v. Haslip,* the Search for the Magic Bullet," Association of Life Insurance Counsel Proceedings (1993-1994). Co-Author: "A Discussion of Insurers' Vicarious Liability for Agents Wrongdoing," 6 Nat'l Ins.Law.Rev. 809 (1992); "AIDS and Life Insurance," AIDS and the Law

(This Listing Continued)

JORDEN BURT LLP, Washington—Continued

(Wiley & Sons, Inc., New York, 2d ed. 1992). Author: "Trifling with the Risk Classification System: A Risky Business," 9 J.Ins.Reg. 544 (1991); "Punitive Damages: Mutiny Over the Bounty," 8 J.Ins.Reg. 4 (1989). Primary Author: "AIDS-Related Testing of Insurance Applicants: Fear vs. Fairness," 5 J.Ins.Reg. 314 (1987). ***PRACTICE AREAS:*** Class Action Litigation; Insurance Law; Regulatory Law. ***Email:*** pes@wdc.jordenusa.com

WILLIAM RANDOLPH THOMPSON, born Oak Hill, West Virginia, 1946; admitted to bar, 1974, Virginia; 1975, District of Columbia. *Education:* Harvard University (A.B., magna cum laude, 1968); Georgetown University (J.D., 1974). Author: "Status of Variable Products Under the Securities Act of 1933," Regulation and Distribution of Variable Insurance Products, Aspen (1999); "A Variable Life Insurance Primer," Journal of Asset Protection (1995); "Getting a Piece of the Variable Life Insurance Action," World Fund Industry, Gestion Collective Internationale, (Feb. 1995). Attorney, U.S. Securities and Exchange Commission, Division of Investment Management, 1976-1978. Chief, Office of Insurance Products and Legal Compliance, 1984-1988; Special Counsel, Office of Investment Company Regulation, 1980-1984. (Also Of Counsel to Jones & Blouch L.L.P.). ***PRACTICE AREAS:*** Securities Law; Mutual Funds; Insurance Products. ***Email:*** wrt@wdc.jordenusa.com

---

MARIE C. BAKER, born Indianapolis, Indiana, 1958; admitted to bar, 2001, New York; practices under the supervision of principals of the firm (Not admitted in District of Columbia). *Education:* University of Maryland (B.A., 1993); American University, Washington College of Law (J.D., 2000). ***PRACTICE AREAS:*** Securities Law; Financial Services; Mutual Funds; Insurance Products; Corporate. ***Email:*** mcb@wdc.jordenusa.com

AUDREY CHENG, born New York, N.Y., 1975; (admission pending). *Education:* University of California, Irvine (B.A., cum laude, 1998); George Washington University (J.D., 2001). ***LANGUAGES:*** Cinese and Taiwanese. ***PRACTICE AREAS:*** Securities; Financial Services; Insurance Products; Mutual Funds; Corporate; Business. ***Email:*** alc@wdc.jordenusa.com

JASON H. GOULD, born New York, N.Y., 1970; admitted to bar, 1996, New York; 1997, District of Columbia. *Education:* Georgetown University (B.A., magna cum laude, 1992; J.D., 1995). *Member:* New York State and American (Member, Sections on: Litigation; Tort and Insurance Practice; Environmental and National Resources) Bar Associations; New York County Lawyers Association. ***PRACTICE AREAS:*** Litigation; General Practice; Insurance Law. ***Email:*** jhg@wdc.jordenusa.com

MICHAEL C. KENTOFF, born Chicago, Illinois, 1964; admitted to bar, 1996, Maryland; 1998, District of Columbia. *Education:* American University (B.A., 1986); Washington College of Law (J.D., 1996). ***PRACTICE AREAS:*** Commercial Litigation; Insurance Law; Products Liability. ***Email:*** mck@wdc.jordenusa.com

WILLIAM GLENN MERTEN, born Summit, New Jersey, 1972; admitted to bar, 1997, Maryland; 2000, District of Columbia. *Education:* University of Richmond (B.A., 1994); George Washington University (J.D., 1997). ***PRACTICE AREAS:*** Litigation; Insurance Law; Labor and Employment Law. ***Email:*** wgm@wdc.jordenusa.com

MIN SUN OH, born Laurel, Maryland, 1965; admitted to bar, 1996, Maryland; 1998, District of Columbia. *Education:* Lehigh University (B.S., 1987); Catholic University of America (J.D., 1995); Georgetown University Law Center (LL.M. in Securities and Financial Regulation, 1999). ***PRACTICE AREAS:*** Securities Law; Mutual Funds; Insurance Products. ***Email:*** mso@wdc.jordenusa.com

SHAUNDA A. PATTERSON, born Philadelphia, Pennsylvania, 1974; admitted to bar, 1998, New Jersey, Maryland and U.S. District Court, District o f New Jersey; 1999, U.S. District Court, District of Maryland; 2000, District of Columbia. *Education:* Hampton University (B.A., 1995); George Washington University Law School (J.D., 1998). *Member:* Bar Association of the District of Columbia; Maryland State Bar Association; American Bar Association (Member, Sections on: Litigation; Tort and Insurance Practice); Defense Research Institute (Member, Committees on: Insurance Law; Life, Health and Disability; Trial Tactics and Techniques). ***PRACTICE AREAS:*** Litigation; Insurance; Civil Practice. ***Email:*** sap@wdc.jordenusa.com

ASSOCIATES

KRISTIN SHEPARD, born San Diego, California, 1975; admitted to bar, 2000, Missouri; 2001, District of Columbia. *Education:* Washington University (B.A., summa cum laude, History and German, 1997; J.D., 2000). Phi Beta Kappa. Semi-Finalist, Wiley Rutledge Moot Court. Finalist, American Bar Association Negotiation Competition. Recipient; Judge Ruby Helen Endowed Merit Scholarship; Honor Scholar Award. Associate Editor, Journal of Law and Policy. ***PRACTICE AREAS:*** Litigation; Insurance. ***Email:*** kas@wdc.jordenusa.com

BENJAMIN L. TOMPKINS, born Springfield, Missouri, 1974; admitted to bar, 2000, Missouri; 2001, Kansas; practices under the supervision of principals of the firm (Not admitted in District of Columbia). *Education:* Pepperdine University (B.A., cum laude, 1997); George Washington University (J.D., with honors, 2000). Order of the Coif. Member, 1998-1999 and Notes Editor, 1999-2000, The George Washington University Law Review. Law Clerk to the Honorable Stephen H. Glickman, D.C. Court of Appeals, 2000-2001. *Member:* Kansas and American Bar Associations; The Missouri Bar. ***PRACTICE AREAS:*** Litigation. ***Email:*** blt@wdc.jordenusa.com

DAVID WHITE, born Palm Beach, 1964; admitted to bar, 1997, South Carolina; 1998, District of Columbia. *Education:* University of North Carolina (B.A., 1986); Washington & Lee University (J.D., 1991). Moot Court Semi Finalist. Moot Court Judge Research Assistant. Dean's List. Recipient, American Jurisprudence Awards. Author: "Disorder in the Court: Annual Survey of Bankruptcy Law, Washington & Lee Law Review. *Member:* South Carolina Bar; The District of Columbia Bar; Federalist Society. ***PRACTICE AREAS:*** Commercial Litigation; Appellate Practice; Federal Jurisdiction; Labor and Employment. ***Email:*** dw@wdc.jordenusa.com

OF COUNSEL

DENISE A. FEE, born Washington, D.C., 1955; admitted to bar, 1990, Maryland; 1991, District of Columbia. *Education:* University of Maryland (B.S., 1977); Catholic University of America (J.D., 1990). ***PRACTICE AREAS:*** Class Action Defense Litigation; General Civil Litigation. ***Email:*** daf@wdc.jordenusa.com

RICHARD KARPINSKI, born 1957; admitted to bar, 1985, Maryland, District of Columbia and U.S. District Court, District of Columbia; 1992, U.S. District Court, District of Maryland. *Education:* University of Maryland (B.A., 1980); Catholic University of America (J.D., 1984). ***PRACTICE AREAS:*** Litigation; Insurance Law; Aviation. ***Email:*** rjk@wdc.jordenusa.com

MARILYN A. SPONZO, born Hartford, Connecticut, 1953; admitted to bar, 1987, Massachusetts (Not admitted in District of Columbia). *Education:* Smith College (B.A., cum laude, 1975); University of Connecticut (J.D., 1987). Recipient, American Jurisprudence Award in Trial Practice. *Member:* American Bar Association. ***PRACTICE AREAS:*** Insurance; Securities. ***Email:*** mas@wdc.jordenusa.com

LEGAL SUPPORT PERSONNEL

SENIOR GOVERNMENT RELATIONS PERSONNEL

MARILYN B. THOMPSON, born Union County, New Jersey, 1946. *Education:* Syracuse University (B.A. Political Science/International Relations, 1968); Graduate Course Work, Rutgers University, Eagleton Institute and New School, New York City. Director of Federal Policy and Governor's Washington Office, State of New Jersey, 1974-1982. Served as a Consultant on White House Staff to Develop the Carter Urban Policy, 1979. Staff Director, National Democratic Governors' Association. Associate Director, Coalition of Northeastern Governors. Co-founder of government relations consulting firm, Meara, Byrne and Thompson, Representing Life Insurance, Savings Industry, University, Medical School and Local Government clients. Senior Vice President, The Keefe Company. Principal, Heron, Burchette, Ruckert and Rothwell; Burchette and Associates. Member: American Association of Universities Council on Federal Relations; National Association of State Universities and Land Grant Colleges Research Leadership Group; American Council on Education Federal Relations Coalition; Committee on Education Funding; Research Universities Network, National League of Cities and the U.S. Conference of Mayors. Represents Major National Research Universities, Medical Schools, Hospitals and Major Cities and Local Government Interests. Specializes in Appropriations, Tax, Budget, Economic Development and Financial Institution Legislation. (Firm Principal, Government Relations Department Head). ***Email:*** mbt@wdc.jordenusa.com

REPRESENTATIVE CLIENTS: Aegon; Aetna Life & Casualty; Ahold USA, Inc.; AIG; Alexander Hamilton Life; Allianz Life Insurance Company; Allmerica; American General Life Insurance Company; Assurant Group; American Council of Life Insurance; Banc One Corporation; Barry University; CIGNA Corporation; Citicorp; Clarica; The Conseco Group; Federal Public Defenders Office; Fortis, Inc.; Franklin Resources, Inc.; Fraternal Order of Police; GE Capital; Giant Food, Inc.; Goldman, Sachs & Co.; Great-West Life Assurance Company; Hartford Life Insurance Company; The ING Group; Jackson National Life Insurance Company; Jefferson Pilot Financial; Kemper Life; Keyport Life Insurance Company; Liberty Life Assurance Company; Life USA; Lutheran Brotherhood; Manufacturers Life; Massachusetts Mutual Life Insurance Co.; Mathias Rath, Inc.; Merrill Lynch & Co., Inc.; City of Miami Beach; Minnesota Life Insurance Company; National Organization of Life and Health Insurance Guaranty Associations; Pacific Life Insurance Company; Pan American Life Insurance Company; Pacific Life Insurance Company; Phoenix Home Life Insurance Company; Police Benevolent Association; Reliastar; Security Life of Denver; Southern Farm Bureau Life Insurance Company; SunAmerica Inc.; Sun Life of Canada; Transamerica Life Insurance Company; University of Miami; Standard Management Corporation; The Voyager Companies; Woodmen Accident and Life Company; Zurich Life.

(For complete biographical data on other personnel, see Professional Biographies in Miami, Florida).

(This Listing Continued)

JOSEPH, McDERMOTT & REINER, P.C.

Established in 1927

1050 SEVENTEENTH STREET, N.W., SUITE 700
WASHINGTON, D.C. 20036
Telephone: 202-331-1955
Facsimile: 202-293-2309

Taxation, Corporations, Real Estate, Estate Planning, Trusts, Probate, Litigation, Aviation, Administrative Law, Adoption, International Law and Domestic Relations.

ALLEN T. JOSEPH, born Brooklyn, New York, July 1, 1941; admitted to bar, 1967, District of Columbia. *Education:* Wharton School of Finance, University of Pennsylvania (B.S. in Econ., 1963); Georgetown University (J.D., 1966; LL.M., in Taxation, 1969). Treasurer, National Prostate Cancer Coalition, 1996-1997. *Member:* The District of Columbia Bar; American Bar Association (Member, Sections on: Taxation; Corporation, Banking and Business Law); Washington, D.C. Estate Planning Council. ***PRACTICE AREAS:*** Corporate Law; Tax Law; Estate Planning Law; Trust Administration; Estate Administration.

MARK T. McDERMOTT, born Indianapolis, Indiana, March 11, 1948; admitted to bar, 1974, Indiana; 1975, District of Columbia; 1978, California; 1980, Virginia; 1982, Maryland. *Education:* Indiana University (B.S., 1970; J.D., cum laude, 1974). Note and Development Editor, Indiana Law Review, 1973-1974. Author: "Pilot Medical Certification—Procedures and Recent Developments," 51 Journal of Air Law & Commerce 119, 1985; "Mandatory Random Drug Testing in the United States Department of Transportation-A Fourth Amendment Analysis," 17 Transportation Law Journal 1, 1988; "Agency versus Independent Adoption: The Case for Independent Adoption," 3 The Future of Children 146, 1993. Trial Attorney, Federal Aviation Administration, 1974-1978. President, American Academy of Adoption Attorneys, 1991-1992. Member, Maryland Governor's Commission on Adoption, 1995. Member of Board of Directors, Families for Private Adoption, 1988—. *Member:* Federal (Member, Air and Space Transportation Law Committee, 1978—) and American (Member, Forum Committee on Air and Space Law, 1983—) Bar Associations; Lawyer-Pilots Bar Association; National Transportation Safety Board Bar Association (President, 1984-1987; Vice President, 1987—). ***REPORTED CASES:*** Witter v. Delta Air Lines, Inc., 138 F.3d 1366 (11th Cir. 1998); Robinson v. NTSB, 28 F.3d 210 (DC Cir. 1994); Heller v. US, 803 F.2d 1558 (11th Cir. 1987); Schwartz v. Helms, 712 F. 2d 633 (DC Cir. 1983); Harr v. US, 705 F.2d 500 (DC Cir. 1983); McHenry v. Bond, 668 F. 2d 1185 (11th Cir. 1982). ***PRACTICE AREAS:*** Litigation; Aviation Law; Adoption Law. ***Email:*** mcdermott@jmr-law.com

ROBERT M. REINER, born New York, N.Y., February 1, 1952; admitted to bar, 1976, Virginia; 1977, District of Columbia; 1985, Maryland. *Education:* Wharton School, University of Pennsylvania (B.S., in Economics, 1973); George Washington University (J.D., with honors, 1976); Georgetown University (LL.M., in Taxation, 1979). *Member:* The District of Columbia Bar; Virginia State Bar; Virginia, Maryland State and American (Member, Sections on: Taxation, Real Property, Probate and Trust Law) Bar Associations; Washington D.C. Estate Planning Council. ***PRACTICE AREAS:*** Tax Law; Estate Planning; Estate Administration; Closely Held Corporations. ***Email:*** reiner@jmr-law.com

PETER J. WIERNICKI, born Washington, D.C., July 12, 1961; admitted to bar, 1987, Maryland; 1990, U.S. Court of Military Appeals and U.S. Court of Appeals, District of Columbia Circuit Fifth Circuit and Eleventh Circuit; 1991, Virginia; 1996, District of Columbia. *Education:* Bucknell University (B.A., 1983); University of Baltimore (J.D., 1987). Member, Moot Court Team. National Finalist, 1985 ABA National Appellate Advocacy Competition. *Member:* Maryland State, Virginia State, Federal and American Bar Associations; National Transportation Safety Board Bar Association (Treasurer, 1996—); American Academy of Adoption Attorneys. [Lieut., USNR, 1986-1990]. ***PRACTICE AREAS:*** Litigation; Aviation Law; Adoption Law; Assisted Reproductive Technologies; Education Law; Guardianship. ***Email:*** pjw@jmr-law.com

---

BRIAN B. SCHIMMING, born South Bend, Indiana, August 23, 1966; admitted to bar, 1992, Maryland; 1994, District of Columbia. *Education:* University of Maryland (B.S., 1988); George Washington University (J.D., 1992). *Member:* Maryland State and American Bar Associations. ***PRACTICE AREAS:*** Trusts and Estates; Tax Law; Corporate Law. ***Email:*** bschimming@jmr-law.com

KAHN AND KAHN

Established in 1936

1730 RHODE ISLAND AVENUE, N.W.
SUITE 810
WASHINGTON, D.C. 20036
Telephone: 202-887-0037
Fax: 202-833-1219
Email: jkahn@erols.com
URL: http://www.lawyers.com/transportation

Transportation Regulation and Administrative Law. Immigration, Customs and Business Law related to Transportation Law.

FIRM PROFILE: For over 65 years, the firm has represented clients ranging from one vehicle operators to publicly traded transportation companies throughout the United States and Canada.

MEMBERS OF FIRM

S. HARRISON KAHN (1911-1980).

JEREMY KAHN, born Washington, D.C., May 14, 1948; admitted to bar, 1974, Virginia and District of Columbia. *Education:* University of Virginia (B.A., with distinction, 1970; J.D., 1974). *Member:* District of Columbia Bar; Virginia State Bar; American Bar Association; Transportation Lawyers Association (Member, Executive Committee, 1988-1990); Canadian Transport Lawyers Association (Non-resident Director, 1990-1992; 1999-2001). ***Email:*** jkahn@erols.com

---

KALBIAN HAGERTY LLP

2001 L STREET NW, SUITE 600
WASHINGTON, D.C. 20036
Telephone: 202-223-5600
Fax: 202-223-6625
URL: http://www.kalbianhagerty.com

General Civil Litigation Practice before all Federal and State Courts, Administrative and Governmental Agencies. Tax Law, Business, Commercial, Corporate, International, Real Estate, Technology, and Venture Capital.

PARTNERS

HAIG V. KALBIAN, born November 19, 1956; admitted to bar, 1985, Pennsylvania; 1986, District of Columbia; 1990, Virginia. *Education:* University of Richmond (B.A., 1979); University of Notre Dame (J.D., 1983). Phi Beta Kappa. Principal, Haig V. Kalbian and Associates, Washington, D.C., 1990. *Member:* Pennsylvania and Virginia Bar Associations; Virginia State Bar. ***LANGUAGES:*** Arabic and French. ***PRACTICE AREAS:*** Commercial Litigation; Personal Injury. ***Email:*** hkalbian@kalbianhagerty.com

JAMES R. HAGERTY, born Quantico, Virginia, September 17, 1957; admitted to bar, 1986, Maryland; 1987, District of Columbia; 1988, U.S. District Court for the District of Columbia; 1992, U.S. Tax Court; 1994, U.S. Supreme Court. *Education:* American University (B.A., 1982); Southwestern University (J.D., 1986); Georgetown University (LL.M., Taxation, 1994). *Member:* Maryland State and American (Chair, Tax, Revenue and Treasury Committee; Member, Administrative Law Section) Bar Associations; District of Columbia Bar;. ***PRACTICE AREAS:*** Federal, State and International Taxation; Corporate Law; Business Law; Exempt Organizations; Government Relations. ***Email:*** jhagerty@kalbianhagerty.com

OF COUNSEL

MARY M. BAKER, born Boston, Massachusetts, December 29, 1964; admitted to bar, 1990, Georgia; 1995, Virginia; 1998, District of Columbia. *Education:* Clemson University (B.A., summa cum laude, 1987) Georgetown University (J.D., cum laude, 1990). Phi Kappa Phi; Pi Sigma Alpha (President, 1986-1987); Blue Key; Phi Alpha Delta; Omicron Delta Kappa (Treasurer, 1986-1987). Recipient, John Engalitcheff Outstanding Young American Award. Staff Member, 1988-1989 and Notes and Comments Editor, 1989-1990, The Journal of Law and Technology. ***PRACTICE AREAS:*** Litigation. ***Email:*** mmb@kalbianhagerty.com

JASON GREEN, born Cleveland, Ohio, August 27, 1943; admitted to bar, 1969, Ohio; 1972, District of Columbia; 1991, Maryland. *Education:* Miami University (B.S., 1965); Cleveland State University (J.D., 1969). Lecturer, Bankruptcy Practice, U.S. Department of Justice, Advocacy Institute, 1987-1991. ***SPECIAL AGENCIES:*** Internal Revenue Service and U.S. Department of Justice. ***PRACTICE AREAS:*** Bankruptcy; Probate; Bankruptcy Litigation; Probate Litigation. ***Email:*** jgreen@kalbianhagerty.com

K. THOMAS SHAHRIARI, born Tehran, Iran, March 24, 1957; admitted to bar, 1983, California (not active) and District of Columbia; 1985, Virginia (not active), U.S. Supreme Court, U.S. District Court Eastern and Western

(This Listing Continued)

KALBIAN HAGERTY LLP, Washington—Continued

Districts of Virginia and U.S. Court of Appeals for the District of Columbia Circuit; U.S. Court of Appeals, Second and Fourth Circuits; U.S. District Court, Eastern and Western Districts of New York. *Education:* State University of New York at Stony Brook (B.A., 1979); American University, Washington College of Law (J.D., 1982). Moot Court Board, 1981. Recent Lectures and Publications: *Getting your Point Across:* A Practicum in Persuasion Using Accessible Technology, Environmental Claims Managers Association, Fall 1996; *Late Notice Under "Occurrence-Based Liability Insurance Policies: When Late May Not Be Late Enough,"* Environmental Claims Journal, Vol 8; No. 3, Spring 1996; *Risks and Benefits of Sophisticated Computer Applications in Environmental Claims,* Environmental Claims Managers Association, Fall 1995. ***LANGUAGES:*** French, Farsi. ***REPORTED CASES:*** American Ins. Co. v. Fairchild Indus., 56 F.3d 435 (2nd Cir. 1995); Eli Lilly & Co. v. Home Ins. Co., 764 F.2nd 876, (DC Cir. 1985); Olin Corp. v. Insurance Co. of North America, 762 F.Supp. 548, (SDNY 1991); Diamond Shamrock Chems. Co. v. Aetna Cas. & Sur. Co., 258 N.J. Super. 167, (1992). ***PRACTICE AREAS:*** Litigation; Insurance. ***Email:*** tshahriari@kalbianhagerty.com

ALFONSO GUIDA, JR., born New Haven, Connecticut, June 4, 1958; admitted to bar, 1987, Pennsylvania (Not admitted in District of Columbia). *Education:* American University (B.A., 1980); Southwestern University (J.D., 1986). ***Email:*** aguida@kalbianhagerty.com

ASSOCIATES

KIMBERLY M. DAVIS, admitted to bar, 1997, Florida; 1999, District of Columbia. *Education:* University of Virginia (B.A., 1993); University of Miami (J.D., 1997). ***PRACTICE AREAS:*** State, Federal and International Taxation; Corporate Law; Business Law. ***Email:*** kimdavis@kalbianhagerty.com

AMJAD H. ATALLAH, born Gary, Indiana, May 3, 1965; admitted to bar, 2000, New York (Not admitted in District of Columbia). *Education:* University of Virginia (M.A., 1995); American University (J.D., 1999). Myers Fellow. Recipient, Equal Justice Foundation Scholarship. ***LANGUAGES:*** Arabic. ***PRACTICE AREAS:*** Litigation; Probate; International Public Law; International Human Rights. ***Email:*** aatallah@kalbianhagerty.com

SALADIN A. ALJURF, born Nablus, West Bank of Jordan, June 3, 1970; admitted to bar, 1998, Virginia (Not admitted in District of Columbia). *Education:* University of Iowa (B.A., 1992; J.D., 1998). Author: "Good Governance and Transparency: Their Impact on Development," and "Participatory Development and NGOs: A Look at the World Bank," 9 Transitional Law and Contemporary Problems, 1999. *Member, American Bar Association.* ***LANGUAGES:*** Arabic. ***Email:*** saljurf@kalbianhagerty.com

CLAIRE A. WOOD, born Irvine, Scotland, June 16, 1976; admitted to bar, 2001, New York (Not admitted in District of Columbia). *Education:* University of Aberdeen, Aberdeen, Scotland (L.L.B., with honors, 1998); American University, Washington College of Law (L.L.M., Law and Government, 2000). Member, European Law Society, 1997-1998; Law and Government Society, 1999-2000. *Member:* New York State and American Bar Associations. ***PRACTICE AREAS:*** Litigation. ***Email:*** cwood@kalbianhagerty.com

KALIJARVI, CHUZI & NEWMAN, P.C.

Established in 1973

SUITE 1011, 1730 K STREET, N.W.
WASHINGTON, D.C. 20006
Telephone: 202-331-9260
FAX: 202-872-9562
Email: kcnlawyers@aol.com

General Civil and Administrative Practice before all Courts, Agencies and Departments. Labor, Equal Opportunity, Civil Service, Contract.

FIRM PROFILE: Kalijarvi, Chuzi & Newman, P.C., concentrates in administrative and civil litigation involving private sector and federal labor and employment, including discrimination. We represent both employees and management, and have a nationwide practice with respect to federal employment.

JUNE D. W. KALIJARVI, born Boston, Massachusetts, May 30, 1941; admitted to bar, 1973, District of Columbia; 1974, U.S. District Court, District of Columbia, U.S. Court of Appeals, District of Columbia, U.S. Tax Court and U.S. Claims Court; 1977, U.S. Supreme Court; 1982, Virginia, U.S. District Court for the District of Maryland and U.S. Court of Appeals for the Fourth Circuit. *Education:* Wellesley College (B.A., 1963); Georgetown University (J.D., 1973; LL.M., 1975). Co-Author, Kalijarvi and Wallace "Executive Authority to Impose Prior Restraint Upon Publication of Information Concerning National Security Affairs: A Constitutional Power," 9 California Western Law Review 468 (1973). *Member:* The District of Columbia Bar; Virginia State Bar; The Bar Association of the District of Columbia; American Bar Association

(This Listing Continued)

(Member, Sections on: Labor and Employment Law). ***PRACTICE AREAS:*** Labor and Employment; Civil Rights; Discrimination. ***Email:*** jkalijarvi@aol.com

GEORGE M. CHUZI, born Bronx, New York, September 17, 1944; admitted to bar, 1980, District of Columbia; 1981, U.S. District Court, District of Columbia, U.S. Court of Appeals, District of Columbia and U.S. Claims Court; 1982, U.S. District Court for the District of Maryland and U.S. Court of Appeals for the Federal Circuit and the Fourth Circuit; 1985, U.S. Supreme Court; 1989, U.S. Court of Appeals, Fifth Circuit. *Education:* Queens College of the City University of New York (B.A., 1966); Georgetown University Law Center (J.D., cum laude, 1980). Member, Editorial Board, American Criminal Law Review, 1979-1980. Member, Executive Board, 1983-1990 and General Counsel, 1986-1990, Federally Employed Women Legal and Education Fund, Inc. *Member:* The District of Columbia Bar; Bar Association of the District of Columbia (Chair, EEO Committee, Young Lawyers Section, 1983-1987; Chair, Pro Bono Prisoner Committee, Young Lawyers Section, 1985-1987; Member, Executive Council, Young Lawyers Section, 1985-1987); American Bar Association (Member, Section of Labor and Employment Law). ***PRACTICE AREAS:*** Labor and Employment; Civil Rights; Discrimination. ***Email:*** GChuzi@aol.com

ELIZABETH L. NEWMAN, born New York, N.Y., April 19, 1948; admitted to bar, 1973, District of Columbia; 1974, U.S. Court of Appeals, District of Columbia; 1977, U.S. District Court, District of Columbia and U.S. Supreme Court; 1983, U.S. Court of Appeals, Federal Circuit; 1987, U.S. District Court, District of Maryland. *Education:* Skidmore College (B.A., 1970); Georgetown Law Center (J.D., 1973). Trial Attorney, U.S. Office of Personnel Management, 1973-1979. Partner, Ambler and Newman, 1980-1983. Of Counsel, Dobrovir and Gebhardt, 1985-1990. Chair, Law Office Management and Economics Section (1985-1986). Member, Executive Board, Federally Employed Women Legal and Education Fund (1979-1982). Member D.C. Bar Membership Benefits Committee (1984-1986). Faculty Member, George Washington University Legal Assistant Program, 1984-1988. *Member:* American Bar Association (Vice Chair, Defense and National Security, 1998—). ***PRACTICE AREAS:*** Labor and Employment; Discrimination; Security Clearances Law. ***Email:*** enewman@aol.com

MARGARET E. JOHNSON, born Royal Oak, Michigan, March 11, 1966; admitted to bar, 1993, Wisconsin; 1996, Massachusetts; 1997, District of Columbia. *Education:* Dartmouth College (B.A., 1987); University of Wisconsin-Madison (J.D., cum laude, 1993). Order of the Coif. Fellow, Women's Law and Public Policy, 1995-1996. Articles Editor, Wisconsin Law Review, 1992-1993. Law Clerk, The Honorable Hector M. Laffitte, U.S. District Court, District of Puerto Rico, 1993-1995. Author: "A Unified Approach to Causation in Disparate Treatment Cases: Using Sexual Harassment by Supervisors as the Causal Nexus for the Discriminatory Motivating Factor in Mixed Motives Cases," Wis. L. Rev. 231, 1993. ***PRACTICE AREAS:*** Employment Discrimination; Federal Employment Law; Employment Law. ***Email:*** johnsonesq@aol.com

E. REYNOLDS WILSON, born Newport News, Virginia, March 31, 1972; admitted to bar, 1998, Virginia and U.S. Court of Appeals, Fourth Circuit; 1999, District of Columbia and U.S. District Court, Eastern District of Virginia; 2000, U.S. Court of Appeals, Federal Circuit and D.C. Circuit; U.S. District Court, District of Columbia and U.S. Court of Federal Claims. *Education:* University of Virginia (B.A., 1994; J.D., 1998). Member, Editorial Board, 1996-1997 and Notes Editor, 1997-1998, Virginia Journal of Social Policy and the Law. Columns Editor, 1996-1997 and Executive Editor, 1997-1998, Virginia Law Weekly. ***PRACTICE AREAS:*** Employment Law; Federal Employment Law; Employment Discrimination. ***Email:*** rwilson@kcnlaw.com

MICHELLE L. PERRY, born Fairfield, California, September 19, 1967; admitted to bar, 1997, Virginia and U.S. Court of Appeals, Fourth Circuit; 1998, Maryland and U.S. District Court, Eastern District of Virginia; 2000, District of Columbia, U.S. Court of Appeals, Federal Circuit and U.S. Court of Federal Claims. *Education:* University of Akron (B.A., 1994); George Washington University (J.D., 1997). *Member:* American Bar Association. ***PRACTICE AREAS:*** Labor and Employment; Civil Rights; Federal Employment Law. ***Email:*** mperry@kcnlaw.com

OF COUNSEL

FRANCINE K. WEISS, born Far Rockaway, New York, August 23, 1949; admitted to bar, 1975, California; 1977, District of Columbia; 1980, U.S. Supreme Court; 1991, Maryland. *Education:* University of California at Berkeley (B.A., with honors, 1971); Loyola University of Los Angeles (LL.B., 1974). Member, Loyola Law Review. Author: "Index to the Legislative History of P.L. 95-555, the Pregnancy Discrimination Act of 1978," February, 1979; "Older Women and Job Discrimination: A Primer," sponsored by The Older Women's League, 1984; "Pay Equity for Older Workers and Women: An Issue of Growing Importance to Public Affairs Officers," Public Affairs Review, 1985; "Employment Discrimination Against Older Women," Lefcourt, C. Women and the Law,

(This Listing Continued)

Clark Boardman Co., Ltd., 1989. Mediator, U.S. District Court for the District of Columbia, 1990—. Director: Women's Bar Association Foundation, 1991-1995; Washington Psychiatric Association Foundation, 1992-1994; Metropolitan Washington Employment Lawyers Association, 1992—. *Member:* District of Columbia Bar (Member, Section on Labor; Co-Chair, EEO Committee, Labor Section); State Bar of California. ***PRACTICE AREAS:*** Labor and Employment; Discrimination.

STEPHEN L. SPITZ, born Chicago, Illinois, February 12, 1947; admitted to bar, 1972, Michigan; 1973, District of Columbia; 1976, U.S. Supreme Court; U.S. Court of Appeals, Fourth, Fifth and Eleventh Circuits; U.S. Court of Appeals for the Federal and District of Columbia Circuits. *Education:* University of Michigan (B.A., with high honors, 1968); University of Chicago (J.D., 1972). Member, Executive Board, Mandel Legal Aid Clinic. Author: "Lawyer's Committee Analysis of the Impact of the Supreme Court Decision in Martin v. Wilks," Daily Labor Report, No. 30, D-1, BNA, Feb. 13, 1990; with James C. Gray, Jr. and Paul Holtzman, "The Supreme Court and Employment Discrimination," Vol. 23 Clearinghouse Review No. 9 1222-1239, National Clearinghouse for Legal Services, Chicago, Jan. 1990; with William L. Robinson, "Affirmative Action: Evolving Case Law and Shifting Philosophy," Vol. 10, Urban League Review No. 2, National Urban League, Wash. D.C., Winter 1986-1987; "Litigation Strategy in Equality Rights-The American Experience," in Weiler and Elliott, eds. The Charter of Rights and Freedoms: Litigating the Values of a Nation, Carswell, Vancouver, B.C. Canada, 1986; with William L. Robinson, "The Civil Rights Record of the Reagan Administration," 71 A.B.A. Journal 39, Oct. 1985; with William L. Robinson, "Did the Stotts Decision Really Spell the End of Race-Conscious Affirmative Action?" Vol. II, Part One, N.Y.L.S. Human Rights Ann. 1-17, fall 1984; also in T. Bagby, ed. The Memphis Firefighters Case: The Impact of the Supreme Court's Stotts Decision on Affirmative Action, Equal Employment Litigation, National Foundation for the Study of Equal Employment Policy, Wash. D.C. 1985, Update on State-Wide School Finance Cases, Lawyer's Committee for Civil Rights Under Law, Wash. D.C., 1980, 1982. Lecturer: University of Michigan Law School, 1972-1973; University of British Columbia Faculty of Law, January-May, 1985. Member, Executive Board, Federally Employed Women Legal and Education Fund, 1985-1990; General Counsel, 1989-1990. *Member:* District of Columbia Bar (Member, Labor and Employment Law Section). ***PRACTICE AREAS:*** Civil Rights; Labor and Employment; Discrimination. ***Email:*** kcnspitz@aol.com

KARALEKAS & NOONE

Established in 1977

1211 CONNECTICUT AVENUE, N.W., SUITE 302
WASHINGTON, D.C. 20036-2603
Telephone: 202-466-7330
Facsimile: 202-955-5879
Email: KN1211CONN@AOL.COM
URL: http://www.lawyers.com/karalekas&noonelaw

Administrative Law Practice. Legislative Law and Lobbying, Government Relations, Civil Litigation, White Collar Crime, Qui Tam, Whistleblower Litigation, Corporate Investigations.

S. STEVEN KARALEKAS, born Boston, Massachusetts, August 10, 1942; admitted to bar, 1970, Massachusetts; 1974, District of Columbia and U.S. Court of Appeals for the District of Columbia Circuit; 1981, U.S. Supreme Court. *Education:* U.S. Naval Academy (B.S., with honors, 1965); Harvard University (M.P.A., cum laude, 1971); Indiana University (J.D., cum laude, 1970). Author: "Discovery in Indiana: An Unanswered Question," 3 Indiana Legal Forum 464, 1970. Law Clerk to Chief Justice Donald H. Hunter, Indiana Supreme Court, 1969-1970. Staff Assistant to President Richard M. Nixon, 1971-1973. Chief Assistant to Congressman Paul W. Cronin, Massachusetts, 1973-1974. *Member:* The District of Columbia Bar; Massachusetts Bar Association. [With U.S. Navy, active duty, 1965-1969; Capt., USNR, Ret.]. ***LANGUAGES:*** French, Greek. ***PRACTICE AREAS:*** Government Relations; Legislative Law; Government Contracts.

JAMES A. NOONE, born Scranton, Pennsylvania, June 8, 1944; admitted to bar, 1985, Pennsylvania and District of Columbia. *Education:* University of Scranton (B.A., cum laude, 1967); American University (M.A., 1974; J.D., 1984). Reporter, *The Scranton Tribune,* 1964-1967, 1969-1970. Staff Correspondent, *The National Journal,* 1972-1974. Writer/Editor, U.S. Information Agency, 1974-1977, 1979-1981. Press Officer, U.S. Consulate General, Rio de Janeiro, Brazil, 1977-1979; Public Relations Manager, ITT Corporation, 1981-1984. *Member:* Bar Association of the District of Columbia; Pennsylvania and American (Member, Section on Public Contract Law) Bar Associations. [With U.S. Navy, Active Duty, 1967-1969; Capt., USNR, 1969—]. ***LANGUAGES:*** Portuguese. ***PRACTICE AREAS:*** Government Relations; Legislative Law; Government Contracts. ***Email:*** janoone123@aol.com

WILLIAM J. HARDY, born Malden, Massachusetts, April 13, 1944; admitted to bar, 1970, Massachusetts; 1971, District of Columbia; 1972, U.S. Court of Military Appeals; 1980, U.S. Supreme Court; 1982, U.S. Court of

(This Listing Continued)

Appeals, Tenth Circuit; 1987, U.S. Court of Appeals, Fifth Circuit; 1988, U.S. Court of Appeals, Ninth Circuit; 1997, Virginia. *Education:* Boston College (B.S., 1965); Georgetown University (J.D., 1970). Member, The Barristers, 1980. Author: "Civil Rico", Litigation Magazine, ABA Vol. 13, No. 4, Summer 1987. Assistant U.S. Attorney, Washington, D.C. 1971-1979. Branch Chief, Criminal Fraud Section U.S. Department of Justice Washington, D.C., 1979-1987; "Attorney-Client Privilege," 5BNA Crim Prac Man 132, 1991; "Brokering a Plea Bargain," 6BNA Crim Prac Man 37, 1991. *Member:* American Bar Association (Member: White Collar Crime Committee; Litigation Committee); National Association of Criminal Defense Lawyers. ***PRACTICE AREAS:*** Federal Civil Litigation; Federal Criminal Law; White Collar Criminal Defense; Qui Tam Litigation; Corporate Investigations. ***Email:*** wmjhardy@hotmail.com

JOHN F. KARL, JR.

ONE FARRAGUT SQUARE
900 17TH AVENUE, N.W., SUITE 1250
WASHINGTON, D.C. 20006
Telephone: 202-293-3200
Fax: 202-429-1851
URL: http://www.lawyers.com/mcdonald&karl

Employment Discrimination, Title 7, A.D.A., Human Rights, Personal Injury, Estate Planning and Medical Malpractice.

JOHN F. KARL, JR., born Utica, New York, November 29, 1947; admitted to bar, 1979, District of Columbia; 1981, Florida; 1984, U.S. Supreme Court. *Education:* University of Toronto (B.A., 1970; M.A., 1971; Ph.D., 1976); American University (J.D., 1979). Professorial Lecturer, Washington College of Law, American University, 1985—. Legislative Assistant, U.S. House of Representatives, 1976-1978. *Member:* The District of Columbia Bar; The Florida Bar; Federal and American Bar Associations; The Association of Trial Lawyers of America; Plaintiff Employment Law Association. ***PRACTICE AREAS:*** Civil Litigation; Employment Litigation; Securities Litigation; Corporate Practice; General Practice.

ASSOCIATE

C. MICHAEL TARONE, born New York, N.Y., July 10, 1945; admitted to bar, 1971, New York; 1972, District of Columbia. *Education;* Georgetown University (B.S.B.A., 1967; J.D., 1970). Law Clerk to the U.S. District Judge, Edward R. Neaher, Eastern District of New York, 1971-1972. Special Counsel to the Administrator, Law Enforcement Assistance Administration, Department of Justice, 1973. President, The Counsellors. *Member:* The District of Columbia Bar; Bar Association of the District of Columbia. ***PRACTICE AREAS:*** Maritime Law; International Law; Automobile Liability; Negligence; Insurance; Civil Practice; Civil Rights Litigation; Employment Law; Labor Law; Federal Election Law; Nonprofit Organizations Law; Commercial Litigation; Torts. ***Email:*** cmtarone@aol.com

KARP, FROSH, LAPIDUS, WIGODSKY & NORWIND, P.A.

1133 CONNECTICUT AVENUE, SUITE 250
WASHINGTON, D.C. 20036
Telephone: 202-822-3777
Fax: 202-822-9722
Email: ronk@karpfrosh.com
URL: http://www.karpfrosh.com

Rockville, Maryland Office: 1370 Piccard Drive, Suite 290. 20850. Telephone: 301-948-3800. Fax: 301-948-5449.

Fairfax, Virginia Office: Karp & Kessel, 11350 Random Hill Road, Suite 700, 22030.

Bethesda, Maryland Office: Karp, Frosh, Lapidus, Wigodsky & Norwind, P.A., 7315 Wisconsin Avenue, Suite 800 West. 20814. Telephone: 301-656-2888. Fax: 301-654-7748.

Frederich, Maryland Office: 110 N. Court Street, 2nd Floor. 21701.

Serious Personal Injury Litigation, Commercial Litigation, Family Law, Estate Planning and Business Law.

FIRM PROFILE: Karp Frosh is a firm of trial lawyers and business lawyers. Three partners are past presidents of the Trial Lawyers Association of Metropolitan Washington, D.C. One division of the firm handles serious personal injury cases (representing victims of malpractice and defective products, serious automobile and trucking accidents). Another division does commercial litigation, business law, estate planning, wills, trusts and family law. Three of the firm's partners have received the prestigious Trial Lawyer of The Tear Award and the firm's partners have numerous million dollar verdicts and settlements. The firm's managing part-

(This Listing Continued)

KARP, FROSH, LAPIDUS, WIGODSKY & NORWIND, P.A., Washington—Continued

ner, Ronald Karp, has been selected to appear in Best Lawyers in America, a publication based upon interviews with lawyers, and which lists less than 1% of the lawyers in the United States.

(For Complete Biographical Data on all Personnel, see Professional Biographies at Rockville, Maryland)

KARR & ALLISON, P.C.

1920 N STREET, N.W., SUITE 300
WASHINGTON, D.C. 20036
Telephone: 202-331-7600
Fax: 202-293-3999
URL: http://www.karrallison.com
Email: tsallison@aol.com
URL: http://www.lawyers.com/karrallison

Corporate, Business, Commercial Litigation, Small Business, General Counselling, Legal Ethics, Medical Ethics, Professional Ethics.

FIRM PROFILE: The firm is primarily engaged in the areas of Business and Commercial Litigation with special emphasis in Business Torts, Employment and Ethics in the Public and Private Sectors; Credit, Collection and Financial Institutions; and Business Transactions.

JOHN W. KARR, born Chicago, Illinois, June 19, 1930; admitted to bar, 1958, District of Columbia. *Education:* Loyola University (B.S., 1952); Georgetown University (LL.B., 1958). Adjunct Professor of Law, Antioch School of Law, 1974-1981. Old Master, Purdue University, 1978. Guest Lecturer, Middlebury College, 1979. Adjunct Professor of Law, Washington College of Law of American University, 1979-1981. Member, District of Columbia Law Revision Commission, 1981-1989. Member, Charles Fabry American Inn of Court. *Member:* District of Columbia Bar. ***PRACTICE AREAS:*** Civil, Criminal Trials; Appellate Practice.

THEODORE S. ALLISON, born Spokane, Washington, 1959; admitted to bar, 1984, California; 1985, Washington; 1993, Maryland; 1994, District of Columbia; 1997, Virginia; U.S. Supreme Court; U.S. Court of Appeals Fourth Circuit; U.S. Court of Appeals, Ninth Circuit; U.S. District Court, Central District of California; U.S. District Court, District of Maryland; U.S. District Court for the District of Columbia; U.S. District Court, Eastern District of Virginia. *Education:* Western Washington University (B.A., 1981); University of Southern California (J.D., 1984). Recipient, American Jurisprudence Award in Contracts, 1982. *Member:* American Bar Association.

MAHMOUD KATIRAI

1050 17TH STREET, N.W., SUITE 700
WASHINGTON, D.C. 20036
Telephone: 202-659-4245
Fax: 202-463-6290
Email: mahmoudkatirai@aol.com
URL: http://www.lawyers.com/mahmoudkatirai

Tehran, Iran Office: Number 4 Second Street, Mir-Emad Avenue, Suite 3. Telephone: 8757887. Fax: 8743911.

General Practice of law with particular attention to Corporate Law, International Law; Serving as an Expert on Iranian Law before Courts and Arbitration Tribunals; Providing Advice on Contract, Transnational Agreements and Investment Arrangements; Iranian Business Formation; Preparing Corporate Legal Documents and Registering both Foreign and Domestic Legal Entities in Iran.

MAHMOUD KATIRAI, born Shiraz, Iran, 1943; admitted to bar, 1969, Iran; 1985, District of Columbia. *Education:* University of Tehran (Licentiate in Law, 1965); National University of Iran (LL.M., 1972); Georgetown University Law School (M.C.L., 1983). Co-Author, "Establishing a Joint Stock Company in Iran," 1971. Instructor, Commercial Law, School of Insurance, Tehran, 1971. Official English Translator, Iranian Ministry of Justice, 1971-1980. Partner: John A. Westberg & Associates, 1975-1979. Law Clerk: Patton, Boggs & Blow, 1972-1973. ***LANGUAGES:*** English and Farsi. ***PRACTICE AREAS:*** International Law; Business Law; Iranian Law.

KATOR, PARKS & WEISER, P.L.L.C.

1020 NINETEENTH STREET, N.W.
SUITE 350
WASHINGTON, D.C. 20036
Telephone: 202-898-4800
Fax: 202-289-1389
Email: KATOR.SCOTT@EROLS.COM
URL: http://www.kator-scott.com

Austin, Texas Office: 812 San Antonio Street, Suite 100, 78701. Telephone: 512-322-0600.

General Practice including Employment, Civil Service, Civil Rights, Civil Trial, Appellate and Administrative Practice before all Courts and Agencies.

FIRM PROFILE: Kator, Scott & Parks is a Washington, D.C.-based law firm with a nationwide practice representing individuals and organizations in public and private employment matters involving civil rights and other personnel issues.

MICHAEL J. KATOR, born Washington, D.C., June 11, 1956; admitted to bar, 1981, Texas; 1982, Maryland and District of Columbia; 1984, U.S. Supreme Court and U.S. Court of Appeals, Fourth, Fifth, Eighth, Tenth, District of Columbia and Federal Circuits. *Education:* University of Texas (B.A., with highest honors, 1977; J.D., 1981). Phi Beta Kappa; Phi Kappa Phi. *Member:* The District of Columbia Bar; State Bar of Texas; Maryland State Bar Association, Inc. ***PRACTICE AREAS:*** Federal Civil Litigation; Federal Employment Law; U.S. Supreme Court Litigation. ***Email:*** mkator@kator-scott.com

JESSICA L. PARKS, born Chattanooga, Tennessee, February 4, 1953; admitted to bar, 1980, North Carolina; 1981, U.S. District Court, Eastern District of North Carolina; 1987, U.S. Court of Appeals, Sixth Circuit (Not admitted in District of Columbia). *Education:* Tulane University of Louisiana (B.A., cum laude, 1974); University of Tennessee (J.D., 1980). Judge George Caldwell Taylor Memorial Scholar. Author: "Creative Settlement Strategies," The Army Lawyer, September 1992; "Remarks on Decisions of the MPSB Under the Whistleblower Protection Act," Federal Merit Systems Reporter, January 1993; "The Merit Systems Protection Board as a Model Forum," The Federal Circuit Bar Journal, Spring 1994. Counsel, Craven County, North Carolina, Department of Social Services, 1981-1982. Administrative Judge, U.S. Merit Systems Protection Board, 1982-1985. Assistant and Associate Regional Counsel, U.S. Department of Housing and Urban Development, 1985-1988. Associate Regional Counsel for Litigation and Program Enforcement, U.S. Department of Housing and Urban Development, 1988-1990. Chairman and Member, U.S. Merit Systems Protection Board, 1990-1995. *Member:* North Carolina State Bar; Federal Bar Association (Appointed Member, National Council, 1992—); Federal Circuit Bar Association. ***PRACTICE AREAS:*** Federal Employment Law; Whistleblower Litigation; Federal Government Law. ***Email:*** jparks@kator-scott.com

DAVID WEISER, born Dallas, Texas, June 28, 1960; admitted to bar, 1989, Texas; 1990, District of Columbia and U.S. Court of Appeals, Fifth Circuit. *Education:* University of Texas (B.A., with highest honors, 1982); Yale University (J.D ., 1986). Phi Beta Kappa. Senior Editor, Yale Law and Policy Review, 1985-1986. Assistant General Counsel for the Governor of Texas. *Member:* The District of Columbia Bar; State Bar of Texas. (Resident Austin, TX). ***PRACTICE AREAS:*** Federal Employment Law; Civil Rights. ***Email:*** dweiser@kator-scott.com

---

LAURA A. STEFANI, born Oak Park, Illinois, July 8, 1969; admitted to bar, 1997, Maryland; 1998, District of Columbia, U.S. Court of Appeals for the Federal Circuit, U.S. District Court, District of Maryland and U.S. District Court for the District of Columbia. *Education:* Lawrence University (B.A., magna cum laude, 1991); George Washington University (J.D., 1997). Author: "Reducing CO and HC Emissions From Small Nonroad Spark-Ignition Engines: How Manufacturers Must Comply With New CAA Regulations," 3 Envtl. Law. 531, 1997. Staff Member, The Environmental Lawyer, 1995-1997. *Member:* District of Columbia Bar (Member, Labor and Employment Law Section); Metropolitan Washington Employment Lawyers Association. ***PRACTICE AREAS:*** Employment Law; Civil Litigation. ***Email:*** lstefani@kator-scott.com

CATHY A. HARRIS, born New York, New York, November 12, 1971; admitted to bar, 1998, New York (Not admitted in District of Columbia). *Education:* Brown University (A.B., 1994); George Washington University (J.D., 1997). Recipient, Michael P. Cooley Award. Articles Editor, George Washington Law Review, 1996-1997. Author: "Outing Privacy Litigation: Toward a Contextual Theory of Lesbian & Gay Civil Rights Litigation," 65, George Washington Law Review, 248, 1997; "Unfair Labor Practices--Pension Plans and the Post-modern Employee," 64 George Washington Law Review, 1354, 1996. Assistant District Attorney, New York County District Attorney's Office, 1997-1999. ***PRACTICE AREAS:*** Employment Law; Civil Rights; Civil Service. ***Email:*** charris@kator-scott.com

(This Listing Continued)

MAIA R. CAPLAN, born Chicago, Illinois, November 7, 1962; admitted to bar, 1989, New York; 1990, District of Columbia; 1992, Pennsylvania. *Education:* University of Michigan (B.A., with high distinction, 1984; J.D., 1988). James B. Angell Scholar. S. Anthony Benton Scholar. Belfield & Bates Fellow. *Member:* The District of Columbia Bar (Member, Labor & Employment Section); New York State Bar Association. ***PRACTICE AREAS:*** Employment; Civil Rights; Litigation.

OF COUNSEL

IRVING KATOR, born Binghamton, New York, March 10, 1920; admitted to bar, 1952, District of Columbia; 1962, U.S. Supreme Court. *Education:* University of Michigan (A.B., 1941); George Washington University (J.D., with honors, 1951). Assistant Executive Director and Assistant to Chairman, U.S. Civil Service Commission, 1969-1975. *Member:* The District of Columbia Bar; Bar Association of the District of Columbia; Federal and American (Chair, 1979-1983 and Vice Chairman, 1984-1985, Government Personnel Law Committee; Vice Chair, Civil Rights and Employment Discrimination Committee, 1986-1988) Bar Associations; Supreme Court Historical Society. ***PRACTICE AREAS:*** Employment Law; Civil Rights; Administrative Law. ***Email:*** ikator@kator-scott.com

JOSEPH B. SCOTT, born San Pedro, California, August 11, 1943; admitted to bar, 1970, California; 1972, U.S. Court of Appeals, Fourth, Sixth, Ninth, Tenth and District of Columbia Circuits; 1975, District of Columbia; 1977, U.S. Supreme Court. *Education:* University of California at Berkeley (A.B., 1966); University of California at Los Angeles (J.D., 1969). Order of the Coif. Member, Board of Editors, UCLA Law Review, 1968-1969. Adjunct Professor, Georgetown University Law Center, 1977-1981. Trial Attorney, U.S. Department of Justice: Civil Rights Division, 1969-1971; Civil Division, 1971-1973. Assistant and Deputy General Counsel, U.S. Civil Service Commission, 1973-1977. Executive Director, Administrative Conference of the U.S., 1977-1978. Senior Trial Attorney, U.S. Department of Justice, Civil Division, Appellate Staff, 1979-1980. Member, Nuclear Regulatory Commission's Advisory Committee on Rights of Employees Under Investigation, 1983. *Member:* The District of Columbia Bar; State Bar of California; American Bar Association (Chairman, Public Personnel Law Committee, 1978-1979). ***Email:*** jscott@kator-scott.com

KATTEN MUCHIN ZAVIS

A Partnership including Professional Corporations

Katten Muchin & Zavis Established in Chicago 1974

1025 THOMAS JEFFERSON STREET, N.W.
EAST LOBBY, SUITE 700

WASHINGTON, D.C. 20007-5201

Telephone: 202-625-3500
Telecopier: 202-298-7570
URL: http://www.kmz.com

Chicago, Illinois Office: 525 West Monroe Street, Suite 1600. Telephone: 312-902-5200. Telecopier: 312-902-1061.

Los Angeles, California Office: 1999 Avenue of the Stars, Suite 1400. Telephone: 310-788-4400. Telecopier: 310-788-4471.

Palo Alto, California Office: 260 Sheridan Avenue, Suite 450. Telephone: 650-330-3650. Telecopier: 310-712-8420.

New York, New York Office: 245 Park Avenue, 39th Floor. Telephone: 212-764-6886. Telecopier: 212-382-3395.

Advertising, Anti-Fraud Counseling and Litigation, Antitrust, Bankruptcy, Reorganization and Creditors' Rights, Business Litigation, Corporate, Corporate Insurance, Customs and International Trade, Employee Benefits and Executive Compensation, Entertainment, Entertainment Finance, Entertainment Litigation, Environmental, Finance and Structured Finance, Financial Institutions, Financial Markets and Products, Financial Services, Franchising, Licensing and Distribution, Governmental Affairs, Health Care, Health Care Compliance, Health Care Insolvency, Health Information and HIPPA Compliance, Intellectual Property, Intellectual Property Litigation, International Transactions and Litigation, Internet and E-Business, Investment Management, Joint Ventures, Strategic Alliances and Partnerships, Labor and Employment, Litigation and Dispute Resolution, Mergers and Acquisitions, Private Equity and Emerging Growth Companies, Product Liability, Public Finance, Publishing, Real Estate, Real Estate Development, Real Estate Finance, Real Estate Investment Fund Formation, Real Estate Litigation, Real Estate Taxation, Securities, Securities Litigation, Shopping Center and Retail Law, Sports Law and Sports Facilities, Tax Planning and Litigation, Taxation of Financial Products, Technology and New Media, Wealth Management and Planning, White Collar Criminal and Civil Litigation.

MEMBERS OF FIRM

RICHARD P. BAUER, born Pittsburgh, Pennsylvania, November 17, 1951; admitted to bar, 1984, Virginia; 1985, District of Columbia; registered to practice before U.S. Patent and Trademark Office. *Education:* United States Military Academy (B.S., Engineering, 1973); Loyola University Law School; Catholic University of America (J.D., 1984). Member, St. Thomas More Law Honor Society. *Member:* The District of Columbia Bar; Virginia State Bar; American Intellectual Property Law Association. ***PRACTICE AREAS:*** Intellectual Property; Intellectual Property Litigation; Internet Law; E-Commerce. ***Email:*** richard.bauer@kmz.com

VIRGINIA A. DAVIS, born Fort Payne, Alabama, April 17, 1966; admitted to bar, 1991, Virginia; 1992, District of Columbia. *Education:* Auburn University (B.A., with highest honors, 1988); Harvard Law School (J.D., 1991). *Member:* District of Columbia Bar; Virginia State Bar; American Bar Association. ***PRACTICE AREAS:*** Commercial Real Estate. ***Email:*** virginia.davis@kmz.com

WENDY L. FIELDS, born New York, N.Y., September 22, 1946; admitted to bar, 1976, District of Columbia. *Education:* George Washington University (B.A., 1968; M.A., 1969; J.D., with honors, 1976). Member, George Washington Law Review, 1975-1976. *Member:* The District of Columbia Bar; American Bar Association. ***PRACTICE AREAS:*** Commercial Real Estate Law. ***Email:*** wendy.fields@kmz.com

ROGER P. FUREY, born Washington, D.C., May 30, 1954; admitted to bar, 1983, District of Columbia; 1984, Virginia; U.S. District Court, Eastern District of Virginia; U.S. District Court for the District of Columbia; U.S. District Court, District of Maryland; U.S. Court of Appeals, Fourth, Sixth, Ninth and District of Columbia Circuits; U.S. Court of Appeals for the Federal Circuit; Virginia Supreme Court. *Education:* George Mason University (B.S., 1979); University of Virginia (J.D., 1983). ***PRACTICE AREAS:*** Intellectual Property; Intellectual Property Litigation. ***Email:*** roger.furey@kmz.com

CHRISTOPHER J. HART, born Little Rock, AR, December 7, 1960; admitted to bar, 1986, Texas; 1992, District of Columbia. *Education:* Harvard University (B.A., 1983); University of Virginia School of Law (J.D., 1986). *Member:* District of Columbia Bar. ***PRACTICE AREAS:*** Real Estate; Finance. ***Email:*** christopher.hart@kmz.com

BRUCE E. KOSUB, born Alice, Texas, May 11, 1962; admitted to bar, 1988, Texas; 1995, District of Columbia. *Education:* University of Texas (B.B.A., 1984; J.D., 1988). Texas Law Review, 1986-1988 (Executive Editor, 1987-1988). Beta Alpha Psi; Delta Sigma Pi. ***PRACTICE AREAS:*** Commercial Finance; Real Estate. ***Email:*** bruce.kosub@kmz.com

S. SCOTT MORRISON, born New Orleans, Louisiana, July 28, 1954; admitted to bar, 1979, District of Columbia; 1980, U.S. Court of Appeals for the District of Columbia Circuit, U.S. District Court for the District of Columbia and U.S. District Court, Northern District of Texas; 1982, U.S. Court of Appeals for the Federal Circuit; 1987, Maryland, U.S. Supreme Court and U.S. Claims Court; 1993, U.S. Court of Appeals, Fourth Circuit. *Education:* Stanford University (A.B., 1976; J.D., 1979). Note Editor, Stanford Law Review, Vol. 31, 1978-1979. *Member:* The District of Columbia Bar; Maryland State and American (Member, Trial Practice Committee, Litigation Section) Bar Associations. ***PRACTICE AREAS:*** Complex Litigation; Defense Litigation; Civil Trial; Construction Law. ***Email:*** scott.morrison@kmz.com

MICHAEL P. MURPHY, born Los Angeles, California, December 24, 1954; admitted to bar, 1981, New York and Florida; 1985, District of Columbia. *Education:* Brown University (A.B., 1977); Fordham University (J.D., 1980). Member, Editorial Board, Fordham International Law Forum, 1979-1980. *Member:* The District of Columbia Bar; New York State Bar Association; The Florida Bar; National Association of Bond Lawyers. ***PRACTICE AREAS:*** Structured Finance; Public Finance. ***Email:*** michael.murphy@kmz.com

ROBERT J. PISANI, born New York, New York, October 13, 1952; admitted to bar, 1979, District of Columbia; 1980, Florida. *Education:* Tulane University of Louisiana (B.A., 1974); American University (J.D., 1978). ***PRACTICE AREAS:*** Customs Law; International Trade. ***Email:*** robert.pisani@kmz.com

STEVEN C. SCHNITZER, born Baltimore, Maryland, April 6, 1962; admitted to bar, 1988, Connecticut; 1989, New York; 1990, District of Columbia. *Education:* University of Maryland (B.A., 1984); Touro College, Jacob D. Fuchsberg Law Center (J.D., cum laude, 1988). Editor-in-Chief, Touro Law Review, 1987-1988. ***PRACTICE AREAS:*** Corporate Law; Finance; Structured Finance; Joint Ventures; Strategic Alliances; Partnership Law; Mergers and Acquisitions. ***Email:*** steven.schnitzer@kmz.com

DAVID SCHWINGER, born Philadelphia, Pennsylvania, November 8, 1956; admitted to bar, 1982, District of Columbia. *Education:* Wharton School of Finance and Commerce, University of Pennsylvania (B.S., summa cum laude, 1977); George Washington University National Law Center (J.D., with high honors, 1982). Order of the Coif. ***PRACTICE AREAS:*** Real Estate and Finance. ***Email:*** david.schwinger@kmz.com

GLORIA B. SOLOMON, born Brooklyn, New York, September 16, 1956; admitted to bar, 1981, District of Columbia. *Education:* Tufts University (B.A., summa cum laude, 1978); Harvard Law School (J.D., cum laude, 1981). Phi

(This Listing Continued)

KATTEN MUCHIN ZAVIS, Washington—Continued

Beta Kappa. *Member:* District of Columbia Bar; American Bar Association. ***PRACTICE AREAS:*** Commercial Litigation; Appellate Litigation. ***Email:*** gloria.solomon@kmz.com

CAROL R. VAN CLEEF, born Point Pleasant, New Jersey, January 10, 1956; admitted to bar, 1985, Virginia; 1986, District of Columbia. *Education:* Georgetown University (B.S.F.S., 1978); The American University Washington College of Law (J.D., 1984). Co-author, "Enhancing the Value of the Thrift Franchise: A Possible Solution for the Dilemma of the FSLIC?" Catholic University Law Review Vol. 37, No. 2, Winter 1988. *Member:* American Bar Association (Administrative Law and Regulatory Practice Section, Vice-Chair, Legislative Process and Lobbying Committee); Women in Housing and Finance (President, 1991-1993). ***PRACTICE AREAS:*** Internet and E-Commerce; Financial Institutions Law; Legislation. ***Email:*** carol.vancleef@kmz.com

JEFFREY M. WERTHAN, born New York, N.Y., September 28, 1954; admitted to bar, 1979, District of Columbia and U.S. District Court for the District of Columbia; 1980, New York; U.S. District Court, Northern District of New York and U.S. Court of Appeals, Sixth and Ninth Circuits. *Education:* The Juilliard School; Tufts University (B.A., cum laude, 1976); Boston University (J.D., 1979). Senior Attorney, Office of General Counsel, Federal Home Loan Bank Board, Federal Savings and Loan Insurance Corporation, 1979-1983. *Member:* New York State and American (Member, Committee on Banking Law) Bar Associations; District of Columbia Bar. ***PRACTICE AREAS:*** Banking Law; Securities Law. ***Email:*** jeff.werthan@kmz.com

EDWARD E. ZUGHAIB, born Baghdad, Iraq, March 31, 1958; admitted to bar, 1986, New York and Virginia; 1988, District of Columbia. *Education:* Colgate University (B.A., 1980); Syracuse University (J.D., 1985). Notes and Comments Editor, Syracuse University College of Law Review, 1984-1985. ***PRACTICE AREAS:*** Real Estate. ***Email:*** edward.zughaib@kmz.com

ASSOCIATES

Myron Paul Barlow
Jennifer S. Beer
Elise A. Cook (Not admitted in DC)
Brian H. Corcoran
Sylvia D. Davis
Oonagh L. Deasy (Not admitted in DC)
Katerina Greenspun (Not admitted in DC)
Gerald P. James (Not admitted in DC)
Richard D. Kelley (Not admitted in DC)
Nicole L. Kobrine
Ann H. Larkin (Not admitted in DC)
Adam V. Lichtenstein
Rori H. Malech
Christine Poulon (Not admitted in DC)
Leta A. Principe
Forrest W. Reid
Eric C. Spencer (Not admitted in DC)

SPECIAL COUNSEL

Thomas A. Brooks.

KATZ, KUTTER, HAIGLER, ALDERMAN, BRYANT & YON

PROFESSIONAL ASSOCIATION

Established in 1987

801 PENNSYLVANIA AVENUE, N.W.
SUITE 750
WASHINGTON, D.C. 20004
Telephone: 202-393-6222
Fax: 202-393-5959
URL: http://www.katzlaw.com

Tallahassee, Florida Office: 106 East College Avenue, 12th Floor, 32301. Mailing address: P.O. Box 1877, 32302-1877. Telephone: 850-224-9634. Fax: 222-0103.
Orlando, Florida Office: 111 North Orange Avenue, Suite 900, 32801. Telephone: 407-841-7100. Fax: 407-648-0660.
Aventura, Florida Office: Suite 409, 2999 N.E. 191st Street, 33180. Telephone: 305-932-0996. Fax: 305-932-0972.

General Civil Practice. Trial and Appellate Practice in all State and Federal Courts. Governmental, Administrative and Legislative Practice, including Insurance Regulation, Banking Regulation, Land Use and Environmental Law, Utility Regulation, Mobile Home Park Regulation, Regulated Professions, Alcoholic Beverages, Life Care, Health Care, and Public Contracts. General Corporate, Business, Real Property and Commercial Law, Mediation and Arbitration, Products Liability, Employment and Labor Law, Alternative Dispute Resolution, Mediation, Antitrust and Trade Regulation, Consumer Regulation.

(This Listing Continued)

OF COUNSEL

RICHARD L. SPEES, JR., born Washington, D.C., June 1, 1954; admitted to bar, 1979, California (Not admitted in District of Columbia). *Education:* University of California at Berkeley (B.A., Economics, 1976); Georgetown University Law Center (J.D., 1979). Author: *The Maverick Spirit:* Building the New Nevada, Chapter on "Paul Laxalt-Man of Political Independence," 1999. Legislative Assistant, Office of Senator Paul Laxalt, 1979-1981. Majority Counsel Senate Judiciary Subcommittee on Regulatory Reform, 1981-1982. Chief Counsel and Staff Director, Senate Appropriations Subcommittee on the Departments of Commerce, Justice and State, The Judiciary and Related Agencies, 1983-1986. General Counsel, Council of American Overseas Research Centers, 1987—. *Member:* State Bar of California. ***PRACTICE AREAS:*** Federal Government Law; International Trade; Transportation; Local Government Law. ***Email:*** rspees@katzlaw.com

REPRESENTATIVE CLIENTS: *Insurance:* American Insurance Association, Inc.; American International Group, Inc.; Aetna US Healthcare; AON Corporation; Humana, Inc.; Cigna Corporation; Cincinnati Insurance Company; Citigroup; Florida Automobile Joint Underwriting Association; Fortis Group; ING Aetna Financial Services; Metropolitan Life Insurance Company; Minnesota Life Insurance Company; Zurich Insurance Co.; Mutual of New York; Mutual of Omaha; Phoenix Home Life Mutual Insurance Company; Physicians Protective Trust; St. Paul Fire and Marine Insurance Company; Travelers; Florida Windstorm Underwriting Assn.; Hartford Life Insurance Co.; Prudential Insurance Company of America; USAA. *Business and Financial:* Amick Construction, Ltd.; Harcourt General; Primax Construction, Inc.; Southern Wine & Spirits; Sun Communities, Inc.; Woerner Companies-Florida; Winn-Dixie Stores; ING Aetna Financial Services, Inc.; AmSouth Bancorporation; Regions Financial Corporation; SouthTrust Bank; PrimeCo Personal Comm.; Joseph E. Seagram & Sons, Inc.; R.J. Reynolds; Amoco Corporation; Sprint Florida; Hometown America, Inc.; Manufactured Housing Communities, Inc.; R.A. Rogers Construction, Inc.; Bruce Building Company, Inc.; TEK Quest Industries, Inc. *Health Care:* Florida Assisted Living Assoc.; American Dental Plan; American Retirement Corporation; Florida Board of Regents/University of Florida Self-Insurance Trust Fund; Florida Health Sciences Center; Florida Pharmacy Association; Health First Health Plan; Jackson Memorial Hospital; Tampa General Hospital; Cardinal Health Systems; Option Care Enterprises, Inc.; Schering Plough, Inc. *Real Estate, Land Use and Environmental:* Bull Run Development; Florida Crystals Corporation; Rudnier Development Company; SkyGen Energy, LLC; City of Cooper City, Florida; City of Kissimmee, Florida; Block Land & Finance Company; Town of Davie, Florida. *Governmental:* City of Miami; City of Tallahassee, Florida; Tallahassee-Leon County Planning Commission; Orange County, Florida; Orlando East-West Expressway Authority; School District of Palm Beach County. *Labor and Employment:* Manpower; U-Haul International; Houghton Mifflin; Company Boca-West Club. *Technology:* Admazing Inc.; Aleff, Inc.; ENRON North America; Gartner Group; Mediacom Cable; Medical Media Technologies. *Telecommunications & Utilities:* Bell South, Tampa Electric, ENRON Broadband Services; Verizon. *Alternative Dispute Resolution:* Dupont; The Toro Company; The Hertz Corp.; Johnson & Johnson; Royal Insurance Company; Tennant Co.

(For complete biographical data on other personnel, see Professional Biographies at other locations)

NEIL B. KATZ

WASHINGTON, D.C.

(See Rockville, Maryland)

Employment Law Practice (primarily plaintiffs civil rights matters including wrongful termination, women's rights, sexual harassment, employee contracts and some employment defense work); Family Law including Divorce and Custody; Commercial and Business Litigation; General Civil Trial Practice.

KATZ & RANZMAN, P.C.

SUITE 801, 1015 EIGHTEENTH STREET, N.W.
WASHINGTON, D.C. 20036
Telephone: 202-659-4656
Fax: 202-659-3145
Email: dankatz@compuserve.com

Labor, ERISA, Civil Rights Law.

DANIEL M. KATZ, born Washington, D.C., October 17, 1944. admitted to bar, 1969, District of Columbia and U.S. District Court for the District of Columbia; 1970, U.S. Court of Appeals for the District of Columbia Circuit and U.S. Court of Appeals, Ninth and Tenth Circuits; 1971, U.S. Court of Appeals, Seventh Circuit; 1973, U.S. Supreme Court; 1975, U.S. Court of Appeals, Second Circuit; 1976, U.S. Court of Appeals, Fifth Circuit; 1977, U.S. Court of Appeals, Eighth Circuit; 1978, Virginia and U.S. District Court, Eastern District of Virginia; 1986, U.S. District Court, District of Maryland including Trial Bar and U.S. Court of Appeals, Third Circuit; 1987, U.S. Court of Appeals, Fourth Circuit; 1990, U.S. Court of Federal Claims; 1996, U.S. District Court, District of Arizona. *Education:* University of Michigan (B.A., 1966); University of Chicago (J.D., 1969). Litigation Attorney, General Counsel's Office, Appellate Court Branch, National Labor Relations Board, 1969-1973. *Member:* The District of Columbia Bar; Virginia State Bar; American Bar Association; AFL-CIO Lawyers Coordinating Committee, 1983—. ***Email:*** dankatz@compuserve.com

ELLEN G. RANZMAN, born Brooklyn, New York, February 28, 1947; admitted to bar, 1980, District of Columbia; 1981, U.S. District Court for the

(This Listing Continued)

District of Columbia and U.S. Court of Appeals for the District of Columbia Circuit; 1983, U.S. Court of Appeals for the Federal Circuit; 1984, U.S. District Court, District of Maryland including Trial Bar; 1990, U.S. Court of Federal Claims; 1992, U.S. Court of Appeals, Tenth Circuit; 1992, U.S. Supreme Court. *Education:* John Carroll University (B.A., 1977); Catholic University of America (J.D., 1980). Attorney, Staff of Chairman John Fanning, National Labor Relations Board, 1980-1981. *Member:* The District of Columbia Bar; AFL-CIO Lawyers Coordinating Committee, 1986—. **Email:** eranzman@compuserve.com

---

NANCY A. DONAHUE, born New York, N.Y., June 26, 1956; admitted to bar, 1982, District of Columbia; 1983, Connecticut; 1987, U.S. Court of Appeals, Fourth Circuit; 1990, U.S. Court of Federal Claims. *Education:* Fairfield University (B.A., 1978); American University (J.D., 1981). *Member:* The District of Columbia Bar; AFL-CIO Lawyers Coordinating Committee, 1986—.

LOUISE P. ZANAR, born Atlanta, Georgia, October 15, 1956; admitted to bar, 1986, Maryland; 1987, District of Columbia. *Education:* Smith College (B.A., cum laude, Phi Beta Kappa, 1978); George Washington University (J.D., cum laude, 1985). Author: Note, "Recent Amendments to the Age Discrimination in Employment Act," 19 George Washington Journal of International Law and Economics 165, 1985. *Member:* The District of Columbia Bar; Maryland State Bar; AFL-CIO Lawyers Coordinating Committee, 1988—. **Email:** lzanar@compuserve.com

OF COUNSEL

IRA M. LECHNER, born New York, N.Y., May 4, 1934; admitted to bar, 1958, New York; 1962, District of Columbia; 1967, Virginia. *Education:* Randolph-Macon College (B.A., 1955); Yale Law School (LL.B., 1958). Treasurer, Executive Committee, Council for Higher Education Accreditation, 1996—. Member, Executive Committee, Sidney Kimmel Cancer Center. Member, Board of Trustees, Randolph Macon College, 1989-1998. Chairman: Arlington County Tenant-Landlord Commission, 1971-1974; Arlington Health Care Commission, 1978-1980. Member, Virginia State Legislature, 1974-1978. Counsel, Employment and Productivity Subcommittee, U.S. Senate Labor and Human Resources Committee, 1987. *Member:* District of Columbia Bar; Virginia State Bar; American Bar Association. [1st Lt. (JAG) U.S. Army, 1959-1962]. **Email:** lechner@connectnet.com

---

KATZ & STONE, L.L.P.

1120 19TH STREET, N.W.
7TH FLOOR
WASHINGTON, D.C. 20036
Telephone: 703-761-3000
Facsimile: 703-761-6179
Email: info@katzandstone.com
URL: http://www.katzandstone.com

Vienna, Virginia Office: Suite 600, 8230 Leesburg Pike. Telephone: 703-761-3000.

Rockville, Maryland Office: 600 East Jefferson Street, Suite 201, 20852. Telephone: 703-761-3000.

Construction, Public Contract, Surety and Alternative Dispute Resolution, Practice before Federal and State Courts.

(For Complete Biographical Data on all Personnel, See Professional Biographies at Vienna, Virginia)

KAYE SCHOLER LLP

A New York Limited Liability Partnership
MCPHERSON BUILDING
901 FIFTEENTH STREET, N.W., SUITE 1100
WASHINGTON, D.C. 20005-2327
Telephone: 202-682-3500
Facsimile: 202-682-3580
URL: http://www.kayescholer.com

New York, N.Y.: 425 Park Avenue, 10022-3598. Telephone: 212-836-8000. Telex: 234860 KAY UR. Facsimile: 212-836-8689.

Los Angeles, California: 1999 Avenue of the Stars, Suite 1600, 90067-6048. Telephone: 310-788-1000. Facsimile: 310-788-1200.

West Palm Beach, Florida Office: Phillips Point, West Tower 900, 777 South Flagler Drive, 33401-6163. Telephone: 561-802-3230. Facsimile: 561-802-3217.

Chicago, Illinois Office: 311 South Wacker Drive, 62nd Floor, 60606. Telephone: 312-583-2300. Facsimile: 312-583-2360.

(This Listing Continued)

Hong Kong: Suite 2006-2010, One International Finance Centre, No. 1 Harbor View Street, Central. Telephone: 011 852-28458989. Facsimile: 011 852-28452389.

Shanghai, Peoples Republic of China: Suite 1504-1506 CITIC Square, 1168 Nanjing Xi Lu, 200041. Telephone: 011 86-21 5298-4266. Facsimile: 011 86-21 5298-4277.

London, England Office: 10th Floor, 88 Wood Street, EC 2V 7RS. Telephone: 011-020-8528-1006. Fax: 011-020-8528-1174.

General and Administrative Practice.

RESIDENT PARTNERS

SYLVIA M. BECKER, admitted to bar, 1987, District of Columbia. *Education:* Georgetown University (B.S.F.S., cum laude, 1980; M.S.F.S. and J.D., magna cum laude, 1987). Order of the Coif. Fellow at Women's Legal Defense Fund through Women's Law and Public Policy Fellowship Program, 1987-1988. Robert Bosch Foundation Fellow, 1990-1991. *Member:* The District of Columbia Bar. ***PRACTICE AREAS:*** Foreign Investment; Commercial Litigation; Intellectual Property; Internet Law.

DAVID O. BICKART, admitted to bar, 1969, New York; 1981, District of Columbia. *Education:* Harvard University (A.B., magna cum laude, 1966); New York University (J.D., cum laude, 1969). Editor in Chief, New York University Law Review, 1968-1969. Adjunct Professor, Georgetown University Law Center. Law Clerk to: Judge Inzer B. Wyatt, U.S. District Court, Southern District of New York, 1969-1970; Chief Justice Warren E. Berger, U.S. Supreme Court, 1970-1971. Deputy Assistant Director, Bureau of Consumer Protection, Federal Trade Commission, 1971-1977. Deputy General Counsel, U.S. Environmental Protection Agency, 1977-1981. *Member:* The District of Columbia Bar. ***PRACTICE AREAS:*** Environmental Law; Trade Regulation; Administrative Law; Litigation.

DONALD B. CAMERON, JR., admitted to bar, 1979, District of Columbia. *Education:* Kenyon College (B.A., 1971); Vanderbilt University School of Law (J.D., 1974); Vrije Universiteit, Brussels, Program on International Legal Cooperation, Brussels, Belgium (LL.M., 1975). *Member:* The District of Columbia Bar; American Bar Association. ***SPECIAL AGENCIES:*** U.S. Department of Commerce; International Trade Commission; Office of the U.S. Trade Representative; World Trade Organization; U.S. Customs Service. ***PRACTICE AREAS:*** International Trade.

G. CHRISTOPHER GRINER, admitted to bar, 1973, Pennsylvania; 1976, District of Columbia. *Education:* Lehigh University (B.A., 1971); Rutgers University (J.D., 1973). *Member:* The District of Columbia Bar. ***PRACTICE AREAS:*** International Transactions; National Security Law; Technology Licensing; Export Regulation; Export Compliance.

RONALD K. HENRY, admitted to bar, 1976, District of Columbia. *Education:* University of Michigan (B.A., 1973; J.D., magna cum laude, 1976). Phi Beta Kappa. Note and Comment Editor, Journal of Law Reform, 1975-1976. *Member:* The District of Columbia Bar; American Bar Association (Member: Public Contracts Section; Litigation Section). ***PRACTICE AREAS:*** Government Contracts; Litigation; Intellectual Property.

MICHAEL P. HOUSE, admitted to bar, 1982, District of Columbia. *Education:* Southern Methodist University (B.F.A., magna cum laude, 1978); University of Texas (J.D., 1981). Managing Editor, Texas Law Review, 1980-1981. Law Clerk to Hon. Walter Ely, Senior U.S. Circuit Judge, U.S. Court of Appeals, Ninth Circuit, 1981-1982. *Member:* The District of Columbia Bar (Member, International Law Section); American Bar Association (Member, Sections on: Administrative Law; International Law and Practice). ***PRACTICE AREAS:*** International Trade; Administrative Law.

JULIE C. MENDOZA, admitted to bar, 1981, District of Columbia. *Education:* Tufts University (B.A., summa cum laude, 1977); Harvard University; Universidad Nacional Autonoma de Mexico, Mexico City, Mexico; University of Chicago Law School (J.D., 1981). ***LANGUAGES:*** Spanish. ***SPECIAL AGENCIES:*** U.S. Department of Commerce; International Trade Commission; Office of the U.S. Trade Representative; World Trade Organization; U.S. Customs Service. ***PRACTICE AREAS:*** International Trade.

C. CHRISTOPHER PARLIN, admitted to bar, 1975, District of Columbia. *Education:* Yale University (B.A., 1971); School of Advanced International Studies (SAIS), Johns Hopkins University (Diploma, 1972); American University (J.D., cum laude, 1975). Managing Editor, Law Review, 1974-1975. Assistant United States Trade Representative (USTR) for the Environment 1994-1995. Deputy Assistant USTR (NAFTA and Mexico), 1994. Deputy Assistant USTR for Multilateral Trade Negotiations, 1993-1994. Legal Advisor, USTR Mission to GATT, Geneva, 1987-1993. Adjunct Professor, Georgetown University Law Center, 1994—. *Member:* District of Columbia Bar; American Bar Association. ***SPECIAL AGENCIES:*** World Trade Organization. ***PRACTICE AREAS:*** International Trade.

MARK S. POPOFSKY, admitted to bar, 1994, California; 1996, District of Columbia. *Education:* Brown University (A.B., magna cum laude, Phi Beta Kappa, 1990); Harvard Law School (J.D., 1993). Executive Editor, ***Harvard***

(This Listing Continued)

KAYE SCHOLER LLP, Washington—Continued

Law Review. Law Clerk, Hon. Dorothy W. Nelson, U.S. Court of Appeals, 9th Circuit, 1993-1994. Attorney, Appellate Section, U.S. Department of Justice, Antitrust Division (Honor's Program), 1994-1997. Special Assistant United States Attorney, Eastern District of Virginia, 1997. Senior Counsel to the Assistant Attorney General, Antitrust Division, U.S. Department of Justice, 1997-1999. Vice Chair, Internet Committee, ABA Antitrust Section, 1997-1998; Vice Chair, Section 2 Committee, ABA Antitrust Section, 2000—; Associate Editor, Computer Industry Committee, U.S. Council for International Business, Antitrust, Intellectual Property, and E-Commerce Committees, 2000—. Adjunct Professor, Advanced Antitrust Seminar, Georgetown University Law Center, 1999—. Author: *Vertical Restraints in the 1990s: Is there a "Thermadonan Reaction" to the Post-Sylvania Orthodoxy?,* 62 Antitrust L.J. 729 (1994). ***PRACTICE AREAS:*** Antitrust and Trade Regulation; Intellectual Property; E-Commerce; Mergers and Acquisitions; Litigation.

KERRY ALAN SCANLON, admitted to bar, 1977, District of Columbia. *Education:* Harvard University (A.B., 1973); University of Freiburg, Germany (Fulbright/DAAD Scholar); Antioch School of Law (J.D., 1977). Law Clerk to Hon. Richard P. Matsch, U.S. District Court, District of Colorado, 1978-1979. Project Director and Staff Attorney, Washington Lawyers' Committee for Civil Rights and Urban Affairs, 1979-1989. Assistant Counsel, NAACP Legal Defense and Educational Fund, Inc., 1989-1994. Deputy Assistant Attorney General, Civil Rights Division, U.S. Department of Justice, 1994-1997. *Member:* The District of Columbia Bar; American Bar Association. ***PRACTICE AREAS:*** Civil Rights; Employment Discrimination.

JASON L. SHRINSKY, admitted to bar, 1963, Virginia; 1964, District of Columbia. *Education:* University of Pittsburgh (B.A., 1959); George Washington University (J.D., 1962). Delta Theta Phi. Attorney-Advisor, Complaints and Compliance Division, Federal Communications Commission, Washington, D.C., 1961-1964. *Member:* The District of Columbia Bar; The Bar Association of the District of Columbia; Virginia State Bar; Federal Communications and American Bar Associations. ***PRACTICE AREAS:*** Sports Law; Mergers and Acquisitions; Telecommunications Law; Communications Law.

RANDALL L. SPECK, admitted to bar, 1977, District of Columbia. *Education:* Abilene Christian University (B.A., 1968); Harvard University (J.D., cum laude, 1977). Equal Employment Opportunity Specialist, Office of Compliance and Office of the General Counsel, U.S. Equal Employment Opportunity Commission, 1969-1974. Special Counsel: California Public Utilities Commission, 1984-1988; Connecticut Department of Public Utilities Control, 1997-1998. ***PRACTICE AREAS:*** Litigation, International Arbitration.

SPECIAL COUNSEL

WILLIAM S. EBERLE, (P.A.), admitted to bar, 1950, Idaho (Not admitted in District of Columbia). *Education:* Stanford University (B.A., 1945); Harvard Business School (M.B.A., 1947); Harvard Law School (LL.B., 1949). Member, 1953-1960 and Speaker, 1961, Idaho House of Representatives. Vice President, Boise Cascade Corporation, 1958-1965. United States Trade Representative and Special Representative of the President of the United States with the Rank of Ambassador, 1971-1975. Chairman and CEO American Standard, 1966-1971. *Member:* Idaho State Bar; American Bar Association. ***PRACTICE AREAS:*** International Trade.

CHRISTOPHER J. KELLY, admitted to bar, 1983, Illinois (Not admitted in District of Columbia). *Education:* Harvard University (A.B.); Columbia University (J.D.).

STEVEN L. SCHWARCZ, admitted to bar, 1975, New York and U.S. District Court, Southern District of New York (Not admitted in District of Columbia). *Education:* New York University School of Engineering and Science (B.S., summa cum laude, 1971); Columbia University (J.D., 1974). Tau Beta Pi; Sigma Gamma Tau. George Granger Brown Scholar. Adjunct Professor of Law, Benjamin N. Cardozo Law School, 1983-1991. Lecturer in Law, Yale and Columbia Law Schools, 1992-1996. Professor of Law, Duke Law School, 1996—. *Member:* The Association of the Bar of the City of New York (Chairman, Committee on Science and Law, 1987-1990); American Law Institute. Fellow, American College of Commercial Finance Lawyers. ***PRACTICE AREAS:*** Asset Securitization; Structured Finance; Bankruptcy and Corporate Reorganization; Commercial Finance; Banking; International Finance.

COUNSEL

CHRISTOPHER R. BREWSTER, admitted to bar, 1975, Missouri; 1988, District of Columbia. *Education:* Dartmouth College (A.B., cum laude with high honors in Government, 1972); University of Virginia (J.D., 1975). Columnist, The National Law Journal, 1993—. Assistant Attorney General, Missouri, 1975-1977. Subcommittee Chief Counsel, U.S. Senate Committee on Governmental Affairs, 1980-1982. Associate Director for Marketing Practices, Bureau of Consumer Protection, Federal Trade Commission Associate, 1982-1984. *Member:* The District of Columbia Bar; The Missouri Bar. ***PRACTICE AREAS:*** Legislation; Consumer Protection; Product Recall; Advertising Law; False Advertising; Public Contracts Law; Government Ethics; Government Affairs; Foreign Investment in the United States; National Security Law; Foreign Transactions.

(This Listing Continued)

DAVID S. CHRISTY JR., admitted to bar, 1991, New York; 1992, District of Columbia and U.S. Court of International Trade; 1993, U.S. Court of Appeals for the Federal Circuit. *Education:* University of Kansas (B.A., with distinction and departmental honors, 1985); University of Chicago (J.D., 1990). Phi Beta Kappa; Pi Sigma Alpha. Adjunct Professor, Georgetown University Law Center, 1998—. *Member:* District of Columbia Bar Association. ***SPECIAL AGENCIES:*** World Trade Organization. ***PRACTICE AREAS:*** Litigation; International Trade.

BRUCE ALAN EISEN, admitted to bar, 1970, District of Columbia. *Education:* Syracuse University (A.B., 1966); American University (J.D., 1969). Adjunct Professor of Administrative Law, Antioch University School of Law, 1979-1980. *Member:* The District of Columbia Bar; American and Federal Communications Bar Associations. ***PRACTICE AREAS:*** Communication Law; Telecommunications Law; Internet Law.

FARHAD JALINOUS, admitted to bar, 1990, Pennsylvania; 1991, District of Columbia. *Education:* Georgetown University (B.A., summa cum laude, 1987; J.D., cum laude, 1990). Phi Beta Kappa. ***LANGUAGES:*** Persian and French. ***PRACTICE AREAS:*** International Transactions; Export Compliance; Export Regulation; National Security Law.

RAYMOND PARETZKY, admitted to bar, 1990, Pennsylvania; 1991, District of Columbia. *Education:* Queens College of the City University of New York (B.A., summa cum laude, 1983); Oxford University, Oxford, England (B.A./M.A., 1985); Yale University (J.D., 1988). Phi Beta Kappa. Rhodes Scholarship. Law Clerk, U.S. District Judge Douglas P. Woodlock, District of Massachusetts, 1988-1989. Member, Washington, D.C. Council, Lawyers Committee for Human Rights. ***PRACTICE AREAS:*** International Trade.

R. WILL PLANERT, admitted to bar, 1987, District of Columbia. *Education:* College of William and Mary (A.B., 1984); University of Michigan (J.D., cum laude, 1987). Phi Beta Kappa. Contributing Editor, University of Michigan Law Review, 1986-1987. *Member:* The District of Columbia Bar. ***PRACTICE AREAS:*** International Trade.

JOHN P. RYNKIEWICZ, admitted to bar, 1981, Pennsylvania (Not admitted in District of Columbia). *Education:* King's College (B.A., magna cum laude, 1978); Dickinson School of Law (J.D., 1981). ***PRACTICE AREAS:*** Trademarks; Intellectual Property; Electronic Commerce; Internet.

RESIDENT ASSOCIATES

Nicole J. Becton (Not admitted in DC); ***Crystal J. Jones*** (Not admitted in DC); ***John R. Miles; Brady W. Mills; Allan Gary Moskowitz; T. Melindah Musa; Margaret Scicluna*** (Not admitted in DC); ***Deborah L. Wengel.***

(For complete biographical data on other personnel, see Professional Biographies at New York, New York, Los Angeles, California, West Palm Beach, Florida, Chicago, Illinois, Hong Kong, China, Shanghai, China and London, England)

KEIL & WEINKAUF

Established in 1947

1101 CONNECTICUT AVENUE, N.W.
WASHINGTON, D.C. 20036
Telephone: 202-659-0100
Telecopier: 202-659-0105

Patent, Trademark, Copyright, Unfair Competition, Licensing and Related Antitrust Law. Litigation.

FIRM PROFILE: Keil & Weinkauf handles all manner of intellectual property, with an emphasis on patent and trademark issues, and a particular concentration on chemical patents.

MEMBERS OF FIRM

HERBERT B. KEIL, born Chicago, Illinois, August 12, 1927; admitted to bar, 1953, Illinois; 1978, U.S. Supreme Court; 1980, District of Columbia; 1982, U.S. Court of Appeals, Federal Circuit. *Education:* North Central College and College of William & Mary (B.S.Chem., 1950); Chicago-Kent College of Law (J.D., 1953). Delta Theta Phi. Author: Papers, "Doctrine of Equivalents," 1963; "Double Patenting and Terminal Disclaimers," 1968; "The Patentability of Chemical Compositions," 1978, "U.S. Antitrust Law," 1988. Adjunct Professor, Patent Law, Trademark Law, Antitrust Law and Trade Regulations, Chicago-Kent College of Law, 1963-1983. *Member:* American Bar Association; Patent Law Association of Chicago; American Intellectual Property Law Association. ***PRACTICE AREAS:*** Chemical Patent Law; Patent; Trademark Law; Litigation. ***Email:*** hkeil555@aol.com

(This Listing Continued)

RUSSELL E. WEINKAUF, born Waukesha, Wisconsin, July 8, 1923; admitted to bar, 1951, Wisconsin (Not admitted in District of Columbia). *Education:* University of Texas; University of Wisconsin-Madison (B.S., 1948; LL.B., 1951). *Member:* State Bar of Wisconsin; American Bar Association. ***PRACTICE AREAS:*** Patent; Trademark Law.

JASON D. VOIGHT, born Arlington, Virginia, April 20, 1968; admitted to bar, 1996, Texas; 1999, District of Columbia; registered to practice before U.S. Patent and Trademark Office. *Education:* Cornell University (B.S., Ch.E., 1990); University of Texas, Austin (J.D., 1996). Tau Beta Pi. *Member:* American Bar Association. ***PRACTICE AREAS:*** Patents; Trademark Law; Litigation. ***Email:*** voightjd@aol.com

SPECIAL COUNSEL

GERALD H. BJORGE, born Sioux Falls, South Dakota, April 27, 1937; admitted to bar, 1966, District of Columbia; 1966-1982, U.S. Court of Customs and Patent Appeals; 1980, U.S. Supreme Court; 1982, U.S. Court of Appeals for the Federal Circuit. *Education:* Northwestern University (B.S., Ch.E., 1959); Princeton University (M.S., Ch.E., 1962); George Washington University (LL.B., 1964). Textile Research Institute Fellow, 1959-1961. Editor-in-Chief, The Federal Circuit Bar Journal, 1990—. Editor-in-Chief, Journal of the Patent and Trademark Office Society, 1975-1986. Author: "35 U.S.C. 103: The PTO, The Courts and Future," 5 APLA Quarterly Journal 137, 1977; "Diamond v. Chakrabarty Puts New Life in The Patent System," III Proceedings 1981 Batelle Conference on Genetic Engineering 3; "Editors Note: in re Wertheim," 63 J. Pat. Off. Soc. 213, 1981. Examiner-in-Chief and Member, Board of Patent Appeals & Interferences, U.S. Patent & Trademark Office, 1983-1986. Associate Solicitor, U.S. Patent & Trademark Office, 1973-1983. Technical Advisor to Chief Judge Eugene Worley, U.S. Court of Customs and Patent Appeals, 1964-1973. *Member:* District of Columbia Bar (Member, Steering Committee, Patent Trademark Copyright Section, 1982-1984); Patent Lawyers Club of Washington (President, 1979-1980); Federal Circuit Bar Association (Member, Board of Governors, 1993—); American Bar Association; American Intellectual Property Law Association; American College of Legal Medicine. ***PRACTICE AREAS:*** Patents; Trademark Law.

NORMAN G. TORCHIN, born Washington, D.C., December 24, 1929; admitted to bar, 1961, District of Columbia. *Education:* George Washington University (B.S., 1951; J.D., 1960). Author: "The Pitfall of Interference Practice: 37 CFR 231," 60J Pat. Off. Soc. 597-594, Sept., 1978. Member, Patent Office Society, 1957-1990. Patent Examiner (Chemical Arts), 1956-1962, Supervisory Primary Examiner, 1971 and Patent Interference Examiner, 1976-1977; Member, Board of Patent Interferences, 1978-1984, U.S. Patent and Trademark Office. Member, Committee on Enrollment, U.S. Patent and Trademark Office, 1977-1989. Examiner-in-Chief and Member, Board of Patent Appeals and Interferences, U.S. Patent and Trademark Office, 1985-1990. *Member:* The District of Columbia Bar. ***PRACTICE AREAS:*** Patents; Trademark Law.

GEORGE F. HELFRICH, born New Orleans, Louisiana, July 22, 1933; admitted to bar, 1970, Louisiana (Not admitted in District of Columbia). *Education:* Tulane University of Louisiana (B.S., Chemistry, 1955); Louisiana State University (J.D., 1970). Phi Beta Kappa. Fulbright Scholar in Chemistry at the Institute of Technology, Karlsruhe, Germany, 1959-1960. Research Chemist, Dow Chemical Company, 1960-1970. Patent Counsel: BASF Corporation, Williamsburg, Virginia, 1970-1986; NASA Langley Research Center, Hampton, Virginia, 1987—. ***LANGUAGES:*** German. ***PRACTICE AREAS:*** Chemical Patents; Litigation; Licensing; Trade Secret and Trademark Law.

RONALD H. SMITH, born Green Bay, Wisconsin, November 26, 1938; admitted to bar, 1976, Maryland; registered to practice before U.S. Patent and Trademark Office (Not admitted in District of Columbia). *Education:* University of Wisconsin-Madison (B.S.Ch.E., 1960); University of Maryland (J.D., 1976). Tau Beta Pi. Member: Patent Office Society, 1965-1999; Board of Patent Appeals and Interferences, U.S. Patent and Trademark Office, 1981-1998. ***PRACTICE AREAS:*** Patents.

ASSOCIATES

DANIEL S. KIM, born South Korea, December 19, 1972; admitted to bar, 2001, District of Columbia. *Education:* Harvard University (A.B., 1995); Emory University (J.D., 2000). *Member:* American Bar Association; The District of Columbia Bar. ***LANGUAGES:*** Korean. ***PRACTICE AREAS:*** Patents. ***Email:*** dankim@post.harvard.edu

DAVID C. LIECHTY, born Salt Lake City, Utah, August 9, 1969; admitted to bar, 1999, Utah; registered to practice before U.S. Patent and Trademark Office (Not admitted in District of Columbia). *Education:* Brigham Young University (B.S., with honors, 1996); University of Utah (J.D., 1999). Reza Ali Khazeni Memorial Fellowship. Marriners Eccles Foundation Graduate Fellowship in Law. Articles Editor, Journal of Law and Family Studies, 1998-1999. *Member:* Utah State Bar. ***PRACTICE AREAS:*** Chemical Patents; Biotechnology Patents. ***Email:*** dcliechty@hotmail.com

(This Listing Continued)

OF COUNSEL

MELVIN GOLDSTEIN, born Philadelphia, Pennsylvania, March 8, 1934; admitted to bar, 1970, Maryland; 1980, California and U.S. Supreme Court; registered to practice before U.S. Patent and Trademark Office (Not admitted in District of Columbia). *Education:* Temple University (A.B., 1955); University of California at Los Angeles (Ph.D., 1962); Georgetown University (J.D., 1970). Member, Board of Patent Appeals and Interferences, U.S. Patent and Trademark Office, 1976-1996. *Member:* State Bar of California. ***PRACTICE AREAS:*** Patents.

PATENT AGENT

HENRY R. JILES, born Washington, D.C., November 30, 1931. *Education:* Delaware State College (B.S., Chemistry, 1955). Registered to practice before U.S. Patent and Trademark Office. *Education:* Delaware State College (B.S., Chemistry, 1955); Federal Executive Institute for Senior Executives in the Federal Service (Session 34, 1976). Commerce-Science Fellow, 1978-1979. Patent Examiner, Chemical Arts, 1955-1967 and Supervisory Primary Examiner, 1968-1987, U.S. Patent and Trademark Office.

EDWARD J. SMITH, born Stuart Florida, Frbruary 10, 1931. *Education:* University of Florida (B.S., chemistry, 1953). registered to practice before U.S. Patent and Trademark Office. Phi Beta Kappa. Patent Agent, Shell Development, 1966-1969. Patent Examiner, Chemical Arts, 1961-1966, 1969-1999, U.S. Patent and Trademark Office.

TECHNICAL AND FOREIGN PATENT ADVISOR

BARBARA A. SCHWALGE, born Dortmund, Germany, May 28, 1956. *Education:* Rheinische Friedrich Wilhelms University, Bonn, Germany (Ph.D., Chemistry, 1986). Institute of Professional Representatives before the European Patent Office, 1995. European Patent Attorney (EPO 1995). ***LANGUAGES:*** German. ***PRACTICE AREAS:*** Chemical Patents; Licensing.

KELLER AND HECKMAN LLP

Established in 1962

SUITE 500 WEST, 1001 G STREET, N.W.

WASHINGTON, D.C. 20001

Telephone: 202-434-4100
Cable Address: "Kelman"
Telex: 49 95551
Telecopier: 202-434-4646
URL: http://www.khlaw.com

San Francisco, California Office: California Street Center, 50 California Street, Suite 1500. Telephone: 415-277-5952. Telecopier: 415-439-5299.

Brussels, Belgium Office: 25 Rue Blanche B-1060. Telephone: 32 (2) 541 05 70. Telecopier: 32 (2) 541 05 80.

Administrative Practice before Federal Departments and Agencies of Federal, State and Foreign Governments; Representation before Congress and State Legislatures; Civil and Criminal Litigation before Federal and State Courts; Trade Associations Representation; Domestic and International Business Transactions. Food and Drug, Telecommunications, Environmental, Occupational Health and Safety, Labor and Employment, Transportation, Litigation, International Trade, Antitrust and Trade Regulation, Product Liability, Advertising and Labeling, Corporate, Contracts, Intellectual Property, Biotechnology, and Internet and E-Commerce.

FIRM PROFILE: Keller and Heckman, founded in 1962 has a broad practice in regulatory law, litigation and business transactions, serving both domestic and foreign clients. The firm has been a pioneer in the use of inter-disciplinary approaches in problem-solving; for example, since 1971 the firm has had an in-house scientific staff, which works closely with the firm's attorneys in matters of great technical complexity. In addition, many of the firm's attorneys have expertise in multiple areas of law, as well as experience in government.

Keller and Heckman represents a wide spectrum of companies, trade associations and individuals. The firm has experience with a range of industries, including food and food additives, plastics and chemicals, drugs and medical devices, transportation and telecommunications. The firm emphasizes creative service to clients involved in the development of new products, services and markets.

MEMBERS OF FIRM

JOSEPH E. KELLER (1907-1994).

JEROME H. HECKMAN, born Washington, D.C., June 7, 1927; admitted to bar, 1953, District of Columbia and U.S. Court of Appeals for the District of Columbia Circuit; 1965, U.S. Supreme Court. *Education:* Georgetown University (B.S.S., 1948; J.D., 1953). Phi Delta Phi. Listed in: Who's Who in America and Who's Who in American Law. Federal Legislation Editor, Georgetown University Law Journal, 1952-1953. President, The Plastics Academy of the

(This Listing Continued)

KELLER AND HECKMAN LLP, Washington—Continued

United States, 1995-1997. Member: Editorial Board, "Regulatory Toxicology and Pharmacology; Council of "International Society of Regulatory Toxicology and Pharmacology," 1981—; Editorial Board, "Food Drug Cosmetic Law Journal," Food and Drug Law Institute, 1985-1988. Author: "Fathoming Food Packaging Regulation: A Guide to Independent Industry Action," 42 Food Drug Cosmetic Law Journal 38 (January, 1987); "Harmonizing Food Packaging Regulations: An American and European Dilemma," 47 Food and Drug Law Journal, 579 (May, 1992); "De Minimis and Harmonization of International Regulations," ICI International "Plastics for Packaging Food" Symposium, Geneva, May, 1994. Inducted into the Plastics Industry Hall of Fame on October 8, 1986. Awarded the National Sanitation Foundation Spes Hominum (Hope of Mankind) award on April 21, 1987. Awarded, William Bradbury Lifetime Achievement Award by Plastics Industry, March 2, 2000. Awarded, Director's Citation, Food & Drug Administration Center for Food Safety and Applied Nutrition, June 23, 2000. *Member:* The District of Columbia Bar; Bar Association of the District of Columbia; American Bar Association; Federal Communications Bar Association. ***PRACTICE AREAS:*** Food and Drug Law; Antitrust Law; Trade Regulation Law. ***Email:*** heckman@khlaw.com

WILLIAM H. BORGHESANI, JR., born Plymouth, Massachusetts, February 21, 1931; admitted to bar, 1957, Massachusetts; 1958, District of Columbia; 1960, U.S. Supreme Court. *Education:* Boston College (A.B., 1952; J.D., 1957). Author, "Truck Transportation Manual for Wholesale Grocers," "Trucking Labor Relations for Wholesale Grocers," and "Private Carrier Options Workbook." Attorney Advisor, Federal Communications Commission, 1957-1958. ***PRACTICE AREAS:*** Transportation Law; Telecommunications Law; Environmental Law. ***Email:*** borghesani@khlaw.com

WAYNE V. BLACK, born Kansas City, Missouri, April 12, 1937; admitted to bar, 1964, Missouri and District of Columbia; 1969, U.S. Court of Appeals, District of Columbia Circuit; 1976, U.S. Supreme Court. *Education:* University of Missouri (B.S., 1959); George Washington University (LL.B., 1964). *Member:* The District of Columbia Bar; Missouri Bar; American Bar Association. ***PRACTICE AREAS:*** Telecommunications Law; Trade Regulation Law; Antitrust Law. ***Email:*** black@khlaw.com

TERRENCE D. JONES, born Washington, D.C., July 10, 1939; admitted to bar, 1966, District of Columbia. *Education:* University of Florida (B.A., 1961); Georgetown University (J.D., 1965). Member, The Georgetown Law Journal, 1962-1964. Attorney, Trade Regulation Rules Division and General Counsel's Office, Federal Trade Commission, 1965-1970. *Member:* The District of Columbia Bar; Bar Association of the District of Columbia; American Bar Association. ***PRACTICE AREAS:*** Transportation Law; Trade Regulation Law. ***Email:*** jones@khlaw.com

MARTIN W. BERCOVICI, born Omaha, Nebraska, November 7, 1942; admitted to bar, 1968, District of Columbia; 1969, California and U.S. Court of Appeals for the District of Columbia Circuit; 1973, U.S. Supreme Court. *Education:* University of Missouri (B.S., cum laude, 1964); New York University (J.D., 1967). Staff Member, 1965 Annual Survey of American Law and Articles Editor, 1966 Annual Survey of American Law, New York University. Clerk, Honorable Joseph A. Waddy, U.S. District Court, District of Columbia, 1968. Vice-Chairman, Federal Advisory Committee for the 1987 World Administrative Radio Conference for the Mobile Services, 1985-1987. Member, U.S. Delegation World Administrative Radio Conference for the Mobile Services, 1987. *Member:* The District of Columbia Bar; American Bar Association; Federal Communications Bar Association. ***PRACTICE AREAS:*** Transportation Law; Telecommunications Law; Import and Export Law. ***Email:*** bercovici@khlaw.com

JOHN S. ELDRED, born Paducah, Kentucky, January 21, 1945; admitted to bar, 1969, Kentucky; 1975, District of Columbia. *Education:* Vanderbilt University (B.A., 1966); University of Kentucky (J.D., 1969). Delta Theta Phi. Staff Member, University of Kentucky Law Journal, 1967-1969. Member: Editorial Board, The Food and Drug Law Journal, 1996-1998; Editorial Advisory Board, World Food Regulation Review, 1990—. Trial Attorney, U.S. Food and Drug Administration, 1970-1975. *Member:* The District of Columbia Bar; Kentucky and American Bar Associations. ***PRACTICE AREAS:*** Food and Drug Law; Trade Regulation Law; Litigation. ***Email:*** eldred@khlaw.com

RICHARD J. LEIGHTON, born New York, N.Y., October 16, 1939; admitted to bar, 1971, Maryland, District of Columbia and U.S. Court of Appeals of Maryland; 1973, U.S. Claims Court; 1975, U.S. Supreme Court; 1977, U.S. Court of Appeals for the District of Columbia Circuit; 1981, U.S. Court of Appeals, 7th Circuit; 1982, U.S. Court of Appeals for the Federal Circuit; 1984, U.S. Court of Appeals, Fourth and Ninth Circuits; 1997, U.S. District Court, District of Maryland. *Education:* Pennsylvania State University (B.A., 1962); American University (J.D., 1970). Member, American University Law Review, 1969-1970. Author, "Lawyers and the Legal Profession," Encyclopedia of the Future, MacMillan, 1996. Co-Author: "The Supreme Court's True Colors—Trade Dress Argued Again," The Strategist, 1993 (with S. Anthony); "U.S. Direct Marketing Law: The Complete Handbook for Managers," Libey, 1993

(This Listing Continued)

(with A. Regnery). Consultant, Subcommittee on Regulatory Reform, Senate Judiciary Committee, U.S. Senate, 1980. Chairman, Council on Administrative Law, Chamber of Commerce of the United States, 1983-1987. Chairman, Adjudication Committee, Administrative Conference of the United States, 1984-1995. Member, Legal Advisory Board, Reagan-Bush 84, 1984-1985. Editorial Advisor, Inside Litigation, Prentice Hall, 1986-1995. Vice Chairman, Adjudication Committee, American Bar Association Section on Administrative Law, 1989. President, Federal American Inn of Court, 1998-2000. Chair, ADR Committee, U.S. Trademark Association, 1998-1999. One of Washington's "50 Best Lawyers," Washingtonian Magazine, 1992. ADR Panel Member, Center for Public Resources - International Trademark Association, 1993—. Instructor and Program Leader, National Institute of Trial Advocacy, 1995—. Member, Panel of Arbitrators and Mediators, CPR, 1993—. *Member:* District of Columbia Bar; Maryland State, Federal and American Bar Associations; Member, Panel of Arbitrators and Panel of Mediators, American Arbitration Association, 1988—. ***PRACTICE AREAS:*** Commercial Litigation; Food, Drug, Cosmetic and Device Litigation; Trade Regulation; Labeling and Advertising; Intellectual Property; Franchise Disputes; Employment Law; General Business Disputes. ***Email:*** leighton@khlaw.com

DOUGLAS J. BEHR, born Cincinnati, Ohio, June 25, 1947; admitted to bar, 1973, District of Columbia, Maryland and U.S. Supreme Court. *Education:* Northwestern University (B.A., 1969); New York University (J.D., 1972); Georgetown University (LL.M., 1975). Root-Tilden Scholar. Member, New York University Law Review, 1971-1972. E. Barrett Prettyman, Legal Intern, Georgetown University Law School, 1972-1974. Author: "Prescription Drug Control Under the Federal Controlled Substances Act: A Web of Administrative, Civil and Criminal Controls," 45 Journal of Urban and Contemporary Law, 41 (1994). Professor, U.S. Department of Agriculture Graduate School, 1986. Assistant U.S. Attorney for the District of Columbia, 1974-1986. Member, American Bar Association Criminal Justice Section Ad Hoc Task Force on Double Jeopardy; American Bar Association Criminal Justice Section White Collar Crime Sub Committee. *Member:* The District of Columbia Bar; Maryland State Bar Association; National Institute of Trial Advocacy (Faculty Member). ***PRACTICE AREAS:*** Commercial Litigation; White-Collar Criminal Defense; General Business Disputes. ***Email:*** behr@khlaw.com

MICHAEL F. MORRONE, born Mount Vernon, New York, July 15, 1946; admitted to bar, 1975, District of Columbia and U.S. Court of Appeals for the District of Columbia. *Education:* Colgate University (B.A., History, with honors, 1968); Georgetown University (J.D., 1974). Phi Alpha Theta. National History Honor Society. Editor, Law and Policy in International Business, 1973-1974. Co-author: "The Michelin Decision: A Possible New Direction for U.S. Countervailing Duty Law," 6 Law and Policy in International Business 1, 1974. *Member:* The District of Columbia Bar; American Bar Association; Federal Communications Bar Association. [U.S. Army, 1969-1971]. ***PRACTICE AREAS:*** Telecommunications Law; Transportation Law. ***Email:*** morrone@khlaw.com

JOHN B. (JACK) RICHARDS, born Sharon, Pennsylvania, December 22, 1950; admitted to bar, 1975, Pennsylvania; 1988, District of Columbia; 1989, U.S. Court of Appeals for the District of Columbia Circuit; 1993, U.S. Supreme Court. *Education:* Pennsylvania State University (B.A., Psychology, with distinction, 1972); Dickinson School of Law (J.D., 1975). Member, Appellate Moot Court Board (1974-1975). Trial Attorney (1976-1978), Chief Enforcement Branch (1978-1980). Deputy Chief (1981-1982) and Chief (1983-1984), Rules Branch, Land Mobile and Microwave Division, Private Radio (now Wireless Telecommunications) Bureau and Legal Assistant (1984-1986), Office of Commissioner Mimi Weyforth Dawson, Federal Communications Commission. *Member:* Federal Communications Bar Association. ***PRACTICE AREAS:*** Telecommunications Law. ***Email:*** richards@khlaw.com

JEAN M. SAVIGNY, born Nogent-le-Rotrou, France, February 28, 1947; admitted to bar, 1976, Paris. *Education:* Faculté de Droit et des Sciences Economiques de Caen (Licence en Droit, 1969); Institut d'Etudes Politiques de Paris (Diplôme Section Economique et Financiére, 1971). Internship, Commission of the European Communities, Brussels, 1970; Associate, Clifford Turner, Paris, 1973-1976; Counsel France, John Deere, Orléans, 1976-1983; Section President, Labour Court, Orléans, 1982-1984; European Counsel, Corning Glass Works, Paris, London, 1984-1988; Partner, Jeantet & Associés, 1988-1992. *Member:* International Bar Association. (Resident, Brussels, Belgium Office). ***LANGUAGES:*** French, German. ***PRACTICE AREAS:*** European and International Practice. ***Email:*** savigny@khlaw.be

JOHN B. DUBECK, born Orange, New Jersey, November 25, 1949; admitted to bar, 1976, Virginia; 1977, District of Columbia and U.S. Court of Appeals for the District of Columbia Circuit; 1980, U.S. Supreme Court. *Education:* Cornell University (B.S., Chem. Eng., with distinction, 1971); Georgetown University (J.D., 1976). Tau Beta Pi. Author: "Food Additives and Packaging Materials," 3 Toxic Substances Journal 197, Winter, 1981/1982; "The Next Pesticide Data Compensation Battleground: Inert Ingredients," Chemical Regulation Reporter, May 8, 2000. *Member:* The District of Columbia Bar; Virginia

(This Listing Continued)

State Bar; American Bar Association. [Lt., USN, Division of Naval Reactors, 1971-1976]. ***PRACTICE AREAS:*** Food and Drug Law; Environmental Law; Trade Regulation Law. ***Email:*** dubeck@khlaw.com

PETER L. DE LA CRUZ, born New York, New York, December 27, 1947; admitted to bar, 1976, Ohio; 1980, U.S. Supreme Court; 1982, District of Columbia. *Education:* Cornell University (A.B., 1969); University of Toledo (J.D., 1976). Associate Editor, Toledo Law Review, 1975-1976. Attorney, Antitrust Division, Department of Justice, 1976-1980. Staff Member, National Commission for the Review of Antitrust Laws and Procedures, 1978-1979. Co-author: "Environmental and Workplace Safety: A Guide for University, Hospital and School Managers," (1996); "Look Both Ways: Trends in Competition Analysis of Retail and Distribution Functions," European Retail Digest (Oxford, 2001). *Member:* The District of Columbia Bar; American Bar Association. ***PRACTICE AREAS:*** Environmental Law; Trade Association Law; Antitrust and Trade Regulation. ***Email:*** delacruz@khlaw.com

MELVIN S. DROZEN, born Buffalo, New York, April 7, 1949; admitted to bar, 1976, New York; 1979, District of Columbia; 1986, U.S. Court of Appeals for the District of Columbia Circuit. *Education:* Georgetown University (B.A., 1971); Brooklyn Law School (J.D., 1975). Associate Chief Counsel, U.S. Food and Drug Administration, 1979-1987. Assistant District Attorney, Brooklyn, New York, 1975-1979. *Member:* The District of Columbia Bar; New York State Bar Association. ***PRACTICE AREAS:*** Food and Drug Law; Trade Regulation Law. ***Email:*** drozen@khlaw.com

LAWRENCE P. HALPRIN, born Philadelphia, Pennsylvania, October 30, 1952; admitted to bar, 1977, Pennsylvania; 1978, District of Columbia. *Education:* University of Pennsylvania (B.S.Ch.E., with honors, 1974); Duquesne University (J.D., 1977); George Washington University (M.B.A. in Finance and Investments, 1984). Beta Gamma Sigma. Staff Member, Duquesne Law Review, 1975-1977. Law Clerk, Honorable Charles R. Johnston, U.S. Tax Court, 1977-1978. Author: "Can OSHA Constitutionally Bring Criminal Charges Against Businesses Based on Evidence Obtained Under an Administrative Inspection Warrant?" Washington Legal Foundation, Legal Backgrounder, Vol. 9 No. 11; "Sixth Circuit Provides Employers with Legal Basis to Challenge OSHA Inspections," Washington Legal Foundation, Legal Backgrounder, Vol. 9 No. 28. *Member:* The District of Columbia Bar; Pennsylvania and American Bar Associations. ***PRACTICE AREAS:*** Occupational Safety and Health Law; Environmental Law; Hazardous Materials and Substances; Commercial Transactions; Employment Law. ***Email:*** halprin@khlaw.com

RALPH A. SIMMONS, born Cheverly, Maryland, January 12, 1952; admitted to bar, 1977, District of Columbia; 1986, U.S. Supreme Court. *Education:* Princeton University (A.B., 1973); University of Virginia (J.D., 1977). Law Clerk to the Hon. George Herbert Goodrich, Superior Court of the District of Columbia, 1977-1979. Author: "Packaging and Environmental Legislation—United States," Packaging, Policy and the Environment, 1999; "Packaging Laws and Regulations in the United States," The Wiley Encyclopedia of Packaging, 2d Ed., 1997. *Member:* The District of Columbia Bar; American Bar Association. ***PRACTICE AREAS:*** Food and Drug Law; Trade Regulation Law. ***Email:*** simmons@khlaw.com

RICHARD F. MANN, born Dallas, Texas, August 17, 1951; admitted to bar, 1977, Maryland; 1978, District of Columbia; 1980, U.S. Court of Appeals, District of Columbia Circuit; 1983, U.S. District Court for the District of Columbia. *Education:* Vanderbilt University (A.B., 1974); American University (J.D., 1977). *Member:* The District of Columbia Bar; Maryland State and American Bar Associations. ***PRACTICE AREAS:*** Advertising and Labeling; Federal and State Trade Regulation; Food, Drug and Device Law. ***Email:*** mann@khlaw.cm

C. DOUGLAS JARRETT, born Jersey City, New Jersey, June 27, 1952; admitted to bar, 1979, District of Columbia. *Education:* College of the Holy Cross and University of Colorado at Boulder (B.A., cum laude, History, 1974); George Washington University (J.D., 1979). *Member:* The District of Columbia Bar; American Bar Association; Federal Communications Bar Association. ***PRACTICE AREAS:*** Telecommunications Law; Environmental Law; Computer Law. ***Email:*** jarrett@khlaw.com

SHEILA A. MILLAR, born Baltimore, Maryland, February 5, 1953; admitted to bar, 1980, District of Columbia, U.S. Court of Appeals, District of Columbia Circuit and U.S. Supreme Court. *Education:* Bryn Mawr College (B.A., cum laude, 1975); American University (J.D., 1980). Author: "More Than Just Luck," IP Worldwide, April/May 2000. Co-Author: "Product Liability: Prevention and Defense Tips for Associations," Association Law and Policy, August 15, 1994; "Product Safety Management Handbook," Society of the Plastics Industry, Inc., 1994; "Liability Prevention: Corporate Policies and Procedures," Personnel Administration, Feb. 1986; "Trademark, Copyright and Related Issues in the Promotional Products Industry," Promotional Products Association International, 1986, 1994. Presenter, "Associations and the Internet," American Society of Association Executives DC Legal Symposium, November 3, 2000. *Member:* The District of Columbia Bar; American Bar Association; Women's Bar Association of the District of Columbia; Women's Council on Energy and the Environment; International Trademark Association

(This Listing Continued)

(Member, Legislation Committee). ***LANGUAGES:*** French. ***PRACTICE AREAS:*** E-Commerce; Privacy Law; Environmental Law; Trade Regulation Law; Trademark Law; Copyright Law. ***Email:*** millar@khlaw.com

GEORGE G. MISKO, born Washington, D.C., September 9, 1955; admitted to bar, 1980, District of Columbia; 1982, Maryland. *Education:* Catholic University of America (B.A., magna cum laude, 1977; J.D., 1980). Author: "Regulatory Update," Food and Drug Packaging Magazine column. Law Clerk to the Hon. Nicholas S. Nunzio, Superior Court of the District of Columbia, 1981-1982. *Member:* The District of Columbia Bar; Maryland State and Federal Bar Associations. ***PRACTICE AREAS:*** Food and Drug Law; Environmental Law; Trade Regulation Law. ***Email:*** misko@khlaw.com

LESLIE T. KRASNY, born Staten Island, New York, August 6, 1947; admitted to bar, 1982, California. *Education:* University of Wisconsin-Madison (B.A., 1969); San Francisco State University (M.A., Molecular Biology, 1974); Hastings College of the Law, University of California (J.D., 1982). *Member:* Bar Association of San Francisco; State Bar of California; American Bar Association. (Resident, San Francisco, California Office). ***PRACTICE AREAS:*** Food and Drug Regulation; Drug and Medical Device Regulation; Advertising and Labeling; Trademark Registration; Biotechnology. ***Email:*** krasny@khlaw.com

DAVID I. READER, born New York, N.Y., January 18, 1958; admitted to bar, 1983, District of Columbia. *Education:* State University of New York at Albany (B.S., 1980); Southwestern University School of Law (J.D., 1983); Georgetown University (LL.M. in Taxation, 1986). Attorney, Tax Law Specialist, Reorganization Branch, Internal Revenue Service, 1983-1985. *Member:* District of Columbia Bar; American Bar Association. ***PRACTICE AREAS:*** Business Planning; Business Organization; Corporate Law; Transactional Law; Mergers and Acquisitions. ***Email:*** reader@khlaw.com

DAVID G. SARVADI, born Erie, Pennsylvania, September 26, 1947; admitted to bar, 1986, Virginia; 1996, District of Columbia. *Education:* Pennsylvania State University (B.S./B.A., 1969); University of Pittsburgh (M.S.C., 1970); George Mason University School of Law (J.D., 1986). Author: "The Occupational Safety and Health Act," Environmental Law Handbook, Government Institutes, 1992. *Member:* Virginia State Bar; The District of Columbia Bar; Virginia and American Bar Associations. ***PRACTICE AREAS:*** Environmental Law; Occupational Health and Safety Law; Pesticides; Hazardous Materials; Transportation; Products Liability. ***Email:*** sarvadi@khlaw.com

CATHERINE ROEMER NIELSEN, born Montgomery, Alabama, February 7, 1962; admitted to bar, 1987, Virginia; 1989, District of Columbia. *Education:* University of Alabama (B.A., summa cum laude, 1984); University of Virginia (J.D., 1987). Phi Beta Kappa. Member, 1985-1986 and Notes Editor, 1986-1987, Virginia Journal of Natural Resources Law. *Member:* The District of Columbia Bar; Virginia State Bar. ***PRACTICE AREAS:*** Food and Drug Law; Environmental Law. ***Email:*** nielsen@khlaw.com

MARK MANSOUR, born Detroit, Michigan, April 23, 1957; admitted to bar, 1988, Michigan (Not admitted in District of Columbia). *Education:* Georgetown University (B.S.F.S., cum laude, 1979); Harvard University (A.M., 1983); Georgetown University (J.D., 1988). Phi Beta Kappa. *Member:* State Bar of Michigan. ***LANGUAGES:*** Arabic and French. ***PRACTICE AREAS:*** International Trade Regulation; Biotechnology; Food and Drug Law. ***Email:*** mansour@khlaw.com

ELLIOT BELILOS, born Far Rockaway, New York, December 14, 1961; admitted to bar, 1988, Maryland; 1989, District of Columbia. *Education:* Cornell University (B.S., 1983); George Washington University (J.D., with honors, 1988). Managing Editor, The George Washington Journal of International Law and Economics, 1987-1988. *Member:* Maryland State and American Bar Associations; The District of Columbia Bar; Federal American Inn of Court (Barrister). ***PRACTICE AREAS:*** Product Safety Law; Employment Law; Business Law; Commercial Law; Litigation. ***Email:*** belilos@khlaw.com

JEAN-PHILIPPE MONTFORT, born Brussels, Belgium, February 9, 1962; admitted to bar, 1989, Brussels (Not admitted in United States). *Education:* Université de Louvain (Licence en Droit, 1984; Diplôme en Administration des Entreprises, 1985); Georgetown University (LL.M., 1988). Associate, Jeantet & Associés, Brussels Office, 1988-1992. (Resident, Brussels, Belgium Office). ***LANGUAGES:*** French. ***PRACTICE AREAS:*** European Union Law; International Law; Food and Drug Law; Chemicals; Environmental Law. ***Email:*** montfort@khlaw.be

ARTHUR S. GARRETT, III, born Philadelphia, Pennsylvania, July 3, 1965; admitted to bar, 1990, Virginia; 1991, District of Columbia; 1994, U.S. Supreme Court. *Education:* Lafayette College (B.A., Chemical Engineering, 1987); University of Richmond (J.D., 1990). Author: "Recovery of Attorneys' Fees When Insurer Refuses to Defend and Indemnify," The Virginia Environmental Law News, Summer, 1995. *Member:* The District of Columbia Bar; Virginia State Bar (Member, Insurance Coverage Litigation Committee); American Bar Association; Federal American Inn of Court (Barrister). ***PRACTICE AREAS:*** Litigation; Insurance Recovery. ***Email:*** garrett@khlaw.com

JOAN SYLVAIN BAUGHAN, born Needham, Massachusetts, September 20, 1962; admitted to bar, 1991, Massachusetts; 1994, District of Columbia.

(This Listing Continued)

KELLER AND HECKMAN LLP, Washington—Continued

Education: University of Massachusetts (B.S., Microbiology, 1984; B.S., Medical Technology, 1985); Catholic University of America (J.D., 1991). Managing Editor, The Catholic University Law Review, 1990-1991. Author: "Michael H. v. Gerald D.: The Presumption of Paternity," The Catholic University Law Review, Volume 40. Member, Board of Advisors, EuroWatch. *Member:* The District of Columbia Bar; Massachusetts State and American Bar Associations. ***PRACTICE AREAS:*** US and EU Food and Drug Law; Product Safety Law. ***Email:*** baughan@khlaw.com

MARTHA E. MARRAPESE, born Franklin, New Hampshire, July 31, 1962; admitted to bar, 1992, New Hampshire; 1994, District of Columbia. *Education:* University of Vermont (B.S., 1984); Columbus School of Law, Catholic University of America (J.D., 1991). Moot Court Associate; Federalist Society (President, 1990-1991). *Member:* The District of Columbia Bar; New Hampshire and American (Member, Section of Natural Resources and Environmental Law) Bar Associations. ***PRACTICE AREAS:*** Environmental Law; Occupational Safety and Health Law. ***Email:*** marrapese@khlaw.com

DAVID R. JOY, born Idaho Falls, Idaho, August 7, 1964; admitted to bar, 1992, Maryland; 1994, District of Columbia. *Education:* University of Maryland (B.S., 1986); George Washington University (J.D., 1992). ***PRACTICE AREAS:*** Food and Drug Law; Environmental Law. ***Email:*** joy@khlaw.com

FREDERICK A. STEARNS, born Syracuse, New York, March 30, 1966; admitted to bar, 1993, Virginia and U.S. Court of Appeals, Fourth Circuit; 1995, District of Columbia. *Education:* Cornell University (B.S., 1988); George Washington University (J.D., with honors, 1993). *Member:* The District of Columbia Bar; Virginia State Bar. ***PRACTICE AREAS:*** Food and Drug Law. ***Email:*** stearns@khlaw.com

JUSTIN C. POWELL, born Chester, Pennsylvania, October 24, 1943; admitted to bar, 1996, District of Columbia. *Education:* Carnegie-Mellon University (B.S., 1965); University of Delaware (Ph.D., 1969); George Mason University (J.D., 1996). National Science Foundation Fellow, 1965-1969. Recipient, Bronze Medal, U.S. Environmental Protection Agency, 1984. Author: "TSCA: It's Better with Polymers," Living with TSCA 2000, March 28, 2000; "A Practical Understanding of the Amended Polymer Exemption," *in Guidance Manual for Amended Polymer Exemption Rule*, published by The Society of the Plastics Industry, Inc., September, 1996. Associate Professor, Chemistry, University of Delaware, 1968-1969. Senior Research Chemist, Texaco, Inc., eighteen U.S. Patents, 1969-1980; Section Chief, New Chemicals Review, U.S. Environmental Protection Agency, 1980-1989; Special Assistant for Compliance and Enforcement to the Director of the Office of Toxic Substances, U.S. Environmental Protection Agency, 1989. Approved by the Environmental Protection Agency as an Auditor for Compliance with the Toxic Substances Control Act, 1995. *Member:* District of Columbia Bar; Bar Association of the District of Columbia; American Bar Association; American Chemical Society. ***PRACTICE AREAS:*** Domestic and International Chemical Control Law; Chemical Regulation; Chemical Nomenclature. ***Email:*** powell@khlaw.com

ASSOCIATES

GEORGE BRENT MICKUM, IV, born Washington, D.C., June 15, 1954; admitted to bar, 1984, Virginia; 1985, District of Columbia. *Education:* George Washington University (B.A., 1978); George Mason University (J.D., 1984). Delta Theta Phi. Member, Board of Editors and Lead Articles Editor, George Mason University, 1983-1984. Judicial Clerk, Fairfax County Circuit Court, 1984-1985. Senior Investigative Counsel, Special Committee on Investigations, U.S. Senate, 1988; Federal Trade Commission, 1990-1995; Special Assistant, United States Attorney, 1995-1998. Vice Chairman, 1993-1998 and Chairman, 1998-2000, Town Council, Village of North Chevy Chase. *Member:* Virginia State Bar; The District of Columbia Bar; American Bar Association. ***PRACTICE AREAS:*** Litigation; Advertising Law; Federal Practice; Criminal Law. ***Email:*** mickum@khlaw.com

THOMAS B. MAGEE, born Orange, New Jersey, August 18, 1959; admitted to bar, 1991, Colorado, District of Columbia and U.S. Court of Appeals for the District of Columbia Circuit. *Education:* Columbia University; University of Colorado at Boulder (B.A., 1982; J.D., 1990). William J. Bowe Scholar. Recipient, American Jurisprudence Award in Contracts. Staff Editor, University of Colorado Law Review, 1989-1990. *Member:* District of Columbia Bar; American Bar Association; Federal Communications Bar Association. ***LANGUAGES:*** French. ***PRACTICE AREAS:*** Communications Law. ***Email:*** magee@khlaw.com

LESA L. BYRUM, born Bristol, Tennessee, June 18, 1962; admitted to bar, 1991, Virginia, U.S. Court of Appeals, Fourth Circuit, U.S. District Court, Eastern District of Virginia and U.S. Bankruptcy Court, Eastern District of Virginia; 1998, Maryland (Not admitted in District of Columbia). *Education:* James Madison University (B.S., 1984); George Mason University (J.D., 1991). Member, Construction Specifications Institute, 1992-2000. *Member:* Virginia State Bar. ***PRACTICE AREAS:*** Occupational Safety and Health; Employment Law. ***Email:*** byrum@khlaw.com

(This Listing Continued)

NEGIN MOHTADI, born Tehran, Iran, November 2, 1967; admitted to bar, 1992, Michigan; 1993, Illinois; 1994, District of Columbia. *Education:* University of Michigan (B.A., 1988); University of Detroit (J.D., 1992); American University (LL.M., 1994). Phi Alpha Delta. Author: "The Federal Toxics Release Inventory: An Important Tool in Identifying Neighborhood Risks From Chemicals," Journal of Environmental Law and Policy, Washington College of Law, Winter, 1996; "Imminent Hazard Provisions and Their Applications in Central and Eastern Europe," Environmental Law Institute, Nov., 1995. Member, National Honor Society, 1986-1988. *Member:* The District of Columbia Bar; American Bar Association (Member, Women's Council on Energy and the Environment, 1999). ***SPECIAL AGENCIES:*** Office of Administrative Law Judges, EPA, 1996-1998. ***PRACTICE AREAS:*** Environmental Law; Transactional Law; International Law. ***Email:*** mohtadi@khlaw.com

NICOLE B. DONATH, born Queens, New York, May 9, 1966; admitted to bar, 1992, Maryland; 1994, District of Columbia. *Education:* Williams College (B.A., magna cum laude, 1988); Harvard University (J.D., magna cum laude, 1992). Phi Beta Kappa. Student Attorney, Harvard Legal Aid Bureau, 1990-1992. *Member:* Federal Communications Bar Association. ***PRACTICE AREAS:*** Telecommunications. ***Email:*** donath@khlaw.com

DAVID J. ETTINGER, born Queens, New York, March 13, 1967; admitted to bar, 1993, New York and Connecticut; 1999, District of Columbia and U.S. District Court, Southern and Eastern Districts of New York. *Education:* State University of New York at Albany (B.A., cum laude, 1989); Pace University School of Law (J.D., 1992); University of London, London School of Economics and Kings College (LL.M., International Law, 1993). Managing Editor, Pace International Law Review, 1991-1992. Author: "Legal Status of the International Olympic Committee," Pace Yearbook of International Law, Volume 4, 1992. Former Assistant District Attorney, Nassau County, New York. Former Trademark Attorney, U.S. Patent and Trademark Office, Crystal City, Virginia. *Member:* District of Columbia Bar; American Bar Association. ***PRACTICE AREAS:*** Food and Drug Law; Litigation; Trademarks. ***Email:*** ettinger@khlaw.com

JOHN F. FOLEY, born Takoma Park, Maryland, December 18, 1958; admitted to bar, 1993, Pennsylvania; 1996, District of Columbia. *Education:* Boston University (B.A., 1984; M.A., 1984); George Washington University (J.D., 1993). ***PRACTICE AREAS:*** Food and Drug Law; Environmental Law. ***Email:*** foleyj@khlaw.com

THOMAS C. BERGER, born Detroit, Michigan, October 9, 1964; admitted to bar, 1993, Pennsylvania; 1995, District of Columbia. *Education:* Wayne State University; Michigan State University (B.S., Ch.E., 1987); George Washington University (J.D., with honors, 1993). Tau Beta Pi. ***PRACTICE AREAS:*** Environmental Law; Occupational Safety and Health Law. ***Email:*** berger@khlaw.com

RACHIDA SEMAIL, born Villacourt, France, July 22, 1964; admitted to bar, 1994, Paris as Avocat. *Education:* University of Social Sciences Sociales of Toulouse (Doctorate of law). Thesis entitled "La Dénomination des Denrées Alimentaires en Droit Communautaire," 1992. Associate, Coutrelis & Associés, 1994-1997. Internship, Commission of the European Communities, Brussels, 1990-1991. (Resident, Brussels, Belgium Office). ***LANGUAGES:*** French, English. ***PRACTICE AREAS:*** EC Food and Drug Law. ***Email:*** rsemail@khlaw.be

ERIC C. NASTASI, born San Diego, California, May 21, 1970; admitted to bar, 1994, Illinois; 1999, District of Columbia. *Education:* University of Maryland (B.A., 1991); Cleveland-Marshall College of Law (J.D., 1994). Member, Moot Court Board of Governors. *Member:* The District of Columbia Bar; Illinois State Bar Association. ***PRACTICE AREAS:*** Telecommunications Law; Corporate Law; Transactional Law; Mergers and Acquisitions. ***Email:*** nastasi@khlaw.com

JOHN DOBINSON, born Birmingham, UK, September 16, 1967; admitted to bar, 1995, England and Wales. *Education:* University of Kent, Canterbury; University of Grenoble (Law Degree, 1990). Research Assistant at the Centre of International Consumer Law, University of Louvain-la-Neuve, Belgium, 1995-1997. (Resident, Brussels, Belgium Office). ***LANGUAGES:*** English, French, Romanian and Spanish. ***PRACTICE AREAS:*** EU; Central and East European Law; Food Law; Consumer Law. ***Email:*** dobinson@khlaw.be

MANESH K. RATH, born Pittsburgh, Pennsylvania, December 17, 1969; admitted to bar, 1995, Virginia and U.S. District Court, Eastern District of Virginia; 1998, District of Columbia. *Education:* Virginia Polytechnic Institute and State University (B.S., Finance, 1991); College of William & Mary (J.D., 1995). Author: "Left Standing at the Altar: How Relocation Affects the Employment at Will Relationship," 37 South Texas Law Review, 813 (June 1996); "How Relocation Affects the Employment at Will Relationship," 12 The Labor Lawyer 207 (1996); "Is OSHA Watching From Afar?" 7 Compliance Magazine No. 4 at 18 (April 2000). *Member:* Virginia State Bar; Virginia Bar Association (Chair, Young Lawyers Division, Mentor Program, 1995-1997); The District of Columbia Bar. ***PRACTICE AREAS:*** Employment and Labor Law; OSHA; Litigation. ***Email:*** rath@khlaw.com

(This Listing Continued)

CARLOS CELESTINO, born Defiance, Ohio, November 25, 1955; admitted to bar, 1995, Texas (Not admitted in District of Columbia). *Education:* Bowling Green State University (B.A.; 1982); University of Toledo (J.D., 1988). *Member:* State Bar of Texas. ***LANGUAGES:*** Spanish. ***PRACTICE AREAS:*** Food and Drug Regulation; Litigation. ***Email:*** celestino@khlaw.com

LYNN LORIS OWENS, born New York, N.Y., August 7, 1961; admitted to bar, 1995, Pennsylvania; 1997, New Jersey; 2000, District of Columbia. *Education:* Columbia University (B.A., 1989); University of Pennsylvania School of Law (J.D., 1995). Phi Beta Kappa. Federal Inn of Court. *Member:* American Bar Association. ***PRACTICE AREAS:*** Commercial Litigation; Unfair Trade Practices; Products Liability; Toxic Torts. ***Email:*** owens@khlaw.com

DEVON WM. HILL, born Akron, Ohio, December 8, 1965; admitted to bar, 1996, South Carolina; 1999, District of Columbia. *Education:* Furman University (B.S., 1987; M.S., 1993); University of South Carolina (J.D., 1996). (Resident, Brussels, Belgium Office). ***PRACTICE AREAS:*** Food and Drug Law; Environmental. ***Email:*** hill@khlaw.be

JoANNA R. SOFFA, born Ann Arbor, Michigan, February 24, 1971; admitted to bar, 1996, California; 1998, District of Columbia. *Education:* Vassar College (B.A., 1993), Phi Beta Kappa; George Washington University (M.P.H., 1996; J.D., with honors, 1996). *Member:* District of Columbia Bar; American Bar Association. (Resident, San Francisco, California Office). ***PRACTICE AREAS:*** Food and Drug Law. ***Email:*** soffa@khlaw.com

JEAN-CYRIL WALKER, born Port-Au-Prince, Haiti, November 1, 1962; admitted to bar, 1996, Maryland (Not admitted in District of Columbia). *Education:* University of Maryland (B.A., waived, 1992; J.D., 1995). Editor, Environmental Law Reporter, 1995-1997. Deputy Manager, Regulatory and Legislative Services, Waste Policy Institute, 1997-1998. Environmental Counsel, Parsons Engineering Science, 1998-2000. Member, Society of American Military Engineers, 1997-1999. *Member:* American (Natural Resource, Energy and Environment Sections) Bar Association; Environmental Law Institute. [U.S. Marine Corps., 1982-1986]. ***LANGUAGES:*** French. ***PRACTICE AREAS:*** Environmental Law. ***Email:*** walker@khlaw.com

ERIC H. SINGER, born Hartford, Connecticut, December 28, 1961; admitted to bar, 1997, Maryland and U.S. District Court, District of Maryland; 2001, District of Columbia. *Education:* Columbia University (B.A., 1983; M.Phil., 1990); Yale University (M.A., 1985); George Mason University (J.D., 1996). Author: "Can Product Certifiers be Held Liable for Economic Loss from Defective Safety Products?" Product Liability Law and Strategy, Feb. 2000; "The Consumer Product Safety Act and the Common Law Product Liability," For the Defense, February, 2000; "Product Sample Solicitation by the Consumer Product Safety Commission and Section 6(b) of the Consumer Product Safety Act - Time for an Overhaul," Product Liability Advisory, August, 2000. Trial Attorney, Consumer Product Safety Commission, 1997-2000. *Member:* Montgomery County and American Bar Associations; The District of Columbia Bar. ***LANGUAGES:*** Spanish. ***PRACTICE AREAS:*** Litigation; Product Safety. ***Email:*** singer@khlaw.com

COLLEEN M. EVALE, born Syracuse, New York, February 13, 1972; admitted to bar, 1997, Pennsylvania and New Jersey; 1998, District of Columbia. *Education:* University of Notre Dame (B.S., 1994); Villanova University School of Law (J.D., 1997). Author: "Sandison v. Michigan High School Athletic Association: The Sixth Circuit Sets Up Age Restrictions as Insurmountable Hurdles for Learning Disabled High School Student Athletes," The Sports Lawyers Journal, Vol. 5, 1998. *Member:* District of Columbia Bar; American Bar Associations. ***PRACTICE AREAS:*** Food and Drug Law. ***Email:*** evale@khlaw.com

PAMELA L. GAUTHIER, born Laconia, New Hampshire, October 23, 1972; admitted to bar, 1997, Maryland; 1999, District of Columbia. *Education:* Villanova University (B.A., magna cum laude, 1994); George Washington University (J.D., 1997). Phi Beta Kappa. Co-author: "New Municipal Waste Combustor Regulations and Their Impact in the Absence of Flow Controls," The Environmental Lawyer, Vol. 3, 1996. *Member:* District of Columbia Bar; Maryland State and American Bar Associations. ***PRACTICE AREAS:*** Food and Drug Law. ***Email:*** gauthier@khlaw.com

SUSANNE VALLUET, born Düsseldorf, Germany, January 15, 1969; admitted to bar, 2000, Dusseldorf, Germany. *Education:* University of Montpellier, (Maîtrise en droit, with honors, 1993); Albert Luwigs University (with honors, 1995); Düsseldorf Higher Court (1998). (Resident, Brussels, Belgium Office). ***LANGUAGES:*** German, English, French, Spanish. ***PRACTICE AREAS:*** Environmental; European Union Law; Food and Drug Law. ***Email:*** valluet@khlaw.be

ALEXA BOONSTRA BARNETT, born Boulder, Colorado, March 16, 1970; admitted to bar, 1998, Florida; 2001, District of Columbia. *Education:* Davidson College (B.A., 1992); University of Florida (J.D., with honors, 1997). Assistant Chief Counsel, Office of the Chief Counsel, Food and Drug Administration, 1998-2000. *Member:* District of Columbia Bar; American Bar Association. ***PRACTICE AREAS:*** Food and Drug. ***Email:*** barnett@khlaw.com

(This Listing Continued)

MICHAEL T. NOVAK, born Perth Amboy, New Jersey, September 25, 1967; admitted to bar, 1998, Illinois and North Carolina; 2001, District of Columbia. *Education:* University of North Carolina (B.S., 1989); University of South Carolina (J.D., 1992). *Member:* Chicago, Illinois State and North Carolina State Bar Associations. ***PRACTICE AREAS:*** Environmental Law. ***Email:*** novak@khlaw.com

KAREN ROTHSCHILD CAVANAUGH, born Washington, D.C., February 17, 1964; admitted to bar, 1998, New York; 2001, District of Columbia. *Education:* Oberlin College (B.A., 1986); Yeshiva University, Benjamin N. Cardozo School of Law (J.D., 1997). Co-author: with Daniel Pollack: "Child Support Obligations of Incarcerated Parents," 7 Cornell L.J. & Pub. Pol. 2 (Winter 1998); "Liability Safeguards for Foster Parents," 17 A.B.A. Child Law Practice 4 (June 1998); "Child Support Responsibilities of Inmates," 23 Corrections Compendium 5 (May 1998); "Liability Protections for Foster Parents," 6 Kansas J.L. & Pun. Pol. 3 (Summer/Fall 1997). Author: Note, "Emerging South Africa: Human Rights Responses in the Post-Apartheid Era," 5 Cardozo J. Int'l & Comp. L. 1 (Spring 1997). *Member:* The District of Columbia Bar; New York State and American Bar Associations. ***PRACTICE AREAS:*** Food and Drug. ***Email:*** cavanaugh@khlaw.com

NATASHA L. DREW, born Manchester, Connecticut, June 15, 1973; admitted to bar, 1998, California (Not admitted in District of Columbia). *Education:* University of California, Riverside (B.A., magna cum laude, 1995); California Western School of Law (J.D., cum laude, 1998). Co-Author: with T. Redick, "Certifying Settlement in Mass Tort Cases After the Amchem Decision," ABA Toxic Torts and Environmental Litigation Committee Newsletter, Spring 1999; with T. Redick, "Precautionary Priority in Approving Imports of Genetically Improved Commodity Crops," Biotech Law Reporter, Fall 2000; with T. Redick and C. Bernstein, "The 'Right Not to Know' Meets the 'Right to Know': Genetic Susceptibility and the 21st Century Genome," Trends, ABA Section of Environment, Energy and Resources Newsletter, January/February 2001. *Member:* State Bar of California; American Bar Association; Federal American Inn of Court. ***PRACTICE AREAS:*** Litigation. ***Email:*** drew@khlaw.com

DEBORAH W. ZIFFER, born Loch Haven, Pennsylvania, October 31, 1969; admitted to bar, 1998, Maryland; 1999, District of Columbia. *Education:* Christopher Newport University (B.S., 1993); American University (J.D., 1998). *Member:* The District of Columbia Bar; Maryland State and American Bar Associations. ***PRACTICE AREAS:*** Food and Drug. ***Email:*** ziffer@khlaw.com

JEFFREY A. KEITHLINE, born Kansas City, Missouri, October 20, 1965; admitted to bar, 1998, Virginia; 1999, District of Columbia. *Education:* Benedictine College (B.A., Physics, magna cum laude, 1988); Washington & Lee University (J.D., cum laude, 1998). Editor-in-Chief, Washington & Lee Law Review. Author: "Emergency Planning and Community Right-to-Know Citizen Suits," 54 Wash & Lee Law Review. *Member:* Virginia State Bar; District of Columbia Bar; American Bar Association. [LT U.S. Navy, 1988-1995]. ***PRACTICE AREAS:*** Food and Drug; Environmental Law. ***Email:*** keithline@khlaw.com

FRANK J. VITOLO, born Livingston, New Jersey, July 20, 1973; admitted to bar, 1998, New Jersey; 1999, District of Columbia, New York and U.S. District Court, District of New Jersey. *Education:* Boston College (B.A., magna cum laude, 1995); George Washington University (J.D., 1998). Phi Beta Kappa; Order of the Cross and Crown (Marshall). *Member:* The District of Columbia Bar; New York State and American Bar Associations; The Federal American Inn of Court. ***PRACTICE AREAS:*** Commercial Litigation; Intellectual Property Litigation; General Litigation. ***Email:*** vitolo@khlaw.com

VANESSA H. BROUSSARD, born St. Louis, Missouri, February 25, 1971; admitted to bar, 1999, Louisiana (Not admitted in District of Columbia). *Education:* Louisiana State University (B.S., 1994; J.D., 1998). Best Closing Argument, Louisiana State University Trial Advocacy Program. Co-Author: *1999 Update Louisiana Construction Law* West, Pub., Holliday/Shreves; *1999 Update Louisiana Corporations* West Pub., Holliday/Norman. Seminars Co-Authored: "Buying and Selling a Louisiana Business"; "Current Issues in Louisiana Construction Law." *Member:* Louisiana State and American (Member, Intellectual Property Section, 1999—) Bar Associations; The Association of Trial Lawyers of America. (Ms. Broussard is provisionally recognized before the United States Patent and Trademark Office). ***LANGUAGES:*** French. ***PRACTICE AREAS:*** Intellectual Property; Electronic Commerce; Internet Law; Advertising Law. ***Email:*** broussard@khlaw.com

JENNIFER B. BENNETT, born Martinsville, Virginia, August 13, 1971; admitted to bar, 1999, Virginia; 2001, District of Columbia. *Education:* University of Richmond (B.A., 1993); Miami University (M.A., 1995); Georgetown University Law Center (J.D., 1999). Phi Beta Kappa. *Member:* Virginia and American Bar Associations; The District of Columbia Bar. ***PRACTICE AREAS:*** Food and Drug; International Regulation; International Trade. ***Email:*** bennett@khlaw.com

CAREN A. GRAU, born Pittsburgh, Pennsylvania, April 7, 1971; admitted to bar, 1999, Pennsylvania and Maryland; 2000, District of Columbia. *Educa-*

(This Listing Continued)

KELLER AND HECKMAN LLP, Washington—Continued

tion: University of Pennsylvania (B.A., 1993); Catholic University of America (J.D., cum laude, 1999). Member, Journal of Contemporary Health Law and Policy. ***LANGUAGES:*** Italian. ***PRACTICE AREAS:*** Food and Drug. ***Email:*** grau@khlaw.com

LUTHER L. HAJEK, born New York, N.Y., April 2, 1970; admitted to bar, 1999, Virginia; 2000, District of Columbia. *Education:* Dartmouth College (B.A., 1992); George Washington University (J.D., cum laude, 1999). ***PRACTICE AREAS:*** Litigation; Unfair Trade; Food and Drug. ***Email:*** hajek@khlaw.com

TRENT M. DOYLE, born Barberton, Ohio, May 28, 1966; admitted to bar, 2000, Virginia; 2001, District of Columbia. *Education:* Colorado School of Mines (B.S., 1988); College of William & Mary (M.A.Ed., 1991; J.D., 2000). Member, Air and Waste Management Association, 1990-2000. *Member:* Virginia State Bar; American Bar Association. ***PRACTICE AREAS:*** Environmental Law. ***Email:*** doyle@khlaw.com

KATHERINE COLLINS LUCAS, born Washington, D.C., January 8, 1973; admitted to bar, 2000, Virginia; 2001, District of Columbia. *Education:* University of Virginia (B.A., 1995); Georgetown University (J.D., 2000). *Member:* Virginia State Bar; The District of Columbia Bar; Virginia Bar Association. ***PRACTICE AREAS:*** Telecommunications Law. ***Email:*** lucas@khlaw.com

MATTHEW T. FREKKO, born Washington, D.C., January 23, 1972; admitted to bar, 2000, Maryland (Not admitted in District of Columbia). *Education:* Colgate University (B.A., 1994); Georgetown University Law Center (J.D., 2000). ***PRACTICE AREAS:*** Food and Drug Regulation. ***Email:*** frekko@khlaw.com

RUXANDRA GRIGORE, born Bucharest, Romania, February 16, 1976; admitted to bar, 2000, Bucharest, Romania. *Education:* University of Paris II Pantheon Sorbonne (Licence en droite, 1998); College of Europe, Bruges, (LL.M.,1999). (Resident, Brussels, Belgium Office). ***LANGUAGES:*** Romanian, English, French. ***PRACTICE AREAS:*** European Union Law; Food Law; Environmental Law. ***Email:*** grigore@khlaw.be

KEVIN G. RUPY, born Cleveland, Ohio, May 2, 1968; admitted to bar, 2001, District of Columbia. *Education:* Fordham University (B.A., 1990); American University Washington College of Law (J.D., 2000). *Member:* The District of Columbia Bar; Federal Communications Bar Association. [Major, U.S. Marine Corps, 1990-1995]. ***PRACTICE AREAS:*** Telecommunications Law; Business Transactions. ***Email:*** rupy@khlaw.com

MATTHEW WRIGHT, born San Francisco, California, August 21, 1975; admitted to bar, 2001, Massachusetts and District of Columbia. *Education:* Princeton University (A.B., Public & International Affairs, cum laude, 1997); Boston College (J.D., 2000). *Member:* Massachusetts Bar Association; Federal Inn of Court. ***PRACTICE AREAS:*** Commercial Litigation; Trademark Litigation; Intellectual Property; Environmental Litigation. ***Email:*** wright@khlaw.com

KEVIN PATRICK BOOT, born Des Moines, Iowa; admitted to bar, 2001, New York (Not admitted in District of Columbia). *Education:* University of Iowa (B.A., 1994); George Washington University (J.D., 2000). ***PRACTICE AREAS:*** Food and Drug Regulation; International Regulatory Law; Litigation. ***Email:*** boot@khlaw.com

SEBASTIEN FRANCOIS LOUVION, born Cambrai-Nord, France, October 26, 1974; admitted to bar, 2001, District of Columbia. *Education:* University of Paris X Nanterre, Nanterre, France (Maîtrise en Droit des Affaires, 1998); University of Richmond (J.D., 2000). *Member:* The District of Columbia Bar; American Bar Association. ***LANGUAGES:*** French and Spanish. ***PRACTICE AREAS:*** Food and Drug Regulation; Intellectual Property. ***Email:*** louvion@khlaw.com

COUNSEL

ALFRED S. REGNERY, born Chicago, Illinois, November 21, 1942; admitted to bar, 1971, Wisconsin; 1987, District of Columbia. *Education:* Beloit College (B.A., 1965); University of Wisconsin (J.D., 1971). Author: "U.S. Direct Marketing Law: The Complete Handbook for Managers," Libey, 1993 (with R. Leighton); "The Mind of Justice Brennan," National Review, May, 1984. Administrator, Office of Juvenile Justice & Delinquency Prevention, Department of Justice, 1983-1986. Deputy Assistant Attorney General, U.S. Department of Justice, 1981-1983. Minority Counsel, U.S. Senate Judiciary Committee, 1978-1981. President, Regnery Publishing, Inc. *Member:* State Bar of Wisconsin; The District of Columbia Bar. [U.S. Coast Guard, 1965-1971]. ***LANGUAGES:*** German. ***PRACTICE AREAS:*** Publishing; Direct Marketing; International Trade. ***Email:*** regnery@khlaw.com

LEGAL SUPPORT PERSONNEL

STAFF SCIENTISTS

HOLLY H. FOLEY, born Washington, D.C., April 24, 1959. *Education:* Massachusetts Institute of Technology (B.S., 1981). Phi Beta Kappa. *Member:* American Chemical Society. ***PRACTICE AREAS:*** Food and Drug Regulatory Analysis and obtaining regulatory clearances for same. ***Email:*** foleyh@khlaw.com

CHARLES V. BREDER, born Atlantic City, New Jersey, February 15, 1940. *Education:* Carson-Newman (B.S., 1962); Vanderbilt University (M.S., 1964; Ph.D., 1968). Recipient, DuPont Fellowship, Vanderbilt University. Member: American Chemical Society; American Society of Testing and Materials; Association of Official Analytical Chemists. Research Chemist, Dupont, 1967-1971. Supervisory Chemist, Food and Drug Administration, 1971-1984. ***PRACTICE AREAS:*** Food and Drug Regulatory Analysis; Polymer and Analytical Chemistry. ***Email:*** breder@khlaw.com

ROBERT A. MATHEWS, born Cincinnati, Ohio, June 27, 1940. *Education:* University of Cincinnati (B.S., 1967); University of Michigan (Ph.D., 1973). Diplomate: American Board of Toxicology (D.A.B.T.); Director, Food Chemicals Codex (1981-1987). *Member:* Society of Toxicology; Society for Risk Analysis; American Chemical Society; American Association Advancement of Science; American Statistical Association. ***PRACTICE AREAS:*** Toxicology; Risk Assessment; Food, Drug and Medical Device regulatory analysis. ***Email:*** mathews@khlaw.com

LESTER BORODINSKY, born Brooklyn, New York, March 6, 1950. *Education:* Brooklyn College (B.S., 1972; M.A., 1976); University of Virginia (Ph.D., 1982). Member: American Chemical Society, 1973; Sigma Xi Society, 1975; Institute of Food Technologists, 1986. Lecturer In Introductory Chemistry, Piedmont Virginia Community College, Charlottesville, VA, 1979-1981. Recipient, FDA Commendable Service Award, 1990. ***Email:*** borodinsky@khlaw.com

THOMAS C. BROWN, born Lancaster, Ohio, May 8, 1940. *Education:* Bowling Green State University (B.S., 1962). Thirty years experience with the U.S. Food and Drug Administration. Former Chief, Indirect Additive Branch, in charge of the regulation of additives for use in food packaging. ***PRACTICE AREAS:*** Food and Drug Regulation; Food Law. ***Email:*** brownt@khlaw.com

MICHAEL T. FLOOD, born Cleveland, Ohio, November 19, 1942. *Education:* College of the Holy Cross (B.S., 1964); Columbia University (Ph.D., 1970). National Academy of Sciences Overseas Research Fellow, Rio de Janeiro, Brazil, 1969. Post doctoral Fellow, Stanford University, 1973. Assistant Professor, Beloit College, 1975. Review Chemist, Food and Drug Administration, 1978. Senior Scientist, U.S. Environmental Protection Agency, 1987. *Member:* American Chemical Society. ***LANGUAGES:*** Portuguese. ***Email:*** flood@khlaw.com

DR. ANNA GERGELY, born Budapest, Hungary, June 15, 1953. *Education:* Technical University of Budapest, Budapest, Hungary (M.Sc., Biochemistry and Microbiology, 1976; Ph.D., Analytical Chemistry and Quantum Chemistry, 1981). Chartered Patent Attorney, Hungary, 1992. Assistant and later Associated Professor, Organic Chemistry and Analytical Chemistry, Technical University of Budapest, Hungary, 1977-1987. Visiting scientist at the University of Notre Dame (US/Indiana) 1982-83 and the University of Antwerp (Belgium) 1987-1990. Over ten years of academic research experience in analytical chemistry, specifically, mass spectrometry; Experience in marketing development and regulatory affairs in the polymer industry. Senior Technical Officer, Analytical Chemistry and Technical Market Development, Monsanto Technical Centre, Europe, 1990-1995. *Member:* Union, European Association of Chartered Patent Attorneys. (Resident, Brussels, Belgium Office). ***LANGUAGES:*** English, German, French, Dutch, Hungarian and Russian. ***PRACTICE AREAS:*** European Regulatory Status Analysis; Analytical Chemistry; Biotechnology. ***Email:*** gergely@khlaw.be

STEFANIE M. CORBITT, born Hagerstown, Maryland, August 29, 1969. *Education:* West Virginia University (B.A., 1991; M.S.E., 1993). Beta Beta Beta. *Member:* American Industrial Hygiene Association; American Conference of Governmental Industrial Hygienists; American Welding Society. ***PRACTICE AREAS:*** Occupational Safety and Health. ***Email:*** corbitt@khlaw.com

ELIZABETH HEGER, born Oakland, Maryland, January 15, 1958. *Education:* University of Maryland (M.S., 1994). Member, American Society of Agronomy, 1991-1996. ***PRACTICE AREAS:*** Pesticide Registrations; OSHA, DOT; Chemical Transport Requirements; Hazardous Materials and Substances Labeling. ***Email:*** heger@khlaw.com

ROBERT J. SCHEUPLEIN, born Long Island, New York, 1932. *Education:* University of Miami, (B.S., 1956); University of Utah at Salt Lake City (Ph.D., Physical Chemistry, 1961). ***PRACTICE AREAS:*** Food and Drug; Health; Safety Compliance. ***Email:*** scheuplein@khlaw.com

ANDREW P. JOVANOVICH, born Denver, Colorado, February 9, 1944. *Education:* Colorado College (B.S., 1965); Northwestern University (Ph.D., 1970); University of Denver (M.B.A., 1974). Political Appointee, U.S. Environmental Protection Agency, 1981-1985. ***PRACTICE AREAS:*** Pesticide Registration. ***Email:*** jovanovich@khlaw.com

KAREN R. OBENSHAIN, born Ft. Hauchuca, Arizona, November 18, 1956. *Education:* Mary Washington College (B.A., 1978); University of Geor-

(This Listing Continued)

gia (M.S., 1981); Tulane University (Sc.D., 1998). *Member:* American Association of Petroleum Geologists; Society for Risk Analysis. ***LANGUAGES:*** Russian. ***Email:*** obenshain@khlaw.com

JOSEPH E. PLAMONDON, born Dubuque, Iowa, March 3, 1941. *Education:* Loras College (B.S., maxima cum laude, 1963); University of California at Berkeley (M.S., 1965); University of California at Davis (Ph.D., 1969). Research Manager, 1969-1982, New Business Development Manager, 1983-1986 and Corporate TSCA Manager, 1987-1991, Rohm & Haas Co. Consultant, Toxic Substances Control Act and Associate Director, Chemicals Division, Technology Sciences Group, 1991-1995. Regulatory Affairs Manager, Akzo Nobel Chemicals, 1995-1999. ***PRACTICE AREAS:*** Toxic Substances Control Act. ***Email:*** plamondon@khlaw.com

JOHN P. MODDERMAN (1944-1998).

RANDALL D. YOUNG, born Centralia, Illinois, January 3, 1948. *Education:* Southern Illinois University (B.A., 1975; Ph.D. candidate, 1979); University of Houston (M.B.A., 1993). Twenty-two years experience in Telecommunications field, including system engineering, planning and performance evaluation. Experience in financial planning, analysis and asset valuation for commercial wireless facilities. ***Email:*** ryoung@khlaw.com

LINDA M. THOMPSON, born Buffalo, New York, June 4, 1975. *Education:* Rochester Institute of Technology (B.S., 1997); University of Maryland (M.S., 2000). Delta Sigma Lambda. *Member:* American Chemical Society. ***PRACTICE AREAS:*** Domestic and International Chemical Control Laws. ***Email:*** thompson@khlaw.com

ROBERT J. KELLER, P.C.

1850 M STREET N.W., SUITE 240
P.O. BOX 33428
WASHINGTON, D.C. 20036
Telephone: 202-223-2100
Facsimile: 202-223-2121
Email: rjk@telcomlaw.com
URL: http://www.lawyres.com/keller

Telecommunications Law, Communications Law, Telecommunications Regulation, FCC Regulation, FCC Licensing.

FIRM PROFILE: Mr. Keller, has over twenty years experience representing companies that are subject to or affected by Federal Communications Commission regulation and policies, including wireless carriers and other mobile radio system operators, telephone companies, long distance carriers, electronic and communications equipment vendors and manufacturers, microwave and satellite system operators, broadcast licensees, internet service providers, etc. Mr. Keller has also served as special communications counsel to banking and investment firms in financial and securities transactions involving such regulated companies. Mr. Keller is an adjunct lecturer at the Institute for Communications Law Studies at Catholic University's Columbus School of Law.

ROBERT J. KELLER, born New Albany, Indiana, February 20, 1953; admitted to bar, 1979, District of Columbia and U.S. District Court for the District of Columbia; U.S. Court of Appeals for the District of Columbia Circuit. *Education:* Catholic University of America (B.A., 1975; J.D., 1979). Member, American Radio Relay League. *Member:* District of Columbia Bar; American Bar Association; Federal Communications Bar Association. (Also Of Counsel to Shainis & Peltzman Chartered).

JAMES H. KELLEY

Established in 1990

9611 SUTHERLAND ROAD
WASHINGTON, D.C. 20901
Telephone: 1-800-294-6372
Email: JHKLawFirm@aol.com

Edgartown, Massachusetts Office: 230 Upper Main Street. P.O. Box, 1288. 02539-1288. Telephone: 508-627-7305. Fax: 508-627-7007. E-Mail: PEVKY@aol.com; JHKLawFirm@aol.com.

Commercial Law, Products Liability and Antitrust.

REPRESENTATIVE CLIENTS: Consolidated Furniture Corporation; Great Harbour Resorts; Connemara Company; A.C.P., Inc.
REFERENCES: Furnished On Request.

(For Complete Biographical Data see Professional Biographies at Edgartown, Massachusetts)

KELLEY DRYE & WARREN LLP

1200 19TH STREET, N.W., SUITE 500
WASHINGTON, D.C. 20036
Telephone: 202-955-9600
Fax: (202) 955-9792
Email: info@kelleydrye.com
URL: http://www.kelleydrye.com

New York, N.Y. Office: 101 Park Avenue. Telephone: 212-808-7800. Fax: (212) 808-7897.
Los Angeles, California Office: 777 South Figueroa Street, Suite 2700. Telephone: 213-689-1300. Fax: (213) 688-8150.
Stamford, Connecticut Office: Two Stamford Plaza, 281 Tresser Boulevard. Telephone: 203-324-1400. Fax: (203) 327-2669; (203) 964-3188.
Parsippany, New Jersey Office: 5 Sylvan Way. Telephone: 973-539-0099. Fax: (973) 539-3167.
Chicago, Illinois Office: 303 West Madison Street, Suite 1400. Telephone: 312-346-6350. Fax: (312) 346-8982.
Vienna, Virginia Office: 8000 Towers Crescent Drive, Suite 1200. Telephone: 703-918-2300. Fax: 703-918-2450.
Brussels, Belgium Office: 106 Avenue Louise, 1050. Telephone: (011) (32-2) 646-1110. Fax: (011) (32-2) 640-0589.
Hong Kong Office: Suite 1602, Fairmont House, 8 Cotton Tree Drive. Telephone: (011) (852) 2869-0821. Fax: (011) (852) 2869-0049.
Affiliated Offices:
Jakarta, Indonesia: Soebagjo, Jatim, Djarot, Plaza DM, 17th Floor, Jalan Jend. Sudirman Kav. 25, Jakarta 12920, Indonesia. Telephone: (011) (62-21) 5229765. Fax: (011) (62-21) 5229752.
Tokyo, Japan: Yumoto & Ota, Kioi Royal Heights, 3-29, Kioi-Cho, Chiyoda-Ku, Tokyo 102, Japan. Telephone: (011) (81-3) 3234-2441. Fax: (011) (81-3) 3262-2729.
Manila, Philippines: Oporto Reyes Suarez & Associates, 2111 BSA Suites, 103 C. Palanca Street, Legaspi Village, Makati City, Metro Manila. Telephone: (011) (63-2) 888-6951; 888-6953. Fax: (011) (63-2) 888-6945. E-Mail: oporto@pacific.net.ph.
Bangkok, Thailand: Dej-Udom & Associates, Charn Issara Tower, 9th Floor, 942/142-3 Rama IV Road, Bangkok 10500 Thailand. Telephone: (011) (66-2) 233-0055. Fax: (011) (66-2) 236-6681. E-Mail: dejudom@loxinfo.co.th.
Mumbai (Bombay) India: Wakhariya & Wakhariya, 41 Bajaj Bhawan, 226 Nariman Point, Mumbai 400021. Telephone: (91-22) 281-0336; 91-22-285-9820. Fax: (91-22) 281-0337. E-Mail: shabbirw@counsellor.com.

Litigation, Commercial Litigation, Emerging Growth Companies, Employee Benefits, Executive Compensation, Environmental Law, Financial Institutions, Health Care, Immigration, Insurance, Intellectual Property, Technology Litigation, International Law, Labor and Employment Law, Mergers and Acquisitions, Private Clients, Products Liability, Project Finance, Infrastructure, Real Estate Law, Restructuring, Creditors Rights, Securities, Securities Industry, Securities Litigation, Telecommunications, Trade Regulation, Antitrust, White Collar Crime, Corporate Investigations, Year 2000, Y2K.

PARTNERS

ROBERT J. AAMOTH, born Bay City, Michigan, November 9, 1956; admitted to bar, 1982, District of Columbia. *Education:* University of Michigan (A.B., 1979); Harvard University (J.D., 1982). Law Clerk, Chief Judge Spottswood W. Robinson, III, U.S. Court of Appeals for the District of Columbia Circuit, 1982-1983. (Resident). ***PRACTICE AREAS:*** Telecommunications Law; Appellate Practice. ***Email:*** raamoth@kelleydrye.com

STEVEN A. AUGUSTINO, born Washington, D.C., June 21, 1966; admitted to bar, 1991, Maryland; 1992, District of Columbia; 1994, U.S. District Court for the District of Columbia and U.S. District Court, District of Maryland. *Education:* University of Virginia (B.A., with highest distinction, 1988); Georgetown University Law Center (J.D., magna cum laude, 1991). Order of the Coif. Criminal Procedure Project Editor, Georgetown Law Journal. ***PRACTICE AREAS:*** Telecommunications Law. ***Email:*** saugustino@kelleydrye.com

JONATHAN E. CANIS, born Hinsdale, Illinois, January 24, 1954; admitted to bar, 1983, New Jersey; 1989, District of Columbia. *Education:* Rutgers University (B.A., with highest honors, 1979); Syracuse University (J.D., 1982; M.P.S. (Masters in Telecommunications Administration), 1984). Staff Attorney, FCC: Tariff Division, 1984-1986; Accounting and Audits Division, 1986-1987. *Member:* The District of Columbia Bar; New Jersey and Federal Communications Bar Association. ***PRACTICE AREAS:*** Communications; Corporate Law. ***Email:*** jcanis@kelleydrye.com

THOMAS C. JACKSON, born Rochester, New York, March 1, 1959; admitted to bar, 1984, District of Columbia. *Education:* Amherst College (B.A., summa cum laude, 1981); Harvard University (J.D., cum laude, 1984). Phi Beta Kappa. Member, 1982-1984 and Research Director, 1983-1984, Harvard Legal Aid Bureau. *Member:* The District of Columbia Bar; American Bar Associa-

(This Listing Continued)

KELLEY DRYE & WARREN LLP, Washington—Continued

tions (Vice-Chairman, Endangered Species Subcommittee). (Resident). ***PRACTICE AREAS:*** Environmental Law; Endangered Species; Litigation. ***Email:*** tjackson@kelleydrye.com

DOUGLAS P. LOBEL, born Glen Cove, New York, 1957; admitted to bar, 1984, New York; 1985, District of Columbia; 1998, Virginia; 1999, Maryland. *Education:* Haverford College (B.A., 1979); George Washington University (J.D., 1983). Assistant District Attorney, Brooklyn, New York, 1983-1987. Trial Attorney, Fraud Section, Criminal Division, U.S. Department of Justice, Member, Dallas Bank Fraud Task Force, 1987-1990. *Member:* The District of Columbia Bar; Virginia State, Maryland State, New York State and American Bar Associations; Edward Bennett Williams Inn of Court. (Resident). ***PRACTICE AREAS:*** Litigation; Telecommunications Law; White Collar Criminal Litigation; Business Crimes; Securities Arbitrations. ***Email:*** dlobel@kelleydrye.com

BRAD E. MUTSCHELKNAUS, born Sioux Falls, South Dakota, December 16, 1954; admitted to bar, 1980, District of Columbia. *Education:* Concordia College (B.A., summa cum laude, 1977); Georgetown University Law Center (J.D., cum laude, 1980). Editor, Law and Policy in International Business, 1980. General Attorney, Satellite Business Systems, 1983-1985. Director, Regulatory Affairs, U.S. Sprint Communications, 1985-1988. Vice President and General Counsel, NTS, 1988-1991. *Member:* Federal Communications Bar Association (Chairperson, State and Local Practice Committee). (Resident). ***PRACTICE AREAS:*** Communications; Antitrust and Trade Regulation; Litigation; Corporate Law. ***Email:*** bmutschelknaus@kelleydrye.com

AILEEN A. PISCIOTTA, born Rochester, New York, November 6, 1951; admitted to bar, 1983, District of Columbia. *Education:* University of Pennsylvania (B.A., 1973); Annenberg School of Communications (M.A., 1977); Georgetown University (J.D., cum laude, 1983). Chief, Planning and Negotiations Division, International Bureau, Federal Communications Commission, 1994-1996. *Member:* District of Columbia Bar; American Bar Association (Section of International Law and Practice: Co-Chair, Communications Committee, 1989-1992; Coordinator, Latin America Administrative Law Project, 1993—; Council Member, 1993—); Federal Communications Bar Association. (Resident). ***PRACTICE AREAS:*** International Communications Law; Administrative Law; Communications Law; Finance. ***Email:*** apisciotta@kelleydrye.com

J. BARTON SEITZ, born San Antonio, Texas, May 29, 1959; admitted to bar, 1987, Pennsylvania; 1988, District of Columbia. *Education:* College of William & Mary (A.B., 1981); Christ's College, Cambridge University, Cambridge, England; George Washington University National Law Center (J.D., 1987). ***PRACTICE AREAS:*** Environmental Law; Environmental Litigation. ***Email:*** jseitz@kelleydrye.com

JUDITH ST. LEDGER-ROTY, born Buffalo, New York, November 8, 1952; admitted to bar, 1979, District of Columbia; U.S. Court of Appeals Eighth Circuit. *Education:* Florida Technological University (B.A., 1974); Cleveland State University, Cleveland Marshall College of Law (J.D., 1979). *Member:* The District of Columbia Bar; American Bar Association; Federal Communications Bar Association (Co-Chair, State and Local Practice Committee). (Resident). ***PRACTICE AREAS:*** Telecommunications Law; Commercial Law. ***Email:*** jstledgerroty@kelleydrye.com

DANIEL M. STEINWAY, born Detroit, Michigan, July 7, 1950; admitted to bar, 1976, Michigan; 1978, District of Columbia. *Education:* University of Michigan (B.S.E. in Engineering Science, cum laude, 1972); George Washington University (J.D., with honors, 1976). Attorney-Advisor, Office of Enforcement, U.S. Environmental Protection Agency, 1976-1978. Minority Counsel, U.S. House of Representatives Committee on Science and Technology (Subcommittees on National Resources, Agricultural Research and the Environment, Energy Development and Applications, 1978-1986). Member: Editorial Board, Real Estate/Environmental Liability News, 1990—. *Member:* Federal (Chairman, Environmental Law Committee, 1988—) and American (Vice Chairman: Alternate Energy Sources Committee, Section of Natural Resources, Energy, and Environmental Law, 1985—; Energy Resources Law Committee, Section of Tort and Insurance Practice, 1991—) Bar Associations. (Resident). ***PRACTICE AREAS:*** Environmental Law; Administrative Law; Litigation. ***Email:*** dsteinway@kelleydrye.com

DAVID L. VAUGHAN, born Jackson, Mississippi, 1946; admitted to bar, 1972, New York; 1973, District of Columbia. *Education:* Mississippi State University (B.A., with special distinction, 1968); Duke University (J.D., 1971); Georgetown (LL.M., 1974). Phi Kappa Phi; Omicron Delta Kappa; Phi Delta Phi. *Member:* The District of Columbia Bar; New York State Bar Association. Asst. Gen. Counsel, Dept. of the Army, 1974-1975. [Capt., U.S. Army, JAGC, 1972-1974]. (Resident). ***PRACTICE AREAS:*** Administrative Law; Aviation Law; International Law; Government Procurement. ***Email:*** dvaughan@kelleydrye.com

EDWARD A. YORKGITIS, JR., born Pittsburgh, Pennsylvania, November 2, 1961; admitted to bar, 1987, Pennsylvania; 1989, District of Columbia; 1990, U.S. District Court, Western District of Pennsylvania; 1992, U.S. District Court for the District of Columbia. *Education:* Princeton University (A.B., cum laude, 1983); Harvard Law School (J.D., cum laude, 1986). *Member:* The District of Columbia Bar; American and Federal Communications Bar Associations. (Resident). ***PRACTICE AREAS:*** Telecommunications Law. ***Email:*** cyorkgitis@kelleydrye.com

RESIDENT OF COUNSEL

JAMES J. FREEMAN, born Norristown, Pennsylvania, December 29, 1940; admitted to bar, 1966, District of Columbia. *Education:* College of the Holy Cross (A.B., 1962); Harvard University (LL.B., 1965). *Member:* The District of Columbia Bar; American and Federal Communications Bar Associations. ***PRACTICE AREAS:*** Telecommunications Law; Communications Law. ***Email:*** jfreeman@kelleydrye.com

GENEVIEVE MORELLI, born New York, N.Y., February 26, 1956; admitted to bar, 1981, District of Columbia. *Education:* New York University (B.A., 1978); George Washington University (J.D., 1981). ***PRACTICE AREAS:*** Telecommunications. ***Email:*** gmorelli@kelleydrye.com

PHILIP V. PERMUT, born Boston, Massachusetts, October 27, 1943; admitted to bar, 1968, Massachusetts; 1977, District of Columbia. *Education:* Ohio Wesleyan University (A.B., 1965); Boston University (J.D., 1968). Trial Attorney, Federal Communications Commission; Broadcast Bureau, 1968-1973; General Counsel's Office, 1973-1974. Special Assistant to Common Carrier Bureau Chief, 1974-1976, Chief, Policy and Rules Division, 1976-1977 and Deputy Chief, Common Carrier Bureau, Federal Communications Commission, 1977-1978. Washington Attorney, RCA Global Communications, 1978-1979. *Member:* The District of Columbia Bar; American Bar Association; Federal Communications Bar Association. (Resident). ***PRACTICE AREAS:*** Communications; Administrative Law; Litigation. ***Email:*** ppermut@kelleydrye.com

RESIDENT SPECIAL COUNSEL

JEFFREY S. LONGSWORTH, born Washington, D.C., January 30, 1962; admitted to bar, 1991, Maryland; 1992, District of Columbia. *Education:* Amherst College (B.A., 1984); Catholic University, Columbus School of Law (J.D., 1991). Member, Catholic University Law Review. Member, EPA Federal Advisory Committee on Urban Wet Weather Flows. Member, Montgomery County (MD) Water Quality Advisory Group. Contributing Editor, "The Stormwater Permit Manual," Thompson Publishing, Inc. *Member:* The District of Columbia Bar; Maryland State and American (Member, Natural Resources, Energy and Environmental Law Section) Bar Associations. ***PRACTICE AREAS:*** Environmental Law. ***Email:*** jlongsworth@kelleydrye.com

ENRICO C. SORIANO, born Manila, Philippines, March 17, 1958; admitted to bar, 1991, Pennsylvania and New Jersey; 1998, District of Columbia. *Education:* University of the City of Manila (B.A., cum laude, 1978); University of Oklahoma (M.A., 1985); Temple University School of Law (J.D., 1991). Spofford Scholar. Klasky Memorial Awardee. Member, Moot Court Board. Editor-in-Chief, International and Comparative Law Journal. ***PRACTICE AREAS:*** Communications Law; Litigation. ***Email:*** esoriano@kelleydrye.com

JOSEPH F. YENOUSKAS, born Cambridge, Massachusetts, March 14, 1960; admitted to bar, 1987, Virginia; 1988, District of Columbia. *Education:* Georgetown University (B.A., 1982); George Washington University (J.D., 1987). Order of the Coif. Law Clerk, Honorable Joyce Hens Green, U.S. District Court for the District of Columbia, 1987-1989. ***PRACTICE AREAS:*** Litigation. ***Email:*** jyenouskas@kelleydrye.com

SENIOR COUNSEL

RONALD J. JARVIS, born Kansas City, Missouri, February 6, 1953; admitted to bar, 1980, District of Columbia; 1982, U.S. District Court for the District of Columbia; 1983, U.S. Court of Appeals for the District of Columbia Circuit. *Education:* Princeton University (A.B., 1975); Duke University (J.D., 1979). Attorney Advisor, Office of Hearings and Appeals, U.S. Department of Energy, 1980-1982. *Member:* The District of Columbia Bar; Federal Communications Bar Association. ***PRACTICE AREAS:*** Telecommunications Law; Technology Law; Export Control. ***Email:*** rjarvis@kelleydrye.com

RESIDENT ASSOCIATES

LEILA M. BAHERI, born September 11, 1967; admitted to bar, 1994, Pennsylvania (Not admitted in District of Columbia). *Education:* Duke University (B.A., 1989); American University (J.D., cum laude, 1994). Author: "Telecommunications Reports International Data Rights and Privacy Principles," in Global E-Commerce. *Member:* American Bar Association. ***LANGUAGES:*** French and Farsi. ***PRACTICE AREAS:*** Telecommunications Law. ***Email:*** lbaheri@kelleydrye.com

KATHERINE ELIZABETH BARKER, admitted to bar, 1997, Massachusetts; 1998, New York (Not admitted in District of Columbia). *Education:* Syracuse University (B.S., 1993); Suffolk University (J.D., 1997). ***Email:*** kbarker@kelleydrye.com

(This Listing Continued)

JOHN M. BRENDEL, born Teaneck, New Jersey, January 28, 1971; admitted to bar, 1996, New Jersey; 1997, U.S. District Court, District of New Jersey; 1998, District of Columbia. *Education:* University of Chicago (B.A., 1992); University of Pennsylvania (J.D., 1995). ***PRACTICE AREAS:*** Telecommunications Law.

ROSS A. BUNTROCK, born Aberdeen, South Dakota, April 12, 1970; admitted to bar, 1995, Virginia and U.S. District Court, Eastern District of Virginia; 1996, District of Columbia. *Education:* South Dakota State University (B.S., with high honors, 1992); University of Nebraska (J.D., 1995). Phi Alpha Delta. Allen Moot Court Board, 1994-1995. ***PRACTICE AREAS:*** Telecommunications Law; Corporate Law. ***Email:*** rbuntrock@kelleydrye.com

ADAM AUGUSTINE CARTER, born Pittsburgh, Pennsylvania, January 20, 1965; admitted to bar, 1991, Virginia and U.S. Court of Appeals, Fourth Circuit; 1992, District of Columbia and U.S. District Court, Eastern District of Virginia; 1993, U.S. Court of Appeals for the District of Columbia Circuit and U.S. District Court for the District of Columbia. *Education:* Georgetown University (A.B., 1987; J.D., 1991). Law Clerk to the Hon. Oliver Gasch, U.S. District Court, District of Columbia, 1991-1992. ***PRACTICE AREAS:*** Litigation. ***Email:*** acarter@kelleydrye.com

MELISSA S. CONWAY, born Madison, Wisconsin, February 25, 1972; admitted to bar, 1997, Maryland; 1998, District of Columbia. *Education:* Princeton University (B.A., Public Affairs, 1994); George Washington University (J.D., 1997). Member, Moot Court Board. *Member:* Federal Communications Bar Association. ***PRACTICE AREAS:*** Telecommunications Law. ***Email:*** mconway@kelleydrye.com

TODD D. DAUBERT, born Manhattan, Kansas, January 19, 1967; admitted to bar, 1994, New York; 1996, Maryland; 1997, District of Columbia. *Education:* Oklahoma State University (B.A.E., 1990); Duke University (J.D., with honors, 1993). Senior Editor, Journal of Law and Contemporary Problems. Law Clerk to Chief Judge Gerald B. Tjoflat, U.S. Court of Appeals, Eleventh Circuit, 1993-1994. ***LANGUAGES:*** German. ***PRACTICE AREAS:*** Telecommunications Law. ***Email:*** tdaubert@kelleydrye.com

JAMES W. DEACON II, born Colorado Springs, Colorado, May 25, 1973; admitted to bar, 1998, Louisiana, U.S. District Court, Eastern and Western Districts of Louisiana and U.S. Court of Appeals, Fifth Circuit; 1999, Virginia (Not admitted in District of Columbia). *Education:* Tulane University (B.A., 1995); Georgetown University (J.D., cum laude, 1998). Recipient, Corpus Juris Secundum Award and CALI's Excellence for Future Award. Member, The Tax Lawyer, 1996-1998. *Member:* Virginia State Bar; Federal and American Bar Associations. ***PRACTICE AREAS:*** Telecommunications Law; Commercial Litigation. ***Email:*** jdeacon@kelleydrye.com

ANDREW M. DUNNAVILLE, admitted to bar, 2000, Maryland (Not admitted in District of Columbia). *Education:* Amherst College (B.A., 1997); University of Virginia (J.D., 2000). Member, Virginia Journal of Social Policy and the Law. ***PRACTICE AREAS:*** Telecommunications. ***Email:*** adunnaville@kelleydrye.com

ERIN WEBER EMMOTT, born Columbus, Ohio, February 3, 1974; admitted to bar, 1999, Massachusetts; 2001, District of Columbia and U.S. District Court, District of Massachusetts. *Education:* University of Richmond (B.A., magna cum laude, 1996); Northeastern University (J.D., 1999). Dean's List. Golden Key. *Member:* Massachusetts and American Bar Association. ***PRACTICE AREAS:*** Telecommunications. ***Email:*** eemmott@kelleydrye.com

MICHAEL C. ENGEL, born Baltimore, Maryland, October 20, 1969; admitted to bar, 2000, New York (Not admitted in District of Columbia). *Education:* Southwest Missouri State University (B.S., 1992); Catholic University of America (J.D., cum laude, 1999). *Member:* Federal Communications Bar Association. ***PRACTICE AREAS:*** Telecommunications. ***Email:*** mengel@kelleydrye.com

MICHAEL J. FRANCESCONI, born Pittsburgh, Pennsylvania, November 30, 1965; admitted to bar, 1997, Virginia; 1999, District of Columbia. *Education:* United States Military Academy (B.S., 1987); Catholic University (J.D., cum laude, 1997). Managing Editor, Catholic University Law Review. *Member:* Virginia State and Federal Communications Bar Associations. [Capt. U.S. Army, 1987-1993]. ***PRACTICE AREAS:*** Telecommunications Law. ***Email:*** mfrancesconi@kelleydrye.com

BRETT HEATHER FREEDSON, born Manhasset, New York, July 10, 1975; admitted to bar, 2000, Virginia; 2001, District of Columbia. *Education:* University of Chicago (B.A., 1997); George Washington University (J.D., 2000). *Member:* American Bar Association; Federal Communications Bar Association. ***PRACTICE AREAS:*** Telecommunications. ***Email:*** bfreedson@kelleydrye.com

JOHN J. HEITMANN, born Port Jefferson, New York, May 28, 1967; admitted to bar, 1995, New York; 1997, District of Columbia. *Education:* University of Notre Dame (B.A., cum laude, 1989); New York University (J.D., cum laude, 1994). ***PRACTICE AREAS:*** Telecommunications Law. ***Email:*** jheitmann@kelleydrye.com

(This Listing Continued)

ERIC D. JENKINS, born Portland, Oregon, July 7, 1973; admitted to bar, 2000, Maryland (Not admitted in District of Columbia). *Education:* Florida A. & M. University (B.S., 1996); George Washington University (M.B.A., 1999; J.D., 1999). ***PRACTICE AREAS:*** Telecommunications. ***Email:*** ejenkins@kelleydrye.com

STEPHANIE A. JOYCE, born Boston, Massachusetts; admitted to bar, 1998, California; 1999, District of Columbia. *Education:* University of Notre Dame (B.A., 1994); George Washington University (J.D., 1998); George Washington University Elliott School of International Affairs (M.A., 1998). ***Email:*** sjoyce@kelleydrye.com

JENNIFER MYERS KASHATUS, born Washington, D.C., August 18, 1972; admitted to bar, 1997, Maryland (Not admitted in District of Columbia). *Education:* Colgate University (B.A., 1994); Case Western Reserve University (J.D., cum laude, 1997). *Member:* Maryland State and American Bar Associations; Federal Communications Bar Association. ***PRACTICE AREAS:*** Telecommunications. ***Email:*** jkashatus@kelleydrye.com

DAVID C. KIRSCHNER, born November 22, 1962; admitted to bar, 1995, New Jersey; 1996, New York; 1998, District of Columbia. *Education:* University of Chicago (B.A., 1986); Benjamin N. Cardozo School of Law (J.D., 1995). *Member:* New York State and American Bar Associations; District of Columbia Bar; Federal Communications Bar Association. ***PRACTICE AREAS:*** Telecommunications. ***Email:*** dkirschner@kelleydrye.com

ANDREW M. KLEIN, born Suffern, New York, May 31, 1967; admitted to bar, 1992, New York, New Jersey, U.S. District Court, Southern District of New York and U.S. District Court, District of New Jersey (Not admitted in District of Columbia). *Education:* Clark University (B.A., 1989); Albany Law School of Union University (J.D., 1992). Member, Board of Directors, ALS Alumni Association, 1992—; President, ALS Student Bar Association, 1991-1992. *Member:* Federal Communications Bar Association. ***PRACTICE AREAS:*** Telecommunications; Litigation. ***Email:*** aklein@kelleydrye.com

DAVID A. KONUCH, born Bethlehem, Pennsylvania, March 25, 1964; admitted to bar, 1994, California; 1996, District of Columbia. *Education:* Stanford University (B.A., 1986); Tulane Law School (J.D., cum laude, 1993). Law Clerk to Hon. Charles Schwartz, Jr., Senior Judge, United States District Court for the Eastern District of Louisiana, 1993-1994. Author: "United States v. R.W. Meyer, Inc.: Sixth Circuit Clarifies Courts' Use of Equitable Discretion in CERCLA Contribution Actions," 5 TUL. ENVTL. L.I. 673 (1992). *Member:* Federal Communications Law Bar Association. ***PRACTICE AREAS:*** Communications Law; Litigation. ***Email:*** dkonuch@kelleydrye.com

CARL F. LETTOW, born Washington, D.C., March 6, 1970; admitted to bar, 1995, Virginia, U.S. District Court, Eastern District of Virginia and U.S. Court of Appeals, Fourth Circuit; 1997, District of Columbia; 2000, U.S. Supreme Court. *Education:* College of William and Mary (B.A., 1992); Wake Forest University School of Law (J.D., 1995). *Member:* Fairfax and Virginia Bar Associations. ***Email:*** clettow@kelleydrye.com

NICHOLAUS G. LEVERETT, born Opelika, Alabama, October 2, 1975; admitted to bar, 2000, Virginia; 2001, District of Columbia. *Education:* Auburn University (B.S., magna cum laude, 1997); Washington & Lee University (J.D., cum laude, 2000). ***PRACTICE AREAS:*** Telecommunications. ***Email:*** nleverett@kelleydrye.com

MICHAEL P. McGOVERN, born Washington, D.C., December 4, 1962; admitted to bar, 1990, Virginia; 1997, District of Columbia and Maryland. *Education:* University of Maryland (B.S., cum laude, 1985); George Washington University (M.B.A., 1987); University of Virginia School of Law (J.D., 1990). ***PRACTICE AREAS:*** Environmental Law. ***Email:*** mmcgovern@kelleydrye.com

ELIZABETH S. NICHOLAS, admitted to bar, 1999, New York and Massachusetts (Not admitted in District of Columbia). *Education:* University of Florida (B.S., 1995); Tulane University of Louisiana (J.D., cum laude, 1998). ***PRACTICE AREAS:*** Environmental Law. ***Email:*** enicholas@kelleydrye.com

M. NICOLE ODEN, born Cincinnati, Ohio, May 15, 1970; admitted to bar, 1999, Maryland; 2001, District of Columbia. *Education:* Washington & Lee University (1988-1991); University of South Florida (B.A., 1992); Georgetown University (J.D., 1999). Phi Gamma Mu. Dean's List. *Member:* Federal Communications Bar Association. ***PRACTICE AREAS:*** Telecommunications. ***Email:*** moden@kelleydrye.com

NEIL FRANCIS O'DONNELL, born 1969; admitted to bar, 1996, Colorado; 2000, New York (Not admitted in District of Columbia). *Education:* Georgetown University (A.B., 1991); University of North Carolina at Chapel Hill (J.D., with honors, 1996). Author: "Dispute Resolution in the Commercial Law Tribunals of the Russian Federation," 22 N.C.L.J. Int'l. L. & Comm. Reg. 795, 1997. Co-Author: with A. Veiksha, "Ukrainian Securities Law," East/West Executive Guide, December 1996. ***LANGUAGES:*** Russian. ***PRACTICE AREAS:*** Corporate Finance; Project Finance. ***Email:*** odonnell@kelleydrye.com

ASPASIA PAROUTSAS, born Washington, D.C., May 1, 1973; admitted to bar, 2000, Maryland (Not admitted in District of Columbia). *Education:* New

(This Listing Continued)

KELLEY DRYE & WARREN LLP, Washington—Continued

York University (B.A., 1993); University of London, Queen Mary and Westfield College (M.S.C. in Public Policy, 1994); Catholic University (J.D., cum laude, 2000). *Member:* American Bar Association; Federal Communications Bar Association. ***PRACTICE AREAS:*** Telecommunications.

TROY D. REYNOLDS, born Danville, Kentucky, October 3, 1967; admitted to bar, 1992, Kentucky and U.S. District Court, Eastern District of Kentucky; 2000, District of Columbia. *Education:* University of Kentucky (B.A., with high distinction, 1989; J.D., with distinction, 1992). Phi Beta Kappa; Order of the Coif. Commissioner, Lexington-Fazette County Historic Preservation 1994-1995. *Member:* Federal and American Bar Associations. ***PRACTICE AREAS:*** Business Law; Commercial Law; Intellectual Property Law; Contracts; Corporate; Trademark. ***Email:*** treynolds@kelleydrye.com

TRISTAN B.L. SIEGEL, admitted to bar, 1996, California; 1997, District of Columbia; 2000, U.S. Supreme Court. *Education:* Niagara University (B.A., 1987); Defense Intelligence College (M.S., 1992); University of Virginia School of Law (J.D., 1996). First Year Council President, Moot Court. [Major, U.S. Army, 1984—]. ***LANGUAGES:*** French and German. ***PRACTICE AREAS:*** Litigation. ***Email:*** tsiegel@kelleydrye.com

RANDALL W. SIFERS, born Cameron, Missouri, June 2, 1957; admitted to bar, 1997, Maryland; 1998, District of Columbia. *Education:* University of Missouri, Columbia (B.S.B.A., 1979); Indiana University (J.D., 1997). Phi Delta Phi. *Member:* District of Columbia Bar; American and Federal Communications Bar Associations. ***PRACTICE AREAS:*** Telecommunications. ***Email:*** rsifers@kelleydrye.com

ERIN R. SWANSIGER, born Bethesda, Maryland, October 20, 1967; admitted to bar, 1995, Maryland; 1996, New Jersey; 1998, District of Columbia. *Education:* University of Maryland (B.A., 1989); Catholic University of America (J.D., 1995). Recipient, Leadership Award, 1994-1995 and Certif. of Comm. Law, The Inst. for Communi. Law Studies. CommLaw Conspectus, 1994-1995. Author: "The Telecommunications Industry in 1993: The Year of the Merger," CommLaw Conspectus, Vol. 2 (1994). ***PRACTICE AREAS:*** Telecommunications Law. ***Email:*** eswansiger@kelleydrye.com

DAVID A. VOGEL, born Berwyn, Illinois, June 22, 1966; admitted to bar, 1992, Illinois; 1994, District of Columbia. *Education:* University of Michigan (B.S.E., summa cum laude, 1987); Stanford Law School (J.D., with distinction, 1991). Tau Beta Pi. Author, "Licensing Software and Technology to the U.S. Government," C.C.M., 2000. ***PRACTICE AREAS:*** Litigation; Government Contracts; Intellectual Property. ***Email:*** dvogel@kelleydrye.com

HEATHER M. WILSON, born Aberdeen, Maryland, February 13, 1970; admitted to bar, 1998, Virginia; 1999, District of Columbia. *Education:* University of Wisconsin (B.A., 1992); College of William and Mary (J.D., 1998). ***PRACTICE AREAS:*** Telecommunications; International Telecommunications. ***Email:*** hwilson@kelleydrye.com

JOSEPH D. WILSON, III, born Los Gatos, California, December 31, 1968; admitted to bar, 1999, Virginia and Maryland; 2001, District of Columbia and U.S. District Court, Eastern District of Virginia. *Education:* Georgetown University (B.S.F.S., cum laude, 1991; J.D., cum laude, 1999). National Political Science Honor Society. Law Clerk to Hon. Gregory E. Mize, Superior Court, District of Columbia, 1999-2000. ***PRACTICE AREAS:*** Litigation. ***Email:*** jwilson@kelleydrye.com

DARIUS B. WITHERS, born Washington, D.C., June 21, 1969; admitted to bar, 1994, Maryland (Not admitted in District of Columbia). *Education:* University of Virginia (B.A., History, 1991); George Washington University (J.D., 1994). Jessup International Law Moot Court, 1992-1993. Extern Law Clerk to the Honorable Luke C. Moore, Superior Court for the District of Columbia, 1992. Equal Opportunity Law Specialist, Division of Civil Rights, U.S. Department of Labor, 1992. *Member:* American and National Bar Associations; Federal Communications Bar Association. ***PRACTICE AREAS:*** Communications; Administrative Law. ***Email:*** dwithers@kelleydrye.com

(For Biographical data on all Personnel, see Professional Biographies at New York, N.Y.).

STEVEN E. KELLIS, P.C.

1411 K STREET N.W.,
SUITE 602
WASHINGTON, D.C. 20005
Telephone: 202-347-2000
Fax: 202-783-7114
URL: http://www.kellislaw.com
Email: kellislaw@mindspring.com
URL: http://www.lawyers.com/kellislaw

New address effective October 30, 2001: 105 Lenox Way, Atlanta, Georgia, 30324.

(This Listing Continued)

Criminal Defense, including DWI/DUI, Driving While Intoxicated, Driving While Under the Influence, Vehicular Homicide, Drivers License Suspension, Drug Crimes, Traffic Violations.

FIRM PROFILE: Steven E. Kellis, P.C. is a firm specializing in Criminal Defense and DWI/DUI law. Mr. Kellis is a former Senior Assistant District Attorney who has been lead counsel in over 80 criminal jury trials. The firm represents individuals throughout Washington, D.C., Maryland and Northern Virginia.

STEVEN E. KELLIS, born Philadelphia, Pennsylvania, October 28, 1965; admitted to bar, 1992, Pennsylvania, Georgia and U.S. Court of Appeals, Eleventh Circuit; 2000, District of Columbia and Maryland. *Education:* Bucknell University (B.A., 1987); Villanova University Law School (J.D., 1991). Assistant Solicitor-City of Atlanta, 1997-1998. Senior Assistant District Attorney, Atlanta Judicial Circuit, 1998-2000. *Member:* Maryland State Bar Association; District of Columbia Bar; State Bar of Georgia; Maryland Trial Lawyers Association; The Association of Trial Lawyers of America; National Association of Criminal Defense Lawyers; National College of DUI Defense. ***LANGUAGES:*** Greek. ***REPORTED CASES:*** Graves v. State, 269 Ga. 772, 504 S.E.2d 679 (1998); Tomko v. State, 233 Ga. App. 20, 503 S.E.2d 300 (1998). ***PRACTICE AREAS:*** Criminal Defense; Driving While Intoxicated; Driving Under the Influence; Vehicular Homicide; Drivers License Suspension; Drug Offenses; Traffic Violations. ***Email:*** kellislaw@mindspring.com

REFERENCE: Nations Bank.

KELLOGG, HUBER, HANSEN, TODD & EVANS, P.L.L.C.

Established in 1993
SUMNER SQUARE
1615 M STREET, N.W.
SUITE 400
WASHINGTON, D.C. 20036-3209
Telephone: 202-326-7900
Fax: 202-326-7999
Telecommunications and Litigation.

MICHAEL K. KELLOGG, born Palo Alto, California, April 18, 1954; admitted to bar, 1983, District of Columbia; 1987, U.S. Supreme Court. *Education:* Stanford University (A.B., 1976); Oxford University, St. Catherine's College (B. Phil., 1979); Harvard Law School (J.D., magna cum laude, 1982). Editor, Harvard Law Review, 1980-1982. Law Clerk: Hon. Malcolm Wilkey, U.S. Court of Appeals, District of Columbia Circuit, 1982-1983; Hon. William H. Rehnquist, U.S. Supreme Court, 1983-1984. Assistant U.S. Attorney, U.S. Department of Justice, Criminal Division, Southern District of New York, 1984-1986. Assistant to the Solicitor General, U.S. Department of Justice, 1987-1989. Co-Author: *Federal Telecommunications Law,* Aspen (2d Ed. 1999); *The Geodesic Network II: 1993 Report on Competition in the Telephone Industry,* Geodesic Publishing (1992); *Federal Broadband Law,* Little, Brown & Co. (1995); *Special Report: The Telecommunications Act of 1996,* Little, Brown & Co. (1996). ***LANGUAGES:*** French. ***PRACTICE AREAS:*** Telecommunications; Supreme Court and Appellate Litigation. ***Email:*** mkellogg@khhte.com

PETER W. HUBER, born Toronto, Canada, November 3, 1952; admitted to bar, 1986, District of Columbia. *Education:* Massachusetts Institute of Technology (Ph.D., 1976); Harvard Law School (J.D., summa cum laude, 1982). Member, Harvard Law Review, 1980-1982. Law Clerk: Hon. Ruth Bader Ginsburg, U.S. Court of Appeals, District of Columbia Circuit, 1982-1983; Hon. Sandra Day O'Connor, U.S. Supreme Court, 1983-1984. Author: *The Geodesic Network: 1987 Report on Competition in the Telephone Industry,* U.S. Department of Justice (1987); *Liability,* Basic Books (1988); *Sandra Day O'Connor,* Chelsea House Publishers (1990); *Galileo's Revenge: Junk Science in the Courtroom,* Basic Books (1991); *Orwell's Revenge: The 1984 Palimpsest,* Free Press (1994); *Law and Order in Cyberspace ... Abolish the FCC and Let Common Law Rule the Telecosm,* Oxford University (1997); *Hard Green, Saving the Environment from the Environmentalists: A Conservative Manifesto,* Basic Books (1999). Co-Author: *Federal Telecommunications Law,* Aspen (2d Ed. 1999); *The Geodesic Network II: 1993 Report on Competition in the Telephone Industry*, Geodesic Publishing (1992); *Federal Broadband Law,* Little, Brown & Co. (1995); *Special Report: The Telecommunications Act of 1996,* Little, Brown & Co. (1996); *Judging Science,* MIT Press (1997). Editor: *The Liability Maze,* Brookings Institution (1991); *Phantom Risk: Scientific Inference and the Law,* MIT Press (1993). ***LANGUAGES:*** French. ***PRACTICE AREAS:*** Telecommunications. ***Email:*** phuber@khhte.com

MARK C. HANSEN, born New York, New York, August 13, 1956; admitted to bar, 1983, Massachusetts; 1990, District of Columbia; 1996, Maryland. *Education:* Dartmouth College (A.B., summa cum laude, with highest distinction, 1978); Harvard Law School (J.D., cum laude, 1982). Phi Beta Kappa. Law Clerk: Hon. William H. Timbers, U.S. Court of Appeals, Second Circuit, 1982-

(This Listing Continued)

1983. Assistant U.S. Attorney, U.S. Department of Justice, Criminal Division, Southern District of New York, 1986-1990. Partner, Johnson & Gibbs, Washington, D.C., 1990-1993. Author including articles in The Wall Street Journal, New York Times and Litigation. Commentator, Court TV. ***PRACTICE AREAS:*** Litigation. ***Email:*** mhansen@khhte.com

K. CHRIS TODD, born Salina, Kansas, August 11, 1946; admitted to bar, 1972, Texas; 1979, District of Columbia; 1988, New York. *Education:* Texas Tech University (B.A., 1969); University of Texas School of Law, Austin (J.D., 1972); Cambridge University, Darwin College (1973-1974). Law Clerk: Hon. William M. Taylor, Jr., U.S. District Court, Northern District of Texas, 1972-1973. Trial Attorney, U.S. Department of Justice, Tax Division, Criminal Section, 1975-1978. Assistant U.S. Attorney, U.S. Department of Justice, Criminal Division, Southern District of New York, 1978-1987. Associate Counsel, Office of Independent Counsel (Iran/Contra Matter), 1987-1989. ***PRACTICE AREAS:*** Litigation. ***Email:*** ctodd@khhte.com

MARK L. EVANS, born Brooklyn, New York, December 2, 1942; admitted to bar, 1968, New York; 1969, District of Columbia; 1972, U.S. Supreme Court. *Education:* Hamilton College (A.B., with honors, 1964); Cornell Law School (J.D., with distinction, 1968). Phi Kappa Phi. Order of the Coif. Editor-in-Chief, Cornell Law Review, 1967-1968. Law Clerk: Hon. John A. Danaher, U.S. Court of Appeals, District of Columbia Circuit, 1968-1969. Assistant to the Solicitor General, U.S. Department of Justice, 1972-1976. General Counsel, Interstate Commerce Commission, 1976-1979. Member, Advisory Committee on Procedures, U.S. Court of Appeals, District of Columbia Circuit, 1987-1993 . ***PRACTICE AREAS:*** Telecommunications; Supreme Court and Appellate Litigation. ***Email:*** mevans@khhte.com

STEVEN F. BENZ, born Baltimore, Maryland, September 16, 1960; admitted to bar, 1990, Iowa and Minnesota; 1991, District of Columbia; 1993, U.S. Supreme Court; 1996, Maryland. *Education:* Johns Hopkins University (B.A., general honors, departmental honors, 1983); Fletcher School of Law & Diplomacy (M.A.L.D., 1985); Stanford Law School (J.D., 1990). Phi Beta Kappa. President, Stanford Law Review, Volume 42, 1989-1990. Deputy Staff Judge Advocate, 113th Fighter Wing (DCANG), Andrews Air Force Base, 1991-1998. Author: "Below-Cost Sales and the Buying of Market Share," 42 Stanford Law Review 695 (1990); "Soviet Nationalities Policies and the Soviet Germans," 16 Heritage Review 11 (1986); "Trade Liberalization and the Global Service Economy," 19 Journal of World Trade Law 95 (1985); "High Technology Occupations Lead Growth in Services Employment," 7 Business America 19 (1984). Co-Author: "The Trigger of Coverage Under CGL Policies, Insurance Coverage Litigation 1993: Critical Issues and Strategies," New York: Practicing Law Institute (1993); "International Competition in Information Technologies: Foreign Government Intervention and the U.S. Response," 22 Stanford Journal of International Law 215 (1987); "The Semiconductor Chip Protection Act - Experience in the Utilization of the Law and Current International Developments," 8 European Intellectual Property Review 229 (1986); "U.S.-Japan Relations - Convergence and Cooperation in a Changing World Economy," Southwestern Legal Foundation (1986); *Private Investors Abroad: Problems and Solutions in International Business in 1986*, Matthew Bender (1986); "Government Procurement of Semiconductors - Economic and Environmental Issues Affecting a Major Strategic Resource, San Jose," Semiconductor Industry Association (1985). [Major, Air National Guard/Air Force Reserve]. ***PRACTICE AREAS:*** Litigation; Antitrust. ***Email:*** sbenz@khhte.com

NEIL M. GORSUCH, born Denver, Colorado, August 29, 1967; admitted to bar, 1992, New York; 1994, Colorado; 1997, District of Columbia; 1998, U.S. Supreme Court. *Education:* Columbia University (B.A., 1988); Harvard Law School (J.D., cum laude, 1991); Oxford University, University College (1992-1995). Phi Beta Kappa. Marshall Scholar. Truman Scholar. Law Clerk: Hon. David B. Sentelle, U.S. Court of Appeals, District of Columbia Circuit, 1991-1992; Hon. Byron R. White, U.S. Supreme Court, 1993-1994. Author: "The Right to Assisted Suicide and Euthanasia," 23 Harvard J. Law & Public Policy 600 (2000). Co-author: "Will the Gentlemen Please Yield? — A Defense of the Constitutionality of State-Imposed Term Limitations," 20 Hofstra Law Review 341 (1991); "The Constitutional Case for Term Limits," The Wall Street Journal, November 4, 1992, at A15. ***PRACTICE AREAS:*** Litigation. ***Email:*** ngorsuch@khhte.com

GEOFFREY M. KLINEBERG, born Cambridge, Massachusetts, November 23, 1963; admitted to bar, 1994, District of Columbia; 1998, U.S. Supreme Court. *Education:* Princeton University, Woodrow Wilson School, Public and International Affairs (A.B., magna cum laude, 1985); Oxford University, Balliol College (M.Phil. in International Relations, with distinction, 1987); Yale Law School (J.D., 1990). Phi Beta Kappa. Articles Editor, Yale Law Journal, 1989-1990. Law Clerk: Hon. José A. Cabranes, U.S. District Court, District of Connecticut, 1990-1991; Hon. Patricia M. Wald, U.S. Court of Appeals, District of Columbia Circuit, 1991-1992; Hon. Harry A. Blackmun, U.S. Supreme Court, 1992-1993. Author: "Remembering Harry Blackmun," ABA Journal, April 1999; "Fighting Words," The Federal Lawyer, June 1995. Co-Author: "Justice Department Contacts with Represented Persons: A Sensible Solution," 78 Judicature 136 (1994). Special Assistant, Deputy Attorney General, U.S. Department of Justice, 1993-1995. ***LANGUAGES:*** French. ***PRACTICE AREAS:*** Telecommunications; Appellate Litigation. ***Email:*** gklineberg@khhte.com

REID M. FIGEL, born San Francisco, California, January 28, 1956; admitted to bar, 1982, Colorado, 1987, New York; 1988, California; 2000, District of Columbia. *Education:* Middlebury College (A.B., cum laude, with honors in Political Science, 1978); New York University School of Law (LL.B., 1982). New York University Law Review, 1980-1981. Thomas J. Watson Fellowship, 1978-1979. Recipient: The Chief Postal Inspector's Special Award (for United States v. Drexel Burnham Lambert, Inc. and United States v. Michael R. Milken), 1990; The Attorney General's Award for Distinguished Service (for United States v. Christopher Drogoul, arising from the multi-billion dollar fraud on Banca Nazionale del Lavoro), 1994; The Attorney General's Award for Distinguished Service (for United States v. The Daiwa Bank, Ltd.), 1996; The U.S. Securities and Exchange Commission "Stanley Sporkin Award" (for outstanding contributions to enforcement of the federal securities laws), 1997. Law Clerk: Hon. George C. Pratt, U.S. Court of Appeals, Second Circuit, 1982-1983; Hon. James R. Browning, U.S. Court of Appeals, Ninth Circuit, 1983-1984. Assistant U.S. Attorney, U.S. Department of Justice, Criminal Division, Southern District of New York, 1987-1998. Deputy Chief, 1993-1995 and Chief, 1995-1998, Securities and Commodities Fraud Unit. ***PRACTICE AREAS:*** Litigation; Securities. ***Email:*** rfigel@khhte.com

HENK BRANDS, born Amsterdam, The Netherlands, April 17, 1964; admitted to bar, 1991, New York; 1995, U.S. Supreme Court; 1996, District of Columbia. *Education:* University of Amsterdam (LL.B., 1987); Columbia University Law School (J.D., 1990). Editor, Columbia Law Review, 1989-1990. Law Clerk: Hon. Stephen Breyer, U.S. Court of Appeals, First Circuit, 1990-1991; Hon. David H. Souter, U.S. Supreme Court, 1991-1992; Hon. Stephen Breyer, U.S. Supreme Court, 1994-1995. ***PRACTICE AREAS:*** Telecommunications; Litigation. ***Email:*** hbrands@khhte.com

SEAN A. LEV, born Brooklyn, New York, November 22, 1966; admitted to bar, 1993, Pennsylvania (inactive); 1996, District of Columbia. *Education:* Williams College (B.A., magna cum laude, 1988); Harvard Law School (J.D., magna cum laude, 1992). Phi Beta Kappa. Supervising Editor, Harvard Law Review, 1991-1992. Law Clerk: Hon. Patricia M. Wald, U.S. Court of Appeals, District of Columbia Circuit, 1992-1993. Attorney, U.S. Department of Justice, Civil Division, Appellate Staff, 1993-1996. ***PRACTICE AREAS:*** Telecommunications; Appellate Litigation; General Litigation. ***Email:*** slev@khhte.com

EVAN T. LEO, born New York, New York, August 24, 1968; admitted to bar, 1994, New York; 1996, District of Columbia. *Education:* University of California at Los Angeles (B.A., 1990); The George Washington University National Law Center (J.D., with honors, 1993). Co-Author: *The Law and Regulation of Telecommunications Carriers,* Artech (1998). ***PRACTICE AREAS:*** Telecommunications. ***Email:*** eleo@khhte.com

ANTONIA M. APPS, born Cambridge, United Kingdom, August 1, 1969; admitted to bar, 1995, New York; 2000, District of Columbia. *Education:* University of Sydney (LL.B., first class honors, 1990); Oxford University, Magdalen College, (B.C.L., with honors, 1993); Harvard Law School (LL.M., 1994). Frank Knox Memorial Fellowship. Commonwealth Scholarship and Fellowship Plan. Law Clerk: Hon. T.W. Waddell, Equity Division, New South Wales Supreme Court, 1991; Hon. Fred I. Parker, U.S. Court of Appeals, Second Circuit, 1997-1998. Author: "The Right to Cure Defective Performance," 94 Lloyd's Maritime & Commercial Law Quarterly 525 (1994); "Verification of Photographs," 9 Australian Bar Review 202 (1992); "Affidavits," 66 Australian Law Journal 163 (1992); "Breavington v. Godleman: A New Choice of Law Rule for Torts," 12 Sydney Law Review 625 (1990). Co-author: "Non-Regulation of Advanced Internet Services," 8 George Mason Law Review 681 (2000). ***LANGUAGES:*** German. ***PRACTICE AREAS:*** Litigation; Telecommunications. ***Email:*** aapps@khhte.com

MICHAEL J. GUZMAN, born San Jose, California, February 6, 1964; admitted to bar, 1994, Pennsylvania; 1995, District of Columbia. *Education:* Brigham Young University (B.A., summa cum laude, University Honors, 1988); Harvard Law School (J.D., magna cum laude, 1991). Book Review and Commentary Editor, Harvard Law Review, 1989-1991. Law Clerk: Hon. Douglas H. Ginsburg, U.S. Court of Appeals, District of Columbia Circuit, 1991-1992. Legal Assistant: Hon. George H. Aldrich, Iran-United States Claims Tribunal, 1992-1993. Author: Note, "Unsecured Creditors of Failed Banks: It's Not a Wonderful Life," 104 Harvard Law Review 1052 (1991). Co-Author: "With Motor-Voter Bill, Congress May Have Invited a Constitutional Challenge," Washington Legal Foundation (1994); "Will the Gentlemen Please Yield? —A Defense of the Constitutionality of State-imposed Term Limitations," 20 Hofstra Law Review 341 (1991); "The Constitutional Case for Term Limits," The Wall Street Journal, p. A15, Nov. 4, 1992. ***PRACTICE AREAS:*** Litigation; Telecommunications. ***Email:*** mguzman@khhte.com

AARON M. PANNER, born Rochester, New York, February 28, 1965; admitted to bar, 1995, Massachusetts; 1996, New York; 1997, District of Columbia. *Education:* Yale University (B.S., summa cum laude, 1986); Harvard Law School (J.D., magna cum laude, 1995). Phi Beta Kappa. Fay Diploma.

(This Listing Continued)

KELLOGG, HUBER, HANSEN, TODD & EVANS, P.L.L.C., Washington—Continued

Primary Editor, Harvard Law Review, 1994-1995. Law Clerk: Hon. Michael Boudin, U.S. Court of Appeals, First Circuit, 1995-1996; Hon. Stephen Breyer, U.S. Supreme Court, 1996-1997. Foreign Service Officer, U.S. Department of State, 1987-1992. ***LANGUAGES:*** French and Spanish. ***PRACTICE AREAS:*** Telecommunications; Litigation. ***Email:*** apanner@khhte.com

DAVID E. ROSS, born Livingston, New Jersey, April 27, 1971; admitted to bar, 1995, Maryland and New Jersey; 1996, District of Columbia. *Education:* Johns Hopkins University (B.A., 1994); Columbia University Law School (J.D., 1995). Harlan Fiske Stone Scholar. James A. Elkins Prize in Constitutional Law; Lawrence S. Greenbaum Prize; Thomas E. Dewey Prize. ***PRACTICE AREAS:*** Litigation. ***Email:*** dross@khhte.com

SILVIJA A. STRIKIS, born Bloomington, Indiana, October 23, 1962; admitted to bar, 1991, U.S. Tax Court (by examination); 1995, Maryland; 1998, U.S. Supreme Court; 2001, District of Columbia. *Education:* University of Maryland (B.S., summa cum laude, 1985); Georgetown University Law Center (J.D., summa cum laude, 1995). Articles Editor, Georgetown Law Journal, 1993-1994. Law Clerk: Hon. Harry T. Edwards, U.S. Court of Appeals, District of Columbia Circuit, 1995-1996; Hon. Sandra Day O'Connor, U.S. Supreme Court, 1997-1998. Bristow Fellow, Office of the Solicitor General, U.S. Department of Justice, 1996-1997. Certified Public Accountant (received Sells Award from American Institute of Certified Public Accountants). Author: "Stopping Stalking," 81 Georgetown Law Journal 2771 (1993); "Double Jeopardy," 22nd Ann'l Rev. of Crim. Procedure, 81 Georgetown Law Journal 853 (1993); "Elements Required For Qualifying as an Innocent Spouse Still Far From Clear," 81 Journal of Taxation 354 (1994); "Service Increases Use of 'Impeding IRS' Provision to Prosecute Tax Professionals," 80 Journal of Taxation 362 (1994). Contributor: *Stalked: Breaking the Silence on the Crime of Stalking in America,* Pocket Books/Simon & Schuster (1995). ***LANGUAGES:*** Latvian. ***PRACTICE AREAS:*** Telecommunications; Litigation. ***Email:*** sstrikis@khhte.com

WILLIAM J. CONYNGHAM, JR., born Washington, D.C., June 28, 1956; admitted to bar, 1985, Pennsylvania; 2001, District of Columbia. *Education:* Georgetown University (A.B., 1978); University of Texas, Austin (M.B.A., 1984); Catholic University of America (J.D., 1985). ***PRACTICE AREAS:*** Telecommunications; Complex Litigation. ***Email:*** bconyngham@khhte.com

DAVID C. FREDERICK, born Shields, Illinois, April 9, 1961; admitted to bar, 1989, Pennsylvania; 1992, District of Columbia; 1996, U.S. Supreme Court. *Education:* University of Pittsburgh (B.A., summa cum laude, 1983); Oxford University, University College (D.Phil., 1987); University of Texas Law School (J.D., with honors, 1989). Phi Beta Kappa. Rhodes Scholar.Truman Scholar. Articles Editor, Texas Law Review, 1988-1989. Law Clerk: Hon. Joseph T. Sneed, U.S. Court of Appeals, Ninth Circuit, 1989-1991; Hon. Byron R. White, U.S. Supreme Court, 1991-1992. Author: "Constitutional Law and Separation of Power Decisions," in *Developments in Administrative Law and Regulatory Practice, 1998-1999,* 2000; "Reforming Congressional Ethics Procedures: Lessons from the Attorney Disciplinary Process," 48 Administrative Law Review 69 (1996); "Commentary on the Congressional Accountability Act of 1995: A Section-by-Section Analysis," in *Lobbying the New Congress: Compliance with the Legal, Regulatory and Ethical Requirements,* Susman and Timmer, 1995; *Rugged Justice: The Ninth Circuit Court of Appeals and the American West, 1891-1941,* University of California Press, 1994; "The Ninth Circuit and the Development of Natural Resources in the Early Twentieth Century," 6 Western Legal History 183 (1993); "Railroads, Robber Barons, and the Saving of Stanford University," 4 Western Legal History 225 (1991); "John Quincy Adams, Slavery, and the Disappearance of the Right to Petition," 9 Law and History Review 113 (1991); "Political Participation and Legal Reform in the International Maritime Rulemaking Process: Lesser Developed Countries and the Hamburg Rules," 22 Journal of Maritime Law and Commerce 81 (1991). Associate, Shearman & Sterling, 1992-1995. Counselor to the Inspector General, U.S. Department of Justice, 1995-1996. Assistant to the Solicitor General, U.S. Department of Justice, 1996-2001. ***PRACTICE AREAS:*** Litigation. ***Email:*** dfrederick@khhte.com

---

SCOTT H. ANGSTREICH, born Philadelphia, Pennsylvania, October 14, 1971; admitted to bar, 1999, New York; 2001, District of Columbia. *Education:* Princeton University (A.B., summa cum laude, 1993); Oxford University, Balliol College (M.Phil., Politics, 1995); Harvard Law School (J.D., magna cum laude, 1998). Phi Beta Kappa. Keasbey Scholar. John M. Olin Fellow in Law, Georgetown University Law Center, 1999-2000. John M. Olin Research Fellow in Law and Economics, Harvard Law School, 1999-2000. Editor, 1996-1997 and Executive Editor, 1997-1998, Harvard Law Review. Law Clerk: Hon. Douglas H. Ginsburg, U.S. Court of Appeals, District of Columbia Circuit, 1998-1999. Author: "Shoring Up Chevron: A Defense of Seminole Rock Deference to Agency Regulatory Interpretations," 34 U.C. Davis Law Review 49 (2000); "The Rules Enabling Act and the Limits of Rule 23," 111 Harvard Law Review 2294 (1998); Case Comment, *Timmons v. Twin Cities Area New Party,* 111 Harvard Law Review 309 (1997). Co-Author, "Multilateral Merger Review," 68 Antitrust Law Journal 219 (2000). ***PRACTICE AREAS:*** Telecommunications. ***Email:*** sangstreich@khhte.com

SCOTT K. ATTAWAY, born Houston, Texas, January 1, 1962; admitted to bar, 1998, Massachusetts; 2001, District of Columbia. *Education:* Berklee College of Music (B.M., magna cum laude, 1993); Boston University (J.D., summa cum laude, 1997). Law Clerk: Hon. Catherine C. Blake, U.S. District Court, District of Maryland, 1997-1998; Hon. Douglas H. Ginsburg, U.S. Court of Appeals, District of Columbia Circuit, 1998-1999. Author: "The Case For Constitutional Discrimination in Taxation of Out-Of-State Municipal Bonds," 76 Boston University Law Review 237 (1996). ***PRACTICE AREAS:*** Telecommunications; Appellate Practice; Litigation. ***Email:*** sattaway@khhte.com

JOSEPH SOLOMON HALL, born New York, New York, August 22, 1973; admitted to bar, 2000, New York (Supervised by Partners of the firm while D.C. Bar application is pending) (Not admitted in District of Columbia). *Education:* Duke University (A.B., with honors, 1995); Georgetown University Law Center (J.D., cum laude, 1999). Member, American Criminal Law Review, 1997-1998. Senior Projects Editor, Fourteenth Survey of White Collar Crime, 1998-1999. Law Clerk: Hon. Fred I. Parker, U.S. Court of Appeals, Second Circuit, 1999-2000; Hon. James Robertson, U.S. District Court, District of Columbia, 2000-2001. Author: "Rule 11(e)(1)(c) and the Federal Sentencing Guidelines: Bargaining Outside the Heartland," Iowa Law Review (2001); "Corporate Criminal Liability," Thirteenth Survey of White Collar Crime, 35 American Criminal Law Review 549 (1998). Co-Author: "Independent Counsel Investigations," Fourteenth Survey of White Collar Crime, 36 American Criminal Law Review 809 (1999); "Guided to Injustice?: The Effect of the Sentencing Guidelines on Indigent Defendants and Public Defense," 36 American Criminal Law Review 1331 (1999). ***PRACTICE AREAS:*** Litigation. ***Email:*** jhall@khhte.com

KEVIN B. HUFF, born Salt Lake City, Utah, September 10, 1971; admitted to bar, 1997, New York; 1999, District of Columbia. *Education:* University of Utah (B.S., summa cum laude, 1993); Columbia University Law School (J.D., 1996). James Kent Scholar. Harlan Fiske Stone Scholar. Articles Editor, Columbia Law Review, 1995-1996. Law Clerk: Hon. Denise Cote, U.S. District Court, Southern District of New York, 1996-1997; Hon. Douglas H. Ginsburg, U.S. Court of Appeals, District of Columbia Circuit, 1997-1998; Hon. Antonin Scalia, U.S. Supreme Court, 1998-1999. Author: Note, "The Role of Corporate Compliance Programs in Determining Corporate Criminal Liability: A Suggested Approach," 96 Columbia Law Review 1252 (1996). ***PRACTICE AREAS:*** Litigation. ***Email:*** khuff@khhte.com

JOSEPH K. LEAHY, born Washington, D.C., April 27, 1972; admitted to bar, 1998, New York; 2000, District of Columbia. *Education:* Swarthmore College (B.A., 1994); New York University School of Law (J.D., magna cum laude, 1997). Order of the Coif. Associate Editor, New York University Law Review, 1996-1997. Law Clerk: Hon. M. Blane Michael, U.S. Court of Appeals, Fourth Circuit, 1997-1998. Trial Attorney, U.S. Department of Justice, Antitrust Division, Criminal Section, 1998-1999. Associate, Debevoise & Plimpton, 1999-2000. ***PRACTICE AREAS:*** Litigation. ***Email:*** jleahy@khhte.com

JOHN H. LONGWELL, born Westfield, New Jersey, September 15, 1970; admitted to bar, 2000, New York; 2001, District of Columbia. *Education:* University of Virginia (B.A., with high distinction, 1993); University of Georgia School of Law (J.D., magna cum laude, 1999). Order of the Coif. Symposium Editor, Georgia Law Review, 1998-1999. Law Clerk: Hon. Vaughn R. Walker, U.S. District Court, Northern District of California, 1999-2000. ***LANGUAGES:*** Spanish. ***PRACTICE AREAS:*** Litigation. ***Email:*** jlongwell@khhte.com

TEAL E. LUTHY, born Seattle, Washington, June 27, 1969; admitted to bar, 2000, District of Columbia. *Education:* Cornell University (B.A., 1991); University of Chicago Law School (J.D., with high honors, 1999). Order of the Coif. John M. Olin Student Fellow in Law and Economics. Bristol Fellow, Office of the Solicitor General, U.S. Department of Justice, 2000-2001. Recipient, Joseph Henry Beale Prize. Articles Editor, 1998-1999 and Member, 1997-1998, University of Chicago Law Review. Law Clerk: Hon. Edward R. Becker, U.S. Court of Appeals, Third Circuit, 1999-2000. Author: "Assigning Common Law Claims for Fraud," (Comment) 65 University of Chicago Law Review 1001 (1998). ***LANGUAGES:*** Spanish. ***PRACTICE AREAS:*** Litigation; Telecommunications Law. ***Email:*** tluthy@khhte.com

KEVIN J. MILLER, born Morristown, Tennessee, January 17, 1971; (admission pending). *Education:* University of Georgia (B.A., cum laude, 1993); University of Chicago Law School (J.D., magna cum laude, 1999). Order of the Coif. John M. Olin Student Fellow in Law and Economics. Comment Editor, 1998-1999 and Member, 1997-1998, University of Chicago Law Review. Law Clerk: Hon. Jerry E. Smith, U.S. Court of Appeals, Fifth Circuit, 1999-2000; Hon. Anthony M. Kennedy, U.S. Supreme Court, 2000-2001. Author: "Lawyers as Venture Capitalists: An Economic Analysis of Law Firms That Invest in Their Clients," 13 Harvard Journal of Law & Technology 435 (2000); "Welfare and Minimum Wage: Are Workforce Participants 'Employees' Under the Fair Labor Standards Act?", (Comment) 66 University of Chicago Law Review 183 (1999). ***PRACTICE AREAS:*** Litigation. ***Email:*** kmiller@khhte.com

(This Listing Continued)

JIDE O. NZELIBE, born Washington, D.C., October 16, 1970; admitted to bar, 1998, Maryland; 2000, District of Columbia. *Education:* St. John's College (B.A., 1993); Princeton University (M.P.A., 1995); Yale Law School (J.D., 1998). Woodrow Wilson Fellow. Ford Foundation Fellow. Law Clerk: Hon. Stephen Williams, U.S. Court of Appeals, District of Columbia Circuit, 1998-1999. Author: "Free Movement: A Federalist Reinterpretation," 49 American University Law Review 433 (1999); "When the Multinational Meets the Patrimonial State: Prospects for Improving Transnational Liability," 5 Journal of International Law 963 (1996). ***PRACTICE AREAS:*** Telecommunications; Litigation. ***Email:*** jnzelibe@khhte.com

EUGENE M. PAIGE, born Philadelphia, Pennsylvania, November 29, 1973; admitted to bar, 1999, California (Supervised by Partners of the firm while D.C. Bar application is pending) (Not admitted in District of Columbia). *Education:* Rice University (B.A., magna cum laude, 1995); Harvard Law School (J.D., magna cum laude, 1998). Phi Beta Kappa. Editor, Harvard Law Review, 1996-1997 and Executive Editor, 1997-1998. Editor, Harvard Journal of Law & Technology, 1995-1997. Law Clerk: Hon. Alex Kozinski, U.S. Court of Appeals, Ninth Circuit, 1998-1999; Hon. Anthony M. Kennedy, U.S. Supreme Court, 2000-2001. Author: "To Bar or Not to Bar: Prosecution History Estoppel After Warner-Jenkinson," (Note) 111 Harvard Law Review 2330 (1998); "The Supreme Court, 1996 Term - Leading Cases," 111 Harvard Law Review 329 (1997); "Recent Case," 110 Harvard Law Review 775 (1997). Co-Author: "Means Plus and Step Plus Function Claims: Do We Only Know Them When We See Them?", 80 Journal of Patent & Trademark Office Society 251 (1998). Associate, Keker & Van Nest, 1999-2000. ***PRACTICE AREAS:*** Litigation. ***Email:*** epaige@khhte.com

EDUARDO MOISÉS PEÑALVER, born Pasadena, California, January 12, 1973; (admission pending). *Education:* Cornell University (A.B., magna cum laude, 1994); Oxford University, Oriel College (M.A., with first class honors, 1996); Yale University Law School (J.D., 1999). Phi Beta Kappa. Rhodes Scholar. Member, Yale Law Journal. Law Clerk: Hon. Guido Calabresi, U.S. Court of Appeals, Second Circuit, 1999-2000; Hon. John Paul Stevens, U.S. Supreme Court, 2000-2001. Author: "Redistributing Property: Natural Law, International Norms, and the Property Reforms of the Cuban Revolution," 52 Florida Law Review 107 (2000); "The Persistent Problem of Obligation in International Law," 36 Stanford Journal of International Law 271 (2000); "Acts of God or Toxic Torts? Applying Tort Principles to the Problem of Climate Change," 38 Natural Resources Journal 563 (1998); "The Concept of Religion," (Note) 107 Yale Law Journal 791 (1997); "Christian Conscience: Where Are You?", America, November 11, 1995. ***LANGUAGES:*** Spanish. ***PRACTICE AREAS:*** Litigation. ***Email:*** epenalver@khhte.com

JOHN CHRISTOPHER ROZENDAAL, born Manhasset, New York, January 30, 1967; admitted to bar, 1997, Virginia; 1999, District of Columbia. *Education:* University of Texas, Austin (B.A., Plan II, with highest honors, 1989; J.D., with highest honors, 1997); Oxford University, Brasenose College (B.A., with first-class honors, 1991; M.A., 1998). Phi Beta Kappa; Friar Society; Chancellors; Order of the Coif. Marshall Scholar. Member, Texas Law Review, 1995-1996 and Articles Editor, 1996-1997. Law Clerk: Hon. Douglas H. Ginsburg, U.S. Court of Appeals, District of Columbia Circuit, 1997-1998; Hon. Anthony M. Kennedy, U.S. Supreme Court, 1998-1999. Author: "Choice of Law in Distinguishing Leases from Security Interests Under the Uniform Commercial Code," 75 Texas Law Review 375 (1996). Associate, McKinsey & Co., Inc., Zurich, Switzerland, 1992-1994. ***LANGUAGES:*** German and French. ***PRACTICE AREAS:*** Litigation; Telecommunications. ***Email:*** jrozendaal@khhte.com

ELI C. SCHULMAN, born Boston, Massachusetts, July 19, 1970; admitted to bar, 1998, Massachusetts and New York; 2001, District of Columbia. *Education:* Columbia University (A.B., summa cum laude, 1993); Harvard Law School (J.D., cum laude, 1997). Phi Beta Kappa. Fulbright Scholar. Editor, Harvard Journal on Legislation, 1995-1997. Law Clerk: Hon. Michael B. Mukasey, U.S. District Court, Southern District of New York, 1999-2000. Associate, Cahill, Gordon & Reindel, New York, New York, 1997-1999. ***LANGUAGES:*** Hebrew. ***PRACTICE AREAS:*** Litigation. ***Email:*** eschulman@khhte.com

DAVID L. SCHWARZ, born Lubbock, Texas, August 31, 1971; admitted to bar, 2000, California; 2001, District of Columbia. *Education:* Harvard University (A.B., magna cum laude, 1993); Oxford University, New College (M.Phil. in Politics, 1995); Harvard Law School (J.D., magna cum laude, 1998). Law Clerk: Hon. Patricia M. Wald, U.S. Court of Appeals, District of Columbia Circuit, 1998-1999. ***PRACTICE AREAS:*** Telecommunications. ***Email:*** dschwarz@khhte.com

COLIN S. STRETCH, born San Francisco, California, April 13, 1969; admitted to bar, 1999, California; 2000, District of Columbia. *Education:* Dartmouth College (A.B., magna cum laude, 1991); Harvard Law School (J.D., magna cum laude, 1996). Editor, Harvard Law Review, 1994-1996. Law Clerk: Hon. Laurence H. Silberman, U.S. Court of Appeals, District of Columbia Circuit, 1996-1997; Hon. Stephen G. Breyer, U.S. Supreme Court, 1998-1999. Co-Author: Note, "Fusion Candidacies, Disaggregation & Freedom of Association," 109 Harvard Law Review 1302 (1996); Case Comment, McIntyre v. Ohio

(This Listing Continued)

Elections Comm'n, 514 U.S. 334 (1995), 109 Harvard Law Review 180 (1995). ***PRACTICE AREAS:*** Telecommunications; Litigation. ***Email:*** cstretch@khhte.com

KARL REMÓN THOMPSON, born Evanston, Illinois, April 27, 1969; (admission pending). *Education:* Harvard University (B.A., 1991); Cambridge University, Trinity College (M.Phil., 1992; Ph.D., 1998); University of Chicago Law School (J.D., with high honors, 2000). Order of the Coif. Articles Editor, 1999-2000 and Member, 1998-1999, University of Chicago Law Review. Law Clerk, Hon. David S. Tatel, U.S. Court of Appeals, District of Columbia Circuit, 2000-2001. ***LANGUAGES:*** Spanish. ***PRACTICE AREAS:*** Litigation.

LEO R. TSAO, born August 2, 1970; admitted to bar, 1999, New York; 2001, District of Columbia. *Education:* Rutgers University (B.A., 1992); Cornell Law School (J.D., magna cum laude, 1998). Order of the Coif. John M. Olin Research Fellow in Law and Economics. Senior Note Editor, Cornell Law Review, 1996-1998. Law Clerk, Hon. Robert Boochever, U.S. Court of Appeals, Ninth Circuit, 1998-1999. Associate, Cravath, Swaine & Moore, New York, New York, 1999-2001. ***LANGUAGES:*** Chinese. ***PRACTICE AREAS:*** Telecommunications; Litigation. ***Email:*** ltsao@khhte.com

OF COUNSEL

RICHARD H. STERN, born New York, New York, September 9, 1931; admitted to bar, 1959, Connecticut; 1970, U.S. Supreme Court; 1980, District of Columbia; registered to practice before U.S. Patent and Trademark Office. *Education:* Columbia College (A.B., cum laude, 1953); Columbia University (B.S.E.E., 1954); Yale University (LL.B., cum laude, 1959). Eta Kappa Nu; Order of the Coif. Law Clerk: Hon. Byron R. White, U.S. Supreme Court, 1962-1963. Attorney/Advisor to Commissioner A.L. Higginbotham and Trial Attorney, Federal Trade Commission, Bureau of Restraint of Trade, 1963-1966. Director, U.S. Department of Commerce, Compliance Division, Office of Foreign Direct Investments, 1966-1969. Chief, U.S. Department of Justice, Antitrust Division, Patent Section, 1970-1977, and Chief, Intellectual Property Section, 1977-1978. Distinguished Visiting Professor of Law, University of Minnesota, 1974. Professorial Lecturer in Law, George Washington University, 1992—. Author: "Semiconductor Chip Protection," Harcourt Brace Jovanovich/Law & Business, 1986. ***PRACTICE AREAS:*** Copyrights; Computer Software Law; Intellectual Property; Antitrust. ***Email:*** rstern@khhte.com

SHANLON WU, born New York, New York, May 13, 1959; admitted to bar, 1990, District of Columbia. *Education:* Vassar College (A.B., 1980); Sarah Lawrence College (M.F.A., 1984); Georgetown University Law Center (J.D., 1988). Order of the Barristers. Law Clerk: Hon. Jerry Buchmeyer, U.S. District Court, Northern District of Texas, 1988-1989; Hon. Eugene A. Wright, U.S. Court of Appeals, Ninth Circuit, 1989-1990. Associate Editor, Law & Policy in International Business, 1986-1987. Managing Editor, Georgetown International Environmental Law Journal, 1987-1988. Assistant U.S. Attorney, U.S. Department of Justice, District of Columbia, 1990-2001. Acting Deputy Chief, Misdemeanor Trial Section, Superior Court Division, 1995-1996. Senior Associate Independent Counsel, Office of Independent Counsel, 1998-1999. Counsel to the Attorney General, U.S. Department of Justice, 1999-2001. ***LANGUAGES:*** Mandarin Chinese. ***PRACTICE AREAS:*** Litigation.

KELLOGG, SACCOCCIA & SIGELMAN

1742 N STREET, N.W.

WASHINGTON, D.C. 20036

Telephone: 202-223-9880
Fax: 202-223-9449
URL: http://www.ksslawfirm.com
Email: webmaster@ksslawfirm.com

Mailing Address: P.O. Box 941668, Atlanta, Georgia 31141-0668

Atlanta, Georgia Office: P.O. Box 941668, 31141-0668. Telephone: 770-220-2465. Telecopier: 770-220-2762.

Personal Injury, Products Liability and Medical Malpractice.

FIRM PROFILE: The firm specializes in representing victims of defective and dangerous pharmaceutical products and medical devices, medical malpractice, professional negligence, products liability cases, consumer class actions, tortious injury and wrongful death. The principal attorneys in the firm have extensive experience at the local, national and international levels in areas of litigation including artificial heart valves, the arthritis drug Oraflex, the sleeping tablet Halcion, the contraceptive Dalkon Shield, the diet drug fen-phen, as well as other national pharmaceutical and product liability suits.

These attorneys are intimately familiar with the process by which the Food and Drug Administration (FDA) regulates pharmaceuticals and medical devices and are very accomplished at evaluating safety data relating to such products and have

(This Listing Continued)

KELLOGG, SACCOCCIA & SIGELMAN, Washington—Continued

access to the leading experts in the world in these matters and the processes by which these experts evaluate and scrutinize these products above and beyond the FDA process.

With registered nurses, computer specialists and paralegal professionals on staff, the firm is well equipped to handle intricate and complex medical, pharmaceutical and products liability litigation. A substantial percentage of the firm's clients are referred to it by other attorneys familiar with the specialized legal representation the firm can offer.

MEMBERS OF FIRM

DANIEL W. SIGELMAN, born Watertown, South Dakota, December 18, 1949; admitted to bar, 1980, District of Columbia; U.S. District Court for the District of Columbia and U.S. Court of Appeals for the District of Columbia Circuit; 1989, Georgia and U.S. District Court, Northern District of Georgia. *Education:* Dartmouth College (A.B., summa cum laude, 1972) Phi Beta Kappa; University of California, Berkeley (M.A., English, 1974); Boalt Hall School of Law, University of California, Berkeley (J.D., 1979). Staff Attorney, Public Citizen Health Research Group, 1979-1981. Counsel, Subcommittee on Human Resources and Intergovernmental Relations, Committee on Government Operations, U.S. House of Representatives, 1981-1988. *Member:* The District of Columbia Bar; State Bar of Georgia; The Association of Trial Lawyers of America; Trial Lawyers Association of Metropolitan Washington, D.C.; Georgia Trial Lawyers Association. ***PRACTICE AREAS:*** Torts; Personal Injury; Toxic Torts; Pharmaceutical Law; Medical Device Litigation. ***Email:*** DanSigel@aol.com

REFERENCE: Trust Company Bank.

KELLOGG, WILLIAMS & LYONS

Established in 1972

1275 K STREET, N.W.

WASHINGTON, D.C. 20005

Telephone: 202-898-0722
Telecopier: 202-371-1257
Email: kwl@elinkisp.com

Vienna, Virginia Office: 246 Maple Avenue, East. Telephone: 703-938-4875. Telecopier: 703-938-4877.

Civil and Criminal Trial and Appellate Practice before all Courts and Agencies. Corporate, International Law, Tax Crimes, Commercial Real Estate Transactions.

FIRM PROFILE: Kellogg Williams & Lyons is devoted to providing high-quality legal work and unmatched personal service to its clientele. The firm's diverse clients range from individuals to corporations with local, national and international needs.

MEMBERS OF FIRM

EDWIN A. WILLIAMS, born Stillwater, Oklahoma, March 5, 1940; admitted to bar, 1966, District of Columbia; 1967, U.S. Court of Military Appeals; 1972, U.S. Supreme Court; 1977, Virginia. *Education:* Oklahoma State University (B.A., 1961); George Washington University (J.D., 1965). Omicron Delta Kappa; Phi Kappa Phi; Phi Delta Phi. Trial Attorney, District of Columbia Public Defender Service, 1967-1969. Assistant U.S. Attorney for the District of Columbia, 1969-1972. Member, Fairfax County Criminal Justice Advisory Board, 1988—. Faculty Member, National Institute of Trial Advocacy, 1980—. *Member:* Bar Association of the District of Columbia; Vienna (President, 1980-1981), Fairfax County and American Bar Associations; Virginia State Bar; Virginia Trial Lawyers Association; The Barristers. [Capt., U.S. Army, Intelligence, 1965-1967]. ***PRACTICE AREAS:*** Civil Litigation; Criminal; Appellate Practice.

PHILIP L. KELLOGG, born Columbus, Ohio, November 13, 1940; admitted to bar, 1968, District of Columbia; 1975, U.S. Supreme Court; 1995, U.S. District Court, District of Maryland. *Education:* University of Illinois (B.S., 1961); University of North Carolina (J.D., with honors, 1967). Order of the Coif. Member, Board of Editors, North Carolina Law Review, 1966-1967. Law Clerk, Circuit Judge Edward A. Tamm, U.S. Court of Appeals for the District of Columbia Circuit, 1967-1968. Assistant U.S. Attorney for the District of Columbia, 1968-1972. Faculty Member, National Institute of Trial Advocacy, 1990-1997. Member: Judicial Conference of the District of Columbia Circuit, 1982-1983; Judicial Conference of the District of Columbia, 1979-1980. [Lieut., U.S. Marine Corps, 1961-1964]. ***PRACTICE AREAS:*** Civil Litigation; Criminal; Corporate Law; Commercial Real Estate; Tax Law; International Law.

JAMES L. LYONS, born South Bend, Indiana, June 26, 1937; admitted to bar, 1968, District of Columbia; 1975, U.S. Supreme Court. *Education:* Wheeling Jesuit University (B.A., summa cum laude, 1962); Georgetown University (J.D., 1967). Alpha Sigma Nu. Co-Author: "Strategy and Tactics in the Prosecution and Defense of Complex Wire-Interception Cases," National Wiretap Commission Report, 1976. Law Clerk to the Honorable Edmund T. Daly, Superior Court of the District of Columbia, 1966-1967. Trial Attorney, District of Columbia Public Defender Service, 1968-1969. Assistant U.S. Attorney for the District of Columbia, 1969-1972. Member, Judicial Conference for the District of Columbia Circuit, 1975-1978, 1982-1983. President, Assistant U.S. Attorney's Association of the District of Columbia, 1977. Lecturer, George Washington University, 1978. Faculty Member, National Institute of Trial Advocacy, 1980-1981. *Member:* Bar Association of the District of Columbia; National Association of Criminal Defense Lawyers; Trial Lawyers Association of Metropolitan Washington, D.C.; The Counsellors. [U.S. Marine Corps, 1956-1959]. ***PRACTICE AREAS:*** Civil Litigation; Criminal; Appellate Practice.

(This Listing Continued)

KELLY & WEAVER

A PROFESSIONAL CORPORATION

Established in 1993

SUITE 700
11 DUPONT CIRCLE

WASHINGTON, D.C. 20036

Telephone: 202-797-7100
Fax: 202-939-6969
Email: weaver@kellyweaver.com
URL: http://www.lawyers.com/kelly&weaver

Environmental Regulation, Federal Grants, Federal Legislative Practice.

WILLIAM G. KELLY, JR., born Chicago, Illinois, November 3, 1944; admitted to bar, 1971, Illinois; 1987, District of Columbia. *Education:* Georgetown University (A.B., 1966); Northwestern University (J.D., cum laude, 1970). Trial Attorney, Antitrust Division, U.S. Department of Justice, 1970-1973. Attorney-Advisor, Division of Energy and Resources, Office of the Solicitor, U.S. Department of the Interior, 1974-1982. Member, Board of Directors, Federal Focus, Inc., 1986—. *Member:* The District of Columbia Bar. ***PRACTICE AREAS:*** Pollution; Endangered Species; Wetlands Regulation; National Environmental Policy Act; Federal Regulatory Law.

ROBERT C. WEAVER, born Lincoln, Nebraska, May 30, 1943; admitted to bar, 1969, Nebraska; 1981, Texas; U.S. Court of Appeals, 4th Circuit; 1988, District of Columbia; 1996, U.S. Supreme Court. *Education:* University of Nebraska (B.A., 1966; J.D., 1969); University of Georgia. Phi Sigma Alpha; Phi Kappa Phi; Phi Delta Phi. Office of The Secretary, U.S. Department of the Interior, 1972-1975. Associate Director, for Environmental, Energy and Land Use, National Association of Counties, 1976-1979. *Member:* Nebraska State and American (Member, Natural Resources Law Section) Bar Associations; State Bar of Texas; The District of Columbia Bar. [Capt., U.S. Army, 1970-1971]. ***PRACTICE AREAS:*** Water Quality; Water Pollution; Clean Water Act; Federal Grants; Environmental Law. ***Email:*** weaver@kellyweaver.com

NON-ATTORNEY MEMBER AND REGULATORY ADVISOR

JIM J. TOZZI. *Education:* Carnegie Institute of Technology (B.S., 1960); University of Pittsburgh (M.R., 1961); University of Florida (Ph.D., 1963). Deputy Administrator, Office of Information and Regulatory Affairs, Office of Management and Budget, 1981-1983. Assistant Director, Office of Management and Budget, Executive Office of the President, 1980-1981. Chief, Environment Branch, Office of Management and Budget, 1972-1980. Director, Systems Analysis Group, Office of the Secretary of the Army, 1965-1972. Program Analyst, Office of the Chairman, Joint Chiefs of Staff, 1964-1965. President, Multinational Business Services, Inc., 1983—. Board of Directors, National Law Library, 1994-1997. Board of Directors, World Environment Council, 1989—. Board of Directors, Federal Focus, Inc., 1986—. Member: EPA Environmental Financial Advisory Board, 1992—; Bretton Woods Committee, 1995—.

LAW OFFICE OF ROBERT KENDALL, JR.

1815 PENNSYLVANIA AVENUE, NW
SUITE 500

WASHINGTON, D.C. 20006

Telephone: 202-457-0516
Fax: 202-457-0537
Email: kendlawoffice@aol.com
URL: http://www.kendalllawoffice.com

Immigration and Citizenship Law.

(This Listing Continued)

ROBERT KENDALL, JR., born Thomaston, Georgia, February 11, 1947; admitted to bar, 1973, Texas; 1974, U.S. Court of Appeals, Fourth and Sixth Circuits; 1976, U.S. Court of Appeals, Nineth and Tenth Circuits; 1981, U.S. Court of Appeals, Fifth and Eleventh Circuits; 1993, U.S. Court of Appeals, First Circuit; U.S. Court of Appeals, Seventh Circuit; 1994, District of Columbia. *Education:* Fort Valley State University (B.S., 1969); Thurgood Marshall School of Law, Texas Southern University (J.D., 1973). Attorney, United States Department of Justice, 1973-1996. *Member:* State Bar of Texas; National Bar Association; American Immigration Lawyers Association. ***PRACTICE AREAS:*** Immigration and Naturalization; Citizenship; Business Immigration; Employment Immigration; Family Immigration Law.

KENNY NACHWALTER SEYMOUR ARNOLD CRITCHLOW & SPECTOR

PROFESSIONAL ASSOCIATION

Established in 1978

1201 PENNSYLVANIA AVENUE, SUITE 300

WASHINGTON, D.C. 20004

Telephone: 305-373-1000

Facsimile: 305-372-1861

Email: admin@knsacs.com

URL: http://www.knsacs.com

Rogersville, Tennessee Office: 107 East Main Street, Suite 301. Telephone: 423-272-5300. Facsimile: 423-272-4961.

Miami, Florida Office: 1100 Miami Center, 201 South Biscayne Boulevard, 33131-4327. Telephone: 305-373-1000. Facsimile: 305-372-1861.

Complex Litigation, Antitrust Litigation, Securities Litigation, Professional Liability Litigation. Trials in all Courts.

FIRM PROFILE: Kenny Nachwalter Seymour Arnold Critchlow & Spector, P.A. was founded in 1978. The firm specializes in complex business litigation, particularly antitrust, securities, intellectual property, lender liability, professional liability litigation and white collar criminal defense. The firm is frequently retained in cases involving complicated legal, economic and factual issues, discovery problems, and substantive issues requiring superior legal scholarship and forensic skills.

REPRESENTATIVE CLIENTS: Albertson's, Inc.; American Bankers Insurance Group; Audesey Partners; Avatar; Braman Motors; Cartier, Inc.; Ethan Allen; Federated Department Stores, Inc.; GTE Florida, Inc.; GTE Directories Corp.; Macmillan, Inc.; J.B. Hanauer & Co.; Mercy Hospital, Inc.; Nestle Food Company; Prince Manufacturing, Inc.; Rolex Watch U.S.A., Inc.; Royce Laboratories, Inc.; Siemens Capital Corp.; State of Florida; Sunbeam Television Corp.; Providence Journal Company; Pepe Jeans USA, Inc.; Tommy Hilfiger USA, Inc.; Ford Motor Company; Republic Engineered Steels, Inc.; General Motors; Chrysler Corporation; U.S. Steel.

(For Complete Biographical Data on all Personnel, see Professional Biographies at Miami, Florida)

KENYON & KENYON

Established in 1879

1500 K STREET, N.W.

SUITE 700

WASHINGTON, D.C. 20005

Telephone: 202-220-4200

Fax: (202) 220-4201, Groups II & III

New York, N.Y. Office: One Broadway, 10004. Telephone: 212-425-7200. Fax: (212) 425-5288.

Munich, Germany Office: Steinsdorfstr. 10, 80538 Munich. Telephone: 49 89 211 134-30. Fax: 49 89 21 134-49.

San Jose, California Office: Riverpark Towers, Suite 600, 333 West San Carlos Street, 95110. Telephone: 408-975-7500. Fax: (408) 975-7501.

Intellectual Property Practice. Patents, Trademarks, Copyrights, Trade Secrets, Unfair Competition, Computer Law, Licensing and related Trade Regulation, Antitrust and International Trade Matters. Sports Marketing, Entertainment Law, Trials, Appeals and Arbitration.

FIRM PROFILE: Kenyon & Kenyon, founded in 1879, specializes in the practice of law relating to intellectual property. Our practice includes the procurement and enforcement of legal rights relating to patents, trademarks and copyrights. This involves counseling clients on intellectual property matters, negotiating and drafting agreements, trial and appellate litigation in the Federal and State Courts in all areas of the country and before the International Trade Commission, as well as preparing applications to obtain patents, trademark registrations, and copyright registrations, and guiding these applications through the appropriate administrative bodies in Washington, D.C. The firm also renders advice and representation in closely allied fields, such as antitrust, trade protection, franchising, entertainment, computer law and product advertising and marketing.

RESIDENT PARTNERS

JOHN C. ALTMILLER, born Hazleton, Pennsylvania, November 5, 1936; admitted to bar, 1971, Pennsylvania; 1972, New York; 1976, New Jersey; 1993, District of Columbia. *Education:* Villanova University (B.E.E., 1959); Cornell University (J.D., 1971). Phi Kappa Phi. *Member:* American Bar Association; New York Intellectual Property Law Association; International Patent and Trademark Association. ***PRACTICE AREAS:*** Intellectual Property. ***Email:*** jaltmiller@kenyon.com

EDWARD T. COLBERT, born New York, N.Y., January 20, 1947; admitted to bar, 1973, Maryland; 1974, District of Columbia; 1975, U.S. Claims Court; 1975-1982, U.S. Court of Customs and Patent Appeals; 1982, U.S. Supreme Court and U.S. Court of Appeals for the Federal Circuit. *Education:* University of Maryland (B.A., 1970; J.D., with honors, 1972). Phi Alpha Delta. Member, University of Maryland Law Review, 1970-1971. Law Clerk to the Hon. Herbert S. Boreman, U.S. Court of Appeals for the Fourth Circuit, 1972-1973. Co-Author with Richard G. Kline, "Roots of the Lemon Tree: Priority Rights in the Registration of Trademarks Under the International Convention for the Protection of Intellectual Property," International Trade Law Journal, Summer 1978. Contributor: "Refusals to Deal and Exclusive Distributorships," ABA Monograph Task Force, No. 9, 1982-1983. Senior Trial Attorney, Federal Trade Commission, Bureau of Competition, 1976-1981. *Member:* The District of Columbia Bar; Maryland State and American (Chair, Sports and Entertainment Committee, Section on Antitrust, 1991-1993) Bar Associations. ***PRACTICE AREAS:*** Intellectual Property Litigation; Trademark Counseling and Prosecution; Unfair Competition and Related Litigation. ***Email:*** ecolbert@kenyon.com

WILLIAM K. WELLS, JR., born Newport, Rhode Island, October 9, 1943; admitted to bar, 1974, New York; 1977, District of Columbia; 1985, Virginia; 1989, Maryland. *Education:* Virginia Polytechnic Institute (B.S., 1966); Rensselaer Polytechnic Institute; University of Virginia (J.D., 1972). Author: "How to Protect New Products, Works and Ideas from Competition," Journal of the Kansas Bar Association, 1984; "Are Registered Marks Open to Attack by Subsequent Users?" Journal of the Patent Office Society, 1990. Member, U.S. Chamber Task Force on Intellectual Property, 1987—. *Member:* The District of Columbia Bar; Virginia State Bar; American Bar Association (Contributing Author, Antitrust Law Developments (Second), Prepared by Section of Antitrust and Law, 1984; Member, Task Force to Study and Comment on EEC Licensing Guidelines, 1978—); Licensing Executive Society; American Intellectual Property Association (Chairman, Industrial Design Committee, 1993-1994); ITC Trial Lawyers Association; International Intellectual Property Association; The Computer Law Association. ***PRACTICE AREAS:*** Intellectual Property. ***Email:*** wwells@kenyon.com

BRIAN S. MUDGE, born Trenton, New Jersey, October 6, 1956; admitted to bar, 1991, New Jersey and Pennsylvania; 1998, District of Columbia; registered to practice before U.S. Patent and Trademark Office. *Education:* University of Pennsylvania (B.S., magna cum laude, 1979; M.S., 1984; J.D., magna cum laude, 1991). Order of the Coif; Tau Beta Pi; Eta Kappa Nu. *Member:* American Bar Association; American Intellectual Property Law Association; Institute of Electrical and Electronic Engineers. ***PRACTICE AREAS:*** Intellectual Property. ***Email:*** bmudge@kenyon.com

JOHN W. BATEMAN, born Fort Belvoir, Virginia, June 14, 1965; admitted to bar, 1991, Virginia; 1998, District of Columbia; registered to practice before U.S. Patent and Trademark Office. *Education:* University of Virginia (B.A., 1987; J.D., 1990). *Member:* American Bar Association; American Intellectual Property Law Association; Federal Circuit Bar Association; ITC Trial Lawyers Association. ***PRACTICE AREAS:*** Intellectual Property. ***Email:*** jbateman@kenyon.com

DOUGLAS E. RINGEL, born Jacksonville, Florida, July 17, 1966; admitted to bar, 1993, Florida; 1994, New York; registered to practice before U.S. Patent and Trademark Office (Not admitted in District of Columbia). *Education:* Cornell University (B.S., with distinction, 1988); The University of Michigan Law School (J.D., cum laude, 1992). Order of the Coif. *Member:* American Intellectual Property Law Association. ***PRACTICE AREAS:*** Intellectual Property. ***Email:*** dringel@kenyon.com

RESIDENT COUNSEL

MICHAEL N. ZACHARY, born 1956; admitted to bar, 1984, California; 2001, District of Columbia. *Education:* Columbia University (A.B., cum laude, 1978); Harvard University (J.D., cum laude, 1983). ***PRACTICE AREAS:*** Intellectual Property. ***Email:*** mzachary@kenyon.com

(This Listing Continued)

KENYON & KENYON, Washington—Continued

RESIDENT ASSOCIATES

MARK M. SUPKO, born 1963; admitted to bar, 1994, New York; 1995, District of Columbia. *Education:* University of Scranton (B.S., 1985); Georgetown University (J.D., 1993). ***PRACTICE AREAS:*** Intellectual Property. ***Email:*** msupko@kenyon.com

JUDITH L. TOFFENETTI, born 1953; admitted to bar, 1994, Maryland; 1996, District of Columbia; registered to practice before U.S. Patent and Trademark Office. *Education:* Barnard College (B.A., 1975); Georgetown University (Ph.D., 1980); George Washington University (J.D., 1993). ***PRACTICE AREAS:*** Intellectual Property. ***Email:*** jtoffenetti@kenyon.com

C. KYLE MUSGROVE, born 1970; admitted to bar, 1996, New York; 1998, District of Columbia; registered to practice before U.S. Patent and Trademark Office. *Education:* Tulane University (B.S., 1992); University of North Carolina (J.D., 1995). ***PRACTICE AREAS:*** Intellectual Property. ***Email:*** cmusgrove@kenyon.com

GARY S. MORRIS, born 1961; admitted to bar, 1996, New York; 1998, District of Columbia; registered to practice before U.S. Patent and Trademark Office. *Education:* Rensselaer Polytechnic Institute (B.S., 1983); State University of New York at Stony Brook (M.A., 1985); Georgetown University Law Center (J.D., 1995). ***PRACTICE AREAS:*** Intellectual Property. ***Email:*** gmorris@kenyon.com

WILLIAM M. MERONE, born 1969; admitted to bar, 1995, Virginia; 1998, District of Columbia; registered to practice before U.S. Patent and Trademark Office. *Education:* University of Southern California (B.S./B.A., cum laude, 1992); University of Virginia (J.D., 1995). ***PRACTICE AREAS:*** Intellectual Property. ***Email:*** wmerone@kenyon.com

JOHN McGROARTY, born 1967; admitted to bar, 1997, New York; 1999, District of Columbia; registered to practice before U.S. Patent and Trademark Office. *Education:* University of Pennsylvania (B.S., magna cum laude, 1989); Cornell University (M.S., 1992); Georgetown University (J.D., 1995). ***PRACTICE AREAS:*** Intellectual Property. ***Email:*** jmcgroarty@kenyon.com

TIMOTHY M. DEVLIN, born 1970; admitted to bar, 1997, New York; 2000, District of Columbia; registered to practice before U.S. Patent and Trademark Office. *Education:* Pennsylvania State University (B.S., with honors, 1993; B.S., with honors, 1993); University of Michigan (J.D., 1996). ***PRACTICE AREAS:*** Intellectual Property. ***Email:*** tdevlin@kenyon.com

JOHN R. HUTCHINS, born 1970; admitted to bar, 1996, New York; 1997, District of Columbia; registered to practice before U.S. Patent and Trademark Office. *Education:* University of Michigan (B.S.E., summa cum laude, 1992); Harvard University (J.D., magna cum laude, 1995). ***PRACTICE AREAS:*** Intellectual Property. ***Email:*** jhutchins@kenyon.com

ROBERT L. HAILS, JR., born 1968; admitted to bar, 1993, Virginia; 1995, District of Columbia; registered to practice before U.S. Patent and Trademark Office. *Education:* University of Maryland (B.S., 1990); George Washington University (J.D., with honors, 1993). ***PRACTICE AREAS:*** Intellectual Property. ***Email:*** rhails@kenyon.com

KAREN L. FEISTHAMEL, born 1965; admitted to bar, 1990, Connecticut; 1996, California; 1998, District of Columbia; registered to practice before U.S. Patent and Trademark Office. *Education:* Brown University (Sc.B., magna cum laude, 1987); Georgetown University (J.D., 1990). ***PRACTICE AREAS:*** Intellectual Property. ***Email:*** kfeisthamel@kenyon.com

TERESA A. LAVENUE, born 1966; admitted to bar, 1998, California; registered to practice before U.S. Patent and Trademark Office (Not admitted in District of Columbia). *Education:* Vanderbilt University (B.S., 1987); Washington University (J.D., summa cum laude, 1997). ***PRACTICE AREAS:*** Intellectual Property. ***Email:*** tlavenue@kenyon.com

BRADLEY J. MEIER, born 1973; admitted to bar, 1999, New York; 2001, District of Columbia; registered to practice before U.S. Patent and Trademark Office. *Education:* Washington & Lee University (B.S., Physics-Engineering/Computer Science, 1995); University of Notre Dame (M.E., Computer Engineering, 1998; J.D., 1998). Phi Beta Kappa. ***PRACTICE AREAS:*** Intellectual Property. ***Email:*** bmeier@kenyon.com

KRISTINA M. CASTELLANO, born 1971; admitted to bar, 1996, Washington; 2000, District of Columbia; registered to practice before U.S. Patent and Trademark Office. *Education:* University of Washington (B.S.Ch.E., 1993); Franklin Pierce Law Center (J.D., M.I.P., 1996). ***PRACTICE AREAS:*** Intellectual Property. ***Email:*** kjahns@kenyon.com

MARK H. NEBLETT, born 1958; admitted to bar, 1994, Virginia; 1995, District of Columbia; registered to practice before U.S. Patent and Trademark Office. *Education:* University of Illinois (B.S., 1980); Georgetown University (J.D., cum laude, 1994). ***PRACTICE AREAS:*** Intellectual Property. ***Email:*** mneblett@kenyon.com

(This Listing Continued)

FRED GRASSO, born 1966; admitted to bar, 1997, Virginia; 1998, District of Columbia; registered to practice before U.S. Patent and Trademark Office. *Education:* University of Virginia (B.S.C.E., 1988); Washington College of Law, American University (J.D., 1997). Member, American University Law Review. ***PRACTICE AREAS:*** Intellectual Property. ***Email:*** fgrasso@kenyon.com

CLINT A. GERDINE, born 1970; admitted to bar, 1998, Virginia; registered to practice before U.S. Patent and Trademark Office (Not admitted in District of Columbia). *Education:* Stanford University (B.S., 1992); Georgia Institute of Technology (M.S., 1993); Rutgers University (J.D., 1998). ***PRACTICE AREAS:*** Intellectual Property. ***Email:*** cgerdine@kenyon.com

KENNETH R. CORSELLO, born 1965; admitted to bar, 1992, Connecticut; 1993, New York; 1994, District of Columbia; registered to practice before U.S. Patent and Trademark Office. *Education:* State University of New York at Stony Brook (B.S., 1987); Catholic University of America (J.D., 1992); George Washington University (LL.M., 1998). Managing Editor, Catholic University Law Review. ***PRACTICE AREAS:*** Intellectual Property. ***Email:*** kcorsello@kenyon.com

DAN SALEHI, born 1967; admitted to bar, 1999, New York; 2000, District of Columbia; registered to practice before U.S. Patent and Trademark Office. *Education:* California Polytechnic State University (B.Sc., 1993); Franklin Pierce Law Center (J.D., 1998). ***PRACTICE AREAS:*** Intellectual Property. ***Email:*** dsalehi@kenyon.com

R. PAUL ZEINEDDIN, born 1966; admitted to bar, 1998, Virginia; 2001, District of Columbia. *Education:* Ohio University (B.S., Electrical Engineering, 1990; M.S., Electrical Engineering, 1993); George Washington University (J.D., 1999). ***PRACTICE AREAS:*** Intellectual Property. ***Email:*** pzeineddin@kenyon.com

MICHAEL M. SHEN, born 1973; admitted to bar, 1998, New York; registered to practice before U.S. Patent and Trademark Office (Not admitted in District of Columbia). *Education:* University of Michigan (B.S.Ch.E., 1995); Georgetown University (J.D., 1998). ***PRACTICE AREAS:*** Intellectual Property. ***Email:*** mshen@kenyon.com

T. CY WALKER, born 1961; admitted to bar, 1992, District of Columbia. *Education:* General Motors Institute (B.S.E.E., 1985); George Washington University (J.D., with high honors, 1992). ***PRACTICE AREAS:*** Intellectual Property. ***Email:*** twalker@kenyon.com

BARRY S. GOLDSMITH, born 1962; admitted to bar, 1994, Florida; 1995, District of Columbia; registered to practice before U.S. Patent and Trademark Office. *Education:* Virginia Polytechnic Institute and State University (B.S.E.E., with honors, 1985); University of Florida (J.D., cum laude, 1994). ***PRACTICE AREAS:*** Intellectual Property. ***Email:*** bgoldsmith@kenyon.com

DAVID J. ZIBELLI, born 1961; admitted to bar, 1993, Virginia; registered to practice before U.S. Patent and Trademark Office (Not admitted in District of Columbia). *Education:* Boston University (B.S.E.E., 1984); Franklin Pierce Law Center (J.D., 1993). ***PRACTICE AREAS:*** Intellectual Property. ***Email:*** dzibelli@kenyon.com

RONALD E. PRASS, JR., born 1963; admitted to bar, 1996, Maryland; 1997, District of Columbia; registered to practice before U.S. Patent and Trademark Office. *Education:* U.S. Naval Academy (B.S., 1987); Troy State University (M.S., 1989); American University (J.D., 1995). ***PRACTICE AREAS:*** Intellectual Property. ***Email:*** rprass@kenyon.com

JENNIFER L. KING, born 1972; admitted to bar, 1999, District of Columbia; registered to practice before U.S. Patent and Trademark Office. *Education:* George Washington University (B.S., magna cum laude, 1994); Georgetown University (J.D., cum laude, 1999). ***PRACTICE AREAS:*** Intellectual Property. ***Email:*** jking@kenyon.com

SUMEET MAGOON, born 1971; admitted to bar, 1999, Virginia; registered to practice before U.S. Patent and Trademark Office (Not admitted in District of Columbia). *Education:* Drexel University (B.S.E.E., 1993); University of Baltimore (J.D., magna cum laude, 1999). ***PRACTICE AREAS:*** Intellectual Property. ***Email:*** smagoon@kenyon.com

RONALD L. SIGWORTH, born 1964; admitted to bar, 1997, Virginia; 1998, New Jersey and District of Columbia. *Education:* University of Virginia (B.S.M.E., 1987); Catholic University of America (J.D., 1997). ***PRACTICE AREAS:*** Intellectual Property. ***Email:*** rsigworth@kenyon.com

MICHAEL I. ANGERT, born 1961; admitted to bar, 1999, Maryland; 2000, District of Columbia; registered to practice before U.S. Patent and Trademark Office. *Education:* Pennsylvania State University (B.S.E.E., 1983); Johns Hopkins University (M.S.E.E., 1989); University of Baltimore (J.D., summa cum laude, 1999). ***PRACTICE AREAS:*** Intellectual Property. ***Email:*** mangert@kenyon.com

JULIE E. STEIN, born 1971; admitted to bar, 2000, California; registered to practice before U.S. Patent and Trademark Office (Not admitted in District of

(This Listing Continued)

Columbia). *Education:* Massachusetts Institute of Technology (B.S., 1993); George Washington University National Law Center (J.D., with honors, 1999). ***PRACTICE AREAS:*** Intellectual Property. ***Email:*** jstein@kenyon.com

ZEBA T. ALI, born 1974; admitted to bar, 2000, North Carolina (Not admitted in District of Columbia). *Education:* Duke University (B.S., 1996); University of North Carolina at Chapel Hill (J.D., 2000). ***PRACTICE AREAS:*** Intellectual Property. ***Email:*** zali@kenyon.com

AMY L. HULINA, born 1964; admitted to bar, 1996, Virginia; registered to practice before U.S. Patent and Trademark Office (Not admitted in District of Columbia). *Education:* Pennsylvania State University (B.S., Ch.E., 1988); American University (J.D., 1996). ***PRACTICE AREAS:*** Intellectual Property. ***Email:*** ahulina@kenyon.com

MICHAEL A. SIEM, born 1973; admitted to bar, 2001, New York; registered to practice before U.S. Patent and Trademark Office (Not admitted in District of Columbia). *Education:* Illinois Institute of Technology (B.S.Ch.E., 1996); University of Michigan (J.D., 2001). ***PRACTICE AREAS:*** Intellectual Property. ***Email:*** msiem@kenyon.com

CEDRIC CHIA YANG TAN, born 1973; admitted to bar, 1997, Tennessee; 1999, District of Columbia. *Education:* University of Alberta (B.Sc., with honors, 1994); Tulane University of Louisiana (J.D., cum laude, 1997). ***PRACTICE AREAS:*** Intellectual Property. ***Email:*** ctan@kenyon.com

WILLIAM E. CURRY, born 1958; admitted to bar, 1997, Maryland; registered to practice before U.S. Patent and Trademark Office (Not admitted in District of Columbia). *Education:* University of Maryland (B.S.E.E., 1987; J.D., with honors, 1997). ***PRACTICE AREAS:*** Intellectual Property. ***Email:*** wcurry@kenyon.com

THU A. DANG, born 1966; admitted to bar, 1995, Virginia (Not admitted in District of Columbia). *Education:* University of Virginia (B.S.E.E., 1989); George Washington University (J.D., 1994). ***PRACTICE AREAS:*** Intellectual Property. ***Email:*** tdang@kenyon.com

B. DELANO JORDAN, born 1970; admitted to bar, 1999, Michigan; 2000, District of Columbia; registered to practice before the U.S. Patent and Trademark Office. *Education:* Virginia Polytechnic Institute (B.S.E.E., 1994); College of William & Mary School of Law (J.D., 1999). ***PRACTICE AREAS:*** Intellectual Property. ***Email:*** djordan@kenyon.com

LALEH JALALI, born 1967; admitted to bar, 1994, Pennsylvania; 1997, District of Columbia; registered to practice before U.S. Patent and Trademark Office. *Education:* University of Maryland (B.S.M.E., 1989); George Washington University (J.D., 1994). ***PRACTICE AREAS:*** Intellectual Property. ***Email:*** ljalali@kenyon.com

DAVID R. SCHAFFER, born 1958; admitted to bar, 1997, Virginia (Not admitted in District of Columbia). *Education:* The College of William and Mary (B.A., 1980); Virginia Polytechnic Institute and State University (M.S., 1988); The Catholic University of America (J.D., 1997). ***PRACTICE AREAS:*** Intellectual Property. ***Email:*** dschaffer@kenyon.com

W. DAVID WALLACE, born 1968; admitted to bar, 1996, Ohio; 1998, District of Columbia; registered to practice before U.S. Patent and Trademark Office. *Education:* Cornell University (B.A., 1990); State University of New York at Buffalo (M.S., 1992); Case Western Reserve University (J.D., cum laude, 1996). ***PRACTICE AREAS:*** Intellectual Property. ***Email:*** dwallace@kenyon.com

(For Biographical data on all Personnel, see Professional Biographies at New York, New York)

STEVEN R. KIERSH

Established in 1983

MARKET SQUARE
717 D STREET, N.W., FOURTH FLOOR
WASHINGTON, D.C. 20004
Telephone: 202-347-0200
Fax: 202-835-1543
Email: stevenkiersh@prodigy.net
URL: http://www.lawyers.com/stevenkiershlaw

Medical Negligence, Product Liability, Civil Litigation and Criminal Defense including Major Felonies, Drug and White Collar Crimes.

FIRM PROFILE: Primarily a litigation law firm, the office of Steven R. Kiersh represents individuals in both criminal and civil trials in Washington, D.C. and Maryland.

Mr. Kiersh has 20 years of trial experience and his office is located 1 block from the courthouse.

STEVEN R. KIERSH, born New York, N.Y., November 7, 1954; admitted to bar, 1980, District of Columbia, U.S. District Court, District of Maryland, U.S. Court of Appeals, Eleventh and Fourth Circuits, U.S. Court of Appeals for the District of Columbia Circuit and U.S. Court of Military Appeals. *Education:* Boston University (B.A., 1976); Antioch School of Law (J.D., 1979). Author: "Medical-Legal Aspects of Intraoperative Monitoring," Seminars in Spine Surgery, W.B. Saunders Co., December 1997. Invited Lecturer, Harvard University, School of Law, "Trial Advocacy Workshop". Annual Lecturer, District of Columbia Criminal Practice Institute. Adjunct Faculty Member, "Trial Practice," Georgetown University Law Center. Qualified as Learned Counsel Pursuant to the Federal Death Penalty Act. *Member:* The District of Columbia Bar.

KILE GOEKJIAN LERNER & REED PLLC

1101 PENNSYLVANIA AVENUE, N.W., SUITE 800
WASHINGTON, D.C. 20004
Telephone: 202-639-1260
Fax: 202-639-1298; 202-639-1299
URL: http://www.kglrlaw.com
Email: info@kglrlaw.com
URL: http://www.lawyers.com/kglr

New York, New York Office: 729 Seventh Avenue, 14th Floor, 10019. Telephone: 212-921-9713. Fax: 212-921-9778.

International Trade and Investment, Commercial Transactions, Telecommunications and Information Technology, Corporation and Securities, Banking and Real Estate Law, Patent, Trademark and Copyright Registration, Licensing and Litigation, Environmental and Natural Resources Law, Governmental Affairs and Administrative Law.

MEMBERS OF FIRM

BRADFORD E. KILE, born Marion, Ohio, August 9, 1943; admitted to bar, 1971, Virginia; 1973, District of Columbia; 1975, U.S. Court of Federal Claims, U.S. Court of Appeals for the Federal Circuit and U.S. Supreme Court; registered to practice before U.S. Patent and Trademark Office. *Education:* The Ohio State University (Bachelor of Mechanical Engineering, 1966); George Washington University (J.D., 1970; LL.M., with highest honors, 1978). Phi Eta Sigma; Delta Theta Phi. Law Clerk, U.S. Court of Federal Claims, 1970-1971. Examiner, U.S. Patent and Trademark Office, 1966-1968. Adjunct Professor, George Mason University School of Law, 1997—. Author: "Legal 'X-Games' Risk: Officer and Director Passive Retention of Personal Liability for Patent Infringement," IP Litigator II (2001); "Lotus v. Borland-Copyright Protection of Computer Software in a State of Transition," Copyright World, 1995. *Member:* District of Columbia Bar; The Bar Association of the District of Columbia; Virginia State Bar; American Bar Association (Member, Section on: Litigation, Patent, Trademark and Copyright Law); American Intellectual Property Law Association; International Trademark Association; Giles Sutherland Rich American Inn of Court (Master). ***PRACTICE AREAS:*** Intellectual Property Litigation; Licensing and Procurement; Products Liability. ***Email:*** bkile@kglrlaw.com

SAMUEL V. GOEKJIAN, born Syra, Greece, August 22, 1927; admitted to bar, 1958, New York; 1960, District of Columbia. *Education:* Syracuse University (B.A., magna cum laude, 1952); Harvard Law School (J.D., 1955). Author: "A Critical Appraisal of United States Investment Guaranty Programs" and "The Role of Export Credits, Guaranties and Insurance in International Trade," *International Financing and Investment,* Oceana, 1963: "What to Do Right and What Not to Do Wrong in Negotiating Concession Agreement in Black Africa," ABA, 1975; "Legal Problems of Transferring Technology to the Third World," Vol. XXV, The American Journal of Comparative Law, 1977; "Specific Problems and Unique Aspects of Doing Business in Egypt," ABA, 1977; "The Role of Arab Public Enterprises in International Transactions," *Public Enterprises and Development in the Arab Countries,* International Legal Center, 1977; "The Conduct of International Arbitration," Vol. II, Lawyer of the Americas, 1980; "ICC Arbitration from a Practitioner's Perspective," Vol. 14. No. 3, The Journal of International Law and Economics, George Washington University National Law Center, 1980. Professorial Lecturer, George Washington University Graduate School of Public Law, 1963-1968. Lecturer, International Law Institute, 1973-1992 and Adjunct Professor of Law, 1979-1982, Georgetown University Law Center. Member, Executive Committee and Counsel, Egypt-United States Business Council, 1977-1983. Senior Consultant, United Nations on Legal and Contractual Aspects of Economic Development, 1971-1991. Board of Trustees, Syracuse University, 1998—. *Member:* Federal and American Bar Associations. ***PRACTICE AREAS:*** International Trade and Investment; Commercial Transactions. ***Email:*** sgoekjian@kglrlaw.com

CHARLES D. REED, born Houston, Texas, May 8, 1935; admitted to bar, 1967, District of Columbia. *Education:* Rice University (B.A., 1956); University of Texas (M.S.CH.E., 1958); Institut Francais de Petrole, Paris, France (certificat, 1959); South Texas College of Law (Texas A&M University;; summa cum laude, 1965). Phi Lambda Upsilon; Omega Chi Epsilon; Sigma Xi. Fulbright Fellow (Paris, France, 1958-1959). Editor-in-Chief, South Texas Law Journal, 1964-1965. Law Clerk, Justice Tom C. Clark, U.S. Supreme Court, 1965-1966. Science Officer, International Scientific and Technological Affairs,

(This Listing Continued)

KILE GOEKJIAN LERNER & REED PLLC, Washington—Continued

Department of State, 1967-1968. Adjunct Professor, Washington College of Law of American University, 1972. Associate Professor, University of the District of Columbia, 1982-1986. Associate, Cadwalader, Wickersham & Taft, Washington, D.C., 1968-1971. Partner, Surrey & Morse, Washington, D.C., 1971-1983. Trustee, National Capital YMCA, 1986-1990. Board of Visitors, South Texas College of Law (Texas A&M University), 1990—. *Member:* District of Columbia Bar; American Bar Association; U.S. Supreme Court Bar. [USAR, Corps of Engineers, 1956-1961, 1st Lieut.]. ***PRACTICE AREAS:*** Corporate Law; Securities; Banking Law; Real Estate. ***Email:*** creed@kglrlaw.com

ROBERT J. McMANUS, born New York, N.Y., August 22, 1940; admitted to bar, 1968, District of Columbia. *Education:* Yale University (B.A., 1961; LL.B., 1968). Member, Board of Editors, Yale Law Journal, 1966-1968. Author: "International Trade in Pesticides," Chap. 10, Pesticides Law Handbook (M.L. Miller, ed., 1999); "Environmental Considerations in Investment Decisions," Chap. 8, Manual of Foreign Investment in the United States (Byam et al., eds. 1993); "Federal Preemption of Local Pesticide Regulation," Washington Legal Foundation Working Paper no. 45, 1991; "Natural Resource Damages," Oil Spills: Management and Legislative Implications, American Society of Civil Engineers, 1990; "Trade in 'Unregistered' Pesticides," 14 Chem. Reg. Rptr. 270, 1990; "Legal Aspects of Land-Based Pollution," Chap. 4, The New Nationalism and the Use of Common Spaces, American Society of International Law (J. Charney, ed., 1982). Attorney-advisor, Office of General Counsel, 1971-1974 and Director, Oceans Division, Office of International Activities, 1974-1977, U.S. Environmental Protection Agency. General Counsel, National Oceanic and Atmospheric Administration, U.S. Department of Commerce, 1981-1985. Senior Counsel, FMC Corporation, Philadelphia, Pennsylvania, 1986-1989. Alternate U.S. Representative, Third United Nations Conference on the Law of the Sea, 1974-1977. *Member:* The District of Columbia Bar; American Society of International Law. [LTJG, U.S. Naval Reserve, 1962-1965]. ***PRACTICE AREAS:*** Environmental and Natural Resources Law.

KARAN SINGH, born New Delhi, India, November 9, 1956; admitted to bar, 1993, New York; 1994, District of Columbia; registered to practice before U.S. Patent and Trademark Office. *Education:* St. Stephen's College (B.Sc., with honors, 1978); Georgetown University Law Center (J.D., cum laude, 1992); Georgetown University School of Business (Certificate, Executive International Finance, 1996). Senior Advisor to the Representative for the State of Oklahoma in India, 1987-1989. (Resident, New York, New York Office). ***PRACTICE AREAS:*** Intellectual Property Litigation; International Trade. ***Email:*** ksingh@kglrlaw.com

ASSOCIATE

EDUARDO M. SILVA, born Lisbon, Portugal, November 29, 1971; admitted to bar, 1996, Rio de Janeiro, Brazil (Not admitted in the United States). *Education:* State University of Rio de Janeiro Law School (LL.B., 1996); Franklin Pierce Law Center (LL.M., 1998). *Member:* Brazilian Bar Association; International Trademark Association; American Intellectual Property Law Association. ***LANGUAGES:*** Portuguese and Spanish. ***PRACTICE AREAS:*** Trademark; Patents; Copyrights; Licensing; Internet. ***Email:*** esilva@kglrlaw.com

OF COUNSEL

ROGER J. LERNER, born New York, New York, March 22, 1954; admitted to bar, 1979, District of Columbia; 1980, U.S. District Court, District of Columbia and U.S. Court of Appeals, District of Columbia Circuit. *Education:* George Washington University (B.A., 1976); Washington University School of Law (J.D., 1979). Washington University Law Quarterly. General Counsel, Interbank Capital Partners, LLC, 2001—. Assistant Director of Resolutions, Resolution Trust Corporation, 1989-1990. Regional Director, Mergers & Acquisitions, Federal Savings and Loan Insurance Corp, 1987-1989. Executive Assistant to the General Counsel, Pension Benefit Guaranty Corp. 1985-1987. *Member:* District of Columbia Bar. ***PRACTICE AREAS:*** Finance; Banking; Litigation; Real Estate; Bankruptcy. ***Email:*** rlerner@kglrlaw.com

BRUCE K. LAGERMAN, born Brooklyn, New York, November 15, 1959; admitted to bar, 1990, Virginia, U.S. District Court, District of Columbia, U.S. District Court, Eastern District of Virginia, and U.S. Court of Appeals, D.C., Fourth and Federal Circuits; registered to practice before the U.S. Patent and Trademark Office (Not admitted in District of Columbia). *Education:* Catholic University of America (B.S., Biomedical Engineering, 1982); Washington College of Law, American University (J.D., 1989). Judicial Law Clerk to the Honorable Randall R. Rader, U.S. Court of Appeals for the Federal Circuit, 1991-1992. (Also with Lagerman & Associates, P.C., Reston, Virginia). ***PRACTICE AREAS:*** Intellectual Property Licensing. ***Email:*** blagerman@kglrlaw.com

RAYMOND E. VICKERY, JR., born Brookhaven, Mississippi, April 30, 1942; admitted to bar, 1968, Maryland; 1969, District of Columbia; 1974, U.S.

(This Listing Continued)

Supreme Court; 1976, Virginia. *Education:* Duke University (A.B., magna cum laude, 1964, Phi Beta Kappa; Omicron Delta Kappa); University of Sri Lanka (Fulbright Fellow, 1965); Harvard University (LL.B., 1968). United States Assistant Secretary of Commerce for Trade Development, 1993-1997. (Also heads Vickery International, an international business consulting firm). ***PRACTICE AREAS:*** International Trade and Transactions; Government Relations. ***Email:*** rvickery@kglrlaw.com

KILPATRICK STOCKTON LLP

Established in 1874

607 14TH STREET, N.W., SUITE 900

WASHINGTON, D.C. 20005-2018

Telephone: 202-508-5800
Facsimile: 202-508-5858
Email: info@KilpatrickStockton.com
URL: http://www.KilpatrickStockton.com

Atlanta, Georgia Office: Suite 2800, 1100 Peachtree Street. Telephone: 404-815-6500. Facsimile: 404-815-6555. Telex: 54-2307.
Augusta, Georgia Office: 1400 First Union Bank Building, P.O. Box 2043, 30903-2043. Telephone: 706-724-2622. Facsimile: 706-722-0219.
Brussels, Belgium Office: Avenue Louise 149, BTE 15, 1050 Brussels. Telephone: 32-2-533-0300. Facsimile: 32-2-534-8638.
Charlotte, North Carolina Office: 301 South College Street, 28202-6001. Telephone: 704-338-5000. Facsimile: 704-338-5125.
Miami, Florida Office: First Union Financial Center, 200 South Biscayne Boulevard, Suite 2000, 33131-2310. Telephone: 786-777-8000. Facsimile: 786-777-8001.
London, England Office: 68 Pall Mall, London SW1Y 5ES. Telephone: 44-171-321-0477. Facsimile; 44-171-930-9733.
Raleigh, North Carolina Office: Suite 400, 3737 Glenwood Avenue, 27612. Telephone: 919-420-1700. Facsimile: 919-420-1800.
Reston, Virginia Office: 11130 Sunrise Valley Drive, Suite 300, 20191-4329. Telephone: 703-648-8500. Facsimile: 703-648-8501.
Stockholm, Sweden Office: Hovslagargatan 5 S-111 48. Telephone: 46-8-505-646-00. Facsimile: 46-8-505-646-99.
Winston-Salem, North Carolina Office: 1001 West Fourth Street, 27101-2400. Telephone: 336-607-7300. Facsimile: 336-607-7500.

General Civil, Trial and Appellate Practice. Administrative, Antitrust, Aviation, Banking, Bankruptcy, Charitable Foundations, Construction Law, Copyright, Corporations, Creditors' Rights, Employee Benefits, Entertainment, Equal Opportunity, Environmental, Estate Planning, Franchising, Health Care Law, Insurance, International, Labor, Medical Malpractice Defense, Municipal Finance, Oil and Gas, Patent, Personal Injury Litigation, Probate, Products Liability Litigation, Public Utility, Real Estate, Securities, Taxation, Trademark, Trust and Unfair Competition.

MEMBERS OF FIRM

THOMAS K. BICK, admitted to bar, 1977, District of Columbia; 1978, Virginia. *Education:* University of Notre Dame (B.S., Chemistry, 1970); Antioch School of Law (J.D., 1977). ***PRACTICE AREAS:*** Environmental; Insurance; Native American Law. ***Email:*** TBick@KilpatrickStockton.com

TESS J. FERRERA, admitted to bar, 1990, Maryland; 1992, District of Columbia. *Education:* George Washington University (B.A., 1980); Georgetown University (J.D., 1990). ***LANGUAGES:*** Spanish. ***PRACTICE AREAS:*** ERISA. ***Email:*** TFerrera@KilpatrickStockton.com

RONALD A. FEUERSTEIN, admitted to bar, 1973, District of Columbia; 1978, U.S. Supreme Court; 1979, U.S. Tax Court. *Education:* Boston University (B.A., 1969); American University (J.D., 1973); New York University (LL.M. in Taxation, 1974). ***PRACTICE AREAS:*** Taxation; Estate Planning; Pension and Profit Sharing. ***Email:*** RFeuerstein@KilpatrickStockton.com

KENNETH A. GODLEWSKI, admitted to bar, 1991, Ohio; 1994, U.S. District Court, Northern District of Ohio and U.S. Court of Appeals for the Federal Circuit; 2000, District of Columbia; U.S. Court of Appeals, Sixth Circuit; U.S. District Court, District of Wisconsin; U.S. District Court, District of Colorado; U.S. District Court, District of Iowa. *Education:* Ohio State University (J.D., 1991). ***PRACTICE AREAS:*** Patent Law; Intellectual Property Litigation; Litigation. ***Email:*** KGodlewski@KilpatrickStockton.com

STANLEY M. GORINSON, admitted to bar, 1974, New York; 1985, Maryland and District of Columbia. *Education:* Brooklyn College of the City University of New York (B.A., 1967); Rutgers University School of Law (J.D., 1973). ***PRACTICE AREAS:*** Antitrust; Litigation. ***Email:*** SGorinson@KilpatrickStockton.com

JOHN C. HARDWICK, JR., admitted to bar, 1992, Massachusetts; 1995, Maryland; 1996, District of Columbia, U.S. Court of Appeals, Fourth Circuit and U.S. District Court, District of Maryland; 1997, U.S. Court of Appeals for the District of Columbia Circuit and U.S. District Court for the District of

(This Listing Continued)

Columbia. *Education:* Duke University (B.A., History, 1988); Boston College Law School (J.D., 1991). ***LANGUAGES:*** French. ***PRACTICE AREAS:*** Employment Law; Labor Law; Immigration Law. ***Email:*** JHardwick@KilpatrickStockton.com

MICHAEL A. HORDELL, admitted to bar, 1973, Massachusetts; 1976, District of Columbia. *Education:* University of Cincinnati (B.B.A., 1970); Boston University (J.D., 1973). ***PRACTICE AREAS:*** Government Contracts; Government; Business. ***Email:*** MHordell@KilpatrickStockton.com

J. VANCE HUGHES, admitted to bar, 1971, Georgia; 1980, U.S. Supreme Court; 1984, District of Columbia. *Education:* Davidson College (A.B., 1968); University of Georgia (J.D., 1971). ***PRACTICE AREAS:*** Environmental; Natural Resources. ***Email:*** VHughes@KilpatrickStockton.com

DAVID R. LEVIN, admitted to bar, 1978, District of Columbia. *Education:* George Washington University (B.A., 1969); Catholic University (J.D., 1978). ***PRACTICE AREAS:*** Employee Benefits; ERISA Counseling; ERISA Litigation. ***Email:*** DLevin@KilpatrickStockton.com

NEIL I. LEVY, admitted to bar, 1972, California (inactive); 1975, District of Columbia; 1980, Maryland. *Education:* Wharton School of Commerce & Finance, University of Pennsylvania (B.S.E., 1969); University of Pennsylvania (J.D., magna cum laude, 1972). ***PRACTICE AREAS:*** Government Contracts; Real Estate; Litigation. ***Email:*** NLevy@KilpatrickStockton.com

GEORGE T. MARCOU, admitted to bar, 1984, District of Columbia; U.S. District Court for the District of Columbia; registered to practice before U.S. Patent and Trademark Office. *Education:* Massachusetts Institute of Technology (B.S.M.E., 1979); Georgetown University (J.D., with honors, 1984). ***PRACTICE AREAS:*** Intellectual Property; Patents. ***Email:*** GMgmarcou@KilpatrickStockton.com

DAVID PICKLE, admitted to bar, 1991, Kansas; 1994, District of Columbia. *Education:* Carleton College (B.A., 1984); University of Kansas (J.D., 1991). ***PRACTICE AREAS:*** Employee Benefits; Labor and Employment. ***Email:*** DPickle@KilpatrickStockton.com

RONALD L. RAIDER, admitted to bar, 1986, New York; 1988, District of Columbia and U.S. Court of Appeals, Tenth Circuit; 1987, U.S. Court of Federal Claims; 1990, U.S. Court of Appeals for the District of Columbia Circuit. *Education:* State University of New York at Albany (B.A., cum laude, 1982); George Washington University (J.D., with honors, 1985). ***Email:*** RRaider@KilpatrickStockton.com

STEVEN J. SACHER, admitted to bar, 1968, District of Columbia. *Education:* University of Wisconsin (B.S., 1964); University of Chicago (J.D., 1967). ***PRACTICE AREAS:*** ERISA; Employee Benefits; Federal Regulatory; Legislative Practice. ***Email:*** SSacher@KilpatrickStockton.com

CHARLES T. SIMMONS, admitted to bar, 1991, Connecticut; 1994, District of Columbia. *Education:* University of Hartford (B.S., magna cum laude, 1976); Institute of Textile Technology (M.S., 1980); University of Connecticut (J.D., 1991). ***PRACTICE AREAS:*** Environmental. ***Email:*** CSimmons@KilpatrickStockton.com

MARK D. WINCEK, admitted to bar, 1977, Massachusetts; 1980, District of Columbia. *Education:* Boston College (B.A., cum laude, 1972; J.D., cum laude, 1976). ***PRACTICE AREAS:*** Employee Benefits; Executive Compensation. ***Email:*** MWincek@KilpatrickStockton.com

COUNSEL

ELLIOTT H. LEVITAS, admitted to bar, 1955, Georgia; 1963, U.S. Supreme Court; 1984, District of Columbia. *Education:* Emory University (A.B., 1952); Oxford University (M.A., (jur.) 1954); University of Michigan Law School, 1955-1956; Emory University Law School (J.D., 1956). ***PRACTICE AREAS:*** Government Contracts; Legislative; Environmental Law; Administrative Law; Constitutional Law. ***Email:*** ELevitas@KilpatrickStockton.com

DEVON LEE MILLER, admitted to bar, 1985, District of Columbia. *Education:* Yale University (B.A., cum laude, 1975); Georgetown University (J.D., 1985). ***PRACTICE AREAS:*** Employee Benefits. ***Email:*** DMiller@KilpatrickStockton.com

ASSOCIATES

JOHN WILLIAM BALL, JR., admitted to bar, 1999, Maryland; 2000, District of Columbia; registered to practice before U.S. Patent and Trademark Office. *Education:* U.S. Naval Academy (B.S., Mechanical Engineering, 1986); University of Arkansas at Little Rock (J.D., with honors, 1999). ***PRACTICE AREAS:*** Intellectual Property. ***Email:*** JBall@KilpatrickStockton.com

DAWN-MARIE BEY, admitted to bar, 1999, Virginia, U.S. District Court, Eastern District of Virginia and U.S. Court of Appeals, Fourth Circuit; 2000, District of Columbia and U.S. Court of Appeals for the Federal Circuit; registered to practice before U.S. Patent and Trademark Office. *Education:* Franklin

(This Listing Continued)

& Marshall College (B.A., Physics, 1994); George Mason University School of Law (J.D., 1999). ***PRACTICE AREAS:*** Intellectual Property. ***Email:*** dbey@kilpatrickstockton.com

ELIZABETH R. BINDER, admitted to bar, 1990, New York (Not admitted in District of Columbia). *Education:* University of Pennsylvania (B.A., 1982); University of Miami School of Law (J.D., 1988). ***PRACTICE AREAS:*** Employee Benefits; Compensation; ERISA Litigation. ***Email:*** EBinder@KilpatrickStockton.com

AMY E. FORTENBERRY, admitted to bar, 1997, Georgia; 1999, District of Columbia. *Education:* Georgia State University (B.A., summa cum laude, 1992); Boston College (J.D., with Environmental Certification, 1997). ***PRACTICE AREAS:*** Environmental Law; Food and Drug. ***Email:*** AFortenberry@KilpatrickStockton.com

AMY D. HEALY, admitted to bar, 1999, Maryland; 2000, District of Columbia. *Education:* Davidson College (B.A., 1994); George Washington University (J.D., 1999). ***PRACTICE AREAS:*** Employee Benefits. ***Email:*** AHealy@KilpatrickStockton.com

LAURA L. HOFFMAN, admitted to bar, 1994, Maryland; 1995, District of Columbia. *Education:* Boston University (B.S., cum laude, 1989); George Washington University Law School (J.D., 1994). ***PRACTICE AREAS:*** Government Contracts; Litigation. ***Email:*** LHoffman@KilpatrickStockton.com

YONCHA L. KUNDUPOGLU, admitted to bar, 1995, California and District of Columbia; registered to practice before U.S. Patent and Trademark Office. *Education:* University of California at Davis (B.S.M.E., and B.S., Aero. Eng., 1988); Golden Gate University (J.D., 1994). ***LANGUAGES:*** Turkish. ***PRACTICE AREAS:*** Patents; Intellectual Property; Litigation. ***Email:*** YKundupoglu@KilpatrickStockton.com

EMMETT H. MILLER, admitted to bar, 1994, Georgia; 1995, District of Columbia. *Education:* Vanderbilt University (B.A., 1990; J.D., 1993). ***PRACTICE AREAS:*** Government Contracts; Commercial Litigation. ***Email:*** MMiller@KilpatrickStockton.com

CHRISTOPHER A. OTT, admitted to bar, 1999, Missouri; 2000, Maryland; 2001, District of Columbia. *Education:* College of Charleston (B.A., 1995); Saint Louis University (J.D., cum laude, 1999). ***PRACTICE AREAS:*** Intellectual Property Litigation. ***Email:*** COtt@KilpatrickStockton.com

RICHARD T. PETERSON, admitted to bar, 1995, Virginia; registered to practice before U.S. Patent and Trademark Office (Not admitted in District of Columbia). *Education:* Columbia University (B.S. in Biochemistry, magna cum laude, 1983); Harvard University (M.S. in Organic Chemistry, 1985); Georgetown University Law Center (J.D., with honors, 1995). ***PRACTICE AREAS:*** Intellectual Property Litigation. ***Email:*** RPeterson@KilpatrickStockton.com

ROBERT V. PAMBIANCO, admitted to bar, 1998, Maryland (Not admitted in District of Columbia). *Education:* LaSalle University (B.A., 1988); Catholic University of America (J.D., 1998). ***PRACTICE AREAS:*** Antitrust. ***Email:*** RPambianco@KilpatrickStockton.com

LEWIS J. SARET, admitted to bar, 1990, District of Columbia. *Education:* Lamar University (B.B.A., 1981); Rice University (M.B.A., 1983); George Washington University (J.D., 1990). ***PRACTICE AREAS:*** Tax; Estate Planning. ***Email:*** LSaret@KilpatrickStockton.com

MARK L. STEMBER, admitted to bar, 1996, Iowa and U.S. District Court, Norhtern and Southern District of Iowa (Not admitted in District of Columbia). *Education:* St. Cloud State University (B.S., Accounting, magna cum laude, 1991); Hamline University (J.D., 1995); University of Missouri, Kansas City (LL.M., Taxation, 1996). ***PRACTICE AREAS:*** Employee Benefits; Executive Compensation. ***Email:*** MStember@KilpatrickStockton.com

(For complete biographical data on all personnel, see Professional Biographies at Atlanta and Augusta, Georgia; Miami, Florida; Charlotte, Raleigh and Winston Salem, North Carolina; Reston, Virginia; Stockholm, Sweden; Brussels, Belgium and London, England).

EDWARD M. KIMMEL

WASHINGTON, D.C.

(See Takoma Park, Maryland)

Bankruptcy.

KING & ATTRIDGE

WASHINGTON, D.C.

(See Rockville, Maryland)

General Civil Litigation. Construction Litigation, Professional Liability, Products Liability, Toxic Tort Litigation, Insurance Coverage, Insurance Defense and Personal Injury Law.

KING & NORDLINGER, L.L.P.

Established in 1933

5028 WISCONSIN AVENUE, N.W.
SUITE 300
WASHINGTON, D.C. 20016
Telephone: 202-833-9310
URL: http://www.knlaw.com

Arlington, Virginia Office: 4350 North Fairfax Drive, Suite 950. Telephone: 703-522-8084. Fax: 703-522-8108.
Gaithersburg, Maryland Office: 806 West Diamond Avenue, Fourth Floor. Telephone: 301-258-4571. Fax: 301-258-4575.

General Practice before Federal and State Courts, Corporate and Business, Litigation, Real Estate, Personal Injury, Employment and Labor Law, Estate Planning and Probate, Condominium and Cooperative Law, Rent Control, Housing Law, Discrimination Law, Commercial Leasing and Landlord-Tenant Law.

FIRM PROFILE: King & Nordlinger was founded in 1933 by Milton W. King and Bernard I. Nordlinger in the District of Columbia and now serves clients with multi-state interests, particularly in the state and federal courts and administrative agencies of the District of Columbia, Northern Virginia and Maryland counties.

(For Complete Biographical Data on all Personnel, see Professional Biographies at Arlington, Virginia)

KING, PAGANO & HARRISON

1730 PENNSYLVANIA AVENUE, N.W.
WASHINGTON, D.C. 20006
Telephone: 202-371-6800
Fax: 202-371-6770
URL: http://www.kph.com

New York, New York Office: 425 Park Avenue, 10022. Telephone: 212-223-4000. FAX: 212-223-4134.
East Hampton Office: 33 Newtown Lane, 11937. Telephone: 631-329-8466. Fax: 631-329-8436.

Complex Civil and Criminal Practice before Federal and State Courts, Domestic and International Management Labor Relations, Antitrust, Employment, Health Care, Managed Care, Government Contracts, Domestic and International Management Labor Relations and Intellectual Property Litigation.

MEMBERS OF FIRM

JEFFREY W. KING, born Suffern, New York, May 14, 1947; admitted to bar, 1977, District of Columbia; 1979, U.S. District Court for the District of Columbia and U.S. Court of Appeals for the District of Columbia Circuit; 1982, U.S. Court of Appeals for the Federal Circuit; 1988, U.S. Supreme Court; 1989, Maryland; 1992, U.S. Court of Federal Claims. *Education:* State University of New York at Brockport (B.A., summa cum laude, 1974); Albany Law School of Union University (J.D., cum laude, 1977). Editor-in-Chief, Albany Law Review, 1976-1977. Editor and Author: "Legal Information Review," Convention Liaison Council, 1984-1996; Co-Author: "Health Care Fraud: The Rising Tide of Enforcement," White Collar Crime Reporter, March 1993. Editor and Co-Author: "Temporary Relief Before the U.S. International Trade Commission," International Trade Commission Trial Lawyers Association, 1985; "Legal Aspects of Running Trade Shows and Expositions," 1986. Author: "Forfeiture: The Anomaly of the Land Sale Contract," 41 Albany Law Review 71, 1976; "When Do You Have to Pay the Band?" ASAE Conventions and Expositions, 1989. *Member:* The District of Columbia Bar; Maryland State and American Bar Associations; National Association of Criminal Defense Lawyers. [With USMC, 1967-1971]. ***PRACTICE AREAS:*** Complex Civil Litigation; Health Care Law; Government Contracts; Criminal Defense; Antitrust. ***Email:*** jking@kph.com

JEFFREY W. PAGANO, born Long Branch, New Jersey, September 19, 1950; admitted to bar, 1976, New Jersey; 1978, District of Columbia; 1985, New York, U.S. Supreme Court, U.S. Court of Appeals, Second, Third, Fourth, Fifth, Sixth, Ninth and Eleventh Circuits; U.S. District Court, District of New Jersey; U.S. District Court, District of Columbia; U.S. District Court, Southern, Eastern and Northern Districts of New York; U.S. District Court, Eastern District of Michigan; U.S. District Court, Eastern District of Wisconsin. *Education:* College de Europe, Brugge, Belgium (EEC Integration, 1971-1972); Ohio University (B.A., cum laude, 1973); Rutgers University School of Law, Newark (J.D., 1976). Contributing Editor, "The Developing Labor Law." Counsel to General Counsel, National Labor Relations Board, Region 9, Cincinnati, Ohio, 1976-1978. *Member:* The District of Columbia Bar; New Jersey State, New York State and American Bar Associations. (New York and East Hampton, New York). ***PRACTICE AREAS:*** Labor and Employment Law; National Labor Relations Act; ERISA; Health Care Litigation; Employment Litigation; Complex Civil Litigation. ***Email:*** jpagano@kph.com

(This Listing Continued)

KEITH J. HARRISON, born Stuttgart, West Germany, October 20, 1958; admitted to bar, 1986, New York; 1989, District of Columbia, U.S. District Court for the District of Columbia, U.S. District Court, District of Maryland, U.S. Court of Appeals, Fifth and Sixth Circuits, U.S. Court of Federal Claims and U.S. Court of Appeals for the Federal Circuit. *Education:* College of William and Mary (B.A., 1981); University of Virginia (J.D., 1984). Assistant District Attorney, County of New York (Manhattan), 1984-1987. Co-Author: "Healthcare Fraud: The Rising Tide of Enforcement," White Collar Crime Reporter, March, 1993. *Member:* The District of Columbia Bar; New York State, American and National Bar Associations; National Health Lawyers Association; Federal Circuit Bar Association (Member, Board of Governors; Chairman, Committee on Minorities in the Federal Circuit). ***PRACTICE AREAS:*** Complex Civil Litigation; Intellectual Property Litigation; Employment Law; Health Care Law; Government Contracts; Year 2000 Computer Conversion. ***Email:*** kharrison@kph.com

JAMES E. KELLETT, born Glen Ridge, New Jersey, June 22, 1948; admitted to bar, 1988, New Jersey; 1989, New York, U.S. District Court, Eastern and Southern Districts of New York and U.S. District Court, District of New Jersey; 1997, U.S. Court of Appeals, Ninth Circuit and U.S. District Court, Northern District of Illinois; 1998, U.S. District Court, Western District of New York; 2000, U.S. Court of Appeals, Second Circuit; 2001, U.S. Court of Appeals, Sixth Circuit. *Education:* Lafayette College (B.A., 1970); Fairleigh Dickinson University (M.B.A., 1982); Fordham University School of Law (J.D., 1988). Staff Member, Fordham Law Review, 1985-1987. Chairman, Ethical Standards Board, Township of Belleville, New Jersey, 1991-1994. *Member:* The Association of the Bar of the City of New York; New Jersey State and American Bar Associations. [1st Lt., U.S. Army Medical Service Corps, 1970-1973]. (Resident, New York, N.Y. Office). ***PRACTICE AREAS:*** Labor and Employment; Litigation; Affirmative Action and Equal Employment Law. ***Email:*** jkellett@kph.com

STEVEN SCHAARS, born Green Bay, Wisconsin, April 15, 1945; admitted to bar, 1970, Wisconsin; 1973, District of Columbia, U.S. District Court for the District of Columbia and U.S. Court of Appeals for the District of Columbia, Third, Fourth, Fifth and Eleventh Circuits; 1978, U.S. Supreme Court; 1986, Virginia and U.S. District Court, Eastern and Western Districts of Virginia. *Education:* University of Wisconsin (B.S., 1967; J.D., 1970). Attorney, U.S. Department of Justice, Criminal Division, 1970-1972; Staff Assistant to Assistant Attorney General, U.S. Department of Justice, Criminal Division, 1972-1973. Assistant U.S. Attorney, Washington, D.C., 1973-1978. *Member:* Virginia State Bar; The District of Columbia Bar; American Bar Association. ***PRACTICE AREAS:*** Criminal Law; Complex and Multi-District Litigation; Health Care; RICO. ***Email:*** sschaars@kph.com

JEFFREY L. POSTON, born Washington, D.C., October 10, 1961; admitted to bar, 1988, Pennsylvania; 1990, District of Columbia, U.S. District Court for the District of Columbia. *Education:* University of Richmond (B.A., magna cum laude, 1984); Georgetown University (J.D., 1988). Phi Beta Kappa. *Member:* District of Columbia Bar; Pennsylvania and American Bar Associations. ***PRACTICE AREAS:*** Complex Civil Litigation; Criminal Litigation; Health Care Law; Employment Law; Government Contracts; Election Law. ***Email:*** jposton@kph.com

IRA M. SAXE, born Bronx, New York, September 24, 1957; admitted to bar, 1989, New York and U.S. District Court, Southern and Eastern Districts of New York; 1996, U.S. District Court, Western District of New York; 2000, U.S. Court of Appeals, Fourth Circuit (Not admitted in District of Columbia). *Education:* State University of New York at Albany (B.A., 1978); New York State School of Industrial and Labor Relations at Cornell University (M.I.L.R., 1981); Fordham University School of Law (J.D., cum laude, 1988). Staff Member, 1985-1987 and Associate Editor, 1987-1988, Fordham Law Review. Recipient, American Jurisprudence Award in: Civil Procedure; Constitutional Law; Contracts. Recipient, CJS Award, Andrew Mark Stillman Memorial Prize. Author: "Constructive Discharge Under the ADEA: An Argument for the Intent Standard," 55 Fordham Law Review, 963, 1987. *Member:* The Association of the Bar of the City of New York; New York State and American Bar Associations. (Resident, New York, N.Y. Office). ***PRACTICE AREAS:*** Labor and Employment Law; Affirmative Action and Equal Employment Law; Litigation. ***Email:*** isaxe@kph.com

CHERYL A. MAIER, born East Orange, New Jersey, May 25, 1959; admitted to bar, 1989, New Jersey and U.S. District Court, District of New Jersey; 1990, District of Columbia; 1991, U.S. District Court for the District of Columbia, U.S. Court of Appeals for the District of Columbia, U.S. Court of Appeals, Third Circuit; 1992, U.S. Court of Appeals, Fifth Circuit; 1994, U.S. Supreme Court; 1996, U.S. Court of Appeals, Fourth Circuit and U.S. District Court, District of Maryland. *Education:* Rutgers University (B.A., 1981); Cornell University; Boston College (J.D., 1989). Co-Author: "Indian Water Settlements & EPA," Natural Resources & Environment, Spring, 1991. Member, Organization of American Historians, 1980—. *Member:* District of Columbia Bar; American Bar Association. ***PRACTICE AREAS:*** Complex Civil Litigation; Civil Law; Criminal; Appellate Practice; Employment Law. ***Email:*** cmaier@kph.com

(This Listing Continued)

CHRISTOPHER FLYNN, born Manchester, New Hampshire, April 7, 1965; admitted to bar, 1992, Maryland; 1995, District of Columbia; U.S. District Court, District of Columbia; 1998, U.S. District Court, District of Maryland, U.S. District Court, District of Massachusetts and U.S. Court of Federal Claims; 1999, U.S. District Court, Eastern District of Michigan. *Education:* George Washington University (B.A., 1987); Columbus School of Law at The Catholic University of America (J.D., 1992). Omicron Delta Kappa. Recipient, American Jurisprudence Awards in Criminal Trial Practice and Estates. *Member:* Maryland State and American Bar Associations; the District of Columbia Bar; National Health Lawyers Association. **PRACTICE AREAS:** Litigation; Health Care Law; Employment Law. **Email:** cflynn@kph.com

OF COUNSEL

HERBERT I. MEYER, born Richmond, Virginia, June 11, 1933; admitted to bar, 1963, Virginia; 1973, U.S. Court of Appeals, Fifth Circuit; 1977, New York; 1980, U.S. District Court, Southern and Eastern Districts of New York; 1988, U.S. Court of Appeals, Second Circuit. *Education:* University of North Carolina (B.S., 1954); University of Richmond (J.D., 1963). (Resident, New York, N.Y. Office). **PRACTICE AREAS:** Labor and Employment Law. **Email:** hmeyer@kph.com

GARY A. STAHL, born New York, N.Y., April 29, 1957; admitted to bar, 1982, New York and U.S. District Court, Southern and Eastern Districts of New York; 1987, U.S. District Court, Northern District of Texas. *Education:* John's Hopkins University (B.A., 1978); Fordham University (J.D., 1981). Member: National Moot Court Team, 1980-1981. (Resident, New York,N.Y. Office). **LANGUAGES:** French.

ASSOCIATES

TRINA L. FAIRLEY, born Alexandria, Virginia, June 21, 1971; admitted to bar, 1997, Maryland, Texas, District of Columbia, U.S. District Court, Northern District of Texas and U.S. District Court for the District of Columbia. *Education:* University of Virginia (B.A., 1993); George Washington University (J.D., 1996). *Member:* American Bar Association. **PRACTICE AREAS:** Management Labor and Employment Law; Commercial Litigation; Litigation.

EMILY B. ZUCKERMAN, born Philadelphia, Pennsylvania, January 22, 1970; admitted to bar, 1996, New Jersey and U.S. District Court, Southern and Eastern Districts of New York; 1997, New York and U.S. District Court, District of New Jersey; 1998, District of Columbia. *Education:* Northwestern University (B.A., with honors, 1991); George Washington University (J.D., with Honors, 1996). *Member:* The Association of the Bar of the City of New York; American Bar Association. (Resident, New York, N.Y. Office). **PRACTICE AREAS:** Labor Law; Employment Law. **Email:** ezuckerman@kph.com

HOWARD SCHRAGIN, born New Hyde Park, New York, January 18, 1970; admitted to bar, 1998, New York and U.S. District Court, Southern and Eastern Districts of New York (Not admitted in District of Columbia). *Education:* University of Wisconsin-Madison (B.S., 1992); Fordham University School of Law (J.D., 1997). Publications: "U.S. Shoe Corp. v. United States: A Victory for U.S.-Canada Maritime Trade," 19 Fordham Int'l L.J. 1764 (April 1996). *Member:* Association of the Bar of the City of New York; New York State Bar Association; New York County Lawyer's Association. **REPORTED CASES:** Cobian v. City of New York, 2000 U.S. Dist. LEXIS 17479 (S.D.N.Y. Dec.6, 2000); Muse v. New York City Dep't of Housing Preservation & Development, 2000 U.S. Dist. LEXIS 12207 (E.D.N.Y. Aug. 22, 2000); Hogarth v. New York City Health & Hospitals Corp., 2000 U.S. Dist. LEXIS 4590 (Apr. 12, 2000); Papeskov v. Brown, 1998 U.S. Dist. LEXIS 8255 (S.D.N.Y. June 8, 1998); Damino v. Stern, 276 A.D.2d 581; 715 N.Y.S.2d 324 (2nd Dep't 2000). **PRACTICE AREAS:** Employment Discrimination; Labor Law; Employee Benefits. **Email:** hschragin@kph.com

FRANK M. ESPOSITO, born New York, N.Y., May 28, 1970; admitted to bar, 1998, New York and U.S. District Court, Eastern and Southern Districts of New York (Not admitted in District of Columbia). *Education:* Boston University (B.A., 1995); Benjamin N. Cardozo School of Law, Yeshiva University (J.D., 1998). Samuel Belkin Memorial Scholar. Order of Barrister. *Member:* Association of the Bar of the City of New York; New York State and American Bar Associations. **LANGUAGES:** Italian. **PRACTICE AREAS:** Employment Law; Commercial Law; Contracts; Constitutional Law. **Email:** fesposito@kph.com

JULIE A. BARNES, born Oak Lawn, Illinois, November 30, 1969; admitted to bar, 1999, Maryland; 2000, District of Columbia. *Education:* University of Iowa (B.A.); Washington College of Law of American University (J.D.). *Member:* American Bar Association; American Health Lawyers Association. **PRACTICE AREAS:** Health Law; Litigation. **Email:** jbarnes@kph.com

REPRESENTATIVE CLIENTS: Air Transport International, LLC; GEO Logistics; G.A.B. Robbins, Inc.; SGS Control Services, Inc.; Foundation Health Plan, Inc.; Brink's, Inc.; BAX Global; The Pittston Co.; Philadelphia National Bank; Kaiser Permanente; Humana Health Plans; Mexicana Health Plans; Pacificare; United Healthcare Inc. of Illinois; Health Net; Magellan Health Services Inc.; TNT USA Inc.; Capital Credit Corp.; Core States Financial; Medlantic Healthcare Group; Human Genome Sciences, Inc.; Weichert, Realtors; Aetna-U.S. Health Care; Humana, Inc.; Health Insurance Plan of Greater New York; Mid-Atlantic Medical Services, Inc.; Sentara Health Plan; American Association of Health Plans; National Rehabilitation Hospital; James Hardie Inc.

KING & SPALDING

1730 PENNSYLVANIA AVENUE, N.W.
WASHINGTON, D.C. 20006-4706
Telephone: 202-737-0500
FAX: 202-626-3737
URL: http://www.kslaw.com/

Atlanta, Georgia Office: 191 Peachtree Street, N.E., 30303-1763. Telephone: 404-572-4600. Fax: 404-572-5100.

New York, N.Y. Office: 1185 Avenue of the Americas, 10036-4003. Telephone: 212-556-2100. Fax: 212-556-2222.

Houston, Texas Office: 1100 Louisiana, Suite 4000, 77002-5213. Telephone: 713-751-3200. Fax: 713-751-3290.

General Practice in all State and Federal Courts, Administrative and Governmental Agencies; Antitrust; Arbitration & Mediation; Bankruptcy & Creditors Rights; Biotechnology & Pharmaceuticals; Capital Markets (Corporate Finance / Private Debt Finance / Structured Finance); Construction & Procurement; Cyberspace & Information Security; E-Commerce & Internet; Emerging Growth Companies); Employee Benefits & Executive Compensation; Energy Industries (Oil & Gas / Power); Environmental; Food, Drug & Medical Devices (Controlled Substances / Consumer Products Safety / FDA Practice / FTC Practice); Franchise & Distribution; Governmental Practice; Healthcare; Intellectual Property (Copyrights / Patents / Trademarks / Trade Secrets); International (German Practice / International Business / Islamic Finance & Investment / Latin American Practice/ Trade & Customs); International Energy; International Arbitration; International Business Law; Joint Ventures & Strategic Alliances; Labor & Employment; Licensing; Contracting & Outsourcing; Litigation (Appellate / Class Action / Commercial Litigation / Corporate Espionage & Competitive Intelligence / Environmental Tort Practice / Product Liability / Shareholders & Securities Litigation); Maritime Law; Mergers & Acquisitions; Private Equity & Investment Fund; Project & Equipment Finance; Public Finance; Real Estate; Special Matters & Government Investigations; Tax; Technology; Telecommunications; Trusts & Estates. (While every area within the Firm may not represented by lawyers resident in each of its offices - for example, the Firm's Food & Drug or Governmental lawyers are solely located in the Firm's Washington, D.C. office - lawyers throughout the entire Firm are nonetheless available to work and support relationships with Firm clients).

FIRM PROFILE: King & Spalding has been in the forefront of providing excellent legal services to its clients for over a century. Since it's establishment in 1885, the firm has had a tradition of attracting and developing many of this country's finest lawyers. Among them are Griffin B. Bell, former Attorney General of the United States: Sam Nunn, former United States Senator; and numerous other lawyers who have held high-level positions in the federal and state governments. The partnership also includes two past presidents and an additional nine members of the American College of Trial Lawyers, two past presidents of the American Health Lawyers Association and three past presidents of the National Association of Bond Lawyers. Today, from offices in Atlanta, Washington, D.C., New York and Houston, the firm continues to provide the highest caliber legal counsel to clients from the United States and abroad. King & Spalding currently represents more than 250 public companies, including over half of the Fortune 100 companies. The firm also represents hundreds of clients with new ventures and mid-sized companies in emerging industries. Long-standing client relationships are one of the surest barometers of a law firm's success in meeting its client's needs for legal services. King & Spalding lawyers pride themselves on developing continuing client relationships that are productive, professional and collegial.

RESIDENT PARTNERS

EDWARD M. BASILE, born New Hyde Park, New York; admitted to bar, 1973, District of Columbia; 1976, U.S. Supreme Court. *Education:* Lafayette College (B.S.M.E., 1969); George Washington University (J.D., 1972). **PRACTICE AREAS:** Food and Drug Regulation.

ANDREW BERG, born Philadelphia, Pennsylvania; admitted to bar, 1980, Pennsylvania; 1982, U.S. District Court, Eastern District of Pennsylvania; 1985, U.S. Supreme Court; 1986, District of Columbia. *Education:* Harvard University (A.B., cum laude, 1977); Vanderbilt University (J.D., 1980). **PRACTICE AREAS:** Litigation and Trade.

WILLIAM BLUMENTHAL, born White Plains, New York; admitted to bar, 1980, District of Columbia. *Education:* Brown University (A.B., 1977; M.A., 1977); Harvard University (J.D., 1980). **PRACTICE AREAS:** Litigation and Trade.

JOHN M. BRAY, born St. Louis, Missouri; admitted to bar, 1962, Missouri; 1965, U.S. Supreme Court; 1968, District of Columbia and U.S. Tax Court. *Education:* St. Louis University (B.A., 1962; LL.B., cum laude, 1962). **PRACTICE AREAS:** Litigation and Trade.

(This Listing Continued)

KING & SPALDING, Washington—Continued

MARK S. BROWN, born Clinton, Maryland; admitted to bar, 1985, Pennsylvania; 1986, Maryland; 1991, U.S. District Court, District of Maryland; 1997, District of Columbia. *Education:* University of Michigan (A.B., 1982); St. Louis University (J.D., 1985). ***LANGUAGES:*** German. ***PRACTICE AREAS:*** Food and Drug Regulation.

GLENN C. CAMPBELL, born Lutherville, Maryland; admitted to bar, 1985, Maryland; 2000, Georgia (Not admitted in District of Columbia). *Education:* Wake Forest University (B.A., magna cum laude, 1981); University of North Carolina (J.D., 1985). ***PRACTICE AREAS:*** Corporate and Finance.

ROBERT E. CULBERTSON, born Washington, D.C.; admitted to bar, 1982, District of Columbia. *Education:* Yale University (B.A., cum laude, 1979); Harvard University (J.D., cum laude, 1982). ***PRACTICE AREAS:*** Tax.

FREDERICK H. DEGNAN, born New Haven, Connecticut; admitted to bar, 1974, Virginia; 1993, District of Columbia. *Education:* College of the Holy Cross (B.A., cum laude, 1970); Georgetown University (J.D., 1973). ***PRACTICE AREAS:*** Food and Drug Regulation.

KEVIN M. DINAN, born Washington, D.C.; admitted to bar, 1985, Virginia; 1987, District of Columbia. *Education:* University of Vermont (B.A., 1980); Emory University (J.D., with distinction, 1985). ***PRACTICE AREAS:*** Litigation and Trade.

JOSEPH W. DORN, born Atlanta, Georgia; admitted to bar, 1974, Georgia; 1976, District of Columbia; 1979, U.S. Supreme Court; 1981, U.S. Court of International Trade. *Education:* University of North Carolina (A.B., 1970); University of Virginia (J.D., 1973). ***PRACTICE AREAS:*** Litigation and Trade.

MICHAEL C. DURST, born Metuchen, New Jersey; admitted to bar, 1981, District of Columbia. *Education:* Williams College (B.A., with highest honors, 1975); Massachusetts Institute of Technology (M.S., 1978); Boalt Hall School of Law, University of California, Berkeley (J.D., 1981); Harvard University (LL.M., 1985). ***PRACTICE AREAS:*** Tax.

DAVID A. GIBBONS, born Charleston, West Virginia; admitted to bar, 1991, Maryland; 1999, District of Columbia. *Education:* University of Virginia (B.A., 1988); Emory University (J.D., 1991). ***PRACTICE AREAS:*** Corporate and Finance.

THOMAS R. GRAHAM, born Shelbyville, Indiana; admitted to bar, 1970, District of Columbia. *Education:* Indiana University (B.A., magna cum laude, 1965); Harvard Law School (J.D., 1968). ***PRACTICE AREAS:*** Litigation and Trade.

SANDRA W. HALLMARK, born Seattle, Washington; admitted to bar, 1984, New York; 1985, U.S. Tax Court; 1986, District of Columbia and Texas. *Education:* Brandeis University (B.A., 1977); Benjamin N. Cardozo School of Law (J.D., 1983); Georgetown University (M.L.T., 1986). ***PRACTICE AREAS:*** Tax.

THEODORE M. HESTER, born Richland, Georgia; admitted to bar, 1970, Georgia; 1999, District of Columbia. *Education:* University of Georgia (A.B., magna cum laude, 1966); Harvard University (J.D., 1969). ***PRACTICE AREAS:*** Governmental Practice.

ELEANOR J. HILL, born Miami Beach, Florida; admitted to bar, 1975, Florida, U.S. District Court, Middle District of Florida and U.S. Court of Appeals, Fifth Circuit; 1999, District of Columbia. *Education:* Florida State University (B.A., magna cum laude, 1972; J.D., magna cum laude, 1974). ***PRACTICE AREAS:*** Special Matters/Government Investigations.

SUSAN JEWETT, born Sudbury, Massachusetts; admitted to bar, 1977, District of Columbia. *Education:* University of Chicago (A.B., 1970); Harvard University (J.D., cum laude, 1977). ***PRACTICE AREAS:*** Tax.

STEPHEN A. JONES, born Wilmington, Delaware; admitted to bar, 1990, District of Columbia; 1991, U.S. Court of International Trade and U.S. Court of Appeals for the Federal Circuit. *Education:* Washington & Lee University (B.A., magna cum laude, 1984); University of Regensburg, Germany (DAAD Scholar, 1985); Georgetown University (J.D., cum laude, 1990; M.S.F.S., with honors, 1990). ***PRACTICE AREAS:*** Litigation and Trade.

DUANE W. LAYTON, born Seattle, Washington; admitted to bar, 1982, California; 1984, Washington; 1990, District of Columbia. *Education:* University of Washington (B.A., 1976); California Western School of Law (J.D., cum laude, 1982); University of Cambridge, Cambridge, United Kingdom (LL.M., 1983). ***PRACTICE AREAS:*** Litigation; Trade.

JACKIE S. LEVINSON, born Lynbrook, New York; admitted to bar, 1973, New York; 1989, District of Columbia. *Education:* Vassar College (A.B., magna cum laude, 1969); Yale University (J.D., 1972). ***PRACTICE AREAS:*** Tax.

JANE C. LUXTON, born Philadelphia, Pennsylvania; admitted to bar, 1976, District of Columbia. *Education:* Harvard University (A.B., with honors, 1973); Cornell University (J.D., 1976). ***PRACTICE AREAS:*** Environmental.

(This Listing Continued)

ANDREW C. LYNCH, born Mount Holly, New Jersey; admitted to bar, 1982, Illinois; 1996, District of Columbia. *Education:* University of Virginia (B.A., 1978; J.D., 1982). ***PRACTICE AREAS:*** Corporate; Finance.

MICHAEL P. MABILE, born Panama City, Florida; admitted to bar, 1977, Florida; 1978, U.S. Court of Appeals, Fifth Circuit; 1980, District of Columbia and U.S. District Court for the District of Columbia; 1985, U.S. Court of International Trade and U.S. Court of Appeals, Federal Circuit. *Education:* Florida State University (B.S., cum laude, 1973; J.D., with honors, 1977). ***PRACTICE AREAS:*** Litigation and Trade.

PATRICIA L. MAHER, born Des Moines, Iowa; admitted to bar, 1982, District of Columbia. *Education:* Brown University (A.B., magna cum laude, 1976); University of Michigan (M.A., Philosophy, 1977); Georgetown University (J.D., cum laude, 1981). ***PRACTICE AREAS:*** Business Litigation.

TODD Y. McARTHUR, born Charlottesville, Virginia; admitted to bar, 1990, Virginia; 1991, District of Columbia and U.S. Tax Court. *Education:* University of Virginia (B.S., Intermediate Honors, 1985; J.D., 1990). ***PRACTICE AREAS:*** Tax.

MARTIN M. McNERNEY, born Detroit, Michigan; admitted to bar, 1980, District of Columbia; 1985, U.S. Court of Appeals, 6th Circuit and U.S. Court of Appeals for the District of Columbia Circuit; 1986, U.S. Court of Appeals, 4th Circuit; 1987, U.S. Court of International Trade and U.S. Court of Appeals, 5th Circuit; 1993, U.S. Court of Appeals for the Federal Circuit. *Education:* Hampden-Sydney College (B.A., magna cum laude, 1977); University of Virginia (J.D., 1980). ***PRACTICE AREAS:*** Litigation and Trade.

JAMES D. MILLER, born College Park, Georgia; admitted to bar, 1975, Georgia and Massachusetts; 1980, District of Columbia. *Education:* New College (B.A., 1972); Yale University (J.D., 1975). ***PRACTICE AREAS:*** Litigation and Trade.

EUGENE M. PFEIFER, born Springfield, Massachusetts; admitted to bar, 1967, District of Columbia; 1979, U.S. Supreme Court. *Education:* Brown University (B.A., 1962); Georgetown University (J.D., 1967). ***PRACTICE AREAS:*** Food and Drug Regulation.

JAMES T. PHALEN, born Jewett City, Connecticut; admitted to bar, 1991, Virginia; 1992, District of Columbia; 1997, U.S. Court of Appeals, 7th Circuit. *Education:* College of the Holy Cross (A.B., cum laude, 1988); Northwestern University (J.D., cum laude, 1991). ***PRACTICE AREAS:*** Litigation; Trade Regulation.

KATHERINE L. RHYNE, born Norfolk, Virginia; admitted to bar, 1980, District of Columbia; 1981, Virginia; 1984, U.S. Supreme Court; 1985, Maryland. *Education:* University of Virginia (B.A., with high distinction, 1977; J.D., 1980). ***PRACTICE AREAS:*** Environmental.

DVORAH A. RICHMAN, born Phoenix, Arizona; admitted to bar, 1983, District of Columbia. *Education:* Arizona State University (B.S., 1973); University of Denver (M.A., 1974); Catholic University of America (J.D., 1983). ***PRACTICE AREAS:*** Food and Drug Regulation.

GRACE M. RODRIGUEZ, born Fort Lauderdale, Florida; admitted to bar, 1987, New York; 1993, District of Columbia. *Education:* Harvard University (B.A., cum laude, 1983); Columbia University (J.D., 1986). ***PRACTICE AREAS:*** Special Matters/Government Investigations.

JOSEPH SEDWICK SOLLERS III, born Baltimore, Maryland; admitted to bar, 1983, District of Columbia. *Education:* Princeton University (A.B., 1977); University of Maryland (J.D., with honors, 1982). ***PRACTICE AREAS:*** Special Matters/Government Investigations.

JEFFREY S. SPIGEL, born Nashville, Tennessee; admitted to bar, 1992, Tennessee and Supreme Court of Tennessee; 1993, District of Columbia and U.S. District Court for the District of Columbia. *Education:* Emory University (B.A., 1989); University of Miami (J.D., 1992); Georgetown University (LL.M., Tax, 1994). ***PRACTICE AREAS:*** Litigation; Trade Regulation.

KEVIN R. SULLIVAN, born Erie, Pennsylvania; admitted to bar, 1975, Pennsylvania; 1987, District of Columbia. *Education:* Gannon University (B.A., 1971); Catholic University of America (J.D., 1975). ***PRACTICE AREAS:*** Litigation and Trade.

RESIDENT COUNSEL

Sandra Cohen Kalter; Christina M. Markus; Lisa L. Poole; Harold M. Shaw; Christopher Sprigman (Not admitted in DC); ***William C. Talmadge*** (Not admitted in DC).

RESIDENT ASSOCIATES

Christopher Kole Agbe-Davies (Not admitted in DC); ***Corey Amundson; Amy M. Angelo; Thomas D. Blanford*** (Not admitted in DC); ***Robert Boyd*** (admission pending); ***Jamie A. Brown*** (admission pending); ***Jeffrey S. Bucholtz; John R. Bunker*** (Not admitted in DC); ***Aileen Hurley Ciampa*** (Not admitted in DC); ***Michael J. Ciatti; Lisa L. Cochrane*** (Not admitted in DC); ***David A. Cohen; James D. Colt*** (admission pending); ***Susan R. Connella;***

(This Listing Continued)

Elizabeth S. Crockett; Melissa Dempsey; Kristen B. Dowd (admission pending); ***Alan F. Enslen; Mark Filpi; Rishona Fleishman*** (Not admitted in DC); ***Peter Carlton Fleming; John H. Fontham; Gary J. Greco*** (Not admitted in DC); ***Reuben Green*** (Not admitted in DC); ***Ann Marie Hart; Elizabeth H. Jafari*** (admission pending); ***Mark Jensen; Andrew Kaplan*** (Not admitted in DC); ***Jaime E. King*** (admission pending); ***M. Alexander Koch; Steven L. Lane; Scott P. McClure; Andrew McCormack*** (Not admitted in DC); ***Amy B. Metzel*** (Not admitted in DC); ***M. Elizabeth Mims*** (Not admitted in DC); ***Philip A. Moffat*** (admission pending); ***Thomas A. Monheim; Stephen A. Myrow; Kelly Nicole Reeves; Kerri L. Ruttenberg; Christine E. Savage; Anne R. Schott; John D. Shakow; Stacy S. Shibao; Jennafer Smoker; Cynthia A.M. Stroman; Jeffrey M. Telep; Dianna Thomsen; Demetria C. Titus*** (admission pending); ***Peter M. Todaro; Elaine H. Tseng; Joseph R. Waala*** (Not admitted in DC); ***Anne K. Walsh; Kathryn E. Walsh*** (Not admitted in DC); ***David R. Weiser*** (Not admitted in DC); ***Jacqueline S. Weiss; Edward H. White; Ashley Whitesides; Craig M. Wolff; Tamara Yakimetz*** (Not admitted in DC).

KIRKLAND & ELLIS

A Partnership including Professional Corporations

Established in 1908

655 FIFTEENTH STREET, N.W., SUITE 1200

WASHINGTON, D.C. 20005

Telephone: 202-879-5000

Telex: 89-2320

Facsimile: 202-879-5200

URL: http://www.kirkland.com

Chicago, Illinois Office: 200 East Randolph Drive. Telephone: 312-861-2000. Telex: 25-4361.

Los Angeles, California Office: 777 South Figueroa Street. Telephone: 213-680-8400. Facsimile: 213-680-8500.

New York, New York Office: Citicorp Center, 153 East 53rd Street. Telephone: 212-446-4800. Facsimile: (212)-446-4900.

London, England Office: International Financial Centre, Old Broad Street. Telephone: 171-816-8700; New Telephone Effective April 1, 2000: 207-816-8700. Facsimile: 171-816-8800.

General Practice including Practice before United States Courts, Administrative Agencies and Departments of the Government and other Litigation.

MEMBERS OF FIRM

JAY I. ALEXANDER, admitted to bar, 1990, Illinois; 1992, District of Columbia. *Education:* Northwestern University (B.S., 1985; J.D., 1990). Law Clerk to the Hon. Pauline Newman, Circuit Judge, United States Court of Appeals for the Federal Circuit, 1990-1992. Patent Examiner, United States Patent and Trademark Office, 1985-1987. ***PRACTICE AREAS:*** Intellectual Property. ***Email:*** jay_alexander@dc.kirkland.com

EUGENE F. ASSAF, admitted to bar, 1989, Pennsylvania; 1996, District of Columbia. *Education:* Dickinson College (B.A., 1984); Essex University (M.A., 1987); University of Notre Dame (J.D., 1989). Law Clerk to Judge Joseph F. Weis, Jr., United States Court of Appeals, Third Circuit, 1989-1991. ***PRACTICE AREAS:*** Commercial Litigation; Trade Secrets; Antitrust; First Amendment. ***Email:*** eugene_assaf@dc.kirkland.com

DANIEL F. ATTRIDGE, admitted to bar, 1980, District of Columbia. *Education:* University of Pennsylvania (B.A., 1976); Georgetown University (J.D., 1979). Law Clerk to the Honorable Oliver Gasch, U.S. District Court for the District of Columbia, 1979-1980. Member, Board of Advisors, Georgetown University Law Center, 1994-2000. *Member:* District of Columbia Bar (Board of Governors, 1996-1999; Co-Chair, Litigation Section, 1993-1996); American Bar Association (Vice Chair, Sherman Act Section 2 Committee, 1999—). Fellow, American Bar Foundation (1997—). ***PRACTICE AREAS:*** Litigation; Antitrust. ***Email:*** daniel_attridge@dc.kirkland.com

PAMELA J. AUERBACH, admitted to bar, 1994, Massachusetts; 1995, District of Columbia. *Education:* Columbia University (B.A., 1989); University of Chicago (J.D., 1993). ***PRACTICE AREAS:*** Litigation; Antitrust. ***Email:*** pamela_auerbach@dc.kirkland.com

JAMES F. BASILE, admitted to bar, 1989, Pennsylvania; 1990, District of Columbia. *Education:* University of Notre Dame (B.A., 1986); Notre Dame Law School (J.D., 1989). Article Editor, Notre Dame Law Review. ***PRACTICE AREAS:*** Commercial Litigation; First Amendment; Libel and Defamation; Antitrust; Intellectual Property; Product Liability. ***Email:*** james_basile@dc.kirkland.com

KENNETH N. BASS, admitted to bar, 1984, South Carolina; 1985, District of Columbia. *Education:* Yale University (B.A., 1980); Georgetown University (J.D., 1983). Law Clerk to the Honorable Elbert P. Tuttle, Circuit Judge, U.S. Eleventh Circuit Court of Appeals, 1983-1984. ***PRACTICE AREAS:*** Commercial Litigation-Corporate; Product Liability. ***Email:*** kenneth_bass@dc.kirkland.com

MICHAEL S. BECKER, admitted to bar, 1994, Virginia; 1995, District of Columbia. *Education:* Macalester College (B.A., 1984); George Mason University (Ph.D., Economics, 1991); University of Virginia (J.D., 1994). ***PRACTICE AREAS:*** Antitrust Law; Litigation. ***Email:*** michael_becker@dc.kirkland.com

TERRANCE L. BESSEY, admitted to bar, 1983, Illinois; 1985, Colorado; 1987, District of Columbia. *Education:* University of Denver (B. Music, 1979); Northwestern University (J.D., 1983). Executive Editor, Northwestern Journal of International Law and Business, 1982-1983. ***PRACTICE AREAS:*** Corporate; Securities. ***Email:*** terrance_bessey@dc.kirkland.com

STEVEN GILL BRADBURY, admitted to bar, 1988, District of Columbia; 1991, U.S. Court of Appeals, District of Columbia Circuit; 1994, U.S. Court of Appeals, Fifth Circuit; 1996, U.S. Supreme Court; 1997, U.S. Court of Appeals, Fourth Circuit; 1998, U.S. Court of Appeals, First Circuit. *Education:* Stanford University (B.A., 1980); University of Michigan (J.D., 1988). Article Editor, Michigan Law Review. Law Clerk to: the Honorable Clarence Thomas, Supreme Court of the United States, 1992-1993; the Honorable James L. Buckley, U.S. Court of Appeals, District of Columbia Circuit, 1990-1991. Attorney Advisor, Office of Legal Counsel, U.S. Department of Justice, 1991-1992. ***PRACTICE AREAS:*** General Litigation; Antitrust; Telecommunications; Appellate Litigation; Constitutional Law. ***Email:*** steven_bradbury@dc.kirkland.com

PAUL F. BRINKMAN, admitted to bar, 1993, Virginia; 1994, District of Columbia. *Education:* Yale College (B.A., 1988); Cambridge University, Cambridge, England (M.Phil., 1989); University of Virginia (J.D., 1993). Law Clerk, Hon. James C. Turk, U.S. District Court, Western District of Virginia. ***PRACTICE AREAS:*** International Trade; Customs; Commercial Litigation. ***Email:*** paul_brinkman@dc.kirkland.com

PAT A. CIPOLLONE, admitted to bar, 1993, Illinois; 1995, District of Columbia. *Education:* Fordham University (B.A., 1988); University of Chicago (J.D., 1991). Managing Editor, The University of Chicago Law Review. Clerk to Judge Danny J. Boggs, U.S. Court of Appeals, Sixth Circuit, 1991-1992. Assistant, to U.S. Attorney General William P. Barr, 1992-1993. ***Email:*** pat_cipollone@dc.kirkland.com

THOMAS A. CLARE, admitted to bar, 1995, Virginia; 1999, District of Columbia. *Education:* University of Notre Dame (B.A., 1992; J.D., 1995). Law Clerk to the Hon. Kenneth F. Ripple, U.S. Court of Appeals, Seventh Circuit, 1995-1996. ***PRACTICE AREAS:*** Litigation. ***Email:*** thomas_clare@dc.kirkland.com

ANDREW B. CLUBOK, admitted to bar, 1994, Ohio; 1997, District of Columbia. *Education:* Harvard College (A.B., 1990); University of Michigan (J.D., 1993). Law Clerk, Hon. Frank J. Battisti, U.S. District Court, Northern District of Ohio. ***PRACTICE AREAS:*** Litigation. ***Email:*** andrew_clubok@dc.kirkland.com

KAREN McCARTAN DeSANTIS, admitted to bar, 1986, Ohio; 1989, District of Columbia. *Education:* Princeton University (A.B., 1983); University of Notre Dame (J.D., 1986). ***PRACTICE AREAS:*** Commercial Litigation; Products Liability. ***Email:*** karen_desantis@dc.kirkland.com

MAUREEN A. DONLEY-HOOPES, admitted to bar, 1980, Pennsylvania; 1985, District of Columbia. *Education:* University of Virginia (B.A., 1976); Georgetown University Law Center (J.D., 1979). ***PRACTICE AREAS:*** Futures Law; Derivative Products; Financial Services. ***Email:*** maureen_donley-hoopes@dc.kirkland.com

EDWARD C. DONOVAN, admitted to bar, 1994, New York and Pennsylvania; 1995, District of Columbia. *Education:* State University of New York at Stony Brook (B.E., 1987); George Washington University (J.D., 1993). Law Clerk to Hon. Glenn L. Archer, Jr., U.S. Court of Appeals, Federal Circuit, 1993-1995. ***PRACTICE AREAS:*** Intellectual Property. ***Email:*** edward_donovan@dc.kirkland.com

STUART A. C. DRAKE, admitted to bar, 1983, District of Columbia. *Education:* Yale College (B.A., 1977); University of Cambridge (M.Litt., 1981); Yale University (J.D., 1981). Law Clerk to the Honorable Louis F. Oberdorfer, U.S. District Court for the District of Columbia, 1981-1982. ***PRACTICE AREAS:*** Environmental and Regulatory Counseling; Government Litigation. ***Email:*** stuart_drake@dc.kirkland.com

JAMES WORTH DRAUGHN, JR., admitted to bar, 1991, Virginia; 1992, District of Columbia. *Education:* University of North Carolina (B.A., 1988); Harvard University (J.D., 1991). ***PRACTICE AREAS:*** Commercial Litigation; Energy Litigation; Antitrust; Product Liability. ***Email:*** james_draughn@dc.kirkland.com

MICHAEL T. EDSALL, admitted to bar, 1986, Virginia; 1989, District of Columbia. *Education:* University of Michigan (B.G.S., 1982; J.D., 1986). ***PRACTICE AREAS:*** Corporate-Mergers and Acquisitions; Venture Capital; Corporate Finance. ***Email:*** michael_edsall@dc.kirkland.com

(This Listing Continued)

KIRKLAND & ELLIS, Washington—Continued

THOMAS L. EVANS, admitted to bar, 1984, Illinois; 1994, Texas; 2001, District of Columbia. *Education:* University of Illinois (B.S., Finance, 1976); University of Chicago (J.D., 1983). Order of the Coif. Professor, Federal Income Tax Law, including Corporate, Partnership, Individual, International and Exempt Organizations, Business Associations and Bankruptcy, University of Texas School of Law. Associate Tax Legislative Counsel, Department of Treasury, Office of Tax Policy, Washington, D.C., 1986-1989. ***PRACTICE AREAS:*** Tax; Corporate. ***Email:*** thomas_evans@dc.kirkland.com

ROBERT R. GASAWAY, admitted to bar, 1994, Illinois; 1996, District of Columbia. *Education:* Northwestern University (B.A., 1981); Yale University (M.Phil., 1989); University of Chicago (J.D., 1992). ***PRACTICE AREAS:*** Appellate Litigation; Environmental Litigation. ***Email:*** robert_gasaway@dc.kirkland.com

JAMES P. GILLESPIE, admitted to bar, 1990, New York; 1991, District of Columbia. *Education:* Grinnell College (B.S., 1985); University of Notre Dame (J.D., 1988). Law Clerk, Hon. George E. MacKinnon, Sr. Circuit Judge, U.S. Court of Appeals, District of Columbia, 1988-1989. ***PRACTICE AREAS:*** Commercial Litigation; Antitrust. ***Email:*** james_gillespie@dc.kirkland.com

MARK E. GRUMMER, admitted to bar, 1976, Illinois; 1979, District of Columbia. *Education:* Northwestern University (B.A., 1973); University of Chicago (J.D., 1976). Trial Lawyer, U.S. Department of Justice, Land and Natural Resources Division, 1983-1989. ***PRACTICE AREAS:*** Environmental Litigation; Environmental Due Diligence; CERCLA. ***Email:*** mark_grummer@dc.kirkland.com

BARBARA MACK HARDING, admitted to bar, 1988, Virginia; 1989, District of Columbia. *Education:* University of Alabama (B.A., 1985); Georgetown University (J.D., 1988). Notes and Comment Editor, Georgetown University Law Journal, 1987-1988. Adjunct Professor, George Washington National Law Center, 1991-1994. ***PRACTICE AREAS:*** Civil Litigation; Criminal Litigation. ***Email:*** barbara_harding@dc.kirkland.com

TIMOTHY S. HARDY, admitted to bar, 1972, Ohio; 1976, District of Columbia. *Education:* Amherst College (B.A., 1969); Yale University (J.D., 1972). Law Clerk to the Honorable Max Rosenn, U.S. Court of Appeals, Third Circuit, 1972-1973. Member, Office of Counsel to the President, 1975-1976. ***PRACTICE AREAS:*** Environmental Law; Toxic Substance Regulation, Litigation and Counseling; Commercial Litigation-Environmental, Product Liability; Product Liability-Product Defect. ***Email:*** timothy_hardy@dc.kirkland.com

MITCHELL F. HERTZ, admitted to bar, 1990, New York; 1991, District of Columbia. *Education:* American University (B.A., 1986); Columbia University (J.D., 1989). ***PRACTICE AREAS:*** Corporate Law; Energy; Communications. ***Email:*** mitchell_hertz@dc.kirkland.com

JOHN S. IRVING, JR., admitted to bar, 1965, New Jersey; 1966, District of Columbia. *Education:* Brown University (A.B., 1962); Georgetown University (J.D., 1965; LL.M., 1967). Appellate Division and Legal Assistant to Board Member, National Labor Relations Board, 1965-1969. Special Assistant to the Solicitor of Labor, 1969-1970. Executive Assistant to Under Secretary of Labor, 1970-1971. Associate General Counsel, 1971-1972, Deputy General Counsel, 1972-1975 and General Counsel, 1975-1979, National Labor Relations Board. Governor, College of Labor and Employment Lawyers. ***PRACTICE AREAS:*** Civil Rights; Labor and Employment. ***Email:*** john_irving@dc.kirkland.com

MICHAEL D. JONES, admitted to bar, 1986, Georgia; 1989, District of Columbia. *Education:* Dillard University (B.A., 1982); Georgetown University (J.D., 1985). Law Clerk to the Honorable Elbert P. Tuttle, Eleventh Circuit Court of Appeals, 1985-1986. ***PRACTICE AREAS:*** Litigation. ***Email:*** michael_jones@dc.kirkland.com

DARYL JOSEFFER, admitted to bar, 1996, Illinois; 1998, District of Columbia. *Education:* Stanford University (A.B., 1992); Harvard Law School (J.D., 1995). Law Clerk to the Hon. Jerry E. Smith, U.S. Court of Appeals, Fifth Circuit, 1995-1996. ***PRACTICE AREAS:*** Appellate; Litigation. ***Email:*** daryl_joseffer@dc.kirkland.com

ANTONY B. KLAPPER, admitted to bar, 1996, New York; 1997, District of Columbia. *Education:* University of Virginia (B.A., 1989); Princeton University (M.P.A., 1991); University of Pennsylvania (J.D., 1994). Executive Editor, The University of Pennsylvania Law Review, 1993-1994. Law Clerk for The Honorable Myron Bright, U.S. Court of Appeals, Eighth Circuit. ***PRACTICE AREAS:*** Litigation. ***Email:*** antony_klapper@dc.kirkland.com

STEPHEN D. KNIGHT, admitted to bar, 1978, Virginia and District of Columbia. *Education:* University of Virginia (B.A., 1975; J.D., 1978). ***PRACTICE AREAS:*** Government Contracts. ***Email:*** stephen_knight@dc.kirkland.com

MARK L. KOVNER, admitted to bar, 1989, Massachusetts; 1991, District of Columbia. *Education:* Brandeis University (B.A., 1986); Georgetown University Law Center (J.D., 1989). Editor-in-Chief, Law and Policy in International Business, 1988-1989. ***PRACTICE AREAS:*** Antitrust; Commercial Litigation. ***Email:*** mark_kovner@dc.kirkland.com

ROBERT G. KRUPKA, (P.C.), admitted to bar, 1974, Illinois; 1991, Colorado and District of Columbia; 1998, California; registered to practice before U.S. Patent and Trademark Office. *Education:* Georgetown University (B.S., 1971); University of Chicago (J.D., 1974). (Also at Chicago, Illinois and Los Angeles, California Offices). ***PRACTICE AREAS:*** Intellectual Property; Litigation; Advertising and Marketing; Antitrust; Trade Regulation; Biotechnology. ***Email:*** robert_krupka@kirkland.com

DAVID L. LAMBERT, admitted to bar, 1993, North Carolina; 1998, District of Columbia. *Education:* Duke University (B.A., 1988); North Carolina Central School of Law (J.D., 1993); New York University School of Law (LL.M. in Taxation, 1995). Law Clerk to Honorable J. Rich Leonard, U.S. Bankruptcy Court, Eastern District of North Carolina, 1995-1996; Honorable Hugh A. Wells, North Carolina Court of Appeals, 1993-1994. ***PRACTICE AREAS:*** Mergers and Acquisitions; Securities. ***Email:*** david_lambert@dc.kirkland.com

BRIAN R. LAND, admitted to bar, 1989, Maryland; 1990, District of Columbia and U.S. District Court, District of Maryland; 1991, Minnesota. *Education:* University of Michigan; Washington University (B.S., 1983); George Washington University (J.D., 1989). ***PRACTICE AREAS:*** Environmental Law. ***Email:*** brian_land@dc.kirkland.com

CHRISTOPHER LANDAU, admitted to bar, 1990, District of Columbia. *Education:* Harvard University (A.B., 1985; J.D., 1989). Law Clerk to: Judge Clarence Thomas, U.S. Court of Appeals, District of Columbia Circuit, 1990; Associate Justice Antonin Scalia, U.S. Supreme Court, 1990-1991; Associate Justice Clarence Thomas, U.S. Supreme Court, 1991-1992. ***PRACTICE AREAS:*** Appellate Litigation; Commercial Litigation; Products Liability. ***Email:*** christopher_landau@dc.kirkland.com

NEIL L. LEVY, admitted to bar, 1990, New Jersey; 1992, District of Columbia; U.S. District Court, District of New Jersey; U.S. Court of Appeals, District of Columbia Circuit, Fifth Circuit, Sixth Circuit; U.S. Supreme Court. *Education:* George Washington University (B.A., 1987); Ohio Northern University (J.D., 1990). Executive Editor, Ohio Northern University Law Review, 1989-1990. ***PRACTICE AREAS:*** Energy Law and Litigation; Utility Regulatory Law. ***Email:*** neil_levy@dc.kirkland.com

GREGG F. LoCASCIO, admitted to bar, 1995, Virginia; 1997, District of Columbia. *Education:* Virginia Polytechnic Institute and State University (B.S.M.E., 1992); University of Notre Dame (J.D., 1995). ***PRACTICE AREAS:*** Intellectual Property; General Litigation. ***Email:*** gregg_locascio@dc.kirkland.com

WALTER H. LOHMANN, JR., admitted to bar, 1983, California; 1988, District of Columbia. *Education:* Cornell University (B.A., 1980); George Washington University (J.D., 1983). ***PRACTICE AREAS:*** Environmental Transaction Support; Environmental Counseling. ***Email:*** walter_lohmann@dc.kirkland.com

DAWN DANZEISEN MARCHANT, admitted to bar, 1990, Virginia; 1991, District of Columbia; 2000, Arizona. *Education:* Lehigh University (B.S., 1987); Harvard Law School (J.D., 1990). ***PRACTICE AREAS:*** Commercial Litigation; Product Liability. ***Email:*** dawn_marchant@dc.kirkland.com

ROBERT G. MARKS, admitted to bar, 1994, Pennsylvania; 1996, District of Columbia. *Education:* Princeton University (A.B., 1991); Harvard Law School (J.D., 1994). ***PRACTICE AREAS:*** Corporate. ***Email:*** robert_marks@dc.kirkland.com

GERALD F. MASOUDI, admitted to bar, 1994, Colorado; 1995, District of Columbia. *Education:* Amherst College (B.A., 1990); The University of Chicago Law School (J.D., 1993). Law Clerk to Hon. Frank H. Easterbrook, 7th Circuit Court of Appeals, 1993-1994. ***PRACTICE AREAS:*** Commercial Litigation; Appellate Litigation. ***Email:*** gerald_masoudi@dc.kirkland.com

SUSAN O'SULLIVAN McGUIRE, admitted to bar, 1987, Virginia; 1988, District of Columbia; 1990, California. *Education:* College of William and Mary (B.A., 1982); University of Virginia (J.D., 1987). ***PRACTICE AREAS:*** Environmental Law; Environmental Litigation. ***Email:*** susan_mcguire@dc.kirkland.com

JOHN GIBSON MULLAN, admitted to bar, 1983, District of Columbia. *Education:* University of Pennsylvania (B.A., 1975); University of Virginia (J.D., 1983). ***PRACTICE AREAS:*** Administrative Law; Environmental Law-Air Pollution Regulation; Appellate Litigation; Regulatory Litigation. ***Email:*** john_mullan@dc.kirkland.com

GRANTA Y. NAKAYAMA, admitted to bar, 1994, Virginia; 1995, District of Columbia. *Education:* Massachusetts Institute of Technology (S.B., S.M., 1981); George Mason University School of Law (J.D., 1994). Adjunct Professor of Law, George Mason University, 1997—. [Lt., Naval Nuclear Propulsion Program, U.S. Navy, 1981-1986]. ***PRACTICE AREAS:*** Environmental Law; Intellectual Property. ***Email:*** granta_nakayama@dc.kirkland.com

(This Listing Continued)

CRAIG S. PRIMIS, admitted to bar, 1996, New York; 1997, District of Columbia. *Education:* Brown University (A.B., 1991); Harvard Law School (J.D., 1994). Law Clerk: Justice Clarence Thomas, U.S. Supreme Court, 1995-1996; Hon. J. Michael Luttig, U.S. Court of Appeals, Fourth Circuit, 1994-1995. ***PRACTICE AREAS:*** Litigation. ***Email:*** craig_primis@dc.kirkland.com

LEWIS T. PUTMAN, JR., admitted to bar, 1994, Illinois; 1998, District of Columbia. *Education:* Colorado School of Mines (B.S., 1986); University of Illinois (J.D., 1994). ***PRACTICE AREAS:*** Environmental Law; Natural Resources Law; Environmental Transaction Support. ***Email:*** lewis_putman@dc.kirkland.com

JEFFREY A. ROSEN, admitted to bar, 1982, District of Columbia. *Education:* Northwestern University (B.A., with highest distinction, 1979); Harvard University (J.D., magna cum laude, 1982). ***PRACTICE AREAS:*** Commercial Litigation; Class Actions; Antitrust. ***Email:*** jeff_rosen@dc.kirkland.com

ROBERT S. RYLAND, admitted to bar, 1988, Maryland; 1989, District of Columbia. *Education:* Swarthmore College (B.A., 1982); University of Chicago (J.D., 1987). Law Clerk to the Honorable Joseph H. Young, U.S. District Court, District of Maryland, 1987-1988. ***PRACTICE AREAS:*** Government Contracts; Health Care Law; White Collar Defense. ***Email:*** robert_ryland@dc.kirkland.com

DAVID P. SANDERS, admitted to bar, 1987, Colorado; 1989, District of Columbia. *Education:* University of Michigan (B.A., 1982); University of Denver College of Law (J.D., 1987). Member, CIT Advisory Committee, 1998—. ***PRACTICE AREAS:*** Customs Law; International Trade. ***Email:*** david_sanders@dc.kirkland.com

MARIMICHAEL O. SKUBEL, admitted to bar, 1979, District of Columbia. *Education:* Indiana University of Pennsylvania (B.A., 1976); Catholic University of America (J.D., 1979). Federal Trade Commission. ***PRACTICE AREAS:*** Antitrust. ***Email:*** marimichael_skubel@dc.kirkland.com

TEFFT W. SMITH, admitted to bar, 1971, Illinois; 1998, District of Columbia. *Education:* Brown University (B.A., 1968); University of Chicago (J.D., 1971). (Also at Chicago, Illinois Office). ***PRACTICE AREAS:*** Competition and Antitrust Law; Sales of Business Disputes; Distribution Litigation. ***Email:*** tefft_smith@dc.kirkland.com

KENNETH W. STARR, admitted to bar, 1973, California; 1979, Virginia and District of Columbia. *Education:* George Washington University (A.B., 1968); Brown University (A.M., 1969); Duke University (J.D., 1973). Counselor to U.S. Attorney General, 1981-1983. Circuit Judge, U.S. Court of Appeals, District of Columbia Circuit, 1983-1989. U.S. Solicitor General, 1989-1993. ***PRACTICE AREAS:*** Appellate Litigation; Commercial Litigation; Antitrust Law. ***Email:*** kenneth_starr@dc.kirkland.com

ROBERT TIMOTHY STEPHENSON, admitted to bar, 1990, Oklahoma and Maryland; 1992, District of Columbia. *Education:* University of Oklahoma (B.A., 1979); Georgetown University (J.D., 1990). ***PRACTICE AREAS:*** Employment Relations; Labor Relations. ***Email:*** timothy_stephenson@dc.kirkland.com

DAVID P. SWENSON, admitted to bar, 1994, Illinois; 1996, Minnesota; 1997, District of Columbia. *Education:* Boston College (B.A., Computer Science, 1990); University of Minnesota (M.A., 1993; J.D., 1994). Law Clerk to Judge Pauline Newman, U.S. Court of Appeals, Federal Circuit, 1997-1998. ***PRACTICE AREAS:*** Intellectual Property; Litigation; Appellate Practice. ***Email:*** david_swenson@dc.kirkland.com

LAURENCE A. URGENSON, admitted to bar, 1976, New York; 1997, District of Columbia. *Education:* City College of the City University of New York (B.B.A., 1968); Brooklyn Law School (J.D., 1975). Member, National Moot Court Team. Senior Editor, Brooklyn Law Review, 1974-1975. Adjunct Professor of Law, Trial Advocacy, Brooklyn Law School, 1986-1989. Chief, Criminal Division; Chief, Economic Crime Section, 1979-1983 and Chief Assistant U.S. Attorney, 1986-1990, U.S. Attorney's Office, Eastern District of New York. Chief, Fraud Section, Executive Director, Economic Crime Council, and Acting Deputy Assistant Attorney General, 1990-1993, Criminal Division, U.S. Department of Justice. ***PRACTICE AREAS:*** White Collar Crime; Commercial Litigation. ***Email:*** laurence_urgenson@dc.kirkland.com

KAREN NATALIE WALKER, admitted to bar, 1987, District of Columbia. *Education:* Bowdoin College (B.A., 1984); Harvard Law School (J.D., 1987). Law Clerk to the Honorable Thomas Penfield Jackson of the U.S. District Court for the District of Columbia, 1987-1988. ***PRACTICE AREAS:*** Commercial Litigation; Antitrust; Product Liability; Healthcare; Intellectual Property. ***Email:*** karen_walker@dc.kirkland.com

EDWARD W. WARREN, (P.C.), admitted to bar, 1969, Illinois; 1970, District of Columbia. *Education:* Yale College (B.A., 1966); University of Chicago (J.D., 1969). Law Clerk to the Honorable Luther M. Swygert, U.S. Court of Appeals, Seventh Circuit, 1969-1970. ***PRACTICE AREAS:*** Appellate Litigation; Administrative; Constitutional Law. ***Email:*** edward_warren@dc.kirkland.com

(This Listing Continued)

KENNETH G. WEIGEL, admitted to bar, 1979, District of Columbia. *Education:* University of Michigan (B.A., 1976); George Washington University (J.D., 1979). ***PRACTICE AREAS:*** International Law; Customs Law; International Trade Law. ***Email:*** kenneth_weigel@dc.kirkland.com

STEVEN M. WELLNER, admitted to bar, 1985, District of Columbia. *Education:* University of Virginia (B.A., 1981); University of Michigan (J.D., 1985). ***PRACTICE AREAS:*** Environmental Law. ***Email:*** steven_wellner@dc.kirkland.com

L. MARK WINE, (P.C.), admitted to bar, 1970, District of Columbia. *Education:* University of Virginia (B.A., 1967); University of Chicago (J.D., 1970). ***PRACTICE AREAS:*** Environmental Law and Hazardous Waste Liability and Compliance; Private Environmental Litigation; Air Pollution Regulation and Enforcement; Toxic Substance Regulation; Litigation and Counseling. ***Email:*** mark_wine@dc.kirkland.com

THOMAS D. YANNUCCI, admitted to bar, 1977, Ohio; 1981, District of Columbia. *Education:* University of Notre Dame (A.B., 1972; J.D., 1976). Editor-in-Chief, Notre Dame Law Review. Law Clerk to the Honorable John A. Danaher, U.S. Court of Appeals for the District of Columbia Circuit, 1976-1977. Trial Attorney, Appellate Attorney, Civil Rights Division, Department of Justice, 1977-1980. Distinguished Service Award, 1978, 1979. ***PRACTICE AREAS:*** Commercial Litigation; Antitrust; Defamation; Intellectual Property. ***Email:*** thomas_yannucci@dc.kirkland.com

MARK D. YOUNG, admitted to bar, 1977, District of Columbia. *Education:* Tufts University (B.A., 1974); Georgetown University (J.D., 1977). Staff Attorney, 1977-1979, Special Counsel, 1979-1980 and Assistant General Counsel, 1980-1982, Commodity Futures Trading Commission. ***PRACTICE AREAS:*** Securities; Derivatives Law; Banking; Legislative. ***Email:*** mark_young@dc.kirkland.com

MARC J. ZWILLINGER, admitted to bar, 1994, Illinois; 1996, District of Columbia. *Education:* Tufts University (B.A., 1991); Harvard University (J.D., 1994). *Member:* American Bar Association (Co-Chair, Subcommittee on Computer and High-Tech Crime, White Collar Crime Committee, 2000-2002). ***PRACTICE AREAS:*** Cyber Law; Information Technology; White Collar Crime; Litigation. ***Email:*** marc_zwillinger@dc.kirkland.com

OF COUNSEL

JOSEPH J. DeSANCTIS, admitted to bar, 1983, Ohio (Not admitted in District of Columbia). *Education:* Duquesne University (B.A., 1980); Case Western Reserve University (J.D., 1983); George Mason University (M.A., 1998). Attorney, U.S. Department of Justice, Washington, D.C., 1989-1995. Senior Legislative Counsel, U.S. Senator Mike DeWine, Washington, D.C., 1995-1997. Senior Legislative Counsel, Senate Judiciary Committee, Washington, D.C., 1997. (Counsel). ***PRACTICE AREAS:*** Litigation. ***Email:*** joseph_desanctis@dc.kirkland.com

LAURA S. HARPER, admitted to bar, 1991, Massachusetts; 1994, District of Columbia; 1998, New York. *Education:* University of Utah (B.S., 1983); Cornell University, Johnson Graduate School of Management (M.B.A., 1990); Cornell University Law School (J.D., 1991). ***PRACTICE AREAS:*** Corporate; Mergers and Acquisitions; Securities; Venture Capital; Private Equity. ***Email:*** laura_harper@dc.kirkland.com

JAMES S. HOSTETLER, admitted to bar, 1958, Ohio; 1962, District of Columbia. *Education:* Yale University (B.A., 1955); Harvard Law School (J.D., 1958). ***PRACTICE AREAS:*** Government Contracts; Association Law; Legislative; Administrative Law. ***Email:*** james_hostetler@dc.kirkland.com

DAVID G. NORRELL, admitted to bar, 1980, District of Columbia. *Education:* Florida State University (B.A., 1974); University of Virginia (J.D., 1977). Law Clerk to: The Honorable Thurgood Marshall, U.S. Supreme Court, 1978-1979; Chief Judge Clement F. Haynsworth, Jr., U.S. Court of Appeals, Fourth Circuit, 1977-1978. ***PRACTICE AREAS:*** International Law; International Trade Regulation; International Acquisitions and Investment; Worldwide Litigation. ***Email:*** david_norrell@dc.kirkland.com

FREDERICK M. ROWE, admitted to bar, 1952, New York; 1953, District of Columbia. *Education:* College of the City of New York (B.B.A., 1949); Yale Law School (LL.B., 1952). Visiting Lecturer: Yale Law School, 1978-1982; Boalt Hall School of Law, University of California, 1981; Yale School of Organization and Management, 1984; Harvard Law School, 1985. Adjunct Professor of Law and Management, Yale School of Organization and Management, 1985-1987. Law Clerk to the Honorable Tom C. Clark, U.S. Supreme Court, 1952-1953. ***PRACTICE AREAS:*** Antitrust; Commercial Litigation; Legislative; International Antitrust and Trade Regulation. ***Email:*** fred_rowe@dc.kirkland.com

JAMES D. SENGER, admitted to bar, 1981, District of Columbia. *Education:* Dartmouth College (A.B., 1978); University of Michigan; Yale University (J.D., 1981). ***PRACTICE AREAS:*** Energy. ***Email:*** james_senger@dc.kirkland.com

(This Listing Continued)

KIRKLAND & ELLIS, Washington—Continued

ASSOCIATES

GARY D. ANDERSON, admitted to bar, 1997, New York; 2001, District of Columbia. *Education:* University of Notre Dame (B.B.A., 1990; J.D., 1996). Note Editor, Notre Dame Law Review. ***PRACTICE AREAS:*** Commercial Litigation; Trademarks. ***Email:*** gary_anderson@dc.kirkland.com

MARYBELLE CAM ANG, (admission pending). *Education:* Stanford University (B.A., 1994); Northwestern University (J.D., 2001). ***PRACTICE AREAS:*** Energy. ***Email:*** marybelle_ang@kirkland.com

LAURA R. BACH, admitted to bar, 1999, Maryland and District of Columbia. *Education:* North Carolina State University (B.A., 1995); Columbia University (J.D., 1998). ***PRACTICE AREAS:*** Litigation. ***Email:*** laura_bach@dc.kirkland.com

REATHA A. BAKER, admitted to bar, 1996, Missouri; 1999, District of Columbia. *Education:* Vanderbilt University (B.A., 1992); St. Louis University School of Law (J.D., 1996). ***PRACTICE AREAS:*** Corporate. ***Email:*** reatha_baker@dc.kirkland.com

JASON BECKERMAN, admitted to bar, 1999, California and District of Columbia. *Education:* University of Connecticut (B.A., 1993); Loyola Marymount University (J.D., 1998). ***PRACTICE AREAS:*** Litigation. ***Email:*** jason_beckerman@dc.kirkland.com

STACEY L. BENNETT, admitted to bar, 1999, Minnesota; 2001, District of Columbia. *Education:* Wheaton College (B.A., 1991); Yale University (J.D., 1999). ***PRACTICE AREAS:*** Litigation. ***Email:*** stacey_bennett@dc.kirkland.com

BRADFORD E. BIEGON, admitted to bar, 1996, Virginia; 1998, District of Columbia. *Education:* Georgetown University (B.S., 1993); University of Virginia (J.D., 1996). ***PRACTICE AREAS:*** Intellectual Property; Litigation. ***Email:*** bradford_biegon@dc.kirkland.com

BRANT W. BISHOP, admitted to bar, 1996, Utah; 1998, District of Columbia. *Education:* Brigham Young University (B.A./M.A., 1993); Harvard (J.D., 1996). Law Clerk to Hon. Paul Niemeyer, U.S. Court of Appeals, 4th Circuit, 1996-1997. ***PRACTICE AREAS:*** Litigation. ***Email:*** brant_bishop@dc.kirkland.com

PAUL J. BOHR, admitted to bar, 1999, Virginia; 2000, District of Columbia. *Education:* Princeton University (A.B., 1988); University of Notre Dame (J.D., 1999). [Captain, U.S. Army, 1988-1995]. ***PRACTICE AREAS:*** Corporate Law; Mergers and Acquisitions; Private Equity; Venture Capital; Securities. ***Email:*** paul_bohr@dc.kirkland.com

JULIE L. BRENNAN, admitted to bar, 2001, Virginia (Not admitted in District of Columbia). *Education:* Emory University (B.A., 1993); George Washington University (J.D., 2001). ***PRACTICE AREAS:*** Antitrust; Litigation. ***Email:*** julie_brennan@dc.kirkland.com

JENNIFER R. BROSNAHAN, admitted to bar, 1999, Maryland, District of Columbia. *Education:* Harvard College (A.B., 1995); Harvard Law School (J.D., 1998). ***PRACTICE AREAS:*** Litigation. ***Email:*** jennifer_brosnahan@dc.kirkland.com

ZHONETTE BROWN, admitted to bar, 1998, Maryland; 1999, District of Columbia. *Education:* University of Colorado (B.A., 1995); Georgetown University Law Center (J.D., 1998). Clerk, Hon. Marvin J. Garbis, U.S. District Court, District of Maryland, 1998-1999. ***PRACTICE AREAS:*** Litigation. ***Email:*** zhonette_brown@dc.kirkland.com

EUGENE F. CHAY, admitted to bar, 1998, Pennsylvania; 1999, New Jersey; 2000, District of Columbia. *Education:* University of Pennsylvania (B.A., 1993); Washington College of Law, American University (J.D., 1998). Board Member, Asian Pacific American Bar Association Educational Fund, 2001. ***PRACTICE AREAS:*** Intellectual Property Litigation; Commercial Litigation. ***Email:*** eugene_chay@dc.kirkland.com

ELIZABETH CHEUNG, (admission pending). *Education:* Columbia University (B.A., 1998); University of Notre Dame (J.D., 2001). ***PRACTICE AREAS:*** Litigation. ***Email:*** elizabeth_cheung@dc.kirkland.com

DAVID A. CODEVILLA, admitted to bar, 1996, Virginia; 1998, District of Columbia. *Education:* University of California at Berkeley (B.A., 1992); George Mason University (J.D., 1996). Member, Federalist Society. Law Clerk to Chief Judge Loren A. Smith, U.S. Court of Federal Claims, 1996-1997. ***PRACTICE AREAS:*** Environmental Transactions. ***Email:*** david_codevilla@dc.kirkland.com

GREGORY F. CORBETT, admitted to bar, 2000, Massachusetts (Not admitted in District of Columbia). *Education:* Harvard University (A.B., 1996); Boston College (J.D., 1999). Law Clerk: Judge Arthur Gajarsa, U.S. Court of Appeals, Federal Circuit, 2000-2001; Judge Edward Harrington, U.S. District Court, District of Massachusetts, 1999-2000. ***PRACTICE AREAS:*** Litigation; Intellectual Property; Environmental; Appellate Practice. ***Email:*** gregory_corbett@kirkland.com

JOANNE COSIOL, (admission pending). *Education:* University of Rochester (B.A., 1997); Georgetown University (J.D., 2001). ***PRACTICE AREAS:*** Corporate. ***Email:*** joanne_cosiol@dc.kirkland.com

JOSEPH E. CULLEITON, admitted to bar, 1998, Pennsylvania; 2001, District of Columbia. *Education:* Georgetown University (B.S.B.A., 1993; J.D., 1998). ***PRACTICE AREAS:*** Litigation. ***Email:*** joseph_culleiton@dc.kirkland.com

ELIZABETH LEE DEELEY, admitted to bar, 1998, Virginia; 2000, District of Columbia. *Education:* University of Georgia (B.B.A., 1992); George Washington University (J.D., 1998). Law Clerk to the Hon. Roger B. Andewelt, U.S. Court of Federal Claims, 1998-1999. ***PRACTICE AREAS:*** Litigation. ***Email:*** elizabeth_deeley@dc.kirkland.com

GRANT M. DIXTON, (admission pending). *Education:* Harvard University (B.A., 1996; J.D., 1999). Law Clerk: Justice Anthony Kennedy, U.S. Supreme Court, 2000-2001; Judge Michael Luttig, U.S. Court of Appeals, 4th Circuit. ***Email:*** grant_dixton@dc.kirkland.com

DANIEL T. DONOVAN, admitted to bar, 1997, Ohio; 1998, District of Columbia. *Education:* Villanova University (B.S., 1993); George Washington University (J.D., 1996). Law Clerk to the Hon. George A. O'Toole, Jr., United States District Court, District of Massachusetts, 1996-1997. ***PRACTICE AREAS:*** Litigation. ***Email:*** daniel_donovan@dc.kirkland.com

CARA TSENG DUFFIELD, admitted to bar, 2000, Illinois (Not admitted in District of Columbia). *Education:* Radcliffe College (A.B., 1996); Chicago Law School (J.D., 2000). Law Clerk, Judge Nancy F. Atlas, U.S. District Court, Southern District of Texas, 2000-2001. ***PRACTICE AREAS:*** Litigation. ***Email:*** cara_duffield@dc.kirkland.com

SUSAN KATHLEEN FITCH, admitted to bar, 1992, Virginia; 1994, District of Columbia. *Education:* University of Texas at Austin (B.A., 1989; J.D., 1991). Law Review. ***PRACTICE AREAS:*** White Collar Crime; Government Contracts; Health Care. ***Email:*** susan_fitch@dc.kirkland.com

ERIC L. FLETCHER, admitted to bar, 1998, Illinois (Not admitted in District of Columbia). *Education:* University of California, Berkeley (B.S., 1995); University of Virginia (J.D., 1998). [Petty Officer, Third Class, U.S. Navy, 1985-1989]. ***PRACTICE AREAS:*** Corporate. ***Email:*** eric_fletcher@dc.kirkland.com

DAVID B. FLORENZO, admitted to bar, 1998, Maryland; 1999, District of Columbia. *Education:* University of Notre Dame (B.A., 1992); Georgetown University (J.D., 1998). ***PRACTICE AREAS:*** Litigation; Antitrust and Trade Regulation. ***Email:*** david_florenzo@dc.kirkland.com

LAURA FRAEDRICH, admitted to bar, 1995, Virginia; 1998, District of Columbia. *Education:* College of William and Mary (B.A., 1983); George Mason University (J.D., 1995). Clerk to Honorable Pauline Newman, U.S. Court of Appeals for the Federal Circuit, 1995-1997. ***PRACTICE AREAS:*** International Trade; Customs Law. ***Email:*** laura_fraedrich@dc.kirkland.com

CHRISTIAN S. GENETSKI, admitted to bar, 1995, Georgia; 2001, District of Columbia. *Education:* Birmingham-Southern College (B.A., 1992); Vanderbilt University (J.D., 1995). Adjunct Professor, Cyberlaw, Georgetown University Law Center, 2000. ***PRACTICE AREAS:*** Cyber Law; Information Technology; Intellectual Property; Litigation. ***Email:*** christian_genetski@dc.kirkland.com

DANIEL J. GERKIN, admitted to bar, 2001, New York and District of Columbia. *Education:* Georgetown University (B.A., 1997); George Washington University (J.D., 2000). ***PRACTICE AREAS:*** Customs Law; International Trade. ***Email:*** daniel_gerkin@dc.kirkland.com

JOHN P. GONSOULIN, admitted to bar, 2001, Texas (Not admitted in District of Columbia). *Education:* University of Texas at Austin (B.A., 1997); Harvard University (J.D., 2001). ***PRACTICE AREAS:*** Litigation; Appellate Practice. ***Email:*** john_gonsoulin@dc.kirkland.com

RYAN W. GOODE, admitted to bar, 2001, Illinois (Not admitted in District of Columbia). *Education:* University of Notre Dame (B.B.A., 1997); Harvard University (J.D., 2000). ***PRACTICE AREAS:*** Litigation. ***Email:*** ryan_goode@dc.kirkland.com

PATRICK EDWARD GROOMES, (admission pending). *Education:* American University (B.A., 1993; J.D., 2001); Harvard University (M.P.P., 1996). ***PRACTICE AREAS:*** Energy; Corporate. ***Email:*** patrick_groomes@dc.kirkland.com

AMY MARIE HARVEY, admitted to bar, 1997, Virginia; 1999, District of Columbia. *Education:* University of Pittsburgh (B.A., 1989); George Washington University (J.D., 1997). ***PRACTICE AREAS:*** Corporate Law. ***Email:*** amy_harvey@dc.kirkland.com

(This Listing Continued)

ROBERT W. IRISH, admitted to bar, 1999, Illinois; 2000, Wisconsin (Not admitted in District of Columbia). *Education:* Tufts University (B.A., 1991); University of Wisconsin - Madison (J.D., 1999). ***PRACTICE AREAS:*** International Trade. ***Email:*** robert_irish@dc.kirkland.com

GEOFFREY S. IRWIN, admitted to bar, 1996, Illinois; 2000, District of Columbia. *Education:* Georgetown University (B.A., 1993); University of Texas, Austin (J.D., 1996). ***PRACTICE AREAS:*** Litigation. ***Email:*** geoffrey_irwin@dc.kirkland.com

SARA KALIN, admitted to bar, 2001, California (Not admitted in District of Columbia). *Education:* University of California, Santa Barbara (B.A., 1997); University of California, Los Angeles (J.D., 2000). ***PRACTICE AREAS:*** Corporate Law. ***Email:*** sara_kalin@dc.kirkland.com

NELLY KARDAKOVA, (admission pending). *Education:* American University (B.A., 1998; J.D., 2001). ***PRACTICE AREAS:*** Intellectual Property. ***Email:*** nelly_kardakova@dc.kirkland.com

COLIN R. KASS, admitted to bar, 1996, Illinois; 1998, District of Columbia. *Education:* University of Chicago (B.A./M.A., 1993); University of Michigan (J.D., 1996). ***PRACTICE AREAS:*** Litigation. ***Email:*** colin_kass@dc.kirkland.com

ANDREW B. KAY, admitted to bar, 1997, Illinois; 1999, District of Columbia. *Education:* Cornell (B.A., 1994); University of Michigan (J.D., 1997). Associate Editor, Michigan Law Review, 1995-1996. Law Clerk to the Hon. Joel M. Flaum, U.S. Court of Appeals, Seventh Circuit, 1997-1998. ***PRACTICE AREAS:*** Litigation. ***Email:*** andrew_kay@dc.kirkland.com

JAMES M. KOUKIOS, admitted to bar, 2000, New York (Not admitted in District of Columbia). *Education:* University of Michigan (B.A., 1996); Harvard University (J.D., 1999). Law Clerk, Judge Edith Brown Clement, U.S. District Court, Eastern District of Louisiana, 1999-2001. ***PRACTICE AREAS:*** Litigation. ***Email:*** james_koukios@dc.kirkland.com

ANTHONY W. LACOSTA, admitted to bar, 1999, Virginia; 2000, District of Columbia. *Education:* Willamette University (B.A., 1991); Boalt Hall School of Law, University of California (J.D., 1999). ***PRACTICE AREAS:*** White Collar Crime; Litigation. ***Email:*** anthony_lacosta@dc.kirkland.com

TONY Y. LAM, admitted to bar, 1998, Pennsylvania and New Jersey; 2001, District of Columbia. *Education:* University of Hong Kong (B.A., 1985); University of London (LL.B., 1997); Seton Hall University (J.D., 1998); New York University (LL.M., 1999). ***PRACTICE AREAS:*** Corporate; Securities. ***Email:*** tony_lam@dc.kirkland.com

JENNIFER G. LEVY, admitted to bar, 1998, New York; 1999, District of Columbia. *Education:* Duke University (B.A., 1994; J.D., 1997). ***PRACTICE AREAS:*** Litigation. ***Email:*** jennifer_levy@dc.kirkland.com

MARK E. McKANE, admitted to bar, 1997, Illinois; 1999, District of Columbia. *Education:* Yale University (B.A., 1993); Northwestern University (J.D., 1997). ***PRACTICE AREAS:*** Litigation. ***Email:*** mark_mckane@dc.kirkland.com

DAVID E. MENDELSON, admitted to bar, 1997, Pennsylvania; 2001, District of Columbia. *Education:* University of Maryland (B.A., 1993); Washington College of Law of American University (J.D., 1997). Staff Attorney, U.S. Court of Appeals, Third Circuit, 1998-2000. ***PRACTICE AREAS:*** Litigation. ***Email:*** david_mendelson@dc.kirkland.com

JUNAID "JAY" MUNIR, admitted to bar, 2001, Florida (Not admitted in District of Columbia). *Education:* Yale University (B.A., 1998); Harvard University (J.D., 2001). ***PRACTICE AREAS:*** Litigation. ***Email:*** jay_munir@dc.kirkland.com

MATTHEW E. PAPEZ, admitted to bar, 1999, Nevada; 2001, District of Columbia. *Education:* University of Nevada at Reno (B.S., 1996); Harvard Law School (J.D., 1999). Notes Editor, Harvard Law Review, 1997-1999. Law Clerk, Chief Judge Procter Hug, U.S. Court of Appeals, Ninth Circuit, 1999-2000. ***PRACTICE AREAS:*** Litigation. ***Email:*** matthew_papez@dc.kirkland.com

ASHLEY CHARLES PARRISH, admitted to bar, 1998, Virginia; 2000, District of Columbia. *Education:* University of Washington (B.A., 1994); University of Chicago (J.D., 1998). ***PRACTICE AREAS:*** Litigation; Appellate Practice. ***Email:*** ashley_parrish@dc.kirkland.com

LARISSA PAULE-CARRES, admitted to bar, 1999, Virginia; 2000, District of Columbia. *Education:* Denison University (B.A., 1993); Benjamin N. Cardozo School of Law (J.D., 1999). ***PRACTICE AREAS:*** Litigation. ***Email:*** larissa_paule-carres@dc.kirkland.com

ELIZABETH S. PETRELA, admitted to bar, 2000, Nevada (Not admitted in District of Columbia). *Education:* Cornell University (B.S., 1995); Harvard Law School (J.D., 1999). ***PRACTICE AREAS:*** Appellate Litigation. ***Email:*** elizabeth_petrela@kirkland.com

RYAN PATRICK PHAIR, (admission pending). *Education:* Boston College (B.A., 1996); University of Chicago (J.D., 2001; M.A., Economics and Public Policy, 2001). ***PRACTICE AREAS:*** Litigation; Appellate Practice. ***Email:*** ryan_phair@dc.kirkland.com

(This Listing Continued)

DAVID PRUITT, admitted to bar, 1999, Virginia; 2000, District of Columbia. *Education:* University of Notre Dame (B.B.A., 1992; J.D., 1999). ***PRACTICE AREAS:*** Civil Litigation. ***Email:*** david_pruitt@dc.kirkland.com

KAREN M. ROBINSON, admitted to bar, 1998, New York; 1999, District of Columbia. *Education:* Georgetown University (B.S.F.S., 1994); University of Texas at Austin (J.D., 1997). ***PRACTICE AREAS:*** Litigation. ***Email:*** karen_robinson@dc.kirkland.com

REBECCA I. RUBY, admitted to bar, 1999, Massachusetts; 2000, District of Columbia; 2001, Virginia. *Education:* Brown University (A.B., 1996); Georgetown University Law Center (J.D., 1999). ***PRACTICE AREAS:*** Litigation. ***Email:*** rebecca_ruby@dc.kirkland.com

CHRISTIAN C. SEMONSEN, admitted to bar, 1999, California; 2001, District of Columbia. *Education:* University of California at Davis (B.A., 1988); George Washington University (J.D., 1999). Managing Editor, The Environmental Lawyer, 1998-1999. ***PRACTICE AREAS:*** Environmental Law. ***Email:*** christian_semonsen@dc.kirkland.com

KANNON K. SHANMUGAM, admitted to bar, 2001, Kansas and District of Columbia. *Education:* Harvard University (A.B., 1993; J.D., 1998); Oxford University, England (M.Litt., 1995). Law Clerk: Hon. Antonin Scalia, U.S. Supreme Court, 1999-2000; Hon. J. Michael Luttig, U.S. Court of Appeals, Fourth Circuit, 1998-1999. ***PRACTICE AREAS:*** Appellate Litigation; Commercial Litigation; Arbitration; Antitrust; Competition; Products Liability Litigation. ***Email:*** kannon@kirkland.com

STEPHANIE M. STERN, (admission pending). *Education:* Brown University (B.A., 1996); Yale University (J.D., 1999). ***PRACTICE AREAS:*** Environmental. ***Email:*** stephanie_stern@dc.kirkland.com

MARTHA PHILLIPS STUART, admitted to bar, 1996, Missouri; 1997, Illinois; 1998, District of Columbia. *Education:* University of Illinois (B.A., 1993); Saint Louis University (J.D., 1996). ***PRACTICE AREAS:*** Corporate Law; Mergers and Acquisitions; Private Equity; Venture Capital. ***Email:*** martha_stuart@dc.kirkland.com

DAVID P. SULLIVAN, admitted to bar, 2000, Maryland; 2001, District of Columbia. *Education:* University of Pennsylvania (B.A., 1994); Washington College of Law of American University (J.D., 2000). Associate Managing Editor, American University Law Review. ***PRACTICE AREAS:*** Commercial Litigation. ***Email:*** david_sullivan@dc.kirkland.com

EDWIN JOHN U, admitted to bar, 1998, California; 1999, District of Columbia. *Education:* Harvard University (B.A., 1995; J.D., 1998). Articles Editor, Vol. 111, and Editor, Vol. 110, Harvard Law Review, 1996-1998. Law Clerk: Hon. Norman Stahl, U.S. Court of Appeals, First Circuit, 1999-2000; Hon. James Cacheris, U.S. District Court, Eastern District of Virginia, 1998-1999. ***PRACTICE AREAS:*** Litigation. ***Email:*** edwin_u@dc.kirkland.com

ELAINE M. WALSH, admitted to bar, 1996, Missouri and U.S. District Court, Eastern District of Missouri; 1997, Illinois and Massachusetts (Not admitted in District of Columbia). *Education:* University of Florida (B.A., 1991); Washington University (M.A., Economics, 1996; J.D., 1996). ***PRACTICE AREAS:*** Energy. ***Email:*** elaine_walsh@dc.kirkland.com

AMY C. WHITEHURST, admitted to bar, 2001, North Carolina (Not admitted in District of Columbia). *Education:* Duke University (B.A., 1998); Harvard University (J.D., 2001). ***PRACTICE AREAS:*** Corporate. ***Email:*** amy_whitehurst@dc.kirkland.com

JEFFREY WILLIAMSON, admitted to bar, 2000, Florida (Not admitted in District of Columbia). *Education:* Georgetown University (B.A., 1995); University of Michigan (J.D., 1999). ***PRACTICE AREAS:*** Energy Law. ***Email:*** jeffrey_williamson@dc.kirkland.com

ERIC B. WOLFF, (admission pending). *Education:* Concordia College (B.A., 1995); Boalt Hall School of Law, University of California (J.D., 1998). Law Clerk: Justice Antonin Scalia, U.S. Supreme Court, 2000-2001; Judge Stephen F. Williams, U.S. Court of Appeals of the District of Columbia, 1999-2000; Judge William A. Fletcher, US. Court of Appeals, 9th Circuit, 1998-1999. ***PRACTICE AREAS:*** Appellate Litigation. ***Email:*** eric_wolff@dc.kirkland.com

(For Biographical Data on Chicago, Illinois, New York, N.Y., Los Angeles, California and London, England, see Professional Biographies at those points Respectively).

KIRKPATRICK & LOCKHART LLP

Established in 1946
1800 MASSACHUSETTS AVENUE, N.W.
2ND FLOOR
WASHINGTON, D.C. 20036-1800
Telephone: 202-778-9000
Telex: 244859
Facsimile: 202-778-9100
URL: http://www.kl.com

Boston, Massachusetts Office: 75 State Street. Telephone: 617-261-3100. Facsimile: 617-261-3175.
Dallas, Texas Office: 3100 Bank One Center, 1717 Main Street. Telephone: 214-939-4900. Facsimile: 214-939-4949.
Harrisburg, Pennsylvania Office: Payne Shoemaker Building, 240 North Third Street. Telephone: 717-231-4500. Facsimile: 717-231-4501.
Los Angeles, California Office: 10100 Santa Monica Boulevard, Suite 700. Telephone: 310-552-5000. Facsimile: 310-552-5001.
Miami, Florida Office: Miami Center, 20th Floor, 201 South Biscayne Boulevard. Telephone: 305-539-3300. Facsimile: 305-358-7095.
Newark, New Jersey Office: The Legal Center, One Riverfront Plaza, Seventh Floor. Telephone: 973-848-4000. Facsimile: 973-848-4001.
New York, New York Office: 1251 Avenue of the Americas, 45th Floor. Telephone: 212-536-3900. Facsimile: 212-536-3901.
Pittsburgh, Pennsylvania Office: Henry W. Oliver Building, 535 Smithfield Street. Telephone: 412-355-6500. Facsimile: 412-355-6501.
San Francisco, California Office: Four Embarcadero Center, 10th Floor. Telephone: 415-249-1000. Facsimile: 415-249-1001.

General Practice including Antitrust; Appellate; Banking and Financial Institutions; Bankruptcy and Business Restructurings; Construction; Corporate; Environmental; ERISA and Executive Compensation; Governmental Affairs and Legislation; Government Contracts; Insurance Coverage; International; Investment Companies and Investment Advisers; Labor and Employment; Litigation; Mergers and Acquisitions; Mortgage Banking and Consumer Finance; Product Liability and Toxic Torts; Real Estate; Securities; Securities Enforcement; Tax; Technology; Trusts and Estates; White Collar Crime and Year 2000 Computer Conversion.

MEMBERS OF FIRM

CLIFFORD J. ALEXANDER, admitted to bar, 1970, Massachusetts; 1977, District of Columbia. *Education:* Rockhurst College (A.B., 1966); Georgetown University (J.D., 1969). ***PRACTICE AREAS:*** Investment Company Law; Investment Management; Broker-Dealer Regulation; Banking Law; Business Organizations.

DIANE E. AMBLER, admitted to bar, 1978, District of Columbia. *Education:* University of Rochester (B.A., 1971); Villanova University (J.D., 1978).

COSTAS A. AVRAKOTOS, admitted to bar, 1987, Maryland; 1995, District of Columbia. *Education:* University of Pittsburgh (B.S., 1973); Catholic University of America (J.D., 1986). ***PRACTICE AREAS:*** Mortgage Banking Law; Consumer Law; Banking Regulation.

ALAN J. BERKELEY, admitted to bar, 1967, District of Columbia; 1981, New York. *Education:* Cornell University (B.S., 1964); Georgetown University (J.D., 1967). ***PRACTICE AREAS:*** Securities; Corporate Law; Business Law.

JOSEPH J. BRIGATI, admitted to bar, 1967, District of Columbia. *Education:* University of Notre Dame (B.A., 1962); Duke University (LL.B., 1965). ***PRACTICE AREAS:*** Government Contracts; Shipbuilding and Repair; Construction Claims; Banking Litigation; Federal Litigation.

MELANIE HIBBS BRODY, admitted to bar, 1994, District of Columbia. *Education:* University of Connecticut (B.A., 1989); Syracuse University (J.D., cum laude, 1992). ***PRACTICE AREAS:*** Privacy; Electronic Commerce; Mortgage Banking Law.

ARTHUR J. BROWN, admitted to bar, 1980, District of Columbia. *Education:* City College of New York (B.S., 1970); New York University (J.D., 1973). ***PRACTICE AREAS:*** Securities Regulation; Investment Company Law; Securities Registration; Investment Regulation; Hedge Funds.

DAVID T. CASE, admitted to bar, 1978, Michigan 1984, District of Columbia. *Education:* University of Michigan (B.A., 1975; J.D., 1978; M.A., 1984). ***PRACTICE AREAS:*** Civil Litigation; Environmental Coverage Litigation; Government Contracts; Construction Claims.

SUSAN M. CASEY, admitted to bar, 1985, New York; 1988, District of Columbia. *Education:* Brown University (A.B., 1975); Yale Law School (J.D., 1984). ***PRACTICE AREAS:*** Financial Services Regulation; Mutual Funds; Banking Regulation; Investment Management.

THOMAS F. COONEY, III, admitted to bar, 1978, District of Columbia. *Education:* Dartmouth College (A.B., 1974); University of Michigan (J.D., 1978). ***PRACTICE AREAS:*** Business Law; Corporate Law; Finance; Mergers, Acquisitions and Divestitures; Securities.

(This Listing Continued)

ARTHUR C. DELIBERT, admitted to bar, 1980, New York; 1982, District of Columbia. *Education:* Cornell University (B.S.E.E., 1968); New York University (J.D., 1978). ***PRACTICE AREAS:*** Investment Company Law; Investment Management; Mutual Funds; Business Trusts; Securities Regulation.

CHARLES LEE EISEN, admitted to bar, 1967, Maryland; 1968, District of Columbia;. *Education:* Princeton University (B.A., 1964); Yale University (LL.B., 1967). ***PRACTICE AREAS:*** Complex Litigation; Federal Civil Litigation; Trial Practice; Securities Fraud; Arbitration.

MAHLON M. FRANKHAUSER, admitted to bar, 1958, District of Columbia; 1985, New York. *Education:* Albright College (A.B., 1954); University of Pennsylvania Law School (LL.B., 1957).

ELINOR W. GAMMON, admitted to bar, 1970, District of Columbia. *Education:* Wellesley College (A.B., 1966); University of Virginia (LL.B., 1969). ***PRACTICE AREAS:*** Investment Company Law; Investment Regulation; Mutual Funds; Securities Regulation.

STEPHEN W. GRAFMAN, admitted to bar, 1965, Virginia; 1969, District of Columbia. *Education:* University of North Carolina (A.B., 1962); University of Virginia (LL.B., 1965). ***PRACTICE AREAS:*** Commercial Litigation; Commercial Arbitration; Federal Criminal Law.

ROBERT C. HACKER, admitted to bar, 1966, District of Columbia. *Education:* University of Illinois (A.B., 1962; J.D., 1965). ***PRACTICE AREAS:*** Financial Services Law; Investment Management; Investment Regulation; Mutual Funds; Broker-Dealer Regulation.

BARRY M. HARTMAN, admitted to bar, 1979, District of Columbia; 1984, Pennsylvania. *Education:* University of Pennsylvania (B.A., 1976); George Washington University (J.D., 1979). ***PRACTICE AREAS:*** Environmental Litigation; Criminal Litigation; Appellate Litigation; Administrative Litigation. **Email:** bhartman@kl.com

BENJAMIN J. HASKIN, admitted to bar, 1991, Illinois; 1992, District of Columbia. *Education:* Princeton University (A.B., 1986); University of Chicago (J.D., 1991). ***PRACTICE AREAS:*** Investment Management; Securities; Mutual Funds; Investment Company Law.

PHILIP H. HECHT, admitted to bar, 1980, District of Columbia; 1984, Virginia. *Education:* Amherst College (B.A., 1975); Oxford University (B.A., 1977; M.A., 1982); University of Michigan (J.D., 1980). ***PRACTICE AREAS:*** Insurance Coverage; Complex Litigation.

DUMOND PECK HILL (1923-1991).

MATTHEW L. JACOBS, admitted to bar, 1982, District of Columbia. *Education:* Princeton University (A.B., 1977, Woodrow Wilson School); University of Virginia (J.D., 1981). ***PRACTICE AREAS:*** Environmental Insurance Coverage; Insurance; Products Liability; Complex Litigation; Year 2000 Computer Conversion.

KATHLEEN D. JAEGER, admitted to bar, 1990, Massachusetts; 1993, District of Columbia. *Education:* University of Rhode Island (B.S., 1987); Catholic University of America (J.D., 1990). ***PRACTICE AREAS:*** Food and Drug Law.

JUDITH STURTZ KARP, admitted to bar, 1982, California; 1983, District of Columbia and New Jersey; 1984, Maryland. *Education:* Cornell University (B.A., 1979); Emory University School of Law (J.D., 1982). ***PRACTICE AREAS:*** Commercial Bankruptcy; Workouts; Business Transactions; Lenders Rights; Commercial Litigation.

REBECCA H. LAIRD, admitted to bar, 1970, District of Columbia. *Education:* University of Pennsylvania (B.A., 1967); Georgetown University (J.D., 1970). ***PRACTICE AREAS:*** Banking Law; Thrift Institutions Law; Investment Company Law; Investment Management; Trust Law.

LAWRENCE COE LANPHER, admitted to bar, 1975, District of Columbia. *Education:* Stanford University (B.A., 1968); Hampton Institute (M.A.T., 1971); Georgetown University (J.D., 1974). ***PRACTICE AREAS:*** Labor and Employment; Disabilities; Litigation; Insurance Coverage.

THOMAS M. LEAHEY, admitted to bar, 1983, District of Columbia. *Education:* Brown University (A.B., 1973); Yale University (J.D., 1976). ***PRACTICE AREAS:*** Financial Institutions Law; Investment Management; Corporate Law; Securities Regulation.

JEFFREY B. MALETTA, admitted to bar, 1979, District of Columbia. *Education:* Harvard University (B.A., 1975); Stanford University (J.D., 1979). ***PRACTICE AREAS:*** SEC Enforcement; Securities Litigation; Corporate Litigation; Insurance Coverage.

CARY J. MEER, admitted to bar, 1983, New York; 1986, District of Columbia. *Education:* University of Pennsylvania (B.S., 1979); Harvard University (J.D., 1982). ***PRACTICE AREAS:*** Securities Offerings; Securities Regulation; Commodities Regulation; Investment Partnerships; Private Placement; Corporate Finance.

(This Listing Continued)

GILBERT C. MILLER, admitted to bar, 1964, District of Columbia. *Education:* Harvard University (B.A., 1959); University of Michigan (J.D., 1963). ***PRACTICE AREAS:*** SEC Enforcement; Securities Litigation; Appellate Practice.

RICHARD CHARLES MILLER, admitted to bar, 1989, District of Columbia. *Education:* Harvard University (B.A., 1980); University of Pennsylvania (J.D., 1985). ***PRACTICE AREAS:*** Investment Company Law; Securities Regulation; Corporate Finance.

CHARLES R. MILLS, admitted to bar, 1977, California; 1979, District of Columbia; 1986, Virginia; 1989, New York; 1990, Maryland. *Education:* Occidental College (B.A., 1974); Georgetown University (J.D., 1977). ***PRACTICE AREAS:*** Securities Litigation; SEC Enforcement; Securities Arbitration; Securities Regulation; Commodities Regulation.

MICHAEL J. MISSAL, admitted to bar, 1982, District of Columbia. *Education:* Washington & Lee University (B.S., 1978); Catholic University of America (J.D., 1982). ***PRACTICE AREAS:*** SEC Enforcement; Blue Sky Law; Broker-Dealer Regulation; Self Regulatory Agency Investment; Securities Arbitration.

A. THOMAS MORRIS, admitted to bar, 1989, Pennsylvania; 1990, District of Columbia. *Education:* Georgetown University (B.S., 1986); Duke University (J.D., with high honors, 1989). ***PRACTICE AREAS:*** Environmental Insurance Coverage; Labor and Employment.

R. DARRELL MOUNTS, admitted to bar, 1988, Virginia; 1989, District of Columbia; 2001, California. *Education:* Washington and Jefferson College (B.A., 1984); College of William and Mary (J.D., 1988). ***PRACTICE AREAS:*** Investment Company Law; Investment Management; Investment Regulation; Mutual Funds; Securities Regulation.

BRUCE H. NIELSON, admitted to bar, 1987, Virginia; 1988, District of Columbia. *Education:* Brigham Young University (B.S., 1984); Harvard University (J.D., 1987). ***PRACTICE AREAS:*** Information Technology Contracts; Information Technology Licensing; Computer Contracts; Software Licensing.

THOMAS J. NOTO, admitted to bar, 1986, Maryland; 1989, District of Columbia. *Education:* Clark University (B.A., 1981); Catholic University (J.D., 1986). ***PRACTICE AREAS:*** Consumer Banking; Fair Lending; Truth in Lending; Consumer Credit Compliance; Lender Regulation.

SUZAN ONEL, admitted to bar, 1990, Pennsylvania; 1991, District of Columbia. *Education:* University of Pennsylvania (B.A., 1986); University of Virginia (J.D., 1990).

LAURENCE E. PLATT, admitted to bar, 1982, District of Columbia. *Education:* University of Pittsburgh (B.A., 1976); George Washington University (J.D., 1982). ***PRACTICE AREAS:*** Housing Law; Banks and Banking; Business Law; Finance; Consumer Law.

ALAN C. PORTER, admitted to bar, 1978, District of Columbia. *Education:* Lehigh University (B.A., 1973); Case Western Reserve University (J.D., 1976); Georgetown University (LL.M., 1980). ***PRACTICE AREAS:*** Investment Company Law; Investment Management; Securities Regulation.

THEODORE L. PRESS, admitted to bar, 1970, District of Columbia and U.S. Tax Court. *Education:* Cornell University (A.B., 1965); Columbia University (J.D., 1968). ***PRACTICE AREAS:*** Federal Income Tax; Corporate Tax Planning; Partnership Taxation; Investment Partnerships; Business Trusts.

GLENN R. REICHARDT, admitted to bar, 1977, District of Columbia; 1983, U.S. Court of International Trade. *Education:* Duke University (A.B., 1973); Harvard University (M.P.P., 1977; J.D., 1977). ***PRACTICE AREAS:*** SEC Enforcement; Antitrust and Trade Regulation; International Trade; Federal Civil Litigation; Alternative Dispute Resolution.

JEFFREY B. RITTER, admitted to bar, 1981, District of Columbia; 1983, Ohio. *Education:* The Ohio State University (B.A., M.A., 1976); Duke University (J.D., 1979). ***PRACTICE AREAS:*** Electronic Commerce; Information and Privacy; Mergers and Acquisitions; Commercial Law; International Trade.

ROBERT H. ROSENBLUM, admitted to bar, 1987, New York; 1992, District of Columbia. *Education:* State University of New York at Binghamton (B.A., 1983); Georgetown University (J.D., 1986). ***PRACTICE AREAS:*** Investment Partnerships; Financial Services Regulation; Broker-Dealer Regulation; Investment Regulation; Private Placements.

WILLIAM AUBREY SCHMIDT, admitted to bar, 1973, Connecticut; 1983, District of Columbia. *Education:* University of Virginia (B.A., 1970; J.D., 1973); Georgetown University Law Center (LL.M., 1983).

PHILLIP L. SCHULMAN, admitted to bar, 1975, Maryland; 1976, District of Columbia. *Education:* Northeastern University (B.A., 1972); Northeastern University School of Law (J.D., 1975). ***PRACTICE AREAS:*** Administrative Law; Finance; Housing Law; Real Estate; Regulatory Law.

LYNN A. SCHWEINFURTH, admitted to bar, 1991, Massachusetts; 1998, District of Columbia. *Education:* Cornell University (B.S., 1988); Boston University School of Law (J.D., cum laude, 1991). ***PRACTICE AREAS:*** Investment Company Law; Investment Management; Investment Regulation; Mutual Funds.

(This Listing Continued)

KEVIN MICHAEL SHEYS, admitted to bar, 1987, District of Columbia. *Education:* Gustavus Adolphus College (B.A., 1984); University of Minnesota (J.D., 1987). ***PRACTICE AREAS:*** Transportation.

DONALD W. SMITH, admitted to bar, 1978, District of Columbia. *Education:* Yale University (B.A., 1966); University of Virginia (M.A., 1969; J.D., 1978). ***PRACTICE AREAS:*** Banking Regulation; Securities Regulation; Investment Company Law; Export Regulation.

RONALD W. STEVENS, admitted to bar, 1973, District of Columbia. *Education:* Carleton College (B.A., 1969); University of Virginia (J.D., 1972). ***PRACTICE AREAS:*** Banking Litigation; Directors and Officers Liability; Securities Fraud Class Actions; Complex Litigation; Trial Practice.

DONALD R. STONE, admitted to bar, 1963, Minnesota; 1987, District of Columbia. *Education:* University of Wisconsin, Madison (B.S., 1960; LL.B., 1963, conferred to J.D., 1966). ***PRACTICE AREAS:*** Food, Drug and Medical Device Law; Products Liability.

IRA L. TANNENBAUM, admitted to bar, 1968, District of Columbia. *Education:* Brown University (A.B., 1962); University of Michigan (J.D., 1967). ***PRACTICE AREAS:*** Thrift Institution Regulation; Banking Regulation; International Banking Law.

DANIEL J. TOBIN, admitted to bar, 1991, Maryland; 1992, District of Columbia. *Education:* Columbia College (B.A., 1982); University of Virginia (M.A., 1987); University of Maryland (J.D., 1991). ***PRACTICE AREAS:*** Civil Litigation; Commercial Litigation; Employment Litigation.

STEPHEN G. TOPETZES, admitted to bar, 1988, Wisconsin; 1990, District of Columbia. *Education:* University of Minnesota (B.A., 1985); Georgetown University (J.D., 1988). ***PRACTICE AREAS:*** Civil Litigation; SEC Enforcement; Trial Practice; Securities Arbitration; Securities Class Actions.

ROBERT A. WITTIE, admitted to bar, 1970, District of Columbia. *Education:* University of Michigan (A.B., 1967); Harvard University (J.D., 1970). ***PRACTICE AREAS:*** Investment Management; Mutual Funds; Electronic Commerce; Privacy; Uniform Commercial Code; Secured Finance.

GARY L. YINGLING, admitted to bar, 1968, Georgia; 1969, District of Columbia. *Education:* University of North Carolina (B.S., 1962); Purdue University (M.S., 1966); Emory University (J.D., 1968). ***PRACTICE AREAS:*** Food and Drug Regulation.

ROBERT J. ZUTZ, admitted to bar, 1979, District of Columbia. *Education:* Tufts University (B.A., 1974); New York University (J.D., 1977). ***PRACTICE AREAS:*** Investment Company Law; Investment Management; Investment Regulation; Mutual Funds; Broker-Dealer Regulation.

OF COUNSEL

CATHERINE S. BARDSLEY, admitted to bar, 1976, District of Columbia. *Education:* Wellesley College (B.A., 1971); Boston University (J.D., 1974); New York University School of Law (LL.M., Taxation, 1975). ***PRACTICE AREAS:*** Investment Company Law; Investment Management; Mutual Funds; Financial Services Regulation; ERISA.

GEORGE L. CHRISTOPHER, admitted to bar, 1961, District of Columbia. *Education:* Harvard College (B.A., 1953); Harvard Law School (LL.B., 1957). ***PRACTICE AREAS:*** Financial Institutions Law; Corporate Law.

PAUL GONSON, admitted to bar, 1954, New York; 1999, District of Columbia. *Education:* University of Buffalo (1949-1951; LL.B., cum laude, 1954). ***PRACTICE AREAS:*** Securities Litigation; Securities Regulation; SEC Enforcement; Insider Trading; U.S. Supreme Court Litigation.

FRANCIS THORNTON GREENE (1908-1992).

KATHY KRESCH INGBER, admitted to bar, 1986, New York and Connecticut; 1988, District of Columbia. *Education:* Cornell University (B.A., 1982); Boston University (J.D., 1985). ***PRACTICE AREAS:*** Investment Management; Corporate; Securities.

HENRY L. JUDY, admitted to bar, 1968, Maryland and District of Columbia; 1969. *Education:* Georgetown University (A.B., 1961; J.D., 1968). ***PRACTICE AREAS:*** Financial Institutions Law; Business; Technology Law; Electronic Commerce; Year 2000 Computer Conversion.

DEAN E. MILLER, admitted to bar, 1960, Illinois; 1999, District of Columbia. *Education:* Drake University (B.A., 1957); Harvard University (J.D., 1960). ***PRACTICE AREAS:*** Financial Institutions Law.

EMALEE G. MURPHY, admitted to bar, 1980, District of Columbia. *Education:* Oberlin College (A.B., 1968); American University (J.D., 1980). ***PRACTICE AREAS:*** Food and Drug Regulation; Medical Devices; Alternative Health Care Products; Personal Care Products; Animal Drug Regulation.

(This Listing Continued)

KIRKPATRICK & LOCKHART LLP, Washington—Continued

CHARLES DIRK PETERSON, admitted to bar, 1990, Pennsylvania; 1996, District of Columbia. *Education:* University of Tulsa (B.A., 1986); Washington University (J.D., 1990). ***PRACTICE AREAS:*** Securities; Corporate.

LESLIE A. SOWLE, admitted to bar, 1990, Illinois; 1999, California (Not admitted in District of Columbia). *Education:* Randolph-Macon Woman's College (B.A., 1980); University of Chicago (M.A., 1983); Northwestern University (J.D., 1990). ***PRACTICE AREAS:*** Intellectual Property; Technology Law.

DICK THORNBURGH, admitted to bar, 1957, Pennsylvania; 1998, District of Columbia. *Education:* Yale University (B.Eng., 1954); University of Pittsburgh (LL.B., 1957). ***PRACTICE AREAS:*** Economic Development; Corporate Investigations; Federal Criminal Law; Americans with Disabilities Act; Government Relations.

LEGISLATIVE CONSULTANT

GEORGE W. KOCH. *Education:* University of Cincinnati (B.B.S., 1948; LL.B., 1950; J.D., 1950).

ASSOCIATES

Alissa Jennifer Altongy
Mark C. Amorosi
Erin K. Ardale (Not admitted in DC)
Angela Y. Ball
Ann Marie Begley
Eric Berger
Michele Levy Berlove
Emily J. Booth
Christopher J. Costello
Rebecca L. Dandeker
James E. Day
Oscar A. Del-Cid (admission pending)
Amy S. Doig (Not admitted in DC)
Christopher E. Dominguez
Courtney Eaton (admission pending)
Eric John Edwardson
Jodi Finder
Edward Fishman
Leigh M. P. Freund
Ranji Martelli Garrett
Suzanne Fay Garwood (Not admitted in DC)
Kari M. Gibbs (admission pending)
Tata Goebel (admission pending)
Jennifer R. Gonzalez
Allison W. Harrison
Benjamin S. Hayes
Kimberley H. Haynes
Jennifer L. Hieb (admission pending)
Lance W. High
Michael Henry Hinckle
Shirley A. Hinton
Ronald A. Holinsky (Not admitted in DC)
Sean R. Hunt
Julia Reynolds Johnson
Steven M. Kaplan
Karsie Kish (admission pending)
Rebecca L. Kline
Ivan B. Knauer
Kristie D. Kully
David A. Kurzweil
Alexandra C. LaFrankie
Stavroula E. Lambrakopoulos
Alicia L. Lewis (Not admitted in DC)
Patricia A. Maxey (Not admitted in DC)
John M. McCann (Not admitted in DC)
Mignon McLemore
Ndenisarya M. Meekins (Not admitted in DC)
Marc Mehrespand
Phillip A. Minnick (Not admitted in DC)
Lucrecia Renea Moore
Krista Patterson (admission pending)
Adam C. Paul
Mark D. Perlow
Francine J. Rosenberger
Tara L. Royal
Lori L. Schneider
Tara C. Sirmans
Sheldon B. Sommer (Not admitted in DC)
Tracie D. Spear
Jon A. Stanley (admission pending)
Fatima Sulaiman
Sean R. Sullivan (Not admitted in DC)
Jon M. Talotta
Nicholas G. Terris
David U. Thomas
Courtney S. Thornton
Carol M. Tomaszczuk
Joseph P. Vitale
Nanci L. Weissgold
Gregory S. Wright
George J. Zornada
Rachael M. Zufall

LARRY H. KIRSCH

5301 WISCONSIN AVENUE, NW, SUITE 640
WASHINGTON, D.C. 20015
Telephone: 202-237-6600
Fax: 202-237-0258
Email: DClawyer@aol.com
URL: http://www.lawyers.com/larrykirschlaw

Commercial Transactions, Commercial Real Estate, Real Estate Acquisitions, Real Estate Sales, Commercial Real Estate Sales, Commercial Real Estate Development, Shopping Center Law, Commercial Leasing, Landlord and Tenant, Lease Finance, Real Estate Litigation, Complex Commercial Litigation, Settlements, Workouts, Bankruptcy, Chapter 7, 11, 13, Commercial Loans.

FIRM PROFILE: For over 15 years, Mr. Kirsch has represented small Business Owners, Lenders, Entrepreneurs, Developers, Mortgage Brokers and International Corporation in a regional Commercial Transaction and Real Estate practice. Mr. Kirsch is well known throughout the Washington, D.C. and Maryland Metro area. His clients have included Retailers Distributors, Restaurants, E-Commerce Businesses, Automotive and Fuel Companies, Manufacturers, and Professional Associations.

LARRY H. KIRSCH, born Brooklyn, New York, May 18, 1959; admitted to bar, 1985, Maryland; 1988, District of Columbia. *Education:* State University of New York at Binghamton (B.A., with honors, 1981); George Washington University (J.D., with honors, 1985). Adjunct Professor, Montgomery College, 1998—. *Member:* The District of Columbia Bar; Maryland State and American Bar Associations. ***PRACTICE AREAS:*** Real Estate Law; Corporate Law; Wills; Probate Law.

KIVITZ & LIPTZ, LLC

WASHINGTON, D.C.

(See Chevy Chase, Maryland)

General Civil and Trial Practice before all Courts and Government Agencies, Business, Corporate, Real Estate, Family, Personal Injury, Banking, Bankruptcy, Medical Malpractice and Landlord/Tenant Law.

K.K.M., P.A.

WASHINGTON, D.C.

(See Bethesda, Maryland)

Business Law, Corporate Law, Commercial Law, Corporate Taxation, Finance, Intellectual Property, Labor and Employment, Personnel Policies, Restrictive Covenants, Executive Contracts, Executive Transfers, Federal Technology Transfer, Federal Trade Secrets.

MORRIS KLEIN

WASHINGTON, D.C.

(See Bethesda, Maryland)

Elder Law, Medicare and Medicaid, Guardianship and Conservatorship, Trusts and Estates, Probate and Wills, Disability Planning and Trusts, Public Policy, Nonprofit Organizations Law.

KLEINFELD, KAPLAN AND BECKER

Established in 1953

SUITE 900, 1140 NINETEENTH STREET, N.W.
WASHINGTON, D.C. 20036
Telephone: 202-223-5120
Telecopier: 202-223-5619
Email: kkb@kkblaw.com
URL: http://www.kkblaw.com

San Francisco, California Office: One Market Street, Steuart Tower, Suite 1450. Telephone: 415-538-0014. Telecopier: 415-538-0016.

Practice before all Courts and Government Agencies. Regulatory and Administrative Law involving Food, Drugs, Cosmetics, Medical Devices, Dictary Supplements, Pesticides, Controlled Substances and Consumer Products.

FIRM PROFILE: Since its founding in 1953, Kleinfeld, Kaplan and Becker has concentrated its practice on regulatory and administrative law involving foods, pharmaceuticals, controlled substances, cosmetics, medical devices, pesticides, consumer products, and health care reimbursement. Several partners were formerly with federal agencies including the United States Department of Health and Human Services and the Food and Drug Administration. The firm frequently rep-

(This Listing Continued)

resents clients in litigation on food, drug and related issues before administrative agencies and the federal courts. It has a national and international practice, and represents a wide variety of clients including manufacturers and trade associations.

Members of the firm teach food and drug law courses at George Washington University and George Mason University. Attorneys from the firm also regularly present speeches, seminars and workshops, and have authored numerous articles on food and drug law topics. From 1949 to 1992, members of the firm edited Federal Food, Drug, and Cosmetic Act Administrative and Judicial Record, a widely used multi-volume compilation of cases and FDA rulings. Since 1992, they have prepared case headnotes for the successor publication, Food and Drug Report, published by the Food and Drug Law Institute. The firm is a member of the Martindale-Hubbell Bar Register of Preeminent Law firms.

VINCENT A. KLEINFELD (1907-1993).

MEMBERS OF FIRM

ALAN H. KAPLAN, born New York City, April 26, 1930; admitted to bar, 1955, New York; 1960, District of Columbia. *Education:* New York University (A.B., 1951; LL.M., 1957); Harvard University (J.D., 1954). Food Law Institute Fellow, 1956-1957. Co-editor, *Federal Food, Drug and Cosmetic Act, Administrative and Judicial Record,* Kleinfeld and Kaplan, 1958-1960, 1961-1964, 1965-1968; Kleinfeld, Kaplan and Weitzman, 1969-1974, 1975-1977; Kleinfeld and Kaplan, 1978-1980, 1981-1982, 1983-1984, 1985-1986, 1987-1988, 1989-1990, 1991-1992. Professorial Lecturer, Food and Drug Law, George Washington University, 1961-1990. Trial Attorney, Food and Drug Division, Office of General Counsel, Department of Health, Education and Welfare, 1957-1960. *Member:* District of Columbia Bar; Bar Association of the District of Columbia; Federal and American Bar Associations. ***PRACTICE AREAS:*** Food, Drug and Cosmetic Law; Food and Drug Regulation; Drug and Medical Device Regulation; Federal Civil Litigation; Federal Administrative Law. **Email:** akaplan@kkblaw.com

THOMAS O. HENTELEFF, born Salt Lake City, Utah, May 24, 1943; admitted to bar, 1969, California; 1970, District of Columbia. *Education:* University of Utah (B.S., magna cum laude, 1965); Boalt Hall School of Law, University of California (J.D., 1968). Phi Beta Kappa. Law Clerk for Honorable David T. Lewis, U.S. Court of Appeals, Tenth Circuit, 1968-1969. FDA Commissioner's Special Citation, 1997. *Member:* District of Columbia Bar; State Bar of California; Federal and American Bar Associations. ***PRACTICE AREAS:*** Food, Drug and Cosmetic Law; Drug and Medical Device Regulation; Controlled Substances Law; Advertising Law; Food Labeling and Inspection; Pesticide Regulation; Federal Regulatory Law; Federal Civil Litigation; Corporate Investigations. **Email:** toh@kkblaw.com

RICHARD S. MOREY, born New York, N.Y., May 6, 1938; admitted to bar, 1966, New York; 1967, District of Columbia. *Education:* University of Pennsylvania (B.S., in Chem.E., 1960); Columbia University (J.D., magna cum laude, 1966). Recipient: James Kent Scholar; Harlan Fiske Stone Scholar. Editor, Columbia Law Review, 1965-1966. Law Clerk to Judge Sterry R. Waterman, U.S. Court of Appeals for the Second Circuit, 1966-1967. Adjunct Professor, Food and Drug Law, George Mason University Law School, 1989—. *Member:* District of Columbia Bar; Federal and American Bar Associations. [Lieut. (j.g.), U.S. Navy, 1960-1963]. ***PRACTICE AREAS:*** Food, Drug and Cosmetic Law; Food and Drug Regulation; Drug and Medical Device Regulation; Controlled Substances Law; Advertising Law. **Email:** rmorey@kkblaw.com

PETER O. SAFIR, born New York, N.Y., April 1, 1945; admitted to bar, 1973, New York; 1975, District of Columbia. *Education:* Princeton University (A.B., cum laude, 1967); Yale University (J.D., 1972). Professorial Lecturer, Food and Drug Law, George Washington University Law School, 1991—. *Member:* District of Columbia Bar; American Bar Association. ***PRACTICE AREAS:*** Food, Drug and Cosmetic Law; Drug and Medical Device Regulation; Advertising Law; Federal Civil Litigation; Corporate Investigations. **Email:** psafir@kkblaw.com

KINSEY S. REAGAN, born Nazareth, Pennsylvania, September 4, 1950; admitted to bar, 1975, Massachusetts; 1979, District of Columbia. *Education:* Rensselaer Polytechnic Institute (B.S., cum laude, 1972); Harvard University (J.D., cum laude, 1975). Attorney, U.S. Department of Health and Human Services, 1975-1980. *Member:* District of Columbia Bar; Massachusetts, Federal and American Bar Associations; American Health Lawyers Association. ***PRACTICE AREAS:*** Food, Drug and Cosmetic Law; Drug and Medical Device Regulation; Controlled Substance Law; Animal Drug Regulation; Food Labeling and Inspection; Pesticide Regulation; Advertising Law; Health Care Reimbursement; Federal Civil Litigation; Corporate Investigations. **Email:** kreagan@kkblaw.com

PETER R. MATHERS, born Camden, New Jersey, January 12, 1955; admitted to bar, 1979, District of Columbia. *Education:* Rensselaer Polytechnic Institute (B.S., cum laude, 1976); Yale University (J.D., 1979). Omicron Delta Epsilon. *Member:* District of Columbia Bar; American Bar Association. ***PRACTICE AREAS:*** Food, Drug and Cosmetic Law; Food and Drug Regulation; Drug and Medical Device Regulation; Controlled Substances Law; Advertising and Labeling; Corporate Investigations. **Email:** pmathers@kkblaw.com

BONNIE A. BEAVERS, born Dallas, Texas, May 19, 1958; admitted to bar, 1983, District of Columbia; 1984, Texas. *Education:* Duke University (B.A., magna cum laude, 1980); University of Texas (J.D., 1983). Pi Sigma Alpha. Member, The Review of Litigation, 1982-1983. Chair, Federal Bar Association, Food and Drug Subcommittee. *Member:* District of Columbia Bar; Women's Bar Association of the District of Columbia; State Bar of Texas; American Bar Association. ***PRACTICE AREAS:*** Food, Drug and Cosmetic Law; Food and Drug Regulation; Drug and Medical Device Regulation; Controlled Substances Law; Advertising Law. **Email:** bbeavers@kkblaw.com

DANIEL R. DWYER, born Jamestown, New York, September 16, 1955; admitted to bar, 1985, Maryland; 1988, District of Columbia. *Education:* State University of New York at Buffalo (B.A., 1977); Georgetown University (J.D., 1984). Phi Beta Kappa. Adjunct Professor, Food and Drug Law, George Mason University Law School, 1996—. Investigator and Legal Advisor to the Vice Chairman, U.S. International Trade Commission, 1984-1987. *Member:* District of Columbia Bar; Maryland State and American Bar Associations. ***PRACTICE AREAS:*** Food, Drug and Cosmetic Law; Drug and Medical Device Regulation; Food Labeling and Inspection; Advertising Law; Corporate Investigations. **Email:** ddwyer@kkblaw.com

GLENN E. DAVIS, born Antioch, California, May 12, 1949; admitted to bar, 1974, California; 1975, District of Columbia. *Education:* London School of Economics; University of the Pacific (A.B., summa cum laude, 1970); University of California, Boalt Hall School of Law (J.D., 1973). Phi Kappa Phi. General Counsel, Pharmaceutical Marketing Research Group, Inc., 1990—. *Member:* State Bar of California; The District of Columbia Bar; American Bar Association (Vice Chair, Committee on Food and Drug Law); Orange County Regulatory Affairs Discussion Group. ***PRACTICE AREAS:*** Food, Drug and Cosmetic Law; Drug and Medical Device Regulation; Advertising Law. **Email:** gdavis@kkblaw.com

PRESCOTT M. LASSMAN, born Lexington, Virginia, February 5, 1963; admitted to bar, 1991, Maryland; 1992, District of Columbia. *Education:* Yale University (B.A., cum laude, 1985); University of Texas (M.A., 1988); University of Virginia (J.D., 1991). Order of the Coif. Member: University of Virginia Law Review; Virginia Environmental Law Journal. Author: "U.S. Device Tracking Regulations," Regulatory Affairs Journal, Vol. 2, No. 2, May, 1994. *Member:* District of Columbia Bar; American Bar Association. ***PRACTICE AREAS:*** Food, Drug and Cosmetic Law; Food and Drug Regulation; Drug and Medical Device Regulation; Advertising Law; Federal Civil Litigation. **Email:** plassman@kkblaw.com

ASSOCIATES

STACY L. EHRLICH, born Syosset, New York, May 18, 1968; admitted to bar, 1994, Georgia; 1995, District of Columbia. *Education:* Emory University (B.A., magna cum laude, 1990); Hebrew University; Harvard University (J.D., cum laude, 1993). Phi Beta Kappa. Deans Scholar. Vice-President, Board of Student Advisors. Law Clerk to the Honorable Alexander B. Denson, U.S. District Court, Eastern District of North Carolina, 1993-1994. Associate, Hogan and Hartson, 1994-1996. *Member:* State Bar of Georgia; Bar Association of the District of Columbia; American Bar Association. ***PRACTICE AREAS:*** Food, Drug and Cosmetic Law; Food and Drug Regulation; Drug and Medical Device Regulation; Advertising Law; Federal Civil Litigation. **Email:** sehrlich@kkblaw.com

JENNIFER A. DAVIDSON, born Bethesda, Maryland, May 31, 1969; admitted to bar, 1994, Maryland; 1995, District of Columbia. *Education:* University of Michigan (B.A., with high distinction, 1991); University of Virginia School of Law (J.D., 1994). Order of Coif. Articles Editor, Virginia Journal of Social Policy and the Law. *Member:* Maryland and American Bar Associations; The District of Columbia Bar. ***PRACTICE AREAS:*** Food, Drug and Cosmetics Law; Food and Drug Regulation; Drug and Medical Device Regulation; Advertising Law; Civil Litigation. **Email:** jdavidson@kkblaw.com

STACEY L. VALERIO, born Burlington, Vermont, August 30, 1970; admitted to bar, 1996, Massachusetts; 1997, District of Columbia. *Education:* University of Pennsylvania (B.A., summa cum laude, 1991); George Washington University (J.D., 1995). Phi Betta Kappa. Member, Journal of International Law and Economics. ***PRACTICE AREAS:*** Food, Drug and Cosmetic Law; Drug and Medical Device Regulation; Advertising Law; Civil Litigation. **Email:** svalerio@kkblaw.com

ROBERT O. WINTERS, born Newton, New Jersey, May 4, 1967; admitted to bar, 2000, Virginia (Not admitted in District of Columbia). *Education:* Haverford College (B.S., Biology, 1989); University of North Carolina School of Public Health (M.S.P.H., Environmental Science/Toxicology, 1994); University of Virginia (J.D., 2000). *Member:* Virginia Bar Association. ***PRACTICE***

(This Listing Continued)

KLEINFELD, KAPLAN AND BECKER, Washington—Continued

AREAS: Food, Drug and Cosmetic Law; Food and Drug Regulation; Drug and Medical Device Regulation; Food Labeling and Inspection; Advertising Law.

KLIMASKI & GRILL, P.C.

Established in 1977

1400 K STREET, N.W.
SUITE 1000
WASHINGTON, D.C. 20005-2409
Telephone: 202-296-5600
Fax: 202-296-5601
URL:http://www.klimaskigrill.com
Email: kgpc@igc.org
URL: http://www.lawyers.com/klimaskilaw

Military Law, Employment Law, Labor Relations, Civil Rights Law, Police Misconduct, Employment Benefits, Security Clearances, Criminal Defense, Personal Injury, Auto Accidents, Bankruptcy, Small Business and Contracts.

FIRM PROFILE: Klimaski & Grill, P.C., is a public interest-oriented litigation and legal counseling practice serving clients in the District of Columbia and Maryland, as well as in the Federal and Military courts of the United States. Because of its small size and diverse practice areas, Klimaski & Grill devotes its full and personalized attention to providing outstanding professional services to meet its clients' legal needs.

JAMES R. KLIMASKI, born Montclair, New Jersey, February 2, 1946; admitted to bar, 1976, District of Columbia; 1977, U.S. District Court, District of Columbia, U.S. District Court, District of Maryland, U.S. Tax Court, U.S. Court of Appeals for the Armed Forces, U.S. Court of Appeals for District of Columbia, Fourth and Federal Circuits and U.S. Supreme Court; 1982, Maryland. *Education:* Spring Hill College (B.S., 1967); New School for Social Research (M.A., 1973); Antioch School of Law (J.D., 1976). Member, National Employment Lawyers Association. *Member:* District of Columbia Bar (Chairperson, Court Rules Committee, 1995-1997); National Lawyers Guild (Regional Vice President, 1984-1986; Member, Steering Committee, Military Law Task Force); Metropolitan Washington Employment Lawyers Association (Member, Board of Directors, 1993—); Judge Advocates Association. ***SPECIAL AGENCIES:*** Government Accountability Project (GAP), Litigation Director. ***PRACTICE AREAS:*** Employment Law; Military Law; Security Clearances; Pension Rights Law; Personal Injury; Criminal Law. ***Email:*** kgpc@igc.org

ANDREA S. GRILL, born Bronx, New York, December 28, 1964; admitted to bar, 1989, Pennsylvania; 1990, District of Columbia, U.S. District Court, District of Columbia, U.S. District Court, District of Maryland, U.S. Court of Appeals, District of Columbia and U.S. Supreme Court. *Education:* Boston University (B.A., cum laude, 1986); Georgetown University (J.D., 1989). Member, The Tax Lawyer. *Member:* American Bar Association; The District of Columbia Bar (Member, Nominating Committee, Board of Governors, 1993); Metropolitan Washington Employment Lawyers Association; National Lawyers Guild. ***SPECIAL AGENCIES:*** U.S. Department of Labor, Civil Rights Division, Trial Attorney; U.S. Department of Justice, Office of Justice Programs, Attorney-Advisor. ***PRACTICE AREAS:*** Employment Law; Labor Relations; Police Misconduct; Civil Rights; Discrimination; Bankruptcy. ***Email:*** kgpc@igc.org

OF COUNSEL

LYNN I. MILLER, born Allentown, Pennsylvania, March 6, 1949; admitted to bar, 1977, District of Columbia; 1987, Maryland; U.S. District Court for the District of Columbia; U.S. District Court, District of Maryland; U.S. Court of Appeals, Fourth, Seventh, Eighth and for the District of Columbia Circuits; U.S. Supreme Court and U.S. Court of Appeals for the Armed Forces. *Education:* Smith College (B.A., 1971); Washington College of Law (J.D., 1977; LL.M., 1992). Member, American University Law Review; Dean's Fellowship, Teaching Assistant in Legal Methods, 1976-1977. Instructor, Legal Writing and Research, Washington College of Law, The American University , Fall 1982. Author: "Fair Use, Biographers and Unpublished Works: Life After H.R. 4412," Journal of the Copyright Society of the USA, Vol. 40. 3, p. 349 (Spring 1993); Reproductive Rights Law Reporter, Editor (1986); "Evolution of Abortion Law in North America," with Roy Lucas. In: Abortion and Sterilization: Medical and Social Aspects, Jane E. Hodgson, M.D., ed., New York, Grune & Stratton (1981). *Member:* National Lawyers Guild. ***PRACTICE AREAS:*** Employment Law; Police Misconduct; Pension Rights Law; Civil Rights.

MARTIN F. KLINGENBERG

1025 THOMAS JEFFERSON STREET, N.W.
SUITE 425 WEST
WASHINGTON, D.C. 20007
Telephone: 202-223-1066
Fax: 202-462-7450
Email: martin6@attglobal.net

U.S., European and Asian Company Law, International Investment, International Commercial Negotiations.

FIRM PROFILE: For over 25 years the firm has advised, counseled and represented European, Asian and U.S. firms in connection with corporate and business issues. Representation includes merger and acquisition, joint venture, licensing, distribution, finance and cross-border commercial issues.

MARTIN F. KLINGENBERG, born Enid, Oklahoma, July 5, 1942; admitted to bar, 1968, Oklahoma, District of Columbia, U.S. Tax Court and U.S. Court of Military Appeals; 1969, U.S. Court of Appeals for the District of Columbia Circuit; 1970, U.S. Court of Appeals, Tenth Circuit; 1974, U.S. Supreme Court; 1987, U.S. Court of International Trade, U.S. Court of Appeals, Fourth Circuit and U.S. District Court, District of Maryland; 1993, New York. *Education:* Phillips University (B.S., 1964); University of Oklahoma (J.D., 1968). Editor in Chief, International Contract Adviser. Kluwer Law International The Hague, 1988-1994. Co-Author, with Pattison: "Soviet Announcement Should Stir Interest of U.S. Corporations," Legal Times, Vol. IX, No. 38, March 2, 1987; "Joint Ventures From the View of Western Investors," Economicheskya Geseta, Moscow, #50, December 1986; "Joint Ventures in the People's Republic of China: The New Legal Environment," Virginia Journal of International Law, Vol. 19, Summer, 1979. Author: "The Canton Trade Fair: The Initiation of United States-Chinese Trade," Virginia Journal of International Law, Vol. 13, Fall, 1972; "Trade with China, The Practical Side of Trade with China," American Management Association, 1972. Lecturer, The Adjunct Faculty, The American University, Washington College of Law, 1974-1975. Trustee, Foundation for National Museums and Galleries, Czech Republic. Member, Advisory Board, The Fund for Arts and Culture in Central and Eastern Europe. *Member:* New York State (Member, Sections on: Tax; Entertainment, Arts and Sports) and Oklahoma Bar Associations; District of Columbia Bar. ***REPORTED CASES:*** U.S. v. Stuver, 845 F 2d 73 (4th Cir. 1988); U.S. v. Harding, 469 F 2d 114 (D.C. Circuit, 1972). ***PRACTICE AREAS:*** International; Mergers and Acquisitions; Finance; Corporate; Antitrust; Import Relief.

BRUCE J. KLORES & ASSOCIATES, P.C.

Established in 1983

915 FIFTEENTH STREET, N.W.
SUITE 300
WASHINGTON, D.C. 20036
Telephone: 202-628-8100
Telecopier: 202-628-1240
URL: http://www.klores.com
Email: office@klores.com
URL: http://www.lawyers.com/klores

Arlington, Virginia Office: Suite 708, 2009 North 14th Street. Telephone: 703-527-0970. Telecopier: 703-522-1250.

Civil Trial Practice with emphasis in Medical Negligence, Birth Trauma, Pediatric Malpractice and Professional Liability.

FIRM PROFILE: The attorneys and staff at Bruce J. Klores & Associates, P.C. are dedicated to zealously, creatively, ethically and compassionately protecting people in need.

BRUCE J. KLORES, born Brooklyn, New York, December 14, 1954; admitted to bar, 1981, District of Columbia; 1982, Maryland and U.S. District Court for the District of Columbia; 1983, U.S. Court of Appeals for the District of Columbia Circuit; 1985, U.S. District Court, District of Maryland and U.S. Supreme Court; 1991, U.S. Court of Appeals, Fourth Circuit; 1992, Virginia and U.S. District Court, Eastern District of Virginia. *Education:* Brandeis University (B.A., in Political Science, 1976); Catholic University of America (J.D., 1981). Recipient, Martin Luther King Jr. Corporate Community Service Award, 2001 (United Planning Organization). Listed in, *The Best Lawyers in America.* Named, Lawyer of the Year, Trial Lawyers Association of Metropolitan Washington, D.C., 1998-1999. Author: *Medical Malpractice in Virginia,* Klores, B., Grad. J. Teaching Appointments: Adjunct Professor of Law, Catholic University of America, 1992-1995. Trial Techniques, Federal Practice Institute; Medical Malpractice in Virginia, National Business Institute; Masters, Trial Program, American Board of Trial Advocates. Faculty Chair, How to Litigate a Medical Malpractice Case, George Washington University, Continuing Legal Education Program, 1994—. Program Director: Medicine For Lawyers, District of Columbia Bar, 1998-1999 and 2000-2001; "How to Try an Effective Civil Case," D.C.

(This Listing Continued)

CLE, August 1999; "Litigation of Federal Tort Claims Cases, Military Bar Association, October, 1999. Vice President, Richmond Teachers' Association, 1977-1978. Mediator, Superior Court of the District of Columbia and the U.S. District Court for the District of Columbia. Arbitrator, Superior Court of the District of Columbia. Member, Judicial Conference, District of Columbia Circuit, 1991 and 1994. Member: Committee on Arrangements, District of Columbia Judicial Conference, 1998; Jury Instruction Revision Committee, District of Columbia, 1998 and 2000. *Member:* District of Columbia Bar (Steering Committee Injury to Persons and Property Section, 1997—; Chair, Medical Malpractice Subcommittee); Maryland State and Virginia Bar Associations; Trial Lawyers Association of Metropolitan Washington, D.C. (Member, Board of Governors, 1988—; President. 1995-1996); The Association of Trial Lawyers of America; International Association of Jewish Lawyers and Jurists; Maryland Trial Lawyers Association; Virginia Trial Lawyers Association; The Counselors. ***REPORTED CASES:*** District of Columbia v. Perez, 694 A2d 882 (1997). ***PRACTICE AREAS:*** Civil Trials; Professional Negligence. ***Email:*** bjk@klores.com

RICHARD J. FOGELSON, born Denville, New Jersey, February 10, 1967; admitted to bar, 1992, Maryland; 1993, Virginia, District of Columbia, Colorado; 1997, U.S. Supreme Court; U.S. Court of Appeals, Fourth Circuit; U.S. District Court, District of Maryland; U.S. District Court for the District of Columbia and U.S. District Court, Eastern District of Virginia. *Education:* Colgate University (B.A., Political Science, 1989); Syracuse University (J.D., with honors, 1992). National Order of the Barristers. Moot Court Board. National Trial Team. Emergency Medical Technician, Commonwealth of Virginia. Author, "The Truth Behind Political Action Committees," 1989 Colgate Political Review. Faculty: Critical Care Medicine, Transports and the Law, University of Maryland Emergency Health Services, 1995-2001. Teaching Appointment, Adjunct Professor, George Washington University Medical Center, Emergency Medicine and the Law. Assistant Program Director, Medicine for Lawyers, District of Columbia Bar, 1999-2001. Member, Board of Directors, McLean Fire Department. *Member:* Fairfax, Arlington, Virginia State, Maryland State and American Bar Associations; District of Columbia Bar; Trial Lawyers Association of Metropolitan Washington; Virginia Trial Lawyers Association; The Association of Trial Lawyers of America. ***PRACTICE AREAS:*** Civil Trial Practice; Professional Negligence; Emergency Medicine.

LESLEY S. ZORK, born Kalabo, Zambia, May 4, 1958; admitted to bar, 1988, District of Columbia; 1996, Maryland. *Education:* Atlantic Union College (A.S., Nursing, 1979); Antioch School of Law (J.D., 1988). Contributing Editor, District of Columbia Trial Lawyers News Publication. Faculty Member, How to Litigate a Medical Malpractice Case, District of Columbia Bar, G.W. University, CLE, 2000. Practicing Registered Nurse, Obstetrics and Gynecology, 1979-1988. Senior Trial Attorney, Public Defender Service for the District of Columbia, 1988-1995. *Member:* District of Columbia Bar (Member, Steering Committee Injury to Persons and Property Section; Chairman, Medical Malpractice Committee); Trial Lawyers Association of Washington, D.C. (Member, Board of Governors); District of Columbia Womens' Bar Association. ***PRACTICE AREAS:*** Civil Trials; Medical Malpractice Law. ***Email:*** elzork@klores.com

PATRICIA C. KARPPI, born Washington, D.C., March 8, 1966; admitted to bar, 1993, Virginia, U.S. District Court, Eastern and Western Districts of Virginia, U.S. Court of Appeals, Fourth Circuit; 1995, District of Columbia, U.S. District Court, District of Columbia and U.S. Court of Appeals, D.C. Circuit. *Education:* University of Virginia (B.A., 1988); Catholic University of America (J.D., with highest honors, 1993). Editor-in-Chief, Journal of Contemporary Health Law & Policy, 1992-1993. Author: "Statutory Caps: Involuntary Contribution to Medical Malpractice Insurance Crisis or a Reasonable Means for Obtaining Affordable Health Care?," 9J. Contemporary Health Law & Policy, 1993. Law Clerk to Hon. John M. Steadman, District of Columbia Court of Appeals, 1993-1994. *Member:* Virginia Bar Association; District of Columbia Bar; Trial Lawyers Association of the District of Columbia. ***LANGUAGES:*** Serbo-Croatian. ***REPORTED CASES:*** Paul v. Bier, 765 A.2d 40 (D.C. App. 2000); Molchon v. Tyler, Virginia Supreme Court, June 2001; Dudley v. Bungee International Corp., 76 F.3d 372 (1996). ***PRACTICE AREAS:*** Professional Negligence; Civil Practice. ***Email:*** pck@klores.com

KNIGHT, MANZI, NUSSBAUM & LAPLACA, P.C.

WASHINGTON, D.C.

(See Upper Marlboro)

General Civil and Criminal Trial and Appellate Practice before State and Federal Courts. Negligence, Corporate, Family, Estate, Administrative, Education, Employment, Banking, Real Estate, Zoning, Commercial, Criminal, Insurance, Municipal Law.

KNOPF & BROWN

Established in 1987

1050 SEVENTEENTH STREET, N.W., SUITE 1200
WASHINGTON, D.C. 20036
Telephone: 202-785-8200
Telecopier: 202-331-0174
URL: http://www.knopf-brown.com
URL: http://www.lawyers.com/knopf&brownlaw

General and Administrative Practice and Litigation, Antitrust and Trade Regulation, Environmental, Land Use and Zoning, Local Government, Energy, Trade Associations, Nonprofit Organizations, Corporate Law.

FIRM PROFILE: The firm provides counseling and litigation services in a broad range of civil matters. Clients are businesses; individuals; local governments; homeowners' associations; and national and local non-profit professional, trade and civic associations. The partners are known for their in-depth expertise in the areas of zoning and land use, planning, environmental, solid waste, antitrust, municipal and administrative law. The firm's practice involves representing clients in federal, state and local courts and agencies, principally in Montgomery County, Maryland and the District of Columbia.

NORMAN G. KNOPF, born Cornwall, New York, May 23, 1939; admitted to bar, 1964, New York; 1968, U.S. Supreme Court; 1970, District of Columbia; 1978, Maryland. *Education:* Cornell University (A.B., 1961); Columbia University (LL.B., 1964). Member, Board of Editors, Columbia Law Review, 1963-1964. Law Clerk to Frederick Bryan, U.S. District Court Judge for the Southern District of New York, 1964-1966. Attorney, U.S. Department of Justice, Civil Division, Appellate Section, 1966-1969. *Member:* Maryland State and American (Member, Section of Antitrust Law) Bar Associations; Association of Maryland Municipal Attorneys. ***PRACTICE AREAS:*** Litigation; Land Use and Zoning; Local Government; Antitrust and Trade Regulation. ***Email:*** knopf@knopf-brown.com

DAVID W. BROWN, born Newton, Massachusetts, December 9, 1944; admitted to bar, 1974, New York; 1988, District of Columbia. *Education:* University of Washington (B.A., 1966); Boston University (J.D., 1973). Victor H. Kramer Foundation Fellow, University of Chicago Law School, 1984-1985. Note Editor, Boston University Law Review, 1972-1973. Law Clerk to Honorable Edward R. Neaher, Eastern District of New York, 1973-1975. Acting Chief and Assistant Chief, Energy Section, Antitrust Division, Department of Justice, 1981-1985. *Member:* Federal Energy and American (Member, Sections of: Antitrust; Litigation) Bar Associations. ***PRACTICE AREAS:*** Antitrust and Trade Regulation; Energy; Trade Associations; Litigation. ***Email:*** brown@knopf-brown.com

BARRY S. SHANOFF, born Chicago, Illinois, August 24, 1943; admitted to bar, 1968, Illinois; 1976, District of Columbia; 1977, Maryland. *Education:* Northwestern University (B.S., 1964; J.D., 1967). Counsel, Office of Enforcement, U.S. Environmental Protection Agency, Washington, D.C., 1975-1977. *Member:* American Bar Association; International Municipal Lawyers Association. ***PRACTICE AREAS:*** Environmental Law; Local Government Law; Solid Waste. ***Email:*** shanoff@knopf-brown.com

SUSAN G. GOLDBERG, born New York, N.Y., May 15, 1955; admitted to bar, 1986, Maryland; 1987, District of Columbia. *Education:* L'Université de Dakar; Bryn Mawr College (A.B., magna cum laude, 1977); Georgetown University Law Center (J.D., 1985). Notes and Comments Editor, The Tax Lawyer, 1984-1985 and Senior Editor, The National Jewish Law Review, Georgetown University, 1984-1985. ***LANGUAGES:*** French, Spanish and Wolof. ***PRACTICE AREAS:*** Non-profit Organizations; Corporate Law; Litigation. ***Email:*** goldberg@knopf-brown.com

KOHN, KOHN & COLAPINTO, P.C.

3233 P STREET, N.W.
WASHINGTON, D.C. 20007
Telephone: 202-342-6980
Fax: 202-342-6984
Email: kkc@kkc.com
URL: http://www.kkc.com

Whistleblower Litigation, Retaliatory Discharge, Civil Litigation, Nuclear Energy, Qui Tam Litigation, Privacy Law, Forensic Science, Congressional Investigations, Labor and Employment, First Amendment Law, Government Contract Fraud, Freedom of Information, False Claims Act.

STEPHEN M. KOHN, born Plainfield, New Jersey, September 6, 1956; admitted to bar, 1985, Pennsylvania; 1987, District of Columbia. *Education:* Boston University (B.S., magna cum laude, 1979); Brown University (M.A., 1981); Northeastern University (J.D., 1984). Student Law Clerk, Honorable A. Leon Higginbotham, Jr., U.S. Court of Appeals, Third Circuit, 1983-1984. Author: *Concepts and Procedures in Whistleblower Law*, Quorum, 2000; *The*

(This Listing Continued)

KOHN, KOHN & COLAPINTO, P.C., Washington—Continued

Whistleblower Litigation Handbook, John Wiley & Sons, 1991; *American Political Prisoners:* Prosecutions under the Espionage and Sedition Act, Praeger, 1994; *The Labor Lawyer's Guide to the Rights and Responsibilities of Employee Whistleblowers*, Quorum Books, 1988; *Jailed for Peace*, Greenwood Press, 1986; *Protecting Environmental & Nuclear Whistleblower*, NIRS, 1985. Adjunct Professor, Antioch School of Law, 1984-1988. Chair, National Whistleblower Center, 1988—. ***PRACTICE AREAS:*** Whistleblower Litigation; Civil Liberties; Qui Tam Litigation; Labor and Employment.

MICHAEL D. KOHN, born Plainfield, New Jersey, December 28, 1954; admitted to bar, 1985, District of Columbia and Pennsylvania; 1990, U.S. Supreme Court. *Education:* Rutgers University (B.S., 1979); Antioch Law School (J.D., 1985). Articles Editor, Antioch Law Journal, 1985. Co-Author: *The Labor Lawyer's Guide to the Rights and Responsibilities of Employee Whistleblowers*, Quorum Books (1988); "An Overview of Federal and State Whistleblower Protections," 4 Antioch Law Journal 99 (Summer 1986). General Counsel, National Whistleblower Center, 1988—. ***PRACTICE AREAS:*** Whistleblower Litigation; Labor and Employment Law; Retaliatory Discharge; Qui Tam Litigation.

DAVID K. COLAPINTO, born Springfield, Massachusetts, December 4, 1958; admitted to bar, 1988, District of Columbia; 1989, Massachusetts. *Education:* Boston University (B.A., 1984); Antioch School of Law (J.D., 1987). General Counsel, Forensic Justice Project, 1998—. *Member:* National Association of Criminal Defense Lawyers. ***PRACTICE AREAS:*** Whistleblower Litigation; Civil Liberties; Privacy Law; Freedom of Information; Forensic Science.

MARY JANE WILMOTH, born Anchorage, Alaska, April 10, 1969; admitted to bar, 1994, District of Columbia. *Education:* George Mason University (B.A., 1989); Franklin Pierce Law Center (J.D., 1992). Trustee, National Whistleblower Center Legal Defense and Education Fund, 1998—. ***Email:*** mjw@whistleblowers.org

CHRISTOPHER J. WESSER, born El Cajon, California, November 4, 1969; admitted to bar, 1999, Virginia (Not admitted in District of Columbia). *Education:* LeMoyne College (B.A., 1996); College of William & Mary (J.D., 1999). [U.S. Army, 1987-1990]. ***PRACTICE AREAS:*** Whistleblower Litigation. ***Email:*** wesserz@widowmaker.com

CHIEF INVESTIGATOR

KRIS J. KOLESNIK, born Waterbury, Connecticut, February 16, 1953. *Education:* University of Dallas (B.A., 1975). Senior Counselor, 1992-2000 and Legislative Assistant, 1982-1992 to U.S. Senator Charles Grassley with responsibility for passage of legislation, False Claims Act Amendments of 1986 and Whistleblower Protection Act of 1989 and oversight hearings. Supervised oversight investigations and hearings, including Defense Contractor Fraud, 1983-1988, Revolving Door Legislation, 1986-1987, Federal Employee Gag Orders, 1988-2000, WACO, Ruby Ridge, 1995, Inspector General Accountability, 1996-2000, FBI Crime Lab, 1997-1998, TWA Flight 800, 1999, Wen Ho Lee, 1999-2000. Advisor on government oversight to the leadership of the U.S. House of Representatives and Senate, 1995-1998. ***PRACTICE AREAS:*** Congressional Investigations; Government Investigations; False Claims Act; Government Contract Fraud. ***Email:*** kjk@whistleblowers.org

KOLTUN & KING, P.C.

Established in 1991

1146 19TH STREET, N.W.

SUITE 250

WASHINGTON, D.C. 20036

Telephone: 202-331-0123

Facsimile: 202-466-5011

Email: koltunlaw@koltunlaw.com

URL: http://www.koltunlaw.com

Securities Offerings, Private Placements, Blue Sky Law, Corporate Finance, Health Care Finance, International Securities, Mergers and Acquisitions, Spin-Offs, Corporate Formation, Buy-Sell Agreements, Corporate Contracts, Employment Contracts, Non-Competition and Non-Solicitation Agreements.

FIRM PROFILE: Koltun & King, P.C. provides corporate, finance, securities and general business representation to established and early stage businesses. The Firm specializes in all phases of capital formation, including public and private securities offerings of U.S. and foreign entities, and in privately negotiated purchases and sales of businesses.

(This Listing Continued)

LAWRENCE W. KOLTUN, born New Orleans, Louisiana, February 3, 1950; admitted to bar, 1975, Louisiana; 1978, U.S. Supreme Court; 1981, District of Columbia. *Education:* Washington University (A.B., magna cum laude, 1972); University of Pennsylvania (J.D., 1975). Phi Beta Kappa. Adjunct Professor, Securities Law, George Mason University School of Law, 1986-1987. Lecturer, Securities Law, Georgetown University District of Columbia Bar Association, Continuing Legal Education, 1988. Counsel, Division of Investment Management and Office of the General Counsel, U.S. Securities and Exchange Commission, 1979-1983. Member, Board of Directors, Association for Corporate Growth, National Capital Chapter. *Member:* The District of Columbia Bar; Louisiana State and American (Member, Corporation, Banking and Business Law Section) Bar Associations. ***PRACTICE AREAS:*** Securities Law; Mergers, Acquisitions and Divestitures; Business Law; International Securities; Corporate Law; Health Care Financings. ***Email:*** lkoltun@koltunlaw.com

SUSAN J. KING, born Wellesley, Massachusetts, September 25, 1956; admitted to bar, 1986, Virginia; 1989, District of Columbia. *Education:* Sweet Briar College (A.B., 1978); George Washington University (J.D., with honors, 1986). *Member:* Virginia State Bar; The District of Columbia Bar. ***PRACTICE AREAS:*** Corporate Law; Mergers and Acquisitions; Business Law; Securities Law; Private Placement; Blue Sky Law. ***Email:*** sking@koltunlaw.com

ARTHUR F. KONOPKA

Established in 1982

4530 WISCONSIN AVENUE, N.W., SUITE 200

WASHINGTON, D.C. 20016

Telephone: 202-686-0600

Maryland 301-983-4040

Fax: 202-686-0896

Email: afk@relawpro.com

URL: http://www.lawyers.com/konopkalaw

Commercial and Residential Real Estate Law, Real Estate Settlements, Real Estate Litigation (including issues involving Titles, Zoning, Tax Assessment and Performance Contracts), Landlord and Tenant Law, Shopping Center Law, Leases, Commercial Real Estate Transactions, Wills and Probate, Trusts and Estates.

FIRM PROFILE: The firm has a regional practice handling real estate and probate matters throughout the District of Columbia, Maryland and Virginia. The firm's clients include individuals, partnerships, corporations and real estate entrepreneurs.

ARTHUR F. KONOPKA, admitted to bar, 1966, New York; 1967, Florida; 1971, District of Columbia; 1981, Maryland. *Education:* Creighton University (B.A., 1961); Goethe Institute, Munich (Arbiture Diplom, 1962); Columbia University (J.D., 1966). Instructor, Licensure of Real Estate Agents, Maryland. Attorney, Office of General Counsel, National Aeronautics and Space Administration, Kennedy Space Center and NASA Headquarters, Washington, D.C., 1966-1971. Program Director, National Science Foundation, 1971-1981. Member: Montgomery County Association of Realtors; Maryland Association of Realtors; Washington, D.C. Association of Realtors. *Member:* Montgomery County (Member, Real Estate Section) and American (Member, Real Property and Probate Section) Bar Associations; District of Columbia Bar (Member, Sections on: Real Estate; Probate); Maryland State Bar Association, Inc. (Member, Sections on: Real Estate; Probate). ***LANGUAGES:*** German. ***PRACTICE AREAS:*** Real Estate; Probate.

ASSOCIATES

WILLIAM J. GESSNER, born Nyack, New York, August 10, 1950; admitted to bar, 1983, Maryland; 1990, U.S. District Court, District of Maryland (Not admitted in District of Columbia). *Education:* Frostburg State University (B.A., 1973); University of Baltimore (J.D., 1982). Licensed Title Insurance Agent, 1996, Maryland. Intern to the Honorable Richard B. Latham, Sixth Judicial District of Maryland, 1980. Member, Parish Council, St. Mary's Catholic Church, Rockville, Maryland, 1996— President, 1997-2001. *Member:* Maryland State (Member, Real Property and Business Sections) and American Bar Associations. ***PRACTICE AREAS:*** Commercial Real Estate; Residential Real Estate; Landlord and Tenant Law; Probate; Lender Representation. ***Email:*** wjg@relawpro.com

WILLIAM W. WALLER, born Seaford, Delaware, March 23, 1952; admitted to bar, 1995, Maryland; 1996, U.S. District Court, District of Maryland; 1997, District of Columbia; 2000, U.S. Supreme Court; 2001, U.S. District Court, District of Columbia. *Education:* University of Delaware (B.A., 1976; M.A., 1981); Washington College of Law of American University (J.D., 1995). Order of the Barristers. *Member:* Montgomery County Bar Association (Member, Real Estate and Public Speakers Sections); District of Columbia Bar (Member, Real Estate Section); American Trial Lawyers Association. ***PRACTICE AREAS:*** Real Estate; Litigation; Probate. ***Email:*** bw@relawpro.com

(This Listing Continued)

OF COUNSEL

QUINN O'CONNELL, JR., born Washington, D.C., 1952; admitted to bar, 1996, District of Columbia; U.S. District Court, District of Columbia. *Education:* Regis College (B.S., 1974); American University (J.D., 1995). Law Clerk, Judge Gardner, Superior Court of the District of Columbia, 1995-1997. *Member:* The District of Columbia Bar (Member, Estates, Trusts and Probate Law Section; Real Estate, Housing and Land Use Section); Bar Association of the District of Columbia; American Bar Association (Member, Real Property, Probate and Trust Law Section); Charlotte E. Ray, American Inn of Court. ***PRACTICE AREAS:*** Real Estate; Probate; Litigation; Criminal Defense.

APPROVED AGENTS FOR: 1st American Title Insurance Company; Lawyers Title Insurance Co.

KOONZ, McKENNEY, JOHNSON, DePAOLIS & LIGHTFOOT

Established in 1979

SUITE 500, 2020 K STREET, N.W.
WASHINGTON, D.C. 20006
Telephone: 202-659-5500
Fax: 202-785-3719
Email: dc@koonz.com
URL: http://www.koonz.com

Greenbelt, Maryland Office: 6301 Ivy Lane, Suite 510. Telephone: 301-345-5700. Fax: 301-474-5578.

Falls Church, Virginia Office: Suite 400, George Mason Square, 103 W. Broad Street. Telephone: 703-237-9300. Fax: 703-533-5974.

Negligence, Medical Malpractice, Workers Compensation, Automobile, Torts, Products Liability, Aviation, Social Security, Federal Employers Liability Law, Industrial and Commercial Accident Liability, Aviation Accidents, Automobile and Public Transportation Accident Liability.

JOSEPH H. KOONZ, JR., born Cornwall, New York, November 27, 1934; admitted to bar, 1960, District of Columbia. *Education:* St. Anselm College (B.A., 1956); Georgetown University (LL.B., 1959). *Member:* The District of Columbia Bar; American Bar Association; The Association of Trial Lawyers of America; Trial Lawyers Association of Metropolitan Washington, D.C. (President, 1988; Trial Lawyer of the Year, 1990). Fellow, American College of Trial Lawyers. ***Email:*** jkoonz@koonz.com

ROGER C. JOHNSON, born Kalamazoo, Michigan, May 31, 1952; admitted to bar, 1977, District of Columbia. *Education:* University of Michigan (B.A., 1974); George Washington University (J.D., 1977). Law Clerk to the Honorable George H. Revercomb, District of Columbia Superior Court, 1977-1978. *Member:* The District of Columbia Bar; American Bar Association (Member, Section on Litigation); The Association of Trial Lawyers of America; The Trial Lawyers Association of Metropolitan Washington, D.C. (Member, Board of Governors, 1992-1998). (Board Certified Civil Trial Specialist by the National Board of Trial Advocacy). ***Email:*** rjohnson@koonz.com

PETER C. DePAOLIS, born Hartford, Connecticut, April 20, 1949; admitted to bar, 1976, Virginia and District of Columbia; 1982, U.S. Supreme Court, U.S. District Court, Eastern District of Virginia; U.S. District Court, District of Columbia; U.S. Court of Appeals, Fourth and District of Columbia Circuits. *Education:* Lafayette College (B.A., magna cum laude, 1971, Phi Beta Kappa); George Washington University (J.D., 1976). Order of the Coif. Law Clerk to the Hon. William E. Stewart, Jr., Associate Judge, Superior Court of the District of Columbia, 1976-1977. Assistant U.S. Attorney, Washington, D.C., 1977-1980. *Member:* Fairfax Bar Association (Board of Directors, 1996-1998; Treasurer, 1998-2000; President, 2000-2001); Virginia State Bar; The District of Columbia Bar; Virginia Trial Lawyers Association; The Association of Trial Lawyers of America. [First Lieutenant, U.S. Army, Infantry (Airborne), Military Intelligence, 1971-1973]. (Resident at Falls Church, Virginia Office). ***Email:*** pdepaolis@koonz.com

WILLIAM P. LIGHTFOOT, JR., born January 3, 1950; admitted to bar, 1977, Pennsylvania; 1980, District of Columbia. *Education:* Howard University (B.A., 1972); Washington University (J.D., 1977). Chairperson, D.C. Cable Television Design Commission, 1983-1984. Lecturer, Continuing Legal Education programs in Personal Injury, 1980—. District of Columbia Council Member at-Large, 1988-1996; Charlotte Rae American Inn of Court. *Member:* The District of Columbia Bar; Bar Association of the District of Columbia; American Bar Association; The Association of Trial Lawyers of America; Trial Lawyers Association of Metropolitan Washington; American Law Institute. (Board Certified, Civil Trial Specialist, by the National Board of Trial Advocacy). ***Email:*** wlightfoot@koonz.com

MARC FIEDLER, born New Haven, Connecticut, May 4, 1955; admitted to bar, 1985, Massachusetts; 1987, U.S. Court of Appeals for the District of Columbia Circuit; 1988, District of Columbia; U.S. District Court for the District of Columbia; U.S. Court of Appeals, Fourth Circuit; U.S. Supreme Court.

(This Listing Continued)

Education: Harvard University (B.A., 1978; J.D., 1984). Recipient, Lawyer of the Year Award, Trial Lawyers Association of Metropolitan Washington, D.C., 1989. Co-Founder and Executive Committee Member, Disability Rights Council of Greater Washington, 1992—. *Member:* The District of Columbia Bar; Bar Association of the District of Columbia; The Association of Trial Lawyers of America (Co-Chairman, 1996-1998, Amicus Committee); Trial Lawyers Association of Metropolitan Washington, D.C. (President, 2001-2002; Chairman, Amicus Curiae Committee, 1992—). ***Email:*** mfiedler@koonz.com

KAREN A. CRIST, born Dallas, Texas, September 22, 1955; admitted to bar, 1987, Virginia, Supreme Court of Virginia and U.S. District Court, Eastern District of Virginia; U.S. Court of Appeals, Fourth Circuit; 1988, District of Columbia, U.S. Court of Appeals for the District of Columbia Circuit and U.S. District Court for the District of Columbia. *Education:* Oberlin College (B.A., 1978); George Washington University (J.D., with honors, 1987). *Member:* The District of Columbia Bar; Fairfax, Arlington and American Bar Associations; Virginia State Bar; Virginia Trial Lawyers Association; Virginia Women's Attorneys Association (Past President). (Resident at Falls Church, Virginia Office). ***Email:*** kcrist@koonz.com

PAULETTE E. CHAPMAN, born Canal Zone, Panama, September 8, 1954; admitted to bar, 1988, District of Columbia. *Education:* George Mason University (B.A., 1976); George Washington University (J.D., with honors, 1988). Adjunct Faculty, Catholic University Law School, 1995 and 1996. *Member:* The District of Columbia Bar; Bar Association of the District of Columbia; The Women's Bar Association of the District of Columbia; The Association of Trial Lawyers of America; Council for Court Excellence; Trial Lawyers Association of Metropolitan Washington, D.C. (Board of Governors, 1998—). ***Email:*** pchapman@koonz.com

DAVID M. SCHLOSS, born Hartford, Connecticut, January 16, 1963; admitted to bar, 1988, District of Columbia. *Education:* Tufts University (B.A., cum laude, 1985); George Washington University (J.D.,1988). *Member:* The District of Columbia Bar; Bar Association of the District of Columbia; American Bar Association; The Association of Trial Lawyers of America; Trial Lawyers Association of Metropolitan Washington, D.C. ***Email:*** dschloss@koonz.com

KEITH W. DONAHOE, born New Brunswick, New Jersey, February 13, 1965; admitted to bar, 1990, New Jersey, Pennsylvania; 1991 District of Columbia and U.S. Court of Claims; 1992, U.S. District Court, District of Columbia and U.S. Court of Appeals for the District of Columbia Circuit; 1993, U.S. Court of Appeals for the Federal Circuit; 1994, U.S. Supreme Court; 1997, Maryland. *Education:* Villanova University (B.S., 1987); Georgetown University (J.D., 1990). *Member:* Prince Georges County and American Bar Associations; The District of Columbia Bar; Maryland Trial Lawyers Association; The Association of Trial Lawyers of America; Charles Fahy American Inns of Court. (Board Certified Civil Trial Specialist by the National Board of Trial Advocacy) (Resident at Greenbelt, Maryland Office). ***Email:*** kdonahoe@koonz.com

WILLIAM A. MUSTO, born Wilkes-Barre, Pennsylvania, February 24, 1961; admitted to bar, 1989, Virginia. *Education:* College of William & Mary (B.B.A., 1984); Howard University (J.D., 1989). *Member:* Arlington and Fairfax Bar Associations; Virginia State Bar; Northern Virginia Young Lawyers Association (Vice-President); Virginia Trial Lawyers Association. (Resident at Falls Church, Virginia Office). ***Email:*** wmusto@koonz.com

JULIE H. HEIDEN, born Ohio, November 6, 1966; admitted to bar, 1992, Virginia and District of Columbia. *Education:* Shepherd College (B.S., 1988); George Mason University (J.D., 1992). Phi Delta Phi; Phi Alpha Theta. Recipient, American Jurisprudence Award in Trial Advocacy. *Member:* Fairfax, Virginia and American Bar Associations; The District of Columbia Bar; Virginia Women's Attorneys Association; Virginia Association of Trial Lawyers; District of Columbia Trial Lawyers. (Resident at Falls Church, Virginia Office). ***Email:*** jheiden@koonz.com

HAROLD E. BRAZIL, admitted to bar, 1973, Ohio; 1974, District of Columbia and U.S. District Court, District of Columbia and District of Maryland. *Education:* Ohio State University (B.A., 1970; J.D., 1973); Georgetown University (LL.M., 1978). Member, District of Columbia City Council. *Member:* The District of Columbia Bar; National and American Bar Associations; The Association of Trial Lawyers of America. ***Email:*** hbrazil@koonz.com

DANIEL S. KOZMA, born Pittsburgh, Pennsylvania, January 16, 1950; admitted to bar, 1977, District of Columbia; 1978, U.S. District Court for the District of Columbia; 1981, U.S. Court of Appeals, Fifth, Eighth, Ninth and Eleventh Circuits; 1982, U.S. Court of Appeals for the District of Columbia Circuit; 1983, U.S. Supreme Court. *Education:* University of Pittsburgh (B.A., 1971); Cornell University (J.D., 1977). *Member:* The District of Columbia Bar; The Association of Trial Lawyers of America; Trial Lawyers Association of Metropolitan Washington, D.C. [U.S. Army, 1971-1974]. ***Email:*** dkozma@koonz.com

FRANK R. KEARNEY, born Chicago, Illinois, October 13, 1967; admitted to bar, 1993, Virginia; 1995, District of Columbia. *Education:* Duquesne University (B.A., cum laude, 1990); George Mason University School of Law (J.D., 1993). *Member:* Alexandria Bar Association; Virginia State Bar; The District of

(This Listing Continued)

KOONZ, McKENNEY, JOHNSON, DePAOLIS & LIGHTFOOT, Washington—Continued

Columbia Bar; The Association of Trial Lawyers of America; District of Columbia Trial Lawyers Association. [Capt., U.S. Army Reserve]. ***Email:*** fkearney@koonz.com

DOUGLAS K. ALLSTON, JR., born Wilmington, Delaware, June 7, 1970; admitted to bar, 1995, Maryland; 1996, Virginia. *Education:* University of Notre Dame (B.A., Government, 1992); Catholic University of America (J.D., 1995). *Member:* Prince Georges County and Montgomery County Bar Associations; Virginia State Bar. (Resident at Greenbelt, Maryland Office). ***Email:*** dallston@koonz.com

STEVEN H. KAMINSKI, born Stamford, Connecticut, February 7, 1969; admitted to bar, 1999, Maryland; 2000, Arizona and District of Columbia. *Education:* George Washington University (B.A., 1992); Catholic University School of Law (J.D., cum laude, 1999). Note and Comment Editor, Catholic University Law Review, 1998-1999. *Member:* Association of Trial Lawyers of America. ***PRACTICE AREAS:*** Consumer Class Actions; Personal Injury; Medical Malpractice; Employment Law. ***Email:*** skaminski@koonz.com

ANGELIA T. ROWE, born Washington, D.C.; admitted to bar, 1992, Maryland. *Education:* Howard University (B.A., 1983); Georgetown University (J.D., 1987). (Resident at Greenbelt, Maryland Office). ***PRACTICE AREAS:*** Personal Injury; Workers Compensation. ***Email:*** arowe@koonz.com

JARVIS F. TAIT, born Dayton, Ohio, April 17, 1972; admitted to bar, 1999, District of Columbia. *Education:* University of Notre Dame (B.B.A., 1994); Duquesne University (J.D., 1998). *Member:* District of Columbia Bar; Association of Trial Lawyers of America; District of Columbia Trial Lawyers Association. ***PRACTICE AREAS:*** Personal Injury. ***Email:*** jtait@koonz.com

DORA MONICA RODRIGUES, born Washington, D.C., May 15, 1971; admitted to bar, 2001, District of Columbia, U.S. District Court, District of Columbia and U.S. Court of Appeals, District of Columbia Circuit. *Education:* American University (B.A., 1993); Stetson University (J.D., 2000). Paramedic License, May 1996. *Member:* Bar Association of the District of Columbia; The District of Columbia Bar; American Bar Association; The Women's Bar Association of the District of Columbia; The Association of Trial Lawyers of America; Trial Lawyers Association of Metropolitan Washington, D.C. ***LANGUAGES:*** Spanish and Portuguese. ***PRACTICE AREAS:*** Personal Injury; Medical Malpractice; Workers Compensation. ***Email:*** drodrigues@koonz.com

LAW OFFICE OF RUPAL G. KOTHARI, P.C.

1900 K STREET NW, SUITE 1050
WASHINGTON, D.C. 20006
Telephone: 202-466-2921
Fax: 202-466-2925
Email: rgkothari@aol.com
URL: http://www.rgkotharilaw.com

Litigation, Nationality Matters, Employment and Family Based Litigations.

RUPAL G. KOTHARI, born Pittsburgh, Pennsylvania, February 27, 1970; admitted to bar, 1997, Maryland; 1998, District of Columbia. *Education:* The Johns Hopkins University (B.A., 1991); American University (J.D., 1996). *Member:* Maryland State and American Bar Associations (Member, Section: International Law); The District of Columbia Bar; South Asian Bar; American Immigration Association; Indian American Bar Association (President). ***LANGUAGES:*** French; Italian; Gujarati. ***PRACTICE AREAS:*** Immigration and Naturalization; Employment; Family Corporations.

KOZUSKO LAHEY HARRIS LLP

1666 K STREET, NW, SUITE 400
WASHINGTON, D.C. 20006
Telephone: 202-457-7200
Fax: 202-457-7201
URL: http://www.lawyers.com/kozlaw

Closely Held Business Taxation, Business Law, Venture Capital, Tax Planning, International Estate Planning, Estate Planning, Charitable Trusts and Non Profit Organizations, Trusts and Estates, Dispute Resolution, Tax Controversy, Tax Litigation.

PARTNERS

DONALD D. KOZUSKO, admitted to bar, 1970, Ohio; 1974, District of Columbia. *Education:* Villanova University (B.A., cum laude, 1967); Harvard University (J.D., cum laude, 1970). ***PRACTICE AREAS:*** Closely Held Business Taxation; Charitable Trusts; Non Profit Organization; International Estate Planning; Venture Capital; Contested Trusts and Estates. ***Email:*** dkozusko@kozlaw.com

(This Listing Continued)

JOHN H. LAHEY, admitted to bar, 1972, Ohio; 1998, District of Columbia. *Education:* Miami University (B.S., 1968); The Ohio State University (J.D., 1971). ***PRACTICE AREAS:*** Taxation; International Law; Nonprofit and Charitable Organizations; Business Law; Trusts and Estates. ***Email:*** jlahey@kozlaw.com

GEORGE N. HARRIS, JR., admitted to bar, 1990, Texas; 1998, District of Columbia. *Education:* Texas A & M University (B.A., 1985); California Western School of Law (J.D., 1990). Member, Advocacy Honors Board. Recipient, Tax Division Outstanding Attorney Award, 1993. Trial Attorney, Tax Division, U.S. Department of Justice, 1990-1997. *Member:* American Arbitration Association. ***PRACTICE AREAS:*** Tax Controversies; Dispute Resolution; Tax Legislation; Tax Planning. ***Email:*** gharris@kozlaw.com

MILES C. PADGETT, admitted to bar, 1994, Missouri; 1995, Illinois; 1999, District of Columbia. *Education:* Cornell University (B.A., 1991); Vanderbilt University (J.D., 1994). Harry Caplan Fellow. ***LANGUAGES:*** Latin and Greek. ***PRACTICE AREAS:*** Closely Held Business Taxation; Business Law; Charitable Trusts and Foundations; Nonprofit Organizations; International Estate Planning; Tax Planning; Estate Planning. ***Email:*** mpadgett@kozlaw.com

STEPHEN K. VETTER, admitted to bar, 1991, California; 1993, Colorado and District of Columbia. *Education:* University of California at Davis (B.S., 1987; J.D., 1991); Georgetown University (LL.M. in Taxation, with distinction, 1995). Tau Beta Pi. Recipient, American Jurisprudence Award in Business Organizations. Law Clerk: Hon. Volney V. Brown, Jr., Chief U.S. Magistrate-Judge, Central District of California, 1991-1993; Hon. Charles E. Clapp II, U.S. Tax Court, 1995-1997. ***PRACTICE AREAS:*** Taxation; Venture Capital; Private Business; Nonprofit Organizations; Estate Planning. ***Email:*** svetter@kozlaw.com

ASSOCIATE

RASHAD WAREH, admitted to bar, 1997, Virginia; 2000, District of Columbia. *Education:* American University (B.A., magna cum laude, 1993); Duke University (J.D., magna cum laude, 1997). ***PRACTICE AREAS:*** Closely Held Business Taxation; Tax Planning; International Estate Planning; Estate Planning; Venture Capital. ***Email:*** rwareh@kozlaw.com

OF COUNSEL

JEFFREY M. BUCHER, admitted to bar, 1958, California; 1975, District of Columbia. *Education:* Occidental College (B.A., 1954); Stanford University (J.D., 1957). Adjunct Banking Law Professor, George Washington University School of Law, 1994-1998. Lecturer, American Institute for Political and Economic Studies, Charles University, Prague, Czech Republic. President, The Vasek and Anna Maria Polak Charitable Foundation, Inc. ***PRACTICE AREAS:*** Financial Institution Regulation. ***Email:*** jbucher@kozlaw.com

KRAMER & ASSOCIATES, P.C.

WASHINGTON, D.C.

(See Arlington, Virginia)

Domestic and International Patent, Trademark, Copyright, Unfair Competition and Related Matters; U.S. and International Patent and Technical Literature Research; Patent Research Groups: Software/Internet/Business Methods Patents; Chemical/Biotechnology/Medical; Electrical/Communications; Mechanical/Design Patents; Printing and Photocopying.

KRAMON & GRAHAM, P.A.

WASHINGTON, D.C.

(See Baltimore, Maryland)

General Civil, Criminal and Appellate Practice. Real Estate, Corporate, Environmental, Health, Construction, Insurance and Surety Law.

KRAUSE & FERRIS

WASHINGTON, D.C.

(See Annapolis, Maryland)

General Civil and Trial Practice in all Courts. Real Estate, Banking, Probate, Corporations, Family Law, Divorce, Custody Support, Business, Criminal, DWI, Traffic Violations, Personal Injury, Automobile Accidents, Zoning and Land Use, Taxation, Military Law and Appellate Litigation.

NINA KRAUT

3815 YUMA STREET, N.W.
WASHINGTON, D.C. 20016-2213
Telephone: 202-745-0300
*Fax: 202-745-0300 * 51*
Email: ninakraut@aol.com
URL: http://www.lawyers.com/kraut

Federal Litigation, Constitutional Law, First Amendment Law, Civil Liberties, Civil Rights, Discrimination, Womens Rights, U.S. Supreme Court Litigation, Complex Litigation, Public Interest Law, Civil Appeals, Freedom of Information, Freedom of Religion.

FIRM PROFILE: Ms. Kraut is a former assistant legal director for the ACLU's D.C. Chapter with over 20 years of trial experience. In her national practice, Ms. Kraut has represented many clients in a variety of civil liberties trials and appeals.

NINA KRAUT, admitted to bar, 1978, Pennsylvania; 1981, District of Columbia. *Education:* New York University (1966, B.S.); Franklin Pierce Law Center (1978, J.D.). ***PRACTICE AREAS:*** Federal Litigation; Constitutional Law; First Amendment Law; Civil Liberties; Civil Rights; Discrimination; Womens Rights; U.S. Supreme Court Litigation; Complex Litigation; Public Interest Law; Civil Appeals; Freedom of Information; Freedom of Religion.

KRAUTHAMER & STAHL

CHARTERED

WASHINGTON, D.C.

(See Chevy Chase, Maryland)

Corporate, Real Estate, Estate Planning, Probate, Wills, Trusts, Elder Law, Americans with Disabilities Act, Contracts, Leases, Prenuptial Agreements and Like-Kind Exchanges.

KROOTH & ALTMAN LLP

Established in 1947

SUITE 400
1850 M STREET, N.W.
WASHINGTON, D.C. 20036-5803
Telephone: 202-293-8200
Telecopier: 202-872-0145, 202-775-5872

General, Administrative and Business Practice. Corporate, Taxation, Securities, Bond Finance, Real Estate, Health Care, Housing and Urban Development, Banking, Mortgage Banking, Creditor's Rights, Entertainment Law. Civil Litigation in all Federal and State Courts and Agencies.

MEMBERS OF FIRM

DAVID L. KROOTH (1907-1978).

NORMAN S. ALTMAN (1912-1997).

E. JOSEPH KNOLL, born Nebraska City, Nebraska, June 5, 1939; admitted to bar, 1964, Nebraska; 1965, District of Columbia. *Education:* University of Nebraska (B.S., 1961); Georgetown University (J.D., 1964). Delta Theta Phi. Attorney, Federal Housing Administration, 1964-1968. *Member:* The District of Columbia Bar; Nebraska State and American Bar Associations. ***Email:*** ejknoll@krooth.com

MICHAEL E. MAZER, born Springfield, Massachusetts, July 18, 1942; admitted to bar, 1967, Massachusetts; 1972, District of Columbia. *Education:* Yale University (B.A., cum laude, 1964); Harvard University (J.D., 1967). *Member:* The District of Columbia Bar; Massachusetts Bar Association. [Lieut., U.S. Navy, 1968-1971]. ***Email:*** mmazer@krooth.com

DONALD F. LIBRETTA, born West Springfield, Massachusetts, March 3, 1938; admitted to bar, 1965, Connecticut; 1966, District of Columbia. *Education:* U.S. Merchant Marine Academy (B.S., 1960); Georgetown University (J.D., 1965). Phi Delta Phi. Associate Editor, Georgetown Law Journal, 1964-1965. *Member:* The District of Columbia Bar; Hartford County and Connecticut Bar Associations. ***Email:*** dlibretta@krooth.com

DANIEL RANDOLPH COLE, JR., born Washington, D.C., May 19, 1941; admitted to bar, 1967, District of Columbia; 1968, Maryland. *Education:* Washington & Lee University (A.B., 1963); George Washington University (J.D., 1966). Attorney, Office of General Counsel, U.S. Department of Housing and Urban Development, 1970-1973. Acting Director (Chief Underwriter), Housing Production and Mortgage Credit Division, District of Columbia Area Office, U.S. Department of Housing and Urban Development, 1973-1976. *Member:* The District of Columbia Bar; Maryland State Bar Association. ***PRACTICE AREAS:*** Real Estate Development and Finance Law; Transactional Law. ***Email:*** rcole@krooth.com

(This Listing Continued)

PATRICK J. CLANCY, born Washington, D.C., May 17, 1945; admitted to bar, 1972, Maryland; 1980, District of Columbia. *Education:* University of Maryland (B.A., cum laude, 1967); Georgetown University (J.D., 1972). Omicron Delta Kappa; Pi Sigma Alpha. Assistant Attorney General, State of Maryland, 1975, 1976, 1978. Director, Community Development Administration, State of Maryland, 1977. Member, Howard County (Md.) Charter Review Commission, 1979. Chairman, Howard County, Maryland, Housing and Community Development Board, 1982-1986. Member, Maryland Governor's Commission on Condominiums, Cooperatives and Homeowners' Associations, 1985-1986. Adjunct Professor, University of Baltimore School of Law, 1982-1990. Lecturer in Entertainment Law, Omega School of Applied Recording Arts and Science, 1991—. *Member:* The District of Columbia Bar; Maryland State Bar Association; National Association of Bond Lawyers; Washington Area Lawyers for the Arts. ***Email:*** pclancy@krooth.com

JAMES F. PERNA, born Greenwich, Connecticut, December 1, 1947; admitted to bar, 1976, California; 1977, Connecticut and U.S. Tax Court; 1980, District of Columbia. *Education:* Cornell University (A.B., 1969); University of California at Berkeley (M.B.A., 1974); Boalt Hall School of Law, University of California at Berkeley (J.D., 1976); Georgetown University (LL.M., 1979). Beta Gamma Sigma. Editor, Industrial Relations Law Journal. Director, American University of Rome; Director, Homestead Mutual Funds. *Member:* National Association of Real Estate Investment Trusts. ***Email:*** jperna@krooth.com

HARRISON C. SMITH, born New York, N.Y., August 3, 1954; admitted to bar, 1979, Virginia and U.S. Court of Appeals, Fourth Circuit; 1980, District of Columbia. *Education:* Cornell University (B.S., 1976); Duke University (J.D., 1979). *Member:* The District of Columbia Bar; Virginia State Bar. ***Email:*** hsmith@krooth.com

DAVID A. BARSKY, born Plainfield, New Jersey, December 31, 1959; admitted to bar, 1986, Maryland; 1988, District of Columbia. *Education:* George Washington University (B.A., 1981; J.D., 1986). *Member:* The District of Columbia Bar; Maryland State and American Bar Associations. ***Email:*** dbarsky@krooth.com

JOHN E. VIHSTADT, born Berwyn, Illinois, June 15, 1952; admitted to bar, 1977, Iowa, Nebraska, U.S. District Court, District of Nebraska and U.S. District Court, District of Iowa; 1995, District of Columbia. *Education:* University of Nebraska (B.A., 1973; J.D., 1976). Delta Theta Phi. Member, Arlington, Virginia Commission on Housing, 1991-1997. Member, Board of Directors, National Housing Conference, 1991—. Member, Arlington, Virginia Planning Commission, 1997—. Minority Counsel, Select Committee on Aging, U.S. House of Representatives, 1981-1985. Executive Assistant to the President, Government National Mortgage Association, 1986-1989. *Member:* District of Columbia Bar; Nebraska State and American Bar Associations. ***PRACTICE AREAS:*** Mortgage Financing; Housing and Urban Development; Legislation. ***Email:*** jvihstadt@krooth.com

BONNIE HOCHMAN ROTHELL, born Brooklyn, N.Y., 1963; admitted to bar, 1988, Maryland; 1989, District of Columbia. *Education:* Brandeis University (B.A., cum laude, 1985); University of Miami (J.D., cum laude, 1988). Society of Wig and Robe. Who's Who Among World Women; Who's Who Among Law Students. Recipient, American Jurisprudence Book Awards: Contracts; Criminal Law; Criminal Procedure; Leadership Award. Articles and Comments Editor, University of Miami Inter-American Law Review, 1986-1988. Legal Intern to Judge William Hoeveler, U.S. District Court, Southern District of Florida, 1987-1988. Member, National Employment Lawyers Association. ***PRACTICE AREAS:*** Litigation; Employment Law; Alternative Dispute Resolution. ***Email:*** brothell@krooth.com

JON I. OPERT, born New York, N.Y., December 18, 1963; admitted to bar, 1989, New Jersey; 1990, New York; 1995, District of Columbia. *Education:* Lehigh University (B.S., 1986); George Washington University (J.D., 1989). ***PRACTICE AREAS:*** Real Estate Transactions. ***Email:*** jopert@krooth.com

OF COUNSEL

WILLIAM S. TENNANT, born Bellevue, Pennsylvania, July 4, 1931; admitted to bar, 1956, Illinois; 1960, U.S. Supreme Court; 1963, District of Columbia; 1966, Virginia. *Education:* Grove City College (A.B., magna cum laude, 1953); Northwestern University (J.D., 1956). Member, Board of Editors, Northwestern Law Review, 1953-1956. Editor, Journal of Air Law and Commerce, 1955-1956. Attorney, 1958-1961, Assistant to the General Counsel, 1961 and Assistant Chief Counsel, Urban Renewal, 1958-1962, Federal Housing Administration. ***Email:*** wtennant@krooth.com

WILLIAM J. DELANY, born Washington, D.C., May 26, 1931; admitted to bar, 1960, District of Columbia; 1961, U.S. Court of Appeals, District of Columbia Circuit; 1962, U.S. Court of Military Appeals, U.S. Claims Court and U.S. Tax Court; 1965, U.S. Supreme Court; 1975, Court of Appeals of Maryland. *Education:* Georgetown University (A.B., 1953; J.D., 1960). Attorney, Federal Housing Administration, Washington, D.C., 1961-1963. Assistant General Counsel, District of Columbia Redevelopment Land Agency, 1963-1964. *Member:* District of Columbia Bar; Maryland State Bar Association, Inc.;

(This Listing Continued)

KROOTH & ALTMAN LLP, Washington—Continued

American Bar Association. ***PRACTICE AREAS:*** Real Estate Law; Real Estate Finance; Affordable Housing Law; Probate Law. ***Email:*** wdelany@krooth.com

MICHAEL J. MILTON, born Washington, D.C., December 22, 1937; admitted to bar, 1964, Maryland; 1995, District of Columbia. *Education:* Harvard University (B.A., 1961; LL.B., cum laude, 1964). Registered Representative, National Association of Securities Dealers, 1984. Partner, Braiterman & Milton, 1966-1972. Assistant Attorney General and Counsel: Maryland Department of Economic Community Development, 1972-1980; U.S. Department of Housing and Urban Development, 1980-1983. Associate General Counsel, National Consumer Cooperative Bank, 1983-1984. *Member:* Maryland State Bar Association (Member, Committee on Municipal Securities, 1974-1987). ***Email:*** mmilton@krooth.com

ROBERT J. SICILIANO, born Neptune, New Jersey, August 31, 1941; admitted to bar, 1967, District of Columbia and U.S. Court of Appeals for the District of Columbia Circuit; 1975, U.S. Supreme Court, U.S. Tax Court; 1979, U.S. Court of Military Appeals. *Education:* Seton Hall University (B.S., 1963); Catholic University of America (J.D., 1966). Attorney, Refund Litigation Division, Office of Chief Counsel, Internal Revenue Service, 1966-1969. Chairman, Bar Association of the District of Columbia, Lawyer Referral Information Service Committee, 1981-1986. Adjunct Lecturer, Catholic University of America, 1981-1985. *Member:* District of Columbia Bar; Bar Association of the District of Columbia. ***PRACTICE AREAS:*** Estate Administration; Real Estate; Tax Audit. ***Email:*** bsiciliano@krooth.com

KENNETH A. LAZARUS, born Passaic, New Jersey, March 10, 1942; admitted to bar, 1967, New Jersey; 1976, District of Columbia. *Education:* University of Dayton (B.A., 1964); University of Notre Dame (J.D., 1967); George Washington University (LL.M., Tax, 1971). Adjunct Professor of Law, Georgetown University Law Center, 1979—. Trial Attorney U.S. Department of Justice, 1967-1971. Counsel, U.S. Senate Judiciary Committee, 1971-1974. Associate Counsel to the President of the United States, 1974-1977. *Member:* International Law Institute (Member, Board of Trustees, 1986—); American Law Institute (1977—). (Also Member, Lazarus & Associates). ***PRACTICE AREAS:*** Litigation; Legislation and Regulation; Foreign Investment.

PATRICIA PRITT TOADVINE, born Charleston, West Virginia, April 20, 1958; admitted to bar, 1985, Maryland; 1995, U.S. District Court, District of Maryland (Not admitted in District of Columbia). *Education:* University of Florida (B.A., 1979); Stetson University (J.D., 1982). ***PRACTICE AREAS:*** Multi-Family Housing; Health Care Facility Regulation; Mortgage Finance. ***Email:*** ptoadvine@krooth.com

ASSOCIATES

H. SCOTT JOHNSON, JR, born Plainfield, New Jersey, May 2, 1972; admitted to bar, 1997, Virginia and U.S. Court of Appeals, Fourth Circuit; 1998, U.S. District Court, Eastern District of Virginia (Not admitted in District of Columbia). *Education:* University of North Carolina at Chapel Hill (B.S., 1994); George Washington University Law School (J.D., 1997). Moot Court Board. Dean's Fellow, George Washington University Law School, 1996-1997. *Member:* American Bar Association. ***PRACTICE AREAS:*** Employment Law; Commercial Litigation. ***Email:*** sjohnson@krooth.com

RODERICK D. OWENS, born Alexandria, Virginia, March 21, 1972; admitted to bar, 1998, Maryland; 2000, District of Columbia. *Education:* University of Maryland (B.A., 1994); Tulane University School of Law (J.D., cum laude, 1998). Member: Federalist Society; International Law Society; Wechsler First Amendment Moot Court Team. ***PRACTICE AREAS:*** Real Estate Finance; Corporate Law. ***Email:*** rowens@krooth.com

MONICA E. MONROE, born Pittsburgh, Pennsylvania, January 17, 1974; admitted to bar, 1999, Maryland; 2000, U.S. District Court, District of Maryland (Not admitted in District of Columbia). *Education:* Boston University (B.A., 1985); George Washington University (J.D., 1998). Member, International Law Society, 1995-1997. Legal Intern to Judge Eugene R. Sullivan, U.S. Court of Appeals for the Armed Forces, 1997-1998. Law Clerk to Judge Linda Turner and Judge Robert Tignor, D.C. Supreme Court, 1998-2000. Chair, National BLSA Midatlantic Regional Convention, 1997. Member, BLSA, 1995-1998. ***PRACTICE AREAS:*** Employment Law; Commercial Litigation. ***Email:*** mmonroe@krooth.com

DEBORAH A. TURNER, born Smithtown, New York, 1972; admitted to bar, 2000, Maryland; 2001, District of Columbia and U.S. District Court, District of Maryland. *Education:* Emory University (B.A., cum laude, 1994); American University (J.D., cum laude, 1999). Pi Sigma Alpha. Member, ABA Administrative Law Review, American University, 1997-1999. *Member:* Maryland State and American Bar Associations; District of Columbia Bar. ***PRACTICE AREAS:*** Real Estate; Commercial Litigation; Employment Litigation. ***Email:*** dturner@krooth.com

ALEXANDRA STEFANOVIC, born Passaic, New Jersey, January 28, 1973; (admission pending). *Education:* Bucknell University (B.A., Political

(This Listing Continued)

Science; B.A., Spanish, 1995); Catholic University of America (J.D., 1999). Editorial Assiatant, The CommLaw Conspectus, Journal of Communications Law and Policy. Associate, Moot Court. Judicial Intern, Hon. Randall R. Rader, U.S. Court of Appeals, Federal Circuit, 1999. Law Clerk, Administrative Judges, Board of Contract Appeals, U.S. Department of Housing and Urban Development, 1999-2000. Author: "Judicial Nuts and Bolts," The Administrative Judiciary, Winter 1999. *Member:* New Jersey State, American and Inter-American Bar Associations. ***LANGUAGES:*** Spanish. ***PRACTICE AREAS:*** Real Estate; Finance. ***Email:*** astefanovic@krooth.com

GORDON C. F. CHIN, born Charleston, West Virginia, May 28, 1973; admitted to bar, 1999, West Virginia and U.S. District Court, Southern District of West Virginia (Not admitted in District of Columbia). *Education:* University of Miami (B.B.A., International Finance and Marketing, 1995); American University, Washington College of Law (J.D., 1998). Phi Delta Phi. First Place, National Corporate Law Competition: Widener University Ruby R. Vale Corporate Moot Court Competition, 1997. Member, American University Moot Court Board, 1997-1998. Legislative Intern to the Honorable John D. Rockefeller, IV, United States Senator, 1998. *Member:* West Virginia and American Bar Associations. ***LANGUAGES:*** Chinese. ***PRACTICE AREAS:*** Real Estate Finance; Mortgage Finance; Multi-Family Housing; Corporate Law. ***Email:*** gchin@krooth.com

AMY B. CONNELLY, born Baltimore, Maryland, February 1, 1970; admitted to bar, 2000, Maryland (Not admitted in District of Columbia). *Education:* Mount St. Mary's College (B.A., 1992); Georgetown University Law Center (J.D., 2000). *Member:* Maryland State Bar Association. ***PRACTICE AREAS:*** Commercial Real Estate; Corporate Law. ***Email:*** aconnelly@krooth.com

KRUKOWSKI & COSTELLO, S.C.

1401 EYE STREET NW, SUITE 1210
WASHINGTON, D.C. 20005
Telephone: 202-898-1031
Facsimile: 202-898-1311
URL: http://www.krukowski.com

Milwaukee, Wisconsin Office: 7111 West Edgerton Avenue, P.O. Box 28999, 53228-0999. Telephone: 414-423-1330. Telefax: 414-423-1694.

Representing Management in Labor and Employment Law.

ELLIOT H. SHALLER, born Brooklyn, New York, May 21, 1952; admitted to bar, 1977, District of Columbia; 1996, Maryland. *Education:* Brooklyn College of the City University of New York (B.A., magna cum laude, 1974); George Washington University (J.D., with honors, 1977; LL.M. in Labor Law, 1979). Law Clerk, U.S. Court of Appeals for the District of Columbia Circuit, 1979-1980. Author: "The Family and Medical Leave Act — Key Provisions and Potential Problems," 19 Employee Relations Law Journal 5 (Summer 1993); "A Guide to the EEOC's Final Regulations on the Americans with Disabilities Act," 17 Employee Relations Law Journal (Winter 1991-1992); "'Reasonable Accomodation' Under the Americans with Disabilities Act — What Does It Mean?" 16 Employee Relations Law Journal 431 (Spring 1991-1992); "Analyses of the Americans with Disabilities Act," 18 Tax Management Compensation Planning Journal (BNA's Tax Management Inc. 287) (1990); "The Availability of Punitive Damages in Breach of Contract Actions Under Section 301 of the Labor Management Relations Act," 50 George Washington University Law Review 219 (1982); "The Constitutionality of a Federal Collective Bargaining Statute for State and Local Employees," 8 Capital University Law Review 59, reprinted in 29 Labor Law Journal 594 (1978). University Fellow and Lecturer in Law, The National Law Center, George Washington University, 1977-1978. Court Appointed Mediator, U.S. District Court for the District of Columbia. *Member:* American Bar Association (Labor and Employment Section, 1980-1997). ***REPORTED CASES:*** Nazaire v. Trans World Airlines, Inc., 807 F.2d 1372 (7th Cir. 1986); Gulf Coast Indus. Workers Union v. Exxon Co., 70 F. 3d 847 (5th Cir. 1995); LeBoutillier v. Air Line Pilots Ass'n Intern., 778 F. 2d 883 (D.C. Cir. 1985); Air Line Pilots Ass'n v. Trans World Airlines, Inc., 729 F. Supp. 888 (D.D.C. 1989); IAM v. Trans World Airlines, Inc., 686 F. Supp. 930 (D.D.C. 988); IAM v. Trans World Airlines, Inc., 663 F. Supp. 230 (D.D.C. 1987); Williams v. Trans World Airlines, Inc., 588 F. Supp. 1037 (W.D. Mo. 1984). ***PRACTICE AREAS:*** Labor and Employment Law. ***Email:*** ehskclegal@elinkisp.com

MARIA PIA TORRETTI GEKAS, born Santiago, Chile, February 11, 1959; admitted to bar, 1995, Virginia (Not admitted in District of Columbia). *Education:* Wellesley College (B.A., 1980); Georgetown University Law Center (J.D., 1995). *Member:* State Bar of Wisconsin. ***LANGUAGES:*** Spanish. ***PRACTICE AREAS:*** Labor and Employment Law; Transportation; Drug Testing; Immigration. ***Email:*** ptgkclegal@elinkisp.com

TIMOTHY P. BLODGETT, born Rochester, New York, June 16, 1966; admitted to bar, 1992, New York; 1994, U.S. District Court, Western District of

(This Listing Continued)

New York (Not admitted in District of Columbia). *Education:* Buffalo State College (B.A., magna cum laude, 1988); American University, Washington College of Law (J.D., 1992). Recipient: National Collegiate Political Science Award; Raymond P. Stone Award; T. Morton McDonald Award for Excellence in Legal Research. Author: "Hiring Standards and the ADA: Police Departments Adapting to a Changing Workforce," The Police Chief Executive, August 1994; "Section 33: Third Party Settlements," Thew Longshore Judges Bench Book, Office of Administrative Law Judges, U.S. Department of Labor; "Pre-trial Practice in Black Lung Cases," Office of Administrative Law Judges Desk Book, U.S. Department of Labor. Former Associate, Harris, Chesworth & O'Brien, Rochester, NY. *Member:* Monroe County and New York State (Member, Labor Section, 1994-2000) Bar Associations. ***PRACTICE AREAS:*** Labor and Employment Discrimination; Litigation. ***Email:*** tpbkclegal@elinkisp.com

(For Complete Biographical Data on all Personnel, see Professional Biographies at Milwaukee, Wisconsin)

KRUPIN O'BRIEN

1156 15TH STREET, NW
SUITE 200
WASHINGTON, D.C. 20005
Telephone: 202-530-0700
Fax: 202-530-0703
Email: info@krupinobrien.com
URL: http://www.krupinobrien.com

Management Side Labor and Employment Law, Business Immigration, Benefits and Related Litigation.

FIRM PROFILE: Exclusive representation of employers and management in the areas of Labor, Employment, Business Immigration and Related Litigation.

JAY P. KRUPIN, born Brooklyn, New York, September 4, 1954; admitted to bar, 1978, District of Columbia; 1982, U.S. Supreme Court. *Education:* George Washington University (B.A., 1975); St. Louis University (J.D., 1978); Georgetown University (LL.M., 1982). Omicron Delta Kappa; Pi Sigma Alpha; Phi Alpha Delta. Member, St. Louis University Law Journal, 1977-1978. Clerk to U.S. District Judge James L. Foreman, 1977-1978. Author: "Sidestepping Congress," *The National Law Journal* (May 15, 1995); "ADA Case Is Food For Thought," *Hotel & Restaurant Industry* (February 1995); "Court to Consider After-Acquired Evidence Case," *Legal Times* (October 24, 1994); "Employee Participation: Changing the Status Quo," *Washington Business Journal* Volume 12, Issue 44 (1994); "Alarming Rise in Sexual Harassment Litigation," *Washington Business Journal* Volume 12, Issue 37 (1994); "Charting a New Course in Labor Law," *Legal Times* (December 13, 1993); "Role of Business in Health-Care Reform," *Washington Business Journal* Volume 12, Issue 25 (1993); "Operating a Law Firm by the Book," *Legal Times* (April 26, 1993). Advisory Board, Lodging HR., American Hotel and Motel Association, 1998—. *Member:* District of Columbia Bar; American Bar Association (Member, Labor and Employment Law Section); American Immigration Lawyers Association. ***PRACTICE AREAS:*** Labor Law; Employment Law. ***Email:*** jpk@krupinobrien.com

JAMES J. O'BRIEN, born Denville, New Jersey, November 26, 1957; admitted to bar, 1987, District of Columbia; 1988, Maryland and U.S. District Court, District of Columbia. *Education:* Fairleigh Dickinson University (B.S., 1983); Columbus School of Law of the Catholic University of America (J.D., 1987). Pi Sigma Alpha. *Member:* District of Columbia Bar; Maryland State Bar Association. ***PRACTICE AREAS:*** Employment Law; Immigration Law. ***Email:*** jjo@krupinobrien.com

CARYN G. PASS, born Baltimore, Maryland, January 23, 1959; admitted to bar, 1985, Ohio; 1991, District of Columbia. *Education:* University of Maryland (B.S., 1982); Case Western Reserve University (J.D., 1985). *Member:* District of Columbia Bar. ***PRACTICE AREAS:*** Labor Law; Employment Law. ***Email:*** cgp@krupinobrien.com

SCOTT V. KAMINS, born Hartford, Connecticut, April 15, 1967; admitted to bar, 1992, Maryland; 1994, U.S. District Court, District of Maryland and U.S. Court of Appeals, Fourth Circuit; 1999, District of Columbia. *Education:* Emory University; Boston University (B.A., cum laude, 1989); University of Maryland (J.D., with honors, 1992). Order of the Coif. *Member:* The District of Columbia Bar. ***PRACTICE AREAS:*** Labor Relations; Employment Law. ***Email:*** svk@krupinobrien.com

SENIOR ASSOCIATES

D. JAY SUMNER, born Nashville, Tennessee, February 19, 1971; admitted to bar, 1998, Tennessee; 1999, District of Columbia. *Education:* Rhodes College (B.A., 1993); University of Tennessee at Knoxville (J.D., summa cum laude, 1997). Phi Alpha Phi. Member, University of Tennessee Law Review. *Member:* The District of Columbia Bar; American Bar Association. ***PRACTICE AREAS:*** Labor Law; Employment Law. ***Email:*** djs@krupinobrien.com

MONIQUE A. VAN STIPHOUT, born Salt Lake City, Utah, November 25, 1970; admitted to bar, 1998, Maryland; 1999, District of Columbia. *Education:* Georgetown University (B.S.F.S., 1993; J.D., 1998). Author, "Immigration Reform on the Hill," Georgetown Immigration L.J. 10:1, March 6, 1996. *Member:* The District of Columbia Bar; American Bar Association; Women in International Trade. ***PRACTICE AREAS:*** Immigration (100%). ***Email:*** mas@krupinobrien.com

ARI KAREN, born Washington, D.C., September 10, 1970; admitted to bar, 1996, Georgia; 1997, Maryland; 1998, District of Columbia. *Education:* University of Maryland (B.A., Economics, cum laude, 1992); Emory University (J.D., with distinction, 1996). *Member:* State Bar of Georgia; The District of Columbia Bar; The Association of Trial Lawyers of America. ***PRACTICE AREAS:*** Securities Fraud; Consumer Fraud; Employment Discrimination. ***Email:*** axk@krupinobrien.com

JEFFREY M. RICAPITO, born Binghamton, New York, February 26, 1973; admitted to bar, 1998, Connecticut (Not admitted in District of Columbia). *Education:* Pennsylvania State University (B.S., 1995); Hofstra University (J.D., 1998). ***Email:*** jmr@krupinobrien.com

NEDA E. BITAR, admitted to bar, 1999, District of Columbia. *Education:* Vassar College (B.A., 1992); St. Louis University School of Law (J.D., 1997); Georgetown University (LL.M., 1999). Member, Law Review, Trial Advocacy. *Member:* District of Columbia Bar; American Immigration Lawyers Association. ***LANGUAGES:*** Spanish, Portuguese, Arabic, French. ***PRACTICE AREAS:*** Immigration Law; Litigation. ***Email:*** neb@krupinobrien.com

ALISON N. DAVIS, born Montreal, Quebec, Canada, May 4, 1966; admitted to bar, 1991, District of Columbia and New York. *Education:* McGill University (B.A., with honors, 1987); Harvard University (J.D., 1990). *Member:* New York State Bar Association; The District of Columbia Bar. (Associate General Counsel, Labor and Employment). ***PRACTICE AREAS:*** Labor and Employment. ***Email:*** and@krupinobrien.com

DANIEL FELDMAN, born Philadelphia, Pennsylvania, December 1, 1972; admitted to bar, 1998, Texas (Not admitted in District of Columbia). *Education:* University of Pennsylvania (B.A., History, 1994); University of Texas (J.D., 1998). *Member:* State Bar of Texas. ***PRACTICE AREAS:*** Labor and Employment. ***Email:*** dxf@krupinobrien.com

SCOTT A. MIRSKY, born Baltimore, Maryland, January 18, 1972; admitted to bar, 1997, Maryland; 1998, U.S. District Court, District of Maryland; 1999, District of Columbia. *Education:* The American University (B.A., Justice, Psychology, 1994); University of Baltimore (J.D., 1997). *Member:* Maryland State Bar Association, Inc.; The District of Columbia Bar. ***PRACTICE AREAS:*** Labor and Employment. ***Email:*** sam@krupinobrien.com

CRAIG SYMONS, born Washington, DC, February 21, 1975; admitted to bar, 2000, District of Columbia. *Education:* Maryville College (B.A., International Studies, 1996); George Washington University Law School (J.D., 2000). *Member:* The District of Columbia Bar. ***PRACTICE AREAS:*** Business Immigration. ***Email:*** cms@krupinobrien.com

KUBOVCIK & KUBOVCIK

THE FARRAGUT BUILDING
900 17TH STREET, N.W., SUITE 710
WASHINGTON, D.C. 20006
Telephone: 202-887-9023
Fax: 202-887-9093
Email: KandK@kubovcik.com
URL: http://www.lawyers.com/kubovciklaw

Intellectual Property Law, Chemical Intellectual Property, Pharmaceutical Intellectual Property, Mechanical Intellectual Property, Patent Interference Practice, Trademarks.

RONALD J. KUBOVCIK, born Washington, Pennsylvania, December 9, 1944; admitted to bar, 1973, Pennsylvania; 1974, District of Columbia; 1974-1982, U.S. Court of Customs and Patent Appeals; 1982, U.S. Court of Appeals for the Federal Circuit; registered to practice before U.S. Patent and Trademark Office. *Education:* University of Pittsburgh (B.S., Ch.E., 1966; M.S., Ch.E., 1968); Duquesne University (J.D., 1973). Sigma Tau; Omega Chi Epsilon: Phi Alpha Delta. *Member:* District of Columbia Bar; American Intellectual Property Law Association; Federation of Industrial Property Attorneys (FICPI); AIPPI. ***PRACTICE AREAS:*** Chemical Intellectual Property; Pharmaceutical Intellectual Property; Mechanical Intellectual Property; Trademarks; Patent Prosecution; Patent Interference Practice.

KEIKO TANAKA KUBOVCIK, born Tokyo, Japan, August 11, 1950; admitted to bar, 1988, Japan; (Not admitted in the United States); registered to practice before U.S. Patent and Trademark Office. *Education:* Tokyo College of Pharmacy (B.A., 1975). Pharmacist, Japan, 1975. Registered Patent Attorney, Japan. *Member:* Japan Patent Attorneys Association. ***LANGUAGES:*** Japanese.

(This Listing Continued)

KUBOVCIK & KUBOVCIK, Washington—Continued

PRACTICE AREAS: Chemical Intellectual Property; Pharmaceutical Intellectual Property; International Intellectual Property.

KUDER, SMOLLAR & FRIEDMAN, P.C.

Established in 1978

SUITE 200, 1925 K STREET, N.W.

WASHINGTON, D.C. 20006

Telephone: 202-331-7522

Fax: 202-331-0388

Email: Lawyers@ksflaw.com

URL: http://www.ksflaw.com

Rockville, Maryland Office: 414 Hungerford Drive, Suite 456. Telephone: 301-340-9090.

General Civil Trial and Family Law Practice, Malpractice and Personal Injury, Association and Health Law, Probate and Estate Planning.

ARMIN U. KUDER, born Philadelphia, Pennsylvania, November 14, 1935; admitted to bar, 1959, District of Columbia; 1962, U.S. Court of Military Appeals; 1987, Maryland. *Education:* Lafayette College (A.B., 1956); Harvard Law School (LL.B., 1959). Phi Beta Kappa; Phi Alpha Theta. President, Arthritis and Rheumatism Association of Metropolitan Washington, 1973-1975. Director, Region III, Arthritis Foundation, 1975-1976. Vice Chairman, 1977-1980, Senior Vice Chairman, 1991-1992 and Chair, 1993-1994, Arthritis and Rheumatism International. Trustee, President, 1997-1998, Treasurer, 1999—. Secretary, Combined Health Appeal of the National Capital Area, 1976-1977, 1984. Chairman, National Health Agencies, National Capitol Area Council, 1977-1978. Chairman, Human Subjects Review Committee, N.I.H., 1980-1983. Member, International Steering Committee, Bone C Joint Decade, 2000-2010. Director, 1976-1985, Chairman, 1981-1983, Center for Environmental Education. Chairman of the Board, Hyde School, Bath, Maine, 1984-1988. Trustee, 1983-1991 and Chairman, 1990-1991, District of Columbia Bar Client's Security Fund. Chairman, Hearing Committee, Board on Professional Responsibility, 1984-1990. Member, Task Force on Family Law Representation, 1997-1998. Vice-Chairman, Board of Directors, The Washington New Art Association, 1985-1986. *Member:* Montgomery County, Maryland State and American Bar Associations; District of Columbia Bar; Bar Association of the District of Columbia (Member, Domestic Relations Committee, 1968—); International Academy of Matrimonial Lawyers. Fellow, American Academy of Matrimonial Lawyers. ***PRACTICE AREAS:*** Domestic Relations Law; Estate Probate; Professional Association Law; Mental Health Law; Civil Litigation. ***Email:*** akuder@ksflaw.com

PAUL R. SMOLLAR, born Washington, D.C., December 10, 1944; admitted to bar, 1969, District of Columbia; 1979, U.S. Claims Court; 1988, Virginia. *Education:* Columbia University (A.B., 1966); Northwestern University (J.D., 1969). Instructor, District of Columbia Bar Continuing Legal Education Course on Divorce Taxation, 1983—; National Business Institute Inc. Course on Divorce Taxation, 1995. Lecturer: Tracing, Virginia CLE, 1996; Valuations of Closely Held Businesses, Virginia, 1996; Family Law Around the Beltway, District of Columbia, 1998, 2000, 2001. Mentor, PSAC Advice and Referral Clinic, District of Columbia Bar. Mediator for Family Law Matters. Television Show Panelist, Separation and Property Settlement Agreements. *Member:* Fairfax and Virginia (Member, Commonwealth of Virginia, 1988) Bar Associations; District of Columbia Bar; Virginia State Bar; Virginia Trial Lawyers Association. Fellow, American Academy of Matrimonial Lawyers (President, District of Columbia Chapter, 1997-1998). ***PRACTICE AREAS:*** Domestic Relations Law; Personal Injury Law; General Civil Litigation. ***Email:*** psmollar@ksflaw.com

SUSAN MEYERS FRIEDMAN, born New York, N.Y., July 4, 1943; admitted to bar, 1982, Maryland; 1983, District of Columbia. *Education:* Brooklyn College (B.A., 1963); George Washington University (M.A., 1968); Georgetown University (J.D., 1982). Instructor, Nuts and Bolts of Divorce, Continuing Legal Education Course, Georgetown University Law Center, 1992. Delegate, District of Columbia Judicial Conference, 1984-1998. *Member:* Montgomery County and American (Member, Family Law Section) Bar Associations; District of Columbia Bar (Member, Section of Family Law) Maryland State Bar Association, Inc.; Woman's Bar Associations of District of Columbia, Montgomery County and Maryland. Mentor, D.C. Bar Pro Bono Program. Member, Fundraising Board, Make the Road By Walking, Brooklyn, New York. Fellow, American Academy of Matrimonial Lawyers. ***PRACTICE AREAS:*** Domestic Relations Law. ***Email:*** sfriedman@ksflaw.com

THERESA M. MIHALIK, born Scranton, Pennsylvania, April 8, 1963; admitted to bar, 1987, Pennsylvania; 1988, District of Columbia; 1989, Virginia and U.S. Court of Appeals for the District of Columbia and Fourth Circuits. *Education:* University of Scranton (B.A., magna cum laude, 1984); Catholic University of America (J.D., 1987). Chancellor, Moot Court, 1986-1987. Law

(This Listing Continued)

Clerk to The Honorable Rufus G. King, III, Superior Court of the District of Columbia, 1987-1989. *Member:* District of Columbia Bar (Member: Section of Family Law; Family Law Steering Committee, Co-Chair, 1996-1998; Program Chair, 1995-1996; Treasurer, 1995-1996); Virginia State Bar; American Bar Association (Member, Family Law Section); Thurgood Marshall American Inn of Court, 1989-1993. ***PRACTICE AREAS:*** Domestic Relations Law. ***Email:*** tmihalik@ksflaw.com

ANDREA E. HIRSCH, born Washington, D.C., March 20, 1956; admitted to bar, 1984, California; 1995, Maryland; 1996, District of Columbia. *Education:* Stanford University (B.A., 1978); University of Santa Clara (J.D., 1984). Articles Editor, Santa Clara Law Review, 1983-1984. Author: "The Impact of Automated Litigation Support Systems on Attorney's Standard of Care," Vol. 23, No. 4, Santa Clara Law Review. *Member:* The State Bar of California; District of Columbia Bar (Member, Family Law Section); Maryland State Bar Association Inc. (Member, Family Law Sect. ***PRACTICE AREAS:*** Domestic Relations; Trust and Estates. ***Email:*** ahirsch@ksflaw.com

KUDON LAW FIRM

Established in 1996

SUITE 200

2000 L STREET, N.W.

WASHINGTON, D.C. 20036

Telephone: 202-965-1602

Fax: 301-294-6407

Mobile: 240-472-1086

Email: kudonlaw@abanet.org

URL: http://www.lawyers.com/kudonlaw

Complex Civil Litigation, Business Torts, Anti-Trust, Unfair Competition, Class Actions, Electronic Banking and Funds Transfer Litigation.

FIRM PROFILE: Mr. Kudon has handled business and class action litigation cases for over 25 years. His clients range from individuals to very large corporations and they have included manufacturers, distributors as well as family-run companies and entrepreneurs from a wide variety of industries.

H. KENNETH KUDON, born Albany, New York, November 13, 1942; admitted to bar, 1971, District of Columbia, Tennessee and U.S. District Court for the District of Columbia; 1974, Pennsylvania and U.S. District Court, Eastern District of Pennsylvania; U.S. Court of Appeals, Third Circuit; 1979, U.S. Court of Appeals, Fifth Circuit; 1983, U.S. Court of Appeals, Fourth Circuit; 1986, U.S. Court of Appeals, Eleventh Circuit; 1995, U.S. District Court, District of Maryland. *Education:* University of Alabama (B.A., 1968); University of Tennessee (J.D., 1970). Phi Delta Phi. Trial Attorney, Antitrust Division, Department of Justice, 1970-1973. Author: "United States v. U.S. Gypsum: Price Verification-Controlling Circumstances or Controlling Prices," 23 Villanova Law Review 688, 1978; "Summary Judgment in Antitrust," Working Paper, American Bar Association, 1992. Contributor, "Antitrust Law Developments," published by the American Bar Association, 1975. *Member:* The District of Columbia Bar (Co-Chairman, Trade Regulation Committee, Computer Law Section, 1986-1988); American Bar Association (Member, Sections on: Antitrust Law; Litigation; Intellectual Property); Center for Public Policy (Board Member, 1996—). ***REPORTED CASES:*** Metrix Warehouse v. Daimler-Benz AG, 828 F.2d 1033 (4th Cir. 1987); Helicopter Support Systems, Inc. v. Hughes Helicopter, Inc., 818 F.2d 1530 (11th Cir. 1987); Commercial Business Systems, Inc. v. BellSouth Serv., Inc., 453 S.E.2d 261 (1995). ***PRACTICE AREAS:*** Business Torts Litigation; Antitrust Litigation; Franchise Law; Unfair Competition Litigation; Electronic Banking. ***Email:*** kudon@sprintmail.com

KURTIS & ASSOCIATES, P.C.

1000 POTOMAC STREET, N.W.

SUITE 200

WASHINGTON, D.C. 20007

Telephone: 202-328-4500

Telecopier: 202-328-1231

Email: RMcgovern@kurtispc.com

URL: http://www.kurtispc.com

Corporate, Communications and Telecommunications Law.

FIRM PROFILE: Kurtis and Associates is a communications law firm with an Engineering Department. The Firm's expertise in communications include cellular, paging, two-way radio, microwave and PCS. The Engineering Department duties include, but are not limited to, working with topographical maps, computer pro-

(This Listing Continued)

grams, propagations predictions, and preparation of documents to be filed with government agencies such as the Federal Communications Commission and Federal Aviation Administration.

MICHAEL K. KURTIS, born Chicago, Illinois, October 3, 1953; admitted to bar, 1978, Indiana; 1979, District of Columbia, U.S. Court of Appeals for the District of Columbia Circuit and U.S. District Court for the District of Columbia; 1981, U.S. Supreme Court. *Education:* Valparaiso University (B.S.E.E., 1975; J.D., 1978). Phi Alpha Delta (President, 1977-1978). *Member:* District of Columbia Bar; Indiana State and American Bar Associations; Institute of Electrical and Electronics Engineers; Federal Communications Bar Association. ***PRACTICE AREAS:*** Cellular Radio; PCS; Telephone Litigation; Arbitration; Business Transactions. ***Email:*** MKurtis@kurtispc.com

---

RHONDA PINES KURTIS, born Chicago, Illinois, November 19, 1952; admitted to bar, 1978, Indiana; 1985, Virginia; 1981 U.S. Supreme Court; 1980, U.S. Court of Appeals for the District of Columbia Circuit; 1982, U.S. Court of Appeals 5th, 6th and 11th Circuits; 1983, U.S. Court of Appeals, 7th, 9th and 10th Circuits; 1984, U.S. Court of Appeals, 3rd Circuit and 8th Circuit (Not admitted in District of Columbia). *Education:* Northwestern University (B.A., 1975); Valparaiso University (J.D., 1978). *Member:* Indiana and Virginia State and Federal Communications Bar Associations. ***PRACTICE AREAS:*** Corporate Law; Communications Law. ***Email:*** RKurtis@kurtispc.com

LISA L. LEIBOW, born Leominster, Massachusetts, July 8, 1966; admitted to bar, 1991, Massachusetts; 1997, District of Columbia. *Education:* George Washington University (B.A., 1988); Suffolk University (J.D., 1991). *Member:* The District of Columbia Bar; Federal Communications Bar Association; American Bar Association; Massachusetts Bar Association. ***PRACTICE AREAS:*** Telecommunications Law; Federal Regulatory Law. ***Email:*** lleibow@kurtispc.com

ANNA E. WARD, born Cocoa Beach, Florida, November 7, 1967; admitted to bar, 2000, Maryland; 2001, District of Columbia. *Education:* American University (B.A., 1989); George Mason University (J.D., 1999). ***PRACTICE AREAS:*** Telecommunications Law (100%). ***Email:*** award@kurtispc.com

OF COUNSEL

JEROME K. BLASK, born Philadelphia, Pennsylvania, September 19, 1951; admitted to bar, 1980, Pennsylvania and District of Columbia; 1981, U.S. District Court for the District of Columbia; 1983, U.S. Supreme Court; 1989, U.S. Court of Appeals for the District of Columbia Circuit. *Education:* Dickinson College (B.A., magna cum laude, 1973); Georgetown University (J.D., 1979). Author: "Indecent Channels: The Supreme Court Reviews the Cable Television Consumer Protection and Competition Act," in the Federalist Society's Telecommunications and Electronic Media News (Fall 1996). *Member:* District of Columbia Bar; Federal Communications Bar Association; The Federalist Society (Past Vice Chairman, Telecommunications & Electronic Media Practice Group). ***PRACTICE AREAS:*** Telecommunications Law. ***Email:*** jblask@kurtispc.com

---

KUTAK ROCK LLP

Established in 1965

SUITE 1000

1101 CONNECTICUT AVENUE, N.W.

WASHINGTON, D.C. 20036-4374

Telephone: 202-828-2400

Fax: 202-828-2488

URL: http://www.kutakrock.com

Atlanta, Georgia Office: Suite 2100, 225 Peachtree Street, NE, 30303-1731. Telephone: 404-222-4600. Facsimile: 404-222-4654.

Denver, Colorado Office: Suite 2900, 717 Seventeenth Street, 80202-3329. Telephone: 303-297-2400. Facsimile: 303-292-7799.

Des Moines, Iowa Office: Suite 124, Highland Building, 4201 Westown Parkway, West Des Moines, 50266-6720. Telephone: 515-224-1266. Facsimile: 515-457-7669.

Fayetteville, Arkansas Office: 2766 Millennium Place, Highway 265 and Joyce Street, 72703-4793. Telephone: 501-973-4200. Facsimile: 501-973-0007.

Kansas City, Missouri Office: Valencia Place, Suite 200, 444 West 47th Street, 64112-1914. Telephone: 816-960-0090. Telefax: 816-960-0041.

Little Rock, Arkansas Office: Suite 1100, 425 West Capitol Avenue, 72201-3409. Telephone: 501-975-3000. Facsimile: 501-975-3001.

New York, New York Office: 650 Fifth Avenue, 10019-6108. Telephone: 212-713-6480. Facsimile: 212-713-6481.

Oklahoma City, Oklahoma Office: Suite 475, 6305 Waterford Boulevard, 73118-1116. Telephone: 405-848-2475. Facsimile: 405-842-5748.

Omaha, Nebraska Office: The Omaha Building, 1650 Farnam Street, 68102-2186. Telephone: 402-346-6000. Facsimile: 402-346-1148.

(This Listing Continued)

Scottsdale, Arizona Office: Suite 300, 8601 N. Scottsdale Road, 85253-2742. Telephone: 480-429-5000. Facsimile: 480-429-5001.

Newport Beach, California Office: Suite 450, 620 Newport Center Drive, 92660-8019. Telephone: 949-718-6700. Facsimile: 949-718-6708.

Pasadena, California Office: Suite 210, 117 East Colorado Boulevard. Telephone: 626-432-1630. Facsimile: 626-432-1614.

Richmond, Virginia Office: Bank of America Center, Suite 800, 1111 East Main Street, 23219-3103. Facsimile: 804-783-6192.

Chicago, Illinois Office: Kutak Rock Illinois LLC, One South Wacker Drive, 60606-4614. Telephone: 312-602-4100. Facsimile: 312-602-4101.

Civil Litigation and Bankruptcy, Public Finance, Corporate and Structured Finance, Banking and Commercial Lending, Real Estate Law, Taxation Law, Health Care and Hospital Law.

FIRM PROFILE: Founded in Omaha in 1965, Kutak Rock conducts a full-service, multidisciplinary practice. While the firm has long had a nationally recognized public and corporate finance practice, we have also developed a sophisticated business and litigation practice representing clients across the country in complex transactions and major litigation. Kutak Rock has represented every major investment banking firm in the United States; major European, Asian and domestic money-center banks; savings and loan associations; insurance companies; national real estate syndicators and developers; major national franchising enterprises; and numerous other financial institutions, businesses and state and local governmental units. The firm's litigation practice group represents corporate and individual clients in federal and state courts nationwide in complex civil litigation matters and represents clients in arbitration, mediation proceedings, antitrust and white collar criminal defense. The Firm's Healthcare/hospital law group represents hospitals and physician organizations in numerous states.

MEMBERS OF FIRM

JOSEPH A. INGRISANO, born Manhattan, New York, July 21, 1955; admitted to bar, 1980, District of Columbia. *Education:* State University of New York at Binghamton (B.A., 1977); American University (J.D., 1980). ***PRACTICE AREAS:*** Securities Litigation and Arbitration; Insurance Defense; General Litigation. ***Email:*** joseph.ingrisano@kutakrock.com

MITCHELL J. BRAGIN, born Philadelphia, Pennsylvania, May 27, 1945; admitted to bar, 1970, Pennsylvania; 1978, District of Columbia, U.S. Court of Appeals ; 1984, U.S. Tax Court. *Education:* Temple University (B.S., 1967; J.D., 1970); Georgetown University (LL.M., Taxation, 1973). ***PRACTICE AREAS:*** Taxation Law; Municipal Finance Law; Asset-Backed Securities Law. ***Email:*** mitchell.bragin@kutakrock.com

JEFFREY S. JACOBOVITZ, born New York, N.Y., April 3, 1955; admitted to bar, 1981, District of Columbia; 1988, Maryland; 1989, New York; U.S. District Court for the District of Columbia and Maryland; U.S. Supreme Court; 1982, U.S. Court of Appeals for the District of Columbia Circuit; 1992, U.S. Court of Appeals, Fourth Circuit. *Education:* State University of New York at Buffalo (B.A., magna cum laude, 1977); American University (J.D., 1980). Contributing Author: "Antitrust Law Developments," Criminal Antitrust Section. Co-Chair, Criminal Antitrust Subcommittee of ABA White Collar Crime Committee of Criminal Justice Section. ***REPORTED CASES:*** U.S. vs. Microsoft, 56 F.3d. 1448 (D.C. Cir. 1995); U.S. vs. Smith, 44 F.3d. 1259 (4th Cir. 1995); U.S. vs. Microsoft, 159 F.R.D. 318 (D.D.C. 1995). ***PRACTICE AREAS:*** Antitrust Law; Criminal Defense; Civil Litigation; Appellate Practice.

GEORGE R. SCHLOSSBERG, born New York, N.Y., March 30, 1952; admitted to bar, 1977, New York and U.S. District Court, Southern and Eastern Districts of New York; 1981, U.S. Supreme Court; 1983, District of Columbia. *Education:* State University of New York at Stony Brook (B.A., 1973); New England School of Law (J.D., 1976). General Counsel, National Association of Installation Developers, 1993—. Senior Counsel, Office of Secretary of Defense, 1980-1990. Counsel: President's Economic Adjustment Committee, 1984-1990; President's Commission on Alternative Utilization of Military Facilities, 1989-1990; Department of Defense Bureau of Prisons Assistance Council, 1989-1990. ***PRACTICE AREAS:*** Construction Law; Military Base Closures. ***Email:*** george.schlossberg@kutakrock.com

BARRY P. STEINBERG, born Richmond, Virginia, July 16, 1941; admitted to bar, 1966, Virginia; 1970, U.S. Supreme Court; 1972, U.S. Court of Military Appeals; 1991, District of Columbia. *Education:* University of Richmond (B.A., 1963); T.C. Williams School of Law (LL.B., 1966). Author: Federal Facilities Environmental Journal, "Long-Term Leases and the Reuse of Base Closure Property--The Reaction of the Courts and Congress," Summer 1996, Vol. 7, No. 2. ***PRACTICE AREAS:*** Environmental; Military Personnel; Municipal. ***Email:*** barry.steinberg@kutakrock.com

GILBERT W. BOYCE, born New York, N.Y.; admitted to bar, 1988, Pennsylvania, District of Columbia and U.S. Tax Court. *Education:* Howard University (B.B.A., 1980); Catholic University (J.D., 1987). Certified Public Accountant, District of Columbia, 1985. ***PRACTICE AREAS:*** Litigation; Securities Law; Taxation Law. ***Email:*** gilbert.boyce@kutakrock.com

(This Listing Continued)

KUTAK ROCK LLP, Washington—Continued

ALAN D. STRASSER, born Fairfield, Connecticut, November 3, 1952; admitted to bar, 1977, Massachusetts and District of Columbia; 1980, U.S. Court of Appeals, District of Columbia Circuit; 1989, U.S. District Court for the District of Columbia. *Education:* Yale University (B.A., cum laude, 1974); Harvard University (J.D., cum laude, 1977). Trial Attorney, Department of Justice, 1977-1979. Assistant U.S. Attorney, 1980-1991 (Chief Felony Trial Division, 1985-1989. Associate Independent Counsel, Clinton Passport Investigation, 1993. ***PRACTICE AREAS:*** Criminal Defense, Employment Law. ***Email:*** alan.strasser@kutakrock.com

PAUL D. BORJA, born Omaha, Nebraska, November 25, 1960; admitted to bar, 1990, Virginia; 2000, District of Columbia. *Education:* University of Notre Dame (B.B.A., 1982); George Washington University (J.D., with honors, 1990); Georgetown University (LL.M. in Taxation, with distinction, 1991). Certified Public Accountant, Guam, 1986 and Virginia, 1989. ***PRACTICE AREAS:*** Corporate Law; Securities Law; Banking Law; Taxation Law. ***Email:*** paul.borja@kutakrock.com

ALICIA A. TERRY, born Washington, D.C., May 30, 1953; admitted to bar, 1987, Maryland; 1988, District of Columbia. *Education:* Howard University (B.M.E., magna cum laude, 1975; M.M.E., 1976); Georgetown University (J.D., 1987). ***PRACTICE AREAS:*** Public Finance Law; Asset-Backed Structured Finance Law. ***Email:*** alicia.terry@kutakrock.com

SETH DAVID KIRSHENBERG, born Miami, Florida, July 28, 1967; admitted to bar, 1992, Florida; 1993, District of Columbia. *Education:* University of Florida (B.S., Business Administration and Finance, 1989); Washington College of Law American University (J.D., 1992). ***PRACTICE AREAS:*** Real Estate; Environmental; Government Affairs.

OF COUNSEL

ROBERT M. DISCH, born Milwaukee, Wisconsin, December 16, 1955; admitted to bar, 1981, District of Columbia. *Education:* Carroll College (B.A., 1978); Northwestern University (J.D., 1981). ***PRACTICE AREAS:*** Litigation; Antitrust. ***Email:*** robert.disch@kutakrock.com

JOHN J. VECCHIONE, born Brooklyn, New York, June 6, 1964; admitted to bar, 1990, New York; 1991, District of Columbia. *Education:* Hamilton College (B.A., 1986); Georgetown University Law Center (J.D., 1989). ***PRACTICE AREAS:*** Commercial Litigation; Employment Law; Corporate Law. ***Email:*** john.vecchione@kutakrock.com

ASSOCIATES

NANCY ELIZABETH NUNAN, born Albany, New York, October 24, 1963; admitted to bar, 1993, New York, Massachusetts and Virginis; 1995, District of Columbia. *Education:* Cornell University (B.A., 1985); Georgetown University Law Center (J.D., 1992). ***PRACTICE AREAS:*** Employment Law; White Collar Crime; Securities; Civil Litigation. ***Email:*** nancy.nunan@kutakrock.com

LESLIE CAREY, born Chicago, Illinois, June 12, 1971; admitted to bar, 1996, Illinois (Not admitted in District of Columbia). *Education:* University of Illinois, Champaign-Urbana (B.A., 1993; J.D., 1996). ***PRACTICE AREAS:*** Public Finance; Corporate Finance. ***Email:*** leslie.carey@kutakrock.com

JENNIFER M. BLUNT, born Fort Belvoir, Virginia, January 13, 1965; admitted to bar, 1991, Maryland; 2000, District of Columbia; 2001, U.S. Tax Court. *Education:* Swarthmore College (B.A., Political Science, 1988); Columbus School of Law of The Catholic University of America (J.D., 1991). ***PRACTICE AREAS:*** Complex Commercial Litigation; Securities; Antitrust; White Collar Crime. ***Email:*** jennifer.blunt@kutakrock.com

JORGE A. DEL RIO, born Los Angeles, California, May 12, 1971; admitted to bar, 1997, Florida; 2000, District of Columbia. *Education:* Loyola University, New Orleans (B.A., 1989); Nova Southeastern University Shepard Broad Law Center (J.D., 1997); University of Miami (LL.M., Taxation, 1998). ***PRACTICE AREAS:*** Tax Law. ***Email:*** jorge.delrio@kutakrock.com

(For biographical data of Atlanta Lawyers, see Professional Biographies at Atlanta, Georgia).
(For biographical data of Chicago Lawyers, see Professional Biographies at Chicago, Illinois).
(For biographical data of Denver Lawyers, see Professional Biographies at Denver, Colorado).
(For biographical data of Des Moines Lawyers, See Professional Biographies at West Des Moines, Iowa).
(For biographical data of Fayetteville Lawyers, see Professional Biographies at Fayetteville, Arkansas).
(For biographical data of Kansas City Lawyers, see Professional Biographies at Kansas City, Missouri)
(For biographical data of Little Rock Lawyers, see Professional Biographies at Little Rock, Arkansas).
(For biographical data of Newport Beach Lawyers, see Professional Biographies at Newport Beach, California).
(For biographical data of New York Lawyers, see Professional Biographies at New York, N.Y.).
(For biographical data of Oklahoma City Lawyers, see Professional Biographies at Oklahoma City, Oklahoma).
(For biographical data of Omaha Lawyers, see Professional Biographies at Omaha, Nebraska).
(For biographical data of Pasadena Lawyers, see Professional Biographies at Pasadena, California).
(For biographical data of Pittsburgh Lawyers, see Professional Biographies at Pittsburgh, Pennsylvania).
(For biographical data of Richmond Lawyers, see Professional Biographies at Richmond, Virginia).
(For biographical data of Scottsdale Lawyers, see Professional Biographies at Scottsdale, Arizona).

LACHTER & CLEMENTS LLP

SUITE 900
1150 CONNECTICUT AVENUE, N.W.
WASHINGTON, D.C. 20036-4192
Telephone: 202-862-4321
Telecopier: 202-835-3219
Email: lachter@starpower.net
URL: http://www.lawyers.com/lachterclementslaw

Antitrust, Aviation Law, including International Aviation Law, Airline Regulation, Administrative Litigation, International Law, Transportation Law, Commercial Litigation.

STEPHEN H. LACHTER, born New York, N.Y., November 21, 1944; admitted to bar, 1969, District of Columbia and U.S. Court of Appeals for the District of the Columbia Circuit; 1971, U.S. Court of Appeals, Second Circuit. *Education:* Syracuse University (A.B., 1966); Georgetown University (J.D., 1969). Adjunct Professor, American University, Washington College of Law, Washington, D.C., 1983-1985. Special Aviation Counsel, U.S. Department of Transportation, 1985. Deputy Director, Bureau of Domestic Aviation, Civil Aeronautics Board, 1982-1985. Executive Assistant to CAB Member, 1978-1982. Trial Attorney, Antitrust Division, U.S. Department of Justice, 1975-1978. *Member:* The District of Columbia Bar; American Bar Association. ***PRACTICE AREAS:*** Civil Litigation; Antitrust Law; Aviation Law; International Aviation; Administrative.

ROXANNE S. CLEMENTS, born Fulton, New York, January 7, 1959; admitted to bar, 1986, District of Columbia and Maryland. *Education:* Cornell University (B.A., 1980); George Washington University National Law Center (J.D., with honors, 1985). Member, Moot Court Board. *Member:* District of Columbia Bar; Maryland State Bar Association. ***LANGUAGES:*** French and German. ***PRACTICE AREAS:*** Antitrust Law; Commercial Litigation.

LALOS & KEEGAN

Established in 1979
1146 NINETEENTH STREET N.W., FIFTH FLOOR
WASHINGTON, D.C. 20036-3723
Telephone: 202-887-5555
Telecopier: (202) 296-1682
Email: laloskeegan@radix.net
URL: http://www.lawyers.com/lalos&keeganlaw

Intellectual Property Law including Patent, Trademark, Copyright, International Trade and Unfair Competition Law, before Federal Trial and Appeal Courts, International Trade Commission, Federal Agencies and State Trial and Appeal Courts.

FIRM PROFILE: The firm is a member of the Martindale-Hubbell Bar Register of Preeminent Lawyers.

(This Listing Continued)

MEMBERS OF FIRM

PETER N. LALOS, born Cleveland, Ohio, June 16, 1934; admitted to bar, 1961, Virginia and Supreme Court of Appeals of Virginia; 1962, District of Columbia, U.S. Court of Appeals for the District of Columbia Circuit; 1982, U.S. Court of Appeals for the Federal Circuit and U.S. Claims Court; registered to practice before U.S. Patent and Trademark Office. *Education:* Rensselaer Polytechnic Institute (B.S.M.E., 1956); American University (LL.B., 1961); Georgetown University (LL.M., 1963). Delta Theta Phi. *Member:* The District of Columbia Bar; Virginia State Bar; American Intellectual Property Law Association. [Lt., USNR, 1956-1958]. ***PRACTICE AREAS:*** Intellectual Property Law; Corporate Law; Litigation; Appellate Practice. ***Email:*** laloskeegan@radix.net

ALFRED A. STADNICKI, born Springfield, Massachusetts, January 3, 1950; admitted to bar, 1978, Massachusetts; 1979, U.S. District Court, District of Massachusetts; registered to practice before U.S. Patent and Trademark Office (Not admitted in District of Columbia). *Education:* Lowell Technological Institute (B.S.C.E., 1971); Western New England College (J.D., 1978). Counsel, Digital Equipment Corporation, 1979-1982. Counsel/Assistant General Counsel, Intelsat, 1982-1993. *Member:* American Bar Association (Patent, Trademark and Copyright, Business Law and Science and Technology Sections); American Intellectual Property Law Association; Society of Satellite Professionals International; Suburban Maryland Technology Council (Member, Steering Committee). ***Email:*** astadnicki_lk@radix.net

ASSOCIATES

STERLING W. CHANDLER, admitted to bar, 1991, Louisiana (Not admitted in District of Columbia). *Education:* Centenary College (B.A., 1988); Tulane University of Louisiana (J.D., 1991); Louisiana Tech University, Ruston, Louisiana (B.S., 1998). ***PRACTICE AREAS:*** Intellectual Property.

KENNETH JOHN WHITTINGTON, born Greenville, Ohio, September 29, 1970; admitted to bar, 2000, South Carolina (Not admitted in District of Columbia). *Education:* University of Northern Colorado (B.A., 1994); University of South Carolina (J.D., 2000). Author, "After April Showers Every Wet Spot May Be Subject to Regulation by the Clean Water Act if a Migratory Bird Stops to take a Drink," South Carolina Environmental Law Journal, Volume 8-1, Spring, 1999. ***PRACTICE AREAS:*** Intellectual Property.

REPRESENTATIVE CLIENTS: ABB Combustion Engineering, Inc.; AGFA Corp.; Audi AG; CheckFree Corp.; CertainTeed Corporation; Dr. O.K. Wack Chemie, GmbH; Niagara Mohawk Power Corp.; Thermwood Corp.; Volkswagen of America; Washington Gas Light Co.; Chem-Lig International, Inc.; Edwards Industries, Inc.; ETC of Henderson, Inc.; Rockland, Inc.; RWC, Inc.; Taylor Cutlery; Unisul, Inc.; U.S. Farathane Corp.; The Young Industries, Inc.; National Oilwell Houston; Mitsubishi Electric, ITA.

DAVID B. LAMB

Established in 1971

1818 N STREET, N.W., 7TH FLOOR

WASHINGTON, D.C. 20036

Telephone: 202-785-4822

Facsimile: 202-785-2210

URL: http://www.washington-office.com

Email: lambdb@wizard.net

URL: http://www.lawyers.com/davidblamb

Rockville, Maryland Office: Suite 200, 255 North Washington Street. Telephone: 301-279-7500.

Fairfax, Virginia Office: 10511 Judicial Drive. Telephone: 703-273-3190.

Civil Trials, Commercial Litigation, Personal Injury, Auto Accidents, Premises Liability, Family Law, Divorce, Separation, Custody, Visitation, Marital Property, Matrimonial Law, White Collar Crime, Securities, Labor, E-Commerce Law, Internet Law, General Civil Litigation in the Federal and Local Courts of Maryland and The District of Columbia.

FIRM PROFILE: Mr. Lamb has over 29 years of court room experience. His clients have included a variety of individuals, families, small businesses and professionals from around the country. The firms' offices are located in the heart of Washington, D.C.'s business district.

DAVID B. LAMB, born Washington, D.C., August 4, 1942; admitted to bar, 1968, Maryland and District of Columbia; 1972, U.S. Supreme Court; 1979, U.S. Tax Court. *Education:* Georgetown University (B.S.B.A., 1964); American University (J.D., 1967). *Member:* The District of Columbia Bar; Montgomery County and Maryland State (Member, Litigation and Family Law Sections) Bar Associations; The Barristers. ***PRACTICE AREAS:*** Civil Litigation; Criminal Litigation; Personal Injury Law; Divorce.

GAIL B. LANDAU, P.C.

WASHINGTON, D.C.

(See Rockville, Maryland)

Family Law, Divorce, Child Custody, Visitation Rights, Marital Property Law, Civil Litigation, Real Estate, Personal Injury.

RON M. LANDSMAN, P.A.

WASHINGTON, D.C.

(See Bethesda, Maryland)

Elder Law, Medicaid Law, Medical Legal Law, Medicaid Hearings, Estate Planning and Tax, Wills, Trust and Probate Law, Disability Planning, Medicaid and Disability Trusts, bot Individual and Pooled Trusts.

LANE, AITKEN & McCANN, L.L.P.

WASHINGTON, D.C.

(See Venable, Attorneys at Law, Venable, Baetjer and Howard, LLP)

CHISWELL D. LANGHORNE, JR.

Established in 1982

1616 H STREET, N.W., SUITE 902

WASHINGTON, D.C. 20006

Telephone: 202-628-5093

Telecopier: 202-628-5932

Email: langhorc@erols.com

General Civil and Administrative Practice. Estate Planning, Probate, Natural Resources, Taxation and Trusts.

CHISWELL D. LANGHORNE, JR., born Lynchburg, Virginia, 1940; admitted to bar, 1966, Virginia and District of Columbia; 1973, U.S. Supreme Court; 1984, U.S. Tax Court. *Education:* University of Virginia (B.A., 1963; J.D., 1966). Co-Author: "Will & Testamentary Trust Forms," 1st Edition, 1974; 2nd Edition, 1981, published by the Bar Association of the District of Columbia. *Member:* The District of Columbia Bar; Bar Association of the District of Columbia; Virginia State Bar; Virginia, Federal and American Bar Associations.

LANKFORD & COFFIELD

WASHINGTON, D.C.

(See Alexandria, Virginia)

Civil and White Collar Criminal Trial and Appellate Practice before all Courts and Government Agencies. Domestic and International Arbitration. International Business Law.

MARK D. LAPONSKY

THE INTERNATIONAL TRADE CENTER

1300 PENNSYLVANIA AVENUE, NW, SUITE 700

WASHINGTON, D.C. 20004

Telephone: 202-789-0990

Facsimile: 202-789-7349

Email: mdlaponsky@laponsky-law.com

URL: http://www.lawyers.com/laponskylaw

Labor and Employment, Disabilities, Civil Rights, Education Law, Constitutional Law, Civil Litigation, Business Law.

MARK D. LAPONSKY, born Niskayuna, New York, May 18, 1958; admitted to bar, 1984, Maryland; 1987, U.S. District Court, District of Maryland; 1990, District of Columbia and U.S. Supreme Court; 1993, U.S. District Court for the District of Columbia, U.S. Court of Appeals for the District of Columbia Circuit, U.S. Court of Appeals for the Federal Circuit and U.S. Court of Appeals, Fourth Circuit. *Education:* Syracuse University (B.A., 1980); Washington College of Law of American University (J.D., 1983). *Member:* Maryland State (Member, Labor and Employment Law Section), Federal (National Council; Chair, Labor and Employment Law Section) and American (Member: Labor and Employment Law Section; Litigation Section; Business Law Section) Bar Associations; The District of Columbia Bar (Member, Labor Relations Section; Chair, Committee on Individual Employee Rights and Responsibilities in the Workplace, 1993-1995). ***PRACTICE AREAS:*** Employment Law; Disabilities; Civil Rights; Education; Constitutional; Civil Litigation; Business Law.

LaROE, WINN, MOERMAN & DONOVAN

Established in 1921

3900 HIGHWOOD COURT, N.W.

WASHINGTON, D.C. 20007

Telephone: 202-298-8100

Telecopier: 202-298-8200

Email: p.m.donovan@worldnet.att.net

Legislative Practice. Civil, Administrative and Appellate Litigation. Antitrust, Transportation, Environment, Occupational Safety and Health Law.

FIRM PROFILE: LaRoe, Winn, Moerman & Donovan was founded in 1921. The firm, which is listed in the Martindale-Hubbell Bar Register of Preeminent Lawyers, specializes in federal litigation, regulation and legislation particularly in the areas of antitrust, transportation and environmental law.

Antitrust functions include litigation before the federal courts and Federal Trade Commission, as well as, legislative activities before the United States Congress. The transportation practice consists primarily of representation before various federal and transportation regulatory agencies and the Congress. The environmental practice involves numerous issues before the Environmental Protection Agency, the Occupational Safety and Health Administration and other federal and state agencies and the Congress.

The work of LaRoe, Winn, Moerman & Donovan involves constant contact with regulatory and executive agencies and the Congress to assist corporate and trade association clients in governmental relations and select litigation problems.

MEMBERS OF FIRM

WILBUR LaROE, JR. (1921-1957).

ARTHUR L. WINN, JR. (1928-1995).

PAUL M. DONOVAN, born Cortland, New York, September 21, 1941; admitted to bar, 1968, District of Columbia and U.S. Court of Appeals for the District of Columbia Circuit; 1973, U.S. Supreme Court; 1976, U.S. Court of Appeals, 4th Circuit; 1979, U.S. Court of Appeals, 5th, 7th and 9th Circuits; 1981, U.S. Court of Appeals, 11th Circuit; 1983, U.S. Court of Appeals, 2nd Circuit; 1986, U.S. Court of Appeals, 3rd Circuit. *Education:* Le Moyne College (B.A., 1964); Boston College (LL.B., 1967). Water Transportation Editor, Transportation Practitioners Journal, 1975-1990. Co-Author: "The Shipping Act of 1984," 51, ICC Prac. J. 463, 1984. *Member:* The District of Columbia Bar; American Bar Association. ***REPORTED CASES:*** Chlorine Institute, Inc. vs. California Highway Patrol, 29 F.3d 495 (9th Cir. 1994). ***PRACTICE AREAS:*** Transportation Law; Environmental Law; Antitrust Law.

OF COUNSEL

SAMUEL H. MOERMAN, born Washington, D.C., September 30, 1913; admitted to bar, 1934, District of Columbia and U.S. Court of Appeals for the District of Columbia Circuit; 1946, U.S. Supreme Court. *Education:* George Washington University Law School (J.D., 1934). *Member:* The District of Columbia Bar.

REPRESENTATIVE CLIENTS: The Port Authority of New York and New Jersey; The Chlorine Institute, Inc.

LARSON & TAYLOR, PLC

WASHINGTON, D.C.

(See Alexandria, Virginia)

Patent, Trademark, Copyright and Unfair Competition Law and related Litigation. International Patent and Trademark Practice.

JOHN L. LASTER

1776 MASSACHUSETTS AVENUE, N.W., SUITE 300

WASHINGTON, D.C. 20036

Telephone: 202-530-0850

Email: TrustToLast@prodigy.com

Bethesda, Maryland Office: Telephone: 301-656-0744.

Falls Church, Virginia Office: 103 Rowell Court, Telephone: 703-538-3600. Fax: 703-538-3601.

Trusts, Estates, Estate Planning and Elder Law.

(For biographical data on Personnel, see Professional Biographies at Falls Church, Virginia)

LATHAM & WATKINS

555 11TH STREET, N.W., SUITE 1000

WASHINGTON, D.C. 20004-1304

Telephone: 202-637-2200

Telecopier: 202-637-2201

URL: http://www.lw.com

Chicago, Illinois; Costa Mesa, California; Frankfurt/Main, Germany Office- Latham & Watkins Schön Nolte; Hamburg, Germany Office- Latham & Watkins Schön Nolte; Hong Kong, China; London, England; Los Angeles, California; Menlo Park, California; Moscow, Russia; Newark, New Jersey; Newton, Massachusetts; New York, N.Y.; Paris, France; Reston, Virginia; San Diego, California; San Francisco, California; Singapore; Tokyo, Japan.

Communications, Corporate, Energy, Environmental, Health Care, Government Contracts, Government Relations, Litigation, Products Liability, Project Finance, Real Estate, Securities, Taxation, White Collar Crime.

PARTNERS

NICHOLAS W. ALLARD, admitted to bar, 1980, New York; 1981, District of Columbia. *Education:* Princeton University (A.B., 1974); Oxford University, Rhodes Scholar (B.A., 1976); Yale University (J.D., 1979). ***PRACTICE AREAS:*** Communications and Media; Election, Campaign and Political Law; Government; Regulatory Law; Privacy Law.

JENNIFER C. ARCHIE, admitted to bar, 1989, Maryland; 1990, District of Columbia. *Education:* St. Lawrence University (B.A., 1983); Cornell Law School (J.D., 1989). ***PRACTICE AREAS:*** Commercial Litigation; Internet Law; Health Care; Government Contract Fraud; Insurance Coverage.

TERESA D. BAER, admitted to bar, 1986, Pennsylvania; 1987, District of Columbia. *Education:* University of Pennsylvania (B.A., 1982); Stanford University (J.D., 1985). ***LANGUAGES:*** Spanish. ***PRACTICE AREAS:*** Communications and Media.

JAMES H. BARKER, III, admitted to bar, 1990, Florida; 1991, District of Columbia. *Education:* Washington & Lee University (B.A., 1987); University of Virginia (J.D., 1990).

JAMES R. BARRETT, admitted to bar, 1991, California; 1994, District of Columbia. *Education:* Pitzer College (B.A., 1984); Georgetown University Law Center (J.D., 1991).

ERIC L. BERNTHAL, admitted to bar, 1970, District of Columbia. *Education:* Columbia University (B.A., 1967); George Washington University (J.D., with honors, 1970). (Resident).

RICHARD P. BRESS, admitted to bar, 1989, Pennsylvania; 1998, District of Columbia. *Education:* Cornell University (B.A., 1982; M.B.A., 1983); Stanford University (J.D., 1987). ***PRACTICE AREAS:*** Appellate Practice; Communications and Media; Constitutional Law; ERISA Litigation; U.S. Supreme Court Litigation.

KAREN BRINKMANN, admitted to bar, 1989, New York (resigned); 1990, District of Columbia. *Education:* Brown University (A.B., 1983); New York University (J.D., 1988). ***LANGUAGES:*** French. ***PRACTICE AREAS:*** Communications Law.

RICHARD A. CONN, JR., admitted to bar, 1982, California; 1996, District of Columbia. *Education:* Dartmouth College (B.A., 1979); Fordham University (J.D., 1982). ***LANGUAGES:*** Russian and Spanish. ***PRACTICE AREAS:*** Bankruptcy; Debtor and Creditor; Insurance; Investment in Russia; Litigation; International Litigation.

GARY M. EPSTEIN, admitted to bar, 1971, District of Columbia. *Education:* Lehigh University (B.S.E.E., 1968); Harvard University (J.D., 1971). ***PRACTICE AREAS:*** Administrative Law; Communications and Media; Corporate Law; Intellectual Property; Technology and Science.

ROGER S. GOLDMAN, admitted to bar, 1980, District of Columbia; 1981, California. *Education:* University of Virginia (B.A., 1977; J.D., 1980). ***PRACTICE AREAS:*** Government Contract Fraud; Health Care Fraud; Bid Protests; Foreign Military Sales.

McGEE GRIGSBY, admitted to bar, 1971, California and District of Columbia. *Education:* Louisiana State University (B.A., 1965); Harvard University (J.D., cum laude, 1970). ***PRACTICE AREAS:*** International Tax Controversies; Tax Controversies; Tax Planning.

JULIA A. HATCHER, admitted to bar, 1987, District of Columbia. *Education:* Mount Holyoke College (B.A., 1982); Georgetown University Law Center (J.D., 1987). ***LANGUAGES:*** French. ***PRACTICE AREAS:*** Environmental Law; Administrative Law; Litigation; Occupational Safety and Health.

CAROLYNE R. HATHAWAY, admitted to bar, 1988, Virginia and District of Columbia. *Education:* Salve Regina College (B.S., 1975); Bryant College (M.B.A., 1984); Georgetown University Law Center (J.D., 1987).

(This Listing Continued)

DAVID J. HAYES, admitted to bar, 1978, District of Columbia. *Education:* University of Notre Dame (B.A., 1975); Stanford University (J.D., 1978). ***PRACTICE AREAS:*** Environmental Law; Natural Resources; Indians and Native Populations; Energy.

DAVID R. HAZELTON, admitted to bar, 1983, District of Columbia; 1985, Virginia. *Education:* Wayne State University (A.B., 1977); University of Michigan (J.D., 1981). ***PRACTICE AREAS:*** Government Contracts; Litigation; Administrative Law; Intellectual Property.

JOHN J. HUBER, admitted to bar, 1975, Wisconsin; 1981, District of Columbia. *Education:* University of Wisconsin (B.A., 1968; J.D., cum laude, 1974); Georgetown University (LL.M., 1978).

PAUL J. HUNT, admitted to bar, 1992, Pennsylvania; 1993, District of Columbia. *Education:* Bucknell University (B.A., 1988); University of Virginia (J.D., 1991). ***PRACTICE AREAS:*** Project Finance; Energy Project Development; Infrastructure Development; Energy Contracts; Independent Power.

JOHN P. JANKA, admitted to bar, 1987, California; 1988, District of Columbia. *Education:* Duke University (A.B., 1984); University of California at Los Angeles (J.D., 1987). ***PRACTICE AREAS:*** Communications and Media Law; Corporate Law; Business Law; Intellectual Property.

EVERETT C. JOHNSON, JR., admitted to bar, 1981, District of Columbia; 1996, Maryland. *Education:* Duke University (A.B., 1978); University of Virginia (J.D., 1981). (Resident).

WILLIAM C. KELLY, JR., admitted to bar, 1972, Maine; 1973, District of Columbia. *Education:* Harvard University (A.B., 1968); Yale University (J.D., 1971). ***PRACTICE AREAS:*** Government; Historic Preservation; Housing Law; Nonprofit and Charitable Organizations; Real Estate.

STUART S. KURLANDER, admitted to bar, 1989, Illinois; 1990, District of Columbia. *Education:* Indiana University (B.A., 1984; Certificate in Public Affairs, 1984); St. Louis University (J.D., 1988; M.H.A., 1988). ***PRACTICE AREAS:*** False Claims Act; Health Care Corporate Law; Health Care Mergers and Acquisitions; Health Care Regulation; Health Care Reimbursement.

DANIEL T. LENNON, admitted to bar, 1990, Maryland; 1991, District of Columbia. *Education:* University of Notre Dame (B.A., 1987); Catholic University (J.D., 1990).

CURTIS P. LU, admitted to bar, 1991, Maryland; 1994, District of Columbia. *Education:* University of Virginia (B.A., 1986); Harvard University (J.D., 1989). ***PRACTICE AREAS:*** Securities Litigation; Health Care Fraud; Commercial Litigation.

MAUREEN E. MAHONEY, admitted to bar, 1978, Illinois; 1980, District of Columbia; 1983, Virginia. *Education:* Indiana University (A.B., 1974); University of Chicago (J.D., 1978).

MARK E. NEWELL, admitted to bar, 1983, District of Columbia. *Education:* Albion College (A.B., 1977); Harvard Law School (J.D., 1981); Kennedy School of Government (M.P.P., 1981). ***PRACTICE AREAS:*** Insurance Coverage; Civil Litigation; Commercial Litigation.

WILLIAM PATRICK O'NEILL, admitted to bar, 1976, Illinois; 1982, District of Columbia. *Education:* University of Kansas (B.A., 1973); University of Michigan at Ann Arbor (J.D., 1976). ***PRACTICE AREAS:*** Mergers, Acquisitions and Divestitures; Securities.

THOMAS L. PATTEN, admitted to bar, 1969, Missouri; 1972, District of Columbia and U.S. Supreme Court; 1983, Virginia. *Education:* University of Missouri (B.S., 1967; J.D., 1969). ***PRACTICE AREAS:*** Arbitration; Qui Tam Litigation; Public Contract Law; Complex Litigation; White Collar Criminal Defense.

WILLIAM K. RAWSON, admitted to bar, 1980, Washington; 1982, District of Columbia. *Education:* Amherst College (B.A., 1975); Stanford Law School (J.D., 1980).

JAMES F. RITTER, admitted to bar, 1986, California; 1997, District of Columbia. *Education:* Dartmouth College (A.B., 1981); University of Virginia (J.D., 1986). ***PRACTICE AREAS:*** Finance; Corporate Law; Business Law; Mergers, Acquisitions and Divestitures; Debtor and Creditor.

JAMES F. ROGERS, admitted to bar, 1981, District of Columbia. *Education:* Yale University (B.A., 1975); Princeton University (M.P.A., 1979); Columbia University (J.D., 1979). ***LANGUAGES:*** Spanish, German, French. ***PRACTICE AREAS:*** Corporate Law; Communications and Media.

JOHN L. SACHS, admitted to bar, 1980, District of Columbia. *Education:* Yale University (B.A., magna cum laude, 1976); Harvard University (J.D., 1980). ***LANGUAGES:*** French and Spanish. ***PRACTICE AREAS:*** Energy; Energy Project Development; Infrastructure Development; Project Finance.

KENNETH A. SCHUHMACHER, born Trenton, New Jersey, September 3, 1965; admitted to bar, 1992, California (inactive); 1994, District of Columbia. *Education:* Dartmouth College (A.B., 1987); University of Michigan (J.D., 1990); Cambridge University (LL.M., 1991). ***PRACTICE AREAS:*** Project Finance.

(This Listing Continued)

DAVID L. SCHWARTZ, admitted to bar, 1989, Pennsylvania; 1990, District of Columbia. *Education:* Bowdoin College (A.B., 1986); American University, Washington College of Law (J.D., 1989). ***LANGUAGES:*** Russian and French. ***PRACTICE AREAS:*** Electric Power; Energy Regulation; Energy Contracts.

EDWARD J. SHAPIRO, admitted to bar, 1981, District of Columbia. *Education:* Princeton University (A.B., 1978); Harvard University (J.D., 1981).

DEMAURICE F. SMITH, admitted to bar, 1989, Maryland; 1990, District of Columbia and U.S. District Court, District of Maryland; U.S. Court of Appeals for District of Columbia. *Education:* Cedarville College (B.S., 1985); University of Virginia (J.D., 1989). ***PRACTICE AREAS:*** White Collar Criminal Defense; Computer Crime; Trial Practice; Litigation; Grand Jury Practice; Government.

ERIC A. STERN, admitted to bar, 1985, Maryland and District of Columbia. *Education:* Dartmouth College (A.B., 1979); Harvard Law School (J.D., 1983).

JOSEPH D. SULLIVAN, admitted to bar, 1985, Maryland; 1986, District of Columbia and U.S. Tax Court. *Education:* Georgetown University (B.A., 1980; J.D., 1985).

ROBERT M. SUSSMAN, admitted to bar, 1974, New York; 1976, District of Columbia. *Education:* Yale University (B.A., 1969; LL.B., 1973). ***PRACTICE AREAS:*** Environmental; Air Quality; Chemical Regulation; Superfund.

KENNETH W. WEINSTEIN, admitted to bar, 1973, Maryland; 1974, District of Columbia. *Education:* City College of the City University of New York (B.S., 1969); Georgetown University (J.D., 1973). ***PRACTICE AREAS:*** Environmental Litigation; Pesticide Regulation; Toxic Substance Regulation.

W. HARRISON WELLFORD, admitted to bar, 1977, District of Columbia. *Education:* Davidson College (B.A., 1962); Cambridge University (M.A., 1964); Harvard University (Ph.D., 1972); Georgetown University (J.D., 1976).

BETH A. WILKINSON, admitted to bar, 1988, New York; 1999, District of Columbia. *Education:* Princeton University (B.A., 1984); University of Virginia (J.D., 1987). ***PRACTICE AREAS:*** White Collar Crime; Civil Litigation.

E. MARCELLUS WILLIAMSON, admitted to bar, 1989, New York; 1999, District of Columbia. *Education:* Swarthmore College (B.A., 1984); Columbia University (M.A., 1985); New York University (J.D., 1988). ***LANGUAGES:*** French. ***PRACTICE AREAS:*** Antitrust; Civil Litigation; EU Competition.

PETER L. WINIK, admitted to bar, 1980, District of Columbia; 1983, Maryland. *Education:* Stanford University (A.B., 1977; J.D., 1980). ***PRACTICE AREAS:*** Complex and Multi-District Litigation; Class Action Defense; Product Safety; Product Recall; Antidumping.

LEONARD A. ZAX, admitted to bar, 1978, District of Columbia and New Jersey. *Education:* University of Chicago (A.B., 1971); Harvard University (M.C.P., 1975; J.D., 1975).

OF COUNSEL

BRUCE BABBITT, admitted to bar, 1965, Arizona (Not admitted in District of Columbia). *Education:* University of Notre Dame (B.A., 1960); University of Newcastle (M.S., 1963); Harvard University (LL.B., 1965). ***PRACTICE AREAS:*** Natural Resources.

DAVID A. BARRETT, admitted to bar, 1988, California; 1991, District of Columbia. *Education:* Pitzer College (B.A., 1984); University of Texas, Austin (J.D., with honors, 1988). ***PRACTICE AREAS:*** Insurance Coverage; Civil Litigation.

EDWARD CORREIA, admitted to bar, 1976, Oklahoma; 1989, District of Columbia. *Education:* University of Oklahoma (B.A., 1970); Harvard University (M.P.P., 1972); University of Oklahoma J.D., 1976). ***PRACTICE AREAS:*** Government Relations; Antitrust; Consumer Protection; Civil Rights.

DAVID M. LEIVE, admitted to bar, 1961, District of Columbia. *Education:* Columbia University (A.B., 1956); Harvard University (LL.B., 1959).

ESTHER R. SCHERB, admitted to bar, 1987, Virginia; 1990, U.S. Court of Appeals, Fourth Circuit; 1994, U.S. Court of Appeals, Ninth Circuit; 1997, U.S. Court of Appeals, Eleventh Circuit; 1998, District of Columbia. *Education:* Brooklyn College (B.S., Chemistry, 1975); Tufts University School of Dental Medicine (D.M.D., 1978); University of Richmond (J.D., 1987). ***PRACTICE AREAS:*** Health Law; Medicare and Medicaid Reimbursement; Federal Administrative Law.

ERIN M. SWEENEY, admitted to bar, 1989, Pennsylvania; 1990, District of Columbia; 1997, New York. *Education:* Ohio University (B.S.B.A., 1986); American University (J.D., 1989; M.A., 1990). ***PRACTICE AREAS:*** ERISA Compliance; ERISA Litigation; Executive Compensation; Health Benefits; Pension and Profit Sharing Plans.

(This Listing Continued)

LATHAM & WATKINS, Washington—Continued

SPECIAL LEGAL CONSULTANT

BETTINA VERONICA FREIRE, admitted to bar, 1991, Argentina; 2000, New York and Special Legal Consultant in the District of Columbia (Not admitted in District of Columbia). *Education:* Universidad de Buenos Aires (Attorney at Law, 1991); Austral University (LL.M., 1995); Columbia University (LL.M., 1999). ***LANGUAGES:*** Spanish. ***PRACTICE AREAS:*** Project Finance; Investment in Latin America; International Finance; International Mergers and Acquisitions; Energy Project Development.

ASSOCIATES

JOEL B. ARD, born Hamilton, Ontario, Canada, September 4, 1973; admitted to bar, 2000, Illinois; 2001, District of Columbia. *Education:* St. John's College (B.A., 1995); University of Chicago (J.D., 2000). ***LANGUAGES:*** German. ***PRACTICE AREAS:*** Litigation.

WENDY ATROKHOV, admitted to bar, 2000, New York and District of Columbia. *Education:* American University (B.A., 1995); Cornell University (J.D., 1999). ***LANGUAGES:*** Russian. ***PRACTICE AREAS:*** Public Finance; Project Finance.

SEUNG W. BAIK, admitted to bar, 2000, Maryland; 2001, District of Columbia. *Education:* Cornell University (B.A., 1996); Northwestern University (J.D., 2000). ***LANGUAGES:*** Korean.

DORI K. BAILEY, admitted to bar, 2000, New York, Maryland and District of Columbia. *Education:* State University of New York at Albany (B.S., 1988); Cornell University (J.D., 1999). ***PRACTICE AREAS:*** Corporate.

VICKY L. BEASLEY, admitted to bar, 1999, Virginia; 2000, District of Columbia. *Education:* University of Virginia (B.A., 1996); Columbia University (J.D., 1999).

DAVID A. BECKER, admitted to bar, 1996, Maryland; 1997, District of Columbia. *Education:* Yale University (B.A., 1991); University of Chicago (J.D., 1996). ***PRACTICE AREAS:*** White Collar Criminal Defense; Congressional Investigations; Health Care Fraud; Insider Trading; Commercial Litigation.

JACOB D. BERNSTEIN, admitted to bar, 2000, California; 2001, District of Columbia. *Education:* University of California at Santa Barbara (B.A., 1997); Georgetown University (J.D., 2000). ***PRACTICE AREAS:*** Corporate Law.

DAVID I. BROWN, admitted to bar, 1999, New York; 2001, District of Columbia. *Education:* University of Virginia (B.A., 1995); Harvard Law School (J.D., 1998). ***PRACTICE AREAS:*** Mergers, Acquisitions and Divestitures; Corporate Law.

ANA MARÍA CABASSA, admitted to bar, 2001, New York (Not admitted in District of Columbia). *Education:* Georgetown University (B.S.B.A., 1995); New York University School of Law (J.D., 2000). ***LANGUAGES:*** Spanish. ***PRACTICE AREAS:*** Corporate Law; Taxation.

RICHARD R. CAMERON, admitted to bar, 1995, New York and Massachusetts; 1996, District of Columbia. *Education:* Cornell University (A.B., 1990); George Washington University (J.D., 1994). ***PRACTICE AREAS:*** Administrative Law; Communications and Media; Federal Legislative Practice; Telephone Utility Regulation.

GEORGE D. CANNON, JR., admitted to bar, 1995, New York; 1996, District of Columbia. *Education:* University of Hamburg, Germany; Tulane University of Louisiana (B.A., cum laude, 1988); Free University of Berlin, Germany; George Washington University (J.D., cum laude, 1994). ***LANGUAGES:*** German. ***PRACTICE AREAS:*** Energy.

WILLIAM S. CARNELL, admitted to bar, 1997, Virginia; 1999, District of Columbia. *Education:* James Madison University (B.A., 1991); George Mason University (M.A., History, 1994); University of Virginia (J.D., 1997). ***PRACTICE AREAS:*** Communications and Media; Broadcasting Law; Communications Law; Telecommunications Competition; Wireless Communications.

RAMONA R. CARROLL, admitted to bar, 1998, Maryland (Not admitted in District of Columbia). *Education:* University of Maryland (B.S., 1995); University of Chicago (J.D., 1998).

SUE J. CHOI, admitted to bar, 1997, New York; 2000, District of Columbia. *Education:* University of California at Berkeley (B.A., 1991); University of California at Los Angeles (J.D., 1996).

ANN CLAASSEN, admitted to bar, 1989, New Mexico; 1991, District of Columbia. *Education:* St. John's College; The Colorado College (B.A., 1975); University of New Mexico (J.D., 1989). ***PRACTICE AREAS:*** Chemical Regulation; Environmental Administrative Law; Environmental Health and Safety; Environmental Regulation; Toxic Substance Regulation.

(This Listing Continued)

BARTON B. CLARK, admitted to bar, 1995, New York; 1996, District of Columbia. *Education:* Harvard College (B.A.., 1990); University of Chicago (J.D., 1994). ***LANGUAGES:*** German. ***PRACTICE AREAS:*** Securities Regulation; Corporate Law.

CHERYL MILLER COE, admitted to bar, 1995, Virginia; 1996, District of Columbia. *Education:* Emory University (B.A., 1990); Georgetown University (J.D., 1995). ***PRACTICE AREAS:*** Taxation; Corporate Taxation; Partnership Taxation; Federal Taxation.

MARCELO N. CORPUZ, III, admitted to bar, 1995, Ohio; 1997, District of Columbia; 1998, Illinois. *Education:* Georgetown University (B.A., 1990); George Washington University (J.D./M.P.H., 1995). ***PRACTICE AREAS:*** Health Care.

DAVID S. DANTZIC, admitted to bar, 1995, California (inactive); 1996, District of Columbia. *Education:* Cornell University (B.A., 1989); Harvard University (J.D., 1994). ***PRACTICE AREAS:*** Mergers and Acquisitions; General Corporate; Venture Capital Financings.

NESTOR M. DAVIDSON, admitted to bar, 1999, New York (Not admitted in District of Columbia). *Education:* Harvard University (A.B., 1990); Columbia Law School (J.D., 1997). ***PRACTICE AREAS:*** Affordable Housing; Commercial Real Estate; Civil Appeals.

KEVIN H. DOUGLAS, admitted to bar, 1998, Tennessee; 2000, District of Columbia. *Education:* University of Virginia (B.A., 1995); Vanderbilt University (J.D., 1998). ***PRACTICE AREAS:*** Mergers and Acquisitions; Corporate Law; Securities.

ALEXANDRA FELDER DUFRESNE, admitted to bar, 1999, Illinois (Not admitted in District of Columbia). *Education:* University of Chicago (J.D., 1999). ***LANGUAGES:*** Spanish and Italian. ***PRACTICE AREAS:*** Litigation.

BART S. EPSTEIN, admitted to bar, 1999, Virginia; 2000, District of Columbia. *Education:* State University of New York at Binghamton (B.A., 1991); University of Virginia (J.D., 1999). ***PRACTICE AREAS:*** Computer Law; Communications Law; Internet Law; Electronic Commerce; Business Law.

ADAM S. FELS, admitted to bar, 2000, Maryland; 2001, District of Columbia. *Education:* Columbia University (A.B., 1993); University of Chicago (J.D., 1998). ***PRACTICE AREAS:*** Litigation.

JILL FRANCE, born Hagerstown, Maryland, July 26, 1971; admitted to bar, 1999, Maryland; 2000, District of Columbia. *Education:* Haverford College (B.A., 1993); George Washington University (J.D., 1999). ***PRACTICE AREAS:*** Corporate Finance; Corporate Governance; Private Placement; Public Offerings.

W. ANDREW H. GANTT, III, admitted to bar, 1994, Maryland; 2000, District of Columbia. *Education:* University of California at Berkeley (B.A., 1987); Harvard University (M.T.S., 1990); University of Virginia (J.D., 1993). ***LANGUAGES:*** French. ***PRACTICE AREAS:*** Health Care; Corporate Law; Intellectual Property; Mergers, Acquisitions and Divestitures; Privacy Law.

ALLEN M. GARDNER, admitted to bar, 1996, Utah; 1997, District of Columbia. *Education:* Brigham Young University (B.A., 1993); Columbia University (J.D., 1996). ***LANGUAGES:*** Mandarin Chinese.

MICHAEL J. GERGEN, admitted to bar, 1993, New York; 1995, District of Columbia and Illinois. *Education:* Antioch College (B.A., 1982); University of California (M.S., 1987); New York University (J.D., 1992). ***PRACTICE AREAS:*** Regulated Industries; Utility Law; Energy; Antitrust and Trade Regulation; Administrative Law.

NICHOLAS B. GERTLER, admitted to bar, 1999, Maryland; 2000, District of Columbia. *Education:* University of Virginia (B.S., 1993); Massachusetts Institute of Technology (M.S., 1995); Harvard University (J.D., 1998). ***LANGUAGES:*** Hungarian. ***PRACTICE AREAS:*** Environmental Law.

BARBARA M. GIBIAN, admitted to bar, 1994, New York; 1995, District of Columbia. *Education:* Hamline University (B.A., 1977); Georgetown University (J.D., 1993). ***LANGUAGES:*** French and Spanish.

BRIAN L. GLASSBERG, born Cheverly, Maryland, May 2, 1974; admitted to bar, 1999, Maryland; 2000, District of Columbia. *Education:* Harvard University (J.D., 1999). ***PRACTICE AREAS:*** Communications Law; Corporate Law; Technology Law.

MICHAEL JOSEPH GOLDEN, admitted to bar, 1998, Virginia; 2000, District of Columbia. *Education:* University of Virginia (B.S., 1995); Georgetown University (J.D., 1998). ***PRACTICE AREAS:*** Litigation; Appellate Practice; Consumer Law; Intellectual Property; Computers and Software.

TODD S. GORDON, admitted to bar, 1999, Maryland; 2000, District of Columbia. *Education:* James Madison University (B.B.A., 1994); Vanderbilt University (J.D., 1999).

JENNIFER L. GOWETSKI, admitted to bar, 1999, Virginia; 2000, District of Columbia. *Education:* Georgetown University (B.S.F.S., 1994; J.D., 1999). ***PRACTICE AREAS:*** Corporate Law; Communications and Media.

(This Listing Continued)

TIMOTHY W. GREGG, admitted to bar, 1999, Maryland; 2001, District of Columbia. *Education:* University of North Carolina (B.A., 1992); Vanderbilt University (J.D., 1999). ***PRACTICE AREAS:*** Corporate Law; Securities.

RAYMOND B. GROCHOWSKI, admitted to bar, 1992, Maryland; 1994, District of Columbia. *Education:* College of William & Mary (B.S., 1975); Georgetown University (J.D., 1991). ***PRACTICE AREAS:*** Telecommunications Regulation; Corporate Finance; Corporate Governance; Venture Capital; Mergers and Acquisitions.

JAMES R. HANNA, admitted to bar, 1996, Georgia; 1998, District of Columbia. *Education:* Texas Christian University (B.A., 1988); University of California, Boalt Hall School of Law (J.D., 1995). ***PRACTICE AREAS:*** Telecommunications; Mergers and Acquisitions; Securities.

CLAUDIA HINSCH, admitted to bar, 1995, Maryland (Not admitted in District of Columbia). *Education:* Carnegie Mellon University (B.A., 1989); Georgetown University (J.D., 1995; LL.M., 1998). ***PRACTICE AREAS:*** Employee Benefits; ERISA.

JULIE K. HOFFMAN, admitted to bar, 1995, Ohio; 2000, District of Columbia. *Education:* Ohio University (B.B.A., 1992); University of Cincinnati (J.D., 1995). ***PRACTICE AREAS:*** Securities.

JOHN G. HOLLAND, admitted to bar, 1995, Arizona; 1996, Colorado and District of Columbia. *Education:* Brigham Young University (B.A., 1991); Columbia University (J.D., 1994). ***LANGUAGES:*** French.

CLAIRE HOLLOWAY, admitted to bar, 2000, Hawaii; 2001, District of Columbia. *Education:* Vanderbilt University (B.S., magna cum laude, 1997); University of Michigan (J.D., 2000). ***LANGUAGES:*** French.

ANDREW D. IRWIN, admitted to bar, 1996, Maryland; 1997, District of Columbia. *Education:* Princeton University (A.B., 1993); University of Edinburgh, Scotland; George Washington University (J.D., 1996). ***PRACTICE AREAS:*** Government Contracts; White Collar Crime; Health Care Fraud; Litigation; Government Ethics.

BENOIT N. JACQMOTTE, admitted to bar, 1999, Maryland; 2000, District of Columbia. *Education:* McGill University (B.A., 1994); New York University (J.D., 1999). ***LANGUAGES:*** French. ***PRACTICE AREAS:*** Communications and Media; Corporate Law.

JARED W. JOHNSON, admitted to bar, 1993, Maryland; 1995, District of Columbia. *Education:* Gonzaga University (B.A., cum laude, 1990); Georgetown University Law Center (J.D., cum laude, 1993). ***LANGUAGES:*** French. ***PRACTICE AREAS:*** Energy; Electric Power.

NANDAN M. JOSHI, born 1971; admitted to bar, 1996, Maryland; 1997, District of Columbia. *Education:* Louisiana State University (B.A., 1993); Georgetown University (J.D., 1996). ***PRACTICE AREAS:*** Communications Law; Telecommunications Competition; Satellite Communications; Mass Media Law; Civil Appeals.

MORENIKE S. KASSIM, admitted to bar, 1999, Maryland; 2000, District of Columbia. *Education:* University of Virginia (B.A., 1996); University of Michigan (J.D., 1999). ***LANGUAGES:*** Dutch. ***PRACTICE AREAS:*** Corporate Law; Finance; Commercial Law; Energy; Communications and Media.

THOMAS J. KIM, admitted to bar, 1996, New York; 1997, District of Columbia; 1998, California. *Education:* Yale University (B.A., 1991); Harvard University (J.D., 1995). ***PRACTICE AREAS:*** Corporate; Securities Law; Entertainment Law.

MARK KLAASSEN, admitted to bar, 1998, Colorado; 1999, District of Columbia and Maryland. *Education:* Oral Roberts University (B.S., 1995); University of Notre Dame (J.D., 1998). ***PRACTICE AREAS:*** Litigation.

TRENA LEE KLOHE, admitted to bar, 1998, Maryland (inactive); 1999, District of Columbia. *Education:* Reed College (B.A., 1989); University of New Mexico (M.A., J.D., 1998). ***LANGUAGES:*** Spanish and Portuguese. ***PRACTICE AREAS:*** Health Care; Medicare and Medicaid Reimbursement; Health Care Regulation; International Law; International Human Rights.

ARTHUR S. LANDERHOLM, admitted to bar, 1996, California; 1997, District of Columbia. *Education:* Pomona College (B.A., 1992); University of California at Los Angeles (J.D., 1996). ***PRACTICE AREAS:*** Communications and Media; Mergers, Acquisitions and Divestitures.

MATTHEW R. LEWIS, admitted to bar, 1996, Arizona; 1998, Utah and District of Columbia. *Education:* University of Utah (B.A., 1993); Columbia University (J.D., 1996). ***LANGUAGES:*** French. ***PRACTICE AREAS:*** Business Arbitration; Business Litigation; Federal Civil Practice.

STEPHANIE SZU-PING LIM, admitted to bar, 2000, Virginia; 2001, District of Columbia. *Education:* Amherst College (B.A., 1992); Duke University (M.A., 1997; J.D, 2000).

JEREMY B. LUSTMAN, born Baltimore, Maryland, May 17, 1973; admitted to bar, 2000, Maryland; 2001, District of Columbia. *Education:* Yeshiva University (B.A., 1996); Georgetown University (J.D., 2000). ***LANGUAGES:*** Hebrew. ***PRACTICE AREAS:*** Telecommunications Law; Corporate Finance; Health Care Corporate Law; Business Acquisitions; Technology Law.

(This Listing Continued)

JULIA MacLAREN, admitted to bar, 2000, Virginia; 2001, District of Columbia. *Education:* Georgetown University (B.A., 1995); University of Virginia (J.D., 2000). ***PRACTICE AREAS:*** Litigation; White Collar Crime.

CHITTARANJAN MALLIK, admitted to bar, 2000, Maryland; 2001, District of Columbia. *Education:* University of Maryland (B.S., 1997); University of Michigan (J.D., 2000). ***PRACTICE AREAS:*** Corporate Law.

GEOFFREY A. MANNE, admitted to bar, 2000, Virginia (Not admitted in District of Columbia). *Education:* University of Chicago (A.B., 1993; J.D., 1997). ***LANGUAGES:*** Spanish and Italian. ***PRACTICE AREAS:*** Antitrust; Appellate Practice; Commercial Litigation.

JOHN R. MANTHEI, admitted to bar, 1994, Wisconsin and Pennsylvania; 1995, District of Columbia. *Education:* Miami University (B.A., magna cum laude, 1990); University of Wisconsin (J.D., 1994). ***PRACTICE AREAS:*** Food and Drug Law; Government Relations.

JEFFREY A. MARKS, admitted to bar, 1998, Maryland; 1999, District of Columbia. *Education:* Franklin & Marshall College (B.A., 1993); George Washington University (J.D., 1998). ***PRACTICE AREAS:*** Communications Common Carrier; Wireless Communications; Satellite Communications; Federal Civil Litigation.

ERICA McFARQUHAR, admitted to bar, 1998, California; 2000, District of Columbia and Virginia. *Education:* Princeton University (A.B., 1980); University of San Diego (J.D., 1997). ***PRACTICE AREAS:*** Litigation; Internet Law; Computer Fraud; Health Care Fraud.

HEATHER M. McPHEE, admitted to bar, 2000, Virginia (Not admitted in District of Columbia). *Education:* Princeton University (A.B., 1992); University of Chicago (J.D., 2000).

DAVID M. McPHERSON, admitted to bar, 1994, Massachusetts; 2000, District of Columbia. *Education:* University of Massachusetts (B.S., 1989); Boston University School of Law (J.D., 1993).

ELLIOTT MILHOLLIN, admitted to bar, 1999, Minnesota; 2001, District of Columbia. *Education:* University of Michigan (B.A., 1993); University of Wisconsin, Madison (J.D., 1999). ***LANGUAGES:*** French. ***PRACTICE AREAS:*** Appellate Practice; Regulatory Law; Environmental Law.

ANDREW D. MORTON, admitted to bar, 2000, Maryland; 2001 District of Columbia. *Education:* University of Maryland (B.A., magna cum laude, 1991); University of Pennsylvania (J.D., cum laude, 2000). ***PRACTICE AREAS:*** Government Relations; Telecommunications Law; Health Care.

ASHLIE MUSS HEGERLE, admitted to bar, 1995, Maryland and Minnesota; 1998, District of Columbia. *Education:* Cornell University (B.A., 1987); New York University School of Law (J.D., 1993). ***PRACTICE AREAS:*** Commercial Financing; Secured Transactions; Mergers and Acquisitions Finance.

LAURA H. NEUWIRTH, admitted to bar, 1993, New York; 1995, District of Columbia. *Education:* Cornell University (B.A., 1986); Yale University (J.D., 1992). ***PRACTICE AREAS:*** Environmental Administrative Law; Product Safety.

CLAUDIA M. O'BRIEN, admitted to bar, 1994, Virginia; 1995, District of Columbia. *Education:* Yale University (B.A., 1987); Georgetown University (J.D., magna cum laude, 1994). ***PRACTICE AREAS:*** Environmental Law.

LYNLEY A. OGILVIE, admitted to bar, 1995, Virginia; 1996, District of Columbia. *Education:* Harvard University (B.A., 1988); Bristol University, Bristol, England; University of Virginia (J.D., 1995). ***LANGUAGES:*** Japanese and French. ***PRACTICE AREAS:*** International Finance.

AMY J. OLIVER, admitted to bar, 2000, Utah; 2001, District of Columbia. *Education:* University of Utah (B.S., 1995); Harvard University (J.D., 2000). ***PRACTICE AREAS:*** Litigation; Labor and Employment.

ELIZABETH R. PARK, admitted to bar, 2000, Virginia; 2001, District of Columbia. *Education:* Tufts University (B.S., 1994); George Washington University (J.D., 2000).

JENNIFER O. PATEL, admitted to bar, 1999, Maryland; 2000, District of Columbia. *Education:* Utah State University (B.A., 1993); Georgetown University (J.D., 1999). ***LANGUAGES:*** Russian.

C. THOMAS POWELL, admitted to bar, 1999, Virginia; 2000, District of Columbia. *Education:* University of North Carolina at Chapel Hill (A.B., 1977; M.A., 1982; Ph.D., 1986; J.D., 1999). ***PRACTICE AREAS:*** Environmental Law; Litigation.

JAMAL QAIMMAQAMI, admitted to bar, 2000, New York and District of Columbia. *Education:* American University (B.A., 1996); University of California at Los Angeles (J.D., 1999).

ABID RIAZ QURESHI, admitted to bar, 1997, Virginia; 2000, District of Columbia. *Education:* Cornell University (B.A., 1994); Harvard Law School (J.D., 1997). ***LANGUAGES:*** Urdu, Punjabi. ***PRACTICE AREAS:*** Technology Law; Internet Litigation.

JUSTIN R. RHOADES, admitted to bar, 2000, Virginia; 2001, District of Columbia. *Education:* Pomona College (B.A., 1997); Harvard University (J.D., 2000). ***PRACTICE AREAS:*** Business Litigation; Antitrust; Intellectual Property Litigation.

(This Listing Continued)

LATHAM & WATKINS, Washington—Continued

KATHRYN H. RUEMMLER, admitted to bar, 1998, Virginia and District of Columbia. *Education:* University of Washington (B.A., 1993); Georgetown University (J.D., 1996). ***PRACTICE AREAS:*** Criminal Litigation; Civil Litigation.

TONYA RUTHERFORD, admitted to bar, 1997, Georgia (Not admitted in District of Columbia). *Education:* Johns Hopkins University (B.A., 1994); George Washington University (J.D., 1997). ***PRACTICE AREAS:*** Communications Common Carrier.

SCOTT E. SCHANG, admitted to bar, 1994, Maryland; 1995, District of Columbia. *Education:* Yale University (B.A., cum laude, 1988); Georgetown University (J.D., magna cum laude, 1994). ***PRACTICE AREAS:*** Environmental Law.

JANICE M. SCHNEIDER, admitted to bar, 1992, Maryland (Not admitted in District of Columbia). *Education:* University of Miami (B.S., 1983); Lewis and Clark College, Northwestern School of Law (J.D., 1992). ***PRACTICE AREAS:*** Natural Resources; Environmental Law; Indians and Native Populations; Administrative Law; Energy.

STEVEN H. SCHULMAN, admitted to bar, 1994, Maryland; 1997, District of Columbia. *Education:* Brandeis University (B.A., 1989); Northwestern University (J.D., 1994). ***PRACTICE AREAS:*** Litigation; Antitrust; White Collar Criminal Defense; Pro Bono Immigration Law; Communications Law.

PATRICK H. SHANNON, admitted to bar, 1999, Virginia; 2000, District of Columbia. *Education:* University of Virginia (J.D., 1999). ***PRACTICE AREAS:*** Corporate Law; Communications Law.

JOSEPH A. SIMEI, admitted to bar, 1998, Maryland; 1999, District of Columbia. *Education:* United States Naval Academy (B.S., 187); Northwestern University (J.D., 1998). ***PRACTICE AREAS:*** Mergers and Acquisitions.

ANDREW R. STEWART, admitted to bar, 1998, Maryland; 1999, District of Columbia. *Education:* Duke University (B.A., cum laude, 1994); University of Virginia (J.D., 1997). ***PRACTICE AREAS:*** Environmental Law.

OLIVIER P. STRAUCH, admitted to bar, 2000, Maryland (Not admitted in District of Columbia). *Education:* Harvard University (A.B., 1994); Georgetown University (J.D., 2000). ***LANGUAGES:*** French. ***PRACTICE AREAS:*** Communications Law; Civil Litigation.

CASSANDRA STURKIE, admitted to bar, 2000, Virginia; 2001, District of Columbia. *Education:* University of South Carolina (B.Ar.Sc., 1995); University of Queensland, Queensland, Australia (P.G. Dip. Sci., 1996); Duke University (J.D., 2000; M.A., 2000). ***PRACTICE AREAS:*** Administrative Litigation; Environmental Law; Political Asylum; Zoning, Planning and Land Use.

AMY LYNN SYPULA, admitted to bar, 2000, Illinois; 2001, District of Columbia. *Education:* University of Chicago (B.A., 1997; J.D., 2000). ***PRACTICE AREAS:*** Environmental Law.

H. BARTON THOMAS, admitted to bar, 1998, Oregon; 2000, District of Columbia and U.S. Tax Court. *Education:* Rollins College (A.B., 1988); Lewis and Clark College (J.D., cum laude, 1998). ***PRACTICE AREAS:*** Tax Controversies; Tax Planning; Civil Litigation.

JOEL H. TROTTER, admitted to bar, 1995, Virginia; 2000, District of Columbia. *Education:* University of Virginia (B.A., 1992; J.D., 1995). ***PRACTICE AREAS:*** Corporate Law.

MATTHEW R. VANDERGOOT, admitted to bar, 2000, Virginia; 2001, District of Columbia. *Education:* University of Notre Dame (B.A., Economics, 1993); University of Michigan (J.D., 2000; M.B.A., 2000). ***PRACTICE AREAS:*** Corporate Law; Communications and Media.

JENNIFER VAN DRIESEN, admitted to bar, 1997, Maryland; 2000, District of Columbia. *Education:* Duke University (B.A., 1990); Georgetown University (J.D., 1997). ***PRACTICE AREAS:*** Secured Financing.

RACHEL WARD, admitted to bar, 1998, Maryland; 1999, District of Columbia. *Education:* University of Virginia (B.A., 1994; J.D., 1998). ***PRACTICE AREAS:*** Mergers, Acquisitions and Divestitures; Corporate Finance.

JOHN W. WESTMORELAND, admitted to bar, 1998, Missouri; 1999, Illinois; 2000, District of Columbia and U.S. Tax Court. *Education:* University of Missouri, Columbia (B.S., 1994; M.A., 1997; J.D., 1997). ***PRACTICE AREAS:*** Taxation.

LIANE N. WILSON, admitted to bar, 1999, New York; 2001, District of Columbia. *Education:* Fordham University (B.A., 1994); Pace University (J.D., cum laude, 1998). ***PRACTICE AREAS:*** Corporate Practice; Mergers and Acquisitions; Securities.

JOEL D. WRIGHT, admitted to bar, 2000, New York (Not admitted in District of Columbia). *Education:* Brigham Young University (B.A., 1996); New York University (J.D., 1999). ***LANGUAGES:*** Portuguese. ***PRACTICE AREAS:*** Project Finance; Energy Project Development; Finance; Infrastructure Development; Independent Power.

(This Listing Continued)

ERIC J. WYCOFF, admitted to bar, 1999, Iowa; 2000, District of Columbia. *Education:* Briar Cliff College (B.A., 1996); University of Notre Dame (J.D., 1999).

LATHROP & GAGE PLLC

SUITE 800, 1200 G STREET, N.W.
WASHINGTON, D.C. 20005
Telephone: 202-434-8984
Facsimile: 202-434-8992
URL: http://www.lathropgage.com

Kansas City, Missouri Office: Lathrop & Gage LC, 2345 Grand Boulevard, Suite 2800. Telephone: 816-292-2000. Facsimile: 816-292-2001.
Overland Park, Kansas Office: 10851 Mastin Boulevard, Building 82, Suite 1000. Telephone: 913-451-5100. Facsimile: 913-451-0875.
St. Louis, Missouri Office: Lathrop & Gage, 1010 Market Street, Suite 1300. Telephone: 314-613-2500. Facsimile: 314-613-2550.
Jefferson City, Missouri Office: Lathrop & Gage LC, 326 East Capitol. Telephone: 573-893-4336. Facsimile: 573-893-5398.
Boulder, Colorado Office: 4845 Pearl East Circle, Suite 302, 80301. Telephone: 303-449-5800. Facsimile: 303-443-6998.
Springfield, Missouri Office: 1845 S. National, P.O. Box 4288. Telephone: 417-886-2000. Facsimile: 417-886-9126.

General and Administrative Practice and Litigation before all Courts and Agencies. Government Contracts, International Trade and Investment Law, Environmental and Energy Law.

PAUL KALCHBRENNER, born Chicago, Illinois, 1968; admitted to bar, 1996, Maryland (Not admitted in District of Columbia). *Education:* Gettysburg College (B.A., 1990); Vermont Law School (J.D., M.S.L., 1995). ***PRACTICE AREAS:*** Environmental; Regulatory; Government Relations. ***Email:*** pkalchbrenner@lathropgage.com

All attorneys are members of the American Bar Association, The Missouri Bar and/or Various local and regional bar associations

(For Complete Biographical Data on all Personnel, see Professional Biographies of Kansas City, Missouri).

LAZARUS & ASSOCIATES

1850 M STREET, SUITE 400
WASHINGTON, D.C. 20036
Telephone: 202-457-0380
fax: 202-452-1822
Email: LazarusLaw@aol.com

Litigation in all courts. Legislation and Regulation. Business Counseling.

KENNETH A. LAZARUS, born Passaic, New Jersey, March 10, 1942; admitted to bar, 1967, New Jersey; 1971, U.S. Supreme Court; 1976, District of Columbia. *Education:* University of Dayton (B.A., 1964); University of Notre Dame (J.D., 1967); George Washington University (LL.M., Tax, 1971). Adjunct Professor of Law, Georgetown University Law Center, 1979—. Trial Attorney and Special Assistant U.S. Attorney, U.S. Department of Justice, 1967-1971. Chief Counsel to Republicans, U.S. Senate Judiciary Committee, 1971-1974. Associate Counsel to the President of the United States (Gerald R. Ford), 1974-1977. Appointed Member, U.S. Advisory Committee on Trade Negotiations by President Ronald Reagan, 1982-1986. *Member:* The District of Columbia Bar; Federal and American Bar Associations; International Law Institute (Member, Board of Trustees, 1986—); American Law Institute (Elected Life Member).

LEBOEUF, LAMB, GREENE & MACRAE L.L.P.

A Limited Liability Partnership including Professional Corporations

Formerly LeBoeuf, Lamb, Leiby & MacRae

1875 CONNECTICUT AVENUE, N.W.
WASHINGTON, D.C. 20009
Telephone: 202-986-8000
Facsimile: 202-986-8102
Telex: 440274
URL: http://www.llgm.com

Eastern United States:
New York, N.Y. Office: 125 West 55th Street. Telephone: 212-424-8000. Facsimile: 212-424-8500. Telex: 423416 or 1561363.

(This Listing Continued)

Albany, New York Office: One Commerce Plaza, 99 Washington Avenue, Suite 2020. Telephone: 518-626-9000. Facsimile: 518-626-9010.
Boston, Massachusetts Office: 260 Franklin Street. Telephone: 617-439-9500. Facsimile: 617-439-0341; 439-0342.
Harrisburg, Pennsylvania Office: 200 North Third Street, Suite 300, P.O. Box 12105. Telephone: 717-232-8199. Facsimile: 717-232-8720.
Hartford, Connecticut Office: Goodwin Square, 225 Asylum Street, 13th Floor. Telephone: 860-293-3500. Facsimile: 860-293-3555.
Newark, New Jersey Office: The Legal Center, One Riverfront Plaza. Telephone: 973-643-8000. Facsimile: 973-643-6111.
Pittsburgh, Pennsylvania Office: One Gateway Center, Fort Duquesne Boulevard, Suite 1600. Telephone: 412-594-2300. Facsimile: 412-594-5237.
Western United States:
Denver, Colorado Office: 633 17th Street, Suite 2000. Telephone: 303-291-2600. Facsimile: 303-297-0422.
Los Angeles, California Office: 725 South Figueroa Street, Suite 3100. Telephone: 213-955-7300. Facsimile: 213-955-7399. Telex: 678982.
Salt Lake City, Utah Office: 1000 Kearns Building, 136 South Main Street. Telephone: 801-320-6700. Facsimile: 801-359-8256.
San Francisco, California Office: One Embarcadero Center, Suite 400. Telephone: 415-951-1100. Facsimile: 415-951-1180; 951-1181. Telex: 470167.
Southern United States:
Houston, Texas Office: 1000 Louisiana Avenue. Telephone: 713-287-2000. Facsimile: 713-287-2100.
Jacksonville, Florida Office: 50 North Laura Street, Suite 2800. Telephone: 904-354-8000. Facsimile: 904-353-1673.
European Offices:
Brussels, Belgium Office: Kunstlaan/Avenue des Arts, 19H, B-1000 Brussels, Belgium. Telephone: 011-32-2-227-0900. Facsimile: 011-32-2-227-0909.
London, England Office: LeBoeuf, Lamb, Greene & MacRae (A London Based Multinational Partnership); One Minster Court, Mincing Lane, 6th Floor, London EC3R 7AA England. Telephone: 011-44-20-7-459-5000. Facsimile: 011-44-20-7-459-5099.
Moscow, Russian Federation Office: Nikitsky Pereulok, 5 (formerly Ulitsa Belinskogo) 103473 Moscow, Russian Federation. Telephone: 011-7-095-737-5000. Facsimile: 011-7-095-737-5050.
Paris, France Office: 30, rue du Faubourg Saint-Honoré 75008 Paris, France. Telephone: 011-33-1-53-93-77-00. Facsimile: 011-33-1-42-56-08-06.
Asian Offices:
Almaty, Kazakhstan Office: Prospect Seyfullin, 531, 5th Floor, 480083, Almaty, Republic of Kazakhstan. Telephone: 011-7-3272-50-7575. Facsimile: 011-7-3272-50-7576.
Bishkek, Kyrgyz Office: Ulitsa Panfilova, 205 Bishkek, Kyrgyz Republic. Telephone: 011-996-3312-22-2994. Facsimile: 011-996-3312-66-2233.
Tashkent, Uzbekistan Office: Ulitsa Turab Tula, 1 700003 Tashkent Republic of Uzbekistan. Telephone: 011-7-3712-40-6050. Facsimile: 011-7-3712-40-6052.
African Office:
Johannesburg, South Africa Office: 11 Alice Lane, 2nd Floor, West Wing, Standard Bank Building, Sandton 2196 Johannesburg, South Africa. Telephone: 27-011-784-0233. Fax: 27-011-784-2855.

General Practice including Administrative, Antitrust, Copyrights, Corporate, EMF Litigation, Energy, Environmental, ERISA, Government Relations, Insurance, International Trade & Customs, Labor, Legislative, Litigation, Maritime, Municipal Bonds, Oil & Gas, Patents, Public Utilities, Reinsurance, Securities, Taxation, Telecommunications, Trademarks, Transportation, Venture Capital.

PARTNERS

GEORGE R. ABRAMOWITZ, born 1946; admitted to bar, 1970, District of Columbia. *Education:* Colgate University (A.B., 1967); Georgetown University Law Center (J.D., 1970). Editor, Georgetown Law Journal, 1969-1970. Adjunct Professor, Georgetown University Law Center, 1977-1979. 1978). ***PRACTICE AREAS:*** Tax; Insurance. ***Email:*** gabramow@llgm.com

LAWRENCE G. ACKER, born 1950; admitted to bar, 1974, Virginia; 1975, District of Columbia; 1988, Minnesota. *Education:* Syracuse University (B.A., 1971); Georgetown University (J.D., 1974). ***PRACTICE AREAS:*** Utilities. ***Email:*** lacker@llgm.com

DENNIS L. ALLEN, born 1954; admitted to bar, 1980, Illinois; 1981, District of Columbia. *Education:* Augustana College (B.A., 1976); University of Notre Dame (J.D., magna cum laude, 1980). Phi Beta Kappa. ***PRACTICE AREAS:*** Taxation; Insurance. ***Email:*** dallen@llgm.com

CYNTHIA T. ANDREASON, born 1953; admitted to bar, 1984, Utah; 1993, District of Columbia. *Education:* Brigham Young University; University of Colorado (B.A., Music, with honors, 1978); University of Southern California; University of Utah (J.D., 1984). Member, Utah Law Review, 1982-1983. ***PRACTICE AREAS:*** Insurance; Litigation. ***Email:*** candreas@llgm.com

(This Listing Continued)

DOUGLAS N. BECK, born 1959; admitted to bar, 1987, Virginia; 1988, District of Columbia. *Education:* Boston University (B.A., 1981); Columbia University (M.A., 1983); University of Virginia School of Law (J.D., 1987). ***Email:*** dxbeck@llgm.com

SAMUEL BEHRENDS, IV, born 1951; admitted to bar, 1979, District of Columbia; 1984, North Carolina. *Education:* Harvard University (B.A., 1974); Wake Forest University (J.D., 1979). ***PRACTICE AREAS:*** Utilities. ***Email:*** sbehrend@llgm.com

MICHAEL A. BELL, born 1949; admitted to bar, 1981, District of Columbia. *Education:* University of Maryland (B.S., 1974) Beta Alpha Psi; Columbus School of Law, Catholic University of America (J.D., 1981). Staff Member, Catholic University Law Review, 1980-1981. ***PRACTICE AREAS:*** Tax. ***Email:*** mabell@llgm.com

D. RANDALL BENN, born 1962; admitted to bar, 1987, North Carolina; 1988, District of Columbia. *Education:* Duke University (B.A., magna cum laude, 1984; J.D., 1987). Phi Eta Sigma. President, Duke Chapter, Phi Delta Phi, 1985-1986. ***PRACTICE AREAS:*** Environmental; Hydropower; Legislative. ***Email:*** dbenn@llgm.com

DOUGLAS G. BONNER, born 1958; admitted to bar, 1983, Florida; 1984, District of Columbia. *Education:* Bucknell University (B.A., 1980); Catholic University of America (J.D., 1983). Member, 1981-1982 and Associate Editor, 1982-1983, Catholic University Law Review. ***LANGUAGES:*** French. ***PRACTICE AREAS:*** Telecommunications; Litigation. ***Email:*** dbonner@llgm.com

DAVID A. COLSON, born 1943; admitted to bar, 1975, California; 1976, District of Columbia. *Education:* California State College (B.A., 1966); Boalt Hall School of Law, University of California, Berkeley (J.D., 1975). [U.S. Marine Corps, 1969-1971]. ***PRACTICE AREAS:*** International Law; Environmental Law. ***Email:*** dacolson@llgm.com

ELIAS G. FARRAH, born 1951; admitted to bar, 1978, Massachusetts; 1981, District of Columbia. *Education:* St. Anselm's College (A.B., 1973); Western New England College (J.D., cum laude, 1978). ***PRACTICE AREAS:*** Energy; Utilities. ***Email:*** efarrah@llgm.com

A. EVERETTE JAMES, admitted to bar, 1995, Florida and District of Columbia. *Education:* University of North Carolina at Chapel Hill; Illinois Institute of Technology (J.D., M.B.A., 1990). ***PRACTICE AREAS:*** Insurance; Emerging Business Law; Corporate. ***Email:*** aejames@llgm.com

CECELIA KEMPLER, born 1940; admitted to bar, 1980, New York and U.S. District Court, Southern and Eastern Districts of New York; 1994, U.S. Supreme Court; 1999, District of Columbia. *Education:* Tufts University; City College of the City University of New York (B.A., 1974); New York Law School (J.D., cum laude, 1979). New York Law School Law Review. (Also in New York, NY Office). ***PRACTICE AREAS:*** Insurance Company Reorganization; Insurance Insolvencies; Market Conduct. ***Email:*** ckempler@llgm.com

L. CHARLES LANDGRAF, born 1952; admitted to bar, 1978, District of Columbia; 1979, U.S. District Court for the District of Columbia; 1980, U.S. Court of Appeals for the District of Columbia Circuit and U.S. Court of Appeals, Fifth Circuit. *Education:* Rice University (B.A., 1975); New York University (J.D., 1978). ***LANGUAGES:*** Thai, Russian. ***PRACTICE AREAS:*** Insurance; Legislation; Intellectual Property. ***Email:*** landgraf@llgm.com

MARY A. LOPATTO, born 1954; admitted to bar, 1986, Pennsylvania; 1988, District of Columbia. *Education:* Princeton University (A.B., 1976); Catholic University of America (J.D., 1986). Associate Editor, Catholic University Law Review. ***PRACTICE AREAS:*** Reinsurance; Insurance; Litigation. ***Email:*** mxlopatt@llgm.com

MICHAEL F. McBRIDE, born 1951; admitted to bar, 1976, Wisconsin and District of Columbia. *Education:* University of Wisconsin-Milwaukee (B.S., 1972); California Institute of Technology (M.S., 1973); University of Wisconsin-Madison (J.D., 1976). ***PRACTICE AREAS:*** Transportation; Litigation; Environmental; Utilities. ***Email:*** mfmcbrid@llgm.com

BRUCE W. NEELY, born 1948; admitted to bar, 1979, Pennsylvania; 1992, District of Columbia. *Education:* College of Wooster (B.A., with honors, 1970); Columbia University (M.A., with honors, 1974); University of Pittsburgh (J.D., with honors, 1978). Phi Beta Kappa. ***PRACTICE AREAS:*** Utilities. ***Email:*** bwneely@llgm.com

BRIAN D. O'NEILL, born 1946; admitted to bar, 1971, Florida; 1975, District of Columbia. *Education:* Florida State University (B.A., 1968; J.D., 1971). ***PRACTICE AREAS:*** Energy Regulation; Administrative Litigation. ***Email:*** boneill@llgm.com

DAVID R. POE, born 1948; admitted to bar, 1975, New York; 1977, North Carolina; 1991, District of Columbia. *Education:* University of Missouri (B.S.M.E., cum laude, 1970) Tau Beta Pi; Duke University (J.D., 1974). ***PRACTICE AREAS:*** Communications; Utilities. ***Email:*** dpoe@llgm.com

M. KRISTAN RIZZOLO, born 1966; admitted to bar, 1991, Virginia; 1993, District of Columbia. *Education:* George Washington University (B.A., magna cum laude, 1988); George Washington University National Law Center

(This Listing Continued)

LEBOEUF, LAMB, GREENE & MACRAE L.L.P., Washington—Continued

(J.D., with honors, 1991); Georgetown University Law Center (LL.M., with distinction, 1992). Phi Beta Kappa. Clerk, The Honorable Charles E. Clapp, II, U.S. Tax Court. ***PRACTICE AREAS:*** Tax. ***Email:*** mkrizzol@llgm.com

DAVIS R. ROBINSON, born 1940; admitted to bar, 1968, New York; 1972, District of Columbia. *Education:* Yale University (B.A., magna cum laude, 1961); Harvard University (LL.B., cum laude, 1967). Foreign Service Officer, 1961-1969 and The Legal Adviser, U.S. Department of State, 1981-1985. Former United States Member, Permanent Court of Arbitration, The Hague. ***PRACTICE AREAS:*** International; Corporate. ***Email:*** drrobins@llgm.com

ELIZABETH BARRY SANDZA, born 1951; admitted to bar, 1979, Delaware; 1981, California; 1988, District of Columbia and Maryland. *Education:* University of Minnesota (B.S., magna cum laude, 1973); Northwestern University (M.A., 1974); Temple University (J.D., 1979). ***PRACTICE AREAS:*** Insurance; Litigation. ***Email:*** ebsandza@llgm.com

MELVIN S. SCHWECHTER, born 1947; admitted to bar, 1975, District of Columbia; 1984, New York. *Education:* Hebrew College (B.J.Ed., 1968); Brandeis University (A.B., magna cum laude, 1969); Harvard University (M.A., Regional Studies-Soviet Union, 1971); New York University (J.D., 1974). ***PRACTICE AREAS:*** International. ***Email:*** myschwec@llgm.com

LAJUANA S. WILCHER, born 1954; admitted to bar, 1980, Kentucky and U.S. District Court, Western District of Kentucky; 1997, District of Columbia. *Education:* Western Kentucky University (B.S., magna cum laude, 1977); Salmon P. Chase College of Law, Northern Kentucky University (J.D., 1980); University of Louisville. ***PRACTICE AREAS:*** Environmental Law and Litigation; Administrative and Regulatory Law. ***Email:*** lwilcher@llgm.com

OF COUNSEL

THOMAS F. BROSNAN, born 1921; admitted to bar, 1949, Connecticut; 1950, District of Columbia. *Education:* Boston University (B.S., cum laude, 1943); Columbia University (LL.B., 1948). Phi Delta Phi. [Active duty, U.S. Naval Reserve, 1943-46; Lieut. Comdr., U.S.N.R.]. ***PRACTICE AREAS:*** Federal Energy Law; Gas Utilities; Rates; Facility Siting; Taxation.

FRANK CUMMINGS (P.C.), born 1929; admitted to bar, 1959, New York; 1963, District of Columbia; 1973, U.S. Tax Court. *Education:* Hobart College (B.A., 1951); Columbia University (M.A., 1955; LL.B., 1958). Phi Beta Kappa; Phi Alpha Delta. Articles Editor, Columbia Law Review, 1957-1958. ***PRACTICE AREAS:*** Employee Benefits; Employment; Labor; Litigation.

JAMES P. FAMA, born 1953; admitted to bar, 1981, Maryland; U.S. Court of Appeals, 9th Circuit; 1989, Florida and U.S. District Court, Middle District of Florida; 1990, District of Columbia; 1993, U.S. Court of Appeals, District of Columbia Circuit. *Education:* University of Virginia (B.A., 1975); University of Baltimore (J.D., 1981). ***PRACTICE AREAS:*** Energy Law; Regulatory Law; Mergers and Acquisitions; Corporate Law. ***Email:*** jfama@llgm.com

CHARLES W. HAVENS III (P.C.), born 1936; admitted to bar, 1961, Virginia and District of Columbia. *Education:* Franklin & Marshall College (A.B., 1958); University of Virginia (LL.B., 1961). ***PRACTICE AREAS:*** Insurance; Antitrust.

CARL D. HOBELMAN, (P.C.), born 1931; admitted to bar, 1960, New York; 1980, District of Columbia; 1993, California. *Education:* Cornell University (B.C.E., 1954); Harvard University (J.D., 1959). ***PRACTICE AREAS:*** Utilities; Trade and Professional Associations.

JOHN W. LAWRENCE, born 1961; admitted to bar, 1993, Maryland; 1994, U.S. Court of Appeals, Fourth Circuit; 1996, District of Columbia and U.S. Court of Appeals, District of Columbia Circuit; 1998, U.S. Court of Appeals, Fifth Circuit. *Education:* Purdue University (B.S., Nuclear Engineering, 1983); Catholic University of America (J.D., 1993). ***PRACTICE AREAS:*** Nuclear Law; Energy Law; Litigation. ***Email:*** jlawrenc@llgm.com

MARTIN G. MALSCH, born 1942; admitted to bar, 1968, Connecticut; 1986, U.S. Court of Appeals for the District of Columbia Circuit; 1997, District of Columbia. *Education:* College of the Holy Cross (B.S., Physics, 1964); University of Connecticut (J.D., 1968). Recipient, American Jurisprudence Award. Meritorious Executive Rank, President Ronald Reagan, 1984, President George Bush, 1990; Distinguished Executive Rank, President George Bush, 1993. ***PRACTICE AREAS:*** Nuclear Energy; Environmental; Administrative; Litigation. ***Email:*** mmalsch@llgm.com

ARNOLD W. REITZE, JR., born 1938; admitted to bar, 1971, District of Columbia; 1979, Virginia. *Education:* Fairleigh Dickinson University (B.A., 1960); Rutgers University (LL.B., 1962); Johns Hopkins University (M.P.H., 1986). ***PRACTICE AREAS:*** Environmental Law.

(This Listing Continued)

COUNSEL

MARY A. MURPHY, born 1964; admitted to bar, 1989, District of Columbia. *Education:* Wheaton College (B.A., magna cum laude, 1986); George Washington University (J.D., 1989). ***PRACTICE AREAS:*** Energy; Utilities. ***Email:*** mmurphy@llgm.com

SUSAN E. SEABROOK, born 1960; admitted to bar, 1986, Arizona and U.S. District Court, District of Arizona; 2001, District of Columbia. *Education:* University of Colorado (B.A., 1982); Gonzaga University School of Law (J.D., 1985). ***Email:*** sseabroo@llgm.com

ROBERT W. WOODY, born 1959; admitted to bar, 1992, Virginia; 1993, District of Columbia. *Education:* James Madison University (B.S., cum laude, 1982); Catholic University of America (J.D., 1992). Pi Gamma Mu. ***PRACTICE AREAS:*** Insurance; Government Relations. ***Email:*** rwoody@llgm.com

(Biographical data on all Members of the Firm, Counsel, Of Counsel and Special Counsel in New York, New York; Washington, D.C.; San Francisco, California; Newark, New Jersey; Boston, Massachusetts; Salt Lake City, Utah; Jacksonville, Florida; Houston, Texas; Hartford, Connecticut; Los Angeles, California; Albany, New York; Harrisburg, Pennsylvania; Pittsburgh, Pennsylvania; Denver, Colorado; London, England; Brussels, Belgium; Almaty, Kazakhstan; Moscow, Russian Federation and Paris, France are listed in the respective Biographical Sections)

LEE & MCSHANE, PC

1211 CONNECTICUT AVENUE N.W., SUITE 425
WASHINGTON, D.C. 20036
Telephone: 202-530-8100
Fax: 202-530-0402
URL: http://www.leemcshane.com
Email: jrb@lee-mcshane.com
URL: http://www.lawyers.com/leeandmcshanelaw

Architecture Law, Engineering Law, Corporate Law.

JAMES F. LEE, JR., born New York, N.Y., September 20, 1950; admitted to bar, 1975, New York and U.S. Court of Military Appeals; 1979, District of Columbia and U.S. Supreme Court; 1981, Maryland. *Education:* Syracuse University (B.A., 1972; J.D., 1974). *Member:* American Bar Association (Member, Forum Committee on Construction Law); Asian Pacific American Bar Association; District of Columbia Defense Lawyers Association (President, 1989-1990); Legal Counsel's Forum of the American Consulting Engineers Council; American Institute of Architects (Northern Virginia, Baltimore, Washington, D.C. and Potomac Valley Chapters) and Consulting Engineers Council (Metropolitan Washington Chapter); Professional Affiliate Member. [Capt., U.S. Army, JAGC, 1975-1979]. ***PRACTICE AREAS:*** Business Transactions; Construction; Architects and Engineers; Commercial Litigation. ***Email:*** jfl@lee-mcshane.com

TERRENCE M. MCSHANE, born San Francisco, California, September 29, 1950; admitted to bar, 1984, New York; 1991, District of Columbia and Maryland. *Education:* Georgetown University (B.S., 1976; J.D., 1983). Assistant District Attorney, New York County, 1983-1989. *Member:* American Bar Association. [U.S. Navy-U.D.T./S.E.A.L. Teams, 1968-1972]. ***PRACTICE AREAS:*** Construction; Architects and Engineers; Products Liability; Real Estate. ***Email:*** tmm@lee-mcshane.com

---

LAURENCE C. FAUTH, born Huntington, New York, March 24, 1964; admitted to bar, 1997, Maryland and District of Columbia. *Education:* Bucknell University (B.A., 1986); George Mason University School of Law (J.D., 1996). Member, George Mason Law School National Moot Court Team, 1995. Law Clerk, Honorable Joseph E. McGuire, U.S. Department of Justice, Executive Office for Immigration Review, 1996-1997. U.S. Attorney's Office for the District of Columbia, Special Assistant, 1998. *Member:* Maryland State Bar Association; The District of Columbia Bar. ***PRACTICE AREAS:*** Commercial Litigation; Architects and Engineers Liability; Construction Law. ***Email:*** lcf@lee-mcshane.com

BRANDON M. GLADSTONE, born Camp Springs, Maryland, March 21, 1968; admitted to bar, 1993, Virginia; 1994, Maryland; 1995, District of Columbia; 1999, U.S. District Court, District of Maryland and U.S. Court of Appeals, Fourth Circuit; 2000, U.S. District Court, Eastern District of Virginia and U.S. District Court, District of Columbia. *Education:* University of Virginia (B.S., Commerce, with distinction, 1990); Indiana University (J.D., 1993). Finalist, Sherman Minton Moot Court Competition, 1992. Assistant Public Defender, Commonwealth of Virginia, 1994-1996. *Member:* Virginia State Bar. ***PRACTICE AREAS:*** Personal Injury; Negligence; Civil Litigation; Insurance Law; Commercial Litigation; Construction Law; Professional Liability; Architects and Engineers Liability; Toxic Torts; Defamation; Contract Law. ***Email:*** bmg@lee-mcshane.com

(This Listing Continued)

KAREN O. SHEEHAN, born Fairborn, Ohio, March 25, 1966; admitted to bar, 1995, Maryland and Virginia; 1997, District of Columbia. *Education:* Bucknell University (B.A., 1988); George Washington University (J.D., with honors, 1995). *Member:* Montgomery County and Maryland State Bar Associations; Women's Bar Association of Maryland(Montgomery County Chapter). ***PRACTICE AREAS:*** Business Transactions; Construction Litigation; Commercial Litigation. ***Email:*** kos@lee-mcshane.com

EUGENE W. POLICASTRI, born Pawtucket, Rhode Island, December 15, 1961; admitted to bar, 1989, Louisiana; 2000, Maryland; 2001, District of Columbia. *Education:* Colgate University (B.A., 1983); Tulane University (J.D., 1989). *Member:* American Bar Association; Defense Research Institute. ***PRACTICE AREAS:*** Construction Litigation; Architects and Engineers; Commercial Litigation; Maritime Law. ***Email:*** ewp@lee-mcshane.com

ARTHUR T. K. NORRIS, born Baltimore, Maryland, October 13, 1964; admitted to bar, 1991, Virginia; 1993, District of Columbia; 2000, Maryland. *Education:* Stanford University (A.B., with distinction, 1986); Duke University School of Law (J.D., 1990). Recipient, James S. Bidlake Award for Legal Research and Writing, 1988. ***PRACTICE AREAS:*** Civil Litigation; Construction Law; Architects and Engineers; Real Estate; Title Insurance. ***Email:*** atn@lee-mcshane.com

LEE & SMITH, P.C.

1101 30TH STREET N.W.,
SUITE 200
WASHINGTON, D.C. 20007
Telephone: 202-293-4584
Fax: 202-293-4588
Email: davidlee@leesmithpc.com
URL: http://www.lawyers.com/federalregulatorylaw

Federal Administrative Law, Federal Regulatory Law, Legislative Lobbying, Defense Contracts, Foreign Military Sales, Army Export Controls and Regulations, High Technology Transfer, Government Affairs, Government Relations, Export Compliance, Public Land Law, Defense Department Trade Controls, Technical Assistance Agreements.

FIRM PROFILE: Lee & Smith, P.C. has a unique administrative, legislative and federal regulatory practice. The firm's partners have top secret security clearance with the Departments of State and Defense. Clients to the firm include universities, research institutions and international entities involved in technology transfer.

DAVID B. LEE, born Salt Lake City, Utah, July 25, 1949; admitted to bar, 1976, Utah; 1980, District of Columbia; 1981, U.S. District Court for the District of Columbia; 1985, U.S. Supreme Court. *Education:* University of Washington; University of Utah (B.A., magna cum laude, 1973); Brigham Young University (J.D., 1976). Phi Kappa Phi. Chief of Staff and Counsel to Congressman Gunn McKay, 1976-1981. Executive Director, United Democrats of Congress, 1986. *Member:* District of Columbia Bar; Utah State Bar; American Bar Association. ***PRACTICE AREAS:*** Federal Legislative Practice; Administrative Law. ***Email:*** davidlee@leesmithpc.com

C. WILLIAM SMITH, born Washington, D.C., September 4, 1942; admitted to bar, 1975, District of Columbia. *Education:* American University (J.D., 1974). Staff Director, Treasury, Postal Service and General Appropriations Subcommittee of the Appropriations Committee, U.S. House of Representatives. Top Secret Security Clearance. *Member:* District of Columbia Bar. [Captain, U.S. Marine Corps, 1964-1968]. ***PRACTICE AREAS:*** Federal Legislative Practice; Administrative Law. ***Email:*** billsmith@leesmithpc.com

OF COUNSEL

GLENDON E. JOHNSON, JR., born Salt Lake City, Utah, August 25, 1951; admitted to bar, 1978, Texas; 1990, District of Columbia. *Education:* University of Utah (B.A., with honors, 1975); University of Texas (J.D., 1978). Member, 1976-1978 and Note and Comment Editor, 1977-1978, Texas Law Review. Co-Author: *The Art of M&A, a Merger/Acquisition Buyout Guide,* Dow Jones-Irwin, 1989. *Member:* State Bar of Texas; District of Columbia Bar; American Bar Association. ***LANGUAGES:*** French. ***PRACTICE AREAS:*** Corporate; Corporate Finance; Mergers and Acquisitions.

LEFTWICH & DOUGLAS, P.L.L.C.

Established in 1970

SUITE 600, 1401 NEW YORK AVENUE, N.W.
WASHINGTON, D.C. 20005
Telephone: 202-434-9100
Facsimile: 202-783-3420
URL: http://www.lawyers.com/leftwich&douglaslaw

General Practice, Commercial Litigation, Telecommunications, Government Contracts, Energy, Construction, Real Estate, Estate Planning, Divorce, Employment Law.

(This Listing Continued)

FIRM PROFILE: For 30 years the law firm of Leftwich & Douglas, P.L.L.C. based in Washington, D.C. has provided legal advice and counsel to a variety of clients from individuals and families to very large corporations and small businesses throughout the mid-Atlantic region of the United States. The firm is known primarily through its successes in the courtroom, and the firm is proud of its heritage as one of Washington, D.C.'s very first minority-owned law firms.

FREDERICK A. DOUGLAS, born New York, N.Y., November 28, 1947; admitted to bar, 1974, New York, District of Columbia, U.S. District Court, Southern District of New York and U.S. Court of Appeals, Second Circuit; 1976, U.S. District Court, District of Columbia and U.S. Court of Appeals, District of Columbia Circuit; 1980, U.S. Supreme Court; 1984, U.S. Court of Appeals, Eleventh Circuit; 1994, U.S. Court of Appeals, Fourth Circuit; 1995, U.S. Court of Appeals, Third Circuit; 1998, U.S. District Court, District of Maryland. *Education:* Fordham University (B.A., cum laude, 1969); New York University (J.D., 1973). Administrative Editor, Moot Court Board, 1972-1973. Adjunct Assistant Professor, George Washington University, 1983-1985. Assistant U.S. Attorney for the District of Columbia, 1974-1978. Assistant Chief Trial Attorney, Enforcement Division, Securities and Exchange Commission, 1978-1980. Supervisory Trial Attorney, Office of Enforcement, Federal Energy Regulatory Commission, 1980-1981. *Member:* The District of Columbia Bar; Bar Association of the District of Columbia (Member and Chairman, 1982-1983, Young Lawyers Section; Member, Board of Directors, 1995-1997); New York State and American Bar Associations; Charlotte Ray American Inns of Court. ***Email:*** fadouglas@ldpllc.com

NICHOLAS S. PENN, born Buckinghamshire, England, August 28, 1959; admitted to bar, 1987, District of Columbia; 1988, U.S. Court of Appeals, District of Columbia Circuit. *Education:* Georgetown University (B.A., 1981; J.D., 1987). Research Editor, American Criminal Law Review, 1986-1987. Author, "Embezzlement," White Collar Crime Survey, Volume 23, American Criminal Law Review, Winter 1986. *Member:* The District of Columbia Bar; American Bar Association. ***Email:*** nspenn@ldpllc.com

NATALIE O. LUDAWAY, born New York, N.Y., May 6, 1961; admitted to bar, 1986, District of Columbia; 1987, U.S. District Court, District of Columbia. *Education:* Hunter College of the City University of New York (B.A., with honors, 1983; M.A., 1983); George Washington University (J.D., 1986). National Institute Trial Advocacy (National Course, 1988). Phi Alpha Delta. U.S. Civil Rights Commission, State Advisory Member for the District of Columbia, 1989-1990. Instructor, Training Program, Notre Dame, 1990. General Counsel, D.C. Chamber of Commerce, 1995-1997. Member: District of Columbia Committee on Admissions; Leadership Washington (Graduate), 1996. *Member:* The District of Columbia Bar (Member, Rules Advisory Committee); American Bar Association; National Bar Association (Member, Greater Washington Area Chapter, Women Lawyers Division); Charlotte E. Ray Inn of Court; American Inn of Court. ***Email:*** noludaway@ldpllc.com

---

CURTIS A. BOYKIN, born Nuremberg, Germany, January 5, 1962; admitted to bar, 1994, Maryland; 1995, District of Columbia. *Education:* Michigan State University (B.A., 1984); George Washington University (M.P.A., 1988; J.D., 1993); National Institute of Trial Advocacy (National Course, 1997). Member, Board of Appeals and Review, District of Columbia Government. *Member:* District of Columbia Bar; National Association of Bond Lawyers. ***PRACTICE AREAS:*** Commercial Litigation; Governmental Affairs; Government Contracts; Domestic Relations. ***Email:*** caboykin@ldpllc.com

THOMAS D. BRIDENBAUGH, born Fullerton, California, May 23, 1965; admitted to bar, 1991, California; 1992, District of Columbia. *Education:* University of California at Berkeley (B.A., 1987); American University (J.D., cum laude, 1991). Author, "FERC and the California State Water Resources Control Board," Administrative Law Journal, Vol. 5 (1991). *Member:* State Bar of California; The District of Columbia Bar; American Bar Association. ***Email:*** tdbridenbaugh@ldpllc.com

CHARNIELE HERRING, born Dominican Republic, September 25, 1969; admitted to bar, 1997, Virginia (Not admitted in District of Columbia). *Education:* George Mason University (B.A., 1993); Catholic University (J.D., 1997). *Member:* The District of Columbia Bar (Young Lawyers Division). ***REPORTED CASES:*** U.S. v. Dollenie 45 NJ 234 Amicus Curiae. ***PRACTICE AREAS:*** Telecommunications; Civil Litigation; Criminal Defense. ***Email:*** clherring@ldpllc.com

NICOLE C. MASON, born Fort Sill, Oklahoma, March 16, 1973; admitted to bar, 1998, Maryland; 1999, District of Columbia. *Education:* Bucknell University (B.A., magna cum laude, 1995); George Washington University (J.D., with honors, 1998). *Member:* Maryland State and American Bar Associations; District of Columbia Bar; Bar Association of the District of Columbia. ***PRACTICE AREAS:*** Telecommunications; Government Contracts; Government Procurement; Litigation; Criminal Law; Energy Regulatory. ***Email:*** ncmason@ldpllc.com

(This Listing Continued)

LEFTWICH & DOUGLAS, P.L.L.C., Washington—Continued

NAT N. POLITO, born Spokane, Washington, December 5, 1969; admitted to bar, 1995, Maryland; 1996, District of Columbia; 1998, U.S. District Court, District of Maryland. *Education:* Georgetown University (A.B., magna cum laude, 1992); George Washington University (J.D., 1995). *Member:* The District of Columbia Bar; American Bar Association; The Association of Trial Lawyers of America. ***PRACTICE AREAS:*** Medical Negligence; Personal Injury; Domestic Relations; Real Property. ***Email:*** nnpolito@ldpllc.com

MALAIKA T. SMITH, born Washington, D.C., September 18, 1971; admitted to bar, 1996, District of Columbia. *Education:* University of Pennsylvania (B.A., International Relations, 1993); George Washington University (J.D., 1996). *Member:* The District of Columbia Bar. ***PRACTICE AREAS:*** Family Law; Estate Litigation; Probate; General Practice.

REBECCA LYNN TAYLOR, born Rocky Mount, Virginia, February 7, 1968; admitted to bar, 1995, Maryland; 1996, District of Columbia. *Education:* University of Maryland College Park (B.A., 1990); George Washington University (J.D., 1994). *Member:* District of Columbia Bar; Federal Bar Association. ***PRACTICE AREAS:*** Employment Law; Estate Litigation; Contracts; Domestic Relations. ***Email:*** rltaylor@ldpllc.com

OF COUNSEL

LEONARD A. SACKS, born New York, N.Y., June 11, 1946; admitted to bar, 1971, Virginia and Virginia Supreme Court; 1972, District of Columbia; 1973, U.S. District Court for the District of Columbia; 1974, U.S. Court of Appeals for the District of Columbia; 1977, Maryland; 1981, New York. *Education:* Lehigh University (B.A., cum laude, 1968); George Washington University (J.D., with honors, 1971; LL.M. in Government Procurement Law, 1973). *Member:* The District of Columbia Bar; Bar Association for the District of Columbia; Virginia, Federal and American (Member, Forum Committee on the Construction Industry, Administrative Law Section, 1977—) Bar Associations; Virginia State Bar. ***PRACTICE AREAS:*** Construction Law.

LEIBNER & POTKIN, P.C.

4725 WISCONSIN AVENUE, N.W. SUITE 250
WASHINGTON, D.C. 20016
Telephone: 202-244-0600
Fax: 202-244-8930
Email: potkin@bellatlantic.net
URL: http://www.lawyers.com/leibner&potkin

Real Estate Law, Residential Development, Settlements, Mortgage Leasing, Landlord and Tenant Law, Leasing, General Civil Practice, Commercial Litigation, Commercial Transactions, Business Law, Corporate Law, Small Business, Estate Planning and Trust Administration, Probate, Tax Law.

ROBERT F. LEIBNER, born Brooklyn, New York, September 4, 1953; admitted to bar, 1979, District of Columbia; 1985, Maryland. *Education:* George Washington University (B.A., with distinction, 1975; J.D., 1978). Phi Beta Kappa. *Member:* District of Columbia Bar. ***PRACTICE AREAS:*** Real Estate Law; Commercial Litigation.

LANE H. POTKIN, born Brooklyn, New York, November 1, 1954; admitted to bar, 1978, District of Columbia; 1984, Maryland. *Education:* George Washington University (B.A., with distinction, 1975; J.D., with Honors, 1978). Phi Beta Kappa. *Member:* District of Columbia Bar. ***PRACTICE AREAS:*** Real Estate Law; Business Law; Trusts and Estates; Probate; Commercial Law.

JOHN E. ARNESS, II, born Bethesda, Maryland, 1957; admitted to bar, 1991, Maryland and District of Columbia. *Education:* Villanova University (B.A., 1979); Georgetown University (J.D., 1989). *Member:* District of Columbia Bar; Maryland State and American Bar Associations. ***PRACTICE AREAS:*** Civil Litigation; Real Estate; Collections; General Practice.

TERRY F. LENZNER, P.C.

1015 FIFTEENTH STREET, N.W., SUITE 400
WASHINGTON, D.C. 20005
Telephone: 202-789-7620
Telecopier: 202-789-7740
Email: tlenzner@igint.com
URL: http://www.lawyers.com/terryflenzner

General Civil, Criminal, Administrative and Trial Practice.

TERRY F. LENZNER, born New York, N.Y., August 10, 1939; admitted to bar, 1966, District of Columbia. *Education:* Harvard University (B.A., cum laude, 1961; LL.B., 1964). Trial Attorney, Civil Rights Division, U.S. Department of Justice, 1964-1967. Assistant U.S. Attorney, Southern District of New York, Organized Crime Unit, 1967-1969. Special Assistant to the President of New York City Board of Education, 1969. Director, Office of Legal Services, U.S. Office of Economic Opportunity, 1969-1970. Assistant Chief Counsel, Select Committee on Presidential Campaign Activities, U.S. Senate, 1973-1974. Special Counsel, Alaska Pipeline Commission, 1976-1977. Special Counsel, State of Alaska, 1978-1986. Special Counsel, Division of Pari-Mutual Wagering, State of Florida, 1978-1980. Special Counsel, City of Boston, Massachusetts, 1978-1984. Adjunct Professor, Criminal Procedure, Georgetown University Law Center, 1976. Member, Harvard University Board of Overseers, 1970-1976. Member, Executive Committee, District of Columbia Lawyers Committee for Civil Rights Under Law, 1970—. Chairman, Board of Directors, Investigative Group International, Inc., 1984—. *Member:* The District of Columbia Bar; American Bar Association. ***PRACTICE AREAS:*** Trial Practice; Administrative; Mergers and Acquisitions; Due Diligence; Internet Investigations.

OF COUNSEL

EDWARD T. FERGUSON, III, born Utica, New York, December 23, 1956; admitted to bar, 1982, New York; 1983, U.S. District Court, Southern and Eastern Districts of New York; 1986, U.S. Court of Appeals, 2nd Circuit; 1996, U.S. Court of Appeals, District of Columbia Circuit (Not admitted in District of Columbia). *Education:* Columbia University (B.A., magna cum laude, 1978); Harvard University (J.D., 1981). Phi Beta Kappa. Assistant U.S. Attorney, Southern District of New York, 1986-1992. Deputy Chief, Civil Division, 1991-1992. Chief Appellate Attorney, 1989-1991. Chairman and Executive Director, New York City Trade Waste Commission, 1996-2000. *Member:* The Association of the Bar of the City of New York. ***PRACTICE AREAS:*** Investigations; Litigation; Transactions.

LEONARD HURT FROST LILLY & LEVIN

A PROFESSIONAL CORPORATION
1701 K STREET, N.W., SUITE 300
WASHINGTON, D.C. 20006-1522
Telephone: 202-223-2500
Telecopy: 202-223-2501
Email: mfassler@leonardhurt.com
URL: http://www.leonardhurt.com

Dallas, Texas Office: 600 North Pearl, Suite 900. Telephone: 214-954-6300. Telecopy: 214-954-6386.
Austin, Texas Office: 816 Congress, Suite 1280. Telephone: 512-477-7161. Telecopy: 512-476-1676.
Houston, Texas Office: 4545 Bissonnet, Suite 131. Telephone: 713-666-6388. Telecopy: 713-666-6454.

General Civil Practice. Municipal Finance, Environmental Finance, Infrastructure Finance, Real Estate, General Litigation, Antitrust, Environmental Law, Bankruptcy, Creditor's Rights, Corporate, Banking, Securities, Government Contract, Legislative, Administrative, Agricultural, Business and Taxation. Alternative Dispute Resolution.

FIRM PROFILE: Member, National Landfill Gas Consortium, L.L.C.

EDMUND B. FROST, born Pueblo, Colorado, December 5, 1942; admitted to bar, 1967, Colorado; 1970, District of Columbia; 1980, U.S. Supreme Court. *Education:* Dartmouth College (B.A., 1964); University of Michigan Law School (J.D., magna cum laude, 1967). Order of the Coif. Assistant Editor, Michigan Law Review, 1966-1967. Member, Board of Directors, 1992-1997 and Advisory Counsel, 1998—, Environmental Law Institute. Senior Vice President and General Counsel, 1994-1999, Clean Sites, Inc. Member, Board of Directors, Vice President and Secretary, 1996—, Center for Land Renewal. Member, Board of Directors and Executive Director, 1994—, Community Council For The Homeless, Inc. Vice President and General Counsel, 1978-1982, Chemical Manufacturers Association. [With U.S. Army, 1967-1969; Capt., 1968-1969]. ***PRACTICE AREAS:*** Environmental Law; Litigation; Antitrust Law; Transportation Law; Real Estate; Nonprofit Law. ***Email:*** ebfrost@leonardhurt.com

MICHAEL H. LEVIN, born Philadelphia, Pennsylvania, November 24, 1942; admitted to bar, 1970, District of Columbia and U.S. Court of Appeals, District of Columbia Circuit; 1973, U.S. Supreme Court. *Education:* University of Pennsylvania (B.A., summa cum laude, 1964); Harvard University (J.D., cum laude, 1969); Oxford University, England (M.Litt., 1970). Phi Beta Kappa. Thouron Fellow, 1964-1966. Executive Branch Congressional Fellowship, 1978-1979. Recipient, EPA Gold Medal for Extraordinary Service, 1982. Listed in: Who's Who In American Law; Who's Who in the East; Who's Who in America. Co-Founder, National Landfill Gas Consortium, LLC, 1996—. Founding Director, Regulatory Reform Staff, U.S. Environmental Protection Agency, 1979-1988. Legislative Aide, U.S. Senate, House of Representatives, 1978-1979. Deputy Director, President's Task Force on Safety & Health, The White House, 1977-1978. Counsel for Appellate Litigation (OSH), U.S. Department of

(This Listing Continued)

(This Listing Continued)

Labor, 1972-1977. Special Assistant, Complex, Constitutional Litigation, Fair Labor Standards, U.S. Department of Labor, 1971-1972. Appellate Attorney, National Labor Relations Board, 1969-1971. Chair, Legal/Liability Committee, 1996-1999 and Vice Chair, U.S. Government Affairs Committee, 1994-1996, U.S. Air and Waste Management Association. Member, National Clean Air Act Compliance/Enforcement Steering Committee, 1996-1999. Member, National Advisory Panel, Integrating Environmental Goals with Product Design, U.S. Congressional Office of Technology Assessment, 1990-1992. Chair, Task Force on Market Approaches, Clean Air Working Group, 1989-1990. Vice Chair, Environmental Values Committee, Administrative Law Section, 1988-1990 and Public Chair, OSHA Committee, Labor Law Section, 1977-1978, American Bar Association. ***LANGUAGES:*** French. ***SPECIAL AGENCIES:*** EPA; CEQ; Treasury Department; Executive Office, White House. ***PRACTICE AREAS:*** Environmental; Environmental Finance; Government Relations; Administrative Law; Appellate Litigation. ***Email:*** mhlevin@leonardhurt.com

OF COUNSEL

MAX A. STOLPER, born Vienna, Austria, September 30, 1924; admitted to bar, 1953, New York; 1975, District of Columbia. *Education:* Harvard University (A.B., magna cum laude, 1948; J.D., magna cum laude, 1952). Phi Beta Kappa. Member, Board of Editors, Harvard Law Review, 1949-1952. *Member:* The District of Columbia Bar; The Association of the Bar of the City of New York; American and Inter-American (Co-Chairman, 1980-1981, 1984-1987 and Chairman, 1981-1984, Committee on Business Law) Bar Associations; American Society of International Law. ***LANGUAGES:*** German, French, Spanish and Portuguese. ***PRACTICE AREAS:*** Securities; Corporate Law; Investment Law. ***Email:*** mastolper@leonardhurt.com

PAULINE C. SHOBACK, born New Brunswick, New Jersey, July 12, 1955; admitted to bar, 1984, Illinois; 1988, District of Columbia. *Education:* Smith College (B.A., 1977); University of Virginia (J.D., 1984). ***PRACTICE AREAS:*** Corporate Law; Securities. ***Email:*** pcshoback@leonardhurt.com

MARSHA R. GREENFIELD, born Bay Shore, New York, July 5, 1948; admitted to bar, 1974, New York; 1979, Michigan (inactive); 1981, U.S. District Court, Eastern District of Michigan; 1989, Maryland and U.S. District Court, District of Maryland (Not admitted in District of Columbia). *Education:* Vassar College (A.B., 1970); Rutgers University Law School (J.D., 1973). Co-Author: "Threats to Fair Trial Rights," in *Jury Work: Systematic Techniques*, Clark Boardman, Second Edition, 1990. Adjunct Professor, University of San Francisco School of Law, 1975. Member, Michigan State Bar, 1979-1988. *Member:* Maryland State Bar Association; American Health Lawyers Association. ***REPORTED CASES:*** Williamson v. Williamson, 333 NW2d6 (Mich.App. 1982); Faler, et. al. v Unawee County Sheriff, 409 NW2d 791 (Mich.App. 1987). ***PRACTICE AREAS:*** Association Law; Corporate Law; Health Law; Energy Law. ***Email:*** mrgreenfield@leonardhurt.com

REPRESENTATIVE CLIENTS: Association for Governmental Leasing and Finance; Banc One Leasing Corporation; Biomass Power Coalition; Can Manufacturers Institute; Chancellor Financial Services, Inc.; Council of Industrial Boiler Owners; Clean Sites, Inc.; The CKD Coalition; Covanta Energy Corp.; Denton County Development District No. 1; Denton County Commissioners Court; Denton County Fresh Water Supply District No. 1-A; Energy Developments, Inc.; Eurotech, Ltd.; Fort Bend County M.U.D. No. 49; Guaranty Federal Bank, F.S.B.; Harris County M.U.D. No. 127; Kaufman County Development District No. 1; Landmark Organization; LaSalle National Leasing Corp.; National Energy Resources Corp.; National Lime Association; Northgate Crossing R.U.D.; CIBC Oppenheimer, Inc.; Periodic Monitoring Coalition; Planning Research Corp.; The Center for Land Renewal, Inc.; The Chemical Manufacturers Assn.; The Scientex Corp.; The SBREFA Coalition; Stephens, Inc.; SDGA, Inc.; Waste Management, Inc.; West Virginia Chamber of Commerce; Williamson County M.U.D. No. 9.

LEONARD, STREET AND DEINARD

PROFESSIONAL ASSOCIATION

Established in 1922

600 PENNSYLVANIA AVENUE, N.W., SUITE 900, SOUTH BUILDING

WASHINGTON, D.C. 20004

Telephone: 202-974-6100

Fax: 202-974-6101

Email: lsd1500@leonard.com

URL: http://www.leonard.com

St. Paul, Minnesota Office: 380 St. Peter Street, Suite 500. Telephone: 651-222-7455. Fax: 651-222-7644.

Mankato, Minnesota Office: 121 East Walnut Street, P. O. Box 967. Telephone: 507-345-1179. Fax: 507-345-1182.

Washington D.C. Office: 601 Pennsylvania Avenue N.W., Suite 900, South Building.

General Civil and Trial Practice, including Administrative Law, Advertising and Sales Promotion, Alternative Dispute Resolution, including Mediation, Antitrust, Architectural Law, Arts Law, Banking Law, Bankruptcy Litigation, Business Law, Business Succession Planning, Commercial Litigation, Communications Law, Computer Law, Condemnation and Valuation Litigation, Construction Law, Copyright and Trademark Law and Litigation, Corporations, Deceptive Trade Practices, Employment Law and Litigation, Employee Benefits, Entertainment Law, Environmental Law, Estate Planning, Family Law, Federal Indian Law, Financial Institutions Law, Financial Reorganization, Franchise Law, Governmental Relations, Health Care Law, Housing Development and Finance, Immigration Law, Income Tax Law, Insurance Disputes, Intellectual Property Law and Litigation, Labor Relations, Land Use, Internet Law, Licensing, Medical Malpractice, Mergers and Acquisitions, Multimedia Law, Online Law, Partnerships, Patent Litigation, Private and Emerging Business Law, Public Finance, Public Utility Law, Probate and Trust Administration, Product Distribution and Marketing, Products Liability and Tort Litigation, Professional Liability, Real Estate Development and Finance, Securities Law and Litigation, Shareholder Disputes, Taxable and Tax-exempt Securities, Trade Secret Law, Unfair Competition and White Collar Crime.

FIRM PROFILE: Leonard, Street and Deinard was founded in 1922 by George Leonard, Arthur Street and Benedict and Amos Deinard. The firm is one of Minnesota's largest and oldest law firms, with more than 150 lawyers practicing from offices in Minneapolis, St. Paul and Mankato, Minn.

Leonard, Street and Deinard's approach to the practice of law is to understand the client's overall business objectives. The practice includes both litigation and transactional matters for small business clients and Fortune 500 companies, including U.S. Satellite Broadcasting, Canadian Pacific Railway and Piper Jaffray, Inc.

Leonard, Street and Deinard has a strong commitment to its clients. In 1993, the firm started its Client Advisory Council to ensure strong lines of communication between the firm and the people and companies it serves. In 1996, a Client Covenant was implemented, guarantying immediate access, predictability, controlled fees and costs, and teamwork.

Leonard, Street and Deinard is also committed to the community. In 1993, the Leonard, Street and Deinard Pro Bono Legal Clinic opened in the Phillips neighborhood, providing legal services to one of Minneapolis' most disadvantaged neighborhoods. The Leonard, Street and Deinard Foundation supports over 100 nonprofit organizations locally, including arts organizations, legal service providers and social service groups.

STEVEN A. WEILER, born Bismarck, North Dakota, March 13, 1957; admitted to bar, 1986, North Dakota; 1987, U.S. District Court, District of Columbia; 1988, District of Columbia and U.S Court of Appeals for the District of Columbia Circuit. *Education:* University of North Dakota (B.A., English, summa cum laude, 1979; M.A., English, summa cum laude, 1982; J.D., 1986). Member, Order of Barristers. Note Editor, North Dakota Law Review, 1985-1986. Legal Writing Instructor, University of North Dakota, 1985-1986. Instructor, Appellate Advocacy, University of North Dakota, Spring, 1986. Member, Federal Energy Regulatory Commission, 1985-1988. *Member:* Bar Association of District of Columbia; Federal Energy Bar Association. ***PRACTICE AREAS:*** Regulated Industries.

ROBERT Y. HIRASUNA, born Rexburg, Idaho, August 19, 1950; admitted to bar, 1978, District of Columbia; 1992, Texas; 1995, New Mexico. *Education:* Brown University (B.A., 1973); Catholic University of America (J.D., 1978). *Member:* The District of Columbia Bar; Federal Energy Bar Association (Member, Tax Developments Committee, 1984-1988). ***PRACTICE AREAS:*** Energy; Public Utility Law.

REPRESENTATIVE CLIENTS: A.O. Smith Harvestore Products, Inc.; Aldrich, Eastman & Waltch, Inc.; Blount Energy Resources Corp.; Business Health Care Action Group; Canadian Pacific Railway; Carlson Real Estate Company; Chase Manhattan Bank, USA, N.A.; Chase Manhattan Mortgage Corporation; Cooper Industries; Dataserv, Inc.; Eaton Corp; Edina Realty, Inc.; Franchise Associates, Inc.; Gabberts, Inc.; Gustavus Adolfus College; Home Savings of America; Honeywell International, Inc.; Horty, Elving & Associates, Inc.; Housing and Redevelopment Authority of the City of Saint Paul, Minnesota; Hubbard Broadcasting, Inc.; Independent Hydro Developers; Lundgren Brothers Construction Co.; Marquette Bank, Minneapolis; Midcontinent Media, Inc.; Midwest Importers of Cannon Falls, Inc.; Midwest Wireless Communications, L.L.C.; Minnesota Bankers Association.; Minnesota Timberwolves Basketball Limited Partnership; Nabisco Brands Inc.; National City Bank of Minneapolis; Packaging Corporation of America; NRG Energy, Inc.; PCL Construction - PCL Enterprises, Inc.; U.S. Bancorp Piper Jaffray, Inc.; Prudential-Bache Securities, Inc.; Quadion, Inc.; Regis Corporation; Bob Ryan Oldsmobile, Inc.; St. Jude Medical, Inc.; Setter, Leach & Lindstrom, Inc.; Symmes Maini and McKee Associates, Inc.; Target Corporation; Taylor Corporation; TCF Bank, fsb; Terra International, Inc.; United of Omaha Life Insurance Co.; Unocal Corp.; Witcher Construction, Inc..

(This Listing Continued)

LERCH, EARLY & BREWER

CHARTERED

1900 M STREET, N.W., SUITE 601

WASHINGTON, D.C. 20005

Telephone: 202-293-5494

URL: http://www.lercheearly.com

Bethesda, Maryland Office: 3 Bethesda Metro Center, Suite 460. Telephone: 301-986-1300. Telecopy: 301-986-0332.

(This Listing Continued)

LERCH, EARLY & BREWER, CHARTERED, Washington—Continued

Fairfax, Virginia Office: 9302 Lee Highway, Suite 1100. Telephone: 703-278-9020.
Frederick, Maryland Office: 228 West Patrick Street.

General Civil and Appellate Practice. Real Estate, Land Use, Historic Preservation and Development, Corporate and Tax, Estate Planning and Probate, Commercial, Banking, Hospital and Health Care, Domestic Relations, Community Associations, Employment and Labor Law, White Collar Criminal Defense and Criminal Trial Practice.

FIRM PROFILE: Since 1950, when our predecessor firm Wallace & Lerch was founded, our law firm has changed with the times. We are proud that many of our current clients have been with the firm for decades, and that our growth has resulted primarily from client referrals. In the years ahead, we hope to further our relationships with long-standing clients and to develop rewarding working relationships with new ones.

While our attorneys practice in specialized areas, much of our practice transcends rigid departmentalization and involves the expertise of more than one specialty group in a manner designed to best meet our clients' legal needs.

(For complete biographical data on all personnel, see Professional Biographies at Bethesda, Maryland)

LEVENTHAL, SENTER & LERMAN, P.L.L.C.

Established in 1982

SUITE 600
2000 K STREET, N.W.
WASHINGTON, D.C. 20006
Telephone: 202-429-8970
Telecopier: 202-293-7783
Email: info@lsl-law.com
URL: http://www.lsl-law.com

General Federal Administrative Practice including Legislative and Governmental Affairs and Federal Court Litigation, International and U.S. Communications Law (including Satellite and Space Technology), Media Contracts and Transactions, Corporate and Commercial, and Intellectual Property Law including Copyright, Trademark, Service Mark and Internet Matters and Related Litigation.

FIRM PROFILE: Leventhal, Senter & Lerman was established in 1982 by Norman P. Leventhal. From our inception, the firm's mission has been to serve the diverse needs of its telecommunications industry clients before the Federal Communications Commission, other regulatory agencies, the United States Congress and the courts. As our client base has expanded and as our clients have diversified their interests, the firm's practice has correspondingly expanded to meet their particular needs. Thus, the firm currently represents a broad range of clients with interest in all facets of the telecommunications industry. Clients include Fortune 500 companies and large media ownership groups, as well as start-up enterprises and new companies or individuals seeking to acquire and operate broadcast media or other telecommunications businesses, both domestic and international.

MEMBERS OF FIRM

NORMAN P. LEVENTHAL, born Washington, D.C., September 7, 1943; admitted to bar, 1968, District of Columbia; 1969, U.S. Court of Appeals for the District of Columbia Circuit; 1972, U.S. Supreme Court; 1980, U.S. Court of Appeals, Fifth Circuit; 1981, U.S. Court of Appeals, Second Circuit. *Education:* University of Maryland (B.A., with honors and high honors in Economics, 1965); Yale University (LL.B., 1968). Author: "Caution: Cigarette Commercials May Be Hazardous to Your License—The New Aspect of Fairness," Federal Communications Bar Journal, Vol. XXII, No. 1, 1968; "Europe Aims at Open Skies," Communications International, August, 1992; "Personal Satellite Communications from Reason to Reality: The Regulatory Impediments," Proceedings of the Tenth European Satellite Communications Conference, December, 1995; "Freedom of Expression and Social Responsibility," presentation to Camara Nacional de la Industria de Radio y Television, Mexico City, 1998. Co-Author, "Outer Space & Worldwide Market Access, Regulatory Issues for Mobile Satellite Service," International Bar Association, Berlin, 1996. U.S. Delegate, International Telecommunication Union World Telecommunication Policy Forum, Geneva, 1996. *Member:* District of Columbia Bar; American and International Bar Associations; American Intellectual Property Law Association; Federal Communications Bar Association (Member, Executive Committee, 1983-1986). [USAR, 1968-1974]. ***PRACTICE AREAS:*** Communications Law; Media Law; Intellectual Property; Internet Law. ***Email:*** nleventhal@lsl-law.com

(This Listing Continued)

MEREDITH S. SENTER, JR., born Lillington, North Carolina, February 28, 1953; admitted to bar, 1978, District of Columbia; 1979, U.S. District Court for the District of Columbia; 1980, U.S. Court of Appeals for the District of Columbia Circuit; 1990, U.S. Supreme Court. *Education:* Duke University (B.A., magna cum laude, 1973); Columbia University (M.A., 1975); Georgetown University (J.D., magna cum laude, 1978). Author or Co-Author: "Private Intracity Data Communications Networks," Federal Bar Journal, November, 1982; "Sounding the Alarm: Sony and the Software Lock-Breaker," Computer Law Reporter, 1986; "Financing Broadcast Transactions: Avoiding the FCC Pitfalls," Broadcast Financial Journal, May-June, 1990; "Thick Books, But Thin Protection," Legal Times, April 22, 1991; "Report of the Subcommittee on Legal Opinions," Federal Communications Law Journal, June 1996. *Member:* District of Columbia Bar; American Bar Association (Chairman, Subcommittee on Registration of Databases, Section on Patent, Trademark and Copyright, 1989-1990; Chairman, Subcommittee on Protection of Databases, 1990-1992); Federal Communications Bar Association (Co-Chair, Committee on Cooperation with Review Board and Administrative Law Judges, 1985-1986; Co-Chair, Ad Hoc Committee on Opinion Letters, 1992-1994; Co-Chair, Transactional Practice Committee, 1993-1994). ***PRACTICE AREAS:*** Communications Law; Media Law. ***Email:*** msenter@lsl-law.com

STEVEN ALMAN LERMAN, born Cambridge, Massachusetts, January 28, 1947; admitted to bar, 1973, District of Columbia, U.S. District Court for the District of Columbia and U.S. Court of Appeals for the District of Columbia Circuit; 1975, U.S. Court of Appeals, 9th Circuit; 1978, U.S. Court of Appeals, Fourth Circuit. *Education:* University of Pennsylvania, Wharton School of Finance and Commerce (B.S., Economics and Finance, 1969); George Washington University Law School (J.D., with honors, 1972). Order of the Coif. Author: "Arming Licensees for Renewal Combat," National Association of Broadcasters Newsletter, 1989. Co-Author: "Equal Employment Opportunity Guidebook: How to Comply with the Requirements of the Federal Communications Commission," published by the National Association of Broadcasters, 1991; "Preventing the Broadcast of Hoaxes and Other False or Deceptive Programming," published by the National Association of Broadcasters, 1992. *Member:* District of Columbia Bar; Federal Communications Bar Association (Member, Committee on Professional Responsibility, 1989-1991). ***PRACTICE AREAS:*** Communications Law; Media Law. ***Email:*** slerman@lsl-law.com

RAUL R. RODRIGUEZ, born Havana, Cuba, September 2, 1948; admitted to bar, 1974, Florida; 1980, District of Columbia; 1981, New York. *Education:* University of South Florida (B.A., 1971); Florida State University (J.D., 1974). Director of International Satellite Policy, National Telecommunications and Information Administration, U.S. Department of Commerce, 1981-1984. U.S. Delegate: World Administrative Radio Conference, Geneva, Switzerland, 1985; Region 2 Administrative Radio Conference, Rio de Janeiro, Brazil, 1988; World Administrative Radio Conference, Malaga-Torremolinos, Spain, 1992. Chairman, U.S. Delegation to 1994 World Telecommunication Development Conference, Buenos Aires, Argentina. *Member:* District of Columbia Bar; The Florida Bar; Federal Communications Bar Association (Secretary, 1984-1985). ***PRACTICE AREAS:*** Communications Law; Media Law. ***Email:*** rrodriguez@lsl-law.com

DENNIS P. CORBETT, born Cincinnati, Ohio, February 18, 1953; admitted to bar, 1979, District of Columbia. *Education:* Harvard University (A.B., magna cum laude, 1975); Georgetown University (J.D., 1979). Case and Note Editor, Law and Policy in International Business, 1978-1979. Trustee: The Barker Foundation, 1995—; Lowell School in Washington, D.C., 1996-2000. *Member:* District of Columbia Bar; Federal Communications Bar Association (Member, Mass Media Committee). ***PRACTICE AREAS:*** Communications Law; Media Law. ***Email:*** dcorbett@lsl-law.com

BRIAN M. MADDEN, born Washington, D.C., March 10, 1949; admitted to bar, 1975, District of Columbia, U.S. District Court, District of Columbia and U.S. Court of Appeals, District of Columbia Circuit. *Education:* University of Pennsylvania (B.A., Political Science, 1971); George Washington University Law School (J.D., with honors, 1974). Attorney, Broadcast Bureau, Federal Communications Commission, 1974-1975. President, Capitol Chapter, Juvenile Diabetes Foundation International, 1989-1992; Board of Directors, 1985-1995, July, 1997-June, 2000. *Member:* District of Columbia Bar; Federal Communications Bar Association (Co-Chair, Transaction Practiace Committee; Member, Mass Media Committee). ***PRACTICE AREAS:*** Communications Law; Media Law. ***Email:*** bmadden@lsl-law.com

BARBARA K. GARDNER, born New Haven, Connecticut, September 11, 1939; admitted to bar, 1982, District of Columbia; 1983, U.S. Court of Appeals for the District of Columbia Circuit. *Education:* Smith College; George Washington University (B.A., 1960); Georgetown University (J.D., 1982). Author, "EEO Compliance Under New FCC 'Tough But Fair ' Enforcement Regime," Communications Lawyer, Spring 1994. Co-author, "Equal Employment Opportunity Guidebook: How To Comply With The Requirements of the Federal Communications Commission," National Association of Broadcasters, 1991. *Member:* District of Columbia Bar; Federal Communications Bar Association

(This Listing Continued)

(Co-Chair, Professional Responsibility Committee, 1993-1995, 1998-1999). ***PRACTICE AREAS:*** Communications Law; Media Law. ***Email:*** bgardner@lsl-law.com

STEPHEN D. BARUCH, born New Brunswick, New Jersey, February 19, 1960; admitted to bar, 1985, Maryland and District of Columbia; 1987, U.S. Court of Appeals for the District of Columbia Circuit and U.S. District Court for the District of Columbia. *Education:* University of Virginia (B.S., 1981); Boston University (J.D., cum laude, 1984). Author: "The Dawning of a New Era of Cooperation: Satellite-Service Issues Prove Worth of Negotiated Rule-Making Process," Legal Times, May 17, 1993. Co-Author: "Satellite Sales and Lease Agreements: A User's Guide," Satellite Communications, July, 1990. Member: U.S. Delegation to World Radiocommunication Conferences, Geneva, Switzerland, 1995 and 1997; World Radiocommunication Conference, Istanbul, Turkey, 2000. *Member:* District of Columbia Bar; Maryland State Bar Association; Federal Communications Bar Association. ***PRACTICE AREAS:*** Communications Law; International and Domestic Satellite Law. ***Email:*** sbaruch@lsl-law.com

SALLY A. BUCKMAN, born Cleveland, Ohio, January 19, 1957; admitted to bar, 1982, District of Columbia; 1983, U.S. District Court for the District of Columbia and U.S. Court of Appeals for the District of Columbia Circuit. *Education:* Wellesley College (B.A., 1979); New York University (J.D., 1982). Wellesley College Scholar. Articles Editor, Annual Survey of American Law, New York University Law School, 1981-1982. Author: "Antitrust Law," Annual Survey of American Law, Volume 4, 1981. Vice-President, Development, American Women in Radio and Television, Washington, D.C. Chapter, 1998-2000. *Member:* District of Columbia Bar; American Bar Association; Federal Communications Bar Association (Secretary, 1997-1998; Trustee, Federal Communications Bar Association Foundation, 1993-1996). ***PRACTICE AREAS:*** Communications Law; Media Law. ***Email:*** sbuckman@lsl-law.com

NANCY L. WOLF, born Bridgeport, Connecticut, June 2, 1952; admitted to bar, 1980, District of Columbia. *Education:* Smith College (B.A., cum laude, 1974); The Fletcher School of Law and Diplomacy (M.A.L.D., 1976); George Washington University Law School (J.D., 1979). *Member:* District of Columbia Bar; Federal Communications Bar Association. ***PRACTICE AREAS:*** Communications Law; Media Law. ***Email:*** nwolf@lsl-law.com

DAVID S. KEIR, born Washington, D.C., November 11, 1962; admitted to bar, 1990, Virginia and U.S. Court of Appeals, Fourth Circuit; 1993, District of Columbia; 1998, U.S. Court of Appeals, District of Columbia Circuit. *Education:* Harvard University (A.B., cum laude, 1985); College of William and Mary (J.D., 1990). Phi Delta Phi. *Member:* District of Columbia Bar; Virginia State Bar; Federal Communications Bar Association; Society of Satellite Professionals International. ***PRACTICE AREAS:*** Communications Law; International and Domestic Satellite Law; Media Law. ***Email:*** dkeir@lsl-law.com

DEBORAH R. COLEMAN, born Washington, D.C., August 12, 1962; admitted to bar, 1989, District of Columbia. *Education:* University of Virginia (B.A., with distinction, 1984); College of William & Mary (J.D., 1989). College of William & Mary Law Review. *Member:* District of Columbia Bar; Federal Communications Bar Association. ***PRACTICE AREAS:*** Communications Law; Media Law. ***Email:*** dcoleman@lsl-law.com

HOWARD A. TOPEL, born New York, New York, February 21, 1948; admitted to bar, 1973, District of Columbia. *Education:* University of Pennsylvania (A.B., 1970; J.D., 1973). *Member:* District of Columbia Bar; American Bar Association; Federal Communications Bar Association. ***Email:*** htopel@lsl-law.com

ASSOCIATES

NANCY A. ORY, born Bedford, Pennsylvania, April 6, 1963; admitted to bar, 1994, Massachusetts and District of Columbia. *Education:* Pennsylvania State University (B.A., with honors, 1985); George Washington University Law School (J.D., with honors, 1993). The George Washington University Journal of International Law and Economics, 1991-1993. *Member:* District of Columbia Bar; Massachusetts Bar Association; Federal Communications Bar Association. ***PRACTICE AREAS:*** Communications Law; Media Law. ***Email:*** nory@lsl-law.com

LINDA DANIELLE FELDMANN, born Bonn, Germany, May 1, 1966; admitted to bar, 1993, Maryland; 1994, District of Columbia. *Education:* The Johns Hopkins University (B.A., with highest honors, 1988); George Washington University Law School (J.D., with honors, 1993). Assistant General Counsel, CBS, 1998-2001. Member, The George Washington Law Review, 1991-1994. *Member:* Maryland State and American Bar Associations; District of Columbia Bar; Federal Communications Bar Association; American Women in Radio and Television. (Assistant General Counsel). ***PRACTICE AREAS:*** Broadcast; Communications. ***Email:*** lfeldmann@lsl-law.com

JOHN D. POUTASSE, born Stuttgart, Germany, December 6, 1964; admitted to bar, 1995, Maryland; 1997, District of Columbia. *Education:* Colgate University (B.A., 1987); Johns Hopkins University (M.A., 1992); George Washington University Law School (J.D., with honors, 1995). Member, George Washington University Journal of International Law and Economics, 1993-1995. *Member:* Federal Communications Bar Association. ***PRACTICE AREAS:*** Communications Law; Media Law. ***Email:*** jpoutasse@lsl-law.com

CHRISTOPHER J. SOVA, born Passaic, New Jersey, November 28, 1962; admitted to bar, 1996, New Jersey; 1997, New York and District of Columbia. *Education:* Seton Hall University (M.B.A., 1990); Rutgers University School of Law (J.D., 1996). Recipient, Allan Axelrod Award in Commercial Law. *Member:* The District of Columbia Bar; Federal Communications Bar Association. ***PRACTICE AREAS:*** Communications Law; Commercial Transactions; Corporate Law; Commercial Law. ***Email:*** csova@lsl-law.com

PHILIP A. BONOMO, born Washington, D.C., September 28, 1960; admitted to bar, 1997, Maryland; 1998, District of Columbia. *Education:* University of Maryland (B.S., 1982); Georgetown University (J.D., cum laude, 1997). Law Fellow, Georgetown University. Member, The Tax Lawyer. Recipient, American Jurisprudence Award, Legal Research and Writing. *Member:* Maryland State Bar Association, Inc; The District of Columbia Bar. ***PRACTICE AREAS:*** Communications Law; Broadcasting Law; Satellite Communications. ***Email:*** pbonomo@lsl-law.com

JENNIFER A. MERRILL, born Houston, Texas, May 18, 1970; admitted to bar, 2000, District of Columbia. *Education:* Texas A & M University (B.A., 1992); University of Texas at Austin (J.D., 2000). Co-Author: "State Class Action Practice and Procedure," New York Chapter of CCM, 2000. *Member:* Federal Communications Bar Association. ***PRACTICE AREAS:*** Broadcast Media Law; Intellectual Property. ***Email:*** jbabin@lsl-law.com

OF COUNSEL

STEPHEN AUSTIN HILDEBRANDT, born Milwaukee, Wisconsin, September 24, 1947; admitted to bar, 1975, District of Columbia. *Education:* Harvard University (A.B., magna cum laude, 1972); Duke University (J.D., 1975). Staff Member, 1973-1974 and Member, Editorial Board, 1974-1975, Duke Law Journal. Author: Note, "Heater v. FTC and the Federal Trade Commission Improvement Act: The FTC's Power to Order Restitution," 1975 8 Duke Law Journal 379; Co-author: "The Additional Expense Test: A Proposal to Help Solve the Dilemma of Mixed Business Personal Expenses," 1974 Duke Law Journal 636. *Member:* District of Columbia Bar; Federal Communications Bar Association. (Associate General Counsel).

BETH-SHERRI AKYEREKO, born Richmond, Virginia, February 10, 1964; admitted to bar, 1995, Virginia; 1996, District of Columbia. *Education:* Princeton University (B.A., 1985); George Washington University National Law Center (J.D., 1995). *Member:* District of Columbia Bar; Virginia State Bar; National Bar Association. ***Email:*** bakyereko@lsl-law.com

S. JENELL TRIGG, born Fort Sill, Oklahoma, September 21, 1957; admitted to bar, 1997, Maryland; 2000, District of Columbia; U.S. District Court, District of Maryland. *Education:* Northwestern University (BS., 1978); Columbus School of Law of the Catholic University of America (J.D., magna cum laude, 1997); Institute for Communications Law Studies (Post Graduate, with honors, 1997). Member, Board of Directors, Minority Media and Telecommunications Council. *Member:* District of Columbia Bar; Federal Communications Bar Association; National and American Bar Associations.

ROBERT N. LEVIN, P.C.

WASHINGTON, D.C.

(See Rockville, Maryland)

Civil and Criminal Litigation in all Courts including Intellectual Property Litigation, Personal Injury, Litigation, Employment Law, Civil Rights, Business Litigation, Real Estate, Construction Litigation.

LEVIN & ROSENSTEIN, P.C.

Established in 1982

1130 SEVENTEENTH STREET, N.W., SUITE 314

WASHINGTON, D.C. 20036

Telephone: 202-429-1795

Fax: 202-429-9729

URL: http://www.lawyers.com/levin&rosenstein

Practice before Federal Courts, Departments and Agencies and Arbitration in matters of Agricultural Insurance Law, Agriculture Law, Government Contract, and Insurance.

JOSEPH B. LEVIN (1918-1985).

LARRY M. ROSENSTEIN (1941-2000).

DANIEL N. ROSENSTEIN, born Winston-Salem, North Carolina, October 8, 1966; admitted to bar, 1991, Maryland; 1992, District of Columbia, U.S. Court of Appeals, District of Columbia Circuit, U.S. Court of Appeals, Fourth Circuit, U.S. District Court for the District of Columbia and U.S. District Court,

(This Listing Continued)

LEVIN & ROSENSTEIN, P.C., Washington—Continued

District of Maryland; 1998, U.S. Court of Appeals, Eleventh Circuit. *Education:* University of North Carolina (A.B., 1988); Catholic University of America (J.D., 1991). Recipient: American Jurisprudence Book Award, Federal Practice and Procedure, 1990. Note and Comment Editor, 1990-1991 and Staff Member, 1989-1990, Catholic University Law Review. Author: Note, "Section 666: The Beast In The Federal Criminal Arsenal," 39 Cath. U.L. Rev. 673, 1990; "Emergency Stabilization for a Wounded COBRA," 9 Issues in Law & Medicine 255, 1993. *Member:* Maryland State and American Bar Associations; District of Columbia Bar. ***PRACTICE AREAS:*** Agricultural Law; Government Contracts; Insurance; Administrative Law.

RAYMOND R. MULERA, born Washington, D.C., October 10, 1965; admitted to bar, 1991, Maryland; 1992, U.S. District Court, District of Maryland; 1998, District of Columbia; 2000, U.S. District court, District of Columbia. *Education:* University of Notre Dame (A.B., 1988); Catholic University of America (J.D., 1991). ***PRACTICE AREAS:*** Agricultural Law; Insurance; Government Contracts; Litigation.

AARON M. LEVINE & ASSOCIATES

Established in 1960

1320 - 19TH STREET, N.W.

WASHINGTON, D.C. 20036

Telephone: 202-833-8040

Fax: 202-833-8046

URL: http://www.aaronlevinelaw.com

Email: aaronlevinelaw@aol.com

URL: http://www.lawyers.com/aaronlevine

Civil Trial Practice. Personal Injury, Medical and Drug Products Liability, Medical Malpractice, LASIK Surgery Malpractice, Diethylstilbestrol (DES) Class Action, "DES" Daughter's Class Action.

FIRM PROFILE: Aaron M. Levine & Associates, located in midtown Washington, D.C., began in 1960, and since then has represented thousands of victims of defective drugs, medical devices, medical and surgical malpractice and all other forms of personal injury in the trial and appellate courts of many states and the federal system. The firm has broadly based associates, physicians, surgeons and other health-care professionals, closely connected consultants and employees, both in the United States and Western Europe. The firm exclusively specializes in personal injury, malpractice, pharmaceutical and medical device products liability, with emphasis on scientific and epidemiologic proof in the courtroom. The firm is also well known nationally for its expertise in cases involving laser eye surgery malpractice and its representation of the daughters of "DES" victims.

AARON M. LEVINE, born Brooklyn, N.Y., October 6, 1934; admitted to bar, 1960, District of Columbia; 1965, Maryland. *Education:* Brooklyn College of the City University of New York; George Washington University (LL.B., 1960). Author: "Products Liability Comes of Age in the District of Columbia," American University Law Review, Vol. 17, No. 2, 1968; "Gilding the Lily-A DES Update," Trial, Vol. 20, No. 12, December 1984; "Identification of Manufacturer of Diethylstilbestrol (DES)," 45 Am Jur Proof of Facts 2d, Lawyers Co-operative Publishing Co., 1986. Co-Author: "The Medicolegal Aspects of Adverse Drug Reactions," The Eye in Systemic Diseases, III, Little, Brown and Co., 1970; "Obstetrical Malpractice - The Last Decade," Contemporary OB/GYN, 1982. Recipient, Plaintiff's Lawyer of the Year, Plaintiff's Trial Attorneys of Washington, D.C., 1980. Lecturer: National College of Trial Advocacy; Association of Trial Lawyers of America; Defense Research Institute; Children's Hospital of Washington, D.C.; Washington Hospital Center; American College of Surgery; D.C. Medical Society. Legislative Assistant, Hon. S. Halpern, Queens, New York, 1958-1960. Appointee, Medical Device Classification Panel Food and Drug Administration, 1977-1978. Member, U.S. Judicial Conference for the District of Columbia Circuit, 1980-1990. Court Appointed Dalkon Shield Creditors Committee, 1985. Court Appointed Steering Committee, Silicone Breast Implant MDL-926, 1993; Co-Chair, Science Committee. Member, Association of Trial Lawyers of America, 1975-1989 (Chair, Aralen Litigation Committee; Chair, Pacemaker Litigation Committee; Chair, DES Litigation Committee). *Member:* The District of Columbia Bar; American Bar Association; The Bar Association of the District of Columbia; Association of Plaintiff's Trial Attorneys of Metropolitan Washington, D.C.; The American Society of Law and Medicine, Inc.; National Health Lawyers Association; Maryland Trial Lawyers Association; American Board of Professional Liability Attorneys; American Board of Trial Attorneys; Trial Lawyers Association of Metropolitan Washington, D.C. (Certified as a Civil Trial Advocate by the National Board of Trial Advocacy). ***PRACTICE AREAS:*** Medical Products Liability; Medical Malpractice; Personal Injury.

(This Listing Continued)

BRANDON J. LEVINE, born Washington, D.C., October 9, 1960; admitted to bar, 1987, District of Columbia; 1988, U.S. District Court for the District of Columbia; 1990, U.S. Court of Appeals for the District of Columbia Circuit; 1994, Maryland; 1995, U.S. District Court, District of Maryland; 1999, U.S. Court of Appeals, Fourth Circuit. *Education:* George Washington University (B.A., 1986); Howard University (J.D., 1987). Recipient, American Jurisprudence Award for Excellence in Evidence. Author, Note, "Banking Law-Federal Reserve Board's Grant of Authority to Enforce Holding Company Act Extends Only to Anticompetitive Considerations-Dimension Financial v. Board of Governors," 30 Howard Law Journal 143, 1987. *Member:* Prince George's County, Maryland State and American Bar Associations; The District of Columbia Bar; Association of the Bar of the District of Columbia; The Association of Trial Lawyers of America; Trial Lawyers Association of Metropolitan Washington, D.C. (Member, Board of Governors). ***PRACTICE AREAS:*** Medical Products Liability; Medical Malpractice; Personal Injury; Drugs and Medical Devices. **Email:** Levbran@aol.com

RENEE L. ROBINSON-MEYER, born Johnstown, Pennsylvania, January 5, 1964; admitted to bar, 1995, Maryland; 1996, U.S. District Court, District of Maryland; 1997, District of Columbia; 1999, U.S. District Court, District of Columbia. *Education:* Duquesne University (B.S.N., 1985); Georgetown University (J.D., 1995). Author, "Hypertrophic Cardiomyopathy: Medical, Surgical and Nursing Management," 7 Journal of Cardiovascular Nursing 13 (1993). Staff Nurse/Assistant Nursing Coordinator, Georgetown University Medical Center, 1989-1996. Staff Nurse, Veterans Administration Medical Centers: Washington, D.C.; Palo Alto, California; Pittsburgh, Pennsylvania, 1985-1989. District of Columbia Nursing License, 1989—. *Member:* Maryland State Bar Association, Inc.; Association of Trial Lawyers of America; American Association of Critical Care Nurses. ***PRACTICE AREAS:*** Medical Malpractice; Products Liability. **Email:** rlmsib@msn.com

STEVEN JAY LEWIS, born Camp Kue, Okinawa, Japan, December 1, 1966; admitted to bar, 2000, Virginia and U.S. Court of Appeals, Fourth Circuit; 2001, U.S. District Court, Eastern District of Virginia (Not admitted in District of Columbia). *Education:* University of California at Santa Barbara (B.S., 1989); George Washington University (J.D., 2000). *Member:* Virginia State Bar; Virginia and American Bar Associations; Virginia Trial Lawyers Association. ***PRACTICE AREAS:*** Personal Injury; Medical Liability; Medical Malpractice. **Email:** lewissj9@aol.com

LEVINE & ASSOCIATES

WASHINGTON, D.C.

(See Arlington, Virginia)

Immigration and Citizenship. International Business Transactions, Forensic Immigration Law, Customs Seizures. Practice before Federal Government Agencies.

LEVINE, BLASZAK, BLOCK & BOOTHBY, LLP

2001 L STREET, N.W., SUITE 900

WASHINGTON, D.C. 20036

Telephone: 202-857-2550

Fax: 202-223-0833

URL: http://www.LB3Law.com

Communications, Telecommunication Regulations, Internet Law, E-Commerce Law, High Technology Law, Administrative Law, Contract Law and Litigation.

FIRM PROFILE: Levine, Blaszak, Block & Boothby specializes in telecommunications law, with emphasis on the representation of large users and issues arising out of innovative uses of emerging technologies. The firm has more experience than any other in negotiating custom network service and internet agreements and network outsourcing arrangements of behalf of large users, and participates in state and federal proceedings involving issues such as local exchange competition, interconnection, internet access, toll fraud, and mobile services, and the implementation of the Telecommunications Act of 1996. The firm also represents the information technology industry on telecommunications matters and advises clients on telecommunications-related mergers and acquisitions, securities offerings, new technology services, and joint ventures.

MEMBERS OF FIRM

HENRY D. LEVINE, born June 7, 1951; admitted to bar, 1977, New York; 1978, District of Columbia. *Education:* Yale University (B.A., magna cum laude, 1972); Harvard University (M.P.P., 1976; J.D., magna cum laude, 1976). Phi Beta Kappa. Listed in "The 25 Most Powerful People in Networking," Network World, Jan. 1996. Editor-in-Chief, *Telematics,* 1984-1989. Chairman,

(This Listing Continued)

Subcommittee on State Regulation of the Telecommunications Committee, Section of Corporation, Banking and Business Law, American Bar Association, 1984-1987. Member, Committee on Technologically Enhanced Buildings, Building Research Board, National Research Council, 1985-1988. Consultant, GSA-FTS2001 1994-1999. *Member:* The District of Columbia Bar; Federal Communications Bar Association. ***PRACTICE AREAS:*** Telecommunications Law; Contracts.

JAMES S. BLASZAK, born January 6, 1946; admitted to bar, 1973, Texas; 1979, District of Columbia. *Education:* University of Dallas (B.A., cum laude, 1967); University of Texas (J.D., 1973). Attorney, Federal Communications Commission, 1973-1979. *Member:* The District of Columbia Bar; State Bar of Texas; Federal Communications Bar Association. ***PRACTICE AREAS:*** Telecommunications Law; Administrative Law; Public Utility Law.

ELLEN G. BLOCK, born January 5, 1948; admitted to bar, 1975, District of Columbia; 1979, U.S. Supreme Court. *Education:* Brandeis University (A.B., magna cum laude, 1969); Johns Hopkins University (M.A.T., 1971); Georgetown University (J.D., 1975). Phi Beta Kappa. *Member:* The District of Columbia Bar; American Bar Association (Vice-Chair, Domestic Telecommunications and Information Services Committee, Comm. Law Division, Science and Technology Section, 1993—); Federal Communications Bar Association. ***PRACTICE AREAS:*** Telecommunications Law; Administrative Law; Litigation.

COLLEEN L. BOOTHBY, born May 4, 1955; admitted to bar, 1980, District of Columbia. *Education:* Pomona College (A.B., 1977); Boalt Hall School of Law, University of California (J.D., 1980). Associate Editor, California Law Review, 1978-1980. Deputy and Associate Chief, Tariff Division. Legal Advisor to Common Carrier Bureau Chief; Attorney-Advisor, International Facilities Division and Tariff Division, Federal Communications Commission, 1983-1993. *Member:* The District of Columbia Bar; Federal Communications (Co-chair, Common Carrier Practice Committee, 1998-1999) and American (Member, Communications Forum, 1994—) Bar Associations. ***PRACTICE AREAS:*** Telecommunications Law.

KEVIN S. DiLALLO, born April 11, 1959; admitted to bar, 1987, Maryland; 1988, District of Columbia; 1990, U.S. District Court, District of Columbia and U.S. Court of Appeals, District of Columbia Circuit; 1998, U.S. Court of Appeals, Fifth Circuit. *Education:* University of Virginia (B.A., with Intermediate honors, 1981); Case Western Reserve University (J.D., 1986). Notes Editor and Executive Board Member, Case Western Reserve Law Review, 1984-1986. *Member:* Bar Association of the District of Columbia (Member, Sections on: Computer and Telecommunications Law; Corporations, Finance & Securities Law; Arts, Entertainment and Sports Law); Federal Communications Bar Association. ***PRACTICE AREAS:*** Telecommunications Law; Commercial Law; Technology Law.

LAURA F. H. McDONALD, born May 10, 1963; admitted to bar, 1988, Virginia; 1990, District of Columbia. *Education:* University of Virginia (B.A., 1985; J.D., 1988). Law Clerk to the Honorable Stanley S. Harris, U.S. District Court, Washington, D.C., 1988-1990. *Member:* The District of Columbia Bar (Member, Court Rules Committee, 1993-1994); Virginia State Bar; Federal Communications and American Bar Associations. ***PRACTICE AREAS:*** Telecommunications Law; Technology; Civil Litigation; Alternative Dispute Resolution.

D.E. BOEHLING, born August 16, 1965; admitted to bar, 1991, Virginia; 1992, District of Columbia. *Education:* University of Virginia (B.A., with high distinction, 1987; J.D., 1991). Author, "PCS Auctions: Who Will Benefit," CMA Review, Spring 1995. Co-Author, "Who Owns Your 800 Numbers?" CMA Review, Fall 1995. *Member:* The District of Columbia Bar; Virginia State Bar; Federal Communications and American Bar Associations. ***PRACTICE AREAS:*** Telecommunications Law; Administrative Law.

ASSOCIATES

JANINE F. GOODMAN, born October 12, 1966; admitted to bar, 1992, Illinois; 1994, District of Columbia. *Education:* Brown University (B.A., magna cum laude, 1988); University of Chicago (J.D., 1992). *Member:* Illinois State, Federal Communications and American Bar Associations; The District of Columbia Bar. ***PRACTICE AREAS:*** Telecommunications Law; Administrative Law; Commercial Law.

MARK G. JOHNSTON, born Berwyn, Illinois, April 24, 1965; admitted to bar, 1993, New York; 2000, District of Columbia. *Education:* University of Illinois (B.A., magna cum laude, 1987); University of Michigan (J.D., cum laude, 1991). Phi Beta Kappa. Member, 1989-1991 and Executive Notes Editor, 1990-1991, Michigan Journal of International Law. ***PRACTICE AREAS:*** Telecommunications Law. ***Email:*** mjohnston@lb3law.com

JUSTIN G. CASTILLO, born Denver, Colorado; admitted to bar, 1994, Pennsylvania; 1996, Colorado; 2000, District of Columbia. *Education:* Yale University (B.A., magna cum laude, 1987; M.A., 1987); Georgetown University (J.D., cum laude, 1993). Assistant Editor, American Criminal Law Review, 1992-1993. Law Clerk to the Hon. John A. Terry, District of Columbia Court of Appeals, 1993-1994. Trial Attorney, Civil Fraud Section, Department of Justice, 1994-1997. ***PRACTICE AREAS:*** Telecommunications Law; Corporate Contracts; International Law. ***Email:*** jcastillo@lb3law.com

(This Listing Continued)

MARC A. LINDSEY, born Bridgeton, New Jersey, January 1, 1966; admitted to bar, 1996, North Carolina; 2000, District of Columbia. *Education:* Howard University (B.S.E.E., 1989); University of Pennsylvania (M.S.E., Systems Engineering, 1992); University of North Carolina (J.D., with honors, 1996). Tau Beta Pi. Member, National Moot Court Team. *Member:* North Carolina State Bar; North Carolina and American (Member: Intellectual Property Law Section; Forum on Communications) Bar Associations; Federal Communications Bar. ***PRACTICE AREAS:*** Technology Law; Software Licensing; Intellectual Property Licensing; Telecommunications Law; Outsourcing; Internet Law; Contracts; Information Technology; Administrative Law; Commercial Litigation. ***Email:*** mlindsey@lb3law.com

ANDREW M. BROWN, born May 26, 1971; admitted to bar, 1998, California; 1999, District of Columbia. *Education:* Georgetown University (B.S., magna cum laude, 1993); University of Virginia (J.D., 1997). Winner, William Minor Lile Moot Court Competition, 1997. Executive Editor, Virginia Journal of International Law, 1996-1997. *Member:* Federal Communications Bar Association. ***PRACTICE AREAS:*** Telecommunications Law; Contracts; Information Technology; Outsourcing. ***Email:*** abrown@lb3law.com

BONNIE R. GERHARDT, born February 7, 1970; admitted to bar, 1997, Maryland; 1999, District of Columbia. *Education:* Williams College (B.A., 1992); Washington & Lee University School of Law (J.D., 1997). Executive Editor, Law Review. ***PRACTICE AREAS:*** Telecommunications. ***Email:*** bgerhardt@lb3law.com

STEPHEN J. ROSEN, born Garden City, New York, July 16, 1962; admitted to bar, 1993, Maryland; 1994, District of Columbia. *Education:* Princeton University (B.A., with honors, 1984); Uniformed Services University of Health Sciences (M.P.H., 1987); The George Washington University (J.D., with highest honors, 1993). Member, The George Washington Law Review. Law Clerk to the Hon. Michael Farrell, District of Columbia Court of Appeals, 1993-1994. *Member:* Federal Communications Bar Association. ***PRACTICE AREAS:*** Communications Law. ***Email:*** srosen@lb3law.com

BENJAMIN HUANG, born Rolla, Missouri, 1969; admitted to bar, 1995, Texas; registered to practice before U.S. Patent and Trademark Office (Not admitted in District of Columbia). *Education:* University of Texas-Austin (B.S., 1992; B.A., 1992); Duke University School of Law (J.D., 1995). Managing Editor, *Duke Journal of Comparative and International Law.* ***PRACTICE AREAS:*** Intellectual Property.

LEVINE SULLIVAN & KOCH, L.L.P.

Established in 1997

1050 SEVENTEENTH STREET, N.W.
SUITE 800
WASHINGTON, D.C. 20036
Telephone: 202-508-1100
Facsimile: 202-861-9888
Email: info@lsklaw.com

Media, Defamation, First Amendment, Publishing and related law, Copyright, and General Civil Litigation.

MEMBERS OF FIRM

LEE LEVINE, born Brooklyn, New York, November 20, 1954; admitted to bar, 1980, District of Columbia. *Education:* University of Pennsylvania (B.A., summa cum laude, 1976; M.A., 1976); Yale University (J.D., 1979). Phi Beta Kappa. Managing Editor, Yale Law Journal, 1978-1979. Partner, Ross, Dixon & Masback, L.L.P., 1987-1996. Co-Author: "Newsgathering and the Law," LEXIS Law Publishing, 2d ed. 1999; "Implied Libel, Defamatory Meaning, and State of Mind," 78 Iowa Law Review 237, 1993; "Branzburg Revisited: Confidential Sources and First Amendment Values," 57 George Washington Law Review 13, 1988; "Judge and Jury in the Law of Defamation," 35 American University Law Review 3, 1985; "Reckless Disregard," 56 George Washington University Law Review, 245, 1987; "The Editorial Function and The Gertz Public Figure Standard," 87 Yale Law Journal 1723, 1978. Law Clerk to Chief Judge Irving R. Kaufman, United States Court of Appeals for the Second Circuit, 1979-1980. Adjunct Professor of Law, Georgetown University Law Center, 1989—. *Member:* District of Columbia Bar; American Bar Association (Past Chair, Forum on Communications Law). ***Email:*** llevine@lsklaw.com

MICHAEL D. SULLIVAN, born Cincinnati, Ohio, September 16, 1955; admitted to bar, 1980, District of Columbia. *Education:* The Ohio State University (B.A., summa cum laude, 1977); Georgetown University (J.D., magna cum laude, 1980). Case and Note Editor, Georgetown Law Journal, 1979-1980. Partner, Ross, Dixon & Masback, L.L.P., 1990-1996, Adjunct Professor: Georgetown University Law Center, 1984; University of Maryland College of Journalism, 1990-1997. Co-Author: "Developments in West Virginia's Insurance

(This Listing Continued)

LEVINE SULLIVAN & KOCH, L.L.P., Washington—Continued

Bad Faith Law—Where Do We Go From Here?" 98 West Virginia Law Review 267, 1995. *Member:* District of Columbia Bar; American Bar Association. **Email:** msullivan@lsklaw.com

ELIZABETH C. KOCH, born New London, Connecticut, May 17, 1961; admitted to bar, 1987, District of Columbia and Maryland. *Education:* Vassar College (A.B., general honors, 1983); University of Michigan (J.D., cum laude, 1986). Partner, Ross, Dixon & Masback, L.L.P., 1994-1996. *Member:* District of Columbia Bar (Member, Steering Committee, Intellectual Property Law Section, 1996-1999); American Bar Association (Co-editor, Forum on Communications Law's Communications Lawyer, 1995-1999; Member, Governing Board, Forum on Communications Law, 2000—; Member, Intellectual Property Law Section). **Email:** bkoch@lsklaw.com

JAMES E. GROSSBERG, born New York, N.Y., August 12, 1956; admitted to bar, 1985, Virginia; 1988, District of Columbia; 1994, California. *Education:* University of Virginia (B.A., 1978; J.D., 1983). Law Clerk, The Honorable Judge William L. Garwood, U.S. Court of Appeals, Fifth Circuit, 1983-1984. Partner, Ross, Dixon & Masback, L.L.P., 1991-1996. *Member:* Libel Defense Resource Center Defense Counsel Section (President, 1996-1997); District of Columbia Bar; Virginia State Bar; State Bar of California. **Email:** jgrossberg@lsklaw.com

CELESTE PHILLIPS, born New York, N.Y., May 27, 1953; admitted to bar, 1981, California (Not admitted in District of Columbia). *Education:* University of California at Berkeley (A.B., 1978); University of California, Hastings College of the Law (J.D., 1981). Phi Beta Kappa; Order of the Coif. Partner, Ross, Dixon & Masback, L.L.P., 1993-1996. *Member:* State Bar of California. **Email:** cphillips@lsklaw.com

SETH D. BERLIN, born Roanoke, Virginia, July 17, 1966; admitted to bar, 1991, Maryland; 1992, District of Columbia; 2001, New York. *Education:* Brown University (B.A., magna cum laude, 1988); Harvard University (J.D., cum laude, 1991). Chair, Young Lawyers Division Law and Media Committee, 1997-1999. *Member:* District of Columbia Bar; American Bar Association (Member, Forum on Communications Law). **Email:** sberlin@lsklaw.com

JAY WARD BROWN, born Minneapolis, Minnesota, September 29, 1964; admitted to bar, 1992, Virginia; 1993, District of Columbia. *Education:* University of Minnesota at Minneapolis (B.A., 1984) Phi Beta Kappa; Columbia University Graduate School of Journalism (M.S., with honors, 1985); New York University (J.D., cum laude, 1992). Member, Order of the Barristers. National Merit Scholar. Arthur Garfield Hays Civil Liberties Fellow. Appointment to Community Services Commission, City of Richfield, Minnesota, 1979-1984. Adjunct Faculty, Media Law, Trinity College, 1999—. *Member:* Virginia State Bar; District of Columbia Bar. **Email:** jbrown@lsklaw.com

OF COUNSEL

CAMERON A. STRACHER, born Brooklyn, New York, July 25, 1961; admitted to bar, 1988, New York; 1989, District of Columbia. *Education:* Amherst College (B.A., magna cum laude, 1983); Harvard University (J.D., 1987); University of Iowa (M.F.A., 1991). Adjunct Professor of Law, University of Iowa College of Law, 1989-1993. Litigation Counsel, CBS Broadcasting, 1994-1999. *Member:* New York State Bar; District of Columbia Bar. **Email:** cstracher@lsklaw.com

ASSOCIATES

ASHLEY I. KISSINGER, born Austin, Texas, March 4, 1968; admitted to bar, 1996, Texas; 1997, California; 1999, District of Columbia. *Education:* Stanford University (A.B., 1990); The University of Texas at Austin (J.D., with honors, 1995). Award for Outstanding Labor Law Note. Dean's Achievement Award in Constitutional Law. Associate Editor, Texas Law Review, 1994-1995. Law Clerk to The Honorable Judge Sam Sparks, U.S. District Court, Western District of Texas, 1995-1997. Author, Note, "Civil Rights and Professional Wrongs: A Female Lawyer's Dilemma," 73 Texas Law Review 1419, 1995. *Member:* American Bar Association; State Bar of Texas; State Bar of California; District of Columbia Bar. **Email:** akissinger@lsklaw.com

AMY E. LEDOUX, born Alexandria, Louisiana, March 22, 1970; admitted to bar, 1997, Illinois; 1998, District of Columbia. *Education:* Washington University (A.B., 1991); Georgetown University (J.D., magna cum laude, 1997). Order of the Coif. Notes and Comments Editor, Georgetown Law Journal. *Member:* District of Columbia Bar; American Bar Association. **Email:** aledoux@lsklaw.com

AUDREY BILLINGSLEY, born Fort Bragg, North Carolina, October 11, 1971; admitted to bar, 1999, Virginia; 2000, District of Columbia. *Education:* University of Chicago (B.A., 1994; M.A., 1996); Georgetown University (J.D., 1999). Law Clerk to The Honorable Judge Andrew Effron, U.S. Court of Appeals for the Armed Forces. **Email:** abillingsley@lsklaw.com

(This Listing Continued)

THOMAS CURLEY, born Long Branch, New Jersey, August 9, 1968; admitted to bar, 2000, Maryland; 2001, District of Columbia. *Education:* Duke University (B.A., magna cum laude, 1990); Georgetown University (J.D., magna cum laude, 2000). **Email:** tcurley@lsklaw.com

LEWIS AND ASSOCIATES

WASHINGTON, D.C.

(See Springfield, Virginia)

Immigration, Immigration Employment, Personal Injury, Automobile Accidents, Wrongful Death, Medical Malpractice, Products Liability, Criminal Law, Traffic Violations, Driving While Intoxicated, Shoplifting, Embezzlement, Family Law, Divorce, Child Custody, Child Support, Adoptions, Spousal Abuse, Small Business Law, Contracts.

THE LEWIS LAW FIRM

A PROFESSIONAL CORPORATION

Established in 1981

805 15TH STREET, N.W.
SUITE 200
WASHINGTON, D.C. 20005
Telephone: 202-408-0655
Fax: 202-408-9826
Email: glewis@lewislawfirm.com
URL: http://www.lewislawfirm.com

Fairfax, Virginia Office: Suite 100, 10306 Eaton Place. Telephone: 703-691-8686.

Rockville, Maryland Office: Suite 402, 11921 Rockville Pike, 20852.

Family Law, Adoptions, Child Custody, Child Support, Divorce, Criminal Law, Business and Transaction Matters, General, Civil and Commercial Litigation, Appellate practice in State and Federal Courts.

GLENN C. LEWIS, born New York, N.Y., October 20, 1952; admitted to bar, 1977, Virginia; U.S. District Court, Eastern District of Virginia and U.S. Court of Appeals, Fourth Circuit; 1978, District of Columbia and U.S. District Court for the District of Columbia and U.S. Court of Appeals, District of Columbia Circuit; 1999, Maryland. *Education:* University of Miami (B.A., Politics and Public Affairs, 1973); George Mason University (J.D., 1977). Listed in The Best Lawyers in America, Family Law, 1994—. Featured in Washingtonian Magazine as one of the top divorce lawyers in the Washington Metro Area. Named the Virginia Liaison to American Bar Association Section on Family Law, January, 1993; Elected Fairfax Bar Delegate to American Bar Association House of Delegates, 1997—; Panelist, Faculty, American Bar Association Section on Taxation, 1996, Orlando, Florida. Named by Chief Justice of Virginia to Advisory Work Group on Legislation for Implementation of the Family Court, 1992. Named to Commission on Youth, Virginia General Assembly Subcommittee on Model Child Custody and Visitation, March, 1993. Member: SJR 64 Work Group with Virginia Supreme Court to develop judge and lawyer training on dealing with issues of Child Visitation, 1994—; Chief Judge's Task Force on Domestic Relations Delay Reduction, Fairfax Circuit Court, 1988-1990; Virginia Supreme Court Symposium on Children and Families, 1993; Virginia Supreme Court Advisory Work Group on Alternative Dispute Resolution. Co-Drafter: New Virginia Mediation Statute (effective July 1, 1994). Executive Producer and Host of "Law Weekly" Cable Television show seen in Washington, D.C. metro area; awards include: "Outstanding Achievement Award" by the Virginia State Bar, June 1990; "Exceptional Service Award" by the Fairfax Bar Association, May 1990; two "Telly Awards" for Outstanding Educational Series and Cultural Nonperformance from Local Cable Television Industry, 1990, and "Outstanding Live Cable Talk Show" by the National Federation of Local Cable Programmers, July, 1991; Finalist, Hometown Video Award for "Outstanding Talk Show," 1995, 1997. Recipient: Award of Merit, Virginia State Bar, 1996; Virginia State Bar Award of Merit, Fairfax Bar Association Diversity Task Force, June, 1996; 20th Annual Human Rights Award, Fairfax County Human Rights Commission for the Fairfax Bar Association's Diversity Task Force, May 6, 1997; 2nd Annual Local Bar Leader of the Year Award, Virginia State Bar, June 19, 1997. *Member:* Fairfax County Bar Association (President, 1995-1996; Member: Board of Directors, 1991—; Family Law Section, 1988—; Budget Committee, 1994—; Chair, Fairfax Cultural Diversity Task Force, 1996—; Moderator, Fairfax Bar Association Conference: "Sanctions -- Love'em or Leave'em;" September, 1994. Member: Child Advocacy Task Force, 1994—; Legislative Committee, 1994—; Member, Town Hall Committee, 1992-1993, recipient of "President's Award" for Outstanding Service; Board Liaison to Circuit Court Committee, 1992—; Member, Judicial Screening and Nominating Committee, 1992—; Member, President's Task Force, Shelter Outreach Program, 1990; Chair, President's Nominating Committee for Bar Officers and Directors, 1989; Member, Circuit Court Committee, 1988-1990; Co-Chair, Domestic Relations Task Force, Circuit Court Committee, 1988-1991; Chair, Sub-

(This Listing Continued)

committee on Motions Day Practice, Circuit Court Committee, 1988-1989; Chair, Public Relations Committee, 1988-1990); Virginia State Bar (Board of Governors, Family Law Section, 1989-1993; Chair, Special Committee on Access to Legal Services; Member, Virginia State Bar Council; Chair, Family Law Section, 1992-1993; Chair, Board of Governors Committee on Attorney's Fees in Family Matters, 1994-1996; Appointed VSB Long Range Planning Committee, 1994; Moderator, VSB YLC Panel: "The Demise of the Nuclear Family, June, 1994; Faculty, VSB Professionalism Course, 1996—; Member, Domestic Relations Counsel; Panelist, Gender Bias in Domestic Relations Cases, Williamsburg, January 1996; Faculty, VSB MCLE - Family Law Issues, 1986-1997); The District of Columbia Bar (Member: Domestic Relations Section; Member, Family Law Committee; Civil Litigation Committee; Nominated and Appointed, Voting Delegate by District of Columbia Court of Appeals to District of Columbia Judicial Conference, 1993, 1994, 1995; Member, Chief Judge's Task Force on Maintaining the Official Court Record, 1994—); Co-Chair, Virginia Bar Association Coalition Committee on Family Law Legislation; Lecturer, Virginia CLE 19th Annual Family Law Seminar 2000 "Going for the Gold: Locating and Using Winning Evidence." Virginia Trial Lawyers Association (Lecturer, "Recent Developments in Family Law, 1990, 1992, 1994, 1995, 1996). Lecturer, Moderator and Author: Richmond, Tysons, Virginia Beach, Norfolk, Roanoke, Lynchburg, Charlottesville, Stauton, Grand Cayman Islands, B.W.I. Member, Virginia Summit on Racial and Ethnic Bias, Richmond, March 1996. Lecturer, "Child Support and Income Tax Rules," "Annual Developments in Family Law and Use of Experts," Virginia Trial Lawyers Association, Falls Church VA and Virginia Beach, VA, July, 1996. Speaker: "Comments on CPA Support in Family Law Practice," Greater Washington Society of Certified Public Accountants, Washington, DC, February, 1997; "Common Sense Rules for Family Law Practice," Fairfax Bar Association CLE, Fairfax, VA, March, 1997; "Client Funds/Trust Accounts," Virginia State Bar, Alexandria, VA, March, 1997; "How To Handle A Crisis," American Bar Association's Bar Leader's Institute, Chicago, IL, March 1997; "Ethical Issues and the Computer Age," Virginia CLE, Richmond, VA, May, 1997. Moderator, "Nuts and Bolts of Bar Leadership," Virginia Bar Leader's Institute, Richmond, VA, March, 1997. Neutral Case Evaluator, Fairfax Circuit Court. Faculty: "Lessons Learned: Practical Ideas for the Practice of Law," Fairfax Bar Association, December 1997; "Recent Developments in Family Law," Arlington County Bar Association, 15th Annual Family Law Seminar, Hitting the Ground Running - Taking A Divorce Case Through the Pendente Lite Hearing, January 1998; CLE Lecture, " Legislative Update, Family Law, Virginia Trial Lawyers Association, Ready for Trial Now and in the Year 2000," The Homestead, April 1998; CLE, "Trying an Equitable Distribution Case; Examining the Expert on Business Valuation," Virginia State Bar, Litigation Section and AICPA, Richmond, VA, May 1998; CLE, "Comparison and Contrast of Family Law Practice in Virginia, District of Columbia and Maryland," 1997 Fairfax Bar Association Annual Convention, Williamsburg, Virginia, September 1997; CLE, "Cohabitation in Custody and Visitation," Virginia Bar Association, 108th Annual Meeting, Williamsburg, VA, January 1998; CLE, "Recent Developments in Family Law," Virginia Law Foundation, 16th Family Law Seminar, Tysons Corner, Norfolk, Virginia, November 1997. Member, William B. Fitzgerald Scholarship Fund (Member, Board of Trustees). (Also at Fairfax, Virginia Office). ***PRACTICE AREAS:*** Family Law. ***Email:*** glewis@lewislawfirm.com

---

WENDY HELENE SCHWARTZ, born Detroit, Michigan, May 24, 1954; admitted to bar, 1990, Maryland; 1991, Pennsylvania; 1992, District of Columbia; 1993, Virginia and U.S. District Court for the District of Columbia. *Education:* Mercy College of Detroit (B.A., cum laude, 1978); Washington College of Law of American University (J.D., 1990). Law Clerk to the Hon. Cheryl M. Long, Associate Judge, District of Columbia Superior Court. Lecturer: "Recent Development in Virginia Family Law," Arlington County Bar Associations Twelfth Annual Family Law Seminar, January, 1995; "Avoiding Malpractice-Family Law," Fairfax Bar Association Annual Convention, September, 1997. Appointed Voting Delegate by the District of Columbia Court of Appeals for Judicial Conference, June, 1994; June, 1995; June, 1996; June 1999; June 2000. Appointed President of the Lewis Law Firm, June 17, 1999. *Member:* The District of Columbia Bar (Member, Family Law Section); Fairfax (Member, Circuit Court Committee and Juvenile and Domestic Relations Committee, 1995-1998) and American (Member, Family Law Section) Bar Associations; Virginia Trial Lawyers Association. (Also at Rockville, Maryland and Fairfax, Virginia Offices). ***PRACTICE AREAS:*** Family Law; Criminal Law. ***Email:*** wschwartz@lewislawfirm.com

DANIEL G. DANNENBAUM, born Philadelphia, Pennsylvania, January 25, 1962; admitted to bar, 1990, Virginia; 1996, District of Columbia. *Education:* Harvard University (A.B., cum laude, 1983); George Washington University (J.D., with high honors, 1990). Order of the Coif. Law Clerk to the Civil Judges of the Circuit Court of the City of Richmond, 1993-1994. Featured in Washingtonian Magazine (March 2000) as one of the Washington Metropolitan Area's Top Divorce Lawyers. Lecturer, "Recent Developments in Virginia Domestic Relations Practice," Virginia CLE, 1995; Fourteenth Annual Family Law Seminar, Arlington County Bar Association, 1997. Panelist, Divorce Mediation

(This Listing Continued)

Seminar, Virginia Bar Association Convention, 1997. *Member:* Fairfax (Member, Continuing Legal Education Committee, 1995-1996; General District Court and Juvenile and Domestic Relations Court Committee, 1995-1997), Arlington County and Virginia Bar Associations; Virginia State Bar; District of Columbia Bar; Virginia Trial Lawyers Association (Continuing Legal Education Committee). (Also at Fairfax, Virginia Office); (Shareholder). ***PRACTICE AREAS:*** Family Law; Civil Litigation. ***Email:*** ddannenbaum@lewislawfirm.com

GREGORY R. NUGENT, born New York, N.Y., May 20, 1962; admitted to bar, 1989, Illinois and U.S. District Court, Northern District of Illinois; 1997, Maryland and District of Columbia. *Education:* Boston College (B.A., 1984); Suffolk University (J.D., 1989). *Member:* Montgomery County (Member, Family Law Section) and Maryland State (Member, Family Law Section) Bar Associations; The District of Columbia Bar (Member, Family Law Section). (Also at Rockville, Maryland Office). ***PRACTICE AREAS:*** Family Law; Criminal Law; Civil Litigation. ***Email:*** gnugent@lewislawfirm.com

CATHERINE M. REESE, born Belleville, New Jersey, May 10, 1963; admitted to bar, 1998 Virginia and U.S. Court of Appeals, 4th Circuit, U.S. District Court and Bankruptcy Court for the Eastern District of Virginia; 1999, District of Columbia and Maryland. *Education:* University of Maryland (B.A., 1995); Catholic University Columbus School of Law (J.D, 1998). Phi Alpha Delta National Capital Alumni Association (Officer). The Virginia State Attorney General's Office Division of Child Support Enforcement Statewide Attorney Training Seminar CLE, Spring Seminar, "Family Law and Legislative Update," 2000. *Member:* Fairfax (Family Law Section and Committee Member), Maryland State (Family Law Section), Virginia (Domestic Relations Section) and American Bar Associations; Virginia State Bar (Member, Family Section); The District of Columbia Bar (Family Law Section); Virginia Trial Lawyers Association (Family Law Section); Association of Trial Lawyers of America; Virginia Women's Attorney Association; Northern Virginia Women's Attorneys Association (Officer). ***PRACTICE AREAS:*** Family Law. ***Email:*** creese@lewislawfirm.com

AMY L. HADLEY, born Portsmouth, Virginia, September 4, 1973; admitted to bar, 1998, Virginia (Not admitted in District of Columbia). *Education:* College of William & Mary (B.A. 1994; J.D., 1998). Law Clerk to the Hon. David G. Lowe, U.S. Magistrate Judge, U.S. District Court, Eastern District of Virginia, Richmond Division, 1998-1999. Speaker: "Family Law and Legislative Update," The Virginia State Attorney General's Office Division of Child Support Enforcement Statewide Attorney Training Seminar, Spring 2000. *Fairfax Bar Association.* ***PRACTICE AREAS:*** Family Law. ***Email:*** asvatek@lewislawfirm.com

SHERRY L. LEICHMAN, born New York, N.Y., April 14, 1954; admitted to bar, 1985, Maryland; 1999, U.S District Court, District of Maryland; 2001, District of Columbia. *Education:* Boston University (B.S., 1976); Antioch School of Law (J.D., 1984). Judicial Law Clerk, Hon. Douglas Moore, Jr. and Hon. John Tracey, Montgomery County Maryland Juvenile Court. In-house counsel, Montgomery County Department of Health and Human Services, Montgomery County Attorney's Office, Rockville, MD., 1988-2000. *Member:* Montgomery County and Maryland State Bar Association; District of Columbia Bar; Womens Bar Association of Maryland. ***PRACTICE AREAS:*** Family Law. ***Email:*** sleichman@lewislawfirm.com

ROBERT C. EUSTICE, born Royal Oak, Michigan, September 4, 1963; admitted to bar, 1988, Michigan; 1989, District of Columbia; 1990, Virginia, U.S. District Court, Eastern District of Virginia and U.S. Court of Appeals, Fourth Circuit; 1993, Maryland; 1996, U.S. Court of Federal Claims, U.S. District Court for the District of Columbia; 1999, U.S. District Court, District of Maryland. *Education:* University of Michigan (A.B., with high distinction, 1985; J.D., 1988). Phi Alpha Delta. Member, Golden Key. *Member:* State Bar of Michigan; District of Columbia Bar; Virginia State Bar; American Bar Association. ***PRACTICE AREAS:*** Family Law; Commercial Litigation. ***Email:*** reustice@lewislawfirm.com

RICHARD F. GIBBONS, JR., born Portsmouth, Virginia, May 1, 1962; admitted to bar, 1987, New York; 1988, District of Columbia and U. S. District Court, Eastern, Southern and Northern Districts of New York; 1990, Virginia; 1991, U. S. District Court for the District of Columbia, U. S. District Court, Eastern District of Virginia and U. S. Court of Appeals, 4th Circuit. *Education:* College of the Holy Cross (A.B., 1984); College of William & Mary (J.D., 1987). Order of the Barristers; National Moot Court Team. Recipient, American Jurisprudence Award for Contracts. Winner, Best Brief, Kaufman Securities Competition. Finalist, Kaufman Securities Competition. ***REPORTED CASES:*** F.D.I.C. v. Hadid, 947 F.2d 1153 (4th Cir., 1991). ***PRACTICE AREAS:*** Family Law (95%); Commercial Litigation (5%). ***Email:*** rgibbons@lewislawfirnm.com

ROBERTA KATHRYN HENAULT, born San Diego, California, February 9, 1968; admitted to bar, 1999, Massachusetts; 2000, Virginia (Not admitted in District of Columbia). *Education:* Stonehill College (B.A., magna cum laude, 1990); Suffolk University (J.D., cum laude, 1999). Psi Chi Honor Society. *Member:* Fairfax, Massachusetts and American Bar Associations. ***PRACTICE AREAS:*** Family Law. ***Email:*** rhenault@lewislawfirm.com

(This Listing Continued)

THE LEWIS LAW FIRM, A PROFESSIONAL CORPORATION, Washington—Continued

LEGAL SUPPORT PERSONNEL

KIM ELLA CLARKSON, born Syracuse, New York, March 31, 1952. *Education:* Keuka College (B.A., 1974); University of Maryland (B.S., 1996); Mansfield State University; Elmira College; Exeter College, Exeter, England. *Member:* The Institute of Legal Executives; Virginia Trial Lawyers Association (VTLA). (Paralegal Coordinator). ***LANGUAGES:*** German. ***PRACTICE AREAS:*** Family Law. ***Email:*** kclarkson@lewislawfirm.com

JACQUELINE ROBINSON, born Washington, D.C., August 7, 1962. *Education:* Howard University; Washington School for Secretaries (A.A., Certificate, honors). *Member:* Association of Office Administrators. (Paralegal). ***PRACTICE AREAS:*** Family Law. ***Email:*** jrobinson@lewislawfirm.com

SHERRIE L. WHITE, born Staten Island, New York, March 27, 1949. *Education:* Wagner College; Rockland Community College (Paralegal Certification). *Member:* Virginia Trial Lawyers Association. (Paralegal). ***PRACTICE AREAS:*** Child Support Enforcement; Family Law; Wills and Estates. ***Email:*** swhite@lewislawfirm.com

DIANA M. FIELDING, born Fort Devons, Massachusetts, Octoer 27, 1955. *Education:* University of Maryland University College (B.A., 2000); American University. Alpha sigma Lamda; Phi Kappa Phi. Member, Virginia Trial Lawyers Association. (Paralegal). ***PRACTICE AREAS:*** Trial and Deposition Preparation; Draft Pleadings and Discovery Documents. ***Email:*** dfielding@lewislawfirm.com

REFERENCE: Franklin National Bank of Washington.

LEWIS & MUNDAY

A PROFESSIONAL CORPORATION

(Formerly Lewis, White & Clay, P.C.)

1120 CONNECTICUT AVENUE N.W., SUITE 280
WASHINGTON, D.C. 20036
Telephone: 202-835-0616
Fax: 202-833-3316
Email: KBrown@lewismunday.com
URL: http://www.lewismunday.com

Detroit, Michigan Office: 1300 First National Building, 660 Woodward Avenue. 48226-3531. Telephone: 313-961-2550. Fax: 313-961-1270.

Boston, Massachusetts Office: 101 Federal Street, Suite 1900. 02110. Telephone: 617-478-0553. Fax: 617-478-0543.

Business, Banking, Bankruptcy, Casualty Insurance, Real Estate, Litigation, Civil Rights, Corporate, Life and Health Insurance, Mortgage, Municipal Bond, Municipal, Urban Affairs and Railroad Law.

KAREN KENDRICK BROWN, born Washington, D.C., March 3, 1954; admitted to bar, 1980, District of Columbia; 1983, U.S. Tax Court; 1994, U.S. District Court for the District of Columbia; 1995, Maryland. *Education:* Boston University (B.A., 1976); George Washington University (J.D., 1979). Certified Public Accountant, Maryland, 1985. *Member:* The District of Columbia Bar; Maryland State Bar Association, Inc.; American Bar Association; National Bar Association (Member, Greater Washington Area Chapter of Women Lawyers); National Association of Bond Lawyers. (Resident). ***PRACTICE AREAS:*** Public Finance; Taxation Law. ***Email:*** KBrown@lewismunday.com

(For Complete Personnel and Biographical Data, see Professional Biographies at Detroit, Michigan).

LEYDIG, VOIT & MAYER, LTD.

700 THIRTEENTH STREET N.W., SUITE 300
WASHINGTON, D.C. 20005-3960
Telephone: 202-737-6770
Telecopier: 202-737-6776
Email: mail@leydig.com
URL: http://www.leydig.com

Chicago, Illinois Office: Two Prudential Plaza, Suite 4900. 180 North Stetson Avenue. Telephone: 312-616-5600. Telecopier: 312-616-5700.

Rockford, Illinois Office: 6815 Weaver Road, Suite 300. Telephone: 815-963-7661. Telecopier: 815-963-7664.

Patent, Trademark, Copyright, Unfair Competition and Related Antitrust and International Trade Law. Trials and Appeals.

JOHN M. BELZ, born East St. Louis, Illinois, December 3, 1948; admitted to bar, 1980, Texas; 1981, Illinois; 1985, District of Columbia; U.S. Court of Appeals for the Federal Circuit; U.S. District Court, District of Columbia; registered to practice before U.S. Patent and Trademark Office. *Education:* University of Missouri (B.S.E.E., 1975; M.S. Nuclear Eng., 1976); University of Texas (J.D., 1980). (Resident). ***Email:*** jbelz@leydig.com

JEFFREY A. WYAND, born Hagerstown, Maryland, November 14, 1942; admitted to bar, 1977, Maryland; 1980, Ohio; 1988, District of Columbia; U.S. Court of Appeals for the Federal Circuit; U.S. District Court, District of Maryland; registered to practice before U.S. Patent and Trademark Office. *Education:* Lehigh University (B.S.E.E., 1964; B.S. Eng. Physics, 1965); Carnegie-Mellon University (M.S.E.E., 1966); University of Maryland (J.D., 1977). (Resident). ***Email:*** jwyand@leydig.com

JEREMY M. JAY, born Hackensack, New Jersey, November 22, 1953; admitted to bar, 1990, Virginia; 1991, District of Columbia; U.S. Supreme Court; U.S. Court of Appeals for the Federal Circuit; U.S. District Court, Eastern District of Virginia; registered to practice before U.S. Patent and Trademark Office. *Education:* University of Connecticut (B.S. in Pre-Veterinary Technology, 1976; M.S., Zoology, 1978); Texas A & M University (Ph.D., Biology, 1985); George Mason University (J.D., 1990). (Resident). ***Email:*** jjay@leydig.com

---

XAVIER PILLAI, born Budhalur, Tamil Nadu, India, December 18, 1952; admitted to bar, 1994, Illinois; U.S. District Court, Northern District of Illinois; registered to practice before U.S. Patent and Trademark Office (Not admitted in District of Columbia). *Education:* Case Western Reserve University (Ph.D., 1984); Chicago-Kent College of Law, Illinois Institute of Technology (J.D., 1994). (Resident). ***LANGUAGES:*** Tamil and Hindi. ***Email:*** xpillai@leydig.com

SHANNON D. SCHEMEL, born Kansas City, Missouri, March 5, 1973; admitted to bar, 2000, Virginia; registered to practice before U.S. Patent and Trademark Office (Not admitted in District of Columbia). *Education:* University of South Carolina (B.S., Chem. Engineering, 1997); George Washington University (J.D., 2000). (Resident). ***Email:*** sschemel@leydig.com

LEAH C. OUBRE, born Stade, Germany, August 11, 1975; admitted to bar, 2000, Virginia; 2001, District of Columbia; registered to practice before U.S. Patent and Trademark Office. *Education:* Louisiana State University (B.S., Chem. Engineering, 1997); University of Richmond (J.D., 2000). (Resident). ***Email:*** loubre@leydig.com

OF COUNSEL

JOHN P. BUNDOCK, JR., born Floral Park, New York, August 3, 1926; admitted to bar, 1951, District of Columbia; 1954, Illinois; U.S. Court of Appeals for the Federal Circuit; U.S. District Court, District of Columbia; registered to practice before U.S. Patent and Trademark Office. *Education:* Tufts University (B.S.E.E., 1948); George Washington University (LL.B., 1950). (Resident).

JOHN D. FOSTER, born Moline, Illinois, February 9, 1943; admitted to bar, 1970, District of Columbia and California; 1977, Illinois; U.S. Court of Appeals for the Federal Circuit; U.S. District Court, Northern District of Illinois; registered to practice before U.S. Patent and Trademark Office. *Education:* Iowa State University (B.S.Ch.E., 1965); Georgetown University (J.D., 1969). (Resident).

LIEFF, CABRASER, HEIMANN & BERNSTEIN, LLP

1100 NEW YORK AVENUE, N.W.
SUITE 1080 - WEST TOWER
WASHINGTON, D.C. 20005-3934
Telephone: 202-582-1000
Facsimile: 202-582-1500
Email: mail@lchb.com
URL: http://www.lchb.com

New York, New York Office: 780 Third Avenue, 48th Floor, 10017-2024. Telephone: 212-355-9500. Facsimile: 212-355-9592.

San Francisco, California Office: Embarcadero Center West, 30th Floor, 275 Battery Street, 94111-3339. Telephone: 415-956-1000. Facsimile: 415-956-1008.

Boston, Massachusetts Office: 175 Federal Street, 7th Floor, 02110-1216. Telephone: 617-720-5000. Facsimile: 617-720-5015.

Nashville, Tennessee Office: 3319 West End Avenue, Suite 600, 37203-1074. Telephone: 615-313-9000. Facsimile: 615-313-9965.

Practice Limited to Class Actions and Multi-Plaintiff Litigation.

FIRM PROFILE: Lieff, Cabraser, Heimann & Bernstein, LLP, a fifty-five attorney firm founded in 1972 with offices in San Francisco, New York, Boston, Nashville and Washington, D.C. For the past 28 years Lieff, Cabraser has concentrated its

(This Listing Continued)

practice in the field of complex civil litigation, representing plaintiffs in securities and investment fraud, products liability, tort, consumer, antitrust, environmental, and employment cases throughout the United States. The firm has tried and/or settled over 200 class actions. Lieff Cabraser has served as court-appointed Plaintiff Lead or Class Counsel in state and federal coordinated, multi-district, and complex litigation in Alabama, Alaska, Arizona, California, Colorado, Florida, Georgia, Hawaii, Illinois, Indiana, Louisiana, Massachusetts, Minnesota, New York, North Carolina, Ohio, Oregon, Pennsylvania, Tennessee, Texas, Utah, Virginia, Washington, Wisconsin, and Wyoming.

RICHARD T. SEYMOUR, born Grand Rapids, Michigan, August 22, 1942; admitted to bar, 1968, District of Columbia; 1969, U.S. Court of Appeals, District of Columbia Circuit; 1971, U.S. Court of Appeals, 4th Circuit; 1972, U.S. Supreme Court; 1975, U.S. District Court, Northern District of Mississippi; 1981, U.S. Court of Appeals, 5th and 11th Circuits; 1993, U.S. Court of Appeals. 3rd and 10th Circuits; 1994, U.S. District Court, Northern District of New York; 1997, U.S. Court of Appeals, 6th and 9th Circuits; U.S. District Court, Southern District of Texas. *Education:* Aquinas College (A.B., 1965); Harvard University (LL.B., 1968). Adjunct Professor, Graduate Program, Georgetown University Law Center, 1991-1993. Member: Law Students Civil Rights Research Council; Law Students Civil Rights Research Council National Board of Directors; Law Students Civil Rights Research Council Local Board of Directors; Law Students Civil Rights Research Council Intern, New Orleans, LA, Summer, 1966; ABA Section of Labor and Employment Law Section, 1998—; Member of Council, 1998—; Co-Chair, CLE Committee, 1995-1998; Co-Chair, Annual Meeting Subcommittee, 1994-1995; Co-Chair, Equal Employment Opportunity Committee, 1991-1994; Co-Chair, Subcommittee on Liaison with Department of Labor, 1988-1991; Council Task Force on Multidisciplinary Practice, 2000-2001; Council Task Force on Government Fellowship Program, 2000-2001; Council Task Force on Investments, 1997-1998; Council Task Force on Law Student Recruitment, 1998-2000; Council Liaison to Task Force on Judicial Law Clerk Education, 2000—; Council Liaison to the Alliance for Education in Dispute Resolution 1998—; The Association of Trial Lawyers of America; Committee on the Courts, 1999-2000; Executive Committee of Employee Rights Division, 199—; College of Labor and Employment Lawyers (Fellow, Governor, 1998-2000); Chair Committee on Standards of Practice, 1998-2000. ***Email:*** rseymour@lchb.com

(For complete biographical data on all personnel, see Professional Biographies at San Francisco, California)

LINIAK, BERENATO, LONGACRE & WHITE, LLC

WASHINGTON, D.C.

(See Bethesda, Maryland)

Patent and Trademark, Copyright, Trade Secret and Unfair Competition Law.

LINKLATERS

900 17TH STREET, N.W.
SUITE 450
WASHINGTON, D.C. 20006
Telephone: 1-202- 296- 8337
Fax: 1-202- 296- 8454
Email: enquiries@linklaters.com
URL: http://www.linklaters.com

OFFICES IN: Alicante, Antwerp, Bangkok, Berlin, Bratislava, Brussels, Bucharest, Budapest, Cologne, Frankfurt am Main, Hong Kong, London, Luxembourg, Madrid, Malmö, Milan, Moscow, Munich, New York, Paris, Prague, São Paulo, Shanghai, Singapore, Stockholm, Tokyo, Warsaw, Washington.

FIRM PROFILE: Linklaters is one of the leading global law firms, with first-class corporate, finance and specialist teams operating throughout the world. Our lawyers work closely with leading corporates, investment banks and other major institutions offering the highest quality advice and innovative use of technology to meet our clients' needs.

In January 2001, Linklaters and Oppenhoff & Rädler merged and now practise under the name Linklaters Oppenhoff & Rädler in Germany. In September 2001, Linklaters merged with Lagerlöf & Leman which practises as Linklaters Lagerlöf in Sweden. In Belgium the firm is known as Linklaters De Bandt and in Luxembourg Linklaters Loesch following a merger in January 2002 with De Bandt, van Hecke, Lagae & Loesch. Other key developments have included in September 2000 a joint venture in Singapore to form Linklaters Allen & Gledhill and in July 2001 a cooperation agreement in Brazil with Goulart Penteado Iervolino e Lefosse.

(This Listing Continued)

ASSISTANT SOLICITOR

PHILIPPA COTTLE, admitted to bar, 1983, England and Wales (Not admitted in the United States). *Education:* Bristol University (1979); College of Law (1981). ***LANGUAGES:*** English, French. ***Email:*** philippa.cottle@linklaters.com

LINOWES AND BLOCHER LLP

SUITE 302, 1150 17TH STREET, N.W.
WASHINGTON, D.C. 20036
Telephone: 202-293-8510
Telecopier: 202-293-8513
Email: inbox@linowes-law.com
URL: http://www.linowes-law.com

Silver Spring, Maryland Office: Suite 1000, 1010 Wayne Avenue. Telephone: 301-588-8580. Telecopier: 301-495-9044.
Greenbelt, Maryland Office: Suite 202, 6411 Ivy Lane. Telephone: 301-982-3382. Telecopier: 301-982-0595.
Annapolis, Maryland Office: 145 Main Street. Telephone: 410-268-0881. Telecopier: 301-261-2603.
Frederick, Maryland Office: 247 West Patrick Street. Telephone: 301-695-0244. Telecopier: 301-663-6656.
Columbia, Maryland Office: Suite B215, 10015 Old Columbia Road. Telephone: 410-312-5457. Fax: 410-290-5285.

Real Estate Development, Zoning and Land Use, Municipal Law, Administrative Law, Banking, Corporate, Environmental Law, Municipal Finance, Bankruptcy/Workouts, Condominium/Community Association Development, Litigation, Real Estate Finance and Taxation, Securities Law.

PARTNER EMERITUS

R. Robert Linowes (Also at Silver Spring, Maryland office) (See biographical data at Silver Spring, Maryland) (Partner Emeritus)

REPRESENTATIVE CLIENTS: See Silver Spring, Maryland Office.

(For complete biographical data on all personnel, see Professional Biographies at Silver Spring, Maryland)

LIOTTA, DRANITZKE & ENGEL, LLP

SUITE 250
1666 CONNECTICUT AVENUE, N.W.
WASHINGTON, D.C. 20009
Telephone: 202-797-7700
Facsimile: 202-797-2354
Email: attys@ldelaw.com

General Practice, Real Estate, Domestic Relations, Litigation, Torts, Business Law, Wills and Estates, Probate, Family Law, Divorce, Criminal Law and Mediation.

MEMBERS OF FIRM

ALAN DRANITZKE, born Patchogue, New York, June 16, 1942; admitted to bar, 1968, District of Columbia; 1969, U.S. Court of Appeals for the District of Columbia Circuit; 1972, U.S. Supreme Court and U.S. Court of Appeals, 4th Circuit; 1999, Virginia. *Education:* Wesleyan University (B.A., cum laude, 1964); Yale Law School (LL.B., 1968). Adjunct Professor, Georgetown University Law School, 1969-1971. Law Clerk, Judge Gerhard A. Gesell, U.S. District Court for the District of Columbia, 1968-1969. Co-Director, Center for Mediation, Inc., 1989-1991. *Member:* The District of Columbia Bar (Member, Real Estate Section); Virginia State Bar. ***PRACTICE AREAS:*** Real Estate; General Practice. ***Email:*** ad@ldelaw.com

ROBERT CASE LIOTTA, born Somerville, New Jersey, January 18, 1942; admitted to bar, 1969, District of Columbia; 1980, U.S. Supreme Court; 1981, U.S. Claims Court; 1988, Maryland. *Education:* Brown University (A.B., 1964); Georgetown University (J.D., 1969). Author: *Child Custody & Visitation, Allegations of Abuse in Child Custody Proceedings,* Matthew Bender, 1987. Lecturer, Family Law, District of Columbia Bar, Continuing Legal Education, 1988-2001. Member: Superior Court District of Columbia, Domestic Relations Rules Committee, 1991-1998; Superior Court Civil Arbitrator. *Member:* District of Columbia Bar (Member, Family Law Steering Committee, 1994-2001; Co-Chair, 2000-2001); Maryland State and American Bar Associations. [Lt., U.S. Navy, 1964-1966]. ***REPORTED CASES:*** Gordon v. Gordon, 675 A.2d 540 (MD 1996); Ferebee v. Chevron Chemical Co., 736 F 2d 1529, cert den. 469 US 1062. ***PRACTICE AREAS:*** Family Law; Domestic Relations; Personal Injury; Tort Law; Criminal Law.

DIANA R. ENGEL, born New York, N.Y., November 2, 1937; admitted to bar, 1984, District of Columbia; 1985, Maryland. *Education:* Barnard College (A.B., 1958); American University (M.A., 1976); Georgetown University (J.D., 1983). Author: "Marital Property in Jewish Law," National Jewish Law Journal,

(This Listing Continued)

LIOTTA, DRANITZKE & ENGEL, LLP, Washington—Continued

Spring 1987. Law Clerk to the Honorable Steffen W. Graae, Superior Court of the District of Columbia, 1983-1984. *Member:* The District of Columbia Bar (Member, Sections of: Family Law; Trusts and Estates); Maryland State and American Bar Associations; SPIDR. ***PRACTICE AREAS:*** Family Law; Wills; Estates; Probate; Mediation.

ASSOCIATE

REGINA A. DEMEO, born New York, N.Y., September 25, 1972; admitted to bar, 1998, Maryland; 1999, District of Columbia. *Education:* Georgetown University (B.S., 1994); George Washington University (J.D., 1998). *Member:* The District of Columbia Bar (Member, Family Law Section); Women's Bar Association of D.C. (Member, Solo and Small Practice Forum). ***LANGUAGES:*** Spanish. ***PRACTICE AREAS:*** Family Law; Wills; Real Estate. ***Email:*** rad@ldelaw.com

LIPPMAN & SEMSKER, PLLC

1120 G STREET, N.W., SUITE 200
WASHINGTON, D.C. 20005-3801
Telephone: 202-824-8100
Fax: 202-824-8199
URL: http://www.lippmansemsker.com
Email: mail@lippmansemsker.com
URL: http://www.lawyers.com/lippman&semskerlaw

Labor and Employment, Wrongful Termination, Civil Rights, Discrimination (age, sex, race, disability), Disabilities, Retaliation, Sexual Harassment, Computers and Software, e-Commerce Law, Technology Law, Small Business Law, Corporate Law, Civil Practice, Appellate Practice.

SOLAMAN G. LIPPMAN, born Chicago, Illinois, July 13, 1912; admitted to bar, 1937, Illinois; 1957, District of Columbia; U.S. Supreme Court; U.S. Court of Appeals, Second, Third, Fourth, Seventh, Ninth, District of Columbia and Federal Circuits. *Education:* University of Chicago (B.A., 1933; J.D., 1936). Associate Editor, University of Chicago Law Review. Staff Attorney, The National Labor Relations Board, 1937-1941. General Counsel: Retail Clerks International Association, 1947-1974; National Organization for Women (NOW), 1981-1984; Associated Fur Manufactures and United Fur Manufacturers, 1978-1984; House Education and Labor Committee, Pension (ERISA) Legislation and Amendments, 1974-1976. Member and Arbitrator, Federal Mediation and Conciliation Services Roster of Arbitrators. *Member:* District of Columbia Bar; American Bar Association (Member, Labor Law Section, Former Chairman and Committee Member, Subcommittee on Practice and Procedures before the National Labor Relations Board). ***REPORTED CASES:*** Retail Clerks Int'l Assoc. v. Schermerhorn II, 375 U.S. 96 (1963); Retail Clerks Int'l Assoc. v. Schermerhorn I, 373 U.S. 746 (1963); Retail Clerks Int'l Assoc. v. Lion Dry Goods, Inc., 369 U.S. 17 (1962); Retail Clerks Int'l Assoc. v. J.J. Newberry Co., 352 U.S. 987 (1957); (Retirement Fund of Fur Manufacturer Indus. v. Getto & Getto, Inc., 714 F.Supp. 651 (S.D.N.Y. 1989); Schmidt v. National Organization for Women, 562 F.Supp. 210 (N.D.Fl. 1983); Underwood v. National Credit Union Admin., 665 A.2d 621 (D.C. 1995). ***PRACTICE AREAS:*** Employment Law; Arbitration. ***Email:*** lippman@lippmansemsker.com

RICHARD H. SEMSKER, born Washington, D.C., November 6, 1960; admitted to bar, 1987, Maryland; 1988, District of Columbia; U.S. District Court for the District of Columbia; U.S. District Court, District of Maryland; U.S. Court of Appeals, District of Columbia Circuit. *Education:* Syracuse University (B.A., 1982); American University, Washington School of Law; Widener University (J.D., 1986). Case Note Writer, Delaware Law Form. Assistant Author, "The Inequities of Section 726(b) of the U.S. Bankruptcy Code," The Commercial Law Journal, December, 1985. *Member:* District of Columbia Bar; Maryland State Bar Association (Member, Labor and Employment Section); Metropolitan Washington Employment Lawyers Association. ***REPORTED CASES:*** Griffin v. Washington Convention Center, 142 F.3d 1308, (D.C.Cir. 1998); Simard v. Resolution Trust Corp. 639 A.2d 540 (D.C. 1994); Cox's Food Center v. Retail Clerk's Assoc., 457 P.2d 418 (Idaho 1969); In re: Amalgamated Food Handlers, 244 Minn. 179 (1955); Smith v. United Parcel Service, Inc., 947 F.Supp. 190 (D.Md. 1996); Underwood v. National Credit Union Admin., 665 A.2d 621 (D.C. 1995). ***PRACTICE AREAS:*** Employment Law; Business Litigation; Technology Law; Civil Litigation; Appellate Practice. ***Email:*** rsemsker@lippmansemsker.com

ASSOCIATE

SHANNON MICAH SALB, born Hartford, Connecticut, May 3, 1969; admitted to bar, 1995, Maryland; 1996, District of Columbia; 1997, U.S. District Court, District of Columbia and U.S. District Court, District of Maryland; 1998, U.S. Court of Appeals, Federal Circuit; 1999, U.S. Court of Appeals, District of Columbia Circuit. *Education:* University of Connecticut (B.A., 1991); Emory University (J.D., 1994). Pi Sigma Alpha. Articles Editor, Bankruptcy Developments Journal. Martin Luther King Fellow, North Carolina Legal Services, 1993. Recipient, Dean's Public Service Award, 1994. Professorial Adjunct, American University College of Law, 1999—. Guest Lecturer, "Employment Issues for Human Resource Professionals", Bowie University, October 1996, January 1997. *Member:* District of Columbia Bar; American Bar Association (Member, Labor and Employment and Litigation Sections); Metropolitan Washington Employment Lawyers Association; Federal Bar Association; Judicature. ***REPORTED CASES:*** Griffin v. Washington Convention Center, 142 F.3d 1308, (D.C.Cir. 1998); Rao v. County of Fairfax, Virginia, 108 F.3d 42 (4th Cir. 1997); Sotabinda v. Hotel Lombardy, 173 F.R.D. 3 (D.D.C. 1997); Van Allen v. Bell Atlantic-Washington, D.C., Inc., 921 F.Supp. 830 (D.D.C. 1996). ***PRACTICE AREAS:*** Employment Law; Business Litigation; Technology Law; Civil Litigation; Appellate Practice. ***Email:*** ssalb@lippmansemsker.com

REPRESENTATIVE CLIENTS: Grand Bank (formerly Women's Bank); The Rural Coalition; Offices of Drs. Schonholtz, Magee and Michaels; Frames by Rebecca.

LIPSHULTZ AND HONE

CHARTERED
SUITE 200, 2000 L STREET, N.W.
WASHINGTON, D.C. 20036
Telephone: 202-872-0909

Silver Spring, Maryland Office: Suite 108 Montgomery Center, 8630 Fenton Street. Telephone: 301-587-8500. Fax: 301-495-9759.

Products Liability Defense, Insurance Agents and Brokers Errors and Omissions Defense, Defense Insurance Law (including coverage opinions and analysis), Environmental, Pollution, Contamination and Toxic Tort Claims and Defense, Property Insurance Law (including Fire, Marine and Inland Marine Claims), Excess, Surplus Lines and Reinsurance Claims and Defense, Employment Law, Workers Compensation Defense, Professional Liability Defense (including medical and professional malpractice), General Civil and Criminal Trial Practice and State Courts, Corporate, Probate and Real Estate.

(For complete biographical data on all personnel, see Professional Biographies at Silver Spring, Maryland)

LIPSTEIN, JAFFE & LAWSON L.L.P.

Established in 1994
1900 M STREET, N.W.
SUITE 700
WASHINGTON, D.C. 20036-3508
Telephone: 202-296-6655
Telecopier: 202-296-0848
Email: Lawinfo@LJLLaw.com
URL: http://www.LJLLaw.com

Practice before Federal and Local Courts, and Federal Agencies, specializing in counseling and litigation in the areas of Antitrust, Corporate, Consumer Protection, International Trade and Intellectual Property.

FIRM PROFILE: The founding partners have significant experience in representing multinational companies in regulatory proceedings before the International Trade Commission, the Department of Commerce, the Antitrust Division of the Department of Justice, and the Federal Trade Commission, and in litigating trade, antitrust and trademark and copyright issues. The firm also provides Multinational clients international trade and customs advice under U.S. law, NAFTA and GATT, and antitrust, corporate and intellectual property law advice to Washington, D.C.-based trade associations, major multinational corporations and local start-up companies.

MEMBERS OF FIRM

ROBERT A. LIPSTEIN, born Wilmington, Delaware, December 6, 1954; admitted to bar, 1978, District of Columbia; 1979, U.S. Court of Appeals for the District of Columbia Circuit and U.S. District Court, District of Columbia; 1984, U.S. Court of International Trade; 1990, U.S. Court of Appeals for the Federal Circuit and U.S. Supreme Court. *Education:* Stanford University (A.B., 1975; J.D., 1978). Phi Beta Kappa. Associate Managing Editor, Stanford Law Review, 1977-1978. Co-Author, with Grace W. Lawson: "Intellectual Property Rights and Antitrust Policy," The United States Antitrust Review, 1998. Author: "Using Antitrust Principles to Reform Antidumping Laws," Global Competition Policy (Editors, E.M. Graham and J.D. Richardson, 1997); "International Antitrust Enforcement by the United States: What the Antitrust Guidelines for International Operations Tell You, and What They Don't," 12 Nihon University Comparative Law 89 (1995); "The U.S. Government's 1994 Draft Antitrust

(This Listing Continued)

Enforcement Guidelines for International Operations - Too Much Enforcement, Too Little Guidelines," 11 Nihon University Comparative Law 75 (1994); "Its Time to Dump the Dumping Laws," International Economics Insights (Nov./ Dec. 1993); Co-Author: (with Douglas E. Rosenthal) "The 1992 Merger Guidelines - Strategies for Managing the Merger Review Process," 16 World Competition 5 (1992); "Competition and Trade Policy in a Global Economy," Testimony Before the Senate Judiciary Committee (June, 1992); "A Global Perspective on Regulation of Mergers;" "Mergers & Acquisitions," (September/ October, 1990); "Using U.S. Antitrust Law to Open Foreign Markets;" "M&A TODAY," (April, 1990). Member, ICC Joint Working Group on Trade and Competition Policy. *Member:* The District of Columbia Bar (Co-Chair, Antitrust Committee, International Law Section, 1989-1990); American Bar Association (Member, Sections on: Antitrust Law and Intellectual Property Law). ***PRACTICE AREAS:*** Antitrust; Trademark & Copyright; Corporate; International Trade. ***Email:*** rlipstein@ljllaw.com

MATTHEW P. JAFFE, born Washington, D.C., December 23, 1955; admitted to bar, 1982, District of Columbia; U.S. Court of International Trade and The Court of Appeals for the Federal Circuit. *Education:* University of Maryland (B.A., 1977); University of Denver (M.B.A., 1981; J.D., 1981). Phi Beta Kappa. Editor-in-Chief, Denver Journal of International Law & Policy, 1980-1981. International Trade Attorney, Office of Chief Counsel for Import Administration, U.S. Department of Commerce, 1987-1990. Attorney, Office of Administrative Law Judges, U.S. International Trade Commission, 1984-1986. Staff Counsel, U.S. Senate, Select Committee to Study Law Enforcement Undercover Activities of Components of the U.S. Department of Justice, 1981-1983. *Member:* The District of Columbia Bar; Maryland State Bar Association, Inc.; American Bar Association (Member, Sections on: Administrative Law and Regulatory Practice, and International Law and Practice). ***PRACTICE AREAS:*** International Trade; Customs; Corporate. ***Email:*** mjaffe@ljllaw.com

GRACE W. LAWSON, born Austin, Texas, December 7, 1967; admitted to bar, 1991, Texas; 1992, District of Columbia; U.S. District Court, District of Columbia; U.S. Court of International Trade; U.S. Court of Appeals for the District of Columbia and Federal Circuits. *Education:* University of Texas at Austin (B.B.A., with highest honors and Business Honors, Beta Gamma Sigma, 1988); University of Chicago (J.D., 1991). Recipient, Mulroy Prize. Co-Author, with Robert A. Lipstein: "Intellectual Property Rights and Antitrust Policy," The United States Antitrust Review, 1998. *Member:* The District of Columbia Bar; American Bar Association (Member, Sections on Antitrust, Intellectual Property Law, International Law and Litigation). ***PRACTICE AREAS:*** Antitrust; Copyright & Trademark; Consumer Protection; International Trade; Corporate. ***Email:*** glawson@ljllaw.com

ASSOCIATE

JOSEPH A. KONIZESKI, born Baltimore, Maryland, October 9, 1967; admitted to bar, 1998, Louisiana; 2001, District of Columbia; U.S. Court of International Trade, Court of Appeals for The Federal Circuit. *Education:* University of Maryland (B.A., 1989); Tulane University (J.D., cum laude, 1997). Law Clerk to the Honorable Mildred Methvin, United States Magistrate Judge for the Western District of Louisiana, 1997-1999. Trial Attorney, Division of Enforcement Commodity Futures Trading Commission, 1999-2000. ***PRACTICE AREAS:*** Antitrust; Intellectual Property; International Trade; Corporate Law; Litigation. ***Email:*** jkonizeski@ljllaw.com

LITMAN LAW OFFICES, LTD.

WASHINGTON, D.C.

(See Arlington, Virginia)

Intellectual Property. Patent, Trademark, Copyright and Unfair Competition Law including U.S. and International Intellectual Property Portfolio Management; Searches, Applications, Prosecution and Registration; Procurement; Licensing; and Protection (Litigation, Interferences, Arbitration, Rights Disputes and Liability Evaluations for Infringement) relating to: Mechanical, Electrical, Electro-Mechanical, and Metallurgical Technology (Aerospace, Aviation, Construction, Electronics, Energy, Explosives, Fiber Optics, Lasers, Mining, Oil and Gas, Physics and Semiconductors); Chemical (Agrochemicals, Coating Technology, Polymers, Inorganic, Organic and Petroleum Chemistry); Health Care, Medical and Life Sciences (Biochemical, Biotechnology, Molecular Biology, Pharmaceutical, Medical Devices, Cosmetics and Food); Communications (Broadcast, Cable, Cellular, Telecommunications and Wireless); Computers, Information Technology and Software (Applications, Architecture, Publishing and Security); Business Methods (Management, Financial, Sales and Marketing); Trade Secrets (Misappropriation and Theft); Internet (Content, Domain Names, E-Commerce and Web Site Development); Designs and Industrial Property Rights in Models; Advertising, Branding and Marketing (Labeling, Product Configuration, Trade Dress, Internet Trademarks, Trade Names and Lanham Act; Art, Literary, Media and Proprietary Rights (Interactive, Multimedia, Motion Pictures, Newspaper, Publishing, Radio, Television, Music, Protection of Personality and Characters). High Technology and Science Law including Contracts (Confidentiality Agreements, Covenants Not to

(This Listing Continued)

Compete, Non-Solicitation Agreements, Outsourcing), Finance (Private Equity, Private Placement, Securities, Venture Capital), Joint Ventures and Strategic Alliances, Licensing and Transfers, Litigation and Protection Strategies, and related Business, Corporate, Commercial and Employment Law (Business Start-ups, Franchises, International Trade, Investments, Joint Ventures and Strategic Alliances, Mergers, Acquisitions and Divestitures, Partnerships and Limited Liability Companies, and Spin-Offs). Intellectual Property relating to: Alcoholic Beverages, Agricultural (Farms, Crops, Livestock) and Food and Drug Law; Asset Protection, Bankruptcy, Debtor And Creditor Rights; Banks, Banking and Real Estate Law; Entertainment, Sports and Leisure Equipment and Facilities); Gambling, Clubs, Golf Courses, Hotels, Resorts and Restaurants); Government Contracts; Municipal and Public Finance Law; Medical Malpractice, Negligence, Personal Injury, and Products Liability; Nonprofit Charitable, and Tax Exempt Organizations (Educational and Religious Institutions, Trade and Professional Associations).

RICHARD LITTELL

1220 NINETEENTH STREET, N.W.
SUITE 400
WASHINGTON, D.C. 20036
Telephone: 202-466-8260
Fax: 202-293-4377
Email: littell@dgs.dgsys.com

Utility Rates, Airline Regulation, Postal Regulation, Gas Utility Regulation, Endangered Species.

RICHARD LITTELL, born Hartford, Connecticut, February 7, 1931; admitted to bar, 1957, California; 1961, U.S. Supreme Court and District of Columbia; 1984, New York. *Education:* Cornell University (A.B., 1953); Harvard University (J.D., 1956). Author: "The Endangered Species Act: Not Just for Environmentalists Anymore," Legal Times, April 14, 1997; "Deregulation's Turbulent Flight," Journal of Commerce, November 3, 1993, p 6A; "Endangered and Other Protected Species," BNA Books, 1992; "'Culling'Ivory, Saving Elephants," Washington Post, Feb. 23, 1992, p. C5; "Reviving Airline Deregulation," Journal of Commerce, Nov. 9, 1988, p. 8A; "Deregulation of Industrial Gas Prices Without Discrimination," Public Utilities Fortnightly, October 27, 1983; "Judicial Review," Chapter 46 in Regulation of the Gas Industry, American Gas Association, 1981. General Counsel, Civil Aeronautics Board, 1973-1974. General Counsel, Postal Rate Commission, 1971-1973. Observer, 6th Meeting (Ottawa) and 8th Meeting (Kyoto) of the Convention on International Trade in Endangered Species. ***SPECIAL AGENCIES:*** U.S. Postal Rate Commission; U.S. Department of Transportation; U.S. Federal Energy Regulatory Commission; D.C. Public Service Commission; U.S. National Transportation Safety Board; U.S. Fish & Wildlife Service; U.S. National Marine Fisheries Service.

LITTLER MENDELSON

A PROFESSIONAL CORPORATION
Established in 1942
1225 I STREET, N.W., SUITE 1000
WASHINGTON, D.C. 20005-3914
Telephone: 202-842-3400
Facsimile: 202-842-0011
Email: info@littler.com
URL: http://www.littler.com

Offices located in: Phoenix, Arizona, California -- Bakersfield, Fresno, Los Angeles, Oakland, Palm Desert, Sacramento, San Diego, San Francisco, San Jose, Santa Maria, Santa Rosa, Stockton and Walnut Creek; Denver, Colorado; Atlanta, Georgia; Chicago, Illinois; Baltimore, Maryland; Minneapolis, Minnesota; Reno and Las Vegas, Nevada (a partnership with Hicks & Walt); Newark, New Jersey; New York, New York; Columbus, Ohio; Philadelphia and Pittsburgh, Pennsylvania; Dallas and Houston, Texas; and Seattle and Yakima, Washington

FIRM PROFILE: Littler Mendelson, a Professional Corporation, is the largest law firm in the United States engaged exclusively in the practice of employment and labor law. The firm has nearly 400 attorneys in 31 offices nationwide who represent and advise management in all major subspecialties of employment and labor law including wrongful termination; sex, race, and age discrimination; wage and hour law; NLRB cases and collective bargaining; workers' compensation; unemployment benefits; workplace violence; substance abuse; employee privacy rights; occupational safety and health; the ADA; FMLA; ERISA; employee benefits; tax issues; and immigration.

PETER A. SUSSER, born New York, N.Y., May 21, 1955; admitted to bar, 1979, Virginia; 1981, District of Columbia; 1982, Maryland; 1984, U.S. Supreme Court. *Education:* Cornell University (B.S., 1976); College of William &

(This Listing Continued)

LITTLER MENDELSON, A PROFESSIONAL CORPORATION, Washington—Continued

Mary (J.D., 1979); Georgetown University (LL.M. in Labor Law, 1983). (Managing Partner). ***PRACTICE AREAS:*** Labor and Employment; Occupational Safety and Health Law. ***Email:*** psusser@littler.com

MARK A. DE BERNARDO, born Rochester, New York, December 27, 1953; admitted to bar, 1979, District of Columbia. *Education:* Marquette University (B.A., cum laude, 1976); Georgetown University (J.D., 1979). ***LANGUAGES:*** Italian. ***PRACTICE AREAS:*** Drug and Alcohol Testing; Labor and Employment. ***Email:*** mdebernardo@littler.com

KEVIN L. WRIGHT, born Knoxville, Tennessee, 1962; admitted to bar, 1987, Virginia; 1988, District of Columbia. *Education:* Harvard University (A.B., 1984); University of Virginia (J.D., 1987). ***PRACTICE AREAS:*** Labor and Employment; Employee Benefits. ***Email:*** klwright@littler.com

JOSEPH P. HARKINS, born Philadelphia, Pennsylvania, April 13, 1954; admitted to bar, 1983, New York; 1985, District of Columbia. *Education:* Princeton University (A.B., 1976); Georgetown University Law Center (J.D., 1982). ***PRACTICE AREAS:*** Labor and Employment; Litigation. ***Email:*** jharkins@littler.com

TODD ANDREW BROMBERG, born New York, N.Y., March 27, 1962; admitted to bar, 1992, New York and Connecticut; 1993, U.S. District Court, Southern and Eastern Districts of New York; 1996, U.S. District Court, Western District of New York; 2001, District of Columbia. *Education:* Oberlin College (B.A., with honors, 1985); Benjamin N. Cardozo School of Law (J.D., 1992). Supervising Editor, Benjamin N. Cardozo Law Review, 1991-1992. ***PRACTICE AREAS:*** Labor and Employment. ***Email:*** tbromberg@littler.com

ANNITA M. RIDDICK, born Tuscumbia, Alabama, June 9, 1961; admitted to bar, 1992, Georgia and U.S. District Court, Northern District of Georgia; 1999, District of Columbia. *Education:* Howard University (B.A., 1983); Duke University (J.D., LL.M., 1992). Ford Foundation Fellow, 1992. ***PRACTICE AREAS:*** Labor and Employment. ***Email:*** ariddick@littler.com

RONALD I. TISCH, born New York, New York, 1944; admitted to bar, 1969, District of Columbia; 1970, U.S. Supreme Court. *Education:* Brooklyn College of the City University of New York (B.A., 1966); George Washington University (J.D., 1969); Harvard University (LL.M., 1970). Phi Alpha Delta; Order of the Coif. ***PRACTICE AREAS:*** Labor and Employment. ***Email:*** rtisch@littler.com

PAUL J. KENNEDY, born Albany, New York, 1959; admitted to bar, 1985, Texas; 1988, Virginia; 1989, District of Columbia. *Education:* Colgate University (B.A., 1981); Washington & Lee University (J.D., 1984). ***PRACTICE AREAS:*** Labor and Employment. ***Email:*** pkennedy@littler.com

JASON M. BRANCIFORTE, born Seneca Falls, New York, October 17, 1965; admitted to bar, 1991, New York and District of Columbia; 1996, Virginia. *Education:* Georgetown University (A.B., cum laude, 1987); Cornell University (J.D., 1990). Pi Sigma Alpha. ***PRACTICE AREAS:*** Labor and Employment; Litigation. ***Email:*** jbranciforte@littler.com

GAREN E. DODGE, born Wausau, Wisconsin, January 2, 1957; admitted to bar, 1982, Wisconsin; 1983, District of Columbia; 1986, U.S. Supreme Court; 1990, Virginia. *Education:* University of Wisconsin, Green Bay (B.A., summa cum laude, 1979); Marshall-Wythe School of Law, College of William and Mary (J.D., 1982). ***PRACTICE AREAS:*** Labor and Employment. ***Email:*** gdodge@littler.com

MARIA A. PERUGINI, born Waterbury, Connecticut, July 26, 1968; admitted to bar, 1993, Maryland; 1995, District of Columbia. *Education:* Providence College (B.A., magna cum laude, 1990); Catholic University of America (J.D., 1993). ***PRACTICE AREAS:*** Labor and Employment; Litigation. ***Email:*** mperugini@littler.com

---

Nancy N. Delogu; Katherine Anne Goetzl; Janis A. Thom; Tessa J. Gelbman; Stacy Holmes Hawkins; Margarita D. Santos (Not admitted in DC); ***Christa Haas; Douglas Cheney Adams*** (admission pending).

OF COUNSEL

JOSEPH E. SCHULER, born Takoma Park, Maryland, October 9, 1954; admitted to bar, 1979, District of Columbia; 1983, Maryland. *Education:* University of Maryland (B.A., magna cum laude, 1976); Georgetown University (J.D., cum laude, 1979). ***PRACTICE AREAS:*** Labor and Employment; Litigation. ***Email:*** jschuler@littler.com

(For biographical data on personnel at other locations, see Professional Biographies at those cities).

THOMAS SAYRE LLEWELLYN

5125 MACARTHUR BOULEVARD, N.W.
SUITE 32A
WASHINGTON, D.C. 20016
Telephone: 202-237-7291
Fax: 202-237-7884
Email: t.llewellyn@worldnet.att.net
URL: http://www.lawyers.com/llewellyn

Environmental law and litigation practice with emphasis on agency proceedings and appellate litigation. Resource Conservation and Recovery Act (RCRA), Clean Air Act, Clean Water Act, and other environmental laws.

FIRM PROFILE: The firm has a national practice representing business trade associations and energy companies in the highly specialized field of environmental regulation. Mr. Llewellyn has significant litigation experience which remains at the center of the firm's practice.

THOMAS SAYRE LLEWELLYN, born 1955; admitted to bar, 1980, District of Columbia; 1998, U.S. Supreme Court; 2001, U.S. Court of Appeals, Ninth Circuit. *Education:* University of Virginia (B.A., 1977); George Washington University (J.D., 1980). Senior Attorney, American Petroleum Institute, 1984-1988. Associate, 1988-1991 and Partner, 1992-1994, Pillsbury Madison & Sutro. Partner, Dorsey & Whitney, 1994-1995. [Captain, U.S. Army, 1981-1984]. ***REPORTED CASES:*** American Petroleum Institute v. EPA, 216 F.3d 50 (D.C. Cir. 2000); Appalachian Power Co. v. EPA, 135 F.3d 791 (D.C. Cir. 1998); Hazardous Waste Treatment Council v. EPA, 886 F.2d 355 (D.C. Cir. 1989). ***PRACTICE AREAS:*** Environmental Law; Federal Administrative Law; Air Pollution; Water Pollution; Hazardous Waste.

LLOYD & MARCOTTE, PLLC

645 PENNSYLVANIA AVENUE SE, 2ND FLOOR
WASHINGTON, D.C. 20003
Telephone: 202-548-0856
Fax: 202-548-2647
Email: lloyer@kreative.net
URL: http://www.lawyers.com/lloyd&marcotte

General Practice, Personal Injury, Criminal Defense, Real Estate, Social Security Disability.

DAVID P. MARCOTTE, born Lowell, Massachusetts, February 11, 1967; admitted to bar, 1997, New Jersey and U.S. District Court, District of New Jersey; 1998, District of Columbia; 1999, U.S. District Court, District of Maryland and U.S. District Court for the District of Columbia. *Education:* Northeastern University (B.S., 1990); District of Columbia School of Law (J.D., 1997). *Member:* District of Columbia Bar; New Jersey State and American Bar Associations; Trial Lawyers Association of Metro Washington, D.C. ***PRACTICE AREAS:*** Personal Injury; Criminal Defense; Real Estate; Social Security Disability. ***Email:*** lloyer@kreative.net

BRIAN D. LLOYD, born New York, N.Y., August 12, 1966; admitted to bar, 1996, Maryland; 1998, District of Columbia. *Education:* University of Rhode Island (B.A., 1988); Washington College of Law, American University (J.D., 1995). *Member:* Prince Georges County, Maryland State and American Bar Associations; District of Columbia Bar; Bar Association of the District of Columbia; Trial Lawyers Association of Metro Washington, D.C. ***PRACTICE AREAS:*** Personal Injury; Criminal Defense. ***Email:*** lloyer@kreative.net

---

LOBEL, NOVINS & LAMONT

Established in 1972

SUITE 770, 1275 K STREET, N.W.
WASHINGTON, D.C. 20005
Telephone: 202-371-6626
Telecopier: 202-371-6643
URL: http://www.lnllaw.com
Email: lobel@lnllaw.com
URL: http://www.lawyers.com/lobelnovinslamont

Civil and Administrative Practice. Energy Law, Communications, Natural Resources, Public Lands Law, Taxation, International Law, Antitrust, Legal Ethics, Litigation in Federal Courts.

FIRM PROFILE: Lobel, Novins & Lamont is devoted to providing high-quality legal work and unmatched personal service to its clients. The firm's diverse clientele range from individuals to corporations with local, national and international needs.

MEMBERS OF FIRM

WILLIAM J. LAMONT (1916-1994).

(This Listing Continued)

MARTIN LOBEL, born Cambridge, Massachusetts, June 19, 1941; admitted to bar, 1965, Massachusetts; 1968, District of Columbia. *Education:* Boston University (A.B., 1962; J.D., cum laude, 1965); Harvard University (LL.M., 1966). Order of the Coif. Member, Boston University Law Review, 1964-1965. Author: "Federal Control of Campaign Contributions," 51 Minn. L.R. 1, 1996; "Elections: An Analysis of the Oklahoma Corrupt Practice Act, 20 Ok. L.R. 381, 1967; "Federal Control of Campaign Contributions," 51 Minn. L.R. 1, 1966; "Elections an Analysis of the Oklahoma Corrupt Practice Act," 20 Ok L.R. 381, 1967; "Billions in Windfall Profits Taxes Still to be Collected," Tax Notes, July 24, 1989, p. 445; "Refunding Unconstitutional Taxes," Tax Notes, July 29, 1991, p. 581; "Political Access Key to Upholding State Taxes," State Tax Notes, May 18,1992; "The Supreme Court as Delphic Oracle," State Tax Notes, Nov. 19, 1992, p. 683; "Barclays: A Test of the Administration's Willingness to Collect Taxes from Multinational Corporations," Tax Notes, June 28, 1993, p. 1841; "Lobbying Disclosure Act of 1995," Tax Notes, June 17, 1996, p. 1699; "Myths, Tax Policy and The Oil Industry," Tax Notes, March 15, 1999, P. 1675. Assistant Professor, University of Oklahoma Law School, 1966-1967. Chairman, Board of Directors, Tax Analyst, 1972—. Congressional Fellow. American Political Science Association, Office of Hon. Gerald R. Ford, 1968. Legislative Assistant to U.S. Senator William Proxmire, 1968-1972. Referee, U.S. District Court for the District of Kansas, to decide claims by resellers to oil overcharge refunds, see In Re Dept. of Energy Stripper Well Exemption Litigation, 853 F.2d 1579 & 1584 (TECA 1988). *Member:* The District of Columbia Bar (Chairman, 1977-1978, Steering Committee, Division of Antitrust and Consumer Affairs); Massachusetts, Federal and American Bar Associations. ***PRACTICE AREAS:*** Entertainment and Art; Civil Litigation; U.S. Supreme Court Litigation. ***Email:*** 110704.3524@compuserve.com

JACK A. BLUM, born Bronx, New York, August 5, 1941; admitted to bar, 1967, District of Columbia; 1976, U.S. Supreme Court. *Education:* Bard College (B.A., 1962); Columbia University (J.D., 1965). Recipient, Lawrence S. Greenbaum Prize, Harlan Fiske Stone Honor Argument. Editor-in-Chief, Columbia Law School News, 1964-1965. Co-Author, "Financial Havens, Banking Secrecy & Money Laundering," UNDCP Technical Series, United Nations, 1998. Legal Assistant, Federal Communications Commission, 1965. Assistant Counsel, Senate Judiciary Committee, Subcommittee on Antitrust and Monopoly, 1965-1972. Associate Counsel, Senate Foreign Relations Committee, 1972-1976; Special Counsel, Senate Foreign Relations Committee, 1987-1989. Senior Editor, Crime, Law and Social Change: An International Journal. *Member:* The District of Columbia Bar; Federal and American (Member, Sections on: International Law; Criminal Law) Bar Associations. ***PRACTICE AREAS:*** International Law and Taxation; Criminal Law; Money Laundering; Financial Fraud. ***Email:*** blumja@lnllaw.com

LEE ELLEN HELFRICH, born Bucyrus, Ohio, February 22, 1955; admitted to bar, 1980, District of Columbia. *Education:* Ohio Wesleyan University (B.A., summa cum laude, 1977); American University (J.D., summa cum laude, 1980); Harvard University (LL.M., 1984). Phi Beta Kappa. Associate Editor, American University Law Review, 1979-1980. Author, "Valuation Under State Leases: State Land Trusts - A Thumb on the Scale of Justice," 16 Petroleum Accounting and Finance Management Journal 28 (1997). Instructor in Legal Methods, American University Law School, 1982. Instructor, Legal Ethics, Mandatory Course for New Admittees, District of Columbia Bar, 1997-1999. Chair, Litigation Section's District of Columbia Digest Committee, 1993-1998. *Member:* The District of Columbia Bar (Member, Continuing Legal Ethics Standing Committee); American Bar Association; Womens Bar Association. ***PRACTICE AREAS:*** Federal Energy; Natural Resources; Public Lands; Oil and Gas; Complex Civil Litigation; Legal Ethics. ***Email:*** 105140.1713@ compuserve.com

HENRY M. BANTA, born Pittsburgh, Pennsylvania, December 30, 1937; admitted to bar, 1966, District of Columbia. *Education:* Georgetown University (B.S., 1960; LL.B., 1965). Co-Author: with H. Robert Field, "FTC Orders Under the Price Discrimination Law: An Evaluation," 3 Antitrust Law and Economics Review 89, 1970; "Billions in Windfall Profits Taxes Still to be Collected," Tax Notes, p. 445, July 24, 1989. Attorney: Federal Trade Commission, Bureau of Consumer Protection, Division of Compliance, 1971-1972; Federal Trade Commission, Bureau of Competition, 1973-1974. Attorney Advisor to Chairman, Federal Trade Commission, 1972-1973. Counsel: U.S. Senate Subcommittee on Antitrust and Monopoly, 1974-1979; U.S. Senate Committee on the Judiciary, 1979-1980. *Member:* The District of Columbia Bar (Member, Antitrust and Consumer Protection Division Steering Committee, 1977-1978); American Bar Association. [First Lieut., U.S. Army, 1960-1962]. ***PRACTICE AREAS:*** Anti-Trust; Federal Energy Law; Pipeline Law. ***Email:*** 110704.3524@compuserve.com

OF COUNSEL

ALAN S. NOVINS, born Rochester, New Hampshire, October 23, 1937; admitted to bar, 1964, New Hampshire; 1970, District of Columbia. *Education:* Harvard University (A.B., 1961); Columbia University (J.D., 1964). Legislative Counsel, U.S. Senator Thomas J. McIntyre, 1964-1970. Assistant Counsel, U.S. Senate Committee on Banking, Housing and Urban Affairs, 1971. Chairman,

(This Listing Continued)

Hearing Committee, District of Columbia Board on Professional Responsibility, 1982-1988. *Member:* The District of Columbia Bar (Chairman, Committee on Specialization, Division of Courts, Lawyers and Administration of Justice, 1975-1976); Bar Association of the District of Columbia (Member, Ethics Committee, 1976-1978). Resident of Jerusalem, Israel. ***PRACTICE AREAS:*** Legal Ethics; Civil Litigation. ***Email:*** novins@compuserve.com

ARTHUR L. FOX, II, born Morristown, New Jersey, March 30, 1943; admitted to bar, 1968, Virginia; 1969, District of Columbia. *Education:* University of Virginia (B.A., 1965; LL.B., 1968). Author: "Title IV's Never-Never Land: When and How Victorious Insurgents Are To Be Installed in Union Office," 4 Hofstra Lab. L. J. 299, 1987; "Showing Workers Who's Boss," The Burger Years, Viking Press, 1987; "Section 301 and Exhaustion of Intra-Union Appeals: A Misbegotten Marriage," 128 U. Pa. L. Rev. 989, 1980; "Teamster Democracy and Financial Responsibility," PROD, 1976. Attorney: Office of General Counsel, NLRB, Washington, D.C., 1968-1972; Public Citizen Litigation Group, 1972-1990. Member, Board of Directors, Association for Union Democracy, 1979—. ***PRACTICE AREAS:*** Litigation; Labor and Employment. ***Email:*** ALFII@aol.com

MARK ZAID, born Manhasset, New York, June 25, 1967; admitted to bar, 1992, Connecticut; 1993, New York and U.S. District Court, Northern District of New York; 1994, District of Columbia; 1995, U.S. District Court, Eastern District of New York. *Education:* University of Rochester (B.A. cum laude, with honors, Pol.Sc. and high honors, History, 1989); Albany Law School of Union College (J.D., 1992). Associate Editor, Albany Law Review, 1991-1992. Author: "The Declassification of Dealey Plaza; After Thirty Years, A New Disclosure Law At Last May Help to Clarify the Facts of the Kennedy Assassination", 34 S.Tex.L.Rev.407 (1993). Member, Board of Directors: Public International Law and Policy Fund, 1994—; Titanic International, Inc., 1993—. *Member:* American Bar Association (Member: International Law Practice Section, 1994— and Criminal Justice Section, 1993—; Chair, Task Force on Proposed Protocols for Evidence and Procedure for Future War Crimes Tribunal, 1993—; Vice Chair, International Criminal Law Committee, 1994—); District of Columbia Bar (Member, International Law Section); International Law Students Association (Member, Board of Directors, 1994—). ***PRACTICE AREAS:*** International; National Security; Freedom of Information.

LOEFFLER, JONAS & TUGGEY, L.L.P.

1801 K STREET NW, SUITE 340K
WASHINGTON, D.C. 20006-0301
Telephone: 202-775-4430
Fax: 202-775-0836

San Antonio, Texas Office: One Riverwalk Place, 700 North Saint Mary's Street, Suite 800, 78205. Telephone: 210-354-4300. Fax: 210-354-4034. Email: info@ljtlaw.com.

Austin, Texas Office: 1005 Congress Avenue, Suite 330, 78701. Telephone: 512-479-6403. Fax: 512-479-8282.

Administrative Law, Appellate Practice, Banks and Banking, Business Law, Commercial Law, Contracts, Corporate Law, Election, Campaign and Political Law, Environmental Law, Finance, Government, Health Care, Litigation, Mergers, Acquisitions and Divestures, Mortgages, Municipal Law, Probate, Real Estate, Securities, Sports Law, Wills.

FIRM PROFILE: A firm of over 25 Attorneys, Loeffler, Jonas & Tuggey is a national law firm that provides clients with comprehensive legal services and creative public strategies.

Our approach reflects our entrepreneurial mindset. We work with clients as a business partner - looking for opportunities, opening doors, resolving problems, constantly providing a practical but broad view of any situation, whether legal, business, or political. And our culture of coordinating efforts ensures that the full power of the firm can be brought to bear for every client.

PARTNERS

THOMAS G. LOEFFLER, born Fredericksburg, Texas, August 1, 1946; admitted to bar, 1971, Texas; 1980, District of Columbia. *Education:* University of Texas (B.B.A., 1968; J.D., 1971). Delta Theta Phi. Member, U.S. House of Representatives, 1978-1986. Vice-Chairman and Chairman, Board of Regents, University of Texas System, 1989-2001. *Member:* State Bar of Texas; District of Columbia Bar. ***PRACTICE AREAS:*** Government Affairs. ***Email:*** tloeffle@ ljtlaw.com

W. JAMES JONAS, III, born Kerrville, Texas, October 13, 1961; admitted to bar, 1987, Texas; 1990, District of Columbia. *Education:* Washington & Lee University (B.A., magna cum laude, with honors in Politics, 1983); University of Texas (J.D., 1987). Phi Alpha Delta, District Justice, 1986-1992, International Executive Board, 1992-1994. National Associate Editor, Harvard Journal of Law and Public Policy (1986 Symposium Edition). *Member:* Travis County, San

(This Listing Continued)

LOEFFLER, JONAS & TUGGEY, L.L.P., Washington—Continued

Antonio and American Bar Associations; State Bar of Texas; The District of Columbia Bar. ***PRACTICE AREAS:*** Governmental Affairs Law. ***Email:*** jjonas@ljtlaw.com

NON-LEGAL PERSONNEL

GOVERNMENT AFFAIRS SPECIALISTS

MARK A. FRANZ, born San Antonio, Texas, October 19, 1962. *Education:* University of Texas at Austin (B.A., 1985; M.A., Public Affairs, 1988). Vice Chancellor, Federal Relations, University of Texas System. Chief of Staff to U.S. Senator Kay Bailey Hutchison and U.S. Congressman Sam Johnson. ***Email:*** mfranz@ljtlaw.com

JON PLEBANI, born October 6, 1947. Former Special Advisor to President Clinton on Haiti. Former Chief of Staff to the Majority Whip, U.S. House of Representatives. Former Staff Director for the Chairman, U.S. House of Representatives Budget Committee. ***Email:*** jplebani@ljtlaw.com

DAN COHEN, born July 16, 1958. Former Member, Senior Staff, Congressman Joseph McDade, U.S. House of Representatives. Senior Legislative Liaison, American Israel Public Affairs Committee, 1986-1993. ***Email:*** dcohen@ljtlaw.com

MICHAEL J. FRAZIER, born August 3, 1956. Former Assistant Secretary of Transportation for Government Affairs to President Bill Clinton. Former Chief of Staff to U.S. Senator Carol Moseley-Braun. Former Legislative Assistant to U.S. Senator Edward M. Kennedy. ***Email:*** mfrazier@ljtlaw.com

EVERETT BIERMAN, born August 16, 1924. U.S. Ambassador to Papua New Guinea, the Solomon Islands and Vanuatu, 1986-1989. ***Email:*** ebierman@ljtlaw.com

JOSÉ MARTINEZ, born August 14, 1941. *Education:* Our Lady of the Lake University (B.A., 1976); Catholic University of America (B.A., 1979). President and CEO, Free Trade Alliance San Antonio. Director, U.S. Trade and Development Agency, 1991-1993. (Resident, San Antonio, Texas Office).

(For complete Biographical Data on all Personnel, see Professional Biographies at San Antonio, Texas)

LOEWINGER & BRAND, PLLC

Established in 1975

471 H STREET, N.W.
WASHINGTON, D.C. 20001
Telephone: 202-789-2382
Fax: 202-789-0939
http://www.loewinger-brand.com
URL: http://www.lawyers.com/loewinger&brandlaw

Landlord-Tenant, Commercial Real Estate Law, including matters dealing with Lead Paint and Oil Tank Storage, Arbitration and Mediation, Bankruptcy, Construction Law, and Complex Corporate and Commercial Litigation.

FIRM PROFILE: Loewinger & Brand has a special reputation in the greater Washington, D.C. community in matters dealing in landlord and tenant law as well as the full spectrum of commercial and residential real estate transactions. The firm's full complement of 10 attorneys represents clients throughout Maryland, Virginia and Washington, D.C.

KENNETH J. LOEWINGER, born Washington, D.C., September 22, 1945; admitted to bar, 1971, District of Columbia and U.S. Court of Appeals for the District of Columbia Circuit; 1972, District of Columbia Court of Appeals; 1979, U.S. Supreme Court. *Education:* Georgetown University (B.A., 1967; J.D., 1971). Delta Theta Phi. *Member:* The District of Columbia Bar; American Judicature Society. ***PRACTICE AREAS:*** Real Property Law; Landlord and Tenant Law; Condominium Law; Cooperative Housing Law; Environmental Law. ***Email:*** KLoewinger@www.loewinger-brand.com

MICHAEL E. BRAND, born New Haven, Connecticut, January 20, 1950; admitted to bar, 1975, District of Columbia and U.S. District Court for the District of Columbia; 1976, Connecticut and U.S. Court of Appeals for the District of Columbia Circuit; 1977, Maryland. *Education:* University of Rochester (A.B., 1971); Catholic University of America (J.D., 1974). Recipient, American Jurisprudence Award in Property. Member, Catholic University of America Law Review, 1973-1974. *Member:* The District of Columbia Bar; Bar Association of the District of Columbia; Connecticut and Maryland State Bar Associations. ***PRACTICE AREAS:*** Real Estate Law; Landlord and Tenant Law; Complex Commercial Litigation. ***Email:*** MBrand@www.loewinger-brand.com

TARRANT H. LOMAX, ESQ., P.C.

Established in 1979

4530 WISCONSIN AVENUE, N.W., SUITE 200
WASHINGTON, D.C. 20016
Telephone: 202-537-7320
Fax: 202-686-0896
Email: tarrantlomax@abanet.org

Annapolis, Maryland Office: 613 Third Street. Telephone: 410-267-6151.

Civil and Commercial Litigation, Contracts, Construction Law, Government Contracts, Business Law, Business Formation, Corporate Law, Maritime Law, Trusts and Estates, Wills, Probate.

TARRANT H. LOMAX, born Los Angeles, California, November 13, 1946; admitted to bar, 1977, Maryland; 1978, District of Columbia, U.S. Court of Appeals for the District of Columbia Circuit, U.S. Court of Appeals, 4th Circuit, U.S. Claims Court, U.S. District Court for the District of Maryland and U.S. District Court for the District of Columbia; 1981, U.S. Supreme Court; 1982, U.S. Court of Appeals, Federal Circuit. *Education:* University of Missouri (B.A., 1969); George Washington University (J.D., 1977). Delta Theta Phi. Member, Panel of Arbitrators, American Arbitration Association. *Member:* The District of Columbia Bar; The Bar Association of District of Columbia, Maryland State and American Bar Associations. [LCDR, USNR]. ***Email:*** tarrantlomax@abanet.org

LONDON & MEAD

1225 NINETEENTH STREET, NORTHWEST
SUITE 320
WASHINGTON, D.C. 20036
Telephone: 202-331-3334
Fax: 202-785-4280
URL: http://www.lawyers.com/london&meadlaw

Civil and Criminal Litigation, Business Litigation, Commercial Litigation, White Collar Criminal Defense, Personal Injury, Wrongful Death, Complex Litigation, Complex and Multi-District Litigation.

FIRM PROFILE: The firm represents clients in litigation matters throughout the country.

MARK LONDON, born New York, N.Y., June 29, 1952; admitted to bar, 1979, District of Columbia; 1989, Maryland. *Education:* Amherst College (B.A., 1974); George Washington National Law Center (J.D., 1979). *Member:* The District of Columbia Bar; Maryland State and American Bar Associations. ***PRACTICE AREAS:*** Civil Litigation. ***Email:*** shark@londonandmead.com

CHRISTOPHER B. MEAD, born Richmond, Virginia, March 20, 1959; admitted to bar, 1985, Maryland; 1986, U.S. Court of Appeals, Fourth Circuit and U.S. District Court, District of Maryland; 1988, District of Columbia; 1995, Virginia. *Education:* Yale University (B.A., magna cum laude, 1981; J.D., 1985). Law Clerk to the Honorable Joseph H. Young, U.S. District Court, District of Maryland, 1985-1986. Author: "Champion: Joe Louis, Black Hero in White America," Chas. Scribner's Sons, 1985. Associate, Williams & Connolly, 1986-1989. Assistant U.S. Attorney, District of Maryland, 1989-1994. Special Assistant U.S. Attorney, District of Columbia, 1994. *Member:* District of Columbia Bar; Maryland State Bar Association; Virginia State Bar. ***PRACTICE AREAS:*** Civil Litigation; White Collar Criminal Litigation. ***Email:*** cmead@londonandmead.com

LONG ALDRIDGE & NORMAN LLP

A Limited Liability Partnership including Professional Corporations

SUITE 600
701 PENNSYLVANIA AVENUE, N.W.
WASHINGTON, D.C. 20004
Telephone: 202-624-1200
FAX: 202-624-1298
Email: dc@lanlaw.com
URL: http://www.lanlaw.com

Atlanta, Georgia Office: Suite 5300, 303 Peachtree Street, 30308. Telephone: 404-527-4000. Telecopier: 404-527-4198.

General Litigation and Appellate Practice before Federal and State Courts and Regulatory Agencies, Antitrust, Public Utilities, Natural Gas and Electric Power Regulations, Federal and State Taxation, Corporate, Commercial, Securities, Real Property, Environmental, Immigration, Government Relations, Communications, Healthcare, Financial Restructurings, Transportation Matters, Intellectual Property and Patent, International Law and Transactions, Technology, Public Finance, Sports and Entertainment Law , Estate Planning and Administration and Employee Benefits.

(This Listing Continued)

MEMBERS OF FIRM

PHILIP D. BARTZ, born Buffalo, New York, July 10, 1956; admitted to bar, 1984, District of Columbia; U.S. Supreme Court; U.S. Court of Appeals for the District of Columbia; U.S. Court of Appeals, Second, Fourth, Fifth and Ninth Circuits. U.S. District Court for the District of Columbia; U.S. District Court, District of Maryland. *Education:* Clark University (B.A., magna cum laude, 1978); Georgetown University Law Center (J.D., magna cum laude, 1982). Phi Beta Kappa. Editor, Georgetown Law Journal, 1981-1982. Law Clerk to Judge Caleb M. Wright, U.S. District Court, District of Delaware, 1982-1983. Assistant Attorney General, Federal Programs Branch, 1998-1999; Office of Consumer Litigation, 1997-1998; Office of Immigration Litigation, 1996-1998. (Resident). ***PRACTICE AREAS:*** Antitrust; Litigation; Administrative Law. ***Email:*** pbartz@lanlaw.com

GASPARE J. BONO, born Philadelphia, Pennsylvania, December 9, 1950; admitted to bar, 1977, New York; 1978, District of Columbia; U.S. District Court, District of Columbia, U.S. District Court, Western District of New York, U.S. District Court, District of Maryland, U.S. Court of Appeals, Third, Fourth, Sixth, Ninth, Eleventh and District of Columbia Circuits and U.S. Supreme Court. *Education:* University of Pennsylvania (B.S. Econ., cum laude, 1972); Georgetown University Law Center (J.D., 1976). (Resident). ***PRACTICE AREAS:*** Antitrust; Complex Litigation; Commercial Litigation. ***Email:*** gbono@lanlaw.com

CAMERON COHICK, born Jefferson City, Missouri, April 21, 1957; admitted to bar, 1985, District of Columbia; 1996, Virginia. *Education:* University of Missouri (B.J., 1979); University of Virginia (J.D., 1985). Member, Editorial Board, Virginia Law Review, 1983-1984. (Resident). ***PRACTICE AREAS:*** Litigation. ***Email:*** ccohick@lanlaw.com

DENNIS A. DAVISON, born New York, New York, August 17, 1948; admitted to bar, 1974, New Jersey; 1976, District of Columbia; 1982, Maryland and U.S. Tax Court. *Education:* George Washington University (B.A., special honors, 1971); Rutgers-Camden School of Law (J.D., cum laude, 1974). Notes and Comments Editor, Rutgers Law Journal. Law Clerk to the Honorable Charles R. Richey, U.S. District Court for the District of Columbia, 1974-1976. (Resident). ***PRACTICE AREAS:*** Real Estate Development; Business Law; Business Litigation. ***Email:*** ddavison@lanlaw.com

GORDON D. GIFFIN, born Springfield, Massachusetts, December 29, 1949; admitted to bar, 1974, Georgia; 1978, District of Columbia. *Education:* Duke University (B.A., 1971); Emory University (J.D., 1974). United States Ambassador to Canada, 1997-2001. ***PRACTICE AREAS:*** Administrative Law; Energy; Utilities; Communications and Media; Contracts; Bid Protests; Election, Campaign and Political Law; Governmental Law. ***Email:*** ggiffin@lanlaw.com

SONG K. JUNG, born Seoul, Korea, March 29, 1965; admitted to bar, 1996, Maryland; 1997, District of Columbia; registered to practice before U.S. Patent and Trademark Office. *Education:* University of Maryland (B.S.E.E., 1987); Johns Hopkins University (M.S.E.E., 1990); Columbus School of Law, The Catholic University of America (J.D., 1995). (Resident). ***PRACTICE AREAS:*** Intellectual Property. ***Email:*** sjung@lanlaw.com

C. RANDALL NUCKOLLS, born 1952; admitted to bar, 1977, Georgia; 1978, District of Columbia. *Education:* University of Georgia (B.S.A., summa cum laude, 1974; J.D., 1977). Member, Executive Board, Moot Court, 1976-1977. (Resident). ***PRACTICE AREAS:*** Legislation; Regulations. ***Email:*** rnuckolls@lanlaw.com

IAN K. PORTNOY, born Philadelphia, Pennsylvania, August 27, 1943; admitted to bar, 1969, Pennsylvania; 1970, District of Columbia; 1973, U.S. Supreme Court. *Education:* University of Michigan (B.A., 1965); Villanova University School of Law (J.D., 1968). (Resident). ***PRACTICE AREAS:*** Real Estate; Intellectual Property Transactions. ***Email:*** iportnoy@lanlaw.com

IRA S. SHAPIRO, born New York, N.Y., October 14, 1947; admitted to bar, 1973, Illinois; 1976, U.S. Supreme Court; 1984, District of Columbia. *Education:* Brandeis University (B.A., magna cum laude with honors, 1969); University of California at Berkeley (M.A., 1970); University of Pennsylvania (J.D., 1973). Editor and Business Manager, University of Pennsylvania Law Review, 1972-1973. Law Clerk to the Honorable Alfred L. Luoago, Judge, U.S. District Court, Eastern District of Pennsylvania, 1973-1974. Office of the United States Trade Representative, 1993-1997, General Counsel, 1993-1995, Ambassador and Chief Negotiator for Japan and Canada, 1995-1997. (Resident). ***PRACTICE AREAS:*** Government Relations; Public Policy; International Trade and Customs. ***Email:*** ishapiro@lanlaw.com

EDGAR H. SIMS, JR. (P.C.), born Atlanta, Georgia, January 3, 1941; admitted to bar, 1965, Georgia; 1980, U.S. Court of Appeals, Sixth Circuit; 1981, U.S. Court of Appeals, Fifth and Eleventh Circuits; 1993, District of Columbia. *Education:* University of Geneva, Geneva, Switzerland; Davidson College (A.B., 1962); Duke University (LL.B., 1965). Law Clerk, Chief Judge, U.S. District Court, Northern District of Georgia, 1965-1966. Chairman, Democratic Party of Georgia, 1990-1995. ***PRACTICE AREAS:*** Banks; Banking; Finance; Government Affairs; Municipal Law; Securities. ***Email:*** esims@lanlaw.com

(This Listing Continued)

RESIDENT ASSOCIATES

KATHERINE R. BLANCHETTE, born Burlington, Vermont, August 11, 1970; admitted to bar, 2000, Maryland (Not admitted in District of Columbia). *Education:* University of Pennsylvania (B.S., 1992); University of North Carolina at Chapel Hill (J.D., with honors, 2000). Editor, North Carolina Law Review, 1999-2000. ***PRACTICE AREAS:*** Real Estate; Litigation. ***Email:*** kblanchette@lanlaw.com

LESLEY E. DAIGLE, born Manchester, New Hampshire, July 10, 1970; admitted to bar, 1998, Georgia; 2000, District of Columbia. *Education:* Yale University (B.A., 1992); University of Texas at Austin (M.A., 1995; J.D., 1997). ***PRACTICE AREAS:*** Commercial Real Estate; Secured Lending. ***Email:*** ldaigle@lanlaw.com

DONNA M. DONLON, born Fort Belvoir, Virginia, November 9, 1970; admitted to bar, 1997, Virginia; 1998, District of Columbia. *Education:* University of Virginia (B.A., 1993); College of William & Mary (J.D., 1996). Order of the Coif. Member, William & Mary Law Review. ***PRACTICE AREAS:*** Litigation. ***Email:*** ddonlon@lanlaw.com

BRIAN E. FINCH, born Troy, New York, July 27, 1974; admitted to bar, 1999, District of Columbia. *Education:* Cornell University (B.S., 1996); George Washington University (J.D., 1999; M.A., 1999). ***PRACTICE AREAS:*** Litigation; Government/Administrative. ***Email:*** bfinch@lanlaw.com

REBECCA A. GOLDMAN, born Dayton, Ohio, January 27, 1967; admitted to bar, 1996, Massachusetts; 1997, Maryland; 1998, District of Columbia; registered to practice before U.S. Patent and Trademark Office. *Education:* Tufts University (B.S.E.E., 1989); California State University (M.S.E.E., 1994); Franklin Pierce Law Center (J.D., 1996). ***PRACTICE AREAS:*** Intellectual Property; Patents; Technology Licensing; Litigation. ***Email:*** rgoldman@lanlaw.com

STEPHEN M. LASTELIC, born Alexandria, Virginia, December 31, 1974; admitted to bar, 2000, Virginia, U.S. Court of Appeals, Fourth Circuit and U.S. District Court, Eastern District of Virginia; 2001, District of Columbia. *Education:* University of North Carolina at Chapel Hill (B.A., 1997); College of William & Mary School of Law (J.D., 2000). ***PRACTICE AREAS:*** Litigation. ***Email:*** slastelic@lanlaw.com

ADRIAN P.J. MOLLO, born Tucson, Arizona, June 29, 1974; admitted to bar, 1999, District of Columbia. *Education:* Winthrop College (B.A., 1996); University of South Carolina (J.D., 1999). Order of the Coif. Research Editor, ABA Real Property, Probate & Trust Journal, Fall 1998 - Spring 1999. ***PRACTICE AREAS:*** Information Technology; Corporate; Litigation. ***Email:*** amollo@lanlaw.com

ANNA W. NICOL, born Sheffield, England, October 3, 1969; admitted to bar, 1998, Maryland; 1999, District of Columbia. *Education:* Boston University (B.A., 1992); Georgetown University (J.D., 1998). Member, American Criminal Law Review, 1996-1998. ***PRACTICE AREAS:*** Litigation. ***Email:*** anicol@lanlaw.com

KENNETH D. SPRINGER, born Manchester, Connecticut, June 28, 1960; admitted to bar, 1994, California and District of Columbia Bar; registered to practice before U.S. Patent and Trademark Office. *Education:* Georgia Institute of Technology (B.E.E., summa cum laude, 1982); University of South Florida (M.S.E.E., 1987); Georgetown University (J.D., magna cum laude, 1994). Order of the Coif. ***PRACTICE AREAS:*** Patents, Trademark, Copyright. ***Email:*** kspringer@lanlaw.com

OF COUNSEL

JOHN M. KELLY, born Akron, Ohio, February 26, 1952; admitted to bar, 1989, Minnesota, 1991, Washington (inactive); 1994, California (Not admitted in District of Columbia). *Education:* Washington State University (B.S., 1980); University of Washington; University of Akron (J.D., cum laude, 1989). Member, University of Akron Law Review, 1988. [With U.S. Coast Guard, 1970-1974]. ***PRACTICE AREAS:*** Intellectual Property. ***Email:*** jkelly@lanlaw.com

(For a complete list of all personnel, see Firm Profile at Atlanta, Georgia)

JOHN S. LOPATTO III

1800 K STREET, NW
SUITE 300
WASHINGTON, D.C. 20006-2202
Telephone: 202-861-5800
1-800-814-3447
1-888-887-6399
Fax: 202-861-5802
Email: JLopatto3@aol.com
URL: http://www.lawyers.com/lopattolaw

Automobile Crash Worthiness, Negligence, Personal Injury, Automobile Accidents, Wrongful Death, Head Trauma, Government Contracts, Professional Malpractice, Medical Malpractice, Products Liability, General Business and Commercial Litigation, Intellectual Property, Black Lung, Venture Capital. Complex Civil Litigation, Toxic Torts.

FIRM PROFILE: The firm represents individuals and businesses in metro District of Columbia, Maryland and Virginia in matters involving litigation. For over 15 years the firm has represented major coal producers in defense of federal black lung cases.

JOHN S. LOPATTO, III, born Kingston, Pennsylvania, October 7, 1951; admitted to bar, 1976, Pennsylvania; 1978, District of Columbia; 1989, Maryland; 1992, Virginia. *Education:* University of Pennsylvania (B.A., 1973); Dickinson School of Law (J.D., 1976). Phi Alpha Delta. Author: "The Federal Black Lung Program: A 1983 Primer," 85 W. Va. Law Review 677, National Coal Issue, 1983. Co-Author: "Hazardous and Solid Waste Laws and Regulations: Effects on the Mining of Coal and Other Minerals," 92 W. Va. Law Review, 1986. Attorney, Office of The Solicitor, U.S. Department of Labor, 1976-1980. Associate, 1980-1986 and Partner, 1986-1988, Freedman, Levy, Kroll & Simonds, Washington, D.C. Solo Practice, 1988-1991, Washington, D.C. Associate, 1991-1996, Paulson, Nace & Norwind. *Member:* The District of Columbia Bar; Maryland Trial Lawyers Association; Trial Lawyers Association of Metropolitan Washington, D.C. (Board of Governors, 1993—); The Association of Trial Lawyers of America; Virginia Trial Lawyers Association.

LOTSTEIN BUCKMAN, LLP

5185 MACARTHUR BOULEVARD, N.W.
WASHINGTON, D.C. 20016-3341
Telephone: 202-237-6000
Facsimile: 202-237-8900
Email: info@lotsteinbuckman.com
URL: http://www.lotsteinbuckman.com

Mortgage Banking, Real Estate, Title, Condominium, Foreclosure, Business Transactions, Commercial Litigation, Probate, and Bankruptcy.

STEVEN M. BUCKMAN, born Spring Valley, Illinois, February 3, 1953; admitted to bar, 1980, District of Columbia; 1987, New York and U.S. District Court, District of Columbia; 1981, U.S. Court of Appeals, District of Columbia Circuit; 1986, U.S. District Court, District of Maryland. *Education:* University of Wisconsin-Madison (B.A., 1975); University of Maryland (J.D., cum laude, 1979). Staff Assistant, Congressman Tim L. Hall (D-Il), 1975-1976. *Member:* District of Columbia Bar (Member, Real Estate, Housing and Land Use Section); Bar Association of the District of Columbia; D.C. Superior Court Panel of Arbitrators; District of Columbia Land Title Association (Vice President, 1994-2000; President-Elect 2000); Maryland Land Title Association; American Land Title Association. ***PRACTICE AREAS:*** Real Estate; Real Estate Title; Real Estate Leasing; Foreclosures; Commercial Litigation. ***Email:*** buckman@lotsteinbuckman.com

ROBERT S. LOTSTEIN, born Hartford, Connecticut, September 26, 1961; admitted to bar, 1987, Maryland; 1988, District of Columbia and U.S. District Court, District of Maryland; 1990, U.S. District Court, District of Columbia; 1991, U.S. Supreme Court. *Education:* American University (B.S.B.A., 1984) Alpha Lambda Delta; Washington College of Law of American University (J.D., 1987). Editor, Mortgage Banking Update. Author: *Lotstein Buckman Mortgage Banking Compliance Manuals*; *1999-2000 State and Federal Mortgage Banking Regulators Guide*. Member, Panel of Arbitrators, American Arbitration Association. *Member:* Montgomery County, Maryland State and American (Member, Real Estate Settlement Procedures Act and Truth-in-Lending Act Subcommittees, Business Law Section) Bar Associations; The District of Columbia Bar; Maryland Trial Lawyers Association; Maryland Land Title Association; American Land Title Association; American Association of Residential Mortgage Regulators (Member, Advisory Counsel); Mortgage Bankers Association (Member, Regulatory Compliance Committee; Legal Issues Committee; State Legislative and Regulatory COmmittee). ***PRACTICE AREAS:*** Mortgage Banking Law; Real Estate; Business Transactions; Commercial Litigation. ***Email:*** lotstein@lotsteinbuckman.com

(This Listing Continued)

STEPHANIE L. SHAW, born Passaic, New Jersey, February 7, 1968; admitted to bar, 1996, Maryland; 1999, District of Columbia. *Education:* Franklin and Marshall College (B.A., 1990); Catholic University of America Columbus School of Law (J.D., 1996). *Member:* Maryland State Bar Association; The District of Columbia Bar. ***PRACTICE AREAS:*** Mortgage Banking Law; Real Estate. ***Email:*** slshaw@lotsteinbuckman.com

PAUL A. MONDOR, born Takoma Park, Maryland, October 16, 1957; admitted to bar, 1989, Maryland; 1990, District of Columbia. *Education:* Catholic University of America (B.A., cum laude, 1979; J.D., 1989). Psi Chi. Author: "Lock-In Laws: Adding More Patches to the Mortgage Lending Quilt," 37 Catholic University Law Review 543, 1988. *Member:* Prince George's County, Maryland State and American Bar Associations; The District of Columbia Bar. ***PRACTICE AREAS:*** Mortgage Banking Law. ***Email:*** pmondor@lotsteinbuckman.com

ANNA CAMPO PANÉ, born Brooklyn, New York, January 23, 1970; admitted to bar, 1997, New York; 1999, District of Columbia. *Education:* Kings College (B.A., 1992); Boston University (J.D., 1996). *Member:* The District of Columbia Bar. ***PRACTICE AREAS:*** Mortgage Banking Law. ***Email:*** pane@lotsteinbuckman.com

CHARLOTTE K. BOONCHAROEN, born New York, N.Y., December 28, 1972; admitted to bar, 1999, New York (Not admitted in District of Columbia). *Education:* University of Michigan (B.A., 1994); George Washington University (J.D., 1998). Co-Author with John Gase: "International Commitment Towards Curbing Global Warming: The Kyoto Protocol," 4 Envtl. Law 917, 1998. *Member:* American Bar Association. ***LANGUAGES:*** French. ***PRACTICE AREAS:*** Mortgage Banking. ***Email:*** booncharoen@lotsteinbuckman.com

LEGAL SUPPORT PERSONNEL

REGINA JOAN REED, born Washington, D.C., November 16, 1963. *Education:* Tulane University (B.S., 1984; M.B.A., 1986). Certified Public Accountant. (Director). ***PRACTICE AREAS:*** Compliance; Operational Consulting. ***Email:*** reed@lotsteinbuckman.com

MARY L. MICHAELS, born Washington, D.C., March 16, 1946. (Compliance Analyst). ***PRACTICE AREAS:*** Licensing Services. ***Email:*** mlmich@lotsteinbuckman.com

VANESSA CARPENTER LOURIE, P.C.

Established in 1982
4400 MACARTHUR BOULEVARD, NW, SUITE 205
WASHINGTON, D.C. 20007-2521
Telephone: 202-342-8000
Facsimile: 202-342-9000
Email: vlourie@vclaw.zyan.net
URL: http://www.lawyers.com/commercialrealestate

Commercial and Real Estate Litigation, Commercial and Real Estate Transactions, Landlord and Tenant Law, Acquisitions, Finance Restructuring, Leasing, Contracts, Collections, Partnerships, Wills, Estates, Trusts, Personal Injury, Domestic Relations.

FIRM PROFILE: The firm has successfully represented contractors, lenders, real estate entrepreneurs, real estate businesses and individuals in commercial litigation and transactions throughout Washington, D.C. and Maryland.

COUNSEL

VANESSA CARPENTER LOURIE, born Richmond, Virginia, April 17, 1953; admitted to bar, 1978, District of Columbia; 1996, Maryland. *Education:* Howard University (B.A.,with honors, magna cum laude,1975); Georgetown University (J.D., 1978). Phi Beta Kappa. Member, Voting Delegant, 16th Annual Judicial Conference of DC, 1991. *Member:* Prince George's County, Maryland and Washington State Bar Associations; District of Columbia Bar; The Association of Trial Lawyers of America. ***PRACTICE AREAS:*** Civil Litigation; Real Estate Law; Corporate Law; Domestic Relations; Personal Injury. ***Email:*** vlorie@vclaw.zyan.net

LOVELLS

401 9TH STREET, N.W., SUITE 1150
WASHINGTON, D.C. 20004
Telephone: +1-202 783-6144
Fax: +1 202 783-6250
Email: information@lovells.com
URL: http://www.lovells.com

REVISERS OF THE GERMAN LAW DIGEST FOR THIS DIRECTORY

(This Listing Continued)

Alicante, Spain Office: Lovells Boesebeck Droste, Bilbao 1, 5° Piso, 03001 Alicante. Telephone: +34 96 514 41 05. Fax: +34 96 514 43 03.
Amsterdam, Netherlands Office: Frederiksplein 42, 1017 XN Amsterdam. Telephone: +31 20 55 33 600. Fax: +31 20 55 33 777.
Beijing, Republic of China Office: Suite 414 Tower B, COFCO Plaza, 8 Jianguomennei Dajie, Beijing 100005. Telephone: +86 10 6526 3490. Fax: +86 10 6526 3492.
Berlin, Germany Office: Lovells Boesebeck Droste, Schlüterstrasse 37, 10629 Berlin. Telephone: +49 30 8 89 19-0. Fax: +49 30 8 89 19-100.
Brussels, Belgium Office: Lovells Boesebeck Droste, Avenue Louise 523, Bte 24, 1050 Brussels. Telephone: +32 -2 647 06 60. Fax: +32-2 647 11 24.
Budapest, Hungary Associated Office: Squarra & Partos, Andrassy ut. 2, 1061 Budapest. Telephone: +36 1 474 2080. Fax: +36 1 474 2081.
Chicago, Illinois Office: One IBM Plaza, 330 North Wabash Avenue, Suite 1900, Chicago, IL 60611. Telephone: +1 312 832 4400. Fax: +1 312 832 4444.
Dresden, Germany Office: Lovells Boesebeck Droste, Heideparkstrasse 4, 01099 Dresden. Telephone: +49 351 829 61-0. Fax: +49 351 829 61-99.
Dusseldorf, Germany Office: Lovells Boesebeck Droste, Kennedydamm 17, 40476 Düsseldorf. Telephone: +49 211 13 68-0. Fax: +49 211 32 44 39.
Frankfurt, Germany Office: Lovells Boesebeck Droste, Darmstädter Landstrasse 125, 60598 Frankfurt am Main. Telephone: +49 69 962 36-0. Fax: +49 69 962 36-100.
Hamburg, Germany Office: Lovells Boesebeck Droste, Warburgstrasse 50, 20354 Hamburg. Telephone: +49 40 419 93-0. Fax: +49 40 419 93-200.
Ho Chi Minh City, Vietnam: 10th Floor, OSIC Building, 8 Nguyen Hue Street, District 1, Ho Chi Minh City. Telephone: +84 8 829 5100. Fax: +84 8 829 5101.
Hong Kong Office: 23rd Floor, Cheung Kong Center, 2 Queen's Road Central, Hong Kong. Telephone: +852 2219 0888. Fax: +852 2219 0222.
London, England Office: 65 Holborn Viaduct, London EC1A 2DY. Telephone: +44 20 7296 2000. Fax: +44 20 7296 2001.
Milan, Italy Office: Via F.lli Gabba 3, 20121 Milan. Telephone: +39 02 7202 521. Fax: +39 02 7202 5252.
Moscow, Russia Office: 5th Floor, Usadba Centre, 22 Voznesensky, Pereulok, Moscow 103032. Telephone: +7 095 933 3000. Fax: +7 095 933 3001.
Munich, Germany Office: Lovells Boesebeck Droste, Marstallstrasse 8, 80539 München. Telephone: +49 89 290 12-0. Fax: +49 89 290 12-222.
New York, N.Y. Office: 900 Third Avenue, 16th Floor, New York, NY 10022. Telephone: +1 212 909 0600. Fax: +1 212 909 0666.
Paris, France Office: 37 Avenue Pierre 1er de Serbie, 75008, Paris. Telephone: +33 1 53 67 47 47. Fax: +33 1 47 23 96 12.
Prague, Czech Republic Office: Slovanský dům, Na Příkopě 22, 110 00 Prague 1. Telephone: +420 2 2141 1700. Fax: +420 2 2421 0004.
Rome, Italy Office: Via Due Macelli 66, 00187 Rome. Telephone: +39 06 675 8231. Fax: +39 06 6758 2323.
Singapore Office: 80 Raffles Place #54-01 UOB Plaza 1, Singapore 048624. Telephone: +65 538 0900. Fax: +65 538 7077.
Tokyo, Japan Office: 3rd Floor, Joware Hanzomon, 2-19 Hayabusa-cho, Chiyoda-ku Tokyo 102-0092. Telephone: +81-3 3221 8511. Fax: +81-3 3221 8560.
Vienna, Austria Associated Office: Graben 29 A, 1010 Vienna. Telephone: +43 1 53 55 744. Fax: +43 1 53 50 649.
Warsaw, Poland Office: Lovells Boesebeck Droste, ul. Nowogrodzka 50, 00695 Warszawa. Telephone: +48 22 529 29 00. Fax: +48 22 529 29 01.
Zagreb, Croatia Associated Office: Mirko Bogdanović & Tin Dolički, ul. Alexandera von Humboldta 4b/III, 10000 Zagreb. Telephone: +385 1 6 15 95 95. Fax: +385 1 6 15 77 33.

Concentrating in consumer financial services, privacy and federal regulatory compliance.

RESIDENT PARTNER

ANNE PRICE FORTNEY, born 1944; admitted to bar, 1969, District of Columbia; 1982, U.S. Supreme Court; 1987, Hawaii. *Education:* Institute for American Universities, Aix-en-Provence, France; Mary Washington College (B.A., 1966); Georgetown University Law Center (J.D., 1969). Associate Director for Credit Practices, Bureau of Consumer Protection, Federal Trade Commission, 1982-1986. Attorney, Bureau of Consumer Protection, Federal Trade Commission, 1973-1976. Attorney-Advisor, Commissioner Mary Gardiner Jones, Federal Trade Commission, 1972-1973. Member, Board of Visitors, Mary Washington College, 1982-1984. Founder and Chair, Hawaii Military Spouse Career Network, 1989-1990. *Member:* The District of Columbia Bar; Hawaii State and American (Member, Business Law Section: Member, Consumer Financial Services Committee, 1982—, Chair, Consumer Communications Subcommittee, 1983-1986; Vice-Chair, 1991-1992 and Chair, 1992-1995, Privacy Subcommittee; Vice-Chair, 1997-2000, FTC Activities Subcommittee; Chair, 2000—, Federal and State Trade Practice Subcommittee; Member, Section of Administrative Law and Regulatory Practice, Vice-Chair, Financial Services Committee, 1992-1995; Member, Section of Antitrust Law; Member: Governing Committee of Conference on Consumer Finance Law, 1995—; Vice President, 1999—) Bar Associations. Founding Member, American College of Consumer Financial Services Lawyers (Member, Board of Regents). ***LANGUAGES:*** French. ***PRACTICE AREAS:*** Consumer Financial Services; Privacy; Federal Regulatory Compliance. ***Email:*** anne.fortney@lovells.com

RESIDENT LAWYER

MARKUS B. HEYDER, born 1962; admitted to bar, 1994, Illinois; 1999, District of Columbia. *Education:* Middlebury College (B.A., summa cum laude, 1989); Columbia University (J.D., 1994). *Member:* American Bar Association. ***LANGUAGES:*** German and Russian. ***PRACTICE AREAS:*** Consumer Financial Services; Privacy; Federal Regulation; Commercial Litigation; Reinsurance. ***Email:*** markus.heyder@lovells.com

JULIA A. NOVINA, born 1970; admitted to bar, 1988, Maryland (Not admitted in District of Columbia). *Education:* Connecticut College (B.A., magna cum laude, 1991); Georgetown University Law Center (J.D., 1997). *Member:* American Bar Association. ***LANGUAGES:*** German, Italian and Spanish. ***PRACTICE AREAS:*** Consumer Financial Services; Privacy Law; Federal Regulatory Compliance. ***Email:*** julia.novina@whitecase.com

ANDREW MACGREGOR SMITH, born 1965; admitted to bar, 1994, Virginia; 1997, District of Columbia. *Education:* Williams College (B.A., 1987); College of William & Mary (J.D., 1994). Acting Assistant General Counsel, 1999-2000, Senior Counsel, 1998-1999, and Staff Attorney, 1997-1998, Office of the General Counsel, U.S. Securities and Exchange Commission. *Member:* District of Columbia Bar; Virginia State Bar. ***PRACTICE AREAS:*** Consumer Financial Services; Privacy Law; Federal Regulatory Compliance. ***Email:*** andrew.smith@lovells.com

REVISERS OF THE GERMAN LAW DIGEST FOR THIS DIRECTORY

(For list of Partners see Professional Biographies at London, England)

JEFFREY A. LOVITKY

Established in 1989
1735 NEW YORK AVENUE N.W., SUITE 700
WASHINGTON, D.C. 20006
Telephone: 202-429-3393
Fascimile: 202-318-4013
URL: http://www.lawyers.com/lovitky
Email: jeff@lovitky.com
URL: http://www.lovitky.com

Health Law, Medicare Law including Reimbursement Disputes and Payment Suspensions; Fraud and Abuse; Health Privacy; Government Contracts Law.

FIRM PROFILE: Mr. Lovitky, Board Certified in Health Law, has a national health-care practice. He represents a broad cross-section of health-care providers, including hospitals, physicians, and skilled nursing facilities. Mr. Lovitky has achieved Martindale-Hubbell's highest possible rating for legal ability and ethical standards. He has further expertise in government contracts law.

JEFFREY A. LOVITKY, born Flint, Michigan, September 22, 1954; admitted to bar, 1980, Michigan; 1982, Connecticut and Florida; 1986, District of Columbia. *Education:* University of Michigan (B.A., 1976); Thomas M. Cooley Law School (J.D., 1980); George Washington University (LL.M., 1988). U.S. Department of Justice, Washington, D.C., 1984-1988; U.S. Army Judge Advocate General Corps, 1981-1983. Contributing Author: *Treatise on Health Care Law;* Contributing Editor, *Federal Contract Management:* Author: Analyzing the Anti-Kickback Act, *Health Care Law Monthly, May 2001;* The National Practitioner Databank, *Journal of Health Law, Spring 2000;* Designing Compliance Programs, *Healthcare Financial Management, March 1999.* Scholar, Mid-Atlantic Health Leadership Institute - Johns Hopkins University, 1997-1998. (Board Certified Health Law Lawyer, Florida Bar Board of Legal Specialization and Education).

LUDWIG & ROBINSON, P.L.L.C.

555 ELEVENTH STREET, N.W.
SUITE 850
WASHINGTON, D.C. 20004-1304
Telephone: 202-289-1800
Telecopier: 202-289-1804
Email: contact@ludwigrobinson.com
URL: http://www.ludwigrobinson.com

Affiliated Law Firm: K ümmerlein, Simon & Partner, Rechtsanwälte, Huyssenallee 58-64, D-45128 Essen, Germany. Telephone: 011-49-201-1756-600. Telecopier: 011-49-201-1756-666. Email: zentrale@Ksup.de

(This Listing Continued)

(This Listing Continued)

LUDWIG & ROBINSON, P.L.L.C., Washington—Continued

Domestic and International Civil Practice, Litigation, Arbitration and Mediation, Administrative, Aviation, Banking, Corporate Finance and Restructuring, Commercial Law, Mergers, Acquisitions and Divestitures, Computer, Technology and Internet. Employment, Export, Customs and Trade. Insurance, Products Liability, Negligence, Securities, Trademark and Telecommunications.

FIRM PROFILE: Ludwig & Robinson, P.L.L.C. has a diverse regional, national and international litigation, business and regulatory practice. The firm represents domestic and international clients before U.S. courts and administrative agencies, and provides advice on corporate and commercial law. Clients range from emerging companies and individuals to major foreign and domestic corporations.

ROBERT W. LUDWIG, JR., born Syracuse, New York, July 20, 1955; admitted to bar, 1982, District of Columbia, U.S. District Court, District of Columbia and U.S. Court of Appeals, District of Columbia, Fourth and Seventh Circuits; 1987, U.S. Supreme Court; 1988, Maryland and U.S. District Court, District of Maryland. *Education:* Colgate University (B.A., 1977); Washington & Lee University (J.D., 1981). Editorial Advisor, German American Law Journal, 1991-1993. Author, "Neue Exportkontrolle f ür Computer, Technologie und Software in den Vereinigten Staaten," Computer und Recht (Dec. 1992). *Member:* District of Columbia Bar; Maryland State and American (Member, Sections on: Litigation; Torts and Insurance Practice; Business; International Law) Bar Associations; German American Law Association (President, Capital Area Chapter, 1993-1995); American Institute for Aeronautics and Astronautics (Member, Legal Aspects Committee, Orbital Debris Launch Vehicle Subcommittee, 1991—); American Society of International Law. ***LANGUAGES:*** German. ***Email:*** rludwig@ludwigrobinson.com

PHILLIP L. ROBINSON, born Phoenix, Arizona, March 29, 1947; admitted to bar, 1986, Maryland; 1987, District of Columbia and U.S. District Court, District of Columbia and U.S. District Court, District of Maryland; 1992, U.S. Court of Appeals, Fourth Circuit and U.S. Court of Appeals, District of Columbia Circuit. *Education:* Whittier College (B.A., with honors, 1969; M.A., with highest honors, 1971); Cornell University (M.A., 1973); George Washington University (J.D., 1986). Professor: Comparative and European Politics, Northwestern University, 1975-1977; Visiting Professor of Comparative Politics and Public Policy, Oberlin College, 1977-1978; Assistant Professor of Comparative Politics, Middle Eastern Politics, and Statistical and Quantitative Research Methods, Williams College, 1978-1979; Adjunct Professor of International Law, George Washington University, 1997—. Special Counsel, American Political Science Association, 1988-1993. *Member:* The District of Columbia Bar; Maryland State Bar Association. ***LANGUAGES:*** Scandinavian and Arabic. ***PRACTICE AREAS:*** Banking Law; Corporate; Mergers and Acquisitions; International Business Law; Offshore Trusts. ***Email:*** probinson@ludwigrobinson.com

MICHAEL H. MOBBS, born Lawrenceburg, Tennessee, December 25, 1948; admitted to bar, 1974, Alabama; 1978, District of Columbia; 1980, U.S. Supreme Court. *Education:* Yale University (B.A., summa cum laude, honors with exceptional distinction in Russian Studies, 1971); University of Chicago (J.D., 1974). Phi Beta Kappa. Author: "Preferences and Problems for Manufacturers Under Russian Law: An Overview," Final Report, Third Annual U.S.-Russian Investment Symposium, John F. Kennedy School of Government, Harvard University, 1999; "The Current Legal Environment for Investment in the Russian Federation," Proceedings, Southwestern Legal Foundation: 1997 Annual Symposium on Private Investments Abroad, Matthew Bender, 1998; "Environmental Protection in the CIS and Eastern Europe: Emerging Trends May Affect Your Business," Counsel to Counsel, Arthur Andersen & Co., 1993; "Remarks on Verification of Arms Control Agreements: New Hope in a New Era," Proceedings, American Society of International Law, 1988. Co-Author: "Overview of the Laws Governing Foreign Investment in the USSR," Doing Business in Eastern Europe and the Soviet Union, Federal Publications Inc., 1990; "An Importer's Roadmap to U.S. Import Restrictions," U.S. Taxation of International Business Operations, Prentice-Hall, 1980. Representative of U.S. Secretary of Defense to: Strategic Arms Reduction Talks (START), 1982-1985; Nuclear and Space Talks (NST), 1985. Assistant Director, Strategic Programs, U.S. Arms Control and Disarmament Agency, 1985-1987. *Member:* Alabama State Bar; District of Columbia Bar; American Bar Association. ***LANGUAGES:*** Russian. ***PRACTICE AREAS:*** International; Commercial Transactions; Corporate; Securities. ***Email:*** mmobbs@ludwigrobinson.com

SALVATORE SCANIO, born New Orleans, Louisiana, March 10, 1965; admitted to bar, 1992, District of Columbia. *Education:* Tulane University of Louisiana (B.A., cum laude with departmental honors in Political Science, 1986; J.D., cum laude, 1991); A.B. Freeman School of Business, Tulane University (M.B.A., 1991). *Member:* The District of Columbia Bar; American Bar Association. ***PRACTICE AREAS:*** Complex Litigation; Banking Law; Corporate Law. ***Email:*** sscanio@ludwigrobinson.com

(This Listing Continued)

OF COUNSEL

ETHAN S. BURGER, born New York, N.Y., February 11, 1959; admitted to bar, 1989, District of Columbia; 1990, U.S. District Court, District of Columbia; 2000, Maryland. *Education:* Leningrad State University (Certificate 1980); Harvard University (A.B., magna cum laude, 1981); Georgetown University Law Center (J.D., cum laude, 1989). Research Associate Professor, American University, School of International Service; Project Director, Transnational Crime and Corruption Center, 2001—. Arbitrator, District of Columbia Bar's Attorney/Client Arbitration Board, 1997—. Special Counsel to Lawyers Committee for Human Rights for Conference on Security and Cooperation in Europe Matters, 1990-1992. *Member:* The District of Columbia Bar; Maryland State Bar Association, Inc. (Also Of Counsel: Russin & Vecchi LLP). ***LANGUAGES:*** Russian. ***PRACTICE AREAS:*** Corporate Law; Commercial Law; Directors and Officers Liability; Professional Negligence; Domestic and International; Arbitration and Mediation; International Trade and Investments.

WILLIAM L. MENARD, born Daytona Beach, Florida, February 15, 1960; admitted to bar, 1992, Pennsylvania; 1995, District of Columbia. *Education:* Williams College (B.A., 1983); Georgetown University Law Center (J.D., magna cum laude, 1992). Order of the Coif. Member, Georgetown Law Review, 1990-1992. Member, Corporations, Finance and Securities Law Section, District of Columbia. ***LANGUAGES:*** Italian. ***PRACTICE AREAS:*** Corporate Law; International Law; Business Transactions; International Contracts; Foreign Corrupt Practices Act; Mergers, Acquisitions and Divestitures; Agency and Distributorships; Offshore Corporations; Corporate Finance; Shareholder Agreements; Securities.

GLENN J. MELCHER, born Baltimore, Maryland, September 24, 1960; admitted to bar, 1987, Maryland and U.S. District Court, District of Maryland; 1989, District of Columbia; 1996, U.S Supreme Court. *Education:* University of Maryland (B.A., 1983); Catholic University of America (J.D., 1987); McGeorge School of Law, University of the Pacific (LL.M., 1988). *Member:* Maryland State and American (Member, Sections on: Litigation, International Law, Taxation) Bar Associations; The District of Columbia Bar. ***LANGUAGES:*** Spanish. ***REPORTED CASES:*** United States v. Sheldon G. Hansel, 42 F. Supp.2d 201 (N.D.N.Y. 199); 83 A.F.T.R.2d 99-1994; 99-1 USTC 50432; Bruce B. Reimer v. United States, 43 F.Supp.2d 232 (N.D.N.Y.1999); 83 A.F.T.R.2d 99-2041; 99-1 USTC 50434; United States v. Sheldon G. Hansel, 999 F.Supp 694 (N.D.N.Y. 1998); 81 A.F.T.R.2d 98-1382; 98-1 USTC 50,293; Mazur v. Commissioner of Internal Revenue, 986 F. Supp. 752 (W.D.N.Y. 1997); 80 A.F.T.R.2d 97-8140; 97-2 USTC 50,981; John N. Hauf v. Internal Revenue Service, 968 F. Supp 78 (N.D.N.Y. 1997); 80 A.F.T.R.2d 97-5430; 97-2 USTC 50,645; City of Keytesville v. Kelco Industries, Inc., et al., 773 F. Supp. 1264 (E.D. Mo. 1991); 68 A.F.T.R.2d 91-5918; 91-2 USTC 50,483; United States v. Sheldon G. Hansel, 182 F.R.D. 7 (N.D.N.Y. 1998); 82 A.F.T.R.2d 98-7014; William J. Zecco v. United States, 211 B.R. 109 (Bankr. D. Mass. 1997); 79 A.F.T.R.2d 97-3131; 97-2 USTC 50,910; United States v. Robert S. Mathews, 209 B.R. 218 (6th Cir. B.A.P. 1997); 79 A.F.T.R. 2d 97-3084; 97-2 USTC 50,851; William J. Brady v. United States, 200 B.R. 178 (Bankr. S.D. Ohio 1996); 78 A.F.T.R.2d 96-5347; Cleveland Indians Baseball Company v. United States, 2001 WL 933593 (N.D. Ohio), 88 A.F.T.R.2d 2001-5338, 2001-2 USTC 50593; Ronald Girvin v. United States, 200 WL 905212 (S.D. Ohio), 85 A.F.T.R.2d 2000-1974; Cleveland Indians Baseball Company v. United States, 1998 WL 180623 (N.D. Ohio); 81 A.F.T.R.2d 98-645; 98-1 USTC 50,197; United States v. Sheldon G. Hansel, 1997 WL 407446 (N.D.N.Y. 1997); 79 A.F.T.R.2d 97-2568; David R. Roberts v. Internal Revenue Service, 1997 WL 401556 (N.D. Ohio 1997); 79 A.F.T.R.2d 97-2362; 97-1 USTC 50,422; Robert Ljungberg v. United States, 1997 WL 222643 (W.D.N.Y. 1997); 79 A.F.T.R.2d 97-1273; Randy S. Mayle v. United States, 1996 WL 857936 (S.D. Ohio 1996); 79 A.F.T.R.2d 97-686; Orvel L. Turner v. Internal Revenue Service, 1996 WL 679465 (S.D. Ohio 1996); 78 A.F.T.R.2d 96-6734; Randy S. Mayle v. United States, 1996 WL 376338 (S.D. Ohio 1996); 77 A.F.T.R.2d 96-2194; United States v. Van Skiver, 1991 WL 12828 (D.Kan. 1991); United States v. Van Skiver, 1990 WL 251738 (D.Kan. 1990); 71 A.F.T.R.2d 93-4063; 91-1 USTC 50,017; In re: Sampson, 1997 WL 1038155 (Bankr. S.D. Ohio 1997); 80 A.F.T.R.2d 97-6778; In re Morgan, 1990 WL 208790 (Bankr. E.D. Okla. 1990); 71 A.F.T.R.2d 93-5025. ***PRACTICE AREAS:*** Complex Litigation; Tax Controversies; International Law.

EDWIN Y. SZETO, born Hong Kong, June 2, 1971; admitted to bar, 1996, Virginia; 1997, District of Columbia and U.S. District Court, Eastern District of Virginia. *Education:* James Madison University (B.B.A., cum laude, 1993); T.C. Williams School of Law, University of Richmond (J.D., 1996). Omicron Delta Epsilon. Managing Editor, Richmond Journal of Law & Technology, 1995-1996. Co-Author: "U.S. Update: Legal Status at Safeguarding Proprietary Information," The Computer Law and Security Report, July-August, 1997. *Member:* Fairfax Bar Association; Bar Association of the District of Columbia. ***LANGUAGES:*** Chinese. ***PRACTICE AREAS:*** Commercial Litigation; Corporate Law; Commercial Law; Customs and International Trade; Electronic Commerce. ***Email:*** eszeto@ludwigrobinson.com

(This Listing Continued)

MICHAEL J. KRESSLEIN, born Baltimore, Maryland, May 23, 1969; admitted to bar, 1994, Maryland; 1995, District of Columbia. *Education:* Georgetown University (B.S.B.A., magna cum laude, 1991); University of Maryland (J.D., 1994). Order of the Coif. Assistant Editor, University of Maryland Law Review, 1993-1994. *Member, The District of Columbia Bar.* ***PRACTICE AREAS:*** Litigation; Corporate Law. ***Email:*** mkresslein@ludwigrobinson.com

EVGENIA V. SOROKINA, born Moscow, Russia, June 14, 1971; admitted to bar, 1999, Russian Federation (Not admitted in District of Columbia). *Education:* InterAmerican University of Costa Rica (Business Administration, 1992-1993); Moscow State Law Academy (J.D, 1999). (Foreign Legal Advisor). ***LANGUAGES:*** Russian, Spanish, Italian. ***PRACTICE AREAS:*** Russian Civil Law; International Law. ***Email:*** esorokina@ludwigrobinson.com

LUKAS, NACE, GUTIERREZ & SACHS

CHARTERED

Established in 1985

1111 19TH STREET, N.W., SUITE 1200
WASHINGTON, D.C. 20036
Telephone: 202-857-3500
Telecopier: 202-842-4485
Email: lmng@fcclaw.com
URL: http://www.fcclaw.com

Telecommunications Law, Business Organizations, Commercial Transactions and Litigation.

FIRM PROFILE: Lukas, Nace, Gutierrez & Sachs Chartered is a member of the Martindale-Hubbell Bar Register of Preeminent Lawyers.

RUSSELL D. LUKAS, born Roslyn, New York, October 15, 1946; admitted to bar, 1975, District of Columbia. *Education:* Syracuse University (B.A., 1968); Georgetown University (J.D., 1975). *Member:* The District of Columbia Bar; Federal Communications Bar Association. ***PRACTICE AREAS:*** Telecommunications Law; Appellate Practice. ***Email:*** rlukas@fcclaw.com

DAVID L. NACE, born Philadelphia, Pennsylvania, July 26, 1949; admitted to bar, 1976, District of Columbia. *Education:* Monmouth College (B.S., 1971); American University (J.D., 1975). Counsel to Fund for Rural Education and Development. *Member:* The District of Columbia Bar; Federal Communications Bar Association. ***PRACTICE AREAS:*** Telecommunications Law; FCC Regulation; Business Transfers. ***Email:*** dnace@fcclaw.com

THOMAS GUTIERREZ, born Washington, D.C., September 18, 1950; admitted to bar, 1979, District of Columbia. *Education:* University of Maryland (B.S., 1972; M.B.A., 1974); Catholic University of America (J.D., 1979). *Member:* The District of Columbia Bar; American Bar Association; Federal Communications Bar Association; Hispanic National Bar Association; Hispanic Bar Association of the District of Columbia. ***PRACTICE AREAS:*** Administration Law; Communications and Media; Contracts. ***Email:*** tgutierrez@fcclaw.com

ELIZABETH R. SACHS, born Newark, New Jersey, June 17, 1949; admitted to bar, 1980, District of Columbia. *Education:* Rosemont College (B.A., 1971); Washington College of Law of American University (J.D., magna cum laude, 1980). *Member:* The District of Columbia Bar; American Bar Association; Women's Bar Association of the District of Columbia; Federal Communications Bar Association. ***PRACTICE AREAS:*** Telecommunications Law; FCC Regulation; Business Transfers. ***Email:*** lsachs@fcclaw.com

GEORGE L. LYON, JR., born Richmond, Virginia, August 19, 1954; admitted to bar, 1979, Virginia; 1985, District of Columbia. *Education:* University of Virginia (B.A., with distinction, 1976); College of William & Mary (J.D., 1979). Phi Delta Phi. Member, William & Mary Law Review, 1978-1979. *Member:* The District of Columbia Bar; Virginia State Bar; Federal Communications Bar Association. ***PRACTICE AREAS:*** Communications; Civil and Appellate Litigation; Transactions. ***Email:*** glyon@fcclaw.com

JOEL R. KASWELL, born Jersey City, New Jersey, December 20, 1937; admitted to bar, 1962, Massachusetts; 1964, District of Columbia. *Education:* Dartmouth College (B.A., magna cum laude, 1959); Harvard University (J.D., 1962). Phi Beta Kappa. Rufus Choate Scholar. Woodbury Law Fellow, 1960. *Member:* The District of Columbia Bar; American Bar Association (Member, Sections on: Antitrust Law; Corporation, Banking and Business Law; General Practice). ***PRACTICE AREAS:*** Securities; Financial; Corporation Law.

PAMELA L. GIST, born Helena, Arkansas, August 12, 1957; admitted to bar, 1980, Arkansas; 1982, District of Columbia. *Education:* Memphis State University (B.F.A., magna cum laude, 1977); University of Arkansas (J.D., 1979); George Washington University (LL.M., Corporations, 1982). *Member:* The District of Columbia Bar; Federal Communications Bar Association. ***PRACTICE AREAS:*** Wireless Communications; Cable TV; Trademark Registration. ***Email:*** pgist@fcclaw.com

DAVID A. LaFURIA, born Erie, Pennsylvania, March 20, 1959; admitted to bar, 1985, Pennsylvania; 1989, District of Columbia. *Education:* Temple University (B.A., cum laude, 1981); Catholic University of America (J.D., 1985). *Member:* The District of Columbia Bar; Federal Communications Bar Association. ***PRACTICE AREAS:*** Telecommunications Law; Wireless Communications; Telecommunications Contracts. ***Email:*** dlafuria@fcclaw.com

OF COUNSEL

JOHN J. McAVOY, born Worley, Idaho, June 28, 1933; admitted to bar, 1958, Idaho; 1963, New York; 1976, District of Columbia. *Education:* University of Idaho (B.A., 1954; LL.B., 1958); Yale University (LL.M., 1959). Member, 1982-1988, Vice Chair, 1986-1987 and Chair, 1987-1988, District of Columbia Legal Ethics Committee. Adjunct Professor, American University School of Law, 1990-1991. ***PRACTICE AREAS:*** Civil Litigation; Antitrust; Legal Ethics. ***Email:*** jmcavoy@fcclaw.com

JOSEPH K. HAGE, III, born Utica, New York, October 17, 1950; admitted to bar, 1979, New York; 1985, Alaska (Not admitted in District of Columbia). *Education:* Hamilton College (B.A., 1972); Oxford University, Oxford, England; University of Madrid, Spain; Albany Law School (J.D., 1978). *Member:* Alaska and New York State Bar Associations. (Also Partner, Hage & Hage, L.L.C., Utica, New York). ***PRACTICE AREAS:*** Public Utility Law; Municipal Law; Business Law; Corporate Law; Partnership Law; Estate Planning; Successions.

MARILYN SUCHECKI MENSE, born Brookline, Massachusetts, October 30, 1964; admitted to bar, 1992, Massachusetts; 1995, District of Columbia. *Education:* University of Massachusetts (B.A., magna cum laude, 1988); Universite de Paris Sorbonne, Paris, France; George Washington University (J.D., 1992). *Member:* The District of Columbia Bar; Federal Communications Bar Association. ***PRACTICE AREAS:*** Telecommunications Law; FCC Regulation; FCC Licensing. ***Email:*** mmense@fcclaw.com

PAMELA C. GAARY-HOLRAN, born October 4, 1965; admitted to bar, 1991, Pennsylvania; 1992, Maryland; 1993, District of Columbia. *Education:* Lafayette College (A.B., 1988); George Washington University (J.D., 1991). *Member:* The District of Columbia Bar. ***PRACTICE AREAS:*** Telecommunications Law; FCC Regulation; FCC Licensing. ***Email:*** gaary@fcclaw.com

B. LYNN F. RATNAVALE, born Washington, D.C., October 2, 1967; admitted to bar, 1993, Maryland; 1994, District of Columbia. *Education:* Boston College (B.A., cum laude, 1989); Columbus School of Law of the Catholic University of America (J.D.,1992). *Member:* The District of Columbia Bar; American Bar Association; Federal Communications Bar Association. ***PRACTICE AREAS:*** Wireless Communications; FCC Regulation; FCC Licensing; Cable TV. ***Email:*** lratnavale@fcclaw.com

TODD R. SLAMOWITZ, born Livingston, New Jersey, April 1, 1966; admitted to bar, 1994, Maryland, New Jersey and District of Columbia. *Education:* University of Wisconsin (B.S., 1988); Catholic University of America (J.D., 1994). *Member:* Federal Communications Bar Association. ***PRACTICE AREAS:*** FCC Regulation; FCC Licensing; Telecommunications Law. ***Email:*** tslamowitz@fcclaw.com

DAVID M. BRIGLIA, born Phillipsburg, New Jersey, February 3, 1970; admitted to bar, 1997, Maryland; 2000, District of Columbia. *Education:* Rutgers University (B.A., 1992); University of Maryland (J.D., with honors, 1997). Recipient: Maryland Alumni Association; Course Award for Outstanding Work in Business Associations. Henry Rutgers Scholar. Articles Editor, Maryland Journal of International Law & Trade. Moot Court Board. *Member:* Montgomery County, Maryland State and American (Member, Antitrust and Business Law Sections) Bar Associations. ***PRACTICE AREAS:*** Corporate Law; Business Transactions; Civil Litigation; Securities. ***Email:*** dbriglia@fcclaw.com

ALLISON M. JONES, born Washington, D.C., March 14, 1973; admitted to bar, 1998, Maryland; 2000, District of Columbia. *Education:* Goucher College (B.A., 1995); University of Maryland (J.D., 1998). *Member:* Federal Communications Bar Association. ***PRACTICE AREAS:*** Communications Law; Commercial Transactions. ***Email:*** ajones@fcclaw.com

STEVEN M. CHERNOFF, born Washington, D.C., June 10, 1969; admitted to bar, 1998, Massachusetts; 2000, District of Columbia. *Education:* Colby College (B.A., 1991); Boston College (J.D., 1998). *Member:* Massachusetts and American Bar Associations; Federal Communications Bar Association. ***LANGUAGES:*** Russian, French and Spanish. ***PRACTICE AREAS:*** Telecommunications Law (100%). ***Email:*** schernoff@fcclaw.com

ENGINEERS

ALI KUZEHKANANI, born January 3, 1960. *Education:* George Washington University (B.S.E.E., 1996). ***Email:*** akuzehkanani@fcclaw.com

LeROY A. ADAM, born October 15, 1939. *Education:* United States Military Academy (B.S., 1965); University of Alabama (M.S.E.E., 1972). Eta Kappa

(This Listing Continued)

LUKAS, NACE, GUTIERREZ & SACHS, CHARTERED, Washington—Continued

Nu; Tau Beta Pi. *Member:* Institute of Electrical and Electronics Engineers; Armed Forces Communications-Electronics Association. **Email:** aadam@fcclaw.com

LEILA REZANAVAZ, born March 24, 1963. *Education:* George Mason University (BSEE., 1989); LCC Incorporated Cellular Institute (1994). Eta Kappa Nu; Golden Key. **Email:** lrezanavaz@fcclaw.com

LUMAN, LANGE & WHEELER

1660 L STREET, N.W., SUITE 506

WASHINGTON, D.C. 20036

Telephone: 202-463-1260

Fax: 202-463-6328

Email: LLW1660@aol.com

URL: http://www.lawyers.com/lumanlange&wheeler

Administrative Law, Antitrust, Business Law, Commercial Law, Education, Food and Drug Litigations, Trade and Professional Associations.

MEMBERS OF FIRM

GENE C. LANGE, born Sac City, Iowa, July 31, 1947; admitted to bar, 1973, District of Columbia; U.S. Court of Appeals for the District of Columbia; U.S. Claims Court. *Education:* Iowa State University (B.S., 1969); Georgetown University (J.D., 1972). Member, Charles Fahy Inn of Court. *Member:* The District of Columbia Bar. **PRACTICE AREAS:** Business Law; Commercial Law; Business Immigration Law; Trade and Professional Associations.

CHRISTOPHER WHEELER, born Topeka, Kansas, January 16, 1957; admitted to bar, 1983, District of Columbia; 1989, Maryland; U.S. Court of Appeals, Fourth Circuit, U.S. Claims Court, U.S. District Court, District of Columbia and U.S. District Court, District of Maryland. *Education:* Northwestern University (B.A., 1979); Washington College of Law, American University (J.D., 1982). *Member:* The District of Columbia Bar; Maryland State Bar Association. **PRACTICE AREAS:** Litigation; Government Contracts; Administrative Law; Creditor Bankruptcy Law.

JOHN W. THOMAS, born Carroll, Iowa, October 9, 1949; admitted to bar, 1974, Virginia; 1975, District of Columbia; 1996, U.S. District Court, Eastern District of Virginia. *Education:* Iowa State University (B.S., with honors, 1971); George Washington University National Law Center (J.D., with honors, 1974). Co-Author: Thomas, J. and Terry, M. "Professional Labeling and Animal Drugs," 56 Journal of Association Food & Drug Officials. *Member:* Fairfax Bar Association; District of Columbia Bar; Virginia State Bar; U.S. Animal Health Association; American Veterinary Medical Law Association; American Society of Association Executives. (Also Of Counsel to Dickinson, Mackaman, Tyler & Hagen, P.C.). **PRACTICE AREAS:** Food and Drug Law; Government Relations; Business Law; Trade and Professional Associations.

ASSOCIATE

SEAN P. McMULLEN, born Plainfield, New Jersey, August 3, 1965; admitted to bar, 1990, Virginia; 1991, U.S. District Court, Eastern District of Virginia; 1994, U.S. Bankruptcy Court, Eastern District of Virginia (Not admitted in District of Columbia). *Education:* Harvard University (A.B., 1987); Marshall-Wythe School of Law, College of William & Mary (J.D., 1990). Order of the Coif. *Member:* Virginia State Bar. **PRACTICE AREAS:** Civil Litigation; Employment; Business Law; Creditor Rights; Bankruptcy.

OF COUNSEL

JOSEPH C. LUMAN, born 1936; admitted to bar, 1972, Virginia; 1987, District of Columbia. *Education:* United States Military Academy (B.S., 1958); Georgetown University (J.D., 1972). With Foreign Service Office, U.S. Department of State (Superior Honor Award), 1962-1966. Subcommittee Staff Director, House Government Operations Committee, 1966-1982. District Governor, Toastmasters International, 1975-1976. *Member:* District of Columbia Bar; Virginia State Bar. [With U.S. Army, 1958-1962]. **PRACTICE AREAS:** Association Law; Government Law. **Email:** jcluman@erols.com

LUSE LEHMAN GORMAN POMERENK & SCHICK

A PROFESSIONAL CORPORATION

Established in 1993

5335 WISCONSIN AVENUE, N.W.

SUITE 400

WASHINGTON, D.C. 20015

Telephone: 202-274-2000

Facsimile: 202-362-2902

Email: john@luselaw.com

URL: http://www.luselaw.com

Banking and Financial Institutions, Savings and Loans, Mergers and Acquisitions, Securities and Corporate Law.

ERIC LUSE, born Paris, France, May 15, 1952; admitted to bar, 1978, New York; 1979, District of Columbia. *Education:* University of Paris, Paris, France; Yale University (B.A., cum laude, 1974); Columbia University (M.B.A., 1978); American University (J.D., 1977). Senior Editor, The American University Law Review, 1976-1977. *Member:* District of Columbia Bar; New York State and American (Member, Section of Corporation, Banking and Business Law) Bar Associations. **PRACTICE AREAS:** Banking and Financial Institutions; Mergers and Acquisitions; Securities; Corporate. **Email:** eric@luselaw.com

JOHN J. GORMAN, born Washington, D.C., June 12, 1954; admitted to bar, 1979, New York; 1985, District of Columbia. *Education:* Brown University (B.A., 1976); Vanderbilt University (J.D., 1979). Special Counsel, Office of Chief Counsel, Division of Corporation Finance, 1982-1984. *Member:* District of Columbia Bar; Association of the Bar of the City of New York. **PRACTICE AREAS:** Banking and Financial Institutions; Mergers and Acquisitions; Corporate Law; Securities.

ROBERT B. POMERENK, born Bayshore, New York, March 29, 1958; admitted to bar, 1984, Georgia; 1986, District of Columbia; 1989, New York. *Education:* Georgetown University (B.S.F.S., magna cum laude, 1980); University of Virginia (J.D., 1984). Phi Delta Phi. Member, Editorial Board, Virginia Journal of International Law, 1983-1984. Attorney Advisor, U.S. Securities and Exchange Commission, Division of Corporation Finance, 1989-1991. *Member:* District of Columbia Bar; State Bar of Georgia. **PRACTICE AREAS:** Corporate Finance; Securities; Financial Institutions. **Email:** bobp@luselaw.com

KENNETH R. LEHMAN, born Manheim, Pennsylvania, January 26, 1959; admitted to bar, 1987, Arizona; 1989, District of Columbia. *Education:* Temple University (B.B.A., magna cum laude, 1982); Hastings College of Law, University of California (J.D., 1987); Georgetown University (LL.M., with distinction, 1991). Staff Attorney, U.S. Securities and Exchange Commission, Division of Corporation Finance, 1988-1992. *Member:* District of Columbia Bar; State Bar of Arizona. **PRACTICE AREAS:** Securities; Corporate.

ALAN SCHICK, born Brooklyn, New York, July 21, 1959; admitted to bar, 1984, New York; 1988, District of Columbia. *Education:* State University of New York at Buffalo (B.A., magna cum laude, 1980); Suffolk University Law School (J.D., 1983); Georgetown University Law Center (LL.M., Securities Regulation, 1987). Staff Attorney, Securities and Exchange Commission, 1986-1988; Attorney Advisor, Department of Transportation, Office of General Counsel, 1983-1986. *Member:* District of Columbia Bar; New York State and American (Member, Section of Business Law) Bar Associations. **PRACTICE AREAS:** Corporate Law; Securities Law; Mergers and Acquisitions; Financial Institutions.

BEVERLY WHITE, born El Paso, Texas, September 1, 1954; admitted to bar, 1984, Virginia; 1985, District of Columbia; 1991, Maryland. *Education:* University of Houston (B.S., 1976); National Law Center, George Washington University (J.D., with honors, 1984); Georgetown University (M.L., Taxation, 1990). Attorney Advisor, U.S. Treasury Department, Office of Tax Policy, Office of Tax Legislative Counsel, 1986-1987. *Member:* District of Columbia Bar; Virginia State Bar; Maryland State Bar Association. **PRACTICE AREAS:** Employee Benefits; Taxation; Executive Compensation; Business Planning and Transactions; Tax-Exempt Organizations.

ROBERT I. LIPSHER, born New Haven, Connecticut, October 29, 1951; admitted to bar, 1977, Connecticut; 1980, District of Columbia. *Education:* Clark University (B.A., 1973); University of Connecticut (J.D., magna cum laude, 1977). Member, Board of Editors, Connecticut Law Review, 1976-1977. Counsel to Commissioner, 1982-1983 and Staff Attorney, 1977-1982, Securities and Exchange Commission. *Member:* The District of Columbia Bar; American Bar Association (Member, Section on Corporation, Banking and Business Law). **Email:** bobl@luselaw.com

EDWARD A. QUINT, born Washington, D.C., July 22, 1969; admitted to bar, 1995, Maryland; 1996, District of Columbia. *Education:* Duke University (B.A., 1991); Vanderbilt University (J.D., 1995). *Member:* Maryland State Bar

(This Listing Continued)

Association; District of Columbia Bar. **PRACTICE AREAS:** Corporate Financing Law; Financial Institutions Law; Securities. **Email:** ned@luselaw.com

LUXENBERG, JOHNSON & DICKENS, P.C.

1244 19TH STREET, N.W.
WASHINGTON, D.C. 20036
Telephone: 202-265-3340
Fax: 202-265-0101
Email: counsel@luxlaw.com
URL: http://www.lawyers.com/luxenbergjohnsondickens

Family Law, Domestic Relations, Gay and Lesbian Family Law, Divorce, Separation, Custody Litigation, Child Support, Adoption, Prenuptial and Marital Agreements, Family Law Mediation, Spousal Abuse, Domestic Violence, Probate, Estate Planning, Family Trusts, Wills, Employment Law (Employee Representation and Advice and Counsel to Management), Employment Discrimination, Wrongful Termination, Business Law, Nonprofit Organizations Law, Chancery and Equity, Federal Civil Practice, Litigation.

FIRM PROFILE: The firm represents individuals, families, small to medium-sized corporations, family businesses and non-profit organizations in Washington, D.C., Virginia, Maryland and other jurisdictions.

DEBORAH LUXENBERG, born 1949; admitted to bar, 1974, Pennsylvania; 1975, District of Columbia; 1982, Maryland. *Education:* Case Western Reserve University (B.A.); Catholic University of America (J.D.). ***PRACTICE AREAS:*** Family Law; Domestic Relations; Gay and Lesbian Family Law; Divorce; Child Custody; Adoption Law; Spousal Abuse; Domestic Violence; Family Mediation. ***Email:*** dluxenberg@luxlaw.com

STEPHEN D. JOHNSON, born 1944; admitted to bar, 1976, Virginia; 1978, District of Columbia. *Education:* University of Washington (B.A., 1968); George Washington University (J.D., 1976). ***PRACTICE AREAS:*** Family Law; Domestic Relations; Gay and Lesbian Family Law; Divorce; Child Custody; Adoption Law; Wills; Probate; Estate Planning; Employment Law; Business Law; Nonprofit Organizations Law. ***Email:*** sjohnson@luxlaw.com

DORRANCE D. DICKENS, born Gulfport, Mississippi, January 20, 1958; admitted to bar, 1996, District of Columbia. *Education:* State University of New York at Albany (B.A., 1988); Mississippi College (J.D., 1996). Phi Alpha Delta. ***PRACTICE AREAS:*** Family Law; Domestic Relations; Gay and Lesbian Family Law; Divorce; Child Custody; Adoption Law; Wills; Probate; Estate Planning; Employment Law; Wrongful Termination. ***Email:*** ddickens@luxlaw.com

LYON & LYON LLP

A Limited Liability Partnership including Professional Corporations
Established in 1919
SUITE 1040, 1701 PENNSYLVANIA AVENUE, N.W.
WASHINGTON, D.C. 20006
Telephone: 202-331-3600
Fax: 202-331-3301
Email: lyon@lyonlyon.com
URL: http://www.lyonlyon.com

Los Angeles, California Office: Suite 4700, 633 West Fifth Street, 90071-2066. Telephone: 213-489-1600.

Irvine, California Office: Sixth Floor, 1900 Main Street, 92614. Telephone: 949-567-2300. Fax: 949-567-6600.

San Jose (Silicon Valley), California Office: Suite 800, 333 West San Carlos Street, 95110. Telephone: 408-993-1555. Fax: 408-287-2664.

La Jolla, California Office: Suite 800, 4225 Executive Square, 92037. Telephone: 858-552-8400. Fax: 858-552-0159.

White Plains, New York Office: Suite 1500, 1 North Lexington Avenue, 10601. Telephone: 914-681-8851. Fax: 914-686-4488.

Intellectual Property, Patents, Trademarks, Copyrights, Technology and Science, Trade Secrets, Unfair Competition, Antitrust, Biomedical Devices, Chemical Compositions, Electrical Devices, Electronic Devices, Mechanical Devices, Biotechnology, Computers and Software, Internet Law, Internet Trademark Law, Software Copyright, Software Licensing, Software Protections, Franchises and Franchising, Patent Litigation, Trademark Litigation, Copyright Litigation, Patent Prosecution, Patents Reexaminations, Patent Reissues, Patent Interferences, Patent Appeals, Trademark Prosecution, Trademark Oppositions, Trademark Appeals, Artistic Design Protections, Trade Dress Protection, International Trade Commission, Intellectual Property Licensing, Technology Transfer, Intellectual Property Audits, Intellectual Property Portfolio Management, Intellectual Property Planning, Intellectual Property Opinion Letters and Intellectual Property General Counseling.

RESIDENT PARTNER

JAMES T. CARMICHAEL, born Chicago, Illinois, April 1, 1962; admitted to bar, 1987, Wisconsin and California; 1990, U.S. Court of Appeals for the Federal Circuit; 1993, U.S. Supreme Court (Not admitted in District of Columbia). *Education:* Yale University (B.A., 1984); University of Wisconsin (J.D., cum laude, 1987); George Mason University (Electrical and Computer Engineering, 1996). Judicial Law Clerk to the Honorable Chief Judge Markey, U.S. Court of Appeals for the Federal Circuit, 1990-1991. Administrative Patent Judge, Board of Patent Appeals and Interferences, 1996-1999. *Member:* American Bar Association (Chair, Intellectual Property Law Committee on Inventors, 1995); American Intellectual Property Law Association. ***REPORTED CASES:*** Recreative Techs. Corp., 95-1337, U.S. Court of Appeals for the Federal Circuit, 83 F.3d 1394, (1996); Aktiebolaget Astra v. Lehman, 94-1388, U.S. Court of Appeals for the Federal Circuit, 71 F.3d 1578 (1995); Gurley, 94-1025, U.S. Court of Appeals for the Federal Circuit, 27 F.3d 551 (1994); Donaldson Co., 91-1386, U.S. Court of Appeals for the Federal Circuit, 16 F.3d 1189 (1994); Gerritsen v. Shoji Shirai, 91-1480, U.S. Court of Appeals for the Federal Circuit, 979 F.2d 1524 (1992); Franchi v. Manbeck, 92-1085, U.S. Court of Appeals for the Federal Circuit, 972 F.2d 1283 (1992); Hallmark Cards, Inc. v. Lehman, Civil Action No. 95-318 SSH, U.S. District Court for the District of Columbia, 959 F. Supp. 539 (1997). ***PRACTICE AREAS:*** Patents; Trademarks; Copyrights; Appellate Practice; Computer Law; Intellectual Property. ***Email:*** jtcarmichael@lyonlyon.com

RESIDENT ASSOCIATE

ROUGET F. HENSCHEL, born New York, N.Y., May 23, 1959; admitted to bar, 2000, Virginia and District of Columbia; registered to practice before U.S. Patent and Trademark Office. *Education:* City College of the City University of New York (B.S., 1981; Ph.D., 1990); Georgetown University Law Center (J.D., 2000). *Member:* Virginia Bar Association; District of Columbia Bar; American Intellectual Property Law Association; Patent and Trademark Office Society. ***LANGUAGES:*** German, French and Spanish. ***PRACTICE AREAS:*** Intellectual Property; Pro Bono. ***Email:*** rfhenschel@lyonlyon.com

RESIDENT OF COUNSEL

SCOTT H. BLACKMAN, born Jenkintown, Pennsylvania, January 30, 1960; admitted to bar, 1989, New York and U.S. District Court, Southern and Eastern Districts of New York; 1992, U.S. Supreme Court; 1997, District of Columbia; U. S. Court of Appeals for the Federal Circuit; registered to practice before U.S. Patent and Trademark Office. *Education:* Philadelphia College of Pharmacy and Science (B.S., Chemistry, 1981; M.S., Medicinal Chemistry, 1984); Cornell University Law School (J.D., cum laude, 1988). Law Clerk to the Honorable S. Jay Plager, U.S. Court of Appeals for the Federal Circuit, 1990-1992. *Member:* New York State and American Bar Associations; Federal Circuit Bar Association; American Intellectual Property Law Association; American Chemical Society. ***PRACTICE AREAS:*** Intellectual Property; Licensing; Litigation and Prosecution. ***Email:*** shblackman@lyonlyon.com

SUET M. CHONG, born Hong Kong, June 29, 1966; admitted to bar, 1991, District of Columbia; registered to practice before U.S. Patent and Trademark Office. *Education:* University of Maryland (B.S. in Chemistry and Economics, cum laude, 1988); George Washington University (J.D., 1991). Phi Beta Kappa; Phi Kappa Phi. *Member:* The District of Columbia Bar; American Bar Association. ***LANGUAGES:*** Cantonese. ***PRACTICE AREAS:*** Patent Prosecution; Litigation; Licensing. ***Email:*** smchong@lyonlyon.com

(For Complete Biographical Data on all Personnel, see Professional Biographies at Los Angeles, California).

MACLEAY, LYNCH, GREGG & LYNCH, P.C.

Established in 1946
SUITE 1150
1629 K STREET, N.W.
WASHINGTON, D.C. 20006
Telephone: 202-785-0123
FAX: 202-393-3390
Email: maclmac@aol.com

General Civil Practice in all Courts and Agencies. General Insurance Defense Practice, Subrogations, Workers Compensation, ERISA, Automobile, Medical and Professional Liability.

FIRM PROFILE: Macleay, Lynch, Gregg & Lynch was founded in 1946 by Donald Macleay and Hugh Lynch, Jr. The firm of fourteen individuals including legal support personnel has grown through the years to become one of Washington D.C.'s best known insurance defense law firms. The hallmark of this firm's success has been its continuous representation of certain insurance carriers since 1946. The firm's insurance defense work has drawn special focus in the areas of ERISA, automobile, professional liability, toxic torts and defense of self-insureds.

The firm is listed in the Martindale-Hubbell Bar Register of Preeminent Lawyers.

DONALD MACLEAY (1908-1994).

(This Listing Continued)

MACLEAY, LYNCH, GREGG & LYNCH, P.C., Washington—Continued

HUGH LYNCH, JR. (1913-1994).

JOHN C. LYNCH, born Washington, D.C., January 11, 1952; admitted to bar, 1979, District of Columbia; 1994, Maryland. *Education:* Lafayette College (B.A., 1974); St. Mary's University (J.D., 1979). Phi Delta Phi. *Member:* The District of Columbia Bar; Maryland State Bar Association, Inc.; Federation of Insurance and Corporate Counsel; Defense Research Institute; District of Columbia Defense Lawyers Association. ***PRACTICE AREAS:*** Insurance Defense; ERISA; Medical and Professional Liability; Product Liability Defense.

ROBERT P. LYNCH, born Washington, D.C., August 10, 1958; admitted to bar, 1985, Pennsylvania; 1988, District of Columbia. *Education:* Villanova University (B.A., 1981); St. Mary's University (J.D., 1985). *Member:* The District of Columbia Bar; Pennsylvania Bar Association. ***PRACTICE AREAS:*** Insurance Liability Defense; Automobile; Subrogation.

ROBERT G. McGINLEY, born Queens, New York, August 18, 1962; admitted to bar, 1988, Maryland, District of Columbia, U.S. District Court, District of Maryland, U.S. District Court, District of Columbia and U.S. Court of Federal Claims. *Education:* University of Scranton (B.A., magna cum laude, 1984); Catholic University of America, Columbus School of Law (J.D., 1987). *Member:* Maryland State Bar Association; The District of Columbia Bar. ***PRACTICE AREAS:*** Insurance Defense.

JAMES C. GREGG, born Ebensburg, Pennsylvania, December 26, 1924; admitted to bar, 1950, District of Columbia; 1953, Virginia. *Education:* George Washington University (LL.B., 1950). *Member:* Bar Association of the District of Columbia; The District of Columbia Bar; Virginia State Bar; District of Columbia Defense Lawyers Association; Virginia Association of Defense Attorneys; Northern Virginia Defense Lawyers Association; Defense Research Institute. ***PRACTICE AREAS:*** Insurance Defense; Architectural and Engineering Law; Insurance Liability.

JACK DAVID LAPIDUS, born Paterson, New Jersey, April 5, 1969; admitted to bar, 1994, Virginia; 1995, Maryland and District of Columbia. *Education:* Rutgers University (B.A., 1991); George Washington University (J.D., 1994). *Member:* Virginia Bar Association. ***PRACTICE AREAS:*** Insurance Defense.

BRETT SCHOEL, born 1971; admitted to bar, 1999, Virginia and Maryland; 2001, District of Columbia. *Education:* University of Maryland (B.A., 1996); George Washington University Law School (J.D., 1999). *Member:* The District of Columbia Bar; Virginia State Bar.

REPRESENTATIVE CLIENTS: Avis Rent-A-Car Systems, Inc.; American International Underwriters; Bakers Life & Casualty; Benefits Trust Co.; CNA Insurance; Continental Insurance Co.; Dominion Bank; Fireman's Fund-American Group; First American Bank; Florists Insurance Co.; Foremost Insurance Co.; Fremont Indemnity Co.; Jefferson Insurance Co.; Keystone Insurance Co.; Liberty Mutual Insurance Co.; MNC Financial, Inc.; Marriott Corporation; Massachusetts General Life Insurance Co.; Metropolitan Life Insurance Co.; National General Insurance Co.; Nautilis Insurance Co.; Northland Insurance Co.; PCM Intermediaries, Ltd.; Prudential Property & Casualty Co.; Reliance Insurance Group; Stonewall Insurance Co.; Transamerica Insurance Group; The Travelers Insurance Co.; Underwriters Adjusting Co.; United Capitol Insurance Co.

MURDAUGH STUART MADDEN AND ROGER A. KINDLER

2100 L STREET, N.W.
WASHINGTON, D.C. 20037
Telephone: 202-833-3360
Fax: 202-778-6126
URL: http://www.lawyers.com/madden-kindler

Tax Exempt Organizations, Wills, Trusts and Estate Law, Wealth Preservation, Immigration Law, International Law.

MURDAUGH STUART MADDEN, born Morgantown, West Virginia, February 26, 1922; admitted to bar, 1948, District of Columbia; 1949, Virginia; 1953, U.S. Supreme Court. *Education:* Oberlin College; George Washington University (B.A., 1942); Harvard University Law School (J.D., 1948). Author, "The Legal Status and Problems of the American Abroad," *The Annals of the American Academy of Political and Social Science,* Philadelphia, Vol. 368, November, 1966. Associate Counsel, Navy Bureau of Aeronautics, 1948-1950. General Counsel, 1958-1990 and Senior Counsel, 1990—, The Humane Society of the United States. Partner, Shaw, Pittman, Potts, Trowbridge & Madden, 1961-1971. Trustee: Institute for Study of National Behavior, Princeton, New Jersey, 1965—; Friends of India Committee, Washington, D.C., 1967—. Vice President, World Society for the Protection of Animals, London, Zurich and Boston, 1979—. *Member:* District of Columbia Bar; Bar Association of the District of Columbia (Chairman, Committees on: Legal Ethics, 1965-1966; Ethics Revision, 1970; Director, 1966-1968); Virginia State Bar; American Bar Association (Chairman, Committee on International Transportation, International and Comparative Law Section, 1968-1971; Chairman, Sub-Committee on Charitable Organizations, Committee on International Property, Estate and Trust Law, Section on International Law Practice, 1984—); Barristers.

(This Listing Continued)

ROGER A. KINDLER, born Wichita, Kansas, January 2, 1950; admitted to bar, 1975, District of Columbia; 1987, Maryland. *Education:* Harvard University (A.B., 1971); Kings College, Cambridge University, England; Georgetown University (J.D., 1975). Associate General Counsel, 1981-1990 and General Counsel, 1990—, The Humane Society of the United States. *Member:* District of Columbia Bar; Maryland State and American Bar Associations; American Immigration Lawyers Association; American Corporate Counsel Association.

MAGGIO & KATTAR, P.C.

Established in 1982

ELEVEN DUPONT CIRCLE, N.W., SUITE 775
WASHINGTON, D.C. 20036
Telephone: 202-483-0053
FAX: 202-483-6801
Email: inquire@maggio-kattar.com
URL: http://www.maggio-kattar.com

Immigration and Nationality Law. Business and Employment Immigration Law.

FIRM PROFILE: Maggio & Kattar, P.C. represents individuals, corporations, and other institutions from across the nation and around the world on all matters related to United States immigration and nationality law. The firm specializes in employment-based cases for executives, scientists, physicians, computer professionals and other highly skilled foreign workers; waivers of the two-year foreign residence requirements for physicians and other exchange visitors; H-1B specialty worker, E-2 investor and L-1 international executive visas; employment certification from the Department of Labor as well as permanent resident status without labor certification or a job offer; defending corporations from charges of knowingly employing unauthorized workers; complex deportation cases, appeals, and federal immigration litigation. The firm is listed in the Martindale-Hubbell Bar Register of Preeminent Lawyers.

MICHAEL MAGGIO, born Philadelphia, Pennsylvania, March 21, 1947; admitted to bar, 1978, District of Columbia; U.S. District Court for the District of Columbia; U.S. Court of Appeals for the District of Columbia Circuit; U.S. Court of Appeals, Third, Fourth, Sixth and Ninth Circuits; 1998, U.S. Supreme Court. *Education:* Georgetown University; Temple University (B.A., 1971); Antioch School of Law (J.D., 1978). Author: "Extreme Hardship For Waivers of Inadmissibility" (with S. Sivaprasad) 21st Annual Immigration Law Update (Florida Bar Association, 2000); "J-1 Waivers for Physicians -The Current State of the Art?" Immigration and Nationality Law, Advanced Practice (AILA, 1999). Co-Author: "The Truth About Immigration Lies," 20th Annual Immigration Law Update (Florida Bar Association, 1999); "Basic Ethical Issues in Labor Certification Cases", Strategic Lawyering: Guiding Business Personnel Through the Minefields Toward Permanent Residency (AILA, 1998): "Qualifying Occupations for H-1B Status," 18th Annual Immigration Law Update (Florida Bar Association, 1997); "International Medical Graduates," (with E. Quinn), Immigration Law and Procedure (Matthew Bender, 1997); "Interested Government Agency Waivers For Physicians," (with E. Quinn), Immigration Options for Doctors, Robert Aronson and George S. Newman, eds. (AILA, April 1995); "Understanding J-1 Visas: When And Why Employers Should Avoid Them," Immigration Law Reports, June, 1994; "When An Immigrant Does Not Assume the Certified Job, the 'Materiality' of Good Intentions," 1994 Immigration Law Update (New York State Bar Association, 1994); "Ethics and Grounds of Excludability - How to Resolve Common Complexities in Preparing Immigration Documents," (with E. Lichtman), Immigration and Nationality Law Handbook Vol. II Advanced Practice (AILA, 1994); "Current Options and Strategies for Obtaining J-1 Waivers," (with A. Brown), Exceptions To The Rule: Winning INA Waivers, Ellen Ma Lee, ed. (AILA 1994); "Changes in Deportation Process: Limits on Discretion," Handbook On The Immigration Act Of 1990, P. Schmidt, ed. (AILA, 1991); "Some Significant Problems in Sanctions Cases," Hiring Foreign Personnel; Immigration Problems And Solutions, D. Sabagh & A. Novick, eds., (AILA, 1988); "Trial Strategies in Immigration Judge Proceedings," Immigration & Nationality Law, Vol. II, R. Juceam & E. Rubin, eds., (AILA, 1987); "Labor Certifications for Domestic Workers," (with C. Kattar), 12 Immigration Newsletter 18 (NLG. 1983); "BIA Appeals: What to Do and Expect," Asylees & Refugees: Strategies for Representation, (NLG, 1982). Adjunct Professor, Immigration Law, American University's Washington College of, 1994—. Chair, INS Central Office Liaison Committee, 1988. Co-Chair, Employment Authorization Committee, 1989-1990. Trustee, NLG Immigration Project, American Immigration Law Foundation. *Member:* District of Columbia Bar; American Immigration Lawyers Association. ***LANGUAGES:*** Spanish. ***PRACTICE AREAS:*** Immigration and Nationality Law. ***Email:*** mmaggio@maggio-kattar.com

(This Listing Continued)

ALISON J. BROWN, born Andrews Air Force Base, Maryland, February 7, 1961; admitted to bar, 1986, Maryland (Not admitted in District of Columbia). *Education:* University of Georgia (B.A., magna cum laude, 1982); American University, Washington College of Law (J.D., 1986). Phi Beta Kappa. Recipient, Judge Horace B. Russell Prize. Author: "Current Options and Strategies for Obtaining J-1 Waivers," (with M. Maggio), Exceptions to the Rule: Winning INA Waivers, Ellen Ma Lee, ed. (AILA, 1994). *Member:* Maryland State and American Bar Associations; American Immigration Lawyers Association. ***LANGUAGES:*** Spanish. ***PRACTICE AREAS:*** Immigration and Nationality Law. ***Email:*** abrown@maggio-kattar.com

ELIZABETH A. QUINN, born Oceanside, New York, March 28, 1966; admitted to bar, 1993, Virginia (Not admitted in District of Columbia). *Education:* College of William & Mary (B.A., 1988); George Washington University (J.D., 1993). Author, "International Medical Graduates," (with M. Maggio), in Immigration Law and Procedure (Matthew Bender, 1997); "Interested Government Agency Waivers For Physicians," (with M. Maggio), Immigration Options for Doctors (AILA, April 1995). *Member:* Virginia State Bar; American Bar Association; American Immigration Lawyers Association. ***LANGUAGES:*** French. ***PRACTICE AREAS:*** Immigration and Nationality Law. ***Email:*** equinn@maggio-kattar.com

ANDRES CAYETANO BENACH, born Mt. Kisco, New York, July 26, 1972; admitted to bar, 1999, New York (Not admitted in District of Columbia). *Education:* Boston College (B.A., 1994); George Washington University (J.D., 1998). Co-Author: "Keeping Battered Noncitizens in the U.S. Until Permanent Residency," with Cyrus Menta, 77 Interpreter Releases 225 (Feb. 28, 2000). Author: "Effective Mehta Advocacy Through Private Immigration Bills," Third Annual New York Chapter Immigration Law Symposium, December 2000: "Asylum Research on the Internet: How to Get Started," Second Annual New York Chapter Immigration Law Symposium, December 1999. Director, Legislative Advocacy Efforts, New York Chapter of the American Immigration Lawyers Association. *Member:* New York State Bar Association; Association of the Bar of the City of New York; American Immigration Lawyers Association. ***LANGUAGES:*** Spanish. ***PRACTICE AREAS:*** Immigration Law. ***Email:*** acbenach@maggio-katter.com

SHOBA SIVAPRASAD, born Dayton, Ohio, January 2, 1975; admitted to bar, 2000, Maryland and New Jersey (Not admitted in District of Columbia). *Education:* Indiana University (B.A., with honors, Political Science, 1996); Georgetown University Law Centre (J.D., 1999). Recipient, William Bryant Prize for Best Senior Thesis in Political Science, 1996; Research Grant, South Africa Public Int. Law Association, 1997.Co-Author: "Extreme Hardship for Waivers of Inadmissibility," with Michael Maggio, *21st Annual Immigration Law Update,* Florida Bar Association. *Member:* Maryland State and New Jersey State Bar Associations; American Bar Association; American Immigration Lawyers Association; National Lawyers Guild Association. ***PRACTICE AREAS:*** Immigration Law; Nationality Law. ***Email:*** ssivaprasad@maggio-kattar.com

JOHN C. MAGINNIS, III

1350 CONNECTICUT AVE., N.W., SUITE 301
WASHINGTON, D.C. 20036
Telephone: 202-659-4420
Fax: 202-775-2463
Email: maginnisdclaw@msn.com

Family Law, Divorce, Custody, Adoption, Visitation, Marital Property, Estate Planning, Wills, Probate, Trusts, Personal Injury, Auto Accidents, Medical Malpractice, Orthopedic Malpractice, Family Business Law, Business Formation, Small Business Litigation.

FIRM PROFILE: Mr. Maginnis has practiced law as a courtroom attorney for over 25 years. His firm represents individuals, families, and businesses from Metropolitan Washington, D.C., Northern Suburban Virginia and Southern Suburban Maryland.

JOHN C. MAGINNIS, III, born Baltimore, Maryland, August 24, 1948; admitted to bar, 1974, District of Columbia; 1978, Virginia; 1984, Maryland. *Education:* University of Michigan (B.B.A., 1970; J.D., 1973). *Member:* The District of Columbia Bar Association; Virginia State Bar Association ; Maryland State Bar Association. ***PRACTICE AREAS:*** Family Law; Estate Planning; Probate; Personal Injury; Medical Malpractice; Business Law.

LAW OFFICES OF GERALD A. MALIA

1660 L STREET, NW
SUITE 506
WASHINGTON, D.C. 20036
Telephone: 202-639-8000
Fax: 202-463-6328
URL: http://www.lawyers.com/malialaw
General Practice.

GERALD A. MALIA, born Blakely, Pennsylvania, August 6, 1933; admitted to bar, 1959, District of Columbia. *Education:* St. Peter's College (B.S., 1954); Georgetown University (J.D., 1958; LL.M., 1959). Phi Delta Phi. Editor, Georgetown Law Journal, 1958. Author: "Maritime Law: The Need for a Comprehensive Maritime Code," Associated Faculty Press, 1983. Adjunct Professor of Maritime Law and Customs Law , Georgetown University Law Center, 1973—. Visiting Professor, World Maritime University, Malmo, Sweden, 1992—. Lecturer, Catholic University Law School, 1979—. *Member:* The District of Columbia Bar; The Bar Association of the District of Columbia; American Bar Association; Maritime Law Association; Maritime Administrative Bar Association (President, 1973-1974).

MALIZIA SPIDI & FISCH, PC

1100 NEW YORK AVENUE, N.W.
SUITE 340 WEST
WASHINGTON, D.C. 20005
Telephone: 202-434-4660
Facsimile: 202-434-4661
Email: mail@malizialaw.com
URL: http://www.malizialaw.com

State College, Pennsylvania Office: 637 Kennard Road, 16801. Telephone: 814-466-6625. Fax: 814-466-6703.

Financial Institutions, Securities, Corporate, Business Start-ups, Employee Benefits, ERISA, Taxation, Business Law. Practice before Federal and State Regulatory Agencies including Securities and Exchange Commission, Office of Thrift Supervision, Federal Deposit Insurance Corporation, Office of the Comptroller of the Currency, Federal Reserve Board, Internal Revenue Service and state banking agencies.

FIRM PROFILE: Malizia Spidi & Fisch, PC ("MS&F") is headed by Samuel J. Malizia, John J. Spidi and Richard Fisch who have collectively concentrated in representing financial institutions for approximately 50 years. Attorneys at the firm have over 90 years experience in the representation of financial institutions, and are actively involved in a broad range of sophisticated transactional and regulatory matters for financial institutions located throughout the country. Attorneys at the firm are members of the District of Columbia, Florida, Texas, Pennsylvania, Ohio, Massachusetts, Maryland and California bars and the Bar of the United States Supreme Court.

The practice includes representing financial institutions, investment bankers, corporations, individuals, and groups in connection with mergers and acquisitions, regulatory and enforcement proceedings, holding company reorganizations, debt and equity offerings, reporting requirements under the Securities Exchange Act of 1934, and executive compensation and employee benefit programs.

SAMUEL J. MALIZIA, born New Castle, Pennsylvania, May 27, 1954; admitted to bar, 1979, District of Columbia; 1980, U.S. Tax Court, U.S. Claims Court and U.S. Court of Appeals for the District of Columbia Circuit; 1996, Pennsylvania. *Education:* Pennsylvania State University (B.S., with distinction, 1976); George Washington University (J.D., 1979). Beta Alpha Psi; Omicron Delta Kappa. Member: Skull and Bones Honor Society; The Lion's Paw. Associate Editor, The Tax Lawyer, 1979-1980. Attorney Advisor to Special Trial Judge Francis J. Cantrel, U.S. Tax Court, 1978-1980. *Member:* The District of Columbia Bar; Pennsylvania, Federal and American Bar Associations; Conference on Consumer Finance Law. ***PRACTICE AREAS:*** Securities; Banking; Corporate; Tax. ***Email:*** malizia@malizialaw.com

JOHN J. SPIDI, born Boston, Massachusetts, June 24, 1957; admitted to bar, 1982, Massachusetts; 1985, District of Columbia; 1986, U.S. Supreme Court. *Education:* Northeastern University (B.A., with honors, 1979); New England School of Law (J.D., cum laude, 1982). Recipient, American Jurisprudence Book Award. Member, 1980-1981 and Research Editor, 1981-1982, New England Law Review. *Member:* The District of Columbia Bar. ***PRACTICE AREAS:*** Securities; Corporate; Banking. ***Email:*** spidi@malizialaw.com

RICHARD FISCH, born Queens, New York, August 9, 1957; admitted to bar, 1985, Maryland; 1986, District of Columbia. *Education:* Cornell University (B.S.I.L.R., 1979; M.B.A., 1980); Georgetown University (J.D., 1984). *Mem-*

(This Listing Continued)

MALIZIA SPIDI & FISCH, PC, Washington—Continued

ber: The District of Columbia Bar; Maryland State and American Bar Associations. ***PRACTICE AREAS:*** Securities; Banking; Corporate; Tax; Employee Benefits. ***Email:*** fisch@malizialaw.com

FELICIA C. BATTISTA, born Washington, D.C., July 14, 1950; admitted to bar, 1993, Pennsylvania; 1999, District of Columbia and U.S. Supreme Court; practice limited to federal agencies. *Education:* George Washington University (B.B.A., 1973); Catholic University (J.D., 1992). Certified Public Accountant, Washington, D.C., 1986. ***PRACTICE AREAS:*** Securities; Corporate; Banking. ***Email:*** battista@malizialaw.com

DANIEL H. BURD, born Berkeley, California, May 11, 1954; admitted to bar, 1983, California; 1987, District of Columbia. *Education:* Stanford University (A.B., 1976); University of California at Los Angeles (M.A., 1978); University of Chicago (J.D., 1983). Attorney, Legal Division, Federal Reserve Board, 1983-1986. *Member:* American Bar Association. ***PRACTICE AREAS:*** Banking Law; Corporate Law. ***Email:*** burd@malizialaw.com

---

TIFFANY A. HENRICKS, born Washington, D.C., September 20, 1972; admitted to bar, 1998, California; 1999, District of Columbia. *Education:* University of California at San Diego (B.A., 1994); Washington College of Law American University (J.D., 1998). ***PRACTICE AREAS:*** Securities; Corporate; Banking. ***Email:*** henricks@malizialaw.com

EVAN M. SEIGEL, born Silver Spring, Maryland, January 1, 1968; admitted to bar, 1993, Maryland; 1994, District of Columbia. *Education:* Indiana University (B.S., 1989); Duquesne University (J.D., 1992); New York University (LL.M., Taxation, 1993). Certified Public Accountant, Maryland, 1996. *Member:* District of Columbia Bar; Maryland State Bar Association. ***PRACTICE AREAS:*** Securities; Banking; Corporate; Tax; Employee Benefits. ***Email:*** seigel@malizialaw.com

JENNIFER E. MARTELLA, born San Diego, California, November 6, 1971; admitted to bar, 1999, District of Columbia. *Education:* University of California at Santa Barbara (B.A., with honors, 1993); Catholic University of America (J.D., 1998). ***PRACTICE AREAS:*** Securities; Corporate; Banking. ***Email:*** martella@malizialaw.com

RACHEL E. MALKIN

WASHINGTON, D.C.

(See Bethesda, Maryland)

Technology Law, Contracts, Licensing, Electronic Commerce, Websites and Domain Names, Privacy, Marketing, Consulting Services and Employment. Internet Law, Emerging Business Law, Small Business Law.

KEITH R. MALLEY, P.C.

WASHINGTON, D.C.

(See Arlington, Virginia)

Business Law, Corporate Law, Technology and Science, Labor and Employment, Government Contracts, Nonprofit and Charitable Organizations.

MALONEY & MOHSEN

4201 CONNECTICUT AVENUE, SUITE 404
WASHINGTON, D.C. 20008-1129
Telephone: 202-237-6800
Fax: 202-966-5270
http://www.mmlegal.com
Email: partners@mmlegal.com
URL: http://www.lawyers.com/maloney&mohsen

Civil Litigation Law and Litigation, Communications Law, Contracts, Labor and Employment Law, Wrongful Termination, Civil Rights, Commercial Landlord and Tenant Law, Professional Liability, Legal Ethics and Professional Responsibility, Medical Malpractice, Child Sexual Abuse Litigation, Personal Injury, Automobile Accidents and Injuries, Products Liability, Criminal Defense, White Collar Crime, Alcoholic and Beverage Control.

FIRM PROFILE: Partners Maloney and Mohsen have combined 26 years of civil and criminal trial experience to provide quality legal counsel to businesses and individuals from the Washington Metropolitan area.

MEMBERS OF FIRM

JAMES T. MALONEY, born Cheverly, Maryland, December 7, 1953; admitted to bar, 1978, District of Columbia; 1978, U.S. District Court, District of Columbia and U.S. Court of Appeals, District of Columbia Circuit; 1980, U.S. Court of Military Appeals; U.S. Court of Appeals, Fifth Circuit; U.S. District Court, District of Maryland. *Education:* University of Maryland (A.B., with honors, 1974); George Washington University (J.D., 1978). *Member:* District of Columbia Bar; Bar Association of the District of Columbia (Member, Criminal Law Section); The Association of Trial Lawyers of America. ***PRACTICE AREAS:*** General Practice. ***Email:*** verdict@bellatlantic.net

ARYA A. MOHSEN, born Washington, D.C., October 23, 1968; admitted to bar, 1994, District of Columbia, U.S. District Court, District of Columbia and U.S. District Court, District of Maryland. *Education:* Bowdoin College (A.B., 1990); Syracuse University (J.D., 1993). *Member:* District of Columbia Bar; Bar Association of the District of Columbia; The Association of Trial Lawyers of America. ***LANGUAGES:*** Farsi (Persian). ***Email:*** mohsen@worldnet.att.net

MANATT, PHELPS & PHILLIPS, LLP

A Limited Liability Partnership including Professional Corporations
Established in 1965
1501 M STREET, N.W., SUITE 700
WASHINGTON, D.C. 20005-1702
Telephone: 202-463-4300
FAX: 202-463-4394
Email: mpp@manatt.com
URL: http://www.manatt.com

Los Angeles, California Office: Trident Center, East Tower, 11355 West Olympic Boulevard. Telephone: 310-312-4000. Fax: 310-312-4224.
Palo Alto, California Office: 1001 Page Mill Road, Building 2. Telephone: 650-812-1300. Fax: 650-213-0260.
Sacramento, California Office: 1215 K Street, Suite 1900. Telephone: 916-552-2300. Fax: 916-552-2323.
Costa Mesa, California Office: 12th Floor, Center Tower, 650 Town Center Drive. Telephone: 714-371-2500. Fax: 714-371-2550.

LITIGATION: Civil Trial Practice in all Courts; Class Action Defense; Energy and Natural Resources; Entertainment; General Commercial; Health Care; Insurance; Intellectual Property; Labor and Employment; National and International Arbitration; Mediation and Preventive Law; Securities; Special Investigations and White-Collar Defense. BUSINESS, FINANCE and REAL ESTATE: Banking and Financial Services; Bankruptcy and Reorganization; Corporate Finance and Securities; Electronic Commerce and Telecommunications; Executive Compensation and Employee Benefits; Real Estate; Tax; Venture Capital and Private Equity. ENTERTAINMENT, MEDIA and INTELLECTUAL PROPERTY: Internet and New Media; Motion Picture and Television; Music; Technology. GOVERNMENT and INTERNATIONAL TRADE and POLICY: Domestic and International Government Affairs; Election and Campaign Law; Global Business Strategies; Government Contracts; International Trade and Customs; Land Use, Energy and Environmental; Latin America and China Advisory; Legislative and Regulatory Advocacy; Political, Economic and Business Risk Assessment.

FIRM PROFILE: Manatt, Phelps & Phillips, LLP is recognized as one of the most influential professional services firms headquartered in the United States, with preeminent capabilities in industries including technology, entertainment, media, financial services, e-commerce, energy and natural resources and health. Approaching 300 professionals in six offices, Manatt provides legal and strategic consulting services to domestic and international clients in the new and traditional economies. For more information on Manatt's services, professionals and business focus, please visit our website or call any of our offices for information.

MEMBERS OF FIRM

CHARLES T. MANATT, (P.C.), admitted to bar, 1962, California; 1967, U.S. Supreme Court; 1985, District of Columbia. *Education:* Iowa State University (B.S., 1958); George Washington University (J.D., 1962).

JUNE LANGSTON (WALTON) DEHART, born Camp Stewart, Georgia, November 14, 1952; admitted to bar, 1981, Mississippi; 1982, District of Columbia. *Education:* Millsaps College (B.A., with honors, 1974); Mississippi College (J.D., with distinction, 1981).

MICHAEL B. ADLIN, born Philadelphia, Pennsylvania, May 17, 1965; admitted to bar, 1991, Pennsylvania; 1993, District of Columbia. *Education:* Duke University (A.B., 1987); Boston University School of Law (J.D., 1991).

JONATHAN E. ALLEN, admitted to bar, 1998, Virginia (Not admitted in District of Columbia). *Education:* University of North Carolina at Chapel Hill (B.A., 1994); University of Virginia (J.D., 1997).

IRWIN P. ALTSCHULER, born Washington, D.C., September 28, 1950; admitted to bar, 1975, Maryland; 1977, District of Columbia; 1980, U.S. Court of Federal Claims; 1981, U.S. Court of International Trade; 1983, U.S. Court of Appeals for the Federal Circuit. *Education:* George Washington University (B.A., 1972); University of Maryland (J.D., 1975).

(This Listing Continued)

DAVID R. AMERINE, born Columbus, Ohio, May 23, 1953; admitted to bar, 1978, District of Columbia; 1979-1982, U.S. Court of Customs and Patent Appeals; 1982, U.S. Court of International Trade and U.S. Court of Appeals for the Federal Circuit. *Education:* Marietta College (B.A., 1975); Catholic University of America (J.D., 1978); Georgetown University (LL.M. in International Law, 1981).

BARRIE D. BERMAN, born New Hyde Park, New York, December 31, 1960; admitted to bar, 1987, Virginia; 1988, District of Columbia; 1990, U.S. Court of Appeals for the District of Columbia Circuit; 1991, U.S. Court of Appeals, Fourth Circuit. *Education:* Johns Hopkins University (B.A., 1983); Washington University, St. Louis (J.D., 1986).

JACK W. BUECHNER, born St. Louis, Missouri, June 4, 1940; admitted to bar, 1965, Missouri, U.S. District Court, Eastern and Western Districts of Missouri and U.S. Court of Appeals, Eighth Circuit; 1998, District of Columbia. *Education:* St. Benedict's College (A.B., 1962); St. Louis University (J.D., 1965).

STEPHEN E. CORAN, admitted to bar, 1986, Virginia; 2001, District of Columbia and U.S. Court of Appeals, District of Columbia Circuit. *Education:* Miami University (B.S., 1983; B.A., 1983); Washington College of Law of American University (J.D., 1986).

DONALD J. FITZGERALD (Also at Los Angeles and Palo Alto, California Offices).

GREGORY A. GEHLMANN, admitted to bar, 1988, Ohio; 1991, District of Columbia; 2000, U.S. Supreme Court. *Education:* University of Dayton (B.A., 1984); The Ohio State University (M.A., 1985; J.D., 1988).

MARY ANN GILLEECE, born Effingham, Illinois, September 3, 1940; admitted to bar, 1972, Massachusetts; 1978, U.S. Supreme Court; 1982, U.S. Court of Federal Claims; 1991, District of Columbia. *Education:* University of Connecticut (B.A., 1962); Suffolk University (J.D., 1972).

JAMES R. JONES, born Muskogee, Oklahoma, May 5, 1939; admitted to bar, 1964, District of Columbia and Oklahoma. *Education:* University of Oklahoma (A.B., 1961); Georgetown University (LL.B., 1964).

ROBERT J. KABEL, born Burbank, California, November 30, 1946; admitted to bar, 1972, Tennessee; 1973, Ohio; 1979, District of Columbia; 1998, U.S. Supreme Court. *Education:* Denison University (B.A., 1969); Vanderbilt University (J.D., 1972); Georgetown University (LL.M., in Taxation, 1979).

STEVEN A. LANCELLOTTA, admitted to bar, 1982, District of Columbia; U.S. Court of Appeals, District of Columbia Circuit. *Education:* University of Rhode Island (B.A., 1979); George Washington University (J.D., 1982).

LIZBETH R. LEVINSON, born May 11, 1956; admitted to bar, 1982, District of Columbia; 1983, Virginia; 1984, U.S. Court of Appeals, District of Columbia; 1985, Court of International Trade; 1986, Court of Appeals, Federal Circuit. *Education:* Wellesley College (B.A., magna cum laude, 1978); Georgetown University (J.D. , 1981). ***LANGUAGES:*** French.

ABBE DAVID LOWELL, born New York, N.Y., April 28, 1952; admitted to bar, 1977, New York; 1981, District of Columbia; 1983, Maryland; U.S. District Court for the District of Columbia; U.S. Court of Appeals, District of Columbia Circuit; U.S. District Court, District of Maryland; U.S. Court of Appeals, 4th Circuit; U.S. Supreme Court. *Education:* Columbia University (B.A., magna cum laude, 1974; J.D., 1977).

PAMELA J. MARPLE, admitted to bar, 1991, Wisconsin; 1999, District of Columbia. *Education:* University of Virginia (B.A., 1986); University of Wisconsin (J.D., 1991). ***PRACTICE AREAS:*** Litigation. **Email:** pjmarple@manatt.com

MARYLIN JENKINS MILNER, born Philadelphia, Pennsylvania, July 22, 1950; admitted to bar, 1979, California; 1985, District of Columbia; 1991, New York; 2000, Texas. *Education:* Wellesley College (B.A., 1972); Loyola Law School, Los Angeles (J.D., 1979); Colorado School of Mines (Certificate in Refinery Processes and Economics, 1996).

STEPHEN L. NEAL JR., admitted to bar, 1994, District of Columbia. *Education:* Duke University (A.B., 1989); University of North Carolina at Chapel Hill (J.D., 1993).

JEFFREY S. NEELEY, born Valparaiso, Indiana, April 12, 1953; admitted to bar, 1979, District of Columbia. *Education:* Northwestern University (B.A., 1975); George Washington University (J.D., with honors, 1979).

B. MICHAEL RAUH, born Washington, D.C., July 11, 1936; admitted to bar, 1961, Virginia and District of Columbia. *Education:* University of Michigan (A.B., 1958); University of Virginia (LL.B., 1961); Georgetown University (LL.M., 1967).

JOHN L. RAY, born Toms Creek, Georgia, May 16, 1943; admitted to bar, 1975, District of Columbia, U.S. District Court for the District of Columbia and U.S. Court of Appeals for the District of Columbia Circuit. *Education:* George Washington University (B.A., 1970; J.D., with honors, 1973).

(This Listing Continued)

STEVEN F. REICH, born New York, N.Y., June 5, 1961; admitted to bar, 1987, New York; 1988, District of Columbia. *Education:* Columbia University (B.A., 1983; J.D., 1986).

ROBERT J. RINI, admitted to bar, 1986, District of Columbia, U.S. District Court, District of Columbia and U.S. Court of Appeals, District of Columbia Circuit. *Education:* State University of New York at Albany (B.A., 1982); Catholic University of America (J.D., 1985).

JAMES H. ROBERTS III, born Omaha, Nebraska, August 11, 1949; admitted to bar, 1974, Iowa; 1981, District of Columbia; 1982, U.S. District Court for the District of Columbia; 1989, U.S. Court of Federal Claims and U.S. Court of Appeals for the Federal Circuit; U.S. Supreme Court. *Education:* University of Notre Dame (B.A., 1971); Saint Louis University (J.D., cum laude, 1974).

STEPHEN M. RYAN, born New York, N.Y., April 19, 1955; admitted to bar, 1980, Pennsylvania; 1991, District of Columbia; U.S. Supreme Court; U.S. Court of Appeals for the District of Columbia and Seventh Circuits. *Education:* Cornell University (B.S., 1977); University of Notre Dame (J.D., cum laude, 1980).

SUSAN M. SCHMIDT, admitted to bar, 1983, Illinois; 1986, California; 1988, District of Columbia. *Education:* University of Wisconsin-Madison (B.A., 1979); Boston University School of Law (J.D., 1982); Foreign Service Institute, Washington, D.C. (Professional Diploma, Economic and Commercial Studies, 1996).

DONALD S. STEIN, born Philadelphia, Pennsylvania, October 28, 1953; admitted to bar, 1981, District of Columbia; 1982, U.S. Court of International Trade, U.S. District Court for the District of Columbia and U.S. Court of Appeals for the District of Columbia; 1983, U.S. Court of Appeals for the Federal Circuit; 1985, U.S. Supreme Court. *Education:* George Washington University (B.A., 1976; M.A., 1979); American University (J.D., 1981); Hebrew University of Jerusalem.

JESSICA A. WASSERMAN, born Chicago, Illinois, February 24, 1959; admitted to bar, 1985, Michigan; 1986, District of Columbia; 1989, U.S. Court of International Trade; 1991, U.S. Court of Appeals for the Federal Circuit. *Education:* St. John's College (B.A., cum laude, 1981); University of Michigan (J.D., 1984).

OF COUNSEL

DAVID G. O'NEIL, admitted to bar, 1987, Pennsylvania; 1988, District of Columbia; U.S. Court of Appeals, District of Columbia Circuit. *Education:* Syracuse University (B.A., 1984); Washington College of Law of American University (J.D., 1987).

RONALD M. WISLA, admitted to bar, 1983, District of Columbia. *Education:* State University of New York at Binghamton (B.A., 1979); George Washington University (J.D., with honors, 1982).

RESIDENT ASSOCIATES

MICHAEL T. BROWN, admitted to bar, 1998, Virginia; 2001, District of Columbia. *Education:* College of William & Mary (B.A., 1990); George Mason University School of Law (J.D., with honors, 1998).

JULIE A. CAMPBELL, admitted to bar, 1998, Virginia (Not admitted in District of Columbia). *Education:* Ohio State University (B.A., magna cum laude, 1995); Georgetown University (J.D., 1998).

LINDSEY W. COOPER, admitted to bar, 2000, Tennessee (Not admitted in District of Columbia). *Education:* American University (B.A., 1997); Washington College of Law of American University (J.D., 2000).

ANDREW N. GENTIN, admitted to bar, 1997, New Jersey; 1998, District of Columbia. *Education:* Amherst College (B.A., 1990); Georgetown University (J.D., 1996).

THEODORE W. JONES, admitted to bar, 1998, California (Not admitted in District of Columbia). *Education:* Vanderbilt University (B.A., 1994); Southern Methodist University (J.D., 1998).

STEPHANIE J. KIM, admitted to bar, 1998, Maryland; 1999, U.S. District Court, Southern District of Maryland and U.S. Court of International Trade; 2001, District of Columbia. *Education:* College of William & Mary (B.A., 1990); George Mason University School of Law (J.D., 1998).

DAVID A. LEIB, admitted to bar, 1997, Maryland; 1998, U.S. Court of Federal Claims and U.S. District Court, District of Maryland; 2001, District of Columbia. *Education:* Miami University (B.A., 1994); University of Maryland (J.D., 1997).

KIMBERLY LINCOLN-STEWART, admitted to bar, 1990, Pennsylvania; 1991, District of Columbia; 1997, Maryland. *Education:* Hampton University (B.A., 1983); Howard University (J.D., 1990).

SARAH J. LOOPE, admitted to bar, 2001, Michigan (Not admitted in District of Columbia). *Education:* Michigan State University (B.A., 1998); University of Michigan (J.D., 2000).

(This Listing Continued)

MANATT, PHELPS & PHILLIPS, LLP, Washington—Continued

RUEL B. PILE, admitted to bar, 1991, Pennsylvania; 1993, Florida; 1994, District of Columbia. *Education:* Western New England College (B.A., 1988); Suffolk University (J.D., 1991); Georgetown University (LL.M., Taxation, 1993).

HOLLY A. ROTH, admitted to bar, 1995, Virginia; 1997, District of Columbia and U.S. District Co urt, Eastern District of Virginia. *Education:* Scripps College (B.A., 1978); University of Illinois (M.B.A., 1980); Washington College of Law of American University (J.D., cum laude, 1995).

SARAH E. STEPHENS, admitted to bar, 1993, Virginia; 1994, District of Columbia. *Education:* Princeton University (A.B., 1988); George Washington University (J.D., 1993).

JAMES A. TARTAL, admitted to bar, 1997, Pennsylvania; 1998, Massachusetts and Maryland; 2001, District of Columbia. *Education:* Johns Hopkins University (B.S., 1993; M.S.E., 1994); Boston College (J.D., 1997).

CHRISTINE H. T. YANG, admitted to bar, 1997, Illinois; 2000, District of Columbia; U.S. Court of Appeals, Federal Circuit and U.S. Court of International Trade. *Education:* University of Michigan (B.A., 1994); University of Illinois (J.D., 1997).

E. LAWRENCE ZOLT, admitted to bar, 1986, Maryland; 1990, District of Columbia. *Education:* Miami University (B.A., 1982); University of Maryland (J.D., 1985).

(For complete Biographical Data on all Personnel, see Professional Biographies at Los Angeles, Palo Alto, Sacramento and Costa Mesa, California)

MANELLI, DENISON & SELTER, P.L.L.C.

2000 M STREET, N.W.
SUITE 700
WASHINGTON, D.C. 20036-3307
Telephone: 202-261-1000
Fax: 202-887-0336
URL: http://www.mdslaw.com

Intellectual Property, Internet Law, Venture Capital.

FIRM PROFILE: Manelli, Denison & Selter, P.L.L.C. provides litigation, counseling, intellectual property prosecution strategies and opinions, and legislative services to domestic and multinational clients that include electronics and telecommunications equipment manufacturers, software firms, makers of pharmaceuticals, medical devices, automotive equipment, foods, beverages and specialty chemicals, trade associations, express couriers, aviation insurers, ocean and non-vessel common carriers, and marine terminal and cruise ship operators.

DANIEL J. MANELLI, born Burlington, Iowa, 1935; admitted to bar, 1962, Illinois; 1963, District of Columbia; 1976, U.S. Supreme Court. *Education:* University of Notre Dame (B.S., 1957; LL.B., 1962). Member, Notre Dame University Law Review, 1961-1962. Trial Attorney, Federal Trade Commission, 1962-1965. Staff Attorney, Special Subcommittee to Investigate the Department of Health, Education and Welfare, House Commerce Committee, 1965-1966. Legal Counsel, Office of State Technical Services, U.S. Department of Commerce, 1966-1967. Staff Attorney, 1967-1972 and Chief Counsel, 1972-1975, Special Subcommittee on Investigations, House Commerce Committee. Vice President, Legal Affairs, The Proprietary Association, 1975-1978. *Member:* Bar Association of the District of Columbia; Federal Bar Association. ***PRACTICE AREAS:*** Food, Drug and Cosmetic Law; Administrative Law; Legislative Law. ***Email:*** dmanelli@mdslaw.com

MARY BONEY DENISON, born Wilmington, North Carolina, 1956; admitted to bar, 1982, New York; 1983, U.S. District Court, Southern and Eastern Districts of New York; 1984, U.S. Court of Appeals, Second Circuit; 1988, District of Columbia, U.S. Court of Appeals for the District of Columbia Circuit and U.S. District Court for the District of Columbia; 1993, U.S. Court of Appeals, Eleventh Circuit; 1994, U.S. Court of Appeals, Fourth Circuit. *Education:* University of Paris IV-Sorbonne, Paris, France (1976-1977); Duke University (A.B., 1978); University of North Carolina (J.D., 1981). Phi Delta Phi. Articles Editor, North Carolina Journal of International Law and Commercial Regulation, 1980-1981. Co-Editor: *Nouveau Guide de l'Implementation aux Etats-Unis,* 1989. *Member:* American Bar Association; International Trademark Association (Vice-Chair, Treaty Analysis Committee). ***LANGUAGES:*** French. ***PRACTICE AREAS:*** Intellectual Property; Trademarks; Copyrights; Commercial Litigation. ***Email:*** mdenison@mdslaw.com

MICHAEL H. SELTER, born New York, New York, 1949; admitted to bar, 1975, Pennsylvania, District of Columbia, U.S. Court of Appeals, Third Circuit and U.S. Court of Appeals for the District of Columbia Circuit; 1980, U.S. Court of Appeals for the Federal Circuit; 1982, U.S. Court of Appeals, Tenth Circuit; 1984, U.S. Court of Appeals, Seventh Circuit; 1985, U.S. Court of Appeals, Ninth Circuit; 1986, U.S. Court of Appeals, Fifth Circuit; 1987, U.S. Court of Appeals, Fourth Circuit; 1988, U.S. Supreme Court; 1989, U.S. Court of Appeals, Sixth Circuit. *Education:* Brown University (A.B., cum laude, 1970); University of Pennsylvania (J.D., magna cum laude, 1974). Sigma Xi. Order of the Coif. Recipient, G. Newton Greene Prize, Torts. Editor, University of Pennsylvania Law Review, 1973-1974. Author: "Selecting Forums for Dispute, Special Report on Commercial Litigation," The Legal Times, October 23, 1995; "Abuse of the Grand Jury Process," Handbook on Grand Jury Investigations," ABA, Section on Antitrust Law (2 ed. 1988). Co-Author: "Do the Sale and Manufacture of Replacement Parts Infringe The Original Equipment Manufacturer's Patent and Trademark Rights?" Intellectual Property Today, December 1999; "Filibuster Halts Product Liability Reform Act," Korean Business News, July 1994; "Getting Your Accident Case Into Federal Court," Aviation Litigation News, June 1994; "Protecting Rights in Intellectual Property," (published in French), French-American Chamber of Commerce, Nouveau Guide de l'Implementation Aux Unis (1989). Visiting Professor, University of Iowa Law School, 1979. Law Clerk to Hon. Max Rosenn, U.S. Court of Appeals, Third Circuit, 1974-1975. *Member:* American Bar Association (Member, Sections on: Litigation; Tort and Insurance Practice, Intellectual Property). ***PRACTICE AREAS:*** Litigation; Appellate Practice; Intellectual Property Litigation. ***Email:*** mselter@mdslaw.com

ELIOT J. HALPERIN, born New York, New York, 1940; admitted to bar, 1965, New York; 1973, District of Columbia. *Education:* Hobart College (B.A., cum laude, 1962); Harvard University (J.D., 1965); New York University (LL.M., in International Law, 1966). Phi Beta Kappa. Legal Assistant to Commissioner and Vice-Chairman, Federal Maritime Commission, 1967-1977. Chairman, Water Transportation Law Committee, Federal Bar Association, 1974-1976. President, Maritime Administrative Bar Association, 1981-1982. *Member:* Bar Association of the District of Columbia; Maritime Administrative Bar Association. ***PRACTICE AREAS:*** Transportation Law; Maritime Law; Legislation; Administrative Law. ***Email:*** ehalperin@mdslaw.com

JEFFREY SCOTT MELCHER, born Pottstown, Pennsylvania, 1961; admitted to bar, 1991, Wisconsin, District of Columbia and U.S. Court of Appeals for the Federal Circuit; registered to practice before U.S. Patent and Trademark Office. *Education:* University of Wisconsin (B.S., Chemistry and Mathematics, 1984); Marquette University Law School (J.D., cum laude, 1991). *Member:* Bar Association of the District of Columbia; State Bar of Wisconsin; Federal Circuit and American Bar Associations; American Intellectual Property Law Association. ***PRACTICE AREAS:*** Patent Litigation; Patent Prosecution; Patent Infringement; Intellectual Property. ***Email:*** melcher@mdslaw.com

WILLIAM H. BOLLMAN, born Plainfield, New Jersey, 1960; admitted to bar, 1993, Maryland; 1994, District of Columbia and U.S. Court of Appeals for the Federal Circuit; registered to practice before U.S. Patent and Trademark Office. *Education:* University of Delaware (B.E.E., 1982); Clemson University (M.E.E.E., 1987); George Washington University (J.D., 1993). *Member:* Maryland State and American Bar Associations; Bar Association of the District of Columbia; American Intellectual Property Law Association; Industrial Designers Society of America. ***PRACTICE AREAS:*** Patent Prosecution; Litigation; Design Patents; Trade Secrets; Trademarks; International Trade; Alternative Dispute Resolution; Electronic Patents; Telecommunications; Internet Law; Computers and Software; Medical Patents. ***Email:*** bollman@mdslaw.com

EDWARD J. STEMBERGER, born Cleveland, Ohio, 1963; admitted to bar, 1991, Ohio; 1992, District of Columbia and U.S. Court of Appeals for the Federal Circuit; registered to practice before U.S. Patent and Trademark Office. *Education:* University of Dayton (B.M.E., 1986); Cleveland-Marshall College of Law, Cleveland State University (J.D., 1991). Tau Beta Pi. *Member:* Bar Association of the District of Columbia. ***PRACTICE AREAS:*** Intellectual Property; Patent Prosecution; Design Patents. ***Email:*** stemberger@mdslaw.com

STUART E. BENSON, born Whittier, California; admitted to bar, 1972, California; 1973, District of Columbia. *Education:* University of California at Berkeley (A.B., 1966); Boalt Hall School of Law, University of California (J.D., 1972). Deputy Assistant Secretary of Commerce for Trade Agreements, 1980-1981. Attorney Adviser and Deputy Assistant Legal Adviser for Economic and Business Affairs, U.S. Department of State, 1976-1980. Professorial Lecturer in Law, The National Law Center, The George Washington University, 1982-1984. *Member:* The District of Columbia Bar (Member, Steering Committee, International Law Section, 1987-1989); State Bar of California; American and International Bar Associations. ***LANGUAGES:*** Italian and French. ***PRACTICE AREAS:*** Trademarks; International Trade. ***Email:*** sbenson@mdslaw.com

W. WARREN TALTAVULL III, born Washington, D.C., July 26, 1943; admitted to bar, 1971, District of Columbia. *Education:* Catholic University of America (B.A., 1966); George Washington University (J.D., 1971). *Member:* The District of Columbia Bar; Bar Association of the District of Columbia; American Intellectual Property Law Association. ***Email:*** wtaltavull@mdslaw.com

LEON R. TURKEVICH, born March 26, 1962; admitted to bar, 1991, Maryland; 1993, District of Columbia and U.S. Court of Appeals for the Federal Circuit; registered to practice before U.S. Patent and Trademark Office. *Educa-*

(This Listing Continued)

tion: University of Maryland (B.S.E.E., 1985); George Washington University (J.D., with honors, 1991). Tau Beta Pi; Eta Kappa Nu. Lecturer: "Dealing with Computer Hardware, Software and Information Services Technology," Virginia CLE High Tech Legal Forum, January 1994. Author, "In re Alappat: The End of 'Mathematical Algorithm' Confusion?" The Computer Lawyer, Vol. 11, No. 9 (Sept. 1994), reprinted in Intellectual Property News Report (Japanese), Vol. 8, Nos. 9-10 (Sept.-Oct., 1994); "An End to the 'Mathematical Algorithm'Confusion? In re Alappat," European Intellectual Property Review, Vol. No. 2 (Feb. 1995). Contributing Author, Donner, Patent Prosecution: Practice and Procedure before the U.S. Patent Office (1996). *Member:* American Bar Association; American Intellectual Property Law Association. ***PRACTICE AREAS:*** Patent Law. ***Email:*** lturkevich@mdslaw.com

PAUL E. WHITE, JR., born Washington, D.C., December 2, 1949; admitted to bar, 1983, Massachusetts; 1984, District of Columbia; registered to practice before U.S. Patent and Trademark Office. *Education:* University of Maryland (B.S., 1971); Clemson University (M.S., 1972); Suffolk University (J.D., 1983). Staff Member, The Advocate, 1982-1983. Instructor, Patent, Trademark and Copyright Law, The George Washington University, 1988-1996. Author and Speaker: Legal Protection for Bioinformatics Technology, 4th Annual Conference on Computational Genomics, Baltimore, Maryland, November, 2000; Adding Commercial Value Through Legal Protection for Your Genomics/ Bioinformatics Technology, Seminar by Virginia Biotechnology Association and Virginia Centers for Innovative Technology, November 2000; Panel Discussion on Strategic Management of Intellectual Property, Maryland Bioscience Forum 2000, October 2000; Patent Protection for Drugs, Biologics and Biotechnology, Annual Conference of the Regulatory Affairs Professionals Society, October 2000; Legal Protection for Genomics/Bioinformatics Technology, Seminar by Northern Virginia Technology Council and Virginia Biotechnology Association, June, 2000. *Member:* The District of Columbia Bar; Massachusetts, Federal Circuit and American (Member, Sections of: Business Law; Patent, Trademark and Copyright Law) Bar Associations; American Intellectual Property Law Association; American Chemical Society. ***PRACTICE AREAS:*** Patent Procurement; Intellectual Property; Patents; Management Labor Law; Commercial. ***Email:*** pwhite@mdslaw.com

GEORGE A. QUADRINO, born Yonkers, New York, 1945; admitted to bar, 1971, District of Columbia; 1981, U.S. Surpreme Court; 1992, U.S. Court of Appeals, Third Circuit. *Education:* Bridgewater Stage College (B.S., 1968); Georgetown University Law Center (J.D., 1971); University of London, UK, (LL.M, International Economic Law, 1972). Notes Editor, "Law and Policy in International Business," Georgetown. Co-Author: *Federal Restrictions Affecting Investment in the Maritime Industries*, District of Columbia Bar, 1980, 1981; Editor: Survey of Maritime Administrative Law, 1992. President, Maritime Administrative Bar Association, 1993-1994. *Member:* District of Columbia and Maritime Administrative (President, 1993-1994) Bar Associations. ***PRACTICE AREAS:*** Maritime Law; Administrative Law; Transportation Regulation. ***Email:*** gquadrino@mdslaw.com

OF COUNSEL

DEANA E. ROSE, born Washington, D.C., 1951; admitted to bar, 1976, Kentucky; 1977, District of Columbia. *Education:* University of Kentucky (B.A., with distinction, 1973); Louis D. Brandeis School of Law, University of Louisville (J.D., 1975). Phi Beta Kappa. Guest Lecturer: U.S. Army Transportation School, Ft. Eustis, Virginia, 1976-1977. Senior Trial Attorney, Federal Maritime Commission, 1976-1983. *Member:* Bar Association of the District of Columbia; Kentucky Bar Association; Maritime Administrative Bar Association. ***PRACTICE AREAS:*** Administrative Law; Admiralty and Maritime Law; Transportation Law; Litigation. ***Email:*** drose@mdslaw.com

MANN BRACKEN, LLC

SUITE 360 CHEVY CHASE PAVILLION
5335 WISCONSIN AVENUE, N.W.
WASHINGTON, D.C. 20015
Telephone: 202-274-2140
Facsimile: 202-686-9709
Email: skramer@mannbracken.com
URL: http://www.mannbracken.com

Atlanta, Georgia Office: Suite 700 Peachtree Center International Tower, 229 Peachtree Street, N.E. Telephone: 404-586-0500. Facsimile: 404-586-0638.

General Civil and Business Litigation, Commercial and Bankruptcy Law. Retail and Commercial Collection Law, Alimony and Child Support Collection Law, Domestic Relations and Family Law, Personal Injury Law. Trials in all State and Federal Courts.

(For Complete Biographical Information on all personnel, see Professional Biographies at Atlanta, Georgia)

MARGOLIUS, MALLIOS, DAVIS, RIDER & TOMAR, LLP

1828 L STREET, N.W., SUITE 500
WASHINGTON, D.C. 20036
Telephone: 202-296-1000
Fax: 202-296-6400
Email: info@mmdrt.com
URL: http://www.lawyers.com/mmdrt

Largo, Maryland Office: 9200 Basil Court, Suite 300, 20774. Telephone: 301-925-4900. Fax: 301-925-9752.

Alexandria, Virginia Office: 120 South Fairfax Street, Suite 300, 22314.

General Civil Practice, Estate Planning and Probate, Matrimonial and Family Law, Personal Injury, Commercial and Residential Landlord and Tenant Law, Negligence and Medical Malpractice, General Civil Commercial Litigation, Real Estate Transactions, Alcoholic Beverage Law, before Courts, Agencies and Departments in the District of Columbia, Maryland and Virginia.

JAMES L. RIDER, born Newburgh, New York, February 11, 1942; admitted to bar, 1966, New York; 1971, District of Columbia and U.S. Supreme Court; 1972, Virginia. *Education:* Lafayette College (B.A., 1963); Fordham University (J.D., 1966). [With JAGC, U.S. Army, 1967-1971]. (Also at Alexandria, Virginia). ***PRACTICE AREAS:*** Family Law; Mediation. ***Email:*** jrider@mmdrt.com

DIMITRI P. MALLIOS, born Wilkes-Barre, Pennsylvania, April 15, 1932; admitted to bar, 1960, District of Columbia; 1964, Maryland; 1966, U.S. District Court, District of Maryland; 1982, U.S. Court of Appeals for the Federal Circuit. *Education:* George Washington University (B.A., 1954; LL.B., 1960). (Also at Largo, Maryland). ***PRACTICE AREAS:*** Liquor Licensing; Alcoholic Beverages; Hospitality Law; Business Law. ***Email:*** dmallios@mmdrt.com

PHILIP N. MARGOLIUS, born Washington, D.C., September 24, 1940; admitted to bar, 1966, District of Columbia; 1978, Maryland. *Education:* Dartmouth College (B.A., 1962); Yale University (LL.B., 1965). *Member:* American Bar Association. (Also at Largo, Maryland). ***PRACTICE AREAS:*** Probate and Estate Planning; Real Estate; Commercial Transactions. ***Email:*** pmargolius@mmdrt.com

RICHARD T. TOMAR, born Camden, New Jersey, March 4, 1945; admitted to bar, 1971, District of Columbia and New Jersey; 1976, Maryland. *Education:* Columbia College (B.A., 1967); University of Pennsylvania (J.D., 1970). Lecturer: "How to Win a Business Jury Trial," ABA National Institute, 1992-1993; National College of Advocacy, Georgetown University Law Center; Bank Administration Institute. (Also at Largo, Maryland). ***PRACTICE AREAS:*** Litigation; Family Law. ***Email:*** rtomar@mmdrt.com

GARY A. STEIN, born New Orleans, Louisiana, November 9, 1948; admitted to bar, 1980, District of Columbia; 1981, Maryland. *Education:* Georgetown University (B.S.F.S., 1970; J.D., cum laude, 1980); University of Iowa (M.F.A., 1972). Cases and Notes Editor, The Tax Lawyer, 1979-1980. Author: "Whose Fault is No Fault: A Guide to the New D.C. Law," District Lawyer, March/April, 1984; "Son of No-Fault," The Washington Lawyer, Nov./Dec., 1987. *Member:* The District of Columbia Bar; Maryland State Bar Association; The Association of Trial Lawyers of America. (Also at Largo, Maryland). ***PRACTICE AREAS:*** Personal Injury; Negligence; Medical Malpractice. ***Email:*** gstein@mmdrt.com

SHARON M. GOLEY, born Suffern, New York, October 12, 1962; admitted to bar, 1989, Virginia; 1991, District of Columbia and U.S. District Court, Eastern District of Virginia; 1992, U.S. Court of Appeals, 4th Circuit. *Education:* University of Charleston (B.A., 1984); Washington College of Law of American University (J.D., 1989). *Member:* The Association of Trial Lawyers of America; District of Columbia Women's Bar Association. ***PRACTICE AREAS:*** Commercial Litigation; Residential and Commercial Landlord-Tenant Law; Employment Law. ***Email:*** sgoley@mmdrt.com

SUSAN M. BUTLER, born Waterbury, Connecticut, January 10, 1966; admitted to bar, 1992, Connecticut; 1994, U.S. District Court, District of Connecticut; 1995, Virginia; 1997, District of Columbia and Maryland. *Education:* Mount Holyoke College (A.B., 1988); Catholic University of America (J.D., 1992). Recipient, American Jurisprudence Award in Alternative Dispute Resolution. *Member:* Fairfax Bar Association; Virginia State Bar; The District of Columbia Bar. ***PRACTICE AREAS:*** Family Law. ***Email:*** sbutler@mmdrt.com

LAURA G. MOLDOWAN, born Washington, D.C., February 10, 1964; admitted to bar, 1994, Florida; 1995, Virginia; 1996, District of Columbia. *Education:* Virginia Polytechnic Institute and State University (B.S., cum laude, 1986); University of Florida (J.D., 1994). Certified Public Accountant, 1987. *Member:* The District of Columbia Bar; Virginia State Bar; The Florida Bar. ***PRACTICE AREAS:*** Estate Planning; Estate Administration; Business Planning. ***Email:*** lmoldowan@mmdrt.com

(This Listing Continued)

MARGOLIUS, MALLIOS, DAVIS, RIDER & TOMAR, LLP, Washington—Continued

CHERYL K. GRAHAM, born Silver Spring, Maryland, May 6, 1967; admitted to bar, 1992, Virginia (Not admitted in District of Columbia). *Education:* George Mason University (B.A., 1989); Catholic University of America (J.D., 1992). *Member:* Fairfax County and American (Member, Adoption Committee) Bar Associations; Virginia State Bar; Virginia Bar Association (Co-Chair, Family Court Committee, 1996); Virginia Trial Lawyers Association. ***PRACTICE AREAS:*** Domestic Relations; Mediation. ***Email:*** cgraham@mmdrt.com

JENNIFER M. BARHAM, born Washington, D.C., December 29, 1970; admitted to bar, 1999, Maryland (Not admitted in District of Columbia). *Education:* University of Maryland (B.A., 1992); Washington College of Law of American University (J.D., 1999). ***Email:*** jbarham@mmdrt.com

MELISSA POLITO, born Washington, Pennsylvania, November 28, 1969; admitted to bar, 1995, Maryland; 1997, District of Columbia. *Education:* Ohio Wesleyan University (B.A., 1992); George Washington University (J.D., 1995). Member: Montgomery County Bar Association, 1998; Maryland State Bar Association, Inc., 1995; Womens Bar Association of D.C., 1997. ***PRACTICE AREAS:*** Litigation; Family Law. ***Email:*** mpolito@mmdrt.com

HARVEY J. COHEN, born Brooklyn, New York, April 21, 1973; admitted to bar, 1998, Connecticut; 1999, New York, Maryland and District of Columbia. *Education:* Binghamton University (B.A., 1995); University of Miami School of Law (J.D., 1998); Washington College of Law, American University (LL.M., 1999). Phi Delta Phi. *Member:* Maryland State and American Bar Associations; New York County Lawyers Association. ***PRACTICE AREAS:*** Real Estate; Real Estate Title Insurance; Commercial Transactions. ***Email:*** hcohen@mmdrt.com

STEPHEN C. LEWIS, born Bellingham, Washington, September 12, 1973; admitted to bar, 2000, Virginia (Not admitted in District of Columbia). *Education:* University of Washington (B.A., 1997); The George Washington University (J.D., 2000). *Member:* Virginia State Bar; American Bar Association. ***PRACTICE AREAS:*** Estate Administration (75%); Estate Planning (10%); Tax Law (10%); Corporate Law (5%). ***Email:*** slewis@mmdrt.com

LARGO, MARYLAND OFFICE

Angelia Merritt Gates ***Alyssa W. Chang***

OF COUNSEL

EUGENE G. HOROWITZ, born Washington, D.C., February 8, 1936; admitted to bar, 1961, District of Columbia. *Education:* George Washington University (B.A., 1958; J.D., 1961). Phi Delta Phi; Order of the Coif; Omicron Delta Kappa. Research Editor, George Washington Law Review, 1959-1960. Lecturer in Law (Estate Planning Seminar), George Washington University Law School, 1970-1977. ***PRACTICE AREAS:*** Commercial Transactions; Federal Income, Estate and Gift Taxation; Estate Planning; Probate; Real Estate.

EDWARD L. WEIDENFELD, born Akron, Ohio, July 15, 1943; admitted to bar, 1968, New York; 1970, U.S. District Court, Southern District of New York; 1976, District of Columbia; 1982, U.S. Court of Appeals, District of Columbia and U.S. Supreme Court; 1986, U.S. Claims Court; 1998, Maryland and U.S. Court of Appeals Fourth Circuit. *Education:* University of Wisconsin (B.S., with honors, 1965); Columbia University (J.D., 1968). Member,The Advisors Board, Tax Management, Estates, Gifts and Trusts Journal, 1999—. Contributing Author: "Generations: Planning Your Legacy," Esperti-Peterson Press,1998. Member, Task Force on the Omnibus Trusts and Estates Amendment Act, 2000. Formerly with, McKenna & Cuneo. *Member:* The District of Columbia Bar (Member: Estate, Trusts and Probate Law Sections). ***PRACTICE AREAS:*** Estate Planning; Business Planning; Trust Administration; Estate Administration; Corporate Transactions; Administrative Law.

REFERENCES: BB&T.

(For complete biographical data on Largo personnel, see Professional Biographies at Largo, Maryland)

MARSH FLEISCHER & QUIGGLE

CHARTERED

WASHINGTON, D.C.

(See Bethesda, Maryland)

General Civil and Trial Practice. Real Estate, Estate Planning, Probate and Tax Law, Arbitration and Mediation.

MARTELL & ASSOCIATES

Established in 1983

1718 CONNECTICUT AVENUE, N.W.

WASHINGTON, D.C. 20009

Telephone: 202-483-3550

Telecopier: 202-483-7159

Mortgage and Related Securities, Financial Institutions, Housing and Urban Development Law.

FIRM PROFILE: The firm specializes in transactional work involving government mortgage product.

MARY MARTELL, born Philadelphia, Pennsylvania, March 10, 1956; admitted to bar, 1980, Georgia and Pennsylvania; 1981, District of Columbia. *Education:* University of Pennsylvania (B.S., 1976); Rutgers University (J.D., 1980); George Washington University (LL.M., 1986). Attorney-Advisor, Office of General Counsel, U.S. Department of Housing and Urban Development, 1980-1983. *Member:* The District of Columbia Bar; State Bar of Georgia; Pennsylvania Bar Association; Women's Bar Association of the District of Columbia. ***PRACTICE AREAS:*** Transactional Law; Housing and Urban Development. ***Email:*** martell@martfour.com

OF COUNSEL

ROBERTA BEARY, born Jamaica Estates, New York, January 27, 1954; admitted to bar, 1979, New York; 1984, District of Columbia. *Education:* Eisenhower College (B.A., 1974); St. John's University (J.D., 1978). Co-Author, "A Guide through the Maze of Shareholder Derivative Lawsuits", Seibunsha, Tokyo (published in Japanese), 1994. Former Senior Attorney, U.S. Department HUD, Office of the General Counsel (1979-1990). *Member:* District of Columbia Bar, New York State and American Bar Associations; Women's Bar Association of the District of Columbia. ***PRACTICE AREAS:*** Real Estate Finance; Mortgage Finance; Housing and Urban Development; Secondary Mortgage Market; International Real Estate. ***Email:*** rbearyesq@aol.com

MARTELL, DONNELLY, GRIMALDI & GALLAGHER, P.A.

Established in 1970

1815 H STREET, N.W., SUITE 420

WASHINGTON, D.C. 20006

Telephone: 202-293-0830

Fax: 202-452-8460

Email: d.gallagher@mdgg.com

URL: http://www.mdgg.com

Rockville, Maryland Office: 9 North Adams Street. Telephone: 301-424-1300. Fax: 301-217-9088.

Fairfax, Virginia Office: 10201 Lee Highway, Suite 490, 22030-2222. Telephone: 703-273-2811. Fax: 703-273-3208.

General and Insurance Practice, Casualty, Professional Malpractice, Products Liability, Life and Health, Aviation and Automobile Law.

DAVID F. GRIMALDI, born Erie, Pennsylvania, January 10, 1939; admitted to bar, 1964, District of Columbia. *Education:* Gannon College (B.A., 1960); Catholic University of America (J.D., 1963). CUA (President Law Alumni, 1989-1990). *Member:* The District of Columbia Bar; Bar Association of the District of Columbia (Secretary, 1983; President, 1987-1988); American Bar Association (Member, House of Delegates, 1986-1988); Federation of Insurance and Corporate Counsel; District of Columbia Defense Lawyers Association (President, 1985-1986); Defense Research Institute (State Chairman, 1988-1994); Barristers (Vice President, 1984; President, 1994); The Counsellors (President, 1985-1986); Trial Attorneys of America (Board Member and Secretary, 1996-1999). ***Email:*** d.grimaldi@mdgg.com

WADE J. GALLAGHER, born Washington, D.C., June 25, 1940; admitted to bar, 1967, District of Columbia; 1977, Maryland. *Education:* Georgetown University (A.B., 1962); Catholic University of America (J.D., 1966). *Member:* Montgomery County and Maryland State Bar Associations; The District of Columbia Bar; Bar Association of the District of Columbia; International Association of Defense Counsel; District of Columbia Defense Lawyers Association; Barristers; The Counsellors. ***Email:*** w.gallagher@mdgg.com

DON F. RYDER, JR., born Harrisburg, Pennsylvania, April 30, 1932; admitted to bar, 1959, Maryland; 1964, District of Columbia; 1971, U.S. Supreme Court. *Education:* Gettysburg College (A.B., magna cum laude, 1954); Georgetown University (J.D., 1958). Delta Theta Phi. *Member:* Montgomery County Bar Association; The District of Columbia Bar. ***Email:*** d.ryder@mdgg.com

(This Listing Continued)

NONA JEAN BONANNO, born Montclair, New Jersey, July 16, 1964; admitted to bar, 1990, Pennsylvania, New Jersey, Maryland and District of Columbia; 1991, U.S. District Court, District of Columbia. *Education:* Catholic University of America (B.A., 1986); Howard University (J.D., cum laude, 1989). Law Clerk to Honorable Judges Nunzio, Doyle, McIntyre and Neilson, Superior Court of the District of Columbia, 1989-1991. *Member:* The District of Columbia Bar; Bar Association of District of Columbia; Maryland and New Jersey State Bar Associations; Italian American Bar Association. ***Email:*** n.bonanno@mdgg.com

DAVID FRANKLIN RYDER, born Washington, D.C., October 19, 1960; admitted to bar, 1986, Maryland; 1988, District of Columbia. *Education:* Gettysburg College (B.A., 1982); Washington College of Law, American University (J.D., 1986). *Member:* Montgomery County Bar Association; District of Columbia Bar. ***Email:*** david.ryder@mdgg.com

ANTHONY E. GRIMALDI, born Punxsutawney, Pennsylvania, August 25, 1930; admitted to bar, 1958, District of Columbia; 1968, Virginia. *Education:* Pennsylvania State University (B.A., 1952); Georgetown University (LL.D., 1957). Delta Theta Phi. Young Lawyer of the Year, Bar Association of The District of Columbia, 1966. *Member:* Fairfax and American Bar Associations; The District of Columbia Bar; Bar Association of the District of Columbia; Virginia State Bar; Northern Virginia Defense Lawyers Association; Virginia Association of Defense Attorneys; Federation of Insurance Counsel; Trial Attorneys of America; Association of Defense Trial Attorneys. ***PRACTICE AREAS:*** Civil Practice; General Liability; Malpractice; Products Liability; Employment Law. ***Email:*** mdgg@erols.com

WILLIAM J. VIRGULAK, JR., born Norwalk, Connecticut, November 21, 1952; admitted to bar, 1977, Virginia; 1978, District of Columbia. *Education:* Providence College (B.A., cum laude, 1974); George Mason University School of Law (J.D., magna cum laude, 1977). Phi Sigma Tau. *Member:* Fairfax, Virginia and American Bar Associations; The District of Columbia Bar; Bar Association of the District of Columbia; Virginia State Bar; Virginia Trial Lawyers Association; Northern Virginia Defense Lawyers Association; District of Columbia Defense Lawyers Association. ***PRACTICE AREAS:*** Civil Practice; Personal Injury Litigation; Defense Litigation; Automobile Liability; Products Liability; Employment Law. ***Email:*** mdgg@erols.com

DANA L. SCOTT, JR., born Takoma Park, Maryland, June 3, 1951; admitted to bar, 1978, Virginia; 1983, District of Columbia; 1997, Maryland. *Education:* University of Virginia (B.A., 1974); George Mason University (J.D., 1978). *Member:* Fairfax, Virginia and American Bar Associations; The District of Columbia Bar; Virginia State Bar; Northern Virginia Defense Lawyers Association; District of Columbia Defense Lawyers Association. ***PRACTICE AREAS:*** Automobile Liability; Civil Practice; Personal Injury Litigation; Commercial Liability; Defense Litigation. ***Email:*** mdgg@erols.com

OF COUNSEL

Frank J. Martell ***William J. Donnelly, Jr.***

REPRESENTATIVE CLIENTS: Armed Forces Insurance Exchange; Borg-Warner Protective Services Corp.; Burns International Security Services; CGU Insurance Companies; Erie Insurance Group; Fidelity and Deposit Co. of Maryland; First Financial Insurance; GEICO; John Deere Insurance Co.; Great West Casualty Company; Independent Fire Insurance Co.; International Chiropractors Association; Kemper Insurance; The May Department Stores Co.; No. Carolina Farm Bureau Insurance Co.; One Beacon Insurance Co.; Ranger Insurance; Richfood Holdings, Inc.; Roadway Services, Inc.; Shoppers Food Warehouse; State Auto Insurance; State Capitol Insurance Co.; Transguard Insurance; Travelers Insurance Co.; United Services Automobile Assn.; Universal Underwriters Insurance Co.; Zurich Insurance.

MARTIN & ADAMS, PLLC

1730 RHODE ISLAND AVENUE, N.W.
SUITE 812
WASHINGTON, D.C. 20036-3114
Telephone: 202-408-1155
Fax: 202-408-7554
URL: http://www.martinadams.com
Email: info@martinadams.com
URL: http://www.lawyers.com/martin&rylanderpc

FIRM PROFILE: Martin & Adams, PLLC offers representation in government contracts, federal litigation, complex civil litigation, intellectual property litigation, business tort litigation, white collar criminal defense, construction litigation, corporate law, software licensing and internet law.

KENNETH A. MARTIN, born Philadelphia, Pennsylvania, 1955; admitted to bar, 1986, Pennsylvania; 1987, Massachusetts; 1990, District of Columbia; U.S. Supreme Court; U.S. Court of Appeals, Federal and District of Columbia Circuits; U.S. District Court, District of Columbia; U.S. Court of Federal

(This Listing Continued)

Claims. *Education:* Albright College (B.A., Economics, 1976); Suffolk University (J.D., cum laude, 1986). Phi Delta Phi. Adjunct Professor, Government Contracting, Middlesex Community College. Author: Martin, Holman and Rylander, "Is This The End Of Federal Minority Contracting?" The Federal Lawyer (Feb. 1995); Kenneth A. Martin and Craig A. Holman, "How To File A Monetary Claim Under The Contract Disputes Act," Acquisition Issues (Jan. 1994). Lectures: Adarand Constructors, Inc. and the 8(a) Contractor; Federal Contract Administration & Accounting; The ABC's of Writing Winning Proposals; Basics of Commercial Contracting and Advanced Commercial Contracting; Electronic Contracting; How to Get Paid on Time by the U.S. Government; Collections & Cost Recovery Workshop; Changes in Government Contracts; Native American Opportunities in Small Business and Government Contracting; Small Business Investment Companies. *Member:* The District of Columbia Bar; Pennsylvania, Massachusetts, Federal and American Bar Associations; Armed Forces Communications and Electronics Association. [Capt., USAF, 1980-1987; Maj. Systems Contracting Officer]. ***REPORTED CASES:*** Amicus Curiae Counsel, Adarand Constructors, Inc. v. Pena, 515 U.S. 100, 115 S. Ct. 2097, 132 L. Ed.2d 158 (1995); DSE, Inc. d/b/a Dayron v. United States, 20 F.Supp. 2d 25 (D.C.C. 1998); DSE, Inc. v. United States, 3 F.Supp. 2d 1464 (D.D.C. 1998); DSE, Inc. v. United States, 169 F.3d 21 (D.C. Cir 1999); TMC Technologies, Inc. v. United States, 1997 U.S. Dist. LEXIS 9793 (D.D.C. 1997); Ellsworth Associates, Inc. v. U.S. Dep't of Commerce, 926 F.Supp. 207 (D.D.C. 1996); Naing International Enterprises v. Ellsworth Associates, Inc., 961 F.Supp. 1 (D.D.C. 1997). ***PRACTICE AREAS:*** Government Contracts; Complex Business Litigation; White Collar Criminal Defense; Intellectual Property Litigation; Construction Law; Surety Law. ***Email:*** ken@martinadams.com

JENNIFER COLLESANO ADAMS, born Buffalo, New York, 1972; admitted to bar, 1997, Virginia; 1999, District of Columbia; U.S. Court of Appeals, Fourth Circuit; U.S. Court of Federal Claims; U.S. District Court, Eastern District of Virginia; U.S. District Court, District of Columbia. *Education:* Cornell University (B.A., 1994); Catholic University of America, Columbus School of Law (J.D., cum laude, 1997). Author, "Choice Influencing Considerations for Determining the Organizational Structure of an Internet Gaming Operation," Gaming Law Review. Lectures: Basics of Commercial Contracting and Advanced Commercial Contracting; Offshore Corporate Structures; Changes in Government Contracts. ***PRACTICE AREAS:*** Government Contracts; Complex Business Litigation; White Collar Criminal Defense; Intellectual Property Litigation; Software Licensing; Internet Law; Copyrights; Trademarks. ***Email:*** jennifera@martinadams.com

JASEN DEAN ADAMS, born Salt Lake City, Utah, 1971; admitted to bar, 1999, Virginia (Not admitted in District of Columbia). *Education:* Cornell University (B.A., 1995); George Mason University School of Law (J.D., 1998). Lecturer, Internet Gaming: Understanding the Impact of U.S Legislation on the Worldwide Market. ***PRACTICE AREAS:*** Government Contracts; Internet Law; Asset Protection; Corporate Law; Civil Litigation; Copyrights; Trademarks. ***Email:*** jasena@martinadams.com

MARTIN, SNYDER & BERNSTEIN, P.A.

WASHINGTON, D.C.

(See Baltimore, Maryland)

Criminal and Civil Trial Practice and Appellate Practice in Federal and State Courts. Emphasis on white collar criminal defense, complex litigation (including multi-district and RICO matters), tax litigation, and commercial litigation. Business planning, corporate and real estate.

MARZOUK & PARRY

1120 NINETEENTH STREET, N.W., SEVENTH FLOOR
WASHINGTON, D.C. 20036
Telephone: 202-463-7293
Telecopier: 202-955-9371
Email: tmarzouk@veriomail.com
URL: http://www.lawyers.com/marzouk&parrylaw

Computer and Software, Internet, Electronic Commerce, Technology Licensing, Copyrights, Trade Secrets, Trademark Law, Litigation and Cyber Law and Emerging Business Law.

TOBEY B. MARZOUK, born August 26, 1952; admitted to bar, 1977, District of Columbia; 1988, Virginia. *Education:* Princeton University (A.B., magna cum laude, 1974); Harvard University (J.D., cum laude, 1977). Consulting Editor: Computer Law Reporter, 1984-1992; Internet Law & Business, 1998—. Author: "Software Licensing and Internet Agreements," 2000 and "Business and Legal Issues in Systems Integration," 1991, Sequoia Press; "Protecting Your Proprietary Rights in the Computer and High Technology Industries," IEEE Computer Society Press, 1988. *Member:* The District of Columbia

(This Listing Continued)

MARZOUK & PARRY, Washington—Continued

Bar; Computer Law Association. ***PRACTICE AREAS:*** Computer Software Law; Technology Law; Copyrights; Trade Secrets; Trademarks. ***Email:*** tmarzouk@veriomail.com

THOMAS M. PARRY, born August 13, 1952; admitted to bar, 1983, District of Columbia; 1987, Maryland. *Education:* Colorado College (B.A., 1975); Rutgers University (M.A., 1978); Georgetown University (J.D., cum laude, 1983). Project Editor, Georgetown Law Journal, 1982-1983. Author: "Counseling High Tech Clients," 1996 and "Software Licensing Agreements," 1992, Sequoia Press. *Member:* The District of Columbia Bar (Co-Chair, Steering Committee, Computer Law Section, 1992-1994); Computer Law Association. ***PRACTICE AREAS:*** Computer Software Law; Software Copyright; Trademark Infringement; Business Law. ***Email:*** tparry@veriomail.com

OF COUNSEL

PAUL G. GASTON, born February 16, 1953; admitted to bar, 1979, District of Columbia. *Education:* Yale University (B.A., magna cum laude, 1974; J.D., 1979). ***PRACTICE AREAS:*** Commercial Litigation; Copyrights; Trademarks.

LAW OFFICE OF PETER R. MASCIOLA

601 INDIANA AVENUE, SUITE 603
WASHINGTON, D.C. 20004
Telephone: 202-628-5680; 1-800-741-5308
Fax: 202-628-5682
Email: petermas@erols.com
URL: http://www.lawyers.com/petermasciola

Medical Malpractice, Military Medical Malpractice, Military Health Care, Military Courts Martial, Military Law, Military Criminal Law, Cerebral Palsy, Catastrophic Injury, Birth Trauma, Serious Personal Injury, Airplane Crashes, Military Accidents and Tort Law.

FIRM PROFILE: Peter R. Masciola established a successful specialized medical law practice representing patients with military medical malpractice claims, airplane crashes, military accidents and tort law suits in federal courts. Mr. Masciola defends military health care providers facing adverse credentials actions including administrative board hearings and professional pay issues. Additionally the firm provides criminal defense representation for service men and women at military courts-martial and adverse administrative proceedings.

PETER R. MASCIOLA, born Boston, Massachusetts, August 3, 1957; admitted to bar, 1983, Massachusetts; 1984, U.S. Court of Appeals for the Armed Forces; 1996, U.S. District Court, District of Maryland and U.S. Court of Veterans Appeals; 1998 District of Columbia; 1999, U.S. District Court for the District of Columbia. *Education:* Stonehill College (B.A., 1979); New England School of Law (J.D., 1983). *Member:* District of Columbia Bar (Former Steering Committee Member, Torts Law Section); Massachusetts, Federal and American Bar Associations; Trial Lawyers Association of Metropolitan Washington, D.C. ; JAA American Inns of Court (Master); Association of Trial Lawyers of America (Chair Elect, Federal Tort Claims Act and Military Advocacy Section); Judge Advocates Military Bar Association (President). [Lt. Col. MA ANG United States Air Force Reserves]

CRAIG MATHEWS

3902 JOCELYN STREET, N.W.
WASHINGTON, D.C. 20015
Telephone: 202-966-8965
Fax: 202-966-8978

General Corporate, Antitrust, Environmental, Trade Associations, Federal Departmental and International Practice.

CRAIG MATHEWS, born Columbus, Ohio, October 19, 1929; admitted to bar, 1954, Ohio; 1959, District of Columbia; 1963, U.S. Supreme Court; 1970, U.S. Court of International Trade. *Education:* Yale University (B.A., 1951); Yale Law School (J.D., 1954); Georgetown Law Center (LL.M., 1967). Phi Delta Phi (Corbey Court); Phi Beta Kappa. Author: "The Constitutional Power of the President to Conclude International Agreements," 64 Yale Law Journal, 345, 1955; "Restrictions on Procurement Under the Economic Assistance Program," 52 Georgetown Law Journal, 457, 1964; "Non-Tariff Import Restrictions: Remedies Available in United States Law," 62 Michigan Law Review, 1295, 1964; "Non-Tariff Import Barriers and the Kennedy Round," Common Market Law Review 403, 1965; "Certificated Air Service at Smaller Communities: The Need for Service as a Determinant of Regulatory Policy," 34 Journal of Air Law and Commerce 27, 1968; "Living with United States Environmental Regulations," Belgian American Trade Review, 1984. Adjunct Professor, Washington College

(This Listing Continued)

of Law, The American University, 1984-1985. Visiting Lecturer, Environmental Regulation, Yale University, 1987. Chairman, Executive Committee, 1973-1983, Chairman of the Board, 1983-1984 and Member of the Board and Executive Committee, 1987-1992, Environmental Law Institute. Member of the Board, Levine School of Music, 1990—. *Member:* The District of Columbia Bar; American Bar Association; American Society of International Law.

EDWARD N. MATISIK

4201 MASSACHUSETTS AVENUE, N.W., SUITE 5047
WASHINGTON, D.C. 20016-4701
Telephone: 202-244-7611
Fax: 202-244-3544
Email: enmatisik@hotmail.com
URL: http://www.stateregistrations.com

Nonprofit and Charitable Organizations Law, Charitable Giving, Nonprofit Tax Law, Charitable Trusts and Foundations, Public Charitites, Private Foundations, Fundraising Legal Consultation, Fundraising Licensing, Taxability Assesment of Charitable Contributions, Education Law.

FIRM PROFILE: Mr. Matisik is a former officer of development and fundraising for the Kennedy Center and the National Symphony Orchestra. He regularly provides fundraising and legal counsel for nonprofit and tax exempt organizations throughout the United States.

EDWARD N. MATISIK, born Johnstown, Pennsylvania, July 18, 1962; admitted to bar, 1999, District of Columbia. *Education:* Boston University (B.S., 1984); American University (M.A., 1991; J.D., 1997); George Washington University. Author: "Obsessive-Compulsive Disorder and the Americans with Disabilities Act," The Obsessive-Compulsive Foundation, 1999; "The Legal Handbook for Pennsylvania School Teachers," Omni Publishers, 2000. *Member:* American Bar Association; The Association of Trial Lawyers of America. ***PRACTICE AREAS:*** Nonprofit Organizations Law; Mental Disability Law; Education Law; Medical Malpractice.

REPRESENTATIVE CLIENTS: DCM, Inc.; N.P.O. Direct Marketing; AB Data; Avalon Consulting Group; Washington Shakespeare Theater; U.S. Marine Corp; A Better Chance; Unitarian Church; Womens Direct Response Group; International Campaign for Tibet.

THOMAS A. MAURO & ASSOCIATES

1050 SEVENTEENTH STREET, N.W.
SUITE 1200
WASHINGTON, D.C. 20036
Telephone: 202-452-9865
Fax: 202-452-0092
URL: http://www.lawyers.com/maurolaw

Complex Commercial Litigation, Patent Litigation, Intellectual Property Law, Electromechanical Patent Law, Computer and Software Patent, Patent Infringement, Trademark Law, Complex Patent Litigation.

FIRM PROFILE: Mr. Mauro is a well known commercial litigator with over 25 years of courtroom experience. He frequently works in conjunction with both large and small law firms involved in complex patent litigation and intellectual property cases.

THOMAS A. MAURO, born Brooklyn, New York, September 29, 1945; admitted to bar, 1973, District of Columbia; 1976, U.S. Supreme Court; 1989, Maryland. *Education:* Polytechnic University (B.S., Physics, 1967); Georgetown University (J.D., 1973). Editor, Georgetown Law Journal. Author: "An Analysis of the Fairness Doctrine," Georgetown Law Journal, 1972; "Unsolicited Merchandise in the Mails: Rights and Remedies," Res Ipsa Loquitur, Fall, 1971; "The Robinson Patman Act," NTDRA Journal, 1978; "Speaking Out," June 1980. Law Clerk to Hon. Thomas A. Flannery, U.S. District Court, District of Columbia, 1973-1974. Design Engineer, Eastman Kodak Co. U.S. Patent Examiner, 1970-1971. Trial Attorney, Honors Program, Antitrust Division, United States Department of Justice, 1974-1975. Member, Antitrust Committee, Small Business Legislative Council, 1977-1982. Issue Editor, ABA Antitrust Law Journal, 1978-1980. *Member:* District of Columbia Bar; Federal and American (Member, Sections of: Antitrust; Government Law; Litigation; Contracts) Bar Associations. ***PRACTICE AREAS:*** Intellectual Property Law.

MAYER, BROWN & PLATT

1909 K STREET, N.W.
WASHINGTON, D.C. 20006-1101
Telephone: (202) 263-3000
Facsimile: (202) 263-3300
Telex: 892603
Cable: LE MAYDC
URL: http://www.mayerbrown.com

Chicago, Illinois Office: 190 South LaSalle Street, 60603-3441. Telephone: (312) 782-0600. Facsimile: (312) 701-7711. Telex: 190404. Cable: LEMAY.

Berlin, Germany Office: Breite Strasse 29, Muehlendamm, 10178. Telephone: 011-49-30-2060-7710. Facsimile: 011-49-30-2060-7744.

Charlotte, North Carolina Office: 100 North Tryon Street, Suite 2400. Telephone: (704) 444-3500. Fax: (704) 377-2033.

Cologne, Germany Office: Kaiser-Wilhelm-Ring 27-29, 50672. Telephone: 011-49-221-5771-100. Facsimile: 011-49-221-5771-199.

Frankfurt/Main, Germany Office: Mayer, Brown, Platt, Gaedertz. Bockenheimer Landstraße 98-100. Telephone: 011-49-69 79 41-0. Facsimile: 011-49-69 79 41-100.

Houston, Texas Office: 700 Louisiana Street, Suite 3600, 77002-2730. Telephone: (713) 221-1651. Facsimile: (713) 224-6410. Telex: 775809. Cable: LEMAYHOU.

London, England Office: Bucklersbury House, 3 Queen Victoria Street, London, EC4N 8EL, England. Telephone: 011-44-207-246-6200. Facsimile: 011-44-207-329-4465. Telex: 8811095. Cable: LEMAYLDN.

Los Angeles, California Office: 350 South Grand Avenue, 25th Floor, 90071-1503. Telephone: (213) 229-9500. Facsimile: (213) 625-0248. Telex: 188089. Cable: LEMAYLA.

New York, New York Office: 1675 Broadway, 10019-5820. Telephone: (212) 506-2500. Facsimile: (212) 262-1910. Telex: 701842. Cable: LEMAYEN.

Representative Offices:

Ashgabat, Turkmenistan: 28 Gogal Street, 744000. Telephone: 011-99-312-355247. Facsimile: 011-99-312-510074.

Mexico City, Mexico, D.F., Independent Mexico Correspondent: Jáuregui, Navarrete, Nader y Rojas, S.C., Torre Arcos, Paseo de los Tamarindos No. 400-B. Col. Bosques de las Lomas, 05120. Telephone: 011-525-267-45-00. Facsimile: 011-525-267-45-99.

Paris, France, Independent Paris Correspondent: Lambert & Lee, 13 Avenue Hoche, 75008. Telephone: 011-33-1-53-53-43-43. Facsimile: 011-33-1-53-96-03-83.

General Practice.

PARTNERS

ROBERT E. BLOCH, born Irvington, New Jersey, March 22, 1947; admitted to bar, 1973, District of Columbia; 1975, U.S. Court of Appeals for the District of Columbia Circuit; 1977, U.S. Supreme Court. *Education:* Franklin & Marshall College (B.A., 1969); George Washington University (J.D., with honors, 1973). Co-Author of "Product Market Definition in Pharmaceutical Mergers," published in *Antitrust Report,* Matthew Bender & Co. (Sept. 1997). Co-author of "A New and Uncertain Future for Managed Care Mergers: An Antitrust Analysis of the Aetna/Prudential Merger, published in *Antitrust Report,* Matthew Bender & Co. (Oct. 1999). Antitrust Division, U.S. Department of Justice: Chief Professions and Intellectual Property Section, 1988-1993; Assistant Chief, Litigation I, 1985-1988; Assistant Chief, Trial Section, 1981-1985; Trial Attorney, 1975-1981. Office of the Attorney General of Ohio, Assistant Attorney General, Antitrust Section, Columbus, 1973-1975. Author: "The Antitrust Division's Amnesty Program," American Bar Association Section on Antitrust Law (February 1995); "State Action Immunity as a Defense in an Antitrust Health Care Context: What Works and What Doesn't," American Bar Association Antitrust Section and Forum on Health Care (October 1994); "Corporate Compliance Programs and Corporate Amnesty: The Perilous Pursuit of Virtue," Antitrust Report, Matthew Bender & Co. (June 1994); "Antitrust Competition and Health Care Reform," Health Affairs (Spring I February 1994); "The Antitrust Division's Corporate Amnesty Program," Antitrust Magazine (American Bar Association, December 1993); "Antitrust Enforcement and Health Care Reform," The National Law Journal (October 11, 1993); "Corporate Compliance Programs, Antitrust Enforcement and the New Organizational Sentencing Guidelines," Antitrust Report. Matthew Bender & Co. (April 1993). Co-author: "Analyzing and Defending HMO Mergers Under the Antitrust Laws," American Association of Health Plans (February 1998); "Analyzing Provider Joint Ventures Outside the Safety Zones: Provider Integration, the Rule of Reason and Messenger Models Under the Health Care Antitrust Policy Statements," National Health Lawyers Association (February 1997); "Responding to Antitrust Criminal Investigations," The American Bar Association Section of Antitrust Law (February 1997); "U.S. Antitrust Law and Its Effect on Copyright Protections for the Music Industry," The Impact of Competitive Law on the Music Industry, MAKLU Publishers (January 1997; "Defending Provider Networks Before the Antitrust Enforcement Agencies," Health Care M & A, Practicing Law Institute (1997); "Most Favored Nation Clauses in Contracts Between Health Care Networks and Providers: The Search for Practical Antitrust Guidance," Antitrust Report, Matthew Bender & Co. (September 1996); "Defending Provider Networks and Hospital Mergers before the Antitrust Enforcement Agencies," National Health Lawyers Association (February 1996); "Innovation Policy and Antitrust Enforcement: The 1995 Antitrust Guidelines for Licensing of Intellectual property," Antitrust Report (Matthew Bender & Co. June 1995). Co-author and Co-editor: *Compendium of Informal Antitrust Enforcement Agency Advice in Health Care* (American Bar Association, 1997); *Handbook on Antitrust Grand Jury Investigations* (American Bar Association, 1988); *Sample Jury Instructions in Civil Antitrust Cases* (American Bar Association, 1987); *Criminal Antitrust Litigation Manual* (American Bar Association, 1984); *Sample Jury Instructions in Criminal Antitrust Cases* (American Bar Association, 1984). ***Email:*** rbloch@mayerbrown.com

DAVID I. BLOOM, born Washington, D.C., March 27, 1954; admitted to bar, 1978, District of Columbia and U.S. District Court, District of Columbia; 1979, U.S. Court of Appeals, District of Columbia Circuit and Temporary Emergency Court of Appeals; 1983, U.S. Court of Appeals, Fifth Circuit; 1984, U.S. Court of Appeals, Seventh Circuit. *Education:* Brown University (A.B., magna cum laude, 1975); Yale University (J.D., 1978). ***Email:*** dbloom@mayerbrown.com

KIM MARIE KOZACZEK BOYLAN, born Newburgh, New York, July 19, 1959; admitted to bar, 1986, Pennsylvania and U.S. Court of Federal Claims; 1987, Massachusetts, District of Columbia and U.S. Tax Court; 1994, U.S. Court of Appeals for the Federal Circuit; 1998, U.S. Court of Appeals for the District of Columbia Circuit. *Education:* Georgetown University (B.S., 1981); Syracuse University (J.D., cum laude, 1986); Georgetown University Law Center (LL.M., with distinction, 1993). Certified Public Accountant. Co-author: "Guide to Transfer Pricing Compliance," 1995 Thompson Publishing Group. ***Email:*** kboylan@mayerbrown.com

ROBERT P. DAVIS, born Syracuse, New York, April 12, 1949; admitted to bar, 1980, District of Columbia. *Education:* Brown University (A.B., 1971); Boston University (M.A., 1972); Syracuse University (M.P.A., 1973); Georgetown University (J.D., magna cum laude, 1980). Solicitor for U.S. Department of Labor, 1989-1991. Chief of Staff to the Secretary of Transportation, 1983-1985. Publication: National Employment Law Institute, Litigation under the Fair Labor Standards Act (2000). ***LANGUAGES:*** French. ***Email:*** rdavis@mayerbrown.com

DAVID F. DOWD, born Worcester, Massachusetts, August 25, 1966; admitted to bar, 1992, Virginia; 1994, District of Columbia. *Education:* Georgetown University (B.A., summa cum laude, 1989; J.D., magna cum laude, 1992). ***PRACTICE AREAS:*** Government Contracts; Litigation. ***Email:*** ddowd@mayerbrown.com

KERRY LYNN EDWARDS, born Bay Shore, New York, February 9, 1957; admitted to bar, 1986, Maryland; 1988, District of Columbia. *Education:* State University of New York at Oneonta (B.S., with highest honors, 1979); Georgetown University (J.D., magna cum laude, 1986). ***Email:*** kedwards@mayerbrown.com

DONALD M. FALK, born San Francisco, California, February 6, 1957; admitted to bar, 1990, California; 1993, District of Columbia; U.S. Court of Appeals for the District of Columbia, Federal, Third, Fourth, Fifth, Sixth, Seventh, Eighth, Ninth and Tenth Circuits; U.S. District Court, Northern, Central and Eastern Districts of California; U.S. District Court for the District of Columbia; U.S. Supreme Court. *Education:* University of California at Berkeley (B.A., 1976); University of Chicago (M.A., 1977); Boalt Hall School of Law, University of California (J.D., 1990). Order of the Coif. Law Clerk to Hon. Douglas H. Ginsburg, U.S. Court of Appeals for the District of Columbia Circuit. Co-Author: with Hon. Douglas H. Ginsburg, "The Court En Banc: 1981-1990," 59 Geo. Wash. L.Rev. 1008 (1991); with Robert E. Bloch, "Antitrust, Competition and Health Care Reform," Health Affairs, Spring 1994, at 206. Author: "Antitrust & Refusals to Deal after *Nynex v. Discon,*" Practical Lawyer, April 2000, at 25. Member, Antitrust and Intellectual Property Sections, American Bar Association. ***Email:*** dfalk@mayerbrown.com

RICHARD J. FAVRETTO, born New York, N.Y., May 16, 1941; admitted to bar, 1966, New York; 1972, District of Columbia. *Education:* Iona College (B.A., cum laude, 1963); Catholic University of America (LL.B., 1966). Student Material Editor, Catholic University Law Review, 1965-1966. Trial Attorney, 1966-1973, Assistant Chief, Trial Section, 1973-1976, Deputy Director of Operations, 1976-1979, Deputy Assistant Attorney General, 1979-1981, Antitrust Division, U.S. Department of Justice. ***Email:*** rfavretto@mayerbrown.com

ANDREW L. FREY, born New York, N.Y., August 11, 1938; admitted to bar, 1962, New York; 1967, District of Columbia; 1972, U.S. Supreme Court. *Education:* Swarthmore College (B.A., with high honors, 1959); Columbia University (LL.B., 1962). Notes and Comments Editor, Columbia Law Review. Author: "Punitive Damages," Business and Commercial Litigation on Federal Courts (ABA 1998); "How to Write a Good Appellate Brief," Litigation Magazine. Deputy Solicitor General of the United States, 1974-1986. *Member:* American Law Institute; American Academy of Appellate Lawyers. (Also at

(This Listing Continued)

MAYER, BROWN & PLATT, Washington—Continued

New York, N.Y. Office). ***PRACTICE AREAS:*** Civil Appeals; Criminal Appeals; Constitutional Law; Complex Civil Litigation; Products Liability. ***Email:*** afrey@mayerbrown.com

KENNETH S. GELLER, born New York, N.Y., September 22, 1947; admitted to bar, 1972, New York; 1986, District of Columbia. *Education:* City College of New York (B.A., magna cum laude, 1968); Harvard University (J.D., magna cum laude, 1971). Co-author: "Supreme Court Practice," (BNA 7th ed., 1993). Contributing Author: "Business and Commercial Litigation in Federal Courts" (Robert L. Haig ed., West Group & ABA 1998). Assistant Special Prosecutor, Watergate Special Prosecution Force, 1973-1975. Assistant to the Solicitor General, U.S. Department of Justice, 1975-1979. Deputy Solicitor General, 1979-1986. ***Email:*** kgeller@mayerbrown.com

MARK H. GITENSTEIN, born Montgomery, Alabama, March 7, 1946; admitted to bar, 1972, District of Columbia. *Education:* Duke University (A.B., 1968); Georgetown University (J.D., 1972). ***Email:*** mgitenstein@mayerbrown.com

JOHN S. HAHN, born Sikeston, Missouri, July 30, 1952; admitted to bar, 1977, District of Columbia; 1978, U.S. Court of Appeals, District of Columbia Circuit; 1981, U.S. Supreme Court. *Education:* Duke University (A.B., magna cum laude, 1974); Yale Law School (J.D., 1977). *Member:* American Bar Association (Natural Resources Section). ***Email:*** jhahn@mayerbrown.com

CAMERON STREET HAMRICK, born Charlotte, North Carolina, November 4, 1958; admitted to bar, 1985, District of Columbia. *Education:* Duke University (B.A., magna cum laude, 1981; J.D., 1985). ***Email:*** chamrick@mayerbrown.com

WERNER J. HEIN, born Neisse, Germany, October 17, 1942; admitted to bar, 1973, Germany; 1986, New York; 1999, District of Columbia. *Education:* Universities at Berlin, Bonn and Nice; Columbia University (LL.M., 1975). Attorney, Wilkinson, Barker & Quinn, Washington, D.C., 1987-1994. (Also at Cologne, Germany Office). ***LANGUAGES:*** French and German. ***Email:*** whein@mayerbrown.com

CHARLES M. HORN, born Boston, Massachusetts, September 28, 1951; admitted to bar, 1976, District of Columbia; 1977, U.S. District Court for the District of Columbia; U.S. Court of Appeals for the District of Columbia Circuit; 1980, U.S. Supreme Court. *Education:* Stanford University; Harvard University (A.B., magna cum laude, 1973); Cornell University (J.D., 1976). ***PRACTICE AREAS:*** Financial Services Law; Securities; Corporate Law. ***Email:*** chorn@mayerbrown.com

ROBERT M. JENKINS, III, born Fort Lauderdale, Florida, January 14, 1947; admitted to bar, 1974, California; 1975, District of Columbia and U.S. District Court, District of Columbia; Court of Appeals, Third, Sixth and District of Columbia Circuits; 1980, Supreme Court; 1981, U.S. Court of Federal Claims. *Education:* Harvard College (B.A., 1969); University of California at Berkeley (J.D., with honors, 1974). Order of the Coif. Chief Note and Comment Editor, California Law Review, 1972-1974. Law Clerk to Hon. Malcolm R. Wilkey, U.S. Court of Appeals for the District of Columbia Circuit, 1974-1975. ***LANGUAGES:*** Spanish. ***Email:*** rmjenkins@mayerbrown.com

ERIKA Z. JONES, born Washington, D.C., June 10, 1955; admitted to bar, 1980, District of Columbia; 1987, U.S. Court of Appeals, District of Columbia Circuit and U.S. Supreme Court; 1992, U.S. Court of Appeals, Fourth Circuit; 1997, U.S. Court of Appeals, Ninth and Seventh Circuits. *Education:* Georgetown University (A.B., magna cum laude, 1976; J.D., 1980). Chief Counsel, 1985-1989 and Special Counsel, 1981-1985, National Highway Traffic Safety Administration, Department of Transportation. ***Email:*** ejones@mayerbrown.com

MICHAEL ("MICKEY") KANTOR, born Nashville, Tennessee, August 7, 1939; admitted to bar, 1968, Florida; 1975, California; 1978, District of Columbia. *Education:* Vanderbilt University (B.A., 1961); Georgetown University (LL.B., 1968). United States Secretary of Commerce, 1996-1997. United States Trade Representative, 1993-1996. Member, Board of Directors: Pharmacia Corporation, Monsanto Company; Korea First Bank; National Association of Public Interest Lawyers. Member, Board of Visitors, Georgetown Law School. Trustee, International Commercial Diplomacy Project. Partner, Manatt, Phelps & Phillips; South Florida Migrant Legal Services; Migrant Legal Action Program. [U.S. Naval Officer, 1961-1965]. ***Email:*** mkantor@mayerbrown.com

TIMOTHY E. KEEHAN, born Houston, Texas, August 14, 1961; admitted to bar, 1987, Virginia (inactive); 1988, District of Columbia. *Education:* University of Virginia (B.A., Honors, 1984); University of Virginia School of Law (J.D., 1987); Reformed Theological Seminary (M.A., 1995). ***PRACTICE AREAS:*** Financial Services Law; E-Commerce. ***Email:*** tkeehan@mayerbrown.com

SIMEON M. KRIESBERG, born Washington, D.C., June 4, 1951; admitted to bar, 1977, District of Columbia; 1978, U.S. District Court, District of Columbia and U.S. Court of Appeals, District of Columbia Circuit; 1979, U.S. Court of International Trade and U.S. Court of Appeals for the Federal Circuit;

(This Listing Continued)

1982, U.S. Supreme Court. *Education:* Harvard College (A.B., magna cum laude, 1973); Woodrow Wilson School of Public and International Affairs, Princeton University (M.P.A., 1977); Yale Law School (J.D., 1977). Author: "Toward the Twenty-First Century: Trends in U.S. Trade Remedies," in Private Investment Abroad, Matthew Bender, 1993. Guest Scholar, Brookings Institution, 1992-1993. Professorial Lecturer, Nitze School of Advanced International Studies, Johns Hopkins University, 1991-1993. Vice President and General Counsel, 1985-1987, Senior Counsel for International Trade, 1983-1985, Sears World Trade, Inc. Associate, Leva, Hawes, Symington, Martin & Oppenheimer, 1977-1983. Member: Roster of Dispute Resolution Panelists Under NAFTA (by appointment of U.S. Government), 1996—; Roster of Dispute Resolution Panelists under U.S. - Canada Free-Trade Agreement (by appointment of U.S. Government), 1990-1992. ***Email:*** skriesberg@mayerbrown.com

KATHRYN A. KUSSKE, born St. Paul, Minnesota, June 16, 1958; admitted to bar, 1986, Maryland; 1987, District of Columbia. *Education:* Georgetown University (B.S.F.S., magna cum laude, 1980); American University (J.D., magna cum laude, 1985). Law Clerk, U.S. Court of Appeals for the District of Columbia Circuit, 1985-1986. Attorney, Clifford & Warnke, 1986-1991. ***Email:*** kkusske@mayerbrown.com

PHILIP ALLEN LACOVARA, born New York, N.Y., July 11, 1943; admitted to bar, 1967, New York; 1974, District of Columbia; 1970, U.S. Supreme Court. *Education:* Georgetown University (A.B., magna cum laude, 1963); Columbia University Law School (J.D., summa cum laude, 1966). Deputy Solicitor General of the United States, 1972-1973. Counsel to Watergate Special Prosecutor (1973-1974). Managing Partner, Washington, D.C. office, Hughes Hubbard & Reed, 1974-1988. Vice President and Senior Counsel for Litigation and Legal Policy, General Electric Co., 1988-1990. Managing Director and General Counsel, Morgan Stanley & Co., 1990-1993. President, District of Columbia Bar, 1988-1989. (Also at New York, N.Y. Office). ***Email:*** placovara@mayerbrown.com

DANIEL A. MASUR, born Jacksonville, Florida, June 9, 1952; admitted to bar, 1977, District of Columbia. *Education:* Marquette University (B.A., cum laude, 1974); Georgetown University (J.D., 1977). Editor, Georgetown Law Journal. Vice President and General Counsel, NET Inc., 1994-1997; Partner, Reed, Smith, Shaw & McClay, 1977-1994. ***Email:*** dmasur@mayerbrown.com

JAMES R. MOGLE, born Niles, Michigan, September 9, 1944; admitted to bar, 1974, Virginia; 1979, District of Columbia, U.S. Tax Court and U.S. Supreme Court; 1982, Illinois; 1984, Michigan. *Education:* Northwestern University (B.S., 1966); Stanford University (M.B.A., 1968); American University (J.D., 1974); George Washington University National Law Center (LL.M., 1979). Alpha Pi Mu. International Tax Counsel, Treasury Department, 1991-1992. Member: Advisory Board for IRS/George Washington University Institute on International Taxation, 1989-1991; IRS Commissioner's Advisory Group, 1990-1991; Board of Advisors, The Journal of International Taxation. *Member:* American Bar Association (Member, Section of Taxation, Foreign Activities of U.S. Taxpayers Committee, Section 482 Subcommittee); American Institute of Certified Public Accountants (Member: Advisory Task Force on IRS Quality Improvement Project for Coordinated Examination Program, 1989; International Tax Committee, 1991); National Council of the International Fiscal Association-U.S.A. Branch. ***Email:*** jmogle@mayerbrown.com

MIRIAM R. NEMETZ, born New York, N.Y., August 26, 1963; admitted to bar, 1990, Pennsylvania; 1992, District of Columbia. *Education:* Harvard University (B.A., 1985; J.D., 1989). Clerk to Judge Edward N. Cahn, E. D. Pennsylvania. Associate Counsel to the President, 1995-1997. ***Email:*** mnemetz@mayerbrown.com

CAROLYN P. OSOLINIK, born Brooklyn, New York, May 18, 1952; admitted to bar, 1977, District of Columbia; 1979, U.S. District Court for the District of Columbia and U.S. Court of Appeals for the District of Columbia Circuit; 1982, U.S. Supreme Court. *Education:* Lindenwood College (B.S., 1973); George Washington University (J.D., 1977). ***Email:*** cosolinik@mayerbrown.com

EILEEN PENNER, born Northridge, California, March 24, 1963; admitted to bar, 1988, California; 1996, District of Columbia. *Education:* University of California at Berkeley (B.A., 1984); Harvard University (J.D., magna cum laude, 1988).

STUART P. PERGAMENT, born New York, N.Y., March 24, 1942; admitted to bar, 1980, New York; 1983, Colorado; 1987, District of Columbia. *Education:* State University of New York at Stony Brook (B.S.E., 1963; Ph.D., 1970); Princeton University (M.S.E., 1966); Fordham University (J.D., 1979). ***Email:*** spergament@mayerbrown.com

SCOTT P. PERLMAN, born Brooklyn, New York, September 15, 1960; admitted to bar, 1987, New York; 1988, District of Columbia; 1991, U.S. District Court for the District of Columbia; 1992, U.S. Court of Appeals for the District of Columbia Circuit. *Education:* University of Pennsylvania (B.A., summa cum laude, 1982); Harvard University (J.D., magna cum laude, 1986). Co-author: Article, "Innovation Policy and Antitrust Enforcement: The 1995 Antitrust Guidelines for the Licensing of Intellectual Property," published in Mathew Bender & Co., Antitrust Report, June 1995; Article, "Most Favored

(This Listing Continued)

Nation Clauses in Contracts Between Health Care Networks and Providers," published in Mathew, Bender & Co., Antitrust Report, September 1996; Article, "A New and Uncertain Future for Managed Care Mergers: An Antitrust Analysis of the Aetna/Prudential Merger," published in *Antitrust Report,* Matthew Bender & Co. (Oct. 1999); "Analysis of Antitrust Issues Raised by B2B Exchanges: Practical Guidelines and Insights from the FTC B2B Workshop," published in Antitrust Report, Matthew Bender & Co., September 2000; "United States v. Microsoft Corporation: Striking a Balance Between Antitrust Enforcement and Intellectual Property Rights in the New Economy," published by Texas Institute of Continuing Legal Education, October 2001. *Member:* Federal Bar Association (Chair, Antitrust & Trade Regulation Section, 1997—). ***TRANSACTIONS:*** Aetna's acquisitions of US Healthcare, NYLCare and Prudential; Dow Chemical's sales of Marion Merrell Dow to Hoescht and DowBrands to S.C. Johnson; the merger of Strong Memorial and Highland Hospitals in Rochester, New York; the merger of St. Joseph's and Candler Hospitals in Savannah, Georgia; formation of a joint venture between Cargill and Monsanto for the development of transgenic seed; formation of a joint venture between Bertelsmann's Doubleday Direct Book Club and Time Warner's Book of the Month Club. ***PRACTICE AREAS:*** Antitrust; Hart-Scott-Rodino; Litigation. ***Email:*** sperlman@mayerbrown.com

MICHAEL W. PUNKE, admitted to bar, 1989, Maryland; 1998, District of Columbia. *Education:* George Washington University (B.A., with distinction, 1986); Cornell University (J.D., International Legal Affairs, 1989). Editor-in-Chief, *Cornell International Law Journal.* Author: "Structural Impediments to U.S.-Japanese Trade: The Collision of Culture and Law," 23 *Cornell International Law Journal* 1 (Winter 1990). Founding Partner, Arrowhead International, 1996-1997. Senior Policy Advisor to U.S. Trade Representative, Washington, D.C., 1995-1996. Director for International Economic Affairs, National Security Council/National Economic Council, The White House, 1993-1995. International Trade Counsel to Senator ax Baucus, Chairman of Finance Committee's International Trade Subcommittee, 1991-1993. Associate, Hogan & Hartson, Washington, D.C., 1989-1991. ***LANGUAGES:*** French. ***PRACTICE AREAS:*** International Law. ***Email:*** mpunke@mayerbrown.com

MITCHELL D. RAUP, born Baltimore, Maryland, May 25, 1959; admitted to bar, 1983, Illinois and U.S. District Court, Northern District of Illinois; 1991, U.S. Court of Appeals, Seventh Circuit; 1997, U.S. Court of Appeals, Sixth Circuit; 1998, District of Columbia; 1999, U.S. Court of Appeals, Third Circuit; 2000, U.S. Supreme Court. *Education:* University of Chicago (B.A., 1980); Duke University (J.D., with honors, 1983). Author: "Medical Boycotts by Health Care Providers: A Noett Pennington Defense," 69 Iowa l. Review 1393 (1984). Adjunct Professor of Antitrust Law, DePaul Law School, 1993-1996. ***Email:*** mraup@mayerbrown.com

LEE H. RUBIN, born Peoria, Illinois, June 8, 1963; admitted to bar, 1989, California; 1991, District of Columbia. *Education:* Duke University (B.A., summa cum laude, 1985); Stanford University (J.D., with distinction, 1988). Phi Beta Kappa. Law Clerk to the Honorable Warren J. Ferguson, United States Court of Appeals for the Ninth Circuit, 1988-1989. Trial Attorney, U.S. Department of Justice, Civil Rights Division, 1989-1995. Assistant U.S. Attorney, District of Columbia, 1995-1997. ***Email:*** lrubin@mayerbrown.com

MARK W. RYAN, born Batavia, New York, October 6, 1955; admitted to bar, 1981, District of Columbia; 1982, U.S. Court of Appeals, District of Columbia Circuit and U.S. District Court, District of Columbia; 1989, U.S. Supreme Court; 1993, Maryland. *Education:* Syracuse University (B.A., magna cum laude, 1977; Phi Beta Kappa); Duke University (J.D., 1981). ***Email:*** mryan@mayerbrown.com

PETER L. SCHER, born New York, N.Y., April 12, 1961; admitted to bar, 1988, New York; 1989, District of Columbia. *Education:* American University (B.A., 1983); Washington College of Law (J.D., 1987). U.S. Special Trade Negotiator (Rank of Ambassador), 1997-2000. Chief of Staff, USTR and Department of Commerce, 1995-1997. Staff Director, U.S. Senate Committee on Environmental and Public Works, 1993-1995. Chief of Staff, U.S. Senator Max Baucus, 1991-1993. ***Email:*** pscher@mayerbrown.com

JOHN P. SCHMITZ, born Cherry Point, North Carolina, April 19, 1955; admitted to bar, 1985, Pennsylvania; 1994, District of Columbia. *Education:* Georgetown University (B.A., magna cum laude, 1976); California Institute of Technology (M.A., Economics, 1978); Stanford University (J.D., 1981). (Also at Cologne, Germany Office). ***LANGUAGES:*** German. ***Email:*** jschmitz@mayerbrown.com

BRIAN W. SMITH, born Queens, New York, February 3, 1947; admitted to bar, 1972, New York; 1975, District of Columbia and U.S. District Court, Southern and Eastern Districts of New York; 1976, U.S. Supreme Court; 1986, U.S. District Court for the District of Columbia. *Education:* St. John's University (B.A., 1968; J.D., 1971); Columbia University Graduate School of Business (M.S., 1981). Co-Author: "Banker or Big Brother?" *Legal Times,* Week of March 1, 1999; "Lender Responsibility for Y2K Compliance," *The Journal of Lending & Credit Risk Management,* January 1999; "Banking vs. The Bug," *Legal Times,* January 25, 1999; "To Certify or Not to Certify? The OCC Opens the Door to Digital Signature Certification," *Ohio Northern University Law*

(This Listing Continued)

Review, Vol. XXIV, No. 4, 1998. Editor, Bank Investment Products Deskbook, New York, Warren, Gorham & Lamont, 1995. Editor, E-commerce in Financial Products and Services, Law Journal Press, 2001. Stroock & Stroock & Lavan, Washington, D.C., 1984-1992, Managing Partner, D.C. Office. Chief Counsel and Member of Policy Group, Office of Comptroller of Currency, U.S. Department of Treasury, Washington, D.C., 1982-1984. Senior Vice President, General Counsel and Corporate Secretary, MasterCard International Inc., New York, 1974-1982; CIT Financial Corporation, New York, 1973-1974; American Express Company, New York, 1970-1973. ***Email:*** bsmith@mayerbrown.com

ADRIAN L. STEEL, JR., born St. Louis, Missouri, January 2, 1950; admitted to bar, 1975, Missouri; 1976, Illinois; 1979, U.S. Supreme Court; 1981, District of Columbia. *Education:* University of Missouri at Columbia (A.B., 1972); University of Michigan (J.D., magna cum laude, 1975). ***Email:*** asteel@mayerbrown.com

JOHN J. SULLIVAN, born Boston, Massachusetts, November 20, 1959; admitted to bar, 1987, New York; 1993, District of Columbia. *Education:* Brown University (A.B., 1981); Columbia University (J.D., 1985). Book Reviews Editor, *Columbia Law Review.* Law Clerk to: Judge John Minor Wisdom, 1985-1986; Justice David H. Souter, 1990-1991. Deputy General Counsel, Bush-Quayle '92, 1992. General Counsel, Phil Gramm for President, 1995. Counselor to Assistant Attorney General J. Michael Luttig, Office of Legal Counsel, U.S. Department of Justice, 1991. Publication: Co-author: "Appeals to the Supreme Court," in Business and Commercial Litigation in Federal Courts (West 1998). . ***Email:*** jsullivan@mayerbrown.com

ROBERT H. SWART, born Grand Rapids, Michigan, November 12, 1946; admitted to bar, 1970, Michigan; 1971, District of Columbia. *Education:* St. Joseph Seminary, St. Norbert College and University of Michigan (A.B., 1968); University of Michigan (J.D., cum laude, 1970). ***Email:*** rswart@mayerbrown.com

EVAN M. TAGER, born Columbia, South Carolina, May 27, 1960; admitted to bar, 1986, New York and U.S. District Court for the District of Maryland; 1987, District of Columbia and U.S. Court of Appeals, Eleventh Circuit; 1988, U .S. District Court for the District of Columbia; 1989, U.S. Court of Appeals for the District of Columbia Circuit and U.S. Court of Appeals, Fourth Circuit; 1990, U.S. Supreme Court; 1993, U.S. Court of Appeals for the Federal Circuit; 1995, U.S. Court of Appeals, Second Circuit; 1996, U.S. Court of Appeals, Seventh Circuit; 2001, U.S. Court of Appeals, Fifth Circuit. *Education:* Princeton University (A.B., magna cum laude, 1982); Stanford University (J.D., 1985). Author: "Reading Between the Lines of Cooper Industries, Inc. v. Leatherman Tool Group, Inc., 121 S. Ct. 1678 (2001)," Mealey's Litigation Report: Insurance Bad Faith, Aug. 8, 2001, at 22; "The Constitutional Limitations on Class Actions," Mealey's Litigation Report: Class Actions, Jan. 2000, at 34; "Tips on Preserving Arguments for Appeal," Mealey's Insurance Law Weekly (Dec. 1, 1997). Co-author: with Frey, "Punitive Damages," in Business and Commercial Litigation in Federal Courts (West 1998). Law Clerk, Honorable Mary M. Schroeder, U.S. Court of Appeals, Ninth Circuit, Phoenix, Arizona, 1985-1986. ***PRACTICE AREAS:*** Appellate Litigation; Constitutional Law. ***Email:*** etager@mayerbrown.com

CHARLES S. TRIPLETT, born Kansas City, Missouri, 1948; admitted to bar, 1975, Missouri; 1993, District of Columbia; U.S. Tax Court. *Education:* Rockhurst College (B.S., 1970); University of Missouri at Kansas City (J.D., 1974; LL.M., 1977). Internal Revenue Service: Deputy Associate Chief Counsel, 1986-1992; Special Assistant to the Chief Counsel, 1992-1993. Member, Business and Industry Advisory Committee, OECD. *Member:* American Bar Association (Chair, Transfer Pricing Committee, 2002—); International Fiscal Association. ***PRACTICE AREAS:*** International Taxation; Tax Controversies. ***Email:*** ctriplett@mayerbrown.com

KEITH J. WILLNER, born Topeka, Kansas, December 10, 1959; admitted to bar, 1984, California; 1988, District of Columbia. *Education:* University of Virginia (B.A., magna cum laude, 1981); University of Virginia School of Law (J.D., 1984). Member, Steering Committee of Real Estate, Housing and Land Use Section, District of Columbia Bar, 1997-2000, Financial Officer, 1998-2000. Chairman, Real Property Transactions Committee, Real Estate, Housing and Land Use Section, District of Columbia Bar, 1996-1997. Chairman, Commercial Transactions Committee, Real Estate, Housing and Land Use Section, District of Columbia Bar, 1995-1996. ***Email:*** kwillner@mayerbrown.com

GARY A. WINTERS, born Baltimore, Maryland, 1963; admitted to bar, 1992, Maryland; 1993, District of Columbia. *Education:* Northwestern University (B.A., 1985); Georgetown University (J.D., 1991). Author: "Unconstitutional Conditions as Nonsubsidiaries: When is Deference Inappropriate," 80 Geo. L.J. 161 (1991). ***PRACTICE AREAS:*** Antitrust; Commercial Litigation. ***Email:*** gwinters@mayerbrown.com

SENIOR COUNSEL

DAVID B. FINNEGAN, born New York, N.Y., July 17, 1933; admitted to bar, 1961, District of Columbia and Massachusetts; 1993, U.S. Supreme Court. *Education:* Boston College (B.S., 1956; J.D., 1960). U.S. House of Representatives, Washington, D.C., 1969-1995. Senior Counsel, Committee on Energy

(This Listing Continued)

MAYER, BROWN & PLATT, Washington—Continued

and Commerce (formerly the Committee on Interstate Foreign Commerce), 1976-1995. Counsel, Committee on Science and Technology, 1975-1976. Associate General Counsel, Committee on Government Operations, 1969-1975. Staff of Congressman Ken Heckler (D-WVA), Washington, D.C., 1969. U.S. Department of the Interior, Washington, D.C., 1960-1969. Assistant Legislative Counsel, 1968-1969. General Attorney, Office of the Legislative Counsel, 1963-1968. General Attorney, Office of the Solicitor, 1961-1963. Law Clerk, Office of the Solicitor, 1960-1961. ***Email:*** dfinnegan@mayerbrown.com

SPECIAL COUNSEL

DAVID HYMAN, born 1961; admitted to bar, 1989, Illinois; 1996, District of Columbia. *Education:* University of Chicago (B.A.; J.D., 1989). ***Email:*** dhyman@law.unmaryland.edu

CHARLES ROTHFELD, born New York, N.Y., November 17, 1956; admitted to bar, 1982, New York; 1983, District of Columbia. *Education:* Cornell University (A.B., 1977); University of Chicago (J.D., cum laude, 1980). Author: "The Surprising Case Against Punitive Damages in Libel Suits Against Public Figures," 19 Yale L. & Pol. Rev. 165 (2000); "Scheiner's Next Wave: Distinguishing Taxes From Fees Under the Commerce Clause," 17 State Tax Notes 1681 (1999);"From Japan Line to Barclays: The Rise and Fall of the Foreign Commerce Clause," 7 State Tax Notes 379 (1994); "Section 1983: The Civil Rights Alternative to Constitutional Challenges," 6 State Tax Notes 751 (1994); "Quill: Confusing the Commerce Clause," 56 Tax Notes 487 (1992); "Federalism in a Conservative Supreme Court," 22 Journal of Federalism 21 (1992); "Rationalizing Removal," 1990 B.Y.U.L. Rev. 221. Law Clerk to: Justice Harry A. Blackmun, U.S. Supreme Court, 1981-1982; Judge Spottswood Robinson, III, U.S. Court of Appeals for the District of Columbia Circuit, 1980-1981. Assistant to the Solicitor General, U.S. Department of Justice, 1984-1988. Deputy Minority Counsel, U.S. House of Representatives Select Committee on the U.S. Role in Iranian Arms Transfers to Croatia and Bosnia, 1996. Board of Advisors, Georgetown University Law Center's Supreme Court Institute, 1999—. Advisory Board, State and Local Legal Center, 1991 —. ***Email:*** crothfeld@mayerbrown.com

COUNSEL

CAROL J. BILZI, born Huntington, New York, August 6, 1954; admitted to bar, 1986, Pennsylvania; 1987, District of Columbia. *Education:* State University of New York at Albany (B.A., magna cum laude, 1976); Georgetown University (J.D., cum laude, 1986). ***Email:*** cbilzi@mayerbrown.com

BRIAN T. BORDERS, born Washington, Indiana, July 8, 1950; admitted to bar, 1980, California; 1981, District of Columbia; 1987, Colorado. *Education:* United States Military Academy (B.S., 1972); University of California, Hastings College of the Law (J.D., 1980). Order of the Coif. Thurston Society. Note and Comment Editor, Hastings Law Journal, 1979-1980. Adjunct Associate Professor, Hastings College of Law, 1986. *Member:* American Bar Association (Member, Business Law Section); National Association of Securities Dealers (Member, Board of Governors); NASD Regulation (Member, Board of Directors). [U.S. Army, 1972-1977]. ***PRACTICE AREAS:*** Federal Regulation and Legislation; Securities Regulatory Policy and Controversies. ***Email:*** bborders@mayerbrown.com

THOMAS B. BURNSIDE, born Columbus, Ohio, March 28, 1958; admitted to bar, 1987, Maryland (Not admitted in District of Columbia). *Education:* Ohio Wesleyan University (B.A., 1981) Phi Alpha Theta; Catholic University of America (J.D., 1987). Associate Editor, Catholic University Law Review. ***Email:*** tburnside@mayerbrown.com

COURTNEY A. DINSMORE, born Washington, D.C., April 13, 1966; admitted to bar, 1993, New York (Not admitted in District of Columbia). *Education:* Swarthmore College (B.A., 1988); University of Virginia (J.D., 1992). Past Associate, Brobeck, Phlegar & Harrison (NY office) and Brown & Wood. ***Email:*** cdinsmore@mayerbrown.com

JULIAN P. GEHMAN, born December 11, 1955; admitted to bar, 1992, Maryland; 1995, District of Columbia. *Education:* University of Southern California (B.A., 1980); Georgetown University Law Center (J.D., cum laude, 1992). Phi Beta Kappa. ***Email:*** jgehman@mayerbrown.com

ANDREW J. MORRIS, born Newport News, Virginia, July 29, 1958; admitted to bar, 1986, Maryland and U.S. Court of Appeals, Third Circuit; 1987, District of Columbia; U.S. Supreme Court; U.S. Court of Appeals for the District of Columbia, Third, Fourth and Eleventh Circuits. *Education:* University of Virginia (B.S., with distinction, 1980; J.D., 1985, Order of Coif); University of Oxford, England (B.C.L., with honors, 1993). Certified Public Accountant. Author: "Clarifying the Imputation Doctrine: Charging Audit Clients With Responsibility for Unauthorized Audit Interference," Colum. Bus. L. Rev. 339, 2001; Jurisdiction in Cyberspace (Book Chapter), in E-Commerce, Law Journal Seminars Press (2000); Avoiding & Defending Against Securities Class Actions, 3 Journal of Internet Law (May 1999). Co-author: "Class Actions," in Federal Practice Manual (Seventh Circuit), Lwyrs Coop. (1998); "Federal Rule of Evidence 404 (b): The Fictitious Ban on Character Reasoning from Other Crimes Evidence," 17 Review of Litigation 181 (1998). Law Clerk to the Honorable Max Rosenn, U.S. Court of Appeals for the Third Circuit, 1985-1986. ***Email:*** amorris@mayerbrown.com

HOWARD A. PARELSKIN, born Milwaukee, Wisconsin, June 20, 1952; admitted to bar, 1977, California; 1987, Florida; 1991, District of Columbia. *Education:* University of Pennsylvania (B.S., magna cum laude, 1974); Stanford University (J.D., 1977). Beta Gamma Sigma; Beta Alpha Psi. Author: "Buying Assets from the RTC," 9 The Practical Real Estate Lawyer 4, 1993. Senior Counsel: Resolution Trust Corporation, 1990-1992; Federal Home Loan Mortgage Corporation, 1995-1998. *Member:* State Bar of California; The Florida Bar; District of Columbia Bar. ***PRACTICE AREAS:*** Real Estate Transactions; Real Estate Finance. ***Email:*** hparelskin@mayerbrown.com

ROGER W. PATRICK, born Youngstown, Ohio, November 26, 1959; admitted to bar, 1984, District of Columbia. *Education:* Carnegie Mellon University (B.S., Chemistry, with University Honors, 1981); Yale University (J.D., 1984). ***PRACTICE AREAS:*** Environmental Law. ***Email:*** rwpatrick@mayerbrown.com

LINDA L. RHODES, born Washington, D.C., August 13, 1962; admitted to bar, 1987, Virginia; 1988, District of Columbia. *Education:* College of William & Mary (B.B.A., 1984); University of Virginia (J.D., 1987). ***Email:*** lrhodes@mayerbrown.com

ADAM C. SLOANE, born Glen Cove, New York, July 24, 1958; admitted to bar, 1993, Pennsylvania; 1994, District of Columbia. *Education:* Haverford College (B.A., 1980); Princeton University (M.A., 1984); University of Michigan (J.D., 1991). ***Email:*** asloane@mayerbrown.com

ASSOCIATES

ROBERT L. BRONSTON, born Mather AFB, California, May 24, 1969; admitted to bar, 1996, Virginia, U.S. District Court, Eastern District of Virginia and U.S. Court of Appeals, Fourth Circuit; 1997, U.S. Court of Appeals, Third Circuit; 1998, District of Columbia and U.S. Court of Appeals, Eighth and Ninth Circuits; 2000, U.S. Supreme Court; 2001, U.S. Court of Appeals for the Federal Circuit. *Education:* University of Pennsylvania (B.S. & B.A., 1991); University of Michigan (J.D., magna cum laude, 1995). ***PRACTICE AREAS:*** Appellate and Trial Litigation; Antitrust. ***Email:*** rbronston@mayerbrown.com

MARY BETH BROOKS, born New London, Connecticut, November 7, 1970; admitted to bar, 2001, New York (Not admitted in District of Columbia). *Education:* Providence College (B.A., magna cum laude, 1993); Georgetown University Law Center (J.D., 2000). ***PRACTICE AREAS:*** Corporate Law. ***Email:*** mbrooks@mayerbrown.com

JAY S. BROWN, born Cleveland, Ohio, June 22, 1970; admitted to bar, 1995, Maryland; 1998, District of Columbia. *Education:* Santa Clara University (B.S., 1992); Syracuse University (J.D., magna cum laude, 1995). ***Email:*** jsbrown@mayerbrown.com

CRAIG W. CANETTI, born Queens, New York, April 15, 1968; admitted to bar, 1996, District of Columbia. *Education:* Yale University (B.A., magna cum laude, 1990); Georgetown University (J.D., cum laude, 1995). Author: "Fifty Years After the Chicago Conference: A Proposal for Dispute Settlement Under the Auspices of the International Civil Aviation Organization," 26 Law & Policy Int'l Bus. 497, 1995. ***Email:*** ccanetti@mayerbrown.com

PETER C. CHOHARIS, born Athens, Greece, April 11, 1961; admitted to bar, 1993, New York and Massachusetts; 1994, District of Columbia. *Education:* Harvard University (B.A., 1984); Yale University (J.D., 1991). Sheldon Fellow. Visiting Lecturer, Yale College, 1991. Adjunct Professor (Remedies), American University, 1996. Author, "A Comprehensive Market Strategy for Tort Reform," 12 Yale J. on Reg. 435 (1995). ***Email:*** pchoharis@mayerbrown.com

STEVEN J. DUFFIELD, admitted to bar, 2001, Texas and U.S. District Court, Southern District of Texas (Not admitted in District of Columbia). *Education:* Georgetown University (B.A., 1992); University of Chicago Law School (J.D., 1999). Phi Beta Kappa. ***PRACTICE AREAS:*** Appellate Practice. ***Email:*** sduffield@mayerbrown.com

MICHAEL J. FARLEY, born Chicago, Illinois, January 5, 1965; admitted to bar, 1992, Wisconsin; 2000, District of Columbia. *Education:* Marquette University (B.A., 1987; J.D., 1992). ***Email:*** mfarley@mayerbrown.com

GREGORY S. FEDER, admitted to bar, 1997, Virginia and U.S. Court of Appeals, Fourth Circuit; 1998, District of Columbia, U.S. District Court for the District of Columbia, U.S. Court of Appeals for the District of Columbia and Seventh Circuits and U.S. District Court, Eastern District of Virginia; 1999, U.S. Court of Appeals, Eleventh Circuit and U.S. Court of Appeals, Federal Circuit. *Education:* University of Virginia (B.A., 1992; J.D., 1997). Author: Note, "Enforcement of Intellectual Property Rights in China: You Can Lead a Horse to Water, But You Can't Make it Drink," 37 Va. J. Int'l L. 223 (1996). Co-author: with Kim Marie Boylan, Brian W. Smith and Joseph E. Yesutis, "Bank-Owned

(This Listing Continued)

Life Insurance: Pre-Purchase Analysis & Post-Purchase Compliance," 118 Banking Law Journal 208 (Mar. 2001); with Thomas H. Odom, "Challenging the Federal Driver's Privacy Protection Act: The Next Step in Developing a Jurisprudence of Process-Oriented Federalism under the Tenth Amendment," 53 U. Miami L. Rev. 71 (1998). ***PRACTICE AREAS:*** Financial Services Law; Regulatory Law; E-Commerce; Privacy Law. ***Email:*** gfeder@mayerbrown.com

DAVID M. GOSSETT, born Chicago, Illinois, July 8, 1969; admitted to bar, 1997, Illinois and U.S. Court of Appeals, Seventh Circuit; 1999, U.S. Court of Appeals, for the District of Columbia and Ninth Circuits; 2000, District of Columbia and U.S. District Court, District of Maryland; 2001, U.S. Supreme Court and U.S. District Court for the District of Columbia. *Education:* Reed College (B.A., 1991); University of Pennsylvania (M.A., 1993); University of Chicago (J.D., with high honors, 1997). National Science Foundation Fellow. Author: Comment: "Chevron, Take Two: Deference to Revised Agency Interpretations of Statutes," 64 U. Chi. L. Rev. 681 (1997); "Dialogue with Archibald Cox: The Case for Campaign Finance Reform," 1 Green Bag 2d 289 (1998); "Dialogue with John Sexton: Legal Education Today and Tomorrow," 3 Green Bag 2d 417 (2000). Co-founder and Executive Editor, The Green Bag, 1997—. Law Clerk, the Honorable Diane P. Wood, U.S. Court of Appeals for the Seventh Circuit, 1997-1998. Attorney, U.S. Department of Justice, Civil Division, 1998-2000. Visiting Associate Professor, Riga Graduate School of Law, Summer, 1999; Summer, 2000. ***Email:*** dgossett@mayerbrown.com

BRITTON B. GUERRINA, born Big Spring, Texas, September 7, 1968; admitted to bar, 1999, Illinois (Not admitted in District of Columbia). *Education:* University of Chicago (B.A., 1990; M.A., 1990; J.D., 1999). ***LANGUAGES:*** French. ***Email:*** bguerrina@mayerbrown.com

SHOUFEN HU, born Taipei, Taiwan, August 18, 1973; admitted to bar, 1997, New York; 1999, District of Columbia. *Education:* National Taiwan University (LL.B., 1995); Tulane Law School (J.D., 1998). Author: "WTO and New Opportunities in Ghina - Financial Services Industries," MBP Financial Services Regulatory Report; "WTO and New Opportunities in China - Telecommunications and Internet Industries," MBP Financial Services Regulatory Report. Contributor: Investment Product Deskbook: Banking Rules and Regulations (1005/Supp. 2001) (Chapter 13 - Ancillary Issues). ***PRACTICE AREAS:*** Financial Services Law; Corporate Law; Mergers and Acquisitions. ***Email:*** shu@mayerbrown.com

JOHN C. C. HUGHES, born East Lansing, Michigan, October 22, 1971; admitted to bar, 1999, Illinois; 2000, District of Columbia. *Education:* Pepperdine University (B.A., 1993); Michigan Law School (J.D., 1999). ***PRACTICE AREAS:*** Tax Controversies. ***Email:*** jhughes@mayerbrown.com

CRAIG ISENBERG, born Albany, New York, April 10, 1970; admitted to bar, 1997, New York; 1999, District of Columbia. *Education:* Amherst College (B.A., 1992); Tulane Law School (J.D., 1996). Law Clerk, Hon. Henry A. Politz, U.S. 5th Circuit Court of Appeals, 1996-1997.

JOHN W. JARRELL, JR., born Woodbury, New Jersey, January 19, 1969; admitted to bar, 1995, Virginia; 1998, District of Columbia. *Education:* Rutgers University (B.A., 1991); George Washington University (J.D., high honors, 1995). Order of the Coif. ***Email:*** jjarrell@mayerbrown.com

DAWN MARIE KAROLICK, born Berea, Ohio, September 15, 1963; admitted to bar, 1999, Virginia; 2001, District of Columbia. *Education:* Bowling Green State University (B.A., 1986); Washington College of Law, American University, (J.D., 1999). ***PRACTICE AREAS:*** Regulated Industries; Litigation. ***Email:*** dkarolick@mayerbrown.com

RICHARD B. KATSKEE, born Omaha, Nebraska, October 3, 1967; admitted to bar, 2000, Maryland; 2001, District of Columbia. *Education:* University of Michigan (A.B., 1989); Yale Law School (J.D., 1996). Author: "Book Review, *John Rawls, Political Liberalism (1993),*" 7 REV. POL. ECON. 242 (1995). ***PRACTICE AREAS:*** Appellate Practice. ***Email:*** rkatskee@mayerbrown.com

MICHAEL E. LACKEY, JR., born Hopkinsville, Kentucky, May 3, 1961; admitted to bar, 1993, Florida; 1994, District of Columbia; 1999, U.S. Supreme Court. *Education:* Massachusetts Institute of Technology (B.S., 1983); George Washington University (J.D., with high honors, 1993). Order of the Coif. Co-Author with Mark Ryan: "Removing Class Actions to Federal Court: Preserve Congress' Intent," (Washington Legal Foundation 1994); Co-Author with Jim Dobkin: "Government Contractor Compliance Program Hotlines and the Attorney Client Privilege," 61 Fed. Cont. Rep. (BNA 1994); Co-Author with Ken Geller: "Supreme Court's 'Kumho' Decision a Boon to Public," Leader's Product Liability Law and Strategy, 1999. Associate Independent Counsel, 1997-1998. [Lieutenant, U.S. Navy, 1983-1990]. ***Email:*** mlackey@mayerbrown.com

LISA L. LEVINE, born Honesdale, Pennsylvania, November 6, 1969; admitted to bar, 1994, Maryland; 1997, District of Columbia. *Education:* University of Pennsylvania (B.A., 1991); Washington College of Law of American University (J.D., cum laude, 1994). Trial Attorney, U.S. Department of Transportation, 1995-1998. ***PRACTICE AREAS:*** Litigation. ***Email:*** llevine@mayerbrown.com

(This Listing Continued)

SUSAN J. LUKEN, born Cincinnati, Ohio, January 23, 1963; admitted to bar, 1988, Ohio; 1998, District of Columbia. *Education:* University of Cincinnati (B.A., 1985); The American University (J.D., cum laude, 1988); Georgetown University Law Center (LL.M. in Taxation & Certificate in Employee Benefits, 1999). Member, American University Law Review, 1986-1988. Counsel, National Organization of Life and Health Insurance Guaranty Associations, 1996-1997. Associate, Dinsmore & Shohl, Cincinnati, 1988-1996. ***Email:*** sluken@mayerbrown.com

ELDAD Z. MALAMUTH, admitted to bar, 2001, Illinois (Not admitted in District of Columbia). *Education:* University of Michigan (B.S., 1997); University of Chicago (J.D., with honors, 2001). ***PRACTICE AREAS:*** Litigation. ***Email:*** emalamuth@mayerbrown.com

JENNIFER C. MALONEY, born Madrid, Spain, December 13, 1966; admitted to bar, 1992, Connecticut; 1995, District of Columbia. *Education:* New England Conservatory of Music (B.M., 1988); Western New England School of Law (J.D., magna cum laude, 1992). ***PRACTICE AREAS:*** Tax Controversies. ***Email:*** jmaloney@mayerbrown.com

JULIE K. McCONNELL, born Pittsburgh, Pennsylvania, October 10, 1971; admitted to bar, 1997, Pennsylvania (Not admitted in District of Columbia). *Education:* Wake Forest University (B.A., cum laude, 1993); American University (J.D., magna cum laude, 1997). Federal Trade Commission. ***Email:*** jmcconnell@mayerbrown.com

JILL K. McDOWELL, born St. Petersburg, Florida, 1968; admitted to bar, 1998, Florida; 1999, District of Columbia. *Education:* University of Florida (B.S., 1990); Catholic University (J.D., magna cum laude, 1998). Author: "Congress Errs in Deregulating Broadcast Ownership Caps: More Monopolies Less Localism, Decreased Diversity and Violations of Equal Protection," 5 Comm. Law Conspectus 269, 1997. ***PRACTICE AREAS:*** Litigation; Government Contracts; Regulated Industries. ***Email:*** jmcdowell@mayerbrown.com

RITA W. MORALES, born Hindman, Kentucky, September 15, 1961; admitted to bar, 1992, Maryland; 1995, District of Columbia. *Education:* Eastern Kentucky University (B.A., 1985); Howard University School of Law (J.D., cum laude, 1992). ***Email:*** rmorales@mayerbrown.com

SCOTT A. MOREHOUSE, born Newport, Rhode Island, November 28, 1967; admitted to bar, 1993, Virginia; 1994, District of Columbia. *Education:* University of Massachusetts (B.A., summa cum laude, 1990); Georgetown University Law Center (J.D., 1993). Phi Beta Kappa. ***PRACTICE AREAS:*** Real Estate; Finance. ***Email:*** smorehouse@mayerbrown.com

WENDY L. MORRIS, born Philadelphia, Pennsylvania, July 6, 1967; admitted to bar, 1993, Pennsylvania; 1996, District of Columbia. *Education:* George Washington University (B.A., 1989); Washington College of Law (J.D., magna cum laude, 1992). ***Email:*** wmorris@mayerbrown.com

J. KEVIN MULDOWNEY, born Richmond, Virginia, August 16, 1964; admitted to bar, 2001, Virginia (Not admitted in District of Columbia). *Education:* Virginia Tech (B.S., 1988); George Mason University School of Law (J.D., magna cum laude, 2000). Certified Public Accountant, Virginia, 1995. ***Email:*** kmuldowney@mayerbrown.com

ANDREW A. NICELY, born Rochester, New York, December 11, 1967; admitted to bar, 1997, Virginia; 1998, District of Columbia, Illinois, U.S. District Court, Eastern District of Virginia and District of Columbia; 1999, U.S. Bankruptcy Court, Eastern District of Virginia; 2001, U.S. Supreme Court. *Education:* Bates College (B.A., cum laude, with high honors, 1990); State University of New York at Buffalo (M.A., 1994); University of Pennsylvania (J.D., cum laude, 1997). Order of the Coif. Recipient, W. Foster Reeves Faculty Award. ***PRACTICE AREAS:*** Commercial Litigation; Labor and Employment; Appellate Practice. ***Email:*** anicely@mayerbrown.com

RONALD D. PARISOTTO, born Sudbury, Ontario, Canada, April 22, 1964; admitted to bar, 1998, New York and District of Columbia. *Education:* University of Waterloo (B.Math., 1988); Syracuse University (J.D., cum laude, 1997). ***LANGUAGES:*** Italian. ***Email:*** rparisotto@mayerbrown.com

JULIE ANNA POTTS, born Birmingham, Alabama, November 9, 1969; admitted to bar, 1997, Virginia; 1999, District of Columbia. *Education:* Bryn Mawr College (A.B., 1991); George Washington University (J.D., with honors, 1997). Law Clerk to the Honorable John M. Facciola, U.S. Magistrate Judge, U.S. District Court for the District of Columbia, 1997-1998. ***PRACTICE AREAS:*** Environmental Law; Litigation. ***Email:*** jpotts@mayerbrown.com

LAURA A. REILLY, born Smithtown, New York, 1970; admitted to bar, 1995, Virginia; 1996, District of Columbia; 1997, Maryland; 1999, New York. *Education:* Lafayette College (B.A., cum laude, 1992); George Washington University (J.D., with honors, 1995). ***PRACTICE AREAS:*** Real Estate. ***Email:*** lreilly@mayerbrown.com

ANDREA ELISA RYAN, born Philadelphia, Pennsylvania, July 7, 1975; admitted to bar, 2001, New York and District of Columbia. *Education:* University of Maryland (B.A., 1996); Georgetown University Law Center (J.D., 2000). ***PRACTICE AREAS:*** Litigation. ***Email:*** aryan@mayerbrown.com

(This Listing Continued)

MAYER, BROWN & PLATT, Washington—Continued

TIMOTHY R. RYAN, born Washington, D.C., October 30, 1970; admitted to bar, 1997, New York; 2000, District of Columbia. *Education:* James Madison University (B.S., magna cum laude, 1992); University of Virginia (J.D., 1996). Omicron Delta Kappa. ***PRACTICE AREAS:*** Finance; Corporate Law; Technology Law. ***Email:*** tryan@mayerbrown.com

KRISTIN HART SMITH, born Meadowbrook, Pennsylvania, March 10, 1969; admitted to bar, 1994, New Jersey; 1995, Pennsylvania; 1996, New York; 1999, District of Columbia. *Education:* Pennsylvania State University (B.S., 1991); University of California, Hastings College of the Law (J.D., 1994). ***Email:*** khsmith@mayerbrown.com

LILY FU SWENSON, born Chicago, Illinois, November 22, 1969; admitted to bar, 1994, Illinois; 1996, District of Columbia. *Education:* University of Wisconsin-Madison (B.A., 1990); University of Minnesota (J.D., 1993). Law Clerk to Hon. Michael S. Kanne, U.S. Court of Appeals for the Seventh Circuit, 1993-1994. ***LANGUAGES:*** Chinese. ***REPORTED CASES:*** U.S. v. Rahseparian, 231 F.3d 1257 (2000). ***PRACTICE AREAS:*** Trial Practice; Appellate Practice; Antitrust; White Collar Crime. ***Email:*** lswenson@mayerbrown.com

JEFFREY P. TAFT, born Haverhill, Massachusetts, January 2, 1967; admitted to bar, 1993, New York; 1994, Ohio; 2001, District of Columbia. *Education:* Tulane University (B.A., 1989); University of Pittsburgh (J.D., 1992); Harvard University (LL.M., 1993). Author: "The Latest Attempt to Make the Fair Credit Reporting Act More Fair," 51 Cons. Fin. L. Q. Rep. 304 (1997); "Credit Screening: The Rest of the Story," 49 Cons. Fin. L. Q. Rep. 391 (1995). Contributor: Investment Products Deskbook: Banking Rules and Regulations (1955 / Supp. 2001); Chapter 10 - Non-Mutual Fund Related Products (Annuities and Insurance); Chapter 12 - Institutional Investment; Chapter 18 - Bank Marketing of Insurance Products. ***PRACTICE AREAS:*** Bank Regulatory; Consumer Financial Services; Privacy Law. ***Email:*** jtaft@mayerbrown.com

JODI L. VALERI, born Leominster, Massachusetts, January 12, 1970; admitted to bar, 1996, Maryland; 1998, District of Columbia. *Education:* University of Florida (B.S., magna cum laude, 1992); Georgetown University Law Center (J.D., 1996). ***Email:*** jvaleri@mayerbrown.com

SHEILA DEARYBURY WALCOFF, born Washington, D.C., February 19, 1969; admitted to bar, 1993, Maryland; 1996, District of Columbia. *Education:* Minot State University (B.A., cum laude, 1990); Georgetown University (J.D., 1993). Majority Counsel, U.S. House of Representatives Armed Services Committee, 1998-1999. ***PRACTICE AREAS:*** Government Relations. ***Email:*** sdearybury@mayerbrown.com

ARTHUR C. WALKER, JR., born Glen Ridge, New Jersey, March 3, 1971; admitted to bar, 1997, California; 1998, District of Columbia. *Education:* Georgetown University School of Business (B.S.B.A., magna cum laude, 1993); Georgetown University Law Center (J.D., cum laude, 1996; LL.M., Taxation, 1999). Author: "Tax Planning Opportunities Using QSSSs as Pass-Through Entities," Taxes, 1998. ***Email:*** awalker@mayerbrown.com

CHRISTOPHER C. WANG, born Washington, D.C., May 18, 1973; admitted to bar, 1998, Maryland; 1999, U.S. Court of Appeals, Fourth Circuit; 2001, District of Columbia. *Education:* Yale University (B.A., cum laude, 1995); University of Chicago (J.D., 1998). ***Email:*** cwang@mayerbrown.com

NICK S. WILLIAMS, born Maisons - Laffitte, France, 1965; admitted to bar, 1999, New York and U.S. District Court, Southern District of New York; 2000, U.S. District Court, Eastern District of New York (Not admitted in District of Columbia). *Education:* George Mason University (B.A., with highest distinction, 1994); University of Virginia School of Law (J.D., 1998). Member, Articles Review Board, Virginia Journal of Internal Law. ***LANGUAGES:*** Spanish. ***PRACTICE AREAS:*** Civil Litigation; Securities Litigation; Professional Liability. ***Email:*** nickwilliams@mayerbrown.com

JOSEPH E. YESUTIS, born Chicago, Illinois, December 23, 1966; admitted to bar, 1994, Alabama and U.S. District Court, Middle District of Alabama; 1996, District of Columbia. *Education:* Harvard University (A.B., magna cum laude, 1989); Tulane University of Louisiana (J.D., 1994). Phi Alpha Delta. ***Email:*** jyesutis@mayerbrown.com

GEORGE E. YORK, born Chicago, Illinois, December 26, 1972; admitted to bar, 2001, Illinois (Not admitted in District of Columbia). *Education:* Brown University (B.A., 1995); Columbia University School of Law (J.D., 2001). Harlan Fiske Stone Scholar. Member, Columbia Journal of European Law. ***PRACTICE AREAS:*** International Trade; Government. ***Email:*** geyork@mayerbrown.com

MCALEESE & ASSOCIATES, P.C.

WASHINGTON, D.C.

(See McLean, Virginia)

Specializing in Federal Procurement Law and Government Contracts in defense and intelligence communities in addition to civilian agencies; including Bid Protests before the General Accounting Office, the Court of Federal Claims and the

(This Listing Continued)

United States District Court; handling of all aspects of claims preparation and prosecution of resulting disputes under the Contract Disputes Act before the Court of Federal Claims and all Boards of Contract Appeals; Defense of defective cost-or-pricing allegations as well as defense of civil False Claims Act whistle-blower suits; negotiation and litigation of rights in Technical Data, Computer Software, Patents Rights, and other facets of high technology law in Federal Procurements; handling of all aspects of environmental compliance, counseling as well as representation with respect to private cost recovery actions under Comprehensive Environmental Response, Compensation, and Liability Act and environmental insurance coverage claims; assists in all aspects of mergers and/or acquisitions in the defense community.

LAW OFFICE OF VIRGINIA A. MCARTHUR

Established in 1992

1101 17TH STREET, N.W.
SUITE 820
WASHINGTON, D.C. 20036
Telephone: 202-857-3434
Fax: 202-463-3060
Email: vmcarthur@mcarthurlaw.com
URL: http://www.lawyers.com/mcarthurlaw

Trusts and Estates, Estate Planning, Estate Administration, Estate and Gift Taxation.

VIRGINIA A. MCARTHUR, born Ottawa, Canada, July 10, 1942; admitted to bar, 1975, District of Columbia; 1988, Maryland; 1989, Virginia. *Education:* Bucknell University (B.A., 1964); University of Edinburgh, Scotland; Georgetown University (J.D., 1975). Co-author: "Disabled Planning-How Laws Thwart Planning for Incapacity of Owners of D.C. Real Property," Washington Lawyer, May/June, 1990; Book, *Wills, Trusts & Estates,* published by Bar Association of the District of Columbia, 1993. *Member:* The District of Columbia Bar (Member, Steering Committee of Estates, Trusts and Probate Law Section, 1988-1992; Chair, 1989-1991; Chair, Committee on Professional and Fiduciary Responsibility, 1992-1995); American Bar Association (Member: Real Property, Probate and Trust Law Section); Washington, D.C. Estate Planning Council (Board of Directors, 1993-1995; President, 2001-2002). Fellow: American College of Trust and Estate Counsel, 1990. ***LANGUAGES:*** Spanish. ***PRACTICE AREAS:*** Trusts and Estates; Estate Planning; Estate Administration.

ANN ST. LAURENT, born Rochester, New Hampshire, February 12, 1944; admitted to bar, 1990, Virginia; 1991, District of Columbia; 1998, Maryland. *Education:* Smith College (B.A., 1966); Tulane University (J.D., cum laude, 1990); Georgetown University Law Center (LL.M, 1997). Author: "Estate Planning with Tax-Deferred Annuities -- Special Problems Under Section 72," 21 Tax Management Estates, Gifts and Trusts Journal 6 (1996); The Monthly Digest of Tax Articles, (July 1997). Co-Author: "Defective Grantor Trusts: Gift Tax Consequences of Payment of Income Tax Liability by Grantor," Vol. 20, No. 5 Tax Management Estates, Gifts and Trusts Journal (1995). *Member:* The District of Columbia Bar; Virginia State Bar; American Bar Association (Member: Real Property, Probate and Trust Law Section and the Section of Taxation). ***LANGUAGES:*** French. ***PRACTICE AREAS:*** Trusts and Estate; Estate Planning; Estate Administration. ***Email:*** astlaurent@mcarthurlaw.com

LEGAL SUPPORT PERSONNEL

JEFFREY L. TRENT, (Legal Assistant). ***PRACTICE AREAS:*** Trusts and Estates. ***Email:*** jtrent@mcarthurlaw.com

JOHN A. MCCAHILL

2021 L STREET, N.W., SUITE 300
WASHINGTON, D.C. 20036
Telephone: 202-861-0070
Fax: 202-861-2939
Email: Artabane@cais.com
URL: http://www.lawyers.com/mccahilllaw

White Collar Criminal Defense, Commercial Fraud, Business Crimes, Electronic Surveillance, Qui Tam, Criminal Appeals, Securities Fraud, International Criminal Defense, Export Crimes, Grand Jury Practice, Personal Injury, Civil Trial Law.

FIRM PROFILE: Mr. John A. McCahill is first and foremost a trial lawyer. His practice is best known for its representation of corporate officers and business owners. The firm concentrates on complex trial work including white collar crime, export crimes and securities fraud. Mr. McCahill is listed in the Martindale-Hubbell Bar Register of Preeminent Lawyers.

(This Listing Continued)

JOHN A. McCAHILL, born Canonsburg, Pennsylvania; admitted to bar, 1970, District of Columbia; 1974, U.S. Supreme Court; 1985, Pennsylvania; 1995, Virginia. *Education:* Columbia University (A.B., 1961); Catholic University of America (J.D., 1969). Assistant U.S. Attorney, District of Columbia, 1970-1973. Assistant Special Counsel to the President, 1973-1974. Special Assistant to the Attorney General, 1974. General Counsel, President's Commission on Olympic Sports, 1975-1977. Special Legislative Counsel to the U.S. Olympic Committee, 1977-1985. *Member:* The District of Columbia Bar; American Bar Association (Member: Criminal Justice Section; White Collar Crimes Committee, 1986—); National Association of Criminal Defense Lawyers; Assistant United States Attorneys Association. (Also Of Counsel, Artabane & Belden, P.C.). ***PRACTICE AREAS:*** Civil Litigation; Legislative Law; Criminal Law; White Collar Crime; Personal Injury.

ROBERT C. McCANDLESS

Established in 1973

618 E STREET, S.E.

WASHINGTON, D.C. 20003

Telephone: 202-547-1200

Fax: 202-543-2931

URL: http://www.lawyers.com/robertcmccandless

Federal Legislative Practice, Financial and Insurance Institutions, Corporate Law, Foreign Governments and Legislative Strategies.

ROBERT C. McCANDLESS, born Hobart, Oklahoma, July 23, 1937; admitted to bar, 1965, Oklahoma and U.S. Court of Appeals, Tenth Circuit; 1967, District of Columbia; 1970, U.S. Supreme Court; 1975, U.S. Court of Appeals, District of Columbia. *Education:* George Washington University (A.A., 1959; B.A., 1961); George Washington University and University of Oklahoma (J.D., 1965). Phi Delta Phi. Assistant to U.S. Senator Robert S. Kerr, 1955-1963. Member, Executive Committee, George Washington University Law Alumni, 1971-1976. Member, Board of Trustees: Ford's Theatre, 1979-1980; Close-up Foundation, 1980-1986. Member, Panel of Arbitrators, Federal Mediation and Conciliation Service, American Arbitration Association. *Member:* The District of Columbia Bar; The Bar Association of the District of Columbia; Oklahoma, Federal and American Bar Associations; American Academy of Political and Social Science; American Judicature Society.

REPRESENTATIVE CLIENTS: Miller and Schroeder Municipals, Inc.; Transamerica Corporation; Transamerica Occidental Life Insurance Company; Transamerica Interway, Inc.; Santa Anita Realty Enterprises, Inc.; Provisional Government of Haiti; First National Bank of Chicago; International Paper Company; Democratic National Committee.

McCARRON & DIESS

Established in 1980

4910 MASSACHUSETTS AVENUE, N.W., SUITE 18

WASHINGTON, D.C. 20016

Telephone: 202-364-0400

Fax: 202-364-2731

URL: http://www.mccarronlaw.com

Perishable Agricultural Commodities Act (PACA) Law.

FIRM PROFILE: The firm limits its practice to representing produce businesses in cases under the Perishable Agricultural Commodities Act (PACA), a federal statute that regulates the produce industry. Mr. McCarron served as a staff attorney with USDA/PACA in Washington, D.C. Since 1980, the firm has concentrated on representing domestic and international produce companies in cases arising under the PACA. The firm also takes an active role in legislative and regulatory matters under the PACA.

MEMBERS OF FIRM

STEPHEN P. McCARRON, born Washington, D.C., August 25, 1951; admitted to bar, 1978, Maryland; 1979, District of Columbia and U.S. Court of Appeals, District of Columbia Circuit and Fourth Circuits; 1981, U.S. Supreme Court. *Education:* Bellarmine College (B.A., 1973); Catholic University of America (J.D., 1977). Staff Attorney, U.S. Department of Agriculture, 1977-1979. Assistant Public Defender, Montgomery County, Maryland, 1980-1982. *Member:* Montgomery County and Maryland State Bar Associations; The District of Columbia Bar. ***SPECIAL AGENCIES:*** U.S. Department of Agriculture, Perishable Agricultural Commodities Act (PACA) Division. ***REPORTED CASES:*** In re Magic Restaurants, Inc., 205 F.3d 108 (3rd Cir. 2000); In re Country Harvest Buffet Restaurants, Inc., 245 B.R. 650 (9th Cir. BAP 2000); Norinsberg v. U.S. Dept. of Agric., 162 F.3d 1194 (D.C. Cir., 1998); In re Kelly Food Products, Inc., 204 B.R. 18 (Bkrptcy. C.D. Ill 1997); In re Kornblum & Co., Inc., 81 F.3d 280 (2d Cir. 1996); John J. Conforti, d/b/a CÆ Produce v. U.S.A., 74 F. 3d 838 (8th Cir. 1996); Frank Tambone, Inc. v. U.S. Dept. of Agriculture, 50 F.3d 52 (D.C. Cir. 1995); Bell v. Department of Agriculture, 39 F.3d 1199 (D.C. Cir. 1994); Consumers Produce Co., Inc. v. Volante Wholesale Produce, Inc., 16 F.3d 1374 (3rd Cir. 1994); In re Lombardo Fruit and Produce Co., 12 F.3d 806, (8th Cir. 1994); Sanzone-Palmisano Company v. M. Seaman Enterprises, Inc., 986 F.2d 1010 (6th Cir. 1993); Six L's Packing Co. v. West Des Moines State Bank, 967 F.2d 256 (8th Cir. 1992); Frio Ice, S.A. v. SunFruit, Inc., 918 F.2d 154 (11th Cir. 1990); Harry Klein Produce Corp. v. U.S.D.A., 831 F.2d 403 (2d Cir. 1987); GÆ Terminal Packing v. Joe Phillips, Inc., 798 F.2d 579 (2d Cir. 1986); Tony Vitrano Co. v. National Produce Co., 815 F.Supp.23, (D.C.D.C., 1993); Stowe Potato Sales, Inc. v. Terry's Inc., 224 B.R. 329 (W.D. Va. 1998); In re Richmond Produce, 112 B.R. 364 DeBruyn Produce Company, et al. v. Olympia Produce Co., Inc., et al., 734 F.Supp. 483 (N.D.Ga. 1989); Willoughby Farms v. Frito-Lay, 863 F.2d 1029 (D.C. Cir. 1988); DeBruyn Produce Co. v. Victor Foods Inc., 674 F.Supp. 1405 (E.D.Mo. 1987). ***PRACTICE AREAS:*** Perishable Agricultural Commodities Act; Food and Agriculture. ***Email:*** smccarron@mccarronlaw.com

LOUIS W. DIESS, III, born Pequannock, New Jersey, April 9, 1967; admitted to bar, 1992, Maryland, New Jersey, U.S. District Court, District of New Jersey and U.S. District Court, District of Maryland (Not admitted in District of Columbia). *Education:* Gettysburg College (B.A., 1989); Widener University (J.D., 1992). Recipient, American Jurisprudence Award for Legal Writing and Analysis. Member, Moot Court Honor Society. *Member:* Maryland State, New Jersey State and American Bar Associations. ***SPECIAL AGENCIES:*** Perishable Agricultural Commodities Act (PACA) Division. ***REPORTED CASES:*** In re Snyder, 184 B.R. 473 (Bkrptcy. D.Md. 1995); Golman-Hayden Co., Inc. v. Fresh Source Produce, Inc., 217 F.3d 348 (5th Cir. 2000). ***PRACTICE AREAS:*** Perishable Agricultural Commodities Act (PACA). ***Email:*** ldiess@mccarronlaw.com

REFERENCE: NationsBank.

McCARTHY, SWEENEY & HARKAWAY, P.C.

Established in 1968

2175 K STREET, N.W.

SUITE 600

WASHINGTON, D.C. 20037

Telephone: 202-393-5710

Telecopier: 202-393-5721

Email: MSH@MSHPC.com

URL: http://www.mshpc.com

Energy, Public Utility, Transportation, Government Contracts and Administrative Practice Areas.

FIRM PROFILE: Since 1968, McCarthy, Sweeney & Harkaway, P.C. has concentrated on providing advice and litigation services in energy, transportation law matters, and government contracts. The firm's energy group includes former high ranking and key staff personnel from the Federal Energy Regulatory Commission. The firm's energy practice includes representing clients in litigation and rulemaking matters before the FERC, the Department of Energy, various state agencies and courts. The firm's transportation group includes former staff personnel from the Interstate Commerce Commission and the Department of Transportation. The firm's transportation practice includes representing clients in litigation and rulemaking matters before the Surface Transportation Board, the Department of Transportation, international regulatory bodies and various federal and state agencies and courts. The firm's government contracts group includes former high ranking personnel from the Department of Defense. The firm's government contracts practice includes counseling and litigation on contract formation, administration, contract compliance programs, equitable adjustments and claims.

CHARLES J. McCARTHY (1907-1995).

STEVEN J. KALISH, born Boston, Massachusetts, June 10, 1946; admitted to bar, 1974, Massachusetts; 1977, District of Columbia. *Education:* University of Massachusetts (B.A., 1968); University of Pennsylvania (J.D., 1973). Staff Attorney, Interstate Commerce Commission, 1973-1976. Author: "Antitrust Considerations for Shippers in a Changing Environment," 52 Transportation Practitioners Journal, Winter 1985; "Civil RICO—A Primer and Some Observations On An Avenue For Relief," 54 TPJ, Spring 1987; "Almost Everything You Wanted to Know About ICC Leasing Regulations," 55 TPJ, Winter 1988. Co-Author: "Transportation Deregulation - What's Deregulated and What Isn't," Nasstrac Publications, 1986. *Member:* Massachusetts, Federal (Chairman, Motor Carrier Committee, 1977-1980), Federal Energy (Chairman, Natural Gas Committee, 1998-1999) and American Bar Associations; Association of Transportation Law, Logistics and Policy (Chairman, Education Committee, 1987-1988; Secretary, 1988-1989). ***PRACTICE AREAS:*** Transportation Law; Energy Law. ***Email:*** SKALISH@MSHPC.com

JOHN M. CUTLER, JR., born Macon, Georgia, July 28, 1947; admitted to bar, 1976, District of Columbia. *Education:* University of the South (B.A., 1969); Georgetown University (J.D., 1976). Co-Author: "Transportation De-

(This Listing Continued)

McCARTHY, SWEENEY & HARKAWAY, P.C., Washington—Continued

regulation—What's Deregulated and What Isn't," Nasstrac Publications, 1986. *Member:* The District of Columbia Bar; Energy Bar Association; Association of Transportation Law, Logistics and Policy (Energy Editor, Association Newsletter). ***PRACTICE AREAS:*** Transportation Law; Energy Law. **Email:** jcutler@mshpc.com

DOUGLAS M. CANTER, born Washington, D.C., December 1, 1954; admitted to bar, 1979, Maryland; 1986, District of Columbia. *Education:* Bucknell University (B.A., 1976); University of Baltimore (J.D., 1979). Author: "Buy/Sell Transactions in The Natural Gas Industry: What's Prohibited and What Isn't," 15 Energy Law Journal 2, 427 (1994). Attorney Adviser to Administrative Law Judges, 1979-1980, Trial Attorney, 1980-1982 and Special Assistant to the Deputy General Counsel for Litigation, 1982-1983, Federal Energy Regulatory Commission. *Member:* The District of Columbia Bar (Steering Committee Administrative Law and Agency Practice Section, 1997-1999 Term); Maryland State (Chairman, Environment Committee, 1986-1987; Vice-Chairman, Ethics Committee, 1991-1992; Vice-Chair, Administrative Practice and Administrative Law Judges, 1998-2000) and American (Member, Administrative Law and Regulatory Practice Section) Bar Associations. ***PRACTICE AREAS:*** Administrative Law; Public Utility Law; Energy Law. **Email:** dmcwash@MSHPC.com

ANDREW P. GOLDSTEIN, born New York, N.Y., December 28, 1934; admitted to bar, 1959, New York; 1965, District of Columbia and U.S. Court of Appeals, District of Columbia Circuit; 1977, U.S. Court of Appeals, Fifth Circuit; 1978, U.S. Court of Appeals, Tenth Circuit; 1979, U.S. Court of Appeals, Eighth Circuit; 1982, U.S. Court of Appeals, Second Circuit; 1987, U.S. Court of Appeals, Fourth Circuit; 1993, U.S. Supreme Court. *Education:* Allegheny College; Boston University (LL.B., 1958). Author: "The Single Product Rule and Rail Freight Transportation," 53 Transp. Prac. J. 151, 1986. Attorney and Assistant to Vice Chairman, Interstate Commerce Commission, 1960-1966. *Member:* American Bar Association; Association of Transportation Law, Logistics and Policy. ***PRACTICE AREAS:*** Transportation Law; Antitrust Law. **Email:** APG@MSHPC.COM

LAWRENCE W. BIERLEIN, born Cleveland, Ohio, May 4, 1942; admitted to bar, 1968, District of Columbia; 1972, U.S. Supreme Court; 1975, U.S. Court of Appeals for the District of Columbia Circuit and U.S. Court of Appeals, Second Circuit; 1979, U.S. Court of Appeals, First Circuit. *Education:* Johns Hopkins University (B.A., 1964); University of Pennsylvania (J.D., 1967). Author: *Red Book on Transportation of Hazardous Materials,* (Cahners, 1976; Van Nostrand Reinhold, 1987); "Increasing Complexity in the Regulation of Hazardous Materials Transportation," Transportation Practitioners Journal, Fall 1986. Attorney, U.S. Department of Transportation, 1968-1972. *Member:* The District of Columbia Bar. ***PRACTICE AREAS:*** Hazardous Materials and Substances; Transportation; Environmental Law. **Email:** LWBIERLEIN@MSHPC.com

RICHARD D. LIEBERMAN, born New York, N.Y., June 13, 1946; admitted to bar, 1988, Maryland; 1989, District of Columbia. *Education:* Cornell (A.B., 1967); University of Wisconsin (M.A., 1968); Georgetown (J.D., 1988). Deputy Inspector General and Assistant Inspector General, Department of Defense, 1982-1988. Professional Staff Member, U.S. Senate Appropriations Committee, 1974-1981. Budget Analyst, Department of Defense, 1968-1974. Co-Author: *Elements of Contract Formation*, CCH-George Washington University, 2000; *Elements of Contract Administration*, CCH-George Washington University, Second Edition, 2001; *Anatomy of an Inspector General Investigation*, Federal Publications, 1991-1994; *Government Contract Compliance*, George Washington University, 1992-2000; "Bid Protests at the Court of Federal Claims and the General Accounting Office: A Comparison," 67 BNA Fed. Contr. Rpt. 383, March 31, 1997. *Member:* Maryland State, Federal and American Bar Associations; National Contract Management Association. ***PRACTICE AREAS:*** Government Contracts; Contract Fraud; Government Investigations. **Email:** rlieberman@mshpc.com

CHANNING D. STROTHER JR., born Washington, D.C., 1952; admitted to bar, 1977, Virginia and Maryland; 1979, District of Columbia. *Education:* University of Virginia (B.A., 1974; J.D., 1977). Author: "FERC Issues Landmark Order No. 2000 on RTOs," Power Insight, Jan. 2000. Co-Author, with David C. Hjelmfelt, "Antitrust Damages for Consumer Welfare Loss," 39 Cleveland State Law Review 505, 1991. Vice Chair, FEBA Committee on Electric Utility Regulation, 1993-1994. *Member:* District of Columbia Bar; Virginia State Bar; Maryland State, Federal, Federal Energy and American Bar Associations. ***PRACTICE AREAS:*** Energy Law; Public Utility Law; Antitrust Law. **Email:** cstrother@mshpc.com

OF COUNSEL

KAREN R. O'BRIEN, born Utica, New York, July 11, 1962; admitted to bar, 1987, Pennsylvania; 1995, District of Columbia. *Education:* Niagara University (B.B.A., 1984); Vermont Law School (J.D., 1987). Co-Author: *Elements of Contract Administration,* CCH-George Washington University, Second Edition, 2001; *Competitive Negotiation: The Source Selection Process,* GWU, CCH second edition, 1999; *The Government Contracts Reference Book,* GWU, CCH second edition, 1998. Co-Author: *Elements of Contract Formation: Practical Advice on Winning Government Contracts,* GWU, CCH 2000. Staff of Section 800 Procurement Panel and Litigation and Appellate Positions, United States Army. *Member:* Pennsylvania Bar Association; The District of Columbia Bar. [U.S. Army, Judge Advocate General's Corps, 1988-1992]. ***PRACTICE AREAS:*** Government Contracts. **Email:** kobrien@mshpc.com

(This Listing Continued)

McCARTHY, WILSON & ETHRIDGE

WASHINGTON, D.C.

(See Rockville, Maryland)

General Civil Trial Practice in State and Federal Courts. Workers Compensation, Negligence, Insurance, Products Liability, Personal Injury.

JERRY J. McCOY

SUITE 1200
1050 CONNECTICUT AVENUE
P.O. BOX 66491
WASHINGTON, D.C. 20035-6491
Telephone: 202-466-6941
Fax: 202-466-6942
Email: mccoylaw@aol.com

Charitable Giving, Charitable Trusts and Foundations, Nonprofit and Charitable Organizations, Nonprofit Tax Law.

FIRM PROFILE: This is a national tax law practice with clients that include universities, colleges, charitable organizations and individuals.

JERRY J. McCOY, born Pittsburgh, Pennsylvania, August 4, 1941; admitted to bar, 1967, New York; 1968, District of Columbia. *Education:* West Virginia University (B.S., 1963); Duke University (LL.B., 1966); New York University (LL.M., Taxation, 1967). Co-Founder and Co-Editor, Charitable Gift Planning News, 1983—. Executive Editor, Estates, Gifts and Trusts, Series of Tax Management (a publication of the Bureau of National Affairs), 1976-1993. Co-Author: "Family Foundation Handbook," Aspen, 2001. Contributing Author: "International Charitable Giving: Laws and Taxation," Kluwer, 1994. Adjunct Faculty: Georgetown University Law Center, 1996—; University of Miami School of Law, 1982—. Member, Advisory Committee, University of Miami Philip E. Heckerling Institute on Estate Planning, 1977—. *Member:* District of Columbia Bar; American Bar Association; American Law Institute. Fellow: American College of Tax Counsel; American College of Trust and Estate Counsel (Chairman, Committee on Charitable Planning and Exempt Organizations).

McDADE WARRAN & ZIMMERMAN

WASHINGTON, D.C.

(See Jason R. Warran, Kensington, Maryland)

Natural Resources, Federal Mineral Law, Oil and Gas, and Public Land Law. Practice before Federal Courts, Departments and Commissions.

McGUINESS NORRIS & WILLIAMS, LLP

Established in 1969

SUITE 1200, 1015 FIFTEENTH STREET, N.W.
WASHINGTON, D.C. 20005
Telephone: 202-789-8600
Telecopier: 202-789-1708
Email: Info@mnwlaw.net
URL: http://www.mnwlaw.net

Practice before the Federal Courts and Administrative Agencies. Employment, Labor, Equal Employment Opportunity, Agricultural Labor, Immigration, Federal Appellate Practice and Government Relations.

FIRM PROFILE: McGuiness Norris & Williams, LLP is a management labor, employment and government relations firm with a unique practice.

Like other management firms, it represents corporate clients in all phases of employment law, from providing advice and counsel in day-to-day human resources administration to litigating cases before the federal agencies and courts.

In addition, McGuiness Norris & Williams, LLP manages and represents several highly-respected national associations that bring together top human resources professionals from many of the nation's leading business organizations. The associations focus on employment law and policy issues before Congress, the federal

(This Listing Continued)

enforcement agencies and the courts. Through this activity, McGuiness Norris & Williams, LLP attorneys maintain close working relationships with key people in government responsible for labor and employment matters.

Also, through an affiliated consulting firm, attorneys and other professionals of McGuiness Norris & Williams, LLP provide a wide range of human resources and affirmative action planning, consulting and training services to employers.

MEMBERS OF FIRM

JEFFREY C. McGUINESS, born Fresno, California, January 21, 1947; admitted to bar, 1979, District of Columbia; 1982, U.S. Supreme Court. *Education:* The Principia College (B.A., 1969); Washington College of Law, American University (J.D., 1978). Author: "Plant Closings and Employee Separations: A Guide to the Law," National Council on Occupational Readjustment, 1984; "Guard Unions and the Problem of Divided Loyalties," The Wharton School, 1986. Special Counsel to U.S. Senator Richard Luger, 1979; Chairman, Civil Rights Reviewing Authority, Department of Health and Human Services, 1981-1984. President, LPA, Inc., 1988—. Fellow, National Academy of Human Resources. *Member:* The District of Columbia Bar. ***PRACTICE AREAS:*** Employment Relations Law.

JEFFREY A. NORRIS, born Chelsea, Massachusetts, January 9, 1945; admitted to bar, 1970, Connecticut; 1977, U.S. Supreme Court; 1978, District of Columbia. *Education:* Bucknell University (B.A., 1967); Cornell University (J.D., 1970). President, Equal Employment Advisory Council. Pi Sigma Alpha; Omicron Delta Kappa. *Member:* The District of Columbia Bar. ***PRACTICE AREAS:*** Labor Relations Law; Equal Employment Opportunity Law.

EDWARD E. POTTER, born Bath, New York, August 7, 1946; admitted to bar, 1979, District of Columbia; 1982, U.S. Supreme Court. *Education:* Michigan State University (B.A., 1968); Cornell University (M.S., 1972); Washington College of Law, American University (J.D., 1978). Phi Beta Kappa. Co-Author, *Keeping America Competitive: Employment Policy for the Twenty-First Century,* Glenbridge Publishing, 1995. Author: "The Impact on U.S. Law and Practice of Ratification of ILO Conventions No. 87 and No. 98," Labor Policy Association, 1984. President, Employment Policy Foundation, 1988—. U.S. Employer Delegate, International Labor Organization Conference, 1997—. Member, National Advisory Committee, North American Agreement on Labor Cooperation, 1997—. Member, Tripartite Advisory Panel on International Labor Standards, 1981—. Fellow, National Academy of Human Resources. *Member:* The District of Columbia Bar; American Bar Association. ***PRACTICE AREAS:*** International Labor Law; Labor Relations Law; Employment Law.

G. JOHN TYSSE, born Chicago, Illinois, May 30, 1946; admitted to bar, 1973, Ohio; 1985, District of Columbia. *Education:* Hope College (B.A., 1968); The Ohio State University (J.D., 1973). Author: "The Immigration Reform and Control Act of 1986 - A Handbook on Employer Sanctions and Nondiscrimination Requirements," EPF, 1988. Co-Author: "Winning the War on Drugs: The Role of Workplace Testing," EPF, 1989; "ADA Compliance Guide," EPF, 1991. Director of Labor Law, U.S. Chamber of Commerce, 1980-1984. President, Employment Advisory Services, Inc., 1990—. Chief Administrative Officer, Equal Employment Advisory Council, 1994—. [U.S. Army, 1968-1970]. ***PRACTICE AREAS:*** Employment Law.

MONTE B. LAKE, born Fresno, California, March 21, 1947; admitted to bar, 1973, California; 1977, District of Columbia. *Education:* University of the Pacific (B.A., with honors, 1969); McGeorge College of the Law of the University of the Pacific (J.D., 1973). Blue Key. Chairman, Moot Court Honors Board, 1973. Editor, "Age Discrimination in Employment Act: A Compliance and Litigation Manual for Lawyers and Personnel Practitioners," 1982. Author: "Avoiding Discriminatory Immigration-Related Employment Practices," Employment Relations Today, Vol. 15, No. 1, p.49, spring 1988; "Immigration Act of 1990: An Employer's Handbook," Employment Policy Foundation, 1992; "Adams Fruit v. Barrett: Restoration of Workers' Compensation as the Exclusive Remedy for Workplace Injuries Under the Federal Migrant Law," San Jauquin Agricultural Law Review, Vol. 6, No. 1, p. 69, 1996. Deputy District Attorney, Sacramento County, 1973-1977. Deputy Attorney General, State of California, 1975-1976. Representative for Labor Affairs, U.S. Secretary of Agriculture's Users' Advisory Board, 1984-1989. *Member:* The District of Columbia Bar (Co-Chair, EEO Subcommittee, 1982-1990); State Bar of California. ***PRACTICE AREAS:*** Agricultural Labor Law; Equal Employment Opportunity Law; Employment Law; Business Immigration Law; Government Relations.

ROBERT E. WILLIAMS, born Elgin, Illinois, November 9, 1942; admitted to bar, 1967, Illinois; 1973, District of Columbia and U.S. Supreme Court. *Education:* Beloit College (B.A., 1964); University of Illinois (J.D., 1967). Member, 1966 and Assistant Editor, 1966-1967, University of Illinois Law Forum. Author: "NLRB Regulation of Election Conduct," Wharton School Industrial Research Unit, 1974 and revised edition, 1985. Trial Attorney, 1967-1970 and Supervisory Attorney, 1970-1972, Appellate Court Branch, National

(This Listing Continued)

Labor Relations Board. *Member:* The District of Columbia Bar; Federal and American Bar Associations. ***PRACTICE AREAS:*** Labor Relations Law; Equal Employment Opportunity Law; Federal Appellate Practice.

ANN ELIZABETH REESMAN, born Somerset, Pennsylvania, November 12, 1956; admitted to bar, 1981, Pennsylvania; 1988, District of Columbia and U.S. Supreme Court. *Education:* University of Pittsburgh (B.A., cum laude, 1978); Dickinson School of Law (J.D., 1981). General Counsel, Equal Employment Advisory Council, 1996—. *Member:* The District of Columbia Bar; Pennsylvania Bar Association. ***PRACTICE AREAS:*** Employment Law; Federal Appellate Practice.

DANIEL V. YAGER, born Wichita, Kansas, December 23, 1950; admitted to bar, 1976, California; 1989, District of Columbia. *Education:* University of Nebraska (B.S., 1972); University of Santa Clara (J.D., 1975). Author: "Has Labor Law Failed? An Examination of Congressional Oversight and Legislative Proposals (1968-1990)," EPF, 1990; "Loading the Scales: Is the Balance Between the Right to Strike and the Right to Operate in Need of Reform?" EPF, 1992; "NLRB: Agency in Crisis," LPA, 1996. Co-Author: "Is the Chevron Deference Standard Too High-Octane For the NLRB?" Employee Relations Law Journal, Spring 1998; "Corporate Campaigns and Card Checks: Creating the Company Unions of the Twenty-First Century," Employee Relations Law Journal, Spring, 1999; "Workplace Cyberspace: Going Where No Board Has Gone Before," Employee Relations Law Journal, Autumn, 1999; "Employee Free Choice: It's Not in the Cards," LPA, 1998. Legislative Director, U.S. Congresswoman Marge Roukema, 1981-1983. Associate Minority Counsel, 1983-1986 and Minority Counsel, 1986-1988, Committee on Education and Labor, U.S. House of Representatives. Senior Vice President and General Counsel, LPA, Inc., 1994—. *Member:* The District of Columbia Bar; State Bar of California. ***PRACTICE AREAS:*** Employment Law and Legislation.

CHRISTINE M. COOPER, born St. Louis, Missouri, October 27, 1965; admitted to bar, 1990, Virginia; 1991, District of Columbia; 1997, U.S. Supreme Court. *Education:* University of Colorado at Boulder (B.S., 1987); George Washington University (J.D., 1990). Law Clerk to Senior Judges, Superior Court of District of Columbia, 1990-1991. *Member:* The District of Columbia Bar (Member, Litigation Steering Committee, 2000—); Virginia State Bar. ***PRACTICE AREAS:*** Civil Litigation; Employment Law; Agricultural Labor Law; Commercial Law; Administrative Law.

MARK E. BAKER, born Winchester, Virginia, April 26, 1960; admitted to bar, 1985, Virginia; 1989, District of Columbia. *Education:* University of Virginia (B.A., 1982; J.D., 1985). Co-Author: With S. Chetlin, Meeting the Challenge at the Mines: The Americans with Disabilities, Act 96 W. Va., Rev. 717 (Spring 1999). Partner, Crowell & Moring, LLP, 1994-2001. ***PRACTICE AREAS:*** Employment Litigation; Equal Employment Opportunity Law; Labor Relations Law; Employment Law.

ASSOCIATES

TIMOTHY J. BARTL, born Milwaukee, Wisconsin, March 9, 1968; admitted to bar, 1993, Minnesota; 1998, Maryland; 1999, District of Columbia. *Education:* Marquette University (B.S., cum laude, 1990); University of Minnesota (J.D., 1993). Associate General Counsel, Labor Policy Association, 1997-1998. Assistant General Counsel, 1998—. Legislative Assistant, 1993-1996. Legislative Director to U.S. Representative Steve Gunderson, 1996. Author: Union Corporate Campaign Tactics: Issues and Examples, LPA, 1997; America Wants Flexible Work, LPA, 1998; Options, Incentives and Sales People: How the FLSA Discriminates Against Non Exempt Employees, Employee Relations L.J. Autumn, 2000. *Member:* Minnesota State, Maryland State and American Bar Associations; District of Columbia Bar. ***PRACTICE AREAS:*** Labor Law; Employment Law; Legislation.

JUDITH A. LAMPLEY, born Teaneck, New Jersey, March 17, 1953; admitted to bar, 1992, Virginia and U.S. Court of Appeals, Fourth Circuit (Not admitted in District of Columbia). *Education:* Marymount College (B.S., summa cum laude, 1984); George Washington University (J.D., 1992). Member, Moot Court Board. *Member:* Virginia State Bar. ***PRACTICE AREAS:*** Human Resources Training; Employment Law; Equal Employment Opportunity Law.

AMY M. HABIB, born Buffalo, New York, June 7, 1968; admitted to bar, 1996, New York; 1997, District of Columbia and U.S. District Court, Western District of New York. *Education:* Boston College (B.A., 1990); University of Buffalo (J.D., 1995). *Member:* Erie County, New York State Bar Associations; The District of Columbia Bar Association. ***PRACTICE AREAS:*** Litigation; Labor Law; Employment Law.

JOSEPH S. LAKIS, JR., born New York, New York, September 30, 1969; admitted to bar, 1994, Connecticut;1996, U.S. District Court, Northern District of Illinois; 1999, New York (Not admitted in District of Columbia). *Education:* Long Island University (1989); Hofstra University (J.D., 1994). *Member:* Connecticut, Illinois State, New York State and American (Member, Labor and Employment Section) Bar Associations. ***PRACTICE AREAS:*** Employment Law; Equal Employment Opportunity Law; Affirmative Action Compliance.

(This Listing Continued)

McGUINESS NORRIS & WILLIAMS, LLP, Washington—Continued

MICHAEL J. EASTMAN, born Nashua, New Hampshire, July 11, 1968; admitted to bar, 1998, Virginia and U.S. Court of Appeals, Fourth Circuit (Not admitted in District of Columbia). *Education:* Colgate University (B.A., 1990); George Mason University School of Law (J.D., 1998). Legislative Assistant, 1992-1998 and Legislative Counsel, U.S. Representative Jim Moran, 1998-2000; Associate Staff, U.S. House Budget Committee, 1999-2000; Counsel and Director, Government Relations, LPA, 2000—. *Member:* Virginia State Bar. ***PRACTICE AREAS:*** Labor Law; Employment Law; Legislative Practice.

RAE T. VANN, born Bay Shore, New York, January 1, 1968; admitted to bar, 1994, Connecticut; 1997, U.S. District Court, District of Connecticut and Federal Circuit; 2001 U.S. Court of Appeals, Fifth Circuit and U.S. Supreme Court (Not admitted in District of Columbia). *Education:* Carnegie Mellon University (B.S., 1990); University of Connecticut School of Law (J.D., 1993). National Merit Commended Scholar. Chair, City of Hartford Permanent Commission on the Status of Hartford Women, 1996-1997. Author: "Preventive Medicine: Avoiding Costly Litigation Related to the Employment-At-Will Doctrine," Connecticut Law Tribune, August, 1997. *Member:* Hartford County (Member, Labor and Employment Law) and Connecticut Bar Associations; George W. Crawford Law Association (NBA Affiliate, 1995-2000). ***LANGUAGES:*** French, Haitian Creole. ***PRACTICE AREAS:*** Employment.

KATHERINE Y.K. CHEUNG, born New York, New York, April 29, 1968; admitted to bar, 1994, New York, Maryland, U.S. District Court, District of Maryland and U.S. Court of Appeals, Fourth Circuit; 1995, District of Columbia. *Education:* Harvard/Radcliffe College (A.B., magna cum laude, 1990); Harvard Law School (J.D., cum laude, 1993). *Member:* The District of Columbia Bar; Asian and Pacific American Bar Association. ***PRACTICE AREAS:*** Labor and Employment.

OF COUNSEL

LORENCE L. KESSLER, born Pittsburgh, Pennsylvania, August 10, 1946; admitted to bar, 1974, Pennsylvania; 1975, District of Columbia; 1980, U.S. Supreme Court; 1995, U.S. District Court, District of Maryland. *Education:* Dickinson College (A.B., 1969); George Washington University (J.D., with honors, 1974). Executive Editor, The George Washington Law Review, 1973-1974. Law Clerk to the Honorable Rabe F. Marsh, U.S. District Court for the Western District of Pennsylvania, 1974-1979. Author: "Managing Diversity in an Equal Opportunity Workplace," EPF, 1990. Co-Author: "A Closer Look at Comparable Worth: A Study of the Basic Questions to be Addressed in Approaching Pay Equity," EPF, 1984. Partner, McGuiness & Williams, 1983-1995. *Member:* The District of Columbia Bar. ***PRACTICE AREAS:*** Equal Employment Opportunity Law.

LYNNETTE CONWAY JACQUEZ, born Moline, Illinois, August 24, 1958; admitted to bar, 1983, District of Columbia. *Education:* L'Universite d'Aix-Marseilles; Northern Illinois University (B.A., magna cum laude, 1979); Notre Dame Law School (J.D., 1983). Phi Theta Kappa. Thomas J. White Scholar. Member, Journal of Legislation. Author: "Under the Knife," Journal of Legislation, Spring 1983. Co-Author: "Avoiding Discriminatory Immigration-Related Employment Practices," Employment Relations Today, Spring 1988. Assistant Counsel, House Subcommittee on Immigration, Refugees and International Law, 1984-1987. Counsel, Judiciary Committee, U.S. House of Representatives, 1984-1987. *Member:* The District of Columbia Bar; American Bar Association; American Immigration Lawyers Association (Co-Chair, Agricultural Workers Committee, 1989—). ***LANGUAGES:*** Spanish and French.

WILLIAM N. LaFORGE, born Durham, North Carolina, April 18, 1950; admitted to bar, 1975, Mississippi and U.S. District Court, Northern District of Mississippi; 1980, U.S. Supreme Court; 1986, District of Columbia. *Education:* Delta State University (B.A., with honors, 1972); University of Mississippi (J.D., 1975); Cambridge University, Cambridge, England (1981); Georgetown University (LL.M., International Law, 1982). Omicron Delta Kappa; Phi Alpha Delta. Fellowships: European Union Visitors Programme, Brussels, 1984; Senior Managers in Government, Kennedy School of Government, Harvard, 1990. Adjunct Professor: Business and Public Policy, Business Representation and Lobbying, Commercial Law, George Washington University, 1982—; Business and Government Relations, Georgetown University Harlow Institute, 1994—. Chief of Staff and Chief Legislative Counsel, U.S. Senator, Thad Cochran, 1983-1990. Chief Counsel, U.S. Senate Appropriations Subcommittee on Agriculture, Rural Development and Related Agencies, 1981-1983. Congressional Liaison, Peace Corps, 1979-1981. Legislative Assistant, Congressman David Bowen, 1976-1979. *Member:* The District of Columbia Bar; The Mississippi Bar; Federal Bar Association (Board of Directors and Deputy Secretary). ***PRACTICE AREAS:*** Legislation; Government Relations; Administrative; International Trade; Commercial Law.

HEATHER L. MacDOUGALL, born Great Lakes, Illinois, January 17, 1969; admitted to bar, 1994, Wisconsin, U.S. District Court, Eastern and Western Districts of Wisconsin and U.S. Court of Appeals, Seventh Circuit; 1998, Virginia; 1999, U.S. Court of Appeals, Sixth and D.C. Circuits; 2000, U.S. Court of Appeals, Third Circuit (Not admitted in District of Columbia). *Education:* University of Wisconsin-Madison (B.A., 1991); Marquette University (J.D., 1994). Associate Member, Marquette Law Review, Marquette University, 1993-1994. Author: "Is the DOL Regulating Through the Back Door?: The Significance of Its Interpretative Letters," 26 Employee Relations L.J. 47 (Summer 2000). Associate General Counsel, LPA, Inc., 2000—. *Member:* State Bar of Wisconsin (Member, Labor and Employment Law Section); Virginia State Bar; American Bar Association (Member, Labor and Employment Law Section). ***PRACTICE AREAS:*** Labor and Employment Law; Human Resources Compliance and Training.

LEGAL SUPPORT PERSONNEL

CONSULTANTS

COLIN CRAIG BENNETT, born Washington, D.C., August 31, 1971. *Education:* Cornell University (B.S., Economics, 1995); American University - Washington College of Law; George Washington University (M.B.A., 2000); Johns Hopkins University (M.S., Business, 2000). Member, National Association of Legal Assistants,1998— National Capitol Area Paralegals Association, 1998— National Federation of Paralegals Association, 1998—.

RONALD BIRD, born Montgomery, Alabama, March 3, 1948. *Education:* University of North Carolina (Ph.D., 1974). Sr. Economist, Dyn Corp. 1990-1999.

MICHELLE FERNANDEZ MOORE, born Los Angeles, California, November 19, 1971. *Education:* Tulane University (B.A., 1993). Pi Sigma Alpha. Member, National Society of Fundraising Executives, 1998—. ***LANGUAGES:*** Spanish.

CHRIS GOKTURK, born Decatur, Georgia, November 1, 1964. *Education:* West Georgia College (B.S., Mathmatics and Computer Science, 1987). Member, American Compensation Society; Society for Human Resource Management. Manager of Compliance, American Express, 1997-2001.

WILLIAM F. HOLMES, born New York, New York, July 14, 1946. *Education:* University of Maryland (B.A., 1970; M.A., 1977). Author: "Managing OFCCP Compliance Reviews," Employment Policy Foundation, 5th ed., 1995. Co-Author: "Corporate Affirmative Action Practices and The Civil Rights Act of 1991," Employment Policy Foundation, 1992. Program Analyst: U.S. Department of Labor, Wage & Hour Division, 1972-1976; Office of Federal Contract Compliance Programs, 1976-1982; Office of Inspector General, 1982-1985. EEO Consultant, Bank of America, 1985-1987. Vice President/Manager, Equal Opportunity Programs, Bank of America, 1987-1990.

JAMES S. HOLT, born July 29, 1938. *Education:* Pennsylvania State University (B.S., 1959; Ph.D., 1963). Instructor, Assistant Professor, Associate Professor and Professor of Agricultural Economics, Pennsylvania State University 1963-1979. Visiting Scholar, Economic Development Division, U.S. Department of Agriculture, 1978-1979. Principal, Holt, Miller and Associates, 1980-1991. Author: "Coverage and Exemption of Agricultural Employment Under the Fair Labor Standards Act," Washington DC, Minimum Wage Study Commission, 1981 (Joshua G. Eltora and Lawrence Burton); "Economic and Social Consideration in Extending Unemployment Insurance to Agricultural Workers," University Park, Pa., The Pennsylvania State University, 1976.

BRUCE D. KUEHNL, born Baltimore, Maryland, January 28, 1948. *Education:* University of California Davis (B.A., 1973); Golden Gate University, San Francisco (M.A., 1979). Adjudication Officer and Educational Benefits Specialist, U.S. Veterans Administration, San Francisco, California, 1973-1979; Equal Opportunity Specialist, U.S. Department of Labor, Office of Federal Contract Compliance Programs, 1979-1985; Assistant District Director, Portland, Oregon: U.S. Department of Labor, Office of Federal Contract Compliance Programs, 1985-1988 and 1990-1993; Special Assistant to Director of Policy: U.S. Department of Labor, Office of Federal Contract Compliance Programs, 1988-1990; District Director (Acting), Portland, Oregon: U.S. Department of Labor, Office of Federal Contract Compliance Programs, 1993-1997. Senior Consultant, Equal Employment Advisory Council and Employment Advisory Services, Inc., 1997—.

DAN LARA, born July 30, 1969. *Education:* Southwestern College (B.A., 1991); University of Kansas (M.S., 1996). Press Secretary, House Education and the Workforce Committee, 1999-2001. Deputy Press Secretary, Joint Economic Committee, 1997-1998. Legislative Correspondent, Office of U.S. Senator Sam Brownback, 1995-1997.

NANCY W. NELKIN, born High Point, North Carolina, September 2, 1967. *Education:* University of Virginia (B.A., 1989); Wake Forest University (M.B.A., 1992). Director of Human Resources, Computer Technology Associates, 1995-1999. Member, World At Work.

DAVID H. RAINWATER, born Jackson, Mississippi, February 26, 1949. *Education:* Stephen F. Austin University (B.S., 1971); Houston Baptist University (M.B.A., 1980). Member, Human Resources, Chevron Corporation, 1971-1997. Employee Relations, Bechtel Corporation, 1997-1999. Sr. Consultant,

(This Listing Continued)

(This Listing Continued)

Equal Employment Advisory Council and Employment Advisory Services, 1999—.

McGUIREWOODS LLP

WASHINGTON SQUARE
1050 CONNECTICUT AVENUE, N.W., SUITE 1200
WASHINGTON, D.C. 20036-5317
Telephone: 202-857-1700
Fax: 202-857-1737
Email: info@mcguirewoods.com
URL: http://www.mcguirewoods.com

REVISERS OF THE VIRGINIA LAW DIGEST FOR THIS DIRECTORY

Atlanta, Georgia Office: The Proscenium, 1170 Peachtree Street, N.E., Suite 2100, 30309-7649. Telephone: 404-443-5500. Fax: 404-443-5599.

Baltimore, Maryland Office: 7 Saint Paul Street, Suite 1000, 21202-1671. Telephone: 410-659-4400. Fax: 410-659-4599.

Charlotte, North Carolina Offices: Bank of America Plaza, 101 South Tryon Street, Suite 3700, 28280. Telephone: 704-373-8999. Fax: 704-373-8980 and Bank of America Corporate Center, Suite 2900, 100 North Tryon Street, 28202. Telephone: 704-373-8999. Fax: 704-373-8935.

Charlottesville, Virginia Office: Court Square Building, 310 Fourth Street, N.E., Suite 300, P.O. Box 1288, 22902-1288. Telephone: 804-977-2500. Fax: 804-980-2222.

Chicago, Illinois Office: 77 West Wacker Drive, Suite 4500, 60601-1635. Telephone: 312-849-3699. Fax: 312-849-3690.

Jacksonville, Florida Office: Bank of America Tower, 50 North Laura Street, 32202-3635. Telephone: 904-798-3200. Fax: 904-798-3207.

McLean, (Tysons Corner) Virginia Office: 1750 Tysons Boulevard, Suite 1800, 22102-3892. Telephone: 703-712-5000. Fax: 703-712-5050.

New York, New York Office: 9 West 57th Street, Suite 1620, 10019. Telephone: 212-548-2100. Fax: 212-548-2150.

Norfolk, Virginia Office: World Trade Center, 101 West Main Street, Suite 9000, 23510-1655. Telephone: 757-640-3700. Fax: 757-640-3701.

Pittsburgh, Pennsylvania Office: Dominion Tower, 23rd Floor, 625 Liberty Avenue, 15222. Telephone: 412-667-6000. Fax: 412-667-6050.

Richmond, Virginia Office: One James Center, 901 East Cary Street, 23219-4030. Telephone: 804-775-1000. Fax: 804-775-1061.

Almaty, Republic of Kazakhstan Office: McGuire Woods Kazakhstan LLP, Park Palace, 41 Kazibek Bi Street, 2nd Floor, 480100. Telephone: 7-3272-608-300. Fax: 7-3272-608-305.

Brussels, Belgium Office: 250 Avenue Louise, Boite 64, 1050. Telephone: 32-2-629-42-11. Fax: 32-2-629-42-22.

Accountants Liability, Affordable Housing and Tax Credits, Antitrust, Appellate, Asset Securitization, Automotive, Aviation Disaster Litigation, Banking, Business Acquisitions, Business Reorganizations and Divestitures, Capital Markets, Charitable Giving and Tax-Exempt Organizations, Class Action Litigation, Commercial Litigation, Complex Commercial Litigation, Construction Equipment, Construction Litigation, Consumer Financial Services, Consumer Products, Corporate Finance and Securities, Corporate Services, Creditors Rights and Bankruptcy, Distribution and Franchising, Document and Discovery Management, e-Commerce, Emerging Growth and Technology, Employee Benefits, Employment Discrimination, Energy and Utilities, Executive Compensation Arrangements, Executive Compensation Litigation, Family Businesses, Fiduciary Litigation, Financial Services, First Amendment, Government Compliance, Government Investigations, Government Relations, Health Care, Higher Education, Immigration, Insurance Coverage Litigation, Intellectual Property, Labor and Employment, Labor Management Relations, Land Use, Leasing, Litigation Management, Medical Devices, Drugs and Pharmaceuticals, Mergers and Acquisitions, Non-compete Litigation, Partnerships and Joint Ventures, Products Liability, Project Finance, Public Finance, Real Estate, REIT's and Financial Products, Resorts and Hospitality, Risk Management, Securities Compliance and Enforcement, Securities Litigation, Sports Law, State and Local Taxation, Taxation, Tax Audits; Toxic Torts, Trade Regulation, Traditional Real Estate Transactions, White Collar Crime, Wrongful Discharge.

FIRM PROFILE: McGuireWoods LLP is redefining the traditional role of law firms by providing innovative legal and consulting solutions. We are entrepreneurial, creative thinkers - creating a dynamic new definition of a law firm by expanding services to keep pace with our clients' varied needs.

Having developed through mergers and a growing client base into one of the largest law firms in the country, we are known for quality legal counsel and the ability to find the right business solutions. We serve public, private, government and nonprofit clients from such industries as automotive, banking and financial services, chemicals, energy resources, food processing, general manufacturing, government, health care, insurance, real estate, retailing, sports and entertainment, technology and telecom, and transportation.

(This Listing Continued)

Our clients' businesses, cultures, perspectives and profitability are important to us - proven by the fact that many of our client relationships have lasted for decades. Whether assisting a small start-up or a Fortune 500 giant, our objective is unwavering - a dedication to service that exceeds all expectations.

MEMBERS OF FIRM

JAMES L. BLASIAK, born Buffalo, New York, June 21, 1951; admitted to bar, 1977, New York; 1979, District of Columbia; U.S. Court of Appeals for the District of Columbia Circuit. *Education:* State University of New York at Buffalo (B.A., cum laude, 1973; J.D., 1976). Senior Editor, Buffalo Law Review. *Member:* Energy Bar Association. ***PRACTICE AREAS:*** Energy Law; Utility Law. ***Email:*** jblasiak@mcguirewoods.com

MARK F. BRZEZINSKI, born New York, N.Y., April 7, 1965; admitted to bar, 1997, Virginia (Not admitted in District of Columbia). *Education:* Dartmouth College (B.A.); Oxford University, Oxford, England (Ph.D.); University of Virginia (J.D.). Member, Washington Board, Council on Foreign Relations. *Member:* American Bar Association (Member, Advisory Board, Central and East European Law Initiative). ***LANGUAGES:*** Polish, French, Spanish. ***PRACTICE AREAS:*** International Transactions; International Law. ***Email:*** mbrzezinski@mcguirewoods.com

NEAL J. CABRAL, born Baltimore, Maryland, May 23, 1959; admitted to bar, 1988, Virginia; 1989, District of Columbia. *Education:* Union College and University (B.A., 1981); College of William & Mary, Marshall-Wythe School of Law (J.D., 1987). *Member:* District of Columbia Bar (Member, Environment, Energy and Natural Resources Section); Water Environment Federation; The Virginia Water Environment Association (Member, Government Affairs Committee); The Chesapeake Water Environment Association;. ***PRACTICE AREAS:*** Environmental Law. ***Email:*** ncabral@mcguirewoods.com

DOUGLAS W. CHARNAS, born Cleveland, Ohio, January 6, 1953; admitted to bar, 1978, Ohio; 1985, District of Columbia. *Education:* Ohio University (A.B., summa cum laude, 1975); Case Western Reserve University (J.D., 1978); Georgetown University Law Center (M.L.T., 1983). Phi Beta Kappa; Pi Gamma Mu. Attorney, Legislation & Regulations Division, Office of Chief Counsel for IRS, 1978-1984. Acting Assistant to IRS Chief Counsel, 1984. Adjunct Professor, Georgetown University Law Center. *Member:* The District of Columbia Bar (Member, Taxation Section; Estate, Trusts and Probate Law Section); American Bar Association (Member, Sections on Taxation and Business Law). ***PRACTICE AREAS:*** Business Acquisitions; Reorganizations; Divestitures; Charitable Giving; Tax Exempt Organizations; Executive Compensation; Family Business Law; Partnerships; Joint Ventures; Trusts and Estates; Civil Tax Litigation; Criminal Tax Litigation; Tax Audits. ***Email:*** dcharnas@mcguirewoods.com

JAMES M. COSTAN, born Asheville, North Carolina; admitted to bar, 1974, Virginia; 1975, U.S. Court of Appeals, Fifth Circuit; 1976, District of Columbia and U.S. District Court for the District of Columbia; 1978, U.S. Supreme Court; 1979, U.S. Court of Appeals, Tenth Circuit. *Education:* University of Virginia (B.A., English, 1970); Washington & Lee University (J.D., cum laude, 1974). Omicron Delta Kappa. Topics and Research Editor, Law Review; Washington and Lee Law Review, 1974. Law Council, Washington and Lee University Law School, 1994—. ***PRACTICE AREAS:*** Energy; Utility Law. ***Email:*** jcostan@mcguirewoods.com

JERRY A. ISENBERG, admitted to bar, 1975, Texas (Not admitted in District of Columbia). *Education:* University of Texas (B.A., with honors, 1972); University of Pennsylvania (J.D., 1975). Editor, University of Pennsylvania Law Review, 1974-1997. U.S. Securities and Exchange Commission: Staff Attorney, 1975-1983; Branch Chief, Division of Enforcement, 1983-1985; Assistant Director, Division of Enforcement, 1985-1994; Principal Assistant Director, Division of Enforcement, 1994-2000. ***PRACTICE AREAS:*** Securities Litigation; Compliance and Enforcement. ***Email:*** jisenberg@mcguirewoods.com

STEVEN D. KITTRELL, born Winfield, Kansas, August 4, 1953; admitted to bar, 1978, District of Columbia; 1979, U.S. Tax Court and U.S. Court of Federal Claims; 1984, U.S. Supreme Court; 1991, Maryland. *Education:* Baylor University (B.A., cum laude, 1974); George Washington University National Law Center (J.D., cum laude, 1978); Georgetown University Law Center (LL.M. in Taxation, 1981). Delta Theta Phi. Legislative Assistant to U.S. Senator Bob Dole (R-Kan.), 1976-1978. *Member:* American Bar Association (Member, Sections on: General Practice and Taxation, 1978—, Chairman, Committee on Domestic Relations Tax Problems, 1984-1986. ***PRACTICE AREAS:*** Employee Benefits; Securities Litigation; Mergers and Acquisitions; Executive Compensation. ***Email:*** skittrell@mcguirewoods.com

THOMAS J. McGONIGLE, born Scranton, Pennsylvania, October 27, 1957; admitted to bar, 1983, New York; 1984, U.S. District Court, Eastern and Southern Districts of New York; 1985, District of Columbia; 1989, U.S. Supreme Court, U.S. Court of Appeals for the District of Columbia Circuit and U.S. District Court for the District of Columbia; 1993, U.S. Court of Appeals, Second Circuit; 1994, U.S. District Court, Western District of Michigan. *Edu-*

(This Listing Continued)

McGUIREWOODS LLP, Washington—Continued

cation: University of Scranton (B.S., magna cum laude, 1979); Georgetown University Law Center (J.D., cum laude, 1982). Staff Attorney, 1984-1986 and Branch Chief, 1986-1988, Enforcement Division, Securities and Exchange Commission. Assistant District Attorney, Kings County District Attorney's Office, 1982-1984. *Member:* District of Columbia Bar (Member, Committee on Broker-Dealer Regulation, Corporate, Finance and Securities Law Section); American Bar Association (Member: Federal Regulation of Securities Committee, Business and Corporate Litigation Committee, Business Law Section; Securities Litigation Committee, Litigation Section; National Society of Compliance Professionals. ***PRACTICE AREAS:*** Consumer Financial Services; Securities Compliance; Securities Litigation. ***Email:*** tmcgonigle@mcguirewoods.com

DAVID H. PANKEY, born Richmond, Virginia, July 22, 1952; admitted to bar, 1976, Virginia; 1985, District of Columbia. *Education:* University of Richmond (B.A., summa cum laude, 1973); Yale University Law School (J.D., 1976). Phi Beta Kappa. ***PRACTICE AREAS:*** Securities Litigation; Corporate Finance; Securities; Energy; Utility Law; Mergers and Acquisitions; Emerging Growth Companies; Technology Law. ***Email:*** dpankey@mcguirewoods.com

JAMES U. TROUP, born Schenectady, New York, October 8, 1958; admitted to bar, 1985, District of Columbia; 1987, Virginia. *Education:* Georgetown University (B.S., 1981); University of Virginia (J.D., 1985). Partner, Arter & Hadden, 1990-2001. ***PRACTICE AREAS:*** Telecommunications; Media. ***Email:*** jtroup@mcguirewoods.com

RETIRED PARTNER

CLIFFORD R. OVIATT JR., born New Haven, Connecticut, May 25, 1926; admitted to bar, 1954, New York; 1955, Connecticut; 1981, District of Columbia; 1986, Virginia. *Education:* Wesleyan University (B.A., 1949); Cornell University Law School (LL.B., 1953). Alpha Delta Phi; Phi Alpha Delta. Member: Panel of Arbitrators, American Arbitration Association; Arbitration Panel, Federal Mediation Conciliation Service; National Labor Relations Board, 1989-1993. Former Partner, Cummings & Lockwood, Stamford, Connecticut, 1965-1981. *Member:* Virginia (Member, Labor and Employment Law Section, 1993—) and American (Member, Section on Labor and Employment Law, Committee on Developing Labor Law, 1988—) Bar Associations; National Association of Manufacturers (Member, Lawyers Advisory Committee). ***PRACTICE AREAS:*** Labor Management Relations. ***Email:*** coviatt@mcguirewoods.com

OF COUNSEL

ROCHELLE S. HALL, born San Francisco, California, February 19, 1958; admitted to bar, 1984, California; 1988, Missouri; 1989, District of Columbia. *Education:* Boston College (A.B., cum laude, 1980); Harvard University (J.D., 1983). ***PRACTICE AREAS:*** Securities. ***Email:*** rshall@mcguirewoods.com

ANITA M. HERRERA, born Washington, D.C., February 11, 1957; admitted to bar, 1992, Pennsylvania (Not admitted in District of Columbia). *Education:* College of William and Mary (B.B.A., 1980); Temple University (J.D., 1992). Chairman, Financial Transactions Committee, Energy Bar Association, 2000-2001. ***PRACTICE AREAS:*** Energy; Utilities; Securities. ***Email:*** aherrera@mcguirewoods.com

ASSOCIATES

KATHRYN B. ALLEN, born San Francisco, California, January 7, 1965; admitted to bar, 1995, Colorado (Not admitted in District of Columbia). *Education:* University of Texas (B.A., 1988; J.D., 1994). *Member:* Energy Bar Association. ***PRACTICE AREAS:*** Energy; Utilities. ***Email:*** kallen@mcguirewoods.com

ADRIAN B. COPIZ, born Takoma Park, Maryland, October 13, 1971; admitted to bar, 1999, Maryland (Not admitted in District of Columbia). *Education:* University of Maryland (B.A., 1995; J.D., with honors, 1999). *Member:* Federal Communications Bar Association. ***LANGUAGES:*** German. ***PRACTICE AREAS:*** Telecommunications; Media. ***Email:*** acopiz@mcguirewoods.com

GEORGE W. ERIKSON JR., born New York, N.Y., April 26, 1972; admitted to bar, 1999, Virginia and District of Columbia. *Education:* University of Virginia (B.A., 1994); Vanderbilt University School of Law (J.D., 1998). ***PRACTICE AREAS:*** Mergers and Acquisitions; Emerging Growth Companies; Technology Law; Corporate Finance; Securities. ***Email:*** gerikson@mcguirewoods.com

ROBERT P. HOWARD, JR., born Fairfax, Virginia, March 4, 1966; admitted to bar, 1996, Virginia and U.S. Court of Appeals, Fourth Circuit; 1997, District of Columbia and U.S. District Court, Eastern and Western Districts of Virginia; 1998, U.S. Court of Appeals for the District of Columbia Circuit. *Education:* University of Pittsburgh (B.A., 1987); University of Virginia (J.D., 1996). Phi Delta Phi, 1994-1996. ***PRACTICE AREAS:*** Securities Litigation; Securities Regulation. ***Email:*** rhoward@mcguirewoods.com

LEYLA GAINIEVNA KALNIAZOVA, (not admitted in the United States) *Education:* Kazak State University (Degree in Law, 1989); Institute of State and Law, Academy of Science of the Republic of Kazakstan (Ph.D., 1991). ***LANGUAGES:*** Russian, Kazakh, English. ***PRACTICE AREAS:*** International; Telecommunications.

STEPHEN A. KATSURINIS, born Houston, Texas, August 4, 1966; admitted to bar, 1992, Virginia and U.S. Court of Appeals, Fourth Circuit; 1999, District of Columbia. *Education:* Southwestern University (B.A., 1988); Franklin Pierce Law Center (J.D., 1991). Staff, Department of Planning and Budget, Commonwealth of Virginia, Richmond, Virginia, 1994-1995. Counsel to Congressman Dana Rohrabacher, Washington, D.C., 1991-1994. ***LANGUAGES:*** Greek. ***PRACTICE AREAS:*** Complex Commercial Litigation. ***Email:*** skatsurinis@mcguirewoods.com

JAMES H. LISTER, born Washington, D.C., July 2, 1969; admitted to bar, 1994, Maryland; 1995, Virginia and District of Columbia. *Education:* College of William & Mary (B.A., with honors, 1991; J.D., 1994). ***PRACTICE AREAS:*** Creditors Rights; Bankruptcy; Telecommunications; Commercial Litigation. ***Email:*** jlister@mcguirewoods.com

IAN C. LOFWALL, born Hays, Kansas; admitted to bar, 1998, Illinois; 2000, District of Columbia. *Education:* Northwestern University (B.A., Political Science, 1995); University of Barcelona (Summer Study Abroad Program, 1996); Chicago-Kent College of Law (J.D., with honors, 1998). ***PRACTICE AREAS:*** Executive Compensation; Employee Benefits. ***Email:*** ilofwall@mcguirewoods.com

AMY E. MILLER, born Newport News, Virginia, January 26, 1968; admitted to bar, 1999, Georgia (Not admitted in District of Columbia). *Education:* College of William & Mary (B.A., 1990); Virginia Commonwealth University (Master of Public Administration, 1994); University of Richmond (J.D., magna cum laude, 1999). Pi Alpha Alpha; McNeill Law Honor Society (Vice Chancellor, 1998-1999; Member, 1997-1998). ***PRACTICE AREAS:*** Labor Management Relations; Employment Discrimination. ***Email:*** amiller@mcguirewoods.com

VINCENT J. MIRAGLIA, born Waterbury, Connecticut, Nov. 24, 1969; admitted to bar, 1995, Georgia (Not admitted in District of Columbia). *Education:* Suffolk University (B.A., cum laude, 1991); Catholic University, Columbus School of Law (J.D., 1995). ***PRACTICE AREAS:*** Employment Discrimination; Labor-Management Relations. ***Email:*** vmiraglia@mcguirewoods.com

JENNIFER L. SCHWITZER, born Cedar Rapids, Iowa, February 9, 1973; admitted to bar, 1998, Oklahoma (Not admitted in District of Columbia). *Education:* Coe College (B.A., 1995); University of Tulsa College of Law (J.D., 1998). Phi Delta Phi. Recipient, National Energy-Environment Law and Policy Institute Award, Outstanding Student in Energy Law, 1997-1998. Editor-in-Chief, Energy Law Journal, 1997-1998. Attorney-Advisor, Federal Energy Regulatory Commission, Office of the General Counsel, Markets, Tariffs and Rates Division, 1998-2000. *Member:* Energy Bar Association. ***PRACTICE AREAS:*** Energy Law; Utility Law. ***Email:*** jschwitzer@mcguirewoods.com

KURT T. SLAWSON, born Waverly, Iowa, February 19, 1966; admitted to bar, 1994, Virginia; 1996, District of Columbia. *Education:* Grinnell College (B.A., with honors, 1988); Brown University (A.M., 1992); University of Michigan (J.D., 1994). Staff Attorney, Office of the General Counsel, Pension Benefit Guaranty Corporation, Washington, D.C., 1994-1997. *Member:* District of Columbia Bar (Member, Sections on: Taxation; Labor and Employment). ***PRACTICE AREAS:*** Employee Benefits; Executive Compensation. ***Email:*** kslawson@mcguirewoods.com

OLEG V. YAROSHIN, born Zyryanovsk, Kazakhstan, December 27, 1961; (admission pending). *Education:* Moscow State University (B.A., 1987); Catholic University of America (M.A., 1992); University of Virginia (J.D., 1999). ***LANGUAGES:*** Russian. ***PRACTICE AREAS:*** Project Finance; Antitrust and Trade Regulation; Securities Compliance. ***Email:*** oyaroshin@mcguirewoods.com

KRISTEN I. ZARENKO, born Pittsburgh, Pennsylvania; admitted to bar, 1999, Virginia; 2000, District of Columbia. *Education:* Georgetown University (B.S.B.A., magna cum laude, 1996); Georgetown University Law Center (J.D., magna cum laude, 1999). Order of the Coif; Beta Gamma Sigma. Member, *The Tax Lawyer*, 1997-1999. ***PRACTICE AREAS:*** Corporate Finance; Securities; Mergers and Acquisitions. ***Email:*** kzarenko@mcguirewoods.com

REVISERS OF THE VIRGINIA LAW DIGEST FOR THIS DIRECTORY

(This Listing Continued)

McINTYRE LAW FIRM, PLLC

MADISON OFFICE BUILDING
1155 FIFTEENTH STREET, NORTHWEST, SUITE 1101
WASHINGTON, D.C. 20005
Telephone: 202-659-3900
Fax: 202-659-5763
Email: mcintyre@mcintyrelf.com

Banking Law, Corporate Organization, Federal Legislative Practice, Environmental Regulation, Trade Association Law and Insurance Regulation.

JAMES T. McINTYRE, born Vidalia, Georgia, December 17, 1940; admitted to bar, 1963, Georgia; 1976, U.S. Court of Military Appeals; 1981, U.S. Supreme Court; 1986, District of Columbia. *Education:* Young Harris College (A.A., 1959); University of Georgia (A.B., 1963; J.D., 1963). General Counsel, Georgia Municipal Association, 1966-1970. Deputy Revenue Commissioner, State of Georgia, 1970-1972. Director, Office of Planning and Budget, State of Georgia, 1972-1977. Acting Director/Deputy Director, U.S. Office of Management and Budget, 1977-1978. Member of President Carter's Cabinet, Director, U.S. Office of Management and Budget, 1978-1981. Member, President Reagan's Commission on Privatization, 1987-1988. *Member:* The District of Columbia Bar; State Bar of Georgia; American Bar Association. ***PRACTICE AREAS:*** Banking Law; Corporate Organization; Federal Legislative Practice; Environmental Regulation; Trade Association Law; Insurance Regulation. ***Email:*** jmcintyre@mcintyrelf.com

CHRYS D. LEMON, born Perryton, Texas, December 13, 1957; admitted to bar, 1991, Virginia; 1992, District of Columbia and Maryland, U.S. District Court, District of Columbia, U.S. District Court, District of Maryland, U.S. District Court, Eastern District of Virginia, U.S. Court of Appeals, District of Columbia Circuit and U.S. Court of Appeals for the Fourth Circuit. *Education:* United States Air Force Academy (B.S., 1980); Oklahoma State University (M.A., 1985); The American University (J.D., cum laude, 1991). *Member:* State Bar of Virginia; State Bar of Maryland; The District of Columbia Bar. [Pilot, U.S. Air Force, 1980-1988.]. ***PRACTICE AREAS:*** Insurance Regulation; Corporate Organization; Environmental Regulation; Banking Law. ***Email:*** clemon@mcintyrelf.com

---

McKAY CHADWELL, P.L.L.C.

WASHINGTON, D.C.

(See Seattle, Washington)

Civil and Criminal Trial Practice in all Courts, Government Law, Criminal Defense, White Collar Crime, Internal Investigations.

McKEE NELSON LLP

1919 M STREET, N.W., SUITE 800
WASHINGTON, D.C. 20036
Telephone: 202-775-1880
Fax: 202-775-8586
Email: info@mckeenelson.com
URL: http://www.mckeenelson.com

Taxation.

FIRM PROFILE: Established in the District of Columbia in November 1999, McKee Nelson LLP is an independent law firm allied with the global professional services firm, Ernst & Young LLP.

J. BRADFORD ANWYLL, born Newport News, Virginia, January 17, 1957; admitted to bar, 1982, District of Columbia. *Education:* Johns Hopkins University (B.A., 1979); Duke University School of Law (J.D., 1982). Member, Editorial Board, Duke Law Journal, 1981-1982. Author, "How to Make Informal Refund Claims," 11 Practical Tax Lawyer 29 (Winter 1997). Law Clerk to Judge Marion T. Bennett, U.S. Court of Appeals for the Federal Circuit, 1982-1983. *Member:* The District of Columbia Bar; American (Chair, Court Procedure and Practice Committee, Section on Taxation, 1997-1999), Federal Circuit, and Court of Federal Claims (Chair, Tax Section, 1993-1994) Bar Associations; American College of Tax Counsel. ***PRACTICE AREAS:*** Tax Litigation. ***Email:*** banwyll@mckeenelson.com

JOHN C. ARNHOLZ, born New York, New York, August 3, 1959; admitted to bar, 1986, New York; 1993, District of Columbia. *Education:* Bowdoin College (B.A., 1981); Georgetown University (J.D., 1985). ***PRACTICE AREAS:*** Structured Finance.

JAMES D. BRIDGEMAN, born Nashville, Tennessee, 1954; admitted to bar, 1981, Georgia; 1990, District of Columbia. *Education:* David Lipscomb College (B.A., magna cum laude, 1976); University of Virginia (J.D., 1981). Order of the Coif. Member, 1979-1981 and Executive Editor, 1980-1981, Virginia Law Review. Attorney-Advisor, Office of Tax Legislative Counsel, U.S.

(This Listing Continued)

Department of the Treasury, 1984-1986. Special Assistant to the Chief Counsel, 1986-1988 and Deputy Associate Chief Counsel (Technical), 1988-1989, Internal Revenue Service. *Member:* American Bar Association (Member, Section on Taxation). Fellow, American College of Tax Counsel. ***PRACTICE AREAS:*** Taxation. ***Email:*** jbridgeman@mckeenelson.com

RITA A. CAVANAGH, born 1951; admitted to bar, 1987, District of Columbia. *Education:* State University of New York at Albany (B.A., Political Science, summa cum laude, 1973); Yale Law School (J.D., 1987). Co-author: Litigation of Federal Civil Tax Controversies, a leading treatise on civil tax litigation (Warren, Gorham & Lamont, 2nd Edition, 1997, with annual supplements). Adjunct Professor of Law, George Washington University National Law Center. *Member:* American Bar Association (Member, Taxation Section; Former Vice-Chair, Court Procedure and Practice Committee). ***PRACTICE AREAS:*** Tax Litigation. ***Email:*** rcavanagh@mckeenelson.com

DAVID J. CURTIN, born St. Louis, Missouri, 1947; admitted to bar, 1972, Missouri; 1979, District of Columbia. *Education:* St. Louis University (B.A., cum laude, 1969; J.D., cum laude, 1972). Alpha Sigma Nu. Member, Order of Woolsack. Recipient: Tax Division Outstanding Attorney Award, 1977; Special Commendation for Outstanding Service from Attorney General, 1978. Lecturer, U.S. Attorney General's Advocacy Institute, 1974-1979. Trial Attorney, Tax Division, U.S. Department of Justice, 1972-1979. Adjunct Professor, Tax Practice and Procedure (Litigation), Graduate Program, Georgetown Law Center, 1983—. Instructor, National Institute for Trial Advocacy. National and SE Regional Programs. J. Edgar Murdock American Inn of Court. *Member:* The District of Columbia Bar: The Missouri Bar: American Bar (U.S. Tax Court) Association (Member, Sections of: Taxation; Litigation). ***PRACTICE AREAS:*** Litigation. ***Email:*** dcurtin@mckeenelson.com

JEFFREY G. DAVIS, born St. Louis, Missouri, 1968; admitted to bar, 1994, California; 1995, Tennessee, District of Columbia and U.S. Court of Appeals, Sixth Circuit; 1998, U.S. Tax Court. *Education:* David Lipscomb College (B.S., summa cum laude, 1991); Pepperdine University (J.D., summa cum laude, 1994); Georgetown University (LL.M., with distinction, 1999). Recipient, Thomas Bradbury Chetwood, S.J. Prize. Member and Articles Editor, The Pepperdine Law Review, 1992-1994. Clerk for the Hon. H. Ted Milburn, U.S. Court of Appeals for the Sixth Circuit, 1994-1995. *Member:* The District of Columbia Bar; American Bar Association (Member, Section on Taxation). ***PRACTICE AREAS:*** Taxation. ***Email:*** jdavis@mckeenelson.com

F. SCOTT FARMER, born High Point, North Carolina; admitted to bar, 1982, North Carolina; 1989, District of Columbia. *Education:* North Carolina State University (B.A., magna cum laude, 1979); University of North Carolina at Chapel Hill (J.D., 1982); George Washington University (LL.M., in Taxation, with highest honors, 1983). Attorney, International Division of Chief Counsel, National Office of Internal Revenue Service, 1983-1988. Vice Chairman, Tax Section, U.S. Council for International Business, 1990—. *Member:* The District of Columbia Bar; The North Carolina State Bar; American Bar Association (Member, Foreign Activities of U.S Tax Payers). ***PRACTICE AREAS:*** Taxation; International Taxation; Tax Litigation. ***Email:*** sfarmer@mckeenelson.com

EDWARD E. GAINOR, born Baltimore, Maryland, August 3, 1954; admitted to bar, 1990, Maryland; 1992, District of Columbia. *Education:* Loyola College (B.A., 1976); George Washington University National Law Center (J.D., highest honors, Order of the Coif, 1990). Projects Editor, George Washington Law Review, 1989-1990. *Member:* District of Columbia Bar (Chairman, Committee on Derivatives and Securitization). ***PRACTICE AREAS:*** Securitization; Securities; Corporate.

JOE GARCIA, JR., born Mason City, Iowa, 1957; admitted to bar, 1986, Texas; 1999, District of Columbia. *Education:* University of North Texas (B.S., magna cum laude, 1981; M.A., 1981); University of Texas at Austin (J.D., 1986). Order of the Coif. ***PRACTICE AREAS:*** Taxation. ***Email:*** jgarcia@mckeenelson.com

JASPER A. HOWARD, born Pineville, Kentucky, November 5, 1962; admitted to bar, 1987, Kentucky; 1989, District of Columbia. *Education:* University of Kentucky (B.S., Accounting, 1984); Duke University (J.D., 1987); New York University (LL.M. in Taxation, 1989). Special Counsel to the Chief Counsel, Internal Revenue Service, 1995-1998. *Member:* The District of Columbia Bar; American Bar Association (Member, Taxation Section, Corporate Tax Committee). ***PRACTICE AREAS:*** Taxation; Federal Taxation. ***Email:*** jhoward@mckeenelson.com

JEFFREY R. JOHNSON, born Winchester, Massachusetts, July 24, 1966; admitted to bar, 1993, Virginia; 1995, District of Columbia. *Education:* University of Vermont (B.S., mahna cum laude, 1988); Georgetown University Law Center (J.D., 1993). ***PRACTICE AREAS:*** Securitization; Structured Finance; Corporate Securities.

GERALD A. KAFKA, born Martins Ferry, Ohio, September 9, 1951; admitted to bar, 1975, Ohio; 1982, District of Columbia; 1984, Maryland. *Education:* Wheeling Jesuit College (B.S., 1972); University of Cincinnati (J.D., 1975); Georgetown University (LL.M., Taxation, 1979). Adjunct Professor of

(This Listing Continued)

McKEE NELSON LLP, Washington—Continued

Taxation, Georgetown University Law Center, 1979—. Author: "Litigation of Federal Tax Controversies," Shepards/McGraw Hill, 1986 and 1995. ***PRACTICE AREAS:*** Tax. ***Email:*** gkafka@mckeenelson.com

ROBERT A. KATCHER, born Cleveland, Ohio; admitted to bar, 1976, Michigan; 1979, District of Columbia and Illinois. *Education:* University of Michigan (B.A., 1972; J.D., 1975); Georgetown University (LL.M. in Taxation, 1979). Branch Chief, Associate Chief Counsel International, Internal Revenue Service, 1986-1991. *Member:* The District of Columbia Bar; American Bar Association. ***PRACTICE AREAS:*** International Income Tax; Tax Planning; Federal Tax Controversies; Transfer Pricing; Taxation. ***Email:*** rkatcher@mckeenelson.com

MARK A. KULLER, born New York, N.Y., 1952; admitted to bar, 1979, California; 1999, District of Columbia. *Education:* New York University (B.S., cum laude, 1975); University of California at Los Angeles (J.D., 1978). Co-Author: Partnerships and Partners: Structuring and Drafting Agreements (2d ed., 1993); Federal Taxation of Debt Instruments. Adjunct Professor, Georgetown University Law Center, 1983-1989. Special Assistant to the Chief Counsel, Internal Revenue Service, 1984-1986. Attorney Advisor, Office of Tax Legislative Counsel, U.S. Department of Treasury, 1982-1984. ***PRACTICE AREAS:*** Tax Planning; Tax Litigation. ***Email:*** mkuller@mckeenelson.com

THOMAS J. LYDEN, born Minneapolis, Minnesota, November 23, 1949; admitted to bar, 1979, Minnesota; 2001, District of Columbia. *Education:* University of Minnesota (B.A., 1975); William Mitchell College of Law (J.D., 1979). ***PRACTICE AREAS:*** Tax.

RAJ MADAN, born New Dehli, India; admitted to bar, 1993, New Jersey, New York and U.S. Tax Court; 1999, District of Columbia. *Education:* New York University (B.A., with honors, 1990); George Washington University (J.D., with honors, 1992). IRS Trial Attorney, New York, N.Y., 1992-1997. *Member:* American Bar Association. ***PRACTICE AREAS:*** Taxation; Federal Tax Controversies; Tax Appeals; Tax Collection; Tax Controversies. ***Email:*** rmadan@mckeenelson.com

JOHN B. MAGEE, born Seattle, Washington; admitted to bar, 1972, Washington; 1977, District of Columbia. *Education:* Pomona College (B.A., 1966); University of Washington (J.D., 1972); Georgetown University (LL.M., 1977). Order of the Coif. *Member:* The District of Columbia Bar; Washington State and American Bar Associations; American Law Institute. ***PRACTICE AREAS:*** Tax Planning; Tax Controversies; Tax Litigation; International Taxation. ***Email:*** jmagee@mckeenelson.com

WILLIAM S. McKEE, born Washington, D.C., 1944; admitted to bar, 1971, Virginia; 1988, District of Columbia. *Education:* Yale University (B.A., cum laude, 1966); Harvard University (J.D., magna cum laude, 1969). Editor, 1968-1969, the Harvard Law Review. Co-Author: Federal Taxation of Partnerships and Partners (3rd ed., 1997); Federal Taxation of Partnerships and Partners: Structuring and Drafting Agreements (2d ed., 1993). Assistant Professor, 1969-1972, Associate Professor, 1969-1981 and Professor of Law, 1975-1983, University of Virginia School of Law. Visiting Professor, New York University School of Law, Graduate Tax Program, 1975-1977. Tax Legislative Counsel, U.S. Department of Treasury, 1981-1983. *Member:* American Law Institute; American College of Tax Counsel; National Institute of Tax Professionals. ***PRACTICE AREAS:*** Taxation. ***Email:*** bmckee@mckeenelson.com

WILLIAM F. NELSON, born Jackson, Mississippi, 1947; admitted to bar, 1972, Georgia; 2000, District of Columbia. *Education:* Mississippi State University (B.S., with highest honors, 1969); University of Virginia (J.D., 1972). Order of the Coif. Member, 1969-1972, and Editor-in-Chief, 1971-1972, Virginia Law Review. Co-Author: Federal Taxation of Partnerships and Partners (2 volumes, 1990); Federal Taxation of Partnerships and Partners: Structuring and Drafting Agreements (2d ed., 1993). Chief Counsel, Internal Revenue Service, 1986-1988. *Member:* The District of Columbia Bar; State Bar of Georgia; American Bar Association; American College of Tax Counsel. ***PRACTICE AREAS:*** Taxation. ***Email:*** wnelson@mckeenelson.com

STEPHEN M. PIPER, born Akron, Ohio, June 8, 1956; admitted to bar, 1981, Virginia; 2000, District of Columbia. *Education:* Davidson College (B.A., 1978); Oxford University, Oxford, England; Washington & Lee University (J.D., 1981); Georgetown University Law Center (LL.M. in Securities Law, 1991). Co-Author, "The Emerging Role of Dutch Auctions," Insights - The Corporate & Securities Law Advisor, August, 1989. In-House Counsel, Lockhead Martin Corporation, 1986-1998. Vice President, General Counsel, Lockhead Martin Global Telecommunications, Inc., 1998-2000. *Member:* Virginia State Bar; The District of Columbia Bar; American Bar Association (Member, Federal Regulation of Securities Committee). ***PRACTICE AREAS:*** Securities; Mergers and Acquisitions; Transactions; Corporate Law; Corporate Finance; Corporate Governance. ***Email:*** spiper@mckeenelson.com

R. NICHOLAS SINGH, born New Delhi, India, March 3, 1959; admitted to bar, 1991, New York; 1992, District of Columbia. *Education:* Carleton College (B.A., 1981); Columbia University (M.A., 1986); American University (J.D., 1990). ***PRACTICE AREAS:*** Corporate; Securities.

(This Listing Continued)

RICHARD C. STARK, born Ann Arbor, Michigan; admitted to bar, 1976, Texas; 1989, District of Columbia. *Education:* Vanderbilt University (B.A., magna cum laude, 1970; J.D., first honors, 1976). Phi Beta Kappa; Order of the Coif. Special Projects Editor, Vanderbilt Law Review, 1975-1976. Recipient, Founder's Medal. Assistant to the Commissioner of Internal Revenue, Internal Revenue Service, 1986-1989. *Member:* The District of Columbia Bar (Member, Steering Committee, Taxation Section, 1994—; Co-Chair, 1996-1999); American Bar Association (Member, 1989—; Chair, 1999—, Administrative Practice Committee, Section of Taxation). Fellow, American College of Tax Counsel. ***PRACTICE AREAS:*** Taxation; Federal Taxation; Federal Income Tax; Federal Tax Controversies; Tax Litigation. ***Email:*** rstark@mckeenelson.com

SANFORD W. STARK, born New York, N.Y.; admitted to bar, 1991, Illinois; 1992, District of Columbia. *Education:* Yale University (B.A., cum laude, 1988); Duke University (J.D., with high honors, 1991). Judicial Clerk to the Honorable Peter Hill Beer, U.S. District Court, Eastern District of Louisiana, 1991-1992. Associate, Hogan & Hartson, 1992-1995. Trial Attorney, Tax Division, U.S. Department of Justice, 1995-1999. Recipient, Outstanding Attorney Award, 1998. Counsel, Miller & Chevalier, 1999-2000. *Member:* District of Columbia Bar; American Bar Association. ***PRACTICE AREAS:*** Tax Litigation; Litigation; Federal Tax Controversies. ***Email:*** sstark@mckeenelson.com

H. JOHN STEELE, born Mineral Wells, Texas, 1955; admitted to bar, 1981, New York and District of Columbia. *Education:* Florida Southern College (B.A., 1977); University of Florida College of Law (J.D., with honors, 1980); New York University (LL.M., Taxation, 1984). Order of the Coif. *Member:* The District of Columbia Bar. ***PRACTICE AREAS:*** Securitization; Structured Finance; Corporate; Securities.

MICHELE E. WILLIAMS, born Torrington, Connecticut, April 26, 1961; admitted to bar, 1991, District of Columbia. *Education:* Georgetown University (B.S.F.S., magna cum laude, 1983; J.D., cum laude, 1990). Phi Beta Kappa. *Member:* The District of Columbia Bar. ***PRACTICE AREAS:*** Corporate Finance; Real Estate Finance; Project Finance; Asset Protection.

OF COUNSEL

GERALD GOLDMAN, born Cambridge, Massachusetts; admitted to bar, 1968, District of Columbia. *Education:* Harvard University (A.B., magna cum laude, 1965; LL.B., magna cum laude, 1968). Phi Beta Kappa. Member, 1966-1968, and Case Editor, 1967-1968, Harvard Law Review. Law Clerk to Mr. Justice William J. Brennan, Jr., U.S. Supreme Court, 1971-1972. Assistant Special Prosecutor, Watergate Special Prosecution Force, 1973-1975. *Member:* The District of Columbia Bar (Member, 1984-1991, and Vice Chair, 1989-1990, Legal Ethics Committee). ***PRACTICE AREAS:*** Tax Litigation; Litigation; Appellate Practice. ***Email:*** ggoldman@mckeenelson.com

PAUL C. HURDLE, III, born Portsmouth, Virginia, March 9, 1948; admitted to bar, 1974, New York; 1977, U.S. Supreme Court; 1978, District of Columbia, U.S. District Court for the District of Columbia and U.S. Court of Appeals for the District of Columbia Circuit; 1988, Virginia; 1996, North Carolina. *Education:* University of Virginia (B.A., with high honors, 1970; J.D., 1973). Phi Beta Kappa; Omicron Delta Kappa; Phi Alpha Delta. Member, Raven Society. *Member:* The Association of the Bar of the City of New York; The District of Columbia Bar; Virginia State Bar; North Carolina State Bar; New York State Bar Association; Commercial Mortgage Securities Association; American College of Mortgage Attorneys. [Lt., U.S. Navy - J.A.G. Corps, 1970-1979, Lieutenant.]. ***PRACTICE AREAS:*** Securitization; Capital Markets; Structured Finance; Commercial Real Estate. ***Email:*** phurdle@mckeenelson.com

TIMOTHY SADLER, born Chicago Heights, Illinois, January 18, 1949; admitted to bar, 1975, District of Columbia; 1979, New York; 1989, California. *Education:* Williams College (B.S., 1971); Georgetown University Law Center (J.D., 1974); New York University (LL.M., Taxation, 1979); Columbia University (M.A., 1986). [Infantry, 1974-1975, 1st Lt.]. ***PRACTICE AREAS:*** Securities.

ASSOCIATES

A. SONNY ABBASI, born Karachi, Pakistan, 1970; admitted to bar, 1996, District of Columbia. *Education:* George Washington University (B.A., 1992); American University (J.D., cum laude, 1995). ***PRACTICE AREAS:*** Securitazation; Structured Finance.

JONATHAN Z. ACKERMAN, admitted to bar, 1999, Colorado and U.S. Tax Court; 2000, District of Columbia. *Education:* University of Arizona (B.S.B.A., 1995); University of Denver (M.T., 1996); University of Chicago (J.D., 1999). ***PRACTICE AREAS:*** Taxation. ***Email:*** jackerman@mckeenelson.com

CRAIG T. BEAZER, born New York, N.Y., April 22, 1967; admitted to bar, 1993, New York (Not admitted in District of Columbia). *Education:* Iona College (B.A., summa cum laude, 1989); New York University (J.D., 1992). Phi Alpha Theta. Casebook Research and Writing Editor. Member, New York Uni-

(This Listing Continued)

versity Moot Court Board. *Member:* New York State Bar Association. ***LANGUAGES:*** Spanish, French. ***PRACTICE AREAS:*** Structured Finance; Lending; General Corporate; Public Finance.

HARTMAN E. BLANCHARD, JR., born New York, New York; admitted to bar, 1994, Maryland; 1996, District of Columbia and U.S. District Court, District of Maryland; 2001, U.S. Court of Appeals, Fourth Circuit. *Education:* Harvard University (B.A., magna cum laude, 1991); The George Washington University (J.D., with honors, 1994). Member, The George Washington Journal of International Law and Economics. Law Clerk, Hon. James C. Turk, U.S. District Judge, Western District of Virginia. *Member:* The District of Columbia Bar; Maryland State and American Bar Associations. ***PRACTICE AREAS:*** Tax Litigation; Taxation; Intellectual Property Litigation. ***Email:*** hblanchard@mckeenelson.com

RONALD L. BUCH,, JR., born Flint, Michigan, September 20, 1965; admitted to bar, 1993, Michigan; 1994, Ohio, Florida, U.S. Court of Federal Claims and U.S. Tax Court; 1996, District of Columbia and U.S. Supreme Court. *Education:* Northwood Institute (B.B.A., 1987); Detroit College of Law (J.D., 1993). Adjunct Professor of Tax Research IRS Office of Chief Counsel, 1997-2001. *Member:* The District of Columbia Bar; J. Edgar Murdock American Inn of Court. Fellow, Ohio Tax Review, 1993-1994. ***PRACTICE AREAS:*** Tax Litigation.

CORINA R. CAPLAN, born Bucharest, Romania, July 29, 1971; admitted to bar, 1996, New Jersey; 1997, New York; 1998, District of Columbia. *Education:* University of California at Berkeley (B.A., cum laude, 1993); Rutgers University School of Law-Newark (J.D., 1996). Member, Order of the Coif. Recipient, West Publishing Prize, Rutgers School of Law-Newark. Articles Editor, Rutgers Law Review. Author: Rutgers Law Review, Volume 48, Number 2. ***LANGUAGES:*** Romanian. ***PRACTICE AREAS:*** Secured Fianace.

NATHAN ELLIOTT CLUKEY, born Fort Monmouth, New Jersey, March 30, 1970; admitted to bar, 1997, Virginia; 1999, District of Columbia. *Education:* Virginia Polytechnic Institute and State University (B.A., 1994); Catholic University of America (J.D., magna cum laude, 1997); Georgetown Law Center (LL.M., with distinction, 2000). ***PRACTICE AREAS:*** Tax Controversies; Tax Litigation. ***Email:*** nclukey@mckeenelson.com

SHANNA MONIQUE COHN, born 1974; admitted to bar, 1999, Tennessee; 2001, District of Columbia. *Education:* Vanderbiit University (B.A.,1996); Yale University Law School (J.D., 1999). ***PRACTICE AREAS:*** Corporate; Securities; Mergers and Acquisitions; Capital Markets.

AMY KATHLEEN TESAR CONTRERAS, admitted to bar, 1995, Texas; 1996, District of Columbia. *Education:* University of Texas at Austin (B.A., 1992); St. Mary's University of San Antonio (J.D., 1995). *Member:* State Bar of Texas; The District of Columbia Bar; American Bar Association. ***LANGUAGES:*** Spanish. ***PRACTICE AREAS:*** Taxation. ***Email:*** acontreras@mckeenelson.com

MICHAEL J. DESMOND, born Santa Monica, California, July 28, 1968; admitted to bar, 1994, California; 2000, District of Columbia. *Education:* University of California, Santa Barbara (B.A., 1990); Catholic University (J.D., magna cum laude, 1994). Managing Editor, Catholic University Law Review. Clerk for the Hon. Ronald S.W. Lew, U.S. District Court, Central District of California, 1994-1995. ***PRACTICE AREAS:*** Tax Controversies; Tax Litigation. ***Email:*** mdesmond@mckeenelson.com

SHERI DILLON, born Stillwater, Oklahoma, 1962; admitted to bar, 1999, Georgia; 2000, District of Columbia. *Education:* University of Missouri at Columbia (B.A., 1984; M.A., 1986); Georgetown University Law Center (J.D., cum laude, 1999). Member, 1997-1999 and Notes Editor, 1998-1999, American Criminal Law Review. Co-Author: Computer Crimes, Project, Thirteenth Survey White Collar Crime (Spring 1998). *Member:* State Bar of Georgia; District of Columbia Bar; American Bar Association. ***PRACTICE AREAS:*** Taxation; Tax Controversies; Tax Litigation. ***Email:*** sdillon@mckeenelson.com

JOHN A. GALOTTO, born Baltimore, Maryland, March 3, 1967; admitted to bar, 1994, New York; 1995, District of Columbia; 2000, Illinois. *Education:* Johns Hopkins University (B.A., with honors, 1988); Columbia University (J.D., 1993). Harlan Fiske Stone Scholar. Senior Editor, Columbia Law Review. Clerk to the Honorable Edward Rafeedie, U.S. District Court, Central District of California. Trial Attorney, U.S. Department of Justice, Tax Division, Civil Trial and Criminal Enforcement Sections, 1995-2000. Special Assistant U.S. Attorney, District of Columbia, 1999. Co-Author , Right To Counsel: Courts Adhere to Bright-Line Limits, ABA Criminal Justice Magazine, Summer, 2001 at 4; Sensible Decision on Admissibility of Witness Guilty Pleas Repudiated in Third Circuit, but Dissenters Offer Hope in Other Circuits, White Collar Crime Reporter, June/July 2000, at 1; The COSO Report on Internal Control: Implications for Public Companies and Executive, Insights, August 1993, at 29. Author, Note, Strict Scrunity for Gender Via Croson, 93 Colum.L.Rev. 508, 513 (1993). ***PRACTICE AREAS:*** Tax Litigation; White Collar Crime.

MATTHEW GENASCI, born Santa Rosa, California, August 23, 1974; admitted to bar, 2001, New York and District of Columbia (Not admitted in District of Columbia). *Education:* Westmont College (B.A., 1996); Stanford University (J.D., 2000). ***PRACTICE AREAS:*** Taxation. ***Email:*** mgenasci@mckeenelson.com

ANTHONY C. GREEN, born St. Albans, England, June 21, 1974; admitted to bar, 1999, Maryland; 2001, District of Columbia. *Education:* University of Pennsylvania (B.A., 1996); Cornell University (J.D./LL.M., 1999). ***PRACTICE AREAS:*** Securities.

GWYNETH E. HAMBLEY, born Minneapolis, Minnesota, January 22, 1960; admitted to bar, 1993, Pennsylvania; 1995, District of Columbia. *Education:* College of William & Mary (B.A., 1981); University of California, Boalt Hall School of Law, Berkeley (J.D., 1993). Member, California Law Review. ***PRACTICE AREAS:*** Corporate Law; Securities. ***Email:*** ghambley@mckeenelson.com

TAE YEOL JEON, born Seoul, Korea, 1971; admitted to bar, 2000, New York; 2001, District of Columbia. *Education:* Yale University (B.A., 1993); New York University (J.D., 1997; LL.M., 1998). ***PRACTICE AREAS:*** Taxation. ***Email:*** tjeon@mckeenelson.com

PHILLIP JOHN KARDIS, born Urbana, Illinois, June 29, 1961; admitted to bar, 1996, Virginia and District of Columbia. *Education:* George Washington University (B.A., 1985; M.A., 1987); George Mason University (M.A., 1992); Georgetown University (J.D., 1996). Phi Beta Kappa; Alpha Epsilon Delta. Recipient: Charles E Gauss Prize; American Jurisprudence Award. ***PRACTICE AREAS:*** Corporate; Securities.

JEFFREY S. KORENBLATT, born Philadelphia, Pennsylvania, October 26, 1969; admitted to bar, 1998, Michigan; 2000, District of Columbia. *Education:* Georgetown University (B.S.F.S., cum laude, 1992); University of Michigan (J.D., 1997). ***PRACTICE AREAS:*** International Taxation; Tax Planning. ***Email:*** jkorenblatt@mckeenelson.com

CHRISTOPHER P. LA PUMA, born San Gabriel, California, February 21, 1969; admitted to bar, 1996, California; 1998, District of Columbia; 1998, U.S. Tax Court. *Education:* Stanford University (A.B., 1991); Georgetown University (J.D., magna cum laude, 1996; LLM., with distinction, 2001). Order of the Coif. *Member:* American Bar Association (Member, Taxation Section Court Procedure and Practice Committee). ***PRACTICE AREAS:*** Federal Taxation; Tax Controversies.

CHRISTINE RUSHIN MISTR, born Greenville, Mississippi, September 16, 1971; admitted to bar, 1998, Virginia; 2000, District of Columbia. *Education:* University of Richmond (B.S./B.A., 1993); University of Virginia School of Law (J.D., 1998). *Member:* Virginia (Member, Taxation Section) and American Bar Associations. ***PRACTICE AREAS:*** Federal Taxation. ***Email:*** cmistr@mckeenelson.com

PETER C. MORREALE, born Brooklyn, New York, October 3, 1969; admitted to bar, 1994, Connecticut; 1995, New York; 1996, District of Columbia. *Education:* Georgetown University (B.A., 1991); Fordham University (J.D., 1994). ***PRACTICE AREAS:*** Securitization; Structured Finance.

MARK DAVID NELSON, born Arlington, Virginia, October 27, 1974; admitted to bar, 2000, Virginia; 2001, District of Columbia. *Education:* University of Alabama at Tuscaloosa (B.A., 1997); Stanford University (J.D., 2000). Phi Beta Kappa. Executive Editor, Stanford Environmental Law Journal. Associate with Swidler, Berlin, Shereff, Friedman, LLP, Washington, D.C., 2000-2001. *Member:* American Bar Association. (practices under the supervision of principals of the firm). ***PRACTICE AREAS:*** Tax Litigation.

NEERAJ D. PAI, born May 3, 1974; admitted to bar, 2000, Pennsylvania (Not admitted in District of Columbia). *Education:* Villanova University (B.S., magna cum laude, 1996); Harvard University (J.D., 1999). ***PRACTICE AREAS:*** Tax Litigation.

ANDREW B. ROSENSTEIN, born Fairfax, Virginia, June 29, 1972; admitted to bar, 1998, Maryland and District of Columbia. *Education:* University of Michigan (B.B.A., high distinction, 1994); George Washington University (M.B.A., 1997; J.D., 1997). *Member:* The District of Columbia Bar (Member, Business Law Section); American Bar Association (Member, Business Law Section).. ***PRACTICE AREAS:*** Securities; Venture Capital; Mergers and Acquisitions; Corporate.

CORNELIA SCHNYDER, born Los Angeles, California, 1971; admitted to bar, 1997, Florida; 1999, District of Columbia and U.S. Tax Court. *Education:* Jacksonville University (B.S., summa cum laude, 1992); University of Florida (J.D., with high honors, 1996; LL.M., 1997). Order of the Coif. Member and Editor, Florida Tax Review, 1996-1997. Attorney-Advisor to Judge Wright, U.S. Tax Court, 1997-1998. ***PRACTICE AREAS:*** Taxation. ***Email:*** cschnyder@mckeenelson.com

ANITA CAROLINE SOUCY, born Melrose, Massachusetts, February 16, 1973; admitted to bar, 1999, Virginia (Not admitted in District of Columbia). *Education:* Wheaton College (B.A., 1995); University of Georgia School of Law (J.D., 1999). Phi Beta Kappa. ***LANGUAGES:*** Spanish. ***PRACTICE AREAS:*** Taxation; Tax Litigation.

(This Listing Continued)

(This Listing Continued)

McKEE NELSON LLP, Washington—Continued

JOSHUA E. SPOONER, born Wahiawa, Hawaii, March 28, 1972; admitted to bar, 2000, Maine; 2001, District of Columbia (Not admitted in District of Columbia). *Education:* George Washington University (B.A., 1994); University of Maine (J.D., 2000). ***PRACTICE AREAS:*** Securitization.

JULIE K. WEINSTEIN, born Baltimore, Maryland, August 10, 1975; admitted to bar, 2000, Pennsylvania (Not admitted in District of Columbia). *Education:* University of Michigan (B.B.A., 1997); George Washington University Law School (J.D., 2000). *Member:* American Bar Association. ***PRACTICE AREAS:*** Securitization; Structured Finance; General Corporate; Mergers and Acquisitions.

McKENNA & CUNEO, L.L.P.

Established in 1940

1900 K STREET, N.W.

WASHINGTON, D.C. 20006

Telephone: 202-496-7500

Telecopier: 202-496-7756

URL: http://www.mckennacuneo.com

Los Angeles, California Office: 444 South Flower Street, 90071. Telephone: 213-688-1000.

San Francisco, California Office: One Market, Steuart Street Tower, Twenty-Seventh Floor, 94105. Telephone: 415-267-4000.

Denver, Colorado Office: 370 Seventeenth Street, Suite 4800, 80203. Telephone: 303-634-4000.

San Diego, California Office: Symphony Towers, Suite 3300, 750B Street, 92101. Telephone: 619-595-5400.

Brussels, Belgium Office: 56, rue des Colonies, Box 14, B-1000. Telephone: 011-322-278-1211.

Devon, Pennsylvania Office: 28 South Waterloo Road, Suite 101. 19333. Telephone: 610-687-9750.

General Civil, Criminal and Trial Practice in all State and Federal Courts, Federal Departments and Agencies. Government Contracts, Construction, Environmental, Food and Drug, Trade Associations; Health Care, Energy, White Collar Crime, Antitrust, International, Trade Regulation, Trademark, Estate Planning, Trust, Probate, Labor and Employment, Product Liability Litigation, Insurance Coverage and Intellectual Property.

ASHLEY SELLERS (1902-1977).

GILBERT A. CUNEO (1913-1978).

RESIDENT PARTNERS

JEFFREY P. ALTMAN, born January 27, 1949; admitted to bar, 1975, District of Columbia. *Education:* Yale University (B.A., 1972); Tulane University (J.D., 1974). Order of the Coif. Associate Editor, Tulane Law Review, 1973-1974. Special Counsel, Grace Commission, 1982-1984. *Member:* The District of Columbia Bar (Past Chair, Not-for-Profit Committee, Corporations Section); American Bar Association; American Society of Association Executives (Past Chair, Legal Section Council). ***PRACTICE AREAS:*** Trade Associations; Non-Profit Organizations; Technology; Insurance; Business; Tax; Election Law; Government Relations. ***Email:*** jeff_altman@mckennacuneo.com

RAY M. ARAGON, born Bethesda, Maryland, October 16, 1959; admitted to bar, 1986, Maryland; 1988, District of Columbia; 1989, California. *Education:* University of Maryland, College Park (B.A., with honors in Economics, 1981); Yale University (J.D., 1986). Co-Author: with Raymond B. Biagini, "Contractor Defense May Fail to Shield Businesses," National Law Journal, September 25, 1995 at B12; with Michael G. Scheininger, "Joint Defense Agreements," Litigation Magazine, Spring 1994 at 11. ***PRACTICE AREAS:*** Business Litigation; Products Liability; Insurance Coverage. ***Email:*** ray_aragon@mckennacuneo.com

TAMI LYN AZORSKY, born Pittsburgh, Pennsylvania, July 29, 1959; admitted to bar, 1984, Pennsylvania; 1985, District of Columbia. *Education:* Pennsylvania State University (B.A., with distinction, 1981); George Washington University (J.D., 1984). Pi Sigma Alpha. *Member:* The District of Columbia Bar (Member, Sections on: Courts, Lawyers and Administration of Justice; Litigation); Pennsylvania and American (Member: Litigation; Environment; Energy; Resources and Public Contract Law Sections) Bar Associations; Women's Bar Association of the District of Columbia. ***PRACTICE AREAS:*** Product Liability; Environmental Tort Litigation; Administrative Procedure Act Litigation; Environmental Claims; Commercial Litigation. ***Email:*** tami_azorsky@mckennacuneo.com

RAYMOND B. BIAGINI, born Pittsburgh, Pennsylvania, March 6, 1954; admitted to bar, 1979, Pennsylvania; 1980, District of Columbia and U.S. Claims Court. *Education:* University of Notre Dame (B.A., magna cum laude, 1976; J.D., 1979). Phi Beta Kappa. Law Clerk to Hon. Philip Nichols, U.S. Court of Claims, 1979-1980. *Member:* The District of Columbia Bar; Pennsylvania Bar Association. ***PRACTICE AREAS:*** Product Liability Litigation; Insurance Coverage Litigation. ***Email:*** ray_biagini@mckennacuneo.com

THOMAS F. BURKE, born San Diego, California, July 12, 1966; admitted to bar, 1991, Maryland; 1993, District of Columbia. *Education:* Brown University (A.B., 1988); George Washington University (J.D., with honors, 1991). Co-Author: "The Present and Future of MAS Contracting," 27 Public Contracts Law Journal 369, Winter, 1998. ***PRACTICE AREAS:*** Government Contracts; Construction Law. ***Email:*** thomas_burke@mckennacuneo.com

J. KEITH BURT, born Chapel Hill, North Carolina, June 30, 1960; admitted to bar, 1985, Maryland; 1986, District of Columbia. *Education:* University of Maryland (B.S., 1982); George Washington University (J.D., with honors, 1985). Member, George Washington University Law Review, 1984-1985. Trial Attorney, U.S. Department of Justice, Civil Division, 1987-1989. ***PRACTICE AREAS:*** Litigation; Government Contracts Law; International. ***Email:*** keith_burt@mckennacuneo.com

ROBERT L. CARTER, JR., born Washington, D.C., February 3, 1965; admitted to bar, 1990, District of Columbia; 1993, Virginia. *Education:* Mount St. Mary's College (B.A.B.S., cum laude, 1987); Catholic University of America, Columbus School of Law (J.D., 1990). Author: "Protection Plan—Insurance Can Give Important Safeguard Against Employee Claims," ABA Journal, June 1997; "Old Insurance for New Liabilities," International Commercial Litigation, January 1997; "Using Insurance to Cover Employment Related Claims," International Commercial Litigation, September 1996. Co-Author: "California Insurer Wins Right to Regain Defense Cost," The National Law Journal, September 8, 1997; "Using Risk Retention Groups and Purchasing Groups to Provide Employment Practices Liability," The Risk Retention Reporter, February 1997; "Tobacco Litigation: Looking for Cover," Legal Times, March 6, 1995. Lecturer: Court T.V.; Federal Publications, Inc; The New York State Bar, Real Property Law Section; Risk Insurance Management Society, Inc.; Mealey's Insurance Conferences; International Risk Management Institute, Inc. Editor, McKenna & Cuneo Insurance Advisor. *Member:* The District of Columbia Bar; Virginia State Bar (Member, Committee on Resolutions); American Bar Association (Member, Property Insurance Law/Committee). ***PRACTICE AREAS:*** Insurance Coverage Litigation; Insurance Recovery. ***Email:*** robert_carter@mckennacuneo.com

JOHN D. CONNER, born Fort Worth, Texas, February 24, 1911; admitted to bar, 1938, District of Columbia. *Education:* Texas Christian University, Baylor University (A.B., 1933); George Washington University (LL.B., 1938). *Member:* The District of Columbia Bar; Bar Association of the District of Columbia (Member, Board of Directors, 1957-1958; Chairman, Administrative Law Section, 1956-1957); American Bar Association (Chairman, Committee on Economics of Law Practice, 1959-1965); American Judicature Society (Member, Board of Directors, 1968-1972); American Law Institute. Fellow, American Bar Foundation. (Partner Emeritus). ***Email:*** john_conner_sr@mckennacuneo.com

JOHN D. CONNER, JR., born Washington, D.C., July 27, 1948; admitted to bar, 1974, Tennessee; 1975, District of Columbia. *Education:* Baylor University and University of Tennessee at Knoxville (B.S., 1970); University of Tennessee at Knoxville (J.D., 1973). Editor-in-Chief, Tennessee Law Review, 1972-1973. Law Clerk to the Hon. Robert L. Taylor, U.S. District Court, Eastern District of Tennessee, 1974-1975. Author: Note, "The Federal Environmental Pesticide Control Act of 1972," 40 Tennessee Law Review 538, 1973; "Federal Indemnification for Losses Resulting from the Suspension of Hazardous Products—The Lessons of FIFRA," 32 Admin. Statute Law Review 441, 1980; "The Reregistration of Products Under 1988 Amendments to the Pesticide Law—Is The Past Prologue to the Future?" Chem. Reg. Reporter 649, Aug. 11, 1989. Co-Author: *Pesticide Regulation Handbook,* 3rd ed, 1991; *TSCA Handbook,* 3d ed, 1997. *Member:* District of Columbia Bar; American Bar Association.

DEL STILTNER DAMERON, born Pikeville, Kentucky, July 12, 1953; admitted to bar, 1977, Ohio; 1978, District of Columbia. *Education:* Pikeville College (B.A., summa cum laude, 1974); University of Cincinnati (J.D., 1977). Order of the Coif. Member, Editorial Board, University of Cincinnati Law Review, 1976-1977. Author: "Extra—Contractual Damages in Suits on Insurance Policies," 46 University of Cincinnati Law Review 170, 1977. Co-Author: "Son of Scanwell: Antitrust Challenges to Government Contract Awards and Related Actions," 92 Dickinson Law Review 281, 1988. *Member:* The District of Columbia Bar; Bar Association of the District of Columbia; American Bar Association; Women's Bar Association of the District of Columbia. ***Email:*** del_dameron@mckennacuneo.com

C. STANLEY DEES, born Tulsa, Oklahoma, June 24, 1938; admitted to bar, 1963, Virginia; 1964, District of Columbia. *Education:* Princeton University (A.B., with honors, 1960); University of Virginia (LL.B., 1963). Order of the Coif. Member, Editorial Board, Virginia Law Review, 1961-1963. Author of articles on topics including unabsorbed overhead, defective specifications, false claims act damages, privatization. Lecturer, University of Virginia Law School. President, Legal Aid Society of the District of Columbia, 1978-1980. *Member:* District of Columbia Bar (Chairman, Government Contracts Division, 1975-

(This Listing Continued)

1977); Virginia State Bar; American Bar Association (Council or Officer, 1981-1987; Chairman, Public Contract Law Section, 1987-1988); National Defense Industrial Association (Vice President or Trustee, 1983-1997). ***PRACTICE AREAS:*** Government Contracts; Litigation. ***Email:*** stanley_dees@mckennacuneo.com

JOSEPH F. DENNIN, born New York, N.Y., June 9, 1943; admitted to bar, 1969, California; 1970, New York; 1987, District of Columbia. *Education:* Stanford University (A.B., with great distinction, 1965; J.D., 1968). Fulbright Scholar, University of Helsinki, 1968-1969. Associate, Simpson Thacher & Bartlett, 1969-1975. Counsel, Senate Select Committee on Intelligence, 1975-1976. Staff Assistant to the President, The White House, 1976-1978. Director of Operations, U.S. International Trade Commission, 1978-1979. Deputy Associate Attorney General, U.S. Department of Justice, 1979-1981. Deputy Assistant Secretary for Finance, Investment and Services, 1981-1982. Deputy Assistant Secretary for Africa, the Near East and South Asia, 1982-1984. Assistant Secretary for International Economic Policy, U.S. Department of Commerce, 1984-1986. Member, NAFTA Disputes Resolution Panel, 1994—. Board of Directors, US-ROC (Taiwan) Business Council. Board of Advisors, "North American Free Trade & Investment Report." General Editor, "Law and Practice Before the World Trade Organization," 1995—. *Member:* American Bar Association. ***PRACTICE AREAS:*** International Trade and Investment; Government Relations. ***Email:*** joseph_dennin@mckennacuneo.com

ALISON L. DOYLE, born Buffalo, New York, November 10, 1955; admitted to bar, 1984, District of Columbia. *Education:* University of Pennsylvania (B.A., magna cum laude, 1977); Georgetown University (M.S.F.S., 1983; J.D., magna cum laude, 1983). Editor, Georgetown Law Journal, 1981-1982. Law Clerk to the Hon. H. Emory Widener, Jr., U.S. Court of Appeals, 4th Circuit, 1983-1984. Co-Author: "Multiple Award Schedules: Guide for Business and Government," Holbrook & Kellog, 1995; "GSA Multiple Award Schedule Audits and Investigations," Acquisition Issues, 1996. *Member:* The District of Columbia Bar; American Bar Association (Member, Section on Public Contract Law; Co-Chair, Conflicts of Interest and Ethics Committee). ***PRACTICE AREAS:*** Government Contracts Law. ***Email:*** alison_doyle@mckennacuneo.com

LAWRENCE S. EBNER, born Jersey City, New Jersey, May 29, 1947; admitted to bar, 1973, District of Columbia. *Education:* Dartmouth College (B.A., cum laude, 1969); Harvard University (J.D., 1972). Phi Beta Kappa. Principal-Author: *Pesticide Regulation Handbook,* McGraw-Hill, Inc and Executive Enterprises Publications Co., Inc., New York, N.Y., 1991 (Third Edition); *TSCA Handbook,* Government Institutes, Inc., 1996 (Third Edition). Author: "The California Supreme Court Weighs In On FIFRA Preemption," BNA Toxics Law Reporter (Vol. 15, No. 24, pp. 627-633)(June 22, 2000); "California Supreme Court Repudiates Federal Government Position on Pesticide Tort Preemption," Product Liability Law & Strategy (Vol. XIII, No. 10) (April 2000). Trial Attorney, Attorney General's Honor Program, Civil Division, U.S. Department of Justice, 1972-1974. *Member:* The District of Columbia Bar; Federal and American Bar Associations. (Chair, Appellate Litigation Group). ***PRACTICE AREAS:*** Appellate Practice; Complex Civil Litigation; Toxic Torts; Product Liability. ***Email:*** larry_ebner@mckennacuneo.com

MICHAEL L. FAYAD, born Detroit, Michigan, May 3, 1945; admitted to bar, 1970, District of Columbia; 1970, Michigan. *Education:* University of Detroit (B.A., 1967; J.D., 1970). Member and Articles Editor, Journal of Urban Law, 1969-1970. Member: E. Barrett Prettyman Legal Intern Program, Georgetown University, 1970-1972; Public Defender Service of D.C., 1972-1977. Visiting Professor of Law, Washington College of Law of American University, 1977-1979. Member, U.S. Department of Justice, Fraud Section, 1979-1989. *Member:* The District of Columbia Bar. ***PRACTICE AREAS:*** Corporate Criminal Law; Civil Fraud Defense; Criminal Trials; Corporate Investigations; Government Contracts; Federal Aviation Regulation; Foreign Military Sales; International Arms Shipment; Foreign Corrupt Practices Act; Banking Regulation; False Claims Act. ***Email:*** michael_fayad@mckennacuneo.com

PETER BUCK FELLER, born Los Angeles, California, August 1, 1937; admitted to bar, 1965, District of Columbia; 1967, U.S. Court of International Trade; U.S. Court of Appeals for the Federal Circuit; U.S. Supreme Court. *Education:* University of Pennsylvania (A.B., 1960); American University Law School (J.D., 1964); George Washington University (LL.M., 1967). Author: "U.S. Customs and International Trade Guide," Matthew Bender & Co., 4 Vol. Treatise, 1979 (current updates). Attorney-Advisor: Office of General Counsel, 1964-1968; Office of Tax International Counsel, 1969-1971, U.S. Treasury Department. *Member:* The District of Columbia Bar; American Bar Association. ***Email:*** peter_feller@mckennacuneo.com

HERBERT L. FENSTER, born New York, N.Y., March 29, 1935; admitted to bar, 1961, Virginia; 1962, District of Columbia; 1965, U.S. Supreme Court; 1993, Colorado. *Education:* University of Pennsylvania (A.B., 1957; B.S., 1958); University of Virginia (LL.B., 1961). *Member:* The District of Columbia Bar; Bar Association of the District of Columbia; Virginia State Bar; American Bar Association; American Law Institute.

(This Listing Continued)

T. MARK FLANAGAN, JR., born Pittsburgh, Pennsylvania, August 25, 1954; admitted to bar, 1981, District of Columbia; 1982, Maryland. *Education:* University of Notre Dame (B.A., with high honors, 1976); University of Virginia (J.D., 1981). Assistant U.S. Attorney, District of Columbia, 1984-1988. Staff Researcher, Select Committee on Assassinations, U.S. House of Representatives, Washington, D.C., 1977-1979. *Member:* The District of Columbia Bar; Maryland State and American Bar Associations. ***PRACTICE AREAS:*** White Collar Criminal Defense Law; General Civil Litigation. ***Email:*** mark_flanagan@mckennacuneo.com

RUTH S. FLYNN, born Washington, D.C., May 1, 1944; admitted to bar, 1983, Illinois; 1993, District of Columbia. *Education:* Northwestern University (B.S., 1965); University of Denver (M.A., 1967); Illinois Institute of Technology/Chicago-Kent College of Law (J.D., 1983). National Team, Moot Court; Notes and Comments Editor, Chicago/Kent Law Review, 1982-1983. *Member:* District of Columbia Bar (Member, Estates, Trusts and Probate and Taxation Sections); Illinois State and American Bar Associations. ***PRACTICE AREAS:*** Estate Planning; Estate Administration; Charitable Giving. ***Email:*** ruth_flynn@mckennacuneo.com

STEPHEN K. GARDNER, born 1949; admitted to bar, 1976, California; 1978, District of Columbia. *Education:* University of Denver (B.A., 1971); University of California, Hastings College of the Law (J.D., 1975). ***PRACTICE AREAS:*** Energy Law. ***Email:*** stephen_gardner@mckennacuneo.com

PETER L. GRAY, born Washington, D.C., May 23, 1957; admitted to bar, 1985, Pennsylvania; 1986, District of Columbia. *Education:* University of Maryland (B.S., with honors, 1979); George Washington University (M.S., 1982; J.D., 1985). Order of the Coif. Author: "Emergency Planning and Community Right-to-Know Act Practice Manual," American Bar Association, 2001. Editor and Principal Author: *Superfund Claims and Litigation Manual*, Executive Enterprises Publications, 1990. Editor and Co-Author, *Wiley Environmental Law Update,* 1998 and 1999 editions. Member, Board of Directors, Chemical Waste Litigation Reporter. *Member:* The District of Columbia Bar; Pennsylvania, Federal and American (Member, Sections on: Natural Resources, Energy and Environmental Law, Vice-Chair, Toxic Torts and Environmental Litigation Committee, 1997-2001; Litigation, Chair, Subcommittee on Environmental Legislation, 1996-1997) Bar Associations. ***Email:*** peter_gray@mckennacuneo.com

KURT J. HAMROCK, born Weymouth, Massachusetts, November 18, 1966; admitted to bar, 1992, Texas; 1994, District of Columbia. *Education:* Southern Methodist University (B.A., 1989); University of Texas at Austin (J.D., with honors, 1992). ***PRACTICE AREAS:*** Appellate Litigation. ***Email:*** kurt_hamrock@mckennacuneo.com

JACQUELINE A. HENSON, born Bethesda, Maryland, October 13, 1955; admitted to bar, 1983, Maryland; 1985, District of Columbia. *Education:* University of Pennsylvania (B.A., magna cum laude, 1977); American University (J.D., 1982); George Washington University (M.B.A., 1983). Certified Public Accountant, Maryland, 1984. Staff Member, American University Law Review, 1980-1981. *Member:* The District of Columbia Bar; Maryland State and American Bar Associations. ***PRACTICE AREAS:*** Nonprofit Organization Law; Taxation Law; Corporation Law. ***Email:*** jackie_henson@mckennacuneo.com

E. SANDERSON HOE, born Plainfield, New Jersey, November 1, 1947; admitted to bar, 1973, District of Columbia; 1977, U.S. Supreme Court. *Education:* Colby College (B.A., 1969); Cornell University (J.D., 1973). Author: "Law for Engineers," George Washington University, 1980; "Flow-Down Clauses in Subcontracts," Federal Publications, 1985. Professorial Lecturer in Engineering Law, George Washington University, 1980-1984. *Member:* The District of Columbia Bar (Co-Chair, Government Contracts and Litigation Section, Steering Committee, 1990-1994); American Bar Association (Member, Sections on Public Contract Law, Co-Chair, Privatization and Outsourcing Committee; Litigation). ***PRACTICE AREAS:*** Governments Contracts; Telecommunications; Litigation. ***Email:*** sandy_hoe@mckennacuneo.com

MICHAEL A. HOPKINS, born Meadville, Pennsylvania, June 22, 1961; admitted to bar, 1993, Georgia; 1995, District of Columbia. *Education:* Assumption College (B.A., 1983); George Washington University (J.D., 1993). ***PRACTICE AREAS:*** Government Contracts; Telecommunications. ***Email:*** mike_hopkins@mckennacuneo.com

DANIEL G. JARCHO, born Salt Lake City, Utah, April 22, 1959; admitted to bar, 1984, Utah; 1985, District of Columbia. *Education:* Harvard University (B.A., cum laude, 1981; J.D., cum laude, 1984). Clerk to Chief Judge Aldon J. Anderson, U.S. District Court, District of Utah, 1984-1985. Trial Attorney, Office of Consumer Litigation, Civil Division, U.S. Department of Justice, 1988-1992. Special Assistant U.S. Attorney, Criminal Division, U.S. Attorney's Office for the Eastern District of New York, 1991. ***PRACTICE AREAS:*** Civil Litigation; Criminal Litigation; Appellate Litigation; Food and Drug Law; Federal Regulatory Law. ***Email:*** dan_jarcho@mckennacuneo.com

DANIEL E. JOHNSON, born Everett, Washington, August 2, 1958; admitted to bar, 1983, District of Columbia. *Education:* Virginia Polytechnic Institute and State University (B.S., magna cum laude, 1980); University of Virginia (J.D., 1983). Phi Sigma; Phi Kappa Phi. *Member:* The District of Columbia Bar

(This Listing Continued)

McKENNA & CUNEO, L.L.P., Washington—Continued

(Member, Sections on: Litigation; Labor and Employment); American Bar Association (Member, Litigation Section). ***PRACTICE AREAS:*** Litigation; Trade Secrets; Employment. ***Email:*** dan_johnson@mckennacuneo.com

DAVID KASANOW, born Philadelphia, Pennsylvania, September 9, 1947; admitted to bar, 1991, Pennsylvania; 1992, District of Columbia and U.S. Court of Federal Claims; 1996, U.S. Court of Appeals for the Federal Circuit. *Education:* University of Pennsylvania (B.A., 1969); Georgetown University (J.D., magna cum laude, 1991). Order of the Coif. *Member:* The District of Columbia Bar; Federal and American (Member, Public Contract Law and Litigation Sections) Bar Associations; U.S. Court of Federal Claims Bar Association. ***PRACTICE AREAS:*** Government Contracts. ***Email:*** david_kasanow@mckennacuneo.com

CHRIS S. LEASON, born Latrobe, Pennsylvania, October 9, 1963; admitted to bar, 1994, Pennsylvania and District of Columbia. *Education:* Pennsylvania State University (B.S., 1987); George Washington University (J.D., 1993). ***PRACTICE AREAS:*** Environmental Law; Transportation Law; Occupational Safety and Health Law; Administrative Law. ***Email:*** chris_leason@mckennacuneo.com

FREDERIC M. LEVY, born Washington, D.C., August 15, 1953; admitted to bar, 1978, District of Columbia. *Education:* Columbia University (B.A., 1975; J.D., 1978). *Member:* The District of Columbia Bar; American Bar Association (Member, Sections on: Administrative Law; Litigation; Public Contract Law; Vice-Chair, Suspension and Debarment Committee; Vice-Chair, Procurement Fraud Committee). ***PRACTICE AREAS:*** White Collar Criminal Defense Law; White Collar Fraud; Government Procurement Law; Commercial Transactions; Commercial Litigation. ***Email:*** fred_levy@mckennacuneo.com

LINO S. LIPINSKY DE ORLOV, born New York, New York, August 5, 1958; admitted to bar, 1983, New York, Colorado, U.S. District Court, District of Colorado and U.S. Court of Appeals, Tenth Circuit; 1989, U.S. Supreme Court; 1998, District of Columbia. *Education:* Brown University (A.B., magna cum laude, 1979); New York University (J.D., 1982). *Member:* Denver, Colorado and American Bar Associations; The District of Columbia Bar. (Also at Denver Office). ***PRACTICE AREAS:*** Civil Practice; Civil Appeals; Trial Practice; Technology Law. ***Email:*** lino_lipinsky@mckennacuneo.com

ROBERT A. MATTHEWS, born New York, N.Y., June 20, 1948; admitted to bar, 1974, New York; 1993, District of Columbia. *Education:* Gettysburg College (A.B., 1970); Fordham University Law School (J.D., 1973). Co-Editor and Principal Author: *Superfund Claims and Litigation Manual*, Executive Enterprise Publication, Inc., 1990. Member, Board of Advisors, Chemical Waste Litigation Reporter. *Member:* American Bar Association (Member, Natural Resources Section). ***Email:*** robert_matthews@mckennacuneo.com

MATTHEW J. McGRATH, born Michigan City, Indiana, August 22, 1956; admitted to bar, 1986, Maryland; 1987, District of Columbia. *Education:* University of Notre Dame (B.A., 1978); George Washington University National Law Center (J.D., 1986). Member, George Washington Law Review, 1985-1986. *Member:* American Bar Association (Co-Chairman, International Procurement Committee, Section of International Law and Practice, 1992-1993, 1995-1996, 1997-1998; Chair, International Procurement Committee, Public Contract Law Section, 1994-1995); The District of Columbia Bar. ***PRACTICE AREAS:*** Government Contracts; International Business Transactions; International Dispute Resolution; International Financing; Foreign Corrupt Practices Act; Agency for International Development; Export-Import Bank; World Bank; Export Controls Law. ***Email:*** matthew_mcgrath@mckennacuneo.com

KELLIE L. NEWTON, born Jamestown, New York, June 6, 1959; admitted to bar, 1984, Ohio; 1985, U.S. District Court, Southern District of Ohio; 1992, Pennsylvania; 1997, District of Columbia. *Education:* City of London Polytechnic University, London, England; Dickinson College (B.A., 1981); Capital University (J.D., 1984). Member, 1982-1983 and Research Editor, 1983-1984, Capital University Law Review. Note, "Detling v. Chockley: Punitive Damages and the Drunk Driver-An Untimely Decision," 12 Capital University Law Review 271, 1983. ***PRACTICE AREAS:*** Corporate; Business. ***Email:*** kellie_newton@mckennacuneo.com

CHARLES A. O'CONNOR, III, born Providence, Rhode Island, April 7, 1942; admitted to bar, 1967, Rhode Island; 1969, District of Columbia; 1970, U.S. Supreme Court. *Education:* Harvard University (A.B., cum laude in English, 1964); Georgetown University (J.D., 1967; M.A., 1985). Principal - Author: *Pesticide Regulation Handbook,* Executive Enterprises Publications, Inc., New York, N.Y., 1991 (Third Edition); *TSCA Handbook,* Government Institutes, Inc., 1997 (Third Edition); *Consumer Product Safety Law,* Government Institutes, Inc., Washington, D.C., 1977. Adjunct Professor of Law, Georgetown Law Center, 1973-1977. Lecturer of Law, Catholic University of America, Columbus School of Law, 1975-1977. *Member:* The District of Columbia Bar; Bar Association of the District of Columbia; Federal and American Bar Associations. [U.S. Navy JAGC, 1967-1969]. ***PRACTICE AREAS:*** Environmental Regulation; Chemical Regulation. ***Email:*** charles_oconnor@mckennacuneo.com

(This Listing Continued)

THOMAS C. PAPSON, born Lebanon, Pennsylvania, September 12, 1951; admitted to bar, 1977, Pennsylvania; 1978, District of Columbia. *Education:* University of Pennsylvania (B.A., 1973); Georgetown University (J.D., 1977). Law Clerk to the Hon. John J. Sirica, U.S. District Court, District of Columbia, 1977-1979. President, DC Legal Aid Society. Fellow, American Bar Foundation. *Member:* American Bar Association (Sections on Litigation and Public Contract Law). ***PRACTICE AREAS:*** Commercial Litigation; Government Contract Litigation; Administrative. ***Email:*** tom_papson@mckennacuneo.com

DON J. PELTO, born Baltimore, Maryland, January 20, 1960; admitted to bar, 1985, Maryland; 1989, California and U.S. District Court, Central District of California; 1990, District of Columbia and U.S. Court of Appeals for the Federal Circuit; registered to practice before U.S. Patent and Trademark Office. *Education:* University of Maryland (B.S., Biological Sciences, 1982); University of Baltimore School of Law (J.D., 1985). Biologist, National Institutes of Health, National Institute on Aging, 1979-1988. *Member:* The District of Columbia Bar; Maryland State and American Bar Associations; State Bar of California; American Intellectual Property Law Association; San Diego Intellectual Property Law Association. ***LANGUAGES:*** Finnish. ***REPORTED CASES:*** In re Ochiai, 71 F.3d 1565, 37 USPQ2d 1127 (Fed.Cir. 1995). ***PRACTICE AREAS:*** Intellectual Property; Biotechnology Patents; Pharmaceutical Patents; Patent Procurement; Patent Litigation; Patent Interferences. ***Email:*** don_pelto@mckennacuneo.com

LARRY R. PILOT, born Detroit, Michigan, April 22, 1940; admitted to bar, 1967, Virginia; 1968, District of Columbia. *Education:* Wayne State University (B.S., 1962); University of Detroit and Catholic University of America (J.D., 1967). Delta Theta Phi; Omicron Delta Kappa. Registered Pharmacist: Michigan, 1963; District of Columbia, 1967. Special Assistant to Assistant Secretary for Health and Scientific Affairs, U.S. Department of Health Education and Welfare, 1969. Special Assistant to Commissioner, 1969-1970 and Associate Commissioner of Medical Affairs, 1970-1971, U.S. Food and Drug Administration. Director, Office of Compliance, Bureau of Medical Devices, U.S. Food and Drug Administration, 1971-1979. *Member:* The District of Columbia Bar; Federal (Chairman, 1979-1981, Health and Welfare Committee) and American Bar Associations; Virginia State Bar. ***Email:*** larry_pilot@mckennacuneo.com

RAYMOND S. E. PUSHKAR, born Sharon, Pennsylvania, September 3, 1938; admitted to bar, 1963, Wisconsin; 1968, U.S. Supreme Court; 1969, District of Columbia; 1976, U.S. Court of Federal Claims; U.S. Court of Appeals for the Federal Circuit. *Education:* Marquette University (A.B., 1960; J.D., 1963). Law Clerk to the Hon. William J. Storey, Delaware Superior Court, 1965-1966. Member: Board of Contract Appeals Association; National Contract Management Association; Northern Virginia Technology Council; Washington, D.C. Technology Council. *Member:* The District of Columbia Bar (Chairman, Government Contracts and Litigation Section, 1982-1988); State Bar of Wisconsin; Federal, Federal Circuit and American Bar Associations. [Judge Advocate, USAF, 1963-1966]. ***PRACTICE AREAS:*** Government Contracts Litigation; Commercial Contracts Litigation; Electronic Commerce; Litigation; International Contracts. ***Email:*** ray_pushkar@mckennacuneo.com

FRANK M. RAPOPORT, born Philadelphia, Pennsylvania, 1950; admitted to bar, 1976, Pennsylvania; 1978, District of Columbia. *Education:* University of Pennsylvania (B.A., magna cum laude, 1973); Temple University (J.D., 1976). Trial Attorney, U.S. Department of Justice, 1977-1982. *Member:* American Bar Association (Section of Public Contract Law: State Chairman for Pennsylvania, 1992—; Co-Chair, Health Care Procurement Committee, 1997—). ***PRACTICE AREAS:*** Government Contracts; Public Health Law; Health Care Fraud. ***Email:*** frank_rapoport@mckennacuneo.com

ANDREW M. REIDY, born Worcester, Massachusetts, November 15, 1962; admitted to bar, 1987, District of Columbia and Massachusetts. *Education:* Boston College (B.A., cum laude, 1984); George Washington University (J.D., 1987). Author: "Is Insurance the Cure for the Millenium Bug?" Insurance Teller, Vol. 4, Summer 1997; "Directors and Officers Insurance: Knowing the Response to Your D&O Insurer's Hardball Tactics," Banking on Insurance, Vol. 1, No. 1, Winter 1994-1995; "The Pitfalls of Fidelity Insurance," The National Law Journal, March 4, 1996. "Tobacco Litigation: Looking for Cover," Legal Times, March 6, 1995. Editor, Insurance Teller. *Member:* The District of Columbia Bar; Massachusetts and American Bar Associations. ***PRACTICE AREAS:*** Commercial Litigation; Insurance Recovery Litigation; Directors and Officers Insurance Coverage; Fidelity Bond Litigation. ***Email:*** andrew_reidy@mckennacuneo.com

MURRAY D. SACKS, born Kansas City, Missouri, April 5, 1961; admitted to bar, 1986, Maryland; 1988, District of Columbia. *Education:* Northwestern University; Washington University (B.S., cum laude, 1983); George Washington University (J.D., with honors, 1986). Author: "Finding a Pot of Gold: Your Liability Policy's Aggregate Limits Probably Don't Apply to Environmental Actions," 6 Environmental Claims Journal 489, Summer 1994; "Insurance for Cyberspace Defamation: A Safe Harbor for Policyholders?" Mealey's Emerging Insurance Disputes, June 5, 1997; "On-Line Defamation—Don't Overlook Your Insurance," 4 Multimedia and Technology Licensing Report, November 1997; "Yes, Virginia, Full Coverage Exists," Legal Times, Jan. 11, 1999. *Member:* The

(This Listing Continued)

District of Columbia Bar; Maryland State and American Bar Associations. ***PRACTICE AREAS:*** Insurance Litigation; Commercial Litigation. ***Email:*** murray_sacks@mckennacuneo. com

MICHAEL G. SCHEININGER, born Newark, New Jersey, April 16, 1947; admitted to bar, 1972, Pennsylvania and District of Columbia; 1978, Maryland. *Education:* Franklin & Marshall College (B.A., magna cum laude, 1969); University of Pennsylvania (J.D., 1972). Phi Beta Kappa. Member, Editorial Board, University of Pennsylvania Law Review, 1971-1972. Adjunct Professor, Trial Practice, Georgetown University Law Center, 1980—. Assistant United States Attorney, District of Columbia, 1972-1976. *Member:* The District of Columbia Bar; American Bar Association (Co-Chair, Washington, D.C. Subcommittee of the Criminal Litigation Committee, Litigation Section, 1988—). ***PRACTICE AREAS:*** Civil Litigation; White Collar Criminal Defense Law; General Liability. ***Email:*** michael_scheininger@mckennacuneo.com

MATTHEW J. SCHLESINGER, born Syracuse, New York, June 29, 1963; admitted to bar, 1989, Maryland; 1990, District of Columbia. *Education:* The American University (B.A., cum laude, 1985); Northwestern University (J.D., 1989). Note and Comment Editor, Northwestern Journal of International Law and Business. *Member:* American Bar Association. ***PRACTICE AREAS:*** Insurance Coverage; Complex Commercial Litigation. ***Email:*** matthew_schlesinger@mckennacuneo.com

JEFF E. SCHWARTZ, born Newark, New Jersey, August 24, 1958; admitted to bar, 1993, Texas; 1994, District of Columbia and U.S. Court of Appeals for the Federal Circuit; 1997, U.S. Court of Veterans Appeals; 1998, U.S. Supreme Court; registered to practice before U.S. Patent and Trademark Office. *Education:* United States Military Academy (B.S., 1980); American Technological University (M.S., 1986); Georgetown University (J.D., magna cum laude, 1993). Order of the Coif. Registered Engineer in Training, Pennsylvania, 1980. Author, "The Acquisition of Technical Data Rights," Public Contract Law Journal, Volume 23, Number 4. Law Clerk to Judge Daniel Friedman, U.S. Court of Appeals for the Federal Circuit, 1993-1994. *Member:* District of Columbia Bar (Member, Sections on Intellectual Property Law, Government Contracts); American Bar Association (Member, Sections on: Patent, Trademark and Copyright; Public Contracts); Federal Circuit Bar Association; American Intellectual Property Law Association; American Society for Mechanical Engineers. [Lieutenant Colonel, U.S. Army Reserves, Ordnance Corps; Engineer, U.S. Navy]. ***LANGUAGES:*** German. ***PRACTICE AREAS:*** Patent Law; Patent Licensing; Mechanical Intellectual Property; Medical Intellectual Property; Aerospace Intellectual Property; Patent Litigation; Patent Interferences; Civil Litigation; Technology Law; Government Contracts; Technical Data Rights; Software. ***Email:*** jeff_schwartz@mckennacuneo.com

CATHERINE J. SERAFIN, born Philadelphia, Pennsylvania, October 12, 1961; admitted to bar, 1986, Delaware; 1987, U.S. District Court, District of Delaware; 1990, U.S. Court of Appeals, Third Circuit; 1992, U.S. Court of Appeals, Fourth Circuit; 1993, U.S. Court of Appeals, Sixth Circuit and U.S. Supreme Court; 1996, District of Columbia. *Education:* King's College (B.A., summa cum laude, 1983); Villanova University (J.D., 1986). *Member:* Delaware State (Member, Section on Women and the Law) and American Bar Associations; The District of Columbia Bar. ***PRACTICE AREAS:*** Insurance Coverage Litigation. ***Email:*** cathy_serafin@mckennacuneo.com

CAROL A. SMOOTS, born Wenatchee, Washington; admitted to bar, 1978, Oregon; 1981, District of Columbia; 1985, U.S. Court of Appeals, District of Columbia Circuit; 1986, U.S. Supreme Court. *Education:* Seattle Pacific University; Central Washington University (B.A., summa cum laude, 1975); University of Washington; Willamette University (J.D., 1978). Editor-in-Chief, The Natural Gas Lawyers Journal, 1985-1988. Reports Editor, Energy Law Journal, 1989-1993. Municipal Judge, Lafayette, Oregon. Attorney: The Bonneville Power Administration, 1979-1984; American Gas Association, 1984-1988. Director, Government Relations, MidCon Corporation, a subsidiary of Occidental Petroleum. *Member:* The District of Columbia Bar; American Bar Association; Federal Energy Bar Association (Officer and Board Member, 1991-2000); International Bar Association. ***PRACTICE AREAS:*** Energy Law; Administrative Law; International Law. ***Email:*** carol_smoots@mckennacuneo.com

DONNA LEE YESNER, born Hartford, Connecticut, 1950; admitted to bar, 1983, District of Columbia. *Education:* University of New Mexico (B.A., 1974); University of Georgia (M.A., 1977); Catholic University (J.D., 1983). Member, Catholic University Law Review. ***PRACTICE AREAS:*** Public Health Law; Government Procurement. ***Email:*** donna_yesner@mckennacuneo.com

CHARLES E. YONKERS, born Kansas City, Missouri, May 12, 1940; admitted to bar, 1966, District of Columbia; 1967, U.S. Claims Court; 1970, U.S. Supreme Court. *Education:* Yale University (A.B., 1963); Harvard University (J.D., 1966). Country Director, Peace Corps, Benin, West Africa, 1972-1976. *Member:* The District of Columbia Bar. ***Email:*** charles_yonkers@mckennacuneo.com

RESIDENT OF COUNSEL

WALTER J. EIDSON, JR., born Mt. Clemens, Michigan, July 30, 1954; admitted to bar, 1986, Pennsylvania; 2000, District of Columbia. *Education:* Georgetown University (B.S., cum laude, 1977); George Washington University (J.D., 1985). Sigma Delta Pi. Certified Spanish English Translator, Georgetown University, Washington, D.C., 1976. General Counsel, Alcatel Data Networks, 1995-1999. Senior Attorney, Sprint International, 1988-1995. Legal Officer, Pan American Health Organization, 1986-1988. *Member:* Inter-American Bar Association; American Immigration Lawyers Association. ***LANGUAGES:*** Spanish and French. ***PRACTICE AREAS:*** Information Technology; Licensing; Corporate; Commercial; International; Joint Ventures. ***Email:*** jay_eidson@mckennacuneo.com

LAWRENCE M. FARRELL, born Niagara Falls, New York, June 10, 1934; admitted to bar, 1966, Virginia; 1967, District of Columbia; 1992, California. *Education:* Canisius College (A.B., 1956); Catholic University of America, Columbus School of Law (LL.B., 1966). Special Counsel to Assistant Secretary of the Navy for Manpower and Logistics, 1976-1977. Professional Lecturer in Engineering Law, George Washington University, 1984-1990. *Member:* The District of Columbia Bar; State Bar of California; Virginia State Bar. [U.S. Navy Line Officer, 1957-1967; U.S. Navy Judge Advocate, 1967-1977]. ***PRACTICE AREAS:*** Government Contracts Law; Litigation. ***Email:*** larry_farrell@mckennacuneo.com

STEPHEN MARK GOLDMAN, born Denver, Colorado, October 28, 1946; admitted to bar, 1971, Colorado; 1991, Pennsylvania and Hawaii; 1999, District of Columbia. *Education:* Duke University (A.B., 1968); University of Michigan (J.D., 1971); Oxford University, England (D.Phil., 1979). Phi Beta Kappa. Bigelow Fellow and Instructor, University of Chicago Law School, 1974-1975. Law Clerk to Judge John Paul Stevens, U.S. Court of Appeals, Seventh Circuit, 1973-1974. *Member:* American Bar Association (Co-Chair, International/London Subcommittee, Insurance Coverage Litigation Committee, Litigation Section). ***PRACTICE AREAS:*** Insurance Coverage. ***Email:*** stephen_goldman@mckennacuneo.com

THOMAS B. JOHNSTON, born Akron, Ohio, February 9, 1954; admitted to bar, 1987, District of Columbia. *Education:* College of William & Mary (B.S., 1976); Ohio State University (M.S., 1979); George Washington University (J.D., with honors, 1986). Ohio State University Fellow. Professorial Lecturer in Law, George Washington University, 1989-1994. Co-Author: *TSCA Handbook,* 3rd Edition, Government Institutes, 1997; *Pesticide Regulation Handbook,* 3rd Edition, Executive Enterprises, 1991. *Member:* District of Columbia Bar (Member, Sections on Administrative Law and Agency Practice, Environment, Energy and Natural Resources); American Bar Association (Member, Sections on Administrative Law, Natural Resources Law). ***PRACTICE AREAS:*** Toxic Substance Control Law; Pesticide Law; Environmental Law. ***Email:*** thomas_johnston@mckennacuneo.com

GEOFFREY T. KEATING, born Washington, D.C., October 4, 1940; admitted to bar, 1967, District of Columbia; 1970, Maryland; 1971, U.S. Supreme Court and U.S. Court of Federal Claims. *Education:* Ohio Wesleyan University (B.A., 1962); George Washington University (J.D., 1966). Author: "Privatization of Public Infrastructure," Federal Publications, Inc., Construction Briefings, July 1993; "Construction Contractor's Right to Early Completion," John Wiley & Sons, 1994; Faculty: Construction Executive Program, Stanford University, 1984; International Law Institute; Faculty, International Procurement, Arbitration and World Bank Contracts, China, 1996 and Uganda, 1997. Board of Governors, American College of Construction Lawyers. *Member:* American Bar Association (Co-Chair, 1988-1992; Chair, 1993, Construction Claims Committee; Vice-Chair, Bonds and Insurance Committee, 2000-2002; Forum Committee on Construction). ***PRACTICE AREAS:*** Construction Law; Government Contracts Law. ***Email:*** geoffrey_keating@mckennacuneo.com

MARY S. WEBSTER, born Bellefonte, Pennsylvania, September 20, 1960; admitted to bar, 1992, Maryland; 1994, District of Columbia; 1995, U.S. Court of Appeals for the Federal Circuit. *Education:* University of Wisconsin (B.S., Bacteriology, 1983); University of South Florida (M.S., Microbiology, 1985); Washington College of Law, American University (J.D., magna cum laude, 1992). ***PRACTICE AREAS:*** Intellectual Property. ***Email:*** mary_webster@mckennacuneo.com

RESIDENT ASSOCIATES

PAUL R. ALMANZA, born Los Angeles, California, December 4, 1966; admitted to bar, 1993, California (Not admitted in District of Columbia). *Education:* Princeton University (A.B., 1988); Boalt Hall School of Law, University of California (J.D., 1992). [Captain, U.S. Army, JAG Corps, 1996-2001]. ***LANGUAGES:*** Italian and German. ***PRACTICE AREAS:*** Litigation. ***Email:*** paul_almanza@mckennacuneo.com

MONICA A. AQUINO, born Lakeland, Florida, May 17, 1974; admitted to bar, 1999, Florida; 2000, District of Columbia. *Education:* University of Miami (B.A., 1996; J.D., 1999). ***PRACTICE AREAS:*** Civil Litigation; Appellate Practice. ***Email:*** monica_aquino@mckennacuneo.com

MICHAEL JAMES BEARMAN, born Auburn, Washington, August 13, 1973; admitted to bar, 2000, Maryland; 2001, District of Columbia. *Education:* University of Washington (B.A., 1997); Georgetown University Law Center

(This Listing Continued)

McKENNA & CUNEO, L.L.P., Washington—Continued

(J.D., cum laude, 2000). ***LANGUAGES:*** Mandarin Chinese. ***PRACTICE AREAS:*** Litigation; Government Contracts; Life Sciences. ***Email:*** michael_bearman@mckennacuneo.com

ANNE D. BERUBE, born New York, New York, September 5, 1968; admitted to bar, 1998, Maryland; 1999, District of Columbia. *Education:* Kenyon College (B.A., 1990); George Washington University (J.D., 1998). ***PRACTICE AREAS:*** Environmental. ***Email:*** anne_berube@mckennacuneo.com

JOHN A. BONELLO, born Lansing, Michigan, April 4, 1966; admitted to bar, 1991, Maryland; 1992, District of Columbia. *Education:* University of Notre Dame (B.B.A., 1988); Catholic University of America (J.D., 1991). ***PRACTICE AREAS:*** Commercial Litigation; Technology Law; Outsourcing; Software Licensing; Internet Law; Privacy Law; Intellectual Property. ***Email:*** john_bonello@mckennacuneo.com

JEFFREY R. BOODMAN, born New York, N.Y., May 22, 1970; admitted to bar, 1999, Virginia; 2000, District of Columbia. *Education:* Washington University (A.B., 1992); Georgetown University (M.A., 1996; J.D., 1999). ***Email:*** jeffrey_boodman@mckennacuneo.com

KAREN A. BORELLI, born Charlotte, North Carolina, March 24, 1975; (admission pending). *Education:* Georgia Institute of Technology (B.M.E., 1998); Catholic University of America (J.D., 2001). Member, American Society of Mechanical Engineers, 1999—. *Member:* American Bar Association; American Intellectual Property Law Association; Giles Rich American Inn of Court. ***PRACTICE AREAS:*** Intellectual Property. ***Email:*** karen_borelli@mckennacuneo.com

MICHAEL BOUCHER, admitted to bar, 1994, New York; 1996, District of Columbia; 1997, U.S. Supreme Court. *Education:* Georgetown University Law Center (J.D., 1993). ***PRACTICE AREAS:*** Environmental Law; Environmental Litigation; Environmental Auditing; International Environmental Law; Joint Ventures; Consumer Product Regulation. ***Email:*** michael_boucher@mckennacuneo.com

CHRISTOPHER C. BOUQUET, born Colorado Springs, Colorado, April 18, 1961; admitted to bar, 1994, Virginia; 1995, District of Columbia. *Education:* Washington & Lee University (B.A., cum laude, 1983); George Mason University (M.B.A., 1990); George Washington University (J.D., with honors, 1994). ***PRACTICE AREAS:*** Government Contracts; Commercial Contracts. ***Email:*** christopher_bouquet@mckennacuneo.com

LORA A. BRZEZYNSKI, born Brooklyn, New York, July 15, 1968; admitted to bar, 1993, Virginia; 1994, Maryland and District of Columbia; U.S. Court of Appeals, Fourth Circuit; U.S. District Court for the District of Columbia; U.S. District Court, Eastern and Western Districts of Virginia; U.S. Bankruptcy Court, Eastern District of Virginia. *Education:* University of Miami (B.A., 1990); Georgetown University Law Center (J.D., cum laude, 1993). *Member:* Fairfax County and American Bar Associations; Virginia State Bar. ***PRACTICE AREAS:*** Civil Litigation; Commercial Litigation; Products Liability. ***Email:*** lora_brzezynski@mckennacuneo.com

CHRISTINA M. CARROLL, born Lowell, Massachusetts, January 24, 1975; admitted to bar, 2001, Maryland and District of Columbia. *Education:* Harvard University (A.B., 1997); Georgetown University (J.D., 2000). ***Email:*** christina_carroll@mckennacuneo.com

PAUL R. CASSELL, born Wytheville, Virginia, October 14, 1971; admitted to bar, 1996, West Virginia; 1999, District of Columbia. *Education:* College of William & Mary (B.A., 1993); University of Virginia (J.D., 1996). ***PRACTICE AREAS:*** Litigation. ***Email:*** paul_cassell@mckennacuneo.com

RICHARD P. CASTIGLIA, JR., born Buffalo, New York, October 19, 1966; admitted to bar, 1992, Virginia; 1999, District of Columbia. *Education:* Case Western Reserve University (B.A., summa cum laude, 1989); University of Virginia (J.D., 1992). ***PRACTICE AREAS:*** Government Contracts. ***Email:*** richard_castiglia@mckennacuneo.com

CASS WALKER CHRISTENSON, born Hammond, Indiana, September 13, 1969; admitted to bar, 1994, Florida; 1995, U.S. District Court, Southern District of Florida; 1997, District of Columbia; 1998, U.S. District Court, Middle District of Florida; 1999, U.S. Court of Appeals, Eleventh Circuit; 2000, U.S. District Court, Northern District of Florida and U.S. Supreme Court. *Education:* University of Tampa (B.A., magna cum laude, 1991); Vanderbilt University (J.D., 1994). ***PRACTICE AREAS:*** Insurance Litigation; Commercial Litigation. ***Email:*** cass_christenson@mckennacuneo.com

JOHN M. CLERICI, born Grand Rapids, Michigan, September 24, 1970; admitted to bar, 1995, Georgia; 2000, District of Columbia. *Education:* Catholic University of America (B.A., 1992); University of North Carolina (J.D., 1995). ***PRACTICE AREAS:*** Government Contracts; Insurance Coverage; Litigation. ***Email:*** john_clerici@mckennacuneo.com

STACEY ANN FELDMAN, born Rochester, New York, September 27, 1974; admitted to bar, 1999, Virginia; 2000, District of Columbia. *Education:* University of Michigan (B.A., with distinction, 1996); American University

(This Listing Continued)

(J.D., cum laude, 1999). ***PRACTICE AREAS:*** Litigation; White Collar Crime; Employment Law; Insurance Recovery. ***Email:*** stacey_feldman@mckennacuneo.com

BRIAN T. FISHER, born Amesbury, Massachusetts, January 2, 1964; admitted to bar, 1994, Massachusetts; 1996, District of Columbia. *Education:* New Hampshire College (B.S., 1990); New England School of Law (J.D., 1994); George Washington University (LL.M., 1998). ***PRACTICE AREAS:*** Government Contracts; Commercial Law; Litigation. ***Email:*** brian_fisher@mckennacuneo.com

GUIDO J. GALVEZ, born Baltimore, Maryland, July 4, 1972; (admission pending). *Education:* University of Maryland (B.S., 1995; M.S., 1997); Catholic University of America (J.D., 2001). *Member:* American Bar Association; American Intellectual Property Law Association. ***PRACTICE AREAS:*** Intellectual Property. ***Email:*** guido_galvez@mckennacuneo.com

KERRI A. GILDOW, born Marietta, Ohio, April 21, 1972; (admission pending). *Education:* Bowling Green State University (B.S.B.A., 1994); Tulane Law School (J.D., magna cum laude, 2001). Order of the Coif. Member, Tulane Law Review, 2000-2001. ***Email:*** kerri_gildow@mckennacuneo.com

RICHARD T. GIRARDS, JR., born Southampton, New York, January 2, 1974; (admission pending). *Education:* Cornell University (B.S., 1996); Catholic University of America (J.D., 2001). ***PRACTICE AREAS:*** Intellectual Property. ***Email:*** richard_girards@mckennacuneo.com

DAVID GLYNN, born Boston, Massachusetts, September 28, 1975; (admission pending). *Education:* Franklin & Marshall College (B.A., 1998); George Washington University (J.D., with honors, 2001). ***PRACTICE AREAS:*** Government Contracts; Litigation; Health Care; White Collar Crime. ***Email:*** david_glynn@mckennacuneo.com

MICHELLE L. HYLTON, born Bossier City, Louisiana, February 6, 1969; admitted to bar, 1997, Virginia; 1998, District of Columbia. *Education:* Boston University (B.A., 1991); Columbus School of Law, Catholic University (J.D., 1997). ***PRACTICE AREAS:*** Commercial Litigation; Civil Litigation. ***Email:*** michelle_hylton@mckennacuneo.com

DONALD O. JOHNSON, born Philadelphia, Pennsylvania, May 18, 1954; admitted to bar, 1994, Maryland, District of Columbia and Pennsylvania; 1995, Virginia. *Education:* Pennsylvania State University (B.A., 1976); Temple University (B.B.A., summa cum laude, 1980; LL.M. in Trial Advocacy, cum laude, 1999); University of Miami (J.D., cum laude, 1993). Computer Systems Analyst, 1987-1993. ***LANGUAGES:*** Spanish and Portuguese. ***PRACTICE AREAS:*** Commercial Litigation; Insurance Litigation; Trade Secrets Litigation; Trademarks. ***Email:*** don_johnson@mckennacuneo.com

TONYA B. JOHNSON, born McKeesport, Pennsylvania, February 15, 1965; (admission pending). *Education:* Robert Morris College (B.S., 1990); University of Pittsburgh (J.D., 2001). Member, Journal of Law and Commerce. ***LANGUAGES:*** English.

LAWRENCE J. JOSEPH, born Greenville, Pennsylvania, November 18, 1960; admitted to bar, 1991, California; 1999, District of Columbia. *Education:* Franklin & Marshall College (B.A., 1984); Harvard University (J.D., 1991). ***PRACTICE AREAS:*** Environmental; Administrative. ***Email:*** larry_joseph@mckennacuneo.com

SCOTT E. KAUFF, born Glen Ridge, New Jersey, February 28, 1971; admitted to bar, 1996, Pennsylvania and New Jersey; 1997, District of Columbia. *Education:* Cornell University (B.A., cum laude, 1993); University of Pennsylvania (J.D., 1996). ***PRACTICE AREAS:*** Environmental Law; Litigation; Administrative Law; Occupational Safety and Health Law. ***Email:*** scott_kauff@mckennacuneo.com

STUART KIM, born Minneapolis, Minnesota, October 28, 1966; admitted to bar, 1999, Wisconsin; 2001, District of Columbia. *Education:* Lafayette College (B.S., honors with thesis, 1988); University of Notre Dame (M.S., 1991); University of Wisconsin (M.S., 1995; J.D., 1999). ***PRACTICE AREAS:*** Food and Drug Regulation; Food, Drug, Medical Device and Cosmetic Law; Unfair Trade Practices. ***Email:*** stuart_kim@mckennacuneo.com

SHARI L. KLEVENS, born Monterey Park, California, July 20, 1972; admitted to bar, 1999, Virginia; 2000, District of Columbia. *Education:* University of Maryland (B.S.B.A., cum laude, 1995); George Washington University (J.D., with honors, 1999). ***PRACTICE AREAS:*** Trademarks; Copyrights; Intellectual Property Litigation. ***Email:*** shari_klevens@mckennacuneo.com

LOUIS H. KOZLOFF, born West Reading, Pennsylvania, January 13, 1971; admitted to bar, 1998, Pennsylvania; 1999, District of Columbia. *Education:* Dartmouth College (A.B., 1993); University of Pittsburgh (J.D., 1998). ***PRACTICE AREAS:*** Litigation. ***Email:*** louis_kozloff@mckennacuneo.com

ILIA LEVITINE, born Moscow, Russia, April 11, 1967; admitted to bar, 1996, New Jersey; 1997, District of Columbia. *Education:* Moscow State University, Faculty of Law, Moscow, Russia (1987-1990); Guilford College (B.S., high honors, 1992); Washington & Lee University (J.D., 1995); Princeton Uni-

(This Listing Continued)

versity (M.P.A., 1996). ***LANGUAGES:*** Russian. ***PRACTICE AREAS:*** Electricity Regulation; Gas; Public Utilities; International Law. ***Email:*** ilia_levitine@mckennacuneo.com

JONATHAN PHILIP LIENHARD, born Fort Ord, California, October 22, 1972; admitted to bar, 1997, Virginia; 2001, District of Columbia. *Education:* University of Notre Dame (B.A., 1994; J.D., 1997). [Lieutenant, United States Navy JAG Corps, 1997-2000.]. ***PRACTICE AREAS:*** Civil Litigation. ***Email:*** jonathan_lienhard@mckennacuneo.com

JANE ANN ROE NEISWENDER, born Baltimore, Maryland, December 7, 1971; admitted to bar, 1999, Maryland; 2000, District of Columbia. *Education:* Princeton University (A.B., cum laude, 1993); Catholic University of America (J.D., cum laude, 1999). Staff Member, 1997-1998 and Associate Editor, 1998, Journal of Contemporary Health Law and Public Policy. ***LANGUAGES:*** French. ***PRACTICE AREAS:*** Litigation. ***Email:*** jane_neiswender@mckennacuneo.com

LISA MICHELE NORRETT, born Philadelphia, Pennsylvania, March 22, 1973; admitted to bar, 1998, New Jersey and Maryland; 1999, District of Columbia. *Education:* College of William & Mary (B.A., 1995); University of Virginia (J.D., 1998). ***PRACTICE AREAS:*** Products Liability Litigation; Civil Litigation. ***Email:*** lisa_norrett@mckennacuneo.com

WILLIAM T. O'BRIEN, born Red Bank, New Jersey, October 22, 1964; admitted to bar, 1994, Maryland; 1996, District of Columbia. *Education:* Boston University (B.S., 1987); Catholic University, Columbus School of Law (J.D., 1994). ***PRACTICE AREAS:*** Litigation. ***Email:*** william_o'brien@mckennacuneo.com

DANA BARRIE PASHKOFF, born Biloxi, Mississippi, December 20, 1972; admitted to bar, 1997, Maryland; 1999, District of Columbia. *Education:* University of Maryland (B.A., magna cum laude, 1994); George Washington University (J.D., with honors, 1997). ***PRACTICE AREAS:*** Government Contracts; Information Security; Privacy. ***Email:*** dana_pashkoff@mckennacuneo.com

MANIK K. RATH, born Pittsburgh, Pennsylvania, December 17, 1969; admitted to bar, 1994, Texas; 1997, Virginia; 1998, District of Columbia. *Education:* University of Virginia (B.A., 1991; J.D., 1994). ***PRACTICE AREAS:*** Labor and Employment Law; Business Litigation. ***Email:*** manik_rath@mckennacuneo.com

CHRISTOPHER ROBINSON, born Buffalo, New York, July 28, 1973; admitted to bar, 2000, New York; 2001, District of Columbia. *Education:* State University of New York at Geneseo (B.S., 1995); University of Notre Dame (J.D., 1999). ***PRACTICE AREAS:*** Corporate Law; Immigration Law; Health Care. ***Email:*** christopher_robinson@mckennacuneo.com

STEPHEN E. RUSCUS, born Washington, D.C., May 13, 1964; admitted to bar, 1991, Maryland; 1996, District of Columbia. *Education:* University of North Carolina, Chapel Hill (B.A., 1986); Catholic University of America (J.D., 1991). ***PRACTICE AREAS:*** Government Contracts; Litigation; Health Care Fraud; Medicaid/VA Compliance Pricing. ***Email:*** stephen_ruscus@mckennacuneo.com

JASON M. SILVERMAN, born New York, N.Y., August 18, 1972; admitted to bar, 2000, Illinois; 2001, District of Columbia. *Education:* Emory University (B.A., magna cum laude, 1994); Northwestern University School of Law (J.D., 2000). Phi Beta Kappa. ***PRACTICE AREAS:*** Litigation. ***Email:*** jason_silverman@mckennacuneo.com

KATHRIN V. SMITH, born Camphill, Pennsylvania, July 7, 1974; admitted to bar, 1999, Pennsylvania; 2001, District of Columbia. *Education:* State University of New York at Buffalo (B.S., cum laude, 1996); University of Pittsburgh School of Law (J.D., 1999). The Order of Barristers. ***PRACTICE AREAS:*** Insurance Litigation. ***Email:*** kathrin_smith@mckennacuneo.com

JODI T. TUER, born Winnipeg, Manitoba, April 17, 1966; admitted to bar, 1994, Pennsylvania; 1996, Virginia; 1998, District of Columbia. *Education:* McGill University (B.A., 1988); Washington College of Law of American University (J.D., 1994). ***PRACTICE AREAS:*** Insurance Recovery; Commercial Litigation. ***Email:*** jodi_tuer@mckennacuneo.com

TRACI MEAKEM VANEK, born Washington, D.C., July 4, 1970; admitted to bar, 1997, Maryland; 1999, District of Columbia. *Education:* College of William and Mary (B.S., 1992); Boston University (J.D., 1997). ***PRACTICE AREAS:*** Environmental Litigation; Products Liability; Appellate Practice; White Collar Crime Litigation. ***Email:*** traci_vanek@mckennacuneo.com

LEAH WARNICK, born Baltimore, Maryland, September 27, 1975; admitted to bar, 2000, Virginia; 2001, District of Columbia. *Education:* College of William & Mary (B.A., 1997); University of Virginia (J.D., 2000). ***PRACTICE AREAS:*** Environmental Law; Environmental Litigation. ***Email:*** leah_warnick@mckennacuneo.com

JASON N. WORKMASTER, born Columbus, Ohio, November 23, 1975; admitted to bar, 2000, Virginia; 2001, U.S. Court of Federal Claims (Not admitted in District of Columbia). *Education:* University of Florida (B.A., magna cum laude, 1997); Regent University (J.D., 2000). Phi Beta Kappa. ***PRACTICE AREAS:*** Contracts; Technology Law.

JOANNE L. ZIMOLZAK, born Nanticoke, Pennsylvania, July 22, 1968; admitted to bar, 1994, Maryland; 1996, District of Columbia. *Education:* University of Maryland (B.A., 1990); Georgetown University Law Center (J.D., 1994). ***Email:*** joanne_zimolzak@mckennacuneo.com

(For Biographical Data on other Firm Personnel, see Professional Biographies at Los Angeles, San Francisco and San Diego, California, Denver, Colorado, Dallas, Texas and Brussels, Belgium).

McLEOD, WATKINSON & MILLER

Established in 1984

EIGHTH FLOOR

ONE MASSACHUSETTS AVENUE, N.W.

WASHINGTON, D.C. 20001

Telephone: 202-842-2345

Telecopy: 202-408-7763

URL: http://www.mwmlaw.com

Agriculture and Agribusiness, Food, Drug and Nutrition, Transportation, Litigation, Employment, Medical Malpractice, International Trade, Real Estate, Corporate and Trade Association, Administrative, Entertainment, Legislation and Government Relations.

FIRM PROFILE: McLeod, Watkinson & Miller represents major agricultural and agribusiness organizations including several of the nation's major commodity promotion organizations. The firm also represents commuter rail and transit agencies and local governments in transactions and in addressing transportation regulatory issues. The practice also includes federal and state court litigation and representation before government agencies on the federal, state and local levels. For more than a decade, the firm has published The Agricultural Law Letter. Located on Capitol Hill, the firm maintains a thriving government relations practice as well as employment and government ethics representation.

MEMBERS OF FIRM

MICHAEL R. McLEOD, born Brooks County, Georgia, August 23, 1941; admitted to bar, 1967, District of Columbia. *Education:* University of Georgia (A.B., 1963); American University (J.D., 1967). Delta Theta Phi. Legislative Assistant to Senator Herman E. Talmadge, 1967-1971. Counsel to Senate Committee on Agriculture and Forestry, 1971-1974. General Counsel and Staff Director, Senate Committee on Agriculture and Forestry, 1974-1978. Editorial Director: "The Agricultural Law Letter," 1984—; "Here's How You Can Have an Impact on the 1990 Farm Bill," Top Producer, Mar. 1990; "Farmers Need a Bill of Rights," Top Producer, Jan. 1990; "Checkoffs Gain Favor," Top Producer, Jan. 1989; "Following the Food Companies," Agrimarketing, Oct. 1987; "Farmers Need a New Kind of Organization," Progressive Farmer, Aug. 1995. Columnist, "U.S. Agriculture, 1992-1993. President, Agriculture Law.com, 1998—. *Member:* District of Columbia Bar; American Bar Association. ***PRACTICE AREAS:*** Agricultural and Trade Association Law. ***Email:*** mmcleod@mumlaw.com

WAYNE R. WATKINSON, born Deep River, Connecticut, January 22, 1956; admitted to bar, 1983, District of Columbia. *Education:* St. Leo College (B.A., 1978); Howard University (J.D., 1983). *Member:* District of Columbia Bar; American Bar Association. **REPORTED CASES:** Goetz v. Glickman, 920 F. Supp. 1173 (D.Kan. 1966)(appeal pending at 10th Circuit). ***PRACTICE AREAS:*** Agricultural and Trade Association Law; Marketing Issues. ***Email:*** wwatkin@mwmlaw.com

MARC ERIC MILLER, born New York, N.Y., February 8, 1947; admitted to bar, 1973, New York; 1978, District of Columbia; 1982, U.S. Supreme Court. *Education:* Princeton University (A.B., 1969); Harvard Law School (J.D., 1972). Administrative Assistant to: Hon. Lester L. Wolff, 1972-1975; Hon. Thomas J. Downey, U.S. House of Representatives, 1975-1977. Author: "Politicians and Their Spouses' Careers," Congressional Management Foundation, 1986. Co-Author: "Answers to Common Legal Questions of Independent Film and Video Makers," Washington Area Lawyers for the Arts, 1991. *Member:* District of Columbia Bar; New York State Bar Association. ***PRACTICE AREAS:*** Government Ethics; Corporate; Entertainment Law. ***Email:*** mmiller@mwmlaw.com

RICHARD T. ROSSIER, born Detroit, Michigan, 1954; admitted to bar, 1980, District of Columbia; 1981, Virginia; 1986, U.S. Supreme Court; 1987, Maryland. *Education:* University of Michigan (B.A., cum laude, with high distinction, 1976); Georgetown University (J.D., cum laude, 1979). Phi Beta Kappa. Topics Editor, American Criminal Law Review, 1978-1979. Author: "Court May Close Rule 11 Loophole," Legal Times, Vol. XII, No. 4, March 12, 1990; "San Jose Law Not Likely to Pass High Court Test," Legal Times, Vol. X, No. 24, Nov. 24, 1987. Co-Author: Note, "Stepping Into the Breach: Basing

(This Listing Continued)

McLEOD, WATKINSON & MILLER, Washington—Continued

Defendants' Rights on State Rather Than Federal Law," 15 Am. Crim. L. Rev. 339, 1978. Law Clerk, Michigan Court of Appeals, 1979-1980. *Member:* District of Columbia Bar; Virginia State Bar; Maryland State and American (Member, Litigation Section) Bar Associations. ***REPORTED CASES:*** Auxier v. Kraisel, 466 A2d 416 (D.C. App. 1983); TVL Associates v. A & M Const. Corp., 474A.2d 156 (D.C. 1984); Vicki Bagley Realty, Inc. v. Laufer, 482 A.2d 359 (D.C. App. 1984); Kaszuk v. Bakery and Confectionery Union, 638 F. Supp. 548 (N.D. Ill. 1984) and 791 F.2d 548 (7th Cir. 1986); Temple v. D.C. Rental Housing Comm., 536 A.2d 1024 (D.C. App. 1987); Ohman v. Kahn, 685 F. Supp. 1302 (S.D.N.Y. 1988); Ohman v. Kahn, 1990, Fed. Sec. L. Rep. (CCH) ¶95,359 (S.D.N.Y. June 27, 1990); American Angus Assn. v. Sysco Corp., 829 F.Supp. 807 (W.D.N.C. 1992); American Angus Assn. v. Sysco Corp., 865 F.Supp. 1174 (W.D.N.C. 1993); American Angus Assn. v. Sysco Corp., 865 F.Supp. 1180 (W.D.N.C. 1993); American Angus Assn. v. Sysco Corp., 158 F.R.D. 372 (W.D.N.C. 1994); Management Information Technologies, Inc. v. Alyeska Pipeline Service Co., 51 F.R.D. 471 (D.D.C. 1993) and 51 F.R.D. 478 (D.D.C. 1993); Goetz v. Glickman, 920 F. Supp. 1173 (D.Kan, 1996); affd. Goetz v. Glickman, 149 F3d 1131 (10th Cir., 1998), cert. denied, 525 U.S. 1102 (1999); Peta v. Doughney, 113 F. Supp. 2nd 915 (S.E.D. Va, 2000), appeal pending. ***PRACTICE AREAS:*** Civil Litigation; Commercial Law; Real Estate Law. ***Email:*** rrossier@mwmlaw.com

CHARLES A. SPITULNIK, born Hornell, New York, December 1, 1951; admitted to bar, 1979, District of Columbia; 1981, Virginia; 1984, Maryland; 1989, U.S. Supreme Court. *Education:* Oberlin College (A.B., with high honors, 1973); Syracuse University (M.S.W., 1975); University of Virginia (J.D., 1979). Commuter Rail Editor: Association of Transportation Law, Logistics and Policy, "Highlights," "Use of Freight Rail Lines for Commuter Operations: Public Interest, Private Property," 26 Trans. L.J. 319, 1999; " Peaceful Co-existence Between Local Governments and Freight Rail Lines: An Impossible Dream?" 40 Municipal Lawyer 10, January/February, 1999. *Member:* The District of Columbia Bar; Virginia and American Bar Associations; Virginia State Bar; Maryland State Bar Association, Inc.; Association of Transportation Practitioners. ***PRACTICE AREAS:*** Transportation Law; Labor Law; Administrative Law; Corporate Law. ***Email:*** cspitulnik@mwmlaw.com

ASSOCIATES

RICHARD E. PASCO, born Nebraska City, Nebraska, February 4, 1955; admitted to bar, 1983, Colorado, Nebraska and U.S. District Court, Districts of Nebraska and Colorado; 1990, District of Columbia. *Education:* University of Washington (B.S., 1977); University of Nebraska (M.S., Agricultural Economics, 1981; J.D., 1982). Co-Author: "Blowing Smoke: Does Congress Lack the Willpower to Reform Federal Tobacco Policies?" Journal of Medicine and Law, Michigan State University, Detroit College of Law, Vol. 3, Issue 2, Spring, 1999. Legislative Assistant to Hon. Edward Zorinsky, U.S. Senate, 1985-1987. Member, Agricultural Technical Advisory Committee for Trade in Livestock and Livestock Products, 1992-1993. Member, National Advisory Council on Commodity Distribution, 1994-1995. *Member:* Nebraska State and Colorado Bar Associations; The District of Columbia Bar. ***PRACTICE AREAS:*** Legislative Practice; Food and Agriculture Law. ***Email:*** rpasco@mwmlaw.com

ALEX MENENDEZ, born Miami Beach, Florida, November 25, 1966; admitted to bar, 1992, Florida; 1995, Maryland; 1996, Virginia; 2000, District of Columbia. *Education:* Princeton University (B.A., 1989); George Washington University (J.D., 1992). *Member:* The Florida Bar; Virginia State Bar; The District of Columbia Bar. ***LANGUAGES:*** Spanish. ***PRACTICE AREAS:*** Commercial Litigation; Corporate Law; Employment Law; Medical Malpractice; Transportation Law. ***Email:*** amenendez@mwmlaw.com

PAUL D. SMOLINSKY, born Madison, New Jersey, July 10, 1967; admitted to bar, 1996, Maryland; 1998, Virginia and District of Columbia. *Education:* Carleton College (B.A., 1990); George Washington University (J.D., 1996). ***Email:*** psmolinsky@mwmlaw.com

LEGAL SUPPORT PERSONNEL

LAURA PHELPS, born Statesville, North Carolina, January 31, 1957. *Education:* University of North Carolina (B.A., 1979). (Government Relations Professional) *CONCENTRATION:* Specializes in Farm Program Policies and Agricultural Issues by Monitoring the Legislative Process and Administrative Actions. ***Email:*** lphelps@mwmlaw.com

STEPHEN FRERICHS, born Dubuque, Iowa, November 10, 1962. *Education:* St. Olaf College, Northfield, Minnesota (B.S., 1985); University of Minnesota (M.S., Agricultural Economics, 1987). ***Email:*** frerichs@mwmlaw.com

ROBERT RANDALL GREEN

MARTIN F. McMAHON & ASSOCIATES

Established in 1978
1150 CONNECTICUT AVENUE, N.W., SUITE 900
WASHINGTON, D.C. 20036
Telephone: 202-862-4343
Telecopier: 202-828-4130
Email: McMahonM@I-opener.net
URL: http://www.lawyers.com/martinmcmahonlaw

Business Law, Commercial Litigation, Complex Civil Trial Practice, Employment Litigation, Corporate Law, White Collar Criminal Defense, Commercial and Securities Fraud. The firm represents individuals and small to mid-size businesses throughout metro D.C., Northern Virginia and Southern Maryland.

MARTIN F. McMAHON, born New York, N.Y., October 1, 1945; admitted to bar, 1970, New York; 1973, District of Columbia. *Education:* City College of the City of New York (B.B.A., 1967); Fordham Law School (J.D., 1970). Senior Trial Attorney, Department of Transportation, 1970-1973. Senior Regulatory Attorney, Securities Investor Protection Corporation, 1975-1978. Formerly with: Proskauer, Rose, Goetz and Mendelsohn, 1973-1974. Speaker, "Punitive Damage Awards," D.C. Trial Lawyers Association, Luncheon, 1989. *Member:* The District of Columbia Bar; New York State Bar Association. ***REPORTED CASES:*** Sorrells v. Garfinkels, 656 A.2d 285 (D.C. App., 1989); Hercules Inc. v. Shama Restaurant and Corporation.

JOSEPH M. McMANUS

Established in 1987
2001 L STREET, N.W., SUITE 400
WASHINGTON, D.C. 20036
Telephone: 202-822-8888
Fax: 202-775-9330
Email: JMM@JMMCMANUS.COM

Tax Law.

JOSEPH M. McMANUS, born Jersey City, New Jersey, February 2, 1946; admitted to bar, 1971, New Jersey; 1976, District of Columbia; 1987, Maryland; 1989, Virginia. *Education:* St. Peter's College (B.S., 1968); Fordham University (J.D., 1971); George Washington University (LL.M. in Taxation, with highest honors, 1975). Associate Editor, Fordham Law Review, 1970-1971. (Also Of Counsel to Ross Marsh & Foster).

McMANUS, SCHOR, ASMAR & DARDEN, L.L.P.

Established in 1997
1301 CONNECTICUT AVENUE, N.W.
SIXTH FLOOR
WASHINGTON, D.C. 20036
Telephone: 202-296-9260
Fax: 202-659-3732
Email: info@msadlaw.com
URL: http://www.msadlaw.com

Construction, Government Contracts, Commercial, Real Estate, Business, Bankruptcy, Corporate and Administrative Law.

FIRM PROFILE: McManus, Schor, Asmar & Darden, L.L.P. provides legal services in the practice specialties of construction law, government contracts, commercial leasing, general business matters and commercial litigation. The firm's clients include many of the largest building contractors in the United States and leading national owners, engineers, architects and government contractors, subcontractors, suppliers and consultants.

Our counsel addresses the management of risk and the resolution of disputes. In our specialized practice areas, we assist in the drafting of effective contracts prior to the beginning of projects. Furthermore, we lend advice during the bidding process, advising and assisting clients in contract modifications, helping to analyze, evaluate and formulate or review claims for presentation or response and assisting in contract close-out. We negotiate, litigate or arbitrate all matters to conclusion and provide full hands-on support for these efforts.

The practice at McManus, Schor, Asmar & Darden, L.L.P. is both regional, to the Washington, D.C. metropolitan area, including both Maryland and Virginia, and national in scope. Approximately 50 percent of the matters handled by the firm involve clients located near the firm's offices in Washington, D.C. with concerns unique to this region. The remaining 50 percent involve clients located throughout

(This Listing Continued)

the United States and overseas. Firm members routinely handle matters before federal and state courts, regulatory agencies and administrative courts across the United States and in International locations.

JOSEPH A. McMANUS (1916-1995).

MEMBERS OF FIRM

JOSEPH A. McMANUS, JR., born New York, N.Y., January 18, 1948; admitted to bar, 1972, North Carolina; 1973, New York; 1974, U.S. Court of Federal Claims; 1977, Georgia; 1981, District of Columbia and U.S. District Court, Northern District of Georgia; 1984, U.S. Court of Appeals for the Federal Circuit; 1988, U.S. District Court, Middle District of North Carolina and U.S. Court of Appeals for the District of Columbia Circuit; 1992, U.S. Court of Appeals, Fourth Circuit; U.S. Court of Appeals, Eleventh Circuit. *Education:* College of the Holy Cross (B.A., 1969); Duke University (J.D., 1972). Author: "Alternate Clauses to Standard Construction Contracts," Chapters 10, 11, 12 and 15, Wiley Law Press, 1990 and 1998; Hospital Construction Projects, Construction Project Formbook, Wiley Press, 1994. Law Clerk, Armed Service Board of Contract Appeals, 1972-1976. General Counsel, Clark Construction, 1979-1984. Fellow, Duke University Private Adjudication Center, 1997—. Chairman, Task Force on Procurement Reform, District of Columbia Council, (1995-1996). Member, Panel of Arbitrators and Mediators, American Arbitration Association. *Member:* The District of Columbia Bar; New York State and American (Member: Public Contract Law Section; Litigation Section; Forum Committee on the Construction Industry, 1982—) Bar Associations; North Carolina State Bar; State Bar of Georgia. Fellow, American College of Construction Lawyers (President, 1996-1997). [Capt., JAGC, USAF, 1972-1976]. ***Email:*** jmcmanus@msadlaw.com

LAURENCE SCHOR, born Brooklyn, New York, May 3, 1942; admitted to bar, 1966, Texas; 1970, District of Columbia; 1993, Maryland. *Education:* Southern Methodist University (B.B.A., 1963); University of Texas (J.D., 1966); George Washington University (LL.M., 1972). Phi Alpha Delta. Lecturer, Construction and Government Contracts, George Washington University, Federal Publications Inc., Engineering News-Record, 1976—. Member, Advisory Board of Editors, The Construction Contractor. Author and Editor, 50 State Construction Lien and Bond Law, D.C. Chapter, 1993-2000 Updates; Editor Vol. 3, Forms, 2000; "The Right to Stop Work," Workplace Safety and Health in the 1990's; "Bid, Bid Errors, Relief from Bids" Chapter Rewrite, 2000. Commentator, MSNBC, 2000. *Member:* The District of Columbia Bar (Vice-Chairman, 1979-1981 and Chairman, 1981-1985, Government Contracts and Litigation Division); Federal and American (Member, Public Contract Law Section; Chair, Region III, 1983-1987; Chair, Construction Committee, 1987-1989; Vice-Chairman, Program Committee, 1987-1988; Budget and Finance Officer, 1990-1995) Bar Associations; American College of Construction Lawyers (Founder; Member, Board of Governors, 1989-1994; Treasurer, 1996-2000; President-elect, 2000-2001; Member, D.C. Council Task Force on Procurement Reform; Chair, Committee on Prevention of Waste, Fraud and Abuse). ***PRACTICE AREAS:*** Government Contracts; Construction Law. ***Email:*** lschor@msadlaw.com

CHARLES M. ASMAR, born Washington, D.C., October 3, 1963; admitted to bar, 1991, Maryland and U.S. District Court, District of Maryland; 1992, District of Columbia and U.S. District Court for the District of Columbia; 1993, U.S. Court of Appeals, 4th Circuit. *Education:* University of Vermont (B.S., 1985); Catholic University of America (J.D., 1991). *Member:* Maryland State and American Bar Associations; The District of Columbia Bar. ***PRACTICE AREAS:*** Construction Law; Commercial Law; Civil Litigation. ***Email:*** casmar@msadlaw.com

ERIC J. DARDEN, born Cheverly, Maryland, May 9, 1963; admitted to bar, 1989, Maryland and U.S. District Court, District of Maryland; 1991, U.S. Court of Appeals for the Federal Circuit; 1995, District of Columbia, U.S. District Court for the District of Columbia and U.S. Court of Appeals, Fourth Circuit. *Education:* University of Maryland (B.A., 1985); Duke University (J.D., 1988). Phi Kappa Phi. Arbitrator, State of Maryland Health Claims Arbitration Office, 1995—. *Member:* The District of Columbia Bar; Maryland State Bar Association. ***PRACTICE AREAS:*** Construction Law; Civil Litigation; Administrative Law. ***Email:*** edarden@msadlaw.com

SUSAN L. SCHOR, born Columbus, Ohio, July 12, 1943; admitted to bar, 1977, Maryland; 1978, District of Columbia; 1988, Virginia; U.S. Court of Federal Claims; U.S. District Court, District of Maryland; U.S. District Court, District of Columbia; U.S. District Court, Eastern District of Virginia; U.S. District Court, Western District of Virginia; U.S. Bankruptcy Court, Eastern District of Virginia; U.S. Bankruptcy Court, Western District of Virginia. *Education:* Tulane University of Louisiana (B.A., 1964); Catholic University of America (J.D., 1977). *Member:* The District of Columbia Bar; Maryland State and Virginia State Bar Associations. ***PRACTICE AREAS:*** Commercial Leasing and Litigation; Government Contracts; Civil Litigation. ***Email:*** sschor@msadlaw.com

(This Listing Continued)

DANIEL K. FELSEN, born Washington, D.C., November 2, 1966; admitted to bar, 1991, Virginia and U.S. Court of Appeals, Fourth Circuit; 1992 Maryland and U.S. District Court, District of Maryland; 1993, District of Columbia and U.S. District Court, Eastern District of Virginia; 1996, U.S. District Court for the District of Columbia; 2000, U.S. Court of Federal Claims. *Education:* University of Virginia (B.A., 1988; J.D., 1991). Co-Author: "Virginia General Conditions for Public Projects," Virginia Law Foundation, 1993; "Design/Build in Virginia: Drafting the Plan," Virginia Law Foundation, 1997; "Overview of Changes in the AIA General Conditions," Construction Risk Management, 1998; "Performance and Payment Bond Claims," 18th Annual Construction Insurance Conference, International Risk Management Institute, Inc., 1998. *Member:* Fairfax County (Virginia) Bar Association. ***PRACTICE AREAS:*** Construction Law; Fidelity and Surety. ***Email:*** dfelsen@msadlaw.com

JOHN J. McKENNA, JR., born Washington, D.C., October 4, 1963; admitted to bar, 1991, Maryland (Not admitted in District of Columbia). *Education:* St. Anselm College (B.A., 1986); Columbus School of Law of The Catholic University of America (J.D., 1991). Law Clerk, Hon. Thomas A. Flannery, U.S. District Court, District of Columbia, 1992-1994. ***PRACTICE AREAS:*** Construction Defects; Construction Claims; Insurance Coverage; Real Estate Title; Contracts. ***Email:*** jmckenna@msadlaw.com

ASSOCIATES

JEREMIAH S. REGAN, born Palo Alto, California, October 27, 1966; admitted to bar, 1996, Maryland; 1997, U.S. District Court, District of Maryland; 1998, U.S. District Court, District of Columbia; 1999, District of Columbia; 2000, U.S. Court of Federal Claims. *Education:* University of Maryland (B.A., 1990); Catholic University of America (J.D., 1994). Member, Moot Court Team. Jessup Cup, International Law Moot Court Competition. *Member:* Maryland State and American Bar Associations; The District of Columbia Bar. ***PRACTICE AREAS:*** Government Contracts; Construction Litigation. ***Email:*** jregan@msadlaw.com

GREGORY H. KOGER, born Washington, D.C., September 7, 1972; admitted to bar, 1999, Maryland (Not admitted in District of Columbia). *Education:* University of Maryland (B.S., 1995); Columbus School of Law of The Catholic University of America (J.D., 1999). Member, Thurgood Marshall Inn of Court, 1998-1999. Law Clerk to the Honorable Durke G. Thompson, Sixth Judicial Circuit of Maryland, 1999-2000. *Member:* Montgomery County and Maryland State Bar Associations; Montgomery County American Inn of Court. ***PRACTICE AREAS:*** Commercial Litigation; Construction Law; Government Contracts. ***Email:*** gkoger@msadlaw.com

JOHN T. BERGIN, born Washington, D.C., August 20, 1968; admitted to bar, 1993, Maryland; 1994, Virginia; 1995, District of Columbia. *Education:* Catholic University of America (B.A., 1990); American University (J.D., 1993). *Member:* Virginia State Bar; The District of Columbia Bar. ***PRACTICE AREAS:*** Construction Law. ***Email:*** jbergin@msadlaw.com

WILLIAM F. GIBSON, II, born Warwick, Rhode Island, April 6, 1968; admitted to bar, 1997, New York; 1998, District of Columbia; 2000, Virginia, U.S. District Court for the Eastern District of Virginia and U.S. Court of Appeals, Fourth Circuit; 2000, U.S. District Court, District of Columbia. *Education:* University of Virginia (B.A., 1990); Hofstra University (J.D., 1996). Formerly with Citak and Citak; Long Aldridge and Norman, LLP. ***PRACTICE AREAS:*** Construction Law; Litigation. ***Email:*** wgibson@msadlaw.com

OF COUNSEL

RICHARD W. SCHWARTZMAN, born Boca Raton, Florida, 1945; admitted to bar, 1969, Massachusetts; 1970, U.S. District Court, District of Massachusetts and U.S. Court of Appeals, First Circuit; 1973, U.S. Court of Federal Claims and U.S. Court of Appeals for the Federal Circuit; 1987, District of Columbia, U.S. District Court for the District of Columbia and U.S. Court of Appeals for the District of Columbia Circuit; 1992, U.S District Court, District of Maryland. *Education:* Pennsylvania Military College (B.A., 1966); New England School of Law (J.D., 1969). Staff Editor, New England Law Review, 1967-1968, 1968-1969. Adjunct Lecturer: Construction Contracts, Engineer Liability, George Washington University National Law Center; Trial Advocacy, Harvard Law School, MCLE, 1978. Contracting Officer, U.S. Department of the Army. Member, National Panel of Arbitrators, American Arbitration Association. *Member:* Massachusetts and American (Member, Sections on: Tort and Insurance Practice; Public Contracts; Litigation; Member, Fidelity and Surety Law Committee, 1977—; Chair, Bonding and Insurance Committee, 1996-1999; Vice Chair, Construction Division, 1999—; Member, Forum Committee on Construction Industry) Bar Associations; The District of Columbia Bar. [Capt., U.S. Army, Quartermaster Corps, JAG, 1966-1973]. ***PRACTICE AREAS:*** Construction Law; Government Contracts; Surety Law; Litigation. ***Email:*** rschwartzman@msadlaw.com

BRETT L. ANTONIDES, born Platteville, Wisconsin, November 22, 1954; admitted to bar, 1980, Pennsylvania and New Jersey; 1985, District of Columbia; 1990, Virginia. *Education:* Princeton University (B.S., Civil Engineering, cum laude, 1977); Villanova University (J.D., 1980); Georgetown University

(This Listing Continued)

McMANUS, SCHOR, ASMAR & DARDEN, L.L.P., Washington—Continued

(LL.M. Taxation, 1984). Member and Editor, Villanova Law Review, 1978-1980. *Member:* Fairfax and American (Member: Business Law Section; Committee on Business and Corporate Litigation; Committee on the Law of Commerce in Cyberspace; Small Business Committee) Bar Associations; The District of Columbia Bar (Member, Computer and Telecommunications Law Section); Virginia State Bar (Member, Sections on: Business Law; Litigation; Member, Committee on Resolution of Fee Disputes). [Capt., JAGC, U.S. Army, 1981-1984]. ***PRACTICE AREAS:*** Business Planning; Commercial Litigation; Government Contracts; Intellectual Property Law; Technology Licensing. ***Email:*** bantonides@msadlaw.com

REPRESENTATIVE CLIENTS: A.E. Mitchell Co., Inc.; A.S. Johnson Company; Associated Specialty Contractors of America; Bahamas Marine Construction Co., Ltd.; Beacon Dioguardi; Boulder Corporation; Brian Cohn, Inc.; Burns and Roe Services Corporation; Cabinet Refacers, Inc.; CareMatrix Corporation; Carilion Health System; CarrAmerica Development and Construction, Inc.; CarrAmerica Realty Corporation; Casetech, Inc.; Cavalier Construction Company, Bahamas; Cellular Telephone Partners Group; Coastal Power Production Company; CPI International; Edmar Construction Co., Inc.; Enserch Corporation; Faison; Glen Construction Company, Inc.; Gould Property Co.; Guardian Realty Management, Inc.; Heidenberger Construction, Inc.; Hess Mechanical Corporation; Hitt Contracting, Inc.; Home Plazza Hotels; Host Marriott Corporation; ING Real Estate; International Monetary Fund; The John Akridge Company; Joseph M. Zimmer, Inc.; Kvaerner Construction, Inc.; K C Company, Inc.; London & Leeds Development Corp.; Manhattan Construction Company; McCarthy; McDonald-Bradley, Inc.; Mona Electric Service, Inc.; Morse Diesel International; Net Zone, Inc.; Oceaneering International; OHM Corporation; Pacific Construction Co., Ltd.; PEC, Inc.; Portland Natural Gas Transmission System; The Port Authority of New York and New Jersey; Ragnar Benson, Inc.; Research Planning, Inc.; Ruppert Landscaping; Satellite Services, Inc.; San Jose Construction; Steele Foundations, Inc.; Superior Foundation, Inc.; Tishman Speyer Properties; Trafalgar House Construction; Trans Island Pavers Co. Ltd.; Wash Net Investors, L.P.; Willco Construction Co., Inc.

McNAMEE, HOSEA, JERNIGAN & KIM, P.A.

WASHINGTON, D.C.

(See Greenbelt, Maryland)

Corporations, Wills, Trusts, Estates, Real Estate and Civil Litigation in all Courts. Business, Banking, Franchise and Trademark Law, Taxation, and Labor and Employment Law.

McNARY, MORRIS & SMALLEY

1712 NEW HAMPSHIRE AVENUE N.W.
WASHINGTON, D.C. 20009
Telephone: 202-265-7200
Fax: 202-265-7530
URL: http://www.visalink.com
Email: MMS@visalink.com
URL: http://www.lawyers.com/mcnarymorris&smalley

Immigration, Nationality Law, Consular Law, Administrative Law, Business Immigration, Information Technology, Computer Technology.

FIRM PROFILE: McNary, Morris & Smalley is a boutique immigration firm concentrating exclusively on the representation of U.S. business and foreign investors, scientists, researchers, athletes and professionals, and on the representation of high-technology clients.

MEMBERS OF FIRM

GENE McNARY, born Muncie, Indiana, September 14, 1935; admitted to bar, 1960, Indiana; 1961 Missouri; 1994, District of Columbia; U.S. District Court, Eastern District of Missouri; U.S. Court of Appeals, Eighth Circuit; U.S. Supreme Court. *Education:* Indiana University (B.S., 1957; J.D., 1960). Assistant Public Defender, 1963-1965, Prosecuting Attorney, 1967-1974 and County Executive, 1974-1989, St. Louis County. Commissioner, Immigration and Naturalization Service, 1989-1993. *Member:* The Missouri Bar; District of Columbia Bar; Missouri Association of Prosecuting Attorneys (President, 1971); American Immigration Lawyer's Association. ***PRACTICE AREAS:*** Immigration Law. ***Email:*** gmcnary@ix.netcom.com

DAVID M. MORRIS, born Suffern, New York, August 21, 1967; admitted to bar, 1992, Massachusetts; 1993, Maryland (Not admitted in District of Columbia). *Education:* State University of New York at Buffalo (B.A., 1989); University of Dayton (J.D., 1992). Judicial Law Clerk, Dayton Municipal Courts, 1990-1991, 1991-1992. Author: "IRCA: Pitfalls and Traps in Existing Hiring Practices," The Labor Lawyer, Fall, 1994. *Member:* American Bar Association. ***PRACTICE AREAS:*** Immigration Law; Litigation. ***Email:*** morris@visalink.com

(This Listing Continued)

ASSOCIATE

NICOLE HUGHES, born Norwood, Massachusetts, May 23, 1973; admitted to bar, 1998, Maryland (Not admitted in District of Columbia). *Education:* Villanova University (B.A., 1995); Columbus School of Law of the Catholic University of America (J.D., 1998). Moot Court Associate. Finalist, Moot Court Spring Trials Competition. Law Clerk, New York Supreme Court, White Plains, New York. Member, Maryland Volunteer Legal Service. *Member:* Montgomery County, Maryland State and American Bar Associations. ***PRACTICE AREAS:*** Immigration Law; Litigation. ***Email:*** hughes@visalink.com

OF COUNSEL

CHARLES W. PLEY, born January 3, 1959; admitted to bar, 1985, Ontario; 1992, New York (Not admitted in District of Columbia). *Education:* Osgoode Hall Law School (LL.B., 1983). Second Secretary, (Immigration), Canadian High Commission, Singapore, 1986-1988. Second Secretary (Immigration) and Vice Consul-Canadian Embassy Bonn Germany, 1988-1991. Litigation Advisor Department of External Affairs, Immigration and Consular Affairs Branch, Ottawa, 1991. *Member:* Canadian Bar Association (Member, Citizenship and Immigration Section); American Immigration Lawyers Association; Organization of Professional Immigration Consultants (President). (Also practicing individually, Missauga, Canada). ***LANGUAGES:*** French, German, Mandarin and Cantonese. ***PRACTICE AREAS:*** Business Immigration; International Immigration; Related Matters.

FREDERICK R. TRONCONE, born Erie, Pennsylvania, March 24, 1957; admitted to bar, 1982, Pennsylvania and U.S. District Court, Western District of Pennsylvania; 1985, District of Columbia; 1986, U.S. Court of Appeals for the Federal Circuit; 1988, Hawaii and U.S. District Court, District of Hawaii; 1990, U.S. Court of Appeals, District of Columbia Circuit. *Education:* Pennsylvania State University (B.A., 1979); University of Toledo (J.D., 1982). Student Articles Editor, University of Toledo Law Review. Speaker, Business Investments and Immigration Programs, Honolulu, Hawaii and Japan. Attorney Consultant, American Life and Business Services, Tokyo, Japan. Former Attorney Advisor to the General Counsel of the National Labor Relations Board in Washington, D.C. *Member:* Erie County, Pennsylvania and Hawaii State Bar Associations; District of Columbia Bar; American Immigration Lawyers Association (Former Chair, Hawaii Chapter). (Also, Practicing individually, Washington, D.C.). ***PRACTICE AREAS:*** Immigration Law; Labor and Employment. ***Email:*** ftroncone@visalink.com

McNEES WALLACE & NURICK LLC

1200 G STREET, N.W., SUITE 800
WASHINGTON, D.C. 20005
Telephone: 202-434-8991
Fax: 202-347-0988
Email: info@mwn.com
URL: http://www.mwn.com

Harrisburg, Pennsylvania Office: 100 Pine Street, P.O. Box 1166, 17108. Telephone: 717-232-8000. Fax: 717-237-5300.
Columbus, Ohio Office: 21 East State Street, 17th Floor, 43215. Telephone: 614-469-8000. Fax: 614-469-4653.
Hazleton, Pennsylvania Office: 1 South Church Street, Suite 302, 18201. Telephone: 570-455-8300. Fax: 570-455-8390.

General Civil Practice. Administrative, Antitrust, Bankruptcy, Corporate, Banking and Finance, ERISA, Tax, Probate, Labor and Employment, Litigation, Real Estate, Securities, Municipal Bonds, Public Utilities, Intellectual Property, Health Care, Environmental, Automotive, Transportation, Trademark, Copyright, Computer, Franchise and Unfair Competition Law.

FIRM PROFILE: McNees Wallace & Nurick, established in 1935, is a firm of over 85 attorneys headquartered in Harrisburg, Pennsylvania. While based in the capital city, our practice represents clients which operate locally, regionally and nationally. With additional offices in Columbus, Ohio, Hazelton, PA and Washington, DC, the practice includes all areas of commercial practice and civil litigation. Our attorneys represent businesses, banks, insurance companies, trade associations, hospitals, public and private non-profit institutions and individuals.

RESIDENT ASSOCIATE

ROBERT A. WEISHAAR, JR., born 1969; admitted to bar, 1995, Pennsylvania; 1996, U.S. Court of Appeals for the District of Columbia Circuit (Practice limited to matters and proceedings before federal courts and agencies) (Not admitted in District of Columbia). *Education:* American University (B.A., magna cum laude, 1991); Georgetown University Law Center (J.D., 1994). Attorney-Advisor, Office of Administrative Law Judges, Federal Energy Regulatory Commission, 1994-1996. *Member:* Pennsylvania (Public Utility Law Section), Federal Energy and American Bar Associations. ***PRACTICE***

(This Listing Continued)

AREAS: Utility Law; Energy Law; Regulatory Law. ***Email:*** rweishaar@mwn.com

DALE E. MCNIEL

1776 EYE STREET, N.W.
NINTH FLOOR
WASHINGTON, D.C. 20006
Telephone: 202-756-1368
Fax: 202-756-1501
Email: dalemcniel@aol.com
URL: http://www.lawyers.com/dalemcniel

Agriculture Law, International Law, International Trade Law, International Agriculture Law.

DALE E. McNIEL, born Duluth, Minnesota, December 4, 1948; admitted to bar, 1976, Illinois; 1977, U.S District Court, Northern District of Illinois; 1998, District of Columbia. *Education:* University of Iowa (B.A., with high distinction and special honors, 1971); University of Chicago (J.D., 1976). Phi Beta Kappa. Recipient: Distinguished Service Award, U.S. Department of Agriculture, 1991; Unit Award for Superior Service, U.S. Department of Agriculture, 1993; Certificate of Merit, International Trade Policy, 1996. Senior Counsel, Office of the General Counsel, U.S. Department of Agriculture, Washington, 1984-1997. *Member:* Illinois State Bar Association; District of Columbia Bar. ***PRACTICE AREAS:*** International Trade; Administrative Law; Agriculture.

MCQUADE & HITE, P.L.L.C.

WASHINGTON, D.C.

(See Alexandria, Virginia)

Family Law including Divorce, Custody, Child Support, Property Division, Prenuptial and Separation Agreements, Adoptions, Negotiations and Litigation, as well as Mediation.

MARY A. MCREYNOLDS, P.C.

Established in 1992

SUITE 300, 1701 PENNSYLVANIA AVENUE, N.W.
WASHINGTON, D.C. 20006
Telephone: 202-835-7455
Telecopier: 202-296-8791
Email: marymcreynolds@aol.com
URL: http://www.lawyers.com/maryamcreynolds

The Firm specializes in complex Commercial and Government Civil Litigation, Civil Appellate Practice and Communications Law (including Broadcast and Common Carrier Regulation).

FIRM PROFILE: The firm routinely handles highly complex multi-jurisdictional litigation, including oversight of local counsel and of substantive and procedural matters. The firm is listed in the Martindale-Hubbell Bar Register of Preeminent Lawyers.

MARY A. McREYNOLDS, born Carthage, Missouri, September 2, 1946; admitted to bar, 1971, District of Columbia and U.S. Court of Appeals for the District of Columbia Circuit; 1975, U.S. Court of Appeals, 2nd Circuit; 1979, U.S. Court of Appeals, 4th Circuit; 1980, U.S. Supreme Court and U.S. Court of Appeals, 1st, 5th, 6th, 9th and 10th Circuits; 1981, U.S. Court of Appeals, 11th Circuit; 1983, U.S. Court of Appeals, 3rd, 7th and 8th Circuits; 1987, U.S. Court of Federal Claims; 1988, U.S. Court of Appeals, Federal Circuit. *Education:* Mt. Holyoke College (B.A., 1968); Georgetown University (J.D., 1971); Harvard University (LL.M., 1973). Judicial Clerkship with Hon. Charles Fahy, U.S. Court of Appeals for the District of Columbia Circuit, 1971-1972. Senior Trial Attorney, Federal Programs Branch, 1977-1979 and Appellate Staff, 1979-1981, U.S. Department of Justice, Civil Division. Member, American Society of Legal History, 1973—. *Member:* The District of Columbia Bar; Bar Association of the District of Columbia; American Bar Association (Member, Litigation Section); Federal Communications Bar Association. ***LANGUAGES:*** Spanish. ***PRACTICE AREAS:*** Communications Law; Complex Civil Litigation.

RICHARD J. MEDALIE

1750 K STREET, N.W., SUITE 1200
WASHINGTON, D.C. 20006-2303
Telephone: 202-659-0880
Telefax: 202-659-5618
Email: rmedalie@worldnet.att.net

Corporate, Commercial and Complex Litigation, Commercial Arbitration and Mediation, Domestic and International Estate Plannings, Wills and Trusts, Charitable Trusts and Foundations, Family Wealth Transfer.

(This Listing Continued)

RICHARD J. MEDALIE, born Duluth, Minnesota, July 21, 1929; admitted to bar, 1958, District of Columbia; 1962, New York. *Education:* University of Minnesota (B.A., 1952); University of London, London, England and Harvard University (A.M., 1955); Harvard University (J.D., 1958). Phi Beta Kappa; Phi Alpha Theta. Member, 1956-1958, Case Editor, 1957-1958, Harvard Law Review. Law Clerk to Honorable G.T. Washington, U.S. Court of Appeals for the District of Columbia Circuit, 1958-1959. Editor and Co-author, "Commercial Arbitration for the 1990's," ABA Press 1991. Author: "Preparing For a Non-administered Arbitration," ABA Section of Litigation, Critical Issues In Arbitration, Tab 5, 1993; "The Libyan Producers' Agreement Arbitration: Developing Innovative Procedures in a Complex Multiparty Arbitration," Journal of International Arbitration, June, 1990, at 7; "The New Appeals Amendment: A Step Forward for Arbitration," AAA Arbitration Journal, June, 1989, at 22. Co-author: "Suits Against State Insurance Commissioners for Misconduct in the Regulation and Liquidation of Insurance Companies," in ABA Nat'l Inst. on Insurer Insolvency, Law and Practice of Insurance Company Insolvency 295, 1986. Member, Friedman and Medalie (and predecessors), 1968-1998. Deputy Director, Institute of Criminal Law and Procedure, 1965-1968, Adjunct Professor of Administrative and Criminal Law, 1966-1969, Georgetown University Law Center. Assistant to the Solicitor General of the United States, 1960-1962. Commissioner, 1975-1987, Member, Executive Committee, 1977-1982 and Chairman, Criminal Law Task Force, 1978-1981, District of Columbia Law Revision Commission. Vice Chairman, 1981-1984, Major Gifts Chairman, 1984-1986, Deputy Chairman, 1986-1987, and Chairman, 1987-1989, Harvard Law School Fund. Member, National Panel of Commercial Arbitrators, American Arbitration Association. *Member:* The Association of the Bar of the City of New York (Secretary, Foreign Law Committee, 1962-1965); The District of Columbia Bar; American (Vice-Chair, Arbitration Committee, Litigation Section, 1991-1994) Bar Associations; American Law Institute. Fellow, American Bar Foundation. (Also Of Counsel, Brock Partners LLC, New York, N.Y.).

MEHRI, MALKIN & ROSS, PLLC

2120 L STREET, NW, SUITE 400
WASHINGTON, D.C. 20037
Telephone: 202-822-5100
Fax: 202-822-4997
Email: mmr@findjustice.com
URL: http://www.lawyers.com/mm&rlaw

Complex and Multi-District Litigation, Class Actions, Commercial Fraud, Employment Discrimination, Consumer Fraud, Antitrust, Securities Fraud, Qui Tam Litigation, Consumer Protection, Civil Rights, Employee Stock Ownership.

FIRM PROFILE: Bringing together decades of front-line experience in litigation, legislation and issue advocacy, the founders of Mehri, Malkin & Ross, PLLC, build upon strong working relationships with public interest, consumer, labor, whistle-blower and civil rights organizations. Invoking private attorney general powers under federal and state law, the firm provides legal representation for employees, consumers, investors, and small businesses in complex litigation.

CYRUS MEHRI, born New York, N.Y., July 14, 1961; admitted to bar, 1988, Connecticut; 1989, District of Columbia; 1990, U.S. Court of Appeals for the District of Columbia. *Education:* Hartwick College (B.A., 1983); Cornell University (J.D., 1988). Pi Sigma Alpha. Associate Editor, 1986-1987 and Article Editor, 1987-1988, Cornell International Law Journal. Semi-Finalist First Year Moot Court Competition. Quarter-Finalist Cuccia Cup Moot Court Competition. Recipient: Finalist, Trial Lawyer of the Year, Trial Lawyers for Public Justice, 1997; Most Outstanding Young Alumnus Award, Hartwick College, 1998. Judicial Law Clerk to the Honorable John T. Nixon, U.S. District Judge for the Middle District of Tennessee, 1988-1989. Author: "Negotiating Cultural Change," The Recorder, 1997. *Member:* The District of Columbia Bar; Connecticut Bar Association. ***PRACTICE AREAS:*** Employment Discrimination; False Claims Act; Consumer Fraud; Securities Fraud; Employee Stock Ownership Plans; Commercial Business Fraud. ***Email:*** cmehri@findjustice.com

ARTHUR N. MALKIN, born Brooklyn, New York, May 30, 1954; admitted to bar, 1979, New York; 1999, District of Columbia. *Education:* State University of New York at Albany (B.A., 1975); Northeastern University (J.D., 1978). Partner, Malkin & Ross (lobbying firm), 1984—. Principal, M&R Strategic Services (government affairs firm), 1991—. Founder, Non-Profit Resource Center, Inc., 1984. Legislative Director, New York Public Interest Research Group, 1978-1984. ***PRACTICE AREAS:*** Lobbying; Governmental Relations. ***Email:*** amalkin@findjustice.com

DONALD K. ROSS, born Bronx, New York, June 30, 1947; admitted to bar, 1970, District of Columbia; 1975, New York and U.S. Court of Appeals for the District of Columbia Circuit. *Education:* Fordham University (B.A., 1965); New York University (J.D., 1970). Partner, Malkin & Ross (lobbying firm), 1984—. Principal, M&R Strategic Services (government affairs firm), 1991—. Chief Executive Officer, Rockefeller Family Fund, 1985-1998. Founder, New

(This Listing Continued)

MEHRI, MALKIN & ROSS, PLLC, Washington—Continued

York Public Interest Research Group, 1973. Member, U.S. Peace Corps, 1965-1967. ***PRACTICE AREAS:*** Lobbying; Governmental Relations. ***Email:*** dross@findjustice.com

---

PAMELA COUKOS, born Indianapolis, Indiana, February 21, 1968; admitted to bar, 1995, New York and U.S. District Court, Eastern and Southern Districts of New York; Massachusetts; 1997, District of Columbia. *Education:* Brown University (A.B., magna cum laude and honors, Political Science, 1990); Harvard Law School (J.D., cum laude, 1994). Phi Beta Kappa. Symposium Editor, Harvard Civil Rights Civil Liberties Law Review. Law Clerk to the Hon. Edward R. Korman, U.S. District Judge, Eastern District of New York. Teaching Associate, Brown University Department of Political Science, 1993-1994. Co-Author, with Julie Goldscheld, "Violence Against Women Act," Merrick T. Rossein, Employment Discrimination Law and Litigation, Ch. 35 Clark-Boardman, 1997. Author, "Deconstructing the Debate over Gender and Hate Crimes Legislation," Georgetown Journal of Gender and the Law II, Inaugural Issue 1999. *Member:* District of Columbia Bar; National Employment Lawyers Association. ***PRACTICE AREAS:*** Employment Discrimination; Civil Rights. ***Email:*** pcoukos@findjustice.com

MICHAEL I. KANOVITZ, born Louisville, Kentucky, October 26, 1968; admitted to bar, 1994, Kentucky and U.S. District Court, Western and Eastern Districts of Kentucky; 1996 U.S. Court of Appeals, Sixth Circuit (Not admitted in District of Columbia). *Education:* Brandeis University (B.A., with honors, cum laude, 1990); Cornell University (J.D., cum laude, 1994). Editor, Cornell Journal of International Law, 1993-1994. Co-Author, "Constitutional Law," 8th Ed. 1998. *Member:* Kentucky, Federal and American Bar Associations; Kentucky Academy of Trial Attorneys; The Association of Trial Lawyers of America. ***PRACTICE AREAS:*** False Claims Act; Commercial Litigation; Consumer Fraud; Securities Act. ***Email:*** mkanovitz@findjustice.com

GOURI BHAT, born East Lansing, Michigan, August 3, 1966; admitted to bar, 1997, Wisconsin and U.S. District Court, Eastern District of Wisconsin; 1998, Illinois; 2000, District of Columbia. *Education:* University of Texas (B.A. English, 1988); University of Wisconsin - Madison (J.D., 1997). Member, Wisconsin Law Review. Law Clerk to the Hon. Lynn Adelman, U.S. District Judge, Eastern District of Wisconsin, 1997-1999. ***PRACTICE AREAS:*** Employment Discrimination; Civil Rights; False Claims Act; Consumer Fraud; Commercial Litigation. ***Email:*** gbhat@findjustice.com

OF COUNSEL

BRADLEY SCOTT WEISS, born Hammond, Indiana, May 28, 1954; admitted to bar, 1988, Illinois; 1991, District of Columbia. *Education:* Loyola University of Chicago (B.A., 1976); Chicago-Kent College of Law (J.D., 1987). Contributing Author: "Qui Tam Litigation Under The False Claims Act," American Bar Association, Section of Public Contract Law (Aug. 1994); "Report on the Law Division," Special Commission (Aug. 1987); Co-Author: "Construction Fraud," Airport Magazine, (Jul./Aug. 1993); The Department of Defense Voluntary Disclosure Program - A Description of The Process," Department of Defense, Office of the Inspector General (Sep. 1987); "Funding Judicial Campaigns in Cook County Circuit Court," 70 JUDICATURE (Jun./Jul. 1986); "Funding Judicial Campaigns in the Circuit Court, JUDICATURE (Feb. 1987). Special Assistant to Assistant Inspector General, Criminal Policy and Oversight, Department of Defense, Office of the Inspector General, 1987-1989. *Member:* District of Columbia Bar; American Bar Association (Member, Section on Public Contract Law; Vice Chair, Procurement Fraud Committee). ***PRACTICE AREAS:*** Qui Tam Litigation; Whistleblower Litigation; Wrongful Termination; Government Contract Fraud; Health Care Fraud. ***Email:*** weiss@bsw-law.com

---

MENARD, MURPHY & WALSH LLP

FARRAGUT PARK
910 17TH STREET, NW,
SUITE 800
WASHINGTON, D.C. 20006
Telephone: 202-293-3500
Telecopier: 202-293-3596
Email: mmw@mmwlaw.com
URL: http://mmwlaw.com

Boston, Massachusetts Office: 60 State Street, 34th Floor, 02109. Telephone: 617-832-2500. Telecopier: 617-832-2550.

Civil Litigation, Management Labor, Employment Law, Corporate Intellectual Property, Finance and Real Estate, Construction and Environmental Law, Eminent Domain, Tax Abatement, Discrimination, Wrongful Discharge, Wage-Hour, Higher Education Law, Domestic Relations.

(For complete biographical data on all personnel see Professional Biographies at Boston, Massachusetts)

LAWRENCE G. MEYER

1735 NEW YORK AVENUE, SUITE 700
WASHINGTON, D.C. 20006-5209
Telephone: 202-661-3910
Fax: 202-331-1024
Email: larry@lawlgm.com

Antitrust Law, Trade Regulations Law, Unfair Competition Law, Food, Drug and Cosmetic Law, Litigation.

LAWRENCE G. MEYER, born East Grand Rapids, Michigan, October 2, 1940; admitted to bar, 1965, Wisconsin and Illinois; 1968, U.S. Supreme Court; 1972, District of Columbia. *Education:* Michigan State University (B.A., with honors, 1961); University of Michigan (J.D., with distinction, 1964). Assistant Editor, *Michigan Law Review*, 1963-1964. Lecturer, University of Michigan Continuing Legal Education Program, 1971-1972. Trial Attorney, Appellate, Evaluation and Special Litigation Sections, Antitrust Division, Department of Justice, 1966-1968. Legal and Legislative Counsel to Senator Robert P. Griffin of Michigan, U.S. Senate, 1968-1970. Director of Policy Planning and Evaluation, Federal Trade Commission, 1970-1972. *Member:* American Bar Association (Chairman, Subcommittee on Competition, Federal Trade Commission Committee, Antitrust Section, 1974-1978). ***PRACTICE AREAS:*** Antitrust Law; Trade Regulations Law; Unfair Competition Law; Food, Drug and Cosmetic Law; Litigation.

MEYER & KLIPPER, PLLC

Established in 1996

923 FIFTEENTH STREET, N.W., 5TH FLOOR
WASHINGTON, D.C. 20005
Telephone: 202-637-0850
Fax: 202-637-0851
Email: meyerklipper@mindspring.com
URL: http://www.lawyers.com/meyer&klipperlaw

Domestic and International Copyright Issues, Trademark Law, Constitutional and Legislative Law Practice.

CHRISTOPHER A. MEYER (1946-1999).

MICHAEL RUSSELL KLIPPER, born New York, N.Y., February 25, 1948; admitted to bar, 1973, District of Columbia and Massachusetts; 1979, U.S. Supreme Court; 1982, U.S. District Court for the District of Columbia; 1983, New York and U.S. Court of Appeals for the District of Columbia Circuit; 1984, U.S. Court of Appeals, Eleventh Circuit. *Education:* Syracuse University (B.A., cum laude, 1969); George Washington University (J.D., with honors, 1972); Harvard University (LL.M., 1973). Counsel, U.S. Senate Judiciary Committee, 1975-1980. Chief Counsel, U.S. Senate Judiciary Subcommittee on Criminal Law, 1981-1982. *Member:* The District of Columbia Bar; American Bar Association; Copyright Society of the U.S.A. ***Email:*** klipper@erols.com

CHRISTOPHER A. MOHR, born New York, NY, September 16, 1969; admitted to bar, 1996, New York; 1999, District of Columbia. *Education:* Haverford College (B.A., 1991); Catholic University of America (J.D., 1996). Comment Editor, Catholic University Law Review, 1995-1996. Moot Court Associate, 1994-1996. Author, "Gray Market Goods and Copyright Law: An End Run Around, K Mart v. Cartier", 45 Catholic University Law Review 561 (1996). *Member:* The District of Columbia Bar; American Bar Association (Member, Section on Intellectual Property Law, 1997—). ***PRACTICE AREAS:*** Copyrights; Electronic Commerce; Trademarks; Unfair Competition. ***Email:*** chrismohr@sprintmail.com

OF COUNSEL

ROBERT A. GORMAN, born New York, N.Y., April 22, 1937; admitted to bar, 1962, New York (Not admitted in District of Columbia). *Education:* Harvard University (B.A., summa cum laude, 1958; LL.B., magna cum laude, 1962). Recipient: Fulbright Scholarship, University College Oxford, 1958-1959. Member, American Law Institute; Copyright Society of the U.S.A. Law Clerk: Hon. Irving R. Kaufman, U.S. Court of Appeals for Second Circuit, 1962-1963. Author, "Copyright: Cases & Materials" (3d cd. 1999); "Labor Law: Cases & Materials" (12th ed. 1996); "Copyright "(Federal Judicial Center)," 1991; "Basic Text on Labor Law: Unionization and Collective Bargaining", 1976. Professor, 1965—, Associate Dean, 1976-1982, 1992-1994, University of Pennsylvania Law School. President, American Association of University Professors, 1981-1982, Association of American Law School, 1991. Member, 1980—, President, 1998—, World Bank Administrative Tribunal. Member, 1995—, Vice-President, 1997—, Asian Development Bank Administrative Tribunal. Associate, 1962-1963 and Consultant, 1987-1993, Proskauer Rose Goetz & Mendelsohn, New York City. ***Email:*** rgorman@law.upcnn.edu

(This Listing Continued)

LEGAL SUPPORT PERSONNEL

REBECCA JOHNSON (Office Manager).

MEYER, SUOZZI, ENGLISH & KLEIN, P.C.

SUITE 600, 1300 CONNECTICUT AVENUE, N.W.
WASHINGTON, D.C. 20036
Telephone: 202-955-6340
Telecopier: 202-223-0358
Email: meyersuozzi@msek.com

Mineola, New York Office: 1505 Kellum Place, 11501. Telephone: 516-741-6565; 212-227-5511. Cable Address: Islandlaw New York. Telecopier: 516-741-6706. Email: meyersuozzi@msek.com.
Albany, New York Office: One Commerce Plaza, 12260. Telephone: 518-465-5551. Telecopier: 518-465-2033. Email: meyersuozzi@msek.com.
New York, N.Y. Office: 1350 Broadway, Suite 501, 10018. Telephone: 212-239-4999. Telecopier: 212-239-1311. Email: meyersuozzi@msek.com.

General Practice before all State and Federal Courts. Appellate and Trial Practice, Antitrust, Banking, Commercial, Corporate, Criminal, Elder Law, Election Law, Governmental Relations, Labor and Employment, Land Use and Environment, Legal, Medical and Professional Liability, Lobbying, Medical and Health Care, Municipal and Public Finance, Personal Injury, Probate, Real Estate, Tax Certiorari, Condemnation and Zoning Law, and Trusts, Estates and Estate Planning.

HAROLD ICKES, born Baltimore, Maryland, September 4, 1939; admitted to bar, 1973, New York; 1978, U.S. District Court, Southern and Eastern Districts of New York (Not admitted in District of Columbia). *Education:* University of Arizona; Stanford University (B.A., 1964); Columbia University School of Law (J.D., 1971). Author: "An Alternative Proposal for the State Debt Provisions of the New York State Constitution," Essays of the New York Constitution, Weinstein, J.B., (ed) 1966. Assistant to the President and Deputy Chief of Staff for Political Affairs and Policy to President Clinton, 1994-1997. White House Coordinator of the Presidential Inaugural, 1997. Director of Summit Affairs for the 1997 Denver Summit of the Eight, 1997. Deputy Director of the Clinton - Gore Presidential Transition Team, 1992-1993. Deputy Chair of the Democratic National Committee, 1992. Director for the Clinton Presidential Campaign of the 1992 Democratic National Convention, 1992. Partner: The Iches an Enright Group, 1997—. *Member:* The Association of the Bar of the City of New York; New York State and American Bar Associations. ***PRACTICE AREAS:*** Government Relations; Employment and Labor Law; Election Law; FEC Law. ***Email:*** hickes@msek.com

(For biographical data on all personnel, see Professional Biographies at Mineola, New York)

MIDLEN LAW CENTER

WASHINGTON, D.C.

(See Chevy Chase, Maryland)

Communications, Trademark, Copyright and Administrative.

MILBANK, TWEED, HADLEY & McCLOY LLP

INTERNATIONAL SQUARE BUILDING
SUITE 1100, 1825 EYE STREET, N.W.
WASHINGTON, D.C. 20006
Telephone: 202-835-7500
Fax: 202-835-7586
Email: postmaster@milbank.com
URL: http://www.milbank.com

New York, New York Offices: 1 Chase Manhattan Plaza, 10005-1413. Telephone: 212-530-5000. Fax: 212-530-5219. ABA/net: MilbankNY.
Midtown Office: 375 Park Avenue, Suite 3601, 10152.
Los Angeles, California Office: 601 South Figueroa Street, 90017. Telephone: 213-892-4000. Fax: 213-629-5063.
Palo Alto, California Office: 630 Hansen Way, 94304-1022. Telephone: 650-739-7000. Fax: 650-739-7100.
Frankfurt am Main, Germany Office: Frankfurter Welle, An Der Welle 4, 60422. Telephone: 011-49-69-7593-7170. Fax: 011-49-69-7593-8303.
Tokyo, Japan Office: Fukoku Seimei Building, 2-2, Uchisaiwai-cho 2-Chome, Chiyoda-ku, Tokyo 100-0011, Japan. Telephone: 011-81-3-3504-1050. Telephone: 011-81-3-3504-1050. Fax: 011-81-3-3595-2790, 011-81-3-3595-2840.
London, England Office: Dashwood House, 69 Old Broad Street, London, EC2M 1QS. Telephone: 44-207-448-3000. Fax: 44-207-448-3029.

(This Listing Continued)

Hong Kong: 3007 Alexandra House, 16 Chater Road. Telephone: 852-2971-4888. Fax: 852-2840-0792, 852-2854-9046.
Singapore Office: 14-00 Caltex House, 30 Raffles Place, 048622. Telephone: 65-428-2400. Fax: 65-428-2500.

General Practice.

PARTNERS

WINTHROP N. BROWN, born Washington, D.C., July 27, 1948; admitted to bar, 1975, District of Columbia. *Education:* Stanford University (B.A., 1970); London School of Economics and Political Science, London, England (M.Sc., 1971); George Washington University (J.D., with honors, 1974). Order of the Coif. ***PRACTICE AREAS:*** Banking; Securities.

GLENN S. GERSTELL, born New York, New York, 1951; admitted to bar, 1977, New York; 1981, District of Columbia. *Education:* New York University (B.A., 1974); Columbia (J.D., 1976).

ROBERT F. LAWRENCE, born Springfield, Illinois, 1955; admitted to bar, 1983, District of Columbia; 2000, New York. *Education:* Dartmouth College (A.B, cum laude, 1977); Georgetown University (J.D., cum laude, 1983).

JONATHAN A. MAIZEL, born New York, New York, 1964; admitted to bar, 1988, New Jersey; 1989, New York (Not admitted in District of Columbia). *Education:* Montclair State University (B.A., 1985); Rutgers University (J.D., 1988).

MICHAEL D. NOLAN, born Boston, Massachusetts, 1965; admitted to bar, 1992, New York, District of Columbia and U.S. District Court, Southern and Eastern Districts of New York; 1993, U.S. Court of Appeals, Second Circuit; 2001, U.S. District Court, District of Columbia, U.S. District Court, Eastern District of Virginia, U.S. District Court, District of Maryland, U.S. Court of Appeals,Third, Fourth and District of Columbia Circuits and U.S. Court of Federal Claims. *Education:* Harvard University (A.B., 1988); University of Chicago (J.D., 1991). Member: Arbitration Committee, U.S. Council for International Business; Institute for Transnational Arbitration.

JOHN E. SHOCKEY, born Corpus Christi, Texas, 1942; admitted to bar, 1967, Texas; 1971, U.S. Supreme Court; 1974, District of Columbia. *Education:* University of Houston (B.B.A., magna cum laude, 1965; J.D., cum laude, 1967). *Member:* Federal Bar Association (Member, Executive Council, Saving Institutions Law Committee, 1978—, and Banking Law Committee, 1978—).

RICHARD C. TUFARO, born New York, New York, 1944; admitted to bar, 1969, New York; 1992, District of Columbia; 1994, Maryland. *Education:* Dartmouth (A.B., magna cum laude, 1965); Harvard (LL.B., cum laude, 1968).

WILLIAM E. WALLACE, III, born 1953; admitted to bar, 1979, Florida and District of Columbia. *Education:* Boston College (B.A., cum laude, 1975); University of Miami School of Law (J.D., cum laude, 1978). Law Clerk to U.S. District Judge José A. Gonzalez, Jr. Southern District of Florida, 1978-1979. Editorial Board, *Trademark Reporter*, 1989—. Member, Antitrust Council, U.S. Chamber of Commerce. *Member:* The Florida Bar; The District of Columbia Bar; Federal and American (Member, Sections on: Litigation; Antitrust; Trademark) Bar Associations; Defense Research Institute; The Association of Trial Lawyers of America; The Academy of Florida Trial Lawyers; International Trademark Association; American Intellectual Property Law Association. ***PRACTICE AREAS:*** Antitrust; Complex Litigation; Intellectual Property.

WILLIAM H. WEBSTER, born St. Louis, Missouri, 1924; admitted to bar, 1949, Missouri; 1981, District of Columbia. *Education:* Amherst College (B.A., 1947); Washington University (J.D., 1949); Awarded LL.D. by Amherst College, 1975 and by Washington University, 1978. Order of the Coif. Fellow, American Bar Foundation. Honorary Fellow, American College of Trial Lawyers.

OF COUNSEL

ORLAN M. JOHNSON, born San José, Costa Rica, 1962; admitted to bar, 1988, Pennsylvania; 2001, District of Columbia. *Education:* Andrews University (B.A., 1984); Howard University (J.D., 1987). Alpha Mu Gamma. Delta Mu Delta. Andrews Scholar. Recipient, American Jurisprudence Award in Contracts. Chairman, Price George's College Foundation Board, 2000—. ***LANGUAGES:*** French.

STEVEN M. KRAMER, born Washington, D.C., 1960; admitted to bar, 1987, Virginia; 1988, Maryland and District of Columbia. *Education:* University of Maryland (B.S., 1982); University of Richmond Law School (J.D., 1987).

(For complete biographical data on all Members of Firm, Of Counsel, Counsel and Senior Attorneys, see Professional Biographies at New York, New York)

MILES & STOCKBRIDGE P.C.

1140 CONNECTICUT AVENUE, N.W., SUITE 1212
WASHINGTON, D.C. 20036-4001
Telephone: 202-737-9600
Facsimile: 202-737-0097
URL: http://www.milesstockbridge.com

Baltimore, Maryland Office: 10 Light Street, Telephone: 410-727-6464. Facsimile: 410-385-3700.
Cambridge, Maryland Office: 300 Academy Street. Telephone: 410-228-4545. Facsimile: 410-228-5652.
Columbia, Maryland Office: 9881 Broken Land Parkway, Suite 400, Telephone: 410-381-6000. Facsimile: 410-381-6430.
Easton, Maryland Office: 101 Bay Street. Telephone: 410-822-5280. Facsimile: 410-822-5450.
Frederick, Maryland Office: 30 West Patrick Street. Telephone: 301-662-5155. Facsimile: 301-662-3647.
McLean, Virginia Office: 1751 Pinnacle Drive, Suite 500. Telephone: 703-903-9000. Facsimile: 703-610-8686.
Rockville, Maryland Office: 22 West Jefferson Street. Telephone: 301-762-1600. Facsimile: 301-762-0363.
Towson, Maryland Office: 600 Washington Avenue, Suite 300. Telephone: 410-821-6565. Facsimile: 410-823-8123.

General Practice.

SAMUEL A. BLEICHER, born Omaha, NE, 1942; admitted to bar, 1966, Nebraska; 1972, Ohio; 1979, District of Columbia; 1989, Virginia; 1991, Maryland. *Education:* Northwestern Univ. (B.A., 1963); Harvard Law School (J.D., 1966). Phi Beta Kappa. Law Professor, Univ. of Toledo College of Law, 1966-1972. Deputy Director for Regulation & Enforcement, Ohio Environmental Protection Agency, 1972-1975. Deputy General Counsel, National Oceanic and Atmospheric Administration, 1980-1981. Author: "Economic and Technical Feasibility in Clean Air Act Enforcement Against Stationary Sources," 89 Harvard L.Rev. 316-54 (1976). (Also at McLean, Virginia Office). ***PRACTICE AREAS:*** Environmental. ***Email:*** sbleicher@milesstockbridge.com

RICHARD D. BENNETT, born Baltimore, MD, 1947; admitted to bar, 1973, Maryland; 1974, U.S. Claims Court; 1975, U.S. District Court, District of Maryland; 1976, U.S. Court of Appeals, Fourth Circuit; 1981, U.S. Tax Court and District of Columbia. *Education:* Univ. of Pennsylvania (B.A., 1969); Univ. of Maryland (J.D., 1973). Staff, Maryland Law Review, 1972-1973. Author: "Self Incrimination: Choosing A Constitutional Immunity Standard," 32 Maryland Law Review 289, 1972. Special Counsel, U.S. House of Representatives, GROC, 1997-1998. U.S. Attorney for Maryland, 1991-1993. Assistant U.S. Attorney, Maryland, 1976-1981. Member, Maryland Bar Foundation. *Member:* Maryland State, Federal (Member, Board of Governors, 1982—) and American (Member, White Collar Crime Section) Bar Associations. [Major, JAGC, Maryland National Guard, 1969-1975; 1983-1997; Retired - U.S. Army Reserve Control Group, 1997]. (Also at Baltimore, Maryland Office). ***PRACTICE AREAS:*** White Collar Criminal Defense Law; Federal Litigation; Internal Investigations. ***Email:*** rbennett@milesstockbridge.com

REPRESENTATIVE CLIENTS: American Paper Institute, Inc.; The Black & Decker Corporation; Honeywell International Inc.; Illinois Tool Works Inc.; Schindler Elevator Corp.; The District of Columbia Public Schools; American Association of Blood Banks.

(For biographical data on firm personnel resident at other locations, see Professional Biographies at those cities).

MILLEN, WHITE, ZELANO & BRANIGAN, P.C.

WASHINGTON, D.C.

(See Arlington, Virginia)
Intellectual Property.

JOHN T. MILLER, JR.

Established in 1962
1001 CONNECTICUT AVENUE, N.W.
WASHINGTON, D.C. 20036
Telephone: 202-331-1630
Fax: 202-331-3806
Email: jtmillerjr@erols.com

Practice before Federal Courts and Federal Administrative Agencies.

JOHN T. MILLER, JR., born Waterbury, Connecticut, August 10, 1922; admitted to bar, 1949, Connecticut (inactive) and District of Columbia; 1952, U.S. Supreme Court. *Education:* Clark University (A.B., cum laude, 1944); Georgetown University (J.D., 1948); University of Geneva (Docteur en Droit, 1951). Note Editor, Georgetown Law Review, 1947-1948. Adjunct Professor, Federal Trade Regulation, Antitrust, Corporate Problems, International Law, Energy Problems, The Deregulated Natural Gas and Electric Industries, Georgetown University Law Center, 1959-2001. Faculty Member, National Judicial College, 1974-1983. Master and President, 1995-1996, Prettyman-Leventhal American Inns of Court. *Member:* District of Columbia Bar; Bar Association of the District of Columbia; American Bar Association (Chairman, Administrative Law Section, 1972-1973; Member, House of Delegates, 1991-1992); Federal Energy Bar Association (President, 1990-1991); Thomas More Society of America (President, 1996-1997). ***PRACTICE AREAS:*** Federal Administrative Law; Energy Regulation.

MILLER, BALIS & O'NEIL, P.C.

Established in 1978
1140 NINETEENTH STREET, N.W.
SUITE 700
WASHINGTON, D.C. 20036
Telephone: 202-296-2960
Fax: 202-296-0166
URL: http://www.mbolaw.com

Practice before Federal and State Regulatory Agencies, State and Federal Courts and Congress. Energy, Environmental, General Administrative Law, Governmental Affairs, Hydroelectric Licensing, International, Litigation, Maritime, Military, and Public Utilities.

FIRM PROFILE: Miller, Balis & O'Neil attorneys are experienced in the legal and regulatory aspects of every phase of both the natural gas and electric power industries. Clients of the firm include hundreds of municipally-owned and county-run natural gas distribution systems, public agencies and associations, consumer-owned electric distribution systems, owners of electric generating facilities, wholesale customers of utilities, and state public utility advocates. Simply put, the firm serves those that serve the public.

WILLIAM T. MILLER, born Charleston, West Virginia, March 9, 1941; admitted to bar, 1966, Virginia; 1967, District of Columbia. *Education:* Princeton University (B.A., cum laude, 1963); University of Virginia (LL.B., 1966). Order of the Coif; Phi Alpha Delta. Law Clerk to Judge E. Barrett Prettyman, U.S. Court of Appeals, Washington, D.C., 1966-1967. ***PRACTICE AREAS:*** Electric Power; Electric Utilities; Municipal Utility Law; Natural Gas; Electric Cooperative Law; Public Utility Law.

STANLEY W. BALIS, born Lock Haven, Pennsylvania, November 21, 1949; admitted to bar, 1975, District of Columbia; 1980, Maryland. *Education:* Boston University (B.S., cum laude, 1971); Beta Gamma Sigma; Georgetown University (J.D., 1974). Editor, Georgetown Law Journal, 1973-1974. Assistant Director for Gas and Oil Pipeline and Producer Enforcement, Federal Energy Regulatory Commission, 1978-1979. ***PRACTICE AREAS:*** Economic Regulatory Law; Energy Contracts; Gas Utilities.

ROBERT A. O'NEIL, born Boston, Massachusetts, August 22, 1946; admitted to bar, 1971, Massachusetts; 1972, U.S. Court of Military Appeals; 1978, District of Columbia. *Education:* Boston College (B.A., 1968; J.D., 1971). Member, Board of Editors, Boston College Industrial & Commercial Law Review, 1970-1971. ***PRACTICE AREAS:*** Energy Contracts; Energy Project Development; Project Finance; Electric Utilities.

JAMES R. CHOUKAS-BRADLEY, born Hartford, Connecticut, September 11, 1950; admitted to bar, 1980, District of Columbia. *Education:* University of Vermont (B.A., cum laude, 1974); Georgetown University (J.D., cum laude, 1980). Phi Beta Kappa. Assistant to the City Manager, City of Berlin, New Hampshire, 1975-1977. ***PRACTICE AREAS:*** Energy Finance; Municipal Solid Waste; Energy Contracts; Natural Resources; Energy Regulation.

JOHN MICHAEL ADRAGNA, born Watertown, New York, August 28, 1953; admitted to bar, 1978, District of Columbia. *Education:* State University of New York at Buffalo (B.A., 1975); George Washington University (J.D., 1978). Phi Beta Kappa. ***PRACTICE AREAS:*** Electric Power; Electric Utilities; Energy Regulation; Energy Contracts; Electric Cooperatives; Public Utility Law.

JAMES H. BYRD, born Owosso, Michigan, June 17, 1954; admitted to bar, 1980, Michigan; 1981, District of Columbia. *Education:* Michigan State University (B.A. and B.S., with high honors, 1976); Wayne State University (J.D., 1980). Law Clerk, Third Judicial Circuit Court of Michigan, 1980-1981. ***PRACTICE AREAS:*** Energy Regulation; Hydroelectricity; Natural Gas Regulation; Energy; Contracts.

JOHN P. GREGG, born Cincinnati, Ohio, April 11, 1957; admitted to bar, 1983, District of Columbia. *Education:* Hobart College (B.A., 1979); American University (J.D., 1982). Note and Comment Editor, American University Law Review, 1981-1982. Author: "Gas Supply Contracting Without a Safety Net," Public Utilities Fortnightly, October, 1992. Lecturer, American University Law

(This Listing Continued)

School, 1984-1987. Assistant General Counsel, Public Service Commission of the District of Columbia, 1986-1988. ***PRACTICE AREAS:*** Energy Contracts; Energy Legislation; Energy Regulation; Public Utility Regulation.

SEAN T. BEENY, born San Diego, California, July 1, 1945; admitted to bar, 1979, District of Columbia. *Education:* Carleton College (B.A., cum laude, with distinction in English, 1967); Georgetown University Law Center (J.D., 1979). Executive Editor, American Criminal Law Review, 1978-1979. American Judicature Society. ***PRACTICE AREAS:*** Antitrust and Trade Regulation; Energy Contracts; Electric Power; Electric Utilities; Economic Regulatory Law.

SUSAN N. KELLY, born Washington, D.C., December 26, 1955; admitted to bar, 1980, District of Columbia. *Education:* University of Missouri (A.B., magna cum laude, 1977); George Washington University (J.D., with high honors, 1980). Phi Beta Kappa; Order of the Coif. *Member:* District of Columbia Bar; Energy Bar Association (Member, Board of Directors, 1995-1998); Women's Bar Association of the District of Columbia. ***PRACTICE AREAS:*** Energy Law.

RANDOLPH LEE ELLIOTT, born Cushing, Oklahoma, February 8, 1957; admitted to bar, 1983, District of Columbia. *Education:* Massachusetts Institute of Technology (S.B., 1979); Harvard University (M.P.P., 1983; J.D., cum laude, 1983). Law Clerk, Judge Thomas Penfield Jackson, U.S. District Court, District of Columbia, 1983-1984. Attorney, Office of the Solicitor, Federal Energy Regulatory Commission, 1991-1995. ***PRACTICE AREAS:*** Energy Law; Antitrust; Judicial Review.

JOSHUA L. MENTER, born Washington, D.C., March 17, 1950; admitted to bar, 1975, District of Columbia. *Education:* Union College-Schenectady (B.A., summa cum laude, 1971); New York University (J.D., 1974). Phi Beta Kappa. ***PRACTICE AREAS:*** Natural Gas Regulation; Electric Power; Energy Contracts.

BENJAMIN L. WILLEY, born Cambridge, Maryland, April 6, 1949; admitted to bar, 1976, Iowa, Maryland and U.S. Court of Military Appeals; 1999, District of Columbia. *Education:* Salisbury State University (B.A., magna cum laude, 1971); University of Maryland (J.D., 1976). Phi Alpha Kappa; Phi Alpha Delta; Phi Alpha Theta. Instructor, City College of Chicago, 1980. Deputy Admiralty Counsel, United States Navy, 1991-1994. *Member:* Wicomico County, Maryland State and American Bar Associations; Judge Advocates' Association. [With U.S. Navy, JAGC, 1974-1994]. ***PRACTICE AREAS:*** Military Law; Federal Administrative Law; Federal Civil Practice; Admiralty Law; Maritime Commercial Law. **Email:** militarylaw@mbolaw.com

COUNSEL

LINDA K. BROWNING, born Nashville, Tennessee, September 26, 1949; admitted to bar, 1982, Alabama (Not admitted in District of Columbia). *Education:* David Lipscomb University (B.A., 1971); Cumberland School of Law of Samford University (J.D., 1982). Writing Editor, Cumberland Law Review, 1981-1982. Instructor, Cumberland School of Law, 1999-2000. *Member:* Alabama State Bar. ***PRACTICE AREAS:*** Energy Law; Natural Gas Transactions; Energy Regulation.

MILTON J. GROSSMAN, born Baltimore, Maryland, February 2, 1936; admitted to bar, 1960, District of Columbia. *Education:* Johns Hopkins University (A.B., 1956); Harvard University (LL.B., magna cum laude, 1959). Article Editor, Harvard Law Review. Law Clerk to the Honorable Henry J. Friendly, U.S. Court of Appeals, Second Circuit, 1959-1960. Trial Attorney, Federal Power Commission, 1960-1964. Legal Assistant to the Honorable Philip Elman, Federal Trade Commission, 1964-1966. Trial Attorney, U.S. Department of Justice, Antitrust Division, 1966-1975. Assistant Chief, Public Counsel Section, 1970-1975. Chief Hearing Counsel, Nuclear Regulatory Commission, 1976-1978. Associate Rail Public Counsel, Office of Rail Public Counsel, 1978-1990. ***PRACTICE AREAS:*** Energy Law; Antitrust Law; Appellate Practice.

MARY A. HEKMAN, born Holland, Michigan, August 27, 1957; admitted to bar, 1984, Virginia; 1985, District of Columbia. *Education:* Calvin College (B.A., 1979); American University (J.D., cum laude, 1984). ***PRACTICE AREAS:*** Cogeneration; Hydroelectricity; Energy Project Development; Electric Power; Electric Utilities.

LISA M. OCHSENHIRT, born Gainesville, Florida, December 17, 1968; admitted to bar, 1994, Virginia (inactive); 1995, Pennsylvania (Not admitted in District of Columbia). *Education:* University of Virginia (B.A., 1990); College of William and Mary (J.D., 1994). Law Clerk and Assistant Consumer Advocate, Pennsylvania Office of Consumer Advocate, 1994-1998.

CRAIG W. SILVERSTEIN, born Pittsburgh, Pennsylvania, March 2, 1972; admitted to bar, 1998, Maryland; 1999, District of Columbia and U.S. Court of Appeals, District of Columbia Circuit. *Education:* American University (B.A., cum laude, 1994); University of Pittsburgh (J.D., 1998).

(This Listing Continued)

PHYLLIS G KIMMEL, born Columbus, Ohio, March 13, 1967; admitted to bar, 1995, New York; 1996, District of Columbia. *Education:* Wesleyan University (B.A., 1989); New York University (J.D., 1994). Phi Beta Kappa.

MILLER, CANFIELD, PADDOCK AND STONE, P.L.C.

A Professional Limited Liability Company

Founded in 1852 by Sidney Davy Miller

1900 K STREET, N.W.
SUITE 1150
WASHINGTON, D.C. 20006
Telephone: 202-429-5575
Fax: 202-331-1118
URL: http://www.millercanfield.com

REVISERS OF THE MICHIGAN LAW DIGEST FOR THIS DIRECTORY

Detroit, Michigan Office: 150 West Jefferson, Suite 2500, 48226-4415. Telephone: 313-963-6420. Fax: 313-496-7500. Cable Address: "Stem Detroit."

Ann Arbor, Michigan Office: 101 North Main Street, 7th Floor, 48104-1400. Telephone: 734-663-2445. Fax: 734-747-7147.

Grand Rapids, Michigan Office: 99 Monroe, N.W., Suite 1200, 49503-2639. Telephone: 616-454-8656. Fax: 616-776-6322.

Howell, Michigan Office: 121 South Barnard Street, Suite 7, 48843-2305. Telephone: 517-546-7600. Fax: 517-546-6974.

Kalamazoo, Michigan Office: 444 West Michigan Avenue, 49007-3751. Telephone: 616-381-7030. Fax: 616-382-0244.

Lansing, Michigan Office: Suite 900, One Michigan Avenue, 48933-1609. Telephone: 517-487-2070. Fax: 517-374-6304.

Monroe, Michigan Office: 214 East Elm Avenue, Suite 100, 48162-2682. Telephone: 734-243-2000. Fax: 734-243-0901.

Troy, Michigan Office: 840 West Long Lake Road, Suite 200, 48098-6358. Telephone: 248-879-2000. Fax: 248-879-2001.

Pensacola, Florida Office: 25 West Cedar Street, Suite 500, 32501. Telephone: 850-469-1088. Fax: 850-432-0677.

New York, New York Office: 1450 Broadway, 41st Floor, 10018. Telephone: 212-704-4400. Fax: 212-704-4410.

Gdynia, Poland Office: ul. Batorego 28-32, 81-366. Telephone: 011 (48-58) 782-0200. Fax: 011 (48-58) 782-0201.

Warsaw, Poland Office: ul. Nowogrodzka 11, 5th Floor, 00-513. Telephone: 011 (48-22) 529-0200. Fax: 011 (48-22) 529-0201.

Katowice, Poland Office: ul. Francuska 35/37, 40-027. Telephone: 011 (48-32) 757-2414. Fax: 011 (48-32) 757-2483.

Accounting Litigation, Administrative, Admiralty/Maritime, Antidumping, Antitrust, Appellate Practice, Banking, Bankruptcy & Reorganization, Commercial Transactions, Computer, Condemnation, Condominiums & Cooperatives, Construction Litigation, Corporate, Domestic Relations, Education, Emerging Business, Environmental, Estate Planning & Administration, Foundations & Nonprofit Organizations, Franchising, Health Care & Hospital, Immigration, Insurance, Intellectual Property, International Law, International Trade & Customs, Labor & Employment, Libel & Slander Litigation, Licensing & High Technology, Litigation & Alternative Dispute Resolution, Litigation Management, Mergers & Acquisitions, Municipal & School Finance & Bond Counsel, Nuclear Power Plant Litigation, Oil & Gas, Pension, Profit-Sharing & Employee Benefits, Product Liability Consulting & Defense, Professional Malpractice Consulting & Defense, Public Law, Real Estate Development & Investment, Securities (Corporate & Municipal), Securities Litigation, State, Finance & Bond Counsel, Taxation, Tax-Exempt Financing, Telecommunications, Toxic Torts Litigation, Transportation, Utilities, Zoning.

FIRM PROFILE: Miller, Canfield, Paddock and Stone, P.L.C. traces its history to 1852 when Sidney Davy Miller (1830-1904) opened a practice on Detroit's Jefferson Avenue. Today Miller Canfield is one of the largest law firms in Michigan with more than 260 attorneys and over 50 legal assistants. We have a growing national practice and a long-established statewide practice. Our Michigan offices are located in Ann Arbor, Detroit, Grand Rapids, Howell, Kalamazoo, Lansing, Monroe, and Troy. We also have offices in New York City, and in Washington, D.C.; and an affiliated office in Pensacola, Florida. Our offices in Gdynia, Katowice, and Warsaw, Poland enable us to serve clients throughout Central and Eastern Europe.

Our practice areas are organized into the following groups: Bankruptcy/Workout; Business and Finance (Commercial Lending, Corporations and Securities, Finance and Development Sections), Environmental and Regulatory; Estate Planning; Federal Tax and Employee Benefits; Health Care; Intellectual Property; International Business; Labor and Employment; Litigation (Commercial Litigation and Dispute Resolution, Product Liability/Tort, State and Local Tax Sections), and Public Law Services and Bond Counsel.

(This Listing Continued)

MILLER, CANFIELD, PADDOCK AND STONE, P.L.C., Washington—Continued

We represent individuals in their personal and business concerns, trusts and estates, publicly traded and multinational companies, and many start-up, small, and medium sized businesses. Clients also include public bodies such as the state of Michigan, and many of its agencies, authorities and universities, cities, counties, townships, school and community college districts, and special authorities throughout Michigan and in other states. We represent many nonprofit, tax-exempt institutions, such as hospitals, charitable corporations, and professional associations.

PRINCIPALS OF FIRM

JOHN O. RENKEN, born Ann Arbor, Michigan, July 28, 1965; admitted to bar, 1990, Michigan (Not admitted in District of Columbia). *Education:* Georgetown University; DePauw University (B.A., Management Fellows Program, 1987); Indiana University (J.D., cum laude, 1990). *Member:* State Bar of Michigan; American Bar Association; National Association of Bond Lawyers; National Multi Housing Council. ***PRACTICE AREAS:*** Municipal Finance or Bond Law; Real Estate Finance; Housing Finance; Health Care Finance; Project Finance. ***Email:*** renken@millercanfield.com

RICHARD A. WALAWENDER, born Hamtramck, Michigan, December 14, 1960; admitted to bar, 1986, Michigan (Not admitted in District of Columbia). *Education:* University of Michigan (B.A., with high distinction, 1982; J.D., 1986). Contributing Editor, University of Michigan Journal of Law Reform, 1985-1986. Director of Firm's International Business Services Group and Automotive Practice Group. Co-Founder of Firm's Polish Operations. Member, Advisory Board, University of Michigan Center for Russian and E. European Studies. *Member:* Detroit and American (Member, International Law Section; Business Law Section; Public Law Section) and International Bar Associations; State Bar of Michigan (Member: International Law Section). (Also in Detroit Office). ***LANGUAGES:*** Polish. ***PRACTICE AREAS:*** Business Law; Finance (Public and Project Financings); International Corporate Law; Automotive Industry; Real Estate Development. ***Email:*** walawender@millercanfield.com

OF COUNSEL/SENIOR COUNSEL

TILLMAN L. LAY, born Knoxville, Tennessee, November 24, 1955; admitted to bar, 1981, District of Columbia; 1983, U.S. Court of Appeals, Fifth Circuit; 1991, U.S. Court of Appeals, Fourth Circuit; 1992, U.S. Court of Appeals, 9th and 11th Circuit; 1993, U.S. Court of Appeals, Sixth Circuit; 2001, U.S. Supreme Court. *Education:* University of Tennessee (B.S., with highest honors, 1977); University of Michigan (J.D., magna cum laude, 1980). Order of the Coif. Articles and Executive Editor, Michigan Law Review, 1979-1980. Faculty Member, Practising Law Institute, Cable Television Law, 1994, 1995 and 1997. Author: "Local Government and Industry: An Uneasy Balance," 2 Telecommunications Reports International Journal 1 (Winter 1998); "Some Thoughts on Federalism in a World of Convergence," 2000 Law Review of Michigan State University Detroit College of Law 223 (Spring 2000). Co-Author: "The Telecommunications Act of 1996; What It Means to Local Governments" (National League of Cities, 1996). Author: "Keeping the Gateway Open," Telematics (Jan. 1988); "A Pragmatic Look at Social Contracts and Price Caps," Telematics (Oct. 1987); "The D.C. Circuit's Detariffing Decision: A Sheep in Wolf's Clothing," Telematics (Aug./Sept. 1985). Judicial Clerk, The Honorable John C. Godbold, U.S. Court of Appeals for the Fifth Circuit, 1980-1981. Attorney, Wilmer, Cutler & Pickering, Washington, D.C., 1981-1988. Partner, Miller & Holbrooke, 1988-1994. *Member:* The District of Columbia Bar; American Bar Association; Federal Communications Bar Association. ***PRACTICE AREAS:*** Communications Law; Appellate Practice; Antitrust Law. ***Email:*** lay@millercanfield.com

DAVID H. JACOBS, born Fort Zama, Japan, February 3, 1962; admitted to bar, 1989, Maryland; 1991, U.S. District Court, District of Maryland; 1994, U.S. Court of Appeals, 4th Circuit; 2000, District of Columbia. *Education:* Syracuse University; University of Maryland (B.A., 1986; J.D., 1989). Law Clerk to the Honorable L.H. Rushworth, Anne Arundel County Circuit Court. *Member:* American Bar Association (Member, Labor and Employment Section); Defense Research Institute; Maryland Association of Defense Trial Counsel. (Also in Detroit Office). ***LANGUAGES:*** German. ***PRACTICE AREAS:*** Labor and Employment Law; Products Liability; Construction Litigation; Commercial Litigation. ***Email:*** jacobs@millercanfield.com

RANDALL E. ROBERTSON, born High Point, North Carolina, January 31, 1953; admitted to bar, 1978, North Carolina; 1981, Texas, U.S. District, Northern District of Texas and Middle District of North Carolina and U.S. Court of Appeals, Fourth Circuit; 1994, District of Columbia. *Education:* Wake Forest University; University of North Carolina (B.S., 1974; J.D., 1978). *Member:* Rutherford County and North Carolina Bar Associations; National Bar Association; American Corporate Counsel Association. (Also in Detroit Office). ***PRACTICE AREAS:*** Employment Litigation; Labor.

(This Listing Continued)

CER GLADWYN GOINS, born Washington, D.C., July 18, 1951; admitted to bar, 1976, Pennsylvania (Not admitted in District of Columbia). *Education:* Case Western Reserve University (B.A., with honors, 1973; J.D., 1976); Georgetown University (LL.M., 1979). Instructor, Stanford University School of Law, 1990-1991. Formerly with U.S. Securities and Exchange Commission. [U.S. Army, Office of Staff Judge Advocate, Fort Belvoir, VA, 1976-1979]. ***PRACTICE AREAS:*** Securities; Banking Law; Litigation. ***Email:*** goins@millercanfield.com

STEVEN C. KAHN, born Buffalo, New York, August 29, 1942; admitted to bar, 1970, California; 1974, Massachusetts; 1981, District of Columbia; 1991, Maryland. *Education:* Yale University (B.A., 1964); University of Pennsylvania (LL.B., 1969). Co-Author: *Legal Guide to Human Resources* (3d. ed. 1994), Enforcement Attorney, National Labor Relations Board. ***PRACTICE AREAS:*** Labor and Employment. ***Email:*** kahn@millercanfield.com

REPRESENTATIVE FIRM CLIENTS: City of Detroit, Michigan; City of Midland, Michigan; Comerica Bank; CMS Energy; DaimlerChrysler Corporation; Denso America, Inc.; Detroit Tigers, Inc.; DTE Energy Company; First of Michigan; Flint Ink Corporation; Ford Motor Company; Ford Credit Company; Henry Ford Hospital; Huntington Banks of Michigan; Kellogg Company; Kelly Services, Inc.; La-Z-Boy Incorporated; Mead Corp.; Michigan State University; Mitsubishi; NCAA; Northwest Airlines; Owens-Illinois; Pharmacia Corporation; Phillips Petroleum; R.L. Polk & Company; Siemens Corporation; Source One Mortgage Services Corporation; Spartan Stores Incorporated; State of Michigan and its authorities; Tecumseh Products Company; The University of Michigan; Wayne County; Xerox Corporation.

REVISERS OF THE MICHIGAN LAW DIGEST FOR THIS DIRECTORY

(For Complete Biographical Data on all Personnel, see Professional Biographies at Detroit, Michigan)

MILLER & CHEVALIER

CHARTERED

Established 1920

655 FIFTEENTH STREET, N.W., SUITE 900

WASHINGTON, D.C. 20005-5701

Telephone: 202-626-5800

Fax: 202-628-0858

Email: inquiries@milchev.com

URL: http://www.millerchevalier.com

Taxation: Federal Taxation, International Taxation, Tax Planning, Tax Litigation, Tax Appeals, Tax Audits, Tax Controversies, Federal Tax Legislation. Government Contracts: Bid Protests, Government Contract Fraud, Government Procurement, Public Contract Law, False Claims Act, Qui Tam Litigation, Legislative Practice, Information Technology Contracts, Government Construction Contracts, Health Care Contracts, Health Care Fraud, Health Care Litigation, Health Insurance, Managed Care, and Medicare Fraud and Abuse. Litigation: Federal Litigation, Complex Litigation, Complex Commercial Litigation, RICO, White Collar Crime, Administrative Litigation, Antitrust, Patent Litigation, Federal Administrative Law, Trial Practice and U.S. Supreme Court Litigation. International Trade: International Law, International Trade Regulation, International Dispute Resolution, International Intellectual Property, Foreign Corrupt Practices Act, North American Free Trade Agreement, Import and Export Law, and Foreign Trade Sanctions.

FIRM PROFILE: Miller & Chevalier specializes in: taxation, government contracts, international and related litigation. In each area, we have developed a thorough understanding of the substantive law, its underlying policies, its institutions, and its institutions' personnel. In each, the standard we set for ourselves is to be among preeminent firms in the country.

Since its founding in 1920, Miller & Chevalier has been based in Washington, D.C., close to administrative and policy developments, as well as the specialized litigation forums vital to our clients' interests.

Most of the legal issues with which we deal on a daily basis relate to U.S. laws and regulations of government agencies. Because of our experience, our U.S. and foreign-based clients have the confidence to trust us for solutions to their most difficult problems. It is not uncommon for the issues on which we work to be without controlling precedent. Our intricate knowledge of the areas in which we practice allows us to provide our clients with solutions to even these issues. Large, complex litigation is a common feature of each area of our practice for issues that cannot practically be resolved otherwise.

MEMBERS

STUART CHEVALIER (1879-1956).

ROBERT NETHERLAND MILLER (1879-1968).

RICHARD H. ABBEY, born Brooklyn, New York, February 20, 1938; admitted to bar, 1963, New York and U.S. Court of International Trade; 1982, U.S. Court of Appeals for the Federal Circuit (Not admitted in District of Columbia). *Education:* Hobart College (B.A., cum laude, 1959); New York

(This Listing Continued)

University (LL.B., 1963). Pi Gamma Mu. Author: "Valuation of Countertrade Merchandise; Countertrade and Trading Companies," Law and Business, Inc., 1984-1990. Lecturer: Court of Customs and Patent Appeals Judicial Conference, 1972 and 1991; Court of International Trade Judicial Conference, 1980 and 1992; United States Trademark Association, 1982; International Anti-Counterfeiting Coalition, 1982; American Bar Association National Institutes, 1983; International Chamber of Commerce, 1983; American Management Association, 1985; Conference on Trade and International Law, Texas Tech University School of Law, 1986; Keidanren, 1992; Court of International Trade Judicial Conference, 1993. Assistant Chief Counsel, 1972-1977, Deputy Chief Counsel, 1977-1980 and Chief Counsel, 1980-1985, U.S. Customs Service. *Member:* Federal and American (Member: Section on Administrative Law and Regulatory Practice; Standing Committee on Customs Law) Bar Associations; Customs and International Trade Bar Association; National Customs Brokers and Forwarders Association of America; Joint Industry Group (Chair, Import Programs Committee). ***PRACTICE AREAS:*** Customs and International Trade. ***Email:*** rabbey@milchev.com

JAMES B. ALTMAN, born Chicago, Illinois; admitted to bar, 1978, District of Columbia. *Education:* Massachusetts Institute of Technology (B.S., 1971; M.S., 1975); Boalt Hall School of Law, University of California (J.D., 1978). Associate Editor, California Law Review, 1977-1978. *Member:* The District of Columbia Bar; American Bar Association. ***PRACTICE AREAS:*** International Technology and Science; Intellectual Property; Federal Tax Controversies Litigation. ***Email:*** jaltman@milchev.com

JOHN D. BATES, born Elizabeth, New Jersey; admitted to bar, 1976, Maryland; 1977, District of Columbia. *Education:* Wesleyan University (B.A., 1968); University of Maryland (J.D., 1976). Order of the Coif. Note and Comment Editor, Maryland Law Review, 1975-1976. Law Clerk to Judge Roszel Thomsen, U.S. District Court for the District of Maryland, 1976-1977. Deputy Independent Counsel, Whitewater Investigation, 1995-1997. Assistant U.S. Attorney, District of Columbia, 1980-1997 (Chief, Civil Division, 1987-1997). Member: D.C. Circuit Advisory Committee on Procedure, 1991-1997; Civil Justice Reform Committee, U.S. District Court for the District of Columbia, 1995—. *Member:* The District of Columbia Bar (Treasurer, 1991; Chairman, Publications Committee, 1994-1997); Federal (Chairman, Litigation Section, 1989) and American Bar Associations. [LT., U.S. Army, 1968-1971]. ***PRACTICE AREAS:*** Federal Civil Litigation; Health Care Fraud; Government Contracts; False Claims Act; White Collar Crime. ***Email:*** jbates@milchev.com

DENNIS P. BEDELL, born Detroit, Michigan; admitted to bar, 1965, District of Columbia; 1980, U.S. Supreme Court. *Education:* Harvard College (A.B., cum laude, 1961); University of Michigan (J.D., 1964). Adjunct Professor, Georgetown University Law Center, 1977—. Recipient of Charles Fahy Distinguished Adjunct Professor Award, 1997-1998. Joint Committee on Internal Revenue Taxation, U.S. Congress, 1967-1972 (Assistant Chief of Staff, 1970-1972). *Member:* The District of Columbia Bar (Chair, Taxation Committee, 1978-1979); American Bar Association (Chair, Committee on Natural Resources, Section on Taxation, 1985-1987). Fellow, American College of Tax Counsel. ***PRACTICE AREAS:*** Taxation; Corporate Taxation; Partnership Taxation; Federal Tax Controversies; Oil and Gas Taxation; Mineral Taxation. ***Email:*** dbedell@milchev.com

JAMES A. BENSFIELD, born Inglewood, California; admitted to bar, 1969, Massachusetts; 1974, District of Columbia, U.S. District Court for the District of Columbia and U.S. Court of Appeals for the District of Columbia Circuit; 1979, U.S. Supreme Court. *Education:* Occidental College (B.A., magna cum laude, 1966); Harvard University (J.D., 1969). Phi Beta Kappa. Editor and Publisher, *The New Mexico Review and Legislative Journal,* Sante Fe, New Mexico, 1970-1973. Adjunct Professor, Trial Practice, Georgetown University Law Center, 1982-1987. Attorney: Center for Law and Education, Harvard University, 1969-1970; National Senior Citizens Law Center, Washington, D.C., 1974. Attorney, 1974-1979 and Director of Training, 1979-1980, Public Defender Service for the District of Columbia. Deputy to Jacob A. Stein, Independent Counsel appointed to investigate Edwin Meese, III, 1984. *Member:* The District of Columbia Bar; American Bar Association; National Association of Criminal Defense Lawyers. ***Email:*** jbensfield@milchev.com

LEONARD BICKWIT, JR., born New York, N.Y.; admitted to bar, 1967, New York; 1980, District of Columbia. *Education:* Yale University (B.A., magna cum laude, 1961); Oxford University (B.A., 1963); Harvard University (LL.B., 1966). Phi Beta Kappa. Counsel, Subcommittee on the Environment, U.S. Senate Committee on Commerce, 1969-1974. Chief Legislative Assistant, Senator John Glenn, 1975-1979. General Counsel, U.S. Nuclear Regulatory Commission, 1979-1983. *Member:* The District of Columbia Bar; Bar Association of the District of Columbia; American Bar Association. ***PRACTICE AREAS:*** Energy; Environmental Law; Taxation; International Trade; Banks and Banking. ***Email:*** lbickwit@milchev.com

DAVID B. BLAIR, born Oslo, Norway; admitted to bar, 1990, Massachusetts and U.S. Court of Appeals, Eleventh Circuit; 1996, District of Columbia. *Education:* Georgetown University (A.B., 1985); Cornell University (J.D., magna cum laude, 1989). Order of the Coif. Articles Editor, Cornell Law Review. Trial Attorney, U.S. Department of Justice, Tax Division, 1990-1995. Law Clerk to The Honorable Frank M. Johnson, Jr., U.S. Court of Appeals, Eleventh Circuit. *Member:* The District of Columbia Bar; Massachusetts and American (Member, Section of Taxation, Court Procedures Committee) Bar Associations. ***PRACTICE AREAS:*** Federal Income Tax; Federal Tax Controversies; Tax Litigation; Tax Appeals; Taxation. ***Email:*** dblair@milchev.com

MICHAEL D. CAMPBELL, born Short Hills, New Jersey; admitted to bar, 1967, District of Columbia; 1969, New York. *Education:* Lafayette College (B.A., 1964); Georgetown University Law Center (J.D., 1967). *Member:* The District of Columbia Bar; American Bar Association. (Member, Executive Director). ***Email:*** mcampbell@milchev.com

JAY L. CARLSON, born Superior, Wisconsin; admitted to bar, 1970, District of Columbia. *Education:* University of Wisconsin (B.S., 1965); The George Washington University (J.D., with honors, 1970). Managing Editor, The George Washington University Law Review, 1969-1970. Assistant General Counsel for Litigation, Federal Energy Administration, 1975-1976. President, The George Washington Law Alumni Association, 1990-1991; Law School's Board of Advisors, 1991-1997. *Member:* The District of Columbia Bar; American Bar Association (Member of the Council, Section of Administrative Law, 1986-1989; Chairman, Committee on Energy, Section of Administrative Law, 1984-1986). Fellow, American Bar Foundation. [Lt., U.S. Navy, 1965-1967, Ret.]. ***PRACTICE AREAS:*** Tax Litigation; International Tax Controversies; Federal Tax Controversies. ***Email:*** jcarlson@milchev.com

CATHERINE L. CREECH, born Richmond, Kentucky; admitted to bar, 1987, Kentucky; 1989, District of Columbia. *Education:* Transylvania University (B.A., summa cum laude, 1984); Harvard University (J.D., 1987). Editor-in-Chief, The Harvard Women's Law Journal, 1986-1987. Attorney-Advisor, Office of Tax Policy, U.S. Treasury Department, 1991-1994. *Member:* Kentucky and American (Member, Tax Section) Bar Associations; The District of Columbia Bar. ***PRACTICE AREAS:*** Employee Benefits; Executive Compensation Taxation; Taxation; Employment Tax; Federal Taxation. ***Email:*** ccreech@milchev.com

DAVID B. CUBETA, born New Haven, Connecticut; admitted to bar, 1978, New York; 1979, District of Columbia. *Education:* Colgate University (B.A., 1974); Albany Law School (J.D., cum laude, 1977). Member, Justinian Honor Society. Chief Notes Editor, Albany Law Review, 1976-1977. Adjunct Professor, Georgetown University Law Center, 1981-1983, 1994—. Attorney Advisor, Office of the Chief Counsel, Internal Revenue Service, 1977-1981. *Member:* The District of Columbia Bar; New York State and American Bar Associations. ***PRACTICE AREAS:*** Taxation; Partnership Taxation; Mineral Taxation; Corporate Law; Business Law. ***Email:*** dcubeta@milchev.com

JOEL DAVIDOW, born Trenton, New Jersey, July 24, 1938; admitted to bar, 1965, District of Columbia; 1981, New York. *Education:* Princeton University (B.A., summa cum laude, 1960); Columbia University (LL.B., 1963). Notes and Comments Editor, Columbia Law Review, 1962-1963. Author: Antitrust Guide for International Commerce, BNA 5th Edition, 2001; "International Competition Rules for the 1990s," The American University Journal of International Law and Policy, Spring 1991. Co-Author: "Antitrust Merger Control and National Security Review of Foreign Acquisitions in the U.S.," 24 J. World Trade 39, 1990. Adjunct Professor, George Mason University International Law School. Chief, Foreign Commerce Section, Antitrust Division, U.S. Department of Justice, 1973-1977. Trial Attorney, Regulated Industries Section, Antitrust Division, U.S. Department of Justice, 1971-1973; U.S. Delegate, U.N. Conference on a Restrictive Business Practices Code of Conduct, 1975-1980; Director, Policy Planning, Antitrust Division, U.S. Department of Justice, 1978-1981. Foreign Editor, The Antitrust Bulletin, 1981—. Member, U.S. Canada FTA Dispute Settlement Panel, 1991-1995. *Member:* The District of Columbia Bar; New York State and American Bar Associations. ***PRACTICE AREAS:*** Antitrust Law; International Litigation; Intellectual Property Litigation; Trade Regulation Law. ***Email:*** jdavidow@milchev.com

F. AMANDA DeBUSK, born Chilhowie, Virginia, December 20, 1955; admitted to bar, 1981, District of Columbia. *Education:* University of Richmond (B.A., summa cum laude, 1976); Harvard University (J.D., 1981). Phi Beta Kappa. Assistant Secretary for Export Enforcement Department of Commerce, Presidential Appointment. *Member:* The District of Columbia Bar; American Bar Association. ***PRACTICE AREAS:*** International Trade. ***Email:*** adebusk@milchev.com

PETER D. EHRENHAFT, born Austria, 1933; admitted to bar, 1958, New York; 1961, District of Columbia. *Education:* Columbia University (A.B., with honors, 1954; LL.B., with honors, 1957; M.I.A., with honors, 1957). Motions Law Clerk, U.S. Court of Appeals for D.C. Circuit, 1957-1958; Senior Law Clerk to Chief Justice Earl Warren, U.S. Supreme Court, 1961-1962. Deputy Assistant Secretary and Special Counsel (Tariff Affairs), U.S. Department of the Treasury, 1977-1979. Member: Advisory Committee on the U.S. Court of Appeals for the Federal Circuit, 1992-1996; U.S. Department of Commerce Industry Sector Advisory Committee on Trade in Services, 1999—; Licensing Executives Society; Advisory Boards, Georgetown University Journal of Law & Policy in International Business, 1970—; Bureau of National Affairs Patent Trademark & Copyright Journal, 1970—; American Society of International

(This Listing Continued)

MILLER & CHEVALIER, CHARTERED, Washington—Continued

Law International Legal Materials, 1979-1987. Professional Lecturer in Law, George Washington University Law School, 1966-1972. Adjunct Professor, University of Pennsylvania Law School, 1980-1985. Member, Panel of Arbitrators, American Arbitration Association. *Member:* American Bar Association (Member: Commission on Multijurisdictional Practice, 2000—; Council of Section on International Law and Practice, 1982-1986, 1989-1997; International Legal Scholar, 1994-1997); Washington Foreign Law Society (President, 1986-1988); American Law Institute (Member: Consultative Group on Restatements of Law of Unfair Competition, 1990-1995; Transnational Rules of Civil Procedure, 1999—); American Society of International Law. ***LANGUAGES:*** German. ***PRACTICE AREAS:*** International Trade Law; Transnational Business Transactions; Licensing Law. ***Email:*** pehrenhaft@milchev.com

F. DAVID FOSTER, born Miami, Florida, June 5, 1946; admitted to bar, 1973, District of Columbia; 1982, U.S. Court of Appeals for the Federal Circuit and U.S. Court of International Trade. *Education:* Arizona State University (B.A., 1969; J.D., 1972); Columbia University (LL.M., 1973). Attorney Adviser, Office of the General Counsel, 1973-1975, Assistant to the Chairman, 1975-1977, U.S. International Trade Commission; International Trade Counsel, U.S. Senate Committee on Finance, 1977-1980. *Member:* The District of Columbia Bar; American Bar Association; ITC Trial Lawyers Association (President, 1988-1989). ***PRACTICE AREAS:*** International Trade Law; Unfair Competition Law. ***Email:*** dfoster@milchev.com

LAWRENCE B. GIBBS, born Hutchinson, Kansas; admitted to bar, 1963, Texas; 1994, District of Columbia. *Education:* Yale University (B.A., magna cum laude, 1960); University of Texas (LL.B., with honors, 1963). Commissioner of Internal Revenue, 1986-1989; Assistant Commissioner (Technical) IRS, 1973-1976; Acting Chief Counsel, IRS, 1973; Deputy Chief Counsel, IRS, 1972-1973. *Member:* The District of Columbia Bar; Federal (Chair, Taxation Section, 1976-1977) and American (Vice Chair, Administration, 1991-1993 and Chair, Administrative Practice Committee, 1981-1983, Section of Taxation) Bar Associations; American College of Tax Counsel; American College of Trust and Estate Counsel (Member, Board of Regents, 1987-1996); American Law Institute; American Tax Policy Institute (Trustee, 1996—); Southern Federal Tax Institute (Trustee, 1989—). ***PRACTICE AREAS:*** Taxation; Tax Litigation; Legislative Practice; Corporate Taxation; International Taxation. ***Email:*** lgibbs@milchev.com

ROBERT E. HERZSTEIN, born Denver, Colorado; admitted to bar, 1955, Colorado; 1959, District of Columbia. *Education:* Harvard University (A.B., magna cum laude, 1952; LL.B., magna cum laude, 1955). Phi Beta Kappa. Editor, Harvard Law Review, 1953-1955. Lecturer in Law, Harvard Law school, 1999. Assistant to General Counsel, Department of the Army, 1955-1958. Under Secretary for International Trade, U.S. Department of Commerce, 1980-1981. Trustee, International Law Institute, 1974—. Chairman, Standing Committee on Customs Law, American Bar Association, 1976-1979. Director, International Human Rights Law Group, 1984—, Council of the Americas, 1995—; Partners for Democratic Change, 1998—; Appleseed Foundation, 1998—. ***PRACTICE AREAS:*** International Trade and Investment; Administrative Law; Litigation; Antitrust. ***Email:*** rherzstein@milchev.com

ALAN I. HOROWITZ, born Pittsburgh, Pennsylvania; admitted to bar, 1977, District of Columbia; 1981, U.S. Supreme Court. *Education:* Massachusetts Institute of Technology (B.S., 1974); Columbia Law School (J.D., 1977). Harlan Fiske Stone Scholar. Articles and Book Reviews Editor, Columbia Law Review, 1976-1977. Assistant to the Solicitor General, 1979-1986; Tax Assistant to the Solicitor General, 1986-1990, U.S. Department of Justice. *Member:* The District of Columbia Bar; American Bar Association. ***PRACTICE AREAS:*** Appellate Practice; Litigation; U.S. Supreme Court Litigation; Tax Appeals; Tax Litigation. ***Email:*** ahorowitz@milchev.com

PETER B. HUTT II, born Washington, D.C.; admitted to bar, 1990, Maryland and District of Columbia. *Education:* Yale University (B.A., cum laude, 1984); Stanford University (J.D., 1989). Senior Articles Editor, Stanford Law Review. Law Clerk to Judge William W. Schwarzer, N.D. California; Judge Vaughn R. Walker, N.D. California. ***PRACTICE AREAS:*** False Claims Act; Qui Tam Litigation; Government Contracts; Health Care Litigation; Federal Civil Litigation. ***Email:*** phutt@milchev.com

THOMAS D. JOHNSTON, born Port Huron, Michigan; admitted to bar, 1976, District of Columbia. *Education:* University of Pennsylvania (B.S., cum laude, 1973); University of Michigan (J.D., magna cum laude, 1976). Managing Editor, University of Michigan Journal of Law Reform, 1975-1976. *Member:* The District of Columbia Bar; American Bar Association. ***PRACTICE AREAS:*** Taxation; Tax Litigation; Tax Appeals; Tax Audits; Litigation; Natural Resources. ***Email:*** tjohnston@milchev.com

KEVIN L. KENWORTHY, born Pampa, Texas; admitted to bar, 1985, Oklahoma; 1987, U.S. Tax Court; 1988, District of Columbia; 1994, U.S. Court of Federal Claims. *Education:* University of Oklahoma (B.B.A., with distinction, 1982); Southern Methodist University (J.D., 1985). Order of the Coif. Managing Tax Editor, Southwestern Law Journal, 1984-1985. Law Clerk to Judge William A. Goffe, U.S. Tax Court, 1985-1987. *Member:* The District of Columbia Bar; Oklahoma and American (Vice-Chair, Court Procedure Committee, Section of Taxation) Bar Associations. ***PRACTICE AREAS:*** Taxation; Federal Income Tax; Federal Tax Controversies; Tax Litigation; Mineral Taxation. ***Email:*** kkenworthy@milchev.com

PHILIP KARTER, born New York, N.Y.; admitted to bar, 1982, Wisconsin; 1984, Connecticut; 1987, New York; 1990, District of Columbia; 1997, Pennsylvania. *Education:* Emory University (B.A., 1979); University of Wisconsin (J.D., 1982); New York University (LL.M in Taxation, 1984). Recipient, Outstanding Attorney Award, 1990. Author, "IRS Access to Computerized Records of Corporate Taxpayers," 87 J. Tax'n., Sept. 1997. Co-Author, "Transfer Pricing for Services," Transfer Pricing Handbook, John Wiley & Sons, 1997. Trial Attorney, Tax Division, Department of Justice, 1986-1992. Barrister, J. Edgar Murdock Inn of Court. ***Email:*** pkarter@milchev.com

CLARENCE T. KIPPS, JR., born Arlington, Virginia; admitted to bar, 1953, District of Columbia; 1954, Virginia. *Education:* American University (B.S., 1951); The George Washington University (J.D., 1953). Member, The George Washington Law Review, 1952-1953. Co-Author: "Living with TINA: A Practical Guide to the Truth in Negotiations Act," Washington Legal Foundation, 1989; "TINA's New Teeth: Why Prosecutors and Plaintiffs Love the Truth in Negotiations Act," Washington Legal Foundation, 1990. Law Clerk, U.S. Court of Claims, 1953-1956. Chairman, Advisory Council to U.S. Court of Federal Claims, 1986—. Member, Procurement Planning Committee of NDIA, 1985—. Chairman, Practice and Procedures Committee of the BCA Bar Association, 1991-1992. Co-Chairman, Ad Hoc Committee for the Enactment of the Contract Disputes Act of 1978 (P.L.95-563). Chairman of a Committee to Restructure the Court of Claims into the Court of Appeals for the Federal Circuit and the U.S. Claims Court (P.L.97-1964). *Member:* The District of Columbia Bar; Bar Association of the District of Columbia (Chairman, Court of Claims Committee, 1976-1977); Virginia, Federal (Chairman, Board of Contract Appeals Committee, 1975-1976) and American (Chairman, Board of Contract Appeals Committee, 1973-1974; Member, Public Contracts Section Council, 1980-1984) Bar Associations; Federal Circuit Bar Association (President, 1990-1991; Chairman, Judicial Selection Committee, 1985-1990); U.S. Claims Court Bar Association (Member, Board of Governors, 1987). Fellow: American Bar Foundation. ***PRACTICE AREAS:*** Government Contracts; Government Construction Contracts; Legislative Practice; Fifth Amendment Law; Government Contract Fraud. ***Email:*** ckipps@milchev.com

PETER J. KOENIG, born Columbus, Ohio, August 5, 1955; admitted to bar, 1982, Pennsylvania (Not admitted in District of Columbia). *Education:* Ohio State University (B.A., 1977; Ph.D., Economics, 1981); University of Michigan (J.D.,.1981). Adjunct Faculty, Law and Economics, American University, 1987—. Office of Policy, Federal Trade Commission, 1983. International Trade Counsel, USX Corporation, 1981-1986. Post Editor, 337 Reporter, ITC Trial Lawyers Association. *Member:* American Bar Association (Member: Customs Committee; U.S. Administrative Conference Advisory Group to U.S. Congress on U.S. Dumping Law). ***PRACTICE AREAS:*** International Trade Law; Unfair Competition Law; Customs. ***Email:*** pkoenig@milchev.com

EMMETT B. LEWIS, born Wilmington, North Carolina; admitted to bar, 1967, Ohio and Georgia; 1974, U.S Supreme Court; 1980, District of Columbia. *Education:* Duke University (B.A., 1964; J.D., 1967). Phi Delta Phi. Trial Attorney, Civil Division, Department of Justice, 1971-1979. Assistant Chief, Admiralty and Shipping Section, U.S. Department of Justice, 1974-1978. Assistant Director, Torts Branch, Civil Division, U.S. Department of Justice, 1978-1979. *Member:* The District of Columbia Bar; Bar Association of the District of Columbia; American Bar Association. ***PRACTICE AREAS:*** Federal Litigation; Tax Controversies and Litigation; Government Contract Litigation. ***Email:*** elewis@milchev.com

ROBERT E. LILES, II, born Pomona, California; admitted to bar, 1978, New York; 1979, District of Columbia. *Education:* Claremont McKenna College (B.A., summa cum laude, 1975); Columbia University (J.D., 1977). Harlan Fiske Stone Scholar, Columbia University, 1975-1977. Associate Editor, Columbia Journal of Transnational Law, 1977. *Member:* The District of Columbia Bar; American Bar Association (Chair, Tax Accounting Committee, 1994-1996, Section of Taxation). ***PRACTICE AREAS:*** Corporate Tax Controversies; Accounting Law; Federal Income Tax; Tax Appeals; Tax Audits; Taxation. ***Email:*** rliles@milchev.com

LUCINDA A. LOW, born Denver, Colorado; admitted to bar, 1977, California; 1979, District of Columbia; 1984, Colorado. *Education:* Pomona College (B.A., 1973); University of California at Los Angeles (J.D., 1977). Member, Mortar Board. Associate Editor, 1975-1976 and Editor in Chief, 1976-1977, University of California at Los Angeles Law Review. Adjunct Professor: International Conflicts of Law, American University Law School, Washington D.C., 1983; International Business Transactions, University of Colorado School of Law, 1987, 1989. Chair, ABA Section of International Law and Practice, 1996-1997. Member, ABA Standing Committee on Law and National Security, 1991-1996. Council Member and ABA Representative, Inter-American Bar Association, 1998-2001. President, International Business Association of the

(This Listing Continued)

Rockies, 1987-1989. Member, Rocky Mountain District Export Council, 1987—. Member, Advisory Board, Procedural Aspects of International Law Institute, 1986-1990. Member, Board of Editorial Reviewers, The International Lawyer, 1987-1988. *Member:* American (Section of International Law and Practice) , Inter-American and International Bar Associations. ***LANGUAGES:*** Portuguese, Spanish, French and Italian. ***PRACTICE AREAS:*** Business Law; Corporate Law; International Law; International Trade; Investments. ***Email:*** llow@milchev.com

DANIEL W. LUCHSINGER, born St. Paul, Minnesota; admitted to bar, 1992, District of Columbia. *Education:* University of Minnesota (B.S., summa cum laude, 1988), Phi Beta Kappa; Georgetown University (J.D., magna cum laude, 1992), Order of the Coif. Sewall Key Prize. Author: "Committee Impeachment Trials: The Best Solution?" 80 Geo. L.J. 163 (1991). *Member:* The District of Columbia Bar (Member: Taxation Section; Young Tax Practitioners Committee); American Bar Association (Member, Taxation Section). ***REPORTED CASES:*** McKean v. United States, 33 Fed. Ct. 535 (1995). ***PRACTICE AREAS:*** Taxation; Federal Income Tax; International Taxation; Tax Planning. ***Email:*** dluchsinger@milchev.com

PHILLIP L. MANN, born Alva, Oklahoma; admitted to bar, 1962, Texas; 1975, District of Columbia. *Education:* University of Oklahoma and University of Texas (B.B.A., 1962); University of Texas (LL.B., 1962). Phi Delta Phi; Beta Gamma Sigma. Deputy Tax Legislative Counsel, 1973-1974 and Tax Legislative Counsel, 1974-1975, U.S. Treasury Department. Internal Revenue Service Commissioner's Advisory Group, Chair, 1987-1988, Member, 1994-1996. *Member:* The District of Columbia Bar; State Bar of Texas; American Bar Association (Chair, Section of Taxation, 1997-1998; Member of Council, Vice-Chair for Government Relations, Section of Taxation, 1992-1993); National Tax Association (Member, Board of Directors, 1991-1994). Fellow: American College of Tax Counsel; American Bar Foundation; American Law Institute. ***PRACTICE AREAS:*** Taxation; Business Taxation; Financial Institutions Taxation; Oil and Gas Taxation; Tax Controversies. ***Email:*** pmann@milchev.com

SAMUEL M. MARUCA, born Trenton, New Jersey; admitted to bar, 1983, District of Columbia; 1984, Connecticut. *Education:* Yale University (B.A., cum laude, 1977); Georgetown University (J.D., cum laude, 1982). Member, Georgetown Law Journal, 1980-1981. *Member:* District of Columbia Bar; International Fiscal Association. ***PRACTICE AREAS:*** Taxation; Tax Controversies; International Taxation; Tax Audits; Tax Planning. ***Email:*** smaruca@milchev.com

CHARLES F. B. McALEER, JR., born Washington, D.C.; admitted to bar, 1984, Virginia; 1985, District of Columbia. *Education:* Georgetown University (A.B., magna cum laude, 1981; J.D., 1984). Phi Beta Kappa; Phi Delta Phi. *Member:* District of Columbia Bar; Virginia State Bar; Alexandria, Fairfax, Virginia and American (Litigation Section) Bar Associations;. ***PRACTICE AREAS:*** Federal Civil Litigation; Complex Commercial Litigation; Professional Malpractice; Technology Law; Litigation. ***Email:*** cmcaleer@milchev.com

WILLIAM M. McGLONE, born Bronx, New York; admitted to bar, 1988, New York; 1989, District of Columbia and U.S. Court of Appeals for the Federal Circuit. *Education:* Harvard University (B.A., cum laude, 1982); Georgetown University Law Center (J.D., magna cum laude, 1987). Order of the Coif. Member, Journal of Law and Policy in International Business, 1985-1987. *Member:* The District of Columbia Bar; New York State, American (Chair, Committee on Export Controls and Economic Sanctions, Section of International Law and Practice, 1998—) and International Bar Associations. ***PRACTICE AREAS:*** International Trade Regulation; Export Regulation; Foreign Trade Sanctions; Import and Export Law; International Trade. ***Email:*** wmcglone@milchev.com

ROBERT L. MOORE, II, born Harrisonburg, Virginia; admitted to bar, 1964, Virginia; 1967, District of Columbia. *Education:* Davidson College (B.A., 1961), Phi Beta Kappa, Omicron Delta Kappa; University of Virginia (LL.B., 1964). Phi Alpha Delta; Order of the Coif. *Member:* The District of Columbia Bar; Bar Association of the District of Columbia; Virginia State Bar; Federal and American Bar Associations. ***PRACTICE AREAS:*** Taxation; Federal Tax Controversies; Tax Appeals; Tax Audits; Tax Controversies; Tax Litigation. ***Email:*** rmoore@milchev.com

HOMER E. MOYER, JR., born Atlanta, Georgia; admitted to bar, 1967, Georgia; 1973, District of Columbia. *Education:* Emory University (B.A., 1964), Phi Beta Kappa; Omicron Delta Kappa; Yale Law School (LL.B., 1967). Co-Author: "Export Controls as Instruments of Foreign Policy," ILI, 1989; "Justice and the Military," PLEI, 1972. Deputy General Counsel, 1976-1978, Counsellor to the Secretary, 1979 and General Counsel, 1980-1981, U.S. Department of Commerce. President, Washington Council of Lawyers, 1977-1978. *Member:* The District of Columbia Bar; American Bar Association (Chairman, 1990-1991, and Vice-Chairman, 1986-1989, Section of International Law and Practice; Chairman, International Trade Committee, 1984-1986; Co-Founder and Chairman, Central and East European Law Initiative, 1990—). [LCDR, U.S. Navy, JAG, 1967-1971]. ***PRACTICE AREAS:*** International Trade Regulation; Foreign Corrupt Practices Act; North American Free Trade Agreement; International Dispute Resolution; International Trade. ***Email:*** hmoyer@milchev.com

(This Listing Continued)

MATTHEW M. NOLAN, born Washington, D.C.; admitted to bar, 1986, Maryland; 1989, District of Columbia; 1994, U.S. Court of International Trade; U.S. Court of Appeals for the Federal Circuit. *Education:* Tufts University (B.A., 1980); George Washington University (M.A., 1983); Georgetown University (J.D., 1986). Author: "Obscure NAFTA Clause Empowers Private Parties," The National Law Journal, April 6, 1998; "U.S. Sanctions Law: A Complex Web for U.S. and Foreign Companies," Oil and Gas Law and Taxation Review, March 1998; "NAFTA and North American Trade in Natural Gas," Natural Gas Contracts, August 1995. *Member:* The District of Columbia Bar; American Bar Association (Member, Sections on: International Law; Taxation). ***LANGUAGES:*** Spanish. ***PRACTICE AREAS:*** Antidumping; Countervailing Duty; Customs Law; Export Compliance; Export Regulation; Foreign Trade Sanctions; Latin American Trade. ***Email:*** mnolan@milchev.com

HERBERT ODELL, born Philadelphia, Pennsylvania; admitted to bar, 1963, Florida; 1968, Pennsylvania (Not admitted in District of Columbia). *Education:* University of Pennsylvania (B.S., 1959); University of Miami Law School (LL.B., magna cum laude, 1962); Harvard University (LL.M., Ford Fellow, 1963). Editor-in-Chief, University of Miami Law Review. Author: "What Constitutes a Change in Business Within the Confines of Section 382(a) of the Internal Revenue Code of 1954," 16 University Miami L.Rev.; "Purchase by Redemption, A Proposed Solution to the Taxation of the Remaining Shareholder," 17 University Miami L.Rev.; "Assessments: What Are They--Ordinary? Immediate? Jeopardy?" 31 NYU Institute on Federal Taxation, 1495; "Deductibility of Greenmail Payments," Tax Management Memoranda, Vol. 31, No. 23, p. 327. Adjunct Professor: University of Miami, 1977-1981; Villanova Law School, 1983-1985. Trial Attorney, Tax Division, U.S. Department of Justice, 1963-1965. ***Email:*** hodell@milchev.com

LYNDA TROUTMAN O'SULLIVAN, born Oil City, Pennsylvania; admitted to bar, 1978, District of Columbia; 1979, U.S. District Court, District of Columbia; 1985, U.S. Court of Federal Claims; 1986, U.S. Court of Appeals for the Federal Circuit; 1991, U.S. Supreme Court. *Education:* Albright College; American University (B.A., 1974); Georgetown University (J.D., 1978). Lecturer, The George Washington University Government Contracts Program, 1993-1998. Recent Publications include: "Deciphering Caldera v. Northrop Worldwide Aircraft Services, Inc. —The Concept of 'Benefit'and Its Role in Cost Allocation and Allowability," The Government Contractor (Fed. Pubs. January 2000); "CAS Board Review Panel Opts for Middle of the Road," The Government Contractor (Fed. Pubs. May 1999); "CAPS on Allowable Executive Compensation Costs: The Bottom Line," Government Contract Audit Report (The Lyman Group, June 1998). Co-author: "Commercial Item Acquisitions," Briefing Papers No. 97-5 (Fed. Pubs., April 1997); "Joint Ventures and Special Business Units A Primer on Cost Allowability, Accounting and Allocability," Government Contract Costs, Pricing and Accounting Report (Fed. Pubs. November 1996). Member, Federal Contracts Report Advisory Board (BNA), 1991-1997. *Member:* The District of Columbia Bar; American Bar Association (Chair, Accounting, Cost and Pricing Committee, 1996—; Council Member, 1993-1995; Chair, Truth in Negotiations Committee, 1991-1994, Section of Public Contract Law); National Contract Management Association; National Defense Industrial Association. ***PRACTICE AREAS:*** Government Contracts; Health Care Contracts; Federal Litigation; Alternative Dispute Resolution. ***Email:*** losullivan@milchev.com

C. FREDERICK OLIPHANT III, born Chattanooga, Tennessee; admitted to bar, 1975, District of Columbia. *Education:* University of North Carolina (A.B., 1971); University of Michigan (J.D., cum laude, 1975). Phi Beta Kappa. Member, University of Michigan Journal of Law Reform, 1973-1975. Member, Board of Advisors of the Journal of Taxation of Employee Benefits, 1993-2000. *Member:* The District of Columbia Bar; Bar Association of the District of Columbia; American Bar Association. ***PRACTICE AREAS:*** Employee Benefits; Qualified Retirement Plans; Executive Compensation; Fringe Benefits; Employment Tax. ***Email:*** foliphant@milchev.com

JEAN A. PAWLOW, born Detroit, Michigan; admitted to bar, 1989, California and District of Columbia. *Education:* University of California at Berkeley (B.S., with high honors, 1985); Harvard Law School (J.D., cum laude, 1988). Phi Beta Kappa; Beta Gamma Sigma. *Member:* The District of Columbia Bar; State Bar of California; American Bar Association (Member, Section of Taxation). ***PRACTICE AREAS:*** Taxation; Tax Controversies; Tax Litigation; Accounting Law; International Taxation. ***Email:*** jpawlow@milchev.com

SCOTT E. PICKENS, born Rochester, New York; admitted to bar, 1981, District of Columbia; U.S. Court of Federal Claims; U.S. Court of Appeals for the Federal Circuit. *Education:* Cornell University (B.S., with distinction, 1978; J.D., cum laude, 1981). Tau Beta Pi; Chi Psi. Editor, *Cornell Law Review*. Law Clerk to Judge John H. Pratt, U.S. District Court for the District of Columbia, 1981-1982. *Member:* The District of Columbia Bar (Member, Section of Government Contracts); American Bar Association (Co-Chair, Research and Development Intellectual Property Committee; Section of Public Contract Law; Member, Sections of Litigation and Business Law); National Defense Industrial

(This Listing Continued)

MILLER & CHEVALIER, CHARTERED, Washington—Continued

Association; National Contract Management Association. ***PRACTICE AREAS:*** Government Contracts; Information Technology Contracts; Intellectual Property; Government Contract Fraud; Bid Protests. ***Email:*** spickens@milchev.com

JOHN LLOYD RICE, born River Falls, Wisconsin; admitted to bar, 1965, Illinois; 1970, District of Columbia. *Education:* Wisconsin State University (B.S., 1962); Harvard Law School (LL.B., 1965). Co-author: "Living with TINA: A Practical Guide to the Truth in Negotiations Act," Washington Legal Foundation. Author: "Federal Circuit Voids Fixed-Price R&D Contract," Government Contractor (October 1997). Attorney, Office of the Secretary of Defense, 1967-1970. *Member:* The District of Columbia Bar; Bar Association of the District of Columbia; U.S. Court of Federal Claims Bar Association; Illinois State and American (Vice Chair, Judicial Remedies Committee, Public Contract Law Section, 1997-1998) Bar Associations. ***PRACTICE AREAS:*** Government Contracts; Government Agency Practice; Contract Litigation; Administrative Litigation; Federal Administrative Law. ***Email:*** jrice@milchev.com

FREDERICK H. ROBINSON, born Chicago, Illinois; admitted to bar, 1973, Virginia; 1974, District of Columbia. *Education:* Cornell University (B.A., 1967); University of Virginia (J.D., 1973). *Member:* The District of Columbia Bar; Bar Association of the District of Columbia; Virginia State Bar; American Bar Association. ***PRACTICE AREAS:*** Taxation; Health Insurance; Tax Litigation; Federal Tax Controversies. ***Email:*** frobinson@milchev.com

STEVEN M. ROSENTHAL, born Miami, Florida, September 30, 1957; admitted to bar, 1985, California; 1986, District of Columbia. *Education:* University of California at Berkeley (A.B., 1979; J.D., 1985). ***PRACTICE AREAS:*** Tax Law. ***Email:*** srosenthal@milchev.com

HAL S. SHAPIRO, born Manhasset, New York; admitted to bar, 1991, Connecticut; 1992, New York; 1994, District of Columbia. *Education:* Columbia College (B.A., summa cum laude, 1988); Columbia Law School (J.D., 1991). Phi Beta Kappa. Harlan Fiske Stone Scholar. Adjunct Assistant Professor, Columbia University Department of Political Science, 1992-1993. Trial Attorney, U.S. Department of Justice, 1993-1996. Associate General Counselor, U.S. Trade Representative, 1996-1998. ***PRACTICE AREAS:*** International Trade; International Trade Agreements; Import and Export Law; Foreign Trade Sanctions; Federal Litigation.

ANTHONY F. SHELLEY, born Buffalo, New York; admitted to bar, 1988, New York; 1989, District of Columbia. *Education:* Canisius College (B.A., summa cum laude, 1984); Harvard Law School (J.D., cum laude, 1987). Associate Editor, 1985-1986 and Recent Developments Editor, 1986-1987, Harvard International Law Journal. *Member:* The District of Columbia Bar; American Bar Association. ***PRACTICE AREAS:*** Federal Litigation; Employee Benefits and ERISA; Health Care. ***Email:*** ashelley@milchev.com

SERENA GRAY SIMONS, born Detroit, Michigan; admitted to bar, 1984, District of Columbia. *Education:* Duke University (B.A., 1971; J.D., with high honors, 1983); University of North Carolina (M.S.L.S., 1973). Executive Editor, Law and Contemporary Problems. Member, Employee Benefits Committee, Section of Taxation: American Bar Association, The District of Columbia Bar and Bar Association of the District of Columbia. ***PRACTICE AREAS:*** ERISA; Executive Compensation; Health Benefits; Qualified Retirement Plans. ***Email:*** ssimons@milchev.com

STURGIS M. SOBIN, born Derby, Connecticut, August 23, 1955; admitted to bar, 1983, District of Columbia; 1984, Virginia. *Education:* Harvard University (B.A., cum laude, 1977); The American University (J.D., 1983). Legislative Assistant, Senator Moynihan, 1978-1980. *Member:* The District of Columbia Bar; Virginia State Bar; Virginia and American Bar Associations. ***PRACTICE AREAS:*** International Trade Law; Antitrust; Unfair Competition Law; Intellectual Property Licensing; Intellectual Property Litigation. ***Email:*** ssobin@milchev.com

MARY LOU SOLLER, born Denver, Colorado; admitted to bar, 1977, Virginia; 1979, District of Columbia. *Education:* Wellesley College (B.A., with honors, 1974); Dartmouth College (Rufus Choate Scholar); Stanford Law School (J.D., 1977). Lecturer, Catholic University School of Law, 1986-1990. Staff Attorney, 1978-1984, Training Director, 1984-1988, Public Defender Service, Washington, D.C. Senior Investigative Counsel, Special Committee on Investigations, Select Committee on Indian Affairs, U.S. Senate, 1988-1989. Member, U.S. Sentencing Commission Practitioner's Advisory Group. *Member:* The District of Columbia Bar (Committee on Judicial Disabilities and Tenure Chair; Past Board of Professional Responsibility; Hearing Committee Chair); Virginia State Bar; American Bar Association (Past Chairman, Sentencing Guidelines Committee, Criminal Justice Section; Chairman, Procurement Fraud Committee, Public Contract Law Section); NACDL. ***PRACTICE AREAS:*** Criminal Law; Litigation; Government Contracts; Health Care. ***Email:*** msoller@milchev.com

(This Listing Continued)

PATRICIA J. SWEENEY, born Cleveland, Ohio; admitted to bar, 1980, Ohio; 1983, District of Columbia. *Education:* University of Michigan (B.A., magna cum laude, 1977); Boston University (J.D., cum laude, 1980); New York University (LL.M. in Taxation, 1983). Phi Beta Kappa. Editor, Boston University Law Review, 1979-1980. *Member:* The District of Columbia Bar; American Bar Association. ***PRACTICE AREAS:*** Taxation; Federal Tax Controversies; Federal Taxation; Nonprofit Tax Law; Natural Resources. ***Email:*** psweeney@milchev.com

ANTHONY J. TRENGA, born Wilmerding, Pennsylvania; admitted to bar, 1974, Virginia; 1975, District of Columbia. *Education:* Princeton University (A.B., 1971); University of Virginia (J.D., 1974). Law Clerk to Hon. Ted Dalton, U.S. District Judge, Western District of Virginia, 1974-1975. Member, 1981-1986 and Chairman, 1983-1985, Alexandria Human Rights Commission. Member, Virginia State Bar Eighth District Disciplinary Committee, 1989 (Secretary, 1990-1991; Chair, 1991-1992); Member, Virginia State Bar Disciplinary Board, 1996—. Master of the Bench, 1991, George Mason American Inn of Court, 1991—. Member: NASD Securities Arbitration Board, 1990—; Member, Virginia State Bar Client Protection Fund Board, 1992-1998. *Member:* The District of Columbia Bar; Virginia and American Bar Associations; Virginia State Bar; Virginia Association of Defense Attorneys. ***PRACTICE AREAS:*** Complex Commercial Litigation; Trial Practice; Professional Liability; Securities Litigation. ***Email:*** atrenga@milchev.com

JOEL C. WEISS, born Brooklyn, New York; admitted to bar, 1979, New York; 1981, Pennsylvania; 1983, New Jersey (Not admitted in District of Columbia). *Education:* Brooklyn College (B.S., Accounting, 1975); Brooklyn Law School (J.D., 1978); New York University Law School (LL.M. in Taxation, 1979). Attorney-Advisor, U.S. Tax Court, 1979-1981. ***Email:*** jweiss@milchev.com

ALEXANDER ZAKUPOWSKY, JR., born Perth Amboy, New Jersey; admitted to bar, 1973, District of Columbia. *Education:* Georgetown University (B.S.B.A., cum laude, 1968; J.D., 1972). Advisor on Tax Accounting Matters, Office of Tax Legislative Counsel, U.S. Treasury Department, 1976-1978. *Member:* The District of Columbia Bar; American Bar Association (Chair, Committee on Tax Accounting Problems, Tax Section, 1986-1988). ***PRACTICE AREAS:*** Taxation; Tax Litigation. ***Email:*** azakupowsky@milchev.com

DAVID W. ZIMMERMAN, born Casper, Wyoming; admitted to bar, 1987, New York; 1990, Texas; 1998, California; 1999, Florida (Not admitted in District of Columbia). *Education:* University of Texas (B.B.A., 1981; J.D., with honors, 1984); New York University (LL.M., Taxation, 1985). Beta Alpha Psi; Phi Delta Phi. Recipient, Wallace Scholarship. Managing Editor, Texas International Law Journal, 1983-1984; Graduate Editor, Tax Law Review, 1984-1985. *Member:* American Bar Association (Member, Corporate Tax Committee, Section of Taxation). ***PRACTICE AREAS:*** Taxation. ***Email:*** dzimmerman@milchev.com

OF COUNSEL

CHARLES T. AKRE, born Algona, Iowa; admitted to bar, 1934, District of Columbia; 1941, Illinois; 1960, Florida. *Education:* University of Iowa (B.A., 1931); The George Washington University (J.D., 1934); Graduate School of Banking, Rutgers University. *Member:* The District of Columbia Bar; Bar Association of the District of Columbia; The Florida Bar; Illinois State and American Bar Associations.

JOHN C. CHIU, born Taipei, Taiwan; admitted to bar, 1992, Pennsylvania (Not admitted in District of Columbia). *Education:* Fu-Jen Catholic University, Taiwan (LL.B., 1984); American University (LL.M., 1989); Tulane University (J.D., 1992). *Member:* Pennsylvania and American Bar Associations; National Asian Pacific American Bar Association. ***LANGUAGES:*** Mandarin Chinese and Taiwanese. ***PRACTICE AREAS:*** International Trade; Corporate Law. ***Email:*** jchiu@milchev.com

TERRY BANCROFT DOWD, born New York, N.Y.; admitted to bar, 1974, Connecticut; 1976, District of Columbia. *Education:* University of Wisconsin at Madison (B.A., 1965); University of Connecticut (J.D., magna cum laude, 1974). Associate Editor, University of Connecticut Law Review, 1974. Deputy General Counsel, Regulation Review, U.S. Department of Health and Human Services, 1979-1981. Attorney-Advisor, Office of General Counsel, U.S. Department of Transportation, 1978-1979. Attorney, Enforcement Division, U.S. Securities and Exchange Commission, 1975-1978. *Member:* The District of Columbia Bar; Connecticut Bar Association; National Health Lawyers Association; American Bar Association. ***PRACTICE AREAS:*** Government Contracts; Government Procurement; Federal Litigation. ***Email:*** tdowd@milchev.com

A. JOHN GABIG, born Washington, Pennsylvania; admitted to bar, 1963, Virginia; 1968, District of Columbia. *Education:* Gettysburg College (A.B., 1957); Dickinson School of Law (LL.B., 1961). *Member:* The District of Columbia Bar; Bar Association of the District of Columbia; Federal and American Bar Associations; Virginia State Bar. ***Email:*** agabig@milchev.com

(This Listing Continued)

PHILIP S. NEAL, born Washington, D.C., April 6, 1933; admitted to bar, 1959, Virginia and District of Columbia. *Education:* University of Colorado (A.B., 1954); The George Washington University (J.D., 1959). Phi Beta Kappa; Order of the Coif. *Member:* The District of Columbia Bar; American Bar Association; National Health Lawyers Association. ***Email:*** pneal@milchev.com

DAVID W. RICHMOND, born Silver Hill, West Virginia; admitted to bar, 1936, District of Columbia; 1946, Illinois; 1950, Maryland. *Education:* Hutchinson, Kansas Junior College; The George Washington University (LL.B., 1937). Member, Advisory Group to Commissioner of Internal Revenue, 1955. *Member:* The District of Columbia Bar; Bar Association of the District of Columbia; Illinois State Bar Association; American Bar Association (former member, Chairman, Section of Taxation, 1955-1957; Member, House of Delegates, 1958-1960); American Law Institute. Fellow, American Bar Foundation; American College of Tax Counsel.

NUMA L. SMITH, JR., born Rock Hill, South Carolina; admitted to bar, 1942, New York; 1947, District of Columbia. *Education:* Furman University (A.B., summa cum laude, 1938); Duke University (LL.B., with distinction, 1941). Order of the Coif. *Member:* The District of Columbia Bar; Bar Association of the District of Columbia; American Bar Association; American Law Institute (Life Member). Fellow: American Bar Foundation.

COUNSEL

KATHRYN CAMERON ATKINSON, born Bellingham, Washington; admitted to bar, 1992, Pennsylvania; 1994, District of Columbia. *Education:* Johns Hopkins University (B.A., 1989); Cornell University (J.D., 1992). Associate, 1990-1991, Executive Editor, 1991-1992, Cornell International Law Journal. ***LANGUAGES:*** German. ***PRACTICE AREAS:*** Foreign Corrupt Practices Act; International Trade Regulation; Federal Litigation. ***Email:*** katkinson@milchev.com

MICHAEL T. BRADY, born Seattle, Washington; admitted to bar, 1983, Washington; 1984, U.S. District Court, Western and Eastern Districts of Washington; 1990, District of Columbia and U.S. Claims Court; 1991, U.S. Supreme Court and U.S. Court of Appeals, First and Federal Circuits; 1993, U.S. Court of International Trade; 1997, U.S. Court of Appeals, Fourth Circuit; 2000, U.S. Court of Appeals, Fifth Circuit. *Education:* Pomona College (B.A., cum laude, with distinction in History, 1978); Yale University (J.D., 1983). Thomas J. Watson Fellowship, 1978-1979. Editor, The Yale Law Journal, 1982-1983. Author: "Executive Discretion and the Congressional Defense of Statutes," 92 Yale Law Journal 970, 1983; "Environmental Review of Military Base Closures: Implications for Affected Governments," II Duke Environmental Law Policy Forum 79, 1992. *Member:* Washington State and American Bar Associations; District of Columbia Bar; American Intellectual Property Association. ***PRACTICE AREAS:*** Litigation; Patent Litigation; Complex Litigation; Intellectual Property Litigation. ***Email:*** mbrady@milchev.com

PAUL CHERECWICH, JR., born Nyack, New York, March 4, 1941; admitted to bar, 1971, Massachusetts; 1985, Michigan; 1987, Pennsylvania; 2001, District of Columbia. *Education:* Rensselaer Polytechnic Institute (B.E.E., 1963); Suffolk University (J.D., 1971). ***PRACTICE AREAS:*** Taxation. ***Email:*** pcherecwich@milchev.com

MITCHELL W. DALE, born Cincinnati, Ohio, May 19, 1949; admitted to bar, 1976, Ohio, District of Columbia and U.S. District Court for the District of Columbia; 1979, Supreme Court; 1993, U.S. Court of International Trade; 1996, Virginia. *Education:* Duke University (B.A., 1971); Georgetown University (J.D., 1975; LL.M., with honors, International and Comparative Law, 1990). Attorney-Advisor, Office of the General Counsel, 1987-1989, and Legal Advisor to the Chairman, 1989-1993, U.S. International Trade Commission. Trial Attorney, Civil Rights Division of the U.S. Department of Justice, 1982-1987. *Member:* Washington International Trade Association; Virginia State Bar (Intellectual Property, International Practice and Litigation Sections); District of Columbia Bar. ***LANGUAGES:*** French. ***PRACTICE AREAS:*** International Trade. ***Email:*** mdale@milchev.com

JOHN E. DAVIS, born Augusta, Georgia; admitted to bar, 1991, Virginia; 1993, District of Columbia. *Education:* University of Virginia (B.A., with distinction, 1987); University of Virginia (J.D., 1991). Phi Alpha Theta. Research and Projects Editor, Virginia Journal of International Law, 1990-1991. *Member:* The District of Columbia Bar; Virginia State Bar; American Bar Association (Member, Section on International Law and Practice). ***PRACTICE AREAS:*** Foreign Corrupt Practices Act; Import and Export Law; International Trade Regulation; Foreign Trade Sanctions; Federal Litigation; International Trade. ***Email:*** jdavis@milchev.com

JANET A. FOREST, admitted to bar, 1978, Minnesota; 1982, New York; 1983, District of Columbia. *Education:* Gustavus Adolphus College (B.A., German, 1973); University of Minnesota Law School (J.D., 1978). Office of the Chief Counsel, U.S. Customs Service, 1980-1983; 1986-1987 and 1995-1996. Office of Tariff Affairs and Trade Agreements, U.S. International Trade Commission, 1983-1986. ***PRACTICE AREAS:*** Customs Law. ***Email:*** jforest@milchev.com

(This Listing Continued)

DAVID R. HAMILL, admitted to bar, 1988, New York; 1989, New Jersey (Not admitted in District of Columbia). *Education:* Bucknell University (B.A., 1981); Georgetown University (J.D., 1988). ***Email:*** dhamill@milchev.com

GEORGE A. HANI, born Washington, D.C.; admitted to bar, 1994, Maryland; 1996, District of Columbia. *Education:* Duke University (A.B., 1987); Harvard University (Ed.M., 1991); Catholic University of America (J.D., magna cum laude, 1994). Honors Attorney, Office of the General Counsel, U.S. Treasury, 1994-1996. *Member:* The District of Columbia Bar; Maryland State and American Bar Associations. ***PRACTICE AREAS:*** Federal Tax Controversies; Corporate Taxation; International Taxation; Employment Tax. ***Email:*** ghani@milchev.com

MARK VAN DYKE HOLMES, born Buffalo, New York; admitted to bar, 1984, New York; 1997, District of Columbia. *Education:* Harvard University (B.A., cum laude, 1979); University of Chicago (J.D., 1983). Law Clerk to the Hon. Alex Kozinski, U.S. Court of Appeals, Ninth Circuit, 1985-1987. Counsel to the Chairman, U.S. International Trade Commission, 1991-1997. ***PRACTICE AREAS:*** Federal Litigation; Tax Litigation; International Trade; Litigation. ***Email:*** mholmes@milchev.com

MARIA O'TOOLE JONES, born Cocoa Beach, Florida; admitted to bar, 1993, Virginia; 1996, District of Columbia. *Education:* University of Delaware (B.S., cum laude, 1988); George Washington University (J.D., with high honors, 1993); Georgetown University (LL.M., with distinction, 1999). Order of the Coif. Executive Articles Editor, George Washington University Journal of International Law and Economics. *Member:* The District of Columbia Bar; American Bar Association. ***PRACTICE AREAS:*** Taxation; Federal Income Tax; Tax Controversies; Tax Exempt Organizations; Employee Benefits. ***Email:*** mjones@milchev.com

JOHN S. LEVIN, born Philadelphia, Pennsylvania; admitted to bar, 1985, Pennsylvania (Not admitted in District of Columbia). *Education:* University of Pennsylvania, (B.S., Econ., magna cum laude, 1982); Phi Beta Kappa; Stanford University, (J.D., 1985). ***PRACTICE AREAS:*** Taxation; Federal; International Taxation; Federal Tax Controversies. ***Email:*** jlevin@mitchev.com

JOEL W. ROGERS, born Bitburg, Germany; admitted to bar, 1992, Virginia; 1995, U.S. Court of Appeals, District of Columbia Circuit; 1996, U.S. Court of Appeals, Federal Circuit, U.S. Court of Federal Claims and U.S. Court of International Trade; 1997, U.S. District Court, Eastern District of Virginia. *Education:* University of Virginia (B.A., 1989); Catholic University of America (J.D., 1992). *Member:* Virginia State Bar; Washington Law Society. ***LANGUAGES:*** Italian. ***PRACTICE AREAS:*** Customs; International Trade; Export Control; Intellectual Property. ***Email:*** jrogers@milchev.com

JERI KAYLENE SOMERS, born Wichita, Kansas; admitted to bar, 1986, Virginia; 1989, District of Columbia; 1999, U.S. Supreme Court. *Education:* George Mason University (B.A., 1983); Washington College of Law of American University (J.D., 1986). *Member:* Virginia State Bar (Member, Disciplinary Committee, 1999-2001); American Bar Association. [USAF, 1986-1991, U.S. Reserve, 1991-1993, DC Army Guard, 1993-1995, D.C. Air National Guard, 1995—, Lt. Col.]. ***PRACTICE AREAS:*** Government Contracts; Litigation. ***Email:*** jksomers@milchev.com

SENIOR ASSOCIATES

JOSEPHINE AIELLO LEBEAU, born Plainview, New York; admitted to bar, 1995, Virginia; 1998, District of Columbia. *Education:* Tulane University (B.S., summa cum laude, 1992; B.A., summa cum laude, 1992); Harvard University (J.D., 1995). Phi Beta Kappa; Pi Sigma Alpha; Upsilon Pi Epsilon. Articles Editor, Harvard Journal of Law and Technology. Technical Editor, Harvard Journal of Legislation. Author: Book Note, 30 Harv. J. on Legis. 553 (1993); "Congressional Cablevision: Turner Broadcasting v. Federal Communications Commission," 8 Harv. J.L. Tech. 231 (1994). *Member:* Virginia State Bar; American Bar Association. ***PRACTICE AREAS:*** Export Regulation; Import and Export Law; Foreign Trade Sanctions; International Trade; International Law. ***Email:*** jalebeau@milchev.com

MARJORIE A. BURNETT, born Oneonta, New York; admitted to bar, 1996, Connecticut; 1997, New York and District of Columbia. *Education:* Wharton School, University of Pennsylvania (B.S., 1977); Fordham University School of Law (J.D., cum laude, 1995). Order of the Coif. Notes and Comments Editor, Fordham Environmental Law Journal. Certified Public Accountant, Maryland, 1978. Law Clerk to Senior Judge Virgil Pittman, U.S. District Court for the Southern District of Alabama, 1995-1997. *Member:* The District of Columbia Bar; American Bar Association. ***PRACTICE AREAS:*** Taxation; Federal Tax Controversies; International Income Tax; Accounting Law; Tax Litigation; Tax Planning. ***Email:*** mburnett@milchev.com

MICHAEL L. BURTON, born New Orleans, Louisiana; admitted to bar, 1997, Maryland; 1998, District of Columbia. *Education:* Brown University (A.B., magna cum laude, 1994); Georgetown University Law Center (J.D., magna cum laude, 1997). Phi Beta Kappa; Order of the Coif. Notes and Comments Editor, Georgetown Law Journal, 1996-1997. Author: Note, " Legalizing the Sublegal: A Proposal for Codifying a Doctrine of Unilateral Humanitarian

(This Listing Continued)

MILLER & CHEVALIER, CHARTERED, Washington—Continued

Intervention," 85 Geo. L.J. 417 (1996). *Member:* American Society of International Law. ***PRACTICE AREAS:*** International Trade; Foreign Asset Control; Foreign Corrupt Practices Act; Foreign Trade Sanctions; World Trade Organization. ***Email:*** mburton@milchev.com

ANNE E. COLLIER, born Glen Cove, New York; admitted to bar, 1992, Michigan; 1993, District of Columbia. *Education:* University of Michigan (B.A., with high distinction, 1988; M.A., Public Policy, 1988; J.D., cum laude, 1991). Docket Attorney, Internal Revenue Service, Office of Chief Counsel, 1991-1995. Legislative Analysis Officer, Internal Revenue Service, 1995. Associate, King & Spalding, 1996-1998. *Member:* The District of Columbia Bar. ***PRACTICE AREAS:*** Taxation; Tax Accounting; Federal Tax Controversies; Tax Litigation; Tax Accounting of Technology; Joint Ventures. ***Email:*** acollier@milchev.com

JEANNETTE DAYAN, born New York, N.Y.; admitted to bar, 1996, New York (Not admitted in District of Columbia). *Education:* Williams College (B.A., summa cum laude, Phi Beta Kappa, 1992); Yale Law School (J.D., 1995). ***PRACTICE AREAS:*** Employee Benefits; Taxation. ***Email:*** jdayan@milchev.com

JACQUELINE DE GRAMONT, born Mexico City, Mexico; admitted to bar, 1998, District of Columbia. *Education:* The American University (B.A., magna cum laude, 1991); Georgetown University (J.D., cum laude, 1997). Public Interest Law Scholar. ***LANGUAGES:*** French and Spanish. ***PRACTICE AREAS:*** International Trade; International Law; International Trade Regulation; Foreign Corrupt Practices Act; Import and Export Law. ***Email:*** jdegramont@milchev.com

PATRICK P. DE GRAVELLES, born Tracy, California; admitted to bar, 1995, California; 1998, District of Columbia. *Education:* Georgetown University (B.S.F.S., magna cum laude, 1987); University of California School of the Law (J.D., 1995). Phi Beta Kappa. ***PRACTICE AREAS:*** Business Litigation; Contract Litigation. ***Email:*** pdegravelles@milchev.com

ADAM P. FEINBERG, born Los Angeles, California; admitted to bar, 1994, Virginia; 1995, District of Columbia and U.S. District Court, Eastern District of Virginia. *Education:* Georgetown University (A.B., cum laude, 1991; J.D., cum laude, 1994). Georgetown Criminal Justice Clinic. *Member:* Virginia State Bar; The District of Columbia Bar; American Bar Association. ***PRACTICE AREAS:*** Government Contract Fraud; White Collar Crime; Government Contracts; False Claims Act. ***Email:*** afeinberg@milchev.com

MYLES S. GETLAN, born Baltimore, Maryland; admitted to bar, 1995, Maryland; 1998, District of Columbia. *Education:* Lafayette College (B.A., 1992); University of Pittsburgh (J.D., 1995); Georgetown University Law Center (LL.M., International and Comparative Law, 1998). Author: "Trips and the Future of Section 301: A Comparative Study in Trade Dispute Resolution," 34 Columbia Journal of Transnational Law 173 (1995); "WTO Dispute Settlement: Issues in Antidumping and Countervailing Duty Law," The Commerce Department Speaks on International Trade and Investment (PLI, 1998). Co-author: "The Globalization of International Trade Litigation," Minutes of the Eleventh Judicial Conference of the U.S. Court of International Trade, December 7, 1999. *Member:* American Bar Association. ***PRACTICE AREAS:*** International Trade. ***Email:*** mgetlan@milchev.com

SHANE T. HAMILTON, born Falls Church, Virginia; admitted to bar, 1997, Virginia; 1998, District of Columbia. *Education:* University of Virginia (B.A., 1993; M.A., 1997; J.D., 1997). Phi Beta Kappa. Executive Editor, Virginia Tax Review. *Member:* The District of Columbia Bar; Virginia State Bar; American Bar Association (Member, Section of Taxation). ***PRACTICE AREAS:*** Taxation; Federal Income Tax; Federal Tax Controversies; Tax Litigation; Tax Exempt Organizations. ***Email:*** shamilton@milchev.com

BRIAN A. HILL, born Benton Harbor, Michigan; admitted to bar, 1996, Missouri; 1997, District of Columbia. *Education:* Southwest Missouri State University (B.A., summa cum laude, 1993); Georgetown University Law Center (J.D., magna cum laude, 1996). Order of the Coif. Notes and Comments Editor, *The Tax Lawyer.* Author: Note, "First Amendment Vagueness and the Methodology Test for Determining Exempt Status," 48 Tax Lawyer 569 (1995). Law Clerk to the Honorable John M. Steadman, Associate Judge, District of Columbia Court of Appeals. *Member:* American Bar Association; Christian Legal Society. ***PRACTICE AREAS:*** Litigation; Defense Contract Fraud; Health Care Fraud; Civil Practice; Appellate Practice. ***Email:*** bhill@milchev.com

ZION LEVI, born Tel Aviv, Israel; admitted to bar, 1996, New York; 1998, District of Columbia. *Education:* Fordham University (B.A., magna cum laude, 1992); Brooklyn Law School (J.D., cum laude, 1995); New York University School of Law (LL.M., Taxation, 1996). Articles Editor, Brooklyn Journal of International Law. *Member:* New York State and American (Member, Foreign Activities of U.S. Taxpayers Section) Bar Associations. ***PRACTICE AREAS:*** Taxation; Tax Planning; Federal Taxation of Consolidated Group; International Taxation; Federal Tax Controversies. ***Email:*** zlevi@milchev.com

(This Listing Continued)

SARAH M. NAPPI, born Washington, D.C.; admitted to bar, 1996, Virginia and U.S. Court of Appeals, Fourth Circuit; 1997, District of Columbia; 1998, U.S. Court of International Trade. *Education:* Cornell University (B.A., 1992); Georgetown University Law Center (J.D., 1996). Editor, Georgetown International Environmental Law Review, 1995-1996. Judicial Clerk to the Honorable Ronna Lee Beck, Superior Court, District of Columbia, 1996-1997. *Member:* Bar Association of the District of Columbia; Virginia and American Bar Associations; Women's Bar Association of the District of Columbia; Women in International Trade. ***LANGUAGES:*** Spanish and Italian. ***PRACTICE AREAS:*** Customs; International Trade. ***Email:*** snappi@milchev.com

ROBIN H. VILLANUEVA, born Miami, Florida; admitted to bar, 1996, Maryland; 1997, District of Columbia and U.S. District Court, District of Maryland; 1998, U.S. District Court for the District of Columbia. *Education:* Hunter College of the City University of New York (B.A., summa cum laude, 1993); George Washington University (J.D., with honors, 1996). Phi Beta Kappa. Member, George Washington Journal of Law and Economics. Author: Note, "Free Trade and the Protection of Cultural Property," 29 Geo. Wash. J. Intl. L. & Econ. 547 (1995). *Member:* Maryland State and American Bar Associations; The District of Columbia Bar. ***PRACTICE AREAS:*** ERISA; Retirement Benefit Plans; Health Benefits; Deferred Compensation; Employee Benefit Taxation. ***Email:*** rvillanueva@milchev.com

ASSOCIATES

CHARLES F. ABERNATHY, born Nashville, Tennessee; admitted to bar, 2000, Maryland and U.S. Court of Appeals, Eighth Circuit (Not admitted in District of Columbia). *Education:* Georgetown University (B.A., 1991; J.D., cum laude, 1998). Executive Editor, Law & Policy in International Business, 1997-1998. *Member:* American Bar Association (Member, International Section, 2000). ***Email:*** cabernathy@milchev.com

TAMARA W. ASHFORD, born Boston, Massachusetts, December 19, 1968; admitted to bar, 1995, North Carolina; 1997, U.S. Court of Appeals, Fourth and Ninth Circuits; 1998, U.S. Supreme Court and U.S. Court of Appeals, Second, Fifth and Tenth Circuits; 2000, U.S. Court of Appeals, First Circuit (Not admitted in District of Columbia). *Education:* Duke University (B.A., 1991); Vanderbilt University (J.D., 1994); University of Miami (LL.M., Taxation, 1997). Phi Alpha Delta. Certificate of Specialization in International Tax, University of Miami. *Member:* American Bar Association (Member, Committees on: Court Procedures and Practice; U.S. Activities of Foreigners and Tax Treaties; Tax Section). ***REPORTED CASES:*** Francisco v. United States, 88 A.F.T.R.2d 2001, 2001 U.S. App. LEXIS 21236, F.3d. (3d Cir. 2001); Malachinski v. Commissioner, 88 A.F.T.R.2d 2001-6169, F.3d (7th Cir. 2001); Benci-Woodward v. Commissioner, 219 F.3d 941 (9th Cir. 2000); Tedori v. United States, 211 F.3d 488 (9th Cir. 2000); Allied Mutual v. Mid-Plains Waste Mgmt., 612 N.W.2d 488 (Neb. 2000). ***PRACTICE AREAS:*** Taxation; Tax Litigation; Tax Controversies; Federal Income Tax; International Taxation. ***Email:*** tashford@milchev.com

THOMAS E. COONY, admitted to bar, 1998, Virginia; 2000, District of Columbia. *Education:* Boston University (B.A., 1987); University of Virginia School of Law (J.D., 1998). ***Email:*** tcoony@milchev.com

LEONARD JON COOPERMAN, born Washington, D.C.; admitted to bar, 1998, Maryland; 1999, District of Columbia; 2000, U.S. District Court, District of Maryland. *Education:* University of Pennsylvania (B.A., 1995); Emory University School of Law (J.D., 1998). *Member:* Baltimore and American Bar Associations; Maryland State Bar Association, Inc.; The District of Columbia Bar. ***LANGUAGES:*** Spanish. ***PRACTICE AREAS:*** Corporate Law; Business Law; International Trade; Investments; Intellectual Property. ***Email:*** lcooperman@milchev.com

CHARLES F. DE JAGER, born Brussels, Belgium, April 21, 1971; admitted to bar, 2000, District of Columbia. *Education:* Brown University (A.B., 1993); Fordham University (J.D., 1996); College of Europe, Bruges (M.A.E.L.S.., European Law, 1997); Georgetown University Law Center (LL.M., 2000). ***LANGUAGES:*** French, Swedish, Italian and German. ***PRACTICE AREAS:*** International Trade; Antidumping; Customs Law; World Trade Organization; Export Control. ***Email:*** cdejager@milchev.com

WILLIAM C. ELWELL, born La Mesa, California, August 17, 1972; admitted to bar, 2001, Maryland (Not admitted in District of Columbia). *Education:* Brigham Young University (B.A., 1998); Georgetown University Law Center (J.D., cum laude, 2001). Executive Editor, Georgetown Law Journal, 2000-2001. Co-Author: "Prisoners Rights: Procedural Means of Enforcement Under 42 U.S.C. § 1983" 88 Georgetown Law Journal, 1753, 2000. ***LANGUAGES:*** Spanish. ***PRACTICE AREAS:*** Corporate Taxation; Technology and Science; International Taxation; Federal Tax Controversies; Exempt Organizations. ***Email:*** welwell@milchev.com

JEANNE K. FALSTROM, born Valparaiso, Indiana, January 8, 1967; admitted to bar, 2000, Virginia (Not admitted in District of Columbia). *Education:* University of Cincinnati (B.A., 1989); University of Virginia (M.A., English, 1995; J.D., 2000). Recipient, John M. Olin Prize in Law and Economics, University of Virginia School of Law, 2000. Articles Review Board Member,

(This Listing Continued)

1999-2000 and Editorial Board Member, 1998-1999, Virginia Law Review, University of Virginia School of Law. Law Clerk, Justice Barbara M. Keenan, Supreme Court of Virginia, 2000-2001. Author: "Give Section 357 the Boot: A Proposal for Taxing Liability Relief in Section 351 Transactions," 85 Va. L. Rev. 1205 (1999). *Member:* Virginia State Bar; Virginia Bar Association. ***PRACTICE AREAS:*** Taxation; Employee Benefits. ***Email:*** jfalstrom@milchev.com

KIMBERLY R. HEIFETZ, born Towson, Maryland, 1971; admitted to bar, 1998, Maryland; 2000, District of Columbia. *Education:* Smith College (B.A., 1993); American University, Washington College of Law (J.D., 1998). Author: "Striking a Balance Between Government Efficiency and Fairness to Contractors; Past Performance in Government Contracts," Administrative Law Review, 50:1. *Member:* American Bar Association (Member, Public Contracts Law Section). ***PRACTICE AREAS:*** Government Contracts; Commercial Law; Government Procurement; Bid Protests. ***Email:*** kheifetz@milchev.com

ALICIA D. LOMBA, born West Palm Beach, Florida; admitted to bar, 1999, New York and District of Columbia. *Education:* University of Miami (B.A., with honors, 1994); Georgetown University (J.D., cum laude, 1998). Member, American Society of International Law, 1998. *Member:* American Bar Association. ***LANGUAGES:*** Spanish. ***PRACTICE AREAS:*** International Law; International Trade; Foreign Asset Control; Customs Law; Export Regulation. ***Email:*** alomba@milchev.com

WILLIAM A. MACDONALD, born Quincy, Massachusetts; admitted to bar, 1999, District of Columbia. *Education:* Harvard University (A.B., 1985); Georgetown University (J.D., 1998). Order of the Coif. Executive Editor, Georgetown Journal of Legal Ethics. ***PRACTICE AREAS:*** Corporate Taxation; Exempt Organizations; International Taxation; Tax Practice; Tax Procedure. ***Email:*** wmacdonald@milchev.com

SASHA A. MASON, born Wilmington, Delaware; admitted to bar, 1999, Maryland (Not admitted in District of Columbia). *Education:* Union College (B.A., 1996); George Washington University (J.D., with honors, 1999). Phi Delta Phi. Member, Moot Court Board. Articles Editor, The George Washington Law Review. Author: "The National Security Council is not an Agency Under the Freedom of Information Act," 66 George Washington L. Rev. 996, 1998. Writing Fellow. ***PRACTICE AREAS:*** Federal Litigation. ***Email:*** smason@milchev.com

SYDNEY H. MINTZER, born Los Angeles, California, December 30, 1969; admitted to bar, 1998, California; 1999, District of Columbia. *Education:* University of California at Berkeley (B.A., 1991); University of California at Los Angeles (M.A., 1994); New York University (J.D., 1998). Phi Beta Kappa. Associate Casebook Editor. Member, Moot Court Board. *Member:* State Bar of California; The District of Columbia Bar. ***PRACTICE AREAS:*** International Trade; Antidumping; Export Regulation; Foreign Asset Control; Customs Law. ***Email:*** smintzer@milchev.com

RAGAN G. REEVES, born Dallas, Texas; admitted to bar, 1997, Texas; 1998, District of Columbia. *Education:* University of Texas, Austin (B.B.A., with highest honors, 1990; M.P.A., 1990; J.D., with honors, 1997). Order of the Coif. Member, Texas Law Review. Certified Public Accountant, Texas, 1992. Author: "IRS Cracks Down on Software Research-It's Tough to Claim Credit," Legal Times (July 5, 1999); "Revisiting the Funding Exclusion of the Research Tax Credit After Lockheed Martin Corp. v. U.S.," The Government Contractor, Vol. 41, N o. 2 (Jan. 13, 1999); "Franchise Blackmail and the NFL: What a City Can Do to Keep its Home Team," Texas Entertainment and Sports Law Journal, Vol. 5, No. 3, Fall 1996. *Member:* American Bar Association. ***LANGUAGES:*** German. ***PRACTICE AREAS:*** Taxation; Technology and Science; Aeronautical Technology; International Taxation; Tax Credits. ***Email:*** rreeves@milchev.com

MATTHEW REINHARD, born Philadelphia, Pennsylvania, March 23, 1974; admitted to bar, 2001, Virginia (Not admitted in District of Columbia). *Education:* Colorado College (B.A., cum laude, 1996); University of Iowa (J.D., with high distinctions, 1999). Order of the Coif. Law Clerk, Honorable Carolyn Dineen-King, U.S. District Court of Appeals for the Fifth Circuit. ***PRACTICE AREAS:*** Commercial Litigation; Government Contracts. ***Email:*** mreinhard@milchev.com

ELIZABETH ROBITSCHEK, admitted to bar, 2000, District of Columbia. *Education:* Florida State University (B.S., magna cum laude, 1996; M.Acc., 1997); Georgetown University (J.D., cum laude, 2000). Publications Director, The State and Local Tax Lawyer. Author: "Application of the Relation-Back Doctrine to Non-Charitable Gifts: Estate of Newman v. Commissioner," The Tax Lawyer, Winter 1999. ***PRACTICE AREAS:*** Taxation. ***Email:*** erobitschek@milchev.com

DAVID A. ROMAN, admitted to bar, 2000, District of Columbia. *Education:* Carleton College (B.A., 1993); Cornell University (J.D., magna cum laude, 1999). Recipient, Olin Scholarship, Study of Law and Economics. Member, Cornell Law Review. ***PRACTICE AREAS:*** Taxation. ***Email:*** droman@milchev.com

KARA N. SCHMIDT, born Hinsdale, Illinois; admitted to bar, 1999, District of Columbia. *Education:* University of Illinois (B.A., 1995); Georgetown University (J.D., cum laude, 1998). Phi Beta Kappa; Golden Key. Senior Editor, Georgetown International Environmental Law Review. *Member:* District of Columbia Bar; American Bar Association; National Environmental Policy Act (NEPA). ***PRACTICE AREAS:*** Qui Tam Litigation; Federal Litigation. ***Email:*** kschmidt@milchev.com

KRISTEN SMITH, born Hartford, Connecticut; admitted to bar, 1995, New Jersey; 1996, New York and District of Columbia; 1998, Illinois. *Education:* Catholic University of America (B.A., 1990); Syracuse University (J.D., 1994); Georgetown University (LL.M., 1995). Import Compliance Specialist, Antidumping and Countervailing Duty Division, International Trade Administration, U.S. Commerce Department, 1996-1998. ***PRACTICE AREAS:*** International Trade; Customs. ***Email:*** ksmith@milchev.com

DUNCAN N. STEVENS, born Doylestown, Pennsylvania, May 16, 1975; admitted to bar, 2001, District of Columbia. *Education:* Swarthmore College (B.A., 1996); Northwestern University (J.D., 2000). Christian Legal Society. Comment Editor, Journal of Criminal Law and Criminology Vol. 89-3. ***PRACTICE AREAS:*** Government Contracts; Litigation. ***Email:*** dstevens@milchev.com

JAMES G. TILLEN, born Thompson, Connecticut; admitted to bar, 1999, District of Columbia. *Education:* University of Connecticut (B.A., magna cum laude, 1996); George Washington University (J.D., with honors, 1999). Member, The George Washington Law Review, 1997-1999. ***PRACTICE AREAS:*** Federal Litigation; International Litigation. ***Email:*** jtillen@milchev.com

CHRISTINE S. TRAFFORD, born Fort Bragg, North Carolina, July 20, 1972; admitted to bar, 1998, Virginia (Not admitted in District of Columbia). *Education:* James Madison University (B.S., 1995); Catholic University (J.D., 1998). Associate Editor, Catholic University Law Review, 1997-1998. *Member:* Virginia State Bar. ***PRACTICE AREAS:*** Government Contracts. ***Email:*** ctrafford@milchev.com

ADAM B. WALKER, born Kansas City, Missouri, February 22, 1971; admitted to bar, 1999, Maryland; 2001, District of Columbia. *Education:* Northwestern University (B.A., 1993); Georgetown University (J.D., 1999). *Member:* American Bar Association. ***PRACTICE AREAS:*** Civil Litigation; Employee Benefits Litigation; Employment Law. ***Email:*** awalker@milchev.com

JEFFREY C. WALKER, born Silver Spring, Maryland; admitted to bar, 1998, Maryland; 1999, District of Columbia. *Education:* State University of New York at Buffalo (B.A., magna cum laude, 1994); George Washington University (J.D., with high honors, 1998). Phi Beta Kappa. Order of the Coif. Senior Notes Editor, Public Contract Law Journal. Law Clerk to Judge Lawrence S. Margolis, U.S. Court of Federal Claims. Author: "Enforcing Grants and Cooperative Agreements as Contracts Under the Tucker Act," 26 Public Contract Law Journal 683, 1997. *Member:* The District of Columbia Bar; Maryland State and American (Member, Section of Public Contract Law) Bar Associations. ***PRACTICE AREAS:*** Government Contracts; Federal Litigation; Qui Tam Litigation. ***Email:*** jwalker@milchev.com

LORI B. WITTLIN, born Dix Hills, New York; admitted to bar, 1998, Georgia; 1999, District of Columbia. *Education:* University of North Carolina (B.A., with distinction, 1995); Emory University School of Law (J.D., with distinction, 1998). Phi Beta Kappa. Executive Managing Editor, Emory Law Journal, 1997-1998. *Member:* State Bar of Georgia; District of Columbia Bar; American Bar Association. ***PRACTICE AREAS:*** Federal Tax Controversies; Corporate Taxation; International Taxation. ***Email:*** lwittlin@milchev.com

FOREIGN CONSULTANT

JOSE DE REYES, born Mexico City, Mexico, September 3, 1973; admitted to bar, 1997, Mexico (Not admitted in District of Columbia). *Education:* Escuela Libre De Derecho (Abogado, 1997); Columbia University School of Law (LL.M, 2000). Fulbright Scholar, Columbia University. Assistant Editor "NAFTA Natural Partners? Five Years of the North American Free Trade Agreement", Co Published by: Itam and Editorial Miguel Angel Porrua, Mexico, 2000. NAFTA Chapter 19 Binational Panel Assistant, 2000. ***LANGUAGES:*** Spanish. ***PRACTICE AREAS:*** International Trade; Investments; Alternative Dispute Resolution. ***Email:*** jdereyers@milchev.com

(This Listing Continued)

MILLER & COMPANY P.C.

1825 I STREET, N.W., SUITE 400
WASHINGTON, D.C. 20006
Telephone: 202-429-2017
Fax: 202-659-6848
Email: intllaw@millerco.com
URL: http://www.millerco.com

Kansas City, Missouri Office: 4929 Main Street, 64112. Telephone: 816-561-4999. Fax: 816-561-5999.
New York, N.Y. Office: 51st Floor, 233 Broadway, 10279. Telephone: 212-608-2707. Fax: 212-513-7206.

International Trade, Customs and Foreign-Trade Zone Law.

(This Listing Continued)

MILLER & COMPANY P.C., Washington—Continued

MARSHALL V. MILLER, admitted to bar, 1971, Missouri; 1978, U.S. Court of International Trade; 1982, U.S. Court of Appeals for the Federal Circuit; 1990, District of Columbia. *Education:* University of Missouri-Kansas City (B.A., 1967); University of Virginia (J.D., 1970). ***PRACTICE AREAS:*** International Trade Law; U.S. Foreign -Trade Zone Law; Customs Law; Government Relations Law. ***Email:*** mmiller@millerco.com

OF COUNSEL

THOMAS L. LOBRED, admitted to bar, 1969, District of Columbia; 1970, U.S. Court of Appeals for the Federal Circuit; 1983, Missouri and U.S. Court of International Trade. *Education:* University of Maryland (B.A., 1963); Northwestern University School of Law (J.D., 1966). ***PRACTICE AREAS:*** International Trade Law; U.S. Foreign -Trade Zones; Customs Law. ***Email:*** tlobred@millerco.com

(For Complete Biographical Data on all Personnel, see Professional Biographies at Kansas City, Missouri).

MILLER, HAMILTON, SNIDER, ODOM & BRIDGEMAN, L.L.C.

SUITE 200, 1925 K STREET, N.W.
WASHINGTON, D.C. 20006
Telephone: 202-429-9223
Telecopier: 202-331-0388

Mobile, Alabama Office: Miller, Hamilton, Snider & Odom, L.L.C., 254-256 State Street. P.O. Box 46. Telephone: 251-432-1414. Telecopier: 251-433-4106.
Montgomery, Alabama Office: Miller, Hamilton, Snider & Odom, L.L.C., Suite 305, One Commerce Street. Telephone: 334-834-5550. Telecopier: 334-265-4533.

Administrative, Admiralty, Antitrust, Aviation, Banking, Bank Regulation, Corporations, Energy, ERISA, Litigation, Securities, Taxation, Transportation and International Trade.

(For complete biographical data, see Professional Biographies at Mobile, Alabama)

MILLER THOMSON WICKENS & LEBOW LLP

Established in 1957

SUITE 610, 1919 PENNSYLVANIA AVENUE, N.W.
WASHINGTON, D.C. 20006
Telephone: 202-775-2400
Telecopier: 202-331-7538
Email: Washington@millerthomson.com

Edmonton, Alberta Office: Miller Thomson, Suite 2700 Commerce Place, 10155 102nd Street, Edmonton, Alberta, T5J 4G8. Telephone: 780-429-1751. Fax: 780-424-5866.
Toronto, Ontario Office: Miller Thomson, 20 Queen Street West, Suite 2500, Toronto, Ontario, M5H 3S1. Telephone: 416-595-8500. Fax: 416-595-8695.
York Region, Ontario Office: Miller Thomson, 60 Columbia Way, Suite 600, Markham, Ontario, L3R 0C9. Telephone: 905-415-6700. Fax: 905-415-6777.
Calgary, Alberta Office: Miller Thomson, 3000, 700 - 9th Avenue S.W., Calgary, Alberta, T2P 3V4. Telephone: 403-298-2400. Fax: 403-262-0007.
Law Firm Affiliations/Associations:
Priel, Stevenson, Hood & Thornton, Saskatoon, Saskatchewan
McCarter Grespan Robson Beynon - Kitchener, Ontario
Azevedo Sette Advogados - Sao Paulo and Belo Horizonte, Brazil, South America
Estudio Faraggi, Sateler & CIA - Santiago, Chile
Davies Arnold Cooper - London, England (Offices also in Manchester, Brussels, Vienna, Zurich, Madrid and Hong Kong)
Schürmann & Partners - Germany (Offices in Frankfurt, Berlin, Bonn, Dresden, Leipzig, Munich, Brussels, Milan, New York, Paris and Prague)

CONTACT: JOHN A. PETERS. Telephone: 403-298-2434. E-mail: jpeters@millerthomson.ca.

Commercial Litigation in all Federal Courts. International Trade and Customs. Administrative Practice before Federal Agencies.

LAW FIRM ALLIANCES/ASSOCIATIONS: **MULTILAW:** *An international association of over forty individual law firms.*

(This Listing Continued)

MEMBERS OF FIRM

WILLIAM E. WICKENS, born Elyria, Ohio, May 29, 1939; admitted to bar, 1964, Ohio; 1969, U.S. District Court, Northern District of Ohio; 1974, District of Columbia; 1975, Temporary Emergency Court of the United States; 1976, U.S. Supreme Court; 1978, U.S. Court of Appeals for the District of Columbia Circuit; 1979, U.S. District Court for the District of Columbia; 1987, U.S. Court of Appeals, Fifth Circuit. *Education:* DePauw University (B.A., 1961); University of Michigan (J.D., 1964). Phi Beta Kappa; Delta Sigma Rho. Winner, Campbell Competition (Appellate Advocacy), 1963; Director of Legislation and Research, Senator Robert Taft, 1971-1973. Counsel to Senator Lowell Weicker, Watergate Investigation, 1973. ***PRACTICE AREAS:*** Commercial Law; Litigation; Administrative Law.

EDWARD M. LEBOW, born Boston, Massachusetts, 1948; admitted to bar, 1974, Massachusetts; 1977, District of Columbia; 1988, New York. *Education:* Harvard (B.A., cum laude, 1970; J.D., 1974). International Honors Program for Study in Asia. Author: "U.S. International Trade Laws," Asia Publishing Company, Seoul, Korea, 1986; "Avoiding U.S. Antidumping Law Problems," Bank of Tokyo, Tokyo, Japan, 1986. Attorney-Advisor, 1976-1980, Acting Chief, Unfair Import Investigations Division, Section 337, 1980 and Assistant General Counsel, 1981, U.S. International Trade Commission. *Member:* The District of Columbia Bar. ***LANGUAGES:*** French and Japanese. ***PRACTICE AREAS:*** International Trade and Customs; Administrative Law; Commercial Law.

OF COUNSEL

JOSEPH S. HOOVER, JR., born Washington, D.C., May 28, 1959; admitted to bar, 1986, Virginia; 1988, U.S. Court of Appeals, Fifth Circuit; 1989, District of Columbia. *Education:* University of Virginia (B.A., with distinction, 1981); National Law Center, George Washington University (J.D., with high honors, 1986). Order of the Coif. Managing Editor, George Washington Law Review, 1985-1986. *Member:* Virginia State Bar. ***PRACTICE AREAS:*** Commercial Law; Environmental Law; Litigation; Administrative Law.

BEVERLY D. ROSS, born Jersey City, New Jersey, 1946; admitted to bar, 1974, District of Columbia; 1976, Virginia. *Education:* New York University (B.A., 1968); George Washington University (J.D., 1974; LL.M., with highest honors, 1993). International Shipping and Trade Attorney, Arent Fox Kintner Plotkin & Klahn, Washington, D.C., 1974-1975. Joint Venture and Project Finance Attorney, FINNFUND, Helsinki, Finland, 1982-1983. Lending Program Legal and Financial Risk Assessment Attorney, Nordic Investment Bank, Helsinki, Finland and Washington, D.C., 1983-1991. Cofinancing and Trust Fund Negotiating Attorney on financing and Private Sector Development Unit, Legal Department, World Bank (International Bank for Reconstruction and Development), Washington, D.C., 1993-1994. Board Member, Washington Foreign Law Society. ***LANGUAGES:*** Finnish, French, German, Italian, Norwegian, Spanish and Swedish. ***PRACTICE AREAS:*** International Banking; International Trade and Finance; Maritime Law.

MILLER & VAN EATON, P.L.L.C.

1155 CONNECTICUT AVENUE, N.W., SUITE 1000
WASHINGTON, D.C. 20036-4320
Telephone: 202-785-0600
Fax: 202-785-1234
Email: info2@millervaneaton.com
URL: http://www.millervaneaton.com

San Francisco, California Office: 400 Montgomery Street, Suite 501, 94104. Telephone: 415-477-3650. Fax: 415-477-3652.

Administrative, Business, Legislative and Litigation Practice in Telecommunications including: Cable Television and Electronic Media (franchise renewal, rate regulation, transfers, municipal system ownership, and public, educational and government (PEG) services), Telephone, Common Carrier and Wireless Services, Broadcasting, Satellite and New Technology Licensing, Consumer Protection and Fair Competition, Financing and Joint Ventures, and Privatization. Additional specialties include First Amendment, Constitutional Law, Intellectual Property Law, Public Utilities Law, Real Estate Law, State Tax Law, Transportation Law and Bankruptcy Law.

FIRM PROFILE: Miller & Van Eaton, P.L.L.C. is a Washington, D.C. law firm that traces its roots to 1985 and the formation of Miller & Holbrooke. Incorporating that practice, the firm today represents public and private sector clients in all types of telecommunications matters both domestically and internationally. Domestically, the firm is active in federal and state courts and before federal and state agencies, the U.S. Congress, and the federal Executive Branch. Firm attorneys combine legal expertise with specialized knowledge of communications technology. Internationally, the firm advises governments and private sector clients on telecommunications regulation, liberalization and privatization.

(This Listing Continued)

NICHOLAS P. MILLER, born Kansas City, Kansas, August 28, 1944; admitted to bar, 1973, Washington; 1978, District of Columbia. *Education:* University of Washington (B.A., 1966; J.D., 1973). Member, Washington Law Review, 1971-1973. Counsel, Senate Committee on Commerce, 1973-1977. Counsel, Senate Communications Subcommittee, 1976-1977. Consultant, Office of Telecommunications Policy, Executive Office of the President, 1977. Author: "Regulating Cable Television," 57 Washington Law Review 85; "Privatizing the National Telephone Company--How Do You Do It?" Pacific Telecommunications Council, PTC '91 Proceedings 12 (D. Wedenmeyer & M. Lofstrom ed., 1991). *Member:* The District of Columbia Bar; Washington State Bar; American Bar Association; Federal Communications Bar Association. ***PRACTICE AREAS:*** International Joint Ventures; Privatization; Communications Law; Media Law; Cable Franchising; Legislative Practice. ***Email:*** nmiller@millervaneaton.com

JOSEPH VAN EATON, born Memphis, Tennessee, August 14, 1953; admitted to bar, 1979, District of Columbia; 1981, U.S. Courts of Appeals for the District of Columbia and 5th Circuits; 1982, U.S. Court of Appeals, 9th Circuit and U.S. District Court for the District of Columbia; 1983, U.S. Court of Appeals, 11th Circuit; 1986, U.S. Supreme Court. *Education:* Syracuse University (B.A., 1975); University of Pennsylvania (J.D., 1979). Phi Beta Kappa. Author: "Denying Renewal Under the First Amendment and the Cable Act," 6 Card. Arts and Ent. L.J. 37, 1987. Board of Directors, Alliance for Community Media, 1983-1987. *Member:* The District of Columbia Bar; Federal Communications Bar Association. ***PRACTICE AREAS:*** Communications Law; Cable Franchising; Telecommunications Law; First Amendment Law; Electric Power. ***Email:*** jvaneaton@millervaneaton.com

WILLIAM R. MALONE, born Terre Haute, Indiana, April 15, 1936; admitted to bar, 1962, Indiana; 1963, District of Columbia; 1981, Connecticut. *Education:* Massachusetts Institute of Technology (Special Student, 1957); Harvard University (A.B., cum laude, 1958; J.D., cum laude, 1962). Vice President and Washington Counsel, GTE Corporation, 1970-1980. Vice President and an Associate General Counsel, GTE, Stamford, Connecticut, 1981-1986. Partner, Murphy & Malone, 1987-1990. Law Clerk to the Honorable Henry W. Edgerton, U.S. Court of Appeals for the District of Columbia Circuit, 1962-1963. Associate, Covington & Burling, 1963-1969. Member, Board of Trustees, Harvard Radio Broadcasting Co., Inc., 1984—. *Member:* The District of Columbia Bar; Federal and American Bar Associations; Computer Law Association; Federal Communications Bar Association (Chairman, Committee on Judicial Practice, 1987-1990); Institute of Electrical and Electronic Engineers (Senior Member, 1958—). ***PRACTICE AREAS:*** Administrative Agency Practice; Municipal Taxation; International Telecommunications Law; Communications Common Carrier; Broadcasting Law; Telephone Utility Regulation; Civil Appeals. ***Email:*** wmalone@millervaneaton.com

FREDERICK E. ELLROD III, born Washington, D. C., January 19, 1953; admitted to bar, 1986, District of Columbia. *Education:* Catholic University of America (B.A., summa cum laude, 1975; M.A., summa cum laude, 1976); Boston University (Ph.D., 1979); Harvard University Law School (J.D., cum laude, 1986). Phi Beta Kappa. *Publications:* Co-Author: *Rate Regulation and the Cable Television Consumer Protection and Competition Act of 1992* (with Lisa S. Gelb), 2 Maine Policy Review 51-56 (December 1993). Member, D.C. Computer Law Forum. *Member:* The District of Columbia Bar; American Bar Association; Federal Communications Bar Association. ***LANGUAGES:*** French, German. ***PRACTICE AREAS:*** Cable Franchising; Local Government Law; Municipal Leasing; Municipal Utility Regulation; Telephone Utilities. ***Email:*** fellrod@millervaneaton.com

MATTHEW C. AMES, born Arlington, Virginia, May 8, 1959; admitted to bar, 1987, Virginia; 1991, District of Columbia. *Education:* College of William & Mary (B.S., 1980); Georgetown University Law Center (J.D., cum laude, 1987). Phi Eta Sigma; Delta Phi Alpha. Staff Member, 1985-1986; Student Editor in Chief, 1986-1987, The Tax Lawyer. Author: "Formal Opinion 352: Professional Integrity and the Tax Audit Lottery," 1 Georgetown Journal of Legal Ethics, 411 (1987). Associate General Counsel, 1991-1992; Acting General Counsel, 1992-1993, Office of National Drug Control Policy, Executive Office of the President. *Member:* The District of Columbia Bar; Virginia State Bar; American Bar Association; Federal Communications Bar Association. [Capt., U.S. Army, 1980-1984]. ***LANGUAGES:*** Spanish and German. ***PRACTICE AREAS:*** Cable Franchising; Communications Law; Local Government Law; Information Technology; Contracts; Fifth Amendment Law; Property Law. ***Email:*** mames@millervaneaton.com

WILLIAM L. LOWERY, born Sharon, Pennsylvania, May 27, 1955; admitted to bar, 1993, California; 1996, District of Columbia. *Education:* Ohio University (B.S.C., 1977); Hastings College of the Law, University of California (J.D., 1993). Recipient, American Jurisprudence Award. Executive Associate Editor, Hastings Communications and Entertainment Law Journal. Extern to Hon. Thelton E. Henderson, Chief Judge, U.S. District Court, Northern District of California, 1991. *Member:* Bar Association of San Francisco; State Bar of California; The District of Columbia Bar; American Bar Association (Member, Forum Committee on Communications Law); Federal Communications Bar Association. (Resident, San Francisco, California Office). ***PRACTICE AREAS:*** Litigation; Local Government Law; Telecommunications Law; Intellectual Property; Cable Franchising; Cable TV. ***Email:*** wlowery@millervaneaton.com

OF COUNSEL

JAMES R. HOBSON, born Atlanta, Georgia, September 13, 1937; admitted to bar, 1972, California; 1973, District of Columbia. *Education:* Cornell University (B.A., 1959); Georgetown University (M.A., 1963); University of San Francisco (J.D., 1971). Co-Author: "Preemption of Local Regulation of Radio Antennas," 46 Fed. Comm. L.J., No 3, June, 1994. Washington Counsel, GTE Corporation, 1978-1990. Federal Communications Commission, 1972-1978. Chief, Cable Television Bureau, 1976-1978. *Member:* District of Columbia Bar; State Bar of California; American Bar Association; Federal Communications Bar Association (Member, Executive Committee, 1984-1987, 1994-1996); American Arbitration Association (Member, National Panel; Trained Mediator). ***PRACTICE AREAS:*** Communications Law; Administrative Law; Public Utilities Law. ***Email:*** jhobson@millervaneaton.com

GERARD L. LEDERER, born Philadelphia, Pennsylvania, April 18, 1958; admitted to bar, 1983, Pennsylvania; 1984, New Jersey (Not admitted in District of Columbia). *Education:* Haverford College (B.A., 1980); Temple University (J.D., 1983). ***PRACTICE AREAS:*** Telecommunications Law; Private Property; Contracts/Licensing; Advocacy. ***Email:*** glederer@millervaneaton.com

ASSOCIATES

MARCI LYNN FRISCHKORN, born New Brighton, Pennsylvania, July 7, 1969; admitted to bar, 1994, Virginia (Not admitted in District of Columbia). *Education:* West Virginia University (B.A., 1991); Dickinson School of Law (J.D., 1994). *Member:* Virginia Bar Association; Federal Communications Bar Association. ***PRACTICE AREAS:*** Cable Franchising; Cable TV; Communications Law; Telecommunications Competition; Telecommunications Regulation; Regulatory Agency Practice. ***Email:*** mfrischkorn@millervaneaton.com

MITSUKO R. HERRERA, born Hollywood, California, August 1, 1969; admitted to bar, 2000, California (Not admitted in District of Columbia). *Education:* University of California at San Diego (B.A., cum laude, 1992); Georgetown University Law Center (J.D., 1998). *Member:* State Bar of California; Federal Communications Bar Association. ***PRACTICE AREAS:*** Telecommunications Law; Cable TV; Local Government Law; Copyrights; Trademarks; Intellectual Property. ***Email:*** mherrera@millervaneaton.com

KENNETH A. BRUNETTI, born Berkeley, California, July 15, 1964; admitted to bar, 1991, California; U.S. Court of Appeals, Ninth Circuit; U.S. District Court, Northern, Central and Eastern Districts of California. *Education:* University of Pennsylvania (B.A., 1986); Hastings College of the Law, University of California (J.D., magna cum laude, 1991). Order of the Coif; Thurston Society. Note Editor, The Hastings Law Journal. Author: "It's Time to Create A Bay Area Regional Government," 42 Hastings Law Journal 1103 (1991). *Member:* Bar Association of San Francisco (Member, Commercial Law and Bankruptcy Section); State Bar of California. (Resident, San Francisco, California Office). ***PRACTICE AREAS:*** Telecommunications Law; Cable TV; Local Government Law; Cable Franchising; Bankruptcy. ***Email:*** kbrunetti@millervaneaton.com

HOLLY LYNN SAURER, born San José dos Campos, Brazil, March 2, 1972; admitted to bar, 2000, Maryland (Not admitted in District of Columbia). *Education:* Syracuse University (B.S., 1993); Washington College of Law of American University (J.D., 2000). ***LANGUAGES:*** French. ***PRACTICE AREAS:*** Telecommunications Law; Cable TV; Cable Franchising; Local Government Law. ***Email:*** hsaurer@millervaneaton.com

MINTZ, LEVIN, COHN, FERRIS, GLOVSKY AND POPEO, P.C.

701 PENNSYLVANIA AVENUE, N.W.
WASHINGTON, D.C. 20004-2608
Telephone: 202-434-7300
Fax: 202-434-7400
Internet: Each Attorney's Internet Address takes the following form: first initial, last name @mintz.com (e.g., rmintz@mintz.com)
URL: http://www.mintz.com

Boston, Massachusetts Office: One Financial Center. Telephone: 617-542-6000. Fax: 617-542-2241.

New York, N.Y. Office: Chrysler Center, 666 Third Avenue. Telephone: 212-935-3000. Fax: 212-983-3115.

New Haven, Connecticut Office: 157 Church Street. Telephone: 203-777-8200. Fax: 203-777-7111.

Reston, Virginia Office: One Fountain Square, 11911 Freedom Drive. Telephone: 703-464-4800. Fax: 703-464-4895.

(This Listing Continued)

MINTZ, LEVIN, COHN, FERRIS, GLOVSKY AND POPEO, P.C., Washington—Continued

Administrative, Antitrust and Trade, Banking, Business Law, Cable Programming, Class Actions, College and University Law, Communications, Copyright Litigation, Copyrights, Corporate Law, Environmental, FCC Regulation, Federal Education Grants, Federal Practice, Finance, Food and Drug, Government, Health Care, Health Care Fraud, Health Care Legislation, Health Care Mergers and Acquisitions, Health Care Reimbursement, Intellectual Property, International, Internet Law, Investments, Legislation, Litigation, Medicare and Medicaid Reimbursement, Mergers and Acquisitions, Municipal Bonds, Real Estate, Regulatory Law, Satellite Communications, Securities, Technology Business Startups, Technology Finance, Telecommunications, Telemedicine, Trademarks, Venture Capital, Wireless Communications.

FRANCIS X. MEANEY, born January 15, 1933; admitted to bar, 1960, Mass.; 1972, D.C.; 1986, N.Y. *Education:* University of Notre Dame (A.B., 1954); Harvard Law School (LL.B., 1960). President, Mintz, Levin, Cohn, Ferris, Glovsky and Popeo, P.C., 1984-1991; Chairman, ML Strategies, Inc., 1991—. *Member:* The District of Columbia Bar; International Bar Association; National Association of Bond Lawyers. ***PRACTICE AREAS:*** Financial Services Law; Federal and State Relations Law; Health Care.

CHARLES D. FERRIS, born April 9, 1933; admitted to bar, 1961, Mass.; 1969, D.C. *Education:* Boston College (A.B., 1954; J.D., 1961). Member, Boston College Law Review, 1960-1961. Trial Attorney, U.S. Department of Justice, 1961-1963; General Counsel to U.S. Senate Majority Leader and Staff Director and General Counsel to Senate Democratic Policy Committee, 1964-1976; Chief Counsel to the Speaker of the U.S. House of Representatives, 1976-1977. Chairman, Federal Communications Commission, 1977-1981. *Member:* The District of Columbia Bar. ***PRACTICE AREAS:*** Litigation; Telecommunications; Legislation.

NATHAN LEWIN, born January 31, 1936; admitted to bar, 1962, N.Y.; 1963, D.C. *Education:* Yeshiva College (B.A., summa cum laude, 1957); Harvard Law School (J.D., magna cum laude, 1960). Editor, 1958-1959 and Treasurer, 1959-1960, Harvard Law Review. Adjunct Professor, Georgetown Law School, 1971-1974, 1975-1977. Visiting Professor, Harvard Law School, 1974-1975. Lecturer: University of Chicago Law School, 1994; Columbia Law School, 1996-2001; George Washington University Law School, 1998, 2001. Law Clerk to: Chief Judge J. Edward Lumbard, U.S. Court of Appeals, Second Circuit, 1960-1961; Justice John M. Harlan, U.S. Supreme Court, 1961-1962. Special Assistant to Assistant Attorney General, Criminal Division, Department of Justice, 1962-1963. Assistant to Solicitor General, Department of Justice, 1963-1967. Deputy Administrator, Bureau of Security and Consular Affairs, Department of State, 1967-1968. Deputy Assistant Attorney General, Civil Rights Division, Department of Justice, 1968-1969. *Member:* The District of Columbia Bar; Bar Association of the District of Columbia; Federal and American Bar Associations; International Association of Jewish Lawyers and Jurists (President, American Section, 1991-1996; Honorary President, 1996-2001). ***LANGUAGES:*** Hebrew and Yiddish. ***REPORTED CASES:*** Barnett Bank of Marion County v. Nelson, 116 S.Ct. 1103 (1996); K-Mart Corp. v. Cartier, 486 U.S. 281 (1988); County of Allegheny v. ACLU, 492 U.S. 573 (1989); Commissioner v. Shapiro, 424 U.S. 614 (1976); Smith v. Our Lady of the Lake Hosp., 960 F.2d 439 (5th Cir. 1992); United States v. Hansen, 772 F.2d 940 (D.C. Cir. 1985); Virgin Islands v. Lee, 775 F.2d 514 (3rd Cir. 1985). ***PRACTICE AREAS:*** U.S. Supreme Court Litigation; Criminal Defense; Constitutional Litigation; Appellate Litigation; Federal Litigation. ***Email:*** nlewin@mintz.com

WILLIAM C. BRASHARES, born June 7, 1939; admitted to bar, 1965, D.C.; 1970, U.S. Supreme Court; 1977, Calif. *Education:* University of Virginia (B.A., 1961); University of Michigan (J.D., 1964). Associate Editor, Michigan Law Review, 1963-1964. General Counsel, Association of Home Appliance Manufacturers, 1983—. Finalist, Campbell Moot Court Competition, 1963. *Member:* The District of Columbia Bar; State Bar of California. ***PRACTICE AREAS:*** Federal and State Litigation; Administrative Litigation; Securities Litigation; Commercial Arbitration; International Arbitration.

FRANK W. LLOYD, born August 5, 1941; admitted to bar, 1968, D.C.; 1986, Mass. *Education:* Williams College (B.A., 1963); University of Michigan (M.A., 1964); Harvard Law School (LL.B., 1967). Editor, Harvard Law Review, 1965-1967. Co-Author: *Cable Television Law:* A Video Communications Practice Guide, Mathew Bender (1983, 1996 update). Assistant to Chairman Federal Communications Commission, 1977-1981. Chairman, Annual Practicing Law Institute on Cable Television Law. *Member:* The District of Columbia Bar; Federal Communications Bar Association. ***PRACTICE AREAS:*** Communications Law; Cable TV.

RAYMOND D. COTTON, born December 8, 1942; admitted to bar, 1968, Mass.; 1972, D.C.; 1976, Florida. *Education:* Monmouth University (A.B., summa cum laude, 1965); Harvard Law School (J.D., 1968); Harvard School of Public Health (M.S. in Health Services Administration, 1969). *Member:* The District of Columbia Bar (Member, Health Law Committee); American Bar Association (Member, Forum on Health Law); American Health Lawyers Association; National Association of College and University Attorneys. ***PRACTICE AREAS:*** Health Law; Public Health Law; Health Care Legislation; Biomedical Technology; College and University Law; Federal Education Grants.

HARVEY I. SAFERSTEIN, born September 27, 1943; admitted to bar, 1969, D.C.; 1971, Ca. *Education:* University of California, Berkeley (B.A., 1965); Harvard University (LL.B., magna cum laude, 1968). Executive Editor, Harvard Law Review, 1967-1968. Author: "An Overview of the Federal and State Law of Price Discrimination," 19th-42nd PLI Annual Antitrust Law Institute, 1978-2001; "Antitrust Issues for Telecom Mergers and Acquisitions," PLI Telecommunications Deals, 1999-2001. Law Clerk to Judge Bailey Aldrich, U.S. Court of Appeals, First Circuit, 1968-1969. Advisor to Philip Elman, Federal Trade Commissioner, 1969-1970. Regional Director, Federal Trade Commission, Los Angeles Regional Office, 1978-1979. *Member:* The District of Columbia Bar; Los Angeles County and American (Vice-Chair, Intellectual Property Committee, Antitrust Law Section, 2000—) Bar Associations; State Bar of California (President, 1992-1993; Access to Justice Commission, 1997—; State Bar Foundation, 1990—); Association of Business Trial Lawyers (President, 1990-1991); Legal Aid Foundation of Los Angeles (President, 1987-1989); Ninth Circuit Judicial Conference (Delegate, 2000—; Chair, 1991). ***PRACTICE AREAS:*** Antitrust; Intellectual Property; Litigation.

HOPE S. FOSTER, born October 22, 1948; admitted to bar, 1973, D.C. *Education:* Wellesley College (B.A., 1970); George Washington National Law Center (J.D., 1973). Co-author: "Laboratory Regulation Manual," Aspen Systems, Inc., 1977-1999. Author: "Avoiding OIG-Imposed Exclusion," American Bar Association, 1997; "Defending a Nationally Orchestrated, Multi-Provider Federal Health Task Force Investigation," American Bar Association, 1997; "Medicare Compliance Guide for Clinical Labs," Washington G-2 Reports, 1997; Hospital Physician Exclusive Arrangements: Antitrust's Next Frontier in Health?" St. Louis L.J., Vol. 26, No. 3 April 1982. *Member:* The District of Columbia Bar; American Bar Association (Member, Committees: White Collar Crime, Health Care and Antitrust; Subcommittee on Health Care Fraud and Abuse); American Health Lawyers Association. ***PRACTICE AREAS:*** Health Care Fraud; Health Care Legislation; Health Care Regulation; Health Care Reimbursement; Health Law.

THOMAS M. ANTONE, IV, born January 31, 1947; admitted to bar, 1975, Md. and D.C. *Education:* North Carolina State University (B.A., magna cum laude, 1968); Duke University (M.H.A., cum laude, 1970); George Washington University (J.D., cum laude, 1974). Phi Beta Kappa; Phi Kappa Phi. Assistant Secretary for Health Legislation, 1980-1982 and Executive Secretary for Health, 1982-1983, U.S. Department of Health and Human Services. *Member:* District of Columbia Bar; Maryland State Bar Association; National Health Lawyers Association. ***PRACTICE AREAS:*** Health Law; Legislation.

BRUCE D. SOKLER, born May 2, 1949; admitted to bar, 1975, D.C.; 1984, Mass. *Education:* Princeton University (A.B., cum laude, 1971); Georgetown University (J.D., 1974). Editor-in-Chief, Georgetown Law Journal, 1973-1974. Clerk to Judge Edward Allen Tamm, U.S. Court of Appeals for the District of Columbia Circuit, 1974-1975. *Member:* The District of Columbia Bar; American Bar Association (Member, Sections on: Administrative Litigation; Antitrust Law); Federal Communications Bar Association. ***PRACTICE AREAS:*** Antitrust Law; Communications Law; Copyright Litigation.

ALVIN J. LORMAN, born October 8, 1945; admitted to bar, 1975, Va; 1976, D.C. *Education:* Long Island University (B.A., 1966); The Ohio State University (M.A., 1968); University of Virginia (J.D., 1975). Member, Editorial Board, Virginia Law Review, 1973-1975. Law Clerk to Hon. Leonard Braman, Superior Court of the District of Columbia, 1975-1976. *Member:* The District of Columbia Bar; American Bar Association (Vice Chair, Committee on Food Drug Cosmetic Law, 1988-1991). ***PRACTICE AREAS:*** Food and Drug; Environmental; Health Care Law.

JAMES L. CASSERLY, born 1951; admitted to bar, 1976, District of Columbia. *Education:* Tufts University (A.B., magna cum laude, 1973); Columbia University (J.D., 1976). Harlan Fiske Stone Scholar. *Member:* Federal Communications Bar Association (Co-Chair, of Committee on Legislation, 1983-1987); District of Columbia. ***PRACTICE AREAS:*** Communications Law; FCC Regulation; Telecommunications Competition.

BENJAMIN J. GRIFFIN, born January 1, 1952; admitted to bar, 1976, South Carolina; 1977, D.C. *Education:* University of South Carolina (B.A., Phi Beta Kappa, 1973; J.D., 1976). *Member:* Federal Communication Bar Association. ***PRACTICE AREAS:*** Communications and Media; Satellite Communications; Cable Programming; Cable Communications.

PETER M. KAZON, born November 20, 1953; admitted to bar, 1978, Maine; 1979, D.C.; 1981, Mass. *Education:* Tufts University (B.A., magna cum laude, 1975); Temple University (J.D., 1978). *Member:* The District of Columbia Bar; Maine State and Massachusetts State Bar Associations; American Health Lawyers Association. ***PRACTICE AREAS:*** Health Law; Health Care Reform; Health Care Reimbursement; Medicare and Medicaid Reimbursement; Medicare and Medicaid Fraud and Abuse.

(This Listing Continued)

CHARLES ALAN SAMUELS, born March 25, 1954; admitted to bar, 1978, Ill. 1981, D.C. *Education:* University of Virginia (B.A., 1975; LL.B., 1978). Special Assistant to the General Counsel, Council on Wage and Price Stability, Executive Office of the President, 1980. *Member:* The District of Columbia Bar; American Bar Association (Member, Section on Administrative Law). ***PRACTICE AREAS:*** Federal Legislation and Regulation; Natural Resources; Antitrust Law.

HOWARD J. SYMONS, born November 14, 1953; admitted to bar, 1978, D.C. *Education:* Yale University (B.A., summa cum laude, 1975); Harvard University (J.D., 1978). Senior Counsel, U.S. House of Representatives Subcommittee on Telecommunications, 1981-1985. ***PRACTICE AREAS:*** Telecommunications Law; Cable TV; Wireless Communications; FCC Regulation.

BRADLEY L. KELLY, born November 27, 1953; admitted to bar, 1979, District of Columbia. *Education:* University of Texas (B.A., with high honors, 1976; J.D., with honors, 1979). Phi Beta Kappa; Phi Kappa Phi. Teaching Quizmaster, 1978-1979. Assistant U.S. Attorney, U.S. Attorney's Office, District of Columbia, 1984-1989. ***PRACTICE AREAS:*** Health Care; Litigation; White Collar.

RUSSELL H. FOX, born March 20, 1957; admitted to bar, 1981, District of Columbia and U.S. District Court, District of Columbia; 1983, U.S. Court of Appeals for the District of Columbia Circuit. *Education:* University of Rochester (B.A., 1978); Duke University School of Law (J.D. , 1981). President, American SMR (Specialized Mobile Radio) Network Association, Inc., 1987-1991. *Member:* The District of Columbia Bar; Federal Communications Bar Association. ***PRACTICE AREAS:*** Telecommunications Law; Telecommunications Licensing; Telecommunications Regulation; Wireless Communications.

DAVID N. BAUMANN, born January 30, 1959; admitted to bar, 1984, Ohio; 1990, District of Columbia. *Education:* University of Rochester (B.A. Political Science and Psychology, with highest honors, with distinction, 1981); Case Western Reserve University (J.D., 1984). President, Phi Alpha Delta Legal Fraternity, 1982-1983. Associate, 1982-1983 and Associate Editor, 1983-1984, Case Western Reserve Law Review. *Member:* The District of Columbia Bar; Bar Association of the District of Columbia; Ohio State, Federal and American Bar Associations. ***TRANSACTIONS:*** A substantial number of the largest technology, telecommunications and outsourcing transactions. ***PRACTICE AREAS:*** Technology Contracts; Outsourcing; Intellectual Property; Telecommunications Law.

RICHARD M. GRAF, born December 13, 1957; admitted to bar, 1984, N.Y; 1987, D.C. *Education:* University of Chicago (B.A., 1979; M.A., 1980); Boston College (J.D., cum laude, 1984). *Member:* American Bar Association. ***PRACTICE AREAS:*** Mergers & Acquisitions; Internet Law; Securities Offerings; Corporate Finance.

SUSAN W. BERSON, born August 13, 1961; admitted to bar, 1986, New York; 1993, Pennsylvania (Not admitted in District of Columbia). *Education:* University of Rochester (B.A., magna cum laude, 1982); Columbia University (J.D., 1985). Phi Beta Kappa; Harlan Fiske Stone Scholar. *Member:* Association of the Bar of the City of New York; New York State and American (Member, Health Law Sections) Bar Associations; American Health Lawyers Association. . ***PRACTICE AREAS:*** Health Law; Health Care Regulation; Health Care Mergers and Acquisitions; Health Care Contracts; Health Care Corporate Law. ***Email:*** sberson@mintz.com

CHRISTOPHER J. HARVIE, born July 16, 1959; admitted to bar, 1986, California; 1998, District of Columbia. *Education:* Brown University (A.B., 1981); University of California at Los Angeles (J.D., 1986). Order of the Coif. Recipient, American Jurisprudence Award, Torts, Constitutional Law. Law Clerk, Judge Hugh H. Bownes, U.S. Court of Appeals, First Circuit, Concord, New Hampshire, 1986-1987. Project Director, Advocacy Institute, Washington, D.C., 1987-1988. Counsel, Senate Judicial Committee, Subcommittee on Antitrust, Monopolies and Business Rights, Washington, D.C., 1988-1993. ***PRACTICE AREAS:*** Communications; Legislation.

SUSAN L. BURKE, born July 30, 1962; admitted to bar, 1987, VA; 1988, DC; 2000, MI. *Education:* Georgetown University's School of Foreign Service (B.S.F.S., 1984); Catholic University (J.D., with highest honors, 1987). ***PRACTICE AREAS:*** Intellectual Property Litigation; Patent Litigation; Civil Litigation; Complex Litigation; Health Care Fraud; Health Care Liability; ERISA Litigation; Complex Commercial Litigation; Unfair Competition.

CHERIE R. KISER, born October 6, 1958; admitted to bar, 1987, Penn.; 1988, D.C. *Education:* University of Minnesota (B.A., 1983); Catholic University of America, Columbus School of Law (J.D., 1987); Certificate conferred by the Institute of Communications Law Studies, Columbus School of Law (1987). Co-Author: "Customized Tariffs: The Dawn of a New Era," Telematics, March, 1986. *Member:* Federal Communications Bar Association (Co-Chair, Ad Hoc Committee on Chapter Development, 1994—; Co-Chair, State and Local Practice Committee, 1991-1993). ***PRACTICE AREAS:*** Communications Law; FCC Regulation.

SARA F. LEIBMAN, born December 7, 1956; admitted to bar, 1987, Pa; 1991, D.C. *Education:* Grinnell College (B.A., 1979); Georgetown University Law Center (J.D., cum laude, 1987). Publications Editor: "Law and Policy in International Business;" Note, "The European Communities Products Liability Directive: is The American Experience Applicable?" 18 Law & Policy Int'l bus. 795, 1986. *Member:* Federal Communications Bar Association. ***PRACTICE AREAS:*** Communications; Wireless Communications.

(This Listing Continued)

WILLIAM A. DAVIS, born February 24, 1963; admitted to bar, 1987, PA; 1990, D.C. *Education:* University of Pittsburgh (B.A., summa cum laude, 1984); Columbia University (J.D., 1987). Phi Beta Kappa. Editor, Columbia Law Review, Note, "The Impeachment Exception to the Sixth Amendment Exclusionary Rule," 87 Colum. L.Rev. 176 (1987). Law Clerk, Hon. Alexander Harvey, U.S. District Court for the District of Maryland, 1987-1988. *Member:* The District of Columbia Bar; American Bar Association. ***PRACTICE AREAS:*** Complex Business Litigation; Intellectual Property Litigation; Telecommunications Litigation; Securities Litigation.

ERIN M. FALK, born November 11, 1960; admitted to bar, 1988, Va. (Not admitted in District of Columbia). *Education:* University of Texas at Austin (B.A., 1983); Washington College of Law of American University (J.D., 1986). ***PRACTICE AREAS:*** Intellectual Property; Intellectual Property Litigation; Intellectual Property Portfolio Management; Trademarks; Trademark Litigation; Trademark Prosecution.

LINDA K. McLEOD, born August 19, 1963; admitted to bar, 1989, Ore.; 1990, D.C. *Education:* Willamette University (B.A., 1984); University of Oregon (J.D., 1988); New York University (LL.M., Trade Regulation, 1989). ***PRACTICE AREAS:*** Intellectual Property; Trademarks; Trademark Clearance; Trademark Prosecution; Trademark Enforcement; Trademark Litigation; Domain Names. ***Email:*** lkmcleod@mintz.com

MICHAEL H. PRYOR, born December 30, 1953; admitted to bar, 1989, Ca.; 1990, D.C. *Education:* Western Washington University (B.S., 1978); Georgetown University (J.D., magna cum laude, 1988). Order of the Coif. Law Clerk to Judge, Harold H. Greene, U.S. District Court, for the District of Columbia. *Member:* District of Columbia Bar; State Bar of California. ***PRACTICE AREAS:*** Communications Law; Policy and Regulation.

LAURA J. OBERBROECKLING, born May 25, 1967; admitted to bar, 1992, Va.; 1994, D.C.; 1998, Md. *Education:* University of Iowa (B.A., with distinction, 1988); Harvard Law School (J.D., 1992). Phi Beta Kappa. Author: "e-health and the Law," in "e-healthcare: Harness the Power of Internet e-Commerce & e-Care," Douglas E. Goldstein, editor, Aspen Publishers, 2000. ***PRACTICE AREAS:*** Health Care; Litigation.

JAMES J. VALENTINO, born March 4, 1963; admitted to bar, 1992, Md.; 1994, D.C. *Education:* Georgetown University (B.S., cum laude, 1985; J.D., cum laude, 1992). ***PRACTICE AREAS:*** Communications; Internet Law.

All of the firm's attorneys are members of the American Bar Association.

(For complete biographical data on Boston, MA, Reston VA, New York, NY and New Haven, CT attorneys, see Professional Biographies at Boston, MA, Reston, VA, New York, NY and New Haven, CT).

MITCHELL AND DUNN

Established in 1991

818 18TH STREET, N.W.
WASHINGTON, D.C. 20006
Telephone: 202-296-6844
Fax: 202-296-6855

Immigration and Nationality and International Law, Criminal and Personal Injury Practice before Government Agencies. Trial, Appellate and Supreme Court Practice.

MEMBERS OF FIRM

ANNE M. MITCHELL, born Belfast, Northern Ireland; admitted to bar, 1985, New York (Not admitted in District of Columbia). *Education:* Methodist College, Belfast; University of Dublin, Trinity College (B.L.Sc., 1980; M.A., 1986). *Member:* American Bar Association; The American Immigration Lawyers Association. ***PRACTICE AREAS:*** Immigration Law; Visas; International Law.

THOMAS F. DUNN, born Atlantic City, New Jersey, June 9, 1935; admitted to bar, 1965, District of Columbia; 1993. Virginia. *Education:* Georgetown University (B.A., 1957; LL.B., 1959). Former FBI Agent Foreign Service Reserve Officer. Assistant Director, Office of Territories. Deputy Legislative Counsel, Federal Energy Administration. Director of Congressional Affairs, Commodities Futures Trading Commission. *Member:* District of Columbia Bar. ***PRACTICE AREAS:*** Criminal; Drug Crimes; Lobbying; Personal Injury.

OF COUNSEL

ROBERT F. CONDON, born Hempstead, New York, November 7, 1936; admitted to bar, 1961, New York; 1972, District of Columbia; 1973, U.S. Court of Federal Claims. *Education:* St. John's University (B.A., 1958); Georgetown

(This Listing Continued)

MITCHELL AND DUNN, Washington—Continued

University (J.D., with honors, 1961). Assistant District Attorney, New York County, 1961-1965. Counsel to Grievance Committee, Association of the Bar of the City of New York, 1965-1966. Associate Counsel for Litigation, New York Life Insurance Co., 1966-1972. Senior Counsel to Board, Merit Systems Protection Board. *Member:* The District of Columbia Bar; American Bar Association (Member, Sections on: Construction Law; Litigation, 1972-1992); Society of Professionals in Dispute Resolution. (Also Member, Artabane & Belden). ***PRACTICE AREAS:*** Commercial Litigation; Employment Law; Real Estate; Construction Law; Professional Ethics; Government Contracts; Administrative Law.

MIZRACK & GANTT

SUITE 850
555 11TH STREET, N.W.
WASHINGTON, D.C. 20004-1304
Telephone: 202-628-1717
Fax: 202-628-1919
Email: jbgantt@attglobal.net
Email: johngantt@aol.com

New York, New York Office: Park Avenue Tower, 31st Floor, 65 East 55th Street, 10022. Telephone: 212-418-0638. Fax: 212-308-5856.

Civil and Commercial Laws, Regulations and Policies related to Outer Space, International Trade and Commercial Matters, Public International Law, Commercial Law, Corporate Law, Business Law, Mergers and Acquisitions Law, Transactional Business Law, Technology Transfers Law and Trade Matters.

FIRM PROFILE: The firm provides advice and assistance to domestic and foreign clients, including multinational companies, governmental agencies, and international organizations, with respect to United States' laws, regulations, and policies, as well as international public and private law.

MEMBERS OF FIRM

RICHARD MIZRACK (See Biographical Data at New York, New York).

JOHN B. GANTT, born Washington, DC, 1939; admitted to bar, 1965, Virginia; 1966, U.S. District Court, Eastern and Western Districts of Virginia; 1972, District of Columbia; 1984, U.S. Supreme Court. *Education:* Carnegie Mellon Univ. (B.S., Physics, 1960); Univ. of Virginia (LL.B., 1965). Attorney/General Attorney/Assistant General Counsel, Communications Satellite Corporation, 1966-1983. Vice President and General Counsel/Secretary, COMSAT General Corporation, 1976-1981. Private Practice, 1983—, including Counsel, Hunton & Williams, 1985-1987. ***PRACTICE AREAS:*** Civil Practice; International Trade; Public International Law; Commercial Law; Space and Telecommunications Law. ***Email:*** jbgantt@attglobal.net

MOIR & HARDMAN

1015 18TH STREET, NW, SUITE 800
WASHINGTON, D.C. 20036-5204
Telephone: 202-872-8680
Fax: 202-872-8698

Telecommunications and Information Services Law, Communication, Antitrust and Trade Regulation Law, Corporate and Commercial Litigation, Practice Before Administrative Agencies, Federal Courts and Legislative Bodies.

BRIAN R. MOIR, born Pasadena, California, May 10, 1945; admitted to bar, 1973, Nebraska; 1979, U.S. Supreme Court; 1981, District of Columbia. *Education:* Parsons College (B.A., 1967); University of Denver (J.D., 1971). Member, University of Denver Journal of International Law, 1970-1971. Recipient, International Legal Studies Concentration Award. Assistant Corporate Counsel, Tele-Communications, Inc., 1972-1973. Staff Attorney, Federal Communications Commission, 1973-1975. Senior Legal Counsel, Committee on Energy and Commerce, U.S. House of Representatives, 1975-1981. Member: U.S. Delegations to the International Maritime Satellite Organization, 1976-1979; Federal Communications Commission Delegations for North Atlantic Facilities Planning, 1977-1979. *Member:* Federal and American (Member, Sections on: Science and Technology; Communications Law Committee) Bar Associations; Federal Communications Bar Association. ***PRACTICE AREAS:*** Telecommunications Law; Communications Law; Antitrust Law; Administrative Law; International Law.

KENNETH E. HARDMAN, born Wabash, Indiana, June 7, 1944; admitted to bar, 1969, District of Columbia; 1975, U.S. Supreme Court. *Education:* Indiana University (A.B., with honors, 1966); Georgetown University (J.D., 1969). Deputy Assistant General Counsel, National Association of Regulatory Utility Commissioners, 1973-1975. Author: "A Primer on Cellular Mobile Telephone Systems," 29 Federal Bar News & Journal 385 (Nov. 1982). *Member:* The District of Columbia Bar; American Bar Association; Federal Communications Bar Association. ***PRACTICE AREAS:*** Telecommunication Law; Communications Law; Antitrust Law; Administrative Law. ***Email:*** kenhardman@ibm.net

(This Listing Continued)

MONTEAU, PEEBLES & CROWELL, LLP

511 C STREET, N.E.
WASHINGTON, D.C. 20002
Telephone: 202-543-5000
Fax: 202-543-7716
Email: ndnlaw@ndnlaw.com
URL: http://www.ndnlaw.com

Omaha, Nebraska Office: 12100 West Center Road, Suite 202, 68144. Telephone: 402-333-4053. Fax: 402-333-4761. E-Mail: ndnlaw@ndnlaw.com
Sacramento, California Office: 1001 Second Street, 95814. Telephone: 916-441-2700. Fax: 916-441-2067. E-Mail: ndnlaw@ndnlaw.com
Kirkland, Washington Office: 1670 10th Street West, 98033. Telephone: 425-828-9070. Fax: 425-828-8978. E-Mail: ndnlaw@ndnlaw.com
Kalispell, Montana Office: 235 Wild Rose Trail, 59901. Telephone: 406-755-3544. Fax: 406-755-3546. E-Mail: hmonteau@ndnlaw.com

Federal Indian Law, Indian Economic Development, Indian Child Welfare Act, Indian Gaming Law, Indian Land Law, Indian Water Claims, Tribal Taxation, Civil Litigation, Appellate Practice, and Administrative Law.

FIRM PROFILE: Monteau, Peebles & Crowell, LLP has a nationwide practice specializing in Federal Indian law, complex governmental negotiations, business transactions in Indian Country and federal lobbying. The internal diversity of the firm's practice of Federal Indian law, gaming, general trial and appellate practice, financing, business transactions in Indian Country, administrative law and employment matters allow it to effectively represent the client's present and future interests. The firm, with extensive experience in Federal Indian law, represents Indian Tribes across the United States. The firm's litigation practice focuses on complex litigation, contracts, gaming and Indian land issues at both trial and appellate levels, but also includes commercial matters. Our attorneys speak at professional seminars relating to Indian issues for various associations.

(For biographical data on all personnel, see Professional Biographies at Omaha, Nebraska)

MOOERS & MOUNT, PLLC

1730 M STREET, N.W., SUITE 905
WASHINGTON, D.C. 20036
Telephone: 202-955-6227
Fax: 202-955-1149
URL: http://www.lawyers.com/mooers_law

Insurance Defense, Auto Negligence Defense, Premises and Products Liability Defense, Workers Compensation Defense. Commercial Litigation, Complex Multi-jurisdictional Litigation, Civil Trial, Medical Malpractice.

FIRM PROFILE: Mooers & Mount, PLLC is best known for its successful trial work. The firm routinely defends major insurance companies, insurance funds, large businesses such as construction companies, hospitals, commercial line insurance underwriters, workers compensation funds as well as individuals and their families. The firm provides litigation expertise and business counsel to clients throughout metropolitan Washington, D.C., suburban Maryland and Baltimore.

THOMAS R. MOOERS, born Washington, D.C., May 9, 1959; admitted to bar, 1989, Maryland; 1990, Pennsylvania; 1991, District of Columbia and U.S. District Court, District of Maryland; 1992, U.S. District Court for the District of Columbia. *Education:* Corcoran School of Art (B.F.A., 1986); University of Baltimore School of Law (J.D., 1989). Team Member, Giles Sutherland Rich Moot Court Competition in Intellectual Property. Member, The Inns of Court. *Member:* District of Columbia Bar; Montgomery County and Maryland State Bar Associations; District of Columbia Defense Lawyers Association. ***PRACTICE AREAS:*** Insurance Defense; Insurance Coverage; Medical Malpractice; Construction Litigation; Civil Litigation; Products Liability. ***Email:*** trm943@aol.com

ROCCO C. NUNZIO, born Washington, D.C., February 1, 1956; admitted to bar, 1982, Maryland; 1983, District of Columbia and U.S. District Court, District of Maryland; 1984, U.S. District Court, District of Columbia. *Education:* George Washington University (B.A., with distinction, 1978); University of Baltimore (J.D., cum laude, 1982). Member, Heuisler Honor Society. Editor, University of Baltimore Law Review, 1981-1982. Author: "Eminent Domain:

(This Listing Continued)

Private Corporations and the Public Use Limitation," University of Baltimore Law Review, Volume 11:2, 1983. Law Clerk to Honorable John P. Moore, Maryland Court of Special Appeals, 1982. *Member:* Maryland State Bar Association; The District of Columbia Bar. ***PRACTICE AREAS:*** Insurance Defense; Premises Liability Defense; Products Liability Defense; Insurance Coverage Litigation; Civil Litigation.

BRIAN C. MALONE, born Guantanamo Bay, Cuba, September 27, 1965; admitted to bar, 1998, Maryland; 1999, District of Columbia. *Education:* Lander University (B.A., 1992); University of South Carolina (Masters Program, History); Georgetown University Law Center (J.D., 1998). Constitutional Research for Children's Rights, University of South Carolina, 1996. *Member:* Maryland State Bar Association. [U.S. Army Res., 1982-1995]. ***PRACTICE AREAS:*** Insurance Defense; Insurance Coverage; Civil Litigation.

REPRESENTATIVE CLIENTS: Maryland Automobile Insurance Fund; Allstate Insurance Company; Royal and SunAlliance Insurance Company, Fireman's Fund Insurance Co.; Budget Rent-A-Car; Sibley Memorial Hospital, Managed Care, U.S.A.; AIG Insurance Co.; Risk Enterprise Management, Ltd.; The Clark Construction Group; State Farm Insurance Co.; Safeway Stores, Inc.

MOONEY, GREEN, BAKER & SAINDON, P.C.

1920 L STREET, N.W., SUITE 400
WASHINGTON, D.C. 20036
Telephone: 202-783-0010
Telecopier: 202-783-6088
Email: pgseen@mooneygreen.com
URL: http://www.mooneygreen.com

Labor Law, Public Sector Labor Relations, Labor Arbitration and Litigation, Collective Bargaining, Employee Benefits, ERISA, Multiemployer Pensions and Benefits, Taft-Hartley Plans, Qualified Pension Plans, Public Employee Retirement, Employee Relations, Equal Opportunity Law, Bankruptcy Law, RICO, Antitrust and General Civil Litigation.

FIRM PROFILE: The Firm was established to serve the interests of working people by assisting their labor representatives (unions) and benefit plans. The Firm represents unions in the private and public sectors, and in many industries and fields, including mining and industrial, service employees, educational, transportation and construction. Services provided to unions range from litigation (including cases involving offensive and defensive RICO and antitrust actions, defending injunction and strike damage suits, and defending member law suits), assisting unions in responding to governmental investigations and audits, assisting in collective bargaining, and advising on such matters as regulatory compliance, internal union affairs, organizing, and strike conduct. The Firm also represents pension and benefit plans of all sizes. Services to these plans include tax qualification, ERISA compliance, employer collection actions, responding to governmental investigations, obtaining rulings and exemptions from the appropriate governmental agencies, defending participant law suits, and general advice. The Firm has also been involved in crafting legislation to address labor issues that could not be adequately resolved in collective bargaining. Finally, the Firm represents individual employees in a wide range of employment-related matters.

JOHN R. MOONEY, born Jersey City, New Jersey, August 19, 1956; admitted to bar, 1982, Virginia; 1983, U.S. District Court, Eastern and Western Districts of Virginia; 1984, District of Columbia and U.S. District Court, District of Columbia; U.S. Supreme Court. *Education:* College of William & Mary (B.A., 1978); Catholic University of America (J.D., 1982). Member, Moot Court Board. Member, Catholic University Law Review, 1980-1982. Author: "RICO and Labor Law: Is Accommodation Possible?" Proceedings of the 7th Annual University of Louisville Labor and Employment Law Symposium, 1990. Co-Author: "Drug Testing Developments in the Private Workplace," Proceedings of the 1990 Section of Labor and Employment Law, American Bar Association. Adjunct Professor: Columbus School of Law, Catholic University of America, 1986-1990; Georgetown University Law Center, 1990-2000. *Member:* The District of Columbia Bar (Co-Chair, Public Employee Subsection, Section on Labor Law, 1986-1987); Virginia State Bar; American Bar Association (Member, Litigation Section). ***PRACTICE AREAS:*** Labor Law; Litigation; Constitutional Law; RICO; Union Organization. ***Email:*** jmooney@mooneygreen.com

PAUL A. GREEN, born Washington, D.C., September 8, 1957; admitted to bar, 1982, Maryland; 1984, District of Columbia. *Education:* University of Chicago (A.B., 1978); University of Maryland (J.D., with honors, 1982). Law Clerk to the Honorable Rita C. Davidson, Court of Appeals of Maryland, 1982-1983. Co-Author: "The Single-Employer Pension Plan Amendments of 1986: An Overview," Charles Spencer and Associates, Inc., Chicago, Illinois, 1986; "Pension-Related Claims in Bankruptcy," Pension Briefings, Federal Publications, Inc., No. 87-7, July, 1987. Author: "Self-Pay Revisited: New Legal Requirements," Digest, International Foundation of Employee Benefit Plans, Vol. 23, No. 6, pp. 7, et seq., June, 1986. Adjunct Professor, Columbus School of Law, Catholic University of America, 1986-1995. Attorney, Office of the General Counsel, Pension Benefit Guaranty Corporation, 1983-1985. *Member:* The District of Columbia Bar (Co-Chair, Employee Benefits Committee, Labor Relations Section, 1985-1990); Maryland State and American Bar Associations. ***PRACTICE AREAS:*** ERISA; Employee Benefits; Health and Welfare Benefit Plans; Qualified Retirement Plans; Multiemployer Plans; Public and Non-Profit Pension Plans. ***Email:*** pgreen@mooneygreen.com

(This Listing Continued)

MARILYN L. BAKER, born Omaha, Nebraska, April 17, 1962; admitted to bar, 1989, Maryland; 1990, U.S. District Court for the District of Maryland; 1991, District of Columbia and U.S. District Court for the District of Columbia. *Education:* Macalester College (B.A., 1984); Washington College of Law of American University (J.D., 1989). *Member:* The District of Columbia Bar; Maryland State Bar Association. ***PRACTICE AREAS:*** ERISA; Employee Benefits; Taft-Hartley Plans; Pension Plans; Health and Welfare Benefit Plans; Bankruptcy. ***Email:*** mbaker@mooneygreen.com

ELIZABETH A. SAINDON, born Ipswich, Massachusetts, June 18, 1967; admitted to bar, 1991, Virginia; 1993, District of Columbia. *Education:* University of Florida (B.S., magna cum laude, 1988); American University (J.D., 1991). Phi Beta Kappa. Managing Editor, The Administrative Law Journal, 1990-1991. Member, Charles Fahy American Inns of Court, 1994-1997. Law Clerk to the Honorable Nan R. Huhn, Superior Court of the District of Columbia, 1991-1992. *Member:* District of Columbia Bar; American Bar Association. ***PRACTICE AREAS:*** ERISA; Employee Benefits; ERISA Collections; Taft-Hartley Plans; Litigation; Bankruptcy. ***Email:*** bsaindon@mooneygreen.com

---

MARK J. MURPHY, born Worcester, Massachusetts, June 30, 1968; admitted to bar, 1996, District of Columbia; 1997, Maryland and U.S. District Court for the District of Columbia. *Education:* College of the Holy Cross (B.A., 1990); Brooklyn Law School (J.D.). *Member:* District of Columbia Bar (Member, Labor and Employment Section, 1996—). ***Email:*** mmurphy@mooneygreen.com

DANIEL E. KORNFELD, born Epsom, England, 1972; admitted to bar, 1998, Maryland; 1999, District of Columbia. *Education:* Cornell University (B.S., with honors, 1995); George Washington University Law School (J.D., with honors, 1998); Georgetown University Law School (LL.M., with distinction, 2001). *Member:* The District of Columbia Bar. ***PRACTICE AREAS:*** Labor; ERISA; Multiemployer Plans; Litigation. ***Email:*** dkornfeld@mooneygreen.com

DOUGLAS L. PARKER, born Bluefield, West Virginia, May 9, 1969; admitted to bar, 1997, Virginia; 1999, District of Columbia. *Education:* James Madison University (B.A., 1991); University of Virginia (J.D., 1997). Recipient, Earle Shawe Labor Relations Award. Co-Author: "Hiding Behind the Corporate Veil; Employer Abuse of the Corporate Form to Avoid or Deny Workers' Collectively Bargained and Statutory Rights," W. Va. Law Rev. Vol. 100 No. 3 (Spring 1998). *Member:* The District of Columbia Bar (Labor and Employment Law Section); Virginia Bar Association. ***PRACTICE AREAS:*** Labor; Labor Arbitration; Litigation; Labor Strikes. ***Email:*** dparker@mooneygreen.com

SPECIAL COUNSEL

ROBERT H. STROPP, JR., born Baltimore, Maryland, September 21, 1947; admitted to bar, 1975, Alabama, U.S. District Court, Northern, Middle and Southern Districts of Alabama and U.S. Court of Appeals, First, Second, Third, Fourth, Fifth, Sixth, Eighth, Tenth, Eleventh and District of Columbia Circuits; 1991, District of Columbia and U.S. Supreme Court. *Education:* University of Maryland (B.A., 1969); Cumberland School of Law of Samford University (J.D., 1975). Delta Theta Phi. Author: "Walkaround Rights For Miners-Representative Under MSHA: A Compatible Statutory Scheme", West Virginia Law Review, Vol. 96, Spring 1994, Number 3. General Counsel Advisory Board, AFL-CIO, 1989-1996. Member, Advisory Panel, National Labor Relations Board. Member, AFL-CIO Lawyers Coordinating Committee. General Counsel of the United Mine Workers of America, 1989-1996. *Member:* Birmingham and American (Member, Labor and Employment Section) Bar Associations; Alabama State Bar; Industrial Relations Research Association. Fellow: College of Labor and Employment Lawyers. ***Email:*** rstropp@mooneygreen.com

MOORE & BRUCE, LLP

1072 THOMAS JEFFERSON STREET, N.W.
WASHINGTON, D.C. 20007
Telephone: 202-965-5300
Facsimile: 202-965-7745
URL: http://www.lawyers.com/moore&brucellp

Wilmington, Delaware Office: 2 East 7th Street, Suite 302. Telephone: 302-655-0582. Fax: 302-655-9321.

London, England Office: 43 Upper Grosvenor Street. Telephone: 011-44-207-493-4840. Fax: 011-44-207-493-4299.

(This Listing Continued)

MOORE & BRUCE, LLP, Washington—Continued

Taxation, Corporate and Commercial Law, International Trade and Customs Law, Trusts and Estates, Civil and Criminal Tax Litigation.

CHARLES M. BRUCE, born Washington, D.C., August 1, 1945; admitted to bar, 1972, District of Columbia; 1973, U.S. Tax Court; 1976, U.S. Supreme Court; 1982, U.S. Claims Court. *Education:* Washington & Lee University (A.B., 1967); George Washington University Law School (J.D., with honors, 1971). Editor: United States Internal Revenue Service International Tax Compliance Series, Kluwer (1998). Author: "U.S. Taxation of Foreign Trusts," Kluwer (1999); "U.S. Taxation of Foreign Trusts: Post-1976 Act Changes and Continued Uses," 17 TMIJ 192 (1988). Co-author: Tax Management Portfolio, 264-5th, "Foreign Sales Corporations" (1998); U.S. Reporter: "Constraints on Cross Border Takeovers and Mergers," A Report by the Section on Business Law, International Bar Association for the International Capital Markets Group, reprinted in International Business Lawyer (1991). Adjunct Professor, Graduate Tax Program, Georgetown University Law Center, 1977-1982. Visiting Professor, Institut Für Auslåndisches und Internationales Finaz- und Steuerwesen, Hamburg University, Spring, 1982. Counsel, Committee on Finance, United States Senate, 1977-1979. Attorney-Advisor to Judge Howard A. Dawson, Jr., U.S. Tax Court, 1971-1973. Chairman, Annual Institute on Multinational Taxation, co-sponsored by Georgetown University Law Center and the Chamber of Commerce of the United States. 1979-1984. International Tax Practitioners Panel, Tax Management International Journal, 1987—. *Member:* District of Columbia Bar; American Bar Association (Member, Section on Taxation, Subcommittee on Foreign Activities of U.S. Taxpayers; Chairman, Subcommittee on FSC/DISC and Task Force on Foreign Trusts); International Bar Association (Member, Section on Business Law); International Fiscal Association. ***Email:*** cbruce@mooreandbruce.com

JONATHON R. MOORE, born Jackson, Mi., January 5, 1947; admitted to bar, 1975, New York and U.S. Court of Appeals, Second Circuit; 1977, U.S. Tax Court; 1978, District of Columbia; 1979, U.S. Court of International Trade; 1980, U.S. District Court, District of Columbia and U.S. Court of Appeals, District of Columbia Circuit; 1982, U.S. Court of Appeals for the Federal Circuit. *Education:* Williams College (B.A., 1969); George Washington University (J.D., with honors, 1974). Articles Editor, Journal of International Law and Economics, 1973-1974. *Member:* District of Columbia Bar (Member, Sections on: International Law; Corporate, Finance and Securities Law); International Trade Commission Trial Lawyers Association. ***Email:*** jmoore@mooreandbruce.com

OF COUNSEL

MICHAEL C. DURNEY, born Piedmont, California, May 20, 1943; admitted to bar, 1969, California; 1972, District of Columbia and U.S. Supreme Court. *Education:* University of California at Berkeley (A.B., 1965); Hastings College of Law, University of California (J.D., 1968). Phi Delta Phi. Member, Editorial Board, Hastings Law Journal, 1967-1968. Trial Attorney, Tax Division, Department of Justice, 1968-1972. Deputy Assistant and Acting Assistant Attorney General, Tax Division, Department of Justice, 1986-1988. Co-Author: "Criminal Tax Procedure," Tax Management Portfolio No. 162-2nd. Member, U.S. Court of Federal Claims Advisory Council, 1993—. *Member:* The District of Columbia Bar; State Bar of California; Federal (Chairman: Court and Tax Procedure Committee, 1977-1982; Section of Taxation, 1982-1984; Senior Advisory Committee, 1984—) and American (Member, Sections of: Taxation; Chairman, Subcommittee on Legislative and Administrative Proposals, 1993—, Litigation) Bar Associations. (Also practicing individually). ***Email:*** mdurney@mooreandbruce.com

WILLIAM MORRIS, born Lakewood, New Jersey; admitted to bar, 1966, Virginia; 1981, District of Columbia. *Education:* Rutgers University (A.B., 1963); Georgetown University Law Center (J.D., 1966; LL.M. in Taxation, 1971). Adjunct Professor of Law, Georgetown University Law Center, 1978-1982. General Counsel to Committee on Finance, U.S. Senate, 1972-1980. Attorney-Advisor to the Hon. Howard A. Dawson, U.S. Tax Court, 1970-1972. Trial Attorney, Office of Chief Counsel, Internal Revenue Service, 1966-1970. Advisor to Georgetown University Law Center, Bi-Annual Institute on State and Local Taxation, 1979-1995. Member, IRS Commissioner's Advisory Group, 1985-1986. *Member:* The District of Columbia Bar; New York State (Member, Section on Taxation) and American (Member, Section on Taxation) Bar Associations.

EDWARD M. LURIA, born Philadelphia, Pennsylvania, December ll, 1941; admitted to bar, 1968, Pennsylvania; 1970, District of Columbia and U.S. Tax Court; 1971, Delaware; 1982, U.S. Claims Court. *Education:* University of Pennsylvania (A.B., 1964; J.D., 1967); New York University (LL.M. in Taxation, 1968). Co-Author: "Tax Court-Trial of Case," Tax Management Portfolio No 153-3rd, 1975; "Cancellation of Indebtedness-Sections 108 and 1017," Tax Management Portfolio No. 88-4th, 1981. Law Clerk to Hon. John W. Kern, Jr., U.S. Tax Court, 1968-1970. Certified Public Accountant, Maryland, 1981. *Member:* The District of Columbia Bar (Member, Section on Taxation); Delaware State, Federal and American (Member, Estate and Gift Tax Committee, Committee on Value Added Taxes and Committee on Closely-Held Corporations, Section on Taxation,1977—) Bar Associations. (Resident, Wilmington, Delaware Office) (Also, Member Alvord and Alvord, and Of Counsel to Damico and Associates, Washington, D.C.). ***LANGUAGES:*** French and German. ***Email:*** eluria@compuserve.com

MORGAN & FINNEGAN, L.L.P.

A Registered Liability Partnership

1775 EYE STREET, N.W., 4TH FLOOR

WASHINGTON, D.C. 20006

Telephone: 202-857-7887

Facsimile: 202-857-7929

URL: http://www.MorganFinnegan.com

New York, N.Y. Office: 345 Park Avenue, 10154. Telephone: 212-758-4800. Cable Address: "Findurpine". Facsimile: (212) 751-6849. Telex: ITT 421792.

Patent and Technology-related law, Trademark, Copyright, Trade Secret and Unfair Competition, Licensing and Related Antitrust, Trade Regulation, Environmental and Food and Drug Law. International Trade Law. Trials and Appeals. Arbitration.

RESIDENT PARTNERS

MICHAEL S. MARCUS, born New York, N.Y., April 8, 1949; admitted to bar, 1984, Virginia, Virginia Supreme Court, U.S. Court of Appeals, Fourth Circuit and U.S. District Court, Eastern District of Virginia; 1985, U.S. Court of Appeals for the Federal Circuit; 1992, District of Columbia; registered to practice before U.S. Patent and Trademark Office. *Education:* City College of the City University of New York (B.Ch.E., 1972); George Mason University (J.D., 1984). Member, American Chemical Society, 1973—. *Member:* Virginia State Bar; The District of Columbia Bar; American Bar Association; American Intellectual Property Law Association. ***PRACTICE AREAS:*** Intellectual Property; Patents; Reexamination and Petition Practice. ***Email:*** msmarcus@morganfinnegan.com

JOHN E. HOEL, born Belleville, Illinois, January 21, 1942; admitted to bar, 1974, Virginia; 1982, U.S. Court of Appeals for the Federal Circuit; registered to practice before U.S. Patent and Trademark Office (Not admitted in District of Columbia). *Education:* University of Missouri (B.S., Physics, 1964); Georgetown University (J.D., 1974). Sigma Pi Sigma (Physics Honor Society); Phi Kappa Phi. President, Kappa Mu Epsilon Math Honor Society, University of Missouri, 1963-1964. *Member:* Virginia State Bar; American Bar Association; Computer Law Society; Institute of Electrical and Electronic Engineers; American Intellectual Property Law Association. ***Email:*** jehoel@morganfinnegan.com

COUNSEL

JOSEPH C. REDMOND, JR., born Camden, New Jersey, June 25, 1924; admitted to bar, 1955, District of Columbia; 1963, New York; 1972, Virginia. *Education:* Tufts University (B.S.E., 1945); George Washington University (J.D., 1954); New Jersey Institute of Technology (M.S.E.E., 1962); Pace University (M.S., Taxation, 1986). *Member:* The District of Columbia Bar; Virginia State Bar; New York State Bar Association. [U.S. Navy, 1943-1946 and 1951-1952, Lt.]. ***PRACTICE AREAS:*** Patents; Copyright; Trademarks; Intellectual Property Law. ***Email:*** jcredmond@morganfinnegan.com

ASSOCIATES

JAMES HWA, born Yokohama, Japan, September 26, 1969; admitted to bar, 1997, New York; registered to practice before U.S. Patent and Trademark Office (Not admitted in District of Columbia). *Education:* Columbia University (B.S., Electrical Engineering, 1991); George Washington University (J.D., 1996). Tau Beta Pi; Eta Kappa Nu. ***LANGUAGES:*** Chinese (Mandarin). ***PRACTICE AREAS:*** Intellectual Property. ***Email:*** jhwa@morganfinnegan.com

JUSTIN L. KRIEGER, born Akron, Ohio, May 20, 1973; (admission pending). *Education:* College of William & Mary (B.S., Chemistry); University of Florida (J.D., 1999). Member: University of Florida Law Review; Moot Court Board. Co-Author, with Andrew Riddles: "The Business Method Patent Controversy," International Legal Strategy, Jan. 2000, at 60-70. ***PRACTICE AREAS:*** Intellectual Property. ***Email:*** jkrieger@morganfinnegan.com

PETER ZURA, born Detroit, Michigan, November 1, 1967; admitted to bar, 1997, Michigan (Not admitted in District of Columbia). *Education:* Oakland University (B.S.E.E., 1990); Michigan State University (J.D., 1997); George Washington University (LL.M., 2000). Recipient: Ralph, Rose & Samuel Helper Award; Eve August Moot Court Award, 1996. Member, Journal of the Patent and Trademark Office Society. Oralist, Coach and Executive Board Member, Moot Court Team. Patent Examiner, U.S. Patent and Trademark Office, 1998-1999. *Member:* American Bar Association; American Intellectual Property Law Association. ***LANGUAGES:*** Ukrainian. ***PRACTICE AREAS:*** Intellectual Property. ***Email:*** pzura@morganfinnegan.com

(This Listing Continued)

KEATS A. QUINALTY, born Monett, Missouri, April 6, 1971; admitted to bar, 1996, Kansas (Not admitted in District of Columbia). *Education:* University of Missouri (B.S.M.E., 1993); Washburn University of Topeka (J.D., 1996). Patent Examiner, U.S. Patent and Trademark Office, 1997-2000. ***PRACTICE AREAS:*** Intellectual Property. ***Email:*** kquinalty@morganfinnegan.com

GREGORY PERRONE, born Westerly, Rhode Island, May 4, 1967; admitted to bar, 1997, Kentucky; 1999, District of Columbia. *Education:* University of Rhode Island (B.S.E.E., 1988); University of Kentucky (J.D., cum laude, 1997). Order of the Coif. Member, Kentucky Law Journal, 1998-1999. Law Clerk to Judge Karl S. Forester, U.S. District Court for the Eastern District of Kentucky, 1997-1999. ***PRACTICE AREAS:*** Intellectual Property. ***Email:*** gperrone@morganfinnegan.com

KENNETH P. WASZKIEWICZ, born Baltimore, Maryland, June 7, 1963; admitted to bar, 1998, Maryland; 1999, District of Columbia; registered to practice before U.S. Patent and Trademark Office. *Education:* University of Maryland (B.S., Computer Science, 1985); George Washington University (M.S., Computer Science, 1988); University of Baltimore (J.D., 1997). Member, University of Baltimore Intellectual Property Law Journal, 1995-1997. *Member:* Maryland State and American Bar Associations; The District of Columbia Bar; Computer Law Association. ***PRACTICE AREAS:*** Intellectual Property; Patents. ***Email:*** kpwaszkiewicz@morganfinnegan.com

THOMAS A. MORRISON, born Takoma Park, Maryland, September 17, 1967; (admission pending), registered to practice before U.S. Patent and Trademark Office. *Education:* North Carolina State University at Raleigh (B.S., Mechanical Engineering, 1991); Franklin Pierce Law Center (J.D., 2000). *Member:* American Bar Association. ***LANGUAGES:*** Japanese. ***PRACTICE AREAS:*** Patents. ***Email:*** tmorrison@morganfinnegan.com

(For complete biographical data on New York, New York personnel, see Professional Biographies at New York, New York)

MORGAN, LEWIS & BOCKIUS LLP

1800 M STREET, N.W.
WASHINGTON, D.C. 20036-5869
Telephone: 202-467-7000
Fax: 202-467-7176
Email: postmaster@morganlewis.com
URL: http://www.morganlewis.com

Philadelphia, Pennsylvania Office: 1701 Market Street, 19103-2921. Telephone: 215-963-5000. Fax: 215-963-5299.
New York, New York Office: 101 Park Avenue, 10178-0060. Telephone: 212-309-6000. Fax: 212-309-6273.
Los Angeles, California Office: 300 South Grand Avenue, 22nd Floor, 90071-3132. Telephone: 213-612-2500. Fax: 213-612-2554.
Miami, Florida Office: 5300 First Union Financial Center, 200 South Biscayne Boulevard, 33131-2339. Telephone: 305-579-0300. Fax: 305-579-0321.
Harrisburg, Pennsylvania Office: One Commerce Square, 417 Walnut Street, 17101-1904. Telephone: 717-237-4000. Fax: 717-237-4004.
Pittsburgh, Pennsylvania Office: One Oxford Centre, 301 Grant Street, 32nd Floor, 15219-6401. Telephone: 412-560-3300. Fax: 412-560-3399.
Princeton, New Jersey Office: 502 Carnegie Center, 08540-6241. Telephone: 609-919-6600. Fax: 609-919-6639.
Northern Virginia Office: 1600 Tysons Boulevard, McLean, Virginia 22102-4824. Telephone: 703-918-1000. Fax: 703-918-1999.
London, England Office: Morgan, Lewis & Bockius, 2 Gresham Street, London EC2V 7PE. Telephone: 44-207-710-5500. Fax: 44-207-710-5600.
Frankfurt, Germany Office: Guiollettstraße 54, 60325 Frankfurt am Main. Telephone: (49-69) 71 40 07-0. Fax: (49-69) 71 40 07-10.
Brussels, Belgium Office: Morgan, Lewis & Bockius, 7 Rue Guimard, B-1040. Telephone: 32-2/507.75.00. Fax: 32-2/507.75.55.
Tokyo, Japan Office: Yurakucho Denki Building S-556, 7-1 Yurakucho 1-chome, Chiyoda-ku, Tokyo 100-0006. Telephone: (81-3) 5219-2500. Fax: (81-3) 5219-2501.

Acquisitions and Mergers, Antitrust, Banking, Bankruptcy, Civil Litigation, Construction, Corporate, Elections and Campaign Financing, Employee Benefits and Pensions, Environmental, Estate Planning, Government Regulation, Health and Biotechnology, Immigration, Intellectual Property, Insurance, International Law, Investment Management and Financial Services, Labor and Employment, Legislative, Litigation, Municipal Finance, Natural Resources, Non-Profit Organizations, Partnerships, Patent Litigation, Personal Injury, Personal Law and Probate, Product Liability, Public Utilities, Real Estate, Savings and Loan, Securities Offerings, Trademarks and Copyrights, Taxation and White Collar Defense.

MEMBERS OF FIRM IN WASHINGTON

JOHN QUARLES, born April 26, 1935; admitted to bar, 1980, District of Columbia; 1965, U.S. Supreme Court. *Education:* Yale University (B.A., 1957); Harvard Law School (LL.B., 1961). General Counsel, 1970-1973 and Deputy Administrator, 1973-1977, Environmental Protection Agency. Assistant to Secretary, U.S. Department of the Interior, 1969-1970. Author: "Federal Regulation of Hazardous Wastes: A Guide to RCRA," 1982; "The New Clean Air Act," 1991. Chairman, Committee on Environmental Quality, Section of Public Utility Law, American Bar Association, 1980-1985. Founder, The Information Network for Superfund Settlements, 1988. Member, Board of Directors, Betz Laboratories, 1992—. ***Email:*** jquarles@morganlewis.com

CHARLES P. O'CONNOR, born September 29, 1940; admitted to bar, 1966, Massachusetts; 1968, District of Columbia; 1974, U.S. Supreme Court. *Education:* College of the Holy Cross (B.S., 1963); Boston College Law School (LL.B., 1966). Attorney, National Labor Relations Board, 1967-1968. ***Email:*** co'connor@morganlewis.com

JOHN H. SHENEFIELD, born January 23, 1939; admitted to bar, 1966, District of Columbia; 1972, U.S. Supreme Court. *Education:* Harvard University (A.B., 1960; LL.B., 1965). Assistant Attorney General, Antitrust Division, U.S. Department of Justice, 1977-1980. Acting Associate Attorney General, 1979-1980 and Associate Attorney General, 1980-1981, Department of Justice. Chairman, National Commission to Review Antitrust Law and Procedure, 1978-1979. Chairman, Standing Committee on Law and National Security, American Bar Association, 1992—. ***Email:*** jshenefield@morganlewis.com

CASWELL O. HOBBS, III, born August 25, 1941; admitted to bar, 1967, District of Columbia; 1972, U.S. Supreme Court. *Education:* University of Kansas (B.S., 1963); University of Pennsylvania Law School (LL.B., 1966). Director, Office of Policy Planning, 1972-1973, Assistant to the Chairman, 1970-1972 and Attorney, 1967-1970, Federal Trade Commission. Author: "The Federal Trade Commission," Antitrust Advisor, Shepards McGraw Hill, Inc., 1975. Chair, Section of Antitrust Law, American Bar Association, 1994-1995. ***Email:*** chobbs@morganlewis.com

RALPH N. ALBRIGHT, JR., born November 24, 1942; admitted to bar, 1968, District of Columbia; 1984, Maryland. *Education:* University of Pittsburgh (B.B.A., 1964); American University, Washington College of Law (J.D., 1968). ***Email:*** ralbright@morganlewis.com

WILLIAM L. GARDNER, born June 3, 1942; admitted to bar, 1968, District of Columbia; 1979, Massachusetts. *Education:* Duke University (A.B., 1964); American University, Washington College of Law (J.D., 1968). Chief, Criminal Civil Rights Section, U.S. Department of Justice, 1976-1979. ***Email:*** wgardner@morganlewis.com

JAMES A. GLASGOW, born April 17, 1945; admitted to bar, 1975, District of Columbia. *Education:* University of Arizona (B.A., 1966; J.D., 1969). Law Clerk to Judge Richard H. Chambers, U.S. Court of Appeals for the Ninth Circuit, 1969-1970. Deputy Assistant General Counsel for International Affairs, U.S. Department of Energy, 1977-1981. Chairman, Board of Directors, Waste Management Symposia, Inc., 1992—. Chairman, Fuel Supply and Trade Issues Task Force of U.S. Council for Energy Awareness, 1987-1993. *Member:* Federal and American Bar Associations; American Nuclear Society; International Nuclear Law Association; Institute of Electrical and Electronic Engineers. ***Email:*** jglasgow@morganlewis.com

KATHRYN B. McGRATH, born September 2, 1944; admitted to bar, 1969, District of Columbia. *Education:* Mount Holyoke College (A.B., 1966); Georgetown University Law Center (J.D., 1969). Director, Division of Investment Management, 1983-1990. Associate Director, Division of Market Regulation, 1977-1978. Assistant and Associate General Counsel, 1976-1977. Assistant Director, Division of Corporation Finance, 1976. Special Counsel and Executive Assistant to Chairman Ray Garrett, Jr., Legal Assistant to Commissioner Philip A. Loomis, Jr., 1970-1975, Securities and Exchange Commission. Staff Attorney, Office of the General Counsel, U.S. Department of the Treasury, 1969-1970. (Resident). ***Email:*** kmcgrath@morganlewis.com

GARY G. QUINTIERE, born November 26, 1944; admitted to bar, 1969, Virginia; 1970, District of Columbia. *Education:* Lafayette College (A.B., 1966); George Washington University National Law Center (J.D., 1969). Law Clerk to Judge Philip Nichols, Jr., U.S. Court of Claims, 1969-1970. ***Email:*** gquintiere@morganlewis.com

HARRY A. RISSETTO, born December 1, 1943; admitted to bar, 1969, New York; 1970, District of Columbia. *Education:* Fairfield University (A.B., 1965); Georgetown University Law Center (J.D., 1968). Law Clerk to Judge John J. Sirica, U.S. District Court, District of Columbia, 1968-1969. Law Clerk to Chief Justice Warren E. Burger, U.S. Supreme Court, 1969-1970. Adjunct Professor of Law, Georgetown University Law Center, 1986-1989. Co-Chairman, Railway Labor Act Committee, Section of Labor and Employment Law, American Bar Association, 1987-1989. ***Email:*** hrissetto@morganlewis.com

THOMAS F. WILLIAMSON, born August 29, 1940; admitted to bar, 1969, District of Columbia. *Education:* Yale University (B.A., 1962); George Washington University National Law Center (J.D., 1968). Associate Administrator for Procurement Law, Office of Federal Procurement Policy, 1977-1979. Assistant General Counsel, U.S. General Accounting Office, 1973-1977. Assistant Counsel, U.S. Commission on Government Procurement, 1971-1973. ***Email:*** twilliamson@morganlewis.com

(This Listing Continued)

MORGAN, LEWIS & BOCKIUS LLP, Washington—Continued

CHARLES I. COHEN, born October 11, 1945; admitted to bar, 1971, Pennsylvania; 1979, District of Columbia; 1980, U.S. Supreme Court. *Education:* Tulane University of Louisiana (B.A., 1967); University of Pittsburgh School of Law (J.D., 1970). Member, National Labor Relations Board, 1994-1996; National Labor Relations Board, 1971-1979 (Various capacities in Washington, DC and Philadelphia, PA). Adjunct Faculty Member, Catholic University of America, 1982-1985. Assistant Editor, The Developing Labor Law, 3rd Edition. *Member:* American Bar Association (Member, Committee on Development of the Law under the National Labor Relations Act, 1982—). Fellow, College of Labor and Employment Lawyers. ***Email:*** ccohen@morganlewis.com

GEORGE L. EDGAR, born November 2, 1941; admitted to bar, 1970, District of Columbia. *Education:* Dartmouth College (A.B., 1963; B.M.E., 1964); George Washington University National Law Center (J.D., 1970). ***Email:*** gedgar@morganlewis.com

WILLIAM H. LEWIS, JR., born November 12, 1942; admitted to bar, 1970, California; 1984, District of Columbia. *Education:* University of North Carolina (A.B., 1965; J.D., 1969). Co-Author, *The New Clean Air Act: A Guide to the Clean Air Program As Amended in 1990.* Lecturer, University of Virginia Law School, 1993—. Director, National Commission on Air Quality, 1978-1981. Executive Officer, California Air Resources Board, 1975-1978. Special Advisor on Environmental Policy, State of California, 1975. ***Email:*** wlewis@morganlewis.com

ALVIN H. GUTTERMAN, born May 12, 1945; admitted to bar, 1972, Tennessee; 1980, District of Columbia. *Education:* University of Massachusetts (B.S., 1969); New York University School of Law (J.D., 1972). ***Email:*** agutterman@morganlewis.com

PETER E. HALLE, born April 29, 1944; admitted to bar, 1973, Florida; 1975, District of Columbia; 1980, U.S. Supreme Court. *Education:* New York University (B.A., 1967); University of Miami School of Law (J.D., 1973). Trial Attorney, Antitrust Division, U.S. Department of Justice, 1973-1976 and 1977-1979. Special Assistant, Office of the Deputy Attorney General, 1976-1977. Assistant Chief, Trial Section, Antitrust Division, 1979-1981. Chair, Health Law Litigation Committee, 1991-1994, and Co-Chair, Antitrust Law Litigation Committee, 1994—, Section of Litigation, American Bar Association. Co-Chair, Antitrust and Trade Litigation Subcommittee of the Committee on Business and Corporate Litigation, American Bar Association, 1994—. Member, American Bar Association Coordinating Group on Bioethics and The Law, 1992-1995. Member, ABA Task Force on Health Care Reform, 1992-1994. Member, Antitrust Council, United States Chamber of Commerce. ***Email:*** phalle@morganlewis.com

LINDA L. GRIGGS, born May 20, 1949; admitted to bar, 1974, Ohio; 1980, District of Columbia. *Education:* Smith College (B.A., 1971); University of Cincinnati College of Law (J.D., 1974). ***Email:*** lgriggs@morganlewis.com

JAMES J. KELLEY, II, born November 22, 1947; admitted to bar, 1974, District of Columbia and Virginia; 1979, U.S. Supreme Court. *Education:* Belmont Abbey College (B.A., 1969); Washington & Lee University School of Law (J.D., 1974). ***Email:*** jkelley@morganlewis.com

KENNETH A. RUBIN, born November 24, 1947; admitted to bar, 1974, District of Columbia; 1992, U.S. Supreme Court. *Education:* Cornell University (B.S., 1969; M.S., 1971; J.D., 1973). Author: Book, "What the Japanese Business Executive Needs to Know About U.S. and E.C. Environmental Laws and Liabilities," NGB Tokyo, 1991; Safe Drinking Water Act - Environmental Law Practice Guide (Matthew Bender) 1992. Attorney, U.S. Department of Justice, 1973-1974. ***Email:*** krubin@morganlewis.com

MICHAEL BERENSON, born October 21, 1948; admitted to bar, 1974, District of Columbia; 1979, U.S. Supreme Court. *Education:* Johns Hopkins University (B.A., 1969); Georgetown University Law Center (J.D., 1973). ***Email:*** mberenson@morganlewis.com

GARY S. SMUCKLER, born January 29, 1949; admitted to bar, 1974, Michigan; 1980, District of Columbia. *Education:* University of Michigan (B.A., 1971); Wayne State University Law School (J.D., 1974). Assistant General Counsel and Deputy General Counsel, Federal Home Loan Mortgage Corporation, 1978-1983. ***Email:*** gsmuckler@morganlewis.com

HARRY W. BURTON, born March 29, 1949; admitted to bar, 1975, District of Columbia. *Education:* Princeton University (A.B., 1971); Georgetown University Law Center (J.D., 1975). ***Email:*** hburton@morganlewis.com

KATHLEEN W. COLLINS, born October 18, 1950; admitted to bar, 1975, Pennsylvania; 1978, District of Columbia. *Education:* Pennsylvania State University (B.A., 1972); Temple University School of Law (J.D., 1975). ***Email:*** kcollins@morganlewis.com

KEVIN P. GALLEN, born April 30, 1946; admitted to bar, 1975, District of Columbia; 1981, New York. *Education:* Villanova University (B.A., 1968; B.S., 1968); Harvard Law School (J.D., 1975). Tau Beta Pi. Registered Professional Engineer, Commonwealth of Pennsylvania, 1972—. Vice-President and General Counsel, Simmonds Precision Products, Inc., 1981-1984. Member, National Panel of Arbitrators, American Arbitration Association. ***Email:*** kgallen@morganlewis.com

ROBERTA L. HALLADAY, born July 6, 1949; admitted to bar, 1975, District of Columbia; 1980, U.S. Supreme Court. *Education:* St. Francis College (A.B., 1971); University of Notre Dame Law School (J.D., 1974). Member, Board of Directors, Foundation of the *Energy Law Journal*. ***Email:*** rhalladay@morganlewis.com

MICHAEL S. KELLY, born August 18, 1948; admitted to bar, 1975, District of Columbia; 1984, U.S. Supreme Court. *Education:* Georgetown University (B.A., 1970); George Washington University National Law Center (J.D., 1974). ***Email:*** mkelly@morganlewis.com

DONALD C. KLAWITER, born February 26, 1950; admitted to bar, 1975, Pennsylvania; 1979, U.S. Supreme Court; 1987, District of Columbia. *Education:* University of Pennsylvania (B.A., 1972; M.A., 1972; J.D., 1975). Trial Attorney, 1975-1978, Special Assistant, Office of Operations, 1978-1980, Chief, Dallas Field Office, 1980-1982 and Senior Trial Attorney, 1982-1986, Antitrust Division, U.S. Department of Justice. ***Email:*** dklawiter@morganlewis.com

STEPHEN PAUL MAHINKA, born June 25, 1949; admitted to bar, 1976, District of Columbia. *Education:* Johns Hopkins University (A.B., 1971); Harvard Law School (J.D., 1974). Law Clerk to Chief Justice Allan M. Hale, Massachusetts Appeals Court, 1974-1975. Chairman, Committee on Labor Exemptions, Section of Antitrust Law, American Bar Association, 1983-1987. Member: Editorial Board, *Food and Drug Law Journal*; Regulatory Affairs Professionals Society. ***Email:*** smahinka@morganlewis.com

FLOYD L. NORTON, IV, born October 23, 1950; admitted to bar, 1975, District of Columbia. *Education:* University of Virginia (B.A., 1972; J.D., 1975). Editor: Electric Power Purchasing Handbook, Executive Enterprises Publishing Co., Inc., 1989; "Electricity: Mandatory Access, Wheeling and Transmission. Energy Law and Transactions, Matthew Bender 1990; The Wholesale Service Obligation of Electric Utilities," Energy Law Journal Vol. 6, No. 2, 1985. *Member:* American Bar Association (Vice-Chairman, Antitrust Committee, Section on Public Utility, Transportation, and Communications Law); Federal Energy Bar Association. ***Email:*** fnorton@morganlewis.com

ROBERT A. DUFEK, born April 11, 1951; admitted to bar, 1976, District of Columbia. *Education:* University of Wisconsin (B.A., 1973); Georgetown University Law Center (J.D., 1976). Member, Adjunct Faculty, Georgetown University Law Center. ***Email:*** rdufek@morganlewis.com

CELIA ROADY, born December 6, 1951; admitted to bar, 1976, District of Columbia. *Education:* Duke University (A.B., 1973; J.D., 1976); Georgetown University Law Center (LL.M. in Taxation, 1979). *Member:* District of Columbia Bar (Member, Steering Committee, Section of Taxation, 1988-1995; Vice Chair, 1990-1991; Co-Chair, 1991-1993; Co-Chair, Exempt Organizations Committee, Section of Taxation, 1988-1991); American Bar Association (Member, Taxation Section; Exempt Organizations Committee, Vice Chair, 1991-1993; Chair, 1993-1995). ***Email:*** croady@morganlewis.com

JOSEPH E. SANTUCCI, JR., born March 5, 1950; admitted to bar, 1976, Virginia; 1978, District of Columbia. *Education:* University of Notre Dame (B.A., 1972); Catholic University of America, Columbus School of Law (J.D., 1976). ***Email:*** jsantucci@morganlewis.com

THOMAS A. SCHMUTZ, born December 28, 1948; admitted to bar, 1978, District of Columbia. *Education:* Fairleigh Dickinson University (B.A., 1972); Washington and Lee University School of Law (J.D., 1976). ***Email:*** tschmutz@morganlewis.com

GEORGE G. YEARSICH, born July 13, 1950; admitted to bar, 1976, Illinois; 1981, District of Columbia. *Education:* Butler University (B.A., 1972); Harvard Law School (J.D., 1976). Law Clerk to Judge Herbert Choy, U.S. 9th Circuit Court of Appeals, 1976-1977. Member, Office of the General Counsel, 1977-1978; Legal Assistant to the Chairman, 1978-1979; Special Counsel to the Chairman, 1979-1981, Securities and Exchange Commission. ***Email:*** gyearsich@morganlewis.com

PETER BUSCEMI, born September 25, 1950; admitted to bar, 1977, New York; 1979, District of Columbia; 1980, U.S. Supreme Court. *Education:* Columbia University (B.A., 1969); Princeton University (M.A., 1971); Columbia University School of Law (J.D., 1976). Law Clerk to Judge Carl McGowan, U.S. Court of Appeals for the District of Columbia Circuit, 1976-1977. Assistant to the Solicitor General, U.S. Department of Justice, 1977-1981. ***Email:*** pbuscemi@morganlewis.com

MICHAEL F. HEALY, born October 1, 1951; admitted to bar, 1977, District of Columbia. *Education:* New York University (B.A., 1973); Harvard Law School (J.D., 1976). Clerk to the Honorable Inzer B. Wyatt, U.S. District Court for the Southern District of New York, 1976-1977. ***Email:*** mhealy@morganlewis.com

(This Listing Continued)

JOHN D. McGRANE, born February 15, 1951; admitted to bar, 1977, District of Columbia; 1980, U.S. Supreme Court; 1982, U.S. Claims Court. *Education:* Cornell College (B.A., 1973); Georgetown University Law Center (J.D., 1976). Law Clerk to Hon. Barrington D. Parker, U.S. District Court for the District of Columbia, 1977-1978. *Member:* Federal Energy and American Bar Associations. ***Email:*** jmcgrane@morganlewis.com

MICHAEL W. STEINBERG, born September 20, 1952; admitted to bar, 1978, District of Columbia. *Education:* Yale University (B.A., 1974); University of Pennsylvania Law School (J.D., 1977). Law Clerk to Hon. Alfred L. Luongo, U.S. District Court, Eastern District of Pennsylvania, 1977-1979. Author: "Civil and Criminal Enforcement," chapter in RCRA Practice Manual, ABA, 1994; "The Demise of EPA's 'Mixture' and 'Derived-From' Rules?" Journal of Environmental Regulation, 1992; "Private-Party Cost Recovery Litigation Under Superfund," 22 Chemical Waste Litigation Reporter 56, 1991; "Can EPA Sue Other Federal Agencies?" Ecology Law Quarterly, 1990. U.S. Department of Justice, Environmental Defense Section, Trial Attorney, 1982-1984. Assistant Section Chief, 1984-1987. ***Email:*** msteinberg@morganlewis.com

HOWARD T. WEIR, III, born May 9, 1949; admitted to bar, 1979, District of Columbia. *Education:* University of California at Berkeley (A.B., 1971); Hollins College (M.A., 1974); University of Alabama Law School (J.D., 1977). Law Clerk to Judge Walter P. Gewin, U.S. Court of Appeals for the Fifth Circuit, 1977-1978. ***Email:*** hweir@morganlewis.com

ROBERT J. GAYBRICK, born May 1, 1950; admitted to bar, 1978, District of Columbia; 1978-1982, U.S. Court of Customs and Patent Appeals; 1982, U.S. Court of Appeals for the Federal Circuit; registered to practice before U.S. Patent and Trademark Office. *Education:* Michigan State University (B.S.E.E. & C.S., 1972); Catholic University of America Columbus School of Law (J.D., 1978). Member, Catholic University Law Review, 1976-1978. Technical Advisor to the Honorable Phillip B. Baldwin, Associate Judge, U.S. Court of Customs and Patent Appeals, 1978-1979. *Member:* The District of Columbia Bar; Bar Association of the District of Columbia; American and International Bar Associations; American Intellectual Property Law Association; American Chamber of Commerce in Japan; Asia-Pacific Lawyers Association; Licensing Executives Society. ***Email:*** rgaybrick@morganlewis.com

MARK N. BRAVIN, born August 11, 1951; admitted to bar, 1979, District of Columbia. *Education:* University of California at Los Angeles (B.A., 1973); John F. Kennedy School of Government, Harvard University (M.P.P., 1978); Harvard Law School (J.D., 1978). Author, "Beyond Aerospatiale: A Commentary on Foreign Discovery Provisions of the Restatement (Third) and the Proposed Amendments to the Federal Rules of Civil Procedure," in *The International Lawyer* (1991). Contributing author and co-editor for litigation of *Doing Business in Mexico* (Matthew Bender, 1990). *Member:* American Immigration Lawyers Association. ***Email:*** mbravin@morganlewis.com

STEVEN P. FRANTZ, born January 12, 1954; admitted to bar, 1979, District of Columbia. *Education:* University of Virginia (B.S.N.E., 1976); University of Virginia School of Law (J.D., 1979). ***Email:*** sfrantz@morganlewis.com

JAY M. GUTIERREZ, born June 10, 1951; admitted to bar, 1991, District of Columbia. *Education:* Georgetown University (B.S., 1973); Rutgers University Law School (J.D., 1979). Hearing Attorney, 1980-1983 and Regional Counsel, 1983-1989, United States Nuclear Regulatory Commission, Region I. ***Email:*** jgutierrez@morganlewis.com

THOMAS P. LEMKE, born July 30, 1954; admitted to bar, 1979, District of Columbia; 1980, New York. *Education:* State University of New York at Albany (B.A., 1976); American University, Washington College of Law (J.D., 1979). Co-Author: "How to Read a Mutual Fund Prospectus," 1999; "Soft Dollars and Other Brokerage Arrangements," 1997; "Regulation of Investment Companies," 1994; "Regulation of Investment Advisers," 1991. Member, NASD Investment Companies Committee. ***Email:*** tlemke@morganlewis.com

ARTHUR B. AXELSON, born February 12, 1955; admitted to bar, 1980, Maryland; 1981, District of Columbia. *Education:* Franklin & Marshall College (B.A., 1977); Villanova University School of Law (J.D., 1980). Editor, Villanova Law Review. Vice Chairman, ABA Subcommittee on Housing Finance, 1994—; Chairman, MBA State Legislative and Regulatory Compliance Committee, 1997. ***Email:*** aaxelson@morganlewis.com

MICHAEL F. CLAYTON, born March 2, 1954; admitted to bar, 1980, District of Columbia; 1981, Virginia; 1988, U.S. Supreme Court. *Education:* Wake Forest University (B.A., 1977); University of Virginia Law School (J.D., 1980). Elizabeth D. and Richard A. Merrill Lecturer in Law, University of Virginia School of Law. Member, Editorial Board, The Trademark Reporter. ***Email:*** mclayton@morganlewis.com

DONALD L. HAVERMANN, born October 11, 1954; admitted to bar, 1980, District of Columbia. *Education:* University of Virginia (B.S., 1976; J.D., 1980). ***Email:*** dhavermann@morganlewis.com

(This Listing Continued)

THOMAS E. REINERT, JR., born September 5, 1954; admitted to bar, 1980, District of Columbia. *Education:* Harvard University (A.B., 1975; J.D., 1980). ***Email:*** treinert@morganlewis.com

DONALD J. SILVERMAN, born February 21, 1955; admitted to bar, 1980, District of Columbia. *Education:* University of Pittsburgh (B.A., 1977; J.D., 1980). ***Email:*** dsilverman@morganlewis.com

KATHRYN L. GLEASON, born November 20, 1956; admitted to bar, 1981, District of Columbia. *Education:* Johns Hopkins University (B.A., 1978); Georgetown University Law Center (J.D., 1981). ***Email:*** kgleason@morganlewis.com

CHARLES C. THEBAUD, JR., born March 13, 1952; admitted to bar, 1981, Pennsylvania; 1987, District of Columbia. *Education:* United States Military Academy (B.S., 1974); Dickinson School of Law (J.D., 1981). ***Email:*** cthebaud@morganlewis.com

FRANCIS L. CASEY, born June 1, 1954; admitted to bar, 1982, District of Columbia. *Education:* Georgetown University (A.B., 1976; J.D., 1980). Law Clerk to Judge H. Emory Widener, Jr., U.S. Court of Appeals for the Fourth Circuit, 1980-1981. ***Email:*** fcasey@morganlewis.com

REID G. ADLER, born May 21, 1954; admitted to bar, 1982, Maryland; 1986, District of Columbia; registered to practice before U.S. Patent and Trademark Office. *Education:* University of Maryland (B.S., 1975); George Washington University National Law Center (J.D., 1982). Technical Law Clerk to Judge Giles S. Rich, U.S. Court of Appeals for the Federal Circuit, 1984. Research Fellow, Max Planck Institute (Munich) for Foreign and International Patent, Copyright and Competition Law, 1985. Founding President, Association of Federal Technology Transfer Executives, 1992-1993. Author: "Genome Research: Fulfilling the Public's Expectations for Knowledge and Commercialization," Science, Vol. 2567, August 1992; "Controlling the Applications of Biotechnology: A Critical Analysis of the Proposed Moratorium on Animal Patenting," 1 Harvard Journal of Law and Technology 1, May 1988, reprinted in Sept.-Oct. 1988 issue of the Biotechnology Law Report. ***PRACTICE AREAS:*** Intellectual Property; Technology Transfer. ***Email:*** radler@morganlewis.com

GRACE E. SPEIGHTS, born February 22, 1957; admitted to bar, 1982, Pennsylvania; 1985, District of Columbia. *Education:* University of Pennsylvania (B.A., 1978); George Washington University National Law Center (J.D., 1982). Law Clerk to the Honorable Aubrey E. Robinson, Jr., Senior Judge, U.S. District Court for the District of Columbia, 1982-1984. Adjunct Professor, American University, Washington College of Law, Products Liability. Member, House of Delegates, American Bar Association, 1989-1990. President, Greater Washington Area Chapter, Women Lawyers Division, National Bar Association, 1991-1993. Vice President, Washington Bar Association, 1988-1995. ***Email:*** gspeights@morganlewis.com

SCOTT A. STEMPEL, born June 10, 1957; admitted to bar, 1982, District of Columbia. *Education:* Northwestern University (B.A., 1979); George Washington University National Law Center (J.D., 1982). ***Email:*** sstempel@morganlewis.com

D. MICHAEL UNDERHILL, born August 27, 1958; admitted to bar, 1982, District of Columbia. *Education:* Carnegie-Mellon University (B.S., 1981); Duke University School of Law (J.D., 1982). ***Email:*** munderhill@morganlewis.com

THOMAS S. HARMAN, born March 5, 1957; admitted to bar, 1984, District of Columbia. *Education:* Duke University (B.A., 1979); University of Virginia School of Law (J.D., 1982); Georgetown University Law Center (Masters of Securities Law, 1988). Author: "Emerging Alternatives to Mutual Funds: Unit Investment Trusts and Other Fixed Portfolio Investment Vehicles," Duke Law Journal (December 1987); "Eligible Foreign Custodians and the Investment Company Act of 1940," The Business Lawyer (August 1991); "Custody Rules for Investment Advisers," The Investment Lawyer, Vol. 1, No. 4 (July 1994); "Arbitration Under the Advisers Act: Is it Here Already," The Investment Lawyer (July 1994); "Arbitration Under the Advisers Act," NSCP Currents (Jan.-Feb., 1995); "Truth in Pricing: The *Askin* Decision," The Investment Lawyer (May/June 1995); "When it's Mutual: The SEC Takes a Look at Investment Companies and Advisers," Business Law Today (July/August 1995); "The Challenge of Cultural Consolidation: SEC-OCC Joint Fund Examinations Agreement," NSCP Currents (September/October 1995), and "Integration and Attribution Issues Affecting Hedge Funds," Review of Securities & Commodities Regulation (December 6, 1995). Adjunct Professor, Georgetown Law Center, 1991—. Attorney, Division of Investment Management, Securities and Exchange Commission, 1982-1985. Special Counsel, Office of Disclosure and Adviser Regulation, 1986-1987. Chief, Office of Disclosure and Adviser Regulation, Division of Investment Management, 1987-1988. Former Chief Counsel, Division of Investment Management, Securities and Exchange Commission, 1988-1994; Associate Director (Chief Counsel), 1992-1994. ***PRACTICE AREAS:*** Mutual Funds; Securities Law; Banking. ***Email:*** tharman@morganlewis.com

(This Listing Continued)

MORGAN, LEWIS & BOCKIUS LLP, Washington—Continued

STANLEY F. LECHNER, born September 6, 1949; admitted to bar, 1983, District of Columbia; 1988, U.S. Supreme Court; 1997, Pennsylvania. *Education:* Pennsylvania State University (B.S., 1971); Georgetown University Law Center (J.D., 1983). ***Email:*** slechner@morganlewis.com

ROBERT S. SCHLOSSBERG, born August 6, 1957; admitted to bar, 1983, District of Columbia. *Education:* Franklin and Marshall College (B.A., 1979); George Washington University National Law Center (J.D., 1982). Co-Author, "Antitrust Considerations in Mergers and Acquisitions," *Business Organizations with Tax Planning*, 1992. Staff Attorney, United States Court of Appeals for the Ninth Circuit, 1982-1983. ***Email:*** rschlossberg@morganlewis.com

SANDRA J.P. DENNIS, born April 14, 1956; admitted to bar, 1984, District of Columbia. *Education:* Pennsylvania State University (B.A., 1978); University of South Carolina Law School (J.D., 1984). ***Email:*** sdennis@morganlewis.com

STEPHANIE M. MONACO, born September 13, 1957; admitted to bar, 1982, Maryland; 1992, District of Columbia. *Education:* University of Maryland (B.A., 1979); University of Baltimore School of Law (J.D., 1982). ***Email:*** smonaco@morganlewis.com

DONNA K. THIEL, born July 26, 1957; admitted to bar, 1982, District of Columbia; 1993, U.S. Supreme Court. *Education:* Drew University (B.A., 1979); Boston University School of Law (J.D., 1982). ***Email:*** dthiel@morganlewis.com

ANTHONY C. ROTH, born September 9, 1957; admitted to bar, 1983, Michigan; 1988, District of Columbia. *Education:* Goshen College (B.A., 1979); University of Notre Dame Law School (J.D., 1983). Law Clerk: Michigan Supreme Court Justice James L. Ryan, 1983-1984; Sixth Court of Appeals Judge Pierce Lively, 1984-1985. ***Email:*** aroth@morganlewis.com

DAVID J. McPHERSON, born March 23, 1959; admitted to bar, 1985, Maryland; 1989, District of Columbia. *Education:* Franklin & Marshall College (B.A., 1981); George Washington University National Law Center (J.D., 1984). Member, George Washington Law Review. ***Email:*** dmcpherson@morganlewis.com

RON N. DREBEN, born March 4, 1961; admitted to bar, 1988, District of Columbia. *Education:* Harvard University (A.B., 1983; J.D., 1986). ***Email:*** rdreben@morganlewis.com

JAMES R. SIMS III, born January 15, 1960; admitted to bar, 1986, Pennsylvania; 1988, District of Columbia. *Education:* Hope College (B.A., 1981); George Washington University National Law Center (J.D., 1986). ***Email:*** jsims@morganlewis.com

RICHARD S. MEYER, born September 11, 1960; admitted to bar, 1988, New York, District of Columbia, U.S. District Court for the District of Columbia and U.S. Court of Appeals for the Federal Circuit; registered to practice before U.S. Patent and Trademark Office. *Education:* Cooper Union School of Engineering (B.E., 1982); Georgetown University Law Center (J.D., cum laude, 1987). *Member:* American Bar Association (Member: Patent, Trademark and Copyright and Litigation Sections); American Intellectual Property Law Association; New York Intellectual Property Law Association. ***PRACTICE AREAS:*** Intellectual Property Law; Patents; Litigation. ***Email:*** rmeyer@morganlewis.com

KATHLEEN M. SANZO, born January 5, 1957; admitted to bar, 1982, Connecticut; 1987, District of Columbia. *Education:* Duke University (A.B., 1979); Emory University School of Law (J.D., 1982); George Washington University National Law Center (LL.M., 1985). ***Email:*** ksanzo@morganlewis.com

STEVEN W. STONE, born February 16, 1960; admitted to bar, 1988, Pennsylvania; 1989, District of Columbia. *Education:* Bates College (B.A., 1983); George Washington University National Law Center (J.D., 1988). ***Email:*** sstone@morganlewis.com

JONATHAN M. RICH, born April 5, 1959; admitted to bar, 1985, New York; 1995, District of Columbia. *Education:* Princeton University (A.B., 1981); Columbia University School of Law (J.D., 1984). ***Email:*** jrich@morganlewis.com

GREGORY L. NEEDLES, born November 25, 1960; admitted to bar, 1987, Florida; 1995, District of Columbia. *Education:* University of Florida (B.S.A.C., 1982); University of Florida School of Law (J.D., 1987); New York University School of Law (LL.M., 1988). ***Email:*** gneedles@morganlewis.com

MARK A. SRERE, born November 26, 1959; admitted to bar, 1988, District of Columbia. *Education:* Reed College (B.A., 1981); University of Texas School of Law (J.D., 1986). ***Email:*** msrere@morganlewis.com

(This Listing Continued)

MARK D. FITTERMAN, born November 1, 1942; admitted to bar, 1974, Ohio; 1975, District of Columbia. *Education:* Oberlin College (A.B., 1964); Wright State University (M.B.A., 1971); Georgetown University Law Center (J.D., 1974). ***Email:*** mfitterman@morganlewis.com

NANCY R. KUHN, born April 28, 1951; admitted to bar, 1985, District of Columbia. *Education:* Wake Forest University (B.A., 1973); University of North Carolina at Chapel Hill (M.P.A., 1975); George Washington University National Law Center (J.D., 1985). ***Email:*** nkuhn@morganlewis.com

MARY ANN K. HUNTINGTON, born March 5, 1964; admitted to bar, 1990, Maryland; 1991, District of Columbia. *Education:* Georgetown University (A.B., 1986; J.D., 1990). ***Email:*** mhuntington@morganlewis.com

JOHN E. MATTHEWS, born August 31, 1964; admitted to bar, 1991, District of Columbia. *Education:* Georgetown University (B.S.F.S., 1986) University of Virginia School of Law (J.D., 1990). ***Email:*** jmatthews@morganlewis.com

JOHN F. RING, born May 29, 1963; admitted to bar, 1989, Connecticut; 1991, District of Columbia. *Education:* Catholic University of America (B.A., 1985; J.D., 1989). ***Email:*** jring@morganlewis.com

DAVID A. SIRIGNANO, born March 5, 1953; admitted to bar, 1979, New York; 2000, District of Columbia. *Education:* Manhattan College (B.A., 1975); Albany Law School (J.D., 1978). ***Email:*** dsirignano@morganlewis.com

LAWRENCE P. STADULIS, born February 5, 1964; admitted to bar, 1990, New York; 1992, District of Columbia. *Education:* Boston College (B.A., 1986; J.D., 1989). ***Email:*** lstadulis@morganlewis.com

PAUL HUEY-BURNS, born November 1, 1956; admitted to bar, 1982, District of Columbia. *Education:* Johns Hopkins University (B.A., 1978); University of Pennsylvania Law School (J.D., 1982). ***Email:*** phuey-burns@morganlewis.com

CHRISTIAN J. MIXTER, born March 13, 1953; admitted to bar, 1978, New York; 1981, District of Columbia. *Education:* Ohio State University (B.A., 1974); Duke University School of Law (J.D., 1977). Chief Litigation Counsel, U.S. Securities and Exchange Commission Division of Enforcement 1997-2000. Co-recipient, Law and Policy Award, 1997. Recipient, Stanley Sporkin Award, 1998. Former Associate Counsel to Independent Counsel Lawrence E. Walsh, Iran/Contra Investigation. ***Email:*** cmixter@morganlewis.com

WILLARD K. TOM, born August 11, 1952; admitted to bar, 1979, District of Columbia. *Education:* Harvard University (A.B., 1975); Harvard Law School (J.D., 1979). ***Email:*** wtom@morganlewis.com

GREGORY P. ASCIOLLA, born February 22, 1965; admitted to bar, 1994, New York; 1996, District of Columbia. *Education:* Boston College (A.B., 1987); Catholic University of America, Columbus School of Law (J.D., 1993). ***Email:*** gasciolla@morganlewis.com

M. ELIZABETH BIERMAN, born October 14, 1955; admitted to bar, 1987, District of Columbia. *Education:* University of Virginia (B.A., 1977); Catholic University of America, Columbus School of Law (J.D., 1986). ***Email:*** mebierman@morganlewis.com

PETER M. BOYLE, born May 11, 1966; admitted to bar, 1994, New Jersey; 1995, District of Columbia and New York. *Education:* Swarthmore College (B.A., 1988); Fordham University School of Law (J.D., 1993). ***Email:*** pboyle@morganlewis.com

KAREN A. BUTCHER, born December 30, 1966; admitted to bar, 1993, Virginia; 1994, District of Columbia. *Education:* University of Virginia (B.S., 1988; J.D., 1993). ***Email:*** kbutcher@morganlewis.com

BRAD FAGG, born November 4, 1962; admitted to bar, 1990, New York; 1992, District of Columbia. *Education:* Wake Forest University (B.A., 1985); Columbia University School of Law (J.D., 1988). ***Email:*** bfagg@morganlewis.com

CAROLE R. KLEIN, born November 16, 1956; admitted to bar, 1991, District of Columbia. *Education:* Georgetown University (B.S.F.S., 1982); University of Virginia School of Law (J.D., 1990). ***Email:*** cklein@morganlewis.com

JEFFREY A. LINDEMAN, born July 18, 1961; admitted to bar, 1992, Virginia; 1995, District of Columbia; 1996, Tennessee; registered to practice before U.S. Patent and Trademark Office. *Education:* West Virginia University (B.A., 1983); University of South Carolina (Ph.D., 1988); Georgetown University Law Center (J.D., 1992). ***Email:*** jlindeman@morganlewis.com

PENELOPE M. "GARI" LISTER, born September 20, 1965; admitted to bar, 1992, Pennsylvania; 1993, District of Columbia. *Education:* Wellesley College (B.A., 1987); George Washington University National Law Center (J.D., 1991). ***Email:*** plister@morganlewis.com

NATHAN W. McCUTCHEON, born June 16, 1965; admitted to bar, 1993, Virginia; 1995, District of Columbia. *Education:* Vanderbilt University (B.S.E., 1987); George Washington University National Law Center (J.D., 1993). ***Email:*** nmccutcheon@morganlewis.com

(This Listing Continued)

NANCY L. ROWE, born February 11, 1964; admitted to bar, 1994, District of Columbia. *Education:* Bucknell University (B.A., 1986); Catholic University of America, Columbus School of Law (J.D., 1992). ***Email:*** nrowe@morganlewis.com

JOHN G. SMITH, born August 28, 1963; admitted to bar, 1991, Maryland; 1992, District of Columbia; 1995, Colorado; registered to practice before U.S. Patent and Trademark Office. *Education:* Marquette University (B.S.E.E., 1987); George Washington University National Law Center (J.D., 1991). ***Email:*** jsmith@morganlewis.com

JOHN H. WILLIAMSON, born June 23, 1963; admitted to bar, 1990, Texas; 1991, District of Columbia; 1995, England and Wales. *Education:* Princeton University (A.B., 1987); University of Texas School of Law (J.D., 1990). ***Email:*** jwilliamson@morganlewis.com

JOHN D. ZELE, born June 18, 1966; admitted to bar, 1993, Virginia; 1996, District of Columbia; registered to practice before U.S. Patent and Trademark Office. *Education:* Princeton University (B.S.E.E., 1988); George Washington University National Law Center (J.D., 1993). ***Email:*** jzele@morganlewis.com

CHRISTOPHER L. WHITE, born March 16, 1963; admitted to bar, 1989, District of Columbia. *Education:* Wake Forest University (B.A., 1985); The Catholic University of America, Columbus School of Law (J.D., 1988). ***Email:*** cwhite@morganlewis.com

MICHAEL R. DZWONCZYK, born November 4, 1962; admitted to bar, 1990, Pennsylvania; 1992, District of Columbia; U.S. Court of Appeals for the Federal Circuit; registered to practice before U.S. Patent and Trademark Office. *Education:* Temple University (B.S., 1984); Dickinson School of Law (J.D., 1990). ***Email:*** mdzwonczyk@morganlewis.com

LYNN E. ECCLESTON, born November 14, 1948; admitted to bar, 1988, District of Columbia; registered to practice before U.S. Patent and Trademark Office. *Education:* Northwestern University (B.A., 1970); Wayne State University (M.A., 1980; J.D., 1986). ***Email:*** leccleston@morganlewis.com

MICHELE VAN PATTEN FRANK, born March 4, 1966; admitted to bar, 1995, Pennsylvania; 1997, District of Columbia; registered to practice before U.S. Patent and Trademark Office. *Education:* Union College (B.S.M.E., 1988); American University, Washington College of Law (J.D., 1994). ***Email:*** mvfrank@morganlewis.com

R. TYLER GOODWYN, IV, born March 3, 1960; admitted to bar, 1994, Virginia; 2000, District of Columbia; registered to practice before U.S. Patent and Trademark Office. *Education:* Virginia Military Institute (B.S.E.E., 1982); College of William & Mary, Marshall-Wythe School of Law (J.D., 1994). ***Email:*** rtgoodwyn@morganlewis.com

MICHAEL C. GRIFFEN, born March 2, 1964; admitted to bar, 1994, New York; 1997, District of Columbia. *Education:* LeMoyne College (B.A., 1986); State University of New York at Binghamton (M.A., 1989); State University of New York at Buffalo School of Law (J.D., 1993). ***Email:*** mgriffen@morganlewis.com

SHELDON M. KLINE, born June 2, 1948; admitted to bar, 1987, Virginia; 1988, District of Columbia. *Education:* University of Massachusetts (B.A., 1970); Virginia Polytechnic Institute (M.A., 1981); George Mason University School of Law (J.D., 1987). ***Email:*** skline@morganlewis.com

W. JOHN McGUIRE, born July 26, 1957; admitted to bar, 1989, District of Columbia. *Education:* Wichita State University (B.A., 1980; M.P.A., 1986); Washburn University School of Law (J.D., 1986). ***Email:*** wjmcguire@morganlewis.com

PAUL J. ZAFFUTS, born January 15, 1960; admitted to bar, 1992, District of Columbia; 1994, California. *Education:* Rensselaer Polytechnic Institute (B.S., 1982; M.E., 1983); Cornell Law School (J.D., 1992). ***Email:*** pzaffuts@morganlewis.com

COUNSEL

SHELDON S. COHEN, born June 28, 1927; admitted to bar, 1952, District of Columbia; 1956, U.S. Supreme Court. *Education:* George Washington University (A.B., 1950; J.D., 1952). Professorial Lecturer, George Washington University Law School, 1957-1982. Adjunct Professor, University of Miami School of Law, 1974-1985. Professorial Lecturer, Howard University Law School, 1956-1957. Chief Counsel, Internal Revenue Service, 1964-1965. Commissioner of Internal Revenue, 1965-1969. President, Inter-American Center of Tax Administrators, 1967-1968. Member, Administrative Conference of the United States, 1974-1982, Chairman, Tax Steering Committee, 1974-1982, and Chairman, Committee on Retirement Benefits, 1970-1973, American Bar Association. Consultant to Comptroller General of the United States, 1982—. *Member:* American Law Institute; American College of Tax Counsel. Executive Committee, The Supreme Court Historical Society. ***Email:*** sscohen@morganlewis.com

RICHARD C. HOTVEDT, born March 4, 1935; admitted to bar, 1962, District of Columbia; 1970, U.S. Supreme Court. *Education:* Marquette University (B.S., 1957); Harvard Law School (LL.B., 1960). Attorney, National Labor Relations Board, 1960-1962. ***Email:*** rhotvedt@morganlewis.com

(This Listing Continued)

ADRIAN L. MORCHOWER, born April 20, 1930; admitted to bar, 1973, District of Columbia. *Education:* Syracuse University (B.A., 1952); Rutgers University (J.D., 1965); Georgetown University Law Center (LL.M., Taxation, 1968). Attorney, Internal Revenue Service, 1965-1969. ***Email:*** amorchower@morganlewis.com

E. CARL UEHLEIN, JR., born May 7, 1941; admitted to bar, 1968, District of Columbia; 1991, U.S. Supreme Court. *Education:* Swarthmore College (B.A., 1962); Boston College Law School (LL.B., 1965). Author, "The NLRA and the Antitrust Laws," NLRA, Law Practice, Matthew Bender, 1995. Attorney, National Labor Relations Board, 1965-1968. Executive Assistant to the Secretary, U.S. Department of Labor, 1971-1973. Co-Chairman, Antitrust and Labor Relations Law Committee, Section of Labor and Employment Law, American Bar Association, 1981-1984. ***Email:*** ecuehlein@morganlewis.com

SPECIAL COUNSEL IN WASHINGTON

EDGAR H. MARTIN, born February 21, 1934; admitted to bar, 1962, District of Columbia; registered to practice before U.S. Patent and Trademark Office. *Education:* Rensselaer Polytechnic Institute (B.Met.E., 1956); Georgetown University Law Center (LL.B., 1962). ***Email:*** ehmartin@morganlewis.com

MONA C. ZEIBERG, born May 23, 1961; admitted to bar, 1991, District of Columbia. *Education:* American University (B.A., 1983); Emory University (J.D., 1986). ***Email:*** mzeiberg@morganlewis.com

OF COUNSEL IN WASHINGTON

WILLIAM E. BAER, JR., born January 24, 1958; admitted to bar, 1983, Virginia; 1984, District of Columbia. *Education:* College of William & Mary (B.A., 1980); Cornell Law School (J.D., 1983). ***Email:*** wbaer@morganlewis.com

CHRISTOPHER J. BARR, born January 25, 1957; admitted to bar, 1983, District of Columbia. *Education:* Yale University (B.A., 1979); George Washington University National Law Center (J.D., 1983). ***Email:*** cbarr@morganlewis.com

JOHN MILLS BARR, born December 2, 1962; admitted to bar, 1989, Virginia; 1990, District of Columbia. *Education:* Wabash College (B.A., 1984); Harvard Law School (J.D., 1987). ***Email:*** jbarr@morganlewis.com

MARY JANE BOSWELL, born July 18, 1957; admitted to bar, 1986, Florida; 1988, District of Columbia; registered to practice before U.S. Patent and Trademark Office. *Education:* Vanderbilt University (B.E./E.E., 1979); DePaul University (J.D., 1986). ***Email:*** mboswell@morganlewis.com

JOSEPH BROOKS, born October 16, 1956; admitted to bar, 1982, District of Columbia; 2000, Massachusetts. *Education:* Indiana University of Pennsylvania (B.A., 1979); University of Virginia School of Law (J.D., 1982). ***Email:*** jbrooks@morganlewis.com

JOHN E. DANIEL, born October 14, 1943; admitted to bar, 1983, U.S. Supreme Court; 1996, District of Columbia. *Education:* University of Alabama (B.S.C.E., 1965; J.D., 1968). Chief of Staff, U.S. Environmental Protection Agency, 1981-1983; Vice President, International Technology Corporation, 1989-1994. ***Email:*** jdaniel@morganlewis.com

JACK P. DROGIN, born February 9, 1963; admitted to bar, 1990, New York (Not admitted in District of Columbia). *Education:* University of Pennsylvania (B.A., 1985); Harvard Law School (J.D., 1989). ***Email:*** jdrogin@morganlewis.com

BARBARA A. FRIEDMAN, born January 18, 1953; admitted to bar, 1983, District of Columbia; 1986, New York. *Education:* State University of New York at Stony Brook (B.A., 1975); George Washington University National Law Center (J.D., 1983). ***Email:*** bfriedman@morganlewis.com

MARGERY SINDER FRIEDMAN, born November 23, 1950; admitted to bar, 1978, District of Columbia. *Education:* Case Western Reserve University (B.A., 1972); Georgetown University Law Center (J.D., 1978). ***Email:*** mfriedman@morganlewis.com

L. DENISE GALAMBOS, born August 12, 1962; admitted to bar, 1990, Wisconsin; 1996, District of Columbia. *Education:* Princeton University (B.A., 1984); University of Wisconsin Law School (J.D., 1990). ***Email:*** ldgalambos@morganlewis.com

ANGELA C. GOELZER, born October 14, 1955; admitted to bar, 1980, District of Columbia. *Education:* Providence College (B.A., 1977); Harvard Law School (J.D., 1980). ***Email:*** agoelzer@morganlewis.com

ALISSA A. HORVITZ, born April 10, 1966; admitted to bar, 1990, Maryland; 1991, District of Columbia. *Education:* Cornell University (B.S., 1987); George Washington University National Law Center (J.D., 1990). ***Email:*** ahorvitz@morganlewis.com

RICHARD F. JACKSON, born November 4, 1962; admitted to bar, 1987, District of Columbia. *Education:* Georgetown University (B.S., 1984); Georgetown University Law Center (J.D., 1987). ***Email:*** rjackson@morganlewis.com

(This Listing Continued)

MORGAN, LEWIS & BOCKIUS LLP, Washington—Continued

MICHAEL A. McCORD, born February 2, 1948; admitted to bar, 1975, District of Columbia and U.S. Supreme Court. *Education:* Indiana University (A.B., 1970); Harvard Law School (J.D., 1974). U.S. Department of Justice, Appellate Section, Attorney, 1974-1981; U.S. Department of Labor, Counsel for Appellate Litigation, 1981-1985; U.S. Department of Justice, Environmental Defense Section, Attorney, 1985-1987; Assistant Section Chief, 1987-1994. ***Email:*** mmccord@morganlewis.com

DAVID M. MORRIS, born March 25, 1959; admitted to bar, 1989, Virginia; 1992, District of Columbia. *Education:* Virginia Commonwealth University (B.A., 1983); University of Virginia School of Law (J.D., 1989). ***Email:*** dmorris@morganlewis.com

THOMAS J. O'BRIEN, born May 14, 1947; admitted to bar, 1984, Virginia; 1985, District of Columbia; 1993, U.S. Supreme Court. *Education:* College of the Holy Cross (A.B., 1969); University of North Carolina at Chapel Hill (M.R.P., 1971); George Washington University National Law Center (J.D., 1984). ***Email:*** to'brien@morganlewis.com

MONICA L. PARRY, born July 6, 1958; admitted to bar, 1996, District of Columbia. *Education:* Marquette University (B.A., 1980); College of William & Mary, Marshall-Wythe School of Law (J.D., 1983). ***Email:*** mparry@morganlewis.com

DARYL M. SHAPIRO, born May 6, 1963; admitted to bar, 1991, Pennsylvania; 1997, District of Columbia. *Education:* Temple University (B.B.A., 1988); University of Miami School of Law (J.D., 1991). ***Email:*** dshapiro@morganlewis.com

DON WALLACE, JR., born April 23, 1932; admitted to bar, 1957, New York; 1978, District of Columbia and U.S. Supreme Court. *Education:* Yale University (B.A., 1953); Harvard University Law School (LL.B., 1957). ***Email:*** dwallace@morganlewis.com

ELIZABETH WEIMAR, born June 26, 1957; admitted to bar, 1986, Virginia; 2001, District of Columbia. *Education:* Georgetown University (B.S., 1979); Catholic University of America, Columbus School of Law (J.D., 1986). ***Email:*** eweimar@morganlewis.com

ROBERT B. WIGGINS, born July 20, 1961; admitted to bar, 1988, District of Columbia. *Education:* University of North Carolina (B.S., 1983; J.D., 1986). ***Email:*** rwiggins@morganlewis.com

KENNETH D. WOODROW, born February 16, 1966; admitted to bar, 1991, Ohio; 1997, District of Columbia. *Education:* University of Virginia (B.A, 1988); Washington & Lee University School of Law (J.D., 1991). ***Email:*** kwoodrow@morganlewis.com

PHILLIP C. ZANE, born September 25, 1961; admitted to bar, 1991, Illinois; 1996, District of Columbia. *Education:* Pomona College (B.A., 1983); New York University School of Law (J.D., 1991). ***Email:*** pzane@morganlewis.com

ASSOCIATES IN WASHINGTON

JOHN V. AYANIAN, admitted to bar, 1993, Illinois; 2000, District of Columbia. *Education:* University of Michigan (B.A., 1990); DePaul University School of Law (J.D., 1993). ***Email:*** jayanian@morganlewis.com

MAYA J. BERMINGHAM, admitted to bar, 2000, District of Columbia. *Education:* Harvard College (B.A., 1990); New York University School of Law (J.D., 1997). ***Email:*** mbermingham@morganlewis.com

JESSICA R. BERNANKE, admitted to bar, 1995, New York; 1997, District of Columbia. *Education:* Boston College (B.A., 1989); College of William and Mary (J.D., 1994). ***Email:*** jbernanke@morganlewis.com

PAUL M. BESSETTE, admitted to bar, 2000, Maryland; 2001, District of Columbia. *Education:* Boston University (B.S., 1982); University of Iowa Law School (J.D., 1999). ***Email:*** pbessette@morganlewis.com

DOROTHY J. BLACK, admitted to bar, 1993, California; 1994, District of Columbia. *Education:* Stanford University (B.A., 1964); Johns Hopkins University (M.A., 1966); Georgetown University Law Center (J.D., 1993). ***Email:*** dblack@morganlewis.com

JEFFREY C. BLOCKINGER, admitted to bar, 1997, New York; 1998, District of Columbia. *Education:* Purdue University (B.A., 1991); University of Miami School of Law (J.D., 1996). ***Email:*** jblockinger@morganlewis.com

CHRISTINE E. BLOOMQUIST, admitted to bar, 1995, Illinois; 1997, District of Columbia. *Education:* Tulane University (B.A., 1991); Washington University (M.H.A., J.D., 1995). ***Email:*** cbloomquist@morganlewis.com

TRAVIS P. BOOZER, admitted to bar, 1998, Florida (Not admitted in District of Columbia). *Education:* Duke University (B.A., 1994); University of Georgia (J.D., 1997). ***Email:*** tboozer@morganlewis.com

(This Listing Continued)

GEORGE BOROVAS, admitted to bar, 1998, New York; 1999, District of Columbia. *Education:* University of Wisconsin (B.S., 1992); George Washington University Law School (J.D., 1996). ***Email:*** gborovas@morganlewis.com

ANNE BRAFFORD, admitted to bar, 1996, Missouri; 2000, District of Columbia. *Education:* Iowa State University (B.S., 1992); University of Iowa College of Law (J.D., 1996). ***Email:*** abrafford@morganlewis.com

DONALD E. BROADFIELD, JR., admitted to bar, 1996, Virginia; 2001, District of Columbia. *Education:* University of Kentucky (B.G.S., 1986); Case Western Reserve University School of Law (J.D., 1996). ***Email:*** dbroadfield@morganlewis.com

ADRIENNE A. BROWN, admitted to bar, 1999, Pennsylvania; 2001, District of Columbia. *Education:* Yale University (B.A., 1996); University of Pennsylvania Law School (J.D., 1999). ***Email:*** abrown@morganlewis.com

BOYD J. BROWN, II, admitted to bar, 1993, Virginia and Maryland; 1996, District of Columbia. *Education:* Swarthmore College (B.A., 1985); University of Virginia School of Law (J.D., 1993); Georgetown University Law Center (LL.M., 1999). ***Email:*** bbrown@morganlewis.com

JAMES A. BUDINETZ, admitted to bar, 1995, Connecticut; 2001, District of Columbia. *Education:* Georgetown University (B.S., 1992); American University, Washington College of Law (J.D., 1995). ***Email:*** jbudinetz@morganlewis.com

VU BUI, admitted to bar, 1999, New York; 2001, District of Columbia. *Education:* George Washington University (B.A., 1995); Fordham University School of Law (J.D., 1998). ***Email:*** vbui@morganlewis.com

GREGORY W. CAMET, admitted to bar, 1996, Maryland; 1998, District of Columbia. *Education:* Tulane University (B.A., 1990); The American University, Washington College of Law (J.D., 1996). ***Email:*** gcamet@morganlewis.com

DANIEL S. CARLINEO, admitted to bar, 1998, California; 1999, District of Columbia. *Education:* State University of New York, Binghamton (B.S.E.E., 1992); University of Cincinnati (J.D., 1998). ***Email:*** dcarlineo@morganlewis.com

MEREDITH A. CARLO, admitted to bar, 1997, Maryland; 2000, District of Columbia. *Education:* James Madison University (B.S., 1994); Harvard Law School (J.D., 1997). ***Email:*** mcarlo@morganlewis.com

G. SCOTT CARTER, admitted to bar, 1993, District of Columbia. *Education:* Lebanon Valley College (B.S., 1989); University of Chicago Law School (J.D., 1992). ***Email:*** gscarter@morganlewis.com

TERRA E. CASTALDI, admitted to bar, 1997, Ohio; 1999, District of Columbia. *Education:* Bowling Green State University-Ohio (B.S., 1994); Ohio State University (J.D., 1997). ***Email:*** tcastaldi@morganlewis.com

MARIA D. CASTNER, admitted to bar, 2000, Maryland (Not admitted in District of Columbia). *Education:* American University (B.A., 1996); University of Miami School of Law (J.D., 2000). ***Email:*** mcastner@morganlewis.com

LISA ANN CHAIKIN, admitted to bar, 1995, Massachusetts; 1998, District of Columbia. *Education:* University of Michigan (B.A., 1991); Suffolk University (J.D., 1995). ***Email:*** lchaikin@morganlewis.com

A. C. BROOKE CLAGETT, admitted to bar, 1997, Maryland; 1998, District of Columbia. *Education:* Macalester College (B.A., 1993); Tulane Law School (J.D., 1997). ***Email:*** bclagett@morganlewis.com

THOMAS P. CONAGHAN, admitted to bar, 1996, Maryland; 1997, District of Columbia; 2000, England and Wales. *Education:* University of Notre Dame (B.A., 1992; J.D., 1995). ***Email:*** tconaghan@morganlewis.com

PATRICK D. CONNER, admitted to bar, 1998, Georgia; 2001, District of Columbia. *Education:* University of Georgia (B.A., 1995; J.D., 1998). ***Email:*** pconner@morganlewis.com

AMY J. CONWAY, admitted to bar, 1993, Maryland; 1994, District of Columbia. *Education:* University of Vermont (B.A., 1990); Catholic University of America, Columbus School of Law (J.D., 1993). ***Email:*** aconway@morganlewis.com

LESLIE SPERLING CRUZ, admitted to bar, 1997, District of Columbia and Maryland. *Education:* University of Maryland (B.A., 1991; J.D., 1995). ***Email:*** lcruz@morganlewis.com

PATRICK M. CURRAN, JR., admitted to bar, 1998, Maryland; 2001, District of Columbia. *Education:* Bowdoin College (A.B., 1991); College of William & Mary (M.A., 1993); Georgetown University Law Center (J.D., 1998). ***Email:*** pcurran@morganlewis.com

RACHEL B. DAMELIN, admitted to bar, 1998, Maryland; 1999, District of Columbia. *Education:* Tufts University (B.A., 1994); Boston College Law School (J.D., 1997). ***Email:*** rdamelin@morganlewis.com

F. NIKKI DAVIS, admitted to bar, 1999, Arkansas (Not admitted in District of Columbia). *Education:* University of Arkansas (B.S., 1996); University of Arkansas School of Law (J.D., 1998). ***Email:*** fdavis@morganlewis.com

(This Listing Continued)

ANN K. DERSTINE, admitted to bar, 2000, Maryland (Not admitted in District of Columbia). *Education:* Messiah College (B.A., 1995); New York University School of Law (J.D., 2000). ***Email:*** aderstine@morganlewis.com

RANI E. DOYLE, admitted to bar, 1995, New Jersey; 1996, New York; 2001, District of Columbia. *Education:* Rutgers University (B.A., 1989); New York Law School (J.D., 1995). ***Email:*** rdoyle@morganlewis.com

SUSAN S. DUNNE, admitted to bar, 1992, Virginia; 1994, District of Columbia. *Education:* Cornell University (B.S., 1989); George Washington University National Law Center (J.D., 1992). ***Email:*** sdunne@morganlewis.com

MAGDA EL GUINDI-ROSENBAUM, admitted to bar, 1996, Maryland; 1997, District of Columbia. *Education:* Smith College (B.A., 1991); Northwestern University School of Law (J.D., 1996). ***Email:*** mer@morganlewis.com

SALMAN H. ELMI, admitted to bar, 2000, Maryland; 2001, District of Columbia. *Education:* University of Michigan (B.A., 1997); Emory University School of Law (J.D., 2000). ***Email:*** selmi@morganlewis.com

DONALD E. ENGLISH, JR., admitted to bar, 2000, Maryland; 2001, District of Columbia. *Education:* United States Air Force Academy (B.S., 1995); George Washington University National Law Center (J.D., 2000). ***Email:*** denglish@morganlewis.com

J. CLAYTON EVERETT, JR., admitted to bar, 1999, Virginia; 2000, District of Columbia. *Education:* University of Virginia (B.A., 1996); University of Virginia School of Law (J.D., 1999). ***Email:*** jeverett@morganlewis.com

ROBERT C. FARLEY, JR., admitted to bar, 1996, Pennsylvania; 1997, New Jersey (Not admitted in District of Columbia). *Education:* University of Tennessee (B.A., 1985); Temple University School of Law (J.D., 1996). ***Email:*** rfarley@morganlewis.com

BARBARA M. FLAHERTY, admitted to bar, 1997, Maryland; 1998, District of Columbia. *Education:* University of Maryland (B.S., 1993); The Catholic University of America, Columbus School of Law (J.D., 1997). ***Email:*** bflaherty@morganlewis.com

COLIN T. FLYNN, admitted to bar, 1993, New Jersey; 1994, District of Columbia. *Education:* Fordham University (B.A., 1987); Catholic University of America, Columbus School of Law (J.D., 1992). ***Email:*** cflynn@morganlewis.com

JOHN M. FORD, admitted to bar, 1994, New Jersey; 1995, Pennsylvania; 2000, District of Columbia. *Education:* St. Joseph's University (B.S., 1991); Rutgers University (J.D., 1994). ***Email:*** jmford@morganlewis.com

STEPHANIE M. FOSTER, admitted to bar, 1994, New York; 2000, District of Columbia. *Education:* Wesleyan University (B.A., 1988); Brooklyn Law School (J.D., 1993). ***Email:*** sfoster@morganlewis.com

PAUL A. FOURNIER, admitted to bar, 1998, Maryland; 1999, District of Columbia; registered to practice before U.S. Patent and Trademark Office. *Education:* University of Maine (B.S.E.E., 1991); George Washington University National Law Center (J.D., 1997). ***Email:*** pfournier@morganlewis.com

MARY J. FRANK, admitted to bar, 2000, Maryland; 2001, District of Columbia. *Education:* Southwest Missouri State University (B.F.A., 1986); University of Utah (M.F.A., 1989); Fordham University School of Law (J.D., 2000). ***Email:*** mjfrank@morganlewis.com

DOUGLAS J. FREE, admitted to bar, 2000, Maryland (Not admitted in District of Columbia). *Education:* Georgetown University (B.A., 1976); University of Maryland (M.A., 1987); The Catholic University of America, Columbus School of Law (J.D., 2000). ***Email:*** dfree@morganlewis.com

JONATHAN C. FRITTS, admitted to bar, 1998, Virginia; 1999, District of Columbia. *Education:* University of Virginia (A.B., 1994); Georgetown University Law Center (J.D., 1998). ***Email:*** jfritts@morganlewis.com

LAWRENCE S. GANSLAW, admitted to bar, 1998, Maryland; 1999, District of Columbia. *Education:* University of Maryland (B.S., 1989); George Washington University (M.B.A., 1991); University of Maryland Law School (J.D., 1998). ***Email:*** lganslaw@morganlewis.com

CYNTHIA M. GAYTON, admitted to bar, 1996, Virginia (Not admitted in District of Columbia). *Education:* George Washington University (B.A., 1982); George Mason University (J.D., 1995). ***Email:*** cgayton@morganlewis.com

LATRICE A. GEORGE, admitted to bar, 2000, Maryland; 2001, District of Columbia. *Education:* Cornell University (B.S., 1997); Columbia University School of Law (J.D., 2000). ***Email:*** lgeorge@morganlewis.com

LANCE E. GIBBONS, admitted to bar, 2000, District of Columbia. *Education:* Miami University (B.S., 1996); Ohio Northern University College of Law (J.D., 1999). ***Email:*** lgibbons@morganlewis.com

MARK A. GOODIN, admitted to bar, 1992, Maryland; 1993, District of Columbia. *Education:* University of Virginia (B.A., 1989); George Washington University National Law Center (J.D., 1992). ***Email:*** mgoodin@morganlewis.com

(This Listing Continued)

GAYLE GRABOW-WALLACE, admitted to bar, 1999, Maryland and Virginia; 2001, District of Columbia. *Education:* State University of New York at Oswego (B.A., 1995); Albany Law School of Union University (J.D., 1998). ***Email:*** ggrabow-wallace@morganlewis.com

LIA SILVA GRASSI, admitted to bar, 1996, New Jersey and Pennsylvania (Not admitted in District of Columbia). *Education:* Virginia Polytechnic Institute and State University (B.A., 1986); Rutgers University School of Law (J.D., 1996). ***Email:*** lgrassi@morganlewis.com

LORA M. GREEN, admitted to bar, 1998, Maryland (Not admitted in District of Columbia). *Education:* Rensselear Polytechnic Institute (B.S., 1985); Johns Hopkins University (Ph.D., 1991); George Washington University Law School (J.D., 1998). ***Email:*** lgreen@morganlewis.com

CHARLES P. GROPPE, admitted to bar, 1997, Virginia; 1999, District of Columbia. *Education:* Georgetown University (B.A., 1981); George Washington University National Law Center (J.D., 1997). ***Email:*** cgroppe@morganlewis.com

FREDERICK J. HAMBLE, admitted to bar, 1997, New York; 1999, District of Columbia; registered to practice before U.S. Patent and Trademark Office. *Education:* Cornell University (B.S., 1993); Fordham University Law School (J.D., 1996). ***Email:*** fhamble@morganlewis.com

JACQUENETTE M. HELMES, admitted to bar, 2000, Maryland (Not admitted in District of Columbia). *Education:* Syracuse University (B.S., 1991); Georgetown University Law Center (J.D., 2000). ***Email:*** jhelmes@morganlewis.com

ROBERT P. HENLEY, admitted to bar, 1999, Virginia (Not admitted in District of Columbia). *Education:* University of Virginia (B.A., 1992); University of Denver School of Law (J.D., 1999). ***Email:*** rphenley@morganlewis.com

LISA D. HERBST, admitted to bar, 1998, Virginia; 1999, District of Columbia. *Education:* Southern Connecticut State University (B.S., 1992); Catholic University of America, Columbus School of Law (J.D., 1998). ***Email:*** lherbst@morganlewis.com

JASON I. HEWITT, admitted to bar, 1997, District of Columbia. *Education:* University of Southern Mississippi (B.A., 1993); University of Texas School of Law (J.D., 1996). ***Email:*** jhewitt@morganlewis.com

DAVID M. HIBEY, admitted to bar, 1998, Maryland; 2000, District of Columbia. *Education:* Georgetown University (B.A., 1994; J.D., 1998). ***Email:*** dhibey@morganlewis.com

ROBERT J. HOLLINGSHEAD, admitted to bar, 1999, Maryland; 2000, District of Columbia; registered to practice before U.S. Patent and Trademark Office. *Education:* University of Maryland (B.S.E.E., B.S.M.A., 1992); Johns Hopkins University (M.S.E.E., 1995); Catholic University of America, Columbus School of Law (J.D., 1999). ***Email:*** rhollingshead@morganlewis.com

RHONDA C. HOLMES, admitted to bar, 1998, New York and New Jersey; 1999, District of Columbia. *Education:* Duke University (A.B., 1982); University of Rochester (M.B.A., 1985); Fordham University Law School (J.D., 1997). ***Email:*** rholmes@morganlewis.com

MARTHA J. HOPKINS, admitted to bar, 1999, Virginia; 2001, District of Columbia. *Education:* West Virginia University (B.S.E.E., 1987); Virginia Polytechnic Institute and State University (M.S.E.E., 1991); Catholic University of America, Columbus School of Law (J.D., 1999). ***Email:*** mhopkins@morganlewis.com

KATHARINE B. HOULIHAN, admitted to bar, 1995, Maryland; 1996, District of Columbia. *Education:* Ohio University (A.B., 1968); Michigan State University (M.S.W., 1970); Georgetown University Law Center (J.D., 1995). ***Email:*** khoulihan@morganlewis.com

JOSEPH R. HOUSE, admitted to bar, 1996, Maryland; 1998, District of Columbia. *Education:* College of the Holy Cross (B.A., 1991); Catholic University of America, Columbus School of Law (J.D., 1995). ***Email:*** jhouse@morganlewis.com

RIMA IDZELIS, admitted to bar, 2001, Wisconsin (Not admitted in District of Columbia). *Education:* Michigan State University (B.A., 1995); Vermont Law School (J.D., 2000). ***Email:*** ridzelis@morganlewis.com

TOMER J. INBAR, admitted to bar, 1997, New York; 1998, District of Columbia. *Education:* State University of New York at Binghamton (B.A., 1988); Cornell University (M.A., 1992); New York University School of Law (J.D., 1996; LL.M., 1998). ***Email:*** tinbar@morganlewis.com

SHANNON M.P. JOHNSON, admitted to bar, 1999, Maryland; 2000, District of Columbia. *Education:* University of Minnesota (B.S., 1993); William and Mary School of Law (J.D., 1999). ***Email:*** sjohnson@morganlewis.com

PAMELA M. KEITH, admitted to bar, 1995, District of Columbia. *Education:* University of California at Davis (A.B., 1990; M.A., 1992); Boston College Law School (J.D., 1995). ***Email:*** pkeith@morganlewis.com

(This Listing Continued)

MORGAN, LEWIS & BOCKIUS LLP, Washington—Continued

TARA R. KELLY, admitted to bar, 2001, Massachusetts and District of Columbia. *Education:* College of William & Mary (B.A., 1995); Boston University School of Law (J.D., 2000). **Email:** tkelly@morganlewis.com

RONA C. KELNER, admitted to bar, 1999, District of Columbia. *Education:* Stanford University (A.B., 1992); University of Virginia School of Law (J.D., 1997). **Email:** rkelner@morganlewis.com

DAVID J. KENEALY, admitted to bar, 1995, Ohio; 1998, District of Columbia; registered to practice before U.S. Patent and Trademark Office. *Education:* University of Cincinnati (B.S.M.E., 1990); American University, Washington College of Law (J.D., 1995). **Email:** dkenealy@morganlewis.com

JENNIFER L. KLASS, admitted to bar, 1998, Pennsylvania; 1999, District of Columbia. *Education:* Lehigh University (B.A., 1992); Widener University (J.D., 1997). **Email:** jklass@morganlewis.com

DANIEL R. KLEINMAN, admitted to bar, 1997, Pennsylvania and New Jersey; 2001, District of Columbia. *Education:* New York University (B.S., 1991); Dickinson School of Law (J.D., 1997). **Email:** dkleinman@morganlewis.com

HEATH K. KNAKMUHS, admitted to bar, 1999, Massachusetts and Illinois; 2000, District of Columbia. *Education:* Northwestern University (B.A., 1995); Boston University School of Law (J.D., 1998). **Email:** hknakmuhs@morganlewis.com

JENNIFER L. KOCHER, admitted to bar, 1995, Virginia; 1998, District of Columbia. *Education:* Hamilton College (B.A., 1990); University of Virginia School of Law (J.D., 1995). **Email:** jkocher@morganlewis.com

GERALD P. KONKEL, admitted to bar, 1998, Maryland (Not admitted in District of Columbia). *Education:* St. Louis University (B.A., 1993); St. Louis University School of Law (J.D., 1996). **Email:** gkonkel@morganlewis.com

CHRISTINE A. LACIAK, admitted to bar, 1999, Illinois; 2000, District of Columbia. *Education:* Catholic University of America (B.A., 1990); University of Chicago Law School (J.D., 1999). **Email:** claciak@morganlewis.com

THOMAS J. LANG, admitted to bar, 1996, New York and District of Columbia. *Education:* Princeton University (A.B., 1988); Georgetown University (M.A., 1992); Cornell Law School (J.D., 1995). **Email:** tlang@morganlewis.com

JENNIFER M. LEE, admitted to bar, 1996, New York; 1997, District of Columbia; registered to practice before U.S. Patent and Trademark Office. *Education:* University of Colorado (B.S., 1992); Syracuse University (J.D., 1995). **Email:** jmlee@morganlewis.com

JEFFERY M. LILLYWHITE, admitted to bar, 2000, Utah (Not admitted in District of Columbia). *Education:* University of Utah (B.S., 1995); Franklin Pierce Law Center (J.D., 2000). **Email:** jlillywhite@morganlewis.com

DAVID R. LIPSON, admitted to bar, 1994, Maryland; 1996, District of Columbia. *Education:* Brandeis University (B.A., 1991); Northwestern University (J.D., 1994). **Email:** dlipson@morganlewis.com

BRIAN Z. LISS, admitted to bar, 1999, Maryland; 2000, District of Columbia. *Education:* University of Rochester (B.A., 1996); George Washington University National Law Center (J.D., 1999). **Email:** bliss@morganlewis.com

HENRY LIU, admitted to bar, 1997, Maryland; 1999, District of Columbia. *Education:* University of Maryland (B.S., 1994); George Washington University National Law Center (J.D., 1997). **Email:** hliu@morganlewis.com

K. KAREN LOEWENSTEIN, admitted to bar, 1998, District of Columbia. *Education:* Peking University (B.S., 1984); Virginia Polytechnic Institute and State University (M.S., 1990; Ph.D., 1991); Georgetown University Law Center (J.D., 1997). **Email:** kloewenstein@morganlewis.com

JASON A. LOMAX, admitted to bar, 1998, District of Columbia; 1999, New York. *Education:* Boston College (B.A., 1992; J.D., 1996). **Email:** jlomax@morganlewis.com

KATHLEEN M. MACPEAK, admitted to bar, 1999, Maryland; 2000, District of Columbia. *Education:* Catholic University of America (B.A., 1996); Catholic University of America, Columbus School of Law (J.D., 1999). **Email:** kmacpeak@morganlewis.com

KENDRA A. MARTELLO, admitted to bar, 2001, Maryland (Not admitted in District of Columbia). *Education:* University of Maryland (B.A., 1992); American University, Washington College of Law (J.D., 2000). **Email:** kmartello@morganlewis.com

MARJAN MASHHADI, admitted to bar, 2001, New York and District of Columbia. *Education:* Washington University (B.A., 1997); Boston University School of Law (J.D., 2000). **Email:** mmashhadi@morganlewis.com

(This Listing Continued)

TIMOTHY P. MATTHEWS, admitted to bar, 1994, Virginia; 1995, District of Columbia. *Education:* U.S. Naval Academy (B.S.M.E., 1983); George Washington University National Law Center (J.D., 1994). **Email:** tmatthews@morganlewis.com

ERIC J. MAURER, admitted to bar, 1997, Pennsylvania; 1998, District of Columbia. *Education:* Johns Hopkins University (B.S., 1993); George Washington University National Law Center (J.D., 1996). **Email:** emaurer@morganlewis.com

JAMES T. McHALE, admitted to bar, 1993, District of Columbia. *Education:* University of South Carolina (B.S., 1988; J.D., 1991). **Email:** jtmchale@morganlewis.com

C. BRIAN MEADORS, admitted to bar, 1999, Virginia; 2000, District of Columbia. *Education:* University of Michigan (B.S.E., 1991); Georgetown University Law Center (J.D., 1999). **Email:** cbmeadors@morganlewis.com

CHRISTOPHER DENNIS MENCONI, admitted to bar, 1994, New Jersey; 1998, New York; 1999, District of Columbia. *Education:* Catholic University of America (B.A., 1990); Catholic University of America, Columbus School of Law (J.D., 1994). **Email:** cmenconi@morganlewis.com

BRETT I. MILLER, admitted to bar, 1995, Georgia; 1997, District of Columbia. *Education:* Emory University (B.A., 1985); University of Virginia School of Law (J.D., 1995);. **Email:** bmiller@morganlewis.com

JENNIFER TETENBAUM MILLER, admitted to bar, 2000, Virginia; 2001, District of Columbia. *Education:* Mount Holyoke College (B.A., 1993); George Washington University (M.A., 1995); Georgetown University Law Center (J.D., 2000). **Email:** jmiller@morganlewis.com

NICHOLAS C. MINSHEW, admitted to bar, 2000, Maryland (Not admitted in District of Columbia). *Education:* Goucher College (B.A., 1994); University of Maryland (M.S.W., 1997); American University, Washington College of Law (J.D., 2000). **Email:** nminshew@morganlewis.com

PRUFESH R. MODHERA, admitted to bar, 1999, New Jersey; 2000, New York; 2001, District of Columbia. *Education:* Rutgers University (B.A., 1986); Georgetown University (M.B.A., 1990); American University, Washington College of Law (J.D., 1999). **Email:** pmodhera@morganlewis.com

PHOEBE MOUNTS, PH.D., admitted to bar, 1999, Maryland; 2001, District of Columbia. *Education:* University of Pittsburgh (B.S., 1971; M.S., 1973); Edinburgh University, Scotland (Ph.D., 1977); Johns Hopkins University (P.D.F., 1980); Georgetown University Law Center (J.D., 1999). **Email:** pmounts@morganlewis.com

NATHAN J. MUYSKENS, admitted to bar, 1995, Virginia; 1997, District of Columbia. *Education:* University of Virginia (B.A., 1992); University of Kansas School of Law (J.D., 1995). **Email:** nmuyskens@morganlewis.com

ARLENE P. NEAL, admitted to bar, 1998, Massachusetts; 2000, District of Columbia. *Education:* Grambling State University (B.S., 1989); New England School of Law (J.D., 1998). **Email:** aneal@morganlewis.com

THOMAS E. NELSON, admitted to bar, 1994, New York; 2000, District of Columbia; registered to practice before U.S. Patent and Trademark Office. *Education:* Pennsylvania State University (B.S.E.E., 1985); Syracuse University (J.D., 1993). **Email:** tnelson@morganlewis.com

CORINNE A. NIOSI, admitted to bar, 1996, New York; 1997, District of Columbia. *Education:* Fairfield University (B.A., 1992); Catholic University of America, Columbus School of Law (J.D., 1995). **Email:** cniosi@morganlewis.com

REGINA A. O'BRIEN, admitted to bar, 1999, Virginia (Not admitted in District of Columbia). *Education:* George Mason University (B.A., 1986); Georgetown University Law Center (J.D., 1999). **Email:** robrien@morganlewis.com

LISA ERIN O'DONALD, admitted to bar, 1998, District of Columbia. *Education:* Villanova University (B.A., 1992); College of William & Mary School of Law (J.D., 1995). **Email:** lo'donald@morganlewis.com

SHANA E. OMMAYA, admitted to bar, 1993, Maryland; 1995, District of Columbia. *Education:* American University (B.A., 1989); Catholic University of America, Columbus School of Law (J.D., 1993). **Email:** sommaya@morganlewis.com

DANIELLE HELEN PARADINE, admitted to bar, 1998, New York; 1999, District of Columbia. *Education:* Indiana University (B.A., 1994); George Washington University National Law Center (J.D., 1997). **Email:** dparadine@morganlewis.com

COLLIN W. PARK, admitted to bar, 1997, Virginia; 2000, District of Columbia; registered to practice before U.S. Patent and Trademark Office. *Education:* University of Virginia (B.E., 1989; M.E., 1991); George Washington University National Law Center (J.D., 1996). **Email:** cpark@morganlewis.com

ALLISON L. PARLIN, admitted to bar, 1995, Pennsylvania and New Jersey; 2001, District of Columbia. *Education:* Tufts University (B.A., 1991); University of Pennsylvania Law School (J.D., 1995). **Email:** aparlin@morganlewis.com

(This Listing Continued)

ROSS H. PARR, admitted to bar, 1999, Pennsylvania; 2001, District of Columbia. *Education:* Michigan State University (B.A., 1994); College of William & Mary School of Law (J.D., 1999). ***Email:*** rparr@morganlewis.com

RALPH A. PHILLIPS, admitted to bar, 2000, Pennsylvania (Not admitted in District of Columbia). *Education:* Pennsylvania State University (B.S., 1993); North Carolina State University (M.S., 1995); University of Pennsylvania Law School (J.D., 2000). ***Email:*** rphillips@morganlewis.com

AMY E. POCINO, admitted to bar, 1999, Pennsylvania; 2001, District of Columbia and Virginia. *Education:* Boston University (B.A., 1996); Rutgers University School of Law (J.D., 1999). ***Email:*** apocino@morganlewis.com

ALEX S. POLONSKY, admitted to bar, 1999, New York and District of Columbia. *Education:* Wesleyan University (B.S., 1992); Vermont Law School (J.D., 1998). ***Email:*** apolonsky@morganlewis.com

ANITA B. POLOTT, admitted to bar, 1996, Maryland; 1998, District of Columbia. *Education:* Washington University (B.A., 1993); American University, Washington College of Law (J.D., 1996). ***Email:*** apolott@morganlewis.com

CRANE M. POMERANTZ, admitted to bar, 1996, Massachusetts and New York; 2001, District of Columbia. *Education:* University of Michigan (B.A., 1992); Boston University School of Management (M.B.A., 1995); Boston University School of Law (J.D., 1995). ***Email:*** cpomerantz@morganlewis.com

BRIAN M. PRIVOR, admitted to bar, 2000, California and District of Columbia. *Education:* Tulane University (B.A., 1995); Harvard Law School (J.D., 1998). ***Email:*** bprivor@morganlewis.com

LAUREL E. QUEENO, admitted to bar, 1995, Ohio; 1998, District of Columbia. *Education:* Michigan State University (B.A., 1992); University of Michigan Law School (J.D., 1995). ***Email:*** lqueeno@morganlewis.com

LIZA M. RAY, admitted to bar, 2000, Kentucky; 2001, District of Columbia. *Education:* University of Miami (B.A., 1995); Catholic University of America, Columbus School of Law (J.D., 2000). ***Email:*** lray@morganlewis.com

JAMES L. REED, admitted to bar, 1999, Maryland; 2000, District of Columbia. *Education:* Boston University (B.S., 1988); Johns Hopkins University (M.S., 1994); American University, Washington College of Law (J.D., 1999). ***Email:*** jreed@morganlewis.com

TARA LEE REINHART, admitted to bar, 1994, Virginia; 1997, Pennsylvania; 1999, District of Columbia. *Education:* University of North Carolina at Chapel Hill (B.A., 1988); Catholic University of America, Columbus School of Law (J.D., 1994). ***Email:*** treinhart@morganlewis.com

CORINNE ANN RICHARDSON, admitted to bar, 1998, New York (Not admitted in District of Columbia). *Education:* Princeton University (A.B., 1988); Georgetown University Law Center (J.D., 1994). ***Email:*** crichardson@morganlewis.com

JEFFREY L. RILEY, admitted to bar, 1996, Maryland; 1997, District of Columbia. *Education:* George Washington University (B.A., 1992; J.D., 1996). ***Email:*** jriley@morganlewis.com

JONATHAN G. ROSE, admitted to bar, 1992, Pennsylvania; 1995, District of Columbia. *Education:* Western Maryland College (B.A., 1986); Catholic University of America, Columbus School of Law (J.D., 1992). ***Email:*** jgrose@morganlewis.com

SCOTT D. SADLER, admitted to bar, 1999, Maryland and District of Columbia. *Education:* University of Maryland (B.A., 1995); Howard University Law School (J.D., 1998). ***Email:*** ssadler@morganlewis.com

JULIAN F. SAENZ, admitted to bar, 1999, Maryland (Not admitted in District of Columbia). *Education:* Yale University (B.A., 1988); Georgetown University Law Center (J.D., 1999). ***Email:*** jsaenz@morganlewis.com

MATTHEW O. SCHAD, admitted to bar, 1998, Virginia (Not admitted in District of Columbia). *Education:* Amherst College (B.A., 1994); Wake Forest University School of Law (J.D., 1998). ***Email:*** mschad@morganlewis.com

ALEX M. SCHNELL, admitted to bar, 1994, Texas; 2001, District of Columbia. *Education:* Boston University (B.S., 1991); University of Texas Law School (J.D., 1994). ***Email:*** aschnell@morganlewis.com

TODD A. SCHROEDER, admitted to bar, 2000, Alabama; 2001, District of Columbia. *Education:* Auburn University (B.S., 1997); University of Alabama (J.D., 2000). ***Email:*** tschroeder@morganlewis.com

LAINE M. SCHWARTZ, admitted to bar, 2001, District of Columbia. *Education:* University of Texas at Austin (B.A., 1996); University of Georgia School of Law (J.D., 2000). ***Email:*** lschwartz@morganlewis.com

AMAAL A.D. SCROGGINS, admitted to bar, 2000, Maryland and New Jersey (Not admitted in District of Columbia). *Education:* Spelman College (B.A., 1995); Washington University (J.D., 1999). ***Email:*** ascroggins@morganlewis.com

(This Listing Continued)

SANGITA A. SHAH, admitted to bar, 2001, New York and District of Columbia. *Education:* Virginia Commonwealth University (B.A., 1997); Howard University Law School (J.D., 2000). ***Email:*** sshah@morganlewis.com

BARBARA ANN SHIRLEY, admitted to bar, 1996, Virginia; 1997, Maryland; 2001, District of Columbia. *Education:* Virginia Polytechnic Institute (B.S., 1993); George Washington University National Law Center (J.D., 1996). ***Email:*** bshirley@morganlewis.com

ROBERT SMYTH, PH.D., admitted to bar, 2000, Maryland; 2001, District of Columbia. *Education:* Syracuse University (B.S., 1989); Temple University School of Medicine (Ph.D., 1995); University of Pennsylvania School of Medicine (Post-doctoral Fellow, 1997); Temple University School of Law (J.D., 1999). ***Email:*** rsmyth@morganlewis.com

YIOTA G. SOURAS, admitted to bar, 2000, New York; 2001, District of Columbia. *Education:* Johns Hopkins University (B.A., 1992); Fordham University School of Law (J.D., 1999). ***Email:*** ysouras@morganlewis.com

DENISE L. SPEAS, admitted to bar, 1992, Colorado; 2001, District of Columbia. *Education:* Creighton University (B.S., 1988); University of Denver Law School (J.D., 1992); Georgetown University Law Center (LL.M., 2000). ***Email:*** dspeas@morganlewis.com

STEPHEN M. SPINA, admitted to bar, 1996, Maryland; 1997, District of Columbia. *Education:* Boston College (B.A., 1989); Tulane University (J.D., 1996). ***Email:*** sspina@morganlewis.com

GORAN P. STOJKOVICH, admitted to bar, 1997, Illinois; 1998, District of Columbia. *Education:* University of Illinois at Urbana-Champaign (B.S., 1989); Chicago-Kent College of Law, Illinois Institute of Technology (J.D., 1997). ***Email:*** gstojkovich@morganlewis.com

VICTORIA L. STROHMEYER, admitted to bar, 2000, Maryland (Not admitted in District of Columbia). *Education:* University of Maryland (B.A., 1992); Georgetown University Law Center (J.D., 2000). ***Email:*** vstrohmeyer@morganlewis.com

MICHAEL STRONG, admitted to bar, 2000, Illinois; 2001, District of Columbia. *Education:* University of California, Irvine (B.S., B.A., 1990; M.S., 1996); Loyola University, Chicago School of Law (J.D., 2000). ***Email:*** mstrong@morganlewis.com

RICHARD A. SUGARMAN, admitted to bar, 2001, District of Columbia and Massachusetts. *Education:* University of Massachusetts (B.A., 1992); Colorado State University (M.B.A., 1996); George Washington University Law School (J.D., 2000). ***Email:*** rsugarman@morganlewis.com

CHARLES SWINBURN, admitted to bar, 1993, Pennsylvania; 1995, District of Columbia. *Education:* Princeton University (B.A., 1963); Harvard University (M.B.A., 1971); University of Pennsylvania Law School (J.D., 1993). ***Email:*** cswinburn@morganlewis.com

KHOI TA, admitted to bar, 2001, Virginia (Not admitted in District of Columbia). *Education:* Virginia Polytechnic Institute (B.S., 1988); George Mason University (J.D., 2000). ***Email:*** kta@morganlewis.com

GREGORY R. TALBOT, admitted to bar, 1998, District of Columbia and Maryland. *Education:* University of Notre Dame (B.A., 1990); Catholic University of America, Columbus School of Law (J.D., 1997). ***Email:*** gtalbot@morganlewis.com

TODD P. TAYLOR, admitted to bar, 2000, Virginia; 2001, District of Columbia. *Education:* University of Notre Dame (B.S., 1988); American University, Washington College of Law (J.D., 2000). ***Email:*** tptaylor@morganlewis.com

JOHN F. TERZAKEN, III, admitted to bar, 2000, Virginia; 2001, District of Columbia. *Education:* American University (B.A., 1996); University of Virginia School of Law (J.D., 2000). ***Email:*** jterzaken@morganlewis.com

ANGELA F. THORNHILL, admitted to bar, 1996, Alabama; 1997, District of Columbia. *Education:* United States Air Force Academy (B.S., 1989); College of William & Mary, Marshall-Wythe School of Law (J.D., 1996). ***Email:*** athornhill@morganlewis.com

JEFFREY N. TOWNES, admitted to bar, 2000, Virginia; 2001, District of Columbia; registered to practice before U.S. Patent and Trademark Office. *Education:* Bucknell University (B.S., 1997); George Mason University School of Law (J.D., 2000). ***Email:*** jtownes@morganlewis.com

JOHN C. TRUONG, admitted to bar, 1999, California; 2000, District of Columbia. *Education:* University of Southern California (B.A., 1993); American University, Washington College of Law (J.D., 1997). ***Email:*** jtruong@morganlewis.com

MICHAEL S. TUSCAN, admitted to bar, 1999, Maryland; 2001, District of Columbia. *Education:* Carroll College (B.S., 1984); Illinois State University (M.S., 1986); Emory University (Ph.D., 1991); Georgetown University Law Center (J.D., 1998). ***Email:*** mtuscan@morganlewis.com

(This Listing Continued)

MORGAN, LEWIS & BOCKIUS LLP, Washington—Continued

ERICH E. VEITENHEIMER, III, admitted to bar, 1999, Maryland; 2001, District of Columbia. *Education:* Washington State University (B.S., 1980); University of Wisconsin-Madison (M.S., 1982; Ph.D., 1985); Georgetown University Law Center (J.D., 1998). ***Email:*** eveitenheimer@morganlewis.com

ANTHONY J. VERDUCCI, admitted to bar, 1990, New Jersey; 2001, District of Columbia. *Education:* U.S. Naval Academy (B.S., 1980); Webster University (M.A., 1985); Seton Hall University Law School (J.D., 1990); Georgetown University Law Center (LL.M., 1997). ***Email:*** averducci@morganlewis.com

MARY D. WALSH, admitted to bar, 1999, District of Columbia and California. *Education:* University of California at Berkeley (B.A., 1994); George Washington University National Law Center (J.D., 1998). ***Email:*** mwalsh@morganlewis.com

EMIL P. WANG, admitted to bar, 2001, Maryland (Not admitted in District of Columbia). *Education:* Johns Hopkins University (B.A., 1993); University of Maryland Law School (J.D., 2000). ***Email:*** ewang@morganlewis.com

CAROLYN O. WARD, admitted to bar, 1995, District of Columbia. *Education:* Duke University (B.A., 1989); American University, Washington College of Law (J.D., 1993); Georgetown University Law Center (LL.M., 1997). ***Email:*** cward@morganlewis.com

JOSEPH E. WASHINGTON, admitted to bar, 2000, New York; 2001, District of Columbia. *Education:* The Citadel (B.A., 1991); Catholic University of America, Columbus School of Law (J.D., 1999). ***Email:*** jwashington@morganlewis.com

ANDREA J. WEINSTEIN, admitted to bar, 1998, Connecticut; 1999, New York; 2000, District of Columbia. *Education:* Washington University (B.A., 1995); American University, Washington College of Law (J.D., 1998). ***Email:*** ajweinstein@morganlewis.com

ROBYN B. WEISS, admitted to bar, 1998, Maryland; 1999, District of Columbia. *Education:* Cornell University (B.S., 1995); George Washington University National Law Center (J.D., 1998). ***Email:*** rweiss@morganlewis.com

GREGORY F. WELLS, admitted to bar, 2001, California (Not admitted in District of Columbia). *Education:* University of California at Davis (B.A., 1997); Georgetown University Law Center (J.D., 2000). ***Email:*** gwells@morganlewis.com

PAMELA R. WILLIAMS, admitted to bar, 1998, Maryland (Not admitted in District of Columbia). *Education:* University of Virginia (B.A., 1995); George Washington University Law School (J.D., 1998). ***Email:*** pwilliams@morganlewis.com

TIMOTHY J. WOLF, admitted to bar, 1997, Maryland; 1999, District of Columbia. *Education:* United States Naval Academy (B.S., 1987); Georgetown University (M.A., 1993); Catholic University of America, Columbus School of Law (J.D., 1997). ***Email:*** twolf@morganlewis.com

Members of the Firm, Counsel, Of Counsel and Associates in Philadelphia, Harrisburg and Pittsburgh, Pennsylvania, New York, New York, Los Angeles, California, Miami, Florida, Princeton, New Jersey, Northern Virginia, London, England, Brussels, Belgium, Frankfurt am Main, Germany and Tokyo, Japan are listed in the Biographical Section respectively.

MORLEY CASKIN

WASHINGTON, D.C.

(See Cameron McKenna LLP)

MORRIS, MANNING & MARTIN, LLP

Established in 1976

THE COLORADO BUILDING

1341 G STREET, N.W., SUITE 610

WASHINGTON, D.C. 20005

Telephone: 202-408-5153

Fax: 202-408-5146

URL: http://www.mmmlaw.com

Atlanta (Buckhead) Office: 1600 Atlanta Financial Center, 3343 Peachtree Road, N.E., Atlanta, Georgia, 30326. Telephone: 404-233-7000.

Atlanta (Northside) Office: Suite 150, 5775-B Peachtree Dunwoody Road, Atlanta, Georgia, 30342. Telephone: 404-255-6900.

Gwinnett County Office: 2180 Satellite Boulevard, Suite 180, Duluth, Georgia, 30097. Telephone: 678-987-2800. Fax: 678-417-0056.

Forsyth County Office: 307 Atlanta Highway, Cumming, Georgia, 30040. Telephone: 770-781-3000. Fax: 770-781-3007.

(This Listing Continued)

Charlotte, North Carolina Office: 600 Fairview Road, Suite 1125, 28210. Telephone: 704-554-7070. Fax: 704-556-9554.

General Commercial Practice including Practice in all Courts. Administrative Law and Litigation, Antitrust, Asset Based Lending, Banking Regulation and RTC, Bankruptcy and Creditor's Rights, Bond Financing, Business Litigation, Real Estate Lending, Real Estate Transactions, Construction Law, Corporate, Employment Law, Environmental Law, ERISA and Employee Benefits, Government Guaranteed Lending, Governmental Relations, Healthcare, Insurance, Insurance Regulatory, International, Liquidation and Rehabilitation of Insurers and Reinsurers, Leasing, Patent, Partnership, Residential Real Estate, Securities, Taxation, Technology and Intellectual Property, Title Insurance, Trusts and Estates.

FIRM PROFILE: The attorneys in the D.C. office specialize in Insurance, Regulatory, Corporate, Antitrust, Healthcare, Privacy, and Trade Association matters. We also provide a window on the activities of Congress and the Executive Branch of the federal government.

MEMBER OF FIRM

THOMAS A. PLAYER, born Orangeburg, South Carolina, February 4, 1940; admitted to bar, 1965, South Carolina; 1968, Georgia (Not admitted in District of Columbia). *Education:* Furman University (B.A., 1962); University of Virginia (LL.B., 1965). Author: "Comparison of U.S. and Foreign Solvency, Rehabilitation and Liquidation Laws," Public Regulation of Insurance Law Newsletter, Summer, 1994; "Insurer Insolvency Laws: Comparisons and Observations," 1995 Organization for Economic Cooperation and Development, Paris, France. Contributing Editor, "Managing for Solvency and Profitability in Life and Health Insurance Companies," published by LOMA, 1996. Chairman, Board of Directors, Federation of Regulatory Counsel, 1995-1996. *Member:* State Bar of Georgia (Chairman, Corporate Counsel Committee); South Carolina Bar; American Bar Association; American Council of Life Insurance (Legal Section); International Insurance Society; Federation of Regulatory Counsel. ***PRACTICE AREAS:*** Corporate Law; Insurance; Reinsurance; Insurance Rehabilitation and Liquidation; Insurance Mergers and Acquisitions; Health Care; Regulatory Law; Administrative Law. ***Email:*** tap@mmmlaw.com

COUNSEL

S. ROY WOODALL, JR., born Paducah, Kentucky, July 8, 1936; admitted to bar, 1962, Kentucky; 1985, District of Columbia. *Education:* University of Kentucky (B.A., 1958; LL.B., 1962). Phi Beta Kappa; Phi Alpha Delta (President). Woodrow Wilson Fellow, Yale University, 1959. Listed in Who's Who in Insurance and Who's Who in America. Editor, University of Kentucky Law Review, 1961-1962. Trustee, Georgia State Educational Foundation, Inc. Member, International Insurance Society. *Member:* Kentucky and American Bar Associations; The District of Columbia Bar; Association of Life Insurance Counsel; Federation of Insurance Counsel. ***PRACTICE AREAS:*** Insurance; Finance; Mergers and Acquisitions; Regulatory Law. ***Email:*** srw@mmmlaw.com

ROBERT H. MYERS, JR., born Washington, D.C., October 8, 1947; admitted to bar, 1972, Maryland; 1973, District of Columbia, U.S. Tax Court and U.S. Supreme Court. *Education:* Princeton University (A.B., with honors, 1969); University of Virginia (J.D., 1972). Member, Virginia Journal of International Law, 1970-1972. Publications: Author: "Financial Services Continuing to Evolve Without Federal Legislation," LOMA Resource, Feb 1998, p. 30; Co-Author: "Tax Advantages of Utilizing a Mutual Structure for a Risk Retention Group," Risk Retention Reporter, July 1997, p 6; "The Interstate Insurance Receivership Compact, A Model for Enhancing State Insurance Regulation," The Examiner, Vol 21, No 3, Winter 1997, p 15; Co-Author, "Where's the Next Stop on the Financial Services Company Train?" LOMA, Resource, Feb. 1997, p 20; "Insurer Licensing, Enhancement of State Regulation by Interstate Compacts," American Bar Association, Torts and Insurance Practice Section, January 12, 1996; Co-Author: "Insurance Regulation in the Public Interest: Where Do We Go From Here?" 12 Journal of Insurance Regulation 285, Spring, 1994 (Recipient of Award for the best Article Published in the Journal of Insurance Regulation during, 1994); "Federal Regulation of Insurance," The Brief, Volume 23, No. 3, Spring, 1994, p. 20; "How Art-Oriented Exempt Organizations Can Skirt the Unrelated Business Income Tax," 49 Journal of Taxation 150, 1978. Author: "An Evolutionary View of Insurance Regulation," Best's Review, p. 50, December, 1994; "Can Interstate Compacts Solve the Insurance Regulation Debate?" Risk Management, p. 52, August, 1993; "A Balanced Approach to Insurance Regulation Reform," Risk Management, p. 14, February, 1993; "The McCarran-Ferguson Act: Why Antitrust is Only Part of the Debate," Risk Management, p. 44, May, 1992; "Regulatory Authority Under the Risk Retention Act," 6 Journal of Insurance Regulation 72, September, 1987; "The Birth of the Foreign Sales Corporation: The Administration Proposes a DISC Substitute That Will Have an Important Impact on Farmers," 5 Journal of Agricultural Taxation and Law 310, 1984. *Member:* The District of Columbia Bar; Bar Association of the District of Columbia; Maryland State and American (Member, Sections on: Torts and Insurance Practice and Antitrust; Vice-Chair, 1993-1996 and Chair, 1996-1997, Public Regulation of Insurance Committee) Bar

(This Listing Continued)

Associations; Federation of Regulatory Counsel. (Resident). ***PRACTICE AREAS:*** Insurance Regulation; General Corporate; Antitrust; Trade Association Law. ***Email:*** rhm@mmmlaw.com

L. CHRIS PETERSEN, born Graettinger, Ohio, September 24, 1956; admitted to bar, 1984, Virginia (Not admitted in District of Columbia). *Education:* Washington University (B.A., with honors, 1980); Georgetown University (J.D., cum laude, 1984). Member, Board of Standards, National Commission on Accreditation of Benefit Advisors. *Member:* Bar Association of the District of Columbia. ***PRACTICE AREAS:*** Insurance Regulation; Health Care. ***Email:*** lcp@mmmlaw.com

---

MORRISON & FOERSTER LLP

Established in 1883

2000 PENNSYLVANIA AVENUE, N.W., SUITE 5500
WASHINGTON, D.C. 20006-1888
Telephone: 202-887-1500
Facsimile: 202-887-0763
URL: http://www.mofo.com

Other offices located in: San Francisco, Los Angeles, New York, London, Brussels, Beijing, Hong Kong, Singapore, Tokyo, Irvine, San Diego, Sacramento, Palo Alto, Walnut Creek, Denver, Northern Virginia (McLean) and Century City.

FIRM PROFILE: Morrison & Foerster is one of the world's largest international law firms with over 1,000 lawyers in 18 offices worldwide. The firm's legal practice encompasses every major area of commercial law, including corporate finance, project finance, institutional lending, financial services, real estate, environmental and land use planning, internet and new media, natural resources, multimedia, intellectual property, energy, communications, computer technology, insurance, alternative dispute resolution, product liability, bankruptcy and workouts, estate planning, probate, trust administration, financial transactions, labor and employment, immigration, civil, criminal and securities litigation, entertainment and sports, food and beverage, health care, hotel and resort, antitrust, international business, international litigation and arbitration, trade regulation, transportation and tax.

LAW FIRM ALLIANCES/ASSOCIATIONS: ***LEX MUNDI***

MEMBERS OF FIRM

LEE S. ADAMS, born June 3, 1949; admitted to bar, 1975, District of Columbia and Missouri; 1995, California. *Education:* Rutgers College (A.B., 1971); Georgetown University Law Center (J.D., 1974). General Counsel, Federal Reserve Bank of Cleveland, 1981-1986. Senior Counsel, Board of Governors, Federal Reserve System, Washington, D.C., 1976-1981. Adjunct Professor, Georgetown University Law Center, 1974-1977. Lecturer, Catholic University School of Law, 1977-1981. Chair, Subcommittee on Payments and Electronic Banking, 1998-2000, Banking Law Committee, American Bar Association. Member, Financial Institutions Committee, State Bar of California, 1996-1999. ***PRACTICE AREAS:*** Financial Services. ***Email:*** ladams@mofo.com

MARCO E. ADELFIO, born October 13, 1956; admitted to bar, 1982, District of Columbia and Massachusetts. *Education:* Bucknell University (B.A., 1978); Boston College Law School (J.D., magna cum laude, 1982). Order of the Coif. (Resident). ***PRACTICE AREAS:*** Investment Management; Corporate Finance; Financial Services. ***Email:*** madelfio@mofo.com

JONATHAN BAND, born November 30, 1959; admitted to bar, 1985, California; 1986, District of Columbia. *Education:* Harvard University (A.B., magna cum laude, 1982); Yale Law School (J.D., 1985); Georgetown University Law Center, Visiting Student, 1984-1985. Phi Beta Kappa. (Resident). ***PRACTICE AREAS:*** Intellectual Property; Internet Regulation; Appellate Litigation. ***Email:*** jband@mofo.com

BARRY E. BRETSCHNEIDER, born 1947; admitted to bar, 1971, Iowa; 1975, District of Columbia; 1976, Texas; registered to practice before U.S. Patent and Trademark Office. *Education:* Princeton University (A.B., 1968); University of Iowa College of Law (J.D., with distinction, 1971); George Washington University National Law Center (LL.M., 1974). Visiting Professor of Law and Acting Director, Patent Law Program, George Washington University National Law Center, 1988-1989. Attorney-Advisor and Trial Counsel, Department of Navy, Office of General Counsel, 1971-1974. Technical Advisor to Judge Giles S. Rich, U.S. Court of Customs and Patent Appeals, 1974-1976. Chairman, Interference, 1986-1988 and Education, 1988-1989, Committees of the American Intellectual Property Law Association. (Resident). ***PRACTICE AREAS:*** Intellectual Property; Patents; Trademarks; Litigation; Interference Practice; Business Counseling. ***Email:*** bbretschneider@mofo.com

ALEX CHARTOVE, born January 21, 1954; admitted to bar, 1980, California; 1984, New York; 1986, District of Columbia; registered to practice before U.S. Patent and Trademark Office. *Education:* Brandeis University (B.A., magna cum laude, 1976); Duke University School of Law (J.D., 1980). Author: 1998 Federal Circuit Yearbook - Patent Law Developments in the Federal Circuit (Practising Law Institute). ***PRACTICE AREAS:*** Intellectual Property; Patent Prosecution. ***Email:*** achartove@mofo.com

STEVEN G. CRAVATH, born Scranton, Pennsylvania, 1959; admitted to bar, 1989, Maryland; 1991, District of Columbia. *Education:* James Madison University (B.A.A., 1983); Catholic University of America, Columbus School of Law (J.D., 1989). (Resident). ***PRACTICE AREAS:*** Investment Management. ***Email:*** scravath@mofo.com

L. RICHARD FISCHER, born March 2, 1943; admitted to bar, 1971, California; 1980, District of Columbia. *Education:* University of San Francisco (A.B., 1965); University of California, Hastings College of the Law (J.D., 1970). Order of the Coif; Thurston Society. (Resident). ***PRACTICE AREAS:*** Financial Services and Administrative Law. ***Email:*** lfischer@mofo.com

WILLIAM D. FREEDMAN, born February 7, 1949; admitted to bar, 1976, Ohio; 1980, District of Columbia; 1985, Massachusetts. *Education:* Boston University (B.S.B.A., cum laude, 1971); University of Cincinnati College of Law (J.D., 1976). Beta Gamma Sigma. Trial Attorney, Safety and Special Radio Services Bureau, 1978. General Attorney and Trial Attorney, Broadcast Bureau, 1978-1981. Attorney Adviser, Office of General Counsel, Federal Communications Commission, 1982. Member, Montgomery County, Maryland, Cable Communications Advisory Committee, 1991-1997. Chairman, Regulatory & Consumer Affairs Subcommittee, 1992-1997. *Member:* District of Columbia Bar; Massachusetts and American Bar Associations; The Federal Communications Bar Association. ***PRACTICE AREAS:*** Communications Law; Litigation; Appellate Advocacy; Business Transactions. ***Email:*** wfreedman@mofo.com

RANDOLPH M. GOODMAN, born July 25, 1948; admitted to bar, 1974, New York; 1977, District of Columbia; 1981, California. *Education:* Franklin & Marshall College (B.A., 1970); Rutgers University (J.D., 1973); New York University (LL.M., 1974). Editor, Rutgers University Law Review, 1972-1973. Editor, The Tax Lawyer, 1977-1979. Author: "Exempt Compensation Arrangements Under ERISA," 28 Catholic University Law Review 445, 1979; "Employee Medical and Other Fringe Benefits," California Society of Certified Public Accountants, 1989; "Retirement and Benefit Planning," Butterworth Legal Publishers, 1991; "Trading Technology for Equity," Matthew Bender, NYU Conference on Tax Planning for 501(c)(3) Organizations, 1999. Adjunct Professor, Public Affairs, Columbia University, 2000—. *Member:* Los Angeles County, Orange County and American (Member, Section of Taxation; Co-Chair, Compensation and Benefits, Exempt Organizations Committee, Section of Taxation, 1995—) Bar Associations; State Bar of California; The District of Columbia Bar; National Association of College and University Attorneys (Co-Chair, Section on Taxation, 1990-1997); Board of Advisors, University of California (Irvine) Graduate School of Management (Health Care Programs, 1991-1995); National Board of Advisors, Financial and Estate Planning (1990-1992). (Washington, D.C. and Irvine, California Offices). ***Email:*** rgoodman@mofo.com

LOUIS GURMAN, born March 24, 1947; admitted to bar, 1974, Virginia; 1975, District of Columbia. *Education:* Harpur College (B.A., 1968); George Washington University National Law Center (J.D., with honors, 1974). *Member:* District of Columbia Bar; Virginia State Bar (Associate Member); Federal Communications Bar Association (Chairman, Mobile Facilities Committee, 1985-1987). ***PRACTICE AREAS:*** PCS and Wireless Communications; Appellate Advocacy; Litigation; Business Transactions. ***Email:*** lgurman@mofo.com

KENNETH W. IRVIN, born September 30, 1964; admitted to bar, 1993, District of Columbia and New York. *Education:* Clarkson University (B.S.E.E., 1987); Syracuse University College of Law (J.D., magna cum laude, 1992). Member, Order of the Coif. Technical Editor, Syracuse Law Review, 1990-1992. *Member:* District of Columbia Bar; Bar Association of the District of Columbia; Court of Federal Claims Bar Association. ***Email:*** kirvin@mofo.com

FREDERICK E. JENNEY, born November 13, 1957; admitted to bar, 1984, New York; 1987, District of Columbia. *Education:* Yale University (B.A., 1979); University of Virginia School of Business Administration (M.B.A., 1983); University of Virginia School of Law (J.D., 1983). ***PRACTICE AREAS:*** Project Development; Project Finance. ***Email:*** fjenney@mofo.com

CHARLES H. KENNEDY, born November 3, 1946; admitted to bar, 1976, Illinois; 1985, Arizona; 1999, District of Columbia. *Education:* Florida State University (B.A., 1968); University of Chicago Law School (J.D., 1976). Associate Editor, University of Chicago Law Review. Author: "An Introduction to U.S. Telecommunications Law," Artech House, 1994; Co-Author: "An Introduction to International Telecommunications Law," Artech House, 1996 (Second Edition, 2001); "Modern Communications Law ," West Pub. Co., 1999. Adjunct Professor, Columbus School of Law, Catholic University of America. ***PRACTICE AREAS:*** Telecommunications; Internet Law. ***Email:*** ckennedy@mofo.com

DOANE F. KIECHEL, III, born June 25, 1958; admitted to bar, 1982, Massachusetts; 1986, District of Columbia. *Education:* Columbia University (B.A., summa cum laude, 1979); Harvard Law School (J.D., cum laude, 1982).

(This Listing Continued)

MORRISON & FOERSTER LLP, Washington—Continued

Phi Beta Kappa. *Member:* District of Columbia Bar; Federal Communications Bar Association. ***PRACTICE AREAS:*** PCS and Wireless Communications; Transactional and Contract Work; Financing Law; Real Estate Law. ***Email:*** dkiechel@mofo.com

ROBERT M. KURUCZA, born May 27, 1948; admitted to bar, 1973, Pennsylvania; 1975, New Jersey (Not admitted in District of Columbia). *Education:* University of Pennsylvania (B.A., cum laude, 1970; J.D., 1973). (Resident). ***PRACTICE AREAS:*** Financial Services. ***Email:*** rkurucza@mofo.com

ROBERT H. LOEFFLER, born May 27, 1943; admitted to bar, 1969, New York; 1970, District of Columbia. *Education:* Harvard University (A.B., magna cum laude, 1965); Columbia University School of Law (J.D., cum laude, 1968). Editor, Columbia Law Review, 1966-1968. Law Clerk to Hon. Harold R. Medina, Senior Circuit Judge, U.S. Court of Appeals for 2nd Circuit, 1968-1969. Vice Chairman, Energy Law Committee, Administrative Law Section, American Bar Association, 1980-1985. President, Columbia Law School Association of Washington, 1993—. Editor, Settlement Chapter, Energy Law and Transactions. *Member:* American Intellectual Property Law Association; Federal Energy Bar Association (Chairman, Oil Pipeline Committee, 1994-1995). (Resident). ***PRACTICE AREAS:*** Alternative Dispute Resolution; Energy; Intellectual Property. ***Email:*** rloeffler@mofo.com

BRADLEY S. LUI, born September 9, 1964; admitted to bar, 1989, California; 1990, District of Columbia. *Education:* Yale University (B.A., cum laude, 1986); University of California, Berkeley, Boalt Hall School of Law (J.D., 1989). Law Clerk to Judge Dickran Tevrizian, U.S. District Court, Central District of California, 1989-1990. Trial Attorney, U.S. Department of Justice, Antitrust Division, 1990-1994. Special Assistant U.S. Attorney, Eastern District of Virginia, 1993-1994. (Resident). ***PRACTICE AREAS:*** Antitrust; Civil Litigation; Criminal Litigation. ***Email:*** blui@mofo.com

KENNETH M. MINESINGER, born 1965; admitted to bar, 1991, Maryland; 1999, District of Columbia. *Education:* University of Maryland (B.A., 1987); George Washington University (J.D., 1990). *Member:* Maryland State Bar Association, Inc. ***PRACTICE AREAS:*** Energy Regulation; Natural Gas Pipelines; Antitrust. ***Email:*** kminesinger@mofo.com

W. STEPHEN SMITH, born July 4, 1956; admitted to bar, 1983, District of Columbia. *Education:* Northwestern University (B.A., 1978; M.B.A., 1979); University of Chicago Law School (J.D., 1983). (Resident). ***PRACTICE AREAS:*** Antitrust; Administrative Law. ***Email:*** ssmith@mofo.com

NICHOLAS J. SPILIOTES, born November 1, 1955; admitted to bar, 1986, New York; 1989, District of Columbia. *Education:* Williams College (B.A., cum laude, 1977); Columbia University (M.I.A., 1979); Columbia University School of Law (J.D., 1985). Junior Staff Member, National Security Council, 1979-1981. Special Assistant, U.S. Mission to the United Nations, 1981. (Resident). ***PRACTICE AREAS:*** Project Finance; Corporate Finance; International. ***Email:*** nspiliotes@mofo.com

MARGARET L. TOBEY, born June 27, 1949; admitted to bar, 1980, Ohio; 1982, District of Columbia. *Education:* University of Iowa (B.A., with distinction and honors, 1974; M.A., with highest distinction, 1980); University of Iowa College of Law (J.D., with high distinction, 1980). Order of the Coif. Editor-in-Chief, Iowa Law Review, 1979-1980. Author: Chapter 1, "Procedures for Awarding, Transferring, Renewing, and Revoking Licenses," *The Communications Act of 1934:* A Legislative History of the Major Amendments 1934-1996, 1999; Comment, "Preferential Burden of Proof Allocation in Indian Land Claims Cases," 64 Iowa Law Review 386, 1979. Co-author with Robert Clinton: "Judicial Enforcement of the Federal Restraint on Alienation of Indian Land," 31 Maine Law Review 17, 1979. Law Clerk to Hon. Roger Robb, U.S. Court of Appeals, District of Columbia Circuit, 1980-1981. *Member:* American Bar Association (Vice-Chair, Communications Subcommittee, Government Functions Committee, Administrative Law Section; Member, Forum Committee on Communications Law); Federal Communications Bar Association (Co-Chair, Adjudicatory Practice Committee, 1990-1992; Executive Committee, 1995-1998; Assistant Secretary, 1998-1999; Secretary, 1999-2000; President-Elect, 2000-2001; President, 2001-2002); Federal Communications Bar Association Foundation (Trustee, 1991-1995; Chair, 1993-1994). (Resident). ***PRACTICE AREAS:*** Communications and Media. ***Email:*** mtobey@mofo.com

CHERYL A. TRITT, born May 8, 1947; admitted to bar, 1976, Illinois; 1993, District of Columbia. *Education:* University of Nebraska (B.S., cum laude, 1969); Northwestern University (M.S., 1970); Northwestern University School of Law (J.D., cum laude, 1976). Phi Beta Kappa. (Resident). ***PRACTICE AREAS:*** Telecommunications; Multimedia and Information Technology. ***Email:*** ctritt@mofo.com

THOMAS J. UMBERG, born September 25, 1955; admitted to bar, 1980, California (Not admitted in District of Columbia). *Education:* University of California, Los Angeles (B.A., cum laude, 1977); University of California, Hastings College of the Law (J.D., 1980). Member, California State Assembly, 1990-1994. Chairman, Assembly Committee on Environmental Safety and

(This Listing Continued)

Toxic Materials. Assistant U.S. Attorney, Criminal Division, Central District of California, 1987-1990. Adjunct Professor of Law, Southwestern University, 1995-1997. Member, California Council on Criminal Justice, 1991-1995. Deputy Director, White House Office of National Drug Control Policy (ONDCP), 1997-2000. [Military Prosecutor, Italy and Korea, U.S. Army, 1980-1985; Col., U.S. Army Reserve]. (Irvine, California and Washington, D.C. Offices). ***PRACTICE AREAS:*** Federal Legislative Practice; State Legislative Practice; Regulatory Law; Project Development; International Project Development; Trade; Investments. ***Email:*** tumberg@mofo.com

BARBARA S. WELLBERY, born December 1, 1948; admitted to bar, 1978, District of Columbia. *Education:* State University of New York at Binghamton (B.A., 1969); Stanford Law School (J.D., 1978). Author: "Privacy and Self-Regulation in the Information Age"; "An Overview of Information Privacy in the United States and European Union, A Compendium of Essays on the Use of Information". *Member:* The District of Columbia Bar; American Bar Association (Vice Chair: Privacy Group and Consumer Protection Group, Project on Transnational Jurisdiction in Cyberspace; Electronic Commerce Subcommittee, International Business Transactions Committee). ***PRACTICE AREAS:*** Financial Services Law; Communications Law. ***Email:*** bwellbery@mofo.com

RESIDENT OF COUNSEL

LINDA A. ARNSBARGER, born September 3, 1957; admitted to bar, 1985, Maryland; 1986, District of Columbia. *Education:* Kenyon College (B.A., summa cum laude, 1979); Duke University School of Law (J.D., with high honors, 1985). Order of the Coif. Phi Beta Kappa. Law Clerk to Judge Kenneth W. Starr, U.S. Court of Appeals, District of Columbia Circuit, 1985-1986. Member, J. Edgar Murdock American Inn of Court, 1988—. ***PRACTICE AREAS:*** Federal Taxation; State Taxation; Tax Controversies. ***Email:*** arnsbarger@mofo.com

PANAGIOTIS C. BAYZ, born September 17, 1962; admitted to bar, 1991, Maryland; 1992, District of Columbia. *Education:* Georgetown University School of Foreign Service (B.S., 1984); London School of Economics (M.Sc., 1985); American University, Washington College of Law (J.D., cum laude, 1991). ***LANGUAGES:*** French, Greek and Italian. ***Email:*** akibayz@mofo.com

JONATHAN F. CAYNE, born January 12, 1962; admitted to bar, 1988, New York and District of Columbia. *Education:* Cornell University (B.S., 1984); Boston University School of Law (J.D., 1987). Member, Board of Editors, Boston University International Law Journal, 1985-1987. ***Email:*** jcayne@mofo.com

LEONARD N. CHANIN, born July 10, 1957; admitted to bar, 1984, Georgia; 2000, District of Columbia. *Education:* American University (B.A., cum laude, 1979); Washington University School of Law (J.D., 1984). Board Member/Editor, Washington University Law Quarterly, 1982-1984. Formerly with Division of Consumer and Community Affairs, Federal Reserve Board, 1985-1999. Member, The American College of Consumer Financial Services Lawyers, 1997—. ***PRACTICE AREAS:*** Financial Services Law. ***Email:*** lchanin@mofo.com

PETER J. DAVIS, born November 28, 1963; admitted to bar, 1994, Maryland; 1999, District of Columbia; registered to practice before U.S. Patent and Trademark Office. *Education:* Cornell University (A.B., 1987); Catholic University of America (J.D., 1993). *Member:* The District of Columbia Bar; American Bar Association; American Intellectual Property Law Association. ***LANGUAGES:*** French. ***PRACTICE AREAS:*** Intellectual Property. ***Email:*** pdavis@mofo.com

DREW S. DAYS, III, born August 29, 1941; admitted to bar, 1966, Illinois; 1970, New York (Not admitted in District of Columbia). *Education:* Hamilton College (A.B., cum laude, 1963); Yale Law School (LL.B., 1966). Associate Professor, Temple Law School, 1973-1975. Professor, Yale Law School, 1981—. Assistant Attorney General for Civil Rights, 1977-1980 and Solicitor General, 1993-1996, U.S. Department of Justice. ***PRACTICE AREAS:*** Civil Appeals; Criminal Appeals. ***Email:*** ddays@mofo.com

MORRIS F. DEFEO, JR., born May 26, 1959; admitted to bar, 1985, Maryland; 1988, District of Columbia. *Education:* University of Pennsylvania (B.A., cum laude, 1981); Boston University (J.D., 1984). Pi Sigma Alpha. Chair, Washington, D.C. Corporate Finance Group. *Member:* The District of Columbia Bar; American and Inter-Pacific Bar Association. ***PRACTICE AREAS:*** Corporate Finance; Securities; Mergers and Acquisitions. ***Email:*** mdefeo@mofo.com

OLIVER I. IRELAND, born 1948; admitted to bar, 1974, Massachusetts (Not admitted in District of Columbia). *Education:* Yale University (B.A., 1970); University of Texas at Austin (J.D., 1974). ***PRACTICE AREAS:*** Financial Services Law.

BARBARA L. KIRSCHTEN, born April 11, 1950; admitted to bar, 1983, New York; 1987, District of Columbia. *Education:* University of Pennsylvania (B.A., summa cum laude, 1972); Cambridge University, England (B.A., with honors, 1974; M.A., 1974); Harvard University (A.M., 1977; Ph.D., 1979); Northwestern University (J.D., 1982). Phi Beta Kappa. Author: *The Nonprofit*

(This Listing Continued)

Corporation Forms Handbook, West Group, 9th ed., 1999. Co-Author: *Federal and State Taxation of Exempt Organizations,* Warren Gorham & Lamont, 1994; "Charitable Contributions: Income Tax Aspects," BNA Tax Management Portfolio Nos. 281-4th and 521, 1997. *Member:* District of Columbia Bar (Member, Steering Committee, Taxation Section; Chair, 1994-1997 and Vice Chair, 1991-1994, Exempt Organizations Committee); New York State and American (Member: Section on Taxation, Committee on Exempt Organizations, Committee Task Forces on Policy Issues and Compliance and State and Local Taxes, 1991-1993; Co-Chair, Subcommittee on Museums and other Cultural Organizations, 1993—) Bar Associations. ***PRACTICE AREAS:*** Nonprofit Organizations; Tax Exempt Organizations. ***Email:*** bkirschten@mofo.com

FRANK W. KROGH, born November 20, 1945; admitted to bar, 1971, New York; 1981, District of Columbia. *Education:* Brown University (A.B., cum laude, 1967); Yale Law School (LL.B., 1970). ***PRACTICE AREAS:*** Telecommunications; Administrative Law. ***Email:*** fkrogh@mofo.com

RAFAEL HERNANDEZ MAYORAL, born September 15, 1960; admitted to bar, 1986, Puerto Rico; 1988, New York (Not admitted in District of Columbia). *Education:* Yale Law School (J.D., 1986).

JOAN E. NEAL, born December 28, 1963; admitted to bar, 1989, Illinois; 1991, District of Columbia. *Education:* University of Michigan (B.A., with distinction, 1986); Yale Law School (J.D., 1989). ***Email:*** jneal@mofo.com

BRYAN A. SCHWARTZ, born June 12, 1960; admitted to bar, 1988, California; 1991, District of Columbia. *Education:* Brown University (B.A., magna cum laude, 1983); Oxford University (B.A., Jurisprudence, 1986, Marshall Scholar); Stanford University Law School (J.D., 1988). Phi Beta Kappa. Author: "Remedy and Bonding Law Under Section 337: A Primer for the Patent Litigator," 29 Computer Law Reporter 673, July 1999; "Beyond the Amendments: Federal and ITC Case Law Developments That May Determine the Long-Term Future of Section 337 Litigation," 22 AIPLA Q.J. 491, 1995; "The Fate of Section 337 Litigation After the Uruguay Round Agreements Act," 27 Law & Pol'y. Int'l. 1, 1995; "Computer Associates Crosses The Atlantic and Lake Ontario: Richardson v. Flanders and Delrina v. Triolet," The International Computer Lawyer, Vol. 1, No. 7 June 1993, with Jonathan Band and Thomas C. Vinje. Editor: Section 337 Reporter, Journal of The ITC Trial Lawyers Association. ***Email:*** bschwartz@mofo.com

EILEEN M. SMILEY, born November 30, 1959; admitted to bar, 1989, California (Not admitted in District of Columbia). *Education:* Trinity College (B.A., 1982); University of California School of Law, Davis (J.D., 1988). Order of the Coif. ***PRACTICE AREAS:*** Investment Management. ***Email:*** esmiley@mofo.com

EDWARD J. TWOMEY, born October 20, 1947; admitted to bar, 1974, District of Columbia. *Education:* University of Minnesota (B.S., summa cum laude, 1969); Georgetown University (J.D., 1974). Phi Beta Kappa. *Member:* The District of Columbia Bar. ***PRACTICE AREAS:*** Litigation; Electric Utilities; Antitrust; Oil and Gas Law. ***Email:*** etwomey@mofo.com

KATHERINE C. ZEITLIN, born October 17, 1957; admitted to bar, 1985, Illinois; 1987, District of Columbia. *Education:* Radcliffe College (A.B., magna cum laude, 1979); University of Chicago (J.D., 1985). *Member:* The District of Columbia Bar. ***PRACTICE AREAS:*** Energy. ***Email:*** kzeitlin@mofo.com

RESIDENT ASSOCIATES

JONATHAN BOCKMAN, born October 28, 1974; admitted to bar, 2000, Colorado; 2001, District of Columbia; registered to practice before U.S. Patent and Trademark Office. *Education:* Cornell University (B.S., 1997); University of Colorado at Boulder (J.D., 2000). ***PRACTICE AREAS:*** Patents. ***Email:*** jbockman@mofo.com

ALLISON G. BOTHELL, born May 8, 1972; admitted to bar, 1998, California; 1999, District of Columbia. *Education:* Georgetown University (B.A., magna cum laude, 1995); University of Washington (J.D., 1998).

TYLER S. BROWN, born February 9, 1968; admitted to bar, 1995, Georgia and Virginia; 1996, Pennsylvania; 1999, District of Columbia; registered to practice before U.S. Patent and Trademark Office. *Education:* The Citadel (B.S.E.E., with honors, 1990); University of Georgia (J.D ., cum laude, 1995). ***PRACTICE AREAS:*** Intellectual Property; Technology Contracts; Litigation.

MICHAEL DASHEFSKY, born September 30, 1970; admitted to bar, 1997, New Jersey (Not admitted in District of Columbia). *Education:* University of Rochester (B.A., magna cum laude, 1992; M.S., 1993); Georgetown University Law Center (J.D., 1996). ***PRACTICE AREAS:*** Antitrust.

RAJ S. DAVÉ, born August 29, 1958; admitted to bar, 1997, Connecticut; 1998, District of Columbia. *Education:* Indian Institute of Technology, School of Engineering (B.S., 1981); Washington State University School of Engineering (M.S., 1983); Washington University School of Engineering (Ph.D., 1986); University of Connecticut School of Law (J.D., 1996).

KRISTA DeLARGY, born December 12, 1969; admitted to bar, 1997, Maryland (Not admitted in District of Columbia). *Education:* University of Missouri (B.S., summa cum laude, 1992); Georgetown University Law Center (J.D., cum laude, 1997). ***PRACTICE AREAS:*** Financial Services. ***Email:*** kdelargy@mofo.com

TINA F. HOFMANN, born October 2, 1960; admitted to bar, 1990, New York; 1996, District of Columbia. *Education:* University of Geneva, Switzerland (1983); Tufts University, Fletcher School of Law and Diplomacy (M.A., 1985); Harvard Law School (J.D., cum laude, 1989). ***LANGUAGES:*** French, German and Spanish. ***Email:*** thofmann@mofo.com

RACHEL HOWELL, born July 30, 1975; admitted to bar, 2001, Virginia (Not admitted in District of Columbia). *Education:* American University (B.A., cum laude, 1997; Washington College of Law of American University (J.D., cum laude, 2000). ***PRACTICE AREAS:*** Financial Services Law.

MELISSA L. IVERS, born September 8, 1971; admitted to bar, 1997, Maryland; 1998, District of Columbia. *Education:* Connecticut College (B.A., 1993); Catholic University of America, Columbus School of Law (J.D., 1997). ***Email:*** mivers@mofo.com

WAYNE C. JAESCHKE, JR., born September 2, 1965; admitted to bar, 1998, Maryland; registered to practice before the U.S. Patent Office (Not admitted in District of Columbia). *Education:* Rensselaer Polytechnic Institute (B.S.Ch.E., 1987); American University (J.D., cum laude, 1998). ***PRACTICE AREAS:*** Patents.

KIMBERLY A. KARCEWSKI, born Norristown, Pennsylvania, June 15, 1971; admitted to bar, 1997, Virginia; 2000, District of Columbia. *Education:* Moravian College (B.A., magna cum laude, 1993); Thomas M. Cooley Law School (J.D., summa cum laude, 1996). ***PRACTICE AREAS:*** Investment Management. ***Email:*** kkarcewski@mofo.com

JANIS FONDA KERNS, born September 24, 1963; admitted to bar, 1994, Maryland (Not admitted in District of Columbia). *Education:* Wake Forest University (B.A., 1985); American University, Washington College of Law (J.D., 1994). ***PRACTICE AREAS:*** Business; Investment Management; Securities. ***Email:*** jfonda@mofo.com

JENNIFER L. KOSTYU, born February 12, 1975; admitted to bar, 2000, Virginia; 2001, District of Columbia. *Education:* University of North Carolina at Chapel Hill (B.A., 1996); Columbus School of Law of the Catholic University of America (J.D., cum laude, 2000). ***PRACTICE AREAS:*** Litigation; Communications Law. ***Email:*** jkostyu@mofo.com

JULIE D. LAWTON, admitted to bar, 1997, Maryland; 1998, District of Columbia. *Education:* Florida A&M University (B.S., magna cum laude, 1993); Howard University School of Law (J.D., cum laude, 1997). ***PRACTICE AREAS:*** Financial Services. ***Email:*** jlawton@mofo.com

CHRISTA PARKER McANDREW, born February 19, 1972; admitted to bar, 2000, New York; 2001, District of Columbia. *Education:* Columbia University (B.A., 1994); Tulane University of Louisiana (J.D., cum laude, 1999). ***LANGUAGES:*** French. ***PRACTICE AREAS:*** Communications Law. ***Email:*** cmcandrew@mofo.com

WILLIAM McCARRON, JR., born January 4, 1966; admitted to bar, 1994, Virginia; 1996, District of Columbia. *Education:* Colgate University (B.A., 1988); Catholic University (J.D., cum laude, 1994). ***PRACTICE AREAS:*** Bankruptcy; Creditors' Rights; Litigation. ***Email:*** wmccarron@mofo.com

THOMAS C. McCORMICK, born May 14, 1971; admitted to bar, 2001, New York (Not admitted in District of Columbia). *Education:* Kenyon College (B.A., 1993); Fordham University (J.D., 1996). ***PRACTICE AREAS:*** Financial Services Law; Banking Law; Legislative Practice; Regulatory Law. ***Email:*** tmccormick@mofo.com

ELISA D. METZGER, born September 15, 1962; admitted to bar, 1987, Pennsylvania; 1989, District of Columbia. *Education:* Valparaiso University (B.S., 1984; J.D., 1987). ***PRACTICE AREAS:*** Investment Management; Investments; Broker-Dealer Regulation. ***Email:*** emetzger@mofo.com

SAMANTHA J. PELOSI, born January 23, 1971; admitted to bar, 1998, Maryland; 2000, District of Columbia. *Education:* Duke University (B.A., magna cum laude, 1993); University of Virginia School of Law (J.D., 1997). ***PRACTICE AREAS:*** Project Finance; Export Compliance; Corporate Law. ***Email:*** spelosi@mofo.com

LOIS K. PERRIN, born October 22, 1971; admitted to bar, 1996, California (Not admitted in District of Columbia). *Education:* Arizona State University (B.A./B.S., summa cum laude, 1992); University of Southern California Law Center (J.D., 1996). ***Email:*** lperrin@mofo.com

BARRY I. PERSHKOW, born April 25, 1966; admitted to bar, 1993, Pennsylvania (Not admitted in District of Columbia). *Education:* Duke University (B.A., 1988); Tulane University Law School (J.D., cum laude, 1992). ***PRACTICE AREAS:*** Investment Management; Financial Services. ***Email:*** bpershkow@mofo.com

(This Listing Continued)

MORRISON & FOERSTER LLP, Washington—Continued

OBREA O. POINDEXTER, born February 16, 1968; admitted to bar, 1994, Pennsylvania (Not admitted in District of Columbia). *Education:* Howard University (B.A., magna cum laude, 1990); Georgetown University (J.D., 1994). ***Email:*** opoindexter@mofo.com

NADJA S. SODOS-WALLACE, born April 5, 1968; admitted to bar, 1993, Georgia; 1995, District of Columbia. *Education:* University of Massachusetts (B.A., summa cum laude, 1990); Georgetown University Law Center (J.D., 1993). ***PRACTICE AREAS:*** Communications Law.

ANDREW N. SPIVAK, born Silver Spring, Maryland, November 24, 1973; admitted to bar, 1998, Maryland and New Jersey; 1999, District of Columbia. *Education:* University of Rochester (B.A., 1995); University of Baltimore (J.D., 1998). ***PRACTICE AREAS:*** Intellectual Property. ***Email:*** aspivak@mofo.com

KEVIN R. SPIVAK, born Silver Spring, Maryland, August 31, 1969; admitted to bar, 1997, New Jersey; 1998, District of Columbia; registered to practice before U.S. Patent and Trademark Office. *Education:* George Washington University (B.S., Computer Engineering, 1992); American University (J.D., 1996). ***PRACTICE AREAS:*** Intellectual Property. ***Email:*** kspivak@mofo.com

NAVID J. TOFIGH, born March 28, 1972; admitted to bar, 1997, Texas; 1999, District of Columbia. *Education:* Santa Clara University (B.S.C., 1994); Southern Methodist University School of Law (J.D., 1997); Georgetown University Law Center (LL.M., 1999). ***PRACTICE AREAS:*** Securities; Business Law; Investment Management. ***Email:*** ntofigh@mofo.com

MICHELLE A. WAKINO, born December 6, 1960; admitted to bar, 1989, California (Not admitted in District of Columbia). *Education:* California State University, Fullerton (B.A., cum laude, 1982); University of Southern California (M.B.T., 1985); Loyola Law School (J.D., cum laude, 1989). ***Email:*** mwakino@mofo.com

VICTORIA Y. WEI, born February 9, 1972; admitted to bar, 1996, Illinois; 2001, District of Columbia. *Education:* Harvard University (A.B., cum laude, 1993); Northwestern University School of Law (J.D., 1996).

GANG XU, born October 13, 1967; admitted to bar, 1995, New York; 1997, Virginia; 1998, District of Columbia. *Education:* Beijing University Law Department (LL.B., 1990); Georgetown University Law Center (LL.M., 1991); Boston University (J.D., 1994). ***PRACTICE AREAS:*** Corporate; Commercial Law; Project Finance. ***Email:*** gxu@mofo.com

JOHN R. ZITKO, born September 24, 1966; admitted to bar, 1997, California; 1999, District of Columbia. *Education:* University of California, Berkeley (B.A., 1988); London School of Economics (M.Sc., 1992); University of Michigan Law School (J.D., 1997). ***PRACTICE AREAS:*** Project Finance; Corporate Finance; International Law. ***Email:*** jzitko@mofo.com

(For biographical data on San Francisco, Los Angeles, Sacramento, Walnut Creek, Palo Alto, San Diego, Irvine and Century City, CA, New York, NY, Denver, CO, London, England, Brussels, Belgium, Buenos Aires, Argentina, Hong Kong, Singapore, Tokyo, Japan and Beijing, China see professional biographies at each of those cities.)

MORRISON & HECKER L.L.P.

Established in 1909

1150 EIGHTEENTH STREET, N.W.
SUITE 800
WASHINGTON, D.C. 20036-3816
Telephone: 202-785-9100
Telefax: 202-785-9163
Email: POSTMASTER@moheck.com
URL: http://www.moheck.com

Kansas City, Missouri Office: 2600 Grand Avenue, 64108-4606. Telephone: 816-691-2600. Telefax: 816-474-4208.

Overland Park, Kansas Office: Corporate Woods, Building 9 Suite 450, 9200 Indian Creek Parkway, 66210-2008. Telephone: 816-691-2600. Telefax: 913-451-6352.

Wichita, Kansas Office: 600 Commerce Bank Center, 150 North Main Street, 67202-1320. Telephone: 316-265-8800. Telefax: 316-265-1349.

Phoenix, Arizona Office: 1850 North Central Avenue, Suite 2100, 85004-4584. Telephone: 602-279-1600. Telefax: 602-240-6925.

Civil Practice, Litigation, Banks and Banking, Commercial Law, Bankruptcy, Public Utility Law, Environmental Law, Administrative, International, Commercial Litigation.

RETIRED PARTNER

RICHARD A. SOLOMON (1917—).

(This Listing Continued)

HARVEY L. REITER, born Detroit, Michigan, December 3, 1950; admitted to bar, 1975, Michigan; 1976, District of Columbia; 1983, U.S. Supreme Court. *Education:* Michigan State University (B.A., 1972); Boston University (J.D., 1975). Phi Kappa Phi; Omicron Delta Epsilon. Trial Attorney, Federal Power Commission, 1975-1978. Special Assistant to the Deputy General Counsel for Litigation, Federal Energy Regulatory Commission, 1979-1984. ***PRACTICE AREAS:*** Federal Energy Regulation; Energy Marketing; Appellate; Telecommunications Law; Litigation. ***Email:*** hlreiter@moheck.com

DAVID D'ALESSANDRO, born Milford, Massachusetts, August 20, 1951; admitted to bar, 1977, Massachusetts; 1982, U.S. Court of Appeals for the District of Columbia Circuit and U.S. Supreme Court (Not admitted in District of Columbia). *Education:* College of the Holy Cross (B.A., 1973); Suffolk University (J.D., cum laude, 1976). Deputy Assistant General Counsel, Federal Energy Regulatory Commission, 1978-1981. President, Federal Energy Bar Association, 1998. ***PRACTICE AREAS:*** Public Utility Regulation; Energy. ***Email:*** dwdalessandro@moheck.com

JANET M. NESSE, born Bronx, New York, April 7, 1958; admitted to bar, 1981, District of Columbia; 1983, Maryland; 1986, Virginia. *Education:* Yale University (B.A., 1978); College of William & Mary (J.D., 1981). Member, Moot Court Team. Notes and Comments Editor, William & Mary Law Review, 1980-1981. Law Clerk to the Hon. Paul Mannes, U.S. Bankruptcy Court for the District of Maryland, 1982. Attorney, Federal Reserve Board, 1982-1983. Member, Chapter 7 Panel Trustee for the District of Maryland. *Member:* The Walter Chandler American Inn of Court; American Inns of Court (Montgomery County Chapter LXI). ***PRACTICE AREAS:*** Bankruptcy; Commercial Law; Government Contracts; Litigation. ***Email:*** jmnesse@moheck.com

STEVEN K. WHITE, born Ottumwa, Iowa, February 11, 1953; admitted to bar, 1982, District of Columbia; 1983, Maryland. *Education:* University of Iowa (B.A., with high distinction, 1974); Stanford University; Georgetown University (J.D., 1982). Phi Beta Kappa. Editor, Law & Policy in International Business. Law Clerk to Hon. Shirley B. Jones, U.S. District Judge, District of Maryland, 1982-1983. ***PRACTICE AREAS:*** Litigation; Banking Law; Professional Liability. ***Email:*** skwhite@moheck.com

MICHAEL E. TUCCI, born Washington, D.C., November 13, 1957; admitted to bar, 1985, Tennessee; 1991, Virginia and District of Columbia. *Education:* University of Tennessee at Knoxville (B.A., with honors, 1980; J.D., 1985). Senior Counsel, Resolution Trust Corporation, 1989-1990. ***PRACTICE AREAS:*** Mortgage and Commercial Banking Law and Litigation; Complex Commercial Litigation; Professional Liability; Federal Regulation. ***Email:*** metucci@moheck.com

KELLY A. DALY, born Yonkers, New York, June 18, 1964; admitted to bar, 1989, Pennsylvania; 1991, Florida and District of Columbia. *Education:* University of Notre Dame (B.A., 1986); Notre Dame Law (J.D., 1989). Member, Gas Industry Standards Board (Executive Committee, 1997-2001). Commissioner of the County Board on Aging. *Member:* Federal Energy Bar Association (Board of Directors, 1998—). ***PRACTICE AREAS:*** Energy; Public Utility Law; Telecommunications Law; Litigation. ***Email:*** kadaly@moheck.com

MARC E. ALBERT, born Philadelphia, Pennsylvania, July 16, 1948; admitted to bar, 1974, Pennsylvania; 1981, District of Columbia; 1984, Maryland; 1986, Virginia. *Education:* George Washington University (B.A., 1970; J.D., with honors, 1973); Georgetown University (M.L.T., 1984). Trustee in Bankruptcy, Washington, D.C., 1983—. ***PRACTICE AREAS:*** Bankruptcy; Tax; Real Estate. ***Email:*** mealbert@moheck.com

DARRELL W. CLARK, born Beverly, Massachusetts, August 29, 1967; admitted to bar, 1993, Maryland; 1994, Missouri; 1996, District of Columbia; 1999, Virginia. *Education:* Connecticut College (B.A., 1987); Washington University (J.D., 1993). Law Clerk to Hon. Barry S. Schermer, U.S. Bankruptcy Court, Eastern District of Missouri, 1993-1995. ***PRACTICE AREAS:*** Bankruptcy; Commercial Law; Real Estate; Banking and Finance. ***Email:*** dwclark@moheck.com

GLEN L. ORTMAN, admitted to bar, 1972, Colorado; 1979, District of Columbia. *Education:* Bowdoin College (A.B., 1969); University of Denver College of Law (J.D., 1972). ***PRACTICE AREAS:*** Energy Law. ***Email:*** glortman@moheck.com

---

JOHN E. McCAFFREY, born Havertown, Pennsylvania, November 16, 1969; admitted to bar, 1995, Massachusetts; 1998, District of Columbia. *Education:* Boston College (B.A., magna cum laude, 1992); George Washington Law School (J.D., 1995). ***PRACTICE AREAS:*** Energy Regulation; Electric Power; Natural Gas; Litigation. ***Email:*** jemccaffrey@moheck.com

LAWRENCE P. BLOCK, born Abington, Pennsylvania, August 25, 1969; admitted to bar, 1995, Maryland; 1996, District of Columbia; 1999, Virginia; U.S. Court of Appeals, Fourth Circuit; U.S. District Court for the District of Columbia; U.S. District Court, District of Maryland; U.S. District Court, East-

(This Listing Continued)

ern District of Virginia; U.S. Court of Federal Claims. *Education:* Connecticut College (B.A., 1991); George Washington Law School (J.D., 1995). ***PRACTICE AREAS:*** Government Contracts; Bankruptcy Reorganization; Business Law; Commercial Litigation. ***Email:*** lpblock@moheck.com

GREGORY O. OLANIRAN, born Lagos, Nigeria, June 20, 1961; admitted to bar, 1995, Maryland; 1997, District of Columbia. *Education:* Morgan State University (B.S., with honors, 1984; M.B.A., 1986); George Washington University, National Law Center (J.D., 1995). Certified Public Accountant, Maryland. ***PRACTICE AREAS:*** Copyright; Communications; Energy; Business Law. ***Email:*** goolaniran@moheck.com

ROBERT L. ESKAY, JR., born Natchez, Mississippi, January 16, 1965; admitted to bar, 1998, Arizona (Not admitted in District of Columbia). *Education:* College of William & Mary (B.A., 1988); Arizona State University (J.D., cum laude, 1997). Note and Comment Editor, 1996-1997, Arizona State Law Journal. Judicial Law Clerk to Chief Justice Thomas A. Zlaket, Arizona Supreme Court, 1997-1998. ***PRACTICE AREAS:*** Commercial Litigation; Appellate Practice; Bankruptcy Litigation; Fraudulent Convergence; Energy Deregulation. ***Email:*** rleskay@moheck.com

CARRIE L. McGUIRE, born New York, N.Y., December 20, 1971; admitted to bar, 2000, Virginia (Not admitted in District of Columbia). *Education:* University of Richmond (B.A., 1994); George Washington University (J.D., 2000). Spanish National Honor Society. ***PRACTICE AREAS:*** Bankruptcy; Communications. ***Email:*** clmcguire@moheck.com

KATHERINE M. SUTCLIFFE BECKER, born Washington, Missouri, June 11, 1976; admitted to bar, 2000, Missouri (Not admitted in District of Columbia). *Education:* Boston College (B.A., 1997); University of Missouri-Kansas City (J.D., 2000). Phi Beta Kappa. ***Email:*** kmbecker@moheck.com

MARIE DENYSE ZOSA, born Quezon City, Philippines, June 23, 1971; admitted to bar, 1999, Virginia; 2000, District of Columbia. *Education:* George Washington University (B.A., 1992); Washington College of Law (J.D., 1998). ***PRACTICE AREAS:*** Litigation; Energy; Foreclosures. ***Email:*** mdzosa@moheck.com

ADRIENNE E. CLAIR, born 1970; admitted to bar, 1996, Maryland; 1999, District of Columbia. *Education:* Hampton University (B.A., 1992); George Washington University (J.D., 1996). Member, Executive Committee, Moot Court Board. ***PRACTICE AREAS:*** Energy. ***Email:*** aeclair@moheck.com

REPRESENTATIVE CLIENTS: American Federal Savings Bank; Arizona Public Service Company; City of New Smyrna Beach, Florida; Federal Deposit Insurance Corporation; Nevada Attorney General - Bureau of Consumer Protection; Citizen Power, Inc.; Michigan Public Service Commission; New Hampshire Public Utilities Commission; Oneok Power Marketing; Public Service Commission of the State of New York; Kentucky Public Service Commission; Kinder Morgan Energy Partners L.P.; Maine Public Utilities Commission; Midwest Energy, Inc.; Missouri Public Service Commission; New England Conference of Public Utilities Commissioners; Sacramento Municipal Utility District; Utilities Commission; Vermont Department of Public Service; Motion Picture Association of America; Ohio National Life Insurance Company; Watkins Consulting, Inc.

MOSES & AIKEN

WASHINGTON, D.C.

(See Rockville, Maryland)

Alcohol Beverage Control, Real Estate Law, Settlements, Commercial and Residential Leases, Corporate Law, Incorporations, Partnerships, Contract Preparation, Negotiation, Commercial Real Estate, Small Business Law, Wills, Estate Planning, General Civil Practice.

RICHARD J. MUDD

2319 PENNSYLVANIA AVENUE, S.E.
WASHINGTON, D.C. 20020
Telephone: 703-360-0941
Fax: 703-360-8770
Email: rich3333@erols.com
URL: http://www.lawyers.com/richardmudd

Civil Trial Practice, Medical Malpractice, Professional Malpractice, Personal Injury, Probate Litigation, Real Estate Litigation, Estate Planning and Administration.

FIRM PROFILE: The firm represents individuals and businesses in suburban Virginia, suburban Maryland and Washington, D.C.

RICHARD J. MUDD, born Washington, D.C., April 4, 1941; admitted to bar, 1972, District of Columbia; 1976, Virginia. *Education:* George Washington University (B.A., 1964; J.D., 1972). *Member:* District of Columbia Bar; Virginia State Bar; The Association of Trial Lawyers of America. ***PRACTICE AREAS:*** Civil Trial Practice; Medical Malpractice; Professional Malpractice; Personal Injury; Probate Litigation; Real Estate Litigation; Estate Planning; Estate Administration.

MULDOON MURPHY & FAUCETTE LLP

Established in 1968

5101 WISCONSIN AVENUE, N.W.
WASHINGTON, D.C. 20016
Telephone: 202-362-0840
Telecopier: 202-966-9409; 202-363-5068
Email: counsel@mmf-law.com
URL: http://www.mmf-law.com

Practice before Federal and State Regulatory Agencies. Savings and Loan, Corporation, Banking, Securities and Administrative Law, Employee Benefits, Taxation, representation of Nonprofit and Charitable Organizations.

MEMBERS OF FIRM

JOSEPH A. MULDOON, JR., born Waltham, Massachusetts, August 24, 1931; admitted to bar, 1957, District of Columbia. *Education:* Georgetown University (B.S., 1953; LL.B., 1956). Phi Alpha Delta. Attorney, Federal Home Loan Bank Board, 1958-1966. *Member:* The District of Columbia Bar; Bar Association of the District of Columbia; Federal Bar Association. ***PRACTICE AREAS:*** Legislative Practice; Congressional; Federal Government; Finance; Savings and Loan.

GEORGE W. MURPHY, JR., born Honesdale, Pennsylvania, December 21, 1929; admitted to bar, 1954, District of Columbia. *Education:* Georgetown University (B.S., 1951; LL.B., 1954; LL.M., 1959). Phi Delta Phi. Attorney, 1958-1967 and Associate General Counsel, 1968-1970, Federal Home Loan Bank Board. *Member:* The District of Columbia Bar; Bar Association of the District of Columbia; Federal (Executive Council, Savings Institution Law Committee, 1976-1986) and American Bar Associations. ***PRACTICE AREAS:*** Financial Institutions; Mergers and Acquisitions; Regulation; Savings and Loan; Savings and Loan Regulation; Nonprofit and Charitable Organizations. ***Email:*** GMurphy@MMF-law.com

DOUGLAS P. FAUCETTE, born Yonkers, New York, October 8, 1946; admitted to bar, 1972, District of Columbia; 1974, New York. *Education:* University of Massachusetts (B.A., 1968); Suffolk University (J.D., 1971). Note Editor, Suffolk University Law Review, 1970-1971. Author: "Recapitalization of Savings Institutions in the Garn-St. Germain Era: The Federal Home Loan Bank Board's New Mutual to Stock Conversion Regulation," XLIX Legal Bulletin, U.S.L.S.I., 107, May, 1983. Co-Author: Faucette and Kneipper, "Income Capital Certificates: FSLIC Creates a Unique Savings and Loan Security," 14 Federal Home Loan Bank Board Journal 10, October, 1981; "Non-Cash Assets for Thrifts," Banking Law Report, Vol. 2, No. 2, May, 1985; Faucette and Gorman, "Self-help financing," Banking Law Report Vol. 2 Nos. 6-7, September-October, 1985. Associate General Counsel and Director, Securities Division, 1977-1980 and Senior Associate General Counsel for Securities and Business Transactions, 1980-1981, Federal Home Loan Bank Board. *Member:* The District of Columbia Bar; New York State, Federal (Member, Executive Council Savings Institution Law Committee, 1982-1984) and American (Member, Section of Corporation, Banking and Business Law) Bar Associations; International Bar Association. ***PRACTICE AREAS:*** Government; Finance; Banks and Banking; Corporate Law; Securities. ***Email:*** DFaucette@MMF-law.com

JOHN R. HALL, born Jackson, Mississippi, November 25, 1946; admitted to bar, 1975, Maryland; 1978, District of Columbia. *Education:* Duke University (B.A., 1968); University of Alabama (M.A., 1969); Washington College of Law, The American University (J.D., 1975). Phi Delta Kappa; Kappa Delta Pi. Attorney, 1976-1979 and Associate General Counsel, 1980-1982, Federal Home Loan Bank Board. *Member:* The District of Columbia Bar; Maryland State and American Bar Associations. ***PRACTICE AREAS:*** Financial Institutions; Thrift Insurance; Corporate Banking; Mergers, Acquisitions and Reorganizations; Federal Regulatory. ***Email:*** JHall@MMF-law.com

THOMAS J. HAGGERTY, born Washington, D.C., August 1, 1944; admitted to bar, 1970, Maryland (Not admitted in District of Columbia). *Education:* Georgetown University (B.S.F.S., 1966; J.D., 1970). Associate General Counsel, Corporate & Regulatory Structure, 1983 and Senior Attorney, Securities and Corporate Analysis, 1980-1983, Federal Home Loan Bank Board. Attorney, Division of Corporation Finance, Securities and Exchange Commission, 1970-1980. ***PRACTICE AREAS:*** Business Law; Banks and Banking; Corporate Law; Mergers, Acquisitions and Divestitures; Securities. ***Email:*** THaggerty@MMF-law.com

JOSEPH P. DALY, born Washington, D.C., January 22, 1957; admitted to bar, 1982, District of Columbia. *Education:* State University of New York at Stony Brook (B.A., 1979); The National Law Center, George Washington University (J.D., 1982). Topics Editor, George Washington Law Review, 1981-1982. Author: "National Banks as General Partners: New Opportunities for Joint Enterprises," 104 Banking Law Journal 516; "Asset Purchases From Affiliates: The Federal Reserve's Interpretive Exemption From Limits on Affiliate Transactions," 113 Banking Law Journal 601. Co-author: *Banking Law in the United States,* Butterworths 1988 and 2nd ed, 1992. Contributing Author: "Banks and Thrifts: Regulatory Enforcement and Receivership Law," Matthew Bender,

(This Listing Continued)

MULDOON MURPHY & FAUCETTE LLP, Washington—Continued

1991. Attorney, Legal Advisory Services Division, U.S. Comptroller of the Currency, 1982-1985. *Member:* The District of Columbia Bar; American Bar Association. ***PRACTICE AREAS:*** Financial Institutions Regulation; Holding Companies Regulation; Regulation; Savings and Loan Regulation; Thrift Institutions Regulation. ***Email:*** JDaly@MMF-law.com

LORI M. BERESFORD, born Bermuda, June 30, 1963; admitted to bar, 1987, Pennsylvania; 1988, District of Columbia. *Education:* University of Mississippi (B.B.A., 1983; M.A., 1984); Catholic University, Columbus School of Law (J.D., 1987). *Member:* The District of Columbia Bar; American Bar Association. ***PRACTICE AREAS:*** Financial Institutions; Corporate Law; Mergers and Acquisitions; Banks and Banking; Securities. ***Email:*** LBeresford@MMF-law.com

CHRISTINA M. GATTUSO, born Wilkes Barre, Pennsylvania, December 7, 1957; admitted to bar, 1984, Maryland; 1995, District of Columbia. *Education:* King's College (B.S., 1979); University of Baltimore (J.D., 1983). Author: "Fair Lending Compliance After Chevy Chase," The Review of Banking & Financial Services, Dec. 7, 1994; "The New CRA Examination Procedures," The Review of Banking & Financial Services, Jan. 31, 1996; "Interagency Interpretations Under the Community Reinvestment Act," The Review of Banking and Financial Services, April 9, 1997; "Guide to Financial Data Privacy," Thompson Publishing Group, 2000. Regulatory Counsel, 1987-1988 and Attorney, 1985-1987, Federal Home Loan Bank Board. Attorney, Division of Market Regulation, Securities and Exchange Commission, 1984-1985. *Member:* Maryland State and American Bar Associations; District of Columbia Bar. ***PRACTICE AREAS:*** Business Law; Financial Institution Regulations; Holding Companies; Nonprofit and Charitable Organizations; Thrift Institutions; Corporate Law; Banks and Banking. ***Email:*** CGattuso@MMF-law.com

LAWRENCE M. F. SPACCASI, born Rochester, New York, June 6, 1962; admitted to bar, 1988, New York (Not admitted in District of Columbia). *Education:* State University of New York at Buffalo (B.A., 1984; J.D., 1987). *Member:* Erie County and New York State Bar Associations. ***PRACTICE AREAS:*** Finance; Banks and Banking; Corporate Law; Securities; Securities and Exchange Commission Regulation. ***Email:*** LSpaccasi@MMF-law.com

PAUL M. AGUGGIA, born Queens, New York, March 15, 1963; admitted to bar, 1989, New York and District of Columbia. *Education:* Colgate University (B.A., cum laude, 1985); Duke University (J.D., 1988). Phi Alpha Theta. Editor-in-Chief, Alaska Law Review (published by Duke University). *Member:* New York State Bar Association; District of Columbia Bar. ***PRACTICE AREAS:*** Financial Institutions; Business Law; Mergers, Acquisitions and Divestitures; Securities. ***Email:*** paguggia@mmf-law.com

ERIC S. KRACOV, born New York, N.Y., June 26, 1957; admitted to bar, 1985, Maryland; 1987, District of Columbia. *Education:* University of Maryland (B.A., 1979); George Washington University (J.D., 1985). Phi Beta Kappa; Phi Kappa Phi. Legal Editor, Tax Notes, 1985-1986. Executive Editor, Washington Tax Review, 1986-1990. Vice-Chairman, Compensation Planning Journal Advisory Board, 1990-1993. *Member:* District of Columbia Bar. ***PRACTICE AREAS:*** Employee Benefits; Federal Taxation; ERISA; Trade Associations; Tax-Exempt Organizations. ***Email:*** ekracov@mmf-law.com

VICTOR L. CANGELOSI, born Queens, New York, November 3, 1961; admitted to bar, 1991, Maryland; 1993, District of Columbia. *Education:* College of the Holy Cross (B.A., cum laude, 1983); University of Dallas (M.B.A., 1985); George Washington University (J.D., 1991). Phi Beta Kappa. *Member:* The District of Columbia Bar; Maryland State Bar Association. ***PRACTICE AREAS:*** Financial Institutions; Securities; Corporate Law. ***Email:*** vcangelosi@mmf-law.com

AARON M. KASLOW, born New Haven, Connecticut, May 21, 1964; admitted to bar, 1991, California; 1994, District of Columbia. *Education:* Yale University (B.A., cum laude, 1986; J.D., 1989). Member, Moot Court Board, 1989. Executive Editor, The Yale Law and Policy Review, 1988-1989. Law Clerk, Hon. Martin L. C. Feldman, U.S. District Court, Eastern District of Louisiana, 1989-1990. *Member:* District of Columbia Bar; State Bar of California. ***PRACTICE AREAS:*** Financial Institutions; Mergers and Acquisitions; Securities; Corporate Law. ***Email:*** akaslow@mmf-law.com

KENT M. KRUDYS, born Kittery, Maine, September 1, 1963; admitted to bar, 1988, Connecticut; 1989, U.S. District Court, District of Connecticut; 1990, New Jersey and U.S. District Court, District of New Jersey; 1991, District of Columbia. *Education:* Baylor University (B.B.A., 1985); University of Bridgeport (J.D., 1988). Sigma Iota Epsilon; Phi Delta Phi. Editor-in-Chief, Bridgeport Law Review. Author: Comment, 8 University of Bridgeport L. Rev. 255, 1987. *Member:* Connecticut Bar Association (Member, Financial Institutions Section); District of Columbia Bar (Member, Financial Institutions Section). ***PRACTICE AREAS:*** Financial Institutions; Corporate Law; Banks and Banking; Securities; Bankruptcy; Commercial and Securities Litigation; Commercial Real Estate; Foreclosures. ***Email:*** kkrudys@mmf-law.com

(This Listing Continued)

THOMAS P. HUTTON, born Denver, Colorado, March 7, 1963; admitted to bar, 1988, Florida; 1991, District of Columbia. *Education:* Auburn University (B.S., 1985); Cumberland School of Law, Samford University (J.D., 1988); University of Florida (LL.M., Taxation, 1989). Attorney Advisor, U.S. Tax Court, 1989-1991. *Member:* District of Columbia Bar; The Florida Bar. ***PRACTICE AREAS:*** Employee Benefits; Federal Taxation; ERISA. ***Email:*** thutton@mmf-law.com

OF COUNSEL

LESLIE ANN MURPHY, born Denver, Colorado, October 22, 1945; admitted to bar, 1982, Alabama; 1989, District of Columbia. *Education:* Hope College (B.A., 1967); Florida State University (M.B.A., 1981; J.D., with honors, 1981). Phi Kappa Phi; Mortar Board. National Endowment Fellowship, Harvard Institute for AICS Administration, 1977. Treasurer, Women's Law Symposium, FSU, 1980-1981. Member, National Association of Corrosion Engineers, 1971-1972. Attorney, 1982-1986 and Legal Assistant to Chairman John Shad, 1986, Securities and Exchange Commission, Division of Corporation Finance. *Member:* The District of Columbia Bar. ***PRACTICE AREAS:*** Securities; Capital Formation; Corporate Law; Business Law; Financial Institutions; Mergers and Acquisitions; Merger Reorganization. ***Email:*** lmurphy@mmf-law.com

ARTHUR D. PERSCHETZ, born Ossining, New York, May 17, 1943; admitted to bar, 1969, New York; 1971, U.S. District Court, Southern and Eastern Districts of New York, U.S. Court of Appeals, Second Circuit and U.S. Supreme Court; 1988, North Carolina; U.S. District Court, Western District of North Carolina (Not admitted in District of Columbia). *Education:* Syracuse University (B.A., 1965; J.D., 1967). Vice President and Assistant General Counsel, Royal Insurance, 1970-1991. Senior Vice President and General Counsel, Maryland Insurance Group, 1991-1996. Member: Industry Advisory Committee to Draft Model Redomestication Law, 1978-1979 and Industry Advisory Committee to the Market Conduct and Consumer Affairs Subcommittee, 1980-1988, National Association of Insurance Commissioners; Board of Directors, Maine Insurance Guaranty Association, 1992-1996; New Hampshire Insurance Guaranty Association, 1992-1996. Trustee, Incorporated Village of Saltaire, New York, 1978-1979. Chairman, Mayor's Committee on Cable Television, Charlotte, North Carolina, 1986-1991. *Member:* New York State, North Carolina and American Bar Associations. [Capt., U.S. Army, 1967-1969]. ***PRACTICE AREAS:*** Insurance Regulation; Corporate. ***Email:*** aperschetz@mmf-law.com

---

MICHAEL R. MURPHEY

SUITE 202, 1320 19TH STREET, N.W.
WASHINGTON, D.C. 20036
Telephone: 202-659-8611
Fax: 202-659-8612
Email: murpheyusa@aol.com
URL: http://www.lawyers.com/murpheylaw

Bankruptcy, Bankruptcy Chapter 7, Bankruptcy Chapter 13 and Bankruptcy Chapter 11, Debtor and Creditor, Consumer Rights, Commercial Bankruptcy, Probate Litigation, Wills, Trust Law, Estate Administration, Inheritance, Probate Taxation, Small Business Law, Business Successions, Business Reorganization, Incorporation, Family Business Law, Family Law.

FIRM PROFILE: For over twenty-five years, Michael R. Murphey has advised and counseled individuals, families, entrepreneurs and small to medium sized businesses throughout Washington, D.C. and suburban Maryland. The firm has successfully and continually provided expert general business counseling and individualized service for all its clients.

MICHAEL R. MURPHEY, born Pensacola, Florida, June 1, 1947; admitted to bar, 1973, District of Columbia; 1976, Maryland. *Education:* Miami University (B.A., 1969); George Washington University (J.D., 1973). *Member:* The District of Columbia Bar; Bar Association of the District of Columbia; Maryland State and American Bar Associations; Trial Lawyers Association of the Superior Court of the District of Columbia.

LAW OFFICES OF
PIERRE E. MURPHY

2445 M STREET, N.W., SUITE 260
WASHINGTON, D.C. 20037
Telephone: 202-872-1679
Fax: 202-872-1725
Email: pmurphy@lopmurphy.com

Aviation, Regulatory and Commercial Law. International Law. Travel Law.

(This Listing Continued)

FIRM PROFILE: The firm specializes in aviation law, representing a wide variety of clients before numerous U.S. and foreign government agencies including FAA, DOT, Dept. of State, Dept. of Defense and Treasury Dept. (OFAC, Customs Service and INS). Clients include scheduled and charter U.S. and foreign airlines, major tour operators/wholesalers, travel agents, airports, defense contractors and other aviation-related businesses. The firm advises clients on a broad range of aviation-related issues, including licensing and regulatory compliance, operations issues, bilateral air service negotiations, aircraft purchase and leasing contracts, overflight customs matters and international route development counsel.

PIERRE E. MURPHY, born Northampton, England, August 16, 1956; admitted to bar, 1979, England and Wales; 1980, Wisconsin; 1983, District of Columbia. *Education:* The Polytechnic, Wolverhampton, England (LL.B., Honors, 1978); Inns of Court School of Law, London, England, Lincoln's Inn, London, England (Barrister, 1979); University of Wisconsin (J.D., 1980). *Member:* The District of Columbia Bar; State Bar of Wisconsin; Federal and American Bar Associations; Bar of England and Wales; Honorable Society of Lincoln's Inn (London, England); Washington Foreign Law Society; Association des Jeunes Avocats; Foreign Lawyers Forum. (Also Of Counsel, Boros & Garofalo, P.C.). ***LANGUAGES:*** French. ***PRACTICE AREAS:*** Aviation Law; Regulatory Law; Commercial Law; International Law.

ASSOCIATE

ANDREA RUIZ, born Ibague, Colombia, January 18, 1967; admitted to bar, 2000, New York and Republic of Colombia (Not admitted in District of Columbia). *Education:* Los Andes University, School of Law (J.D., 1991); Georgetown University (LL.M., 1993). *Member:* New York State and American Bar Associations. ***LANGUAGES:*** Spanish. ***PRACTICE AREAS:*** Aviation Law; International Law. ***Email:*** aruiz@lopmurphy.com

MURPHY ELLIS WEBER

818 CONNECTICUT AVENUE, N.W., SUITE 700
WASHINGTON, D.C. 20006-2702
Telephone: 202-833-9211
Fax: 202-833-6570
URL: http://www.MurphyEllisWeber.com
Email: mew@MurphyEllisWeber.com

Associated Offices: Fact Law Group (Helsinki & Washington) and Kiskalt, Dielmann & Schoenberger (Frankfurt).

International Business Law, Litigation, Administrative Law and Government Relations, Export Controls. Defense Trade/Technology Transfer, Encryption, Economic Sanctions, E-Commerce/Telecommunications, Intellectual Property Law, Antitrust and Trade Regulation.

FIRM PROFILE: International business Law firm advising multinational and domestic enterprises. Business, litigation and regulatory advice. Extensive experience on export controls and technology transfer.

MEMBERS OF FIRM

COURTENAY ELLIS, born January 4, 1946; admitted to bar, 1970, Solicitor, England and Wales; 1973, District of Columbia. *Education:* Oxford University (B.A., 1967; M.A., 1974); George Washington University (LL.M., 1972). President, British-American Business Association, 1999-2001. Chair, Federal Bar Association International Law Section, 1996-1998. President, Washington Foreign Law Society, 1997-1998. ***PRACTICE AREAS:*** International Business Law; Litigation; Administrative Law; Government Relations. ***Email:*** CEllis@MurphyEllisWeber.com

CHARLES A. WEBER, born September 8, 1959; admitted to bar, 1985, District of Columbia. *Education:* University of Michigan (A.B., 1981); University of Iowa (J.D., 1984). Associate Editor, Iowa Law Review, 1983-1984. Counsel, British-American Business Association. Vice Chairman, International Law Committee, American Bar Association Administrative Law Section, 1997—. ***PRACTICE AREAS:*** Export Compliance; E-Commerce; International Business Law; Corporate. ***Email:*** CWeber@MurphyEllisWeber.com

SENIOR COUNSEL

TERENCE MURPHY, born October 20, 1937; admitted to bar, 1967, District of Columbia. *Education:* Harvard College (A.B., 1959); University of Michigan (J.D., cum laude, 1966). Honorary O.B.E., 1993. Member, U.S. Department of Commerce, Advisory Committee on Export Regulations, 2001—. Member, Munitions Exports Working Group, Center for Strategic and Intenational Studies, 2000-2001. ***PRACTICE AREAS:*** Export Compliance; Intellectual Property; Administrative Law. ***Email:*** TMurphy@MurphyEllisWeber.com

REPRESENTATIVE CLIENTS: Allergan; American Association of Exporters and Importers; American Express; British-American Business Association; Carl Zeiss Jena; Embraer; Malta Financial Services Centre.; Nokia; OneTravel.com.

MURRELL & BROWN

1401 I STREET N.W.
SUITE 250
WASHINGTON, D.C. 20005
Telephone: 202-289-9001
Fax: 202-289-9094
Email: ATTYTRAV@aol.com

Special Education Law, Disability Rights, Psychological Evaluation, Individual Education Programs.

FIRM PROFILE: The law firm of Murrell & Brown represents children with disabilities and their parents in matters dealing primarily with the Federal laws involving special education. The firm has both a national and local practice with significant experience in litigation for the advocacy of learning disabled children.

MEMBERS OF FIRM

TRAVIS A. MURRELL, born Camden, New Jersey, January 19, 1942; admitted to bar, 1976, Washington, D.C. *Education:* Yale University; Georgetown University (B.S.L., 1971; J.D., 1975). Associate Professor, University of the District of Columbia, 1994-1999. Hearing Officer for special education matters, 1988-1996. *Member:* The District of Columbia Bar. [U.S. Air Force, 1959-1963]. ***LANGUAGES:*** Chinese and Japanese. ***PRACTICE AREAS:*** Special Education.

JAMES E. BROWN, born May 26, 1938; admitted to bar, 1969, Virginia; 1970 District of Columbia. *Education:* Norfolk State University (B.S., 1967); Howard University (J.D., 1969). Instructor, Antioch Law School, Washington, D.C., 1973-1974. *Member:* The District of Columbia Bar; Virginia State Bar. [Army, 1960-1963]. ***PRACTICE AREAS:*** Disabilities; Special Education.

ASSOCIATES

DOMIENTO C.R. HILL, born Washington, D.C., May 20, 1972; admitted to bar, 2000, Maryland (Not admitted in District of Columbia). *Education:* University of Maryland (B.S., 1995; J.D., 1999). ***LANGUAGES:*** Spanish. ***PRACTICE AREAS:*** Complex Litigation; Class Actions.

MYERS LAZRUS TECHNOLOGY LAW GROUP

1990 M STREET, NW, SUITE 200
WASHINGTON, D.C. 20036
Telephone: 202-296-0626
Fax: 202-296-1680
URL: http://www.lawyers.com/myerskeller
URL: http://www.myerslazrus.com

Telecommunications Law (Broadcast, Common Carrier, Cellular Radio, Satellite, MDS, and Private Radio). Litigation Practice before the Federal Communications Commission and Federal Courts.

FIRM PROFILE: Myers Lazurus Technology Law Group ("MLTLG") is a Washington, D.C. law firm specializing in technology law matters, including structural and financing issues for early-stage ventures, nondisclosure agreements, transaction planning, joint ventures, strategic partnering, business contracts, and government regulation. MLTLG is prepared to assist clients with their copyright and trademark matters. The firm has easy access to the U.S. Copyright Office and the resources necessary to register copyrighted material as well as research and register trademarks. MLTLG has established special expertise in the field of telecommunications law and matters before the Federal Communications Commission, encompassing FCC litigation, rulemakings, licensing, spectrum auctions and commercial transactions in services such as cellular radio, SMR, PCS, MDS, private land mobile radio, microwave, experimental, common carrier, satellite and wireless data. MLTLG attorneys have served clients in the wireless communications and other industries by assisting in the negotiation and/or drafting a large number and variety of contracts necessary for the conduct of their business, such as contracts involving interconnection and financing. MLTLG also represents clients engaged in the purchase and sale of businesses and in accessing the capital marketplace. MLTLG also provides in-house engineering services such as wireless system designs, propagation studies and frequency coordination.

RICHARD S. MYERS, born Bloomington, Illinois, June 24, 1958; admitted to bar, 1984, District of Columbia; 1989, U.S. Court of Appeals, District of Columbia Circuit; 1993, U.S. Court of Federal Claims; 1994, U.S. Supreme Court. *Education:* University of Illinois (B.A., 1980); American University (M.A., 1984); Washington College of Law of American University (J.D., 1984). *Member:* The District of Columbia Bar; Federal Communications Bar Associa-

(This Listing Continued)

MYERS LAZRUS TECHNOLOGY LAW GROUP, Washington—Continued

tion. ***LANGUAGES:*** French. ***PRACTICE AREAS:*** Cellular Communications; FCC Licensing; Federal Litigation. ***Email:*** myers@myerslazrus.com

JAY N. LAZRUS, born Tacoma Park, Maryland, May 16, 1957; admitted to bar, 1981, Maryland; 1982, Virginia (Not admitted in District of Columbia). *Education:* University of Maryland (B.A., General Honors, 1978; J.D., 1981); Georgetown University (Masters, Tax, with honors, 1992). Member, Maryland Committee of Dispute Resolution. *Member:* Maryland State Bar Association; Virginia State Bar. ***PRACTICE AREAS:*** Communications and Media; Business Law; Litigation. ***Email:*** lazrus@myerslazrus.com

ENGINEERING CONSULTANT

JAMES J. KELLER, born Fitchburg, Massachusetts, May 26, 1964. *Education:* University of Kentucky (B.S.E.E., 1989). *Member:* Federal Communications Bar Association. (Consulting Engineer).

RONALD M. NADITCH, P.A.

WASHINGTON, D.C.

(See Annapolis, Maryland)

Family Law, Mediation, General Civil and Criminal Trial Practice in all State Courts.

LAW OFFICES OF KUROSH NASSERI

3207-A M ST., NW, 3RD FLOOR
WASHINGTON, D.C. 20007
Telephone: 202-457-0808
Fax: 202-457-0909
Email: mail@kurosh.net
URL: http://www.kurosh.net

Entertainment Law, Licensing, Publishing, Entertainment Business Counselling, Electronic Music, International Licensing, Contract Licensing.

FIRM PROFILE: The firm's primary focus is the international licensing of electronic music.

KUROSH NASSERI, born Bonn, West Germany, June 25, 1959; admitted to bar, 1986, New York and District of Columbia. *Education:* American University (B.A., 1980; M.A.; 1981); Georgetown University Law Center (J.D., 1984; LL.M., 1987). Lead Articles Editor, The Tax Lawyer, 1983-1984. Author: "The Multimodal Transport Convention," 19 Journal of Maritime Law and Commerce 231, 1988. *Member:* The District of Columbia Bar; New York State Bar Association. ***LANGUAGES:*** German and Farsi. ***PRACTICE AREAS:*** Entertainment Law; Contracts.

TERRIE M. BJORKLUND, MS., born Minneapolis, Minnesota, March 26, 1952; admitted to bar, 1984, Pennsylvania; 1985, District of Columbia. *Education:* Augsburg College; Pacific Lutheran University; The Evergreen State College (B.A., 1972); Antioch School of Law (J.D., 1982). *Member:* Pennsylvania Bar Association; District of Columbia Bar. ***PRACTICE AREAS:*** Entertainment Law; Copyrights; Trademarks.

NATH & ASSOCIATES, PLLC

1030 15TH STREET, N.W.
6TH FLOOR
WASHINGTON, D.C. 20005
Telephone: 202-775-8383 or 202-775-9393
Facsimile: 202-775-8396 or 202-882-9409
Email: IP@NATHLAW.COM
URL: http://www.NATHLAW.COM

San Diego, California Office: 110 West C Street, Suite 1300, 92101. Telephone: 619-645-5290. Facsimile: 619-645-5289.

Patent, Trademark, Copyright, Licensing Litigation, International Patents, General Counsel Services.

FIRM PROFILE: The law firm of Nath & Associates represents clients in all aspects of intellectual property law, focusing on securing, protecting, defending and licensing of national and international rights in patents, trademarks, copyrights, computer law, and trade secrets, including unfair competition and related issues, creating and managing patent portfolios and estates, and providing overall general services and other advice.

MEMBERS OF FIRM

GARY M. NATH, born Trenton, New Jersey, August 3, 1944; admitted to bar, 1975, New Jersey, U.S. Court of Appeals for the Federal Circuit; 1999, District of Columbia; registered to practice before U.S. Patent and Trademark Office. *Education:* Rider College (B.S. in Biology and Chemistry, with honors, 1966); American University (J.D., with honors, 1972). Examiner, U.S. Patent and Trademark Office, 1969-1973. Patent Attorney, FMC Corporation, 1973-1976. Senior Patent Attorney, NL Industries, 1977-1982. Warner-Lambert Company Consumer Products Patent Counsel, 1982-1989. *Member:* New Jersey State and American Bar Associations; The District of Columbia Bar; American Intellectual Property Law Association (Member, Chemical Practice Committee, 1975—). ***PRACTICE AREAS:*** Patent and Trademark Prosecution and Litigation; Trade Secrets; Licensing; Acquisitions, Divestitures and Mergers; Joint Ventures. ***Email:*** gnath@nathlaw.com

HAROLD L. NOVICK, born Philadelphia, Pennsylvania, December 29, 1942; admitted to bar, 1973, Maryland and District of Columbia; 1975, U.S. Supreme Court; 1982, U.S. Court of Appeals, Federal Circuit; registered to practice before U.S. Patent and Trademark Office. *Education:* Miami University, Ohio (B.A., in physics, 1964); U.S. Naval Nuclear Power Training Schools (Qual. Nuc. Eng. Off. of Watch, 1965); George Washington University (J.D., with honors, 1972). *Member:* American Intellectual Property Law Association; Computer Law Association; D.C. Computer Law Forum (Director, 1986-1992; President, 1991); International Association for the Protection of Industrial Property. ***PRACTICE AREAS:*** Electro-Mechanical Patents; Prosecution; Intellectual Property Licensing; Trademark Prosecution; Copyright Prosecution; Intellectual Property Litigation; Computer Law. ***Email:*** hnovick@nathlaw.com

TODD L. JUNEAU, born Portland, Oregon, July 24, 1966; admitted to bar, 1995, Illinois; 1997, District of Columbia and U.S. Court of Appeals, Federal Circuit; registered to practice before U.S. Patent and Trademark Office. *Education:* University of Minnesota (B.A., Microbiology, 1992); The John Marshall Law School (J.D., 1995). Intern, Office of Unfair Import Investigations, International Trade Commission. Research Assistant to the Honorable Paul R. Michel, U.S. Court of Appeals, Federal Circuit, John Marshall Law School. *Member:* Bar Association of the District of Columbia; American Bar Association; The District of Columbia Bar; American Society of Microbiologists; American Intellectual Property Law Association, Patent and Trademark Office Society. ***LANGUAGES:*** Mandarin Chinese, Danish. ***PRACTICE AREAS:*** Intellectual Property Law; Patents; Trademarks; Copyrights. ***Email:*** tjuneau@nathlaw.com

ROSS A. EPSTEIN, born Philadelphia, Pennsylvania, August 7, 1961; admitted to bar, 1987, California (Not admitted in District of Columbia). *Education:* Princeton University (A.B., History, minor Premedical Studies, 1983); Boston University (J.D., cum laude, 1987). Law Clerk, Federal Court, S. Dist. California, 1987-1988. Associate Attorney, Brobeck, Phleger & Harrison, 1988-1992. President & CEO, BCH Communications (Telephone and Telecom Service and Equipment Provider) in Prague and Warsaw, 1992-2001. Member: San Diego Software and Internet Council; UCSD Connect; San Diego Regional Technology Allaince; San Diego Regional Chamber of Commerce. *Member:* LaJolla and San Diego County Bar Associations; State Bar of California. ***PRACTICE AREAS:*** Corporate Law; Business Transactions; Intellectual Property; Business Formation; Real Estate. ***Email:*** rae@nathlaw.com

ASSOCIATES

MICHELLE L. HARTLAND, admitted to bar, 1997, Virginia (Not admitted in District of Columbia). *Education:* College of William and Mary (C.B.A.E., Economics, 1986); Washington College of Law of American University (J.D., 1996). *Member:* International Trademark Association. ***PRACTICE AREAS:*** Trademarks; Copyrights. ***Email:*** mhartland@nathlaw.com

LEE C. HEIMAN, born Alhambra, California, February 10, 1958; admitted to bar, 1985, California; 1986, U.S. District Court, Southern, Central and Eastern Districts of California; 1987, U.S. Court of Appeals, Ninth Circuit; registered to practice before U.S. Patent and Trademark Office (Not admitted in District of Columbia). *Education:* California Institute of Technology; Stanford University (A.B., 1980); New York Law School; Loyola Marymount University of Los Angeles (J.D., 1985); George Washington University (B.S., Biology, 1997). *Member:* Los Angeles County and American Bar Associations; State Bar of California (Member, Intellectual Property Section); American Intellectual Property Law Association. ***PRACTICE AREAS:*** Civil Litigation; Probate Litigation. ***Email:*** lheiman@nathlaw.com

JERALD L. MEYER, admitted to bar, 1998, Virginia; registered to practice before U.S. Patent and Trademark Office (Not admitted in District of Columbia). *Education:* University of Michigan (B.S.C.E., 1992); Franklin Pierce Law Center (J.D., 1998). Phi Alpha Delta. *Member:* American Intellectual Property Law Association. ***Email:*** jmeyer@nathlaw.com

MARVIN C. BERKOWITZ, born Boston, Massachusetts, July 6, 1952; admitted to bar, 1995, Georgia, U.S. District Court, Northern District of Georgia and U.S. Court of Appeals, 11th Circuit, Registered to practice before the

(This Listing Continued)

U.S. Patent and Trademark Office (Not admitted in District of Columbia). *Education:* Georgia Institute of Technology (B.I.E., 1974; B.E.E., 1977; M.S.O.R., 1981); Georgia State University (J.D., 1995). Registered Professional Engineer, Georgia, 1984—. Member, Institute of Electrical and Electronics Engineers. Member, Board of Equalization, Dekalb County, Georgia, 1985-1986. Member, Atlanta Bar Association, 1996-1998. *Member:* State Bar of Georgia (Member, Intellectual Property Section). ***REPORTED CASES:*** Rapps v. Cooke, 505 S.E.2d 566 (Ga. App. 1998); Bodymasters v. Wimberley, 501 S.E.2d 556 (Ga. App. 1998); Rapps v. Cooke, 540 S.E.2d 241 (Ga. App. 2000). **Email:** mberkowitz@nathlaw.com

TANYA E. HARKINS, born Pensacola, Florida, November 7, 1968; admitted to bar, 1999, Maryland (Not admitted in District of Columbia). *Education:* Virginia Commonwealth University (B.A., English, 1992); Catholic University of America (J.D., 1998). ***LANGUAGES:*** French. ***PRACTICE AREAS:*** Patent Prosecution; Trademark Prosecution; Copyright Prosecution. ***Email:*** tej@nathlaw.com

JOSHUA L. GOLDBERG, admitted to bar, 1999, Virginia; registered to practice before the Bar of the Commonwealth of Virginia (Not admitted in District of Columbia). registered to practice before U.S. Patent and Trademark Office. *Education:* Washington University (B.S., Chemical Engineering, 1996); George Washington University (J.D., 1999). ***Email:*** IP@NATHLAW.COM

TODD W. KUNZ, born Harvey, Illinois, May 19, 1965; admitted to bar, 2000, Illinois (Not admitted in District of Columbia). *Education:* University of Illinois (B.S., Psychology, minors in Chemistry, Mathematics, 1988); Illinois Institute of Technology - Kent College of Law (J.D., 2000). ***PRACTICE AREAS:*** Patents. ***Email:*** twk@nathlaw.com

JOSEPH K. HEMBY JR., born Washington D.C., April 7, 1958; admitted to bar, 1999, Maryland; Registered to practice before the U.S. Patent and Trademark Office (Not admitted in District of Columbia). *Education:* Hampton University (B.A., Biology, 1981); George Washington University Law School (J.D., 1997). Author: "Meghrig v. K.F.C. Western, Inc.," The Environmental Lawyer, Vol. 3, No. 1, Sept. 96, pp. 285-296; "Development of Alternate P-1099 Plasticizer," Chemical Propulsion Information Agency (CPIA) PNB 548 of Dec 90; "Characterization of Polyethylene and Polypropylene," Chemical Propulsion Information Agency (CIPA) PNB 578 of April 92. Licensing Specialist, National Institute of Health, 1996-1999. Patent Advisor, Naval Medical Research Center, 1995-1996. *American Intellectual Property Association; Government Intellectual Property Law Association.* [First Lieutenant, Army, 4]. ***PRACTICE AREAS:*** Patent Prosecution. ***Email:*** jkh@nathlaw.com

PATENT AGENT

ALVIN E. TANENHOLTZ, registered to practice before the U.S. Patent and Trademark Office. *Education:* University of Massachusetts (B.S., Microbiology, 1956). Participated in the Conference on Patenting of Life Forms at Cold Spring Harbor and the Biotechnology Patent Conference at American Type Culture Collection. Instructor, Korean International Property Training Institute in Seoul, 1987. ***Email:*** IP@NATHLAW.COM

RETIRED

Irvin A. Lavine ***Donald M. Sandler*** (Not admitted in DC)

NEALON & MORAN, LLP

WASHINGTON, D.C.

(See Alexandria, Virginia)

Criminal Defense, Business Law, Contracts, Family Law, Divorce, Child Custody, Child Support, Real Estate, Traffic Violations, Driving While Intoxicated, Juvenile, Technology Law, Commercial Civil Litigation, Small Business Formation.

MARILYN E. NELSON

WASHINGTON, D.C.

(See Bethesda, Maryland)

Estate and Gift Taxation, Estate Planning, Wills, Trusts, Probate, Estate Administration, Business Planning, Wealth Preservation, Business Succession Planning, Small Business Law, Taxation.

NELSON & NELSON LLP

WASHINGTON, D.C.

(See Bethesda, Maryland)

Probate and Estate Planning, Trust Law, Marital Contracts, Negligence, Arbitration and Mediation.

BARRY S. NEUMAN, P.L.L.C.

1752 N STREET, N.W., SUITE 800
WASHINGTON, D.C. 20036
Telephone: 202-466-2886
Fax: 202-887-8044
Email: bneuman@neumanpllc.com
URL: http://www.lawyers.com/neumanlaw

Environmental Law.

BARRY S. NEUMAN, born Jersey City, New Jersey, April 7, 1949; admitted to bar, 1975, New York; 1986, District of Columbia. *Education:* University of Rochester (B.A., with high distinction, 1971); University of California, Boalt Hall School of Law (J.D., 1974). Phi Beta Kappa. Attorney-Advisor, Environmental Protection Agency, Office of General Counsel, Water and Solid Waste Division, 1978-1980. Trial Attorney, U.S. Department of Justice, Land and Natural Resources Division, Environmental Defense Section, 1980-1985. Recipient: Special Commendation of Assistant Attorney General, 1984; Special Achievement Award of the Attorney General, 1983. Developments Editor, Ecology Law Quarterly, 1973-1974. Editorial Board, EPA Administrative Law Reporter, 1994—. *Member:* The District of Columbia Bar; New York State Bar Association. ***PRACTICE AREAS:*** Environmental Law; Complex Litigation; Administrative Law; Trade Association Law.

NEVILLE, PETERSON LLP

Established in 1989

1233 20TH STREET, N.W., SUITE 500
WASHINGTON, D.C. 20036
Telephone: 202-861-2959
Fax: 202-861-2924
Email: info@npwtradelaw.com
URL: http://www.npwtradelaw.com

New York, N.Y. Office: Neville, Peterson & Williams, 80 Broad Street, 10004. Telephone: 212-635-2730. Facsimile: (212) 635-2734. Internet: info@npwtradelaw.com

Customs, International Trade, Antitrust, Trade Regulation, Trade Association, Franchise, Government Contract Litigation, International Commercial Law, Administrative and Admiralty Law. Litigation in all Courts. Federal Practice.

GEORGE THOMPSON, born Brooklyn, New York, July 2, 1956; admitted to bar, 1982, New York; 1983, U.S. Court of International Trade and U.S. Claims Court; 1984, U.S. Court of Appeals for the Federal Circuit; 1988, District of Columbia. *Education:* State University of New York at Oneonta (B.S., magna cum laude, 1978); Cornell University (J.D., 1981). Co-Author: de Kieffer and Thompson, "Political and Policy Dimensions of Foreign-Trade Zones," 18 Vanderbilt Journal of Transnational Law 481, 1985; "Made in USA, Should a Pre-1970 FTC Legal Standard Govern Product Claims for the Year 2000 and Beyond?," 9 Association Law and Policy 16, 1995; "Exporting: Regulations, Documentation, Procedures," Global Training Institute, 1997. Customs Law and Administrations, Oceana Publications, Inc.; Transnational Contracts, Oceana Publications; International Ocean and Air Transportation, Global Training Center, 1998. Adjunct Professor, The School of Public Policy, George Mason University. *Member:* The District of Columbia Bar. ***PRACTICE AREAS:*** International Trade; Administrative Practice; Litigation. ***Email:*** gthompso@npwdc.com

OF COUNSEL

MICHAEL K. TOMENGA, born Port Byron, New York, April 14, 1953; admitted to bar, 1978, District of Columbia, U.S. Court of Appeals for the District of Columbia Circuit and U.S. District Court for the District of Columbia; 1979, U.S. Court of International Trade; 1979-1982, U.S. Court of Customs and Patent Appeals; 1982, U.S. Court of Appeals for the Federal Circuit; 1992, U.S. Supreme Court. *Education:* St. Lawrence University (B.A., 1975); Catholic University of America (J.D., 1978). Phi Beta Kappa; Phi Sigma Alpha; Delta Sigma Rho; Tau Kappa Alpha; Omicron Delta Kappa. Chairman, International Department. Author: "Laws Regulating the Operation of Foreign Fish Processing Vessels off the Coast of the United States," Federal Bar News and Journal, June, 1982. Co-Author: "U.S. Import Classification Under the Harmonized Tariff Schedule," 1989. Attorney, Office of Regulations and Rulings, U.S. Customs Service, 1978-1984. Contributor, U.S. Customs and International Trade Guide, Authored by Peter Buck Feller. Speaker on Customs Topics, American Association of Exporters and Importers and the Practicing Law Institute. *Member:* The District of Columbia Bar; American (International Section) and Customs and International Trade Bar Associations; Customs Lawyers Association (Former Vice President); Joint Industry Group. ***PRACTICE AREAS:*** Customs Law; International Trade Law. ***Email:*** mtomenga@npwdc.com

LAWRENCE J. BOGARD, born Champaign, Illinois, July 12, 1952; admitted to bar, 1977, District of Columbia; 1981, U.S. Court of International

(This Listing Continued)

NEVILLE, PETERSON LLP, Washington—Continued

Trade; 1987, U.S. Court of Appeals for the Federal Circuit. *Education:* Vassar College (A.B., 1974); Georgetown University (J.D., 1977). *Supervisory Editor:* Customs Law and Administration, Oceana Publications, Inc., New York, 1998. Faculty Member, Practicing Law Institute Symposia on Antidumping and Countervailing Duty Procedures, 1984, 1992. Attorney: Office of Chief Counsel, U.S. Customs Service, 1977-1979; Office of General Counsel, Department of Commerce, 1980, 1984. U.S.-Canada Free Trade Agreement Bi-National Dispute Panel Roster, Member, 1991-1994, Panelist, 1992, Panel Chair, 1993-1994. Member, NAFTA Dispute Panel Roster, 1994—. *Member:* The District of Columbia Bar. ***PRACTICE AREAS:*** International Trade; Customs Law; Administrative Law. ***Email:*** lbogard@npwdc.com

JOHN A. DETZNER, born Chicago, Illinois, March 31, 1955; admitted to bar, 1980, Illinois and U.S. District Court, Northern District of Illinois; 1989, District of Columbia; 1990, U.S. District Court for the District of Columbia, U.S. Court of International Trade, U.S. Court of Appeals for the District of Columbia and U.S. Court of Appeals for the Federal Circuit; 1993, U.S. Supreme Court and U.S. Court of Federal Claims. *Education:* Harvard University (A.B., 1977; J.D., 1980). Author: "Foreign Investment in Chile," Corporate Counsel's International Adviser, September 1994; "Doing Business in Post-Devaluation Mexico," Inter-American Trade and Investment Law, February 1995; "Chile's Environmental Framework Law: Considerations of Foreign Investors," NAFTA and the Environment, Martinus Nijhoff Publishing, 1996. Member, Board of Advisors, Foreign Corrupt Practices Act Reporter. *Member:* The District of Columbia Bar (Member, International Section); American (Member, International Law and Practice Section; Co-Chair, Task Force on Foreign Corrupt Practices; Steering Group, Export Controls and Economic Sections Committee) and Inter-American (Member, Committee of Commercial Law and Procedure) Bar Associations. (Resident). ***LANGUAGES:*** Spanish. ***PRACTICE AREAS:*** International Trade Regulation; International Transactions. ***Email:*** jdetzner@npwdc.com

ASSOCIATE

JULIA S. PADIERNA-PERALTA, born Puebla, Pue., Mexico, May 24, 1964; admitted to bar, 2000, Florida, U.S. Court of International Trade, U.S. Court of Federal Claims and U.S. Court of Appeals for the Federal Circuit (Not admitted in District of Columbia). *Education:* Universidad de las Americas, Puebla, Mexico (1982-1983); L'Universite de Fribourg, Switzerland (1985-1986); Georgetown University (B.S.F.S., magna cum laude, 1987); The London School of Economics and Political Science (M.Sc., 1989); Washington College of Law, American University (J.D., cum laude, 1999). Official Liaison of the Mexican Senate on NAFTA at the Mexican Embassy in the United States, 1991-1994. Consultant to the Secretariat of Industry, Trade and Tourism of the State of Tamaulipas, Mexico, 1994-1995. Contributor to the North American Free Trade & Investment Report, and El Financiero, International Edition, newspaper. *Member:* The Florida Bar; American Bar Association; Inter-American Bar Association; Women in International Trade. ***LANGUAGES:*** Spanish, French and Portuguese. ***PRACTICE AREAS:*** Mexico Trade; Customs Law; Regulatory Law; Trade Law; International Trade Law; Litigation. ***Email:*** jpadierna@npwdc.com

(For Biographical data on all Personnel, see Professional Biographies at New York, New York).

NEWMAN & McINTOSH

WASHINGTON, D.C.

(See Bethesda, Maryland)

Medical Malpractice, Birth Trauma, Oncology Law, Plastic Surgery, Brain Injury, Catastrophic Injury, Neurolaw, Wrongful Death, Expert Witnessing, Products Liability, Auto Accidents, Business Fraud, White Collar Crimes, Drug Crimes, Bribery, Theft, Homicide, Gun Crimes, Federal Crimes, Personal Injury. Managed Care Issues, Hospital Peer Review, Investigational Review Board, Mass Tort Litigation, Medical Devices, Criminal law and Civil Litigation.

ROY I. NIEDERMAYER

WASHINGTON, D.C.

(See Bethesda, Maryland)

Business Litigation, Alternative Dispute Resolution, Entrepreneurial Business Law, Commercial Litigation, Construction Litigation.

NIXON PEABODY LLP

401 9TH STREET, N.W.
SUITE 900
WASHINGTON, D.C. 20004-2128
Telephone: 202-585-8000
Fax: 202-585-8080
Email: nixonpeabody@nixonpeabody.com
URL: http://www.nixonpeabody.com

Rochester, New York Office: Clinton Square. Telephone: 716-263-1000. Fax: 716-263-1600.
New York, N.Y. Office: 437 Madison Avenue. Telephone: 212-940-3000. Fax: 212-940-3111.
Albany, New York Office: Omni Plaza, 30 South Pearl Street. Telephone: 518-427-2650. Fax: 518-427-2666.
Garden City, New York Office: 990 Stewart Avenue. Telephone: 516-832-7500. Fax: 516-832-7555.
Buffalo, New York Office: 1600 Main Place Tower. Telephone: 716-853-8100. Fax: 716-853-8109.
Hartford, Connecticut Office: City Place, 185 Asylum Street. Telephone: 860-275-6820. Fax: 860-275-6821.
Boston, Massachusetts Office: 101 Federal Street. Telephone: 617-345-1000. Fax: 617-345-1300.
Manchester, New Hampshire Office: 889 Elm Street. Telephone: 603-628-4000. Fax: 603-628-4040.
Providence, Rhode Island Office: One Citizens Plaza. Telephone: 401-454-1000. Fax: 401-454-1030.
McLean, Virginia Office: 8180 Greensboro Drive, Suite 800. Telephone: 703-790-9110. Telecopier: 703-883-0370.
Costa Mesa, California Office: 600 Anton Boulevard, Suite 1600, 92626. Telephone: 714-241-0101. Fax: 714-241-0105.
San Francisco, California Office: Two Embarcadero Center, Suite 2700, 94111-3996. Telephone: 415-984-8200. Fax: 415-984-8300.

FIRM PROFILE: Nixon Peabody LLP is a general practice law firm that offers services in complex multijurisdictional and International matters involving antitrust, corporate and business law, bank regulatory law, bankruptcy, commercial lending, commercial litigation, employee benefits and labor and employment law, environmental law, estate planning and administration, franchising, healthcare law, housing and community development and syndication, loan enforcement, project finance, public finance, public utilities and energy law, real estate, securities law, tax law, and technology and intellectual property.

PARTNERS

VERONICA M. AHERN, born New York, N.Y., 1946; admitted to bar, 1973, District of Columbia. *Education:* Rosemont College (B.A., 1968); Georgetown University (J.D., 1972). Director, International Affairs, National Telecommunications and Information Administration, 1978-1982. *Member:* The District of Columbia Bar; American Bar Association; Federal Communications Bar Association. ***PRACTICE AREAS:*** Communications and Media; Alternative Dispute Resolution (ADR); Antitrust; Nonprofit and Charitable Organizations. ***Email:*** vahern@nixonpeabody.com

WILLIAM S. ANDREWS, born Rockville Centre, New York, 1949; admitted to bar, 1978, Florida; 1979, New York; 1984, District of Columbia. *Education:* Lafayette College (A.B., 1971); University of Pennsylvania (A.M., 1974); University of Virginia (J.D., 1978). *Member:* The Florida Bar; The District of Columbia Bar. (Also at New York, N.Y. Office). ***PRACTICE AREAS:*** Energy Finance; Project Finance. ***Email:*** wandrews@nixonpeabody.com

LESLIE P. ARRINGTON, born Syracuse, New York, 1967; admitted to bar, 1993, Virginia; 1995, District of Columbia. *Education:* Virginia Polytechnic Institute and State University (B.A., summa cum laude, 1989); University of Virginia (J.D., 1993). Phi Beta Kappa. *Member:* Virginia State Bar; The District of Columbia Bar. ***PRACTICE AREAS:*** Litigation; Labor and Employment. ***Email:*** larrington@nixonpeabody.com

GARY A. BAND, born Washington, D.C., 1965; admitted to bar, 1990, Maryland; 1991, District of Columbia. *Education:* Tulane University (B.S.M., 1987); Washington College of Law, American University (J.D., 1990). Certified Public Accountant, Washington, D.C., 1993. *Member:* The District of Columbia Bar. ***PRACTICE AREAS:*** Real Estate Syndication; Taxation. ***Email:*** gband@nixonpeabody.com

EDWARD C. BERKOWITZ, born Perth Amboy, New Jersey, 1935; admitted to bar, 1960, New Jersey; 1966, District of Columbia. *Education:* Cornell University (B.A., 1956); Harvard University (LL.B., 1959). Attorney-Advisor, National Labor Relations Board, 1964-1966. General Attorney, Communications Satellite Corporation, 1966-1970. *Member:* The District of Columbia Bar; American Bar Association. ***PRACTICE AREAS:*** Business Law; Real Estate; Litigation. ***Email:*** eberkowitz@nixonpeabody.com

(This Listing Continued)

ROBERT C. BERNIUS, born Brooklyn, New York, 1946; admitted to bar, 1973, New York; 1985, District of Columbia; 1987, Maryland. *Education:* Brown University (Sc.B.E.E., magna cum laude, 1968) Tau Beta Pi, Sigma Xi; Yale University (J.D., 1972). *Member:* The District of Columbia Bar. Fellow, American College of Trial Lawyers. ***PRACTICE AREAS:*** Appellate Practice; Labor and Employment; Litigation; Media Law. ***Email:*** rbernius@nixonpeabody.com

ROBERT L. BODANSKY, born New York, N.Y., 1952; admitted to bar, 1978, Maryland and District of Columbia; 2000, Virginia. *Education:* Syracuse University (A.B., 1974); George Washington University (J.D., with honors, 1977). *Member:* The District of Columbia Bar; Maryland State, Virginia and American (Chairman, Subcommittee on Foreign and International Business Law, Young Lawyers Section, 1979-1981) Bar Associations. ***PRACTICE AREAS:*** Business; Bankruptcy; Real Estate; Mergers and Acquisitions. ***Email:*** rbodansky@nixonpeabody.com

JOHN M. BRADHAM, born Charleston, South Carolina, 1962; admitted to bar, 1989, Pennsylvania and District of Columbia. *Education:* Davidson College (B.A., 1984); Cornell Law School (J.D., 1987). *Member:* The District of Columbia Bar. (Also at New York, New York Office). ***PRACTICE AREAS:*** Civil Litigation; Corporate. ***Email:*** jbradham@nixonpeabody.com

WILLIAM F. CAUSEY, born Baltimore, Maryland, 1949; admitted to bar, 1979, District of Columbia; 1984, Maryland. *Education:* The American University (B.A., 1971); University of Maryland (J.D., 1975). Adjunct Professor of Trial Practice: Georgetown University Law Center, 1984—. Judicial Conference for the District of Columbia Circuit, 1983—. Mediator, U.S. District Court for the District of Columbia, 1990—. *Member:* The District of Columbia Bar (Board of Governors, 1996-1999; Chairman, Litigation Section, 1988-1991). Fellow, American Bar Foundation. ***PRACTICE AREAS:*** Trial Practice; Appellate Practice. ***Email:*** wcausey@nixonpeabody.com

J. WILLIAM CODINHA, (P.C.), born New York, N.Y., 1947; admitted to bar, 1972, Massachusetts; 1994, District of Columbia. *Education:* Ohio Wesleyan University (B.A., 1969); Boston University (J.D., 1972). Chief Counsel/ Deputy Staff Director, United States Senate Select Committee on POW/MIA Affairs, 1991-1992. Special Counsel, United States Senate Committee on Banking, Housing and Urban Affairs "Whitewater Investigation," June 1994-December 1994. *Member:* The District of Columbia Bar. (Also at Boston, Massachusetts Office). ***PRACTICE AREAS:*** White Collar Criminal Litigation; Civil Litigation; Environmental Litigation. ***Email:*** jcodinha@nixonpeabody.com

JEFF M. COHEN, born Brooklyn, New York, 1959; admitted to bar, 1984, District of Columbia. *Education:* State University of New York at Albany (B.A., magna cum laude, 1981); George Washington University (J.D., 1984). Phi Beta Kappa. *Member:* The District of Columbia Bar (Member, Corporate, Finance and Securities Section). ***PRACTICE AREAS:*** Corporate Finance; Energy Finance; Project Finance; Mergers and Acquisitions. ***Email:*** jcohen@nixonpeabody.com

SUSAN O. CUNNINGHAM, born Dell Rapids, South Dakota, 1962; admitted to bar, 1987, Wisconsin; 1990, Colorado; 1996, District of Columbia. *Education:* University of Iowa (B.B.A., with Distinction, 1984; J.D., 1987). *Member:* State Bar of Wisconsin; The District of Columbia Bar. ***PRACTICE AREAS:*** Real Estate; Affordable Housing; Small Business Representation; Commercial Transactions. ***Email:*** scunningham@nixonpeabody.com

ROBERT L. DAILEADER, JR., born New York, N.Y., 1954; admitted to bar, 1980, New York; 1997, District of Columbia. *Education:* University of Notre Dame (B.B.A., 1976); Albany Law School of Union University (J.D., 1979). *Member:* The District of Columbia Bar. ***PRACTICE AREAS:*** Energy Finance; Project Finance. ***Email:*** rdaileader@nixonpeabody.com

GEORGE L. DAVES, born Dalton, Georgia, 1943; admitted to bar, 1967, Georgia; 1988, District of Columbia. *Education:* University of Georgia (B.B.A., 1965; J.D., 1968). *Member:* State Bar of Georgia; The District of Columbia Bar. ***PRACTICE AREAS:*** Real Estate; Real Estate Finance; Housing and Urban Affairs. ***Email:*** gdaves@nixonpeabody.com

CHARLES L. EDSON, born St. Louis, Missouri, 1934; admitted to bar, 1959, Missouri; 1967, District of Columbia. *Education:* Harvard University (A.B., magna cum laude, 1956; J.D., 1959). Phi Beta Kappa. Vice Chair, Maryland Historical Trust. *Member:* The Missouri Bar; The District of Columbia Bar; American Bar Association (Founding Chair, Forum Committee on Affordable Housing and Community Development, 1991-1993). ***PRACTICE AREAS:*** Affordable Housing; Community Development. ***Email:*** cedson@nixonpeabody.com

ROBERT P. FLETCHER, born Kansas City, Missouri, 1958; admitted to bar, 1983, District of Columbia; 1994, Maryland. *Education:* Princeton University (A.B., summa cum laude, 1980); Duke University (J.D., with honors, 1983). Phi Beta Kappa. *Member:* The District of Columbia Bar; American Bar Association (Member, Litigation Section). ***PRACTICE AREAS:*** Litigation; Labor and Employment; Employment Litigation; Contracts; Contract Litigation; Commercial Law; Appellate Practice; Banks and Banking; Business Law. ***Email:*** rfletcher@nixonpeabody.com

(This Listing Continued)

RICHARD S. GOLDSTEIN, born Buffalo, New York, 1948; admitted to bar, 1974, Massachusetts; 1985, District of Columbia. *Education:* State University of New York at Buffalo (B.A., 1970); Boston College (J.D., 1974). *Member:* The District of Columbia Bar. ***PRACTICE AREAS:*** Real Estate; Housing Law; Real Estate Securities. ***Email:*** rgoldstein@nixonpeabody.com

RAYMOND J. GUSTINI, born New London, Connecticut, 1943; admitted to bar, 1970, Virginia; 1971, Connecticut; 1978, District of Columbia. *Education:* University of Connecticut (B.A., 1965; J.D., 1968). *Member:* Virginia State Bar; The District of Columbia Bar; Federal (Chairman, Thrift Institutions Law Committee, 1977-1980) and American (Member, Banking Law Committee; Co-Chair, Joint Financial Services Privacy Task Force) Bar Associations. ***PRACTICE AREAS:*** Banking Law; Privacy Law. ***Email:*** rgustini@nixonpeabody.com

KENNETH G. HANCE, JR., born Ann Arbor, Michigan, 1940; admitted to bar, 1966, Michigan; 1980, District of Columbia. *Education:* DePauw University; Michigan State University (B.A., with honors, 1962); Northwestern University (J.D., 1965). *Member:* State Bar of Michigan; The District of Columbia Bar. ***PRACTICE AREAS:*** Real Estate; Real Estate Finance; Housing and Urban Development. ***Email:*** khance@nixonpeabody.com

JOHN C. HAYES, JR., born Utica, New York, 1947; admitted to bar, 1973, District of Columbia; 1982, Maryland. *Education:* Williams College (B.A., 1969); George Washington University (J.D., with honors, 1973). *Member:* The District of Columbia Bar; Bar Association of the District of Columbia; American Bar Association; International Association of Defense Counsel; Defense Research Institute. ***PRACTICE AREAS:*** Litigation. ***Email:*** jhayes@nixonpeabody.com

MARC S. KAUFMAN, born Cleveland, Ohio, 1962; admitted to bar, 1992, Pennsylvania; 1993, District of Columbia; registered to practice before U.S. Patent and Trademark Office. *Education:* Boston University (B.S.M.E., 1984); Catholic University of America (J.D., 1991). *Member:* The District of Columbia Bar (Member, Intellectual Property Law Section). ***PRACTICE AREAS:*** Patent Law; Copyright Law; Trademark Law; Licensing. ***Email:*** mkaufman@nixonpeabody.com

HARRY J. KELLY, born Worcester, Massachusetts, 1956; admitted to bar, 1982, Massachusetts; 1983, Texas; 1985, District of Columbia. *Education:* Williams College (B.A., magna cum laude, 1978); Harvard University (M.C.R.P., 1982); Boston University (J.D., 1982). Phi Beta Kappa. *Member:* State Bar of Texas; The District of Columbia Bar. ***PRACTICE AREAS:*** Bankruptcy; Environmental Law; Litigation; Housing. ***Email:*** hkelly@nixonpeabody.com

MARY JO KELLY, born High Point, North Carolina, 1955; admitted to bar, 1984, Virginia; 1998, District of Columbia. *Education:* University of North Carolina at Chapel Hill (B.A., 1977); College of William & Mary (J.D., 1984). Order of the Coif. Attorney-Fellow, Securities and Exchange Commission, 1995-1997. *Member:* Virginia State Bar; District of Columbia Bar; National Association of Bond Lawyers. ***PRACTICE AREAS:*** Public Finance; Securities. ***Email:*** mjkelly@nixonpeabody.com

BRUCE S. LANE, born New London, Connecticut, 1932; admitted to bar, 1955, Ohio; 1966, District of Columbia. *Education:* Boston University; Harvard College (A.B., magna cum laude, 1952); Harvard University (J.D., 1955). Phi Beta Kappa. *Member:* The District of Columbia Bar; American Bar Association (Chairman, Committee on Court Procedure, Taxation Section, 1967-1969); American College of Real Estate Lawyers (President, 1986-1987); American Law Institute. ***PRACTICE AREAS:*** Tax; Real Estate; Business Law. ***Email:*** blane@nixonpeabody.com

GORDON L. LANG, born Chicago, Illinois, 1951; admitted to bar, 1976, Illinois; 1977, District of Columbia; 1989, New York. *Education:* University of Michigan (B.A., 1973); Harvard University (J.D., 1976). Phi Beta Kappa. *Member:* The District of Columbia Bar (Member, Sections on: Antitrust; Litigation); American Bar Association. ***Email:*** glang@nixonpeabody.com

JEFFREY S. LESK, born Syracuse, New York, 1954; admitted to bar, 1980, Arizona; 1982, District of Columbia. *Education:* Stanford University (B.A., 1976); University of Arizona (J.D., 1979). Attorney-Real Estate Specialist, Office of Urban Development Action Grants, H.U.D., 1982-1984. *Member:* State Bar of Arizona; The District of Columbia Bar. ***PRACTICE AREAS:*** Real Estate; Housing and Urban Development. ***Email:*** jlesk@nixonpeabody.com

CHRISTIAN M. McBURNEY, born Kingston, Rhode Island, 1959; admitted to bar, 1986, New York; 1988, District of Columbia; 1996, Virginia and Maryland. *Education:* Brown University (A.B., magna cum laude, 1981); New York University School of Law (J.D., 1985); Georgetown University Law School (Masters in Taxation, high honors, 1992). Phi Beta Kappa. *Member:* The District of Columbia Bar (Chair, Committee on State and Local Taxation); Virginia, Maryland State and New York State Bar Associations. ***PRACTICE AREAS:*** Taxation; Mergers and Acquisitions. ***Email:*** cmcburney@nixonpeabody.com

TIMOTHY R. McTAGGART, born Philadelphia, Pennsylvania, 1960; admitted to bar, 1985, Massachusetts; 1987, District of Columbia. *Education:*

(This Listing Continued)

NIXON PEABODY LLP, Washington—Continued

Harvard University (A.B., cum laude, 1982; J.D., 1985). Delaware State Bank Commissioner, 1994-1998. ***PRACTICE AREAS:*** Banks and Banking; Corporate; Legislative. ***Email:*** tmctaggart@nixonpeabody.com

LAURA ARIANE MILLER, born New York, N.Y., 1954; admitted to bar, 1988, Virginia; 1989, District of Columbia. *Education:* University of Michigan (B.A., 1974); Harvard University (M.P.P., 1976); Yale University (J.D., 1988). Phi Beta Kappa. Member, The Barristers. *Member:* The District of Columbia Bar; Virginia State Bar; American Bar Association (Co-Chair, Criminal Litigation Committee); Edward Bennett Williams Inn of Court. ***PRACTICE AREAS:*** Litigation; Affordable Housing; Environmental Law; White Collar Crime. ***Email:*** lmiller@nixonpeabody.com

LAURIN H. MILLS, born Raleigh, North Carolina, 1957; admitted to bar, 1989, Maryland; 1991, District of Columbia; 1992, Colorado. *Education:* University of Maryland (B.A./B.S.); Georgetown University Law Center (J.D., cum laude, 1989). *Member:* The District of Columbia Bar. ***PRACTICE AREAS:*** Litigation; White Collar Crime; Intellectual Property Litigation; Internet and Media Law. ***Email:*** lmills@nixonpeabody.com

SCOTT M. NEMEROFF, born Baltimore, Maryland, 1959; admitted to bar, 1985, Maryland; 1988, District of Columbia and U.S. District Court, District of Columbia; U.S. Court of Appeals for the Distict of Columbia. *Education:* Georgetown University (B.A., 1981); University of Maryland Law School (J.D., cum laude, 1984). *Member:* The District of Columbia Bar. ***PRACTICE AREAS:*** Securities; Corporate Law; Affordable Housing. ***Email:*** snemeroff@nixonpeabody.com

JOHN C. PARTIGAN, born Rochester, New York, 1959; admitted to bar, 1986, New York; 2001, District of Columbia. *Education:* Willamette University (B.S., cum laude, 1981); Albany Law School of Union University (J.D., magna cum laude, 1985). ***PRACTICE AREAS:*** Business Law; Securities; Mergers and Acquisitions; Telecommunications Law. ***Email:*** jpartigan@nixonpeabody.com

BARRY J. POLLACK, born Youngstown, Ohio, 1964; admitted to bar, 1991, Maryland; 1992, District of Columbia. *Education:* Indiana University (B.S., with high honors, 1986); Georgetown University Law Center (J.D., magna cum laude, 1991). Order of the Coif. Law Clerk to the Hon. Thomas A. Flannery, U.S. District Court, District of Columbia, 1991-1992. Formerly with Miller, Cassidy, Larroca and Lewin, 1992-1998. Assistant Federal Public Defender, District of Maryland, 1998-2000. *Member:* Edward Bennett Williams Inn of Court.; National Association of Criminal Defense Lawyers. ***PRACTICE AREAS:*** White Collar Criminal Defense; Civil Litigation. ***Email:*** bpollack@nixonpeabody.com

RICHARD M. PRICE, born Queens, New York, 1964; admitted to bar, 1988, Pennsylvania; 1989, Maryland and District of Columbia. *Education:* George Washington University (B.A., 1985; J.D., 1988). Commissioner, Montgomery County, Commission on Common Ownership Communities, 1995—. *Member:* The District of Columbia Bar. ***PRACTICE AREAS:*** Litigation; Housing; Community Development; Administrative Law; Commercial Real Estate. ***Email:*** rprice@nixonpeabody.com

MITCHELL H. RAPAPORT, born Brooklyn, New York, 1958; admitted to bar, 1983, New York (Not admitted in District of Columbia). *Education:* Hofstra University (B.B.A., magna cum laude, 1979); George Washington University (J.D., with high honors, 1982); Georgetown University (M.L.T., with distinction, 1988). Order of the Coif. ***PRACTICE AREAS:*** Public Finance. ***Email:*** mrapaport@nixonpeabody.com

ROBERT F. REKLAITIS, born Elizabeth, New Jersey, 1953; admitted to bar, 1978, Illinois; 1982, District of Columbia; 1993, Maryland. *Education:* LeMoyne College (B.A., summa cum laude, 1975); University of Virginia (J.D., 1978). Alpha Sigma Nu. *Member:* The District of Columbia Bar; American Bar Association (Member, Litigation Section); National Association of College and University Attorneys. ***PRACTICE AREAS:*** Litigation; Antitrust; Insurance; Securities; Telecommunications Law. ***Email:*** rreklaitis@nixonpeabody.com

JOSEPH H. REYNOLDS, born Wilmington, Delaware, 1946; admitted to bar, 1977, New York; 1985, District of Columbia. *Education:* Lehigh University (B.A., 1968; M.A., 1972); Albany Law School of Union University (J.D., 1976). *Member:* The District of Columbia Bar. ***PRACTICE AREAS:*** Corporate Finance; Mergers and Acquisitions. ***Email:*** jreynolds@nixonpeabody.com

EDWARD M. ROGERS, born Long Island, New York, 1960; admitted to bar, 1987, New York; 1988, District of Columbia. *Education:* University of Virginia (B.A., 1982; J.D., 1986). *Member:* The District of Columbia Bar. ***PRACTICE AREAS:*** Real Estate; Real Estate Leasing; Real Estate Finance. ***Email:*** erogers@nixonpeabody.com

RUTH BORSUK ROSENBERG, born Plainfield, New Jersey, 1935; admitted to bar, 1964, Pennsylvania; 1967, New York; 1986, District of Columbia; 1987, Maryland; 1994, Virginia; 1995, Massachusetts. *Education:* Douglass College (A.B., 1956, Phi Beta Kappa); University of Pennsylvania (J.D., cum laude, 1963). *Member:* Maryland State and American Bar Associations; The District of Columbia Bar; Virginia State Bar. ***PRACTICE AREAS:*** Leases and Leasing; Real Estate; Zoning, Planning and Land Use. ***Email:*** rrosenberg@nixonpeabody.com

KENNETH H. SILVERBERG, born Cleveland, Ohio, 1946; admitted to bar, 1973, Virginia; 1995, District of Columbia. *Education:* University of Michigan (B.A., 1968); Georgetown University (J.D., 1973). Certified Public Accountant Licensed in Virginia and District of Columbia, 1973. *Member:* Virginia and American (Member, Tax Section) Bar Associations; District of Columbia Bar. ***PRACTICE AREAS:*** Business; Nonprofit and Charitable Organizations; Tax Law; Litigation; Trusts and Estates. ***Email:*** ksilverberg@nixonpeabody.com

JOHN STUART SMITH, born Rochester, New York, 1943; admitted to bar, 1968, New York; 1986, District of Columbia. *Education:* Harvard University (A.B., magna cum laude, 1965; LL.B., cum laude, 1968). ***PRACTICE AREAS:*** Antitrust Law; Litigation. ***Email:*** jssmith@nixonpeabody.com

HERBERT F. STEVENS, born Philadelphia, Pennsylvania, 1948; admitted to bar, 1975, District of Columbia. *Education:* Massachusetts Institute of Technology (S.B., 1970); Catholic University (J.D., 1974); Georgetown University (Master of Laws in Taxation, 1983). *Member:* The District of Columbia Bar. ***PRACTICE AREAS:*** Tax; Real Estate; Syndication; Housing Law. ***Email:*** hstevens@nixonpeabody.com

KATHLEEN F. SULLIVAN, born Rio de Janeiro, Brazil, 1949; admitted to bar, 1981, District of Columbia. *Education:* Newton College (B.A., 1970); Catholic University (J.D., 1981). *Member:* The District of Columbia Bar. ***PRACTICE AREAS:*** Taxation; Real Estate; Partnerships. ***Email:*** ksullivan@nixonpeabody.com

MONICA HILTON SUSSMAN, born New York, N.Y., 1952; admitted to bar, 1977, Virginia; 1978, District of Columbia. *Education:* Syracuse University (B.A., cum laude, 1973); Hofstra University (J.D., 1977). President, 1997-2000 and Member, National Housing Conference. *Member:* Virginia State Bar; The District of Columbia Bar. ***PRACTICE AREAS:*** Real Estate; Affordable Housing; Real Estate Finance; Legislation; Corporate. ***Email:*** msussman@nixonpeabody.com

KENDAL TYRE, JR., born 1967; admitted to bar, 1993, New York and Illinois; 1995, District of Columbia. *Education:* University of Minnesota (J.D., 1992). ***PRACTICE AREAS:*** Business; Energy Finance; Project Finance Law. ***Email:*** ktyre@nixonpeabody.com

GARY L. VALBY, born Rochester, New York, 1948; admitted to bar, 1974, New York; 1989, District of Columbia. *Education:* Middlebury College (B.A., 1970); New York University (J.D., Root-Tilden Scholar, 1973). *Member:* The District of Columbia Bar. ***PRACTICE AREAS:*** Energy Finance; Project Finance. ***Email:*** gvalby@nixonpeabody.com

G. JOSEPH VOTAVA, JR., born Elmira, New York, 1954; admitted to bar, 1981, New York; 2000, U.S. Tax Court; 2001, District of Columbia. *Education:* Siena College (B.B.A., 1976); University of Dayton (J.D., 1980). Certified Public Accountant, New York, 1983. Certified Financial Planner, 1994. AICPA - Personal Financial Specialist, 1996. President, National Board of Directors, International Association for Financial Planning, 1999. Chairman, National Board of Financial Planning Association, 2000. (Also at Rochester, New York Office). ***PRACTICE AREAS:*** Employee Benefits; Investments; Taxation; Trusts and Estates. ***Email:*** jvotava@nixonpeabody.com

MARIE JOHNSON WADLER, born Georgetown, South Carolina, 1963; admitted to bar, 1988, Florida; 1990, District of Columbia. *Education:* Duke University (A.B., 1985); Emory University (J.D., 1988). Member, D.C. Commercial Real Estate Women, Inc. *Member:* The Florida Bar; The District of Columbia Bar. ***PRACTICE AREAS:*** Real Estate Law; Finance Law; Commercial Leasing; Real Estate Syndication. ***Email:*** mwadler@nixonpeabody.com

STEPHEN J. WALLACE, born Rockville Centre, New York, 1957; admitted to bar, 1985, New York; 1988, District of Columbia. *Education:* Fordham University (B.A., 1979); Hofstra University (J.D., 1983). *Member:* The District of Columbia Bar. ***PRACTICE AREAS:*** Federal Legislation; Housing and Urban Development; Real Estate Finance. ***Email:*** swallace@nixonpeabody.com

ELIZABETH WARD WHITTLE, born Washington, D.C., 1964; admitted to bar, 1990, Maryland; 1991, District of Columbia. *Education:* Colgate University (A.B., 1986); Washington College of Law, The American University (J.D., 1990). *Member:* The District of Columbia Bar; Maryland State and American Bar Associations; Energy Bar Association. ***PRACTICE AREAS:*** Energy; Project Finance. ***Email:*** ewhittle@nixonpeabody.com

JUSTINE E. WILCOX, born New York, N.Y., 1949; admitted to bar, 1978, Massachusetts; 1979, District of Columbia. *Education:* Goucher College (B.A., 1971); Suffolk University (J.D., cum laude, 1978). *Member:* The District of Columbia Bar. ***PRACTICE AREAS:*** Real Estate; Real Estate Finance; Syndication; Housing Law. ***Email:*** jwilcox@nixonpeabody.com

(This Listing Continued)

DEBRA D. YOGODZINSKI, born Somerville, New Jersey, 1953; admitted to bar, 1978, District of Columbia. *Education:* Pennsylvania State University (B.A., 1975); Catholic University of America (J.D., 1978). *Member:* The District of Columbia Bar. ***PRACTICE AREAS:*** Real Estate; Real Estate Finance. ***Email:*** dyogodzinski@nixonpeabody.com

COUNSEL

RICHARD P. STANTON, born Lakewood, Ohio, 1964; admitted to bar, 1990, Pennsylvania and U.S. District Court, Northern District of Ohio; 1993, U.S. Court of Appeals, Fourth Circuit; 1998, District of Columbia. *Education:* Boston College (B.A., 1986); Georgetown University (J.D., 1989). Law Clerk to Chief Judge Thomas D. Lambros, N.D. Ohio, 1989-1991. Legislative Assistant: Committee on Banking, Finance and Urban Affairs, U.S. House of Representative, 1989; Judiciary Committee, U.S. House of Representatives, 1988. Special Counsel to Attorney General, State of Ohio, 1995—. Associate Independent Counsel, 1995-1997. Counsel, U.S. House of Representatives, Office of General Counsel, 1991-1995. ***PRACTICE AREAS:*** Government Relations; Intellectual Property Law. ***Email:*** rstanton@nixonpeabody.com

ASSOCIATES

ELIZABETH A. ALLEN, born 1969; admitted to bar, 1996, Virginia; 1998, District of Columbia. *Education:* Harvard University (B.A., 1991); Georgetown University (J.D., 1996). *Member:* Virginia State Bar; The District of Columbia Bar. ***PRACTICE AREAS:*** Litigation; Antitrust; Employment Law; Telecommunications. ***Email:*** eallen@nixonpeabody.com

HOLLIS BRYAN BREWER III, born Bethesda, Maryland, 1967; admitted to bar, 1994, Pennsylvania; 1995, District of Columbia. *Education:* College of William & Mary (B.A., 1990); Catholic University of America (J.D., 1993). Pi Sigma Alpha. *Member:* The District of Columbia Bar; American Bar Association. ***PRACTICE AREAS:*** Corporate; Emerging Growth Companies; Securities; Intellectual Property; Mergers and Acquisitions. ***Email:*** bbrewer@nixonpeabody.com

TRACY L. BRUEHS, born 1969; admitted to bar, 1999, New York; 2001, District of Columbia. *Education:* State University of New York at Plattsburgh (B.S., 1991); University of Rochester (M.S., 1995); Albany Law School of Union College (J.D., cum laude, 1998). *Member:* New York State and American Bar Associations; The District of Columbia Bar. ***PRACTICE AREAS:*** Business Law. ***Email:*** tbruehs@nixonpeabody.com

MOLLY R. BRYSON, born Washington, D.C., 1971; admitted to bar, 1998, Maryland; 1999, District of Columbia. *Education:* Catholic University of America (B.A., magna cum laude, 1993); Columbus School of Law of The Catholic University of America (J.D., 1998). Phi Beta Kappa. Editor-in-Chief, Catholic University Law Review, 1997-1998. *Member:* The District of Columbia Bar. ***PRACTICE AREAS:*** Real Estate Syndication; Taxation. ***Email:*** mbryson@nixonpeabody.com

MARGARET J. CHRISS, born 1969; admitted to bar, 1995, Georgia; 1996, District of Columbia. *Education:* Rice University (B.A., cum laude, 1988); Emory University (J.D., with distinction, 1994). *Member:* State Bar of Georgia; The District of Columbia Bar. ***PRACTICE AREAS:*** Litigation. ***Email:*** mchriss@nixonpeabody.com

LOUIS E. DOLAN, JR., born Columbus, Ohio, 1964; admitted to bar, 1992, Virginia; 1994, District of Columbia. *Education:* Colgate University; Georgetown University (B.S., 1986); George Mason University School of Law (J.D., with distinction, 1992). *Member:* Virginia State Bar; The District of Columbia Bar. ***PRACTICE AREAS:*** Corporate Litigation; Commercial Litigation; Real Estate. ***Email:*** ldolan@nixonpeabody.com

SUSAN E. EGGERS, admitted to bar, 1995, Illinois; 1999, District of Columbia. *Education:* Boston College (B.A., magna cum laude, 1990); University of Illinois (J.D., magna cum laude, 1995); Georgetown University (LL.M., 2000). ***PRACTICE AREAS:*** Affordable Housing; Real Estate. ***Email:*** seggers@nixonpeabody.com

MARK M. FOSTER, born Seattle, Washington, 1963; admitted to bar, 1996, Maryland; 1999, District of Columbia. *Education:* Embry-Riddle Aeronautical University (B.S., magna cum laude, 1993); Gonzaga University (J.D., magna cum laude, 1996); Georgetown University (LL.M., Taxation, 1998). *Member:* Maryland State (Member, Tax Section) and American Bar Associations. ***PRACTICE AREAS:*** Business; Nonprofit and Charitable Organizations; Tax Law. ***Email:*** mfoster@nixonpeabody.com

MONICA O. FRAZER, born Fort Collins, Colorado, 1975; admitted to bar, 2000, Virginia; 2001, District of Columbia. *Education:* University of Colorado (B.A., with honors, 1997); Georgetown University (J.D., with honors, 2000). *Member:* Virginia and American Bar Associations. ***PRACTICE AREAS:*** Business Law. ***Email:*** mfrazer@nixonpeabody.com

RAY A. JOHNSON, admitted to bar, 1999, Virginia; 2000, District of Columbia. *Education:* Wesleyan University (B.A., 1977); University of Rochester (M.B.A., 1979); Howard University (J.D., 1998). *Member:* Virginia State

(This Listing Continued)

Bar; The District of Columbia Bar; American and National Bar Associations. ***PRACTICE AREAS:*** Real Estate; Corporate Law; Zoning, Planning and Land Use. ***Email:*** rjohnson@nixonpeabody.com

VALERIE S. JOHNSON, born Stamford, Connecticut, April 12, 1961; admitted to bar, 1994, New South Wales, Australia; 2001, New York (Not admitted in District of Columbia). *Education:* Duke University (B.A., 1983); University of Sydney (LL.B., 1994; LL.M., 1999). ***PRACTICE AREAS:*** Business Law; Mergers and Acquisitions; Technology Law. ***Email:*** vsjohnson@nixonpeabody.com

RANDALL KELLY, born Louisiana, Missouri, 1970; admitted to bar, 1996, Missouri; 2000, District of Columbia. *Education:* University of Missouri (B.A., magna cum laude, 1993); Washington University (J.D., 1996). Co-Chair, Homestart Advisory Committee for a DC City Council member, 2000-2001. *Member:* The Missouri Bar; The District of Columbia Bar; Mortgage Bankers Association. ***PRACTICE AREAS:*** Affordable Housing; Mortgage Banking; Real Estate. ***Email:*** rkelly@nixonpeabody.com

DAVID K. KOEHLER, admitted to bar, 1995, New York; 1999, Virginia; 2000, District of Columbia. *Education:* Princeton University (A.B., 1991); State University of New York at Buffalo (J.D., cum laude, 1994). *Member:* Virginia State Bar; The District of Columbia Bar. (Also at McLean, VA Office). ***PRACTICE AREAS:*** Intellectual Property; Trademarks; Media Law; Litigation. ***Email:*** dkoehler@nixonpeabody.com

LESLIE P. MACHADO, born 1970; admitted to bar, 1997, New York, Massachusetts, Maryland and District of Columbia. *Education:* Fordham University (B.A., 1992); University of Buffalo (J.D., cum laude, 1996). ***PRACTICE AREAS:*** Litigation; Media Law. ***Email:*** lmachado@nixonpeabody.com

BRIAN MULFORD, born Rochester, New York, 1973; admitted to bar, 1999, Virginia; 2000, District of Columbia. *Education:* University of Rochester (B.A., 1996); University of Virginia (J.D., 1999). *Member:* Virginia State Bar. ***PRACTICE AREAS:*** Corporate Law. ***Email:*** bmulford@nixonpeabody.com

ANDREW S. POTTS, born Indianapolis, Indiana, 1967; admitted to bar, 1993, Indiana; 1994, Illinois; 2001, District of Columbia. *Education:* Indiana University (B.A., 1989; J.D., 1992). *Member:* The District of Columbia Bar; American Bar Association. ***PRACTICE AREAS:*** Real Estate; Affordable Housing; Tax; Historic Preservation. ***Email:*** apotts@nixonpeabody.com

MICHAEL H. REARDON, born Winthrop, Massachusetts, 1950; admitted to bar, 1977, Massachusetts (Not admitted in District of Columbia). *Education:* Georgetown University (B.S.F.S., 1972); Suffolk University (J.D., 1977). Chief Counsel's Office, Washington, D.C., U.S. Department of Housing and Urban Development, 1985-1991. Assistant General Counsel for Assisted Housing, U.S. Department of Housing and Urban Development, 1991-2000. ***PRACTICE AREAS:*** Real Estate; Affordable Housing. ***Email:*** mreardon@nixonpeabody.com

ANTHONY D. RUVOLO, born Elizabeth, New Jersey, 1960; admitted to bar, 1987, California; 1989, District of Columbia. *Education:* University of Pennsylvania (B.A., cum laude, 1982); Georgetown University Law Center (J.D., cum laude, 1986). *Member:* State Bar of California; The District of Columbia Bar. ***PRACTICE AREAS:*** Affordable Housing; Real Estate. ***Email:*** aruvolo@nixonpeabody.com

DAVID F. SCHON, born Detroit, Michigan, 1966; admitted to bar, 1992, Michigan; 1993, Illinois; 1994, District of Columbia. *Education:* University of Michigan (B.A., 1988); Wayne State University (J.D., 1992). *Member:* State Bar of Michigan; The District of Columbia Bar. ***PRACTICE AREAS:*** Real Estate; Affordable Housing; Partnership Law; Corporate Law. ***Email:*** dschon@nixonpeabody.com

SCOTT D. SERGIO, born Philadelphia, Pennsylvania, 1970; admitted to bar, 1999, Pennsylvania; 2000, District of Columbia. *Education:* University of Richmond (B.A., 1992); Temple University (J.D., magna cum laude, 1998). ***PRACTICE AREAS:*** Real Estate; Syndication; Affordable Housing. ***Email:*** ssergio@nixonpeabody.com

LAMONT H. SILAS, born Flushing, New York, 1967; admitted to bar, 1995, New York; 1996, Pennsylvania; 1999, District of Columbia. *Education:* Blackburn College (B.A.); Georgetown University (J.D., 1994). *Member:* The District of Columbia Bar. ***PRACTICE AREAS:*** Public Finance; Tax. ***Email:*** lsilas@nixonpeabody.com

JULIA A. SOLO, born Buffalo, New York; admitted to bar, 1996, New York (Not admitted in District of Columbia). *Education:* University of Michigan (B.A., 1988); State University of New York at Buffalo (J.D., magna cum laude, 1995). *Member:* The Association of the Bar of the City of New York; American Bar Association (Member, Forum on Affordable Housing). (Also at New York, N.Y. Office). ***PRACTICE AREAS:*** Syndication; Affordable Housing; Real Estate. ***Email:*** jsolo@nixonpeabody.com

SARAH A. STONE, born Clark Air Force Base, Manila, Philippine Islands, 1956; admitted to bar, 1982, Texas; 1990, Massachusetts; 1999, District of Columbia. *Education:* Georgetown University, School of Foreign Service (B.S.F.S., 1978); University of Virginia (J.D., 1982). *Member:* State Bar of

(This Listing Continued)

NIXON PEABODY LLP, Washington—Continued

Texas; The District of Columbia Bar. ***PRACTICE AREAS:*** Tax Credits; Syndication; Affordable Housing; Bankruptcy; Workouts; Litigation. ***Email:*** sstone@nixonpeabody.com

DWAYNE M. TOLIVER, born Washington, D.C., 1958; admitted to bar, 1995, Maryland; 1997, District of Columbia. *Education:* LaSalle University (B.S., 1980); Columbus School of Law of The Catholic University of America (J.D., 1995). *Member:* The District of Columbia Bar. ***PRACTICE AREAS:*** Commercial Real Estate; Nonprofit and Charitable Organizations; Leases and Leasing. ***Email:*** dtoliver@nixonpeabody.com

LYDIA P.A. TURNIPSEED, born Texarkana, Texas, 1969; admitted to bar, 1996, New Jersey; 1997, District of Columbia. *Education:* Vanderbilt University (B.A., 1991); Georgetown University (J.D., cum laude, 1995). Law Clerk to Judge Gilbert S. Merritt, United States Court of Appeals for the Sixth Circuit, 1995-1996. ***PRACTICE AREAS:*** Litigation; White Collar Crime; Insurance Law. ***Email:*** lturnipseed@nixonpeabody.com

SUSAN L. WILDER, born Philadelphia, Pennsylvania, 1967; admitted to bar, 1992, Pennsylvania; 1993, New Jersey; 1994, District of Columbia. *Education:* University of Pennsylvania (B.A., cum laude, 1989); George Washington University Law School (J.D., with honors, 1992). *Member:* The District of Columbia Bar. ***PRACTICE AREAS:*** Affordable Housing; Community Development; Real Estate; Syndication; Public Finance Law. ***Email:*** swilder@nixonpeabody.com

(For biographical data on other personnel, see Professional Biographies at Rochester, New York, New York, New York, Albany, New York, Garden City, New York, Buffalo, New York, Hartford, Connecticut, Boston, Massachusetts, Manchester, New Hampshire, Providence, Rhode Island and McLean, Virginia)

NIXON & VANDERHYE P.C.

WASHINGTON, D.C.

(See Arlington, Virginia)

United States and International Patent, Trademark, Copyright and Unfair Competition Law, Other Matters Involving Technology and Related Litigation in all Courts and Administrative Agencies Including the U.S. International Trade Commission.

NORDHAUS, HALTOM, TAYLOR, TARADASH & BLADH, LLP

Established in 1979

816 CONNECTICUT AVENUE, N.W., SUITE 300

WASHINGTON, D.C. 20006

Telephone: 202-530-1270

Telecopier: 202-530-1920

Albuquerque, New Mexico Office: 500 Marquette Avenue, N.W., Suite 1050. Telephone: 505-243-4275. Telecopier: 505-243-4464.

Santa Fe, New Mexico Office: 200 West De Vargas, Suite 9. Telephone: 505-982-3622. Telecopier: 505-982-1827.

Indian Affairs, Litigation, Energy, Oil and Gas, Water, Environmental Law, Natural Resources, Commercial Transactions, State and Tribal Taxation, Business and General Civil Practice.

FIRM PROFILE: Established in 1979 Nordhaus, Haltom, Taylor, Taradash & Bladh has steadily grown in size and in areas of expertise. The Firm maintains offices in Albuquerque, Santa Fe and Washington, D.C., serving clients throughout the United States. The law firm provides a wide array of legal services to its clients and has developed notable experience in all areas of Indian affairs, Indian taxation, environmental, water and natural resources (oil and gas, coal, gravel and uranium), business transactions, housing development, economic development, gaming, banking, real estate, commercial and construction law. The law firm handles major litigation primarily in federal courts.

JILL ELISE GRANT, born New York, N.Y., November 22, 1955; admitted to bar, 1981, District of Columbia; 1982, U.S. Court of Appeals for the District of Columbia Circuit; 1993, New Mexico; 1994, U.S. Court of Federal Claims; 1996, U.S. Supreme Court; 1997, U.S. Court of Appeals, Tenth Circuit. *Education:* Yale University (B.A., summa cum laude, 1976); Harvard University (J.D., 19 81). Phi Beta Kappa. Vice Chair, SONREEL, Air Quality Committee, 1993-1995. *Member:* State Bar of New Mexico; District of Columbia Bar; Federal Energy and American Bar Associations. ***LANGUAGES:*** French. ***PRACTICE AREAS:*** Administrative Law; Environmental Law; Indian Law; Federal Litigation. ***Email:*** jgrant@nordhauslaw.com

(This Listing Continued)

REPRESENTATIVE CLIENTS: AK Chin Indian Community; Jicarilla Apache Nation; Pueblo of Laguna; Pueblo of San Juan; Pueblo of Santa Ana; Taos Pueblo; Navajo Nation; Red Lake Band of Chippewa Indians; Seneca Nation of Indians; Delaware Tribe of Indians; Hualapai Indian Tribe; Absentee Shawnee Tribe of Indians of Oklahoma; Gila River Indian Community; ASCG, Inc.; Cochiti Community Development Corporation; Indian Pueblos Federal Development Corporation; Indian Pueblo Marketing, Inc.; Laguna Development Corporation; Laguna Housing Development and Management Enterprises; Laguna Rainbow Corporation; National Indian Business Association; National Tribal Environmental Council; Navajo Nation Hospitality Enterprise; Navajo Nation Oil & Gas Company; Sandia Peak Ski & Tramway; Santa Fe Ski Area; Santa Ana Golf Corporation; Southern Sandoval Investments Ltd.; Santa Ana Hospitality Corporation; Tsay Corporation; Turner Environmental.

(For complete biographical data on Albuquerque and Santa Fe, New Mexico personnel, see Professional Biographies, Albuquerque and Santa Fe, New Mexico)

NOSSAMAN, GUTHNER, KNOX & ELLIOTT, LLP

C/O FRENCH & COMPANY

THE HOMER BUILDING

SUITE 370-S, 601 13TH STREET, N.W.

WASHINGTON, D.C. 20005

Telephone: 202-783-7272

Los Angeles, California Office: Thirty-First Floor, Union Bank Square, 445 South Figueroa Street. Telephone: 213-612-7800.

San Francisco, California Office: Thirty-Fourth Floor, 50 California Street. Telephone: 415-398-3600.

Orange County, California Office: Suite 1800, 18101 Von Karman Avenue, Irvine, California. Telephone: 714-833-7800.

Sacramento, California Office: Suite 1000, 915 L Street. Telephone: 916-442-8888.

Legislative Law. General Civil Practice, including Administrative and Regulatory, Antitrust, Trade Regulation and Unfair Competition, Appellate Practice, Bankruptcy and Creditors Rights, Business and Corporate, Communications, Construction and Construction Litigation, Eminent Domain, Environmental, Estate Planning, Probate and Trusts, Financial Institutions, Franchise, Hazardous Waste, Health Care, Health Maintenance Organizations and Medical Groups, Infrastructure, Insurance Coverage, Land Use, Legislative Advocacy, Litigation, Natural Resources, Oil and Gas, Physician and Professional Licensure and Discipline, Labor and Employment Counseling and Litigation, Municipal and Public Agency Law, Public Finance, Public Utility Regulation, Real Estate, Tax, Transportation, Securities, Sports, Water Rights, White Collar Criminal Defense.

OF COUNSEL

WARREN G. ELLIOTT, born Pueblo, Colorado, January 3, 1927; admitted to bar, 1952, Colorado; 1976, Connecticut; 1978, District of Columbia. *Education:* University of Colorado at Boulder (A.B., 1949); University of Michigan (LL.B., 1952). General Counsel, Aetna Life & Casualty Co., 1968-1978. Associate General Counsel, Life Insurance Association of America, 1961-1968. Legislative Counsel and Administrative Assistant to U.S. Senator Gordon Allott, Colorado, 1955-1960. *Member:* District of Columbia Bar. [With U.S. Army Air Corps, 1944-1946]. ***PRACTICE AREAS:*** Government Relations. ***Email:*** welliott@nossaman.com

MURRAY ZWEBEN, born Elizabeth, New Jersey, May 9, 1930; admitted to bar, 1959, Virginia; 1980, District of Columbia. *Education:* Clarkson College of Technology; State University of New York at Albany (B.S., 1952; M.S., 1953); George Washington University (LL.B., 1959). Member, George Washington University Law Review, 1958-1959. Law Clerk, U.S. Court of Claims, 1959-1960. Professorial Lecturer in Law, George Washington University Law School, 1971-1981. Assistant Parliamentarian, 1963-1975, Parliamentarian, 1975-1981 and Parliamentarian Emeritus, 1983—, U.S. Senate. *Member:* District of Columbia Bar. [U.S. Naval Officer, 1953-1956]. ***PRACTICE AREAS:*** Legislative Law. ***Email:*** mzweben@nossaman.com

(For Biographical Data of other Firm Personnel, see Professional Biographies at Los Angeles, San Francisco, Irvine and Sacramento California).

NOTO & OSWALD, P.C.

Established in 1983
1850 M STREET, NW
SUITE 920
WASHINGTON, D.C. 20036
Telephone: 202-331-2883
Fax: 202-261-2835
Email: rscottoswald@compuserve.com
URL: http://www.lawyers.com/noto&oswald

Civil and Criminal Trial Practice before all Courts and International Practice, Legislative Practice, Immigration Law, Business Immigration, Employment Visas, Religious Visas, Deportation, Political Asylum, Refugee Law, Civil Service, Commercial Transactions, Corporate Law.

MARIO T. NOTO, born New York, N.Y., December 1, 1917; admitted to bar, 1940, New York; 1960, U.S. Supreme Court; 1971, District of Columbia and U.S. District Court for the District of Columbia. *Education:* St. Johns University; Fordham University (LL.B., 1939). Deputy and Assistant Commissioner, U.S. Immigration & Naturalization Service, 1942-1968 and 1977-1979. Special Counsel and Staff Director, U.S. Senate Labor and Public Welfare Committee, 1971-1974. *Member:* The District of Columbia Bar; Federal Bar Association. [U.S. Air Corps, 1942-1945]. ***LANGUAGES:*** Italian and Spanish. ***PRACTICE AREAS:*** International Law; Immigration Law.

ROBERT L. OSWALD, born Los Angeles, California, October 31, 1937; admitted to bar, 1981, Pennsylvania; 1982, District of Columbia and U.S. District Court for the District of Columbia; 1984, U.S. Court of Appeals for the Federal Circuit; 1985, U.S. District Court, District of Maryland. *Education:* University of Maryland (B.A., with distinction, 1960); George Washington University (J.D., 1964). Delta Theta Phi. Recipient, Outstanding Law Student Award, 1964. Administrative Assistant to U.S. Representative William S. Mailliard, 1966-1970. Congressional Relations Officer of the Interstate Commerce Commission, 1970-1971. Secretary and Congressional Relations Officer at Interstate Commerce Commission, 1971-1978. *Member:* The District of Columbia Bar; Pennsylvania and American Bar Associations; The Association of Trial Lawyers of America; National Association of Criminal Defense Lawyers; American Immigration Lawyers Association (President, Washington, D.C., Baltimore Chapter, 1990-1991). [With U.S. Air Force, 1954-1957]. ***PRACTICE AREAS:*** Immigration Law.

DANIELLE L. C. BEACH, born Bruxelles, Belgium, April 14, 1955; admitted to bar, 1991, Maryland and U.S. District Court, District of Maryland (Not admitted in District of Columbia). *Education:* Loma Linda University (B.A., English, cum laude, 1975); University of California, Riverside (M.A., Comparative Literature, 1981); University of Baltimore School of Law (J.D., 1991). Phi Alpha Delta; Delta Kappa Gamma. Professor, English: California State University, 1987; Columbia Union College, 1987-1988. *Member:* Maryland State Bar Association; Maryland Trial Lawyers Association; Washington Foreign Law Society; American Association of University Women; American Immigration Lawyers Association. ***LANGUAGES:*** French, Italian, German. ***PRACTICE AREAS:*** Immigration Law.

R. SCOTT OSWALD, born Washington, D.C., December 21, 1967; admitted to bar, 1997, Virginia; 1997, U.S. District Court, Eastern District of Virginia and U.S. Court of Appeals, Fourth Circuit; 1998, Maryland, District of Columbia, Florida, U.S. District Court, District of Columbia, U.S. District Court, District of Maryland and U.S. Court of Appeals, District of Columbia; 1999, U.S. District Court, Northern and Southern Districts of Florida; 2000, U.S. Court of Appeals, Fifth Circuit. *Education:* University of Virginia (B.A., 1990); Howard University (J.D., 1997). *Member:* The District of Columbia Bar; Maryland State Bar Association, Inc.;The Florida Bar; Virginia State Bar; Virginia Trial Lawyers Association; Maryland Trial Lawyers Association; American Immigration Lawyers Association; Metropolitan Washington Employment Lawyer Association (Board Member). (Also Member, Employment Law Group). ***REPORTED CASES:*** Avery v. Va. Ret, Sys., 520 S.E.2d 831 (Va. 1999), aff'd, en banc, 532 S.E.2d 348 (2000), aff'd 551 S.E.2d 612 (2001). ***PRACTICE AREAS:*** Labor and Employment; Immigration Law; Corporate Law. **Email:** soswald@employmentlawgroup.net

LAW OFFICES OF DAVID NOVELLO, LLC

1752 N STREET NW, SUITE 800
WASHINGTON, D.C. 20036
Telephone: 202-857-9708
Fax: 202-887-8044
Email: dnovello@novellolaw.com
URL: http://www.novellolaw.com

Environmental Law, Clean Air Act, Environmental Litigation, Environmental Compliance, Environmental Permitting, Environmental Regulation, Environmental Legislative Practice, Administrative Law, Appellate Litigation.

(This Listing Continued)

FIRM PROFILE: Law Offices of David Novello, LLC is a Washington, D.C. based law firm that focuses on environmental law and regulation. The firm's particular expertise is the Clean Air Act and the emerging climate change area. The firm assists business clients in compliance counseling, regulatory development, permitting, appellate litigation, environmental enforcement, and other aspects of environmental law. Clients include large and small corporations and trade associations.

DAVID P. NOVELLO, born Elizabeth, New Jersey, 1957; admitted to bar, 1985, Massachusetts; 1986, U.S. District Court, District of Massachusetts; 1987, U.S. Court of Appeals, First Circuit; 1988, U.S. Court of Appeals, District of Columbia Circuit; 1991, District of Columbia. *Education:* Dartmouth College (B.A., magna cum laude, 1979); Columbia Law School (J.D., 1984). Harlan Fiske Stone Scholar. Attorney, General Counsel's Office, U.S. Environmental Protection Agency, 1987-1990; Senior Attorney, 1991-1992. Law Clerk to Judge Edith Fine, Massachusetts Court of Appeals, 1984-1985. Co-editor: The Clean Air Act Handbook, published by American Bar Association in 1998. Author: "Proposed Reforms of New Source Review Under the Clean Air Act," Environmental Law and Practice, 1996; "The New Title III Air Toxics Program," guide published by Air and Waste Management Association, 1994; "Capturing the Market's Power," The Environmental Forum, 1994; "The New Clean Air Act Operating Permit Program," Environmental Law Reporter, 1993; Adjunct Professor, Georgetown University Law Center, 1994-1997; University of Maryland School of Law, 2001— *Member:* District of Columbia Bar Association; American Bar Association (Member, Sections on: Natural Resources, Energy and Environmental Law, 1985-1989 and 1991—; Vice-Chair: Committee on Climate Change and Sustainable Development, 1997—; Air Quality Committee, 1993—; Editor, Trends Publication, 2000—); Air and Waste Management Association, 1992—. ***PRACTICE AREAS:*** Environmental Law; Clean Air Act; Environmental Litigation; Environmental Compliance; Environmental Permitting; Environmental Regulation; Environmental Legislative Practice; Administrative Law; Appellate Litigation. **Email:** dnovello@novellolaw.com

NUSSBAUM & WALD

WASHINGTON, D.C.

(See Baach Robinson & Lewis PLLC)

OBER, KALER, GRIMES & SHRIVER

A PROFESSIONAL CORPORATION

SUITE 500
1401 H STREET, N.W.
WASHINGTON, D.C. 20005-2110
Telephone: 202-408-8400
Facsimile: 202-408-0640
Email: info@ober.com
URL: http://www.ober.com

Baltimore, Maryland Office: 120 East Baltimore Street. Telephone: 410-685-1120. Facsimile: 410-547-0699.
Falls Church, Virginia Office: 254 North Washington Street. Telephone: 703-237-0126. Facsimile: 703-237-2644.

Admiralty, Shipping and Transportation, Business and Corporate, Commercial Financing, Construction, Creditors' Rights Workouts, and Bankruptcy, Employee Benefits, Employment and Labor Matters, Equipment Finance, Estates and Trusts, Financial Institution/Regulatory, Health Law, Intellectual Property, Litigation, Real Estate, Tax, and White-Collar Criminal Defense.

LAWRENCE D. HOLLMAN, admitted to bar, 1956, MA; 1957, DC. *Education:* Harvard Univ. (A.B., 1953); Harvard Law School (LL.B., 1956). **Email:** ldhollman@ober.com

STEPHEN L. PARKER, admitted to bar, 1967, Pacific Islands; 1968, NY; 1969, DC; 1982, MD. *Education:* Amherst College (B.A., 1963); Columbia Univ. (LL.B., 1966). **Email:** slparker@ober.com

PAUL M. VINCENT, admitted to bar, 1970, VA and DC; 1984, MD. *Education:* Harvard Univ. (B.A., 1967); Univ. of Virginia (J.D., 1970). **Email:** pmvincen@ober.com

HARRY R. SILVER, admitted to bar, 1972, NY; 1973, DC. *Education:* Temple Univ. (B.A., 1968); Columbia Univ. (J.D., 1971). **Email:** hrsilver@ober.com

JOHN J. MILES, admitted to bar, 1973, VA; 1982, DC. *Education:* Virginia Tech (B.S., 1968; M.A., 1971); Washington & Lee Univ. (J.D., 1973). **Email:** jjmiles@ober.com

PATRICK K. O'HARE, admitted to bar, 1973, DC. *Education:* Brown Univ. (B.A., 1968); Stanford Univ. (J.D., 1971). **Email:** pkohare@ober.com

(This Listing Continued)

OBER, KALER, GRIMES & SHRIVER, A PROFESSIONAL CORPORATION, Washington—Continued

JOHN S. GRAHAM III, admitted to bar, 1974, VA; 1975, DC; 1992, MD. *Education:* Washington & Lee Univ. (B.A., 1967); Univ. of St. Andrews, Scotland (B.Phil., 1969); Yale Law School (J.D., 1974). ***Email:*** jsgraham@ober.com

ROBERT L. ASH, admitted to bar, 1975, MD; 1979, DC. *Education:* Univ. of Maryland (B.S., 1972; J.D., 1975); Georgetown Univ. (M.L.T., 1981). ***Email:*** rlash@ober.com

MARTHA PURCELL ROGERS, admitted to bar, 1977, DC. *Education:* Univ. of Texas (B.A., 1966); George Washington Univ. (J.D., 1977). ***Email:*** mrogers@ober.com

JOHN N. RODOCK, admitted to bar, 1982, DC; 1983, VA. *Education:* Univ. of Notre Dame (B.B.A., 1978); Univ. of Virginia (J.D., 1982). ***Email:*** jnrodock@ober.com

THOMAS K. HYATT, admitted to bar, 1982, DC; 1989, PA. *Education:* Boston College (B.A., 1979); Univ. of Pittsburgh (J.D., 1982). ***Email:*** tkhyatt@ober.com

LEON RODRIGUEZ, admitted to bar, 1989, NY (Not admitted in District of Columbia). *Education:* Brown Univ. (B.A., 1984); Boston College (J.D., 1988). ***Email:*** lrodriguez@ober.com

E. JOHN STEREN, admitted to bar, 1989, MD; 1991, DC. *Education:* Univ. of Maryland (B.A., 1986); Georgetown Univ. (J.D., 1989). ***Email:*** ejsteren@ober.com

EDWIN G. DAVILA-BLOISE, admitted to bar, 1984, VA; 1985, DC; 1996, MD. *Education:* Georgetown Univ. (B.S.B.A., 1978; J.D., 1984; LL.M., 1988). ***Email:*** egdavila@ober.com

NIKOLAUS F. SCHANDLBAUER, admitted to bar, 1990, MD; 1992, DC. *Education:* Univ. of Virginia (B.A., 1986); Dickinson School of Law (J.D., 1990). ***Email:*** nfschandlbauer@ober.com

---

HAROLD G. BELKOWITZ, admitted to bar, 1994, VA; 1995, MD; 1996, DC. *Education:* Brandeis Univ. (B.A., 1989); Syracuse Univ. College of Law (J.D., 1994). ***Email:*** hgbelkowitz@ober.com

OF COUNSEL

JAMES R. WORSLEY, JR., admitted to bar, 1949, NC and DC. *Education:* East Carolina Univ. (B.S., 1944); Harvard Graduate School of Business Administration (M.O.C., 1944-1945); Harvard Law School (LL.B., 1949). ***Email:*** jrworsley@ober.com

CARLYLE C. RING, JR., admitted to bar, 1956, DC; 1972, VA. *Education:* Hamilton College (B.A., 1953); Columbia Law School and Duke Law School (LL.B., 1956). ***Email:*** ccring@ober.com

(For biographical data on personnel at Baltimore, Maryland, see Professional Biographies at that location)

OBLON, SPIVAK, McCLELLAND, MAIER & NEUSTADT, P.C.

WASHINGTON, D.C.

(See Arlington, Virginia)

Patent Law; Patent Prosecution; Patent Litigation; Patent Infringement; Patent Licensing; Patent Protection; Chemical Patents; Biotechnology Patents; Biotechnology Licensing; Biochemical Technology; Genetics; Mechanical Patents; Electrical Patents; Computer and Software Patents; Computer Technology; Software Copyright; Software Leasing; Software Protection; Trademark Law; Trademark Infringement; Trademark Licensing; Trademark Litigation; Trademark Prosecution; Trademark Registration; Copyright Law; Copyright Infringement; Copyright Prosecution; Copyright Registration; Trade Dress; Trade Names; Unfair Competition Law; International Trademarks; International Copyright Law; International Intellectual Property.

O'BRIEN, BUTLER, McCONIHE & SCHAEFER, PLLC

SUITE 1000 BRAWNER BUILDING
888 SEVENTEENTH STREET, N.W.
WASHINGTON, D.C. 20006-3967
Telephone: 202-298-6161
Fax: 202-293-1640
Email: schae001@winstarmail.com

General Civil Practice before the Courts of the District of Columbia, Maryland, Virginia and before the Federal Departments and Commissions. Civil Litigation, Non-Profit Organizations Law, Association Law, Insurance Law, Health Care Law, Estates and Trusts.

FIRM PROFILE: The firm has been engaged in the continuous practice of law in the Washington, D.C., metropolitan area (including Virginia and Maryland) for more than 50 years. We emphasize quality, personalized and responsive legal services at a reasonable cost. As a medium sized firm, we specialize our practice in the areas of association, litigation, insurance, health care and estate law.

MEMBERS OF FIRM

WILLIAM J. BUTLER, JR., born Washington, D.C., November 26, 1933; admitted to bar, 1962, Virginia; 1963, District of Columbia, U.S. Supreme Court, U.S. Court of Appeals for the District of Columbia Circuit and U.S. Court of Appeals, Third Circuit. *Education:* University of Virginia (B.A., 1955; LL.B., 1962). Phi Alpha Delta. *Member:* District of Columbia Bar; Virginia State Bar; Bar Association of the District of Columbia; American Bar Association. ***PRACTICE AREAS:*** Nonprofit Organizations Law. ***Email:*** butle001@winstarmail.com

MICHAEL H. McCONIHE, born Washington, D.C., April 7, 1940; admitted to bar, 1965, Maryland; 1966, District of Columbia and U.S. Court of Military Appeals; 1969, U.S. Supreme Court; 1980, U.S. Claims Court and U.S. Court of Appeals for the District of Columbia Circuit. *Education:* Princeton University (A.B., 1962); Georgetown University (LL.B., 1965). Assistant Director, Division of Enforcement, Securities and Exchange Commission, 1974-1977. *Member:* District of Columbia Bar Association; Maryland State Bar Association, Inc. [Lieut., JAGC, USNR, 1965-1968]. ***Email:*** mmcconihe@aol.com

JEROME C. SCHAEFER, born Medina, Ohio, October 9, 1946; admitted to bar, 1972, Maryland; 1974, U.S. District Court, District of Maryland; 1976, District of Columbia and U.S. Supreme Court; 1977, U.S. Court of Appeals, Fourth Circuit. *Education:* John Carroll University (B.A., 1969); Catholic University of America (J.D., 1972). Assistant State's Attorney, Montgomery County, Maryland, 1973-1975. *Member:* District of Columbia Bar; Montgomery County (Secretary, 1976-1977), Maryland State and American Bar Associations. (Resident). ***REPORTED CASES:*** Passer v. American Chemical Soc., 935 F.2d, 322 C.A.D.C., 1999; Brice v. Nkaru, 220 F.3d, 233 C.A. 4, 2000. ***PRACTICE AREAS:*** Tort Defense; Indemnity; Nonprofit Organizations Law; Civil Rights Defense; Media and First Amendment. ***Email:*** schae001@winstarmail.com

STEVEN P. BENSON, born Corona, California, May 18, 1956; admitted to bar, 1981, Massachusetts; 1985, District of Columbia. *Education:* University of Massachusetts (B.A., 1978); George Washington University (J.D., 1981). *Member:* District of Columbia Bar; American Bar Association. ***PRACTICE AREAS:*** Nonprofit and Charitable Organizations. ***Email:*** benso001@winstarmail.com

ASSOCIATES

A. STATTON HAMMOCK, JR., born Charlottesville, Virginia, November 26, 1967; admitted to bar, 1995, Virginia and U.S. Court of Appeals, Fourth Circuit; 1996, Maryland and District of Columbia; 1998, U.S. District Court, Eastern District of Virginia; 1999, U.S. Court of Appeals for the Federal Circuit; 2000, U.S. Supreme Court. *Education:* University of Virginia (B.A., 1990); University of Maine School of Law (J.D., 1995). Member, Moot Court Board. Law Clerk to the Honorable Donald L. Ivers, U.S. Court of Appeals for Veterans Claims. *Member:* Maryland State Bar Association; Virginia State Bar; District of Columbia Bar; American Bar Association. ***PRACTICE AREAS:*** Media Libel; Corporate Law; Nonprofit Organizations Law; Trademarks; Copyrights; Civil Litigation; Estate Planning. ***Email:*** hammo001@winstarmail.com

MARK B. SANDGROUND, JR., born Washington, D.C., May 2, 1960; admitted to bar, 1985, Virginia (Not admitted in District of Columbia). *Education:* Stanford University (B.A., 1982); University of Virginia (J.D., 1985); Institute Superior d'Administration, H.E.C., Jouy-en-Josas, France (1991); University of California at Los Angeles (M.B.A., 1992). *Member:* Virginia State Bar; American Bar Association. ***PRACTICE AREAS:*** Nonprofit Organizations Law; Corporate Law; Real Estate; Restaurant Law; Civil Litigation. ***Email:*** sandg001@winstarmail.com

(This Listing Continued)

STEPHEN M. SCHAEFER, born Silver Spring, Maryland, April 18, 1974; admitted to bar, 1999, Maryland; 2000, District of Columbia; 2001, U.S. District Court, District of Maryland. *Education:* Villanova University (B.A., 1996; J.D., 1999). ***PRACTICE AREAS:*** Media and First Amendment; Nonprofit Organizations Law; Corporate Law; Civil Litigation. ***Email:*** schae004@winstarmail.com

KEVIN A. KERNAN, born Rochester, New York, January 2, 1967; admitted to bar, 1995, Pennsylvania; 1996, Maryland; 1997, District of Columbia, 1998, Virginia. *Education:* State University of New York at Albany (B.S., 1989); Widener University School of Law (J.D., 1995). Phi Delta Phi. Moe Levine Trial Advocacy Honor Society. Listed in: Who's Who American Law Students. Publications: Defense Research Institute, (Winter 1999); Texas Risk Management Program for Interstate Ins. Group, (Summer 2000). *Member:* Maryland State and American Bar Associations; Virginia State Bar; District of Columbia Bar. ***PRACTICE AREAS:*** Civil Litigation; Nonprofit Organizations Law. ***Email:*** kerna001@winstarmail.com

OF COUNSEL

HARRY TETER, born Frostburg, Maryland, December 24, 1940; admitted to bar, 1966, Maryland; 1981, District of Columbia. *Education:* Washington & Lee University (B.A., 1962); Georgetown University (J.D., 1965). Author: "Rule Making verses Adjudication in the Federal Trade Commission," Georgetown Law Review, 1966. Director, Appalachian Regional Commission, 1973-1978. *Member:* Maryland State Bar Association, Inc.; American Bar Association; District of Columbia Bar.

PAUL L. O'BRIEN, born Holyoke, Massachusetts, March 15, 1926; admitted to bar, 1953, District of Columbia, U.S. Supreme Court, U.S. Court of Appeals for the District of Columbia Circuit, U.S. Claims Court and U.S. Court of Military Appeals. *Education:* Wesleyan University (B.A., 1949); University of Virginia (LL.B., 1952). *Member:* District of Columbia Bar; Bar Association of the District of Columbia; American Bar Association.

O'BRIEN & LONG

SUITE 208
2600 VIRGINIA AVENUE, N.W.
WASHINGTON, D.C. 20037
Telephone: 202-625-7700
Fax: 202-625-7706
URL: http://www.lawyers.com/obrienandlong

Alcoholic Beverage Licensing, Liquor Licensing, Municipal Law, Commercial Litigation, Business Planning.

STEPHEN J. O'BRIEN, born Mount Vernon, New York, November 5, 1946; admitted to bar, 1975, District of Columbia; 1976, U.S. District Court, District of Columbia; 1978, U.S. Court of Appeals, District of Columbia Circuit; 1980, U.S. District Court, District of Maryland; 1995, Virginia; 1996, U.S. Bankruptcy Court, Eastern District of Virginia; 1998, U.S. Court of Appeals, Fourth Circuit. *Education:* Georgetown University (A.B., 1969); Catholic University of America (J.D., 1974). Member, District of Columbia Board of Appeals and Review, 1984-1985. *Member:* District of Columbia Bar; Virginia State Bar. [U.S. Army, 1969-1971]. (Also Of Counsel, Odin, Feldman & Pittleman, P.C., Fairfax, Virginia). ***PRACTICE AREAS:*** Alcoholic Beverage Licensing; Liquor Licensing; Commercial Litigation; Business Planning; Municipal Law. ***Email:*** stephen.obrien@obrienandlong.com

STUART J. LONG, born January 21, 1942; admitted to bar, 1968, U.S. District Court, District of Columbia; 1969, District of Columbia; 1975, U.S. Court of Appeals for the District of Columbia; 1979, U.S. Supreme Court. *Education:* College of the Holy Cross (B.A., 1964); George Washington University (J.D., 1967). Member: District of Columbia Armory Board, 1979-1993. *Member:* District of Columbia Bar; American Bar Association. ***PRACTICE AREAS:*** Municipal Law.

MICHAEL D. FONSECA, born Tampa, Florida, July 7, 1954; admitted to bar, 1982, District of Columbia; 1990, U.S. District Court for the District of Columbia. *Education:* City College of the City University of New York (B.A., 1977); Georgetown University (J.D., 1981). Staff Director, District of Columbia Alcholic Beverage Control Board, 1987-1990. *Member:* District of Columbia Bar. ***LANGUAGES:*** Spanish. ***PRACTICE AREAS:*** Alcoholic Beverage Licensing; Liquor Licensing; Municipal Law.

BARBARA LEE SMITH, born 1944; admitted to bar, 1985, District of Columbia, U.S. District Court, District of Maryland and U.S. District Court for the District of Columbia. *Education:* Howard University (B.A., 1966; J.D., 1973; Ph.D., Forensic Counseling Psychology, 1978); University of the District of Columbia (M.A., Counseling,1969). Recipient, District of Columbia Bar Arbitration Board Special Arbitration Merit Award, 2001. *Member:* The Association of Trial Lawyers of America; Women's Bar Association. ***PRACTICE AREAS:*** Civil (General Civil) Law; Landlord and Tenant Law; Domestic Law; Probate; Divorce; Child Custody; Child Support; Spousal Support.

(This Listing Continued)

LAURANCE J. OCHS

1748 N STREET, N.W.
WASHINGTON, D.C. 20036
Telephone: 202-331-9009
Facsimile: 202-785-0066
Email: llochs@aol.com
URL: http://www.lawyers.com/llochs

General Practice. Litigation, Counseling, Commercial, Computer, Corporate, Intellectual Property Rights, E-Commerce Law, Internet Law..

LAURANCE J. OCHS, born Buffalo, New York, February 10, 1944; admitted to bar, 1970, District of Columbia; 1991, U.S. District Court, District of Maryland; 1992, U.S. Court of Appeals, Fourth Circuit. *Education:* State University of New York at Buffalo (B.A., 1966); Howard University Law School (J.D., 1969); George Washington University Law School (LL.M., 1970). Author: "Computer Fraud Insurance," ABA Banking Journal, Oct., 1983. Special Counsel to the Secretary of Transportation for the Rail Valuation Case, 1979. *Member:* The District of Columbia Bar; American Bar Association (Member, Litigation, Business and Science and Technology Sections); The Association of Trial Lawyers of America; Computer Law Association.

O'CONNELL & ASSOCIATES

Established in 1977
1730 RHODE ISLAND AVENUE, N.W.
SUITE 809
WASHINGTON, D.C. 20036
Telephone: 202-466-8200
Fax: 202-466-4663
Email: maoc@oconnell-associates.com
URL: http://www.lawyers.com/oconnell&associates

Tax, Family Law, Estate Planning, and Employee Benefits.

MARJORIE A. O'CONNELL, born Worcester, Massachusetts, November 17, 1948; admitted to bar, 1973, District of Columbia; 1974, U.S. Court of Appeals for the District of Columbia Circuit, U.S. District Court for the District of Columbia and U.S. Tax Court; 1977, U.S. Supreme Court. *Education:* Catholic University of America (B.A., magna cum laude, 1970); Georgetown University (J.D., 1973). Phi Beta Kappa; Kappa Beta Pi. Student Editor-in-Chief, *The Tax Lawyer,* 1973. Author: *Divorce Taxation,* Warren, Gorham Lamont, 1982—. Member, Board of Directors, National Conference of Women's Bar Associations, 1990—. *Member:* The District of Columbia Bar (Member, Tax and Family Law Divisions); Bar Association of The District of Columbia (Member, Executive Committee, Board of Directors, 1994-1995) Member and Chair, Taxation Committee, 1988—); Foundation of the Bar Association of the District of Columbia (President, 1994-1996; Director, 1992—); Women's Bar Association of the District of Columbia (Member, Board of Directors, 1980-1981); Women's Bar Association Foundation (Member and President, 1980-1984, Vice President, 1984-1986 and Board of Directors, 1989-1992); International (Vice Chair, Family Law Committee, 1988—), Federal (Member, Council on Taxation, 1977-1987) and American (Member of Council, 1986-1990 and Assistant Secretary, Executive Committee, 1986-1987, Taxation Section; Chair, Domestic Relations Tax Problems Committee, 1980-1982; General Practice Section, Editorial Board Member and Tax Committee Vice-Chairman, 1979-1985; Family Law Section, Vice Chair, 1980-1987 and Chair, 1987-1989 Tax Committee; Member, House of Delegates, 1997—) Bar Associations. Fellow: American College of Tax Counsel; American Academy of Matrimonial Lawyers; International Academy of Matrimonial Lawyers. ***PRACTICE AREAS:*** Family Law; Taxation; Divorce Taxation; Estate and Gift Taxation; Estate Planning; Employee Benefits.

PETE M. MURCHISON, born Roswell, New Mexico, February 7, 1945; admitted to bar, 1980, Virginia, District of Columbia, U.S. Court of Appeals, Fourth Circuit and U.S. Court of Appeals for the District of Columbia. *Education:* University of Texas (B.A., 1968); The Ohio State University (M.A., 1973); George Mason University School of Law (J.D., 1980). Delta Theta Phi. *Member:* Fairfax, Virginia and American Bar Associations; The Association of Trial Lawyers of America. [With USAF, 1963-1969]. ***PRACTICE AREAS:*** Litigation; Family Law.

ASSOCIATE

JESSICA ADLER, born Toledo, Ohio, February 10, 1975; admitted to bar, 2000, Ohio; 2001, District of Columbia. *Education:* University of Wisconsin-Madison (B.A., with honors, 1997); The Ohio State University (J.D., 2000). Associate Editor, Journal on Dispute Resolution, Ohio State University. *Mem-*

(This Listing Continued)

O'CONNELL & ASSOCIATES, Washington—Continued

ber: Ohio State and American (Member, Sections on: Family Law; Taxation) Bar Associations. ***PRACTICE AREAS:*** Family Law; Taxation; Divorce Taxation; Estate and Gift Taxation; Estate Planning; Employee Benefits. ***Email:*** jea@oconnell-associates.com

O'CONNELL & GLOCK, P.C.

1100 CONNECTICUT AVENUE, N.W. 9TH FLOOR
WASHINGTON, D.C. 20036-4114
Telephone: 202-293-7909
Telecopier: 202-293-7907
URL: http://www.lawyers.com/oconnell&glock

General Practice. Real Estate, Commercial Law, Corporate, Small Business Law, Taxation and International.

JOHN W. O'CONNELL, born Flandreau, South Dakota, August 18, 1921; admitted to bar, 1960, District of Columbia. *Education:* Georgetown Foreign Service School (B.S.F.S., 1946); Georgetown University (Ph.D., 1958; J.D., 1948); Punjab University, Lahore, Pakistan (M.A., 1952). Recipient, Fulbright Fellowship, Punjab University. *Member:* The District of Columbia Bar. ***PRACTICE AREAS:*** International Law.

EARL F. GLOCK, born Johnstown, Pennsylvania, December 15, 1952; admitted to bar, 1980, Virginia, District of Columbia, U.S. Court of Appeals, Fourth Circuit and U.S. Court of Federal Claims; 1981, U.S. District Court for the District of Columbia, U.S. Court of Appeals for the District of Columbia Circuit and U.S. Tax Court; 1982, U.S. Court of Appeals for the Federal Circuit; 1985, U.S. District Court, Eastern District of Virginia and U.S. Supreme Court; 2000, Maryland. *Education:* University of Notre Dame (B.A., with honors, 1974); Georgetown University (M.S.F.S., 1980; J.D., 1980; M.L. in Taxation, 1988). Pi Sigma Alpha. *Member:* District of Columbia Bar; Virginia State Bar; American Bar Association (Member: International Law Section; U.S. Activities of Foreigners and Tax Treaties Committee, Taxation Section). ***PRACTICE AREAS:*** Real Estate; Taxation; Corporate; International Law. ***Email:*** earlglock@oconnellglock.com

O'CONNELL & O'CONNELL

WASHINGTON, D.C.
(See Rockville, Maryland)

Civil Litigation, Insurance Defense, Workers Compensation, Personal Injury, Insurance Coverage, Products Liability, Employment Law, Contracts, Wills.

BRIAN M. O'CONNOR

WASHINGTON, D.C.
(See Reston)

General Civil, Criminal and Trial Practice in all Courts. Personal Injury, Medical Malpractice, Commercial Litigation and Construction Litigation, Family Law, Divorce, Driving While Intoxicated.

O'CONNOR & HANNAN, L.L.P.

SUITE 500, 1666 K STREET, N.W.
WASHINGTON, D.C. 20006
Telephone: 202-887-1400
Telecopy: 202-466-2198
Email: oh@oconnorhannan.com
URL: http://www.oconnorhannan.com

Vienna, Virginia Office: 8300 Boone Boulevard, Suite 554. Telephone: 703-714-6670. Fax: 703-848-4586.
Madrid, Spain Office: Veláquez 21-4°. Telephone: +(011) 34-91-575-0944; +(011) 34-91-357-2251. Fax: +(011) 34-91-577-0822.

General Practice before United States Courts, Administrative Agencies, Government Departments and the Congress. Environmental and Natural Resources, Associations, White Collar Crime, Employment, Corporate, Health, Communications, Taxation, Probate. Customs, Immigration Law, Export Control, and International Trade.

MEMBERS OF FIRM

PATRICK J. O'CONNOR, born Eden Valley, Minnesota, 1920; admitted to bar, 1945, Minnesota; 1964, District of Columbia. *Education:* Creighton University (Ph.B., 1942); University of Minnesota (LL.B., 1945). Treasurer, 1967-1971 and Director, 1971—, Democratic National Committee. President, University of Minnesota Law School Alumni Association. *Member:* The District of Columbia Bar; Hennepin County, Minnesota State, Federal and American Bar Associations.

JOE A. WALTERS, born Youngstown, Ohio, 1920; admitted to bar, 1947, Minnesota; 1964, District of Columbia; U.S. Supreme Court; U.S. Court of Appeals, 8th Circuit; U.S. Court of Appeals for the District of Columbia; U.S. District Court, District of Minnesota; U.S. District Court, District of Columbia. *Education:* University of Minnesota (B.S.L., 1946; LL.B., 1947). *Member:* Hennepin County, Minnesota State and American Bar Associations. (Civil Trial Specialist Certified by the Civil Litigation Section, Minnesota State Bar Association).

DAVID R. MELINCOFF, born Boston, Massachusetts, 1932; admitted to bar, 1961, Massachusetts; 1970, District of Columbia. *Education:* Bowdoin College (A.B., 1954); Boston College Law School (LL.B., 1961). Editor, Boston College Industrial and Commercial Law Review, 1960-1961. Member, Trial Section, Antitrust Division, U.S. Department of Justice, 1961-1969. *Member:* Massachusetts and American Bar Associations; The District of Columbia Bar; Bar Association of the District of Columbia. [U.S. Army, 1954-1957]

F. GORDON LEE, born Johnson City, Tennessee, 1953; admitted to bar, 1978, District of Columbia; 1979, Virginia, U.S. District Court, District of Columbia and U.S. Claims Court; 1982, U.S. Court of International Trade; U.S. District Court, Eastern District of Virginia; U.S. Court of Appeals for the District of Columbia; Supreme Court of Virginia. *Education:* East Tennessee State University (B.S., magna cum laude, 1975); George Washington University (J.D., 1978). Phi Kappa Phi. Recipient, Outstanding Philosophy Student Award. *Member:* The District of Columbia Bar; American Bar Association; American Immigration Lawyers Association. ***Email:*** fglee@oconnorhannan.com

GEORGE J. MANNINA, JR., born Washington, D.C., 1949; admitted to bar, 1980, District of Columbia; U.S. District Court for the District of Columbia; U.S. Court of Appeals, for the District of Columbia; U.S. Supreme Court, U.S. Court of Appeals, Seventh Circuit, U.S. Claims Court; U.S. Court of Appeals for the Federal Circuit; U.S. Court of International Trade. *Education:* Cornell University (B.S., 1971); Washington College of Law (J.D., 1979). Author: "The Law Enforcement Assistance Administration: A Symposium On Its Operation and Impact," Columbia Human Rights Law Review, Vol. 5, Spring, 1973; "Is There a Legal and Conservation Basis for Individual Fishing Quotas?" Ocean and Coastal Law Journal, Vol. 3, Nos. 1&2, 1997; "Changing Judicial Review Standard for Resource Damage Claims Sets a Dangerous Precedent," Legal Backgrounder (Washington Legal Foundation), Vol. 12, No. 39, Oct. 24, 1997; "Is Soil a 'Navigable Water' Under the Clean Water Act?" Legal Backgrounder (Washington Legal Foundation), Vol. 13, No. 12, Mar. 20, 1998; "The Clean Water Act, By Its Terms, Does Not Directly Cover Wildlife, But the Army Corps of Engineers is Trying to Extend the Act To Protect Migratory Birds," The National Law Journal, p. B6, Nov. 10, 1997. Administrative Aide, Congressman Gilbert Guide, 1971-1973. Legislative Assistant, Congressman Edwin B. Forsythe, 1973-1975. Counsel, House of Representatives Subcommittee on Fisheries, Wildlife Conservation and the Environment, 1975-1983. Chief Minority Counsel, House of Representatives Merchant Marine and Fisheries Committee, 1983-1985. *Member:* Bar Association of the District of Columbia; American Bar Association. ***Email:*** gmannina@oconnorhannan.com

ROBERT M. ADLER, born Toledo, Ohio, October 2, 1943; admitted to bar, 1969, District of Columbia; 1994, Maryland. *Education:* Oberlin College (B.A., 1965); University of Michigan (J.D., 1968). Adjunct Professor of Law: Oil and Gas Law, Income Taxation of Trusts and Estates and Accounting, Georgetown University Law Center, 1974-1976. Trial Attorney, Tax Division, U.S. Department of Justice, 1968-1974. Special Assistant to the Attorney General, 1976-1977. *Member:* The District of Columbia Bar; Maryland State Bar Association. ***Email:*** radler@oconnorhannan.com

TIMOTHY W. JENKINS, born Washington, D.C., 1957; admitted to bar, 1985, Virginia; 1986, District of Columbia; U.S. Court of Appeals for the Federal Circuit. *Education:* Trinity College (B.A., 1979); Marshall-Wythe School of Law, College of William and Mary (J.D., 1985). Member, National Moot Court Team. Investigator, Subcommittee on Investigations and General Oversight, U.S. Senate, Labor Committee, 1980-1982. *Member:* Virginia State Bar; The District of Columbia Bar. ***Email:*** tjenkins@oconnorhannan.com

STEPHEN N. SHULMAN, born New Haven, Connecticut, April 6, 1933; admitted to bar, 1958, Connecticut; 1960, District of Columbia and U.S. Court of Appeals, District of Columbia Circuit; 1962, U.S. Supreme Court; 1974, U.S. Court of Appeals, Fourth Circuit and U.S. Court of Federal Claims; 1976, U.S. Court of Appeals, Fifth Circuit; 1978, U.S. Court of Appeals, First and Sixth Circuits; 1981, U.S. Court of Appeals, Eleventh Circuit; 1982, U.S. Court of Appeals, Federal Circuit; 1994, U.S. Court of Appeals, Second Circuit and Tax Court. *Education:* Harvard University (A.B., 1954); Yale University (LL.B. cum laude, 1958). Order of the Coif. Editor-in-Chief, Yale Law Journal, 1957-1958. Law Clerk to Justice John M. Harlan, U.S. Supreme Court, 1958-1959. Author: "The Law of Equal Employment Opportunity," by Stephen N. Shulman and Charles F. Abernathy. Visiting Assistant Professor of Law, University of Michigan, 1959. Assistant U.S. Attorney, District of Columbia, 1960-1961. Executive

(This Listing Continued)

Assistant to Secretary of Labor, 1961-1962. Deputy Assistant Secretary of Defense, 1962-1965. General Counsel of the Air Force, 1965-1966. Chairman, Equal Employment Opportunity Commission, 1966-1967. *Member:* The District of Columbia Bar. ***PRACTICE AREAS:*** Litigation; Associations; Employment Law. ***Email:*** sshulman@oconnorhannan.com

JAMES W. SYMINGTON, born Rochester, New York, 1927; admitted to bar, 1954, Missouri; 1960, District of Columbia; 1962, U.S. Supreme Court; U.S. District Court, District of Missouri. *Education:* Yale University (B.A., 1950); Columbia University (LL.B., 1954). Phi Delta Phi. Associate, Cobbs, Armstrong, Teasdale & Roos, St. Louis, Mo., 1955-1958. Attache, U.S. Embassy, London, England, 1958-1960. Deputy Director, Food For Peace, White House, 1961-1962. Administrative Assistant to U.S. Attorney General, 1962-1963. Associate, Arnold, Fortas & Porter, Washington, D.C., 1963-1965. Executive Director, President's Committee on Juvenile Delinquency & Youth Crime, 1964-1966. Recipient, National Science Foundation Award for Distinguished Service as Chairman of Science, Research and Technology Subcommittee, 1977. Chairman, Fund for the Improvement of Post Secondary Education, 1977-1981. Secretary, Atlantic Council, 1986—. Chairman, National Rehabilitation Hospital, 1989-1992. President, United States Association of Former Members of Congress, 1993—. [With U.S. Marine Corps, 1945-1946]

LARRY PRESSLER, born Humboldt, South Dakota, March 29, 1942; admitted to bar, 1972, District of Columbia; 1998, New York. *Education:* University of South Dakota (B.A., 1964); Oxford University (Oxford Diploma, 1966); Harvard University (J.D., 1971). Rhodes Scholar. Member, United States Senate from South Dakota, January 1979 - January 1997. Member, United States House of Representative from South Dakota, January 1975- January 1979. Principal author, Telecommunications Act of 1996. Chairman, Committee on Commerce, United States Senate 1992-1996. *Member:* The Association of the Bar of the City of New York; New York State and American Bar Associations; The District of Columbia Bar; United States Association of Former Members of Congress; American Association of Rhodes Scholars. [Lieutenant, U.S. Army, 1996-1968]. ***PRACTICE AREAS:*** Telcom; Corporate Law; International Law. ***Email:*** lpressler@oconnorhannan.com

J. CRAIG POTTER, born December 23, 1943; admitted to bar, 1973, Wyoming; 1988, District of Columbia. *Education:* University of Illinois (A.B., 1967); University of Wyoming (J.D., 1972). Assistant Administrator, Air and Radiation, EPA, 1986-1988; Pr. Deputy Assistant Secretary, Fish and Wildlife and Parks, Department of Interior, 1982-1985. *Member:* Wyoming State Bar; American Bar Association (Vice Chairman, Environment Quality Committee, Natural Resources Section, 1984-1986). ***PRACTICE AREAS:*** Natural Resources Law; Environmental Law. ***Email:*** jcpotter@oconnorhannan.com

CHRISTINA W. FLEPS, born Alexandria, Virginia, 1952; admitted to bar, 1978, District of Columbia. *Education:* Pomona College (B.A., cum laude, 1973); Boalt Hall School of Law, University of California at Berkeley (J.D., 1978); George Washington University (M.B.A., 1986). Recipient, International Business Award. Author: "Medicare, Prepping for the 1990s," American Society of Ophthalmic Administrators, September 1990; "New Developments in Blood Donor Confidentiality," Council of Community Blood Centers Newsletter, October, 1985; "Health Facility Financing," Advanced Legal Education, September, 1985; "Country of Origin Rule Changes," International Business Forum, November, 1984. *Member:* The District of Columbia Bar. ***Email:*** cfleps@oconnorhannan.com

GARY C. ADLER, born Hempstead, New York, 1957; admitted to bar, 1985, Maryland; 1988, District of Columbia and U.S. District Court, District of Maryland; 1989, U.S. District Court for the District of Columbia. *Education:* George Washington University (B.A., 1980); Columbus University; Catholic University of America (J.D., 1985). Recipient, American Jurisprudence Award, Property. *Member:* Maryland State Bar Association; The District of Columbia Bar. ***Email:*** gadler@oconnorhannan.com

JOHN M. HIMMELBERG, born Washington, D.C., July 9, 1946; admitted to bar, 1975, Maryland; 1976, District of Columbia. *Education:* College of the Holy Cross (A.B., 1968); Catholic University of America (J.D., 1974). Adjudicator, Claims Division, United States General Accounting Office, 1970-1972. Law Clerk to Judge James A. Belson, Superior Court of the District of Columbia, 1974-1975. Deputy Director, Hearings and Appeals, Commodity Futures Trading Commission, 1975-1976. Co-Author: "The 1984 PACA Amendments After Six Year: Producing Sellers' Trust and Lenders' Disgust," 43 Arkansas Law Review 523 (1990). Member, Board of Editors, Federal Bar Journal, 1978-1979. *Member:* The District of Columbia Bar; Bar Association of the District of Columbia (Member, Agricultural Technical Advisory Committee, U.S. Secretary of Agriculture, U.S. Trade Representative, 1992-1995). ***Email:*** jhimmelberg@oconnorhannan.com

ROY C. COFFEE III, born Dallas, Texas, January 6, 1964; admitted to bar, 1992, California; 1993, Texas (Not admitted in District of Columbia). *Education:* University of Texas (B.J., 1986); Pepperdine University (J.D., 1992). ***Email:*** rcoffee@oconnorhannan.com

KURT E. BLASE, born 1953; admitted to bar, 1979, District of Columbia. *Education:* Furman University and Clemson University (B.A., 1975); Georgetown University (J.D., 1979). Member, Georgetown Law Journal, 1977-1979. Author: "Habeas Relief for State and Federal Prisoners," 66 Georgetown Law Journal 647-73, 1977. Member, Georgetown Legal Aid Society, 1976-1977. *Member:* The District of Columbia Bar. ***PRACTICE AREAS:*** Environmental; Occupational Safety and Health. ***Email:*** kblase@oconnorhannan.com

EDWARD A. BECK III, born New York, N.Y., October 12, 1944; admitted to bar, 1974, Virginia; 1979, District of Columbia. *Education:* Davidson College (B.A., 1967); University of Manchester, Manchester, England (M.A., Econ., 1971); University of Virginia (M.A., Govt., 1973); University of Richmond (J.D., 1974); George Washington University (LL.M., Taxation, 1978). Pi Alpha Delta. Member, University of Richmond Law Review, 1973-1974. Law Clerk, Chief Justice Harold F. Snead, Justice A.C. Compton, 1974-1975. Tax Counsel, Subcommittee on Taxation and Debt Management, Senate Finance Committee, 1977-1982. Tax Counsel, National Association of Home Builders, 1982-1985. Washington Representative, American Petroleum Institute, 1985-1992. *Member:* Virginia State Bar; District of Columbia Bar; Federal (Past Chairman, Tax Section) and American Bar Associations. ***PRACTICE AREAS:*** Legislation; Taxation Law; International Trade; Estate Planning; Probate. ***Email:*** ebeck@oconnorhannan.com

ALBERT P. LINDEMANN, JR., born Providence, Rhode Island, December 3, 1937; admitted to bar, 1962, District of Columbia; 1975, New York. *Education:* University of Rhode Island (B.S., 1959); Boston University (LL.B., 1962). Adjunct Professor of International Law, T.C. Williams School of Law, University of Richmond, 1990-1994. Trial Attorney: Antitrust Division, U.S. Department of Justice, Washington, D.C., 1962-1966; Exxon Corporation Law Department, 1966-1988. Member, Panel of Arbitrators, American Arbitration Association. *Member:* Association of the Bar of the City of New York; American Bar Association (Member, Sections on: Antitrust; Litigation; International Law). ***PRACTICE AREAS:*** Litigation; International Law; Trade Regulation. ***Email:*** alindemann@oconnorhannan.com

JED L. BABBIN, born New York, N.Y., March 16, 1950; admitted to bar, 1973, Alabama; 1978, District of Columbia. *Education:* Stevens Institute of Technology (B.S., 1970); Cumberland School of Law (J.D., 1973); Georgetown University School of Law (LL.M., 1978). Listed in Who's Who in American Law. Member, Panel of Arbitrators, American Arbitration Association. Associate, McKenna, Conner & Cuneo, 1977-1981. Author: "Government Contracts Reform: A Critical Analysis of the Administration's Proposal," Washington Legal Foundation, May 1995; "Real Defense Conversion Requires Tax Relief for R&D," *Aviation Week & Space Technology Magazine,* August 8, 1994. Member, Board of Directors, National Lawyers Association, 2000—. Vice President and General Counsel, Shipbuilders Council of America, 1981-1985. Director of Contract Policy, Lockheed Corporation, 1985-1990. Deputy Under Secretary of Defense Acquisition Planning, Department of Defense, 1990-1991. Partner, McGuire Woods Battle & Boothe, 1991-1994. Partner, Tighe, Patton & Babbin, LLC (1994-2000). ABA Public Contracts Law Section; Vice Chairman, Judicial Remedies Committee (1995-1996); Vice Chairman, Truth in Negotiations Act Committee (1993-1994). Fellow and Member, Board of Advisors National Contract Management Association; Air Force Association (Counsel, National Capital Chapter). [Judge Advocate, U.S. Air Force (1973-1977)]. ***PRACTICE AREAS:*** Government Contracts; Complex Civil and Criminal Litigation. ***Email:*** jbabbin@oconnorhannan.com

SHARON L. BABBIN, born Plainfield, New Jersey, February 19, 1954; admitted to bar, 1977, Virginia; 1979, District of Columbia; 1980, U.S. Court of Appeals for the District of Columbia Circuit and U.S. Supreme Court; 1997, U.S. District Court for the District of Columbia, U.S. District Court, District of Maryland, U.S. District Court, Eastern District of Virginia, U.S. Court of Federal Claims and U.S. Court of Appeals for the Federal Circuit. *Education:* Indiana University (B.S., 1974); Georgetown University (J.D., 1977). Associate, James E. Ritchie and Associates, 1977-1978. Vice-President and Associate General Counsel, Marriott International, Inc. Formerly Marriott Corporation, 1979-1996. Of Counsel, Tighe, Patton, Babbin LLC, 1998-2000. Shareholder, Hillyer & Irwin, P.C., 1997-1998. ***PRACTICE AREAS:*** Commercial Litigation; Corporate Transactions; Intellectual Property; Antitrust; Construction Law; Federal Government Law. ***Email:*** sbabbin@oconnorhannan.com

EMIL HIRSCH, born Bistrita, Romania, June 11, 1951; admitted to bar, 1976, Maryland; 1977, District of Columbia. *Education:* University of Maryland (B.S., 1973; J.D., 1976). *Member:* Maryland State and American Bar Associations; District of Columbia (Member, Litigation and Corporation, Finance and Securities Law Sections). ***LANGUAGES:*** German, Romanian and Hungarian. ***PRACTICE AREAS:*** Business Litigation; Bankruptcy Law; Corporate Law. ***Email:*** ehirsch@oconnorhannan.com

FREDERICK T. DOMBO III, born New York, New York, August 12, 1967; admitted to bar, 1993, New York; 1995, District of Columbia. *Education:* Drew University (B.A., 1989); Widener University School of Law (J.D., 1992). Counsel to Honorable Michael P. Forbes, April 1997-May 1999. Member, Federalist Society, 1994—. *Member:* The District of Columbia Bar; New York State Bar Association. ***PRACTICE AREAS:*** Lobbying; Administrative Law. ***Email:*** fdombo@oconnorhannan.com

(This Listing Continued)

(This Listing Continued)

O'CONNOR & HANNAN, L.L.P., Washington—Continued

PAUL L. KNIGHT, born Palo Alto, California, June 26, 1949; admitted to bar, 1975, District of Columbia; U.S. District Court, District of Columbia; U.S. Court of Appeals, District of Columbia Circuit; U.S. Court of Appeals, Fourth Circuit; U.S. Court of Appeals, Fifth Circuit; U.S. Court of Appeals, Federal Circuit; U.S. Court of Appeals, Armed Forces; 1980, U.S. Supreme Court. *Education:* University of California at Berkeley (A.B., 1971); Hastings College of the Law, University of California (J.D., 1975). Prettyman Program, Georgetown University Law Center, 1975-1977. Assistant, U.S. Attorney, District of Columbia, 1977-1989. Special Assistant U.S. Attorney, Western District of Texas and District of Maryland. Associate Director, President's Task Force on Victims of Crime, 1982-1983. Member, 1997— and Hearing Committee Member, 1991-1997, District of Columbia Court of Appeals Board on Professional Responsibility. ***PRACTICE AREAS:*** White Collar Criminal Defense; Civil Litigation; Criminal Law. ***Email:*** pknight@oconnorhannan.com

MICHAEL J. WING, born Tucson, Arizona, July 1, 1959; admitted to bar, 2000, Texas (Not admitted in District of Columbia). *Education:* University of Colorado at Boulder (B.A., 1981); Denver University (M.B.A., 1986); Georgetown University (M.A., Public Policy, 1988); University of Houston (M.A., Political Science, 1998; Ph.D., Political Science/Privatization, 2002); South Texas College of Law (J.D., 1999); Wheaton College (M.A., Theology, 2000). White House Fellow, 1992-1993. Member, American Political Science Association, 1998—. *Member:* Houston and American Bar Associations; State Bar of Texas. ***LANGUAGES:*** Spanish. ***PRACTICE AREAS:*** Corporate Law; Commercial Transactions; Mergers and Acquisitions; International Business Law; Privatization; Oil and Gas Law. ***Email:*** mwing@oconnorhannan.com

D. LEE ANTTON, born Milwaukee, Wisconsin, June 17, 1959; admitted to bar, 1986, District of Columbia; 1992, U.S. District Court for the District of Columbia and U.S. Court of Appeals for the Federal Circuit; registered to practice before U.S. Patent and Trademark Office. *Education:* University of Wisconsin-Madison (B.S., Physics, Astronomy, 1982); Georgetown University (J.D., 1985). Author: "The Significance of Lotus v. Borland," The Computer Lawyer, October 1992; "Is the United States Automating a Patent Registration System for Software? A Critical Review of Information Management in the U.S.P.T.O." Journal of the Patent and Trademark Office Society, September 1990; "Copyright Protection and Innovation: The Impact of Lotus Development v. Paperback Software," The Computer Lawyer, August 1990. *Member:* The District of Columbia Bar. ***PRACTICE AREAS:*** Patents; Trademarks; Copyrights. ***Email:*** lantton@oconnorhannan.com

NON-ATTORNEY MEMBER

THOMAS J. CORCORAN, born Ottawa, Illinois, May 23, 1939. *Education:* University of Notre Dame (B.A., 1961); University of Illinois; University of Chicago; Northwestern University. U.S. Congressman, 1977-1985. [1st Lt., U.S. Army Artillery]. ***Email:*** tcorcoran@oconnorhannan.com

ASSOCIATE

JAMES P. RYAN, born Houston, Texas, May 28, 1965; admitted to bar, 1997, Florida and Massachusetts; 1999, Virginia (Not admitted in District of Columbia). *Education:* University of Central Florida (B.A., 1992); University of Miami (J.D., 1997). *Member:* The Florida Bar; American Bar Association. ***PRACTICE AREAS:*** Intellectual Property Litigation; Commercial Litigation; Bankruptcy; Trademarks; Copyrights. ***Email:*** jryan@oconnorhannan.com

OF COUNSEL

KENNETH A. MAYFIELD, born Kadena, Okinawa, December 10, 1950; admitted to bar, 1980, Texas (Not admitted in District of Columbia). *Education:* University of Texas at Arlington (B.A., 1976); St. Mary's University (J.D., 1980). Dallas County District Attorney Office, 1980-1988; Dallas County Commissioner, 1995. *Member:* State Bar of Texas.

CHARLES R. McCARTHY, JR., born Tully, New York, September 22, 1938; admitted to bar, 1966, District of Columbia. *Education:* LeMoyne College (B.S., 1960); Georgetown University (J.D., 1965). Member, Georgetown Law Journal, 1962. Faculty Member, George Mason University School of Law, 1974-1978. Law Clerk, Honorable Edward A. Beard, Superior Court of the District of Columbia, 1965-1966. Deputy Director of Criminal Justice Act for the District of Columbia, 1966-1967. Assistant Corporation Counsel for the District of Columbia (Civil Division), 1967-1968. Trial Attorney (Finance) for the Securities and Exchange Commission, 1968-1970. Director of Securities for the District of Columbia, 1970. Member, The District of Columbia Securities Advisory Committee, 1974-1984. General Counsel, National Association of Corporate Directors, 1990-1995. *Member:* The District of Columbia Bar; American Bar Association. ***Email:*** cmccarthy@oconnorhannan.com

WILLIAM W. NICKERSON, born Chelsea, Massachusetts, May 13, 1944; admitted to bar, 1980, Massachusetts; 1985, District of Columbia; U.S. Circuit Court, First, Fourth and Federal Circuits. *Education:* University of Massachusetts (B.A., 1969); American University (J.D., 1980). Deputy Assistant Secretary, U.S. Treasury Department, 1979-1981. Director, National Technical Assistance Program, U.S. Department of Justice, 1977-1979. Commissioner, City of Boston, 1974-1977. *Member:* The District of Columbia Bar; Massachusetts Bar Association.

STEPHEN M. SOBLE, born Rochester, New York, August 15, 1951; admitted to bar, 1978, District of Columbia and U.S. District Court for the District of Columbia; 1979, U.S. Court of Appeals for the District of Columbia Circuit; 1985, U.S. Supreme Court and U.S. Court of International Trade; 1989, New York. *Education:* Syracuse University (B.A., summa cum laude, 1972); London School of Economics and Political Science, London, England; School of Oriental and African Studies, University of London; Harvard University (J.D., 1978). Phi Beta Kappa. Author: "Proposal for the Administrative Compensation of Victims of Toxic Substance Pollution: A Model Act," 14 Harvard Journal on Legislation 683, 1977. Lecturer, Seminar, U.S. Income Tax for Students in the Harvard International Tax Program, 1977-1978. General Counsel: U.S. ASEAN Council, 1984-1996; The Utility PhotoVoltaic Group, 1993—; United BioEnergy Commercialization Association, 1993—. Senior Editor, *East Asian Executive Reports,* 1979—. Editor: *Middle East Executive Reports,* 1980—. *Member:* The District of Columbia Bar; New York State and American Bar Associations; American Society of International Law. ***LANGUAGES:*** Chinese and French. ***PRACTICE AREAS:*** International Infrastructure Development; International Project Finance; International Government Relations. ***Email:*** ssoble@oconnorhannan.com

THOMAS J. SCHNEIDER, born Marshall, Michigan, 1951; admitted to bar, 1980, District of Columbia; U.S. District Court, District of Columbia. *Education:* Harvard University (A.B., magna cum laude with highest honors, 1973; J.D., 1980); Nuffield College, Oxford University, Oxford, England (D.Phil., 1977). Author: "NLRB at Fifty: Quality of Worklife Programs and the National Labor Relations Act," A BNA Special Report, 1985. Member, White House Conference on Productivity/APC Conference on Cooperation in the Workplace, 1983. *Member:* The District of Columbia Bar; American Bar Association (Member, Labor and Employment Law Section).

A list of representative clients at Washington, D.C. will be furnished upon request.

(For complete biographical data on other personnel, see Professional Biographies at Vienna, Virginia)

O'DONNELL, SCHWARTZ & ANDERSON, P.C.

Established in 1981

1300 L STREET, N.W.
SUITE 1200
WASHINGTON, D.C. 20005
Telephone: 202-898-1707
FAX: 202-682-9276

Other Washington, D.C. Office: Suite 707, 1900 L Street, N.W., 20036. Telephone: 202-898-1824. Fax: 202-429-8928.

Labor Relations Law, Aviation and Railroad Law, Employee Benefits, Civil Rights and Torts.

FIRM PROFILE: O'Donnell, Schwartz & Anderon, P.C., specializes in union side labor law, employee benefits law, civil rights law and tort law. The firm is general counsel to several national labor unions and performs a variety of services for other national unions, local unions, and individual and institutional clients. The firm's practice involves every aspect of traditional labor law with a nationwide litigation practice. The firm also serves as general counsel to a variety of pension and welfare funds and advises a number of unions on benefits-related topics as well as federal contract procurement laws and regulations.

JOHN F. O'DONNELL (1907-1993).

DARRYL J. ANDERSON, born Berea, Ohio, September 7, 1944; admitted to bar, 1970, Michigan; 1971, U.S. Court of Appeals, 6th Circuit; 1973, District of Columbia; 1975, U.S. Supreme Court; 1976, U.S. Court of Appeals, 4th and 8th Circuits; 1981, U.S. Court of Appeals, 5th Circuit and U.S. Court of Appeals for the District of Columbia Circuit; 1985, U.S. Court of Appeals, 11th Circuit; 1987, U.S. Court of Appeals, 2nd Circuit; 1988, U.S. Court of Appeals for the Federal Circuit; 1989, U.S. Court of Appeals, 9th Circuit. *Education:* University of Michigan (B.B.A., with distinction, 1966; M.B.A., 1970; J.D., cum laude, 1970). Law Clerk to the Hon. Wade H. McCree, Jr., U.S. Court of Appeals, 6th Circuit, 1970-1972. Counsel to U.S. Senate Committee on Labor and Human Resources, 1977-1981. *Member:* State Bar of Michigan; District of Columbia Bar; American Bar Association (Member, Labor and Employment Law Section). ***Email:*** danderson@odsalaw.com

MARTIN R. GANZGLASS, born New York, N.Y., April 1, 1941; admitted to bar, 1964, New York; 1969, U.S. District Court, Southern District of New York; 1971, District of Columbia and U.S. Court of Appeals for the District of Columbia Circuit; 1976, U.S. Court of Appeals, 5th Circuit; 1980, U.S. Court of

(This Listing Continued)

Appeals, 10th Circuit. *Education:* City College of the City University of New York (B.A., 1961), Phi Beta Kappa; Harvard University (LL.B., 1964). Author: "The Somali Penal Code Cases, Commentary and Examples," Rutgers University Press, 1971; "Constitutions of the Countries of the World, Somali Democratic Republic," Oceana Publications, 1971, 1979, 1981. Associate, 1968-1971 and Partner, 1971-1987, Delson & Gordon. Legal Advisor as Peace Corps Volunteer, Somali National Police Force, 1966-1968. Attorney, National Labor Relations Board, Washington D.C., Office of the General Counsel, Division of Enforcement Litigation, Appellate Court Branch, 1964-1966. Special Consultant, U.S. Department of State Operation Restore Hope, 1993. General Counsel, Graphic Communications International Union, AFL-CIO. Participated in drafting a Penal Code and Criminal Procedure Code for the Eritrean Ministry of Justice. *Member:* The District of Columbia Bar; New York State and American Bar Associations. ***Email:*** mganzglass@odsalaw.com

LEE W. JACKSON, born Natchez, Mississippi, September 16, 1950; admitted to bar, 1975, Mississippi, U.S. Court of Appeals, Fourth and Ninth Circuits; 1980, Pennsylvania; 1981, U.S. Supreme Court and U.S. Court of Appeals, Fifth and Eleventh Circuits; 1983, Pennsylvania and U.S. Court of Appeals, Third Circuit; 1984, U.S. District Court, Eastern District of Pennsylvania; 1992, District of Columbia. *Education:* Jackson State College (B.A. with honors, 1972); National Law Center, George Washington University (J.D., with honors, 1975). Field Attorney, National Labor Relations Board Region 15, New Orleans, Louisiana, 1975-1978. Attorney, National Labor Relations Board, Washington, D.C. Office of the General Counsel, Division of Enforcement Litigation, Appellate Court Branch, and Contempt Litigation Section, 1978-1982. Associate, 1982-1987 and Partner, 1987-1991, Kirschner, Walters & Willig, Philadelphia, Pennsylvania. *Member:* Magnolia (Member, Labor and Employment Law Sections), Pennsylvania and American Bar Associations; Mississippi State Bar; National Bar Association (Member, Labor and Employment Law Sections). ***PRACTICE AREAS:*** Labor Law; Civil Rights Law. ***Email:*** ljackson@odsalaw.com

ARTHUR M. LUBY, born New Haven, Connecticut, August 6, 1953; admitted to bar, 1980, Michigan; 1982, District of Columbia; 1983, U.S. Court of Appeals, Sixth Circuit; 1985, U.S. Court of Appeals for the District of Columbia Circuit; 1987, U.S. Court of Appeals, Ninth Circuit. *Education:* Brown University (B.A., magna cum laude, 1975); University of Michigan (J.D., 1979). Phi Beta Kappa. Recipient, American Jurisprudence Book Award for Constitutional Law. Counsel to U.S. Senate Labor and Human Resources Committee, 1980-1981. *Member:* State Bar of Michigan; District of Columbia Bar; American Bar Association (Member, Labor and Employment Law Section; Co-chair, Task Force on Supreme Court Litigation of Employee Benefits Committee, 1988-1989). ***PRACTICE AREAS:*** Labor Law; Employee Benefits Law; Transportation Law. ***Email:*** aluby@odsalaw.com

ANTON G. HAJJAR, born New York, N.Y., September 12, 1947; admitted to bar, 1975, Louisiana; 1979, U.S. Court of Appeals, Fifth Circuit; 1981, U.S. Supreme Court and U.S. Court of Appeals, Eleventh Circuit; 1982, District of Columbia and U.S. Court of Appeals for the District of Columbia Circuit; 1984, U.S. Court of Appeals for the Federal Circuit and U.S. Court of Appeals, 4th, 9th and 10th Circuits; 1987, Maryland and U.S. District Court of the District of Columbia and Maryland including Trial Bar; 1991, U.S. Court of Appeals, Second Circuit. *Education:* Fordham University (B.A., 1969); Tulane University of Louisiana (J.D., 1975). Order of the Coif. Recipient, American Jurisprudence Awards in Contracts and Administrative Process and Mitchell Franklin Award. Member, Board of Editors, Tulane Law Review, 1973-1975. Law Clerk to Judge John Minor Wisdom, U.S. Court of Appeals for the Fifth Circuit, 1974-1975. Field Attorney, National Labor Relations Board Region 15, New Orleans, Louisiana, 1975-1979. Attorney, National Labor Relations Board, Washington, D.C., Office of the General Counsel, Division of Enforcement Litigation, Appellate Court Branch and Contempt Litigation Section, 1979-1981. *Member:* District of Columbia Bar; Maryland State Bar Association. ***PRACTICE AREAS:*** Labor and Employment Law. ***Email:*** ahajjar@odsalaw.com

SUSAN L. CATLER, born Boston, Massachusetts, August 13, 1956; admitted to bar, 1982, District of Columbia; 1984, U.S. District Court, District of Columbia; 1987, U.S. Court of Appeals, Third and Eleventh Circuits; 1988, U.S. Court of Appeals, Second Circuit and U.S. Supreme Court; 1989, U.S. Court of Appeals, Fourth and Sixth Circuits; 1990, U.S. Court of Appeals for the District of Columbia Circuit; 1991, U.S. Court of Appeals, Seventh and Federal Circuits and U.S. District Court, Eastern District of Wisconsin; 1992, U.S. Court of Appeals, Eighth Circuit; 1994, U.S. District Court, Eastern District of Michigan; 1995, U.S. Court of Appeals, Fifth Circuit; 1997, U.S. Court of Appeals, Tenth Circuit; 2000, U.S. Court of Appeals, First Circuit; 2001, U.S. Court of Appeals, Ninth Circuit and U.S. District Court, District of Colorado. *Education:* Harvard University (B.A., magna cum laude, 1978; J.D., cum laude, 1982). Author: "The Case Against Proposals to Eliminate the Employment At Will Rule," 5 Industrial Relations Law Journal 471, 1983. *Member:* District of Columbia Bar; American Bar Association (Member, Administrative Law and Labor and Employment Law Sections). ***Email:*** scatler@odsalaw.com

RICHARD S. EDELMAN, born New York, N.Y., March 2, 1953; admitted to bar, 1979, New York; 1989, District of Columbia; U.S. Supreme Court; U.S. Court of Appeals for the First, Third, Fourth, Fifth, Sixth, Seventh, Eighth, Tenth, District of Columbia, and Federal Circuits. *Education:* Cornell University (B.S., 1975); Boston University (J.D., 1978). Associate, Mozer and Gulmi, P.C., 1979-1981; Assistant Counsel, 1981-1983, and Assistant Counsel for Litigation, 1983-1986, National Treasury Employees Union; Associate, 1986-1990, and Principal, 1990-1998, Highsaw, Mahoney and Clarke, P.C., Washington, D.C. *Member:* District of Columbia Bar. ***SPECIAL AGENCIES:*** Surface Transportation Board; Federal Labor Relations Authority; National Mediation Board; Equal Employment Opportunity Commission; Merit Systems Protection Board. ***PRACTICE AREAS:*** Labor Law; Administrative Law; Transportation Law; Employment Discrimination Law; Federal District Court and Appellate Litigation. ***Email:*** redelman@odsalaw.com

PETER J. LEFF, born Niles, Illinois, July 23, 1971; admitted to bar, 1996, Virginia; 1998, District of Columbia Bar, U.S. District Court, Eastern District of Virginia and U.S. Court of Appeals for the Tenth Circuit; 1999, U.S. Court of Appeals for the Fourth and Eleventh Circuits and U.S. District Court for the District of Columbia; 2000, U.S. Court of Appeals for the Sixth and First Circuits and U.S District Court, Eastern District of Wisconsin; 2001, U.S. Court of Appeals for the Ninth Circuit and U.S. District Court for the District of Colorado and U.S. District Court, Central District of Illinois. *Education:* Washington University (B.A., magna cum laude, 1993), Phi Beta Kappa; University of Michigan (J.D., 1996). *Member:* Virginia State Bar; District of Columbia Bar; American (Member, Labor and Employment Law Sections) Bar Associations. ***Email:*** pleff@odsalaw.com

MELINDA K. HOLMES, born Milwaukee, Wisconsin, August 16, 1970; admitted to bar, 1996, Pennsylvania; 1998, District of Columbia and U.S. District Court, District of Columbia. *Education:* Northwestern University (B.A., 1992); Georgetown University Law Center (J.D., cum laude, 1996). Article Editor, Georgetown Journal on Fighting Poverty, 1995-1996. Law Clerk to the Hon. Robert I. Richter, D.C. Superior Court, 1996-1997. *Member:* Pennsylvania and American (Member, Labor and Employment Law, Litigation, and D.C. Affairs Sections) Bar Associations; District of Columbia (Co-Chair, Community Outreach Committee, D.C. Bar Labor and Employment Section, 2000-2002). ***Email:*** mholmes@odsalaw.com

MURSHED ZAHEED, born Dhaka, Bangladesh, November 13, 1973; admitted to bar, 1999, Massachusetts (Not admitted in District of Columbia). *Education:* University of California at Los Angeles (B.A., 1996); Boston University (J.D., 1999). *Member:* Massachusetts Bar Association.

DANIEL B. SMITH, born Saint Paul, Minnesota, April 3, 1972; admitted to bar, 2001, Maryland (Not admitted in District of Columbia). *Education:* Johns Hopkins University (B.A., 1994); Georgetown University Law Center (J.D., cum laude, 2001). Member, National Lawyers Guild, 1998-2001. ***LANGUAGES:*** Spanish. ***Email:*** dsmith@odsalaw.com

OF COUNSEL

ASHER W. SCHWARTZ, born New York, N.Y., September 23, 1911; admitted to bar, 1935, New York; 1942, U.S. Supreme Court; 1947, District of Columbia; 1957, U.S. Court of Appeals, Third Circuit; 1959 U.S. Court of Appeals, Second Circuit; 1972, U.S. Court of Appeals, Ninth Circuit; 1974, U.S. Court of Appeals, Fifth Circuit; 1975, U.S. Court of Appeals, District of Columbia Circuit; 1982, U.S. Court of Appeals, Eleventh Circuit. *Education:* Williams College (A.B., 1932); Harvard University (LL.B., 1935). Special Assistant to U.S. Attorney General, 1947-1948. Member, National Panel of Arbitrators, American Arbitration Association, 1964—. *Member:* The Association of the Bar of the City of New York (Member: Committee on: Aeronautics, 1965-1966; Committee on: Labor Law, 1967-1972); American Bar Association (Member, Section on: Labor Relations Law). (Also Member, O'Donnell Schwartz & Glanstein).

LEGAL SUPPORT PERSONNEL

PATRICIA RICE. *Education:* George Washington University (B.A., 1981). (Employee Benefits Specialist).

O'DONOGHUE & O'DONOGHUE

Established in 1940

4748 WISCONSIN AVENUE, N.W.

WASHINGTON, D.C. 20016

Telephone: 202-362-0041

Telecopier: 202-362-2640

Philadelphia, Pennsylvania Office: Constitution Place, Suite 515, 325 Chestnut Street. Telephone: 215-629-4970. Telecopier: 215-629-4996.

General Practice, Labor Law and Employee Benefits Law.

(This Listing Continued)

O'DONOGHUE & O'DONOGHUE, Washington—Continued

FIRM PROFILE: O'Donoghue & O'Donoghue is a Washington, D.C. and Philadelphia, Pa. based Labor Relations & Employment law firm.

MEMBERS OF FIRM

MARTIN F. O'DONOGHUE (1903-1973).

PATRICK C. O'DONOGHUE (1930-1979).

JOSEPH P. BOYLE (1954-1998).

DONALD J. CAPUANO, born Troy, New York, September 26, 1934; admitted to bar, 1958, District of Columbia; 1962, U.S. Court of Appeals, District of Columbia Circuit; 1971, U.S. Supreme Court. *Education:* State University of New York at Albany (B.S. in Comm., 1955); Georgetown University (J.D., 1958). Phi Delta Phi. Member, Georgetown Law Journal, 1956-1958. Law Clerk to Judge Charles F. McLaughlin, U.S. District Court, District of Columbia, 1959-1960. Member, Judicial Conference of the District of Columbia Circuit, 1971. *Member:* The District of Columbia Bar; The Bar Association of the District of Columbia (Chair, Labor Law Committee, 1973-1974); American Bar Association (Chair, Section of Labor and Employment Law, 1991-1992; Chair-Elect, 1990-1991, Member of Council, 1984-1990 and Section Governance Liaison, 1996—; Subcommittee Co-Chair, 1971-1979 and Co-Chair, 1979-1982, Committee on Development of Law Under the National Labor Relations Act; Co-chair, 1982-1984 Institutes and Meetings Committee). ***Email:*** dcapuano@odonoghuelaw.com

JAMES R. O'CONNELL, born Washington, D.C., May 8, 1943; admitted to bar, 1968, Maryland; 1972, District of Columbia and Virginia. *Education:* University of Maryland (B.A., 1965); Georgetown University (J.D., 1968). Omicron Delta Kappa; Phi Alpha Theta; Pi Sigma Alpha. *Member:* The District of Columbia Bar; The Bar Association of the District of Columbia; Maryland State and American Bar Associations. [Capt., USMC, 1969-1972]. ***Email:*** joconnell@odonoghuelaw.com

ROBERT MATISOFF, born Boston, Massachusetts, April 16, 1949; admitted to bar, 1974, Virginia; 1975, District of Columbia. *Education:* Harvard University (A.B., 1971); George Washington University (J.D., 1974). Member, George Washington Law Review, 1972-1973. Author: Note, 41 George Washington Law Review 106, October, 1972. *Member:* The District of Columbia Bar; American Bar Association (Subcommittee Co-Chairman, Committee on Development of Law Under the National Labor Relations Act, 1982-1989, 1994-1996); Virginia State Bar. Fellow: College of Labor and Employment Lawyers. ***Email:*** bmatisoff@odonoghuelaw.com

JOYCE A. MADER, born Harrisburg, Pennsylvania, September 13, 1951; admitted to bar, 1976, Pennsylvania; 1977, District of Columbia; 1980, U.S. Court of Appeals, District of Columbia Circuit and U.S. Supreme Court. *Education:* Dickinson College (B.A., 1973); Catholic University of America (J.D., 1976). *Member:* The District of Columbia Bar (Member, Steering Committee of Division 13, Labor Law, 1983-1987); American Bar Association (Member, Section of Labor and Employment Law, Employee Benefits Committee, Sub-Committee Co-Chair, 1990—). ***Email:*** jmader@odonoghuelaw.com

SALLY M. TEDROW, born Boston, Massachusetts, March 1, 1947; admitted to bar, 1977, District of Columbia. *Education:* Wellesley College (B.A., 1969); Catholic University of America (J.D., 1977). Staff Member, 1975-1976 and Note Editor, 1976-1977, Catholic University Law Review. Author: Casenote, "Warth v. Seldin," 25 Catholic University Law Review 417, 1976. *Member:* The District of Columbia Bar; American Bar Association. ***Email:*** stedrow@odonoghuelaw.com

BRIAN A. POWERS, born New York, N.Y., September 27, 1950; admitted to bar, 1977, North Carolina; 1979, District of Columbia and U.S. Court of Appeals, District of Columbia Circuit; 1984, U.S. Court of Appeals, Third Circuit; 1985, U.S. Court of Appeals, Fourth Circuit; 1986, U.S. Court of Appeals, Seventh and Ninth Circuits; 1986, U.S. Supreme Court. *Education:* State University of New York at Oneonta (B.A., 1972); London School of Economics, London, England (M.Sc., 1973); University of North Carolina (J.D., 1977). Staff Member, 1975-1976 and Staff Editor, 1976-1977, University of North Carolina Law Review. Author: "Admiralty Law/Workmen's Compensation-on the waterfront: The Fourth Circuit draws the line at the point of rest in a narrow interpretation of the Longshoremen's and Harbor Workers Compensation Act," 54 NCL Rev. 925, 1976; "Defining the Relationship Between Antitrust Law and Labor Law: Professional Sports and the Current Legal Battleground," 19 W & M L. Rev. 345, 1978. Attorney, National Labor Relations Board, 1977-1979. *Member:* The District of Columbia Bar; North Carolina Bar; American Bar Association. ***Email:*** bpowers@odonoghuelaw.com

JOHN L. BOHMAN, born Dayton, Ohio, September 8, 1951; admitted to bar, 1980, District of Columbia. *Education:* St. Louis University (A.B., 1973); University of Pittsburgh (M.S.W., 1977); Catholic University of America (J.D., 1980). Phi Beta Kappa; Alpha Sigma Nu. Associate Editor, Catholic University Law Review, 1979-1980. *Member:* The District of Columbia Bar; American Bar Association. ***Email:*** jbohman@odonoghuelaw.com

FRANCIS J. MARTORANA, born Brooklyn, New York, January 4, 1951; admitted to bar, 1982, District of Columbia; 1989, U.S. Court of Appeals, District of Columbia; 1988, U.S. Supreme Court. *Education:* LeMoyne College (B.S., 1972); University of Massachusetts (M.S. in Labor Studies, 1974); Catholic University of America (J.D., 1982). Member, 1980-1981 and Senior Staff Member, 1981-1982, Catholic University Law Review. Author: "Federal Preemption: State Strikebreaking Laws and the National Labor Policy," 30 Catholic University Law Review 521, 1981. Assistant General Counsel, International Association of Machinists, 1982-1983. *Member:* The District of Columbia Bar; American Bar Association (Member: Section of Labor and Employment Law; Committee on Labor Arbitration and the Law of Collective Bargaining Agreements). ***Email:*** fmartorana@odonoghuelaw.com

NICHOLAS R. FEMIA, born Weehawken, New Jersey, January 24, 1958; admitted to bar, 1985, New Jersey and U.S. District Court, District of New Jersey; 1986, Pennsylvania and U.S. Court of Appeals, Sixth and Tenth Circuits; 1987, District of Columbia; 1988, U.S. District Court, District of Maryland; U.S. Court of Appeals, Fourth Circuit; 1989, U.S. District Court, District of Columbia; U.S. Court of Appeals, District of Columbia and Eighth Circuits; 1995, U.S. Court of Appeals, Fifth Circuit; 1999, U.S. Court of Appeals, Seventh Circuit; 2000, U.S. Court of Appeals, First Circuit. *Education:* Princeton University (A.B., with honors, 1980); Columbia University (M.A., 1981); New York University (J.D., 1984). Staff Member, 1982-1983 and Articles Editor, 1983-1984, Journal of International Law and Politics, New York University. *Member:* The District of Columbia Bar; New Jersey, Pennsylvania and American (Chapter Co-Chair, Supplements to Employment Discrimination Law, 3rd Edition; assisted in planning and development of American Bar Association EEO Basics Program; Speaker at American Bar Association sponsored programs) Bar Associations. ***PRACTICE AREAS:*** Labor and Employment Law. ***Email:*** nfemia@ononoghuelaw.com

ELLEN O. BOARDMAN, born Washington, D.C., September 30, 1957; admitted to bar, 1983, District of Columbia; 1984, U.S. Court of Appeals, Ninth and Eleventh Circuits; 1985, U.S. Court of Appeals for the District of Columbia Circuit; 1986, U.S. Court of Appeals, First, Second and Fourth Circuits and U.S. District Court for the District of Columbia; 1999, U.S. Supreme Court. *Education:* Catholic University (B.A., magna cum laude, 1979; J.D., 1983). Attorney, Appellate Court Branch, Division of Enforcement Litigation, National Labor Relations Board, 1983-1986. *Member:* The District of Columbia Bar (Member, Labor Law Section); American Bar Association. ***Email:*** eboardman@odonoghuelaw.com

CHARLES W. GILLIGAN, born Salem, Massachusetts, February 2, 1960; admitted to bar, 1985, District of Columbia; 1986, Maryland, District of Columbia Court of Appeals; U.S. District Court, District of Maryland, U.S. District Court for the District of Columbia and U.S. Court of Appeals, Second and Fourth Circuits. *Education:* Brandeis University (B.A., 1982); Catholic University (J.D., 1985). *Member:* The District of Columbia Bar (Member, Sections on Labor and Employment Law); Maryland State and American Bar Associations. ***PRACTICE AREAS:*** Labor and Employment. ***Email:*** cgilligan@odonoghuelaw.com

LOUIS P. MALONE III, born Detroit, Michigan, November 29, 1954; admitted to bar, 1980, Michigan; 1982, District of Columbia and U.S. District Court, Eastern District of Michigan; 1983, U.S. Court of Appeals, Fifth Circuit; 1984, U.S. Court of Appeals, First Circuit; 1985, U.S. Court of Appeals, Third Circuit; 1987, U.S. District Court, District of Columbia; 1989, U.S. Court of Appeals, Fourth Circuit; U.S. District Court for the District of Maryland. *Education:* Aquinas College; Michigan State University (B.A., 1976); Detroit College of Law (J.D., 1980). Member, Moot Court Board. Instructor, Legal Research and Writing, Detroit College of Law, 1981. *Member:* State Bar of Michigan; The District of Columbia Bar; American Bar Association (Member, Section on Labor and Employment; Co-Chairman, Committee on Railway and Airline Labor Law, 1985-1988; Committee on Employee Benefits, Co-Chairman, Sub Committee on ERISA Preemption, 1988—). ***Email:*** lmalone@odonoghuelaw.com

MARY CAPUANO FELLER, born Washington, D. C., December 28, 1961; admitted to bar, 1986, Pennsylvania; 1987, U.S. District Court, District of Maryland; 1992, District of Columbia; 1993, U.S. Supreme Court. *Education:* University of South Carolina (B.S., cum laude, 1983); Catholic University of America (J.D., 1986). Phi Beta Kappa. Member and Senior Staff Member, Catholic University Law Review, 1984-1986. *Member:* Pennsylvania and American Bar Associations; District of Columbia Bar. ***Email:*** mfeller@odonoghuelaw.com

JOHN LEARY, born Abington, Pennsylvania, September 20, 1949; admitted to bar, 1987, Pennsylvania; 1988, U.S. District Court, District of Maryland; 1999, District of Columbia. *Education:* St. Joseph's College (B.A., 1971); University of Maryland (M.A., 1974; Ph. D., 1981); Catholic University of America School of Law (J.D., 1987). Alpha Sigma Nu; Phi Kappa Phi. Attorney, Division

(This Listing Continued)

(This Listing Continued)

of Advice, National Labor Relations Board, 1987-1988. Adjunct Professor, Columbus School of Law, Catholic University of America, 1995-2001. *Member:* Pennsylvania and American Bar Associations; The District of Columbia Bar. ***Email:*** jleary@odonoghuelaw.com

JOHN R. HARNEY, born Boston, Massachusetts, August 31, 1955; admitted to bar, 1989, Wisconsin, U.S. District Court, Eastern and Western Districts of Wisconsin and U.S. District Court, District of Maryland; 1990, District of Columbia; 1997, Virginia; 1998, Maryland. *Education:* University of California, Berkeley (B.A., 1978); University of Wisconsin, Madison (M.S., 1981; J.D., 1989). Author, "Perhaps Because They Are Deadbeats: The Use of Injunctive Relief in ERISA Collection Cases," 22 Employee Benefits Journal 31 (March 1997). *Member:* Maryland and American Bar Associations; The District of Columbia Bar; State Bar of Wisconsin; Virginia State Bar. ***PRACTICE AREAS:*** Employee Benefits. ***Email:*** jharney@donoghuelaw.com

R. RICHARD HOPP, born Seattle, Washington, August 3, 1964; admitted to bar, 1990, Maryland, U.S. District Court, District of Maryland and U.S. Court of Appeals, Fourth Circuit; 1992, District of Columbia, U.S. District Court, District of Columbia and U.S. Court of Appeals, District of Columbia; 1995, U.S. Supreme Court. *Education:* University of Washington (B.A., 1986); University of Maryland (J.D., with honors, 1989). Order of the Coif. Author: "Cartier v. K-Mart: The Supreme Court Decides The Gray Market Problem" 13 Md. J. Intl. & Td. (1990). Law Clerk to United States District Court Judge Joseph C. Howard. *Member:* Maryland State Bar Association, Inc.; American Bar Association (Member, Labor and Litigation Sections). ***Email:*** rhopp@odonoghuelaw.com

GERARD M. WAITES, born Levittown, Pennsylvania, April 13, 1959; admitted to bar, 1989, Pennsylvania (Not admitted in District of Columbia). *Education:* Allentown College of St. Francis De Sales (B .A., cum laude, 1983); University of Baltimore (J.D., 1989). Member, University of Baltimore Law Forum, 1988-1989. Author: "Revitalizing The Maryland Wage Compensation Law," The Law Form, Univ. of Baltimore School of Law, Summer 1989, Vol 19. 3. *Member:* Pennsylvania and American (Member, Sections on Labor & Employment, Public Contract Law; Former Co-Chairman, Committee on Federal Legislative Development, 1993-1995) Bar Associations; Pennsylvania Trial Lawyers Association (Member, Section on Public Contract Law). ***Email:*** gwaites@odonoghuelaw.com

MARK W. KUNST, born Grafton, West Virginia, February 11, 1959; admitted to bar, 1989, Maryland; 1991, District of Columbia. *Education:* University of Delaware (B.A.A.S., 1986); Delaware Law School of Widener University (J.D., 1989); Georgetown University Law Center (LL.M., in Tax, 1995). ***Email:*** mkunst@odonoghuelaw.com

ROBERT P. CURLEY, born Philadelphia, Pennsylvania, December 30, 1953; admitted to bar, 1989, Pennsylvania, New Jersey, U.S. District Court, Eastern District of Pennsylvania and U.S. District Court, District of New Jersey (Not admitted in District of Columbia). *Education:* George Washington University (B.A., 1975); Temple University School of Law (J.D., 1989). Recipient, American Jurisprudence Award in Federal Courts and Jurisdiction. Law Clerk to the Honorable Lowell A. Reed Jr., U.S. District Court for the Eastern District of Pennsylvania, 1989-1991. Professor; Advisory Board Member, St. Joseph's University. President: Philadelphia Chapter, Lorney Institute; Industrial Relations Research Association, 2001-2002. *Member:* Philadelphia, Pennsylvania and American Bar Associations. ***PRACTICE AREAS:*** Labor and Employment; ERISA.

ASSOCIATES

DANIEL JAMES McNEIL, born Livonia, Michigan, January 20, 1971; admitted to bar, 1998, District of Columbia and U.S. District Court, District of Maryland. *Education:* Michigan State University (B.A., International Relations, 1993); Georgetown University (J.D., 1997). ***PRACTICE AREAS:*** Labor and Employment Law; ERISA. ***Email:*** dmcneil@odonoghuelaw.com

TERESA WHITE MURRAY, born Cincinnati, Ohio, April 12, 1972; admitted to bar, 1998, Maryland, District of Columbia, U.S. District Court, District of Maryland , U.S. District Court, District of Columbia, U.S. Court of Appeals, Fourth Circuit and U.S. Court of Appeals for the District of Columbia. *Education:* Howard University (B.A., 1994); George Washington University (J.D., 1997). *Member:* District of Columbia Bar; Maryland State, Federal and American Bar Associations. ***PRACTICE AREAS:*** Labor and Employment Law; EEO; Employee Benefits. ***Email:*** tmurray@odonoghuelaw.com

DINAH S. LEVENTHAL, born Bethesda, Maryland, October 24, 1966; admitted to bar, 1996, Maryland; 1997, District of Columbia. *Education:* Harvard University (A.B., cum laude,1988); University of Maryland (J.D., with honors, 1996). Member, Maryland Law Review (1994-1995). Notes and Comments Editor, Maryland Law Review (1995-1996). Member, Maryland Chapter Order of the Coif. Law Clerk, Hon. William M. Nickerson, U.S. District Court, District of Maryland, 1996-1997. *Member:* Maryland State and American Bar Associations; District of Columbia Bar. ***REPORTED CASES:*** Lee v. Vance Exec. Protection Inc., 2001 U.S. App. Lexis 1849 (4th Cir); Tradesource, Inc. v. NLRB, 2001 U.S. App. Lexis 19285 (4th Cir.); Waldinger Corp. v. NLRB, 2001 U.S. App. Lexis 19053 (11th Cir.). ***PRACTICE AREAS:*** Labor and Employment; Employee Benefit Law. ***Email:*** dleventhal@odonoghuelaw.com

(This Listing Continued)

JEAN M. KELLY, born Glen Ridge, New Jersey, March 19, 1967; admitted to bar, 1996, New York, New Jersey, and U.S. District Court, Southern and Eastern Districts of New York and District of New Jersey; 1997, District of Columbia. *Education:* University of Notre Dame (B.A., 1989); Fordham University (J.D., 1995). *Member:* American Bar Association. ***PRACTICE AREAS:*** Labor and Employment Law; Employee Benefits. ***Email:*** jkelly@odonoghuelaw.com

KEITH R. BOLEK, born Cleveland, Ohio, May 15, 1972; admitted to bar, 1998, Maryland; 1999, District of Columbia and U.S. District Court, District of Maryland; U.S. Court of Appeals, Fourth, Fifth and Eleventh Circuits; 2000, U.S. District Court, District of Columbia; U.S. Court of Appeals, Third, Sixth, Seventh, Eighth Circuits. *Education:* American University (B.A., magna cum laude, 1994); Washington College of Law, American University (J.D., magna cum laude, 1998). Contributing Editor, Developing Labor Law; Assistant Editor, How to Take a Case Before the NLRB. *Member:* Bar Association of the Fifth Circuit; District of Columbia Bar Association (Member, Lawyers Coordinating Committee); Maryland State and American Bar Associations. ***PRACTICE AREAS:*** Labor and Employment Law; ERISA. ***Email:*** kbolek@odonoghuelaw.com

GREGORY F. MOORE, born Astoria, New York, August 31, 1960; admitted to bar, 1996, Maryland; 2000, District of Columbia. *Education:* Loyola University (B.A., 1982); Seattle University School of Law (J.D., 1994). *Member:* American Bar Association (Member Sections On: Labor and Employment; Employee Benefits Committee). ***PRACTICE AREAS:*** Employee Benefits; Labor and Employment. ***Email:*** gmoore@odonoughelaw.com

DAVID D. CAPUANO, born Washington, D.C., June 17, 1967; admitted to bar, 1994, Pennsylvania and U.S. District Court, District of Maryland (Not admitted in District of Columbia). *Education:* James Madison University (B.A., 1990); Catholic University of America (J.D., 1993). *Member:* Philadelphia Bar Association. ***PRACTICE AREAS:*** Employee Benefits; Labor. ***Email:*** ddcapuano@odonoghuelaw.com

TODD BITNER CASTLETON, born Salt Lake City, Utah, January 18, 1969; admitted to bar, 1996, Virginia; 1998, District of Columbia. *Education:* University of Utah (B.S., with honors, 1993); George Mason University School of Law (J.D., 1996); Georgetown University National Law Center (LL.M., 1999). Dean's Scholar. Phi Alpha Delta. George Mason Law Review, Board of Editors. Law Clerk, Fourth Judicial Circuit Court of Virginia (1996-1997). Author, "Compounding Fraud", 4 Geo. Mason L. Rev., 1996. Adjunct Professor, George Mason University School of Law (1999-2000). *Member:* Virginia, District of Columbia and American Bar Associations. [U.S.M.C., 1988]. ***PRACTICE AREAS:*** Employee Benefits; ERISA; Labor and Employment; Litigation. ***Email:*** tcastleton@odonoghuelaw.com

JOHN M. McINTIRE, born Cheverly, Maryland, 1963; admitted to bar, 1993, Maryland; 1994, District of Columbia and U.S. District Court, District of Maryland; 1997, U.S. Court of Appeals, Fourth Circuit; 2000, U.S. District Court, District of Columbia. *Education:* University of Maryland (B.A., 1989; J.D., with Honors, 1993). *Member:* District of Columbia Bar; Maryland and American Bar Associations. ***Email:*** jmcintire@odonoghuelaw.com

JAMIE PRICE, born New York, August 15, 1976; (admission pending). *Education:* University of Michigan (B.A., 1998); George Washington University (J.D., 2001). ***PRACTICE AREAS:*** ERISA; Labor Law. ***Email:*** jprice@odonoghuelaw.com

OF COUNSEL

PHYLLIS C. BORZI, born Port Jefferson, New York, August 10, 1946; admitted to bar, 1978, District of Columbia. *Education:* Ladycliff College (B.A., 1968); Syracuse University (M.A., 1970); Catholic University of America (J.D.). Editor-in-Chief, Law Review, 1977-1978. Member, Advisory Board, BNA Pension and Benefits Reporter. Research Professor, Center for Health Services Research and Policy, School of Public Health and Health Services, The George Washington University. Member, Pension Benefit Guaranty Corporation Advisory Committee. *Member:* American Bar Association; American Health Lawyers Association; Women's Bar Association. Charter Fellow: American College of Employee Benefit Counsel. ***PRACTICE AREAS:*** Employee Benefits (ERISA); Health Law. ***Email:*** pborzi@odonoghuelaw.com

OGLETREE, DEAKINS, NASH, SMOAK & STEWART, P.C.

FIFTH FLOOR, 2400 N STREET, N.W.
WASHINGTON, D.C. 20037
Telephone: 202-887-0855
Facsimile: 202-887-0866
Email: Washington@odnss.com
URL: http://www.ogletreedeakins.com

Atlanta, Georgia Office: 600 Peachtree Street, N.E., Suite 2100. Telephone: 404-881-1300.
Birmingham, Alabama Office: 1900 SouthTrust Tower, 420 North 20th Street. Telephone: 205-328-1900.
Charleston, South Carolina Office: 134 Meeting Street, Suite 500, P.O. Box 1808. Telephone: 843-853-1300.
Chicago, Illinois Office: Twenty-Fifth Floor, Two First National Plaza, 20 South Clark Street. Telephone: 312-558-1220.
Columbia, South Carolina Office: 1501 Main Street, Suite 600, P.O. Box 11206. Telephone: 803-252-1300.
Dallas, Texas Office: 700 Preston Commons, 8117 Preston Road. Telephone: 214-987-3800.
Greenville, South Carolina Office: The Ogletree Building, 300 North Main Street, P.O. Box 2757. Telephone: 864-271-1300.
Houston, Texas Office: One Allen Center, 500 Dallas Street, Suite 3000. Telephone: 713-655-0855.
Indianapolis, Indiana Office: Suite 2300, One Indiana Square. Telephone: 317-916-1300.
Nashville, Tennessee Office: SunTrust Center, Suite 800, 424 Church Street. Telephone: 615-254-1900.
Raleigh, North Carolina Office: 2301 Sugar Bush Road, P.O. Box 31608. Telephone: 919-787-9700.
San Antonio, Texas Office: 100 West Houston Street, Suite 1700. Telephone: 210-354-1300.
St. Thomas, U.S. Virgin Islands Office: The Tunick Building, 1336 Beltjen Road, Suite 202. Telephone: 340-714-1235.

Labor Relations, Employment, Employee Benefits, Occupational Safety and Health, Environmental, Construction and Immigration Law, Legislation. Civil Litigation in all State and Federal Courts and before Administrative Agencies.

J. FRANK OGLETREE, JR. (1930-1985).

PETER G. NASH (1937-1993).

DIXIE L. ATWATER (1948-1992).

JOHN A. PENELLO (1909-1998).

PETER H. KIEFER, born Leoben, Austria, April 25, 1948; admitted to bar, 1975, Virginia; 1976, District of Columbia; 1980, U.S. Supreme Court. *Education:* Georgetown University, School of Foreign Service (B.S.F.S., 1970); International School of Law (J.D. 1975). *Member:* The District of Columbia Bar; Virginia State Bar; American Bar Association. ***PRACTICE AREAS:*** Management Labor Law; Employment Law. ***Email:*** peter.kiefer@odnss.com

DAVID S. FORTNEY, born Lafayette, Indiana, December 8, 1954; admitted to bar, 1980, Pennsylvania; 1997, District of Columbia. *Education:* Pennsylvania State University (B.A., 1977); Duquesne University School of Law (J.D., 1980). Acting Solicitor, 1991, Deputy Solicitor, 1990-1992 and Associate Deputy Solicitor, 1989-1990, U.S. Department of Labor, Office of the Solicitor. *Member:* American Bar Association (Equal Employment Opportunity Committee); National Association of Manufacturers; Employment Lawyers Advisory Committee. ***PRACTICE AREAS:*** Labor; Employment; Litigation. ***Email:*** david.fortney@odnss.com

HAROLD P. COXSON, JR., born Camden, New Jersey, October 26, 1947; admitted to bar, 1972, New Jersey; 1981, District of Columbia. *Education:* Franklin & Marshall College (A.B., 1969); American University (J.D., 1972). Principal, Ogletree Governmental Affairs, Inc. Managing Editor, American University Law Review, 1971-1972. U.S. Employer Advisor, International Labor Conference, 1980-1985. Employer Representative, President's Tripartite Advisory Panel on International Labor Standards, 1980-1988. Member, NLRB's Advisory Panel (Management), 1994—. Member, Labor Relations Committee, and Chairman, Sub-Committee on Workplace Trends and International Perspectives, U.S. Chamber of Commerce. Member, Committee on Employment Law, National Retail Federation, 1992—. Labor Law Attorney, 1975-1977 and Director of Labor, 1977-1980, U.S. Chamber of Commerce. Appellate Attorney, Office of the Solicitor, U.S. Department of Labor, 1972-1974. Board of Editors, HR Advisor (Warren, Gorham & Lamont). *Member:* District of Columbia and New Jersey Bars; American Bar Association (Chairman, Labor Law Committee, International Law Section, 1986-1987). ***PRACTICE AREAS:*** Labor Legislation; Labor and Employment Law; Alternative Dispute Resolution; International Labor Law; Trade and Professional Associations. ***Email:*** hal.coxson@odnss.com

(This Listing Continued)

BERNARD P. JEWELER, born Washington, D.C., November 14, 1945; admitted to bar, 1970, Maryland; 1974, U.S. Supreme Court; 1989, District of Columbia; 1990, New York. *Education:* University of Maryland (B.A., 1967); George Washington University (J.D., with honors, 1970). Attorney, National Labor Relations Board Appellate Court Branch, 1976-1982. Deputy Assistant General Counsel, National Labor Relations Board, 1982-1988. Assistant General Counsel for Contempt Litigation, National Labor Relations Board, 1988-1989. *Member:* Maryland State Bar, New York State and American Bar Associations; The District of Columbia Bar. ***PRACTICE AREAS:*** Labor and Employment; Collective Bargaining; Labor Arbitration; Labor Litigation. ***Email:*** bernard.jeweler@odnss.com

MICHAEL J. MURPHY, born Philadelphia, Pennsylvania, April 1, 1963; admitted to bar, 1989, District of Columbia. *Education:* Lafayette College (B.A., 1985); Catholic University (J.D., 1989). Recipient: American Jurisprudence Award in Labor Law; Plato Papps Labor Law Scholarship. Contributor, *Americans With Disabilities Act: Employee Rights And Employer Obligations,* Matthew Bender, 1992. *Member:* The District of Columbia Bar; American Bar Association. ***PRACTICE AREAS:*** Labor and Employment; Employment Litigation; Equal Employment Opportunity Law; Employment Contracts; Fair Labor Standards; National Labor Relations Act. ***Email:*** michael.murphy@odnss.com

BURTON J. FISHMAN, born Los Angeles, California, December 17, 1942; admitted to bar, 1979, District of Columbia; 1986, New York; 1992, Maryland. *Education:* Occidental College (B.A., magna cum laude, 1964); Cambridge University, Cambridge, England (B.A., Hons., 1966); Princeton University (Ph.D., 1969); Yale University (J.D., 1979). Phi Beta Kappa. Author: "Working With AIDS," HR Advisor, Jan/Feb 1998; "Psychological Disabilities," HR Advisor, Sept/Oct 1997; "ADA and Workers Compensation," HR Advisor, May/June 1997. Co-Author: "Collective Bargaining in the 1980s: A Prospective Analysis," Hofstra L. Rev. (1983). Contributor to Employment Discrimination Law: Schlei and Grossman, Second Edition ("Reverse Discrimination"), 1983. Principal Editor: Legal Dilemmas in the Changing Workplace, Nat'l Legal Center for the Public Interest (1988). General Editor, A Comparison of Labor Law in the U.S. and Mexico: An Overview, (1992), Editorial Board, HR Advisor. Deputy Solicitor, National Operations, U.S. Dept. of Labor, 1992-1993. *Member:* Bar Association of the District of Columbia; Maryland State, New York State and American (Co-Chair, Mgt., Federal Legislative Developments Committee; Member, Equal Employment Opportunity Committee of Labor and Employment Section) Bar Associations; Maryland Bar Association Inc. ***PRACTICE AREAS:*** Labor Law; Employment Discrimination Law; ERISA. ***Email:*** info@odnss.com

J. ROBERT BRAME, III, born Hopkinsville, Kentucky, April 18, 1942; admitted to bar, 1968, Virginia (Not admitted in District of Columbia). *Education:* Vanderbilt University (B.A., cum laude, 1964); Yale University (LL.B., 1967). Phi Beta Kappa. Author: "Significant Developments in Robinson-Patman Act Law Relating to Injury to Competition and Proof of Damage Standards," American Bar Association, 39th Antitrust Spring Meeting, 1991; "How to Maintain the Labor Peace," in Allen *How to Keep Your Company Out of Court,* Prentice Hall, 1984. Co-Author: "The Immunity of Local Governments and Their Officials to Antitrust After City of Boulder," 16 U Rich L. Rev. 705, 1982; "Equal Opportunity Law: Defending Fair Employment Cases," DRI 1976. Chairman, Tenth Amendment Committee, Governor's Council on Self-Determination and Federalism, 1994—. General Counsel, Republican Party of Virginia, 1993-1996. Third District Committee of Virginia State Bar, 1980-1983; Co-Chairman, 1982-1983. Fellow, American Bar Foundation. *Member:* Virginia State Bar; American Bar Association. (Richmond and Charlottesville Offices). ***PRACTICE AREAS:*** Labor; Employment; Litigation. ***Email:*** robert.brame@odnss.com

REGINALD E. JONES, born Youngstown, Ohio, June 25, 1950; admitted to bar, 1977, New York; 1990, District of Columbia. *Education:* Yale University (B.A., 1972); New York University (M.B.A., 1976; J.D., 1976). Goldman Sacks Fellow. Author: "The Future of Employment Discrimination Law: The Views of a Former EEOC Commissioner," The Metropolitan Corporate Counsel, March 2001; "Are We Witnessing a Kinder, Gentler EEOC? The EEOC's Task Force Report on Best Private Sector EEO and Diversity Practices and Other Agency Trends," The Labor Lawyer, Vol. 14, No. 2, Fall 1998. Co-Author, with Leibold and Sola, "Civil Rights Act of 1991: Race to the Finish -- Civil Rights, Quotas and Disparate Impact in 1991," Rutgers Law Journal, Vol. 45, No. 4, Summer 1993. Chairman, Task Force Report on Best Equal Employment Opportunity Policies, Programs and Practices in the Private Sector, Equal Employment Opportunity Commission, September 1997, December, 1997, February 1998. *Member:* The District of Columbia Bar; National Bar Association; National Employment Law Council. ***PRACTICE AREAS:*** Labor and Employment; Equal Employment Opportunity Law; Alternative Dispute Resolution. ***Email:*** reg.jones@odnss.com

STEVEN R. SEMLER, born New York, N.Y., May 7, 1945; admitted to bar, 1971, District of Columbia. *Education:* Hunter College (B.A., 1967); George Washington University (J.D., 1970). National Moot Court Competition, 1968. National Labor Relations Board, Enforcement Litigation Division. *Member:*

(This Listing Continued)

The District of Columbia Bar; American Bar Association (Member: Section on Labor and Employment Law; Committee on Practice and Procedure before the National Labor Relations Board, 1979—). ***PRACTICE AREAS:*** Labor Law; Employment Discrimination Law; OSHA. ***Email:*** steven.semler@odnss.com

---

YOORA KIM, born Kwangju, South Korea, March 30, 1970; admitted to bar, 1995, Virginia; 2000, District of Columbia. *Education:* Cornell University (B.S., 1992); George Washington University (J.D., 1995; LL.M., International and Comparative Law, 2001). ***PRACTICE AREAS:*** Labor and Employment; Litigation; Employment Discrimination; Employment Litigation; Labor Law. ***Email:*** yoora.kim@odnss.com

CONSUELA A. PINTO, born Belleville, New Jersey, August 4, 1970; admitted to bar, 1995, Maryland; 1996, New Jersey; 1998, District of Columbia. *Education:* Boston University (B.S., 1992); Syracuse University College of Law (J.D., cum laude, 1995). U.S. Department of Labor, Office of the Solicitor, 1995-1998. ***PRACTICE AREAS:*** Labor and Employment; Litigation; Employment Discrimination; Employment Litigation; Labor Law. ***Email:*** consuela.pinto@odnss.com

RAFAEL E. MORELL, born San Juan, Puerto Rico, April 19, 1973; admitted to bar, 1999, District of Columbia. *Education:* University at Albany (B.A., 1995); Cornell Law School (J.D., 1998). Arthur S. Chatman Labor Law Prize, Cornell Law School. *Member:* Labor and Employment Law Section, District of Columbia Bar. ***PRACTICE AREAS:*** Labor and Employment. ***Email:*** rafael.morell@odnss.com

OF COUNSEL

STANLEY R. STRAUSS, born New York, New York, June 3, 1915; admitted to bar, 1941, New York; 1964, District of Columbia; 1965, U.S. Supreme Court. *Education:* Williams College (B.A., cum laude, 1936); Columbia University (LL.B., Horn Scholar, 1940). National Labor Relations Board: Supervising Attorney, 1953-1959 and Chief Counsel, 1959-1963. Co-author: *Practice and Procedure Before the National Labor Relations Board,* American Law Institute-American Bar Association, 1980, 1987 and 1996. *Member:* The District of Columbia Bar; American Bar Association. ***PRACTICE AREAS:*** Labor and Employment; National Labor Relations Act; Management Labor Law; Appellate Practice. ***Email:*** stanley.strauss@odnss.com

REPRESENTATIVE CLIENTS: AMCAST Industrial Corporation; American Red Cross; American Textile Manufacturers Institute; American Academy of Adoption Attorneys; American University; AmeriVision Communications, Inc.; Asplundh Tree Expert Co.; Associated General Contractors of America; Atlantic Research Corp.; Barclays Global Investors; BASF Corp.; Becon Construction Co.; The Budd Co.; Burlington Industries, Inc.; Burns Security Services International; The Business Roundatable; Century Aluminum (Ravenswood); Chevron USA Products Co.; Cingular Wireless; Coalition on Occupational Safety and Health; Collins & Aikman; Coors Brewing Company; Council on Labor Law Equality; Deere & Co.; Duke Energy Corp.; Dynatech Corp.; Eastman Chemical Company; Eastman Kodak Co.; Eka Chemicals, Inc.; Electronic Industries Alliance; Emery Worldwide; Fluor Corporation; Gallaudet University; General Electric Co.; W.R. Grace & Co.; John Hancock Life Insurance Co.; Hitachi Electronics Devices, Inc.; Hoechst Celanese Corp.; Kobe Steel USA, Inc.; Laidlaw Waste Systems, Inc.; Lockheed Martin Corp.; McGraw-Edison Co.; Mercedes-Benz U.S. International, Inc.; Michelin Tire Corporation; Minnesota Mining and Manufacturing Co.; National Arborists Association; Nissan North America, Inc.; Oracle Corporation; Penske Truck Leasing Corp.; Pfizer, Inc.; Pitt-Des Moines, Inc.; Printing Industries of America; Quebecor Printing (U.S.A.) Inc.; Richfood, Inc.; Roadway Services, Inc.; Rockwell International; Ryobi Motor Products, Inc.; Sallie Mae, Inc.; Schlumberger; Society for Human Resource Management; Sysco, Corp.; U.S. Chamber of Commerce; Valero Energy Corp.; Winn-Dixie Stores, Inc.; YKK (USA), Inc.

OLDAKER & BIDEN, LLP

818 CONNECTICUT AVENUE, N.W.
SUITE 1100
WASHINGTON, D.C. 20006
Telephone: 202-728-1010
Facsimile: 202-728-4044
Email: rhb@aldaker-biden.com
URL: http://www.oldaker-biden.com

Federal Administrative and Legislative Practice, Elections, Campaign Finance, Lobbying Disclosures and Ethics, Transportation, Communications, Internet Law, Intellectual Property.

FIRM PROFILE: Oldaker & Biden, formerly Oldaker & Harris is one of the nation's leading legislative lobbying and campaign finance law firms. The firm represents trade associations, corporations, campaign organizations, and state and local governments throughout the United States.

WILLIAM C. OLDAKER, born Evanston, Illinois, May 8, 1941; admitted to bar, 1966, Iowa; 1969, District of Columbia; 1970, U.S. Court of Appeals for the District of Columbia Circuit ; 1973, Colorado and The U.S. Supreme Court. *Education:* University of Iowa (LL.B., 1966). Attorney, Federal Communications Commission, 1968-1969; Special Assistant to the Chairman of the Equal Employment Opportunity Commission, 1969-1973. General Counsel, Federal Election Commission, 1976-1979. Counsel/Treasurer, Kennedy for President Committee, 1979-1980. General Counsel, Biden for President Committee, 1987-1988. *Member:* District of Columbia Bar.

R. HUNTER BIDEN, born Wilmington, Delaware, February 4, 1970; admitted to bar, 1996, Connecticut (Not admitted in District of Columbia). *Education:* Georgetown University (B.A., 1992); Yale University (J.D., 1996). Presidential Appointee, U.S. Department of Commerce, Executive Director for E-Commerce Policy Coordination under Secretaries Daley and Mineta, 1998. ***PRACTICE AREAS:*** Internet Law; International Trade; Information Technology; Intellectual Property. ***Email:*** rhb@oldaker-biden.com

---

JACK H. OLENDER AND ASSOCIATES, P.C.

Established in 1961
888 17TH STREET, N.W., 4TH FLOOR
WASHINGTON, D.C. 20006
Telephone: 202-879-7777
Fax: 202-393-2245
URL: http://www.olender.com
Email: jhopc@olender.com
URL: http://www.lawyers.com/olenderlaw

Malpractice Law, Personal Injury, General Negligence Trials and Appeals, Products Liability.

FIRM PROFILE: Jack H. Olender and Associates represents victims of medical malpractice and other catastrophically injured individuals in the courts of the District of Columbia and the surrounding metropolitan Washington, D.C. jurisdictions. The firm is recognized in obstetrical negligence cases, failure to diagnose cancer cases, anesthesia cases, infectious disease cases, and many other areas of medical practice. The attorneys at Jack H. Olender and Associates frequently lecture the legal and medical professions on medical-legal issues of importance to both professions.

JACK H. OLENDER, born McKeesport, Pennsylvania, September 8, 1935; admitted to bar, 1961, District of Columbia; 1965, U.S. Supreme Court; 1966, Maryland; 1985, Pennsylvania. *Education:* University of Pittsburgh (A.B., summa cum laude, 1957; J.D., 1960); George Washington University (LL.M., 1961). Phi Beta Kappa. Recipient: 1994 Distinguished Alumnus Award, George Washington University National Law Center; 1993 Golden Apple Award, Howard University Law School; Presidential Award 1996, National Bar Association; Ollie May Cooper Award 1996, Washington Bar Association; Outstanding Leader Award, Trial Lawyers Association of Metropolitan Washington, D.C., 1998. Distinguished Alumnus of the Year, 1996, University of Pittsburgh Law School. Article Editor, University of Pittsburgh, 1959-1960. Author: " "Obstetric Negligence," An Introduction to a High-Risk Specialty, TRIAL Magazine, May 1984; "Lessons in Malpractice: 12 Ways to Prevent Lawsuits," Group Practice Journal, May/June 1986; "The Great Insurance Fraud of the '80s," The National Law Journal, July 21, 1986; "Medical Malpractice—A Plan for its Cure," Medical Malpractice Prevention, Nov./Dec. 1987; "How to Avoid Problems with Doctors," Every Day Law, March 1989; "Medical Negligence Can Invite Legal Negligence," TRIAL Magazine, May 1989; "Medical Malpractice and the Shroud of Secrecy," NBA Magazine, Vol. 4 No. 11, November 1990. Trial Lawyer of the Year, Trial Lawyers Association of Metropolitan Washington, D.C., 1972. Lawyer of the Year, Bar Association of the District of Columbia, 1991. Member, District of Columbia Judicial Conference, 1976-1991, 1994—. President, Washington Area Chapter, George Washington University Law School Alumni, 1986-1988. Member: Board of Advisors, Anesthesia Malpractice Prevention, 1996—; Greater Washington Urban League, 1985—; Board of Directors, African-American Civil War Memorial Freedom Foundation, 1994—; Board of Visitors, Pittsburgh University Law School; Board of Visitors, Howard University School of Law. *Member:* District of Columbia Bar (Chairman, Personal Injury Law Division, 1974-1982); Bar Association of the District of Columbia (President, 1999-2000); Maryland Trial Lawyers Association; The Association of Trial Lawyers of America (Member, Board of Governors, 1973-1976); Trial Lawyers Association of Metropolitan Washington, D.C. (President, 1969-1970); George Washington American Inns of Court (President, 1991-1992); Trial Lawyers for Public Justice (Member, Board of Directors, 1991—); International Association of Jewish Lawyers and Jurists (Member, Board of Directors, 1992—); World Peace Through Law Center; American Board of Professional Liability Attorneys (Secretary, 1989—); American College of Legal Medicine; The Inner Circle of Advocates; American Board of Trial Advocates (President, D.C. Chapter, 1993-1995). Fellow: American College of Trial Lawyers; International Academy of Trial Lawyers; American Bar Foundation. Certified as a Civil Trial Advocate by the National Board of Trial Advocacy. ***PRACTICE AREAS:*** Malpractice; Products Liability; Personal Injury. ***Email:*** jhopc@olender.com

(This Listing Continued)

JACK H. OLENDER AND ASSOCIATES, P.C., Washington—Continued

HARLOW R. CASE, born Ilion, New York, November 6, 1953; admitted to bar, 1979, District of Columbia. *Education:* Syracuse University (B.A., magna cum laude, 1974); George Washington University (J.D., 1979). Phi Beta Kappa; Phi Kappa Phi; Phi Alpha Theta; Pi Sigma Alpha. Recipient, Trial Lawyer of the Year, Trial Lawyers Association of Metropolitan Washington, D.C., 1996-1997. Member: Judicial Conference of the District of Columbia, 1983-1988, 1991; Judicial Conference of the District of Columbia Circuit, 1990—; U.S. District Court, District of Columbia Civil Justice Reform Act Advisory Group, 1992; Frederick B. Abramson Memorial Foundation, Board of Directors, 1996—; The Roscoe Pound Foundation. Volunteer Mediator and Arbitrator: Superior Court, District of Columbia; U.S. District Court, District of Columbia; U.S. Court of Appeals, District of Columbia. Trustee, The Washington Opera, 1996-1998. Member, Board of Directors, Washington Concert Opera, 1997—. *Member:* The District of Columbia Bar (Co-Chair, Personal Injury Section Steering Committee, 1986, 1992; Member: Alternate Dispute Resolution Committee, 1987-1990; Nominating Committee, 1997; Service to Members Task Force, 1997-1998); Bar Association of the District of Columbia (Vice Chair, Civil Jury Instructions Committee, 1985-1987); Trial Lawyers for Public Justice; The Association of Trial Lawyers of America (State Delegate, 1994; Member, Board of Governors, 1995—; Vice-Chair, National Law Student Trial Advocacy Committee, 1998; Coordinating Host, Moot Court National Championships, 1998); Trial Lawyers Association of Metropolitan Washington, D.C. (President, 1987-1988). ***PRACTICE AREAS:*** Malpractice; Personal Injury. ***Email:*** harlowcase@olender.com

SANDRA H. ROBINSON, born Lynchburg, Virginia, July 17, 1951; admitted to bar, 1983, Maryland; 1985, District of Columbia. *Education:* Oberlin College (B.A., 1973); Catholic University of America (J.D., 1982). Recipient: Presidential Award, National Bar Association, 1996; Charlotte E. Ray Award, Greater Washington Area Chapter, Women's Division, National Bar Association, 1998; Trial Lawyer of the Year, Trial Lawyers Association of Metropolitan Washington, D.C., 2000-2001. Senior Attorney, Federal Election Commission, 1987-1990. Faculty, National Institute for Trial Advocacy, Georgetown Law School, 1999. *Member:* Washington, Maryland State, National (Past Chair, Legal and Legislative Committees, 1995-1996) and American Bar Associations; Bar Association of the District of Columbia (Member, Board of Directors, 1998-2000); District of Columbia Bar; The Association of Trial Lawyers of America (Member, Board of Directors, 1998; Delegate, Minority Caucus, 1997—); Maryland Trial Lawyers Association; Trial Lawyers for Public Justice (Member, Board of Directors, 1999—); Trial Lawyers Association of Metropolitan Washington, D.C. (President, 1997-1998); Women's Bar Association Foundation (Member, Board of Governors, 1997—; Treasurer, 1998-2000; President, 2000—); Charlotte E. Ray American Inn of Court (Master, 1994—); Women's Bar Association. ***PRACTICE AREAS:*** Medical Malpractice; Personal Injury; Products Liability. ***Email:*** shrobinson@olender.com

KIM KEENAN SOLOMON, born Buffalo, New York, January 19, 1962; admitted to bar, 1988, Virginia; 1989 District of Columbia; 1994, Maryland. *Education:* Georgetown University (B.S., 1983); University of Virginia (J.D., 1987). Recipient: Presidential Award, Washington Bar Association, 1999; Presidential Award, National Bar Association, 1998; Student Support Award, National Association of Black Women Attorneys, 1989; Special Project of the Year Award, Bar Association of the District of Columbia, 1997; Marvin E. Preis Outstanding Committee Chair of the Year Awards, Bar Association of the District of Columbia, Young Lawyers Section, 1997; Outstanding Achievement Award, Washington Bar Association, 1997. Adjunct Professor, George Washington University Law Center, 1999—. Member, District of Columbia Bar Association Civility Implementation Committee, 1999—. Member, Edward Bennett Williams Inn of Court, 1991-1994. Barrister, Charlotte Ray Inn of Court, 1994-1997; Master, 1997—. Mediator, Superior Court, District of Columbia; United States District Court for the District of Columbia. Member: Judicial Conference of the District of Columbia Circuit, 1990-1991, 1996; Rule 711 Committee, U.S. District Court, District of Columbia, 1997—. *Member:* Washington (Director, 1995-1997; Vice-President, 1997-1999; Vice President, 1997-1999; Vice-President and Chairman of the Board, 1999—; Chair, Law Day, 1996-1997), Virginia, Maryland State, National (Member, Executive Committee, 1998—, Board of Governors; Member-At-Large, 1997—; Deputy Regional Director-Region XII; Vice-Chair, Trial Advocacy Section) and American Bar Associations; Bar Association of the District of Columbia (Member, Board of Directors, 1998-1999; Chair, New Admittee Committee, 1999-2000; Director, 1994-1996 and Chair, 1996-1999, Fair Employment Council); Virginia State Bar; The Association of Trial Lawyers of America (Member, Keyperson Committee, 1996—); Trial Lawyers Association of Metropolitan Washington, D.C. (Member, Board of Governors, 1997—); National Association of Black Women Attorneys (Recording Secretary, 1991-1993; Director, 1994—); Judicial Conference of the District of Columbia, 1994, 1996-1999; Member, Committee on Arrangements, 1997); Trial Lawyers for Public Justice; Women's Bar Association. ***REPORTED CASES:*** McNeil v. District of Columbia. ***PRACTICE AREAS:*** Medical Malpractice; Personal Injury; Complex Civil Litigation. ***Email:*** kkeenansolomon@olender.com

(This Listing Continued)

MELISSA RHEA, born Poughkeepsie, New York, January 7, 1957; admitted to bar, 1982, District of Columbia; 1983, Maryland, U.S. Court of Appeals, Fourth Circuit, U.S. District Court, District of Maryland, U.S. Court of Appeals for the District of Columbia Circuit, U.S. District Court, District of Columbia and U.S. Bankruptcy Court, District of Maryland. *Education:* Washington University (A.B., cum laude, 1979); Washington College of Law of American University (J.D., 1982). Faculty, National Institute for Trial Advocacy, Georgetown Law School, June 1998, June 1999, June 2000; Mediation Trainer, District of Columbia Superior Court Mediation Program, 1995, 1997. Teaching Team Member, Harvard Law School Winter Trial Advocacy Workshop, January 1996, January 1997, January 1998, January 1999, January 2000. Alternative Dispute Resolution Trainer: Republic of Tanzania, August-September 1996, February 1998; Republic of Zambia, April 2000. Volunteer Case Evaluator/Mediator: District of Columbia Superior Court, 1991—. Arbitrator, District of Columbia Superior Court Mandatory Arbitration Program, 1994—. *Member:* District of Columbia Bar; Bar Association of the District of Columbia; Maryland State Bar Association, Inc.; Women's Bar Association; Trial Lawyers Association of Metropolitan Washington, D.C. (Member, Board of Governors, 1996—; Co-Chair, Membership Committee, 1997-1999; Chair, 1999—); The Association of Trial Lawyers of America (Sustaining Member, 1996—); Maryland Trial Lawyers Association. ***PRACTICE AREAS:*** Medical Malpractice; Personal Injury. ***Email:*** mrhea@olender.com

KAREN E. EVANS, born Wilmington, North Carolina, April 12, 1958; admitted to bar, 1990, District of Columbia; 1997, Virginia and Maryland. *Education:* East Carolina University (B.S.N., 1980); Texas Tech University; University of North Carolina at Chapel Hill (J.D., 1990). Registered Nurse, North Carolina, 1981-1990. Member, Texas Tech University Law Review, 1987. *Member:* Fairfax, (Member, Diversity Task Force Subcommittee on The Inclusion of Minorities in the Activities of the Fairfax Bar Association), Virginia, Maryland, American and National Bar Associations; District of Columbia Bar; Bar Association of The District of Columbia (Member, Sections on: Litigation and Health Law); Virginia State Bar; American and National Bar Associations; Virginia Association of Defense Attorneys. [Capt., U.S. Air Force, 1981-1987]. ***PRACTICE AREAS:*** Medical Malpractice; Personal Injury. ***Email:*** kevans@olender.com

ELIZABETH JESUKIEWICZ FREY, born Winchester, Massachusetts, December 29, 1958; admitted to bar, 1987, Maryland and Pennsylvania; 1989, U.S. District Court, District of Maryland; 1990, District of Columbia. *Education:* York Hospital (Diploma, 1979); University of Maryland (B.S.N., 1982); University of Baltimore (J.D., 1987). *Member:* Bar Association of the District of Columbia; American Bar Association; Trial Lawyers Association of the District of Columbia; Maryland Trial Lawyers' Association (Member, Board of Directors); Chesapeake Nurse Attorneys, Inc.; The Association of Trial Lawyers of America. ***PRACTICE AREAS:*** Civil Trial Practice; Medical Malpractice; Personal Injury. ***Email:*** efrey@olender.com

NARDA M. NEWBY, born Kingston, Jamaica, May 10, 1969; admitted to bar, 1995, Maryland; 1996, District of Columbia, U.S. District Court, District of Maryland, U.S. District Court, District of Columbia and U.S. Court of Appeals, District of Columbia Circuit. *Education:* George Washington University (B.B.A., 1991); University of Pennsylvania (J.D., 1995). Recipient: Washington Bar Association Presidential Award, 1999. Secretary, Charlotte E. Ray American Inn of Court, 1997-1998. Firm Coordinator, D.C. Street Law Program, 1996-1998. *Member:* Washington (Member, Young Lawyers Division), Maryland State, National (Member: Young Lawyers Division; Greater Washington Area Chapter, Women Lawyers' Division) and American (Member, Young Lawyers Division) Bar Associations; Bar Association of the District of Columbia (Chair, 2000-2001, Chair-Elect, 1999-2000, Secretary, 1998-1999 and Co-Chair, Professional Development Committee, 1997-1998, Young Lawyers Section); The District of Columbia Bar (Member, Steering Committee, Injury to Persons and Property Section); The Association of Trial Lawyers of America (Member, Key Person Committee); National Association of Black Women Attorneys; Trial Lawyers Association of Metropolitan Washington, D.C.; Womens Bar Association; Maryland Trial Lawyers Association; Trial Lawyers for Public Justice. ***PRACTICE AREAS:*** Medical Malpractice; Personal Injury; Products Liability. ***Email:*** nnewby@olender.com

OF COUNSEL

ROBERT S. CHABON, born New York, N.Y., December 2, 1938; admitted to bar, 1976, Pennsylvania (Not admitted in District of Columbia). *Education:* George Washington University (B.S., 1959); Georgetown University (M.D., with honors, 1963); University of Maryland (J.D., with honors, 1976); University of Pittsburgh (M.P.H., 1979). Licensed M.D.: Maryland, 1969; Pennsylvania, 1976. Adjunct Professor of Law, Duquesne University Law School, 1977-1982. Diplomate, American Board of Pediatrics.

OLIFF & BERRIDGE, PLC

WASHINGTON, D.C.

(See Alexandria, Virginia)

Intellectual Property Law including Chemical Intellectual Property, Electrical Intellectual Property, Electronic Intellectual Property, Industrial Property, Intellectual Property Arbitration, Intellectual Property Infringement, Intellectual Property Licensing, Intellectual Property Litigation, International Intellectual Property, International Licensing, Mechanical Intellectual Property, Medical Intellectual Property, New Media Law, Pharmaceutical Intellectual Property, Piracy, Proprietary Rights, as well as Patent, Trademark, Copyright, Antitrust and International Trade Law, and Trials and Appeals before Federal and State Courts and U.S. Administrative Agencies.

OLIVER & OLIVER, P.C.

Established in 1984

SUITE 800
1090 VERMONT AVENUE, N.W.
WASHINGTON, D.C. 20005
Telephone: 202-371-5656
Telecopier: 202-289-8113

General and Administrative Practice before Federal and State Courts, Departments and Agencies, including Energy, Business and Public Utility Law. Legislative Practice.

RICHARD A. OLIVER, born Chicago, Illinois, October 14, 1947; admitted to bar, 1973, District of Columbia; 1996, Virginia; 1997, Maryland. *Education:* Dartmouth College (B.A., cum laude, 1969); Boston College (J.D., 1973). Member: Annual Survey of Massachusetts Law, 1971-1972; Uniform Commercial Code Digest, 1972-1973. Attorney, Federal Power Commission, 1973-1976. *Member:* District of Columbia Bar; Virginia State Bar Association; Federal Energy (Secretary, 1979-1981) and American Bar Associations.

MARY ANN OLIVER, born Tampa, Florida, August 25, 1948; admitted to bar, 1973, District of Columbia; 1975, Virginia. *Education:* University of Massachusetts (B.A., magna cum laude, 1970); Boston College (J.D., 1973). Phi Beta Kappa; Phi Kappa Phi. Deputy Assistant Director, Division of Corporate Regulation, Office of Public Utility Regulation, Securities and Exchange Commission, 1981-1984. Attorney: Securities and Exchange Commission, 1977-1981; Rural Electrification Administration, 1973-1977. *Member:* District of Columbia Bar; Virginia State Bar; Federal Energy and American Bar Associations.

LAW OFFICES OF ROGER M. OLSEN

Established in 1989

1201 CONNECTICUT AVENUE, SUITE 600
WASHINGTON, D.C. 20036
Telephone: 202-887-6820
Fax: 202-887-9073

Federal and State Taxation Law, Civil and Criminal Tax Litigation.

ROGER M. OLSEN, admitted to bar, 1969, California; 1977, District of Columbia. *Education:* University of California at Berkeley (A.B., 1964); Boalt Hall School of Law, University of California (J.D., 1968); George Washington University (LL.M., Taxation, 1977). Recipient, U.S. Justice Department Edmund J. Randolph Award, 1987. Deputy Assistant Attorney General, Criminal Division, U.S. Department of Justice, Washington D.C., 1981-1983. Trial Attorney, 1972-1976, Deputy Assistant Attorney General, 1983-1985 and Assistant Attorney General, 1985-1987, Tax Division, U.S. Department of Justice. Deputy District Attorney, Alameda County District Attorneys Office, 1969-1972. Author: "Criminal Tax Procedure," Commerce Clearing House Tax Transactions Library, Vol. I 1989, Vol. II 1990; "Criminal Tax Procedure," Little, Brown & Co., 1995; "What Every Tax Lawyer Should Know About Representing Clients Accused of Tax Fraud, The Receipt of Illegal Income, or the Failure to Report Income," 40th U.S.C. Law Center Tax Institute, 1988, Advisor, The Department of Justice Manual, Prentice Hall Law and Business. *Member:* American Bar Association; State Bar of California (Member, Executive Committee, Taxation Section, 1992-1995). Fellow, American College of Tax Counsel.

OLSSON, FRANK AND WEEDA, P.C.

Established in 1979

SUITE 400, 1400 SIXTEENTH STREET, N.W.
WASHINGTON, D.C. 20036
Telephone: 202-789-1212
Telecopier: 202-234-3550
Email: info@ofwlaw.com
URL: http://www.ofwlaw.com

General Administrative and Trade Regulation Practice. Agriculture, Food and Drug, International Trade, Litigation and Legislation.

FIRM PROFILE: Our firm has become a leader in the food, drug, medical device, and agricultural law field since its founding in 1979. The firm's original regulatory practice has been expanded to include federal and state lobbying on agriculture, food and drug, and related issues, litigation, insurance/risk retention, agriculture risk management, environmental health and policy, Indian and trademark law.

PRINCIPALS

PHILIP C. OLSSON, born Brockton, Massachusetts, April 1, 1939; admitted to bar, 1965, Massachusetts; 1973, District of Columbia. *Education:* Harvard University (A.B., cum laude, 1962; LL.B., 1965). Author: "Meat and Poultry Inspection: Wholesomeness, Integrity and Productivity," 75th Anniversary Commemorative Volume of Food and Drug Law, 1984. Legislative Assistant to Congressman Hastings Keith, 1967 and to Congressman Bob Mathias, 1967-1969. Assistant to Assistant Secretary of Agriculture for Marketing and Consumer Services, 1969-1971. Deputy Assistant Secretary of Agriculture for Marketing and Consumer Services, 1971-1973. *Member:* The District of Columbia Bar; American Bar Association (Vice-Chairman, Agriculture Committee, Section on Administrative Law and Regulatory Practice). ***SPECIAL AGENCIES:*** Food Safety and Inspection Service; Agricultural Marketing Service; Packers and Stockyards Administration; Farm Service Agency; Animal and Plant Health Inspection Service; Office of Management and Budget. ***REPORTED CASES:*** American Meat Inst. v. USDA, 646 F.2d 125, (4th Cir. 1981); Community Nutrition Inst. v. Dávila, 749 F.2d 50 (D.C. Cir. 1984); United Egg Producers v. Dávila, 871 F.Supp. 106 (D.P.R. 1994), aff'd, 77 F.3d 567 (1st Cir. 1996); Nat. Risk Retention Assn. v. Brown, 927 F. Supp. 195 (M.D. La., 1996), affirmed 114 F.3d 1183 (5th Cir., 1997). ***PRACTICE AREAS:*** Agriculture Law; Food and Drug Law; International Trade Law. **Email:** polsson@ofwlaw.com

RICHARD L. FRANK, born Elizabeth, New Jersey, June 25, 1951; admitted to bar, 1976, Michigan; 1977, District of Columbia. *Education:* University of Michigan (B.A., 1972; J.D., 1976). Phi Beta Kappa. Member, Michigan Law Review, 1975-1976. Adjunct Law Professor, Columbus School of Law, Catholic University of America, 1985-1986. Author: "Food Labeling and Inspection Issues--1981-1983: Living with the Regulators," Food Drug Cosmetic Law Journal, Vol. 38, October, 1983; Note, "Some Observations on the Disposition of CCW Cases in Detroit," Michigan Law Review, Vol. 74, No. 3, January, 1976; "Food Labeling-The Case for National Uniformity," Food, Drug, Cosmetic Law Journal, Commerce Clearing House Publication, Vol. 34, No. 10, October, 1979. Co-Author: "Antitrust Consequences of United States Corporate Payment to Foreign Officials," Vanderbilt Law Review, Vol. 30, No. 2, March, 1977; "USDA Pre-Market Label Approval Process Criticized," Legal Times of Washington, Vol. III, No. 22, November 2, 1981; "The USDA's Compliance and Enforcement Program," 44 Food, Drug and Comm. L.J. 205, 1989; "History of Health Claims Regulation," 45 Food Drug Comm. L.J. 655, Nov. 1990; "Regulators Dish It Out on Food Labeling," Legal Times of Washington, Vol. XIV, No. 36, January 27, 1992; "Final Round of the Fight Over Food Labels," Legal Times of Washington, Vol. XV, No. 34, January, 1993; "Complying With the Nutrition Labeling and Education Act," The Food Institute Press, 1993; "The FDA Under Siege," New Directions in Health Care and Food and Drug Law, Legal Times, July 17, 1995. *Member:* The District of Columbia Bar; American Bar Association. ***SPECIAL AGENCIES:*** Food and Drug Administration; Federal Trade Commission; Food Safety and Inspection Service; Food and Nutrition Service; Occupational Safety and Health Administration; Consumer Product Safety Commission. ***PRACTICE AREAS:*** Food and Drug Law; Advertising Law; Agriculture Law. **Email:** rfrank@ofwlaw.com

DAVID F. WEEDA, born Washington, D.C., April 18, 1948; admitted to bar, 1976, Maryland; 1984, District of Columbia. *Education:* Biscayne College (B.A., cum laude, 1970); Loyola University of New Orleans School of Law (J.D., 1976). Associate Chief Counsel, Food and Drug Administration, 1976-1981. Adjunct Law Professor, Columbus School of Law, Catholic University of America, 1985-1989. Author: "FDA Seizure and Injunction Actions; Judicial Means of Protecting the Public Health," Food, Drug & Cosmetic Law Journal, Vol. 35, No. 2, February, 1980; "Food Safety Regulation-Time for Change and Compromise," Food, Drug and Cosmetic Law Journal, Vol. 40, No. 3, July, 1985; "Food and Drug Administration Regulation of Blood Bank Software: The New Regulatory Landscape for Blood Establishments and Their Vendors," 38 Transfusion 86 (1998); "The Legal Framework for the Regulation of Bulk

(This Listing Continued)

OLSSON, FRANK AND WEEDA, P.C., Washington—Continued

Pharmaceutical Chemicals," Chapter 3 of Validation of Bulk Pharmaceutical Chemicals Eds. Berry and Harpaz, (1997). Counsel to the National Association of Pharmaceutical Manufacturers. *Member:* Maryland State Bar Association; The District of Columbia Bar. ***SPECIAL AGENCIES:*** Food and Drug Administration; Department of Justice; Drug Enforcement Administration. ***PRACTICE AREAS:*** Food and Drug Law; Litigation; White Collar Criminal Defense. ***Email:*** dweeda@ofwlaw.com

DENNIS R. JOHNSON, born Morristown, New Jersey, May 19, 1952; admitted to bar, 1981, District of Columbia. *Education:* George Washington University (B.A., 1978); Catholic University of America (J.D., 1981); George Washington University (LL.M., 1982). Fellow, Food and Drug Law Institute, 1981-1982. Author: "American Public Health Association v. Veneman: Why?" Food Drug Cosmetic Law Journal, Vol. 39, April, 1984; "Guide to HACCP & Food Safety," The Food Institute Press, 1996. *Member:* The District of Columbia Bar. ***SPECIAL AGENCIES:*** Food, Safety and Inspection Service; Food and Drug Administration. ***PRACTICE AREAS:*** Agriculture Law; Food and Drug Law; Administrative Law. ***Email:*** djohnson@ofwlaw.com

ARTHUR Y. TSIEN, born New York, N.Y., July 22, 1949; admitted to bar, 1978, Washington; 1987, District of Columbia. *Education:* Tufts University (B.S., magna cum laude, 1971); University of Washington (J.D., 1978). Law Clerk to Chief Judge Frank D. James, Washington Court of Appeals, 1978-1980. Co-Author: "Regulators Dish It Out on Food Labeling," Legal Times of Washington, Vol. XIV, No. 36, January 27, 1992; "Final Round of the Fight Over Food Labels," Legal Times of Washington, Vol. XV, No. 34, January, 1993; "Complying With the Nutrition Labeling and Education Act," The Food Institute Press, 1993. Associate Chief Counsel for Veterinary Medicine and Enforcement, Food and Drug Administration, 1980-1985. *Member:* The District of Columbia Bar; Washington State and American Bar Associations. ***SPECIAL AGENCIES:*** Food and Drug Administration; Department of Justice. ***PRACTICE AREAS:*** Food and Drug Law; Litigation. ***Email:*** atsien@ofwlaw.com

JOHN W. BODE, born Oklahoma City, Oklahoma, January 24, 1955; admitted to bar, 1983, Oklahoma (Not admitted in District of Columbia). *Education:* United States Naval Academy; University of Oklahoma (B.A., 1977); George Mason University (J.D., 1983). Assistant Secretary of Agriculture for Food and Consumer Services, 1985-1989. Director, Commodity Credit Corporation, 1986-1989. Director, Rural Telephone Bank, 1987-1989. *Member:* Oklahoma and American Bar Associations. ***SPECIAL AGENCIES:*** U.S. Department of Agriculture; Food and Drug Administration; U.S. Congress; Federal Election Commission; Office of Management and Budget. ***PRACTICE AREAS:*** Agriculture Law; Food and Drug Law; Legislation. ***Email:*** jbode@ofwlaw.com

STEPHEN D. TERMAN, born Washington, D.C., June 16, 1951; admitted to bar, 1976, Maryland; 1979, District of Columbia, U.S. District Court, District of Columbia and District of Maryland, U.S. Court of Appeals, 4th, 7th, 8th, 9th and District of Columbia Circuits and U.S. Supreme Court. *Education:* University of Maryland (B.S., 1973; J.D., 1976). Phi Kappa Phi. Author: Chapters, Biomedical Instrumentation and Technology on the: "Safe Medical Devices Act of 1989" and "Complying with the Medical Device Reporting Regulation," *The Medical Device Industry, Science Technology and Regulation in a Competitive Environment,* 1990; Article, "The Medical Device Amendments of 1976 and 1990 - A Statutory Overview," Sterilization Technology, published by Van Nostrand Reinhold-New York, 1993; "Bard Case Sets Bad Precedents," 14 Food Drug Cosm. & Med. Devices L. Dig. No. 1: 1-8 (N.Y. St. Bar Assn., Jan 1997); "Food and Drug Administration Regulation of Blood Bank Software: The New Regulatory Landscape for Blood Establishments and Their Vendors," Transfusion, Volume 38: 86-89, January 1998. *Member:* The District of Columbia Bar. ***SPECIAL AGENCIES:*** Food and Drug Administration; Department of Justice. ***PRACTICE AREAS:*** Medical Device Law; Litigation; Food and Drug Law. ***Email:*** sterman@ofwlaw.com

MARSHALL L. MATZ, born Cambridge, Massachusetts, July 13, 1946; admitted to bar, 1971, Connecticut; 1979, District of Columbia. *Education:* University of Connecticut (B.A., 1968); University of Louisville (J.D., 1971). Reginald Heber Smith Community Law Fellowship, South Dakota Legal Services, 1971-1972. Counsel and General Counsel, U.S. Senate Select Committee on Nutrition and Human Needs, 1973-1977. Special Counsel, U.S. Senate Committee on Agriculture, Nutrition and Forestry, 1978-1980. Member, Board of Directors: Food Research Action Center; Friends of the World Food Programme; Congressional Hunger Center. *Member:* The District of Columbia Bar; Connecticut and American (Member, Committee on Agriculture Law) Bar Associations. ***SPECIAL AGENCIES:*** U.S. Department of Agriculture; U.S. Congress; Bureau of Indian Affairs; Federal Election Commission; Office of Management and Budget. ***PRACTICE AREAS:*** Legislation; Agriculture Law; Indian Law; Trade Association Law. ***Email:*** mmatz@ofwlaw.com

MICHAEL J. O'FLAHERTY, born Chicago, Illinois, June 11, 1956; admitted to bar, 1987, Illinois; 1988, District of Columbia. *Education:* Northwestern University (B.S., 1978); Loyola University of Chicago School of Law (J.D., 1987). Co-author: "History of Health Claims Regulation," 45 Food Drug Comm. L.J. 655, Nov. 1990; U.S. Food Labeling Guide, The Food Institute Press, 1998. *Member:* The District of Columbia Bar; Illinois State Bar Association. ***SPECIAL AGENCIES:*** Food and Drug Administration; Patent and Trademark Office; U.S. Customs Service. ***PRACTICE AREAS:*** Food and Drug Law; Trademark Law; Customs Law. ***Email:*** moflaherty@ofwlaw.com

DAVID L. DURKIN, born Cleveland, Ohio, July 10, 1959; admitted to bar, 1988, New York; 1989, District of Columbia. *Education:* John Carroll University (A.B., 1981); Catholic University of America (J.D., 1986). Staff Member, 1984-1985, and Publication Editor, 1985-1986, The Catholic University Law Review. Author: Comment, "Employment at Will in the Unionized Setting," 34 Catholic University Law Review 943, 1985. Law Clerk to Honorable Jaime Pieras, Jr., Judge U.S. District Court for the District of Puerto Rico, 1986-1988. *Member:* The District of Columbia Bar. ***SPECIAL AGENCIES:*** Food and Drug Administration; Drug Enforcement Administration; U.S. Department of Agriculture; Patent and Trademark Office; International Trade Commission; Animal and Plant Health Inspection Service. ***REPORTED CASES:*** United Egg Producers v. Dávila, 871 F. Supp. 106 (D.P.R. 1994), aff'd, 77 F.3d 567 (1st. Cir. 1996); Texas Food Industry Ass'n v. U.S. Department of Agriculture, 842 F. Supp. 254 (W.D. Tex. 1993), aff'd, 81 F.3d 578 (5th Cir. 1996). ***PRACTICE AREAS:*** Food, Drug and Medical Device Law; Litigation. ***Email:*** ddurkin@oflaw.com

NEIL F. O'FLAHERTY, born Chicago, Illinois, February 2, 1965; admitted to bar, 1990, Illinois; 1991, District of Columbia. *Education:* University of Notre Dame (B.A., 1987); Loyola University of Chicago School of Law (J.D., 1990). Author: "Comments on FDA Guidelines for In Vitro Diagnostic Products," Regulatory Affairs, Volume 6: 79-86 (Fall 1994). Co-Author: "The Legal Framework for the Regulation of Bulk Pharmaceutical Chemicals," Chapter 3 of Validation of Bulk Pharmaceutical Chemicals Eds. Berry and Harpaz, 1997; "Changing Regulatory Climate for Blood Establishments and Their Vendors," IVD Technology, Volume 3, Number 7:22-29, November/December 1997; "Food and Drug Administration Regulation of Blood Bank Software: The New Regulatory Landscape for Blood Establishments and Their Vendors," Transfusion, Volume 38:86-89, January 1998. *Member:* Illinois State and American Bar Associations; The District of Columbia Bar. ***SPECIAL AGENCIES:*** Food and Drug Administration; Department of Justice; Health and Human Services Office of Inspector General. ***PRACTICE AREAS:*** Medical Device Law; Food and Drug Law. ***Email:*** noflaherty@ofwlaw.com

PAMELA J. FURMAN, born Rochester, New York, June 8, 1966; admitted to bar, 1995, New York; 1996, District of Columbia. *Education:* Yale University (B.A., summa cum laude, 1988); Stanford University (J.D., 1994). Phi Beta Kappa. Author: "The Impact of FDA Medical Device Regulation on Hospitals," Health Law Digest, Volume 29, Number 1:3-13 (January 2001); "Third-Party Reprocessing of Endoscopic Accessories," Gastrointestinal Endoscopy Clinics of North America, Volume 10, Number 2:385-392 (April 2000); "Reprocessing Devices Labeled for Single Use," Infection Control Today, Volume 3, Number 9:44-46 (September 1999); "Reprocessing Devices Labeled for Single Use: The Great Misunderstanding," Infection Control Today, Volume 3, Number 4: 30-34 (April 1999); "Third-Party Reprocessing: Conserving Health-Care Resources," Medical Device and Diagnostic Industry, Volume 20, Number 10: 26-30 (October 1998); "Association of Medical Device Reprocessors' Position on Reprocessing Single-Use Medical Devices," Surgical Services Management, Volume 4, Number 7: 42-43 (July 1998). *Member:* The District of Columbia Bar. ***PRACTICE AREAS:*** Medical Device Law; Food, Drug and Cosmetics Law. ***Email:*** pfurman@ofwlaw.com

OF COUNSEL

JUR T. STROBOS, born New York, New York, May 5, 1952; admitted to bar, 1988, Pennsylvania and District of Columbia; 1989, California. *Education:* Johns Hopkins University (B.A., cum laude, 1974); University of Chicago (M.D., 1978); University of Pennsylvania (J.D., 1987). Medical Doctor: New York, 1979; Pennsylvania, 1981; Maryland, 1983. Director, Policy Research Staff/Office of Policy in the Commissioner's Office. Fellow, American College of Emergency Physicians, 1986-1996. *Member:* The District of Columbia Bar; State Bar of California. ***SPECIAL AGENCIES:*** Food and Drug Administration. ***PRACTICE AREAS:*** Food and Drug Law; Health Law; Patent Litigation. ***Email:*** jstrobos@ofwlaw.com

JACQUELINE H. EAGLE, born Des Moines, Iowa; admitted to bar, 1978, District of Columbia. *Education:* Duke University (B.A., 1961); Georgetown University Law Center (J.D., 1977). ***SPECIAL AGENCIES:*** Food and Drug Administration; Department of Justice. ***PRACTICE AREAS:*** Litigation. ***Email:*** jeagle@ofwlaw.com

KENNETH D. ACKERMAN, born Albany, New York, October 25, 1951; admitted to bar, 1976, District of Columbia. *Education:* Brown University (B.A., 1973); Georgetown University Law Center (J.D., 1976). ***SPECIAL AGENCIES:*** U.S. Department of Agriculture, Risk Management Agency; Federal Crop Insurance Corporation. ***PRACTICE AREAS:*** Agricultural Risk Management; Litigation. ***Email:*** kackerman@ofwlaw.com

(This Listing Continued)

(This Listing Continued)

MARK L. ITZKOFF, born New York, New York, April 29, 1955; admitted to bar, 1989, District of Columbia. *Education:* University of Rochester (B.A., 1977); John Marshall Law School (J.D., 1988). *Member:* The District of Columbia Bar. ***SPECIAL AGENCIES:*** Food and Drug Administration; Environmental Protection Agency. ***PRACTICE AREAS:*** Food and Drug Regulation; Administrative Law; Environmental Law. ***Email:*** mitzkoff@ofwlaw.com

SENIOR ATTORNEY

RICHARD D. SIEGEL, born Lewistown, Pennsylvania, October 13, 1939; admitted to bar, 1965, Pennsylvania; 1973, District of Columbia; 1976, U.S. Supreme Court. *Education:* University of Pennsylvania (B.A., 1960); Harvard University (J.D., 1963). Special Assistant to Congressman Richard S. Schweiker, 1966-1968. Legislative Counsel to U.S. Senator Richard S. Schweiker, 1969-1971. Associate Minority Counsel, U.S. Senate Committee on Labor and Public Welfare, 1971-1973. Deputy Assistant Secretary of Agriculture for Natural Resources and Environment, 1981-1987. Author: "Bumper Crop of Farm Controls," Journal of Commerce, September 24, 1987; "The Lobby for a Bailout," National Law Journal, July 10, 1989; "Owls or Jobs?," Washington Times, September 4, 1990; "A Candidate to Handle Spotted Owls," Sacramento Bce, September 25, 1992; "Deadwood Environmental Policies," Washington Times, August 31, 1995; "New Federal Agriculture Legislation Affects Farmers in Pennsylvania," Agricultural Law Committee Newsletter, Pennsylvania Bar Association, June 1996. *Member:* District of Columbia Bar; Pennsylvania (Member, Agricultural Law Committee), Federal and American Bar Associations. ***SPECIAL AGENCIES:*** U.S. Department of Agriculture; U.S. Forest Service; U.S. Congress; Small Business Administration. ***PRACTICE AREAS:*** Agriculture Law; Food and Drug Regulation; Medical Law; Legislative Practice; Forestry Law. ***Email:*** rsiegel@ofwlaw.com

ASSOCIATES

TISH EGGLESTON PAHL, born Pasadena, California, October 3, 1961; admitted to bar, 1988, Minnesota; 1990, District of Columbia. *Education:* Northwestern University (B.S., 1983; J.D., cum laude, 1988). *Member:* The District of Columbia Bar (CEELI Liaison to Romania). ***PRACTICE AREAS:*** Food and Drug Law; Dietary Supplements; Advertising; Litigation. ***Email:*** tpahl@ofwlaw.com

BRETT T. SCHWEMER, born Grosse Point, Michigan, April 17, 1967; admitted to bar, 1992, Maryland; 1995, District of Columbia. *Education:* James Madison University (B.B.A., 1989); Ohio Northern University (J.D., with distinction, 1992). *Member:* Maryland State Bar Association; District of Columbia Bar. ***PRACTICE AREAS:*** Agriculture Law; Food and Drug Law; Litigation. ***Email:*** bschwemer@ofwlaw.com

KAREN R. HARNED, born Ft. Hood, Texas, January 17, 1967; admitted to bar, 1995, Oklahoma; 1997, District of Columbia. *Education:* University of Oklahoma (B.A., 1989); George Washington University (J.D., 1995). *Member:* Oklahoma Bar Association; The District of Columbia Bar. ***PRACTICE AREAS:*** Legislation; Food and Drug Law; Agriculture Law. ***Email:*** kharned@ofwlaw.com

ROBERT A. HAHN, born New Hyde Park, New York, December 4, 1958; admitted to bar, 1985, New York; 2001, District of Columbia. *Education:* Brown University (A.B., magna cum laude, 1980); Columbia University (J.D., 1984). Phi Beta Kappa. ***PRACTICE AREAS:*** Banking Law; Food and Drug Regulation; Lobbying. ***Email:*** rhahn@ofwlaw.com

NAOMI JOY LEVAN HALPERN, born Philadelphia, Pennsylvania, December 31, 1963; admitted to bar, 1992, Maryland; 1995, District of Columbia. *Education:* University of Michigan (B.A., with high honors and distinction, 1985); George Washington University (J.D., with honors, 1992). Staff Member, The George Washington University Law Review. *Member:* The District of Columbia Bar. ***PRACTICE AREAS:*** Food, Drug and Cosmetic Law. ***Email:*** nhalpern@ofwlaw.com

STEPHEN L. LACEY, born Syracuse, New York, December 27, 1967; admitted to bar, 1999, Maryland; 2001, District of Columbia. *Education:* University of Vermont (B.A., 1990); Catholic University, Columbus School of Law (J.D., 1999). ***PRACTICE AREAS:*** Agriculture Law; Food and Drug Regulation; Administrative Law; Legislation. ***Email:*** slacey@ofwlaw.com

JAN M. BRUNNER, born Bluefield, West Virginia, December 20, 1968; admitted to bar, 1999, Maryland (Not admitted in District of Columbia). *Education:* Trinity College (B.A., magna cum laude, 1991); University of Leeds (M.A., International Relations, 1992); University of Virginia (J.D.,1999). Phi Beta Kappa. Fulbright Scholar, 1992. ***PRACTICE AREAS:*** Food and Drug Regulation.

SUSAN PAGE GRYMES, born Richmond, Virginia, July 3, 1969; admitted to bar, 2000, Virginia; 2001, District of Columbia. *Education:* University of Virginia (B.A., 1992); George Mason University (J.D., 2000). ***PRACTICE AREAS:*** Legislation; Food and Drug Law; Litigation. ***Email:*** sgrymes@ofwlaw.com

(This Listing Continued)

SHARON D. BROOKS, born Stamford, Connecticut; admitted to bar, 2000, Maryland; 2001, District of Columbia. *Education:* University of Illinois (B.A); Georgetown University (J.D.). *Member:* The District of Columbia Bar. ***PRACTICE AREAS:*** Agricultural Law; Medical Device Law; Food and Drug Law.

RYAN W. STROSCHEIN, born Mansfield, South Dakota, February 4, 1970; admitted to bar, 2000, South Dakota (Not admitted in District of Columbia). *Education:* South Dakota State University (B.A., 1993); University of Nebraska (J.D., 1998). ***PRACTICE AREAS:*** Agricultural Law; Indian Law; Forestry Law. ***Email:*** rstroschein@ofwlaw.com

EVAN PHELPS, born Washington, D.C., November 17, 1965; admitted to bar, 2001, Virginia (Not admitted in District of Columbia). *Education:* Trinity University (B.A., 1987); George Mason University School of Law (J.D., 2001). *Member:* Virginia State Bar. ***PRACTICE AREAS:*** Food and Drug Law; Medical Device Law; Litigation. ***Email:*** ephelps@ofwlaw.com

O'MELVENY & MYERS LLP

555 13TH STREET, NW
WASHINGTON, D.C. 20004-1109
Telephone: 202-383-5300
Facsimile: 202-383-5414
Cable: MOMSWSH
Telex: 89622
Email: omminfo@omm.com
URL: http://www.omm.com

Los Angeles, CA Office: 400 South Hope Street, 90071-2899. Cable: MOMS. Telex: 674122. Tel: 213-430-6000. Fax: 213-430-6407. E-mail: omminfo@omm.com.

Century City, CA Office: 1999 Avenue of the Stars, Los Angeles, 90067-6035. Telex: 674097. Tel: 310-553-6700. Fax: 310-246-6779.

Irvine, CA Office: 114 Pacifica, Suite 100, 92618-3318. Tel: 949-737-2900. Fax: 949-737-2300.

Newport Beach, CA Office: 610 Newport Center Drive, 92660-6429. Telex: 4722088. Tel: 949-760-9600. Fax: 949-823-6994.

Menlo Park, CA Office: 990 Marsh Road, 94025-1949. Telephone: 650-473-2600. Facsimile: 650-473-2601.

San Francisco, CA Office: Embarcadero Center West, 275 Battery Street, 94111-3305. Tel: 415-984-8700. Fax: 415-984-8701.

New York, NY Office: Citigroup Center, 153 East 53rd Street, 10022-4611. Telex: 129165. Tel: 212-326-2000. Fax: 212-326-2061.

McLean, VA Office: 1650 Tysons Boulevard, 22102. Tel: 703-287-2400. Fax: 703-287-2404.

London Office: O'Melveny & Myers, 3 Finsbury Square, London, EC2A 1LA, England. Tel: 44-20-7256-8451. Fax 44-20-7638-8205.

Tokyo Office: Akasaka Twin Tower, East 14F, 2-17-22, Akasaka, Minato-ku, Tokyo 107-0052, Japan. Tel: 81-3-5562-2800. Fax: 81-3-5575-3840.

Hong Kong Office: O'Melveny & Myers, Suite 1905, Tower Two, Lippo Centre, 89 Queensway, Central, Hong Kong. Tel: 852-2523-8266. Fax: 852-2522-1760.

Shanghai Office: Kerry Centre, 20F, 1515 Nanjing Road West, Shanghai, 200040 People's Republic of China. Tel: 86-21-5298-5600. Fax: 86-21-5298-5500.

General Civil Litigation, Appellate Practice, and Criminal Trials Practice in all State and Federal Courts. Administrative; Antitrust; Banking; Bankruptcy; Commercial; Communications; Construction; Corporation and Corporate Financing; Environmental; Immigration and Naturalization; Insurance Coverage Defense; Intellectual Property; Internet Law; International Business; Labor and Employment; Employment Benefits; Media and Entertainment; Municipal, Municipal Zoning and Municipal Finance; Natural Resources; Oil and Gas; Patent, Trademark, Copyright and Unfair Competition; Probate, Trusts and Estate Planning; Public Utilities; Real Estate; Securities; Telecommunications; and Tax Law.

FIRM PROFILE: O'Melveny & Myers LLP, founded over 115 years ago on January 2, 1885, is the oldest law firm in Los Angeles. Since that time, we have grown from two attorneys in two rooms, specializing in the local concerns of a frontier community, to a firm of more than 700 lawyers involved in matters of regional, national and global concern.

Initially, the growth of our firm paralleled the growth of Los Angeles. Under founder Henry O'Melveny, the firm benefited from the first great California land and population booms that transformed a small outpost into one of the nation's most important cities. Our practice kept pace with the region's growth, and the early decades of the century saw O'Melveny attorneys working on behalf of clients in the aircraft, oil, motion picture and utility sectors. In the post-World War II period, leadership passed to John O'Melveny, who presided over the development of the modern firm until 1970. The ensuing years have seen a dramatic acceleration of our practice on both the national and international fronts. Today O'Melveny ranks as one of the largest law firms in the world.

(This Listing Continued)

O'MELVENY & MYERS LLP, Washington—Continued

Each of our thirteen offices - Los Angeles, Century City, Newport Beach, Irvine, Menlo Park, and San Francisco, CA; New York, NY; McLean, VA; Washington, DC; Tokyo, Japan; London, England; Hong Kong, SAR of China; and Shanghai, People's Republic of China - is specifically located both to provide service affecting a particular region and to contribute important strengths and specializations to the firm as a whole.

Office-to-office collaborations are the norm, with attorneys on different coasts and different continents working together to structure complex transactions and to resolve important controversies.

Among our lawyers are many who have distinguished themselves through their leadership at the Bar or in public service. Our ranks include former Executive Branch and Capitol Hill policymakers; some of the nation's leading litigators and labor lawyers; recognized experts in public finance, financial institutions, corporate, securities, entertainment, real estate, bankruptcy, constitutional and tax law; and the nation's foremost practitioners in representations concerning Europe, Latin America, and the Pacific Rim. This combination of highly skilled lawyers and a strategic presence in key economic centers enables O'Melveny to offer our clients the highest level of legal service and consultation.

CHAIRMAN

ARTHUR B. CULVAHOUSE, JR., born Athens, TN, July 4, 1948; admitted to bar, 1973, Tennessee; 1977, California and District of Columbia; 1988, U.S. Supreme Court. *Education:* University of Tennessee (B.S., with high honors, 1970); New York University (J.D., 1973). Root Tilden Scholar. Editor-in-Chief, NYU Annual Survey of American Law, 1972-1973. Chief Legislative Assistant to Senator Howard H. Baker, Jr., 1973-1976. Counsel to the President of the United States, 1987-1989. (Chairman). ***PRACTICE AREAS:*** Litigation; Corporate Law. ***Email:*** aculvahouse@omm.com

PARTNERS

KERMIT W. ALMSTEDT, born St. Louis County, MO, May 24, 1945; admitted to bar, 1970, Missouri; 1971, U.S. Courts of Appeals, Eighth Circuit; 1974, U.S. District Court, Western District of Missouri; 1979, U.S. Supreme Court; 1981, District of Columbia and Court of International Trade; 1988, Courts of Appeals for the Federal Circuit. *Education:* Southeast Missouri University (B.S., 1967); University of Missouri-Kansas City (J.D., with honors, 1970). Member, Bench and Robe. Member, University of Missouri Law Review, 1969-1970. Trial Attorney, Anti-Trust Division, U.S. Department of Justice (honors program), 1970-1971. Assistant Attorney General, Chief Counsel, Antitrust Division, State of Missouri, 1971-1977. Legislative Assistant to U.S. Senator John C. Danforth, 1977-1981. *Member:* The District of Columbia Bar; The Missouri Bar. ***PRACTICE AREAS:*** Antitrust; Customs Law; International Trade. ***Email:*** kalmstedt@omm.com

BRIAN C. ANDERSON, born Berkeley, CA, October 27,1959; admitted to bar, 1986, California; 1987, U.S. Courts of Appeals, District of Columbia Circuit; 1988, District of Columbia; 1989, U.S. Court of International Trade; 1990, U.S. District Court, District of Columbia; 1994, U.S. Courts of Appeals, Second Circuit; 1995, U.S. Courts of Appeals, Eleventh Circuit; 1996, U.S. Courts of Appeals, Fifth Circuit. *Education:* University of California at Berkeley (B.A., magna cum laude, 1982); Stanford University (J.D., with honors, 1986). Phi Beta Kappa. Note Editor, Stanford Law Review, 1984-1986. Law Clerk to Honorable Laurence H. Silberman, U.S. Courts of Appeals, D.C. Circuit, 1986-1987. Special Assistant to the General Counsel, U.S. Department of Education, 1987-1989. ***PRACTICE AREAS:*** Litigation; Class Action Litigation. ***Email:*** banderson@omm.com

DAVID T. BEDDOW, born Logan, WV, April 13, 1955; admitted to bar, 1979, District of Columbia; 1982, U.S. Courts of Appeals, Third Circuit; 1983, U.S. District Court, District of Columbia Circuit; 1985, U.S. Courts of Appeals, District of Columbia Circuit and U.S. Claims Court. *Education:* Colgate University (A.B., magna cum laude, with high honors in History, 1976); University of Virginia (J.D., 1979). Phi Beta Kappa; Phi Alpha Theta. Member, University of Virginia Law Review, Editorial Board, 1977-1979. Co-Author: "Should The Shipping Act of 1984 Be Amended To Eliminate Conference Antitrust Immunity?" Federal Bar News & Journal-volume 36, no. 8, Oct, 1989, pg. 357. *Member:* The District of Columbia Bar; Federal (Former Chairman, Transportation Law Section) and American (Member, Clayton Act Committee and Transportation Industry Committee) Bar Associations. ***PRACTICE AREAS:*** Antitrust; Aviation; Transportation. ***Email:*** dbeddow@omm.com

JOHN H. BEISNER, born Salina, KS, February 24, 1953; admitted to bar, 1978, California and U.S. District Court, Central District of California; 1980, District of Columbia and U.S. District Court, District of Columbia; 1985, U.S. Supreme Court. *Education:* University of Kansas (B.A., with distinction, 1975); University of Michigan (J.D., 1978). Phi Beta Kappa. Associate Editor, 1976-1977 and Administrative Editor, 1977-1978, Michigan Law Review. Author: "Conflicts of Interest and The Changing Concept of Marriage: The Congressional Compromise," 75 Michigan Law Review 1647, 1977. Member, State Colleges Coordinating Committee, Kansas Board of Regents, 1974-1975. *Member:* The District of Columbia Bar; State Bar of California; Federal and American Bar Associations; American Law Institute; Federal Communications Bar Association. ***PRACTICE AREAS:*** Complex Civil Litigation; Class Actions; Communications Law. ***Email:*** jbeisner@omm.com

DONALD T. BLISS, JR., born Norwalk, CT, November 24, 1941; admitted to bar, 1967, Trust Territory of the Pacific Islands; 1969, New York; 1970, District of Columbia and U.S. Supreme Court. *Education:* Principia College (B.A., with highest honors, 1963); Harvard University (J.D., cum laude, 1966). Peace Corp Volunteer Lawyer, Micronesia, 1966-1968. Assistant to the Secretary of Health, Education and Welfare, 1969-1973. Special Assistant to the Administrator of the Environmental Protection Agency, 1973-1974. Assistant to the Administrator, Agency for International Development, U.S. Department of State, 1974-1975. Deputy General Counsel, U.S. Department of Transportation, 1975-1977. Acting General Counsel, U.S. Department of Transportation, 1976-1977. President, Harvard Law School Association of D.C., 1985-1986. *Member:* The District of Columbia Bar (Co-Chair, Section on Administrative Law and Agency Practice, 1989-1990); Federal (Chair, Transportation Law Section, 1988-1990) and American (Chairman, Air and Space Law Forum, 1999—) Bar Associations; Lawyers for Shakespeare Theatre (Executive Council). ***PRACTICE AREAS:*** Aviation Law; Transportation Law; Healthcare Law; Appellate Litigation; Administrative Law; Constitutional Law. ***Email:*** dbliss@omm.com

BRIAN D. BOYLE, born Covina, CA, July 27, 1960; admitted to bar, 1986, California; 1989, District of Columbia. *Education:* Georgetown University (A.B., summa cum laude, 1982); Harvard University (J.D., magna cum laude, 1986). Board of Editors, Harvard Law Review, 1984-1986. Law Clerk to: Justice Antonin Scalia, U.S. Supreme Court, 1991-1992; Judge Laurence H. Silberman, U.S. Court of Appeals for the District of Columbia Circuit, 1988-1989. [Assistant to the General Counsel, U.S. Army, 1986-1988 and 1989-1991]. ***PRACTICE AREAS:*** Class Action Litigation; Health Care Litigation; Insurance Liability; Product Liability; Appellate Litigation. ***Email:*** bboyle@omm.com

NADIA ST. GEORGE BURGARD, born St. Paul, MN, 1960; admitted to bar, 1992, New York; 1999, District of Columbia. *Education:* Wesleyan University (B.A., 1982); Fordham Law School (J.D., 1991). Articles Editor, Fordham Urban Law Journal, 1990-1991. *Member:* The Association of the Bar of the City of New York. ***LANGUAGES:*** French. ***PRACTICE AREAS:*** Loan Restructuring; Loan Workouts; Leveraged Acquisitions; Mergers and Acquisitions. ***Email:*** nburgard@omm.com

WALTER E. DELLINGER, born Charlotte, NC, May 15, 1941; admitted to bar, 1970, North Carolina (Not admitted in District of Columbia). *Education:* University of North Carolina, Chapel Hill (A.B., with honors, 1963); Yale University (J.D., 1966). ***Email:*** wdellinger@omm.com

ROBERT N. ECCLES, born Madison, WI, May 13, 1947; admitted to bar, 1972, Wisconsin; 1981, District of Columbia; 1982, U.S. Court of Appeals, Ninth Circuit; 1990, U.S. Court of Appeals, Tenth Circuit; 1991, U.S. Court of Appeals, Sixth Circuit and U.S. District Court, Eastern District of Michigan and Northern District of California; 1992, U.S. Court of Appeals, Fourth Circuit and U.S. District Court, District of Columbia; 1994, U.S. Supreme Court and U.S. Court of Appeals, Second, Third and Eleventh Circuits; 1995, U.S. Court of Appeals, Fifth and District of Columbia Circuits; 1997, U.S. District Court, Central District of Illinois; 1998, U.S. District Court, District of Maryland. *Education:* Harvard University (A.B., magna cum laude, 1969; J.D., 1972). Trial Attorney, U.S. Department of Justice, 1972-1977. Trial Attorney, 1977-1980, Deputy Associate Solicitor, 1980-1982, and Associate Solicitor, 1982-1988, U.S. Department of Labor. Editor, ERISA Litigation Reporter (1991—). ***PRACTICE AREAS:*** ERISA; ERISA Litigation; Employee Benefits; Employee Benefits Litigation. ***Email:*** beccles@omm.com

CLIFF H. FONSTEIN, born Los Angeles, CA, July 20, 1957; admitted to bar, 1984, California; 1994, District of Columbia and New York; U.S. District Court, Central, Northern and Eastern Districts of California, and Southern District of New York. *Education:* University of California at Berkeley (B.A., 1979); University of California at Los Angeles (J.D., 1983). *Member:* Los Angeles County and American Bar Associations; New York County Lawyers' Association. (Also at New York, NY Office). ***PRACTICE AREAS:*** Labor and Employment. ***Email:*** cfonstein@omm.com

STEPHEN J. HARBURG, born Philadelphia, PA, October 8, 1960; admitted to bar, 1985, Pennsylvania; 1987, District of Columbia. *Education:* Yale University (B.A., magna cum laude, 1982); University of Pennsylvania (J.D., magna cum laude, 1985). Order of the Coif. Associate Editor, University of Pennsylvania Law Review, 1983-1985. Law Clerk to Hon. Donald W. Van Artsdalen, U.S. District Judge, Eastern District of Pennsylvania, 1985-1986. *Member:* Pennsylvania and American Bar Associations; The District of Columbia Bar. ***PRACTICE AREAS:*** Antitrust; Class Action Litigation; Insurance Coverage. ***Email:*** sharburg@omm.com

(This Listing Continued)

BRUCE A. HILER, born Watervliet, MI, June 4, 1952; admitted to bar, 1977, Illinois; 1995, District of Columbia. *Education:* University of Notre Dame (B.A., magna cum laude, 1974); University of Michigan (J.D., cum laude, 1977). Author: *Dirks v. SEC:* A Study in Cause and Effect," 43 Md. L. Rev. 292 (1984); "The Judiciary Considers the Nature of Confidential Relationships in Insider Trading Cases - A Look at *United States v. Reed,* 13 Sec. Reg. L. J. 128 (1985); "Confidential Relationships and Insider Trading," 18 Rev. Sec. Reg. 135 (June 19, 1985); "The SEC and the Courts' Approach to Disclosure of Earnings Projections, Asset Appraisals and Other Soft Information: Old Problems, Changing Views," 46 Md. L. Rev. 1401 (1987), cited in *Basic Inc. v. Levinson,* 485 U.S. 224 (1988); "*Basic Inc. v. Levinson:* The Supreme Court's Opinion on Disclosure of Merger Negotiations, in Theory and Practice," 7 Corp. Counsel Rev. 1 (May 1988); "The SEC and the Insider Trader/Tipper," N.Y.L.J., August 29, 1991; "The Central Bank of Denver Decision and the SEC: Effects of the Decision and the SEC's Possible Response," 8 Corp. Counsel Rev. 1 (May 1994); "Management's Discussion and Analysis: Known Trends In SEC Enforcement," 8 (2) Insights (Dec. 1994); "Retail Broker Compensation," Insights (Vol. 9, No. 10; October, 1995); "The SEC's Use of Its Cease-and-Desist Authority," Survey Securities Regulations Law Journal (Fall, 1995); "Enforcement Issues and Litigation," Securities Regulation Law Journal, Vol. 25, No. 1 (Spring, 1997); "SEC Sends Warning Signals Regarding Supervision at Remote Locations," Insights, Vol. 11, No. 4, April 1997; "*United States v. O'Hagan:* The Supreme Court Upholds the Misappropriation Theory of Insider Trading Liability," Insights, Vol. 11, No. 9, September 1997; "The Evolving Standards for Board Oversight," Insights, Vol. 12, No. 1, January 1998; "The SEC's New Materiality Regime" Securities & Commodities Regulation, (Vol. 32, No. 17, Oct. 13, 1999); "Dealing with Securities Analysts; Recent Guidance," Securities Regulation Law Journal, Vol. 28, No. 3 (Fall 2000); "The SEC's New Public Disclosure Rule: Regulation FD," Securities Regulation Law Journal, Vol. 29, No. 1 (Spring 2001). Instructor, Civil Procedure, George Washington University Legal Assistant Program, Spring 1987. Adjunct Professor, Securities Law, Georgetown University Law Center, 1992-1998. Staff Attorney, August 1978 to December 1980, Special Counsel, January 1981 to June 1981, Branch Chief, July 1981 to January 1985, Assistant Director, January 1985 to March 1990 and Associate Director, March 1990 to March 1994, U.S. Securities and Exchange Commission, Division of Enforcement, Washington, D.C. Member, American Bar Association Task Force SEC Settlements. Member, Federal Regulations of Securities Committee, Business Law Section, American Bar Association. Member: Advisory Board of the Securities Regulation Law Journal. ***PRACTICE AREAS:*** Securities Law; Securities Regulation and Enforcement; Litigation. ***Email:*** bhiler@omm.com

GARY N. HORLICK, born Washington, DC, March 12, 1947; admitted to bar, 1974, Connecticut; 1975, District of Columbia. *Education:* Dartmouth College (A.B., 1968); Cambridge University, Cambridge, England (M.A., Diploma of International Law, 1970); Yale University (J.D., 1973). Phi Beta Kappa. Visiting Lecturer: Yale Law School, 1983-1986, 2001—; Georgetown Law Center, 1986—. Assistant Representative (Santiago, Chile and Bogota, Columbia), Ford Foundation, 1973-1976. International Trade Counsel, U.S. Senate Committee on Finance, 1981. Deputy Assistant Secretary of Commerce for Import Administration, 1981-1983. Member, Permanent Group of Experts (SCM Agreement), World Trade Organization, 1996-2001; Chairman, 1996-1997. *Member:* The District of Columbia Bar (Member, Steering Committee, International Division, 1983-1985; Chairman, 1984-1985); American (Member, Committee on International Aspects of Antitrust Law, International Law Section, 1972—) and International (Vice Chairman, Antitrust and Trade Law Committee, 1987-1989) Bar Associations; American Branch, International Law Association (Member, Executive Council, 1984—); American Society of International Law (Member, Board of Review, 1987-1991; Executive Council, 1998-1999); U.S. Court of International Trade (Advisory Committee, 1993-1997); Council on Foreign Relations. ***LANGUAGES:*** Spanish. ***REPORTED CASES:*** Certain Table Wines from France and Italy, 49 Fed. Reg. 10,587 (Int'l Trade Comm'n 1984) (anti-dumping and countervailing duty allegations) (negative preliminary), USITC Pub. No. 1502 (March 1984) (Represented Commission of the European Communities); Carbon and Certain Alloy Steel Products, 49 Fed. Reg. 30,807 (Int'l Trade Comm'n 1984) (Section 201), USITC Pub. No. 1553 (July 1984) (Represented Japan Iron and Steel Exporters Association); Certain Table Wines from W. Germany, France and Italy, 50 Fed. Reg. 45,174 (Int'l Trade Comm'n 1985) (anti-dumping and countervailing duty allegations) (neg. prelim.), USITC Pub No. 1771, appealed GATT Panel, SCM/71 (March 24, 1986) (Represented Commission of the European Communities); Steel Wheels From Brazil, 54 Fed. Reg. 21,456, (Dep't. Comm. 1989) (anti-dumping and countervailing duty allegations) (final, affirm. in part and neg. in part), USITC Pub. No. 2193 (May 1989) (neg. final) (Represented Rockwell International); Certain Fresh Atlantic Groundfish from Canada, 51 Fed. Reg. 10,041 (Dep't Comm. 1986) (countervailing duty allegation) (final affirm.), USITC Pub. No. 1844 (May 1986) (final, affirm. in part and neg. in part) (Counsel to Government of Canada); Canada - United States Free Trade Agreement, Jan. 2, 1988, U.S.T., T.I.A.S. No., reprinted in 27 I.L.M. 281 (1988) (Counsel to the Government of Canada); Fresh, Chilled, or Frozen Pork from Canada, 12 I.T.R.D. 1302 (1989) (appeal of Dep't of Comm. decision) 12 I.T.R.D. 1380 (1989) (appeal of Int'l Trade Comm'n decision), 13 I.T.R.D. 1859 (1991) (Extraordinary Challenge Committee) (Counsel to Government of Alberta); Flat Panel Displays and Subassemblies from Japan, 56 Fed. Reg. 32, 376 (Dep't Comm. 1991) (anti-dumping allegation) (final, affirm. in part and neg. in part), USITC Pub. No. 2413 (August 1991) (Counsel to International Business Machines Co. [IBM]); Fresh and Chilled Atlantic Salmon from Norway, 56 Fed. Reg. 7, 661 (Dep't Comm. 1991) (anti-dumping allegation) (final affirm.), appeal filed with GATT Panel, Request by Norway for the Establishment of a Panel Under Article 15:5 of the Agreement (Sept. 25, 1991); 56 Fed. Reg. 7, 678 (Dep't Comm. 1991) (countervailing duty allegation) (final affirm.), appeal filed with GATT Panel, Request by Norway for the Establishment of a Panel Under Article 17:3 of the Agreement (Aug. 28, 1991) (Counsel to the Government of Norway); Canada-Mexico-United States: North American Free Trade Agreement, December 1992, U.S.T., T.I.A.S. No., Reprinted in 32 I.L.M. 289 (1993) (Counsel to Government of Mexico); Agreement Establishing the World Trade Organization, in Final Act Embodying the Results of the Uruguay Round of Multilateral Trade Negotiations 9 (General Agreement on Tariffs and Trade) (April 15, 1994) (Counsel to Emergency Committee For American Trade); In the Matter of Tariffs Applied by Canada to Certain U.S.-Origin Agricultural Products (North American Free Trade Agreement Arbitral Panel Established Pursuant to Article 2008) (No. CDA-95-2008-01, December 2, 1996) (Counsel to Government of Canada); Fresh Atlantic Salmon From Chile, 62 Fed. Reg. 61803 (Dep't Comm. 1997) (negative countervailing duty determination) (Counsel to Government of Chile); Brazil-Measures Affecting Desiccated Coconut (World Trade Organization) (No. AB-1996-4, February 21, 1997) (Counsel to Government of Brazil); First Anti-dumping Duty Case in China:. Imported Newsprint Originally Manufactured in Canada, South Korea and the U.S. (1998) (Ministry of Foreign Trade and Economic Cooperation of People's Republic of China, "MOFTEC") (Counsel to Bowater Inc.); European Communities-Measures Concerning Meat and Meat Products (Hormones) (World Trade Organization) (No. 99-2855, July 12, 1999) (Counsel to National Cattlemen's Beef Association); Certain Crude Petroleum Oil Products From Iraq, Mexico, Saudi Arabia, and Venezuela, 64 Fed. Reg. 44480 (Dep't Comm. 1999) (neg. initiation determ.) (Counsel to Pemex) Certain Steel Beams from Germany and Spain (antidumping allegations), neg. prelim., USITC Pub. 3225 (1999) (Counsel to Trade Arbed); Mexico Measures Affecting Telecommunications Services: Request for the Establishment of a Panel by the United States (World Trade Organization) (November 16, 2000). ***PRACTICE AREAS:*** International Trade Law. ***Email:*** ghorlick@omm.com

TOM A. JERMAN, born Salt Lake City, UT, August 1, 1955; admitted to bar, 1981, California and U.S. District Court, Central District of California (Not admitted in District of Columbia). *Education:* University of Utah (B.S., magna cum laude, 1978; J.D., 1981). Member, Order of the Coif. Staff Member, 1979-1980 and Executive Editor, 1980-1981, Utah Law Review. Senior Editor, "The Railway Labor Act" (Bureau of National Affairs, 1995). *Member:* District of Columbia Bar; American Bar Associations. ***PRACTICE AREAS:*** Labor and Employment. ***Email:*** tjerman@omm.com

RONALD KLAIN, born Indianapolis, IN, August 8, 1961; admitted to bar, 1992, Pennsylvania; 1999, District of Columbia. *Education:* Georgetown University (A.B., summa cum laude, 1983); Harvard Law School (J.D., magna cum laude, 1987). Sears Prize Winner. Editor, Harvard Law Review, 1985-1986. Assistant to the President and Chief of Staff to the Vice President, 1995-1999. Chief of Staff to the Attorney General, 1994-1995. ***PRACTICE AREAS:*** Appellate Litigation; Strategic Counseling; Government Relations. ***Email:*** rklain@omm.com

DAVID G. LITT, born Boston, MA, October 10, 1962; admitted to bar, 1989, California, U.S. Courts of Appeals, Ninth Circuit and U.S. District Court, Central District of California; 1991, District of Columbia. *Education:* Yale University (B.A., in Economics, summa cum laude, 1984); University of Chicago (J.D., with honors, 1988). Phi Beta Kappa; Order of the Coif. Recipient, Floyd R. Mechem Scholarship and William R. Massee Award. Member, University of Chicago Law Review, 1986-1987. Law Clerk for: Chief Judge Alfred T. Goodwin U.S. Courts of Appeals, Ninth Circuit, 1988-1989; Hon. Anthony M. Kennedy, Associate Justice, U.S. Supreme Court, 1990-1991. Co-Author, with Macey, Miller and Rubin, "Politics, Bureaucracies and Financial Markets: Bank Entry Into Commercial Paper Underwriting in the United States and Japan," 139 U. Pa. L. Rev. 369 (1990). Author: "Work in Progress at the Ministry of Finance: Proposals for Restructuring the Japanese Financial Services Industry," 12 U. Pa. J. Int'l. Bus. L. 711 (1991). *Member:* American Bar Association (Business Law Section). ***LANGUAGES:*** Japanese. ***PRACTICE AREAS:*** Mergers and Acquisitions; Joint Ventures; Finance; International Business Law. ***Email:*** dlitt@omm.com

RICHARD G. PARKER, born St. Paul, MN, June 27, 1948; admitted to bar, 1974, California; 1980, District of Columbia. *Education:* University of California at Davis (A.B., summa cum laude, with highest honors, 1970); University of California at Los Angeles (J.D., 1974). Phi Beta Kappa; Phi Kappa Phi; Order of the Coif. Comment Editor, U.C.L.A. Law Review, 1973-1974. Law Clerk to the Hon. William Matthew Byrne, Jr., U.S. District Court, Central District of California, 1974-1975. Co-Author: "The Merger Wave:

(This Listing Continued)

(This Listing Continued)

O'MELVENY & MYERS LLP, Washington—Continued

Trends in Merger Enforcement and Litigation," 55 The Business Lawyer 351 (1999); "The Evolving Approach to Merger Remedies," Antitrust Report, May 2000. Former Director, Bureau of Competition. Formerly with Federal Trade Commission. *Member:* The District of Columbia Bar; American Bar Association (Annual Meeting Chair, 1996-1998 and Spring Meeting Chair, 2002, Antitrust Section). ***PRACTICE AREAS:*** Litigation. ***Email:*** rparker@omm.com

DAVID G. POMMERENING, born Milwaukee, WI, March 22, 1960; admitted to bar, 1986, New York; 1992, District of Columbia. *Education:* Duke University (A.B., magna cum laude, 1982); University of Virginia (J.D., 1985). *Member:* New York State Bar Association; The District of Columbia Bar. (Also at McLean, VA Office). ***PRACTICE AREAS:*** Corporate Law; Corporate Transactions. ***Email:*** dpommerening@omm.com

IRA H. RAPHAELSON, born Chicago, IL, July 3, 1953; admitted to bar, 1977, Illinois and U.S. District Court, Northern District of Illinois; 1981, U.S. Courts of Appeals, Seventh Circuit; 1983, U.S. District Court, Trial Bar of Northern District of Illinois; 1993, U.S. Supreme Court; 1996, District of Columbia and U.S. District Court, District of Maryland and District of Columbia; 1998, U.S. Court of Appeals for the District of Columbia and Fourth Circuits. *Education:* Northwestern University (B.A., 1974; J.D., 1977). First Presidentially-appointed Special Counsel for Financial Institutions Crime U.S. Department of Justice, 1991-1993. Counselor to the Attorney General of the United States, 1992-1993. Chairman (Banking), Senior Interagency Group, 1991-1993. United States Attorneys Office, Northern District of Illinois: United States Attorney, 1989-1990; First Assistant U.S. Attorney, 1989-1991; Chief, Special Prosecutions Division, 1987-1989; Chief, Criminal Litigation Division, 1987; Deputy Chief, Special Prosecutions Division, 1986-1987; Assistant U.S. Attorney, 1980-1991. Adjunct Faculty, John Marshall Law School, 1979-1990, Attorney General's Advocacy Institute, 1988-1993. Assistant States Attorney, Cook County, Illinois, 1978-1980. ***PRACTICE AREAS:*** Complex Litigation; Corporate Compliance and Special Investigations; Antitrust; White Collar Defense; Health Care; Financial Institutions. ***Email:*** iraphaelson@omm.com

ROBERT A. RIZZI, born Madison, WI, December 25, 1949; admitted to bar, 1978, California; 1997, District of Columbia. *Education:* Dartmouth College; Princeton University (A.B., 1972); Oxford University, Oxford, England (M.Litt., 1975); Harvard University (J.D., cum laude, 1978). Phi Beta Kappa. Member: Harvard Board of Student Advisers, 1975-1978; Board of Contributing Editors, Journal of Corporate Taxation, 1987— and Mergers & Acquisitions: The Monthly Tax Journal, 1999— . Adjunct Faculty, Golden Gate University Law School, 1991-1994. Adjunct Faculty, Catholic University Law School (1997-1998). *Member:* American Bar Association (Tax Section). (Also at Menlo Park, CA Office). ***PRACTICE AREAS:*** Tax Law. ***Email:*** rrizzi@omm.com

WILLIAM H. SATCHELL, born San Francisco, CA, March 24, 1953; admitted to bar, 1979, California; 1992, District of Columbia. *Education:* University of Chicago; University of California at Berkeley (A.B., 1974); University of Southern California (J.D., 1979). (Also at New York, NY Office). ***PRACTICE AREAS:*** Banking. ***Email:*** bsatchell@omm.com

CARL R. SCHENKER, JR., born Portland, OR, February 28, 1949; admitted to bar, 1974, California; 1977, District of Columbia; 1978, U.S. Supreme Court. *Education:* Stanford University (B.A., with great distinction, 1971; J.D., 1974). Phi Beta Kappa. President, Stanford Law Review, 1973-1974. Law Clerk to: Hon. Shirley M. Hufstedler, U.S. Courts of Appeals, Ninth Circuit, 1974-1975; Hon. Lewis F. Powell, Jr., U.S. Supreme Court, 1975-1976. *Member:* The District of Columbia Bar; State Bar of California; American Bar Association. ***PRACTICE AREAS:*** Civil Practice; Appellate Practice. ***Email:*** cschenker@omm.com

HENRY C. THUMANN, born Chicago, IL, January 6, 1935; admitted to bar, 1961, California (Not admitted in District of Columbia). *Education:* University of Illinois (B.A., with honors, 1957); Harvard University (LL.B., magna cum laude, 1960). Member, Board of Editors, Harvard Law Review, 1958-1960. Listed in *The Best Lawyers in America. Member:* Los Angeles County and American Bar Associations. Fellow, American College of Trial Lawyers. (Also at Los Angeles, CA Office). ***PRACTICE AREAS:*** General Business Litigation; Antitrust; Securities.

DEBRA A. VALENTINE, born Cleveland, OH, April 16, 1953; admitted to bar, 1980, District of Columbia; 1983, U.S. Court of Appeals, District of Columbia Circuit; 1988, U.S. Supreme Court; 1990, U.S. District Court, District of Columbia. *Education:* Princeton University (A.B., magna cum laude, 1976); Munich University, Munich, Germany; Yale University (J.D., 1980). Phi Beta Kappa. Fulbright Scholar. Editor, Yale Law Review, 1979-1980. Law Clerk to the Hon. Arlin M. Adams, U.S. Court of Appeals, Third Circuit, 1980-1981. Author: "The Logic of Secession," 89 Yale Law Journal 802, 1980; "Building a Cooperative Framework for Oversight in Mergers - The Answer to Extraterritorial Issues in Merger Review," 6 Geo. Mason L. Rev. 525 (1998); "Privacy on the Internet: The Evolving Legal Landscape," 16 Santa Clara Computer & High Tech L.J. 401 (2000). Co-Author, "Working with U.S. Trade Laws: The Practitioner's Perspective," Part One, 29 Swiss Rev. Int'l Comp. L. 5 (1987), Part Two, 30 Swiss Rev. Int'l Comp. L. 7 (1987). Speaker: "Merger Enforcement: Multijurisdictional Review and Restructuring Remedies," Third Regional Conference, International Bar Association, Santiago, Chile, March 24, 2000; "B2Bs: Distribution Efficiencies and Antitrust Issues," 2000 Annual Meeting, ABA Section of Antitrust Law, New York, N.Y., July 10, 2000; "Issues at the Intersection of Antitrust and Intellectual Property," Houston Intellectual Property Association and University of Houston Law Center Institute for Intellectual Property and Information Law, Galveston, Tex., October 7, 2000; "Retailer Buyer Power: Abusive Behavior and Merger/Acquisitions Roundtable," Fordham Corporate Law Institute, Fordham University School of Law, New York, N.Y., October 20, 2000. Teaching Assistant to Prof. Joseph Goldstein, Yale Law School, 1979-1980. Attorney Advisor, Office of Legal Counsel, Department of Justice, 1981-1985. Former General Counsel, Former Assistant Director for International Antitrust and Former Deputy for Policy Planning, Federal Trade Commission. *Member:* The District of Columbia Bar; American Bar Association (Co-Chair, International Antitrust and Foreign Competition Laws Committee, Antitrust Section, 2000—); American Law Institute; Council on Foreign Relations. ***LANGUAGES:*** German and French. ***REPORTED CASES:*** Collins v. Weinberger, 707 F.2d 1518 (D.C. Cir. 1983); Kendall v. Ferren, 1992 U.S. App. LEXIS 28627; Trans Union Corp. v. FTC, 245 F.3d 809 (D.C. Cir. 2001); FTC v. Heinz, 246 F.3d 708 (D.C. Cir. 2001). ***PRACTICE AREAS:*** Litigation; Antitrust and Trade Regulation. ***Email:*** dvalentine@omm.com

KAREN MARY WAHLE, born Chicago, Illinois, February 18, 1959; admitted to bar, 1992, Virginia; 1994, District of Columbia. *Education:* University of Illinois (B.S., with highest distinction, 1980); Stanford University (J.D., 1992). ***Email:*** kwahle@omm.com

SENIOR COUNSELLOR

WILLIAM T. COLEMAN, JR., born Philadelphia, PA, July 7, 1920; admitted to bar, 1947, Pennsylvania; 1955, U.S. Supreme Court; 1977, District of Columbia. *Education:* University of Pennsylvania (A.B., summa cum laude, 1941); Harvard Law School (LL.B., magna cum laude, 1946). Phi Beta Kappa; Pi Gamma Mu. Editor, Harvard Law Review, 1942-1943 and 1946-1947. Law Secretary to: Judge Herbert F. Goodrich, 1947-1948; Justice Felix Frankfurter, 1948-1949. Trustee, Trilateral Commission. Secretary, U.S. Department of Transportation, 1975-1977. Officer, de la Légion d' Honneur, 1980. Recipient, Presidential Medal of Freedom, 1995. Recipient, Thurgood Marshall Lifetime Achievement Award from NAACP Legal Defense and Educational Fund, 1997 and the American Law Institute's Henry J. Friendly Medal (May 2000). *Member:* Pennsylvania, Federal Power and American Bar Associations; District of Columbia Bar. Fellow, American College of Trial Lawyers. Fellow, American College of Appellate Lawyers, American Law Institute Council. ***PRACTICE AREAS:*** Constitutional Law; Appellate Practice; Trial Litigation; Corporate Law; Business Law; Transactional International Law.

SENIOR COUNSEL

JOEL S. BURTON, born New York, NY, May 31, 1935; admitted to bar, 1961, New York; 1962, District of Columbia. *Education:* Hobart & William Smith Colleges (B.A., 1957); Georgetown University Law School (LL.B., 1960). ***Email:*** jburton@omm.com

OF COUNSEL

SUSAN S. RICHARDSON, born Sewickley, PA, July 18, 1946; admitted to bar, 1981, California; 1983, District of Columbia. *Education:* Smith College (B.A., 1968); Harvard University (M.C.P., 1972); Boalt Hall School of Law, University of California, Berkeley (J.D., 1981). Order of the Coif. Associate Editor, Ecology Law Quarterly, 1979-1981. Law Clerk to Hon. William A. Norris, U.S. Court of Appeals, Ninth Circuit, 1981-1982. *Member:* The District of Columbia Bar; State Bar of California (inactive). ***PRACTICE AREAS:*** Corporate Law; Banking; Project Finance; Mergers and Acquisitions. ***Email:*** srichardson@omm.com

SPECIAL COUNSEL

EVELYN BECKER, born Philadelphia, Pennsylvania, April 12, 1968; admitted to bar, 1994, California; 1996, District of Columbia. *Education:* University of Southern California (A.B., cum laude, 1990); University of Chicago (J.D., 1993). ***Email:*** ebecker@omm.com

PEGGY ANN CLARKE, born New York, NY, 1957; admitted to bar, 1991, District of Columbia and New York. *Education:* George Washington University (B.A., 1979); Johns Hopkins University (M.A., 1982); Georgetown University (J.D., magna cum laude, 1990). Order of the Coif. *Member:* The District of Columbia Bar; American Bar Association. ***LANGUAGES:*** Italian and Spanish. ***PRACTICE AREAS:*** International Trade. ***Email:*** pclarke@omm.com

TERESA E. DAWSON, born Arlington Heights, IL, 1962; admitted to bar, 1991, Illinois; 1992, District of Columbia; 1993, U.S. Court of International

(This Listing Continued)

Trade. *Education:* Bradley University (B.A., magna cum laude, 1984); Georgetown University (M.S.F.S., 1991; J.D., 1991). Phi Kappa Phi; Omicron Delta Epsilon. Staff Member and Articles Editor, Georgetown Immigration Law Journal, 1989-1991. *Member:* American Bar Association. ***LANGUAGES:*** French. ***PRACTICE AREAS:*** Litigation; Regulatory Law. ***Email:*** tdawson@omm.com

SUZANNE RICH FOLSOM, born Honolulu, HI; admitted to bar, 1994, New York; 1995, District of Columbia. *Education:* Duke University (A.B., 1983); Georgetown University (J.D., cum laude, 1993). ***PRACTICE AREAS:*** Strategic Alliances; Litigation; Trade Association Law. ***Email:*** sfolsom@omm.com

NEIL K. GILMAN, born New York, NY, 1968; admitted to bar, 1995, New York; 1996, District of Columbia. *Education:* Amherst College (B.A., 1990); University of Michigan (J.D., magna cum laude, 1993). Order of the Coif. Law Clerk to the Hon. A. Raymond Randolph, U.S. Court of Appeals, District of Columbia Circuit, 1993-1994. Co-Author, with Bruce Hiler, "The SEC's Use of Its Cease-and-Desist Authority: A Survey," 23 SEC Regulation L. Jour. 256, 1995. ***PRACTICE AREAS:*** Antitrust; Securities; Litigation. ***Email:*** ngilman@omm.com

PAMELA A. HARRIS, born Hartford, CT, 1962; admitted to bar, 1992, Pennsylvania; 1994, District of Columbia. *Education:* Yale University (B.A., summa cum laude, 1985; J.D., 1990). Phi Beta Kappa. Current Topics Editor, Yale Law & Policy Review, 1989-1990. Law Clerk to Hon. Harry T. Edwards, U.S. Court of Appeals, District of Columbia, 1990-1991 and to Hon. John Paul Stevens, U.S. Supreme Court, 1992-1993. Assistant Professor, University of Pennsylvania Law School, 1996-1999: Church and State; Law and Literature; Criminal Procedure. ***PRACTICE AREAS:*** Appellate Practice. ***Email:*** pharris@omm.com

LYNN E. PARSEGHIAN, born Silver Spring, MD, 1965; admitted to bar, 1992, District of Columbia and New York. *Education:* University of Pennsylvania (B.A., cum laude, 1987); University of Chicago (J.D., 1991). Member, University of Chicago Law Review, 1991. Author: "Defining the 'Public Act' Requirement in the Act of State Doctrine" 58 University of Chicago L. Rev. 1151, 1991. *Member:* The District of Columbia Bar; New York State and American Bar Associations. ***PRACTICE AREAS:*** Litigation; Administrative Law. ***Email:*** lparseghian@omm.com

PATRICK ROBERT RIZZI, born New Milford, CT, 1968; admitted to bar, 1993, Pennsylvania; 1994, District of Columbia. *Education:* Georgetown University (B.S.B.A., magna cum laude, 1990); New York University School of Law (J.D., 1993). Beta Gamma Sigma. Articles Editor, New York University Law Review, 1992-1993. *Member:* The District of Columbia Bar; American Bar Association. ***PRACTICE AREAS:*** Aviation Regulation; Class Action Defense; Commercial Litigation. ***Email:*** prizzi@omm.com

IAN SIMMONS, born Toronto, Ontario, Canada, July 13, 1963; admitted to bar, 1992, Pennsylvania; 1993, District of Columbia. *Education:* McGill University (B.A., 1986); Yale University (M.A., 1988); University of Pennsylvania (J.D., 1991). Guy Drummond Fellow. University Scholar. Judicial Clerk to Hon. Gustave Diamond, Chief Judge, Western District of Pennsylvania, 1991-1992. U.S. Department of Justice, 1994-1997. Counsel, U.S. Senate Governmental Affairs Committee, 1997-1998. ***LANGUAGES:*** French.

GARY S. TELL, born Pittsburgh, PA, 1967; admitted to bar, 1992, Pennsylvania; 1993, District of Columbia and U.S. District Court, District of Columbia; 1995, U.S. District Court, District of Maryland. *Education:* Brown University (A.B., magna cum laude, 1989); University of Chicago (J.D., 1992). Associate Editor, University of Chicago Legal Forum, 1992. Co-Author with Stephen M. Saxon: and "Shifting the Liability Noose, Fiduciary Liability Under ERISA" 30 Pension Management 69 (Oct 1994); "Key Issues for Pension Plan Investments in the '90s" NYU 53rd Institute on Federal Taxation (1995). Trial Attorney, Office of the Solicitor, U.S. Department of Labor, 1995-1999. *Member:* American Bar Association. ***PRACTICE AREAS:*** Employee Benefits; Litigation. ***Email:*** gtell@omm.com

GREGG H. VICINANZA, born Belleville, NJ, October 6, 1965; admitted to bar, 1992, New York; 1994, U.S. District Court, Southern and Eastern Districts of New York; 1998, District of Columbia. *Education:* Rutgers College (B.A., 1987); New York University (J.D., 1991). Member, Moot Court. Research and Writing Editor, Moot Court Casebook Division, 1990-1991. Co-Author, "The 1992 Merger Guidelines as Applied to Mergers of Significant Competitors in Highly Concentrated Industries," Clayton Act Newsletter, Vol. 1, No. 2 (Spring 2001). Staff Attorney in Mergers II, 1998-1999 and Attorney Advisor to Chairman Robert Pitofsky, 1999-2001, Federal Trade Commission. *Member:* The Association of the Bar of the City of New York (Secretary, Committee on Antitrust and Trade Regulation Section, 1997-1998); The District of Columbia Bar (Member, Antitrust, Trade Regulation and Consumer Affairs Section); American Bar Association (Member, Antitrust Section). ***PRACTICE AREAS:*** Litigation; Antitrust and Trade Regulation. ***Email:*** gvicinanza@omm.com

(This Listing Continued)

ASSOCIATES

David Applebaum; Elizabeth H. Baird; Shannon M. Barrett (Not admitted in DC); ***Jeremy B. Bash*** (Not admitted in DC); ***Sean G. Blackman*** (Not admitted in DC); ***K. Lee Blalack II; Benjamin G. Bradshaw; Brian P. Brooks; William T. Buffaloe*** (Not admitted in DC); ***Nathan Garrett Bush*** (Not admitted in DC); ***Danielle L. Cannata*** (Not admitted in DC); ***Charles F. Connolly; John J. Donoghue*** (Not admitted in DC); ***Richard J. Dyer; Leslie A. Fahrenkopf*** (Not admitted in DC); ***Daniel E. Farrington; Rebecca H. Farrington; Theodore H. Frank; Richard D. Gardner*** (Not admitted in DC); ***Paul G. Griffin; CarrieLyn D. Guymon; Jonathan Hacker; Katharine B. Hazlett; Paul Horwitz; Benjamin R. Jacewicz; Sital Kalantry*** (Not admitted in DC); ***Laura M Kam*** (Not admitted in DC); ***Amy H. Kay*** (Not admitted in DC); ***Kathleen P. Kelly*** (Also at McLean, VA Office); ***Kerry A. Krentler*** (Not admitted in DC); ***Thomas A. Kuczajda; Veronique Lanthier; Elisabeth Layton; Alan Lefkowitz*** (Not admitted in DC); ***Goodwin H. Liu*** (Not admitted in DC); ***John P. Maloney, Jr.; Jeremy Maltby*** (Not admitted in DC); ***James V. Martin*** (Also at New York, NY Office); ***Jessica D. Miller; Kristin H. Mowry; John F. Niblock*** (Not admitted in DC); ***Matthew L. Olmsted; Shannon M. Pazur*** (Not admitted in DC); ***K. David Phan*** (Not admitted in DC); ***Gregory Y. Porter; Kelly Riordan; Rachel A. Shapiro*** (Not admitted in DC); ***Matthew M. Shors*** (Not admitted in DC); ***Srikanth Srinivasan*** (Not admitted in DC); ***Robert Stern*** (Not admitted in DC); ***William J. Stuckwisch; Morgen A. Sullivan*** (Not admitted in DC); ***Scott A. Thompson*** (Not admitted in DC); ***Andrew J. Trask; Darren S. Tucker; Andrew J. Varner*** (Also at McLean, VA Office); ***Joshua Waldman*** (Not admitted in DC); ***Robert E. Winter; Andrea Worden; Garrett Wotkyns*** (Not admitted in DC).

(For Complete Personnel and Biographical Data, see Professional Biographies at Los Angeles, California).

OPPENHEIMER WOLFF & DONNELLY LLP

1620 L STREET, N.W.
SUITE 600
WASHINGTON, D.C. 20036
Telephone: 202-312-8000
FAX: 202-312-8100
For attorney e-mails use: First initial of first name, last name, firm name, e.g., bkeil@oppenheimer.com
Email: info@oppenheimer.com
URL: http://www.oppenheimer.com

Minneapolis, Minnesota Office: 3300 Plaza VII, 45 South Seventh Street, 55402. Telephone: 612-607-7000. FAX: 612-607-7100.
Brussels, Belgium Office: Avenue Louise 240, Box 5, 1050. Telephone: 32-2-626-0500. FAX: 32-2-626-0510.
Newport Beach, California Office: 840 Newport Center Drive, Suite 700, 92660. Telephone: 949-823-6000. FAX: 949-823-6100.
New York, N.Y. Office: The Chrysler East Building, Suite 1900, 666 Third Avenue, 10017. Telephone: 212-884-4500. FAX: 212-884-4600.
Paris, France Office: 35 Boulevard des Capucines, 75002. Telephone: (33/1) 53 45 40 00. FAX: (33/1) 53 45 40 10.
Los Angeles, California Office: 2029 Century Park East, Suite 3800, 90067. Telephone: 310-788-5000. FAX: 310-788-5100.
Palo Alto, California Office: 1400 Page Mill Road, 94304. Telephone: 650-320-4000. FAX: 650-320-4100.

International Trade and Corporate Law, Taxation, Government Contracts, Environmental Law, Litigation, Immigration, Agency and Regulatory Law.

RESIDENT PARTNERS

HARRY W. CLADOUHOS, born March 9, 1925; admitted to bar, 1955, District of Columbia. *Education:* Georgetown University (B.S.F.S., magna cum laude, 1951); Harvard University (LL.B., 1954). ***PRACTICE AREAS:*** Government Relations.

JOHN H. KORNS, born March 20, 1945; admitted to bar, 1970, Louisiana; 1972, District of Columbia. *Education:* Harvard University (A.B., 1967; J.D., 1970). Law Clerk to the Hon. John Minor Wisdom, U.S. Court of Appeals, 5th Circuit, 1970-71; Hon. Warren E. Burger, Chief Justice, U.S. Supreme Court, 1971-72. ***PRACTICE AREAS:*** Litigation; International Trade Regulation.

PAUL M. LAURENZA, born March 31, 1948; admitted to bar, 1974, Missouri; 1975, District of Columbia. *Education:* University of New Hampshire (B.S., 1969); Brown University (M.A., 1971); Washington University (J.D., 1974). ***PRACTICE AREAS:*** Litigation.

THOMAS LAWRENCE, III, born February 19, 1951; admitted to bar, 1987, Virginia (Not admitted in District of Columbia). *Education:* State University of New York at Albany (B.A., 1973); George Mason University School of Law (J.D., 1987). ***PRACTICE AREAS:*** Transportation Law.

(This Listing Continued)

OPPENHEIMER WOLFF & DONNELLY LLP, Washington—Continued

BRIAN R. COLEMAN, born 1967; admitted to bar, 1998, California; registered to practice before the U.S. Patent and Trademark Office (Not admitted in District of Columbia). *Education:* University of California at San Diego (B.S.E.E., 1990; M.S.E.E., 1991); Hastings College of the Law, University of California (J.D., 1998). ***PRACTICE AREAS:*** Intellectual Property.

RESIDENT ASSOCIATES

DAPHNE L. BURTON, born 1967; admitted to bar, 1995, Texas; registered to practice before Patent and Trademark Office (Not admitted in District of Columbia). *Education:* University of Texas (B.S.M.E., 1990; J.D., 1994). ***PRACTICE AREAS:*** Intellectual Property.

CHAD SMITH, born 1967; admitted to bar, 1996, Minnesota (Not admitted in District of Columbia). *Education:* University of Minnesota (B.S., Aerospace Engineering/Mechanics, 1990); William Mitchell College of Law (J.D., 1996). ***PRACTICE AREAS:*** Intellectual Property. ***Email:*** chads@oppenheimer.com

DAVID BOGART DORT, born February 14, 1968; admitted to bar, 1998, New York; 2000, District of Columbia and U.S. District Court, Eastern and Southern Districts of New York. *Education:* Brown University (B.A., Logic and Philosophy of Science, 1993); Case Western Reserve University (J.D., 1997). ***PRACTICE AREAS:*** Intellectual Property.

RONALD S. GRUBB, JR., born Peoria, Illinois, 1966; admitted to bar, 2000, Tennessee; 2001, District of Columbia, registered to practice before Patent and Trademark Office. *Education:* Christian Brothers University (B.S.E.E., 1990); University of Memphis (M.B.A., 1994; J.D., 1999). ***PRACTICE AREAS:*** Intellectual Property.

(For biographical information on resident attorneys in Brussels, Los Angeles, Minneapolis, New York, Newport Beach, Palo Alto or Paris, please see the specific city and state listing)

LAW OFFICES OF JOHN T. O'ROURKE

801 PENNSYLVANIA AVENUE, N.W.
FIFTH FLOOR
WASHINGTON, D.C. 20004
Telephone: 202-662-4720
Fax: 202-662-4748

General Practice, Banking and Financial Institutions, Legislative, Tax, Telecommunications, International Transactions and International Trade.

FIRM PROFILE: Boutique law firm specializing in the representation of U.S. businesses in domestic and international business and trade matters. The firm is engaged in legislative and executive branch representation of clients with respect to banking and financial services, telecommunications and international trade/transactional matters.

JOHN T. O'ROURKE, born Lowell, Massachusetts, September 22, 1949; admitted to bar, 1981, District of Columbia. *Education:* Georgetown University (A.B., in Economics with distinction, 1972; J.D., 1980). Member, Industry Sector Advisory Committee on Services (ISAC 13), U.S. Department of Commerce, 1991-1993. Vice President and Counsel, Securities Industry Association, 1984-1990. Minority Staff Member, House Banking Committee, 1982-1984. Legislative Assistant to Rep. Ed Bethune, 1981-1982. Economist, U.S. Department of Labor, 1974-1977. *Member:* District of Columbia Bar. ***PRACTICE AREAS:*** Legislative; Banking; Securities; Telecommunications; International Trade and Transactions.

ASSOCIATE

MAGGI A. LAZARUS, born South Bend, Indiana, May 12, 1967; admitted to bar, 1993, Virginia; 1996, District of Columbia. *Education:* University of Virginia (B.A., 1989); Tulane University (J.D., cum laude, 1993). Member, Tulane Law Review, 1992-1993. Author: "Life After Lampf: The Constitutionality of New Section 27A," 68 Tul. L. Rev. 975 (1994); "United States v. Byrd: Scope of 'A Crime of Violence' for Preventative Detention Purposes," 67 Tul. L. Rev. 1693 (1993). *Member:* Virginia State Bar; District of Columbia Bar; American Bar Association. ***PRACTICE AREAS:*** Legislative.

ORRICK, HERRINGTON & SUTCLIFFE LLP

Established in 1863
WASHINGTON HARBOUR
3050 K STREET, N.W.
WASHINGTON, D.C. 20036
Telephone: 202-339-8400
Telecopier: 202-339-8500
URL: http://www.orrick.com

San Francisco, California Office: Old Federal Reserve Bank Building, 400 Sansome Street. Telephone: 415-392-1122. Telecopier: 415-773-5759.
Los Angeles, California Office: 777 South Figueroa Street. Telephone: 213-629-2020. Telecopier: 213-612-2499.
New York, New York Office: 666 Fifth Avenue. Telephone: 212-506-5000. Telecopier: 212-506-5151.
Sacramento, California Office: 400 Capitol Mall. Telephone: 916-447-9200. Telecopier: 916-329-4900.
Menlo Park, California Office: 1020 Marsh Road. Telephone: 650-614-7400. Fax: 650-614-7401.
Singapore Office: 10 Collyer Quay, #23-08 Ocean Building, Singapore. Telephone: 011-65-538-6116, Telecopier: 011-65-538-0606.
Tokyo, Japan Office: 11th Floor, Main Tower, Akasaka Twin Towers, 17-22 Akasaka 2-Chome, Minato-Ku. Telephone: 011-81-3-3224-2900. Telecopier: 011-81-3-3224-2901.
London, England Office: 1st Floor, 4 Broadgate, London EC2M 2DA. Telephone: 011-44-20-7638-1584. Telecopier: 011-44-20-7628-0078.
Seattle, Washington Office: 719 Second Avenue, Suite 900. Telephone: 206-839-4300. Fax: 206-839-4301.

General Practice, including Corporate and Municipal Finance, Domestic and International Commercial Law, Banking and Commercial Finance, Project Finance, Structured Finance, Mergers and Acquisitions, Commercial Litigation, Insurance, Insurance Insolvency, White Collar Criminal Defense, Tax, Employee Benefits and Personal Estates, Antitrust, Distribution, and Trade Regulation, Intellectual Property, Real Estate, Environmental and Energy and Labor and Employment Law and Bankruptcy.

RESIDENT PARTNERS

CAMERON L. COWAN, born Ontario, Canada, 1951; admitted to bar, 1982, New York and New Jersey; 1984, Connecticut; 1985, District of Columbia. *Education:* Syracuse University (B.A., magna cum laude, 1973); Columbia University (M.B.A., 1975); University of Virginia (J.D., 1981). *Member:* The Association of the Bar of the City of New York; The District of Columbia Bar; American Bar Association. ***PRACTICE AREAS:*** Corporate Finance Law; Structured Finance Law.

FELICIA B. GRAHAM, born Philadelphia, Pennsylvania, 1952; admitted to bar, 1978, District of Columbia. *Education:* Barnard College (B.A., magna cum laude, 1974); Vermont Law School (J.D., magna cum laude, 1978). *Member:* The District of Columbia Bar. ***PRACTICE AREAS:*** Structured Finance Law; Public Finance Law.

MICHAEL D. HORNSTEIN, born New York, New York, 1954; admitted to bar, 1981, New York; 1987, District of Columbia. *Education:* State University of New York at Albany (B.A., 1976); St. John's University (J.D., 1980). ***PRACTICE AREAS:*** Project Finance; Energy Regulation.

THOMAS J. HORTON, born New York, N.Y., 1955; admitted to bar, 1981, Ohio; 1987, District of Columbia. *Education:* Harvard University (A.B., cum laude, 1977); Case Western Reserve University (J.D., 1981).

DAVID S. KATZ, born New York, N.Y., 1955; admitted to bar, 1984, New York; 1988, District of Columbia. *Education:* University of Vermont (B.A., 1976); State University of New York at Binghamton (M.A., 1979); Boston University (J.D., 1983). Paul J. Liacos Scholar. Staff Member, 1981-1982 and Editor, 1982-1983, Annual Review of Banking Law. Author: "Irrevocability of Inter-Bank Electronic Fund Transfers: Delbruck & Co. v. Manufacturers Hanover Trust Co.," 3 Annual Review of Banking Law, 1984. Attorney, Office of General Counsel, Federal Home Loan Bank Board, 1983-1984. *Member:* The District of Columbia Bar; New York State and American (Member, Section on Corporation, Banking and Business Law) Bar Associations.

KEITH W. KRIEBEL, born Lansdale, Pennsylvania, 1958; admitted to bar, 1983, District of Columbia. *Education:* Dickinson College (B.A., summa cum laude, 1980); University of Pennsylvania (J.D., cum laude, 1983). Phi Beta Kappa; Omicron Delta Kappa; Phi Delta Phi. Executive Editor, University of Pennsylvania Law Review, 1982-1983. Author: Comment, "Gottfried v. FCC: The Public Interest Standard and Broadcaster Responsibility to the Hearing-Impaired," 130 University of Pennsylvania Law Review 957, April 1982; "Financing Merchant Power Plants," Project Finance 1999, Supplement to International Financial Law Review, July 1999. *Member:* The District of Columbia Bar; American Bar Association (Member, Section of Business Law). ***PRACTICE AREAS:*** Project Finance; Corporate Law.

(This Listing Continued)

DOUGLAS L. MADSEN, born Bradenton, Florida, 1961; admitted to bar, 1991, New York; 1992, District of Columbia. *Education:* Brigham Young University (B.A., magna cum laude, 1987); Harvard University (J.D., 1990). Author: "Judge versus Professor: Frank Easterbrook and the Wisconsin Anti-Takeover Statute," Harvard Journal of Law Public Policy, Volume 13. ***PRACTICE AREAS:*** Corporate; Structured Finance.

MICHAEL HOYT MITCHELL, born San Diego, California, 1961; admitted to bar, 1987, California; 1989, District of Columbia. *Education:* Siena College (B.S., magna cum laude, 1983); Georgetown University Law Center (J.D., 1986).

EDWIN G. OSWALD, born Queens, New York, 1959; admitted to bar, 1989, New York and Connecticut (Not admitted in District of Columbia). *Education:* St. John's University (B.S., 1983; J.D., 1988); New York University (LL.M., Taxation, 1992). Member, St. John's Law Review, 1986-1988. Certified Public Accountant, Maryland. Attorney Advisory, U.S. Treasury Department, Office of Tax Legislative Counsel, Dec., 1997 - July, 1999. Co-author: "IRS Revises Rules for Private Business Use of Facilities Financed by Tax-Exempt Bonds," The Journal of Taxation, Vol. 82, No. 5, May 1995. *Member:* American Bar Association (Committee on Tax-Exempt Financing); National Association of Bond Lawyers. ***PRACTICE AREAS:*** Tax Law; Tax Exempt Bonds.

DIANA WEISS, born Buffalo, New York, 1966; admitted to bar, 1992, New York; 1993, U.S. District Court, Southern and Eastern Districts of New York; 1996, U.S. Court of Appeals, Third Circuit (Not admitted in District of Columbia). *Education:* Ohio State University (B.A., 1988); Cornell University (J.D., 1991).

RESIDENT OF COUNSEL

MICHELE E. BEASLEY, born Washington, D.C., 1964; admitted to bar, 1992, Massachusetts; 1993, District of Columbia. *Education:* Smith College (B.A., cum laude, with high honors, 1986); Georgetown University (J.D., cum laude, 1991). Recipient, American Jurisprudence Award in Administrative Law. Author: "Guilty Pleas," 20th Ann. Rev. Crim. Pro., 79 Georgetown L.J. 879, 1991; "Wrongful Birth Wrongful Life: The Tort Progeny of Legalized Abortion," in Abortion Medicine of the Law, N.Y., 1992; "Punishing the Victim: Rape and Mistreatment of Asian Maids in Kuwait," Human Rights Watch, N.Y., 1992; "Domestic Violence As A Human Rights Issue," 15 Hum. Rts., Jan., 1993. Member, Board of Directors, Women's Commission for Refugee Women and Children, 1996—. *Member:* Massachusetts and American Bar Associations.

JONATHAN W. HADDON, born Albany, New York, 1958; admitted to bar, 1985, New York; 1998, District of Columbia. *Education:* University of Pennsylvania (B.A., 1980); Boston University School of Law (J.D., 1984). Member, 1982-1983 and Editor, 1983-1984, Boston University Law Review. Author, "Three Exceptions to the Per Se Rule Against Boycotts," Boston University Law Review, Vol. 65 (1985). ***LANGUAGES:*** French and German.

DIANNE L. STODDARD, born Humboldt, Nebraska, 1946; admitted to bar, 1975, Nebraska; 1991, District of Columbia; 1995, Virginia. *Education:* University of Nebraska (B.A., 1969); Creighton University (J.D., cum laude, 1975). Member, Board of Editors, Creighton Law Review. Law Clerk to The Honorable Hale McCown, Nebraska Supreme Court, 1975-1976. ***PRACTICE AREAS:*** Municipal Law; Public Finance; Structured Finance.

SANDRA E. TRIMBLE, born Buffalo, Wyoming, 1952; admitted to bar, 1989, Maryland; 1990, District of Columbia. *Education:* Colorado State University (B.A., with highest distinction, 1974); Sul Ross State University (M.Ed., 1977); Georgetown University (J.D., cum laude, 1989). Associate Articles Editor, Georgetown Law Journal, 1988-1989. *Member:* The District of Columbia Bar; Maryland State and American Bar Associations. ***PRACTICE AREAS:*** Corporate; Structured Finance.

PATRICIA R. ZEIGLER, born Freeport, New York, 1957; admitted to bar, 1983, California; 1986, District of Columbia. *Education:* Oberlin College (B.A., 1980); University of San Francisco (J.D., 1983).

RESIDENT ASSOCIATES

REAGEN BECK, born 1970; admitted to bar, 1997, Maryland; 2000, District of Columbia. *Education:* Johns Hopkins University (B.A., 1992); Washington College of Law, American University (J.D., 1997).

MARK S. DOLA, born New Brunswick, New Jersey, 1958; admitted to bar, 1994, New York; 1996, District of Columbia. *Education:* Yale University (B.A., 1980); Georgetown University Law Center (J.D., 1994).

KYLE W. DREFKE, born Cherokee, Iowa, 1969; admitted to bar, 1994, Iowa and Missouri; 1998, New York (Not admitted in District of Columbia). *Education:* University of Iowa (B.B.A., with distinction, 1991; J.D., with high distinction, 1994). Member, Iowa Law Review.

JOHANNA EADIE, born 1969; admitted to bar, 2000, New York and Maryland (Not admitted in District of Columbia). *Education:* University of California, Berkeley (B.A., 1992); University of Miami (J.D., 1999).

(This Listing Continued)

WELLS ENGLEDOW, born Lancaster, Pennsylvania, 1973; admitted to bar, 2000, New York and District of Columbia. *Education:* James Madison University (B.S., magna cum laude, 1996); Georgetown University Law Center (J.D., 1999).

CRAIG FISHMAN, born 1960; admitted to bar, 1988, New York; 2000, District of Columbia. *Education:* Cornell University (B.A., 1982); University of Virginia (J.D., 1987).

MICHAEL H. FREEDMAN, born New York, N.Y., 1967; admitted to bar, 1995, New York; 1996, District of Columbia. *Education:* Duke University (B.A., 1989); American University, Washington College of Law (J.D., 1994). Member, American University Law Review.

PREETHA P. GIST, born Kerala, India, 1973; (admission pending). *Education:* University of Virginia (B.A., 1995); Duke University (J.D., 2001).

SHAZMAH HAKIM, born Karachi, Pakistan, 1969; admitted to bar, 1999, New York (Not admitted in District of Columbia). *Education:* Scripps College (B.A., 1991); New York University (M.A., in International Politics and Business, 1993); George Washington University (J.D., with honors, 1998). Member, Journal of International Law and Economics.

STEPHEN L.M. LARSEN, born Cheverly, Maryland, 1977; (admission pending). *Education:* University of Baltimore (B.A., 1999); Georgetown University Law Center (J.D., 2001).

MICHAEL J. McELROY, born Oxnard, California, 1969; admitted to bar, 1997, Virginia (Not admitted in District of Columbia). *Education:* Kenyon College (B.A., magna cum laude, 1991); Georgetown University (J.D., 1997). Phi Beta Kappa.

J. RUSSELL MILLER, born Houston, Texas, 1966; admitted to bar, 1996, Texas; 1998, District of Columbia. *Education:* University of Washington (B.A., magna cum laude, 1991); University of Washington School of Law (J.D., 1995). Phi Beta Kappa. Phi Delta Phi. Member, Texas Young Lawyers Association, 1996-1998.

LAUREN C. MULLEN, born Southampton, New York, 1966; admitted to bar, 1992, Virginia; 1993, District of Columbia; 1995, Maryland. *Education:* Columbia University (A.B., 1988); College of William & Mary (J.D., 1992).

MARGARET PRYOR, born Boston, Massachusetts, 1972; (admission pending). *Education:* Trinity College (B.A., 1994); American University (J.D., 1999). Senior Editor, American University Law Review.

HEATHER L. QUINTER, born Reading, Pennsylvania, 1976; (admission pending). *Education:* George Washington University (B.A., 1998); Georgetown University Law Center (J.D., 2001).

MARK R. RICCARDI, born Albany, New York, 1969; admitted to bar, 1994, Maryland; 1996, District of Columbia. *Education:* Hamilton College (A.B., summa cum laude, 1991); Georgetown University (J.D., 1994). Phi Beta Kappa. Executive Editor, Georgetown Journal of Legal Ethics, 1993-1994. *Member:* District of Columbia Bar; Maryland State and American Bar Associations.

HINA SHAIKH, born 1972; admitted to bar, 1999, New York; 2000, England and Wales (Not admitted in District of Columbia). *Education:* Tulane University (B.A., 1994); Tulane University Law School (J.D., 1998).

SCOTT A. STENGEL, born Fort Wayne, Indiana, 1971; admitted to bar, 1996, Virginia; 1997, District of Columbia. *Education:* University of Notre Dame (B.A., 1993); University of Notre Dame Law School (J.D., 1996). ***PRACTICE AREAS:*** Bankruptcy; Commercial Law; Structured Finance.

BARBARA STETTNER, born Los Gatos, California, 1962; admitted to bar, 1996, District of Columbia. *Education:* University of California, Davis (B.A., 1989); Pepperdine University (J.D., 1994).

MICHAEL R. TROCCHIO, born 1971; admitted to bar, 1998, New York (Not admitted in District of Columbia). *Education:* Georgetown University (B.A., 1993); St. John's University (J.D., 1997).

KENNETH J. YELLEN, born 1969; admitted to bar, 1996, New York (Not admitted in District of Columbia). *Education:* University of California, San Diego (B.A., 1991); Boston University School of Law (J.D., 1995). ***PRACTICE AREAS:*** Structured Finance.

ANDREW P. ZARNOWIECKI, born 1973; (admission pending). *Education:* Syracuse University (B.A., 1996); American University (M.B.A., 2000); Washington College of Law, American University (J.D., 2000).

LONDON, ENGLAND
MEMBERS OF THE FIRM

R. Michael Bacon	***Paul S. Stock***
Martin Stewart-Smith	***Paul Weiffenbach***

LOS ANGELES, CALIFORNIA
MEMBERS OF FIRM

Alan G. Benjamin	***W. Douglas Kari***
J. Keith Biancamano	***Linda S. Koffman***

(This Listing Continued)

ORRICK, HERRINGTON & SUTCLIFFE LLP, Washington—Continued

LOS ANGELES, CALIFORNIA
MEMBERS OF FIRM (Continued)

William W. Bothwell
Lori A. Bowman
Eugene Carron
Gerald L. Chaleff
Blase P. Dillingham
Greg Harrington
Paul A. Webber
Michael A. McAndrews
Richard C. Mendelson
Mary H. Neale
William W. Oxley
Gary D. Samson
Larry D. Sobel
Bradley S. White
Neal L. Wolf

MENLO PARK, CALIFORNIA
MEMBERS OF FIRM

William L. Anthony
W. Reece Bader
Scott D. Blickenstaff
Brian C. Burr
William Sloan Coats
Peter Cohn
Scott D. Elliott
Vickie L. Feeman
Robert E. Freitas
G. Hopkins Guy, III
Lynne C. Hermle
Craig R. Kaufman
Amy Landers
Geoffrey P. Leonard
Christopher R. Ottenweller
Robert S. Shwarts
Gary E. Weiss
Eric L. Wesenberg
Thomas H. Zellerbach

NEW YORK, NEW YORK
MEMBERS OF FIRM

Peter A. Bicks
Charles W. Bradley
Bradford S. Breen
Mary Rose Brusewitz
Peter Bucci
Fred C. Byers, Jr.
William R. Campbell
James J. Capra, Jr.
Michael B. Carlinsky
Richard Chirls
J. Peter Coll, Jr.
Jeffrey A. Conciatori
Peter J. Connors
Robert A. Cote
Katharine I. Crost
Duncan Darrow
Michael Delikat
Edward M. DeSear
Laurie Dix
Lauren Elliot
Joseph Evall
Rubi Finkelstein
Robert A. Fippinger
Lawrence B. Fisher
Stephen G. Foresta
Charles W. Gerdts, III
Lawrence B. Goodwin
F. Susan Gottlieb
Arnold Gulkowitz
Eileen B. Heitzler
Robert M. Isackson
David R. Jewell
Mitchell S. Kaplan
John J. Keohane
Alan M. Knoll
Martin H. Levenglick
Herbert J. Levine
Carl F. Lyon, Jr.
John A. MacKerron
Joseph E. Maloney
Richard W. Mark
Daniel Mathews
Lorraine S. McGowen
Michael R. Meyers
Robert B. Michel
Sam Scott Miller
Christopher J. Moore
Barbara Moses
P. Quinn Moss
James J. Murtha
David Nirenberg
Perry A. Pappas
Anthony Princi
Joshua E. Raff
Clayton Reynolds
Jill L. Rosenberg
Ira G. Rosenstein
Al B. Sawyers
Stephen K. Sawyier
Albert Simons, III
Louis H. Singer
Elaine F. Stein
James L. Stengel
Daniel J. Thomasch
Michael Voldstad
L. Mark Weeks
Robert S. Whitman
Neil T. Wolk

SACRAMENTO, CALIFORNIA
MEMBERS OF FIRM

Norman C. Hile
Perry E. Israel
Cynthia J. Larsen
Marc A. Levinson
Timothy J. Long
Virginia C. Magan
Iain Mickle
John R. Myers
Thomas J. Welsh

SAN FRANCISCO, CALIFORNIA
MEMBERS OF FIRM

William F. Alderman
David T. Alexander
Denise Alter
Mary A. Collins
Dean E. Criddle
Roger L. Davis

(This Listing Continued)

SAN FRANCISCO, CALIFORNIA
MEMBERS OF FIRM (Continued)

Ralph H. Baxter, Jr.
Elaine R. Bayus
Daniel R. Bedford
William D. Berry
Paul C. Borden
Fred A. Brown
Colman J. Burke
Charles C. Cardall
Thomas Y. Coleman
Robert J. Gloistein
Richard Grey
Richard D. Harroch
John M. Hartenstein
Dolph M. Hellman
Gary A. Herrmann
Richard I. Hiscocks
Leslie P. Jay
Lawrence T. Kane
John H. Knox
Mark R. Levie
Michael H. Liever
Peter Lillevand
Sean A. Lincoln
Gary Louie
Joseph M. Malkin
Steven C. Malvey
Dora Mao
Jesse W. Markham
Thomas C. Mitchell
William G. Murray
Noel W. Nellis
Ana Marie Del Rio
Stanley J. Dirks
William M. Doyle
Raymond G. Ellis
Robert P. Feyer
Grant Finlayson
Carlo S. Fowler
Kathy Woeber Gardner
Richard A. Gilbert
Jonathan M. Ocker
Tracy Preston
M. J. Pritchett
Greg R. Riddle
Marie B. Riehle
William L. Riley
Peter E. Root
William R. Sawyers
Paul J. Sax
John F. Seegal
Gary R. Siniscalco
Richard V. Smith
Stephen A. Spitz
Alan Talkington
James V. Telfer
Ralph C. Walker
Jeffrey S. White
Kenneth G. Whyburn
Jeffrey D. Wohl
George G. Wolf
Cameron W. Wolfe Jr.
George A. Yuhas

SINGAPORE
MEMBERS OF FIRM

Marie-Anne Jacoba Birken
Bruce R. Schulberg

TOKYO
MEMBER OF FIRM

Howard M. Goldwasser
Christopher Lewis
Dennis P. Martin

SEATTLE, WASHINGTON
MEMBERS OF FIRM

Keith C. Cochran
Stephen M. Graham
Scott J. Moore

ORTMAN, LOVE & HUCKABAY

WASHINGTON, D.C.

(See Bethesda, Maryland)

General and Civil Practice before all Courts and Governmental Agencies, Probate and Trust Law, Taxation, Casualty and General Negligence Law, Insurance and Corporation Law.

OSBORNE AND DEUTSCH

Established in 1988

SUITE 550
1666 CONNECTICUT AVENUE, N.W.
WASHINGTON, D.C. 20009
Telephone: 202-728-0820
Fax: 202-234-1270
URL: http://www.lawyers.com/osborne&deutsch

General Practice, Specializing in Immigration and Nationality Law, Civil Litigation, Labor and Employment, Domestic Relations Mediation.

WOODLEY B. OSBORNE, born Milwaukee, Wisconsin; admitted to bar, 1965, New York; 1966, District of Columbia; 1978, U.S. Supreme Court; 1988, Maryland; U.S. Court of Appeals, District of Columbia, First, Fourth and Federal Circuits. *Education:* Trinity College (A.B., 1960); New York University (J.D., 1965). Author, "The Need for Legislation after Yeshiva" (NLRB v. Yeshiva University, U.S. 100 S.Ct. 856, 1980), Journal of Law & Education, 1980. Co-Author: "A Primer on Collective Bargaining for College & University Faculty," Published by American Association of University Professors, 1974; "The Effect of the Americans With Disabilities Act on Employer-Sponsored Health

(This Listing Continued)

Plans," District of Columbia Bar, Labor Relations Sections (Commerce Clearing House, Sept. 1993); "Whistle Blowers and D.C.'s Public Policy Tort," The Washington Lawyer, July/August 1992. Mediator, District of Columbia Superior Court, 1989-1999. *Member:* District of Columbia Bar (Member, 1988-1995 and Co-Chair, 1991-1993, Steering Committee of Labor Relations Section); Maryland State Bar Association; National Employment Lawyers Association; Metropolitan Washington Employment Lawyers Association (President, 2000—; Member, Board of Directors, 1988—; Chair, Amicus Brief Committee, 1988—). ***REPORTED CASES:*** Gary V. Long, 59F.3d 1391 CD.C.Cir. 1995; Swanks v. Washington Metropolitan Area Transit Authority, 179 F.3d 929 (D.C. Cir. 1999), cert. denied, 120 S.Ct. 614. ***PRACTICE AREAS:*** Litigation; Civil Rights; Labor and Employment. ***Email:*** wbolaw@erols.com

MORRIS H. DEUTSCH, born Detroit, Michigan, January 15, 1953; admitted to bar, 1982, Massachusetts, Virginia and U.S. District Court, Eastern District of Virginia; 1983, U.S. Court of Appeals, Fourth Circuit; 1986, District of Columbia and U.S. Supreme Court; 1987, U.S. District Court, District of Columbia and U.S. District Court, District of Maryland. *Education:* Boston University (B.A., magna cum laude, 1979); Boston College Law School (J.D., cum laude, 1982). Recipient, Special Achievement Award (Litigation) from Attorney General, U.S. Department of Justice, 1985. Editor, B.C. Int'l & Comp. L.R., 1981-1982. Judicial Law Clerk, U.S. Court of Appeals, Fourth Circuit, 1982-1984. Trial and Appellate Attorney, Civil Division, U.S. Department of Justice, 1984-1986. Author: "Advising Employers on the New Immigration Reform and Control Act," Published by The District of Columbia Bar, May/June, 1987; "A Family on the Edge," Lawyers' Committee for Civil Rights Under Law, Spring 1987; "Obtaining Evidence in the United States for Use in Foreign or International Tribunal," B.C. Int'l & Comp. L.R., 1981. Chair, Asylum Office Liaison Committee, District of Columbia American Immigration Lawyers Association, 1994-1995. Chair, Legal Committee, 1989-1991 and Co-Chair, Fund Raising Committee, 1991-1996, District of Columbia Jewish Community Center. *Member:* District of Columbia Bar; Virginia State Bar; American Immigration Lawyers Association. ***PRACTICE AREAS:*** Immigration and Nationality; General Business Law. ***Email:*** morrisdeutsch@compuserve.com

REPRESENTATIVE CLIENTS: American Automobile Association; Cincinnati Bell Information Systems; Eurocentres, Inc.; Gallaudet University; Gardner Merchant Food Services, Inc.; International Reading Association; Textron, Inc.; TV Answer, Inc., CACI; COMSYS Technical Services.

OSBORNE LAW OFFICES, P.C.

4301 CONNECTICUT AVENUE, NW
SUITE 108
WASHINGTON, D.C. 20008
Telephone: 202-243-3200
Fax: 202-243-3207
Email: Lawfirm@OsborneLaw.com

General Civil Litigation, Labor, Pension and Employee Relations Law, Equal Opportunity Law and Bankruptcy Law.

FIRM PROFILE: The firm advises and counsels individuals, unions and associations in a local and national employment law practice.

WILLIAM W. OSBORNE, JR., born Syracuse, New York, December 9, 1948; admitted to bar, 1975, District of Columbia, U.S. Court of Appeals, Second, Fourth, Fifth, Ninth, Tenth, Eleventh, Federal and the District of Columbia Circuits and U.S. Supreme Court. *Education:* Williams College (B.A., 1971); Catholic University of America (J.D., 1975). Adjunct Professor: Labor Law, Georgetown University Law Center, 1978-1990; Internal Union Affairs, National Law Center, George Washington University, 1985-1988; Catholic University of America, 1981, 1990. Lecturer: George Meany Center for Labor Studies, 1980—; University of the District of Columbia, 1987-1991. Author: "The Union's Preservation of the Bargaining Unit Against Double-Breasted Operations and Similar Contrivances," (Pacific Coast Labor Law Conference, 1986); "Salvaging the Section 10 (e) Injunction," (1995 Annual Meeting, ABA). Attorney, National Labor Relations Board, Washington, D.C., 1975-1976. *Member:* District of Columbia Bar (Co-Chair, Labor Law Division, 1982-1983); American Bar Association (Member, Labor and Employment Law Section; Co-Chair, Committee on Union Administration, 1994—). ***PRACTICE AREAS:*** Labor and Employment Law; Pension Plans; Equal Employment Opportunity Law; Bankruptcy Law. ***Email:*** B.OSBORNE@OsborneLaw.com

JASON J. VALTOS, born Scranton, Pennsylvania, August 22, 1974; admitted to bar, 1999, Washington; 2000, U.S. District Court, Western and Eastern Districts of Washington and U.S. Court of Appeals, Ninth Circuit (Not admitted in District of Columbia). *Education:* The Pennsylvania State University (B.S., Finance, 1996); Widener University School of Law (J.D., 1999). Contributing Editor, The Developing Labor Law, 2000—. Vice President, Negotiation Client Counseling Society, 1998-1999. Member, AFL-CIO Lawyers Coordinating Committee. *Member:* Washington State and American (Member, Labor and Employment Law Sections) Bar Associations. ***REPORTED CASES:*** Nader Spahi, d/b/a/ Emperor West Associates v. Hughes Northwest, Inc. 27 P.3d 1233, 2001 Wash. App. Lexis 1740. ***PRACTICE AREAS:*** Union Labor Law; Litigation. ***Email:*** jvaltos@erols.com

LAW OFFICES OF
R. DENNIS OSTERMAN, PLLC

1901 PENNSYLVANIA AVENUE, SUITE 1005
WASHINGTON, D.C. 20006
Telephone: 202-861-4297
Fax: 202-463-2039
Email: rdostermanpllc@aol.com

Compensation and Insurance Benefits, Sex Discrimination, Wrongful Termination, Race Discrimination, Employment Law, Litigation Medical Malpractice Law, Personal Injury, Automobile Accidents, Wrongful Death, White Collar Crime, Federal Criminal Law, Criminal Defense, Assaults, Felonies.

R. DENNIS OSTERMAN, born Pittsburgh, Pennsylvania, February 19, 1947; admitted to bar, 1977, Virginia; 1978, District of Columbia; 1982, Pennsylvania; 1985, Nebraska; 1989, Maryland. *Education:* Grove City College (B.S., 1969); American University (M.S., 1976; J.D., cum laude, 1977). Member, Editorial Staff, American University Law Review, 1976-1977. Adjunct Instructor in Law, American University, 1978-1982. Adjunct Faculty: Creighton Law School, 1985-1988; American University Law School, Trial Practice, 1988—. University Faculty Award for Outstanding Teaching, 1994. Member, Character Committee, Maryland Court of Appeals, 1996-2000. Assistant U.S. Attorney, District of Columbia, 1978-1982. Partner, Lerch, Early & Brewer, Bethesda, Maryland, 1988-2000. General Trial Counsel, Union Pacific Railroad Company, 1984-1988. *Member:* Montgomery County, Maryland State, Virginia and American Bar Associations; District of Columbia Bar. ***PRACTICE AREAS:*** Employment Law; Litigation; Medical Malpractice Law; White Collar; Criminal Defense.

OSTROLENK, FABER, GERB & SOFFEN, LLP

1725 K STREET NW
WASHINGTON, D.C. 20006
Telephone: 202-457-7785
Fax: 202-429-8919
Email: email@ostrolenk.com

New York, New York Office: 1180 Avenue of the Americas. 10036. Telephone: 212-382-0700. Facsimile: 212-382-0888.

Patent, Trademark, Copyright and Unfair Competition.

STEPHEN A. SOFFEN, born Princeton, New Jersey, June 23, 1956; admitted to bar, 1983, New York and U.S. Court of Appeals for the Federal Circuit; 1988, District of Columbia; registered to practice before U.S. Patent and Trademark Office. *Education:* Cornell University (B.S.E.E., 1978); Washington School of Law of American University; Suffolk University (J.D., 1982). Technical Law Clerk to Hon. Helen W. Neis, U.S. Court of Appeals for the Federal Circuit, 1983-1985. *Member:* The District of Columbia Bar; American Intellectual Property Law Association. (Resident). ***PRACTICE AREAS:*** Patent; Trademark; Copyright; Unfair Competition. ***Email:*** ssoffen@ostrolenk.com

ASSOCIATES

PETER McGEE, born Cambridge, Massachusetts, October 29, 1955; admitted to bar, 1985, Pennsylvania; 1991, District of Columbia; registered to practice before U.S. Patent and Trademark Office. *Education:* Cornell University (B.S., 1979); Columbia School of Law, Catholic University (J.D., 1984). (Resident). ***PRACTICE AREAS:*** Patent Law. ***Email:*** pmcgee@ostrolenk.com

ELLEN S. TAO, born Chicago, Illinois, December 2, 1969; admitted to bar, 1995, Illinois; 1997, District of Columbia; registered to practice before U.S. Patent and Trademark Office. *Education:* Washington University, St. Louis (B.S., Chemical Engineering, 1992); American University (J.D., 1995). Former Patent Examiner, Medical and Surgical Arts, U.S. Patent and Trademark Office. *Member:* The District of Columbia Bar; Illinois State and American Bar Associations; Asian Pacific American Bar Association; American Intellectual Property Law Association. (Also at New York, New York Office). ***PRACTICE AREAS:*** Patent Prosecution.

OF COUNSEL

LEON ZITVER, born New York, N.Y., November 27, 1913; admitted to bar, 1942, District of Columbia; 1975-1982, U.S. Court of Customs and Patent Appeals; 1975, U.S. Court of Appeals for the District of Columbia Circuit; 1972, District of Columbia Court of Appeals; registered to practice before U.S.

(This Listing Continued)

OSTROLENK, FABER, GERB & SOFFEN, LLP, Washington—Continued

Patent and Trademark Office. *Education:* City College of the City University of New York (B.S. in Enginnering,1935); George Washington University (J.D., 1942). *Member:* District of Columbia Bar; Federal Bar Association; American Association for the Advancement of Science; Patent and Trademark Office Society. ***PRACTICE AREAS:*** Patent Law. ***Email:*** lzitver@ostrolenk.com

LAW OFFICES OF MICHAEL J. PANGIA

1717 N STREET, N.W.
WASHINGTON, D.C. 20036
Telephone: 202-955-6450
Fax: 202-955-9444
Email: Michael.Pangia@Verizon.Net
URL: http://www.lawyers.com/aviation

Aviation, Automobile, Maritime, Railroad and Transportation Litigation, Medical Malpractice, Product Liability, Negligence, Civil and Administrative Trials and Appeals in all Courts including Multi-National and Multi-District Tort Disasters, U.S. and Foreign Personal Injuries and Wrongful Deaths.

FIRM PROFILE: Since 1982, Pangia & Hansen has had an expertise in aviation trials and appeals with an emphasis on negligence and products liability in foreign and domestic aviation accidents and on the defense of pilots and operators charged with FAA violations. The firm routinely handles other litigation including foreign and domestic auto, rail, and maritime/admiralty as well as general negligence and products liability matters.

MICHAEL J. PANGIA, born Brooklyn, New York, January 5, 1942; admitted to bar, 1967, New York; 1977, District of Columbia, U.S. Supreme Court and U.S. Claims Court. *Education:* United States Merchant Marine Academy (B.S. in Engineering, 1963); St. John's University (J.D., 1967). Recipient: The John Marshall Award by U.S. Attorney General for Outstanding Achievement in the Development of Aviation Law; Meritorious Award from FAA for Chicago DC-10 Hearings; Highest Professional Achievement Award for USMMA Class '63. Author: "Posttraumatic Stress Disorder, Litigation Strategies," Journal of Air Law & Commerce, 1999; "Litigating Air Crash Cased, "The Digest, Syracuse University School of Law, 1999; "Pilot Judgement: Training, Current Development and Future Issues in Aviation Cases," Journal of Air Law and Commerce, Spring 1983; "A Clear Approach to Aviation Cases," Trial Magazine, Vol. 17, No. 2, 1981; "Handling FAA Enforcement Proceedings, A View From the Inside," Journal of Air Law and Commerce, Spring 1981; "Aviation Accident Investigation in a Litigation Environmental," Lawyer Pilots Bar Association Journal, Fall, 1981; "Use of Demonstrative Evidence," Trial Lawyer's Guide, Spring 1981; "Discovery of the Government in Aviation Cases," Trial Lawyer's Guide, Fall 1980; "Application of the Freedom of Information Act on Discovery," New York Bar Journal, 1979; "Unique Aspects of Discovery in Aviation Cases," American Bar Association, Forum, Vol. XIII, No. 1, Fall 1977. Adjunct Professor, Business Law, Long Island University, 1969-1971. Airline Transport Pilot Certificate, Single, Multiengine, Instrument Rated, Flight and Ground School Instructor, FAA Certificated Aircraft and Powerplant Mechanic. Trial Attorney, Admiralty, Senior Trial Attorney, Aviation and Chief of Aviation Unit, U.S. Department of Justice, 1970-1979. Chief of Litigation Counsel and Accident Investigation Spokesman of Federal Aviation Administration, 1979-1982. FAA Designated Accident Prevention Counselor, 1982—. Director of Air Safety of Congressional Squadron of Civil Air Patrol, 1983. General Counsel and Member of the Board of National Aviation Club, 1984—. Member, Experimental Aircraft Association Advisory Council, 1989-1992. Advisor to Airline Passenger Association, 1989-1990. Member and Counsel, International Society of Air Safety Investigators. *Member:* District of Columbia Bar; Bar Association of the District of Columbia Bar; Association of the Bar of the City of New York; Federal (Chairman, Aviation Committee, 1986—) and American Bar Associations; The Association of Trial Lawyers of America; National Head Injury Foundation; Lawyer-Pilots Bar Association; National Transportation Safety Board Bar Association (Founding Member; President, 1988-1990). Certified as a Civil Trial Advocate by the National Board of Trial Advocacy. ***PRACTICE AREAS:*** Aviation Accidents; Aviation Injuries; Aviation Torts; Helicopter Litigation; Marine Law; Products Liability; Medical Malpractice and Administrative Proceedings.

PARADISO, DACK, TAUB & OLER, P.C.

SIXTH FLOOR, 1201 CONNECTICUT AVENUE, N.W.
WASHINGTON, D.C. 20036
Telephone: 301-986-7900

Bethesda, Maryland Office: Suite 640, 3 Bethesda Metro Center. Telephone: 301-986-7900. Fax: 301-986-4001.

(This Listing Continued)

Vienna, Virginia Office: Suite 540, 8045 Leesburg Pike. Telephone: 703-917-9030. Fax: 703-917-9060.

Family Law, Domestic Relations, Divorce, Custody, Marital Property, Adoption, Domestic Violence, Visitation, Marital Agreements, Separation Agreements, Name Changes, Paternity, Alimony, Arbitration and Mediation, Negligence, Personal Injury.

FIRM PROFILE: Paradiso, Dack, Taub & Oler, P.C., established in 1994, is a boutique practice concentrating in family law and personal injury. The firm consists of seven lawyers and several support personnel serving clients from its three office locations in Montgomery County, Maryland, Washington, D.C., and Fairfax County, Virginia.

(For Complete Biographical Data on all Personnel, see Professional Biographies at Bethesda, Maryland)

THE PARROTT FIRM

WASHINGTON, D.C.

(See Annapolis, Maryland)

Civil Litigation, Insurance Defense, Personal Injury, Products Liability, Banking Law, Business Law, Corporate, Contracts, Family Law, Divorce, Child Custody, Child Support, Adoptions, Criminal Law, Bankruptcy, Commercial Law, Appeals, Mediation.

PASCAL & WEISS, P.C.

Established in 1971
1008 PENNSYLVANIA AVENUE, S.E.
WASHINGTON, D.C. 20003
Telephone: 202-544-2200
Fax: 202-544-5839
Email: pascalweis@aol.com

General and Civil Litigation. Bankruptcy, Commercial, Corporate, Creditors Rights, Banking, Landlord and Tenant and Real Estate Law, City and Government Regulations, Labor and Employment, Alcoholic Beverage Control, Personal Injury.

FIRM PROFILE: A long-standing legal practice concentrated in the representation of small to mid-size business entities. Its clients reflect the diversity of the metropolitan area and include commercial and savings banks, mortgage companies, food and beverage distributors, property management firms and trade associations. The firm handles a variety of legal matters for its clients, including business formations, business financing, lease negotiations, labor/union negotiations, collection of delinquent accounts, workouts with debtors, foreclosures, evictions, creditor rights in bankruptcy, business legal audits, estate planning, government lobbying, alcoholic beverage regulatory matters, and general litigation. The firm believes that its small size contributes to its accessibility to its clients and its speed and flexibility in responding to client's needs.

PAUL L. PASCAL, born Washington, D.C., June 18, 1937; admitted to bar, 1966, District of Columbia; 1976, Maryland. *Education:* University of Maryland (B.A., 1961); George Washington University (J.D., 1965). General Counsel, Transportation Federation, D.C., 1985—. General Counsel, Lincoln Group of the District of Columbia, 1987—. *Member:* The District of Columbia Bar; Bar Association of the District of Columbia; Association of Plaintiffs' Trial Attorneys (President, 1975-1976). ***PRACTICE AREAS:*** Lobbying; Labor; Employment; Alcoholic Beverage Control.

ANTON M. WEISS, born New York, N.Y., November 6, 1942; admitted to bar, 1968, District of Columbia, U.S. District Court for the District of Columbia and U.S. Court of Appeals for the District of Columbia Circuit; 1973, Maryland and U.S. Supreme Court; 1975, U.S. District Court, District of Maryland; U.S. Court of Appeals, Fourth Circuit. *Education:* Harpur College, State University of New York at Binghamton (B.A., 1964); Georgetown University (J.D., 1967). General Counsel, Tara Shores Property Owners Association. *Member:* The District of Columbia Bar; Montgomery County (Member, Banking and Commercial Law Section), Maryland State and American Bar Associations. ***PRACTICE AREAS:*** Commercial Litigation; Commercial Collections; Creditors Rights; Probate.

KATHLEEN I. ANDREWS, born New Orleans, Louisiana, March 22, 1964; admitted to bar, 1989, Virginia and U.S. Bankruptcy Court, Eastern District of Virginia; 1990, U.S. District Court, Eastern and Western Districts of Virginia; 1992, District of Columbia. *Education:* George Mason University (B.S., 1986); George Mason University School of Law (J.D., 1989). *Member:* The District of Columbia Bar; Virginia Bar Association; Virginia State Bar. ***PRACTICE AREAS:*** Labor; Lobbying; Bankruptcy; Alcoholic Beverage Control; Commercial Litigation; Commercial Collections; Creditors Rights; Landlord and Tenant Law.

(This Listing Continued)

REPRESENTATIVE CLIENTS: Greater Washington Food Wholesalers Assn.; Greater Baltimore Food Service Assn.; District of Columbia Association of Beverage Alcohol Wholesalers.

PASSMAN & KAPLAN, PC

1090 VERMONT AVENUE, N.W., SUITE 500
WASHINGTON, D.C. 20005
Telephone: 202-789-0100
Fax: 202-789-0101
Email: inquiry@passmanandkaplan.com
URL: http://www.lawyers.com/passman&kaplan

Federal Government Civil Service Law, D.C. Civil Service, Civil Rights, Employment Law, Employee Benefits, Labor Law, Unfair Labor Practices, Wrongful Termination, Age Discrimination, Sexual Harassment, Wage and Hour Law, Security Clearances, Family and Medical Leave Act, congressional Accountability Act, Personnel Policies, Grievances, Disability Discrimination, Employment Contracts, Executive Compensation, ERISA, Health Benefits, Retirement Benefits.

FIRM PROFILE: Founded in 1989, Passman & Kaplan, P.C., practices federal employment and labor law at the highest level of professionalism. The firm's clients are diverse and include government workers, private sector employees, unions, union members, professionals and executives. Passman & Kaplan attorneys are the authors of the Federal Employees Legal Survival Guide and are approved by the Fraternal Order of Police (FOP), Legal Defense Plan, The American Association of Retired Persons' (AARP), Lawyers Referral Program and the Union Privilege Legal Service (UPLS).

EDWARD H. PASSMAN, admitted to bar, 1968, District of Columbia; 1981, Maryland. *Education:* Pace University (B.B.A., 1961); Harvard University (J.D., 1964); University of California, Los Angeles (M.B.A., 1966). Author, annual chapter in *A Guide to Merit Systems Protection Board Law and Practice.* Co-Author, *Federal Employees Legal Survival Guide. Member:* District of Columbia Bar (Member, Labor and Employment Law Section Steering Committee); National Employment Lawyers Association (Co-Chair, Federal Employee Rights Committee). ***PRACTICE AREAS:*** Federal Employment Law; Federal Civil Service; Equal Employment Opportunity Law; Labor Law; Retirement. ***Email:*** ehpassman@passmanandkaplan.com

JOSEPH V. KAPLAN, admitted to bar, 1978, Pennsylvania; 1981, District of Columbia; 1992, Maryland. *Education:* Pennsylvania State University (B.A., 1975); Gonzaga University (J.D., 1978); George Washington University (LL.M., 1979). Author, *Federal Merit Systems Year Book.* Editor and Co-Author, *Federal Employees Legal Survival Guide. Member:* Metropolitan Washington Employment Lawyers Association (Board of Directors). ***PRACTICE AREAS:*** Employment Law; Federal Civil Service; Equal Employment Opportunity Law; Labor Law; Security Clearances. ***Email:*** jkaplan@passmanandkaplan.com

JAMES M. EISENMANN, admitted to bar, 1991, Maryland; 1992, District of Columbia. *Education:* West Virginia University (B.A., 1986); Columbus School of Law of The Catholic University of America (J.D., 1991). Author: Family and Medical Leave Act of 1993, The Bureau of National Affairs' *Employment Discrimination Report* (Vol. 45, No. 15, April 12, 1995) and Labor Relations Press' *Federal Pay and Benefits Reporter,* April 1995; Recovery Attorney Fees, *Federal Merit Systems Reporter,* (Vol. 96, Issue 6D, July 29, 1996). Co-Author: "Contingent Workers and Employment Law," *Contingent Work:* American Employment Relations in Transition, University Press, 1998; "Federal Employees Legal Survival Guide." Advisory Board of the D.C. Employment Justice Center. *Member:* District of Columbia Bar (Chair, Labor and Employment Law Section Equal Employment Opportunity and Individual Rights Committee; Coordinator of Continuing Legal Education). ***PRACTICE AREAS:*** Employment Law; Federal Civil Service; Equal Employment Opportunity Law; Labor Law; Security Clearances. ***Email:*** jeisenmann@passmanandkaplan.com

SENIOR ASSOCIATES

KRISTIN D. ALDEN, admitted to bar, 1992, Virginia; 1993, Maryland; 1995, District of Columbia. *Education:* Johns Hopkins University (B.A., 1989); American University (J.D., 1992). Co-Author: Federal Employees Legal Service Guide (1999). Contributing Author, *Employment Discrimination Law,* District of Columbia Bar and Chair, Labor and Employment Section, Public Sector Committee. *Member:* Women's Bar Association of DC; Metropolitan Washington Employment Lawyers Association. ***PRACTICE AREAS:*** Employment Law; Federal Civil Service; Equal Employment Opportunity Law; Labor Law.

SANDRA MAZLIAH, admitted to bar, 1993, New York; 1994, District of Columbia. *Education:* Queens College of the City University of New York (B.A., 1987); Georgetown University Law Center (J.D., cum laude, 1992). Author, "The Congressional Accountability Act, Meandering the Mandatory Administrative Maze," 6 Fed. Cir. B.J. 5 (1996). *Member:* American Bar Association; National Employment Lawyers Association; Metropolitan Washington Employment Lawyers Association. ***Email:*** smazliah@passmanandkaplan.com

ASSOCIATES

TANISHA M. COLE, admitted to bar, 1998, Maryland; 1999, District of Columbia. *Education:* Washington University (B.A., 1994; J.D., 1997). *Member:* District of Columbia Bar (Labor and Employment Law Section); National Bar Association; Greater Washington Area Chapter Women Lawyers Division. ***PRACTICE AREAS:*** Employment Law; Federal Civil Service; Equal Employment Opportunity Law; Labor Law. ***Email:*** tcole@passmanandkaplan.com

DANIEL A. PEREZ, admitted to bar, 2000, Florida (Not admitted in District of Columbia). *Education:* University of Central Florida (B.A., 1996); George Washington University (J.D., 2000). ***PRACTICE AREAS:*** Employment Law; Federal Civil Service; Equal Employment Opportunity Law; Labor Law. ***Email:*** dperez@passmanandkaplan.com

PATRICK HENRY CAPPELL & LEWIS, LLP

WASHINGTON, D.C.
(See Alexandria, Virginia)

Corporate, Business Acquisitions, Contracts, Commercial Litigation, Civil Rights, Discrimination, Military Law, Court Martials & Discharges, Domestic Relations, Divorce, Child Custody, Child Support, Adoptions, Guardianships, Personal Injury, Automobile Accidents, Medical Malpractice, Products Liability, Labor and Employment, Franchise Negotiation, Non-Profit, Consumer Protection, Immigration, Bankruptcy, Criminal Law Defense, Driving While Intoxicated, Traffic Violations, Juvenile, Estate Planning, Wills & Probate.

PATTISHALL, McAULIFFE, NEWBURY, HILLIARD & GERALDSON

WASHINGTON, D.C.
(See Alexandria, Virginia)

PATTON BOGGS LLP

2550 M STREET, N.W., SUITE 500
WASHINGTON, D.C. 20037-1350
Telephone: 202-457-6000
Telecopier: 202-457-6315
Email: info@pattonboggs.com
URL: http://www.pattonboggs.com

Anchorage, Alaska Office: Suite 504, 1031 W. Fourth Avenue, 99501. Telephone: 907-277-4900. Facsimile: 907-277-4117.
Louisville, Colorado Office: Suite 200, 867 Coal Creek Circle, 80027. Telephone: 303-379-1100. Facsimile: 303-379-1155.
Dallas, Texas Office: 2001 Ross Avenue, Suite 3000, 75201-2774. Telephone: 214-758-1500. Facsimile: 214-758-1550.
Denver, Colorado Office: Suite 1900, 1660 Lincoln Street, 80264. Telephone: 303-830-1776. Facsimile: 303-894-9239.
McLean, Virginia Office: 8484 Westpark Drive, Suite 900, 22102. Telephone: 703-744-8000. Facsimile: 703-744-8001.

General Practice. Administrative Law, Antitrust and Economic Regulation, Business Law, Construction Law, Environment and Natural Resources, Government Contracts, Health and Consumer Safety, International, Legislative Advocacy, Litigation, Tax, Transportation and Energy.

MEMBERS OF FIRM

JAMES R. PATTON, JR., born Durham, North Carolina, October 27, 1928; admitted to bar, 1951, District of Columbia; 1963, U.S. Supreme Court. *Education:* University of North Carolina (A.B., cum laude, 1948); Yale University, Graduate School of Forestry; Harvard University (J.D., 1951). Phi Beta Kappa; Alpha Epsilon Delta. Lecturer on International Law, Cornell Law School, 1963-1964; U.S. Army War and Staff and Command Colleges, 1967-1970. Attache of Embassy and Special Assistant to the American Ambassador, Indochina, 1951-1954. Director, Lawyers Committee for Civil Rights Under Law, 1973—. Member, Board of Trustees, Legal Aid Society of D.C., 1980-1983. *Member:* The District of Columbia Bar; American and Inter-American Bar Associations; International Law Association; American Society of International Law (Treasurer, 1976-1983; Member, Executive Council, 1976-1983); Washington Institute of Foreign Affairs.

GEORGE BLOW (Retired).

JOSEPH L. BRAND, born Urbana, Ohio, August 11, 1936; admitted to bar, 1963, Ohio; 1964, District of Columbia. *Education:* University of Michigan

(This Listing Continued)

PATTON BOGGS LLP, Washington—Continued

(A.B., 1958); Ohio State University (M.A., 1959); George Washington University (J.D., with honors, 1963). Order of the Coif (President, George Washington Chapter, 1970-1971). Managing Editor, George Washington Law Review, 1962-1963. Adjunct Professor of Comparative Law, George Washington University, 1983-1994. President, George Washington University Law Alumni Association, 1988-1990. Member, National Panel of Arbitrators, American Arbitration Association. Board of Advisors, George Washington University Law School, 1991—. Trustee, George Washington University, 1994—(Chairman, Committee on Academic Affairs). Member, Board of Directors, ACDI/VOCA. Chairman, Washington Council and Director of the Lawyers Committee for Human Rights. Chairman, National Kidney Foundation, 1997-1999. Governor, Middle East Institute. Director, Center for Justice and Accountability, San Francisco, California. *Member:* The District of Columbia Bar; American (Vice-Chair, New Independent States of the Former Soviet Union Law Committee, 1992-1997) and International Bar Associations; American Society of International Law; The American Foreign Law Association; Washington Institute of Foreign Affairs; Washington Foreign Law Society. ***Email:*** jbrand@pattonboggs.com

THOMAS HALE BOGGS, JR., born New Orleans, Louisiana, September 18, 1940; admitted to bar, 1965, District of Columbia and U.S. Supreme Court; U.S. Court of Appeals for the District of Columbia Circuit. *Education:* Georgetown University (A.B., 1961; J.D., 1965). Delta Theta Phi. Coordinator, National Defense Executive Reserve, Executive Office of the President, 1965-1966. Economist, Joint Economic Committee, U.S. Congress, 1961-1965. Presidential Delegate to the Independence of the Solomon Islands, 1978. Presidential Delegate, People's Republic of China Trade Mission, 1979. Member, Presidential Commission on Executive Exchange, 1979-1981. Member, Chesapeake Bay Board of Trustees, 1988—. Member, Board of Directors: Eastern Airlines Incorporated, 1983-1994; Washington Bancorporation, 1984-1985; Suburban Mortgage Association Incorporated, 1986—; Chemfix Technologies, 1988-1995. Member: Duke University Board of Visitors, 1989—; University of Maryland Foundation Board of Trustees, 1984-1995; National Board of Directors, Congressional Award Foundation, 1995—. *Member:* The District of Columbia Bar; Bar Association of the District of Columbia; Maritime Bar Association; Federal and American (Chairman, Committee on Foreign Relations, 1970-1971, Administrative Law Section) Bar Associations; American Judicature Society; Federal City Council. ***Email:*** tboggs@pattonboggs.com

TIMOTHY J. MAY, born Denver, Colorado, August 3, 1932; admitted to bar, 1957, District of Columbia; 1961, U.S. Supreme Court. *Education:* Catholic University of America (B.A., 1954); Georgetown University (J.D., 1957; LL.M., 1960). Blue Key; Phi Delta Phi. Editor-in-Chief, Georgetown Law Journal, 1956-1957. Law Clerk to Judge John Danaher, U.S. Court of Appeals, District of Columbia Circuit, 1957-1958. Consultant, Executive Office of the President, 1961-1962. Acting Chief Counsel, National Stockpile Investigation Subcommittee, U.S. Senate, 1962-1963. Managing Director, Federal Maritime Commission, 1963-1966. United States Representative to International Maritime Conferences, Paris, London, 1964-1965; Chairman of Delegation, 1966. General Counsel, U.S. Post Office Department, 1966-1969. Recipient of: Presidential Award from President Johnson, 1964; Jump Award for Achievement in Public Administration, 1965, 1966 and 1967; Arthur Flemming Award, Ten Outstanding Young Men in Government, 1966; Federal Bar Association Award as Young Lawyer of the Year, 1967; Benjamin Franklin Award, 1969. Member: Judicial Conference of the District of Columbia Circuit, 1966, 1967 and 1968, 1991, 1992; Administrative Conference of the United States, 1968-1969. Trustee, Legal Aid Society of the District of Columbia, 1983—. Legal Aid Society, "Servant of Justice Award," 1997. Chairman, Board of Regents, Catholic University of America, 1991-1993, Trustee, 1993—; Executive Committee and President, Council for Court Excellence, 1992—. *Member:* The District of Columbia Bar; Bar Association of the District of Columbia (President, 1991-1992; Member, Board of Directors, 1986-1993; Lawyer of the Year, 1999); Federal (Chairman, General Counsel's Committee, 1967-1968) and American (House of Delegates, 1990-1992; Chairman: Special Committee on Association Program for Lawyers in Government, 1969-1972; Postal Matters Committee, 1969—, Administrative Law Section) Bar Associations. Fellow, American Bar Foundation. ***Email:*** tmay@pattonboggs.com

ELLIOT H. COLE, born Lynn, Massachusetts, July 13, 1932; admitted to bar, 1960, Massachusetts; 1961, District of Columbia. *Education:* Boston University (B.S., 1954; J.D., 1960). Trustee, Boston University, 1978-2001. *Member:* The District of Columbia Bar. ***Email:*** ecole@pattonboggs.com

J. GORDON ARBUCKLE, born College Station, Texas, June 23, 1942; admitted to bar, 1968, District of Columbia; 1991, Colorado. *Education:* University of Maryland (B.A., with high honors, 1963); George Washington University (LL.B., 1967). *Member:* Colorado Bar Association; The District of Columbia Bar. ***Email:*** garbuckle@pattonboggs.com

DAVID C. TODD, born Muskegon, Michigan, May 3, 1936; admitted to bar, 1962, District of Columbia; 1963, U.S. Court of Military Appeals; 1965, U.S. Claims Court. *Education:* Macalester College (B.A., 1958); University of Michigan (LL.B., 1961). General Counsel, United Planning Organization, Washington, D.C., 1966-1969. *Member:* The District of Columbia Bar; American Bar Association. ***Email:*** dtodd@pattonboggs.com

RICHARD ALAN EARLE, born New York, N.Y., April 30, 1941; admitted to bar, 1968, Michigan and U.S. Supreme Court; 1969, District of Columbia and U.S. Court of Appeals, District of Columbia Circuit. *Education:* University of Michigan (B.B.A., 1963; M.B.A., 1964; J.D., 1968). Editor, *Prospectus, A Journal of Law Reform,* University of Michigan, 1968-1969. Honor Graduate, U.S. Naval Justice School, Newport, Rhode Island, 1965. *Member:* The District of Columbia Bar; State Bar of Michigan; American Society of International Law; Washington Foreign Law Society. ***Email:*** rearle@pattonboggs.com

DAVID B. ROBINSON, born Bellefonte, Pennsylvania, August 17, 1943; admitted to bar, 1970, New York; 1971, District of Columbia and U.S. Court of Appeals, District of Columbia; 1975, U.S. Court of Appeals, 5th Circuit; 1978, U.S. Supreme Court; 1979, U.S. Court of Appeals, 10th Circuit; U.S. Court of Appeals, 4th Circuit. *Education:* Hamilton College (B.A., 1965); Union Theological Seminary (Rockefeller Fellow, 1965-1966); Yale University (J.D., 1969). Phi Beta Kappa. Fellow, Robert F. Kennedy Memorial Foundation, 1969-1970. *Member:* The District of Columbia Bar; Federal Energy Bar Association. ***Email:*** drobinson@pattonboggs.com

JOHN H. VOGEL, born Milwaukee, Wisconsin, February 20, 1944; admitted to bar, 1970, New York; 1971, District of Columbia; 1973, U.S. Supreme Court; 1987, Maryland; 1988, U.S. Court of International Trade and U.S. Court of Appeals for the Federal Circuit. *Education:* Princeton University (A.B., cum laude, 1965); University of Michigan (J.D., 1968). Phi Delta Phi. Fulbright Scholar, Institut des Etudes Européenes and European Economic Communities, Brussels, 1968-1969. *Member:* Association of the Bar of the City of New York; District of Columbia Bar; Bar Association of the District of Columbia; Maryland State, New York State, American and International Bar Associations; American Society of International Law; Union des Avocats Internationales. ***Email:*** jvogel@pattonboggs.com

ALLAN ABBOT TUTTLE, born Orange, New Jersey, June 6, 1939; admitted to bar, 1966, New York; 1971, U.S. Supreme Court; 1976, District of Columbia. *Education:* Yale College (B.A., magna cum laude, 1961); Yale University (LL.B., 1965). Note and Comment Editor, Yale Law Journal, 1964-1965. Assistant U.S. Attorney, Southern District of New York, 1969-1971. Assistant to the Solicitor General, 1971-1975. Solicitor, Federal Power Commission, 1975-1977. General Counsel, Gucci Group N.V., 1997—. *Member:* The District of Columbia Bar; Federal Energy Bar Association.

JOHN L. OBERDORFER, born Lewes, Delaware, February 19, 1944; admitted to bar, 1969, Ohio; 1972, District of Columbia. *Education:* Dartmouth College (A.B., 1966); Yale University (LL.B., 1969). Reginald Heber Smith Law Fellow, 1969-1971. Attorney, Office of the General Counsel, U.S. Department of Transportation, 1971-1974. Trustee, Washington Lawyers Committee for Civil Rights Under Law, 1981—. Board Member, Washington Airports Task Force, 1988—. *Member:* The District of Columbia Bar (Member, Litigation Section); Ohio State Bar Association (Inactive). ***Email:*** joberdorfer@pattonboggs.com

TIMOTHY A. VANDERVER, JR., born Birmingham, Alabama, January 25, 1944; admitted to bar, 1969, District of Columbia; 1978, U.S. Supreme Court. *Education:* Washington & Lee University (B.A., 1965); Oxford University, Oxford, England (B.A., 1967; M.A., 1983); Harvard University (J.D., 1969). Phi Beta Kappa; Omicron Delta Epsilon. Rhodes Scholar. Adjunct Professor of Law, Land Use Planning, Delaware Law School, 1974-1975. Attorney: Office of the Solicitor, U.S. Department of the Interior, 1972-1973; Office of the General Counsel and New Communities Administration, U.S. Department of Housing and Urban Development, 1973-1976. *Member:* The District of Columbia Bar. ***Email:*** tvanderver@pattonboggs.com

MIDDLETON A. MARTIN, born Milwaukee, Wisconsin, September 15, 1943; admitted to bar, 1976, District of Columbia. *Education:* Princeton University (A.B., 1966); Johns Hopkins University (M.A., 1968); Georgetown University (J.D., 1976). *Member:* The District of Columbia Bar. ***Email:*** mmartin@pattonboggs.com

GARRET G. RASMUSSEN, born Bronxville, New York, November 14, 1949; admitted to bar, 1974, Massachusetts; 1977, District of Columbia; 1982, U.S. Supreme Court; U.S. Court of Appeals, District of Columbia, Second, Fourth, Fifth and Sixth Circuits. *Education:* Dartmouth College (A.B., summa cum laude, 1971); Harvard Law School (J.D., 1974). Phi Beta Kappa. Trial Attorney, Federal Trade Commission, 1976-1977. *Member:* The District of Columbia Bar; American Bar Association (Member, Antitrust Section); The American Law Institute. ***Email:*** grasmussen@pattonboggs.com

JAMES B. CHRISTIAN, JR., born Little Rock, Arkansas, July 6, 1947; admitted to bar, 1973, Arkansas; 1977, District of Columbia. *Education:* Vanderbilt University (B.A., 1969); University of Arkansas (J.D., 1973). Legislative Counsel and Professional Staff, Senate Appropriations Committee, 1975-1977. *Member:* The District of Columbia Bar; Arkansas Bar Association. ***Email:*** jchristian@pattonboggs.com

(This Listing Continued)

DAVID E. DUNN, III, born Birmingham, Alabama, July 21, 1949; admitted to bar, 1975, Alabama; 1977, District of Columbia. *Education:* University of Alabama (B.A., 1971; J.D., 1974). Assistant Attorney General, State of Alabama, 1975-1976. Assistant to President, Overseas Private Investment Corporation, U.S. Government, 1977. Presidential Delegate to the Independence Ceremonies for the New Hebrides Islands, 1980. Member, Board of Trustees, Middle East Institute, 1984-1989, 1991-1995. Board Member, American Chamber of Commerce, Paris, France, 2001. *Member:* The District of Columbia Bar. **Email:** ddunn@pattonboggs.com

RONALD S. LIEBMAN, born Baltimore, Maryland, October 11, 1943; admitted to bar, 1969, Maryland; 1970, U.S. District Court, District of Maryland; 1972, U.S. Court of Appeals, Fourth Circuit; 1977, District of Columbia; 1982, U.S. Court of Appeals, District of Columbia Circuit and U.S. District Court, District of Columbia; 1985, U.S. Court of Appeals, Fifth Circuit; 1988, U.S. Court of Appeals, Second Circuit; 1992, U.S. Court of Appeals, Ninth Circuit; 1994, U.S. District Court, Northern District of California; 1995, U.S. Supreme Court; 1996, U.S. Court of Appeals, Seventh Circuit; 1999, U.S. District Court, Eastern District of Texas. *Education:* Western Maryland College (B.A., 1966); University of Maryland (J.D., 1969). Law Clerk to Hon. R. Dorsey Watkins, Chief Judge, U.S. District Court, District of Maryland, 1969-1970. Assistant U.S. Attorney, District of Maryland, 1972-1978. Recipient, Special Commendation Award, U.S. Department of Justice, 1978. *Member:* The District of Columbia Bar; Maryland State and American (Member, Prosecution and Defense of Economic Crimes Committee, Criminal Justice Section, 1980-1982) Bar Associations. **Email:** rliebman@pattonboggs.com

J. KIRK WADE, born Dallas, Texas, January 8, 1945; admitted to bar, 1973, District of Columbia; 1977, Texas. *Education:* Southern Methodist University (B.A., 1967); George Washington University (J.D., 1972). Attorney-advisor, Interpretative Division, Chief Counsel of the Internal Revenue Service, 1972-1976. Attorney-advisor, Tax Legislative Counsel, Department of the Treasury, 1976-1977. *Member:* The District of Columbia Bar; State Bar of Texas. **Email:** kwade@pattonboggs.com

STUART M. PAPE, born Paterson, New Jersey, December 24, 1948; admitted to bar, 1973, Virginia; 1975, U.S. Court of Appeals, 6th Circuit; 1976, U.S. Supreme Court; 1980, District of Columbia. *Education:* University of Virginia (B.A., 1970); University of Virginia School of Law (J.D., 1973). Recipient, Food and Drug Commendable Service Award, 1979. Law Clerk to Judge Leonard Braman, Superior Court of the District of Columbia, 1973-1974. Executive Assistant to the Commissioner, Food and Drug Administration, 1979. *Member:* The District of Columbia Bar; Virginia State Bar; American Bar Association (Member, Committee on Food and Drug Law, Section on Administrative Law, 1973-1998). **Email:** spape@pattonboggs.com

STEVEN M. SCHNEEBAUM, born New York, N.Y., October 29, 1948; admitted to bar, 1978, District of Columbia. admitted to bar, 1978, District of Columbia and U.S. District Court for the District of Columbia; 1980, U.S. Court of Appeals for the District of Columbia Circuit; 1981, U.S. Court of International Trade and U.S. Court of Appeals, 10th Circuit; 1982, U.S. Court of Appeals, 7th Circuit; 1983, U.S. Claims Court; 1984, U.S. Court of Appeals for the Federal Circuit; 1985, U.S. Court of Appeals, 4th Circuit; 1987, U.S. Court of Appeals, 9th Circuit and U.S. District Court for the District of Maryland including Trial Bar; 1988, U.S. Court of Appeals, 3rd Circuit; 1989, U.S. Supreme Court; 1992, U.S. Court of Appeals, 5th Circuit; 1999, U.S. Court of Appeals, 6th Circuit; 2000, U.S. Court of Appeals, 2nd Circuit. *Education:* Yale University (B.A., magna cum laude, 1969); Oberlin College (M.A., 1970); Oxford University, Oxford, England (B.A., First Class Honors, 1976); George Washington University (M.C.L., A.P., 1978). Professorial Lecturer, Johns Hopkins School of Advanced International Studies, 1990—. Professorial Lecturer, The George Washington University Law School, 1992-2000. Member, Board of Directors, International Human Rights Law Group, 1988-1997. Member, 1982-1987 and Chairman, 1987, Policy Board, Legal Counsel for the Elderly. Chairman, Board of Directors, International Law Students Association, 1996-2001. Member, Board of Visitors, U.S. Western Hemishpere Institute for Security Cooperation, 1997—. Member, 1989—, and Chairman, 2001—, Archdiocesan Legal Network. *Member:* District of Columbia Bar; American Bar Association; American Society of International Law; Washington Foreign Law Society. **Email:** sschneebaum@pattonboggs.com

CLIFF MASSA III, born Cookeville, Tennessee, September 9, 1949; admitted to bar, 1975, District of Columbia. *Education:* Northwestern University (B.S., 1971); George Washington University (J.D., with honors, 1974). Director of Taxation, National Association of Manufacturers, 1975-1979. Vice President, Taxation and Fiscal Policy Department, National Association of Manufacturers, 1979-1981. *Member:* The District of Columbia Bar; Bar Association of the District of Columbia; American Bar Association (Member, Taxation Section; Past Chairman, Committee on Alternative Tax Systems). **Email:** cmassa@pattonboggs.com

SHAOUL ASLAN, born Tehran, Iran, November 29, 1949; admitted to bar, 1976, District of Columbia. *Education:* Queens College (B.A., magna cum laude, 1971); London School of Economics, London, England (M.Sc., 1972); Georgetown University (J.D., 1975). Phi Beta Kappa. Senior Editor, Student Editorial Board, The Tax Lawyer, 1974-1975. *Member:* The District of Columbia Bar; American Bar Association; American Immigration Lawyers Association. **Email:** saslan@pattonboggs.com

DONALD V. MOOREHEAD, born Baltimore, Maryland, April 10, 1943; admitted to bar, 1968, District of Columbia; 1969, U.S. Court of Appeals for the District of Columbia Circuit; 1971, U.S. Tax Court; 1982, California. *Education:* University of Virginia (B.A., 1965); George Washington University (J.D., with honors, 1968). Order of the Coif; Phi Delta Phi. Member, Editorial Staff, George Washington University Law Review, 1967-1968. Adjunct Professor of Law, Georgetown University School of Law, 1974-1980. Chief Republican Counsel, Committee on Finance, U.S. Senate, 1975-1976. Vice President and General Counsel, Kaiser Aluminum & Chemical Corporation, 1981-1984. *Member:* The District of Columbia Bar; American Bar Association (Member, Section of Taxation); State Bar of California. **Email:** dmoorehead@pattonboggs.com

FRANK R. SAMOLIS, born Cleveland, Ohio, July 25, 1951; admitted to bar, 1976, Ohio; 1978, District of Columbia; 1982, U.S. Court of International Trade; 1984, U.S. Court of Appeals for the Federal Circuit. *Education:* Georgetown University (B.S.F.S., cum laude, 1973; J.D., 1976). Legislative Assistant to Representative Charles A. Vanik, Ohio, 1976. Member, Professional Staff, Committee on Ways and Means, Subcommittee on Trade, U.S. House of Representatives, 1977-1980. Private Sector Advisor to the GATT Multilateral Trade Negotiations, 1982-1991. *Member:* The District of Columbia Bar; American Bar Association (Section on International Law); American Society of International Law. **Email:** fsamolis@pattonboggs.com

GEORGE M. BORABABY, born Brooklyn, New York, August 29, 1950; admitted to bar, 1979, District of Columbia; 1993, U.S. Supreme Court. *Education:* Cornell University (B.A., magna cum laude, 1972); Oxford University, England (B.A., 1976); Harvard University (J.D., cum laude, 1979). Phi Beta Kappa. *Member:* The District of Columbia Bar (Member, Sections on: Litigation; Intellectual Property),. **Email:** gborababy@pattonboggs.com

JEFFREY T. SMITH, born Orange, New Jersey, March 22, 1953; admitted to bar, 1979, District of Columbia. *Education:* Amherst College (B.A., magna cum laude, 1975); Stanford University (M.B.A ., 1979; J.D., 1979). Phi Beta Kappa. Editor, Stanford Journal of International Studies, 1976-1977. *Member:* The District of Columbia Bar. **Email:** jsmith@pattonboggs.com

KATHARINE R. BOYCE, born Princeton, New Jersey, February 17, 1949; admitted to bar, 1980, District of Columbia. *Education:* Wheaton College (B.A., magna cum laude, 1971); Catholic University of America (J.D., 1979). Member, Catholic University Law Review, 1979. Legislative Aide to Representative James G. O'Hara, Michigan, 1972-1973. Legislative Assistant and Press Secretary to Representative Brock Adams, Washington, 1973-1977. *Member:* The District of Columbia Bar; Federal (Member, Indian Law and Election Law Divisions) and American Bar Associations; Women's Bar Association of the District of Columbia; Native American Bar Association. **Email:** kboyce@pattonboggs.com

GEORGE J. SCHUTZER, born San Antonio, Texas, February 8, 1955; admitted to bar, 1980, District of Columbia; 1981, U.S. Court of Federal Claims and U.S. Tax Court. *Education:* Williams College (B.A., magna cum laude, 1977); Yale University (J.D., 1980). Phi Beta Kappa. *Member:* The District of Columbia Bar; American Bar Association (Member, Taxation Section). **Email:** gschutzer@pattonboggs.com

SCOTT N. STONE, born Bridgeport, Connecticut, February 23, 1952; admitted to bar, 1979, District of Columbia; 1980, U.S. District Court for the District of Columbia and U.S. Court of Appeals for the District of Columbia Circuit; 1985, U.S. District Court, District of Maryland; 1989, U.S. Court of Appeals, Third Circuit and U.S. Court of Federal Claims; 1992, U.S. Court of Appeals, Ninth Circuit; 1995, U.S. Supreme Court. *Education:* Yale University (B.A., summa cum laude, 1974; J.D., 1979). Phi Beta Kappa. *Member:* The District of Columbia Bar. **Email:** sstone@pattonboggs.com

JOHN F. JONAS, born St. John's, Quebec, May 3, 1950; admitted to bar, 1976, District of Columbia. *Education:* Clark University (B.A., 1972); Cornell University (J.D., 1976). Tax Counsel, Committee on Ways & Means, U.S. House of Representatives, 1981-1986. Legislative Director, Office of Congressman Bob Schmansky, 1980-1981. Legislative Counsel, Office of Congresswoman Elizabeth Holtzman, 1978-1980. Office of General Counsel, Department of Health, Education and Welfare, 1976-1978. *Member:* The District of Columbia Bar. **Email:** jjonas@pattonboggs.com

DUANE ALAN SILER, born Greeley, Colorado, January 18, 1949; admitted to bar, 1978, District of Columbia; 1985, U.S. Court of Appeals, District of Columbia Circuit; 1989, U.S. Court of Appeals, Eleventh Circuit; 1992, U.S. Court of Appeals, Second Circuit; 1994, U.S. Court of Appeals, Fourth Circuit. *Education:* University of Colorado (B.A., 1971); Duke University (M.A., 1973); Boalt Hall School of Law, University of California at Berkeley (J.D., 1978). Phi Beta Kappa; Order of the Coif. Member, 1976-1978 and Managing Editor, 1977-1978, California Law Review. *Member:* The District of Columbia Bar. **Email:** dsiler@pattonboggs.com

(This Listing Continued)

PATTON BOGGS LLP, Washington—Continued

RUSSELL V. RANDLE, born New Bedford, Massachusetts, September 26, 1955; admitted to bar, 1980, District of Columbia. *Education:* Princeton University (A.B., magna cum laude, 1977); Yale University (J.D., 1980). Recipient, Gale F. Johnston Prize, June 7, 1977. Editor, Yale Law Journal, 1979-1980. Law Clerk to Judge John H. Pratt, U.S. District Court for the District of Columbia, 1980-1981. Awarded, Distinguished Instructor in Environmental Training, Government Institutes, Inc., 1990. *Member:* The District of Columbia Bar. ***Email:*** rrandle@pattonboggs.com

JEAN VEEDER MACHARG, born Albany, New York, April 20, 1956; admitted to bar, 1981, District of Columbia; 1982, U.S. Court of Appeals, Fifth Circuit, Fourth Circuit, U.S. District Court for the District of Columbia; 1983, U.S. District Court for the Eastern District of Texas; 1988, U.S. Court of Appeals for the District of Columbia Circuit. *Education:* Wellesley College (A.B., with highest honors, 1978); University of Chicago (J.D., 1981). Phi Beta Kappa. Durant Scholar. *Member:* The District of Columbia Bar. ***Email:*** jmacharg@pattonboggs.com

DEAN M. DILLEY, born Columbus, Ohio, August 2, 1955; admitted to bar, 1980, District of Columbia; 1981, U.S. District Court for the District of Columbia; 1982, U.S. Court of Federal Claims and U.S. Court of Appeals for the Federal Circuit. *Education:* Cornell University (A.B., 1977); Catholic University (J.D., 1980). Member, Catholic University Law Review, 1978-1980. Attorney, Office of the General Counsel of the Air Force, 1980-1984. *Member:* The District of Columbia Bar. ***Email:*** ddilley@pattonboggs.com

JOHN C. MARTIN, born Sheridan, Wyoming, April 17, 1953; admitted to bar, 1979, Wyoming; 1980, U.S. District Court, District of Wyoming; 1981, District of Columbia; 1986, U.S. District Court for the District of Columbia and U.S. District Court, Eastern District of Kentucky; 1987, U.S. Court of Appeals for the District of Columbia Circuit; 1989, U.S. Court of Appeals for the Sixth Circuit; 1992, U.S. District Court, Western District of Michigan; 1993, U.S. Court of Appeals, Fourth Circuit; 1994, U.S. Court of Appeals, Eighth Circuit. *Education:* University of Wyoming (B.S., with high honors, 1974); Georgetown University (J.D., 1979). Trial Attorney: Land and Natural Resources Division, Environmental Enforcement Section, Department of Justice, 1982-1985; Office of Solicitor, Department of Interior, 1981-1982. *Member:* The District of Columbia Bar; Wyoming State Bar; American Bar Association (Member, Natural Resources Section). ***Email:*** jmartin@pattonboggs.com

DEBORAH M. LODGE, born Providence, Rhode Island, April 22, 1951; admitted to bar, 1977, Massachusetts; 1978, New York; 1982, U.S. District Court, Southern District of New York; 1984, U.S. District Court, Eastern District of New York; 1985, District of Columbia; 1989, U.S. District Court, District of Maryland; 1990, U.S. District Court for the District of Columbia; 1992, U.S. Supreme Court. *Education:* Wellesley College (B.A., 1973); Boston College (J.D., magna cum laude, 1976). Order of the Coif. Wellesley Scholar. Articles Editor, Boston College Law Review, 1975-1976. *Member:* The District of Columbia Bar; American Bar Association (Member, Sections on: Litigation; Intellectual Property Law). ***Email:*** dlodge@pattonboggs.com

MITCHELL R. BERGER, born New York, N.Y., December 19, 1954; admitted to bar, 1980, New York; 1985, District of Columbia. *Education:* University of Pennsylvania (B.A., summa cum laude, 1976; M.A., 1976); Harvard Law School (J.D., cum laude, 1979). Phi Beta Kappa. Assistant U.S. Attorney, District of Columbia, 1982-1985. Trial Attorney, Tax Division, U.S. Department of Justice, 1981-1982. *Member:* The District of Columbia Bar. ***Email:*** mberger@pattonboggs.com

DONALD H. PEARLMAN, born Portland, Oregon, December 8, 1935; admitted to bar, 1960, Oregon; 1962, U.S. Court of Appeals, Ninth Circuit and U.S. District Court, District of Oregon; 1996, District of Columbia. *Education:* Harvard University (A.B., cum laude, 1957); Yale University (J.D., 1960). Executive Assistant to U.S. Secretary of Energy, 1982-1985. Executive Assistant to U.S. Secretary of the Interior, 1985-1989. Law Clerk to Hon. John R. Ross, Chief Judge, U.S. District Court of Nevada, 1960-1961. Public Member, Bonneville Power Administration Regional Advisory Council, 1971-1978. *Member:* American Bar Association; Oregon (inactive) State Bar. ***Email:*** dpearlman@pattonboggs.com

JEFFREY L. TURNER, born Rapid City, South Dakota, February 11, 1955; admitted to bar, 1982, District of Columbia. *Education:* Tulane University of Louisiana (B.A., 1977); Georgetown University (J.D., 1982; M.S.F.S., 1982). Phi Beta Kappa. Article Editor, Georgetown Law Journal, 1981-1982. *Member:* The District of Columbia Bar. ***Email:*** jturner@pattonboggs.com

CHARLES E. TALISMAN, born Washington, D.C., June 13, 1957; admitted to bar, 1982, District of Columbia; 1986, U.S. District Court for the District of Columbia; 1987, U.S. Court of Appeals, 10th Circuit; 1989, U.S. Court of Appeals, 4th Circuit; U.S. Court of Federal Claims and U.S. Claims Court; 1992, U.S. Court of Appeals, 9th Circuit; 1995, U.S. Supreme Court; 1998, U.S. Court of Appeals, 5th Circuit; 1999, U.S. Court of Appeals, District of Columbia Circuit and U.S. Court of Appeals, 2nd Circuit. *Education:* Brandeis University; Duke University (B.A., summa cum laude, with honors, 1979); Stanford University (J.D., 1982). Phi Beta Kappa. *Member:* The District of Columbia Bar. ***Email:*** ctalisman@pattonboggs.com

W. CAFFEY NORMAN III, born Montgomery, Alabama, February 1, 1953; admitted to bar, 1977, Alabama; 1979, District of Columbia. *Education:* University of Alabama (A.B., cum laude, 1974); University of Virginia Law School (J.D., 1977). Editor, Virginia Journal of International Law, 1975-1976. Law Clerk to Hon. Walter P. Gewin, U.S. Court of Appeals for the Fifth Circuit, 1977-1978. Senior Counsel for Banking, Department of the Treasury, 1986. *Member:* The District of Columbia Bar; Alabama State Bar. ***Email:*** cnorman@pattonboggs.com

PAUL A. J. WILSON, born Urbana, Illinois, December 31, 1949; admitted to bar, 1983, District of Columbia; U.S. Supreme Court; U.S. District Court for the District of Columbia, U.S. Court of Appeals for the District of Columbia, Fifth and Eleventh Circuits and U.S. District Court for the Eastern, Northern and Southern Districts of Texas and Western District of Michigan. *Education:* University of Massachusetts (B.A., magna cum laude, 1972); Northwestern University (M.A., 1974); University of Virginia (J.D., 1983). Phi Kappa Phi. Executive Editor, Virginia Journal of Natural Resources Law, 1982-1983. *Member:* The District of Columbia Bar. ***Email:*** pwilson@pattonboggs.com

MARY ELIZABETH BOSCO, born Jersey City, New Jersey, February 23, 1956; admitted to bar, 1983, District of Columbia; 1985, U.S. Court of Federal Claims. *Education:* Yale University (B.A., cum laude, 1978); George Washington University (J.D., with honors, 1983). *Member:* The District of Columbia Bar; Court of Federal Claims Bar; Federal Circuit Bar. ***Email:*** mbbosco@pattonboggs.com

READ KEMP McCAFFREY, born Baltimore, Maryland, June 1, 1943; admitted to bar, 1971, Maryland; 1973, U.S. District Court, District of Maryland; 1980, U.S. Supreme Court; 1981, U.S. Court of Appeals, 4th Circuit; 1987, U.S. Court of Appeals for the District of Columbia Circuit; 1988, District of Columbia 1992, U.S. Court of Appeals, 11th Circuit. *Education:* University of Virginia (B.A., 1965); University of Baltimore (J.D., 1969). Lecturer, Basic Civil Trial Practice for Continuing Professional Education of Lawyers. Assistant Public Defender, Baltimore City, 1972-1973. Mediator, U.S. District Court, District of Columbia, 1989—. Member, Inquiry Panel, Attorney Grievance Commission of Maryland, 1985-1992. *Member:* Maryland State (Chairman, Editorial Advisory Committee, 1975-1984; Member, Board of Governors, 1981-1983) and American (Vice Chairman, Products General Liability and Consumer Law Committee, 1984-1989) Bar Associations. Fellow, American College of Trial Lawyers.

ROSS E. EICHBERG, born Boston, Massachusetts, April 13, 1959; admitted to bar, 1985, Maryland and U.S. District Court, District of Maryland; 1987, District of Columbia Court of Appeals. *Education:* Duke University (B.A., magna cum laude, 1980); University of Virginia (J.D., 1984). Member, University of Virginia Tax Review, 1983-1984. *Member:* The District of Columbia Bar (Member: Real Estate Section); Maryland State Bar Association. ***Email:*** reichberg@pattonboggs.com

GEOFFREY G. DAVIS, born Arlington, Virginia, March 24, 1958; admitted to bar, 1985, New York; 1993, District of Columbia. *Education:* Amherst College (B.A., 1980); Cambridge University, England (LL.B., 1982; LL.M., 1987); University of Virginia (J.D., 1984). Fellow: Evan Carroll Commager, 1980-1981; John Woodruff Simpson, 1981. *Member:* The District of Columbia Bar; New York State Bar Association. ***Email:*** gdavis@pattonboggs.com

MARTHA M. KENDRICK, born Syracuse, New York, September 10, 1949; admitted to bar, 1985, Maryland; 1986, District of Columbia. *Education:* Newton College of the Sacred Heart (B.A., 1971); Bowling Green University (M.A., 1972); Georgetown University Law Center (J.D., 1985). Editor, Law and Policy in International Business, 1984-1985. U.S. Department of Health and Human Services, 1973-1985. HHS Exceptional Achievement Award, 1984. *Member:* The District of Columbia Bar; Maryland State Bar Association; American Health Lawyers Association; Women in Health Policy Coalition; Leadership Washington. ***Email:*** mkendrick@pattonboggs.com

KENNETH A. GRIGG, JR., born Cincinnati, Ohio, February 4, 1959; admitted to bar, 1984, District of Columbia; 1985, U.S. District Court for the District of Columbia and U.S. Court of Appeals for the District of Columbia Circuit; 1988, Maryland and U.S. District Court, District of Maryland; 1989, U.S. Court of Appeals, Fourth Circuit. *Education:* Columbia University (B.A., 1981); Wake Forest University (J.D., 1984). Member, International Law Society, 1983-1984. *Member:* The District of Columbia Bar; Maryland State Bar Association. ***Email:*** kgrigg@pattonboggs.com

MICHAEL A. CURTO, born Takoma Park, Maryland, February 15, 1958; admitted to bar, 1983, District of Columbia. *Education:* Georgetown University (A.B., 1980); Catholic University (J.D., 1983). Pi Sigma Alpha. Recipient, American Jurisprudence Award for Family Law, 1981. Associate Editor, The Catholic University of America Law Review, 1982-1983. Judicial Clerk to the Honorable Julia Cooper Mack, Associate Judge of the District of Columbia Court of Appeals, 1983-1984. *Member:* District of Columbia Bar. ***Email:*** mcurto@pattonboggs.com

(This Listing Continued)

(This Listing Continued)

JAMES A. REEDER, born Baton Rouge, Louisiana, June 29, 1933; admitted to bar, 1960, Texas; 1961, Louisiana; 1992, District of Columbia. *Education:* Washington & Lee University (B.A., cum laude, 1955); University of Texas at Austin (LL.B., 1960); Louisiana State University (J.D.S., 1961). Omicron Delta Kappa; Phi Alpha Delta. *Member:* Louisiana (Chairman, Young Lawyers Section, 1965) and American (Director, Young Lawyers Section, 1969) Bar Associations. **Email:** jareeder@pattonboggs.com

PHILIP S. KAPLAN, born New Britain, Connecticut, March 28, 1937; admitted to bar, 1963, California; 1995, District of Columbia. *Education:* University of Connecticut (B.A., 1959); Boalt Hall School of Law, University of California (J.D., 1962); Stanford University and University of California, Berkeley (Advanced International Studies, 1963-1965). Counsel, California Legislature, 1962-1963. U.S. Foreign Service Officer, 1967-1994, with Assignments at European Community/Brussels, 1968-1970, Bonn Germany, 1970-1974, Vienna, 1974-1975 and U.S. State Department, Washington, 1975-1980. Deputy Assistant Secretary of State for Policy Planning, 1981-1985. U.S. Minister/ Charge d'affaires, Manila, Philippines, 1985-1987. U.S. Ambassador, Vienna Disarmament Conference, 1989-1991. U.S. State Department Distinguished Service Award. Professor at Brown, George Washington and American Universities, 1991-1994. Fellow, Center for Strategic and International Studies, Washington, 1995—. **Email:** pkaplan@pattonboggs.com

DANIEL E. WALTZ, born Philadelphia, Pennsylvania, November 1, 1957; admitted to bar, 1986, California; 1987, U.S. Court of International Trade; 1988, District of Columbia. *Education:* University of California at Santa Cruz (B.A., 1980); Boalt Hall School of Law, University of California (J.D., 1986). Adjunct Professor of International Business Transactions, Columbus School of Law, Catholic University, 1992-1993. *Member:* The District of Columbia Bar; State Bar of California. **Email:** dwaltz@pattonboggs.com

JOHN F. FITHIAN, born Lincoln, Nebraska, December 15, 1961; admitted to bar, 1987, District of Columbia. *Education:* College of William and Mary (B.A., with high honors, 1984); University of Virginia (J.D., 1987). Phi Beta Kappa. *Member:* The District of Columbia Bar. **Email:** jfithian@pattonboggs.com

TIMOTHY B. MILLS, born Long Beach, California, February 18, 1951; admitted to bar, 1986, California and U.S. District Court, Southern District of California; 1990, U.S. Court of Federal Claims; 1994, U.S. Court of Appeals for the Federal Circuit; 1995, District of Columbia. *Education:* University of California at Santa Cruz (B.A., 1980; M.A., 1982); University of California, Hastings College of the Law, San Francisco (J.D., 1986). Chief Research Editor, International and Comparative Law Review, 1985-1986. Law Clerk to the Honorable John S. Rhoades, U.S. District Judge, Southern District of California, 1986-1987. *Member:* American Bar Association (Public Contract Law and Criminal Justice Sections); Federal Bar Association (Chair, Government Contracts Section, Procurement Ethics Subcommittee, 1993-1994). **Email:** tmills@pattonboggs.com

BENJAMIN L. GINSBERG, born New York, N.Y., May 3, 1951; admitted to bar, 1983, District of Columbia. *Education:* University of Pennsylvania (B.A., 1974); Georgetown University (J.D., 1982). Adjunct Professor of Law, Georgetown University Law Center, 1993-1997 . General and Chief Counsel, Republican National Committee, 1989-1993. Legal Counsel, National Republican Senatorial Committee, 1987-1988. Legal Counsel, National Republican Congressional Committee, 1985-1986. *Member:* American Bar Association (Member: Committee on Election Law and the Electoral Process, 1987-1992; Advisory Committee). **Email:** bginsberg@pattonboggs.com

HENRY CHAJET, born Camaguey, Cuba, December 9, 1950; admitted to bar, 1976, Pennsylvania, Florida and U.S. Court of Appeals, Third Circuit; 1981, U.S. Court of Appeals, Tenth Circuit; 1980, U.S. Court of Appeals for the District of Columbia Circuit; 1982, U.S. Supreme Court; 1989, District of Columbia; 1991, U.S. Court of Appeals, Fourth Circuit; 1997, U.S. Court of Appeals, Second and Sixth Circuits; 1998, U.S. Court of Appeals, Fifth Circuit. *Education:* Case Western Reserve University (B.A., 1972); Duquesne University (J.D., cum laude, 1976). Recent Decision Editor, Duquesne University Law Review. Associate Professor, Occupational Safety and Health Law, Johns Hopkins University Graduate School of Public Health, 1984-1999. Advisor to U.S. House of Representatives Republican Task Force on OSHA Reform, 1990-1992. *Member:* Pennsylvania and American Bar Associations; Florida Bar; The District of Columbia Bar. **Email:** hchajet@pattonboggs.com

MARK N. SAVIT, born Los Angeles, California, October 10, 1949; admitted to bar, 1976, District of Columbia. *Education:* University of Southern California (B.A., 1970); Georgetown University (J.D., 1976). *Member:* The District of Columbia Bar; Bar Association of the District of Columbia; American Bar Association (Member: Committee on Emergency Economic Controls, 1976-1980; Section of Natural Resources Law; Marine Resources Committee, 1985—). **Email:** msavit@pattonboggs.com

ROBERT S. BRAMS, born Wilmington, Delaware, October 10, 1959; admitted to bar, 1985, Pennsylvania and District of Columbia. *Education:* Muhlenberg College (B.A., 1981); Georgetown University Law Center; University of Bridgeport (J.D., 1984). Law Clerk to the Honorable Christine C. Nettesheim, United States Claims Court, 1985-1986. Lecturer, Catholic University, Graduate School of Construction Management, 1997—. Faculty, Educational Services Institute, George Washington University, 1991-1992. Chair, DCBIA Commercial Construction Committee, 1997—. Chair, Government Contracts Committee, Federal Circuit Bar Association, 1997—. Chair, Trial Advocacy Committee, American Bar Association, Section of Public Contract Law, 1991-1996. Vice Chair, Information Systems Committee, Section of Public Contract Law, 1991-1993. Member, Editorial Board, Public Contract Law Journal, 1994—. *Member:* Pennsylvania and American Bar Associations; The District of Columbia Bar. **Email:** rbrams@pattonboggs.com

DAVID J. FARBER, born New York, N.Y., August 13, 1961; admitted to bar, 1988, New York and District of Columbia. *Education:* New York University (B.A., 1983); Georgetown University (J.D., 1987). *Member:* The District of Columbia Bar; New York County Bar Association. **Email:** dfarber@pattonboggs.com

DANIEL A. KRACOV, born New York, N.Y., July 30, 1963; admitted to bar, 1988, Virginia; 1989, District of Columbia. *Education:* University of Maryland (B.A., magna cum laude, 1985); University of Virginia (J.D., 1988). Phi Beta Kappa. Member, Editorial Board, Virginia Journal of International Law, 1987-1988. *Member:* The District of Columbia Bar; Virginia State Bar. **Email:** dkracov@pattonboggs.com

BENJAMIN G. CHEW, born Washington, D.C., September 8, 1961; admitted to bar, 1988, Virginia; 1989, District of Columbia and U.S. District Court, Eastern District of Virginia; 1994, U.S. Court of Appeals, Fourth Circuit; 1995, U.S. Bankruptcy Court for the Eastern District of Virginia; 1996, U.S. District Court for the District of Columbia; 1998, U.S. District Court, Western District of Virginia; 2000, U.S. Supreme Court. *Education:* Princeton University (B.A., 1984); University of Virginia (J.D., 1988). Member, Editorial Board, Journal of Law and Politics. *Member:* Inter-American Bar Association. **Email:** bchew@pattonboggs.com

ROBERT C. JONES, born Washington, D.C., November 8, 1961; admitted to bar, 1986, Virginia; 1994, District of Columbia. *Education:* Virginia Polytechnic Institute and State University (B.A., 1983); University of Mississippi School of Law (J.D., 1986). Phi Alpha Delta. *Member:* Virginia State Bar; The District of Columbia Bar; American Bar Association. **Email:** rjones@pattonboggs.com

RICHARD M. STOLBACH, born New York, N.Y., August 17, 1952; admitted to bar, 1976, Virginia; 1977, District of Columbia; 1996, Florida. *Education:* Tufts University (B.A., magna cum laude, 1973); National Law Center, George Washington University (J.D., with honors, 1976). Assistant General Counsel, 1976-1977 and Special Counsel to the Executive Director, 1978, Appalachian Regional Commission. *Member:* The District of Columbia Bar; Virginia State Bar; The Florida Bar. **Email:** rstolbach@pattonboggs.com

PAUL C. BESOZZI, born New York, N.Y., August 22, 1947; admitted to bar, 1972, Virginia; 1973, District of Columbia; 1977, U.S. Supreme Court; 1978, U.S. Court of Appeals, Third and Fourth Circuits. *Education:* Georgetown University (B.S.F.S., cum laude, 1969; J.D., 1972); George Washington University (M.B.A., 1977). Phi Beta Kappa; Phi Alpha Theta; Pi Sigma Alpha. Member, Georgetown Law Journal, Vol. 60, 1971-1972. General Counsel and Minority Counsel, U.S. Senate Committee on Armed Services, 1980-1984. Director, Procurement Round Table. Member, Board of Governors, Georgetown University Alumni Association. Member, Board of Visitors, Georgetown University School of Foreign Service. *Member:* The District of Columbia Bar; Virginia State Bar; Federal Communications Bar Association. **Email:** pbesozzi@pattonboggs.com

STEPHEN DIAZ GAVIN, born Los Angeles, California, November 2, 1955; admitted to bar, 1984, Pennsylvania; 1985, U.S. Court of Appeals for the District of Columbia Circuit; 1994, District of Columbia; 1995, U.S. Supreme Court; 1996, U.S. District Court, District of Columbia. *Education:* Wesleyan University (B.A., cum laude and honors in History, 1977); School of Advanced International Studies, The John Hopkins University (M.A., 1980); Catholic University (J.D., 1984). Delegate to International Election Observer Mission, Republic of Bulgaria, April 1997 Parliamentary Election. Member, Board of Directors, Catholic Youth Organization of Archdiocese of Washington, 1998—; Treasurer, 1999-2000; Chairman, 2001. Chairman, Cuba Task Force, Sovereign Military Order of Malta, Federal Association U.S.A., 2000—. The Federalist Society. *Member:* Pennsylvania Bar Association; The District of Columbia Bar; Federal Communications Bar Association; Hispanic Bar Association. **Email:** sgavin@pattonboggs.com

J. JEFFREY CRAVEN, born Reynoldsburg, Ohio, September 16, 1959; admitted to bar, 1988, Pennsylvania; 1989, District of Columbia; 1995, U.S. Supreme Court. *Education:* Georgetown University (A.B., 1981; J.D., 1987). Alpha Sigma Nu. George F. Baker Scholar. Legislative Assistant, Congressman Gregory W. Carman, 1981. *Member:* The District of Columbia Bar; Federal Communications Bar Association. **Email:** jcraven@pattonboggs.com

JOSEPH E. SCHMITZ, born Milwaukee, Wisconsin, August 28, 1956; admitted to bar, 1988, Pennsylvania; 1989, District of Columbia; 1995, Maryland. *Education:* United States Naval Academy (B.S., with distinction, 1978);

(This Listing Continued)

PATTON BOGGS LLP, Washington—Continued

Stanford University (J.D., 1986). Associate Managing Editor, Stanford Law Review, 1985-1986. Judicial Clerk, Hon. James L. Buckley, U.S. Court of Appeals, District of Columbia Circuit, 1986-1987. Special Assistant to the Attorney General of the United States, Hon. Edwin Meese III, 1987. Adjunct Professor of Law, Georgetown University Law Center, 1995—. ***Email:*** jschmitz@pattonboggs.com

PENELOPE S. FARTHING, born New Castle, Indiana, June 2; admitted to bar, 1970, Indiana; 1971, District of Columbia Circuit Court of Appeals; 1975, U.S. Supreme Court; 1976, District of Columbia. *Education:* Purdue University (B.A., 1967); Indiana University-Bloomington (J.D., 1970). Staff Attorney, Federal Communications Commission, 1970-1972. Consumer Affairs Counsel American Retail Federation, 1972-1974. Congressional Liaison, Federal Trade Commission, 1974-1977. Special Assistant to the Administrator Food Safety and Quality Service, U.S. Department of Agriculture, 1977-1978. Law Department, Allstate Insurance Company, 1978-1980. Member, Board of Directors, 1981— and President, 1985-1987, American League of Lobbyists. Vice President, Edes Home, Washington D.C., 1993-1996, 1998—. Senior Counsel, American Insurance Association, 1980-1984. Member, Board of Visitors, Indiana University School of Law, 1994—. *Member:* The District of Columbia Bar; Indiana State, Federal (Chairman, Young Lawyers Council, 1975; Program Chairman, Antitrust Council, 1976-1980; Distinguished Service Award, 1975 and 1981) and American (Editorial Board, *Barrister,* 1975-1976; Standing Committee on Lawyer Competence, 1992-1994; Special Committee on Governmental Affairs, 1996—) Bar Associations; Women's Bar Association of the District of Columbia; Federal Communications Bar Association (Co-Chairman, Legislation Committee, 1996-1997). ***Email:*** pfarthing@pattonboggs.com

EDWARD J. NEWBERRY, born Schenectady, New York, September 25, 1962; admitted to bar, 1989, Virginia and U.S. Court of Appeals, Fourth Circuit; 1992, District of Columbia. *Education:* George Mason University (B.A., 1984; B.S., 1984); Georgetown University Law Center (J.D., 1989). *Member:* District of Columbia Bar. ***Email:*** enewberry@pattonboggs.com

MICHAEL J. SCHAENGOLD, born Washington, D.C., November 6, 1959; admitted to bar, 1986, Maryland; 1988, District of Columbia. *Education:* Dickinson College (B.A., summa cum laude, 1981); University of Virginia School of Law (J.D., 1986). Phi Beta Kappa. Law Clerk to Judge H. Robert Mayer, U.S. Claims Court, 1986-1987, and U.S. Court of Appeals for the Federal Circuit, 1987-1988. Member, Advisory Committee on Rules for the U.S. Court of Appeals for the Federal Circuit (by appointment of the Chief Judge). *Member:* Federal Circuit Bar Association (Member, Board of Governors; Chair, Government Contracts Committee); American Bar Association (Public Contract Law Section; Associate Editor, The Public Contract Law Journal); U.S. Court of Federal Claims Bar Association. ***Email:*** mschaengold@ pattonboggs.com

JOHN J. DESCHAUER, JR., born Brooklyn, New York, December 30, 1950; admitted to bar, 1978, New Jersey; 1995, District of Columbia. *Education:* University of Notre Dame (B.A., with honors, 1972); New York University (J.D., 1978). Legislative Counsel, Office of the Secretary of the Navy, 1988-1990. Director of Senate Affairs, Department of Defense, 1990-1994. [Commander, Judge Advocate General's Corps, U.S. Navy, 1972-1994]. ***Email:*** jdeschauer@pattonboggs.com

MICHAEL J. NARDOTTI, JR., born Brooklyn, New York, April 30, 1947; admitted to bar, 1977, New York, U.S. District Court, Southern and Eastern Districts of New York and U.S. Court of Appeals for the Armed Forces; 1980, U.S. Supreme Court; 1982, U.S. Court of Appeals, Second Circuit; 1998, District of Columbia. *Education:* U.S. Military Academy (B.S., 1969); Fordham University School of Law (J.D., 1976). Jessup International Moot Court Team. Best Speaker - 1976 National Competition. Moot Court Board. Assistant Judge Advocate General, Civil Law and Litigation, 1991-1993. The Judge Advocate General, United States Army, 1993-1997. *Member:* Federal Bar Association; Association of the United States Army; Judge Advocates Association. ***Email:*** mnardotti@pattonboggs.com

G. KENDRICK MACDOWELL, born Austin, Texas, July 27, 1959; admitted to bar, 1990, Texas; 1992, District of Columbia. *Education:* University of Texas at Austin (B.A., 1980; M.A., 1986; J.D., 1990). Phi Beta Kappa. Mortar Board. Friar Society. Law Clerk to Judge Thomas Reavley for the U.S. Court of Appeals for the Fifth Circuit. ***Email:*** kmacdowell@pattonboggs.com

DARRYL D. NIRENBERG, born Middletown, New York, September 23, 1959; admitted to bar, 1987, Pennsylvania; 1988, District of Columbia. *Education:* Colgate University (B.A., 1981); George Washington University (J.D., 1987). Member, Moot Court Board. Chief of Staff, U.S. Senator Jesse Helms, 1991-1995. Counsel, U.S. Senate Foreign Relations Committee, 1987-1991. Prof. Staff, U.S. Senate Agriculture Committee, 1983-1986. *Member:* American Bar Association. ***Email:*** dnirenberg@pattonboggs.com

MARY M. SJOQUIST, born Simcoe, Ontario, Canada; admitted to bar, 1982, District of Columbia. *Education:* University of Waterloo, Canada (B.A., 1966); Catholic University of America (J.D., 1982). Staff Attorney and Special Counsel, Division of Corporation Finance, United States Securities and Exchange Commission, 1982-1986. *Member:* The District of Columbia Bar (Member, Steering Committee, Corporation, Finance and Securities Law Section, 1998-2000); American Bar Association (Member: Federal Regulation of Securities Committee and Small Business Committee). ***Email:*** msjoquist@ pattonboggs.com

JOSEPH G. PASSAIC, JR., born Newark, New Jersey, August 23, 1953; admitted to bar, 1979, Pennsylvania; 1985, District of Columbia Bar. *Education:* Pennsylvania State University (B.A., 1975); Delaware Law School of Widener University (J.D., 1979). Attorney, 1979-1982 and Senior Attorney, 1982-1983, Office of the General Counsel, Federal Deposit Insurance Corporation. *Member:* The District of Columbia Bar; Pennsylvania Bar Association (Member, Corporations and Banking Subdivision). ***Email:*** jpassaic@ pattonboggs.com

FLORENCE WEATHERLY PRIOLEAU, born Salisbury, Maryland, January 10, 1952; admitted to bar, 1979, District of Columbia. *Education:* Goucher College (B.A., 1974); Georgetown University (J.D., 1979). Assistant Director, Domestic Policy Staff, The White House, 1979-1981. Member: Professional Staff, Committee on Ways and Means, U.S. House of Representatives, 1976-1979; Board of Directors of the Children's Inn of the National Institutes of Health, 1993—; Member, D.C. Court of Appeals, Committee on Unauthorized Practice. *Member:* The District of Columbia Bar; National and American Bar Associations. ***Email:*** fprioleau@pattonboggs.com

TIMOTHY A. CHORBA, born Yonkers, New York, September 23, 1946; admitted to bar, 1973, New York; 1977, District of Columbia. *Education:* Georgetown University (B.A., magna cum laude, 1968); University of Heidelberg, West Germany; Harvard Law School (J.D., 1972). Phi Beta Kappa. Fulbright Scholar in International Law and International Relations, University of Heidelberg, West Germany, 1968-1969. Legislative Counsel to Hon. Jonathan B. Bingham, U.S. House of Representatives, 1972-1973. U.S. Ambassador to Singapore, 1994-1998. Member, Council of American Ambassadors. *Member:* The District of Columbia Bar.

LANNY J. DAVIS, born Jersey City, New Jersey, December 12, 1945; admitted to bar, 1970, Connecticut; 1972, District of Columbia. *Education:* Yale University (B.A., cum laude, 1967; LL.B., 1970). Chairman, Yale Daily News, 1966-1967. Member, Yale Law Journal, 1971-1972. Winner, Thurmond Arnold Moot Court Prize. Chairman, 1981-1982 and Vice Chairman, 1983, Washington Suburban Transit Commission. Co-Chairman, Georgetown University Continuing Legal Education Computer Contracts Negotiations Conferences, 1983. Co-Chairman, Computer Contracts Conference, Law & Business, Inc., New York, Chicago, San Francisco; Washington, D.C. and Boston 1984, 1985, 1992; Co-Chair, Computer Contracts Conference, Informatics, Inc., London, England, 1984-1992, Amsterdam, 1988. Member, Democratic National Committee, Maryland, 1980-1992, DNC Executive Committee and Chair of Eastern Regional Caucus, 1986-1988 and Regional Floor Whip and Convention Delegate, 1992, Democratic National Convention. Chairman, Montgomery County Commission on the Reorganization of County Governments, 1987. Maryland Commentator, WAMU/FM, National Public Radio D.C. affiliate, 1992—. Special Counsel to the President, 1996-1998. *Member:* The District of Columbia Bar (Chairman, Division on Computer Law, 1985-1986; Vice-Chair, 1987); Connecticut, Federal and American (Member, Committee on Computer Law, Science and Technology Section, 1980; Chairman, Subcommittee on Computer Contracts, 1981) Bar Associations. ***Email:*** ldavis@pattonboggs.com

JONATHAN R. YAROWSKY, born Kansas City, Missouri, May 23, 1949; admitted to bar, 1978, District of Columbia. *Education:* University of Michigan (A.B., with high distinction, 1971); Cornell University (M.S., 1974); University of California at Los Angeles (J.D., 1977). Phi Beta Kappa. Chief Comment Editor, UCLA Law Review. Chief Counsel, House Judiciary Subcommittee on Economic and Commercial Law, 1988-1990. General Counsel, House Judiciary Committee, 1990-1995. Commissioner, National Commission on Crime, 1995-1996. Special Associate Counsel to the President, 1995-1998. ***Email:*** jyarowsky@pattonboggs.com

JOSEPH V. COLAIANNI, born Detroit, Michigan, March 19, 1935; admitted to bar, 1962, Michigan; 1963, Ohio; 1964, District of Columbia; 1966, U.S. Court of Federal Claims; 1982, U.S. Court of Appeals for the Federal Circuit and U.S. Supreme Court; registered to practice before U.S. Patent and Trademark Office. *Education:* University of Detroit, College of Engineering (B.S.E.E., 1956); Wayne State University; George Washington University (J.D., with honors, 1961). Eta Kappa Nu; Omicron Delta Kappa. Member, George Washington Law Review, 1960-1961. Adjunct Professor of Law: American University, 1984-1986; Catholic University of America, 1997—. Trial Attorney, U.S. Department of Justice, Civil Division, 1966-1970. Trial Judge, U.S. Court of Federal Claims, Washington, D.C., 1970-1984. Appointed by Federal Judicial Center to Science Liaison Committee Re Science Court, 1976-1982. Member: Advisory Board, Patent, Trademark and Copyright Journal, 1985-1991; Advisory Committee to the Commissioner of Patents and Trademarks, Donald J. Quigg, 1986-1989; Advisory Council, U.S. Claims Court, 1987—. Co-President, University of Maryland College Park Association, 1991-1997. Senior

(This Listing Continued)

Advisor, U.S. Claims Court Advisory Counsel, 1991—. *Member:* Ohio State, Federal and American Bar Associations; State Bar of Michigan; The District of Columbia Bar. ***Email:*** jcolaianni@pattonboggs.com

MICHAEL T. PLATT, born Brooklyn, New York, September 12, 1935; admitted to bar, 1961, District of Columbia; 1967, New York and U.S. Supreme Court; 1982, U.S. Court of Appeals for the Federal Circuit; registered to practice before U.S. Patent and Trademark Office. *Education:* Rensselaer Polytechnic Institute (B.E.E., 1957); George Washington University (J.D., with honors, 1961). Phi Alpha Delta. Patent Examiner, U.S. Patent Office, 1957-1959. Trial Attorney, U.S. Department of Justice, 1961-1966. *Member:* The District of Columbia Bar; American Bar Association; American Intellectual Property Law Association; International Association for the Protection of Industrial Property. ***Email:*** mplatt@pattonboggs.com

GEORGE P. LEVENDIS, born Washington, D.C.; admitted to bar, 1974, New York; 1980, District of Columbia. *Education:* Yale University (B.A.); University of Virginia (J.D.). Clerk, The Honorable Albert V. Bryan, U.S. Court of Appeals, Fourth Circuit. ***Email:*** glevendis@pattonboggs.com

SALLY D. GARR, born Atlanta, Georgia, June 10, 1952; admitted to bar, 1980, District of Columbia and Georgia. *Education:* Georgia State University (B.A., 1977); University of Georgia (J.D., 1980).

STEPHEN J. KOTT, born Rutherfordton, North Carolina, September 23, 1962; admitted to bar, 1989, North Carolina and U.S. District Court, Middle District of North Carolina; U.S. District Court, Northern District of Texas; 1993, U.S. Court of Appeals, Fourth Circuit; U.S. District Court, Western District of North Carolina; 1999, District of Columbia. *Education:* University of North Carolina (B.A., with distinction, 1986; J.D., 1989). Member, Editorial Board, National Institute of Construction Law, Inc., 1989—. ***Email:*** skott@pattonboggs.com

WILLIAM E. SLADE, born Syracuse, New York, October 6, 1959; admitted to bar, 1984, South Carolina; 1985, U.S. Army Court of Military Review and U.S. Court of Military Appeals; 1990, U.S. Court of Federal Claims and U.S. Court of Appeals, Federal Circuit; 1992, District of Columbia; 1998, U.S. Court of Appeals, Fourth Circuit. *Education:* St. Lawrence University (B.A., 1981); Vermont Law School (J.D., 1984); George Washington University (LL.M., 1992). Thomas M. Debevoise Moot Court Honors Competition; Member, Moot Court Honor Board, 1983. Trial Attorney, U.S. Army Contract Appeals Division, Office of the Judge Advocate General, 1989-1992. *Member:* District of Columbia Bar; South Carolina Bar. [U.S. Army J.A.G. Corps, 1984-1992]. ***Email:*** wslade@pattonboggs.com

ERIC A. KUWANA, born Cleveland, Ohio, February 23, 1966; admitted to bar, 1991, Missouri; 1992, U.S. Court of Appeals for the Fourth Circuit; 1993, District of Columbia; 1997, U.S. District Court, District of Columbia; 1998, U.S. District Court, District of Maryland; 2001, U.S. District Court, District of Colorado. *Education:* University of Chicago (A.B., 1988); University of Kansas (J.D., 1991). Attorney: U.S. Department of Transportation, Office of Motor Carrier Law, 1991-1992; Office of Counsel to the President, The White House, 1992-1993; Office of General and Contract Law, Federal Highway Administration, 1993-1995. Counsel, 2000 Republic National Convention Foreign Relations Platform Subcommittee; Deputy General Counsel, 2001 Presidential Inaugural Committee. ***Email:*** ekuwana@pattonboggs.com

PETER D. ROBERTSON, born Kansas City, Missouri, November 18, 1955; admitted to bar, 1987, District of Columbia; 1989, U.S. Court of Appeals, 5th and 6th Circuits, District of Columbia. *Education:* University of Oklahoma (B.A., with distinction, 1978); University of Virginia; Georgetown University (J.D., cum laude, 1987). Phi Beta Kappa. Legislative Assistant to Congressmen James R. Jones, 1979-1980. Professional Staff Member, Committee on the Budget, U.S. House of Representatives, 1980-1985. Acting Deputy Administrator, Chief of Staff U.S. Environmental Protection Agency, 1995-1999. *Member:* The District of Columbia Bar; Bar Association of the District of Columbia. ***Email:*** probertson@pattonboggs.com

SUSAN B. BASTRESS, born Wilmington, North Carolina, May 1, 1952; admitted to bar, 1981, Maryland; 1982, District of Columbia; 1987, U.S. Virgin Islands. *Education:* Duke University (B.S., magna cum laude, 1974); George Washington University (J.D., with honors, 1981). Member, Board of Governors, Virgin Island Bar Association, 1994-1995. *Member:* The District of Columbia Bar; Maryland State Bar Association (Member, Commercial Real Estate Section). ***Email:*** sbastress@pattonboggs.com

SUSAN MATHIASCHECK, born Des Moines, Iowa, December 14, 1962; admitted to bar, 1988, Massachusetts; 1990, District of Columbia. *Education:* Harvard College (A.B., 1985); Boston University (J.D., 1988). ***Email:*** smathiascheck@pattonboggs.com

ROBERT D. LUSKIN, born Chicago, Illinois, January 21, 1950; admitted to bar, 1979, District of Columbia and U.S. District Court, District of Columbia; 1981, U.S. Court of Appeals, District of Columbia, First, Fourth, Fifth, Sixth, Seventh, Eighth, Ninth, Eleventh and Federal Circuits; 1984, U.S. Supreme Court. *Education:* Harvard College (A.B., magna cum laude, 1972); Oxford University, Oxford England (1972-1975); Harvard Law School (J.D., magna cum laude, 1979). Phi Beta Kappa. Rhodes Scholar. Supreme Court Note Editor, Harvard Law Review, 1978-1979. Lecturer in Law: University of Virginia School of Law, 1992—; Faculty Georgetown University Law Center, Continuing Legal Education Center, National Institute for Trial Advocacy, 1993—. Law Clerk to Judge Louis F. Oberdorfer, U.S. District Court for the District of Columbia, 1979-1980. Special Counsel, Organized Crime and Racketeering Section, U.S. Department of Justice, 1980-1982. President, Harvard Law School Association of the District of Columbia, 1991—. *Member:* The District of Columbia Bar; American Bar Association (Past Chairman, RICO, Forfeiture and Civil Remedies Committee, Criminal Justice Section, 1990-1994; Member, Complex Crimes Committee, Litigation Section; Vice-Chairman, Tasks Force on Forfeiture, 1993); National Association of Criminal Defense Lawyers; California Attorneys for Criminal Justice.

(This Listing Continued)

DOUGLAS C. PROXMIRE, born Washington, D.C., October 12, 1961; admitted to bar, 1987, Virginia and U.S. District Court, Eastern District of Virginia; U.S. Court of Appeals, Federal Circuit; 1997, District of Columbia. *Education:* Wake Forest University (B.A., cum laude, Political Science, 1984); Georgetown University (J.D., 1987). *Member:* District of Columbia Bar; Virginia State Bar; American Bar Association; Court of Federal Claims Bar Association. ***Email:*** dproxmire@pattonboggs.com

STEPHEN H. SHERMAN, born Lancaster, Pennsylvania, November 1, 1961; admitted to bar, 1986, Pennsylvania; 1987, New Jersey and U.S. Tax Court; 1988, District of Columbia; 1992, U.S. Supreme Court. *Education:* Drexel University (B.S.B.A., with high honors, 1983); Dickinson School of Law (J.D., 1986); Georgetown University (LL.M., Taxation, 1991). Articles Editor, Dickinson Journal of International Law, 1985-1986. Senior Trial Attorney and Attorney Advisor, Internal Revenue Service, Office of Associate Chief Counsel (Employee Benefits and Exempt Organizations), 1988-1993. Adjunct Professor of Law (Graduate Tax Program), Georgetown University Law Center, 1993—. *Member:* The District of Columbia Bar (Member, Section on Taxation). ***Email:*** ssherman@pattonboggs.com

DENISE A. VANISON, born Washington, D.C., February 11, 1966; admitted to bar, 1992, Pennsylvania; 1994, District of Columbia. *Education:* University of Virginia (B.A., 1988); Georgetown University (J.D., 1991). ***Email:*** dvanison@pattonboggs.com

JAMIE S. GARDNER, born Miami, Florida, April 8, 1958; admitted to bar, 1983, District of Columbia; 1996, Massachusetts, U.S. District Court, District of Columbia and U.S. Supreme Court. *Education:* Tufts University (B.A., magna cum laude, 1980); Georgetown University (J.D., cum laude, 1983). Visiting Professor, Georgetown University Law Center, 1994-1995. Clinical Instructor, Criminal Justice Institute, Harvard Law School, 1996-1999. Chief, Trial Division, Public Defender Service, District of Columbia, 1984-1996. *Member:* The District of Columbia Bar (Co-Chair, Steering Committee, Criminal Law & Individual Rights Section, 1988-1990). ***Email:*** jgardner@pattonboggs.com

JOSEPH S. TRAPASSO, born Branford, Connecticut, September 27, 1965; admitted to bar, 1991, Connecticut; 1992, District of Columbia. *Education:* Connecticut College (B.A., summa cum laude, 1987); University of Pennsylvania (J.D., 1990). Phi Beta Kappa. Assistant Counsel to the President of the United States, Office of Presidential Personnel, 1993. Legislative Affairs Officer, U.S. Department of State, 1993-1994. ***Email:*** jtrapasso@pattonboggs.com

MARK D. COWAN, born Kankakee, Illinois, December 4, 1949; admitted to bar, 1977, Virginia; 1980, District of Columbia. *Education:* University of Minnesota (B.A., 1971); Columbus School of Law of The Catholic University of America (J.D., 1976). Deputy Assistant Secretary of Labor-OSHA, 1981-1982. Chief of Staff and Counsellor to The Secretary of Labor, 1982-1984. Commissioner, National Commission on Employment Policy, 1990-1992. *Member:* Virginia State Bar; The District of Columbia Bar. ***Email:*** mcowan@pattonboggs.com

LESLIE T. THORNTON, born Philadelphia, Pennsylvania, May 2, 1958; admitted to bar, 1983, District of Columbia, U.S. District Court, District of Columbia and U.S. Supreme Court. *Education:* University of Pennsylvania (B.A., 1980); Georgetown University (J.D., 1983). Member and Associate Editor, American Criminal Law Review, Georgetown University, 1982-1983. Senior Associate, Brand & Lowell, 1989-1992. Associate Counsel to the 1992 Presidential and Vice-Presidential Transition, 1992-1993. Deputy Chief-of-Staff and Counselor, 1993-1997 and Chief-of-Staff, 1997-2000, U.S. Department of Education. *Member:* The District of Columbia Bar; Washington State Bar Association (Member, Board of Directors, Greater Washington Area Chapter, Women Lawyers Division, 1990); National Bar Association. ***Email:*** lthornton@pattonboggs.com

JOHN W. SCHRYBER, born Morristown, New Jersey, January 7, 1957; admitted to bar, 1984, New York; 1994, District of Columbia. *Education:* University of Florida (B.S., 1979); New York Law School (J.D., magna cum laude, 1983). Member, New York Law School Law Review, 1982-1983. *Member:* American Bar Association. ***Email:*** jschryber@pattonboggs.com

C. DONALD JOHNSON, JR., born Atlanta, Georgia, January 30, 1948; admitted to bar, 1973, Georgia and District of Columbia; 1978, Illinois. *Edu-*

(This Listing Continued)

PATTON BOGGS LLP, Washington—Continued

cation: University of Georgia (A.B., 1970; J.D., 1973); The London School of Economics and Political Science (LL.M., 1978); The Hague Academy of International Law (Certificate, 1972). Articles Editor, Georgia Journal of International Comparative Law, 1972-1973. Ambassador and Chief Textile Negotiator, Office of United States Trade Representative, 1998-2000. Member, U.S. Congress, Tenth District of Georgia, 1993-1994. Georgia State Senator, 1987-1992. Chairman, Georgia Senate Appropriations Committee, 1990-1992. Legislative Counsel on Trade, Professional Staff, U.S. House of Ways and Means Committee, 1973. *Member:* The District of Columbia Bar; State Bar of Georgia (Member, Board of Governors, 1986-1992). [Capt., JAG, USAF, 1973-1977]. ***Email:*** cdjohnson@pattonboggs.com

DANIEL R. ADDISON, born Los Angeles, California, March 12, 1960; admitted to bar, 1989, District of Columbia. *Education:* Claremont McKenna College (B.A., 1982); Claremont Graduate (M.A., 1983); Catholic University (J.D., 1987). Special Assistant, Senator Pete Wilson, 1987-1988. Special Counselor, NOAA, 1989-1993. Assistant Director, CA Department of Conservation, 1994-1995. Governor, Board of Governors, Rose Institute of State and Local Government, 1991—. *Member:* American Bar Association (Member, Section of Natural Resources, Energy and Environmental Law). ***Email:*** daddison@pattonboggs.com

PHILIP A. BANGERT, born Washington D.C., November 14, 1961; admitted to bar, 1991, Maryland; 1998, District of Columbia. *Education:* St. Mary's College of Maryland (B.A., in Economics, 1983); Catholic University of America (J.D., 1991). Member, Catholic University Law Review. *Member:* Maryland State Bar Association. ***Email:*** pbangert@pattonboggs.com

PHILIP G. FEIGEN, born Silver Spring, Maryland, June 15, 1965; admitted to bar, 1993, Maryland; 1995, District of Columbia. *Education:* Boston University (B.S., 1987); Catholic University of America (J.D., 1993). Member, Catholic University Law Review, 1991-1993. ***Email:*** pfeigen@pattonboggs.com

RODNEY A. GRANDON, born Des Moines, Iowa, August 13, 1960; admitted to bar, 1985, Iowa; 1992, U.S. Supreme Court; 1996, District of Columbia. *Education:* Iowa State University (B.A., 1982); Drake University (J.D., 1985); U.S. Army Judge Advocate General's School (LL.M., 1992). Recipient, Ernest M. Brannon Award for the Highest Standing in Government Contract Law. [Major, JAGC, U.S. Army, 1985-1995]. ***Email:*** rgrandon@pattonboggs.com

ROBERT A. HAGER, born Dayton, Ohio, September 20, 1965; admitted to bar, 1991, Virginia; 1994, District of Columbia. *Education:* Georgetown University (B.S.F.S., cum laude, 1987; J.D., 1991). Member, 1989-1991 and Senior Article Editor, 1990-1991, Georgetown International Environmental Law Review. ***Email:*** rhager@pattonboggs.com

CLAYTON LEE HOUGH, born Clark AFB, Philippines, November 10, 1958; admitted to bar, 1990, Maryland; 1993, District of Columbia; 1994, U.S. Supreme Court. *Education:* University of California at Los Angeles (B.A., 1982); Georgetown University (J.D., 1990). Phi Eta Sigma; Sigma Nu. ***Email:*** chough@pattonboggs.com

AUBREY A. ROTHROCK, III, born High Point, North Carolina, May 8, 1968; admitted to bar, 1993, North Carolina; 1996, District of Columbia. *Education:* University of North Carolina at Chapel Hill (B.A., with honors in English, 1990; J.D., 1993). ***Email:*** arothrock@pattonboggs.com

PAUL D. RUBIN, born Brooklyn, New York, June 24, 1967; admitted to bar, 1992, Pennsylvania; 1993, District of Columbia. *Education:* Wharton School, University of Pennsylvania (B.S., magna cum laude, 1989); University of Pennsylvania (J.D., cum laude, 1992). ***Email:*** prubin@pattonboggs.com

ANNE SLAUGHTER ANDREW, born Evansville, Indiana, September 23, 1955; admitted to bar, 1983, Indiana; 2001, District of Columbia. *Education:* Georgetown University (B.A., 1977); Indiana University - Indianapolis (J.D., cum laude, 1983). *Member:* American Bar Association (Chair, 1996-1998); Environmental Quality Control. ***Email:*** asandrew@pattonboggs.com

V. HEATHER SIBBISON, born Cheyenne, Wyoming, May 12, 1961; admitted to bar, 1989, Virginia and District of Columbia. *Education:* Tufts University (B.A., magna cum laude, 1983); Columbia University (J.D., 1988). Recipient, Frederick Melvin Ellis Prize. Special Assistant to the Secretary, 1993-1999, Counselor to the Deputy Secretary, 1996-1999 and Vice-Chairman, Indian Arts and Crafts Board, 1999—, U.S. Department of the Interior. Counsel to the Assistant Attorney, Environment and Natural Resources, U.S. Department of Justice, 1999-2001. ***Email:*** hsibbison@pattonboggs.com

RODNEY E. SLATER, born Tutwyler, Mississippi, February 23, 1955; admitted to bar, 1980, Arkansas (Not admitted in District of Columbia). *Education:* Eastern Michigan University (B.S., 1977); University of Arkansas (J.D., 1980). U.S. Secretary of Transportation, 1997-2001. ***Email:*** rslater@pattonboggs.com

(This Listing Continued)

MARIO V. MIRABELLI, born Elizabeth, New Jersey, July 5, 1939; admitted to bar, 1966, District of Columbia. *Education:* Georgetown University (A.B., 1961); American University, Washington College of Law (J.D., 1964). Trial Attorney: Bureau of Deceptive Practices, Federal Trade Commission, 1967-1969; Division of Corporation Finance, Branch of Administrative Proceedings, Securities and Exchange Commission, 1969-1973. ***Email:*** mmirabelli@pattonboggs.com

LAURENCE E. HARRIS, born Baltimore, Maryland, March 24, 1936; admitted to bar, 1974, Pennsylvania (Not admitted in District of Columbia). *Education:* Columbia University (B.A., 1958); Georgetown University Law Center (J.D., 1965). Board of Editors, Law Review, 1965. Chief, Mass Media Bureau, FCC, 1980-1982. Member, Board of Visitors, Georgetown Law Center, 1986—. ***Email:*** lharris@pattonboggs.com

SINGLETON B. McALLISTER, born Baltimore, Maryland, March 25, 1952; admitted to bar, 1985, Pennsylvania; 1986, District of Columbia. *Education:* University of Maryland (B.A., 1975); Howard University (J.D., 1984). President, Women in Government Relations, Inc., 1994-1995. Senior Counsel, Committee on the Budget, U.S. House of Representatives, 1986-1988. Law Clerk to the Honorable Jack E. Tanner, Federal District Court, 9th Circuit, 1984-1986. Special Assistant to Congressman Mickey Leland, U.S. House of Representatives, 1981-1983. Legislative Director to Congressman William H. Gray, U.S. House of Representatives, 1978-1981. Legislative Assistant to Congressman Parren Mitchell, U.S. House of Representatives, 1975-1978. *Member:* District of Columbia Bar; Pennsylvania Bar Association. ***Email:*** smcallister@pattonboggs.com

ROBERT J. HORN, born New York, New York, August 23, 1943; admitted to bar, 1967, New York (Not admitted in District of Columbia). *Education:* City College of the City University of New York (B.A., 1964); Fordham University (J.D., 1967). ***Email:*** rhorn@pattonboggs.com

IRA FISHMAN, born Chicago, Illinois, November 6, 1957; admitted to bar, 1982, District of Columbia. *Education:* Yale College (B.A., 1979); Harvard University (J.D., 1982). Export-Import Bank of the United States, Vice President for Congressional and External Affairs, 1993-1995. Executive of the President of the United States, Deputy Assistant for Legislative Affairs, 1995-1996. Federal Communications Commission, Special Counsel and Director of Task Force on Education, 1996. ***Email:*** ifishman@pattonboggs.com

ASSOCIATES

ELIZABETH E. RING, born Tampa, Florida, July 13, 1967; admitted to bar, 1992, Florida; 1994, District of Columbia. *Education:* University of Virginia (B.A., with high distinction, 1989); University of Texas (J.D., with honors, 1992). Phi Beta Kappa; Raven Society; Omicron Delta Kappa; Pi Sigma Alpha. Associate Editor, Texas Law Review, 1988-1989. *Member:* The District of Columbia Bar; The Florida Bar. ***Email:*** ering@pattonboggs.com

EDWARD S. WISNESKI, born Washington, D.C., June 15, 1968; admitted to bar, 1994, Maryland; 1995, U.S. District Court for the District of Maryland (Not admitted in District of Columbia). *Education:* University of Delaware (B.A., 1990); University of Maryland (J.D., with honors, 1994). Phi Alpha Delta. *Member:* Maryland State Bar Association. ***Email:*** ewisneski@pattonboggs.com

JEANNE M. LIEDTKA, born Silver Spring, Maryland, September 28, 1969; admitted to bar, 1994, Virginia and The Supreme Court of Virginia; 1995, District of Columbia and District of Columbia Court of Appeals and U.S. District Court, Eastern District of Virginia; 1996, U.S. Court of Appeals for the Fifth Circuit; 2000, U.S. Supreme Court. *Edueation:* University of Virginia (B.A., 1991; J.D., 1994). Phi Beta Kappa. John Bassett Moore International Legal Society, 1993-1994. *Member:* Bar Association of the District of Columbia; American Bar Association. ***Email:*** jliedtka@pattonboggs.com

THOMAS C. DOWNS, born St. Johnsbury, Vermont, January 19, 1961; admitted to bar, 1995, North Carolina; 1996, District of Columbia. *Education:* Brown University (A.B., 1983); Washington College of Law, American University (J.D., 1994). Staff Member, The American University Law Review. Legislative Director and Chief of Staff, Representative George J. Hochbrueckner (NY), 1987-1995. Legislative Assistant, Representative Martin Olav Sabo (MN), 1985-1987. ***Email:*** tdowns@pattonboggs.com

MICHAEL T. WOOD, born Schenectady, New York, May 18, 1967; admitted to bar, 1996, Maryland and U.S. District Court, District of Maryland; 1997, District of Columbia; 1999, U.S. District Court for the District of Columbia. *Education:* University of Vermont (B.A., with honors in Political Science, 1989); Washington College of Law (J.D., cum laude, 1995). ***Email:*** mwood@pattonboggs.com

JANET FITZPATRICK MORAN, born Plainfield, New Jersey, August 23, 1963; admitted to bar, 1991, Maryland; 1992, New Jersey; 1994, District of Columbia. *Education:* James Madison University (B.A., cum laude, 1985); Georgetown University (J.D., cum laude, 1991). *Member:* District of Columbia Bar; Federal Communications Bar Associations; Women's Bar Association. ***Email:*** jfitzpatrick@pattonboggs.com

(This Listing Continued)

HAROLD H. KIM, born Las Vegas, Nevada, April 8, 1970; admitted to bar, 1995, Maryland; 1997, District of Columbia. *Education:* University of California, Irvine (B.A., 1991); Catholic University of America (J.D., 1995). ***Email:*** hkim@pattonboggs.com

JON PAUL MORRIS, born Washington, D.C., May 26, 1958; admitted to bar, 1995, Maryland and U.S. District Court, District of Maryland; 1997, District of Columbia. *Education:* St. Peter's College (B.S., 1983); Georgetown University Law Center (J.D., 1994). ***Email:*** jpmorris@pattonboggs.com

ELIZABETH C. MOELLER, born Modesto, California, October 29, 1970; admitted to bar, 1996, California; 1997, District of Columbia. *Education:* University of California at Berkeley (B.A., highest honors, 1992); University of California at Los Angeles (J.D., 1996). Phi Beta Kappa. ***Email:*** bmoeller@pattonboggs.com

WILLA B. PERLMUTTER, born New Haven, Connecticut, December 7, 1958; admitted to bar, 1983, Connecticut; 1994, Alaska; 1998, District of Columbia. *Education:* Mount Holyoke College (B.A., 1980); University of Connecticut (J.D., 1983). ***Email:*** wperlmutter@pattonboggs.com

SEAN PATRICK CLANCY, born Abington, Pennsylvania, November 6, 1971; admitted to bar, 1996, New Jersey and Pennsylvania; 1998, District of Columbia. *Education:* Lehigh University (B.A., with honors, 1993); Widener University School of Law (J.D., cum laude, 1996); Georgetown Law Center (LL.M., Taxation, 1997). Adjunct Professor of Law, Graduate Tax Program, Georgetown University Law Center, 2000—. ***Email:*** sclancy@pattonboggs.com

ANDREW M. ROSENBERG, born Norristown, Pennsylvania, January 28, 1968; admitted to bar, 1997, Maryland; 2000, District of Columbia. *Education:* Amherst College (B.A., 1990); University of Virginia (M.P., 1997; J.D., 1997). ***Email:*** arosenberg@pattonboggs.com

AMY C. DAVINE, born Mineola, New York, October 9, 1972; admitted to bar, 1997, Minnesota; 1998, District of Columbia; 1999, U.S. District Court, District of Columbia. *Education:* Pepperdine University (B.A., cum laude, 1994); University of Notre Dame (J.D., 1997). Member: National Honor Society; Notre Dame Concannon Programme of International Law, London, England. Articles Editor, Journal of Legislation, 1995-1997. Member, Women's Legal Forum, 1994-1997. ***Email:*** adavine@pattonboggs.com

STEPHEN S. (TODD) ANDERSON, JR., born Summit, New Jersey, August 1, 1969; admitted to bar, 1998, California; 1999, District of Columbia. *Education:* University of Pennsylvania (B.A., summa cum laude, 1992); John F. Kennedy School of Government (M.P.P., 1997); Harvard Law School (J.D., cum laude, 1997). Phi Beta Kappa. Teaching Fellow, Economics, Harvard University, 1995-1997. *Member:* The District of Columbia Bar; State Bar of California (inactive); American Bar Association (Member, Antitrust Section). ***Email:*** sanderson@pattonboggs.com

JENNIFER J. SPOKES, born Burlington, Vermont, December 26, 1970; admitted to bar, 1998, Massachusetts; 1999, District of Columbia. *Education:* Duke University (A.B., cum laude, with distinction in Biology, 1992); Boston University (J.D., magna cum laude, 1997). Editor, Boston University Law Review, 1997. ***Email:*** jspokes@pattonboggs.com

JOHN SPITALERI SHAW, born New York, N.Y., June 16, 1969; admitted to bar, 1995, Maryland; 1996, District of Columbia. *Education:* Syracuse University (B.S., 1991); Catholic University of America (J.D., 1995). Member, Board of Governors, Capitol Hill Club, 1996—. Majority Counsel, Special Investigation, U.S. Senate Committee on Governmental Affairs, 1997. ***Email:*** jshaw@pattonboggs.com

MICHAEL T. PALMER, born Baton Rouge, Louisiana, January 30, 1965; admitted to bar, 1993, Louisiana; 1999, District of Columbia. *Education:* Louisiana State University (B.G.S., 1990); Loyola University School of Law (J.D., 1993). Omicron Delta Kappa; Phi Alpha Theta. Member, Moot Court Staff. ***Email:*** mpalmer@pattonboggs.com

MICHELE J. BIANCO, born New York, N.Y., July 8, 1965; admitted to bar, 1993, Florida; 1998, District of Columbia. *Education:* Goucher College (B.A., 1987); Nova Southeast University (J.D., 1993); Georgetown University (LL.M., 1994). ***Email:*** mbianco@pattonboggs.com

MARCUS E. ROSENLEHNER, born Munich, Bavaria, Germany, January 19, 1961 (Not admitted in the United States). *Education:* London University College; Ludwig-Maximilian University (J.D.); American University (LL.M.). (Foreign Associate). ***Email:*** mrosenlehner@pattonboggs.com

BING XU, born Beijing, China, December 10, 1965; admitted to bar, 1999, Maryland; 2000, District of Columbia. *Education:* Foreign Affairs College (B.A., 1989); University of Texas at Dallas (M.A., 1991); Catholic University of America (J.D., 1998). *Member:* American Bar Association (Vice-Chair, China Law Committee, Section of International Law and Practice, 1999-2002). ***Email:*** bxu@pattonboggs.com

LAURENCE E. STEIN, born Denver, Colorado, August 20, 1955; admitted to bar, 1993, Virginia, registered to practice before U.S. Patent and Trademark Office (Not admitted in District of Columbia). *Education:* Old Dominion University (B.S.E.E., 1982); George Mason University School of Law (J.D., 1993); Virginia Polytechnic Institute (M.S.E.E., 1997). ***Email:*** lstein@pattonboggs.com

JAY L. EIZENSTAT, born Atlanta, Georgia, August 2, 1970; admitted to bar, 1998, Georgia (Not admitted in District of Columbia). *Education:* Syracuse University (B.A., 1993); Emory University School of Law (J.D., 1997). ***Email:*** jeizenstat@pattonboggs.com

ANDREW M. FRIEDMAN, born Manchester, New Hampshire, June 7, 1966; admitted to bar, 1994, New Hampshire; 1997, Massachusetts and Pennsylvania; 1999, District of Columbia. *Education:* Brown University (A.B., 1988); University of Minnesota (J.D., cum laude, 1993). Law Clerk to: Judge Richard J. Menke, Minnesota District Court, 1993-1994; the Honorable Donald E. Ziegler, U.S. District Court, Western District of Pennsylvania, 1997-1998. New Hampshire Public Defender, 1994-1997. ***Email:*** afriedman@pattonboggs.com

AMY B. CHASANOV, born Wilmington, Delaware, September 15, 1966; admitted to bar, 1998, Maryland (Not admitted in District of Columbia). *Education:* University of Pennsylvania (B.A., magna cum laude, B.S., magna cum laude, 1988; M.A., 1988); University of Michigan (J.D., with honors, 1998). ***Email:*** achasanov@pattonboggs.com

LISA A. HUNT, born Landstuhl, Germany, July 8, 1969; admitted to bar, 1996, New York; 2000, District of Columbia. *Education:* University of Virginia (B.A., 1991); American University (J.D., 1995). ***Email:*** lhunt@pattonboggs.com

ALYSSA T. SENZEL, born New York, N.Y., April 19, 1968; admitted to bar, 1995, California; 1996, District of Columbia. *Education:* University of Pennsylvania (B.A., 1990); University of Virginia (J.D., 1995). Executive Editor, Virginia Environmental Law Journal. *Member:* District of Columbia Bar; State Bar of California (Member, Labor and Employment Section); American Bar Association. ***Email:*** asenzel@pattonboggs.com

LISA LAVELLE BURKE, born Pittsburgh, Pennsylvania, September 24, 1967; admitted to bar, 1992, California; 1993, District of Columbia. *Education:* Saint Mary's College (B.A., 1989); University of Notre Dame (J.D., cum laude, 1992). Clerk Intern, The Honorable Robert L. Byer, Commonwealth Court of Pennsylvania, 1990. Managing Editor, Notre Dame Law Review. *Member:* State Bar of California; District of Columbia Bar; American Bar Association. ***Email:*** llavelle@pattonboggs.com

ROBERT K. TOMPKINS, born Atlanta, Georgia, May 3, 1968; admitted to bar, 1994, Virginia, U.S. District Court, Eastern District of Virginia, U.S. Court of Appeals, Fourth Circuit and U.S. Court of Federal Claims; 1995, Maryland; 1996, District of Columbia and U.S. Tax Court; 1997, U.S. Supreme Court. *Education:* Washington and Lee University (B.A., 1990; J.D., 1994). *Member:* Virginia and American Bar Associations; Virginia State Bar. ***Email:*** rtompkins@pattonboggs.com

JENNIFER A. GOLDSTEIN, born Norfolk, Virginia, February 18, 1971; admitted to bar, 1996, Virginia; 1998, District of Columbia. *Education:* University of Virginia (B.A., 1993); College of William & Mary (J.D., 1996). ***Email:*** jgoldstein@pattonboggs.com

MICHAEL BLOOMQUIST, born Royal Oak, Michigan, March 18, 1969; admitted to bar, 1995, Illinois; 1999, District of Columbia. *Education:* Hamilton College (B.A., 1991); Washington University (J.D., 1995); George Washington University (LL.M., Environmental, 1997). ***Email:*** mbloomquist@pattonboggs.com

ANDREW ZIMMITTI, born Meriden, Connecticut, October 2, 1969; admitted to bar, 1995, Connecticut; 1999, District of Columbia. *Education:* University of Chicago (B.A., 1991); Georgetown University (J.D., 1995). Phi Beta Kappa. *Member:* Connecticut Bar Association; The District of Columbia Bar. ***Email:*** azimmitti@pattonboggs.com

WILLIAM McGINLEY, born Encino, California, March 14, 1967; admitted to bar, 1997, Maryland (Not admitted in District of Columbia). *Education:* University of California at Los Angeles (B.A., 1992); California State University (M.A., 1994); George Washington University (J.D., with honors, 1997). ***Email:*** wmcginley@pattonbogg.com

CHRISTOPHER HELLMICH, born Detroit, Michigan, August 23, 1967; admitted to bar, 1993, Nebraska (Not admitted in District of Columbia). *Education:* Marquette University (B.S., 1989); Creighton University (J.D., 1993). ***Email:*** chellmich@pattonboggs.com

KAREN L. MARANGI, born Pasadena, California, August 1, 1966; admitted to bar, 1996, California; 1999, District of Columbia. *Education:* Stanford University (B.A., 1988; J.D., 1995). Counsel, U.S. Senate Judiciary Committee, 1997-1999. *Member:* The District of Columbia Bar; State Bar of California. ***Email:*** kmarangi@pattonboggs.com

DAVID M. TAFURI, born Cincinnati, Ohio, February 8, 1970; admitted to bar, 1996, Ohio; 1999, District of Columbia. *Education:* Emory University

(This Listing Continued)

PATTON BOGGS LLP, Washington—Continued

(B.A., magna cum laude, 1992); Georgetown University (J.D., 1996). John Gordon Stipe Society of Scholars. Member, Tax Lawyer Law Journal, 1994-1996. Barrister's Council. ***Email:*** dtafuri@pattonboggs.com

JONATHAN C. PAVONY, born Miami, Florida, May 7, 1971; admitted to bar, 1997, Florida; 1998, District of Columbia. *Education:* University of Florida (B.S., 1993); Catholic University of America (J.D., 1997). *Member:* The Florida Bar (Member, Business Law Section, 1997—); The District of Columbia Bar (Member, Corporation, Finance and Securities Law Section, 1997—); American Bar Association. ***Email:*** jpavony@pattonboggs.com

STEPHANIE J. PETERS, born Akron, Ohio, August 5, 1964; admitted to bar, 1991, Pennsylvania; 2000, District of Columbia. *Education:* Ohio State University (B.A., 1986); Georgetown University (J.D., 1990). ***Email:*** speters@pattonboggs.com

MATTHEW F. STOWE, born Fairfax, Virginia, August 3, 1972; admitted to bar, 1999, Texas (Not admitted in District of Columbia). *Education:* Dartmouth College (A.B., summa cum laude, 1993); Harvard University (J.D., magna cum laude, 1996). Law Clerk to: Honorable Sandra Day O'Connor, U.S. Supreme Court, 1997-1998; Honorable J. Michael Luttig, U.S. Court of Appeals, Fourth Circuit, 1996-1997. Assistant Professor of Law, Cornell Law School, 1999. ***Email:*** mstowe@pattonboggs.com

PATRICK J. SLEVIN, born Washington, D.C., December 8, 1961; admitted to bar, 1988, Pennsylvania; 1990, District of Columbia. *Education:* Georgetown University (A.B., 1983; J.D., cum laude, 1988). Law Clerk to: Honorable Bruce D. Beaudin, D.C. Superior Court, 1989-1991; Hono rable June L. Green, U.S. District Court, District of Columbia, 1994-1996. ***Email:*** pslevin@pattonboggs.com

ALEXANDRA V. BUTLER, born Wilmington, Delaware; admitted to bar, 1996, Idaho; 2000, District of Columbia. *Education:* Cornell University (A.B., 1993); College of William & Mary (J.D., 1996). Order of the Coif. ***Email:*** abutler@pattonboggs.com

COURTNEY COLLINS NOWELL, born Laguna Beach, California, July 19, 1971; admitted to bar, 1996, Virginia; 1997, District of Columbia. *Education:* Wellesley College (B.A., 1993); College of William & Mary (J.D., 1996); Georgetown University (LL.M., Taxation, 1999). ***Email:*** cnowell@pattonboggs.com

CRYSTAL GOTHARD, born Washington, D.C., February 25, 1966; admitted to bar, 1997, Colorado; 1999, District of Columbia. *Education:* University of Denver (B.A., 1993; J.D., 1996). ***Email:*** cgothard@pattonboggs.com

J. YOST CONNER, JR., born Clifton Forge, Virginia, April 27, 1963; admitted to bar, 1997, Virginia and U.S. District Court, Eastern District of Virginia; 2000, District of Columbia. *Education:* Virginia Polytechnic Institute and State University (B.Arch., 1986); University of Virginia (J.D., 1997). ***Email:*** yconner@pattonboggs.com

VINCENTE L. MARTINEZ, born Casper, Wyoming, November 10, 1969; admitted to bar, 1999, New York and U.S. District Court, Southern and Eastern Districts of New York; 2000, District of Columbia. *Education:* Georgetown University (B.A., 1993); University of California, Berkeley (J.D., 1997). *Member:* District of Columbia Bar; New York State Bar Association. ***Email:*** vmartinez@pattonboggs.com

GAL N. KAUFMAN, born Washington, D.C., July 9, 1966; admitted to bar, 1992, Maryland; 1999, District of Columbia. *Education:* University of Maryland (B.S., 1988); American University (J.D., cum laude, 1992); Georgetown University Law Center (LL.M., Taxation, 1993). ***Email:*** gkaufman@pattonboggs.com

MICHAEL GUIFFRE, born Las Cruces, New Mexico, February 19, 1969; admitted to bar, 1993, New Mexico; 2000, District of Columbia. *Education:* New Mexico State University (B.A., 1990); Georgetown University (J.D., 1993). ***Email:*** mguiffre@pattonboggs.com

MATTHEW D. CUTTS, born Washington, D.C., August 30, 1971; admitted to bar, 1997, Maryland (Not admitted in District of Columbia). *Education:* University of Virginia (B.A., 1994); University of Virginia School of Law (J.D., 1997). *Member:* Bar Association for the District of Columbia (Member, Young Lawyers Division, 1999—); District of Columbia Bar (Member, Young Lawyers Division, 1999—).

DANIEL R. VOLKMUTH, born Rochester, New York, July 1, 1968; admitted to bar, 1997, Ohio (Not admitted in District of Columbia). *Education:* Rochester Institute of Technology (B.S., 1991); University of Chicago (J.D., 1995). Law Clerk to Justice Marsha K. Ternus, Iowa Supreme Court, 1995-1996. ***Email:*** dvolkmuth@pattonboggs.com

MICHAEL E. KLEIN, born New Britain, Connecticut, October 21, 1961; admitted to bar, 1993, Pennsylvania; 1997, U.S. Supreme Court; 2000, District of Columbia. *Education:* United States Military Academy (B.S., 1985); University of Virginia (J.D., 1993); The Judge Advocate General's School, Army (LL.M., 1997). ***Email:*** mklein@pattonboggs.com

(This Listing Continued)

UZOAMAKA S. EMEKA, born Lagos Lagos, Nigeria, September 27, 1975; admitted to bar, 2000, New York; 2001, District of Columbia. *Education:* Northwestern University (B.S., 1996); New York University (J.D., 1999). Member, National Society of Black Engineers, 1992—. *Member:* National Bar Association. ***Email:*** uemeka@pattonboggs.com

J. ALEXANDER HERSHEY, born Pittsburgh, Pennsylvania, May 31, 1972; admitted to bar, 1999, Pennsylvania; 2000, District of Columbia. *Education:* Oberlin College (B.A., with highest honors, 1994); George Washington University (J.D., with honors, 1999). Notes Editor, George Washington Law Review, 1998-1999. *Member:* District of Columbia Bar; Pennsylvania and American Bar Associations. ***Email:*** ahershey@pattonboggs.com

LISA M. DWYER, born Killeen, Texas, October 17, 1971; admitted to bar, 1999, Pennsylvania and Massachusetts; 2001, District of Columbia. *Education:* Wesleyan University (B.A., cum laude, 1993); George Washington University (J.D., with honors, 1998). *Member:* American Bar Association. ***Email:*** ldwyer@pattonboggs.com

DEBRA M. LABOSCHIN, born Los Angeles, California, January 1, 1971; admitted to bar, 1999, California (Not admitted in District of Columbia). *Education:* University of Pennsylvania (B.A., 1993); University of California, Hastings College of the Law (J.D., 1999). Member, Thurston Society. ***Email:*** dlaboschin@pattonboggs.com

RAPHAEL J.A. LARSON, born Portland, Oregon, May 23, 1972; admitted to bar, 1999, Maryland (Not admitted in District of Columbia). *Education:* Portland State University (B.S., 1996); Georgetown University (J.D., 1999). ***Email:*** rlarson@pattonboggs.com

R. BRIAN HENDRIX, born Jefferson City, Tennessee, August 30, 1973; admitted to bar, 1999, Tennessee; 2000, District of Columbia; 2001, U.S. District Court for the District of Columbia. *Education:* University of Tennessee at Knoxville (B.A., summa cum laude, 1996); Vanderbilt University (J.D., 1999). Phi Beta Kappa. ***Email:*** bhendrix@pattonboggs.com

SHANNON W. CONWAY, born Washington, D.C., October 19, 1968; admitted to bar, 1999, Virginia (Not admitted in District of Columbia). *Education:* Towson State University (B.S., 1992); Catholic University of America (J.D., 1999). Phi Delta Phi. *Member:* American Bar Association.

ROBYN M. UNDERWOOD, born Baton Rouge, Louisiana, November 28, 1958; admitted to bar, 1989, Louisiana; 1999, District of Columbia. *Education:* University of Louisiana (B.A., 1984); Louisiana State University (J.D., 1989). *Member:* Louisiana State Bar Association. ***Email:*** runderwood@pattonboggs.com

MATTHEW E. PAUL, born New York, N.Y., November 30, 1965; admitted to bar, 1993, California; 1996, District of Columbia. *Education:* Wesleyan University (B.A., with honors, 1987); University of Virginia (J.D., 1993; M.B.A., 1993). Law Clerk to Honorable Susan Ilston, U.S. District Court, Northern District of California, San Francisco, California, 1995-1996. *Member:* The District of Columbia Bar. ***Email:*** mpaul@pattonboggs.com

UGO COLELLA, born Astoria, New York, November 29, 1966; admitted to bar, 1997, New Jersey; 2001, District of Columbia. *Education:* Stanford University (B.A., 1989); Tulane University of Louisiana (J.D., 1996). Trial Attorney, Civil Division Torts Branch, U.S. Department of Justice, 1997-2000. ***Email:*** ucolella@pattonboggs.com

BABAK BAGHERI, born Akron, Ohio, August 10, 1973; admitted to bar, 1998, Maryland; 2000, District of Columbia. *Education:* Case Western Reserve University (B.A., 1995); George Washington University (J.D., 1998). *Member:* The District of Columbia Bar (Member, Corporation, Finance and Securities Law Section); Maryland State Bar Association (Member, Business Law Section). ***Email:*** bbagheri@pattonboggs.com

MICHAEL GOLD, born Doylestown, Pennsylvania, May 15, 1973; admitted to bar, 2000, New York (Not admitted in District of Columbia). *Education:* Brandeis University (B.A., 1995); University of Pennsylvania (J.D., 1998). ***Email:*** mgold@pattonboggs.com

WILLIAM L. NASH, III, born Fort Bragg, North Carolina, March 27, 1972; admitted to bar, 2000, Virginia (Not admitted in District of Columbia). *Education:* Vanderbilt University (B.A., 1994); George Washington University (J.D., 2000; M.A., Security Policy Studies, 2000). Order of the Coif. ***Email:*** wnash@pattonboggs.com

MAREK DRELL GOOTMAN, born Philadelphia, Pennsylvania, October 23, 1970; admitted to bar, 2000, Maryland (Not admitted in District of Columbia). *Education:* University of Pennsylvania (B.S.E., cum laude, 1992; M.G.A., cum laude, 1993); Georgetown University (J.D., magna cum laude, 2000). Order of the Coif. Member, Mortar Board. Order of the Coif. U.K. Atlantic Fellow in Public Policy. ***Email:*** mgootman@pattonboggs.com

JOHN A. ROSANS, born West Chester, Pennsylvania, June 23, 1975; admitted to bar, 2000, Virginia (Not admitted in District of Columbia). *Education:* Cornell University (B.A., 1997); University of Michigan (J.D., 2000). ***Email:*** jrosans@pattonboggs.com

(This Listing Continued)

JONATHAN EDGAR, born Washington, D.C., October 6, 1974; admitted to bar, 2000, Virginia (Not admitted in District of Columbia). *Education:* Princeton University (A.B., 1997); George Washington University (J.D., with honors, 2000). Member, George Washington International Law Review. **Email:** jedgar@pattonboggs.com

DONALD M. DENG, born Stockholm, Sweden, November 7, 1973; admitted to bar, 2000, Maryland (Not admitted in District of Columbia). *Education:* Amherst College (B.A., 1996); Yale University (J.D., 2000). **Email:** ddeng@pattonboggs.com

DARREN P. RILEY, born Cincinnati, Ohio, May 9, 1972; admitted to bar, 2000, Maryland (Not admitted in District of Columbia). *Education:* Washington University (B.A., 1994); Howard University (J.D., cum laude, 2000). **Email:** driley@pattonboggs.com

KEY REID, born Las Vegas, Nevada, August 19, 1974; admitted to bar, 1999, Nevada (Not admitted in District of Columbia). *Education:* University of Virginia (B.A., 1996); George Mason University (J.D., 1999). **Email:** kreid@pattonboggs.com

KEVIN M. O'NEILL, born Washington, D.C., December 4, 1969; admitted to bar, 1999, Virginia (Not admitted in District of Columbia). *Education:* Syracuse University (B.A., 1992); College of William and Mary (J.D., 1999). Notes and Comments Editor, William and Mary Law Review, 1998-1999. Law Clerk to Hon. David A. Lowe, U.S. Magistrate Judge, Eastern District of Virginia, 1999-2000. **Email:** koneill@pattonboggs.com

KATRINA C. GLEBER, born Tallahassee, Florida, December 9, 1972; (admission pending). *Education:* Boston University (B.S./B.A., 1994); George Washington University (J.D., 2000). **Email:** kgleber@pattonboggs.com

KATHRYN W. HAMBRICK, born Southfield, Michigan, November 4, 1966; admitted to bar, 1994, Virginia (Not admitted in District of Columbia). *Education:* Drexel University (B.S., 1988); College of William and Mary (J.D., 1994). Certified Public Accountant, Pennsylvania, 1990. *Member:* Virginia State Bar; American Bar Association; American Institute of Certified Public Accountants; Pennsylvania Institute of Certified Public Accountants. **Email:** khambrick@pattonboggs.com

KATHLEEN J. LESTER, born Indianapolis, Indiana, April 5, 1971; admitted to bar, 1998, Indiana, U.S. District Court, Northern and Southern Districts of Indiana and U.S Court of Appeals, Seventh Circuit; 1999, Maryland; 2000, District of Columbia. *Education:* DePauw University (B.A., 1993); Johns Hopkins University (M.P.H., 1998); Georgetown University Law Center (J.D., 1998). Phi Beta Kappa. Adjunct Professor, Georgetown University Law Center, 2000. Clerk to Michael S. Kanne, U.S Court of Appeals, Seventh Circuit, 1998-1999. *Member:* Indiana State, Maryland State, Seventh Circuit and American Bar Associations; American Public Health Association. **Email:** klester@pattonboggs.com

JULIE K. STAPEL, born Mount Pleasant, Michigan, April 3, 1970; admitted to bar, 1996, Maryland; 1997, District of Columbia. *Education:* University of Michigan (B.A., 1992); Indiana University School of Law (J.D., magna cum laude, 1996). Order of the Coif. **Email:** jstapel@pattonboggs.com

BENJAMIN WOOD, born Minneapolis, Minnesota, July 6, 1972; admitted to bar, 2001, Maryland (Not admitted in District of Columbia). *Education:* Yale University (B.A., 1995); University of Virginia (J.D., 2001). **Email:** bwood@pattonboggs.com

KENNETH P. JONES, born Smithtown, New York, January 5, 1972; admitted to bar, 1999, Florida; 2000, District of Columbia. *Education:* Florida State University (B.S., 1994); University of Florida (J.D., 1998). Deputy Counsel, Republican National Committee, 1999-2001. Counsel, 2001 Presidential Inaugural Committee for the Inauguration of President George W. Bush. *Member:* The Florida Bar; The District of Columbia Bar. **Email:** kjones@pattonboggs.com

ALEXANDER ANNETT, born Houston, Texas, June 15, 1970; (admission pending). *Education:* Franklin & Marshall College (B.A., 1993); Georgetown University Law Center (J.D., 2001). **Email:** aannett@pattonboggs.com

GORDON F. PEERY, born Salt Lake City, Utah, April 23, 1967; admitted to bar, 1996, California; 2001, District of Columbia. *Education:* University of Southern California (B.A., magna cum laude, 1991), Vanderbilt Law School (J.D., 1995). Phi Beta Kappa; Phi Kappa Phi; Golden Key; Recipient, Bennett Douglas Bell Honor. President, Vanderbilt Law School Honor Society. **Email:** gpeery@pattonboggs.com

DAVID J. WEILER, born Houston, Texas, July 28, 1965; admitted to bar, 1990, Pennsylvania; 1991, District of Columbia. *Education:* University of Maryland (B.A., Economics, magna cum laude, 1987); Georgetown University (J.D., cum laude, 1990; LL.M., with distinction, 1993). Adjunct Professor, American University, Washington College of Law, 1998-1999. *Member:* The District of Columbia Bar. **Email:** dweiler@pattonboggs.com

DANIEL S. BATES, born Portland, Oregon, December 22, 1975; (admission pending). *Education:* Houghton College (B.A., 1998); University of Virginia (J.D., 2001). **Email:** dbates@pattonboggs.com

(This Listing Continued)

BRET M. KOPLOW, born Cleveland, Ohio; (admission pending). *Education:* Miami University (B.A., 1981); University of Chicago (J.D., 2001). License in Clinical Psychology, 1994. **Email:** bkoplow@pattonboggs.com

GREGORY F. POLK, born Washington, D.C., January 16, 1976; (admission pending). *Education:* University of Virginia (B.A., 1998); Emory University (J.D., 2001). Member, Moot Court Team, 2000-2001. **Email:** gpolk@pattonboggs.com

CATHERINE SUN, born Taipei, Taiwan, May 30, 1973; admitted to bar, 1998, New York; 2000, U.S. District Court, Southern and Eastern Districts of New York (Not admitted in District of Columbia). *Education:* George Mason University (B.A., with high distinction, 1994); American University (J.D., cum laude, 1997).

FOREIGN ASSOCIATE

WANG ZHANG, born Keramay, Xinjiang Province, China, August 8, 1974; admitted to bar, 1998, China (Not admitted in the United States). *Education:* China University of Political Science & Law, Beijing, China (LL.B., 1997); University of Pennsylvania (LL.M., 2001). *Member:* Chinese Bar Association. **Email:** kelamayi2000@yahoo.com

OF COUNSEL

JOHN C. CAMP, born Arab, Alabama, September 23, 1923; admitted to bar, 1948, Louisiana; 1974, District of Columbia. *Education:* Birmingham-Southern College; University of Alabama; Auburn University; Louisiana State University (J.D., 1948). Member, Board of Editors, Louisiana Law Review, 1947-1948. Participant: International Top Management Roundtable Discussions (London, Milan, Amsterdam, Brussels, Frankfurt, Rome, Düsseldorf, Ditchley Park, Stockholm and Toronto), 1982-1987. Presidential Delegate, People's Republic of China Trade Mission, 1979. Member: Board of New York Trustees of the Athens College (Athens, Greece), 1985-1991; Board Executive Committee, Wolf Trap Foundation, 1984-1991; Vice Chairman of the Board, Executive Committee, Meridian House International, 1984-1995. Assistant Attorney General, Louisiana, 1972-1980. Special Counsel to the Governor of Louisiana (Energy Matters), 1974-1980. Past President, 1982-1989 and Member, Executive Committee, Washington Area United Service Organization (USO). Member, The George Washington University Medical Center Advisory Council, 1990-1997. *Member:* The District of Columbia Bar; Louisiana State Bar Association. **Email:** jcamp@pattonboggs.com

GREGORY H. LAUGHLIN, born Bay City, Texas, January 21, 1942; admitted to bar, 1967, Texas (Not admitted in District of Columbia). *Education:* Texas A & M University (B.A., 1964); University of Texas (LL.B., 1967). U.S. Representative, 14th District of Texas, 1989-1997. *Member:* State Bar of Texas (Board of Directors, 1981-1984). **Email:** glaughlin@pattonboggs.com

THOMAS P. O'DONNELL, born Philadelphia, Pennsylvania, January 31, 1959; admitted to bar, 1992, California; 1993, District of Columbia. *Education:* Yale University (B.A., 1981); University of Texas (J.D., 1992). Special Assistant to the President and Chief of Staff, The White House National Economic Council, 1995-1997. Chief of Staff and General Counsel, The President's Council of Economic Advisers, 1993-1995. Managing Director, Democratic National Convention, Los Angeles, 2000. Registered Agent: Sultanate of Oman; Republic of Costa Rica. *Member:* State Bar of California; The District of Columbia Bar; American Bar Association. **Email:** todonnell@pattonboggs.com

ANNE M. MIANO, born Flushing, New York, July 21, 1953; admitted to bar, 1979, New York; 1999, District of Columbia. *Education:* Adelphi University (B.A., 1975); St. John's University (J.D., 1978). **Email:** amiano@pattonboggs.com

GRAHAM G. WISNER, born Washington, D.C., June 15, 1950; admitted to bar, 1981, Maryland; 1982, District of Columbia; 1996, U.S. District Court, District of Columbia. *Education:* Antioch College (B.A., 1975); Georgetown University (J.D., 1978). Instructor, American University, 1988-1995. *Member:* District of Columbia Bar; Council on Foreign Relations. **Email:** gwisner@pattonboggs.com

BRIAN C. LOPINA, born Chicago, Illinois, March 25, 1955; admitted to bar, 1980, Illinois; 1998, District of Columbia. *Education:* University of Notre Dame (B.A., 1977); De Paul University (J.D., 1980). Administrative Assistant, Rep. Ernest Istook (OK-5), 1993-1995. **Email:** blopina@pattonboggs.com

LANSING B. LEE, III, born Augusta, Georgia, February 26, 1948; admitted to bar, 1974, Georgia; 1989, District of Columbia. *Education:* University of North Carolina (B.A., 1969); Emory University (J.D., 1974). Special Assistant/Administrative Assistant to Governor Jimmy Carter, 1971-1972. Law Assistant to Supreme Court of Georgia Justices William Gunter and Conley Ingram, 1975. Assistant District Attorney, Augusta Judicial Circuit, 1975-1976. *Member:* The District of Columbia Bar; State Bar of Georgia; American Bar Association.

GREGORY S. WALDEN, born Champaign, Illinois, June 26, 1955; admitted to bar, 1981, California; 1982, District of Columbia. *Education:* Wash-

(This Listing Continued)

PATTON BOGGS LLP, Washington—Continued

ington & Lee University (B.A., cum laude, 1977); University of San Diego (J.D., magna cum laude, 1980). Adjunct Professor of Aviation Law, George Mason University School of Law, 1998—. Court Law Clerk, U.S. Court of Appeals for the District of Columbia, 1980-1982. Law Clerk to Robert H. Bork, U.S. Court of Appeals for the District of Columbia, 1982. Special Assistant to Assistant Attorney General, Civil Division, 1983-1986. Associate Deputy Attorney General, U.S. Department of Justice, 1986-1988. Chief Counsel, Federal Aviation Administration, 1988-1990. Associate Counsel to the President, 1990-1993. Transition Ethics Counsel, Bush-Cheney Transition, 2000-2001. Member, Interstate Commerce Commission, 1993. ***Email:*** gwalden@pattonboggs.com

THOMAS L. SIEBERT, born Cleveland, Ohio, May 2, 1946; admitted to bar, 1974, Pennsylvania; 1975, District of Columbia. *Education:* Georgetown University (A.B., 1968); Georgetown University Law Center (J.D., 1972). Editor, Law & Policy in International Business, Georgetown University, 1972. U.S. Ambassador to Sweden, 1994-1998. Chairman, International Telecommunication Plenipotentiary Conference, 1998. *Member:* The District of Columbia Bar; Bar Association of the District of Columbia; American Bar Association; Federal Communications Bar Association. ***Email:*** tsiebert@pattonboggs.com

SEAN P. MURPHY, born Rochester, New York, August 22, 1963; admitted to bar, 1990, New York; 1991, District of Columbia, U.S. District Court , Southern District of New York and U.S. Court of Federal Claims; 1994, U.S. Court of Appeals, Ninth Circuit; 1995, Florida, U.S. Supreme Court, U.S. Court of Appeals, Eleventh Circuit and U.S. District Court, Middle and Southern Districts of Florida; 1996, U.S. District Court, Northern District of Florida; 1997, U.S. Court of Appeals, Federal Circuit; 1998, Maryland; 1999, U.S. Court of Appeals, Fourth Circuit. *Education:* Georgetown University (B.S., Foreign Service, 1985; J.D., 1989). Formerly with Dewey Ballentine, New York, New York, 1989-1991. Trial Attorney, U.S. Department of Justice, Civil Division, 1991-1995. *Member:* Federal and American Bar Associations; William Glen Terrell Inn of Court (Barrister). ***Email:*** smurphy@pattonboggs.com

JOHN D. AUSTIN, JR., born Chickasha, Oklahoma, December 8, 1946; admitted to bar, 1973, Tennessee; 1974, U.S. Court of Appeals for the District of Columbia Circuit; 1978, U.S. Supreme Court; 1985, District of Columbia; 1986, U.S. District Court, District of Columbia. *Education:* The Ohio State University (B.A., 1969); University of Tennessee (J.D., 1973). Phi Alpha Delta. Attorney-Advisor, U.S. Department of the Interior, 1973-1977. Acting Regional Solicitor, Philadelphia, 1976-1977. Vice President-Environment and Assistant Chief Counsel, American Mining Congress, 1977-1986. Contributing Author: D.C. Superior Court Digest. *Member:* District of Columbia Bar (Member, Environment Energy and Natural Resources Division), Tennessee (Member, Environment Law Section), Federal (Former Chairman, Energy Environment and Natural Resources Section) and American (Member, Sections on: Natural Resources; Administrative Law) Bar Associations. [Capt., U.S. Army, 1970-1971]. ***Email:*** jaustin@pattonboggs.com

NANCY A. MURRAY, born Glen Cove, New York, January 10, 1955; admitted to bar, 1979, District of Columbia; 1980, U.S. District Court for the District of Columbia; 1984, U.S. Court of Appeals for the District of Columbia and Federal Circuits. *Education:* Ithaca College (B.A., 1976); University of Dayton (J.D., 1979). Phi Alpha Delta. With United States Department of Housing and Urban Development, Washington, D.C., 1985-1989. Executive Assistant to the Deputy Assistant Secretary, Multifamily Housing Programs, 1985-1986. Executive Assistant to the Assistant Secretary for Housing, Federal Housing Commissioner, 1986-1987. Executive Assistant to the Under Secretary, 1987-1989. *Member:* The District of Columbia Bar. ***Email:*** nmurray@pattonboggs.com

ERIC N. OLSEN, born Minneapolis, Minnesota, December 24, 1961; admitted to bar, 1989, Minnesota (Not admitted in District of Columbia). *Education:* University of Minnesota (B.A., summa cum laude, 1985; J.D., cum laude, 1989). Phi Beta Kappa. Legislative Counsel, U.S. Congressman David Minge, 1993-1994. Chief of Staff, Counsel to Secretary for Domestic Policy, U.S. Department of Agriculture, 1994-2001.

PARKER E. BRUGGE, born Martinsville, Virginia, March 6, 1963; admitted to bar, 1988, Virginia; 1989, District of Columbia. *Education:* University of Virginia (B.S.Ch.E., 1985); Marshall-Wythe School of Law (J.D., 1988). Judicial Law Clerk, The Honorable Edward S. Smith, U.S. Court of Appeals for the Federal Circuit, 1988-1989. Counselor to the Assistant Administrator at the U.S. Environmental Protection Agency, 1993-1997. ***Email:*** pbrugge@pattonboggs.com

PUBLIC SERVICE COUNSEL

MELANIE K. GERBER, born Jersey City, New Jersey, May 27, 1947; admitted to bar, 1989, Pennsylvania and District of Columbia. *Education:* University of Maryland (B.A., 1973); Catholic University; Georgetown University Law Center (J.D., 1988). Member: Capitol Area Immigrants Rights Coalition; Board of Directors, Legal Resource Center for Housing and Community Development; Operating Committee, Whitman-Walker Legal Services; American Bar Association Law Firm Pro Bono Project Advisory Editorial Board. ***Email:*** mgerber@pattonboggs.com

LEGAL SUPPORT PERSONNEL

TRANSPORTATION POLICY CONSULTANT

CAROLINA L. MEDEROS, born Rochester, Minnesota, July 1, 1947. *Education:* Vanderbilt University (B.A., 1969); University of Chicago (M.A., 1971). Administrative Assistant, Lt. Governor of Illinois, Chicago, 1972; Senior Research Associate, University of Chicago, 1972; Project Manager, Consultant, Urban Dynamics, Inner City Fund and Community Programs Inc., Chicago, 1972-1973; Legislative Assistant to Senate President, Illinois State Senate, Chicago and Springfield, 1973-1976; Program Analyst, Department of Transportation, Washington, 1976-1979; Chief, Transportation Assistance Programs Division, 1979-1981; Director, Programs and Evaluation, 1981-1988; Chairwoman, Secretary's Safety Review Task Force, 1985-1988; Deputy Assistant Secretary for Safety and Deputy Assistant Secretary for Policy and International Affairs, Department of Transportation, 1988-1989. Recipient: award for Meritorious Achievement, Secretary of Transportation, 1980; Superior Achievement Award, U.S. Department of Transportation, 1981; Secretary's Gold Medal Award for Outstanding Achievement, 1986; Presidential Rank award, 1987. Member: Womens Transportation Seminar; International Aviation Club; AERO Club. ***Email:*** cmederos@pattonboggs.com

CHIEF ECONOMIC CONSULTANT

DAVID G. RABOY, born Harvey, Illinois, March 13, 1952. *Education:* George Washington University (M.A., Economics, 1981; Ph.D., Economics, 1986); State University of New York at Buffalo (B.A., cum laude, Economics, 1978); New York School of Industrial and Labor Relations, Certificate in Labor Studies (Cornell University, Buffalo Extension, 1978). Experience: Senator William V. Roth, Jr. (R-De.), Legislative Director, 1983-1986; The Institute for Research on the Economics of Taxation (IRET), Executive Director, 1981-1983; National Association of Manufacturers (NAM), Associate Director of Tax Analysis, 1979-1981; Bethlehem Steel Corporation - United Steelworkers of America, Steelworker and Assistant Grievance Committeeman, USW Local 2602, 1974-1977. Affiliations: National Association of Business Economists (National Capital Chapter, President, 1984); American Economic Association, National Tax Association Tax Institute of America; Omicron Delta Epsilon (Honor Society in Economics). ***Email:*** draboy@pattonboggs.com

ECONOMICS CONSULTANT

TERI L. SIMPSON, born Wichita Falls, Texas, December 12, 1959. *Education:* University of Virginia (B.A. 1982, Majors: Foreign Affairs, French Language, 1982); The Fletcher School, Tufts University (M.A.L.D., International Trade and Development Economics, 1988). Founder, Section on Industrialized Country/Developing Country Trade Issues, Women in International Trade. Member: Society for International Development; European Union Young Leaders Program, 1997; National Association of Business Economists. Previous Employment: Lloyd Bentsen 1988 Vice-Presidential Campaign National Advance Staff; International Trade Consultant, Massachusetts Office of International Trade and Investment, 1987-1988; Assistant Director of Government Relations, National Mass Retailing Institute, 1985-1986. Research Assistant for International Issues, Office of Senator Lloyd Bentsen, 1983-1985. ***Email:*** tsimpson@pattonboggs.com

SENIOR HEALTH POLICY ADVISOR

JOANN V. WILLIS, born Tokyo, Japan, August 17, 1953. *Education:* University of Virginia (B.A., 1975); George Washington University (M.A., 1983). ***Email:*** jwillis@pattonboggs.com

PUBLIC POLICY SPECIALISTS

MICHAEL A. BROWN, born Kassel, West Germany, March 4, 1965. *Education:* Clark University (B.A., 1987); Widener University, Delaware Law School (J.D., 1991). President, CEO Ronald H. Brown Foundation, 1996. Boxing and Wrestling Commissioner, Washington, D.C., 1996. Political Director of America's Fund. Member, University of District of Columbia Steering Committee. Member, Council on Foreign Relations. Board Member, Constituency for Africa. Member, Washington, D.C. Recreation Wish List Committee. ***Email:*** mbrown@pattonboggs.com

ELENA M. GIBERGA, born St. Thomas, Virgin Islands, September 10, 1970. *Education:* Vanderbilt University (B.S., 1992). (Legislative Affairs Specialist). ***Email:*** egiberga@pattonboggs.com

JOSEPH W. WESTPHAL, born Santiago, Chile, January 26, 1948. *Education:* Adelphi University (B.A., 1970); University of Missouri (Ph.D., 1980). Pi Sigma Alpha. Assistant Secretary of the Army, 1998-2001; Acting Secretary of the Army, 2001. ***Email:*** jwestphal@pattonboggs.com

(This Listing Continued)

Languages: Farsi, French, German, Italian, Spanish, Arabic, Indonesian, Portuguese, Persian.

(For biographical data on other personnel at Anchorage, Alaska, Denver and Louisville, Colorado, Dallas, Texas and Seattle, Washington, see Professional Biographies at those locations)

PAUL, HASTINGS, JANOFSKY & WALKER LLP

A Limited Liability Partnership including Professional Corporations

Established in 1951

1299 PENNSYLVANIA AVENUE, N.W.

WASHINGTON, D.C. 20004-2400

Telephone: 202-508-9500

Fax: 202-508-9700

URL: http://www.paulhastings.com

Atlanta, Georgia Office: 24th Floor, 600 Peachtree Street, N.E. Telephone: 404-815-2400.

Los Angeles, California Office: 555 South Flower Street. Telephone: 213-683-6000.

New York, New York Offices: 399 Park Avenue. Telephone: 212-318-6000 and 75 East 55th Street. Telephone: 212-318-6000.

Orange County, California Office: 695 Town Center Drive, Costa Mesa. Telephone: 714-668-6200.

San Francisco, California Office: 345 California Street. Telephone: 415-835-1600.

Stamford, Connecticut Office: 1055 Washington Boulevard. Telephone: 203-961-7400.

Tokyo, Japan Office: 27F Ark Mori Building, 12-32, Minato-Ku, Akasaka 1-Chome, P.O. Box 577 . Telephone: (03) 3586-4711.

London, England Office: Tower 42, 25 Old Broad Street. Telephone: +44 (0) 20 7562-4000.

Aircraft Finance Practice, Asia-Pacific, Banking and Financial Services, Computer Law, Creditor's Rights and Bankruptcy, Customs, International Trade and Export Control, Emerging Growth and Technology, Energy, Federal Legislative, Healthcare, International Energy/Utility/Infrastructure, International Trade, Internet and Electronic Commerce, Investment Management, Japan Practice for United States-Based Clients, Latin America, Lease and Asset-Based Finance, Mergers and Acquisitions, Project and Infrastructure Finance, Structured Finance and Asset Securitization, Telecommunications and Media, Timber, Paper and Packaging, Trade Regulation and Proprietary Rights, Year 2000, Employee Benefits, Executive Practice, Immigration, Railroad Labor and Employment Law, Accountant's Liability, Alternative Dispute Resolution (ADR), Antidumping, Countervailing Duty and Related Trade Proceedings, Antitrust Litigation and Government Enforcement, Appellate, Entertainment, Environmental, Government Contracts, Insurance Coverage, Intellectual Property, Technology Licensing and Litigation, Trade Secret, Patent Litigation, Securities and Corporate Finance Litigation, White Collar Corporate Criminal Defense, Affordable Housing, Land Use, Real Estate Acquisition and Disposition, Resort, Restaurant and Recreation, Retail Leasing, International Tax and Tax Litigation.

MEMBERS OF FIRM

E. LAWRENCE BARCELLA, JR., born Washington, D.C., May 23, 1945; admitted to bar, 1971, District of Columbia. *Education:* Dartmouth College (A.B., 1967); Vanderbilt University (J.D., 1970). Assistant U.S. Attorney, D.C., 1970-1986. Chief Counsel, U.S. House of Representatives October Surprise Task Force, 1992-1993. Special Master to Judge Stanley Sporkin and Judge William Howeler, 1995-1998. Member: Vice Chair, White Collar Crime Committee, Criminal Justice Section; Complex Crimes Committee, Litigation Section, American Bar Association. Fellow, American College of Trial Lawyers. ***PRACTICE AREAS:*** White Collar Corporate Defense; Complex Litigation; White-Collar Criminal Investigation and Litigation; Bribery; Ethics Offenses; Political Corruption; Fraud; Government Contract Violations; Health Care Fraud and Abuse; Securities Violations; Money Laundering; Banking Offenses; Tax Violations; Export Violations; Classified Intelligence Procedures Act Law; Foreign Intelligence Surveillance Act Law; Office of Government Ethics (OGE); Ethics in Government Act; Board of Directors Breach of Fiduciary Duty; Corporate Compliance Programs; Arms Export and Munitions Control Act; Foreign Judicial Systems; Treaty Negotiations; Extraditions; Congressional Investigations and Testimony.

KIRBY D. BEHRE, born New Haven, Connecticut, March 29, 1960; admitted to bar, 1985, Maryland; 1986, District of Columbia. *Education:* George Washington University (B.A., with special honors and distinction, 1982); Georgetown University (J.D., cum laude, 1985). Phi Beta Kappa. Assistant U.S. Attorney for the District of Columbia, 1989-1994. Chair 1999— and Member, Judicial Evaluation Committee, Bar Association of the District of Columbia, 1998—. General Counsel, 1996— and Director, Big Brothers of the National Capitol Area, 1989—. ***PRACTICE AREAS:*** Corporate Criminal Defense; Corporate Compliance; Government Investigations; Government Contract Law.

BARBARA BERISH BROWN, born Washington, D.C., June 26, 1946; admitted to bar, 1971, Connecticut; 1972, Pennsylvania; 1981, District of Columbia. *Education:* Radcliffe College (B.A., 1968); Yale University (J.D., 1971). Phi Beta Kappa. Editor, Yale Law Journal, 1969-1971. Law Clerk, Hon. J. Joseph Smith, U.S. Court of Appeals, 2d Cir., 1971-1972. Co-Author: *Legal Guide to Human Resources,* Warren, Gorham & Lamont, 3d-Rev. Ed., (Supp. 2001); *Equal Employment Law Update* (BNA, 6th ed., Fall, 1999). Section Council Member, Co-Chair, EEO Committee, ABA, 1998-2000, Labor and Employment Law Section, American Bar Association. Fellow, American College of Labor and Employment Lawyers. ***PRACTICE AREAS:*** Employment Law; Sexual Harassment; Employment Discrimination; Class Actions; Wrongful Discharge; Office of Federal Contract Compliance Programs Audits; Americans with Disabilities Act; Mediation; Arbitration.

WILLIAM D. DeGRANDIS, born Drexel Hill, Pennsylvania, February 14, 1955; admitted to bar, 1980, District of Columbia. *Education:* Pennsylvania State University (B.A., with highest distinction, 1977); University of California at Los Angeles (J.D., 1980). Phi Beta Kappa. Member, 1978-1979 and Comments Editor, 1979-1980, UCLA Law Review. ***PRACTICE AREAS:*** Energy Regulatory and Transactions; Project Finance and Privatizations; Federal Energy Regulatory Commission Matters.

R. BRUCE DICKSON, born Arlington, Virginia, June 24, 1947; admitted to bar, 1973, New York; 1975, District of Columbia. *Education:* Columbia College (B.A., 1969); Columbia University (J.D., 1973). Member, Board of Directors, Asthma and Allergy Foundation of America. ***PRACTICE AREAS:*** False Advertising Litigation; Lanham Act; Intellectual Property Litigation; Food and Drug Law; Federal Trade Commission; Environmental Law; Consumer Product Safety Commission.

E. DONALD ELLIOTT, born Chicago, Illinois, 1948; admitted to bar, 1975, District of Columbia. *Education:* Yale University (B.A., summa cum laude, 1970; J.D., 1974). Phi Beta Kappa. General Counsel, U.S. Environmental Protection Agency, 1989-1991. Vice Chair, Committee on Second Generation Issues of Energy and Environmental Law, Section on Natural Resources, American Bar Association. Law Clerk to: U.S. District Judge Gerhard Gesell, Washington, D.C., 1974-1975; Hon. David Bazelon, U.S. Court of Appeals, District of Columbia Circuit, 1975-1976. Professor of Law, Yale Law School, 1981—. ***PRACTICE AREAS:*** International Environmental Law; Clean Air Act; Toxic Torts; Resource Conservation and Recovery Act; National Environmental Policy Act; Superfund; Environmental Legislative Practice; Domestic and International Green Procurement; Labeling and Packaging Issues.

RALPH B. EVERETT, born Orangeburg, South Carolina, June 23, 1951; admitted to bar, 1977, North Carolina; 1979, District of Columbia. *Education:* Morehouse College (B.A., with honors, 1973); Duke University (J.D., 1976). Phi Beta Kappa. Chief Counsel and Staff Director, U.S. Senate Committee on Commerce, Science and Transportation, 1987-1989. Minority Chief Counsel and Staff Director, U.S. Senate Committee on Commerce, Science and Transportation, 1983-1987. Legislative Assistant to U.S. Senator Ernest F. Hollings, 1977-1983. Member, Board of Visitors, Duke University Law School, 1993—. U.S. Ambassador to 1998 International Telecommunication Union (ITU) Plenipotentiary Conference; Head of U.S. Delegation to ITU Second Telecommunication Development Conference, 1998. ***PRACTICE AREAS:*** Federal Legislative Practice; Independent Regulatory Agencies; Administrative Policy Initiatives; Preparing Witnesses for Congressional Hearings; Federal Communications Commission; National Telecommunications and Information Administration; Domestic and International Telecommunications.

SCOTT M. FLICKER, born Chicago, Illinois, May 29, 1963; admitted to bar, 1988, California; 1990, District of Columbia. *Education:* University of California at Berkeley (B.A., 1985); University of California at Los Angeles (J.D., 1988). Order of the Coif. ***PRACTICE AREAS:*** International Trade; Commercial Regulation; Competition Law; Antidumping; Trade Agreements and Disputes; Export Licensing; Foreign Investment; Import-Export; Aviation Law; Insurance Coverage on behalf of Corporate Insureds.

JOHN J. GALLAGHER, born Scranton, Pennsylvania, October 1, 1947; admitted to bar, 1972, Pennsylvania; 1974, District of Columbia. *Education:* University of Scranton (B.S., 1969); Cornell University (J.D., with distinction, 1972). Order of the Coif. Member, Board of Editors, Cornell Law Review, 1971-1972. Member, Board of Trustees: The Key School of Annapolis, Maryland, 1989-2000; University of Scranton, 1991-1997.

JON A. GEIER, born Indianapolis, Indiana, March 25, 1955; admitted to bar, 1985, District of Columbia. *Education:* Carnegie Mellon University (B.A., with honors, 1977; M.A., 1977); George Washington University (J.D., with honors, 1985). Member, George Washington University Law Review, 1984-1985. ***PRACTICE AREAS:*** Labor and Employment Law; Title VII; Age Discrimination; Fair Labor Standards Act; Family Medical Leave Act; Americans with Disabilities Act; Office of Federal Contract Compliance Programs; Affirmative Action Plans; National Labor Relations Act; Railway Labor Act; Union Organizing Campaigns; Corporate Campaigns; Collective Bargaining; Strike

(This Listing Continued)

PAUL, HASTINGS, JANOFSKY & WALKER LLP, Washington—Continued

Settlement; Back to Work Agreements; Interrelationship between Federal Labor Law and Bankruptcy Law; Air Carrier Representation before National Mediation Board.

JUDITH RICHARDS HOPE, born Cincinnati, Ohio, November 30, 1940; admitted to bar, 1964, Ohio; 1965, District of Columbia; 1968, California. *Education:* Wellesley College (A.B., magna cum laude, 1961); Harvard University (J.D., 1964; LL.D., 2000). Voting Member, Judicial Conference of the District of Columbia Circuit, 1988-2000. Associate Director, The Domestic Council, The White House, 1975-1977. Vice-Chairman, President's Commission on Organized Crime, 1983-1986. Member, The Harvard Corporation, 1989-2000. Chairman, National Housing Partnership Foundation. Trustee, U.S. Supreme Court Historical Society. Member, National Board, American Arbitration Association. Member, American Law Institute. ***PRACTICE AREAS:*** Corporate Law; Alternative Dispute Resolution; Biotechnology; Privatization Transactions.

JOHN GRIFFITH JOHNSON, JR., born Winston-Salem, North Carolina, July 28, 1950; admitted to bar, 1976, District of Columbia. *Education:* Princeton University (A.B., summa cum laude, 1972; Phi Beta Kappa); Georgetown University (J.D., 1976). Editor, The Georgetown Law Journal, 1975-1976. Co-Chair, Committee on Professional Responsibility, 1992-1994 and 1999-2000, Chair, "Ex Parte" Rules Committee, 1994-1997, Co-Chair, Transactional Practice Committee, 1997-1999, Federal Communications Bar Association. ***PRACTICE AREAS:*** Federal Regulation of Broadcasting; Legal Ethics; Telecommunications Law; Commercial and Non-Commercial Television and Radiobroadcast Station Representation; Broadcast Industry Lender Representation; Federal Communications Commission related Regulations; Applications; Rule Making and Administrative Litigation.

G. HAMILTON LOEB, born New Orleans, Louisiana, June 22, 1951; admitted to bar, 1979, California; 1980, District of Columbia. *Education:* University of Virginia (B.A., with highest distinction, 1973); Harvard University (J.D., magna cum laude, 1978). Phi Beta Kappa. Articles Editor, Harvard Law Review, 1977-1978. Law Clerk, Hon. James R. Browning, Chief Judge, U.S. Court of Appeals, Ninth Circuit, 1978-1979. Chairman, Washington Area Lawyers for the Arts, 1987-1995, Secretary, 1998-2000; Section on International Law and Practice, American Bar Association, Co-chair, International Trade Committee, 1994-1998. ***PRACTICE AREAS:*** Commercial Litigation; Technology Litigation; Intellectual Property Litigation; Financial Litigation; Patent Litigation; Trade Secret; Imports of Infringing Items; International Commercial Arbitration; International Trade; Economic Sanctions; Export Controls on Encryption Technologies; RICO; Right to Financial Privacy Act; Electronic Commerce-Trade Policy; Antidumping; Countervailing Duty; Customs Litigation and Investigations.

NEAL D. MOLLEN, born Richmond, Virginia, July 1, 1956; admitted to bar, 1985, Virginia; 1988, District of Columbia. *Education:* Virginia Commonwealth University (B.S., 1981); University of Richmond (J.D., with honors, 1985). Notes and Comments Editor, University of Richmond Law Review, 1983-1985. ***PRACTICE AREAS:*** Appellate Practice; Labor Law; Employment Law; Litigation; Reductions in Force; Covenants not to Compete; Discrimination; Wage and Hour Law.

THOMAS R. MOUNTEER, born Albany, New York, September 1, 1961; admitted to bar, 1986, New York; 1988, District of Columbia; 1998, U.S. Supreme Court. *Education:* Union College (B.A., cum laude, 1982); George Washington University (J.D., 1986; LL.M., Environmental Law, with highest honors, 1994). Author: "*The Inherent Worthiness of the Struggle:* The Emergence of Mandatory Pollution Prevention Planning as an Environmental Regulatory Ethic," 19 Columbia Journal of Environmental Law 215 (Spring 1994); "Proposed European Community Directive for Damage to the Environment Caused by Waste," 23 Environmental Law 107, (1993); "How to Pay for Cleaning Up Co-Disposal Sites: Enlarging the Scope of the Debate," 23 Environment Reporter 1520 (BNA October 2, 1992) "The 'General Duty' Under the Clean Air Act To Prevent Accidental Releases of Extremely Hazardous Substances," 22 Environment Reporter 141 (BNA, May 17, 1991); "Codifying Basel Convention Obligations Into U.S. Law: The Waste Export Control Act," 22 Environmental Law Reporter News & Analysis 10085 (Feb. 1991). Co-Author: "Air Toxics," "The Clean Air Act Amendments: BNA's Comprehensive Analysis of the New Law," (June 1991). Adjunct Professor, Control of Solid and Hazardous Wastes and Environmental Aspects of Business Transactions, The George Washington University Law School, 1997—. *Member:* The District of Columbia Bar; New York State and American Bar Associations. ***PRACTICE AREAS:*** Environmental Law.

CARL W. NORTHROP, born New Jersey, September 30, 1950; admitted to bar, 1976, District of Columbia. *Education:* University of Michigan (B.B.A., high distinction, 1972); Georgetown University (J.D., 1976). Editor, Georgetown Law Journal, 1975-1976. ***PRACTICE AREAS:*** Wireless Telecommunications Industry; Radio Paging (common and private carrier); Cellular Telephones (MSA, RSA and unserved area licensees); Specialized Mobile Radio (standard and enhanced); Personal Communications Service (wideband PCS and narrowband PCS); Wireless Local Loop; Wireless Competitive Access; Federal Regulatory Issues; Licensing Auction Proceedings; Communications-related Litigation; Telecommunications Transactions (mergers and acquisitions, equipment contracts, finance; intercarrier, interconnection, agency and resale agreements).

CHARLES A. PATRIZIA, born Erie, Pennsylvania, August 10, 1950; admitted to bar, 1976, District of Columbia. *Education:* University of North Carolina (A.B., 1972); Yale University (J.D., 1975). Phi Beta Kappa. Member, Board of Editors, Yale Law Journal, 1974-1975. Legal Advisor, Special Mid East Peace Negotiator and to Ambassador at Large, U.S. Department of State, 1982-1985. Chair, Environmental Law Committee, Section on Public Utility, Telecommunications and Transportation Law, American Bar Association, 1994—. ***PRACTICE AREAS:*** Environmental and Energy Law; Federal and State Regulatory and Permitting Requirements; Electric Utilities; International Trade and Regulation; Commercial Litigation; Government Contracts.

BRUCE D. RYAN, born Buffalo, New York, December 26, 1952; admitted to bar, 1979, District of Columbia. *Education:* Indiana University (A.B., 1974); George Washington University (J.D., with highest honors, 1979). Order of the Coif. Topics Editor, George Washington Law Review, 1978-1979. ***PRACTICE AREAS:*** Antitrust; Communications Transactions, Regulation and Litigation.

KENNETH M. WILLNER, born Topeka, Kansas, February 2, 1962; admitted to bar, 1987, Virginia; 1988, District of Columbia. *Education:* University of Virginia (B.A., with distinction, 1984; J.D., 1987). Order of the Coif. Member, Editorial Board, University of Virginia Law Review, 1985-1987. ***PRACTICE AREAS:*** Employment Law and Litigation; Employment Discrimination; Labor Law; Wrongful Discharge; Discrimination; Sexual Harassment; Disability Law; Class Actions; EEOC; OFCCP; Executive Contract Negotiations; Wage and Hour Law; Noncompetition Covenants; Drug and Alcohol Testing; Unfair Labor Practice Charges; Protection of Employer Intellectual Property.

OF COUNSEL

DAVID D. BURNS, born Bridgeport, Connecticut, September 1, 1960; admitted to bar, 1988, Virginia; 1989, District of Columbia. *Education:* Fordham University (B.A., 1982); University of Virginia (J.D., 1988). Member, Editorial Board, Virginia Law Review, 1986-1988.

CLAUDIA TREADWELL CALLAWAY, born Phoenix, Arizona, August 15, 1966; admitted to bar, 1992, Pennsylvania; 1993, District of Columbia; 1995, Maryland. *Education:* Bryn Mawr College (A.B., 1988); Georgetown University (J.D., 1991). Editor in Chief, Georgetown Law Weekly, 1991. Recipient, American Jurisprudence Award for Excellence in Oral Advocacy. ***PRACTICE AREAS:*** Commercial Litigation; Complex Litigation; Class Action Defense; Consumer Finance; Employment Law; Appellate Practice.

MICHELLE WEISBERG COHEN, born Boston, Massachusetts, September 24, 1967; admitted to bar, 1992, New Jersey; 1993, New York; 1994, District of Columbia. *Education:* Brandeis University (B.A., magna cum laude, highest honors, 1989); Emory University (J.D., with distinction, 1992). Editor-in-Chief, Emory Law Journal, 1991-1992. Executive Committee, Law Firms Division, United Way, National Capital Area. ***PRACTICE AREAS:*** Telecommunications Law.

CHRISTOPHER A. COLE, born New York, New York, January 25, 1966; admitted to bar, 1994, Massachusetts (inactive) and District of Columbia. *Education:* Yale University (B.S., 1987); University of Miami (M.S., 1989); Boston University (J.D., magna cum laude, 1992). Articles Editor, Boston University Law Review, 1991-1992. ***PRACTICE AREAS:*** Litigation; Environmental Law; False Advertising.

EDWIN I. COLODNY, born Burlington, Vermont, June 7, 1926; admitted to bar, 1951, New York; 1958, District of Columbia. *Education:* University of Rochester (A.B., with distinction, 1948); Harvard University (LL.B., 1951). President and Chief Executive Officer, USAir, Inc., 1975-1991. Chairman of the Board, Comsat Corporation, 1997-2000. Interim President, University of Vermont, 2001—. ***PRACTICE AREAS:*** Business Law; Marketing; Advertising; Sales Promotion Law; Aviation Law; Global Satellite Services; Digital Networking Services; Corporate Legal Affairs Advice.

WENDELL M. FARIA, born Trinidad and Tobago, West Indies, June 12, 1955; admitted to bar, 1988, Pennsylvania; 1995, District of Columbia. *Education:* Baruch College (B.B.A., cum laude, 1983); University of California, Boalt Hall (J.D., 1987). Attorney, Division of Investment Management, U.S. Securities and Exchange Commission, 1987-1994. ***PRACTICE AREAS:*** Investment Management Regulation; Securities Law.

INTRA L. GERMANIS, born Cleveland, Ohio, April 20, 1967; admitted to bar, 1992, Illinois; 1994, District of Columbia. *Education:* Cornell University (B.S., 1989); University of Virginia (J.D., 1992). Order of the Coif. ***PRACTICE AREAS:*** Employment Law.

(This Listing Continued)

GEORGE R. A. JONES, born Beverly, Massachusetts, June 25, 1958; admitted to bar, 1985, Massachusetts; 1986, Maryland; 1995, District of Columbia. *Education:* Middlebury College (B.A., cum laude, 1981); Cornell University (J.D., 1985). ***PRACTICE AREAS:*** Real Estate Law.

THOMAS J. KNAPP, born Chicago, Illinois, August 27, 1952; admitted to bar, 1977, Illinois; 1978, Florida; 1979, District of Columbia; 1986, Texas. *Education:* University of Illinois (B.A., with honors, 1974); Loyola University of Chicago (J.D., 1977). ***PRACTICE AREAS:*** Labor and Employment; Litigation; Transportation; Executive Compensation.

P. SUSAN LIVELY, born Baton Rouge, Louisiana, December 26, 1958; admitted to bar, 1990, Louisiana; 1998, District of Columbia. *Education:* Louisiana State University Medical Center (B.S., cum laude, 1980); Tulane University (J.D., cum laude, 1990). Managing Editor, Tulane Law Review, 1989-1990. Law Clerk to Hon. Jacques L. Weiner, Jr., 5th Circuit Court of Appeals, 1990-1991. Managing Editor, Tulane Law Review. ***PRACTICE AREAS:*** Environmental Law; Food and Drug Law; Health Care.

ROBERT S. PLOTKIN, born Plainfield, New Jersey, May 6, 1946; admitted to bar, 1971, Ohio; 1973, District of Columbia. *Education:* University of Cincinnati (B.A., cum laude, 1968; J.D., 1971); New York University (LL.M., 1972). Article Editor, University of Cincinnati Law Review, 1970-1971. Order of the Coif. Chief, Special Litigation Section, Civil Rights Division, U.S. Department of Justice, 1980-1981. Former President, National Capital Area, Civil Liberties Union. ***PRACTICE AREAS:*** White Collar Defense; Securities Enforcement; Health Care Fraud; Complex Federal Civil and Criminal Litigation; Fraud; Ethics; Bribery; Securities Violations; RICO; Domestic and International Financial Institutions (real estate bankruptcy fraud; global money laundering); Health Care/Pharmaceutical Litigation (homicide charges, falsifying government reports); Pyramid Schemes; Parallel Investigations (administrative, civil, congressional, and criminal); Public Official (White-Collar Criminal Violations); Civil Rights Law.

JOSEPH MARK POERIO, born Endicott, New York, March 7, 1958; admitted to bar, 1985, New York; 1989, Massachusetts; 2000, District of Columbia. *Education:* University of Virginia (B.A., cum laude, 1980); Boston University Law School (1982); Cornell Law School (J.D., cum laude, 1984). ***PRACTICE AREAS:*** Executive Compensation; Employee Benefits; ERISA.

MARGARET H. SPURLIN, born Wilmington, Delaware, July 26, 1947; admitted to bar, 1979, District of Columbia. *Education:* Smith College (B.A., 1970); State University of New York (M.S., 1976); Syracuse University (J.D., summa cum laude, 1978). Order of the Coif. Articles Editor, Syracuse Law Review, 1977-1978. ***PRACTICE AREAS:*** Labor Law; Airline Labor Law; Railway Labor Law; Labor Issues Relating to Corporate Mergers/Restructurings/Bankruptcies; Formation of Non-union Subsidiaries and Double-breasted Operations; Collective Bargaining; Concessionary Bargaining; Interest Arbitration; Self-help; Strike Injunctions and Operation.

MARK A. STACHIW, admitted to bar, 1985, California; 1990, Texas; 2001, District of Columbia. *Education:* University of California at Davis (A.B., with honors, 1982; J.D., with honors, 1985). Phi Beta Kappa; Phi Kappa Phi; Order of the Coif. Member, University of California Law Review. ***PRACTICE AREAS:*** Telecommunications Law; Corporate; Interconnection Regulatory.

GREGORY R. WATCHMAN, born July 21, 1959; admitted to bar, 1986, District of Columbia and New York. *Education:* Williams College (B.A., cum laude, 1981); Cornell University (J.D., magna cum laude, 1985). Phi Beta Kappa; Order of the Coif. Member, Cornell Law Review, 1984-1985. Deputy Assistant Secretary of Labor, 1995-1998 and Acting Secretary of Labor, 1997, U.S. Occupational Safety and Health Administration. Associate Counsel, House Education and Labor Committee, 1989-1991. Counsel, 1991-1993 and Chief Labor Counsel, 1993-1995, Senate Labor Subcommittee. ***PRACTICE AREAS:*** Labor Law; Employment Law; OSHA; Title VII; ADEA; ADA; FMLA; NLRA; RLA; FLSA; Warn Act; ERISA; Congressional Testimony relating to Employment Legislation and Regulatory Issues.

JENNY C. WU, born New York, New York, November 18, 1967; admitted to bar, 1992, Virginia; 1993, District of Columbia. *Education:* Princeton University (A.B., cum laude, 1988); University of Virginia (J.D., 1992).

GERALD H. YAMADA, born Jerome Center, Arkansas, May 5, 1944; admitted to bar, 1974, District of Columbia; 1977, California. *Education:* University of California at Berkeley (B.A.); San Francisco State University (B.A.); George Washington University (J.D., 1974). Principal Deputy General Counsel, 1982-1995, Acting General Counsel, 1985, 1989, 1993, U.S. Environmental Protection Agency. Member: Environmental Policy Executive Committee, National Defense Industrial Association; Member, Board of Directors, American Judicature Society. Adjunct Professor of Law, George Washington University Law School. Pro Bono General Counsel, National Japanese American Memorial Foundation. ***PRACTICE AREAS:*** Environmental Law; Federal Procurement Law; Administrative Law; Regulatory Law; Public Safety; Government Contract Matters; Inspector General Investigations and Audits.

(This Listing Continued)

ASSOCIATES

QUISAIRA Y. ALMANZAR, born February 28, 1969; admitted to bar, 1996, New York; 1998, District of Columbia. *Education:* Cornell University (B.A., 1991); New York University (J.D., 1995).

KATHRINE L. CALDERAZZI, born November 5, 1970; admitted to bar, 1997, Maryland; 1998, District of Columbia. *Education:* James Madison University (B.A., magna cum laude, 1992); University of Virginia (J.D., 1997). ***PRACTICE AREAS:*** Telecommunications Law.

CHRISTOPHER T. CLOUTIER, born 1972; admitted to bar, 2000, New York (Not admitted in District of Columbia). *Education:* University of Michigan (B.A., with honors, 1995); George Washington University (J.D., 1999). ***PRACTICE AREAS:*** International Trade; E-Commerce; Commercial Litigation.

DIANNE C. COOMBS, born Kingston, Jamaica, West Indies, February 27, 1963; admitted to bar, 1995, Maryland; 1997, District of Columbia. *Education:* George Washington University (B.A., 1984; J.D., with honors, 1995). Member, George Washington Law Review, 1993-1995. ***PRACTICE AREAS:*** Employment Law.

CHRISTINE M. CROWE, born Jamaica, New York, July 15, 1967; admitted to bar, 1992, Connecticut; 1993, District of Columbia. *Education:* University of Rhode Island (B.A., with honors, 1989); George Washington University (J.D., with honors, 1992). Phi Beta Kappa. ***PRACTICE AREAS:*** Communications Law.

BEHNAM DAYANIM, born Norfolk, Virginia, December 4, 1967; admitted to bar, 1993, Maryland; 1995, District of Columbia. *Education:* Yeshiva College (B.A., summa cum laude, 1989); Harvard University (J.D., cum laude, 1993). ***PRACTICE AREAS:*** Technology and Electronic Commerce Law and Policy; International Trade; Intellectual Property; False Advertising.

DIANA L. EMBREY, born December 29, 1969; admitted to bar, 1996, Maryland; 1997, District of Columbia. *Education:* University of Maryland (B.A., summa cum laude, 1992); Harvard Law School (J.D., cum laude, 1995). Law Clerk to the Honorable Thomas Penfield Jackson, United States District Court for the District of Columbia, 1995-1996.

JUDITH A. FARRAND, born Detroit, Michigan, June 7, 1971; admitted to bar, 1997, Vermont; 1999, District of Columbia. *Education:* Southern Methodist University (B.A., magna cum laude, 1993); Vermont Law School (J.D., cum laude, 1996); M.S.E.L., magna cum laude, 1996). *Member:* The District of Columbia Bar; American Bar Association (Member, Natural Resources, Energy and Environmental Law Section). ***LANGUAGES:*** French. ***PRACTICE AREAS:*** Environmental Law.

RACHEL GAGNEBIN, born Boston, Massachusetts, January 28, 1971; admitted to bar, 1999, New York (Not admitted in District of Columbia). *Education:* Hamilton College (B.A., 1993); Benjamin N. Cardozo School of Law, Yeshiva University (J.D., 1998). ***PRACTICE AREAS:*** Corporate.

LAUREN T. HOLLANDER, born Bronx, New York, October 18, 1974; admitted to bar, 2001, New York (Not admitted in District of Columbia). *Education:* Tufts University (B.A., 1996); Emory University School of Law (J.D., 2000). Member, Moot Court Society. ***PRACTICE AREAS:*** Employment Law.

JENNIFER L. HONG, born St. Joseph, Michigan, May 1, 1969; admitted to bar, 1996, Virginia; 1998, District of Columbia. *Education:* George Washington University (B.A., 1991); Georgetown University (J.D., 1996). ***PRACTICE AREAS:*** Energy; Administrative Law.

PATRICIA E. HURT, born La Mesa, California, December 27, 1965; admitted to bar, 1999, Virginia (Not admitted in District of Columbia). *Education:* George Mason University (B.S., 1988); Wake Forest University (M.B.A., 1990); The Catholic University of America (J.D., 1999). Law Clerk, Hon. William J. Cowan, Hon. Carmen A. Cintron, Federal Energy Regulatory Commission. *Member:* Energy Bar Association. ***LANGUAGES:*** German. ***PRACTICE AREAS:*** Energy; Federal Energy Regulatory Commission Matters. ***Email:*** patriciahurt@paulhastings.com

A. JEFF IFRAH, born Buffalo, New York, March 24, 1968; admitted to bar, 1993, New York and New Jersey; 1998, District of Columbia. *Education:* Yeshiva University (B.A., 1989); Benjamin N. Cardozo School of Law (J.D., 1992). Special Assistant U.S. Attorney, New Jersey, U.S. Army, Trial Counsel, Communications-Electronics Command, Fort Monmouth, 1994-1997. ***PRACTICE AREAS:*** White Collar Criminal Litigation; Government Contracts; International Trade Litigation.

JOHN P. ISA, born Fairfax, Virginia, May 16, 1971; admitted to bar, 1999, Maryland; 2001, District of Columbia. *Education:* George Mason University (B.A., with honors; M.A. summa cum laude); American University (J.D., cum laude, 1999). Judicial Clerk, Honorable Glenn T. Harrell, Jr., Court of Appeals of Maryland, 1999-2000. ***PRACTICE AREAS:*** Employee Benefits; ERISA; Employment Law.

ERIC R. KELLER, born Columbus, Ohio, July 3, 1969; admitted to bar, 1996, Ohio (inactive) and U.S. Tax Court; 1999, District of Columbia. *Educa-*

(This Listing Continued)

PAUL, HASTINGS, JANOFSKY & WALKER LLP, Washington—Continued

tion: Ohio University (B.B.A., cum laude, 1992); Capital University (J.D., magna cum laude, 1995); New York University (LL.M. in Taxation, 1996). Editor-in-Chief, Capital University Law Review, 1994-1995. Law Clerk, Hon. Maurice B. Foley, U.S. Tax Court, 1996-1998. ***PRACTICE AREAS:*** Employee Benefits; Executive Compensation.

ERIN PATTEN LANE, born Oxford, Mississippi, July 30, 1975; admitted to bar, 2000, Mississippi; 2001, District of Columbia. *Education:* University of Mississippi (B.A., magna cum laude, 1996); Harvard University (J.D., 2000). ***PRACTICE AREAS:*** Litigation.

RIKKI McCOY, born New Brighton, Pennsylvania, December 29, 1975; admitted to bar, 2000, New York and New Jersey; 2001, U.S. Court of Appeals, Ninth Circuit (Not admitted in District of Columbia). *Education:* Rutgers University (B.S., 1997); Howard University School of Law (J.D., 2000). ***PRACTICE AREAS:*** Litigation. ***Email:*** rikkimccoy@paulhastings.com

JENNIFER LEVY RAPPAPORT, admitted to bar, 1999, Pennsylvania and New Jersey (Not admitted in District of Columbia). *Education:* Brown University (A.B., honors, 1996); New York University School of Law (J.D., 1999). ***PRACTICE AREAS:*** Employment Law.

MICHELLE I. ROZOF, born October 6, 1973; (admission pending). *Education:* State University of New York at Binghamton (B.A., 1995); Emory University (J.D., 1999).

LISA K. RUSHTON, admitted to bar, 1994, Florida; 1996, Illinois; 1997, District of Columbia. *Education:* Bucknell University (B.A., 1989); Tulane University Law School (J.D., cum laude, 1994). *Member:* Illinois State Bar Association; The Florida Bar; The District of Columbia Bar; Women in Energy and the Environment Association. ***PRACTICE AREAS:*** Litigation; Environmental.

WILLIAM P. SCHARFENBERG, born New Brunswick, New Jersey, March 4, 1967; admitted to bar, 1996, Virginia; 2000, District of Columbia. *Education:* Princeton University (A.B., with honors, 1989); George Mason Law School (J.D., 1995). Member, George Mason Independent Law Review. ***PRACTICE AREAS:*** Energy Law.

MELISSA CALES SCHWARTZ, born Norfolk, Virginia, February 17, 1970; admitted to bar, 1996, Georgia (Not admitted in District of Columbia). *Education:* The College of William and Mary (B.A., 1992); Emory University (J.D., 1996). Order of the Coif. Member, Emory Law Journal. ***PRACTICE AREAS:*** Corporate; Corporate Finance.

ANNA LINCOLN SPRADLIN, born Detroit, Michigan, May 4, 1971; admitted to bar, 1997, New York; 1999, District of Columbia. *Education:* Michigan State University (B.A., 1993); University of Michigan (J.D., cum laude, 1995). ***PRACTICE AREAS:*** Employment Law.

JOCELYN M. STURDIVANT, born Baltimore, Maryland, June 5, 1966; admitted to bar, 1994, Pennsylvania; 1995, District of Columbia and New York. *Education:* Brown University (B.A., 1987); Harvard University (J.D., 1993).

STEPHEN A. WEISBROD, born New Haven, Connecticut, December 22, 1965; admitted to bar, 1992, Illinois; 1993, District of Columbia; 2000, New York. *Education:* University of Michigan (B.A., with high honors and high distinction, 1987); Harvard University (J.D., cum laude, 1991). Faculty, Georgetown University Law Center National Institute of Trial Advocacy, 1999—. Member, National Association of Securities Dealers Board of Arbitrators, 1999—. ***PRACTICE AREAS:*** Litigation; Criminal Defense; Government Investigations; Bankruptcy.

PAUL, WEISS, RIFKIND, WHARTON & GARRISON

1615 L STREET, NW
SUITE 1300
WASHINGTON, D.C. 20036-5694
Telephone: 202-223-7300
TDD 202-223-7490
Facsimile: 202-223-7420
Email: mailbox@paulweiss.com
URL: http://www.paulweiss.com

New York, N.Y. Office: 1285 Avenue of the Americas, 10019-6064. Telephones: 212-373-3000, TDD 212-373-2000. Facsimile: 212-757-3990.
Paris, France Office: 62, rue du Faubourg Saint-Honor é, 75008. Telephone: (33-1) 53.43.14.14. Facsimile: (33-1) 53.43.00.23.
Tokyo, Japan Office: Fukoku Seimei Building, 2-2 Uchisaiwaicho 2-chome, Chiyoda-ku, Tokyo 100-0011, Japan. Telephone: (81-3) 3597-8101. Facsimile: (81-3)3597-8120.

(This Listing Continued)

Beijing, China Office: 2918 China World Tower II, No.1 Jianguomenwai Dajie, 100004. Telephone: (86-10) 6505-6822. Facsimile: (86-10) 6505-6830.
Hong Kong, China Office: 12th Floor, Hong Kong Club Building, 3A Chater Road, Central Hong Kong. Telephone: (011-852) 2536-9933. Facsimile: 011 (852) 2536-9622.

International Trade Policy and Regulation, Telecommunications, Multimedia, Computer Law, Internal Corporate Investigations, International and Domestic Project Finance, Corporate and Aircraft Finance, Leasing and Federal Administrative, Legislative and Litigation Matters. Foreign Investment, Government Procurement, Antitrust, Energy, Appellate, Education and Civil Rights Law, Intellectual Property.

RESIDENT PARTNERS

TERENCE J. FORTUNE, born Watertown, New York, December 27, 1946; admitted to bar, 1975, District of Columbia; 1976, U.S. Court of Appeals for the District of Columbia Circuit; 1977, U.S. Court of Appeals, Sixth Circuit; 1989, New York. *Education:* Georgetown University (B.A, 1969; J.D., 1974). Assistant Legal Adviser, U.S. Department of State, 1977-1983. *Member:* The District of Columbia Bar; New York State Bar Association; American Society of International Law. ***PRACTICE AREAS:*** International Trade; International Telecommunications; Government Procurement; Federal Administrative Law. ***Email:*** tfortune@paulweiss.com

ROBERT E. MONTGOMERY, JR., born Pittsburgh, Pennsylvania, March 15, 1939; admitted to bar, 1970, California; 1975, U.S. Supreme Court; 1976, District of Columbia; 1984, New York. *Education:* United States Military Academy (B.S., 1960); Rhodes Scholar, Magdalen College of Oxford University, Oxford, England (M.A., 1963); Boalt Hall School of Law, University of California (J.D., 1969). Editor-in-Chief, California Law Review, 1968-1969. Assistant to General Counsel, Department of Army, 1969-1971. General Counsel, Office of Consumer Affairs, Executive Office of the President, 1971-1972. Assistant General Counsel, Federal Trade Commission, 1973. General Counsel, Federal Energy Administration, 1974-1975. [With U.S. Army, Inf., Capt., 1960-1966 and JAGC, Major, 1967-1971]. ***PRACTICE AREAS:*** International Trade and Arbitration; Intellectual Property; Antitrust; Energy. ***Email:*** remontgomery@paulweiss.com

ROBERT P. PARKER, born Philadelphia, Pennsylvania, August 2, 1960; admitted to bar, 1984, Pennsylvania; 1985, District of Columbia; 1986, U.S. Supreme Court. *Education:* Johns Hopkins University (B.A., with honors, 1981); Johns Hopkins School of Advanced International Studies (1980-1981); University of Pennsylvania (J.D., cum laude, 1984). Law Clerk, Hon. Oscar H. Davis, Circuit Judge, U.S. Court of Appeals for the Federal Circuit (1984-1985). Counsel to the Chairman, U.S. International Trade Commission, 1988-1991. Adjunct Professor, George Mason University Law School (1996-1997), Officer (1995-1998) and President (1999), International Trade Commission Trial Lawyers Association. ***PRACTICE AREAS:*** Litigation; International Trade; Federal Administrative Law. ***Email:*** rparker@paulweiss.com

WARREN B. RUDMAN, born Boston, Massachusetts, May 18, 1930; admitted to bar, 1960, New Hampshire; 1994, District of Columbia. *Education:* Syracuse University (B.S., 1952); Boston College of Law (J.D., 1960). U.S. Senator from New Hampshire, 1981-1992. Member, Board of Directors: Chubb Corporation, 1993—; Raytheon Corporation, 1993—; Board of Directors of several funds of the Dreyfus Corporation, 1993—; Collins Aikman, 1995—; Boston Specific, 1999—; Allied Waste Industries, Inc., 1997; American Stock Exchange, 1998. Co-founder, Concord Coalition, a non-profit organization set up as a grass-roots movement to awaken the American people to the gravity of our nation's fiscal crisis, 1992—. Member: Chairman, (PFIAB) President's Foreign Intelligence Advisory Board; The Brookings Institution, Council on Foreign Relations and Valley Forge Military Academy. Senior Advisory Committee, Institute on Politics at the John F. Kennedy School of Government at Harvard. *Member:* New Hampshire Bar Association; District of Columbia Bar Association. [Captain, U.S. Army, 1952-1954]. (Also in New York, New York Office). ***Email:*** wrudman@paulweiss.com

DALE M. SARRO, born Lawrence, New York, December 7, 1956; admitted to bar, 1985, New York; 1988, U.S. District Court, Southern and Eastern Districts of New York; 1999, District of Columbia. *Education:* Amherst College (A.B., magna cum laude, 1979); Harvard Law School (J.D., cum laude, 1984). Director, Office of Investment, U.S. Agency for International Development, 1993-1994. Counsel, U.S. Agency for International Development, 1989-1993. ***PRACTICE AREAS:*** International and Domestic Project Finance; Telecommunications; Corporate Finance. ***Email:*** dsarro@paulweiss.com

PHILLIP L. SPECTOR, born Los Angeles, California, July 15, 1950; admitted to bar, 1976, California; 1978, District of Columbia; 1984, U.S. Supreme Court. *Education:* University of Birmingham, England and University of California at Santa Barbara (B.A., with highest honors, 1972); Harvard University (J.D., magna cum laude, 1976); Kennedy School of Government, Harvard University (M.P.P., 1976). Phi Beta Kappa. Staff Member, 1972-1973, and Articles Editor, 1973-1974, Harvard Civil Rights, Civil Liberties Law Review. Editor, 1974-1975, and Supreme Court Note Editor, 1975-1976, Harvard Law

(This Listing Continued)

Review. Author: "Current Telecom Developments" (Weekly Newsletter), 1994—; "The Internet and the Federal Government: The Continued Battle Over Regulation," E-Commerce Law & Strategy, Vol. 17, No. 7, November 2000; "The US Export Control Regime: Challenges in Sourcing Satellites," Satellite Finance, March 8, 2000 (Co-author); "The SkyBridge System," McGraw Hill Yearbook of Science & Technology 2000 (Co-author); "FCC Regulation of the Internet: Fact or Fiction?," 6 Telecommunications & Space Journal 281, 1999 (Co-author); "Internet Regulation," New York Law Journal, June 1, 1999 (Co-author); "Vendor Financing in Satellite Projects," Satellite Finance, May 13, 1999 (Co-author); "FCC Acts to Promote Spectrum Sharing," 13 Satellite Finance 10 (1999) (Co-Author); "Spectrum Sharing and Non-Geostationary Satellite Systems," Via Satellite, February 1998; "The World Trade Organization Agreement on Telecommunications," 32 The International Lawyer 217, 1998; "The Internet and Intellectual Property: Toward a New Model for the Economics of Content," 4 Telecommunications and Space Journal 155, 1997; "Survey of National Broadcasting, Cable and DTH Satellite Laws," 5 Cardozo Journal of International and Comparative Law 715, 1997 (Co-Author); "Developing & Financing Telecommunication Satellite Projects in Asia," 1997 (Co-Author); "International Communications," 31 The International Lawyer 2, 1997 (Co-Author); "Reed Hundt's Legacy at the FCC," Legal Times, June 9, 1997; "Communications and Technology Alliances: Business and Legal Issues," 1996 (Co-Author); "The Telecommunications Act of 1996: An Analysis," 2 Information & Technology Law 26, 1996; "The International Telephony Market," Phone +, Jan. 1996; "The Supreme Court: Deciding What to Decide," Perspectives on Contemporary American Government, 1996; "The Internet Goes International," Proceedings of the Pacific Telecommunications Council, 1996; "Communications Satellite Regulation," Chapter 6 of Communications Law and Practice, 1995; "Strategic, Business, and Legal Issues in Multimedia," The Interactive Media Sourcebook, 1995; "U.S. Telecommunications Law and Multimedia Development," 1 Multimedia Strategist No. 3, 1995; "Joint Venturing in Multimedia," Multimedia and Interactive Technology Licensing, 1994; "Satellite and Mobile Solutions for Telecommunications Development," Proceedings of the Pacific Telecommunications Council, 1994; "Frequency Allocation and New Technologies," New Technology in Mobile Communications, 1993; "Joint Venturing in Multimedia," Multimedia & Technology Licensing, 1993; "Wireless Communications and Personal Freedom," Telecommunications Policy, August 1993; "Recent Changes in the FCC's Rules," 8 Via Satellite No. 9, 1993 (Co-Author); "Legal and Regulatory Aspects of Media Integration," Proceedings of the Pacific Telecommunications Council, 1992; "U.S. Earth Station Regulation," 7 Via Satellite No. 8, 1992; "Computers and RF Emissions: The FCC's New Rules," 6 The Computer Lawyer No. 7, 1989 (Co-Author); "Emerging Opportunities in International Telecommunications," 4 Telematics No. 8, 1987; "Launch Failures and the Future of the Satellite Industry," 3 Telematics No. 8, 1986; "Satellite Transponder Sales: The Emerging Issues," 2 Telematics No. 7, 1985; "Transborder Satellite Services," 1 Telematics No. 3, 1984; "Ma Bell's Children Grow Up," 1 Telematics No. 1, 1984; "Cable Television, Government Regulation and the First Amendment," 3 Comm/Ent 577, 1981 (Co-Author); "Least Cost Achievement of Environmental Quality Objectives," Decision Making in the EPA, Vol. IIB, National Academy of Sciences, 1977 (Co-Author); "Regulation of Pesticides by the Environmental Protection Agency," 5 Ecology Law Quarterly 233, 1976; "Financing the Courts Through Fees," 58 Judicature 330, 1975. Award Recipient, University of California Medal for Distinguished Achievement in the Field of Public Service, 1981; Supreme Court Recognition Award, National Association of Attorneys General, 1993. Listed in: Who's Who in the World; Who's Who in America; Who's Who in American Law; Chambers Guide to the World's Leading Lawyers; Euromoney Guide to the World's Leading Telecommunications Lawyers; An International Who's Who of Telecoms Lawyers. Law Clerk to: Judge James L. Oakes, United States Court of Appeals for the Second Circuit, 1976-1977; Justice Thurgood Marshall, United States Supreme Court, 1977-1978. Associate Assistant to the President, The White House, 1978-1980. *Member:* The District of Columbia Bar; State Bar of California; American Bar Association (Member, Section of International Law and Practice; Chairman, 1995-1997, Committee on International Communications); Federal Communications Bar Association (Member, International Practice Committee). ***PRACTICE AREAS:*** Communications and Media; Internet Law; Computers and Software. ***Email:*** pspector@paulweiss.com

STUART G. STEINGOLD, born New York, N.Y., April 6, 1945; admitted to bar, 1971, New York; 1984, District of Columbia. *Education:* Princeton University (B.A., with honors, 1966); Institut d'Etudes Politiques de Paris (C.d'E.P., 1967); Harvard Law School (J.D., with honors, 1970). Phi Beta Kappa. *Member:* The District of Columbia Bar; American Bar Association (Member, Section of International Law and Practice and Business Law). ***LANGUAGES:*** French. ***PRACTICE AREAS:*** International and Domestic Project Finance; International and Domestic Aircraft Finance; Corporate Finance; Leasing. ***Email:*** ssteingold@paulweiss.com

COUNSEL

RICHARD S. ELLIOTT, born New York, N.Y., November 8, 1955; admitted to bar, 1981, District of Columbia; 1988, U.S. Court of International Trade and U.S. Court of Appeals for the Federal Circuit; 1990, New York. *Education:*

(This Listing Continued)

Trinity College (B.A., 1977); Princeton University (M.P.A., 1981); Columbia University (J.D., 1981). Phi Beta Kappa; Pi Gamma Mu. Harlan Fiske Stone Scholar. Attorney-Adviser, U.S. Department of State, 1981-1984. *Member:* The District of Columbia Bar (Member, Sections on International Law); American Bar Association (Member, Sections on International Law Practice); Washington Foreign Law Society; Washington International Trade Association; Consumers for World Trade. ***PRACTICE AREAS:*** International Trade; International Investment; International Finance; Intellectual Property. ***Email:*** relliott@paulweiss.com

CARL W. HAMPE, born London, England, August 4, 1960; admitted to bar, 1992, California; 1994, District of Columbia, U.S. District Court, District Court of Columbia, U.S. Court of Federal Claims and U.S. Court of Appeals, District of Columbia Circuit. *Education:* Stanford University (B.A., with honors and distinction, 1982); Georgetown University (J.D., magna cum laude, 1991). Deputy Assistant Attorney General, Office of Legislative Affairs, U.S. Department of Justice, 1992-1993. Counsel and Professional Staff Member, United States Senate Committee on the Judiciary, Subcommittee on Immigration, 1983-1992. ***PRACTICE AREAS:*** Legislative; Immigration. ***Email:*** champe@paulweiss.com

JEFFREY H. OLSON, born Ottumwa, Iowa, June 11, 1950; admitted to bar, 1975, Ohio; 1978, U.S. Supreme Court; 1979, District of Columbia. *Education:* Wittenberg University (B.A., 1972); Cleveland State University (J.D., cum laude, 1975). Chairman, Moot Court, 1974-1975. National Order of Barristers. Recipient, West Publishing Company Moot Court Award, 1975. Co-Author: "Computers and RF Emissions: The FCC's New Rules," 6 The Computer Lawyer No. 7, 1989. Co-Author: "Recent Changes in the FCC's Earth Station Rules," Via Satellite (Sept. 1993). Lecturer in Law, Cleveland State University College of Law, 1975-1976; Appellate Practice, Cuyahoga County Bar Association, 1977-1978. Adjunct Professor, Cleveland State University College of Law, 1976-1978. Clinical Professor, Georgetown University Law Center, 1981-1983. *Member:* The District of Columbia Bar; Federal Communications Bar Association (Member, 1980-1996 and Chairman, 1984-1985, 1991-1992, Committee on Judicial Practice; Member, Subcommittees on: Broadcast Matters, 1981-1984; Non-Broadcast Matters, 1982-1984, Committee on Practice and Procedure; Member: Committee on Legislation, 1985-1987, 1991-1995; Committee on International Practice, 1986—). ***REPORTED CASES:*** *FCC* v. *WNCN Listeners Guild,* 450 U.S. 582 (1981); *FCC* v. *Midwest Video Corp.,* 440 U.S. 689 (1979); *Columbia Communications Corp.* v. *FCC,* 832 F.2d 189 (D.C-.Cir. 1987); *NY State Comm. on Cable Television* v. *FCC,* 749 F.2d 804 (D.C. Cir. 1984); *Black Citizens for a Fair Media* v. *FCC,* 719 F.2d 407 (D.C.Cir. 1983); *Office of Communication of United Church of Christ* v. *FCC,* 707 F.2d 1413 (D.C.Cir. 1983); *New South Media Corp.* v. *FCC,* 685 F.2d 708 (D.C.Cir. 1982); *Central Florida Enterprises, Inc.* v. *FCC,* 683 F.2d 503 (D.C.Cir. 1982); *NAACP* v. *FCC,* 682 F.2d 993 (D.C.Cir. 1982); *U.S.* v. *Western Electric Co.,* 569 F. Supp. 1057 (D.D.C. 1983); *U.S.* v. *American Tel. & Tel. Co.,* 552 F. Supp. 131 (D.D.C. 1982). ***PRACTICE AREAS:*** Communications. ***Email:*** jolson@paulweiss.com

LAURA B. SHERMAN, born New York, New York, 1951; admitted to bar, 1986, New York; 1987, District of Columbia. *Education:* Cornell University (B.A., 1973); Georgetown University (J.D., 1985). Author: "WTO: Agreement on Basic Telecommunications," International Legal Materials, Vol. 26; "Wildly Enthusiastic About the First Multilateral Agreement on Trade in Telecommunications Services," Federal Communications Law Journal, Dec. 1998. Paul, Weiss, Rifkind, Wharton & Garrison, 1985-1990. Office of Legal Advisor, Department of State, 1990-1992; Office of the U.S. Trade Representative, 1992-1997; Federal Communications Commission, 1997-1998. ***PRACTICE AREAS:*** Communications Law; International Trade Law; Corporate Law. ***Email:*** lsherman@paulweiss.com

RESIDENT ASSOCIATES

Patrick S. Campbell; Matthew Chavez; Diane C. Gaylor; Gaela K. Gehring-Flores; Ji Lu; Paul Martin (Not admitted in DC); ***Douglas C. Melcher; Kira A. Merski; Jesse A. Nicol; Kathleen McAuliffe Smith; Anthony A. Stenger*** (admission pending); ***Matthew H. Wheelock.***

(For Biographical data of all Personnel, see Professional Biographies at New York, N.Y.).

PAULSON & NACE

Established in 1978

1814 N STREET, N.W.
WASHINGTON, D.C. 20036-2404
Telephone: 202-463-1999
Fax: 202-223-6824
Email: p&n@lawtort.com
URL: http://www.lawyers.com/lawtort

Martinsburg, West Virginia Office: 1444 Edwin Miller Boulevard, P.O. Box 1938, 25402. Telephone: 888-529-2628.

(This Listing Continued)

PAULSON & NACE, Washington—Continued

Negligence, Medical Malpractice, Legal Malpractice, Product Liability and Insurance Law. Trials, Administrative Law. Appellate Advocacy.

FIRM PROFILE: Paulson & Nace and its predecessors (Paulson and Humphreys and Davis and Nace) have been dedicated to representing injured people for more than thirty years. It has been dynamic in its representation of medical malpractice victims, those injured by defective products, especially pharmaceutical products, and those who survive the wrongful death of a loved one. The firm is also active in numerous organizations dedicated to the rights of consumers and the protection of trial by jury. The firm has gained not only a local, but also a national reputation for successfully handling the most difficult malpractice cases and product liability cases from trial to appellate courts.

MEMBERS OF FIRM

RICHARD S. PAULSON (1928-1986).

BARRY J. NACE, born York, Pennsylvania, November 28, 1944; admitted to bar, 1970, Maryland; 1971, Pennsylvania; 1972, District of Columbia; 1974, U.S. Supreme Court; U.S. District Courts, District of Maryland, District of Columbia and Eastern District of Pennsylvania; U.S. Court of Appeals, District of Columbia, Third and Fourth Circuits; registered to practice before U.S. Patent and Trademark Office; 1997, West Virginia. *Education:* Dickinson College (B.S., in Chemistry, 1965); University of Pittsburgh; Dickinson School of Law (J.D., 1969; LL.D., 1994). Recipient, Special Recognition Award, District of Columbia Trial Lawyers Association, 1988. Metropolitan Washington, D.C., Plaintiff's Attorney of the Year, 1976. Attorney of the Year, District of Columbia Trial Lawyers Association, 1976. Vice President, Alumni Association, Dickinson School of Law, 1978-1984. *Member:* The District of Columbia Bar (Co-Chairman, Medical and Legal Malpractice Committee, Section on Negligence Law, 1975-1976; Chairman, Wrongful Death Committee, Section on Negligence Law, 1976-1978; Steering Committee Member, Negligence Division, 1976-1982); Montgomery County and Maryland State Bar Associations; The Association of Trial Lawyers of America (Member, Board of Governors, 1978-1987; State Delegate, 1987-1989; Vice Chair, 1988; Treasurer, 1989-1991; Vice President, 1991; President-Elect, 1992; President, 1993; Chairman, Public Relations Committee, 1980-1982; Home Office and Budget Committee, 1985-1987; 1989-1995); Trial Lawyers Association of Metropolitan Washington, D.C. Member, Board of Governors, 1974; Secretary, 1975; Vice President, 1976; President, 1977, 1986; Maryland Trial Lawyers Association; West Virginia Trial Lawyers Association; Association of Personal Injury Lawyers (United Kingdom); International Academy of Trial Lawyers; American Inns of Court (Master); Counsellors; Trial Lawyers for Public Justice (Founder; Member, Board of Governors, 1988); International Academy of Trial Lawyers; Roscoe Pound Foundation Fellow (Trustee, 1993-1995); Tom Lambert Society; American Board of Trial Advocates; American Board of Professional Liability Attorneys; American Law Institute; American Trial Lawyers Association PAC (Board, 1992—; Chair, 1995-1997). (Also Of Counsel, Burke•Schultz & Harman, Martinsburg, West Virginia). ***REPORTED CASES:*** Nimetz vs. Capadonna, 596 A.2d 603 (D.C. App. 1991); Oxendine vs. Merrell Dow, 506 A.2d 1100 (D.C. App. 1986); 563 A.2d 330 (D.C. App. 1989); 593 A.2d 1023 (D.C. App. 1991); 649 A.2d 825 (D.C. App. 1994); Adkins vs. Morton, 494 A.2d 652 (D.C. App. 1985); Quin vs. George Washington University, 407 A.2d 580 (D.C. App. 1979); Daubert vs. Merrell Dow, 509 US 579, 113 S.Ct., 2786 (1993); Ambrosini vs. Labarraque, 966 F2d 1464 (D.C. Cir. 1992); Sindorff vs. Jacron, 27 Md. App. 53, 341 A.2d 856 (1975); 276 Md. 580, 350 A.2d 688 (1976); Hudson vs. Crisler, 239 Va. 101, 387 S.E.2d 750 (1990); LaMade vs. Wilson, 512 F.2d 1348, 168 U.S. App. D.C. 108 (D.C. Cir. 1975); Havner vs. Merrell Dow, 907 S.W.2d 548 (1994). ***PRACTICE AREAS:*** Medical Malpractice; Products Liability; Wrongful Death; Automobile. ***Email:*** bjn@lawtort.com

ASSOCIATE

BARRY W. WALKER, born Birmingham, Alabama, January 24, 1969; admitted to bar, 1999, Alabama; 2000, Maryland (Not admitted in District of Columbia). *Education:* Birmingham-Southern College (B.A., History, 1992); Cumberland School of Law, Samford University (J.D., 1997). Phi Alpha Delta. Vice President, Student Bar Association, 1997. Member, Birmingham Inns of Court. Federal Judicial Clerkship, Honorable, U. W. Clemon-Chief Judge, Northern District of Alabama, 1997-1998. *Member:* American Bar Association. (Also at Washington, DC and Baltimore, MD Offices).

PAYNE & ASSOCIATES

1250 24TH STREET, N.W., SUITE 300
WASHINGTON, D.C. 20037
Telephone: 202-835-1610
Fax: 202-835-1697
Email: Paynelegal@aol.com

General Business Law practice including Corporate Transactions, Contracts, Franchising, Licensing, Trademarks, Business Torts, Civil Litigation, Finance, State and Federal Securities Law, Estate Planning and Administration, Labor, Employment.

FIRM PROFILE: The firm serves individuals and small and medium-size businesses throughout the metropolitan Washington, D.C. area.

PATRICIA L. PAYNE, born Detroit, Michigan, January 3, 1954; admitted to bar, 1980, District of Columbia; 1993, Virginia. *Education:* University of Michigan (A.B., 1976); Georgetown University (J.D., 1979). Member, Law and Policy in International Business, Georgetown Law Review, 1978-1979. Attorney: Securities and Exchange Commission, Division of Market Regulation, 1980-1981; Division of Corporation Finance, 1982-1983. *Member:* The District of Columbia Bar; Bar Association of the District of Columbia; Virginia and American (Member, Section of Corporation, Banking and Business Law) Bar Associations; Metropolitan Washington Employment Lawyers Association; The Association of Trial Lawyers of America. ***PRACTICE AREAS:*** Finance; Securities Law; Corporate Law; Business Law; Labor and Employment; Civil Litigation.

PAUL D. PEARLSTEIN & ASSOCIATES

Established in 1962
1730 RHODE ISLAND AVENUE, N.W., SUITE 505
WASHINGTON, D.C. 20036
Telephone: 202-223-5848
Fax: 202-223-8737
Email: merraul@aol.com
URL: http://www.pearlstein-law.com

Real Estate, Bankruptcy, Estate Planning, Probate, Litigation and Appeals.

PAUL D. PEARLSTEIN, born Berlin, New Hampshire, January 3, 1938; admitted to bar, 1962, Virginia; 1963, District of Columbia; 1970, U.S. Supreme Court; 1990, Maryland. *Education:* University of Pennsylvania (A.B., 1959); University of Virginia (LL.B., 1962). Author: "The Tao of Arbitration," Commercial Law Bulletin, July/August 1991; "Fraudulent Conveyances and Preferences," Chapter 21, Real Property Practice and Litigation, Shepards/McGraw-Hill, 1990; "The Arcane Impact of the Bankruptcy Law Upon Real Estate Transactions," Probate and Property, ABA, 1987. Editor, "Real Estate Practice in D.C., MD. and Va.," 2 Vol., Bar Association of District of Columbia, 1995. Member, Advisory Rules Committee, U.S. Bankruptcy Court for the District of Columbia, 1984—. Member, Board of Directors, Council for Court Excellence, 1988—. Chair, D.C. Probate Reform Study, 1990-1993. *Member:* The District of Columbia Bar (CLE Lecturer, Real Estate and Bankruptcy, 1982—); Bar Association of the District of Columbia (Treasurer, 1996-1998, Secretary, 1986-1987, Board of Directors, 1991-1993 and 2000-2002, and President, 1990-1991, Research Foundation); Virginia State Bar; Maryland State, Federal and American Bar Associations; Trial Lawyers Association of Washington, D.C. (Board of Governors, 1985-1991); The George Washington American Inn of Court (President, 1992-1993). Fellow, American Bar Foundation. [Capt., USAR, Signal Corps; active duty, 1962-1964]. (Certified in Business Bankruptcy Law by the American Board of Certification). ***PRACTICE AREAS:*** Real Estate; Bankruptcy; Trials; Estate Planning.

OF COUNSEL

ALAN H. YAMAMOTO, born Dinuba, California, October 13, 1945; admitted to bar, 1973, Ohio; 1978, District of Columbia; 1986, Virginia. *Education:* University of California (B.S., 1967); Case Western Reserve University (J.D., 1973). *Member:* The District of Columbia Bar; Fairfax, Virginia State and American Bar Associations. (Also practicing individually in Alexandria, Virginia). ***PRACTICE AREAS:*** Criminal Defense; Trials; Appeals; Business Law; Corporate Law. ***Email:*** ahyama@erols.com

LEGAL SUPPORT PERSONNEL

ANN M. BISTODEAU, born Guam, M.I., December 4, 1956. *Education:* Virginia Polytechnic Institute and State University (B.A., 1978); George Washington University (Paralegal Certificate, Legal Assistance Program, 1982). Notary Public for the District of Columbia. *Member:* American Society of Notaries. Excellent singer, songwriter and guitar accompanist. ***Email:*** merraul@aol.com

(This Listing Continued)

REFERENCES: American Arbitration Assn.; Anacostia Garden Club, Inc.; Branch Banking and Trust Co.; Capital Rowing Club; Eastern Caribbean Investment Promotion Service; Grady Management, Inc.; Jacks Boats; National Assn. of Security Dealers; The Printers Devil.

PEDERSON & FREEDMAN, L.L.P.

A Registered Limited Liability Partnership of Professional Corporations

2001 L STREET, N.W., SUITE 601

WASHINGTON, D.C. 20036-4910

Telephone: 202-785-1960

Telecopier: 202-785-3815

URL: http://www.ilw.com/pederson

URL: http://www.lawyers.com/dcimmigrationlaw

Immigration and Nationality Law. Visas for Business and High Tech Professionals, Foreign Health Care Workers, and for J-1 Physicians, Consular Visa Processing at American Embassies and Counsular Posts. Permanent Residency.

JAN M. PEDERSON, (P.C.), born Minnedosa, Manitoba, Canada, December 3, 1949; admitted to bar, 1975, District of Columbia. *Education:* University of Washington (B.A., in Economics, cum laude, 1971); Howard University (J.D., cum laude, 1974). Recipient: The Edith Lowenstein Award by the American Immigration Lawyers Association in 1997 for excellence in the advancement of the practice of immigration law. Editor, The Visa Processing Guide (1st-5th Editions), The American Immigration Lawyers Association, Washington, DC. Author: "Consular Processing of Nonimmigrant Visas: A Roundtable Discussion," 90-9 Immigration Briefings, Federal Publications, Inc. (September 1990); "Representation of Nonimmigrant Visa Applicants at American Embassies and Consulates," 2 American Immigration Lawyers Association (AILA), Washington, DC, Immigration and Nationality Law 313 (1990); "Processing Visas for Iranian Nationals at U.S. Embassies and Consular Posts," 63 Interpreter Releases, Federal Publications, Inc. (October 10, 1986). Contributing Author, AILA Monthly Mailing, 1993—. Speaker, AILA National Conferences, 1980—. Member: IMMLAW-The National Consortium of Immigration Law Firms. Co-Chair, Alien Physician Task Force, 1993—; American Immigration Lawyers Association (Chairperson, District of Columbia Chapter, 1978-1980; Board of Governors, 1980-1984; Visa Office Liaison Committee, 1987-1988; Co-Chairperson, Visa Practice Advisory Committee, 1989-1990; USIA Liaison Committee, 1999-2000). *Member:* District of Columbia Bar; American Immigration Lawyers Association; Women's Bar Association. ***PRACTICE AREAS:*** Immigration and Naturalization. ***Email:*** jpederson@usvisainfo.com

ROBERTA FREEDMAN, (P.C.), born Chanute A.F.B., Illinois, June 22, 1958; admitted to bar, 1983, Maryland; 1985, District of Columbia. *Education:* Syracuse University (A.B., Political Science, Spanish Language and Literature, 1980); University of Baltimore (J.D., 1983). Recipient: Outstanding Volunteer Services to the Latin Community Award, Ayuda, Inc., 1981; Community Service Award, UJA Federation of Greater Washington for Project Citizenship, Attorneys Community Resettlement Program, 1998. Contributing Author: "The Visa Processing Guide," American Immigration Lawyers Association (AILA), Washington, DC. (1st - 5th editions); "Immigration & Nationality Law Handbook," AILA, Washington, DC., 1995-1996; 2000-2001. Volunteer: Project Citizenship, UJA Federation of Greater Washington; National Institute of Justice Peer Review Panel; Ayuda. *Member:* The District of Columbia Bar; Maryland State and American (Member, Coordinating Committee on Immigration Law, 1999—; Immigration Law Committee, General Practice Section, Chair, 2000—; Immigration Law Committee General Practice Section, Vice-Chair, 1998-1999) Bar Associations; American Immigration Lawyers Association Member, Washington, DC. Chapter, President, 1991-1993; Secretary, 1988-1991; Court Liaison, 1997-1998; District Council Liaison, 1998-1999; Baltimore District Office Liaison, 2000-2001; AILA National Appointments: Board of Governors, Elected Director, 1995-1998; Physicians Task Force, Co-Chair, 1991-1992; INS Headquarters Liaison, Co-Chair, 1993-1994; Improved Adjudications Task Force, Chair, 1994-1995; Social Security Liaison Committee, Chair, 1995-1996, 2000-2001; Information and Technology Committee, Chair, 1996-1997; Department of State Visa Office Liaison Committee, Chair, 1998-1999, Member, 1999-2000; Technology and InfoNet Committee, 1999—). ***LANGUAGES:*** Spanish. ***PRACTICE AREAS:*** Immigration and Nationality Law; Consular Issues. ***Email:*** rfreedman@usvisainfo.com

SENIOR ASSOCIATE

MONTSERRAT C. MILLER, born Ft. Belvoir, Virginia, March 28, 1969; admitted to bar, 1997, Maryland; 1999, District of Columbia. *Education:* George Mason University (B.A., Government and Politics, Spanish Language and Literature, 1992); American University, Washington College of Law (J.D., 1996). Editor, Washington College of Law Journal of Gender and the Law. Volunteer: City of Gaithersburg Recreation Department; One in Ten; DC Scores. *Member:* The District of Columbia Bar; Maryland State and American Bar Associations; American Immigration Lawyers Association. ***LANGUAGES:*** Spanish. ***Email:*** mmiller@usvisainfo.com

(This Listing Continued)

Languages: Spanish, Chinese, Korean, Bulgarian, French, Russian, Arabic and Portuguese.

PEHRSON & ASSOCIATES, P.L.L.C.

4517 FOXHALL CRESCENT

WASHINGTON, D.C. 20006

Telephone: 202-298-5614

Fax: 202-298-9292

Email: gopehrson@aol.com

URL: http://www.lawyers.com/pehrson

Tax Law, Tax Controversies, Tax Planning, Life Insurance, Insurance Companies, Mergers and Acquisitions.

GORDON O. PEHRSON, born San Antonio, Texas, February 18, 1943; admitted to bar, 1968, Illinois; 1969, District of Columbia; U.S. Supreme Court. *Education:* College of William & Mary (A.B., 1964); University of Michigan (J.D., cum laude, 1967); University of London, United Kingdom. Pi Delta Epsilon; Order of the Coif; Omicron Delta Kappa. Ford Foundation Scholar. Co-Author: "BNA Portfolio #546, Annuities, Life Insurance and Long-Term Care Products," Tax Management, Inc., 1999; "Mutual Holding Companies as a Strategic Alternative for Mutual Insurers," Bowne, 1998; "Demutualization of Insurance Companies," Bowne, 1991; "Federal Taxation of Foreign Investment in the United States," *Manual of Foreign Investment in the United States*, Shepard McGraw-Hill, Inc., 1984; "Foreign and International Transactions — Section 367 and 1491," BNA Tax Management Portfolio, 1978. Bi-Monthly Columnist, Life Associated News. Founder, Editor, 1986-1994 and Member, Board of Advisors, 1986—, The Insurance Tax Review. Adjunct Professor, Georgetown University Law Center, 1977-1981. Trustee, U.S. Supreme Court Historical Society, 1993—. Special Advisor to President of the Humane Society of the United States. Member, Advisory Council and Chair, Planning Committee, Hartford Institute on Insurance Taxation, 1993—. Member, Advisory Board, The College of William and Mary's Thomas Jefferson Program on Public Policy. Member, Board of Directors: American League of Lobbyists; Automated Correspondence Systems, Inc.; Food for Christmas. Member, Board of Advisors, New World Telesites. Member: The Economic Club of Washington; The Metropolitan Club; The National Press Club; Washington Board of Trade. Member, Board of Directors and General Counsel, Inside Knowledge, Inc. Founder and President, Pehrson & Associates, P.L.L.C., 2000. Senior Partner, Hopkins & Sutter, Washington, D.C., 1997-2000. Senior Partner, Partner and Associate, Sutherland, Asbill & Brennan, Washington, D.C., 1970-1997. *Member:* Federal Circuit (Chair, Tax Appeals Committee, 1994-1995), Federal (Coordinator, Annual Tax Seminar) and American (Vice Chair, Committee of Insurance Taxation, 1990-1994 and Chair, Investment, Financial Services and Taxation Committee, Tort and Insurance Practice Section, 1994-1996; Chair, Committee on Tax Procedure, Administrative Law and Regulatory Practice Section, 1994-1996) Bar Associations; American Law Institute (Elected Member, 1990). [Lieutenant, U.S. Navy, JAGC, 1968-1970]. ***LANGUAGES:*** French. ***Email:*** gopehrson@aol.com

JOHN D. PELLEGRIN, P.C.

WASHINGTON, D.C.

(See Burke, Virginia)

Communications, Intellectual Property, Copyright, Trademark, Computer, Trade Regulation, Administrative Agency Practice including practice before the F.C.C., state P.U.C.s and other regulatory agencies, Business Law, Employment Law, Franchising.

PENNIE & EDMONDS LLP

1667 K STREET, N.W.

WASHINGTON, D.C. 20006

Telephone: 202-496-4400

Facsimile: 202-496-4444

Email: pennie@info.pennie.com

URL: http://www.pennie.com

New York, New York Office: 1155 Avenue of the Americas. Telephone: 212-790-9090. Facsimile: (212) 869-9741, (212) 869-8864.

Palo Alto, California Office: 3300 Hillview Avenue. Telephone: 650-493-4935. Facsimile: 650-493-5556.

Intellectual Property and Technology Litigation including Patent, Trademark, Trade Secrets, Copyright and Unfair Competition Causes, Environmental Law, Communications Law and Related Government Agency Proceedings, Licensing, Arbitration and International Trade Matters. Trials and Appeals in all Federal and State Courts.

JOHN C. PENNIE (1858-1921).

(This Listing Continued)

PENNIE & EDMONDS LLP, Washington—Continued

DEAN S. EDMONDS (1879-1972).

PARTNERS

STANTON T. LAWRENCE, III, born Glen Ridge, New Jersey, January 27, 1945; admitted to bar, 1973, New York; 1996, District of Columbia; registered to practice before U.S. Patent and Trademark Office. *Education:* Middlebury College and Colorado State University (B.S., Chemistry, 1967); George Washington University (J.D., 1971). (Also at New York, New York Office); (Litigation Practice Group Head). ***PRACTICE AREAS:*** Intellectual Property Litigation. ***Email:*** lawrences@pennie.com

PAUL J. ZEGGER, born Schenectady, New York, June 12, 1959; admitted to bar, 1987, Connecticut; 1988, New York; 1989, U.S. District Court, Southern and Eastern Districts of New York and U.S. Court of Appeals for the Federal Circuit; 1998, U.S. District Court for the District of Columbia; registered to practice before U.S. Patent and Trademark Office (Not admitted in District of Columbia). *Education:* University of Massachusetts (B.S., Chemical Engineering, 1982); Albany Law School of Union University (J.D., 1987). ***PRACTICE AREAS:*** Intellectual Property; Intellectual Property Litigation. ***Email:*** zeggerp@pennie.com

MARCIA H. SUNDEEN, born Cleveland, Ohio, November 5, 1954; admitted to bar, 1981, Ohio and U.S. District Court, Northern District of Ohio; 1983, District of Columbia; 1986, U.S. Court of Appeals for the Federal Circuit; 1990, U.S. Court of International Trade; 1992, U.S. District Court, District of Columbia; 1994, U.S. Court of Appeals for the District of Columbia Circuit; registered to practice before U.S. Patent and Trademark Office. *Education:* Marquette University (B.S., Chemistry, 1976); Case Western Reserve University (J.D., 1981). ***PRACTICE AREAS:*** Intellectual Property; Intellectual Property Litigation; International Trade. ***Email:*** sundeenm@pennie.com

TODD A. WAGNER, born Tucson, Arizona, July 5, 1966; admitted to bar, 1991, New York; 1994, U.S. Court of Appeals, Ninth Circuit; U.S. Court of Appeals for the Federal Circuit; 1995, U.S. District Court, Southern and Eastern Districts of New York and Northern District of California; registered to practice before U.S. Patent and Trademark Office (Not admitted in District of Columbia). *Education:* University of Oregon, Honors College (B.A., Biochemistry, 1987); Albany Law School of Union University (J.D., 1990). *Member:* New York State Bar (Member, Intellectual Property Law Section); and American Bar Associations; New York Intellectual Property Law Association. ***PRACTICE AREAS:*** Intellectual Property; Litigation. ***Email:*** wagnert@pennie.com

WILLIAM G. PECAU, born Mineola, New York, September 12, 1951; admitted to bar, 1977, New York; 1995, California (Not admitted in District of Columbia). *Education:* University of the South (B.A., History, cum laude, 1973); Vanderbilt University (J.D., 1976). Phi Beta Kappa. Chair, Publications Committee, International Trademark Association. ***PRACTICE AREAS:*** Intellectual Property; Intellectual Property Litigation. ***Email:*** pecauw@pennie.com

ASSOCIATES

NANDA K. ALAPATI, born Tenali, A.P., India, November 19, 1959; admitted to bar, 1994, Maryland; 1996, Virginia and District of Columbia; registered to practice before U.S. Patent and Trademark Office. *Education:* Marquette University (B.S., Electrical Engineering, 1982); Carnegie-Mellon University (M.S., Electrical Engineering, 1985); Georgetown University Law School (J.D., 1994). ***PRACTICE AREAS:*** Intellectual Property; Patent. ***Email:*** nalapati@pennie.com

CARL P. BRETSCHER, born Valparaiso, Indiana, November 26, 1962; admitted to bar, 1993, Illinois; 1995, U.S. District Court, Northern District of Illinois; 1999, District of Columbia, U.S. Court of Appeals, Federal Circuit, and U.S. District Court, District of Columbia; registered to practice before U.S. Patent and Trademark Office. *Education:* University of Illinois (B.S., magna cum laude, 1984); Harvard University (M.P.A., 1987); George Washington University (J.D., 1993). Phi Beta Kappa. Member, George Washington Law Review. *Member:* American Intellectual Property Law Association; Federal Circuit Bar Association; International Trade Commission Trial Lawyers Association. ***PRACTICE AREAS:*** Patent Law; Intellectual Property. ***Email:*** bretscher@pennie.com

GREG P. ROGGIN, born Boston, Massachusetts, May 29, 1969; admitted to bar, 1994, Maryland; 1997, District of Columbia and U.S. District Court, District of Maryland; registered to practice before U.S. Patent and Trademark Office. *Education:* University of Michigan (B.A., Political Science and Japanese, 1991); Washington University (M.A., Japanese and East Asian Studies, 1994; J.D., 1994); George Washington University (LL.M., Patent and Intellectual Property Law, 1996). ***LANGUAGES:*** Japanese. ***PRACTICE AREAS:*** Patent Litigation; Intellectual Property Licensing; Intellectual Property Litigation. ***Email:*** rogging@pennie.com

ERIC J. FUES, born Dallas, Texas, May 24, 1962; admitted to bar, 1995, New York and U.S. Court of Appeals for the Federal Circuit; 2000, District of

(This Listing Continued)

Columbia; registered to practice before U.S. Patent and Trademark Office. *Education:* Northwestern University (B.S., Chemical Engineering, 1984; M.M., Marketing, Finance, 1989); Loyola University, Chicago (J.D., 1994). Member, Loyola University of Chicago Law Journal. ***PRACTICE AREAS:*** Intellectual Property; Patent Litigation. ***Email:*** fuese@pennie.com

GEORGE A. WILLINGHAN, III, born Baltimore, Maryland, November 6, 1965; admitted to bar, 1997, Virginia; registered to practice before U.S. Patent and Trademark Office (Not admitted in District of Columbia). *Education:* Hampden-Sydney College (B.S., Physics and Computer Science, 1987); Johns Hopkins University (M.E., Environmental Engineering, 1994); Georgetown University Law Center (J.D., 1997). ***PRACTICE AREAS:*** Intellectual Property; Patent Prosecution; Patent Litigation. ***Email:*** willinghang@pennie.com

GREGORY J. GONSALVES, born Fall River, Massachusetts, June 21, 1960; admitted to bar, 1997, Virginia; 1998, U.S. Court of Appeals, Fourth Circuit; U.S. District Court, Eastern District of Virginia; registered to practice before U.S. Patent and Trademark Office (Not admitted in District of Columbia). *Education:* Northeastern University (B.S., Electrical Engineering, 1982); Syracuse University (M.S., Electrical Engineering, 1987; Ph.D., Computer Engineering, 1991); Georgetown University Law Center (J.D., cum laude, 1997). ***PRACTICE AREAS:*** Intellectual Property. ***Email:*** gonsalvesg@pennie.com

CHRISTOPHER G. HAYDEN, born Chicago, Illinois, November 16, 1957; admitted to bar, 1997, Texas; registered to practice before U.S. Patent and Trademark Office (Not admitted in District of Columbia). *Education:* University of Illinois (B.S., in Chemistry, 1980); University of Houston (B.S., in Chemical Engineering, magna cum laude, 1994; J.D., cum laude, 1997). Tau Beta Pi. *Member:* Houston Young Lawyers Association. ***PRACTICE AREAS:*** Intellectual Property. ***Email:*** haydenc@pennie.com

NANCY H. LUTZ, born Columbus, Ohio, April 4, 1959; admitted to bar, 1995, Illinois; 1996, District of Columbia. *Education:* DePauw University (B.A., English Composition, 1981); The John Marshall Law School (J.D., 1995). Student Editor, The John Marshall Journal of Computer and Information Law, 1994. ***PRACTICE AREAS:*** Litigation; Trademark Law; Copyright Law; Unfair Competition Law; Advertising Law; Intellectual Property.

MAX BACHRACH, born Ellensburg, Washington, May 16, 1968; admitted to bar, 1998, Virginia; registered to practice before U.S. Patent and Trademark Office (Not admitted in District of Columbia). *Education:* Columbia University (B.A., 1990); California Institute of Technology (Ph.D., 1996); University of Virginia (J.D., 1998). ***PRACTICE AREAS:*** Patent Prosecution; Patent Litigation; Pharmaceutical Patents. ***Email:*** bachrachm@pennie.com

PAUL E. DIETZE, born Nassau County, New York, August 29, 1953; admitted to bar, 1999, Virginia; 2000, District of Columbia; registered to practice before U.S. Patent and Trademark Office. *Education:* Queens College of the City University of New York (B.S., 1976); New York University (Ph.D., 1980; M.S., 1983); University of Maryland (J.D., with honors, 1998). Order of the Coif. Member, American Chemical Society. ***PRACTICE AREAS:*** Intellectual Property; Patents. ***Email:*** dietzep@pennie.com

SERGE SIRA, born Birmingham, England, February 21, 1961; admitted to bar, 1999, Maryland; 2000, District of Columbia; registered to practice before U.S. Patent and Trademark Office. *Education:* University of Toronto (Ph.D., 1992); University of Maryland (J.D., 1998). *Member:* American Intellectual Property Law Association. ***PRACTICE AREAS:*** Intellectual Property. ***Email:*** siras@pennie.com

GARY ZHANG, born Shenyang, China, December 7, 1962; admitted to bar, 1999, Virginia (Not admitted in District of Columbia). *Education:* Tsinghua University, Beijing, China (B.S., 1986); Georgetown University (J.D., 1999). ***LANGUAGES:*** English and Chinese. ***PRACTICE AREAS:*** Intellectual Property. ***Email:*** zhangg@pennie.com

SETH ALAIN WATKINS, born New Rochelle, New York, March 10, 1970; admitted to bar, 1999, Virginia and U.S. Court of Appeals for the Federal and Fourth Circuits; 2000, District of Columbia and U.S. District Court, Eastern District of Virginia. *Education:* Duke University (B.S.E., 1992; M.S., 1993; Ph.D., 1996; J.D., 1999). ***PRACTICE AREAS:*** Intellectual Property. ***Email:*** watkinss@pennie.com

DAVID CHAN LEE, born Seoul, South Korea, May 4, 1972; admitted to bar, 1999, Virginia and U.S. Court of Appeals, Fourth Circuit; 2000, District of Columbia, U.S. District Court, Eastern District of Virginia and U.S. Court of Appeals for the Federal Circuit. *Education:* University of North Carolina at Chapel Hill (B.A., 1995); Emory University School of Law (J.D., 1999). ***LANGUAGES:*** Korean. ***PRACTICE AREAS:*** Intellectual Property. ***Email:*** leed@pennie.com

BRIAN JOSEPH MALM, born San Pedro, California, February 18, 1972; (admission pending). *Education:* University of California at Los Angeles (B.S., 1994); Georgetown University (J.D., 1999). ***LANGUAGES:*** Spanish. ***PRACTICE AREAS:*** Intellectual Property; Patent. ***Email:*** malmb@pennie.com

(This Listing Continued)

MEHUL R. JANI, born Poughkeepsie, New York, August 28, 1975; (admission pending). *Education:* Boston University (B.S., 1997); George Washington University (J.D., 2000). ***LANGUAGES:*** Gujarati. ***PRACTICE AREAS:*** Intellectual Property. ***Email:*** janim@pennie.com

STEVEN J. SCHWARZ, born Abington, Pennsylvania, January 4, 1975; registered to practice before U.S. Patent and Trademark Office; (admission pending). *Education:* Lehigh University (B.S.M.E., 1997); Franklin Pierce (J.D., 2000). Phi Alpha Delta. Author: "Signing Your John Hancock in the 21st Century," NH Bar Journal, Fall, 1999. Member, Society of Automotive Engineers, 1996—. *Member:* American Intellectual Property Law Association. ***PRACTICE AREAS:*** Intellectual Property. ***Email:*** schwarz@pennie.com

KAREN G. HOROWITZ, born New York, New York, October 10, 1968; admitted to bar, 1995, New York; registered to practice before U.S. Patent and Trademark Office (Not admitted in District of Columbia). *Education:* Princeton University (B.S.E., 1990); Fordham University (J.D., cum laude, 1995). Order of the Coif. ***LANGUAGES:*** Hebrew, Spanish. ***PRACTICE AREAS:*** Patent Prosecution; Patent Opinions. ***Email:*** horowitzk@pennie.com

MATTHEW GUTTMAN, born Huntington, New York, October 31, 1972; (admission pending). *Education:* State University of New York at Binghamton (B.S., 1995); Fordham University (J.D., 2001). ***PRACTICE AREAS:*** Trademarks. ***Email:*** guttmanm@pennie.com

MARK ANTHONY CHARLES, born Johnson City, Tennessee, February 25, 1975; (admission pending). *Education:* University of Tennessee at Knoxville (B.S., 1995); Duke University (J.D., 1998; M.S., Mechanical Engineering, 1998). Tau Beta Pi. ***PRACTICE AREAS:*** Patents. ***Email:*** charlesm@pennie.com

KENT E. BASSON, born Gadsden, Alabama, July 18, 1958; (admission pending); admitted to bar, registered to practice before U.S. Patent and Trademark Office. *Education:* University of Alabama (B.S.M.E., 1979); Washington & Lee University (J.D., 2001). Member, National Moot Court Team. Licensed Professional Engineer: Alabama, 1988; Michigan, 1989; Ohio, 1991; Illinois, 1997. [U.S. Navy, 1983-1987, Lt.]. ***Email:*** bassonk@pennie.com

TRACY G. PARKER, born Kalamazoo, Michigan, January 19, 1975; (admission pending). *Education:* Florida A & M University (B.S., cum laude, 1998); George Washington University (J.D., 2001). Author, National Law Journal, July 2000. *Member:* American Bar Association; American Intellectual Property Law Association. ***Email:*** parkert@pennie.com

(For Complete personnel and biographical data, see New York, New York Professional Biographies).

PEPPER & CORAZZINI, L.L.P.

Established in 1957

1776 K STREET, N.W.
SUITE 200
WASHINGTON, D.C. 20006
Telephone: 202-296-0600
Telecopier: 202-296-5572
Email: pepcor@commlaw.com
URL: http://www.commlaw.com

Communications Law, International Telecommunications, Radio, Television, CATV, MMDS, CLEC, ITFS Satellite and Microwave, Mobile Radio, Internet Law, General Practice before Federal Courts and Administrative Agencies.

FIRM PROFILE: Pepper & Corazzini, L.L.P. is one of the nation's preeminent boutique law firms, specializing in communications, telecommunications, Internet and online services law. During its over forty years of practice, the firm has expanded its expertise from radio, television and cable matters to include satellite, MMDS, radio common carrier, and, most recently, Internet and on-line services. Pepper & Corazzini's attorneys routinely appear on behalf of clients before the Federal Communication Commission and other federal agencies, the federal courts, the Congress and Executive Branch. Our very dedicated staff of 10 attorneys and 11 legal support personnel are at the center of the firm's tradition of excellence in the representation of each of our clients.

MEMBERS OF FIRM

VINCENT A. PEPPER, born Philadelphia, Pennsylvania, May 28, 1927; admitted to bar, 1951, District of Columbia. *Education:* Seattle University (B.S., cum laude, 1947); University of Washington; Georgetown University (J.D., 1951). Phi Delta Phi; Pi Gamma Mu. Staff Member, Georgetown Law Journal, 1949-1951. Co-Winner, National Appellate Moot Court Competition, 1950. *Member:* The District of Columbia Bar; Bar Association of the District of Columbia; American Bar Association; Federal Communications Bar Association. ***PRACTICE AREAS:*** Communications and Media; Broadcast Television; International Telecommunications Law; Telecommunications Contracts. ***Email:*** vap@commlaw.com

(This Listing Continued)

ROBERT D. L'HEUREUX (1912-1969).

ROBERT F. CORAZZINI, born Greenport, New York, November 22, 1936; admitted to bar, 1961, District of Columbia. *Education:* Mount St. Mary's College (B.S., S.S., cum laude, 1958); Georgetown University (J.D., 1961). Staff Member, Georgetown Law Journal, 1959-1961. *Member:* The District of Columbia Bar; American Bar Association; Federal Communications Bar Association. [Captain, Judge Advocate General Corps, United States Air Force, 1963-1965]. ***PRACTICE AREAS:*** Communications and Media; Cable Communications; FCC Licensing; FCC Regulation.

FREDERICK W. FORD (1909-1986).

PETER GUTMANN, born Kew Gardens, New York, August 3, 1949; admitted to bar, 1978, District of Columbia. *Education:* Wesleyan University (B.A., cum laude, 1971); University of North Carolina (M.A., Communications, 1974); George Washington University (J.D., 1978). *Member:* The District of Columbia Bar; American Bar Association; Federal Communications Bar Association. ***PRACTICE AREAS:*** Telecommunications Law; Broadcast Station Transfers; Broadcast Applications; Telecommunications Contracts; Broadcast Television. ***Email:*** pg@commlaw.com

JOHN F. GARZIGLIA, born Washington, D.C., January 16, 1950; admitted to bar, 1979, District of Columbia. *Education:* St. Louis University (B.A., 1972); Washington University (J.D., 1979). Phi Delta Phi. Attorney-Advisor, AM Branch, 1983-1984 and Trial Attorney, 1984, Hearing Branch, Mass Media Bureau, Federal Communications Commission. *Member:* The District of Columbia Bar; American Bar Association; Federal Communications Bar Association. ***PRACTICE AREAS:*** Broadcast Radio; Broadcast Station Transfers; Broadcast Applications; FCC Regulation; FCC Licensing; Internet Law. ***Email:*** jfg@commlaw.com

GREGG P. SKALL, born El Paso, Texas, March 28, 1944; admitted to bar, 1969, Ohio; 1971, District of Columbia; 1977, U.S. Supreme Court. *Education:* The Ohio State University (B.S., 1966); University of Cincinnati (J.D., 1969). Co-Author: *The Broadcasters Survival Guide,* A Handbook of FCC Rules and Regulations for Radio and TV Stations, Scripps Howard Books (An Imprint of Pharos Books), 1988; "The Regulation of Electronic Publishing," Federal Communications Law Journal, Vol. 33, No. 3, Summer 1981; "Direct International and Domestic Television Broadcasting by Satellite-A Myth or Potential Reality," Proceedings of the Seventh Communications Satellite Systems Conference of the American Institute of Aeronautics and Astronautics, April 1978; "Legal Barriers to Electronic Mail," Proceedings of the International Telecommunications Exposition, 1977, Vol. 3, Horizon House International, 1978; "Regulation and Your Industry," Telco-Digest, the Magazine for Independent Telcos, August/September 1976; "Competition in Telecommunications--The Telephone Industry Bill," Hearing on Competition in the Telecommunications Industry, before the Subcommittee on Communications of the House Committee on Interstate and Foreign Commerce, 94th Cong, 2d Sess., ser 94-129 at 1040 (1976); "Summary of Current Law Relating to Cable Television Systems," XLVI, Ohio Bar 1031 (1973). Professorial Lecturer, Telecommunications Law, George Washington University, 1979-1983. Acting General Counsel, 1977-1978, Office of Telecommunications Policy, Executive Office of the President. Chief Counsel, National Telecommunications and Information Administration, U.S. Department of Commerce, 1978-1981. *Member:* The District of Columbia Bar; Federal (Chairman: Regulated Industries Committee, 1979-1981; Telecommunications Committee, 1982) and American Bar Associations; Federal Communications Bar Association. ***PRACTICE AREAS:*** International Telecommunications Law; Communications Common Carrier; Broadcast Radio; Telecommunications Licensing; Telecommunications Regulation.

HOWARD J. BARR, born Brooklyn, New York, December 10, 1961; admitted to bar, 1986, Maryland; 1989, District of Columbia. *Education:* Oglethorpe University (B.A., 1983); University of Louisville (J.D., 1986). Law Clerk to the Honorable Vincent J. Femia. *Member:* The District of Columbia Bar; Maryland State and American Bar Associations; Federal Communications Bar Association. ***PRACTICE AREAS:*** Cable TV; Cable Communications; Wireless Communications; Broadcast Radio.

ASSOCIATES

SUZANNE SPINK GOODWYN, born Closter, New Jersey, January 10, 1964; admitted to bar, 1994, Virginia; 1999, District of Columbia. *Education:* Tulane University of Louisiana (B.A., 1986); New York Law School (J.D., 1993). *Member:* Virginia State Bar; American Bar Association (Member, Communications Law Forum); Federal Communications Bar Association. ***PRACTICE AREAS:*** Cable Communications; FCC Licensing; FCC Regulation; Communications and Media; Wireless Communications. ***Email:*** scs@commlaw.com

PATRICIA M. CHUH, born Seoul, Korea, August 11, 1964; admitted to bar, 1996, Maryland; 1997, District of Columbia. *Education:* Rutgers University (B.A., 1987); Catholic University of America (J.D., 1996). Author, CommLaw Conspectus, Vol. 3, No 2. *Member:* The District of Columbia Bar; American Bar Association; Federal Communications Bar Association. ***PRACTICE AREAS:*** Broadcast Communications. ***Email:*** pmc@commlaw.com

(This Listing Continued)

PEPPER & CORAZZINI, L.L.P., Washington—Continued

JOAN D. STEWART, born Portland, Oregon, November 18, 1972; admitted to bar, 1999, Virginia. *Education:* George Mason University (B.A., 1995); American University Washington College of Law (J.D., 1999). *Member:* Federal and American Bar Associations. ***PRACTICE AREAS:*** Communications. **Email:** jds@commlaw.com

MARK ERIC BLACKNELL, born 1976; admitted to bar, 2000, Virginia (Not admitted in District of Columbia). *Education:* Georgia State University (A.B., 1996); George Washington University (J.D., 2000). **Email:** mb@commlaw.com

PEPPER HAMILTON LLP

Established in 1890

HAMILTON SQUARE

600 FOURTEENTH STREET, N.W.

WASHINGTON, D.C. 20005-2004

Telephone: 202-220-1200

Telecopy: 202-220-1665

Email: phinfo@pepperlaw.com

URL: http://www.pepperlaw.com

Philadelphia, Pennsylvania Office: 3000 Two Logan Square, Eighteenth and Arch Streets, 19103-2799. Telephone: 215-981-4000. Fax: 215-981-4750.

Detroit, Michigan Office: 100 Renaissance Center, 36th Floor, 48243-1157. Telephone: 313-259-7110. Fax: 313-259-7926.

New York, New York Office: 1180 Avenue of the Americas, 14th Floor, 10036-8401. Telephone: 212-899-5090. Fax: 212-899-5091.

Pittsburgh, Pennsylvania Office: 500 Grant Street, 50th Floor, 15219-2502. Telephone: 412-454-5000. Fax: 412-281-0717.

Berwyn, Pennsylvania Office: 1235 Westlakes Drive, Suite 400, 19312-2401. Telephone: 610-640-7800. Fax: 610-640-7835.

Cherry Hill, New Jersey Office: LibertyView Building, Suite 420, 457 Haddonfield Road, 08002-2220. Telephone: 856-910-7200. Fax: 856-665-7743.

Harrisburg, Pennsylvania Office: 200 One Keystone Plaza, North Front and Market Streets, P.O. Box 1181, 17108-1181. Telephone: 717-255-1155. Fax: 717-238-0575.

Princeton, New Jersey Office: 300 Alexander Park, 08543-5276. Telephone: 609-452-0808. Fax: 609-452-1147.

Tysons Corner, Virginia Office: 8280 Greensboro Drive, Suite 800, 22102-3807. Telephone: 703-748-3900. Fax: 703-356-0005.

Wilmington, Delaware Office: 1201 Market Street, Suite 1600, P.O. Box 1709, 19899-1709. Telephone: 302-777-6500. Fax: 302-656-8865.

General Practice.

PARTNERS

GEORGE A. LEHNER, born Cleveland, OH, 1948; admitted to bar, 1977, Michigan; 1979, District of Columbia. *Education:* Wesleyan University (B.A., 1971); University of Michigan (J.D., cum laude, 1976; M.U.P., 1977); Hague Academy of International Law. Phi Beta Kappa. Adjunct Professor, Georgetown University Law Center, 1990-1993. Attorney-Advisor, U.S. Department of State, 1977-1980. (Chair, Washington Office Management Committee) (Member, Firm Executive Committee). ***LANGUAGES:*** French. ***PRACTICE AREAS:*** Litigation; International Dispute Resolution. **Email:** lehnerg@pepperlaw.com

CHARLES H. CARPENTER, born Hartford, CT, 1958; admitted to bar, 1991, Montana; 1992, District of Columbia. *Education:* University of California at Berkeley; Montana State University (B.S., 1983); Catholic University (J.D., with honors, 1991). Member, Catholic University Law Review. ***PRACTICE AREAS:*** Civil Litigation; Government Contracts; Administrative Law. **Email:** carpenterc@pepperlaw.com

GREGORY C. DORRIS, born Douglasville, GA, 1961; admitted to bar, 1986, Georgia; 1988, District of Columbia and U.S. Court of International Trade. *Education:* University of Georgia (B.A., summa cum laude, 1983; J.D., cum laude, 1986). Phi Beta Kappa. Editor, Georgia Journal of International and Comparative Law. Law Clerk to Hon. Dominick L. DiCarlo, U.S. Court of International Trade, 1986-1988. ***PRACTICE AREAS:*** Customs Law; International Trade Regulation. **Email:** dorrisg@pepperlaw.com

K. STEWART EVANS, JR., born Charlottesville, VA, 1945; admitted to bar, 1972, Virginia; 1998, Maryland; 1999, District of Columbia. *Education:* University of Virginia (B.A., 1968; J.D., 1972). Law Clerk to Hon. Robert J. Kelleher, U.S. District Court, Central District of California, 1972-1973. (Also at Tysons Corner, Virginia Office). ***PRACTICE AREAS:*** Intellectual Property Litigation; Noncompetition and Non-Solicitation Agreements; Business Torts. **Email:** evansks@pepperlaw.com

(This Listing Continued)

STEVEN J. FOX, born Baltimore, MD, 1950; admitted to bar, 1974, Maryland; 1976, District of Columbia. *Education:* University of Maryland (B.A., with honors, 1971; J.D., 1974). **Email:** foxsj@pepperlaw.com

DONALD H. GREEN, born Elizabeth, NJ, 1929; admitted to bar, 1957, Florida; 1958, New York; 1963, District of Columbia. *Education:* Syracuse University (A.B., 1951); Harvard University (LL.B., 1954). Faculty Member, U.S. Department of Justice Legal Education Institute, 1987-1992. Adjunct Professor, Georgetown University Law Center, 1992—. Attorney-Advisor, Office of Legal Counsel, U.S. Department of Justice, 1958-1960. Trial Attorney, Appellate Section, Civil Division, U.S. Department of Justice, 1960-1961. *Member:* Federal (Chairman, Young Lawyers Committee, 1961-1962) and American (Chairman, Committee on Indian Affairs, Section of Administrative Law, 1969-1970) Bar Associations; Defense Research Institute. [Col., USMCR, Ret.]. ***PRACTICE AREAS:*** Litigation; Mediation; Arbitration. **Email:** greendh@pepperlaw.com

ROBERT B. JOSELOW, born New York, NY, 1944; admitted to bar, 1969, District of Columbia. *Education:* New York University (B.A., cum laude, 1966); George Washington University (J.D., 1969). ***PRACTICE AREAS:*** Real Estate Finance; Multi-Family Housing; Secondary Mortgage Market. **Email:** joselowr@pepperlaw.com

MARC D. MACHLIN, born St. Louis, MO, 1957; admitted to bar, 1981, District of Columbia. *Education:* Brown University (A.B., magna cum laude, 1978); Harvard University (J.D., cum laude, 1981). Phi Beta Kappa. Board of Editors, Harvard Environmental Law Review. ***PRACTICE AREAS:*** Environmental Law; Antitrust; Public Utility Regulation. **Email:** machlinm@pepperlaw.com

EDWARD A. McCULLOUGH, born Springfield, OH, 1955; admitted to bar, 1979, Virginia; 1986, District of Columbia. *Education:* University of Virginia (B.A., with distinction, 1976); College of William & Mary (J.D., 1979). Order of the Coif. Editor, William & Mary Law Review. Law Clerk to Hon. Thomas J. Lydon, U.S. Court of Claims, 1979-1980. ***PRACTICE AREAS:*** Public Finance; Municipal Bonds; Federal Taxation. **Email:** mcculloughe@pepperlaw.com

JOHN WILL ONGMAN, born Chicago, IL, 1951; admitted to bar, 1976, Illinois; 1984, District of Columbia; 1990, New York. *Education:* Purdue University (B.S., summa cum laude, 1972); University of Illinois (M.S., 1973); Northwestern University (J.D., cum laude, 1976). Order of the Coif. Editor, Northwestern University Law Review. Law Clerk to Hon. Walter J. Cummings, Chief Judge, U.S. Court of Appeals, Seventh Circuit, 1976-1977. (Chairman, Firm Government Relations and Regulatory Compliance Department). ***PRACTICE AREAS:*** Antitrust; Economic Regulatory Law; Technology and Science. **Email:** ongmanj@pepperlaw.com

DANIEL I. PRYWES, born Philadelphia, PA, 1957; admitted to bar, 1980, District of Columbia; 1997, Maryland. *Education:* University of Pennsylvania (B.A., magna cum laude, 1976; J.D., cum laude, 1980). Editor, University of Pennsylvania Law Review. ***PRACTICE AREAS:*** Commercial Litigation; Regulatory Law. **Email:** prywesd@pepperlaw.com

RICHARD A. ROSSMAN, born Albany, NY, 1939; admitted to bar, 1964, Michigan (Not admitted in District of Columbia). *Education:* University of Michigan (A.B., 1961; J.D., 1964). Chief of Staff to Assistant Attorney General in Charge of Criminal Division, U.S. Department of Justice, 1998-1999. U.S. Attorney, Eastern District of Michigan, 1980-1981. (Also at Detroit, Michigan Office). ***PRACTICE AREAS:*** Commercial Litigation; White Collar Crime. **Email:** rossmanr@pepperlaw.com

SHELDON L. SCHREIBERG, born Minneapolis, MN, 1942; admitted to bar, 1974, Maryland; 1975, District of Columbia. *Education:* University of Michigan; University of Minnesota (B.A., summa cum laude, 1964); Princeton University (M.P.A., 1966); Harvard University (J.D., 1969). Phi Beta Kappa. Assistant to Vice President of the United States, 1968. Executive Assistant to Federal Housing Commissioner, U.S. Department of Housing and Urban Development, 1977-1978. Counsel, Committee on Banking, Finance and Urban Affairs, Subcommittee on Housing and Community Development, U.S. House of Representatives, 1978-1980. ***LANGUAGES:*** Hebrew and Spanish. ***PRACTICE AREAS:*** Real Estate; Affordable Housing; Project Finance. **Email:** schreibergs@pepperlaw.com

MICHAEL B. STAEBLER, born Washington, DC, 1943; admitted to bar, 1969, Michigan (Not admitted in District of Columbia). *Education:* Harvard University (B.A., magna cum laude, 1966); University of Michigan (J.D., with distinction, 1969). (Also at Detroit, Michigan Office). ***PRACTICE AREAS:*** Business Acquisitions; Securities; Venture Capital. **Email:** staeblerm@pepperlaw.com

MARTIN D. TECKLER, born Syracuse, NY, 1946; admitted to bar, 1973, District of Columbia. *Education:* Boston University (B.A., with distinction, 1968); George Washington University (J.D., with honors, 1972). Deputy General Counsel, U.S. Small Business Administration, 1984-1997. ***PRACTICE AREAS:*** Venture Capital; Small Business Law; Securities. **Email:** tecklerm@pepperlaw.com

(This Listing Continued)

STEPHEN M. TRUITT, born Washington, DC, 1939; admitted to bar, 1966, District of Columbia. *Education:* Harvard University (A.B., 1963); Yale University (LL.B., 1966). Trial Attorney, Civil Division, U.S. Department of Justice, 1966-1969. ***PRACTICE AREAS:*** Litigation. ***Email:*** truitts@pepperlaw.com

WILLIAM J. WALSH, born New York, NY, 1946; admitted to bar, 1978, District of Columbia. *Education:* Manhattan College (B.S., cum laude, 1968); George Washington University (J.D., 1978). Order of the Coif. Enforcement Attorney, Environmental Protection Agency, Section Chief in Charge of "Love Canal" cases, 1978-1986. ***PRACTICE AREAS:*** Superfund; Environmental Administrative Law; Environmental Litigation. ***Email:*** walshw@pepperlaw.com

DAVID A. WORMSER, born Kansas City, MO, 1955; admitted to bar, 1980, District of Columbia. *Education:* Miami University (B.S., cum laude, 1977); Ohio State University (J.D., 1980). Assistant General Counsel, ADAPSO (The Information Technology Association of America), 1982-1985. (Also at Tysons Corner, Virginia Office). ***PRACTICE AREAS:*** Corporate Law; Computer Law; Intellectual Property. ***Email:*** wormserd@pepperlaw.com

OF COUNSEL

CYNTHIA A. METZLER, born Pittsburgh, PA, 1948; admitted to bar, 1974, Indiana; 1980, Florida; 1998, District of Columbia. *Education:* Purdue University (B.A., 1970); Indiana University (J.D., 1974); American University (M.S., 1985). Acting Secretary of Labor, U.S. Department of Labor, 1997. ***PRACTICE AREAS:*** Employment; Labor. ***Email:*** metzlerc@pepperlaw.com

ASSOCIATES

EDWARD M. ANDRIES, born Southfield, MI, 1967; admitted to bar, 1996, Maryland; 1998, District of Columbia. *Education:* University of Michigan (B.B.A., 1989); George Washington University (J.D., 1996); Catholic University (M.A., 1997). ***PRACTICE AREAS:*** Commercial Litigation. ***Email:*** andriese@pepperlaw.com

CHRISTINE WALDMANN CARMODY, born Boston, MA, 1967; admitted to bar, 1995, Maryland; 1998, District of Columbia. *Education:* Wellesley College (B.A., cum laude, 1989); Georgetown University (J.D., 1995). Editor, American Criminal Law Review. ***PRACTICE AREAS:*** Real Estate; Housing Finance; Affordable Housing. ***Email:*** waldmannc@pepperlaw.com

DENNIS P. CAWLEY, born Scranton, PA, 1969; admitted to bar, 2000, New Jersey and Pennsylvania; registered to practice before U.S. Patent and Trademark Office (Not admitted in District of Columbia). *Education:* University of Scranton (B.S., 1992); Georgia Institute of Technology (M.S., 1994); Franklin Pierce Law Center (J.D., 2000). ***PRACTICE AREAS:*** Intellectual Property; Patents; Trademarks. ***Email:*** dcawley@pepperlaw.com

SCOTT E. FIREISON, born Chicago, IL, 1967; admitted to bar, 1996, Maryland; 1999, District of Columbia. *Education:* University of Maryland (B.S., 1992); George Washington University (J.D., 1996). Certified Public Accountant, Maryland, 1994. ***PRACTICE AREAS:*** Real Estate; Finance; Affordable Housing. ***Email:*** fireisons@pepperlaw.com

KENING LI, born Jiangsu, China, 1963; admitted to bar, 1998, Wisconsin and California; registered to practice before U.S. Patent and Trademark Office (Not admitted in District of Columbia). *Education:* Nanjing University, China (B.S., 1983; M.S., 1986); University of Wisconsin-Madison (Ph.D., 1995; J.D., 1998). ***PRACTICE AREAS:*** Intellectual Property. ***Email:*** lik@pepperlaw.com

O'KELLY E. McWILLIAMS, III, born Washington, DC, 1968; admitted to bar, 1993, Virginia; 1994, Maryland; 1995, District of Columbia. *Education:* Longwood College (B.S.B.A., 1990); George Mason University (J.D., 1993). Law Clerk to Hon. Gerald Bruce Lee, Fairfax County (Virginia) Circuit Court, 1993-1995. *Member:* Virginia State Bar (President, Young Lawyers Conference, 2001—). (Also at Tysons Corner, Virginia Office). ***PRACTICE AREAS:*** Labor and Employment; Business Litigation; Commercial Litigation. ***Email:*** mcwilliamso@pepperlaw.com

HYUN S. OH, born Seoul, Korea, 1970; admitted to bar, 1998, Maryland, Massachusetts, New York (Not admitted in District of Columbia). *Education:* University of North Carolina (B.A., 1993); Emory University School of Law (J.D., 1997). Law Clerk to Hon. Susan Maze-Rothstein, Massachusetts Court of Appeals, 1996. ***PRACTICE AREAS:*** Intellectual Property. ***Email:*** ohh@pepperlaw.com

JAMES R. PECK, born Palm Springs, CA, 1964; admitted to bar, 2000, Virginia (Not admitted in District of Columbia). *Education:* University of California at Riverside (B.A., 1989); Wheaton College (M.A., 1993); University of California at Los Angeles (M.A., 1995; C.Phil., 1996); College of William and Mary (J.D., 2000). Editor, William and Mary Bill of Rights Journal. ***PRACTICE AREAS:*** Mortgage Finance; Real Estate; Housing Law. ***Email:*** peckj@pepperlaw.com

(This Listing Continued)

CORINNE M. POULIQUEN, born Paris, France, 1965; admitted to bar, 1993, Virginia; 1994, Maryland; 1995, District of Columbia; registered to practice before U.S. Patent and Trademark Office. *Education:* University of Maryland (B.S., 1988); Franklin Pierce Law Center (J.D., 1992). ***LANGUAGES:*** French. ***PRACTICE AREAS:*** Patents; Intellectual Property. ***Email:*** pouliquenc@pepperlaw.com

ELIZABETH D. RODRIGUEZ, born Bridgeport, CT, 1967; admitted to bar, 1994, Maryland; 1995, District of Columbia. *Education:* Yale University (B.A., cum laude, 1989); University of Michigan (J.D., 1993; M.P.P., 1993). ***LANGUAGES:*** Spanish. ***PRACTICE AREAS:*** Intellectual Property; Corporate Law; Securities. ***Email:*** rodrigueze@pepperlaw.com

DAWN M. SIMS, born Baltimore, MD, 1970; admitted to bar, 1996, Maryland; registered to practice before U.S. Patent and Trademark Office (Not admitted in District of Columbia). *Education:* Howard University (B.S.E.E., 1992; J.D., 1996). ***PRACTICE AREAS:*** Intellectual Property; Patents. ***Email:*** simsd@pepperlaw.com

JEFFREY S. TIBBALS, born Dallas, TX, 1973; admitted to bar, 1999, Maryland; 2000, Virginia; 2001, District of Columbia. *Education:* Washington and Lee University (B.A., 1995); Tulane University (J.D., cum laude, 1999). ***LANGUAGES:*** French. ***PRACTICE AREAS:*** Commercial Litigation. ***Email:*** tibbalsj@pepperlaw.com

EDNA VASSILOVSKI, born Boston, MA, 1965; admitted to bar, 1995, Maryland; 1996, District of Columbia; registered to practice before U.S. Patent and Trademark Office. *Education:* Stanford University (B.S., with distinction, 1988); Harvard University (A.M., 1990); Columbia University (J.D., 1995). Phi Beta Kappa. Member, Columbia Journal of Gender and Law. ***LANGUAGES:*** Hebrew. ***PRACTICE AREAS:*** Intellectual Property; Chemical Patents; Patent Prosecution. ***Email:*** vassilovskie@pepperlaw.com

RACHEL H. WILSON, born Pullman, WA, 1971; admitted to bar, 1998, Connecticut; 2000, Maryland (Not admitted in District of Columbia). *Education:* Hampton University (B.A., with high honors, 1992); University of Virginia (J.D., 1996). ***Email:*** wilsonr@pepperlaw.com

---

JOHN PERAZICH

Established in 1973

1701 Q STREET, N.W.
WASHINGTON, D.C. 20009-2455
Telephone: 202-986-7500
Facsimile: 202-986-2386
URL: http://www.lawyers.com/perazichlaw

General Civil and Criminal Litigation Practice before Federal and State Courts. Family Law.

FIRM PROFILE: The firm represents individuals and small to medium-sized corporations seeking counsel in criminal, domestic and civil litigation matters. The firm also represents, banks with bankruptcy and/or foreclosure issues and business entities in complex commercial litigation throughout the District of Columbia and Maryland.

JOHN PERAZICH, born Buffalo, New York, March 20, 1941; admitted to bar, 1967, District of Columbia; 1969, U.S. Supreme Court; 1982, Maryland. *Education:* Oberlin College (A.B., 1963); George Washington University School of Law (J.D., 1967); Georgetown University Law Center (LL.M., 1969). Certificate For Proficiency in Trial Advocacy, 1969 and Recipient, E. Barrett Prettyman Fellowship, Georgetown University Law Center, 1967-1969. Staff Attorney and Chief, Superior Court Division, 1969-1973 and Member, Board of Trustees, 1984-1990, Public Defender Service. Assistant Professorial Lecturer, George Washington University School of Law, 1971-1974. Lecturer, Domestic Relations Bar Review Institute, 1978-1984. Faculty Member: National Institute for Trial Advocacy, 1978, 1987; Harvard Law School Trial Advocacy Workshop, 1989-1994. Member, Judicial Nomination Commission, 1996—. *Member:* The District of Columbia Bar.

PERKINS COIE LLP

607 FOURTEENTH STREET, N.W.
WASHINGTON, D.C. 20005
Telephone: 202-628-6600
Facsimile: 202-434-1690
Email: perkins@perkinscoie.com
URL: http://www.perkinscoie.com

REVISERS OF THE WASHINGTON LAW DIGEST FOR THIS DIRECTORY

Anchorage, Alaska Office: 1029 West Third Avenue, Suite 300, 99501-1981. Telephone: 907-279-8561. Facsimile: 907-276-3108.

Menlo Park, California Office: 101 Jefferson Drive, 94025-1114. Telephone: 650-838-4300. Facsimile: 650-838-4350.

(This Listing Continued)

PERKINS COIE LLP, Washington—Continued

San Francisco, California Office: 180 Townsend Street, 3rd Floor, 94107-1909. Telephone: 415-344-7000. Facsimile: 415-344-7050.
Santa Monica, California Office: 1620 26th Street, Sixth Floor, 90404. Telephone: 310-788-9900. Facsimile: 310-788-3399.
Denver, Colorado Office: 1899 Wynkoop, Suite 700, 80202-1043. Telephone: 303-291-2300. Facsimile: 303-291-2400.
Boise, Idaho Office: 251 East Front Street, Suite 400, 83702-7310. Telephone: 208-343-3434. Facsimile: 208-343-3232.
Portland, Oregon Office: 1211 Southwest Fifth Avenue, Suite 1500, 97204-3715. Telephone: 503-727-2000. Facsimile: 503-727-2222.
Bellevue, Washington Office: One Bellevue Center, Suite 1800, 411 - 108th Avenue N.E., 98004-5584. Telephone: 425-453-6980. Facsimile: 425-453-7350.
Olympia, Washington Office: 1110 Capitol Way South, Suite 405, 98501-2251. Telephone: 360-956-3300. Facsimile: 360-956-1208.
Seattle, Washington Office: 1201 Third Avenue, Suite 4800, 98101-3099. Telephone: 206-583-8888. Facsimile: 206-583-8500.
Spokane, Washington Office: North 221 Wall Street, Suite 600, 99201-0826. Telephone: 509-624-2212. Facsimile: 509-458-3399.
Beijing, R.O.C. Office: 1018, Tower 2, China World Trade Center, 1 Jianguomenwai Avenue. 100004. Telephone: 86 10 6505-6399. Facsimile: 86 10 6505-6390.
Hong Kong Office: 17/F, Standard Charter Bank Building, 4 Des Voeux Road Central. Telephone: 852-2878-1177. Facsimile: 852-2524-9988.

Trial and Appellate Practice, Congressional and Administrative Representation, Government Ethics, Election, Campaign Finance and Lobbying Law, International Trade Law, Aircraft Finance and Leasing, Non-Profit Tax Law, Electronic Commerce, Telecommunications Law, Securities Law, Antitrust, Government Contracts, Environmental, Energy and Natural Resources, International Commercial Transactions, White Collar Crime, Employment Law, Product Liability and Intellectual Property Law.

FIRM PROFILE: Perkins Coie-DC is home to Washington's most connected legal experts in the city. Renowned for its integrated legal, government relations and litigation strategies, we help clients navigate antitrust, communications, energy, environmental, finance, high tech, international trade, natural resource, and political issues. Clients include Fortune 500 companies, members of Congress, multinational corporations, associations and nonprofits and federal, state and local governments and cities.

PARTNERS

ROBERT F. BAUER, born New York, N.Y., February 22, 1952; admitted to bar, 1976, Pennsylvania; 1977, District of Columbia. *Education:* Harvard University (B.A., magna cum laude, 1973); University of Virginia (J.D., 1976). Author: "Paying the Political Price: A Practical Guide to Changes in the Federal Lobbying, Ethics and Campaign Laws," (1996). ***PRACTICE AREAS:*** Federal Election Law; Government Ethics; White Collar Criminal Law.

DONALD C. BAUR, born Meriden, Connecticut, October 31, 1954; admitted to bar, 1979, Pennsylvania; 1985, District of Columbia. *Education:* Trinity College (B.A., with highest honors, 1976); University of Pennsylvania (J.D., 1979). General Counsel, U.S. Marine Mammal Commission, 1984-1987. Attorney, Office of the Solicitor, U.S. Department of the Interior, 1979-1984. ***PRACTICE AREAS:*** Environmental Law; Litigation.

ALLEN CANNON III, born Portsmouth, Virginia, August 19, 1952; admitted to bar, 1987, Pennsylvania; 1988, District of Columbia. *Education:* Old Dominion University (B.A., 1973); University of Arizona (M.A., 1976); Georgetown University (J.D., 1987). National Slavic Honor Society. Graduate Teaching Fellow. Author: "Recovering the Costs of DOL Wage Increases Under the Service Contract Act," Hofstra Labor & Employment Law Journal, Vol. 14, No. 2, May 1998. ***LANGUAGES:*** Russian. ***PRACTICE AREAS:*** Government Contracts; Litigation. ***Email:*** canna@perkinscoie.com

RICHARD B. CLIFFORD, JR., born Paterson, New Jersey, September 23, 1965; admitted to bar, 1990, Maryland; 1991, District of Columbia. *Education:* Franklin & Marshall College (B.A., Economics, 1987); George Washington University (J.D., 1990). Omicron Delta Epsilon; Phi Alpha Theta. Lecturer, George Washington Law School, 1996—. ***PRACTICE AREAS:*** Government Contracts; Litigation; International Law. ***Email:*** clifr@perkinscoie.com

JUDITH L. CORLEY, born Columbia, Missouri, August 14, 1952; admitted to bar, 1985, Maryland; 1986, District of Columbia. *Education:* University of Leningrad; University of Haute Bretagne, Rennes, France; University of Washington (B.A., 1974); George Washington University (J.D., with honors, 1985). ***PRACTICE AREAS:*** Federal and State Election Law; Government Ethics; Non Profit Corporations; Congressional Investigations.

LEE P. CURTIS, born Wilkinsburg, Pennsylvania, April 8, 1953; admitted to bar, 1978, Pennsylvania; 1988, District of Columbia. *Education:* Pennsylvania State University (B.A., 1975); University of Pittsburgh (J.D., 1978). Member, Office of General Counsel, Department of the Navy, 1978-1986. ***PRACTICE AREAS:*** Government Contract Law; Commercial Law and Litigation. ***Email:*** curtl@perkinscoie.com

JOHN M. DEVANEY, born New Rochelle, New York, July 28, 1957; admitted to bar, 1983, District of Columbia. *Education:* Boston College (B.A., magna cum laude, 1979); Catholic University of America (J.D., 1983). Note Editor, Catholic University Law Review, 1982-1983. Judicial Clerk, District of Columbia Court of Appeals, 1983-1984. Trial Attorney, U.S. Department of Justice, Civil Rights Division, 1984-1988. ***PRACTICE AREAS:*** Commercial Litigation; Telecommunications Law; Employment Litigation; Environmental Insurance Coverage.

JEFFREY N. EISENSTEIN, born Brooklyn, New York, July 24, 1948; admitted to bar, 1975, Massachusetts; 1988, California; U.S. District Court, Central District of California; U.S. Court of Federal Claims; U.S. Court of Appeals for the Federal Circuit (Not admitted in District of Columbia). *Education:* Cornell University (B.S., 1969); Suffolk University (J.D., 1975). ***PRACTICE AREAS:*** Government Contracts Law. ***Email:*** eisej@perkinscoie.com

DONALD J. FRIEDMAN, born Chicago, Illinois, July 24, 1945; admitted to bar, 1973, Oregon; 1988, District of Columbia. *Education:* Harvard University (A.B., magna cum laude, 1967); Yale University (J.D., 1973). Editor, Yale Law Journal. Law Clerk to Hon. Alfred T. Goodwin, Ninth Circuit, 1973-1974. [Lt., U.S. Navy, 1967-1970]. ***PRACTICE AREAS:*** Computer Law; Civil Litigation; Commercial Arbitration; Telecommunications Law.

MARY ROSE HUGHES, born Cleveland, Ohio, November 2, 1950; admitted to bar, 1979, Washington; 1985, District of Columbia. *Education:* Georgetown University (B.S., summa cum laude, 1973); Catholic University (J.D., 1979). Member, Catholic University Law Review. Deputy Assistant Secretary of State for Environment, Health and Natural Resources, U.S. Department of State, 1982-1984. ***PRACTICE AREAS:*** Product Liability Litigation; General Civil Litigation.

GUY R. MARTIN, born Denver, Colorado, April 25, 1942; admitted to bar, 1967, Colorado; 1968, Alaska; 1971, District of Columbia. *Education:* University of Colorado (B.A., 1964; J.D., 1967). Commissioner, Natural Resources, State of Alaska, 1975-1977. Assistant Secretary of the Interior for Land and Water Resources, 1977-1981. ***PRACTICE AREAS:*** Natural Resource Law; Public Lands Law; Environmental Law; Energy Law; Federal Legislative Practice; Indian Law.

BARRY J. REINGOLD, born New York, N.Y., May 29, 1951; admitted to bar, 1977, District of Columbia. *Education:* Amherst College (B.A., 1973); George Washington University (J.D., with honors, 1977). Assistant to the Director, Bureau of Competition, Federal Trade Commission, 1979-1980. ***PRACTICE AREAS:*** Civil Litigation; Antitrust and Consumer Protection Litigation; Litigation; Federal Trade Commission; Internet Law.

KARA M. SACILOTTO, born Washington, D.C., April 17, 1964; admitted to bar, 1990, Virginia; 1991, District of Columbia. *Education:* University of Virginia (B.A., with distinction, 1986; J.D., 1990). ***PRACTICE AREAS:*** Telecommunications Law; Civil Litigation; Commercial Litigation. ***Email:*** sacik@perkinscoie.com

YOSHIHIRO SAITO, born Takamatsu, Japan, February 7, 1941; admitted to bar, 1981, District of Columbia; 1983, U.S. Court of International Trade; 1993, U.S. Court of Appeals for the Federal Circuit. *Education:* International Christian University, Tokyo, Japan (B.A., 1963); Washington College of Law, American University (J.D., 1980). ***LANGUAGES:*** Japanese. ***PRACTICE AREAS:*** International Trade; International Business Law; Import and Export Law.

BENJAMIN S. SHARP, born Bridgeton, New Jersey, September 14, 1944; admitted to bar, 1973, Pennsylvania; 1974, District of Columbia. *Education:* Lafayette College (B.A., 1966); Dickinson Law School (J.D., magna cum laude, 1973). Editor-in-Chief, Dickinson Law Review. Law Clerk to Justice Harry A. Blackmun, U.S. Supreme Court, 1973-1974. Assistant Director, Deputy Director and Acting Director, Bureau of Competition, Federal Trade Commission, 1978-1982. ***PRACTICE AREAS:*** Antitrust Law; Civil Litigation; Federal Criminal Law; Federal Trade Commission.

THOMAS V. VAKERICS, born Lorain, Ohio, March 26, 1944; admitted to bar, 1968, District of Columbia; U.S. Court of International Trade. *Education:* Bowling Green State University (B.A., 1965); George Washington University Law School (J.D., 1968). Author: "Antitrust Basics," Law Journal Seminars-Press, 1985. Co-Author: "Antidumping, Countervailing Duty and Other Trade Actions," Practising Law Institute, 1987. Trial Attorney, Bureau of Competition, Federal Trade Commission, 1969-1973. ***PRACTICE AREAS:*** Antitrust Law; International Trade Law.

MARTIN P. WILLARD, born Louisville, Kentucky, August 16, 1955; admitted to bar, 1987, Virginia; 1991, District of Columbia. *Education:* Georgetown University (A.B., 1977); Johns Hopkins University (Ph.D., 1984); University of Virginia (J.D., 1987). ***PRACTICE AREAS:*** Government Contract Law; Commercial Litigation.

(This Listing Continued)

JEFFREY A. WOOL, born New York, N.Y., April 6, 1963; admitted to bar, 1988, Washington (Not admitted in District of Columbia). *Education:* Florida State University (B.A., summa cum laude, 1985); Columbia University (J.D., 1988). Consultant to Unidroit's aircraft finance matters. Counsel to Aerospace Industry group at work on international commercial law reform, 1994—. ***PRACTICE AREAS:*** International Commercial Law; International Business Law; Financial Transactions; Aircraft Finance; Project Finance. ***Email:*** woolj@perkinscoie.com

OF COUNSEL

MARGOT F. BESTER, born Buffalo, New York, May 7, 1954; admitted to bar, 1979, District of Columbia. *Education:* State University of New York at Binghamton (B.A., with highest honors, 1976); Albany Law School of Union University; Washington College of Law, American University (J.D., 1979). Listed in Who's Who of American Women, 1997-1998. ***PRACTICE AREAS:*** Telecommunications Law; Electronic Commerce; Wireless Communications; Electronic Surveillance; Information and Privacy. ***Email:*** bestm@perkinscoie.com

WILFORD H. "BUZZ" FAWCETT, born New Orleans, Louisiana, July 19, 1953; admitted to bar, 1980, Idaho; 1987, California; 1998, District of Columbia. *Education:* University of Southern California (B.A., 1976); Southwestern University School of Law (J.D., 1979). Office of U.S. Senator Dirk Kempthorne, Washington, D.C., Legislative Director and Counsel, 1993-1998. City of Boise, Idaho, City Attorney, 1985-1993. (Also at Boise, Idaho Office). ***PRACTICE AREAS:*** Government; Environmental Law; Natural Resources; Endangered Species; Water Rights; Mining Law; Electronic Commerce; Technology Law.

CASSANDRA F. LENTCHNER, born N.Y., N.Y., May 27, 1964; admitted to bar, 1989, New Jersey; 1990, New York (Not admitted in District of Columbia). *Education:* Rutgers College at New Brunswick (B.A., 1986); Rutgers University of Law at Newark (J.D., 1989). Order of the Coif. ***PRACTICE AREAS:*** White Collar Criminal; Political Law; Congressional Investigation; Securities. ***Email:*** lentc@perkinscoie.com

HELEN P. STARR, born Washington, D.C., February 16, 1947; admitted to bar, 1979, District of Columbia; 1988, Maryland. *Education:* Chatham College (B.A., 1969); Georgetown University Law Center (J.D., 1979). Editor, The Tax Lawyer. ***PRACTICE AREAS:*** Corporate Law; Executive Compensation; Nonprofit Associations; Mergers and Acquisitions.

ELLEN L. WEINTRAUB, born Queens, New York, June 9, 1957; admitted to bar, 1985, New York; 1987, District of Columbia. *Education:* Yale College (B.A., cum laude, 1978); Harvard Law School (J.D., 1984). Editor in Chief, *House Ethics Manual,* 102d Congress, 2d Session (1992). ***PRACTICE AREAS:*** Government Ethics; Lobbying Regulation; Election and Campaign Finance; Congressional Investigations.

LIS WIEHL, born Seattle, Washington, August 19, 1961; admitted to bar, 1987, Washington; 1990, U.S. Court of Appeals, Ninth Circuit and U.S. District Court, Western District of Washington (Not admitted in District of Columbia). *Education:* Barnard College (B.A., summa cum laude, 1983); University of Queensland, Australia (M.A., 1985); Harvard University (J.D., 1987). Editor, Harvard Journal on Legislation. Principal Deputy, Chief Minority Investigative Counsel, U.S. House of Representatives, Committee on the Judiciary, William Jefferson Clinton Impeachment Inquiry, Washington, D.C., 1998-1999. Professor of Law and Director of the Trial Advocacy Program, 1995—. Assistant U.S. Attorney, 1990-1995, Executive Assistant, U.S. Attorney, 1998, United States Attorney's Office, Seattle, Washington. (Also at Seattle, Washington Office). ***LANGUAGES:*** Danish and Swedish. ***PRACTICE AREAS:*** Complex Litigation; Criminal Law; Ethics; Corporate Compliance. ***Email:*** wiehl@perkinscoie.com

SLOANE ANDERS WILDMAN, born New York, New York, August 1, 1965; admitted to bar, 1991, California; 1992, District of Columbia. *Education:* Dartmouth College (A.B., cum laude, 1987); University of Virginia (J.D., 1991). Notes Editor, Virginia Tax Review. ***PRACTICE AREAS:*** Environmental Law. ***Email:*** wilds@perkinscoie.com

RESIDENT ASSOCIATES

KELLY A. CAMERON, born Fullerton, California, October 26, 1967; admitted to bar, 1995, Maryland; 1998, District of Columbia. *Education:* Brigham Young University (B.A., 1992); Washington & Lee University (J.D., 1995). ***PRACTICE AREAS:*** Litigation; Telecommunications Law. ***Email:*** camek@perkinscoie.com

DONALD J. CARNEY, born Bronxville, New York, December 3, 1963; admitted to bar, 1996, Pennsylvania; 1999, District of Columbia. *Education:* George Washington University (B.A., International Affairs, 1985); Defense Intelligence College (M.S., 1991); Georgetown University Law Center (J.D., 1996). [Lt. Comr., U.S. Navy Reserve, 1986-1995]. ***PRACTICE AREAS:*** Government Contracts; Commercial Litigation. ***Email:*** carnd@perkinscoie.com

(This Listing Continued)

ALYSSA CHUMNANVECH, born Minnesota, May 8, 1970; admitted to bar, 1996, Maryland; 1997, District of Columbia. *Education:* Bucknell University (B.A., 1992); George Washington University (M.B.A., 1996; J.D., 1996). ***PRACTICE AREAS:*** International Trade. ***Email:*** chuma@perkinscoie.com

JOHN F. CLARK, born Salt Lake City, Utah, June 22, 1948; admitted to bar, 1974, Utah (Not admitted in District of Columbia). *Education:* Yale University (B.A., 1970); University of Utah (J.D., 1974); Harvard University John F. Kennedy School of Government (M.P.A., 1996). Co-Author, Article with S. Hultberg, "Historic Preservation and Communications," Telecom Land Manager Law Report, Vol. 2, Nos. 5 and 6 Pike and Fisher, Inc., March-April 2000. Counsel to Utah Attorney General, 1989-1994. Department Division Chief, Federal Communications Commission, 1996-2000. *Member:* The Association of Trial Lawyers of America. ***LANGUAGES:*** Russian. ***PRACTICE AREAS:*** Telecommunications Licensing; Environmental Regulation; Telecommunications Contracts; Digital Communications; Environmental Litigation. ***Email:*** clarq@perkinscoie.com

JAMES F. COBB, JR., born Dallas, Texas, December 30, 1971; admitted to bar, 1999, Utah (Not admitted in District of Columbia). *Education:* Brigham Young University (B.A., Economics, 1996); George Washington University (J.D., with honors, 1999). Managing Editor, George Washington Journal of International Law and Economics. *Member:* Utah State Bar; American Bar Association. ***PRACTICE AREAS:*** Commercial Litigation; Telecommunications. ***Email:*** cobbj@perkinscoie.com

SUZETTE W. DERREVERE, born Panorama City, California, February 13, 1970; admitted to bar, 1998, New York; 1999, District of Columbia. *Education:* Smith College (B.A., 1992); Cornell University (J.D., 1997). ***PRACTICE AREAS:*** Government Contracts; Construction Litigation. ***Email:*** derrs@perkinscoie.com

MARC E. ELIAS, born New York, N.Y., February 1, 1969; admitted to bar, 1993, Pennsylvania; 1994, District of Columbia. *Education:* Hamilton College (A.B., 1990); Duke University (M.A., 1993; J.D., with honors, 1993). ***PRACTICE AREAS:*** White Collar Criminal Defense; Election and Campaign Finance; Election Law; Administrative Litigation.

REBECCA H. GORDON, born Farmington, Maine, June 15, 1975; admitted to bar, 2001, Virginia (Not admitted in District of Columbia). *Education:* College of William & Mary (B.A., 1997); George Washington University (J.D., with honors, 2001). ***PRACTICE AREAS:*** Political Law. ***Email:*** gordr@perkinscoie.com

JUNHEE KIM, born 1966; admitted to bar, 2000, District of Columbia; 2001, U.S. Court of International Trade and U.S. Court of Appeals, Federal Circuit. *Education:* Georgetown University (B.S.F.S., 1989); University of Pennsylvania (M.A., 1991); Georgetown University Law Center (J.D., 2000). [1st Lt., R.O.K. Army, 1992-1995]. ***LANGUAGES:*** Korean. ***PRACTICE AREAS:*** International Trade; Telecommunications; Litigation. ***Email:*** kimju@perkinscoie.com

JENNIFER ALLISON MacLEAN, born Oberlin, Ohio, July 31, 1971; admitted to bar, 2001, Virginia and District of Columbia. *Education:* Princeton University (A.B., 1993); University of Virginia (J.D., 2001). ***Email:*** maclj@perkinscoie.com

LALITHA MANI, born Chennai Tamil Nadu, India, December 7, 1950; admitted to bar, 1986, Ohio; 2000, Washington (Not admitted in District of Columbia). *Education:* Bangalore University (B.A., 1970; M.A., 1972); University of Pennsylvania (M.A., 1976); Case Western Reserve University (J.D., 1986). ***LANGUAGES:*** Tamil, Hindi, Kannada, Malayalam. ***PRACTICE AREAS:*** Intellectual Property; Trademarks; Copyrights. ***Email:*** manil@perkinscoie.com

JASON C. RYLANDER, born Bronxville, New York, September 28, 1971; admitted to bar, 2000, Virginia (Not admitted in District of Columbia). *Education:* Cornell University (B.A., cum laude, 1993); College of William & Mary (J.D., 2000). Order of Barristers. Member, Moot Court. Editor, William & Mary Law Review, 1999-2000. Author: "The Emerging Federal Role in Growth Management," 15 J. Land Use & Envtl. L. 277 (2000); "Accounting for Nature," 14 Renewable Resources Journal 8 (Fall 1996). Member, Society of Environmental Journalists, 1994-1998. *Member:* Virginia State Bar. ***PRACTICE AREAS:*** Campaign Ethics; Business Law; White Collar Crime; Natural Resources; Environmental Law. ***Email:*** rylaj@perkinscoie.com

ODIN A. SMITH, born Agua Prieta, Sonora, Mexico, August 11, 1973; (admission pending). *Education:* University of Arizona (B.S., Geosciences, summa cum laude, 1995); Massachusetts Institute of Technology (S.M., Geology, 1999) George Washington University (J.D., magna cum laude, 2001). ***LANGUAGES:*** Spanish. ***PRACTICE AREAS:*** Litigation; Environmental Law; Natural Resources. ***Email:*** smit1@perkinscoie.com

BRIAN G. SVOBODA, born Lincoln, Nebraska, May 26, 1967; admitted to bar, 1994, Pennsylvania; 1996, District of Columbia. *Education:* University of Nebraska (B.A., with distinction, 1989); University of Virginia (J.D., 1993). Phi Beta Kappa. ***PRACTICE AREAS:*** Election Law; Administrative Law; Litigation. ***Email:*** svobb@perkinscoie.com

(This Listing Continued)

PERKINS COIE LLP, Washington—Continued

MARK T. WASDEN, born Colorado Springs, Colorado, August 6, 1966; admitted to bar, 1993, Maryland; 1994, District of Columbia, U.S. Court of International Trade and U.S. Court of Appeals for the Federal Circuit. *Education:* Brigham Young University (B.A., 1990); George Washington University (J.D., 1993). ***LANGUAGES:*** Japanese. ***PRACTICE AREAS:*** International Trade.

W. HARTMANN YOUNG, born Richmond, Virginia, December 10, 1967; admitted to bar, 1996, Texas; 1999, District of Columbia. *Education:* College of William & Mary (B.A., International Relations, 1990); George Mason University School of Law (J.D., 1996). Member, George Mason Law Review. ***PRACTICE AREAS:*** Government Contracts; Litigation. ***Email:*** younw@perkinscoie.com

REPRESENTATIVE CLIENTS: Amazon.com; American Hospital Association; American Petroleum Institute; Bay Delta Urban Coalition; The Boeing Co.; BP Exploration (Alaska) Inc.; Calpine Corp.; Compliance Management Policy Group; Delta Wetland Project; Democratic Congressional Campaign Committee; Democratic Leadership Council; Democratic Senatorial Campaign Committee; The Doe Run Mining Company; East Bay Municipal Utility District; Emily's List; Fort James Corp.; FPL Energy, Inc.; Geothermal Energy Assoc.; Huntsman Corp.; Investment Company Institute; Louisiana-Pacific Corp.; Mars Inc.; MediaOne Group, Inc.; The Metropolitan Water District of Southern California; Mid-American Energy Holdings; National Association of Homebuilders; Outokumpu Copper Strip BV; Oxbow Power Services Inc.; Puget Sound Energy, Inc.; Qwest; 13th Regional Corp. (Alaska); SSAB Svenskt Stål AB; Start Technologies, Inc.; Towers Perrin; Walt Disney Co.; Western Urban Water Coalition; Weyerhaeuser Company; Yahoo!.

REVISERS OF THE WASHINGTON LAW DIGEST FOR THIS DIRECTORY

(For biographical data on other Perkins Coie personnel, see Professional Biographies for those offices)

PERKINS, SMITH, COHEN & CROWE, LLP

1001 PENNSYLVANIA AVENUE, N.W., SUITE 450N
WASHINGTON, D.C. 20004
Telephone: 202-789-8787
Fax: 202-789-4242
Email: dcoffice@pscboston.com
URL: http://www.pscboston.com

Boston, Massachusetts Office: Perkins, Smith & Cohen, LLP, One Beacon Street, 02108. Telephone: 617-854-4000. Fax: 617-854-4040. E-Mail: psc@pscboston.com.

Providence, Rhode Island Office: Tillinghast Licht Perkins Smith & Cohen, LLP, Ten Weybosset Street, 02903. Telephone: 401-456-1200. Fax: 401-456-1210. Email: tlsprov@tlslaw.com.

General Practice, Litigation (All Courts and Agencies), Antitrust, Banking and Finance, Bankruptcy, Biotechnology, Commercial, Computer Law, Copyright, Corporate, Criminal Defense, Domestic Relations, Employment Law, Entertainment, Environmental, Estate Planning, Exempt Organizations, Government Contracts (Federal and State), Government Relations, Immigration, Insurance, Intellectual Property, International Business, Investor Fraud, Patent, Probate, Publishing, Real Estate, Scientific Misconduct, Securities, Taxation, Technology, Telecommunications and Electronic Commerce, Trademark, Trusts and Estates.

PARTNER

ROBERT B. CROWE, (P.C.), born Springfield, Massachusetts, March 24, 1947; admitted to bar, 1973, Massachusetts; 1997, District of Columbia. *Education:* Boston College High School; Fairfield University; Suffolk University (J.D., 1973); Boston University (LL.M., 1979). Chairman, The Commonwealth Group. Trustee, Suffolk University, 1987—. Assistant District Attorney, Norfolk County, 1973-1974. Member, Panel of Arbitrators, American Arbitration Association. *Member:* Boston, Massachusetts and American Bar Associations. ***PRACTICE AREAS:*** Business Law; Corporate; Tax; Real Estate; Government Relations. ***Email:*** Robert_Crowe@pscboston.com

OF COUNSEL

HARVEY KAYE, born Brooklyn, New York, October 19, 1934; admitted to bar, 1960, Virginia; 1961, District of Columbia; 1964, U.S. Supreme Court; 1990, Maryland; registered to practice before U.S. Patent and Trademark Office. *Education:* Lowell Technological Institute (B.S.T.E., 1956); George Washington University (J.D., 1960). Co-Author: *International Trade Practice,* 2 volumes, 1997, with annual supplements, West Group. Patent, Trademark & Copyright Journal, BNA, member of advisory board, 1975-1989. *Member:* American Bar Association; American Intellectual Property Law Association; International Trade Commission Trial Lawyers Association. (Resident). ***PRACTICE AREAS:*** Intellectual Property Law; Litigation; International Law. ***Email:*** Harvey_Kaye@pscboston.com

CHARLES D. ABLARD, born Enid, Oklahoma, 1930; admitted to bar, 1954, Oklahoma; 1958, U.S. Supreme Court; 1959, District of Columbia; 1960, U.S. Court of Federal Claims. *Education:* University of Oklahoma (B.A., 1952; J.D., 1954); George Washington University (LL.M., 1959). Associate Deputy Attorney General, Department of Justice, 1972-1974. General Counsel, U.S. Information Agency, 1969-1972. Arbitrator, American Arbitration Association, 1962—. *Member:* District of Columbia Bar; American Bar Association. (Resident). ***PRACTICE AREAS:*** Administrative Law; Government Contracts Law; Arbitration Law; Mediation Law. ***Email:*** Charles_Ablard@pscboston.com

(For complete biographical data on all personnel, see Professional Biographies at Boston, Massachusetts)

JOSÉ PERTIERRA

Established in 1988
1010 VERMONT AVENUE, N.W.
SUITE 620
WASHINGTON, D.C. 20005
Telephone: 202-783-6666
FAX: 202-347-1925
Email: josepertierra@aol.com
URL: http://www.lawyers.com/pertierra

Immigration Law, Civil Litigation, International Human Rights Law. Business Visas, Business Immigration.

JOSÉ PERTIERRA, born Habana, Cuba, October 23, 1951; admitted to bar, 1984, District of Columbia. *Education:* Loyola University of Los Angeles (B.A., 1975); Georgetown University (M.A., 1978); George Washington University (J.D., 1984). Graduate Fellowship, Georgetown University, 1975-1979. American Immigration Lawyers Association 1996 Human Rights Award Winner. Recipient: Humanitarian Award from MAPAVI Foundation, 1998; Hispanic Democratic Club of Montgomery County, Maryland Law and Justice Award, 1999. Talk Show Host, Nationally Syndicated Immigration Radio Program, "Bienvenidos America". *Member:* District of Columbia Bar; American Immigration Lawyers Association. ***LANGUAGES:*** Spanish.

PETRILLO & POWELL, P.L.L.C.

Established in 1988
1101 15TH STREET, N.W., SUITE 605
WASHINGTON, D.C. 20005-2207
Telephone: 202-887-4848
Fax: 202-887-1121
URL: http://www.petrillopowell.com

Administrative, Litigation and Legislative Practice including Government Contracts, International Trade and Information Law.

FIRM PROFILE: Petrillo & Powell, P.L.L.C. concentrates its practice in the area of Federal Government contracting. The firm advises and represents clients on all legal aspects of government contracts, including regulatory compliance, solicitation and contract interpretation, bid protests, claims, disputes, appeals, alternative dispute resolution, information disclosure, labor standards, small business programs, data rights, and cost accounting. The firm serves clients from a variety of different industries, with considerable involvement in information processing and healthcare.

JOSEPH J. PETRILLO, born Brooklyn, New York, 1948; admitted to bar, 1973, District of Columbia. *Education:* Georgetown University (B.S.F.S., 1970; J.D., 1973); New York University. Editor, Georgetown Law Journal, 1972-1973. Law Clerk to Judge Oscar H. Davis, U.S. Court of Claims, 1973-1974. Author: "Government Information Systems Procurement," Federal Publications, 1981-1996. Co-Author: "Facing A Fraud Investigation," Federal Publications, 1986; "Government Health Care Contracting," Federal Publications, 1993-1994; "*From Torncello to Krygoski:* 25 Years of the Government's Termination for Convenience Power," 7 Fed. Cir. Bar J. 337 (1997); "Where To File The Protest? Implications of The Expanded Bid Protest Jurisdiction of The Court of Federal Claims," 38 Gov. Contractor 3 (1996). Columnist, "Federal Contract Law," Government Computer News, 1984—. Member, Advisory Board, BNA Federal Contracts Report, 1987—. *Member:* The District of Columbia Bar; The Bar Association of the District of Columbia; Federal (Chairman: Government Contracts Committee, 1987-1990; Government Contracts Section, 1990-1992; Chair, Working Group on District Court Bld. Protest Jurisdiction, 1999-2000) and American (Member, Sections on Public Contract Law and Administrative Law; Associate Editor, Public Contracts Law Journal, 1978-1979; Chairman, Subcommittee on Rules and Court Administration, Claims Court Committee, 1984-1985; Vice Chairman, Information Systems Committee, 1987-1993) Bar Associations; Computer Law Association. ***PRACTICE AREAS:*** Government Contracts; Bid Protests; Federal Contracts; Information Technology Contracts; Health Care; Commercial Litigation. ***Email:*** jp@petrillopowell.com

(This Listing Continued)

KAREN D. POWELL, born Paris, France, 1961; admitted to bar, 1989, Massachusetts; 1991, District of Columbia. *Education:* Trinity College, Dublin; University of California at Santa Cruz (B.A., cum laude, 1983); Fletcher School of Law and Diplomacy; Boston College (J.D., 1989). Author: "Proposed DFARS Revisions on the Treatment of Computer Software: a Partial Success," Contract Management, March 1995. Co-Author: "Defense Department to Boost Health Contracting," Washington Business Journal, August 1998; "Free and Open? Preferences for Domestic Products in International Procurement," Contract Management, June 1991. *Member:* The District of Columbia Bar; American Bar Association (Member, Sections on: Public Contracts; Dispute Resolution; Chair, Government Procurement Committee, 1998-2000); American Society of International Law; Prettyman Leventhall Inn, American Inns of Court. ***LANGUAGES:*** French. ***PRACTICE AREAS:*** Public Contract Law; Alternative Dispute Resolution; International Government Contracts; International Trade; Intellectual Property. ***Email:*** kdplawyer@aol.com

CYRUS E. PHILLIPS, IV

SUITE 660
1828 L STREET, N.W.
WASHINGTON, D.C. 20036-5104
Telephone: 202-466-7008
Fax: 202-822-6665
URL: http://www.procurement-lawyer.com
Email: lawyer@procurement-lawyer.com
URL: http://www.lawyers.com/procurementlawyer

Government Contracts, Federal Contracts, Bid Protests, Government Procurement, Computer Contracts, Computer and Software Law, Information Technology, Contracts, Internet Law, e-Commerce, Federal Procurement, Emerging Business Law.

FIRM PROFILE: Mr. Phillips is a former administrative judge and vice-chairman of the G.S.A. Board of Contract Appeals. His practice represents over 30 years of federal contract and procurement experience.

CYRUS E. PHILLIPS, IV, born Charlottesville, Virginia, October 2, 1944; admitted to bar, 1968, Virginia; 1998, District of Columbia. *Education:* University of Illinois (B.A., with honors, 1966); Marshall-Wythe School of Law, College of William & Mary (J.D., 1968). Research Editor, William & Mary Law Review, 1967-1968. Attorney, Defense Logistics Agency's Defense Construction Supply Center, 1968-1980. Administrative Judge, 1980-1987 and Vice Chairman, 1986-1987, General Services Administration Board of Contract Appeals. ***PRACTICE AREAS:*** Government Contracts; Federal Procurement; Computers and Software; Federal Civil Practice.

PHILLIPS & COHEN LLP

2000 MASSACHUSETTS AVENUE, N.W., 1ST FLOOR
WASHINGTON, D.C. 20036
Telephone: 202-833-4567
Facsimile: 202-833-1815
URL: http://www.phillipsandcohen.com
URL: http://www.whistleblowers.com

San Diego, California Office: 705 12th Avenue. Telephone 619-231-6655. Facsimile: 619-231-9777. Web Site: http://www.whistleblowers.com; http://www.phillipsandcohen.com.
San Francisco, California Office: 131 Steuart Street, Suite 501. Telephone: 415-836-9000. Facsimile: 415-836-9001.

FIRM PROFILE: Phillips & Cohen LLP has the nation's largest and longest standing qui tam (Plaintiff's False Claims Act) practice. John R. Phillips worked with U.S. Senator Charles Grassley and U.S. Rep. Howard Berman from 1984 to 1986 in a successful effort to strengthen and modernize the Act. The firm has a national qui tam practice and works with a network of litigation firms throughout the country. Areas of qui tam litigation include: health care, military and other government procurement, customs, royalty underpayments, financial fraud, bid rigging, environmental cleanup and testing, defective products, electric power sales, water supply systems and transportation and construction projects.

JOHN R. PHILLIPS, born Pennsylvania, December 15, 1942; admitted to bar, 1970, California; 1993, District of Columbia. *Education:* University of Notre Dame (A.B., 1966); Boalt Hall School of Law, University of California (J.D., 1969). Member, Board of Editors, California Law Review, 1968-1969. Speaker, ABA Conference on Health Care Fraud, Defense Contractor Fraud and the False Claims Act. Lawyer Representative, Ninth Circuit Judicial Conference, 1989-1992. Co-founder and Director, Center for Law in the Public Interest, Los Angeles, 1971-1988. Appointee, Commission on White House Fellowships, 1997—. ***PRACTICE AREAS:*** False Claims; Qui Tam. ***Email:*** JPhillips@phillipsandcohen.com

(This Listing Continued)

MARY LOUISE COHEN, born Fayetteville, North Carolina, November 22, 1952; admitted to bar, 1977, Georgia; 1979, District of Columbia; 1989, California. *Education:* University of North Carolina (A.B., 1974); Harvard University (J.D., cum laude, 1977). Phi Beta Kappa. Chief Counsel, Senate Subcommittee on Juvenile Justice, 1983-1984. Counsel, Subcommittee on Antitrust, Monopolies and Business Practices, U.S. Senate Judiciary Committee, 1987-1988. Speaker, ABA Conference on Health Care Fraud, Defense Contractor Fraud and the False Claims Act. ***PRACTICE AREAS:*** False Claims; Qui Tam. ***Email:*** mlc@phillipsandcohen.com

PETER WILSON CHATFIELD, born New Brunswick, New Jersey, October 25, 1961; admitted to bar, 1988, Maryland; 1989, District of Columbia. *Education:* Wesleyan University (B.A., 1983); Yale University (J.D., 1986). Phi Beta Kappa. Editor, Yale Law Journal, 1985-1986. Coker Fellow. Law Clerk to Hon. Alvin B. Rubin, U.S. Court of Appeals, Fifth Circuit, 1986-1987. ***PRACTICE AREAS:*** False Claims Act; Qui Tam Litigation. ***Email:*** peter@phillipsandcohen.com

ERIKA ARMITAGE KELTON, born Los Angeles, California; admitted to bar, 1987, California; 1989, District of Columbia. *Education:* University of California (B.A., 1979); Boalt Hall School of Law (J.D., 1987). Articles Editor, California Law Review. Speaker, ABA Conference on Financial Fraud, Medicare Fraud, Employment Law and the False Claims Act. ***Email:*** ekelton@phillipsandcohen.com

STEPHEN L. MEAGHER, born Louisville, Kentucky, May 12, 1958; admitted to bar, 1985, California. *Education:* Dartmouth College (A.B., magna cum laude, 1980); University of Virginia (J.D., 1983). Member, Editorial and Managing Boards, Virginia Law Review. Law Clerk to Hon. Harrison L. Winter, U.S. Court of Appeals, Fourth Circuit. Speaker, ABA Conference on Health Care Fraud, Qui Tam Litigation and the False Claims Act. Adjunct Faculty, Stanford Law School, 1996-1998. Assistant U.S. Attorney: Civil Division, 1987-1989; Criminal Division, 1989-1994. Founder and Chair, Health Care Fraud Task Force of Northern California, 1993-1994. (Resident, San Francisco Office). ***PRACTICE AREAS:*** False Claims; Qui Tam. ***Email:*** slm@pcsf.com

ERIC R. HAVIAN, born Beverly, Massachusetts, May 3, 1955; admitted to bar, 1981, California. *Education:* Stanford University (B.A., with distinction, 1977) Phi Beta Kappa; Harvard University (J.D., cum laude, 1981). Speaker, ABA Conference on Defense Contractor Fraud, Qui Tam Litigation and the False Claims Act. Adjunct Faculty, Stanford Law School, 1996-1998. Assistant U.S. Attorney, Criminal Division, 1987-1994. Lead Attorney, Defense Procurement Fraud Prosecutions, San Francisco U.S. Attorneys Office, 1988-1994. Member, Common Cause National Governing Board, 1996-1998. Board Member, California Common Cause, 1994—. (Resident, San Francisco Office). ***PRACTICE AREAS:*** False Claims; Qui Tam. ***Email:*** erh@pcsf.com

ASSOCIATES

BONNY HARBINGER, born Fort Dix, New Jersey, August 21, 1951; admitted to bar, 1997, Maryland; 2000, District of Columbia. *Education:* Tel Aviv University (B.A., 1976); United States International University (Ph.D., 1982); Georgetown University Law Center (J.D., 1997). Associate Editor, American Criminal Law Review. [Lt., Israeli Air Force, 1974-1978]. ***LANGUAGES:*** Hebrew. ***PRACTICE AREAS:*** False Claims Act; Qui Tam Litigation. ***Email:*** BHarbinger@phillipsandcohen.com

MARY A. INMAN, born Houlton, Maine, August 29, 1968; admitted to bar, 1995, California; 1996, Maine. *Education:* Bowdoin College (B.A., summa cum laude, 1990); University of Pennsylvania (J.D., cum laude, 1994). Phi Beta Kappa. Associate Editor, 1992-1993 and Articles Editor, 1993-1994, University of Pennsylvania Law Review. Recipient: Benjamin R. Jones Award in Humanity in Law. Author: "CPR Change Through Proportional Representation: Resuscitating A Federal Electoral System," 141 U. PA. L. Rev. 1991 (1993). Law Clerk to: Hon. D. Brock Hornby, U.S. District Court, District of Maine, Portland, ME. (1994-1995); Hon. Norman H. Stahl, First Circuit Court of Appeals, Concord, NH. (1995-1996). *Member:* American Bar Association. (Resident, San Francisco Office). ***LANGUAGES:*** Russian and French. ***PRACTICE AREAS:*** False Claims Act; Qui Tam Litigation. ***Email:*** mai@pcsf.com

OF COUNSEL

GERALD M. STERN, born Chicago, Illinois, April 5, 1937; admitted to bar, 1961, District of Columbia; 1964, U.S. Supreme Court; 1992, California. *Education:* University of Pennsylvania (B.S., 1958); Harvard University (LL.B., cum laude, 1961). Member, Harvard Legal Aid Bureau, 1959-1961. Author: *The Buffalo Creek Disaster-The Story of the Survivors' Unprecedented Lawsuit,"* Random House, 1976; *Southern Justice,* Panthoon, 1965; *Outside the Law, Narratives on Justice,* Beacon Press, 1997. Lecturer, Health Care Fraud and Financial Institution Fraud, Harvard Law School. Associate, 1964-1968 and Partner, 1969-1976, Arnold & Porter. Founding Partner, Rogovin, Stern & Huge, 1976-1981. General Counsel, Executive Vice President, Secretary and Member Board of Directors, Occidental Petroleum Corporation, Los Angeles, California, 1981-1992. Member, Board of Directors, Capital Bancorp, 1996-1997. Special Counsel for Financial Institution on Fraud and Health Care Fraud,

(This Listing Continued)

PHILLIPS & COHEN LLP, Washington—Continued

U.S. Department of Justice, 1993-1995. *Member:* The District of Columbia Bar; State Bar of California; American Bar Association. ***PRACTICE AREAS:*** False Claims Act; Qui Tam Litigation. ***Email:*** GMS37@aol.com

LISA FOSTER, born San Diego, California, July 29, 1957; admitted to bar, 1985, California. *Education:* Stanford University (B.A., 1979); Harvard University (J.D., magna cum laude, 1984). Editor, Harvard Law Review. Law Clerk to Hon. Mariana R. Pfaelzer, U.S. District Court, Central District of California. Adjunct Professor, University of San Diego Law School. Staff Attorney: Center for Law in the Public Interest, 1985-1988; Legal Aid Foundation of Los Angeles, 1988-1990. Executive Director, California Common Cause, 1990-1993. Member, Lawyers' Club of San Diego, 1992. *Member:* San Diego County Bar Association; State Bar of California. (Resident, San Diego Office). ***PRACTICE AREAS:*** False Claims Act; Qui Tam Litigation. ***Email:*** Lfoster@cts.com

(For Complete Biographical Data on all Personnel, See Professional Biographies at San Francisco, California)

PICKARD AND DJINIS LLP

Established in 1978

1990 M STREET, N.W.
WASHINGTON, D.C. 20036
Telephone: 202-223-4418
Telecopier: 202-331-3813
Email: pickdjin@aol.com

Securities, Corporate, Litigation, Arbitration and Banking.

FIRM PROFILE: Pickard and Djinis, founded in 1978, renders legal services to the financial community, primarily broker-dealers, investment advisers, mutual funds and banks in the areas of securities regulation and litigation. Many of the lawyers in the firm were previously affiliated with the Securities and Exchange Commission. The firm represents clients before the SEC, NYSE, NASD and other federal and state government agencies having regulatory authority over the financial services industry.

MEMBERS OF FIRM

LEE A. PICKARD, born Syracuse, New York, November 5, 1938; admitted to bar, 1963, New York; 1965, U.S. District Court, Southern District of New York; 1972, U.S. Supreme Court; 1978, District of Columbia. *Education:* Colgate University (A.B., 1960); Harvard University (LL.D., 1963). Phi Beta Kappa. Adjunct Professor, American University Law School, 1976-1977. Faculty, International Law Institute, 1991—. Special Counsel to Chairman, Securities and Exchange Commission, 1971-1973. Director, Division of Market Regulation, Securities and Exchange Commission, 1973-1977. Member, Advisory Committee on Central Market System, 1974-1975 and Member, National Market Advisory Board, 1975-1976, Securities and Exchange Commission. *Member:* American Bar Association (Member, Subcommittee on Securities, Business Law Section, 1988—; Member, Subcommittees on Securities Activities of Banks and Fiduciaries and on Market Regulation, Committee on Federal Regulation of Securities, 1990—; Member, The Nasdaq Stock Market, Inc., Market Operations Review Committee, 1996—).

ANTHONY W. DJINIS, born Rhinebeck, New York, December 7, 1949; admitted to bar, 1975, New York; 1976, Florida and U.S. District Court, Southern and Eastern Districts of New York; 1977, District of Columbia and U.S. Court of Appeals, Second Circuit; 1983, U.S. District Court for the District of Columbia; 1987, U.S. Supreme Court; 1994, U.S. Court of Appeals, District of Columbia. *Education:* Rensselaer Polytechnic Institute (B.S. Physics, with honors, 1971); St. John's University (J.D., with honors, 1974). Author: "The SEC Administrative Proceeding," Chapter 89 Securities Laws Techniques, Matthew Bender, 1985. Co-Author: "The Regulation of Changes in Corporate Control," Fifteenth Annual Institute on Securities Regulation, Volume One, pp. 493-628, 1983; "NASD Disciplinary Proceedings: Practice and Procedure," Vol. 37, No. 3, The Business Lawyer, pp. 1213-1246, April, 1982. General Editor, Securities Arbitration: Practice and Forms, Matthew Bender, 1991. Trial Attorney, 1977-1980 and Special Counsel, 1981-1983, Division of Enforcement, Securities and Exchange Commission. *Member:* American Bar Association (Member, Committee on Federal Regulation of Securities, 1987—).

MARI-ANNE PISARRI, born Troy, New York, March 11, 1956; admitted to bar, 1981, New York and U.S. Court of Federal Claims; 1982, District of Columbia and U.S. Court of International Trade; 1984, U.S. District Court for the District of Columbia and U.S. Court of Appeals for the Federal Circuit; 1988, U.S. District Court, Southern and Eastern Districts of New York; 1995, U.S. Court of Appeals for the District of Columbia Circuit. *Education:* St. Lawrence University (B.A., summa cum laude, 1977); Cornell University (J.D., magna cum laude, 1980). Phi Beta Kappa; Pi Sigma Alpha; Order of the Coif.

(This Listing Continued)

Faculty, International Law Institute, 1991—. Author: "The Arbitration Agreement," Chapter 3, Securities Arbitration: Practice and Forms, Matthew Bender, 1991. Law Clerk for Hon. John P. Wiese, U.S. Claims Court, 1980-1981. ***Email:*** mappertry@aol.com

PAUL J. BAZIL, born Flushing, New York, December 7, 1962; admitted to bar, 1988, California; 1989, U.S. District Court, Northern, Southern, Eastern and Central Districts of California and U.S. Court of Appeals, Ninth Circuit; 1990, District of Columbia; 1998, U.S. District Court for the District of Columbia. *Education:* Dartmouth College (A.B., 1985); Boston University (J.D., 1988). Co-Author: "The SEC Administrative Proceeding, Chapter 89, Securities Law Techniques," Matthew Bender, 1996. Senior Counsel, Division of Enforcement, U.S. Securities and Exchange Commission, 1990-1994. Special Assistant United States Attorney, Northern District of California, 1991-1994. *Member:* District of Columbia Bar; American Bar Associations; State Bar of California. ***Email:*** pjbazil@pickdjin.com

OF COUNSEL

CRAIG L. LANDAUER, born Baltimore, Maryland, April 16, 1951; admitted to bar, 1985, Maryland and U.S. Court of Appeals for the District of Columbia; 1998, District of Columbia. *Education:* University of Virginia (B.A., 1973; M.B.A., 1976); University of Baltimore (J.D., 1984). Associate General Counsel, 1997-1992, Assistant General Counsel, 1992-1990, Senior Attorney, 1990-1987, Attorney, 1987-1984 and Registered Representative, 1981-1976, NASD. Maryland Revised Uniform Securities Act Task Force, 1986-1989. Formerly associated with: Alex Brown & Sons, Baltimore, Maryland; Maryland Division of Securities, Baltimore, Maryland. *Member:* Maryland State and American (Sections on Business Law) Bar Associations. ***PRACTICE AREAS:*** Statutory Disqualification and other NASD Administrative Proceedings; NASD Membership and Registration Issues; Broker-Dealer Compliance. ***Email:*** pickdjin@aol.com

ASSOCIATE

WILLIAM D. EDICK, born Pontiac, Michigan, October 23, 1966; admitted to bar, 1994, Maryland; 1996, District of Columbia; 1998, U.S. Court of Appeals, District of Columbia Circuit. *Education:* American University (B.S.B.A., 1988; J.D., summa cum laude, 1994); Georgetown University (LL.M., Securities and Financial Regulation, with Distinction, 1997). Recipient, Thomas B. Chetwood, S.J. Prize for Most Distinguished Academic Performance in Securities and Financial Regulation, 1998. Member, American University Law Review, 1993-1994. *Member:* The District of Columbia Bar.

PILIERO, MAZZA & PARGAMENT, PLLC

Established in 1991

FARRAGUT SQUARE
888 SEVENTEENTH STREET, N.W., SUITE 1100
WASHINGTON, D.C. 20006
Telephone: 202-857-1000
Fax: 202-857-0200
Email: pmp@pmplawfirm.com
URL: http://www.pmplawfirm.com

New York, N.Y. Office: 292 Madison Avenue, 10017. Telephone: 212-213-8200.

General Civil and Appellate Practice in all State and Federal Courts. Governmental Departments and Federal Agencies, Government Contracts, Administrative Law, Corporate Counseling, Commercial Transactions, Employment Law, Government Relations, Trade Associations and Native American Law.

FIRM PROFILE: Piliero, Mazza & Pargament maintains a nationwide practice providing legal services to commercial businesses, government contractors, non-profit organizations, trade associations and tribal entities. The firm's practice areas include business and corporate law, government contracts law, government relations, litigation, trade association law and Native American law. It has developed a national reputation for its work with small, women, and minority-owned federal and state government contractors. The firm also has a significant practice in other interrelated areas, including legislative and agency advocacy and general and civil appellate litigation before various federal and state courts and administrative agencies. The firm represents clients, on nationwide basis, in a wide array of industries, including construction, engineering, environmental sciences, facilities management, convenience stores and gas stations, security services, health care, information technology and computer-related services and transportation.

MEMBERS OF FIRM

DANIEL J. PILIERO II (1942-1990).

PAMELA J. MAZZA, born Washington, Pennsylvania, April 25, 1958; admitted to bar, 1984, Virginia; 1986, District of Columbia; 1990, U.S. Court of Appeals, District of Columbia; 1991, U.S. District Court, Eastern District of

(This Listing Continued)

Virginia; 1993, U.S. District Court, District of Columbia; U.S. Supreme Court; U.S. Court of Federal Claims. *Education:* Indiana University of Pennsylvania (B.A., 1980); George Washington University (J.D., 1984). Member: Washington, D.C. District Advisory Council of the U.S. Small Business Administration; Small Business Adminstration's Regulatory Fairness Board for Region III. Contributor, Set Aside-Alert. *Member:* The District of Columbia Bar (Member, Government Contracts Section); Virginia State Bar; American Bar Association; Contract Services Association; Greater Washington Society of Association Executives; American Society of Association Executives. ***PRACTICE AREAS:*** Government Contracts; Corporate Law; Small Business Programs; Administrative Law; Indian Law; Alaska Native Law. ***Email:*** pmazza@pmplawfirm.com

JEFFREY J. PARGAMENT, born New York, N.Y., July 16, 1957; admitted to bar, 1984, Pennsylvania (inactive); 1985, U.S. Court of Appeals, Eleventh Circuit; 1988, District of Columbia; 1990, U.S. Court of Appeals, Ninth Circuit; 1991, U.S. District Court, District of Columbia; 1992, U.S. Court of Appeals, District of Columbia Circuit and U.S. Supreme Court; 1995, Maryland; 1996, U.S. Court of Appeals, Fourth Circuit. *Education:* Cornell University (B.A., 1980); George Washington University (J.D., 1984). Field Examiner, National Labor Relations Board, Washington, D.C., 1980-1984. President, Shady Grove Adventist Hospital Foundation. *Member:* The District of Columbia Bar (Member, Labor Relations Section); Maryland State Bar Association; Greater Washington Society of Association Executives; American Society of Association Executives; Gaithersburg-Germantown Chamber of Commerce. ***PRACTICE AREAS:*** Labor and Employment; Civil Litigation; Trade and Professional Associations. ***Email:*** jpargament@pmplawfirm.com

ANDREW P. HALLOWELL, born Rochester, New York, December 27, 1959; admitted to bar, 1986, Maryland; 1988, District of Columbia; 1994, U.S. District Court, District of Columbia; 1996, U.S. District Court, District of Maryland. *Education:* Indiana University (B.A., 1982) Phi Beta Kappa; American University, Washington College of Law (J.D., 1985). Law Clerk to Hon. Donald S. Smith, Superior Court of the District of Columbia, 1985-1987. *Member:* The District of Columbia Bar (Member, Government Contracts and Litigation Section); Maryland State Bar Association; Contract Services Association; American Society of Association Executives. ***PRACTICE AREAS:*** Corporate Law; Government Contracts; Trade Association Law; Native American Law; Civil Litigation. ***Email:*** ahallowell@pmplawfirm.com

ANTONIO R. FRANCO, born Victoria de las Tunas, Cuba, November 21, 1960; admitted to bar, 1987, Florida and U.S. District Court, Southern District of Florida; 1988, District of Columbia; 1992, U.S. District Court, District of Columbia; 1999, Maryland and U.S. Court of Federal Claims. *Education:* University of Madrid; Tulane University (B.A., cum laude, 1983); Georgetown University (J.D., 1986). Member, Hispanic Chamber of Commerce, Montgomery County (Vice President, Corporate Board); Commissioner, Montgomery County Human Relations Commission. *Member:* The District of Columbia Bar; The Florida Bar; Latin American Bar Association (Treasurer, 1988-1989). ***LANGUAGES:*** Spanish. ***PRACTICE AREAS:*** Government Contracts; Civil Litigation; Minority Business. ***Email:*** afranco@pmplawfirm.com

PHILIP M. DEARBORN III, born Cleveland, Ohio, January 11, 1960; admitted to bar, 1987, Virginia; 1988, District of Columbia; 1992, U.S. District Court, District of Columbia; U.S. Court of Appeals, District of Columbia; 1994, U.S. Court of Federal Claims; 1995, U.S. District Court, Eastern District of Virginia; U.S. Court of Appeals, Fourth Circuit. *Education:* Davis and Elkin College (B.A., cum laude, 1983); College of William and Mary (J.D., 1987). Law Clerk to Hon. Richard S. Gebelin, Delaware Superior Court. *Member:* The District of Columbia Bar; Virginia State Bar; Contract Services Association. ***PRACTICE AREAS:*** Government Contracts; Employment Law; Commercial Leasing; Native American Law; Civil Litigation. ***Email:*** pdearborn@pmplawfirm.com

ASSOCIATES

FRANK C. GULIN, born Brooklyn, New York, September 11, 1963; admitted to bar, 1991, New York; 1993, California; 1994, District of Columbia. *Education:* Colgate University (A.B., 1985); American University, Washington College of Law (J.D., cum laude, 1990). Articles Editor, The American University Law Review. Law Clerk, Hon. Malcolm Muir, U.S. District Court, Middle District of Pennsylvania, 1990-1992. ***PRACTICE AREAS:*** Labor and Employment; Government Contracts; Civil Litigation. ***Email:*** fgulin@pmplawfirm.com

JUDITH M. BARGER, born San Francisco, California, April 16, 1968; admitted to bar, 1993, Virginia; 1998, U.S. Supreme Court; 1999, District of Columbia and U.S. District Court for the District of Columbia; 2000, U.S. District Court, Eastern District of Virginia. *Education:* Wright State University (B.S., magna cum laude, Accounting, Minor - Political Science, 1990); Georgetown University Law Center (J.D., 1993). Editor, Tribal Advocate. *Member:* Federal (Member, Indian Law Section) and Virginia Bar Associations; District of Columbia Bar; American Inns of Court (William B. Bryant Inn, 1992-1993). ***REPORTED CASES:*** Martin M. Miller v. Commonwealth of Virginia, 25 V.A. App. 727, 492 SE 2d 482 (1997). ***PRACTICE AREAS:*** Civil Litigation; Criminal Litigation; Native American Law; Labor and Employment; Government Contracts. ***Email:*** jbarger@pmplawfirm.com

JOSEPH J. SUMMERILL IV, born Toms River, New Jersey, August 12, 1966; admitted to bar, 1993, District of Columbia; 1995, U.S. Court of Federal Claims. *Education:* Colby College (B.A., 1989); Franklin Pierce Law Center (J.D., Masters of Intellectual Property Joint Degree, 1993); George Washington University Law School (LL.M., 1997); U.S. Army Judge Advocate General's School; Harvard University John F. Kennedy School of Government. Associate Managing Editor, Public Contract Law Journal (1995-1996). Editor, Corrections Contractor. Instructor: Anne Arundel Community College (1996-2001); University of Maryland (1998). Author: "The Judgement Fund: When Can It Be Used?"; "The Use of UCC Implied Warranties in Public Contracts,"; "Tips for Drafting Takeover Agreements in Federal Construction Contracts,"; "Deregulating Government Sponsored R&D." Member: American Correctional Association; American Jail Association; National Juvenile Detention Association; American Correctional Food Service Association; American Correctional Health Services Association. *Member:* American Bar Association (Member, Government Contracts and Litigation Section). ***SPECIAL AGENCIES:*** U.S. Department of Justice, Federal Bureau of Prisons; United States Marshal Service; Immigration and Naturalization Service. ***PRACTICE AREAS:*** Government Contracts; Corrections Law; Corporate Law; Intellectual Property; Civil Litigation; Employment Law. ***Email:*** jsummerill@pmplawfirm.com

EDITH MOORE McGEE, born Chattanooga, Tennessee, November 23, 1957; admitted to bar, 1999, Virginia; 2000, Maryland (Not admitted in District of Columbia). *Education:* Furman University (B.A., summa cam laude, 1979); Vanderbilt University (M.A., 1981); George Mason University (J.D., magna cum laude, 1999). Phi Beta Kappa. Member, George Mason Law Review, 1996-1999. Dean's Scholar, 1997-1999. Recipient, First Prize, Fairfaz Bar Association Technology Essay Competition, 1998 and 1999. Law Clerk to the Honorable Raymond G. Thieme, Jr., Maryland Court of Special Appeals, 1999-2001. Author: Note, "Morse v. Republican Party of Virginia: Political Costs or Benefits?"; "Virtual Houses and Digital Papers: Rethinking the Fourth Amendment Expectation of Privacy in Cyberspace"; "Big Brother is Watching: Using Technology to Monitor Employee Behavior and Performance in the Workplace". Adjunct Professor, George Mason University School of Law, 2000-2001. *Member:* Virginia State Bar; Federalist Society. ***PRACTICE AREAS:*** Employment Law; Government Contracts; Corporate Counseling. ***Email:*** emcgee@pmplawfirm.com

REPRESENTATIVE CLIENTS: Adventist HealthCare, Inc.; Akima Corporation; APICS, The Educational Society for Resource Management; Parallax, Inc.; Space Mark, Inc.; Intellisource Information Systems, Inc.; CTA Incorporated; Environmental Chemical Corp.; Hebrew Home of Greater Washington; Information Systems & Services, Inc.; Enterprise Advisory Services, Inc.; Ysleta del Sur Pueblo Tigua Indian Tribe.

(This Listing Continued)

PILLSBURY WINTHROP LLP

1133 CONNECTICUT AVENUE, N.W.
WASHINGTON, D.C. 20036
Telephone: 202-775-9800
Fax: 202-833-8491
URL: http://www.pillsburywinthrop.com

San Francisco, California Office: 50 Fremont Street, 94105-2228. Telephone: 415-983-1000. Fax: 415-983-1200.

New York, New York Office: One Battery Park Plaza, 10004-1490. Telephone: 212-858-1000. Fax: 212-858-1500.

Los Angeles, California Office: 725 South Figueroa Street, Suite 2800, 90017-5406. Telephone: 213-488-7100. Fax: 213-629-1033.

Other Los Angeles, California Office: Century City, 10100 Santa Monica Boulevard, Suite 2300.

Orange County, California Office: 650 Town Center Drive, Seventh Floor, Costa Mesa, California 92626-7122. Telephone: 714-436-6800. Fax: 714-436-2800.

McLean, Virginia Office: 1600 Tysons Boulevard, 22102. Telephone: 703-905-2000. Fax: 703-905-2500.

Palm Beach, Florida Office: 125 Worth Avenue, 33480. Telephone: 561-655-7297. Fax: 561-833-6726.

Sacramento, California Office: 400 Capitol Mall, Suite 1700, 95814-4419. Telephone: 916-329-4700. Fax: 916-441-3583.

San Diego, California Office: 101 West Broadway, Suite 1800, 92101-8219. Telephone: 619-234-5000. Fax: 619-236-1995.

Other San Diego, California Office: 11975 El Camino Real, Suite 200, 92130-5000. Telephone: 619-234-5000. Fax: 858-509-4010.

Silicon Valley, California Office: 2550 Hanover Street, Palo Alto, California 94304-1115. Telephone: 650-233-4500. Fax: 650-233-4545.

Stamford, Connecticut Office: Financial Centre, 695 East Main Street, 06904-6760. Telephone: 203-348-2300. Fax: 203-965-8226.

London, England Office: 54 Lombard Street, EC3V 9DH. Telephone: +44-171-648-9200. Fax: +44-171-283-1656.

(This Listing Continued)

PILLSBURY WINTHROP LLP, Washington—Continued

Sydney, Australia Office: Level 10, 7 Macquarie Place, NSW2000. Telephone: +612-8214-2200. Fax: 612-8214-2211.

Tokyo, Japan Office: Fuerte Kojimachi Building, 5th Floor, 1-7-25 Kojimachi, Chiyoda-ku, 102-0083. Telephone: +011-81-3-5226-7260. Fax: +011-81-3-5226-7261.

Other Tokyo, Japan Office: 6 Gaikokuho Jimu Bengoshi Jimusho, Fifth Floor, Samon Eleven Building, 3-1, Samon-cho, Shinjuku-ku, 160. Telephone: +813-3354-3531. Fax: +813-3354-3534.

Hong Kong, China Office: 2504-6 Asia Pacific Finance Tower, Citibank Plaza, 3 Garden Road, Central Hong Kong. Telephone: +852-2530-3400. Fax: +852-2530-3355.

Singapore Office: 6 Battery Road #38-01B, 049909. Telephone: +65-227-4700. Fax: +65-227-4711.

General Practice with an emphasis on Administrative, Admiralty and Maritime, Alternative Dispute Resolution, Antitrust and Trade Regulation, Appellate Practice, Art, Aviation and Aerospace, Bankruptcy, Banking, Biotechnology, Business, Civil, Class Actions, Commerce & Technology, Commercial, Communications and Media, Complex and Multi-District Litigation, Construction, Contracts, Corporate, Creditor's Rights, E-Commerce, Emerging Companies, Employee Benefits, Energy, Environmental, Equipment Finance and Leasing, Executive Compensation, Finance, Guardianship and Conservatorship, Health Care and Hospital, International, International Trade, Internet, Labor and Employment, Leases and Leasing, Licensing, Life Sciences, Litigation, Medicare and Medicaid, Mergers, Acquisitions and Divestitures, Natural Resources, Nonprofit and Charitable Organizations, Partnership, Patents, Planning and Land Use, Political, Probate, Products Liability, Project Finance, Real Estate, Regulatory, RICO, Securities, Taxation, Torts, Toxic Torts, Trademark, Trust and Estates, Utility, White Collar Crime, Wills and Zoning Law.

FIRM PROFILE: Formed in 2001 by the merger of Pillsbury Madison & Sutro and Winthrop, Stimson, Putnam & Roberts, our experience spans three centuries. Today, Pillsbury Winthrop has more than 860 lawyers in 16 locations, including 350 corporate and securities lawyers, 250 intellectual property and technology lawyers and 250 lawyers in complex and international litigation. With 16 locations in major capital finance and technology centers throughout the world, Pillsbury Winthrop is uniquely positioned to counsel clients on all aspects of global business, technology transactions, and intellectual property protection.

MEMBERS OF FIRM

ISAAC D. BENKIN, born July 5, 1935; admitted to bar, 1960, New York; 1962, U.S. Court of Military Appeals; 1964, U.S. Supreme Court and U.S. Court of Appeals for the Federal Circuit; 1982, District of Columbia. *Education:* Harvard University (A.B., cum laude, 1956; LL.B., 1959). Professorial Lecturer, George Washington University Law School, 1990-1999. Deputy Chief Administrative Law Judge, Federal Energy Regulatory Commission, 1974-1990. Articles Editor, Energy Law Journal. *Member:* Federal Energy and American Bar Associations. ***PRACTICE AREAS:*** Energy Law. ***Email:*** ibenkin@pillsburywinthrop.com

TERRY CALVANI, born Carlsbad, New Mexico, January 29, 1947; admitted to bar, 1972, New Mexico and California; 1978, Tennessee; 1985, U.S. Supreme Court; 1992, District of Columbia. *Education:* University of New Mexico (B.A., 1970); Cornell University (J.D., 1972). Lecturer in Law, Antitrust, Harvard Law School, 1998-2001. Commissioner, 1983-1990 and Acting Chairman, 1984-1985, U.S. Federal Trade Commission. Member, Administrative Conference of the United States, 1985-1990. (Also at San Francisco, California Office). ***PRACTICE AREAS:*** Antitrust. ***Email:*** tcalvani@pillsburywinthrop.com

DONALD A. CARR, born August 29, 1948; admitted to bar, 1975, District of Columbia; 1979, U.S. Supreme Court. *Education:* Cornell University (B.A., 1970); George Washington University (J.D., with honors, 1974). Author: *Emerg. Reporting Req. for Env. Spills and Releases,* (Prentiss Hall 1990) (with A. Macbeth and K. Berlin); *European Com. Env. Law,* Int'l Fin. L. Rev., February 1991 (with S. Tupper and M. Wheeler); *The Law And Policy Of Endangered Species Act Reauthorization: Noah's Choices and Ecological Mandarins,* 25 Envtl. L. 1281 (1995) (with W. Thomas). *Env. Criminal Liability - Avoiding And Defending Enforcement Actions* (1995); *The Kyoto Protocol and U.S. Climate Change Policy: Implications for American Industry,* 7 Rev. of Eur. Community & Int'l Envtl. L. 189 (1998). Counselor to the Ass. Att. Gen., 1987-1989 and Acting Ass. Att. Gen., 1989, Dep. of Justice, Env. Nat. Resources Div. ***PRACTICE AREAS:*** Environmental Law; Natural Resources. ***Email:*** dcarr@pillsburywinthrop.com

JOHN E. GILLICK, born August 13, 1945; admitted to bar, 1971, New York; 1976, District of Columbia and U.S. Court of Appeals, District of Columbia Circuit; 1979, U.S. Court of Appeals, Fifth and Fourth Circuits; 1980, U.S. Supreme Court. *Education:* Colgate University (A.B., 1967); Georgetown University (J.D., 1970). Phi Alpha Delta. Editor, Georgetown Law Journal,

(This Listing Continued)

1969-1970. *Member:* The District of Columbia Bar; American Bar Association. ***PRACTICE AREAS:*** Aviation Law; Regulatory Law; International Law. ***Email:*** jgillick@pillsburywinthrop.com

JAY L. HALPERN, born Brooklyn, N.Y., November 26, 1964; admitted to bar, 1989, Pennsylvania and New Jersey; 1990, District of Columbia; 2001, Virginia. *Education:* Emory University (B.A., with honors, 1986); Duke University (J.D., with honors, 1989). Member, Board of Directors, Legal Resource Center for Nonprofit Housing Sponsors, Inc., 1991-1998. *Member:* American Bar Association. ***PRACTICE AREAS:*** Finance; Venture Capital; Mergers and Acquisitions; Corporate Structuring; Joint Ventures; General Corporate Law. ***Email:*** jhalpern@pillsburywinthrop.com

GERALD D. MORGAN, JR., born March 1, 1937; admitted to bar, 1966, New York; 1977, District of Columbia. *Education:* Amherst College (A.B., 1959); Oxford University, Oxford, England (A.B., 1961); Columbia University (LL.B., 1965). Phi Beta Kappa. Rhodes Scholar. Attorney, 1971-1974, Deputy Vice-President for Insurance, 1974-1975, Vice-President and General Counsel, 1975-1976, Overseas Private Investment Corporation. General Counsel, Agency for International Development, 1976-1977. *Member:* The District of Columbia Bar; Association of the Bar of the City of New York; Federal and American Bar Associations; American Society of International Law. ***PRACTICE AREAS:*** Construction Law; Real Estate; Project Development. ***Email:*** gmorgan@pillsburywinthrop.com

ROXANE A. POLIDORA, born Madison, Wisconsin, December 7, 1960; admitted to bar, 1988, California (Not admitted in District of Columbia). *Education:* University of California at Davis (B.A., 1984); University of California, Hastings College of the Law (J.D., 1988). ***PRACTICE AREAS:*** Class Actions; Antitrust; Unfair Competition; Litigation. ***Email:*** roxane.polidora@pillsburywinthrop.com

KENNETH P. QUINN, born November 12, 1960; admitted to bar, 1985, Illinois (Not admitted in District of Columbia). *Education:* Northern Illinois University (B.S., 1982); DePaul University College of Law (J.D., with honors, 1985). Article and Notes Editor, DePaul Law Review, Volume 34. Articles Editor, A.S.I.L.S. International Law Journal. Chief Counsel, Federal Aviation Administration, 1991-1993. Counselor to the Secretary, U.S. Department of Transportation, 1989-1991. Senior Advisor, Office of the President-elect, 1988-1989. Editor-in-Chief, *The Air & Space Lawyer*, 1998—. Member, Board of Advisors, CCH Aviation Law Reporter, 1998—. *Member:* American Bar Association (Chair, 1996-1998, and Member, 1993— of Governing Committee, Forum on Air and Space Law; Member, Antitrust Law Section). ***PRACTICE AREAS:*** Aviation Law; Transportation; Antitrust. ***Email:*** kquinn@pillsburywinthrop.com

JOSHUA I. ROMANOW, born 1964; admitted to bar, 1992, Pennsylvania; 1993, District of Columbia. *Education:* Brandeis University (B.A.); Tulane University of Louisiana (J.D., 1991). Author: "Knowing How to Read Those Low-Fare Ads," The New York Law Journal, October, 1999; "Know the Facts Before Taking A Charter," New York Law Journal, March, 1999; Who's Watching The Skies? A Discussion Of U.S. Department of Transportation Casino Junket Flight Regulations; Gaming Law Review, Winter 1997; "Tour Packages: Know Your Rights," The Sunday Record, March 31, 1996; "Charter Flights Are Cheaper Way To Go, But Use Caution," The Atlantic City Press, April, 1995. ***PRACTICE AREAS:*** Aviation Law; Travel Law; Advertising Law; Media Law; Maritime Law. ***Email:*** romanow@pillsburywinthrop.com

RAYMOND L. SWEIGART, admitted to bar, 1973, OHIO ; 1975, Conecticut ; 1980, New York ; 1995, District of Columbia. admitted to bar, 1973, Ohio; 1975, Connecticut; 1978, U.S. Supreme Court; 1980, New York; 1995, District of Columbia. *Education:* St. Joseph's College (B.A., 1967); University of Cincinnati (J.D., 1972); University of London, London, England (LL.M., 1973). (Also at McLean, Virginia Office). ***PRACTICE AREAS:*** Intellectual Property; Complex and Multi-District Litigation; Commercial Law; Technology and Science; Creditors Rights. ***Email:*** rsweigart@pillsburywinthrop.com

MARY ANN WALKER, born 1953; admitted to bar, 1979, Virginia and U.S. Supreme Court; 1988, District of Columbia. *Education:* University of Virginia (B.A., 1975); University of Richmond (J.D., 1979). Phi Delta Phi. *Member:* Federal Energy Bar Association; Midwest Energy Association. ***PRACTICE AREAS:*** Federal and State Energy and Utility Regulatory Matters. ***Email:*** mwalker@pillsburywinthrop.com

CHRISTOPHER R. WALL, born October 6, 1952; admitted to bar, 1980, New York; 1986, District of Columbia. *Education:* Yale University (B.A., summa cum laude, 1974); Oxford University, England (B.A., 1976); University of Virginia (J.D., 1979). Phi Beta Kappa. *Member:* The District of Columbia Bar; The Association of the Bar of the City of New York; American Bar Association (Chair, Special Advisory Committee on International Activities, 1995-1997; Section of International Law and Practice. Vice Chair, 1994-1997, Co-Chair, Foreign Investment in the U.S. Committee, 1992-1994; Section of Litigation, Co-Chair, International Litigation Committee, 1993-1995); Swedish-American Chamber of Commerce, Washington, D.C. (Chair); British-American

(This Listing Continued)

Business Council (Chair, Trade and Investment Policy Committee). ***PRACTICE AREAS:*** International Trade; International Law. ***Email:*** cwall@pillsburywinthrop.com

COUNSEL

ROBERT REED GRAY, born November 10, 1921; admitted to bar, 1948, New York; 1955, District of Columbia; 1957, U.S. Court of Federal Claims; 1960, U.S. Supreme Court. *Education:* Dartmouth College (A.B., 1943); Harvard Law School (LL.B., 1948). Author: "Aviation Safety: Fact of Fiction," Technology Review, Massachusetts Institute of Technology, 1987. Staff of General Counsel, 1951-1952 and Assistant Chief, International & Rules Division, 1953-1955, Civil Aeronautics Board. Legal Assistant to Deputy Chief of Naval Operations (Air), 1952-1953. *Member:* The District of Columbia Bar. [Naval Aviator, 1943-1946]. ***PRACTICE AREAS:*** Aviation Law. ***Email:*** rgray@pillsburywinthrop.com

AILEEN MEYER, born November 24, 1948; admitted to bar, 1981, New York; 1986, District of Columbia. *Education:* Smith College (A.B., 1970); Brooklyn Law School (J.D., magna cum laude, 1980). Senior Editor, Brooklyn Law Review, 1979-1980. *Member:* The District of Columbia Bar; American Bar Association. ***PRACTICE AREAS:*** Environmental Law; Antitrust. ***Email:*** ameyer@pillsburywinthrop.com

PETER S. WATSON, born February 28, 1953; admitted to bar, 1979, California (Not admitted in District of Columbia). *Education:* Auckland University School of Law (LL.B., 1976); McGill University School of Law (LL.M., 1982). Visiting Professor, International Economic Relations, St. Peter's College, Oxford University and George Mason University, 1994—. Chairman, U.S. International Trade Commission, 1994-1996. Director, Asian Affairs, National Security Counsel, 1989-1991. Special Advisor, Office of the President, Overseas Private Investment Corporation, 1989. *Member:* American Bar Association (Co-Chairman, Committee on Senior International Appointments, International Law and Practice Section, 1992—). (Resident, Other Washington, D.C. Office). ***Email:*** pwatson@pillsburywinthrop.com

SENIOR ATTORNEYS

HENRY J. DALEY, born Boston, Massachusetts; admitted to bar, 1997, Massachusetts and District of Columbia; registered to practice before the U.S. Patent and Trademark Office. *Education:* Worcester Polytechnic Institute (B.S.); University of Arizona (Ph.D., Physics, 1984); Northeastern University (J.D., 1996). ***PRACTICE AREAS:*** Intellectual Property; Patent Prosecution; Patent Litigation. ***Email:*** hdaley@pillsburywinthrop.com

THOMAS P. HILLIARD, born Hartford, Connecticut, June 23, 1965; admitted to bar, 1996, Connecticut; 1997, District of Columbia; registered to practice before the U.S. Patent and Trademark Office. *Education:* Catholic University of America (B.M.E., 1987; M.M.E., 1991; J.D., 1995). Patent Examiner, U.S. Patent and Trademark Office, 1990-1996. *Member:* American Bar Association; American Intellectual Property Law Association. ***PRACTICE AREAS:*** Intellectual Property Law; Patent Law. ***Email:*** thilliard@pillsburywinthrop.com

WILLIAM L. THOMAS, born November 5, 1963; admitted to bar, 1990, New York; 1992, District of Columbia; 1993, U.S. Court of Appeals, Fourth Circuit. *Education:* St. Olaf College (B.A., magna cum laude, with distinction, 1986); Georgetown University (J.D., 1989). Phi Beta Kappa. Executive Editor, Georgetown Journal of Legal Ethics, 1988-1989. Author: "The Green Nexus: Financiers and Sustainable Development," 13 Geo. Int'l Envtl. L. Rev., (2001); "Select Bibliography of Articles and Books on International Environmental Law," 1997—, 13 Geo. Int'l Envtl. L. Rev. 47, (2000); Crafting Superior Environmental Enforcement Solutions, (Environmental Law Institute 2000); "The Kyoto Protocol and U.S. Climate Change Policy: Implications for American Industry," 7 Rev. of Eur. Community & Int'l Envtl. L. 189 (1998); "Devising a Compliance Strategy under the ISO 14000 International Environmental Management Standards," 15 Pace Envtl. L. Rev. 201 (1997). *Member:* The District of Columbia Bar (Member, Sections on: Environment; Energy and Natural Resources; Member, IUCN Commission of Environmental Law) American Bar Association (Chair, International Environmental Law Committee, 1999-2001; Member, Sections on: International; Litigation); International Bar Association; Inter-Pacific and Inter-American Bar Associations. ***PRACTICE AREAS:*** Environmental Law; Litigation; International Law. ***Email:*** wthomas@pillsburywinthrop.com

ASSOCIATES

Sophy Chen
Cecil S. Chung
Thomas M. deButts
William H. Espinosa
James L. Gallagher
David M. Hernandez
Christopher M. Heywood
Paul W. Terry
Jiyul Yoo

(This Listing Continued)

(For biographical data on San Francisco, CA, New York, NY, Los Angeles, CA, Vienna, VA, Costa Mesa, CA, Palm Beach, FL, Sacramento, CA, San Diego, CA, Palo Alto, CA, Stamford, CT, London, England, Sydney, Australia, Tokyo, Japan, Hong Kong, China and Singapore personnel, see Professional Biographies at each of those cities)

PINKOWSKI & ASSOCIATES

WASHINGTON, D.C.

(See Fairfax, Virginia)

Business Law, Construction Law, Consumer Law, Contracts, Criminal Law, Traffic Violations, Driving While Intoxicated, Debtor and Creditor, Franchise Law, General Practice, Immigration Law, Investments, Trusts and Estates, Wills and Probate, Real Estate, Landlord and Tenant Law, Residential Real Estate, Commercial Real Estate, Government Contracts, Litigation, Computer Law, Internet Law, High Tech Law.

PIPER MARBURY RUDNICK & WOLFE LLP

1200 NINETEENTH STREET, N.W.
WASHINGTON, D.C. 20036-2430
Telephone: 202-861-3900
FAX: 202-223-2085
Email: info@piperrudnick.com
URL: http://www.piperrudnick.com

Chicago, Illinois Office: Piper Marbury Rudnick & Wolfe, 203 North La Salle Street, Suite 1800, 60601-1293. Telephone: 312-368-4000. Telecopier: 312-236-7516. Telex: 754347.

Tampa, Florida Office: 101 East Kennedy Boulevard, Suite 2001, 33602-5149. Telephone: 813-229-2111. Telecopier: 813-229-1447.

Baltimore, Maryland Office: 6225 Smith Avenue, 21209-3600. Telephone: 410-580-3000. FAX: 410-580-3001.

Other Baltimore, Maryland Office: 111 South Calvert Street, Suite 1950, 21202-6174. Telephone: 410-580-3000. FAX: 410-580-3665.

Dallas, Texas Office: 1717 Main Street, Suite 4600, 75201-2605. Telephone: 214-743-4500. FAX: 214-743-4545.

New York, N.Y. Office: 1251 Avenue of the Americas, 10020-1104. Telephone: 212-835-6000. FAX: 212-835-6001.

Philadelphia, Pennsylvania Office: 3400 Two Logan Square, 18th & Arch Streets, 19103-2762. Telephone: 215-656-3300. FAX: 215-656-3301.

Princeton, New Jersey Office: 116 Village Boulevard, Suite 200, Princeton Forrestal Village, 08540. Telephone: 609-951-2252. FAX: 609-951-2216.

Easton, Maryland Office: Piper Marbury Rudnick & Wolfe LLP, 117 Bay Street, 21601-2703. Telephone: 410-820-4460. FAX: 410-820-4463.

Reston, Virginia Office: 1775 Wiehle Avenue, Suite 400, 20190. Telephone: 703-773-4000. FAX: 703-773-5000.

Los Angeles, California Office: 9255 Sunset Boulevard, Suite 710, 90069-3309. Telephone: 310-288-8110. FAX: 310-288-8111.

Advertising, Promotion and Trade Practices, Antitrust, Bankruptcy and Business Reorganization, Biotechnology, Business Tax, Class Action Litigation, Communications, Construction, Corporate and Securities, Domain Names, ERISA and Employee Benefits, Electronic Commerce and Privacy, Energy and Public Utilities, Environmental, Finance, Financial Services, Franchise and Distribution, Franchise Litigation, Gaming Law, Government Contracts, Health Care, Information Technology, Insurance and Reinsurance, Intellectual Property, International Transactions, Labor and Employment Law, Land Use and Development, Leasing, Life Sciences, Litigation, Lodging and Timeshare, Medical Malpractice Defense, Mergers and Acquisitions, Multi-Family Housing, Patent Litigation, Patent Prosecution; Pesticide, Private Client Services (Estates and Trusts), Product Liability and Toxic Torts, Professional Liability, Project Finance, Public Finance, REIT and Real Estate Securitizations, Real Estate, Real Estate Finance, Secured Lending, Securities Litigation, Sports Facilities Development, State Legislation and Public Policy, Venture Capital and Emerging Companies, White Collar.

FIRM PROFILE: Piper Marbury Rudnick & Wolfe LLP has over 800 lawyers and operates out of offices in Chicago, Washington, Baltimore, New York, Reston, Tampa, Philadelphia, Dallas and Los Angeles.

The firm's practice is focused on:

Business and Technology, including communications, intellectual property, information technology, e-commerce, life sciences and corporate IPOs, mergers and acquisitions and other major transactions for companies of all sizes; Litigation, including a white collar group led by a former Watergate prosecutor and national products liability, securities litigation and government regulatory practices and they have one of the largest Real Estate practices in the U.S., covering every aspect of industrial, commercial and residential property transactions, finance and securities.

(This Listing Continued)

PIPER MARBURY RUDNICK & WOLFE LLP, Washington—Continued

These core practice areas embrace other disciplines that cross these boundaries, such as business tax, bankruptcy, labor, employee benefits, health care, insurance, public finance and estate planning.

MEMBERS OF FIRM

PERRY C. AUSBROOK, born Little Rock, Arkansas, July 1, 1932; admitted to bar, 1961, District of Columbia. *Education:* University of Pennsylvania (B.S. in Econ., 1954); Harvard University (LL.B., 1960). Beta Gamma Sigma; Pi Gamma Mu. Contributing Author: *Legal Aspects of Selling and Buying,* West Group, 1983, 2d Ed., 1992, Supplement, 2001. Co-Author: "Franchising: Regulation of Buying and Selling a Franchise," Bureau of National Affairs/Corporate Practice Series, 1983. *Member:* The District of Columbia Bar; The Bar Association of the District of Columbia; American and International Bar Associations. ***PRACTICE AREAS:*** International Franchising. ***Email:*** perry.ausbrook@piperrudnick.com

DAVID H. BAMBERGER, born Baltimore, Maryland, February 15, 1948; admitted to bar, 1981, Maryland; 1982, District of Columbia. *Education:* Trinity College (B.A., 1970); University of Toronto (M.A., 1971); George Washington University (J.D., with high honors, 1981). Order of the Coif. ***PRACTICE AREAS:*** Litigation; Antitrust Law. ***Email:*** david.bamberger@piperrudnick.com

WILLIAM D. BLAKELY, born Darien, Wisconsin, October 15, 1945; admitted to bar, 1977, Michigan; 1980, District of Columbia; 1984, Virginia. *Education:* University of Wisconsin-Madison (B.A., 1968); University of Detroit (J.D., 1977). Editor-in-Chief, University of Detroit Law Review. Trail Counsel, Civil Division U.S. Department of Justice, 1977-1982. ***PRACTICE AREAS:*** Aviation Litigation; Commercial Litigation; Construction; Government Contracts Litigation. ***Email:*** william.blakely@piperrudnick.com

GARY P. BLITZ, born New York, New York, December 6, 1958; admitted to bar, 1984, New York; 1986, District of Columbia. *Education:* University of Michigan (B.B.A., with distinction, 1980); New York University (J.D., 1983). Certified Public Accountant, Maryland, 1986 (inactive). Author: "Financial Comfort If a Seller Doesn't Tell the Truth," Mergers and Acquisitions, September/October, 1999; "M&A Insurance: Extra Protections in Risk Management," Mergers & Acquisitions, November/December, 1996; "Executive Compensation Insurance: What to Make of PLR9344038," Journal of Pension Planning and Compensation, Summer, 1994. *Member:* The District of Columbia Bar; New York State and American Bar Associations. ***PRACTICE AREAS:*** Financial Risks; Taxation; Insurance Law. ***Email:*** gary.blitz@piperrudnick.com

BENJAMIN S. BOYD, born Springfield, Missouri, November 1, 1961; admitted to bar, 1987, Arkansas; 1988, District of Columbia and Virginia; 1991, Maryland. *Education:* University of Arkansas (B.S.B.A., 1984; J.D., with high honors, 1987). ***PRACTICE AREAS:*** Business Litigation; Products Liability Law. ***Email:*** benjamin.boyd@piperrudnick.com

DANIEL J. CARRIGAN, born Arlington, Virginia, October 31, 1949; admitted to bar, 1976, Iowa; 1981, Wisconsin; 1984, Pennsylvania; 1996, District of Columbia. *Education:* College of William & Mary; Georgetown University (B.A., cum laude, Phi Beta Kappa, 1971; J.D., 1976). Law Clerk, Hon. Henry D. Evans, U.S. Bankruptcy Court, District of Maryland, 1980-1981. Co-Author: "Demystifying Bankruptcy - A Practice Primer," Pennsylvania Bar Institute; "Insurance Company Insolvencies and Bankruptcy Codes," American Bar Association, Business Bankruptcy Committee, Business Law Section; "Bankruptcy and Environmental Liability," George Washington University Environmental Law and Policy Program. *Member:* Philadelphia, Pennsylvania and American (Member, Business Bankruptcy Committee, Chapter 11 Subcommittee Task Force on State and Regulatory Insolvency Proceedings, Co-Chairman, 1989-1991) Bar Associations; Walter Chandler American Inn of Court (Master, 1990—). ***PRACTICE AREAS:*** Bankruptcy Law; Insolvency Law. ***Email:*** daniel.carrigan@piperrudnick.com

EMILIO W. CIVIDANES, born Petersburg, Virginia, June 5, 1956; admitted to bar, 1983, District of Columbia. *Education:* Haverford College (B.A., 1979); University of Pennsylvania (J.D., 1983). Member, 1981-1982, and Comment Editor, 1982-1983, University of Pennsylvania Law Review. Counsel, Subcommittee on Technology and the Law, Committee on the Judiciary, U.S. Senate, 1987-1988. ***PRACTICE AREAS:*** E-Commerce; Privacy Law; Litigation; Legislative Practice. ***Email:*** emilio.cividanes@piperrudnick.com

DAVID CLARKE, JR., born Baltimore, Maryland, December 6, 1956; admitted to bar, 1981, Maryland; 1986, District of Columbia. *Education:* Harvard University (A.B., 1978; J.D., 1981). *Member:* The District of Columbia Bar. ***PRACTICE AREAS:*** Securities Litigation; Business Litigation. ***Email:*** david.clarke@piperrudnick.com

PHILIP L. COHAN, born Philadelphia, Pennsylvania, July 21, 1939; admitted to bar, 1967, Pennsylvania; 1969, District of Columbia; 1983, Maryland. *Education:* Williams College (B.A., 1961); University of Pennsylvania (J.D., 1966). Assistant U.S. Attorney, District of Columbia, 1969-1972. *Member:* American College of Trial Lawyers. ***PRACTICE AREAS:*** Commercial Litigation; Patent Infringement Litigation; Product Liability; Defense Litigation. ***Email:*** philip.cohan@piperrudnick.com

JOHN E. CORETTE, III, born Butte, Montana, June 24, 1936; admitted to bar, 1961, Montana; 1965, California; 1975, District of Columbia. *Education:* Stanford University and University of Montana (B.S., Business, 1958); University of Virginia (J.D., 1961). Member, Business Board, University of Virginia Law Review, 1959-1961. Adjunct Professor of International Economic Law, Georgetown University Law School, 1983-1985. General Counsel, Export-Import Bank of the United States, 1969-1975. *Member:* The District of Columbia Bar; State Bar of Montana; State Bar of California; American Bar Association (Chairman, Subcommittee on Current Legislation Involving East-West Trade, International Law Section, 1976; Chairman, Subcommittee on Export Import Bank of the United States, International Law Section, 1982-1984); American Society of International Law. ***PRACTICE AREAS:*** International Business Law; Domestic Business Law; Financial Law; Trade Law. ***Email:*** john.corette@piperrudnick.com

JAY A. EPSTIEN, born Newark, New Jersey, May 23, 1951; admitted to bar, 1976, District of Columbia. *Education:* Case Western Reserve University (B.S., magna cum laude, 1973); Cornell University (J.D., magna cum laude, 1976). Order of the Coif. Editor, Cornell Law Review, 1975-1976. Member, Board of Governors, American College of Real Estate Lawyers. Member, Law Conference Program Committee, International Council of Shopping Centers. Listed in Best Lawyers in America and International Who's Who of Real Estate Lawyers. ***PRACTICE AREAS:*** Real Estate. ***Email:*** jay.epstien@piperrudnick.com

STEVEN B. FEIRMAN, born New York, N.Y., April 2, 1955; admitted to bar, 1981, District of Columbia; 1982, New Jersey. *Education:* Colgate University (A.B., magna cum laude, with honors in Economics, 1977); Washington University (J.D., 1980). Senior Editor, *Washington University Law Quarterly,* 1979-1980. Trial Attorney/Senior Trial Attorney, Bureau of Competition, Federal Trade Commission, 1980-1989. Recipient, FTC Meritorious Service Award, 1983. Editor: "Franchise Legal Digest," 1993, 1995; "Franchise Law Journal," 1998—. Author: "Supreme Court Decision Permits Franchisors to Set Price Ceilings," *The Franchise Lawyer* (1998); "Intergovernmental Group Recommends Franchising Policy," *Global Franchising* (1994). Co-Author: "Effects of *State Oil Co. v. Khan* On Franchising," Franchise Law Journal (1998); "Franchising in South Africa Faces New Challenges," *Franchising World* (1995); "OECD Report Recommends Policy Rules for Franchising," *Franchise Legal Digest* (1994); "Franchising and the Federal Trade Commission: Recent Developments," *Franchise Legal Digest* (1993). *Member:* The District of Columbia Bar; New Jersey State and American (Vice Chairman, Franchise and Dealership Committee, Antitrust Section, 1993-1996; Forum on Franchising) Bar Associations. ***PRACTICE AREAS:*** Antitrust; Franchising and Distribution; Litigation. ***Email:*** steven.feirman@piperrudnick.com

JAY GARY FINKELSTEIN, born Riverdale, Maryland, July 22, 1953; admitted to bar, 1978, District of Columbia. *Education:* Princeton University (A.B., magna cum laude, 1975); Harvard University (J.D., magna cum laude, 1978). ***PRACTICE AREAS:*** Corporate Law; Corporate Partnerships; Workouts; Securities Regulation Law; Mergers and Acquisitions Law. ***Email:*** jay.finkelstein@piperrudnick.com

DAVID J. FISHER, born Arlington, Virginia, 1959; admitted to bar, 1985, New York (Not admitted in District of Columbia). *Education:* State University of New York at Albany (B.A., 1981); Georgetown University (J.D., 1984). (Also in New York, New York Office). ***PRACTICE AREAS:*** Finance; Corporate; Securities. ***Email:*** david.fisher@piperrudnick.com

ANN K. FORD, born Cleveland, Ohio, July 12, 1954; admitted to bar, 1981, District of Columbia; 1987, New York. *Education:* Georgetown University (B.A., 1976); Case Western Reserve University and Duke University (J.D., 1980). Associate Editor, Law and Contemporary Problems, 1978-1980. Co-Author: "Review of the 1989 Trademark Decisions of the Court of Appeals for the Federal Circuit," 39 Am. U. L. Rev. 1233, 1990; "What's In A Name: Protecting Yours Is Good Business," Phone and The Monthly Journal for the Public Communications Industry, October 1994. *Member:* District of Columbia Bar; American (Member: Patent, Trademark and Copyright Section; ABA IPL Committee 308-Government Relations to Copyright) and Federal Communications Bar Associations (Online Communications Committee); Women in Film and Video; International Trademark Association (Member, Meetings Committee, 1995); NATPE International. ***PRACTICE AREAS:*** Intellectual Property.

MARY E. GATELY, born Washington, D.C., September 19, 1963; admitted to bar, 1988, Virginia; 1989, District of Columbia. *Education:* Boston College (B.A., summa cum laude, 1985); Harvard University (J.D., cum laude, 1988). ***PRACTICE AREAS:*** Commercial Litigation. ***Email:*** mary.gately@piperrudnick.com

LEONARD L. GORDON, born Sea Isle, New Jersey, March 31, 1963; admitted to bar, 1988, Maryland; 1999, District of Columbia. *Education:*

(This Listing Continued)

George Washington University (B.A., with honors, 1985; J.D., with honors, 1988). ***PRACTICE AREAS:*** Antitrust and Trade Regulation. ***Email:*** leonard.gordon@piperrudnick.com

DOUGLAS H. GREEN, born New York, N. Y., October 19, 1956; admitted to bar, 1983, District of Columbia. *Education:* Connecticut College (B.A., cum laude, 1979); George Washington University (J.D., with honors, 1983). ***PRACTICE AREAS:*** Environmental. ***Email:*** douglas.green@piperrudnick.com

JAMES J. HALPERT, born New York, July 29, 1963; admitted to bar, 1990, Pennsylvania; 1992, District of Columbia. *Education:* Yale University (B.A., magna cum laude, 1985); Harvard University (J.D., cum laude, 1989). (Resident). ***LANGUAGES:*** French. ***PRACTICE AREAS:*** Electronic Commerce; Privacy; Communications; Intellectual Property. ***Email:*** james.halpert@piperrudnick.com

THOMAS L. HANLEY, born New York, N.Y., May 14, 1959; admitted to bar, 1985, Virginia; 1989, District of Columbia; 1997, Maryland. *Education:* Univ. of Virginia (B.A., with distinction, 1981); College of William and Mary (J.D., 1985); Univ. of Michigan (M.B.A., with distinction, 1993). Attorney, Div. of Corporation Finance, U.S. Securities and Exchange Commission, 1985-1989. ***PRACTICE AREAS:*** Finance; Corporate Law; Securities; Mergers and Acquisitions; Business Law. ***Email:*** thomas.hanley@piperrudnick.com

LARRY D. HARRIS, born Tifton, Georgia, July 18, 1950; admitted to bar, 1975, New Jersey and U.S. District Court, District of New Jersey; 1976, U.S. Court of Military Appeals; 1980, District of Columbia and U.S. Supreme Court. *Education:* University of Dayton (B.S., 1972); George Washington University (J.D., with honors, 1975). Law Clerk to the Chairman, Armed Services Board of Contract Appeals, 1978-1980. *Member:* District of Columbia Bar; New Jersey State, Federal and American (Member: Sections on: Public Contract Law; Litigation; Forum on Construction) Bar Associations; National Bar Association. Fellow, American Bar Association Foundation. [Capt., JAGC, U.S. Army, 1976-1980]. ***PRACTICE AREAS:*** Government Contracts; Construction; Commercial Litigation. ***Email:*** larry.harris@piperrudnick.com

BARRY M. HELLER, born Bridgeport, Connecticut, August 12, 1953; admitted to bar, 1977, District of Columbia. *Education:* New York University (B.A., summa cum laude, 1974); Georgetown University (J.D., 1977). Phi Beta Kappa; Justinian Honor Society. Member, 1975-1976 and Managing Editor, 1976-1977, American Criminal Law Review. Teaching Fellow, Legal Writing and Research Seminar, 1975-1976. Law Clerk to The Presidential Clemency Board, The White House, 1975. Law Clerk to Hon. Charles R. Richey, U.S. District Court, District of Columbia, 1977-1979. Co-Chair of 1998 ABA Forum on Franchising Mid-Year Program on Mergers and Acquisitions in Franchising. Co-Author of *Franchise Litigation Claims* for seminar for the Litigation Section of the District of Columbia Bar Association; Co-Author: "Sheraton Adds to the Uncertainty in the Encroachment Area," *The Franchise Lawyer* (Summer 1998); "Territorial Encroachment," *Franchise Law Journal* (Summer 1994); "Defining A Franchise: The 'Community of Interest' Element," *Of Interest* (March 1992). Contributor to the *IFA Insider,* a newsletter of the International Franchise Association. Invited to the United States Judicial Conference for the District of Columbia Circuit (1994). *Member:* The District of Columbia Bar; American Bar Association (Member, Forum on Franchising, Litigation and Antitrust Sections; Former Member of Steering Committee, and Former Director of Litigation and Alternative Dispute Resolution Division, ABA Forum on Franchising). ***PRACTICE AREAS:*** Litigation; Franchising; Antitrust. ***Email:*** barry.heller@piperrudnick.com

ADAM S. HOFFINGER, born New York, N.Y., October 22, 1956; admitted to bar, 1983, New York; 1984, U.S. District Court, Southern and Eastern Districts of New York; 1986, U.S. Court of Appeals, Second Circuit; 1990, U.S. Court of Appeals, District of Columbia Circuit; 1992, District of Columbia, U.S. District Court, District of Columbia and U.S. Supreme Court. *Education:* Trinity College (B.A., 1978); Fordham University (J.D., 1982). Recipient, Director's Award for Superior Performance As An Assistant U.S. Attorney, 1990. Adjunct Professor, George Mason University School of Law, 1992-1994. Instructor, National Institute for Trial Advocacy, Georgetown University Law Center, 1991—. Assistant U.S. Attorney, Southern District of New York, 1985-1990. *Member:* The District of Columbia Bar; The Association of the Bar of the City of New York; American Bar Association (Member: Sections on Litigation, Business Law and Criminal Justice; White Collar Crime Committee). ***PRACTICE AREAS:*** White Collar Crime; Securities; Health Care; Complex Civil Litigation. ***Email:*** adam.hoffinger@piperrudnick.com

E. LESLIE HOFFMAN III, born Charleston, West Virginia, August 8, 1947; admitted to bar, 1972, West Virginia, U.S. District Court, Northern and Southern Districts of West Virginia and U.S. Court of Appeals, 4th Circuit; 1984, U.S. Court of Appeals, 9th Circuit (Not admitted in District of Columbia). *Education:* West Virginia University (B.A., 1969; J.D., 1972). Assistant U.S. Attorney, Southern District of West Virginia, 1976-1981. U.S. Department of Justice: Assistant Director, Attorney Generals Advocacy Institute, 1981-1982. Litigation Branch Chief, Fraud Section, Criminal Division, 1985-1987; Deputy Chief, Fraud Section, 1987-1988. ***PRACTICE AREAS:*** Litigation; White Collar Crime; White Collar Defense. ***Email:*** leslie.hoffman@piperrudnick.com

(This Listing Continued)

DEBORAH J. ISRAEL, born Atlantic City, New Jersey, November 10, 1964; admitted to bar, 1990, Maryland and New Jersey; 1991, Virginia and District of Columbia. *Education:* Rutgers University (B.A., with honors, 1986; J.D., 1990); Exeter College, Oxford University, England. Stratton Advanced Moot Court Competition Winner and Best Brief, Rutgers Law National Moot Court Team. *Member:* Fairfax County, Maryland, New Jersey and Virginia State Bar Associations; District of Columbia Bar; Women's Bar Association Foundation Board of Directors (President, 1996-1998; Vice President, 1995-1996); Women's Bar Association (Chairperson, Community Projects Committee, 1991-1995). ***PRACTICE AREAS:*** Commercial Litigation; Business Litigation; Intellectual Property. ***Email:*** deborah.israel@piperrudnick.com

SANDRA JARVA-WEISS, born Highland Park, Michigan, April 20, 1958; admitted to bar, 1983, Connecticut, U.S. Supreme Court and U.S. District Court, District of Connecticut; 1998, Maryland and District of Columbia. *Education:* George Washington University (B.A., with honors, 1980; J.D., with honors, 1983). Phi Beta Kappa. General Counsel, Bridgeport Hospital, a member of Yale-New Haven Health Services Corporation. *Member:* Connecticut, Maryland State and American Bar Associations; The District of Columbia Bar. (Also at Baltimore, Maryland Office). ***PRACTICE AREAS:*** Health Care Law; Hospital Law; Corporate Law. ***Email:*** sandra.jarvaweiss@piperrudnick.com

DEBORAH E. JENNINGS, born Washington, D.C., February 8, 1949; admitted to bar, 1974, Maryland; 1984, District of Columbia. *Education:* University of Maryland (B.A., with honors, 1970); Georgetown University Law Center (J.D., 1974). Assistant State's Attorney for Montgomery County, Maryland, 1975-1977. Assistant Attorney General of Maryland, 1977-1980. Chief, Criminal Investigations Division, 1978-1980. Fellow, American Bar Foundation. (Also in Baltimore, Maryland Office). ***PRACTICE AREAS:*** Environmental Law; Litigation; Mergers and Acquisitions Law; Commercial Finance. ***Email:*** deborah.jennings@piperrudnick.com

LEANN M. JOHNSON-KOCH, born Grosse Pointe, Michigan, January 11, 1964; admitted to bar, 1990, Pennsylvania; 1991, District of Columbia, U.S. District Court for the District of Columbia and U.S. District Court, District of Maryland. *Education:* Boston University (B.A., 1987); Syracuse University (J.D., 1990). Notes and Comments Editor, Syracuse University Journal of International Law and Commerce, 1988-1990. *Member:* District of Columbia Bar; Pennsylvania and American (Planning Committee, Solid and Hazardous Waste Committee, Section of Natural Resources, Energy and Environmental Law) Bar Associations. ***REPORTED CASES:*** Rossaki v. NUS Corp., et al., 695 A.2d 203 (Md.App. 1997). ***PRACTICE AREAS:*** Environmental Litigation; Environmental Law. ***Email:*** leann.johnson@piperrudnick.com

E. ASHTON JOHNSTON, born Richmond, Virginia, November 13, 1960; admitted to bar, 1991, Virginia; 1993, District of Columbia. *Education:* James Madison University (B.A., 1982); Catholic University (J.D., 1991). Member, Catholic University Law Review, 1989-1991. ***PRACTICE AREAS:*** Telecommunications Law; Business Law; Technology Law. ***Email:*** ashton.johnston@piperrudnick.com

PAULA M. JUNGHANS, born Baltimore, Maryland, September 3, 1949; admitted to bar, 1976, Maryland; 1977, U.S. District Court, District of Maryland and U.S. Tax Court; 1980, U.S. Court of Appeals, Fourth Circuit and U.S. Supreme Court; 1987, U.S. Court of Appeals, Tenth Circuit; 2000, U.S. Court of Appeals, Fifth Circuit; 2001, District of Columbia. *Education:* College of Notre Dame of Maryland (B.A., cum laude, 1971); University of Maryland (J.D., 1976). Co-Author, with Becker, "Federal Tax Litigation," Warren Gorham & Lamont, 1992 & Supps. Member, Trial Courts Judicial Nominating Commission, 8th Judicial Circuit, Baltimore City, 1986-1996. Member, 1988-1998, Treasurer, 1994-1996, Member, Board of Governors, 1994-1998, President-Elect, 1996-1997 and President, 1997-1998, Maryland Criminal Defense Attorneys Association. Member: Attorney Grievance Commission Inquiry Panel, 1988-1992; Review Board, 1993-1997. Deputy Assistant Attorney General, 1998-1999 and Acting Assistant Attorney General, 2000-2001, Tax Division, U.S. Department of Justice. *Member:* Maryland State (Member, Board of Governors, 1984-1986) and American (Vice-Chair, 1993-1995 and Chair, 1995-1997, Committee on Criminal and Civil Tax Penalties and Member, Tax Section; Member, Sections on: Litigation; Criminal Justice) Bar Associations; Maryland Criminal Defense Attorneys Association (President, 1997-1998). Fellow: American Bar Foundation; Maryland Bar Foundation; American College of Tax Counsel. ***PRACTICE AREAS:*** Tax Litigation; White Collar Criminal Defense; Litigation. ***Email:*** paula.junghans@piperrudnick.com

JEFFREY R. KEITELMAN, born New London, Connecticut, February 18, 1960; admitted to bar, 1986, Connecticut; 1987, New York and District of Columbia. *Education:* Brown University (B.A., magna cum laude, 1982); Columbia University (J.D., 1986). Phi Beta Kappa. Harlan Fiske Stone Scholar. Founder and Chair Emeritus of Greater D.C. Cares, Inc., 1989—. Founding Board Member, City Cares of America, Inc., 1991—. *Member:* The District of Columbia Bar; Connecticut, New York State and American (Member: Real Property, Trust and Probate Law; Young Lawyers Division) Bar Associations. ***PRACTICE AREAS:*** Commercial Real Estate; General Business. ***Email:*** jeffrey.keitelman@piperrudnick.com

(This Listing Continued)

PIPER MARBURY RUDNICK & WOLFE LLP, Washington—Continued

STEVEN B. KELBER, born Chicago, Illinois, January 3, 1956; admitted to bar, 1981, District of Columbia and U.S. District Court for the District of Columbia; 1983, U.S. Court of Appeals for the Federal Circuit; 1999, U.S. Supreme Court; registered to practice before U.S. Patent and Trademark Office. *Education:* Rensselaer Polytechnic Institute; University of Maryland (B.A., magna cum laude, 1978); George Washington University (J.D., with honors, 1981). Phi Kappa Phi. Author: "Manufacturing Engineers, Patents and Trade Secrets," SME 1986; New Patent Interference Practice (1996), "The Taking of Testimonial Depositions in Japan for Use in the U.S. Patent Interferences," 78 JPTOS No. 2 (1996); "U.S. Litigation and International Competition," International Legal Strategy Magazine (1996), New Laws on Interference (1995). *Member:* The District of Columbia Bar (Member, Patent, Trademark and Copyright Law Section); American Bar Association (Member, Patent, Trademark and Copyright Law Section); American Chemical Society; Society for the Advancement of Materials and Process Engineering; Society of Manufacturing Engineers; American Intellectual Property Law Association. ***LANGUAGES:*** French. ***Email:*** steven.kelber@piperrudnick.com

JILL K. KERXTON, born Washington, D.C., October 5, 1962; admitted to bar, 1987, Maryland; 1991, District of Columbia. *Education:* Wake Forest University (B.S., 1984); The Columbus School of Law, Catholic University of America (J.D., 1987). Author: "Financial Comfort If a Seller Doesn't Tell The Truth," Mergers and Acquisitions, September/October, 1999; "M&A Insurance: Extra Protections in Risk Management," Mergers and Acquisitions, November/December, 1996. *Member:* Maryland State Bar Association; The District of Columbia Bar. ***PRACTICE AREAS:*** Corporate; Taxation; Insurance Law. ***Email:*** jill.kerxton@piperrudnick.com

MARK A. KIRSCH, born Washington, D.C., September 25, 1958; admitted to bar, 1985, Maryland, District of Columbia, U.S. District Court for the District of Maryland and U.S. District Court for the District of Columbia. *Education:* University of Rochester (B.A., cum laude, 1980); George Washington University (J.D., 1984). Author: "Extranets -- Getting Inside Your Website: Practice Tips" *Maryland Bar Journal,* November 2000; "Franchisor Liability for Failure by Franchises to Comply with the Americans with Disabilities Act," *Franchise Law Journal,* Vol. 19, No. 4, Spring, 2000; "Healthcare Services: An Accidental Franchise?" *Maryland Bar Journal,* November 1999. Co-author: "The Accidental Franchise," ABA Forum on Franchising, October 2001; "Dual Branding: The New Franchising Phenomenon," Leader's Franchising Business and Law Alert, Nov. and Dec., 1995. *Member:* The District of Columbia Bar; Maryland State (Chairman, Franchise and Distribution Law Committee, 1999-2001) and American (Section on Business Law, Forum on Franchising) Bar Associations. ***PRACTICE AREAS:*** Franchise Law; Licensing and Distribution Law; Corporate and Commercial Transactions. ***Email:*** mark.kirsch@piperrudnick.com

FREDERICK L. KLEIN, born New Bedford, Massachusetts, October 20, 1954; admitted to bar, 1979, District of Columbia; 1980, Florida. *Education:* Duke University (A.B., 1976); University of Miami (J.D., 1979). Articles and Comments Editor, University of Miami Law Review, 1978-1979. Law Clerk to The Honorable Paul H. Roney, United States Court of Appeals for the Fifth Circuit, 1979-1980. ***PRACTICE AREAS:*** Real Estate - Commercial. ***Email:*** frederick.klein@piperrudnick.com

SHELDON KRANTZ, born Omaha, Nebraska, June 5, 1938; admitted to bar, 1970, Massachusetts; 1988, California; 1990, District of Columbia. *Education:* University of Nebraska (B.S., 1960; J.D., cum laude, 1962). Order of the Coif. Editor-in-Chief, University of Nebraska Law Review, 1961-1962. Trial Attorney, Organized Crime and Racketeering Section, Criminal Division, U.S. Department of Justice, 1962-1965; Professor of Law, Boston University School of Law, 1970-1981; Dean, University of San Diego School of Law, 1981-1989. Adjunct Professor, American University-Washington College of Law (Corporate and White Collar Crime). Chair American Bar Association Criminal Justice Section, 1989-1990. Co-Chair, White Collar Crime Group. ***PRACTICE AREAS:*** Business Crime Law; Criminal Trial Practice and Federal Practice; White Collar Crime. ***Email:*** sheldon.krantz@piperrudnick.com

MARC R. LABGOLD, born Los Angeles, California, July 15, 1964; admitted to bar, 1995, Georgia; 1996, U.S. Court of Appeals for the Federal Circuit; registered to practice before U.S. Patent and Trademark Office (Not admitted in District of Columbia). *Education:* New York University (B.A., 1986); California Institute of Technology (Ph.D., 1990); George Washington University (J.D., 1995). Author: *Winning Patent Battles in Court* Managing Intellectual Property, Patent Yearbook 1998 at 61; "Electronic Management of Litigation," lecture and paper presented at the American Bar Association, Section on Intellectual Property Law Conference, Washington, D.C., April 11-12, 1996. Co-author: with Kevin M. Bell: "Courts Begin to CD Light on CD Briefs," National Law Journal, November 3, 1997 at B8; "High Tech Solutions To Complex Litigation Problems: (DI)-Document Imaging," The Law Works, June and July 1995; "CD-ROM for Document Handling Creates a Powerful Litigation Tool," New York Law Journal, January 31, 1995, Vol. 213, No. 20. *Member:* American Bar Association; The Association of Trial Lawyers of America. ***REPORTED CASES:*** Ajinomoto Co. v. Archer-Daniel-Midland Co., 228 F.3d 1338 (Fed. Cir. 2000), aff'g 1998 U.S. Dist. LEXIS 3833 (D.Del. 1998); Biacore AB and Biacore, Inc. v. Thermo BioAnalysis Corp., 79 F.Supp.2d 422 (D.Del. 1999); Life Technologies, Inc. v. Clontech Laboratories, Inc., 224 F.3d 1320 (Fed. Cir. 2000); Regents of the University of California v. Eli Lilly & Co., 119 F.3d 1559 (Fed. Cir. 1997), 39 USPQ2d 1225 (S.D.Ind. 1995). ***PRACTICE AREAS:*** Patent Litigation; Patent Prosecution; Biotechnology Patents; Intellectual Property. ***Email:*** marc.labgold@piperrudnick.com

JEFFREY F. LISS, born Baltimore, Maryland, June 10, 1951; admitted to bar, 1975, District of Columbia; 1981, Maryland. *Education:* University of Michigan (B.A., with high honors, 1972; M.A., 1975; J.D., 1975). Special Government Employee, Office of the White House Counsel, 1996-1997. Treasurer, Friends of Lt. Gov. Kathleen Kennedy Townsend (D. Md.). Member, American Law Institute. Fellow, American Bar Foundation. Board Member and Executive Committee, Baltimore Symphony Orchestra. Board Member and Oral Historian, D.C. Circuit Historical Society. ***PRACTICE AREAS:*** Litigation; Insurance Law; Environmental Law. ***Email:*** jeffrey.liss@piperrudnick.com

H. BRET LOWELL, born Brooklyn, New York, August 5, 1953; admitted to bar, 1978, District of Columbia. *Education:* State University of New York at Buffalo (B.A., magna cum laude, 1975); Georgetown University (J.D., 1978). Phi Beta Kappa; Omicron Delta Epsilon. Editor: American Criminal Law Review, 1977-1978; Franchise Law Journal, 1984-1988. Co-Author: "Franchising: Regulation of Buying and Selling a Franchise," Bureau of National Affairs, Corporate Practice Series, 1983, 1997; "The Application of U.S. Franchise Laws to International Franchise Sales," Vol. 1, No. 7, Global Franchise Alert, 1994. Editor, "Franchise Law Compliance Manual," American Bar Association, 2000. Author: "Multiple Unit Franchising: the Key to Rapid System Growth," International Franchise Association, 1991. Franchise Advisor, Franchise and Business Opportunities Committee, North American Securities Administrators Association, 1989—. Listed: Best Lawyers in America; Who's Who in American Law. *Member:* The District of Columbia Bar; American (Governing Committee, 1988-1992; Chair, 1992-1995, Forum on Franchising; Vice Chair, 1985-1989, 1990-1992 and Co-Chair, 1989-1990, Franchise Law Committee, Section of General Practice) and International Bar Associations; American Intellectual Property Law Association; Licensing Executives Society. ***PRACTICE AREAS:*** Franchising; Trade Regulation; Corporate; Trademarks. ***Email:*** bret.lowell@piperrudnick.com

STEVEN J. MANDELL, born Passaic, New Jersey, August 23, 1958; admitted to bar, 1983, Maryland; 1984, District of Columbia and New York. *Education:* University of Richmond (B.A., magna cum laude, 1980); Catholic University of America (J.D., 1983); Georgetown University (LL.M. 1986). (Also in Baltimore, Maryland Office). ***PRACTICE AREAS:*** Health Care and Hospital Law; Corporate Law; Venture Capital. ***Email:*** steven.mandell@piperrudnick.com

MITCHELL S. MARDER, born Boston, Massachusetts, 1961; admitted to bar, 1986, Massachusetts; 1995, District of Columbia. *Education:* George Washington University (B.A., 1983; J.D., 1986). Phi Beta Kappa. ***LANGUAGES:*** French. ***PRACTICE AREAS:*** Corporate Finance; Venture Capital; Banking Law. ***Email:*** mitchell.marder@piperrudnick.com

PETRINA M. MARKOWITZ, born Baltimore, Maryland, January 11, 1957; admitted to bar, 1981, District of Columbia; 1989, Maryland. *Education:* Hood College (B.A., magna cum laude, 1978); University of Strasbourg, Strasbourg, France (Cours Moyen & Cours Superieur Degrees, 1977); Georgetown University (J.D., cum laude, 1981). Phi Kappa Phi; Pi Delta Phi. Editor, American Criminal Law Review, 1980-1981. *Member:* The District of Columbia Bar. ***Email:*** petrina.markowitz@piperrudnick.com

RICHARD J. MARKS, born Washington, D.C., July 5, 1967; admitted to bar, 1993, Maryland; 1999, District of Columbia. *Education:* Northwestern University (B.S.E.E., 1989); University of Maryland (J.D., 1993). Order of the Coif. *Member:* National Association of Bond Lawyers. ***PRACTICE AREAS:*** Banking; Finance; Business Reorganization; Business Taxation; Business; Technology; Corporate; Securities; Public Finance; Venture Capital; Emerging Growth Companies. ***Email:*** richard.marks@piperrudnick.com

EDWIN M. MARTIN, JR., born Washington, DC, 1942; admitted to bar, 1966, Massachusetts; 1982, District of Columbia. *Education:* Harvard University (A.B., cum laude, 1963; LL.B., magna cum laude, 1966). Co-Chairman, Venture Capital and Emerging Companies Practice Group. ***PRACTICE AREAS:*** Securities Regulation Law; Venture Capital Law; Technology Law; Mergers and Acquisitions. ***Email:*** edwin.martin@piperrudnick.com

ANDREA M. MATTEI, born Worcester, Massachusetts, March 10, 1954; admitted to bar, 1983, Massachusetts; 1984, Maryland; 1993, Virginia (Not admitted in District of Columbia). *Education:* Mount Holyoke College (B.A., magna cum laude, 1976); Johns Hopkins University (M.A., 1980); University of Maryland (J.D., 1983). Waddell Fellow, The University of North Carolina at Chapel Hill, 1977-1978. Formerly with: Piper & Marbury, Baltimore, Maryland, 1986-1994; Niles, Barton & Wilmer, Baltimore, Maryland, 1984-1986.

(This Listing Continued)

Member: Virginia State Bar; American Bar Association (Member, Sections on: Real Property; Commercial Law). ***PRACTICE AREAS:*** Finance; Real Estate Finance; Corporate; Securities. ***Email:*** andrea.mattei@piperrudnick.com

JOHN McJUNKIN, born Kingsport, Tennessee, January 5, 1962; admitted to bar, 1987, North Carolina; 1989, District of Columbia; 1990, Virginia; 1993, Maryland. *Education:* Hampden-Sydney College (B.A., summa cum laude, 1984); University of Cincinnati (J.D., 1987). Phi Beta Kappa. Order of the Barristers. *Member:* North Carolina State Bar; Virginia State Bar; District of Columbia Bar; American Bar Association. ***PRACTICE AREAS:*** Commercial Litigation; Bankruptcy; General Business; Workouts; Telecommunications Law. ***Email:*** john.mcjunkin@piperrudnick.com

DEBORAH R. MESHULAM, born Lancaster, Pennsylvania, November 25, 1956; admitted to bar, 1982, New York; 1998, District of Columbia. *Education:* University of Virginia (B.A., magna cum laude, 1978); Columbia University School of Law (J.D., 1981). Harlan Fiske Stone Scholar. Assistant Chief Litigation Counsel, Securities and Exchange Commission Division of Enforcement, 1990-1997. *Member:* District of Columbia Bar; American Bar Association; Women's Bar Association. ***LANGUAGES:*** French. ***PRACTICE AREAS:*** Securities Litigation; Business Litigation; Mergers and Acquisitions Litigation; Financial Litigation; Accounting Litigation. ***Email:*** deborah.meshulam@piperrudnick.com

CYNTHIA J. MORRIS, born Little Rock, Arkansas, June 13, 1952; admitted to bar, 1981, Maryland and District of Columbia. *Education:* University of Miami and California State University at Sonoma (B.A., 1974); University of Maryland (J.D., with honors, 1981). Order of the Coif. ***PRACTICE AREAS:*** Environmental Law; Environmental Litigation; Commercial Litigation; Insurance Coverage. ***Email:*** cynthia.morris@piperrudnick.com

RAYMOND G. MULLADY, JR., born Elizabeth, New Jersey, March 20, 1957; admitted to bar, 1983, Maryland, U.S. Supreme Court, U.S. Court of Appeals, Fourth, Sixth and Eighth Circuits, U.S. District Court, District of Maryland, U.S. District Court, District of Columbia and U.S. District Court, District of Arizona; 2001, District of Columbia. *Education:* University of Maryland (B.S., 1979; J.D., 1983). Notes and Comments Editor, Maryland Law Review, 1982-1983. Author: "Everything You Wanted to Know About Black Box Warnings," Defense Counsel Journal, Vol. 68, No. 1 (January 2001); "The Federal Preemptive Effect of FDA Pre-Market Approval on Product Liability Claims for Regulated Prescription Drugs and Medical Devices," Food, Drug, Cosmetic and Medical Device Law Digest, Vol. 11, No. 3, Food, Drug and Cosmetic Law Section, New York State Bar Association (October 1994). Contributor and speaker, Defense Research Institute Drug & Medical Device Litigation Seminar: "Everything You Wanted to Know About Black Box Warnings," Washington, D.C., April 7, 2000. *Member:* Defense Research Institute (Drug & Medical Device Committee); Maryland Association of Defense Trial Counsel; Maryland Bar Foundation; Bar Association of Baltimore City, Inc. (Board of Trustees). ***PRACTICE AREAS:*** Litigation; Products Liability Law; Food and Drug; Libel and Slander Law. ***Email:*** raymond.mullady@piperrudnick.com

KEVIN P. MULLEN, born Washington, D.C., October 20, 1961; admitted to bar, 1988, Georgia; 1990, District of Columbia and U.S. District Court, Northern District of Georgia; 1994, U.S. Court of Federal Claims; 1996, U.S. Court of Appeals, Federal Circuit; 1998, U.S. Supreme Court; 2000, U.S. District Court, District of Maryland; 2001, U.S. Court of Appeals, Fourth Circuit. *Education:* University of Virginia (B.A., with distinction, 1984; J.D., 1988). *Member:* American Bar Association (Vice Chair, Public Contracts Section, Bid Protest Committee and Emerging Issues Committee; Litigation Section); National Contract Management Association; National Defense Industrial Association. ***PRACTICE AREAS:*** Government Contracts; Construction Law. ***Email:*** kevin.mullen@piperrudnick.com

ROBERT B. MURPHY, born Flushing, New York, February 26, 1956; admitted to bar, 1983, Pennsylvania; 1990, District of Columbia. *Education:* University of Notre Dame (B.A., 1978); University of Minnesota (M.B.A., 1980); Villanova University School of Law (J.D., 1983); Georgetown University (LL.M., Securities Regulation, 1987). Attorney-Adviser, U.S. Securities and Exchange Commission, Div. of Corporation Finance, Washington, D.C., 1983-1987. *Member:* The District of Columbia Bar; American Bar Association. ***PRACTICE AREAS:*** Finance; Corporate Law; Securities. ***Email:*** bob.murphy@piperrudnick.com

STEPHEN R. MYSLIWIEC, born Portland, Oregon, August 15, 1948; admitted to bar, 1976, Texas; 1977, District of Columbia. *Education:* University of Notre Dame (B.A., 1970; M.A., 1973); Yale University (J.D., 1975). Note Editor, Yale Law Journal. Author: "Insurance Coverage for Claims of Latent Defects: What Protection is a Builder Buying?" (March 2000) Journal of Insurance Coverage. ***PRACTICE AREAS:*** Construction Law; Insurance Law; Litigation. ***Email:*** stephen.mysliwiec@piperrudnick.com

LEWIS A. NOONBERG, born Baltimore, Maryland, April 26, 1938; admitted to bar, 1962, Maryland; 1992, District of Columbia. *Education:* Dartmouth College (A.B., 1959); University of Maryland (LL.B., 1962). Order of the Coif. Assistant Attorney General, State of Maryland, 1967-1969. *Member:*

(This Listing Continued)

American Law Institute. Fellow, American College of Trial Lawyers. ***PRACTICE AREAS:*** Antitrust; Trade Regulation Law; Litigation. ***Email:*** lewis.noonberg@piperrudnick.com

RICHARD J. OPARIL, born Syracuse, New York, March 1, 1960; admitted to bar, 1986, New York and U.S. District Court, Southern and Eastern Districts of New York; 1987, District of Columbia and U.S. Court of Appeals, Fourth Circuit; 1988, U.S. District Court for the District of Columbia; 1990, U.S. Supreme Court and U.S. Court of Appeals for the District of Columbia; 1996, U.S. District Court, District of Maryland; 1997, U.S. Court of Federal Claims; 2001, U.S. Court of Appeals, Federal Circuit, U.S. District Court, District of Colorado, U.S. District Court, Northern District of Texas and U.S. District Court, Northern District of New York. *Education:* Syracuse University (B.A., 1981); Case Western Reserve University (J.D., magna cum laude, 1985). Order of the Coif. Associate, Case Western Reserve Law Review, 1983-1984. Recipient: American Jurisprudence Award in Criminal Procedure; First Place, Ault Moot Court Competition. Author: "Making the Defendant's Case: How Much Assistance Must the Prosecutor Provide?," 23 Am. Crim. L. Rev. 447, 1986; "Waiver of Sovereign Immunity in the United States and Great Britain by an Arbitration Agreement," 3 J. Int'l Arb. 61, 1986; "The Coming Impact of the False Claims Act," 22 Akron L. Rev. 525, 1989; "Preemption and the Federal Arbitration Act," 13 Geo. Mason U. L. Rev. 325, 1991; "Immunity of International Organizations in United States Courts: Absolute or Restrictive?," 24 Vanderbilt J. Transnational L. 689, 1991; "Obtaining Federal Court Trial Testimony From Nonresident Corporate Officials: The Rules Need Revision," 25 Akron L. Rev. 571, 1992; "If At First You Don't Succeed: Impediments To A Second Removal To Federal Court Of A Previously Remanded Case," 37 S. D. L. Rev. 523, 1992. *Member:* The District of Columbia Bar (Member: Litigation Section); American Bar Association (Member, Criminal Justice and Litigation Sections; Co-Chair, Experts Subcommittee, Trial Practice Committee, Litigation Section; Member, Editorial Board, ABA Commercial and Banking Litigation Committee Newsletter); D.C. Attorney-Client Arbitration Board. ***PRACTICE AREAS:*** White Collar Crime; Complex Litigation; Civil Litigation; Patent Litigation. ***Email:*** richard.oparil@piperrudnick.com

CAROLINE E. PETRO, born Buffalo, New York, August 27, 1964; admitted to bar, 1989, Virginia and U.S. Court of Appeals, Fourth Circuit; 1991, District of Columbia; 1994, U.S. District Court, District of Maryland; 1995, Maryland and U.S. District Court, District of Columbia; 1996, U.S. District Court, Eastern and Western Districts of Virginia; 1997, U.S. Bankruptcy Court, Eastern and Western Districts of Virginia and U.S. Court of Appeals, District of Columbia Circuit; 2000, U.S. Supreme Court. *Education:* Princeton University (A.B., cum laude, 1986); University of Michigan (J.D., 1989). *Member:* Women's Bar Association Foundation of the District of Columbia (President, 2001-2002; Vice President, 2000-2001; Director, 1999-2002). ***PRACTICE AREAS:*** Commercial Litigation; Employment; Bankruptcy. ***Email:*** caroline.petro@piperrudnick.com

LEE J. PLAVE, born Brooklyn, New York, June 22, 1958; admitted to bar, 1984, New York; 1987, District of Columbia. *Education:* Clark University (B.A., 1980); New York Law School (J.D., cum laude, 1983). Recipient, American Jurisprudence Award for Excellence in the Law of Debtors' and Creditors' Rights (Bankruptcy), 1983. Listed in International Who's Who of Franchise Lawyers (1st ed. and 2nd ed). Member, 1981-1983 and Associate Editor, 1982-1983, New York Law School Journal of International and Comparative Law. Attorney, U.S. Federal Trade Commission, Bureau of Consumer Protection, Enforcement Division, 1983-1987. Author/Co-Author: "FAQ's for Franchising About the Gramm-Leach-Bliley Act and the FTC Rule on Privacy of Consumer Financial Information," Franchise Update (Fall 2001); "Franchisors and Franchisees Face the Reality: The Gramm-Leach-Bliley Act Applies," Franchise World (Oct. 2001); "Essentials of E-commerce," ABA Forum on Franchising Legal Symposium (Oct. 2001); "Protection of Domain Names, Cybersquatting, and Cybergripe Sites," ABA Forum on Franchising Legal Symposium (Oct. 2000); "How to Implement Dot.com Franchising Solutions," Franchise World (Oct. 2000); "E-Sign and the FTC Rule," 4 The Franchise Lawyer 1 (Sept. 2000); "Franchisors Gain Powerful New Weapon In War Against Cybersquatters," 6 Leader's Franchise & Business Alert 4, at 1 (Jan. 2000); "Technology and Franchising," ABA Forum on Franchising Legal Symposium (Oct. 1999); "Intellectual Property, the Internet and Franchising," International Franchise Association Annual Legal Symposium (May 1998); "Communication in the Electronic Age," ABA Forum on Franchising Legal Symposium (Mar. 1996); "It's a Small, Small E-World, Franchise World UK (Sept. 1996); "The Application of US Franchise Laws to International Franchise Sales," 1 Global Franchise Alert 7 (CCH) (June 1994); "Point/Counterpoint: Do US Franchise Laws Cover Intentional Franchise Sales," 1 Global Franchise Alert 11 (CCH) (Oct. 1994); "Franchising and the Federal Trade Commission: Recent Developments (1991-93)," 2 Franchise Legal Digest (Spring 1993) at 13; "Extra-territorial Application of US Franchise Registration and Disclosure Laws in International Franchise Transactions," 7 J. International Franchise and Distribution Law 1, at 8 (1993); "Software Licensing for Franchisors," Franchise Update (Sept. 1991); "Franchising and the Federal Trade Commission: Recent Developments," 2 Franchise Legal Digest (Spring 1991) at 8; "The Form and Content of Unit Franchise Agreements within the Context of International Master Franchising,"

(This Listing Continued)

PIPER MARBURY RUDNICK & WOLFE LLP, Washington—Continued

International Bar Association Franchising Committee Annual Legal Symposium (May 1991); "Franchising and the Federal Trade Commission: A Review of Current Developments," Franchise Legal Digest 3 (May 1989) at 10. Co-Chair, American Conference Institute Symposium on Online Automotive Sales (Oct. 2000 and Oct. 2001—). *Member:* The District of Columbia Bar; American Bar Association (Forum on Franchising); International Bar Association (Section on Business Law; Committee on Franchising). ***PRACTICE AREAS:*** Franchising; Trade Regulation; Technology Licensing. ***Email:*** lee.plave@piperrudnick.com

RONALD L. PLESSER, born Queens, New York, May 28, 1945; admitted to bar, 1971, New York; 1972, District of Columbia. *Education:* George Washington University (B.A., 1967; J.D., with honors, 1970). Appointed General Counsel of United States Privacy Protection Study Commission, 1975-1977. Adjunct Professor of Law, George Washington University, 1982-1988. Chair, Individual Rights Section, ABA. ***PRACTICE AREAS:*** Information and Privacy (33%); Communications Law (33%); Intellectual Property Law (33%). ***Email:*** ronald.plesser@piperrudnick.com

JAMES P. RATHVON, born Port Chester, New York, June 11, 1951; admitted to bar, 1982, District of Columbia; 1991, Maryland. *Education:* Tufts University (B.S., 1973; M.Ed., 1974); State University of New York at Stony Brook (M.A., 1978); George Washington University (J.D., magna cum laude, 1982). ***PRACTICE AREAS:*** Environmental; Commercial Litigation. ***Email:*** james.rathvon@piperrudnick.com

RICHARD P. RECTOR, born Baltimore, Maryland, December 15, 1959; admitted to bar, 1987, Maryland; 1995, District of Columbia. *Education:* University of Maryland (B.A., 1981; J.D., 1986). ABA Public Contract Law Section, Chair, Regulatory Coordinating Committee, 2002, Chair, Federal Claims and Remedies Committee, 1997-2000, Managing Editor, Public Contract Law Journal, 1994-1997. Lecturer, Intensive Program on Trial Advocacy, 1994, 1996; Columnist, Washington Technology, "InfoTech & Law," 1999-2002. *Member:* Maryland State (Board of Contract Appeals) and American (Public Contract Law Section) Bar Associations; The District of Columbia Bar. ***PRACTICE AREAS:*** Government Contracts. ***Email:*** richard.rector@piperrudnick.com

ANTHONY H. RICKERT, born Salisbury, Maryland, May 28, 1955; admitted to bar, 1982, Maryland and District of Columbia. *Education:* University of Maryland (B.A., cum laude, 1977); Georgetown University (J.D., magna cum laude, 1981). ***PRACTICE AREAS:*** Business Law; Commercial Law; Corporate Financing Law; Health Care. ***Email:*** anthony.rickert@piperrudnick.com

ROBERT A. SALERNO, born Newark, New Jersey, September 14, 1961; admitted to bar, 1990, Virginia; 1991, District of Columbia. *Education:* Brown University (B.A., with honors, 1983); University of Virginia (J.D., 1990). *Member:* American Bar Association (Member, Sections on: Litigation; Criminal Justice); Edward Bennett Williams American Inn of Court. ***LANGUAGES:*** Spanish. ***PRACTICE AREAS:*** Commercial Civil Litigation; White Collar Criminal Litigation. ***Email:*** robert.salerno@piperrudnick.com

JEROLD I. SCHNEIDER, born Newark, New Jersey, December 22, 1942; admitted to bar, 1970, Michigan and Virginia; 1989, District of Columbia; U.S. Supreme Court; U.S. Court of Appeals, for the Federal, Fourth, Sixth, Ninth and Eleventh Circuits; U.S. District Court, Eastern District of Virginia; U.S. District Court for the District of Columbia; U.S. District Court, District of Maryland; U.S. District Court, Eastern and Western Districts of Michigan; U.S. Court of Federal Claims; registered to practice before U.S. Patent and Trademark Office. *Education:* Newark College of Engineering (B.S.E.E., 1964); George Washington University (J.D., cum laude, 1970). Author: "What Clients Expect An Attorney to Know About Patents," 55 Michigan State Bar Journal, 418 (1976); Patents, Trademarks and Copyrights for the General Practitioner, 83 Case and Comment, 1977. Editor, Patents, Trademarks and Copyrights, West's Legal Forms 2d, vol 25 (1986). Lecturer: Patent Resources Group, (1993—) National Association of Home Builders (1994-1996), American Intellectual Property law Association (1990); Member, The Association of Trial Lawyers of America, 1994-1998. *Member:* Bureau of National Affairs, United States Patents Quarterly (Member, Advisory Board, 1995—); American Intellectual Property Law Association; International Association for Protection of Industrial Property; District of Columbia; State Bar of Michigan; Virginia and American Bar Associations; Institute of Electrical and Electronic Engineers. ***REPORTED CASES:*** Alpha Industries Inc. v. Alpha Sportswear Ltd., NO. 97-1825-A, 1998 WL 766708, 48 U.S.P.Q.2d 1448 (E.D. Va., Aug 13, 1998); Glaverbel Societe Anonyme v. Northlake Marketing & Supply Inc., NO. 2, 96-CV-32-TS, 1998 WL 750351, 48 U.S.P.Q.2d 1344 (N.D.Ind., Mar 31, 1998); Northlake Mktg. & Supply v. Glaverbel S.A., No. 92 C 2732, 1997 WL 835203, 45 U.S.P.Q.2d 1541 (N.D.Ill. December 19, 1997); Northlake Mktg. & Supply v. Glaverbel S.A., 986 F.Supp 471, 45 U.S.P.Q.2d 1113 (N.D.Ill. November 13, 1997); Glaverbel Societe Anonyme v. Northlake Marketing et al, 45 F.3d 922 (Fed. Cir. 1995); Northlake Mktg. & Supply, Inc. v. Glaverbel S.A., No. 92-C 2732, 1995 WL 534290, 36 U.S.P.Q.2d 1758 (N.D.Ill. September 1, 1995); Northlake Mktg. & Supply v. Glaverbel S.A., 861 F.Supp. 653 (N.D.Ill. 1994), Supplemental Opinion No. 92-C 2732, 1994 U.S. Dist. LEXIS 13990 (N.D.Ill. September 29, 1994); Sig Swiss Indus. Co. v. Fres-Co System USA, Inc., No.Civ.A. 92-0699, 1992 WL 23446, 22 U.S.P.Q.2d 1601 (E.D.Pa. Feb 3, 1992); SmithKline Diagnostics, Inc. Helena Laboratories, Corp., 926 F.2d 1161 (Fed. Cir. 1991); Robert R. Jones Assoc. Inc. v. Nino Homes et al, 858 F.2d 274 (6th Cir. 1988); SmithKline Diagnostics, Inc. Helena Laboratories Corp., 859 F.2d 878 (Fed. Cir. 1988). ***PRACTICE AREAS:*** Intellectual Property Law; Patent; Trademark; Copyright; Internet Law.

THEODORE D. SEGAL, born Washington, D.C., August 7, 1955; admitted to bar, 1985, Maryland; 1986, District of Columbia. *Education:* Duke University (B.A., magna cum laude, 1977); Georgetown University (J.D., magna cum laude, 1984). Law Clerk, Chief Judge William C. Pryor, District of Columbia, 1984-1986. (Also at Baltimore, Maryland Office). ***PRACTICE AREAS:*** Corporate and Securities; Venture Capital; Health Care; Life Sciences; Biotechnology. ***Email:*** theodore.segal@piperrudnick.com

EARL J. SILBERT, born Boston, Massachusetts, March 8, 1936; admitted to bar, 1960, Massachusetts; 1963, District of Columbia; 1975, U.S. Supreme Court; 1983, U.S. Claims Court; 1985, U.S. Tax Court. *Education:* Harvard University (B.A., magna cum laude, Phi Beta Kappa, 1957; LL.B., cum laude, 1960). Tax Division, U.S. Department of Justice, 1960-1964. Assistant U.S. Attorney, 1964-1969. Office of Deputy Attorney General, Department of Justice, 1969-1970. Principal Assistant U.S. Attorney, 1972-1973 and U.S. Attorney, 1974-1979, Schwalb, Donnenfeld, Bray & Silbert, District of Columbia. President, National Association of Former United States Attorneys, 1985-1986. President, Assistant U.S. Attorney's Association for the District of Columbia, 1985-1986. Member, Advisory Committee for Review of the Admissions Process, District of Columbia Court of Appeals, 1986-1987. Member, Practitioners Advocacy Group to U.S. Commissioner for Sentencing Guidelines, 1989—. *Member:* The District of Columbia Bar; American Bar Association (Member: Criminal Justice Section; Litigation Section; Standing Committee on Minimum Standards for Criminal Justice, 1976-1980; Consultant, Standing Committee on Law and National Security, 1979-1985; Member, 1980-1982 and Chairperson, 1983-1986, Hearing Committee, Board on Professional Responsibility, District of Columbia; Member, 1980-1986 and Chairperson, 1989-1994, Federal District Court Committee on Grievances; Chairperson, Ethics in Government Act, White Collar Crime Committee, 1989-1990); National Association of Criminal Defense Lawyers; Charles Fahy American Inn of Court (Master of Bench, 1984-1987); Edward Bennett Williams Inn of Court (Master of Bench, 1989—). Fellow, American College of Trial Lawyers (Chairperson, District of Columbia, 1989-1990; Regent, 1993-1998; Treasurer, 1996-1998; President-Elect, 2000; President, 2001). ***PRACTICE AREAS:*** Corporate Litigation; White Collar Crime Defense; Legal Ethics Advice, Discipline and Malpractice; Securities Enforcement; Tax; Defense Procurement; Health Care; Environmental Litigation. ***Email:*** earl.silbert@piperrudnick.com

GREGORY A. SMITH, born Chicago, Illinois, November 25, 1947; admitted to bar, 1972, Virginia; 1973, District of Columbia. *Education:* Miami University (A.B., 1969); University of Virginia (J.D., 1972). Clerk to Honorable Marion T. Bennett, Judge, U.S. Court of Claims, (now the United States Court of Appeals for the Federal Circuit) (1972-1973). Chair, ABA Section of Public Contracts Law, 2000-2001. Chair, Steering Committee, D.C. Bar Government Contract & Litigation Section, 1992-1993. President, Court of Federal Claims Bar Association, 1994. Member, Court of Federal Claims Advisory Council, 1990. ***PRACTICE AREAS:*** Government Contracts. ***Email:*** gregory.smith@piperrudnick.com

NANCY A. SPANGLER, born Clarion, Iowa, 1963; admitted to bar, 1989, Virginia; 1990, District of Columbia. *Education:* Iowa State University (B.A., with distinction, 1985); University of Virginia (J.D., 1989). (Also in Reston, Virginia Office). ***PRACTICE AREAS:*** Venture Capital; Emerging Growth Companies; Corporate Finance and Securities Law. ***Email:*** nancy.spangler@piperrudnick.com

KENNETH G. STARLING, born High Point, North Carolina, January 16, 1948; admitted to bar, 1973, North Carolina; 1974, District of Columbia. *Education:* University of North Carolina (A.B., with honors, 1969); University of Virginia; Duke University (J.D., 1973). Omicron Delta Epsilon. Adjunct Professor, Antitrust Law, Georgetown University Law Center, 2001. Minority Counsel, Subcommittee on Monopolies and Commercial Law, Committee on the Judiciary, U.S. House of Representatives, 1975-1976. Assistant U.S. Attorney, U.S. Department of Justice, Western District of North Carolina, 1977. Trial Attorney, Bureau of Competition, 1973-1975, Attorney-Adviser to Acting Chairman, David A. Clanton, 1979-1982 and Assistant Director, Bureau of Competition, 1982-1985, Federal Trade Commission. Chief Antitrust Counsel, Committee on the Judiciary, U.S. Senate, 1985-1987. Deputy Assistant Attorney General, Antitrust Division, U.S. Department of Justice, 1987-1989. *Member:* American Bar Association (Chair, 1995-1997, Vice-Chair, 1992-1995, Legislation Committee, Section of Antitrust Law). ***PRACTICE AREAS:*** Antitrust; Litigation; Mergers and Acquisitions. ***Email:*** kenneth.starling@piperrudnick.com

(This Listing Continued)

ERNEST M. STERN, born Port Elizabeth, South Africa, 1950; admitted to bar, 1975, Virginia; 1976, District of Columbia; 1980, U.S. Supreme Court. *Education:* Bowdoin College (A.B., summa cum laude, 1972); Georgetown University (J.D., 1975; LL.M., in Taxation, 1986). Phi Beta Kappa. Member, Board of Editors, Law and Policy in International Business, 1974-1975. *Member:* The District of Columbia Bar (Member: Chairman, Emerging Business Committee of the Committee on Corporation, Finance and Securities Law, 1989—; Committee on Broker Dealer Regulation); American Bar Association (Member, Committee on Federal Regulation of Securities); International Association of Financial Planners. (Resident). ***LANGUAGES:*** French. ***PRACTICE AREAS:*** Corporate Law; Securities. ***Email:*** ernest.stern@piperrudnick.com

JANE KWOK PING TAM, born Hong Kong, 1965; admitted to bar, 1989, Massachusetts; 1990, New York; 1997, District of Columbia. *Education:* University of Michigan; University of Leeds; Albany Law School (J.D., 1989); Georgetown Law Center (LL.M., 1992). ***LANGUAGES:*** Chinese. ***PRACTICE AREAS:*** Corporate; Securities; Venture Capital. ***Email:*** jane.tam@piperrudnick.com

MARK J. TAUBER, born Detroit, Michigan, March 25, 1949; admitted to bar, 1973, District of Columbia; 1974, Maryland. *Education:* University of Michigan (B.A., with honors, 1970); George Washington University (J.D., with honors, 1973). ***PRACTICE AREAS:*** Communications Law; Copyright Law; Trademark Law. ***Email:*** mark.tauber@piperrudnick.com

JOHN M. TIFFORD, born New York, N.Y., March 5, 1942; admitted to bar, 1965, New York; 1977, Virginia; 1978, District of Columbia. *Education:* The City College of New York (B.A., 1962); Cornell University (LL.B., 1965). Member, Moot Court Team, 1964-1965. Program Advisor for Franchising, Federal Trade Commission, 1978-1988. *Member:* The District of Columbia Bar; New York State, Virginia and American Bar Associations. ***PRACTICE AREAS:*** Franchising; Licensing; Distribution; Consumer Protection; Advertising Law. ***Email:*** john.tifford@piperrudnick.com

CARL L. VACKETTA, born Danville, Illinois, August 3, 1941; admitted to bar, 1965, Illinois; 1968, District of Columbia. *Education:* University of Illinois (B.S., magna cum laude, 1963; J.D., 1965). Phi Alpha Delta. Adjunct Professor of Law, Georgetown Law Center, 1973—. Fellow, American Public Contract Law Section; National Contract Management Association. *Member:* Illinois State, Federal and American (Vice Chair, Commercial Products and Services Committee, 1994—; Secretary, Section on: Public Contract Law, 1978-1979; Council Member, 1979, 1982) Bar Associations; District of Columbia Bar. Fellow, National Contract Management Association. ***PRACTICE AREAS:*** Contract Law; Government Contracts. ***Email:*** carl.vacketta@piperrudnick.com

CHARLES B. WAYNE, born Los Angeles, California, January 10, 1951; admitted to bar, 1976, North Carolina; 1977, District of Columbia; 1985, Virginia. *Education:* Wesleyan University (B.A., cum laude, 1973); University of North Carolina (J.D., with honors, 1976). Member, North Carolina Law Review, 1975-1976. *Member:* The District of Columbia Bar; North Carolina State Bar; Virginia State Bar; American Bar Association. ***PRACTICE AREAS:*** Commercial Litigation; Employment and Employee Benefits Litigation; White Collar Criminal Litigation. ***Email:*** charles.wayne@piperrudnick.com

WILLIAM R. WEISSMAN, born New York, N.Y., August 16, 1940; admitted to bar, 1965, New York; 1969, District of Columbia. *Education:* Columbia University (B.A., 1962; J.D., cum laude, 1965). Trial Attorney, Antitrust Division, U.S. Department of Justice, 1966-1969. Special Assistant U. S. Attorney, District of Columbia, 1967. ***PRACTICE AREAS:*** Environmental Law; Administrative Law; Appellate Litigation. ***Email:*** william.weissman@piperrudnick.com

JOHN T. WESTERMEIER, JR., born West Point, New York, September 14, 1941; admitted to bar, 1974, Virginia; 1975, District of Columbia; 1978, U.S. Supreme Court; 1982, Maryland and U.S. District Court, District of Columbia; 1983, U.S. District Court, Eastern District of Virginia; 1987, U.S. District Court, District of Maryland; 1990, U.S. Court of Federal Claims. *Education:* United States Military Academy (B.S., 1963); George Washington University (M.B.A., ADP Management, 1969; LL.M., 1978); American University (J.D., 1974). Recipient: Distinguished Information Sciences Award, Data Processing Management Association, 1987; Burton Award, 2001. Articles Editor, American University Law Review, 1973-1974. Adjunct Professor, American University, Washington College of Law, 1985-1986. President, Data Processing Management Association, D.C. Chapter, 1981. Co-Chair: Advanced Computer and Internet Law Institute, Georgetown University Law Center Continuing Legal Education Division, 1987—; Committee on Professionalism of Computer Specialists, Computer Law Division, ABA Science and Technology Section, 1977—. Member: Board of Directors, 1992-1998 and President, 1998, Computer Law Association; Steering Committee, D.C. Bar Computer Law Section, 1986-1992; Advisory Board, E-Commerce Law & Strategy, 1985—; Advisory Board, The Computer Law Reporter, 1989—; Advisory Board, Information Strategies: The Executives Journal, 1986—; Advisory Board, Intellectual Property Counselor, 1999; Advisory Board, Internet Law & Business, 1999; Advisory Board, BNA's Computer Technology Law Reporter, 1999. *Member:* Virginia and Maryland State Bar Associations; The District of Columbia Bar. Fellow, American Bar Foundation. ***PRACTICE AREAS:*** Computer Law; Litigation; Intellectual Property; Corporate. ***Email:*** jay.westermeier@piperrudnick.com

THOMAS C. WHEELER, born Chicago, Illinois, March 18, 1948; admitted to bar, 1973, District of Columbia; 1976-1981, U.S. Court of Claims; 1978, U.S. Supreme Court; 1982, U.S. Court of Federal Claims and U.S. Court of Appeals for the Federal Circuit. *Education:* Gettysburg College (B.A., 1970); Georgetown University (J.D., 1973). *Member:* American Bar Association (Member, Sections on: Public Contract Law; Litigation). ***PRACTICE AREAS:*** Government Contracts. ***Email:*** thomas.wheeler@piperrudnick.com

ANTHONY L. YOUNG, born Santa Monica, California, April 5, 1944; admitted to bar, 1973, California; 1974, District of Columbia. *Education:* University of Southern California (A.B., 1965); Georgetown University (J.D., 1973). Law Clerk, Honorable George R. Gallagher, District of Columbia Court of Appeals, 1973-1974. Co-Author: "Product Liability Considerations in Prescription Drug Labeling," Drug Information Journal, Vol. 27, pp. 915-920, 1993; "Dietary Supplement Health and Education Act: A Legislative History and Analysis," 1996 Food and Drug Law Institute Book. *Member:* Federal Bar Association. ***PRACTICE AREAS:*** Food and Drug Law; Environmental Law; Toxics Law; Litigation. ***Email:*** anthony.young@piperrudnick.com

PHILIP F. ZEIDMAN, born Birmingham, Alabama, May 2, 1934; admitted to bar, 1958, Alabama; 1960, Florida; 1968, District of Columbia; 1981, New York and U.S. Supreme Court. *Education:* Yale University (B.A., cum laude, 1955); Harvard University (LL.B., 1958). Recipient, Younger Federal Lawyer of the Year Award, 1965. Trial Attorney, Federal Trade Commission, 1960-1961. Staff Assistant, White House Committee on Small Business, 1961-1963. Special Assistant to Administrator, 1961-1963, Assistant General Counsel, 1963-1965 and General Counsel, 1965-1968, Small Business Administration. Special Assistant to the Vice-President of the United States, 1968. Government Relations Manager, National Alliance of Businessmen, 1968. Member: Administrative Conference of United States, 1968; Food Industry Advisory Committee, Department of Energy, 1974-1981 (Chairman, 1979-1981). Member: President's Commission on Executive Exchange, 1978-1981; Advisory Board, *Antitrust and Trade Regulation Report,* 1978-1985; President's Advisory Committee, John F. Kennedy Center for the Performing Arts, 1981. Co-Author: *Franchising: Regulation of Buying and Selling a Franchise,* Bureau of National Affairs/Corporate Practice Series, 1997. Author, Franchising, Aspects of the Market Economy, Verlag Stam (1996). Editor: *Survey of Foreign Laws and Regulations Affecting International Franchising,* American Bar Association, 1982; 2nd edition, 1989; General Editor, *Legal Aspects of Selling and Buying,* West Group, 1983; 2d Ed., 1992, Supplement 2001. Contributing Editor, Antitrust and Trade Regulation, Legal Times, 1978-1985. Associate Editor, *International Journal of Franchising and Distribution Law, 1986*—. Consulting Editor, *Global Franchising Alert,* CCH, Inc., 1993—. General Counsel, American Business Conference, 1980—. General Counsel, International Franchise Association, 1968—. Special Counsel, Japan Franchise Association, 1973—. Founding Principal, East Europe Law, Ltd., 1990. Director, The Appleseed Foundation, 1994—; Executive Committee, 1996—. Member, Advisory Board of the DeWitt Wallace Center for Communications and Journalism, Sanford Institute for Public Policy, Duke University, 1994-1998. Member Advisory Board, Yale University School of Organization and Management, 1982-1989. Trustee, Yale-China Association, 1983-1989. Contributing Author, International Franchising, 2001—. *Member:* The District of Columbia Bar; Bar Association of the District of Columbia (Member, International Law Section); Federal and American (First Chairman, Franchising Committee, Antitrust Section, 1977-1981; Forum on Franchising) and International (Vice Chairman, 1983-1986, Chairman, 1986-1990, Chairman Emeritus, 1990-1992, International Franchising Committee, Section of Business Law; Vice-Chairman, Asia-Pacific Forum, 1992-1994; Member, Council, 1996-2000; President, International Bar Foundation, 2000—) Bar Associations; Alabama State Bar; The Florida Bar; American Intellectual Property Law Association (Chairman, Franchise Law Committee, 1987-1990). ***PRACTICE AREAS:*** Antitrust; Franchise and Distribution Law; International Franchising; Trade Regulation; International Law. ***Email:*** philip.zeidman@piperrudnick.com

OF COUNSEL

LUCINDA J. BACH, born Peoria, Ill.; admitted to bar, 1981, Massachusetts; 1983, District of Columbia. *Education:* Northwestern University (B.S., 1977); Boston University (J.D., 1981). Recipient, American Jurisprudence Award for Constitutional Law. Member, 1979-1980 and Note and Case Editor, 1980-1981, Boston University Law Review. Partner, Schwalb Donnenfeld Bray & Silbert, 1989-1998. *Member:* The District of Columbia Bar; Massachusetts and American Bar Associations. ***PRACTICE AREAS:*** Civil and Commercial Litigation; Professional Liability Litigation; White Collar Criminal Litigation. ***Email:*** lucinda.bach@piperrudnick.com

KEVIN M. BELL, born Kirkwood, Missouri, January 5, 1968; admitted to bar, 1999 Maryland, U.S. District Court, District of Maryland and U.S. Court of Appeals for the Federal Circuit and Fourth Circuit (Not admitted in District of Columbia). *Education:* University of Miami (B.A., 1990); George Mason Uni-

(This Listing Continued)

(This Listing Continued)

PIPER MARBURY RUDNICK & WOLFE LLP, Washington—Continued

versity School of Law (J.D., 1998). Author: "CD-ROM for Document Handling Creates a Powerful Litigation Tool," New York Law Journal, Vol. 213, No. 20, January 31, 1995; "High Tech Solutions to Complex Litigation Problems: (DI)-Document Imaging," The Law Works, Vol. 2, No. 6, June 1995; "Courts Begin to CD Lights on CD Briefs," The National Law Journal, November 3, 1997. *Member:* Maryland State and American (Chair, Imaging and Infobase Interest Group; Member, Law Practice Management Section) Bar Association; The Association of Trial Lawyers of America; American Intellectual Property Law Association. ***PRACTICE AREAS:*** Intellectual Property Litigation; Technology Law. ***Email:*** kevin.bell@piperrudnick.com

CHARLES A. BERARDESCO, born Lakewood, New Jersey, October 1, 1958; admitted to bar, 1983, Maryland; 2000, District of Columbia. *Education:* Duke University (A.B., magna cum laude, 1980); George Washington University (J.D., with high honors, 1983). Order of the Coif. Managing Editor, George Washington Law Review, 1982-1983. Co-Author: "Defrauded Tax Shelter Investors' Recovery Under Securities Laws Need Not Be Reduced by Tax Benefits," Tax Management Real Estate Journal, Vol. 2, No. 10, p. 229, October, 1986. Contributor, *The Entrepreneurs Almanac.* Assistant Professor of Law, Villa Julie College, 1987-1991. *Member:* Bar Association of Baltimore City; Maryland State Bar Association. ***PRACTICE AREAS:*** Securities Law; Corporate Law; Intellectual Property Law; Venture Capital; Technology; Mergers and Acquisitions. ***Email:*** charles.berardesco@piperrudnick.com

WIB CHESSER, born 1964; admitted to bar, 1993, Maryland; 1996, District of Columbia; registered to practice before U.S. Patent and Trademark Office. *Education:* University of Pennsylvania (B.A., 1986); University of Maryland (J.D., 1993). Managing Editor, Maryland Journal of Contemporary Legal Issues. Author: "RCRA's Mens Rea Requirement Under Section 3008(d)(2)," National Environmental Enforcement Journal, October 1993. Co-Author: "Preserving State Authority in the Integration of Overlapping Environmental Statutes at Federal Facilities," National Environmental Enforcement Journal, November 1995. Adjunct Professor, Nuclear Regulation, University of Maryland School of Law. ***PRACTICE AREAS:*** Business Law; Technology Law; Intellectual Property; Patent Prosecution. ***Email:*** wib.chesser@piperrudnick.com

F. MARTIN DAJANI, born Bowling Green, Ohio, October 26, 1966; admitted to bar, 1991, Missouri; 2001, District of Columbia. *Education:* University of Kansas (B.A., 1988); University of Missouri (J.D., 1991). Assistant Attorney General, State of Missouri, 1993-1998. Federal Trade Commission - Bureau of Competition, 1998-2000. *Member:* The Missouri Bar; The District of Columbia Bar; American Bar Association. ***PRACTICE AREAS:*** Antitrust and Trade Regulation; Litigation. ***Email:*** martin.dajani@piperrudnick.com

ELIZABETH R. DEWEY, born Phoenix, Arizona, November 29, 1967; admitted to bar, 1993, Maryland; 1995, District of Columbia. *Education:* University of Tulsa (B.A., cum laude, 1990); Washington College (J.D., summa cum laude, 1993). Phi Beta Kappa; Mortar Board. ***LANGUAGES:*** Spanish. ***PRACTICE AREAS:*** Commercial Litigation; White Collar Crime. ***Email:*** elizabeth.dewey@piperrudnick.com

CARY M. FELDMAN, born Newark, New Jersey, March 26, 1949; admitted to bar, 1975, District of Columbia; 1980, U.S. Supreme Court; 1995, Maryland. *Education:* University of Rochester (B.A., 1971); George Washington University (J.D., with honors, 1974). Order of the Coif. Deputy Independent Counsel (In re: Secretary of Interior Bruce Babbitt, 1998-2000). Partner, Schwalb Donenfeld, Bray & Silbert, 1988-1998. Assistant U.S. Attorney, Washington, D.C., 1978-1984. Associate, Hundley and Cacheris, 1974-1977. President, Assistant U.S. Attorney's Association for the District of Columbia, 1999-2000. Contributor: The Grand Jury of Tomorrow Final Report of the District of Columbia Grand Jury Study Committee, sponsored by the Council for Court Excellence; Criminal Jury Instructions for the District of Columbia, The Red Book. Civil I Mediator, Superior Court of the District of Columbia. Faculty: District of Columbia Bar Continuing Legal Education Trial Skills Series. *Member:* District of Columbia Bar (Co-Chairman, Criminal Law and Individual Rights Section, 1986-1988); American Bar Association (Member: Sections on Litigation and Criminal Justice; White Collar Crime Committee); Council for Court Excellence (Chairman, Criminal Justice Committee, 1996-1998; Board of Directors). ***PRACTICE AREAS:*** White Collar Crime; Litigation; Commercial Litigation. ***Email:*** cary.feldman@piperrudnick.com

DANIEL S. GOLDBERG, born New York, N.Y., February 26, 1947; admitted to bar, 1972, New York; 1973, District of Columbia and U.S. Tax Court; 1984, Maryland; U.S. Court of Appeals, Third and Fourth Circuits. *Education:* University of Rochester (A.B., with high honors, 1968); Harvard University (J.D., cum laude, 1971). Phi Beta Kappa. Recipient, John Dows Mairs Prize for Excellence in Economics and Honors Program of Independent Study in Economics. Member, Editorial Board, Harvard Law Review, 1970-1971. Author: "Nonrecourse Debt in Excess of Fair Market Value: The Confluence of Basis, Realization, Subchapter K and the Need for Consistency," 51 Tax Lawyer 41-82

(This Listing Continued)

(1997); "Government Precommitment to Tax Incentive Subsidies: The Impact of U.S. v. Winstar Corp. et al. on Retroactive Tax Legislation," 14 American Journal of Tax Policy 1-34 (1997); "The Tax Treatment of Limited Liability Companies: Law in Search of Policy," 50 Bus. Lawyer 995-1017 (1995); "Tax Subsidies: One Time vs. Periodic - An Economic Analysis of the Tax Policy Alternatives," 49 Tax Law Review 305-347 (1994). Professor of Law (Taxation), University of Maryland School of Law, 1978—. Voted Outstanding Teacher, University of Maryland, 1993. Professor in Residence, Internal Revenue Service, 1982-1983. *Member:* District of Columbia Bar; American Bar Association (Member, Taxation Section); AALS (Tax Section). ***PRACTICE AREAS:*** Business Taxation; Business; Technology; Venture Capital; Emerging Growth Companies. ***Email:*** daniel.goldberg@piperrudnick.com

ROBERT M. HALL, born Augusta, Maine, January 15, 1950; admitted to bar, 1975, Pennsylvania and U.S. District Court, Eastern District of Pennsylvania; 1984, New York; 1996, District of Columbia; 1999, Virginia. *Education:* University of Notre Dame (B.A., 1972); Villanova School of Law (J.D., 1975). Publications: *Cut-Throughs and Guarantee Clauses,* X Mealey's Lit. Rep. No. 21 at 18 (2000); *Drawing Down Letters of Credit in an Insurer Receivership Context,* XI Mealey's Lit. Rep. No. 21 at 22 (2000); *Alternatives to Estimation of Claims and Acceleration of Reinsurance Receivables: The Uniform Receivership Law,* X Mealey's Insolv. Rep. No. 17 at 16 (1999); *Recent Case Developments with Arbitration in Receiverships* Intl. Journal of Ins. Law, Part 1 of 5 (1998); *Mediation of Reinsurance Disputes,* Mealey's Rein. Rep. Vol. 8, Iss. 10 (1997) at 20; *Direct Actions and Set Off: The Next Generation,* Mealey's Rein. Rep. Vol. 8, Iss. 7 (1997) et 15; *Partiality Among Distribution Panelists,* Mealeys Rein. Rep. Vol. 8, Iss. 3 (1997) at 18; *Reinsurers, Receivers and Abstention,* Mealey's Reins. Rep. Vol 7, Iss. 18 (1997) at 18; Reinsurance Editor, Merritt Insurance Report (1996-1997); *Mission Receiver Suffers Judicial Setbacks,* 2 Merritt Ins. Rpt. No. 23 at 8 (1996); Casenote: *Quackenbush v. Allstate Ins. Co,* Intl. J. of Ins. Law, P. 4, 323 (1996); *Is Reinsurance the 'Business of Insurance?',* Mealey's Reins. Rep., Vol. 7, Iss. 9 (1996) at 18; *When The Other Side Will Not Arbitrate: Judicial Appointment of Umpires and Arbitrators,* Mealey's Reins. Rep., Vol. 6, Iss. 24 (1996) at 15; *Lloyd's of London: Reconstruction and Renewal, Credit for Reinsurance and Equitas,* PLI Conference on Lloyd's and the London Insurance Market (1996); *Changes to Lloyd's U.S. Trust Funds: Considerable Improvement Noted;* The Intl. Journal of Ins. Law (July 1996). *Member:* American Bar Association (Member, Tort and Insurance Practice Section). ***PRACTICE AREAS:*** Reinsurance; Insurance; Insolvency. ***Email:*** robert.hall@erols.com

SHERWIN KAPLAN, born Chicago, Illinois, April 24, 1941; admitted to bar, 1966, Illinois; 1969, U.S. Court of Appeals, Ninth Circuit and U.S. District Court, Northern District of Illinois; 1973, U.S. Supreme Court and U.S. Court of Appeals, Seventh Circuit; 1974, District of Columbia and U.S. District Court, District of Columbia; 1997, U.S. District Court, District of Colorado. *Education:* University of Chicago (B.A., 1963; J.D., 1966). Charter Fellow of the American College of Employee Benefits Counsel; Chair, Employee Benefits Committee of the Labor and Employment Law Section of the District of Columbia Bar; Member, BNA National ERISA Advisory Committee; Formerly, Deputy Associate Solicitor of Labor, U.S. Department of Labor. ***PRACTICE AREAS:*** Employee Benefits. ***Email:*** sherwin.kaplan@piperrudnick.com

PAUL C. KIMBALL, PH.D., born January 26, 1946; admitted to bar, 1993, Maryland; 2000, District of Columbia and U.S. Supreme Court; registered to practice before U.S. Patent and Trademark Office. *Education:* Massachusetts Institute of Technology (B.S., Life Sciences, 1968); University of California, Berkeley (Ph.D., Molecular Biology, 1972); Catholic University of America (J.D., 1993). *Member:* The District of Columbia Bar; American Bar Association (Member, Intellectual Property Section); American Intellectual Property Lawyers Association. ***PRACTICE AREAS:*** Intellectual Property; Patent Law; Patent Interference Practice; Patent Licensing; Patent Litigation; Patent Prosecution. ***Email:*** paul.kimball@piperrudnick.com

JOHN L. MOORE, JR., born New Orleans, Louisiana, December 7, 1960; admitted to bar, 1986, District of Columbia. *Education:* Georgetown University (B.A., magna cum laude, 1982); George Washington University (J.D., with honors, 1986). Phi Beta Kappa. Member, George Washington Law Review. ***LANGUAGES:*** French and German. ***PRACTICE AREAS:*** Customs Law; Insurance Law. ***Email:*** john.moore@piperrudnick.com

SHEILA STARK, born Pennsylvania, July 21, 1964; admitted to bar, 1988, Virginia; 1989, District of Columbia. *Education:* College of William and Mary (B.A., 1985); George Washington University (J.D., 1988). ***PRACTICE AREAS:*** Government Contracts; Litigation Counseling; Contract Law. ***Email:*** sheila.stark@piperrudnick.com

PARTNER EMERITUS

TONI K. ALLEN, born New York, N.Y., August 6, 1940; admitted to bar, 1964, New York; 1972, District of Columbia. *Education:* Wellesley College (B.A., 1960); New York University (LL.B., cum laude, 1964). Order of the Coif.

(This Listing Continued)

Fellow, American Bar Association. ***PRACTICE AREAS:*** Public Utility Law; Environmental Law; Administrative Law. ***Email:*** toni.allen@piperrudnick.com

NATHAN B. FEINSTEIN, born Philadelphia, Pennsylvania, November 13, 1929; admitted to bar, 1955, Pennsylvania; 1988, Maryland and District of Columbia. *Education:* Pennsylvania State College (B.A., 1951); Yale Law School (LL.B., 1954). Chairman, Business Bankruptcy Committee, ABA Business Law Section, 1989-1993. Chairman, Joint Ad Hoc Committee on Bankruptcy Court Structure and Insolvency Processes, ABA Litigation and Business Law Sections, 1994—. Fellow, American College of Bankruptcy. ***PRACTICE AREAS:*** Bankruptcy Law. ***Email:*** nathan.feinstein@piperrudnick.com

J. BRIAN MOLLOY, born New York, N.Y., January 15, 1943; admitted to bar, 1971, Virginia; 1972, District of Columbia. *Education:* Manhattan College (B.C.E., 1963); New York University (M.S., 1967); Georgetown University (J.D., 1971). Director, United States Environmental Protection Agency, Enforcement Division, 1974-1980. ***PRACTICE AREAS:*** Environmental Law. ***Email:*** brian.molloy@piperrudnick.com

RESIDENT ASSOCIATES

ALLISON LESLIE ALEXANDER, born Washington, D.C., September, 7, 1969; admitted to bar, 1999, Maryland; 2000, District of Columbia. *Education:* Syracuse University (B.S., summa cum laude, 1991); University of Maryland (J.D., with honor, 1999). Editor, Maryland Law Review. ***PRACTICE AREAS:*** Corporate Finance; Securities; Venture Capital; Emerging Companies; Mergers, Acquisitions and Divestitures. ***Email:*** allison.alexander@piperrudnick.com

REGINA B. AMOLSCH, admitted to bar, 1996, Georgia; 1999, District of Columbia. *Education:* University of Miami (B.A., with honors, 1993); Emory University (J.D., 1996). ***PRACTICE AREAS:*** Franchise Law; Distribution. ***Email:*** regina.amolsch@piperrudnick.com

J. DARREL BARROS, born Taunton, Massachusetts, December 19, 1960; admitted to bar, 1995, Michigan; 2001, District of Columbia. *Education:* Tufts University (B.S., 1983); Dartmouth College (M.B.A., 1992); University of Michigan (J.D., 1995). *Member:* Wolverine and American Bar Associations; State Bar of Michigan. ***PRACTICE AREAS:*** Venture Capital; Emerging Growth Companies. ***Email:*** darrel.barros@piperrudnick.com

ALISA M. BERGMAN, born Philadelphia, Pennsylvania, September 29, 1972; admitted to bar, 1998, California; 1999, District of Columbia. *Education:* University of California (B.A., 1994); Georgetown University (J.D., 1998). *Member:* State Bar or California. ***PRACTICE AREAS:*** Privacy Law; Electronic Commerce. ***Email:*** alisa.bergman@piperrudnick.com

CHRISTOPHER J. BLAGG, born Leeds, England, 1966; admitted to bar, 1992, Virginia; 1995, District of Columbia. *Education:* Georgetown University (B.S.F.S., 1988); University of Virginia (J.D., 1992). *Member:* The District of Columbia Bar; Virginia State Bar. ***LANGUAGES:*** Russian and French. ***PRACTICE AREAS:*** Venture Capital; Emerging Growth Companies. ***Email:*** christopher.blagg@piperrudnick.com

R. TIMOTHY BRYAN, born Roanoke, Virginia, April 29, 1957; admitted to bar, 1992, California; 2001, District of Columbia. *Education:* North Carolina State University (B.A., summa cum laude, 1987); University of North Carolina, Chapel Hill (J.D., 1991). Research Editor, North Carolina Journal of International Law and Commercial Regulation, 1990-1991. *Member:* American Bar Association. ***PRACTICE AREAS:*** Bankruptcy; Creditors Rights; Commercial Finance; Corporate Law; Mergers and Acquisitions. ***Email:*** timothy.bryan@piperrudnick.com

DAVID CARL, born Springfield, Massachusetts, April 3, 1974; (admission pending). *Education:* Tufts University (B.A., 1996). ***PRACTICE AREAS:*** Venture Capital. ***Email:*** david.carl@piperrudnick.com

JIM CARLSON, born Philippines, November 27, 1952; admitted to bar, 1999, Minnesota (Not admitted in District of Columbia). *Education:* U.S. Air Force Academy (B.S., 1975); Gonzaga University (M.S., 1979); University of Minnesota Law School (J.D., 1999). *Member:* Minnesota State Bar Association. [U.S. Air Force, 1975-1982; U.S. Naval Reserves, 1985-2000]. ***PRACTICE AREAS:*** Business Law; Technology Law; Military Aviation; Computer Programming; Web Site Development; Financial Brokerage; Business and Technology Consulting; Division and Project; Management; Strategic Planning; Human Resource Development. ***Email:*** jim.carlson@piperrudnick.com

MARK WAYNE CARMEAN, born Seaford, Delaware, October 24, 1971; admitted to bar, 1997, Maryland; 1999, District of Columbia. *Education:* Duke University (B.A., cum laude, 1994); University of Maryland (J.D., with honors, 1997). Order of the Coif. Notes and Comments Editor, Maryland Law Review, 1996-1997. ***LANGUAGES:*** French. ***PRACTICE AREAS:*** Telecommunications Litigation; Products Liability; Antitrust. ***Email:*** mark.carmean@piperrudnick.com

EMILY S. CHEN, born New York, New York; admitted to bar, 2001, New York (Not admitted in District of Columbia). *Education:* Dartmouth College

(This Listing Continued)

(B.A., 1997); Boston College (J.D., 2000). ***LANGUAGES:*** Mandarin, Taiwanese, French. ***PRACTICE AREAS:*** Corporate Law; Franchise Distribution. ***Email:*** emily.chen@piperrudnick.com

KHARI M. CLAY, born 1972; admitted to bar, 1998, New York (Not admitted in District of Columbia). *Education:* Swarthmore College (B.A., 1994); Harvard University (J.D., 1997). ***PRACTICE AREAS:*** Venture Capital; Commercial Litigation; Intellectual Property Litigation. ***Email:*** khari.clay@piperrudnick.com

SULEE J. CLAY, admitted to bar, 1998, New York; 2001, District of Columbia. *Education:* Harvard College (A.B., 1992); Harvard Law School (J.D., 1997). ***PRACTICE AREAS:*** Corporate Finance; Securities; Venture Capital; Mergers and Acquisitions. ***Email:*** sulee.clay@piperrudnick.com

SCOTT P. COLLINS, born Rochester, New York, November 28, 1971; admitted to bar, 1997, Virginia and U.S. Court of Appeals, Fourth Circuit; 2001, District of Columbia. *Education:* University of Rochester (B.A., 1993); Syracuse University College of Law (J.D., 1997). Executive Editor, Syracuse University Law Review, 1996-1997. *Member:* District of Columbia Bar; Virginia State Bar. ***PRACTICE AREAS:*** Real Estate; Commercial Leasing. ***Email:*** scott.collins@piperrudnick.com

WILLIAM J. CROWLEY, born Rutland, Vermont, July 22, 1969; admitted to bar, 1997, Maryland and U.S. Court of Federal Claims; 2000, District of Columbia. *Education:* Williams College (B.A., 1991) George Mason University School of Law (J.D., 1996). (Also at Baltimore, Maryland Office). ***PRACTICE AREAS:*** Government Contracts; Litigation; Alternative Dispute Resolution. ***Email:*** william.crowley@piperrudnick.com

MARY JANE DEWEESE, born Ft. Worth, Texas, May 20, 1967; admitted to bar, 1993, Illinois; 1999, District of Columbia. *Education:* Oberlin College (B.A., magna cum laude, 1989); University of Chicago (J.D., 1993). *Member:* Bar Association of the District of Columbia; American Bar Association. ***PRACTICE AREAS:*** Real Estate. ***Email:*** maryjane.deweese@piperrudnick.com

AMY L. DUVALL, born Buffalo, New York, July 26, 1973; admitted to bar, 1999, New Jersey; 2001, District of Columbia. *Education:* Washington University (B.S., 1995); State University of New York at Buffalo (J.D., 1998). Member, Buffalo Moot Court Board. Recipient, Oral Advocacy Scholarship, 1997-1998. Book Review Editor and Articles Editor, Buffalo Environmental Law Journal. Author: "Cleanup Processes and Standards of CERCLA and RCRA: Shortcomings and Recommendations," 4 Buff. Envtl. L.J. 225, 1997. Co-Author: "Recycling: Anything but Garbage," 5 Buff. Envtl. L.J., 101, 1997. Member, Society of Women Engineers, 1991-1996. *Member:* New Jersey State and American Bar Associations; District of Columbia Bar. ***LANGUAGES:*** Spanish. ***PRACTICE AREAS:*** Solid Waste Regulation; Hazardous Waste Regulation; Legislative Practice; Regulatory Law; Appellate Practice; Administrative Law. ***Email:*** amy.duvall@piperrudnick.com

JOHN J. DWYER, born Mendon, Massachusetts, October 15, 1964; admitted to bar, 1990, Virginia; 1996, District of Columbia. *Education:* Providence College (B.A., cum laude, 1986); Georgetown University Law Center (J.D., cum laude, 1990). ***PRACTICE AREAS:*** Litigation; Franchise. ***Email:*** john.dwyer@piperrudnick.com

TERESA E. DYKES, born Chattanooga, Tennessee, August 12, 1966; admitted to bar, 1998, Georgia; 1999, District of Columbia; registered to practice before U.S. Patent and Trademark Office. *Education:* Georgia Institute of Technology (B.Ch.E., 1989); Washington College of Law, American University (J.D., 1997). *Member:* State Bar of Georgia; The District of Columbia Bar; American Bar Association. ***PRACTICE AREAS:*** Environmental. ***Email:*** teresa.dykes@piperrudnick.com

KESHA D. EVANS, born Detroit, Michigan, November, 1973; admitted to bar, 1999, California and District of Columbia. *Education:* University of California, Berkeley (B.A., 1995); Stanford University (J.D., 1998). Member, Stanford Law Review, 1996-1998. ***Email:*** kesha.evans@piperrudnick.com

ERIK M. FEIG, born New York, N.Y., July 18, 1971; admitted to bar, 1997, New Jersey and New York; 1999, District of Columbia. *Education:* Cornell University (B.S., Mechanical Engineering, 1993); Fordham University (J.D., 1996). Technical Editor, Fordham Environmental Law Journal. *Member:* Computer Law Association; The Association of the Bar of the City of New York (Member, Committee on Patents, 1996-1998); The District of Columbia Bar; Copyright Society of the U.S.A.; American Bar Association. ***PRACTICE AREAS:*** Business Law; Technology Law; Information Technology; Venture Capital; Emerging Growth Companies; Intellectual Property. ***Email:*** erik.feig@piperrudnick.com

MARJORIE P. FISHER, born Baltimore, Maryland, July 7, 1968; admitted to bar, 1997, California (Not admitted in District of Columbia). *Education:* Wesleyan University (B.A., with honors, 1990); University of California School of Law, Los Angeles (J.D., 1997). Member, UCLA Law Review. ***PRACTICE AREAS:*** Commercial Real Estate. ***Email:*** marjorie.fisher@piperrudnick.com

BRANDON M. FITZGERALD, born Baltimore, Maryland; admitted to bar, 1997, Maryland; 1998, District of Columbia. *Education:* University of Pennsylvania (B.A., 1993); University of Virginia School of Law (J.D., 1996).

(This Listing Continued)

PIPER MARBURY RUDNICK & WOLFE LLP, Washington—Continued

Co-Author: with Thomas P. Vartanian, Robert H. Ledig and James S. Kennell, "Results of Y2K Litigation Are Beginning to Emerge," Electronic Banking Law and Commerce Report, February 1999. Previous Employment: Patton Boggs, LLP, 1996-1998; Fried, Frank, Harris, Shriver & Jacobson, 1998-2000. *Member:* The District of Columbia Bar; Maryland State Bar Association, Inc.; American Bar Association. ***LANGUAGES:*** Spanish. ***PRACTICE AREAS:*** Mergers and Acquisitions; Venture Capital; Securities. ***Email:*** brandon.fitzgerald@piperrudnick.com

BRIDGET M. FITZPATRICK, admitted to bar, 2000, California (Not admitted in District of Columbia). *Education:* Cornell University (B.A., with honors, 1997); Georgetown University (J.D., cum laude, 2000). *Member:* State Bar of California. ***PRACTICE AREAS:*** Litigation; White Collar Crime. ***Email:*** bridget.fitzpatrick@piperrudnick.com

DAVID E. FLETCHER, born Manassas, Virginia, November 27, 1971; admitted to bar, 2001, Virginia (Not admitted in District of Columbia). *Education:* College of William & Mary (A.B., 1993; M.Ed., 1995); University of Illinois (J.D., cum laude, 2001). ***PRACTICE AREAS:*** Government Contracts. ***Email:*** david.fletcher@piperrudnick.com

STEVEN E. FRIEDMAN, born 1971; admitted to bar, 1996, Maryland; 1999, District of Columbia. *Education:* Washington University (B.A., 1993); George Washington University (J.D., with honors, 1996). Member, The Environmental Lawyer. Participant: Street Law Program; Project for Older Prisoners. *Member:* Maryland State and American Bar Associations. ***PRACTICE AREAS:*** Business Law; Technology Law; Corporate Finance. ***Email:*** steven.friedman@piperrudnick.com

LORRIE A. GIVENTER, born New York, New York, August 16, 1969; admitted to bar, 1995, Florida; 1996, Maryland and District of Columbia. *Education:* Brown University (B.A., with honors, 1991); University of Virginia (J.D., 1995). Law Clerk to Stanley S. Harris, U.S. District Court of the District of Columbia, 1995-1997. ***PRACTICE AREAS:*** Civil Litigation; Criminal Litigation. ***Email:*** lorrie.giventer@piperrudnick.com

KELLY D. GOLDSTEIN, admitted to bar, 1998, California (Not admitted in District of Columbia). *Education:* University of Rochester (B.A., cum laude, 1995); George Washington University (J.D., 1998). ***PRACTICE AREAS:*** Business; Technology; Venture Capital; Emerging Growth Companies. ***Email:*** kelly.goldstein@piperrudnick.com

KEARA M. GORDON, born Bronxville, New York, May 13, 1968; admitted to bar, 1994, New York; 1995, District of Columbia. *Education:* Iona College (B.A., summa cum laude, 1990); Georgetown University (J.D., magna cum laude, 1993). ***PRACTICE AREAS:*** Securities Litigation; Business Litigation. ***Email:*** keara.gordon@piperrudnick.com

STEVEN J. GROSECLOSE, born Baltimore, Maryland, July 11, 1967; admitted to bar, 1994, Texas; 1999, District of Columbia. *Education:* Rice University (B.A., B.S.M.E., 1990); Johns Hopkins University (M.S.E., 1994); University of Maryland (J.D., with honors, 1994). *Member:* State Bar of Texas. ***LANGUAGES:*** German. ***PRACTICE AREAS:*** Environmental. ***Email:*** steven.groseclose@piperrudnick.com

CAROL GUY-JACKSON, born Springfield, Massachusetts, November 4, 1965; admitted to bar, 1994, Pennsylvania; 1995, District of Columbia. *Education:* Howard University (B.B.A., 1987); University of District of Columbia (J.D., 1993). ***PRACTICE AREAS:*** Litigation; Real Estate. ***Email:*** carol.guy-jackson@piperrudnick.com

ALFRED M. HAAS, born Albany, New York, October 22, 1971; admitted to bar, 1997, New Jersey; 1998, District of Columbia; 2000, New York; registered to practice before the U.S. Patent and Trademark Office. *Education:* Duke University (B.A., 1993); George Washington University (J.D., 1997). Member, Moot Court Board. *Member:* The District of Columbia Bar; New Jersey State, New York State and American Bar Associations. ***PRACTICE AREAS:*** Patent Law; Intellectual Property.

JAMES B. HALLMARK, born El Paso, Texas, March 14, 1967; admitted to bar, 1993, Texas; 2001, District of Columbia. *Education:* University of Texas, Austin (B.A., 1989; J.D., 1993). Phi Delta Phi. *Member:* American Bar Association. ***LANGUAGES:*** Spanish. ***PRACTICE AREAS:*** Business and Technology; Corporate and Securities; Venture Capital and Emerging Companies; Mergers and Acquisitions; Intellectual Property. ***Email:*** james.hallmark@piperrudnick.com

HEATHER D. HAMILTON, admitted to bar, 1997, Maryland; 1998, District of Columbia. *Education:* Miami University (B.A., 1992); Valparaiso University (J.D., 1996). *Member:* The District of Columbia Bar. ***LANGUAGES:*** German. ***PRACTICE AREAS:*** Electronic Commerce; Privacy Law; Health Care; State Legislative Practice; Public Policy. ***Email:*** heather.hamilton@piperrudnick.com

(This Listing Continued)

JEFFREY J. HEINS, admitted to bar, 1994, New York; 2000, District of Columbia. *Education:* Le Moyne College (B.A., 1988); Syracuse University (J.D., 1993). ***PRACTICE AREAS:*** Business; Technology; Communications. ***Email:*** jeffrey.heins@piperrudnick.com

JAMES M. HEINTZ, born Syosset, New York, December 7, 1965; admitted to bar, 1997, New York and District of Columbia; 1998, U.S. District Court, District of Columbia, U.S. Court of Appeals, Federal and District of Columbia Circuits; registered to practice before U.S. Patent and Trademark Office. *Education:* State University of New York at Stony Brook (B.E.E.E., 1988); St. John's University School of Law (J.D., magna cum laude, 1996). Member, St. John's University Law Review, 1995-1996. *Member:* District of Columbia Bar; American Bar Association; American Intellectual Property Law Association. ***PRACTICE AREAS:*** Patent; Trademark; Trade Secrets; Intellectual Property Licensing. ***Email:*** jim.heintz@piperrudnick.com

CATHY A. HINGER, born Westwood, New Jersey, September 17, 1973; admitted to bar, 2001, District of Columbia and Virginia. *Education:* University of Maryland (B.A., cum laude, 1996; J.D., with honors, 1999). Order of the Coif. Member, Maryland Law Review. ***Email:*** cathy.hinger@piperrudnick.com

DANIEL M. HORRIGAN, born Washington, D.C., March 31, 1965; admitted to bar, 1992, District of Columbia. *Education:* Georgetown University (A.B., 1987); George Washington University (J.D., 1992). ***PRACTICE AREAS:*** Venture Capital. ***Email:*** daniel.horrigan@piperrudnick.com

TAMI J. HOWIE, born Maryland, January 5, 1972; admitted to bar, 1997, Maryland (Not admitted in District of Columbia). *Education:* Towson State University (B.S., magna cum laude, 1994); University of Maryland (J.D., with honors, 1997). Recipient: The Roger Howell Achievement Award; Health and Elder Law Clinic Award. Member, University of Maryland Trial Team. Runner-Up, American Bar Association Criminal Law Trial Competition. Articles Editor, "The Business Lawyer," 1996-1997. *Member:* American Bar Association (Member, Business Law Section); The Association of Trial Lawyers of America. ***PRACTICE AREAS:*** Corporate; Venture Capital. ***Email:*** tami.howie@piperrudnick.com

STUART P. INGIS, born May 24, 1971; (admission pending). *Education:* Hamilton College (B.A., Government, 1993); Villanova University School of Law (J.D., 1997). Fellow, Center for Information Law and Policy. Advisor, Global Law and Policy Initiative, Chicago Kent College of Law. Former Co-Director, Project Bosnia. ***PRACTICE AREAS:*** Communications; Intellectual Property; Information Technology; Internet Law. ***Email:*** stuart.ingis@piperrudnick.com

CHARLES M. INOKON, born Lagos, Nigeria, May 13, 1971; admitted to bar, 1999, New York; 2001, District of Columbia. *Education:* University of Maryland (B.S., 1993); Cornell Law School (J.D., 1997). President, Black Law Students Association. Editor, Cornell Law Review. Certified Public Accountant, Maryland, 1994. *Member:* New York State and American Bar Associations; American Institute of Certified Public Accountants. ***PRACTICE AREAS:*** Venture Capital; Emerging Technologies. ***Email:*** charles.inokon@piperrudnick.com

PAUL W. JAMIESON, born Trenton, New Jersey, April 27, 1969; admitted to bar, 1998, District of Columbia. *Education:* Yale University (B.A., 1991); University of Virginia (J.D., 1998). *Member:* The District of Columbia Bar; Federal Communications Bar Association. ***PRACTICE AREAS:*** Communications. ***Email:*** paul.jamieson@piperrudnick.com

KEVIN JOSEPH JOYCE, born 1974; admitted to bar, 2000, Virginia; 2001, District of Columbia. *Education:* Princeton University (A.B., 1996); University of Virginia (J.D., 2000). *Member:* Virginia State Bar. ***PRACTICE AREAS:*** Corporate Law. ***Email:*** kevin.joyce@piperrudnick.com

HARVEY KELLMAN, born Brooklyn, New York, November 27, 1962; admitted to bar, 1997, New York (Not admitted in District of Columbia). *Education:* Hunter College of the City University of New York (B.A., 1993); Pace University (J.D., 1996). *Member:* Federal Communications Bar Association. ***PRACTICE AREAS:*** Broadcasting; Internet; Wireless Communications; Multichannel Video; Information Technology; Electronic Commerce; Privacy; E-Business Strategic Alliances; Emerging Growth Companies; Software Licensing. ***Email:*** harvey.kellman@piperrudnick.com

SEAN J. KLEIN, born Lake Grove, New York, May 21, 1970; admitted to bar, 1995, Illinois (Not admitted in District of Columbia). *Education:* Georgetown University (B.S., B.A., 1992); Northwestern University (J.D ., 1995). Attorney Advisor, U.S. Securities and Exchange Commission, 1996-1999. ***PRACTICE AREAS:*** Securities; Venture Capital; General Corporate. ***Email:*** sean.klein@piperrudnick.com

MICHAEL R. LAIDHOLD, born Pittsburgh, Pennsylvania, May 19, 1972; admitted to bar, 1999, Pennsylvania and U.S. District Court, Western District of Pennsylvania; 2001, District of Columbia. *Education:* Miami University (B.A., 1994); University of Pittsburgh (M.P.I.A., J.D., 1999). *Member:* American Bar Association. ***PRACTICE AREAS:*** Franchise Law; Distribution; International Law; Corporate Law. ***Email:*** michael.laidhold@piperrudnick.com

(This Listing Continued)

MICHAEL G. LANGAN, born Syracuse, New York, February 27, 1968; admitted to bar, 1998, District of Columbia; 1999, New York; 2000, U.S. District Court for the District of Columbia. *Education:* Colgate University (B.A., cum laude, 1991); George Mason University (M.F.A., 1995; J.D., 1998). Notes Editor, George Mason Law Review, 1997-1998. Author, "Why A Fixed Salary for Developmental Squad Players Does Not Hurt The Game: Defending The Decision no to Argue Consumer Injury In Brown v. Pro Football," 5 Geo. Mason L. Rev. 559, 1997. Associate Justice, George Mason Moot Court Board, 1996-1998. Member, George Mason Inn of Court, 1997-1998. *Member:* The District of Columbia Bar; New York State and American Bar Associations. ***PRACTICE AREAS:*** White Collar Crime; Civil Litigation; Criminal Litigation; Commercial Litigation. ***Email:*** michael.langan@piperrudnick.com

AMY SUSAN LEAVENS, born Danville, Pennsylvania, October 13, 1972; admitted to bar, 1998, Pennsylvania; 1999, California and District of Columbia. *Education:* Georgetown University (B.A., 1994); Pepperdine University (J.D., 1997). *Member:* American Bar Association. ***LANGUAGES:*** French. ***PRACTICE AREAS:*** Corporate and Securities Law; Venture Capital. ***Email:*** amy.leavens@piperrudnick.com

TASHIR J. LEE, born Ithaca, New York, August 7, 1971; admitted to bar, 1997, New York; 1998, District of Columbia. *Education:* Cornell University (B.S., 1993); University of Pennsylvania (J.D., 1996). *Member:* New York State Bar Association; The District of Columbia Bar; Federal Communications Bar Association. ***PRACTICE AREAS:*** Communications. ***Email:*** tashir.lee@piperrudnick.com

ALAN R. LEWINE, born Columbus, Ohio, May 14, 1955; admitted to bar, 1999, New York; 2000, District of Columbia. *Education:* University of New Mexico (B.S., 1985); Georgetown University (J.D., 1998). Author: "Safe Songs: Copyright Law, Digital Rights Management and the Technology Arms Race," Internet Audio (July, 2001); "Napster, Copyright, and the Pig Encoder," Cyberspace Lawyer (April, 2001); "The E-Audit: Internet Law for Electronic Commerce," (February, 2001). Book: WEB-LINKING AGREEMENTS: CONTRACTING STRATEGIES AND MODEL PROVISION, Published by ABA Committee on the Law of Commerce in Cyberspace, Subcommittee on Interactive Services, ABA Section of Business Law, (ABA Books, 1997), Co-author. Law Review and Law Related Articles: *Copyrights For The Digital Millennium,* 2-3 Telecommunications and Electronic Media News 1 (Winter, 1998); *Making Cyberspace Safe for Children(?): A First Amendment Analysis Of The Communications Decency Act Of 1996,* 18 Journal of Public Law and Policy 78 (Fall 1996); *Burning Down the House to Roast the Pig: The U.S. Congress Takes on Internet Indecency,* 29-4 LAW/TECHNOLOGY JOURNAL OF THE WORLD JURIST ASSOCIATION 16 (Dec. 1996); MODEL WEBSITE DEVELOPMENT AGREEMENT, Interactive Services Subcommittee, Committee of Commerce in Cyberspace, ABA Section on Business Law (ABA Books 1998), Contributor; *Copyrights for a World Without Borders,* (1997)(draft available at http: //www.dcez.com/~alewine/copyright.html); CYBERSPACE LAW AUTHORITIES REPORTS, Contributing Editor (published by Legal Authorities Network, L.L.C.)(1997); CYBERSPACE LAW FOR NON-LAWYERS, Editor and List Manager. Online seminar authored by Professors David Post, Eugene Volokh, and Larry Lessig and sponsored by the CYBERSPACE LAW INSTITUTE, distributed as a listserv to over 20,000 subscribers in some 80 countries (available at http://www.ssrn.com/cyberlaw)(1996-1997); E. Kirsh, D. Phillips, D. McIntyre, *Recommendations for the Evolution of Cyberlaw:* Protecting Informational Privacy in a Digital Age, 2-2 JOURNAL OF COMPUTER MEDIATED COMMUNICATION (Fall 1996). Acknowledged contributor to editorial, research, and drafting; *Collecting Mousedroppings: Legitimate Uses of Individual Web Usage Information* (available at http: //www.dcez.com/~alewine/mousedrop.html)(1996, revised 1997); Course Materials: Articles included in required reading for *Law of Cyberspace Seminar,* Prof. David Post, Georgetown University Law Center (1996); Articles and excerpts from web site included in *The Internet: Business, Law, and Strategy,* Prof. Joan Camp, Harvard University, John F. Kennedy School of Government (2000); CYBERLAW HOME PAGE regular column in *Georgetown Law Weekly* (1994-1996); WORLD WIDE WEB SITE: Designed and maintain personal web site covering legal resources and issues in cyberspace, with special attention to First Amendment issues (available at http://www.dcez.com/~alewine) (since Summer, 1995). Public Broadcasting Service, 1996-1999. *Member:* American Bar Association; American Intellectual Property Law Association; Federal Communications Bar Association; Washington Area Lawyers for the Arts. ***PRACTICE AREAS:*** Technology Transactions; Internet Technology; Electronic Commerce; Software Licensing; Strategic Alliances; Venture Capital; Emerging Growth Companies; General Corporate; Entertainment Law; Intellectual Property; Life Sciences; Biotechnology. ***Email:*** alan.lewine@piperrudnick.com

FRANK A. MARINO, born Baltimore, Maryland, December 20, 1951; admitted to bar, 1980, Maryland; 1981, District of Columbia; 1982, Pennsylvania; 1983, U.S. District Court, District of Maryland and U.S. Court of Appeals, Fourth and District of Columbia Circuits. *Education:* University of Miami, Coral Gables (B.A., 1976); University of Baltimore School of Law (J.D., cum laude, 1980); Georgetown University Law Center (LL.M., International Trade Law, 1982). Member: Heuisler Honor Society; International Law Institute. Fellow, American Express Foundation. *Member:* The District of Columbia Bar; Maryland State Bar Association, Inc. ***LANGUAGES:*** German. ***PRACTICE AREAS:*** Real Estate; Commercial Leasing. ***Email:*** frank.marino@piperrudnick.com

BRADLEY K. McCONNELL, born Toronto, Ontario, Canada, November 27, 1968; admitted to bar, 1995, Maryland; 1998, District of Columbia. *Education:* Princeton University (A.B., 1990); George Washington University (J.D., 1995). ***PRACTICE AREAS:*** Business and Technology; Corporate; Venture Capital; Emerging Growth Companies. ***Email:*** bradley.mcconnell@piperrudnick.com

ROBERT L. McKAY, JR., born Murray, Utah; admitted to bar, 1998, New York and District of Columbia. *Education:* Brigham Young University (B.A., Honors, 1994); Columbia Law School (J.D., 1997). Harlan Fiske Stone Scholar. Editor-in-Chief, Columbia Journal of Environmental Law, 1996-1997. *Member:* The District of Columbia Bar; New York State and American (Member, Venture Capital Task Force) Bar Associations. ***LANGUAGES:*** German. ***PRACTICE AREAS:*** Venture Capital; Emerging Companies; Securities; Mergers and Acquisitions. ***Email:*** robert.mckay@piperrudnick.com

AMY L. MILLER, born Huntingdon, Pennsylvania, April 16, 1971; admitted to bar, 1996, Virginia; registered to practice before U.S. Patent and Trademark Office (Not admitted in District of Columbia). *Education:* University of Richmond (B.S., Chemistry, 1993); T.C. Williams School of Law (J.D., 1995). Gamma Sigma Epsilon; Beta Beta Beta. *Member:* Virginia State Bar. ***PRACTICE AREAS:*** Intellectual Property; Patent Prosecution; Domestic and Foreign Prosecution; Biochemical Patents; Chemical Patents; Patent Interference Practice. ***Email:*** amy.miller@piperrudnick.com

KARIN M. MILLER, admitted to bar, 2001, Maryland (Not admitted in District of Columbia). *Education:* University of Michigan (B.A., with high distinction, 1989; J.D., 2000). Angell Scholar. ***PRACTICE AREAS:*** Franchise Law. ***Email:*** karin.miller@piperrudnick.com

SARA Z. MOGHADAM, admitted to bar, 1998, Maryland (Not admitted in District of Columbia). *Education:* Bucknell University (B.A., 1994); University of Maryland (J.D., 1998). ***PRACTICE AREAS:*** Business Litigation; Securities Litigation. ***Email:*** sara.moghadam@piperrudnick.com

JOHN D. MUIR, JR., born Washington, D.C., March 6, 1967; admitted to bar, 1996, New York; 1998, District of Columbia. *Education:* Vanderbilt University (B.A., 1989); Brooklyn Law School (J.D., 1995). ***PRACTICE AREAS:*** Commercial Real Estate. ***Email:*** john.muir@piperrudnick.com

LAURA D. NAMMO, born Schenectady, New York, June 30, 1968; admitted to bar, 1995, Illinois and U.S. District Court, Northern District of Illinois; 2000, District of Columbia; registered to practice before the U.S. Patent and Trademark Office. *Education:* North Carolina State University (B.S., in Chemistry summa cum laude, 1991); George Washington University (J.D., 1995). *Member:* Illinois State Bar Association; American Intellectual Property Law Association; American Chemical Society; Christian Legal Society. ***PRACTICE AREAS:*** Intellectual Property; Patent Prosecution; Patent Litigation; Opinion Work; Client Counseling. ***Email:*** laura.nammo@piperrudnick.com

ZACHARY N. NOFFSINGER, born Winfield, Illinois, August 17, 1972; admitted to bar, 1999, New York (Not admitted in District of Columbia). *Education:* Duke University (B.A., cum laude, 1994; J.D., with honors, 1998). Alaska Law Review. *Member:* New York State Bar Association. ***LANGUAGES:*** Spanish. ***PRACTICE AREAS:*** Corporate Law; Business; Technology; Venture Capital; Emerging Companies. ***Email:*** zachary.noffsinger@piperrudnick.com

LISA K. NORTON, born Salt Lake City, Utah; admitted to bar, 1994, Utah; 1999, District of Columbia; registered to practice before U.S. Patent and Trademark Office. *Education:* Brigham Young University (B.S., 1991; J.D., 1994). Editor-in-Chief, Brigham Young University Journal of Public Law, 1993-1994. ***LANGUAGES:*** French. ***PRACTICE AREAS:*** Intellectual Property. ***Email:*** lisa.norton@piperrudnick.com

ALAN M. NOSKOW, born Columbia, Maryland, December 23, 1975; admitted to bar, 2000, Maryland; 2001, District of Columbia. *Education:* University of Rochester (B.A., History, 1997); University of Miami (J.D., 2000). Articles & Comments Editor, University of Miami Law Review, 1999-2000. *Member:* District of Columbia Bar; Maryland State Bar Association, Inc. ***PRACTICE AREAS:*** Bankruptcy; Business Reorganization; Creditors Rights; Finance; Financial Services Law. ***Email:*** alan.noskow@piperrudnick.com

REID A. PAGE, born 1975; admitted to bar, 2000, Virginia (Not admitted in District of Columbia). *Education:* Mercer University (B.A., 1997); Georgetown University (J.D., 2000). *Member:* Virginia State Bar. ***PRACTICE AREAS:*** Litigation. ***Email:*** reid.page@piperrudnick.com

KIM K.S. PAGOTTO, born Inchon, South Korea, July 3, 1973; admitted to bar, 2000, Michigan (Not admitted in District of Columbia). *Education:* University of Michigan (B.A., with honors, 1996; J.D., 2000). Associate Editor, Journal of Law Reform, 1998-1999. *Member:* Women's Law Student Association. ***LANGUAGES:*** Italian. ***PRACTICE AREAS:*** Real Estate. ***Email:*** kim.pagotto@piperrudnick.com

(This Listing Continued)

(This Listing Continued)

PIPER MARBURY RUDNICK & WOLFE LLP, Washington—Continued

SONG H. PAK, born 1969; admitted to bar, 1994, Texas (Not admitted in District of Columbia). *Education:* Southern Methodist University (B.A., 1991); University of Texas (J.D., 1994). Member, Texas International Law Journal. ***PRACTICE AREAS:*** Business; Technology; Venture Capital; Emerging Growth Companies. ***Email:*** song.pak@piperrudnick.com

VINCENT M. PALADINI, born New Brunswick, New Jersey; admitted to bar, 1997, New Jersey; 2000, New York (Not admitted in District of Columbia). *Education:* Rutgers University (B.A., 1986); Boston University (J.D., 1997). Eugene C. Bowler Scholar in Telecommunications Law. Federal Communications Commission. *Member:* American Bar Association; Federal Communications Bar Association. ***PRACTICE AREAS:*** Communications Law; Federal Regulatory Law; Administrative Law; International Trade. ***Email:*** vincent.paladini@piperrudnick.com

MARC O. PEISERT, born Berlin, Germany, April 12, 1972; admitted to bar, 1998, Germany; 2000, New York (Not admitted in District of Columbia). *Education:* University of Passau; America University (LL.M., 1999). ***LANGUAGES:*** German and French. ***PRACTICE AREAS:*** Corporate Law; Venture Capital; Mergers and Acquisitions. ***Email:*** marc.peisert@piperrudnick.com

SCOTT M. PERRY, born Paterson, New Jersey, October 23, 1972; admitted to bar, 1997, Maryland; 1998, New Jersey and District of Columbia; U.S. District Court for the District of Columbia; U.S. District Court for the District of Maryland. *Education:* Rutgers University (B.S., with honors, 1994); Catholic University of America (J.D., cum laude, 1997). Associate Editor, Catholic University Law Review. *Member:* Maryland State and American Bar Associations; District of Columbia Trial Lawyers Association. ***PRACTICE AREAS:*** Litigation; Telecommunications; Internet. ***Email:*** scott.perry@piperrudnick.com

SUSAN H. POPE, born Durham, North Carolina, December 28, 1966; admitted to bar, 1996, Maryland; 2001, District of Columbia. *Education:* University of North Carolina at Chapel Hill (B.A., 1989); George Mason University School of Law (J.D., 1996). ***PRACTICE AREAS:*** Antitrust and Trade Regulation. ***Email:*** susan.pope@piperrudnick.com

ANDREW M. PRICE, admitted to bar, 1995, Colorado; 1996, U.S. Court of Federal Claims; 1997, District of Columbia and U.S. District Court for the District of Columbia; 2000, U.S. Court of Appeals for the Federal Circuit. *Education:* Rensselaer Polytechnic Institute; University of Colorado at Boulder (B.S., 1992); George Mason University (J.D., 1995); National Law Center, George Washington University (LL.M., 1996). Member, George Mason University Law Review. Recipient, American Jurisprudence Award for Professional Responsibility. Senior Staff Attorney, Armed Services Board of Contract Appeals, 1996-1999. *Member:* The District of Columbia Bar. ***PRACTICE AREAS:*** Government Contracts. ***Email:*** andrew.price@piperrudnick.com

TILGHMAN EARLE PRICE, born Annapolis, Maryland, January 12, 1966; admitted to bar, 1995, Maryland; 2001, District of Columbia. *Education:* University of Virginia (B.A., 1989); University of Baltimore (LL.D., 1995). ***PRACTICE AREAS:*** Real Estate Development; Finance; Securities. ***Email:*** tilghman.price@piperrudnick.com

JOHN M. PURCELL, admitted to bar, 2000, New York; 2001, District of Columbia. *Education:* University of Wisconsin-Madison (B.A., with distinction, 1995); Georgetown University (J.D., 1999). ***LANGUAGES:*** German. ***PRACTICE AREAS:*** Corporate Law; Securities; Mergers and Acquisitions; Venture Capital; Emerging Growth Companies. ***Email:*** john.purcell@piperrudnick.com

DEEPIKA REDDY, born Queens, New York, August 26, 1974; admitted to bar, 2001, Massachusetts (Not admitted in District of Columbia). *Education:* Tufts University (B.A., 1996); Boston University School of Law (J.D., 2000). Annual Review of Banking Law. ***PRACTICE AREAS:*** Litigation; Intellectual Property. ***Email:*** deepika.reddy@piperrudnick.com

ADAM D. RESNICK, born Washington, D.C., November 20, 1971; admitted to bar, 1998, Maryland and District of Columbia. *Education:* Syracuse University (B.A., 1993); University of Baltimore (J.D., cum laude, 1998). ***PRACTICE AREAS:*** Intellectual Property Law; Electronic Commerce. ***Email:*** adam.resnick@piperrudnick.com

WILLIAM F. REYNOLDS, JR., born New York, N.Y., March 11, 1962; admitted to bar, 1995, New York; 1996, District of Columbia. *Education:* University of Iowa (B.S., 1987); Harvard University (M.A., 1990; Ph.D., 1992); Harvard Law School (J.D., 1995). *Member:* The District of Columbia Bar; American Psychological Association, NHLA/AAHA. ***PRACTICE AREAS:*** Corporate Financing Law; Mergers and Acquisitions. ***Email:*** bill.reynolds@piperrudnick.com

SUSAN B. ROSS, born Cleveland, Ohio, 1960; admitted to bar, 1994, Arizona; 1999, District of Columbia. *Education:* Duke University (B.S.E., cum laude, 1982); Arizona State University (J.D., magna cum laude, 1994). Order of the Coif. Senior Note and Comment Editor, Arizona State Law Journal, 1993-1994. Author: "Legal Ethics, Malpractice and the Internet," The Internet Guide for Michigan Lawyers, 1996, 1992, 1998, 1999. *Member:* The District of Columbia Bar; State Bar of Arizona; American Bar Association (Member, Law Practice Management Section; Vice Chair, Tech Show, 1998; Vice Chair, Computer and Technology Division, 1999—). ***PRACTICE AREAS:*** Information Technology; Venture Capital; Emerging Growth Companies. ***Email:*** susan.ross@piperrudnick.com

LOUIS J. ROULEAU, admitted to bar, 1997, Maryland (Not admitted in District of Columbia). *Education:* University of Connecticut (B.A., magna cum laude, 1992); American University (J.D., 1997). ***LANGUAGES:*** French. ***PRACTICE AREAS:*** Litigation. ***Email:*** louis.rouleau@piperrudnick.com

DAVID M. RUBENSTEIN, born New York, New York, June 30, 1972; admitted to bar, 1997, Virginia; 1998, District of Columbia. *Education:* Emory University (B.A., 1994); Duke Law School (J.D., magna cum laude, 1997). Phi Beta Kappa. ***PRACTICE AREAS:*** Corporate Law. ***Email:*** david.rubenstein@piperrudnick.com

EDWARD S. SCHEIDEMAN, admitted to bar, 1998, Maryland (Not admitted in District of Columbia). *Education:* Hobart and William Smith College (B.A., 1993); Washington University (J.D., 1998). ***PRACTICE AREAS:*** Antitrust and Trade Regulation. ***Email:*** edward.scheideman@piperrudnick.com

MARK I. SCHWARTZ, born New York, N.Y., April 8, 1963; admitted to bar, 1991, Quebec, Canada (inactive); 1996, California; 1999, District of Columbia. *Education:* McGill University (B.S., 1986); University of Sherbrooke (LL.B., with honors, 1989); Duke University (J.D., 1995). ***PRACTICE AREAS:*** Venture Capital; High Technology; Emerging Business Law. ***Email:*** mark.schwartz@piperrudnick.com

REED P. SEXTER, born Louisville, Kentucky, May 5, 1967; admitted to bar, 1992, New Jersey; 1993, New York and District of Columbia. *Education:* University of Michigan (B.A., 1989); Hofstra University School of Law (J.D., 1992). Notes and Comments Editor, Hofstra University School of Law Labor Law Journal. Law Clerk, Hon. Paul Mannes, Chief U.S. Bankruptcy Judge, District of Maryland, 1992-1994. ***PRACTICE AREAS:*** Real Estate; Bankruptcy. ***Email:*** reed.sexter@piperrudnick.com

EMILY C. SEXTON, born Springfield, Missouri, June 5, 1974; admitted to bar, 1999, Maryland; 2000, District of Columbia and U.S. District Court, District of Maryland. *Education:* University of Illinois (B.A., magna cum laude, with high departmental honors, 1996); Harvard University (J.D., 1999). Phi Beta Kappa. James Scholar. *Member:* Maryland State and American (Member, Intellectual Property Section) Bar Associations; The District of Columbia Bar. ***PRACTICE AREAS:*** Intellectual Property. ***Email:*** emily.sexton@piperrudnick.com

ANOOP G. SHROFF, born Ontario, Canada, February 22, 1969; admitted to bar, 1995, Maryland; 1997, District of Columbia. *Education:* Cornell University (A.B., 1991); University of Pennsylvania (J.D., 1995). Member, Board of Directors, Indian American Bar Association, 1996-1998. ***PRACTICE AREAS:*** Corporate; Securities; Mergers and Acquisitions; Venture Capital. ***Email:*** anoop.shroff@piperrudnick.com

CRISTEN E. SIKES, born Jacksonville, Florida, October 20, 1973; admitted to bar, 1999, Maryland (Not admitted in District of Columbia). *Education:* Georgetown University (B.A., cum laude, 1996); William and Mary University (J.D., 1999). Pi Sigma Alpha; Order of the Coif. Moot Court. Law Review. ***Email:*** cristen.sikes@piperrudnick.com

JOSEPH E. SPRINGSTEEN, admitted to bar, 2000, Maryland; 2001, District of Columbia. *Education:* University of North Carolina at Chapel Hill (B.A., 1996); American University (J.D., cum laude, 2000). ***PRACTICE AREAS:*** Franchise Law; Distribution. ***Email:*** joseph.springsteen@piperrudnick.com

AMY L. SCHANER STANLEY, born Washington, D.C., July 22, 1968; admitted to bar, 1996, Maryland (Not admitted in District of Columbia). *Education:* Bowdoin College (B.A., 1990); American University Law School (J.D., summa cum laude, 1996). ***PRACTICE AREAS:*** Environmental; Litigation. ***Email:*** amy.stanley@piperrudnick.com

JAMES MICHAEL SULLIVAN, born Middletown, Connecticut, January 28, 1970; admitted to bar, 1998, New Jersey; 1999, District of Columbia. *Education:* College of the Holy Cross (B.A., 1992); Catholic University of America (J.D., 1997). ***PRACTICE AREAS:*** Commercial Litigation; White Collar Litigation. ***Email:*** james.sullivan@piperrudnick.com

PATRICE J. HARRIS TALBOTT, born Washington, D.C., December 2, 1970; admitted to bar, 1995, Maryland; 2000, Illinois (Not admitted in District of Columbia). *Education:* Stanford University (A.B., 1992); Georgetown University Law Center (J.D., 1995); John Marshall Law School (LL.M. in Real Estate, 1999). *Member:* Maryland State and Illinois State Bar Associations. ***Email:*** patrice.harris@piperrudnick.com

(This Listing Continued)

RACHEL TAUSEND, admitted to bar, 2001, Virginia (Not admitted in District of Columbia). *Education:* Bowdoin College (B.A., 1989); University of Michigan (J.D., 2001). ***PRACTICE AREAS:*** Litigation. ***Email:*** rachel.tausend@piperrudnick.com

LISA R. TROVATO, born Rochester, New York, May 5, 1971; admitted to bar, 1997, Maryland; 1998, District of Columbia. *Education:* Cornell University (B.S., 1993); University of Michigan (J.D., cum laude, 1996). *Member:* Maryland State Bar Association; American Bar Association; International Trademark Association. ***PRACTICE AREAS:*** Intellectual Property. ***Email:*** lisa.trovato@piperrudnick.com

KENNETH Y. TURNBULL, born Baltimore, Maryland, February 13, 1969; admitted to bar, 1999, Maryland and U.S. District Court, District of Maryland; 2001, District of Columbia. *Education:* St. John's College (B.A., 1990); University of Maryland (J.D., 1999); Pennsylvania State University (M.A., 1993; Ph.D., 1995). Order of the Coif. Executive Articles Editor, Maryland Law Review, 1999. Law Clerk to the Honorable Lawrence F. Rodowsky, 1999-2000, Maryland Court of Appeals. ***PRACTICE AREAS:*** Litigation; Products Liability. ***Email:*** kenneth.turnbull@piperrudnick.com

JOSHUA UDLER, born Washington, D.C.,; admitted to bar, 2000, Maryland; 2001, District of Columbia. *Education:* State University of New York at Binghamton (B.A., cum laude, 1996); University of Maryland, Robert H. Smith School of Business (M.B.A., 2000); University of Maryland (J.D., with honors, 2000). *Member:* American Bar Association (Member, Business Law Section). ***Email:*** josh.udler@piperrudnick.com

ANNE MAGEE VAUGHAN, born Virginia Beach, Virginia, December 28, 1967; admitted to bar, 1997, Louisiana (inactive); 2001, Virginia (Not admitted in District of Columbia). *Education:* Harvard University (A.B., 1990); University of Virginia (J.D., 1996). *Member:* Virginia State Bar; American Bar Association. ***PRACTICE AREAS:*** Corporate; Securities; Finance. ***Email:*** maggie.vaughan@piperrudnick.com

KENNETH K. D. VU, born Saigon, Vietnam, February 26, 1966; admitted to bar, 1996, Illinois; registered to practice before U.S. Patent and Trademark Office (Not admitted in District of Columbia). *Education:* Virginia Polytechnic Institute and State University (B.S.E.E., 1988); Johns Hopkins University (M.S., 1991); George Washington University (J.D., 1996). *Member:* American Bar Association; American Intellectual Property Law Association. ***LANGUAGES:*** Vietnamese. ***PRACTICE AREAS:*** Intellectual Property.

JANICE L. WEINER, born Hartford, Connecticut, April 10, 1973; admitted to bar, 1997, Maryland; 1999, District of Columbia. *Education:* Georgetown University (A.B., summa cum laude, 1994); Harvard Law School (J.D., cum laude, 1997). Phi Beta Kappa. ***PRACTICE AREAS:*** Pharmaceutical Products Liability Litigation; Health Care; Food and Drug Regulation. ***Email:*** janice.weiner@piperrudnick.com

GREGORY A. WERKHEISER, born 1973; admitted to bar, 2000, Virginia; 2001, District of Columbia. *Education:* College of William & Mary (B.A., 1996); University of Virginia (J.D., 2000). ***PRACTICE AREAS:*** Litigation. ***Email:*** gregory.werkheiser@piperrudnick.com

ROBIN A. WILLIAMS, born Providence, Rhode Island, October 17, 1968; admitted to bar, 1994, Michigan, U.S. District Court, Eastern and Southern Districts of Michigan; 1999, District of Columbia. *Education:* Boston University (B.S., 1990); Suffolk University Law School (J.D., 1993). ***PRACTICE AREAS:*** Business; Technology; Venture Capital; Emerging Growth Companies. ***Email:*** robin.williams@piperrudnick.com

(For Complete Biographical data on all Personnel, see Professional Biographies at Other Office Locations)

PLEDGER & FEORD P.L.C.

WASHINGTON, D.C.

(See McLean, Virginia)

General Practice. Civil Litigation, Insurance Law, Insurance Defense and Medical Malpractice.

L. HARVEY POE, JR.

Established in 1966

SUITE 514
2600 VIRGINIA AVENUE, N.W.
WASHINGTON, D.C. 20037
Telephone: 202-337-3080
Facsimile: 202-337-1185
Email: LHPOE@AOL.COM

General Practice before Federal and Local Courts, Governmental Departments and Regulatory Agencies, Aviation, Banking, Corporation, Financing, International Business and Finance, Education, Real Estate and Investments Law, Aviation Aerospace Law, International Law.

(This Listing Continued)

L. HARVEY POE, JR., born Richmond, Virginia, January 29, 1916; admitted to bar, 1940, Virginia; 1967, District of Columbia and U.S. Court of Appeals, District of Columbia Circuit; 1969, U.S. Supreme Court; 1972, U.S. Court of Federal Claims; 1974, Maryland. *Education:* University of Virginia (B.S., 1938; J.D., 1941); Oxford University, England (D.Phil., 1957). Rhodes Scholar, Oxford University. Phi Beta Kappa; Phi Delta Phi. Editor, University of Virginia Law Review, 1940-1941. Associate, Cravath, Swain & Moore, New York, N.Y., 1941-1942. Assistant Chairman, National Citizens Committee for Kennedy and Johnson and Chairman, Citizens' Committee, John F. Kennedy's Inaugural Committee, 1960-1961. Chairman, Zoning Board of Appeals, Annapolis, Maryland, 1966-1976. Consultant: National Endowment for the Arts and Humanities, 1967-1969; Department of Transportation, 1968-1970. Member, Governor's Commission on the Capital City of Maryland, 1970-1975. Member, Board of Directors, First American Bank of Maryland, 1979-1991. Organizer, University of Virginia Liberal Arts Program, 1991—. *Member:* Virginia and Maryland State Bar Associations; District of Columbia Bar; Virginia State Bar. [Lieut. Comdr., U.S. Navy, 1942-1946]. (Also Of Counsel to Franch & Jarashow, P.A., Annapolis, Maryland). ***SPECIAL AGENCIES:*** Department of Transportation.

PORTER WRIGHT MORRIS & ARTHUR LLP

Established in 1846

1919 PENNSYLVANIA AVENUE, N.W.
SUITE 500
WASHINGTON, D.C. 20006-3434
Telephone: 202-778-3000; (800-456-7962)
Fax: 202-778-3063
Email: washington@porterwright.com
URL: http://www.porterwright.com

Columbus, Ohio Office: 41 South High Street, 43215-6194. Telephones: 614-227-2000; (800-533-2794). Fax: 614-227-2100. Internet: columbia@porterwright.com.

Dayton, Ohio Office: One Dayton Centre, One South Main Street, Suite 1600, 45402-2028. Telephones: 937-449-6810; (800-533-4434). Fax: 937-449-6820. Internet: dayton@porterwright. com.

Cincinnati, Ohio Office: 250 E. Fifth Street, Suite 2200, 45202-4199. Telephones: 513-381-4700; (800-582-5813). Fax: 513-421-0991. Internet: cincinnati@porterwright.com.

Cleveland, Ohio Office: 925 Euclid Avenue, Suite 1700, 44115-1483. Telephones: 216-443-9000; (800-824-1980). Fax: 216-443-9011. Internet: cleveland@porterwright.com.

Naples, Florida Office: 5801 Pelican Bay Boulevard, Suite 300, 34108-2709. Telephones: 941-593-2900; (800-876-7962). Fax: 941-593-2990. Internet: naples@porterwright.com.

Alternative Dispute Resolution, Business and Corporate, Construction, Employee Benefits, Energy and Utilities, Environment, Federal Contracting and Procurement, Financial Institutions, General Practice, Governmental Affairs, Health Care, Insurance, Intellectual Property, International Business, Labor and Employment, Litigation, Public Law, Public Finance, Real Estate, Securities, Taxation, Technology, Trusts and Estates.

FIRM PROFILE: Porter, Wright, Morris & Arthur is an internationally known business law firm delivering creative solutions for large, mid-size and entrepreneurial businesses. Porter Wright's Washington presence began in 1979 and concentrates on the areas of international business transactions, government affairs and a wide range of litigation matters, including health care fraud recovery, white collar criminal defense, mass tort, insurance coverage and international commercial litigation. The Firm, which traces its origins to 1846, has over 260 lawyers practicing in Cincinnati, Cleveland, Columbus, and Dayton, Ohio; Washington, D.C.; and Naples, Florida.

MEMBERS OF FIRM

DAVID L. DOUGLASS, born Brooklyn, New York, July 16, 1959; admitted to bar, 1985, Massachusetts; 1995, District of Columbia. *Education:* Yale University (B.A., 1981); Harvard University (J.D., cum laude, 1985). Adjunct Faculty, Advanced Evidence, The George Washington Law School. Assistant United States Attorney, United States Attorney's Office, 1988-1991. Trial Attorney, Civil Rights Division, Criminal Section, U.S. Department of Justice, 1991-1993. Assistant Project Director, U.S. Department of Treasury investigation of the Bureau of Alcohol, Tobacco, and Firearms assault on the compound of David Koresh near Waco, Texas, 1993. Executive Director, White House Security Review, 1994-1995. ***Email:*** ddouglas@porterwright.com

ALISON MacDONALD DUNCAN, born Alyth, Scotland, November 3, 1953; admitted to bar, 1984, Maryland; 1985, District of Columbia. *Education:* University of Aberdeen, Scotland (B.Ed., with distinction, 1975); Rotary International Scholar, 1975; University of Maryland (M.A., 1976); George Washington University (J.D., cum laude, 1984). *Member:* The District of Columbia

(This Listing Continued)

PORTER WRIGHT MORRIS & ARTHUR LLP, Washington— Continued

Bar; Maryland State Bar Association. ***PRACTICE AREAS:*** Health Care Fraud; White Collar Crime; Government Contracts. ***Email:*** aduncan@porterwright.com

E. JAY FINKEL, born Philadelphia, Pennsylvania, June 21, 1931; admitted to bar, 1966, District of Columbia and U.S. Court of Appeals for the District of Columbia Circuit; 1980, U.S. Supreme Court; 1983, U.S. Court of International Trade; 1985, U.S. Court of Appeals for the Federal Circuit. *Education:* Swarthmore College (B.A., cum laude, 1952); George Washington University (M.A., economics, 1961; J.D., with honors, 1965). U.S. Director, Inter-American Development Bank, 1977-1981. Director: Developing National Finance, U.S. Treasury, 1970-1974; World Bank/IMF Development Committee, 1975-1977. ***LANGUAGES:*** Spanish. ***PRACTICE AREAS:*** Bank and Thrift Regulation Law; International Finance and Trade Law. ***Email:*** jfinkel@porterwright.com

LESLIE ALAN GLICK, born New York, N.Y., May 22, 1946; admitted to bar, 1971, New York and District of Columbia; 1974, Maryland; U.S. Court of International Trade and 1971-1982; U.S. Supreme Court and U.S. Court of Appeals for the Federal Circuit. *Education:* Cornell University (B.A., 1967; J.D., 1970). Author: *Understanding the North American Free Trade Agreement* (Kluwer Law and Taxation Publishers, second edition, 1994); *Guide to U.S. Customs and International Trade Laws* (Kluwer Law International, second edition, 1997); *Multilateral Trade Negotiations: World Trade After The Tokyo Round* (Littlefield, Adams—1984). Co-Editor and Contributing Author, *Manual for the Practice of United States Import Law* (Kluwer, 1990). Adjunct Professor of Law, University of Baltimore School of Law, 1989-1990. *Member:* The District of Columbia Bar; Federal Bar Association (Chairman, International Law Section, 1986-1989; Chairman, International Trade and Customs Law Committee, 1982-1985); Inter-American Bar Foundation (Chairman, Legal Education and Communications Committee, 1985). ***LANGUAGES:*** Spanish. ***PRACTICE AREAS:*** International Trade Law; Customs Law; Imports and Exports; Food, Drug and Cosmetic Law; NAFTA Anti Dumping; Latin America Trade. ***Email:*** lglick@porterwright.com

THOMAS O. GORMAN, born Cleveland, Ohio, June 13, 1948; admitted to bar, 1973, Ohio; 1974, U.S. District Court, Northern District of Ohio; 1982, U.S. Supreme Court and U.S. Court of Appeals, Ninth Circuit; 1986, District of Columbia; 1990, New York; 1992, U.S. District Court for the District of Columbia and U.S. Court of Appeals, Third Circuit; 1994, U.S. Tax Court and U.S. Court of Federal Claims; 1995, U.S. Court of Appeals for the District of Columbia Circuit. *Education:* John Carroll University (A.B., 1970); Cleveland State University (J.D., cum laude, 1973); Georgetown University (LL.M., 1982). Editor, Cleveland State University Law Review, 1972-1973. Member, Moot Court Board and Order of the Barristers. Selected one of Five Best Litigators 54 Washington Business Journal, February, 1996. Author: Forward to: Williams, *Manipulation on Trial, Economic Analysis And The Hunt Silver Case* (1995); "Current Issues in Securities Litigation," *Securities Litigation,* ACI (1994); "Who's Afraid of 10b-5? The Scope of a Section 10(b) Cause of Action After Central Bank of Denver," 22 Sec. Reg. L.J., August, 1994. Co-Author: "Squeezing Silver," 17 Litigation No. 4, Summer, 1991; "A Case Study in Foreign Discovery: Minpeco S.A. v. Nelson Bunker Hunt," Jan. 1990. Adjunct Professor of Law, Cleveland State University, 1974-1976. Assistant Public Defender, 1973-1975. Special Trial Counsel Office of General Counsel, Securities and Exchange Commission, 1981-1985. Attorney, 1978-1979 and Senior Counsel, 1979-1981, Division of Enforcement, Securities and Exchange Commission. *Member:* American Bar Association (Sections on: Litigation, Business Law, and Committee on SEC Enforcement Matters and Litigation). ***PRACTICE AREAS:*** Complex Litigation; Antitrust; Securities; Commercial; International; Federal Agency Practice; SEC; CFTC. ***Email:*** tgorman@porterwright.com

JUDD L. KESSLER, born Newark, New Jersey, April 10, 1938; admitted to bar, 1963, New Jersey; 1967, U.S. Supreme Court; 1972, District of Columbia; 1989, Maryland. *Education:* Oberlin College (A.B., 1960); Harvard University (LL.B., 1963). Phi Beta Kappa. Assistant General Counsel, 1975-1982, Chief Counsel for Legislative Affairs, 1975-1976, Chief Counsel for Latin American and Caribbean Affairs, 1976-1980 and Chief Counsel for Near East Programs, 1980-1982, U.S. Agency for International Development. *Member:* The District of Columbia Bar; Federal and American Bar Associations; American Society of International Law; Inter-American Bar Foundation (President); Cosmos Club of Washington, D.C.; Roster of International Arbitrators; American Arbitration Association. ***PRACTICE AREAS:*** International Business Transactions; Project Finance; Complex Commercial and International Arbitration; Public Contracting. ***Email:*** jkessler@porterwright.com

WILLIAM P. McGRATH, JR., born Kittery, Maine, April 11, 1961; admitted to bar, 1987, Massachusetts; 1990, District of Columbia; 1991, U.S. District Court, District of Columbia; 1992, U.S. Court of Appeals, District of Columbia Circuit and U.S. Court of Appeals, Third Circuit, 1994, U.S. Tax Court and U.S. Court of Federal Claims; 1995, U.S. District Court, District of

(This Listing Continued)

Maryland. *Education:* Syracuse University (B.A., magna cum laude, 1983); George Washington University (J.D., 1986). Phi Beta Kappa. ***PRACTICE AREAS:*** Litigation. ***Email:*** wmcgrath@porterwright.com

W. SCOTT SIMMER, born Marlborough, Massachusetts, June 22, 1951; admitted to bar, 1985, Iowa; 1998, District of Columbia. *Education:* Cornell College (B.A., with honors, 1973); University of Arkansas (M.F.A., 1978); University of Iowa (J.D., 1985). Fellow, Life Office Management Association, 1994. Associate, Managed Care, Health Insurance Association of America, 1995. ***PRACTICE AREAS:*** Health Care; Health Care Fraud; ERISA; Employee Benefits; Litigation. ***Email:*** ssimmer@porterwright.com

MITCHELL A. STEARN, born New York, N.Y., November 5, 1958; admitted to bar, 1985, Pennsylvania; 1986, District of Columbia; U.S. Court of Appeals, Second, Third, Fourth, Fifth and District of Columbia Circuits; U.S. District Court, for the District of Columbia, District of Maryland and Eastern District of Wisconsin. *Education:* George Washington University (B.A., 1980; J.D., 1985). Law Clerk to Senior Judges John F. Doyle, Nicholas S. Nunzio, Samuel B. Block and Fred L. McIntyre, Superior Court of the District of Columbia, 1985-1987. Author: Late Notice Under "Occurrence-Based" Liability Insurance Policies: When Late May Not Be Late Enough, Environmental Claims Journal, Spring 1996. *Member:* District of Columbia Bar; American Bar Association (Member, Committee on Insurance Coverage Litigation). ***PRACTICE AREAS:*** Complex Litigation; Insurance; Environmental; Professional Liability; Mass Torts; Entertainment Law. ***Email:*** mstearn@porterwright.com

RESIDENT ASSOCIATES

DAVID TIMOTHY FISCHER, born Cincinnati, Ohio, March 31, 1974; admitted to bar, 1999, Ohio; 2001, District of Columbia and U.S. Court of Appeals, District of Columbia Circuit. *Education:* Miami University (B.A.,1996); Georgetown University (J.D., 1999). ***PRACTICE AREAS:*** Complex Litigation; Commercial Litigation. ***Email:*** dfischer@porterwright.com

KEVIN M. GRACE, born Paramus, New Jersey, September 24, 1963; admitted to bar, 1993, Louisiana (Not admitted in District of Columbia). *Education:* Loyola University (B.B.A., 1985; J.D., cum laude, 1993). Member, Loyola Law Review, 1992-1993. Author: Comment, "Protectability of Descriptive Trademarks Acquiring Secondary Meaning: Has Anything Changed Since Straus Frank," 34 Loy. L. Rev. (1993). *Member:* New Orleans, Louisiana State, Federal and American Bar Associations. ***PRACTICE AREAS:*** Insurance Coverage Litigation. ***Email:*** kgrace@porterwright.com

JOHN E. HEDSTROM, born Newton, Massachusetts, July 3, 1970; admitted to bar, 1998, Wisconsin and U.S. District Court, Eastern District of Wisconsin; 1999, District of Columbia and U.S. Court of Appeals, Tenth Circuit. *Education:* Washington & Lee University (B.A., 1993); Marquette University (J.D., 1998). Associate Editor, Marquette Law Review. *Member:* State Bar of Wisconsin; The District of Columbia Bar; American Bar Association; The Association of Trial Lawyers of America. ***Email:*** jhedstrom@porterwright.com

CATHERINE L. HESS, born Charleston, South Carolina, April 10, 1973; admitted to bar, 2000, North Carolina; 2001, District of Columbia. *Education:* University of North Carolina at Charlotte (B.S.W., 1995); Case Western Reserve University (J.D., magna cum laude, 2000). Order of the Coif. ***PRACTICE AREAS:*** Litigation; Government Investigations; Health Care Fraud. ***Email:*** chess@porterwright.com

JENNIFER J. ILLINGWORTH, born Watertown, New York, October 26, 1972; admitted to bar, 1998, New York; 1999, Virginia (Not admitted in District of Columbia). *Education:* Cornell University (B.S., Industrial and Labor Relations, 1994; J.D., 1997). *Member:* New York State and Virginia Bar Associations. ***PRACTICE AREAS:*** Litigation. ***Email:*** jillingworth@porterwright.com

THOMAS J. POULIN, born Farmington, Maine, June 30, 1960; admitted to bar, 1988, Maine and U.S. District Court, District of Maine (Not admitted in District of Columbia). *Education:* Ohio State University (B.A., 1985); University of Maine School of Law (J.D., 1988). *Member:* Maine State Bar Association; Maine Trial Lawyers Association. ***Email:*** tpoulin@porterwright.com

ROBERT T. RHOAD, born Portsmouth, Virginia, April 4, 1967; admitted to bar, 1994, Vermont; 1996, U.S. Court of Appeals for the Armed Forces; 1997, District of Columbia; 1998, U.S. Supreme Court, U.S. Court of Appeals, Fourth Circuit, U.S. District Court, District of Maryland, U.S. Court of Federal Claims and U.S. Tax Court. *Education:* University of Vermont (B.A., 1989); Vermont Law School (J.D., 1994); The George Washington University Law School (LL.M., summa cum laude, 1999). *Member:* Vermont and American (Member, Sections on: Litigation; Torts and Insurance Practice; Administrative Law) Bar Associations; Bar Association of the District of Columbia. [Trial Atty./Lt., US Navy JAG Corps, 1994-1999]. ***PRACTICE AREAS:*** Complex Litigation; Health Care Fraud; White Collar Crime. ***Email:*** rrhoad@porterwright.com

HEATHER J. STEWART, born Buffalo, New York, September 25, 1971; admitted to bar, 1996, Maryland; 1997, District of Columbia. *Education:* Uni-

(This Listing Continued)

versity of Notre Dame (B.S., magna cum laude, 1993); University of Michigan Law School (J.D., cum laude, Order of the Coif, 1996). **PRACTICE AREAS:** Health Care Fraud. **Email:** hstewart@porterwright.com

RENATA S. VASCONCELLOS, born Rio de Janeiro, Brazil, December 21, 1970; admitted to bar, 1992, Brazil; 1998, New York (Not admitted in District of Columbia). *Education:* Universidade Federal Fluminense (J.D., 1992); American University (LL.M., 1994). *Member:* Brazilian Bar Association (Ordem dos Advogados do Brasil). ***LANGUAGES:*** Portuguese, Spanish and English. ***PRACTICE AREAS:*** Federal Practice; International Trade; Customs Law; Import and Export Law; Antidumping; North American Free Trade Agreement; Brazilian Law; International Law. **Email:** rvasconcellos@porterwright.com

JASON E. WOEHRMYER, born St. Marys, Ohio, February 8, 1972; admitted to bar, 1999, Maryland (Not admitted in District of Columbia). *Education:* University of Cincinnati (B.B.A., 1995); Georgetown University Law Center (J.D., 1999). *Member:* Maryland State Bar Association, Inc. ***PRACTICE AREAS:*** Corporate Law; Mergers and Acquisitions. **Email:** jwoehrmyer@porterwright.com

(See Listings at Dayton, Cincinnati, Cleveland and Columbus, Ohio and Naples, Florida for professional biographies on attorneys resident in those offices)

POWELL, GOLDSTEIN, FRAZER & MURPHY LLP

6TH FLOOR, 1001 PENNSYLVANIA AVENUE, N.W.
WASHINGTON, D.C. 20004
Telephone: 202-347-0066
Fax: 202-624-7222
URL: http://www.pgfm.com

Atlanta, Georgia Office: Sixteenth Floor, 191 Peachtree Street, N.E., 30303. Telephone: 404-572-6600. Fax: 404-572-6999.

Reston, Virginia Office: Suite 1375, 11951 Freedom Drive, 20190. Telephone: 703-251-4828.

Geneva, Switzerland Office: Sixth Floor, Rue de Lausanne 139, 1202 Geneva. Telephone: +41-22-908 25 25.

Administrative Advocacy, Antitrust and Trade Regulation, Banking, Litigation, Corporate Finance and Securities, Employee Benefits, Executive Compensation, Environmental, Estate Planning, Financial Institutions, Lending and Securitization, Government Contracts and Construction Litigation, Healthcare, Immigration, Intellectual Property and Technology, International Business, International Trade, Labor and Employment, Legislative and Public Policy Advocacy, Litigation, Mergers and Acquisitions, Public Finance, Real Estate and Housing, Securities, Secured Transactions, Tax, Technology Litigation, Trade Associations, Software, Trademarks, Patents and Copyrights, White Collar Crime, Workouts, Bankruptcy and Insolvency, Y2K.

LAW FIRM ALLIANCES/ASSOCIATIONS: **TECHLAW GROUP**

BUSINESS COUNCIL, INC.

UNITED STATES LAW FIRM GROUP: *(see www.uslfg.com).*

RESIDENT MEMBERS

JESSICA C. ABRAHAMS, born Staten Island, New York, May 5, 1965; admitted to bar, 1990, Ohio; 1992, District of Columbia and U.S. Court of Appeals for the Federal Circuit; 1994, U.S. Court of Federal Claims; 1996, U.S. District Court, Eastern District of Maryland; 1996, U.S. Court of Appeals, Fourth Circuit; 1997, U.S. Court of Appeals for the District of Columbia Circuit and Sixth Circuit; 1998, U.S. Supreme Court. *Education:* Wellesley College (B.A., cum laude, 1987); Université de Provence (Aix-Marseille I), Aix-en-Provence, France; Case Western Reserve University School of Law (J.D., 1990). Member, Order of the Barristers. *Member:* The District of Columbia Bar; Federal and American (Vice Chair, Information Technology and Regulatory Coordinating Committees, Member, Sections on Public Contracts and Young Lawyers) Bar Associations; National Contract Management Association; Women's Bar Association. ***LANGUAGES:*** French. ***PRACTICE AREAS:*** Government Contracts; International Government Contracts; Federal Litigation; Bid Protests. **Email:** jabraham@pgfm.com

J. GAIL BANCROFT, born Cherokee, Iowa, December 9, 1949; admitted to bar, 1977, New York; 1995, District of Columbia. *Education:* St. Olaf College (B.A., magna cum laude, 1972); University of Iowa (J.D., with honors, 1976). *Member:* Association of the Bar of the City of New York; The District of Columbia Bar; American Bar Association; Women's Bar Association of the District of Columbia; World International Trade Association. ***PRACTICE AREAS:*** Corporate Law; Project Finance. **Email:** gbancrof@pgfm.com

RICHARD M. BELANGER, born Lewiston, Maine, March 8, 1947; admitted to bar, 1975, Massachusetts; 1979, District of Columbia; 1980, U.S. Court of International Trade; 1982, U.S. Court of Appeals for the Federal Circuit. *Education:* University of New Hampshire (B.A., 1972); Boston University (J.D., 1975); Georgetown University. *Member:* District of Columbia Bar; American, International and Customs and International Trade Bar Associations. ***PRACTICE AREAS:*** Customs; International Trade; Export Controls. **Email:** rbelange@pgfm.com

JOSEPH M. BERL, born Brooklyn, New York, October 1, 1942; admitted to bar, 1968, New York; 1972, District of Columbia and U.S. Supreme Court. *Education:* Columbia University (A.B., 1964); George Washington University (J.D., with honors, 1967). Phi Delta Phi. *Member:* The District of Columbia Bar; American Bar Association (Member, Section of Corporation, Banking and Business Law). ***PRACTICE AREAS:*** Corporate Law; Business Law; Securities Law. **Email:** jberl@pgfm.com

JEROME A. BREED, born Hammond, Indiana, March 12, 1952; admitted to bar, 1978, New York; 1982, Colorado; 1989, District of Columbia. *Education:* Columbia College (A.B., 1974); Harvard University (J.D., 1977). Staff Editor, International Law Journal, 1976-1977. *Member:* American Bar Association. ***PRACTICE AREAS:*** Taxation Law. **Email:** jbreed@pgfm.com

RALPH J. CACCIA, born Brooklyn, New York, August 22, 1961; admitted to bar, 1987, New York; 1988, District of Columbia. *Education:* Fordham University (B.A., summa cum laude, 1983) Phi Beta Kappa; Georgetown University (J.D., 1986). Assistant U.S. Attorney, U.S. Attorneys's Office, 1990-1995. *Member:* The District of Columbia Bar; American Bar Association. ***PRACTICE AREAS:*** White Collar Criminal Defense; Health Care Fraud; Government Enforcement Litigation; Complex Civil Litigation. **Email:** rcaccia@pgfm.com

KELLY CAMERON, born New York, N.Y., October 24, 1958; admitted to bar, 1983, District of Columbia; 1984, U.S. Court of Appeals, District of Columbia Circuit. *Education:* Tufts University (B.A., summa cum laude, 1980); Georgetown University (J.D., 1983). Staff Attorney, Federal Communications Commission, 1983-1997. ***PRACTICE AREAS:*** Telecommunications; International Trade. **Email:** kcameron@pgfm.com

ANNE B. CAMPER, born Roanoke, Virginia, November 4, 1955; admitted to bar, 1981, District of Columbia; 1982, U.S. District Court, District of Columbia. *Education:* University of Virginia (B.A., with honors, 1977; M.B.A., 1981; J.D., 1981). *Member:* The District of Columbia Bar; American Bar Association; Women's Bar Association of District of Columbia; American Health Lawyers Association. ***PRACTICE AREAS:*** Health Care; Corporate. **Email:** acamper@pgfm.com

MICHAEL H. CHANIN, born Atlanta, Georgia, November 11, 1943; admitted to bar, 1968, Georgia; 1980, District of Columbia. *Education:* University of North Carolina (A.B., 1965); Emory University (J.D., 1968). Omicron Delta Kappa; Phi Delta Phi. Editor, Journal of Public Law, 1967-1968. Deputy Assistant to the President of the United States, 1978-1981. *Member:* The District of Columbia Bar; Atlanta and American Bar Associations; State Bar of Georgia. (Also at Reston, Virginia Office). ***PRACTICE AREAS:*** Corporate; Corporate Finance; Government Contracts. **Email:** mchanin@pgfm.com

WILLIAM C. CRENSHAW, born Red Bank, New Jersey, September 20, 1953; admitted to bar, 1977, Virginia, Florida and U.S. District Court, Southern District of Florida; 1978, District of Columbia; 1981, U.S. Court of Appeals, Fifth and Eleventh Circuits; 1984, U.S. District Court, Middle District of Florida 1993, Maryland and U.S. District Court, Eastern District of Virginia; 1996, U .S. Court of Appeals, District of Columbia Circuit; 1997, U.S. Court of Appeals, Fourth Circuit. *Education:* Tufts University (B.A., 1974); University of Virginia (J.D., 1977). Research and Projects Editor, Virginia Journal of International Law, 1976-1977. *Member:* Dade County and American Bar Associations; The Florida Bar; The District of Columbia Bar; Virginia State Bar. (Also at Reston, Virginia Office). ***PRACTICE AREAS:*** Commercial Litigation; Bankruptcy. **Email:** wcrensha@pgfm.com

BUTLER C. DERRICK, JR., born Springfield, Massachusetts, September 30, 1936; admitted to bar, 1965, South Carolina; 1980, District of Columbia; U.S. Supreme Court. *Education:* University of South Carolina; University of Georgia (J.D., 1965). Phi Kappa Phi; Phi Beta Kappa. U.S. Congressman, 1975-1995. Chief Deputy Whip and Vice Chairman, House Rules Committee. Member, Secretary of Energy Advisory Board, Russia Task Force. Member, National Trust Council of the National Trust for Historic Preservation. Chairman, South Carolina Governor's Task Force on Low Level Nuclear Waste. ***PRACTICE AREAS:*** Administrative. **Email:** bderrick@pgfm.com

ROBERT W. DOYLE, JR., born Philadelphia, Pennsylvania, May 22, 1947; admitted to bar, 1976, Pennsylvania; 1978, District of Columbia; 1988, U.S. Supreme Court. *Education:* Temple University (B.A., 1970; M.A., 1971; J.D., 1976). ***PRACTICE AREAS:*** Antitrust; Mergers and Acquisitions; Litigation.

WILLIAM GERALD DRIGGERS, born Florence, Alabama, January 12, 1955; admitted to bar, 1991, Pennsylvania; 1993, District of Columbia. *Education:* University of Texas (B.A., magna cum laude, 1977; M.A., 1985); Georgetown University (J.D., magna cum laude, 1990). Phi Beta Kappa; Phi Kappa Phi. Member, Georgetown Law Journal, 1989-1990. ***PRACTICE AREAS:*** Real Estate; Tax Law. **Email:** wdrigger@pgfm.com

(This Listing Continued)

POWELL, GOLDSTEIN, FRAZER & MURPHY LLP, Washington—Continued

NEIL R. ELLIS, born Cleveland, Ohio, April 13, 1955; admitted to bar, 1981, District of Columbia; 1982, U.S. Court of Appeals, Fifth and Tenth Circuits; 1983, U.S. Court of Appeals, Fourth and District of Columbia Circuit; 1986, U.S. Court of Appeals for the Federal Circuit and U.S. Court of International Trade. *Education:* Cornell University (A.B., cum laude, 1976); Yale University (J.D., 1980). Phi Beta Kappa. Editor, Yale Law Journal, 1979-1980. *Member:* The District of Columbia Bar; American and International Bar Associations. ***PRACTICE AREAS:*** International Trade Regulation; Antitrust. ***Email:*** nellis@pgfm.com

MICHAEL E. FINE, born Toledo, Ohio, September 12, 1954; admitted to bar, 1983, District of Columbia; 1984, U.S. District Court for the District of Columbia and U.S. Court of Appeals for the District of Columbia Circuit; 1987, U.S. Supreme Court. *Education:* Rutgers College (B.A., magna cum laude, 1977); Boston University (J.D., magna cum laude, 1982). Member, 1980-1981 and Executive Editor, 1981-1982, Boston University Law Review. *Member:* The District of Columbia Bar; American Bar Association. ***PRACTICE AREAS:*** Legislative; International Trade; Government Ethics. ***Email:*** mfine@pgfm.com

LAWRENCE R. FULLERTON, born Stuttgart, Germany, February 6, 1952; admitted to bar, 1978, District of Columbia. *Education:* Princeton University (A.B., cum laude, 1974); University of Virginia (M.A., Economics, 1978; J.D., 1978). Order of the Coif. Deputy Assistant Attorney General, U.S. Department of Justice, 1995-1998. Counsel, U.S. Senate Committee on Commerce, Science and Transportation, 1981-1985. *Member:* American Bar Association (Council, 1992-1995; Chairman, FTC Committee, 1989-1992). ***PRACTICE AREAS:*** Antitrust. ***Email:*** lfullert@pgfm.com

LARRY S. GAGE, born Hollywood, California, August 9, 1947; admitted to bar, 1973, District of Columbia. *Education:* Harvard College (B.A., cum laude, 1968); Columbia University (J.D., 1972). Co-Author: "Managed Care Manual: Medicare, Medicaid & State Health Reform," West Group. President, National Association of Public Hospitals, 1981—. Chairman, Board of Directors, American International Health Alliance, 2000—. Member, Board of Directors and Executive Committee, University HealthSystem Consortium, 1997—. Deputy Assistant Secretary, Health Legislation, U.S. Department of Health and Human Services, 1978-1981. Staff Director, U.S. Senate Subcommittee on Alcoholism and Drug Abuse, 1975-1977. Counsel, U.S. Senate Subcommittee on Employment, Poverty and Migratory Labor, 1973-1975. *Member:* The District of Columbia Bar; American Health Lawyers Association. ***LANGUAGES:*** Spanish. ***PRACTICE AREAS:*** Health Care; Administrative Law; Government Relations. ***Email:*** lgage@pgfm.com

RONALD S. GART, born Middletown, New York, December 7, 1954; admitted to bar, 1979, District of Columbia; 1994, Maryland; 1996, Virginia. *Education:* George Washington University (B.A., with distinction, 1976; J.D., with honors, 1979). Phi Beta Kappa; Phi Eta Sigma; Omicron Delta Kappa. *Member:* District of Columbia Bar; Virginia State Bar; Maryland State Bar Association; D.C. Building Industry Association; Greater Washington Board of Trade. (Also at Reston, Virginia Office). ***PRACTICE AREAS:*** Real Estate; Finance Law; Securitization; Real Estate Law; Condominium Law; Real Estate Development Law; Corporate Banking Law; Commercial Leasing Law. ***Email:*** rgart@pgfm.com

ELIZABETH COLE HAFNER, born Sacramento, California, February 15, 1960; admitted to bar, 1988, Pennsylvania; 1991, District of Columbia. *Education:* University of California at Berkeley (B.A., 1982); Boston University Law School (J.D., 1988); The Fletcher School of Law and Diplomacy (M.A.L.D., 1988). *Member:* The District of Columbia Bar; Pennsylvania and American Bar Associations. ***LANGUAGES:*** French. ***PRACTICE AREAS:*** International Trade Law; Customs Law. ***Email:*** bhafner@pgfm.com

DAVID C. HAMMOND, born Ft. Wayne, Indiana, March 1, 1959; admitted to bar, 1988, Michigan; 1989, District of Columbia; 1992, U.S. Court of Appeals, Federal Circuit and U.S. Court of Federal Claims. *Education:* Albion College (B.A., 1981); University of Michigan (J.D., cum laude, 1988). *Member:* The District of Columbia Bar; American Bar Association. (Also at Reston, Virginia Office). ***PRACTICE AREAS:*** Government Contracts Law; Health Care Procurement Law; Legislative Law. ***Email:*** dhammond@pgfm.com

HARRY HUGE, born Deshler, Nebraska, September 16, 1937; admitted to bar, 1963, Illinois; 1966, District of Columbia; 1967, U.S. Court of Appeals, Ninth Circuit; 1982, U.S. Supreme Court; 1985, South Carolina. *Education:* Nebraska Wesleyan University (A.B., 1959); Georgetown University (J.D., 1963). Phi Delta Phi. Member, Georgetown Law Journal, 1962-1963. Chairman, Board of Trustees, United Mine Workers of America Health and Retirement Funds, 1973-1977. Member, Board of Director's, 1992— and Chairman, 1992-1995, Hollings Cancer Center, Medical University of South Carolina. ***PRACTICE AREAS:*** Commercial Litigation; Civil and Criminal Litigation; Corporate and International Transactions. ***Email:*** hhuge@pgfm.com

(This Listing Continued)

BRENDA A. JACOBS, born New York, N.Y., January 18, 1955; admitted to bar, 1980, District of Columbia; 1982, California; 1988, U.S. Court of International Trade and U.S. Court of Appeals for the Federal Circuit. *Education:* Cornell University (B.S., 1976); George Washington University (J.D., with honors, 1980). Author: "Talking Textiles: A New Four-Year Pact Comes With a 12 Year Punch," The China Business Review, March-April 1997; Attorney-Advisor, Office of the General Counsel, U.S. International Trade Commission, 1983-1985. Senior Counsel, Textiles and Trade Agreements, Office of the General Counsel, U.S. Department of Commerce, 1985-1989. *Member:* The District of Columbia Bar (Member, Section on International Law); State Bar of California; American Bar Association (Member, Section on International Law and Practice); Customs and International Trade Bar Association. ***PRACTICE AREAS:*** Customs and International Trade Law. ***Email:*** bjacobs@pgfm.com

BRETT G. KAPPEL, born New York, N.Y., July 11, 1958; admitted to bar, 1990, Virginia; 1992, District of Columbia. *Education:* State University of New York at Albany (B.A., summa cum laude, 1980) Phi Alpha Theta; Signum Laudis; University of Virginia (J.D., 1990). Dillard Fellow, 1988-1989. Notes Editor, Journal of Law & Politics, 1989-1990. Co-author: "Lender Liability Under the Comprehensive Environmental Response, Compensation and Liability Act," 41 S.C.L. Rev. 705, Summer, 1990; "Nowhere to Run, Nowhere to Hide: Criminal Liability for Violations of Environmental Statutes in the 1990's," 16 Colum J. Envtl. L. 201, 1991. *Member:* Virginia State Bar; The District of Columbia Bar; American Bar Association. (Also at Reston, Virginia Office). ***PRACTICE AREAS:*** Internet Law; Legislative Advocacy; Aviation Law; Election Law. ***Email:*** bkappel@pgfm.com

JOHN J. KNAPP, born New York, N.Y., September 15, 1934; admitted to bar, 1962, New York; 1969, Rhode Island; 1988, District of Columbia; 1990, Maryland. *Education:* Manhattan College (B.S., 1958); Fordham University (J.D., 1961). Articles Editor, Fordham Law Review, 1960-1961. General Counsel, U.S. Department of Housing & Urban Development, 1981-1986. *Member:* The District of Columbia Bar; American Bar Association. ***PRACTICE AREAS:*** Federal Housing Programs; Administrative; Corporate Lending Law. ***Email:*** jknapp@pgfm.com

JEFFREY P. KUSHAN, born Atlanta, Georgia, October 3, 1963; admitted to bar, 1992, Virginia; 1998, District of Columbia; registered to practice before U.S. Patent and Trademark Office. *Education:* College of William and Mary (B.S., 1985); University of North Carolina (M.A., 1987); George Washington University (J.D., with honors, 1992). Author: "Protein Patents and the Doctrine of Equivalents: Limits on Expansion of Patent Rights," 6 Technology L.J. 109 (1992). *Member:* American Bar Association; American Intellectual Property Law Association; National Patent Board. ***LANGUAGES:*** French. ***PRACTICE AREAS:*** Intellectual Property; International Trade; Public Policy; Government Affairs. ***Email:*** jkushan@pgfm.com

SIMON LAZARUS, III, born Cincinnati, Ohio, March 30, 1941; admitted to bar, 1968, District of Columbia. *Education:* Harvard University (B.A., magna cum laude, 1963); Yale University (M.A., 1967; LL.B., 1967). Note and Comment Editor, Yale Law Journal, 1966-1967. Associate Director, White House Domestic Policy Staff, 1977-1981. Secretary, Computer and Business Equipment Manufacturers Association, 1988-1994. Secretary, Competitive Long Distance Coalition, Inc., 1994-1996. Member, Board of Trustees, Center for Law and Social Policy, 1985—. President, American Jewish Committee, D.C. Chapter, 1993-1995. Member, National Board of Governors, American Jewish Committee, 1997—. *Member:* The District of Columbia Bar. ***PRACTICE AREAS:*** Legislation; Electronic Commerce; Telecommunications; Antitrust. ***Email:*** slazarus@pgfm.com

ROBERT E. MADDEN, born Buffalo, New York, November 27, 1943; admitted to bar, 1970, New York; 1971, District of Columbia; 1989, Virginia. *Education:* Cornell University (B.S., 1966; J.D., with distinction, 1969). Author: "Tax Planning for Highly Compensated Individuals," (Warren, Gorham & Lamont - 3rd Ed., 1996). Fellow, American College of Trust and Estate Counsel. *Member:* American Bar Association (Member, Taxation Section). (Also at Reston, Virginia Office). ***PRACTICE AREAS:*** Trusts and Estates; Executive Compensation; Federal Taxation; Corporate. ***Email:*** rmadden@pgfm.com

NIALL P. MEAGHER, born Dublin, Ireland, March 17, 1965; admitted to bar, 1988, District of Columbia. *Education:* Trinity College, Dublin University, Ireland (LL.B., 1987); University of Chicago (LL.M., 1988). *Member:* The District of Columbia Bar. ***LANGUAGES:*** French. ***PRACTICE AREAS:*** International Trade Law. ***Email:*** nmeagher@pgfm.com

RICHARD A. MEDWAY, born Washington, D.C., October 6, 1967; admitted to bar, 1992, Virginia; 1993, Maryland; 1994, District of Columbia. *Education:* Ealing College, London, England (1988); University of Wisconsin-Madison (B.A., 1989); Catholic University, Columbus School of Law (J.D., 1992). Member, 1990-1992; Associate Editor, 1991-1992, Catholic University Law Review. Member, Catholic University Moot Court Team. *Member:* Maryland State Bar Association; Virginia State Bar; District of Columbia Bar. ***PRACTICE AREAS:*** Bankruptcy; Commercial Litigation. ***Email:*** rmedway@pgfm.com

(This Listing Continued)

JAMES E. MENDENHALL, admitted to bar, 1993, New York; 1994, District of Columbia. *Education:* University of Notre Dame (B.A., with highest honors, 1989); Harvard University (J.D., cum laude, 1992). Phi Delta Kappa. *Member:* American Bar Association. ***PRACTICE AREAS:*** International Trade; International Arbitration. ***Email:*** jmendenh@pgfm.com

THOMAS T. MOGA, born Detroit, Michigan, February 5, 1957; admitted to bar, 1985, Illinois and Iowa; 1988, Michigan; 1990, District of Columbia; U.S. Court of Appeals, Federal Circuit and U.S. Supreme Court; registered to practice before U.S. Patent and Trademark Office. *Education:* University of Michigan (B.A., English Literature and Political Science, 1978; M.A., English Literature, 1980); St. Louis University (J.D., 1983); Madonna University (B.S., Biochemistry, cum laude, 1994). Fulbright Scholar, Jilin University, Changchun, People's Republic of China, 1997. Recipient, Certificate of Training, World Intellectual Property Organization Workshop for Mediators, New York, 1999. Honoree, 1996 Crain's Detroit Business "Top 40 Under 40." Author: "Patent Practice & Policy in the Pacific Rim," Oceana Publications, Inc. (treatise); "Patent Practice in the United States," Tianjin (China) Technical News, 1990; "Japanese Patent Practice & American Business," *Collected Speeches Before The Policy Study Group,* Tokyo, Japan, 1993; "Transgenic Animals as Intellectual Property (or the Patented Mouse that Roared)," Journal of the Patent and Trademark Office Society, Volume 76, No. 7, 1994. Foreign Instructor, Xiamen University School of Law, Xiamen, China, 1990. Adjunct Professor of Law, Detroit College of Law at Michigan State University, 1996-1999. Resident Foreign Expert, Saint Island Patent and Trademark Law Office, Taipei, Taiwan, 1983-1984. Honorary Member, Advisory Committee, Journal of International Law and Practice, Detroit College of Law at Michigan State University, 1995—. Foreign Advisor, Patent Office of the People's Republic of China, May-June 1997. Proofreader, Commissioner's Report of the Chinese Patent Office, 1997-1998. Director, Joint U.S.-China Copyright Symposium, Shenyang, China, 1998. Delegation Member, Sino-U.S. Intellectual Property Rights Enforcement Exchange Program, sponsored by the U.S. Department of State, 2001. *Member:* State Bar of Michigan; American Bar Association; American Intellectual Property Law Association (Member, International Education Committee, 1998—); American Chemical Society. ***PRACTICE AREAS:*** Intellectual Property; International Business Law. ***Email:*** Tmoga@pgfm.com

N. DAVID PALMETER, born Elmira, New York, January 29, 1938; admitted to bar, 1963, New York; 1967, U.S. Supreme Court; 1969, District of Columbia; 1976, U.S. Court of International Trade; 1976-1982, U.S. Court of Customs and Patent Appeals; 1982, U.S. Court of Appeals for the Federal Circuit. *Education:* Syracuse University (A.B., 1960); University of Chicago (J.D., 1963). Author: Dispute Settlement in the World Trade Organization: Practice and Procedure (1999); "National Sovereignty and the World Trade Organization," Journal of World Intellectual Property (1999); "The WTO Legal System: Sources of Law," American Journal of International Law (1998); The WTO Appellate Body Needs Remand Authority," Journal of World Trade (1998); "The Need for Due Process in WTO Proceedings," Journal of the World Trade (1997); The WTO Appellate Body's First Decision," Leiden Journal of International Law (1996); "A Commentary on the WTO Antidumping Code," Journal of World Trade (1996); "International Trade Law in the Twenty-First Century," Fordham International Law Journal (1995). Trial Attorney, Civil Division, U.S. Department of Justice, 1966-1968. *Member:* The District of Columbia Bar; Federal, American and International (Chairman, Subcommittee on Trade and Customs Law, 1989-1993) Bar Associations; Washington Foreign Law Society (President, 1992-1993); American Society of International Law; Canadian Council on International Law; British Institute of International and Comparative Law. ***PRACTICE AREAS:*** International Trade Law. ***Email:*** dpalmete@pgfm.com

ALAN K. PARVER, born New York, N.Y., March 4, 1951; admitted to bar, 1977, New York and U.S. District Court, Eastern and Southern Districts of New York; 1978, District of Columbia; 1983, U.S. District Court for the District of Columbia; 1985, U.S. Supreme Court. *Education:* American University (B.A., magna cum laude, 1973) Phi Kappa Pi; Pi Sigma Alpha; Cornell University (J.D., 1976). *Member:* The District of Columbia Bar; New York State Bar Association. ***PRACTICE AREAS:*** Health Care Law; Governmental Relations Law. ***Email:*** aparver@pgfm.com

DANIEL M. PRICE, born St. Louis, Missouri, August 23, 1955; admitted to bar, 1981, District of Columbia; 1986, Pennsylvania; 1999, U.S. Supreme Court. *Education:* Haverford College (B.A., 1977); Cambridge University, England (Diploma, 1979); Harvard University (J.D., 1981). Phi Beta Kappa. Articles Editor, Harvard Law Review, 1980-1981. Author: "An Overview of the NAFTA Investment Chapter," North American Free Trade Agreement: A New Frontier in International Trade and Investment in the Americas, Bello, Holmer & Norton eds. (1994). Principal Deputy General Counsel, Office of the U.S. Trade Representative, Washington, D.C., 1989-1992. Counsel, Organization for International Investment. Member, Panel of Arbitrators, American Arbitration Association. *Member:* American Bar Association (Chair, Task Force on the Multinational Agreement on Investment; Co-Chair, North American Free Trade Agreement Subcommittee); American Society of International Law (Member, Council on Foreign Relations). ***PRACTICE AREAS:*** International Business Transactions; International Arbitration. ***Email:*** dprice@pgfm.com

(This Listing Continued)

CHARLES H. ROISTACHER, born New York, N.Y., February 5, 1943; admitted to bar, 1968, District of Columbia and U.S. District Court, District of Columbia; 1969, U.S. Court of Appeals, District of Columbia Circuit; 1972, U.S. Supreme Court. *Education:* University of Virginia (B.A., 1964); University of Miami (J.D., 1968). Member, University of Miami Law Review, 1966-1968. Assistant United States Attorney, 1969-1989 and Executive Assistant United States Attorney, 1985-1988, District of Columbia. Co-Author: with Jack Chorowsky, "End of Cold War Frees FBI to Target Health Care Fraud and Abuse," HealthSpan The Report of Health and Business and Law, June 1993; "A Practitioner's Guide: Voluntary Disclosure in 1998," (1998); "A Practitioner's Guide: Representing Clients in Health Care Fraud Investigations in 1999," (1999); "Voluntary Disclosure by Healthcare Providers," (2000); "Federal Sentencing Guidelines and Organizational Defendants," (2000); "Advising Clients in the Wake of *United States v. Anderson*: Are You at Risk?" (2000). *Member:* The District of Columbia Bar; American Bar Association (Member, White Collar Crime Committee). ***PRACTICE AREAS:*** White Collar Crime; Congressional Investigations; Internal Corporate Investigations; Government Enforcement Litigation; Complex Civil Litigation; Health Care Litigation. ***Email:*** croistac@pgfm.com

LEONARD J. RUBIN, born New York, N.Y., June 29, 1941; admitted to bar, 1968, District of Columbia; 1970, California. *Education:* Hofstra University (B.A., 1964); American University (J.D., 1967). Author: "Operating Guide to Supervision and Regulation of Financial Institutions," A.S. Pratt, 1996; "Financial Modernization," Alex Information Services, 2000. [Capt., U.S. Army, 1967-1969]. ***PRACTICE AREAS:*** Financial Institution Regulation; Corporate; Nonprofit Organizations. ***Email:*** lrubin@pgfm.com

ALLEN S. RUGG, born Denver, Colorado, July 4, 1949; admitted to bar, 1975, District of Columbia, Virginia, U.S. District Court for the District of Columbia and U.S. District Court, Eastern District of Virginia. *Education:* Miami University; George Washington University (B.A., 1971; J.D., with honors, 1974). (Also at Reston, Virginia Office). ***PRACTICE AREAS:*** Civil Litigation; Business Litigation. ***Email:*** arugg@pgfm.com

MICHAEL I. SANDERS, born Brooklyn, New York, December 23, 1938; admitted to bar, 1964, New York; 1965, U.S. Court of Federal Claims and U.S. Tax Court; 1968, U.S. Supreme Court; 1970, District of Columbia. *Education:* New York University (B.S., summa cum laude, 1960; LL.B., 1964); Georgetown University (LL.M. in Taxation, 1967). Phi Delta Phi; Beta Gamma Sigma. Certified Public Accountant, New York, 1964. Author: *Joint Ventures Involving Tax-Exempt Organizations,* (2nd Edition), John Wiley & Sons; Georgetown University Law Center/Continuing Legal Education. Adjunct Professor of Law: Exempt Organizations, Georgetown Law Center, 1977—; Taxation of Partnership and Sub-Chapter S Corporations, George Washington Law Center, 1997—. Attorney-Advisor to Assistant Secretary of Tax Policy, Office of Tax Legislature Counsel, 1968-1970. Trial Attorney, U.S. Department of Justice (Attorney General's Honors Program), 1964-1968. Course Chairman, The District of Columbia Bar, Real Estate Syndication, 1979, 1984. *Member:* District of Columbia Bar (Member, Steering Committee, Division 16, 1981—); American Bar Association (Chairman, Special Committee on Tax Shelter Study, Taxation Section, 1984-1985; Past Chairman and Special Advisor to Exempt Organization Committee, 1977—; Chairman, IRS Audit and Appeals Subcommittee, 1980—; Member, Ad Hoc Committee on Audit of Partnerships, 1981—; Chairman, Technical Review Committee, 1982 and 1983; Chairman, Special Committee on Tax Shelter Study, 1984-1985; Member, Internal Revenue Commissioner's Exempt Organization Advisory Group, 1987-1988); Master of the Bench, First American Inn of Court; American Institute of Certified Public Accountants. [With USAR, 1959-1965]. ***PRACTICE AREAS:*** Taxation Law; Real Estate Law. ***Email:*** msanders@pgfm.com

PETER W. SEGAL, born Boston, Massachusetts, April 17, 1943; admitted to bar, 1969, District of Columbia; 1973, U.S. Supreme Court. *Education:* Tufts University (B.A., 1965); Boston University (J.D., 1968). *Member:* The District of Columbia Bar. ***PRACTICE AREAS:*** Real Estate Development and Financing Law; Corporate Law; Mortgage Banking Law; Commercial Leasing Law; Housing and Urban Development. ***Email:*** psegal@pgfm.com

W. BRUCE SHIRK, born Kansas City, Missouri, May 9, 1940; admitted to bar, 1969, Massachusetts and U.S. District Court, District of Massachusetts; 1970, District of Columbia and U.S. District Court for the District of Columbia; 1972, U.S. Court of Appeals, District of Columbia Circuit; 1976, U.S. Court of Federal Claims; 1996, U.S. Court of Appeals for the Federal Circuit. *Education:* Harvard University (B.A., cum laude, 1962; J.D., 1969). Author: "D.C. False Claims Act—A Comparison to the Federal Statute," The Procurement Lawyer, Vol. 32, No. 3, Spring 1997; "Appropriations Lapses, Debt Ceilings and Train Wrecks," Government Contractor, Vol. 37, ¶471, September 27, 1995. *Member:* District of Columbia Bar; Massachusetts, Federal (Member and Co-Chairman, Research and Development Committee, Public Contracts Section, 1992-1998) and American (Member, 1975— and Chairman, Committees on Debarment and Suspension, 1988-1991 and Health Care Procurement, 1994-1997, Section of Public Contract Law) Bar Associations. ***PRACTICE AREAS:*** Health Care; Government Contract; Construction Contracts; Administrative Law. ***Email:*** bshirk@pgfm.com

(This Listing Continued)

POWELL, GOLDSTEIN, FRAZER & MURPHY LLP, Washington—Continued

ANDREW W. SHOYER, born Philadelphia, Pennsylvania, June 29, 1960; admitted to bar, 1986, Pennsylvania; 1987, District of Columbia. *Education:* University of Pennsylvania (B.A., cum laude, 1981); Georgetown University (M.S.F.S., with distinction, 1986; J.D., cum laude, 1986); Johns Hopkins University School of Advanced International Studies; Georgetown University School of Foreign Service. Adjunct Professor, Duke University/University of Geneva Institute in Transnational Law, 1997-1998. *Member:* The District of Columbia Bar; American Bar Association; American Society of International Law. ***LANGUAGES:*** Spanish, French. ***PRACTICE AREAS:*** International Trade and Investment Law; International Dispute Settlement. ***Email:*** ashoyer@pgfm.com

STEVEN K. STRANNE, admitted to bar, 1994, Illinois; 1996, District of Columbia. *Education:* Duke University (B.S.E., 1986; M.D., 1990); Harvard Law School (J.D., 1994). Medical License, North Carolina, 1991. ***PRACTICE AREAS:*** Health Care. ***Email:*** sstranne@pgfm.com

ANDREW J. STRENIO, JR., born Erie, Pennsylvania, April 3, 1952; admitted to bar, 1980, District of Columbia; 1992, U.S. Supreme Court. *Education:* Princeton University (A.B., in Public and International Affairs, 1974); John F. Kennedy School of Government at Harvard University (M.P.P., 1978); Harvard University (J.D., cum laude, 1978). Author: "The Testing Trap," Rawson & Wade, 1981. Recipient, FTC Special Award for Excellence, 1983. Senior Staff Economist and sole lawyer, President's Council of Economic Advisers, 1980-1981. Assistant Director for Regulatory Evaluation, Bureau of Consumer Protection, Federal Trade Commission, 1982-1984. Commissioner: Interstate Commerce Commission, 1984-1985; Federal Trade Commission, 1986-1991. Chair, Transportation Industry Committee, 1995-1996 and Member, FTC-DOJ Working Group of the Section of Antitrust Law, 1995-1997, Co-Editor of the Consumer Protection Committee Newsletter, 1994-1996, American Bar Association. Elected Member of the Steering Committee of the Antitrust, Trade Regulation and Consumer Affairs Section, 1992-1998, Section Co-Chair, 1994-1997, The District of Columbia Bar. *Member:* Federal Bar Association. ***PRACTICE AREAS:*** Antitrust; Intellectual Property. ***Email:*** astrenio@pgfm.com

ROBERT TORRESEN, JR., born New York, N.Y., July 20, 1957; admitted to bar, 1983, District of Columbia; 1984, U.S. Court of International Trade; 1988, U.S. Court of Appeals for the Federal Circuit. *Education:* Hope College (B.A., 1979); George Washington University (J.D., 1983). Articles Editor, George Washington Journal of International Law and Economics, 1982-1983. *Member:* The District of Columbia Bar; American Bar Association; Customs and International Trade Bar Association; ITC Trial Lawyers Association. ***PRACTICE AREAS:*** International Trade; Customs Law; Export Control Law. ***Email:*** rtorrese@pgfm.com

MARK TRAPHAGEN, born Wayland, New York, March 23, 1959; admitted to bar, 1985, New York; 1989, District of Columbia and U.S. Court of Appeals, Federal Circuit. *Education:* University of Dayton (B.A., magna cum laude, 1981); University of Denver College of Law (J.D., 1984). Vice President and Counsel, Software Publishers Association, 1993-1999. Trademark Attorney, U.S. Patent & Trademark Office, 1985-1989. Copyright Chairman, Working Party on Intellectual Property and Electronic Commerce, International Chamber of Commerce, 2000—. Steering Committee, U.S. Patent and Trademark Office Conference on Fair Use (CONFU), 1994-1998. Assistant, Copyright Office Advisory Committee on Copyright Registration and Deposit (ACCORD), 1993. Consultant to Malaysian Trade Marks Registry, World Intellectual Property Organization, 1987. *Member:* American Bar Association (Chairman, Committee on Copyright and The Internet, Intellectual Property Section, 1998-2000); Copyright Society of the United States (Trustee, 2000—; Secretary, D.C. Chapter, 1999—); International Trademark Association (Industry Advisory Council, 1998-2000). ***PRACTICE AREAS:*** Intellectual Property; Copyright; Trademark; Electronic Commerce; New Media; Computer Software; International Trade; Public Policy. ***Email:*** mtraphagen@pgfm.com

COLIN W. UCKERT, born Huntington, New York, October 6, 1961; admitted to bar, 1986, Virginia; 1988, District of Columbia; 1993, Maryland. *Education:* The American University (B.A., with distinction, 1983); College of William & Mary (J.D., 1986). Pi Sigma Alpha; Phi Alpha Delta. Member, Mortar Board. *Member:* The District of Columbia Bar; Arlington County, Maryland State and American Bar Associations; Virginia State Bar. (Also at Reston, Virginia Office). ***PRACTICE AREAS:*** Real Estate; Banking; Workouts and Foreclosures. ***Email:*** cuckert@pgfm.com

WILLIAM H.E. VON OEHSEN, born Charlottesville, Virginia, October 18, 1958; admitted to bar, 1988, Pennsylvania; 1990, District of Columbia. *Education:* Princeton University (A.B., 1981); Harvard University (M.T.S., 1984); Georgetown University (J.D., 1988). Annual Scholar, Food and Drug Law Institute, 1987-1988. *Member:* District of Columbia Bar; Food and Drug Law Institute; American Health Lawyers Association. ***PRACTICE AREAS:*** Food and Drug Law; Health Care; Managed Care. ***Email:*** bvonoehs@pgfm.com

(This Listing Continued)

LAWRENCE R. WALDERS, born Chicago, Illinois, 1935; admitted to bar, 1960, District of Columbia; 1984, U.S. Supreme Court, U.S. Court of Appeals for the Federal Circuit and U.S. Court of International Trade. *Education:* University of Michigan (B.A., with distinction, 1957); Harvard University (LL.B., 1960). *Member:* American Bar Association (Member, Section on International Law and Practice); Customs and Internation Trade Bar Association. ***PRACTICE AREAS:*** International Trade Law. ***Email:*** lwalders@pgfm.com

RICHARD C. WILDER, born Seattle, Washington, June 8, 1955; admitted to bar, 1984, New Hampshire; registered to practice before U.S. Patent and Trademark Office (Not admitted in District of Columbia). *Education:* University of Washington (B.S.M.E., 1979); Franklin Pierce Law Center (J.D., 1984). Lecturer in Law, Faculty of Law, University of Malaya, Kuala Lumpur, Malaysia, 1986-1987. Senior Legal Officer, World Intellectual Property Organization, Geneva, Switzerland, 1990-1991. ***PRACTICE AREAS:*** Intellectual Property; International Trade; International Business Law. ***Email:*** rwilder@pgfm.com

OF COUNSEL

ANDREW I. GAVIL, born New York, N.Y., June 24, 1957; admitted to bar, 1981, Illinois and U.S. District Court, District of Illinois; 1982, U.S. Court of Appeals, Seventh Circuit; 1985, U.S. Supreme Court; 1986, Colorado (currently inactive), U.S. District Court, District of Colorado and U.S. Court of Appeals, Tenth Circuit; 1992, District of Columbia. *Education:* Queens College of the City University of New York (B.A., magna cum laude, 1978); Northwestern University (J.D., 1981). Professor of Law, Howard University School of Law, 1994—; Associate Professor, 1991-1994. Editor, Antitrust Magazine. Former Chairman, Antitrust and Economic Regulation, Association of American Law Schools. *Member:* American and Federal Bar Associations. ***PRACTICE AREAS:*** Antitrust Law; Civil Litigation. ***Email:*** agavil@pgfm.com

DAVID GINSBURG, born New York, N.Y., April 20, 1912; admitted to bar, 1935, West Virginia; 1948, District of Columbia. *Education:* West Virginia University (B.A., 1932); Harvard University (LL.B., 1935). General Counsel, Office of Price Administration, 1940-43. U.S. Deputy, Austrian Treaty Commission, 1947. Adviser, Council of Foreign Ministers, London, 1947. Administrative Assistant, Senator M.M. Neely (W.Va.), 1950. Member, Presidential Emergency Board 166, 1966; Chairman, Emergency Board 169, 1967. Member, Commission on Postal Organization, 1967. Executive Director, National Advisory Commission on Civil Disorders, 1967-1968. General Counsel, Democratic National Committee, 1968-1970. Member: Overseers Committee, Kennedy School of Government, 1971-1977; Harvard Law School Association Council, 1972-1976. *Member:* The District of Columbia Bar; Bar Association of the District of Columbia; Cabell County (West Virginia), West Virginia, Federal and American Bar Associations; American Law Institute (Member, Council on Foreign Relations, 1974—). [A.U.S., 1943-46]. ***PRACTICE AREAS:*** International Law; Corporate Law. ***Email:*** dginsburg@pgfm.com

AMBER WONG HSU, born Statesboro, Georgia, September 23, 1969; admitted to bar, 1995, Maryland; 1997, District of Columbia; U.S. Tax Court; U.S. Court of Appeals for the Eleventh and District of Columbia Circuits. *Education:* Rice University (B.A., 1991); Georgetown University Law Center (J.D., 1994). *Member:* American Bar Association; Asian Pacific American Bar Association. ***LANGUAGES:*** Taiwanese, Mandarin. ***PRACTICE AREAS:*** Tax Exempt Organizations; Tax Exempt Litigation. ***Email:*** ahsu@pgfm.com

NANCY ORTMEYER KUHN, born Lake City, Iowa, November 23, 1955; admitted to bar, 1988, Colorado (Not admitted in District of Columbia). *Education:* Cornell College (B.S.S., 1978); University of Minnesota (M.F.A., 1981); University of Colorado (J.D., 1988); University of Denver (LL.M. in Tax, 1989). Fullbright Scholar, University of Trondheim, Norway, 1981-1982. *Member:* Colorado and American Bar Associations. ***PRACTICE AREAS:*** Federal Tax; Tax Exempt Organizations; Litigation. ***Email:*** nkuhn@pgfm.com

SUSAN LEAHY, born Buffalo, New York, June 17, 1964; admitted to bar, 1998, Virginia; 1999, District of Columbia; U.S. Tax Court, U.S. Court of Appeals for the Fifth and District of Columbia Circuits. *Education:* St. Bonaventure University (B.B.A., 1986); Catholic University of America (J.D., 1998). *Member:* Virginia State Bar; The District of Columbia Bar; American Bar Association. ***PRACTICE AREAS:*** Charitable Giving; Tax Exempt Organizations; Private Foundations; Public Charities. ***Email:*** sleahy@pgfm.com

WILLIAM J. LEHRFELD, born Brooklyn, New York, June 14, 1936; admitted to bar, 1966, District of Columbia; U.S. Supreme Court, U.S. Court of Federal Claims and U.S. Tax Court; U.S. Court of Appeals, First, Fourth, Fifth, Sixth, Seventh, Ninth, Tenth, Eleventh, Federal and District of Columbia Circuits. *Education:* Lehigh University (B.S.B.A., 1958); Catholic University of America (J.D., 1965). Tax Law Specialist, Exempt Organizations and Pension Trust Division, Internal Revenue Service, 1960-1966. *Member:* The District of Columbia Bar; American Bar Association (Chairman, Exempt Organizations Committee, Section of Taxation, 1971-1973; Vice Chairman, Committee on Charitable Deductions, Section of Real Property, Probate and Trust Law, 1987-1991). ***PRACTICE AREAS:*** Charitable Giving; Private Foundations; Public Charities; Tax Exempt Organizations Litigation. ***Email:*** wlehrfeld@pgfm.com

(This Listing Continued)

AMELIA PORGES, admitted to bar, 1980, District of Columbia. *Education:* Cornell University (A.B., 1973); Harvard University (M.P.P., 1980; J.D., 1980). ***PRACTICE AREAS:*** World Trade Organization; International Trade; International Investment; International Arbitration. ***Email:*** aporges@pgfm.com

G. LEE SKILLINGTON, born Clearfield, Pennsylvania, April 1, 1950; admitted to bar, 1981, District of Columbia. *Education:* Pennsylvania State University (B.S., 1972); George Washington University (J.D., 1981). ***PRACTICE AREAS:*** Intellectual Property. ***Email:*** lskillin@pgfm.com

DAVID W. WOODWARD, born Buffalo, New York, February 5, 1964; admitted to bar, 1992, Virginia; 1994, District of Columbia; U.S. Court of Appeals, Fourth and Federal Circuits; registered to practice before U.S. Patent and Trademark Office. *Education:* Virginia Polytechnic Institute and State University (B.S., Chemical Engineering and Chemistry, 1986); George Washington University (J.D., with highest honors, 1992). Examiner, U.S. Patent and Trademark Office. *Member:* American Bar Association (Member, Intellectual Property Section); American Intellectual Property Lawyers Association; Patent and Trademark Office Society; American Chemical Society. ***PRACTICE AREAS:*** Patents; Intellectual Property. ***Email:*** Dwoodward@pgfm.com

COUNSEL

SUSAN A. COBB, born Boston, Massachusetts, October 12, 1947; admitted to bar, 1979, District of Columbia. *Education:* Goucher College; University of New Hampshire (B.A., magna cum laude, 1969); Harvard University (M.A.T., 1972); University of Dayton (J.D., magna cum laude, 1979). Phi Beta Kappa. *Member:* District of Columbia Bar; American Bar Association. ***PRACTICE AREAS:*** Tax Exempt Organizations. ***Email:*** scobb@pgfm.com

CHARLOTTE COLLINS, admitted to bar, 1977, Maryland; 1981, Tennessee (Not admitted in District of Columbia). *Education:* Morgan State University (B.A., 1973); Georgetown University (J.D., 1976). *Member:* National Bar Association; American Health Lawyers Association. ***PRACTICE AREAS:*** Health Care. ***Email:*** ccollins@pgfm.com

BARBARA D.A. EYMAN, born Stamford, Connecticut, April 4, 1960; admitted to bar, 1990, Massachusetts; 1993, District of Columbia. *Education:* Middlebury College (B.A., summa cum laude, 1982); Harvard Law School (J.D., magna cum laude, 1990). Phi Beta Kappa. Member, Harvard Law Review, 1988-1990. ***PRACTICE AREAS:*** Health Law. ***Email:*** beyman@pgfm.com

ROBERT N. FALK, born Greensboro, North Carolina, May 4, 1963; admitted to bar, 1990, Pennsylvania; 1991, District of Columbia. *Education:* Princeton University (A.B., summa cum laude, 1985); Yale University (J.D., 1990). Fulbright Scholar. ***LANGUAGES:*** French, Spanish. ***PRACTICE AREAS:*** Health Care. ***Email:*** rfalk@pgfm.com

MICHAEL J. GRACE, born Joliet, Illinois, January 10, 1954; admitted to bar, 1981, California; 1982, U.S. Tax Court; 1983, Illinois; 1992, District of Columbia. *Education:* University of Illinois at Urbana-Champaign (B.S., highest honors, 1976), Beta Gamma Sigma, Bronze Tablet Scholar, Edmund J. James Scholar; University of Michigan Law School (J.D., 1981). Journal of Law Reform, Case Club Junior Clerk. American Jurisprudence Award (Debtors Reorganization). Certified Public Accountant, Illinois, 1976. Senior Attorney-Advisor, Office of Chief Counsel, Internal Revenue Service National Office, 1985-1990. Board of Advisors and Contributors, *Journal of Real Estate Taxation, Journal of Passthrough Entities. Member:* The District of Columbia Bar; State Bar of California; Illinois State and American (Vice Chair, Real Estate Committee, Section of Taxation) Bar Associations. ***PRACTICE AREAS:*** Taxation Law; Business Succession Planning. ***Email:*** mgrace@pgfm.com

MARY BAROODY LOWE, born 1962; admitted to bar, 1991, Virginia; 1993, District of Columbia. *Education:* University of Virginia (B.A., 1984); College of William & Mary, Marshall-Wythe School of Law (J.D., 1991). ***PRACTICE AREAS:*** Government Contracts Law. ***Email:*** mlowe@pgfm.com

RESIDENT ASSOCIATES

JILL M. ABRAMS, admitted to bar, 1999, Virginia; 2000, District of Columbia. *Education:* University of Pennsylvania (B.A., 1994); University of Michigan (J.D., 1999). ***PRACTICE AREAS:*** Health Law. ***Email:*** jabrams@pgfm.com

KEVIN I. BABITZ, (admission pending). *Education:* Swarthmore College (B.A., 1994); New York University (J.D., 2001). ***PRACTICE AREAS:*** Taxation. ***Email:*** kbabitz@pgfm.com

ANDRE BARLOW, admitted to bar, 1997, Virginia (Not admitted in District of Columbia). *Education:* West Virginia University (B.A., 1993); George Washington University (J.D., 1997). ***PRACTICE AREAS:*** Antitrust. ***Email:*** abarlow@pgfm.com

MARINN F. CARLSON, admitted to bar, 1998, New York; 1999, District of Columbia. *Education:* Dartmouth College (B.A., 1993); Yale Law School (J.D., 1997). ***PRACTICE AREAS:*** Antitrust; International Corporate Law; International Trade. ***Email:*** mcarlson@pgfm.com

(This Listing Continued)

JUNE CASALMIR, admitted to bar, 1999, Georgia (Not admitted in District of Columbia). *Education:* Duke University (B.A., 1995); Washington University (J.D., 1999). *Member:* State Bar of Georgia; American Bar Association. ***PRACTICE AREAS:*** Antitrust. ***Email:*** jcasalmir@pgfm.com

ROBERT G. COBERLY, admitted to bar, 1990, Pennsylvania; 1991, District of Columbia. *Education:* Pennsylvania State University (B.A., 1976; M.P.A., 1977); George Washington University (J.D., 1990). ***PRACTICE AREAS:*** Tax; Affordable Housing. ***Email:*** rcoberly@pgfm.com

LISA ANN CROSBY, admitted to bar, 1995, Florida; 1996, District of Columbia and U.S. Court of International Trade; 1997, U.S. District Court for the District of Puerto Rico. *Education:* Linfield College (B.A., magna cum laude, 1984); Purdue University (M.A., 1986); Georgetown University (J.D., magna cum laude, 1995). ***PRACTICE AREAS:*** Customs; International Trade. ***Email:*** lcrosby@pgfm.com

MARIA T. DIGIULIAN, admitted to bar, 1999, Virginia (Not admitted in District of Columbia). *Education:* Hamilton College (B.A., 1988); George Washington University Elliott School of International Affairs (M.A., 1993); George Mason University School of Law (J.D., 1999). ***PRACTICE AREAS:*** International Trade; Litigation; Health. ***Email:*** mdigivli@pgfm.com

CHRISTA L. DOMMERS, admitted to bar, 1997, Connecticut; 1998, New York (Not admitted in District of Columbia). *Education:* Albertus Magnus College (B.A., magna cum laude, 1990); Quinnipiac College (J.D., summa cum laude, 1997). ***PRACTICE AREAS:*** Real Estate; Environmental. ***Email:*** cdommers@pgfm.com

LORENZO F. EXPOSITO, admitted to bar, 1994, Maryland; 1996, District of Columbia. *Education:* University of Connecticut (B.A., 1988); Catholic University of America, Columbus School of Law (J.D., cum laude, 1994). ***PRACTICE AREAS:*** Public Contract Law; Construction Contracts; Litigation. ***Email:*** lexposit@pgfm.com

DAVID L. FITZGERALD, (admission pending). *Education:* University of California at Davis (B.S., Biochemistry, 1981); Northwestern University (M.S., Chemistry, 1982); George Washington University (J.D., with honors, 2000). ***PRACTICE AREAS:*** Patents; International Business Law; International Intellectual Property. ***Email:*** dfitzgerald@pgfm.com

LEIGH FRAISER, admitted to bar, 1996, Virginia; 1998, District of Columbia. *Education:* Georgetown University (B.S., 1992); Vanderbilt University (J.D., 1996). *Member:* Virginia State Bar (Member, International Law Section); The District of Columbia Bar (Member, International Law Section); Customs and International Trade Bar Association. ***PRACTICE AREAS:*** Customs Law; Export Regulation. ***Email:*** Lfraiser@pgfm.com

ROBERT L. GALBREATH, admitted to bar, 1991, Virginia and U.S. Court of Appeals, Fourth Circuit; 1998, District of Columbia. *Education:* Wesleyan University (B.A., 1987); Washington & Lee University (J.D., 1991). ***PRACTICE AREAS:*** Communications Law. ***Email:*** rgalbrea@pgfm.com

DIANE GREENLEE, admitted to bar, 1981, District of Columbia. *Education:* Brandeis University (B.A., 1978); Georgetown University (J.D., 1981). ***PRACTICE AREAS:*** Law Income Housing Tax Credit Transactions. ***Email:*** dgreenle@pgfm.com

JENNIFER L. HAWORTH, admitted to bar, 1998, California (Not admitted in District of Columbia). *Education:* Whitman College (B.A., 1988); Harvard University, Graduate School of Education (M.Ed., 1992); Tufts University, The Fletcher School of Law & Diplomacy (M.A.L.D., 1997); Hastings College of the Law, University of California (J.D., 1997). ***PRACTICE AREAS:*** International Law; International Trade; Customs Law. ***Email:*** jhaworth@pgfm.com

ROBIN HEIMANN-MCGHEE, admitted to bar, 1989, Virginia; 1990, District of Columbia. *Education:* University of Virginia (B.A., 1986); Marshall-Wythe School of Law, College of William & Mary (J.D., 1989). ***PRACTICE AREAS:*** Real Estate Law; Commercial Lending; Tax Credits. ***Email:*** rheimann@pgfm.com

KYRA FISCHBECK HOWELL, admitted to bar, 1997, New York (Not admitted in District of Columbia). *Education:* Manhattanville College (B.A., 1990); Fordham University (J.D., 1996). ***PRACTICE AREAS:*** Government Relations; Internet Law; Election Law. ***Email:*** kfischbe@pgfm.com

THOMAS E.M. HUTTON, admitted to bar, 2000, Maryland (Not admitted in District of Columbia). *Education:* Connecticut College (B.A., cum laude, 1989); University of Hawaii (Graduate Certificate in Public Administration, 1999); Georgetown University (J.D., magna cum laude, 2000). Member, Coalition for Nonprofit Housing and Economic Development. *Member:* Maryland State and American Bar Associations. ***PRACTICE AREAS:*** Tax Exempt Organizations. ***Email:*** Thutton@pgfm.com

ALEXANDER KOFF, admitted to bar, 1997, New York and District of Columbia. *Education:* University of Michigan (B.A., 1992; J.D., 1996); Cambridge University, Cambridge, England (M.Phil., 1993). ***PRACTICE AREAS:*** International. ***Email:*** akoff@pgfm.com

SHERYL KRONGOLD, admitted to bar, 1984, New York; 1989, District of Columbia. *Education:* Barnard College, Columbia University (B.A., cum laude,

(This Listing Continued)

POWELL, GOLDSTEIN, FRAZER & MURPHY LLP, Washington—Continued

1980); Yeshiva University (J.D., 1983). *Member:* The District of Columbia Bar; American Bar Association. ***PRACTICE AREAS:*** Litigation; Antitrust. ***Email:*** skrongol@pgfm.com

ANNE M. LEWIS, admitted to bar, 1995, Maryland; 1996, District of Columbia. *Education:* Mary Washington College (B.A., summa cum laude, 1987); University of Virginia (J.D., 1995). ***PRACTICE AREAS:*** Health Care Law; Food and Drug; Legislative Law; Advocacy; Pharmacy Law. ***Email:*** alewis@pgfm.com

CHARLES A. LUBAND, admitted to bar, 1997, Massachusetts and New York; 1998, District of Columbia. *Education:* Brown University (B.A., 1990); Harvard Law School (J.D., 1996). *Member:* American Health Lawyers Association. ***PRACTICE AREAS:*** Health Law. ***Email:*** cluband@pgfm.com

ROBERT L. MAGIELNICKI, JR., admitted to bar, 1997, New York (Not admitted in District of Columbia). *Education:* University of Virginia (B.A., 1992); Stetson College of Law (J.D., 1996). Articles & Symposia Editor, Stetson Law Review, 1995-1996. *Member:* New York State and American Bar Associations. ***Email:*** rmagieln@pgfm.com

SUSAN M. MATHEWS, admitted to bar, 1991, Pennsylvania; 1992, District of Columbia and U.S. Court of International Trade; 1993, U.S. Court of Appeals for the Federal Circuit. *Education:* Ohio State University (B.A., summa cum laude, 1988); Yale Law School (J.D., 1991). ***PRACTICE AREAS:*** Customs; International Trade Policy and Litigation; International Law; Legislative Advocacy. ***Email:*** smathews@pgfm.com

CAMELIA C. MAZARD, admitted to bar, 1999, District of Columbia. *Education:* University of Southern California (B.S., Business Administration, summa cum laude, 1994); University of California at Berkeley, Boalt Hall School of Law (J.D., 1998); Tufts University (M.A., Law and Diplomacy, 1999). Member, Golden Key. *Member:* Bar Association of the District of Columbia; American Bar Association. ***LANGUAGES:*** French and Spanish. ***PRACTICE AREAS:*** International Trade. ***Email:*** cmazard@pgfm.com

JOCELYN C. NIEVA, admitted to bar, 1997, Maryland (Not admitted in District of Columbia). *Education:* George Washington University (B.A., 1982); American University (J.D., summa cum laude, 1997). Phi Beta Kappa. ***LANGUAGES:*** Spanish. ***PRACTICE AREAS:*** Health Care. ***Email:*** jnieva@pgfm.com

PAUL D.A. PIQUADO, admitted to bar, 1999, Massachusetts (Not admitted in District of Columbia). *Education:* Williams College (B.A., 1993); Fletcher School of Law & Diplomacy (M.A.L.D., 1999); New York University (J.D., 1999). ***PRACTICE AREAS:*** International; Litigation. ***Email:*** ppiquado@pgfm.com

WILLIAM COMPTON POLING, JR, admitted to bar, 1995, Maryland; 1997, District of Columbia. *Education:* Clemson University (B.A., 1991); Case Western Reserve University (J.D., magna cum laude, 1995). Order of the Coif. Editor, Case Western Reserve Law Review, 1993-1995. *Member:* Montgomery County and Maryland State Bar Associations. ***PRACTICE AREAS:*** Litigation; Corporate Transactions. ***Email:*** wpoling@pgfm.com

DAVID C. QUAM, admitted to bar, 1993, Maryland; 1995, District of Columbia. *Education:* Duke University (B.A., 1990); Vanderbilt University (J.D., 1993). ***PRACTICE AREAS:*** Government Relations; Intellectual Property; International Business. ***Email:*** dquam@pgfm.com

KELLY J. ROCK, (admission pending). *Education:* St. John's University (B.A., 1994); Columbia University (M.A., 1995); University of Texas (J.D., 2000). ***PRACTICE AREAS:*** Litigation. ***Email:*** krock@pgfm.com

J. CHRISTOPHER RODGERS, admitted to bar, 1994, Maryland; 1995, U.S. District Court, District of Maryland; 1998, Virginia (Not admitted in District of Columbia). *Education:* University of Maryland (B.S., 1989); George Washington University Law School (J.D., with honors, 1994). ***PRACTICE AREAS:*** Corporate Finance; Real Estate. ***Email:*** crodgers@pgfm.com

DONNA MARIE RODNEY, admitted to bar, 1992, Maryland; 2000, District of Columbia. *Education:* Howard University (B.A., summa cum laude, 1989); Boalt Hall School of Law, University of California at Berkeley (J.D., 1992). Phi Beta Kappa; Golden Key Honor Society. *Member:* Maryland State, American and National Bar Associations. ***PRACTICE AREAS:*** Housing Law; Real Estate Law. ***Email:*** drodney@pgfm.com

STEPHEN R. SMITH, admitted to bar, 1994, Rhode Island; 1996, Massachusetts and District of Columbia. *Education:* Villanova University (B.A., 1991); George Washington University (J.D., cum laude, 1994). ***PRACTICE AREAS:*** Litigation. ***Email:*** stsmith@pgfm.com

DAVID A. STEFFES, admitted to bar, 1998, Virginia and Wisconsin; registered to practice before U.S. Patent and Trademark Office (Not admitted in District of Columbia). *Education:* University of Wisconsin-La Crosse (B.S., with honors, Microbiology, 1994); University of Wisconsin-Madison (J.D., 1998). ***PRACTICE AREAS:*** Patents; Intellectual Property; Technology Transfers; Technology Licensing. ***Email:*** dsteffes@pgfm.com

BART T. VALAD, admitted to bar, 1998, Virginia; 1999, District of Columbia. *Education:* American University (B.S., 1983); George Mason University School of Law (J.D., 1998). ***PRACTICE AREAS:*** Antitrust; Litigation. ***Email:*** bvalad@pgfm.com

ADAM W. WALSH, admitted to bar, 1997, New Jersey; 1998, New York; 2000, District of Columbia. *Education:* University of Notre Dame (B.A., 1994); College of William and Mary (J.D., 1997). Phi Delta Phi. Member, Administrative Law Review. *Member:* New Jersey State, New York State and American Bar Associations. ***PRACTICE AREAS:*** Corporate; Real Estate; Banking. ***Email:*** awalsh@pgfm.com

CYNTHIA Y. WONG, admitted to bar, 1995, New York; 1998, Pennsylvania (Not admitted in District of Columbia). *Education:* New York University (B.A., with honors, 1991); Rutgers University School of Law (J.D., 1994). ***Email:*** cwong@pgfm.com

ANIE ELIZABETH WULKAN, admitted to bar, 1999, Maryland and U.S. Court of Appeals, Fifth Circuit; 2000, District of Columbia, U.S. District Court, District of Maryland and U.S. District Court, District of Columbia. *Education:* Georgetown University (B.A., 1996; J.D., 1999). *Member:* The District of Columbia Bar (Member, Criminal Law and Individual Rights Section); American Bar Association (Member: Practice Development Subcommittee, White Collar Crime Committee, Criminal Justice Section; Steering Committee); National Association of Criminal Defense Lawyers; Edward Bennett Williams Inn of Court. ***PRACTICE AREAS:*** White Collar Criminal Defense.

FOREIGN COUNSEL

STANIMIR A. ALEXANDROV, born Sofia, Bulgaria, April 14, 1955. *Education:* Moscow Institute for International Relations, International Law Department (J.D., 1981); George Washington University (LL.M., with highest honors, 1993; S.J.D., 1994). Senior Fellow, International Rule of Law Institute, George Washington University. Author: "Self Defense Against the Use of Force in International Law," Kluwer Law International, 1996; "Reservations in Unilateral Declarations Accepting the Compulsory Jurisdiction of the International Court of Justice," (The Hague, 1995); "Non-Appearance before the International Court of Justice," 33 Columbia Journal of Transnational Law 41 (1995); "Delimitation of the Continental Shelf in an Enclosed Sea," 1992 Hague Yearbook of International Law 3. Formerly Deputy Minister of Foreign Affairs of Bulgaria. Deputy Chief of Mission of Bulgaria in the United States. Director of the Bureau for European Integration in the Bulgarian Foreign Ministry and Deputy Legal Advisor of the Bulgarian Foreign Service. ***PRACTICE AREAS:*** International Business Transactions; Dispute Settlement. ***Email:*** salexand@pgfm.com

NICOLAS LLOREDA, (admission pending). *Education:* Colegio Mayor de Nuestra Senora del Rosario, Colombia (J.D., 1987); New York University (LL.M., 1988). ***LANGUAGES:*** Spanish. ***PRACTICE AREAS:*** International Trade; International Business Law; Investments; Arbitration. ***Email:*** Nlloreda@pgfm.com

LAURO LOCKS, admitted to bar, 1989, Brazil (Not admitted in the United States). *Education:* Federal University of Santa Catarina, Brazil (LL.B., 1989); Superior School of Magistrates, Brazil (Diploma, 1990); Tufts University (M.A.L.D., 1999); George Washington University (LL.M., Intellectual Property, 2001). *Member:* Brazilian Bar Association. ***PRACTICE AREAS:*** Intellectual Property; Trademarks; Copyrights; E-Commerce; International Business Law. ***Email:*** llocks@pgfm.com

MAURITS J.F. LUGARD. *Education:* Leiden University (J.D., 1988); Johns Hopkins University (M.A., 1991); University of Michigan (LL.M., 1997). ***PRACTICE AREAS:*** International Trade; World Trade Organization. ***Email:*** mlugard@pgfm.com

FOREIGN ASSOCIATE

PATRICIO GRANÉ LABAT, admitted to bar, 1996, Costa Rica (Not admitted in the United States). *Education:* Universidad de Costa Rica (Bachillerato en Derecho, 1994; Licenciado en Derecho, 1995); Georgetown University (LL.M., 2001). ***PRACTICE AREAS:*** GATT; World Trade Organization; International Trade. ***Email:*** pgrane@pgfm.com

PATENT AGENT

BERNARD RHEE, admitted to bar, registered to practice before U.S. Patent and Trademark Office. *Education:* University of Maryland (B.S., Pharmacy, 1991); University of Baltimore (J.D., 2000). Licensed Pharmacist. (Patent Agent and Analyst). ***PRACTICE AREAS:*** Intellectual Property. ***Email:*** brhee@pgfm.com

(For complete biographical data on other personnel, see Professional Biographies at Atlanta, Georgia, Reston, Virginia and Geneva, Switzerland)

(This Listing Continued)

POWER & POWER

4721 MACARTHUR BOULEVARD
WASHINGTON, D.C. 20007
Telephone: 202-659-9061
Email: tpower@erols.com

Arlington, Virginia Office: Courthouse Plaza, Suite 1107, 2300 Clarendon Boulevard. Telephone: 703-841-1330. Facsimile: 703-841-1822. E-Mail: power@erols.com.

Practice before Federal and State Courts, Agencies and Departments. Labor and Employment, Wage and Hour, Tax, Tax Litigation.

(For Complete biographical data on all personnel, see Professional Biographies at Arlington, Virginia).

POWERS, PYLES, SUTTER & VERVILLE, P.C.

Established in 1983

TWELFTH FLOOR
1875 EYE STREET, N.W.
WASHINGTON, D.C. 20006-5409
Telephone: 202-466-6550
Fax: 202-785-1756
Email: ppsv@ppsv.com
URL: http://www.ppsv.com

Health Care and Hospital Law, Education Law, Antitrust, Taxation and Corporate Law, Litigation, Legislative Law.

FIRM PROFILE: Powers Pyles Sutter & Verville, P.C., provides sophisticated and specialized legal services to a national base of clients in the health and education sectors of the American economy. The firm's health care clients include hospitals, multihospital systems, physician groups, home health agencies, long term care institutions, provider associations, and the newer, evolving forms of health care delivery. The firm's higher education clients include public and private, profit and non-profit, traditional and web-based institutions of higher education, as well as investors in and providers to education. The firm provides legislative services, federal and state regulatory advice, advocacy before federal and state regulatory agencies, transactional representation, including mergers and acquisitions of health care and educational institutions, defense of administrative, civil, criminal and Congressional investigations, and representation in administrative and judicial litigation.

GALEN D. POWERS, born Pleasant Lake, Indiana, September 16, 1936; admitted to bar, 1962, Michigan; 1981, District of Columbia; 1985, Pennsylvania. *Education:* University of Michigan (A.B., 1959; LL.B., 1962). Member and President, National Health Lawyers Association, 1990-1991. Assistant General Counsel for Health Care Financing, Health, Education and Welfare, 1977-1979. *Member:* State Bar of Michigan; The District of Columbia Bar; American Bar Association; American Academy of Hospital Attorneys. ***PRACTICE AREAS:*** Health Care Law; Hospital Law; Corporate Law; Joint Ventures Law. ***Email:*** galen.powers@ppsv.com

JAMES C. PYLES, born Winston-Salem, North Carolina, December 27, 1945; admitted to bar, 1972, Tennessee; 1975, Maryland; 1985, District of Columbia. *Education:* University of Virginia (B.A., 1968); University of Tennessee (LL.B., 1972). Litigation Attorney, Office of the General Counsel, Department of Health and Human Services, 1972-1979. *Member:* The District of Columbia Bar; Maryland State, Tennessee, Federal and American Bar Associations; American Health Lawyers Association; American Academy of Hospital Attorneys. ***PRACTICE AREAS:*** Health Care Law; Hospital Law; Litigation; Administrative Law. ***Email:*** jim.pyles@ppsv.com

RONALD N. SUTTER, born Carmel, California, January 1, 1947; admitted to bar, 1975, California; 1978, U.S. Supreme Court; 1981, District of Columbia. *Education:* University of Santa Clara (B.A., 1968); Boalt Hall School of Law, University of California (J.D., 1974); New York University (LL.M., in Taxation, 1980). *Member:* The District of Columbia Bar; State Bar of California. ***PRACTICE AREAS:*** Health Care Law; Hospital Law; Litigation; Administrative Law. ***Email:*** ron.sutter@ppsv.com

RICHARD E. VERVILLE, born Haverhill, Massachusetts, March 21, 1939; admitted to bar, 1965, Massachusetts; 1973, District of Columbia and U.S. District Court of Massachusetts. *Education:* Williams College (B.A., 1961); Columbia University (LL.B., 1964). Special Assistant to Secretary of Health, Education and Welfare, 1970. Deputy Assistant Secretary for Legislation, Department of Health, Education and Welfare, 1971-1973. *Member:* The District of Columbia Bar; Boston and American (Chairperson, Committee on Health and Human Services, 1978-1980) Bar Associations. ***PRACTICE AREAS:*** Health Care Law; Legislative Law. ***Email:*** dick.verville@ppsv.com

MARY SUSAN PHILP, born Mt. Vernon, Illinois, December 12, 1954; admitted to bar, 1979, District of Columbia; 1984, California; 1988, U.S. Supreme Court. *Education:* MacMurray College (B.S., summa cum laude, 1976); Duke University (J.D., 1979). Member, Editorial Board, Duke Law Journal, 1978-1979. Co-Author: "Hospitals Caught in the Antitrust Net: An Overview," 24 Duquesne Law Review 489, 1985. *Member:* The District of Columbia Bar; State Bar of California; American Bar Association; American Health Lawyers Association. ***PRACTICE AREAS:*** Health Care Law; Hospital Law; Antitrust Law; Medical-Legal Law. ***Email:*** susan.philp@ppsv.com

ROBERT J. SANER, II, born Springfield, Illinois, May 3, 1947; admitted to bar, 1973, District of Columbia; 1979, U.S. District Court, District of Columbia and U.S. Court of Appeals, D.C. Circuit. *Education:* Princeton University (A.B., cum laude, 1969); Harvard University (J.D., 1972). Assistant to the Administrator; Social and Rehabilitation Service Department of Health, Education and Welfare, 1972-1973; Office of Health, Cost of Living Council, 1973-1974. Member, Education Appeal Board, U.S. Department of Education, 1976-1984. *Member:* The District of Columbia Bar. ***PRACTICE AREAS:*** Health Care Law; Environmental Law. ***Email:*** robert.saner@ppsv.com

STANLEY A. FREEMAN, born Knoxville, Tennessee, October 15, 1956; admitted to bar, 1982, District of Columbia; 1983, Maryland and U.S. District Court for the District of Columbia; 1984, U.S. Court of Appeals for the District of Columbia Circuit; 1985, Virginia. *Education:* University of Michigan (B.A., with distinction, 1978); Georgetown University (J.D., 1982). *Member:* The District of Columbia Bar; Maryland State and American (Member, Administrative Law Section) Bar Associations; Virginia State Bar. ***PRACTICE AREAS:*** Education Law; Litigation; Administrative Law. ***Email:*** stan.freeman@ppsv.com

PETER W. THOMAS, born Northport, New York, January 12, 1964; admitted to bar, 1990, New York; 1992, U.S. District Court, District of Columbia. *Education:* Boston College (B.A., 1986); Georgetown University Law Center (J.D., 1989). Author: "Complying with the Americans with Disabilities Act: A Guidebook for Management and People with Disabilities," Greenwood Publishing Group, Westport, Connecticut, 1992. Member, President's Advisory Commission on Consumer Protection and Quality in the Health Care Industry. Chair, Subcommittee on Consumer Rights, Protections and Responsibilities. Member, National Advisory Council of the Agency for Healthcare Research and Quality, formerly the Agency for Health Care Policy, Research and Evaluation of the U.S. Department of Health and Human Services. Advisory Board Member, National Center for Medical Rehabilitation Research, National Institutes of Health. ***PRACTICE AREAS:*** Health Care Law and Legislation; Disability and Rehabilitation; Americans with Disabilities Act. ***Email:*** peter.thomas@ppsv.com

THOMAS HYLDEN, born St. Cloud, Minnesota, June 27, 1946; admitted to bar, 1976, District of Columbia; 1977, U.S. Court of Appeals for the District of Columbia Circuit; 1980, U.S. Supreme Court; 1981, U.S. Court of Appeals, Fourth Circuit; 1986, U.S. Court of Appeals, Eleventh Circuit. *Education:* Rice University (B.A., 1969; M.E.E., 1969); George Washington University (J.D., with honors, 1976). *Member:* The District of Columbia Bar; American Bar Association (Member, Sections of: Administrative Law; Litigation; Criminal Law). ***PRACTICE AREAS:*** Education Law; Mergers, Acquisitions and Divestitures; Administrative Law; Litigation. ***Email:*** thomas.hylden@ppsv.com

CHRISTOPHER L. KEOUGH, born Holyoke, Massachusetts, December 5, 1964; admitted to bar, 1991, Maryland; 1993, District of Columbia. *Education:* Franklin & Marshall College (B.A. in Economics, 1987); George Washington University (J.D., 1991). Notes Editor, The George Washington Law Review, George Washington University, 1991. Law Clerk to the Honorable Patrick J. Attridge, U.S. District Court, District of Columbia, 1991-1992. *Member:* The District of Columbia Bar; Maryland State and American Bar Associations; American Health Lawyers Association; Healthcare Financial Management Association. ***PRACTICE AREAS:*** Health Care Law; Reimbursement; Litigation; Administrative Law. ***Email:*** chris.keough@ppsv.com

HAROLD DAMELIN, born Malden, Massachusetts, September 15, 1946; admitted to bar, 1972, Massachusetts; 1975, District of Columbia. *Education:* Boston College (B.A., magna cum laude, 1969; J.D., cum laude, 1972). Tax Attorney, Office of the Chief Counsel, Legislation and Regulations Section, Internal Revenue Service, 1972-73. Trial Attorney, Public Integrity Section, Criminal Division, U.S. Department of Justice, 1973-78. Assistant U.S. Attorney, Office of U.S. Attorney for the District of Columbia, 1978-81. Branch Chief, Government Fraud Branch, Fraud Section, Criminal Division, U.S. Department of Justice, 1981-82. Assistant U.S. Attorney Deputy Chief, Superior Court Grand Jury Section, Office of the U.S. Attorney for the District of Columbia, 1982-86. Staff Director and Chief Counsel, United States Senate Permanent Subcommittee on Investigations, 1995-1996. Senior Counsel, United States Senate, Special Investigation, Committee on Governmental Affairs, 1996-1997. ***PRACTICE AREAS:*** Criminal Law; Health Care Fraud; Grand Jury Practice; Administrative Law. ***Email:*** harry.damelin@ppsv.com

JOEL M. HAMME, born York, Pennsylvania, January 15, 1949; admitted to bar, 1973, Pennsylvania; 1975, District of Columbia. *Education:* Dickinson College (B.A., magna cum laude, 1970); University of Pennsylvania (J.D., 1973). Phi Beta Kappa. Law Clerk to Hon. Alexander F. Barbieri, Common Pleas Court of Philadelphia County, 1973-1974. Law Clerk to Hon. John Biggs,

(This Listing Continued)

POWERS, PYLES, SUTTER & VERVILLE, P.C., Washington—Continued

Jr., Senior Judge, U.S. Court of Appeals, Third Circuit, 1974-1975. Associate Professorial Lecturer in Law, Health Care Delivery Systems, The National Law Center, George Washington University, 1985-1990. ***PRACTICE AREAS:*** Health Care Law; Litigation. ***Email:*** joel.hamme@ppsv.com

JOEL M. RUDNICK, born Washington, District of Columbia, March 30, 1966; admitted to bar, 1991, Maryland; 1994, District of Columbia. *Education:* New York University (B.A., 1988); Georgetown University (J.D., 1991). Member, D.C. Law Students in Court, 1990-1991. *Member:* The District of Columbia Bar; Maryland State Bar Association. ***PRACTICE AREAS:*** Education Law; Administrative Law; Litigation. ***Email:*** joel.rudnick@ppsv.com

DIANE S. MILLMAN, born March 27, 1955; admitted to bar, 1981, District of Columbia; 1982, Massachusetts. *Education:* Franklin & Marshall College (B.A., magna cum laude, 1977); Harvard Law School (J.D., cum laude, 1980). Phi Beta Kappa. *Member:* Massachusetts Bar Association; District of Columbia Bar; National Health Lawyers Association. ***PRACTICE AREAS:*** Health Law. ***Email:*** diane.millman@ppsv.com

---

MARLA P. SPINDEL, born Washington, D.C., November 27, 1968; admitted to bar, 1993, Virginia; 1994, District of Columbia. *Education:* Cornell University (B.A., 1990); George Washington University (J.D., with honors, 1993). *Member:* The District of Columbia Bar (Member, Health Law Section); American Bar Association; Virginia State Bar; American Health Lawyers Association. ***PRACTICE AREAS:*** Health Care Law; Fraud; Managed Care; Administrative Law; Corporate Law. ***Email:*** marla.spindel@ppsv.com

C. ANTHONY RUSSO, born New York, N.Y.; admitted to bar, 1999, Florida; 2000, District of Columbia. *Education:* University of Florida (B.A., with honors, 1996); George Washington University (J.D., 1999). Member, The Environmental Lawyer, American Health Lawyers Association, 1997-1999. ***LANGUAGES:*** Spanish. ***PRACTICE AREAS:*** Health Care Law; Administrative Law; Corporate Law; Litigation. ***Email:*** anthony.russo@ppsv.com

ADAM H. GREENE, born January 28, 1976; admitted to bar, 2000, Maryland (Not admitted in District of Columbia). *Education:* Johns Hopkins University (B.A., 1997); George Washington University Law School (J.D., M.P.H., 2000). ***PRACTICE AREAS:*** Medicare and Medicaid; Health Care; Administrative Law. ***Email:*** adam.greene@ppsv.com

AMY E. NORDENG, born Grand Forks, North Dakota, October 23, 1970; admitted to bar, 2001, District of Columbia. *Education:* Oberlin College (B.A., 1993); University of Michigan (J.D., 2000). *Member:* American Bar Association (Member, Health Law Section); American Health Lawyers Association. ***PRACTICE AREAS:*** Health Care; Privacy Law; Education Law; Administrative Law. ***Email:*** amy.nordeng@ppsv.com

JUSTIN R. HUNTER, born Sikeston, Missouri, October 1, 1968; admitted to bar, 2000, Tennessee (Not admitted in District of Columbia). *Education:* Mississippi State University (B.A., 1992); University of Memphis (J.D., 2000). ***Email:*** justin.hunter@ppsv.com

OF COUNSEL

REBECCA L. BURKE, born Princeton, New Jersey, December 1, 1953; admitted to bar, 1982, District of Columbia; 1983, U.S. District Court, District of Columbia. *Education:* Brown University (B.A., 1975); Georgetown University (J.D., cum laude, 1982). Member, American Criminal Law Review, 1980-1982. *Member:* The District of Columbia Bar. ***LANGUAGES:*** French, Italian. ***PRACTICE AREAS:*** Health Care Law. ***Email:*** rebecca.burke@ppsv.com

DONALD W. AARONSON, born Chicago, Illinois, June 21, 1933; admitted to bar, 1975, Illinois, U.S. District Court, Northern District of Illinois and U.S. Court of Appeals, Seventh Circuit; 1976, District of Columbia. *Education:* University of Illinois (B.A., with honors, 1957; B.S., 1959; M.D., 1961); DePaul University (J.D., cum laude, 1975). Phi Alpha Theta. Medical Doctor: Illinois, 1961; California, 1973. Liaison, Illinois State Medical Society, 1980-1981. President, ACAI, 1988-1989. *Member:* Chicago, Illinois State and American Bar Associations; The District of Columbia Bar; American Medical Association; American Association for Artificial Intelligence. [With U.S. Army. 1953-1955]. (Also Counsel to Epstein, Zaideman & Esrig, P.C., Chicago, Illinois and James P. Chapman & Associates, Ltd., Chicago, Illinois).

D. BENSON TESDAHL, born Fayetteville, North Carolina, June 30, 1952; admitted to bar, 1984, Oregon; 1985, Washington; 1986, U.S. Court of Appeals, Ninth Circuit; 1989, U.S. Supreme Court; 1990, District of Columbia. *Education:* U.S. Military Academy (B.S., 1977); University of Southern California (M.S., 1981); University of Oregon (J.D., 1984); Georgetown University (LL.M. in Taxation, with distinction, 1992). Order of the Coif. Associate Editor, Oregon Law Review, 1983-1984. Recipient: Oregon Law Review Award for Editorial Excellence, 1984; Oregon Law Review Award for Outstanding Achievement, 1984; American Jurisprudence Awards for Torts, Trusts and Estates, Conflict of Laws and Professional Responsibility. Co-Author: Intermediate Sanctions: Curbing Nonprofit Abuse (Wiley & Sons, 1997). Contributing Author: "Charity, Advocacy and the Law," (Wiley & Sons, 1992); "Washington Administrative Law Practice Manual," (Butterworths Legal Publishers, 1990). Author: "Are Emergency Room Physicians Always Employees?," Healthcare Financial Management (May, 1994); "Improved Fund-Raising Through Commercial Co-Ventures," 7 Exempt Org. Tax Review 619 (Apr. 1993); "IRS Guidance on Election Year Issues -- Too Little, Too Late," 6 Exempt Org. Tax Review 1119 (Nov. 1992); "The Disclosure of Nondeductibility -- Has Your Organization Complied?," 6 Exempt Org. Tax Review, 726 (Sept. 1992); "Taxation and Representation -- How to Use Political Organizations," 4 J. Tax'n of Exempt Organizations 29 (Spring 1992); "Intervention in Political Campaigns After the Pickle Hearings -- A Proposal of the 1990s," 4 Exempt Org. Tax Review 1165 (Nov. 1991). Adjunct Professor of Law, Georgetown University, 1995-2000. *Member:* The District of Columbia Bar; American Bar Association (Member, Committee on Exempt Organizations; Co-Chair, Exempt Organizations Subcommittee on Non-501(c)(3) Entities, 1995-1996); American Health Lawyers Association. [Lieutenant Colonel, Retired, JAGC, U.S. Army Reserve]. ***LANGUAGES:*** German. ***PRACTICE AREAS:*** Tax Exempt Organizations; Health Care Law; Corporate Law. ***Email:*** ben.tesdahl@ppsv.com

(This Listing Continued)

EDITH S. MARSHALL, born Boston, Massachusetts, October 30, 1952; admitted to bar, 1977, Massachusetts; 1980, District of Columbia and U.S. District Court for the District of Columbia. *Education:* Harvard/Radcliffe College (A.B., magna cum laude, 1974); University of Michigan (J.D., with honors, 1977). Phi Delta Phi Legal Fraternity. Recipient, Gerda Richards Crosby Award, Harvard. Faculty Member, Continuing Legal Education Program, District of Columbia Bar, 1998—. Consultant and Faculty Member, Pro-Ethics, Inc., 1998—. Assistant U.S. Attorney, Washington, D.C., 1984-1998. Deputy Chief, Civil Division, USAO for Washington, D.C., 1994-1998. Senior Litigation Counsel, Special Litigation Section, Civil Rights Division, U.S. Department of Justice, 1983-1984. Attorney, Office of General Counsel, U.S. Department of Health and Human Services, 1977-1983. *Member:* The District of Columbia Bar. ***PRACTICE AREAS:*** Health Care Law; Litigation; Administrative Law; Information and Privacy; Health Insurance Portability and Accountability Act (HIPAA). ***Email:*** edith.marshall@ppsv.com

SHERRY MASTROSTEFANO GRAY, born Providence, Rhode Island; admitted to bar, 1990, Massachusetts; 1991, District of Columbia. *Education:* Boston University (B.A., cum laude, 1987); George Washington University (J.D., with honors, 1990). Member, George Washington University Law Review. Judicial Clerkship with Chief Judge James C. Turk of the Western District of Virginia, 1990-1991. *Member:* The District of Columbia Bar; American Bar Association. ***LANGUAGES:*** Spanish. ***PRACTICE AREAS:*** Education Law; Administrative Law. ***Email:*** sherry.gray@ppsv.com

---

ELINA HUM PRATT

1120 G STREET N.W., SUITE 200

WASHINGTON, D.C. 20005

Telephone: 202-347-3773; 877-460-6372

Fax: 202-347-3861

URL: www.prattlaw.com

Email: epratt@prattlaw.com

URL: http://www.lawyers.com/prattlaw

Taxation, Trusts and Estates, Wills, Probate, Income Tax, Estates, Gift Taxation, International Taxation, Corporate Taxation and Business Planning.

ELINA HUM PRATT, born Hong Kong, November 29, 1956; admitted to bar, 1983, New York; 1987, District of Columbia; 1988, U.S. Tax Court; 1989, U.S. Court of Federal Claims; 1997, Maryland. *Education:* Cornell University (A.B., 1979); Georgetown University (J.D., 1982); New York University (LL.M., Taxation, 1985). Law Clerk to Judge William M. Fay, U.S. Tax Court, 1985-1987. *Member:* The District of Columbia Bar (Member, Sections on: Taxation; Estates, Trusts and Probate Law); American Bar Association; District of Columbia Women's Bar Association; Asian Pacific American Bar Association of the Greater Washington, D.C. Area. ***LANGUAGES:*** Chinese (Cantonese). ***PRACTICE AREAS:*** Taxation Law; Trusts and Estates; Probate; Income Tax; Estate and Gift Taxation; Wills; International Taxation; Corporate Taxation; Business Planning.

Cantonese and Chinese

PRESTON GATES ELLIS & ROUVELAS MEEDS LLP

1735 NEW YORK AVENUE, N.W.
SUITE 500
WASHINGTON, D.C. 20006-5209
Telephone: 202-628-1700
Facsimile: 202-331-1024
Email: info@prestongates.com
URL: http://www.prestongates.com

Anchorage, Alaska Office: Preston Gates & Ellis LLP, 420 L Street, Suite 400, 99501-1937. Telephone: 907-276-1969. Facsimile: 907-276-1365.

Coeur d'Alene, Idaho Office: Preston Gates & Ellis LLP, 1200 Ironwood Drive, Suite 315, 83814. Telephone: 208-667-1839. Facsimile: 208-765-2494.

Irvine, California Office: Preston Gates & Ellis LLP, Four Park Plaza, Suite 1900, 92614-5925. Telephone: 949-253-0900. Facsimile: 949-253-0902.

Los Angeles, California Office: Preston Gates & Ellis LLP, 725 South Figueroa Street, Suite 2100, 90017. Telephone: 213-624-2395. Facsimile: 213-624-5924.

Palo Alto, California Office: Preston Gates & Ellis LLP, 100 Hamilton Avenue, Suite 100, 94301-1656. Telephone: 650-325-8088. Fax: 650-325-8388.

Portland, Oregon Office: Preston Gates & Ellis LLP, 222 S.W. Columbia Street, 1400 KOIN Tower, 97201-6632. Telephone: 503-228-3200. Facsimile: 503-248-9085.

San Francisco, California Office: Preston Gates & Ellis LLP, One Maritime Plaza, Suite 2400, 94111. Telephone: 415-788-8822. Facsimile: 415-788-8819.

Seattle, Washington Office: Preston Gates & Ellis LLP, 701 Fifth Avenue, Suite 5000, 98104-7078. Telephone: 206-623-7580. Facsimile: 206-623-7022.

Spokane, Washington Office: Preston Gates & Ellis LLP, 601 West Riverside Drive, Suite 1400, 99201-0636. Telephone: 509-624-2100. Facsimile: 509-456-0146.

Hong Kong Office: Preston Gates & Ellis LLP, 1001 Hutchison House, 10 Harcourt Road. Telephone: 852-2511-5100. Facsimile: 852-2511-9515.

Federal Legislative, Administrative and Litigation Practice. Transportation, Telecommunications, Fisheries, Reinsurance and Insurance, High Technology, Antitrust, International Trade, Tax Policy, Forest Products and Natural Resources, Government Contract Law and Federal Procurement Policy, Environmental, Energy and Native American Issues.

RESIDENT PARTNERS

JONATHAN BLANK, born Hartford, Connecticut, December 11, 1944; admitted to bar, 1971, Washington; 1975, District of Columbia and Maryland. *Education:* Hobart College (B.A., magna cum laude, 1966); Harvard University (J.D., cum laude, 1971). ***PRACTICE AREAS:*** Aviation; Maritime. ***Email:*** jblank@prestongates.com

PAMELA JEANNE GARVIE, born Victoria, British Columbia, November 8, 1948; admitted to bar, 1976, Oregon; 1978, District of Columbia. *Education:* University of Oregon (B.A., with honors, 1970); University of Washington (M.A.T., with honors, 1971); University of Oregon (J.D., 1976). Phi Delta Phi (Chapter President, 1975-1976). Member, Mortar Board. Chief Counsel of Subcommittees on Aviation, Surface Transportation and Business, Trade and Tourism of the U.S. Senate Commerce Committee, 1986-1987. Counsel for the U.S. Senate Commerce Committee, 1981-1986. Assistant Legislative Counsel for the Interstate Commerce Commission, 1978-1980. Counsel for U.S. Congressman Robert B. Duncan of Oregon, 1976-1978. Author: "Spill Response Planning--All Modes of Transportation Feel The Impact of The Oil Pollution Reform Act of 1990," Transportation Practitioners Journal, Spring, 1994; "Congressional Task Force Review $35 Billion in Transportation Excise Taxes," Intermodal Insights, February 1997; "Showdown Expected Over EPA's Proposed Clean Air Rules," Intermodal Insights, April 1997; "Intermodal Traffic Jams Our Economic Health," Legal Times, August 18, 1997. ***PRACTICE AREAS:*** Transportation Law; Governmental Relations Law; Administrative Law. ***Email:*** pamelag@prestongates.com

SUSAN B. GEIGER, born Fulton, New York, October 24, 1947; admitted to bar, 1983, District of Columbia. *Education:* University of Rochester (B.A., 1969); Syracuse University (M.S.L.S., 1970); George Washington University (M.A., 1974); Georgetown University (J.D., magna cum laude, 1983). Author: "Spill Response Planning--All Modes of Transportation Feel the Impact of The Oil Pollution Reform Act of 1990," Transportation Practitioners Journal, Spring, 1994; "Preparing the Worst: The Law Dealing With Prevention and Cleanup of Oil Spills Has Created Some Sticky Problems," Legal Times, December 7, 1992; "Criminal Law Goes to Sea," Seatrade Review Monthly, August, 1995. Speeches: "Financial Responsibility Requirements Under the Oil Pollution Act of 1990," National Propeller Club Annual Meeting, 1991; "Tank Vessel Response Plans: Implementation Questions," Oil Spill Prevention and Response Expo, 1992; "Federal Insurance Solvency Legislation," Independent Reinsurance Underwriters Association, 1993; "Federal Legislation Affecting

(This Listing Continued)

The Solid Waste Industry," Waste Expo, 1996; "Financing Issues Underlying the ISTEA Debate," Transportation Funding Seminar, 1997. *Member:* District of Columbia Bar; Federal Bar Association. ***Email:*** susang@prestongates.com

BRUCE J. HEIMAN, born Yonkers, New York, March 8, 1956; admitted to bar, 1980, District of Columbia. *Education:* Brandeis University (B.A., magna cum laude, 1976); Kennedy School of Government, Harvard University (M.P.P., 1980); Harvard University (J.D., 1980). Phi Beta Kappa. Legislative Director and Trade Counsel to Senator Daniel Patrick Moynihan, 1984-1987. Author: "Business Will Benefit From 1996 Telecommunications Law," Washington CEO Magazine, May, 1996; "Does Anyone Care About High-Tech?" Journal of Commerce, March 26, 1996; "Tracking The Clinton Approach To International Trade," Seattle Times, January 25, 1992; "The Conduct of International Economic Relations in the Bush Administration," Fletcher Forum of World Affairs, Vol. 13, No. 1, Winter, 1989. Member: Steering Committee, International Trade Subcommittee, ABA; Editorial Board, Journal of Maritime Law and Commerce. ***PRACTICE AREAS:*** Technology; Trade; Transportation; Federal Policy. ***Email:*** bruceh@prestongates.com

CHRISTOPHER S. HUTHER, born Falls Church, Virginia, September 29, 1966; admitted to bar, 1992, Virginia and U.S. Court of Appeals, Fourth Circuit; 1994, District of Columbia and U.S. District Court, Eastern District of Virginia; 1995, U.S. District Court for the District of Columbia; 1997, U.S. Court of Appeals, District of Columbia Circuit. *Education:* Radford University (B.S., cum laude, 1988); Georgetown University Law Center (J.D., 1992). Executive Director, Georgetown University Law Center Moot Court Program. First Place, 1991 National Corporate Law Moot Court Competition. *Member:* District of Columbia Bar; Virginia State Bar; American Bar Association. ***PRACTICE AREAS:*** Telecommunications; Litigation. ***Email:*** chuther@prestongates.com

GLENN F. IVEY, born Boston, Massachusetts, February 27, 1961; admitted to bar, 1987, Maryland; 1988, District of Columbia. *Education:* Princeton University (A.B., cum laude, 1983); Harvard Law School (J.D., 1986). Adjunct Professor, University of Maryland School of Law, 1995—. Chairman, Maryland Public Service Commission, 1998-2000. ***PRACTICE AREAS:*** Legislative; Utilities Regulation; Criminal Litigation; Telecommunications Law. ***Email:*** givey@prestongates.com

DONALD A. KAPLAN, born New Brunswick, New Jersey, October 18, 1945; admitted to bar, 1971, New York; 1972, U.S. Court of Appeals, Second Circuit and U.S. District Court, Southern and Eastern Districts of New York; 1977, U.S. Supreme Court; 1983, U.S. Court of Appeals, District of Columbia Circuit; 1990, District of Columbia and U.S. District Court, District of Maryland. *Education:* Rutgers College (A.B., summa cum laude, 1967); Harvard Law School (J.D., cum laude, 1970). Legislative Editor, Harvard Journal on Legislation, Harvard Law School, 1969-1970. Law Clerk to Hon. John F. Dooling, Jr., U.S. District Court, Eastern District of New York, 1970-1971. Trial Attorney: Foreign Commerce Section, Antitrust Division, U.S. Department of Justice, 1975-1977; Regulated Industries Section, Antitrust Division, U.S. Department of Justice, 1977. Assistant Chief, Energy Section, Antitrust Division, U.S. Department of Justice, 1977-1978. Chief, Energy Section, Antitrust Division, U.S. Department of Justice, 1978-1981. Special Litigation Counsel, Antitrust Division, U.S. Department of Justice, 1981-1990. *Member:* Federal Energy (Chair, Antitrust Committee, 1992-1993; 1994-1995) and American (Member: Sections of Antitrust Law; Public Utility Law; Administrative Law; Litigation; Natural Resources, Energy Environmental Law) Bar Associations. ***PRACTICE AREAS:*** Antitrust Law; Economic Regulation; Energy Law; Public Utility Law; Litigation. ***Email:*** donk@prestongates.com

JOHN L. LONGSTRETH, born Phoenix, Arizona, October 11, 1956; admitted to bar, 1982, District of Columbia; 1985, U.S. Court of Appeals for the Federal Circuit; 1986, U.S. District Court for the District of Columbia and U.S. Court of Appeals for the District of Columbia Circuit; 1988, U.S. Court of Appeals, Fourth Circuit; U.S. District Court, Eastern District of Michigan. *Education:* Haverford College (B.A., magna cum laude, 1978); Harvard University (M.P.P., 1982; J.D., cum laude, 1982). Phi Beta Kappa. Law Clerk to U.S. District Judge Raymond J. Broderick, 1982-1984. ***PRACTICE AREAS:*** Antitrust; Aviation; Litigation. ***Email:*** johnl@prestongates.com

ROLF MARSHALL, born Cadillac, Michigan, November 15, 1940; admitted to bar, 1991, Virginia; 1992, District of Columbia. *Education:* University of Michigan (B.A., with honors, 1963); Michigan State University (M.A., 1971); George Washington University (J.D., with honors, 1991). Phi Kappa Phi. Author: "The Maritime Reform Act of 1992?" Journal of Maritime Law and Commerce, Vol. 23, No. 4, Oct. 1992. [Cmdr., U.S. Navy, 1964-1991]. ***PRACTICE AREAS:*** Maritime Law; Government Procurement; Litigation. ***Email:*** rolfm@prestongates.com

EUGENE P. MILLER, born Winchester, Virginia, 1937; admitted to bar, 1962, District of Columbia. *Education:* University of Virginia (B.A., with honors, 1959); Harvard University (J.D., 1962). Phi Beta Kappa. Trial Attorney, Department of Justice, 1962. Counsel, Export-Import Bank of The United States, 1966-1973. *Member:* The District of Columbia Bar; Federal (Deputy Chair, Transportation Law Section) and American Bar Associations. [Capt., U.S. Air Force, 1963-1966]. ***PRACTICE AREAS:*** Maritime and Shipping Regulation Law; Corporate Finance Law. ***Email:*** eugenem@prestongates.com

(This Listing Continued)

PRESTON GATES ELLIS & ROUVELAS MEEDS LLP, Washington—Continued

WILLIAM N. MYHRE, born Spokane, Washington, November 25, 1949; admitted to bar, 1976, Washington; 1977, District of Columbia. *Education:* Stanford University (B.A., with distinction, 1972); University of Pennsylvania (M.C.P., 1976; J.D., 1976). Phi Beta Kappa. Co-author, "The Commercial Fishing Industry Vessel Act: Reducing Regulatory Obstacles to the Full Development of the American Fisheries," 17 Journal of Maritime Law and Commerce 327, July 1986. Author, "The Law of Unintended Consequences: Putting Theory into Practice," in *Conserving America's Fisheries*, National Coalition for Marine Conservation (1994). ***PRACTICE AREAS:*** Maritime. ***Email:*** billm@prestongates.com

MICHAEL J. O'NEIL, born Pensacola, Florida, November 11, 1946; admitted to bar, 1971, Ohio; 1972, District of Columbia. *Education:* College of the Holy Cross (A.B., 1968); Georgetown University (J.D., 1971; M.L., Taxation, 1976); London School of Economics and Political Science (M.Sc. in Economics, 1973). Chief Counsel, Permanent Select Committee on Intelligence, U.S. House of Representatives, 1977-1989. Counsel to the Speaker, U.S. House of Representatives, 1989-1994. Counselor to the Secretary and Deputy Secretary Department of Defense, 1995. Chief of Staff, Central Intelligence Agency, 1995-1996. General Counsel, Central Intelligence Agency, 1996-1997. *Member:* American Bar Association (Member, Standing Committee on Law and the National Security, 1997—). ***Email:*** mikeo@prestongates.com

TIM L. PECKINPAUGH, born Los Angeles, California, April 19, 1959; admitted to bar, 1986, District of Columbia. *Education:* Claremont McKenna College (B.A., magna cum laude, 1981); Georgetown University (J.D., cum laude, 1985). Research Associate, House Republican Study Committee, 1981-1982. Legislative Assistant to Congressman Sid Morrison, 1982-1984. Technical Consultant on House Science and Technology Committee, 1985. Author: "An Analysis of Regional Interstate Compacts For The Disposal of Low Level Radioactive Waste," Low-Level Radioactive Waste Regulation, (Book Chapter), 1987. ***PRACTICE AREAS:*** Energy Law; Nuclear Power; Environmental Law; Hazardous Waste Cleanup; Legislative Law; Government Ethics. ***Email:*** timp@prestongates.com

EMANUEL L. ROUVELAS, born Seattle, Washington, September 10, 1944; admitted to bar, 1973, District of Columbia. *Education:* University of Washington (B.A., with honors, 1965); Harvard University (J.D., cum laude, 1968); Harvard Business School (A.M.P., 1996). Chief Counsel: U.S. Senate Subcommittees on Merchant Marine and Foreign Commerce and Tourism, 1969-1973. Member, Transition Advisory Committees for Presidents Carter, 1976, Regan, 1980-1981 and Advisory Congressional Maritime Caucus, 1985-1987. Vice-Chairman, American College of Greece, 1993—. Member, Board of Directors, American Classic Voyages Co. ***PRACTICE AREAS:*** Governmental Relations Law; Maritime; Transportation. ***Email:*** mannyr@prestongates.com

MARK H. RUGE, born Kenosha, Wisconsin, January 7, 1958; admitted to bar, 1993, Virginia (Not admitted in District of Columbia). *Education:* Northern Michigan University (B.A., with highest honors, 1980); Georgetown University Law Center (J.D., 1992). Chief of Staff to Representative Bob Davis, 1988-1990, 1993. Deputy Staff Director to Merchant Marine and Fisheries Committee, 1990-1992. ***PRACTICE AREAS:*** Federal Practice; Policy; Maritime Law; Tax; Health Care. ***Email:*** markr@prestongates.com

MELANIE SABO, born January 24, 1959; admitted to bar, 1991, Florida; 1999, District of Columbia. *Education:* Boston University (B.S., cum laude, 1981); University of Michigan (J.D., cum laude, 1989). ***PRACTICE AREAS:*** Antitrust; Litigation. ***Email:*** melanies@prestongates.com

WILLIAM A. SHOOK, born Loma Linda, California, November 25, 1952; admitted to bar, 1986, Pennsylvania; 1992, District of Columbia. *Education:* Brigham Young University (B.A., magna cum laude, 1977); George Washington University (J.D., with honors, 1986). Articles and Speeches: "Commercial Products Contracting," The George Washington University, Educational Services Institute, 1988; "Contracting For Commercial Off The Shelf Products COTS," Technology Training Corp., 1991, 1992, 1993,1994; "Commercial Product Acquisition: Current Impediments and Recommendations For Improvement," Commercial Product Acquisition Team, 1987; "Congressional and Agency Perspectives On Recent Developments in Commercial Products Contracting," Section of Public Contract Law, American Bar Association, 1990; "The GSA Multiple Awards Schedule Program: Current Issues and Future Trends," March, 1994; "Commercial Item Acquisitions," Federal Publications, April, 1996. *Member:* American Bar Association (Member, Public Contracts Law Section). ***PRACTICE AREAS:*** Governmental Contract Law; Procurement Policy. ***Email:*** billsh@prestongates.com

MARTIN L. STERN, born Manhasset, New York, July 16, 1957; admitted to bar, 1984, New York; 1987, District of Columbia. *Education:* University of Rochester (B.A., cum laude, 1979; M.B.A., 1980); Georgetown University (J.D., cum laude, 1983). Senior Editor, Law and Policy in International Business, 1982-1983. Author: "Communications Satellites and the Geostationary Orbit: Reconciling Equitable Access with Efficient Use," 14:3 Law Pol'y Int'l Bus. (1982); Transactional Activity Under Telecom Act of 1996," National Law Journal, February 10, 1997; "Applying for ETC Status: Utilities Move into the Telecom Market," (UTC 1997). Trial Attorney, Communications and Finance Section, Antitrust Division, U.S. Department of Justice, 1984-1986. Deputy Chief, Competition Division, Federal Communications Commission, Office of General Counsel, 1994-1996. Vice Chair, Communications Industries Committee, ABA Antitrust Section, 1997—. ***PRACTICE AREAS:*** Telecommunications; Information Technology; Competition. ***Email:*** mstern@prestongates.com

LISA HELPERT TUCKER, born Princeton, New Jersey, July 14, 1963; admitted to bar, 1991, Washington (Not admitted in District of Columbia). *Education:* Duke University (A.B., cum laude, 1985); University of California, Hastings College of the Law (J.D., 1991). Member, University of California Hastings Moot Court Board, 1989-1991. ***PRACTICE AREAS:*** Litigation; Energy; Transportation. ***Email:*** lisat@prestongates.com

JAMES R. WEISS, born Munich, Germany, October 27, 1949; admitted to bar, 1974, Pennsylvania; 1985, Maryland and District of Columbia. *Education:* Northwestern University (B.A., 1971); Catholic University (J.D., 1974). Recipient, Justice Dept.: "Harold M. Stephens Award," 1988; Award of Distinction, 1984. Chief and Assistant Chief, Transportation, Energy and Agriculture Section, Antitrust Division, U.S. Department of Justice, 1980-1988. Trial Attorney, Antitrust Division, 1974-1980. *Member:* American Bar Association. ***Email:*** jimwe@prestongates.com

RESIDENT ASSOCIATES

JULIE J. CRAIN, born New York, New York, September 7, 1969; admitted to bar, 1994, New Jersey; 1995, New York and District of Columbia. *Education:* Tufts University (B.A., 1991); American University (J.D., cum laude, 1994). Note and Comment Editor, American University Journal of International Law and Policy, 1993-1994. Clerk, Senior Judges, District of Columbia Court of Appeals, 1994-1995. ***PRACTICE AREAS:*** Litigation; Telecommunications; Antitrust. ***Email:*** julilec@prestongates.com

KELLEY PATRICK DORAN, born Waterbury, Connecticut, August 1, 1967; admitted to bar, 1993, Virginia; 1996, District of Columbia. *Education:* Bates College (B.A., cum laude, 1989); Washington & Lee University (J.D., 1993). Phi Beta Kappa; National Moot Court Team. *Member:* Virginia and American Bar Associations; Virginia State Bar. ***PRACTICE AREAS:*** Government Contracts. ***Email:*** kelleyd@prestongates.com

LISA L. FRIEDLANDER, born Washington, D.C., April 23, 1969; admitted to bar, 1996, Maryland; 1997, District of Columbia. *Education:* University of Pennsylvania (B.A., 1991); The American University-Washington College of Law (J.D., summa cum laude, 1995). ***PRACTICE AREAS:*** Telecommunications Law; Litigation. ***Email:*** lisaf@prestongates.com

CARYN BLYTHE HOUCK, born Wiesbaden, Germany, April 9, 1971; admitted to bar, 1999, Virginia (Not admitted in District of Columbia). *Education:* Smith College (A.B., 1993); University of Virginia (J.D., 1999). Editor-in-Chief, Virginia Environmental Law Journal, 1998-1999. ***PRACTICE AREAS:*** Litigation; Maritime Law. ***Email:*** carynh@prestongates.com

KRISTIE JACKSON, born Garden City, Michigan, January 29, 1972; admitted to bar, 2000, Virginia (Not admitted in District of Columbia). *Education:* Stetson University (B.A., 1994); George Mason University School of Law (J.D., 2000). ***PRACTICE AREAS:*** Litigation. ***Email:*** kristiej@prestongates.com

MARYBETH BRENNAN MAGEE, born Rockville Centre, New York, January 18, 1974; admitted to bar, 2000, New York (Not admitted in District of Columbia). *Education:* Boston College (B.A., 1996); St. John's University (J.D., 1999). ***Email:*** marybethm@prestongates.com

BRIAN K. McCALMON, born Norman, Oklahoma, March 23, 1969; admitted to bar, 1996, Maryland; 1998, District of Columbia. *Education:* University of Oklahoma (B.A., 1992); Georgetown University (J.D., 1996; M.S.F.S., 1996). Author: Note, "States, Refugees, and Self-Defense," Georgetown Immigration Law Journal, Vol. 10, No. 2. ***LANGUAGES:*** French. ***PRACTICE AREAS:*** Antitrust; Litigation. ***Email:*** brianm@prestongates.com

HONG J. PARK, born Seoul, South Korea, January 11, 1973; admitted to bar, 2000, Maryland (Not admitted in District of Columbia). *Education:* Yale University (B.A., cum laude, 1995); Columbia University (J.D., 2000). ***PRACTICE AREAS:*** Antitrust; Litigation. ***Email:*** hongp@prestongates.com

DANIEL RITTER, born New York, New York, November 24, 1966; admitted to bar, 1992, New York (Not admitted in District of Columbia). *Education:* Amherst College (B.A., 1988); Yale University (J.D., 1991). Phi Beta Kappa. Editor, Yale Law and Policy Review. Counsel, U.S. Senate Subcommittee on Education, Arts and Humanities, 1993-1995. ***PRACTICE AREAS:*** Policy; Government Relations. ***Email:*** danielr@prestongates.com

JORGE ROMERO, born La Habana, Cuba, 1954; admitted to bar, 1984, New York; 1993, District of Columbia. *Education:* Columbia University (B.A., cum laude, 1976; J.D., 1983). *Member:* District of Columbia Bar. ***LAN-***

(This Listing Continued)

GUAGES: Spanish. ***PRACTICE AREAS:*** Corporate; Finance; International Project Finance; International Investments; Maritime and Shipping Regulation Law. ***Email:*** jorger@prestongates.com

DANIEL A. SILIEN, born Silver Spring, Maryland, December 11, 1970; admitted to bar, 1997, New York; 1998, District of Columbia. *Education:* American University (B.A., magna cum laude, 1992); New York University (J.D., cum laude, 1996). Editor, Harvard Journal of Law and Public Policy. Law Clerk to the Hon. Moody R. Tidwell, U.S. Court of Federal Claims, 1996-1997. ***PRACTICE AREAS:*** Litigation; Technology and Science; Antitrust. ***Email:*** dans@prestongates.com

W. DAVID THOMAS, born Westminster, Maryland, April 26, 1972; admitted to bar, 1998, Maryland; 1999, District of Columbia. *Education:* Dickinson College (B.A., English, magna cum laude, 1994); University of Maryland (J.D., 1998). Phi Beta Kappa; Omicron Delta Kappa. Senior Articles Editor, Maryland Journal of International Law & Trade, 1997-1998. ***PRACTICE AREAS:*** Legislative; Regulatory; Environmental; Transportation. ***Email:*** davidth@prestongates.com

MEGAN H. TROY, born San Francisco, California, March 31, 1971; admitted to bar, 1997, California (Not admitted in District of Columbia). *Education:* University of California (B.A., 1993); Georgetown University (J.D., 1997). ***PRACTICE AREAS:*** Telecommunications Law; Federal Policy. ***Email:*** megant@prestongates.com

OF COUNSEL

JOHN A. BASTEK, admitted to bar, 1974, Florida; 1977, New Jersey (Not admitted in District of Columbia). *Education:* United States Coast Guard Academy (B.S.); University of Miami (J.D.). ***PRACTICE AREAS:*** Military Law. ***Email:*** johnb@prestongates.com

ARTHUR DIMOPOULOS, born Thessalonica, Greece, August 6, 1958; admitted to bar, 1991, California; 1992, U.S. District Court, Central District of California; 1993, Maryland, U.S. District Court, District of Maryland, and U.S. Court of Appeals, Fourth Circuit; 1999, District of Columbia. *Education:* Catholic University of America (B.F.A., 1980); Southwestern University School of Law (J.D., 1990); Georgetown University Law Center (LL.M., in International Law, with distinction, 1993). Phi Alpha Delta (Marshal, 1988-1991). Recipient: American Jurisprudence Awards, Intellectual Property; Best Achievement, Constitutional Law Seminar. Adjunct Professor of Law, "U.S. Legal Research, Waiting & Analysis for Foreign Lawyers," Georgetown University Law Center, 1993-1997. Chairman, Water Transportation Committee, Federal Bar Association, 1996—. Member, American Hellenic Education Progressive Association (Chapter Vice President). ***LANGUAGES:*** Greek. ***PRACTICE AREAS:*** Transportation; Maritime Law. ***Email:*** artd@prestongates.com

ELIZABETH WALLACE FLEMING, admitted to bar, 1981, Georgia; 1992, Michigan; 1999, District of Columbia. *Education:* University of Georgia (B.A., magna cum laude, 1978; J.D., 1981); Judge Advocate General's School (LL.M., 1988). Former: Assistant U.S. Attorney, Eastern District of Michigan, 1990-1996; Trial Attorney, U.S. Air Force, 1997-1980; Trial Attorney, Department of Justice, 1998-1999. *Member:* American Bar Association (Member: Public Contract Law Section, Legislative Coordinating Committee; Criminal Justice Section, White Collar Committee); American Health Lawyers Association; Women in Defense. ***PRACTICE AREAS:*** Litigation; Health Care Fraud; Government Contracts. ***Email:*** elizabeth@prestongates.com

HARRISON D. HUTSON, born Walthall County, Mississippi, 1926; admitted to bar, 1951, District of Columbia. *Education:* Southeastern Louisiana College (A.B., 1948); The George Washington University (J.D., 1951); London School of Economics, University of London, England. Member, Board of Editors, George Washington Law Review, 1950-1951. Clerk to Chief Judge, U.S. Claims Court, 1952-1954. Counsel: Export-Import Bank of the United States, 1954-1956; International Finance Corporation, 1966-1969. *Member:* The District of Columbia Bar; Federal, American and International Bar Associations. ***PRACTICE AREAS:*** Maritime and Shipping Regulation Law; Environmental Law; Corporate Finance Law. ***Email:*** harrisonh@prestongates.com

G. MATTHEW KOEHL, born Nampa, Idaho, October 24, 1967; admitted to bar, 1993, Maryland (Not admitted in District of Columbia). *Education:* Colgate University (B.A., with honors in History, 1989); Washington & Lee University (J.D., cum laude, 1993). ***PRACTICE AREAS:*** Government Contracts; Litigation. ***Email:*** mkoehl@micronpc.com

LLOYD MEEDS, born Dillon, Montana, December 11, 1927; admitted to bar, 1958, Washington; 1965, U.S. Supreme Court; 1978, District of Columbia. *Education:* Everett Junior College; Gonzaga University (LL.B., 1958). Deputy Prosecuting Attorney, Spokane and Snohomish Counties, 1958-1960. Snohomish Prosecuting Attorney, 1962-1964. Member, U.S. Congress, 1965-1979. ***PRACTICE AREAS:*** Legislative Advocacy; Procedures of the House of Representatives. ***Email:*** lloydm@prestongates.com

SANDRA E. RIZZO, born Philadelphia, Pennsylvania, September 15, 1968; admitted to bar, 1992, Illinois, New Jersey and U.S. District Court, District of New Jersey; 1993, District of Columbia; 1996, U.S. District Court

(This Listing Continued)

for the District of Columbia, U.S. Court of Appeals for the District of Columbia Circuit and U.S. Supreme Court. *Education:* George Washington University (B.A., 1989); College of William & Mary, Marshall-Wythe School of Law (J.D., 1992). Phi Alpha Delta (District Justice, 1998-1999; Alumni Chapter Justice, 1996-1998). *Member:* The District of Columbia Bar; Federal Energy and American Bar Associations. ***PRACTICE AREAS:*** Energy; Administrative Litigation. ***Email:*** sandrar@prestongates.com

STEVEN RICHARDS VALENTINE, born Memphis, Tennessee, January 30, 1956; admitted to bar, 1983, Illinois; 1985, District of Columbia; 1986, U.S. Supreme Court. *Education:* Indiana University (B.G.S., with distinction, 1979; J.D., 1982). Co-Author: with Michael I. Spak, "Objectors Without Recourse: The Rights of Conscience and Military Draft Registration," 13 Seton Hall Law Review 667, 1983. Counsel, 1983 and Chief Counsel and Staff Director, 1983-1985, Subcommittee on the Separation of Powers, Committee on the Judiciary, United States Senate, Washington, D.C.; Chief Counsel and Staff Director, Subcommittee on the Courts, Committee on the Judiciary, United States Senate, Washington, D.C., 1985; Administrative Assistant to Senator John P. East of North Carolina, United States Senate, Washington, D.C., 1985-1986; Director, Office of Policy Development and Communications, Legal Services Corporation, Washington, D.C., 1986-1987; Senior Special Assistant to the Assistant Attorney General, Civil Division, United States Department of Justice, Washington, D.C., 1987; Counselor to the Assistant Attorney General, Civil Division, United States Department of Justice, Washington, D.C., 1987-1988; Deputy Assistant Attorney General, Civil Division, United States Department of Justice, Washington, D.C., 1988-1993; General Counsel, 1993-1999, and Legislative Director, 1996-1999, to Senator Robert C. Smith of New Hampshire, United States Senate, Washington, D.C. ***REPORTED CASES:*** Rafeedie v. Immigration and Naturalization Service, 880 F.2d 506 (D.C. Cir. 1989); Purba v. Immigration and Naturalization Service, 884 F.2d 516 (9th Cir. 1989); American Friends Service Committee v. Thornburgh, 941 F.2d 808 (9th Cir. 1991); American-Arab Anti-Discrimination Committee v. Thornburgh, 970 F.2d 501 (9th Cir. 1991); Xiao v. Barr, 979 F.2d 152 (9th Cir. 1992). ***PRACTICE AREAS:*** Federal Legislative Practice; Federal Regulatory Law. ***Email:*** stevenv@prestongates.com

STAFF ATTORNEY

DAVID M. GILMORE, born Royal Oak, Michigan, May 13, 1969; admitted to bar, 1997, Michigan; 1999, District of Columbia. *Education:* California State University, San Bernardino (B.A., 1992); Michigan State University (J.D., 1997); Georgetown University (LL.M.). ***PRACTICE AREAS:*** Maritime Regulation; Shipping Regulation; Corporate Finance. ***Email:*** davidg@prestongates.com

KENNETH S. KNOX, born San Angelo, Texas, January 17, 1962; admitted to bar, 1996, Maryland; 1999, District of Columbia. *Education:* University of Alaska (B.A., 1991); Howard University (J.D., cum laude, 1995). ***PRACTICE AREAS:*** Litigation. ***Email:*** kennethk@prestongates.com

REPRESENTATIVE CLIENTS: Brown-Forman Corp.; Burlington Northern Santa Fe Corp.; Delta Air Lines, Inc.; Delta Queen Steamboat Co.; Domino Sugar; Microsoft Corp.; PepsiCo Foods and Beverages International; PP&L Resources, Inc.; Schlumberger Wireline and Testing; Simpson Investment Co.; Business Software Alliance; Dredging Contractors of America; Hazardous Waste Action Coalition; Ocean Common Carrier Coalition; Greater Orlando Aviation Authority; Massachusetts Port Authority; Snohomish County P.U.D.; Verizon; MPA; PPL; Sierra Wireless Inc.; RCN; Western Wireless/Voicestream.

(For complete Biographical data on all Personnel, see Professional Biographies at Seattle and Spokane, Washington; Anchorage, Alaska; Portland, Oregon; Coeur d'Alene, Idaho; Los Angeles, Irvine, Palo Alto and San Francisco, California and Hong Kong)

PROSKAUER ROSE LLP

Established in 1875

1233 TWENTIETH STREET, N.W.
SUITE 800
WASHINGTON, D.C. 20036-2396
Telephone: 202-416-6800
FAX: 202-416-6899
URL: http://www.proskauer.com

New York, New York Office: 1585 Broadway. Telephone: 212-969-3000. Fax: 212-969-2900.

Los Angeles, California Office: 2049 Century Park East, Suite 3200. Telephone: 310-557-2900. Fax: 310-557-2193.

Boca Raton, Florida Office: One Boca Place, Suite 340 West, 2255 Glades Road. Telephone: 407-241-7400. Fax: 561-241-7145.

Newark, New Jersey Office: One Newark Center. Telephone: 973-274-3200. Fax: 973-274-3299.

Paris, France Office: Proskauer Rose, 68, rue du Faubourg Saint-Honoré. Telephone: +33-1-53-05-60-00. Fax: +33-1-53-05-60-05.

General Practice.

(This Listing Continued)

PROSKAUER ROSE LLP, Washington—Continued

MEMBERS OF FIRM

JON A. BAUMGARTEN, born New York, New York, October 26, 1942; admitted to bar, 1968, New York; 1977, U.S. Court of Appeals, Fourth Circuit; 1980, District of Columbia; 1982, U.S. Supreme Court; 1983, U.S. District Court, District of Columbia; 1994, U.S. Court of Appeals, Sixth Circuit. *Education:* City College of the City University of New York (B.A., 1964); New York University School of Law (LL.B., 1967). Research Editor, New York University Law Review, 1966-1967. General Counsel, United States Copyright Office, 1986-1989. ***Email:*** jabaumgarten@proskauer.com

MARK J. BIROS, born Wilkes-Barre, Pennsylvania, September 13, 1948; admitted to bar, 1973, District of Columbia; 1974, Pennsylvania; 1977, U.S. District Court, District of Columbia; 1979, U.S. Court of Appeals, District of Columbia Circuit; 1995, U.S. Court of Appeals, Seventh Circuit; 1996, Maryland and U.S. District Court, District of Maryland. *Education:* Princeton University (B.A., cum laude, 1970); Georgetown University Law Center (J.D., 1973). Editor, American Criminal Law Review, 1973. Deputy Chief, Felony Trial Division, United States Attorney's Office, Washington, DC, 1984-1985. Assistant United States Attorney, United States Attorney's Office, Washington, DC, 1977-1988. Assistant Attorney General, Commonwealth of Pennsylvania, 1974-1976. Assistant Counsel, United States Senate Select Committee on Presidential Campaign Activities, 1973-1974. Adjunct Professor of Law, Georgetown University Law Center, 1982—. ***Email:*** mbiros@proskauer.com

JOSEPH E. CASSON, born New York, New York, May 24, 1943; admitted to bar, 1969, District of Columbia and U.S. Court of Appeals, District of Columbia Circuit; 1972, U.S. District Court, District of Maryland; 1977, U.S. Court of Federal Claims and U.S. Supreme Court; 1985, U.S. Court of Appeals, Fifth Circuit. *Education:* Fairfield University (B.A., 1965); Georgetown University Law Center (J.D., 1968; LL.M., 1969). Articles Editor, Georgetown University Law Review, 1967-1968. ***Email:*** jcasson@proskauer.com

WARREN L. DENNIS, born Toms River, New Jersey, September 24, 1948; admitted to bar, 1972, Pennsylvania; 1975, District of Columbia; 1976, U.S. Supreme Court; 1978, U.S. Court of Appeals, District of Columbia Circuit and U.S. District Court, District of Columbia; 1981, U.S. Court of Appeals, Third Circuit; 1984, U.S. Court of Appeals, Federal Circuit; 1988, U.S. Court of Appeals, Fourth Circuit; 1991, U.S. Court of Federal Claims. *Education:* University of Pennsylvania (B.A., 1969); University of Pennsylvania Law School (J.D., 1972). Director, Task Force on Discrimination in Financing, United States Department of Justice, 1975-1977. Trial Attorney, Honors Law Program, United States Department of Justice, Civil Rights Division, 1972-1977. ***Email:*** wdennis@proskauer.com

MALCOLM J. HARKINS, III, born Bryn Mawr, Pennsylvania, October 30, 1951; admitted to bar, 1976, Pennsylvania; 1977, U.S. District Court, Eastern District of Pennsylvania; 1978, District of Columbia; 1979, U.S. Court of Appeals, District of Columbia Circuit and U.S. Court of Federal Claims; 1981, U.S. Court of Appeals, Ninth Circuit; 1982, California; 1983, U.S. Court of Appeals, Seventh Circuit; 1985, U.S. District Court, Eastern District of Wisconsin. *Education:* St. Joseph's University (A.B., 1973) Alpha Sigma Nu; Saint Louis University School of Law (J.D., cum laude, 1976). Member, Saint Louis University Law Journal, 1974-1976. ***Email:*** mharkins@proskauer.com

LAWRENCE Z. LORBER, born Brooklyn, New York, January 16, 1947; admitted to bar, 1970, District of Columbia; 1971, New York; 1970, U.S. Court of Appeals, District of Columbia Circuit and U.S. District Court, District of Columbia; 1976, U.S. Supreme Court; 1983, U.S. District Court, Southern District of New York; 1985, U.S. District Court, Eastern District of New York; 1987, U.S. Court of Appeals, Fifth Circuit; 1990, U.S. Court of Appeals, Third Circuit; 1995, U.S. Court of Appeals, Sixth Circuit. *Education:* Brooklyn College of the City University of New York (B.A., 1967); University of Maryland Law School (J.D., 1970). Executive Assistant to the Solicitor of Labor, 1974-1975. Director, Office of Federal Contract Compliance Programs and Deputy Assistant Secretary of Labor, U.S. Department of Labor, 1976-1977. Member, Board of Directors, Office of Congressional Compliance, 1995-1998. ***Email:*** llorber@proskauer.com

RICHARD H. ROWE, born Waltham, Massachusetts, January 2, 1937; admitted to bar, 1965, District of Columbia, U.S. Court of Appeals, District of Columbia Circuit and U.S. District Court, District of Columbia; 1968, U.S. Supreme Court; 1980, New York. *Education:* Bates College (A.B., 1957); Harvard Law School (J.D., 1964). Director, United States Securities and Exchange Commission, Division of Corporate Finance, Washington, DC, 1976-1979. Attorney, United States Securities and Exchange Commission, Washington, DC, 1964-1969, 1970-1975. ***Email:*** rrowe@proskauer.com

CHRISTOPHER WOLF, born Washington, D.C., February 8, 1954; admitted to bar, 1980, District of Columbia; 1981, U.S. Court of Appeals, District of Columbia and U.S. District Court, District of Columbia; 1985, U.S. District Court, Eastern District of Wisconsin and U.S. Court of Federal Claims; 1989, U.S. Supreme Court; 1991, U.S. Court of Appeals, Federal Circuit and U.S. Court of International Trade; 1993, U.S. District Court, Northern District of California; 1995, U.S. Court of Appeals, Fourth Circuit; 1996, New York. *Education:* Bowdoin College (A.B., cum laude, 1976); Washington & Lee University School of Law (J.D., magna cum laude, 1980). Order of the Coif. Burks Scholar, Teaching Fellow in Law, 1980. Member, Washington & Lee Law Review, 1979. Law Clerk, Hon. Aubrey E. Robinson, Jr., United States District Court, District of Columbia, 1980-1982. ***Email:*** cwolf@proskauer.com

WASHINGTON, D.C.
SENIOR COUNSEL

THOMAS H. BROCK, born Des Moines, Iowa, June 12, 1953; admitted to bar, 1977, District of Columbia; 1979, U.S. District Court, District of Columbia; 1982, U.S. Court of Appeals, Ninth Circuit, U.S. Court of Federal Claims, U.S. Court of Appeals, Federal Circuit and U.S. Court of Appeals, District of Columbia Circuit; 1983, U.S. Court of Appeals, Sixth and Tenth Circuits; 1984, U.S. Court of Appeals, Seventh and Eleventh Circuits and U.S. Supreme Court; 1985, U.S. Court of Appeals, Fifth Circuit; 1986, U.S. Court of Appeals, Eighth Circuit. *Education:* University of Iowa (B.A., 1974) Phi Beta Kappa; George Washington University National Law Center (J.D., 1977). Managing Editor, George Washington Law Review, 1976-1977. ***Email:*** tbrock@proskauer.com

ALEC W. FARR, born Berkeley, California, September 17, 1966; admitted to bar, 1991, Maryland; 1992, District of Columbia; 1994, U.S. District Court for the District of Columbia and U.S. Court of Appeals, Fourth Circuit; 1995, U.S. District Court, District of Maryland and U.S. Court of Appeals, District of Columbia Circuit. *Education:* Georgetown University (B.A., cum laude, 1988); Georgetown University Law Center (J.D., cum laude, 1991). ***Email:*** afarr@proskauer.com

JAMES P. HOLLOWAY, born Buffalo, New York, May 4, 1961; admitted to bar, 1986, California; 1988, District of Columbia. *Education:* Boston University (B.A., magna cum laude, 1983); Hastings College of the Law, University of California (J.D., 1986). ***Email:*** jholloway@proskauer.com

LIONEL E. PASHKOFF, born Port Jefferson, New York, February 27, 1943; admitted to bar, 1968, District of Columbia; 1969, U.S. District Court, District of Columbia; 1993, U.S. District Court, District of Maryland. *Education:* University of Maryland (B.A., 1965); George Washington University National Law Center (J.D., 1968) Phi Delta Phi. Chief Enforcement Attorney, Securities and Exchange Commission, Washington, DC, 1973-1974. Special Assistant, U.S. Attorney, United States Department of Justice, Washington, DC, 1971-1972. ***Email:*** lpashkoff@proskauer.com

STEPHEN D. SOLOMON, born New York, N.Y., February 8, 1956; admitted to bar, 1987, New York and U.S. District Court, Eastern and Southern Districts of New York; 1998, District of Columbia; 2001, U.S. Court of Appeals, Eleventh Circuit. *Education:* State University of New York at Binghamton (B.A., 1977) Phi Beta Kappa; New York Law School (J.D., magna cum laude, 1986). Research Editor, New York Law School Journal of International and Comparative Law, 1985-1986. ***Email:*** ssolomon@proskauer.com

SUSAN A. TURNER, born Munich, Germany, December 22, 1955; admitted to bar, 1990, Virginia, District of Columbia and U.S. Court of Appeals, Fourth Circuit. *Education:* George Washington University (B.S., 1976); Catholic University of America (J.D., 1990). Member, National Appellate Advocacy Competition. Senior Staff Member, Journal of Contemporary Health Law and Policy. *Member:* Virginia State Bar; The District of Columbia Bar. **PRACTICE AREAS:** Health Care Law. ***Email:*** sturner@proskauer.com

WASHINGTON, D.C. ASSOCIATES

Margaret J. Babb
Christine D. Bachman
Anita M. Bahauddin (Not admitted in DC)
Richard S. Basile (Not admitted in DC)
Bruce E. Boyden
Susan Brinkerhoff
Amy J. Dilcher (Not admitted in DC)
Brian Elsbernd
Amybeth Garcia-Bokor
Gretchen E. Lamberg (admission pending)
Stephanie L. Marn
Mark A. McAndrew
Julia McMillen
Richard E. Ramsay
Cheralyn E. Schessler
Megan H. Tinker
Andrew L. Wexton

PROVOST & UMPHREY LAW FIRM, L.L.P.

Established in 1996

SUITE 410
1155 15TH STREET, N.W.
WASHINGTON, D.C. 20005
Telephone: 202-466-0900
Fax: 202-637-2977
Email: provost@erols.com
URL: http://www.provostumphrey.com

Port Arthur, Texas Office: 2901 Turtle Creek Drive, Suite 250, 77643. Telephone: 409-721-6260. Fax: 409-721-9579.

(This Listing Continued)

Beaumont, Texas Office: 490 Park Street, 77701. Telephone: 409-838-8821. Fax: 409-813-8655.
Nashville, Tennessee Office: 3343 Perimeter Hill, Suite 110. Telephone: 615-242-0199. Fax: 615-256-5922.
Albuquerque, New Mexico Office: 9621 Fourth Street NW. Telephone: 505-792-8500. Fax: 505-792-8700.
Denver, Colorado Office: 4155 East Jewell Avenue, Suite 707. Telephone: 303-756-3335. Fax: 303-756-9334.
Little Rock, Arkansas Office: 124 West Capitol Avenue, Suite 1805. Telephone: 501-374-3655. Fax: 501-374-4279.
Atlanta, Georgia Office: 181 14th Street, N.E., Suite 425. Telephone: 404-876-8100; 1-800-340-7862.
Friendswood, Texas Office: 211 East Parkwood, Suite 2017, 77546. Telephone: 281-992-1550. Fax: 281-992-2617.

General Civil and Trial Practice. False Claims Act Litigation, Antitrust Litigation, Securities Litigation, Commercial Litigation, Employment and Labor Litigation, Environmental Litigation, First Amendment Litigation and Civil Rights Litigation.

MEMBER OF FIRM

REUBEN A. GUTTMAN, born New York, N.Y., August 21, 1959; admitted to bar, 1985, Georgia; 1988, District of Columbia; 1991, U.S. District Court, Northern District of Georgia, U.S. District Court, Western District of Michigan, U.S. Court of Appeals, Third and Eleventh Circuits, New Jersey, Pennsylvania and U.S. District Court, District of New Jersey. *Education:* University of Rochester (B.A., History, 1981); Emory University (J.D., 1985). Author: "The Dormant Commerce Clause and Interstate Transportation of Waste," University of Pennsylvania, Journal of Resource Management and Technology, June 1993; "Impact of OSHA Bloodbourne Disease Rule," Medical Waste, Vol. 1, No. 1, Oct. 1992; "Supreme Court Holdings Benefit Landfill and Incinerator Operators," Medical Waste, Vol. 1, No. 3, Dec. 1992; "Supreme Court Upholds Preemptive Powers of OSH Act," Medical Waste, Vol. 1, No. 4, Jan. 1993; "EPA Dialogue May Result in Rules for Commercial Buildings," 2 Nat'l Journal of Asbestos in Buildings Litigation, 13, 1989; "The Asbestos Model: Labor and Citizens Groups and a Multi-Pronged Approach to Regulatory Change," paper first presented at the Annual Meeting of the American Political Science Association, Chicago, Ill., Sept. 1, 1987; published as a chapter in Conflict Resolution and Public Policy, edited by Miriam K. Mills, Greenwood-Quorum Press, October 1990; "At Issue: Should Congress Pass Legislation That Would Extent The Asbestos Hazard Energy Response Act To All Public and Commercial Buildings," Congressional Quarterly's Editorial Research Reports, Vol. 1, No. 9, 1990; "Representation Campaigns and the Future of Labor: a Legal and Theoretical Perspective," paper presented at the Annual Meeting of the Midwest Political Science Association, Chicago, Ill., April 4, 1988. Consulting Editor: The Regulatory Analyst: Medical Waste, a monthly publication, Warren Gorham Lamont, New York, N.Y., 1992-1994. Chapter Author and Advisory Board Member, "Environmental Management in Healthcare Facilities," W.B. Saunders Company, April 1998. *Member:* Bar Association of the District of Columbia; The District of Columbia Bar; State Bar of Georgia; Pennsylvania Bar Association; Association of Trial Lawyers of America. (Manager, Washington, D.C. Office). ***PRACTICE AREAS:*** General Civil and Trial Practice; False Claims Act Litigation; Antitrust Litigation; Securities Litigation; Commercial Litigation; Employment and Labor Litigation; Environmental Litigation; First Amendment Litigation; Civil Rights Litigation.

ASSOCIATES

Brian P. McCafferty (Not admitted in DC)
Traci L. Buschner
Katherine B. Bornstein (Not admitted in DC)

QUAGLIANO & SEEGER

3243 P STREET, N.W.
WASHINGTON, D.C. 20007
Telephone: 202-822-8838
Fax: 202-822-6982
Email: info@quagseeg.com

Commercial Litigation, Construction Law, Government Contracts, Bankruptcy and Creditors' Rights.

JULIE QUAGLIANO WESTEMEIER, born Kewanee, Illinois, May 7, 1959; admitted to bar, 1985, Pennsylvania, District of Columbia; 1991, Maryland; 1994, Virginia. *Education:* University of Notre Dame (B.B.A., with highest honors, 1981); Georgetown University (J.D., 1984). Beta Gamma Sigma. Co-Author: "My Sub Just Went Bankrupt," Constructor (AGC). Participant, Washington Building Congress, Contract Document Workshop. Co-Author and Lecturer, "Working in a Troubled Environment," Washington Building Congress. Speaker and Participant, "Smaller Law Firm Leadership," Fulcrum Information Services. Lecturer, Executive Advancement Program, Associated Builders and Contractors, Metropolitan Washington Chapter. ***REPORTED***

(This Listing Continued)

CASES: U.S.A. u/b/o Allied Building Products Corp. v. Federal Insurance, 729 F.Supp. 477 (D.Md. 1990); In re: Kora & Williams Corp., 97 B.R. 258 (Bankr. D.Md. 1988). ***PRACTICE AREAS:*** Commercial Law; Civil Litigation; Bankruptcy. ***Email:*** quagliano@quagseeg.com

STEPHEN M. SEEGER, born Cleveland, Ohio, May 28, 1963; admitted to bar, 1990, Maryland; 1991, U.S. District Court, District of Maryland; 1992, District of Columbia, U.S. District Court, District of Columbia, U.S. Court of Federal Claims and U.S. Court of Appeals, Federal Circuit; 1996, Virginia and U.S. Court of Appeals, Fourth Circuit; 1998, U.S. District Court, Eastern District of Virginia; 1999, U.S. Supreme Court. *Education:* Lehigh University (B.A., cum laude, 1985); George Washington University (J.D., 1990). Member: Chamber of Commerce; Washington Building Congress. *Member:* District of Columbia Bar. ***REPORTED CASES:*** Gen. Ins. Co. of Am. v. Interstate Serv. Co., 118 Md. App. 126, 701 A. 2d. 1213 (1997) cert den. 349 Md. 103 (1998); Chambco, a Division of Chamberlin Waterproofing & Roofing System, Inc. v. Urban Masonry Corporation, 101 Md. App. 664, 647 A.2d 1234 (1994). ***PRACTICE AREAS:*** Government Contracts; Construction Law; Civil Litigation. ***Email:*** seeger@quagseeg.com

JAMES J. FAUGHNAN, born Brooklyn, New York, August 24, 1958; admitted to bar, 1990, Virginia; 1991, District of Columbia. *Education:* Pace University (B.B.A., cum laude, 1980); George Washington University (J.D., with high honors, 1990). Order of the Coif. Certified Public Accountant, Virginia, 1985-1989. Certified Information Systems Auditor, 1985. *Member:* Virginia State Bar; The District of Columbia Bar; American Bar Association. ***PRACTICE AREAS:*** Commercial Litigation; Corporate. ***Email:*** faughnan@quagseeg.com

ASSOCIATE

NICOLA Y. WHITEMAN, born London, England, November 1, 1973; admitted to bar, 2000, Virginia and U.S. Court of Appeals, Fourth Circuit; 2001, District of Columbia and Maryland. *Education:* Georgetown University (B.A., 1995); Villanova University School of Law (J.D., 1999). *Member:* Virginia State Bar; Virginia Women Attorneys Association. ***PRACTICE AREAS:*** Civil Litigation; Commercial Law. ***Email:*** whiteman@quagseeg.com

SETH ADAM ROBBINS, born New Haven, New York, June 21, 1974; admitted to bar, 2000, Virginia; 2001, District of Columbia, U.S. Court of Federal Claims and U.S. Court of Appeals. *Education:* Susquehanna University (B.S., 1996); George Mason University School of Law (J.D., 2000). Director, National Contract Management Association. *Member:* Virginia State Bar and District of Columbia Bar. ***PRACTICE AREAS:*** Construction Law; Government Contracts; Bankruptcy; Civil Litigation. ***Email:*** robbins@quagseeg.com

OF COUNSEL

ALTON K. BURTON, born Toms River, New Jersey, July 3, 1956; admitted to bar, 1990, Maryland; 1992, District of Columbia; 1995, Virginia. *Education:* University of Maryland (B.S., 1978; M.B.A., 1981); George Washington University (J.D., with honors, 1989). Certified Public Accountant, 1985. *Member:* American Association of Attorney-Certified Public Accountants. ***PRACTICE AREAS:*** Small Business Law; Estate Planning; Estate Administration; Taxation; Intellectual Property.

QUINN, RACUSIN & GAZZOLA CHARTERED

Established in 1982

1400 K STREET, N.W.
SUITE 1010
WASHINGTON, D.C. 20005-2403
Telephone: 202-842-9300
Facsimile: 202-682-0148
URL: http://www.qrg-law.com
Email: qrg@qrg-law.com
URL: http://www.lawyers.com/quinnracusin&gazzola

General, Corporate, Business and Administrative Practice, Securities, Tax, Estate Planning and Administration, Elder Law.

FIRM PROFILE: Quinn, Racusin & Gazzola Chartered was founded in 1982. The firm represents start-up and seasoned domestic and international businesses as general or special counsel. It is experienced in handling a wide range of business issues including corporation and partnership creation, mergers, acquisitions, and financing, as well as day-to-day matters such as contract and lease review and negotiation, taxes, intellectual property, immigration, employee relations and employee benefits.

The firm advises individuals in estate planning, trust, probate and estate administration, and represents individuals seeking the court appointment of guardians and conservators for incapacitated persons. The firm represents clients in estate

(This Listing Continued)

QUINN, RACUSIN & GAZZOLA CHARTERED, Washington—Continued

and fiduciary litigation and arbitration, including will contests. Firm members also serve clients in fiduciary capacities such as attorney in fact, and as court-appointed guardians and conservators.

Members of the firm regularly practice before courts in the District of Columbia, Maryland and Virginia. The firm also has experience with arbitration and other alternative dispute resolution methods as well as extensive experience in business negotiations.

AARON J. RACUSIN (1915-1998).

JOHN H. QUINN, JR., born Memphis, Tennessee, July 16, 1936; admitted to bar, 1961, Virginia and Tennessee; 1962, U.S. Court of Appeals, 4th Circuit; 1963, District of Columbia and U.S. Court of Appeals, District of Columbia Circuit; 1964, U.S. Supreme Court; 1967, U.S. Court of Appeals, 2nd Circuit; 1982, U.S. Court of Appeals for the Federal Circuit; 1989, Maryland. *Education:* Rhodes College (B.A., with honors, 1958); University of Virginia (J.D., 1961). Order of the Coif; Phi Delta Phi. Instructor in Contract and Antitrust Law, Temple University, 1968-1971. Law Clerk to Judge Herbert S. Boreman, U.S. Court of Appeals, Fourth Circuit, 1961-1962. *Member:* The District of Columbia Bar; Maryland State and American (Member, Sections on: Antitrust; Business Law; Real Property, Probate and Trust Law and Tax Law) Bar Associations; Virginia State Bar; National Academy of Elder Law Attorneys, Inc. ***PRACTICE AREAS:*** Business Law; Corporate Law; Estate Planning; Fiduciary Law; Elder Law. ***Email:*** jhq@qrg-law.com

ROBERT A. GAZZOLA, born New York, N.Y., January 3, 1938; admitted to bar, 1984, Virginia, U.S. District Court, Eastern District of Virginia, U.S. Court of Appeals, 4th Circuit, U.S. Court of Appeals, District of Columbia Circuit and U.S. Court of Appeals for the Federal Circuit; 1985, District of Columbia and U.S. Claims Court; 1993, Maryland. *Education:* Fordham University (B.A., 1959); University of Southern California (M.S., 1971); George Washington University (J.D., 1984); National War College (1977). Member, National Panel of Arbitrators (Commercial), American Arbitration Association; D.C. Superior Court Probate Task Force, 1993-1994; Task Force, The District of Columbia Omnibus Trusts and Estates Act, 1999-2000; Washington, D.C. Estate Planning Council. *Member:* The District of Columbia Bar (Co-Chair, Estates, Trust and Probate Law Section, 1999—); Virginia State Bar; Maryland State Bar Association, Inc.; American Bar Association (Member, Section of: Real Property, Probate and Trust Law); National Academy of Elder Law Attorneys. [Colonel, USAF Retired, 1981]. ***PRACTICE AREAS:*** Estate Planning; Fiduciary Law; Probate Law; Elder Law; Business Law. ***Email:*** rag@qrg-law.com

ASSOCIATE

MARK R. GALBRAITH, born 1960; admitted to bar, 1993, Virginia (Not admitted in District of Columbia). *Education:* University of Minnesota (B.A., 1984); George Mason University School of Law (J.D., 1993). ***Email:*** mrg@qrg-law.com

LEGAL SUPPORT PERSONNEL

FRANCISCA I. OTERO, born Alexandria, Virginia. *Education:* University of Virginia (B.A., 1995); American University, Washington, DC (J.D., 2002). (Paralegal). ***Email:*** fio@qrg-law.com

ANDREW C. MARTIN, born Syracuse, New York, April 11, 1978. *Education:* American University, Washington, DC (B.A., 2000). Alpha Kappa Psi. (Paralegal). ***Email:*** acm@qrg-law.com

BRIAN M. BOYLE, born Silver Spring, Maryland, March 19, 1978. *Education:* James Madison University, Harrisonburg, Virginia (B.B.A., 2000). Beta Gamma Sigma; Golden Key. ***Email:*** bmb@qrg-law.com

ANGELA MUSSAR, born Lynchburg, Virginia, October 15, 1973; (admission pending). *Education:* Millersville University (B.A., 1995). (Paralegal). ***Email:*** amm@qrg-law.com

LOUIS RABIL

Established in 1962

SUITE 700
1700 K STREET, N.W.
WASHINGTON, D.C. 20006
Telephone: 202-466-4944
Fax: 202-223-3260
Email: lrabil@aol.com

General Practice in all Courts and before Federal and Local Governmental Departments. Corporation Law, Real Estate, Personal Injury, Probate, Employment Law, Business Litigation and Commercial Transactions, Appellate Practice.

(This Listing Continued)

FIRM PROFILE: For over thirty-five years the firm's clients have been diverse, ranging from individuals to associations and corporations in both business and litigation matters.

LOUIS RABIL, born Weldon, North Carolina, January 17, 1930; admitted to bar, 1957, District of Columbia and North Carolina; 1961, Virginia; 1962, U.S. Supreme Court. *Education:* University of North Carolina (B.S., 1952); Georgetown University (J.D., 1957). Delta Theta Phi. *Member:* The District of Columbia Bar; Bar Association of the District of Columbia; American Bar Association (Member, Section on Litigation; Subcommittee Chairman, Section of International and Comparative Law, 1967-1971); North Carolina State Bar; Virginia State Bar. [Lt., j.g., U.S.N.R., 1953-1956]. ***PRACTICE AREAS:*** Corporate; Business Litigation; Civil Litigation; Appellate Practice; General Practice.

RADER, FISHMAN & GRAUER PLLC

1233 20TH STREET, SUITE 501
WASHINGTON, D.C. 20036
Telephone: 202-955-3750
Fax: 202-955-3751
Email: info@raderfishman.com
URL: http://www.raderfishman.com

Bloomfield Hills, Michigan Office: 39533 Woodward, Suite 140, 48304. Telephone: 248-594-0600. Fax: 248-594-0610.

Englewood, Colorado Office: 383 Inverness Drive South, Suite 140, 80112. Telephone: 303-991-1200. Fax: 303-991-1210.

Salt Lake City, Utah Office: 10653 S. River Front Parkway, Suite 150, South Jordan, 84095. Telephone: 801-572-0185. Fax: 801-572-7666.

Patent, Trademark, Copyright, Computer Law, Unfair Competition, Trial and Appellate Practice.

RONALD P. KANANEN, born Conneaut, Ohio, October 29, 1937; admitted to bar, 1964, Ohio; 1970, District of Columbia; U.S. Court of Appeals for the Federal Circuit; registered to practice before U.S. Patent and Trademark Office. *Education:* Case Western Reserve University (B.S.E.E., 1959; J.D., 1964). Delta Theta Phi. Member, Western Reserve University Law Review, 1962-1963. Law Clerk to Arthur M. Smith, Associate Judge, U.S. Court of Customs and Patent Appeals, 1967-1968. *Member:* The District of Columbia Bar (Member: Patent Trademark & Copyright Section; Steering Committee, 1985, Chairman, 1986); The Bar Association of the District of Columbia (Chairman, PTC Section, 1988-1989); Federal Circuit Bar Association; American Intellectual Property Law Association. ***Email:*** rpk@raderfishman.com

YOICHIRO YAMAGUCHI, admitted to bar, 1988, Japan (as Patent Attorney); registered to practice before Japanese Patent Office and Appear as Patent Counsel before the Courts; 1994, New York; 2000, District of Columbia; U.S. Court of Appeals for the Federal Circuit. *Education:* College of Technology and School of Law, Waseda University, Japan (LL.B., 1974); George Washington University (LL.M., 1992). Co-Author: "Official Commentary of Industrial Property Laws," in Japanese, 1986; "Discovery and Strategy," in Japanese, 1994. Author: "U.S. Intellectual Property Court Document Retrieval Manual," in Japanese, 1993; "Crisis to Japanese Patent Attorney System Caused by U.S. Attorney-Client Privilege/Proposal of Changes to the Patent Attorney Law," in Japanese, 1994; Over 30 articles concerning U.S. intellectual property laws for publications including monthly journal of Japanese Group of AIPPI. Lecturer, Japanese Patent Law and Policy, George Washington University National Law Center, 1994—. Patent Examiner of Japanese Patent Office, 1974-1988; Appeal Examiner, Board of Appeals of the Japanese Patent Office, 1988. *Member:* New York State and American Bar Associations; American Intellectual Property Law Association. ***LANGUAGES:*** Japanese. ***PRACTICE AREAS:*** Intellectual Property Law. ***Email:*** yy@raderfishman.com

ELLEN A. EFROS, born New York, N.Y., January 18, 1950; admitted to bar, 1978, District of Columbia; 1979, New York; 1990, Maryland; U.S. Supreme Court, U.S. Court of Appeals, Second, Fourth, Fifth, Sixth and Ninth Circuits and Federal Circuit. *Education:* Case Western Reserve University (B.A., with honors, 1971); St. John's University (M.A., with honors, 1973); Hofstra University (J.D., with honors, 1978). Member, Hofstra University Inter School Trial Team, 1977-1978. Hofstra University Moot Court Team, 1978. Listed in Who's Who in America; Who's Who in American Law and Women in American Law. Former Editor, Antitrust Law Journal, American Bar Association, 1986-1989. *Member:* Maryland, New York State and American Bar Associations; The District of Columbia Bar. ***PRACTICE AREAS:*** Antitrust Law; Federal Civil Litigation; Commercial Litigation; Intellectual Property Litigation. ***Email:*** eae@raderfishman.com

DAVID T. NIKAIDO, born Santa Monica, California, December 20, 1934; admitted to bar, 1963, Colorado; 1965, Michigan; 1968, Missouri; 1974, District of Columbia; registered to practice before U.S. Patent and Trademark Office. *Education:* University of Colorado (B.A., Chem., 1957); University of

(This Listing Continued)

Denver (J.D., 1963). Phi Alpha Delta (President, 1962-1963). Symposium Editor, University of Denver Law Review, 1962-1963. Author: "Essentials for the Drafting of U.S. Patent Specifications and Claims," Published by the Japanese Group of AIPPI, Tokyo, Japan, 1975, 1980, 1986. *Member:* The District of Columbia Bar; Colorado and American (Member: Section on Patent, Trademark and Copyright Law) Bar Associations; American Intellectual Property Law Association; International Patent and Trademark Association (AIPPI). ***LANGUAGES:*** Japanese. ***PRACTICE AREAS:*** U.S./Japan Negotiations; Patent Licensing.

ASSOCIATE

ROBERT S. GREEN, born New York, New York, February 2, 1961; admitted to bar, 1995, Virginia and U.S. Court of Appeals, Fourth Circuit; 1997, District of Columbia and U.S. Court of Appeals, Federal Circuit; registered to practice before U.S. Patent and Trademark Office. *Education:* Rochester Institute of Technology (B.S., Chemistry, 1983); Washington College of Law of American University (J.D., 1994). *Member:* The District of Columbia Bar; Virginia State Bar; American Bar Association (Member: Section on: Intellectual Property Law); American Institute of Aeronautics and Astronautics (Senior Member). ***PRACTICE AREAS:*** Patent Law. ***Email:*** rsg@raderfishman.com

BRIAN KEITH DUTTON, born Philadelphia, Pennsylvania, July 21, 1958; admitted to bar, 2000, Kansas and U.S. Court of Appeals, Federal Circuit; 2001, District of Columbia; registered to practice before U.S. Patent and Trademark Office. *Education:* Drexel University (B.S.E.E., 1981); George Washington University (J.D., 1995). Patent Examiner, U.S. Patent and Trademark Office, 1993-2000 (Office of Petitions, 1998). *Member:* The District of Columbia Bar, Kansas and American Bar Associations; American Intellectual Property Law Association. ***Email:*** bkd@raderfishman.com

DAVID K. BENSON, born Phoenix, Arizona, May 29, 1969; admitted to bar, 2001, Michigan (Not admitted in District of Columbia). Registered to practice before U.S. Patent and Trademark Office. *Education:* Arizona State University (B.S., Biochemistry); George Mason University School of Law (1999). Member, Journal of International Legal Studies. *Member:* American Intellectual Property Law Association. ***Email:*** dkb@raderfishman.com

CARL SCHAUKOWITCH, born Pittsburgh, Pennsylvania, February 14, 1951; admitted to bar, 1980, Colorado; 1996, District of Columbia; registered to practice before U.S. Patent and Trademark Office. *Education:* Pennsylvania State University (B.S., 1973); University of Denver (J.D., 1980; Finance, 1984). *Member:* The Colorado Bar Association; District of Columbia Bar; American Intellectual Property Law Association. ***PRACTICE AREAS:*** Patents.

OF COUNSEL

PAUL W. FISH, born Ligonier, Pennsylvania, April 12, 1933; admitted to bar, 1965, District of Columbia; 1966, New York; 1967, Michigan; 1976, Wisconsin; 1983, Illinois; 1993, Pennsylvania; registered to practice before U.S. Patent and Trademark Office. *Education:* Catholic University of America (B.S.E.E., 1959; M.S.E.E., 1961); George Washington University (J.D., 1965). Listed in *Who's Who in America* and *Who's Who in American Law* . Assistant Corporate Secretary and Director of Patents, Burroughs Corporation, 1969-1976. Vice President, General Counsel and Corporate Secretary, Jos. Schlitz Brewing Co., 1976-1982. Senior Vice President/Legal, Comdisco, Inc., 1982-1990. Adjunct Professor, Columbus School of Law, CUA, 1997—. Member: Advisory Counsel of the United States Court of Federal Claims; Board of Visitors, Columbus School of Law; Board of Regents, Catholic University of America. *Member:* American Intellectual Property Law Association (Member, Alternate Dispute Resolution Committee). ***Email:*** pwf@raderfishman.com

PATENT AGENTS

EUGENE G. BYRD, born Easton, Pennsylvania, July 2, 1971; admitted to bar, registered to practice before the U.S. Patent and Trademark Office. *Education:* Howard University (B.S., Mechanical Engineering, 1995). Patent Examiner, U.S. Patent and Trademark Office, 1995-2000. *Member:* American Society of Mechanical Engineers; American Intellectual Property Law Association. ***Email:*** egb@aderfishman.com

(For complete biographical data on all personnel, see Professional Biographies at Bloomfield Hills, Salt Lake City, Utah and Denver, Colorado)

LAW OFFICES OF CATHERINE MARY RAFFERTY

4801 YUMA STREET NW
WASHINGTON, D.C. 20016
Telephone: 202-244-0608
Fax: 202-244-2967
Email: c-rafferty-11@alumni.uchicago.edu
URL: http://www.lawyers.com/rafferty

Estate Planning and Probate Administration with special emphasis on Estate Taxation and Collateral Estate Planning Matters.

(This Listing Continued)

FIRM PROFILE: Law Offices of Catherine Mary Rafferty represents clients ranging from individuals to small and medium-sized companies seeking counsel for estate taxation matters, estate planning, probate administration, and general business matters throughout the District of Columbia and Maryland.

CATHERINE MARY RAFFERTY, born Washington, D.C., August 20, 1966; admitted to bar, 1991, District of Columbia; 1992, U.S. Tax Court, U.S. District Court for the District of Columbia and U.S. Court of Appeals for the District of Columbia Circuit; 1994, Maryland. *Education:* University of Chicago (B.A., 1988; M.A., 1988); Catholic University of America (J.D., 1991); Georgetown University (LL.M., Taxation, 1994). Attorney, Internal Revenue Service, Office of Associate Chief Counsel (International), 1991-1992. Associate, Kelly and Nicolaides, 1992-1994. Managing Member, Rafferty & Rafferty, PLLC, 1995-2000. Chairman, 1998-2001, Member, Steering Committee, 1996—, Montgomery County and Prince George's County Tax Study Group. Executive Board Member, 1999—; Assistant Treasurer, 1999-2001 and Treasurer, 2001—, Philoptochos Society of Saint Sophia Greek Orthodox Cathedral. *Member:* Montgomery County Bar Association; District of Columbia Bar; Maryland State (Council Member, Vice Chair, Technology, Tax Section, 2001—) and American Bar Associations; Washington, D.C. Estate Planning Council; American Hellenic Institute; Hellenic American Women's Council. ***PRACTICE AREAS:*** Trusts and Estates; Probate; Estate Planning; Wills; Living Wills; Estate Administration; Taxation.

RAVDIN & WOFFORD

A PROFESSIONAL CORPORATION

Established in 1974

1700 K STREET, N.W., SUITE 650
WASHINGTON, D.C. 20006
Telephone: 202-429-5551
Fax: 202-429-5553
URL: http://www.lawyers.com/ravdin-wofford

Family Law, Trusts and Estates, Divorce Taxation. Practicing in District of Columbia, Maryland, Virginia and Texas.

LINDA J. RAVDIN, born Richmond, Virginia, August 10, 1948; admitted to bar, 1974, Virginia and District of Columbia; 1984, Maryland; U.S. Supreme Court. *Education:* The Ohio State University (B.A., with honors, 1970); George Washington University (J.D., with honors, 1974). Member, Hearing Committee, District of Columbia Board on Professional Responsibility, 1983-1989. *Member:* The District of Columbia Bar (Co-Chair, Solo and Small Firm Practitioners Committee; Member, Committee on MCLE; Member, Sections of: Family Law; Law Practice Management; Steering Committee, 1995—; Member: Legal Ethics Committee, 1985-1991; Chair, 1989-1991; Litigation Section, Steering Committee, 1986-1988; Editor, Superior Court Digest, 1986-1987; Litigation Section Committee on Proposed Rules of Professional Conduct, 1986); Bar Association of the District of Columbia; Virginia State Bar (Member, Section of: Family Law); Maryland State and American (Member, Sections on: Family Law; Member, Ethical Practices Committee, 1993—; Law Practice Management; Member, Governing Council, 1991—) Bar Associations; Virginia Trial Lawyers Association (Member, Family Law Section). ***PRACTICE AREAS:*** Domestic Relations; Trusts and Estates; Civil Litigation. ***Email:*** ljravdin@ravdin-wofford.com

CINDY LYNN WOFFORD, born Athens, Texas, February 3, 1952; admitted to bar, 1978, Texas; 1988, District of Columbia and Maryland; U.S. Tax Court. *Education:* Stephen F. Austin University (B.A., magna cum laude, 1974); University of Texas (J.D., 1978); Southern Methodist University (LL.M., Taxation, 1986). Delta Theta Phi. Author: "Laws and Policies Affecting Handicapped Children in Texas, A Guidebook," Texas Department of Public Affairs and Texas Education, Agency, 1977; BNA Tax Management Portfolio, Divorce and Separation, 515 T.M. (1995 ed.); "Disposition of the Marital Home—Divorce Tax Traps," Journal of Asset Protection, March/April 1996; "Recent Developments—Domestic Relations," The Tax Lawyer, Summer 1996 and Summer, 1997; "When Alimony Isn't Alimony, Keeping Spousal Support Deductible," Legal Times June 2, 1997. *Member:* The District of Columbia Bar (Member, Sections of: Estates and Trusts; Taxation); State Bar of Texas; American Bar Association (Member, Tax Section, Domestic Relations Committee). ***PRACTICE AREAS:*** Trusts and Estates; Divorce Taxation; Domestic Relations. ***Email:*** clwofford@ravdin-wofford.com

KELLY J. CAPPS, born Waco, Texas, August 14, 1965; admitted to bar, 1993, Virginia; 1995, District of Columbia. *Education:* University of Texas (B.B.A., 1986); American University (J.D., with honors, 1993). *Member:* Fairfax and American (Member, Section of Family Law) Bar Associations; Virginia State Bar (Member, Section of Family Law); The District of Columbia Bar.

(This Listing Continued)

RAVDIN & WOFFORD, A PROFESSIONAL CORPORATION, Washington—Continued

PRACTICE AREAS: Domestic Relations; Trusts and Estates. **Email:** kjcapps@ravdin-wofford.com

REA, CROSS & AUCHINCLOSS

Established in 1954

1707 L STREET, N.W., SUITE 570
WASHINGTON, D.C. 20036
Telephone: 202-785-3700
Fax: 202-659-4934
Email: RCALaw@Erols.com

General and Administrative Law. Practice before all Courts and Federal Administrative Agencies. Interstate Commerce, Trucking, Railroad, Maritime, Government Contracts and Claims, Antitrust Law.

MEMBERS OF FIRM

EDGAR WATKINS (1903-1959).

BRYCE REA, JR., born New York, N.Y., January 22, 1918; admitted to bar, 1941, Virginia; 1953, District of Columbia and U.S. Supreme Court. *Education:* Washington & Lee University (A.B., 1940; LL.B., 1942); Queen's University. Order of the Coif. Assistant Professor of Law, Mercer University, Macon, Georgia, 1948-1949. Associate Professor of Law, American University, Washington, D.C., 1949-1951. Lecturer in Law, George Washington University, 1954-1955. Counsel, Transportation, Public Utilities and Fuels, Office of Price Stabilization, 1951-1953. *Member:* The District of Columbia Bar; Bar Association of the District of Columbia; Virginia State Bar; American Bar Association; American Law Institute; American Judicature Society. **PRACTICE AREAS:** Administrative Law; Interstate Commerce; Transportation.

DONALD E. CROSS (1923-1986).

THOMAS M. AUCHINCLOSS, JR., born Elizabeth, New Jersey, December 13, 1934; admitted to bar, 1968, District of Columbia, U.S. District Court, District of Columbia and U.S. Court of Appeals, District of Columbia Circuit. *Education:* Georgetown University (B.S. in B.A., 1960); Catholic University of America (J.D., 1967). Delta Theta Phi. *Member:* The District of Columbia Bar; Bar Association of the District of Columbia; American Bar Association. **PRACTICE AREAS:** Administrative Law; Interstate Commerce; Transportation; Freight Loss and Damage; Government Contracts.

LEO C. FRANEY, born Washington, D.C., October 8, 1938; admitted to bar, 1964, Virginia; 1971, District of Columbia. *Education:* Georgetown University (B.A., 1960); University of Virginia (LL.B., 1963). *Member:* The District of Columbia Bar; Virginia State Bar. **PRACTICE AREAS:** Administrative Law; Interstate Commerce; Transportation.

BRIAN L. TROIANO, born New York, N.Y., June 12, 1948; admitted to bar, 1973, Tennessee; 1975, District of Columbia. *Education:* Ohio University (B.B.A., 1970); University of Tennessee, College of Law (J.D., 1973). Delta Theta Phi. *Member:* The District of Columbia Bar; American Bar Association. **PRACTICE AREAS:** Administrative Law; Interstate Commerce; Transportation; Freight Loss and Damage; Government Contracts.

KEITH G. O'BRIEN, born San Bernardino, California, May 23, 1937; admitted to bar, 1963, California; 1966, U.S. Supreme Court; U.S. Court of Appeals, Fifth, Sixth and Seventh Circuits; U.S. Court of Appeals for the District of Columbia Circuit; 1989, District of Columbia. *Education:* University of Southern California (B.A., 1957; LL.B., 1962). *Member:* The District of Columbia Bar; State Bar of California; Federal Bar Association. [With USN, active duty, 1963-1967; Capt. USNR]. **PRACTICE AREAS:** Administrative Law; Interstate Commerce; Transportation; Railroads.

JOHN D. HEFFNER, born New York, N.Y., July 22, 1945; admitted to bar, 1972, District of Columbia; U.S. District Court for the District of Columbia and U.S. Court of Appeals for the District of Columbia Circuit; 1984, U.S. Court of Appeals, Third Circuit; 1988, U.S. Court of Appeals, Seventh Circuit. *Education:* University of Virginia (B.A., 1967); Emory University (J.D., 1971). Phi Alpha Delta. Author: "Shortline Railroads," Traffic World, January 1983. Contributing Writer: "Modern Railroads, Shortlines and Regionals". Lecturer: Annual Meeting of the National Conference of State Railway Officials, August, 1990; The American Public Transit Association Commuter Rail Conference, April, 1991; "Railroading for NonRailroaders", The Railroad Financial Corporation Conference, June, 1991. Attorney Advisor: Office of Proceedings, Interstate Commerce Commission, 1971-1974; Office of General Counsel, U.S. Railway Association, 1974-1976. *Member:* The District of Columbia Bar; Association for Transportation Law, Logistics and Policy (President, D.C. Chapter); National Association of Railroad Passengers (Board Member). **PRACTICE AREAS:** Administrative Law; Interstate Commerce; Transportation; Railroads.

JOHN DANIEL REAVES

1225 19TH STREET N.W., SUITE 450
WASHINGTON, D.C. 20036
Telephone: 202-296-4950
Fax: 202-296-4951
Email: jdreavesoffice@yahoo.com
URL: http://www.lawyers.com/johndanielreaves

Business Counselling, E-Commerce Law, Internet Law, Trade Association Law, Emerging Business Law, Antitrust Regulation, Trade Regulation, Unfair Trade, Consumer Protection, Regulatory Law, Federal Trade Commission, Corporate Law, Small Business Law, Emerging Growth Law, Strategic Alliances, Complex Litigation.

FIRM PROFILE: Mr. Reaves is presently the General Counsel to the United States Conference of Mayors. His national practice is based in Washington, D.C. and provides representation for a variety of businesses and associations, including trade groups, metal, textile, wood products manufacturers. high tech companies, aeronautical manufacturers, exporters, food products, transportation and medical suppliers and producers.

JOHN DANIEL REAVES, born Camp Hill, Alabama, March 14, 1939; admitted to bar, 1965, Alabama; 1972, District of Columbia; 1977, U.S. Supreme Court. *Education:* Auburn University (B.S., 1961); University of Virginia (LL.B., 1964). Phillip Frances Dupont Scholar. Member, Editorial Board, Virginia Law Review, 1963-1964. Author: "The Application of the United States Arbitration Act to Miller Act Claims," Virginia Law Review, January 1964; "The Federal Anti-Injunction Statute in the Aftermath of Atlantic Coast Line Railroad," Georgia Law Review, 1971. Assistant Professor of Law, 1965-1968 and with Tenure, 1968-1971, University of Georgia Law School. Visiting Professor of Law, George Washington University National Law Center, Summer, 1975. Law Clerk to the late Honorable Richard T. Rives, United States Court of Appeals, Fifth Circuit, 1964-1965. Attorney, Bureau of Competition, Federal Trade Commission, 1972-1973. Legal Advisor, The Honorable Elizabeth Hanford Dole, Commissioner, Federal Trade Commission, 1973-1976. Senior Fellow, Federal Judicial Center, Washington, D.C., 1971-1972. General Counsel, United States Conference of Mayors, 1987—. Partner, Baker & Hostetler, 1986-1995. Chairman of the Board, Smithsonian Early Enrichment Center. Junior Warden, 1998— and Member of the Vestry, 1991-1994, St. Alban's Church. Member, Board of Directors, The Woolly Mammoth Theater Company and Leadership Council, 1993—. *Member:* District of Columbia Bar; Alabama State Bar; American Bar Association. **PRACTICE AREAS:** Antitrust; Trade Regulation Law.

REBOUL, MACMURRAY, HEWITT, MAYNARD & KRISTOL

SUITE 406, 1111 NINETEENTH STREET, N.W.
WASHINGTON, D.C. 20036
Telephone: 202-429-0004
Telecopier: 202-429-8743; 202-296-0627
Email: lawyers@reboul.com
URL: http://www.reboul.com

New York, N.Y. Office: 45 Rockefeller Plaza, 10111. Telephone: 212-841-5700.

General Practice. Corporate, Corporate Finance/Securities, Mergers and Acquisitions, Venture Capital/Buyouts, Start-Ups, International, Banking, Litigation, Commercial Litigation, Bankruptcy, Reorganization and Restructuring, ERISA, Telecommunications, Product Liability Defense, Labor/Employment, Alternative Dispute Resolution, Criminal Defense and Tax.

RESIDENT PARTNER

JAMES E. MAGEE, born Newport, Rhode Island, June 15, 1949; admitted to bar, 1975, District of Columbia; 1979, Rhode Island and Massachusetts; 1993, Maryland. *Education:* University of Rhode Island (B.A., 1971); Georgetown University (J.D., 1974). Editor, Georgetown Law Journal, 1973-1974. *Member:* The District of Columbia Bar; Bar Association of the District of Columbia; Rhode Island, Massachusetts and American Bar Associations; Federal Communications Bar Association. **PRACTICE AREAS:** Regulatory; Telecommunications and Energy; Tort Defense/Product Liability. **Email:** jmagee@reboul.com

RESIDENT ASSOCIATE

KRISTIE S. HASSETT, born Milford, Delaware, July 29, 1961; admitted to bar, 1986, Pennsylvania; 1990, New York; 1993, District of Columbia. *Education:* Swarthmore College (B.A., 1983); University of Pennsylvania Law

(This Listing Continued)

School (J.D., 1986). *Member:* American Bar Association; Federal Communications Bar Association. ***PRACTICE AREAS:*** Regulatory; Telecommunications and Energy; Tort Defense/Product Liability. ***Email:*** khassett@reboul.com

STAFF ATTORNEYS

JENNIFER ANN NEWBERRY, born Pasadena, Texas, May 19, 1972; admitted to bar, 1997, Virginia; 1999, District of Columbia. *Education:* Texas A & M University (B.A., 1994); George Mason University (J.D., 1997). *Member:* Virginia State Bar; District of Columbia Bar; American Bar Association; Federal Communications Bar Association. ***PRACTICE AREAS:*** Regulatory; Telecommunications and Energy. ***Email:*** jnewberry@reboul.com

BERNARD M. SCHULTE, born New Brunswick, New Jersey, November 29, 1962; admitted to bar, 1987, Ohio; 1990, District of Columbia; 1993, Maryland. *Education:* Bucknell University (B.A., 1984); Ohio State University College of Law (J.D., 1987). *Member:* Maryland State and American Bar Associations; The District of Columbia Bar; Federal Communications Bar Association. ***PRACTICE AREAS:*** Regulatory; Telecommunications and Energy; Tort Defense/Product Liability. ***Email:*** bschulte@reboul.com

(For Biographical data on all Personnel, see Professional Biographies at New York, New York)

REDDY, BEGLEY & McCORMICK, LLP

Established in 1968

2175 K STREET, N.W., SUITE 350
WASHINGTON, D.C. 20037-1803
Telephone: 202-659-5700
Facsimile: 202-659-5711
Email: rbm@rbmfcclaw.com
URL: http://www.lawyers.com/rbmfcclaw

Communications, Administrative, Copyright and Trademark Law, Broadcasting Law, Satellite Communications, FCC Regulations, FCC Licensing, Broadcast Station Transfers, Music Licensing.

MEMBERS OF FIRM

DENNIS F. BEGLEY, born Brooklyn, New York, April 13, 1943; admitted to bar, 1972, Virginia; 1973, District of Columbia; registered to practice before U.S. Patent and Trademark Office. *Education:* Rensselaer Polytechnic Institute (B.E.E., 1964); George Washington University (M.S.B.A., 1969); American University (J.D., 1972). Member, American University Law Review, 1970-1971. Law Clerk to the Honorable Frank Q. Nebeker, Associate Judge, Court of Appeals, District of Columbia, 1972-1973. *Member:* The District of Columbia Bar; Virginia State Bar; American Bar Association; Federal Communications Bar Association. [1st Lt., U.S. Army Security Agency, 1964-1966]. ***PRACTICE AREAS:*** Communications Law; Administrative Law. ***Email:*** dbegley@rbmfcclaw.com

MATTHEW H. McCORMICK, born Medford, Oregon, May 31, 1950; admitted to bar, 1979, Oregon and U.S. Court of Appeals for the District of Columbia Circuit; 1980, District of Columbia. *Education:* University of Oregon (B.S., 1976; J.D., 1979). Managing Editor, Oregon Law Review, 1978-1979. *Member:* The District of Columbia Bar (Member, Administrative Law Section); Oregon State Bar (Member, House of Delegates, 2000-2001); American Bar Association; Federal Communications Bar Association. ***PRACTICE AREAS:*** Communications Law; Copyright and Trademark Law. ***Email:*** mmccormick@rbmfcclaw.com

REED SMITH LLP

SUITE 1100 - EAST TOWER
1301 K STREET, N.W.
WASHINGTON, D.C. 20005-3317
Telephone: 202-414-9200
FAX: 202-414-9299
Email: reedsmith@reedsmith.com
URL: http://www.reedsmith.com

Pittsburgh, Pennsylvania Office: 435 Sixth Avenue, 15219-1886. Telephone: 412-288-3131. FAX: 412-288-3063.
Philadelphia, Pennsylvania Office: 2500 One Liberty Place, 19103-7301. Telephone: 215-851-8100. FAX: 215-851-1420.
Harrisburg, Pennsylvania Office: 213 Market Street, 17101-2132. Telephone: 717-234-5988. FAX: 717-236-3777.
Princeton, New Jersey Office: 136 Main Street, Suite 250, 08540-5799. Telephone: 609-987-0050. FAX: 609-951-0824.
New York, N.Y. Office: 375 Park Avenue, 17th Floor, 10152. Telephone: 212-521-5400. FAX: 212-521-5450.
Newark, New Jersey Office: The Legal Center, One Riverfront Plaza, First Floor, 07102-5400. Telephone: 973-621-3200. FAX: 973-621-3199.

(This Listing Continued)

Wilmington, Delaware Office: 1201 Market Street, Suite 1500, 19801. Telephone: 302-778-7500. FAX: 302-778-7575.
McLean, Virginia Office: Suite 1100, 8251 Greensboro Drive, 22102-3844. Telephone: 703-734-4600. FAX: 703-734-4699.
Falls Church, Virginia Office: Suite 1400, 3110 Fairview Park Drive, 22042. Telephone: 703-641-4200. FAX: 703-641-4340.
Leesburg, Virginia Office: 44084 Riverside Parkway, Suite 300. 20176. Telephone: 703-729-8500. Metro: 703-478-1992. FAX: 703-478-8003.
Richmond, Virginia Office: Riverfront Plaza, West Tower, 901 East Byrd Street, Suite 1700, 23219-4069. Telephone: 804-344-3400. FAX: 804-344-3410.
London, England Office: Reed Smith Warner Cranston, Pickfords Wharf, Clink Street, SE1 9DG. Telephone: +44-20-7403-2900. FAX: +44-20-7403-4221.
Coventry, England Office: Reed Smith Warner Cranston, Park House, Station Square, CV1 2FL. Telephone: +44 24 7629 3000. FAX: +44 24 7629 3030. DX: 11203 Coventry 1.

Antitrust and Trade Regulation, Asbestos, Bank Regulatory, Bankruptcy, China/Asia, Communications, Construction, Consumer Financial Services, Corporate and Securities, E-Commerce, Eminent Domain/Condemnation, Employee Benefits, Employment Discrimination Litigation, Employment Law, Energy and Natural Resources, Environmental, Equipment Leasing, Family Business, Financial Services, Financial Services Insurance, Financial Services Litigation, First Amendment, Food, Drug & Device, Franchise, Government Contracts & Export Compliance, Government Relations, Health Care, Higher Education, Immigration, Information Technology, Insurance, Insurance Coverage, Intellectual Property, International, Land Use, Litigation, Media and Entertainment, Mergers and Acquisitions, Non-Profit Organizations, Product Liability, Professional Liability, Project Finance, Public Finance, Real Estate, Restrictive Covenants/Trade Secrets, Satellite Transactions, Tax, Technology, Telecommunications, Tissue Engineering and Biomedical Applications, Trusts & Estates, Venture, White Collar Crime, Year 2000.

FIRM PROFILE: Founded nearly 125 years ago, Reed Smith has been handling the interests of clients both large and small in a broad spectrum of areas. Our client base has expanded from some of Pittsburgh's leading companies and founding families to include a wide variety of Fortune 500 companies, privately held companies and emerging technology businesses.

From our beginnings in Pittsburgh we have expanded to 12 offices in the United States and two in the United Kingdom, and currently include the experience of more than 650 attorneys. Reed Smith is now a global top 30 law firm, and is ranked among the top 100 patent firms. We are counsel to 23 of the top 25 United States banks; 14 of the Fortune e-50 companies; seven of the top 10 pharmaceutical companies; and 50 of the world's leading drug and device manufacturers.

From pharmaceutical companies to financial institutions, from intellectual property dilemmas to complex health care issues, our clients look to us to help them navigate through changing industry environments.

Knox & Reed	1877-1902
Reed Smith Shaw & Beal	1902-1922
Reed Smith Shaw & McClay	1922-2000

MEMBERS OF FIRM

KEVIN R. BARRY, admitted to bar, 1981, D.C. *Education:* Fairfield University (B.A., 1974); Catholic University of America (J.D., 1981). ***PRACTICE AREAS:*** Health Care. ***Email:*** kbarry@reedsmith.com

A. SCOTT BOLDEN, admitted to bar, 1988, N.Y.; 1990, Il.; 1991, D.C. *Education:* Morehouse College (B.A., cum laude, 1984); Howard University School of Law (J.D., cum laude, 1987). ***PRACTICE AREAS:*** Litigation. ***Email:*** abolden@reedsmith.com

ELIZABETH B. CARDER, admitted to bar, 1979, D.C. *Education:* Brown University (A.B., magna cum laude, 1975); Marshall-Wythe School of Law, College of William & Mary (J.D., 1978). ***PRACTICE AREAS:*** Health Care. ***Email:*** ecarder@reedsmith.com

BERNARD J. CASEY, admitted to bar, 1967, R.I.; 1972, D.C. *Education:* Providence College (A.B., 1964); Catholic University of America (J.D., 1967). ***PRACTICE AREAS:*** Litigation. ***Email:*** bcasey@reedsmith.com

DONALD O. CLARK, admitted to bar, 1963, S.C.; 1964, Ga.; 1997, D.C. *Education:* University of South Carolina (A.B., 1956; J.D., cum laude, 1963); University of Illinois (M.A., 1957). ***PRACTICE AREAS:*** International. ***Email:*** dclark@reedsmith.com

GEORGE R. CLARK, admitted to bar, 1972, Il.; 1973, D.C. *Education:* University of Notre Dame (B.S., 1969); University of Illinois (J.D., 1972). ***PRACTICE AREAS:*** Litigation. ***Email:*** gclark@reedsmith.com

FRANCIS P. DICELLO, admitted to bar, 1966, Ct.; 1967, D.C.; 1982, Va.; 1984, Md. *Education:* University of Notre Dame (A.B., 1963); Fordham University (LL.B., 1966). ***PRACTICE AREAS:*** Bankruptcy. ***Email:*** fdicello@reedsmith.com

(This Listing Continued)

REED SMITH LLP, Washington—Continued

ERIC A. DUBELIER, admitted to bar, 1981, La.; 1986, N.Y.; 1989, D.C. *Education:* Tulane University (B.A., with honors, 1977; M.B.A., J.D., 1981). ***PRACTICE AREAS:*** White Collar Crime; Government Contracts; Export Compliance; Civil Litigation. ***Email:*** edubelir@reedsmith.com

DAVID C. EVANS, admitted to bar, 1971, Indiana; 1972, District of Columbia. *Education:* Indiana University (B.S., 1968; J.D., 1971). ***PRACTICE AREAS:*** Government Relations. ***Email:*** devans@reedsmith.com

DONALD A. FARMER JR., admitted to bar, 1970, D.C. and Calif. *Education:* Stanford University (B.A., 1966); Stanford University School of Law (J.D., 1969). ***PRACTICE AREAS:*** Antitrust; Litigation. ***Email:*** dfarmer@reedsmith.com

THOMAS C. FOX, admitted to bar, 1966, Va.; 1967, D.C. *Education:* Muskingum College (B.A., 1963); George Washington University (LL.B., 1966). ***PRACTICE AREAS:*** Health Care. ***Email:*** tfox@reedsmith.com

JUDITH L. HARRIS, admitted to bar, 1973, Oh.; 1974, D.C. *Education:* University of Michigan (B.A., highest honors, 1970); Yale University (J.D., 1973). ***PRACTICE AREAS:*** Communications; Antitrust; Litigation. ***Email:*** jlharris@reedsmith.com

HENRY A. HART, admitted to bar, 1975, Maryland; 1976, District of Columbia; 1983, Virginia. *Education:* Amherst College (B.A., cum laude, 1972); Georgetown University (J.D., 1975). ***PRACTICE AREAS:*** Government Relations; Trade Association Law; Banking Law; Business Law. ***Email:*** hhart@reedsmith.com

GORDON W. HATHEWAY, JR., admitted to bar, 1968, D.C.; 1969, U.S. Court of Military Appeals. *Education:* Bucknell University (B.S., 1965); George Washington University (J.D., 1968; LL.M., 1973). ***PRACTICE AREAS:*** Litigation. ***Email:*** ghatheway@reedsmith.com

ROBERT J. HILL, admitted to bar, 1988, D.C. *Education:* University of Michigan (B.A., 1984; J.D., 1987). ***PRACTICE AREAS:*** Health Care. ***Email:*** rhill@reedsmith.com

JAMES K. KEARNEY, admitted to bar, 1976, Virginia; 1977, District of Columbia. *Education:* University of Pittsburgh (B.A., 1973); University of Virginia (J.D., 1976). ***PRACTICE AREAS:*** Government Contracts; Export Compliance. ***Email:*** jkearney@reedsmith.com

HELEN G. KIRSCH, admitted to bar, 1988, Md.; 1990, D.C. *Education:* Georgetown University (A.B., 1983); Villanova University (J.D., 1988). ***PRACTICE AREAS:*** Litigation. ***Email:*** hkirsch@reedsmith.com

CAROL COLBORN LOEPERE, admitted to bar, 1985, D.C. and Md. *Education:* Radcliffe College (B.A., 1981); New York University (J.D., 1984). ***PRACTICE AREAS:*** Health Care. ***Email:*** cloepere@reedsmith.com

NANCY A. LUQUE, admitted to bar, 1976, Ca., 1989, D.C. *Education:* San Diego State University (B.A., 1973); University of San Diego (J.D., 1976). ***PRACTICE AREAS:*** Litigation; Government Contracts; Export Compliance. ***Email:*** nluque@reedsmith.com

MICHAEL C. LYNCH, admitted to bar, 1983, D.C. *Education:* Williams College (B.A., 1979); Georgetown University (J.D., 1983). ***PRACTICE AREAS:*** Labor and Employment. ***Email:*** mlynch@reedsmith.com

DORN C. McGRATH III, admitted to bar, 1982, Va.; 1985, D.C. *Education:* Davidson College (A.B., 1978); George Washington University (J.D., 1982). ***PRACTICE AREAS:*** Government Contracts; Export Compliance. ***Email:*** dmcgrath@reedsmith.com

KATHLEEN H. McGUAN, admitted to bar, 1981, D.C. *Education:* American University (B.A., 1975); University of Pennsylvania (M.A., 1978); Catholic University of America (J.D., 1981). ***PRACTICE AREAS:*** Litigation. ***Email:*** kmcguan@reedsmith.com

JOSEPH W. METRO, admitted to bar, 1989, Pa.; 1991, D.C. *Education:* Dickinson College (B.A., 1986); George Washington University (J.D., 1989). ***PRACTICE AREAS:*** Health Care. ***Email:*** jmetro@reedsmith.com

RICHARD L. MOORHOUSE, admitted to bar, 1982, Ma.; 1984, D.C. *Education:* University of Massachusetts (B.A., 1969); Suffolk University (M.A., 1972; J.D., 1982). ***PRACTICE AREAS:*** Government Contracts; Export Compliance. ***Email:*** rmoorhouse@reedsmith.com

STEPHEN P. MURPHY, admitted to bar, 1976, D.C. *Education:* Boston College (A.B., cum laude, 1972); Catholic University of America (J.D., 1976). ***PRACTICE AREAS:*** Litigation. ***Email:*** smurphy@reedsmith.com

DONALD J. MYERS, admitted to bar, 1968, N.Y.; 1975, D.C. *Education:* City College of the City University of New York (B.A., 1964); Cornell University (J.D., 1967); Georgetown University (LL.M. in Taxation, 1973). ***PRACTICE AREAS:*** Employee Benefits. ***Email:*** dmyers@reedsmith.com

(This Listing Continued)

JOSEPH A. RIESER, JR., admitted to bar, 1974, Pennsylvania; 1976, District of Columbia. *Education:* Princeton University (A.B., 1969); Harvard University (M.P.P., 1974; J.D., cum laude, 1974). ***PRACTICE AREAS:*** Tax. ***Email:*** jrieser@reedsmith.com

CHRISTOPHER L. RISSETTO, admitted to bar, 1973, Wi.; 1980, D.C.; 1981, Va. *Education:* San Francisco State University (B.A., 1968); University of California at Davis (M.A., 1970); University of Wisconsin (J.D., 1973). ***PRACTICE AREAS:*** Government Contracts; Export Compliance. ***Email:*** crissetto@reedsmith.com

GORDON B. SCHATZ, admitted to bar, 1980, Pa.; 1982, D.C.; 1983, Md. *Education:* Haverford College (B.A., 1974); Temple University (J.D., 1980). ***PRACTICE AREAS:*** Health Care. ***Email:*** gschatz@reedsmith.com

MARC J. SCHEINESON, admitted to bar, 1980, Oh.; 1983, D.C. *Education:* University of Cincinnati (B.A., 1977; J.D., 1980); Georgetown University Law Center (M.L.T., 1987). ***PRACTICE AREAS:*** Health Care; Food, Drug and Cosmetic Law. ***Email:*** mschein@reedsmith.com

C. STEVENS SEALE, admitted to bar, 1987, Ms., 1999, D.C. *Education:* University of Mississippi (B.A., 1975; J.D., 1987). ***LANGUAGES:*** Spanish. ***PRACTICE AREAS:*** Government Relations. ***Email:*** sseale@reedsmith.com

OLIVIA SHAY-BYRNE, admitted to bar, 1982, Tex.; 1984, Md. and Oh.; 1989, D.C. *Education:* Vanderbilt University; Bowdoin College (B.A., 1979); University of Toledo (J.D., 1982); Georgetown University (LL.M. in Tax, 1987). ***PRACTICE AREAS:*** Real Estate. ***Email:*** oshay@reedsmith.com

DOUGLAS K. SPAULDING, admitted to bar, 1977, Va; 1978, D.C. *Education:* Marquette University (B.A., 1970); University of Virginia (J.D., 1977). ***PRACTICE AREAS:*** Litigation. ***Email:*** dspaulding@reedsmith.com

EUGENE TILLMAN, admitted to bar, 1976, Ca.; 1979, D.C. *Education:* University of California at Los Angeles (B.A., cum laude, 1973; J.D., 1976). ***PRACTICE AREAS:*** Health Care. ***Email:*** etillman@reedsmith.com

COUNSEL

KENNETH S. BARR, admitted to bar, 1980, Ga.; 1981, D.C. *Education:* Boston University (B.A., 1977); Mercer University (J.D., 1980); Georgetown University (M.L.T., 1984). ***PRACTICE AREAS:*** Corporate; Finance. ***Email:*** kbarr@reedsmith.com

LINDA A. BAUMANN, admitted to bar, 1975, D.C.; 1998, N.J. *Education:* Brown University (B.A., magna cum laude, 1972); Columbia University (J.D., 1975). ***PRACTICE AREAS:*** Health Care. ***Email:*** lbaumann@reedsmith.com

JOHN A. BECK, admitted to bar, 1951, D.C., Mo. and Va.; 1962, Md. *Education:* University of Tulsa (B.A., 1949); George Washington University (J.D., 1950). ***PRACTICE AREAS:*** Corporate; Finance. ***Email:*** jbeck@reedsmith.com

AMY B. BERGNER, admitted to bar, 1983, D.C. *Education:* Smith College (B.A., 1978); American University (J.D., 1983). ***PRACTICE AREAS:*** Employee Benefits. ***Email:*** abergner@reedsmith.com

MARY E. BUCKLES, admitted to bar, 1981, Ma.; 1986, D.C.; registered to practice before U.S. Patent and Trademark Office. *Education:* Wellesley College (B.A., 1978); American University (J.D., 1981). ***PRACTICE AREAS:*** Intellectual Property; Copyrights; Patents; Trademarks; Trade Secrets. ***Email:*** mbuckle@reedsmith.com

ROBERT D. CLARK, admitted to bar, 1981, D.C. *Education:* University of Maryland (B.A., 1976); Howard University (J.D., 1981). ***PRACTICE AREAS:*** Health Care. ***Email:*** rclark@reedsmith.com

WILLIAM R. COWDEN, admitted to bar, 1988, Il.; 1989, Ca.; 1990, D.C. *Education:* University of Michigan (B.A., 1984); University of Notre Dame (J.D., cum laude, 1988). ***PRACTICE AREAS:*** Health Care. ***Email:*** wcowden@reedsmith.com

JOSÉ A. FUENTES, admitted to bar, 1981, U.S. District Court, District of Puerto Rico; 1989, U.S. Supreme Court; 1999, D.C. *Education:* University of Tampa (B.S., 1977); Inter-American University School of Law, Puerto Rico (J.D., 1980). ***LANGUAGES:*** Spanish and English. ***PRACTICE AREAS:*** Government Relations. ***Email:*** jfuentes@reedsmith.com

ROBERT H. JACKSON, admitted to bar, 1976, Mn.; 1977, Ne.; 1980, Ia.; 1985, D.C. *Education:* University of St. Thomas (B.A., summa cum laude, 1973); University of Minnesota (J.D., cum laude, 1976). ***PRACTICE AREAS:*** Communications. ***Email:*** rjackson@reedsmith.com

ROBERT M. MARINO, admitted to bar, 1986, Va.; 1987, D.C. *Education:* Le Moyne College (B.A., summa cum laude, 1983); Georgetown University Law Center (J.D., cum laude, 1986). ***PRACTICE AREAS:*** Bankruptcy. ***Email:*** rmarino@reedsmith.com

GRANT E. MITCHELL, admitted to bar, 1965, D.C.; 1989, Md. *Education:* State University of New York (B.S., 1958); University of Florida (M.A., 1961); Tulane University (J.D., 1964). ***PRACTICE AREAS:*** Financial Services. ***Email:*** gmitchell@reedsmith.com

(This Listing Continued)

DAVID OBER, admitted to bar, 1991, Md.; 1993, D.C. *Education:* Tulane University (B.A., 1977); American University (J.D., cum laude, 1991). ***PRACTICE AREAS:*** Litigation. ***Email:*** dober@reedsmith.com

PHILLIPS S. PETER, admitted to bar, 1959, Ca. (Not admitted in District of Columbia). *Education:* University of Virginia (B.A., 1954; J.D., 1959). ***PRACTICE AREAS:*** Government Relations. ***Email:*** ppeter@reedsmith.com

LEE A. RAU, admitted to bar, 1966, Calif.; 1972, D.C.; 1986, Va. *Education:* University of Minnesota (B.S.B., 1962); University of California at Los Angeles (J.D., 1965). ***PRACTICE AREAS:*** Antitrust; Litigation. ***Email:*** llee@reedsmith.com

MICHAEL B. RICHMAN, admitted to bar, 1988, Md.; 1989, D.C. *Education:* Princeton University (A.B., 1985); Columbia University (J.D., 1988). ***PRACTICE AREAS:*** Employee Benefits. ***Email:*** mrichman@reedsmith.com

HENRY SANCHEZ, JR., admitted to bar, 1984, Pa., N.J. and U.S. Dist. Ct., Dist. of N.J.; 1987, Fla.; 1990, U.S. Dist. Ct., Middle Dist. of Fla. (Not admitted in District of Columbia). *Education:* Pennsylvania State University; Richard Stockton State College (B.A., 1977); Rutgers University (J.D., 1984); Georgetown University (LL.M., Securities Regulation, 1988). ***PRACTICE AREAS:*** Corporate Law. ***Email:*** hsanchez@reedsmith.com

ANN E. SCHMITT, admitted to bar, 1981, Va.; 1985, D.C.; 1986, Md. *Education:* College of Mount St. Vincent (B.S., 1969); American University (J.D., 1981). ***PRACTICE AREAS:*** Bankruptcy. ***Email:*** aschmitt@reedsmith.com

STEPHEN M. SORETT, admitted to bar, 1976, Md.; 1977, D.C. *Education:* Yale University (B.A., 1971); George Washington University (J.D., 1976). ***PRACTICE AREAS:*** Government Contracts; Export Compliance. ***Email:*** ssorett@reedsmith.com

JOHN H. STERNE, JR., admitted to bar, 1993, Va.; 2000, D.C. *Education:* Old Dominion University (B.A., 1987); Washington and Lee University (J.D., 1993). ***PRACTICE AREAS:*** Government Relations. ***Email:*** jsterne@reedsmith.com

PATRICIA H. WITTIE, admitted to bar, 1977, D.C. *Education:* Washington University (B.A., 1972); George Washington University (J.D., with honors, 1977). ***PRACTICE AREAS:*** Government Contracts; Export Compliance. ***Email:*** pwittie@reedsmith.com

ASSOCIATES

SUELYN SMITH ATHEY, admitted to bar, 1986, Md. (Not admitted in District of Columbia). *Education:* University of Maryland (B.A., 1980); Western New England College of Law (J.D., 1986). ***PRACTICE AREAS:*** Corporate; Finance. ***Email:*** sathey@reedsmith.com

BRAD P. BENDER, admitted to bar, 2001, Pa. (Not admitted in District of Columbia). *Education:* University of North Carolina at Chapel Hill (B.A., 1997); Pennsylvania State University-Dickinson School of Law (J.D., 2000). ***Email:*** bbender@reedsmith.com

JACQUELINE E. BENNETT, admitted to bar, 1991, Md.; 1993, Va. (Not admitted in District of Columbia). *Education:* Harvard University (A.B., 1986); Georgetown University (J.D., 1991). ***PRACTICE AREAS:*** Litigation. ***Email:*** jbennet@reedsmith.com

DAVID J. BLOCH, admitted to bar, 1993, N.J.; 1994, Pa.; 1995, D.C. *Education:* Columbia University (B.A., cum laude, 1990); University of Pennsylvania (J.D., 1993). ***PRACTICE AREAS:*** Health Care. ***Email:*** dbloch@reedsmith.com

DANIELLE R. CESARANO, admitted to bar, 1999, Md. and D.C. *Education:* University of Richmond (B.A., cum laude, 1993); American University, Washington College of Law (J.D., cum laude, 1998; M.S., 1999). ***LANGUAGES:*** French. ***PRACTICE AREAS:*** Litigation. ***Email:*** dcesarano@reedsmith.com

JIWEN CHEN, admitted to bar, 1997, China; 2001, N.Y. (Not admitted in District of Columbia). *Education:* Tianjin University in Tianjin, China (B.E. and B.A., 1995); Fudan University Law School in Shanghai, China (LL.B., with honors, 1997); George Washington University (LL.M., 2000). ***PRACTICE AREAS:*** Intellectual Property; Patents; Copyrights; Trademarks; Trade Secrets. ***Email:*** jchen@reedsmith.com

DANIEL A. CODY, admitted to bar, 1999, New York; 2001, District of Columbia. *Education:* Swarthmore College (B.A., 1993); College of William & Mary (J.D., 1998). ***PRACTICE AREAS:*** Health Care. ***Email:*** dcody@reedsmith.com

GAIL L. DAUBERT, admitted to bar, 1999, Il. (Not admitted in District of Columbia). *Education:* Northwestern University (B.S., with distinction, 1991); Loyola University School of Law (M.S., 1995); American University (J.D., cum laude, 1999). ***PRACTICE AREAS:*** Health Care. ***Email:*** gdaubert@reedsmith.com

(This Listing Continued)

BRIDNETTA D. EDWARDS, admitted to bar, 1991, Md. and Pa.; 1992, D.C. *Education:* Howard University (B.B.A., 1986); Catholic University of America (J.D., 1989). ***PRACTICE AREAS:*** Labor and Employment. ***Email:*** bedwards@reedsmith.com

KURT D. FERSTL, admitted to bar, 1999, Va. (Not admitted in District of Columbia). *Education:* College of William & Mary (B.A., 1990); George Mason University School of Law (J.D., cum laude, 1999). ***PRACTICE AREAS:*** Government Contracts; Export Compliance. ***Email:*** kferstl@reedsmith.com

PHILIP J. FICK, admitted to bar, 1998, Va.; 2000, D.C. *Education:* St. Louis University (B.S.B.A., 1978); Georgetown University (J.D., 1998). ***PRACTICE AREAS:*** Real Estate. ***Email:*** pfick@reedsmith.com

KELLY CALL GRIFFITH, admitted to bar, 1998, N.Y.; 1999, Va. (Not admitted in District of Columbia). *Education:* State University of New York at Binghamton (B.A., 1990); St. John's University School of Law (J.D., 1997). ***PRACTICE AREAS:*** Bankruptcy. ***Email:*** kgriffith@reedsmith.com

SCOT T. HASSELMAN, admitted to bar, 1998, Ca.; 2000, D.C. *Education:* University of California at Santa Cruz (B.A., 1991); American University (J.D., cum laude, 1998). ***PRACTICE AREAS:*** Health Care. ***Email:*** shasselman@reedsmith.com

JASON M. HEALY, admitted to bar, 1999, Md.; 2000, D.C. *Education:* Colgate University (B.A., 1994); Catholic University of America (J.D., 1999). ***PRACTICE AREAS:*** Health Care. ***Email:*** jhealy@reedsmith.com

DAVID T. HICKEY, admitted to bar, 1998, Va. (Not admitted in District of Columbia). *Education:* Virginia Military Institute (B.A., 1988); Catholic University (J.D., 1997). ***PRACTICE AREAS:*** Government Contracts; Export Compliance. ***Email:*** dhickey@reedsmith.com

ANDREW L. HURST, admitted to bar, 1996, Va. and N.J.; 1997, D.C. *Education:* Seton Hall University (B.A., magna cum laude, 1993); Georgetown University Law Center (J.D., cum laude, 1996). ***PRACTICE AREAS:*** Litigation. ***Email:*** ahurst@reedsmith.com

RICHARD F. JOHNS, admitted to bar, 1999, Md.; 2000, D.C. *Education:* Morehouse College (B.S., 1994); George Washington University (M.S., 1995; J.D., 1999);. ***PRACTICE AREAS:*** Litigation. ***Email:*** rjohns@reedsmith.com

ROBBIE N. KOCH, admitted to bar, 1998, Md. and D.C. *Education:* San Diego State University (B.A., 1993); Universität Tübingen; American University (J.D., 1997). ***LANGUAGES:*** Spanish, German. ***PRACTICE AREAS:*** Government Relations. ***Email:*** rkoch@reedsmith.com

ELIZABETH A. MACKENZIE, admitted to bar, 1999, California (Not admitted in District of Columbia). *Education:* University of California (B.A., 1994); Tulane University (J.D., cum laude, 1998). ***PRACTICE AREAS:*** Health Care. ***Email:*** emackenzie@reedsmith.com

EDWARD J. MCANDREW, admitted to bar, 1995, N.J. and Pa.; 1998, D.C. *Education:* College of New Jersey (B.A., 1992); The Catholic University of America (J.D ., 1995). ***PRACTICE AREAS:*** Litigation. ***Email:*** emcandrew@reedsmith.com

LORRAINE T. MULLINGS, admitted to bar, 2000, Ct. and N.Y. (Not admitted in District of Columbia). *Education:* Georgetown University (B.A., 1995); George Washington University (J.D., 1998). ***PRACTICE AREAS:*** Government Contracts; Export Compliance. ***Email:*** lmullings@reedsmith.com

DEXTER U. NUTALL, admitted to bar, 1996, Md.; 1997, D.C. *Education:* Mount St. Mary's College (B.S., 1991); Howard University (J.D., 1995). ***PRACTICE AREAS:*** Litigation. ***Email:*** dnutall@reedsmith.com

FRANK T. PIMENTEL, admitted to bar, 1995, N.Y.; 2000, D.C. *Education:* University of Notre Dame (B.A., 1987; J.D., cum laude, 1994). ***PRACTICE AREAS:*** Litigation; Criminal Law. ***Email:*** fpimentel@reedsmith.com

JAMES P. SCHULZ, admitted to bar, 1996, Fla.; 1997, D.C. *Education:* Florida State University (B.A., 1979); Catholic University of America (J.D., 1996). ***PRACTICE AREAS:*** Communications; Satellite Communications; Telecommunications. ***Email:*** pschulz@reedsmith.com

TAMARA V. SCOVILLE, admitted to bar, 1994, Md.; 1995, D.C. *Education:* Gettysburg College (B.A., 1988); Catholic University of America-The Columbus School of Law (J.D., 1994). ***PRACTICE AREAS:*** Health Care. ***Email:*** tscoville@reedsmith.com

EVAN D. SELIG, admitted to bar, 1999, Md. (Not admitted in District of Columbia). *Education:* Colgate University (B.A., cum laude, 1994); George Washington University (J.D., 1999). ***Email:*** eselig@reedsmith.com

DONNA M. SHEINBACH, admitted to bar, 2001, Pa. and N.J. (Not admitted in District of Columbia). *Education:* Miami University (B.A., 1994); Catholic University of America (J.D., 2000). ***Email:*** dsheinbach@reedsmith.com

DAVID L. TANENHOLZ, admitted to bar, 2000, Md. (Not admitted in District of Columbia). *Education:* University of Maryland (B.S., magna cum laude, 1994); George Washington University (J.D., 2000). ***Email:*** dtanenholz@reedsmith.com

(This Listing Continued)

REED SMITH LLP, Washington—Continued

NIGEL L. WILKINSON, admitted to bar, 2001, Va. (Not admitted in District of Columbia). *Education:* George Mason University (B.A., 1995); Catholic University of America (J.D., 2000). ***PRACTICE AREAS:*** Labor and Employment. ***Email:*** nwilkinson@reedsmith.com

JARRELL E. WILLIAMSON, admitted to bar, 2000, Tx. (Not admitted in District of Columbia). *Education:* University of Texas at Austin (B.A., 1995; J.D., 2000). ***PRACTICE AREAS:*** Government Relations. ***Email:*** jwilliamson@reedsmith.com

(For biographical data on personnel in Pittsburgh, Philadelphia and Harrisburg, Pennsylvania, Falls Church, Leesburg, McLean and Richmond, Virginia, New York, New York, Princeton and Newark, New Jersey, Wilmington, Delaware and London, England, see Professional Biographies at those locations)

REES, BROOME & DIAZ, P.C.

WASHINGTON, D.C.

(See Vienna, Virginia)

Alternative Dispute Resolution, Bankruptcy, Commercial Transactions, Community Associations, Construction Law, Corporate Law, Employment Law, Estate Planning, Immigration, Intellectual Property, Land Use, Litigation, Professional Liability Defense, Real Estate, Taxation and Zoning.

REGAN, HALPERIN & LONG, P.L.L.C.

Established in 1997

PRESIDENTIAL PLAZA
900 NINETEENTH STREET, N.W., SUITE 200
WASHINGTON, D.C. 20006
Telephone: 202-463-3030
Fax: 202-463-0667
Email: rhllaw.com
URL: http://www.rhllaw.com

Fairfax, Virginia Office: Suite 140, 10680 Main Street, 22030. Telephone: 703-549-9663.

Negligence, Medical Malpractice, Product Liability, Automobile Torts, Aviation Accidents, Construction Site Accidents, Industrial and Commercial Liability, Public Transportation Accidents Liability, Tap Water Scald Cases, Elevator and Escalator Accidents, Defective Consumer Product's Claims, Contingency Commercial Litigation, Bad Faith Claims and Private Sector Workers' Compensation.

PATRICK M. REGAN, born Quantico, Virginia, April 23, 1955; admitted to bar, 1980, Virginia, District of Columbia, U.S. Court of Appeals for the District of Columbia Circuit and U.S. Court of Appeals, Fourth Circuit; 1983, U.S. Supreme Court; 1985, Maryland. *Education:* Hamilton College (B.A., 1977); Catholic University of America (J.D., 1980). Member, Catholic University Law Journal, 1979-1980. Master of the Bench, Thurgood Marshall Inn of Court, 1989—. Named Washington, D.C. Trial Lawyer of the Year, 1993. Author: "High Speed Pursuit," Trial Magazine, December, 1985. Adjunct Faculty, Catholic University Law School, 1985-1987, 1991—. Lecturer, Continuing Legal Education Programs in Professional Negligence, District of Columbia Bar, 1986—. Delegate, Judicial Conference for the D.C. Circuit, 1991-1992. Mediator, U.S. District Court for the District of Columbia Alternate Dispute Resolution Program. Mediator and Arbitrator, Superior Court for the District of Columbia Alternate Dispute Resolution Program. *Member:* District of Columbia Bar (Chairman, Injury to Persons and Property Section, 1988-1989); Bar Association of the District of Columbia; Washington Bar Association; Virginia, Maryland State and American (Member, Section on Litigation) Bar Associations; Virginia State Bar (Member, Young Lawyers Conference, 1980); The Association of Trial Lawyers of America (Member, Board of Governors, 1994—); The Trial Lawyers Association of Metropolitan Washington, D.C. (Member, Board of Governors, 1985—; Vice President, 1990; President-Elect, 1991; President, 1992); Maryland Trial Lawyers Association; Virginia Trial Lawyers Association; American Board of Trial Advocates; Trial Lawyers for Public Justice. Fellow, Roscoe Pound Foundation. (Board Certified, Civil Trial Advocacy, National Board of Trial Advocacy). ***PRACTICE AREAS:*** Medical Malpractice; Product Liability; Personal Injury; Wrongful Death; Construction Accidents; Commercial Litigation; Toxic Torts. ***Email:*** pregan@rhllaw.com

JONATHAN E. HALPERIN, born Allentown, Pennsylvania, June 19, 1964; admitted to bar, 1991, Virginia; 1992, Maryland and District of Columbia, U.S. Court of Appeals for the District of Columbia Circuit and U.S. Court of Appeals, Fourth Circuit; 1993, U.S. District Court for the District of Columbia. *Education:* George Washington University (B.A., 1987); Catholic University of America (J.D., 1991). Member, Moot Court, 1989-1991. Recipient, American Jurisprudence Award in Evidence. Member: The Journal of Contemporary Health Law & Policy, 1990-1991. Pro-bono, Appointed Deputy State's Attorney, State of Vermont, Essex County, 1992-1995; Barrister, Thurgood

(This Listing Continued)

Marshall Inn of Court, 1992—. Author: "Spoiling for Another Fight - The Rise of Spoliation of Evidence as a Separate Tort," Legal Times, February, 1997. Adjunct Professor, Advanced Federal Practice and Procedure, Catholic University Law School, 1997—. *Member:* Virginia and American (Member, Sections on: Litigation; Tort and Insurance Practice) Bar Associations; District of Columbia Bar (Elected to Steering Committee, Injury to Persons and Property Section; Member, Young Lawyers Section); Virginia State Bar; The Association of Trial Lawyers of America; Trial Lawyers of Association of Metropolitan Washington, D.C. (Member, Board of Governors, 1997—); Virginia Trial Lawyers Association; Maryland Trial Lawyers Association. ***PRACTICE AREAS:*** Personal Injury; Aviation Accidents; Medical Malpractice; Wrongful Death; Legal Malpractice; Premises Liability; Product Liability; Automobile Injuries; Construction Accidents; Toxic Torts; Police Misconduct; Contingent Commercial Litigation; Sexual Harassment; Private Sector Workers' Compensation Law. ***Email:*** jhalperin@rhllaw.com

VICTOR E. LONG, born Syracuse, New York, April 3, 1954; admitted to bar, 1980, District of Columbia. *Education:* Johns Hopkins University (B.A., 1976); Northeastern University (J.D., 1979). Member: U.S. Department of Labor, Office of Solicitor, 1979-1984; U.S. Department of Justice, 1984-1986; District of Columbia Office of Corporation Counsel, 1986-1989. Mediator and Arbitrator, District of Columbia Superior Court, Alternative Dispute Resolution Program. President, Board of Directors, Friendship House Association, Treasurer Friendship-Edison Public Charter School, Vice President, Friendship House Community Development Corporation. *Member:* District of Columbia Bar (Member, Section on Litigation); The Association of Trial Lawyers of America; Trial Lawyers Association of Metropolitan D.C.; National Bar Association; Maryland State Bar Association. (Board Certified, Civil Trial Advocacy, National Board of Trial Advocacy). ***REPORTED CASES:*** Fiedler vs. American Multi-Cinema, Inc., 871 F.Supp. 35 (D.D.C. 1994); Oates vs. D.C., 824 F.2d 87 (1987); Wilson vs. Group Hospital and Medical Service, 791 F.Supp 309 (1992); Rivero vs. D.C., 1990 WL 52431 D.D.C., 1990; Waters vs. Barry, 711 F.Supp 1125 (1989); Hedgman vs. D.C. Hacker's License Appeal Board, 549 A.2d, 720; Marshall vs. D.C. Rental Housing Commission, 533 A.2d 1271 (1987); United Planning Organization vs. D.C. Commission Human Rights 530 A.2d 674 (1987); Ford vs. Turner, 531 A.2d 233 (1987); Szego vs. Police and Firefighter's Retirement & Relief Board, 528 A.2d 1233 (1987); Lillian Pazmino Washington Area Transit Authority, 638 A.2d 627 (D.C., 1994); Donald Sanders vs. Stephen C. Wright, 642 A.2d (D.C. 1994); District of Columbia v. Walker 689 A.2d 40 (D.C. 1977); Holder v. District of Columbia 700 A.2d 738 (D.C., 1997). ***PRACTICE AREAS:*** Medical Malpractice; Personal Injury; Construction Accidents; Wrongful Death; Automobile Injuries. ***Email:*** vlong@rhllaw.com

SALVATORE J. ZAMBRI, born Long Island, New York, October 3, 1967; admitted to bar, 1992, New Jersey and U.S. District Court, District of New Jersey; 1993, New York, Maryland and District of Columbia; 1995, U.S. District Court for the District of Columbia and U.S. Court of Appeals for the District of Columbia; 1996, U.S. District Court, District of Maryland; 1997, U.S. Supreme Court. *Education:* College of William and Mary (B.A., 1989); George Washington University National Law Center (J.D., 1992). President, 1992 and Member, 1990-1992, Moot Court Board. Recipient, First Place Award, Intrascholastic Negotiations Competition, 1992. Awarded Academic All-American, College of William and Mary. Adjunct Professor, Advanced Federal Practice and Procedure, Catholic University of America School of Law, 1998—. Pro bono: Legal Counsel for Small Businesses, 1992; Legal Counsel for the Elderly, 1994. Co-Founder, Project Smile. *Member:* New York State, Maryland State, New Jersey State and American Bar Associations; The District of Columbia Bar (Co-Chair of Steering Committee of Injury to Persons and Property Section, 1999-2001, Member of Steering Committee, 1999—); Trial Lawyers Association of Metropolitan Washington, D.C. (Member, Board of Governors, 2000, Co-Chair, Membership Committee, 2001—); The Association of Trial Lawyers of America; Italian-American Bar Association. ***LANGUAGES:*** Spanish. ***PRACTICE AREAS:*** Personal Injury; Medical Malpractice; Private Sector Worker's Compensation; Wrongful Death; Automobile Torts; Construction Accidents; Sexual Harassment; Products Liability; Playground Safety; Premises Liability. ***Email:*** szambri@rhllaw.com

---

KAREN M. DOHERTY, born Kenmore, New York, February 13, 1961; admitted to bar, 1994, Maryland; 1995, District of Columbia and Virginia; 1996, U.S. Court of Appeals for the District of Columbia Circuit and U.S. Court of Appeals, Fourth Circuit; 2001, U.S. Supreme Court. *Education:* University of Rochester (B.S.N., 1981); Catholic University of America (M.S., 1987); University of Maryland (J.D., with honors, 1993). Sigma Theta Tau, Recipient, American Jurisprudence Awards in Insurance, Torts, Property and Criminal Procedure. Member: National Nursing Honors Society; National Association of Pediatric Nurse Practitioners; Association of Pediatric Oncology Nurses. *Member:* Montgomery County, Maryland State and American Bar Associations; District of Columbia Bar; Womens' Bar Association of the District of Columbia; Trial Lawyers Association of Metropolitan Washington, D.C.; The Associa-

(This Listing Continued)

tion of Trial Lawyers of America; Maryland Trial Lawyers Association. ***PRACTICE AREAS:*** Medical Malpractice; Wrongful Death; Products Liability. ***Email:*** kdoherty@rhllaw.com

THANOS BASDEKIS, born Oneonta, New York, December 18, 1971; admitted to bar, 1998, New York; 1999, District of Columbia; 2000, U.S. District Court for the District of Columbia and U.S. Court of Appeals, District of Columbia Circuit; 2001 U.S. Dsitrict Court for the Southern District of New York. *Education:* Columbia University (B.A., summa cum laude, 1994); Yale University (J.D., 1997). Phi Beta Kappa. Author: "Perfection By Nullification," 105 Yale Law Journal 2285, 1996. Law Clerk to the Hon. Leonard B. Sand, U.S. District Judge, Southern District of New York, 1997-1998. Adjunct Professor, Advanced Federal Practice and Procedure, Catholic University Law School, 2000—. *Member:* New York State Bar Association; The Association of Trial Lawyers of America; District of Columbia Trial Lawyers Association. ***LANGUAGES:*** Greek. ***PRACTICE AREAS:*** Personal Injury; Product Liability; Aviation Accidents; Medical Malpractice; Wrongful Death; Legal Malpractice; Premises Liability; Automobile Injuries; Products Liability; Construction Accidents; Toxic Torts; Police Misconduct; Contingent Commercial Litigation; Sexual Harassment; Worker's Compensation Law. ***Email:*** tbasdekis@rhllaw.com

THOMAS P. SILIS, born Washington, D. C., March 20, 1969; admitted to bar, 2000, New York; 2001, Maryland (Not admitted in District of Columbia). *Education:* George Washington University (B.A., 1992); New York Law School (J.D., cum laude, 1999). *Member:* Maryland State and New York State Bar Associations; The Association of Trial Lawyers of America; District of Columbia Trial Lawyers Association. ***LANGUAGES:*** Greek. ***PRACTICE AREAS:*** Personal Injury; Medical Malpractice; Premises Liability; Products Liability. ***Email:*** TSilis@RHLlaw.com

RENO & CAVANAUGH, PLLC

Established in 1977

SUITE 900

1250 EYE STREET, N.W.

WASHINGTON, D.C. 20005-3922

Telephone: 202-783-2800

Fax: 202-783-0550

URL: http://www.renocavanaugh.com

Affordable Housing and Real Estate Transactions, Public Housing, Community Development, Legislation, Administrative Law, Nonprofit Organizations, Captive Insurance, and Litigation.

FIRM PROFILE: Reno & Cavanaugh was formed in 1977 with the goal to provide quality legal services to nonprofit organizations dedicated to improving the housing conditions of low-income people throughout the country. Since then, the firm's practice has expanded to provide a broad range of legal and legislative advocacy services to nonprofit organizations, public agencies, consultants and small businesses. While the firm's practice focuses on the development of affordable and public housing and related issues, its general counseling of nonprofit organizations and small businesses involves it in a much broader range of legal issues including corporate formation and governance, government contracts and procurement, federal income tax exemptions and low-income housing tax credits, alternative insurance mechanisms (captive insurance entities and risk retention groups), administrative and legislative lobbying, and employment matters. The nine lawyer firm represents clients who are located throughout the United States and abroad.

MEMBERS OF FIRM

LEE P. RENO, born Allegan, Michigan, December 26, 1940; admitted to bar, 1970, District of Columbia; 1974, U.S. Court of Appeals for the District of Columbia Circuit; 1993, U.S. District Court, Western District of Michigan. *Education:* Western Michigan University (B.S., 1963); Howard University (J.D., 1968). *Member:* The District of Columbia Bar; National and American (Member: Administrative Law Section; Affordable Housing and Community Development Law Forum) Bar Associations. ***PRACTICE AREAS:*** Affordable Housing; Real Estate Finance Transactions; General Corporate; Nonprofit Organizations; Captive Insurance Company Regulation. ***Email:*** lreno@renocavanaugh.com

MEGAN GLASHEEN, born North Adams, Massachusetts, July 28, 1966; admitted to bar, 1991, Maryland; 1992, District of Columbia; 1994, California. *Education:* University of Rhode Island (B.A., with distinction, 1987); Howard University School of Law (J.D., 1991). Member, Howard University Law Journal, 1989-1991. Recipient: Howard University Merit Scholarship; Earl Davis Award for Advocacy; Dean's Recognition Award for Real Estate Finance; American Jurisprudence Award for Evidence. Author: "Patronage Employment Practices and the First Amendment," 34 Howard Law Journal 663, 1991. Co-Author: "PHAs and HOPE 1: Questioning HUD's Giveaway," Journal of Affordable Housing & Community Development Law, Spring 1992; "Public

(This Listing Continued)

Housing Authorities HOPE 1: May HUD Give Away What It Does Not Own?" 25 The Urban Lawyer 69, Winter 1993. *Member:* American Bar Association (Chair, Public Housing Practice Division of the Forum on Affordable Housing and Community Development Law; Member, Section on Urban, State and Local Government Law). ***PRACTICE AREAS:*** Affordable Housing; Real Estate Transactions; General Corporate; Nonprofit Organizations; Administrative Law. ***Email:*** mglasheen@renocavanaugh.com

SHARON WILSON GÉNO, born St. Louis, Missouri, January 25, 1967; admitted to bar, 1992, Missouri; 1998, District of Columbia. *Education:* Newcomb College of Tulane University (B.A., 1988); Georgetown University (J.D., 1991); St. Louis University (M.A., Urban Affairs, 1995). Member, Georgetown Journal of Legal Ethics. Graduate Fellowship, Department of Public Policy Studies, St. Louis University. Vice President, Family Selection, Law Committee, Habitat for Humanity, St. Louis, 1992-1995. *Member:* The District of Columbia Bar; The Missouri Bar; American Bar Association (Member, Forum on Affordable Housing and Community Development Law; Urban, State and Local Government Law Section). ***PRACTICE AREAS:*** Legislative Practice; Administrative Law; Affordable Housing; Real Estate Transactions; Corporate Law; Nonprofit Organizations. ***Email:*** sgeno@renocavanaugh.com

ASSOCIATES

JULIE S. McGOVERN, born Evanston, Illinois, September 5, 1969; admitted to bar, 1996, Pennsylvania and New Jersey; 1997, District of Columbia. *Education:* University of Virginia (B.A., with distinction, 1991); University of Pennsylvania (J.D., 1996). Editor, Journal of International Business Law, 1994-1996. Member, Managing Committee, Hybrid—The University of Pennsylvania Journal of Law & Social Change, 1993-1996. Author and Presenter, "Peer Group Lending: Using Community Norms to Achieve Minimal Default Rate on Loans to the Poor," Annual Law and Society Association, 1995. Co-Author, "Sources of Capital: Public Housing Funds," in Ben L. Hecht, Developing Affordable Housing: A Practical Guide for Nonprofit Organizations, 2 ed. 1999. *Member:* The District of Columbia Bar; Pennsylvania and American Bar Associations (Member: Forum on Affordable Housing Committee and Community Development; Administrative Law Section). ***PRACTICE AREAS:*** Real Estate Transactions; Administrative Law; Affordable Housing. ***Email:*** jmcgovern@renocavanaugh.com

ROBERT A. GRAHAM, born Coral Gables, Florida, January 8, 1968; admitted to bar, 1994, Kentucky; 1996, District of Columbia; 1997, U.S. Supreme Court; 1998, U.S. Court of Appeals, Sixth Circuit and U.S. District Court for the District of Columbia; 2000, U.S. Court of Appeals, District of Columbia Circuit. *Education:* University of North Carolina (A.B., 1990); University of Michigan (J.D., 1993). Contributing Editor, Michigan Law Review, 1993. Author: "The Constitution, the Legislature, and Unfair Surprise: Toward a Reliance-Based Approach to the Contract Clause," 92 Michigan Law Review 398 (1993). Judicial Clerk, Honorable Eugene E. Siler, Jr., U.S. Court of Appeals, Sixth Circuit, 1997-1998. Staff Attorney, Center for Auto Safety, 1994-1997. *Member:* Kentucky Bar Association; The District of Columbia Bar. ***PRACTICE AREAS:*** Litigation; Administrative Agency Practice; Nonprofit Organizations Law; Affordable Housing. ***Email:*** rgraham@renocavanaugh.com

SHARON M. WEATHERS, born Chicago, Illinois; admitted to bar, 1988, Illinois, Michigan and U.S. District Court, Eastern District of Michigan; 1994, U.S. District Court, Northern District of Illinois; 1999, Pennsylvania (Not admitted in District of Columbia). *Education:* Kansas Wesleyan University (B.A., Education); University of Iowa, College of Law (J.D.). Prior Experience: 1998-1999, General Counsel, The Philadelphia Housing Authority; 1997-1998, Supervising Assistant Corporation Counsel, The Detroit Housing Commission; 1996-1997, Attorney, National Equity Fund; 1992-1996, Attorney, Commonwealth Edison Company; 1990-1992, Section Chief and Attorney, The Resolution Trust Corporation; 1988-1990, Attorney, Ford Motor Company. ***PRACTICE AREAS:*** Real Estate Transactions; Affordable Housing; Corporate Transactional. ***Email:*** sweathers@renocavanaugh.com

TIFFANI K. WHITTAKER, born Cincinnati, Ohio, May 13, 1973; admitted to bar, 1998, Maryland; 1999, District of Columbia. *Education:* University of Pennsylvania (B.A., 1995); Georgetown University Law Center (J.D., 1998). Recipient: Keller Scholarship. Student Attorney: Street Law Clinic; Juvenile Justice Clinic. Student Bar Association Delegate. Tutor, Georgetown Outreach. *Member:* American and National Bar Associations; Young Lawyers Association of District of Columbia (Member, Board of Directors). ***PRACTICE AREAS:*** Affordable Housing; Real Estate; Structured Finance. ***Email:*** twhittaker@renocavanaugh.com

OF COUNSEL

GORDON CAVANAUGH, born Philadelphia, Pennsylvania, April 3, 1928; admitted to bar, 1954, Pennsylvania; 1957, U.S. District Court, Eastern District of Pennsylvania; 1988, District of Columbia. *Education:* Fordham University (A.B., cum laude, 1950); University of Pennsylvania (LL.B., 1953). Member, University of Pennsylvania Law Review, 1952-1953. Author: "Ending Severely Distressed Public Housing-a Congressional Initiative, a HUD Challenge," ABA

(This Listing Continued)

RENO & CAVANAUGH, PLLC, Washington—Continued

Journal of Affordable Housing & Community Development Law, Vol.3, November 1, Fall, 1993. General Counsel to the Council of Large Public Housing Authorities, 1981—. Administrator, Farmers Home Administration, U.S. Department of Agriculture, 1977-1981. Executive Director, Housing Assistance Council, 1971-1977. Housing Director, 1968-1971 and Commissioner of Licenses and Inspections, 1966-1968, Philadelphia, Pennsylvania. Private and public law practice, 1953-1966. Chair, Cooperative Housing Foundation. *Member:* The District of Columbia Bar (Member, D.C. Affairs Steering Committee); Pennsylvania and American (Member: Administrative Law Section; Affordable Housing and Community Development Forum) Bar Associations. **PRACTICE AREAS:** Legislation; Administrative Law; Public Housing. **Email:** gcavanaugh@renocavanaugh.com

REPRESENTATIVE CLIENTS: Amerind Risk Management Corp.; Community Transportation Association of America, Inc.; Cooperative Housing Foundation; Council of Large Public Housing Authorities; Housing Assistance Council; Housing Authority Insurance, Inc.; Housing Authority Risk Retention Group, Inc.; Housing Authority Property, Ins.; Housing Environmental Services, Inc.; Housing Research Foundation; Rural Housing Services, Inc.; Receiver of the District of Columbia Housing Authority and many individual Housing Authorities.

RESNICK, ABRAHAM & SCHWARTZMAN, L.L.C.

SUITE 304
1730 K STREET, N.W.
WASHINGTON, D.C. 20006
Telephone: 201-452-1411
URL: http://www.ra-atty.com

Baltimore, Maryland Office: One East Franklin Street, 21202. Telephone: 410-539-6087.

Fairfax, Virginia Office: 12600 Fair Lakes Circle, Suite 220. Telephone: 703-818-0223.

Syosset, New York Office: 485 Underhill Boulevard, Suite 302. Telephone: 515-364-5300

Wilmington, Delaware Office: 100 East 14th Street. Telephone: 302-655-1943.

Glen Mills, Pennsylvania Office: 30 Regency Plaza. Telephone: 610-358-9600.

Burlington, New Jersey Office: 505 High Street, P.O. Box 1427. Telephone: 609-386-1911.

Roswell, Georgia Office: 1265 Minihinette Drive, Suite 150, P.O. Box 1870. Telephone: 770-840-8482.

Los Angeles, California Office: 2049 Century Park East, Suite 460. Telephone: 310-557-2599.

Deerfield Beach, Florida Office: 1701 West Hillsboro Boulevard, Suite 303. Telephone: 954-480-6220.

Charlotte, North Carolina Office: 1721 Norland Road. Telephone: 704-535-8440.

Cary, North Carolina Office: 140 Preston Executive Drive. Telephone: 919-781-1880.

Commercial and Collection Law. Admiralty, Personal Injury, Immigration, Naturalization, Bankruptcy Law.

Murray I. Resnick **Philip Abraham**

(For Complete Personnel and Biographical Data, see Professional Biographies at Baltimore, Maryland)

RESOLUTION LAW GROUP, P.C.

5335 WISCONSIN AVENUE, N.W., SUITE 305
WASHINGTON, D.C. 20015
Telephone: 202-686-4844
Fax: 202-686-4843
Email: firm@reslawgrp.com
URL: http://www.reslawgrp.com

Lafayette, California Office: 3717 Mt. Diablo Boulevard, Suite 200, 94549. Telephone: 925-284-0840. Fax: 925-284-0870. Email: firm@reslawgrp.com. URL: http://ww.,reslawgrp.com

Civil Litigation, Insurance Coverage, Insurance Bad Faith Litigation, Environmental Law, Environmental Litigation, Toxic Torts Litigation, Securities Litigation and Arbitration.

MICHAEL D. GOODSTEIN, born Freeport, New York, May 8, 1959; admitted to bar, 1984, Florida; 1985, U.S. District Court, Southern District of Florida; U.S Court of Appeals, Eleventh Circuit; 2000, District of Columbia; 2001, Maryland and U.S. District Court, District of Columbia. *Education:* Brown University (B.A., with honors, 1981); Cornell University (J.D., 1984). Recipient, U.S. Attorney General's John Marshall Award for Outstanding Legal Achievement, 1998 and 2000. *Member:* The Florida Bar; District of Columbia Bar; Maryland State Bar Association, Inc. **PRACTICE AREAS:** Environmental Litigation. **Email:** mdg@reslawgrp.com

(This Listing Continued)

DEANNA J. CHANG, born Winston-Salem, North Carolina, August 2, 1970; admitted to bar, 1996, Maryland; 1998, District of Columbia; 2001, U.S. District Court, District of Columbia. *Education:* Mount Holyoke College (B.A., 1992); Boston University (J.D., 1995). *Member:* Maryland State and American Bar Associations; District of Columbia Bar. **PRACTICE AREAS:** Environmental Litigation; Civil Litigation; Toxic Torts. **Email:** djc@reslawgrp.com

(For Complete Biographical Data on all Personnel, see Professional Biographies at Lafayette, California)

SIDNEY WHITE RHYNE

3250 ARCADIA PLACE, N.W.
WASHINGTON, D.C. 20015-2330
Telephone: 202-244-6248
Fax: 202-244-4279
Email: swrhyne@abanet.org

Communications Law, Broadcasting Law, Estate Administration.

SIDNEY WHITE RHYNE, born Charlotte, North Carolina, April 2, 1931; admitted to bar, 1955, Pennsylvania; 1957, District of Columbia; 1959, U.S. Supreme Court; 1987, Maryland. *Education:* Roanoke College (A.B., cum laude, 1952); University of Pennsylvania (LL.B., 1955); Georgetown University (LL.M., 1961). Member, Blue Key. Editor, University of Pennsylvania Law Review, 1953-1955.Recipient, Presidential Award, 2001, 2001. Lecturer, Georgetown University Law Center, 1964-1970. President, Legal Aid Society of the District of Columbia, 1976-1978. Chairman, Committee on Admissions and Grievances, U.S. Court of Appeals, District of Columbia Circuit, 1978-1979. *Member:* The District of Columbia Bar; Bar Association of the District of Columbia (Secretary, 1969-1971; Member, Board of Directors, 1967-1968, 1970-1973, 1992-1994, 1998-2002; Chairman, Young Lawyers Section, 1966-1967); American Bar Association (Member, House of Delegates, 1972-1973, 1975, 1976-1978, 1998-2001); Federal Communications Bar Association (Recipient, Distinguished Service Award, 1992; President, 1994-1995). E. Barrett Prettyman Fellow, Georgetown University, 1960-1961; Life Fellow, American Bar Foundation.

RICH GREENBERG ROSENTHAL & COSTLE, LLP

WASHINGTON, D.C.

(See Alexandria, Virginia)

Federal and State Criminal and Civil Litigation, Appellate Practice, Domestic Relations, Personal Injuries, Wills, Trusts and Estates, Business Transactions, Corporate, Employment and Land Use, Civil Rights, Criminal Law, Estate Planning, Commercial Law, Business Law, Corporate Law, Real Estate, Products Liability, Debtor and Creditor, Contracts, Family Law, Children, Adoption Law, Child Support, Child Custody, Divorce, Collections, Constitutional Law, Tax-Exempt Organizations, Bankruptcy.

RICH AND HENDERSON, P.C.

WASHINGTON, D.C.

(See Annapolis, Maryland)

General Civil Litigation and Trial Practice in all Courts, Environmental Law and Regulation, Toxic Tort, Land Use, Real Estate, Construction and Labor Law.

RICHARDS SPEARS KIBBE & ORBE

1775 EYE STREET, N.W.
WASHINGTON, D.C. 20006-2401
Telephone: 202-261-2960
Fax: 202-261-2999
Email: info@rsko.com

New York City, New York Office: One Chase Manhattan Plaza, 10005-1413. Telephone: 212-530-1800. Fax: 212-530-1801.

FIRM PROFILE: Richards Spears Kibbe & Orbe provides litigation, international securities and transactional services and advice. The litigation group represents corporations and individuals in a wide variety of civil and criminal litigation and administrative proceedings, arbitrations and internal and other investigations. The firm's practice includes a focus on international and domestic securities regulation

(This Listing Continued)

and enforcement. The firm's transactional group represents financial institutions, hedge funds and investment partnerships in high yield, special situation and venture capital investments, mergers and acquisitions, commercial loans and loan restructuring.

The firm of Richards Spears Kibbe & Orbe has received from Martindale Hubbell the highest rating available.

MEMBERS OF FIRM

MICHAEL D. MANN, born Chicago, Illinois, May 4, 1953; admitted to bar, 1981, District of Columbia, U.S. District Court, District of Columbia. *Education:* Hampshire College (B.A., 1975); Antioch Law School (J.D., 1981). Author, "Jurisdiction in Cyberspace, International Implications of Electronic Markets," Glasser Legal Workers, 2000; "Developments in International Securities Law Enforcement and Regulation," 29 *The International Lawyer* 4, Winter 1995. Director, Office of International Affairs, Securities and Exchange Commission, 1989-1996; Associate Director, Division of Enforcement, Securities and Exchange Commission, 1988-1989; Chief, Office of International Legal Assistance, Division of Enforcement, Securities and Exchange Commission, 1985-1988; Trial Attorney, Division of Enforcement, Securities and Exchange Commission, 1984-1985; Attorney, Division of Enforcement, Securities and Exchange Commission, 1981-1984. Hampshire College (Trustee); Federation of American Scientists (Treasurer); Council on Foreign Relations (Member). ***Email:*** mmann@rsko.com

LUCINDA O. McCONATHY, born Henderson, Kentucky, September 8, 1949; admitted to bar, 1974, Illinois; 1979, District of Columbia; U.S. Court of Appeals, Second, Fourth, Fifth, Seventh, Ninth, Tenth and District of Columbia Circuits; U.S. Supreme Court. *Education:* Wellesley College (A.B., with honors, 1971); University of Chicago (J.D., 1974). Senior Special Counsel and Special Counsel for Appellate Litigation, Securities and Exchange Commission, 1987-1990; Assistant General Counsel for Appellate Litigation, Securities and Exchange Commission, 1990-1997. *Member:* The District of Columbia Bar. ***Email:*** lmcconathy@rsko.com

OF COUNSEL

PAUL A. LEDER, born Hudson, New York, May 7, 1957; admitted to bar, 1981, District of Columbia. *Education:* University of Michigan (B.A., cum laude, 1978; J.D., cum laude, 1981). Assistant Director, 1990-1993 and Deputy Director, 1993-1999, Office of International Affairs, Securities and Exchange Commission. Senior Advisor to the Chairman for International Issues, Securities and Exchange Commission, 1997-1999. Assistant Chief Litigation Counsel, Division of Enforcement, Securities and Exchange Commission, 1987-1990. Staff Attorney, Public Defender Service for the District of Columbia, 1981-1987. ***Email:*** pleder@rsko.com

JOHN C. RICHOWSKY

WASHINGTON, D.C.

(See Friendship, Maryland)

Trial and Appellate Litigation in State and Federal Courts, Complex Legal and Factual Research, Business Law, Regulatory, Legislative Matters.

RICHTER, MILLER & FINN

A Partnership including Professional Corporations

1815 H STREET, N.W., SUITE 410

WASHINGTON, D.C. 20006

Telephone: 202-467-6200

Fax: 202-293-4395

Email: info@rlaw.com

URL: http://www.rlaw.com/rmf

Litigation, Administrative and Transactional Practice including Business, Taxation, Intellectual Property, Corporate, International Business, Government Contract, Business Crimes Law, and Estate Planning.

PAUL S. RICHTER, (P.C.), born Woodbury, New Jersey, April 25, 1946; admitted to bar, 1971, District of Columbia and U.S. Tax Court; 1972, Connecticut and U.S. Claims Court; 1973-1982, U.S. Court of Customs and Patent Appeals; 1975, Virginia; 1982, U.S. Court of Appeals for the Federal Circuit; 1992, Florida. *Education:* Massachusetts Institute of Technology (B.S. in Econ., B.S.E.E. and M.S.E.E., 1968); George Washington University (J.D., with honors, 1971; LL.M., 1972). Co-Author: The Engineer and Federal Taxes, 1977. Eta Kappa Nu. Tau Beta Pi. *Member:* The District of Columbia Bar; The Florida Bar; Virginia State Bar; American Bar Association; American Intellectual Property Law Association; Institute of Electrical and Electronic Engineers; American Institute of Aeronautics and Astronautics. ***Email:*** richter@rlaw.com

(This Listing Continued)

THOMAS P. MILLER, born Martins Ferry, Ohio, July 23, 1964; admitted to bar, 1990, Pennsylvania; 1991, District of Columbia; 1992, Virginia; 1994, U.S. Tax Court. *Education:* Ohio University (B.A., 1987); Ohio Northern University (J.D., 1990). Delta Theta Phi. *Member:* The District of Columbia Bar; Virginia State Bar; American Bar Association. ***Email:*** miller@rlaw.com

KELLEY A. FINN, (P.A.), born Riverdale, Maryland, September 19, 1958; admitted to bar, 1986, Florida; 1987, U.S. Tax Court (Not admitted in District of Columbia). *Education:* University of Florida (B.S. in Accounting, 1981); Stetson University (J.D., 1984). *Member:* The Florida Bar. (Also practicing individually at Miami Beach, Florida). ***Email:*** finn@rlaw.com

JOHN M. WIDDER, born Oshkosh, Wisconsin, August 5, 1952; admitted to bar, 1978, Wisconsin; 1981, District of Columbia. *Education:* University of Wisconsin-Madison (B.A., 1975); Stanford University (J.D., 1978). Phi Kappa Phi; Phi Beta Kappa. ***Email:*** widder@rlaw.com

RIDBERG, PRESS & SHERBILL, LLP

WASHINGTON, D.C.

(See Bethesda, Maryland)

Corporate and Commercial Law, Litigation in Federal and State Courts, Arbitration and Dispute Resolution, Commercial Real Estate and Finance, Taxation, Government Contracts, Antitrust, Administrative Law, Trusts and Estates.

JOHNNY M. RIDDICK & ASSOCIATES

505 CAPITOL COURT N.E., SUITE 100

WASHINGTON, D.C. 20002

Telephone: 202-371-1933

Fax: 202-371-8332

Email: jriddick@bellatlantic.net

URL: http://www.lawyers.com/johnnyriddicklaw

Family Law, Divorce, Custody, Visitation, Marital Property, Separation Agreements, Pre-nuptial Agreements, Family Mediation, Personal Injury, Auto Accidents, Medical Negligence, Wrongful Death, Premises Liability, Employment Discrimination, Small Business Law, Minority Business Law, Corporate, Commercial Litigation.

JOHNNY M. RIDDICK, born Bronx, New York, September 21, 1956; admitted to bar, 1983, District of Columbia. *Education:* Allentown College of St. Francis de Sales (B.A., Political Science, 1978); Antioch School of Law (J.D., 1981). Director, Kids Corporations, St. Charles Borromeo School, 1975. Legislative Assistant, Committee on Judiciary, District of Columbia City Council. Member, North Portal Estates Civic Association. *Member:* District of Columbia Bar (Member, Sections on: Family Law; Injuries to Persons and Property); Bar Association of the District of Columbia; American Bar Association.

ASSOCIATES

SHARON R. HERRON, born Denver, Colorado, May 12, 1963; admitted to bar, 1998, Maryland (Not admitted in District of Columbia). *Education:* University of Denver (B.A., 1985); University of Maryland (J.D., 1997). Member, Golden Key National Honor Society. Listed in: Who's Who of American Law Students, 1995, 1996. *Member:* Maryland State and American Bar Associations. ***PRACTICE AREAS:*** Family Law; Personal Injury; Medical Malpractice; Disability Benefits; Managed Care Contracts.

JASMIN A. DABNEY, born Queens, New York, May 15, 1963; admitted to bar, 1996, Maryland; 1997, U.S. District Court, District of Maryland; 1999, District of Columbia; 2000, U.S. District Court, District for the District of Columbia. *Education:* Pennsylvania State University (B.A., 1986); Washington College of Law of American University (J.D., 1996). Adjunct Professor, University of the District of Columbia, 1999—. Member, American Bar Association, 1996-1999. *Member:* Prince George's County and National (Greater Washington Area Chapter, 1995-1999) Bar Associations; Charlotte E. Ray American Inn of Court; J. Franklyn Bourne Association; Association of Trial Lawyers of America. ***LANGUAGES:*** Spanish. ***PRACTICE AREAS:*** Employment Discrimination (30%); Family Law (30%); Personal Injury (25%); Corporate Law (10%); General Practice (5%). ***Email:*** jazziejazz@msn.com

RILEY ROUMELL & CONNOLLY, P.C.

Established in 1968

1707 N STREET, N.W.

WASHINGTON, D.C. 20036

Telephone: 202-331-0660

Telefax: 202-223-4884

Email: rrlaw@tir.com

URL: http://www.rrc-law.com

Detroit, Michigan Office: 7th Floor Ford Building, 48226. Telephone: 313-962-8255. Fax: 313-962-2937.

(This Listing Continued)

RILEY ROUMELL & CONNOLLY, P.C., Washington—Continued

Harbor Springs, Michigan Office: 151 East Bay Street, 49740. Telephone: 231-526-2300. Fax: 231-526-6787.

General Practice, Trials and Appeals in State and Federal Courts and Administrative Agencies, Arbitration, Labor and Employment Relations Law and Litigation in the Private and Public Sectors, Employment Discrimination, Corporate, Taxation, Commercial/Business Litigation, Environmental Law, Natural Resources, Occupational Safety and Health, Product Liability, Real Estate, Estate Planning, Probate, Civil Rights, Domestic Relations, Family Law, Education and School Law, Workers' Compensation, Health Care Law, Construction Law, Banking Law, Admiralty and Maritime Law, Trademark Law and Entertainment Law.

MICHAEL J. CONNOLLY, born Detroit, Michigan, March 26, 1949; admitted to bar, 1973, Mississippi and Michigan (Not admitted in District of Columbia). *Education:* Regis College (B.A., 1970); University of Mississippi (J.D., 1973); Wayne State University (LL.M., 1977). Author: *A Practical Guide to Equal Employment Opportunity,* published by Law Journal Seminars-Press, 1979; *Work Stoppages and Union Responsibility,* published by Practicing Law Institute, 1977; "Equal Employment Opportunities: Case Law Overview," Mercer Law Review, Walter F. George School of Law, 1978; "Qualifying Title VII Class Action Discrimination Suits, A Defendant's Perspective," St. Mary's Law Journal, 1977; "Employer's Rights Relative to Sympathy Strikes," Duquesne Law Review, Winter 1975-1976; "The Prevention and Defense of Sexual Harassment Claims," Prentice-Hall, 1984; "An Employer's Introduction to Comparable Worth," Prentice Hall, 1985; "OSHA and Collective Bargaining: The Dynamics of Confrontation and Resolution," Prentice Hall, 1984; *Recent Developments in the EEO Law,* published by the Southwestern Legal Foundation, 1982; "Use of Statistics in Equal Employment Opportunity Litigation," Law Journal Seminars Press, 1987; *Serious Questions Raised by OSHA Reform,* Washington Legal Foundation, May 1992; *OSHA--An Historical Perspective,* Washington Legal Foundation, February 19, 1988; *Understanding the Family and Medical Leave Act's Regulatory Requirements,* Washington Legal Foundation March, 1995. Co-Author: "Supreme Court Decisions Broaden Standards for Imposing Employer Liability for Sexual Harassment," Washington Legal Foundation, August 21, 1998; *Employment Law in Michigan, An Employer's Guide,* published by The Institute of Continuing Legal Education, 1997; U.S. Supreme Court Gives Employers A Chance To Avoid Costly Litigation, Washington Legal Foundation, June 2001. General Counsel, U.S. Equal Employment Opportunity Commission, 1981-1982. *Member:* State Bar of Michigan; American Bar Association (Member, Section on Labor Law). ***PRACTICE AREAS:*** Labor and Employment; Employment Benefits; Occupational Safety and Health; Gaming Law. ***Email:*** rrlaw@tir.com

MARC K. SHAYE, born Detroit, Michigan, December 14, 1942; admitted to bar, 1969, Michigan, U.S. District Court, Eastern District of Michigan, U.S. Court of Appeals, Sixth Circuit and U.S. Supreme Court; 1970, District of Columbia; 1996, Ohio (Not admitted in District of Columbia). *Education:* University of Michigan (B.A., 1965); Wayne State University (J.D., 1969). Editor, The Wayne Law Review, Environmental Law, Winter, 1989. Publications of Note include: "A Safety Valve for Oil and Hazardous Substance Cleanup Costs," Michigan Environmental Law Journal, Winter 1988; "Analysis of Federal Standard Covering Safety and Health Measures for Hazardous Waste Remediation and Emergency Response Workers," Spill Control Association of America Press, 1992 (ISBN 0-929253-00-0); "Wayne Law Review Environmental Law," Vol. 35, No. 2, Winter 1989; "Executives Who Cheat on OSHA Can End Up in Jail," The Complete Lawyer, American Bar Association, Winter 1990; "Analysis and Commentary Regarding Pending or Enacted Oil Spill Liability Legislation Since the Exxon Valdez Spill," Conference Proceedings, 7th National RCRA/Superfund Conference, May 1990. Author and General Editor: Michigan Environmental Law, Lawyers Cooperative Publishing, 1993. Consulting Editor, Environmental Law, Michigan Civil Jurisprudence, Lawyers Cooperative Publishing, 1993. Co-Author, OSHA/MIOSHA Chapter, Employment Law in Michigan, ICLE, 1997. Member, Environmental Auditing Roundtable. Member, Oil Spill Response Plan Negotiation Committee to develop federal regulations pursuant to the Oil Pollution Act of 1990. Certified by the State of California as an Environmental Assessor. Lecturer, Master of Science Program, Hazardous Waste Management, Wayne State University. *Member:* The District of Columbia Bar; State Bar of Michigan (Member, Board of Commissioners, 1979-1981; Chairperson, Young Lawyers Section, 1979); American Bar Association (Vice-Chair, General Practice Section, Natural Resource Committee, 1987-1994). ***PRACTICE AREAS:*** Environmental Law; Natural Resources; Occupational Safety and Health; Entertainment Law. ***Email:*** rrlaw@tir.com

CLIFFORD J. SCHARMAN, born Baulmholder, West Germany, August 12, 1955; admitted to bar, 1980, Michigan and U.S. District Court, Eastern District of Michigan; 1981, U.S. District Court, Western District of Michigan and U.S. Court of Appeals, Sixth Circuit; 1984, District of Columbia; 1985, U.S. District Court for the District of Columbia and U.S. Court of Appeals for the District of Columbia Circuit. *Education:* Cornell University (B.S., 1977); University of Michigan (J.D., cum laude, 1980). Author: "Sexual Harassment in the Workplace and What It Means," Michigan Business Vol. 1, No. 4, August 1981; "Interest Arbitration in the Private Sector," The Arbitration Journal, Vol. XXXVI, No. 3, 1981; "Employment At Will: Do Exceptions Overwhelm the Rule?" Boston College Law Review, Vol XXIII, No. 2, March, 1982; "Implication for An Employers Personnel Policies and Handbooks," Preventive Law Reporter, Vol. II, No. 1, December 1983; "Interest Arbitration - The Current Legal Issues," Society of Professionals in Dispute Resolution, 1982 Proceedings, Tenth Annual Conference. Co-Author, "Supreme Court Decisions Broaden Standards for Imposing Employer Liability for Sexual Harassment," Washington Legal Foundation, August 21, 1998. Co-Editor, Asbestos Abatement Regulatory Service, 1988-1990; "Serious Questions Raised by OSHA Reform," Washington Legal Foundation, May 1992; "Understanding the Family and Medical Leave Act's Regulatory Requirements," Washington Legal Foundation, March, 1995; U.S. Supreme Court Gives Employers A Chance to Avoid Costly Litigation, Washington Legal Foundation, June 2001. *Member:* The District of Columbia Bar; State Bar of Michigan; American Bar Association. (Resident). ***PRACTICE AREAS:*** Labor and Employment. ***Email:*** csscharman@cs.com

REPRESENTATIVE CLIENTS: Bank West; Community Bank of Dearborn; Dearborn Federal Credit Union; Blue Cross Blue Shield of Michigan; Detroit Medical Center; National Tech Team, Inc.; General Motors Corp.; Daimler Chrysler Corp.; Chrysler Financial Corp.; Detroit Edison; Hercules Corp.; The Budd Co.; Lomac, L.L.C.; Baxter International; McLaren Engines, Inc.; Triad Performance Technologies; Jay Enn Corp.; Bertram Yacht, Inc.; Marsh Plating Co.; Advance Stamping Co.; Michigan Marine Terminal; Roadway Express, Inc.; Ryder Systems; A.H. Peters Funeral Home of Grosse Pointe; John H. Santeiu & Son Funeral Home, Inc.; White Chapel Memorial Assn.; YWCA of Metro Detroit; SCOR S.A.; The Accident Fund Company; Chubb Insurance Group; Kemper Insurance Co.; Federal National Mortgage Assn.; Federal Home Loan Mortgage Corp.; GE Capital Mortgage Services, Inc.; Spill Control Association of America; Board of Education of the City of Detroit; County of Wayne; City of Livonia; City of Sterling Heights; Independence Township; The Thomas M. Cooley Law School; Lake Superior State University; Michigan Department of Transportation; Lapeer County Road Commission; Coloma, MI Public School District. *Standard Federal Bank.*

(For Complete Biographical Data on firm personnel see Professional Biographies, Detroit, Michigan)

JOHN A. RITCHIE

1320 19TH STREET, N.W., SUITE 202
WASHINGTON, D.C. 20036
Telephone: 202-887-9690
Fax: 202-659-8612
Email: jritch8@aol.com

General Civil and Trial Practice in all Courts. Business Planning and Counseling; Copyright, Trademark, Trade Secrets, Internet Law, Tax-Exempt Organizations, Estate Planning and Probate Law, Business Immigration Law.

JOHN A. RITCHIE, born Torrington, Connecticut, August 30, 1948; admitted to bar, 1979, Massachusetts; 1980, District of Columbia; 1991, Virginia; 1992, U.S. District Court, District of Columbia; 1993, Maryland; 1994, U.S. District Court, Eastern District of Virginia. *Education:* Princeton University (A.B., 1970); Suffolk University (J.D., cum laude, 1979). Phi Delta Phi. Articles Editor, Suffolk University Law Review, 1978-1979. *Member:* Bar Association of the District of Columbia; American Bar Association (Member, Sections on: Business Law; International Law; Real Property; Probate and Trust; Taxation); American Immigration Lawyers Association. ***LANGUAGES:*** French. Spanish. ***PRACTICE AREAS:*** Business Law; Intellectual Property; Estate Planning; Business Immigration Law.

REPRESENTATIVE CLIENTS: Carfax.com; Health Systems Research, Inc.; Association of Imaging Technology & Sound.
REFERENCE: Bank of America, N.A.

RITTER EICHNER & NORRIS, PLLC

THE JEFFERSON BUILDING
1225 19TH STREET, N.W., 7TH FLOOR
WASHINGTON, D.C. 20036
Telephone: 202-973-0100
Fax: 202-296-6990

Public Finance Law. Federal Income Taxation. Housing, Non-Profit Organizations.

FIRM PROFILE: Established in 1991 by former partners of Haynes & Miller, the firm maintains a national practice in all areas of public finance, representing underwriters, issuers, developers, credit enhancers, real estate investment trusts and Section 501(c)(3) organizations in primary and secondary marketing programs, multi-family and single family mortgage bond financings, refinancings and restructurings, and complex federal income tax questions related to tax-exempt bond issues. As market conditions have changed, the firm's practice has evolved to include taxable municipal and non-municipal debt and tax-exempt derivative products.

(This Listing Continued)

(This Listing Continued)

MEMBERS OF FIRM

C. WILLIS RITTER, born Baltimore, Maryland, February 18, 1940; admitted to bar, 1965, Maryland; 1968, U.S. Tax Court; 1972, District of Columbia and U.S. Supreme Court. *Education:* Cornell University (A.B., 1962); University of Virginia (J.D., 1965). Member, Editorial Board, University of Virginia Law Review, 1963-1965. Senior Attorney Advisor, Office of Tax Legislative Counsel, U.S. Treasury Department, 1969-1972. Author: "Federal Arbitrage Law and Advance Refunding of Municipal Indebtedness," 271-2nd Tax Management, 1978; "Advance Refunding of Municipal Indebtedness," The Urban Lawyer, Spring 1977. "History of Federal Arbitrage Law," National Association of Bond Lawyers, 1985. Editor, *Section 103 Source Book,* 1992 edition. *Member:* The District of Columbia Bar; American Bar Association (Member, Section on Taxation; Chairman, Subcommittee on Federal Arbitrage Law, 1978-1985; National Association of Bond Lawyers (Founding Director, 1978-1979 and Treasurer, 1981-1982). Fellow, American College of Bond Counsel, 1995—. ***PRACTICE AREAS:*** Public Finance Law; Federal Income Taxation; Housing. ***Email:*** writter@renbonds.com

RICHARD A. EICHNER, born Richmond, Virginia, April 6, 1953; admitted to bar, 1980, District of Columbia. *Education:* Cornell University (B.A., 1975); University of Virginia (M.B.A., 1980; J.D., 1980). Member, Editorial Board, University of Virginia Law Review, 1978-1980. *Member:* The District of Columbia Bar; American Bar Association; National Association of Bond Lawyers. ***PRACTICE AREAS:*** Public Finance Law; Federal Income Taxation; Housing. ***Email:*** aeichner@renbonds.com

R. WADE NORRIS, born Gastonia, North Carolina, August 12, 1947; admitted to bar, 1974, Georgia (Not admitted in District of Columbia). *Education:* Duke University (B.A., 1969; J.D., with distinction, 1974); Stanford University (M.B.A., 1971). Editor-in-Chief, Duke Law Journal, 1973-1974. Consultant, U.S. Department of Housing and Urban Development, Washington, D.C., on bond refunding policies, 1994. *Member:* State Bar of Georgia; American Bar Association (Member, Sections on: Corporation, Banking and Business Law; Local Government Law); National Association of Bond Lawyers. ***PRACTICE AREAS:*** Public Finance Law; Housing. ***Email:*** wnorris@renbonds.com

ASSOCIATES

MATTHEW J. BISSONETTE, born San Antonio, Texas, March 26, 1968; admitted to bar, 1995, Virginia; 1998, District of Columbia. *Education:* University of Virginia (B.A., 1990); College of William and Mary (J.D., 1995). Member, Moot Court Board. Recipient, Marshall-Wythe Gambrell Professionalism Award. *Member:* Virginia State and American Bar Associations; National Association of Bond Lawyers. ***PRACTICE AREAS:*** Public Finance Law. ***Email:*** mbissonette@renbonds.com

ROBERT A. WRZOSEK, born Hartford, Connecticut, January 29, 1972; admitted to bar, 1997, Connecticut; 1998, New York; 1999, District of Columbia. *Education:* Ithaca College (B.A./B.S., 1994); Duke University (J.D., 1997). ***PRACTICE AREAS:*** Public Finance Law; Tax. ***Email:*** rwrzosek@renbonds.com

KENT S. NEUMANN, born Stanford, California, June 29, 1971; admitted to bar, 1999, District of Columbia. *Education:* University of California at San Diego (B.M., 1995); Tulane Law School (J.D., 1998). ***PRACTICE AREAS:*** Public Finance Law; Housing. ***Email:*** kneumann@renbonds.com

RYAN L. GEORGE, born Pittsburgh, Pennsylvania, June 10, 1973; admitted to bar, 1999, Pennsylvania; 2001, District of Columbia. *Education:* Washington & Jefferson College (B.A., 1995); University of Pittsburgh (M.B.A., J.D., 1998). *Member:* American Bar Association (Section on Taxation). ***PRACTICE AREAS:*** Public Finance; Federal Income Tax. ***Email:*** rgeorge@renbonds.com

REPRESENTATIVE CLIENTS: American Housing Foundation, Inc.; Banc One Capital Corporation; B.C. Christopher, A Division of Fahnestock & Co., Inc.; Berkshire Hathaway, Inc.; Dain Bosworth, Inc.; Dougherty, Dawkins, Strand & Bigelow, Inc.; Ferris, Baker Watts, Inc.; General Electric Corporation; George K. Baum & Company; Lehman Brothers; Miller & Schroeder Financial, Inc.; Morgan Keegan & Co., Inc.; Nations Bank; Newman and Associates, Inc.; PaineWebber Incorporated; Prudential Securities Incorporates; Rauscher Pierce Refsnes, Inc.; Raymond Tousand Associates, Inc.; Security Capital Realty, Inc.; Stephens Inc.; The First Boston Corporation; The Sumitomo Trust & Banking Co., Ltd.; Robert Trent Jones Golf Club.

RITZERT & LEYTON, P.C.

WASHINGTON, D.C.

(See Fairfax, Virginia)

General Practice, including Administrative Law, Higher Education Law, Taxation, Estate Planning and Administration, Trusts, Estates, Wills and Probate, Corporate and Business Law, Employment Law, Real Estate, Financial Institutions and Banking, Bankruptcy and Creditors' Rights, Criminal Law, Immigration and Naturalization, Military Law, DWI Traffic Violations, Litigation and Appeals in Federal and State Courts.

ROBBINS, RUSSELL, ENGLERT, ORSECK & UNTEREINER LLP

1801 K STREET, N.W., SUITE 411
WASHINGTON, D.C. 20006
Telephone: 202-775-4500
Fax: 202-775-4510
URL: http://www.robbinsrussell.com

Antitrust, Civil Trial Practice, Criminal Trial Practice, Appellate Litigation, Telecommunications Litigation, Administrative Law.

FIRM PROFILE: Robbins, Russell, Englert, Orseck & Untereiner LLP was founded on May 1, 2001, by four former partners of the Washington office of Mayer, Brown & Platt and a 24-year veteran of the Antitrust Division of the U.S. Department of Justice. Our lawyers have extensive experience in trial and appellate litigation, both civil and criminal, and in all types of antitrust and telecommunications work, including litigation, transactions, counseling, and appearances before administrative agencies.

LAWRENCE S. ROBBINS, born Washington, D.C., January 28, 1952; admitted to bar, 1980, New York; 1989, District of Columbia; 1986, U.S. Supreme Court. *Education:* Yale University (B.A., summa cum laude, 1974); Harvard University (J.D., magna cum laude, 1978). Phi Beta Kappa. Editor, 1976-1977 and Developments Editor, 1977-1978, Harvard Law Review. Law Clerk to Hon. John J. Gibbons, U.S. Court of Appeals, Third Circuit, 1978-1979. Assistant U.S. Attorney, Criminal Division, U.S. Attorney's Office, Eastern District of New York, 1983-1986. Assistant to the Solicitor General, U.S. Department of Justice, 1986-1990. Associate Independent Counsel (In re Samuel R. Pierce, Jr.), 1990-1992. Partner, Mayer, Brown & Platt ,Washington, D.C., 1992-2001. Fellow, American College of Trial Lawyers. ***Email:*** lrobbins@robbinsrussell.com

DONALD J. RUSSELL, born Stuttgart, Germany, May 23, 1952; admitted to bar, 1977, Massachusetts (Not admitted in District of Columbia). *Education:* University of Nebraska (B.A., with high distinction, 1974); Harvard University (J.D., cum laude, 1977). U.S. Department of Justice, Antitrust Division, 1977-2001. Assistant Chief, Communications and Finance Section, 1986-1992. Chief, Telecommunications Task Force, 1995-2001. ***Email:*** drussell@robbinsrussell.com

ROY T. ENGLERT, JR., born Alexandria, Virginia, December 5, 1958; admitted to bar, 1981, District of Columbia; 1986, U.S. Supreme Court. *Education:* Princeton University (A.B., 1978); Harvard University (J.D., cum laude, 1981). Editor, 1979-1980 and Executive Editor, 1980-1981, Harvard Law Review. Co-author: (with A. Frey) "How to Write a Good Appellate Brief," Litigation Magazine, Winter 1994. Court Law Clerk, U.S. Court of Appeals, D.C. Circuit, 1981-1982. Assistant to the Solicitor General, U.S. Department of Justice, Washington, D.C., 1986-1989. Associate, 1989-1990, and Partner, 1991-2001, Mayer, Brown & Platt, Washington, D.C. ***Email:*** renglert@robbinsrussell.com

GARY A. ORSECK, born Miami, Florida, May 9, 1963; admitted to bar, 1989, California; 1990, Florida; 1992, District of Columbia. *Education:* Brown University (B.A., magna cum laude, 1985); Stanford University (J.D., with distinction, 1988). Phi Beta Kappa. Notes Editor, 1987-1988, Stanford Law Review. Law Clerk to Hon. Peter T. Fay, U.S. Court of Appeals, Eleventh Circuit, 1988-1989. Trial Attorney, 1989-1995, Civil Division, U.S. Department of Justice. Associate, 1995-1997, and Partner, 1998-2001, Mayer, Brown & Platt, Washington, D.C. ***Email:*** gorseck@robbinsrussell.com

ALAN E. UNTEREINER, born Boston, Massachusetts, December 28, 1960; admitted to bar, 1990, Pennsylvania; 1991, District of Columbia; 1995, U.S. Supreme Court. *Education:* Harvard University (A.B., magna cum laude, 1984); University of Munich, Munich, Germany (1984-1985); Yale University (J.D., 1988). Phi Beta Kappa. Notes Editor, Yale Law Journal, 1988-1989. Law Clerk to Judge J. Clifford Wallace, U.S. Court of Appeals, Ninth Circuit, 1988-1989. Co-Author (with K. Geller and J. Sullivan), "Appeals to the Supreme Court," in Business and Commercial Litigation in Federal Courts (Robert L. Haig ed., West Group & ABA 1998 & Supp. 2000); (with E. Tager and E. Penner); "Bad Faith Experts After Kumho," Mealey's Litigation Report, Insurance Bad Faith (1999); (with K. Geller), "Is There A Noncompliance Exception to Federal Preemption?" 24 Prod. Safety & Liab. Rptr. 57 (1996). Associate, Onek, Klein & Farr, Washington, D.C., 1989-1991. Associate, 1991-1996 and Partner, 1997-2001, Mayer, Brown & Platt, Washington D.C. ***LANGUAGES:*** German. ***Email:*** auntereiner@robbinsrussell.com

COUNSEL

ARNON D. SIEGEL, born New York, N.Y., September 17, 1963; admitted to bar, 1990, New York; 1995, District of Columbia. *Education:* Brown University (A.B., 1985); Yale University (J.D., 1988). Law Clerk to: Hon. Judge Robert P. Patterson, Jr., U.S. District Court, Southern District of New York., 1988-1989; Hon. Clarence Thomas, U.S. Court of Appeals, District of Colum-

(This Listing Continued)

ROBBINS, RUSSELL, ENGLERT, ORSECK & UNTEREINER LLP, Washington—Continued

bia Circuit, 1990-1991; Supreme Court of the United States, 1991-1992. [Judge Advocate General's Corps, U.S. Army (res.), 1993—]. ***Email:*** asiegel@robbinsrussell.com

ASSOCIATES

KATHRYN SCHAEFER ZECCA, born Los Angeles, California, March 1, 1969; admitted to bar, 1995, California; 1998, District of Columbia; U.S. District Court, District of Columbia. *Education:* Georgetown University (B.S.F.S., cum laude, 1991); University of Chicago (J.D., with honors, 1994). Member, University of Chicago Law Review. Law Clerk to Honorable Harold H. Greene, 1994-1995. Associate, Irell & Manella LLP, 1995-1998. Associate, Mayer, Brown & Platt. 1998-2001. ***Email:*** kzecca@robbinsrussell.com

SHERRI LYNN WOLSON, born Minneapolis, Minnesota, September 29, 1971; admitted to bar, 1998, Illinois (Not admitted in District of Columbia). *Education:* Stanford University (A.B., with distinction, 1993; J.D., with distinction, 1997). Editor, 1995-1996, Managing Editor, 1996-1997, Stanford Law Review. Law Clerk to Hon. Barbara Jacobs Rothstein, U.S. District Court, W.D., Wash., 1997-1999. Trial Attorney, Antitrust Division, U.S. Department of Justice, 1999-2001. ***Email:*** swolson@robbinsrussell.com

ROBERTS & HOLLAND LLP

Established in 1955

2175 K STREET, N.W.

SUITE 800

WASHINGTON, D.C. 20037-1827

Telephone: 202-293-3400

Telecopier: 202-293-0479

Email: rhtax.com

URL: http://www.robertsandholland.com

New York, N.Y. Office: Worldwide Plaza, 825 Eighth Avenue. Telephone: 212-903-8700.

Federal, State and International Tax Practice, Related Litigation in Federal and State Courts, Estate Planning, Trusts, Probate, Employee Benefits, Executive Compensation and International Business.

FIRM PROFILE: Roberts & Holland concentrates its practice in tax matters. With offices in New York City and Washington, D.C., Roberts & Holland is the largest law firm in the nation engaged exclusively in tax planning and tax controversy work. By reason of its broad experience in every major area of tax practice, including international, federal, and state and local tax matters, Roberts & Holland has developed a national reputation for solving complex and difficult tax planning problems, and for litigating major tax disputes.

RESIDENT PARTNER

HOWARD J. LEVINE, born Buffalo, New York, November 15, 1947; admitted to bar, 1973, New York; 1975, U.S. Tax Court; 1976, District of Columbia. *Education:* Hunter College of the City University of New York (B.A., 1969); State University of New York at Buffalo (J.D., cum laude, 1972); Georgetown University (LL.M., 1976). Recipient, Tax Management Distinguished Author Award, 2001. Associate Editor, Buffalo Law Review, 1971-1972. Adjunct Professor, Georgetown University Law School, LL.M. Tax Program, 1993-1998. Professorial Lecturer, George Washington University Law School, 1983-1993. Member, Editorial Advisory Board, Tax Management International Journal, 1987—. Contributing Editor, The Journal of Real Estate Taxation, 1981—. Member, Editorial Board, Journal of Taxation of Global Transactions (CCH). Author: 567 T.M., "Taxfree Exchanges Under Section 1031," Tax Management Inc., 2001. Attorney, Office of Chief Counsel, Internal Revenue Service, 1972-1976. *Member:* American Bar Association (Chairman, Committee on Sales, Exchanges and Basis, Section of Taxation, 1992-1994; Chairman, Subcommittee on Customs and Tax, Section of Taxation, 1994—); International Fiscal Association. ***PRACTICE AREAS:*** Taxation; International Taxation; Like Kind Exchanges; Federal Tax Controversies. ***Email:*** hlevine@rhtax.com

OF COUNSEL

LOUIS TIGER, JR., born St. Louis, Missouri, September 18, 1931; admitted to bar, 1958, Massachusetts; 1966, District of Columbia. *Education:* Harvard College (A.B., 1953); Harvard University (LL.B., 1958). Tax law specialist, Reorganization Branch, Internal Revenue Service, 1958-1963. *Member:* The District of Columbia Bar; Federal and American Bar Associations. ***PRACTICE AREAS:*** Taxation; Corporate Taxation.

(This Listing Continued)

THEODORE D. PEYSER, born Washington, D. C., April 16, 1929; admitted to bar, 1955, District of Columbia and U.S. Court of Appeals for the District of Columbia Circuit; 1960, U.S. Supreme Court; 1982, U.S. Court of Appeals for the Federal Circuit and U.S. Court of Federal Claims. *Education:* Princeton University (B.A., 1950); Yale Law School (LL.B., 1955). Author: 631, T.M., "Refund Litigation," Tax Management, Inc., 1995; 627 T.M., "Limitation Periods, Interest on Underpayments and Overpayments, and Mitigation," Tax Management, Inc., 1994. Co-Author: 630 T.M., "Tax Court Litigation," Tax Management, Inc., 1992. Trial Attorney, Tax Division, 1955-1973, Chief of Claims Court Section, 1974-1984 and Special Litigation Counsel, 1985-1987, U.S. Department of Justice. *Member:* U.S. Court of Federal Claims Bar Association (Board Member). ***PRACTICE AREAS:*** Taxation; Tax Litigation.

DAVID A. WEINTRAUB, born Buffalo, New York, December 13, 1954; admitted to bar, 1994, New York; 1997, District of Columbia and U.S. Tax Court. *Education:* State University of New York at Buffalo (B.S., cum laude, 1976; M.B.A., 1977); Albany Law School of Union University (J.D., magna cum laude, 1993); New York University School of Law (LL.M. in Taxation, 1994). Member, Justinian Society. Member, Albany Law Review, 1992. Certified Public Accountant, Texas, 1981, New York, 1985. *Member:* New York State and American Bar Associations. ***PRACTICE AREAS:*** Taxation. ***Email:*** dweintraub@rhtax.com

(For Complete Biographical Data on all Personnel, see Professional Biographies at New York, N.Y.)

ROBERTS & HUNDERTMARK, LLP

WASHINGTON, D.C.

(See Chevy Chase, Maryland)

General Civil and Administrative Practice. Government Contracts, Transportation, Travel, Trade Association Law, Intellectual Property.

ROBERTS & WOOD

WASHINGTON, D.C.

(See Riverdale, Maryland)

Civil Trials, Business Litigation, Small Business Law, Construction Litigation, Civil Rights, Discrimination, Criminal Defense, Homicide, Drug Crimes, Sex Crimes, DWI, Traffic Violations, Police Misconduct, Police Brutality, Serious Felonies, Misdemeanors, Personal Injury, Negligence, Automobile Accidents, Motorcycle Accidents, Truck Accidents, Wrongful Death, Medical Malpractice.

ROBERTSON, MONAGLE & EASTAUGH

A PROFESSIONAL CORPORATION

WASHINGTON, D.C.

(See Arlington, Virginia)

General Civil and Trial Practice. Administrative, Insurance, Construction, Aviation, Mining, Maritime, Municipal, Professional Liability, Products Liability, Admiralty, Natural Resources and Environmental Law, Legislative Law, Communications Law, Fisheries, Family Law.

ROBINS, KAPLAN, MILLER & CIRESI L.L.P.

Established in 1938

SUITE 1200, 1801 K STREET, N.W.

WASHINGTON, D.C. 20006

Telephone: 202-775-0725

Fax: 202-223-8604

URL: http://www.rkmc.com

Atlanta, Georgia Office: 2600 One Atlanta Plaza, 950 East Paces Ferry Road NE. Telephone: 404-233-1114. Fax: 404-233-1267.

Boston, Massachusetts Office: 111 Huntington Avenue, Suite 1300. Telephone: 617-267-2300. Fax: 617-267-8288.

Costa Mesa, California Office: 600 Anton Boulevard, Suite 1600. Telephone: 714-540-6200. Fax: 714-545-6915.

Los Angeles, California Office: 2049 Century Park East, Suite 3700. Telephone: 310-552-0130. Fax: 310-229-5800.

Minneapolis, Minnesota Office: 2800 LaSalle Plaza, 800 LaSalle Avenue. Telephone: 612-349-8500. Fax: 612-339-4181.

Naples, Florida Office: Suite 201, 711 5th Avenue South. Telephone: 941-430-7070. Fax: 941-213-1970.

(This Listing Continued)

Trials and Appeals in all Federal and State Courts. Administrative, Antitrust, Appellate, Banking, Bankruptcy and Reorganization, Construction, Communications, Corporate, Employment and Employee Benefits, Environmental, Estate Planning and Probate, Franchising, Finance, Health, Insurance Law, Intellectual Property, International Litigation and Trade, Medical Malpractice, Personal Injury, Products Liability, Real Estate, Securities, Tax, Transportation.

FIRM PROFILE: The Washington, D.C. office provides representation in federal regulatory/legislative affairs and international trade along with its general, commercial, employment, intellectual property and business litigation practices. Particular areas of emphasis include government contracts, environmental, corporate finance, military base closing and privatization, and maritime/transportation law as well as tax and real estate law. The office represents both U.S. and foreign entities, including multi-national companies, in a wide variety of commercial and governmental matters.

PARTNERS

STACY E. COSTELLO, born Chicago, Illinois, September 18, 1964; admitted to bar, 1990, Maryland; 1992, District of Columbia. *Education:* Brandeis University (B.A., 1986); American University (J.D., 1989). *Member:* District of Columbia Bar; Maryland State and American (Member, Sections of: Taxation; Business Law) Bar Associations. ***PRACTICE AREAS:*** Business Transactions; Real Estate; Taxation; Wills; Trusts Planning; Estate Planning; Probate; Exempt Organizations.

BRIAN R. DINNING, born Fairfax, Virginia, April 20, 1965; admitted to bar, 1990, Virginia and U.S. Court of Claims; 1991, U.S. Court of Federal Claims; 1993, District of Columbia; 1994, U.S. Tax Court. *Education:* Grove City College (B.A., Political Science, 1987); Regent University (J.D., 1990); Georgetown University (LL.M., Taxation, 1993). Member, Law Review. *Member:* Norfolk and Portsmouth Bar Associations; Virginia State Bar; District of Columbia Bar. ***PRACTICE AREAS:*** Mergers, Acquisitions and Consolidations; Business Law; Emerging Growth Companies; Tax and Employee Benefits.

SHARON CUMMINGS GILES, born Holly Hill, South Carolina; admitted to bar, 1985, Pennsylvania; 1986, U.S. District Court, District of Maryland, U.S . Court of Appeals, Fourth Circuit and Florida; 1987, District of Columbia; 1991, U.S. District Court for the District of Columbia; 1995, U.S. Supreme Court. *Education:* University of South Carolina (B.A., magna cum laude, 1981); Georgetown University Law Center (J.D., 1984). Phi Beta Kappa; Phi Delta Phi. Articles and Notes Editor, Editorial Board, American Criminal Law Review, 1983-1984. Clerk, Honorable Herbert F. Murray, U.S. District Court, District of Maryland. *Member:* The District of Columbia Bar; American Bar Association (Member, Litigation and Employment Law Sections); National Bar Association. ***PRACTICE AREAS:*** Commercial Litigation; Business Litigation; Employment Law; Civil Litigation; Antitrust.

ROBERT E. FALB, born New York, N.Y., January 23, 1943; admitted to bar, 1968, District of Columbia, U.S. District Court, District of Columbia and U.S. Court of Appeals, District of Columbia Circuit; 1971, U.S. Tax Court; 1975, U.S. Court of Appeals, Second Circuit; 1976, U.S. Court of Federal Claims. *Education:* Brown University (B.A., magna cum laude, 1964); Harvard University (LL.B., 1967). Phi Beta Kappa. *Member:* The District of Columbia Bar; American Bar Association (Member, Sections on: Real Property, Probate and Trust Law; Taxation). ***PRACTICE AREAS:*** Taxation; Real Estate; Trusts; Estate Planning; Probate; Business Transactions.

CHARLES A. HUNNICUTT, born LaGrange, Georgia, December 7, 1950; admitted to bar, 1975, Georgia; 1978, District of Columbia and U.S. Court of Appeals for the District of Columbia Circuit; 1980, U.S. Court of International Trade; 1981, U.S. Supreme Court, 1982, U.S. Court of Appeals for the Federal Circuit. *Education:* American University (B.S., 1972); University of Georgia (J.D., 1975); Hague Academy of International Law (Certificate, 1975); Vrije Universiteit, Brussels (LL.M., International and Comparative Law, 1976). Editor in Chief, Georgia Journal of International and Comparative Law. Assistant Secretary, Transportation for Aviation and International Affairs, 1996-1999. *Member:* American Bar Association (Member, Steering Committee for International Trade); Federal Bar Association; International Bar Association; American Society of International Law (Member, Executive Council); Washington Foreign Law Society. ***PRACTICE AREAS:*** Government Affairs; Transportation; Maritime; Aviation; International Trade.

ERIC S. JACKSON, born Milwaukee, Wisconsin, January 20, 1966; admitted to bar, 1993, Wisconsin, Minnesota and U.S. District Court, Districts of Wisconsin and Minnesota; 1995, District of Columbia and U.S. District Court, District of Columbia. *Education:* Stanford University (A.B., 1988); University of Wisconsin (J.D., 1993). President, Moot Court Board and Student Bar Association. *Member:* District of Columbia Bar; State Bar of Wisconsin; Minnesota State, American and National Bar Associations; Charlotte E. Ray American Inn of Court. ***PRACTICE AREAS:*** Business Litigation; Intellectual Property Litigation; Employment Law; Civil Litigation.

(This Listing Continued)

HAROLD E. MESIROW, born Washington, D.C., October 25, 1932; admitted to bar, 1957, District of Columbia and U.S. District Court, District of Columbia; 1958, U.S. Court of Appeals, District of Columbia Circuit; 1965, U.S. Supreme Court. *Education:* George Washington University (A.B., 1954; LL.B., 1957). Phi Delta Phi; Order of the Coif; Phi Beta Kappa. *Member:* The District of Columbia Bar; The Bar Association of the District of Columbia; American Bar Association; Maritime Administrative Bar Association. ***PRACTICE AREAS:*** Transportation Law; Administrative Law; Federal Government; Environmental Law; Maritime Law; Marine Insurance Law.

RICHARD B. NETTLER, born New York, N.Y., June 11, 1952; admitted to bar, 1977, District of Columbia and U.S. Court of Appeals for the District of Columbia; 1979, U.S. District Court, District of Columbia; 1980, U.S. Supreme Court; 1982, U.S. Court of Appeals for the Federal Circuit and U.S. Court of Claims; 1987, Maryland; 1992, U.S. District Court, District of Maryland and U.S. Court of Appeals, Fourth Circuit; 1993, U.S. Court of Appeals, Ninth Circuit. *Education:* George Washington University (B.A., 1974); Golden Gate University Law School (J.D., 1977). Editor-in-Chief, Golden Gate University Law Review, Ninth Circuit Survey, 1976-1977. Associate Editor, Appellate Practice Manual for the D.C. Court of Appeals, 1985. Assistant Corporation Counsel for the District of Columbia, 1978-1986. Chairman, Preservation Action, 1996-2001. Trustee, Council for Court Excellence. Chairman, District of Columbia Court of Appeals Committee on Admissions. *Member:* The District of Columbia Bar (Co-Chair, Court Subcommittee Technology Task Force); Maryland Bar Association; National Association of Installation Developers; American Planning Association. (Regional Managing Partner). ***PRACTICE AREAS:*** Litigation; Land Use Law; Zoning Law; Administrative Law; Government Contracts.

KEITH R. STYLES, born Santa Monica, California, July 9, 1957; admitted to bar, 1983, District of Columbia; 1987, U.S. Court of Appeals for the Federal Circuit and U.S. Supreme Court; 1988, Virginia; U.S. District Court, Eastern District of Virginia; U.S. District Court, District of Columbia. *Education:* Yale University (B.A., cum laude, 1979); Georgetown University (J.D., 1982). Editor, Law and Policy in International Business, 1981-1982. *Member:* The District of Columbia Bar; Virginia State Bar; Bar Association of the District of Columbia; Federal Circuit and American Bar Associations. ***PRACTICE AREAS:*** Business and Large Project Financing; Mergers and Acquisitions; Technology Law; General Business Counseling.

DIRK D. THOMAS, born Salisbury, Maryland, November 5, 1959; admitted to bar, 1986, Pennsylvania; 1988, District of Columbia; registered to practice before U.S. Patent and Trademark Office. *Education:* University of Maryland (B.S.M.E., 1982); The George Washington University National Law Center (J.D., 1986). Teaching Faculty, Patent Litigation, Patent Resource Group, 1999—. *Member:* The District of Columbia Bar; American Bar Associations; American Intellectual Property Law Association; Licensing Executives Society. ***PRACTICE AREAS:*** Intellectual Property.

BARBARA WACHTER NEEDLE, born Baltimore, Maryland, September 20, 1962; admitted to bar, 1987, Maryland; 1988, District of Columbia; 1995, U.S. Supreme Court. *Education:* University of Maryland (B.S., magna cum laude, 1984); George Washington University (J.D., 1987). Omicron Delta Kappa. *Member:* The District of Columbia Bar (Member, Real Estate, Housing and Land Use Section; Corporation, Finance and Securities Law Sections); Maryland State (Member, Sections of: Business Law; Real Property, Planning and Zoning) and American (Member, Sections of: Real Estate; Women Rainmakers) Bar Associations; Women's Bar Association; National Network of Commercial Real Estate Women; International Council of Shopping Centers. ***PRACTICE AREAS:*** Real Estate Law; Corporate Law; Commercial Real Estate Development; Commercial Real Estate Finance; Business Law; Business Transactions.

ASSOCIATES

G. BRENT CONNOR, born Presque Isle, Maine, August 28, 1962; admitted to bar, 1992, Maryland; 1996, U.S. District Court, District of Maryland; 1998, District of Columbia and U.S. Court of Federal Claims. *Education:* Clark University (B.A., 1986); Catholic University of America (J.D., 1992). Member and Senior Staff Member, Catholic University Law Review, 1990-1992. *Member:* Maryland State and American Bar Associations; The District of Columbia Bar. ***LANGUAGES:*** French. ***PRACTICE AREAS:*** Governmental Affairs; Administrative Law; Military Base Closures; Military Base Conversions; Maritime; Aviation; Government Contracts.

B. GERARD CORDELLI, born Harrisburg, Pennsylvania, June 11, 1957; admitted to bar, 1983, California; 1984, U.S. District Court, Central District of California; 1986, U.S. Court of Appeals, Ninth Circuit; 1992, District of Columbia, U.S. Court of International Trade and U.S. Court of Appeals, Federal Circuit; 1993, Virginia and Maryland; 1997, U.S. District Court, Eastern District of Virginia and U.S. Court of Appeals, Fourth Circuit; 1999, U.S. Court of Appeals, Eleventh Circuit; 2000, U.S. District Court, District of Maryland. *Education:* George Washington University (B.B.A., with distinction, 1979); University of California School of Law, Los Angeles (J.D., 1983). Member,

(This Listing Continued)

ROBINS, KAPLAN, MILLER & CIRESI L.L.P., Washington—Continued

UCLA-Alaska Law Review. *Member:* State Bar of California; District of Columbia Bar (Member, Litigation Section); American Bar Association. ***PRACTICE AREAS:*** Commercial Insurance Litigation; Counseling and Litigation/Rehabilitation; Business and Commercial Litigation.

DAVID L. FINCH, born Short Hills, New Jersey, May 9, 1968; admitted to bar, 1994, Maryland; 1998, District of Columbia. *Education:* Grove City College (B.A., 1991); Gonzaga University (J.D., magna cum laude, 1994). Member: Gonzaga University Law Review; National Moot Court Team. Clerkship for Honorable Stephen J. Swift, U.S. Tax Court. *Member:* Maryland State Bar Association. ***PRACTICE AREAS:*** Taxation; Partnerships; Corporations.

BRADLEY J. OLSON, born Hartford, Connecticut, September 10, 1957; admitted to bar, 1994, District of Columbia and U.S. Court of Appeals, Federal Circuit; 1997, U.S. District Court, District of Columbia; 1998, U.S. District Court, Eastern District of Wisconsin; registered to practice before U.S. Patent and Trademark Office. *Education:* Central Connecticut State College (B.A., in Biology, 1979); University of Connecticut (M.S., in Zoology, 1985); Franklin Pierce Law Center (J.D., M.I.P., 1994). *Member:* American Bar Association (Member, Intellectual Property Section); American Intellectual Property Law Association; Giles S. Rich American Inn of Court (Barrister); Licensing Executives Society; Swedish-American Chamber of Commerce (Member, Board of Directors). ***PRACTICE AREAS:*** Intellectual Property.

JEANNINE RUSTAD ZIGNER, born Keflavik, Iceland, December 26, 1969; admitted to bar, 1995, Virginia and U.S. Court of Appeals, 4th Circuit; 1996, District of Columbia; 1997, U.S. Bankruptcy Court, Eastern District of Virginia; 1999, U.S. District Court, District of Columbia. *Education:* Bentley College (B.S., Science, 1991); Catholic University of America (J.D., cum laude, certificate in International and Comparative Law, 1994). *Member:* Virginia and American Bar Associations; District of Columbia Bar. ***PRACTICE AREAS:*** Real Estate.

MATTHEW J. THOMAS, born Nyack, New York, 1968; admitted to bar, 1992, Virginia; 1998, U.S. Court of Appeals for the District of Columbia Circuit; 1999, U.S. Court of Appeals, Fourth Circuit (Not admitted in District of Columbia). *Education:* University of Virginia (B.A., 1989; J.D., 1992). Federal Maritime Commission Attorney, Assistant General Counsel, International Affairs, 1992-2000. *Maritime Administrative Bar Association.* ***PRACTICE AREAS:*** Administrative Law; Government-Federal; Transportation Law; International Trade.

OF COUNSEL

JEFFREY J. DOWNEY, born Long Island, New York, February 14, 1963; admitted to bar, 1989, New York and Connecticut; 1991, Virginia and District of Columbia. *Education:* State University of New York at Albany (B.A., 1985); Hofstra Law School (J.D., 1988). *Member:* American Bar Association; Virginia Trial Lawyers Association; Association of Trial Lawyers of America; D.C. Trial Lawyers Association. ***PRACTICE AREAS:*** Personal Injury; Medical Malpractice.

(For other biographical data, see Professional Biographies at all other offices)

RONDA ROBINSON

631 CONSTITUTION AVENUE, N.E., SUITE 3
WASHINGTON, D.C. 20002-6082
Telephone: 202-547-5699
Fax: 202-332-0503
Email: rrr.entlaw@prodigy.net

Communications and Media Law, Broadcast Licensing, Radio, Broadcast Station Transfers, FCC Licensing and Regulation, Wireless Communications, Telecommunications, Information Technology Licensing, Internet Licensing, Software Licensing, Broadcast Property Acquisition, Music Law, Video Law, Multimedia Law, Music Copyright and Publishing, Entertainment Litigation, Contracts.

FIRM PROFILE: Ms. Robinson has a well known national practice representing a special segment of the entertainment industry. Her clients include musicians, recording labels, on-air radio talent and radio broadcast companies.

RONDA ROBINSON, born Miami, Florida, November 28, 1957; admitted to bar, 1990, Florida; 1992, District of Columbia. *Education:* Howard University (B.A. in Journalism, 1979); University of Miami (J.D., 1989). Author: "The Agent-Athlete Relationship: Legal and Regulatory Schemes in the Sports Industry". National Bar Association Magazine, November, 1990. Lecturer, Communications Law, Howard University, Washington, D.C., 1990—. *Member:* American Bar Association; Black Entertainment and Sports Law Association. ***PRACTICE AREAS:*** Entertainment Law; Communications Law.

VINCENT J. ROCQUE

SUITE 400
1155 CONNECTICUT AVENUE, N.W.
WASHINGTON, D.C. 20036
Telephone: 202-429-6659
Telecopy: 202-872-1575
Email: vinrocque@aol.com

Federal Regulatory Law and Enforcement, International Business Transactions, Corporate Investigations, Legislation, Import and Export Law, Foreign Trade Sanctions, Antiboycott Compliance.

VINCENT J. ROCQUE, born Franklin, New Hampshire, November 27, 1945; admitted to bar, 1971, District of Columbia; 1974, U.S. Supreme Court. *Education:* Georgetown (B.A., magna cum laude, 1967); Columbia (J.D., 1970). Phi Beta Kappa. Counsel to Commissioner Barbara Franklin, U.S. Consumer Product Safety Commission, 1973-1977. Assistant Director, Bureau of Trade Regulation, U.S. Department of Commerce, 1977-1980. Counsel, 1980-1981 and Partner, 1981-1990, Sullivan & Worcester. *Member:* The District of Columbia Bar; Federal and American Bar Associations.

RODRIGUEZ O'DONNELL FUERST GONZALEZ & WILLIAMS

1710 RHODE ISLAND AVENUE, N.W.
TENTH FLOOR
WASHINGTON, D.C. 20036-3007
Telephone: 202-293-3300
Facsimile: 202-293-3307
URL: http://www.rofgw.com
Email: rodriguez@rofgw.com
URL: http://www.lawyers.com/transportationlaw

Chicago, Illinois Office: 20 North Wacker Drive, Suite 1416, 60606. Telephone: 312-372-7000. Fax: 312-372-1719.
Miami, Florida Office: 1200 Brickell Avenue, 33131. Telephone: 305-350-5690. Fax: 305-371-8989.
New York, New York Office: 61 Broadway, 10006. Telephone: 212-344-6600. Fax: 212-509-4066.

International Transportation, Trade, Customs, Maritime, Commercial Transactions Law, Government Relations, Tax and Tax Litigation.

FIRM PROFILE: Attorneys of the firm regularly practice before the Federal Maritime Commission, Surface Transportation Board, United States Court of Claims, United States District Courts, United States Court of Appeals, various state courts and various governmental agencies that have jurisdiction over international trade, transportation and tax activities.

Transportation matters handled include: litigation; transportation service contracts; shipper, forwarder, vessel-operating common carrier, and non-vessel-operating common carrier responsibilities and liabilities; corporate forms and transfers; and state and federal regulatory compliance for ocean and air shippers, forwarders, and carriers, and Customs brokers.

CARLOS RODRIGUEZ, born San Antonio, Texas, May 7, 1941; admitted to bar, 1975, New Jersey; 1976, U.S. Court of Appeals, District of Columbia Circuit; 1977, District of Columbia; 1980, U.S. Court of Appeals, First Circuit. *Education:* University of Texas (B.A., 1964); Fairleigh Dickinson University (M.A., 1970); Seton Hall University (J.D., 1975). *Member:* Bar Association of the District of Columbia; New Jersey State and American Bar Associations; Maritime Administrative Bar Association; Washington International Trade Association. [Lt., U.S. Navy, 1964-1968]. ***LANGUAGES:*** Spanish. ***PRACTICE AREAS:*** Transportation; Admiralty Law; Regulatory Law; Maritime Law; International Commercial Transactions; Litigation; Export Compliance. ***Email:*** rodriguez@rofgw.com

THOMAS J. O'DONNELL, born Chicago, Illinois, April 19, 1946; admitted to bar, 1973, Illinois and U.S. District Court, Northern District of Illinois; 1974, U.S. Court of Appeals, Federal Circuit and U.S. Court of International Trade; 1977, New York; 1988, District of Columbia; 1995, U.S. Supreme Court. *Education:* University of Miami; Florida Atlantic University (B.S., cum laude, 1967); Loyola University (J.D., 1973). Licensed Customs Broker. *Member:* Chicago and American Bar Associations; The District of Columbia Bar; Customs and International Trade Bar Association. (Resident, Chicago, Illinois Office). ***PRACTICE AREAS:*** Customs Law; International Trade; Administrative Law. ***Email:*** todonnell@rofgw.com

MITCHELL S. FUERST, born New York, N.Y., January 7, 1953; admitted to bar, 1978, Florida and U.S. Tax Court; 1978, U.S. District Court, Southern District of Florida; 1979, U.S. Court of Appeals, Fifth Circuit (Not admitted in District of Columbia). *Education:* American University (B.S.B.A., 1975); Uni-

(This Listing Continued)

versity of Miami (J.D., cum laude, 1978). Member, University of Miami Tax Law Review, 1977-1978. Author: "Partnership Level Tax Audits and The Tax Matters Partner," Lecture Outlines and Program, The Florida Bar, 1984; "Procedure and Administrative Contracts of Florida Sales Taxes," Dade County Division, FICPA, 1987. Co-Author: "Tax Procedures and I.R.S. Controversies," Lecture Outlines and Program, FICPA, 1990. Adjunct Professor, University of Miami School of Law, Master in Taxation Program, 1986—. Attorney, Office of District Counsel, Internal Revenue Service, 1978-1983. *Member:* Dade County, Federal and American (Member, Sections on: Taxation; Litigation) Bar Associations; The Florida Bar; Tax Litigation Association of South Florida; Florida Academy of Trial Lawyers; The Association of Trial Lawyers of America. ***PRACTICE AREAS:*** Income Tax; Federal Income Tax; Excise Tax; Tax Litigation; Administrative Law; Tax Controversies. ***Email:*** mfuerst@rofgw.com

HENRY P. GONZALEZ, born New York, N.Y., January 31, 1955; admitted to bar, 1986, New York; 1995, U.S. District Court, Southern District of New York; 1996, U.S. Court of Federal Claims; 1997, U.S. Court of International Trade; 2000, U.S. District Court, Eastern District of New York (Not admitted in District of Columbia). *Education:* Fordham University (B.A., 1978); Antioch School of Law (J.D., 1981); Georgetown University (LL.M., 1991). Office of General Counsel, Federal Maritime Commission, 1987-1994. *Member:* Maritime Administrative Bar Association; International Association of Young Lawyers. ***LANGUAGES:*** Spanish. ***PRACTICE AREAS:*** International Transportation; Admiralty and Maritime Law; Export Regulation; International Commercial Transactions; Surety Bonds; Alternative Dispute Resolution; Civil Litigation. ***Email:*** gonzalez@rofgw.com

R. KEVIN WILLIAMS, born Carmi, Illinois, March 23, 1954; admitted to bar, 1987, Illinois; 1988, U.S. Court of Appeals, Federal Circuit and U.S. Court of International Trade; 1989, U.S. District Court, Northern District of Illinois (Not admitted in District of Columbia). *Education:* University of Illinois (B.S., 1976; J.D., 1987); McGeorge School of Law, Salzburg, Austria (Diploma in Advanced International Legal Studies, 1987). Delta Theta Phi (Treasurer, 1985-1986; Dean, 1986-1987). Author, Review, "Mitsubishi Motors Corp. v. Chrysler-Plymouth, Inc.," Illinois Bar Journal, 1986. *Member:* American Bar Association (Member, Sections on: Taxation; International Law). Resident, Chicago, Illinois Office). ***LANGUAGES:*** German. ***PRACTICE AREAS:*** Customs Law; International Trade; Administrative Law. ***Email:*** kwilliams@rofgw.com

ASSOCIATES

USBALDO ANGEL, born Chicago, Illinois, July 27, 1975; (admission pending). *Education:* University of Pennsylvania (B.A., 1997); George Washington University (J.D., 2000). *Member:* American Bar Association (Member, International Law and Practice Section); International Law Society. ***LANGUAGES:*** Spanish. ***PRACTICE AREAS:*** International Transportation Law; Transportation; Litigation. ***Email:*** uangel@rofgw.com

ASHLEY WILLIAM CRAIG, born Santa Monica, California, December 8, 1970; (admission pending). *Education:* American University (B.A., 1992); Columbus School of Law of The Catholic University of America (J.D., 2000; Certificate in Comparative and International Law, 2000). *Member:* American Bar Association (Member, Sections on: Regulatory and Administrative Law; Antitrust); Transportation Law, Logistics and Policy Association; Transportation Lawyers Association; International Law Society; Society for International Affairs. ***PRACTICE AREAS:*** Export Regulation; International Trade; International Transportation Law; Customs Law; Admiralty and Maritime Law; Government Relations. ***Email:*** acraig@rofgw.com

KEVIN L. KELLY, admitted to bar, 1993, Oregon; 1999, Illinois (Not admitted in District of Columbia). *Education:* Washington & Jefferson College (B.S., 1987); Northwestern School of Law, Lewis & Clark College (J.D., 1993). Member, Moot Court. Review Board Member, Northwestern School of Law, Law Review. Deputy District Attorney, Washington County District Attorney's Office, Hillsboro, Oregon. (Resident, Chicago, Illinois Office). ***PRACTICE AREAS:*** Litigation; Customs Law; International Trade.

LARA A. RUTENBERG-AUSTRINS, admitted to bar, 1999, Illinois (Not admitted in District of Columbia). *Education:* Case Western Reserve University (B.A., 1991); Cleveland-Marshall College of Law (J.D., 1999). (Resident, Chicago, Illinois Office). ***PRACTICE AREAS:*** Customs Law; International Trade.

ELLEN C. SMITH, born Chestnut Hill, Pennsylvania, October 15, 1967; admitted to bar, 1999, Illinois (Not admitted in District of Columbia). *Education:* Dickinson College (B.A., 1989); John Marshall Law School (J.D., 1998). Co-Author: Medical Malpractice Notebook, 1989-1999. *Member:* Chicago and Lake County Bar Associations. (Resident, Chicago, Illinois Office). ***PRACTICE AREAS:*** Customs Law; International Trade.

OF COUNSEL

TODD C. FINEBERG, born Philadelphia, Pennsylvania, January 22, 1944; admitted to bar, 1968, Ohio; 1969, U.S. District Court, Northern District of

(This Listing Continued)

Ohio; 1972, California; 1975, U.S. District Court, Eastern District of California; 1989, District of Columbia and U.S. Court of International Trade; 1994, Maryland; 1995, U.S. District Court for the District of Columbia. *Education:* Cornell University (A.B., 1965); Boston University (J.D., 1968); George Washington University (LL.M., International Law, 1988). *Member:* The District of Columbia Bar; State Bar of California. ***LANGUAGES:*** Spanish. ***PRACTICE AREAS:*** International Trade; International Transactions; International Investment; Business; Trusts and Estates. ***Email:*** tcfineberg@rofgw.com

MICHAEL A. JOHNSON, born Philadelphia, Pennsylvania, September 14, 1948; admitted to bar, 1977, New York and U.S. Court of International Trade; 1978, U.S. Court of Appeals, Federal Circuit; 1983, U.S. District Court, Southern and Eastern Districts of New York; 1989, Illinois (Not admitted in District of Columbia). *Education:* Yale University (B.A., summa cum laude, 1970; M.A., 1972); Columbia University (J.D., 1976). Phi Beta Kappa. *Member:* Chicago and New York State Bar Associations; Customs and International Trade Bar Association (Member, Trial and Appellate Practice Committee, 1987—). (Resident, Chicago, Illinois Office). ***LANGUAGES:*** French, German and Italian. ***PRACTICE AREAS:*** Customs Law; International Trade. ***Email:*** mjohnson@rofgw.com

DONALD W. LEWIS, born Brooklyn, New York, September 15, 1931; admitted to bar, 1957, New York; 1965, U.S. District Court, Southern and Eastern Districts of New York; U.S. Court of International Trade; 1973-1982, U.S. Court of Customs and Patent Appeals; 1981, District of Columbia; 1982, U.S. Court of Appeals for the Federal Circuit. *Education:* Queens College of the City University of New York (B.A., 1953); Brooklyn Law School (LL.B., 1957). U.S. Customs Service, 1957-1987: Director: Office of Regulations and Rulings, 1979-1982; Entry Procedures and Penalties Division, 1982-1987. Former partner, Freeman, Wasserman and Schneider, 1988-June 1994. *Member:* The District of Columbia Bar; Customs and International Trade Bar Association. (Also practicing individually at same address). ***PRACTICE AREAS:*** Customs; International Trade. ***Email:*** dlewis@intr.net

LEGAL SUPPORT PERSONNEL

EDDIE L. EDWARDS, born Jamaica, New York, June 8, 1963. *Education:* LaGuardia College (B.S., 1985). [Non-Commissioned Officer (E5), U.S. Marine Corps, 1980-1985]. ***PRACTICE AREAS:*** Transportation; Administrative Law. ***Email:*** eedward@rofgw.com

MEL CHAVEZ, Licensed Customs Broker. (Resident, Chicago, Illinois Office).

ROEDER AND ASSOCIATES, P.C.

WASHINGTON, D.C.

(See McLean, Virginia)

Corporate Law, Business Law, Real Estate, Banking Law, Municipal Law, Construction Law, Commercial Litigation.

STEPHEN C. ROGERS

SUITE 200
1120 G STREET, N.W.
WASHINGTON, D.C. 20005-3801
Telephone: 202-737-0629
Fax: 202-737-0920
Email: SRogersLaw@aol.com
URL: http://www.lawyers.com/stephencrogers

Transportation, Railroad Law, Arbitration, Contracts, Arbitration and Interstate Commerce.

FIRM PROFILE: Stephen C. Rogers conducts a national practice representing clients in matters involving arbitration, litigation and contract negotiations and disputes. The firm offers general counselling and advice to railroads, public agencies and suppliers.

STEPHEN C. ROGERS, born New York, N.Y., April 23, 1941; admitted to bar, 1969, District of Columbia; 1977, U.S. Court of Appeals, Third Circuit; 1983, U.S. Supreme Court; 1985, U.S. Court of Appeals, Second Circuit. *Education:* Harvard College (A.B., 1962); Georgetown University (J.D., 1968). Case and Note Editor, Georgetown Law Journal, Vol. 55, 1967-1968. Law Clerk to Judge James R. Browning, U.S. Court of Appeals, Ninth Circuit, 1968-1969. General Counsel: U.S. Railway Association, 1981-1983; National Railroad Passenger Corp., 1991-1995. Associate, Covington & Burling, 1969-1976. *Member:* The District of Columbia Bar; Roster of Neutrals (Commercial Panel), American Arbitration Association.

ROGERS & KILLEEN

WASHINGTON, D.C.

(See Carter Ledyard & Milburn)

ROLLER & BAUER, PLLC

1020 NINETEENTH STREET, N.W.
SUITE 400
WASHINGTON, D.C. 20036
Telephone: 202-331-3300
Fax: 202-331-3322
Email: airlaw@rollerbauer.com
URL: http://www.lawyers.com/roller&bauerairlaw

Aviation Regulation, Federal Aviation Licenses, (Dept. of Transportation (DOT), Federal Aviation Administration (FAA), Customs, Immigration (INS), Agriculture (APHIS), etc.), International Aviation Law, Airline Contracts, Aviation Tax (Property, Excise Tax, User Fees, etc.), Aircraft Financing and Leasing, Aircraft Sales, Aircraft Title, Aviation Litigation, Aviation-related Trademark and Copyright.

FIRM PROFILE: Messrs. Roller and Bauer have extensive experience handling legal matters related to aviation. They have represented the interests of U.S. and foreign airlines for many years. Their clientele is worldwide and includes airlines and other aviation-related interests from the United States, Mexico, the Middle East and Africa, among others. Together their aviation-related experience totals more than 80 years.

MEMBERS OF FIRM

MOFFETT B. ROLLER, born Luray, Virginia, 1951; admitted to bar, 1976, Virginia and District of Columbia; 1977, New York, U.S. District Court for the District of Columbia, U.S. District Court, Southern and Eastern Districts of New York and U.S. District Court, Eastern District of Virginia; 1980, U.S. Supreme Court. *Education:* Virginia Polytechnic Institute and State University (B.S., 1973); University of Virginia (J.D., 1976). *Member:* The District of Columbia Bar; Virginia State Bar; New York State Bar Association. ***PRACTICE AREAS:*** Airline Regulation; International Aviation Law; Air Cargo; Aviation Tax; Aircraft Finance and Leasing. ***Email:*** mroller@rollerbauer.com

LEE ANTHONY BAUER, born Sycamore, Illinois, May 31, 1944; admitted to bar, 1991, Virginia; 1993, District of Columbia. *Education:* Southern Illinois University (B.A., 1967); Pepperdine University (M.A., 1978); George Washington University (J.D., with honors, 1991). Member: University Moot Court Honors Board. Editor, Journal of International Law and Economics. Commercial Pilot, instrumented rated, 1969—. *Member:* District of Columbia Bar; Virginia Bar Association. [USAF, 1967-1988]. ***PRACTICE AREAS:*** Aviation Regulation; Aeronautical Regulation; Aviation Law; Federal Aviation Licenses; Customs Overflight Law. ***Email:*** lbauer@rollerbauer.com

ROPER & QUIGG

WASHINGTON, D.C.

(See Arlington, Virginia)

Intellectual Property, Patent, Trademark, Copyright, Trade Secret and Unfair Competition Law, Associated Antitrust Matters and Complex Technology.

ROPES & GRAY

ONE FRANKLIN SQUARE
1301 K STREET, NW, SUITE 800 EAST
WASHINGTON, D.C. 20005-3333
Telephone: 202-626-3900
Telecopy: 202-626-3961
Email: postmaster@ropesgray.com
URL: http://www.ropesgray.com

Boston, Massachusetts Office: One International Place. Telephone: 617-951-7000. Fax: 617-951-7050.
Providence, Rhode Island Office: 30 Kennedy Plaza. Telephone: 401-455-4400. Fax: 401-455-4401.
New York, New York Office: 885 Third Avenue, Suite 3200. Telephone: 646-840-6800. Fax: 646-840-6850.

Antitrust, Banking, Bankruptcy and Creditors' Rights, Corporate, Employee Benefits, Environmental, Financial Institutions, Government Contracts, Legislative and Regulatory, Litigation and Appeals in all Courts, Securities, Taxation, Healthcare, Intellectual Property Information, Privacy.

(This Listing Continued)

RESIDENT MEMBERS

MICHAEL NUSSBAUM, born Berlin, Germany, March 26, 1935; admitted to bar, 1962, New York; 1964, District of Columbia; 1971, U.S. Supreme Court. *Education:* Dartmouth College and Hofstra College (B.A., 1957); University of Chicago (J.D., 1961; M.C.L., French Law, 1963). Intern, Legal Service of European Economic Community, Brussels, Belgium, 1963. Instructor, University of Michigan Law School, 1963-1964. Member, Panel of Arbitrators, American Arbitration Association. Member, Judicial Conference, D.C. Circuit, 1972—. *Member:* Bar Association of the District of Columbia; The District of Columbia Bar; American Bar Association; American Society of International Law. Fellow, American College of Trial Lawyers (D.C. State Committee, 1996—). ***Email:*** mnussbau@ropesgray.com

THOMAS M. SUSMAN, born Houston, Texas, February 24, 1943; admitted to bar, 1967, Texas; 1968, District of Columbia; 1985, Massachusetts. *Education:* Yale University (B.A., 1964); University of Texas (J.D., with high honors, 1967). Editor-in-Chief, Texas Law Review, 1966-1967. Law Clerk, Judge John Minor Wisdom, U.S. Court of Appeals, Fifth Circuit, 1967-1968. Visiting Professor of Law, University of Texas at Austin, 1999; Adjunct Professor of Law, Washington College of Law of the American University, 2000—. Special Assistant to Assistant Attorney General, Office of Legal Counsel, U.S. Department of Justice, 1968-1969. General Counsel, U.S. Senate Antitrust Subcommittee, 1977-1978. General Counsel, U.S. Senate Judiciary Committee, 1979-1980. Member, Advisory Council and General Counsel, U.S. Court of Federal Claims, 1988—. Editor: The Lobbying Manual, 1993. *Member:* The District of Columbia Bar (Chairman, Antitrust Section, 1983-1986); American Bar Association (Member, Latin American Legal Initiative Council, 2000—; Member, CEELI Executive Board, 1995-1997, Advisory Board, 1998—; Member, Board of Governors, 1995-1998; House of Delegates, 1995-1998; Chairman, Section on Administrative Law and Regulatory Practice, 1991-1992; Chair, Committee on Legislative Process and Lobbying, 1989-1990; Chair, Committee on Government Information and Privacy, 1985-1989; Council Member, 1982-1985); American Law Institute; Administrative Conference of the U.S.; Council on Legal Education Opportunity; American League of Lobbyists (Board of Directors, 1995—; Chair, Committee on Professional Ethics and Standards, 1995—). ***Email:*** tsusman@ropesgray.com

RUSSELL A. GAUDREAU, JR., born Boston, Massachusetts, February 25, 1943; admitted to bar, 1968, Massachusetts; 1991, District of Columbia. *Education:* University of Massachusetts (B.A., 1965); Suffolk University Law School (J.D., cum laude, 1968); New York University Law School (LL.M., Taxation, 1969). Editor-in-Chief, Suffolk University Law Review, 1967-1968. Law Clerk, Judge Harold R. Tyler, Jr., U.S. District Court, Southern District of New York. Adjunct Professor of Law, Georgetown University Law Center, 1991—; Adjunct Professor of Law, Boston University Law School, 1980—. Author, Chapter 23, *Benders Federal Tax Service,* "Tax-Sheltered Annuities, Church, Governmental and Qualified Bond Purchase Plans," *Member:* Boston and American Bar Associations; District of Columbia Bar. ***PRACTICE AREAS:*** Employee Benefits. ***Email:*** rgaudrea@ropesgray.com

MARTIN E. LYBECKER, born Lincoln, Nebraska, February 11, 1945; admitted to bar, 1970, Washington; 1972, District of Columbia; 1982, Pennsylvania; 1985, U.S. District Court for the District of Columbia and U.S. Court of Appeals, District of Columbia Circuit. *Education:* University of Washington (B.A., 1967; J.D., 1970); New York University (LL.M., 1971); University of Pennsylvania (LL.M., 1973). Graduate Fellow, University of Pennsylvania Law School, Center for the Study of Financial Institutions, 1971-1972. Attorney, Office of Chief Counsel, Division of Investment Management, Securities and Exchange Commission, 1972-1975. Associate Director, Division of Investment Management, Securities and Exchange Commission, 1978-1981. Associate Professor of Law, State University of New York-Buffalo, 1975-1978 (on leave, 1977-1978). Visiting Associate Professor of Law, Duke University, 1977-1978. Visiting Professor of Law, University of North Carolina, 1977. Adjunct Professor of Law, Georgetown University, 1974-1975, 1980-1981. Senior Lecturing Fellow in Law, Duke University, 2000—. *Member:* The District of Columbia Bar; American Bar Association (Member: Subcommittee on Bank Securities, 1980—; Subcommittee on Investment Companies and Investment Advisers, 1980—; Chair, Subcommittee on Financial Holding Companies, 1994—; Subcommittee on Fiduciary Law, 1988—; EC 1992 Task Force Committee on Investment Services and Products, 1989—; Chair, Committee on Developments in Investment Services, 1993—; Business Law Section). ***Email:*** mlybecker@ropesgray.com

SAMUEL J. BUFFONE, born New Kensington, Pennsylvania, October 3, 1946; admitted to bar, 1971, Pennsylvania; 1973, District of Columbia; 1978, U.S. Supreme Court; U.S. Court of Appeals, 1st, 2nd, 3rd, 4th, 5th, 9th, 11th and District of Columbia Circuits. *Education:* University of Pittsburgh (B.A., 1968); Georgetown University (J.D., 1971). Member, Editorial Board, Georgetown Law Review, 1970-1971. Author: "The Offenses of Richard M. Nixon," Quadrangle, 1974; "Defending A Civil RICO Case: Defenders Strategies and Tactics," PLI, 1984; "The Businessman's Guide to the Comprehensible Crime Control Act," ABA, 1985; "Departures from Federal Sentencing Guidelines in

(This Listing Continued)

White Collar Cases," ABA, 1989; "The RICO Debate," Constitution Vol. 2, No. 2, Winter 1990; "The Federal Sentencing Commission and the Importance of Process," 5 Fed. Sent. Rpt. No. 4 (1992); "Organizational Sanctions under The Federal Sentencing Guidelines: The Importance of Compliance Programs," (1991) (Prentice Hall). Adjunct Professor, Washington College of Law, American University, 1989. Law Clerk, Frances L. Van Dusen, U.S. Court of Appeals, Third Circuit, 1971-1972. Member, Committee on Appellate Advocacy of the Appellate Judges Conference, 1984. Member, Advisory Board, RICO Litigation Reporter, 1984—. Chairman, Practitioners Advisory Committee, United States Sentencing Commission, 1989-1992. Vice Chairman, Prentice Hall RICO Litigation Update, 1989-1993. *Member:* The District of Columbia Bar; American Bar Association (Chairperson, Committee on Forfeiture, 1986—; Committee on Sentencing Commission, 1986-1990; Vice Chairman, Committee on RICO, 1986-1988; Member, White Collar Crime Committee, 1984—, Criminal Justice Section). ***PRACTICE AREAS:*** White Collar Crime Law; RICO; Complex Litigation. ***Email:*** sbuffone@ropesgray.com

MARK L. LEZELL, born Detroit, Michigan, April 20, 1947; admitted to bar, 1973, District of Columbia. *Education:* Michigan State University (B.A., 1969); American University (J.D., 1972); Georgetown University (LL.M., in Taxation, 1976). Law Clerk, Chief Judge A. E. Robinson, Jr., U.S. District Court, 1971. Attorney, Office of Chief Counsel, Division of Corporation Finance, 1972-1976 and Legal Assistant to the Hon. I. M. Pollock, Commissioner, 1975, Securities and Exchange Commission. *Member:* The District of Columbia Bar (Chairman, Committee on Partnership, 1991-1992). ***PRACTICE AREAS:*** Business Law; Corporation Law; Finance, Technology and Securities. ***Email:*** mlezell@ropesgray.com

COLBURN T. CHERNEY, born Green Bay, Wisconsin, July 16, 1948; admitted to bar, 1974, Wisconsin and U.S. District Court, Western District of Wisconsin; 1979, District of Columbia. *Education:* DePauw University; University of Wisconsin (B.A., with honors, 1970; J.D., with honors, 1974). Author: "State and Federal Roles Under the Clean Water Act," Natural Resources Environment, Vol. 1, No. 4, 1986. Assistant General Counsel for Superfund, 1981-1983; Associate General Counsel for Water, 1983-1986, U.S. Environmental Protection Agency. *Member:* The District of Columbia Bar; American Bar Association (Vice-Chairman, Water Quality Committee, Natural Resource Section, 1986-1988; Chairman, 1989-1991); State Bar of Wisconsin. ***Email:*** ccherney@ropesgray.com

J. DANIEL BERRY, born Pittsburgh, Pennsylvania, October 11, 1951; admitted to bar, 1977, Maryland; 1978, District of Columbia. *Education:* University of Maryland (B.A., 1973); George Washington University National Law Center (J.D., high honors, 1977). Order of the Coif. Co-Author: "EPA's Pesticides in Groundwater Policy Will It Work?" 4 Natural Resources & Environment 16, 1989. Professorial Lecturer in Law, Control of Toxic and Hazardous Substances, George Washington University, National Law Center, 1987-1990. U.S. Environmental Protection Agency: Associate General Counsel for Grants, Contracts and General Law, 1987-1988; Assistant General Counsel for Superfund, 1983-1987. ***PRACTICE AREAS:*** Environmental Law. ***Email:*** dberry@ropesgray.com

MARK A. GREENWOOD, admitted to bar, 1978, District of Columbia. *Education:* University of Michigan (B.A., Phi Beta Kappa, 1974; J.D., 1978; Master of Public Policy, 1978). Assistant General Counsel, USEPA, 1983-1988. Associate General Counsel, USEPA, 1988-1990. Director, Office of Pollution Prevention and Toxics, USEPA, 1990-1994. ***Email:*** mgreenwo@ropesgray.com

JAMES M. SPEARS, born San Benito, Texas, 1952; admitted to bar, 1978, Texas; 1998, District of Columbia. *Education:* Texas Tech University (B.B.A., 1975); University of Texas, Austin (J.D., 1978); McGill University. Author: "Federal Merger Enforcement in Bankruptcy," Antitrust Magazine, Spring, 1992; "Government Regulation and the Environment: The Role of the Civil Code," Meredith Memorial Lecture Series, McGill University, 1989. Deputy Assistant Attorney General, Lands and Natural Resources Division, 1983-1984 and Civil Division, 1985-1988, U.S. Department of Justice. General Counsel, Federal Trade Commission, 1993-1994. *Member:* The District of Columbia Bar; American Bar Association. ***LANGUAGES:*** French. ***PRACTICE AREAS:*** Litigation; Administrative Law; Antitrust and Trade Regulation; International Law. ***Email:*** jspears@ropesgray.com

DAVID O. STEWART, born Washington, D.C., April 2, 1951; admitted to bar, 1980, District of Columbia; 1983, U.S. Supreme Court; 1986, Maryland. *Education:* Yale University (B.A., summa cum laude, 1973; J.D., 1978). Article and Book Review Editor, Yale Law Journal, 1977-1978. Author: "Raising the Stakes: Resisting the Upward Transformation of Antitrust and Fraud Charges," 20 Journal of American Criminal Law 207 (1993); "Basics of Criminal Liability for Corporations and Their Officials, and Use Compliance Programs and Internal Investigations," 22 Public Contract Law Review 81 (Winter 1993); contributor, *The Supreme Court and Its Justices* (J. Chaper, ed., 2001). Law Clerk to: Judge David Bazelon, U.S. Court of Appeals, District of Columbia Circuit, 1978; Judge J. Skelly Wright, U.S. Court of Appeals, District of Columbia Circuit, 1978-1979; Justice Lewis F. Powell, Jr., U.S. Supreme Court, 1979-1980. Author: "Supreme Court Report," ABA Journal, 1985-1997. *Member:*

(This Listing Continued)

The District of Columbia Bar; American Bar Association. ***PRACTICE AREAS:*** Complex Litigation; White Collar Crime; Appellate Practice; Supreme Court Litigation. ***Email:*** dstewart@ropesgray.com

ALAN G. PRIEST, born Rochester, New York, May 18, 1952; admitted to bar, 1979, District of Columbia; 1982, U.S. District Court for the District of Columbia and U.S. Court of Appeals, District of Columbia Circuit. *Education:* Boston College; State University of New York at Buffalo (B.A., magna cum laude, 1974); George Washington University (J.D., with high honors, 1979). Order of the Coif. *Member:* The District of Columbia Bar; American Bar Association (Member, Business Law Section). ***Email:*** apriest@ropesgray.com

PETER M. BRODY, born Bethlehem, Pennsylvania, August 24, 1958; admitted to bar, 1985, Pennsylvania; 1986, District of Columbia; 1992, Maryland. *Education:* Princeton University (A.B., magna cum laude, 1980); Harvard University (J.D., cum laude, 1984). Executive Editor, Harvard Law Review, 1983-1984. Law Clerk, Honorable Carl McGowan, U.S. Court of Appeals, District of Columbia Circuit, 1984-1985. Author: "Semi-Generic Geographical Wine Designations," 89 Trademark Reporter 979 (1999); "Protection of Geographical Indications in the Wake of TRIPs," 84 Trademark Rep 520 (1994); "Confidentiality Clauses in Research Contracts and Grants: Are They 'Unconstitutional Conditions'?" 22 Public Contract L.J. 447 (1993); "The First Amendment, Governmental Censorship, and Sponsored Research," 19 J. College & University L. 199 (1992). Co-Author: (with Prof. Clark Havighurst) "Accreditation and the Sherman Act," 57 L. & Contemp. Probs 199 (1994). Contributing Author: *Trademark Insights:* The First Circuit (International Trademark Association, 1995). *Member:* The District of Columbia Bar; Maryland State, Pennsylvania and American (Member, Intellectual Property Section); International Trademark Association (Member, Projects Editorial Board). ***Email:*** pbrody@ropesgray.com

GREGORY J. GLOVER, admitted to bar, 1989, D.C. *Education:* Harvard College (B.S., 1981); Harvard Law School (J.D., 1986); Duke University (M.D., 1987). ***Email:*** gglover@ropesgray.com

THOMAS B. SMITH, born Arlington, Virginia, November 7, 1954; admitted to bar, 1986, Pennsylvania; 1987, District of Columbia. *Education:* Dickinson College (B.A., magna cum laude, 1976); Georgetown University (J.D., magna cum laude, 1986). Phi Beta Kappa; Order of the Coif. Executive Editor, Georgetown Law Journal, 1986. Court Law Clerk, United States Court of Appeals for the District of Columbia Circuit, 1986-1987. Author: "Reexamining the Reasonable Access and Equal Time Provisions of the Federal Communications Act: Can These Provisions Stand if the Fairness Doctrine Falls?" 74 Geo. L.J. 1491 (1986); "FCC's New Program Access Rules Designed To Strengthen Cable Competitors," National Law Journal (July 5, 1993); "Udder Truth: Labels for Genetically Engineered Food," Legal Times (Aug. 1, 1994); "Programs Needed to Comply with Privacy Law," American Banber (Aug. 13, 1999). *Member:* The District of Columbia Bar. ***PRACTICE AREAS:*** Communications; Trade Regulation; First Amendment; Privacy Law. ***Email:*** tbsmith@ropesgray.com

KATHLEEN MARIE DELANEY, admitted to bar, 1987, Pennsylvania; 1988, District of Columbia. *Education:* University of Virginia (B.A., cum laude, 1982; J.D., 1987).

DINA L. MICHELS, born Los Angeles, California, March 22, 1961; admitted to bar, 1987, Massachusetts; 1990, District of Columbia; 1992, Maryland. *Education:* Harvard University (A.B., 1983); Georgetown University Law Center (J.D., cum laude, 1987). Notes and Comments Editor, Georgetown Law Journal, 1986-1987. Author: "Rate Regulation," McAlee, R. and Michels, D., Hall, M., Ed., Health Care Corporate Law Financing and Liability, Little, Brown & Co. 1994. *Member:* National Health Lawyers Association; American Academy of Hospital Attorneys. ***Email:*** dmichels@ropesgray.com

RESIDENT ASSOCIATES

J. STEVEN BAUGHMAN, born Charlottesville, Virginia, April 22, 1968; admitted to bar, 1994, N.Y.; 1996, D.C.; registered to practice before the U.S. Patent & Trademark Office. *Education:* Princeton University (B.S.E., 1990); Harvard Law School (J.D., 1993). ***Email:*** sbaughma@ropesgray.com

ALYSSA ALBERTELLI, born February 16, 1965; admitted to bar, 1995, Massachusetts; 1996, New York; 1997, District of Columbia. *Education:* Simmons College (B.A., with distinction, 1987); Boston University (M.B.A., 1992; J.D., cum laude, 1995). ***Email:*** aalberte@ropesgray.com

JENNIFER D. McNASBY, born New Brunswick, New Jersey; admitted to bar, 1996, Massachusetts; 1998, District of Columbia. *Education:* University of North Carolina, Chapel Hill (B.A., 1993); Boston College Law School (J.D., 1996). ***Email:*** jmcnasby@ropesgray.com

DAVID J. BAUM, born Torrance, California, November 11, 1967; admitted to bar, 1996, Maryland; 1998, District of Columbia. *Education:* Georgetown University School of Foreign Service (B.S.F.S., 1989); American University (J.D., summa cum laude, 1996). Note and Comment Editor, The American University Law Review. Author, "The Aftermath of Central Bank of Denver:

(This Listing Continued)

ROPES & GRAY, Washington—Continued

Private Aiding and Abetting Liability". *Member:* The District of Columbia Bar; American Bar Association. ***PRACTICE AREAS:*** Investment Management; Financial Services Law. ***Email:*** dbaum@ropesgray.com

KELLY B. KRAMER, born Philadelphia, PA, April 20, 1972; admitted to bar, 1998, N.Y.; 1999, D.C. *Education:* College of William & Mary (A.B., 1994); University of Pennsylvania (J.D., 1997). ***Email:*** kkramer@ropesgray.com

TODD M. RICHMAN, born Framingham, Massachusetts, January 26, 1970; admitted to bar, 1997, Virginia; 1999, District of Columbia. *Education:* Middlebury College (1992); Georgetown Law Center (J.D., magna cum laude, 1997). ***Email:*** trichman@ropesgray.com

LINDA L. LECRAW, born Mount Lebanon, Pennsylvania, January 11, 1971; admitted to bar, 1997, Maryland and U.S. Court of Appeals, Fourth Circuit; 1998, District of Columbia. *Education:* Harvard College (A.B., 1993); Harvard Law School (J.D., 1996). ***PRACTICE AREAS:*** Corporate Transactional; Biotechnology Transactional. ***Email:*** llecraw@ropesgray.com

BENJAMIN J. PRIESTER, admitted to bar, 1999, Conn. (Not admitted in District of Columbia). *Education:* Harvard University (A.B., 1996); Duke University (J.D., summa cum laude, 1998). Order of the Coif. ***Email:*** bpriester@ropesgray.com

ASHLEY N. BAILEY, admitted to bar, 1999, VA; 2000, D.C. *Education:* Georgetown University (B.A., 1996); Georgetown University Law Cemter (J.D., 1999). ***Email:*** abailey@ropesgray.com

PATRICIA L. BLOCK, born Lancaster, Pennsylvania, August 21, 1962; admitted to bar, 1999, Md. (Not admitted in District of Columbia). *Education:* Indiana University of Pennsylvania (B.A., 1984); Columbus School of Law, Catholic University of America (J.D., 1999). Phi Alpha Delta. ***LANGUAGES:*** French and German. ***PRACTICE AREAS:*** Business.

AMY SOBBA DIAZ, born Boise, Idaho, April 1, 1975; admitted to bar, 2000, Maryland (Not admitted in District of Columbia). *Education:* Linfield College (B.A., magna cum laude, 1997); Georgetown University (J.D., 2000). ***LANGUAGES:*** French. ***PRACTICE AREAS:*** Corporate Law; Financial Services Law. ***Email:*** adiaz@ropesgray.com

JEFFREY PEARLMAN, born Washington, D.C., April 18, 1971; admitted to bar, 1999, New York; 2000, District of Columbia. *Education:* Washington University (B.A., magna cum laude, 1993); George Washington University (J.D., with honors, 1998). Notes Editor, George Washington Law Review, 1997-1998. Clerk to the Honorable Robert Yock, U.S. Court of Federal Claims, 1998-1999. Author, Casenote, "Establishing the Correct Rate Within the Zone of Reasonableness: How Far Can FERC Go?," George Washington Law Review, Vol. 65, 1997. ***PRACTICE AREAS:*** Litigation.

(For Complete Biographical Data on all Personnel, see Professional Biographies at Boston, Massachusetts)

ROSE & ROSE

1320 19TH STREET NW, SUITE 601
WASHINGTON, D.C. 20036
Telephone: 202-331-8557
Fax: 202-331-0996
URL: http://www.lawyers.com/rose&rose
URL: http://www.rose&rose.com

Employment Discrimination, Employment Law, Civil Rights Litigation, Environmental Law, Superfund and Hazardous Waste Issues, Administrative Law, Civil Litigation.

FIRM PROFILE: Rose & Rose, P.C. is a four lawyer firm with a national practice based in Washington, D.C. The firm specializes in federal court litigation and appellate work, particularly in the areas of equal employment opportunity and environmental law. David L. Rose started the firm in December, 1987, following his departure from the U.S. Department of Justice. The firm maintains an active administrative and court practice representing individuals and groups with claims of race, religion, handicap, age, sex and national origin discrimination in employment. The firm has also successfully defended against large civil rights claims. The firm's environmental practice includes the representation of potentially responsible parties under hazardous waste laws and of citizen groups seeking to enforce environmental laws against polluting industries, litigation involving hazardous waste, environmental justice matters and toxic tort litigation.

DAVID L. ROSE, born Gardner, Massachusetts, April 26, 1931; admitted to bar, 1956, Massachusetts and District of Columbia; 1959, U.S. District Court, Southern Districts of District of Columbia, Maryland, Ohio and Illinois. *Education:* Harvard University (B.A. cum laude, 1953; LL.B., cum laude, 1956). Trial lawyer, 1956-1959 and appellate lawyer, 1959-1967, Civil Division, Department of Justice. Special Assistant to the Attorney General, 1967-1969. Chief, Employment Litigation Section, Civil Rights Division, Department of Justice, 1969-1987. Staff Representative and Chairman, Interagency Staff Committee, which developed the "Uniform Guidelines on Employee Selection Procedures," 1972-1980. *Member:* Maryland State, American (Committee On: Landlord Employment Law) and Federal Bar Associations. Fellow: College of Labor and Employment Lawyers. [Active Duty, U.S. Army Reserve, March-August, 1957]. ***REPORTED CASES:*** Griggs vs. Duke Power Co.; Local 189, United Papermakers vs. United States, Contractors Association of Eastern Pennsylvania vs. Secretary of Labor; Moody vs. Albermarle Paper Co.; EEOC and United States vs. A.T.&T.; United States vs. Fairfax County, Virginia; Bazemore vs. Friday; NAACP v. Town of Harrison. ***PRACTICE AREAS:*** Equal Employment Opportunity Law; Appellate Litigation.

JOSHUA N. ROSE, born Washington, D.C., April 2, 1962; admitted to bar, 1987, Missouri 1988, Illinois; 1989, District of Columbia. *Education:* Washington University (A.B., cum laude, 1984); University of North Carolina (J.D., 1987). Author: "Forum non Conveniens and Multinational Corporations: A Government Interest Approach," 11 North Carolina Journal of International Law & Commercial Regulation 694-714, 1986. ***LANGUAGES:*** French. ***PRACTICE AREAS:*** Environmental Litigation; Environmental Cost Recovery; Water Quality; Civil Rights; Employment Litigation; Discrimination. ***Email:*** josh@roselawyers.com

DAVID M. WACHTEL, born New Haven, Connecticut, August 17, 1962; admitted to bar, 1990, California; 1991, District of Columbia; 1997, Maryland. *Education:* Washington University (B.A., 1984); University of Texas (J.D., with honors, 1989). Notes Editor, Texas Law Review, 1988-1989. *Member:* The District of Columbia Bar; Maryland State Bar Association, Inc.; Metropolitan Washington Employment Lawyers Association; National Employment Lawyers Association. ***PRACTICE AREAS:*** Employment Discrimination; Americans with Disabilities Act; Federal Employment Law; Employment Contracts; FOIA & Privacy Act. ***Email:*** davew@roselawyers.com

ASSOCIATE

LINDA Y. SROUFE, born Covington, Kentucky, June 22, 1951; admitted to bar, 1986, District of Columbia; 1989, U.S. District Court, District of Columbia; 1995, Maryland and U.S. District Court, District of Maryland. *Education:* Northwestern University (B.A., 1972); George Washington University National Law Center (J.D., 1986). *Member:* The District of Columbia Bar; Maryland State Bar Association, Inc. ***PRACTICE AREAS:*** Employment Litigation. ***Email:*** linda@roselawyers.com

ROSEN & DE MARTINO

WASHINGTON, D.C.

(See De Martino Finkelstein Rosen & Virga)

LAW OFFICE OF HAROLD ROSEN

WASHINGTON, D.C.

(See Potomac, Maryland)

Construction Law, Government Contract Law, Alternative Dispute Resolution, Construction Litigation.

MERYL BERGER ROSENBERG

WASHINGTON, D.C.

(See Potomac, Maryland)

Surrogacy Law, Adoption Law.

ROSENMAN & COLIN LLP

805 15TH STREET, N.W., 9TH FLOOR
WASHINGTON, D.C. 20005-2212
Telephone: 202-216-4600
Facsimile: (202) 216-4700
URL: http://www.rosenman.com

New York, N.Y. Office: 575 Madison Avenue, 10022. Telephone: 212-940-8800. Facsimiles: (212) 940-8776; (212) 935-0679. Website: http://www.rosenman.com.

Newark, New Jersey Office: Suite 2600, 1 Gateway Center, 07102-5397. Telephone: 973-645-0572. Facsimile: 973-645-0573.

Charlotte, North Carolina Office: 401 South Tryon Street, Suite 2600, 28202-1935. Telephone: 704-444-2000. Facsimile: 704-444-2060.

General Practice.

(This Listing Continued)

(This Listing Continued)

RESIDENT PARTNERS

HOWARD J. BRAUN, born Oceanside, New York, June 30, 1937; admitted to bar, 1963, District of Columbia. *Education:* Brown University (A.B., cum laude, 1959); New York University (LL.B., 1962). Co-Author: "The Federal Communications Commission," *West's Federal Practice Manual* 2nd Edition, 1970. Chairman, Editorial Advisory Board, *Commlaw Conspectus*, The Columbus School of Law, Catholic University of America, Institute for Communications Law Studies, 1992-1999. Attorney, Office of the General Counsel, Federal Communications Commission, 1962-1965. *Member:* The District of Columbia Bar; Federal Communications Bar Association (Member, Executive Committee, 1976-1979). ***SPECIAL AGENCIES:*** FCC. ***PRACTICE AREAS:*** Telecommunications Law. ***Email:*** hjbraun@rosenman.com

RICHARD A. GROSS, born Chicago, Illinois, January 6, 1949; admitted to bar, 1973, Massachusetts; 1980, District of Columbia. *Education:* Wesleyan University (B.A., 1970); Harvard Law School (J.D., 1973). National Merit Scholar, 1966. Horace Reed Baldwin Fellow, 1970. Author: "Making Bankruptcy Work For Consumers," 12 N.E. L. Rev. 1, 1976. Teaching Fellow, Harvard University Law School, 1976-1978. Lecturer, Massachusetts Continuing Legal Education, 1978-1979. Assistant Attorney General and Chief, Consumer Protection Division, Massachusetts Department of the Attorney General, 1974-1978. Executive Director, United States Consumer Product Safety Commission, 1979-1981. General Counsel, National Consumer Cooperative Bank, 1982-1983. Trustee, University of District of Columbia, 1990-1995. *Member:* The District of Columbia Bar. ***LANGUAGES:*** Spanish. ***REPORTED CASES:*** Berk v. Sherman, 682 A2d 209 (1996); GPG v. Georgetown, 836 A.2d 1 (1982); McDonald v. Lawyers Title, 79 F.3d 1141 (1996). ***Email:*** ragross@rosenman.com

TIMOTHY J. LYNES, born New York, N.Y., 1959; admitted to bar, 1984, New Jersey and U.S. District Court, District of New Jersey; 1985, District of Columbia and U.S. District Court for the District of Columbia; 1990, Virginia and U.S. District Court, Eastern District of Virginia; 1991, Maryland and U.S. District Court, District of Maryland; 1995, U.S. Supreme Court. *Education:* Fairfield University (B.A., 1981); Gonzaga University Law School (J.D., cum laude, 1984). Associate Editor, Gonzaga Law Review, 1983-1984. Law Secretary to Judge Richard Newman, Superior Court, New Jersey, 1984-1985. *Member:* The District of Columbia Bar; Virginia State Bar; Federal and American Bar Associations; Defense Research Institute. ***Email:*** tjlynes@rosenman.com

MICHAEL J. METZGER, born Saginaw, Michigan, April 29, 1960; admitted to bar, 1985, Indiana and Florida; 1989, District of Columbia. *Education:* University of Michigan (B.B.A., 1982); Valparaiso University (J.D., 1985); Georgetown University (LL.M., 1990). Associate Editor, Valparaiso University Law Review. U.S. Securities and Exchange Commission: Attorney Advisor, Division of Market Regulation, 1987-1990; Senior Counsel, Office of International Affairs, 1990-1993. ***PRACTICE AREAS:*** Finance; Securities; Banks and Banking. ***Email:*** mjmetzger@rosenman.com

SPECIAL COUNSEL

MICHAEL DEAN GAFFNEY, born New York, N.Y., May 24, 1961; admitted to bar, 1987, Massachusetts; 1994, District of Columbia. *Education:* University of California at Los Angeles (B.A., 1984); Suffolk University Law School (J.D., cum laude, 1987). Editor, Suffolk University Law Review, 1986-1987. Law Clerk to Justice Joseph R. Nolan, Supreme Judicial Court of Massachusetts, 1987-1988. ***Email:*** mgaffney@rosenman.com

SHELLEY SADOWSKY, born Baltimore, Maryland, August 18, 1952; admitted to bar, 1984, Maryland (Not admitted in District of Columbia). *Education:* George Washington University (B.A., 1974); University of Maryland (J.D., 1983). Board of Directors, American Women in Radio and Television, 2000—. *Member:* Maryland State Bar Association; Federal Communications Bar Association. ***PRACTICE AREAS:*** Telecommunications. ***Email:*** ssadowsky@rosenman.com

LEE WARNER SHUBERT, born Cleveland, Ohio, February 11, 1945; admitted to bar, 1973, Ohio (inactive); 1974, District of Columbia; 1993, Virginia; U.S. Supreme Court; U.S. Court of Appeals for the District of Columbia. *Education:* Miami University (A.B., 1966; M.A., 1967); Chase Law School of Northern Kentucky State University (J.D., 1973). Managing Member, Haley, Bader & Potts, P.L.C., 1993-1996; Ballston Aero Trust Services, L.C., 1996—; Ballston Trust Services, L.C., 1992—. Trustee, President and Director, Atmor Properties, Inc.; Trustee, Pinnacle Broadcasting Company, Inc. *Member:* The District of Columbia Bar; Virginia State Bar. ***PRACTICE AREAS:*** Administrative Law; Business Law; Communications Law; Covenants Not To Compete; Entertainment Law; Media Trustee/Receiverships.

SANDRA L. SPALLETTA, born Troy, New York, February 3, 1954; admitted to bar, 1980, New York; 1985, District of Columbia. *Education:* Dickinson College (B.A., summa cum laude, 1976); Harvard Law School (J.D., 1979). *Member:* The District of Columbia Bar. ***PRACTICE AREAS:*** Corporate Law; Real Estate Law. ***Email:*** sspalletta@rosenman.com

(This Listing Continued)

RESIDENT ASSOCIATES

LAURA A. OTIS, born New York, New York; admitted to bar, 1998, Maryland and District of Columbia. *Education:* Georgetown University (B.S.F.S., 1992); American University, Washington College of Law (J.D., 1997). Recipient, Fulbright Scholarship, 1993-1994. Member, Administrative Law Review. Author, "Cellular Telephones and the Potential Hazards of RF Radiation: Responses to the Fear and Controversy," Virginia Journal of Law and Technology (Spring 1998). *Member:* District of Columbia Bar; Maryland State and Federal Communications Bar Associations. ***LANGUAGES:*** Finnish, Spanish, Portuguese.

JAMES A. ZEMBRZUSKI, born February 10, 1975; (admission pending). *Education:* University of Virginia (B.S., 1997); George Washington University (J.D., with honors, 2001). ***Email:*** jazembrzuski@rosenman.com

(For complete biographical data on all personnel, see Professional Biographies at New York, New York)

ROSENZWEIG LAW OFFICE, L.L.P.

516 C STREET NORTHEAST, SUITE 300

WASHINGTON, D.C. 20002

Telephone: 202-543-9370

Fax: 202-543-9372

URL: http://www.rosenzweiglaw.com

Email: psr@rosenzweiglaw.com

URL: http://www.lawyers.com/rosenzweiglawoffice

Supreme Court and Federal Appeals, White Collar Crimes, Grand Jury Practice, Legal Ethics, Legal and Professional Malpractice, Administrative Law, Legislative Practice, Environmental Law and Environmental Criminal Defense.

FIRM PROFILE: The firm's practice builds on the experience of Paul Rosenzweig who was formerly Senior Litigation Counsel in the Office of the Independent Counsel (In re: Madison Guaranty Savings & Loan Association), and has served as Counsel (Investigations) for the House of Representatives Committee on Transportation and Infrastructure. The firm's national practice includes a special emphasis on appellate litigation, legislative investigations, legal ethics and federal trial practice.

PAUL S. ROSENZWEIG, born New York, N.Y., October 31, 1959; admitted to bar, 1987, Pennsylvania; 1988, District of Columbia and U.S. Court of Appeals, Eleventh Circuit; 1990, U.S. Court of Appeals, Fifth and Sixth Circuits; 1991, U.S. Supreme Court. *Education:* Haverford College (B.A., 1981); Scripps Institution of Oceanography, University of California at San Diego (M.S., 1982); University of Chicago (J.D., cum laude, 1986). Order of the Coif. Comment Editor, The University of Chicago Law Review, 1985-1986. Law Clerk to Judge R. Lanier Anderson, III, U.S. Court of Appeals for the Eleventh Circuit, 1986-1987. Author: "Abusing the Canons," Legal Times, July 30, 2001, S0. Co-Author with Nathan A. Fishbach, "EPA Finally is Giving Guidance on its Probes," National Law Journal, August 22, 1994 at A21. Adjunct Professor of Law, White Collar and Corporate Crime, George Madison University School of Law, 2000_. Lecturer: "Trial Techniques in Environmental Criminal Cases," ALI-ABA Environmental Crimes Seminar, Washington, D.C., October 1993; "Small Business Regulatory Enforcement and Fairness Act and Congressional Oversight," ABA, Washington, D.C., September 1995; "Attorney-Client Privilege, Perjury and the Independent Counsel," Chemical Manufacturer's Association, General Counsel's Network, Washington, D.C., November 1999. Trial Attorney, Environmental Crimes Section, U.S. Department of Justice, 1987-1994. Associate, Comey, Boyd & Luskin, Washington, D.C., 1994-1995. Counsel (Investigations), House Committee on Transportation and Infrastructure, Washington, D.C., 1995-1997. Associate Independent Counsel, 1997-1999 and Senior Litigation Counsel, 1999-2000, Office of the Independent Counsel, Madison Guaranty Savings & Loan. *Member:* The District of Columbia Bar; American Bar Association. ***REPORTED CASES:*** United States v. Hubbell, 120 S.Ct. 2037 (2000); In re: Sealed Case No. 99-3091, 192 F.3d 995 (D.C. 1999). ***PRACTICE AREAS:*** Appellate Practice; Legal Ethics; Environmental Criminal Law; Federal Criminal Law; Federal Civil Litigation.

ROSS, DIXON & BELL, L.L.P.

2001 K STREET, N.W.

WASHINGTON, D.C. 20006-1040

Telephone: 202-662-2000

Fax: 202-662-2190

Email: info@rdblaw.com

URL: http://www.rdblaw.com

Irvine, California Office: 5 Park Plaza, Suite 1200, 92614. Telephone: 949-622-2700. Fax: 949-622-2739.

San Diego, California Office: 550 West B Street, Suite 400, 92101-3538. Telephone: 619-235-4040. Fax: 619-231-8796.

(This Listing Continued)

ROSS, DIXON & BELL, L.L.P., Washington—Continued

Chicago, Illinois Office: 3 First National Plaza, 70 West Madison Street, Suite 525, 60602-4261. Telephone: 312-759-1920. Fax: 312-759-1939.

General Trial and Appellate Practice before State and Federal Courts, Insurance Coverage Litigation and Counseling, Directors and Officers Liability, Professional Liability, Environmental/Mass Tort Coverage, White Collar Criminal Defense, Antitrust.

PARTNERS

LESLIE S. AHARI, born Danbury, Connecticut, October 30, 1963; admitted to bar, 1988, Virginia; 1989, District of Columbia. *Education:* Duke University (A.B., magna cum laude, 1985); Harvard University (J.D., cum laude, 1988). Phi Beta Kappa. *Member:* The District of Columbia Bar; Virginia State Bar; American Bar Association. ***Email:*** lahari@rdblaw.com

DANIEL ARONOWITZ, born Cincinnati, Ohio, June 3, 1967; admitted to bar, 1991, California; 1994, District of Columbia. *Education:* The Ohio State University (B.A., 1988); Vanderbilt University (J.D., 1991). Phi Beta Kappa. Mortarboard Honorary. Phi Kappa Phi. Associate Editor, Vanderbilt Law Review, 1989-1991. Author: Note, "Retracing the Antitrust Roots of Section 1972 of the Bank Holding Company Act," 44 Vanderbilt Law Review 865. *Member:* The District of Columbia Bar; State Bar of California. ***Email:*** daronowitz@rdblaw.com

ALEC M. BARINHOLTZ, born Chicago, Illinois, October 20, 1957; admitted to bar, 1988, California. *Education:* Northern Illinois University (B.S., 1979); Southwestern University School of Law (J.D. magna cum laude, 1988). Articles Editor, Southwestern University Law Review, 1987-1988. Author: "False Light Invasion of Privacy: False Tort?" 17 Southwestern University Law Review 135, 1987. *Member:* State Bar of California; American Bar Association. (Resident, Irvine, California). ***Email:*** abarinholtz@rdblaw.com

ROY MORROW BELL, born Pittsburgh, Pennsylvania, April 27, 1944; admitted to bar, 1974, California; 1988, New York. *Education:* United States Naval Academy (B.A., 1966); California Western School of Law (J.D., with honors, 1974). Phi Alpha Delta. Lead Articles Editor, California Western Law Journal, 1972-1973. Associate Professor, California Western School of Law, 1974-1976. Trial Lawyer of the Month, San Diego Trial Lawyers Association, March, 1977; Litigator of the Month, The National Law Journal, February, 2000. President, California Western School of Law Alumni Association, 1987-1990. Chairman, Board of Trustees, California Western School of Law, 1995-1997 and Chairman Emeritus. *Member:* San Diego County, New York State and American Bar Associations; State Bar of California. (Irvine and San Diego, California). ***Email:*** rbell@rdblaw.com

CHARLES T. BLAIR, born Harrisonburg, Virginia, August 10, 1965; admitted to bar, 1990, Virginia; 1991, District of Columbia. *Education:* University of Virginia (B.A., with high distinction, 1987; J.D., 1990). Phi Beta Kappa; Order of the Coif. Executive Editor, Virginia Law Review, 1989-1990. Law Clerk to the Honorable H. Emory Widener, Jr., U.S. Court of Appeals, Fourth Circuit, 1990-1991. Co-Author: "Developments in West Virginia's Insurance Bad Faith Law—Where Do We Go From Here?" 98 West Virginia Law Review 267, 1995. Author: Comment, "Spencer v. Commonwealth and Recent Developments in the Admissibility of DNA Fingerprint Evidence," 76 Virginia Law Review 853, 1990. *Member:* The District of Columbia Bar; Virginia State Bar; American Bar Association. ***Email:*** tblair@rdblaw.com

EILEEN KING BOWER, born Naperville, Illinois, November 27, 1964; admitted to bar, 1988, Illinois and U.S. District Court, Northern District of Illinois. *Education:* Loyola University (B.A., cum laude, 1987; J.D., 1988). *Member:* Chicago, Illinois State and American Bar Associations. (Resident, Chicago, Illinois). ***Email:*** ebower@rdblaw.com

WILLIAM H. BRIGGS, JR., born Statesville, North Carolina, September 11, 1944; admitted to bar, 1969, North Carolina; 1972, District of Columbia. *Education:* Davidson College (A.B., 1966); Duke University (J.D., with honors, 1969). Member, Duke Law Journal, 1968-1969. Assistant U.S. Attorney, 1976-1984. Solicitor, Nuclear Regulatory Commission, 1984-1989. *Member:* The District of Columbia Bar; North Carolina Bar Association. [Field Artillery, U.S. Army, 1969-1971]. ***Email:*** wbriggs@rdblaw.com

WALLACE A. CHRISTENSEN, born Jamaica, New York, September 6, 1950; admitted to bar, 1976, New York and District of Columbia. *Education:* Boston College (A.B., summa cum laude, 1972); Harvard University (J.D., cum laude, 1975); The National Institute for Trial Advocacy (1977-2001). Phi Beta Kappa. *Member:* Bar Association of the District of Columbia; New York State and American Bar Associations; The Professional Liability Underwriting Society. ***Email:*** wchristensen@rdblaw.com

GARY V. DIXON, born Pittsburgh, Pennsylvania, December 5, 1950; admitted to bar, 1975, Virginia; 1977, Virgin Islands and District of Columbia. *Education:* Duke University; Bucknell University (B.S.B.A., magna cum laude, 1972); University of Virginia (J.D., 1975). Phi Beta Kappa. Order of the Coif. Law Clerk to the Honorable Warren H. Young, U.S. District Judge, Virgin Islands, 1975-1976. *Member:* The District of Columbia Bar. ***Email:*** gdixon@rdblaw.com

(This Listing Continued)

JOHN W. DUCHELLE, born Hamden, Connecticut, August 8, 1950; admitted to bar, 1990, Ohio; 1996, District of Columbia. *Education:* University of California at Berkeley (B.A., 1973); University of Virginia (J.D., 1990). *Member:* The District of Columbia Bar. ***Email:*** jduchelle@rdblaw.com

DAVID R. DWARES, born Wilmington, Delaware, April 20, 1963; admitted to bar, 1988, Pennsylvania; 1990, District of Columbia. *Education:* Vanderbilt University (B.A., summa cum laude, 1985); University of Pennsylvania (J.D., 1988). Phi Beta Kappa. *Member:* The District of Columbia Bar; Pennsylvania and American Bar Associations. ***Email:*** ddwares@rdblaw.com

BARBARA E. ETKIND, born Elmira, New York, September 30, 1950; admitted to bar, 1975, Ohio; 1976, Pennsylvania; 1990, District of Columbia. *Education:* Brandeis University (B.A., magna cum laude, 1972); University of Michigan (J.D., cum laude, 1975). Note Editor, Michigan Law Review, 1974-1975. Law Clerk to the Honorable George C. Edwards, Jr., U.S. Court of Appeals, Sixth Circuit, 1975-1976. Assistant to the Solicitor General of the United States, 1980-1984. *Member:* The District of Columbia Bar. ***Email:*** betkind@rdblaw.com

ELIZABETH SARAH GERE, born Rochester, New York, September 14, 1947; admitted to bar, 1973, Maryland and District of Columbia; 1980, Ohio. *Education:* Denison University (B.A., with high honors, 1969); George Washington University (J.D., with honors, 1972). Phi Beta Kappa. Adjunct Professor, Georgetown University Law Center, 1993—. American Inns of Court (Master, 1984-1996; Secretary-Treasurer, 1986-1987; Counselor, 1987-1988, 1994-1996). Member, D.C. Board on Professional Responsibility Hearing Committee, 1994-2000. Chair, U.S. District Court Committee on Pro Se Litigation, 1996-1998. Member, D.C. Court of Appeals Committee on Admissions, 1995—. Member, Judicial Conference for the District of Columbia Circuit, 1975-1980, 1984-2000. Law Clerk to the Honorable June L. Green, U.S. District Judge, District of Columbia, 1972-1974. U.S. Department of Justice-Trial Attorney and Senior Trial Counsel, 1975-1980, 1986-1987. Assistant U.S. Attorney, Southern District of Ohio, 1980-1985 (Chief Civil Division). Instructor, 1981-1985 and Assistant Director, 1985-1986, Attorney General Advocacy Institute. Fellow: American Bar Foundation. *Member:* The District of Columbia Bar; American Bar Association (Member, Sections of Litigation; Tort and Insurance Practice). ***Email:*** egere@rdblaw.com

JOHN R. GERSTEIN, born Washington, D.C., May 5, 1951; admitted to bar, 1975, District of Columbia. *Education:* University of Michigan (A.B., with high distinction and honors, 1972; J.D., magna cum laude, 1975). Order of the Coif; Phi Beta Kappa. *Member:* The District of Columbia Bar; Defense Research Institute. ***Email:*** jgerstein@rdblaw.com

DAVID M. GISCHE, born Los Angeles, California, November 4, 1949; admitted to bar, 1978, District of Columbia. *Education:* Harvard University (A.B., magna cum laude, 1971); Stanford University (M.A., 1974); Yale University (J.D., 1978). Author: "The New York City Banks and the Development of the National Banking System," The American Journal of Legal History, Vol. XXIII. Special Assistant to the Mayor of the City of Boston, 1974-1975; Chairman, Board of Directors, Microlog Corporation. . *Member:* The District of Columbia Bar; American Bar Association. ***Email:*** dgische@rdblaw.com

CHARLES I. HADDEN, born Chicago, Illinois, June 4, 1950; admitted to bar, 1975, Michigan; 1979, District of Columbia. *Education:* Michigan State University (B.S., with high honors, 1972); University of Michigan (J.D., 1975). Author: "Transportation Insurance Co. v. Moriel: Texas Restricts Grounds for Punitive Damages," Coverage, Vol. 4, No. 2 (March/April 1994). Contributing Author: "Occupational Safety and Health Law," The Bureau of National Affairs, Inc., 1988. *Member:* The District of Columbia Bar; State Bar of Michigan. ***Email:*** chadden@rdblaw.com

SEAN M. HANIFIN, born Orange, New Jersey, December 21, 1957; admitted to bar, 1981, District of Columbia. *Education:* Swarthmore College (B.A., with high honors, 1978); University of Chicago (J.D., 1981). Phi Beta Kappa; Phi Delta Phi. *Member:* The District of Columbia Bar; American Bar Association (Member, Sections of Litigation, Tort and Insurance Practice; Committees on Insurance Coverage and Professional Officers' and Directors' Liability Law; Forum Committee on the Construction Industry). ***Email:*** shanifin@rdblaw.com

VAN E. HAYNIE, born Logan, Utah, July 2, 1956; admitted to bar, 1984, California. *Education:* University of Utah (B.A., cum laude, 1981); Brigham Young University (J.D., cum laude, 1984). Member, 1982-1984 and Director, 1983-1984, Board of Advocates. Vice Chairman, San Diego Biotechnology Forum, 1988-1989. *Member:* San Diego County (Member, Sections on: Business Law; Computer Law and High Technology; International Law; Real Property) and American (Member, Sections on: Corporation; Banking and Business Law; Taxation) Bar Associations; State Bar of California (Member, Sections on: Business Law; Tax; Real Property). (Resident, San Diego, California). ***Email:*** vhaynie@rdblaw.com

(This Listing Continued)

MERRIL JAY HIRSH, born Trenton, New Jersey, October 30, 1957; admitted to bar, 1982, District of Columbia. *Education:* Oberlin College (B.A., with high honors in Government, 1979); Harvard University (J.D., magna cum laude, 1982). Phi Beta Kappa, 1978. Recipient, Comfort Starr Award for Excellence in Government, 1979. Trial Attorney, U.S. Department of Justice, Civil Division, 1982-1989. Author: "Can an Insurer and an Insured Settle an Insurance Policy?" *Mealey's Litigation report* 15 (Oct. 28, 1997). Co-Author: with David M. Gische, "Settlement Allocation Under Directors' and Officers' Liability Policies: A Return to Basics," *Coverage* 20 (Mar./April, 1995); with Gary V. Dixon and David M. Gische, "The Nordstrom Decision and Settlement Allocation Under D & O Policies," *Coverage* 1 (May/June 1995). *Member:* The District of Columbia Bar. ***Email:*** mhirsh@rdblaw.com

TIMOTHY P. IRVING, born San Diego, California, December 18, 1955; admitted to bar, 1983, California. *Education:* University of California, Davis (B.S., with honors, 1978; J.D., 1982). Co-chair, Moot Court Board, 1980-1982. Extern Law Clerk, Justice Roger G. Connor, Alaska Supreme Court, 1981. *Member:* San Diego County and American Bar Associations; State Bar of California. (Irvine and San Diego, California). ***Email:*** tirving@rdblaw.com

CARMEN R. KELLEY, born Memphis, Tennessee, November 11, 1963; admitted to bar, 1990, Tennessee; 1992, District of Columbia; 1995, U.S. District Court for the District of Columbia; 1996, U.S. Tax Court; 1997, U.S. Court of Appeals for the District of Columbia Circuit. *Education:* Baylor University (B.S.Ed., cum laude, 1984; M.S.Ed., 1985); Memphis State University (J.D., with honors, 1990). Phi Alpha Delta. Recipient, American Jurisprudence Awards: Torts I, Torts, II, Contracts, II, Civil Procedure II, Criminal Law and Moot Court. Staff Member, Memphis State Law Review, 1988-1990. Assistant Chief Justice, Moot Court Board, 1989-1990. Champion and Best Oral Advocate, Advanced Moot Court Competition, 1988. Member, National Mock Trial Team, Regional Semifinals, 1990. Author: Article, "Substantial Assistance Litigation From The Defense Perspective--An Update," ABA, Section of Criminal Justice, White Collar Crime Newsletter, December, 1995. Instructor, National Institute for Trial Advocacy, Georgetown University: Deposition Skills Program, 1995; Advanced Trial Advocacy Seminar, 2000. Executive Council Member, Assistant United States Attorneys Association, 1998—. *Member:* The District of Columbia Bar; Tennessee and American (Member: Complex Litigation Committee, 1994-1997; White Collar Crime Committee, 1994-1997) Bar Associations; Edward Bennett Williams American Inn of Court (Pupil, 1993; Associate-at-Large, 1994-1998; Barrister, 1998—). ***Email:*** ckelley@rdblaw.com

THOMAS T. LOCKE, born Oxnard, California, April 25, 1960; admitted to bar, 1991, Maryland; 1997, District of Columbia. *Education:* University of New Mexico (B.S.E.E., 1982); George Washington University (J.D., with high honors, 1990). Order of the Coif. Member, The George Washington Law Review. Law Clerk to the Honorable Fredric N. Smalkin, U.S. District Judge, District of Maryland, 1990-1991. *Member:* The District of Columbia Bar; Maryland State Bar Association, Inc. [Lt., U.S. Navy, 1982-1987]. ***Email:*** tlocke@rdblaw.com

LEWIS K. LOSS, born New York, N.Y., March 17, 1958; admitted to bar, 1983, District of Columbia. *Education:* University of Michigan (B.A., with honors, 1980); Harvard University (J.D., 1983). Member, The Professional Liability Underwriting Society. *Member:* The District of Columbia Bar; American Bar Association. ***Email:*** lloss@rdblaw.com

STACEY L. McGRAW, born Nashua, New Hampshire, March 27, 1968; admitted to bar, 1993, Pennsylvania; 1996, District of Columbia. *Education:* University of Virginia (B.A., with distinction, 1990); University of Michigan (J.D., cum laude, 1993). *Member:* The District of Columbia Bar; American Bar Association. ***Email:*** smcgraw@rdblaw.com

TERRENCE R. McINNIS, born Seattle, Washington, July 19, 1966; admitted to bar, 1991, California; 1992, District of Columbia. *Education:* Whitman College (B.A., with honors, 1988); Columbia University (J.D., 1991). Harlan Fiske Stone Scholar. Managing Editor, Columbia Journal of Law and Social Problems, 1990-1991. Law Clerk to the Honorable John T. Nixon, Chief Judge, U.S. District Court, Middle District of Tennessee, 1991-1992. *Member:* The District of Columbia Bar; Orange County and American (Vice Chair, Professionals', Officers' and Directors' Liability Committee, Tort and Insurance Practice Section, 1998—; Member, Editorial Board, Bad Faith Law Report, 2000-2001; Insurance Litigation Reporter, 2001—) Bar Associations; State Bar of California. (Irvine and San Diego, California). ***Email:*** tmcinnis@rdblaw.com

FLETCHER W. PADDISON, born Washington, D.C., March 29, 1950; admitted to bar, 1977, California. *Education:* Allegheny College (B.A., 1972); California Western School of Law (J.D., magna cum laude, 1977). Phi Alpha Delta. Member, Board of Editors, 1976-1977, California Western Law Review. *Member:* San Diego County and American Bar Associations; State Bar of California. (Resident, San Diego, California). ***Email:*** fpaddison@rdblaw.com

ROBERT M. POZIN, born Chicago, Illinois, November 2, 1954; admitted to bar, 1980, District of Columbia; 1994, California. *Education:* Yale University (B.A., cum laude, 1976); Harvard University (J.D., cum laude, 1979). Developments Editor, Harvard Law Review, 1978-1979. Co-Author: "Bankruptcy and Its Impact on D & O Insurance," ABA Torts and Insurance Practice Professionals', Officers' and Directors' Liability Committee News, Fall 2000; "Internal Corporate Investigations," Securities Law Techniques, Matthew Bender, 1985; "Bankruptcy Trustee and Examiner Investigations," Securities Law Techniques, Matthew Bender, 1985; "Computer Evidence at Trial," ABA National Institutes, 1985. Author: Note, "Intracorporate Conspiracies Under 42 U.S.C. Section 1985 (c)," 92 Harvard Law Review 470, 1978. Law Clerk to the Honorable Lloyd F. MacMahon, Chief Judge, U.S. District Court, Southern District of New York, 1979-1980. *Member:* The District of Columbia Bar; Orange County and American Bar Associations; State Bar of California. (Irvine and San Diego, California). ***Email:*** rpozin@rdblaw.com

RICHARD J. PRATT, born Alliance, Ohio, October 11, 1965; admitted to bar, 1991, Pennsylvania; 1994, District of Columbia. *Education:* Duke University (A.B., magna cum laude, 1988); University of Pennsylvania (J.D., cum laude, 1991). Member, University of Pennsylvania Law Review, 1990-1991. Author: "Unilateral Modification of Employment Handbooks: Further Encroachments on the Employment-at-Will Doctrine," 139 University of Pennsylvania Law Review, 197, 1990. *Member:* Pennsylvania Bar Association; The District of Columbia Bar. ***Email:*** rpratt@rdblaw.com

REBECCA L. ROSS, born Lexington, Nebraska, March 16, 1951; admitted to bar, 1976, Nebraska; 1979, Minnesota; 1980, District of Columbia. *Education:* Colby College (B.A., 1973); University of Nebraska (J.D., with distinction, 1976). Order of the Coif; The Order of Barristers. Member, National Moot Court Team, 1974-1975. Associate Editor, Nebraska Law Review, 1975-1976. Author: Note, "The Supreme Court Avoids Considering Sex-Based Classifications," 55 Nebraska Law Review 133, 1976. Co-Author: "Developments in West Virginia's Insurance Bad Faith Law—Where Do We Go From Here?" 98 West Virginia Law Review 267, 1995. Attorney: U.S. Department of Justice, Civil Division, 1976-1979; Briggs & Morgan, 1979-1980; U.S. Attorneys' Office, Civil Division, Washington, D.C., 1980-1987. *Member:* The District of Columbia Bar; Nebraska State and Minnesota State Bar Associations. (Resident, Chicago, Illinois). ***Email:*** rross@rdblaw.com

STUART PHILIP ROSS, born Newark, New Jersey, July 3, 1940; admitted to bar, 1967, District of Columbia. *Education:* George Washington University (A.B., 1963; LL.B., 1966). Law Clerk to Mr. Justice Tom C. Clark, U.S. Supreme Court, 1966-1967. *Member:* The District of Columbia Bar; American Bar Association. ***Email:*** sross@rdblaw.com

CATHY ANN SIMON, born New York, N.Y., September 14, 1950; admitted to bar, 1976, Maryland; 1977, District of Columbia. *Education:* Tufts University (B.A., cum laude, 1972); George Washington University (J.D., high honors, 1976). Order of the Coif. *Member:* The District of Columbia Bar; Maryland State and American Bar Associations. ***Email:*** csimon@rdblaw.com

RICHARD A. SIMPSON, born Providence, Rhode Island, February 9, 1952; admitted to bar, 1978, Illinois; 1987, District of Columbia; 1991, Virginia; 2000, Maryland. *Education:* Wesleyan University (B.A., magna cum laude, 1974); University of North Carolina (J.D., 1977). First in Class, University of North Carolina School of Law. Order of the Coif. Articles Editor, North Carolina Law Review, 1976-1977. Law Clerk to the Honorable John D. Butzner, Jr., U.S. Court of Appeals, Fourth Circuit, 1977-1978. Assistant U.S. Attorney, Southern District of New York, 1982-1984. Attorney-Adviser, Office of Legal Counsel, U.S. Department of Justice, 1984-1985. Deputy Independent Counsel, Office of Independent Counsel Curtis Emery von Kann, 1996-1997. Associate Independent Counsel, Office of Independent Counsel James C. McKay, 1987-1988. *Member:* The District of Columbia Bar; Virginia and American Bar Associations. ***Email:*** rsimpson@rdblaw.com

JAMES W. STUBBLEFIELD, born Omaha, Nebraska, November 6, 1946; admitted to bar, 1989, Kansas; 1993, California. *Education:* Brigham Young University (B.A., 1970; M.Ed., 1976; J.D., 1989). *Member:* Kansas and American Bar Associations; State Bar of California. [1st Lt., USMC, 1971-1974; Lt., USN, 1976-1979]. (Resident, San Diego, California). ***LANGUAGES:*** Spanish. ***Email:*** jstubblefield@rdblaw.com

VAN A. TENGBERG, born Salt Lake City, Utah, August 11, 1957; admitted to bar, 1982, California. *Education:* University of California at Davis (B.A., 1979); McGeorge School of the Law (J.D., 1982); University of San Diego (LL.M. in Taxation, cum laude, 1987). *Member:* San Diego County and American Bar Associations; State Bar of California (Member, Sections on: Real Estate Law; Business Law; Taxation). (Resident, San Diego, California). ***Email:*** vtengberg@rdblaw.com

PETER G. THOMPSON, born Cincinnati, Ohio, May 15, 1954; admitted to bar, 1979, Ohio (Inactive); 1988, District of Columbia. *Education:* College of Wooster; Washington University (A.B., 1976; J.D., 1979). Articles Editor, Washington University Urban Law Annual, 1978-1979. Recipient, Cincinnati Bar Association Volunteer Lawyer of the Year Award, 1983. *Member:* The District of Columbia Bar; American Bar Association. ***Email:*** pthompson@rdblaw.com

(This Listing Continued)

ROSS, DIXON & BELL, L.L.P., Washington—Continued

MICHAEL P. TONE, born Washington, D.C., August 31, 1949; admitted to bar, 1974, Illinois. *Education:* Denison University (B.A., 1971); University of South Carolina (J.D., 1974). *Member:* Illinois State and American Bar Associations. (Resident, Chicago, Illinois). ***Email:*** mtone@rdblaw.com

KAREN HAHN VENTRELL, born Passaic, New Jersey, February 2, 1958; admitted to bar, 1984, Maryland; 1985, California; 1993, North Carolina; 1999, Texas; 2000, District of Columbia. *Education:* Rutgers University (B.A., 1980); Washington College of Law, American University (J.D., 1983). Attorney, Office of the Legal Adviser, U.S. Department of State, 1984-1985. *Member:* The District of Columbia Bar; State Bar of California; State Bar of Texas; American Bar Association (Member, Section on Tort and Insurance Practice); Defense Research Institute; The Professional Liability Underwriting Society. ***REPORTED CASES:*** Shell Oil Co. v. Winterthur Swiss Co., 12 Cal. App. 4th 715 (1993); In Re Mor-ben Ins. Markets Corp., 73 B.R. 644 (B.A.P. 9th Cir. 1987). ***Email:*** kventrell@rdblaw.com

MICHAEL J. WHITTON, born Quantico, Virginia, April 15, 1967; admitted to bar, 1992, California. *Education:* University of Notre Dame (B.B.A., 1989; J.D., 1992). *Member:* San Diego County and American Bar Associations; State Bar of California; Bar Association of Northern San Diego County; National Contract Management Association. (Resident, San Diego, California). ***Email:*** mwhitton@rdblaw.com

SOLOMON LOUIS WISENBERG, born Houston, Texas, June 8, 1954; admitted to bar, 1980, Texas; 1981, Illinois; 1999, District of Columbia. *Education:* Washington University (A.B., 1976); University of Texas at Austin (J.D., 1980). Law Clerk to the Honorable Tom G. Davis, Texas Court of Criminal Appeals, 1982-1985; Law Clerk to the Honorable J. Daniel Mahoney, United States Court of Appeals, Second Circuit, 1986-1987. Associate, Van Duzer, Gershon, Jordan & Peterson, Chicago, 1980-1981; Attorney Advisor, Office of Legal Policy, U.S. Department of Justice, Washington D.C., 1985-1986; Assistant United States Attorney, Eastern District of North Carolina, 1987-1989; Assistant United States Attorney, Western District of Texas, 1989-1997; Chief, Financial Institution Fraud Unit, Western District of Texas, 1993-1995; Health Care Fraud Coordinator, Western District of Texas, 1994-1996; Associate Independent Counsel, Whitewater Investigation, 1997-1998; Deputy Independent Counsel, Whitewater Investigation, 1998-1999. *Member:* American Bar Association Member, Criminal Justice Section and White Collar Crime Committee); National Association of Criminal Defense Attorneys. ***REPORTED CASES:*** U.S. v. Pettigrew et al, 77 F.3d 1500; U.S. v. Waldrip, 981 F.2d 1309; U.S. v. Kelly et al, 973 F.2d 1145; U.S. v. Huntress, 956 F.2d 1309; U.S. v. Hooten, 933 F.2d 293; U.S. v. Talbott, 902 F.2d 1129. ***Email:*** swisenberg@rdblaw.com

OF COUNSEL

MICHAEL G. BRUTON, born Chicago, Illinois, May 6, 1960; admitted to bar, 1985, Illinois; 1986, U.S. District Court, Northern District of Illinois and U.S. District Court, Northern District of Indiana; 1987, U.S. District Court, Eastern District of Michigan and U.S. Court of Appeals, Seventh Circuit; 1992, U.S. District Court, Central District of Illinois, U.S. District Court, Eastern District of Wisconsin, and U.S. Supreme Court. *Education:* University of Notre Dame (B.A., 1982; J.D., magna cum laude, 1985). Member, National Moot Court Team, 1984-1985. Judicial Law Clerk to the Honorable Kenneth F. Ripple, United States Court of Appeals for the Seventh Circuit, 1985-1986. Argued on Behalf of Petitioner Before U.S. Supreme Court in Milwaukee Brewery Workers v. Joseph Schlitz Brewing Co. No. 93-768. (Resident, Chicago, Illinois). ***Email:*** mbruton@kdblaw.com

CLINTON E. CAMERON, born Indianapolis, Indiana, November 22, 1965; admitted to bar, 1991, Michigan; 1993, District of Columbia; 2001, Illinois. *Education:* University of Michigan (A.B., 1988; J.D., 1991); London Business School, University of London (M.S., 1999). Sloan Fellow. Articles Editor, Michigan Journal of International Law, 1990-1991. (Resident, Chicago, Illinois). ***Email:*** ccameron@rdblaw.com

HALLIE MILLER FAHEY, born McHenry, Illinois, July 2, 1965; admitted to bar, 1990, Illinois and U.S. District Court, Northern District of Illinois. *Education:* Butler University (B.S. in Accountancy, cum laude, 1987); Boston College (1987-1988); University of Illinois (J.D., cum laude, 1990). Delta Theta Phi. Harno Scholar. Recipient: American Jurisprudence Award, Legal Process. Member, University of Illinois Law Review. Editor, Illinois Bar Journal, 1989-1990. Author: Note, "DeBartolo Corp. v. Florida Gulf Building and Trades Council, 108 S. Ct. 1392, (1988)," 77 Ill. B.J. 613 (1989). Co-Author: "Tenders of Defense: Practical Solutions to Insurance Coverage Problems," IDC Journal (Spring 1994). *Member:* Chicago, Illinois State and American Bar Associations. (Resident, Chicago, Illinois). ***Email:*** hfahey@rdblaw.com

MICHELE L. LYNCH, born Stanford, California, October 3, 1968; admitted to bar, 1993, California. *Education:* University of California, Los Angeles (B.A., 1990); Hasting College of the Law, University of California (J.D., magna cum laude, 1993). Order of the Coif. Production Editor, Hastings Law Journal, 1992-1993. Author: "The Right to Write In: Voting Rights and the First Amendment," 44 Hastings Law Journal 727, 1993. *Member:* State Bar of California; American Bar Association. (Resident, Irvine, California). ***Email:*** mlynch@rdblaw.com

HAROLD E. MASBACK, III, born White Plains, New York, February 20, 1951; admitted to bar, 1976, District of Columbia. *Education:* Williams College (B.A., cum laude, 1973); Columbia University (J.D., 1976). Phi Beta Kappa. Harlan Fiske Stone Scholar. Assistant General Counsel, Democratic National Committee, 1982-1985. *Member:* The District of Columbia Bar; Defense Research Institute.

JAMES T. WARING, born Leonardtown, Maryland, August 6, 1947; admitted to bar, 1974, California. *Education:* University of Southern California (B.S., 1971); University of San Diego (J.D., 1974). Member, Board of Trustees:, River Network; San Diego National History Museum. *Member:* San Diego County and American Bar Associations; State Bar of California (Member, Sections on: Business Law; Taxation). (Resident, San Diego, California). ***Email:*** jwaring@rdblaw.com

ASSOCIATES

CALANDRA A. ALMOND, born Carrollton, Georgia, September 12, 1974; admitted to bar, 1998, Georgia (Not admitted in District of Columbia). *Education:* Harvard University (A.B., 1995; J.D., 1998). ***PRACTICE AREAS:*** Insurance. ***Email:*** calmond@rdblaw.com

CHRISTOPHER P. "HAWK" BARRY, born Brockton, Massachusetts, August 29, 1970; admitted to bar, 1995, California. *Education:* Duke University (B.A., 1992); University of Southern California (J.D., 1995). *Member:* San Diego County and American Bar Associations; State Bar of California; William L. Todd, Jr. American Inn of Court. (Resident, San Diego, California). ***Email:*** cbarry@rdblaw.com

KIMBERLY E. BLAIR, born Pontiac, Illinois, July 30, 1975; admitted to bar, 2000, Illinois. *Education:* University of Illinois (B.A., 1997); Vanderbilt University (J.D., 2000). Phi Beta Kappa. *Member:* Chicago and Illinois State Bar Associations. (Resident, Chicago, Illinois). ***Email:*** kblair@rdblaw.com

JULIE L. BURGENER, born Joliet, Illinois, April 2, 1970; admitted to bar, 1999, Illinois. *Education:* Northern Illinois University (B.A., 1993); University of Illinois (J.D., magna cum laude, 1999). (Resident, Chicago, Illinois). ***Email:*** jburgener@rdblaw.com

SHEILA R. CAUDLE, born Reno, Nevada, February 20, 1950; admitted to bar, 1987, California (Not admitted in District of Columbia). *Education:* University of Nevada, Reno (B.A. in Jour, 1971); Catholic University of America (J.D., 1986). *Member:* State Bar of California; Defense Research Institute (Member, 1999—). ***Email:*** scaudle@rdblaw.com

PATRICIA E. CHARLES, born Las Cruces, New Mexico, December 16, 1972; admitted to bar, 1999, Illinois; 2000, U.S. District Court, Northern District of Illinois; 2001, U.S. District Court, Southern District of Illinois. *Education:* University of Texas at Austin (B.A., Government, 1995); Vanderbilt University (J.D., 1999). Member, Vanderbilt Moot Court, 1997-1999. Associate Justice, Moot Court Executive Board, 1998-1999. Co-founder, Vanderbilt Trial Lawyers Association, 1998. Chair and Co-founder, 1st Annual Vanderbilt Mock Trial Competition, 1999. (Resident, Chicago, Illinois). ***Email:*** pcharles@rdblaw.com

JODI L. CLEESATTLE, born Columbus, Ohio, June 17, 1968; admitted to bar, 1994, Maryland; 1996, District of Columbia. *Education:* American University (B.A., cum laude, 1990; J.D., summa cum laude, 1994). Phi Kappa Phi; Golden Key; Order of the Barristers. Member, Society of Professional Journalists, 1986—. Executive Editor, The National Jurist, 1991-1998. Co-Author: "Police Records: A Guide to Effective Access in the 50 States & D.C.," The News Media & The Law, Fall 1992. Law Clerk to the Honorable Alan Kay, U.S. Magistrate Judge, 1994-1995. *Member:* The District of Columbia Bar; Maryland State Bar Association. ***Email:*** jcleesattle@rdblaw.com

DANIEL J. CROSS, born California, February 25, 1965; admitted to bar, 1999, California. *Education:* San Diego State University (B.A., cum laude, 1996); University of San Diego (J.D., cum laude, 1999). Order of the Coif. *Member:* State Bar of California. (Resident, San Diego, California). ***Email:*** dcross@rdblaw.com

JACQUELINE K. CUNCANNAN, born Grand Rapids, Michigan, February 13, 1967; admitted to bar, 1997, Michigan; 1999, District of Columbia. *Education:* University of Michigan (A.B., 1989); Grand Valley State University (M.S.W., 1994); Washington University (J.D., 1997). *Member:* The District of Columbia Bar; State Bar of Michigan; American Bar Association. ***Email:*** jcuncannan@rdblaw.com

JAMES J. DALESSIO, born New Haven, Connecticut, October 26, 1961; admitted to bar, 1990, California. *Education:* University of California at San Diego (B.A., 1984); University of San Diego (J.D., magna cum laude, 1990). Executive Comments Editor, University of San Diego Law Review. Professor at Law, University of San Diego Law School, 1994-1998; California Western

(This Listing Continued)

School of Law, 1998-1999. *Member:* San Diego County Bar Association; State Bar of California. (Resident, San Diego, California). **Email:** jdalessio@rdblaw.com

J. KIRK DONNELLY, born Honolulu, Hawaii, December 27, 1967; admitted to bar, 1995, California and U.S. District Court, Southern District of California; 1996, U.S. District Court, Central District of California; 1999, U.S. District Court, Northern District of California; 2000, U.S. District Court, Eastern District of California and U.S. Court of Appeals, Ninth Circuit. *Education:* College of William & Mary (B.A., 1989); University of San Diego (J.D., cum laude, 1995). Order of the Coif; Order of the Barristers. Appellate Moot Court Board. *Member:* Orange County and American Bar Associations; State Bar of California. (Resident, Irvine, California). **Email:** kdonnelly@rdblaw.com

BENJAMIN C. EGGERT, born Alexandria, Virginia, January 4, 1974; admitted to bar, 2000, Virginia; 2001, District of Columbia. *Education:* University of Virginia (B.A., 1996; J.D., 2000). **Email:** beggert@rdblaw.com

VICKI BAJEFSKY FISHMAN, born Washington, D.C., September 1, 1971; admitted to bar, 1997, Maryland; 1998, District of Columbia. *Education:* Swarthmore College (B.A., 1993); University of Michigan (J.D., 1997). *Member:* The District of Columbia Bar; American Bar Association. **Email:** vfishman@rdblaw.com

MONIQUE M. FUENTES, born Monterey Park, California, August 28, 1974; admitted to bar, 1999, California. *Education:* California Polytechnic State University (B.A., 1996); University of Southern California (J.D., 1999). *Member:* Orange County Bar Association; State Bar of California. (Resident, Irvine, California). **Email:** mfuentes@rdblaw.com

JENNIFER L. GATES, born Oconomowoc, Wisconsin, February 26, 1975; admitted to bar, 2001, Virginia (Not admitted in District of Columbia). *Education:* University of Iowa (B.A., 1997; J.D., with honors, 2001); University of Iowa Graduate College of Urban & Regional Planning (M.A., 2001). *Member:* Virginia Bar Association. **Email:** jgates@rdblaw.com

STEPHEN M. HALL, born Seattle, Washington, August 10, 1965; admitted to bar, 1999, Virginia; 2000, District of Columbia. *Education:* College of William & Mary (B.A., 1986); University of Virginia (J.D., 1998). Law Clerk to Hon. Albert B. Bryan, Jr., U.S. District Court, Eastern District of Virginia, 1998-1999. *Member:* Federal Bar Association. **Email:** shall@rdblaw.com

DAVID A. HARRINGTON, born Washington, D.C., April 24, 1965; admitted to bar, 1994, Virginia; 1996, District of Columbia. *Education:* University of Virginia (B.A., 1987; J.D., 1994). Articles Editor, Journal of Law and Politics, 1993-1994. *Member:* The District of Columbia Bar; Virginia State Bar; American Bar Association. **Email:** dharrington@rdblaw.com

JASON S. HARTLEY, born Anaheim, California, 1971; admitted to bar, 1997, California. *Education:* University of California at San Diego (B.A., with honors, 1993); Tulane University (J.D., cum laude, 1997). Provost's Honor List. Washington Scholar. Assistant Executive Editor, Tul. Jnl. Int'l. & Comp. Law, 1995-1997. *Member:* San Diego County and American Bar Associations; State Bar of California. (Resident, San Diego, California). **Email:** jhartley@rdblaw.com

CAROL SCHANNO JOHNSON, born Hastings, Minnesota, October 18, 1962; admitted to bar, 1998, Virginia; 1999, District of Columbia and U.S. Supreme Court. *Education:* St. Cloud State University (B.A., summa cum laude, 1984); University of Minnesota (M.A., 1987); Georgetown University (J.D., 1997). *Member:* The District of Columbia Bar. **Email:** cjohnson@rdblaw.com

CHARLES A. JONES, born Fairfax, Virginia, May 28, 1969; admitted to bar, 1994, Virginia; 1996, District of Columbia. *Education:* University of Virginia (B.A., 1991); Georgetown University Law Center (J.D., cum laude, 1994). Notes Editor, Georgetown Law Journal, 1993-1994. Recipient, American Jurisprudence Award in Administrative Law. *Member:* The District of Columbia Bar; Virginia State Bar; American Bar Association. **Email:** tjones@rdblaw.com

CHRISTOPHER A. JONES, born Ann Arbor, Michigan, May 19, 1972; admitted to bar, 2000, Virginia; 2001, District of Columbia. *Education:* James Madison University (B.S., Sociology, 1997); University of Virginia (J.D., 2000). Presiding Justice, First Round William Minor Lile Moot Court Board. **Email:** cjones@rdblaw.com

THOMAS J. JUDGE, born Pt. Pleasant, New Jersey, March 3, 1964; admitted to bar, 1995, Maryland; 1996, District of Columbia. *Education:* United States Naval Academy (B.S., 1986); George Washington University (J.D., with high honors, 1995). Order of the Coif. *Member:* The District of Columbia Bar; Maryland State Bar Association. **Email:** tjudge@rdblaw.com

KEVIN FOMASI KIEFFER, born Placentia, California, July 17, 1971; admitted to bar, 1997, California; 1999, Nevada. *Education:* University of California, Irvine (B.A., magna cum laude, 1993); McGeorge School of Law (J.D., with great distinction, 1997). Order of the Coif; Traynor Honor Society. Recipient, American Jurisprudence Award for Constitutional Law and Employment Law. Articles Editor and Comment Writer, Pacific Law Journal. Vice

(This Listing Continued)

President, Student Body Association, 1996-1997. *Member:* Orange County and American Bar Associations; State Bar of California; State Bar of Nevada (inactive). (Resident, Irvine, California). **Email:** kkieffer@rdblaw.com

G. SCOTT KIRKPATRICK, born Charleston, West Virginia, October 23, 1965; admitted to bar, 1994, Virginia; 1997, U.S. Court of Appeals, Fifth Circuit; 1999, U.S. District Court, Eastern District of Virginia; 2001, District of Columbia. *Education:* Indiana University (B.A., 1990); George Washington University (J.D., 1994). [Lieutenant, U.S. Navy Reserve, 1985]. **Email:** skirkpatrick@rdblaw.com

PETER D. LINDAU, born New York, N.Y., September 18, 1963; admitted to bar, 1996, Illinois. *Education:* University of Vermont (B.A., 1985); Boston College (J.D., 1996). National Moot Court Team. (Resident, Chicago, Illinois). **Email:** plindau@rdblaw.com

JASON M. LINDNER, born Anaheim, California, January 14, 1975; admitted to bar, 2000, California. *Education:* University of Miami (B.A., cum laude, 1997); University of Pennsylvania (J.D., 2000). *Member:* State Bar of California (Member, Antitrust Section). (Resident, San Diego, California). **Email:** jlindner@rdblaw.com

JENNIFER MATHIS, born Salt Lake City, Utah, May 30, 1968; admitted to bar, 1997, California. *Education:* University of Utah (B.A., cum laude, 1989); Georgetown University (J.D., cum laude, 1996). Phi Beta Kappa; Phi Kappa Phi; Golden Key. Associate Editor, American Criminal Law Review. First Place, Beaudry Appellate Moot Court Competition. National Moot Court Team. *Member:* Orange County and American Bar Associations; State Bar of California. (Resident, Irvine, California). **Email:** jmathis@rdblaw.com

HEATHER E. McINTYRE, born South Bend, Indiana, September 25, 1971; admitted to bar, 1997, Virginia (Not admitted in District of Columbia). *Education:* College of William & Mary (B.A., 1993); Washington University (J.D., 1997). Order of the Coif. **Email:** hmcintyre@rdblaw.com

JOSHUA A. MOONEY, born San Antonio, Texas, November 3, 1971; admitted to bar, 2000, Pennsylvania; 2001, District of Columbia. *Education:* Loyola College (B.A., cum laude, 1993); Cambridge University, Girton College, U.K. (M. Phil., 1994); Georgetown University (J.D., magna cum laude, 2000). Order of the Coif. Recipient, Whiteford Medal for History, Loyola. Project Editor, American Criminal Law Review, 1998-1999. Co-Author: "Securities Fraud," *Thirteenth Survey of White Collar Crime,* 35 Am. Crim. L. Rev. 1167 (1998). **Email:** jmooney@rdblaw.com

KIM S. ORBECK, born Inglewood, California, June 7, 1957; admitted to bar, 1997, California. *Education:* California State University, Long Beach (B.A., with great distinction, 1982); University of California, Los Angeles (J.D., 1997). Associate Editor, UCLA Journal of Environmental Law and Policy. *Member:* Orange County and American Bar Associations; State Bar of California. (Resident, Irvine, California). **Email:** korbeck@rdblaw.com

ERIK PRITCHARD, born San Bernardino, California, October 13, 1971; admitted to bar, 1999, Maryland; 2001, District of Columbia. *Education:* University of California at Riverside (B.A., cum laude, 1994); University of Virginia (J.D., 1999). Editor-in-Chief, Journal of Law and Politics, 1998-1999. **Email:** epritchard@rdblaw.com

SASHA L. RANSOM, born Berkeley, California, May 28, 1971; admitted to bar, 1998, California and U.S. District Court, Central, Northern and Southern Districts of California. *Education:* University of California at Berkeley (B.A., 1993); Southwestern University School of Law (J.D., cum laude, 1998). Author: "How Far Is Too Far? Balancing Sexual Harassment Policies and Reasonableness in the Primary and Secondary Classrooms," 27 Southwestern Law Review 265, 1997. *Member:* Los Angeles and Orange County Bar Associations; State Bar of California. (Resident, Irvine, California). **Email:** sransom@rdblaw.com

PAUL A. RAUNER, born Mason, Michigan, July 10, 1968; admitted to bar, 1998, Illinois. *Education:* Calvin College (B.A., Philosophy, 1992); University of Iowa (J.D., 1997). *Member:* Chicago and American Bar Associations. (Resident, Chicago, Illinois Office). **LANGUAGES:** German. **Email:** prauner@rdblaw.com

GABRIELA A. RICHEIMER, born Bethesda, Maryland, February 19, 1972; admitted to bar, 1997, Maryland; 1999, District of Columbia. *Education:* Long Island University (B.A., 1994); Washington College of Law (J.D., 1997). **Email:** gricheimer@rdblaw.com

STACEY ENGELBRECHT RUFE, born Stuttgart, Germany, August 22, 1971; admitted to bar, 1998, Virginia; 2000, District of Columbia. *Education:* Georgetown University (A.B., 1993; J.D., 1998). Member, American Criminal Law Review, 1996-1998. Law Clerk to the Honorable Andrew Effron, U.S. Court of Appeals for the Armed Forces, 1998-1999. **Email:** sengelbrecht@rdblaw.com

AMY K. SAVAGE, born Norfolk, Virginia, February 14, 1970; admitted to bar, 2000, Virginia; 2001, District of Columbia. *Education:* Eastern New Mexico University (B.A., cum laude, 1994); Georgetown University (J.D., cum laude, 2000). Dean's List. Member, Barristers' Council, 1998-2000. Recipient, CALI Awards, Civil Discovery and Trial Advocacy. Editorial Board Member,

(This Listing Continued)

ROSS, DIXON & BELL, L.L.P., Washington—Continued

1998-1999, and Articles and Notes Editor, 1999-2000, American Criminal Law Review. Author; "Environmental Crimes," 36 Am. Crim. L. Rev. 515 (1999). *Member:* The District of Columbia Bar; Virginia State Bar; American Bar Association; Virginia Trial Lawyers Association. ***Email:*** asavage@rdblaw.com

STEPHANIE T. SCHMELZ, born San Francisco, California; admitted to bar, 1996, Pennsylvania; 1999, District of Columbia. *Education:* Haverford College (B.A., magna cum laude, 1990); University of Michigan (J.D., 1996). Phi Beta Kappa. *Member:* American Bar Association. ***LANGUAGES:*** French. ***Email:*** sschmelz@rdblaw.com

PRAGNA SONI, born London, England, March 17, 1970; admitted to bar, 1997, Virginia; 1998, District of Columbia. *Education:* Colgate University (B.A., cum laude, 1992); University of Iowa (J.D., with distinction, 1997). Member, National Moot Court Team. Editor and Founder, University of Iowa College of Law Journal of Gender, Race and Justice, 1995-1997. ***Email:*** psoni@rdblaw.com

CATHLENE A. THARP, born Cincinnati, Ohio, November 18, 1969; admitted to bar, 1997, Maryland; 1998, District of Columbia, U.S. District Court, District of Maryland and U.S. District Court for the District of Columbia. *Education:* Miami University (B.Phil., 1992); University of Minnesota (J.D., 1997). *Member:* The District of Columbia Bar. ***Email:*** ctharp@rdblaw.com

SCOTT E. TURNER, born Phoenix, Arizona, October 9, 1968; admitted to bar, 1995, Illinois; 1997, U.S. Court of Appeals, Seventh Circuit; 2000, U.S. District Court, Northern District of Illinois including Trial Bar (Not admitted in District of Columbia). *Education:* University of Arizona (B.A., summa cum laude, 1990); University of Chicago (M.A., 1992); Northwestern University (J.D., 1995). Phi Beta Kappa. *Member:* Chicago Bar Association. (Resident, Chicago, Illinois). ***Email:*** sturner@rdblaw.com

PAUL C. VITRANO, born Atlantic City, New Jersey, November 3, 1969; admitted to bar, 1995, New Jersey, Pennsylvania and U.S. District Court, District of New Jersey; 1999, District of Columbia and U.S. District Court, Eastern District of Pennsylvania; 2001, U.S. District Court for the District of Columbia. *Education:* Villanova University (B.A., magna cum laude, 1992); George Washington University (J.D., with honors, 1995). Member, George Washington University Journal of International Law & Economics. Certified Contract Advisor, National Football League Players Association, 1998; Registered Contract Advisor, Canadian Football League Players Association, 1998. *Member:* Association of Trial Lawyers of America. ***Email:*** pvitrano@rdblaw.com

CHRISTOPHER L. WALTERS, born Long Beach, California, July 16, 1973; admitted to bar, 1999, California and U.S. District Court, Southern and Central Districts of California. *Education:* University of California at Berkeley (B.A., 1996); University of Southern California (J.D., 1999). Member, Southern California Law Review, 1997-1998. *Member:* State Bar of California; American Bar Association. (Resident, San Diego, California). ***Email:*** cwalters@rdblaw.com

JEFFREY J. WARD, born Syracuse, New York, September 11, 1970; admitted to bar, 1997, Maryland; 1998, District of Columbia. *Education:* Trinity College (B.A., 1992); George Washington University (J.D., with honors, 1997). Order of the Coif. Author: Case Note, "Transportation Law: Agency Interpretation of Regulations for Awarding International Air Carrier Routes," 64 George Washington University Law Review. ***Email:*** jjward@rdblaw.com

JULIA C. WEISSMAN, born Los Angeles, California; admitted to bar, 1991, Illinois; 1992, U.S. District Court, Central District of Illinois; 1998, California and U.S. District Court, Southern District of California; 1999, U.S. District Court, Central District of California. *Education:* University of Chicago (B.A., 1986); Indiana University (J.D., magna cum laude, 1991). Order of the Coif. Member and Note Editor, Indiana Law Journal, 1989-1991. Law Clerk to the Honorable Harold A. Baker, U.S. District Court, Central District Court of Illinois, 1991-1992. *Member:* State Bar of California. (Resident, Irvine, California). ***Email:*** jweissman@rdblaw.com

JON R. WILLIAMS, born Phoenix, Arizona, September 16, 1966; admitted to bar, 1992, California and U.S. District Court, Southern, Central and Eastern Districts of California. *Education:* San Diego State University (B.A., 1988); California Western School of Law (J.D., cum laude, 1992). Recipient, American Jurisprudence Award for Advanced Legal Research, 1992. Notes and Comments Editor, California Western Law Review/International Law Journal, 1992. Past President, Board of Directors, California Western School of Law Alumni Association. *Member:* San Diego County Bar Association; State Bar Of California; Consumer Attorneys of California; Consumer Attorneys of San Diego; The Association of Trial Lawyers of America. (Resident, San Diego, California). ***Email:*** jwilliams@rdblaw.com

LAURA COHEN ZIMMITTI, born Chicago, Illinois, August 22, 1969; admitted to bar, 1994, Illinois; 1997, District of Columbia and Virginia. *Education:* Colgate University (B.A., 1991); Georgetown University (J.D., 1994). ***Email:*** lzimmitti@rdblaw.com

(This Listing Continued)

STAFF ATTORNEYS

JO ANN ABRAMSON, born Philadelphia, Pennsylvania, November 17, 1952; admitted to bar, 1980, District of Columbia; 1983, Maryland; 1985, Pennsylvania. *Education:* University of Pennsylvania (B.A., 1973); Bryn Mawr College (M.S.W., 1975); Catholic University of America (J.D., 1980). ***Email:*** jabramson@rdblaw.com

SHARON LYNN GIBSON, born Fort Worth, Texas, October 1, 1963; admitted to bar, 1992, Georgia; 1994, District of Columbia. *Education:* Texas A & M University (B.S., 1987); Emory University (J.D., 1992). *Member:* The District of Columbia Bar. ***Email:*** sgibson@rdblaw.com

MARCUS B. HOLLADAY, born Anniston, Alabama, October 6, 1966; admitted to bar, 1992, Georgia; 1999, District of Columbia. *Education:* Birmingham-Southern College (B.S., magna cum laude, 1989); Emory University (J.D., with distinction, 1992). Omicron Delta Kappa. Psi Chi. Who's Who in American Colleges and Universities. Order of the Barristers. Member, Emory Moot Court Society, 1990-1992. Recipient: James C. Pratt Memorial Award, Outstanding Moot Court Member; Federal Bar Association Law Day Award; American Jurisprudence Award. *Member:* State Bar of Georgia; The District of Columbia Bar; American Bar Association. ***Email:*** mholladay@rdblaw.com

BECKI FOMASI KIEFFER, born Santa Cruz, California, May 28, 1970; admitted to bar, 1998, California; 1999, U.S. District Court, Northern and Central Districts of California. *Education:* San Jose State University (B.A. in Economics, 1993); Santa Clara University (J.D., 1998). Recipient, Dean Emory Academic Scholarship, 1996-1998. *Member:* Orange County Bar Association (Member, Committee for Gender Equality, 1999—); State Bar of California. (Resident, Irvine, California). ***Email:*** bfomasi@rdblaw.com

BETH A. KOEHLER, born Detroit, Michigan, July 11, 1972; admitted to bar, 1997, Maryland; 2000, District of Columbia. *Education:* Michigan State University (B.A., with high honors, 1993); Georgetown University (J.D., 1997). Semi-Finalist, Moot Court. *Member:* Montgomery County Bar Association. ***LANGUAGES:*** French. ***Email:*** bkoehler@rdblaw.com

JENNI R. WALLACE, born Florence, Alabama, January 11, 1969; admitted to bar, 1993, Ohio; 1997, District of Columbia. *Education:* Auburn University (B.A., 1990); Case Western Reserve University (J.D., 1993). ***Email:*** jwallace@rdblaw.com

ROSS & HARDIES

A Partnership including Professional Corporations

888 - 16TH STREET, N.W.

WASHINGTON, D.C. 20006-4103

Telephone: 202-296-8600

Fax: 202-296-8791

Email: marketing@rosshardies.com

URL: http://www.rosshardies.com

Chicago, Illinois Office: Suite 2500, 150 North Michigan Avenue. Telephone: 312-558-1000. Fax: 312-750-8600.

New York, N.Y. Office: 65 East 55th Street. Telephone: 212-421-5555. Fax: 212-421-5682.

General Practice before all Courts, Departments and Administrative Agencies. Antitrust and Litigation, Communications and Telecommunications, Corporate, Customs and International Trade, Employment and Labor Law, Banking, Insurance and Financial Services, Health Care, Housing, Immigration, Securities, Taxation, White Collar Criminal Defense and Technology and eCommerce.

RESIDENT PARTNERS

JOHN R. FORNACIARI, born Milford, Massachusetts, October 27, 1946; admitted to bar, 1971, Massachusetts and District of Columbia. *Education:* Providence College (A.B., cum laude, 1968); Boston College (J.D., 1971). Partner, Eckert, Seamans Cherin & Mellott, 1989-1992. Partner, Steele & Fornaciari, Washington, D.C., 1984-1989. Partner, 1978-1984 and Associate, 1971-1977, Howrey & Simon. *Member:* The District of Columbia Bar; Massachusetts Bar Association. ***Email:*** jack.fornaciari@rosshardies.com

CHARLES W. PETTY, JR., born Durham, North Carolina, January 16, 1938; admitted to bar, 1964, California; 1967, District of Columbia. *Education:* Wheaton College (B.S., 1960); Duke University (LL.B., 1963). Editor-in-Chief, Duke Law Journal, 1962-1963. *Member:* The District of Columbia Bar; State Bar of California; American Bar Association; The American Law Institute. ***PRACTICE AREAS:*** Corporate Law; Finance; Insurance Regulation; Financial Services Law; Nonprofit and Charitable Organizations; Securities. ***Email:*** charles.petty@rosshardies.com

JAMES A. STENGER, born Baltimore, Maryland, March 16, 1952; admitted to bar, 1978, District of Columbia. *Education:* University of Glasgow, Glasgow, Scotland (M.A. with honors, 1975); Georgetown University (J.D., magna cum laude, 1978). *Member:* The District of Columbia Bar; Federal

(This Listing Continued)

Communications Bar Association. ***PRACTICE AREAS:*** Communications and Media; Intellectual Property; Litigation; Mergers, Acquisitions and Divestitures; Real Estate. ***Email:*** james.stenger@rosshardies.com

OF COUNSEL

PAULA DIMEO GRANT, born Bridgeport, Connecticut, August 3, 1943; admitted to bar, 1985, District of Columbia and U.S. District Court, District of Columbia; 1989, U.S. Supreme Court; 1994, U.S. District Court, District of Maryland. *Education:* Boston College (B.S., Nursing, cum laude, 1975); Northern Virginia Law School (J.D., 1982); New York University (M.A., Nursing Education, 1994). Registered Nurse, Connecticut, 1973. Co-Author: "Connecticut Statutes Affecting Nursing Practice," Professional Education Systems, Inc., 1988. Author: Chapter on "Expert Nurse Witness Liability Issues in Perinatal Nursing," Lippincott-Raven, 1998. Adjunct Professor of Nursing, Sacred Heart University, 1997-1999. Clinical Assistant Professor of Community and Preventative Medicine, New York Medical College, 1991-1997. Adjunct Assistant Professor of Nursing, Masters Program, Teachers College, Columbia University, 1993-1995. Member: Sigma Theta Tau International, 1998; Advisory Counsel, College of Education and Health Professions, Sacred Heart University, 1998—. Recipient, Board of Directors Award, American Association of Nurse Attorneys, 1995. Mediator, Superior Court, District of Columbia, 1991—. *Member:* Association of the Bar of the City of New York; Bar Association of the District of Columbia; American Bar Association; The American Association of Nurse Attorneys, Inc. (Member, Board of Directors, 1996—; Chairman, Committees on: Awards, 1998—; Archives, 1996-1999); American Association of Nurse Attorneys Foundation, Inc. (President, 1998—); Connecticut Nurses' Association (Chairman, Cabinet on Economic and General Welfare, 1986-1989). ***Email:*** paula.grant@rosshardies.com

(For complete biographical data on personnel at the New York, N.Y. and Chicago, Ill. offices, see Professional Biographies at those locations)

ROSS, MARSH & FOSTER

Established in 1953

2001 "L" STREET, N.W.

SUITE 400

WASHINGTON, D.C. 20036

Telephone: 202-822-8888

Fax: 202-775-9330

Email: rmfmarsh@aol.com

General Civil Practice. Corporate, Administrative, Health Care, Energy, Real Estate, Probate, Tax, Exempt Organizations and Litigation.

MEMBERS OF FIRM

BERNARD A. FOSTER, JR. (1909-1968).

RICHARD S. T. MARSH, born Washington, D.C., 1922; admitted to bar, 1948, District of Columbia; 1956, Maryland. *Education:* Yale University (A.B., 1946); George Washington University Law School (LL.B., 1948). Phi Delta Phi. Member: Committee on Admissions, District of Columbia Court of Appeals, 1977-1984; Judicial Conference of the District of Columbia, 1977-1991, 1993-2001; Judicial Conference of the District of Columbia Circuit, 1982-1983, 1985-1987. Estate Planning Council, Washington, District of Columbia. Former Member, Advisory Committee of District of Columbia Superior Court Rules of Probate and Fiduciary Procedure. *Member:* District of Columbia Bar; Bar Association of the District of Columbia; Maryland State and American Bar Associations; American Law Institute. Fellow: American College of Trust and Estate Counsel; American Bar Foundation. ***PRACTICE AREAS:*** Estate Planning; Trust and Estate Administration; Tax Law; Real Estate Law. ***Email:*** rossmarsh1@aol.com

JAMES D. MCKINNEY, JR., born Muscatine, Iowa, 1931; admitted to bar, 1958, Iowa; 1960, District of Columbia. *Education:* State University of Iowa (B.A., 1956; LL.B., 1958). Delta Sigma Rho. Trial Attorney, Federal Power Commission, 1958-1960. *Member:* The District of Columbia Bar; Federal Energy and American Bar Associations. ***PRACTICE AREAS:*** Energy Law; Utility Law; Litigation; Administrative Law. ***Email:*** rmfmckinne@aol.com

BERNARD A. FOSTER, III, born Washington, D.C., 1942; admitted to bar, 1968, District of Columbia. *Education:* University of the South (A.B., 1964); George Washington University (LL.B., 1967). *Member:* The District of Columbia Bar; Federal Energy and American Bar Associations. ***PRACTICE AREAS:*** Energy Law; Administrative Law.

JOHN M. LYNHAM, JR., born Washington, D.C., 1952; admitted to bar, 1983, District of Columbia; 1992, Maryland. *Education:* Trinity College (B.S., 1975); University of Maryland (M.B.A., 1979); George Washington University (J.D., 1983); Georgetown University (LL.M., 1990). Member: D.C. Superior Court Advisory Committee on Probate and Judiciary Rules (2001); D.C. Task Force on the OmniBus Trusts and Estates Amendment Act (Chair); D.C. Bar LLE Committee (1998—) *Member:* The District of Columbia Bar (Contributor, Practice Manual, Wills and Estates Section; Member, Estates, Trusts and Probate Steering Committee, 1997—); Maryland State Bar Association Inc.; American Bar Association. ***PRACTICE AREAS:*** Real Estate Law; Tax Law; Estate Planning; Trust Law. ***Email:*** rmflynham@aol.com

DONALD B. ROBERTSON, born Washington, D.C., 1931; admitted to bar, 1959, District of Columbia; 1962, U.S. Supreme Court; 1971, Maryland. *Education:* Oberlin College (A.B., 1953); Columbia University (LL.B., 1958). Member, Maryland House of Delegates, 1971-1989 (Speaker Pro Tem, 1987-1989; Majority Leader, 1979-1987). *Member:* The District of Columbia Bar; Bar Association of the District of Columbia; Montgomery County, Maryland State, American and Federal Bar Associations. ***PRACTICE AREAS:*** Estate Planning; Estate and Trust Administration; Taxation Law; Election Law; Real Estate Law. ***Email:*** rmfroberts@aol.com

JOHN MOURER BIXLER, born Washington, D.C., October 14, 1927; admitted to bar, 1954, District of Columbia; 1960, Maryland. *Education:* University of Pennsylvania (B.S., 1949); Harvard Law School (LL.B., 1954). Trustee, D.C. Legal Aid Society, 1975-1992. *Member:* The District of Columbia Bar; Bar Association of the District of Columbia; Maryland State, Federal and American (Member of the Council, Section of Taxation, 1979-1982) Bar Associations. Fellow: American College of Tax Counsel; American College of Trusts and Estate Counsel (Regent, 1987-1994 ; D.C. State Chairman, 1983-1987; Estate and Gift Tax Committee, 1986—). Fellow, American Bar Foundation. ***PRACTICE AREAS:*** Taxation; Tax Litigation; Trusts and Estates; Tax Exempt Organizations. ***Email:*** rmfjbixler@aol.com

WILLIAM E. DAVIS, born Northampton County, North Carolina, March 3, 1943; admitted to bar, 1968, North Carolina; 1971, District of Columbia; 1984, Maryland. *Education:* University North Carolina (A.B., 1965); William & Mary (J.D., 1968). Phi Delta Phi. Fellow, Washington D.C. Estate Planning Council, American College of Trust and Estate Counsel. Member: District of Columbia Superior Court, Advisory Committee on Probate and Fiduciary Procedure; Council for Court Excellence; George Washington american Inns of Court. *Member:* The District of Columbia Bar; Bar Association of the District of Columbia (Chair, Probate and Estate Planning Committee); North Carolina State Bar; Maryland State Bar and American Bar Associations. ***PRACTICE AREAS:*** Estate Planning; Estate Administration; Real Estate; Small Business Corporations. ***Email:*** rmfdavis@aol.com

RAYMOND L. GOOCH, admitted to bar, 1964, Virginia; 1969, District of Columbia. *Education:* Washington University (B.S. ChE., 1960); Georgetown University J.D., 1964). Member: Washington, Virginia Town Council, elected office, 1987-1998; Washington, D.C., Advisory Commissioner and Commission Chairman, 1975-1977. ***PRACTICE AREAS:*** Real Estate Law (50%); Decedents Estates (25%); Estate Planning Law (25%). ***Email:*** raygooch@aol.com

OF COUNSEL

JOSEPH M. MCMANUS, born Jersey City, New Jersey, 1946; admitted to bar, 1971, New Jersey; 1976, District of Columbia; 1987, Maryland; 1989, Virginia. *Education:* St. Peter's College (B.S., 1968); Fordham University (J.D., 1971); George Washington University (LL.M. in Taxation, with highest honors, 1975). Associate Editor, Fordham Law Review, 1970-1971. Author: "Judicial Law Making: The Liquidation of a Corporation Treated as an F Reorganization," 2 Journal of Corporate Taxation 273, 1975. Attorney, Tax Division, Department of Justice, 1971-1976. (Also Practicing Individually). ***PRACTICE AREAS:*** Taxation Law. ***Email:*** jmcmanus@tidalwave.net

(This Listing Continued)

ROTHWELL, FIGG, ERNST & MANBECK

A PROFESSIONAL CORPORATION

SUITE 701 EAST TOWER

555 THIRTEENTH STREET, N.W.

WASHINGTON, D.C. 20004

Telephone: 202-783-6040

Facsimile: 202-783-6031

Email: info@rothwellfigg.com

URL: http://www.rothwellfigg.com

Omaha, Nebraska Office: 13906 Gold Circle, Suite 204, 68144. Telephone: 402-333-1550. Fax: 402-333-1510.

Intellectual Property Law, Practice and Related Litigation, including Patent, Trademark, Copyright, Unfair Competition, Trade Secrets, Licensing and Related Antitrust Law. Defamation Law and other First Amendment Issues.

FIRM PROFILE: Rothwell, Figg, Ernst & Manbeck is a full service intellectual property law firm. The firm is active in counseling and the procurement of patent and trademark rights for its clients as well as significant litigation and licensing. The firm serves a wide variety of domestic and international clients, ranging from small business enterprises to multinational corporations.

(This Listing Continued)

ROTHWELL, FIGG, ERNST & MANBECK, A PROFESSIONAL CORPORATION, Washington—Continued

In connection with its patent practice, Rothwell, Figg, Ernst & Manbeck has special expertise in the fields of pharmaceuticals, biotechnology, health care and electronics (including computers and interactive technology). In addition, the firm has an active trademark and copyright practice, including such fields as grey market goods, character protection and domain names. The firm also provides advice and representation with respect to a wide range of First Amendment issues, including defending entities (and individuals) that have been sued for defamation.

G. FRANKLIN ROTHWELL, born Moberly, Missouri; admitted to bar, 1956, District of Columbia; 1959, U.S. Supreme Court; 1964, Maryland; 1982, U.S. Courts of Appeals for the Federal, District of Columbia, First, Second, Third, Fourth, Fifth, Sixth, Seventh and Ninth Circuits; registered to practice before U.S. Patent and Trademark Office. *Education:* University of Missouri (B.S.M.E., 1949); George Washington University (J.D., with Honors, 1956). Order of the Coif; Pi Tau Sigma. *Member:* The District of Columbia Bar; American Bar Association; American Intellectual Property Law Association; International Trademark Association; International Association for the Protection of Intellectual Property; Federal Circuit Bar Association; American Inns of Court; George Washington University Law School Dean's Board of Advisors. ***PRACTICE AREAS:*** Intellectual Property. ***Email:*** grothwel@rothwellfigg.com

E. ANTHONY FIGG, born Terre Haute, Indiana, March 20, 1946; admitted to bar, 1973, Indiana; 1981, District of Columbia; 1984, U.S. Court of Appeals for the Federal Circuit; U.S. Supreme Court; registered to practice before U.S. Patent and Trademark Office. *Education:* Rose-Hulman Institute of Technology (B.S., 1968); Indiana University (J.D., 1973). Faculty, American Law Institute, American Bar Association, 1981-1985. Author: "Biotechnology: Science Fiction Becomes a Legal Reality," The Compleat Lawyer, Vol. 3, No. 1, 1986; "Intellectual Property—Special Considerations in the Biotechnology Field," Chemtech, May 1986; "Patent Infringement Issues Unique to Biotechnology," Proceedings of the Joint Educational Program at the Section of Patent, Trademark and Copyright Law and the Section of Science and Technology, American Bar Association, August 1987; "Bioscience Patent Prosecution Developments," Proceedings of the 3rd Annual Spring Educational Program, American Bar Association Section of Patent, Trademark and Copyright Law, March 1988; Case Comment, "Burroughs Wellcome Co. v. Barr Laboratories," *Patent World,* October 1993; "Intellectual Property Protection for Plant Research in the USA: A Cornucopia of Opportunity," Curr. Opinion Biotechnology, 6 (2), 135-41, April 1995; "The Impact of GATT on U.S. Patent Protection Laws," The Biotechnology Report 1995/96, p. 37, Camden Publ., Ltd. *Member:* The District of Columbia Bar (Member, Patent, Trademark and Copyright Law Section); American Bar Association (Member, Intellectual Property Law Section; Chairman: Committee 110-Biosciences, 1985-1987; 1992-1993; Committee 554—Special Committee on Biotechnology, 1987; Chairman, Division X—Biosciences, 1991-1992, 1994-1995; Chairman, Division I-Patents, 1995-1996; Council, 1996-2000; Member, Bioethics Coordinating Committee); American Intellectual Property Law Association; Licensing Executive Society; International Trade Commission Trial Lawyers Association; International Intellectual Property Law Association (Member Executive Committee, 1999—); Georgetown University Law School Advisory Board, 1999—. ***PRACTICE AREAS:*** Intellectual Property. ***Email:*** efigg@rothwellfigg.com

BARBARA G. ERNST, born Olney, Maryland, December 31, 1955; admitted to bar, 1980, Maryland; 1981, Ohio; 1984, District of Columbia; 1986, U.S. Court of Appeals for the Federal Circuit; registered to practice before U.S. Patent and Trademark Office. *Education:* Western Maryland College (B.A., summa cum laude, 1977); University of Maryland (J.D., with honors, 1980). Phi Beta Kappa. *Member:* The District of Columbia Bar (Member, Patent, Trademark and Copyright Law Section); American Bar Association (Member, Intellectual Property Law Section); American Intellectual Property Law Association. ***PRACTICE AREAS:*** Intellectual Property. ***Email:*** bernst@rothwellfigg.com

HARRY F. MANBECK, JR., born Honesdale, Pennsylvania, June 26, 1926; admitted to bar, 1955, Kentucky; 1961, Indiana; 1965, Massachusetts; 1989, Connecticut; U.S. District Court, Northern District of Indiana and U.S. Court of Appeals for the Federal Circuit; 1992, District of Columbia; registered to practice before U.S. Patent and Trademark Office. *Education:* Lehigh University (B.S.E.E., with highest honors, 1949); University of Louisville Law School (LL.B., with honors, 1955). Eta Kappa Nu. Assistant Secretary of Commerce and United States Commissioner of Patents and Trademarks, 1990-1992. General Patent Counsel, General Electric Company, 1970-1990. *Member:* Federal Circuit Bar Association (Director, 1985-1988); American Bar Association (Chairman. Patent, Trademark and Copyright Section, 1989-1990); American Intellectual Property Law Association. [Lt., US Army, 1944-1947]. ***Email:*** hmanbeck@rothwellfigg.com

GEORGE R. REPPER, born Topeka, Kansas, December 22, 1954; admitted to bar, 1982, New York and District of Columbia; 1989, U.S. Court of Appeals for the Federal Circuit; registered to practice before U.S. Patent and Trademark Office. *Education:* State University of New York at Albany (B.S., cum laude, 1977); Albany Law School (J.D., 1981). Author: "Patent Perspective: Strategies for Marketing Products," International Business Communications, 1992; "Interference Rules," Patent World, February, 1996. Lecturer: Conference on International Patent Protection for Biotechnology Companies, Washington, D.C., 1992. *Member:* The District of Columbia Bar (Member, Patent, Trademark and Copyright Law Section); American Bar Association (Member, Intellectual Property Law Section; Chairman, Bioethics Subcommittee, 1993-1994); American Intellectual Property Law Association; International Intellectual Property Association (AIPPI); International Federation of Industrial Property Attorneys (FICPI); Intellectual Property Owners Association; International Trademark Association. ***Email:*** grepper@rothwellfigg.com

STEVEN LIEBERMAN, born New York, N.Y., April 19, 1959; admitted to bar, 1985, New York; 1994, District of Columbia; U.S. District Court, Southern, Eastern and Northern Districts of New York; U.S. Court of Appeals, Second, District of Columbia and Federal Circuits and U.S. Supreme Court. *Education:* Princeton University (A.B., summa cum laude, 1980); Columbia University (J.D., 1984). Stone Scholar, 1982-1984. Member, Columbia Journal of Law and Social Policy, 1982-1984. Editor, Libel Defense Resource Center Cyberlaw Project. Author: "LDRC 50-State Survey of Media Privacy and Related Law," (District of Columbia Section), 1995-1996, 1997-1998, 1998-1999, 1999-2000 and 2000-2001; Chapter on Defamation, "Internet and the Law: Legal Fundamentals for the Internet User," 1995; "Defamation Claims in Cyberspace: Liability of Owners and Operators of Electronic Bulletin Boards for Statements Uploaded by Subscribers," Libel Defense Resource Center Newsletter, May 1994; Case Comment, "Burroughs Wellcome Co. v. Barr Laboratories," Patent World, October 1993. Clerk to Hon. Edmund L. Palmieri, Southern District of New York, 1984-1985. Member, Libel Defense Resource Center, Chairman, Cyberspace Committee, 1997-1999. *Member:* The Association of the Bar of the City of New York (Member, Communications Law Committee, 1990-1993); New York State (Member, Media Law Committee; Chairman, Subcommittee on Defamation and New Technologies, 1994-1998) and American Bar Associations; The District of Columbia Bar (Member, Media Law Committee); Giles S. Rich American Inn of Court (Program Chair). ***SPECIAL AGENCIES:*** Pro Bono Special Counsel to the Departmental Disciplinary Committee of the New York Appellate Division, First Department, 1990-1992. ***PRACTICE AREAS:*** Intellectual Property; Litigation; Constitutional Law. ***Email:*** slieberm@rothwellfigg.com

VINCENT M. DeLUCA, born Yonkers, New York, March 4, 1960; admitted to bar, 1987, Virginia; 1991, U.S. Court of Appeals for the Federal Circuit; 1993, District of Columbia; registered to practice before U.S. Patent and Trademark Office. *Education:* Columbia University (B.S.E.E., 1982); George Mason University School of Law (J.D., 1987). Patent Examiner, U.S. Patent and Trademark Office, 1982-1986. *Member:* The District of Columbia Bar (Member, Intellectual Property Law Section); Virginia State Bar; American Bar Association (Member, Intellectual Property Law Section); American Intellectual Property Law Association; Federal Circuit Bar Association; Intellectual Property Owners Association. ***PRACTICE AREAS:*** Intellectual Property. ***Email:*** vdeluca@rothwellfigg.com

JOSEPH A. HYNDS, born Kokomo, Indiana, January 16, 1964; admitted to bar, 1991, Virginia; 1993, District of Columbia, U.S. Court of Appeals for the Federal Circuit and U.S. District Court, District of Columbia; registered to practice before U.S. Patent and Trademark Office. *Education:* Wabash College (B.A. in Physics, 1986); George Washington University (J.D., with honors, 1991). Patent Examiner, U.S. Patent and Trademark Office, 1986-1989. *Member:* District of Columbia Bar (Member, Intellectual Property Law Section); Virginia State Bar; American Bar Association (Member, Section on Patent, Trademark and Copyright Law); American Intellectual Property Law Association; American Inns of Court. ***PRACTICE AREAS:*** Intellectual Property. ***Email:*** jhynds@rothwellfigg.com

ROBERT J. JONDLE, born Iowa City, Iowa, August 8, 1946; admitted to bar, 1991, Maryland, District of Columbia and Nebraska; 1992, U.S. Court of Appeals, Federal Circuit; 1999, U.S. Supreme Court; registered to practice before U.S. Patent and Trademark Office. *Education:* Iowa State University (B.S., with distinction, 1968; Ph.D., 1974); Georgetown University (J.D., 1991). Phi Kappa Phi; Gamma Sigma Delta; Phi Eta Sigma. Member: Crop Science Society of America; American Seed Trade Association; American Society of Horticultural Science (Member and Past Chair, Intellectual Property Rights Committee). *Member:* Nebraska State and American (Member and Chairman, Plant Subcommittee, Division X, Biosciences, 1994, 1995, 1996) Bar Associations; The District of Columbia Bar (Member, Patent, Trademark and Copyright Law Section); American Society of Agronomy; American Intellectual Property Law Association. (Resident, Omaha, Nebraska Office). ***PRACTICE AREAS:*** Intellectual Property. ***Email:*** rjondle@rothwellfigg.com

ELIZABETH A. LEFF, born Albany, New York, May 28, 1957; admitted to bar, 1987, Washington; 1991, Florida; 2001, District of Columbia; U.S. District Court, Northern, Southern and Middle Districts of Florida; U.S. District Court, Western District of Washington; U.S District Court, District of Colorado; U.S.

(This Listing Continued)

Court of Appeals, Ninth and Federal Circuits; U.S. Supreme Court;. *Education:* Bowdoin College; University of Massachusetts (B.S., Microbiology, cum laude, 1979); Cambridge University (B.A., Economics, with honors, 1981); Stanford Law School (J.D., 1987). Author, "LDRC 50-State Survey of Media Privacy and Related Law," District of Columbia Section, 1998-1999, 1999-2000, 2000-2001. *Member:* Washington State and American Bar Associations; The Florida Bar; American Intellectual Property Law Association. ***PRACTICE AREAS:*** Intellectual Property; Litigation. ***Email:*** eleff@rothwellfigg.com

---

MARTHA CASSIDY, born Washington, D.C., February 25, 1958; admitted to bar, 1997, District of Columbia; registered to practice before U.S. Patent and Trademark Office. *Education:* Grinnell College (B.A., Chemistry, 1980); Georgetown University (Ph.D., Biology, 1991); University of Virginia (J.D., 1997). Sigma XI Scientific Honor Society. Dillard Fellowship, Legal Research and Writing, University of Virginia. *Member:* American Bar Association; American Intellectual Property Lawyers Association. ***LANGUAGES:*** French. ***Email:*** mcassidy@rothwellfigg.com

GREGG L. JANSEN, born Ogallala, Nebraska, June 12, 1961; admitted to bar, 1998, Nebraska; registered to practice before U.S. Patent and Trademark Office (Not admitted in District of Columbia). *Education:* University of Nebraska at Lincoln (B.S.E.E., 1990); Indiana University (J.D., 1997). Author: "The United States Moves Ahead of the European Union in Patent Protection for Computer Software," 741 Indiana Int'l & Comparative L.J. 6 No. 3 (1996). *Member:* American Intellectual Property Law Association. (Resident, Omaha, Nebraska Office). ***Email:*** gjansen@rothwellfigg.com

NANCY T. MORRIS, born Omaha, Nebraska; admitted to bar, 1983, Iowa and Nebraska; 1984, Texas; 1999, U.S. District Court, District of Nebraska; registered to practice before U.S. Patent and Trademark Office (Not admitted in District of Columbia). *Education:* University of Nebraska at Omaha (B.A., 1967; M.A., 1975); Creighton University (J.D., 1982). *Member:* Nebraska State and Iowa State Bar Associations; State Bar of Texas; American Intellectual Property Law Association (Member, Biotechnology Committee). (Resident, Omaha, Nebraska Office). ***Email:*** nmorris@rothwellfigg.com

LISA A. FAHIEN ULDRICH, born Bethesda, Maryland, June 8, 1965; admitted to bar, 1994, Missouri; 1995, U.S. District Court, Eastern District of Missouri; 1998, Nebraska; registered to practice before U.S. Patent and Trademark Office (Not admitted in District of Columbia). *Education:* University of Wisconsin-Madison (B.S., Natural Sciences, with honors, 1987); Washington University School of Law (J.D., 1992). Alpha Zeta; Phi Delta Phi. *Member:* Bar Association of Metropolitan St. Louis (Vice-Chair, Patent, Trademark, Copyright Section, 1996-1997; Chair, Trademark, Copyright, Unfair Competition Section, 1995-1996); International Trademark Association (Brand Names Education Foundation Committee, 1995-1996). (Resident, Omaha, Nebraska Office). ***LANGUAGES:*** French. ***PRACTICE AREAS:*** Intellectual Property. ***Email:*** luldrich@rothwellfigg.com

ROBERT H. CAMERON, born Philadelphia, Pennsylvania, June 8, 1969; admitted to bar, 1998, New York; 1999, District of Columbia. *Education:* Duke University (B.A., cum laude, 1991); George Washington University (J.D., with honors, 1997). *Member:* New York State Bar Association; American Intellectual Property Law Association; International Trademark Association. ***Email:*** rcameron@rothwellfigg.com

RICHARD WYDEVEN, born Appleton, Wisconsin, September 3, 1963; admitted to bar, 1994, Texas; 1995, District of Columbia; registered to practice before U.S. Patent and Trademark Office. *Education:* University of Wisconsin-Madison (B.S.E.M., with highest distinction, 1986); George Washington University (M.S. Aeronautics, 1988); University of Texas (J.D., with honors, 1994). Order of the Coif; Tau Beta Pi; Phi Eta Sigma. Member, The Review of Litigation, 1992-1994. Author: "The Foreign Sovereign Immunities Act of 1976: A Contemporary Look at Jurisdiction Under the Commercial Activity Exception," The Review of Litigation, Vol. 13, Fall 1993. *Member:* State Bar of Texas; District of Columbia Bar; American Bar Association; American Intellectual Property Law Association. ***PRACTICE AREAS:*** Intellectual Property. ***Email:*** rwydeven@rothwellfigg.com

THOMAS EDWARD McKIERNAN, born Detroit, Michigan, March 25, 1962; admitted to bar, 1995, Michigan; registered to practice before U.S. Patent and Trademark Office (Not admitted in District of Columbia). *Education:* General Motors Institute (B.S.M.E., 1985); University of Michigan (M.B.A., 1990); University of Detroit (J.D., cum laude, 1994); Wayne State University (M.S.E.E., 1998). Professional Engineer, Michigan, 1990. ***PRACTICE AREAS:*** Intellectual Property. ***Email:*** tmckiern@rothwellfigg.com

JASON M. SHAPIRO, born Red Bank, New Jersey, September 2, 1964; admitted to bar, 1994, Maryland; registered to practice before U.S. Patent and Trademark Office (Not admitted in District of Columbia). *Education:* Johns Hopkins University (B.S., 1986; M.S., 1987); University of Baltimore (J.D., cum laude, 1994). Member, 1991-1992 and Assistant Editor, 1992, University of Baltimore Law Forum. *Member:* Baltimore County, Maryland State and

(This Listing Continued)

American (Member, Intellectual Property Law Section) Bar Associations; American Society of Mechanical Engineers. ***PRACTICE AREAS:*** Intellectual Property. ***Email:*** jshapiro@rothwellfigg.com

MICHAEL JOHN MORAN, born Mineola, New York, July 27, 1953; admitted to bar, 1995, Arizona; 1996, U.S. District Court, District of Arizona; 1997, U.S. Court of Appeals, Ninth Circuit; registered to practice before U.S. Patent and Trademark Office (Not admitted in District of Columbia). *Education:* University of Arizona (B.S., 1982; M.S., 1985; Ph.D., 1990; J.D., 1995). First Author, "Variable Region Genes of Human Monoclonal Antibodies: Evidence of Non-restricted Gene Use and Sonatic Mutation," Molecular Immunology 30, 1545-1551 (1993). *Member:* State Bar of Arizona. ***PRACTICE AREAS:*** Intellectual Property. ***Email:*** mmoran@rothwellfigg.com

ANNE M. STERBA, born Pittsburgh, Pennsylvania, May 14, 1973; admitted to bar, 1998, Virginia; 1999, District of Columbia. *Education:* Westminster College (B.A., with honors, 1995); George Mason University School of Law (J.D., 1998). Phi Alpha Delta. Recipient, Best Oral Advocate in First Year Moot Court Competition, 1996. Listed, Who's Who in American Law Students, 1997. *Member:* American Bar Association; American Intellectual Property Law Association (Member, Trademark Committee); International Trademark Association. ***Email:*** asterba@rothwellfigg.com

LISA N. PHILLIPS, born Spangler, Pennsylvania, September 4, 1964; admitted to bar, 2001, Pennsylvania (Not admitted in District of Columbia). *Education:* Pennsylvania State University (B.S., 1987); George Mason University School of Law (J.D., 2000). *Member:* American Bar Association. ***PRACTICE AREAS:*** Patent Prosecution; Patent Litigation. ***Email:*** lphillips@rothwellfigg.com

LEIGH M. ZANOWSKI, born Ridgewood, New Jersey, December 16, 1969; admitted to bar, 2000, Maryland (Not admitted in District of Columbia). *Education:* Rollins College (A.B., 1993); American University (M.A., 1997); George Washington University (M.F.S., 1997); Catholic University of America (J.D., 2000). *Member:* Maryland State and American Bar Associations; American Intellectual Property Law Association. ***PRACTICE AREAS:*** Pharmaceutical Patent Litigation; Biotechnology Patent Prosecution. ***Email:*** lzanowsk@rothwellfigg.com

C. NICHOLE GIFFORD, born Kingsport, Tennessee, August 19, 1974; admitted to bar, 1999, Tennessee; registered to practice before the U.S. Patent and Trademark Office (Not admitted in District of Columbia). *Education:* Tennessee Technological University (B.S., 1996); University of Memphis (J.D., 1999); George Washington University. Phi Delta Phi. Author: "The Sonny Bono Copyright Term Extension Act", 30 University of Memphis Law Review 363, 2001, reprinted in Intellectual Property Law Review, West, 2001. *Member:* American Bar Association. ***PRACTICE AREAS:*** Intellectual Property. ***Email:*** ngifford@rothwellfigg.com

OF COUNSEL

DON M. KERR, born Lubbock, Texas, October 23, 1936; admitted to bar, 1965, Delaware; 1981, U.S. District Court, District of Delaware; 1982, U.S. Court of Appeals for the Federal Circuit; registered to practice before U.S. Patent and Trademark Office (Not admitted in District of Columbia). *Education:* Texas Tech University (B.Ch.E., 1960); George Washington University (LL.B., 1964). *Member:* Delaware State Bar Association; American Intellectual Property Lawyers Association. ***PRACTICE AREAS:*** Intellectual Property. ***Email:*** dkerr@rothwellfigg.com

JEFFREY L. IHNEN, born Carroll, Iowa, August 2, 1951; admitted to bar, 1980, District of Columbia; 1985, U.S. Court of Appeals for the Federal Circuit; 1987, U.S. Supreme Court; registered to practice before U.S. Patent and Trademark Office. *Education:* Wartburg College (B.A., Chem., 1973); University of Iowa (M.S., Biochem., 1976); George Washington University (J.D., 1980). Faculty Member, Intellectual Property Symposium, Inc., 1988-1990. *Member:* The District of Columbia Bar; American Bar Association (Member, Sections on: Patent, Intellectual Property Law; Science and Technology); American Intellectual Property Law Association; American Association for Advancement of Science; American Society of Human Genetics; New York Academy of Science. ***PRACTICE AREAS:*** Intellectual Property Law. ***Email:*** jihnen@rothwellfigg.com

GLENN E. KARTA, born Bronx, New York, 1957; admitted to bar, 1982, New York; 1985, Connecticut; registered to practice before U.S. Patent and Trademark Office; 1993, District of Columbia. *Education:* Rensselaer Polytechnic Institute (B.S., 1978); Illinois Institute of Technology, Chicago-Kent College of Law (J.D., 1981). *Member:* New York State and American Bar Associations; American Intellectual Property Law Association. ***PRACTICE AREAS:*** Intellectual Property. ***Email:*** gkarta@rothwellfigg.com

MARK I. BOWDITCH, born Ripon, Wisconsin, September 22, 1963; admitted to bar, 1993, Virginia; 1996, District of Columbia; U.S. District Court, District of Columbia and U.S. Court of Appeals, Federal Circuit; registered to practice before U.S. Patent and Trademark Office. *Education:* George Washington University (B.S., with distinction, 1986; M.S., 1988; J.D., 1993). *Member:*

(This Listing Continued)

ROTHWELL, FIGG, ERNST & MANBECK, A PROFESSIONAL CORPORATION, Washington—Continued

American Bar Association; American Intellectual Property Law Association; Intellectual Property Owners Association; International Trademark Association. ***LANGUAGES:*** Italian, French. ***Email:*** mbowditc@rothwellfigg.com

MINAKSI BHATT, born Naini Tal, U.P., India, July 23, 1963; admitted to bar, 1990, California; 1992, District of Columbia; 2000, Washington; registered to practice before the U.S. Patent and Trademark Office. *Education:* Wellesley College (B.A., 1985); George Washington University (J.D., 1990). *Member:* American Bar Association; American Intellectual Property Law Association. ***PRACTICE AREAS:*** Intellectual Property Litigation. ***Email:*** mbhatt@rothwellfigg.com

MICHAEL G. SULLIVAN, born Washington, D.C., October 14, 1963; admitted to bar, 1991, Maryland; 1992, District of Columbia; registered to Practice before the U.S. Patent and Trademark Office. *Education:* Indiana University (B.S., Biology, 1986); University of Baltimore (J.D., 1990); Johns Hopkins University (M.S., Biotechnology, 2001). *Member:* American Bar Association. ***PRACTICE AREAS:*** Intellectual Property. ***Email:*** msulliva@rothwellfigg.com

LAW OFFICES OF SYLVIA ROYCE

5505 CONNECTICUT AVENUE, NW, SUITE 243
WASHINGTON, D.C. 20015
Telephone: 202-362-3445
Fax: 202-686-4271
Email: sylvia_royce@hotmail.com
URL: http://www.lawyers.com/sylviaroyce

International Prisoner Transfer, Prisoner Exchange, Hague Convention, Proceedings, International Child Abduction, Post Conviction Remedies, Expungement of Records, International Post Conviction Remedies.

FIRM PROFILE: Sylvia Royce is a former Assistant U.S. Attorney for the District of Columbia, and the former Chief of International Prisoner Transfer at the U.S. Department of Justice. She represents individuals and families and works closely with foreign embassies from around the world.

SYLVIA ROYCE, born Tulsa, Oklahoma, September 28, 1945; admitted to bar, 1977, District of Columbia; 1980, U.S. Supreme Court. *Education:* Tufts University (B.S.,1972); Antioch School of Law (J.D., 1976). Chief, International Prisoner Transfer Program 1995-2000 and Member, Criminal Division and Civil Division 1982-2000, U.S. Department of Justice; Assistant United States Attorney, District of Columbia, 1977-1982. *Member:* District of Columbia Bar; American Bar Association (Member, Sections on International Law); Women's Bar Association of the District of Columbia. ***LANGUAGES:*** French. ***PRACTICE AREAS:*** International Treaty Law; International Criminal Law; International Child Abduction; Post-Conviction Remedies.

ROYLANCE, ABRAMS, BERDO & GOODMAN, L.L.P.

Established in 1954
1300 19TH STREET, N.W., SUITE 600
WASHINGTON, D.C. 20036-1649
Telephone: 202-659-9076
Facsimile: 202-659-9344
Email: RABG@roylance.com
URL: http://www.roylance.com

Patent, Trademark, Copyright and Unfair Competition Law. International Patent and Trademark Practice. Litigation in all Federal Courts.

FIRM PROFILE: Founded in 1954, the firm is dedicated to providing quality legal services across the full range of intellectual property law in the United States and worldwide. The firm advises on the protection, enforcement, and licensing of intellectual property rights including inventions, designs, trademarks, trade secrets and artistic works. The firm has extensive experience, skill and expertise in litigation in the federal courts, as well as negotiation and settlement of inter parties controversies and drafting and negotiating of licenses; in prosecution of patents, trademarks and copyrights and inter party matters before the U.S. Patent and Trademark Office and the U.S. Copyright Office, as well as the corresponding offices abroad; and in all major technologies.

D. C. ROYLANCE (1920-1995).

DAVID S. ABRAMS, born Washington, D.C., August 27, 1937; admitted to bar, 1964, Maryland; 1964-1982, U.S. Court of Customs and Patent Appeals; 1965, District of Columbia; 1971, U.S. Supreme Court; 1982, U.S. Court of Appeals for the Federal Circuit; registered to practice before U.S. Patent and Trademark Office. *Education:* University of Maryland (B.S., Ch.E., 1960); American University (J.D., 1963). Patent Examiner, U.S. Patent Office, 1960-1965. *Member:* The District of Columbia Bar; Bar Association of the District of Columbia; Maryland State and American Bar Associations; American Intellectual Property Law Association; Maryland Patent Law Association. ***PRACTICE AREAS:*** Litigation; Patent Law; Trademark Law. ***Email:*** dabrams@roylance.com

ROBERT H. BERDO, born Washington, Iowa, January 28, 1930; admitted to bar, 1960, District of Columbia; 1960-1982, U.S. Court of Customs and Patent Appeals; 1965, U.S. Supreme Court; 1982, U.S. Court of Appeals for the Federal Circuit; registered to practice before U.S. Patent and Trademark Office. *Education:* State University of Iowa (B.S., Chemistry, 1956); George Washington University (J.D., 1960). Phi Lambda Upsilon. Patent Examiner, U.S. Patent Office, 1956-1959. *Member:* The District of Columbia Bar; Bar Association of the District of Columbia; American Bar Association; American Intellectual Property Law Association; American Chemical Society. ***PRACTICE AREAS:*** Patent Law; Pharmaceutical Patent Law; Chemical Patent Law. ***Email:*** rberdo@roylance.com

ALFRED N. GOODMAN, born New York, N.Y., January 21, 1945; admitted to bar, 1970, New York; 1971, District of Columbia, U.S. District Court for the District of Columbia and U.S. Court of Appeals, District of Columbia Circuit; 1972-1982, U.S. Court of Customs and Patent Appeals; 1974, U.S. Supreme Court; 1982, U.S. Court of Appeals for the Federal Circuit; 1990, U.S. Court of Appeals, Sixth Circuit; 1992, U.S. Court of Appeals, Fifth Circuit; 1996, U.S. Court of Appeals, Eleventh Circuit; registered to practice before U.S. Patent and Trademark Office. *Education:* University of Rochester (B.S.M.E., 1966); Georgetown University (J.D., 1969). Patent Examiner, U.S. Patent Office, 1969-1971. *Member:* The District of Columbia Bar; Bar Association of the District of Columbia (Member, Board of Directors, 1985-1986; Chairman, Patent, Trademark and Copyright Section, 1984-1985); American Bar Association; American Intellectual Property Law Association. ***PRACTICE AREAS:*** Litigation; Patent Law; Trademark Law; Copyright Law; Mechanical Patent Law. ***Email:*** agoodman@roylance.com

MARK S. BICKS, born New York, N.Y., May 19, 1948; admitted to bar, 1977, Virginia; 1977-1982, U.S. Court of Customs and Patent Appeals; 1978, District of Columbia; 1979, U.S. Court of Appeals, Fourth Circuit; 1982, U.S. Court of Appeals for the Federal Circuit; 1983, U.S. Supreme Court; 1990, U.S. Court of Appeals, Sixth Circuit; 1992, U.S. Court of Appeals, Fifth Circuit; registered to practice before U.S. Patent and Trademark Office. *Education:* Northeastern University (B.S.M.E., 1971); Catholic University of America (J.D., 1977). Recipient, Corpus Juris Secundum Award, Catholic University of America, 1977. Author: "Threatening to Sue for Patent Infringement: Unfair Competition and Antitrust Consequences," 59 Journal of the Patent Office Society 302, May, 1977. Patent Examiner, U.S. Patent and Trademark Office, 1972-1977. *Member:* The District of Columbia Bar; Bar Association of the District of Columbia; Virginia State and American Bar Associations; American Intellectual Property Law Association. ***PRACTICE AREAS:*** Litigation; Patent Law; Trademark Law; Copyright Law; Mechanical Patent Law. ***Email:*** mbicks@roylance.com

RICHARD A. FLYNT, born Alexandria, Virginia, October 10, 1946; admitted to bar, 1973, Mississippi; 1973-1982, U.S. Court of Customs and Patent Appeals; 1975, District of Columbia; 1982, U.S. Court of Appeals for the Federal Circuit. *Education:* University of Virginia (B.A., 1970); University of Mississippi (J.D., 1973). Co-Author: "Recapturing Trademarks from Unauthorized Domain Name Registrants," The Franchise Lawyer, Vol. 4, No. 4, Spring, 2001. *Member:* The District of Columbia Bar; The Bar Association of the District of Columbia (Member, Board of Directors, 1989-1990; 1991-1992; Chairman, Patent, Trademark and Copyright Section, 1990-1991; Chairman, Trademark Committee, 1987-1989); Mississippi State Bar; American Bar Association; American Intellectual Property Law Association; International Trademark Association (formerly, United States Trademark Association). ***PRACTICE AREAS:*** Trademark Law; Litigation; Copyright Law. ***Email:*** rflynt@roylance.com

JOHN E. HOLMES, born New York, N.Y., November 2, 1953; admitted to bar, 1978, District of Columbia; registered to practice before U.S. Patent and Trademark Office. *Education:* Rensselaer Polytechnic Institute (B.S.E.E., cum laude, 1975); George Washington University (J.D., with high honors, 1978). Tau Beta Pi; Eta Kappa Nu; Order of the Coif. *Member:* The District of Columbia Bar; American Bar Association (Member, Section of Intellectual Property Law); American Intellectual Property Law Association. ***PRACTICE AREAS:*** Patent, Trademark and Copyright Law; Technology Licensing; Electrical and Computer Patent Law. ***Email:*** jholmes@roylance.com

MICHAEL T. MURPHY, born New York, N.Y., October 23, 1958; admitted to bar, 1983, Maryland; 1985, District of Columbia; 1989, U.S. District Court, District of Columbia and U.S. District Court, District of Maryland. *Education:* University of Maryland at College Park (B.A., 1980); University of Baltimore (J.D., 1983); Georgetown University (LL.M., 1986). Member, University of Baltimore Law Review, 1982-1983. Author: Casenote, "In Re Appli-

(This Listing Continued)

cation of G.L.S. to the Bar of Maryland," 12 University of Baltimore Law Review 359 (1983). Attorney, U.S. Patent and Trademark Office, 1983-1989. *Member:* The District of Columbia Bar; The Bar Association of the District of Columbia; Maryland State and American Bar Associations. ***PRACTICE AREAS:*** Patents; Trademarks; Copyright Law; Litigation; Unfair Competition Law. ***Email:*** mmurphy@roylance.com

LANCE G. JOHNSON, born Janesville, Wisconsin, October 7, 1959; admitted to bar, 1987, Virginia; 1989, District of Columbia; registered to practice before U.S. Patent and Trademark Office. *Education:* Iowa State University (B.S. in Ch.E., 1982); George Washington University (J.D., 1987). Associate Editor, "Bulletin of Law, Science and Technology," published by the ABA Section on Science and Technology. U.S. Patent Examiner, 1982-1987. Member, ABA Science and Technology Section. Program Chair, Long Range Planning Committee and Internet Policy Committee. Chairman, Young Lawyers Committee of Science and Technology Section. *Member:* District of Columbia Bar; Virginia State Bar; American Bar Association. ***PRACTICE AREAS:*** Preparation; Prosecution; Litigation and Licensing of Patents and Trademarks. ***Email:*** ljohnson@roylance.com

DEAN H. NAKAMURA, born Honolulu, Hawaii, August 18, 1952; admitted to bar, 1993, Maryland; 2000, District of Columbia; registered to practice before U.S. Patent and Trademark Office. *Education:* University of Hawaii (B.S., 1974; M.S., 1979); Cornell Graduate School of Medical Sciences (Ph.D., 1983); George Washington University (J.D., 1993). National Institute of Health Fellow. Cornell University Scholar, March of Dimes Scholar. National Science Foundation Awardee. Member: American Society of Human Genetics; American Society of Animal Sciences. *Member:* Maryland State and American Bar Associations; The District of Columbia Bar; American Intellectual Property Law Association. ***PRACTICE AREAS:*** Intellectual Property Law; Biotechnology. ***Email:*** dnakamura@roylance.com

STACEY J. LONGANECKER, born Washington, D.C., October 2, 1965; admitted to bar, 1993, Maryland; 2000, District of Columbia; registered to practice before the U.S. Patent and Trademark Office. *Education:* University of Maryland (B.S.E.E., 1988); Catholic University of America (J.D., 1993). Eta Kappa Nu. *Member:* Maryland State and American Bar Associations; American Intellectual Property Law Association; Institute of Electrical and Electronics Engineers. ***PRACTICE AREAS:*** Patent, Trademark and Copyright Law; Electrical Patent Law; Computer Law. ***Email:*** slonganecker@roylance.com

JOSEPH J. BUCZYNSKI, born Wilkes-Barre, Pennsylvania, November 22, 1964; admitted to bar, 1994, Pennsylvania; 1995, Maryland; 1996, District of Columbia; registered to practice before U.S. Patent and Trademark Office. *Education:* Wilkes College (B.S.E.E., 1986); George Washington University (J.D., 1994). *Member:* Pennsylvania and Maryland State Bar Associations; The District of Columbia Bar; American Intellectual Property Law Association. ***PRACTICE AREAS:*** Intellectual Property Law; Electrical Patents; Mechanical Patents; Computer Law. ***Email:*** jbuczynski@roylance.com

GARRETT V. DAVIS, born Augusta, Georgia, May 7, 1954; admitted to bar, 1984, Maryland; 1987, District of Columbia; registered to practice before U.S. Patent and Trademark Office. *Education:* West Virginia University (B.S., 1977); University of Baltimore (J.D., 1984). *Member:* The District of Columbia Bar; Maryland State and American (Member, Patent, Trademark and Copyright Section) Bar Associations; American Intellectual Property Law Association. ***PRACTICE AREAS:*** Patent Law; Chemical Patent Law. ***Email:*** gdavis@roylance.com

ASSOCIATES

ANTIGONE E. JUVELIS, born Silver Spring, Maryland, November 19, 1964; admitted to bar, 1995, Virginia; U.S. Court of Appeals, Fourth Circuit; Virginia Supreme Court (Not admitted in District of Columbia). *Education:* University of Maryland (B.A., in Government and Politics, Russian Studies, 1986); Columbus School of Law at Catholic University of America (J.D., 1995). *Member:* Virginia Bar Association. ***PRACTICE AREAS:*** Trademarks; Copyrights; Entertainment Law; Multimedia Law. ***Email:*** ajuvelis@roylance.com

TARA LASTER HOFFMAN, born Washington, D.C., December 29, 1971; admitted to bar, 1999, Virginia; registered to practice before the U.S. Patent and Trademark Offices (Not admitted in District of Columbia). *Education:* Virginia Polytechnic Institute and State University (B.S., 1994);Columbus School of Law at Catholic University of America (J.D., cum laude, 1999). Patent Examiner, the U.S. Patent and Trademark Office, 1994-1996. *Member:* Virginia and American (Member, Intellectual Property Section) Bar Associations. ***PRACTICE AREAS:*** Intellectual Property; Intellectual Property Litigation. ***Email:*** thoffman@roylance.com

JEFFREY J. HOWELL, born Annapolis, Maryland, January 12, 1970; admitted to bar, 1999, Maryland; registered to practice before the U.S. Patent and Trademark Office (Not admitted in District of Columbia). *Education:* John Hopkins University (B.S.M.E., 1992); University of Baltimore (J.D., magna cum laude, 1999). Patent Examiner, the U.S. Patent and Trademark Office, 1998-1999. *Member:* Maryland State and American Bar Associations; American Intellectual Property Law Association. ***PRACTICE AREAS:*** Patent Law; Patent Litigation. ***Email:*** jhowell@roylance.com

AISHA AHMAD, born Bihar, India, August 10; admitted to bar, 1997, Maryland (Not admitted in District of Columbia). *Education:* University of Maryland (BSEE, 1989); Cleveland Marshall College of Law (J.D., 1997). *Maryland State Bar Association.* ***PRACTICE AREAS:*** Patent Prosecution. ***Email:*** aahmad@roylance.com

MARCUS R. MICKNEY, born Washington, D.C. August 17, 1969; admitted to bar, 2000, Virginia (Not admitted in District of Columbia). *Education:* Virginia Tech (BSAE, 1991); George Mason University (J.D., 1999). *Member:* American Bar Association; American Intellectual Property Law Association. ***PRACTICE AREAS:*** Patents; Trademarks; Copyrights. ***Email:*** mmickney@roylance.com

CHRISTIAN C. MICHEL, born Camden, New Jersey, March 5, 1970; admitted to bar, 1999, Pennsylvania; registered to practice before U.S. Patent and Trademark Office (Not admitted in District of Columbia). *Education:* Lafayette College (B.S.E.E., 1992); Villanova University Law School (J.D., 1999). *Member:* Pennsylvania State Bar Association. ***PRACTICE AREAS:*** Electrical Patent Law; Trademark; Computer Law. ***Email:*** cmichel@roylance.com

MARK V. SPARACINO, born Pittsburgh, Pennsylvania, July 7, 1964; admitted to bar, 1996, Colorado (Not admitted in District of Columbia). *Education:* Pennsylvania State University (B.S., 1986); University of Colorado at Boulder (J.D., 1996). *Member:* Colorado Bar Association. [Captain, U.S. Air Force, 1986-1992]. ***PRACTICE AREAS:*** Trademarks; Copyrights. ***Email:*** msparacino@roylance.com

MARK W. HROZENCHIK, born Stamford, Connecticut, September 5, 1962; admitted to bar, 1997, Connecticut; 1998, New York; 2000, District of Columbia; registered to practice before U.S. Patent and Trademark Office. *Education:* Stevens Institute of Technology (B.E.E.E., 1984); Brooklyn Polytechnic Institute (M.S.E.E., 1992); Quinnipiac College School of Law (J.D., 1997). *Member:* Connecticut and American Bar Associations; Bar Association of the District of Columbia. ***PRACTICE AREAS:*** Electronics; Intellectual Property.

PATENT AGENTS

JULIE R. KELLER. *Education:* University of Virginia (Biology and Chemistry). Phi Beta Kappa. registered to practice before the U.S. Patent Office. (Patent Agent). ***PRACTICE AREAS:*** Chemical Patent Prosecution; Chemical Searching. ***Email:*** jkeller@roylance.com

DARYL A. BASHAM, born St. Albans, New York, November 13, 1960. *Education:* Howard University (B.S., Microbiology; Ph.D., Biochemistry); George Washington University. Patent Examiner, U.S. Patent and Trademark Office, 1996-1998. (Patent Agent). ***PRACTICE AREAS:*** Biotechnology Patent Law. ***Email:*** dbasham@roylance.com

PETER L. KENDALL, born British Guyana, December 12, 1965; (admission pending), registered to practice before the U.S. Patent and Trademark Office. *Education:* New York Institute of Technology (B.S.E.E., 1989); Polytechnic University (M.S., 1994); Brooklyn Law School (J.D., 1999). FCC License, U.S.A. (Patent Agent). ***PRACTICE AREAS:*** Patent Prosecution. ***Email:*** pkendall@roylance.com

RUBEN & ARONSON, LLP

3299 K STREET, SUITE 403
WASHINGTON, D.C. 20036
Telephone: 202-965-3600
Fax: 202-965-3700
Email: laronson@randalaw.com
URL: http://www.lawyers.com/rubenandaronsonlaw

Corporate Law, Commercial Transactions, Securities Law, Mergers and Acquisitions, Real Estate, Tax, Labor and Employment, Business Law, Small Business Law, Emerging Business Law, Business Formation.

FIRM PROFILE: Rubin & Aronson is a boutique transactional business law firm. Clients to the firm include the better NASDQ small to mid cap issuers, entrepreneurs, wealthy individuals and hedge funds making direct investments in those companies. The firm also represents many closely held commercial real estate developers and well managed and capitalized e-commerce companies.

ROBERT L. RUBEN, born Norfolk, Virginia, January 28, 1962; admitted to bar, 1986, Pennsylvania; 1988, District of Columbia. *Education:* University of Virginia (B.A., 1983); Dickinson School of Law of the Pennsylvania State University (J.D., 1986). Staff Member, Dickinson Law Review, 1985-1986. Author: "Legislative and Judicial Confusion Concerning Executory Contracts in

(This Listing Continued)

RUBEN & ARONSON, LLP, Washington—Continued

Bankruptcy," 89 Dickinson Law Review 1029, Winter, 1984. Member, Woolsack Society. ***PRACTICE AREAS:*** Securities Law; Corporate Finance; Securities Fraud. ***Email:*** rruben@randalaw.com

LOUIS M. ARONSON, born Providence, Rhode Island, November 21, 1965; admitted to bar, 1991, New York; 1992, District of Columbia and Maryland. *Education:* University of Michigan (B.A., 1987); Syracuse University (J.D., 1990). Member, Syracuse Law Review, 1989-1990. *Member:* New York State, Maryland State and American Bar Associations; District of Columbia Bar. ***PRACTICE AREAS:*** Corporate Finance; Securities; Transactional; Corporate Law; Real Estate; E-Commerce. ***Email:*** laronson@randalaw.com

ASSOCIATES

LAWRENCE ALAN LONDON, born Baltimore, Maryland, February 10, 1961; admitted to bar, 1986, New York (Not admitted in District of Columbia). *Education:* Wharton School of Law (B.A., Economics, 1982); Stanford University (J.D., 1986). ***PRACTICE AREAS:*** Corporate Law; Mergers and Acquisitions; Tax Law. ***Email:*** llondon@randalaw.com

WILLIAM T. NESBITT, born April 7, 1971; admitted to bar, 1998, Maryland (Not admitted in District of Columbia). *Education:* New College of the University of South Florida (B.A., 1995); University of Baltimore (J.D., magna cum laude, 1998). Recipient, High Merit Scholarship. Member, Heuisler Society. Articles Editor, University of Baltimore Law Review, 1997-1998. ***Email:*** tnesbitt@randalaw.com

OF COUNSEL

EDWARD A. FRIEDMAN, born Montreal, Quebec, Canada, September 19, 1956; admitted to bar, 1985, Israel; 1987, New York (Not admitted in District of Columbia). *Education:* Tel Aviv University (LL.B., 1985); George Washington University (M.C.L., 1988). ***PRACTICE AREAS:*** Securities; Mergers and Acquisitions; International Transactions; Corporate; Business. ***Email:*** e1friedman@aol.com

MARSHALL F. BERMAN, born Portsmouth, Virginia, 1939; admitted to bar, 1967, Virginia; 1971, District of Columbia and U.S. Supreme Court. *Education:* University of Virginia (B.A., 1961); American University (J.D., 1967); George Washington University (LL.M. in Labor Law, with highest honors, 1970). Staff Member, American University Law Review, 1965-1966. Author: "The Changing Face of Union Organizing," Synergy (Epstein Becker & Green, New York, N.Y.), Spring 1993, at 1; "Commentary: White Collar Overtime Exemption in Confusion," Synergy (Epstein Becker & Green, New York, N.Y.) Fall 1992, at 1; "New Faces, Old Demands," Small Business Reports, April 1993, at 11. Co-Author, Berman and Garafalo: "Aviation Drug Testing Operating Manual," 1989; "Aviation Drug Testing Handbook," 1990. Attorney, Member's and Chairman's Staff, National Labor Relations Board, 1968-1971. ***PRACTICE AREAS:*** Labor; Employment Relations. ***Email:*** mberman@randalaw.com

RUBIN & RUBIN, P.C.

WASHINGTON, D.C.

(See Silver Spring, Maryland)

Litigation, Hospital Law, Insurance Litigation, Personal Injury, Automobile Accidents and Injuries, Wills, Trusts, Estates, Family Wealth Transfer, Probate, Wealth Preservation, Insurance Claims, Hospital Collection.

RUBIN, WINSTON, DIERCKS, HARRIS & COOKE, L.L.P.

A Limited Liability Partnership including a Professional Corporation

Established in 1981

1155 CONNECTICUT AVENUE, N.W., SIXTH FLOOR
WASHINGTON, D.C. 20036
Telephone: 202-861-0870
Telecopier: 202-429-0657
Email: administrator@rwdhc.com
URL: http://www.rwdhc.com

Litigation before Federal and State Courts. Practice before United States Courts, Governmental Departments and Agencies. Civil and White Collar Criminal Litigation. Trade Regulation, Communications, Media, Land Use and Zoning, Advertising and Franchise Regulation, Corporate, Banking, Construction, Government Contract, Public Utility, Legislative and Sports Law Practice.

ERIC M. RUBIN, (P.C.), born Passaic, New Jersey, March 29, 1943; admitted to bar, 1967, New Jersey; 1970, District of Columbia. *Education:* George Washington University (B.A., 1964); Rutgers University (J.D., 1967). Phi Delta Phi. Adjunct Professor of Law, Antioch School of Law, Antitrust Law, 1976-1978. Trial Attorney, Department of Justice, 1967-1969. Staff Counsel, Executive Office of the President, Council on Executive Reorganization, (establishing the Environmental Protection Agency) 1969-1970. Assistant to Chairman, New York State Public Service Commission, 1970-1972. Deputy Assistant Director, 1972-1974, Assistant Director, 1974-1977 and Associate Director, 1978, Bureau of Consumer Protection, Federal Trade Commission. Member, Legal Advisory Committee, American Advertising Federation, 1990—. *Member:* The District of Columbia Bar; American Bar Association (Member, Antitrust Law Section; Member, Forum Committees on: Entertainment and Sports Industries, 1983—; Communications; Franchising). ***PRACTICE AREAS:*** Outdoor Advertising Law; Media; Advertising; Trade Regulation; Sports; Legislative. ***Email:*** erubin@rwdhc.com

JAMES L. WINSTON, born Pittsburgh, Pennsylvania, August 24, 1947; admitted to bar, 1973, Massachusetts; 1974, New York; 1977, District of Columbia. *Education:* University of Pennsylvania (B.S.E.E., 1969); Harvard University (J.D., 1972). Legal Assistant to Commissioner Robert E. Lee, Federal Communications Commission, 1978-1980. President and General Counsel, National Association of Black-Owned Broadcasters. *Member:* The District of Columbia Bar; Federal and American (Member, Public Utility Law Section) Bar Associations; National Bar Association; Federal Communications Bar Association (Member, Executive Committee, 1993-1996). ***PRACTICE AREAS:*** Communications; Legislative; Public Utility. ***Email:*** jwinston@rwdhc.com

WALTER E. DIERCKS, born Irvington, New Jersey, July 6, 1945; admitted to bar, 1972, Virginia; 1973, District of Columbia; 1984, U.S. Supreme Court. *Education:* Rensselaer Polytechnic Institute (B.Ch.E., 1967); University of Virginia (J.D., 1972). Phi Delta Phi. Staff Attorney, 1972-1976 and Deputy Assistant Director, 1976-1977, Bureau of Consumer Protection, Federal Trade Commission. General Counsel, The Washington Star Company, 1977-1981. *Member:* The District of Columbia Bar; Virginia State Bar; American Bar Association; Federal Communications Bar Association. ***PRACTICE AREAS:*** Media; Civil Litigation; Trade Regulation; General Corporate. ***Email:*** wdiercks@rwdhc.com

JEFFREY HARRIS, born Brooklyn, New York, March 20, 1944; admitted to bar, 1969, New York; 1976, U.S. Supreme Court; 1977, District of Columbia; 1990, Virginia. *Education:* New York University (B.S., 1965); Syracuse University (J.D., 1968). Instructor of Trial Advocacy, National Institute of Trial Advocacy, Programs at: Harvard University; Hastings College of Law. Legal Officer, U.S. Navy, 1968-1971. Assistant U.S. Attorney, Southern District of New York, 1972-1976. Chief, Attorney General's Investigation Review Unit, U.S. Department of Justice, 1976-1977. Deputy Chief Counsel, Committee on Standards of Official Conduct, U.S. House of Representatives (Koreagate Investigation), 1977-1979. Assistant Director for Marketing Abuses, Federal Trade Commission, 1980-1981. Executive Director, Attorney General's Task Force on Violent Crime, U.S. Department of Justice, 1981. Deputy Associate Attorney General, U.S. Department of Justice, 1981-1983. General Counsel, Capital Bancorp., 1983-1985. *Member:* The District of Columbia Bar; Virginia State Bar. ***PRACTICE AREAS:*** White Collar Crime; Criminal Antitrust; Civil Litigation; Construction; Banking; General Corporate; Commercial Speech. ***Email:*** jharris@rwdhc.com

FREDERICK D. COOKE, JR., born Washington, D.C., May 26, 1947; admitted to bar, 1973, District of Columbia. *Education:* Howard University (B.S., 1969; J.D., cum laude, 1972). Phi Alpha Delta. Managing Editor, Howard Law Journal, 1971-1972. Chairman National Conference of Law Reviews, 1971-1972. Adjunct Professor, Howard University School of Law, 1986—. Law Clerk to Judge George W. Draper II, D.C. Superior Court, 1972-1973. Corporation Counsel of the District of Columbia, 1987-1989. *Member:* The District Bar (Member, Board of Governors, 1996-1997); National Bar Association; Federal Communications Bar Association; National Institute of Municipal Law Officers (Trustee, 1989); National Association of Attorneys General. [Capt., U.S. Air Force, Judge Advocate General's Department, 1973-1977]. ***PRACTICE AREAS:*** Communications; Legislative; Government Contracts. ***Email:*** fcooke@rwdhc.com

STEVEN J. STONE, born New York, N.Y., October 12, 1960; admitted to bar, 1986, District of Columbia. *Education:* George Washington University (B.A., 1982); Catholic University of America (J.D., 1986). Note Editor, Journal of Contemporary Health Law & Policy, 1985-1986. *Member:* The District of Columbia Bar; American Bar Association; Federal Communication Bar Association. ***LANGUAGES:*** French. ***PRACTICE AREAS:*** Communications; Corporate Law; Real Estate; Litigation. ***Email:*** sstone@rwdhc.com

ASSOCIATES

PAUL M. BREAKMAN, born Encino, California, April 10, 1972; admitted to bar, 1998, Maryland, New Jersey and U.S. District Court, District of New Jersey; 2000, District of Columbia. *Education:* University of California, San Diego (B.A., cum laude, 1993); Tulane University of Louisiana (J.D., Maritime Law, 1997). Member, Tulane Journal of International and Comparative Law,

(This Listing Continued)

1995-1997. Law Clerk to the Honorable John M. Vittone, Chief Administrative Law Judge, U.S. Department of Labor, 1997-1999. Deputy Secretary to the Board of Alien Labor Certification Appeals, U.S. Department of Labor, 1998-1999. *Member:* Maryland State and American Bar Associations. ***PRACTICE AREAS:*** Communications Law; Media Law; Corporate Law. ***Email:*** pbreakman@rwdhc.com

RUDDY & MUIR, LLP

1730 K STREET, N.W.
SUITE 304
WASHINGTON, D.C. 20006
Telephone: 202-835-0055
Fax: 202-337-6459
URL: http://www.lawyers.com/ruddy&muir

Energy Law, International Law, Corporate Law and Securities Law, Telecommunications Law, Environmental Law, Litigation.

FRANK RUDDY, born New York, N.Y., September 15, 1937; admitted to bar, 1967, District of Columbia; 1972, New York; 1975, Texas. *Education:* College of the Holy Cross (A.B., 1959); New York University (M.A., 1962; LL.M., 1967); Loyola University (LL.B., 1965); Cambridge University, (Ph.D., 1969). Senior Attorney, Office of Telecommunications Policy, Executive Office of the President, 1972-1973. Counsel, Exxon Corporation, USA, 1974-1981. Assistant Administrator for Africa, U.S. Agency for International Development, 1981-1984. U.S. Ambassador to Equatorial Guinea, 1984-1988. General Counsel, U.S. Department of Energy, 1988-1989. ***LANGUAGES:*** French and Spanish. ***PRACTICE AREAS:*** Environmental Law; Energy Law; International Law. ***Email:*** global@globalltd.com

J. DAPRAY MUIR, born Washington, D.C., November 9, 1936; admitted to bar, 1964, District of Columbia, Maryland and Virginia; 1967, U.S. Supreme Court. *Education:* Williams College (A.B., 1958); University of Virginia (J.D., 1964). Assistant Legal Advisor for Economic and Business Affairs, U.S. State Department, 1972-1974. Member, 1982-1985 and Chairman, 1983-1985, District of Columbia Securities Advisory Committee. Member, Panel of Commercial Arbitrators, American Arbitration Association. *Member:* District of Columbia Bar (Chairman: Division of Energy, Natural Resources and Environmental Law, 1985-1986). ***PRACTICE AREAS:*** Corporate Law; Securities Law; Mergers and Acquisitions. ***Email:*** muirlaw@aol.com

OF COUNSEL

EUGENE P. KOPP, born Charleston, West Virginia, November 20, 1934; admitted to bar, 1961, West Virginia; 1977, District of Columbia; 1980, Texas. *Education:* University of Notre Dame (B.A., 1957; M.A., 1958); West Virginia University (J.D., 1961). Editor-in-Chief, West Virginia Law Review, 1960-1961. Trial Attorney, U.S. Department of Justice, Tax Division, 1962-1969. Associate General Counsel, Champlin Petroleum Company, 1977-1981. Vice President, Union Pacific Corporation, 1982-1987. Deputy Director and Acting Director, U.S. Information Agency, 1989- 1993. Executive Director, MFJ Task Force, 1993-1994. ***PRACTICE AREAS:*** Telecommunications Law; Government Affairs; Tax Disputes.

THOMAS P. GROSS, born Cleveland, Ohio, September 4, 1949; admitted to bar, 1979, District of Columbia; 1988, Virginia. *Education:* Case Institute of Technology (B.S., magna cum laude, Physics, 1971); Stanford University (M.S., Applied Physics, cum laude, 1973); Case Western Reserve University (J.D., 1977). Attorney, Office of General Counsel: Patent Division, U.S. Department of Energy, 1977-1979; Federal Energy Regulatory Commission, 1979-1987. Deputy Assistant General Counsel for Rulemaking, Federal Energy Regulatory Commission, 1982-1984. Counsel for projects in Asia, Europe and N.I.S., 1993—. ***LANGUAGES:*** Russian. ***PRACTICE AREAS:*** Energy; Environmental; Project Finance; International; Intellectual Property. ***Email:*** tpgross@hotmail.com

RUSSIAN-UKRAINIAN LEGAL GROUP, P.A.

1200 19TH STREET, N.W.,
SUITE 201
WASHINGTON, D.C. 20036
Telephone: 202-822-1620
Fax: 202-822-1622
Email: general@rulg.com
URL: http://www.rulg.com

With affiliated offices in Moscow, Russia and Kiev, Ukraine.

Corporate, commercial, oil and gas, customs and administrative law, intellectual and industrial property practice, telecommunications, energy, commercial litigation in the Russian Federation and Ukraine. International Arbitration and Mediation.

(This Listing Continued)

RUSSIAN-UKRAINIAN LEGAL GROUP

SENIOR COUNSEL AND PRESIDENT

IRINA PALIASHVILI, born Moscow, Russia, March 1, 1961; admitted to bar, 1983, U.S.S.R.; 1992, Ukraine; 1995, Russia. Licensed to Practice Russian and Ukrainian Law in the District of Columbia as a Special Legal Consultant, 1995. *Education:* Kiev State University School of International Law (with high honors, 1983; Ph.D., International Law, 1987); George Washington University (LL.M., 1993). Internship: six month assignment with a major Chicago law firm, American Bar Association's Soviet Lawyer Internship Program, 1991; four month assignment in Frankfurt with German law firm, EEC-sponsored project for restructuring the banking system of Ukraine, 1993. Law Professor, Kiev State University, School of International Law, Kiev Business Management School, 1989-1992. General Counsel: International Kiev Electronmash, 1987-1990; Microprocessor, Kiev, Ukraine, 1990-1992. Advisor, Ukrainian Chamber of Commerce and Industry, 1992. Member: Ukrainian Chamber of Independent Foreign Investment Experts under the President of Ukraine; Model Form Provisions Committee of Association of International Petroleum Negotiators; Russian International Law Association, 1982—; Foreign Lawyers Forum, Washington D.C., 1993—; Board of Governors, Washington Foreign Law Society (Board of Governors, 1994—); Advisory Group on Ukraine of the Business and Industry Advisory Committee to the OECD (BIAC). *Member:* Kiev Bar. (Also Of Counsel, Hills & Stern, Washington, DC and Member, Russin & Vecchi L.L.P., Washington, DC). ***LANGUAGES:*** English, Russian, Ukrainian, Georgian, Spanish. ***PRACTICE AREAS:*** Corporate Law; International Business Law; Foreign Investment; Oil and Gas Law.

SENIOR COUNSEL

RICHARD H. SMITH, III, admitted to bar, 1994, Maryland; 2001, District of Columbia. *Education:* College of William & Mary (B.A., International Relations, 1991); University of Baltimore (J.D., with honors, 1994). Team Captain, Jessup International Law Moot Court, 1996. Author, "Laws Clash on Executive Firing," The Moscow Times, 1998 and "The Licensing Law," Russia/Central Europe Executive Guide, Vol.9, No.7, 1999. International Contracts Director, Tver InterContact Group, 1995-1996. Associate, Clifford Chance, 1996-1999. ***LANGUAGES:*** English, Russian. ***PRACTICE AREAS:*** Corporate Law; International Business Law; Labor Law; Data Protection; Intellectual Property. ***Email:*** rsmith@rulg.com

OF COUNSEL

PROFESSOR LEVAN ALEXIDZE, Chair, Department of State Law and International Law, 1969-1970. Chief: Department of International Law and Fundamentals of Soviet Law, 1977-1980; Department of International Law, Tbilisi State University, 1980—. Vice President, Tbilisi State University, 1985-1993. Member, Executive Board, Soviet Association of International Law, 1962-1970; 1981-1990. Served as Senior Human Rights Officer, Division of Human Rights at United Nations in New York and Geneva, 1970-1977. Publication, "The Contemporary International Law Manual," 1994. Recipient, State Prize, monograph, Some Theoretical Problems of Contemporary International Law (Jus Cogens), Georgia, 1982. Member: Editorial Board, Georgian Constitutional Committee; Georgian Parliament and State Council, 1991-1994; World International Law Association; Georgian Association of Lawyers. Co-Authored, draft of the Law "On Production Sharing Agreements," for Georgia. ***LANGUAGES:*** Georgian, Russian and English. ***PRACTICE AREAS:*** International and Business Law.

ETHAN S. BURGER, born New York, N.Y., February 11, 1959; admitted to bar, 1989, District of Columbia; 2000, Maryland; U.S. District Court, District of Columbia. *Education:* Leningrad State University (Certificate 1980); Harvard University (A.B., magna cum laude, 1981); Georgetown University Law Center (J.D., cum laude, 1989). Project Director and Research Associate Professor, American University. Arbitrator, District of Columbia Bar's Attorney/Client Arbitration Board, 1997—. Special Counsel to Lawyers Committee for Human Rights for Conference on Security and Cooperation in Europe Matters, 1990-1992. Member: American Bar Association's Task Force on International Standards for Corrupt Practices, 1995—; Executive Committee and Board of Trustees, Foundation for Peaceful Settlement of International Business Disputes (UK). *Member:* The District of Columbia Bar; Maryland State Bar Association, Inc. (Also Of Counsel: Russin & Vecchi LLP; Ludwig & Robinson, P.L.L.C.). ***LANGUAGES:*** Russian. ***PRACTICE AREAS:*** Corporate Law; Commercial Law; Directors and Officers Liability; Professional Negligence; Domestic and International; Arbitration and Mediation; International Trade and Investments.

GALINA DMITRIEVA. *Education:* Leningrad State University Law School (Law Degree, 1964). Professor of Law, Moscow State University and Moscow State Law Academy. Member, Advisory Council, Constitutional Court of Russian Federation. Author of more than 50 professional publications. *Member:* Russian International Law Association; Kiev Bar. ***LANGUAGES:*** Russian, English. ***PRACTICE AREAS:*** Corporate Law; International Business Transactions.

(This Listing Continued)

RUSSIAN-UKRAINIAN LEGAL GROUP, P.A., Washington—Continued

EVGENY A. DANILOV, born Russia, April 28, 1947; admitted to bar, 1977, Russian Arbitration Courts and Courts of General Jurisdiction; 1991, Constitutional Court of Russia. *Education:* Peoples' Friendship University of Russia (1971); Academy of Economy with the Russian Government (1994); Russian Doctorate in Law. Senior Legal Analyst, Institute of State and Law. Head of Legal Division of the Council for Mutual Economic Assistance, 1989-1991. Chief Legal Specialist and Deputy Director, Legal and Federative Relations Department of Parliament of the Supreme Soviet of the Russian Federation. Head of the Legal Department, State Duma (lower house of the Russian Parliament). Associate Professor in Law, Law Faculty Technological University of Moscow, 1985. *Member:* Russian Association of International Law. (Also Member of Aros Advokater, Aarhus, Denmark). ***LANGUAGES:*** Russian and English. ***PRACTICE AREAS:*** Corporate Law; International Business Law; Oil and Gas Law.

(PROFESSOR) IGOR LUKASHUK, Researcher in the Institute of State and Law of the Russian Academy of Science, 1985—. Chief, Chairs of International Law in Saratov Law Institute and Kiev State University. Authored and Co-Authored more than 300 works in the field of International Law, including the UNESCO Course of International Law, 1991, and a 7-volume Course of International Law published in Moscow in 1991. Member: Advisory Council, Foreign Ministry of Russia; Permanent Court of Arbitration in The Hague. Member, Vienna Conference on the Law of International Treaties, 1968-1969. Official Representative of President Yeltsin to the State Duma on the draft of the Law "On International Treaties". Science Editor, International Law Volume of the multi-volume Encyclopedia Law. *Member:* Russian International Law Association (Board Member); United Nations International Law Commission. ***LANGUAGES:*** Russian, Ukrainian, English, German, Slovakian, Bulgarian. ***PRACTICE AREAS:*** International Law.

PROFESSOR APOLLON PALIASHVILI, (admission pending); admitted to bar, (Not admitted in United States). *Education:* Moscow (Ph.D., 1958); Tbilisi (Doctorate of Law, 1968). Recipient, State Medal of Glory by President Shevardnadze. Elected Academician of the Georgian Academy of Liberal Arts and Sciences. Professor, 1960— and Chairman, 1985—, Tbilisi State University Law School, Department of Criminal Procedure and Forensic Sciences. Participant in Georgian Legal Reform.Chairman, Georgian Government's Commission on the Elaboration of a Criminal Procedure Code. Member, Advisory Councils of the Georgian Procurator General's Office and Ministry of Internal Affairs. ***LANGUAGES:*** Georgian and Russian. ***PRACTICE AREAS:*** Criminal Law; Forensic Science.

UKRAINIAN LEGAL GROUP

SENIOR COUNSEL

VICTOR KOVALENKO, admitted to bar, Kiev. *Education:* Kiev State University (Law Degree, High Honors, 1986); George Washington University National Law Center (LL.M., 1993); Studied at Taiwan Institute for Economic Research, 1992. Acting Director of Law Department, Ukrainian Chamber of Commerce & Industry, 1989-1992. CIS Counsel, Latham & Watkins, Washington, D.C. and Moscow offices, 1993-1994. ***LANGUAGES:*** Russian, Ukrainian, English. ***PRACTICE AREAS:*** Corporate Law; Anti-Monopoly Law; International Investment; International Leasing; Securities; Bankruptcy; Labor Law; Customs Regulations; Business Law; Taxes; Energy Legislation; Telecommunications Law; Agricultural Law; Intellectual Property Law. **Email:** Victor.Kovalenko@ulg.kiev.ua

TAMARA LUKANINA, admitted to bar, 1992, Ukraine; Certified by the Ukrainian State Property Fund as a counsel on privatization matters. *Education:* Kiev State University Law School, 1980. Legal Counsel, Ukrtelecom and Electronmash. Consultant to the Ukrainian Ministry of Justice. ***LANGUAGES:*** Ukrainian and Russian. ***PRACTICE AREAS:*** Ukrainian Civil and Business Law; Labor Law; Corporate Law; Tax Law; Transactions; Civil Litigation; Commercial Litigation; Oil and Gas Law; Copyright; Neighboring Rights; Intellectual Property; Environmental Law; Subsoil Use Law; Law Drafting. ***Email:*** Tamara.Lukanina@ulg.kiev.ua

ALEXANDER PADALKA, admitted to bar, 1992, Kiev. *Education:* Kiev State University (Law Degree, 1988). Counsel, Regional State Executive Committee, City of Nikolaev. Legal Director of Business Agency, "Trade House in Kiev". Partner, Legis Law Offices. Editor, Legislation Bulletin, "Ukrainian Business Law," 1994-1997. *Member:* Kiev Regional Bar. ***LANGUAGES:*** Russian, Ukrainian, English. ***REPORTED CASES:*** Defending the interests of foreign investors at the Constitutional Court of Ukraine. ***PRACTICE AREAS:*** Securities Regulation; International Investment; Commercial Litigation; Antimonopoly Law; Export-Import Law; Corporate Law; Agricultural Law; Oil and Gas Law. ***Email:*** Alexander.Padalka@ulg.kiev.ua

(This Listing Continued)

COUNSEL

VYACHESLAV NOVAK, admitted to bar, 1995, Kiev. *Education:* Kiev State University Law School (Business Law, 1995). Manager and Contributing Editor, "Ukrainian Business Law," 1993-1997. Paralegal, Legis Law Offices, 1990-1993. Attorney, Legis Law Offices, 1993-1996. Member, Kiev Regional Bar, 1995. ***LANGUAGES:*** Russian, Ukrainian, English. ***PRACTICE AREAS:*** Arbitrage; Export-Import Law; Corporate Law; International Investment Law; Civil Law; Labor Law; Business Law; Tax; Anti-Monopoly Law; International Leasing; Enforcement; Agricultural Law; Pharmaceutical Law. ***Email:*** Vyacheslav.Novak@ulg.kiev.ua

ALENA VASILENKO, (admission pending); admitted to bar, (Not admitted in United States). *Education:* Taras Shevchenko Kiev State School of Law (Financial Law, 1999). Paralegal, Ukrainian Legal Group, 1996. ***LANGUAGES:*** Ukrainian, Russian, English. ***PRACTICE AREAS:*** Corporate Law; Foreign Investment.

OF COUNSEL

PYTOR M. BOGDANOVITCH, born Kyiv, Ukraine, May 9, 1949. *Education:* Kiev Technology University (Ph.D., 1972); Kiev Public Institute (Patent Attorney, 1972); All-Russian Institute of Industrial Property and Innovation, Moscow (1992). Author: "Does Trademark Register?" Feeding Products, No. 9-10, KYIV, 1999. Head: Patent Division of the Scientific-Research Institute of Electric-Household Machines and Appliances; Patent and Trademark Law Expert at "UBN Kristina". Member, All-Ukrainian Association of Patent Attorneys, 1992—. (Also Of Counsel to Shevchenko, Didkovskiy & Partners). ***LANGUAGES:*** Ukrainian, Russian and English. ***PRACTICE AREAS:*** Industrial Property; Patents; Trademarks. ***Email:*** general@ulg.kiev.ua

SERGEI DENISENKO. *Education:* Kiev State University School of Journalism, 1972. Deputy Editor in Chief, Ukrainian Business Newspaper, "Business Ukraine." Senior Editor at UkrInform and at *Kievskaya Pravada*. ***LANGUAGES:*** Russian, Ukrainian, English. ***PRACTICE AREAS:*** Corporate; Trade; Investment.

RUSSIN & VECCHI L.L.P.

International Legal Counsellors

815 CONNECTICUT AVENUE, N.W.

SUITE 650

WASHINGTON, D.C. 20006

Telephone: 202-822-6100

Fax: 202-822-6101

Email: lawyers@russinvecchi.com

URL: http://www.russinvecchi.com

Bangkok, Thailand Office: International Legal Counsellors Thailand, Ltd., Sathorn City Tower, 175 South Sathorn Road, 18th Floor, 10120. Telephone: 662-679-6005, 662-679-6015. Fax: 662-679-6041, 662-679-6042. e-mail: ilct@mozart.inet.co.th.

Hanoi, Vietnam Office: Russin & Vecchi, L.L.C., Hanoi Central Office Building, 44B Ly Thuong Kiet Street, 11/F. Telephone: (84-4) 825-1700. Fax: (84-4) 825-1742. e-mail: rusvechn@hn.vnn.vn.

Ho Chi Minh City, S.R. Vietnam Office: Russin & Vecchi, L.L.C., 8 Nguyen Hue Boulevard, 15th Floor, Q1. Telephone: (84-8) 8243-026/243-114. Fax: (84-8) 8243-113. e-mail: rusvec@hcm.vnn.vn.

Moscow, Russia Office: Russin & Vecchi L.L.C., Ulitsa Bolshaya Ordynka, 60/2, Moscow 109017. Telephone: 7-095-959-1288/1294. Fax: 7-095-959-1290. e-mail: lawyers@russinvecchi.ru.

New York, New York Office: Russin, Vecchi & Berg L.L.P., 15th Floor, 605 Third Avenue, 10158. Telephone: 212-490-6644. Fax: 212-490-1809. e-mail: lawyers@rvbnewyork.com.

Puerto Plata, Dominican Republic Office: Russin Vecchi & Heredia Bonetti L.L.P., Plaza Turisol Local #11A. Telephone: 809-586-5535. Fax: 809-586-5861. e-mail: rmedina@rvhb.com.

Yuzhno-Sakhalinsk, Russia Office: Russin & Vecchi L.L.C., 32 Kommunisticheski Pr. 693000. Telephone: 7-4242-726-786/87. Fax: 7-4242-726-758. e-mail: russinvecchi@snc.ru.

Santo Domingo, Dominican Republic Office: Russin Vecchi & Heredia Bonetti L.L.P., Edificio Monte Mirador, Calle El Recodo No 2, Tercer Piso, Ensanche Bella Vista, Apartado Postal 425. Telephone: 809-535-9511. Fax: 809-535-6649. e-mail: rvhb@rvhb.com.

Taipei, Taiwan Office: Russin & Vecchi, Bank Tower 9th Floor, 205 Tun Hwa N. Road. Telephone: (886-2) 2712-8956. Fax: (886-2) 2713-4711. e-mail: rusvectp@ms2.hinet.net.

Vladivostok, Russia Office: Russin & Vecchi L.L.C., Sukhanova Street, 3A, 690091. Telephone: 7-4232-260-465; 261-015. Fax: 7-4232-226-505. e-mail: russinvecchi@stl.ru.

(This Listing Continued)

Yangon, Myanmar Office: Russin & Vecchi, Ltd., 8C Bogyoke Museum Rd., Bahan Township. Mailing Address: Box No. 729 G.P.O., Yangon, Myanmar. Telephone (951) 541794/540995. Fax: (951) 548835. e-mail: burmalaw@mptmail.net.mm

General Practice, including International Business and Trade, Foreign Investment and Finance, Transaction Structuring, Corporate Law and Taxation, Foreign Joint Ventures and Branch Operations, Agencies and Distributorships, Export Finance, Civil Litigation and Arbitration, International Programs of Educational Organizations and Religious Institutions.

FIRM PROFILE: Russin & Vecchi, L.L.C., International Legal Counsellors is an international law firm with eleven independent but affiliated offices spanning the globe. The firm was founded in 1969 in Bangkok, Saigon, Santo Domingo, and Washington, D.C. to create an international practice serving the developing commercial environments of Asia and Latin America. The firm's offices now offer a full range of domestic and international business and commercial legal services. The firm's most recent expansion into Moscow and Vladivostok, Russia is coordinated from our Washington, D.C. office, and responds to the need for commercial legal services in that emerging and changing economy. The office in Vladivostok is the first by a U.S. firm, and serves the needs of clients in the Russian Far East. Our clients in Russia are involved in investment transactions, market expansion, and mineral extraction. We are knowledgeable about the frequently changing laws on currency, taxation, customs, labor, and other issues unique to doing business in Russia.

MEMBERS OF FIRM

JONATHAN RUSSIN, born Kingston, Pennsylvania, 1937; admitted to bar, 1964, District of Columbia. *Education:* Yale University (B.A., 1959; J.D., 1963). Recipient, Order of Prince St. Vladimir, Russian Orthodox Church. Co-Author: "Forming A Russian Company," sponsored by the Embassy of the Russian Federation in Washington, D.C., 1994; "Forming A Dominican Company," 10th Edition, American Chamber of Commerce of the Dominican Republic, 1987; "The Powers That Be, The Constitutional Court of the Russian Federation," American Chamber of Commerce in Russia, Vol. 7, No. 33, Jan-Feb. 2000; "Laws Affecting Franchise Operations in Spain," American Bar Association, 1982. With Office of the General Counsel, Agency for International Development, U.S. Department of State, 1964-1969 (Regional Legal Adviser, Caribbean Area, 1967-1969). Chair, Advisory Council, Institute for European, Russin and Eurasian Studies, George Washington University, 1991-1993. General Counsel, Orthodox Church in America. Washington Representative, Russian Orthodox Church. *Member:* The District of Columbia Bar; American Bar Association; Inter-American Bar Association. (Resident, Moscow Office). ***LANGUAGES:*** Spanish and Russian. ***PRACTICE AREAS:*** Investment in Russia; Russia Trade; International Investment; International Finance; Emerging Markets; Investment in Latin America; International Corporate Law; International Business Law.

WILLIAM R. WHITE, born Dayton, Ohio, 1941; admitted to bar, 1967, Ohio; 1968, U.S. District Court, Southern District of Ohio; 1984, U.S. Court of Appeals, Sixth Circuit; 1985, District of Columbia, U.S. Supreme Court, U.S. District Court for the District of Columbia and U.S. Court of Appeals for the District of Columbia Circuit. *Education:* Ohio State University (B.S., 1964; J.D., 1967). Phi Delta Phi. Member, Moot Court, Honor Council. Author: "Debt for Development and the University Role," Midwest Universities Consortium for International Activities, March, 1992. Associate and Partner, Power, Jones & Schneider, Columbus, Ohio, 1967-1974. Deputy Director, Legal and Enforcement, Ohio Department of Natural Resources, 1972-1973. General Counsel, Midwest Universities Consortium for International Activities, 1986—. General Counsel, Governor's Task Force on Environmental Protection, 1971-1972. Chief of Staff, U.S. Senator John Glenn, 1975-1984. *Member:* The District of Columbia Bar; Columbus, Ohio State and American Bar Associations. ***LANGUAGES:*** Spanish. ***PRACTICE AREAS:*** International Business Law; Corporate Commercial Law; International Joint Ventures; Offshore Corporations; Computer Law; Nonprofit Organizations; Information Technology; Software Licensing; College and University Law; Church Law; Religious Nonprofit Corporations Law.

IRINA PALIASHVILI, born Moscow, Russia, March 1, 1961. *Education:* Kiev State University School of International Law (with honors, 1983; Ph.D., International Law, 1987); George Washington University (LL.M., 1993). admitted to practice, 1983, U.S.S.R.; 1992, Ukraine; 1995, Russia (Not admitted in the United States). Licensed to Practice Russian and Ukrainian Law in the District of Columbia as a Special Legal Consultant, 1995. *Education:* Kieve University School of International Law (with high honors, 1983; Ph.D., International Law, 1987); George Washington University (LL.M., 1993). Law Professor, Kiev State University, School of International Law, Kiev Business Management School, 1989-1992, General Counsel: International Kiev Electronmash,1987-1990; Microprocessor, Kiev, Ukraine, 1990-1992. Advisor, Ukrainian Chamber of Commerce and Industry, 1992. Member: Ukrainian Chamber of Independent Foreign Investment Experts under the President of Ukraine; Model Form Provisions Committee of Association of International Petroleum Negotiators; Russian International Law Association, 1982—; Foreign Lawyers Forum, Washington D.C., 1993—; Board of Governors, Washington Foreign Law Society (Board of Governors, 1994—). *Member:* Kiev Bar. (Also Of Counsel, Hills & Stern, Washington, DC and President, Russian-Ukrainian Legal Group, Washington, DC). ***LANGUAGES:*** Russian, Ukrainian, Georgian, Spanish. ***PRACTICE AREAS:*** Corporate Law; International Business Law; Foreign Investment; Oil and Gas Law.

OF COUNSEL

ETHAN S. BURGER, born New York, N.Y., February 11, 1959; admitted to bar, 1989, District of Columbia. *Education:* Leningrad State University (Certificate 1980); Harvard University (A.B., magna cum laude, 1981); Georgetown University Law Center (J.D., cum laude, 1989). Arbitrator, District of Columbia Bar's Attorney/Client Arbitration Board, 1997—. Special Counsel to Lawyers Committee for Human Rights for Conference on Security and Cooperation in Europe Matters, 1990-1992. Member, American Bar Association's Task Force on International Standards for Corrupt Practices, 1995—. *Member:* The District of Columbia Bar. (Also Member, Ludwig & Robinson). ***LANGUAGES:*** Russian. ***PRACTICE AREAS:*** Corporate Law; Commercial Law; Directors and Officers Liability; Professional Negligence; Domestic and International; Arbitration and Mediation; International Trade and Investments. **Email:** ethans@yahoo.com

B. THOMAS MANSBACH, born Norfolk, Virginia, 1939; admitted to bar, 1964, District of Columbia and Virginia. *Education:* Yale University (B.A., cum laude, 1961); Harvard University (LL.B., 1964). Overseas Private Investment Corporation ("OPIC"), 1967-1993: Managing Director: Major Markets, emphasizing independent power, 1992-1993; Central Europe/Former Soviet Union/China/Southeast Asia, 1990-1992; Africa/Middle East/Europe/South Asia and Petroleum/Financial Services, 1986-1990; Natural Resources and Financial Services, 1981-1986; Senior Director for Minerals and Energy, 1978-1981; Director, Latin America/Africa, 1972-1978; Office of the General Counsel and Special Assistant, 1967-1972. Co-Editor, *Investment Incentive Programs in Western Europe.* The Chamber of Commerce of the United States. ***PRACTICE AREAS:*** International Investment; International Finance; Emerging Markets; Political Risk Insurance; Project Finance; Asia-Pacific Investment; Investment in Eastern Europe; Investment in Latin America.

REPRESENTATIVE CLIENTS: Alico; Baltimore Orioles; Bankers Trust; Bausch & Lomb; Baxter Travenol; Bristol Myers Squibb; Brooks Sports, Inc.; Burson Marsteller; Colgate-Palmolive; Consolidated Freightways; Dole Dominicana; Emery Worldwide; Eurasia Foundation; General Electric; HAZ-X Holdings, Ltd.; Honeywell; Konica Business Machines, U.S.A.; Midwest Universities Consortium for International Activities; NACCO Materials Handling Group; North Atlantic Trading Co.; Ramada International; Royal Group; Ryland Trading; Sea-Land; South African Breweries; Timberland; Wartsila Diesel; Russian Orthodox Church; Orthodox Church in America; Joseph E. Seagram & Sons; General Motors Company.

(For Biographical Data on other Personnel, see Professional Biographies at Bangkok, Thailand; Hanoi and Ho Chi Minh City, Vietnam; Moscow, Russia; New York, N.Y.; Puerto Plata and Santo Domingo, Dominican Republic; Sakhalin, Russia; Taipei, Taiwan; Vladivostok, Russia; Yangon, Myanmar)

RYBERG & SMITH, LLP

CANAL SQUARE
1054 31ST STREET, N.W.
WASHINGTON, D.C. 20007
Telephone: 202-333-4000
Fax: 202-965-3445

Federal Legislative and Regulatory Practice focusing on International Trade, Federal Regulation of Real Estate Services and Native American Law, Commercial Litigation, and Commercial Transactions.

PAUL RYBERG, JR., born Salina, Kansas, April 9, 1952; admitted to bar, 1977, District of Columbia. *Education:* Wichita State University (B.A., summa cum laude, 1974); Harvard University (J.D., cum laude, 1977). *Member:* The District of Columbia Bar; American Bar Association. **Email:** pr@his.com

DAVID F. B. SMITH, born Hanover, Pennsylvania, November 3, 1952; admitted to bar, 1977, District of Columbia. *Education:* Georgetown University (B.S.F.S., cum laude, 1974; J.D., 1977). Research Editor, Georgetown Law Journal, 1976-77. *Member:* The District of Columbia Bar; American Bar Association. **Email:** dfbs@his.com

SACKS & CHAPIN, P.C.

748 EXECUTIVE BUILDING
1030 FIFTEENTH STREET, N.W.
WASHINGTON, D.C. 20005
Telephone: 202-659-1200
Fax: 202-659-1029
Email: schapinpc@aol.com

Litigation Practice. Personal Injury, Family and Corporate Law.

(This Listing Continued)

SACKS & CHAPIN, P.C., Washington—Continued

FIRM PROFILE: The firm primarily represents individuals, local businesses and entrepreneurs throughout Metropolitan Washington, D.C. and Southern Maryland.

FRED C. SACKS (1913-1990).

PETER A. CHAPIN, born Atlantic City, New Jersey, February 3, 1945; admitted to bar, 1971, District of Columbia; 1974, U.S. Supreme Court; 1977, Maryland. *Education:* University of Akron (B.A., 1968; J.D., 1970). Member, Honors Program, Appellate Section, Criminal Division, U.S. Department of Justice, 1970-1971. Assistant U.S. Attorney, District of Columbia, 1971-1976. *Member:* District of Columbia Bar; Prince Georges County, Maryland State and American Bar Associations; The Association of Trial Lawyers of America; Maryland Trial Lawyers Association. ***PRACTICE AREAS:*** Personal Injury Law; Family Law; Corporate Law.

SAIDMAN DesignLaw Group

1201 CONNECTICUT AVENUE, SUITE 750
WASHINGTON, D.C. 20036
Telephone: 202-223-0800
Fax: 202-223-6607
Email: Group@designlaw.com

Silver Spring, Maryland Office: 1110 Bonifant Street, Suite 510, 20910. Telephone: 301-585-8601. Fax: 301-585-0138.

Industrial Designs, Design Protection, Industrial Design Law, Industrial Design Registrations, Design Patents, Design Law, Design Law Expert, Design Law Consulting, Design Patent Prosecution, Design Patent Infringement, Trade Dress, Product Configurations, Trademark Law, Trademark Infringement, Trademark Registration, Unfair Competition Law, Intellectual Property, Patent Protection, Royalty Agreements, Licensing Agreements, Expert Witness, Design Copyrights, Designer Agreements, Hague Agreement, Utility Patents, PCT Applications, Utility Patent Infringement, Copyright Law, Copyright Registration, Mediation.

FIRM PROFILE: We specialize in legal issues involving designs and product configurations.

REPRESENTATIVE CLIENTS: Imperial Schrade Corp.; Toyota; Boston Acoustics; The Burdick Group; Design Ideas, Ltd.; Virginia Plastics Co.; Altitude; Zircon Corporation; Ore Originals; Jerry Stubblefield; Paoli, Inc.; Becker Design, Inc.; Inca Solarware; Umbra, Ltd.; Dr. Martens.

(For complete biographical data on all personnel, see Professional Biographies at Silver Spring, Maryland)

SALGADO & ASSOCIATES

Established in 1982

1220 L STREET, N.W., SUITE 540
WASHINGTON, D.C. 20005-4018
Telephone: 202-408-1800
Fax: 202-898-0566
Email: salgadolf@aol.com
URL: http://www.for-a-visa.com

Business Immigration, Deportation, Family Immigration, Religious Visas, Political Asylum, Consular Law, Immigration and Discrimination, Employment Visas and Nationality Law.

FIRM PROFILE: Salgado & Associates process cases involving immigrant visas, work authorizations, political asylum, employer sanctions, federal taxes, deportation defense, criminal conviction consequences and naturalization issues. Nonimmigrant visas include visas for business, temporary work, training, trade, investing and tourism. Immigrant visas include visas obtained through employment, amnesty, the lottery, investing and the relations of U.S. citizens and permanent residents. The firm provides representation before the Immigration and Naturalization Service, the Department of Labor and the Department of State in the U.S. and abroad at U.S. consulates. The ARM conducts business in English and Spanish. Memberships include: American Immigration Lawyers Association; IWFU — American Bar Association; American Bar Association; Hispanic Bar Association; Federal Bar Association; District of Columbia Bar; Maryland State Bar Association; and the Maryland Hispanic Bar Association.

LUIS F. SALGADO, born Manati, Puerto Rico, 1948; admitted to bar, 1980, District of Columbia. *Education:* Massachusetts Institute of Technology (B.S., 1970); Georgetown University (J.D., 1980). Dean's List, Georgetown University, 1976-1977. Counsel, The Embassy of El Salvador, 1995-1996. Chairman, District of Columbia Board of Appeals and Review, 1990-1994. Director, Office of the Secretary, Division of Spanish Surnamed Americans, U.S. Department of Health and Human Services, 1979-1982. Board Member, 1981-1989, Ayuda, Washington, D.C. Board Member, D.C. Public Defender Service, Washington, D.C., 1989-1997. Recognized International, National and Local Expert and Presenter, Matters regarding U.S. Immigration, 1990—. *Member:* Federal, 1988-1992 and American, 1980-1985 Bar Associations; The District of Columbia Bar, 1987—; American Immigration Lawyers Association, 1987—; Inter-American Bar Association, 1990-1991; Hispanic Bar Association, 1982-1988; Computer Law Association, 1980-1984. ***LANGUAGES:*** Spanish. ***PRACTICE AREAS:*** Immigration Law; Visas; Political Asylum; Deportation; Consular Law.

ASSOCIATES

MARIBEL LaFONTAINE, born Brooklyn, New York, April 28, 1967; admitted to bar, 1997, Maryland; 1999, District of Columbia. *Education:* Fordham University (B.A., 1989); Catholic University (J.D., 1994). *Member:* The District of Columbia Bar; Maryland State Bar Association, Inc.; American Bar Association; American Immigration Lawyers Association. ***LANGUAGES:*** Spanish. ***PRACTICE AREAS:*** Immigration; Visas; Political Asylum; Deportation.

JUAN CARLOS FREIRE, born Brooklyn, New York, August 10, 1972; admitted to bar, 2000, Florida (Not admitted in District of Columbia). *Education:* City College of the City University of New York (B.A., 1996); St. Thomas University School of Law (J.D., 1999). *Member:* Florida State Bar; American Bar Association. ***LANGUAGES:*** Spanish. ***PRACTICE AREAS:*** Immigration; Visas; Political Asylum; Deportation.

SALTMAN & STEVENS, P.C.

Established in 1980

1801 K STREET, N.W.
SUITE M-110
WASHINGTON, D.C. 20006
Telephone: 202-452-2140
Fax: 202-775-8217

Practice before Administrative Agencies and Federal Courts, Government Contract, Timber and Logging, Construction, Antitrust, Environmental, Corporate and Commercial Law, Business.

FIRM PROFILE: Saltman & Stevens, P.C., specializes in government contracts, timber and logging law, and natural resources law. The firm advises and represents clients in numerous areas of federal law including contract negotiations, bid protests, small business issues, regulatory and antitrust compliance, claims and equitable adjustments, cost and pricing data, suspension and debarment Fifth Amendment takings and natural resource/endangered species act issues. The firm regularly represents clients in a variety of industries including defense and NASA contractors, computer hardware and software vendors, federal timber purchasers, environmental service companies and construction contractors.

The firm is listed in the Martindale-Hubbell Bar Register of Preeminent Lawyers.

ALAN I. SALTMAN, born Lynn, Massachusetts, January 23, 1948; admitted to bar, 1973, Massachusetts; 1974, District of Columbia; 1976, Maryland; 1982, U.S. Court of Appeals for the Federal Circuit; 1984, U.S. Court of Appeals, Ninth Circuit; 1992, U.S. Court of Federal Claims. *Education:* Northeastern University (A.B., cum laude, 1969); Boston College (J.D., 1973). Attorney-Advisor, U.S. General Accounting Office, 1973-1976. *Member:* The District of Columbia Bar (Government Contract and Litigation Division, 1974—); Federal and American (Chairman, Committee on Natural Resources Sale, 1976—; Member, Sections on: Natural Resources Law; Public Contract Law) Bar Associations. [With USAR, JAGC, 1970-1976]. ***PRACTICE AREAS:*** Government Contract Law; Timber and Logging; Litigation. ***Email:*** asaltman@saltmanandstevens.com

GARY G. STEVENS, born Corpus Christi, Texas, November 18, 1945; admitted to bar, 1973, District of Columbia and U.S. Court of Appeals for the District of Columbia Circuit; 1976, U.S. Supreme Court; 1982, U.S. Court of Appeals for the Federal Circuit; 1992, U.S. Court of Federal Claims; 1984, U.S. Court of Appeals, Ninth Circuit. *Education:* Fordham University (B.A., magna cum laude, 1968); Oxford University, England (B.A., 1970); University of Michigan (J.D., cum laude, 1973). Phi Beta Kappa. *Member:* The District of Columbia Bar (Member, Government Contract and Litigation Division); Federal and American (Chairman, Subcommittee on Timber Sales, Committee on Natural Resources Sales, 1980; Member, Forum Committee on the Construction Industry, 1983—; Member, Sections on: Litigation; Antitrust Law; Public Contract Law; Natural Resources Law) Bar Associations. ***PRACTICE AREAS:*** Government Contract Law; Timber and Logging; Construction Law; Antitrust Law; Natural Resources; Litigation. ***Email:*** gstevens@saltmanandstevens.com

RUTH G. TIGER, born Philadelphia, Pennsylvania, September 8, 1958; admitted to bar, 1985, District of Columbia, Maryland and U.S. District Court

(This Listing Continued)

(This Listing Continued)

for the District of Columbia; 1986, U.S. Court of Appeals for the Federal Circuit; 1992, U.S. Court of Federal Claims; 2000, U.S. Court of Appeals for the District of Columbia Circuit. *Education:* Dickinson College (B.A., cum laude, 1979); Washington College of Law, The American University (J.D., 1984). Articles Editor, American University Law Review, 1983-1984. *Member:* The District of Columbia Bar (Member, Government Contract and Litigation Division); American Bar Association (Member, Sections on: Public Contract Law; Natural Resource, Energy and Environmental Law). ***PRACTICE AREAS:*** Government Contracts; Timber and Logging; Litigation. **Email:** rtiger@saltmanandstevens.com

KEVIN GARDEN, born Atlanta, Georgia, October 9, 1964; admitted to bar, 1989, Virginia; 1990, District of Columbia and U.S. Court of Appeals for the Federal Circuit; 1992, U.S. District Court for the District of Columbia and U.S. Court of Federal Claims; 2001, U.S. Court of Appeals, Ninth Circuit. *Education:* University of Notre Dame (B.A., 1986); Washington College of Law, The American University (J.D., 1989). Member, American University Law Review, 1988-1989. Author: "Fifth Amendment Takings of Rights Arising from Agreements with the Federal Government," 29 Pub. Con. L.J. 187 (2000); Note, "CTS Corp. v. Dynamics Corp. of America: A State's Right to Tend to its Tender Offers," 37 Am. U. L. Rev. 947 (1988). Past Editor, Environmental Liability Enforcement & Penalties Reporter. *Member:* The District of Columbia Bar (Member, Energy and Environmental Law Section); Virginia State Bar; American Bar Association (Member, Section of Natural Resources, Energy and Environmental Law). ***PRACTICE AREAS:*** Government Contracts; Environmental Law; Natural Resources Law; Timber and Logging Law; Corporate Law; Litigation. **Email:** kgarden@saltmanandstevens.com

RICHARD W. GOEKEN, born Davenport, Iowa, November 13, 1963; admitted to bar, 1991, Illinois, U.S. District Court, Northern District of Illinois; 1994, District of Columbia; 1996, U.S. Court of Federal Claims; 1998, U.S. Court of Appeals for the Federal Circuit. *Education:* Marquette University (B.A., cum laude, 1986); College of William & Mary (J.D., 1991). *Member:* The District of Columbia Bar. ***PRACTICE AREAS:*** Government Contracts; Timber and Logging; Litigation; Natural Resources Law. **Email:** rgoeken@saltmanandstevens.com

---

WILLIAM B. KINNER, born Annapolis, Maryland, March 5, 1968; admitted to bar, 1999, Maryland; 2000, District of Columbia. *Education:* Towson University (B.S., 1990); University of Maryland Graduate School, Baltimore (Master of Policy Sciences, MPS Regulatory Policy, 1996); University of Baltimore (J.D., magna cum laude, 1999). Heisler Honor Society. Recipient: Highest Grade, Moot Court, Recent Supreme Court Decisions, Appellate Advocacy and Constitutional Criminal Procedure II. *Member:* District of Columbia Bar Association (Member, Government Contract and Litigation Division); Maryland State and American (Sections on: Litigation; Administrative & Regulatory Practice; Public Contract) Bar Associations. ***PRACTICE AREAS:*** Litigation; Government Contracts; Natural Resources Law. **Email:** wkinner@saltmanandstevens.com

SANDERS & SANDERS

WASHINGTON, D.C.

(See Upper Marlboro, Maryland)

Civil Litigation, Commercial Bankruptcy, Consumer Bankruptcy, Divorce, Child Custody, Child Support, Family Law, Adoptions, Wrongful Termination, Employment Law, Employment Discrimination, Commercial Contracts, Government Contracts, Business Formation, Business Litigation, Non-profit Corporations, Employment Defense.

SANDERS, SCHNABEL & BRANDENBURG, P.C.

Established in 1923

SUITE 900

900 SEVENTEENTH STREET, N.W.

WASHINGTON, D.C. 20006-2501

Telephone: 202-638-2241

Telecopier: 202-293-3419

Email: ssb@ssblegal.com

URL: http://www.ssblegal.com

Pension and Profit Sharing, Employee Benefits, Taxation, Corporate Law, Professional Corporations, Tax Exempt Organizations, Employment Law (Management), Estate Planning, Trusts, Probate, Litigation and Administrative Law.

FIRM PROFILE: Sanders, Schnabel & Brandenburg P.C. is a successor to a firm founded in the 1920's. The firm's practice primarily encompasses advice and representation in the employee benefits, employment law, estate planning and probate and exempt organization areas of law, and includes employee benefits, (such as qualified plans, health plans, non-qualified plans, executive compensation, and association member service programs), employment law, corporate and business formations, and taxation. The firm works with individuals in estate planning, trust matters and estate administration. The firm represents clients in state and federal courts and in alternative dispute resolution matters, resolving primarily employee benefits and probate and trust matters. The firm is listed in the Martindale-Hubbell Bar Register of Preeminent Lawyers.

JOHN A. SANDERS (1924-1998).

DAN S. BRANDENBURG, born Landsberg am Lech, Germany, August 30, 1949; admitted to bar, 1975, District of Columbia. *Education:* Rutgers University (B.A. and B.S., 1972); Georgetown University (J.D., 1975; LL.M., in Taxation, 1978). Tau Beta Pi. U.S. Editor, International Pension and Employee Benefits Lawyers Newsletter, 1997—. Adjunct Professor of Law, Georgetown University Law Center, 1981-1984. *Member:* The District of Columbia Bar; American Bar Association (Member, Section on Taxation, Committee on Employee Benefits, 1978—; Liaison on Small Business Issues, 1992—; Chair of Party Task Force, 1989-1992; Member, Tort and Insurance Practice Section; Committee on Employee Benefits; Chair, 1990-1991, 2000-2001; Vice-Chair, 1996-1999; Chair Elect, 1999-2000; Chair, 2000-2001; Member of Task Force on Long Term Care, 1991-1992). Charter Fellow, American College of Employee Benefits Counsel, Inc. ***LANGUAGES:*** German. ***PRACTICE AREAS:*** Employee Benefits Law; Personal Service Organizations; Estate Planning. **Email:** dbrandenburg@ssblegal.com

DAVID WEINGARTEN, born New York, N.Y., May 7, 1951; admitted to bar, 1975, Illinois; 1977, District of Columbia; 1981, New York. *Education:* University of Wisconsin (B.A., with honors, 1972); University of Chicago (J.D., 1975). Adjunct Professor, Georgetown University School for Summer and Continuing Education, 1990. *Member:* The District of Columbia Bar; Illinois State (Member, Employee Benefits Committee, 1983—) and American (Member, Employee Benefits Committee, Labor and Employment Law Section, 1983—; Co-Chairman, Subcommittee on PBGC Corporate Plan Terminations and Benefit Insurance, 1983—) Bar Associations. ***PRACTICE AREAS:*** Employee Benefits. **Email:** dweingarten@ssblegal.com

CHERYL RISLEY HUGHES, born Alexandria, Virginia, July 19, 1969; admitted to bar, 1996, New York and District of Columbia. *Education:* State University of New York at Geneseo (B.A., Political Science, 1991); The Ohio State University (J.D., cum laude, 1995); Georgetown University Law Center (LL.M. Taxation Certificate of Study in Employee Benefits Law, 1996). Contributing Editor, "Cafeteria Plans", Employee Benefits Institute of America, 2001. Member, 1993-1994 and Chief Managing Editor, 1994-1995, The Ohio State Journal on Dispute Resolution. Public Service Fellow, 1993. *Member:* The District of Columbia Bar; New York State and American Bar Associations. ***PRACTICE AREAS:*** Employee Benefits. **Email:** crhughes@ssblegal.com

---

STACEY A. BRADFORD, born Silver Spring, Maryland, February 5, 1967; admitted to bar, 1994, New Jersey; 1996, District of Columbia. *Education:* Lafayette College (B.A., cum laude, 1989); Washington College of Law of American University (J.D., cum laude, 1994). *Member:* The District of Columbia Bar; American Bar Association. ***LANGUAGES:*** French. ***PRACTICE AREAS:*** Employee Benefits; Trusts and Estates; Corporate. **Email:** sbradford@ssblegal.com

JOANNE G. JACOBSON, born Regina, Canada, April 24, 1961; admitted to bar, 1988, New York; 1989, Maryland; 2000, District of Columbia. *Education:* University of British Columbia (B.Sc., 1982; LL.B., 1985); George Washington University (LL.M., Taxation, 1989). Phi Alpha Delta. Editor, University of British Columbia Law Review, 1982-1985. Member, Jessup Moot Court Competition, 1984. *Member:* Maryland State and American Bar Associations; District of Columbia Bar. ***PRACTICE AREAS:*** ERISA; Employee Benefits Law; Tax Law. **Email:** jjacobson@ssblegal.com

SUSAN YODER TORRES, born New York, N.Y., July 3, 1962; admitted to bar, 1990, Virginia; 1993, District of Columbia. *Education:* University of Virginia (B.A., 1984); George Mason University School of Law (J.D., 1990). Echols Scholar. *Member:* Virginia State Bar; The District of Columbia Bar; American Bar Association. ***PRACTICE AREAS:*** Business Law; Corporate Law; Estate Planning; Fiduciary Law; Probate Law; Elder Law. **Email:** storres@ssblegal.com

LINCOLN WEED, born Baltimore, Maryland, January 3, 1954; admitted to bar, 1980, Alabama; 1989, District of Columbia; U.S. Court of Appeals, Sixth and Eleventh Circuits. *Education:* Hamilton College (A.B., magna cum laude, 1977); Boston University (J.D., 1980). Staff Attorney, Pension Benefit Guaranty Corporation, 1983-1987. *Member:* District of Columbia Bar. ***PRACTICE AREAS:*** Health Care; Employee Benefits. **Email:** lweed@ssblegal.com

(This Listing Continued)

SANDERS, SCHNABEL & BRANDENBURG, P.C., Washington—Continued

OF COUNSEL

ROBERT V. SCHNABEL, born Washington, D.C., July 25, 1931; admitted to bar, 1955, District of Columbia and Virginia; 1963, Maryland. *Education:* University of Virginia (B.A., 1953; LL.B., 1955). Phi Delta Phi. *Member:* The District of Columbia Bar; Virginia State and American Bar Associations. ***PRACTICE AREAS:*** Real Estate Law; Taxation; Corporate Law; Estates.

WILLIAM H. BRADFORD, JR., born St. Petersburg, Florida, February 11, 1937; admitted to bar, 1962, District of Columbia; 1972, Maryland. *Education:* Duke University (A.B., 1959; J.D., 1962); George Washington University (LL.M., 1964). Phi Beta Kappa; Order of the Coif. Member, Board of Editors, Duke University Law Journal, 1961-1962. Commissioner, 1979-1982 and Chairman, 1980-1981, Montgomery County, Maryland Commission on Landlord Tenant Affairs. Adjunct Professor, George Washington University Law School, 1991-1997. *Member:* The District of Columbia Bar; Maryland State and American (Member, Sections on: Taxation, Real Property, Probate and Trust Law) Bar Associations. ***PRACTICE AREAS:*** Taxation; Estate Planning; Probate; Business Law; Real Estate.

CAROL V. CALHOUN, born Frankfurt, Germany, October 6, 1953; admitted to bar, 1980, District of Columbia. *Education:* Johns Hopkins University (B.A., 1976); Georgetown University Law Center (J.D., 1980). Associate Editor, The Tax lawyer, 1978-1979. Editor, Employee Benefits Site, http://benefitsattorney.com. Author: *Governmental Plans Answer Book,* Panel Publishing, 2001; *Tobacco Divestment and Fiduciary Responsibility, A Legal Analysis,* Investor Responsibility Research Center, 2000. Chair: Subcommittees on: Governmental Plans, 1994-1995, 403(b), 457 and Exempt Organization Plans, 1994, Government Submissions, 1989-1993, Distributions, 1986-1989, American Bar Association Section on Taxation. *Member:* American College of Employee Benefits Counsel; National Association of Public Pension Attorneys; National Council on Teacher Retirement. (Also practicing individually, Calhoun Law Group, Washington, D.C.). ***PRACTICE AREAS:*** Employee Benefits; Taxation. ***Email:*** cvcalhoun@benefitsattorney.com

---

SANDGROUND BARONDESS WEST & NEW, P.C.

WASHINGTON, D.C.

(See Vienna, Virginia)

Family Law, Divorce, Child Custody and Child Support, Criminal Law, Civil Litigation and Commercial Litigation.

SANDLER, REIFF & YOUNG, P.C.

50 E STREET, S.E., SUITE 300
WASHINGTON, D.C. 20003
Telephone: 202-479-1111
Fax: 202-479-1115
Email: sandler@sandlerreiff.com
URL: http://www.sandlerreiff.com

Election, Campaign and Political Law, Nonprofit and Charitable Organizations, Nonprofit Tax Law, Government Law, Commercial Law and Litigation.

JOSEPH E. SANDLER, born Baltimore, Maryland, November 15, 1953; admitted to bar, 1978, District of Columbia. *Education:* Harvard College (A.B., summa cum laude, 1975); Harvard University (J.D., cum laude, 1978). Phi Beta Kappa. Author: "Foreign Agents Registration Act," and "Congressional Ethics," Chapters in The Lobbying Manual, American Bar Association, 1993. Co-Author, "Election Law," Developments in Administrative Law and Regulatory Practice, 2000-2001. Counsel, Democratic National Committee, 1986-89. Counsel, Partner, Arent Fox, 1989-1993. General Counsel, Democratic National Committee, 1993-1998. *Member:* American Bar Association (Member: Advisory Committee; Co-Chair, Election Law Subcommittee, Administrative Law Section). ***PRACTICE AREAS:*** Election, Campaign and Political Law; Nonprofit and Charitable Organizations; Nonprofit Tax Law; Election and Campaign Finance; Commercial Law. ***Email:*** sandler@sandlerreiff.com

NEIL P. REIFF, born Brooklyn, New York, May 1, 1968; admitted to bar, 1993, Maryland; 1995, District of Columbia. *Education:* State University of New York, College at Binghamton (B.A., Political Science, 1989); George Washington University (J.D., 1992). Phi Beta Kappa. Counsel, Democratic National Committee, In House, 1993-1998. *Member:* American Bar Association; American Association of Political Consultants. ***PRACTICE AREAS:*** Election, Campaign and Political Law; Election and Campaign Finance. ***Email:*** reiff@sandlerreiff.com

JOHN HARDIN YOUNG, born Washington, D.C., April 25, 1948; admitted to bar, 1973, Virginia; 1974, District of Columbia; 1976, Pennsylvania and U.S. Supreme Court. *Education:* Colgate University (A.B., 1970); University of Virginia (J.D., 1973); Exeter College, Oxford University (B.C.L., 1976). Author, "Federal Rules of Evidence," Went Pub. 6th ed, 2001, Co-Author, "Mastering Discovery," Lexis, 2000. Member: Chair, Virginia Retirement Review Board, 1990-1994; Secretary of State, Advisory Committee on Private International Law, 1984-1995; Certified Mediator, Virginia Supreme Court, 1997-2000. *Member:* American Bar Association (Chair, Section on Administration Law and Regulatory Practice, 1999-2000); Commercial Bar Association (U.K.); American Law Institute; George Mason Inn of Court (President, 2001-2002). ***PRACTICE AREAS:*** Litigation; Administrative Law; Antitrust Law; Technology Law; Business Law. ***Email:*** young@sandlerreiff.com

---

SANDLER, TRAVIS & ROSENBERG, P.A.

Established in 1977
1300 PENNSYLVANIA AVENUE, SUITE 400
WASHINGTON, D.C. 20004
Telephone: 202-216-9307
Fax: 202-842-2247
Email: info@strtrade.com
URL: http://www.strtrade.com

Miami, Florida Office: The Waterford, 5200 Blue Lagoon Drive, Suite 600, 33126-2022. Telephone: 305-267-9200. Fax: 305-267-5155.
New York, New York Office: 551 Fifth Avenue, Suite 614, 10176. Telephone: 212-883-1300. Fax: 212-883-0068.
Baltimore, Maryland Office: 111 South Calvert Street, Suite 2700, 21202. Telephone: 410-385-5208. Fax: 410-837-2441.
San Francisco, California Office: Sandler, Travis & Rosenberg and Glad & Ferguson, P.C., 1 Sutter Street, 10th Floor, 94014. Telephone: 415-986-1088. Fax: 415-986-2271.
Chicago, Illinois Office: Sandler, Travis & Rosenberg LLC, 200 West Madison Street, Suite 2670, 60606. Telephone: 312-236-6555. Telecopier: 312-236-6568.
Houston, Texas Office: 440 Louisiana, Suite 900, 77002. Telephone: 713-236-7715. Fax: 713-236-7768.
Los Angeles, California Office: Sandler, Travis & Rosenberg and Glad & Ferguson, P.C., 5230 Pacific Concourse Drive, Suite 200, 90045. Telephone: 310-643-4494. Telecopier: 310-643-4493.

Customs Law, International Trade and Transportation Law. International Corporate, Copyright and Trademark Law. Trial, Appellate, Federal and Administrative Practice. Immigration and Nationality Law. International Labor Law, NAFTA, Government Relations, Trade Negotiations, International Trade Policy, Intellectual Property, Import and Export Law, Foreign Trade Sanctions, Shipping Law, Surety.

GILBERT LEE SANDLER, born Jacksonville, Florida, January 9, 1944; admitted to bar, 1969, Florida and U.S. Court of International Trade; 1970-1982, U.S. Court of Customs and Patent Appeals; 1975, New York; 1982, U.S. Court of Appeals for the Federal Circuit (Not admitted in District of Columbia). *Education:* Dartmouth College (A.B., with honors, 1966); New York University (J.D., 1969). Author: Articles, "Liquidated Damages" Fordham Law Journal (1990-1991); "Gray Market Goods: The Controversy Will Continue," Brooklyn Journal of Law, Vol. XIII, No. 2, 1987. Trial Attorney, U.S. Department of Justice, Customs Section, 1969-1975. Member, Treasury Department Advisory Committee on Commercial Operations of U.S. Customs Service, 1999—. *Member:* The Florida Bar (Editor, International Law Quarterly, 1982-1987; Chairman, International Law Section, 1987-1988); American Bar Association; Customs and International Trade Bar Association (Treasurer, 1980-1990). ***PRACTICE AREAS:*** Customs Law; International Trade Law; Intellectual Property Law. ***Email:*** lsandler@strtrade.com

THOMAS G. TRAVIS, born New York, N.Y., April 4, 1947; admitted to bar, 1973, New Jersey; 1974, New York and U.S. Court of International Trade; 1975, Florida; 1976-1982, U.S. Court of Customs and Patent Appeals; 1982, U.S. Court of Appeals for the Federal Circuit and U.S. Supreme Court; 1991, District of Columbia. *Education:* Princeton University (A.B., with honors, 1969); Columbia University (J.D., 1972). Member, U.S. Treasury Department's Advisory Committee on Commercial Operations of the United States Customs Service, 1991—. *Member:* New Jersey State and American Bar Associations; The Florida Bar (Chairman, International Law Section, 1983); Customs and International Trade Bar Association. ***PRACTICE AREAS:*** Customs Law; International Trade Law.

LEONARD L. ROSENBERG, born New York, N.Y., January 3, 1946; admitted to bar, 1971, Maryland and District of Columbia; 1974, U.S. Supreme Court; 1981, Florida and U.S. Court of International Trade; 1982, U.S. Court of Appeals for the Federal Circuit. *Education:* Queens College of the City University of New York (B.A., 1967); George Washington University (J.D., with honors, 1971). President, Customs Lawyers Association, 1977-1978. Attorney, 1975-1978 and Senior Attorney, 1978-1980, Office of Regulations and Rulings,

(This Listing Continued)

U.S. Customs Service. *Member:* Maryland State Bar Association; The District of Columbia Bar; The Florida Bar (Editor, International Law Quarterly, 1987-1992; Chair, 1993-1994, International Law Section); Customs and International Trade Bar Association. ***REPORTED CASES:*** Pagoda Trading Co. v. U.S., 617 F.Supp. 96 (CIT 1985), aff'd, 804 F.2d 665 (Fed. Cir. 1988); E.C. McAfeev. U.S., 842 F.2d 314 (Fed. Cir. 1988). ***PRACTICE AREAS:*** Customs Law; Trade Regulation Law; International Law. ***Email:*** lrosenberg@strtrade.com

RONALD W. GERDES, born Dayton, Ohio, March 1, 1947; admitted to bar, 1972, Texas; 1979-1982, U.S. Court of Customs and Patent Appeals; 1979, U.S. Court of International Trade; 1982, U.S. Court of Appeals for the Federal Circuit; 1987, District of Columbia; 1998, U.S. Supreme Court. *Education:* University of Dayton (B.A., 1967); University of Michigan (J.D., 1972). Assistant Chief Counsel, Administration and Legislation, U.S. Customs Service, 1980-1985. Senior Attorney, Office of Regulation and Rulings, U.S. Customs Service, 1973-1980. *Member:* Customs International Trade Bar Association; Customs Lawyers Association. ***PRACTICE AREAS:*** Customs Law; International Trade Law. ***Email:*** rgerdes@strtrade.com

TERESA M. POLINO, born Omaha, Nebraska, May 24, 1952; admitted to bar, 1978, District of Columbia; 1981, U.S. Court of International Trade; 1982, U.S. Court of Appeals for the Federal Circuit. *Education:* State University of New York at Plattsburg (B.A., magna cum laude, 1974); Georgetown University Law Center (J.D., 1977). Attorney-Advisor, Office of the General Counsel (Assistant General Counsel for Enforcement and Operations), U.S. Department of the Treasury, 1983-1984. Senior Attorney, Office of the Chief Counsel, U.S. Customs Service, 1980-1983. Legal Intern, 1976 and Customs Attorney, Office of Regulations and Rulings, 1977-1980, U.S. Customs Service. Co-Author: "The Impact of the Court on I.T.A. Policies and Procedures - Too Much or Too Little?" 10 Boston College International and Comparative Law Review 241, 1987. *Member:* District of Columbia Bar; Customs and International Trade Bar Association; Customs Lawyers Association (Treasurer, 1979-1980). ***PRACTICE AREAS:*** Customs Law; International Trade Law; Administrative Agency Practice. ***Email:*** tpolino@strtrade.com

PEGGY LOUIE CHAPLIN, born Guantanamo Bay Naval Base, Cuba, 1940; admitted to bar, 1973, Maryland; 1981, U.S. Court of International Trade; 1988, District of Columbia. *Education:* Johns Hopkins Univ. (B.S., 1971); Univ. of Maryland (J.D., 1973); Georgetown Univ. (LL.M. in International Commercial Law, 1983). Author: "Legal Aspects of Doing Business Abroad," *Exporter's Encyclopedia*, 2000-2001; "Harbor Maintenance Fee," *Official Export Guide*, 1995-1996; "Regulating International Commerce," *Maryland Bar Journal*, September 1992; "An Introduction To The Harmonized System," *North Carolina Journal of International Law and Commercial Regulation,* Summer, 1987; "The Custom House Broker as Importer of Record," *Journal of Maritime Law and Commerce*, April, 1982. Chair, International Commercial Law Committee, Maryland State Bar Association, Business Law Section, 1998-1999. Counsel, Transportation Committee of American Association of Exporters and Importers, 1993-2001. Fellow, Maryland Bar Foundation, 1991—. (Also in Baltimore, Maryland Office). ***PRACTICE AREAS:*** Customs Law; Administrative Agency Practice; International Commercial Law; Shipping and Transportation Law. ***Email:*** pchaplin@strtrade.com

PHILIP S. GALLAS, born Kansas City, Missouri, July 23, 1953; admitted to bar, 1978, District of Columbia; 1982, U.S. Court of International Trade and U.S. Court of Appeals for the Federal Circuit. *Education:* Washington University (A.B., 1975); American University (J.D., 1978). Customs Attorney, Office of Regulations and Rulings, U.S. Customs Service Headquarters, 1978-1980. Import Administration Specialist, Antidumping Order Compliance Division, International Trade Administration, U.S. Department of Commerce, 1980-1984. Guest Lecturer, New York University, Customs Law Survey, 1986. Instructor, NAFTA Seminar before the Cosmetic, Toiletry and Fragrance Association, 1994. *Member:* The District of Columbia Bar; Customs and International Trade Bar Association; Washington Custom Brokers and Freight Forwarders Association (Associate Member). ***LANGUAGES:*** French. ***PRACTICE AREAS:*** International Trade; Customs Law; Export Law. ***Email:*** pgallas@strtrade.com

CHANDRI NAVARRO-BOWMAN, born Panama, Republic of Panama, March 22, 1964; admitted to bar, 1993, Pennsylvania; 1994, District of Columbia. *Education:* College of William & Mary (B.A., 1986); American University (J.D., 1993). *Member:* American Bar Association (Member, International Law Section); Customs and International Trade Bar Association; Women in International Trade. ***LANGUAGES:*** Spanish and French. ***SPECIAL AGENCIES:*** Cotton Board, 1992-1995. ***PRACTICE AREAS:*** International Trade; Customs Law; International Law. ***Email:*** cnavarro-bowman@strtrade.com

---

DAVID E. COHEN, born Milwaukee, Wisconsin, May 31, 1967; admitted to bar, 1992, Wisconsin and U.S. District Court, Eastern District of Wisconsin; 1999, District of Columbia. *Education:* University of Wisconsin-Madison (B.B.A., 1989); Marquette University (J.D., 1992). Author: "The Community Reinvestment Act, Asset or Liability?" Marquette Law Review, Spring, 1992.

(This Listing Continued)

Attorney, Office of Regulations and Rulings, U.S. Customs Service, 1993-1999. *Member:* State Bar of Wisconsin. ***PRACTICE AREAS:*** Customs Law; International Trade. ***Email:*** dcohen@strtrade.com

MARK R. LUDWIKOWSKI, born Kraków, Poland, March 4, 1971; admitted to bar, 1997, Maryland; U.S. Court of International Trade and U.S. Court of Appeals for the Federal Circuit (Not admitted in District of Columbia). *Education:* Catholic University of America (B.A., 1993); Jagiellonian University School of Law, Kraków, Poland (Certificate, International Trade and Business Law Program, 1994); Catholic University of America, Columbus School of Law (J.D., 1996). Member, CommLaw Conspectus, The Columbus School of Law Journal of Communications Law and Policy. International Trade Analyst, U.S. Department of Commerce, International Trade Administration, 1998-2000. *Member:* Maryland State Bar Association. ***LANGUAGES:*** Polish, French. ***PRACTICE AREAS:*** International Trade; Customs Regulation; International Business Law. ***Email:*** mludwikowski@strtrade.com

SUSAN L. RENTON, born Pittsburgh, Pennsylvania, November 10, 1960; admitted to bar, 1989, Pennsylvania; 1990, District of Columbia. *Education:* Southern Methodist University (B.A., cum laude, 1982); Whittier College School of Law (J.D., 1985); George Washington University National Law Center (LL.M., International and Comparative Law, 1988). Member, Women in International Trade, Customs Section; Co-Chair D.C. Chapter. ***SPECIAL AGENCIES:*** U.S. Customs Service Office of Regulations and Rulings, 1989-1994. ***PRACTICE AREAS:*** Trade Regulation; Customs; Export Regulation. ***Email:*** srenton@strtrade.com

OF COUNSEL

PAUL G. GIGUERE, born Lewiston, Maine, January 23, 1931; admitted to bar, 1959, District of Columbia; 1960, Maine; 1973, U.S. Supreme Court. *Education:* Assumption College (B.A., 1953); Georgetown University (LL.B., 1958). U.S. Customs Service: Director, International Nomenclature Staff, 1983-1989; Deputy Director, Classification and Value Division, 1979-1983; Chief, Special Projects and Programs Branch, Office of Regulations and Rulings, 1975-1979; Attorney-Advisor, Tariff Classification Division, 1970-1975. *Member:* District of Columbia Bar; American Bar Association; Washington International Trade Association. ***PRACTICE AREAS:*** Customs Law; International Trade Law. ***Email:*** pgiguere@strtrade.com

ANDREW JAMES SAMET, born Boston, Massachusetts, June 29, 1957; admitted to bar, 1983, District of Columbia and Massachusetts. *Education:* Yale University (B.A., 1978); Georgetown University (J.D., 1983). Adjunct Professor, George Washington University Law School, 2001. Associate Deputy Undersecretary, 1993-1998 and Deputy Undersecretary, 1998-2001, U.S. Department of Labor. ***PRACTICE AREAS:*** International Trade; International Labor Law. ***Email:*** asamet@strtrade.com

(For Complete Biographical Data on all Personnel, See Professional Biographies at Miami, Florida)

SAUNDERS & SCHMIELER, P.C.

1050 17TH STREET, N.W.
SUITE 600
WASHINGTON, D.C. 20036
Telephone: 202-833-2999
Email: schmielj@sslawfirm.com
URL: http://www.sslawfirm.com

Silver Spring, Maryland Office: 8737 Colesville Rd., Suite L-200. Telephone: 301-588-7717. Facsimile: 301-588-5073.

Baltimore, Maryland Office: Suite 2700, 111 South Calvert Street. Telephone: 410-235-7558.

Arlington, Virginia Office: 2111 Wilson Boulevard, Suite 700. Telephone: 703-243-1100.

General Civil, Trial and Appellate Practice in all Courts, Insurance Defense, Trial and Litigation, Insurance Coverage, Self-Insurance Defense, Liability Defense Litigation, Intellectual Property Law, Products Liability Defense, Premises Liability Defense, Construction Liability Defense, Personal Injury Defense, Civil Rights Litigation, Discrimination Claims, Errors and Omissions, Professional Malpractice Defense, Advice and Consultation, Insurance Risk Management, Corporate Law, Commercial Litigation, Environmental Law, Toxic Tort Defense, Personal Injury Defense, Real Estate Law, Advertising Injury Defense, Labor Relations, Workers' Compensation, Mass Tort and Litigation Defense.

(For complete biographical data on all personnel, see Professional Biographies at Silver Spring, Maryland)

SCHAGRIN ASSOCIATES

Established in 1984

1100 FIFTEENTH STREET, NW
SUITE 700
WASHINGTON, D.C. 20005
Telephone: 202-223-1700
Fax: 202-429-2522
Email: schagrin@erols.com

International Trade Practice before the Civil Courts, Government Departments and Congressional Committees. International Corporate and Customs Law. Antitrust, Administrative and Civil Litigation Law.

MEMBER OF FIRM

ROGER B. SCHAGRIN, born Middletown, New York, March 12, 1957; admitted to bar, 1981, District of Columbia; 1982, Florida; 1983, U.S. Court of International Trade. *Education:* Yale University (B.A., magna cum laude, 1977); University of Virginia (J.D., 1981). Author: "Result-Neutral Efficiencies by the Department of Commerce in an Era of Budget Austerity," 25 L & Poly Int'l Bus. US (1993). *Member:* The District of Columbia Bar (Member, International Trade Section); The Florida Bar; Customs and International Trade Bar Association. ***LANGUAGES:*** French, Spanish and Portuguese. ***PRACTICE AREAS:*** International Trade; Legislative Law. ***Email:*** schagrin@erols.com

DIRECTOR OF GOVERNMENTAL AFFAIRS

TAMARA L. BROWNE, born Gary, Indiana, July 3, 1958. *Education:* Ripon College (B.A., 1980); Indiana University. Member: Women in International Trade, 1991; National Fire Protection Association, 1990-1991. Legislative Assistant to U.S. Rep. Peter Visclosky, 1985, Washington D.C. and Legislative Director to Rep. Visclosky, 1985-1988. (Lobbyist). ***PRACTICE AREAS:*** International Trade; Fire Protection/Fire Safety; General Legislative Affairs.

SCHIFF HARDIN & WAITE

A Partnership including Professional Corporations

Founded 1864

1101 CONNECTICUT AVENUE, N.W.
WASHINGTON, D.C. 20036
Telephone: 202-778-6400
Facsimile: 202-778-6460
Email: attorneys@schiffhardin.com
URL: http://www.schiffhardin.com

Chicago, Illinois Office: 6600 Sears Tower, 60606-6473. Telephone: 312-258-5500. Facsimile: 312-258-5600. TWX: 910-221-2463.
Merrillville, Indiana Office: 8585 Broadway, Suite 842, 46410. Telephone: 219-738-3820. Facsimile: 219-738-3826.
New York, New York Office: 150 East 52nd Street, Suite 2700, 10022. Telephone: 212-753-5000. Facsimile: 212-753-5044.
Dublin, Ireland Office: The Enterprise Building, 5 Harbourmaster Place, International Financial Services Centre. Telephone: +353-1-670-2980. Facsimile: +353-1-670-2988.

General Practice.

LAW FIRM ALLIANCES/ASSOCIATIONS: **TERRALEX**

UNITED STATES LAW FIRM GROUP

RESIDENT PARTNERS

BARBARA K. HEFFERNAN, born Baltimore, Maryland, January 14, 1953; admitted to bar, 1978, District of Columbia; 1979, Maryland and U.S. Court of Appeals for the District of Columbia Circuit; 1980, U.S. Court of Appeals, Fifth Circuit; 1981, U.S. Court of Appeals, Eleventh Circuit; 1982, U.S. Supreme Court; 1989, U.S. Court of Appeals, Third Circuit. *Education:* University of Maryland (B.A., 1975); Catholic University of America (J.D., 1978). Managing Editor, Catholic University Law Review. ***PRACTICE AREAS:*** Energy; Energy Regulatory; Administrative Law. ***Email:*** bheffernan@schiffhardin.com

ANDREW M. KLEIN, born New Rochelle, New York, December 28, 1941; admitted to bar, 1967, New York; 1980, District of Columbia. *Education:* University of Chicago (B.A., 1963; J.D., 1966). Securities and Exchange Commission, Division of Market Regulation, Director, 1977-1979, Associate Director, 1975-1977, Assistant Director, 1974-1975, Special Counsel, 1973-1974, Washington, D.C. ***PRACTICE AREAS:*** Securities Regulation; Broker-Dealer Regulation; Investment Management. ***Email:*** aklein@schiffhardin.com

GEAROLD L. KNOWLES, born Sullivan, Indiana, June 7, 1946; admitted to bar, 1973, Indiana; 1977, District of Columbia and U.S. Supreme Court. *Education:* Indiana University (B.S., 1968; J.D., 1973). Attorney, Division of

(This Listing Continued)

Corporate Regulation, Securities and Exchange Commission, 1973-1976. Senior Attorney, Office of the General Counsel, U.S. Railway Association, 1976-1977. ***PRACTICE AREAS:*** Federal Energy Regulation; Natural Gas Regulation; Electric Power; Energy Project Development; International Telecommunications Law. ***Email:*** gknowles@schiffhardin.com

HOWARD L. KRAMER, born Baltimore, Maryland, May 27, 1955; admitted to bar, 1981, District of Columbia. *Education:* University of Michigan (B.A., 1977; M.A., 1979; J.D., cum laude, 1980). Phi Beta Kappa. Member, The Michigan Yearbook of International Legal Studies. ***PRACTICE AREAS:*** Securities; Commodities. ***Email:*** hkramer@schiffhardin.com

SHIRLEY M. LUKITSCH, born Pittsburgh, Pennsylvania, October 22, 1950; admitted to bar, 1986, Illinois and U.S. District Court, Northern District of Illinois (Not admitted in District of Columbia). *Education:* University of Pittsburgh (B.A., summa cum laude, 1971); University of Wisconsin-Madison (M.A., 1972); University of California at Berkeley (J.D., 1986). Phi Beta Kappa. Member, California Law Review. ***PRACTICE AREAS:*** Corporate; Securities; Banking. ***Email:*** slukitsch@schiffhardin.com

ANDRÉ E. OWENS, born Hartford, Connecticut, October 9, 1963; admitted to bar, 1988, Connecticut; 1989, District of Columbia. *Education:* Providence College (B.S., cum laude, highest honors, 1985); Harvard University (J.D., 1988). ***PRACTICE AREAS:*** Securities Regulation; Broker-Dealer Regulation. ***Email:*** aowens@schiffhardin.com

SPECIAL PARTNER

DREXEL D. JOURNEY

RESIDENT OF COUNSEL

JOHN W. GLENDENING, JR., born Jackson, Michigan, January 15, 1917; admitted to bar, 1941, New York; 1959, U.S. Court of Appeals for the District of Columbia Circuit; 1962, U.S. Supreme Court; 1967, U.S. Tax Court; 1973, U.S. Court of Appeals, Fifth Circuit; 1975, District of Columbia. *Education:* Colgate University (A.B., 1938); Cornell University (J.D., 1941). Phi Beta Kappa. Member, Editorial Board, Cornell Law Quarterly. ***Email:*** jglenden@schiffhardin.com

EDWIN S. ROCKEFELLER

RESIDENT ASSOCIATES

DEBRA ANN PALMER

JAMES L. EASTMAN

KEVIN D. RYAN (Not admitted in District of Columbia).

(For additional biographical data, see Professional Biographies at Chicago, Illinois and Merrillville, Indiana).

WILLIAM G. SCHIFFBAUER

SUITE 700, NORTH TOWER
1300 PENNSYLVANIA AVE., N.W.
WASHINGTON, D.C. 20004-3002
Telephone: 202-204-3030
Fax: 202-789-7349
Email: wgslaw@erols.com
URL: http://www.lawyers.com/healthcareregulation

Health Care Regulation, Health Maintenance Organizations, Managed Care, Health Care Contracts, Health Care Fraud, Health Insurance Defense, Alternative Health Care Delivery Systems, Patients Rights, Government Relations, State Legislative Practice, COBRA, ERISA, Health Benefits.

FIRM PROFILE: Mr. Schiffbauer has a national Health Care Insurance and Regulatory Practice. In over 20 years, Mr. Schiffbauer has represented a broad cross-section of corporations and associations including Health & Life Insurance Associations, Employee Benefit Trade Associations, Health Insurance Companies, Managed Care Providers and Dental Insurance Associations.

WILLIAM G. SCHIFFBAUER, born Columbia, South Carolina, February 17, 1954; admitted to bar, 1979, Nebraska; 1981, U.S. Claims Court; U.S. Tax Court; 1988, District of Columbia. *Education:* University of Nebraska (B.S., 1976); Creighton University (J.D., 1979); George Washington University (LL.M. in Environmental Law, 1987). Member, Environmental Law Institute, 1985—. Counsel and Legislative Assistant for Tax, Energy and Environment, U.S. Senator J. James Exon, U.S. Senate, 1979-1985.

AARON SCHILDHAUS

Established in 1975
1101 NEW HAMPSHIRE AVENUE, N.W.
WASHINGTON, D.C. 20037
Telephone: 202-775-4570
Fax: 202-887-1912
URL: http://www.lawyers.com/aaronschildhaus
Email: schildhaus@aol.com
URL: http://www.schildhaus.com

Business and Corporate Law, Contracts, Joint Ventures, Foreign Corrupt Practices Act, International Financial Transactions, Aviation Law, Aerospace Law, Privatization, Export Controls, International Trade, International Commercial Law, Dispute Resolution, International: Non Governmental Organizations (NGO'S), Non Profit Organizations, Europe, Africa, Asia, EU, Russia, China, India.

AARON SCHILDHAUS, born Burlington, Vermont, July 23, 1943; admitted to bar, 1969, District of Columbia and U.S. Court of Appeals, District of Columbia Circuit; 1986, U.S. Supreme Court; 1988, U.S. Court of Appeals, Federal Circuit and U.S. Court of International Trade. *Education:* University of Vermont (B.A., 1965); Washington College of Law, American University (J.D., 1968). Phi Alpha Delta. Author: "International Legal Developments in Review 1997-2000, International Aviation and Aerospace Law," The International Lawyer, Summer 1998, 1999, 2000. *Member:* The District of Columbia Bar (Member, International Law Section); American Bar Association (Vice Chair, General Practice Section, International Law Committee, 1993-1999; Member, Business Law and Alternative Dispute Resolution Sections; Section of International Law and Practice; Co-Chair: International Aviation and Aerospace Law Committee, 1997—; Chair, International NGO and Non Profit Organization Committee); International Bar Association; American Society of International Law. ***LANGUAGES:*** French and German.

SCHMELTZER, APTAKER & SHEPARD, P.C.

Established in 1976
THE WATERGATE
SUITE 1000, 2600 VIRGINIA AVENUE, N.W.
WASHINGTON, D.C. 20037-1922
Telephone: 202-333-8800
Cable Address: "Ship"
Telex: 440517
Facsimile: 202-337-6065
Email: sas@saslaw.com
URL: http://www.saspc.com

Los Angeles, California Office: 10880 Wilshire Boulevard, Suite 2070, 90024-4121. Telephone: 310-234-5688. FAX: 310-234-5699.

Labor and Employment Law, Franchise, Maritime, Equal Employment Opportunity, Civil Litigation, Employee Benefits, Health Care, Business and Transactional Law, Legislative Law, Municipal, Natural Resources, Antitrust and Corporate Law.

FIRM PROFILE: The firm was founded in 1976 by members of one of the nation's largest firms who believed that a smaller firm emphasizing specialization and cost effective service had the most to offer to lawyers and clients alike. The firm's counselling and litigation practice is international in scope, representing domestic and foreign public and private concerns, as well as governments. Schmeltzer, Aptaker & Shepard, P.C. has grown to meet the needs of its clientele while remaining true to its original concept.

IRA M. SHEPARD, born Troy, New York, January 8, 1947; admitted to bar, 1972, New York and District of Columbia; 1975, U.S. Supreme Court. *Education:* Cornell University (B.S., 1968; J.D., 1971). Articles Editor, Cornell International Law Journal, 1970-1971. Author: "Without Just Cause: An Employer's Practical and Legal Guide on Wrongful Discharge," published by BNA, 1988; "Thieves at Work: An Employer's Guide to Combating Workplace Dishonesty," published by BNA, 1988; "Workplace Privacy: A Bureau of National Affairs Special Report," published by BNA, 1987; "Employment At-Will: A Management Guide," published by College & University Personnel Association, 1987; "Health Care Labor Law," published by University of Michigan, 1981; "A Compliance Guide to Prudence Under ERISA," Journal of Pension Planning and Compliance, 1977. Counsel to the Minority Members, U.S. Senate Labor and Public Welfare Committee, 1975-1976. Chairman, Executive Committee, Cement, Quarry and Mineral Aggregate Section of National Safety Council, 1982-1983. *Member:* The District of Columbia Bar; American Bar Association (Member, Section on Labor Relations Law). ***REPORTED CASES:*** Emeronye v. CACI Int'l Inc., 2001 U.S. Dist. LEXIS 5335 (D.D.C. April 17, 2001); Almonte v. Coca-Cola Bottling Company of New York, 959 F. Supp. 569 (D.Comm. 1997); Camillo v. The Coca-Cola Bottling Company of New York, Inc., 776 F. Supp. 662 (N.D.N.Y. 1991), aff'd, 962 F.2d 2 (2d Cir. 1992); Gray v. Citizens Bank of Washington, 602 A.2d 1096 (D.C.), reh'g en banc granted, 602 A.2d 1096 (D.C.), reh'g en banc vacated, 609 A.2d 1143 (D.C. 1992); United Steelworkers v. Libby, McNeill & Libby, Inc., 895 F.2d 421 (7th Cir. 1990); International Brotherhood of Firemen and Oilers v. Nestle Co., Inc., 630 F.2d 474 (6th Cir. 1980); Seafarers Union (American Pacific Container Lines, Inc.) 105 L.R.R.M. 155 (1980). ***PRACTICE AREAS:*** Management Labor Law; Employment Law; Employee Benefits Law. ***Email:*** ims@saslaw.com

J. THOMAS ESSLINGER, born Ephrata, Pennsylvania, August 11, 1943; admitted to bar, 1973, District of Columbia; 1977, U.S. Supreme Court. *Education:* Yale University (B.A., 1965); Georgetown University (J.D., 1973). Lead Articles Editor, Georgetown Law Journal, 1972-1973. Associate, Morgan, Lewis & Bockius, 1973-1976. *Member:* The District of Columbia Bar; Bar Association of the District of Columbia; American Bar Association; Maritime Administrative Bar Association. [Capt., U.S. Marine Corps, 1966-1970]. ***PRACTICE AREAS:*** Litigation; Business Law; Business Transactions; Corporate Law; Maritime Law. ***Email:*** jte@saslaw.com

PAUL M. HEYLMAN, born Cleveland, Ohio, December 6, 1952; admitted to bar, 1978, District of Columbia; 1991, Maryland. *Education:* St. John's College (B.A., 1974); American University (J.D., 1978). Member, American University Law Review. Author: "Extraterritorial Impact of United States Labor Unions and United States Labor Laws on the Maritime Industry," Journal of Maritime Law and Commerce, Vol. 29 No.1, pp. 59-77, January 1998; "Without Just Cause: An Employer's Practical and Legal Guide on Wrongful Discharge," published by BNA, 1988; "Employee Relations in an Unorganized Facility," Health Care Labor Law, University of Michigan, 1981. *Member:* The District of Columbia Bar; American Bar Association (Member, Labor and Employment Law Section). ***REPORTED CASES:*** The Coca-Cola Bottling Co. of New York (CCNY) (IBT Locals 125 and 812), Case 22-UC-267 (NLRB 2000); NPR v. New Orleans, Dkt. 98-23 (FMC 3/16/00); Farkas v. Rumore and CCNY, 881 F. Supp. 884 (S.D.N.Y. 1995), appeal dismissed, 101 F.3d 20 (2d Cir.1996); Phoenix v. NECA, 867 F. Supp 924 (D.Or. 1994), aff'd, 81 F.3d 858 (9th Cir. 1996); Regan v. CCNY and Local 812, IBT, 149 LRRM 2545 (S.D.N.Y.), aff'd, 89 F.3d 826 (2d Cir. 1995); Wurst v. Nestle Foods, 791 F. Supp. 123 (W.D. Pa. 1991), aff'd, in rel. part, 975 F.2d 1553 (3d Cir. 1992); Less v. Nestle, 705 F. Supp. 110 (W.D.N.Y. 1988); Labeach v. Nestle, 658 F. Supp. 676 (S.D.N.Y. 1987); Boutillier v. Libby, 713 P.2d 110 (Wash. App. 1986). ***PRACTICE AREAS:*** Management Labor and Employment Law; ERISA; Maritime Law. ***Email:*** pmh@saslaw.com

RALPH H. JOHNSON, born Tremonton, Utah, April 2, 1949; admitted to bar, 1975, Utah; 1980, U.S. Supreme Court and U.S. Court of Appeals, Tenth Circuit; 1987, U.S. Court of Appeals for the District of Columbia Circuit; 1988, District of Columbia and U.S. Court of Appeals, Ninth Circuit. *Education:* Weber State University (B.A., 1972); University of Utah (J.D., 1975). Phi Kappa Phi. Recipient: Special Commendation Award, U.S. Department of Justice, 1987; Five Special Achievement Awards from the United States Attorney General, 1983-1988. Instructor, Attorney General's Advocacy Institute, 1981-1987. Ogden City Prosecutor, 1975-1980. Assistant United States Attorney, 1980-1983. Trial Attorney, U.S. Department of Justice, 1983-1985. Senior Trial Attorney, U.S. Department of Justice, 1985-1986. Assistant Director, Torts Branch, U.S. Department of Justice, 1986-1988. ***LANGUAGES:*** German. ***REPORTED CASES:*** Johnston v. United States, 597 F.Supp. 374 (D.Kansas 1984); Timothy v. United States, 612 F.Supp. 160 (D. Utah 1985); Prescott v. United States, 858 F. Supp. 1461 (D. Nevada 1994). ***PRACTICE AREAS:*** Litigation; Radiation Law. ***Email:*** rhj@saslaw.com

GARY L. LIEBER, born Scranton, Pennsylvania, May 28, 1949; admitted to bar, 1974, Pennsylvania; 1975, District of Columbia; 1978, U.S. Supreme Court. *Education:* The American University (B.A., 1971); Washington College of Law, The American University (J.D., 1974); Georgetown University (LL.M., 1979). Articles Editor, The American University Law Review, 1973-1974. Adjunct Faculty, Washington College of Law, The American University, 1985-1987. Attorney, National Labor Relations Board, Division of Enforcement Litigation, 1974-1976; Baltimore Regional Office, 1976-1978. President, Washington Region, Jewish National Fund. *Member:* The District of Columbia Bar; Pennsylvania Bar Association. ***REPORTED CASES:*** National Elec. Contractors Ass'n v. Kansas Chapter, Nat'l Elec. Contractors Ass'n, 46 F. Supp. 2d 1174 (D. Kan., 1999), aff'd 203 F.3d 835 (10th Cir., 2000); Building & Constr. Trades Dep't v. Reich, 40 F.3d 1275 (D.C. Cir., 1994); F.E. Hazard, Ltd. v. NLRB, 917 F.2d 736 (2nd Cir., 1990); Kozera v. Westchester-Fairfield Chapter of Nat'l Elec. Contractors Ass'n, 909 F.2d 48 (2nd Cir., 1990); Community Elec. Serv., Inc. v. National Elec. Contractors Ass'n, 869 F.2d 1235 (9th Cir., 1989); EEOC v. Hansa Products, Inc., 844 F.2d 191 (4th Cir., 1988); Berger v. Iron Workers Reinforced Rodmen Local 201, 843 F.2d 1395 (D.C. Cir., 1988); Aeronautical Indus. Dist. Lodge 91 of the Int'l Ass'n of Machinists & Aero Workers v. United Technologies Corp., 2000 U.S. Dist. LEXIS 2237 (D. Conn., Jan. 6, 2000); Cunliffe v. Sikorsky Aircraft Corp., 9 F. Supp. 2d 125 (D. Conn., 1998); Phoenix Elec. Co. v. National Elec. Contractors Ass'n, 81 F.3d 858 (9th Cir., 1996); T & G Constr. Co. v. Sheet Metal Workers' Int'l Ass'n Local 100, 791 F. Supp. 127 (D. Md., 1992); Kesselring v. United Technologies Corp., 753 F. Supp. 1359 (S.D. Ohio, 1991). ***PRACTICE AREAS:*** Management Labor Law; Employment Law; Employee Benefits Law. ***Email:*** gll@saslaw.com

(This Listing Continued)

(This Listing Continued)

SCHMELTZER, APTAKER & SHEPARD, P.C., Washington—Continued

EDWARD R. LEVIN, born Norfolk, Virginia, March 18, 1943; admitted to bar, 1968, Virginia; 1969, District of Columbia; 1973, U.S. Supreme Court; 1969, U.S. Court of Appeals, Fourth Circuit and U.S. Court of Appeals for the District of Columbia Circuit; 1979, U.S. Court of Appeals, Fifth Circuit. *Education:* Brown University (A.B., 1965); University of Virginia (LL.B., 1968). Contributor, "Employment Discrimination Law," Annual Supplements, BNA, 1984-2001. Law Clerk to Chief Judge Walter E. Hoffman, U.S. District Court for the Eastern District of Virginia, 1968-1969. Member, Labor Policy Committee, U.S. Chamber of Commerce. *Member:* The District of Columbia Bar (Member, Labor Relations and Litigation Divisions); American Bar Association (Member: Sections on Labor and Employment Law, Litigation); Virginia State Bar. Fellow, College of Labor and Employment Lawyers. ***REPORTED CASES:*** Astarita v. Urgo Butts Co., 74 Fair Empl. Prac. Cas. (BNA) 585 (S.D.N.Y., 1997); Ferguson v. Giant Food Inc., 914 F.2d 1490 (D.C. Cir., 1990); Thompson v. Giant Food Inc., 787 F.2d 675 (D.C. Cir., 1986); Hall v. Giant Food Inc., 175 F.3d 1074 (D.C. Cir., 1999); Greenhoot Inc., 205 NLRB 250 (1973); Gray v. Greyhound, 545 F.2d 169 (D.C. Cir., 1976); North American Soccer League v. NLRB, 613 F.2d 1379 (5th Cir., 1980). ***PRACTICE AREAS:*** Management Labor Law; Employment Law; Employee Benefits Law. ***Email:*** erl@saslaw.com

ROBERT L. ZISK, born New York, N.Y., August 12, 1957; admitted to bar, 1983, District of Columbia; U.S. Court of Appeals for the District of Columbia, Second, Third, Fourth, Eighth and Tenth Circuits; U.S. District Court for the District of Columbia; U.S. District Court, District of Maryland. *Education:* Cornell University (B.S., 1980); Duke University (J.D., with honors, 1983). Co-author: "Practical Considerations in Enforcing Standards," 12 Franchise Law Journal 97 (1993); "Criminal Liability for Violations of Federal Hazardous Waste Law: The 'Knowledge' of Corporations and Their Executives," 23 Wake Forest L. Rev. 203 (1988). Attorney, Division of Fair Labor Standards, U.S. Department of Labor, 1983-1985. *Member:* The District of Columbia Bar; American Bar Association. ***REPORTED CASES:*** Yankee Enters., Inc. v. Dunkin' Donuts Inc., Bus. Franchise Guide (CCH) ¶ 11,291, 1997 U.S. App. LEXIS 23330 (5th Cir. July 8, 1997), cert. denied, 522 U.S. 1076 (1998); Goldhammer v. Dunkin' Donuts Inc., 59 F. Supp. 2d 248 (D. Mass. 1999); Dunkin' Donuts Inc. v. Taseski, 47 F. Supp. 2d 867 (E.D. Mich. 1999); Chu v. Dunkin' Donuts Inc., 27 F. Supp. 2d 171 (E.D.N.Y. 1998); Dunkin' Donuts Inc. v. Panagakos, 5 F. Supp. 2d 57 (D. Mass 1998); Dunkin' Donuts Inc. v. NJS, Inc., 889 F. Supp. 1074 (N.D. Ill. 1995); Dunkin' Donuts Inc. v. Guang Chyl Liu, 1999 U.S. Dist. Lexis 71617 (E.D. Pa., Nov. 16, 1999); Dunkin' Donuts Inc. v. Dowco, Inc., 1998 U.S. Dist. LEXIS 4526 (N.D.N.Y., March 31, 1998); Dunkin' Donuts Inc. v. Benita Corp., 1998 U.S. Dist. LEXIS 1716 (N.D. Ill. Feb. 10, 1998); Dunkin' Donuts Inc. v. Taseski, Bus. Franchise Guide (CCH) ¶ 11, 375 (E.D. Mich. Feb. 5, 1998); Dunkin' Donuts Inc. v. Chetminal, Inc., Bus. Franchise Guide (CCH) ¶ 11, 290 (S.D. Fla. Oct. 30, 1997; Dunkin' Donuts Inc. v. Panagakos, Bus. Franchise Guide (CCH) ¶ 11,174 (D. Mass. May 13, 1997); Dunkin' Donuts Inc. v. Mercantile Ventures, Inc., Bus. Franchise Guide (CCH) ¶ 10, 521, 1994 U.S. Dist. LEXIS 19753 (W.D. Tex. Aug 11, 1994); Fritz v. Honda Motor Co., 818 F.2d 924 (D.C. Cir. 1987). ***PRACTICE AREAS:*** Civil Litigation; Franchise Law. ***Email:*** rlz@saslaw.com

ROBERT L. DUSTON, born Detroit, Michigan, November 25, 1960; admitted to bar, 1984, Virginia; 1985, District of Columbia; U.S. Supreme Court, U.S. Court of Appeals for the District of Columbia Circuit, U.S. Court of Appeals, Third, Fourth, Sixth, Ninth and Eleventh Circuits, U.S. District Court for the District of Columbia, U.S. District Court, Eastern and Western Districts of Virginia and U.S. District Court, Northern District of New York. *Education:* George Mason University (B.A., with distinction, 1981); University of Virginia (J.D., 1984). Co-Author: *IMRA's Family & Medical Leave Act Compliance Guide,* IMRA, 1993; *ADA Audit, Transition Plan and Policy Statement for Higher Education,* ACCT and ACCA, 1992; *ADA Compliance Manual for Higher Education,* CUPA, 1992; *ADA Compliance Manual for Mass Retailers,* IMRA, 1992; *Workplace Privacy, Second Edition,* BNA, 1989; "*Without Just Cause:* An Employer's Practical and Legal Guide on Wrongful Discharge," BNA, 1988; "*Thieves at Work:* An Employer's Guide to Combating Workplace Dishonesty," BNA, 1988; "*Gilmer v. Interstate Johnson Lane,*" The Labor Lawyer, 1992; "RICO and Employment Law," *The Labor Lawyer,* 1987. Law Clerk to the Honorable Jackson L. Kiser, United States District Judge for the Western District of Virginia, 1984-1985. *Member:* The District of Columbia Bar; Virginia State Bar; Virginia and American Bar Associations. ***REPORTED CASES:*** Davis v. Target Stores Div. of Dayton Hudson Corp. 87 F. Supp.2d 492 (D. Md. 2000); Dowd v. ILA, 138 LRRM 2453 (1991), aff'd., 975 F.2d 779 (11th Cir. 1992); Jevic v. The Coca-Cola Bottling Company of New York, Inc., 118 Lab. Cas. P 56,591, 5 IER Cas. 765 (D.N.J. 1990); Anderson v. The Coca-Cola Bottling Company of New York, Inc., 772 F. Supp. 77 (D. Conn. 1991); LaBeach v. Nestle Foods Corp., 658 F. Supp. 676 (S.D.N.Y. 1987). ***PRACTICE AREAS:*** Management Labor Law; Employment Law; Employee Benefits Law; Civil Rights Law; School Law. ***Email:*** rld@saslaw.com

(This Listing Continued)

LEON B. TARANTO, born Atlanta, Georgia, March 29, 1951; admitted to bar, 1976, Georgia and U.S. District Court, Northern District of Georgia; 1978, U.S. Court of Appeals, Fifth Circuit; 1980, District of Columbia and U.S. Supreme Court; 1985, U.S. Court of Appeals, First Circuit; 1996, U.S. Court of Appeals, Sixth Circuit; 1997, U.S. District Court, District of Maryland. *Education:* Tulane University (B.A., with honors, 1973); Emory University (J.D., 1976). Recipient, S. Walter Stern Memorial Medal for Best Essay on American Government. Member, Editorial Board, Emory Law Journal, 1975-1976. National Mock Trial Competition, Southern Region. Author: "The Discretionary Function Exception to the Federal Tort Claims Act-An Overview," Federal Tort Claims Act Seminar, 1990, Office of Legal Education, U.S. Department of Justice, 1990; "Litigating Tort Claims Against The Federal Government," Trial Evidence, Civil Practice and Effective Litigation Technique In States and Federal Courts, pp. 695-758, American Law Institute - American Bar Association, 1990; "The Discretionary Function Exception: Part IV - A Torts Branch Monograph, U.S. Department of Justice, 1990; "The Discretionary Function Exception: Part III - A Torts Branch Monograph," U.S. Department of Justice, 1989; "Alternative Exclusive Remedies," Federal Torts Claims Act Seminar, 1989, Office of Legal Education, U.S. Department of Justice, 1989; "The Discretionary Function Exception: Part I, A Torts Branch Monograph," U.S. Department of Justice, 1988; "The Sum Certain Requirement and The Ad Damnum Limitation - A Torts Branch Monograph," U.S. Department of Justice, 1985. Lecturer and Rotating Instructor, Attorney General's Advocacy Institute and Legal Education Institute of U.S. Dept. of Justice's Office of Legal Education, 1985-1991. Member of Faculty, American Law Institute - American Bar Association Course of Study on Trial Evidence, Civil Practice, and Effective Litigation Techniques in Federal and State Court, 1990. Trial Attorney, Torts Branch, Civil Division, U.S. Department of Justice, 1977-1983, 1992-1994. Special Attorney to the U.S. Attorney General, 1992-1994. ***REPORTED CASES:*** Prescott v. United States, 858 F. Supp. 1461 (D. Nev. 1994); Chernock v. United States, 718 F. Supp. 900 (N.D. Fla. 1989); Kitchen v. United States, 741 F. Supp. 182 (D. Alas. 1989); Merricks v. Henderson, 1989 WL 15851 (D. D.C. 1989); Williams v. United States, 665 F. Supp. 1466 (D. Ore. 1987); Hammond v. United States, 786 F.2d 8 (1st Cir. 1986); Canavan v. Washington Chemical Sales of California, 630 F. Supp. 1189 (S.D. Fla. 1986); In re Consol, United States Atmospheric Testing Litig., 616 F. Supp. 759 (N.D. Cal. 1985), aff'd, 820 F.2d 982 (9th Cir. 1987), cert. denied, sub nom., Konizeski v. United States, 485 U.S. 905, 108 S.Ct. 1076 (1988); In re Agent Orange Product Liab. Litig., 603 F. Supp. 239 (S.D. N.Y. 1985), aff'd, 818 F. 2d 194 (2d Cir. 1987); In re Swine Flu Immunization Products Liability Litig., 89 F.R.D. 695 (D. D.C., 1981); Ducharme v. Merrill-National Labs., 574 F.2d 1307 (8th Cir.,), cert. denied, 439 U.S. 1002 (1978). ***PRACTICE AREAS:*** Radiation; Toxic Tort; Environmental Contamination; Workers Compensation Litigation. ***Email:*** lbt@saslaw.com

MARK I. GRUHIN, born New York, N.Y., August 15, 1956; admitted to bar, 1981, District of Columbia; U.S. District Court for the District of Columbia. *Education:* Rutgers College, Rutgers University (B.A., with honors, 1978) Phi Beta Kappa; Washington College of Law, American University (J.D., magna cum laude, 1981). Member, Washington College of Law Honor Society. Member, American University Law Review, 1980-1981. Author: "Jerusalem: Legal and Political Dimensions in a Search for Peace," Case Western Reserve Journal of International Law, Middle East Symposium, Winter, 1980. Member: Northern Virginia Technology Council; High Technology Council of Maryland; Advisory Board, Metro Washington Chapter, The Entrepreneurship Institute. Recognized as a Top Ten Internet Lawyer in *Inside the Minds, Internet Lawyers,* ISBN 1587620065. *Member:* The District of Columbia Bar; New Jersey State Bar Association. ***PRACTICE AREAS:*** Business Law; Transactions; High Technology; Biotechnology; Venture Capital; Real Estate. ***Email:*** mig@saslaw.com

J. ANTHONY SMITH, born Poughkeepsie, New York, September 10, 1942; admitted to bar, 1971, Alaska, District of Columbia and U.S. Court of Appeals, 9th Circuit; 1975, U.S. Supreme Court. *Education:* Cornell University (B.S., 1964; J.D., 1971). Commissioner of Commerce and Economic Development for Alaska, , 1986-1988. Chairman: Board of Municipal Bond Bank, 1989-1991; Industrial Development and Export Authority, 1986-1988; Alaska Housing Finance Corporation, 1986-1988; Alaska Center for International Business, 1987-1991. Professor, Criminal Justice, University of Alaska, 1977-1979. Member: The Board of Directors of the Center for National Policy; Trade Policy Group, Inter-American Dialogue. Chair of the Board of International Advisors Zamorano University, Honduras, Central America. *Member:* Anchorage Bar Association; Bar Association of the District of Columbia; The Association of Trial Lawyers of America (Member, Admiralty Section). (Also Of Counsel, Baker, Brattain & Huguelet, A Professional Corporation, Anchorage, Alaska). ***PRACTICE AREAS:*** International Business Law; Public Policy; Natural Resources; Municipal; Civil Litigation; Trade; Administrative. ***Email:*** jas@saslaw.com

HENRY A. PLATT, born New York, N.Y., June 21, 1964; admitted to bar, 1989, California; 1990, District of Columbia; U.S. Court of Appeals, Second, Third, Fourth, Ninth, Eleventh and District of Columbia Circuits; U.S. District Court, District of Columbia; U.S. District Court, District of Maryland; U.S. District Court, Northern, Central and Eastern Districts of California. *Education:*

(This Listing Continued)

Cornell University (B.A., 1986); University of California at Los Angeles (J.D., 1989). Editor, UCLA Law Review, 1988-1989. Member, Federal Communications Law Journal. *Member:* The District of Columbia Bar; State Bar of California (Member, Sections of: Labor and Employment Law; Litigation); Society for Human Resource Management. ***REPORTED CASES:*** National Elec. Contractors Ass'n v. Kansas Chapter, Nat'l Elec. Contractors Ass'n, 46 F. Supp. 2d 1174 (D. Kan., 1999), aff'd, 203 F.3d 835 (10th Cir., 2000); Cino v. Sikorsky Aircraft Corp., 182 F.3d 898 (2nd Cir., 1999); Yurevich v. Sikorsky Aircraft Corp., 51 F. Supp. 2d 144 (D. Conn., 1999); Farkas v. Rumore, 101 F.3d 20 (2d Cir. 1996); Riesbeck Food Mkts. v. NLRB, 91 F.3d 132 (4th Cir. 1996); Phoenix Elec. Co. v. National Elec. Contractors Ass'n. 81 F.3d 858 (9th Cir. 1996); Coca-Cola Bottling Co. of New York, Inc., 39 F.3d 408 (2d Cir. 1994); Almonte v. Coca-Cola Bottling Co. of New York, Inc., 959 F.Supp. 569 (D. Conn. 1997); Regan v. Coca-Cola Bottling Co. of New York Inc., 149 L.R.R.M. (BNA) 4221 (S.D.N.Y. 1995), aff'd., 89 F.3d 826 (2d Cir. 1996); Tigard Elec., Inc. v. National Elec. Contractors Ass'n, 790 F. Supp. 1498 (D. Or. 1992); Anderson v. The Coca-Cola Bottling Co. of New York, Inc., 772 F. Supp. 77 (D. Conn. 1991); Jevic v. The Coca-Cola Bottling Company of New York, Inc., 5 I.E.R. Cases (BNA) 765 (D.N.J. 1990). ***PRACTICE AREAS:*** Management Labor Law; Employment Law. ***Email:*** hap@saslaw.com

LYNN K. McKAY, born Bedford, Pennsylvania, April 17, 1966; admitted to bar, 1991, Pennsylvania; 1993, District of Columbia. *Education:* College of William and Mary (B.A., 1988); Indiana University (J.D., cum laude, 1991). *Member:* Pennsylvania Bar Association; The District of Columbia Bar. ***PRACTICE AREAS:*** Radiation Litigation; Oilfield NORM Defense; Civil Litigation. ***Email:*** lkm@saslaw.com

MICHAEL C. WHITE, born San Francisco, California, April 22, 1944; admitted to bar, 1986, Maryland; 2000, District of Columbia. *Education:* George Mason University (B.S., 1971); University of Maryland (M.S., 1976; Ph.D., 1979); Catholic University of America (J.D., 1985). *Member:* Bar Association of the District of Columbia; Maryland State Bar Association. ***PRACTICE AREAS:*** Environmental Law; Radiation Litigation. ***Email:*** mcw@saslaw.com

ANESSA ABRAMS, born New York, N.Y., April 28, 1970; admitted to bar, 1995, Maryland; 1996, District of Columbia and U.S. District Court, District of Maryland; 1997, U.S. District Court for the District of Columbia; 1999, U.S. Court of Appeals for the Tenth and Fourth Circuits. *Education:* University of California, San Diego (B.A., magna cum laude, 1992); George Washington University (J.D., with honors, 1995). Phi Beta Kappa. Author: "The First Lady: Federal Employee or Citizen Representative under FACA?" 62 George Washington Law Review 855, 1994. ***REPORTED CASES:*** Yurevich v. Sikorsky Aircraft Div., 51 F. Supp. 2d 144 (D. Conn., 1999); Cino v. Sikorsky Aircraft, 42 F. Supp. 2d 147 (D. Conn., 1998); Cunliffe v. Sikorsky Aircraft Corp., 9 F. Supp. 2d 125 (D. Conn., 1998). ***PRACTICE AREAS:*** Management Labor and Employment. ***Email:*** aa@saslaw.com

DAVID WORTHEN, born Ithaca, New York, April 2, 1963; admitted to bar, 1988, Connecticut; 1994, District of Columbia. *Education:* Syracuse University (B.A., 1985; J.D., cum laude, 1988). Justinian Honor Society. Author: "Asbestos Abatement (The Insurance Crisis): The Problem is Up in the Ambient Air," 38 Syracuse L. Rev. 1343, 1987. ***REPORTED CASES:*** Keating v. Baskin-Robbins USA, Inc., 2001 WL 407017 (E.D.N.C., March 27, 2001); Dunkin' Donuts Inc. v. Donuts, Inc., 2000 U.S. Dist. LEXIS 17927 (N.D. Ill., Dec. 6, 2000); Dunkin' Donuts Inc. v. Alhireh Donuts, Inc., 96 F. Supp. 2d 146 (N.D.N.Y., 2000); Dunkin' Donuts Inc. v. Priya Enter., Inc., 89 F. Supp. 2d 319 (E.D.N.Y., 2000); Yankee Enters., Inc. v. Dunkin' Donuts Inc., 1998 U.S. App. LEXIS 23330 (5th Cir., July 8, 1997), cert. denied, 522 U.S. 1076 (1998); Dunkin' Donuts Inc. v. Benita Corp., 1998 U.S. Dist. LEXIS 1716 (N.D. Ill., Feb. 10, 1998); Dunkin' Donuts Inc. v. Chetminal, Inc., Bus. Franchise Guide (CCH) ¶11,174 (D. Mass., May 13, 1997). ***PRACTICE AREAS:*** Franchise Law; Civil Litigation. ***Email:*** dew@saslaw.com

KATHERINE BREWER, born New York, N.Y., December 7, 1955; admitted to bar, 1983, District of Columbia; 1993, Pennsylvania. *Education:* Yale University (B.A., cum laude, 1978); Duke University (J.D., 1983). Attorney-Advisor, National Labor Relations Board, 1983-1987. *Member:* The District of Columbia; American Bar Association. ***REPORTED CASES:*** T & G Construction Co. v. Sheet Metal Workers' Intern. Ass'n, Local 100, 791 F. Supp. 127 (D. Md. 1992); Grant v. Coca-Cola Bottling Co. of New York, 780 F. Supp. 246 (D. N.J. 1991); Gray v. Citizens Bank of Washington, 602 A.2d 1096 (D.C. App. 1992), rehearing denied, 609 A.2d 1143 (D.C. App. 1992). ***PRACTICE AREAS:*** Labor and Employment Law; Litigation.

CARLOS M. PAZ-SOLDAN, born Lima, Peru, May 14, 1967; admitted to bar, 1994, Pennsylvania; 1996, District of Columbia. *Education:* Occidental College (B.A., 1989); George Washington University (J.D., 1993). Listed in Who's Who Among College and Universities, 1989. Author: "Peru—Restructuring for Growth," Chapter 11 on Legal Environment, Euromoney Publications, 1994. Member, OAS Observer Delegation to Presidential Elections in

(This Listing Continued)

Haiti, 1995 and the Dominican Republic, 1996. International Supervisor, OSCE Delegation to Municipal Elections in Bosnia-Herzegovina, 1997. ***LANGUAGES:*** Spanish, French and Portuguese. ***PRACTICE AREAS:*** Legislative Practice; Natural Resources; Municipal Law. ***Email:*** cps@saslaw.com

LINDA G. HILL, born Plainfield, New Jersey, November 11, 1965; admitted to bar, 1993, Virginia; 1994, District of Columbia. *Education:* Rutgers University (B.S./B.A., with high honors, 1988); University of Virginia (J.D., 1993). Phi Beta Kappa. Member, Virginia Journal of Social Policy and the Law. ***PRACTICE AREAS:*** Employment Law; Management Labor Law. ***Email:*** lgh@saslaw.com

ANNEMARIE BRENNAN RICE, born Atlantic City, New Jersey, July 13, 1962; admitted to bar, 1997, Georgia and U.S. District Court, Northern District of Georgia; 1999, District of Columbia. *Education:* University of Rhode Island (B.A., 1984); Vermont Law School (J.D., 1996). Moot Court Advisory Board, 1995-1996. Member, 1994-1996 and Notes Editor, 1995-1996, Vermont Law Review. Author: Note, "Is All Privacy Created Equal?" 20 Vt. L. Rev. 815, 1996. *Member:* State Bar of Georgia. ***PRACTICE AREAS:*** Business Law; Business Transactions; Commercial Litigation. ***Email:*** ab@saslaw.com

ROLAND B. NINOMIYA, born Washington, D.C., December 11, 1962; admitted to bar, 1997, Virginia (Not admitted in District of Columbia). *Education:* Middlebury College (B.A., cum laude, 1985); George Mason University School of Law (J.D., with high honors, 1997). Author: "Under the Westfall Act, a Plaintiff Can Obtain Judicial Review of the Attorney General's Certification that the Defendant-Employee was Acting within the Scope of Her Employment," Gutierrez de Martines v. Lamagno, 4 Geo. Marshall L. Rev., 485, 1996. ***PRACTICE AREAS:*** Litigation; Franchise Law. ***Email:*** rbn@saslaw.com

STEPHEN J. VAUGHAN, born Minneapolis, Minnesota, February 6, 1973; admitted to bar, 1998, Maryland; 1999 District of Columbia, U.S. District Court for the District of Columbia and U.S. District Court, District of Maryland; 2000, U.S. Court of Appeals, District of Columbia Circuit. *Education:* The Ohio University (B.S., summa cum laude, 1995); The Catholic University of America (J.D., 1998). Member, Catholic University Law Review. Member, Columbus School of Law's National Trial Team. Member, Thurgood Marshall Inn of Court, 1999—. *Member:* Maryland State Bar Association; Bar Association of the District of Columbia. ***PRACTICE AREAS:*** Commercial Litigation; Franchise Law; Corporate Transactions. ***Email:*** sjv@saslaw.com

ELIZABETH THOMAS, born Miami, Florida, June 16, 1972; admitted to bar, 1998, Florida (Not admitted in District of Columbia). *Education:* Cornell University (B.A., 1994); Boalt Hall School of Law, University of California, Berkeley (J.D., 1998). Recipient, Prosser Award in Contracts and Constitutional Law. Assistant State Attorney, Eleventh Judicial District, Dade County, Florida, 1998-2000. ***PRACTICE AREAS:*** Labor and Employment Litigation. ***Email:*** eat@saslaw.com

MATTHEW I. VAN HORN, born Fairfax, Virginia, December 12, 1971; admitted to bar, 1999, North Carolina and Oklahoma; 2001, District of Columbia. *Education:* Hampden-Sydney College (B.A., 1994); University of Tulsa (J.D., 1998; M.B.A., 1998). Author Relations Editor, Tulsa Comparative and International Law Journal. ***PRACTICE AREAS:*** Civil Litigation; Commercial Litigation; Franchise Law. ***Email:*** mvh@saslaw.com

CRAIG M. CIBAK, born Pittsburgh, Pennsylvania, September 4, 1965; admitted to bar, 1996, Virginia; 1998, District of Columbia. *Education:* Shepherd College (B.S., cum laude, 1987); George Washington University (J.D., with honors, 1996). Member, The George Washington University Law Review, 1994-1996. Law Clerk to the Hon. Brook Hedge, Associate Judge, Superior Court of the District of Columbia, 1996-1997. *Member:* The District of Columbia Bar; Virginia State Bar. ***PRACTICE AREAS:*** Commercial Litigation. ***Email:*** cmc@saslaw.com

REBECCA A. HIRSELJ, born Cleveland, Ohio, February 7, 1974; admitted to bar, 1999, Maryland; 2000, Illinois and Missouri (Not admitted in District of Columbia). *Education:* University of Dayton (B.A., 1995); Washington University (J.D., 1999). Phi Alpha Delta; Mu Alpha Omega; Phi Sigma Tau; Golden Key. Member, Mock Trial Competition Team. *Member:* East St. Louis, St. Clair County, Maryland State and Illinois State Bar Associations. ***PRACTICE AREAS:*** Commercial Litigation; Franchise Law. ***Email:*** rah@saslaw.com

GREGORY ZINI, born Buffalo, New York, September 7, 1971; admitted to bar, 1998, New York (Not admitted in District of Columbia). *Education:* State University of New York at Buffalo (B.A., 1993); University of Tulsa (J.D., with honors, 1997). Phi Delta Phi (Historian, 1995-1996). Author: Comment, "The Arbitration Clause Controversy in Oklahoma," 32 Tulsa L.J. 163. *Member:* American Bar Association (Member, Litigation Section). ***PRACTICE AREAS:*** Commercial Litigation; Franchise Law. ***Email:*** gz@saslaw.com

MICHAEL C. GRIFFIN, born Birmingham, Alabama, February 12, 1969; admitted to bar, 2000, Virginia; 2001, District of Columbia. *Education:* The Citadel (B.A., 1991); George Washington University Law Center (J.D., 2000). [Capt., U.S.M.C., 1991-1997; U.S.M.C.R., 1997-1999]. ***PRACTICE AREAS:*** Labor and Employment. ***Email:*** mg@saslaw.com

(This Listing Continued)

SCHMELTZER, APTAKER & SHEPARD, P.C., Washington—Continued

NADÁ MELISSA MOEINY, born Long Beach, California, June 18, 1975; admitted to bar, 2000, Colorado (Not admitted in District of Columbia). *Education:* University of California, Berkeley (B.A., 1997); University of Colorado at Boulder (J.D., 2000). Phi Beta Kappa. Phi Alpha Delta. *Member:* American Bar Association (Member, Labor and Employment Law Section, 2001). ***PRACTICE AREAS:*** Labor and Employment. ***Email:*** nmm@saslaw.com

CHRISTOPHER M. LOVELAND, born Baltimore, Maryland, October 28, 1974; admitted to bar, 2000, Maryland; 2001, District of Columbia. *Education:* LaSalle University (B.A., summa cum laude, 1997); Boston University (J.D., 2000). Participant: Edward C. Sone Moot Court; Homer Albers Prize Moot Court. Edward F. Hennessey Scholar, Boston University. Editor-in-Chief, Legislative Services. ***PRACTICE AREAS:*** Commercial Litigation; Franchise Law; Election and Campaign Finance. ***Email:*** cml@saslaw.com

CHRISTOPHER J. WALLACE, born Newport, Rhode Island, September 3, 1970; admitted to bar, 1998, New York and U.S. District Court, Southern and Eastern Districts of New York (Not admitted in District of Columbia). *Education:* Colgate University (B.A., 1992); Pace University School of Law (J.D., 1997). Articles Editor, Pace Law Review, 1996-1997. ***PRACTICE AREAS:*** Litigation. ***Email:*** cjw@saslaw.com

TIMOTHY H. GOODMAN, born January 14, 1970; admitted to bar, 1999, Ohio, U.S. District Court, Northern District of Ohio and U.S. Court of Appeals, Sixth Circuit; 2000, District of Columbia. *Education:* School of Foreign Service, Georgetown University (B.S., Foreign Service, 1992); Case Western Reserve University (J.D., cum laude, 1999). Pi Sigma Alpha National Honor Society in Political Science. Executive Articles Editor, Case Western Reserve Journal of International Law. Author: "Leaving the Corsair's Name to Other Times: How to Enforce the Law of Sea Piracy in the 21st Century through Regional International Agreements," 31 Case Western Reserve Journal of International Law 139, Winter, 1999. *Member:* American Bar Association. [Lieutenant, U.S. Navy, 1992-1996]. ***PRACTICE AREAS:*** Litigation; Civil Litigation; Business Law; Franchise Law. ***Email:*** THG@saslaw.com

COUNSEL

JOHN A. McGUINN, born Hartford, Connecticut, 1934; admitted to bar, 1959, Connecticut; 1960, District of Columbia. *Education:* College of the Holy Cross (A.B., 1956); Georgetown University (J.D., 1959; LL.M., 1961). Phi Alpha Delta. Editor-in-Chief, Georgetown Law Journal, 1958-1959. Law Clerk to Circuit Judge Charles Fahy, 1959-1960. Adjunct Professor of Law, Georgetown University Law Center, 1964-1972. *Member:* The District of Columbia Bar; American Bar Association. ***REPORTED CASES:*** Detroit Edison Co. v. NLRB, 440 U.S. 301 (1979). ***PRACTICE AREAS:*** Management Labor Law; Employment Law; Employee Benefits Law. ***Email:*** jam@saslaw.com

EDWARD SCHMELTZER, born New York, N.Y., August 22, 1923; admitted to bar, 1954, District of Columbia; 1957, U.S. Supreme Court. *Education:* Hunter College (B.A., 1950); Columbia University (M.A., 1951); George Washington University (J.D., 1954). Recipient, Federal Maritime Commission Distinguished Service Award, 1969. Economist, PHA, 1951-1953. Trial Attorney, Federal Maritime Board, Maritime Administration, 1955-1960. Director, Bureau of Domestic Regulation, 1961-1966 and Managing Director, 1966-1969, Federal Maritime Commission. Of Counsel, 1969-1970 and Partner, 1970-1976, Morgan Lewis & Bockius. U.S. Representative: 12th Diplomatic Conference on International Maritime Law, Brussels, 1967; 13th Diplomatic Conference on International Maritime Law, Brussels, 1968. *Member:* The District of Columbia Bar; Federal Bar Association; Maritime Administrative Bar Association (President, 1971-1973). [With USAF, 1943-1946]. ***PRACTICE AREAS:*** Maritime Law; Aviation Law.

EDWARD APTAKER, born Boston, Massachusetts, August 29, 1922; admitted to bar, 1948, Massachusetts; 1957, U.S. Supreme Court; 1970, District of Columbia. *Education:* Harvard University (B.A., 1943; LL.B., 1948). Attorney, Interstate Commerce Commission, 1949-1951. Staff Attorney, 1951-1958; Assistant General Counsel, 1958-1961; Chief, Office of Government Aid, 1961-1969; Assistant Administrator for Maritime Aids, 1969-1970; Maritime Administration. Of Counsel, 1970-1971 and Partner, 1971-1976, Morgan, Lewis & Bockius. *Member:* The District of Columbia Bar; Massachusetts Bar Association; Maritime Administrative Bar Association. [Col., USAFR, Ret.]. ***PRACTICE AREAS:*** Maritime Law; Administrative Law; Equipment Financing Law.

STEPHEN HORN, born New York, N.Y., September 12, 1946; admitted to bar, 1974, District of Columbia; 1982, Maryland. *Education:* Rutgers University (B.S., 1968); Seton Hall University (J.D., cum laude, 1973). Editor-in-Chief, Seton Hall University Law Review, 1972-1973. Author: "Restricting the Use of General Aptitude Tests as Employment Criteria," Vol. 3, p. 143, Seton Hall Law Review, 1971; "Should Lack of Diligence in Diagnosis Resulting in Loss of Chance to Live Be a Compensable Injury?" Vol. 3, p. 505, Seton Hall Law Review, 1972. Trial Attorney, U.S. Department of Justice, Civil Rights Division, 1973-1978. *Member:* The District of Columbia Bar; American Bar Association (Chairman, RICO Committee, 1981-1984; Member, Litigation Section). [1st Lt., U.S. Army, Infantry, 1968-1970]. (Senior Vice President and General Counsel, Allied Domecq, QSR). ***PRACTICE AREAS:*** Civil Litigation; Franchise Law.

DENISE BONN, born New York, N.Y., October 5, 1952; admitted to bar, 1977, Pennsylvania; 1981, District of Columbia. *Education:* State University of New York at Buffalo (B.A., summa cum laude, 1974); New York University (J.D., 1977). *Member:* The District of Columbia Bar; Women's Bar Association of District of Columbia. ***PRACTICE AREAS:*** Health Care Law. ***Email:*** dcb@saslaw.com

DANIEL P. BEN-ZVI, born Newark, New Jersey, November 25, 1956; admitted to bar, 1981, Connecticut; 1983, New Jersey; 1983, District of Columbia; 1984, New York; 1990, California. *Education:* Hebrew University, Jerusalem, Israel; Rutgers University (B.A., 1978); Yeshiva University (J.D., 1981). Omicron Delta Epsilon. Mediator and Arbitrator, Supreme Court of California. *Member:* State Bar of California; District of Columbia Bar; New York State, New Jersey State, Connecticut and American Bar Associations. (Resident, Los Angeles, California Office).

MARTIN JAY GAYNES, born New York, N.Y., January 6, 1933; admitted to bar, 1960, New York and District of Columbia. *Education:* University of Michigan (A.B., 1954); New York University (LL.B., 1959). Articles and Survey Editor, New York University Law Review, 1958-1959. John Norton Pomeroy Scholar. Editor, Civil Money Penalties Reporter, 1986. Co-Author, "Mass Communications Law," West Publishing Co., 1986. Adjunct Professor, Temple University Law School, 1976-1978. *Member:* The District of Columbia Bar; American Society of Hospital Attorneys; National Health Lawyers Association; Federal Communications Bar Association. ***PRACTICE AREAS:*** Health Care Law. ***Email:*** mjg@saslaw.com

LARRY H. MITCHELL, born New York, N.Y., October 14, 1949; admitted to bar, 1974, Maryland; 1975, District of Columbia. *Education:* Lafayette College (A.B., 1971); Georgetown University (J.D., 1974). Phi Alpha Theta. Editor, American Criminal Law Review, 1972-1974. Author, "Willfulness in Federal Income Tax Evasion: *United States v. Bishop* and The Proposed Federal Criminal Code," 12 American Criminal Law Review 381, 1974. Attorney, Office of the General Counsel, U.S. General Accounting Office, 1974-1975. *Member:* The District of Columbia Bar; Maryland State and American Bar Associations; Association of Transportation Practitioners. ***PRACTICE AREAS:*** Civil Litigation; Franchise Litigation. ***Email:*** lhm@saslaw.com

JEFFREY L. KARLIN, born Los Angeles, California, July 29, 1959; admitted to bar, 1989, California; 1992, U.S. Court of Appeals, Ninth Circuit; 1998, District of Columbia and U.S. Court of Federal Claims; 2000, U.S. District Court for the District of Columbia; 2001, U.S. Court of Appeals, District of Columbia Circuit. *Education:* University of California, Santa Barbara (B.A., cum laude, 1984); University of Maryland (M.A., History, 1986); Washington College of Law, American University (J.D., 1989). President, Moot Court Board, 1988-1989. Law Clerk to the Hon. Alvin I. Krenzler, United States District Court for the Northern District of Ohio, 1989-1990. Trial Attorney, Civil Division, Torts Branch, U.S. Department of Justice, 1990-1997, 1998-2000. Barrister, Charles Fahy American Inn of Court. *Member:* State Bar of California; Bar Association of the District of Columbia. ***REPORTED CASES:*** Hong Wu v. Dunkin' Donuts Inc., 2001 U.S. App. LEXIS 2544 (2nd Cir., Feb. 20, 2001); Kaplan v. United States, 1998, U.S. App. LEXIS 26209 (9th Cir., Oct. 14, 1998); Doe v. United States, 83 F. Supp. 2d 833 (S.D. Tex., 2000); Haney v. Castle Meadows, 868 F. Supp. 1233 (D. Colo., 1994); Schneider v. United States, 1993 U.S. Dist. LEXIS 20139 (D. Minn., 1993); Fahl v. United Staes, Dep't of Interior, 792 F. Supp. 80 (D. Ariz., 1992). ***PRACTICE AREAS:*** Franchise Law; Commercial Litigation. ***Email:*** jlk@saslaw.com

ERIC L. YAFFE, born Boston, Massachusetts, February 14, 1960; admitted to bar, 1986, Massachusetts; 1993, District of Columbia. *Education:* Oberlin College (B.A., 1981); University of Chicago (J.D., 1986). Assistant U.S. Attorney, District of Columbia. Trial Attorney, Public Integrity Section, 1996-2000 and Deputy, Chief, Campaign Financing Task Force, 1999-2000, U.S. Department of Justice. *Member:* District of Columbia Bar; American Bar Association. ***REPORTED CASES:*** United States v. Hsia, 176 F.3d 517 (D.C. Cir., 1999); United States v. Williams, 980 F.2d 1463 (D.C. Cir., 1992); United States v. Ramos, 960 F.2d 1065 (D.C. Cir., 1992); Dunkin' Donuts Inc. v. Gav-Stra Donuts, Inc., 2001 U.S. Dist. LEXIS 4750 (D. Mass., April 10, 2001); Morris v. United States, 922 A.2d 1116 (D.C. Cir., 1993); Barvenik v. Board of Aldermen, 33 Mass. App. Ct. 129 (1992). ***PRACTICE AREAS:*** Civil Litigation; White Collar Criminal Defense; Franchise Law; Election and Campaign Finance Law. ***Email:*** ely@saslaw.com

TÈRESE M. CONNERTON, born Washington, D.C., December 2, 1951; admitted to bar, 1980, Ohio; 1981, District of Columbia; 1985, U.S. District Court, District of Maryland; 1989, U.S. Court of Appeals, Seventh Circuit; 1991, U.S. District Court for the District of Columbia; 1992, U.S. Supreme Court; 1995, U.S. Court of Appeals for the Federal Circuit. *Education:* Ohio State University (B.A., 1974); Capital University of Law (J.D., 1980); George-

(This Listing Continued)

town University School of Law (LL.M., Tax, 1990). Member, 1987— and President, 1993, Worldwide Employee Benefits Network (WEB). *Member:* District of Columbia Bar (Member, Sections on: Tax; Labor and Litigation); Ohio State and American (Member, Sections on: Litigation; Labor and Employment Law; Co-Chairman: Employee Benefits Committee, 1993-1996; Subcommittee on Criminal Law, 1988-1991; Subcommittee on Civil Practice and Procedure, 1991-1993; Senior Editor, Employee Benefits Law, BNA, 1996-1999). ***PRACTICE AREAS:*** Employee Benefits Law; Labor Law; Tax Exempt Entities. ***Email:*** tmc@saslaw.com

DAVID L. SMITH, born Bethlehem, Pennsylvania, March 22, 1960; admitted to bar, 1988, Massachusetts; 1998, District of Columbia. *Education:* Dickinson College (B.A., 1982); Boston University (J.D., 1987). Assistant U.S. Attorney, District of Columbia, 1991-2000. ***REPORTED CASES:*** Iceland Steamship v. Dep't of Army, 201 F.3d 451 (D.C.Cir 2000). ***PRACTICE AREAS:*** Franchise Law; Employment Litigation; White Collar Defense. ***Email:*** dls@saslaw.com

SCHNADER HARRISON SEGAL & LEWIS LLP

11TH FLOOR EAST
1300 I STREET, N.W.
WASHINGTON, D.C. 20005-3314
Telephone: 202-216-4200
Fax: 202-775-8741
URL: http://www.schnader.com

Philadelphia, Pennsylvania Office: Suite 3600, 1600 Market Street. Telephone: 215-751-2000. Fax: 215-751-2205.

Other Philadelphia, Pennsylvania Office: Suite 3800, 1735 Market Street, 19103-7598.

New York, N.Y. Office: 140 Broadway, Suite 3100. Telephone: 212-973-8000. Fax: 212-972-8798.

San Francisco, California Office: 601 California Street, 12th Floor. Telephone: 415-364-6700. Fax: 415-364-6785.

Harrisburg, Pennsylvania Office: Suite 700, 30 North Third Street. Telephone: 717-231-4000. Fax: 717-231-4012.

Norristown, Pennsylvania Office: Suite 901, One Montgomery Plaza. Telephone: 610-277-7700. Fax: 610-277-3211.

Pittsburgh, Pennsylvania Office: Suite 2700, Fifth Avenue Place, 120 Fifth Avenue. Telephone: 412-577-5200. Fax: 412-765-3858.

Canonsburg (Southpointe), Pennsylvania Office: Suite 200, Summit Corporate Center, Southpointe Commercial Park, 1001 Corporate Drive, 15317. Telephone: 724-873-2870. Fax: 724-743-2901.

Cherry Hill, New Jersey Office: Suite 200, Woodland Falls Corporate Park, 220 Lake Drive East. Telephone: 856-482-5222. Fax: 856-482-6980.

Atlanta, Georgia Office: Suite 2800, SunTrust Plaza, 303 Peachtree Street, N.E. Telephone: 404-215-8100. Fax: 404-223-5164.

Boston, Massachusetts: Schnader Harrison Goldstein & Manello, 265 Franklin Street. Telephone: 617-946-8000. Fax: 617-946-8100.

Administrative, Antitrust and Trade Regulation, Aviation and Aerospace, Appellate Practice, Business, Commercial Law, Constitutional Law, Contracts, Corporate Law, Government Contracts, Government, Health and Hospital Law, Intellectual Property, International Law, International Trade, Labor and Employment, Insurance, Litigation, Media Law, Mergers and Acquisitions, Personal Injury, Products Liability, Real Estate, Securities, Technology and Science.

FIRM PROFILE: Schnader Harrison Segal & Lewis LLP is a law firm with a national and international practice. Founded in 1935, the firm has grown to include approximately 350 attorneys in offices in Philadelphia, Pittsburgh, Harrisburg, Norristown and Washington, PA; New York, NY; Atlanta, GA; Cherry Hill, NJ; Washington, D.C.; San Francisco, CA and Boston, MA. Our common bond is a commitment to excellence and hard work, and a dedication to serving the firm's clients.

Our lawyers have been leaders in government and the profession. They have served in high government posts at the federal, state and local levels. Our lawyers have also held leadership positions in the bar, including President of the American Bar Association, President of the Pennsylvania Bar Association and Chancellors of the Philadelphia Bar Association. Our lawyers have taught in leading law schools and have written numerous legal treatises and articles. They have played a significant role in developing our nation's law, most notably in the 30-year development of the Uniform Commercial Code, now in effect across the nation, and in the development of the Uniform Probate Code. They hold leadership positions in national and local civic, cultural, political and charitable institutions, and have a reputation for outstanding pro bono service to the profession and the community.

(This Listing Continued)

Schnader Harrison's clients range from large, international corporations to individual entrepreneurs. They include companies based in the United States as well as those from other countries. We represent clients in many industries including transportation, manufacturing, communications, insurance, banking and finance, health care, computers, construction, as well as service organizations.

PARTNERS OF THE FIRM IN WASHINGTON, D.C.

ROBERT L. MAGIELNICKI, born 1947; admitted to bar, 1971, N.Y.; 1972, U.S. Court of Military Appeals; 1990, D.C. *Education:* Rutgers Univ. (A.B., with honors, 1967); Cornell Law School (J.D., with distinction, 1970). Phi Beta Kappa. Order of the Coif. Editor, Cornell Law Review, 1969-1970. *Member:* The District of Columbia Bar; New York State and American (Member: Antitrust Section; International Section) Bar Associations. ***PRACTICE AREAS:*** Antitrust Law; Commercial Law; Corporate Law; International Law; Litigation. ***Email:*** rmagielnicki@schnader.com

GREGGORY B. MENDENHALL, born 1945; admitted to bar, 1972, D.C. *Education:* Brigham Young Univ. (B.A., 1968); George Washington Univ. Law School (J.D., 1971). Lecturer, Financing Marine Assets and Operations, Euromoney Institute of Finance Law Program, 1995 and 1996. (Also at New York, N.Y. Office). ***PRACTICE AREAS:*** International Maritime; Marine Finance and Contracts; Corporate Law; Finance; Internet Law; Federal Legislative and Administrative. ***Email:*** gmendenhall@schnader.com

EDWARD F. SCHIFF, born 1944; admitted to bar, 1969, Va.; 1970, D.C.; 1993, Md. *Education:* Pennsylvania State Univ. (B.A., 1966); Washington & Lee Univ. (J.D., magna cum laude, 1969). Order of the Coif; Phi Alpha Delta. Editor-in-Chief, Washington & Lee Law Review, 1968-1969. Law Clerk to Judge John Minor Wisdom, U.S. Court of Appeals, Fifth Circuit, 1969-1970. *Member:* The District of Columbia Bar; Maryland State, Virginia State and American Bar Associations. ***PRACTICE AREAS:*** Corporate Transactions; Real Estate Finance; Debt Restructuring. ***Email:*** eschiff@schnader.com

COUNSEL TO THE FIRM IN WASHINGTON, D.C.

M. ROY GOLDBERG, born 1962; admitted to bar, 1987, Colo.; 1989, D.C.; 1999, Md. *Education:* Univ. of Kansas (B.A., 1984) Pi Sigma Alpha; Univ. of Colorado (J.D., 1987). Order of the Coif. Staff Editor, University of Colorado Law Review, 1986-1987. Law Clerk to Judge Carrigan, U.S. District Court, District of Colorado, 1987-1989. Author: "ABA Monograph Predatory Pricing," (Section 2) (1995); "When Unimportant is Interesting: The Negligible Import Exception to Cumulation in Antidumping and Countervailing Duty Investigations," 25 The George Washington Journal of International Law and Economics 721 (1992); "Responsible Export Controls or Nets to Catch the Wind? The Commerce Department's New U.S. Controls on Exports of Chemical Precursors, Equipment and Technical Data Intended to Prevent Development of Chemical and Biological Weapons," 22 California Western International Law Journal 193 (1991); "National Security Review of Foreign Investment in the United States: An Update on Exxon-Florio and the Final Regulations Which Implement In," 2 Florida Journal of International Law 191 (1991); "State Restrictions on Public Procurement," Manual on Foreign Investment (1994). *Member:* American Bar Association (Member: Sections on Antitrust and International; Antitrust Transportation and Predatory Pricing Monograph Committees). ***LANGUAGES:*** Dutch. ***PRACTICE AREAS:*** Civil Litigation; Administrative Law; Antitrust Law; Media Law; Aviation Law; Maritime Law; International Law. ***Email:*** rgoldber@shsl.com

JONATHAN M. STERN, born 1959; admitted to bar, 1987, Md.; 1988, D.C.; 1997, Va. *Education:* Embry-Riddle Aeronautical Univ. (B.S., 1981); American Univ. (J.D., magna cum laude, 1986). Author: "Flying on Instruments with Flight Simulator," Compute Books, 1987; "Microsoft Flight Simulator Handbook" MacMillan, 1995 (English, French and Dutch); "Taking the Wind From the Sails: Deflating Damage Experts," ABA Litigation Magazine, 1995; "Defending Damages in Death Actions," ABA Litigation Magazine, Summer 1997; "The Discovery Plan," ABA Litigation Magazine, Spring 1998. Instrument Flying Columnist, Microwings Magazine. *Member:* The District of Columbia Bar; American Bar Association (Member, Litigation Section, 1987; Editor, Aviation Litigation Quarterly); Aircraft Owners and Pilots Association. ***PRACTICE AREAS:*** Civil Litigation; Aviation Litigation; Insurance Coverage; Insurance Litigation. ***Email:*** jstern@schnader.com

RETIRED MEMBER OF THE FIRM IN WASHINGTON, D.C.

Paul G. Dembling

ASSOCIATES IN WASHINGTON, D.C.

BRYANT ROBINSON, III, born 1964; admitted to bar, 1991, D.C.; 1997, Pa. *Education:* Tufts Univ. (B.A., cum laude, 1987); Univ. of Virginia (J.D., 1990). Special Assistant within the Office of the Secretary of Education, 1994-1996. Associate Counsel to the Office of the Vice President, Feb.-July, 1996. ***PRACTICE AREAS:*** Corporate; Commercial Transactions; Real Estate Transactions. ***Email:*** brobinson@schnader.com

(This Listing Continued)

SCHNADER HARRISON SEGAL & LEWIS LLP, Washington—Continued

KI JUN SUNG, born 1967; admitted to bar, 1993, Va; 1999, D.C. *Education:* Cornell Univ. (B.A., magna cum laude, 1990); Univ. of Virginia (J.D., 1993). Director, Asian Pacific American Bar Association Educational Fund, 1997-1999; President, Asian American Bar Association of Virginia, 1998; District of Columbia Bar Election Board, 2000-2003. ***LANGUAGES:*** Korean. ***PRACTICE AREAS:*** Commercial Litigation; Products Liability; Construction Law; Real Estate. ***Email:*** ksung@schnader.com

STEVEN B. WEINBERG, born 1964; admitted to bar, 2000, California (Not admitted in District of Columbia). *Education:* Vanderbilt Univ. (B.A. in Political Science and History, 1986); Catholic Univ. of America, Columbus School of Law (J.D., 2000). Member: Commlaw Conspectus Journal; Journal of Communications Law. [With U.S. Marine Corps, 1986-1996]. ***PRACTICE AREAS:*** Litigation. ***Email:*** sweinberg@schnader.com

GORDON S. WOODWARD, born 1968; admitted to bar, 1995, Minn.; 1996, Md. and D.C.; 1998, Va. *Education:* Univ. of Minnesota (B.A., 1990); George Washington Univ. (J.D., with honors, 1995). Author: "Wrongful Death Claims amd the Federal Tort Claims Act: Avoiding the Pitfalls of Presentment." Published in the American Bar Association's Aviation Litigation Quarterly. *Member:* Maryland State, Virginia State and Minnesota State Bar Associations; District of Columbia Bar. ***PRACTICE AREAS:*** Civil Litigation; Products Liability; Aviation Law; Construction Law; Premises Liability; Personal Injury; Insurance Coverage; Insurance Defense Litigation. ***Email:*** gwoodward@schnader.com

(For biographical data of other attorneys of the Firm, see Professional Biographies at Atlanta, Georgia, Boston, Massachusetts, Cherry Hill, New Jersey, New York, New York, San Francisco, California, Canonsburg, Harrisburg, Norristown, Philadelphia and Pittsburgh, Pennsylvania)

SCHOCHOR, FEDERICO AND STATON, P.A.

Established in 1984

10 G STREET, N.E., SUITE 650
WASHINGTON, D.C. 20002
Telephone: 202-408-3300
Toll Free: 888-234-0001
URL: http://www.sfspa.com

Baltimore, Maryland Office: The Paulton, 1211 St. Paul Street, 21202. Telephone: 410-234-1000. Fax: 410-234-1010.

Medical Malpractice, General, Negligence, Products Liability, Personal Injury Law, Lead Paint Poisoning and Civil Trial.

FIRM PROFILE: The firm of Schochor, Federico and Staton, P.A. was established to fulfill the need for the highest quality of plaintiffs' representation in medical malpractice cases. Since its inception, the firm has concentrated on the investigation, preparation and trial of medical negligence cases, and is believed to hold the record for the highest recovery in a medical malpractice case in Maryland's history. Additionally, the firm created a Maryland precedent, establishing a right of recovery for patients wrongfully exposed to HIV by an AIDS infected surgeon. The firm has offices in Maryland and Washington, D.C., and has been involved in medical negligence cases in other jurisdictions including Pennsylvania, New Jersey, North Carolina and Georgia.

Due to the firm's depth of experience, its members have regularly been called upon to testify before the Maryland State Legislature in areas of medical negligence and tort reform, have appeared and lectured at various panel presentations, seminars and continuing legal education courses involving medical negligence and trial practice, and have appeared on radio and television programs involving medical negligence and tort reform.

JONATHAN SCHOCHOR, born Suffern, New York, September 9, 1946; admitted to bar, 1971, District of Columbia; 1972, U.S. District Court, District of Columbia, U.S. Court of Appeals, District of Columbia Circuit; 1974, Maryland; 1975, U.S. District Court, District of Maryland; 1976, U.S. Court of Appeals, Fourth Circuit; 1986, U.S. Supreme Court. *Education:* Pennsylvania State University (B.A., 1968); Washington College of Law of American University (J.D., 1971). Phi Alpha Delta. Associate Editor-in-Chief, American University Law Review, 1970-1971. Listed: "Bar Register of Preeminent Lawyers". Co-Author: "Structured Settlements in Maryland," Maryland Institute for Continuing Professional Education of Lawyers, Inc., 1989; "Structured Settlements in Maryland," Maryland Institute for Continuing Professional Education of Lawyers, Inc., revised edition, 1997. Faculty: Seminar on Structured Settlements in Maryland for Lawyers; "Medicine for Lawyers"; "Nine Day Intensive Trial Workshop"; "Depositions and Discovery," Maryland Institute for Continuing Professional Education of Lawyers, Inc. Invited Speaker, "How to Avoid Being Sued for Malpractice," John Hopkins University School of Medicine and

(This Listing Continued)

Johns Hopkins Hospital, 1998, 2000. Faculty, "Nuts and Bolts for Lawyers" and Invited Lecturer on evaluation of damages and settlements, course on civil litigation, Maryland Trial Lawyers Association, 1997, 2000. Invited Speaker, courses in forensic economics, health administration and philosophy of law and Invited Member of Panel, "College of Liberal Arts Prelaw Night and Preprofessional Career Information Session," Pennsylvania State University, 1998. Member, Circuit Court, Baltimore City, Task Force Civil Docket Management System. *Member:* The Bar Association of Baltimore City (Member: Legislative Committee, 1987; Committee on Tort Reform, 1987); The District of Columbia Bar; Maryland State (Member: Special Committee on Health Claims Arbitration, 1983; Member, Medico-Legal Committee, 1989-1990) and American Bar Associations; Bar Association of the District of Columbia; The Association of Trial Lawyers of America (State Delegate 1991, State Governor, 1992-1995); American Board of Trial Advocates (Advocate; Membership Committee, 1994—); American Judicature Society; Maryland Trial Lawyers Association (Member, 1986; Secretary, 1987-1988; Vice President, 1988-1989, President-Elect, 1989-1990; President, 1990-1991; Immediate Past President, 1992; Board of Governors; Chairman, Legislative Committee, 1986-1987); Maryland Institute for Continuing Professional Education of Lawyers, Inc. ***PRACTICE AREAS:*** Medical Malpractice Law; Products Liability Law; Civil Litigation. ***Email:*** jschochor@sfspa.com

PHILIP C. FEDERICO, born Baltimore, Maryland, April 27, 1957; admitted to bar, 1983, Maryland; 1984, U.S. District Court, District of Maryland; 1985, District of Columbia; 1991, U.S. District Court for the District of Columbia; 1998, U.S. Supreme Court. *Education:* Johns Hopkins University (B.S., 1980); University of Baltimore (J.D., 1983). Member, MICPEL Faculty, Deposition Course, 1994—. Lecturer: "Use of a Life Care Plan Expert", Maryland Institute for Continuing Professional Education of Lawyers, Inc., 1993; "Anatomy of A Personal Injury Trial", Maryland Trial Lawyers Association, 1991; "How to Avoid Malpractice", Anne Arundel Western Shore Dental Association, 1991 and Surgical Grand Rounds Union Memorial Hospital, 1990. *Member:* The Bar Association of Baltimore City (Member: Products Liability Committee, 1991—; Medical Legal Committee, 1987-1989); Bar Association of the District of Columbia; Maryland State (Member: Medical Legal Committee, 1987-1989; Committee of Membership and Service to the Bar, 1983-1985; Young Lawyers Section, 1983-1992) and American (Judge: Negotiation Competition Final, 1996 and Client Counseling Competition, Law Student Division, 1984-1989; Vice Chairperson, Membership Sub-Committee, Professional Liability Committee, Litigation Section, 1994-1995; Member: Professional Liability Committee, Litigation Section, 1990—; Litigation Section, Professional Liability Committee and Medical Malpractice Sub Committee, 1992—; Secretary of Litigation, Professional Liability Committee, 1990—) Bar Associations; Maryland Trial Lawyers Association (Member: Legislative Committee, Medical Negligence Procedure Group, 1989; Medical Records Committee, 1989-1990 and Membership Services Committee; Chairman, Deposition Bank Committee, 1994—); The Association of Trial Lawyers of America (State Representative, Young Lawyers Section 1992); American Judicature Society; Maryland Volunteer Lawyers; Maryland Institute for Continuing Professional Education of Lawyers, Inc. ***PRACTICE AREAS:*** Medical Malpractice; Product Liability Law; Civil Litigation. ***Email:*** pfederico@sfspa.com

KERRY D. STATON, born New Rochelle, New York, August 30, 1954; admitted to bar, 1980, Maryland and U.S. District Court, District of Maryland; 1988, District of Columbia; 1990, U.S. District Court, District of Columbia. *Education:* Oberlin College (B.A., 1976); University of Maryland (J.D., 1980). Phi Alpha Delta. Instructor, Course on Professionalism and Deposition Training, University of Maryland School of Law, 1985-1986. Invited Faculty, Maryland Institute for the Continuing Education of Lawyers. Lecturer: Medical Negligence Case Evaluation, National Bar Association; Risk Management Seminars, Johns Hopkins Hospital. Invited Lecturer: Western Shore Dental Society; "Evaluating the Medical Malpractice Case: Is It Worth the Risk?" Maryland Trial Lawyers Association. Member, Inquiry Panel, 1987-1991 and Review Board, 1991-1994, Vice-Chairman, 1995-1996 and Chairman, 1996-1997, Attorney Grievance Commission. Invited Member, Circuit Court for Baltimore City Ad Hoc committee to develop Alternative Dispute Resolution Procedures. Member, Howard Community College Foundation Board. *Member:* The Bar Association of Baltimore City (Member, Committee on Civility, 1996); Maryland State (Member, Special Committee on Audit Procedures, 1985-1986) and American Bar Associations; National Bar Association; Monumental City Bar Association; Maryland Trial Lawyers Association (Member, Board of Governors, 1988-1995); The Association of Trial Lawyers of America (Maryland State Delegate; Member, Minority Caucus); American Judicature Society; Fourth Circuit Judicial Conference (Permanent Member). Fellow: Maryland Bar Foundation; Reginald Heber Smith Law Fellowship. ***PRACTICE AREAS:*** Medical Malpractice Law; Products Liability Law; Civil Litigation. ***Email:*** kstaton@sfspa.com

CHRISTOPHER P. KENNEDY, born Philadelphia, Pennsylvania, June 25, 1963; admitted to bar, 1989, Maryland; 1991, U.S. District Court, District of Maryland; 1994, U.S. Supreme Court; 1995, U.S. Court of Federal Claims; 1997, District of Columbia. *Education:* University of Maryland (B.S., 1985); Catholic University of America (J.D., 1989). Law Clerk to the Honorable John

(This Listing Continued)

F. McAuliffe, Associate Judge, Court of Appeals of Maryland, 1989-1990. Contributing Editor: Maryland Institute of Continuing Professional Education of Lawyers Form Pleadings Book, 1991; Article, "Guardianship Law in Maryland," Maryland Institute of Continuing Professional Education of Lawyers, 1991. Author: Article, "Fifteen Things You Should Know About New Maryland Laws When Making Health Care Decisions," Maryland Medical Journal, March 1994; Article, "Paging, the Police and Privacy," Telocator International Trade Journal of Telecommunications, 1988. Co-Author: "Annual Review of Changes in Medical Malpractice Law," International Association of Defense Counsel, Annual Journal, June 1993; "Medical Malpractice Committee Newsletter," International Association of Defense Counsel, February 1993; "Product Liability Committee Newsletter," International Association of Defense Counsel, February 1992. Judge, Law Student Division, Negotiation Competition National Final, American Bar Association, 1996. Oral Arguments Judge, Catholic University of America Moot Court Association, 1996. Faculty Assistant, 1992 and Participant, 1991, Nine Day Trial Advocacy Course, Maryland Institute of Continuing Professional Education of Lawyers. Participant, Advance Medical Directives Seminar, The Deaton Specialty Hospital and Home, October 1991. *Member:* The Bar Association of Baltimore City (Young Lawyers Section Chairman: Review and Reform Committee, 1995, 1996, 1997; Long Range Planning Committee, 1993, 1994, 1995; Nominating Committee, 1997-1998); Maryland State and American Bar Associations; Maryland Trial Lawyers Association. ***PRACTICE AREAS:*** Medical Malpractice Law; Products Liability Law; Civil Litigation. ***Email:*** ckennedy@sfspa.com

SCHRAUB & COMPANY, CHTD.

A PROFESSIONAL LAW CORPORATION

WASHINGTON, D.C.

(See McLean, Virginia)

Professional Liability Defense, Product Liability Defense, Insurance Coverage, Legal Malpractice, Employment Law (Employer Defense) and General Civil Litigation.

JAMES M. SCHUETTE AND ASSOCIATES

Established in 1955

1111 19TH STREET, N.W., SUITE 209

WASHINGTON, D.C. 20036

Telephone: 301-948-5555; 202-955-5581

Fax: 202-659-1610

Negligence Law, Product Liability, Personal Injury, Automobile Accidents.

FIRM PROFILE: For over forty years the law firm of James M. Schuette and Associates have represented individuals who have been injured physically or mentally against responsible parties. The firm has a national practice.

JAMES M. SCHUETTE, born Highland Park, Illinois, June 22, 1931; admitted to bar, 1955, District of Columbia; 1958, New York; 1970, Maryland. *Education:* Georgetown University (B.S., in Economics, 1953; J.D., 1955; LL.M. in Labor Relations, 1959). Phi Delta Phi. Author: "Auto Accidents: How Can the Public be Protected?" Medical Annals of the District of Columbia, June, 1968. *Member:* The District of Columbia Bar; The Association of Trial Lawyers of America; Plaintiffs' Trial Attorneys of Metropolitan Washington, D.C. ***PRACTICE AREAS:*** Defective Products; Product Liability Law; Negligence Law.

JAMES M. SCHUETTE, JR., born Washington, D.C., July 12, 1960; admitted to bar, 1988, Pennsylvania; 1989, District of Columbia; 1998, Maryland. *Education:* Loyola College (B.A. in Philosophy, 1984); University of Dayton (J.D., 1987). *Member:* The District of Columbia Bar; American Bar Association; The Association of Trial Lawyers of America; The Association of the District of Columbia Trial Lawyers. ***PRACTICE AREAS:*** Defective Products; Products Liability Law; Negligence Law.

REFERENCE: The Palmer National Bank, Washington, D.C.

SCHULTZ & TROMBLY, PLLC

Established in 1976

SUITE 1250

1050 17TH STREET, N.W.

WASHINGTON, D.C. 20036-5510

Telephone: 202-887-5000

Fax: 202-457-0343

URL: http://www.injurycases.com

Email: trombly@erols.com

URL: http://www.lawyers.com/injurycases

Plaintiffs Trial Practice. Personal Injury, Automobile Accidents and Injuries, Wrongful Death, Negligence, Premises Liability, Product Liability, Medical Malpractice, Police Misconduct, Civil Rights.

DANIEL E. SCHULTZ, born Forest Park, Illinois, October 18, 1941; admitted to bar, 1967, Illinois, 1968, Maryland and District of Columbia; 1971, U.S. Supreme Court; 1976, U.S. District Court, District of Maryland; 1983, U.S. Court of Appeals, Fourth Circuit. *Education:* Ripon College (B.A., with honors, 1963); Northwestern University (J.D., cum laude, 1966). Faculty Member, National Institute of Trial Advocacy (Washington Program), 1988. Speaker: 1989 Civil Litigation Conference co-sponsored by Bureau of National Affairs and Law Education Institute, Topic - "The Use of Mental Health Professionals in Death and Personal Injury Cases"; 1989 Friedman & Fuller Risk Management Executive Seminar, Topic - "Civil Liability Concepts and Trends,"; 1989 Philadelphia Bar Association Bench-Bar Conference, Plenary Session; Topic - "Winning at Trial: Selecting a Theme and Theory; 1990 Grand Rounds, Children's Hospital, Topic - "How to Survive Your Deposition". Moderator: 1990 American Bar Association Annual Meeting. Author: "Will Jury Nullification Save Ollie North," Legal Times, March 1989. Vice President, 1985 and President, 1986, Springbrook Forest Citizen's Association. Member, Steering Committee for ABA and Ripon College, Co-Sponsored four day Interdisciplinary Conference, "Family Law and the Best Interests of the Child," 1991. Listed in: Who's Who in American Law, 1989—; The Best Lawyers in America, 1983—. Basketball Coach, Montgomery County, Maryland, Elementary and Junior High Recreational Leagues, 1984—. President, Kennedy High School Football Booster's Club, 1994-1995. *Member:* The District of Columbia Bar; Bar Association of the District of Columbia; Maryland State and American Bar Associations; The Association of Trial Lawyers of America; Trial Lawyers Association of Metropolitan Washington, D.C.; Maryland Trial Lawyers Association. ***Email:*** schultzd@sprintmail.com

KENNETH M. TROMBLY, born Boston, Massachusetts, January 31, 1949; admitted to bar, 1973, Maryland; 1974, District of Columbia; 1975, U.S. District Court for the District of Columbia; 1977, U.S. Court of Appeals, Fourth Circuit; 1978, U.S. Supreme Court. *Education:* George Washington University (A.B., 1970); Catholic University of America (J.D., 1973). Staff Member, Catholic University Law Review, 1972-1973. Author: U.S. District Court Digest, Digested Opinions of the Honorable Charles R. Richey, 1989-1990. Co-Author: 1996 Revisions, "D.C. Bar Practice Manual," Chapter on Personal Injury Practice. Speaker: Motor Vehicle Torts in the District of Columbia Trial Lawyers Seminar, 1992; Communication: The Key to Litigation in the 90's, Trial Lawyers Seminar, 1994; Winning Techniques for Winning Lawyers, Georgetown University Law Center, CLE, 1995; Moderator, Managing Defense Experts, Trial Lawyers Seminar, 1995; Presenter, Uncivil Depositions, D.C. Bar Annual Convention, 1997; Speaker: "Nuts & Bolts of Automobile Cases," American University Law School, 1997 and 1999. Participant, Traumatic Brain Injury Trial Demonstration, 1998 ATLA Convention, Washington, D.C.; Moderator, Voir Dire Techniques, ABOTA Masters in Trial Seminar, New Orleans, LA, 1998; Delegate, 1995, 1998 and 1999, D.C. Judicial Conference; Moderator, D.C. Superior Court Annual Bench & Bar Meeting, 1998; Speaker, D.C. Bar Seminar, "Preparing the Injury Case for Trial," 1998, 1999, 2000. Member, Review Panel, D.C. Civil Jury Instructions Revisions, 1996. Volunteer Arbitrator, District of Columbia Superior Court and Prince George's County, MD, Circuit Court. *Member:* The District of Columbia Bar (Member, Sections of: Litigation; Personal Injury and Property; Co-Chair, Steering Committee, 1996-1997); and American (Member: Litigation Section) Bar Association; The Association of Trial Lawyers of America; Trial Lawyers Association of Metropolitan Washington, D.C. (Recipient, Special Recognition Award, 1990; Member, Board of Governors, 1986-1990; President, 1994-1995); District of Columbia Trial Lawyers Foundation, President, 1995-1996; Maryland Trial Lawyers Association; American Board of Trial Advocates; Trial Lawyers for Public Justice; The Counsellors.

SCHWABE, WILLIAMSON & WYATT

A Partnership including Professional Corporations
Established in 1892
600 THIRTEENTH STREET, N.W.
SUITE 790
WASHINGTON, D.C. 20005
Telephone: 202-628-6870
Fax: 202-628-7804
Email: info@schwabe.com
URL: http://www.schwabe.com

Portland, Oregon Office: Suites 1600-1900 Pacwest Center, 1211 S.W. Fifth Avenue. Telephone: 503-222-9981. Fax: 503-796-2900.
Bend, Oregon Office: 600 S.W. Columbia, Suite 3210, 97702. Telephone: 541-330-0904. Fax: 541-330-1153.
Seattle, Washington Office: U.S. Bank Centre, Suite 3500, 1420 Fifth Avenue. Telephone: 206-622-1711. Fax: 206-292-0460.
Vancouver, Washington Office: Suite 410, Main Place Building, 1111 Main Street. Telephone: 360-694-7551; 696-0241.

Administrative Hearings and Appeals, Federal Administrative Law, Government Relations, Health Care Legislation, Health Care Reform, Health Care Regulation.

FIRM PROFILE: Schwabe, Williamson & Wyatt is one of the top law firms serving the needs of businesses in the Pacific Northwest. The firm's attorneys provide a broad range of transaction and litigation services to many of the Northwest's leading companies, from Fortune 500 industry leaders, to emerging and small, family-owned businesses. With over 130 attorneys, Schwabe, Williamson & Wyatt is the second largest law firm in Oregon, with offices in Portland and Bend. The firm also serves clients from offices in Seattle and Vancouver, Washington, and Washington D.C.

RESIDENT SHAREHOLDER

MARTIN B. GOLD, born New York, N.Y., January 17, 1947; admitted to bar, 1976, Maryland; 1976, District of Columbia. *Education:* American University (B.A., 1968); Washington College of Law (J.D., 1975). *Member:* The District of Columbia Bar. ***LANGUAGES:*** Spanish and Russian. ***PRACTICE AREAS:*** Legislation. ***Email:*** mgold@legstrat.com

(For complete biographical data on personnel at Portland, Oregon, Bend, Oregon, Seattle, Washington and Vancouver, Washington, see Professional Biographies at those locations)

SCHWALB, DONNENFELD & SCHWALB A PROFESSIONAL CORPORATION

Established in 1999
1155 21ST STREET, N.W., SUITE 210
WASHINGTON, D.C. 20036
Telephone: 202-965-7910
202-337-0676
URL: http://www.schwalblaw.com
URL: http://www.lawyers.com/schwalblaw

Federal, State and Administrative Trial Practice, Appellate Practice, Commercial. Tax, Securities, Real Estate, Regulatory, Insurance Coverage, Government Contracts, Zoning, Business Litigation, Arbitration and Mediation.

FIRM PROFILE: Like the previous law firm of Schwalb, Donnenfeld, Bray & Silbert, P.C., Schwalb, Donnenfeld & Schwalb, P.C. enjoys a sophisticated litigation practice that has encompassed local, national and international matters. The attorneys in the Firm have diverse professional backgrounds in the litigation field, both in government and private practice. They are veterans of the Department of Justice. The Firm prides itself on managing complex litigation in a way that is significantly less costly for the client and is committed to staffing cases in the most efficient manner consistent with top professional service. The Firm counts among its clients national and local corporations, partnerships and individuals. The Firm also serves as referral counsel from other law firms that do not litigate or that have either a conflict or some other problem that warrants referral to litigation counsel.

BURTON A. SCHWALB, born Boston, Massachusetts, January 2, 1936; admitted to bar, 1960, Massachusetts; 1962, U.S. Court of Federal Claims; 1964, U.S. Tax Court and U.S. Supreme Court; 1965, District of Columbia; 1984, U.S. Court of Appeals for the Federal Circuit. *Education:* Harvard University (A.B., magna cum laude, 1957; LL.B., cum laude, 1960). Phi Beta Kappa. Trial Attorney, Tax Division, U.S. Department of Justice, 1960-65. Partner, Arent, Fox, Kintner, Plotkin & Kahn, Washington, D.C. to March 1, 1978. Principal, Schwalb, Donnenfeld, Bray & Silbert, P.C., Washington, D.C. to November 1999. *Member:* The District of Columbia Bar; Federal and American Bar Associations. Fellow, American College of Trial Lawyers. ***PRACTICE AREAS:*** Commercial Litigation. ***Email:*** baschwalb@schwalblaw.com

BRIAN L. SCHWALB, born Washington, D.C., September 24, 1967; admitted to bar, 1992, Virginia; 1993, Maryland, U.S. Court of Appeals, Fourth Circuit and U.S. District Court, District of Maryland; 1998, District of Columbia, U.S. District Court, District of Columbia, U.S. Court of Appeals for the District of Columbia Circuit and U.S. Supreme Court; 2000, U.S. District Court, Eastern District of Virginia. *Education:* Duke University (A.B., magna cum laude, 1989); Harvard University (J.D., cum laude, 1992). Phi Beta Kappa. Law Clerk, Honorable John R. Hargrove, U.S. District Court for the District of Maryland, 1992-1994. Trial Attorney, Tax Division, U.S. Department of Justice, 1994-1998. *Member:* Maryland State, Virginia and American Bar Associations; District of Columbia Bar. ***PRACTICE AREAS:*** Commercial Litigation. ***Email:*** blschwalb@schwalblaw.com

ASSOCIATE

DAVID N. GEIER, born Mount Vernon, N.Y., November 3, 1963; admitted to bar, 1989, Florida; 2000, District of Columbia and U.S. Supreme Court. *Education:* Washington University, St. Louis, Missouri (B.S.B.A., 1985); University of Florida (J.D., with honors, 1988; LL.M., Taxation, 1989). Trial Attorney, Tax Division, U.S. Department of Justice, 1989-2000. ***PRACTICE AREAS:*** Commercial Litigation. ***Email:*** dgeier@schwalblaw.com

SENIOR COUNSEL

CHARLES R. DONNENFELD, born Brooklyn, New York, August 15, 1935; admitted to bar, 1960, New York; 1964, District of Columbia. *Education:* Brooklyn College (B.S., cum laude, 1956); Columbia University (LL.B., 1960). Trial Attorney, Civil Division, U.S. Department of Justice, 1960-64. Partner, Arent, Fox, Kintner, Plotkin & Kahn, Washington, D.C., 1973-1978. Chair, Board on Professional Responsibility of the District of Columbia Court of Appeals, 1991-1993. ***Email:*** cdonnenfeld@schwalblaw.com

SCHWANINGER & ASSOCIATES, P.C

1331 H STREET, N.W., SUITE 500
WASHINGTON, D.C. 20005
Telephone: 202-347-8580
Facsimile: 202-347-8607
Email: rschwaninger@sa-lawyer.net
URL: http://www.lawyers.com/schwaningerandassociates

Communications, Transactional, Contract, Valuation of Telecommunications Properties, Commercial Litigation, Federal Appellate, Business Formation, Federal Communications, Intellectual Property, Small Business Law.

ROBERT H. SCHWANINGER, JR., born St. Louis, Missouri, October 10, 1952; admitted to bar, 1982, District of Columbia; U.S. Court of Appeals for the District of Columbia Circuit; 2001, U.S. District Court, District of Columbia Circuit. *Education:* University of Missouri (B.J., 1978; J.D., 1981). *Member:* The District of Columbia Bar; Federal Communications Bar Association. ***PRACTICE AREAS:*** Communications; Contracts; Administrative Law.

GREGORY J. SCHWARTZ

INTERNATIONAL SQUARE
1825 I STREET, N.W., SUITE 400
WASHINGTON, D.C. 20006
Telephone: 202-429-2094
Fax: 202-429-2094
Email: gsesquire@aol.com

United States and International Private Investments, Offshore Investment, Offshore Finance, Private Finance, International Business Law, Venture Capital, Mergers and Acquisitions.

GREGORY J. SCHWARTZ, born Rochester, Pennsylvania, October 10, 1958; admitted to bar, 1986, Maryland and U.S. District Court, District of Maryland; 1987, District of Columbia. *Education:* University of Maryland (B.A., cum laude, with special honors in Government and Politics, 1981); Catholic University of America (J.D., 1985); Georgetown University Law Center. Phi Alpha Delta; Omicron Delta Kappa. Listed in: Who's Who Among Students in American Colleges and Universities; Who's Who in the World, 2001; Who's Who in American Law, 2001. Member, Catholic University Law Review. Author: undergraduate honors thesis, "The Effect of Political Pollsters on Presidential Elections"; "Regulation of Leveraged Buyouts to Protect the Public Shareholder and Enhance the Corporate Image," 35 Cath. U.L. Rev. 489 (1986). Speaker and Legal Counselor, SBA/SCORE/ACE. Legal Counsel, Board of Directors, Washington, D.C. Downtown Jaycees, 1988-1989. Former Member and Rapporteur, Board of Governors, Washington Foreign Law Soci-

(This Listing Continued)

ety. *Member:* The District of Columbia Bar (Member, Sections on: Corporation, Finance and Securities Law; International Law); Maryland State Bar Association, Inc.; American Bar Association (Former Member, Central and Eastern European Law Initiative); Suburban Maryland International Trade Association (President, Board of Directors); International Trade Networking Group of Washington (Founder).

REPRESENTATIVE CLIENTS: Accredited and Sophiscated Investors (U.S. & International).

SCHWARTZ & BALLEN

SUITE 500, 1990 M STREET, N.W.
WASHINGTON, D.C. 20036-3418
Telephone: 202-776-0700
Fax: 202-776-0720
URL: http://www.schwartzandballen.com

Banking, Financial Services, E-Commerce and Payments Law.

MEMBERS OF FIRM

GILBERT T. SCHWARTZ, born Philadelphia, Pennsylvania, December 17, 1946; admitted to bar, 1974, Pennsylvania; 1978, U.S. Supreme Court; 1985, District of Columbia; 1989, Maryland. *Education:* Temple University (B.B.A., 1967; J.D., 1974); Columbia University (M.B.A., 1969). Beta Gamma Sigma. Associate General Counsel, Federal Reserve Board, 1974-1985. ***PRACTICE AREAS:*** Banking; Financial Services. ***Email:*** gschwartz@schwartzandballen.com

ROBERT G. BALLEN, born Bridgeport, Connecticut, December 20, 1956; admitted to bar, 1981, District of Columbia; 1988, U.S. Supreme Court. *Education:* Princeton University (B.A., magna cum laude, 1978); Harvard Law School (J.D., cum laude, 1981). Phi Beta Kappa. Member, Legal Division, Federal Reserve Board, 1981-1985. *Member:* American Bar Association (Past Chairman, Payments Subcommittee). ***PRACTICE AREAS:*** Financial Services; Payments Law; International Banking; E-Commerce and Payments. ***Email:*** rballen@schwartzandballen.com

THOMAS A. FOX, born Rochester, Minnesota, March 31, 1966; admitted to bar, 1991, Maryland; 1993, District of Columbia. *Education:* Duke University (A.B., cum laude, 1988); Georgetown University Law Center (J.D., magna cum laude, 1991). Order of the Coif. ***PRACTICE AREAS:*** Banking; Financial Services; E-Commerce and Payments. ***Email:*** tfox@schwartzandballen.com

ASSOCIATE

BRANDON M. DELL'AGLIO, born Atlanta, Georgia, November 30, 1974; admitted to bar, 2000, Maryland (Not admitted in District of Columbia). *Education:* George Washington University (B.A., 1997); Georgetown University (J.D., 2000). ***PRACTICE AREAS:*** Banking; Financial Services.

SCHWARTZ, WOODS & MILLER

Established in 1970

SUITE 300 THE DUPONT CIRCLE BUILDING
1350 CONNECTICUT AVENUE, N.W.
WASHINGTON, D.C. 20036-1717
Telephone: 202-833-1700
Cable Address: "SWMLAW"
Telecopier: 202-833-2351
Email: watts@swmlaw.com

Communications, Telecommunications Law (Radio, Television, Common Carrier, Private Radio). Copyright and Trademark Law. Broadcast Program Production and Distribution Law. Practice before the Federal Courts and Administrative Agencies.

FIRM PROFILE: Schwartz, Woods & Miller represents radio and television stations licensees (commercial and public) and non-broadcast licensees of the Federal Communications Commission. The firm assists in licensing, regulatory compliance, and station sales and purchases. We also provide counsel on copyright and trademark matters affecting program production and distribution.

OF COUNSEL

LOUIS SCHWARTZ (Retired).

ROBERT A. WOODS, born Beverly, Massachusetts, June 3, 1931; admitted to bar, 1958, Massachusetts; 1961, District of Columbia, U.S. District Court for the District of Columbia and U.S. Court of Appeals for the District of Columbia Circuit; 1966, U.S. Supreme Court. *Education:* Harvard University (B.A., 1953; LL.B., 1958). Phi Beta Kappa. *Member:* The District of Columbia Bar; Federal Communications Bar Association. ***PRACTICE AREAS:*** Communications Law; Telecommunications Law; Copyright and Trademark Law; Broadcast Production and Distribution Law. ***Email:*** woods@swmlaw.com

MEMBERS OF FIRM

LAWRENCE M. MILLER, born Philadelphia, Pennsylvania, June 26, 1946; admitted to bar, 1973, District of Columbia, U.S. District Court for the District of Columbia and U.S. Court of Appeals for the District of Columbia Circuit; 1976, U.S. Supreme Court. *Education:* Dickinson College (A.B., 1968); George Washington University (J.D., with honors, 1972). *Member:* The District of Columbia Bar; American Bar Association; Federal Communications Bar Association. ***Email:*** Miller@swmlaw.com

STEVEN C. SCHAFFER, born Newark, New Jersey, April 8, 1951; admitted to bar, 1976, District of Columbia; 1983, U.S. Court of Appeals for the District of Columbia Circuit. *Education:* University of Wisconsin-Madison (B.A., 1972); George Washington University (J.D., 1975). Phi Kappa Phi. Community Legal Clinic Fellow. *Member:* The District of Columbia Bar; Federal Communications Bar Association. ***PRACTICE AREAS:*** Communications Law; Telecommunications Law; Copyright and Trademark Law; Broadcast Production and Distribution Law. ***Email:*** schaffer@swmlaw.com

MALCOLM G. STEVENSON, born Washington, D. C., September 28, 1953; admitted to bar, 1980, District of Columbia; 1983, U.S. Court of Appeals for the District of Columbia Circuit. *Education:* University of California at Berkeley (B.A., 1974); George Washington University (J.D., 1980). *Member:* The District of Columbia Bar; Federal Communications Bar Association. ***LANGUAGES:*** French. ***PRACTICE AREAS:*** Communications Law; Telecommunications Law; Copyright and Trademark Law; Broadcast Production and Distribution Law. ***Email:*** stevenson@swmlaw.com

COUNSEL

CAMILLE M. CUNNINGHAM, born June 27, 1973; admitted to bar, 2001, District of Columbia. *Education:* Colgate University (B.A., 1996); George Washington University (J.D., 1999). ***PRACTICE AREAS:*** Trademarks; Communications Law; Contracts.

MARK B. WEINBERG, (P.C.), born Chicago, Illinois, October 8, 1946; admitted to bar, 1971, District of Columbia; 1981, Maryland. *Education:* Arizona State University (B.A., with distinction, 1967); University of Chicago (J.D., 1970). Assistant Branch Chief, Interpretative Division, Office of the Chief Counsel, Internal Revenue Service, 1975-77. *Member:* The District of Columbia Bar; Maryland State and American (Member: Exempt Organizations Committee, 1973—; Section on Taxation) Bar Associations. (Also Member Weinberg & Jacobs, Rockville, Maryland).

SCOPELITIS, GARVIN, LIGHT & HANSON, P.C.

1500 "K" STREET, N.W., SUITE 910
WASHINGTON, D.C. 20005-1209
Telephone: 202-783-9222
Fax: 202-783-9230
Email: washingtondc@scopelitis.com
URL: http://www.scopelitis.com

Indianapolis, Indiana Office: 10 West Market Street, Suite 1500. Telephone: 312-637-1777. Fax: 317-687-2414.

Chicago, Illinois Office: 120 South LaSalle Street, Suite 1700. 60603-3419. Telephone: 312-422-1200. Fax: 312-422-1224.

General Civil Practice. Litigation in all State and Federal Courts, including Appellate Practice, Transportation, Motor Carrier, Corporate, Administrative, Antitrust and Trade Regulation, Business, Insurance Defense, Negligence, Labor and Employment, Environmental, Workers Compensation, Probate and Estate Planning and Public Utility Law.

FIRM PROFILE: Scopelitis, Garvin, Light & Hanson is a full-service law firm that offers a wide range of legal services to clients in many industries, including manufacturing, pharmaceutical, e-commerce, retail products, construction, and environmental concerns. Of particular note is the firm's knowledge of the transportation industry and its long-standing history of service to motor carriers, shippers, brokers and insurance companies nationwide. From its offices in Indianapolis, Chicago and Washington, D.C., the firm offers clients knowledge and experience in many business-related disciplines and also seeks to meet its clients' more individual needs in such areas as personal injury litigation, estate planning and probate administration.

DANIEL R. BARNEY, born Concord, New Hampshire, January 27, 1951; admitted to bar, 1975, Massachusetts; 1980, U.S. Supreme Court and U.S. Court of Appeals, District of Columbia Circuit; 1981, District of Columbia; 1982,

(This Listing Continued)

SCOPELITIS, GARVIN, LIGHT & HANSON, P.C., Washington—Continued

U.S. District Court for the District of Columbia; 1994, Virginia; 1994, U.S. Court of Appeals, 4th Circuit; 1998, U.S. Court of Appeals, 6th and 8th Circuit. *Education:* Harvard University (A.B., 1972); University of Texas (J.D., 1975). Senior Vice President & General Counsel, American Trucking Association, 1993-1998; Co-Founder & Chief Counsel, ATA Litigation Center, 1985-1998. Associate, Weil, Gotshal & Manges, Washington, DC, 1981-1985. Attorney Advisor to Commissioner Robert Pitofsky, 1979-1981 and Antitrust Trial Attorney, 1975-1979, Federal Trade Commission. *Member:* Virginia State Bar; American Bar Association (Vice Chairman, Transportation Committee, Section of Antitrust, 2000—); Association of Transportation Law, Logistics and Policy; Transportation Lawyers Association. ***PRACTICE AREAS:*** Antitrust; Trade Regulation; Advertising and Marketing; Transportation; Transportation Safety; Air Cargo; Independent Contractors; E-Commerce; Litigation; State Taxes. ***Email:*** dbarney@scopelitis.com

LAURIE T. BAULIG, born Rome, New York, June 27, 1958; admitted to bar, 1984, Florida; 1988, District of Columbia. *Education:* University of Florida (B.A., 1980; J.D., 1984). Phi Beta Kappa. Board Member, University of Florida Law Review, 1983-1984. General Attorney, Federal Trade Commission, 1984-1986. *Member:* The Florida Bar; The District of Columbia Bar. (Resident). ***Email:*** lbaulig@scopelitis.com

ASSOCIATE

SYLVIA F. JAMES, born Long Island, New York, November 8, 1970; admitted to bar, 1996, Maryland; 1998, District of Columbia. *Education:* Vassar College (A.B., 1993); Duke University (J.D., 1996). *Member:* American Bar Association; The District of Columbia Bar; Black Law Students Association (Secretary, 1993-1996). (Resident). ***LANGUAGES:*** Spanish. ***PRACTICE AREAS:*** Employment; Labor. ***Email:*** sjames@scopelitis.com

SCRIBNER, HALL & THOMPSON, LLP

1875 I STREET, N.W.
SUITE 1050
WASHINGTON, D.C. 20006
Telephone: 202-331-8585
Telecopier: 202-331-2032
Email: lawfirm@scribnerhall.com
URL: http://www.scribnerhall.com

Federal Tax Practice before Government Departments and Courts.

FIRM PROFILE: Scribner, Hall & Thompson's clients are principally large corporate groups that provide insurance and other financial services. The emphasis of the firm's practice is on the federal taxation of life and property and casualty insurance companies and their policyholders, including representation in tax planning, on legislative tax matters and in civil tax controversies before the Internal Revenue Service and in the Federal courts.

FRED C. SCRIBNER, JR. (1908-1994).

LEONARD W. HALL (1900-1979).

MEMBERS OF FIRM

THOMAS C. THOMPSON, JR., born Washington, D.C., December 14, 1926; admitted to bar, 1950, District of Columbia; 1951, U.S. Court of Appeals for the District of Columbia; 1953, U.S. Tax Court; 1964, U.S. Supreme Court; 1971, U.S. Claims Court. *Education:* University of Pennsylvania (B.S., 1948); George Washington University (LL.B., 1950). Phi Delta Phi. Attorney: Appeals Division of the Chief Counsel's Office, 1951-1953; Legal Advisory Staff of Treasury Department, 1953-1955; Staff of Joint Committee on Internal Revenue Taxation, 1955-1957. *Member:* American Bar Association (Member, Taxation Section); The Barristers.

MARK H. KOVEY, born Boston, Massachusetts, October 12, 1942; admitted to bar, 1967, Massachusetts; 1973, District of Columbia, U.S. Claims Court, U.S. Tax Court and U.S. Supreme Court. *Education:* Columbia University (A.B., 1964); New York University (J.D., 1967); George Washington University (LL.M., 1970). Tax Law Specialist, Reorganization Branch, National Office, Internal Revenue Service, 1969-1973. Co-Author: "New Law Revamps Life Insurance Company Taxation," Part I, 62 Journal of Taxation 292, Part II, 63 Journal of Taxation 48, 1985. Contributor: Journal Of Taxation, 1973-1995; TAXES, The Tax Magazine, 1976; The Journal of Corporate Taxation, 1978; The Insurance Tax Review, 1991-1999. Coordinator, Insurance Tax Seminar, 1988—. *Member:* Federal (Chairman, Section on Taxation, 1985-1987) and American (Member, Taxation Section) Bar Associations.

STEPHEN P. DICKE, born Philadelphia, Pennsylvania, September 3, 1942; admitted to bar, 1967, Pennsylvania; 1978, District of Columbia; 1979,

(This Listing Continued)

U.S. Claims Court. *Education:* Princeton University (A.B., cum laude, 1964); University of Pennsylvania School of Law (J.D., 1967). Attorney-Advisor, Office of Tax Legislative Counsel, U.S. Treasury Department, 1974-1977. *Member:* American Bar Association (Member, Taxation Section).

PETER H. WINSLOW, born Wakefield, Rhode Island, May 18, 1950; admitted to bar, 1975, Ohio; 1976, District of Columbia. *Education:* Tufts University (B.A., magna cum laude, 1972); Case Western Reserve University (J.D., 1975; Order of the Coif); Georgetown University (LL.M., 1978). Co-Author: "New Law Revamps Life Insurance Company Taxation," Part I, 62 Journal of Taxation 292, Part II, 63 Journal of Taxation 48, 1985. Author: "Exempt Organizations Declaratory Judgments," Tax Management Portfolio, 421. Contributor: Journal of Taxation, 1978-1985; The Insurance Law Journal, 1980. Attorney, Interpretative and Refund Litigation Divisions, Chief Counsel's Office, Internal Revenue Service, 1975-1979. Member, IRS Information Reporting Program Advisory Committee, 1992-1993. *Member:* Federal and American (Member, Taxation Section) Bar Associations.

SUSAN J. HOTINE, born Roslyn, New York, March 2, 1948; admitted to bar, 1974, New York; 1975, District of Columbia; 1976, Virginia; 1978, U.S. Supreme Court. *Education:* Wells College (B.A., 1970); Cornell University (J.D., 1973). Phi Beta Kappa. Attorney and Assistant Branch Chief, Interpretative Division, Chief Counsel's Office, Internal Revenue Service, 1973-1981. Legislative Attorney, Staff of Joint Committee on Taxation, 1981-1985. *Member:* American Bar Association (Member, Taxation Section).

BIRUTA P. KELLY, born Waterbury, Connecticut, June 17, 1953; admitted to bar, 1981, District of Columbia; 1983, U.S. Tax Court. *Education:* Boston University (B.A., magna cum laude, 1975); George Washington University (J.D., cum laude, 1981). Attorney-Advisor, Judge Howard A. Dawson, Jr., U.S. Tax Court, 1983-1985. Attorney, Interpretative Division, Chief Counsel's Office, Internal Revenue Service, 1982-1983. Contributor, The Insurance Tax Review, 1994; Journal of Taxation, 1995. *Member:* Federal (Member, Taxation Section) and American Bar Associations.

GREGORY K. OYLER, born Moses Lake, Washington, September 16, 1953; admitted to bar, 1978, Pennsylvania; 1979, U.S. Tax Court; 1981, District of Columbia; 1982, U.S. Supreme Court; 1993, U.S. Court of Claims. *Education:* Princeton University (A.B., 1975); Georgetown University (J.D., 1978); New York University (LL.M. in Taxation, 1981). Attorney Advisor, U.S. Tax Court, 1978-1980. Member, IRS Information Reporting Program Advisory Committee, 1993-1994. *Member:* Federal and American Bar Associations (Member, Taxation Section).

LORI J. BROWN, born Queens, New York, November 22, 1961; admitted to bar, 1988, Virginia; 1995, District of Columbia. *Education:* State University College at Oswego (B.S., cum laude, 1983); George Mason University School of Law (J.D., 1988); Georgetown University (LL.M., with distinction, 1993). Author: "Can Indemnity Reinsurance Be Used in Insurance Save the Charter Transactions?" The Insurance Tax Review, April 1996. Contributor, The Insurance Tax Review, 1998-1999; "Major Tax Planning," 42nd Tax Institute, 1990. Attorney Advisor, Office of Chief Counsel, Internal Revenue Service, Corporate Division, 1988-1992. *Member:* Federal (Member, Taxation Section) and American Bar Associations.

THOMAS D. SYKES, born Rice Lake, Wisconsin, July 26, 1954; admitted to bar, 1979, Wisconsin; 1989, U.S. Court of Federal Claims; 1990, U.S. Court of Appeals for the Federal Circuit; 1998, District of Columbia and U.S. Tax Court. *Education:* University of Wisconsin at Eau Claire (B.A., magna cum laude, 1976); The Ohio State University (J.D., 1979). Recipient, Outstanding Attorney Award, U.S. Department of Justice, 1986, 1988, 1991, 1997. Author: "Chart v. General Motors Corp.: Did It Chart the Way for Admission of Evidence of Subsequent Remedial Measures in Products Liability Actions?" 41 Ohio St. L.J. 211, 1980; "Powerful New Arguments Against The Duplicated Loss Provisions of the LDR," Tax Notes, 2001. Assistant District Attorney, 1979-1980 and District Attorney, 1980-1982, Barron County, Wisconsin. Assistant U.S. Attorney, Western District of Wisconsin, Madison, 1982-1984. Trial Attorney, Senior Trial Attorney, Reviewer and Assistant Chief, Tax Division, U.S. Department of Justice, Washington, D.C., 1984-1998. *Member:* Federal and American Bar Associations; Court of Federal Claims Bar Association (Board of Governors, 2000—).

SAMUEL A. MITCHELL, born Durango, Colorado, May 5, 1965; admitted to bar, 1991, Colorado; 1999, District of Columbia. *Education:* Bob Jones University (B.S., magna cum laude, 1986); University of Denver (J.D., 1990). Order of St. Ives. Recipient, Outstanding Attorney Award, U.S. Department of Justice, 1998. Editor-in-Chief, Denver University Law Review, 1989-1990. Law Clerk to Hon. Bobby R. Baldock, U.S. Court of Appeals, Tenth Circuit, 1991-1992. Trial Attorney, U.S. Department of Justice, Antitrust Division, 1992-1995, Tax Division, 1995-1999. *Member:* Colorado and American Bar Associations.

OF COUNSEL

G. NORRIS WATSON, born Washington, D.C., May 1, 1931; admitted to bar, 1957, Virginia; 1958, West Virginia (Not admitted in District of Columbia). *Education:* University of Richmond (B.A., 1954); University of Virginia

(This Listing Continued)

(LL.B., 1957); Georgetown University (LL.M., Taxation, 1962). Assistant to Director, Refund Litigation Division and Assistant Director, Interpretative Division, Chief Counsel's Office, Internal Revenue Service, 1960-1981. Counsel to Chief Judge, U.S. Tax Court, 1981-1992. *Member:* Virginia State Bar.

DAVID L. SCULL

WASHINGTON, D.C.

(See Bethesda, Maryland)

General Civil Practice. Estate Planning, Wills and Trusts, Estate Litigation.

THE M.H. SEARS LAW FIRM, CHARTERED

910 SEVENTEENTH STREET, N.W., SUITE 800
WASHINGTON, D.C. 20006
Telephone: 202-463-3892
Facsimile: 202-463-4852
URL: http://www.searshahn.com
Email: mhsears@mhsears.com
URL: http://www.lawyers.com/mhsearslaw

Litigation, Counseling and Procurement of Rights in all areas of Intellectual Property, including Patents, Trademarks, Copyrights, Trade Secrets and general Unfair Competition matters.

FIRM PROFILE: The M.H. Sears Law Firm, Chartered, has more than forty years of experience in the representation of diverse clients, based in the United States and elsewhere, including, inter alia, Japan, Italy, Germany, Great Britain and various Latin American countries. This experience has encompassed a wide spectrum of technology. Legal reasoning and analysis we presented in briefs before it has been adopted by the United States Supreme Court in several of its significant patent law decisions since 1964. The firm is proud of having successfully steered many of its clients through litigation and of having helped entrepreneurial developers of outstanding technology to protect it in ways that maximized its financial value, both domestically and internationally. The firm strives to do its best for each of its clients in all matter, whether large or small. It also makes a conscientious effort to render advice and recommend courses of action based on each clients' individual needs and circumstances.

The firm is listed in the Bar Register of Preeminent Lawyers.

MEMBERS OF FIRM

MARY HELEN SEARS, born Syracuse, New York; admitted to bar, 1960, Virginia; 1961, District of Columbia; 1963, U.S. Supreme Court; registered to practice before U.S. Patent and Trademark Office. *Education:* Cornell University (A.B., 1950); George Washington University (J.D., with honors, 1960). Phi Alpha Delta; Order of the Coif. Author of numerous articles on various aspects of patent law, Named in *Euromoney Guide to the World's Leading Patent Law Experts* as one of the best patent lawyers in the United States, 1995 and 1997. Listed in *Who's Who in America,* 1993-2002. Member: Cornell University Council, 1980-1987, 1989—; Administrative Board, 1984-1987; George Washington University Law School Law Alumni Board 1996-2001. *Member:* The District of Columbia Bar; Virginia State Bar; American Bar Association (Co-Chair, Appellate Practice Committee, Section of Litigation, 1989-1992); American Intellectual Property Association; American Society of International Law; AIPPI; Licensing Executives Society; International Trademark Association. **PRACTICE AREAS:** Intellectual Property; Patents; Trademarks; Copyrights; Trade Secrets; Unfair Competition. **Email:** mhsears@mhsears.com

SEIDMAN & ASSOCIATES, P.C.

WASHINGTON, D.C.

(See Vienna, Virginia)

Government Contracts, Administrative Law, Federal Litigation.

THE LAW FIRM OF DIANE A. SELTZER

1730 K STREET, NORTHWEST
SUITE 1107
WASHINGTON, D.C. 20006
Telephone: 202-331-3338
Fax: 202-298-9194
Email: diseltz@erols.com

Labor and Employment, Civil Rights, Discrimination, Litigation.

FIRM PROFILE: Diane A. Seltzer represents employees and employers in employment, disability rights and civil rights matters.

(This Listing Continued)

DIANE A. SELTZER, born Brooklyn, New York, August 6, 1967; admitted to bar, 1991, Maryland; 1992, District of Columbia; 1994, U.S. District Court, District of Maryland; 1995, U.S. District Court, District of Columbia and U.S. Court of Appeals, Fourth Circuit; 1996, U.S. Court of Appeals for the District of Columbia Circuit. *Education:* Tufts University (B.A., cum laude, 1988); American University, Washington College of Law (J.D., 1991). Staff Member, American University Law Review. Judicial Clerk to Honorable Frederick C. Wright III, John P. Corderman and Daniel Moylan, Circuit Court for Washington County, Maryland, 1991-1992. National Plaintiffs' Co-Chair, Regional EEO Liaison Program of American Bar Association Labor and Employment Law Section's EEO Committee, 1998-1999 and Co-Chair, EEO Subcommittee of American Bar Association Litigation Section's Labor and Employment Law Committee, 2000—. *Member:* Montgomery County (Chair, Employment Law Section, 1996-1998), Maryland State and American (Member, Sections on: Labor and Employment; Torts and Insurance Practice; Law Practice Management) Bar Associations; District of Columbia Bar (Member, Steering Committee, Law Practice Management Section, 1998-2000; Co-Chair, Solo and Small Firm Committee, 1999-2000); Metropolitan Washington Employment Lawyer's Association (Vice President, 1998-1999 and 2000—; Board Member, 1995—; Newsletter Editor, 1995-1997); National Employment Lawyers Association; Women's Bar Association of Maryland (Member, Executive Committee, Montgomery County Chapter, 1994-1997). Pupil, Montgomery County, Maryland Chapter of American Inns of Court, 1994-1995.

SEMMES, BOWEN & SEMMES

A PROFESSIONAL CORPORATION
Established in 1887
SUITE 1100
1001 CONNECTICUT AVENUE, N.W.
WASHINGTON, D.C. 20036
Telephone: 202-822-8250
Facsimile: 202-822-8258
Email: semmes@mail.semmes.com
URL: http://www.semmes.com

Baltimore, Maryland Office: 250 West Pratt Street, 16th Floor. Telephone: 410-539-5040.
Hagerstown, Maryland Office: 322 East Antietam Street. Telephone: 301-739-4558.
Salisbury, Maryland Office: 231 West Main Street. Telephone: 410-749-1710.
McLean, Virginia Office: Suite 410, 6862 Elm Street. Telephone: 703-760-9473.

General Practice. Litigation in all Courts and Tribunals. Alternative Dispute Resolutions. Representation in all aspects of Corporate and Partnership Planning and Transactions. Specialties include Administrative Law, Admiralty and Maritime, Antitrust, Banking, Bankruptcy and Creditors' Rights, Commercial and Consumer Lending, Construction, Consumer Product Safety, Corporate, Criminal, Environmental, Estate Planning and Probate, Family Law, Government Contracts and Regulation, Health Care, Immigration, Insurance, Intellectual Property (Copyrights, Trademarks), International Trade and Business, Labor Relations and Employment, Legislative, Mergers and Acquisitions, Pension and Profit Sharing, Product Liability, Professional Malpractice, Real Estate, Securities, Small Business Investment Companies, Taxation, Toxic Torts, Venture Capital, Workers' Compensation and Zoning.

PRINCIPALS

ALAN N. GAMSE, born Baltimore, Maryland, 1942; admitted to bar, 1967, Maryland; 1982, District of Columbia. *Education:* Massachusetts Institute of Technology (B.S., 1964); University of Maryland (J.D., 1967). Recent Developments Editor, Maryland Law Review, 1966-1967. Law Clerk to Judge Reuben Oppenheimer, 1967 and Judge Frederick J. Singley, Jr., Court of Appeals of Maryland, 1967-1968. Member, Tort and Insurance Practice Section (Section Council, 1990-1993; Chairman, 1984-1985 and Senior Vice Chairman, 1987-1990, Public Regulation of Insurance Law Committee; Member, Task Force on Insurance Insolvency, 1995-2000) American Bar Association. Chair, Governor's Advisory Panel on Insurance Fraud, 1993-1995. *Member:* Federation of Regulatory Counsel; International Association of Insurance Receivers. ***PRACTICE AREAS:*** Insurance Corporate and Regulatory Law; Insurance Coverage; Insurance Insolvency; Administrative Law. **Email:** angamse@mail.semmes.com

THOMAS G. HAGERTY, born Philadelphia, Pennsylvania, 1950; admitted to bar, 1978, District of Columbia; 1980, U.S. District Court for the District of Columbia; 1987, Maryland. *Education:* Bucknell University (B.S., 1972); Washington College of Law, American University (J.D., 1978). Omicron Delta Kappa. *Member:* The District of Columbia Bar; Maryland State Bar Association; Association of Compensation Insurance Attorneys (President, 1995-1997); District of Columbia Defense Lawyers' Association; Maryland Defense Counsel; Defense Research Institute. **PRACTICE AREAS:** Litigation; Insurance Defense Law; Workers Compensation Law. **Email:** thagerty@mail.semmes.com

(This Listing Continued)

SEMMES, BOWEN & SEMMES, A PROFESSIONAL CORPORATION, Washington—Continued

JONATHAN R. TOPAZIAN, born Vellore, South India, July 2, 1961; admitted to bar, 1991, Maryland; 1993, District of Columbia; 1995, Virginia. *Education:* Central Connecticut State University (B.A., 1987); American University (J.D., cum laude, 1990). Law Clerk to the Honorable Peter H. Wolf, Civil Division of the Superior Court of the District of Columbia, 1990-1991. *Member:* Maryland State Bar Association, Inc.; District of Columbia Bar; Virginia State Bar. ***PRACTICE AREAS:*** Employment Law; Complex Litigation; Labor. ***Email:*** jtopazian@mail.semmes.com

R. MICHAEL HAYNES, born Safford, Arizona, October 3, 1940; admitted to bar, 1969, New York; 1973, U.S. District Court, Southern and Eastern Districts of New York, U.S. Court of Appeals, Second Circuit and U.S. Supreme Court; 1977, New Jersey and U.S. District Court, District of New Jersey; 1992, District of Columbia and U.S. District Court for the District of Columbia. *Education:* Rutgers University (B.A., 1963; J.D., 1968). Phi Delta Phi, Graduate of the Year. Justice Ackerson Distinguished Graduate Award; Attorney General's Special Achievement Award, Department of Justice, 1977. Co-Author: "Historical and Program Highlights of the SBIC Program and Private Venture Capital Investment," 1988; "Should Pension Funds Invest in SBICs? Consideration of Unrelated Business Taxable Income (UBTI)," 1989. Assistant District Attorney, New York County, Deputy Chief of Rackets Bureau, 1969-1974. Executive Assistant District Attorney, Special Narcotics Prosecutors Office, New York City, 1974-1976. Assistant U.S. Attorney, District of New Jersey, Section Chief and Senior Trial Attorney of Criminal Division and Fraud and Public Protection Divisions, 1976-1979. Special Counsel and Minority Counsel, U.S. Senate Committee on Small Business, 1979-1981. Chief Counsel, U.S. Senate Committee on Small Business, 1981-1986. General Counsel, National Association of Small Business Investment Companies, 1986-1990. Law Offices of R. Michael Haynes, 1990—. Member, U.S. Chamber of Commerce, Council of Small Business, 1987-1989. Executive Committee Member, SEC Government-Business Forum on Capital Formation, 1988-1989. *Member:* The District of Columbia Bar; New York State, New Jersey State, Federal (Chairman, Small Business Committee, Financial Institutions and the Economy Section, 1988-1989) and American (Member and Chairman, SBIC Subcommittee of Small Business Committee, 1986-1989) Bar Associations. ***PRACTICE AREAS:*** Venture Capital; Small Business Investment Companies; Government Regulation; White Collar Crime. ***Email:*** rmhaynes@lawyer.com

OF COUNSEL

RICHARD H. GIMER, born Eagle Grove, Iowa, March 24, 1940; admitted to bar, 1965, Iowa; 1966, District of Columbia. *Education:* Iowa State University (B.S., 1962); George Washington University (J.D., with honors, 1965). Administrative Assistant to U.S. Representative William J. Scherle, Iowa, 1967-1969. United States Alternate Representative to the 25th Session of the General Assembly of the United Nations, 1970. Member, Administrative Conference of the United States, 1970-1972. Member, African Affairs Advisory Council, U.S. Department of State, 1971-1972. Member, Foreign Service Officer Selection Board U.S. Department of State, 1973. *Member:* The District of Columbia Bar; American Bar Association. ***PRACTICE AREAS:*** Insurance Coverage; Trade Associations; Trade Regulation. ***Email:*** rgimer@mail.semmes.com

(For complete biographical data on other personnel, see Professional Biographies at Baltimore, Maryland)

JOHN GIBSON SEMMES

WASHINGTON, D.C.

(See Potomac, Maryland)

Intellectual Property Law Practice including Patent, Trademark, Unfair Competition, Copyright Law.
The firm has local, national and international practice serving primarily small to medium corporations and individual entrepreneurs.

SEWARD & KISSEL LLP

(Smith & Martin 1890)

1200 G STREET, N.W.
SUITE 350
WASHINGTON, D.C. 20005
Telephone: 202-737-8833
Cable Address: "Sewkis New York"
Telex: 23-9046; 62-0982
Facsimile: 202-737-5184
URL: http://www.sewkis.com

New York, New York Office: One Battery Park Plaza. Telephone: 212-574-1200. Facsimile: 212-480-8421.

(This Listing Continued)

General Practice including Corporate Finance and Capital Markets, Investment Management, Litigation, Real Estate, Tax and Employee Benefits, Individual Client Matters, Legislative and Regulatory Representation.

RESIDENT PARTNERS

ANTHONY C. J. NULAND, born New York, N.Y., 1943; admitted to bar, 1969, New York; 1977, District of Columbia; 1978, Georgia. *Education:* Princeton University (A.B., cum laude, 1965); New York University (J.D., 1968). Assistant Director, 1975-1976 and Associate Director, 1976-1977, Division of Market Regulation, Securities and Exchange Commission. ***PRACTICE AREAS:*** Investment Companies; Brokers and Dealers; Corporations; Securities; Banking. ***Email:*** nuland@sewkis.com

PAUL T. CLARK, born Long Beach, California, 1954; admitted to bar, 1980, District of Columbia. *Education:* University of California at Berkeley (A.B., high honors, 1976); Boalt Hall School of Law, University of California (J.D., 1980). Legislative Assistant to Hon. Mark W. Hannaford, 1976-1977. ***PRACTICE AREAS:*** Banking; Securities; Legislative and Regulatory Representation. ***Email:*** Clark@sewkis.com

RESIDENT COUNSEL

KATHLEEN K. CLARKE, born Colorado Springs, Colorado, 1943; admitted to bar, 1976, District of Columbia. *Education:* Colorado College (B.A., 1965); George Washington University (J.D., with honors, 1976). Special Counsel, 1990-1991, Division of Corporation Finance, Special County and Deputy Chief, 1991-1997, Assistant Director Division of Investment Management, Securities and Exchange Commission. *Member:* The District of Columbia Bar; American Bar Association. ***PRACTICE AREAS:*** Investment Companies; Securities; Corporations. ***Email:*** clarke@sewkis.com

KEVIN M. BROADWATER, born Buffalo, New York, 1964; admitted to bar, 1989, Pennsylvania; 1991, District of Columbia. *Education:* State University of New York at Buffalo (B.A., cum laude, 1986); American University (J.D., 1989). Member, Journal of International Law & Policy, American University, 1988-1989. ***PRACTICE AREAS:*** Investment Company Regulation; Investment Adviser Regulation. ***Email:*** broadwater@sewkis.com

RESIDENT ASSOCIATES

ANDREW C. BAEK, born Philadelphia, Pennsylvania, 1969; admitted to bar, 1995, New York; 2001, District of Columbia. *Education:* New York University (B.S., Finance/Information Systems, 1991); Brooklyn Law School (J.D., 1994). Vice-President, Republic National Bank of New York, 1997-1998. *Member:* Pennsylvania and American Bar Associations. ***PRACTICE AREAS:*** Securities; Banking; Derivative Products. ***Email:*** baek@sewkis.com

PAUL M. MILLER, born Charlotte, North Carolina,1971; admitted to bar, 1998, Virginia; 1999, District of Columbia. *Education:* University of North Carolina at Chapel Hill (B.S.B.A., 1994); Syracuse University (J.D., 1998). ***PRACTICE AREAS:*** Securities.

NORA L. SHEEHAN, born Bayside, New York,1965; admitted to bar, 1993, Virginia; 1999, District of Columbia. *Education:* Mary Washington College (B.A., 1987); Catholic University of America (J.D., 1990). ***PRACTICE AREAS:*** Mutual Funds; Investment Regulation; Securities Regulation. ***Email:*** sheehan@sewkis.com

JENNIFER REIK, admitted to bar, 2000, Maryland (Not admitted in District of Columbia). *Education:* Western Kentucky University (B.A., 1992); Widener University (J.D., 2000); Georgetown University. Phi Delta Phi. Author: "Physician Assisted Suicide: Is There a Right to Die?" Journal of Medicine and the Law at Michigan State University, 2000. ***PRACTICE AREAS:*** Securities. ***Email:*** reik@sewkis.com

(For biographical data on all Personnel, see Professional Biographies at New York, N.Y.).

HARRY B. SEWELL, JR.
ATTORNEY AT LAW,

CHARTERED

WASHINGTON, D.C.

(See Kensington, Maryland)

Elder Law, Trusts and Estates, Asset Protection, Wealth Preservation, Wills, Probate, Estate Litigation, Guardianship, Medicaid Applications, Nursing Home Placement, Living Trusts, Business Succession Planning, Closely Held Business, Estate Planning, Small Business Law, Non-Profit Corporations, Real Estate, Construction, Business Contracts, Financial Planning, Real Estate Closings.

SEYFARTH SHAW

Established in 1971

815 CONNECTICUT AVENUE, N.W.
WASHINGTON, D.C. 20006-4004
Telephone: 202-463-2400
Facsimile: 202-828-5393
Email: mailbox@seyfarth.com
URL: http://www.seyfarth.com

Chicago, Illinois Office: 55 E. Monroe Street, Suite 4200. Telephone: 312-346-8000. Facsimile: 312-269-8869.

Los Angeles, California Office: 2029 Century Park East. Telephone: 310-277-7200. Facsimile: 310-201-5219.

New York, N.Y. Office: 1270 Avenue of the Americas, Suite 2500. Telephone: 212-218-5500. Facsimile: 212-218-5526.

San Francisco, California Office: Suite 2900, 101 California Street. Telephone: 415-397-2823. Facsimile: 415-397-8549.

Sacramento, California Office: 400 Capitol Mall, Suite 2350. Telephone: 916-448-0159. Facsimile: 916-558-4839.

Houston, Texas Office: 700 Louisiana Street, Suite 3850. Telephone: 713-225-2300. Facsimile: 713-225-2340.

Atlanta, Georgia Office: 1545 Peachtree Street, N.E., One Peachtree Pointe, Suite 700. Telephone: 404-885-1500. Facsimile: 404-892-7056.

Boston, Massachusetts Office: Two Seaport Lane, Suite 300. Telephone: 617-946-4800. Facsimile: 617-946-4801.

Brussels, Belgium Office: Avenue Louise 500, Box 8. Telephone: (32) (2) 647.60.25. Fax: (32) (20 640.70.71.

Labor and Employment Law, Employee Benefits, Employment Discrimination, Employment-at-Will, Health Care, Occupational, Safety and Health, Worker's Compensation. Government Contracts. White-Collar Criminal. Litigation, Administrative Law, Business Contract Disputes, Construction, Corporations and Partnerships, General Tort, Insurance, Intellectual Property, Product Liability, Professional Liability, Securities and Commodities. Corporate, Acquisitions, Antitrust, Bankruptcy and Creditors' Rights, Commercial and Financial Transactions, Contracts, Divestitures, Joint Ventures, Mergers, Real Estate, Tax Law, Trust and Probate. Environmental, Safety and Health.

PARTNERS

DONALD M. BARNES, born 1943; admitted to bar, 1970, District of Columbia. *Education:* Pennsylvania State University (B.S., 1965); George Washington University (J.D., cum laude, 1970). ***PRACTICE AREAS:*** Antitrust Law; Complex Litigation; Agricultural Law; Trade Association Law. ***Email:*** dbarnes@dc.seyfarth.com

ANITA BARONDES, born 1950; admitted to bar, 1977, District of Columbia. *Education:* Bucknell University (B.A., cum laude, 1972); George Washington University (J.D., with honors, 1977). ***PRACTICE AREAS:*** Labor and Employment. ***Email:*** abarondes@dc.seyfarth.com

SUSAN CAROL BENNER, born 1962; admitted to bar, 1988, Maryland; 1990, District of Columbia. *Education:* University of Maryland (B.A., 1984); Catholic University of America (J.D., 1988). ***PRACTICE AREAS:*** Labor and Employment Law. ***Email:*** sbenner@dc.seyfarth.com

STEVEN L. BRIGGERMAN, born 1943; admitted to bar, 1968, Virginia; 1969, District of Columbia. *Education:* University of Chicago (A.B., 1965); George Washington University (J.D., with honors, 1968; LL.M., 1969). Graduate Fellow in Government Procurement Law, George Washington University, 1968-1969. ***Email:*** sbriggerman@dc.seyfarth.com

PETER CHATILOVICZ, born 1946; admitted to bar, 1974, Florida; 1975, District of Columbia. *Education:* Beloit College (B.A., 1969); University of Miami School of Law (J.D., magna cum laude, 1974). ***PRACTICE AREAS:*** Labor Law; Employment Law. ***Email:*** pchatilovicz@dc.seyfarth.com

KEVIN P. CONNELLY, born 1960; admitted to bar, 1985, Maryland; 1988, District of Columbia. *Education:* University of Maryland (B.A., 1982); George Washington University (J.D., 1985). ***PRACTICE AREAS:*** Government Contract Litigation and Counseling; Commercial Contract Litigation and Counseling. ***Email:*** kconnelly@dc.seyfarth.com

JOSEPH R. DAMATO, born 1956; admitted to bar, 1981, District of Columbia. *Education:* Providence College (B.A., summa cum laude, 1978); George Washington University (J.D., with honors, 1981). ***PRACTICE AREAS:*** Labor Law; Employment Law. ***Email:*** jdamato@dc.seyfarth.com

JOSEPH J. DYER, born 1954; admitted to bar, 1979, Maryland (Not admitted in District of Columbia). *Education:* University of Maryland (B.A., 1976; J.D., with honors, 1979); National Law Center, George Washington University. ***PRACTICE AREAS:*** Government Contracts Law; International Law. ***Email:*** jdyer@dc.seyfarth.com

SARA BEIRO FARABOW, born 1963; admitted to bar, 1990, Virginia, 1993, District of Columbia. *Education:* Virginia Polytechnic Institute & State University (B.S., 1986); College of William & Mary (J.D., 1990); Georgetown University (LL.M., with distinction, International and Comparative Law, 1997). ***PRACTICE AREAS:*** Contract Law; International Litigation. ***Email:*** farabow@dc.seyfarth.com

MARTIN J. GOLUB, born 1947; admitted to bar, 1977, Massachusetts; 1980, District of Columbia. *Education:* Princeton University (A.B., cum laude, 1969); Boston College (J.D., cum laude, 1977). ***LANGUAGES:*** English, French. ***PRACTICE AREAS:*** Government Contracts Law; International Commercial Transactions; International Arbitration and Litigation. ***Email:*** golub@seyfarth.be

BENNETT D. GREENBERG, born 1956; admitted to bar, 1981, District of Columbia. *Education:* State University of New York at Buffalo (B.A., summa cum laude, 1978); Georgetown University Law Center (J.D., 1981). ***PRACTICE AREAS:*** Construction Law; Government Contracts Law. ***Email:*** bgreenberg@dc.seyfarth.com

KARLA GROSSENBACHER, born 1967; admitted to bar, 1992, Maryland; 1993, District of Columbia. *Education:* Marquette University (B.A., 1989); Georgetown University Law Center (J.D., cum laude, 1992). ***LANGUAGES:*** French. ***PRACTICE AREAS:*** Employment and Labor Law; Litigation. ***Email:*** kgrossenbacher@dc.seyfarth.com

ABBEY GAIL HAIRSTON, born 1955; admitted to bar, 1982, Florida; 1994, District of Columbia and Maryland. *Education:* Drake University (B.A., 1976); University of Iowa (J.D., 1980). ***PRACTICE AREAS:*** Litigation; Labor and Employment Law; Education Law. ***Email:*** ahairston@dc.seyfarth.com

MICHAEL B. HUBBARD, born 1954; admitted to bar, 1979, Virginia; 1982, Wyoming; 1988, District of Columbia. *Education:* Washington and Lee University (B.A., cum laude, 1976; J.D., 1979). ***PRACTICE AREAS:*** Government Contract Law; Commercial Contract Law; Contract Litigation. ***Email:*** mhubbard@dc.seyfarth.com

STEVEN J. KMIECIAK, born 1953; admitted to bar, 1979, Maryland; 1981, Texas; 1991, District of Columbia; 1995, California. *Education:* University of Notre Dame (B.A., 1975); University of Maryland (J.D., 1979). ***PRACTICE AREAS:*** Construction Law; Government Contracts Law. ***Email:*** mkmieciak@dc.seyfarth.com

ALAN R. MALASKY, born 1944; admitted to bar, 1968, District of Columbia. *Education:* University of Pittsburgh (B.B.A., 1965); George Washington University (J.D., 1968). ***PRACTICE AREAS:*** Agriculture Law; Antitrust and Trade Regulation Law; Administrative Law; Litigation. ***Email:*** amalasky@dc.seyfarth.com

JAMES M. McHALE, born 1946; admitted to bar, 1972, New York and District of Columbia. *Education:* Wesleyan University (B.A., 1968); Université de Paris and Université de Montpellier, France (1965); Cornell University (J.D., 1971). ***PRACTICE AREAS:*** Civil Litigation; Government Contracts Law; International Contracts Law; Administrative Law. ***Email:*** jmchale@dc.seyfarth.com

JOHN T. MITCHELL, born 1952; admitted to bar, 1988, Kentucky; 1989, District of Columbia. *Education:* Georgetown College (B.A., 1974); Southern Baptist Theological Seminary (M.R.E., 1976); University of Louisville (M.S.S.W., 1977; J.D., magna cum laude, 1987). ***PRACTICE AREAS:*** First Amendment Law; Legislative Practice; Franchise and Distributorship Litigation; Trade Associations; Antitrust. ***Email:*** jmitchell@dc.seyfarth.com

STUART B. NIBLEY, born 1953; admitted to bar, 1979, Virginia and District of Columbia. *Education:* Washington & Lee University (B.A., magna cum laude, 1975; J.D., cum laude, 1979). ***PRACTICE AREAS:*** Government Contracts Law; Construction Contracts Law; Administrative Law. ***Email:*** snibley@dc.seyfarth.com

LAWRENCE P. POSTOL, born 1951; admitted to bar, 1976, Connecticut; 1977, District of Columbia ; 1979, 1982, Virginia. *Education:* Cornell University (B.S., with distinction, 1973; J.D., cum laude, 1976). ***PRACTICE AREAS:*** Labor and Employment Law; Environmental Litigation; Worker's Compensation Law. ***Email:*** lpostol@dc.seyfarth.com

RICHARD McKIM PRESTON, born 1947; admitted to bar, 1976, Virginia and District of Columbia. *Education:* Washington & Lee University (B.A., 1969; J.D., cum laude, 1976). ***PRACTICE AREAS:*** Construction Contracts Law; Government Contracts Law; International Contracts Law. ***Email:*** rpreston@dc.seyfarth.com

SALVATORE A. ROMANO, born 1940; admitted to bar, 1965, New York; 1971, District of Columbia. *Education:* St. John's University (B.A., 1961; LL.B., 1964). ***PRACTICE AREAS:*** Litigation. ***Email:*** sromano@dc.seyfarth.com

DONALD L. ROSENTHAL (1950-2001).

FREDRIC S. SINGERMAN, born 1959; admitted to bar, 1982, Illinois; 1993, District of Columbia. *Education:* Oberlin College; University of Cincinnati (B.A., magna cum laude, 1979); University of Chicago (J.D., 1982). ***PRACTICE AREAS:*** Employee Benefits Law; ERISA Litigation. ***Email:*** fsingerman@dc.seyfarth.com

(This Listing Continued)

SEYFARTH SHAW, Washington—Continued

MICHAEL A. VICCORA, born 1963; admitted to bar, 1990, Virginia 1992, District of Columbia. *Education:* Dartmouth College (B.A., 1985); George Washington University National Law Center (J.D., with high honors, 1990). ***PRACTICE AREAS:*** Labor and Employment Law. ***Email:*** mviccora@dc.seyfarth.com

CHRISTOPHER A. WEALS, born 1959; admitted to bar, 1985, Illinois; 1988, District of Columbia. *Education:* Denison University (B.A., summa cum laude, 1982); Northwestern University (J.D., with honors, 1985). ***PRACTICE AREAS:*** Labor and Employment; ERISA Litigation; Immigration. ***Email:*** cweals@dc.seyfarth.com

WILLIAM KARL WILBURN, born 1948; admitted to bar, 1978, Maryland; 1986, District of Columbia. *Education:* Johns Hopkins University (B.A., 1970); University of Baltimore (J.D., 1977). ***LANGUAGES:*** German. ***PRACTICE AREAS:*** Construction Law; Litigation; International Practice. ***Email:*** wwilburn@dc.seyfarth.com

OF COUNSEL

GRACE A. BATEMAN, born 1943; admitted to bar, 1981, District of Columbia. *Education:* St. John's College (B.A., 1965); Catholic University of America (J.D., 1980). ***PRACTICE AREAS:*** Government Contract Law; Commercial Contract Law; Administrative Law. ***Email:*** gbateman@dc.seyfarth.com

NATHANIEL H. GOODRICH, born 1914; admitted to bar, 1936, New York; 1954, District of Columbia. *Education:* Cornell University (A.B., 1934; LL.B., 1936). Counsel, President's Scientific Research Board, 1946-1947. Counsel and Executive Secretary, President's Special Board of Inquiry on Air Safety, 1947-1948. Counsel to Assistant Secretary of Defense, General Counsel and Deputy General Counsel, Department of Defense, 1948-1953. [Lt. Col., USAFR, Retired; Military Service, 1941-1946]. ***Email:*** mgoodrich@dc.seyfarth.com

RUSSELL H. GORE, born Fort Lauderdale, Florida, November 10, 1968; admitted to bar, 1993, California (inactive); 1996, District of Columbia. *Education:* Furman University (B.A., summa cum laude, 1990), Phi Beta Kappa; Georgetown University Law Center (J.D., cum laude, 1993). ***PRACTICE AREAS:*** Labor and Employment. ***Email:*** rgore@seyfarth.com

RONALD A. LINDSAY, born 1952; admitted to bar, 1980, District of Columbia. *Education:* Georgetown University (A.B., 1974; M.A., 1976; Ph.D., 1996); University of Virginia (J.D., 1980). ***PRACTICE AREAS:*** Labor Law; Employment Law; Fair Housing Law. ***Email:*** rlindsay@dc.seyfarth.com

RESIDENT ASSOCIATES

RAYMOND C. BALDWIN, born 1963; admitted to bar, 1996, Maryland (Not admitted in District of Columbia). *Education:* Univ. of Maryland (B.A., 1985; J.D., 1996). ***PRACTICE AREAS:*** Labor and Employment. ***Email:*** rbaldwin@dc.seyfarth.com

DAVID A. BLAKE, born 1969; admitted to bar, 1994, Washington (Not admitted in District of Columbia). *Education:* Catholic University of America (B.S., Architecture, 1991; J.D., cum laude, 1994). ***PRACTICE AREAS:*** Construction; Government Contracts; Litigation. ***Email:*** dblake@dc.seyfarth.com

ANNE D. BOLLING, born November 14, 1957; admitted to bar, 1983, Maryland; 1988, District of Columbia; U.S. Court of Appeals, Fourth Circuit. *Education:* College of William & Mary (B.A., 1980); University of Virginia (J.D., 1983). Member, WEB Network of Professionals. *Member:* The District of Columbia Bar. ***PRACTICE AREAS:*** Employee Benefits. ***Email:*** abolling@dc.seyfarth.com

PAUL R. BROCKMEYER, born 1966; admitted to bar, 1992, Illinois (Not admitted in District of Columbia). *Education:* Vassar College (B.A., magna cum laude, 1988); University of Michigan (J.D., 1992). ***PRACTICE AREAS:*** Labor Litigation. ***Email:*** pbrockmeyer@dc.seyfarth.com

DAVID MICHAEL BURNS, born 1974; admitted to bar, 1999, Maryland (Not admitted in District of Columbia). *Education:* University of Maryland, College Park (B.A., 1996); Catholic University (J.D., magna cum laude, 1999). ***PRACTICE AREAS:*** Labor and Employment. ***Email:*** dburns@dc.seyfarth.com

SUSAN JEANBLANC COHEN, born 1970; admitted to bar, 1995, Maryland; 1997, District of Columbia. *Education:* University of Delaware (B.S.B.A., magna cum laude, 1992); University of Miami (J.D., magna cum laude, 1995). ***PRACTICE AREAS:*** Labor and Employment Law. ***Email:*** scohen@dc.seyfarth.com

EMILY R. FRIEDMAN, born South Weymouth, Massachusetts, June 9, 1975; admitted to bar, 2000, Maryland (Not admitted in District of Columbia). *Education:* Tufts University (B.A., cum laude, 1997); Georgetown University (J.D., magna cum laude, 2000). Order of the Coif. *Member:* Maryland State and American Bar Associations. ***PRACTICE AREAS:*** Litigation; Employment Law; Labor Law. ***Email:*** efriedman@dc.seyfarth.com

SUZANNE HARNESS, born 1945; admitted to bar, 1998, Virginia (Not admitted in District of Columbia). *Education:* Catholic University (B.S., cum laude, Architecture, 1978; M.Arch., 1979); George Washington University (J.D., 1998). ***PRACTICE AREAS:*** Construction; Government Contracts. ***Email:*** sharness@dc.seyfarth.com

HOWARD C.M. HOBBS, born Kansas City, Missouri, April 19, 1949; admitted to bar, 1976, Florida (Not admitted in District of Columbia). *Education:* Loyola University (B.A., 1971; J.D., 1976). *Member:* The Florida Bar. ***PRACTICE AREAS:*** Labor and Employment.

JEFFREY M. HUMMEL, born 1967; admitted to bar, 1995, Virginia; 1996, District of Columbia. *Education:* James Madison University (B.S., 1989); University of Virginia (J.D., 1995). ***PRACTICE AREAS:*** Construction Law; Government Contracts. ***Email:*** jhummel@dc.seyfarth.com

KELLY S. JENNINGS, born Pittsburgh, Pennsylvania, August 19, 1971; admitted to bar, 1996, Maryland and U.S. District Court, District of Maryland; 2000, District of Columbia. *Education:* Denison University (B.A., 1993); George Washington University (J.D., 1996). ***PRACTICE AREAS:*** Employment Law; Employment Discrimination; Affirmative Action. ***Email:*** kjennings@dc.seyfarth.com

JAMES M. MESNARD, born 1953; admitted to bar, 1986, Maryland and District of Columbia. *Education:* Virginia Military Institute (B.A., with distinction, 1975); University of Maryland (J.D., with honors, 1985). ***PRACTICE AREAS:*** Litigation. ***Email:*** jmesnard@dc.seyfarth.com

LOWELL H. PATTERSON, III, born 1959; admitted to bar, 1998, Virginia and Maryland; 1999, District of Columbia. *Education:* Hampden-Sydney College (B.A., 1981); College of William and Mary (M.B.A., 1983); T. C. Williams School of Law, University of Richmond (J.D., 1998). ***PRACTICE AREAS:*** Creditors Rights; Bankruptcy; Commercial Law. ***Email:*** lpatterson@dc.seyfarth.com

ROBERT F. PEZZIMENTI, born 1973; (admission pending). *Education:* State University of New York at Buffalo (B.A., 1996); George Washington University (J.D., 2000). ***PRACTICE AREAS:*** Government Contracts; Antitrust. ***Email:*** rpezzimenti@dc.seyfarth.com

JESSICA R. SCHNEIDER, born 1974; admitted to bar, 1999, Virginia (Not admitted in District of Columbia). *Education:* Stanford University (B.A., 1996; M.A., 1996); Georgetown University (J.D., 1999). ***PRACTICE AREAS:*** Labor and Employment. ***Email:*** jschneider@dc.seyfarth.com

ZACHARY TAYLOR SHULTZ, born Bedford, Texas, August 9, 1975; (admission pending). *Education:* Washington & Lee University (B.A., magna cum laude, 1998); University of Texas at Austin (J.D., 2001). ***PRACTICE AREAS:*** Government Contracts. ***Email:*** tshultz@dc.seyfarth.com

MARK STEVENSON, born 1968; admitted to bar, 1999, Maryland; 2000, District of Columbia. *Education:* Georgetown University (B.S.F.S., 1990); American University (J.D., 1999). ***LANGUAGES:*** German. ***PRACTICE AREAS:*** Employee Benefits. ***Email:*** mstevenson@dc.seyfarth.com

CHARLES FREDERICK WALTERS, born 1963; admitted to bar, 1994, District of Columbia. *Education:* University of Toronto, Ontario (B.S.C., 1988); Cornell University (M.I.L.R.,1990); Catholic University of America, Columbus School of Law (J.D., cum laude, 1994). ***PRACTICE AREAS:*** Labor Law; Employment Law. ***Email:*** cwalters@dc.seyfarth.com

(For complete biographical data on personnel at Chicago, Illinois, Los Angeles, California, New York, New York, San Francisco, California, Sacramento, California, Houston, Texas, Atlanta, Georgia, Boston, Massachusetts, and Brussels, Belgium, see Professional Biographies at those locations)

THOMAS G. SHACK, JR., P.C.

Established in 1971

1150 CONNECTICUT AVENUE, N.W., SUITE 900

WASHINGTON, D.C. 20036

Telephone: 202-293-5900

Telecopier: 202-659-3493

URL: http://www.lawyers.com/thomasshacklaw

General Litigation Practice before all Courts, Departments, Commissions and Federal Agencies. Specializing in International Trade and Commercial Transactions, International Arbitration and in all areas of Telecommunications.

THOMAS G. SHACK, JR., born Boston, Massachusetts, November 27, 1933; admitted to bar, 1958, Massachusetts; 1960, District of Columbia; 1965, U.S. Supreme Court. *Education:* Boston College (B.S., 1955; J.D., 1958). *Member:* The District of Columbia Bar; Bar Association of the District of Columbia; Massachusetts, Federal, American (Member, Sections on: Health Law; Litigation; Intellectual Property Law) and Federal Communications Bar Associations;

(This Listing Continued)

The Association of Trial Lawyers of America; National Health Lawyers Association. ***REPORTED CASES:*** Dames & Moore v. Regan, 101 S.Ct 2972 (1981). ***PRACTICE AREAS:*** International Trade; Commercial Transactions; Arbitration; Communications.

SHAFFER, RAPAPORT & SCHMIDT, L.L.P.

1225 I STREET N.W., SUITE 500
WASHINGTON, D.C. 20005
Telephone: 202-789-8188
Fax: 202-312-2203

New York, NY Office: 1501 Broadway, 31st Floor, 10036. Telephone: 212-382-1600. Fax: 212-382-0920.
Jersey City, NJ Office: 574 Newark Avenue, Suite 211, 07306. Telephone: 201-418-4888. Fax: 212-382-0920.

Labor and Employment Law, Commercial Litigation, Matrimonial Law, Personal Injury, Social Security Law, Medical Malpractice.

DAVID J. SHAFFER, born Springfield, Ohio, July 30, 1958; admitted to bar, 1984, California; 1988, District of Columbia; 1994, Maryland. *Education:* Wittenberg University (B.A., summa cum laude, 1980); Stanford University (J.D., 1983). Order of the Coif. Author: "The Civil Rights Act of 1991," Federal Bar News and Journal 100 (Jan 1992); "Defense Strategies Under Civil Rights Act of 1991," Federal Bar Association, April 1992 (Bethesda, Maryland); "Defending Cases Under the New Civil Rights Act," FBA Annual Briefing Conference (Philadelphia, Pennsylvania, November 1992). Editor, *The Labouring Oar,* the newsletter of the Labor Law and Labor Relations Section of the FBA. Law Clerk, Hon. Betty B. Fletcher, U.S. Court of Appeals, Ninth Circuit, 1983-1984. *Member:* District of Columbia Bar; State Bar of California; Maryland State, Federal (Chair, EEO Committee, Labor Law and Labor Relations Section, 1992-1994; Chair, Individual Rights and Responsibilities Committee, 1994-1995; Chair, Alternative Dispute Resolution, 1995-1996) and American (Member, Labor and Employment Law Section) Bar Associations. ***PRACTICE AREAS:*** Labor and Employment Law.

MARC A. RAPAPORT, born Cleveland, Ohio, June 2, 1967; admitted to bar, 1992, New Jersey; 1993, New York; 1994, U.S. District Court, Eastern and Southern Districts of New York; 1995, District of Columbia; 1997, U .S. District Court, District of New Jersey. *Education:* University of Wisconsin; New York University (B.A., 1989); Georgetown University (J.D., 1992). Staff Attorney, U.S. Department of Justice, Foreign Claims Settlement Commission, 1992-1994. *Member:* Queens County, New York State and American Bar Associations; Association of the Bar of the City of New York; National Association of Social Security Claimants. ***LANGUAGES:*** Spanish.

RONALD A. SCHMIDT, born Louisville, Kentucky, September 2, 1965; admitted to bar, 1995, Nebraska; 1997, Colorado; 1999, U.S. Court of Appeals, Third Circuit; 2000, District of Columbia. *Education:* University of Louisville (B.A., 1991); University of Nebraska (J.D., with distinction, 1995; M.A., Industrial-Organizational Psychology, 1996). Phi Delta Phi. Law Clerk to Honorable D. Nick Caporale, Nebraska Supreme Court, 1995-1996. Author: "The Plaintiff's Burden in Disparate Treatment Cases: Discrimination Vel Non," 73 Neb. L. Rev. 953 (1994). Co-author: with David Shaffer, "Personality Testing in Employment," SHRM Legal Report , Sept-Oct Issue (1999); "The HR Manager 5 Guide to Employment Practices Liability Insurance," SHRM Legal Report, July-August, 2000; "The Top 10 HR Mistakes Tech and Other Emerging Companies Make," SHRM Tech Know Report, 2nd Quarter, 2000. *Member:* Society of Human Resources Management. ***PRACTICE AREAS:*** Labor and Employment; Class Actions; Commercial Litigation.

SHAINIS & PELTZMAN

CHARTERED
1850 M STREET, N.W., SUITE 240
WASHINGTON, D.C. 20036
Telephone: 202-293-0011
Fax: 202-293-0810
Email: shainis-peltzman@s-plaw.com
URL: http://www.lawyers.com/s&plaw

Telecommunications Law, Communications Law, Telecommunications Regulation, FCC Regulation, FCC Licensing.

FIRM PROFILE: Combining over 46 years of experience, the firm specializes in the representation of telecommunications clients including broadcasters, radio and TV stations, cable companies, commercial and non-commercial telecommunications and program distributors. The firm has both a local and national practice and continues to represent both small and large corporations in general commercial transactions, formations, labor and business matters.

(This Listing Continued)

AARON SHAINIS, born Washington, D.C., February 7, 1948; admitted to bar, 1973, Tennessee; 1974, District of Columbia. *Education:* The Ohio State University (B.A., 1969; University of Tennessee at Knoxville (J.D., 1973). Phi Alpha Delta. Attorney, Federal Communications Commission, 1974-1980. *Member:* The District of Columbia Bar; American Bar Association; Federal Communications Bar Association. ***PRACTICE AREAS:*** Communications Law; Corporate Law; Appellate Practice; Telecommunications. ***Email:*** aaron@s-plaw.com

LEE J. PELTZMAN, born Philadelphia, Pennsylvania, October 29, 1948; admitted to bar, 1973, Pennsylvania; 1983, District of Columbia. *Education:* Temple University (B.A., 1970); Columbia University (J.D., 1973). Harlon Fiske Stone Scholar. Attorney, Federal Communications Commission, 1974-1981. *Member:* The District of Columbia Bar; Federal Communications Bar Association. ***PRACTICE AREAS:*** Communications Law; Corporate Law; Appellate Practice. ***Email:*** lee@s-plaw.com

OF COUNSEL

WILLIAM H. DuROSS, III, born Lakewood, Ohio, August 3, 1941; admitted to bar, 1968, District of Columbia; 1973, U.S. Supreme Court. *Education:* Yale University (B.A., 1965); George Washington University (J.D., 1968; LL.M., Labor Law, 1971). Professorial Lecturer in Law, George Washington Law School, 1979-1985. Head Delegate, United States Delegation, International Labor Organization, Geneva, Switzerland, September 1983. ***PRACTICE AREAS:*** Labor and Employment Law; Employment Discrimination; Employee Benefits. ***Email:*** bill@s-plaw.com

ROBERT J. KELLER, born New Albany, Indiana, February 20, 1953; admitted to bar, 1979, District of Columbia and U.S. District Court for the District of Columbia; U.S. Court of Appeals for the District of Columbia Circuit. *Education:* Catholic University of America (B.A., 1975; J.D., 1979). Member, American Radio Relay League. *Member:* District of Columbia Bar; American Bar Association; Federal Communications Bar Association. (Also practicing individually).

THE SHANAHAN LAW FIRM LLC

SUITE 510
1725 K STREET N.W.
WASHINGTON, D.C. 20006
Telephone: 202-785-2940
Fax: 202-785-2941

Cleveland, Ohio Office: 1750 Huntington Building, 925 Euclid Avenue, 44115-1483. Telephone: 216-363-1700. Fax: 216-363-1096.

Business, Litigation and Transactional Practice, Acquisitions and Divestitures, Antitrust, Banks and Banking, Business Law, Civil Litigation, Collective Bargaining, Commercial Law, Computers and Software, Construction Law, Contracts, Corporate Law, Entertainment Law, Environmental Law, Finance, Intellectual Property, Investments, Labor and Employment, Leases and Leasing, Mergers, Mortgages, Partnership Law, Real Estate, Securities, Taxation, Technology, Trusts and Estates, and Venture Capital.

TERRANCE L. RYAN, born Toledo, Ohio, April 25, 1947; admitted to bar, 1976, Ohio (Not admitted in District of Columbia). *Education:* Washington University; University of Toledo (B.A., 1973; J.D., 1976). Associate Editor, University of Toledo Law Review. *Member:* Ohio State (Member, Sections on: Antitrust Law; Labor and Employment Law; Litigation) and American (Member, Sections on: Antitrust Law; Environment, Energy and Resources; Labor and Employment Law; Litigation) Bar Associations. ***PRACTICE AREAS:*** Civil Litigation; Labor (Management) Law; Employment Discrimination; Collective Bargaining. ***Email:*** tryan@ShanahanFirm.com

J. KEARNEY SHANAHAN, born Washington, D.C., July 29, 1944; admitted to bar, 1972, Ohio; 1981, District of Columbia; 1999, Florida. *Education:* Princeton University (A.B., 1966); Georgetown University (J.D., 1971). Member, 1983-1994 and Chair, 1983-1993, Ohio Development Financing Advisory Board. Member, 1983-1993 and Co-Chair, 1991-1993, Ohio Development Financing Policy Board. State of Ohio Representative, Interstate Oil Compact Commission, 1983-1991. *Member:* District of Columbia Bar (Member, Sections on: Antitrust; Trade Regulation and Consumer Affairs; Corporation, Finance and Securities Law; Environment, Energy and Natural Resources; Estates, Trusts and Probate Law; International Law; Labor and Employment Law; Intellectual Property Law; Real Estate, Housing and Land Use; Taxation); The Florida Bar (Member, Sections on: Business Law; Environmental and Land Use Law; International Law; Labor & Employment Law; Real Property Probate and Trust Law; Tax; Trial Lawyers); American Bar Association (Member, Sections on: Business Law; Real Property; Probate and Trust; Taxation). ***Email:*** kshanahan@ShanahanFirm.com

SHANKS & HERBERT

WASHINGTON, D.C.

(See Alexandria, Virginia)

Intellectual Property Law including Patent, Copyright, Industrial Design, Trademark, Trade Secrets and Unfair Competition, Licensing and Litigation, Chemical, Biochemical, Biotechnology, Computer Software, Electronics, Pharmaceutical and Medical Instrumentation Patent Law.

SHANLEY AND BAKER

Established in 1947

GEORGETOWN BUILDING, SUITE 235
2233 WISCONSIN AVENUE, N.W.
WASHINGTON, D.C. 20007
Telephone: 202-333-5800
Facsimile: 202-333-5803

Intellectual Property, Patent, Trademark and Copyright Law.

MEMBERS OF FIRM

JAMES J. SHANLEY (1906-1995).

RAYMOND N. BAKER, born Pittsburgh, Pennsylvania, September 29, 1924; admitted to bar, 1959, District of Columbia; 1968, U.S. Supreme Court; 1982, U.S. Court of Appeals for the Federal Circuit; registered to practice before U.S. Patent and Trademark Office. *Education:* Duquesne University and U.S. Naval Academy (B.S., 1946); Georgetown University and George Washington University (J.D., 1958). Phi Alpha Delta. Examiner, U.S. Patent Office, 1955-1958. *Member:* The Bar Association of the District of Columbia; American Bar Association; American Intellectual Property Law Association; The Newcomer Society of the United States; International Trademark Association; U.S. Naval Academy Alumni Association. [Lieut., U.S. Navy, 1943-1949]. ***PRACTICE AREAS:*** Patents; Trademarks; Copyrights; Patent Licensing; Patent Protection.

SHAPIRO, LIFSCHITZ AND SCHRAM, P.C.

THE EVENING STAR BUILDING
1101 PENNSYLVANIA AVENUE N.W.
SUITE 1050
WASHINGTON, D.C. 20004
Telephone: 202-347-4111
Facsimile: 202-347-8341
URL: http://www.slslaw.com

Greenbelt, Maryland Office: 6411 Ivy Lane, Suite 116, 20770. Telephone: 202-347-4111. Facsimile: 202-347-8341.

Business, Corporate, Real Estate, Litigation, Commercial Transactions, Arbitration, Mediation and Alternative Dispute Resolution, Construction, Government Contracts, Creditors Rights and Remedies, Technology Licensing, Civil Fraud, Appellate Practice, Taxation, Estate Planning.

RONALD S. SHAPIRO, born Washington, D.C., April 27, 1947; admitted to bar, 1973, District of Columbia. *Education:* University of Maryland (B.S., Accounting, 1969); George Washington University (J.D., with honors, 1972). Phi Delta Phi. Former Editor, National Property Law, Finance Law and Environmental Law Digests. *Member:* The District of Columbia Bar. ***PRACTICE AREAS:*** Real Estate; General Business Law; Finance; Creditors Rights. ***Email:*** shapiro@slslaw.com

JUDAH LIFSCHITZ, born New York, N.Y., November 28, 1952; admitted to bar, 1977, Maryland; 1978, District of Columbia, U.S. District Court, District of Columbia, U.S. Court of Appeals for the District of Columbia Circuit and U.S. Claims Court; 1980, U.S. Court of Appeals, Fourth Circuit; 1982, U.S. Court of Appeals for the Federal Circuit; 1985, U.S. Supreme Court, U.S. Court of Appeals, Fifth and Ninth Circuits. *Education:* Yeshiva University (B.A., magna cum laude, 1974); George Washington University (J.D., 1977). Co-Author: "Mechanics' Liens," Construction Briefings, 82-5; "Little Miller Acts," Construction Briefings, 84-8; "Delay and Disruption in International Construction," Construction Briefings, 86-9; "Tort Liability in Construction Contracting," Construction Briefings, 2001; "Misappropriation of Contract Funds," 10; "Handling Environmental Incidents at the Jobsite," Construction Briefings, 91-10, "Construction Supervision," Construction Briefings, 93-10, "Construction Trust Fund Statutes And the Misappropriation of Contract Funds/Edition 11," Construction Briefings, 99-12, Federal Publications, Inc.; "Risky Business: The Extraordinary Products Liability Exposure of the Government Contractor," 1985 ABA Section of Public Contract Law; "Contractor Licensing Laws," Wiley Construction Law Update, 1993. Author: "Heaven Sent Stories of Faith and Effort," Targum/Feldhiem, 1997; "Stories for Shauli," Targum/-Feldhiem, 1999. Proffesorial Lecturer, Construction Law, American University, Washington College of Law. Lecturer: Practical Contract Law Series, Georgetown University Law School Continuing Legal Education Program, 1984-1988; Delay and Disruption, 1984—; International Delay and Disruption, Crown Eagle Communications, Inc., 1985—; Environmental Problems on the Jobsite, Federal Publications, Inc., 1990. Proving Claims Under the FIDIC Conditions of Contract, Hawksmere plc., 1994. Member, Editorial Advisory Board, Construction Business Review, 1992. *Member:* Prince George's County Bar Association; The District of Columbia Bar; Maryland State Bar Association; American Bar Association, Construction Industry Forum. ***LANGUAGES:*** Hebrew. ***PRACTICE AREAS:*** Construction; Government Contracts; Business Litigation. ***Email:*** lifschitz@slslaw.com

STEVEN H. SCHRAM, born Teaneck, New Jersey, February 3, 1953; admitted to bar, 1979, District of Columbia. *Education:* University of Pennsylvania (B.S., magna cum laude, 1975); Georgetown University Law Center (J.D., cum laude, 1978). Beta Gamma Sigma. Author: "Death of a Partnership," 37 N.Y.U. Institute on Federal Tax, 1978. Chief Operating Officer/Chief Financial Officer, Marlo Furniture Company, 1988-1992. Member, Regional Governing Board and Regional Leadership Development Chairperson for Anti-Defamation League. *Member:* The District of Columbia Bar. ***PRACTICE AREAS:*** Business Law; Commercial Finance; Commercial Transactions; Technology Licensing; Corporate Law; Health Care; Limited Liability Company Law; Finance; Partnership Law. ***Email:*** schram@slslaw.com

---

ROBERT A. FOSTER, born Dixon, Illinois, August 4, 1958; admitted to bar, 1983, District of Columbia. *Education:* Northwestern University (B.A., 1979); University of Illinois (M.B.A., 1983; J.D., cum laude, 1983). Phi Beta Kappa. *Member:* The District of Columbia Bar. ***PRACTICE AREAS:*** Commercial Real Estate; Commercial Transactions. ***Email:*** foster@slslaw.com

RANDAL W. WAX, born Nagoya, Japan, March 24, 1959; admitted to bar, 1984, District of Columbia and Massachusetts; 1986, U.S. District Court, District of Columbia, U.S. Claims Court, U.S. Court of Appeals, Fifth, Eighth, Ninth, Eleventh, District of Columbia and Federal Circuits; 1987, U.S. Court of Appeals, Third, Sixth, Seventh and Tenth Circuits; 1988, Virginia and U.S. Court of Appeals, Fourth Circuit; 1992, Maryland; 1993, U.S. District Court, District of Maryland and U.S. District Court, Eastern District of Virginia. *Education:* Massachusetts Institute of Technology (B.S., Biology; B.S., Philosophy, 1980); Georgetown University Law Center (J.D., 1983). Jurist, Germany Academic Exchange Service, University of Tübingen, Baden-Württemberg (1983). Fellow, German Academic Exchange Service, Federal Court of Appeals, Düsseldorf, North-Rhine/Westphalia (1984). Author: "Maryland's Collateral Order Doctrine," PGCBA News Journal, Feb. 2000. Co-Author: "Tort Liability in Construction Contracting," Construction Briefing, 2001, "Mechanics' Liens/ Edition II", Construction Briefings, 2000-u Construction Briefings, West Group; "Construction Trust Fund Statutes and the Misappropriation of Contract Funds," Construction Briefings, 99-12 Construction Briefings, West Group; "Ownership and Reuse of Design Professional's Designs," Architect and Engineer Liability Claims Against Design Professionals, Second Edition, Wiley 1995; "Proving Claims Under the FIDIC Conditions of Contract," Hawksmere, plc, 1994; "Contractor Licensing Laws," Wiley Construction Law Update, 1993; "Misappropriation of Contract Funds," Construction Briefings, 90-10 Federal Publications, Inc. Lecturer, "Fundamentals of Construction Law," MICPEL 1996, 1998, 1999. Co-Editor, "Practice Manual for the Maryland Lawyer," 1996 Edition, MICPEL, 1998. Mediator, Alternative Dispute Resolution Program, District of Columbia Court of Appeals, 1994—; Construction Law Mediator, Prince George County Circuit Court, Maryland. *Member:* Prince George's County (Chairman, Appellate Practice Committee), Maryland State (Member, Sections on: Construction Law and Education) and Massachusetts Bar Associations; The District of Columbia Bar; Virginia State Bar (Member, Section on Construction Law). ***LANGUAGES:*** German. ***PRACTICE AREAS:*** Government Contracts; Construction Claims and Disputes; Commercial Litigation. ***Email:*** wax@slslaw.com

JAMES D. McMICHAEL, born Baton Rouge, Louisiana, October 17, 1956; admitted to bar, 1982, Louisiana; 1995, District of Columbia; 1998, Maryland. *Education:* Louisiana State University (B.A., 1979); University of Texas School of Law (J.D., with honors, 1982). Order of the Coif. Member, Texas Law Review, 1981-1982. *Member:* The District of Columbia Bar; Louisiana State, Maryland and American Bar Associations. ***PRACTICE AREAS:*** Construction Litigation; Government Contracts; Business Litigation. ***Email:*** mcmichael@slslaw.com

THOMAS R. BARTMAN, born Frankfurt/Main, Germany, November 8, 1953; admitted to bar, 1982, District of Columbia; 1999, Maryland. *Education:* Haverford College (B.A., 1975); Yale University (M.Phil., 1979) ; University of Virginia (J.D., 1982). Phi Beta Kappa. Virginia Journal of Natural Resources Law, 1981-1982. Law Clerk to the Hon. Dortch Warriner, U.S. District Court, Eastern District of Virginia, 1982-1983. Attorney, U.S. Department of Justice, Environment Division, 1988-1990. ***LANGUAGES:*** German. ***PRACTICE AREAS:*** Environmental Regulation; Litigation; Environmental Compliance Counseling; General Litigation. ***Email:*** bartman@slslaw.com

(This Listing Continued)

JONATHAN A. BELDON, born San Antonio, Texas; admitted to bar, 1995, Texas; 2000, District of Columbia; 2001, Maryland. *Education:* University of Pennsylvania (B.A., cum laude, 1992); University of Texas (J.D., 1995). [Captain, USAF Dept. of J.A.G., 1995-1999.]. ***PRACTICE AREAS:*** Civil Litigation; Construction Law; Trial Practice. ***Email:*** beldon@slslaw.com

HELMUT E. GERLACH, born Pirmasens, Germany, May 31, 1964; admitted to bar, 1997, Maryland; 1998, U.S. District Court, District of Maryland; 1999, District of Columbia; 2001, U.S. District Court, District of Columbia. *Education:* Towson University (B.A., cum laude, 1994); University of Maryland (J.D., 1997). Phi Alpha Theta. Phi Alpha Delta. Contract Editor, Maryland Law Review, 1996-1997. Member, International Moot Court Board and Team. Author, "Bankruptcy in the Czech Republic, Hungary, and Poland and Section 304 of the U.S. Bankruptcy Code, Proceedings Ancillary to Foreign Proceedings," 22 Md. J. Int'l L. & Trade 81 (1998). Associate Editor, The German American Law Journal, 1996-1998. *Member:* Maryland State and American Bar Associations; District of Columbia Bar; German American Law Association. ***LANGUAGES:*** German. ***PRACTICE AREAS:*** Real Estate; Business Law; Commercial Transactions; Secured Lending; Commercial Loans; Commercial Litigation. ***Email:*** gerlach@slslaw.com

SUZANNE MARIE LEWIS, born Alexandria, Virginia, June 20, 1969; admitted to bar, 1994, Maryland; 1995 Virginia and U.S. Court of Appeals, Fourth Circuit; 1997, District of Columbia; 1998, U.S. District Court of Appeals, D.C. Circuit; U.S. District Court, District of Maryland; U.S. District Court, District of Columbia. *Education:* University of Virginia (B.A., 1991); George Mason University (J.D., 1994). Phi Alpha Delta 1992-1993. Co-Author: "Tort Liability in Construction Contracting," Construction Briefs, 2001. Law Clerk to: Hon. Dale R. Cathell, Maryland Court of Special Appeals, 1994-1996; Hon. Robert L. Karwacki, Maryland Court of Appeals, 1996-1997. *Member:* Maryland State (Co-Chair, Public Service Committee, Young Lawyers' Section, 1997-1999; Chairman, Special Projects Committee, Young Lawyers Section, 1999-2000) and American (Member, Young Lawyers Division, 1994-2000) Bar Associations; District of Columbia; Virginia State Bar. ***LANGUAGES:*** Italian. ***PRACTICE AREAS:*** Labor and Employment Law; Debtor Bankruptcy; Creditor Bankruptcy; Creditor Rights; Commercial Real Estate Law; Commercial Leasing. ***Email:*** lewis@slslaw.com

SHAPIRO AND OLANDER

WASHINGTON, D.C.

(See Shapiro Sher & Guinot, P.A.)

SHAPIRO SHER & GUINOT, P.A.

Established in 1972

(Formerly known as Shapiro and Olander)

1800 K STREET, N.W., SUITE 716
WASHINGTON, D.C. 20006
Telephone: 202-331-0200
FAX: 202-331-7457
Email: lg@shapirosher.com
URL: http://www.shapirosher.com

Baltimore, Maryland Office: Suite 2000, 36 South Charles Street, 21201. Telephone: 410-385-0202. Fax: 410-539-7611.

Administrative Law, Alternative Dispute Resolution, Arbitration, Asset Based Finance, Banking, Bankruptcy, Bankruptcy Chapter 7, Bankruptcy Chapter 11, Bankruptcy Litigation, Bankruptcy Reorganization, Biotechnology, Blue Sky Law, Business Law, Civil Litigation, Civil Rights Litigation, Commercial Bankruptcy, Commercial Insolvency, Commercial Law, Commercial Leasing, Commercial Litigation, Commercial Real Estate, Commercial Transactions, Commercial Workouts, Complex Commercial Litigation, Complex Litigation, Computer Law, Computer Software Law, Computers and Software, Contracts, Copyrights, Corporate Law, Creditor Bankruptcy, Creditors Rights, Creditors Rights in Bankruptcy, Debtor Bankruptcy, Debtor and Creditor, Debtor and Creditor Remedies, Debtor and Creditor Reorganization, Debtor and Creditor Rights, Debtor Rights, Defense Litigation, Employment Litigation, Federal Civil Litigation, Federal Litigation, Finance, Financial Institution Regulation, Financial Institutions Law, Franchises and Franchising, Franchise Law, Fraudulent Conveyance, Government Relations, Initial Public Offerings, Intellectual Property, International Commercial Law, International Law, International Trade, Internet Law, Internet Trademark Law, Land Development, Land Use, Liquidations, Litigation, Mediation, Mergers and Acquisitions, Municipal Bonds, Municipal Civil Rights, Municipal Corporation Law, Municipal Defense, Municipal Finance, Municipal Law, Municipal Liability, Out of Court Debt Restructuring, Pre-Bankruptcy Workouts, Products Liability, Products Liability Defense, Public Offerings, Real Estate, Real Estate Development, Real Estate Finance, Real Estate Secured Lending, Receiverships, Retail Financing, Secured Creditors Rights, Securities, Securities Regulation, Software Copyright, Start-Up Organization and Financing, Taxation, Technology Transfer, Trademarks, Trial Practice, Venture Capital, Workouts, U.S. Supreme Court Litigation, Uniform Commercial Code, Unsecured Creditors Rights, Zoning.

(This Listing Continued)

FIRM PROFILE: Shapiro Sher & Guinot is a 27-lawyer firm based in Baltimore, Maryland, with an office in Washington, D.C. Formerly known as Shapiro and Olander, the Firm was founded in 1972 by Ronald M. Shapiro, who is now Counsel to the Firm. Known for its business law, bankruptcy, banking, and commercial litigation practice areas, in recent years the Firm has developed a growing practice in international trade and commerce law, with emphasis on Latin American, the Caribbean and Western Europe.

Concurrent with its name change in mid-year 2000, SS&G adopted an innovative management structure-the first of its kind in the region-by hiring a non-lawyer business executive as Chief Operating Officer to manage the day-to-day business of the Firm.

Practice areas are grouped into four departments, each chaired by a senior partner. Integrated services involving multiple practice areas are readily provided to ensure effective use of a broad range of talents and experience.

With its new name, Shapiro Sher & Guinot proudly reflects its linkage to a strong heritage of excellence in the practice of law, focusing on the core strengths that are its future.

Corporate / Business: Corporate and Securities, Commercial Real Estate, Public Companies and Underwriters, Franchising, Tax Law and Biotechnology - Technology Transfers.

Litigation: Corporate and Commercial, Securities Litigation, Employment Law, Product Liability, Public and Governmental Disputes.

Bankruptcy and Financial Services: Counseling Debtor and Creditors' Committees, Workouts and Restructuring, Insolvency and Bankruptcy Litigation, Lenders' and Creditors' Rights, Banking and Financial Services.

International Trade and Commerce: Bilateral International Trade Relations, NAFTA and World Trade Organization Agreements, Investments and Regulatory Compliance, Latin American and Caribbean Government Relations.

PARTNER

LUIS GUINOT, JR., born San Juan, Puerto Rico, April 8, 1935; admitted to bar, 1968, Virginia, District of Columbia, U.S. District Court, Eastern and Western Districts of Virginia, U.S. Court of Appeals, First, Second and Fourth Circuits and U.S. Court of Military Appeals. *Education:* New York University (B.A., 1957); Catholic University of America (J.D., 1968). Recipient, Order of Juan Mora (Silver Plaque) Republic of Costa Rica. Administrator, Office of Commonwealth of Puerto Rico, 1969-1972. Assistant General Counsel, U.S. Department of Agriculture, 1972-1974. United States Ambassador to the Republic of Costa Rica, 1991-1993. Fellow, American Bar Foundation. Chairman of the Board of Trustees of the Puerto Rico Conservation Trust. Member, U.S. Advisory Commission on Civil Disorders (Kerner Commission). Delegate, 1972 Republican National Convention. Member: United States International Agribusiness Promotion Council; Board of Directors, United States Legal Services Corporation; Board of Directors, TECO Energy and TECO Electric Company. *Member:* Virginia State Bar; The District of Columbia Bar. [Commissioned Officer, U.S. Navy, 1957-1967]. ***LANGUAGES:*** Spanish, Italian, French and English. ***PRACTICE AREAS:*** International Law; Commercial Law. ***Email:*** lg@shapirosher.com

RESIDENT MEMBERS, BALTIMORE, MARYLAND OFFICE

CHARLES S. FAX, born Baltimore, Maryland, September 12, 1948; admitted to bar, 1974, New York and District of Columbia; 1990, Maryland, U.S. District Court, District of Columbia, U.S. District Court, District of Maryland, U.S. District Court, Southern District of New York, U.S. Court of Appeals, First, Second, Fourth, Sixth, Ninth, Eleventh and District of Columbia Circuits, U.S. Claims Court and U.S. Supreme Court. *Education:* The Johns Hopkins University (B.A., 1970); George Washington University (J.D., with honors, 1973). Member, National Moot Court Team, 1972-1973. Assistant District Attorney, Bronx County, New York, 1974. *Member:* The District of Columbia Bar; Maryland State Bar Association. ***PRACTICE AREAS:*** Civil Litigation. ***Email:*** csf@shapirosher.com

JOEL I. SHER, born Baltimore, Maryland, December 22, 1952; admitted to bar, 1978, Maryland, U.S. District Court, District of Maryland, U.S. Bankruptcy Court, District of Maryland, U.S. Court of Appeals, Fourth Circuit and U.S. Supreme Court. *Education:* University of Maryland (B.A., 1974); Villanova University (J.D., 1978). Panel Trustee, U.S. Bankruptcy Court for the District of Maryland, 1985—. *Member:* Baltimore City, Baltimore County, Maryland State and American Bar Associations; Commercial Law League of America; Association of Commercial Finance Attorneys; Bankruptcy Bar Association of

(This Listing Continued)

SHAPIRO SHER & GUINOT, P.A., Washington—Continued

Maryland (Chair, Baltimore Chapter, 1994). ***PRACTICE AREAS:*** Bankruptcy; Creditors Rights; Workouts; Commercial Litigation. ***Email:*** jis@shapirosher.com

WILLIAM E. CARLSON, born Baltimore, Maryland, July 23, 1957; admitted to bar, 1983, Maryland; 1984, U.S. District Court, District of Maryland and U.S. Court of Appeals, Fourth Circuit. *Education:* The Johns Hopkins University (B.A., 1979); University of Maryland (J.D., with honors, 1983). Order of the Coif. Articles Editor, Maryland Law Review, 1982-1983. Law Clerk to Hon. Norman P. Ramsey, U.S. District Court, District of Maryland, 1983-1984. Author: "The Work of the Court of Appeals: A Statistical Miscellany," 42 Md. L. Rev. 610, 1983; "Business Organizations," Practice Manual for the Maryland Lawyer, 1988. Lecturer: Business Organizations and Corporations, The Maryland Institute for Continuing Professional Education of Lawyers, Inc., 1986—. Community Relations Commission of Baltimore City, Member, 1990-1996 and Vice Chair, 1994-1996. *Member:* Baltimore City, Maryland State and American (Business Law Section) Bar Associations. ***PRACTICE AREAS:*** Corporate Law; Biotechnology; Municipal Law. ***Email:*** wec@shapirosher.com

LONNIE M. RITZER, born Brooklyn, New York, October 13, 1954; admitted to bar, 1979, Maryland, U.S. District Court, District of Maryland and U.S. Tax Court. *Education:* Brooklyn College of the City University of New York (B.S., summa cum laude, 1976); University of Maryland (J.D., 1979). Order of the Coif. Co-Author: "Maryland Limited Liability Company Forms and Practice Manual." Lecturer: Maryland Sales and Use Taxes and Income Taxation of Maryland Corporations, National Business Institute, Baltimore, Maryland, 1988-1994; Tax Aspects of Partnership Agreements, 1990-1991 and Maryland Limited Liability Companies, 1993—, Maryland Institute for Continuing Professional Education of Lawyers. *Member:* Baltimore City, Maryland State (Tax Section) and American (Tax Section, Low Income Housing Committee) Bar Associations; National Association of Bond Lawyers; Baltimore Association of Tax Counsel (Vice-President, 1989-1990; President, 1990-1991). ***PRACTICE AREAS:*** Taxation; Corporate Law; Real Estate. ***Email:*** lmr@shapirosher.com

SHERYL N. STEPHENSON, born Dallas, Texas, August 20, 1963; admitted to bar, 1992, Maryland. *Education:* University of North Texas (B.B.A., 1986); University of Baltimore (J.D., 1992). Heuisler Honor Society. Author: "Who Owns the Copyright for Specifically Related Computer Software," http://www.sando.com/busart13.htm; "Facing a Corporate Change: A Director's Duty," http://www.sando.com/busart14.htm; Note, "Securities Law-Uncollateralized Promissory Notes are Considered 'Securities' to be Regulated Under Federal Securities Laws, Reves v. Ernst & Young, 494 U.S. 56 (1990)", University of Baltimore Law Review, Vol. 20, Spring, 1991. ***PRACTICE AREAS:*** Corporate Law; Mergers and Acquisitions; Computers and Software; Securities Regulation; Trademarks; Copyrights. ***Email:*** sns@shapirosher.com

SHARRETTS, PALEY, CARTER & BLAUVELT, P.C.

SUITE 725, 1707 L STREET, N.W.
WASHINGTON, D.C. 20036
Telephone: 202-223-4433
Cable Address: "Customlex" Washington
Fax: 202-659-3904
Email: 102160.3466@compuserve.com
URL: http://www.sharretts-paley.com/index.htm

New York, N.Y. Office: 75 Broad Street, 26th Floor. Telephone: 212-425-0055.

Customs Law, International Trade, Imports and Exports, Anti-Dumping and Countervailing Duties.

M. BARRY LEVY, born Bronx, New York, February 1, 1936; admitted to bar, 1961, New York, U.S. Court of International Trade and U.S. Court of Customs and Patent Appeals; 1967, U.S. Supreme Court and U.S. Court of Military Appeals; 1970, U.S. District Court, Southern and Eastern Districts of New York; 1982, U.S. Court of Appeals for the Federal Circuit (Not admitted in District of Columbia). *Education:* College of William & Mary (B.A., 1957); Fordham University (J.D., 1961). Eta Sigma Phi, President, 1961. Pi Lambda Phi, President, 1956. Co-editor: *Handbook on Customs and International Trade Law,* New York County Lawyers Association, 1988. Co-Editor, Revised Handbook on Customs and International Trade Law, N.Y. County Lawyers Association, 1996. Instructor, World Trade Institute, New York and New Jersey Port Authority, 1974-1976. *Member:* New York County Lawyers Association (Member, Board of Directors, 1997—; Member of the Executive Committee, 1998—; Co-Chair, Committee on Multidisciplinary Practice; Co-Chair, Committee on Senior Lawyers, 1998—; Chairman, Committee on Customs Customs and International Trade Law, 1984-1991; 1993-1997; Chairman, Committee on Committees, 1999—); Federal Bar Association (Vice President, Empire State Chapter, 1996-1999; President, 1999—; National Council 1999—; National Secretary, Committee on Customs Law, 1969-1971; Deputy Chair, Committee on Customs Law, 1971); American Bar Association (Member, Committee on Customs and International Trade Law, 1990—); National Conference of Bar Presidents, 1999—); International Bar Association (Member, Committee of Secretaries, 1968-1970); Association of The Customs Bar (Secretary and Director, 1965-1969; Treasurer, 1976-1978; Vice President, 1978-1990 and President, 1980-1981; Chair, Special Committee on Reform of Customs Law Pertaining to Fraud, 1975-1979); Customs and International Trade Bar Association (President, 1981, 1982; U.S. Government Industry Trade Advisor Consumer Goods, 1976— U.S. Government Industry Functional Advisor, Intellectual Property Rights Committee, 1998—; U.S. Functional Advisor, Customs, 1999—; Network of Bar Lenders, Executive Council, 2001—). ***PRACTICE AREAS:*** Customs Law; International Trade; Imports and Exports; Antidumping; Countervailing Duties. ***Email:*** mbarrylevy@spcblaw.com

GAIL T. CUMINS, born New York, N.Y., June 6, 1939; admitted to bar, 1963, New York; 1964, U.S. Court of International Trade; 1967 , U.S. Court of Customs and Patent Appeals; 1970, U.S. District Court, Southern and Eastern Districts of New York; 1982, U.S. Court of Appeals for the Federal Circuit (Not admitted in District of Columbia). *Education:* University of Geneva, Geneva, Switzerland; University of Michigan (A.B., 1960); Harvard University (J.D., 1963). Phi Sigma Alpha. Author: "The Role of Respondent's Counsel in an Antidumping Proceeding Before the International Trade Administration of the United States Department of Commerce," The Commerce Department Speaks on Import Administration, Practising Law Institute, 1984. Senior Adjunct Professor, Brooklyn Law School, 1995—; Adjunct Professor of Law, Brooklyn Law School, 1990, 1992. Member, Advisory Committee, U.S. Court of International Trade, 1994-1998. *Member:* New York State (Member, Committee on International Trade and Transactions, 1978-1984) and American (Member, Standing Committee on Customs Law, 1979-1984) Bar Associations; Customs and International Trade Bar Association (Member: Membership Committee, 1966—; Committee on Practice, Procedure and Legislation, 1972—; Special Committee on Specialization, 1970—; Chairman, Committee on Nominations, 1975-1976; Member, Committee on Nominations, 1996; Director, 1990-1996; Chairman, Committee on Meetings and Special Events, 1990-1992; Chairman, Memberships, 1992-1996); American Society of International Law; American Association of Exporters and Importers (Director, 1990—; Chairman, Committee on Trade Restrictions, 1988—; Chairman, Committee on Textiles, 1990—). ***LANGUAGES:*** French. ***PRACTICE AREAS:*** Customs Law; International Trade; Imports and Exports; Antidumping; Countervailing Duties. ***Email:*** gcumins@spcblaw.com

DUNCAN A. NIXON, born Batavia, New York, November 3, 1947; admitted to bar, 1976, New York and U.S. Court of International Trade; 1982, U.S. Court of Appeals for the Federal Circuit and U.S. Court of Federal Claims (Not admitted in District of Columbia). *Education:* State University of New York at Albany (B.A., 1969); University of Iowa; St. John's University (J.D., 1975). Associate Editor: *Handbook on Customs and International Trade Law,* Oceana Publications, 1988. *Member:* New York County Lawyers Association (Member: Committee on Customs Law, 1980-1984; Committee on Customs and International Trade Law, 1984-1989); Customs and International Trade Bar Association (Member, Committee on Administrative Practice, 1981-1990; Committee on Unfair Trade and Trade Adjustment, 1990-1994; Committee on Customs and Tariffs, 1990—). (Resident). ***PRACTICE AREAS:*** Customs Law; International Trade; Imports and Exports; Antidumping; Countervailing Duties. ***Email:*** dnixon@spcblaw.com

BEATRICE A. BRICKELL, born New York, N.Y., 1944; admitted to bar, 1973, District of Columbia. *Education:* University of Maryland (B.A., 1966); American University (J.D., 1972); Georgetown University (LL.M., 1977). Editor, American University Law Review, 1971-1972. Author: "The Two Hundred Mile Territorial Sea: The Case for the Littoral State," 21 American University Law Review, 1972. *Member:* The District of Columbia Bar. (Resident). ***PRACTICE AREAS:*** Customs Law; International Trade; Imports and Exports; Antidumping; Countervailing Duties. ***Email:*** bbrickell@spcblaw.com

(For Biographical Data on all Personnel see Professional Biographies at New York City).

SHAW, BRANSFORD, VEILLEUX & ROTH

A PROFESSIONAL CORPORATION
Established in 1982
1100 CONNECTICUT AVENUE, N.W., SUITE 900
WASHINGTON, D.C. 20036-4101
Telephone: 202-463-8400
Telecopier: 202-833-8082
Email: sbvr@shawbransford.com
URL: http://www.shawbransford.com

Administrative, Associations, Legislative, Litigation, Corporation, Taxation, Estate Planning, Probate, Employment Law, EEO and Federal Personnel Law.

(This Listing Continued)

FIRM PROFILE: Shaw, Bransford, Veilleux & Roth has developed a national reputation for effectively representing federal managers, professionals and executives with their employer and their professional associations before Congress and Executive Branch agencies. It handles complex litigation on behalf of public employees and retirees concerning their rights and benefits. In addition, its continuous access to federal and congressional offices allows it to represent effectively the interests of a variety of corporations, associations and individuals seeking lobbying efforts or relief in regulatory and tax matters.

†G. JERRY SHAW, JR., born Helena, Montana, November 16, 1940; admitted to bar, 1970, Texas; 1980, U.S. Supreme Court; 1981, District of Columbia. *Education:* Gonzaga University (B.B.A., 1962); St. Mary's University (J.D., 1970). Member, Law Review, 1969-1970. Attorney, Branch Chief and Director, General Legal Services Division, Office of Chief Counsel, Internal Revenue Service, 1970-1981. President, 1980-1983 and General Counsel, 1983—, Senior Executives Association. Chairman, Public Employees Roundtable, 1983—. President, Federal Employees Education and Assistance Fund, 1986—. *Member:* The District of Columbia Bar; State Bar of Texas; Federal Bar Association. **PRACTICE AREAS:** Administrative Law; Legislative Law; Association Law; Employment Law.

WILLIAM L. BRANSFORD, born Bethesda, Maryland, August 21, 1947; admitted to bar, 1975, Ohio; 1979, District of Columbia; 1984, U.S. Supreme Court. *Education:* University of Maryland (B.S., 1968); Cleveland State University (J.D., cum laude, 1975); Georgetown University (LL.M. in Labor Law, 1983). Attorney-Adviser, Office of Chief Counsel, Bureau of the Public Debt, Department of the Treasury, 1978-1981. Attorney, Office of Chief Counsel, Internal Revenue Service, 1981-1983. *Member:* The District of Columbia Bar; Ohio State and Federal Bar Associations. **PRACTICE AREAS:** Federal Employment Law; Employment Law; Litigation.

DIANA J. VEILLEUX, born Washington, D.C., May 6, 1958; admitted to bar, 1986, Maryland; 1989, District of Columbia. *Education:* Boston University (B.S., 1980); Georgetown University Law Center (J.D., 1985). Member, American Criminal Law Review, 1984-1985. Attorney, Office of Labor Law, U.S. Postal Service, 1985-1990. *Member:* The District of Columbia Bar; Maryland State Bar Association; Women's Bar Association. **PRACTICE AREAS:** Federal Employment Law; Employment Law; Litigation.

DEBRA L. ROTH, born Newark, New Jersey, March 14, 1962; admitted to bar, 1989, New Jersey; 1990, District of Columbia. *Education:* Boston University (B.A., cum laude, 1984); American University (J.D., 1988). Note and Comment Editor, The Administrative Law Journal, 1987-1988. Law Clerk, Hon. Virginia Long, State of New Jersey, Superior Court, Appellate Division, 1988-1989. *Member:* The District of Columbia Bar; New Jersey State Bar Association. **PRACTICE AREAS:** Employment Law; Litigation.

LORI E. KLINE, born Bethesda, Maryland, December 28, 1970; admitted to bar, 1995, Maryland; 2000, District of Columbia. *Education:* University of Maryland, Honors Program (B.S., cum laude, 1992); William and Mary (J.D., 1995). Mortar Board. Order of Omega. Golden Key. Honor's Certificate Public Service Fund Fellowship. Associate Editor, William & Mary Journal of Women and the Law. Author: Discrimination Laws and Unionized Employee - The Trouble With Collective Bargaining Agreements in the Wake of Austin v. Owens-Brockway Glass Container Inc., Maryland Bar Newsletter, Spring, 1998. *Member:* Montgomery County Bar Association; Women's Bar Association of Montgomery County. **REPORTED CASES:** Maron v. United States, 126 F.3d 317 (4th Cir. 1997). **PRACTICE AREAS:** Employment Discrimination; Federal Personnel Law; Employment Law. **Email:** lkline@shawbransford.com

BERNARD E. DOYLE, born Hazel Green, Wisconsin, July 14, 1955; admitted to bar, 1985, Maryland; 1999, D.C. *Education:* George Washington University (B.A., 1978); University of Maryland (J.D., with honor, 1984). Order of the Coif. *Member:* Maryland State and American Bar Associations; District of Columbia Bar. [Judge Advocate, U.S. Air Force, 1985-1998]. **REPORTED CASES:** Reported Cases: Worthy v. Widnall, 138 F. 3d 885 (10th Cir. 1998); Bullock v. Widnall, 953 F.Supp. 1461 (M.D. Ala. 1996); Gonzagowski v. Widnall, 115 F. 3d 744 (10 Cir. 1997); U.S. v. Maio, 34 MJ 215 (CMA 1992); U.S. v. Button, 34 MJ 139 (CMA 1992); U.S. v. Rhea, 33MJ 413 (CMA 1991); U.S. v. Appel, 31MJ 314 (CMA 1990); U.S. v. Gregory, 31MJ 236 (CMA 1990); U.S. v. Berry, 30MJ 134 (CMA 1990); U.S. v. Beehler, 35MJ 502 (AFCMR 1992); U.S. v. Blackshire, 33 MJ 501 (AFCMR 1991); U.S. v. Bragg, 30MJ 1147 (AFCMR 1990); U.S. v. Woods, 38 MJ 694 (AFCMR 1989); U.S. v. Bair, 29 MJ 862 (AFCMR 1989); U.S. v. Johnson, 28 MJ 693 (AFCMR 1989). **PRACTICE AREAS:** Federal Employment Law; Employment Law; Military Law; Litigation. **Email:** bdoyle@shawbransford.com

JOHN P. MAHONEY, born Worcester, Massachusetts, October 29, 1968; admitted to bar, 1993, Maryland; 1994, District of Columbia. *Education:* Assumption College (A.B., cum laude, 1990); Catholic University of America (J.D., 1993). Delta Theta Phi. Moot Court. Editor, Catholic University of America Law Review, 1992-1993. Associate Editor of the Year (1993). Co-Author: "The Federal Employees' Legal Survival Guide" (National Employee Rights Institute, 1999); "MSPB Non-Local Attorney Fees Awards: Recognizing the Strong Interest of Geographic Latitude in the Selection of Counsel", 95 Fed. Merit Sys. Rep. 38 (Aug. 28, 1995). Co-Author: "Reckless Disregard: Intentional and Willful Violations of the Privacy Act's Investigatory Requirements", Fed. L. Mag., May 1997, at 38; "EEOC's New Federal Sector Regulations and Management Directive 110: an Overview", The D.C. B. Lab & Employment L. Section's Newsl., No.3. (Winter 1999-2000), at 13. *Member:* District of Columbia Bar (Vice-Chair, Council on Section, 2000-2001; Co-Chair, Labor and Employment Section , 1998-2000; Chairman, Public Sector Committee, 1997-1998); Metropolitan Washington Employment Lawyers Association. **REPORTED CASES:** Van Wersch v. Department of Health and Human Services, 197 F.3d 1144 (Fed. Cir. 1999); Dong v. Smithsonian Institution, 125 F.3d 877 (D.C. Cir. 1997), reh'g denied, No. 96-503 (1997), cert. denied, 524 U.S. 922 (1998); Begley v. OPM, 60 F.3d 804 (Fed. Cir. 1995); Dong v. Smithsonian Institution, 943 F.Supp. 69 (1996); Flythe v. Caldera, Secretary Department of the Army, EEOC Appeal No. 01972258 (2000). **PRACTICE AREAS:** Federal Employment Law; Employment Law; Federal Personnel Law; Employment Discrimination; Civil Litigation. **Email:** jmahoney@shawbransford.com

(This Listing Continued)

ANJALI KUMAR, born Winnipeg, Manitoba, Canada, January 9, 1967; admitted to bar, 1992, District of Columbia and U.S. Court of Appeals, Fourth Circuit; 1993, Maryland, U.S. District Court, District of Maryland, U.S. District Court, District of Columbia and U.S. Court of Appeals for the District of Columbia; 1997, U.S. Supreme Court. *Education:* George Washington University (B.A., with special honors, 1988); Georgetown University (J.D., 1992). Barristers' Council. Pace Environmental Law Moot Court Team. *Member:* District of Columbia Bar; Maryland State Bar Association; South Asian Bar Association (Secretary 2000—); Asian Pacific American Legal Resource Center (Board Member, 2001—); Metropolitan Washington Employment Lawyers Association (Secretary, 1999—). **LANGUAGES:** Spanish, Hindi. **PRACTICE AREAS:** Labor and Employment; Federal Employment Law; Employment Discrimination; Civil Litigation; Mediation; Equal Employment Opportunity Law. **Email:** akumar@shawbransford.com

JANICE A. SIMONS, born Bronxville, New York, March 12, 1968; admitted to bar, 1995, Maryland; 1996, District of Columbia. *Education:* Wellesley College (B.A., 1990); Washington College of Law (J.D., 1995). Recipient, Best Brief and Best Oralist. Co-Editor, *Journal of Gender and the Law. Member:* Metropolitan Washington Employment Lawyers Association; National Employment Lawyers Association.. **PRACTICE AREAS:** Employment. **Email:** jsimons@shawbransford.com

ANTHONY VERGNETTI, born Lancaster, Pennsylvania, May 30, 1967; admitted to bar, 1995, Maryland; 1997, District of Columbia. *Education:* Arizona State University (B.A., 1992); Widener University School of Law (J.D., 1995); Georgetown University Law Center (L.L.M., Employment Law, 1999). Moot Court Honor Society; Order of the Barristers; First Place, M. Marshal Federal Bar Moot Court Competition, 1994. *Member:* The District of Columbia Bar (Member, Labor and Employment Section); Maryland State Bar Association (Member, Labor and Employment Section). [U.S. Air Force, 1985-1991, Staff Sergeant]. **PRACTICE AREAS:** Employment Law; Litigation; Federal Employment Law. **Email:** avergnet@shawbransford.com

OF COUNSEL

THOMAS J. O'ROURKE, born Hastings, Pennsylvania, November 8, 1946; admitted to bar, 1973, Pennsylvania; 1985, District of Columbia; 1992, Maryland; 1992, U.S. Supreme Court. *Education:* Indiana University of Pennsylvania (B.S., 1968); Notre Dame Law School (J.D., 1973); Georgetown University (M.L.T. in Taxation Law, 1981). Pi Gamma Mu. Author: *The Ways of Wills:* Trust and Estate Planning for Government Employees (MPC Publications, 1991); *Independent Contractor or Employee?* Management Accounting, (December, 1990). Adjunct Professor of Taxation, George Mason University, 1980-1983. Attorney, IRS Office of Chief Counsel, 1974-1983. *Member:* The District of Columbia Bar (Member, Tax and Estate/Probate Sections); Pennsylvania and American (Member, Taxation Section) Bar Associations; National Academy of Elder Law Attorneys. (Also practicing individually, Rockville, Maryland). **PRACTICE AREAS:** Estate Planning; Probate; Taxation Law; Associations Law; Corporate Law.

† Professional Corporation

SHAW PITTMAN LLP

A Limited Liability Partnership Including Professional Corporations

2300 N STREET, N.W.

WASHINGTON, D.C. 20037

Telephone: 202-663-8000
Cable Address: "Shawlaw"
Telex: 89-2693 (Shawlaw Wsh)
Telecopier: 202-663-8007
Email: postmaster@sppt.com
URL: http://www.shawpittman.com

McLean, Virginia Office: 1650 Tysons Boulevard. Telephone: 703-770-7900. Telecopier: 703-821-2397.

New York, N.Y. Office: 335 Madison Avenue. Telephone: 212-603-6800. Facsimile: 212-603-6801.

Los Angeles, California Office: 2029 Century Park East. Telephone: 310-551-4500. Facsimile: 310-551-4501.

London, England Office: Regis House, 45 King Street. Telephone: 011-44-171-337-9400. Fax: 011-44-171-337-9401.

General Federal, Corporate, Commercial, Administrative, International Practice, Litigation, Technology Transactions, Real Estate, Securities, Tax, Financial Institutions, Communications (including broadcast, common carrier, cellular telephone, paging, cable, satellite and business radio), Entertainment, Copyright, Intellectual Property and Trademark Law.

FIRM PROFILE: One of the largest full-service firms in the Washington, D.C. area, Shaw Pittman LLP almost forty years of experience representing local, national, and international clients in a full array of legal practice areas. Using the firm's extensive interdisciplinary resources, Shaw Pittman's 450 attorneys work closely with clients to develop creative and cost-effective approaches to their legal questions. Shaw Pittman LLP is proud of its commitment to its clients and of the legislative, administrative and judicial strategies it develops to help them meet their objectives.

The firm has developed a national and international reputation for representing a broad range of clients in real estate, construction, corporate, tax, and securities matters; in complex criminal and civil litigation; in administrative and regulatory advocacy; on issues pertaining to banking and financial institutions; and in government contracting, high technology industry, intellectual property, international trade, transportation, employment and energy and environmental matters.

MEMBERS OF FIRM

GEORGE F. TROWBRIDGE (1919-1989).

JAMES L. ALBERG, born New York, N.Y., July 11, 1952; admitted to bar, 1978, New York; 1979, District of Columbia; 1986, Massachusetts; 1994, Georgia (inactive). *Education:* Union College (B.A., cum laude, with distinction, 1974); Boston University (J.D., 1977). Senior Vice President and General Counsel, Dun & Bradstreet Software, 1989-1996. *Member:* The District of Columbia Bar; State Bar of Georgia; American Bar Association; Computer Law Association. ***PRACTICE AREAS:*** Information Technology; Corporate Law. ***Email:*** james.alberg@shawpittman.com

WALTER J. ANDREWS, born Washington, D.C., February 13, 1957; admitted to bar, 1982, District of Columbia; 1990, U.S. District Court, District of Maryland; 2000, Virginia. *Education:* Swarthmore College (B.A., 1979); University of Chicago (J.D., 1982). Author: "Policyholder Claims for Tobacco-Related Liability," Tort and Insurance Law Journal (Vol. 36, No. 1, Fall 2000); "Curing the Fever for Virus Coverage Under Traditional Property Policies," Mealey's Cyber Tech Litigation Report (August 2000); "Lloyd's of London: Playing the Name Game in Federal Court," Mealey's Litigation Report: Insurance (July 18, 2000); "Gun Makers Miss Target: Insurers Do Not Owe Coverage for Recent Firearm Litigation," Legal Times, March 13, 2000; "Bug Fixes Aren't Insured; 'Sue and Labor ' Provisions Don't Cover Upgrade Costs," Legal Times, December 6, 1999; "Gunning for Insurers: Who Will Pay Threatened Liability Against the Gun Industry," Vol. 9, No. 5, September/October, 1999; "Coverage for Natural and Unnatural El Niños," Tort & Insurance Law Journal 34, No. 3, Spring, 1999; "Is Daubert Limited to Scientific Testimony?" For The Defense, at 4, February, 1999. *Member:* American Bar Association (Vice-Chair, Litigation Section, Insurance Coverage Committee; Editor, Coverage Journal); Defense Research Institute (Chair, Insurance Coverage Professional Liability Sub-Committee; Editorial Board, Y2K Handbook). (Resident, McLean, Virginia Office). ***PRACTICE AREAS:*** Insurance; Litigation. ***Email:*** walter.andrews@shawpittman.com

SCOTT A. ANENBERG, (P.C.), born Brooklyn, New York, December 4, 1953; admitted to bar, 1978, District of Columbia. *Education:* Washington University (B.A., magna cum laude, 1975); George Washington University (J.D., with high honors, 1978). Phi Beta Kappa; Order of the Coif. Attorney, Honors Program, Office of the General Counsel, Federal Deposit Insurance Corporation, 1978-1980. Contributing Editor and Member, Editorial Advisory

(This Listing Continued)

Board, Electronic Banking Law and Commerce Report (Glasser LegalWorks). Author: "Lender Regulatory Aspects of Real Estate Workouts," The Real Estate Workout Deskbook, Probus Publishing Company, 1992. Co-Author: "E-Commerce in the Financial Services Sector," IBC Global Conferences Limited, 2000; "Traps for the Unwary Lender: State Law Issues Related to Internet Lending," Electronic Banking and Commerce Report, Glasser LegalWorks, 1998; "Regulation of Foreign Banks in the United States," International Banking: U.S. Laws and Regulations, American Bankers Association, 1984. ***PRACTICE AREAS:*** Banking; International Transactions; Corporate Law. ***Email:*** scott.anenberg@shawpittman.com

DEAN D. AULICK, (P.C.), born Fort Dodge, Iowa, August 18, 1945; admitted to bar, 1974, District of Columbia. *Education:* Indiana University (A.B., with highest distinction, 1967); Yale University (J.D., 1972). Phi Beta Kappa. Member, Board of Editors, Yale Law Journal, 1971-1972. Law Clerk, Hon. Jesse Eschbach, U.S. District Court for the Northern District of Indiana, 1972-1973. ***PRACTICE AREAS:*** Technology Outsourcing; Energy; Contracts. ***Email:*** dean.aulick@shawpittman.com

ASLAN BAGHDADI, born Cairo, Egypt, October 20, 1943; admitted to bar, 1990, Maryland; 1991, District of Columbia; 2001, Virginia. *Education:* Rensselaer Polytechnic Institute (B.S., 1966); Brown University (Ph.D., 1972); George Washington University (J.D., 1990). Moot Court Board. Member, George Washington University Law Review, 1988-1990. *Member:* Virginia State Bar. (Resident, McLean, Virginia Office). ***PRACTICE AREAS:*** Intellectual Property Litigation; Patent Prosecution; Trademark Prosecution; Intellectual Property Licensing; Trade Secrets; Copyright Protection. ***Email:*** aslan.baghdadi@shawpittman.com

DEBORAH BRAND BAUM, born New Haven, Connecticut, December 26, 1959; admitted to bar, 1983, Ohio (inactive); 1985, District of Columbia. *Education:* College of William and Mary (B.A., 1980); University of Virginia (J.D., 1983). Phi Beta Kappa. Trustee, Legal Aid Society. Hearing Committee Chair, DC Board on Professional Responsibility. *Member:* The District of Columbia Bar; American Bar Association. ***PRACTICE AREAS:*** Litigation. ***Email:*** deborah.baum@shawpittman.com

THOMAS A. BAXTER, (P.C.), born Decatur, Indiana, August 30, 1946; admitted to bar, 1971, District of Columbia; 1980, U.S. Supreme Court. *Education:* Purdue University (B.A., 1968); George Washington University (J.D., with honors, 1971; LL.M., Administrative Law-Economic Regulation, 1977). Special Assistant for Litigation, Price Commission and Cost of Living Council, Executive Office of the President, 1972-1973. ***PRACTICE AREAS:*** Information Technology. ***Email:*** thomas.baxter@shawpittman.com

STEPHAN E. BECKER, born Chicago, Illinois, June 29, 1957; admitted to bar, 1982, District of Columbia. *Education:* Yale University (B.A., 1979); Columbia University (J.D., 1982). Notes and Comments Editor, Columbia Law Review, 1981-1982. *Member:* The District of Columbia Bar. ***PRACTICE AREAS:*** International Trade. ***Email:*** stephan.becker@shawpittman.com

MICHAEL D. BEDNAREK, born Chicago, Illinois, September 28, 1960; admitted to bar, 1987, Virginia; 1988, District of Columbia. *Education:* Marquette University (B.S.E., 1982); George Washington University (J.D., 1987). Patent Examiner, U.S. Patent and Trademark Office, 1982-1986. (Resident, McLean, Virginia Office). ***PRACTICE AREAS:*** Computer and Software Patents; Business Methods Patents; Mechanical Patents; Electrical Patents; Trademarks; Intellectual Property Licensing. ***Email:*** michael.bednarek@shawpittman.com

LON A. BERK, born Brooklyn, New York, 1955; admitted to bar, 1985, Massachusetts; 1986, U.S. District Court, District of Massachusetts; 1991, U.S. Court of Appeals, First Circuit and District of Columbia; 1993, U.S. District Court, District of Maryland, U.S. Court of Appeals, Eighth Circuit and U.S. Court of Appeals for the Federal Circuit. *Education:* Washington University (B.A., magna cum laude, 1977); Massachusetts Institute of Technology (Ph.D., 1982); Harvard Law School (J.D., cum laude, 1985). Phi Beta Kappa. (Resident, McLean, Virginia Office). ***PRACTICE AREAS:*** Insurance; Civil Litigation. ***Email:*** lon.berk@shawpittman.com

CHARLES G. BERRY, born New York, N.Y., 1950; admitted to bar, 1978, New York; 1979, District of Columbia. *Education:* Yale University (B.A., summa cum laude, 1972); Cambridge University (B.A., M.A., 1974); Columbia University (J.D., 1977). (Resident, New York, N.Y. Office). ***PRACTICE AREAS:*** Litigation. ***Email:*** charles.berry@shawpittman.com

ROBERT BISHOP, admitted to bar, 1995, Solicitor of the Supreme Court of England and Wales. *Education:* University of Exeter (B.A., 1991); College of Law, Chester (1993). *Member:* Law Society of England and Wales. (Resident, London, England Office). ***PRACTICE AREAS:*** Corporate Law; Securities; Joint Ventures; Strategic Alliances; Mergers and Acquisitions. ***Email:*** robert.bishop@shawpittman.com

ERNEST L. BLAKE, JR. (P.C.), born Portland, Maine, January 22, 1942; admitted to bar, 1973, District of Columbia; 1992, Colorado. *Education:* United

(This Listing Continued)

States Naval Academy (B.S., 1964); Duke University (J.D., 1972). Research and Managing Editor, Duke Law Journal, 1971-1972. ***PRACTICE AREAS:*** Energy; Administrative Law. ***Email:*** ernest.blake@shawpittman.com

JAMES A. BLALOCK III, born Austin, Texas, 1958; admitted to bar, 1983, Texas; 1987, California; 1992, District of Columbia. *Education:* University of California, Los Angeles (B.A., 1980); Tulane University (J.D., 1983). Member, 1981-1983 and Senior Notes and Comments Editor, 1982-1983, Tulane Law Review. *Member:* State Bar of Texas; State Bar of California; The District of Columbia Bar. ***PRACTICE AREAS:*** Securitization; Structured Finance; Public Offerings; Securities Registration; Corporate Finance. ***Email:*** trey.blalock@shawpittman.com

BRIAN M. BLUM, born Columbus, Ohio, February 9, 1963; admitted to bar, 1988, Illinois and U.S. District Court, Northern District of Illinois; 1989, U.S. Tax Court; 1998, District of Columbia. *Education:* St. Louis University (B.S.B.A., summa cum laude, 1985); University of North Carolina (J.D., 1988). Beta Gamma Sigma; Order of the Coif. Senior Technical Reviewer, Office of the assistant Chief Counsel, Internal Revenue Service, 1997-1998. *Member:* The District of Columbia Bar. ***PRACTICE AREAS:*** Tax Law.

EILEEN L. BROWNELL, (P.C.), born Evanston, Illinois, March 7, 1954; admitted to bar, 1982, District of Columbia. *Education:* University of Virginia (B.S., 1976); Harvard University (J.D., cum laude, 1982). *Member:* The District of Columbia Bar; American Bar Association (Member, Taxation Section). ***PRACTICE AREAS:*** Tax; Corporate. ***Email:*** eileen.brownell@shawpittman.com

DENISE R. CADE, born Washington, D.C., October 31, 1962; admitted to bar, 1990, Illinois; 1992, District of Columbia. *Education:* Marquette University (B.A., 1984); Georgetown University (J.D., 1990). ***Email:*** denise.cade@shawpittman.com

CECELIA A. CALABY, born Washington, D.C., October 12, 1960; admitted to bar, 1991, Pennsylvania; 1993, District of Columbia. *Education:* Rice University (B.A., 1982); George Washington University (J.D., with honors, 1990). ***Email:*** cecelia.calaby@shawpittman.com

JOHN L. CARR, JR., born Madison, Georgia, August 31, 1946; admitted to bar, 1978, Georgia; 1979, District of Columbia. *Education:* Auburn University (B.S., 1969); University of Georgia (J.D., 1978). Staff Member, 1976-1977 and Senior Editor, 1977-1978, Georgia Law Review. Author: "Fine-Tuning The DISC: Evaluation and Framework," 11 Georgia Law Review 902, 1977 and 7 Georgia Journal of International and Comparative Law 629, 1977. Co-Author: "Regulation of Foreign Bank Operations in the United States," International Financial Law, 1980 and 1984; "Developments in the Regulation of Foreign Bank Operations in the United States," University of Illinois Law Review Vol. 1988, No. 2, pg. 235; "Conditions of Entry and Forms of Doing Business," Regulation of Foreign Banks, United States and International Butterworth Legal Publishers, 1991; "Form of Entry, Operation, Expansion, and Supervision of Foreign Banks in the United States," Butterworth Legal Publishers 1995; "The Indirect Foreign Tax Credit," a BNA Tax Management Portfolio, 1997. ***PRACTICE AREAS:*** International Tax; Banking; Corporate. ***Email:*** john.carr@shawpittman.com

KENNETH A. CARUSO, born Passaic, New Jersey, 1952; admitted to bar, 1978, New York. *Education:* Rutgers University (B.A., 1974); Columbia University (J.D., 1977). Law Clerk to the Hon. L.F. MacMahon, Judge, U.S. District Court, Southern District of New York, 1977-1978. Deputy Associate Attorney General, 1982-1983, Special Assistant to the Associate Attorney General, 1981-1982, U.S. Department of Justice. Assistant U.S. Attorney, Southern District of New York, 1983-1984. With Shearman & Sterling, New York, N.Y., 1984-1994. Director, Metropolitan Transit Authority. (Resident, New York, N.Y. Office). ***PRACTICE AREAS:*** Litigation. ***Email:*** kenneth.caruso@shawpittman.com

THOMAS J. CATLIOTA, born Cleveland, Ohio, May 20, 1953; admitted to bar, 1984, District of Columbia. *Education:* Marquette University (B.S., 1977); Catholic University (J.D., 1983); Georgetown University (LL.M., 1985). Recipient, Faculty Award, 1983. Editor, Fourth Circuit and District of Columbia Bankruptcy Court Reporter, 1993-1996. ***PRACTICE AREAS:*** Bankruptcy Law; Business Reorganization. ***Email:*** thomas.catliota@shawpittman.com

CRAIG E. CHASON, born Washington, D.C., January 30, 1955; admitted to bar, 1983, Texas (inactive); 1984, Virginia; 1989, District of Columbia. *Education:* University of Virginia (B.A., with high honors, 1977); University of Chicago, Graduate School of Business; University of Virginia (J.D., 1983). *Member:* The District of Columbia Bar; State Bar of Texas; Virginia State Bar. (Resident, McLean, Virginia Office). ***PRACTICE AREAS:*** Corporate; Securities; Mergers and Acquisitions. ***Email:*** craig.chason@shawpittman.com

HOWARD L. CLEMONS, born Memphis, Tennessee, September 18, 1956; admitted to bar, 1981, Tennessee (inactive); 1982, Texas (inactive); 1985, District of Columbia; 1998, Virginia. *Education:* University of Memphis (B.B.A., cum laude, 1978; J.D., 1981); New York University School of Law (LL.M. in Taxation, 1982). Staff Member, University of Memphis Law Review, 1979-1981. *Member:* The District of Columbia Bar; American Bar Association

(This Listing Continued)

(Member, Sections on: Taxation; Business Law). (Resident, McLean, Virginia Office). ***PRACTICE AREAS:*** Tax; Corporate; Executive Compensation. ***Email:*** howard.clemons@shawpittman.com

MARC R. COHEN, born October 15, 1959; admitted to bar, 1985, Connecticut; 1991, District of Columbia. *Education:* Yale University (B.A., 1981; J.D., 1984). Editor, Yale Journal of International Law. Clerk to Judge Jose A. Cabranes, D. Connecticut. Author, *Commercial Bank Lending to LDC's: Balancing Bank Overexposure and Credit Undersupply*, 8 Yale Journal of World Public Order 201 (1983). ***PRACTICE AREAS:*** Banks & Banking. ***Email:*** marc.cohen@shawpittman.com

ROBERT E. COHN, born Brooklyn, New York, 1945; admitted to bar, 1969, District of Columbia. *Education:* Syracuse University (B.A., 1966); Georgetown University (J.D., 1969). Senior Trial Attorney, Civil Aeronautics Board, 1970-1976. Executive Assistant to Chairman and Board Members, Civil Aeronautics Board 1976-1977. Partner, Butler and Binion, 1977-1984. General Counsel, People Express Airlines, 1984-1986. ShawPittman Partner since 1984. Chairman: Transportation Practice Group; Lateral Partner Committee. ***PRACTICE AREAS:*** Aviation; Administrative; Transportation. ***Email:*** robert.cohn@shawpittman.com

H. GUY COLLIER, born Richmond, Virginia, June 16, 1950; admitted to bar, 1976, Virginia; 1978, District of Columbia. *Education:* University of Virginia (B.A., with distinction, 1972); University of Richmond (J.D., 1976); Johns Hopkins University (M.P.H., 1978). Member, Raven Society. Attorney-Advisor, Office of the General Counsel, U.S. Department of Health and Human Services, 1978-1981. *Member:* The District of Columbia Bar (Member: Health Law Section; Steering Committee, 1989-1991); Virginia State Bar (Member: Health Law Section); American Health Lawyers Assn. ***PRACTICE AREAS:*** Health Law. ***Email:*** guy.collier@shawpittman.com

ALAN S. COOPER, born Louisville, Kentucky, June 13, 1942; admitted to bar, 1968, Tennessee (inactive); 1969, District of Columbia; 1975-1982, U.S. Court of Customs and Patent Appeals; 1980, U.S. Supreme Court; 1982, U.S. Court of Appeals for the Federal Circuit. *Education:* Vanderbilt University (B.A., magna cum laude, 1964; J.D., 1968). Phi Beta Kappa. Law Clerk to the Hon. Frank Gray, Jr., Chief Judge, U.S. District Court, Middle District of Tennessee, 1967-1968. Author: "Managing the Board's Increasing Workload: The Creative Use of Sanctions," 88 Trademark Reporter 43, 1998; "Limitations on Trademark Advocacy: Ethic, Procedure and Substantive Law," 85 Trademark Reporter 161, 1995; "The Application of Rule 11 Sanctions in Trademark Cases," 78 Trademark Reporter 427, 1988. Adjunct Professor, Georgetown University Law Center, 1985—. Member of Faculty, American Bar Association National Institute on Trademark Litigation, 1978 and 1979. Advisor on Trademark Law to United States Delegation to Diplomatic Conference for Revision of Paris Convention, Nairobi, Kenya, 1981. *Member:* The District of Columbia Bar; Bar Association of the District of Columbia; American Bar Association; International Trademark Association; American Intellectual Property Law Association. ***Email:*** alan.cooper@shawpittman.com

B. SCOTT CUSTER, JR., born San Diego, California, October 12, 1937; admitted to bar, 1965, District of Columbia; 1967, New York; 1976, U.S. Tax Court; 1991, U.S. Court of Appeals, Fourth Circuit. *Education:* Harvard College (A.B., magna cum laude, 1959); University of Paris; Harvard Graduate School of Arts and Sciences; Columbia University, International Fellows Program; Harvard Law School (LL.B., cum laude, 1964). Government Service: Executive Assistant to Deputy Secretary of State, Washington, D.C., 1970-1973 and to U.S. Ambassador to France, Paris, 1973. *Member:* The Association of the Bar of the City of New York; The District of Columbia Bar; American and International Bar Associations; American Society of International Law; Union Internationale des Avocats. ***LANGUAGES:*** French; Spanish. ***PRACTICE AREAS:*** Technology and Telecommunications Outsourcing; International Transactions; Project Finance; Privatization; Corporate Law. ***Email:*** scott.custer@shawpittman.com

DAVID J. CYNAMON, (P.C.), born Philadelphia, Pennsylvania, January 27, 1949; admitted to bar, 1973, District of Columbia. *Education:* Brown University (A.B., 1970); Harvard University (J.D., 1973). ***PRACTICE AREAS:*** Litigation. ***Email:*** david.cynamon@shawpittman.com

THOMAS J. DELANEY, born January 28, 1957; admitted to bar, 1987, New Jersey and Pennsylvania; 1995, District of Columbia. *Education:* Georgetown University (B.A., 1979); American University (J.D., 1986). Author, *Special Report: Interstate Banking and Community Development Acts*, Warren, Gorham & Lamont, 1995. Co-author, "The Community Development Banking Act: New Opportunities, Limited Compliance Costs," 112 Banking Law Journal 4 (1985). Special Counsel to the Chief Counsel, Office of Thrift Supervision, 1988-1990. ***PRACTICE AREAS:*** Banks & Banking.

CRAIG A. DE RIDDER, born Adelaide, South Australia, December 1, 1954; admitted to bar, 1981, South Australia; 1984, New York; 1990, District of Columbia. *Education:* University of Adelaide (B.A., with honors, 1975; LL.B., with honors, 1980); Yale University (LL.M., 1983). ***PRACTICE AREAS:***

(This Listing Continued)

SHAW PITTMAN LLP, Washington—Continued

Technology Transactions; Technology Outsourcing; Telecommunications and Broadband; Technology; Partnership Law; Strategic Alliances; Real Estate; Finance. ***Email:*** craig.deridder@shawpittman.com

ROBERT M. DI GIOVANNI, born Philadelphia, Pennsylvania, December 12, 1958; admitted to bar, 1984, District of Columbia; 2000, California. *Education:* University of Pennsylvania (B.S., cum laude, 1980); University of North Carolina (J.D., with high honors, 1984). Order of the Coif. Executive/Articles Editor, University of North Carolina Law Review, 1983-1984. (Resident, Los Angeles, California Office). ***PRACTICE AREAS:*** Outsourcing; Technology; Energy; Arbitration; Contracts; ADR. ***Email:*** robert.digiovanni@shawpittman.com

MARIE N. DOLAND, born Pittsburgh, Pennsylvania, September 30, 1949; admitted to bar, 1977, Virginia; 1978, District of Columbia. *Education:* Smith College (B.A., 1971); George Washington University (J.D., with high honors, 1977). Order of the Coif. Member, George Washington University Law Review, 1976-1977. *Member:* The District of Columbia Bar. ***PRACTICE AREAS:*** Outsourcing; Technology. ***Email:*** marie.doland@shawpittman.com

RICHARD C. DONALDSON, born Cleveland, Ohio, December 28, 1959; admitted to bar, 1985, Virginia (Not admitted in District of Columbia). *Education:* Cornell University (B.A., cum laude, 1982); University of Chicago (J.D., 1985). *Member:* Virginia State Bar; American Bar Association. (Resident). ***PRACTICE AREAS:*** Tax; REIT; Corporate Finance.

MARIO F. DOTTORI, born New Haven, Connecticut, November 8, 1961; admitted to bar, 1987, Connecticut (inactive); 1988, District of Columbia. *Education:* Denison University (B.A., 1984); University of Bridgeport School of Law (J.D., 1987). ***Email:*** mario.dottori@shawpittman.com

MAUREEN ELLEN DWYER, born Mount Vernon, New York, May 4, 1951; admitted to bar, 1979, District of Columbia. *Education:* Smith College (B.A., 1973); Fordham University and Catholic University (J.D., 1978). Member, Business Advisory Council, Commercial Real Estate Women (CREW), President, 1989-1991. Vice Chair, The Eugene and Agnes Meyer Foundation. *Member:* The District of Columbia Bar (Section on Real Estate, Housing and Land Use); American Bar Association (Section on Urban, State and Local Government Law); DC Chamber of Commerce; The Greater Washington Board of Trade; The Barristers; Leadership Washington; Urban Land Institute (Associate Member); Lamda Alpha International; DC Business Coalition; DC Building Industry Association. ***PRACTICE AREAS:*** Real Estate; Zoning, Planning and Land Use; Municipal Law; Historic Preservation; Lobbying. ***Email:*** maureen.dwyer@shawpittman.com

JOHN ENGEL, (P.C.), born New York, N.Y., March 8, 1943; admitted to bar, 1971, District of Columbia; 1984, Virginia. *Education:* Yale University (B.A., 1965); Georgetown University (J.D., 1971). Chair, Real Estate Group. ***PRACTICE AREAS:*** Commercial Real Estate. ***Email:*** john.engel@shawpittman.com

GREGORY S. FEIS, born June 22, 1956; admitted to bar, 1981, California; 1987, District of Columbia. *Education:* University of California, Berkeley (A.B., 1978); University of California School of Law, Los Angeles (J.D., 1981). ***Email:*** gregory.feis@shawpittman.com

PHIL T. FEOLA, born Paterson, New Jersey, May 5, 1947; admitted to bar, 1979, District of Columbia; 1980, Maryland and U.S. District Court for the District of Columbia. *Education:* University of Notre Dame (B.A., 1969); Florida State University (M.U.R.P., 1971); Catholic University of America (J.D., 1979). Member, Lambda Alpha International. Adjunct Professor, George Washington University Law School, 1980—. Author: "Housing Incentives A National Perspective," Urban Lawyer, Vol. 21, No. 2, 1989. Board Member, Four Walls Development, Inc. *Member:* The District of Columbia Bar; American Planning Association; Urban Land Institute; Washington Architectural Forum (Board Member); Center for Dispute Settlement (Board Member). ***PRACTICE AREAS:*** Real Estate; Zoning, Planning and Land Use; Municipal Law. ***Email:*** phil.feola@shawpittman.com

CHARLES S. FIEDLER, born Grand Rapids, Michigan, October 22, 1947; admitted to bar, 1973, California. *Education:* University of Pennsylvania (B.S.Ec., 1969); University of San Francisco (J.D., 1973). (Resident, Los Angeles, California Office). ***PRACTICE AREAS:*** Corporate Law; Securities Law; Health Care Law.

ERIC T. FINGERHUT, born Passaic, New Jersey, July 29, 1965; admitted to bar, 1990, Pennsylvania (inactive); 1992, District of Columbia; 1996, U.S. Supreme Court. *Education:* Boston University College of Communications (B.S., 1987); Benjamin N. Cardozo School of Law (J.D., 1990). Author: "Protection of Domain Names in the U.S.," Managing Intellectual Property - The Trademark Yearbook, March 1997; "We're Entering a New Domain," Legal Times, October 6, 1997; "The GTLD-Mou: A Yellow Flag for Trademark Owners on the Information Superhighway," IDEA The Journal of Law and Technology, Vol. 38, No. 2, January 1989. *Member:* The District of Columbia Bar

(This Listing Continued)

(Co-Chair, Intellectual Property Law Section Steering Committee); American Bar Association; American Intellectual Property Law Association. (Resident, McLean, Virginia Office). ***Email:*** eric.fingerhut@shawpittman.com

DAVID G. FISKE, born Parris Island, South Carolina, July 7, 1944; admitted to bar, 1969, Maryland; 1975, Virginia; U.S. District Court, Eastern District of Virginia; U.S. District Court, District of Maryland; U.S. Court of Appeals, Fourth Circuit; 1998, District of Columbia. *Education:* Johns Hopkins University (B.A., 1966); Georgetown University (J.D., 1969). Pi Sigma Alpha. Special Assistant to Senator Harry F. Byrd, Jr., of Virginia, 1967-1970 and 1973-1974. Member, Civil Justice Reform Act Advisory Group, U.S. District Court for Eastern District of Virginia. *Member:* Alexandria, Virginia, Maryland State and American Bar Associations; Virginia State Bar (Member, 1982-1985 and Chairman, 1984-1985, Eighth District Grievance Committee; Member, Special Committee on Continuing Professional Competence, 1984-1985); The District of Columbia Bar; Virginia Association of Defense Attorneys. [Capt., USMC, Judge Advocate Division, 1970-1973]. ***PRACTICE AREAS:*** Commercial Litigation; Federal Practice. ***Email:*** david.fiske@shawpittman.com

LAUREN LYNCH FLICK, born Martinsville, New Jersey, June 28, 1965; admitted to bar, 1990, Maryland; 1991, U.S. District Court, District of Maryland; 1992, District of Columbia, U.S. District Court, District of Columbia and U.S. Court of Appeals, Eighth Circuit. *Education:* Georgetown University (B.A., 1987); The Catholic University of America (J.D., 1990). Member, Catholic University Law Review, 1988-1990. Legal Intern, Felony Trial Division, United States Attorney's Office, Washington, DC, 1989-1990. Legal Intern to U.S. District Judge John Garrett Penn, Washington, D.C., 1989. Congressional Intern, U.S. Representative Peter W. Rodino, Jr., 1987. Co-Author: "Stations Face Regs for Kids' Programming," The National Law Journal, January 20, 1997. *Member:* District of Columbia Bar; Maryland State, American and Federal Communications Bar Associations. ***LANGUAGES:*** Spanish. ***PRACTICE AREAS:*** Communications; Litigation; Intellectual Property. ***Email:*** lauren.lynch.flick@shawpittman.com

SCOTT R. FLICK, born Evansville, Indiana, August 31, 1963; admitted to bar, 1988, California; 1990, District of Columbia. *Education:* Indiana University (B.A., summa cum laude, 1985); University of California at Los Angeles (J.D., 1988). Phi Beta Kappa. Editor, UCLA Law Review, 1987-1988. Editor-in-Chief, 1987-1988 and Assistant Managing Editor, 1986-1987, Federal Communications Law Journal. Author: "The Life, Death and Rebirth of Section 319(a): The Prohibition on Premature Construction of Communications Facilities," 40 Fed. Comm. L. J. 235, 1988. Co-Author: "Review of the 1989 Trademark Decisions of the Court of Appeals for the Federal Circuit," 39 Am. U. L. Rev. 1233, 1990; "Stations Face Regs for Kids' Programming," The National Law Journal, January 20, 1997. *Member:* District of Columbia Bar; State Bar of California; Federal Communications Bar Association. ***PRACTICE AREAS:*** Communications. ***Email:*** scott.flick@shawpittman.com

BRUCE M. FRIED, born Coral Gables, Florida, September 10, 1949; admitted to bar, 1975, Florida; 1981, District of Columbia. *Education:* University of Florida (B.A., 1971; J.D., 1974). Director, Center for Health Plans and Providers, Health Care Financing Administration, US DHHS, 1995-1998. *Member:* The Florida Bar; The District of Columbia Bar. ***PRACTICE AREAS:*** Health Care. ***Email:*** bruce.fried@shawpittman.com

PAUL A. GAUKLER, born Lidgerwood, North Dakota, February 3, 1947; admitted to bar, 1975, North Dakota (inactive) and U.S. District Court, District of North Dakota; 1984, U.S. Court of Appeals, Ninth Circuit; 1988, District of Columbia. *Education:* University of North Dakota (B.S., 1969); Massachusetts Institute of Technology (M.S., 1971); Harvard University (J.D., 1975). Phi Beta Kappa. Attorney: U.S. Nuclear Regulatory Commission, 1975-1977; U.S. Department of Justice, Civil Division, 1977-1984. *Member:* The District of Columbia Bar. ***PRACTICE AREAS:*** Energy; Administrative; Litigation. ***Email:*** paul.gaukler@shawpittman.com

GREGORY M. GIAMMITTORIO, born Washington, D.C., April 16, 1962; admitted to bar, 1988, Virginia; 1990, District of Columbia. *Education:* University of Virginia (B.A., 1984; J.D., 1988). *Member:* District of Columbia Bar (Chairman, Project Finance Committee of the Corporation, Finance and Securities Law Section); American Bar Association (Chairman, Subcommittee on Emerging Companies, Small Business Committee, Section of Business Law). (Resident, McLean, Virginia Office).

JEFFERSON C. GLASSIE, born Washington, D.C., March 1, 1953; admitted to bar, 1985, Maryland; 1986, District of Columbia. *Education:* University of Virginia (B.A., 1975); George Washington University (J.D., with honors, 1985). Recipient, Francis O. Deak Award of Association of Student International Law Societies. Articles Editor, George Washington Journal of International Law and Economics, 1984-1985. Chairman, Law and Legislative Committee, Greater Washington Society of Association Executives, 1986-1987. Chairman, Legal Section Council, American Society of Association Executives, 2000-2001. ***PRACTICE AREAS:*** Association Law; International Law; Government Relations; Nonprofit Organizations. ***Email:*** jeff.glassie@shawpittman.com

(This Listing Continued)

BARRY H. GOTTFRIED, born New York, N.Y., March 8, 1948; admitted to bar, 1977, New York; 1979, District of Columbia; 1990, Maryland. *Education:* Wesleyan University (B.A., summa cum laude, 1970); Oxford University, England (B.A., 1972); Harvard University (J.D., cum laude, 1976). Phi Beta Kappa. Trial Attorney, Civil Rights Division, Office of the General Counsel, Department of Health, Education and Welfare, 1976-1978. *Member:* District of Columbia Bar; Maryland State and American Bar Associations; Washington Council of Lawyers (Director, 1982-1992). ***PRACTICE AREAS:*** Litigation; Communications. ***Email:*** barry.gottfried@shawpittman.com

LAWRENCE J. GOTTS, born Washington, D.C., April 18, 1958; admitted to bar, 1985, Virginia; 1989, District of Columbia. *Education:* University of Maryland (B.S.M.E., 1980); George Washington University (J.D., 1985). Patent Examiner, U.S. Patent and Trademark Office, 1981-1983. (Resident, McLean, Virginia Office). ***PRACTICE AREAS:*** Intellectual Property Litigation and Counseling; Intellectual Property Transactions; Intellectual Property Administrative; Commercial Litigation-Intellectual Property; Government Contracts. ***Email:*** larry.gotts@shawpittman.com

EDMUND D. GRAFF, born Red Wing, Minnesota, February 28, 1964; admitted to bar, 1989, Texas; 1997, District of Columbia. *Education:* Washington & Jefferson College (B.A., magna cum laude, 1985); University of Virginia (J.D., 1989). ***Email:*** edmund.graff@shawpittman.com

R. TIMOTHY HANLON, (P.C.), born St. Louis, Missouri, February 23, 1937; admitted to bar, 1961, Missouri (inactive); 1965, District of Columbia. *Education:* St. Louis University (B.A., magna cum laude, 1958); Harvard Law School (J.D., cum laude, 1961). Honors Program, Office of the General Counsel, Department of the Air Force, 1961-1964. Consultant, President's Advisory Council on Executive Organization, 1970. ***PRACTICE AREAS:*** Government Contracts; Outsourcing Contracts; Dispute Resolution. ***Email:*** timothy.hanlon@shawpittman.com

EDWARD J. HANSEN, born Staten Island, New York, May 20, 1961; admitted to bar, 1990, New Jersey; 1991, New York. *Education:* New York University (B.A., 1987); St. John's University (J.D., 1990). (Resident, New York, N.Y. Office). ***Email:*** edward.hansen@shawpittman.com

ELISABETH J. HARPER, born Somerville, New Jersey, April 17, 1961; admitted to bar, 1987, Maryland; 1988, District of Columbia. *Education:* Duke University (B.A., magna cum laude, 1983); University of Virginia (J.D., 1986). *Member:* The District of Columbia Bar; Maryland State and American Bar Associations. (Resident, McLean, Virginia Office). ***PRACTICE AREAS:*** Emerging Growth Companies; Corporate Transactions; Securities Law. ***Email:*** elisabeth.harper@shawpittman.com

JOHN S. HARPER, born Virginia Beach, Virginia, April 24, 1953; admitted to bar, 1978, District of Columbia. *Education:* Miami University (B.A., magna cum laude, 1975); Georgetown University Law Center (J.D., magna cum laude, 1978; LL.M., 1982). Phi Beta Kappa. Student Editor, Tax Lawyer, 1977. Adjunct Faculty, Georgetown University Law Center, 1989-1992. Tax Law Specialist, IRS National Office Corporate Division, 1978-1982. *Member:* The District of Columbia Bar. (Resident, McLean, Virginia Office). ***PRACTICE AREAS:*** Federal Taxation Law. ***Email:*** john.harper@shawpittman.com

CLIFFORD M. HARRINGTON, born Lafayette, Louisiana, November 20, 1947; admitted to bar, 1972, Colorado; 1975, District of Columbia. *Education:* University of Southwestern Louisiana (B.A., with distinction, 1969); University of Colorado (J.D., 1972). Office of Opinions and Review, Federal Communications Commission, 1972-1974. Task Force on Adjudicatory Reregulation, 1974-1975. Society of Satellite Professionals Internationals (Assistant Treasurer, 1986-1988; Treasurer, 1988-1996). *Member:* District of Columbia Bar; American and Federal Communications Bar Associations. ***PRACTICE AREAS:*** Communications. ***Email:*** clifford.harrington@shawpittman.com

ELLEN K. HARRISON, born March 2, 1946; admitted to bar, 1973, District of Columbia; 1984, U.S. Tax Court and U.S. Supreme Court; 1996, Maryland. *Education:* University of Michigan (B.A., 1968); Harvard Law School (J.D., 1971). Adjunct Professor, Advanced Estate Planning, Georgetown University Law Center, 1986-1989, 1993-1995. Trustee: Arena Stage; Longview Foundation. *Member:* American Bar Association (Supervisory Council Member, Real Property, Probate and Trust Law Section); American College of Trusts and Estate Counsel (Chair, International Estate Planning Committee); D. C. Estate Planning Council. ***PRACTICE AREAS:*** Tax Law; Estate Planning; Estate Administration; Tax Controversies. ***Email:*** ellen.harrison@shawpittman.com

SHEILA McC. HARVEY, born Ridgewood, New Jersey, June 28, 1954; admitted to bar, 1979, District of Columbia. *Education:* Bryn Mawr College (A.B., summa cum laude, 1976); University of Michigan (J.D., 1979). *Member:* American Bar Association (Member, Natural Resources, Energy and Environmental Law Section). ***PRACTICE AREAS:*** Environmental. ***Email:*** sheila.harvey@shawpittman.com

ROBERT E. HASTY, born Coral Gables, Florida, May 9, 1964; admitted to bar, 1990, Virginia; 1992, District of Columbia; 1993, Florida. *Education:* Duke University (B.S.E., 1986); University of Virginia (J.D., 1990). ***Email:*** robert.hasty@shawpittman.com

(This Listing Continued)

DEVON ELIZABETH HEWITT, born Buenos Aires, Argentina, September 3, 1964; admitted to bar, 1989, District of Columbia; 1996, Virginia. *Education:* Smith College (B.A., magna cum laude, Phi Beta Kappa, 1986); University of Virginia (J.D., 1989). Editor, Journal of Law and Politics. (Resident, McLean, Virginia Office). ***Email:*** devon.hewitt@shawpittman.com

J. PATRICK HICKEY, (P.C.), born Iron Mountain, Michigan, October 20, 1939; admitted to bar, 1963, District of Columbia; 1967, U.S. Supreme Court. *Education:* Carroll College (B.A., maxima cum laude, 1959); Harvard University (LL.B., 1963); Georgetown University (LL.M., 1966). Attorney, 1965-1967, 1970-1979 and Director, 1975-1979, D.C. Public Defender Service. ***PRACTICE AREAS:*** Litigation; Internal Investigations; Employment Litigation; White-Collar Crime; Criminal Law. ***Email:*** patrick.hickey@shawpittman.com

THOMAS C. HILL, (P.C.), born New York, N.Y., June 11, 1950; admitted to bar, 1976, District of Columbia. *Education:* Princeton University (A.B., magna cum laude, 1972); Cornell University (J.D., magna cum laude, 1976). Order of the Coif. Note and Comment Editor, Cornell Law Review, 1975-1976. Adjunct Professor of Law, Washington College of Law, American University, 1979-1982. Assistant United States Attorney for the District of Columbia, 1978-1983. ***PRACTICE AREAS:*** Litigation. ***Email:*** thomas.hill@shawpittman.com

CHRISTOPHER HOLDER, admitted to bar, 1991, Supreme Court of England and Wales. *Education:* Bristol University (LL.B., 1987). (Resident, London, England Office). ***PRACTICE AREAS:*** Outsourcing; Systems Integration; Computer Software Licensing.

JEFFREY D. HUTCHINGS, born Chicago, Illinois, October 12, 1957; admitted to bar, 1983, Washington (inactive); 1986, Virginia; 1987, District of Columbia. *Education:* Duke University (A.B., magna cum laude, 1979; J.D., 1983). Order of the Coif. Editorial Board, Duke Law Journal, 1982-1983. *Member:* The District of Columbia Bar; Washington State Bar Association; Virginia State Bar; American Bar Association. ***PRACTICE AREAS:*** Technology; Corporate. ***Email:*** jeffrey.hutchings@shawpittman.com

STEPHEN B. HUTTLER, (P.C.), born Newport, Rhode Island, September 19, 1949; admitted to bar, 1975, District of Columbia; 1980, U.S. Supreme Court. *Education:* Syracuse University (B.A., cum laude, 1971); Georgetown University (J.D., 1974). Editor, Law and Policy in International Business, 1973-1974. Co-Author: "The Legal Response to the Illicit Movement of Cultural Property," 5 Law and Policy in International Business, 932, 1973. ***PRACTICE AREAS:*** Commercial Real Estate. ***Email:*** stephen.huttler@shawpittman.com

REBECCA L. JACKSON, born September 16, 1951; admitted to bar, 1978, District of Columbia; U.S. Claims Court. *Education:* University of Missouri (B.S., with honors, 1972); Georgetown University (J.D., cum laude, 1978). Law Clerk to the Honorable John Lewis Smith, Jr., U.S. District Court for the D.C., 1978-1979. *Member:* The District of Columbia Bar (Health and Corporate Sections); Bar Association of the District of Columbia (Chair, Young Lawyers Section, 1987-1988; Board Member, 1987-1991); American Bar Association (Health, Antitrust, Business, Insurance and Tort Sections). ***PRACTICE AREAS:*** Health Care; Technology; Corporate. ***Email:*** rebecca.jackson@shawpittman.com

BRUCE D. JACOBS, born Springfield, Illinois, January 4, 1955; admitted to bar, 1980, District of Columbia; 1983, Maryland. *Education:* New College of the University of South Florida (B.A., 1976); Harvard University (J.D., 1980). Member, District of Columbia Cable Design Commission, 1982-1984. *Member:* District of Columbia Bar; Maryland State and Federal Communications Bar Associations. ***PRACTICE AREAS:*** Communications; Internet and World Wide Web. ***Email:*** bruce.jacobs@shawpittman.com

JERALD A. JACOBS, born Waukegan, Illinois, February 26, 1945; admitted to bar, 1971, District of Columbia. *Education:* Georgetown University (A.B., 1967; J.D., 1970); University of Fribourg, Switzerland. Author: "Association Law Handbook," 3d Edition, American Society of Association Executives, 1996. Co-Author: "Legal Risk Management for Associations," ASAE, 1995. Co-Author and Editor: "Federal Lobbying," 2d Edition, ASAE, 1993; "Certification and Accreditation Law Handbook," ASAE, 1992. General Counsel, American Society of Association Executives, 1995—. ***PRACTICE AREAS:*** Association Law; Health Care Law; Antitrust Law. ***Email:*** jerald.jacobs@shawpittman.com

CHRISTOPHER G. JANNEY, born Bethesda, Maryland, February 14, 1964; admitted to bar, 1991, Maryland; 1993, District of Columbia. *Education:* University of Maryland (B.A., summa cum laude, 1986); Harvard University (J.D., cum laude, 1991).

JOHN E. JENSEN, born Syosset, New York, November 9, 1960; admitted to bar, 1987, District of Columbia. *Education:* Cornell University (B.A., 1982); George Washington University (J.D., with honors, 1987). Co-Author: The Adjudicatory Arm of Congress - The GAO's Sixty-Year Role In Deciding Government Contract Bid Protests Comes Under Renewed Attack By The Department of Justice, Harvard Journal on Legislation, 1992. Attorney Advisor, Office of General Counsel, U.S. Environmental Protection Agency, 1987-1990. *Member:*

(This Listing Continued)

SHAW PITTMAN LLP, Washington—Continued

The District of Columbia Bar (Government Contracts and Litigation Section); American Bar Association (Public Contract Law Section); Federal Bar Association (Government Section). (Resident, McLean, Virginia Office). ***PRACTICE AREAS:*** Government Contracts. ***Email:*** john.jensen@shawpittman.com

CHRISTINE NICOLAIDES KEARNS, born Washington, D.C., August 30, 1960; admitted to bar, 1987, Maryland; 1988, District of Columbia. *Education:* Duke University (B.A., cum laude, 1982); Vanderbilt University (J.D., 1987). ***PRACTICE AREAS:*** Employment; Litigation. ***Email:*** christine.kearns@shawpittman.com

JOSEPH E. KENDALL, born Cleveland, Ohio, November 23, 1957; admitted to bar, 1984, District of Columbia. *Education:* Yale University (B.A., magna cum laude, 1979); Harvard Law School (J.D., cum laude, 1984). Recipient: At Yale, John Addison Porter Prize for Senior Thesis; At Harvard, Irving R. Oberman Memorial Award for Third Year Thesis. *Member:* The District of Columbia Bar (Member, Sections on: Intellectual Property Law and Computer Law); American Bar Association (Member, Sections on: Intellectual Property Law; Science and Technology and Business Law). ***PRACTICE AREAS:*** Technology Transactions; Outsourcing Transactions; Software Development; Licensing Transactions; Systems Integration Transactions; Real Estate Transactions. ***Email:*** joseph.kendall@shawpittman.com

ALLEN J. KLEIN, born East Orange, New Jersey, November 8, 1953; admitted to bar, 1979, New York; 1985, District of Columbia. *Education:* Cornell University (B.A., 1975); State University of New York at Buffalo (J.D., 1978). Senior Editor, Buffalo Law Review, 1977-1978. Legislation Attorney, U.S. Congress Joint Committee on Taxation, 1983-1984. ***PRACTICE AREAS:*** Outsourcing; Technology; Corporate. ***Email:*** allen.klein@shawpittman.com

ERIC A. KLEIN, born New York, New York, July 3, 1959; admitted to bar, 1986, California and U.S. District Court, Northern District of California. *Education:* Princeton University (A.B., magna cum laude, Certificate in Russian Studies, 1981); Boston University School of Law (J.D., 1985). Executive Committee Member, CalTech/MIT Enterprise Forum, 1992-1995. Chair, San Francisco Barristers Soviet Law Committee, 1991. Co-Author, "The Subjective Element of Infringement-Advice for the Counselor and Litigator," Intellectual Property Section of the State Bar of California. Seminar, "Crossing the Line: Competing Without Infringing the Rights of Others," 1991. *Member:* State Bar of California (Member, Sections on: Business Law; Intellectual Property; International Law); American Bar Association (Member, Sections on: Business Law; International Law; Patent, Trademark and Copyright Law; Science and Technology; Member, Young Lawyers Division, Patent, Trademark and Intellectual Property Committee; Member, Committee on Soviet and East European Law). (Resident, Los Angeles, California Office).

THOMAS J. KNOX, born Stamford, Connecticut, 1963; admitted to bar, 1987, Maryland; 1988, District of Columbia; 2000, Virginia. *Education:* Middlebury College (A.B., cum laude, 1984); University of Michigan (J.D., 1987). Contributing Editor, University of Michigan Journal of Law Reform, 1986-1987. Adjunct Professor of Law, Georgetown University Law Center, 1993-1995. Co-Chair, Computer & Telecommunications Law Section, D.C. Bar, 1998-1999. Treasurer, Technology Lawyers' Consortium, 1995-1999. *Member:* The District of Columbia Bar; Virginia State Bar; Maryland State and American Bar Associations. (Resident, McLean, Virginia Office). ***PRACTICE AREAS:*** Technology Law; Business Law. ***Email:*** tom.knox@shawpittman.com

M. DAVID KROHN, born Oak Ridge, Tennessee, March 16, 1959; admitted to bar, 1983, Virginia; 1985, District of Columbia; 1986, Illinois (inactive); 2000, New York. *Education:* Georgetown University (B.S.B.A., magna cum laude, 1980; J.D., cum laude, 1983). Editor, Law and Policy in International Business, 1982-1983. (Resident, New York, N.Y. Office). ***PRACTICE AREAS:*** Commercial Finance; Structured Finance; Asset Securitization; Banking. ***Email:*** david.krohn@shawpittman.com

CHARLES J. LANDY, born Wilmington, Delaware, 1944; admitted to bar, 1973, Pennsylvania (inactive); 1975, District of Columbia. *Education:* University of Pennsylvania (B.A., 1966); Temple University (J.D., 1973). Editor, Temple Law Quarterly, 1972-1973. Attorney, Division of Enforcement of the Securities and Exchange Commission, 1974-1977. *Member:* The District of Columbia Bar. ***PRACTICE AREAS:*** Securities Enforcement; Securities Litigation; Corporate Securities. ***Email:*** charles.landy@shawpittman.com

KURT L.P. LAWSON, born Davenport, Iowa, November 10, 1958; admitted to bar, 1985, District of Columbia. *Education:* Yale University (B.A., 1982; M.A., 1982); University of Virginia (J.D., 1985). ***Email:*** kurt.lawson@shawpittman.com

MARTIN R. LEADER, born Boston, Massachusetts, July 9, 1940; admitted to bar, 1967, District of Columbia. *Education:* Tufts University (A.B., 1962); Vanderbilt University (J.D., 1965). Office of Opinions and Review, Federal Communications Commission, 1965-1967. *Member:* District of Columbia Bar; Federal Communications Bar Association. ***PRACTICE AREAS:*** Communications. ***Email:*** martin.leader@shawpittman.com

(This Listing Continued)

WARREN U. LEHRENBAUM, born New York, N.Y., December 18, 1963; admitted to bar, 1989, Maryland; 1998, District of Columbia. *Education:* State University of New York at Binghamton (B.A., with honors, 1985); George Washington University (J.D., with honors, 1989).

J. THOMAS LENHART, (P.C.), born Cambridge, Massachusetts, November 3, 1946; admitted to bar, 1973, New York; 1974, District of Columbia. *Education:* University of Edinburgh (Cert. in History, 1967); Columbia University (A.B., 1968); Columbia University Law School (J.D., 1972). Harlan Fiske Stone Scholar. Law Clerk, Hon. Edward C. McLean, United States District Court for the Southern District, now deceased, 1972; Hon. Kevin Thomas Duffy, United States District Court for the Southern District of New York, 1972-1973. Instructor in Law, Washington College of Law of American University, 1976-1978. Adjunct Professor, Cornell Law School, 1992. Author: "A Modest Proposal To Encourage Wider Participation In Investigations," 9 Air Law 50, 1984. *Member:* American Bar Association; American Law Institute. ***PRACTICE AREAS:*** Litigation; Corporate Investigations. ***Email:*** thomas.lenhart@shawpittman.com

DAVID R. LEWIS, born Washington, D.C., February 11, 1953; admitted to bar, 1982, District of Columbia. *Education:* Massachusetts Institute of Technology (B.S., 1979); George Washington University (J.D., with high honors, 1982). Order of the Coif. Notes Editor, George Washington Journal of International Law and Economics, 1981-1982. Author: Note, "The Proposed Export Trading Company Act of 1980: An Amendment to the Webb Pomerene Act," 15 Journal of International Law and Economics 465-491, 1981; "Report on the Renewal of Nuclear Power Plant Operating Licenses," Committee on Nuclear Technology and Law of the Association of the Bar of the City of New York (May 1991); "The Renewal of Nuclear Power Plant Operating Licenses — Executive Summary," 46 Rec. A.B. City N.Y. 899 (1991). Attorney, Atomic Safety and Licensing Board, U.S. Nuclear Regulatory Commission, 1982-1983. Member, American Nuclear Society. ***PRACTICE AREAS:*** Energy; Administrative; Environmental. ***Email:*** david.lewis@shawpittman.com

JACK L. LEWIS, born New York, N.Y., December 19, 1944; admitted to bar, 1969, District of Columbia and Virginia. *Education:* Brown University (A.B., cum laude, 1965); Cornell University (J.D., 1969). *Member:* The District of Columbia Bar; Virginia State Bar. (Resident, McLean, Virginia Office). ***PRACTICE AREAS:*** Corporate Law; Securities; Technology Law; Corporate Finance Law; Business Planning Law. ***Email:*** jack.lewis@shawpittman.com

ROBERT Y. LEWIS, born Garden City, Kansas, September 8, 1958; admitted to bar, 1988, New York; 1991, California. *Education:* Grinnell College (B.A., 1980); Stanford University (J.D., 1984). Phi Beta Kappa. Notes Editor, Stanford Law Review. Law Clerk to the Honorable Harlington Wood, Jr., Judge, U.S. Court of Appeals, Seventh Circuit, 1984-1985. Rotary Fellow, Max Planck Institute for Comparative and International Criminal Law, Freiburg, Germany, 1985-1986. Assistant United State Attorney, Central District of California, 1990-1994. (Resident, New York, N.Y. Office). ***Email:*** robert.lewis@shawpittman.com

SYLVIA M. MAHAFFEY, (P.C.), born Boston, Massachusetts, October 17, 1955; admitted to bar, 1980, Texas; 1984, District of Columbia. *Education:* Bryn Mawr College (A.B., summa cum laude, 1977); University of Texas (J.D., with honors, 1980). ***PRACTICE AREAS:*** Corporate Securities. ***Email:*** sylvia.mahaffey@shawpittman.com

DAVID C. MAIN, born Des Moines, Iowa, February 29, 1948; admitted to bar, 1977, District of Columbia. *Education:* DePauw University (B.A., 1970); Harvard University (M.T.S., 1973); Georgetown University (J.D., 1976). Phi Beta Kappa. Author, "Leadership Will Make Health Reform War," Modern Healthcare, 1993; "Forming Physician Networks," American Medical Association, 1993. Rockefeller Fellow. Professional Staff Member, Minority Policy Committee, 1974-1976. Health Counsel to Senator Richard S. Schweiker, 1976-1979. Minority Counsel, Subcommittee on Health and Scientific Research, U.S. Senate, 1977-1979. Founder and Coordinator, Health Technology Network of Greater Washington. Chairman of the Board, David A. Winston Health Policy Fellowship. Co-Chair, ALI-ABA Annual Course on Health Care Law and Litigation. *Member:* The District of Columbia Bar; Health Management Academy. ***PRACTICE AREAS:*** Health Law. ***Email:*** david.main@shawpittman.com

CLARA RUYAN MARTIN, born Seattle, Washington, February 3, 1964; admitted to bar, 1989, California and U.S. District Court, Southern District of California. *Education:* University of California at Berkeley (B.A., high honors, 1985); University of Michigan Law School (J.D., 1989). Speaker: "Computer Law and the Internet," Computer Law Conference, 1996; "Computer Law and the Internet," Computer Law Conference, 1997; "Advanced Seminar on Drafting Licensing Agreements," Practising Law Institute, 1997. *Member:* State Bar of California (Member, Sections on: Business Law, Real Property Law); American Bar Association (Member, Sections on: Business Law and Real Property Law). (Resident, Los Angeles, California Office).

MILES S. MASON, born Washington, D.C., January 10, 1961; admitted to bar, 1986, New York; 1988, District of Columbia. *Education:* City of London Polytechnic; Wesleyan University (B.A., 1983); Georgetown University Law Center (J.D., 1986). Summer Clerk, Securities and Exchange Commission, Of-

(This Listing Continued)

fice of General Counsel, 1985. *Member:* New York State and Federal Communications Bar Associations; District of Columbia Bar; Bar Association of the District of Columbia. ***PRACTICE AREAS:*** Communications; Corporate; Business. ***Email:*** miles.mason@shawpittman.com

JENNIFER LYNN MATTINGLY, born Tulsa, Oklahoma, March 11, 1965; admitted to bar, 1993, New York; 1994, Florida; 1995, District of Columbia; 1996, Georgia. *Education:* Emory University (B.A., 1988; J.D., 1991); McGeorge School of Law (LL.M. in Transnational Business Law, 1992). Author: "The Banking Market, Competition and Banking Mergers in the United States and European Community," LL.M. Thesis, 1992; "Is Your Shrinkwrap License Enforceable?" Fort Knox Forum: Updates in International Technology Issues, 1996. Co-Author: "Negotiating Multimedia Agreements: Issues Associated with Acquiring Multiple Rights from Multiple Parties," Practising Law Institute, January, 1997. *Member:* Intellectual Property Association of New York State Bar; Computer Law Association of Florida Bar. (Resident, London, England Office).

ALISTAIR MAUGHAN, born Shipley, England, August 22, 1963; admitted to bar, 1987, Solicitor, Supreme Court of England and Wales; 1990, New York. *Education:* Leicester University, England (LL.B., 1984). (Resident, London, England Office). ***Email:*** alistair.maughan@shawpittman.com

THOMAS H. McCORMICK, born New York, N.Y., May 6, 1950; admitted to bar, 1977, District of Columbia. *Education:* Manhattan College (B.E., 1972); Georgetown University (J.D., 1977). Editor, Law and Policy in International Business, 1976-1977. Adjunct Professor of Law, Georgetown University Law Center, 1981-1986, 1989. ***PRACTICE AREAS:*** Corporate Securities; Technology. ***Email:*** thomas.mccormick@shawpittman.com

JOHN M. McDONALD, born Pikeville, Kentucky, July 31, 1963; admitted to bar, 1990, Virginia; 1996, District of Columbia. *Education:* University of Notre Dame (B.A., 1985); University of Kentucky School of Law (J.D., 1990). ***Email:*** john.mcdonald@shawpittman.com

JACK McKAY, (P.C.), born Blytheville, Arkansas, March 24, 1946; admitted to bar, 1970, Virginia; 1972, District of Columbia. *Education:* Vanderbilt University (B.A., 1967); University of Virginia (J.D., 1970). Order of the Coif. Research and Projects Editor, Virginia Law Review, 1969-1970. Law Clerk to Hon. Collins J. Seitz, Chief Judge, U.S. Court of Appeals for the Third Circuit, 1974-1975. [U.S. Navy JAG Corps, 1970-1974]. ***PRACTICE AREAS:*** Commercial Litigation. ***Email:*** jack.mckay@shawpittman.com

KATHY J. McKNIGHT, born Rome, Georgia, November 14, 1949; admitted to bar, 1983, District of Columbia; 1984, U.S. Court of Appeals for the Federal Circuit; 1988, U.S. Supreme Court. *Education:* Auburn University (B.S., summa cum laude, 1971); Georgetown University (J.D., cum laude, 1983). Phi Kappa Phi. Adjunct Professor, George Mason University School of Law, 1996. Author: "Section 33(b) of the Lanham Act: What Effect in Trademark Infringement Litigation?" 72 Trademark Reporter 329, 1982; "Incontestability Revisited - The Rock of Gibralter and MarCon Cases," 73 Trademark Reporter, 561, 1983. Lecturer, Various INTA and CLE Seminars. *Member:* The District of Columbia Bar; American Bar Association; Women's Bar Association of the District of Columbia; International Trademark Association. ***Email:*** kathy.mcknight@shawpittman.com

STEVEN L. MELTZER, (P.C.), born Rochester, New York, September 6, 1946; admitted to bar, 1973, Maryland; 1974, District of Columbia; 1997, Virginia. *Education:* Brown University (A.B., cum laude, 1968); Harvard Law School (J.D., 1973); Harvard Business School (M.B.A., with high distinction, Baker Scholar, 1973). Chairman, 1989-2000 and Trustee, 1972-1989, New England Institute of Technology. Advisor, Technology Executives Roundtable, 1990-1994. General Counsel: High Technology Council of Maryland, 1995—; Maryland Information Technology Center, 1993-1997. Vice Chairman, Standing Committee on Globalization of the Legal Profession, International Bar Association, 1996-1999. Judge, Entrepreneur of the Year Awards, Washington Region, 1995. Member: Information Technology Association of America; Northern Virginia Technology Council. Chairman, Corporate Practice Group, 1995-1996. (Senior Partner, McLean, Virginia Office). ***PRACTICE AREAS:*** Corporate; Technology. ***Email:*** steven.meltzer@shawpittman.com

DAVID E. MENOTTI, born Chicago, Illinois, May 20, 1942; admitted to bar, 1967, New York; 1972, District of Columbia. *Education:* Syracuse University (A.B., 1964); University of Pennsylvania (J.D., magna cum laude, 1967). Order of the Coif. Member, University of Pennsylvania Law Review, 1965-1967. EPA Associate General Counsel, Pesticides, 1978-1980; Toxic Substances, 1980; Air, Noise and Radiation, 1981-1982. *Member:* The District of Columbia Bar. [Capt., U.S. Army, JAGC, 1969-1973]. ***PRACTICE AREAS:*** Environmental Law. ***Email:*** david.menotti@shawpittman.com

PAUL F. MICKEY, JR., born Washington, D.C., September 25, 1949; admitted to bar, 1974, District of Columbia; 1975, U.S. Court of Appeals for the District of Columbia Circuit; 1979, U.S. Court of Appeals, Tenth Circuit; 1981, U.S. Supreme Court; 1982, U.S. Court of Appeals, Seventh Circuit. *Education:* Princeton University (A.B., summa cum laude, 1971); University of Virginia (J.D., 1974). Articles Editor, Virginia Law Review, 1973-1974. Law Clerk to the Hon. George E. MacKinnon, U.S. Court of Appeals for the District of Columbia

(This Listing Continued)

Circuit, 1974-1975. Attorney, Office of Legal Adviser, U.S. Department of State, 1975-1977. Vice President-General Counsel, 1979-1983 and Executive Vice President-Law and Public Affairs, 1983-1985, National Railroad Passenger Corp. ("Amtrak"). *Member:* The District of Columbia Bar (Chair, Subcommittee on Individual Employee Rights and Responsibilities in the Workplace, 1990-1993); American Bar Association. ***PRACTICE AREAS:*** Labor and Employment Law; Transportation; Appellate Litigation. ***Email:*** paul.mickey@shawpittman.com

DAVID L. MILLER, (P.C.), born Brooklyn, New York, November 4, 1954; admitted to bar, 1979, District of Columbia; 1986, Virginia. *Education:* George Washington University (B.A., with distinction, 1976); University of Michigan (J.D., magna cum laude, 1979). Phi Beta Kappa; Order of the Coif. *Member:* The District of Columbia Bar; Virginia State Bar; American Bar Association. (Resident, McLean, Virginia Office). ***PRACTICE AREAS:*** Commercial Real Estate; Corporate. ***Email:*** david.miller@shawpittman.com

MICHAEL C. MOETELL, born Pittsburgh, Pennsylvania, April 5, 1961; admitted to bar, 1985, District of Columbia. *Education:* Villanova University (B.S., cum laude, 1982); Harvard University (J.D., cum laude, 1985). *Member:* The District of Columbia Bar (Member, Taxation Section); American Bar Association (Member, Taxation Section). ***PRACTICE AREAS:*** Commercial Tax. ***Email:*** mitch.moetell@shawpittman.com

FRANCISCO R. MONTERO, born Brooklyn, New York, February 8, 1960; admitted to bar, 1987, New York, New Jersey, District of Columbia and Virginia. *Education:* University of Michigan (B.A., with honors in Political Science, 1982); George Washington University (J.D., 1986). Phi Alpha Delta. Member, George Washington Law Review, 1985-1986. Board of Directors, Minority Media and Telecommunications Council, 1995-1999. General Counsel: American Hispanic Owned Radio Association; Puerto Rico Radio Broadcasters Association. Member, United States Senior Executive Director, FCC Office of Service, 1999-2000; Communications Business Opportunities, 1999-2000; Advisory Board, Hispanic Internet Summit, 2001. *Member:* District of Columbia Bar; New York State, New Jersey State, National Hispanic and Federal Communications Bar Associations; Virginia State Bar. ***LANGUAGES:*** Spanish. ***Email:*** frank.montero@shawpittman.com

THOMAS D. MORTON, born Queens, New York, June 8, 1959; admitted to bar, 1985, New York; 1989, District of Columbia. *Education:* Manhattan College (B.S., 1981); Cornell University (J.D., 1984); New York University (LL.M., 1989). Delta Mu Delta; Epsilon Sigma Pi. Order of the Coif. *Member:* The District of Columbia Bar (Member, Taxation Section). ***PRACTICE AREAS:*** Partnership Taxation; Affordable Housing; Equipment Leasing. ***Email:*** thomas.morton@shawpittman.com

ANDREW C. MOYLE, born Australia, May 28, 1964; admitted to bar, 1989, Supreme Court Victoria, Australia and High Court of Australia; 1996, Supreme Court New South Wales. *Education:* University of Melbourne (B.Comm., 1988; LL.B., 1988). (Resident, London, England Office). ***PRACTICE AREAS:*** Intellectual Property; Electronic Commerce; Technology; Outsourcing; Telecommunications. ***Email:*** andrew.moyle@shawpittman.com

J. E. MURDOCK III, born Washington, D.C., March 26, 1947; admitted to bar, 1973, District of Columbia; 1977, Illinois (inactive). *Education:* Princeton University (A.B., 1969); Northwestern University (M.M., 1980); Columbia University (J.D., 1972). Author: "The Congressional Mandate Against A Federal Strike," Journal Air Law and Commerce, 1982; "Report from the United States of America," German Journal of Air and Space Law, 1984. Chief Counsel, 1981-1985 and Acting Deputy Administrator, 1984, Federal Aviation Administration. Member, International Civil Aviation Organization Panel of Arbiters and Experts, 1987—; Co-Chairman, Board of Editors, Av Lex, 1991-1992; President, Air & Space Heritage Council, Inc., 1992-2000; Chairman, Business Aviation Coalition Political Action Committee, 1988-1991. Member, Board of Trustees and Past President, Aero Club of Washington, 1982-1988. Deputy Chairman-Section Liaison, Federal Bar Association, 1991-1994; Secretary, Transportation Law Section, Federal Bar Association, 1999—; Executive Committee, 1995-2000. Chairman, Forum Committee on Air and Space Law, American Bar Association, 1987-1990. Chairman, Aeronautical Law Committee, International Bar Association, 1984-1988. *Member:* The District of Columbia Bar; Illinois State Bar Association. ***PRACTICE AREAS:*** Transportation Law; Aviation Law; Administrative Law; Lobbying; Environmental Law; Antitrust Law. ***Email:*** sandy.murdock@shawpittman.com

MICHAEL T. MURPHY, born Winton, Queensland, Australia, February 15, 1963; admitted to bar, 1987, Victoria, Australia; 1996, New York. *Education:* University of Melbourne (B.Com., 1986; LL.B., 1986). (Resident, Los Angeles, California Office). ***PRACTICE AREAS:*** Technology; Corporate; Transactions. ***Email:*** michael.murphy@shawpittman.com

TREVOR W. NAGEL, born Adelaide, Australia, 1951; admitted to bar, 1985, Barrister, New South Wales, Australia and Barrister, High Court of Australia; 1986, Massachusetts; 1996, District of Columbia. *Education:* University of Adelaide (B.A., with honors, 1973; Dip.Ed., 1974; LL.B., with honors, 1980); University of Chicago (LL.M., 1981); Harvard University (S.J.D., 1984). Member, University of Adelaide Law Review, 1977-1980. *Member:* American

(This Listing Continued)

SHAW PITTMAN LLP, Washington—Continued

and International Bar Associations. ***PRACTICE AREAS:*** Information Technology; Telecommunications; Intellectual Property; Infrastructure Development; International. ***Email:*** trevor.nagel@shawpittman.com

JOYCE L. OLINER, born Wakefield, Yorkshire, England, March 29, 1957; admitted to bar, 1984, District of Columbia. *Education:* Lady Margaret Hall, Oxford University, Oxford, England (B.A., Hons. Jurisprudence, 1978); University of Virginia (LL.M., 1979); University of Wisconsin (J.D., cum laude, 1983). ***PRACTICE AREAS:*** Employment.

JOHN H. O'NEILL, JR. (P.C.), born Bainbridge, Maryland, October 20, 1946; admitted to bar, 1976, Maryland; 1977, District of Columbia. *Education:* United States Naval Academy (B.S., with distinction, 1968); Yale University (J.D., 1976). ***PRACTICE AREAS:*** Energy; Nuclear Energy; Electric Utility; International Energy Transactions. ***Email:*** john.o'neill@shawpittman.com

AARON M. OSER, born Orlando, Florida, February 22, 1961; admitted to bar, 1990, New York; 1996, District of Columbia. *Education:* State University of New York at Albany (B.A., 1983); New York University (M.P.A., 1985); St. John's University (J.D., 1989). ***Email:*** aaron.oser@shawpittman.com

DAVID D. OXENFORD, born Point Pleasant, New Jersey, December 1, 1954; admitted to bar, 1980, Georgia and District of Columbia. *Education:* College of William & Mary (B.A., 1977); Emory University (J.D., with distinction, 1980). Order of the Coif. *Member:* District of Columbia Bar; State Bar of Georgia; American and Federal Communications (Co-Chair Adjudicatory Practice Committee, 1992-1994; Co-Chair, Mass Media Practice Committee, 1994-1999; Co-Chair, Continuing Legal Education Committee, 1996-1998; Co-Chair, Transactional Practice Committee, 1998-1999; Co-Chair, Committee on Relations With Other Bar Associations, 2000-2001) Bar Associations. ***PRACTICE AREAS:*** Communications; Intellectual Property; Internet and World Wide Web. ***Email:*** david.oxenford@shawpittman.com

THOMAS J. PAX, born St. Marys, Ohio, January 20, 1958; admitted to bar, 1987, New York; 1993, District of Columbia. *Education:* Harvard University (A.L.B., 1983); Boston College Law School (J.D., 1986); New York University School of Law (LL.M., 1990). Editor in Chief, Boston College International and Comparative Law Review, 1985-1986. Author: "Nicaragua v. United States in the International Court of Justice: Compulsory Jurisdiction or Just Compulsion?," 8 B.C. Int'l. Comp. L. Rev. 471 (1985); Old Bonds and New Law: Misunderstanding Foreign Sovereign Immunity in the Chinese Railroad Case," 5 U. Conn. J. Int'l L. 625 (1990). Co-Author: "Forms of Entry, Operation, Expansion, and Supervision of Foreign Banks in the United States," Regulation of Foreign Banks: United States and International, Lexis Law Publishing, 1995, 1998, 2000. *Member:* The District of Columbia Bar; New York State Bar Association. ***SPECIAL AGENCIES:*** Federal Reserve, 1986-1989. ***PRACTICE AREAS:*** Financial Institutions Law. ***Email:*** thomas.pax@shawpittman.com

MARC A. PEARL, born Detroit, Michigan, April 26, 1950; admitted to bar, 1979, Georgia; 1996, District of Columbia. *Education:* Case Western Reserve University (B.A., 1972); Emory University School of Law (J.D., 1979). ***Email:*** marc.pearl@shawpittman.com

VICTORIA J. PERKINS, (P.C.), born Morristown, New Jersey, August 15, 1945; admitted to bar, 1976, District of Columbia. *Education:* Douglass College (B.A., with honors, 1967); Monmouth College (M.A.T., magna cum laude, 1973); Harvard University (J.D., cum laude, 1976). Phi Beta Kappa. ***PRACTICE AREAS:*** Real Estate; Corporate; Commercial Finance. ***Email:*** victoria.perkins@shawpittman.com

WILLIAM J. PETERS, admitted to bar, 1994, California. *Education:* University of California at Los Angeles (B.A., 1990); Loyola University of Los Angeles (J.D., 1994). (Resident, Los Angeles, California Office). ***Email:*** bill.peters@shawpittman.com

CHARLES H. PETERSON, born May 8, 1938; admitted to bar, 1974, California; 1996, District of Columbia. *Education:* United States Naval Academy (B.S., 1960); Stanford University (M.B.A., 1971; J.D., 1974).

PAUL S. PILECKI, (P.C.), born Norristown, Pennsylvania, September 12, 1950; admitted to bar, 1978, Pennsylvania (inactive); 1985, District of Columbia. *Education:* St. Joseph's College (A.B., 1972); Temple University (J.D., 1978). Contributor: *Banking Law* Volume II, "International Banking," Matthew Bender. Chairman, International Subcommittee, Banking Law Committee, American Bar Association. Senior Counsel, Legal Division, Board of Governors of the Federal Reserve System, 1978-1984. ***PRACTICE AREAS:*** Banking. ***Email:*** paul.pilecki@shawpittman.com

ANNE K. PLANNING, born Minneapolis, Minnesota, July 26, 1960; admitted to bar, 1988, Virginia; 1989, District of Columbia. *Education:* Iowa State University (B.A., 1982); George Washington University (J.D., 1988). *Member:* Virginia State Bar; The District of Columbia Bar. ***PRACTICE AREAS:*** Real Estate. ***Email:*** anne.planning@shawpittman.com

(This Listing Continued)

PATRICK JOHN POTTER, born Lapeer, Michigan, March 25, 1964; admitted to bar, 1989, Michigan; 1991, District of Columbia; 1996, Virginia; 1998, U.S. Supreme Court. *Education:* Michigan State University (B.A., high honors, 1986); University of Michigan (J.D., cum laude, 1989). Law Clerk to Honorable Ray Reynolds Graves, U.S. Bankruptcy Court, Eastern District of Michigan, 1989-1990. *Member:* State Bar of Michigan; The District of Columbia Bar; Virginia State Bar.

GLENN S. RICHARDS, born Brooklyn, New York, May 9, 1961; admitted to bar, 1986, New York; 1987, U.S. District Court, Southern District of New York; 1989, U.S. Court of Appeals for the District of Columbia Circuit; 1992, District of Columbia. *Education:* West Virginia University (B.S., Journalism, cum laude, 1982); New York Law School (J.D., cum laude, 1985). *Member:* District of Columbia Bar; New York State, American and Federal Communications Bar Associations. ***PRACTICE AREAS:*** Communications. ***Email:*** glenn.richards@shawpittman.com

DIANE SHAPIRO RICHER, born Cleveland, Ohio, May 21, 1959; admitted to bar, 1985, New York and District of Columbia. *Education:* University of Pennsylvania (B.A., cum laude, 1981); Georgetown University (J.D., cum laude, 1984). Associate Editor, Law Review, The Tax Lawyer, 1983-1984. *Member:* The District of Columbia Bar (Member, Real Estate, Housing and Land Use Section); New York State and American (Member, Sections on: Real Property, Probate and Trust Law; Business Law) Bar Associations. ***PRACTICE AREAS:*** Commercial Real Estate. ***Email:*** diane.richer@shawpittman.com

ROBERT B. ROBBINS, (P.C.), born Canton, Ohio, August 31, 1951; admitted to bar, 1975, District of Columbia. *Education:* Cornell University (A.B., magna cum laude, 1972); Harvard Law School (J.D., cum laude, 1975). Court Law Clerk, U.S. Court of Appeals for the District of Columbia Circuit, 1975-1976. Author: "Private Offering Liabilities and Due Diligence, Post-*Gustafson,*" Insights, May 1998; "The Effect of Stock Exchange Roles on Corporate Disclosure Obligations," Rev. of Sec. & Comm. Reg., Oct. 23, 1996; "SEC Expands Offshore Funds' Access to U.S. Markets," Insights, September 1996; "Due Diligence in Private Placement Offerings," Rev. of Sec. & Comm. Reg., June 14, 1995; "Ensuring Mandatory Indemnification of Corporate Officers and Directors," Insights, October 1994; "Informal Communications with Securities Analysts," Insights, April 1994; "Directors' Fiduciary Duties to Preferred Stockholders," Insights, November 1993; "Fiduciary Duty of Directors of Corporate General Partners," Rev. of Sec. and Comm. Reg., August 1992; "Takeovers of Limited Partnerships," Insights, December 1990; "Limited Partnership Distress Situations: Resales, Restructuring, Rescission" Insight August 1990; "Closing Unsuccessful Offerings: The New Scope of Rule 10b-9," Insights, May 1990; "All-or-None Offerings Under Rule 106-9," 13 ALI-ABA Journal 77, February 1989; "All or None Offerings," 19 Rev. Sec. Reg. 59, March 19, 1986; "All or None Offerings: An Update," 19 Rev. of Sec. Reg. 181, August 27, 1986; "Structuring Limited Partnership Offerings: Recent Developments," 43 Wash. & Lee L. Rev. 829, 1986. Co-Chair, ALI-ABA Annual Course of Study on Private Placements and Regulation D, 1991—. *Member:* The District of Columbia Bar (Chair: Steering Committee, Section of Corporation, Finance and Securities Law, 1993-1994; Standing Committee on Broker-Dealer Regulation, 1985-1991). ***PRACTICE AREAS:*** Corporate Securities. ***Email:*** robert.robbins@shawpittman.com

JANE SULLIVAN ROBERTS, born New York, N.Y., December 3, 1954; admitted to bar, 1988, District of Columbia. *Education:* College of the Holy Cross (A.B., magna cum laude, 1976); Melbourne University (Dip.Ed., 1977); Brown University (M.Sc., 1981); Georgetown University (J.D., cum laude, 1984). Law Clerk to the Honorable James M. Sprouse, U.S. Court of Appeals, Fourth Circuit. *Member:* The District of Columbia Bar; Virginia State Bar. ***PRACTICE AREAS:*** Technology Transactions. ***Email:*** jane.roberts@shawpittman.com

MICHELE D. ROSS, born Lower Merion, Pennsylvania, May 14, 1956; admitted to bar, 1983, California and U.S. District Court, Northern District of California; 1985, District of Columbia; 1986, New York. *Education:* American University (B.A., 1978); New York Law School; London School of Economics and Political Science (Dip. Int'l. Law, 1981); University of San Francisco (J.D., 1983). Author: "The Spirit of Uppsala—International Organization for a New World Order," Atle Grahl-Madsen and Jiri Toman, de Gruyter, New York, 1984. Junior Co-Chair, Legal Aide Society Associates Campaign, 1989-1990. *Member:* The Association of the Bar of The City of New York. ***PRACTICE AREAS:*** Corporate Finance; Securities. ***Email:*** michele.ross@shawpittman.com

BARBARA M. ROSSOTTI (P.C.), born Englewood, New Jersey, February 28, 1940; admitted to bar, 1964, Massachusetts (inactive); 1966, District of Columbia. *Education:* Mount Holyoke College (B.A., magna cum laude, 1961); Harvard Law School (LL.B., 1964). Phi Beta Kappa. *Member:* International Law Association (American Branch); American Society of International Law. ***PRACTICE AREAS:*** Corporate; Technology; International Transactions. ***Email:*** barbara.rossotti@shawpittman.com

GARY D. ROTH, born New York, N.Y., June 3, 1955; admitted to bar, 1981, New York; 1984, U.S. District Court, Southern District of New York.

(This Listing Continued)

Education: Franklin & Marshall College (B.A., 1977); University of Pittsburgh (J.D., 1980). Member, University of Pittsburgh Law Review, 1978-1979. Member, Manufacturers Hanover Trust Company, New York, N.Y., Legal Department, 1981-1986. Associate, Booth & Baron, New York, N.Y., 1986-1989. Partner, Beller & Keller, New York, N.Y., 1989-1996. *Member:* American Bar Association (Chairman, Asset-Backed Securitization and Structured Finance Subcommittee of the Section of International Law and Practice, 1989-1991; Member, Documentation Committee and Drafting Subcommittee, 1984-1986; International Swap Dealers Association). (Resident, New York, N.Y. Office). ***PRACTICE AREAS:*** Structured Finance; Asset Securitization; Corporate Finance. ***Email:*** gary.roth@shawpittman.com

DAVID R. SAHR, born Minneapolis, Minnesota, January 19, 1953; admitted to bar, 1982, District of Columbia. *Education:* Georgetown School of Foreign Service (B.S.F.S., magna cum laude, 1976); London School of Economics and Political Science (M.Sc., 1977); Georgetown University (J.D., magna cum laude, 1982). Associate Editor, Georgetown Law Journal, 1980-1982. ***PRACTICE AREAS:*** International; Banking; Financial Services. ***Email:*** david.sahr@shawpittman.com

KATHRYN R. SCHMELTZER, born Newark, New Jersey, September 18, 1946; admitted to bar, 1974, District of Columbia. *Education:* Smith College (A.B., 1968); University of Virginia (J.D., 1973). Law Clerk to Judge Dyer Justice Taylor, Superior Court for the District of Columbia, 1973-1974. Attorney, Review Board, Federal Communications Commission, 1974-1976; Broadcast Bureau Hearing Division, 1976-1978. President, D.C. Chapter, 1987-1988 and Vice President, Government/Industry Affairs, 1988-1989, American Women in Radio and Television. Recipient, FCBA Distinguished Service Award, 1996. *Member:* District of Columbia Bar; American and Federal Communications (Treasurer, 1997-1998, Assistant Treasurer, 1996-1997, Executive Committee Member, 1990-1993) Bar Associations; Supreme Court Bar. ***PRACTICE AREAS:*** Communications. ***Email:*** kathryn.schmeltzer@shawpittman.com

LAWRENCE A. SCHULTIS, born Alexandria, Virginia; admitted to bar, 1992, Virginia; 1996, District of Columbia. *Education:* George Washington University (B.B.A., 1985; J.D., 1992).

CHARLES SEVERS, admitted to bar, 1994, Solicitor of the Supreme Court of England and Wales. *Education:* College of Law, Guildford (1991); University of Briston (LL.B., 1990). *Member:* Law Society of England and Wales. (Resident, London, England Office). ***PRACTICE AREAS:*** Corporate Law; Securities; Joint Ventures; Strategic Alliances; Mergers and Acquisitions. ***Email:*** charles.severs@shawpittman.com

JAY E. SILBERG, (P.C.), born Weehawken, New Jersey, April 5, 1941; admitted to bar, 1966, New Jersey (inactive); 1968, District of Columbia. *Education:* Amherst College (B.A., cum laude, 1963); Harvard University (J.D., 1966). With Office of General Counsel, Atomic Energy Commission, 1966-1969. ***PRACTICE AREAS:*** Energy; Nuclear; Litigation; Administrative. ***Email:*** jay.silberg@shawpittman.com

LYNN A. SOUKUP, (P.C.), born New York, N.Y., June 20, 1956; admitted to bar, 1981, District of Columbia. *Education:* Bucknell University (B.A., magna cum laude, 1978); Georgetown University Law Center (J.D., magna cum laude, 1981). Senior Lead Articles Editor, 1980-81, Law & Policy in International Business. Clerk, The Honorable Lloyd Fletcher, United States Court of Claims, 1981-82. Member, ABA Section of Business Law, Commercial Financial Services Committee, Subcommittee on Loan Documentation and Uniform Commercial Code Committee, Investment Securities Subcommittee, Subcommittee Chair, 2000—. ***PRACTICE AREAS:*** Corporate; Structured Finance; Asset Securitization; Commercial Finance; Securities. ***Email:*** lynn.soukup@shawpittman.com

DEBBIE BEECHER SPARTIN, (P.C.), born Washington, D.C., June 30, 1962; admitted to bar, 1987, Virginia; 1988, District of Columbia. *Education:* University of Virginia (B.A., with high distinction, 1984); Harvard Law School (J.D., 1987). *Member:* The District of Columbia Bar; Virginia State Bar. ***PRACTICE AREAS:*** Commercial Real Estate. ***Email:*** debbie.spartin@shawpittman.com

THOMAS J. SPULAK, born New York, N.Y., February 23, 1956; admitted to bar, 1982, Florida; 1984, District of Columbia. *Education:* University of Miami (B.A., 1977); Florida State University (J.D., 1982). General Counsel, U.S. House of Representatives. General Counsel and Staff Director, House Rules Committee. ***Email:*** thomas.spulak@shawpittman.com

AKIBA STERN, born Brooklyn, New York, March 3, 1955; admitted to bar, 1979, Massachusetts; 1981, New York; 1988, Connecticut. *Education:* Yeshiva University (B.A., 1976); Boston University (J.D., 1979; M.B.A., 1980). Author: "Entrepreneurship: When a User Organization Markets Its Own Software," 5 The Computer Lawyer 6, 1988. *Member:* American Bar Association; Computer Law Association. (Resident, New York, N.Y. Office). ***LANGUAGES:*** Hebrew.

ELIZABETH ESPIN STERN, born Prince Georges County, Maryland, June 21, 1961; admitted to bar, 1986, Virginia; 1988, District of Columbia. *Education:* University of Virginia (B.A., with high distinction, 1983; J.D., 1986). Phi Beta Kappa. Semifinalist, University of Virginia Lile Moot Court Competition. Listed in: *Who's Who in American Law; Outstanding Young Women In America.* Member: Information Technology Association of America (Immigration Policy Committee); Editorial Board, Business Laws Inc.; French-American Chamber of Commerce (Contributing Author, Speaker); Institute of International Human Resources. *Member:* The District of Columbia Bar (Member, International Law Section); Bar Association of the District of Columbia (Treasurer-Elect, 1998-1999; Secretary, 1997-1998, Board, 1994-1995 and Chair, 1993-1994, Young Lawyers Section); Virginia (Member, International Law Section) and American ("Under 35" Delegate for the District of Columbia, 1994-1995) Bar Associations; American Immigration Lawyers Association (Mentor, Business Visas For Professionals); Washington International Trade Association. ***LANGUAGES:*** Spanish and French. ***PRACTICE AREAS:*** Business Immigration. ***Email:*** elizabeth.stern@shawpittman.com

CHARLES B. TEMKIN, (P.C.), born Providence, Rhode Island, June 19, 1948; admitted to bar, 1973, District of Columbia. *Education:* Columbia University (B.A., summa cum laude, 1969); Harvard University (J.D., magna cum laude, 1972). Phi Beta Kappa. Articles Editor, Vol. 85, Harvard Law Review, 1971-1972. Attorney Advisor, Office of Tax Legislative Counsel, United States Treasury, 1974-1976. ***PRACTICE AREAS:*** Tax. ***Email:*** charles.temkin@shawpittman.com

ALEXANDER D. TOMASZCZUK, born St. Joseph, Missouri, December 4, 1955; admitted to bar, 1981, Missouri; 1982, District of Columbia, U.S. Court of Appeals for the Federal Circuit and U.S. Court of Federal Claims; 1983, U.S. District Court for the District of Columbia; 1989, California (inactive); 1991, U.S. Court of Appeals, District of Columbia Circuit; 1996, Virginia. *Education:* Stanford University (B.A., 1977); University of Missouri (J.D., 1981); Columbia University (LL.M., 1987). Lead Articles Editor, Missouri Law Review, 1980-1981. Author: "The Adjudicatory Arm of Congress—The GAO's Sixty-Year Role in Deciding Government Contract Bid Protests Comes Under Renewed Attack by the Department of Justice," 29 Harvard Journal on Legislation 399, Summer 1992. Law Clerk to Judge Robert L. Kunzig, U.S. Court of Claims, 1981-1982. Attorney, Office of the Legal Advisor, U.S. Department of State, 1987-1990. Director, Diplomatic Law and Litigation Division, U.S. Department of State, 1989-1990. *Member:* The District of Columbia Bar; The Missouri Bar; State Bar of California; Virginia Bar; Federal and American (Member, Public Contracts Law Section) Bar Associations; American Society of International Law. (Resident, McLean, Virginia Office). ***LANGUAGES:*** French. ***PRACTICE AREAS:*** Contracts; International Law. ***Email:*** alexander.tomaszczuk@shawpittman.com

MATIAS F. TRAVIESO-DIAZ, (P.C.), born Havana, Cuba, February 21, 1943; admitted to bar, 1976, District of Columbia. *Education:* University of Miami (B.S.E.E., 1966; M.S.E.E., 1967); The Ohio State University (Ph.D., 1971); Columbia University (J.D., 1976). Tau Beta Pi; Eta Kappa Nu; Sigma Xi. Harlan Fiske Stone Scholar. ***PRACTICE AREAS:*** Energy; Litigation; International; Cuba. ***Email:*** matias.travieso-diaz@shawpittman.com

ANDREW M. TUCKER, born Brooklyn, New York, July 25, 1962; admitted to bar, 1987, New Jersey; 1988, New York; 1995, Georgia; 1999, District of Columbia; 2000, Virginia. *Education:* University of Notre Name (B.A., with honors, 1984); Georgetown University (J.D., cum laude, 1987). Lead Articles Editor, The Tax Lawyer, 1986-1987. *Member:* State Bar of Georgia; The District of Columbia Bar; Virginia State Bar; Virginia Bar Association. (Resident, McLean, Virginia Office). ***PRACTICE AREAS:*** Securities; Venture Capital; Mergers and Acquisitions. ***Email:*** andy.tucker@shawpittman.com

TIMOTHY HANSEN WATKINS, born Montgomery County, Maryland, March 23, 1958; admitted to bar, 1986, New York; 1988, District of Columbia. *Education:* Georgetown University School of Foreign Service (B.S.F.S., cum laude, 1980); Georgetown University Law Center (J.D., cum laude, 1984). Phi Beta Kappa. Editor, Law and Policy in International Business, 1983-1984. ***LANGUAGES:*** French. ***PRACTICE AREAS:*** Commercial Real Estate; Corporate Lending. ***Email:*** timothy.watkins@shawpittman.com

GADI WEINREICH, born Tel Aviv, Israel, April 25, 1962; admitted to bar, 1987, Massachusetts; 1988, District of Columbia. *Education:* Brown University (A.B., magna cum laude, 1983); Harvard University (J.D., cum laude, 1987); Cambridge University (LL.M., 1992). *Member:* The District of Columbia Bar (Member, Health Law Section); American Bar Association; American Health Lawyers Association. ***PRACTICE AREAS:*** Health Law; Health Care Regulation; Health Care Fraud and Abuse; Health Care Compliance; Health Care Litigation. ***Email:*** gadi.weinreich@shawpittman.com

ROBERT N. WEINSTOCK, born New York, N.Y., May 5, 1946; admitted to bar, 1971, Pennsylvania (inactive); 1975, District of Columbia; 1979, Virginia. *Education:* University of Pennsylvania (B.S., 1968; J.D., 1971). *Member:* The District of Columbia Bar; Virginia State Bar; American Bar Association. ***PRACTICE AREAS:*** Commercial Real Estate. ***Email:*** robert.weinstock@shawpittman.com

SHELDON J. WEISEL, (P.C.), born Detroit, Michigan, December 18, 1945; admitted to bar, 1970, California (inactive); 1976, District of Columbia. *Education:* University of California at Los Angeles (B.A., 1966; J.D., 1969).

(This Listing Continued)

SHAW PITTMAN LLP, Washington—Continued

Order of the Coif. Senior Editor, U.C.L.A. Law Review, 1968-1969. Co-Author: "Marijuana Laws: An Empirical Study of Enforcement and Administration in Los Angeles County," 15 U.C.L.A. Law Review 1499, 1968. ***PRACTICE AREAS:*** Commercial Real Estate. ***Email:*** sheldon.weisel@shawpittman.com

WENDELIN A. WHITE, born Coral Gables, Florida, December 31, 1952; admitted to bar, 1981, Florida (inactive) and District of Columbia. *Education:* Sweet Briar College (B.A., 1974); University of California at Irvine (M.F.A., 1977); University of Miami (J.D., cum laude, 1981). Member: Moot Court Board; University of Miami Law Review, 1980-1981. Author: Note, "'Some Measure' of Protection: Due Process in the Balance in Greenholtz," 34 University of Miami Law Review 357, 1980. Member, Federal City Council; Economic Club. *Member:* The Florida Bar; The District of Columbia Bar; American Bar Association; National Association of Real Estate Investment Trusts; National Network of Commercial Real Estate Women; Commerical Real Estate Women of Washington, D.C. (Past President). ***PRACTICE AREAS:*** Commercial Real Estate. ***Email:*** wendelin.white@shawpittman.com

MILTON B. WHITFIELD, born Norfolk, Virginia, March 10, 1951; admitted to bar, 1979, District of Columbia, U.S. District Court, District of Columbia and U.S. Court of Appeals, District of Columbia Circuit; 1980, Virginia, U.S. District Court, Eastern District of Virginia and U.S. Court of Appeals, Fourth Circuit; 1984, U.S. Supreme Court; 1985, U.S. Court of International Trade. *Education:* University of Virginia (B.S., summa cum laude, 1974); Georgetown University (J.D., 1979); George Washington University (M.B.A., with high honors, 1984). Editor, Georgetown International Law Journal, Law and Policy in International Business, 1977-1978. Special Assistant to Admiral Rickover, Division of Naval Reactors, Department of Energy, 1974-1979. *Member:* Virginia State Bar; Federal Energy and American (Member, Litigation Section) Bar Associations. ***PRACTICE AREAS:*** Administrative Law; Customs Law; Energy Law; Environmental Law; Technology Outsourcing. ***Email:*** milton.whitfield@shawpittman.com

JAMES H. WILKINS, JR., born Torrance, California, June 3, 1945; admitted to bar, 1972, Arkansas (inactive); 1996, District of Columbia. *Education:* Iowa State University; University of Arkansas (B.A., 1967); University of Texas (J.D., 1972). Delta Theta Phi (Dean, Sam Houston Senate, 1972). *Member:* Pulaski County, Arkansas and American Bar Associations; The District of Columbia Bar. ***PRACTICE AREAS:*** Corporate Transactions; Outsourcing; Technology Transactions; Strategic Alliances; Electronic Commerce Transactions; Software Licensing. ***Email:*** james.wilkins@shawpittman.com

FRANK WINSTON, JR., born Bristol, Tennessee, January 23, 1957; admitted to bar, 1986, Virginia and U.S. Court of Appeals, Fourth Circuit; 1988, District of Columbia and U.S. Court of Appeals for the District of Columbia Circuit; 1990, U.S. District Court, District of Maryland. *Education:* Duke University (B.A., cum laude, 1979); University of Virginia (J.D., 1986). (Resident, McLean, Virginia Office). ***PRACTICE AREAS:*** Insurance; Litigation. ***Email:*** frank.winston@shawpittman.com

D. CRAIG WOLFF, born Billings, Montana, February 20, 1954; admitted to bar, 1987, Virginia; 1988, District of Columbia. *Education:* University of Montana (B.A., with honors, 1976); Harvard University (M.C.R.P., with distinction, 1981); Georgetown University (J.D., magna cum laude, 1987). *Member:* The District of Columbia Bar; Virginia State Bar; Bar Association of the District of Columbia; Virginia and American Bar Associations. ***PRACTICE AREAS:*** Technology Law; Technology Contracts; Outsourcing; Computer; Software; Telecommunications. ***Email:*** craig.wolff@shawpittman.com

ANDREW L. WOODS, born Gainesville, Florida, September 13, 1962; admitted to bar, 1990, North Carolina and Maryland; 1991, District of Columbia; 1994, Florida. *Education:* North Carolina State University (B.A., magna cum laude, 1985) Phi Kappa Phi; University of North Carolina at Chapel Hill (J.D., 1988). ***Email:*** andrew.woods@shawpittman.com

JEFFERY L. YABLON, (P.C.), born Chicago, Illinois, June 28, 1948; admitted to bar, 1974, California (inactive); 1975, District of Columbia. *Education:* University of Wisconsin (B.A., with honors, 1970); Stanford University (J.D., 1973). Fulbright Scholar, 1976. Developments Editor, Stanford Law Review, 1972-1973. Law Clerk to Judge Cynthia Holcomb Hall, U.S. Tax Court, 1973-1975. ***PRACTICE AREAS:*** Taxation. ***Email:*** jeffery.yablon@shawpittman.com

LAWRENCE T. YANOWITCH, born Rochester, New York, March 26, 1962; admitted to bar, 1987, Pennsylvania; 1988, District of Columbia; 1998, New York. *Education:* Georgetown University (B.A., cum laude, 1984; J.D., cum laude, 1987). *Member:* The District of Columbia Bar (Chairman, Corporate Finance Committee, 1996—). (Resident, McLean, Virginia Office). ***PRACTICE AREAS:*** Corporate; Securities; Mergers and Acquisitions; Corporate Finance; Venture Capital. ***Email:*** lawrence.yanowitch@shawpittman.com

GINO ZACCARDELLI, born Hartford, Connecticut, March 21, 1961; admitted to bar, 1986, Florida; 1988, District of Columbia. *Education:* Boston College (B.A., summa cum laude, 1983); Georgetown University (J.D., magna cum laude, 1986). Phi Beta Kappa; Alpha Sigma Nu. Administrative Editor, Georgetown Law Journal, 1985-1986. *Member:* The District of Columbia Bar; The Florida Bar. (Also at McLean, Virginia Office). ***PRACTICE AREAS:*** Trusts; Estates.

ROBERT E. ZAHLER, (P.C.), born New York, N.Y., August 4, 1950; admitted to bar, 1975, District of Columbia. *Education:* Massachusetts Institute of Technology (S.B., 1972); Harvard University (J.D., cum laude, 1975). Sigma Xi. Articles Editor, Harvard Journal on Legislation, 1974-1975. ***PRACTICE AREAS:*** Outsourcing; Technology Licensing; Technology Transactions; Corporate. ***Email:*** robert.zahler@shawpittman.com

RICHARD R. ZARAGOZA, born Worcester, Massachusetts, April 3, 1944; admitted to bar, 1969, Massachusetts; 1970, District of Columbia. *Education:* Georgetown University (A.B., 1966); Boston College (J.D., 1969). Attorney, Broadcast Bureau, Federal Communications Commission, 1969-1970. Office of the General Counsel, Appellate Litigation Division, 1970-1972. *Member:* District of Columbia Bar; American and Federal Communications (Co-Chairman, Continuing Legal Education Committee, 1979-1981; Chairman, Committee on Cooperation with Review Board and Administrative Law Judges, 1981-1982; Assistant Secretary, 1982-1983; Secretary, 1983-1984; Member, Executive Committee, 1984-1987; Chairman, FCC Relocation Committee, 1987-1988; Co-Chairman, Access to Records Committee, 1987-1988; President-Elect, 1988-1989; President, 1989-1990; Delegate to the ABA House of Delegates, 1993-1995) Bar Associations. ***PRACTICE AREAS:*** Communications. ***Email:*** richard.zaragoza@shawpittman.com

SENIOR COUNSEL

RICHARD S. BEATTY, born Washington, D.C., May 6, 1934; admitted to bar, 1962, District of Columbia. *Education:* Williams College (B.A., 1955); Georgetown University (LL.B., 1961). Trial Attorney, Civil Division, Department of Justice, 1962-1966. Associate Chief Counsel, Office of the Comptroller of the Currency of the United States, 1966-1967. *Member:* American Law Institute. [U.S. Army, 1956-1959]. ***PRACTICE AREAS:*** Corporate Law; Non-Profit Organizations; Trusts and Estates.

NATHANIEL P. BREED, JR. (P.C.), born Boston, Massachusetts, September 26, 1937; admitted to bar, 1967, District of Columbia. *Education:* Harvard University and Babson College (B.S.B.A., 1963); University of Michigan (J.D., 1966). Phi Delta Phi. Member, Board of Governors, International Aviation Club, 1985-1990. ***PRACTICE AREAS:*** Aviation; Administrative. ***Email:*** nathaniel.breed@shawpittman.com

GERALD CHARNOFF, (P.C.), born Brooklyn, New York, April 18, 1930; admitted to bar, 1957, New York (inactive); 1961, U.S. Supreme Court; 1966, District of Columbia. *Education:* Brooklyn College (A.B., 1951); Columbia University (M.S., 1952); New York University Law School (LL.B., 1957). Phi Beta Kappa. Associate Editor, New York University Law Review, 1956-1957. Lecturer in Administrative Law, New York University, 1964-1966. With Office of General Counsel, Atomic Energy Commission, 1957-1960. Assistant to the Director, Division of Licensing and Regulation, 1960. Counsel, Atomic Industrial Forum, 1960-1966. Partner, Shaw Pittman, 1966—. ***PRACTICE AREAS:*** International Transactions; Litigation; Energy; Administrative. ***Email:*** gerald.charnoff@shawpittman.com

MARY JANE DODSON, born Augusta, Georgia, August 23, 1954; admitted to bar, 1982, New York; 1989, District of Columbia. *Education:* Princeton University (A.B., magna cum laude, 1976); University of Virginia (J.D., 1981). *Member:* The District of Columbia Bar; Bar Association of the City of New York; New York State Bar Association. ***PRACTICE AREAS:*** Corporate Finance. ***Email:*** mary.jane.dodson@shawpittman.com

BEN C. FISHER, born Coos Bay, Oregon, February 6, 1923; admitted to bar, 1951, District of Columbia. *Education:* University of Illinois (A.B., 1948); Harvard University (J.D., magna cum laude, 1951). Phi Beta Kappa. Member, Board of Editors, Harvard Law Review, 1950-1951. Law Clerk to Judge Learned Hand, 2nd Circuit, 1951-1952. President, Society of Satellite Professionals, 1983-1985. Member, U.S. Delegation, ITU Plenipotentiary Conference, Nice, France, 1989. Member, U.S. Delegation, CCIR Plenary Assembly, Dusseldorf, Germany, 1990. Member, FCC Industry Advisory Committee on WARC-92 Preparation (Chairman, Informal Working Group II), 1990. Member, U.S. Delegation, 1992 WARC, Torremolinos, Spain. Co-Chair, Combined Task Force of U.S. CCIs on Review of the International Telecommunications Union Structure and Functioning. Member, U.S. Delegation, 1992 Additional Plenipotentiary Conference, Geneva, Switzerland. Member, U.S. Delegation, ITU Plenipotentiary Conference, Kyoto, Japan, 1994. *Member:* District of Columbia Bar; Federal Communications (President, 1967) and American (Chairman, Administrative Law Section, 1968-1969; Delegate to House of Delegates, 1970-1972; 1973-1975) Bar Associations; American Law Institute. Fellow, American Bar Foundation. ***PRACTICE AREAS:*** Communications. ***Email:*** ben.fisher@shawpittman.com

ELLEN CANAN GRADY, born Rochester, New York, November 18, 1960; admitted to bar, 1985, Maryland; 1987, District of Columbia; 1999, Virginia. *Education:* Allegheny College (B.A., magna cum laude, 1982); University of

(This Listing Continued)

Pennsylvania (J.D., 1985). *Member:* The District of Columbia Bar; Maryland State, Virginia and American Bar Associations. (Resident, McLean, Virginia Office). ***PRACTICE AREAS:*** Corporate and Securities. ***Email:*** ellen.grady@shawpittman.com

STEUART L. PITTMAN, (P.C.), born Albany, New York, June 6, 1919; admitted to bar, 1948, New York; 1954, District of Columbia. *Education:* Yale University (B.A., cum laude, 1941); Yale Law School (J.D., 1948). Phi Delta Phi, Corbey Court. Assistant General Counsel, Foreign Operations Administration, 1953-1954. Consultant, International Lending and Investment, Hoover Commission, 1954. Assistant Secretary of Defense, 1961-1964. ***PRACTICE AREAS:*** International Transactions; Banking.

RAMSAY D. POTTS, (P.C.), born Memphis, Tennessee, October 24, 1916; admitted to bar, 1948, Tennessee (inactive); 1954, District of Columbia; 1957, U.S. Supreme Court. *Education:* University of North Carolina (B.S., 1941); Harvard Law School (J.D., 1948). Phi Beta Kappa. ***PRACTICE AREAS:*** Transportation; Aviation; Government; Legislation; Commercial.

JOHN B. RHINELANDER, (P.C.), born Boston, Massachusetts, June 18, 1933; admitted to bar, 1964, New York; 1967, U.S. Supreme Court; 1971, District of Columbia. *Education:* Yale University (B.A., 1955); University of Virginia (LL.B., 1961). Editor in Chief, Virginia Law Review, 1960-1961. Law Clerk to Associate Justice John M. Harlan, U.S. Supreme Court, 1961-1962. Lecturer, University of Virginia Law School, 1982-1985, 1989-1991. Adjunct Professor, Georgetown University School of Foreign Service and Law Center, 1991-1994. Special Civilian Assistant to Secretary of Navy, 1966-1968. Chief Counsel, Acting Deputy Director, Office of Foreign Direct Investments, Department of Commerce, 1968-1969. Deputy Legal Adviser, Department of State, 1969-1971. Legal Adviser to U.S. SALT Delegation, Arms Control and Disarmament Agency, 1971-1972. General Counsel, Department of Health, Education and Welfare, 1973-1975. Under Secretary, Department of Housing and Urban Development, 1975-1977. ***PRACTICE AREAS:*** Government; Health Care.

GEORGE M. ROGERS, JR. (P.C.), born Washington, D.C., May 23, 1933; admitted to bar, 1959, District of Columbia. *Education:* Princeton University (A.B., 1955); University of Virginia (LL.B., 1958). Sigma Nu Phi. ***PRACTICE AREAS:*** Corporate Securities; Tax; Real Estate. ***Email:*** george.rogers@shawpittman.com

LESLIE SRAGER, born New York, N.Y., 1935; admitted to bar, 1963, New York and U.S. District Court, Eastern and Southern Districts of New York; 1968, District of Columbia; 1984, Connecticut (inactive). *Education:* City College of New York (B.B.A., 1956); Boston University (LL.B., cum laude, 1961). Recipient: John Ordronaux Award as Outstanding Student; Alumni Academic Achievement Award as First in Class. Notes Editor, Boston University Law Review. Author: "PLI," Computer Law Institute, New York Law Journal, 1984. Lecturer, Administrative Law, Catholic University Law School, 1973. Consultant, Strategic Arms Limitation Talks. Panel of Arbitrators, A.A.A., 1991—. *Member:* The District of Columbia Bar; American Bar Association. (Resident, New York, N.Y. Office). ***PRACTICE AREAS:*** Computer Law; Corporate Law; International Law.

COUNSEL

SCOTT E. BARAT, born Bellmore, New York, December 24, 1959; admitted to bar, 1985, District of Columbia; 1987, Virginia. *Education:* University of Virginia (B.A., with distinction, 1982); University of Michigan (J.D., 1985). *Member:* Fairfax, Virginia and American Bar Associations. (Resident, McLean, Virginia Office). ***PRACTICE AREAS:*** Construction; Commercial Litigation; Government Contracts.

MAUREEN BYRNE BEAHN, born Baltimore, Maryland, July 30, 1964; admitted to bar, 1989, Virginia; 1990, District of Columbia. *Education:* Georgetown University (B.A., summa cum laude, 1985); University of Virginia (J.D., 1989). (Resident, McLean, Virginia Office).

MINDY BUREN, born Newark, New Jersey, August 22, 1955; admitted to bar, 1980, District of Columbia and New Jersey (inactive). *Education:* University of Pennsylvania (B.S. in Economics, 1977); New York University (J.D., 1980). *Member:* The District of Columbia Bar; Bar Association of the District of Columbia; New Jersey State Bar Association. ***PRACTICE AREAS:*** Utility Regulation; Nuclear Waste Issues; Environmental Law.

LISA M. BYINGTON, born Bristol, Pennsylvania, March 21, 1965; admitted to bar, 1991, Maryland (inactive); 1992, District of Columbia. *Education:* Pennsylvania State University (B.A., with high distinction, 1988); George Washington University (J.D., with high honors, 1991). ***Email:*** lisa.byington@shawpittman.com

GRAEME A. CHAMBERS, born 1955; admitted to bar, 1983, New York. (Resident, New York, N.Y. Office).

ALVIN DUNN, born Dallas, Texas, September 8, 1962; admitted to bar, 1989, Texas (inactive); 1990, District of Columbia. *Education:* University of Texas at Austin (B.A., with highest honors, 1984); Harvard University (J.D., cum laude, 1987). Law Clerk, the Honorable Richard A. Gadbois, Jr., U.S.

(This Listing Continued)

District Court, Central District of California, 1987-1988. *Member:* The District of Columbia Bar; American Bar Association. ***PRACTICE AREAS:*** Litigation; Antitrust.

LORI VAUGHN EBERSOHL, born De Ridder, Louisiana, January 14, 1964; admitted to bar, 1990, Maryland; 1991, District of Columbia; 1995, Virginia. *Education:* McNeese State University (B.A., summa cum laude, 1985); George Washington University (J.D., 1990). (Resident, McLean, Virginia Office).

JOHN C. EICHENBERGER, born Oceanside, New York, October 12, 1962; admitted to bar, 1990, New York; 1991, District of Columbia. *Education:* State University of New York at Albany (B.A., magna cum laude, 1984); Georgetown University Law Center (J.D., 1989).

JOHN T. EPTING, born Florence, South Carolina, December 1, 1950; admitted to bar, 1982, District of Columbia. *Education:* Clemson University (B.A., 1973); Florida State University (M.U.R.P., 1975); University of Oregon; American University (J.D., with honors, 1982). *Member:* The District of Columbia Bar (Member, Real Estate Section; Housing and Land Use); American Bar Association (Section on Urban, State and Local Government Law); American Planning Association; American Institute of Architects; National Alcoholic Beverage Control Association (NABCA). ***PRACTICE AREAS:*** Real Estate; Zoning, Planning and Land Use; Municipal Law; Historic Preservation; Building Codes; Permitting; Alcoholic Beverage Control. ***Email:*** john.epting@shawpittman.com

NANCY A. FISCHER, born Covington, Kentucky, October 4, 1967; admitted to bar, 1993, New York; 1994, District of Columbia. *Education:* University of Georgia (B.B.A., cum laude, 1989); Syracuse University (J.D., magna cum laude, 1992). Staff Member, Syracuse Law Review.

JENNIFER A. GIBLIN, born Providence, Rhode Island, October 16, 1966; admitted to bar, 1992, Massachusetts; 1993, District of Columbia. *Education:* Yale University (B.A., cum laude, 1988); University of Pennsylvania (J.D., 1991).

CYNTHIA D. GREER, born New Orleans, Louisiana, April 29, 1966; admitted to bar, 1990, Pennsylvania; 1998, District of Columbia. *Education:* Centenary College (B.A., Economics, 1987); American University, Washington College of Law (J.D., 1990). Trademark Attorney, U.S. Patent and Trademark Office, U.S. Department of Commerce, 1990-1995. *Member:* District of Columbia Bar; Pennsylvania and American Bar Associations. ***PRACTICE AREAS:*** Intellectual Property; Internet and World Wide Web; Communications. ***Email:*** cynthia.greer@shawpittman.com

JAMES M. GROSSER, born Philadelphia, Pennsylvania, March 10, 1966; admitted to bar, 1993, Pennsylvania; 1995, Maryland; 1998, District of Columbia. *Education:* Dartmouth College (A.B., cum laude, 1988); University of Pennsylvania Law School (J.D., 1992); New York University School of Law (LL.M. in Taxation, 1993).

DAVID S. HOUSTON, born Jacksonville, North Carolina, February 12, 1956; admitted to bar, 1981, District of Columbia; 1985, U.S. Supreme Court; 1987, Virginia. *Education:* University of Virginia (B.P., 1978); George Washington University (J.D., 1981). *Member:* American Institute of Certified Planners; International Council of Shopping Centers; American Planning Association. (Resident, McLean, Virginia Office). ***PRACTICE AREAS:*** Land Use; Commercial Leasing; Real Estate; Retailing. ***Email:*** david.houston@shawpittman.com

SHERYL R. ISRAEL, born Brooklyn, New York, April 13, 1961; admitted to bar, 1987, New York (inactive); 1994, District of Columbia. *Education:* Newcomb College, Tulane University (B.A., 1983); Boston University (J.D., 1986). *Member:* The District of Columbia Bar; New York State Bar Association. ***PRACTICE AREAS:*** Transportation; Aviation; Administrative Law.

MARVIN R. LANGE, born Bronx, New York, March 25, 1948; admitted to bar, 1972, New York; 1975, U.S. District Court, Southern and Eastern Districts of New York and U.S. Court of Appeals, Second Circuit; 1980, U.S. Supreme Court; 1986, U.S. Court of Appeals, Sixth Circuit; 1998, District of Columbia. *Education:* Queens College of the City University of New York (B.A., cum laude, 1968); Harvard University (J.D., magna cum laude, 1971). Member, Harvard Law Review, 1969-1971. *Member:* The Association of the Bar of the City of New York (Member, Antitrust and Trade Regulation Committee, 1990-1993); American Bar Association (Member, Sections on: Litigation; Antitrust); American Health Lawyers Association. (Resident New York, N.Y. Office). ***PRACTICE AREAS:*** General Litigation; Antitrust Law.

MICHAEL G. LEPRE, born Madison, New Jersey, July 30, 1963; admitted to bar, 1988, New Jersey; 1990, District of Columbia. *Education:* University of Notre Dame (B.A., with honors, 1985); George Washington University (J.D., 1988). ***PRACTICE AREAS:*** Energy Transactions; Energy; Public Utility Regulatory Law.

JOSEPHINE S. LO, born Hong Kong, June 30, 1957; admitted to bar, 1988, Maryland; 1989, District of Columbia. *Education:* Mississippi University

(This Listing Continued)

SHAW PITTMAN LLP, Washington—Continued

for Women (B.A., magna cum laude, 1979); Columbia University (M.A., 1981; M.Ed., 1982); Georgetown University (J.D., cum laude, 1988). ***PRACTICE AREAS:*** Tax. ***Email:*** josephine.lo@shawpittman.com

CHARLES B. LOBSENZ, born New York, N.Y., August 21, 1963; admitted to bar, 1992, New York; 1994, District of Columbia; 1998, Texas; registered to practice before U.S. Patent and Trademark Office. *Education:* Bucknell University (B.S., 1985); Albany Law School of Union University (J.D., cum laude, 1991). Justinian Society. Associate Editor, Albany Law School Journal of Science and Technology, 1990-1991. *Member:* New York State and American Bar Associations; The District of Columbia Bar; American Intellectual Property Law Association. (Resident, McLean, Virginia Office). ***PRACTICE AREAS:*** Intellectual Property; Patents; High Technology Law; Software Licensing. ***Email:*** charles.lobsenz@shawpittman.com

T. LANE MACALESTER, born Memphis, Tennessee, April 13, 1957; admitted to bar, 1984, Missouri; 1986, Minnesota; 1998, District of Columbia. *Education:* Emory University (B.A., 1979); Washington University (J.D., 1982). Law Clerk to the Honorable Albert J. Stephan, Missouri Court of Appeals, 1982-1984. Author: "Havens Realty Corp. v. Coleman: Extending Standing in Racial Steering Cases to Housing Associations and Testers," Journal of Urban and Contemporary Law (formerly Urban Law Annual) Vol. 22, 1981. *Member:* The District of Columbia Bar; The Missouri Bar; Minnesota State and American Bar Associations. ***PRACTICE AREAS:*** Technology Law; Health Law.

BRYAN T. McGINNIS, born Bellefontaine, Ohio, December 13, 1949; admitted to bar, 1989, New York; 1997, U.S. District Court, Southern and Eastern Districts of New York; 1998, District of Columbia. *Education:* Harvard College (B.A., Government, 1972); Stanford University Law School (J.D., 1987). Author: "R.I.A.A. v. Diamond Multimedia, A Recent Court Decision Accelerates Change in the World of Digital Music and the Internet," E-Commerce Law Report, August, 1999. Private law practice, 1988-1990; 1995-1999. Senior Counsel, Westinghouse Broadcasting Company, Inc., 1990-1995. Television producer and political consultant, 1973-1984. *Member:* New York State and Federal Communications Bar Associations; The District of Columbia Bar. ***PRACTICE AREAS:*** Communications Transactions; Media Law. ***Email:*** bryan.mcginnis@shawpittman.com

JOHN J. MOLLOY, III, born San Antonio, Texas, August 8, 1946; admitted to bar, 1972, California and U.S. Tax Court; 1973, U.S. District Court, Southern District of California; 1975, U.S. Court of Appeals, Ninth Circuit; 1976, U.S. Supreme Court. *Education:* University of Southern California (B.S., 1968; J.D., 1972). *Member:* Los Angeles County and American Bar Associations; State Bar of California. [Sgt., California National Guard, 1969-1975]. (Resident, Los Angeles, California Office).

THOMAS R. PETTY, born Newport News, Virginia, December 13, 1957; admitted to bar, 1983, District of Columbia. *Education:* Boston College (A.B., magna cum laude, 1980); Washington & Lee University (J.D., 1983). ***Email:*** thomas.petty@shawpittman.com

THOMAS J. PLOTZ, born Brooklyn, New York, March 3, 1953; admitted to bar, 1978, Missouri; 1985, District of Columbia. *Education:* Columbia University (B.A., 1976); New York University (J.D., 1978). Attorney-Advisor, Division of Corporation Finance, Securities and Exchange Commission, 1980-1983. *Member:* The Missouri Bar; The District of Columbia Bar. ***PRACTICE AREAS:*** Securities Offerings; Corporate Financing Law.

ALLISON C. PRINCE, born Brighton, Massachusetts, September 13, 1958; admitted to bar, 1984, Virginia; 1986, District of Columbia. *Education:* Bucknell University (B.A., with honors, 1980); Columbus School of Law, Catholic University of America (J.D., 1983). *Member:* The District of Columbia Bar; Bar Association of the District of Columbia; Women's Bar Association; Greater Washington Commercial Association of Realtors; Commercial Real Estate Women. ***PRACTICE AREAS:*** Real Estate; Zoning, Planning and Land Use; Municipal Law. ***Email:*** allison.prince@shawpittman.com

ELIZABETH M. ROESEL, born Albany, New York, February 1, 1962; admitted to bar, 1987, Ohio (inactive); 1988, District of Columbia. *Education:* State University of New York at Binghamton (B.S., 1984); Duke University (J.D., 1987). Phi Beta Kappa. Law Clerk to Judge Mayer, U.S. Court of Appeals, Federal Circuit, 1989-1990. (Resident, McLean, Virginia Office).

JORDANA G. SCHWARTZ, born March 7, 1964; admitted to bar, 1992, New York; 1998, District of Columbia. *Education:* University of Chicago (B.A., 1986); Fordham University (J.D., cum laude, 1991). Associate Editor, Fordham Law Review. Author: "Analyzing the 1993 Amendments to the Federal Rules of Civil Procedure," ALI-ABA Course Materials, Vol. 18, No. 2, 1993; "Standing to Challenge Tax-Exempt Status: The Second Circuit's Competitive Political Advocate Theory," 58 Fordham Law Rev. 723, 1990.

DAWN M. SCIARRINO, born Rochester, New York, February 11, 1963; admitted to bar, 1991, New York and U.S. Court of Appeals for the District of Columbia Circuit; 1992, Virginia and U.S. Court of Appeals, Fourth Circuit; 1997, District of Columbia. *Education:* Ithaca College (B.A. in History, 1985); Institute for Communications Law Studies, Columbus School of Law, The Catholic University of America (J.D., 1990). Co-Author: "A Broadcaster's Guide to PCB and Underground Storage Tank Regulation," National Association of Broadcasters, 1992. Law Clerk and Intern, Fairness/Political Programming Branch, Enforcement Division, Mass Media Bureau, Federal Communications Commission, 1988. Principal, Brockmeyer Media Group (political consultants), 1994-1995. *Member:* New York State and Federal Communications Bar Associations; Virginia State Bar; American Association of Political Consultants. ***PRACTICE AREAS:*** Communications. ***Email:*** dawn.sciarrino@shawpittman.com

GREG SHORT, born Liverpool, England, October 22, 1961; admitted to bar, 1994, California; 1996, District of Columbia (inactive). *Education:* University of Kent (B.S., Honors, 1984); Virginia Polytechnic Institute (M.A., 1986); Santa Clara University (J.D., 1994). Research Editor, Santa Clara Computer and High Technology Law Journal. *Member:* Santa Clara County and American (Member, Section on Science and Technology) Bar Associations; Computer Law Association. (Resident, Los Angeles, California Office). ***PRACTICE AREAS:*** Intellectual Property; Litigation.

JOHN C. SIMONS, admitted to bar, 1977, Texas (inactive); 1987, New York. *Education:* University of Texas (B.A., cum laude, 1974); University of Texas School of Law (J.D., 1977). Phi Beta Kappa. *Member:* New York State (Associate Member; Member, Banking, Corporation and Business Law Section) and American (Member, Business Law Section) Bar Associations. (Resident, New York, N.Y. Office). ***PRACTICE AREAS:*** Financial Institutions. ***Email:*** john.simons@shawpittman.com

DANIELLE R. SROUR, born New York, N.Y., 1957; admitted to bar, 1982, District of Columbia. *Education:* Mount Holyoke College (A.B., magna cum laude, 1979); University of Pennsylvania (J.D., 1982). Phi Beta Kappa. *Member:* The District of Columbia Bar. ***PRACTICE AREAS:*** Securities; Corporate.

MICHELE N. TANAKA, born Washington, D.C., November 27, 1955; admitted to bar, 1983, District of Columbia. *Education:* Princeton University (A.B., cum laude, 1978); Georgetown University Law Center (J.D., 1982). Co-Author: "Licensing Technology Packages to Japan." East Asian Executive reports, Vol. 4, No. 12. *Member:* The District of Columbia Bar. ***PRACTICE AREAS:*** International Trade; Intellectual Property; Corporate; Transactional; Litigation. ***Email:*** michele.tanaka@shawpittman.com

BETH MEZOFF WILSON, born New Rochelle, New York, May 4, 1962; admitted to bar, 1988, California. *Education:* Brown University (A.B., 1984); University of California at Los Angeles (J.D., 1987). *Member:* Los Angeles County Bar Association. (Resident, Los Angeles, California Office).

CARROLL JOHN YUNG, born Washington, D.C., November 26, 1956; admitted to bar, 1982, District of Columbia. *Education:* Massachusetts Institute of Technology (S.B. in Mathematics, 1979); Cornell University (J.D., 1982). Sigma Xi. *Member:* District of Columbia Bar; American and Federal Communications Bar Associations. ***PRACTICE AREAS:*** Communications. ***Email:*** carroll.yung@shawpittman.com

MARYELENA ZACCARDELLI, born Indianapolis, Indiana, April 22, 1963; admitted to bar, 1988, Massachusetts; 1990, District of Columbia. *Education:* Indiana University (B.S., with high honors, 1985); University of Michigan (J.D., cum laude, 1988). Recipient, School of Public and Environmental Affairs Book Award. Associate Editor, University of Michigan Law Review, 1986-1987. Law Clerk, The Honorable Conrad K. Cyr, U.S. District Court, District of Maine.

JANICE HELEN ZIEGLER, born Brooklyn, New York, January 25, 1962; admitted to bar, 1987, Massachusetts; 1989, District of Columbia. *Education:* Cornell University (B.S., with honors, 1984); Harvard University (J.D., magna cum laude, 1987). Law Clerk to the Honorable John H. Pratt, U.S. District Court, District of Columbia, 1987-1988.

ASSOCIATES

MATTHEW A. ANZALDI, born Passaic, New Jersey, October 14, 1971; admitted to bar, 1996, Virginia; 1997, District of Columbia. *Education:* Duke University (A.B., 1993); Vanderbilt University (J.D., 1996). Student Writing Editor, Vanderbilt Journal of Transactional Law.

THOMAS E. AREND, JR., born Chicago, Illinois, December 12, 1963; admitted to bar, 1994, Maryland and District of Columbia. *Education:* Kenyon College (B.A., magna cum laude, 1986); Fletcher School of Law and Diplomacy, Tufts University (M.A.L.D., 1990); Washington College of Law, American University (J.D., 1994). Phi Beta Kappa. ***LANGUAGES:*** Spanish and Portuguese.

STEVEN P. ARNHEIM, born Tallahassee, Florida, November 10, 1970; admitted to bar, 1999, Maryland; registered to practice before U.S. Patent and Trademark Office. *Education:* University of Pennsylvania (B.S.E., 1992); University of Maryland (J.D., 1999). (Resident, McLean, Virginia Office). ***Email:*** steven.arnheim@shawpittman.com

(This Listing Continued)

RAINEY L. ASTIN, born Danville, Virginia, February 23, 1967; admitted to bar, 1995, Georgia; 1997, District of Columbia. *Education:* University of North Carolina at Chapel Hill (B.A., 1989); University of Georgia (J.D., cum laude, 1995). Member, University of Georgia Law Review. *Member:* State Bar of Georgia.

GERARD M. BABENDREIER, admitted to bar, 1998, Maryland (Not admitted in District of Columbia). *Education:* Columbia University (B.A., 1984); Harvard University (J.D., 1998). Phi Beta Kappa. Member, Roscoe Pound Society for Law, Life and Religion.

GAELA BAILEY, (admission pending). *Education:* Cardiff University (LL.B., 1996); Nottingham Law School (LPC, 1999). (Resident, London, England Office). ***PRACTICE AREAS:*** Technology Transactions; Internet Law; Outsourcing; Computer Software Licensing.

ERIC M. BAIM, born Pittsburgh, Pennsylvania, January 23, 1972; admitted to bar, 2001, Virginia (Not admitted in District of Columbia). *Education:* University of North Carolina at Chapel Hill (B.A., with distinction, 1994); University of Cincinnati (M.A., Psychology, 1998); Duke University (M.A., Public Policy, 2001); Duke University School of Law (J.D., 2001). Phi Beta Kappa. *Member:* American Health Lawyers Association.

SUSAN E. BALDWIN, born Baltimore, Maryland, August 16, 1974; admitted to bar, 2001, Virginia (Not admitted in District of Columbia). *Education:* Washington & Lee University (B.S., magna cum laude, 1996); University of Virginia School of Law (J.D., 2001). Phi Beta Kappa. Member, Virginia Tax Review, Washington & Lee University.

THOMAS J. BALL, JR., born Rochester, New York, March 24, 1966; admitted to bar, 1997, Virginia. *Education:* Princeton University (B.A., with honors, 1988); Catholic University of America (J.D., 1997). Recipient, Corpus Juris Secundum Award. (Resident, McLean, Virginia Office).

LAURIE G. BALLENGER, born Spartanburg, South Carolina, September 2, 1967; admitted to bar, 1994, Virginia; 1996, District of Columbia. *Education:* Davidson College (B.A., 1989); University of North Carolina (M.R.P., J.D., with honors, 1994). Articles Editor, North Carolina Law Review, 1993-1994.

D. SEAN BARNETT, born Clearfield, Pennsylvania, September 1, 1963; admitted to bar, 1997, Virginia and U.S. Court of Appeals, Fourth Circuit (Not admitted in District of Columbia). *Education:* Purdue University (B.S.N.E., 1985); Massachusetts Institute of Technology (Ph.D., 1989); Georgetown University Law Center (J.D., cum laude, 1997). *Member:* Virginia State Bar.

JOHN L. BARTON, born Long Island, New York, June 19, 1973; admitted to bar, 1999, California (Not admitted in District of Columbia). *Education:* University of Texas at Austin (B.A., History, 1995); University of Virginia (J.D., 1999). Phi Beta Kappa. Member, Virginia Law Review. ***PRACTICE AREAS:*** Technology. ***Email:*** john.barton@shawpittman.com

MARGARET M. BATEMAN, admitted to bar, 2000, New York and Massachusetts. *Education:* Boston College (B.A., 1994); St. John's University (J.D., 1999). (Resident, New York, N.Y. Office).

BART E. BEALS, admitted to bar, 2000, Illinois (Not admitted in District of Columbia). *Education:* Howard University (J.D., 2000). Member, Howard Law Journal.

BEVERLY A. BOBAN, admitted to bar, 1998, New York. *Education:* City College of the City University of New York (B.S., 1987); Brooklyn Law School (J.D., 1997). Recipient, Professor Samuel Hoffman Memorial Prize for Excellence in Corporate Law. (Resident, New York, N.Y. Office).

JAMES P. BOBOTEK, born Champaign-Urbana, Illinois, July 31, 1962; admitted to bar, 1995, Virginia; 1998, District of Columbia; 1999, Maryland. *Education:* George Mason University (B.A., with distinction, 1992); Columbus School of Law, Catholic University of America (J.D., 1995). Phi Delta Phi. Recipient, American Jurisprudence Award, Torts, 1992-1993. Member, Catholic University Law Review, 1994-1995. Captain, National Civil Rights Moot Court Team, 1994-1995. Member, American Inns of Court, Thurgood Marshall Chapter, 1994-1995. Student Attorney, D.C. Law Students in Court Program, 1994-1995. Clerk/Intern, The Honorable James C. Cacheris, United States District Court for the Eastern District of Virginia, 1993-1994. *Member:* Alexandria and American Bar Associations; Virginia State Bar (Member, Construction Law and Public Contracts Section); The District of Columbia Bar. (Resident, McLean, Virginia Office). ***PRACTICE AREAS:*** Construction Law; Architects and Engineers Liability; Professional Liability; Products Liability; Commercial Litigation; Civil Litigation. ***Email:*** james.bobotek@shawpittman.com

BRIAN R. BODOR, born Warren, Ohio, December 6, 1970; admitted to bar, 1996, Arizona; 1997, District of Columbia. *Education:* Cornell University (B.A., with distinction, 1993); University of Michigan School of Law (J.D., 1996). Associate Editor, 1994-1995 and Contributing Editor, 1995-1996, University of Michigan Journal of Law Reform.

SUSAN J. BORSCHEL, born Bloomington, Indiana, February 24, 1959; admitted to bar, 1998, Virginia and District of Columbia. *Education:* University of California at Davis (B.A., 1981); California State University at Fullerton (M.B.A., 1984); Cornell University (M.P.A., 1992); George Mason University

(This Listing Continued)

Law School (J.D., 1997). [Active duty, 1985-1995; reserve duty, Maj., Natl. Military Joint Intelligence Ctr., J-2, 1995—]. (Resident, McLean, Virginia Office).

LAUREN W. BRIGHT, admitted to bar, 1997, New Jersey; 1999, District of Columbia. *Education:* Gettysburg College (B.A., 1990); Villanova University (J.D., 1994). *Member:* The District of Columbia Bar.

JOSEPH S. BROWN, born 1974; admitted to bar, 1999, Virginia (Not admitted in District of Columbia). *Education:* University of Rochester (B.A., 1996); University of Virginia (J.D., 1999). *Member:* Virginia State Bar.

LESLIE S. BROWN, born Washington, D.C., June 2, 1975; admitted to bar, 2000, Virginia. *Education:* Carnegie Mellon University (B.S., 1997); George Washington University (J.D., 2000). Member, Environmental Lawyer Journal. (Resident, McLean, Virginia Office). ***PRACTICE AREAS:*** Corporate Law; Technology Transactions; Securities. ***Email:*** leslie.brown@shawpittman.com

M. SCOTT BROWN, born Shreveport, Louisiana, September 16, 1969; admitted to bar, 1994, Maryland and New Jersey; 1997, District of Columbia. *Education:* Florida State University (B.A., magna cum laude, 1991); George Washington University (J.D., 1994). Phi Beta Kappa. *Member:* District of Columbia Bar; Maryland State and American Bar Associations. (Resident, McLean, Virginia Office). ***PRACTICE AREAS:*** Corporate; Securities; Mergers and Acquisitions.

STEPHENIE L. BROWN, born Cullman, Alabama, 1967; admitted to bar, 1993, Alabama; 1997, New York. *Education:* University of Alabama (B.A., summa cum laude, 1990); Columbia University School of Law (J.D., 1993). Articles Editor, Journal of Chinese Law. Law Clerk to the Honorable Virgil Pittman, U.S. District Judge, Southern District of Alabama, 1993-1995. (Resident, New York, N.Y. Office).

CHRISTIAN A. BUERGER, born Bad Kreuznach, Germany, May 25, 1972; admitted to bar, 1996, Virginia; 1997, District of Columbia. *Education:* Princeton University (A.B., 1993); Harvard Law School (J.D., cum laude, 1996).

ANN MARIE BURKE, born Fairfax, Virginia, March 19, 1969; admitted to bar, 1998, Virginia; 1999, District of Columbia. *Education:* University of Virginia (B.A., 1991; J.D., 1997). Recipient, University Achievement Award Scholarship. *Member:* Virginia State Bar; The District of Columbia Bar.

MICHELE M. BURRIS, born San Diego, California, August 26, 1964; admitted to bar, 1998, Virginia; 1999, District of Columbia. *Education:* Washington State University (B.S., 1985); Boston University (M.S., 1992); Georgetown University (J.D., 1998). Staff Member, Georgetown International Environmental Law Review, 1995-1998. (Resident, McLean, Virginia Office). ***Email:*** michele.burris@shawpittman.com

ROBERT W. BUSBY JR., born Detroit, Michigan, January 27, 1965; admitted to bar, 1997, Virginia; 1998, District of Columbia; registered to practice before U.S. Patent and Trademark Office. *Education:* United States Naval Academy (B.S.E.E., with merit, 1989); George Washington University (J.D., with high honors, 1997). Order of the Coif. Member, George Washington Journal of International Law and Economics. Author: "The United States' Failure to Establish A High Level Nuclear Waste Disposal Facility is Threatening its Ability to Effectively Promote Nuclear Nonproliferation," 30:1. *Member:* Virginia Bar Association; Fourth Circuit Bar Association; Federal Circuit Bar Association. [Lieutenant, U.S. Navy, 1982-1993]. (Resident, McLean, Virginia Office). ***PRACTICE AREAS:*** Patents; Trademarks; Copyrights; Patent Licensing. ***Email:*** bob.busby@shawpittman.com

DAISY M. BYGRAVE, born Toronto, Ontario, November 30, 1974; admitted to bar, 2000, Maryland (Not admitted in District of Columbia). *Education:* Seton Hall University (B.A., magna cum laude, 1997); Harvard University Law School (J.D., 2000).

COLETTE M. CAPRETZ, born Frankfurt, West Germany, January 19, 1969; admitted to bar, 1995, Virginia; 1996, District of Columbia. *Education:* The University of Texas at Austin (B.S., Advertising, with high honors, 1990); Concannon Programme of International Law, London, England; University of Notre Dame Law School (J.D., cum laude, 1995). Recipient, Dean's Awards in Administrative and Family Law. Legal Intern to U.S. District Judge Richard T. Haik, Lafayette, Louisiana, 1993. *Member:* District of Columbia Bar; Virginia State Bar; Federal Communications Bar Association. ***PRACTICE AREAS:*** Communications. ***Email:*** colette.capretz@shawpittman.com

CHRISTINA M. CARLSON, born San Diego, California, November 30, 1963; admitted to bar, 1994, California, U.S. District Court, Southern, Eastern, Northern and Central Districts of California and U.S. Court of Appeals, Ninth Circuit. *Education:* University of California, Los Angeles (B.A., 1987); Loyola Law School, Los Angeles (J.D., 1994). Member, Loyola's International & Comparative Law Journal. Author: "Quasi In Rem Jurisdiction: Obtaining Control Over Assets of A Foreign Corporation," Buchalter's *Quarterly Perspective*; "Congress Decreases Burdens & Costs Associated with Transaction in Securities," *ECJ's Legal Update*, Summer 1997. *Member:* Beverly Hills Bar Associa-

(This Listing Continued)

SHAW PITTMAN LLP, Washington—Continued

tion; Financial Lawyer's Conference. (Resident, Los Angeles, California Office). ***PRACTICE AREAS:*** Technology Transactions; Technology Outsourcing; Health Care. ***Email:*** christina.carlson@shawpittman.com

LEE C. CARTER, born Washington, D.C., July 2, 1967; admitted to bar, 1993, Illinois; 1995, District of Columbia. *Education:* Denison University (B.A., with high honors, 1989); University of Chicago (J.D., with honors, 1993).

DAVA CASONI, born Cortland, New York, October 26, 1969; admitted to bar, 1996, New York and Massachusetts; 1998, District of Columbia; U.S. Court of Federal Claims. *Education:* Boston University (B.A., B.S., 1991); Cornell University (J.D., LL.M., 1996). Law Clerk to the Honorable Judge James T. Turner, U.S. Court of Federal Claims. *Member:* New York State and American Bar Associations. ***PRACTICE AREAS:*** Corporate Law; Securities; Entrepreneurial Law; Entertainment Law. ***Email:*** dava.casoni@shawpittman.com

GINA M. CAVALIER, born Long Beach, California, January 19, 1971; admitted to bar, 1997, New York (Not admitted in District of Columbia). *Education:* Boston University (B.A., summa cum laude, 1993); Georgetown University (J.D., cum laude, 1996). ***PRACTICE AREAS:*** Health Care. ***Email:*** gina.cavalier@shawpittman.com

G. A. "JAY" CHADWICK, IV, born Chicago, Illinois; admitted to bar, 1996, Kentucky; 1999, District of Columbia. *Education:* College of William and Mary (B.A., History, 1993); University of Virginia (J.D., 1996). ***PRACTICE AREAS:*** Commercial Real Estate Loans; Commercial Real Estate Leasing; Commercial Real Estate Development; Business.

INDRA SEHDEV CHALK, born Toronto, Ontario, Canada, June 18, 1965; admitted to bar, 1993, Texas (Not admitted in District of Columbia). *Education:* Stanford University (B.A., English Literature, with honors and distinction, 1987; M.A., English Literature, 1987); University of Chicago (M.A., U.S. and Latin American History, 1989); University of Virginia (J.D., 1993). Congressional Intern, U.S. Representative Jim Slattery, 1985. Senate Intern, U.S. Senator Robert Dole, 1985. Legislative Assistant, U.S. Representative Jan Meyers, 1990. *Member:* State Bar of Texas. ***LANGUAGES:*** Spanish. ***PRACTICE AREAS:*** Communications; Corporate; Business. ***Email:*** indra.chalk@shawpittman.com

DAVID J. CHARLES, born March 31, 1966; admitted to bar, 1993, Pennsylvania; 1995, District of Columbia. *Education:* Johns Hopkins University (B.A., 1988; M.A., 1989); Georgetown University (J.D., 1993). Editor, Georgetown Law Journal. Clerk to Judge Lawrence S. Margolis, U.S. Court of Federal Claims, Washington, D.C. (Resident, McLean, Virginia Office).

ALBERT S. CHO, admitted to bar, 2000, New York and District of Columbia. *Education:* Brown University (B.A., 1994); Cornell University (J.D., 1999). Member, Asian American Law Students Association.

JACK Y. CHU, born Taipa, Taiwan, September 1, 1974; admitted to bar, 2001, Virginia. *Education:* Stanford University (B.A., 1996); New York University School of Law (J.D., 2001). (Resident, McLean, Virginia Office).

POH C. CHUA, born Port Klang, Malaysia, November 1, 1965; admitted to bar, 1998, New York and District of Columbia. *Education:* George Washington University School of Engineering and Applied Science (B.S.C.E., 1988); George Washington University (J.D., 1997). Tau Beta Pi. Executive Managing Editor, George Washington Journal of International Law and Economics, 1996-1997. Registered Professional Engineer, Commonwealth of Virginia. (Resident, McLean, Virginia Office). ***Email:*** poh.chua@shawpittman.com

PAUL A. CICELSKI, born Nuremberg, Germany, July 7, 1969; admitted to bar, 1999, District of Columbia. *Education:* University of Virginia (B.A., Foreign Affairs, 1991); Vanderbilt University (J.D., 1999). Recipient, University of Virginia J. Sargeant Reynolds Political Achievement Award, 1991. Legal Intern, Office of the Chairman, Federal Communications Commission, 1997. Intern, U.S. Senator John F. Kerry, 1991. *Member:* The District of Columbia Bar; Federal Communications Bar Association. ***PRACTICE AREAS:*** Communications. ***Email:*** paul.cicelski@shawpittman.com

KAREN L. CIPRIANI, born Boston, Massachusetts, March 28, 1969; admitted to bar, 1996, Maryland; 1997, District of Columbia. *Education:* Stanford University (B.A., with distinction, 1991); Georgetown University Law Center (J.D., 1995). Author: "The Numbers Don't Add Up: Challenging the Premise of J.E.B. v. Alabama ex re T.B.," American Criminal Law Review, Summer, 1994. Co-Author: "Implications of the Privatization of Sallie Mae," Journal of Public Budgeting, Accounting and Financial Management, Spring 1999. *Member:* American Bar Association (Vice Chair, Section on Administrative and Regulatory Practice, Education Committee, 1997-1998); American Society of Association Executives.

KEVIN E. COLANGELO, born Norman, Oklahoma, March 1, 1967; admitted to bar, 1994, New Jersey and U.S. District Court, District of New Jersey; 1995, New York and U.S. District Court, Southern District of New York; ; 1997, U.S. Court of International Trade. *Education:* Hamilton College (B.A., in History, 1989); Vermont Law School (J.D., cum laude, 1994). *Member:* Morris County, New Jersey State, New York State and American Bar Associations. (Resident, New York, N.Y. Office).

DAMON D. COLBERT, born Washington, D.C., September 2, 1976; admitted to bar, 2001, Virginia (Not admitted in District of Columbia). *Education:* Davidson College (B.A., 1998); Georgetown University Law Center (J.D., 2001).

MICHAEL K. COLBY, born San Diego, California, March 13, 1969; admitted to bar, 1998, Virginia; 2000, District of Columbia; registered to practice before U.S. Patent and Trademark Office. *Education:* University of Washington (B.S., Cer. E., 1991; M.S.M.E., 1995); Duke University School of Law (J.D., 1998). President, Christian Legal Society, Duke Chapter, 1996-1997. Member, Keramos Honor Society. Member, American Society of Military Engineers, 1987-1991. *Member:* American Intellectual Property Law Association. (Resident, McLean, Virginia Office). ***PRACTICE AREAS:*** Technology Transactions; Intellectual Property; Patent Licensing; Patent Litigation; Trade Secrets; Corporate Law.

KRISTEN M. COLSTON, born Fort Polk, Louisiana, April 2, 1969; admitted to bar, 1997, New York and District of Columbia. *Education:* Mount Holyoke College (A.B., 1991); New York University (J.D., 1996; LL.M. in Taxation, 1997). Editor-in-Chief, NYU Environmental Law Journal.

MARTIN COTTERILL, (admission pending). *Education:* University of Wales (B.Eng., Biochemical Engineering, 1990); Sussex University (CPE, 1994); De Montford University (Postgraduate Diploma in Law, 1995). (Resident, London, England Office). ***PRACTICE AREAS:*** Technology Transactions; Outsourcing; Computer Software Licensing.

CHERYL R. COVELLO, born Lackawanna, New York, June 15, 1968; admitted to bar, 1996, Connecticut; 1997, New York. *Education:* Fordham University (B.A., 1990); Brooklyn Law School (J.D., 196). Notes and Comments Editor, Brooklyn Law School. (Resident, New York, N.Y. Office). ***PRACTICE AREAS:*** Litigation.

LARA CRELLIN, (admission pending). *Education:* University of Manchester (LL.B., 1995); College of Law, London (J.D., 1997). (Resident, London, England Office).

CHRISTOPHER A. CROUCH, admitted to bar, 1999, District of Columbia. *Education:* Texas Christian University (B.A., 1992); New York University (LL.M., 1999).

KIMBERLY A. CROWDER, born Norfolk, Virginia, January 25, 1969; admitted to bar, 1995, Virginia; 1997, District of Columbia. *Education:* University of Virginia (B.A., 1992; J.D., 1995); New York University (LL.M., Taxation, 1996). ***PRACTICE AREAS:*** Tax; Real Estate.

BROOKE DANIELS, born Manassas, Virginia, July 6, 1976; admitted to bar, 2001, Virginia (Not admitted in District of Columbia). *Education:* University of Chicago (B.A., 1997); University of Tulane Law School (J.D., cum laude, 2001).

BRAD M. DASHOFF, born Baltimore, Maryland, December 28, 1975; admitted to bar, 2000, Maryland (Not admitted in District of Columbia). *Education:* University of Michigan (B.A., 1997); University of Pennsylvania (J.D., 2000). Order of the Coif; Pi Sigma Alpha; Mortar Board. ***PRACTICE AREAS:*** Corporate Law; Securities. ***Email:*** brad.dashoff@shawpittman.com

RICHARD J. DAVIS, born Columbus, Ohio, October 24, 1968; admitted to bar, 1998, Virginia. *Education:* James Madison University (B.B.A., 1991); Detroit College of Law at Michigan State University (J.D., cum laude, 1997); University of Miami (LL.M., 1998). *Member:* Virginia State Bar. (Resident, McLean, Virginia Office). ***PRACTICE AREAS:*** Commercial Real Estate.

BENJAMIN MASUR DEAN, born New Orleans, Louisiana, November 3, 1971; admitted to bar, 1998, Maryland; 1999, District of Columbia. *Education:* Dartmouth College (A.B., magna cum laude, 1994); University of Virginia (J.D., 1997). Phi Beta Kappa. Editor in Chief, Virginia Journal of Social Policy & The Law, 1996-1997. Law Clerk to the Honorable Donald E. Walter, U.S. District Court for the Western District of Louisiana, 1997-1998. Author, "The Age-Based Ratings System: An Unfortunate Response to the V-Chip Legislation," 4 VA J. Soc. Pol'y & L. 743.

BIANCA M. DEGAUDENZI, born New York, N.Y., December 26, 1969; admitted to bar, 1994, New York. *Education:* St. John's University (B.S., magna cum laude, 1991; J.D., 1994). (Resident, New York, N.Y. Office).

SEAN DENNISON, born Washington, DC, January 29, 1974; admitted to bar, 2000, Maryland (Not admitted in District of Columbia). *Education:* Virginia Commonwealth University (B.S., 1996); University of Pennsylvania (J.D., 2000). ***PRACTICE AREAS:*** Real Estate. ***Email:*** sean.dennison@shawpittman.com

ROUX DE VILLIERS, born Stellenbosch, South Africa, September 3, 1968; admitted to bar, 1998, South Africa. *Education:* University of Stellenbosch (B.Eng., 1990; M.Eng., Electronic Engineering, 1994; LL.B., 1996); University of London (LL.M., Computer & Communications Law, 2000). *Mem-*

(This Listing Continued)

ber: Law Society of the Cape of Good Hope. (Resident, London, England Office). ***LANGUAGES:*** Afrikaans. ***PRACTICE AREAS:*** Information Technology; Internet Law; Intellectual Property; Commercial Law.

ELIZABETH J. DILLON, born Washington, D.C., August 26, 1964; admitted to bar, 1995, Maryland. *Education:* Georgetown University (B.A., 1986); Catholic University of America (J.D., magna cum laude, 1995). (Resident, McLean, Virginia Office).

BROOKE AMY DOMBEK, born Olney, Maryland, June 14, 1975; admitted to bar, 2001, New York (Not admitted in District of Columbia). *Education:* Northwestern University (B.A., cum laude, 1997; M.A., 1997); New York University (J.D., 2000). Pi Sigma Alpha; Golden Key; Moot Court, Marden Competition Winner. ***PRACTICE AREAS:*** Technology Transactions; Technology Licensing; Intellectual Property; Commercial Transactions; Internet Law. ***Email:*** brooke.dombek@shawpittman.com

MILDRED DOMENECH, born Brooklyn, New York, November 10, 1973; admitted to bar, 2000, Maryland (Not admitted in District of Columbia). *Education:* Georgetown University (B.S.F.S., 1995); Columbia University (J.D., 2000). Managing and Production Editor, Columbia Journal of Gender and Law. *Member:* Maryland State and Federal Communications Bar Associations. ***LANGUAGES:*** Spanish. ***PRACTICE AREAS:*** Communications Law; Technology Law. ***Email:*** millie.domenech@shawpittman.com

JEANNE M. MOORE DUROSS, born 1968; admitted to bar, 1996, Virginia; 1998, District of Columbia. *Education:* Pomona College (B.A., 1989); University of Pennsylvania (M.G.A., 1993); George Washington University (J.D., 1996). Order of the Coif. Articles Editor, The George Washington Law Review. Legal Research and Writing Fellow, 1995-1996. *Member:* Virginia State Bar. ***PRACTICE AREAS:*** Environmental; Litigation; Antitrust.

JESSE EGGERT, born Portland, Maine, January 30, 1976; admitted to bar, 2001, Virginia (Not admitted in District of Columbia). *Education:* Cornell University (A.B., with distinction, 1997; J.D., magna cum laude, 2001).

JULIE EHINGER, born Richmond, Virginia, December 27, 1973; admitted to bar, 1999, Virginia. *Education:* Cornell University (B.S., 1996); Vanderbilt University (J.D., 1999). (Resident, McLean, Virginia Office). ***PRACTICE AREAS:*** Venture Capital; Emerging Business Law; Technology Licensing. ***Email:*** julie.ehinger@shawpittman.com

LAWRENCE D. EISEN, born Montreal, Quebec, Canada, July 9, 1966; admitted to bar, 1996, Virginia; registered to practice before U.S. Patent and Trademark Office. *Education:* University of Texas at Austin (B.S., Electrical Engineering, 1989); University of Baltimore School of Law (J.D., 1996). Staff Member, Intellectual Property Law Journal, 1994-1995. (Resident, McLean, Virginia Office). ***Email:*** lawrence.eisen@shawpittman.com

JOSEPH A. EISERT, admitted to bar, 1997, Virginia; 1998, District of Columbia. *Education:* U.S. Naval Academy (B.S., 1989); Georgetown University (M.A., 1993); George Mason University (J.D., 1997). [Lt., Naval Nuclear Propulsion Program, U.S. Navy, 1989-1996]. (Resident, McLean, Virginia Office). ***PRACTICE AREAS:*** Corporate; Securities; Mergers and Acquisitions; Emerging Companies.

SHEILA T. EVANS, born May 25, 1970; admitted to bar, 1995, Florida; 1996, U.S. District Court, Southern District of Florida; 1999, District of Columbia. *Education:* Vanderbilt Univ. (B.A., 1992); Univ. of Miami (J.D., cum laude, 1995). Phi Delta Phi. Recipient: Corpus Juris Secundum Award for Scholastic Excellence in Contracts; American Jurisprudence Book Award in Criminal Procedure. Member, Inter-American Law Review, 1993-1995. *Member:* The District of Columbia Bar; The Florida Bar; American Bar Association.

ALEJANDRO FERRATE, born Guatemala City, Guatemala, March 28, 1969; admitted to bar, 1995, Virginia; 1997, District of Columbia. *Education:* Roanoke College (B.A., 1991); George Mason University School of Law (J.D., 1995). Staff Member, George Mason Law Review.

THOMAS P. FITZGERALD, born Norwich, Connecticut, April 2, 1966; admitted to bar, 1995, Maryland; 1998, District of Columbia. *Education:* Trinity College (B.A., Economics, 1988); American University (J.D., 1995). *Member:* Maryland State and American Bar Associations; The District of Columbia Bar. (Resident, McLean, Virginia Office). ***PRACTICE AREAS:*** Corporate Law; Computer/Technology Law; Securities Law.

JOSHUA D. FITZHUGH, born Cambridge, Massachusetts, June 30, 1970; admitted to bar, 1998, California; 1999, District of Columbia. *Education:* Colby College (B.A., 1992); Georgetown University Law Center (J.D., 1998). Phi Beta Kappa. *Member:* The District of Columbia Bar (Member, International Law Section); American Bar Association. ***LANGUAGES:*** French.

LAUREN L. FRANCIS, born New York, New York, May 27, 1972; admitted to bar, 1998, New York; 2000, District of Columbia. *Education:* University of Pennsylvania (B.A., 1994); University of Michigan (J.D., 1997). ***PRACTICE AREAS:*** Corporate Law. ***Email:*** lauren.francis@shawpittman.com

PETER G. FREEMAN, born Silver Spring, Maryland, February 12, 1974; admitted to bar, 1999, Maryland; 2000, District of Columbia. *Education:* Columbia University (B.A., 1996); George Washington University (J.D., 1999).

(This Listing Continued)

Member, Moot Court Board. Book Review Editor, The George Washington Journal of International Law & Economics. ***PRACTICE AREAS:*** Corporate Law; Securities.

NORMAN J. FRY, born Chicago, Illinois, July 8, 1950; admitted to bar, 1994, Pennsylvania; 1995, New Jersey, New Hampshire and Virginia; 1996, District of Columbia. *Education:* University of Illinois (A.B., 1973); University of Rhode Island (M.A., 1991); George Washington University (J.D., with highest honors, 1994).

RUDY FUENTES, born Houston, Texas, January 26, 1966; admitted to bar, 1990, Texas (Not admitted in District of Columbia). *Education:* Stanford University (B.A., 1988); Boalt Hall School of Law, University of California at Berkeley (J.D., 1992). *Member:* State Bar of Texas.

JONATHAN W. GANNON, born New York, N.Y., May 31, 1973; admitted to bar, 2001, Virginia (Not admitted in District of Columbia). *Education:* College of the Holy Cross (B.A., 1995); Vanderbilt University (J.D., 2000). Phi Delta Phi; Fulbright Scholar. ***LANGUAGES:*** German. ***PRACTICE AREAS:*** Litigation. ***Email:*** jonathan.gannon@shawpittman.com

CRAIG H. GARNETT, born Norfolk, Virginia, December 12, 1964; admitted to bar, 1996, New York. *Education:* Amherst College (A.B., 1987); University of Virginia (J.D., 1995). (Resident, New York, N.Y. Office).

TAMMY GERSHONI, born Petah-Tikva, Israel, June 10, 1959; admitted to bar, 2000, Virginia (Not admitted in District of Columbia). *Education:* New York University (B.S., 1980); George Washington University (J.D., 2000). ***PRACTICE AREAS:*** Communications Law. ***Email:*** tammy.gershoni@shawpittman.com

JENNIFER G. GLASS, born Staten Island, New York, May 1, 1973; admitted to bar, 1998, Virginia; 1999, District of Columbia. *Education:* Cornell University (B.S., 1995); George Washington University (J.D., 1998). Note Editor, George Washington Journal of International Law and Economics, 1997-1998.

AMY GOLDFRANK, born Rochester, New York, May 7, 1972; admitted to bar, 2000, Maryland (Not admitted in District of Columbia). *Education:* Carleton College (B.A., 1994); University of Chicago (J.D., 2000). ***PRACTICE AREAS:*** Litigation. ***Email:*** amy.goldfrank@shawpittman.com

CHRISTINE M. GOLLATZ, admitted to bar, 2000, District of Columbia. *Education:* Syracuse University (B.A., 1994); University of Pennsylvania (J.D., 1999). Gold Key.

RONALD B. GRABER, born New York, N.Y., July 6, 1970; admitted to bar, 1995, New Jersey and U.S. District Court, District of New Jersey; 1996, New York. *Education:* Tufts University (B.A., 1992); Fordham University (J.D., 1995). *Member:* The Association of the Bar of the City of New York; New Jersey State Bar Association. ***PRACTICE AREAS:*** Securitization.

EDWARD J. GRASS, born New Brunswick, New Jersey, September 18, 1968; admitted to bar, 1994, Maryland; 1996, District of Columbia. *Education:* College of the Holy Cross (B.A., 1990); George Washington University (J.D., with honors, 1994). (Resident, McLean, Virginia Office).

ERIC M. GREEN, born Detroit, Michigan, February 2, 1972; admitted to bar, 2000, Virginia (Not admitted in District of Columbia). *Education:* University of Pennsylvania (B.A., 1994; J.D., 2000). ***PRACTICE AREAS:*** Securities; Corporate Law. ***Email:*** eric.green@shawpittman.com

KEVIN GREEN, admitted to bar, 1992, South Africa; 1999, England and Wales. *Education:* University of Witwatersrand, South Africa (B.A., 1990; LL.B., 1992); Bond University, Australia (M.B.A., 1998). *Member:* Law Society of England and Wales; Law Society of Tranvaal, South Africa. (Resident, London, England Office). ***PRACTICE AREAS:*** Outsourcing; Internet Law; Computer Software Licensing; Technology Transactions.

ANDREW B. GREENFIELD, born Philadelphia, Pennsylvania, March 30, 1967; admitted to bar, 1992, Pennsylvania, New Jersey and U.S. District Court, District of New Jersey; 1993, Maryland and District of Columbia. *Education:* University of Pennsylvania (B.A., cum laude, 1989); George Washington University (J.D., 1992). *Member:* Maryland State Bar Association; District of Columbia Bar; American Immigration Lawyers Association (Young Lawyers Division: National Steering Committee, 1996-1998; Chair, D.C. Chapter Committee, 1996-1997). ***PRACTICE AREAS:*** Immigration and Nationality Law.

JEFFREY B. GRILL, born Queens, New York, July 7, 1971; admitted to bar, 1995, Maryland; 1996, District of Columbia. *Education:* State University of New York at Albany (B.A., summa cum laude, 1992); University of Pennsylvania Law School (J.D., 1995).

ALLISON S. GROFF, born Washington, D.C., September 15, 1973; admitted to bar, 2001, Virginia. *Education:* University of Virginia (B.A., 1995); University of Michigan School of Law (J.D., cum laude, 2001). (Resident, McLean, Virginia Office).

LUKE GRUBB, born December 9, 1966; admitted to bar, 1998, Solicitor of England and Wales. *Education:* Manchester University (B.A., 1989); Notting-

(This Listing Continued)

SHAW PITTMAN LLP, Washington—Continued

ham Law School (Postgraduate Diploma in Law, 1994). *Member:* Law Society of England and Wales. (Resident, London, England Office). ***PRACTICE AREAS:*** Corporate Law; Mergers and Acquisitions; Venture Capital.

ROBERT HAEMER, born Trenton, New Jersey, October 13, 1961; admitted to bar, 1999, Virginia (Not admitted in District of Columbia). *Education:* University of Washington (B.S., cum laude, 1983); Georgetown University Law Center (J.D., magna cum laude, 1999). Order of the Coif, Georgetown Chapter, 1999. [U.S. Navy, 1983-1999]

SUSAN M. HAFELI, born Detroit, Michigan, October 26, 1955; admitted to bar, 1987, Texas; 1988, California; 1998, District of Columbia. *Education:* University of Michigan (B.A., Economics, 1977); University of Texas at Austin (J.D., 1987). Assistant General Counsel, Telecommunications, Public Utility Commission of Texas, 1989-1993. Attorney, Office of Consumer Advocate, U.S. Postal Rate Commission, 1995. *Member:* State Bar of Texas; State Bar of California; Federal Communications Bar Association. ***PRACTICE AREAS:*** Communications. ***Email:*** susan.hafeli@shawpittman.com

ALEXANDER HAMILTON, born London, England, September 18, 1971; admitted to bar, 1997, Solicitor in England and Wales. *Education:* Nottingham University (B.A., in Philosophy, 1993); College of Law, London (Legal Practice Course, 1994). Speaker: Internet Security and Ecryption; Regulation of Trusted Third Parties. Treasurer, Liberty (the National Council of Civil Liberties). Member, Executive Committee and Trustee, Civil Liberties Trust. (Resident, London, England Office).

ATINA S. HARLEY-BOYCE, born Cheverly, Maryland, September 13, 1969; admitted to bar, 1994, Maryland; 1996, District of Columbia. *Education:* Virginia Polytechnic Institute & State University (B.S., 1991); Yale Law School (J.D., magna cum laude, 1994). *Member:* The District of Columbia Bar. ***PRACTICE AREAS:*** Litigation.

ELIZABETH A. HARRIS, born Poughkeepsie, New York, June 26, 1972; admitted to bar, 1998, Maryland and District of Columbia. *Education:* Columbia University (B.A., 1994; J.D., 1997). *Member:* Maryland State Bar Association, Inc.; The District of Columbia Bar. ***LANGUAGES:*** French and Spanish. ***PRACTICE AREAS:*** Taxation; Corporate Law.

MICHAEL L. HENTREL, born Memphis, Tennessee, August 20, 1966; admitted to bar, 1992, Maryland; 1993, District of Columbia. *Education:* University of Michigan (B.A., 1989); Howard University (J.D., cum laude, 1992).

RITA M. HERSCOVICI, born Bucharest, Romania, 1960; admitted to bar, 1996, California; 1997, U.S. District Court, Central District of California; 1998, U.S. District Court, Northern District of California. *Education:* University of Southern California (B.A., 1983); University of Southern California School of Law (J.D., 1996). Order of The Coif. Writing Instructor, University of Southern California School of Law, 1994-1996. *Member:* Los Angeles County and American Bar Associations (Intellectual Property Section); California State Bar. (Resident, Los Angeles, California Office). ***LANGUAGES:*** Spanish, French, Romanian and Hungarian.

ELISABETH M. HERTZBERG, born Washington, D.C., February 15, 1971; admitted to bar, 1998, Maryland (Not admitted in District of Columbia). *Education:* University of Virginia (B.S., 1993); George Washington University (J.D., 1998). ***PRACTICE AREAS:*** Technology Law; Corporate Law.

WAYNE G. HESS, born Syosset, New York, May 24, 1963; admitted to bar, 1995, New Jersey; 1996, New York (Not admitted in District of Columbia). *Education:* Cornell University (B.S., 1985); Hofstra University (M.B.A., 1991); St. John's University (J.D., cum laude, 1995). (Resident, McLean, Virginia Office). ***PRACTICE AREAS:*** Corporate.

ANTHONY S. HIGGINS, born Steubenville, Ohio, September 27, 1969; admitted to bar, 1995, Maryland; 1998, District of Columbia. *Education:* Michigan State University (B.S., 1992); University of Baltimore (J.D., cum laude, 1995); Georgetown University (LL.M., with distinction, 1997). Contributing Author: "21st Century Money, Banking & Commerce," NACHA, 1998. ***PRACTICE AREAS:*** Financial Institutions; Investment Companies; Securities Regulation; Electronic Commerce; Year 2000 Computer Conversion.

BRENDAN HOLLAND, born Arlington, Virginia, May 8, 1973; admitted to bar, 1999, District of Columbia. *Education:* University of Virginia (B.A., English and History, 1995); College of William and Mary (J.D., 1998). Phi Alpha Theta; Gold Key. Member, Moot Court Bar, 1996-1998. Member, William and Mary Bill of Rights Journal, 1996-1998. *Member:* District of Columbia Bar; Federal Communications Bar Association. ***PRACTICE AREAS:*** Communications. ***Email:*** brendan.holland@shawpittman.com

M. JENNIFER HOPEMAN, born Minneapolis, Minnesota, 1970; admitted to bar, 1996, Minnesota; 1999, Massachusetts (Not admitted in District of Columbia). *Education:* Carleton College (B.A., magna cum laude, 1992); Harvard Law School (J.D., cum laude, 1996). Phi Beta Kappa. Executive Editor, Harvard Women's Law Journal, Volume 19. *Member:* Boston, Hennepin County,

(This Listing Continued)

Minnesota State, Massachusetts and American Bar Associations. ***LANGUAGES:*** French. ***PRACTICE AREAS:*** Litigation; Labor and Employment Law; Antitrust.

WILLIAM L. HORTON, JR., born Stone Mountain, Georgia, November 29, 1969; admitted to bar, 1996, New York; 1997, District of Columbia. *Education:* Wake Forest University (B.A., 1991); University of Pennsylvania (M.G.A., 1993); University of Virginia (J.D., 1995).

SHANTELLE DENISE HUGHES, born Rochester, New York, March 12, 1973; admitted to bar, 1998, Maryland; 1999, District of Columbia. *Education:* Hampton Institute (B.A., in Sociology, 1995); George Washington University (J.D., 1998). *Member:* The District of Columbia Bar. ***PRACTICE AREAS:*** Commercial Real Estate. ***Email:*** shantelle.hughes@shawpittman.com

MICHELLE M. HUHNKE, born Staten Island, New York, November 12, 1966; admitted to bar, 1995, Virginia; 1996, District of Columbia. *Education:* Barnard College of Columbia University (B.A., 1989); National Law Center, George Washington University (J.D., 1995). (Resident, McLean, Virginia Office).

SOL L. IRVINE, born Bath, England, June 8, 1973; admitted to bar, 1999, New York. *Education:* Franklin & Marshall College (B.A., 1995); Tulane Law School (J.D., 1998). (Resident, New York, N.Y. Office). ***PRACTICE AREAS:*** Copyrights; Trademarks; Trade Secrets; Software Licensing; Entertainment Law; High Technology; Employment Contracts.

DAVID C. ISAACSON, born Baltimore, Maryland, August 2, 1963; admitted to bar, 1996, Maryland; 1998, District of Columbia. *Education:* University of Delaware (B.S.E.E., 1985); Johns Hopkins University (M.S., 1991); University of Maryland (J.D., 1996). Associate Editor, Maryland Law Review, 1995-1996. (Resident, McLean, Virginia Office). ***Email:*** david.isaacson@shawpittman.com

D. DAVID JACKSON, admitted to bar, 1997, New York and Massachusetts. *Education:* Birmingham-Southern College (B.A., 1982); New York Law School (J.D., 1995). (Resident, New York, N.Y. Office).

PAUL E. JANASKIE, born Shamokin, Pennsylvania, April 16, 1961; admitted to bar, 1993, Illinois; 1995, District of Columbia. *Education:* Carnegie-Mellon University (B.S., with honors, 1984); University of Rochester (M.A., 1987); Northwestern University (J.D., cum laude, 1993). Member, Northwestern University Law Review. (Resident, McLean, Virginia Office).

HELEN JERRY, born United Kingdom; admitted to bar, 1991, England. *Education:* Trinity College, Oxford University (1987); College of Law London (LSF, 1989). *Member:* Law Society of England and Wales; Employment Lawyers' Association. (Resident, London, England Office). ***LANGUAGES:*** French. ***PRACTICE AREAS:*** Employment Law.

LARA JOHNSON, born Singapore, March 3, 1974; admitted to bar, 2001, Virginia (Not admitted in District of Columbia). *Education:* College of William & Mary (B.A., magna cum laude, 1996); University of Virginia School of Law (J.D., 2001).

SHARON Y. JOHNSON, born Newport News, Virginia, October 5, 1973; admitted to bar, 1998, California (Not admitted in District of Columbia). *Education:* George Mason University (B.A., 1995); Pepperdine University School of Law (J.D., 1998). ***PRACTICE AREAS:*** Financial Institution Regulation. ***Email:*** sharon.johnson@shawpittman.com

JULIA EDEN JUDISH, born Annapolis, Maryland, February 19, 1968; admitted to bar, 1997, Maryland; 1999, District of Columbia. *Education:* Swarthmore College (B.A., magna cum laude, 1989); Harvard Law School (J.D., 1996).

NIKI A. KAPLAN, born New York, N.Y.; admitted to bar, 1990, New York. *Education:* Brandeis University (B.A., 1985); Boston University School of Law (J.D., 1989); Boston University College of Communication (M.S., 1989). Attorney: Paramount Pictures Corporation, New York, N.Y., 1994-1995; Thirteen/WNET, New York, N.Y., 1993-1994. Associate, Sullivan, Donovan, Bond & Bonner, 1989-1993. (Resident, New York, N.Y. Office). ***Email:*** niki.kaplan@shawpittman.com

CHARLES W. KATZ, born St. Louis, Missouri, June 6, 1967; admitted to bar, 1992, Virginia. *Education:* The Episcopal Academy; Lafayette College (A.B., 1989); Washington and Lee University (J.D., 1992); Georgetown University (LL.M., with distinction, Securities Regulations, 1993). (Resident, McLean, Virginia Office). ***PRACTICE AREAS:*** Securities; Mergers and Acquisitions; Venture Capital; Corporate Law.

ELIZABETH J. KELLEY, admitted to bar, 1999, Georgia; 2000, District of Columbia. *Education:* Emory University (B.A., 1993); University of Georgia (J.D., 1999).

ALISA C. KEY, born Washington, D.C., 1970; admitted to bar, 1999, Maryland. *Education:* Skidmore College (B.A., 1992); University of Baltimore (J.D., 1998). Sigma Delta Kappa. Law Clerk to Hon. John J. Farley, III, U.S. Court of Veterans Appeals, 1998-2000. (Resident, McLean, Virginia Office). ***PRACTICE AREAS:*** Intellectual Property; Trademarks.

(This Listing Continued)

DAVID W. KIEFER, born Perth Amboy, New Jersey; admitted to bar, 1998, New Jersey; 1999, North Carolina (Not admitted in District of Columbia). *Education:* Lafayette College (B.A., Political Science, 1995); George Washington University (J.D., 1998). Pi Sigma Alpha.

AMY B. KIESEL, born January 11, 1965; admitted to bar, 1999, New York (Not admitted in District of Columbia). *Education:* Georgetown University (B.S.N., 1986); Yale University School of Nursing (M.S.N., 1988); Yale University School of Medicine (M.P.H., 1990); Duke University (J.D., 1998). Registered Nurse, Washington, D.C., 1986. *Member:* Health Law Society.

JEFFREY A. KNIGHT, born Morristown, Tennessee, June 3, 1971; admitted to bar, 1996, Virginia; 1997, District of Columbia. *Education:* Amherst College (B.A., magna cum laude, 1993); University of Chicago Law School (J.D., 1996).

PETER G. KOBACK, born Providence, Rhode Island, November 10, 1968; admitted to bar, 1993, Massachusetts; 1996, District of Columbia. *Education:* University of Massachusetts at Amherst (B.A., cum laude, 1990); Stanford Law School (J.D., 1993).

MARK R. KOEHN, born Englewood, New Jersey, December 16, 1962; admitted to bar, 1991, Maryland; 1992, District of Columbia; registered to practice before U.S. Patent and Trademark Office. *Education:* Cornell University (B.S., 1985); Georgetown University (J.D., 1991). Tau Beta Pi. (Resident, McLean, Virginia Office).

ADAM M. KOHN, born Bronx, New York, February 23, 1973; admitted to bar, 1999, New York (Not admitted in District of Columbia). *Education:* University of Pennsylvania (B.S., 1995); Benjamin N. Cardozo, Yeshiva University (J.D., 1998). *Member:* American Bar Association (Member, Health Law Section); American Health Lawyers Association. ***PRACTICE AREAS:*** Health Law. ***Email:*** adam.kohn@shawpittman.com

DAVID S. KONCZAL, born Westwood, New Jersey, January 25, 1972; admitted to bar, 1997, Maryland; 1998, District of Columbia. *Education:* Duke University (A.B., Economics and Political Science, cum laude, 1994); The George Washington University (J.D., with honors, 1997). Managing Editor, The George Washington Law Review, 1996-1997. Author: "Ruing Rufo: Ramifications of a Lenient Standard for Modifying Antitrust Consent Decrees and an Alternative," 65 Geo. Wash. L. Rev. 130, 1997; "Obscuring Notice Through Footnotes in FCC Rulemaking Proceedings," 64 Geo. Wash. L. Rev. 974, 1996. Intern, AT&T Corp., Basking Ridge, New Jersey, 1991-1995. *Member:* District of Columbia Bar; Maryland State and Federal Communications Bar Associations. ***PRACTICE AREAS:*** Communications. ***Email:*** david.konczal@shawpittman.com

JOSHUA B. KONVISSER, born Columbus, Ohio, May 27, 1970; admitted to bar, 1997, Massachusetts; 1998, New York and District of Columbia. *Education:* University of Pennsylvania (B.A.B.S., 1992); Harvard University (J.D., 1997). (Resident, New York, N.Y. Office).

KEITH R. KOST, born Canton, Ohio, January 22, 1968; admitted to bar, 1995, Ohio; 1996, U.S. District Court, Northern District of Ohio; 1999, U.S. Tax Court. *Education:* University of Akron (B.S., Accounting, magna cum laude, 1992; M.Tax., 1994; J.D., cum laude, 1995). (Resident, McLean, Virginia Office). ***PRACTICE AREAS:*** Employee Benefits; ERISA; Federal Taxation.

LINDSAY B. KRAUSE, born Bethesda, Maryland, August 6, 1976; admitted to bar, 2001, Virginia. *Education:* University of Virginia (B.A., with distinction, 1998; J.D., 2001). (Resident, McLean, Virginia Office).

CYNTHIA R. KRIPS, born Washington, D.C., June 14, 1969; admitted to bar, 1998, Maryland. *Education:* University of Maryland (B.A., 1991); American University, Washington College of Law (J.D., magna cum laude, 1997). (Resident, McLean, Virginia Office). ***PRACTICE AREAS:*** Trusts and Estates; Estate Administration. ***Email:*** cynthia.kripps@shawpittman.com

STUART M. KUNTZ, born Philadelphia, Pennsylvania, April 27, 1973; admitted to bar, 1999, Maryland and District of Columbia. *Education:* Emory University (B.A., 1995); New York University (J.D., 1998). ***Email:*** stuart.kuntz@shawpittman.com

KARIN J. KYSILKA, admitted to bar, 1998, Pennsylvania (Not admitted in District of Columbia). *Education:* Pennsylvania State University (B.A., with highest distinction, 1995); Harvard Law School (J.D., cum laude, 1998). Phi Beta Kappa. ***PRACTICE AREAS:*** Real Estate.

ALEX LAKATOS, born March 25, 1970; admitted to bar, 1996, California; 1997, District of Columbia. *Education:* University of Maryland (B.A., 1992); Hastings College of Law, University of California (J.D., Valedictorian, 1995). Associate Articles Editor, Hastings Law Journal. Clerk to Judge Mary Schroeder, 9th Circuit.

EDWARD W. LAM, born Chicago, Illinois, August 2, 1966; admitted to bar, 1995, New York and Illinois; 1997, U.S. Tax Court (Not admitted in District of Columbia). *Education:* Southern Illinois University (B.A., 1989); Syracuse University (J.D., 1994). ***PRACTICE AREAS:*** Federal Income Tax.

NANCY S. LAPIDUS, admitted to bar, 1995, Pennsylvania; 1997, District of Columbia and U.S. District Court, Eastern District of Pennsylvania. *Education:* Washington University (B.A., 1992); George Washington University (J.D., 1995). The George Washington University Law Review. Law Clerk, The Honorable Lowell A. Reed, U.S. District Court, Eastern District of Pennsylvania, 1995-1997. ***PRACTICE AREAS:*** Intellectual Property; Food and Drug Regulation.

DAVID LASHWAY, born Middlebury, Connecticut, February 7, 1971; admitted to bar, 1996, New York; 1997, District of Columbia. *Education:* Dickinson College (B.A., cum laude, 1993); Vermont Law School (J.D./Masters Degree, magna cum laude, 1996). Omicron Delta Kappa; Pi Sigma Alpha. Law Clerk, U.S. District Court, District of Vermont, 1996. *Member:* New York State and American Bar Associations. ***PRACTICE AREAS:*** Food and Drug; Trade; Environmental.

KEVIN R. LEARNED, born Carmichael, California, March 26, 1973; admitted to bar, 1999, New York; 2000, District of Columbia. *Education:* George Washington University (B.A., 1995); University of Chicago (J.D., 1998). ***PRACTICE AREAS:*** Corporate; Securities.

BRIAN K. LEE, born Sacramento, California, December 25, 1971; admitted to bar, 1997, Maryland; 1998, District of Columbia. *Education:* Vanderbilt University (B.A., 1993); Washington College of Law of American University (J.D., cum laude, 1997). Notes and Comment Editor, Administrative Law Review, 1994-1997. (Resident, McLean, Virginia Office).

MICHAEL S. LEE, born Seoul, South Korea, January 4, 1968; admitted to bar, 1995, Maryland; 1998, District of Columbia. *Education:* Lehigh University (B.S.M.E., 1990); Catholic University (J.D., 1995). Patent Examiner, U.S. Patent and Trademark Office, 1990-1996. (Resident, McLean, Virginia Office). ***Email:*** michael.lee@shawpittman.com

ANDREA LISA LEEB, born New York, N.Y., March 15, 1959; admitted to bar, 1990, New York. *Education:* Georgetown University (B.S.N., 1981); Benjamin Cardozo Law School, Yeshiva University (J.D., cum laude, 1989). Associate Editor, Cardozo Law Review, 1988-1989. Registered Nurse, New Jersey. Author: "Future Disability Under New York Human Rights Law," 10 Cardozo Law Review 769, 1989. *Member:* New York State and American Bar Associations; The Florida Bar. [LTJG, U.S. Public Health Service, 1981-1984]. (Resident, Los Angeles, California Office).

KATHERINE LEH, born Riverside, California, June 16, 1976; admitted to bar, 2000, California. *Education:* University of California at Santa Barbara (B.A., 1997); Loyola Law School (J.D., 2000). St. Thomas More Honor Society. *Member:* State Bar of California; American Bar Association. (Resident, Los Angeles, California Office). ***PRACTICE AREAS:*** Outsourcing; Technology Transactions. ***Email:*** katherine.leh@shawpittman.com

MICHAEL S. LEVINE, born Queens, New York, February 28, 1966; admitted to bar, 1995, New York; 1996, District of Columbia; 1997, Massachusetts; 1999, U.S. District Court for the District of Columbia. *Education:* State University of New York at Stony Brook (B.A., 1988); Franklin Pierce Law Center (J.D., 1994). Co-Author: "Negligent Supervision: To Be...Or Not To Be," 34 NHBJ 39 (1993); "Insurance Coverage Is Available For Property Losses Resulting From The Blizzard of '96," VA. Lawyers Weekly, April 1996. *Member:* New York State, Massachusetts and American Bar Associations; The District of Columbia Bar. (Resident, McLean, Virginia Office). ***PRACTICE AREAS:*** Insurance Coverage Litigation; Business Litigation; Defense Law.

TIMOTHY J. LEVY, born Trenton, New Jersey, June 20, 1970; admitted to bar, 1997, New Jersey; 1998, District of Columbia. *Education:* Columbia University (B.A., 1992); George Washington University (J.D., with honors, 1996). Member, Journal of International Law. (Resident, McLean, Virginia Office). ***PRACTICE AREAS:*** Litigation.

TONY LIN, born Anderson, South Carolina, July 17, 1969; admitted to bar, 1998, Iowa; 1999, District of Columbia. *Education:* University of Virginia (B.A., Economics and Mathematics, 1991); University of Iowa (J.D., with high distinction, 1995; M.A., Economics, 1996; Ph.D., Economics, 1997). University of Virginia McDermott Scholar, 1987-1991. University of Iowa Foundation Fellow, 1991-1992. Law Opportunity Fellow, University of Iowa College of Law, 1992-1995. Member, Journal of Corporation Law, 1993-1995. Author: "Distinguishing Kodak Lock-in and Franchise Contractual Lock-in," 23 So. Ill. U. L. J. 87, 1998. Lecturer, Economics, Southern Illinois University, 1997-1998. *Member:* The District of Columbia Bar; Iowa State and Federal Communications Bar Associations. ***PRACTICE AREAS:*** Communications. ***Email:*** tony.lin@shawpittman.com

ROBERT SCOTT LOGAN, born Richmond, Virginia, October 29, 1962; admitted to bar, 2000, Virginia (Not admitted in District of Columbia). *Education:* University of Maryland (B.S., 1986); George Washington University Law School (J.D., 2000).

ERIC R. LoPRESTI, born Los Angeles, California, February 10, 1969; admitted to bar, 1998, Virginia; 1998, District of Columbia. *Education:* Rutgers University (B.S., 1991); Georgetown University (J.D., cum laude, 1998). *Member:* Virginia State Bar; The District of Columbia Bar. (Resident, McLean, Virginia Office). ***PRACTICE AREAS:*** Tax Law.

(This Listing Continued)

SHAW PITTMAN LLP, Washington—Continued

ANDREW J. LOVE, born Plainview, New York, March 12, 1972; admitted to bar, 1997, Maryland; 1998, District of Columbia and U.S. District Court, District of Maryland. *Education:* State University of New York at Binghamton (B.A., cum laude, 1994); Georgetown University Law Center (J.D., 1997). Author: "Replacing Our Current System of Organ Procurement with a Futures Market: Will Supply Be Maximized?" Jurimetrics Journal, Spring, 1997; "S Corporation Indebted & Indirect Shareholder Lending, Hitchins v. Commissioner," 49 The Tax Lawyer, 1996. *Member:* Maryland State Bar Association, Inc.; Bankruptcy Bar Association. ***LANGUAGES:*** Spanish. ***PRACTICE AREAS:*** Bankruptcy; Creditors Rights; Litigation.

MARTA T. LOWE, born Olympia, Washington, February 12, 1971; admitted to bar, 1996, Illinois; 1998, District of Columbia. *Education:* University of Washington (B.A., 1993); University of Chicago (J.D., 1996).

ALISON B. MACDONALD, born Royal Oak, Michigan, February 23, 1973; admitted to bar, 2001, Virginia (Not admitted in District of Columbia). *Education:* Bryn Mawr College (A.B., cum laude, 1995); University of Michigan (J.D., 2000). Executive Editor, Michigan Journal of Law Reform, 1999-2000. ***PRACTICE AREAS:*** Litigation. ***Email:*** alison.macdonald@shawpittman.com

JOHN P. MALLOY, born Plainfield, New Jersey, March 15, 1965; admitted to bar, 1994, Pennsylvania; 1995, New Jersey; 1999, District of Columbia. *Education:* Williams College (B.A., 1987); Brooklyn Law School (J.D., 1994). Member, Moot Court Honor Society. Assistant District Attorney, Philadelphia, Pennsylvania, 1994-1997. (Resident, McLean, Virginia Office).

MICHAEL ANDREW MANCUSI, born Washington, D.C., August 12, 1972; admitted to bar, 1997, Virginia (Not admitted in District of Columbia). *Education:* University of Virginia (B.S., 1994); University of Richmond (J.D., 1997; M.B.A., 1997). *Member:* Virginia State Bar; American Bar Association.

KIMBERLY V. MANN, born Salisbury, Maryland, November 15, 1959; admitted to bar, 1995, Maryland; 1998, District of Columbia. *Education:* University of Delaware (B.S., 1981); University of Maryland (J.D., with honors, 1995). Staff Member, Maryland Journal of Contemporary Legal Issues. ***LANGUAGES:*** Spanish.

NICOLE E. MARCSON, born 1974; admitted to bar, 2000, Virginia (Not admitted in District of Columbia). *Education:* Duke University (A.B., summa cum laude, 1997); Vanderbilt University (J.D., 2000). ***PRACTICE AREAS:*** Technology Law. ***Email:*** nicole.marcson@shawpittman.com

LUIS MARINI, born San Juan, Puerto Rico, February 19, 1975; admitted to bar, 2001, Virginia (Not admitted in District of Columbia). *Education:* University of Michigan (B.B.A., with high distinction, 1997); Georgetown University Law Center (J.D., 2001).

C. TODD MARKS, born Cincinnati, Ohio, July 16, 1970; admitted to bar, 2001, Virginia. *Education:* University of Cincinnati (B.B.A., 1996); George Mason University School of Law (J.D., cum laude, 2001). Symposium Editor, George Mason Law Review. (Resident, McLean, Virginia Office).

MICHELLE S. MARKS, admitted to bar, 1996, Maryland; 1998, District of Columbia; registered to practice before U.S. Patent and Trademark Office. *Education:* Pitzer College (B.A., 1978); Tufts University, Sackler School of Graduate Biomedical Sciences Cellular Biology (Ph.D., 1987); University of Maryland (J.D., cum laude, 1996). Awarded The Food and Drug Law Institute's Vincent A. Kleinfeld Scholarship, 1995-1996. Author: "How Will the 'Equitable Remuneration' Payment Within the New Patent Term Be Interpreted?" The Federal Circuit Bar Journal 5: 261-292 (1995) and Intellectual Property Law Review (1997); "The Impact of the 1994 Uruguay Round Agreements Act (URAA) Patent Term Provisions on the Drug Price Competition and Patent Term Restoration Act of 1984," The Food and Drug Law Journal 51:445-470 (1996); "Expression and Functional Analysis of the Hyaluronate-Binding Region of Cartilage Proteoglycan," Journal of Cellular Biochemistry 13:44 (1989); "Hyaluronate-Binding Proteins of Murine Brain," Journal of Neurochemistry 54:171-180 (1990). Formerly with Foley and Lardner, Washington, D.C., 1996-1999. *Member:* American Intellectual Property Law Association; The Federal Circuit Bar Association; American Society for Cell Biology. ***PRACTICE AREAS:*** Intellectual Property.

CATHERINE E. MARSHALL, born Prince George, Maryland, June 9, 1971; admitted to bar, 1998, New York and New Jersey (Not admitted in District of Columbia). *Education:* Georgetown University (B.A., 1997; LL.M., 1999); Columbus School of Law of the Catholic University of America (J.D., 1998).

MARY MARTIN, born Baton Rouge, Louisiana, June 19, 1974; admitted to bar, 2000, Virginia (Not admitted in District of Columbia). *Education:* Louisiana State University (B.A., summa cum laude, 1996); Washington & Lee University (J.D., 1999). Member, Capital Defense Journal. Clerkship with Judge LeRoy S. Millette, Jr., Thirty-First Judicial Circuit Court of Prince William County, Virginia. *Member:* American Bar Association. (Resident, McLean, Virginia Office).

(This Listing Continued)

JOAN E. MASTERS, born Plattsburgh, New York, June 18, 1968; admitted to bar, 1996, Maryland (Not admitted in District of Columbia). *Education:* Columbia University (B.A., 1990); American University (J.D., 1996). Articles Editor, American University Administrative Law Journal, 1995-1996. *Member:* Maryland State Bar Association, Inc.; Federal Communications Bar Association. ***PRACTICE AREAS:*** Communications.

DANIEL MAX, born New York, New York, May 6, 1968; admitted to bar, 1994, New Jersey; 1996, New York. *Education:* Columbia University (B.A., 1990); Fordham University (J.D., 1994). Member, Urban Law Journal. (Resident, McLean, Virginia Office).

JENNIFER P. McCLENAN, born Jacksonville, Florida, October 29, 1965; admitted to bar, 1992, Maryland; 1994, District of Columbia; registered to practice before U.S. Patent and Trademark Office. *Education:* University of Virginia (B.S., 1987); University of Notre Dame (J.D., 1992).

JAMES T. McCORMICK, admitted to bar, 2000, Virginia. *Education:* Oxford University, England (B.A., 1985); Harvard Law School (J.D., 2000). (Resident, McLean, Virginia Office). ***PRACTICE AREAS:*** Corporate; Technology Law; Securities. ***Email:*** james.mccormick@shawpittman.com

VERONICA D. McLAUGHLIN, born Petersburg, Virginia, October 10, 1968; admitted to bar, 1994, Maryland and U.S. Court of Appeals, Fourth Circuit; 1995, District of Columbia. *Education:* University of Richmond (B.A., Mathematics and Journalism, summa cum laude, 1990); Yale Law School (J.D., 1993). Phi Beta Kappa. Coker Fellow, Yale Law School, 1992-1993. University Scholar, 1986-1990 and CIGNA Scholar, 1986-1990, University of Richmond. Member, Yale Journal on Regulation, 1991-1993. Law Clerk, Honorable Richard L. Williams, United States District Court, Eastern District of Virginia, 1993-1994. *Member:* District of Columbia Bar; Maryland State and Federal Communications Bar Associations. ***PRACTICE AREAS:*** Communications. ***Email:*** veronica.mclaughlin@shawpittman.com

SAMANTHA MILLER, born New Orleans, Louisiana, June 21, 1974; admitted to bar, 1999, Maryland; 2001, Virginia. *Education:* University of Texas at Austin (B.A., 1996; J.D., 1998). *Member:* American Bar Association. (Resident, McLean, Virginia Office).

FRANK J. MIRKOW, born Bogota, Colombia, February 4, 1965; admitted to bar, 2001, New York (Not admitted in District of Columbia). *Education:* University of Maryland (B.A., 1987); Harvard University (M.P.A., 1990); Cornell University (J.D., 2000). *Member:* International Law Society. ***PRACTICE AREAS:*** Corporate Law; International Trade. ***Email:*** frank.mirkow@shawpittman.com

LISA-MARIE C. MONSANTO, born St. Thomas, U.S. Virgin Islands, April 29, 1965; admitted to bar, 1997, New York (Not admitted in District of Columbia). *Education:* McGill University (B.A., 1987); Columbia University (J.D., 1996).

H. CARL MOULTRIE, III, born Gary, Indiana, June 26, 1977; admitted to bar, 2001, Virginia (Not admitted in District of Columbia). *Education:* Cornell University (B.S., 1998); Georgetown University Law Center (J.D., 2001).

SANJAY JOSE MULLICK, born Washington, D.C., March 8, 1969; admitted to bar, 1998, District of Columbia. *Education:* Georgetown University (B.S.F.S., 1991; J.D., 1996). Member, Georgetown International Environmental Law Review. *Member:* The District of Columbia Bar.

JAMES E. MYERS, admitted to bar, 1999, California; 2000, District of Columbia. *Education:* Duke University (B.A., 1993); University of Michigan (J.D., 1998). Member, Michigan Law Review.

ANTHONY NAGLE, admitted to bar, 1995, England and Wales. *Education:* Thames Valley University (LL.B., 1994); Nottingham Law School (LPC, 1995). (Resident, London, England Office). ***PRACTICE AREAS:*** Technology Transactions; Outsourcing; Computer Software Licensing; Systems Integration.

NADIA B. NEJAIME, born Maaser El Chouf, Lebanon, March 19, 1967; admitted to bar, 1994, Maryland; 1996, District of Columbia. *Education:* American University (B.A., 1989); George Washington University (J.D., 1994). ***LANGUAGES:*** French. ***PRACTICE AREAS:*** Technology and Science; Contracts. ***Email:*** nadia.nejaime@shawpittman.com

KAREN FAYE NEWMAN, born Hackensack, New Jersey, March 21, 1976; admitted to bar, 2001, Virginia (Not admitted in District of Columbia). *Education:* Johns Hopkins University (B.A., 1997); University of Pennsylvania Law School (J.D., 2001).

STEFAN C. NICHOLAS, born Pontiac, Michigan, May 24, 1968; admitted to bar, 1998, New York (Not admitted in District of Columbia). *Education:* Georgetown University (B.A., 1991); University of Virginia (J.D. and Master's of Foreign Affairs, 1997). ***LANGUAGES:*** German. ***PRACTICE AREAS:*** Corporate; Banking Law; Technology Law.

JOHN LESLIE NICHOLSON, admitted to bar, 1996, Maryland (Not admitted in District of Columbia). *Education:* Williams College (B.A., 1989); Vanderbilt University (J.D., 1995).

(This Listing Continued)

VIPUL N. NISHAWALA, born Bombay, India, July 1, 1970; admitted to bar, 1995, New York; 1998, District of Columbia. *Education:* University of North Carolina (B.A., with distinction, 1992); George Washington University (J.D., 1995). Phi Beta Kappa. Articles Editor, The George Washington Law Review. *Member:* The District of Columbia Bar. (Resident, New York, N.Y. Office).

MICHAEL A. OBLON, born Philadelphia, Pennsylvania, June 10, 1970; admitted to bar, 1997, Massachusetts; 1998, District of Columbia; registered to practice before U.S. Patent and Trademark Office. *Education:* University of Virginia (B.S.E.E., 1992); Harvard University (J.D., 1996). Tau Beta Pi. Law Clerk to Judge Schall, U.S. Court of Appeals for the Federal Circuit, 1996-1997. Patent Examiner, U.S. Patent and Trademark Office, 1992-1993. (Resident, McLean, Virginia Office). ***Email:*** michael.oblon@shawpittman.com

BARBARA J. O'CONNELL, born 1956; admitted to bar, 1995, New York; 1996, District of Columbia. *Education:* State University of New York at Stony Brook (B.A., summa cum laude, 1990); Yale University (J.D., 1993). Phi Beta Kappa; Phi Theta Kappa; Phi Sigma Tau. *Member:* The District of Columbia Bar. (Resident, McLean, Virginia Office). ***PRACTICE AREAS:*** Corporate Law; Securities Law.

DAVID B. OSHINSKY, born New York, N.Y., June 23, 1969; admitted to bar, 1997, California. *Education:* Yale College (B.A., 1991); Columbia Law School (J.D., 1996). Member, Columbia Law Review. *Member:* State Bar of California. (Resident, Los Angeles, California Office).

ERIK ANDERS PETERSEN, born New York, New York, October 17, 1971; admitted to bar, 1996, Virginia; 1998, District of Columbia. *Education:* University of Virginia (B.A., 1993; J.D., 1996). Omicron Delta Kappa; Phi Eta Sigma (Virginia Chapter). Treasurer, Alpha Delta Phi. Golden Key. Editor in Chief and Managing Editor, Corks & Curls, 1991-1993. ***PRACTICE AREAS:*** Intellectual Property; Licensing; Trademarks; Copyrights; Licensing.

JAQUALIN FRIEND PETERSON, born Salt Lake City, Utah, July 13, 1966; admitted to bar, 1992, Utah; 1995, California; 1996, District of Columbia. *Education:* University of Utah (B.S. in Political Science, magna cum laude, 1989; Undergraduate Certificate in Public Administration; J.D., 1992). William H. Leary Scholar, University of Utah College of Law, Spring, 1991. Articles Editor, Journal of Energy, Natural Resources and Environmental Law, 1991-1992. Author: "Nephi City v. Hansen: The Utah Supreme Court Side Steps Public Trust Principle in Allowing Forfeiture of Municipal Water Rights," 11:2 J. Energy Nat. Resources & Envtl. L., 1991. Judicial Law Clerk, Honorable Philip G. Espinosa, Arizona State Court of Appeals, 1994-1995. *Member:* Utah State Bar; State Bar of California; District of Columbia Bar; Federal Communications Bar Association. ***PRACTICE AREAS:*** Communications. ***Email:*** jaqualin.peterson@shawpittman.com

LILYANNA L. PEYSER, born Taipei, Taiwan, September 5, 1973; admitted to bar, 1998, Virginia and Massachusetts; 1999, District of Columbia. *Education:* University of Virginia (B.A., summa cum laude, 1995); Harvard Law School (J.D., cum laude, 1998). Phi Beta Kappa. Echols Scholar. Editor, Harvard Environmental Law Review, 1995-1997. *Member:* Virginia and American Bar Associations; Bar Association of the District of Columbia. ***LANGUAGES:*** Greek and Spanish. ***PRACTICE AREAS:*** Corporate Law; Securities; Mergers and Acquisitions.

GREGORY JAMES PHILLIPS, born Washington, D.C., October 25, 1970; admitted to bar, 1998, Virginia; 1999, District of Columbia. *Education:* Princeton University (A.B., 1993); University of Virginia (J.D., 1998). Recipient, Best Brief Award: Lile Moot Court Competition, Domestic Violence Project. Pro Bono Criminal Adjustication Project.

V. ELIZABETH POWELL, born Durham, North Carolina, October 10, 1961; admitted to bar, 2000, Maryland (Not admitted in District of Columbia). *Education:* Middlebury College (B.A., 1983); George Washington University (M.A.. Soviet and East European Studies, 1987); Washington & Lee University (J.D., 1995). Phi Alpha Delta. *Member:* Maryland State Bar Association. ***LANGUAGES:*** German, Russian, French. ***PRACTICE AREAS:*** Financial Institutions Law. ***Email:*** elizabeth.powell@shawpittman.com

TIFFANY L. POWERS, born Hackensack, New Jersey, November 15, 1973; admitted to bar, 1999, Georgia. *Education:* Vanderbilt University (B.S., 1995); University of Georgia (J.D., 1999). (Resident, McLean, Virginia Office). ***PRACTICE AREAS:*** Employment Law; Insurance Coverage; Government Enforcement; Internal Investigations. ***Email:*** tiffany.powers@shawpittman.com

ALICIA A. PRATHER, born Denver, Colorado; admitted to bar, 1995, Illinois; 1998, Missouri. *Education:* Earlham College (B.A., with high honors, 1992); Chicago-Kent College of Law (J.D., 1995). Order of the Coif. Notes and Comments Editor, Chicago-Kent Law Review. (Resident, McLean, Virginia Office). ***PRACTICE AREAS:*** Securities; Corporate.

DENNIS E. PRYBA II, born Washington, D.C., September 20, 1974; admitted to bar, 1999, Virginia. *Education:* George Mason University (B.S., Finance, 1996); George Mason University School of Law (J.D., magna cum laude,

(This Listing Continued)

1999). (Resident, McLean, Virginia Office). ***PRACTICE AREAS:*** Government Contracts Litigation; Corporate Law; Internet Law. ***Email:*** dennis.pryba@shawpittman.com

GENNET PURCELL, born Toronto, Ontario, May 3, 1974; admitted to bar, 1999, Virginia and Maryland. *Education:* York University (B.A., 1996); Howard University (J.D., 1999). (Resident, McLean, Virginia Office). ***PRACTICE AREAS:*** Corporate Law; Securities. ***Email:*** gennet.purcell@shawpittman.com

SHANNON M. PYSHER, born Salina, Kansas, November 28, 1969; admitted to bar, 1997, Maryland; 1999, District of Columbia. *Education:* Harvard University (B.A., cum laude, 1992); University of Virginia (J.D., 1997). Speaker, AHLA's "E-Health and the Information Age," December 2000 seminar. Author: "Legal Prescription for an E-Healthy Web Site," Health Information & Technology News (American Health Lawyers Association publication), Spring 2001. Co-Author: with B. Fried and E. Baim, "Six Steps to E-Healthy Web Site," Healthcare Business, Nov./Dec. 2000; with D. Main, "Taking Responsibility for Medical records," Healthcare Business, May 2000; with C. Papavizas, "Compliance Tide Leaves Issues Open," National Law Journal, Jul. 6, 1998; with B. Jones, "Prepare to Negotiate Your Next Employment Agreement," VA Med. Q., 1997. *Member:* The District of Columbia Bar (Member, Health Law Section Steering Committee; Attorney Coordinator, Healthcare Decision making Project). ***PRACTICE AREAS:*** Technology Transactions; Health Law. ***Email:*** shannon.pysher@shawpittman.com

MATTHEW C. RAMPY, born Midland, Michigan, April 29, 1971; admitted to bar, 1996, California; 1998, District of Columbia. *Education:* University of Michigan (B.A., 1993); University of San Diego (J.D., M.B.A., 1996). ***PRACTICE AREAS:*** Corporate; Mergers and Acquisitions; Technology Law. ***Email:*** matthew.rampy@shawpittman.com

MAX M. REYNOLDS, born St. Louis, Missouri, May 24, 1970; admitted to bar, 1996, Virginia; 1997, District of Columbia. *Education:* Emory University (B.A., summa cum laude, 1992); University of Virginia (J.D., 1996).

TINA R. REYNOLDS, born Warsaw, Virginia, December 23, 1970; admitted to bar, 1996, New York and U.S. District Court, Southern and Eastern Districts of New York; 1997, District of Columbia; 1998, Virginia. *Education:* College of William & Mary (B.A., Government, 1992); St. John's University (J.D., 1995). Pi Sigma Alpha; Phi Delta Phi. Dean's List, 1992-1995. Recipient, American Jurisprudence Award for Excellence, 1994. Member: Society of Collegiate Journalists, 1991-1992; St. John's Law Review, 1993-1995. Author: "Pimental v. Ltd. Canadian," Admiralty Law Society Newsletter, Fall 1992. *Member:* The Association of the Bar of the City of New York; District of Columbia Bar; New York State Bar Association. ***PRACTICE AREAS:*** Litigation; Corporate; Business. ***Email:*** tina.reynolds@shawpittman.com

MICHAEL RICHARDS, born Chicago, Illinois, June 24, 1958; admitted to bar, 2000, Maryland; 2001, District of Columbia. *Education:* Clark University (B.A., 1980); Columbia University (M.S., Journalism, 1981); Georgetown University Law Center (J.D., cum laude, 2000). Recipient, Dupont-Columbia Award for Broadcasting Journalism, 1990-1991. *Member:* Maryland State and American Bar Associations; District of Columbia Bar; Federal Communications Bar Association.

MARC L. ROBINSON, (admission pending). *Education:* University of Virginia (B.A., 1993); University of Michigan (J.D., 1999). Member, Environmental Law Society.

DOUGLAS J. ROSINSKI, born Utica, New York, October 3, 1959; admitted to bar, 1997, Georgia and South Carolina; 1998, U.S. District Court, Southern District of Georgia and U.S. District Court, District of South Carolina (Not admitted in District of Columbia). *Education:* University of Rochester (B.S., with distinction, 1981); University of South Carolina (J.D., 1997). Order of the Coif; Order of the Wig and Robe. Author: "The Environmental Impact on Foreign Territory from a Proposed Federal Action," South Carolina Environmental L.J., 1995; "South Carolina's Battles with the Department of Energy Over Storage of Spent Nuclear Fuel at the Savannah River Site," South Carolina Environmental L.J., 1997. Member, American Nuclear Society. *Member:* State Bar of Georgia; South Carolina Bar; American Bar Association; Institute of Electrical and Electronics Engineers; American Society of Mechanical Engineers. [with U.S. Navy, 1981-1985]. ***PRACTICE AREAS:*** Energy Law.

JAMES M. ROSS, born 1965; admitted to bar, 1995, Virginia; 1997, District of Columbia. *Education:* Stanford University (B.A.S., 1988); University of Chicago (J.D., with honors, 1995). (Resident, McLean, Virginia Office). ***PRACTICE AREAS:*** Intellectual Property.

JOSEPH M. RYAN, born Danbury, Connecticut, September 4, 1971; admitted to bar, 2001, Virginia. *Education:* George Washington University (B.A., 1993); Georgetown University Law Center (J.D., 2000). [U.S. Marine Corps, 1993-1998; Captain]. (Resident, McLean, Virginia Office). ***PRACTICE AREAS:*** Corporate; Technology. ***Email:*** joseph.ryan@shawpittman.com

V. ANN SANDOR, born Pasco, Washington, May 14, 1962; admitted to bar, 1994, Georgia. *Education:* University of Michigan (B.S.E., 1984); Georgia State University (J.D., cum laude, 1994). Outer Barrister's Guild. Recipient, Am Jur Award and West Publishing Award for Property I & II, May 1992. Student

(This Listing Continued)

SHAW PITTMAN LLP, Washington—Continued

Writing Editor, 1993-1994 and Member, 1992-1993, Georgia State University Law Review. Author: "Byte After Byte, The Courts Nibble Away at Copyright Protection of Software," 10 Georgia State University Law Review 543, March, 1994. *Member:* Atlanta and American Bar Associations; State Bar of Georgia (Member, Sections on: Corporate and Banking; Corporate Counsel). (Resident, McLean, Virginia Office). ***PRACTICE AREAS:*** Corporate Law; Securities; Technology Law.

SAMANTHA E. SCHRADER, (admission pending). *Education:* Griffith University (B.A., 1985); University of Queensland, Australia (J.D., 1991). (Resident, New York, N.Y. Office).

STACY A. SCHULTZ, admitted to bar, 1997, California. *Education:* Georgetown University (B.S.F.S., 1990); Georgetown University Law Center (J.D., 1997). *Member:* American Bar Association. (Resident, Los Angeles, California Office). ***PRACTICE AREAS:*** Health Care. ***Email:*** stacy.schultz@shawpittman.com

WENDY B. SCHRECKINGER, born Brooklyn, New York, April 10, 1967; admitted to bar, 1993, New Jersey; 1994, Pennsylvania; 1999, New York. *Education:* State University of New York at Oneonta (B.A., summa cum laude, 1989); Rutgers School of Law at Newark (J.D., with high honors, 1993). Order of the Coif. Member, Essex Inns of Court, William J. Brennan Chapter, 1996-1997. Law Clerk to the Honorable Joel A. Pisano, U.S.M.J., 1994-1995; Law Clerk to the Honorable Alvin Weiss, A.J.S.C., Essex County, 1995-1996. *Member:* Essex County and New Jersey State Bar Associations. (Resident, New York, N.Y. Office). ***PRACTICE AREAS:*** Internet Law; Electronic Commerce.

ISABELLE SCOTT, born Washington, D.C., October 16, 1940; admitted to bar, 1992, Pennsylvania; 1993, Maryland and District of Columbia. *Education:* University of Virginia (Ph.D., with high distinction, 1969); Catholic University, Columbus School of Law (J.D., 1992). Author: "Domestic Violence Practice and Procedure," Clark Boardman Callaghan (1996). *Member:* The District of Columbia Bar; American Bar Association. ***Email:*** isabelle.scott@shawpittman.com

SARAH E. SHAW, born Royal Oak, Michigan, June 23, 1972; admitted to bar, 1997, Illinois; 1999, District of Columbia. *Education:* University of Michigan (B.A., with distinction, 1994); George Washington University (J.D., with honors, 1997). Dean's Fellow, The George Washington University Legal Research and Writing Program. Law Clerk to U.S. Department of Justice, Civil Division, Torts Branch. Member, The George Washington Journal of International Law and Economics. ***PRACTICE AREAS:*** Real Estate; Zoning, Planning and Land Use; Municipal Law.

PATRICK J. SHEA, admitted to bar, 1999, Virginia. *Education:* Princeton University (A.B., 1996); University of Virginia (J.D., 1999). Member, The Federalist Society. (Resident, McLean, Virginia Office).

ROBERT PUTMAN SHERLEY, born N.Y., N.Y., July 27 1966; admitted to bar, 1992, New York; 1998, District of Columbia. *Education:* University of Pennsylvania (B.A., magna cum laude, 1988); Cornell University (J.D., cum laude, 1991).

WILLIAM A. SHREINER, JR., born Albany, New York, September 21, 1970; admitted to bar, 1998, New York; 2000, Louisiana. *Education:* State University of New York at Oswego (B.A., 1992); New York University School of Law (J.D., 1997). *Member:* Louisiana State Bar Association. (Resident, McLean, Virginia Office).

ERIC J. SHUFFLEBARGER, born Louisville, Kentucky, August 29, 1975; admitted to bar, 2000, Virginia (Not admitted in District of Columbia). *Education:* Transylvania University (B.A., 1997); University of North Carolina at Chapel Hill (J.D., 2000). ***PRACTICE AREAS:*** Corporate Law; Securities. ***Email:*** eric.shufflebarger@shawpittman.com

REBECCA L. SHWAYDER, born Portsmouth, Virginia, August 16, 1974; admitted to bar, 2000, Virginia. *Education:* Stanford University (B.A., 1996); University of Virginia (J.D., 2000). *Member:* Virginia and American Bar Associations. (Resident, McLean, Virginia Office). ***PRACTICE AREAS:*** Corporate; Technology. ***Email:*** rebecca.shwayder@shawpittman.com

JARED R. SILVERMAN, born Glendale, Arizona, September 25, 1971; admitted to bar, 1997, Illinois (Not admitted in District of Columbia). *Education:* University of Michigan (B.A., with high distinction, 1993); University of Pennsylvania (J.D., 1996). Phi Kappa Phi; Phi Beta Kappa; Mortar Board. James B. Angell Scholar. Articles Editor, University of Pennsylvania Environmental Law Journal, 1995-1996. Law Clerk to Hon. James G. Carr, District Judge, Northern District of Ohio, 1996-1997. *Member:* Illinois State Bar Association. ***PRACTICE AREAS:*** Litigation.

ERICA SAPPER SIMPSON, born Amarillo, Texas, October 20, 1972; admitted to bar, 2000, Maryland (Not admitted in District of Columbia). *Education:* Austin College (B.A., 1994); American University (J.D., magna cum laude, 2000). Editor, International Law Review. Author: "Islam in Uzbekistan: Why Freedom of Religion is Fundamental for Peace and Stability in the Region," Journal of Arabic and Islamic Studies, Vol. II, April 2000. ***PRACTICE AREAS:*** Litigation. ***Email:*** erica.simpson@shawpittman.com

P.L. SKIP SINGLETON, JR., born January 19, 1959; admitted to bar, 1999, Maryland; 2000, District of Columbia. *Education:* University of Mississippi at Oxford (B.A., 1981); Franklin Pierce Law Center (M.I.P., 1998; J.D., 1998). Law Clerk to the Honorable Randall R. Rader, U.S. Court of Appeals, Federal Circuit. *Member:* American Bar Association; American Intellectual Property Law Association; The Association of Trial Lawyers of America.

DAVID SKINNER, born September 25, 1963; admitted to bar, 1995, Solicitor of England and Wales. *Education:* Oxford University, Exeter College (M.A., Modern History, 1985); College of London (Law Society Finals, 1993); Bristol University (Diploma Intellectual Property Law and Practice, 1995). Author, Articles: Wurobond Sales Specialising in Japanese Bonds, UBS Phillips & Drew, London; Organic Farming, Stockadon Farm Devon; Foreign Exchange and Interest Rate Swaps Dealer, Chemical Bank, London. (Resident, London, England Office).

CAROLINE C. SMITH, born Summit, New Jersey, January 11, 1969; admitted to bar, 1997, Maryland; 1998, District of Columbia. *Education:* Washington & Lee University (B.S., 1990); American University (J.D., 1997). *Member:* Federal Energy Bar Association; American Intellectual Property Law Association.

RACHEL E. SMITH, born Rockville Center, New York, July 17, 1972; admitted to bar, 1997, Maryland; 1998, District of Columbia. *Education:* James Madison University (B.A., cum laude, 1994), Honors Scholar; Catholic University, Columbus School of Law (J.D., cum laude, 1997). Note and Comment Editor, Catholic University Law Review. (Resident, McLean, Virginia Office).

CRAIG A. SPERLING, born Manhasset, New York, August 9, 1972; admitted to bar, 1997, New Jersey; 1998, District of Columbia. *Education:* Cornell University (B.A., 1994); New York University (J.D., 1997). (Resident, McLean, Virginia Office).

MICHAEL A. SPIELMAN, born Hollywood, Florida, March 10, 1970; admitted to bar, 1996, Connecticut and New York; 1998, District of Columbia and U.S. Tax Court. *Education:* Washington University (A.B., Political Science, 1991); Case Western Reserve University (J.D., magna cum laude, 1995; M.B.A., 1995); New York University School of Law (LL.M., Taxation, 1997). Beta Gamma Sigma; Beta Alpha Psi; Order of the Coif. Certified Public Accountant, Maryland, 1995. Author: "Whole Loan Repurchase Agreements: An Assessment of Investment Transaction Risks in Light of Continuing Legal Uncertainty," 99 Commercial Law Journal 476, 1994. Attorney-Advisor, Judge Renato Beghe, United States Tax Court, 1998-1999. International Tax Counsel, MCI WorldCom, 1999. *Member:* Connecticut, New York State and United States Tax Court Bar Associations; The District of Columbia Bar. ***PRACTICE AREAS:*** Taxation; Corporate; Business. ***Email:*** michael.spielman@shawpittman.com

MATTHEW L. STEIMEL, born Millersburg, Ohio, 1957; admitted to bar, 1982, California; 1987, New York. *Education:* Miami University (B.S., 1979); The Ohio State University (J.D., 1982). (Resident, Los Angeles, California Office). ***PRACTICE AREAS:*** Corporate Law; Business Law; Technology Law.

KATHERINE TONG-SHIN SUH, born Washington, D.C., November 23, 1972; admitted to bar, 1999, District of Columbia. *Education:* University of Virginia (B.A., Foreign Affairs, 1994); Washington and Lee University (J.D., 1998). Judicial Clerk, Hon. George E. Honts, Twenty-Fifth Judicial Circuit of Virginia, 1997-1998. Research Assistant, Professor Allan W. Vestal, Washington and Lee University School of Law, 1996-1998. Intern, Committee on Rules and Administration, United States Senate, 1996. Staff Assistant, Office of Senator John Warner, United States Senate, 1994-1995. *Member:* District of Columbia Bar; Federal Communications Bar Association. ***PRACTICE AREAS:*** Communications. ***Email:*** katherine.suh@shawpittman.com

SEAN M. SULLIVAN, born Raleigh, North Carolina, June 28, 1976; admitted to bar, 2001, Virginia (Not admitted in District of Columbia). *Education:* University of Miami (B.S., 1998); American University Washington College of Law (J.D., cum laude, 2001).

AMY D. TICHENOR, born Roseburg, Oregon, February 19, 1972; admitted to bar, 1998, California. *Education:* Oregon State University (B.S., 1994); University of California at Los Angeles (J.D., 1998). (Resident, Los Angeles, California Office). ***Email:*** amy.tichenor@shawpittman.com

MELDA A. TISOGLU, born Istanbul, Turkey, May 9, 1972; admitted to bar, 1998, New York. *Education:* Bogazici University (B.A., 1993); New York University (LL.M., 1998). (Resident, N.Y., N.Y. Office).

LISA J. TOMASETTI, admitted to bar, 1997, Virginia. *Education:* College of William & Mary (B.A., 1993); George Mason University School of Law (J.D., 1997). Law Clerk to the Honorable Martin V.B. Bostetter, Jr., Chief Judge, U.S. Bankruptcy Court, Eastern District of Virginia. (Resident, McLean, Virginia Office). ***PRACTICE AREAS:*** Corporate; Technology. ***Email:*** lisa.tomasetti@shawpittman.com

(This Listing Continued)

RICHARD F. TRIMBER, born Washington, D.C., 1969; admitted to bar, 1998, Maryland (Not admitted in District of Columbia). *Education:* George Mason University (B.A., English, 1994); Catholic University of America (J.D., cum laude, 1997). ***PRACTICE AREAS:*** Asset Securitization; Private Placements; Corporate; Mergers and Acquisitions. ***Email:*** richard.trimber@shawpittman.com

PAUL A TUMMONDS, JR, born St. Albans, New York, March 26, 1970; admitted to bar, 1995, Maryland; 1996, District of Columbia. *Education:* University of Michigan (B.A., 1992); Wayne State University (J.D., 1995). *Member:* The District of Columbia Bar; Maryland State Bar Association. ***PRACTICE AREAS:*** Real Estate; Zoning, Planning and Land Use; Municipal Law.

JOANNA S. VALDES, born Grosse Pointe, Michigan, January 6, 1972; admitted to bar, 1997, Ohio; 1998, Florida. *Education:* Duke University (A.B., 1994); George Washington University (J.D., 1997). (Resident, McLean, Virginia Office).

LEE VAN BLERKOM, born Washington, D.C., April 9, 1970; admitted to bar, 1996, Maryland; 1997, District of Columbia. *Education:* Amherst College (B.A., 1992); University of Virginia (J.D., 1996).

AMY VAN DE KERCKHOVE, born Chicago, Illinois, May 22, 1973; admitted to bar, 1999, District of Columbia. *Education:* University of Salamanca, Salamanca, Spain; University of Notre Dame in London; University of Notre Dame (B.A., Psychology, magna cum laude, 1995); Georgetown University (J.D., 1999). Member, Georgetown Journal of Legal Ethics, 1997-1999. Legal Intern, Wireless Telecommunications Bureau, Federal Communications Commission, 1997. Congressional Liaison, National Endowment for the Arts, 1995. *Member:* The District of Columbia Bar; Federal Communications Bar Association. ***PRACTICE AREAS:*** Communications. ***Email:*** amy.van.de.kerckhove@shawpittman.com

ALEXANDER M.R. VAN DER BELLEN, born Saginaw, Michigan, May 15, 1966; admitted to bar, 1994, Pennsylvania; 1995, District of Columbia. *Education:* Hamilton College (A.B., 1988); Tulane Law School (J.D., cum laude, 1994). Moot Court Appellate Competition. Member, Environmental Law Society.

ERIK J. VELAPOLDI, born Jerusalem, Israel, November 2, 1970; admitted to bar, 1995, Maryland; 1997, U.S. District Court, District of Maryland. *Education:* University of Virginia (B.A.,1992; J.D., 1995). *Member:* Maryland State (Young Lawyers and Business Law Sections) and American Bar Associations. (Resident, McLean, Virginia Office). ***LANGUAGES:*** Norwegian. ***PRACTICE AREAS:*** Corporate; Securities.

COLLEEN KOTYK VOSSLER, born Meriden, Connecticut, April 24, 1971; admitted to bar, 1998, Maryland (Not admitted in District of Columbia). *Education:* Harvard University (A.B., cum laude, 1993); College of William & Mary (J.D., 1998). William & Mary National Moot Court Team. Champion, Bushrod T. Washington Moot Court Tournament, 1996. Student Note Editor, William & Mary Bill of Rights Journal, 1997-1998. Winner, The American Academy of Matrimonial Lawyers Annual Law School Writing Competition, 1998. Co-Author: "To Be, Or Not To Be: The Undiscovered Country of Claims Estimation in Bankruptcy," Journal of Bankruptcy Law and Practice, Vol.8, No.3, March/April 1999. Author: "Tearing Down the House: Weakening the Foundation of Divorce Mediation Brick by Brick," William & Mary Bill of Rights Journal, Vol.6, Issue 1, Winter 1997. *Member:* Maryland State and American Bar Assns. ***Email:*** colleen.vossler@shawpittman.com

WANJI WALCOTT, born April 22, 1970; admitted to bar, 1994, New Jersey; U.S. District Court, District of New Jersey. *Education:* Howard University (B.A., 1991; J.D., 1994). *Member:* New Jersey State Bar Association.

TOM CHIA-KAI WANG, born Taipei, Taiwan, January 26, 1975; admitted to bar, 2001, Virginia (Not admitted in District of Columbia). *Education:* University of South Carolina (B.A., 1997); University of Virginia (J.D., 2001).

JEFFREY I. WASSERMAN, admitted to bar, 1999, New Jersey and U.S. District Court, District of New Jersey; 2000, New York and U.S. District Court, Southern and Eastern District of New York. *Education:* Lafayette College (A.B., 1996); Fordham University (J.D., 1999). (Resident, New York, N.Y. Office). ***Email:*** jeffrey.wasserman@shawpittman.com

MEREDITH R. WEINBERG, born Valley Stream, New York, February 29, 1976; admitted to bar, 2001, Virginia (Not admitted in District of Columbia). *Education:* Duke University (A.B., cum laude, 1998); Georgetown University Law Center (J.D., cum laude, 2001).

ELIZABETH WEIR, (admission pending). *Education:* Cambridge University (M.A., 1992); College of Law, Chester. (Resident, London, England Office).

JEREMIAH WOLSK, born August 20, 1968; admitted to bar, 1996, Maryland; 1998, District of Columbia. *Education:* The Johns Hopkins University (B.A., 1991); Washington University School of Law (J.D., 1996).

TIM WRIGHT, admitted to bar, 1994, as Solicitor, England and Wales. *Education:* Sussex University (B.A., 1990); Bristol University (LL.M., 1991);

(This Listing Continued)

York College of Law (LSF, 1992). (Resident, London, England Office). ***PRACTICE AREAS:*** Technology Transactions; Outsourcing; Computer Software Licensing.

YUCHONG C. YI, born Seoul, South Korea, December 29, 1970; admitted to bar, 1996, Illinois (Not admitted in District of Columbia). *Education:* Amherst College (B.A., 1993); University of Virginia (J.D., 1996). ***LANGUAGES:*** Korean. ***PRACTICE AREAS:*** Real Estate.

SYLVIA S. YU, born White Plains, New York, November 10, 1971; admitted to bar, 2000, Massachusetts (Not admitted in District of Columbia). *Education:* Yale University (B.A., 1993); Harvard University (J.D., 1999). Contributing Writer, Harvard Journal of Law, Medicine and Ethics, 1997-1999.

RESTITUTO E. YUSON, III, born Manila, Philippines, April 15, 1967; admitted to bar, 1995, New Jersey; 1996, New York. *Education:* Rutgers University (B.S., 1989; J.D., 1995). Articles Editor, Rutgers Law Review. (Resident, New York, NY Office). ***LANGUAGES:*** Spanish and Filipino.

JOHN A. ZALOOM, born Houston, Texas, December 31, 1968; admitted to bar, 1996, New York. *Education:* Texas A & M University (B.A., magna cum laude, 1991); University of Texas (J.D., with honors, 1994); University of London (LL.M., with merit, 1995). Phi Kappa Phi; Sigma Phi Epsilon. Recipient, Academic Excellence and Distinguished Student Award. Texas Environmental Law Journal. (Resident, New York, NY Office).

JON T. ZEIDLER, born Los Angeles, California, August 12, 1962; admitted to bar, 1998, Oregon; 1999, District of Columbia. *Education:* Hampshire College (B.A., 1986); Georgetown University (J.D., 1998). ***PRACTICE AREAS:*** Real Estate.

JASON M. ZUCKERMAN, born Baltimore, Maryland, July 23, 1974; admitted to bar, 2000, Virginia; 2001, District of Columbia. *Education:* Georgetown University (B.A., 1996); University of Virginia (J.D., 2000). Phi Beta Kappa; Alpha Sigma Nu; Pi Sigma Alpha; Theta Alpha Kappa. *Member:* Virginia State Bar. ***PRACTICE AREAS:*** Government Investigations; Employment Law; Commercial Litigation; Insurance Coverage Litigation. ***Email:*** jason.zuckerman@shawpittman.com

SHAWE & ROSENTHAL, LLP

WASHINGTON, D.C.

(See Baltimore, Maryland)

Labor Relations, Equal Employment Opportunity, Occupational Safety and Health, Wrongful Discharge, Wage and Hour, ERISA, Immigration, and all Employment Related Litigation, Exclusively on Behalf of Management.

SHEA & GARDNER

1800 MASSACHUSETTS AVENUE, N.W.
WASHINGTON, D.C. 20036
Telephone: 202-828-2000
Fax: 202-828-2195
URL: http://www.sheagardner.com

Admiralty and Maritime Law, Antitrust and Trade Regulation, Aviation and Aerospace, Bankruptcy, Banks and Banking, Business Law, Civil Rights, Class Actions, Communications and Media, Constitutional Law, Corporate Law, Employee Benefits, Environment Law, Finance, General Practice, Government Contracts, Insurance Regulation, Intellectual Property, International Trade, Investments, Labor and Employment, Legal Ethics and Professional Responsibility, Natural Resources, Nonprofit and Charitable Organizations, Occupational Safety and Health, Products Liability, Professional Liability, Railroad Law, Regulatory Law, Securities, Taxation, Toxic Torts, Transportation, Trusts and Estates, Utility Law and White Collar Crime.

FIRM PROFILE: Shea & Gardner is a mid-sized law firm with a national practice advising on and litigating novel and complex matters, generally brought to us because of their critical significance to the client. The firm was founded in 1947 in Washington, D.C. and all of its attorneys work out of the Washington, D.C. office.

We emphasize quality, responsiveness, and creativity. Experienced partners work directly with clients and are supported by associates of a quality that can hardly be found at the big firms. Ours is a partnership of the traditional mold, virtually all of our partners have trained here and have spent most of their professional lives with the firm. We believe that this stability and continuity make an invaluable contribution to our clients.

We pride ourselves in our ability quickly to master new fields and develop innovative and winning strategies. We train our lawyers as generalists comfortable in several fields and have within the firm a range of expertise and experience, including in general civil and criminal litigation, administrative law, domestic and

(This Listing Continued)

SHEA & GARDNER, Washington—Continued

international corporate advice and transactions, and legislative representation. We nevertheless believe we have developed a national reputation and substantial expertise in the following fields:

Toxic tort and product liability litigation, class actions and complex litigation, claims management, and remediation strategies (including asbestos and various environmental hazards).

Representation of financial institutions (including insurance companies and mutual funds) with regard to regulatory obligations (state and federal), strategies for dealing with information system and back-office operational issues, and management of complex litigation (involving liability and coverage issues).

Counseling and litigation on behalf of corporations, law firms, accounting firms, and other entities in connection with professional standards, ethical requirements and investigations of alleged misconduct and malpractice.

Environmental counseling and litigation under all of the major federal environmental laws and their state analogues (including TSCA, RCRA, CERCLA, SMCRA, NEPA, and the Clean Air and Clean Water Acts).

Representation of the railroad industry in labor matters and major maritime carriers and terminals in maritime regulatory matters.

The firm also has as strong pro bono practice as recognized by the District of Columbia Bar which named Shea & Gardner Pro Bono Law Firm of the Year in 1996, and by the ABA which awarded the firm its Pro Bono Publico Award in 1997.

MEMBERS OF FIRM

FRANCIS M. SHEA (1905-1989).

ROBERT T. BASSECHES, born New York, N.Y., January 24, 1934; admitted to bar, 1962, District of Columbia. *Education:* Amherst College (B.A., 1955); Yale Law School (LL.B., 1958). Order of the Coif; Phi Beta Kappa. Comment Editor, Yale Law Journal, 1958. Law Clerk: Judge David L. Bazelon, U.S. Court of Appeals, District of Columbia Circuit; 1958-1959; Justice Hugo L. Black, U.S. Supreme Court, 1959. *Member:* The District of Columbia Bar; Maritime Administrative Bar Association (President, 1969-1971). ***PRACTICE AREAS:*** Transportation Regulation; Administrative; Civil Litigation. ***Email:*** rbasseches@sheagardner.com

BENJAMIN W. BOLEY, born Brooklyn, New York, October 29, 1934; admitted to bar, 1960, California; 1961, New York; 1962, District of Columbia. *Education:* Amherst College (B.A., 1956); Yale University (LL.B., 1959). Member, Board of Editors, Yale Law Journal, 1959. Co-Author: with William Sheehan and Stephen Hadley, "Discovery of Computerized Litigation Support Systems in Federal Court," 72 Complex Crimes Journal, 1991; with Thomas Mikula and Timothy Lynch, "Legislative and Judicial Efforts to Mandate Parity Between Health Care and Disability Income Benefits for Physical and Mental Illnesses," 24 Journal of Pension Planning & Compliance, Spring 1998; with Valerie Ross, "Full-Time to Part-Time to Termination: What Does COBRA Require?" 12 Benefits Law Journal, Spring 1999. Law Clerk, Judges William Healy, Homer T. Bone and Albert Lee Stephens, Sr., U.S. Court of Appeals, Ninth Circuit, 1959-1960. *Member:* The District of Columbia Bar; The State Bar of California. ***PRACTICE AREAS:*** Employee Benefits; Corporate Law. ***Email:*** bboley@sheagardner.com

RALPH J. MOORE, JR., born St. Paul, Minnesota, September 29, 1932; admitted to bar, 1961, California; 1965, District of Columbia; 1972, Maryland. *Education:* Yale University (B.A., 1954); University of California at Berkeley (LL.B., 1959); Cambridge University. Phi Alpha Delta; Order of the Coif; Phi Beta Kappa. Article Editor, California Law Review, 1958-1959. Law Clerk, Chief Justice Earl Warren, U.S. Supreme Court, 1959-1960. *Member:* The District of Columbia Bar; The State Bar of California; Maryland State and American Bar Associations; American College of Trust and Estate Counsel; National Academy of Elder Law Attorneys. (Also practicing at 7009 West Greenvale Parkway, Chevy Chase, Maryland, 20815). ***PRACTICE AREAS:*** Labor; Employment Law; Transportation Law; Trusts and Estates. ***Email:*** rmoore@sheagardner.com

MARTIN J. FLYNN, born Des Moines, Iowa, October 30, 1937; admitted to bar, 1962, Indiana; 1964, District of Columbia. *Education:* Indiana University (A.B., 1959; J.D., 1962). Order of the Coif; Phi Beta Kappa. Editor-in-Chief, Indiana Law Journal, 1961-1962. Law Clerk, Justice Tom C. Clark, U.S. Supreme Court, 1962-1963. Professorial Lecturer, Catholic University School of Law, 1972-1973. *Member:* The District of Columbia Bar; American Bar Association. ***PRACTICE AREAS:*** Banking; Corporate; Commercial Litigation. ***Email:*** mflynn@sheagardner.com

STEPHEN J. POLLAK, born Chicago, Illinois, March 22, 1928; admitted to bar, 1956, Illinois; 1957, District of Columbia. *Education:* Dartmouth College (A.B., 1950); Yale University (LL.B., 1956). Assistant to the Solicitor

(This Listing Continued)

General, U.S. Department of Justice, 1961-1964. Deputy General Counsel, U.S. Office of Economic Opportunity, 1964-1965. First Assistant, 1965-1967 and Assistant Attorney General, 1968-1969, Civil Rights Division, U.S. Department of Justice. Advisor to the President for National Capital Affairs, 1967. Special Master, Vitamins Antitrust Litigation, U.S. District Court, District of Columbia, 1999—. ADR: Member, Panels of Mediators, U.S. Court of Appeals and U.S. District Court, District of Columbia Circuit, 1989—; Member, CPR Panel of Distinguished Neutrals, 1998—; Member, AAA Panel of Arbitrators and Mediators, 1989—. Member, 1984-1990, 1994-1996 and Chairman, 1989-1990, District of Columbia Judicial Nomination Commission. Director, Oral History Project, Historical Society of the District of Columbia Circuit, 1995—. *Member:* The District of Columbia Bar (President, 1980-1981); Bar Association of the District of Columbia; American Bar Association; American Law Institute. ***PRACTICE AREAS:*** Civil Litigation; Trial Practice; Appellate Practice; ERISA; Labor Law; Mediation; Arbitration. ***Email:*** spollak@sheagardner.com

DAVID BOOTH BEERS, born New Haven, Connecticut, October 19, 1935; admitted to bar, 1961, California and Connecticut; 1962, District of Columbia; 1970, U.S. Supreme Court. *Education:* Trinity College (B.A., 1957); University of California at Berkeley (M.A., 1960; LL.B., 1960). Law Clerk, Judge Fred Kunzel, U.S. District Court, Southern District of California, 1960-1961. Chancellor (Legal Counsel) to the Presiding Bishop of the Episcopal Church, 1991—. *Member:* The District of Columbia Bar; The State Bar of California; American Bar Association. ***PRACTICE AREAS:*** Litigation; Environmental; Products; Nonprofits. ***Email:*** dbeers@sheagardner.com

JOHN D. ALDOCK, born Silver Spring, Maryland, January 20, 1942; admitted to bar, 1968, District of Columbia; 1973, Maryland. *Education:* Northwestern University (B.S., 1964); University of Pennsylvania (LL.B., 1967). Beta Gamma Sigma. Editor, University of Pennsylvania Law Review, 1965-1967. Author: "The Georgine Settlement Class Action: What It Is, Where It May Lead and The Ethical Considerations Presented," Defense Research Institute, 1995; "Constitutional and Other Legal Hurdles to Classwide Resolution of 'Future' Personal Injury Claims," ABA Tort and Insurance Practice Section, 1996; "The Use of Settlement Class Actions to Resolve Future Claims in Mass Tort Litigation," ABA National Institute on Class Actions, 1997; "The Future Use of Settlement Class Actions to Resolve Mass Tort Claims," ABA Annual Meeting, 1997. Law Clerk, Judge Luther W. Youngdahl, U.S. District Court, District of Columbia, 1967-1968. Assistant U.S. Attorney for the District of Columbia, 1968-1971. Member: Judicial Conference for D.C. Circuit; District of Columbia Judicial Conference; U.S. District Court of D.C. Civil Justice Reform Act Advisory Group. Chairman, Advisory Committee on Rules to the U.S. District Court, 1987—; Vice-Chairman, Committee on Unauthorized Practice of Law, D.C. Court of Appeals, 1979-1983. Deputy Independent Counsel, 1984. President, Assistant U.S. Attorneys Association for the District of Columbia, 1975. Member, CPR Institute for Dispute Resolution Panel of Distinguished Neutrals. Arbitrator, American Arbitration Association. Mediator, U.S. District Court, District of Columbia. *Member:* The District of Columbia Bar; Maryland State and American (Fellow; Member, Board of Directors, Washington Legal Clinic for the Homeless) Bar Associations; American Law Institute. Fellow, American College of Trial Lawyers. ***REPORTED CASES:*** In Re Humana, Inc. Managed Care Litigation, S.D. Fla, CA 00-1334, MDL No. 1334 (pending) (client: Prudential Insurance Company of America); Recupito v. Prudential Securities, Inc., et al, 112 F. Supp. 2d 448 (D. Md 2000) (client: Arthur Andersen LLP); Georgine v. Amchem Products, 157 F.R.D. 246, rev'd 83 F2d 610 (3d Cir. 1996), aff'd Amchem v. Windsor, 521 US 591 (1997) (client: 20 CCR companies). ***PRACTICE AREAS:*** Complex Litigation; Class Actions; Products Liability; Toxic Torts; Legal Malpractice; Accountants Malpractice; Insurance; Criminal Defense. ***Email:*** jaldock@sheagardner.com

WILLIAM S. MOORE, born Washington, D.C., November 5, 1944; admitted to bar, 1972, District of Columbia; 1977, Maryland. *Education:* University of Illinois (B.A., 1966); University of Michigan (J.D., 1969). Order of the Coif; Phi Beta Kappa. Note and Comment Editor, 1968-1969, Michigan Law Review. Author: *The Estate Plan Book*, American Institute of Economic Research, 2000; "How to Produce Savings in the Administration of an Estate," American Institute of Economic Research, 1999. Law Clerk, Judge Edward A. Tamm, U.S. Court of Appeals, District of Columbia Circuit, 1970-1971. *Member:* The District of Columbia Bar; Bar Association of the District of Columbia; Maryland State Bar Association. ***PRACTICE AREAS:*** Estate Planning; Trusts and Estates; Litigation. ***Email:*** wmoore@sheagardner.com

JOHN TOWNSEND RICH, born Lansing, Michigan, March 10, 1943; admitted to bar, 1970, New York; 1972, District of Columbia. *Education:* Harvard University (A.B., 1965); Yale University (LL.B., 1969); University College, Oxford, England, 1969-1970. Phi Beta Kappa; Order of the Coif. Editor-in-Chief, Yale Law Journal, 1968-1969. Law Clerk: Chief Judge David L. Bazelon, U.S. Court of Appeals, District of Columbia Circuit, 1970-1971; Justice Harry A. Blackmun, U.S. Supreme Court, 1971-1972. Adjunct Professor, Georgetown University Law Center, 1972-1975. Special Master, U.S. District Court, Northern District of Texas, 1985-1988. Associate Independent Counsel, 1989-1990. *Member:* The District of Columbia Bar (Co-Chairperson, Publications Committee, 1989-1991; Secretary, 1984-1985; Member, Steering Com-

(This Listing Continued)

mittee, Division IV, 1983-1984; Co-Chairperson, Division IV Court Rules Committee, 1981-1983; Co-Chairperson, D.C. Affairs Division, 1976-1978); Bar Association of the District of Columbia; American Bar Association (Member, Sections on: Antitrust Law; International Law; Labor and Employment Law; Litigation; Natural Resources, Energy and Environmental Law); American Society of International Law; Washington Council of Lawyers. ***PRACTICE AREAS:*** Civil Litigation; Appeals; Administrative Law; Antitrust; Transportation. ***Email:*** jrich@sheagardner.com

JAMES R. BIEKE, born Detroit, Michigan, September 7, 1945; admitted to bar, 1973, District of Columbia. *Education:* Sacred Heart Seminary (B.A., 1967); University of Michigan (M.A., 1970; J.D., 1970); New York University (LL.M., 1971). Order of the Coif. Editor-in-Chief, Michigan Law Review, 1969-1970. Law Clerk: Judge J. Edward Lumbard, U.S. Court of Appeals, Second Circuit, 1970-1971; Justice John M. Harlan, U.S. Supreme Court, 1971; Justice Potter Stewart, U.S. Supreme Court, 1972-1973. *Member:* The District of Columbia Bar. ***PRACTICE AREAS:*** Environmental Law; Natural Resources Law. ***Email:*** jbieke@sheagardner.com

WILLIAM F. SHEEHAN, born Baltimore, Maryland, March 11, 1947; admitted to bar, 1973, District of Columbia. *Education:* Yale University (B.A., 1968); University of Pennsylvania (J.D., 1971). Editor-in-Chief, University of Pennsylvania Law Review, 1970-1971. Co-Author: with Celestine McConville, "FIRREA's Cross Guarantee Provision, Solvent Banks, and the Fifth Amendment," The Banking Law Journal, June 1995; with Benjamin Boley and Stephen Hadley, "Discovery of Computerized Litigation Support Systems in Federal Court," 72 Complex Crimes Journal, 1991. Law Clerk, Judge J. Edward Lumbard, U.S. Court of Appeals, Second Circuit, 1971-1972. Assistant to the Solicitor General, Department of Justice, 1975-1978. Deputy General Counsel, Department of Defense, 1995-1997. *Member:* The District of Columbia Bar. ***PRACTICE AREAS:*** Complex Business Litigation; Mass Torts; Appellate Practice. ***Email:*** wsheehan@sheagardner.com

R. JAMES WOOLSEY, born Tulsa, Oklahoma, September 21, 1941; admitted to bar, 1969, California; 1970, District of Columbia. *Education:* Stanford University (B.A., 1963); Oxford University, Oxford, England (M.A., 1965); Yale University (LL.B., 1968). Phi Beta Kappa. Rhodes Scholar. Managing Editor, Yale Law Journal, 1967-1968. Adviser on U.S. Delegation to U.S./USSR Strategic Arms Limitation Talks, 1969-1970. General Counsel, U.S. Senate Committee on Armed Services, 1970-1973. Under Secretary of the Navy, 1977-1979. Delegate at Large, U.S.-USSR Nuclear and Space Arms Talks, 1983-1986. Ambassador and U.S. Representative to Negotiation on Conventional Armed Forces in Europe (CFE), 1989-1991. Director of Central Intelligence, 1993-1995. Member: President's Commission on Strategic Forces (Scowcroft Commission), 1983; President's Blue Ribbon Commission on Defense Management (Packard Commission), 1985-1986; President's Commission on Federal Ethics Law Reform (Wilkey Commission), 1989. Regent, The Smithsonian Institution, 1989-1993. Trustee: Stanford University, 1972-1974. *Member:* The District of Columbia Bar. ***PRACTICE AREAS:*** International Arbitration; Mediation; Commercial Law. ***Email:*** rwoolsey@sheagardner.com

FREDERICK C. SCHAFRICK, born Detroit, Michigan, September 20, 1948; admitted to bar, 1973, District of Columbia. *Education:* University of Michigan (A.B., 1970; J.D., 1973). Phi Beta Kappa; Order of the Coif. Administrative Editor, Michigan Law Review, 1972-1973. Author: "Product Liability Suits and Regulated Products," 32 Tort & Ins L 833, 1997. Law Clerk, Judge J. Edward Lumbard, U.S. Court of Appeals, Second Circuit, 1973-1974. *Member:* The District of Columbia Bar; American Bar Association; Defense Research Institute. ***PRACTICE AREAS:*** Appellate Practice; Aviation; Product Liability; Administrative. ***Email:*** fschafrick@sheagardner.com

DAVID B. COOK, born Washington, D.C., December 28, 1946; admitted to bar, 1972, District of Columbia. *Education:* Princeton University (A.B., 1968); Yale University (J.D., 1971). Phi Beta Kappa. Note and Comment Editor, Yale Law Journal, 1970-1971. Law Clerk, Judge Carl McGowan, U.S. Court of Appeals, District of Columbia Circuit, 1971-1972. Attorney, Office of General Counsel, Council on Environmental Quality, 1972-1975 (On detail from JAGC, USNR). Member, U.S. Delegation to United Nations Law of the Sea Conference, 1973-1975. *Member:* The District of Columbia Bar. ***PRACTICE AREAS:*** Transportation Regulation; Administrative; Civil Litigation. ***Email:*** dcook@sheagardner.com

FRANKLIN D. KRAMER, born Liberty, New York, November 13, 1945; admitted to bar, 1971, New York; 1972, District of Columbia; 1975, U.S. Supreme Court. *Education:* Yale University (B.A., 1967); Harvard University (J.D., 1971). Executive Editor, Harvard Law Review, 1970-1971. Law Clerk, Honorable Judge J. Edward Lumbard, U.S. Court of Appeals, Second Circuit, 1971-1972. Special Assistant to the Assistant Secretary of Defense for International Security Affairs, 1977-1979. Principal Deputy Assistant Secretary of Defense for International Security Affairs, 1979-1981. Deputy Assistant Secretary of Defense for NATO/Europe, 1996. Assistant Secretary of Defense for International Security Affairs, 1996-2001. President, World Affairs Council of Washington, D.C., 1992—. Member, Panel of Arbitrators, (Commercial), American Arbitration Association. *Member:* The District of Columbia Bar; American Bar Association (Chairman, Committee on Arms Control and Disar-

(This Listing Continued)

mament, 1984-1985) ; International Institute for Strategic Studies. ***PRACTICE AREAS:*** Corporate Law; International Trade and Transactions; Government Contracts; Commercial Law. ***Email:*** fkramer@sheagardner.com

PATRICK M. HANLON, born Akron, Ohio, August 20, 1946; admitted to bar, 1978, District of Columbia; 1983, Virginia. *Education:* University of Chicago (A.B., 1967); Harvard University (Ph.D., 1974); Harvard Law School (J.D., 1976). Phi Beta Kappa. Article Editor, Harvard Law Review, 1975-1976. Law Clerk, Chief Judge Irving R. Kaufman, U.S. Court of Appeals, Second Circuit, 1976-1977. Fairfax County (Virginia) Planning Commissioner, 1987-1995. Board Member; Northern Virginia Community College Educational Foundation, 1996—; United States Association for the UN High Commissions for Refugees, 2000—. *Member:* The District of Columbia Bar; Virginia State Bar; American Bar Association (Member, Sections on: Natural Resources Law; Litigation; Tort and Insurance Law; International Law). ***PRACTICE AREAS:*** Environmental; Toxic Torts; Legislative Practice; Civil Litigation; International. ***Email:*** phanlon@sheagardner.com

TIMOTHY K. SHUBA, born Aurora, Illinois, September 24, 1949; admitted to bar, 1977, Pennsylvania; 1979, District of Columbia. *Education:* Davidson College (A.B., 1971); Princeton Theological Seminary (M.Div., 1974); University of Pennsylvania (J.D., 1977). Phi Beta Kappa; Order of the Coif. Executive Editor, University of Pennsylvania Law Review, 1976-1977. Law Clerk, Judge Edward R. Becker, U.S. District Court, Eastern District of Pennsylvania, 1977-1978. *Member:* The District of Columbia Bar; Pennsylvania and Federal Energy Bar Associations. ***PRACTICE AREAS:*** Energy Law; Commercial Law. ***Email:*** tshuba@sheagardner.com

MICHAEL S. GIANNOTTO, born Newark, New Jersey, June 14, 1953; admitted to bar, 1979, District of Columbia and New Jersey. *Education:* University of Pennsylvania (B.A., summa cum laude, 1975); Harvard University (J.D., magna cum laude, 1978). Phi Beta Kappa. Senior Editor, Harvard Law Review, 1976-1978. Co-Author: Giannotto and Katz, "EPA's Developing Strategy for Increased Regulation and Oversight of the Hardrock Mining Industry," 43 Rocky Mtn. Mineral Law Inst., Chapter 14, 1997. Author: "The Uncertain Effects of Environmental Justice on the Mining Industry," 1999 Mining Lawyers Conference (National Mining Association 1999). Co-Author: Giannotto and Mikula, "Environmental Justice and the Mining and Energy Industries," 21 Energy and Min. L. Inst., Chapter 4, 2001; Giannotto and Ross, "New 3809 Requirements Relating to Financial Guarantees, Inspection, Enforcement and Appeals," in Review and Analysis of the New BLM Surface Management (Section 3809) Regulations, Rocky Mountain Mineral Law Foundation, Mineral Law Series, Vol. 2001, No. 1, 2001. Law Clerk, Justice Morris Pashman, New Jersey Supreme Court, 1978-1979. Member: 1997 Panel of Outside Experts Investigating Water Quality Program of the Commonwealth of Virginia's Department of Environmental Quality. *Member:* The District of Columbia Bar; American Bar Association; Rocky Mountain Mineral Law Foundation. ***REPORTED CASES:*** Harmon Industries, Inc. v. Browner, 191 F.3d 394 (8th Cir. 1998); Johnson Controls World Services v. United States, Nos. 98-626C and 99-73C, Fed. C1._(Court Fed. Claims Jan. 26, 2001); Newmont Mining Corporation v. Babbitt, No. 01-CV-00023 (D.D.C. filed January 2001). ***PRACTICE AREAS:*** Environmental Law; Environmental Litigation; Complex Insurance Litigation; Products Liability Litigation; Government Contracts Litigation. ***Email:*** mgiannotto@sheagardner.com

JEFFREY C. MARTIN, born Columbus, Ohio, December 5, 1953; admitted to bar, 1979, Indiana; 1981, District of Columbia. *Education:* Indiana University (A.B., 1975); University of Chicago (J.D., 1978). Phi Beta Kappa; Order of the Coif. Articles and Book Review Editor, University of Chicago Law Review, 1977-1978. Law Clerk, Judge Spottswood W. Robinson, III, U.S. Court of Appeals, District of Columbia Circuit, 1978-1979. Special Advisor, Secretary of Education, 1991. General Counsel, U.S. Department of Education, 1991-1992. Senior Vice President, Compliance and Government Affairs, Saks Incorporated, 1999—. *Member:* The District of Columbia Bar. ***PRACTICE AREAS:*** Insurance Law; Securities; Retail Law; Complex Litigation; Government Relations. ***Email:*** jmartin@sheagardner.com

WILLIAM R. HANLON, born Abington, Pennsylvania, February 10, 1953; admitted to bar, 1981, District of Columbia. *Education:* College of William and Mary (B.A., 1975); St. John's College, Oxford University, England (B.A., Honours, Jurisprudence, 1977); University of Pennsylvania (J.D., cum laude, 1979). Associate Editor, University of Pennsylvania Law Review, 1978-1979. Law Clerk, Judge Arlin M. Adams, U.S. Court of Appeals, Third Circuit, 1979-1980. *Member:* The District of Columbia Bar. ***PRACTICE AREAS:*** Complex Litigation; Class Actions; Mass Torts; Professional Malpractice; Products Liability. ***Email:*** whanlon@sheagardner.com

ELIZABETH RUNYAN GEISE, born St. Joseph, Michigan, October 24, 1955; admitted to bar, 1981, District of Columbia; 1991, Maryland. *Education:* University of Michigan (A.B., History, with high distinction and high honors in History, 1977); Harvard University (J.D., magna cum laude, 1980). Phi Beta Kappa. Note Editor, Harvard Law Review, 1979-1980. Law Clerk, Justice Benjamin Kaplan, Massachusetts Supreme Judicial Court, 1980-1981. *Member:*

(This Listing Continued)

SHEA & GARDNER, Washington—Continued

The District of Columbia Bar; Maryland State Bar Association. ***PRACTICE AREAS:*** Toxic Torts; Environmental; Insurance Coverage. ***Email:*** egeise@sheagardner.com

COLLETTE C. GOODMAN, born Boston, Massachusetts, March 14, 1944; admitted to bar, 1975, District of Columbia; 1983, New York. *Education:* Wellesley College (B.A., 1966); Massachusetts Institute of Technology (M.C.P., 1968); Harvard University (J.D., 1975). Phi Beta Kappa; Sigma Xi. Wellesley College Scholar. Attorney-Advisor, Office of Tax Policy, Treasury Department, 1978-1980. Special Assistant to the Assistant Secretary for Tax Policy, Treasury Department, 1980-1981. *Member:* The District of Columbia Bar; New York State, Federal (Member, Council of Officers, Section of Taxation) and American (Member, Section of Taxation) Bar Associations. ***PRACTICE AREAS:*** Domestic Taxation; International Taxation. ***Email:*** cgoodman@sheagardner.com

LAURA S. WERTHEIMER, born New York, N.Y., November 26, 1955; admitted to bar, 1982, New York and District of Columbia. *Education:* Yale University (B.A., 1977); Columbia University (J.D., 1981). Phi Beta Kappa. Editor, Columbia Law Review, 1980-1981. Court Law Clerk, U.S. Court of Appeals, District of Columbia Circuit, 1981-1982. Law Clerk, Chief Judge Spottswood W. Robinson III, U.S. Court of Appeals, District of Columbia Circuit, 1982-1983. *Member:* The District of Columbia Bar; New York State Bar Association. ***PRACTICE AREAS:*** Civil Practice; Legal Ethics and Professional Responsibility; Products Liability. ***Email:*** lwertheimer@sheagardner.com

RICHARD M. WYNER, born New York, N.Y., July 8, 1957; admitted to bar, 1983, District of Columbia. *Education:* Harvard University (B.A., 1979; J.D., magna cum laude, 1982). Editor, Harvard Law Review, 1980-1982. Law Clerk, Chief Judge Harrison L. Winter, U.S. Court of Appeals, Fourth Circuit, 1982-1983. Deputy General Counsel, U.S. Department of Education, 1991-1992. *Member:* The District of Columbia Bar. ***PRACTICE AREAS:*** Civil Litigation; Insurance Law; Environmental Law. ***Email:*** rwyner@sheagardner.com

THOMAS J. MIKULA, born Allentown, Pennsylvania, July 30, 1959; admitted to bar, 1984, Pennsylvania; 1986, District of Columbia. *Education:* University of Notre Dame (B.A., 1981); George Washington University (J.D., 1984). Order of the Coif. Senior Articles Editor, George Washington Law Review, 1983-1984. Law Clerk, Judge Phyllis A. Kravitch, U.S. Court of Appeals, Eleventh Circuit, 1984-1985. *Member:* The District of Columbia Bar; Pennsylvania Bar Association. ***PRACTICE AREAS:*** Products Liability; Insurance; Environmental Law; Labor Law. ***Email:*** tmikula@sheagardner.com

EUGENIA LANGAN, born Miami, Florida, December 10, 1952; admitted to bar, 1985, Pennsylvania; 1986, District of Columbia. *Education:* Columbia University (B.A., summa cum laude, 1981); University of Chicago (J.D., with honors, 1984). Phi Beta Kappa; Order of the Coif. Comment Editor, University of Chicago Law Review, 1983-1984. Contributing Editor: "The Railway Labor Act," BNA 1995. Member, Editorial Board, The Railway Labor Act, Cumulative Supplement, BNA 1997. Law Clerk, Judge James Hunter III, U.S. Court of Appeals, Third Circuit, 1984-1985. *Member:* The District of Columbia Bar; Pennsylvania and American (Member, Railway and Airlines Labor Law Committee, Section on Labor Law) Bar Associations. ***PRACTICE AREAS:*** Civil Litigation; Labor Law; Transportation Law. ***Email:*** elangan@sheagardner.com

NANCY B. STONE, born Wilmington, Delaware, May 16, 1959; admitted to bar, 1986, Pennsylvania; 1988, District of Columbia. *Education:* Swarthmore College (B.A., with distinction, 1981); University of Pennsylvania (J.D., magna cum laude, 1985). Phi Beta Kappa. Order of the Coif. Articles Editor, University of Pennsylvania Law Review, 1984-1985. Law Clerk, Judge Arlin M. Adams, U.S. Court of Appeals, Third Circuit, 1985-1986. *Member:* The District of Columbia Bar. ***PRACTICE AREAS:*** Civil Litigation; Products Liability. ***Email:*** nstone@sheagardner.com

CHRISTOPHER E. PALMER, born Minneapolis, Minnesota, July 18, 1960; admitted to bar, 1986, Minnesota; 1988, District of Columbia. *Education:* St. John's University (B.A., 1982); Georgetown University (J.D., 1986). Court Law Clerk, U.S. Court of Appeals, District of Columbia Circuit, 1986-1987. *Member:* The District of Columbia Bar; American Bar Association. ***PRACTICE AREAS:*** Securities; Insurance; Litigation. ***Email:*** cpalmer@sheagardner.com

MARK S. RAFFMAN, born Morristown, New Jersey, March 15, 1960; admitted to bar, 1986, Pennsylvania; 1988, District of Columbia. *Education:* Williams College (B.A., 1982); Harvard University (J.D., 1986). Member, Harvard Law Review, 1984-1986. Law Clerk, Judge Anthony M. Kennedy, U.S. Court of Appeals, Ninth Circuit, 1986-1987. International Commercial Arbitration Advocate. *Member:* The District of Columbia Bar; American Bar Association (Member, Section on: Litigation and Natural Resources, Energy and Environmental Law); U.S. Supreme Court Bar. ***PRACTICE AREAS:*** Civil Litigation; Arbitration; Environmental; Labor. ***Email:*** mraffman@sheagardner.com

VALERIE ELLEN ROSS, born Elmira, New York, February 14, 1966; admitted to bar, 1993, New York; 1995, District of Columbia. *Education:* Michigan State University (B.S., 1988); University of Chicago (J.D., 1991). Phi Beta Kappa. Law Clerk to the Honorable Ralph K. Winter, U.S. Court of Appeals, Second Circuit, 1991-1992. *Member:* The District of Columbia Bar; New York State Bar Association. ***PRACTICE AREAS:*** Civil Litigation; Environmental Law; Professional Practices. ***Email:*** vross@sheagardner.com

MICHAEL K. ISENMAN, born Dhaka, Bangladesh, April 12, 1966; admitted to bar, 1993, District of Columbia. *Education:* Harvard University (A.B., cum laude, 1988); University of Michigan (J.D., cum laude, 1991). Order of the Coif. Article Editor, Michigan Law Review, 1990-1991. Law Clerk, Judge David M. Ebel, U.S. Court of Appeals, Tenth Circuit, 1991-1992. *Member:* The District of Columbia Bar. ***PRACTICE AREAS:*** Securities; Litigation. ***Email:*** misenman@sheagardner.com

JOHN MOUSTAKAS, born Elizabeth, New Jersey, April 17, 1964; admitted to bar, 1992, Massachusetts; 1994, District of Columbia. *Education:* Boston University (B.A., magna cum laude, 1986); Cornell University (J.D., cum laude, 1989). Note Editor, Cornell Law Review, 1988-1989. Law Clerk: Judge Joseph L. Tauro, U.S. District Court, District of Massachusetts, 1989-1990; Judge Robert Boochever, U.S. Court of Appeals, Ninth Circuit, 1990-1991. *Member:* The District of Columbia Bar (Co-Chair, Courts, Lawyers and Administration of Justice Steering Committee, 1999-2001). ***REPORTED CASES:*** U.S. v. Moore, 97 F.2d 561 (D.C. Cir. 1996); U.S. v. Myles, 96 F.3d 491 (D.C. Cir. 1996); Thomas v. U.S., 685 A.2d 745 (D.C. 1996); Cole v. U.D., 678 A.2d 554 (D.C. 1996). ***PRACTICE AREAS:*** Complex Civil Litigation; White Collar Criminal Defense. ***Email:*** jmoustakas@sheagardner

SENIOR COUNSEL

WARNER W. GARDNER, born Richmond, Ind., September 25, 1909; admitted to bar, 1935, New York; 1947, District of Columbia. *Education:* Swarthmore College (A.B., 1930); Rutgers University (M.A., 1931); Columbia University (LL.B., 1934). Phi Beta Kappa. Law Clerk, Justice Harlan F. Stone, U.S. Supreme Court, 1934-1935; Office of Solicitor General of U.S., 1935-1941; Solicitor of U.S. Dept. of Labor, 1941-1942; Solicitor, U.S. Dept. of Interior, 1942-1943, 1945-1946; Assistant Secretary of the Interior, 1946-1947. Chairman, Informal Action Committee, Administrative Conference of the U.S., 1968-1976. *Member:* The District of Columbia Bar; American Bar Association; American Law Institute. ***Email:*** wgardner@sheagardner.com

LAWRENCE J. LATTO, born Brooklyn, N.Y., September 23, 1920; admitted to bar, 1948, New York; 1949, District of Columbia; 1954, Virginia. *Education:* College of the City of New York (B.S., 1941); Columbia University (LL.B., 1948). Editor-in-Chief, Columbia Law Review, 1948. Trustee, 1975-1995 and Chairman, 1980-1988, Center for Law & Social Policy. Author: "Federal Regulations of Insurance Contracts on Financial Services Revolution," Irwin Prof. Publishers, 1996. *Member:* The District of Columbia Bar (Chairman, Board on Professional Responsibility, 1979-1982); Virginia State Bar; American Bar Association; American Law Institute. ***PRACTICE AREAS:*** Securities Law; Professional Responsibility. ***Email:*** llatto@sheagardner.com

OF COUNSEL

RICHARD T. CONWAY, born Lake City, Florida, December 4, 1926; admitted to bar, 1952, Kentucky; 1954, District of Columbia. *Education:* Indiana University (A.B., 1950; LL.B., 1952). Phi Beta Kappa; Order of the Coif. Note Editor, Indiana Law Journal, 1951-1952. Law Clerk, Justice Sherman Minton, U.S. Supreme Court, 1953-1954. *Member:* The District of Columbia Bar; Kentucky State Bar Association. ***Email:*** rconway@sheagardner.com

WILLIAM H. DEMPSEY, born New Ulm, Minnesota, December 1, 1930; admitted to bar, 1955, District of Columbia. *Education:* University of Notre Dame (A.B., 1952); Yale University (LL.B., 1955). Notes and Comments Editor, Yale Law Journal. Law Clerk: Judge Charles Fahy, U.S. Court of Appeals, District of Columbia Circuit, 1955-1956; Chief Justice Earl Warren, U.S. Supreme Court, 1959-1960. Chairman, National Railway Labor Conference, 1972-1977. President, Association of American Railroads, 1977-1991. *Member:* The District of Columbia Bar; American Law Institute. [Capt., U.S. Army, 1956-1959]. ***Email:*** wdempsey@sheagardner.com

ANTHONY A. LAPHAM, born San Francisco, California, August 22, 1936; admitted to bar, 1962, District of Columbia; 1967. *Education:* Yale University (B.A., 1958); Georgetown University (J.D., 1961). Assistant U.S. Attorney, District of Columbia, 1962-1965. General Counsel, Central Intelligence Agency, 1976-1979. *Member:* The District of Columbia Bar. ***Email:*** alapham@sheagardner.com

ERIC C. JEFFREY, born New York, N.Y., August 26, 1953; admitted to bar, 1978, District of Columbia; 1979, New Jersey. *Education:* Cornell University (B.A., 1975); University of Pennsylvania Law School (J.D., 1978). Order of the Coif; Phi Beta Kappa; Pi Mu Epsilon. Editor, University of Pennsylvania Law Review, 1977-1978. Law Clerk, Justice Morris Pashman, Supreme Court of New Jersey, 1978-1979. *Member:* The District of Columbia Bar; New Jersey State Bar Association. ***Email:*** ejeffrey@sheagardner.com

(This Listing Continued)

ASSOCIATES

HEATHER H. ANDERSON, born Washington, D.C., November 16, 1967; admitted to bar, 1995, Virginia; 1997, District of Columbia. *Education:* Yale University (B.A., 1989); University of Virginia (J.D., 1993). Order of the Coif. Law Clerk to the Honorable Mary M. Schroeder, U.S. Court of Appeals, Ninth Circuit, 1993-1994. ***Email:*** handerson@sheagardner.com

REENA N. GLAZER, born Englewood, New Jersey, November 19, 1969; admitted to bar, 1995, Georgia; 1996, District of Columbia. *Education:* Barnard College (B.A., magna cum laude, 1990); The Jewish Theological Seminary of America (B.A., with honors and distinction, 1991); Duke University (J.D., with high honors, 1994). Phi Beta Kappa; Order of the Coif. Editor-in-Chief, Duke Law Journal, 1993-1994. Law Clerk, Judge Gerald Bard Tjoflat, U.S. Court of Appeals, Eleventh Circuit, 1994-1995. *Member:* The District of Columbia Bar; State Bar of Georgia. ***Email:*** rglazer@sheagardner.com

DONALD J. MUNRO, born Baltimore, Maryland, January 12, 1969; admitted to bar, 1996, Maryland; 1997, District of Columbia. *Education:* Johns Hopkins University (B.A., 1990); University of Virginia (J.D., 1994). Phi Beta Kappa; Order of the Coif. Articles Editor, University of Virginia Law Review. Author: "The Continuing Evolution of Affirmative Action Under Title VII: New Directions After the Civil Rights Act of 1991," 81 Virginia Law Review 565, 1995; "Draft Rules of Procedure and Evidence for the International Criminal Court," ABA Working Group, Section of International Law, 1999. Law Clerk to Judge J. Harvie Wilkinson, U.S. Court of Appeals, Fourth Circuit, 1994-1995. *Member:* Commercial Bar of England. ***Email:*** dmunro@sheagardner.com

HOWARD R. RUBIN, born Fort Lauderdale, Florida, December 18, 1969; admitted to bar, 1996, Maryland; 1997, District of Columbia and U.S. Court of Appeals, Fourth Circuit; 1999, U.S. Court of Federal Claims; 2001, U.S. Court of Appeals for the District of Columbia Circuit. *Education:* University of Miami (B.A., summa cum laude, 1991); Duke University (J.D., with high honors, 1994). Phi Beta Kappa; Order of the Coif. Co-Author: with J. Edmond, "When Talk Isn't Cheap: Scrutinizing Fiduciaries' Communications to ERISA Plan Participants," Journal of Pension Planning and Compliance, Summer 1997. Law Clerk, Chief Judge Sam J. Ervin, III, U.S. Court of Appeals, Fourth Circuit, 1994-1995. ***Email:*** hrubin@sheagardner.com

TIMOTHY G. LYNCH, born Binghamton, New York, November 17, 1967; admitted to bar, 1997, New York and District of Columbia; U.S. District Court, District of Maryland; U.S. Court of Appeals, Sixth Circuit and District of Columbia Circuit. *Education:* University of Rochester (B.A., 1990); Georgetown University Law Center (J.D., cum laude, 1995). Editor-in-Chief, Georgetown Law Journal, 1994-1995. Law Clerk, Judge Cornelia G. Kennedy, U.S. Court of Appeals, Sixth Circuit, 1995-1996. Legislative Assistant to Congressman John J. LaFalce, 1990-1992. ***Email:*** tlynch@sheagardner.com

MATTHEW M. HOFFMAN, born New York, N.Y., March 21, 1969; admitted to bar, 1996, New York; 1998, District of Columbia. *Education:* Harvard University (A.B., 1991); Yale University (J.D., 1995). Author: "The Illegitimate President: Minority Vote Dilution and the Electoral College," 105 Yale L.J., 935, 1996. Law Clerk to: the Honorable Allyne R. Ross, U.S. District Court, Eastern District of New York, 1995-1996: the Honorable Judith W. Rogers, U.S. Court of Appeals, District of Columbia Circuit, 1996-1997. ***Email:*** mhoffman@sheagardner.com

JAMES CHADWICK OPPENHEIMER, born Washington, D.C., June 10, 1968; admitted to bar, 1997, Maryland; 1998, District of Columbia. *Education:* Trinity College (B.A., 1990); University of Chicago (J.D., with honors, 1997). ***Email:*** joppenheimer@sheagardner.com

JEFFREY M. KLEIN, born Detroit, Michigan, November 2, 1971; admitted to bar, 1997, Maryland; 1999, District of Columbia. *Education:* Yale University (B.A., cum laude with distinction, 1993); Harvard Law School (J.D., magna cum laude, 1997). Notes Editor, Harvard Law Review, 1996-1997. Law Clerk, Judge Paul V. Niemeyer, U.S. Court of Appeals, Fourth Circuit. ***Email:*** jklein@sheagardner.com

CHRISTOPHER L. SAGERS, born Maquoketa, Iowa, March 25, 1970; admitted to bar, 1998, New York and District of Columbia. *Education:* University of Iowa (B.A., 1992); University of Michigan (J.D., 1997). Order of the Coif. Executive Editor, Michigan Law Review. Author: "Waiting With Brother Thomas," 46 U.C.L.A. L.Rev. 461 (1998); Book Review, "Postmodern Legal Movements, by Gary Minda," 95 Mich. L.Rev. 1927 (1997); Note, "An Implied Cause of Action Under the Real Estate Settlement Procedures Act," 95 Mich. L.Rev. 1381 (1997); Note, "Due Process Review Under the Railway Labor Act," 94 Mich. L.Rev. 466 (1995). ***Email:*** csagers@sheagardner.com

JILL ILAN BERGER INBAR, born Philadelphia, Pennsylvania, April 17, 1969; admitted to bar, 1997, New York; 1998, District of Columbia. *Education:* Cornell University (B.A., 1991); Benjamin N. Cardozo School of Law (J.D., cum laude, 1996). Notes Editor, Cardozo Law Review, 1995-1996. ***Email:*** jinbar@sheagardner.com

M. DAVID DOBBINS, born St. Joseph, Missouri, November 18, 1970; admitted to bar, 1998, District of Columbia and Missouri. *Education:* University of Missouri (B.A., cum laude, 1993); University of Michigan (J.D., magna cum laude, 1996). Order of the Coif. Articles Editor, Michigan Law Review, 1995-1996. Law Clerk, Chief Judge J. Harvie Wilkinson III, U.S. Court of Appeals, Fourth Circuit, 1996-1997. Author: Note, "Computer Bulletin Board Operator Liability for Users Infringing Acts," 94 Univ. of Mich. L.Rev. 217, October 1995. ***Email:*** ddobbins@sheagardner.com

LISA M. HARRISON, born Providence, Rhode Island, September 18, 1972; admitted to bar, 1998, Michigan; 1999, Massachusetts; 2000, District of Columbia. *Education:* Williams College (B.A., 1993); Harvard University (J.D., 1997). Phi Beta Kappa. Law Clerk to: Justice Margaret H. Marshall, Massachusetts Supreme Judicial Court, 1997-1998; the Honorable Henry H. Kennedy, Jr., U.S. District Court, District of Columbia, 1998-1999. ***LANGUAGES:*** Italian and Spanish. ***Email:*** lharrison@sheagardner.com

ADAM MICHAEL CHUD, born Philadelphia, Pennsylvania, August 16, 1972; admitted to bar, 2000, District of Columbia and New York. *Education:* American University (B.A., cum laude, 1994); Cornell University (M.P.S., 1997; J.D., cum laude, 1999). Senior Note Editor, Cornell University Law Review. Author: Note, "In Defense of the Government Attorney - Client Privilege," 84 Cornell Law Review; "Six-Member Juries: Does Size Really Matter?" 67 Tennessee Law Review. ***Email:*** achud@sheagardner.com

MICHELE L. SVONKIN, born Hartford, Connecticut, January 24, 1971; admitted to bar, 1999, Maryland; 2000, District of Columbia. *Education:* Brandeis University (B.A., magna cum laude, 1993); Cornell Law School (J.D., cum laude, 1998). Law Clerk to the Honorable Ronald Lee Gilman, U.S. Court of Appeals, Sixth Circuit, Memphis, Tennessee, 1998-1999. Lead Note Editor, Cornell International Law Journal, 1997-1998. ***Email:*** msvonkin@sheagardner.com

ELENA A. BAYLIS, born Portland, Oregon, June 21, 1972; admitted to bar, 1999, California; 2000, District of Columbia. *Education:* University of Oregon (B.A., summa cum laude, 1993); Yale University (J.D., 1998). Phi Beta Kappa. Law Clerk to the Honorable Mariana R. Pfaelzer, U.S. District Court, Central District of California, 1998-1999. *Member:* American Bar Association (Member, International Law Section); California Young Lawyers Association. ***Email:*** ebaylis@sheagardner.com

ROSS E. DAVIES, born June 21, 1962; admitted to bar, 1997, Ohio; 2000, District of Columbia. *Education:* Washington University (B.A., 1984); University of Chicago (J.D., 1997). Editor-in-Chief, University of Chicago Law Review, 1996-1997. Editor-in-Chief, The Green Bag, 1997—. Law Clerk, Hon. Diane P. Wood, U.S. Court of Appeals, 7th Circuit.

RICHARD A. PASCHAL, born Raleigh, North Carolina, January 13, 1965; admitted to bar, 2000, North Carolina and District of Columbia. *Education:* University of North Carolina (A.B., 1988); University of Virginia (M.A., 1992; J.D., 1998). Articles Editor, Virginia Law Review, 1997-1998. Author: "The Continuing Colloquy: Congress and the Finality of the Supreme Court," 8 J.L. and Pol. 143, 1991. Law Clerk, The Honorable James L. Dennis, U.S. Court of Appeals, Fifth Circuit, 1998-1999. ***Email:*** rpaschal@sheagardner.com

RICHARD L. MATHENY, born Columbia, South Carolina, October 18, 1969; admitted to bar, 2000, Maryland and District of Columbia. *Education:* Duke University (B.A., 1991); University of California, San Diego (M.A., 1996); University of Pennsylvania (J.D., 1999). Author: Comment, "In the Wake of the Flood: 'Like Products' and Cultural Products After the World Trade Organization's Decision in Canada: Certain Measures Concerning Periodicals," 147 U. Pa. L.Rev. 245, 1998. Law Clerk to the Honorable Robert E. Payne, U.S. District Judge, Eastern District of Virginia, 1999-2000. ***Email:*** rmatheny@sheagardner.com

(This Listing Continued)

SHEARMAN & STERLING

801 PENNSYLVANIA AVENUE, N.W., SUITE 900
WASHINGTON, D.C. 20004-2604
Telephone: (202) 508-8000
Fax: (202) 508-8100
URL: http://www.shearman.com

New York, N.Y. Office: 599 Lexington Avenue, New York, New York, 10022-6069. Telephone: (212) 848-4000. Telex: 667290. Num Lau. Fax: (212) 848-7179.

Abu Dhabi, United Arab Emirates Office: Butti Al Otaiba Building, 13th Floor, Suite 1301-1302, Sheikh Khalifa Street, P.O. Box 2948. Telephone: (971-2) 6274477. Fax: (971-2) 6268933.

Beijing, People's Republic of China Office: Suite 2318, China World Tower II, 1 Jianguomenwai Dajie, Chaoyang District, 100004 Beijing. Telephone: (86-10) 6505-3399. Fax: (86-10) 6505-1818.

Brussels, Belgium Office: Avenue des Artes 53, 1000 Bruxelles. Telephone: (32 02) 500-9800. Fax: (32 02) 500-9801.

Düsseldorf, Federal Republic of Germany Office: Breite Strasse 69, 40213 Düsseldorf. Telephone: (49 211) 178 88-0. Fax: (49 211) 178 88-88.

(This Listing Continued)

SHEARMAN & STERLING, Washington—Continued

Frankfurt, Federal Republic of Germany Office: Gervinusstrasse 17, 60322 Frankfurt am Main. Telephone: ++49 69 9711 1000. Fax: ++49 69 9711 1100.
Hong Kong Office: 12/F Gloucester Tower, The Landmark, 11 Pedder Street, Central. Telephone: (852) 2978-8000. Fax: (852) 2978-8099.
London, England Office: Broadgate West, 9 Appold Street, London EC2A 2AP. Telephone: 44-20-7655-5000. Fax: 44-20-7655-5500.
Mannheim, Federal Republic of Germany Office: Otto-Beck-Strasse 42, 68165 Mannheim. Telephone: 49 621-4257-0. Fax: 49 621-4257-280.
Menlo Park, California Office: 1080 Marsh Road, 94025-1022. Telephone: (650) 838-3600. Fax: (650) 838-3699.
Munich, Federal Republic of Germany Office: Oberanger 28, 80331 München. Telephone: (49 089) 23888-200. Fax: (49 089) 23888-201.
Paris, France Office: 114, avenue des Champs-Elysées, 75008. Telephone: (33-1) 53-89-7000. Fax: (33-1) 53-89-7070.
San Francisco, California Office: 555 California Street, 94104-1522. Telephone: (415) 616-1100. Fax: (415) 616-1199.
Singapore Office: Shearman & Sterling Stamford, 6 Battery Road #19-02. Singapore 049909. Telephone: (65) 230-3800. Fax: (65) 230-3899.
Tokyo, Japan Office: Fukoku Seimei Building, 5th Floor 2-2-2, Uchisaiwaicho, Chiyoda-ku, Tokyo 100-0011. Japan. Telephone: (81 3) 5251-1601. Fax: (81 3) 5251-1602.
Toronto, Ontario, Canada Office: Commerce Court West, Suite 4405, P.O. Box 247, M5L 1E8. Telephone: (416) 360-8484. Fax: (416) 360-2958.

General Practice.

FIRM PROFILE: Shearman & Sterling, founded in 1873, has more than 1000 lawyers in 15 offices throughout the world. The firm's practice encompasses most major areas of business law, including: Antitrust and Trade Regulation; Banking; Bankruptcy and Corporate Reorganization; Compensation and Benefits; Environmental; Finance (including Corporate Finance, Domestic Private Finance, Financial Institutions, International Private Finance and Project Finance); Individual Clients, Trusts and Estates; Insurance; Intellectual Property; International Trade and Government Relations; Litigation and Arbitration; Mergers and Acquisitions; Oil and Gas; Privatizations; Real Estate; and Tax. The Firm is also engaged in the practice of French, German and English law through its offices in France, Germany and England.

RESIDENT PARTNERS

THOMAS S. MARTIN, born New York, New York, 1946; admitted to bar, 1973, District of Columbia. *Education:* King's College (B.A., 1968); University of Chicago (J.D., 1972). U.S. Department of Justice - Special Assistant to Assistant Attorney General, Civil Division, 1975-1976, Assistant to Solicitor General, 1976-1978, Deputy Assistant Attorney General, Civil Division, 1978-1981, Acting Assistant Attorney General, Civil Division, 1981. Chairman, U.S. Court of Appeals, District of Columbia Circuit Committee on Admissions and Grievances, 1990—. Member: Advisory Committee on the Federal Rules of Civil Procedure, 1980-1984, American Bar Association. (Managing Partner). ***Email:*** tmartin@shearman.com

ABIGAIL ARMS, born New York, New York, 1947; admitted to bar, 1984, Connecticut; 1998, District of Columbia. *Education:* American University (B.A., 1970); New School for Social Research (M.A., 1972); Pace University School of Law (J.D., 1984). ***Email:*** aarms@shearman.com

LAURENCE M. BAMBINO, born New York, N.Y., 1955; admitted to bar, 1983, New York (Not admitted in District of Columbia). *Education:* Columbia University (B.A., 1978); Syracuse University (J.D., 1982); New York University School of Law (LL.M., Taxation, 1990). (Also at New York Office). ***Email:*** lbambino@shearman.com

ROGER J. BANEMAN, born New York, N.Y., 1951; admitted to bar, 1977, New York (Not admitted in District of Columbia). *Education:* Yale University (B.A., 1972); Harvard University (J.D., 1976). Attorney-Advisor, Office of Tax Legislative Counsel, Treasury Department, 1980-1982. Acting Associate Tax Legislative Counsel, 1982. ***Email:*** rbaneman@shearman.com

BARRY P. BARBASH, born Lawrence, Massachusetts, 1953; admitted to bar, 1978, Massachusetts; 1982, New York; 1997, District of Columbia. *Education:* Bowdoin College (A.B., summa cum laude, 1975); Cornell Law School (J.D., 1978). Phi Beta Kappa. Director, Division of Investment Management, U.S. Securities and Exchange Commission, 1993-1998. *Member:* District of Columbia Bar; New York State, Massachusetts and American Bar Associations. ***Email:*** bbarbash@shearman.com

ROBERT A. BERGQUIST, born Grafton, North Dakota, 1940; admitted to bar, 1964, Ohio; 1981, New York; 1994, District of Columbia. *Education:* University of North Dakota (B.A., 1960); University of Michigan (M.A., 1961); Harvard University (LL.B., 1964). Chairman, Corporate Tax Committee, Section on Taxation, American Bar Association, 1992-1993. ***Email:*** rbergquist@shearman.com

JONATHAN L. GREENBLATT, born New Britain, Connecticut, 1955; admitted to bar, 1981, New York; 1996, District of Columbia. *Education:* University of Connecticut (B.A., 1977); George Washington University (J.D., 1980). (Also at New York Office). ***Email:*** jgreenblatt@shearman.com

STEPHEN JAMES MARZEN, born Royal Oak, Michigan, 1960; admitted to bar, 1985, New York; 1988, District of Columbia. *Education:* University of Pittsburgh (B.A., summa cum laude, 1981); Harvard University (J.D., magna cum laude, 1984). Law Clerk to the Hon. Malcolm R. Wilkey, U.S. Court of Appeals for the District of Columbia Circuit, 1984-1985. Law Clerk to the Hon. John P. Stevens, U.S. Supreme Court, 1985-1986. Consultant, McKinsey & Co., Inc., 1986-1989. Assistant to the Solicitor General, U.S. Department of Justice, 1989-1991. ***Email:*** smarzen@shearman.com

R. CHARLES MILLER, born Savannah, Georgia, 1957; admitted to bar, 1986, Pennsylvania; 1989, District of Columbia. *Education:* Harvard University (B.A., cum laude, 1980); University of Pennsylvania (J.D., cum laude, 1985). Order of the Coif. Editor-in-Chief, University of Pennsylvania Law Review, 1984-1985. Author: Note, "Rendering Unto Caesar: Religious Publishers and the Public Benefit Rule," 134 U. Penn. L. Rev. 433, 1986. Law Clerk to Judge Spottswood W. Robinson, III, U.S. Court of Appeals, District of Columbia Circuit, 1986-1987. Law Clerk to Chief Justice William H. Rehnquist, U.S. Supreme Court, 1987-1988. Special Counsel, Office of General Counsel, Securities & Exchange Commission, 1992-1994. *Member:* District of Columbia Bar.

LINDA C. QUINN, born 1948; admitted to bar, 1973, New York and District of Columbia. *Education:* Mount Holyoke College (B.A.); Georgetown University (J.D.). (Also at New York Office). ***Email:*** lquinn@shearman.com

ROBERT A. RUDNICK, born Bronx, New York, 1948; admitted to bar, 1973, New York; 1975, U.S. Tax Court; 1984, District of Columbia. *Education:* Colby College (B.A., 1969); Cornell University (J.D., 1972). *Member:* The District of Columbia Bar. ***Email:*** rrudnick@shearman.com

MICHAEL BRADLEY SHULMAN, born Cleveland, Ohio, July 18, 1968; admitted to bar, 1994, New York; 1996, District of Columbia. *Education:* University of Chicago (B.A., 1990); Vanderbilt University (J.D., 1993); New York University (LL.M., 1997). Senior Articles Editor, Vanderbilt Law Review. **LANGUAGES:** Russian. ***Email:*** mshulman@shearman.com

FRANK R. STRONG, born Lawrence, Kansas, 1964; admitted to bar, 1990, Washington and Pennsylvania; 1991, District of Columbia; 1992, California. *Education:* Carleton College (B.A., 1986); Arizona State University (J.D., 1989); New York University (LL.M., 1990). Phi Beta Kappa; Order of the Coif. ***Email:*** fstrong@shearman.com

STEVEN C. SUNSHINE, born Buffalo, New York, 1959; admitted to bar, 1985, New York; 1996, District of Columbia. *Education:* Brown University (B.A., 1981); Boston College (J.D., 1984). U.S. Department of Justice, Deputy Assistant Attorney General in Charge of Merger Enforcement, Antitrust Division, 1993-1995. ***Email:*** ssunshine@shearman.com

B. JOHN WILLIAMS, JR., born 1949; admitted to bar, 1975, District of Columbia; 1976, Pennsylvania and U.S. Tax Court; 1977, U.S. Claims Court; 1984, U.S. Supreme Court. *Education:* George Washington University (B.A., 1971; J.D., 1974). Law Clerk to Hon. Bruce M. Forrester, U.S. Tax Court, 1974-1976. Special Assistant to IRS Chief Counsel, 1981-1983. Deputy Assistant Attorney General, Tax Division, Department of Justice, 1983-1984. Judge, U.S. Tax Court, 1985-1990. *Member:* American Law Institute. Fellow, American College of Tax Counsel. ***Email:*** bjwilliams@shearman.com

THOMAS B. WILNER, born Toronto, Canada, 1944; admitted to bar, 1969, Pennsylvania; 1971, New York; 1973, District of Columbia; 1975, U.S. Supreme Court; 1992, Tokyo, Japan. *Education:* Yale University (B.A., 1966); University of Pennsylvania (LL.B., 1969). Law Clerk to the Hon. William H. Hastie, Chief Judge, U.S. Court of Appeals for the Third Circuit, 1969-1970. ***Email:*** twilner@shearman.com

JEFFREY M. WINTON, born 1961; admitted to bar, 1985, District of Columbia. *Education:* Princeton University (A.B., 1982); Harvard University (J.D., 1985). ***Email:*** jwinton@shearman.com

OF COUNSEL

EDWARD BRANSILVER, born Fort Wayne, Indiana, 1927; admitted to bar, 1960, New York; 1988, District of Columbia. *Education:* University of Pennsylvania (B.S., 1951); Indiana University (M.B.A., 1952); University of Michigan (LL.B., 1959). General Counsel, Federal Deposit Insurance Corporation, 1973-1975. ***Email:*** ebransilver@shearman.com

COUNSEL

WENDY E. ACKERMAN, born 1962; admitted to bar, 1990, Pennsylvania; 1991, District of Columbia. *Education:* Barnard College (B.A.); University of Chicago (J.D.). ***Email:*** wackerman@shearman.com

(This Listing Continued)

KAREN HESS McMILLAN, born Washington, D.C., 1961; admitted to bar, 1987, Texas; 1989, District of Columbia. *Education:* College of William & Mary (B.A., 1983); University of Virginia (J.D., 1987). Phi Beta Kappa. ***Email:*** kmcmillan@shearman.com

EMANUEL D. STRAUSS, born New York, New York, April 21, 1960; admitted to bar, 1986, Massachusetts and New York; 1989, District of Columbia. *Education:* Cornell University (B.A., 1982; J.D., cum laude, 1985). Member, Cornell Law Review. *Member:* American Bar Association. ***PRACTICE AREAS:*** Corporate; Securities. ***Email:*** estrauss@shearman.com

ANTHONY A. VERTUNO, born Oak Park, Illinois, October 3, 1936; admitted to bar, 1961, Illinois; 1999, District of Columbia. *Education:* St. Mary's University of Minnesota (B.A., 1958); Northwestern University (J.D., 1961). Adjunct Professor, Georgetown University Law Center, 1994—. Member, U.S. Securities and Exchange Commission, 1968-1998. *Member:* The District of Columbia Bar; American Bar Association. ***PRACTICE AREAS:*** Securities; Financial Services Law.

JAMES F. WARREN, born Manaus, Brazil, October 12, 1956; admitted to bar, 1990, North Carolina; 1991, U.S. Tax Court; 1996, District of Columbia. *Education:* Cambridge University (B.A., M.A., 1978); Harvard Law School (J.D., magna cum laude, 1990). ***PRACTICE AREAS:*** Federal Income Tax. ***Email:*** jwarren@shearman.com

(For Biographical data of the New York partners, see Professional Biographies at New York, N.Y.).

SHER & BLACKWELL LLP

1850 M STREET, N.W., SUITE 900
WASHINGTON, D.C. 20036-5820
Telephone: 202-463-2500
Facsimile: 202-463-4950
URL: http://www.sherblackwell.com

Administrative, Antitrust, Commercial, Corporate, Environmental, Government Contracts, Government Relations, International, Legislative, Litigation, Marine Resources, Maritime, Telecommunications, Transportation.

MARK W. ATWOOD, born Lancaster, California, November 6, 1952; admitted to bar, 1979, California; 1983, District of Columbia. *Education:* Loyola College (A.B., magna cum laude, 1974); University of Southern California (J.D., 1978). Phi Alpha Delta. Author: "The Consequences of Airline Mergers," Civil Aeronautics Board, 1982. Trial Attorney, Civil Aeronautics Board, 1978-1981. Attorney-Advisor, Office of the General Counsel, Civil Aeronautics Board, 1981-1982. *Member:* District of Columbia Bar; State Bar of California; Inter-American Bar Association. **LANGUAGES:** Spanish. **TRANSACTIONS:** Member, U.S. Delegation, U.S. - Colombia and U.S. - Brazil Aviation Negotiation, 1996. ***PRACTICE AREAS:*** Transportation; Aviation; Administrative Law. ***Email:*** matwood@sherblackwell.com

ROBERT J. BLACKWELL, born New York, N.Y., February 26, 1925; admitted to bar, 1954, New York; 1977, District of Columbia. *Education:* Mohawk College; Syracuse University (B.S., magna cum laude, 1950); Harvard University (J.D., 1954). Assistant Secretary of Commerce for Maritime Affairs, 1972-1979. *Member:* The District of Columbia Bar; Maritime Administrative Bar Association; Society of Naval Architects and Marine Engineers. [With U.S. Navy, 1943-1946]. ***PRACTICE AREAS:*** Transportation; Government Relations.

JOHN W. BUTLER, born Richmond, Virginia, November 11, 1961; admitted to bar, 1991, Maryland; 1993, District of Columbia and U.S. District Court for the District of Columbia. *Education:* Colorado College (B.A., 1984); George Washington University (J.D., with honors, 1991). *Member:* The District of Columbia Bar. ***PRACTICE AREAS:*** Transportation; Telecommunications; Litigation. ***Email:*** jbutler@sherblackwell.com

EARL W. COMSTOCK, admitted to bar, 1996, Alaska (Not admitted in District of Columbia). *Education:* University of California (B.A., 1988); George Mason University School of Law (J.D., 1992). ***PRACTICE AREAS:*** Telecommunications; Government Relations; Legislative Practice; Marine Law; Environmental Law. ***Email:*** ecomstock@sherblackwell.com

MARC J. FINK, born New York, N.Y., March 19, 1947; admitted to bar, 1973, District of Columbia. *Education:* State University of New York (B.A., 1967); George Washington University (J.D., with honors, 1973). Law Clerk, Trial Division, U.S. Court of Claims, 1973-1974. Trial Attorney, Civil Division, U.S. Department of Justice, 1974-1977. *Member:* The District of Columbia Bar. ***PRACTICE AREAS:*** Transportation; Maritime Law; Antitrust; Government Relations. ***Email:*** mfink@sherblackwell.com

JEFFREY F. LAWRENCE, born Newark, New Jersey, February 3, 1952; admitted to bar, 1977, New Jersey; 1978, District of Columbia. *Education:* University of Pennsylvania (B.A., cum laude, 1973); Rutgers University (J.D., 1977). Staff Counsel, 1977-1978 and Legal Assistant to Commissioner, 1978-1979, U.S. Nuclear Regulatory Commission. *Member:* The District of Columbia Bar; Maritime Administrative Bar Association (President, 1991-1992). ***PRACTICE AREAS:*** Transportation; Maritime Law; International Law; Corporate Law; Commercial Law. ***Email:*** jlawrence@sherblackwell.com

ANNE E. MICKEY, born Washington, D.C., February 4, 1951; admitted to bar, 1976, District of Columbia; 1986, Maryland. *Education:* Smith College (B.A., 1973); George Washington University (J.D., with honors, 1976). Author: "Maritime Law and the World Trade in Forest Products," World Trade in Forest Products 2, Gerald F. Schrueder Edition, University of Washington Press, 1986. General Counsel's Office, Federal Maritime Commission, 1977-1980. *Member:* The District of Columbia Bar; Maryland State Bar; Maritime Administrative Bar Association (President, 1985-1986). ***PRACTICE AREAS:*** Transportation; Corporate Law; Commercial Law; Maritime Law. ***Email:*** amickey@sherblackwell.com

STANLEY O. SHER, born Milwaukee, Wisconsin, June 3, 1935; admitted to bar, 1959, Wisconsin; 1960, District of Columbia. *Education:* University of Wisconsin (B.S., 1956); Harvard Law School (LL.B., 1959). Phi Beta Kappa. Member, Billig, Sher and Jones, P.C., 1973-1986. President, Maritime Administrative Bar Association, 1977-1978. *Member:* The District of Columbia Bar. ***PRACTICE AREAS:*** Transportation; Litigation; Antitrust; Maritime Law. ***Email:*** ssher@sherblackwell.com

DAVID F. SMITH, born Amherst, Massachusetts, October 2, 1953; admitted to bar, 1981, District of Columbia. *Education:* Duke University (B.A., magna cum laude, 1975); George Washington University (J.D., with honors, 1981). Recipient, Jennie Hassler Walburn Prize in Civil Procedure. *Member:* The District of Columbia Bar. ***PRACTICE AREAS:*** Transportation; Litigation; Administrative Law; Maritime Law. ***Email:*** dsmith@sherblackwell.com

PAUL M. TSCHIRHART, born Detroit, Michigan, September 22, 1940; admitted to bar, 1968, Michigan; 1970, District of Columbia; 1979, Illinois; 1999, New Jersey. *Education:* University of Notre Dame (B.S., 1963); Wayne State University (J.D., 1968). Assistant U.S. Attorney, Washington, D.C., 1973-1976. Senior Vice President and General Counsel, The Hertz Corporation, 1986-1998. Senior Trial Attorney, United Airlines, 1977-1986. *Member:* State Bar of Michigan; The District of Columbia Bar. [U.S. Navy Reserve, Active Duty, 1963-1965; Capt., Retired]. ***PRACTICE AREAS:*** Administrative Law; Aviation Law; Corporate Law; Commercial Law; Litigation; Transportation. ***Email:*** ptschirhart@sherblackwell.com

---

WAYNE R. ROHDE, born Park Ridge, Illinois, July 7, 1962; admitted to bar, 1989, District of Columbia. *Education:* Lake Forest College (B.A., Magna Cum Laude, 1984); Middlebury College (M.A., 1985); Georgetown University (M.S., J.D., 1989). Phi Beta Kappa. *Member:* The District of Columbia Bar. ***PRACTICE AREAS:*** Transportation; Maritime Law; Administrative Law; Antitrust. ***Email:*** wrohde@sherblackwell.com

HEATHER SPRING, born Brockport, New York, June 21, 1971; admitted to bar, 1997, New York; 1998, District of Columbia. *Education:* State University of New York at Binghamton (B.A., 1993); Washington College of Law (J.D., magna cum laude, 1996). *Member:* New York State Bar Association. ***PRACTICE AREAS:*** Transportation; Maritime Law; Litigation; Administrative Law; Government Contracts. ***Email:*** hspring@sherblackwell.com

ANTILLA E. TROTTER, III, born St. Louis, Missouri, March 18, 1961; admitted to bar, 2001, District of Columbia. *Education:* Howard University (B.A., cum laude, 1987); Catholic University of America (J.D., 1997). Moot Court. Vice President, Entertainment Law Society, 1996-1997. Member, Federal Communications Bar Association, 1996-1997 and 2000-2001. Treasurer, National Black Law Student Association, 1994-1995. *Member:* Washington (Young Lawyers Section) and National Bar Associations. ***PRACTICE AREAS:*** Telecommunications Law; Government Relations; Health Care; Animal Welfare; Transportation; Maritime Law. ***Email:*** atrotter@sherblackwell.com

SARAH M. SHARMA, born New York, New York, November 23, 1973; admitted to bar, 2001, New York (Not admitted in District of Columbia). *Education:* American University (B.A., cum laude, 1995); Tulane Law School (J.D., 2000). Member: Moot Court Board, 1998-2000; Public Interest Law Foundation, 1997-2000. ***PRACTICE AREAS:*** Transportation; Maritime Law; Corporate Law; Commercial Law. ***Email:*** ssharma@sherblackwell.com

SHERMAN, DUNN, COHEN, LEIFER & YELLIG, P.C.

Established in 1947
SUITE 801, 1125 FIFTEENTH STREET, N.W.
WASHINGTON, D.C. 20005
Telephone: 202-785-9300
Fax: 202-775-1950
Email: shermandunn@shermandunn.com

Labor and Employment Law, Occupational Safety and Health Law, Pensions and Trusts.

(This Listing Continued)

SHERMAN, DUNN, COHEN, LEIFER & YELLIG, P.C., Washington—Continued

FIRM PROFILE: Sherman, Dunn, Cohen, Leifer & Yellig, P.C. has been in existence as a practitioner of union-side labor and employment law continuously since 1947. The Firm specializes in all areas of such a practice, and appears before courts and administrative agencies throughout the United States. The Firm supports the principles and goals of the organized labor movement in the U.S.

LOUIS SHERMAN (1912-1996).

THOMAS X. DUNN (1911-1991).

LAURENCE J. COHEN, born Washington, D.C., May 15, 1932; admitted to bar, 1959, District of Columbia; 1963, U.S. Supreme Court. *Education:* University of Pennsylvania (B.S., in Econ., 1954); Yale University (LL.B., 1959). Phi Alpha Delta. Author: "The NLRB and Section 10(k); A Study of the Reluctant Dragon." 14 CCH Labor Law Journal 905, 1963; "Two Years under Mallindrodt: A Review of the Board's Latest Craft Unit Policy," 20 CCH Labor Law Journal, 1969; "Labor and the Antitrust Laws: A New Look at a Recurring Issue," 22nd Annual Institute on Labor, the Southwestern Legal Foundation, 1975; "Labor Law and Antitrust Law: The Impact of *Connell Construction,*" New York University 32nd National Conference on Labor, 1979. Co-author: "Efforts to Apply the Federal Crime of Extortion to Labor-Related Violence," 72 Northwestern Journal of Criminal Law and Criminology 499, 1981; "The National Labor Relations Act Under Siege: A Labor View of the Reagan Board," 31st Annual Institute on Labor, The Southwestern Legal Foundation, 1985. Co-Editor, The Developing Labor Law, Bureau of National Affairs, 2nd Edition, 1983. Legal Assistant and Supervising Attorney, National Labor Relations Board, 1964-1967; Alternate Member, Chairman's Task Force on the National Labor Relations Board, 1976-1977. *Member:* The District of Columbia Bar; American Bar Association (Member, Labor and Employment Law Section; Co-Chairman, Committee on Development of Law Under NLRA, 1973-1976; Member of Council, 1976-1984; Section Chairman, 1985-1986); National Labor Relations Board Advisory Committee on Agency Procedure, 1994-1998. Fellow, College of Labor and Employment Lawyers. ***PRACTICE AREAS:*** Labor and Employment Law; Union Labor Law.

ELIHU I. LEIFER, born Brooklyn, New York, March 16, 1940; admitted to bar, 1965, District of Columbia; 1966, U.S. Court of Appeals, District of Columbia Circuit; 1970, U.S. Supreme Court. *Education:* Princeton University (A.B., 1961); Harvard University (LL.B., 1964). Attorney, Civil Rights Division, U.S. Department of Justice, 1964-1967. Member, Institutional Review Board, IBPAT Occupational Safety and Health Project, 1983-1986. *Member:* The District of Columbia Bar; American Bar Association (Member, Sections on: Labor and Employment Law; Litigation; Co-Chairman, Committee on Federal Service Labor-Management Relations Law, 1979-1982). Fellow, College of Labor and Employment Lawyers. ***PRACTICE AREAS:*** Labor and Employment Law; Union Labor Law. ***Email:*** leifer@shermandunn.com

TERRY R. YELLIG, born Pittsburgh, Pennsylvania, August 3, 1946; admitted to bar, 1973, Pennsylvania; 1978, District of Columbia. *Education:* American University (B.A., 1968); University of Pittsburgh (J.D., 1972). Co-author: "Efforts to Apply the Federal Crime of Extortion to Labor-Related Violence," 72 Northwestern Journal of Criminal Law and Criminology 499, 1981. Editor: "The Fair Labor Standards Act," Bureau of National Affairs, 1999. U.S. Department of Labor, Office of the Solicitor, 1972-1977. *Member:* The District of Columbia Bar; American Bar Association (Co-Chairman, Committee on Federal Labor Standards, Labor and Employment Law Section, 1980-1983, 1986-1997; Member: Sections on: Administrative Law; Public Contracts Law). ***PRACTICE AREAS:*** Labor and Employment Law; Union Labor Law. ***Email:*** yellig@shermandunn.com

RICHARD M. RESNICK, born New York, N.Y., May 23, 1951; admitted to bar, 1976, Maryland; 1977, District of Columbia; 1980, U.S. Supreme Court. *Education:* Cornell University (B.S., 1973); George Washington University (J.D., 1976). Assistant Editor, The Developing Labor Law. Author: "Project Agreements in the Construction Industry," Fourth Annual Labor and Employment Law Institute, School of Law, University of Louisville, 1988. Administrator, Plan for the Settlement of Jurisdictional Disputes in the Construction Industry, 1992—. *Member:* The District of Columbia Bar; American Bar Association (Member, Section on Labor and Employment Law). Fellow, College of Labor and Employment Lawyers. ***PRACTICE AREAS:*** Labor and Employment Law; Union Labor Law. ***Email:*** resnick@shermandunn.com

ROBERT D. KURNICK, born Philadelphia, Pennsylvania, January 3, 1952; admitted to bar, 1976, District of Columbia; 1980, U.S. Supreme Court. *Education:* University of Pennsylvania (B.A., 1973); George Washington University (J.D., 1976). Notes Editor, George Washington Law Review, 1975-1976. Assistant Editor, The Developing Labor Law, Bureau of National Affairs, 2nd Edition, 1983. *Member:* The District of Columbia Bar. ***PRACTICE AREAS:*** Labor and Employment Law; Union Labor Law. ***Email:*** kurnick@shermandunn.com

VICTORIA L. BOR, born Washington, D.C., April 10, 1952; admitted to bar, 1980, District of Columbia. *Education:* University of Wisconsin (B.A., 1974); Columbia Law School (J.D., 1979). Co-Editor-In-Chief, Cumulative Supplement, OSHA Treatise (BNA), 1987-1993. Author: "Exclusionary Employment Practices in Hazardous Industries: Protection or Discrimination?" 5 Columbia Journal of Environmental Law 97, 1978; "Fetal Protection Policies and Title VII," 2 The Labor Lawyer 683, 1986. Co-author: "The National Labor Relations Act Under Siege: A Labor View of the Reagan Board," 31st Annual Institute of Labor, the Southwestern Legal Foundation, 1985. Law Clerk to Hon. John P. Fullam, U.S. District Court, Eastern District of Pennsylvania, 1979-1980. *Member:* The District of Columbia Bar; American Bar Association (Member, Section on Labor and Employment Law; Co-Chair, Committee on Occupational Safety and Health, 1989-1992). Member of Section Council, 1994-2002. ***PRACTICE AREAS:*** Labor and Employment Law; Union Labor Law. ***Email:*** bor@shermandunn.com

NORA H. LEYLAND, born Troy, New York, December 30, 1952; admitted to bar, 1989, Pennsylvania; 1991, District of Columbia. *Education:* Boston University (B.A., with distinction, 1976) Phi Beta Kappa; American University of Washington College of Law (J.D., cum laude, 1988). Staff Member, American University Law Review, 1987-1988. Member, Washington College of Law Honor Society. *Member:* The District of Columbia Bar; American Bar Association; National Lawyers Guild. ***PRACTICE AREAS:*** Labor and Employment Law; Union Labor Law. ***Email:*** leyland@shermandunn.com

MARTIN J. CRANE, born Wyandotte, Michigan, September 18, 1963; admitted to bar, 1990, Maryland; 1993, District of Columbia. *Education:* Eastern Michigan University (B.S., cum laude, 1986); George Washington University (J.D., cum laude, 1990). Notes Editor, George Washington Law Review, 1989-1990. Author: "Equal Access in NLRB Elections: Determining The Voting Eligibility of Economic Strikers," 58 George Washington Law Review 549, 1990. Contributing Author: "Employee and Union Member Guide to Labor Law"; Contributing Editor: "Discipline & Discharge in Arbitration," Bureau of National Affairs, 1998. *Member:* American Bar Association (Member, Section on Labor and Employment Law. ***PRACTICE AREAS:*** Labor and Employment Law; Union Labor Law. ***Email:*** crane@shermandunn.com

SUE D. GUNTER, born Tuscaloosa, Alabama, September 2, 1954; admitted to bar, 1979, Georgia; 1983, District of Columbia. *Education:* Emory University (B.S.,1975; J.D., with distinction, 1979). Phi Beta Kappa. Order of the Coif. Director-in-Chief, Moot Court Society. Order of the Barristers. Attorney, National Labor Relations Board, 1979-1988. Senior Trial Attorney, U.S. Department of Justice, 1988-1991. *Member:* District of Columbia Bar; American Bar Association (Member, Sections on: Labor and Employment; Litigation). ***PRACTICE AREAS:*** Labor and Employment Law; Union Labor Law. ***Email:*** gunter@shermandunn.com

JONATHAN D. NEWMAN, born Manhasset, New York, September 6, 1967; admitted to bar, 1994, Ohio; 1997, District of Columbia. *Education:* Hamilton College (B.A., 1989); University of Maryland (J.D., with honors, 1994). Order of the Coif. Notes and Comments Editor, Maryland Journal of Contemporary Legal Issues, 1993-1994. Author: "Lechmere, Inc. v. NLRB: Plain Meaning and the Supreme Administrative Agency," 4 Md. J. Comtemp. Legal Issues 297, 1993. *Member:* American Bar Association (Member, Sections on: Labor and Employment Law; Litigation). ***PRACTICE AREAS:*** Labor and Employment Law; Union Labor Law. ***Email:*** newman@shermandunn.com

SHERMAN, MEEHAN, CURTIN & AIN

A PROFESSIONAL CORPORATION

Established in 1968

SUITE 600, 1900 M STREET, NW

WASHINGTON, D.C. 20036-3565

Telephone: 202-530-3300
Facsimile: 202-530-4411
Email: info@smcalaw.com
URL: http://www.smcalaw.com

FIRM PROFILE: Sherman, Meehan, Curtin & Ain was formed in 1968 and engages in a full-service general practice, including general business, trusts and estates, corporate and individual taxation, domestic relations, real estate, antitrust, employee benefits, and commercial, personal injury and aviation litigation.

PETER R. SHERMAN, born South Bend, Indiana, April 14, 1939; admitted to bar, 1965, District of Columbia; 1968, U.S. Supreme Court. *Education:* Indiana University (B.S., with distinction, 1961); Georgetown University (LL.B., 1964; LL.M., 1966). Member, Board of Editors, Georgetown Law Journal, 1963-1964. Law Clerk to Honorable L. W. Youngdahl, U.S. District Court, District of Columbia, 1965-1966. Recipient, E. Barrett Prettyman Fellowship, 1965-1966. Adjunct Professor of Law, Family Law, Trial Practice, The American University Washington College of Law, 1977-1980; 1993—. Member, District of Columbia Superior Court Rules Revision Committee, 1991-1996. Mem-

(This Listing Continued)

ber, Task Force on Race and Ethnic Bias in The District of Columbia Courts, 1990-1991. Fellow, American Academy of Matrimonial Lawyers. ***PRACTICE AREAS:*** Family Law. ***Email:*** psherman@smcalaw.com

MICHAEL F. CURTIN, born Hackensack, New Jersey, December 9, 1940; admitted to bar, 1966, District of Columbia; 1974, U.S. Supreme Court. *Education:* Le Moyne College (B.S., 1962); Catholic University of America (J.D., 1965). Author: "Probate Practice in the District of Columbia," 1981 Supplement to Mersch. Adjunct Professor of Law, Columbus School of Law, Catholic University of America, 1973-1980. Lecturer, Georgetown University Law Center, 1969-1970. Chairperson, Unauthorized Practice of Law Committee, District of Columbia Court of Appeals, 1978-1984. Deputy Register of Wills, U.S. District Court for the District of Columbia, 1966-1969. Member, Judicial Conference, District of Columbia Circuit, 1969-1974, 1979, 1983, 1987, 1992. Member, District of Columbia Judicial Conference, 1976-2000. Reporter, 1972-1984; Member, 1972-1994, Advisory Committee on Probate Division Rules, Superior Court of the District of Columbia. Member, Research Foundation of the Bar Association of the District of Columbia, 1984-1988. Member, District of Columbia Retirement Board, 1992-1996. Member, Board of Trustees (Chair, 1995-1999), LeMoyne College, Syracuse, New York, 1988-2000. *Member:* The District of Columbia Bar (Vice Chairman, Steering Committee for Estates, Trust and Probate Division, 1975-1976; Chairman, 1976-1979); Bar Association of the District of Columbia (Treasurer, 1976-1979; Member of Executive Council, 1969-1971 and Treasurer, 1970-1971, Young Lawyers Section); Federal and American (Member, House of Delegates, 1977-1978) Bar Associations. Fellow, American College of Trust and Estate Counsel (State Chair for the District of Columbia, 1993-1998). ***PRACTICE AREAS:*** Probate; Estate Planning; Trust and Estate Litigation.

SANFORD K. AIN, born Glen Cove, New York, July 24, 1947; admitted to bar, 1972, Virginia; 1973, District of Columbia; 1982, Maryland. *Education:* University of Wisconsin (B.A., cum laude, 1969); Georgetown University (J.D., 1972). Author of Numerous Articles, Publications and Presentations including: "Divorce-The Valuation and Division of Stock Options," D.C. Bar, Jan. 2001; "Complex Family Matters, Editorial on Troxel v. Granville, U.S. Supreme Court," The National Law Journal, January 2000; "How to Value Goodwill as Marital Asset," The National Law Journal, March 1998; What You Should Know About Divorce Taxation Involving the Elderly," The Practical Tax Lawyer, Spring 1994; "Taxation Issues Affecting the Older Divorce Client," American Bar Association Family Advocate, Summer 1993. Lecturer: "Classifying and Valuing Employee Stock Options Upon a Marital Dissolution," Virginia State Bar Presentation, April 1999; "A Comparison of the Domestic Relations Laws- Maryland, Washington D.C. and Virginia," January 1999; "Professional, Personal and Celebrity Goodwill Valuation: Forecasting an Uncertain Future," American Academy of Matrimonial Lawyers Presentation Annual Meeting, November 1998; "The Use of Professional Consultants, Advisors and Experts in Pre-Litigation Resolution of Marital and Custody Disputes," District of Columbia Bar Presentation, September 1993. *Member:* Montgomery County Bar Association (Member, Continuing Legal Education Faculty, 1985—); The District of Columbia Bar (Continuing Legal Education Faculty Member, 1979—); Bar Association of the District of Columbia (Director of Executive Council, Y.L.S., 1978-1981); Virginia State Bar (Continuing Legal Education Faculty Member, 1983—); Maryland State (Member, Continuing Legal Education Faculty, 1985—) and American Bar Associations; Virginia Trial Lawyers Association (Continuing Legal Education Faculty Member); Montgomery County, Maryland Bar Continuing Legal Education Faculty Member. Fellow, American Academy of Matrimonial Lawyers (Counsel, 1999-2000; President, District of Columbia Chapter, 1991-1994; President, 1999-2000). Diplomate, American College of Family Trial Lawyers. ***PRACTICE AREAS:*** Family Law; Commercial Transactions; Business Successions; Real Property. ***Email:*** sain@smcalaw.com

THOMAS E. DUNIGAN, born Queens, New York, November 1, 1950; admitted to bar, 1976, Maryland; 1977, District of Columbia. *Education:* Georgetown University (B.A., summa cum laude, 1972; J.D., 1976). Phi Beta Kappa; Pi Sigma Alpha. Law Clerk: to The Honorable Plummer M. Shearin, Associate Judge, Montgomery County, Maryland Circuit Court; to The Honorable Howard F. Corcoran, Senior District Judge, U.S. District Court, District of Columbia. Adjunct Faculty, Catholic University School of Law, 1985-1987. *Member:* The District of Columbia Bar; Montgomery County, Maryland State and American Bar Associations. ***PRACTICE AREAS:*** Real Property; Corporate Law; Estate Planning. ***Email:*** tdunigan@smcalaw.com

DAVID BRADFORD LAW, born Washington, D.C., September 29, 1950; admitted to bar, 1978, District of Columbia; 1979, Maryland, U.S. District Court for the District of Columbia and U.S. Court of Appeals for the District of Columbia Circuit; 1980, U.S. Claims Court; 1983, U.S. Supreme Court. *Education:* Harvard University (A.B., cum laude, 1972); Christ Church, Oxford University, Oxford, England (B.A., 1975; M.A., 1979); Washington College of Law of The American University (J.D., 1978). Harvard College Scholar. *Member:* The District of Columbia Bar; Maryland State and American (Member, Sections on: Business Law and Real Property, Probate and Trust Law) Bar Associations. ***PRACTICE AREAS:*** Real Property; Corporate Law.

(This Listing Continued)

RANDELL C. OGG, born Evansville, Indiana, July 2, 1952; admitted to bar, 1977, Indiana; 1980, District of Columbia; 1983, Virginia; 1995, Maryland. *Education:* Indiana University (B.A., 1974; J.D., cum laude, 1977). Writer, Indiana Law Journal, 1976-1977. Author: Note, "Due Process and the Automatic Fuel Adjustment Clause," 52 Indiana Law Journal 637, 1977; "Epidural Abscess: The Missed Diagnosis," Trial, Sept. 1997). Trial Attorney, Federal Trade Commission, 1977-1982. Faculty Member, National Institute of Trial Advocacy, Washington, D.C. Program, 1990-1997, 2000. *Member:* The District of Columbia Bar; Virginia State Bar; Maryland State and American Bar Association (Member, Section on Litigation); District of Columbia Trial Lawyers Association; The Association of Trial Lawyers of America; American Board of Trial Advocates. ***PRACTICE AREAS:*** Civil Litigation; Personal Injury.

FAITH D. DORNBRAND, born Amityville, New York, December 27, 1952; admitted to bar, 1979, California; 1980, District of Columbia; 1983, Maryland. *Education:* Yale University (B.A., magna cum laude, 1975; Phi Beta Kappa); Boalt Hall School of Law, University of California (J.D., 1979). Associate Editor, California Law Review, 1977-1979. *Member:* The District of Columbia Bar (Member, Task Force on Family Law Representation, 1992-1995); Montgomery County, Maryland State and American (Member, Subcommittee on Federal Civilian Retirement Legislation, 1991-1993) Bar Associations; The Women's Bar Association of the District of Columbia; Women's Bar Association of Maryland; American Inn of Court (Charles Fahy, 1989-1991). Fellow, American Academy of Matrimonial Lawyers (President, DC Chapter, 2000-2001). ***PRACTICE AREAS:*** Family Law; Civil Litigation. ***Email:*** fdornbrand@smcalaw.com

MARK S. CARLIN, born New York, N.Y., June 25, 1953; admitted to bar, 1977, District of Columbia; 1984, Maryland; 1986, Virginia. *Education:* State University of New York at Buffalo (B.A., summa cum laude, 1974); Yale University (J.D., 1977). Phi Beta Kappa. Editor, Criminal Practice Institute Trial Manual, 1982, 1983. Law Clerk to Honorable James A. Belson, Associate Judge, D.C. Superior Court, 1977-1978. Member, 1994— and Vice Chair, 2000—, District of Columbia Court of Appeals Committee on Admissions. Barrister, Charles Fahy American Inn of Court, 1983-1986. Staff Attorney, 1977-1983 and Assistant Chief, Appellate Division, 1984-1985, District of Columbia Public Defender Service. Faculty Member, National Institute of Trial Advocacy, 1999—. *Member:* The District of Columbia Bar; Bar Association of the District of Columbia; Maryland State Bar Association; Virginia State Bar; Maryland Trial Lawyers Association; Association of Trial Lawyers of America; District of Columbia Judicial Conference. ***PRACTICE AREAS:*** Civil Litigation; Family Law; Professional Malpractice.

CLAUDIA ANNE POTT, born Ann Arbor, Michigan, October 29, 1949; admitted to bar, 1985, Maryland; 1986, District of Columbia. *Education:* University of Michigan (A.B., with high distinction, 1973; M.S.W., 1977); George Washington University (J.D., with high honors, 1985). Order of the Coif. *Member:* Montgomery County and Maryland State Bar Associations; The District of Columbia Bar (Member, Steering Committee, Family Law Section, 1994-2000; Co-Chair, 1995-1997); Women's Bar Association of Maryland; The Women's Bar Association of the District of Columbia. ***PRACTICE AREAS:*** Family Law; Estate Planning.

SAM H. ROBERSON, born Nashville, Georgia, December 7, 1958; admitted to bar, 1984, Georgia; 1988, District of Columbia and U.S. Tax Court. *Education:* University of Georgia (B.B.A., 1981); Mercer University (J.D., 1984); University of Florida (LL.M. in Taxation, 1985). Attorney-Advisor to the Honorable Mary Ann Cohen, United States Tax Court, 1985-1987. *Member:* The District of Columbia Bar (Member, Taxation Section); American Bar Association (Member, Taxation and Health Care Sections). ***PRACTICE AREAS:*** Employee Benefits; Corporate Law; Tax Planning; Estate Planning. ***Email:*** sroberson@smcalaw.com

DOUGLAS E. FIERBERG, born Detroit, Michigan, May 21, 1959; admitted to bar, 1988, Maryland; 1989, District of Columbia, U.S. District Court, District of Maryland and District of Columbia and U.S. Court of Appeals for the District of Columbia Circuit. *Education:* University of Michigan (B.A., with class honors, 1981); George Washington University (J.D., with honors, 1988). Member: Moot Court Board; George Washington University Journal of International Law and Economics, 1987-1988. Recipient, Logan Circle Community Association, Community Advocate and Public Defense Awards, 1993, 1996. Barrister, William B. Bryant American Inn of Court, No. 41, 1996-1997. Author, "Liability for Hazing after Jones v. Kappa Alpha," Synthesis Law and Policy in Higher Education, Vol. 10, No. 3, (Winter 1999); "High School Hazing: Prevention and Risk Management Issues for School Administrators," The School Administrator, Vol. (Fall 2000). Speaker, Maryland State Bar Association Speakers Bureau. *Member:* The District of Columbia Bar; Maryland State Bar Association; The Association of the Trial Lawyers of America; The District of Columbia Trial Lawyers Association; The National Crime Victim Bar Association. ***PRACTICE AREAS:*** Commercial Litigation; Products Liability; Hazing; Campus; Personal Injury. ***Email:*** dfierberg@smcalaw.com

LAURENCE E. SALANS, born Chicago, Illinois, November 23, 1960; admitted to bar, 1987, Virginia; 1988, District of Columbia; 1995, Maryland. *Education:* University of Arizona (B.S.B.A., 1983); George Washington Uni-

(This Listing Continued)

SHERMAN, MEEHAN, CURTIN & AIN, A PROFESSIONAL CORPORATION, Washington—Continued

versity (J.D., with honors, 1987). Notes Editor, George Washington University Journal of International Law and Economics, 1986-1987. Certified Public Accountant, Maryland, 1986. Author: "Retirement Plans: Avoid Seven Expensive Mistakes," Tax Saving Report, December 1999/January 2000; "Using Charitable Remainder Trusts: Doing Well by Doing Good," Legal Times, April 14, 1997. Member, Washington, D.C. Estate Planning Council, 1998. *Member:* Virginia State Bar (Member, Trusts and Estates Section); The District of Columbia Bar (Member, Estates Trusts and Probate Law and Taxation Sections; Elected to Steering Committee, Estates, Trusts and Probate Law Section, 1999-2001); Maryland State (Member, Estates and Trusts Law Section) and American (Member, Real Property ane Probate Law Section) Bar Associations. ***PRACTICE AREAS:*** Estate Planning; Estate Administration; Estate Litigation; Charitable Giving; Business Planning.

LAUREN E. SHEA, born Malden, Massachusetts, August 24, 1958; admitted to bar, 1987, New York; 1989, District of Columbia; 1991, Virginia. *Education:* University of Southern Maine (B.S., 1980); City University of New York (J.D., 1986). *Member:* Fairfax County Bar Association; District of Columbia Bar (Member: Family Law Section); Virginia State Bar. ***PRACTICE AREAS:*** Family Law.

MATTHEW P. MALONEY, born Washington, D.C., April 30,1962; admitted to bar, 1991, Maryland; 1992, District of Columbia and U.S. District Court, District of Columbia; 1994, U.S. District Court, District of Maryland; 2000, Virginia. *Education:* University of Vermont (B.S., 1984); George Washington University (J.D., with honors, 1991). Law Clerk to the Honorable J. James McKenna, Sixth Judicial Circuit of Maryland, 1991-1992. *Member:* Montgomery County Bar Association; The District of Columbia Bar; Virginia State Bar. The Trial Lawyers Association of Metropolitan Washington, D.C.; The Association of Trial Lawyers of America. ***PRACTICE AREAS:*** Civil Litigation; Personal Injury; Medical Malpractice; Toxic Tort. ***Email:*** mmaloney@smcalaw.com

OF COUNSEL

THOMAS P. MEEHAN, born Teaneck, New Jersey, August 15, 1940; admitted to bar, 1965, District of Columbia; 1969, Maryland; 1986, U.S. Supreme Court. *Education:* Middlebury College (B.A., 1962); Duke University (LL.B., 1965). Order of the Coif. Member, Board of Editors, Duke Law Journal, 1964-1965. Recipient, E. Barrett Prettyman Trial Advocacy Fellowship, Georgetown Law Center, 1965-1966. Faculty Member, National Institute of Trial Advocacy, Georgetown University Law Center, 1982-1995, 1997. Court Appointed Member of Plaintiffs' Steering Committee in Northwest Flight 255 Air Disaster Multi District Litigation in Detroit, Michigan, 1988-1991. Founding Member and Master of the Bench, William B. Bryant American Inn of Court, No. 41, 1987-1995. Fellow, The Roscoe Pound Foundation, 1995—. *Member:* The District of Columbia Bar; Bar Association of the District of Columbia; Maryland State, Federal and American Bar Associations; The Association of Trial Lawyers of America.

JEANMARIE LoCOCO NICHOLSON, born New Orleans, Louisiana, November 15, 1958; admitted to bar, 1981, Louisiana (inactive); 1996, District of Columbia; 1997, Virginia. *Education:* Loyola University (B.A., magna cum laude, 1978; J.D., 1981); Boalt Hall School of Law, University of California (LL.M., 1992). Phi Delta Phi. Member, Mock Trial Team. Law Clerk, Hon. Charles Schwartz, Jr., U.S. District Judge, Eastern District of Louisiana. Author: "Admiralty, Fifth Circuit Symposium," 30 Loyola L. Rev. 467, 1984 and 31 Loyola L. Rev., 1985. Lecturer, Loyola University School of Law, 1987-1988 and 1990-1991. *Member:* Fairfax County and Maryland State Bar Associations; The District of Columbia Bar (Member, Family Law Section); Virginia State Bar. ***PRACTICE AREAS:*** Family Law; Civil Litigation. ***Email:*** jnicholson@smcalaw.com

---

NANCY L. WALSH, born Pensacola, Florida, February 5, 1963; admitted to bar, 1988, Virginia; 1992, District of Columbia; 1994, Colorado. *Education:* University of Notre Dame (B.A., 1985); University of Virginia (J.D., 1988). *Member:* District of Columbia Bar; Virginia State Bar; American Bar Association. ***PRACTICE AREAS:*** Business Law; Real Estate; Corporate Law. ***Email:*** nwalsh@smcalaw.com

ANNE MARIE JACKSON, born Rhinebeck, New York, June 23, 1969; admitted to bar, 1994, Maryland; 1995, Virginia; 1997, District of Columbia. *Education:* Emory University (B.A., 1991); Washington College of Law, American University (J.D., cum laude, 1994). Senior Federal Circuit Editor, American University Law Review, 1993-1994. Law Clerk to the Honorable Theodore G. Bloom, Maryland Court of Special Appeals, 1994-1995. Author: "The Coming of Age of Grandparent Visitation Rights," 43 American University Law Review 563 (1994). *Member:* The Montgomery County Bar Association (Family Law Section; Co-Chair, 2000-2001); Maryland State and American (Member, Family

(This Listing Continued)

Law Section) Bar Associations; Virginia State Bar; District of Columbia Bar; Montgomery County Women's Bar Association (Member, Executive Committee, 1997—); Women's Bar Association of Maryland. ***PRACTICE AREAS:*** Family Law. ***Email:*** ajackson@smcalaw.com

JAMES W. KOCH, born Arlington Heights, Illinois, May 11, 1964; admitted to bar, 1989, Pennsylvania; 1991, District of Columbia; 2000, Maryland. *Education:* Duke University (A.B., 1986); Syracuse University College of Law (J.D., cum laude, 1989). Associate Editor, Syracuse Law Review, 1988-1989. Member, Justinian Honor Society. *Member:* District of Columbia Bar (Member, Estate, Trusts and Probate Law Section); Maryland State (Member, Estates and Trusts Law Section) and Pennsylvania Bar Associations. ***PRACTICE AREAS:*** Estate Planning; Estate Administration; Estate Litigation; Business Planning; Charitable Giving. ***Email:*** jkoch@smcalaw.com

DARRYL ALAN FELDMAN, born Merced, California, July 16, 1969; admitted to bar, 1994, Maryland; 1995, U.S. District Court, District of Maryland; 1996, District of Columbia. *Education:* Tulane University of Louisiana (B.S.M., 1991); University of Baltimore (J.D., 1994). *Member:* The District of Columbia Bar; Montgomery County Bar Association. ***PRACTICE AREAS:*** Family Law. ***Email:*** dfeldman@smcalaw.com

TRACY ANETTE MEYER, born Denver, Colorado, January 7, 1970; admitted to bar, 1996, Virginia; 2001, District of Columbia. *Education:* University of Northern Colorado (B.A., magna cum laude, 1992); American University-Washington College of Law (J.D., 1995). *Member:* Arlington Bar Association (Chairman, Law Day, 1999). ***PRACTICE AREAS:*** Family Law. ***Email:*** tmeyer@smcalaw.com

JASON A. DZUBOW, born Philadelphia, Pennsylvania, May 21, 1969; admitted to bar, 1997, Maryland; 2001, District of Columbia. *Education:* Temple University (B.A., summa cum laude, 1991); Georgetown University Law Center (J.D., 1996). ***PRACTICE AREAS:*** Litigation. ***Email:*** jdzubow@smcalaw.com

REPRESENTATIVE CLIENTS: Bank of Nova Scotia; Catholic University of America; NRI, Inc.; Titanium Development Assn.; Marsh & McLennan Companies, Inc.; Devon Properties, Inc.; Victor Stanley, Inc.; Overseas Service Corp.; Winwood Child Care Centers; Occasions Caterers, Inc.; International Gourmet Foods, Inc.; Westlake Internet Training, Inc.

SHOOK, HARDY & BACON L.L.P.

HAMILTON SQUARE
600 14TH STREET, N.W., SUITE 800
WASHINGTON, D.C. 20005-2004
Telephone: 202-783-8400
Facsimile: 202-783-4211
URL: http://www.shb.com

Kansas City, Missouri Office: One Kansas City Place, 1200 Main Street, 64105-2118. Telephone: 816-474-6550. Facsimile: 816-421-5547.
Overland Park, Kansas Office: 84 Corporate Woods, 10801 Mastin, Suite 1000, 66210-1671. Telephone: 913-451-6060. Facsimile: 913-451-8879.
Houston, Texas Office: Chase Tower, 600 Travis Street, Suite 1600, 77002-2911. Telephone: 713-227-8008. Facsimile: 713-227-9508.
Miami, Florida Office: Miami Center, Suite 2400, 201 South Biscayne Boulevard, 33131-4332. Telephone: 305-358-5171. Facsimile: 305-358-7470.
Tampa, Florida Office: 100 North Tampa Street, Suite 2900, 33602-5810. Telephone: 813-202-7100. Facsimile: 813-221-8837.
San Francisco, California Office: 333 Bush Street, 94104-2828. Telephone: 415-544-1900. Facsimile: 415-391-0281.
London, England Office: 25 Cannon Street, EC4M 5SE. Telephone: 011-44-02-07-332 4500. Facsimile: 011-44-02-07-332 4501.
Geneva, Switzerland Office: 118, rue du Rhône, 1204. Telephone: 011-41-22-787-2000. Facsimile: 011-41-22-786-5008.

Acquisitions, Administration, Agriculture, Antitrust, Banking and Commercial Law, Bankruptcy and Creditor's Rights, Broadcasting, Communications, Compensation Planning, Construction Law, Copyright, Corporate, Employment Rights, Energy, Environmental, ERISA, Estate Planning, Federal Communications Commission Issues, Federal Trade Commission Issues, Financial Institution Regulation, Franchise and Professional Corporation Law, General Civil, Trial and Appellate Practice, Health Law, Intellectual Property, International, Labor and Employment, Libel, Mergers and Acquisitions, Municipal, Negligence, Patent, Probate, Products Liability, Real Estate, Restructuring and Reorganization, Securities, Syndications, Taxation, Technology Law, Trade Secret Law, Trademark, Unfair Competition and Workers Compensation Litigation.

PARTNERS

MARK A. BEHRENS, born Cincinnati, OH, 1965; admitted to bar, 1990, Virginia and U.S. Court of Appeals, Fourth Circuit; 1991, District of Columbia and U.S. District Court, Eastern District of Virginia; 1992, U.S. District Court, Western District of Virginia; 1993, U.S. District Court for the District of Columbia; 1994, U.S. Court of Appeals for the District of Columbia Circuit and

(This Listing Continued)

U.S. Supreme Court. *Education:* University of Wisconsin-Madison (B.A., 1987); Vanderbilt University School of Law (J.D., 1990). Recipient, American Jurisprudence Award, Torts. Associate Articles Editor, Vanderbilt Law Review. Adjunct Professorial Lecturer in Law, The American University, Washington College of Law, Spring 1999; Fall 1995. ***PRACTICE AREAS:*** Torts; Insurance; Products Liability; Legislative Practice; Public Policy. ***Email:*** mbehrens@shb.com

KEITH T. BORMAN, born Pasadena, CA., 1948; admitted to bar, 1973, California; 1976, Oregon; 1990, Missouri; 1999, District of Columbia; 2000, U.S. Supreme Court. *Education:* Occidental College (B.A., cum laude, 1970); University of Michigan (J.D., 1972). Phi Beta Kappa. [Capt., USAFR, 1968-1978]. ***PRACTICE AREAS:*** Products Liability. ***Email:*** kborman@shb.com

BARKLEY CLARK, born Denver, CO., 1939; admitted to bar, 1965, Colorado; 1971, Kansas; 1991, Missouri; 2000, District of Columbia. *Education:* Amherst College (B.A., 1962); Harvard University (LL.B., 1965). Phi Beta Kappa. Author: *The Law of Bank Deposits, Collections and Credit Cards,* Warren, Gorham & Lamont, Inc., Revised Edition, 1999, supplemented (with B. Clark); *The Law of Secured Transactions under the Uniform Commercial Code,* Warren, Gorham & Lamont, Inc., Third Edition, 1999, supplemented; *The Law of Product Warranties,* Warren, Gorham & Lamont, Inc., 1984, supplemented (with C. Smith); *Cases and Materials on Consumer Protection,* (with F. Miller), Michie/Bobbs-Merrill, 1980; *Warranties in the Sale of Business Equipment and Consumer Products,* Practicing Law Institute, 1980-1985. Co-Author, *Regulation CC: Funds Availability and Check Collection,* Warren, Gorham & Lamont, Inc., 1988. Co-Author: "Truth in Savings: Legal Analysis and Compliance Strategies," Warren, Gorham & Lamont, Inc., 1992. Visiting Professor of Law, University of Colorado, 1967-1968. Associate Professor of Law, 1969-1972 and Professor of Law, 1972-1982, University of Kansas. Schroeder Distinguished Professor Law, University of Kansas, 1982-1985. Professor of Law, National Law Center, George Washington University, 1985-1989. Visiting Professor of Law, University of Michigan, 1991. Adjunct Professor of Law, Georgetown University Law Center, 2000—. Member, City Commission, 1973-1983 and Mayor, 1975-1979, Lawrence, Kansas. Co-Chair, UCC Article 9 Subcommittee, 1986-1988 and Member, Business and Banking Law Section; Member, ALI-ABA Committee to Revise UCC Article 9, American Bar Association. Best Lawyers in America, 2001-2002. *Member:* Colorado Bar Association; American College of Commercial Finance Attorneys; American College of Consumer Financial Services Lawyers. ***PRACTICE AREAS:*** Banking; Commercial Law; Uniform Commercial Code. ***Email:*** bclark@shb.com

WILLIAM F. DEMAREST, JR., born Newark, N.J., 1947; admitted to bar, 1973, Massachusetts; 1979, District of Columbia; 1996, U.S. Supreme Court; U.S. Court of Appeals, District of Columbia, Fifth, Tenth, Eleventh and Federal Circuits; U.S. Court of International Trade and U.S. Court of Claims. *Education:* University of Scranton (B.S., cum laude, 1969); Boston College (J.D., magna cum laude, 1972). Order of the Coif. Law Clerk, Hon. Ruggero J. Aldisert, U.S. Court of Appeals, Third Circuit, 1972-1973. Counsel, Subcommittee on Energy and Power, U.S. House of Representatives, 1975-1979. Member, Editorial Board, Natural Gas Policy Act Information Service, 1981—. *Member:* Massachusetts Bar Association; Federal Energy Bar Association. ***PRACTICE AREAS:*** Energy; Natural Gas Regulation and Litigation; Legislation; Environment. ***Email:*** wdemarest@shb.com

BARRY P. GOLOB, born Miami, FL., 1961; admitted to bar, 1991, Pennsylvania; 1993, District of Columbia. *Education:* University of Miami (B.S., 1983); Washington College of Law at American University (J.D., 1991). Author: "Patent Damages: The Basics," *IDEA-The Journal of Law and Technology,* Vol. 31, No. 1 (1993). ***PRACTICE AREAS:*** Patent, Trademark, Copyright and Trade Secret Litigation; Intellectual Property Counseling. ***Email:*** bgolob@shb.com

PETER W. GOWDEY, born Middletown, New York, April 10, 1943; admitted to bar, 1969, New York; 1972, North Carolina; 1975, District of Columbia; 1980, U.S. Supreme Court. *Education:* Clarkson University (B.S., 1965); Albany Law School of Union University (J.D., 1968). *Member:* Greensboro, North Carolina, New York State and American Bar Associations; The District of Columbia Bar; Bar Association of the District of Columbia (Council Member, Patent, Trademark and Copyright Section, 1983—); North Carolina State Bar; American Intellectual Property Law Association; Washington Patent Lawyers Club (Vice President, 1983-1984; President, 1984-1985); ITC Trial Lawyers Association. ***PRACTICE AREAS:*** Intellectual Property Litigation; Intellectual Property Audits; International Law. ***Email:*** pgowdey@shb.com

THOMAS A. HART, JR., born Washington, DC, 1956; admitted to bar, 1981, District of Columbia; 1985, U.S. Court of Appeals, Eighth, Tenth and District of Columbia Circuits; 1989, U.S. Supreme Court. *Education:* Brown University (B.A., 1977); Georgetown University (J.D., 1980). Law Clerk, Hon. Theodore McMillian, U.S. Court of Appeals, Eighth Circuit, 1980-1981. Author: "A Review of WARC-79 and its Implications for the Development of Satellite Communications Services," 12 Lawyer of Americas, Journal of International Law 460-75; "The Evolution of Telco Constructed Broadband Services for CATV Operators," Cath. U.L. Rev.; "The Case for Minority Broadcast Ownership," Gannett Center Journal; "The Cable Bill of 1992-Potential for

(This Listing Continued)

Small Business and Programing Suppliers," Presented to U.S. Department of Commerce, Minority Enterprise Development Week, September, 1992; "Keys to Venture Capital Financing in the Telecommunications Industry," Presentation to the National Capital Formation Symposium; "A Retreating Commitment from International Telecommunications Policy," Remarks before Conference on Transborder Data Flow sponsored by the Boston University Journal of International Law; "How to Buy a Radio Station," Drafted section on government financing, National Association of Broadcasters. Director, Telecommunications Development Fund. *Member:* The District of Columbia Bar; American Bar Association; Federal Communications Bar Association; National Bar Association. ***PRACTICE AREAS:*** Telecommunications; Entertainment; Legislative; Corporate. ***Email:*** thart@shb.com

BRUCE O. JOLLY, JR., born Gary, IN., 1946; admitted to bar, 1973, North Carolina; 1974, Virginia; 1976, District of Columbia; 1981, U.S. Supreme Court; 1988, Maryland. *Education:* University of North Carolina (A.B., 1969; J.D., 1973). *Member:* The District of Columbia Bar; Virginia State Bar; North Carolina State Bar; Maryland State, Federal and American (Member, Consumer Financial Services and Credit Union Committees, 1978—, Section of Business Law, 1974—) Bar Associations. ***PRACTICE AREAS:*** Financial Institution Law. ***Email:*** bjolly@shb.com

RODNEY L. JOYCE, born Garden City, KS, 1951; admitted to bar, 1976, Kansas; 1978, District of Columbia. *Education:* Washburn University (B.A., with honors, 1973; J.D., with honors, 1976). Minority Communications Counsel, U.S. House of Representatives, 1981-1985. Deputy Assistant Secretary of Commerce and Acting Assistant Secretary of Commerce for Communications and Information, 1985-1986. *Member:* The District of Columbia Bar; American Bar Association; Federal Communications Bar Association. ***PRACTICE AREAS:*** Communications Law. ***Email:*** rjoyce@shb.com

JEREMIAH D. LAMBERT, born New York, N.Y., 1934; admitted to bar, 1960, New York; 1964, District of Columbia; 1971, U.S. Supreme Court. *Education:* Harvard University; Princeton University (A.B., magna cum laude, 1955); Yale University (LL.B., 1959). Phi Beta Kappa; Phi Alpha Delta. Recipient, Fulbright Scholar, University of Copenhagen, Denmark, 1955-1956. Member, Board of Editors, Yale Law Journal, 1958-1959. Co-author: with Robert N. Jensen, "FERC Policy on Escalator Clauses Under the Natural Gas Policy Act," Public Utilities Fortnightly, March 15, 1979 and "FERC Policy on Price Escalator Clauses Under the Natural Gas Policy Act: An Update," Public Utilities Fortnightly, May 10, 1979; with William D. Coston, "Friendly Foes in the Iranian Assets Litigation," 7 Yale Journal of World Public Order 88, 1980; "Price Relief under Existing Gas Purchase Contracts: The Indefinite Price Escalator Tangle," Eastern Mineral Law Institute, Proceedings of the Second Annual Institute, Matthew Bender, 1981; with Lawrence White, *Handbook of Modern Construction Law,* Prentice-Hall, 1981 and 1982; with Nathalie P. Gilfoyle, "Reforming Natural Gas Markets: The Antitrust Alternative," Public Utilities Fortnightly, May 12, 1983; with Jay D. Pedelty, "Mandatory Contract Carriage: The Changing Role of Pipelines in Competitive Natural Gas Markets," Public Utilities Fortnightly, February 7, 1985; Bypass in the Natural Gas Industry: The Fruit of Regulatory Change," Public Utilities Fortnightly, April 3, 1986; with J. Richard O'Neill, "Privatization of Municipal Hydroelectric Facilities Under Current Law," Public Utilities Fortnightly, February 4, 1988; "Assessing The Impact of the U.S. Canada Free Trade Agreement," Natural Gas, May 1988; "Privatizing Electricity in Britain: The Role of the National Grid," Public Utilities Fortnightly, March 30, 1989; "Gas Supply for Independent Power Projects," Public Utilities Fortnightly, October 11, 1990; "ISOs and Market Regulators: 'The Emerging Debate,'" Public Utilities Fortnightly, April 15, 1998. Co-Editor: with Fereidun Fesharaki, "Economic and Political Incentives to Petroleum Exploration," International Law Institute, 1990. Trustee, International Law Institute, Washington, D.C., 1984-1988. Contributing Editor, World Cogeneration; Member, Electricity Futures Contracts Advisory Committee, New York Mercantile Exchange. *Member:* The District of Columbia Bar; The Association of the Bar of the City of New York; Bar Association of the District of Columbia; New York State, Federal and American Bar Associations; American Society of International Law. ***PRACTICE AREAS:*** Energy; Corporate Law. ***Email:*** jlambert@shb.com

EDWIN N. LAVERGNE, born Chicago, IL., 1954; admitted to bar, 1980, District of Columbia; 1984, U.S. Court of Appeals, Fifth Circuit; 1986, U.S. Supreme Court. *Education:* Ithaca College (B.S., summa cum laude, 1976; M.S., 1977); Georgetown University (J.D., 1980). Author: "AT&T's Entry Into Electronic Publishing: Boon of Burden for IPS?" InfoText, September 1989; "900 Promotional Give-Aways: What's Legal and What's Not?" InfoText, December 1989; "Marketing With ANI: Invasion of Privacy?" InfoText, July 1991; "Telemarketing: Consumer Privacy and Commerce," InfoText, August 1992; "Bell Entry Into Information Services: Will Newspaper Opposition Backfire?" InfoText, November 1992; "Don't Call Us, Or We'll Sue You," InfoText, February 1993; "N11 Services: It's As Easy As 1,2,3," InfoText, July 1993; "Are Service Bureaus Responsible For Program Content?" Voice Processing, November 1993; "1-800-VANITY: Who's Number Is It Anyway?" Voice Processing, February 1994; "New Targets of Toll Fraud," Voice Processing, April 1994; "Telecommunications Reform and Number Portability," InfoText, October

(This Listing Continued)

SHOOK, HARDY & BACON L.L.P., Washington—Continued

1995; "A New Look for Toll Free Numbers," InfoText, December 1995; "Keeping It Legal In Cyberspace," Purchasing Today, April 1996; "Online Privacy: What is the Law," The Multimedia Law Report, April 1996; "Cyberspace Sweepstakes: New Legal Issues," The Multimedia Law Report, July 1996; "Should Tobacco and Alcohol Advertising Be Restricted on the Internet," Digitrends, Winter 1996-1997; "Promoting and Advertising with Email/Fax, Telephone/Telemarketing," Promotion Marketing Association, Inc., Summer 1999. Co-Author: "The Interactive Marketplace Regulatory Handbook," Thompson Publishing Group, June 1994; "Net Success," Adams Publishing, May 1999. *Member:* The District of Columbia Bar. ***PRACTICE AREAS:*** Advertising and Marketing; Telecommunications; Business Law. ***Email:*** elavergne@shb.com

MARK N. LIPP, born Washington, D.C., 1949; admitted to bar, 1974, Maryland; 1994, District of Columbia. *Education:* University of Maryland (B.A., 1971); University of Baltimore (J.D., cum laude, 1974). Staff Writer, University of Baltimore Law Review, 1973-1974. Author: "Due Process in Forfeiture Proceedings," 3 University of Baltimore Law Review 270, 1974. Attorney, Federal Communications Commission Mass Media Bureau, Legal Branch, 1974-1982, Chief, Allocations Branch, 1982-1988. Member, Montgomery County (Maryland) Cable Advisory Committee, 1987-1993. *Member:* Maryland State and American Bar Associations; Federal Communications Bar Association. ***PRACTICE AREAS:*** Communications Law; Administrative Law. ***Email:*** mlipp@shb.com

MICHELLE R. MANGRUM, born St. Louis, MO., 1955; admitted to bar, 1986, Missouri; 1987, U.S. District Court, Eastern District of Michigan; 1991, U.S. Court of Appeals, Sixth Circuit; 1993, U.S. Court of Appeals, Tenth Circuit; 2001, District of Columbia. *Education:* University of Missouri (B.S., cum laude, 1978; J.D., cum laude, 1986). Order of the Coif. Member, 1984-1985 and Note and Comment Editor, 1985-1986, Missouri Law Review. Registered Nurse, Missouri, 1978. Author: "The Seat Belt Defense: Must the Reasonable Man Wear a Seat Belt?" 50 Missouri Law Review 968, 1985; "Informal Discovery with Plaintiff's Treating Physician," 44 J.Mo. Bar 249 (1988). ***PRACTICE AREAS:*** Pharmaceutical/Medical Device Litigation. ***Email:*** mmangrum@shb.com

RICHARD M. MOLLISON, born Portland, OR., 1944; admitted to bar, 1969, Oregon; 1974, U.S. District Court, District of Oregon; 1975, United States Court of Appeals for the Armed Forces; 1997, U.S. Supreme Court; 1998, District of Columbia. *Education:* University of Oregon (B.A., 1966; J.D., 1969); George Washington University (LL.M. in Environmental Law, 1981). *Member:* Oregon State Bar; The District of Columbia Bar. ***PRACTICE AREAS:*** Products Liability. ***Email:*** rmollison@shb.com

JAY S. NEWMAN, born Brooklyn, N.Y., 1965; admitted to bar, 1990, Maryland; 1993, District of Columbia. *Education:* Brandeis University (B.A., magna cum laude, 1987); University of Pennsylvania (J.D., 1990). Phi Beta Kappa. Author: "Korea and the American Generalized System of Preference: Was Graduation a Proper Response?" University of Pennsylvania Journal of International Business Law, Volume 11, Number 3; "Congress Hears Privacy Rights Bill," InfoText, June 1991; "Senate Committee Approves Consumer Protection Act," InfoText, September 1991; "Surrendering to the Attorneys General," InfoText, October 1991; "FTC Tackles Telemarketing Fraud," InfoText, February 1993; "Fantasy Sports Leagues: Not All Fun and Games," Digitrends, Jan. 2001; "Tuning Into Internet Radio," Digitrends, March 2001. Co-Author with Edwin N. Lavergne: "Cyberspace Sweepstakes: New Legal Issues," The Multimedia Law Report, July 1996; "Should Tobacco and Alcohol Advertisements be Restricted on the Internet?" Digitrends, Winter 1996-1997. ***PRACTICE AREAS:*** Communications Law; Advertising; Promotions Law; E-Commerce. ***Email:*** jnewman@shb.com

JOSEPH D. PIORKOWSKI, JR., born Chester, Pennsylvania, November 21, 1956; admitted to bar, 1988, Maryland; 1989, District of Columbia, U.S. District Court, District of Maryland, U.S. Court of Appeals, Fourth Circuit, U.S. District Court for the District of Columbia and U.S. Court of Appeals for the District of Columbia Circuit; 1997, Texas. *Education:* Hofstra University (B.A., cum laude, 1976); Philadelphia College of Osteopathic Medicine (D.O., 1980); Georgetown University (J.D., magna cum laude, 1988); The Johns Hopkins University (M.P.H., 1992). Psi Chi; Order of the Coif; Delta Omega. Licensed Physician, Maryland, 1984 and District of Columbia, 1989. Articles Editor, Georgetown Law Journal, 1987-1988. Author: "Medical Testimony and The Expert Witness," in Legal Medicine (3d ed., 4th ed., 5th ed.); Note, "Between A Rock and a Hard Place: AIDS and the Conflicting Physician's Duties of Preventing Disease Transmission and Safeguarding Confidentiality," 76 Georgetown Law Journal 169, 1987; Note, "Professional Conduct and the Preparation of Witnesses for Trial: Defining the Acceptable Limitations of 'Coaching,'" 1 Georgetown Journal of Legal Ethics 389, 1987. Law Clerk to the Honorable Oliver Gasch, U.S. District Court for the District of Columbia, 1988-1989. Adjunct Professor, Georgetown University Law Center, 1992—. Clinical Assistant Professor, Department of Surgery, Georgetown University Medical Center, 1995—. *Member:* The District of Columbia Bar; Maryland State and American Bar Associations; Aerospace Medical Association; American College of Family

(This Listing Continued)

Physicians. Fellow: American College of Legal Medicine; American College of Preventive Medicine. Diplomate: American Board of Legal Medicine; American Board of Preventive Medicine (Aerospace Medicine). [Active Duty, Commander, U.S. Naval Reserve (Medical Corps), 1980-1988; 1990-1991]. ***Email:*** jpiorkowski@shb.com

HENRY M. RIVERA, born Albuquerque, NM, 1946; admitted to bar, 1973, New Mexico; 1982, District of Columbia. *Education:* University of New Mexico (B.A., 1968); University of Albuquerque (B.B.A., 1980); University of New Mexico (J.D., 1973). Recipient: New Mexico's Outstanding Young Lawyer Award, 1981; Outstanding Leadership in Government Award, 1985. Publications: "Judgments: New Mexico and the Additur," 2 New Mexico Law Review 101, 1972; "On Building Better Laws for New Mexico's Environment," 4 New Mexico Law Review, 105, 1973; "The Wheel of Fortune: Federal Licensing by Lottery," Administrative Law Review, 1983; "The New Interexchange Marketplace: A Consistent View of the Regulatory Outlook," 9th Annual Rate Symposium, University of Missouri-Columbia; "Telecommunications: Currents of Change," 22nd Annual Iowa State University Regulatory Conference; "New Television Services and the FCC's Classification Magic," IEEE Transactions on Broadcasting, Vol. BC-30, #4 (1984); "Changing Directions in the Telecommunications Industry," Public Utilities Fortnightly, Vol. 115, #5 (1985); "The Greening of the FCC: Getting from Here to There," Rural Telecommunications, Vol. 4, #3 (1985); "Hispanics and the Communications Industry," The State of Hispanic America, Vol. V (1985); "Minorities and Telecommunications," Hispanic Review of Business (September, 1983); "A Brief Look at Computer III," Technology Transfer News, Vol. 4, No. 2, 1986; "Separate Systems and International Communications," IEEE Communications Magazine, Vol. 15, No. 1 (January 1987); "Perspective: Are BOC Accounting Safeguards Really Sufficient?" Communications Week, 129, February 2, 1987; "Computer III: How Will It Affect the RHCs?" Telematics, January 1987; "Perspective: FCC's Open Network Architecture: Quo Vadis?" Communications Week, 137, March 30, 1987; "Unleashing the BOC's," Answer, July/August, 1987; "A College Education: No Longer Optional," The College Digest, Special Issue, 1990-1991; "Loose Ends: A Tale of Three FCC Proceedings," PCS: The Quest for 2 GHZ Spectrum, 1990; "Local Exchange Competition," 14th Annual Institute on Telecommunications Policy and Regulation, 1996; The Changing Face of Telecommunications," 15th Annual Institute on Telecommunications Policy and Regulation, 1997; "The Future of Telecommunications: Will Alternative Networks Provide the Competition the 1996 Telecommunications Act Did Not?" 16th Annual Institute on Telecommunications Policy and Regulation, 1998; "Developments in Wireline Telephony," 17th Annual Institute on Telecommunications Policy and Regulation, 1999; "Developments in Wireline Telephony 2000," 18th Annual Institute on Telecommunications Policy and Regulation, 2000. Trustee, Board of Trustees, University of New Mexico Law School Foundation, 1980. Commissioner, Federal Communications Commission, 1981-1985. Supervisory Commissioner, FCC Industry Advisory Group on Revision of the Uniform System Accounts, 1983-1985. Member, Federal-State Joint Board, 1982-1985. Member, Board on Telecommunications & Computer Applications, an agency of the National Research Council, 1986-1990. Telecommunications Advisor, U.S. Department of State, 1987. Member, US West-New Mexico Executive Board, 1987-1996. Vice-Chairman, Foundation for Minority Interests in Media, Inc., 1987—. Vice-Chairman, FCC High Definition Television Advisory Group 2 (Consumer/Trade Issues) 1987-1996. Senior Advisor, U.S. Delegation, International Telecommunications Union Plenipotentiary Conference, Nairobi, Kenya, 1982. Senior Advisor, U.S. Delegation, Space World Administrative Radio Conference Preparatory Meeting, Geneva, Switzerland, 1984. Senior Advisor, U.S. Delegation, Space World Administrative Radio Conference, 1985. Member, U.S. Delegations, U.S.-Mexico and U.S.-Japan Bilateral Consultations on Telecommunications Issues, Mexico City and Tokyo, 1984. President, New Mexico Bar Association Young Lawyers Division, 1976-1977. President-Elect, Albuquerque Bar Association, 1980-1981. Member, National Diabetes and Digestive and Kidney Diseases Advisory Council of the National Institute of Health, 1989-1992. Chairman, District of Columbia, Mayoral Transition Team for D.C. Public Service Commission and Office of the People's Counsel, 1990. Member, Vice President and General Counsel, Executive Board and Board of Management, International Diabetes Foundation, 1994-2000. Member, Board of Directors and Treasurer, Benton Foundation, 1993—. Member, Advanced Television Field Test Technical Oversight Committee, 1992. Member, Advisory Council, Archdiocesan Legal Network, 1993—. INTELSAT Panel of Legal Experts, 1997—. Member: Board of Directors of STARSYS Global Positioning, Inc., 1993-1995; Board of Directors, 1999— and Chairman of the Board, 2001-2002, Catholic Charities of Washington, D.C.; Board of Trustees, Legal Aid Society of D.C., 1995—. Chairman of the Board, Minority Media & Telecommunications Council, 1994—. *Member:* American Bar Association (Member, House of Delegates, 1999-2001); Federal Communications Bar Association (President, 1995-1996). ***PRACTICE AREAS:*** Communications Law; Corporate Law; Commercial Law. ***Email:*** hrivera@shb.com

PAUL S. SCHLEIFMAN, born New York, N.Y., 1954; admitted to bar, 1982, District of Columbia, 1983, U.S. Tax Court; 1984, Virginia; 1985, U.S. District Court, Eastern District of Virginia and U.S. District Court for the District of Columbia; 1989, Maryland and U.S. Court of Appeals, Ninth Circuit;

(This Listing Continued)

1990, U.S. District Court, District of Maryland; 1991, U.S. Court of Appeals, Fourth Circuit. *Education:* State University of New York at Oswego (B.S., 1976); George Mason University School of Law (J.D., with distinction, 1982). Delta Theta Phi. *Member:* The District of Columbia Bar (Member, Sections on: Taxation; Litigation); Virginia State Bar; American Bar Association (Member, Sections on: Litigation; Tort and Insurance Practice; Business Law); Defense Research Institute. ***PRACTICE AREAS:*** Commercial Litigation; Antitrust Litigation; Complex Litigation; Insurance Coverage Litigation. ***Email:*** pschleifman@shb.com

VICTOR E. SCHWARTZ, born 1940; admitted to bar, 1965, New York; 1973, Ohio; 1986, District of Columbia; U.S. Supreme Court; U.S. Court of Appeals for the District of Columbia; U.S. Court of Appeals, Second, Third, Fourth, Fifth and Sixth Circuits; U.S. District Court for the District of Columbia. *Education:* Boston University (A.B., 1962); Columbia University Law School (J.D., 1965). Twice named, one of the 100 most influential attorneys in the U.S., National Law Journal and top 50 lobbyists in the Nation's capital, Washingtonian Magazine. Co-Author: W. Prosser, J. Wade and V. Schwartz, "Cases and Materials on Torts," 8th edition, Foundation Press, 10th ed, 2000; V. Schwartz, P. W. Lee, K. Kelly, "Guide to Multistate Litigation," Shepards McGraw-Hill, 1985. Author: "Comparative Negligence," 2d edition, Michie Co., 1986. Adjunct Professor and Member, Board of Visitors, University of Cincinnati College of Law. General Counsel, American Tort Reform Association. *Member:* American Bar Association (Chair, Legislative Subcommittee, Product Liability Committee); American Legislative Exchange Council (Co-Chair, Civil Justice Reform Committee). Life Member, American Law Institute (Former Member, Advisory Committee to the Third Restatement of Torts: Products Liability; Apportionment of Liability Projects; Member, General Principles Project). ***PRACTICE AREAS:*** Torts; Products Liability; Insurance; Legislative Practice; Public Policy. ***Email:*** vschwartz@shb.com

JACOLYN A. SIMMONS, born Muskogee, OK, 1954; admitted to bar, 1982, District of Columbia; 1984, U.S. District Court for the District of Columbia, U.S. Court of Appeals, Fifth Circuit and U.S. Court of Appeals for the District of Columbia Circuit. *Education:* University of London; American University School of International Service (B.A., 1976); Howard University School of Law (J.D., cum laude, 1981). ***PRACTICE AREAS:*** Energy Law; Environmental Law. ***Email:*** jasimmons@shb.com

LARRY S. SOLOMON, born Hartford, CT., 1949; admitted to bar, 1975, District of Columbia; 1978, U.S. Supreme Court; 1987, Virginia; 1988, Maryland; U.S. Court of Appeals for the District of Columbia, Second and Fourth Circuits, U.S. District Court, District of Columbia and Eastern and Western Districts of Virginia. *Education:* George Washington University (B.A., 1971); Boston College (J.D., 1974). *Member:* The District of Columbia Bar; American Bar Association; Federal Communications Bar Association. ***PRACTICE AREAS:*** Telecommunications Law; Litigation. ***Email:*** lsolomon@shb.com

D. EDWARD WILSON, JR., born New Orleans, LA., 1951; admitted to bar, 1976, Louisiana; 1977, District of Columbia and U.S. Claims Court. *Education:* University of Virginia (B.A., 1973); Georgetown University Law Center (J.D., 1976). Recipient: Distinguished Service Award, U.S. Department of the Treasury; General Counsel's Award, Department of the Treasury; Chief Counsel's Award, Internal Revenue Service, April, 1988. Editor, Law and Policy in International Business, 1975-1976. Law Clerk, Hon. Robert L. Kunzig, U.S. Court of Appeals for the Federal Circuit, 1976-1977. Author: "A Bank's Response to a U.S. Subpoena for Documents Located Abroad and Avoiding a Contempt Citation," 7 Department of Justice Manual 9-52.16 (1991); "Foreign Investment in United States Securities Firms," Practising Law Institute, International Securities Markets, September 17, 1987, New York, N.Y. Associate Counsel to the President of the United States, 1981-1984. Special Assistant to the President for Administration and General Counsel, Office of Administration, White House, 1984-1985. Principal Deputy Assistant Secretary for Management, 1985-1986 and Deputy General Counsel, 1986-1988, Department of the Treasury. *Member:* The District of Columbia Bar; Louisiana State and American Bar Associations; Washington Institute on Foreign Affairs. ***PRACTICE AREAS:*** U.S. and International Regulatory and Corporate. ***Email:*** dwilson@shb.com

ROBERT J. WOODY, born Bartlesville, OK., 1944; admitted to bar, 1969, Kansas; 1973, U.S. Supreme Court; 1975, District of Columbia. *Education:* University of Kansas (B.A., 1966; J.D., 1969); University of Exeter, England. Strickland Award Graduate, 1966. Legislative Assistant to U.S. Senator James B. Pearson, 1969-1971. Counsel, Committee on Commerce, U.S. Senate, 1971-1973. Special Counsel, U.S. Delegation to the 33rd General Assembly of the United Nations, 1978. Appointed by U.S. Secretary of State as Member-at-Large, U.S. National Commission on UNESCO, 1983-1986. Member, Advisory Council, Center for the Study of Values in Public Life, Harvard Divinity School, 1994-1996. Co-Author: with Richard A. Drom, "Barriers to the Development and Expanded Use of Natural Gas Resources," commissioned and published by the Interstate Oil and Gas Compact Commission, June 22, 1992. *Member:* The District of Columbia Bar; Kansas, Federal Energy and American (Member, Section on Natural Resources Law) Bar Associations. ***PRACTICE AREAS:*** Energy; Corporate Law. ***Email:*** rwoody@shb.com

(This Listing Continued)

OF COUNSEL

PETER S. GLASER, born New York, N.Y., 1953; admitted to bar, 1980, District of Columbia; U.S. District Court for the District of Columbia; U.S. Court of Appeals for the District of Columbia Circuit; U.S. Court of Appeals, Tenth Circuit. *Education:* Middlebury College (B.A., cum laude, 1975); George Washington University (J.D., with honors, 1980). *Member:* District of Columbia Bar; Federal Energy and American (Member, Natural Resources, Energy, and Environmental Law Section) Bar Associations. ***PRACTICE AREAS:*** Energy Law; Utility Law; Environmental Law; Litigation. ***Email:*** pglaser@shb.com

ROBERT M. GURSS, born Cleveland, OH, 1957; admitted to bar, 1982, District of Columbia; 1984, U.S. Court of Appeals for the District of Columbia Circuit. *Education:* University of Michigan (B.A., with distinction, 1979; J.D., 1982). Member, Radio Club of America. President, Land, Mobile Communications Council, 2001-2002. *Member:* Federal Communications Bar Association. ***PRACTICE AREAS:*** Telecommunications Law. ***Email:*** rgurss@shb.com

LEAH LORBER, born Salt Lake City, UT, 1964; admitted to bar, 1994, Illinois; 1997, District of Columbia. *Education:* Indiana University (B.A., 1989); Indiana University School of Law (J.D., 1994). Order of the Coif. Articles Editor, Indiana Law Journal. ***PRACTICE AREAS:*** Torts; Insurance Litigation. ***Email:*** llorber@shb.com

CHRISTOPHER P. MURPHY, born Havre de Grace, MD., 1961; admitted to bar, 1994, Virginia; 1995, Maryland and District of Columbia. *Education:* Stevens Institute of Technology (B.E.M.E., 1983); University of Maryland (M.S., 1990); Indiana University School of Law (J.D., magna cum laude, 1994). Order of the Coif. Member, Indiana Law Journal, 1992-1994. Recipient, American Jurisprudence Prize Award. Author, "Experts Liars and Guns for Hire: A Different Perspective on the Qualification of Technical Expert Witnesses," 69 Ind. L.J. 637. ***PRACTICE AREAS:*** Patent, Trademark, Copyright and Trade Secret Litigation; Intellectual Property Counseling. ***Email:*** cpmurphy@shb.com

GARY M. NATEMAN, born Columbus, Ohio, March 27, 1938; admitted to bar, 1966, District of Columbia. *Education:* Ohio University (B.S.C., 1959); George Washington University (LL.B., 1962). Delta Theta Phi. ***PRACTICE AREAS:*** Alcoholic Beverages. ***Email:*** gnateman@shb.com

RAMSEY L. WOODWORTH, born Syracuse, NY., 1941; admitted to bar, 1967, New York; 1968, District of Columbia. *Education:* Brown University (A.B., 1964); Syracuse University (LL.B., cum laude, 1967). Order of the Coif. Member, Board of Editors, Syracuse Law Review, 1966-1967. *Member:* The District of Columbia Bar; American Bar Association; Federal Communications Bar Association (Treasurer, 1989-1990, Executive Committee, 1986-1989; Chairman, Committee on Professional Responsibility, 1984-1986); Federal Communications Bar Association/Foundation (Trustee, 1991-1994; Chairman, 1992-1993; Treasurer, 1991-1992); President, Broadcast Pioneers Educational Fund, Inc. ***PRACTICE AREAS:*** Telecommunications Law; Technology Law. ***Email:*** rwoodworth@shb.com

ASSOCIATES

PHILLIP R. ANDERSON, admitted to bar, 1997, Missouri; 1998, Kansas; 2000, District of Columbia. *Education:* Kansas State University (B.S., 1992); University of Kansas School of Law (J.D., 1997). ***Email:*** panderson@shb.com

PETER D. BERNSTEIN, admitted to bar, 1995, Massachusetts, District of Columbia, U.S. Court of International Trade and U.S. Court of Appeals for the Federal Circuit; 1998, U.S. District Court for the District of Columbia and U.S. Supreme Court. *Education:* George Washington University (B.A., 1991); University of Akron (J.D., 1994); Boston College Law School (Visiting Student, 1994); American University (LL.M., 1995). ***Email:*** pbernstein@shb.com

CURTIS D. BLANC, admitted to bar, 1999, Virginia and District of Columbia. *Education:* Washington University (B.S.B.A., 1996); George Washington University (J.D., 1999). ***Email:*** cblanc@shb.com

TAMARA Y. BROWN, admitted to bar, 1991, Texas; 1992, District of Columbia; U.S. District Court for the District of Columbia. *Education:* Baylor University (B.A., 1988); Howard University (J.D., 1991). ***LANGUAGES:*** Spanish. ***Email:*** tybrown@shb.com

JANINE A. CARLAN, admitted to bar, 1998, California; 1999, District of Columbia; registered to practice before U.S. Patent and Trademark Office. *Education:* North Carolina State University (B.S., magna cum laude, 1990); Widener University (J.D., cum laude, 1998). ***Email:*** jcarlan@shb.com

EDGAR CLASS III, admitted to bar, 1996, Maryland; 1998, District of Columbia. *Education:* American University (B.A., 1993); Washington College of Law (J.D., cum laude, 1996). ***Email:*** eclass@shb.com

JOHN P. FOLEY, admitted to bar, 1989, Ontario; 1995, North Carolina; 1997, District of Columbia. *Education:* Concordia University (B.A., 1984); University of Toronto (J.D., 1987). ***Email:*** jfoley@shb.com

JOHN K. HSU, admitted to bar, 2000, Virginia; registered to practice before U.S. Patent and Trademark Office (Not admitted in District of Columbia).

(This Listing Continued)

SHOOK, HARDY & BACON L.L.P., Washington—Continued

Education: Johns Hopkins University (B.A., 1990); University of Maryland (Ph.D., 1997); University of Maryland School of Law (J.D., 2000). ***Email:*** jhsu@shb.com

JOHN C. MONICA, JR., admitted to bar, 1991, Virginia; 1992, Maryland; 1994, District of Columbia. *Education:* Northwestern University (B.A., 1987); George Washington University (J.D., with honors, 1991). ***Email:*** jcmonica@shb.com

ELISABETH R. MYERS-KERBAL, admitted to bar, 1993, Virginia and U.S. Court of Appeals, Fourth Circuit; 1994, District of Columbia and U.S. Court of Appeals, District of Columbia Circuit; 1998, U.S. Court of Appeals, Fifth Circuit; 2000, U.S. Supreme Court. *Education:* Hunter College of the City University of New York (B.A., summa cum laude, 1988); American University, Washington College of Law (J.D., 1993). ***Email:*** emyerskerbal@shb.com

J. THOMAS NOLAN, admitted to bar, 1995, Maryland; 1997, District of Columbia. *Education:* University of Rochester (B.A., high distinction, 1974); Georgetown University (J.D., magna cum laude, 1995). ***Email:*** jnolan@shb.com

BRIAN J. PERETTI, admitted to bar, 1992, Maryland, New Jersey, U.S. District Court, District of New Jersey and U.S. Court of Appeals, Third Circuit; 1993, District of Columbia and U.S. District Court, District of Maryland; 1994, Virginia, U.S. Court of Appeals, Fourth Circuit and U.S. District Court for the District of Columbia; 1997, U.S. Supreme Court. *Education:* Rider University (B.A., cum laude, 1989); American University, Washington College of Law (J.D., cum laude, 1992). ***Email:*** bperetti@shb.com

SEAN M. REILLY, admitted to bar, 1993, Virginia (Not admitted in District of Columbia). *Education:* University of Richmond (B.S., 1990); University of Notre Dame (J.D., 1993). ***Email:*** sreilly@shb.com

CARY SILVERMAN, admitted to bar, 2000, Maryland (Not admitted in District of Columbia). *Education:* State University of New York College at Geneseo (B.S., 1997); George Washington University (M.P.A., 2000; J.D., with honors, 2000). ***Email:*** csilverman@shb.com

ROCHELLE M. TEDESCO, admitted to bar, 2001, Massachusetts (Not admitted in District of Columbia). *Education:* Hope College (B.A., 1997); University of Michigan School of Law (J.D., 2000). ***Email:*** rtedesco@shb.com

STAFF ATTORNEY

JOHN C. COOTS, admitted to bar, 1994, Nebraska; 1996, Missouri; 1999, District of Columbia. *Education:* University of Kansas (B.A., 1991); Creighton University (J.D., 1994). ***Email:*** jcoots@shb.com

(For complete Biographical Data on other personnel see Professional Biographies at Kansas City, Missouri, San Francisco, California, Miami and Tampa, Florida, Overland Park, Kansas, Houston, Texas, London, England and Geneva, Switzerland. For a list of Representative Clients, see Professional Biographies at Kansas City, Missouri)

SHULMAN, ROGERS, GANDAL, PORDY & ECKER, P.A.

Established in 1972

WEST TOWER, SUITE 500
1100 NEW YORK AVENUE, N.W.
WASHINGTON, D.C. 20005-3934
Telephone: 202-872-0400
Email: lawfirm@srgpe.com
URL: http://www.shulmanrogers.com

Rockville, Maryland Office: 11921 Rockville Pike. Telephone: 301-230-5200. Telecopier: 301-230-2891.
McLean, Virginia Office: 8180 Greensboro Drive, Suite 750. Telephone: 703-684-5200.
Greenbelt, Maryland Office: 6404 Ivy Lane, Suite 718. Telephone: 301-699-9883.

General Practice including Trial and Administrative practice before U.S. Courts and State Courts, Government Departments, Commissions and Federal Agencies. Antitrust, Banking, Bankruptcy, Civil Rights, Commercial Law, Commercial Litigation and Commercial Transactions, Construction, Corporate, Disabilities, Employment, Entertainment, Environmental, Estate Planning and Administration, Family Law, Federal Tort Claims Act, Franchising, Government Contracts, Health Care, Hotels, Housing and Urban Development, Immigration, Insurance, Intellectual Property, International, Interstate Land Sales, Landlord/Tenant, Leasing, Media, Medical Malpractice, Mergers and Acquisitions, Mortgage banking, Municipal Finance, Pension Plans, Partnerships, Personal Injury, Professional Liability, Real Estate, Reorganizations, Securities, Shopping Center, Taxation and Zoning, Tax Exempt Bond Financing, Telecommunications.

(This Listing Continued)

(For personnel and biographical data, see Professional Biographies, Rockville, Maryland)

IRA S. SIEGLER

1616 H STREET, N.W., SUITE 900
WASHINGTON, D.C. 20006
Telephone: 202-737-0220
Telecopier: 202-347-2075
Email: ira_s_siegler@prodigy.net

Estate Planning, Taxation, Trusts, Estates, Wills and Probate Law.

IRA S. SIEGLER, born New York, N.Y., February 16, 1928; admitted to bar, 1951, New York; 1954, District of Columbia; 1964, Maryland. *Education:* Princeton University (B.A., magna cum laude, 1948); Harvard Law School (LL.B., cum laude, 1951). Phi Beta Kappa. Member, Board of Editors, Harvard Law Review, 1950-1951. Secretary (Permanent), Class of 1951, Harvard Law School. Attorney-Advisor, Tax Court of the United States, 1954-1956. *Member:* The District of Columbia Bar (Trustee, 1978-1983 and Chairperson, 1982-1983, Clients' Security Trust Fund; Chairperson, Trusts, Estates and Probate Division, 1981-1983); Bar Association of the District of Columbia; American Bar Association. Fellow, American College of Trust and Estate Counsel.

RICHARD F. SILBER

3221 M STREET, N.W.
WASHINGTON, D.C. 20007
Telephone: 202-338-0687
Fax: 202-333-0858
Email: info@injury-law1.com
URL: http://www.lawyers.com/richardsilberlaw

Personal Injury Law, Automobile Accidents and Injuries, Liability, Product Liability, Premises Liability, Medical and Professional Malpractice, Construction Accidents, Wrongful Death, Nursing Home Negligence, Obstetric Malpractice, Pediatric Malpractice, Lead Poisoning, Head Trauma, Spinal Cord Injuries, Baycol Drug Usage, Drowning, Swimming Accidents.

FIRM PROFILE: Mr. Silber has been practicing law since 1981. He is admitted in Massachusetts and Missouri. Mr. Silber started his own firm in 1991, and his practice to plaintiffs personal injury and medical malpractice. Mr. Silber represented a plaintiff in a wrongful death case that was well publicized. The family was awarded $2.9 million.

RICHARD F. SILBER, born Baltimore, Maryland, April 16, 1952; admitted to bar, 1981, Massachusetts and U.S. Claims Court; 1985, District of Columbia; 1987, Missouri. *Education:* Beloit College (B.S., 1975); Franklin Pierce Law Center (J.D., 1981). Recipient: Distinguished Service Award, 1999; Department of Justice, Outstanding Services as Trial Attorney, Civil Division, 1981-1985. Trial Attorney, Commercial Litigation Branch, Civil Division, U.S. Department of Justice, 1981-1985. Member, The Association of Trial Lawyers D.C. and Board of Governors.

SILVER, FREEDMAN & TAFF, L.L.P.

A Partnership including Professional Corporations

Established in 1971

1100 NEW YORK AVENUE, N.W., SUITE 700
WASHINGTON, D.C. 20005-3934
Telephone: 202-414-6100
Telecopier: 202-682-0354
URL: http://www.sftlaw.com

Practice before Federal and State Regulatory Agencies, including Securities and Exchange Commission, Office of Thrift Supervision, Office of the Comptroller of the Currency, Federal Reserve Board, Federal Deposit Insurance Corporation, National Credit Union Administration and the Internal Revenue Service Emphasis on Banking, Corporate, Securities, Employee Benefits, Taxation, Syndication, Business, Trial and Appellate Court Practice.

FIRM PROFILE: Silver, Freedman & Taff, LLP is nationally recognized for providing its clients with the highest quality representation on complex corporate transactions. During our more than 30 year history, we have pioneered many types of new transactions, particularly within the areas of securities transactions and banking. Our practice is divided into four areas: (i) Securities and Ventures, (ii) Financial Institutions, (iii) Benefits and Taxation and (iv) Commercial Business Law.

(This Listing Continued)

Our Securities and Venture Law Group specializes in representing clients on the sale of equity and debt securities to fund and expand their businesses. We represent a broad spectrum of clients ranging from developmental stage companies to mature public companies.

We also have a unique expertise in mergers and acquisitions and have represented a wide variety of companies on such transactions. As a result of our expertise and reputation in this area, we are frequently engaged by companies with which we have had no prior relationship to represent them on merger and acquisition transactions.

Our Financial Institutions Group focuses on representing depository institutions, including commercial banks, savings associations, credit unions, non-bank banks, specialty lenders and trust companies on a variety of regulatory matters before various federal and state agencies. In addition, members of the Financial Institutions Group work closely with members of the Securities and Venture Group on complex bank reorganizations, securities offerings, and mergers and acquisitions.

Our Firm represents non-financial companies, both public and non-public, national and international, and individuals in corporate, securities, real estate, leasing, financing, income tax and estate planning matters.

Our Firm also maintains a practice specializing in pensions, executive compensation and employee benefits, including qualified plans of all types (including 401(k) plans and ESOPs), non-qualified deferred compensation, fringe benefits and welfare benefits (including cafeteria plans, welfare benefit plans, VEBAs, corporate owned life insurance, group life and medical plans).

MEMBERS OF FIRM

SIDNEY J. SILVER, (P.C.), born Hartford, Connecticut, March 30, 1934; admitted to bar, 1962, Virginia; 1963, District of Columbia; 1965, U.S. Tax Court; 1968, U.S. Court of Appeals, District of Columbia Circuit; 1996, U.S. Supreme Court. *Education:* Lehigh University (B.S., with honors, 1957; M.B.A., 1959); Georgetown University (J.D., 1962). Beta Gamma Sigma; Beta Alpha Psi. Certified Public Accountant, District of Columbia, 1962. Author: "Income Tax Rules Make Trusts an Ideal Tax-Shifting Vehicle," Taxation for Accountants, March 1971. *Member:* The District of Columbia Bar (Member, Taxation Section and Estates and Trusts Section); Virginia State Bar; District of Columbia Institute of Certified Public Accountants; Washington D.C. Estate Planning Council. ***PRACTICE AREAS:*** Taxation; Corporate and Partnership; Mergers, Acquisitions and Reorganizations; Real Estate Leasing; Estate and Gift Tax; Business and Financial Planning. ***Email:*** sjs@sftlaw.com

ROBERT L. FREEDMAN, (P.C.), born Washington, D.C., August 10, 1939; admitted to bar, 1964, Maryland; 1965, District of Columbia. *Education:* University of Maryland (A.B., 1961); University of Michigan (J.D., 1964). Tau Epsilon Rho. Author: "S&L Mergers and Acquisitions: Negotiating With the Bank Board," The Review of Financial Services Regulation, September 1988; "Assisted Acquisitions of Thrift Institutions Insured By The Federal Savings and Loan Insurance Corporation," Consumer Finance Law, Spring, 1989. Frequent speeches on topics relating to Federal and State Regulations of Banks, Thrifts and Credit Unions. *Member:* The District of Columbia Bar; Maryland State and American (Member, Corporation, Banking and Business Law Section) Bar Associations. ***PRACTICE AREAS:*** Financial Institutions Law; Securities Law; Mergers and Acquisitions. ***Email:*** bfreedman@sftlaw.com

BARRY P. TAFF, (P.C.), born Washington, D.C., November 21, 1945; admitted to bar, 1972, Maryland; 1973, District of Columbia. *Education:* University of Maryland (B.A., 1968); American University (J.D., with high honors, 1972). Associate Editor, American University Law Review, 1971-1972. Author: "Civil Rights Removal Under 28 U.S.C., Section 1443(1); 100 Years of Inutility," 21 American University Law Review, 375, 1972; "Paulsen Triggers Supreme Court Review of Stock-to-Mutual Merger Taxability," 1 Banking Law Report 77, 1984. *Member:* The District of Columbia Bar; Maryland State Bar Association. ***PRACTICE AREAS:*** Corporate; Corporate and Financial Institutions Taxation; Mergers, Acquisitions and Reorganizations; Business and Real Estate Debt Restructuring. ***Email:*** btaff@sftlaw.com

JAMES S. FLEISCHER, (P.C.), born Youngstown, Ohio, November 14, 1951; admitted to bar, 1976, Colorado; 1977, Ohio; 1979, District of Columbia. *Education:* Dartmouth College (B.A., with distinction, 1973); Duke University (J.D., 1976). Senior Staff Attorney, Securities Division, Office of General Counsel, Federal Home Loan Bank Board, 1979-1981. *Member:* The District of Columbia Bar; Colorado, Ohio State and American (Member, Section on Corporation, Banking and Business Law) Bar Associations. ***PRACTICE AREAS:*** Securities Law; Mergers and Acquisitions; Banking Law; Corporate Law. ***Email:*** jfleischer@sftlaw.com

MARTIN L. MEYROWITZ, (P.C.), born Washington, D.C., March 7, 1955; admitted to bar, 1980, District of Columbia; 1982, Maryland, Florida, U.S. District Court for the District of Columbia and U.S. Court of Appeals for the District of Columbia Circuit; 1983, U.S. Tax Court. *Education:* University of Maryland (B.S., 1977); University of Miami (J.D., 1980); Georgetown University (M.L.T., 1985). Phi Alpha Delta. Special Counsel, Division of Corporate Finance, Securities and Exchange Commission, 1982-1985. *Member:* The District of Columbia; The Florida Bar; American Bar Association (Member, Section of Young Lawyers Division). ***PRACTICE AREAS:*** Financial Institutions; Securities Law; Mergers and Acquisitions; Financial Institutions; Corporate Law. ***Email:*** mmeyrowitz@sftlaw.com

DAVE M. MUCHNIKOFF, (P.C.), born New York, N.Y., May 13, 1958; admitted to bar, 1986, New York and New Jersey; 1988, District of Columbia. *Education:* Georgetown University (B.S.B.A., 1979); American University (J.D., cum laude, 1985). Certified Public Accountant, New York, 1982. Assistant Branch Chief, Division of Corporation Finance, U.S. Securities and Exchange Commission, 1985-1988. *Member:* The District of Columbia Bar; American Bar Association (Member, Section of Corporation, Banking and Business Law). ***PRACTICE AREAS:*** Securities Law; Financial Institutions Law; Corporate Finance Law. ***Email:*** dmm@sftlaw.com

STEVEN M. ABRAMSON, (P.C.), born Newark, New Jersey, December 28, 1960; admitted to bar, 1986, New Jersey and U.S. District Court, District of New Jersey; 1987, Maryland and New York; 1993, District of Columbia. *Education:* George Washington University (B.B.A., with distinction, 1983; J.D., with honors, 1986). Phi Eta Sigma; Beta Gamma Sigma. Co-Author: Chapter on Strategies for Negotiating Commercial Leases, *The Franchising Handbook,* AMACOM Books, 1993. Registered Representative, National Association of Securities Dealers, 1984. *Member:* New Jersey State, Maryland State and New York State Bar Associations; The District of Columbia Bar. ***PRACTICE AREAS:*** Real Estate Leasing; Corporate Law. ***Email:*** sma@sftlaw.com

BRIAN L. ALPERT, (P.C.), born New Bedford, Massachusetts, March 6, 1959; admitted to bar, 1987, Maryland; 1988, District of Columbia; 1996, U.S. Supreme Court. *Education:* Dartmouth College (A.B., 1981); Georgetown University (J.D., 1986). *Member:* The District of Columbia Bar; Maryland State Bar Association; Dartmouth Lawyers Association. ***PRACTICE AREAS:*** Corporate Law; Probate Law; Estates and Trusts; Trademark Law. ***Email:*** bla@sftlaw.com

MICHAEL S. SADOW, (P.C.), born New York, N.Y., September 13, 1962; admitted to bar, 1989, Maryland; 1990, District of Columbia. *Education:* Muhlenberg College (A.B., magna cum laude, 1984); London School of Economics and Political Science; The Washington College of Law, American University (J.D., cum laude, 1989). Certified Public Accountant, New Jersey, 1991. *Member:* Maryland State and American Bar Associations; The District of Columbia Bar. ***PRACTICE AREAS:*** Securities; Corporate Law; Financial Institutions. ***Email:*** msadow@sftlaw.com

NANCY M. STILES, (P.C.), born Boston, Massachusetts, August 29, 1949; admitted to bar, 1978, District of Columbia. *Education:* Barnard College (A.B., 1971); Columbia University (M.S., 1972); George Washington University (J.D., 1978). *Member:* The District of Columbia Bar; Federal and American (Member: Section of Administrative Law and Regulatory Practice; Banking, Currency and Treasury Committee; Financial Services Committee) Bar Associations; Women's Bar Association. ***PRACTICE AREAS:*** Regulation of Financial Institutions; Federal Regulatory Law. ***Email:*** nstiles@sftlaw.com

BETH A. FREEDMAN, born Washington, D.C., December 29, 1966; admitted to bar, 1992, Maryland; 1999, District of Columbia. *Education:* Vassar College (B.A., 1988); American University Washington College of Law (J.D., 1991). *Member:* Maryland State and American Bar Associations; District of Columbia Bar. ***PRACTICE AREAS:*** Financial Institutions; Regulatory & Securities Law. ***Email:*** beth@sftlaw.com

ASSOCIATES

CRAIG M. SCHEER, born Washington, D.C., June 29, 1970; admitted to bar, 1995, Virginia and U.S. Court of Appeals, Fourth Circuit; 1996, District of Columbia. *Education:* Syracuse University (B.A., cum laude, 1992); George Washington University (J.D., 1995). Notes Editor, The George Washington Journal of International Law and Economics, 1994-1995 (Member, 1993-1995). Member, The George Washington University Moot Court Board, 1994-1995. Author: "Note, The Second Banking Directive and Deposit Insurance In the European Union: Implications for U.S. Banks," 28 Geo. Wash. J. Int'l. L. & Econ. 171 (1994). *Member:* Virginia State Bar; The District of Columbia Bar; American Bar Association. ***PRACTICE AREAS:*** Financial Institutions Law; Securities Law. ***Email:*** cscheer@sftlaw.com

AGATA SZYPSZAK, born Gdynia Poland, December 4, 1974; admitted to bar, 2001, Massachusetts (Not admitted in District of Columbia). *Education:* Boston University (B.S.B.A., magna cum laude, 1997); Georgetown University Law Center (J.D., 2000). Articles and Notes Editor, The Georgetown Journal of Legal Ethics, 1999-2000. Author: "Where in the World is Dr. Detchakandi?" Clinical Law Review, Vol. 6, Num. 2, 2000. *Member:* District of Columbia Bar. ***LANGUAGES:*** Polish. ***PRACTICE AREAS:*** Securities; Corporate; Financial Institutions Law. ***Email:*** agata@sftlaw.com

(This Listing Continued)

(This Listing Continued)

SILVER, FREEDMAN & TAFF, L.L.P., Washington—Continued

OF COUNSEL

JOHN F. BREYER, JR., born New York, N.Y., July 19, 1953; admitted to bar, 1979, Pennsylvania; 1980, District of Columbia. *Education:* Wharton School of Finance and Commerce, University of Pennsylvania (B.S., 1974); Tulane University School of Law (J.D., 1979). Attorney, Office of General Counsel, Federal Deposit Insurance Corporation, Honors Program, 1979-1981. *Member:* District of Columbia Bar; American Bar Association (Member, Section on Corporation, Banking and Business Law). ***Email:*** bank@clark.net

LAWRENCE J. EISENBERG, born Baltimore, Maryland, September 18, 1957; admitted to bar, 1982, Maryland; 1988, District of Columbia. *Education:* George Washington University (B.B.A., summa cum laude, 1979; J.D., 1982). Certified Public Accountant, Maryland and D.C. Co-Author: *Pension Plan Fix-It Handbook,* Thompson Publishing, 1993. *Member:* The District of Columbia Bar; American Bar Association (Member, Committee on Employee Benefits). (Also practicing individually).

JOHN B. SELMAN, born Brenham, Texas, May 29, 1931; admitted to bar, 1957, Texas (Not admitted in District of Columbia). *Education:* University of Texas (B.B.A., 1953; LL.B., 1958). *Member:* Travis County Bar Association; State Bar of Texas. (Also with Selman & Munson, Austin, Texas). ***PRACTICE AREAS:*** Financial Institutions; Corporate Financing; Mergers and Acquisitions.

JAMES W. LANCE, born Little Rock, Arkansas, July 26, 1943; admitted to bar, 1973, Arkansas and U.S. District Court, Eastern District of Arkansas; 1979, U.S. Supreme Court; 1983, U.S. Court of Appeals, Eighth Circuit (Not admitted in District of Columbia). *Education:* University of Arkansas (B.S.B.A., 1965; J.D., 1973). Beta Gamma Sigma; Beta Alpha Psi; Phi Alpha Delta. Blue Key. Member: U.S. League of Savings Associations; Mortgage Bankers Association of America. *Member:* Arkansas (Member, Financial Institutions Section; Chairman, 1978-1980) and American (Member, Section of Corporation, Banking and Business Law-Committee on Savings and Loan Associations) Bar Associations. [U.S. Army Finance Corps, 1967-1969]. ***PRACTICE AREAS:*** Financial Institution Law.

MARTIN J. O'RIORDAN, born Cambridge, Massachusetts, June 12, 1959; admitted to bar, 1985, Massachusetts (Not admitted in District of Columbia). *Education:* Providence College (B.A., 1982); Boston University (J.D., 1985). *Member:* Massachusetts (Member, Business Law Section, 1990-1994) and American Bar Associations. ***PRACTICE AREAS:*** Banking; Corporate Law; Derivative Products.

E. PRESTON RUTLEDGE, born Knoxville, Tennessee, April 21, 1954; admitted to bar, 1984, Texas; 1985, District of Columbia; 1994, Virginia. *Education:* University of Idaho (B.S. in Business, cum laude, 1976); George Washington University (J.D., with high honors, 1984). Order of the Coif. Member, George Washington Law Review, 1982-1984. Author: "When Insurers Go Broke: A Defense Perspective on Annuity and GIC ERISA Litigation," The Brief (A.B.A.) Vol. 24, No 3, Spring 1995; "The Government's ERISA Litigation Theories in Annuity Purchase Cases: A Defense Perspective," Tort and Insurance Practice Section, ABA, National Institute on Life Insurer Insolvency, 1993; "ERISA Annuity Litigation Implicates Pension Consulting Firm," The Pension Actuary, Vol. 18, No. 5, 1993; "What are the Standards for Purchasing Insurance Contracts After Executive Life?" Tort and Insurance Practice Section, ABA, Annual Meeting, 1992; "Purchasing Annuities for Pension Plan Participants: New Rules are Coming," The Defense Research Institute Life and Health News, 1991; Note, "Amended Returns and the Limitations Period for Tax Fraud," 52 George Washington Law Review 600, 1983. Co-author: "The Proactive Plan Administrator: Handling Employee Benefit Claims and Disclosing Plan Amendments," 1998 Update: West Virginia Employment - Practical Solutions, The Cambridge Institute, 1998. Law Clerk to Judge Henry A. Politz, U.S. Court of Appeals, Fifth Circuit, 1984-1985. *Member:* State Bar of Texas; The District of Columbia Bar; Virginia State Bar; American Bar Association; The Defense Research Institute. [Lt., U.S. Navy, SC, 1976-1980]. ***REPORTED CASES:*** Penn Allegh Coal Co., Inc. v. Holland, 183 F. 3d 860 (D.C. Cir. 1999). ***Email:*** prutledge@sftlaw.com

SILVER & SILVER, P.C.

1612 K STREET, NW, SUITE 1204
WASHINGTON, D.C. 20006-2802
Telephone: 202-861-1200
Fax: 202-861-1268
Email: silverpc@aol.com
URL: http://www.lawyers.com/silverpc

Real Estate, Corporate and Business Planning and Transactions.

(This Listing Continued)

JOEL Z. SILVER, born Jersey City, New Jersey, September 22, 1946; admitted to bar, 1971, District of Columbia. *Education:* New York University (B.A., 1968); George Washington University (J.D., 1971). Order of the Coif. Member, George Washington University Law Review, 1970-1971. *Member:* District of Columbia Bar; American Bar Association. ***PRACTICE AREAS:*** Real Estate Law; Corporate Law; Business Law.

LESLIE CARTER SILVER, born Washington, D.C., August, 7, 1949; admitted to bar, 1975, District of Columbia. *Education:* Vassar College (A.B., 1971); George Washington University (J.D., 1974). Phi Beta Kappa. *Member:* The District of Columbia Bar. ***PRACTICE AREAS:*** Real Estate Law; Corporate Law; Business Law.

SILVERBERG, GOLDMAN AND BIKOFF, L.L.P.

SUITE 120
1101 THIRTIETH STREET, N.W.
WASHINGTON, D.C. 20007
Telephone: 202-944-3300
Telecopier: 202-944-3306
URL: http://www.lawyers.com/bagileosilverberg&goldman

Aviation, Commercial Transportation Law, Administrative Law, Antitrust, International Trade, Customs, Litigation, Import and Export Control, Intellectual Property, including Trademarks, Copyrights and Trade Secrets, Internet and Technology Law.

FIRM PROFILE: Silverberg, Goldman & Bikoff, L.L.P. specializes in aviation and intellectual property and technology law. The firm represents its aviation clients before the Department of Transportation, Federal Aviation Administration, the National Transportation Safety Board, the Department of State, the Department of Commerce, state regulatory agencies and before the courts. It also represents clients in connection with the protection, management, licensing and enforcement of U.S. and foreign intellectual property rights concentrating on trademarks, copyrights trade secrets, unfair competition, false advertising, domain names and internet issues. In the transportation field the firm represents major U.S. and foreign air carriers, regional air carriers, cargo air carriers, airport authorities, on demand air taxi operators, fixed base operators, repair stations, aeronautical parts suppliers and aircraft owners and operators. In the intellectual property and technology fields, it represents clients in the sports, entertainment, multimedia telecommunications, broadcast, automotive, clinical testing, insurance and computer software/hardware sectors. In addition to, and in connection with its transportation and intellectual property specialties, the firm practices in the fields of administrative law, antitrust, export control law, customs, international trade law, corporate law and general commercial litigation.

ROBERT P. SILVERBERG, born Wilmington, Delaware, November 13, 1945; admitted to bar, 1971, District of Columbia, U.S. District Court for the District of Columbia and U.S. Court of Appeals, District of Columbia Circuit. *Education:* Tulane University of Louisiana (B.B.A., 1967); George Washington University Law Center (J.D., with honors, 1971). Member, Order of the Coif. Attorney, Civil Aeronautics Board, 1971-1973. *Member:* District of Columbia Bar; American Bar Association (Chairman, Governing Committee, Air and Space Law Forum, 1992-1994; Governing Committee, Air and Space Law Forum, 1990-1996); National Transportation Safety Board Bar Association. ***SPECIAL AGENCIES:*** Department of Transportation; Federal Aviation Administration; National Transportation Safety Board. ***PRACTICE AREAS:*** Air Transportation Law; Commercial Transportation Law; International Air Law. ***Email:*** rsilverberg@sgbdc.com

MICHAEL F. GOLDMAN, born Philadelphia, Pennsylvania, August 27, 1946; admitted to bar, 1971, District of Columbia and U.S. District Court for the District of Columbia; U.S. Court of Appeals, Fifth Circuit and District of Columbia Circuit. *Education:* Temple University (B.A., 1968); Harvard University (J.D., 1971). *Member:* District of Columbia Bar; American Bar Association (Air and Space Law Forum). ***LANGUAGES:*** Spanish and French. ***SPECIAL AGENCIES:*** Department of Transportation; Federal Aviation Administration; Department of State; Department of Commerce. ***PRACTICE AREAS:*** Air Transportation Law; Commercial Transportation Law; Airport Law; International Air Law; Export Controls. ***Email:*** mgoldman@sgbdc.com

JAMES L. BIKOFF, born New York, N.Y., May 26, 1940; admitted to bar, 1967, Michigan; 1972, District of Columbia. *Education:* University of Cincinnati (B.A., cum laude, 1962); Columbia University (LL.B., 1965); New York University (LL.M., 1966). Phi Alpha Theta. Member, Royal Photographic Society. Author: "Protection Against Counterfeiters," U.S. Trademark Association Newsletter No. 40, 1983; "Commercial Counterfeiting: A New Consumer Fraud," Mobius Vol. 2 No. 2, 1983; "Analysis of the Trademark Counterfeiting Act of 1984," Southern International Business Conference, 1984; "New Weapons in the Battle Against Product Counterfeiting," International Business Law

(This Listing Continued)

Reporter, Vol. 2 No. 2, 1986; "Customs Remedies for Intellectual Property Infringement in Pacific Rim Countries," 1994; "Multilateralization of Intellectual Property Protection Under NAFTA and TRIPS and the Future of U.S. Bilateral Intellectual Property Initiatives," (1994); "Gray Market and Parallel Imports. Recent Case Law and Practical Considerations," (1995). Co-author, with David Wilson: "'Imitation' Fragrances," The Merchandizing Reporter, January, 1988; "U.S. Customs Remedies Against Infringing Imports," Trademark World, 1988; "Customs Remedies for Intellectual Property Infringement in Pacific Rim Countries," (1993); "Intellectual Property Protection Under NAFTA and Trips and the Future of Bilateral Intellectual Property Initiatives," 44 Copyright World 27 (1994); "Protection At The Border," The American Lawyer's Corporate Counsel Magazine, (September 1995); with David I. Wilson: "Remedies for Licensors Against Gray Market Imports," The Licensing Journal (1995); with David A. Wilson & Elizabeth R.P. Bowen: "Business As Usual: Section 337 Practice Unfettered by Amendments," IP Litigator (1995); "ITC and Customs Actions," IP Litigator (1995-1996); with David Wilson, "Special 301: An Effective Remedy to Secure Foreign Intellectual Property Protection," IPWW Outlook (1996); with David Wilson and Courtney Bailey, "Copyright Treaties Adopted Regarding Treatment of Internet and Digital Works," IP Litigator (1997); with David Wilson and Curtis McKenzie, "Protecting Intellectual Property Through the World Trade Organization," Corporate Counsel Magazine (1997). President, International Anticounterfeiting Coalition, 1982-1986. Member, Editorial Board, International Quarterly Columnist Intellectual Property Litigation on Internet Domain Names Issues. *Member:* The District of Columbia Bar (Co-Chairman, Patent, Trademark and Copyright Section, 1988-1991); Association of the Bar of the City of New York; American Bar Association; International Trademark Association; American Intellectual Property Law Association; International Bar Association (IBA); European Community Trademark Association (ECTA); Computer Law Association. ***LANGUAGES:*** French and Spanish. ***PRACTICE AREAS:*** Intellectual Property Law; Internet Law; Technology Law; Customs and Trade Law. ***Email:*** jbikoff@sgbdc.com

DAVID I. WILSON, born St. Louis, Missouri, May 24, 1941; admitted to bar, 1968, District of Columbia; 1973, U.S. Supreme Court. *Education:* Southern Illinois University (B.A., 1963); George Washington University (J.D., 1967). Associate Editor, Journal of Law and Economics, 1966-1967. Publications: Columnist for the *Intellectual Property Litigator* on Internet/Domain Name Trademark Disputes in Federal Court and Before Uniform Name Dispute Resolution Panels; Co-author: "Liberalization of Foreign Participation in the United States Telecommunications Market," World Telecom Law Report 37 (Mar. 1998); "Multilateralization of Intellectual Property under NAFTA and TRIPS and the Future of U.S. Bilateral Intellectual Property Initiatives," 7 Intl. Quarterly 1 (1995); "'Imitation' Fragrances: A Growing Threat to the Goodwill of the Trademark of Famous Fragrances," 7 Merchandizing Reporter 3, 1988; "A Trade Policy Goal for the 1980's: Improving Adequacy and Effectiveness of Intellectual Property Protection in Foreign Countries," 1 Transnational Lawyer 421 (1988); "Intellectual Property Provisions of the Omnibus Trade and Competitiveness Act of 1988," Corporate Counsels International Advisor; "Antidumping Countervailing Duty and Other Trade Actions," PLI, 1987; "The Impact of the Gray Market on Licensing," 21 Les Nouvelles 91 (1986); "The Growing Importance of Trademark Litigation before the International Trade Commission under Section 337," 76 Trademark Rep. 1 (1986); "A Preliminary Analysis," 67 J. Pat. Off. Soc. 57 (1985); "The Semiconductor Chip Protection Act of 1984"; "Litigating Intellectual Property Cases at the ITC," 2 Merchandising Reporter 12 (1983). Chief, Unfair Import Investigation Division (Section 337 litigation), U.S. International Trade Commission, 1982-1984. Attorney and Assistant Director, Bureau of Competition, Federal Trade Commission, 1967-1981. FTC Meritorious Service Award for the Investigation and Trial of Complex Restraint of Trade Cases During 1970-1971. *Member:* District of Columbia Bar; American Bar Association. ***PRACTICE AREAS:*** Intellectual Property Law; Customs and Trade; Antitrust Law. ***Email:*** wilsond@sgbdc.com

---

MICHAEL W. AMBROSE, JR., born Alexandria, Virginia, July 13, 1965; admitted to bar, 1991, Virginia, U.S. District Court, Eastern District of Virginia and U.S. Court of Appeals, Fourth Circuit; 1992, District of Columbia; U.S. Court of Appeals, Federal Circuit. *Education:* University College, Dublin, Ireland; Marquette University (B.A., 1987); Georgetown University (J.D., 1990). Assistant Attorney General, Commonwealth of the Northern Mariana Islands, 1996-1998. *Member:* Virginia State Bar; District of Columbia Bar. ***PRACTICE AREAS:*** Air Transportation Law; Civil Rights Law; Litigation. ***Email:*** ambrosem@sgbdc.com

DAVID K. HEASLEY, born Baltimore, Maryland, October 9, 1953; admitted to bar, 1981, Maryland; 1983, District of Columbia. *Education:* The Johns Hopkins University (B.A., 1978); University of Maryland (J.D., with honors, 1981). Law Clerk, Maryland Court of Special Appeals, 1982-1984. ***PRACTICE AREAS:*** Trademarks; Civil Litigation.

LAW OFFICES OF GARY J. SILVERSMITH

THE WATERGATE
2600 VIRGINIA AVENUE, N.W., SUITE 606
WASHINGTON, D.C. 20037
Telephone: 202-337-7300
Fax: 202-429-5290
Email: nebagamon@aol.com
URL: http://www.lawofficesofgaryjsilversmith.com

Newark, Deleware Office: 131 Continental Drive, Suite 108. 19713. Telephone: 302-368-3100. Fax: 302-368-2255.

Toxic Torts, Asbestos Law, Lead Paint Poisoning, Mold, Environmental Law, Collections.

GARY J. SILVERSMITH, born Denver, Colorado, 1956; admitted to bar, 1981, District of Columbia; 1982, Colorado. *Education:* University of Colorado at Boulder (B.S., magna cum laude, 1977); Georgetown University Law Center (J.D., 1981). Member, Journal of Law & Policy, 1980-1981. Supreme Court of the U.S. (2001—). *Member:* District of Columbia Bar; Colorado and American (Member, Annual Report Committee, Taxation Section, 1982—) Bar Associations.

SILVERSTEIN AND MULLENS

Established in 1960
A Division of Buchanan Ingersoll
1776 K STREET, N.W., SUITE 800
WASHINGTON, D.C. 20006
Telephone: 202-452-7900
Telecopier: 202-452-7989
Email: info@silmul.bipc.com
URL: http://www.silmul.bipc.com

Pittsburgh, Pennsylvania Office: Buchanan Ingersoll, One Oxford Centre, 301 Grant Street, 20th Floor. Telephone: 412-562-8800.
Philadelphia, Pennsylvania Office: Buchanan Ingersoll, Eleven Penn Center, 14th Floor, 1835 Market Street. Telephone: 215-665-8700.
Bryn Mawr, Pennsylvania Office: Buchanan Ingersoll, 937 East Haverford Road, Suite 201. Telephone: 610-581-7004.
Harrisburg, Pennsylvania Office: Buchanan Ingersoll, One South Market Square, 213 Market Street, 3rd Floor. Telephone: 717-237-4800.
Tampa, Florida Office: Buchanan Ingersoll, SunTrust Financial Centre, 401 East Jackson Street, Suite 2500. Telephone: 813-222-8180.
Aventura, Florida Office: Buchanan Ingersoll, One Turnberry Place, 19495 Biscayne Boulevard, Suite 606. Telephone: 305-933-5600.
Miami, Florida Office: Buchanan Ingersoll, Bank of America Tower, 100 S.E. Second Street, Suite 2100. Telephone: 305-347-4080.
Princeton, New Jersey Office: Buchanan Ingersoll, 700 Alexander Park, Suite 300. Telephone: 609-987-6800.
Buffalo, New York Office: Buchanan Ingersoll, 268 Main Street, Suite 201. Telephone: 716-853-2330.
New York, New York Office: Buchanan Ingersoll, 140 Broadway, 35th Floor. Telephone: 646-458-2340.
McLean, Virginia Office: Buchanan Ingersoll, 8280 Greensboro Drive, Suite 601. Telephone: 703-749-6060.
London, England Office: Buchanan Ingersoll, Tower 42, International Financial Centre, Old Broad Street, EC2N 1HQ. Telephone: 44-171-629-7343.
Dublin, Ireland Office: Buchanan Ingersoll, Level 1, 4 Custom House Plaza, IFSC, Dublin 1. Telephone: 011-353-1611-7266. Fax: 3531-836-9305.

Federal Taxation, International Taxation, Commercial Real Estate, Legislative Matters, Corporate Law, Litigation, Bankruptcy, Municipal Finance, Estate Planning, Partnerships, Pension and Retirement Planning, Charitable Giving and Tax-exempt Organizations.

FIRM PROFILE: Founded in 1960 by Leonard L. Silverstein and Richard A. Mullens, Silverstein and Mullens became a division of Buchanan Ingersoll in 2000 when the firms merged. Silverstein and Mullens is internationally recognized for its experience in federal taxation, employee benefits and compensation planning, nonprofit and charitable organizations and trade associations, estate planning, commercial real estate, government relations and litigation. The firm provides representation to local, national and multinational corporations, partnerships, trade associations, government entities and foreign governments.

Silverstein and Mullens also has overall editorial responsibility for the highly regarded Tax Management Portfolios and other products published by Tax Management, a subsidiary of the Bureau of National Affairs (BNA). The portfolios, which Leonard Silverstein originally developed and edited, have set the standard for topic-based tax research tools and cover all areas of taxation.

(This Listing Continued)

SILVERSTEIN AND MULLENS, Washington—Continued

Founded in 1850, Buchanan Ingersoll (www.bipc.com) is a top 100 law firm in the nation. The firm's level of business has grown 17-fold since 1980.

MEMBERS OF FIRM

LEONARD L. SILVERSTEIN, born Scranton, Pennsylvania, January 21, 1922; admitted to bar, 1949, Pennsylvania; 1953, District of Columbia. *Education:* Yale University (A.B., 1943); Harvard University (LL.B., 1948). Attorney, Office of Chief Counsel, Internal Revenue Service, Washington, D.C., 1951-1952. Member, Legal Advisory Staff, Treasury Department, Washington, D.C., 1952-1954. Lecturer in Law, New York University, New York City, 1954-1960. Member, Advisory Group, House Ways and Means Committee, 85th Congress, 1957-1958. Special Tax Counsel, Small Business Administration, Washington, D.C., 1958-1959. Chief Editor, Tax Management, Inc., 1959—. Adjunct Professor, Georgetown University Law School, Washington, D.C., 1960-1961. Member, Task Force on Taxes, President-Elect Nixon, 1968-1969. Member, Task Force on Taxes, Council on Environmental Quality, Washington, D.C., 1970-1971. Member, 1971— and President, 1980-1983, Board of Directors, National Symphony Orchestra Association. Executive Director, Commission on Private Philanthropy and Public Needs, Washington, D.C., 1973-1977. Member, Board of Directors: North American Watch Corporation, 1975—; American Security Bank, 1977-1991. Trustee, Corcoran Gallery of Art, Washington, D.C., 1974-1990. Member, 1980-1983 and Chairman, 1981-1982, U.S. Advisory Commission on Public Diplomacy. Member, Presidential Task Force on Arts and Humanities, 1981-1985. Member, 1982—and Chairman, Tax Working Group, 1982—, President's Committee on the Arts & Humanities, 1982-1989. Member, Board of Directors, French American Foundation, 1983—. Member, Vice Chairman, and Honorary Member, Board of Trustees, John F. Kennedy Center for the Performing Arts, 1985—. Member, Commissioner's Exempt Organizations Advisory Group, 1987-1988. Treasurer, American Committee on the French Revolution, 1987-1989. President, Alliance Française de Washington, 1990-1994. Member, Board of Directors: Bureau of National Affairs, 1985-1989; White House Historical Association, 1991—. Member, Board of Directors: The Choral Arts Society of Washington, 1992—; Yosemite Park and Curry Company, 1992-1993; Chevy Chase Savings Bank, F.S.B., 1994—. *Member:* The District of Columbia Bar; Pennsylvania and American Bar Associations; American Law Institute. ***LANGUAGES:*** French. ***Email:*** silversteinll@silmul.bipc.com

GERALD H. SHERMAN, born Brooklyn, New York, August 29, 1932; admitted to bar, 1959, New York; 1960, District of Columbia. *Education:* College of the City of New York (B.B.A., 1953); Harvard University (LL.B., 1958). Deputy Chief Editor and Member, Advisory Board, *Tax Management,* 1960—. Member, Advisory Board, BNA Pension Reporter, 1975-1981. Adjunct Professor, Georgetown University Law Center, 1973-1987. Lecturer, Federal Taxation and Life Insurance: University of New Hampshire; New York University; Purdue University; College of William and Mary; American College of Life Insurance. *Member:* The District of Columbia Bar; American Bar Association. ***PRACTICE AREAS:*** Taxation. ***Email:*** shermangh@silmul.bipc.com

STUART M. LEWIS, born McLean, Virginia, September 17, 1945; admitted to bar, 1970, Virginia and District of Columbia. *Education:* University of Virginia (B.A., 1967; J.D., 1970). Order of the Coif; Phi Delta Phi. Member, Virginia Law Review, 1968. Member, Advisory Board (Secretary), Tax Management, Inc., 1985—. Counsel: Association for Advanced Life Underwriting; Commission on Private Philanthropy and Public Needs, 1973-1; Commission on Private Philanthropy and Public Needs, 1973-1978. Adjunct Professor, Georgetown University Law Center, 1973-1976. Member, Board of Directors, Tax Management, Inc., 1997—. Chair, Employee Benefits CD Advisory Board, BNA, 1996—. Member: Board of Advisors, New York University Law School, 1991—; Editorial Advisory Board, The Journal of Compensation and Benefits, 1985-1990; Board of Advisors, Virginia Tax Review, 1985—; Editorial Board, The Practical Accountant, 1982—. Chairman, Compensation Advisory Board, Tax Management, Inc. Member: 401 (k) Alert Advisory Board; Corporate Board, The International Foundation of Employee Benefit Plans, 1983-1986. Editor, Compensation Planning Journal. *Member:* The District of Columbia Bar; Virginia State Bar; American Bar Association (Council Director, Section of Taxation, 2000—; Chair, Committee on Employee Benefits, Section of Taxation, 1994-1995; Chair-Elect, 1993-1994; Vice-Chair, 1990-1993). Fellow: American College of Tax Counsel, 1995—; American Bar Foundation, 2000—. Charter Fellow, The American College of Employee Benefits Counsel, Inc., 2000—. ***Email:*** lewissm@silmul.bipc.com

RONALD D. ABRAMSON, born Washington, D.C., April 15, 1949; admitted to bar, 1975, District of Columbia. *Education:* New York University (B.A., magna cum laude, 1971); Georgetown University (J.D., 1974). Phi Beta Kappa. Member, Law & Policy in International Business, 1973-1974. Co-Author: "The Legal Response to the Illicit Movement of Cultural Property," 5 Law & Policy in Int'l Business 932, 1973. Adjunct Professor, Georgetown University Law Center, 1979-1987. Chairman, Board of Trustees, Corcoran Gallery of Art. *Member:* The District of Columbia Bar; American Bar Association; United State Supreme Court Bar. ***PRACTICE AREAS:*** Business Planning; Taxation; Real Estate; Estate Planning. ***Email:*** abramsonrd@silmul.bipc.com

JOHN P. WARNER, born Port Chester, New York, March 8, 1949; admitted to bar, 1978, California; 1980, District of Columbia. *Education:* George Washington University (B.A., 1971); Boalt Hall School of Law, University of California (J.D., 1977). Articles Editor, Industrial Relations Law Journal, 1976-1977. Author: "Statutory, Regulatory and Common Law Anti-Abuse Weapons," in Tax Strategies for Corporate Acquisitions, Dispositions, Spin-Offs, Joint Ventures, Reorganizations 2000 (Practicing Law Institute); "Control, Causality and Section 482," 28 Tax Management International J. 408, 1999. Contributing Author and Editor, Tax Management Transfer Pricing Portfolio Series. *Member:* The District of Columbia Bar; State Bar of California; American Bar Association; United States Supreme Court Bar. ***REPORTED CASES:*** Oak Industries, Inc. v. Commissioner, 96 T.C.559; Libbey v. Commissioner, T.C. Memo 1988 - 254. ***PRACTICE AREAS:*** Federal Income Taxation; Taxation of International Transactions; Transfer Pricing; Mediation of Tax Disputes. ***Email:*** warnerjp@silmul.bipc.com

DONALD B. REYNOLDS, JR., born Mt. Kisco, New York, April 17, 1954; admitted to bar, 1979, District of Columbia. *Education:* Hamilton College (B.A., magna cum laude, 1976); Georgetown University (J.D., magna cum laude, 1979). Senior Case and Note Editor, Law and Policy in International Business, 1978-1979. Editor, Tax Management Real Estate Journal, 1992—. *Member:* The District of Columbia Bar. ***PRACTICE AREAS:*** Federal Tax; Real Estate; Business Transactions. ***Email:*** reynoldsdb@silmul.bipc.com

DAVID I. KEMPLER, born January 30, 1942; admitted to bar, 1966, Connecticut; 1974, District of Columbia and U.S. Tax Court. *Education:* University of Pennsylvania (B.S., 1963); University of Connecticut (J.D., 1966); Georgetown University (LL.M. in Taxation, 1967). Editor, Corporate Tax and Business Planning Review. Associate Professor of Law, George Washington University National Law Center, 1980-1984. Visiting Associate Professor of Law, Columbus School of Law, Catholic University, 1993-1995. Attorney, Internal Revenue Service, 1967-1974. Of Counsel, McKenna, Conner and Cuneo, 1974-1984. Partner, Epstein, Becker & Green, P.C., 1984-1989. *Member:* The District of Columbia Bar; Federal (Chairman, Taxation Section, 1987-1988) and American (Member, Corporate-Shareholder Relationships and Exempt Organizations Committees, Section of Taxation, 1974—) Bar Associations. ***PRACTICE AREAS:*** Taxation; Business Planning; Exempt Organizations; Mergers and Acquisitions. ***Email:*** kemplerdi@silmul.bipc.com

DAVID H. DICKIESON, born Dearborn, Michigan, November 20, 1955; admitted to bar, 1980, District of Columbia; 1981, U.S. District Court for the District of Columbia; 1985, U.S. Claims Court; 1990, Maryland, Virginia and U.S. Court of Appeals, Fourth Circuit; 1991, U.S. District Court, Eastern District of Virginia, District of Maryland; 1992, U.S. Bankruptcy Court, Eastern District of Virginia; 1993, U.S. Court of Appeals for the Federal Circuit 1994, U.S. Tax Court; 2000, Pennsylvania. *Education:* Cornell University (B.A., cum laude, 1977); University of Michigan (J.D., 1979). Trial Attorney, Tax Division, U.S. Department of Justice, 1984-1988; Senior Trial Attorney, Office of Special Litigation, Tax Division, U.S. Department of Justice, 1988-1989. ***PRACTICE AREAS:*** Litigation; Tax Controversies; Bankruptcy. ***Email:*** dickiesondh@silmul.bipc.com

JAMES J. FREEDMAN, born Cleveland, Ohio, September 13, 1958; admitted to bar, 1984, New York and Florida; 1985, District of Columbia. *Education:* Kenyon College (A.B., cum laude, 1980); The Ohio State University (J.D., 1983). Phi Delta Phi. Author: "Commercial Law Chapter," D.C. Practice Manual, 1987 and 1993 editions. *Member:* American and New York State Bar Associations; District of Columbia Bar; The Florida Bar. ***PRACTICE AREAS:*** Real Estate; Banking Law. ***Email:*** freedmanjj@silmul.bipc.com

AEN W. WEBSTER, born Washington, D.C., December 31, 1957; admitted to bar, 1988, California; 1989, District of Columbia; 2000, Virginia. *Education:* Yale University (B.A., summa cum laude, with distinction, 1979); Stanford University (J.D., 1988). Phi Beta Kappa. Associate Editor, Stanford Law Review, 1987-1988. Editor, Tax Management, Estates, Gifts and Trust Journal. Deputy Technical Editor, Tax Management, Estates, Gifts and Trusts Portfolio series. Law Clerk, to Hon. James A. Belson, D.C. Court of Appeals, 1988-1989. Special Assistant to U.S. Secretary, Health and Human Services, 1983-1985. *Member:* The District of Columbia Bar; State Bar of California; Virginia State Bar. ***LANGUAGES:*** French. ***Email:*** websteraw@silmul.bipc.com

LOUIS H. DIAMOND, born Washington, D.C., May 10, 1932; admitted to bar, 1957, District of Columbia. *Education:* George Washington University (B.A., 1954; J.D., cum laude, 1957); Georgetown University (LL.M. in Taxation, 1965). Member, George Washington University Law Review. Certified Public Accountant, Washington, D.C. Adjunct Professor of Taxation, Georgetown University Law Center, 1971-1978. Attorney-Advisor, U.S. Tax Court, 1960-1962. Member, Benefits and Compensation Editorial Advisory Board of the Journal of Accountancy, 1992-1995. Charter Member, American College of Benefits Counsel. *Member:* American Bar Association (Section on Taxation: Committee on Employee Benefits, 1975-1986; Special Adviser, Chairman and

(This Listing Continued)

Vice-Chairman, Committee on Tax Accounting Problems, 1968-1974); American College of Tax Counsel. ***PRACTICE AREAS:*** Taxation; Employee Benefits; Employee Stock Ownership Plans (ESOPs); Business; Estate Planning. ***Email:*** diamondlh@silmul.bipc.com

LINDA K. SHORE, born Detroit, Michigan, April 28, 1959; admitted to bar, 1984, Florida; 1989, District of Columbia. *Education:* Boston University (B.A., summa cum laude, 1980); University of Michigan (J.D., 1983); Georgetown University (LL.M., Labor, 1989). Phi Beta Kappa. Adjunct Professor, Georgetown University Law Center, 1994—. Attorney, Office of Regulations and Interpretations, Pension and Welfare Benefits Administration, U.S. Department of Labor, Washington, D.C., 1984-1988. *Member:* District of Columbia Bar; The Florida Bar; American Bar Association (Section on Taxation). ***PRACTICE AREAS:*** Employee Benefits Law; Securities. ***Email:*** shorelk@silmul.bipc.com

GARY K. BAHENA, born Montebello, California, September 27, 1959; admitted to bar, 1985, District of Columbia; 1991, Virginia and U.S. Supreme Court; U.S. Court of Appeals, Fourth, Federal and District of Columbia Circuits; U.S. Court of Appeals for the Armed Services; U.S. Claims Court; U.S. District Court, District of Columbia and Eastern District of Virginia; U.S. Bankruptcy Court, Eastern District of Virginia; U.S. Tax Court. *Education:* Boston University (B.A., with distinction, 1981; M.A., 1981); University of Pennsylvania School of Law (J.D., 1984). *Member:* The District of Columbia Bar; Virginia State Bar; American Bar Association (Member, Sections on: Real Estate; Taxation; Government Contracts Committee; State and Local Government Committee). ***LANGUAGES:*** Spanish. ***PRACTICE AREAS:*** Commercial Real Estate; Construction; Commercial Finance; Commercial Contracts; Real Estate Taxation; Partnership Taxation; Corporate. ***Email:*** bahenagk@silmul.bipc.com

KEITH A. MONG, born Buffalo, New York, August 28, 1962; admitted to bar, 1987, Maryland; 1991, District of Columbia. *Education:* University of Maryland (B.A., 1984); Catholic University School of Law (J.D., 1987); Georgetown University Law Center (LL.M., Taxation, 1990). Author, Articles: "Executive Compensation and Employee Benefit Implication of the Taxpayer Relief Act 1997," 39 TMM, Page 3, January 5, 1998; "Discounted Options as an alternative to Deferred Compensation," 39 TMM, Page 167, May 25, 1998; "IRS Notice 98-S2- Your (k) and (m) Safe Harbor Guidance," 40 TMM Page 19, January 18, 1999. Co-Author, "The BIG (Built-in Gain) Tax on S Corporations: Big is Definitely Not Better," 1 S Corporation: The Journal of Tax, Legal and Business Strategies, Page 3, 1988. Member, Advisory Board for Compensation Planning, Tax Management Inc. Deputy Co-Chair, Management's Compensation Planning Journal, 16. ***PRACTICE AREAS:*** Employee Benefits; Executive Compensation; Federal Taxation; ERISA. ***Email:*** mongka@silmul.bipc.com

COUNSEL

DEBORAH M. BEERS, born Pittsburgh, Pennsylvania, December 27, 1949; admitted to bar, 1976, Maryland; 1978, District of Columbia. *Education:* Barnard College (A.B., magna cum laude, 1971, Phi Beta Kappa); Columbia University (J.D., 1976). Harlan Fisk Stone Scholar. Associate Editor, Journal of Law & Social Problems, Columbia University, 1975-1976. Town Council, 1981-1987, 1989-1992 and Mayor, 1992—, Glen Echo, Maryland. *Member:* The District of Columbia Bar; Maryland State and American Bar Associations. ***LANGUAGES:*** French. ***PRACTICE AREAS:*** Tax Exempt Organizations; Estate Planning; Federal Taxation. ***Email:*** beersdm@silmul.bipc.com

CARMEN IRIZARRY-DÍAZ, born Puerto Rico, May 4, 1956; admitted to bar, 1982, Puerto Rico; 1983, U.S. Tax Court and U.S. Court of Appeals for the District of Columbia Circuit; 1984, District of Columbia; 1985, U.S. District Court for the District of Columbia. *Education:* University of Puerto Rico (B.B.A., magna cum laude, 1978; J.D., magna cum laude, 1981); New York University (LL.M., in Taxation, 1984). Attorney-Advisor to Judge Jules G. Körner III, United States Tax Court, 1984-1986. *Member:* The District of Columbia Bar (Member: Taxation and Estate, Trust and Probate Law Sections); Bar Association of Puerto Rico; American Bar Association (Member: Taxation Section; Estate and Gift Taxes Committee). ***LANGUAGES:*** Portuguese and Spanish. ***PRACTICE AREAS:*** Estate Planning. ***Email:*** irizarry-diazc@silmul.bipc.com

H. GRACE KIM, born Seoul, Korea, December 3, 1963; admitted to bar, 1989, Maryland; 1991, District of Columbia. *Education:* Georgetown University (B.S.F.S., cum laude, 1985; J.D., 1988; LL.M., 1991). Notes and Comments Editor, The Tax Lawyer, 1987-1988. Assistant to the Branch Chief, Associate Chief Counsel, Passthroughs and Special Industries. Office of Chief Counsel, Internal Revenue Service. Author: "Defining an In Lieu Tax: Western Air Lines v. Board of Equalization," 41 The Tax Lawyer 603, 1988; Tax Management Memorandum: "Recent Developments in Passthroughs Taxation: Guidance on Partnerships," February 12, 2001. *Member:* The District of Columbia Bar (Member, Taxation Section); American Bar Association (Member: Taxation Section; Partnerships Committee; S Corporations Committee). ***LANGUAGES:*** Korean and French. ***PRACTICE AREAS:*** Federal Income Taxation. ***Email:*** kimhg@silmul.bipc.com

(This Listing Continued)

SPECIAL TAX COUNSEL

PATRICIA R. LESSER, born Buenos Aires, Argentina, June 18, 1953; admitted to bar, 1980, District of Columbia. *Education:* University of Paris II, Pantheon-Assas (Licence en Droit, 1975; Maitrise en Droit, 1976); University of Paris I, Pantheon-Sorbonne (D.E.S.S., European Community Law, 1977); George Washington University (M.C.L., 1979). *Member:* The District of Columbia Bar; American, International and Inter-American Bar Associations; International Fiscal Association. ***LANGUAGES:*** French and Spanish. ***PRACTICE AREAS:*** International Taxation. ***Email:*** lesserpr@silmul.bipc.com

JOHN S. ROSS, III, born Philadelphia, Pennsylvania, March 18, 1957; admitted to bar, 1983, District of Columbia and U.S. Tax Court. *Education:* Yale University (A.B., 1979); University of Virginia (J.D., 1982); New York University (LL.M. in Taxation, 1983). Co-Author: *District of Columbia Practice Manual* Taxation Section. Law Clerk to Honorable William M. Drennen, U.S. Tax Court, 1983-1985. Attorney, Office of Chief Counsel, Internal Revenue Service, 1985-1987; Vice Chairman, Tax Management Real Estate Journal, 1992—. *Member:* The District of Columbia Bar; American Bar Association (Member, Real Estate Committee, Section of Taxation). ***REPORTED CASES:*** Truck & Equipment Corporation of Harrisonburg vs. Commissioner, 98 T.C. 141 (1992). ***PRACTICE AREAS:*** Federal and State Taxation; Tax Controversies; Real Estate. ***Email:*** rossjs@silmul.bipc.com

RICHARD S. MARSHALL, born El Paso, Texas, June 13, 1953; admitted to bar, 1981, District of Columbia; 1983, Virginia. *Education:* Tufts University (B.A., 1975); National Law Center George Washington University (J.D., 1981; Masters in Taxation, 1984). *Member:* The District of Columbia Bar (Member, Tax Section); Virginia State Bar. ***PRACTICE AREAS:*** Taxation; Tax Controversies. ***Email:*** marshallrs@silmul.bipc.com

CAROL P. TELLO, born Washington, D.C., January 18, 1946; admitted to bar, 1981, Maryland, U.S. Tax Court and U.S. Court of Federal Claims; 1982, District of Columbia. *Education:* College of William and Mary (B.A., 1968); University of Maryland (J.D., 1981); Georgetown University (LL.M., Taxation, 1983). Author: "Income Tax Withholding On Aliens and U.S. Citizens and Residents Abroad," 14 Payroll Exchange 4, 1989. Office of Associate Chief Counsel (International), Internal Revenue Service, 1983-1997. *Member:* The District of Columbia Bar; Federal and American (Section on Taxation) Bar Associations; International Fiscal Association. ***PRACTICE AREAS:*** International Taxation. ***Email:*** tellocp@silmul.bipc.com

GITA KHADIRI, born Tehran, Iran, March 8, 1965; admitted to bar, 1990, Virginia; 1992, District of Columbia; 1996, U.S. Supreme Court. *Education:* University of Virginia (B.A., 1987); American University, Washington College of Law (J.D., 1990). Topics Editor, American University Journal of International Law and Policy, 1989. Author: Comment, "The Effect of the U.S.-Japan Treaty of Friendship, Commerce and Navigation on Japanese Investment in U.S. Real Estate," 4 Am. U. J. Int'l L. & Pol'y 591 (1989). Office of Chief Counsel, Internal Revenue Service, 1990-1998. *Member:* American Bar Association (Taxation Section). ***LANGUAGES:*** Farsi; French. ***PRACTICE AREAS:*** Taxation. ***Email:*** khadirig@silmul.bipc.com

ASSOCIATES

RUTH C. SHAW, born St. Louis, Missouri, March 21, 1947; admitted to bar, 1973, District of Columbia. *Education:* Barnard College (A.B., 1969); George Washington University (J.D., 1972). ***PRACTICE AREAS:*** Trusts and Estates. ***Email:*** shawrc@silmul.bipc.com

NORMA M. SHARARA, born Pittsburgh, Pennsylvania, July 11, 1963; admitted to bar, 1994, Maryland; 1995, U.S. District Court, District of Maryland (Not admitted in District of Columbia). *Education:* American University (B.A., cum laude, 1985); University of Maryland (J.D., with honors, 1994). *Member:* Maryland State and American (Member, Section on Taxation, Employee Benefits Committee) Bar Associations. ***LANGUAGES:*** Arabic and French. ***PRACTICE AREAS:*** Employee Benefits; Executive Compensation. ***Email:*** shararanm@silmul.bipc.com

LAURA A. BAEK, born Plainview, New York, May 12, 1970; admitted to bar, 1996, New York; 2000, District of Columbia. *Education:* New York University, Stern School of Business (B.S., 1992); Hofstra University School of Law (J.D., 1995); New York University School of Law (LL.M., 1998). Certified Public Accountant, Maryland, 1998. *Member:* American Bar Association. ***PRACTICE AREAS:*** Tax Law; Estate Planning. ***Email:*** baekla@silmul.bipc.com

OF COUNSEL

RICHARD A. MULLENS, born Cheyenne, Wyoming, April 15, 1918; admitted to bar, 1942, Wyoming; 1946, U.S. Supreme Court; 1954, District of Columbia and U.S. Tax Court. *Education:* University of Wyoming (B.A., 1940; J.D., 1942). *Member:* The District of Columbia Bar; Bar Association of the District of Columbia; American Bar Association.

(This Listing Continued)

SILVERSTEIN AND MULLENS, Washington—Continued

HARRISON B. McCAWLEY, born Washington, D.C., September 4, 1923; admitted to bar, 1955, District of Columbia. *Education:* Princeton University (A.B., 1948); Harvard University (LL.B., 1951). Author of Portfolios published by Tax Management, Inc.: T.M. 184, Transactions in Stock, Securities and Other Financial Instruments; T.M. 535, Time Value of Money: OID and Imputed Interest; T.M. 441, Civil Tax Penalties, T.M. 230, Section 482 Allocations; T.M. 115, Section 482: The Statute and the Regulations; T.M. 116, Section 482. Co-Author: T.M. 279, Interest Expense Deductions; T.M. 887, Transfer Pricing: The Code and the Regulations. Attorney, Tax Division, Department of Justice, 1955-1960. Staff Attorney, 1960-1972 and Senior Refund Counsel, 1972-1980, Joint Committee on Taxation. *Member:* The District of Columbia Bar. **Email:** mccawleyhb@silmul.bipc.com

LAW OFFICES OF DAVID L. SIMON

SUITE 412, 1000 CONNECTICUT AVENUE, NW
WASHINGTON, D.C. 20006
Telephone: 202-481-9000
Fax: 202-481-9010
URL: http://www.dlsimon.com
Email: dlsimon@dlsimon.com
URL: http://www.lawyers.com/davidsimonlaw

International Trade Law, Antidumping, Asia Trade, Customs Law, Countervailing Duties, Import and Export Law, Middle East Trade, Foreign Trade Sanctions, Pacific Rim Trade.

FIRM PROFILE: For over 20 years, David L. Simon has practiced in antidumping, countervailing duty, customs, and related law fields, with highly impressive results for his clients.

DAVID L. SIMON, born Carlisle, Pennsylvania, January 23, 1947; admitted to bar, 1977, Maryland; 1979, District of Columbia and U.S. Court of International Trade; 1979-1982, U.S. Court of Customs and Patent Appeals; 1982, U.S. Court of Appeals for the Federal Circuit. *Education:* St. John's College (B.A., 1969); University of Maryland (J.D., 1977). President, Maryland International Law Society, 1976-1977. Adjunct Faculty, International Trade, University of Maryland Law School, 1984-1990. Member, American-Turkish Council, Atatürk Society of America. Author: "Implications of the Taiwan Relations Act for US-ROC Economic Relations," 13 American Studies 85, Taipei: Academia Sinica, 1983; "Annual Survey of US-Taiwan Trade Law," Chinese Yearbook of International Law and Affairs, 1981-1990; "Trade with the United States," Mitchell Silk, ed. Taiwan and International Trade, Oxford Univ. Press, 1993. *Member:* The District of Columbia Bar. ***REPORTED CASES:*** Chung Ling Co. v. US, 805 F. Supp. 45, 829 F. Supp. 1353 (Ct. Int'l Trade 1993), aff'd per curiam, No. 94-1028 (Fed. Cir. June 15, 1994); Chang Tieh Ind. Co. v. US, 840 F. Supp. 141 (Ct. Int'l Trade 1993); Torrington Co. v. US, 790 F. Supp. 220 (Ct. Int'l Trade 1992), aff'd per curiam, Nos. 92-1383, 1392 (Fed. Cir. March 5, 1993); China Nat'l Arts & Crafts Import & Export Corp., Tianjin Branch v. US, 771 F. Supp. 407 (Ct. Int'l Trade 1991); Far East Machinery Co. v. US, 688 F. Supp. 610 (Ct. Int'l Trade 1998); Textron, Inc. v. Int'l Trade Comm'n, 753 F.2d 1019 (Fed. Cir. 1985). ***PRACTICE AREAS:*** International Trade Law; Customs Law.

AYLA ÖNDER, admitted to bar, 1969, Izmr, Turkey (Not admitted in District of Columbia). *Education:* Istanbul University Law School (1968). General Counsel, Export-Import Manager and Secretary General, Maktas Makarnacilik ve Ticaret T.A.S., Izmir, Turkey, 1971-1996. *Member:* Izmir Bar; Atatürk Society of America (Director, 1997); American-Turkish Association; Assembly of American-Turkish Associations. ***LANGUAGES:*** Turkish, German. ***REPORTED CASES:*** Chung Ling Co. v. US, 805 F. Supp. 45, 829 F. Supp. 1353 (Ct. Int'l Trade 1993), aff'd per curiam, No. 94-1028 (Fed. Cir. June 15, 1994); Chang Tieh Ind. Co. v. US, 840 F. Supp. 141 (Ct. Int'l Trade 1993); Torrington Co. v. US, 790 F. Supp. 220 (Ct. Int'l Trade 1992), aff'd per curiam, Nos. 92-1383, 1392 (Fed. Cir. March 5, 1993); China Nat'l Arts & Crafts Import & Export Corp., Tianjin Branch v. US, 771 F. Supp. 407 (Ct. Int'l Trade 1991); Far East Machinery Co. v. US, 688 F. Supp. 610 (Ct. Int'l Trade 1998); Textron, Inc. v. Int'l Trade Comm'n, 753 F.2d 1019 (Fed. Cir. 1985). **Email:** aylaonder@dlsimon.com

SIMON & ASSOCIATES

1742 N STREET, N.W.
WASHINGTON, D.C. 20036
Telephone: 202-429-0094
Fax: 202-429-0075
Email: ron@lawtort.com
URL: http://www.lawyers.com/ronaldsimonlaw

Toxic Torts, Environmental Law, Class Actions, Environmental Diseases, Contamination, Groundwater Contamination, Nuclear Waste, Federal Insecticide, Fungicide and Rodenticide Act (FIFRA).

FIRM PROFILE: Mr. Simon's law practice focuses exclusively on plaintiff's toxic tort litigation. In this area of practice, Mr. Simon has over 27 years of trial experience.

RONALD SIMON, born Philadelphia, Pennsylvania, April 7, 1947; admitted to bar, 1973, Massachusetts; 1974 Rhode Island; 1978, District of Columbia, U.S. Supreme Court. *Education:* Harvard University (A.B., summa cum laude, 1969; J.D., 1973). Author: "Managing Complex Toxic Tort Litigation," Trial, June 1987; "Tort Litigation, A Goal, a Source of Polarization, and a Possible Tool for Prevention," N.Y. Acad. Sc., December 29, 1989; "Preparing Experts in Toxic Tort Cases," Trial, October 1989; D.C. Bar Article: "How to Win the Battle of the Experts," Trial, October, 1992; "Some Answers to the Daubert Puzzle," St. John's Journal of Legal Commentary, at 37, (1993); "High Court Throws out Rigid Rules Evidence, Says Focus Must be on Methods, Principals," 21 Product Safety & Liability Rep. (BNA) No. 30 at 11-15, (Summer-Fall, 1993); Amicus Brief, Daubert vs. Merril Dow Pharmaceuticals, Inc. (on subject of peer review of scientific literature); "Pubic Health Policy Forum Commentary: Integrating Epidemiologic Data into Risk Assessment," American Journal of Public Health, Vol. 85, No. 4, April 1995. Professor, American University Law School, 1973-1974. Counsel to: Center for Health, Environment and Justice, 1981—; American Legion, Washington, D.C. National Headquarters, 1983—. Vice Chair, ABA Sections on Veterans Rights Benefits; Vice Chair Section on Environmental Law. Member: Board of Advisors, Tulane University Law School, Environmental Law Clinic. *Member:* American Bar Association; The Association of Trial Lawyers of America (Newsletter Editor, Sections on, Toxics, Environmental & Pharmaceuticals); American Law Institute. ***LANGUAGES:*** Spanish. ***PRACTICE AREAS:*** Environmental Law.

SIMON, TURNBULL & MARTIN

CHARTERED

2000 PENNSYLVANIA AVENUE, N.W., SUITE 4600
WASHINGTON, D.C. 20006-1812
Telephone: 202-785-2202
Fax: 202-785-2273
Email: info@stmlaw.com

Corporate Mergers and Acquisitions, Financial Transactions, Tax Law, Government Contract Law, Federal Regulatory Practice, Export Controls, Copyright, Trademark, Franchise, and Commercial and Corporate Litigation.

WILLIAM D. SIMON, born Abington, Pennsylvania, October 13, 1947; admitted to bar, 1979, District of Columbia. *Education:* Yale University (B.A., cum laude, 1969; J.D., 1978). Law Clerk to the Hon. Edward R. Becker, U.S. District Court for the Eastern District of Pennsylvania, 1978-1979. *Member:* District of Columbia Bar; American Bar Association (Member, Sections on: Taxation; Business Law). ***PRACTICE AREAS:*** Corporate Law; Business Transactions; Mergers, Acquisitions and Divestitures; Taxation. ***Email:*** Bill@stmlaw.com

LOWELL D. TURNBULL, born Albany, New York, September 16, 1947; admitted to bar, 1973, District of Columbia. *Education:* Harvard University (B.A., magna cum laude, 1969; J.D., magna cum laude, 1972). Phi Beta Kappa. *Member:* District of Columbia Bar. ***LANGUAGES:*** French. ***PRACTICE AREAS:*** Corporate Law; Mergers and Acquisitions; Government Procurement. ***Email:*** LDT@stmlaw.com

JEFFREY L. SQUIRES, born Cleveland, Ohio, April 23, 1946; admitted to bar, 1973, District of Columbia and Wisconsin; 1977, U.S. Supreme Court; 1983, Maryland; 1995, Virginia. *Education:* Washington University (B.A., cum laude, 1968); University of Wisconsin-Madison (J.D., 1973). Editor, Wisconsin Law Review, 1972-1973. Author: "Copyright and Compilations in the Computer Era: Old Wine in New Bottles," 24 Bulletin of the Copyright Society of the U.S.A. 18, 1976; "Notice, Deposit and Registration: The Importance of Being Formal," 24 U.C.L.A. Law Review 1232, 1977 (with Arthur J. Levine); "Can We Stop Software Theft," 2 IEEE Micro 12, 1982 (with Richard H. Stern). Instructor, American University Law School, 1978. Member, Panel of Arbitrators, National Association of Securities Dealers. Member, Panel of Arbitrators, American Arbitration Association. *Member:* The District of Columbia Bar;

(This Listing Continued)

Maryland State Bar Association; Virginia State Bar. ***PRACTICE AREAS:*** Commercial Litigation; Corporate Litigation; Information Technology; Copyrights; Trademarks. ***Email:*** JLS@stmlaw.com

JOHN A. KNAB, born Buffalo, New York, September 19, 1963; admitted to bar, 1993, Maryland; 1995, District of Columbia. *Education:* State University of New York at Albany (B.A., 1986); Washington College of Law of American University (J.D., cum laude, 1992); American University (M.A., Law in International Relations, 1993). Dean's Fellow, Legal Methods, Washington College of Law, 1990-1992. Staff Member, 1990-1991 and Associate Executive Editor, 1991-1992, American University Journal of International Law & Policy. Co-Author, "Forming A Russian Company," Ventus Publishing, 1993. *Member:* The District of Columbia Bar; American Bar Association (Member, Sections on: Business; International Law). ***LANGUAGES:*** Russian. ***Email:*** jknab@stmlaw.com

OF COUNSEL

ROBERT MARTIN, born New York, N.Y., March 24, 1927; admitted to bar, 1949, New York; 1953, District of Columbia; 1963, U.S. Supreme Court; 1994, U.S. District Court, District of Maryland. *Education:* Dartmouth College (A.B., cum laude, 1946); Columbia University (LL.B., 1949). Cases Editor, Columbia Law Review, 1948-1949. Co-Author: "A Guide to the Air Quality Act of 1967," Duke University Law and Contemporary Problems, Spring 1968; "Planning for the Negotiated Settlement of Claims," Federal Contracts Report, May 31, 1982. Law Clerk to the Hon. George T. Washington, U.S. Court of Appeals for the District of Columbia Circuit, 1949-1951. Assistant U.S. Attorney, Southern District, New York, 1951-1953. Member: President's Air Quality Advisory Board, 1968-1969; Board of Visitors, Columbia University Law School, 1974-1977, 1981-1996. *Member:* District of Columbia Bar; Bar Association of the District of Columbia; Federal and American Bar Associations. ***PRACTICE AREAS:*** Government Procurement; International Transactions; Mergers and Acquisitions. ***Email:*** info@stmlaw.com

MICHAEL B. SHEPPARD, born Orangeburg, South Carolina, June 5, 1939; admitted to bar, 1965, South Carolina; 1970, District of Columbia, U.S. District Court, District of Columbia, U.S. Court of Appeals, District of Columbia Circuit and U.S. Court of Federal Claims. *Education:* Furman University (B.A., summa cum laude, 1961); Harvard University (LL.B., cum laude, 1964). Editor, Harvard Law Review, 1963-1964. *Member:* The District of Columbia Bar; South Carolina Bar. [Captain, U.S. Army, 1965-1966]. ***PRACTICE AREAS:*** Corporate Law; Government Contracts. ***Email:*** info@stmlaw.com

GARY HOWARD SIMPSON

WASHINGTON, D.C.

(See Bethesda, Maryland)

Employment Law, False Claim Act (Qui Tam Cases), Wrongful Termination, Wage and Hour Law.

SINGLEY & BEAL, P.L.L.C.

1730 RHODE ISLAND AVENUE, N.W., SUITE 806
WASHINGTON, D.C. 20036
Telephone: 202-463-3090
Fax: 202-463-3095
URL: http://www.lawyers.com/singley&beallaw

Antitrust and Trade Regulation, Telecommunications Law.

FIRM PROFILE: Singley & Beal provides advice on antitrust, telecommunications and other regulatory issues to institutional investors, corporations, trade associations and other law firms. The founding partners have significant experience, representing clients before the Federal Trade Commission, Department of Justice and the Federal Communications Commission and regularly provide advice on mergers and acquisitions, distribution practices, trade association issues, and the application of the Hart-Scott-Rodino Antitrust Improvements Act.

MARK A. SINGLEY, born Takoma Park, Maryland, September 9, 1961; admitted to bar, 1987, New York; 1991, District of Columbia. *Education:* College of William & Mary (B.A., 1983); Stanford University (J.D., with distinction, 1986). Phi Beta Kappa. *Member:* The District of Columbia Bar. ***PRACTICE AREAS:*** Antitrust; Trade Regulation; Telecommunications Law. ***Email:*** msingley@aol.com

W. ASHBY BEAL, JR., born Washington, D.C., March 29, 1958; admitted to bar, 1986, District of Columbia. *Education:* Yale University (B.A., 1980); Georgetown University (J.D., cum laude, 1986). Law Clerk to Judge Richey, U.S. District Court for the District of Columbia, 1987 term. *Member:* The District of Columbia Bar. ***PRACTICE AREAS:*** Antitrust; Trade Regulation; Telecommunications Law. ***Email:*** wabeal@elinkisp.com

(This Listing Continued)

SKADDEN, ARPS, SLATE, MEAGHER & FLOM LLP

1440 NEW YORK AVENUE, N.W.
WASHINGTON, D.C. 20005
Telephone: 202-371-7000
Fax: 202-393-5760
URL: http://www.skadden.com

Firm/Affiliate Offices:

New York, New York: Four Times Square, 10036. Telephone: 212-735-3000. Fax: 212-735-2000.
Boston, Massachusetts: One Beacon Street, 02108. Telephone: 617-573-4800. Fax: 617-573-4822.
Wilmington, Delaware: One Rodney Square, P.O. Box 636, 19899. Telephone: 302-651-3000. Fax: 302-651-3001.
Los Angeles, California: 300 South Grand Avenue, 90071. Telephone: 213-687-5000. Fax: 213-687-5600.
Chicago, Illinois: Skadden, Arps, Slate, Meagher & Flom (Illinois), 333 West Wacker Drive, 60606. Telephone: 312-407-0700. Fax: 312-407-0411.
San Francisco, California: Four Embarcadero Center, 94111. Telephone: 415-984-6400. Fax: 415-984-2698.
Houston, Texas: 1600 Smith Street, Suite 4400, 77002. Telephone: 713-655-5100. Fax: 713-655-5200.
Newark, New Jersey: One Newark Center, 07102. Telephone: 973-639-6800. Fax: 973-639-6858.
Palo Alto, California: 525 University Avenue, Suite 1100, 94301. Telephone: 650-470-4500. Fax: 650-470-4570.
Reston, Virginia: 11911 Freedom Drive, Suite 550, 20190. Telephone: 703-796-2345. Fax: 703-796-2344.
Tokyo, Japan: ATT Main Tower 12F, 2-17-22, Akasaka, Minato-ku, 107-0052. Telephone: 011-813-3568-2600. Fax: 011-813-3568-2626.
London, England: One Canada Square, Canary Wharf, E14 5DS. Telephone: 011-44-20-7519-7000. Fax: 011-44-20-7519-7070.
Hong Kong, China: 30/F Tower Two, Lippo Centre, 89 Queensway, Central. Telephone: 011-852-2820-0700. Fax: 011-852-2820-0727.
Sydney, New South Wales 2000, Australia: Skadden, Arps, Slate, Meagher & Flom (International), Level 13, 131 Macquarie Street. Telephone: 011-61-2-9253-6000. Fax: 011-61-2-9253-6044.
Toronto, Ontario, Canada: Suite 1820, North Tower, P.O. Box 189, Royal Bank Plaza, M5J 2J4. Telephone: 416-777-4700. Fax: 416-777-4747.
Brussels, Belgium: 523 avenue Louise, Box 30, 1050. Telephone: 011-32-2-639-0300. Fax: 011-32-2-639-0339.
Frankfurt am Main, Germany: MesseTurm, 27th Floor, 60308. Telephone: 011-49-69-742200. Fax: 011-49-69-74220300.
Paris, France: 68, rue du Faubourg Saint-Honoré, 75008. Telephone: 011-331-55-27-11-00. Fax: 011-331-55-27-11-99.
Beijing, China: East Wing Office, Level 4, China World Trade Center, No. 1, Jian Guo Men Wai Avenue, 100004. Telephone: 011-86-10-6505-5511. Fax: 011-86-10-6505-5522.
Moscow, Russia: Degtyarniy Pereulok 4, Building 1, 103009. Telephone: 011-7-501-797-4600. Fax: 011-7-501-797-4601.
Singapore, Singapore: Skadden, Arps, Slate, Meagher & Flom (International), 9 Temasek Boulevard, Suite 29-01, Suntec Tower Two, 038989. Telephone: 011-65-434-2900. Fax: 011-65-434-2988.

General Practice.

PARTNERS

LYNN R. COLEMAN, born Vernon, TX, 1939; admitted to bar, 1964, Texas; 1973, District of Columbia. *Education:* Abilene Christian College (B.A., 1961); University of Texas (LL.B., with honors, 1964). Order of the Coif; Chancellors. Editor, Texas Law Review, 1963-1964. Law Clerk, Hon. John R. Brown, U.S. Court of Appeals for the Fifth Circuit (1964-1965).

LESLIE J. GOLDMAN, born Chicago, IL, 1945; admitted to bar, 1970, Illinois; 1980, District of Columbia. *Education:* University of Michigan (B.A., 1967; J.D., 1970).

DOUGLAS G. ROBINSON, born Hamilton, MT, 1943; admitted to bar, 1969, District of Columbia. *Education:* University of Washington (B.A., 1965); George Washington University (J.D., 1969). Editor-in-Chief, George Washington Law Review (1968-1969).

C. BENJAMIN CRISMAN, JR., born New York, NY, 1948; admitted to bar, 1975, Nebraska; 1978, District of Columbia; 1983, New York. *Education:* Syracuse University (B.A., 1970); Creighton University (J.D., 1975).

(This Listing Continued)

SKADDEN, ARPS, SLATE, MEAGHER & FLOM LLP, Washington—Continued

MICHAEL P. ROGAN, born Tiffin, OH, 1948; admitted to bar, 1974, Connecticut; 1980, District of Columbia. *Education:* Oberlin College (B.A., 1970); University of Connecticut (M.A., 1973; J.D., 1974). Editor-in-Chief, Connecticut Law Review, 1973.

ROBERT E. LIGHTHIZER, born Ashtabula, OH, 1947; admitted to bar, 1973, District of Columbia. *Education:* Georgetown University (B.A., 1969; J.D., 1973).

FRED T. GOLDBERG, JR., born St. Louis, MO, 1947; admitted to bar, 1974, California; 1988, District of Columbia. *Education:* Yale University (B.A., 1969; J.D., 1973). Editor, Yale Law Journal, 1972-1973. Commissioner, Internal Revenue Service, 1989-1992.

RONALD C. BARUSCH, born Oakland, CA, 1953; admitted to bar, 1978, Massachusetts; 1981, District of Columbia; 1988, New York; 2000, Virginia. *Education:* Harvard College (A.B., magna cum laude, Economics, 1974); Harvard Law School (J.D., magna cum laude, 1978); Kennedy School of Government, Harvard University (M.P.P., 1978). (Also at Reston, VA).

STEPHEN W. HAMILTON, born San Antonio, TX, 1952; admitted to bar, 1978, Iowa; 1983, District of Columbia. *Education:* Harvard University (A.B., cum laude, 1975); University of Iowa (J.D., cum laude, 1978). Editor-in-Chief, The Journal of Corporation Law, 1977-1978.

WILLIAM J. SWEET, JR., born Oklahoma City, OK, 1951; admitted to bar, 1978, District of Columbia. *Education:* Bucknell University (B.A., 1974); Georgetown University (J.D., 1978). Editor, American Criminal Law Review, 1977-1978.

ERICA A. WARD, born Okayama, Japan, 1950; admitted to bar, 1976, California and District of Columbia; 1991, Michigan. *Education:* Stanford University (B.A., 1972); University of Michigan (J.D., 1975). Managing Editor, Michigan Law Review, 1974-1975.

GLENN J. BERGER, born New York, NY, 1953; admitted to bar, 1979, New York; 1983, District of Columbia. *Education:* Cornell University (B.S., 1975); Vermont Law School (J.D.,1978).

CLIFFORD M. NAEVE, born Rapid City, SD, 1947; admitted to bar, 1984, District of Columbia. *Education:* University of Texas (B.S., 1970; M.A., 1972); George Washington University (J.D., with highest honors, 1984). Order of the Coif.

MARTIN KLEPPER, born New York, NY, 1947; admitted to bar, 1973, New Jersey; 1974, District of Columbia. *Education:* University of Pennsylvania (B.S., 1969); Rutgers University (J.D., 1973). Articles Editor, Rutgers Law Review, 1972-1973.

PAUL W. OOSTERHUIS, born Fort Dodge, IA, 1946; admitted to bar, 1973, Massachusetts; 1979, District of Columbia. *Education:* Brown University (B.A., magna cum laude, 1969); Harvard University (J.D., cum laude, 1973). Phi Beta Kappa.

RICHARD L. BRUSCA, born Queens, NY, 1956; admitted to bar, 1982, District of Columbia and New York. *Education:* State University of New York at Binghamton (B.A., 1978); American University (J.D., summa cum laude, 1981). Pi Sigma Alpha. Managing Editor, American University Law Review, 1980-1981.

MARCIA R. NIRENSTEIN, born Macon, GA, 1956; admitted to bar, 1980, District of Columbia. *Education:* American University (B.A., summa cum laude, 1977); Georgetown University (J.D., cum laude, 1980). Case and Note Editor, Georgetown Law Journal, 1979-1980.

ROBERT S. BENNETT, born Brooklyn, NY, 1939; admitted to bar, 1964, Virginia; 1965, District of Columbia. *Education:* Georgetown University (B.A., 1961; LL.B., 1964); Harvard University (LL.M., 1965). Law Clerk, Hon. Howard F. Corcoran, U.S. District Judge for the District of Columbia (1965-1967).

JANET L. GOETZ, born New York, NY, 1954; admitted to bar, 1982, New York; 1986, District of Columbia; 1991, Massachusetts. *Education:* Cornell University (B.S., 1976); New York University (J.D., 1981).

ALAN KRIEGEL, born New York, NY, 1947; admitted to bar, 1977, District of Columbia. *Education:* Rutgers University (B.A., 1968); Georgetown University (J.D., 1977). Editor-in-Chief, American Criminal Law Review, 1976.

JEANINE L. MATTE, born Ridgewood, NJ, 1949; admitted to bar, 1974, North Carolina; 1978, District of Columbia. *Education:* Virginia Polytechnic Institute (B.S., 1971); University of North Carolina (J.D., 1974).

CARL S. RAUH, born Washington, DC, 1940; admitted to bar, 1966, District of Columbia. *Education:* Columbia University (A.B., 1962); University of Pennsylvania (LL.B., 1965); Georgetown University (LL.M., 1968).

(This Listing Continued)

JOHN J. MANGAN, born Mineola, NY, 1941; admitted to bar, 1968, Pennsylvania; 1990, District of Columbia. *Education:* Cornell University (B.C.E., 1964; J.D., 1967).

WILLIAM S. SCHERMAN, born Brooklyn, NY, 1958; admitted to bar, 1984, District of Columbia. *Education:* George Washington University (B.A., 1980); University of Louisville (J.D., 1984). Articles Editor, University of Louisville Law Review.

ALBERT H. TURKUS, born Newark, NJ, 1945; admitted to bar, 1971, District of Columbia; 1978, Maryland. *Education:* University of Pennsylvania (B.S., cum laude, 1967); Harvard Law School (J.D., 1971). Beta Gamma Sigma.

KENNETH BERLIN, born New York, NY, 1947; admitted to bar, 1974, New York; 1982, District of Columbia. *Education:* University of Pennsylvania (B.A., 1969); Columbia University (J.D., 1973). Assistant Editor, Columbia Journal of Law and Social Problems, 1972-1973.

MITCHELL S. ETTINGER, born Passaic, NJ, 1958; admitted to bar, 1983, Maryland; 1988, District of Columbia. *Education:* Northern Arizona University (B.S., magna cum laude, 1980); Catholic University (J.D., 1983).

KENNETH A. GROSS, born New York, NY, 1951; admitted to bar, 1975, Georgia; 1976, District of Columbia. *Education:* University of Bridgeport (B.A., 1977); Emory University (J.D., 1980).

JAMES V. ALPI, born Mt. Kisco, NY, 1958; admitted to bar, 1988, New York and District of Columbia. *Education:* State University of New York at Oswego (B.S., 1980); Pace University (M.S., 1982); Georgetown University (J.D., 1986).

C. KEVIN BARNETTE, born Frankfurt, Germany, 1959; admitted to bar, 1987, Pennsylvania; 1988, District of Columbia. *Education:* Yale University (B.A., 1983; J.D., 1987).

JEFFREY S. CHRISTIE, born Philadelphia, PA, 1954; admitted to bar, 1979, District of Columbia. *Education:* Bucknell University (B.A., 1976); George Washington University (J.D., with honors, 1979); Georgetown University (LL.M., 1985).

ANDREW L. SANDLER, born Brooklyn, NY, 1956; admitted to bar, 1983, Pennsylvania; 1985, District of Columbia; 1991, Maryland. *Education:* Union College (B.A., magna cum laude, 1979); University of Pennsylvania (J.D., 1982; M.B.A., 1983); University of Warwick, Coventry, England (M.A., 1984). Rotary International Scholar.

JOHN C. QUALE, born Boston, MA, 1946; admitted to bar, 1971, Massachusetts; 1972, District of Columbia. *Education:* Harvard College (A.B., cum laude, 1968); Harvard Law School (J.D., cum laude, 1971).

JOHN N. ESTES, III, born New Orleans, LA, 1957; admitted to bar, 1983, Louisiana; 1989, District of Columbia. *Education:* Tulane University of Louisiana (B.A., summa cum laude, 1979); Louisiana State University (J.D., 1983).

CLIFFORD R. GROSS, born Lakewood, OH, 1963; admitted to bar, 1989, New York; 1990, District of Columbia; 1991, U.S. Tax Court. *Education:* Yale University (B.S. in Electrical Engineering, 1985); The University of Chicago (J.D., 1988).

EDWARD J. MEEHAN, born Wilkes-Barre, PA, 1954; admitted to bar, 1985, Pennsylvania; 1988, District of Columbia. *Education:* Boston College (B.A., 1977); Northeastern University (M.A., 1979); George Washington University (J.D., high honors, 1984).

PANKAJ K. SINHA, born Bihar, India, 1964; admitted to bar, 1990, District of Columbia. *Education:* Columbia University (A.B., 1986); Georgetown University (J.D., M.B.A., 1990).

COLLEEN P. MAHONEY, born Cleveland, OH, 1957; admitted to bar, 1981, District of Columbia. *Education:* American University (B.A., 1978; J.D., 1981).

LANCE T. BRASHER, born Albuquerque, NM, 1960; admitted to bar, 1990, New Mexico; 1991, District of Columbia. *Education:* U.S. Naval Academy (B.S., 1982); Harvard University (J.D., 1990).

JAMES A. LOSEY, born Detroit, MI, 1953; admitted to bar, 1990, Pennsylvania; 1991, District of Columbia. *Education:* Oberlin College (B.A., honors, 1975); Princeton University (M.P.A., 1979); Stanford Law School (J.D., 1990).

GARY A. MACDONALD, born Royal Oak, MI, 1958; admitted to bar, 1989, District of Columbia. *Education:* Michigan State University (B.A., 1980); University of Michigan (M.B.A., 1982); University of Michigan Law School (J.D., 1988).

STACIE E. MCGINN, born Little Rock, AR, 1959; admitted to bar, 1991, New York; 1992, District of Columbia. *Education:* Baylor University (B.B.A., 1981); Georgetown University (J.D., cum laude, 1990). Omicron Delta Epsilon.

JOHN S. MOOT, born Rochester, NY, 1961; admitted to bar, 1988, Maryland; 1991, District of Columbia. *Education:* St. Lawrence University (B.A., 1983); American University, Washington College of Law (J.D., cum laude, 1988). Editor-in-Chief, The Administrative Law Journal, 1987-1988.

(This Listing Continued)

SAUL M. PILCHEN, born Chicago, IL, 1957; admitted to bar, 1983, District of Columbia. *Education:* University of Michigan (B.A., 1979); Northern Illinois University; Georgetown University (J.D., 1983). Editor-in-Chief, American Criminal Law Review, 1982-1983. Law Clerk, Hon. William C. Pryor, District of Columbia Court of Appeals (1983-1984).

KENNETH W. GIDEON, born 1946; admitted to bar, 1971, Texas; 1984, District of Columbia. *Education:* Harvard University (A.B., 1968); Yale University (J.D., 1971).

KENNETH M. KAUFMAN, born New York, NY, 1948; admitted to bar, 1972, California; 1975, District of Columbia; 1983, New York. *Education:* Harvard University (A.B., magna cum laude, 1969); Yale University (J.D., 1972).

JAMES C. HECHT, born 1966; admitted to bar, 1991, Texas; 1993, District of Columbia. *Education:* University of Virginia (B.A., with distinction, 1988); Yale Law School (J.D., 1991).

AMY R. SABRIN, born New York, NY, 1951; admitted to bar, 1986, Maryland; 1987, District of Columbia. *Education:* Wellesley College (B.A., 1972); Stanford University (M.A., 1975); George Washington University (J.D., 1985). Law Clerk, Hon. Oliver Gasch, District of Columbia, 1985-1986.

LAWRENCE ROBERTS, born Abington, PA, 1956; admitted to bar, 1981, District of Columbia; 1991, U.S. Supreme Court. *Education:* University of Virginia (B.A., with distinction, 1979); Georgetown University (J.D., 1981).

OF COUNSEL

CURTIS H. BARNETTE, born St. Albans, WV, 1935; admitted to bar, 1962, Connecticut; 1968, Pennsylvania; 1988, District of Columbia; 1990, West Virginia. *Education:* West Virginia University (B.A., 1956); Yale University (J.D., 1962).

SAMUEL H. GILLESPIE, III, born New York, NY, 1942; admitted to bar, 1973, New York (Not admitted in District of Columbia). *Education:* Middlebury College (B.A., 1966); Vanderbilt University (J.D., 1972).

PHILIP McBRIDE JOHNSON, born Springfield, OH, 1938; admitted to bar, 1962, Illinois; 1983, District of Columbia; 1984, New York. *Education:* Indiana University (A.B., with honors, 1959); Yale University (LL.B., 1962). Managing Editor, Yale Law Journal, 1961-1962.

NEAL S. McCOY, born Winfield, KS, 1940; admitted to bar, 1965, California; 1978, District of Columbia. *Education:* University of Kansas (A.B., 1962); Harvard Law School (LL.B., 1965).

MARY LOU STEPTOE, born Washington, DC, 1949; admitted to bar, 1974, Virginia; 1996, District of Columbia. *Education:* Occidental College (B.A., magna cum laude, 1971); University of Virginia (J.D., 1974). Phi Beta Kappa.

COUNSEL

JOHN A. AMODEO, born New York, NY, 1952; admitted to bar, 1977, New Jersey; 1979, District of Columbia. *Education:* Rutgers University (B.A., 1974; J.D., 1977).

JODY J. BREWSTER, born El Paso, TX, 1955; admitted to bar, 1983, Montana; 1986, California; U.S. Tax Court, U.S. District Court, Central District of California and U.S. District Court, District of Montana, 1993, District of Columbia. *Education:* University of Montana (B.S., with highest honors, 1976; B.A., with highest honors, 1982, J.D., with highest honors, 1983); New York University (LL.M., 1986). Graduate Editor, Tax Law Review, New York University, 1985-1986. Certified Public Accountant, Montana, 1980. Law Clerk, Hon. Russell E. Smith, U.S. District Court for the District of Montana (1983-1985).

JUNE BROADSTONE, born Cleveland, OH, 1951; admitted to bar, 1977, Ohio; 1978, District of Columbia. *Education:* The Ohio State University (B.A., 1974); Capital University (J.D., cum laude, 1977).

GERARD A. CLARK, born Washington, DC, 1962; admitted to bar, 1987, Maryland; 1989, District of Columbia. *Education:* Duke University (B.A., cum laude, 1983); Georgetown University Law Center (J.D., cum laude, 1987).

ARTHUR A. COHEN, born New York, NY, 1954; admitted to bar, 1979, New Jersey; 1980, New York; 1999, District of Columbia. *Education:* Yale University (B.A., 1976); Columbia University (J.D., 1979). Harlan Fiske Stone Scholar.

ROSEANN M. CUTRONE, born Syosset, NY, 1961; admitted to bar, 1986, Massachusetts; 1988, District of Columbia. *Education:* Bucknell University (B.A., summa cum laude, 1983); Harvard Law School (J.D., cum laude, 1986). Editor, 1984-1985 and Managing Editor, 1985-1986, Harvard Journal on Legislation.

MARK C. DEL BIANCO, born Washington, DC, 1956; admitted to bar, 1980, District of Columbia; 1984, Maryland. *Education:* University of Maryland (B.A., 1977); Yale University (J.D., 1980). Phi Beta Kappa; Phi Kappa Phi.

(This Listing Continued)

MONA E. EHLENBERGER, born Paterson, NJ, 1956; admitted to bar, 1983, New York; 1988, District of Columbia. *Education:* University of Rochester (B.A., 1978; M.A., 1979); University of Pennsylvania (J.D., 1982). Phi Beta Kappa.

HENRY C. EISENBERG, born Providence, RI, 1959; admitted to bar, 1985, Massachusetts; 1986, District of Columbia. *Education:* Wesleyan University (B.A., 1981); Harvard University (J.D., cum laude, 1985). Phi Beta Kappa.

CARL R. ERDMANN, born 1966; admitted to bar, 1996, New Jersey and Pennsylvania; 1998, District of Columbia. *Education:* James Madison University (B.B.A., cum laude, 1988); Rutgers University (J.D., 1996).

MATTHEW W. S. ESTES, born Charlottesville, VA, 1958; admitted to bar, 1984, District of Columbia. *Education:* Duke University (B.A., 1980); University of Virginia (J.D., 1984).

CHERYL M. FOLEY, born Warren, OH, 1947; admitted to bar, 1978, Texas and Indiana (Not admitted in District of Columbia). *Education:* Mount Holyoke College, Massachusetts (B.A., cum laude, with honors, 1969); Bates College of Law, University of Houston; Capital University Law School, Ohio (J.D., summa cum laude, 1978).

JAMES A. FRAZER, born New Jersey, 1956; admitted to bar, 1987, District of Columbia. *Education:* Brown University (B.A., 1979); University of Chicago (J.D., 1985).

DON JOAQUIN FROST, JR., born San Diego, CA, 1961; admitted to bar, 1989, District of Columbia. *Education:* Carleton College (B.A., 1983); Duke University (J.D., 1988).

DAVID J. HILL, born Olean, New York, October 19, 1948; admitted to bar, 1973, District of Columbia; 1977, U.S. District Court for the District of Columbia and U.S. Supreme Court; U.S. Court of Appeals for the District of Columbia Circuit. *Education:* Georgetown University (B.S.F.S., magna cum laude, 1970); Harvard University (J.D., 1973). Phi Beta Kappa. *Member:* Federal and American (Antitrust and Litigation Sections) Bar Associations. ***PRACTICE AREAS:*** Energy; Litigation; Antitrust. ***Email:*** djhill@skadden.com

RICHARD A. HINDMAN, born Ottumwa, IA, 1953; admitted to bar, 1990, District of Columbia. *Education:* University of Iowa (B.A., 1980); Catholic University of America (J.D., 1989).

KI P. HONG, born 1967; admitted to bar, 1993, New York; 1994, District of Columbia. *Education:* Cornell University (B.A., 1989); Harvard Law School (J.D., cum laude, 1992).

JERRY L. JACKSON, born Atlanta, GA, 1952; admitted to bar, 1977, Georgia; 1981, District of Columbia. *Education:* Emory University (B.A., 1974); University of Georgia (J.D., 1977).

BENJAMIN B. KLUBES, born Washington, DC, 1965; admitted to bar, 1990, Maryland; 1991, District of Columbia. *Education:* George Washington University (B.A., summa cum laude, 1986); Harvard Law School (J.D., magna cum laude, 1990). Executive Editor, Harvard Journal on Legislation.

KIMBERLY T. MAJURE, born Baltimore, Maryland, May 14, 1968; admitted to bar, 1993, Maryland; 1994, District of Columbia. *Education:* University of Virginia (B.A., with honors, 1990); Harvard University (J.D., 1993); Georgetown University (LL.M., Taxation, 1996). Phi Beta Kappa. Managing Editor, Harvard Civil Rights-Civil Liberties Law Review. Summer Research Fellow, International Monetary Fund, 1993. *Member:* Maryland State (Member, Taxation Section), Federal (Member, Taxation Section) and American (Member, Taxation Section) Bar Associations; The District of Columbia Bar; U.S. Tax Court Bar. ***PRACTICE AREAS:*** International Taxation. ***Email:*** kmajure@skadden.com

MOLLY A. MEEGAN, born Buffalo, NY, 1966; admitted to bar, 1992, New York; 1993, District of Columbia. *Education:* Cornell University (B.S., Developmental Psychology, 1988); Georgetown University (J.D., magna cum laude, 1992).

BRIAN C. MOHR, born White Plains, NY, 1949; admitted to bar, 1979, New York; 1985, District of Columbia. *Education:* Harpur College of the State University of New York at Binghamton (B.A., 1971); Pace University (J.D., 1979). Editor-in-Chief, Pace University Law Review, 1978-1979.

TIMOTHY J. MORAN, born Manchester, NH, 1967; admitted to bar, 1993, New York; 2000, District of Columbia. *Education:* University of Virginia (B.A., 1989; J.D., 1992).

MAUREEN NELSON, born St. Joseph, MO, 1955; admitted to bar, 1981, District of Columbia; 1985, Maryland. *Education:* American University (B.A., 1977; J.D., 1980). Law Clerk, Hon. Mary Ann Cohen, U.S. Tax Court (1982-1984).

LEONARD RAWICZ, born Montreal, Canada, 1931; admitted to bar, 1960, Virginia; 1979, District of Columbia. *Education:* Newark College of Engineering; University of Connecticut (B.S.E.E., 1953); George Washington University (LL.B., 1960; LL.M., 1964).

(This Listing Continued)

SKADDEN, ARPS, SLATE, MEAGHER & FLOM LLP, Washington—Continued

JAMES A. ROSSI, born Masontown, PA, 1936; admitted to bar, 1969, District of Columbia; 1974, New York. *Education:* Tufts University and Pennsylvania State University (B.S.I.E., 1958); New York University (J.D., 1968).

SUZANNE E. ROTHWELL, born New Rochelle, NY, 1945; admitted to bar, 1981, District of Columbia. *Education:* George Washington University (B.B.A., with distinction, 1976; M.B.A., 1981); National Law Center, George Washington University (J.D., 1981).

NANCY G. RUBIN, born Frankfurt, Germany, 1961; admitted to bar, 1986, New Jersey; 1987, New York; 1988, District of Columbia. *Education:* Harvard University (A.B., magna cum laude, 1983); University of Michigan (J.D., cum laude, 1986). Executive Note Editor, Michigan Law Review.

IVAN A. SCHLAGER, born Los Angeles, CA, 1961; admitted to bar, 1989, California (Not admitted in District of Columbia). *Education:* Northwestern University (B.A., 1986); Georgetown University (J.D., 1987).

ELLEN J. SCHNEIDER, born 1948; admitted to bar, 1977, New York; 1999, District of Columbia. *Education:* New York University (B.A. 1970); Brooklyn Law School (J.D., 1976); New York University (LL.M., 1990).

ERICH T. SCHWARTZ, born Rochester, MN, 1958; admitted to bar, 1983, District of Columbia; 1984, Massachusetts and Maryland. *Education:* University of Maryland (B.A., 1980); George Washington University (J.D., 1983).

FRANK C. SHAW, born Binghamton, NY, 1963; admitted to bar, 1989, New York; 1989, District of Columbia. *Education:* Harvard College (A.B., cum laude, 1985); Harvard University (A.M., 1985); University of Michigan (J.D., cum laude, 1988).

MATTHEW A. STEVENS, born Kansas City, MO, 1964; admitted to bar, 1990, Missouri; 1992, District of Columbia. *Education:* University of Kansas (B.A., with highest distinction, 1987); Harvard University (J.D., magna cum laude, 1990).

DOUGLAS W. SWALINA, born Richmond, VA, 1968; admitted to bar, 1998, Florida; 2000, U.S. Court of Appeals, Fifth Circuit (Not admitted in District of Columbia). *Education:* Virginia Polytechnic Institute and State University (B.S., 1993); Stetson University (J.D., magna cum laude, 1997). Phi Delta Phi. Adjunct Professor, University of Houston. *Member:* The Florida Bar; Federal and American Bar Associations. ***PRACTICE AREAS:*** Litigation.

CHARLES F. WALKER, born Wilmington, DE, 1957; admitted to bar, 1985, New York; 1990, District of Columbia; 1994, Delaware. *Education:* Boston University (B.A., magna cum laude, 1979); Northwestern University (M.A., 1980); New York University (J.D., 1984).

SPECIAL COUNSEL

KENNETH KRAUS, born New York, NY, 1942; admitted to bar, 1967, New York; 1989, District of Columbia. *Education:* St. John's University (B.B.A., 1964; LL.B., 1966).

EDWARD D. ROSS, JR., born Evergreen Park, IL, 1945; admitted to bar, 1970, District of Columbia. *Education:* College of St. Thomas (B.A., 1967); Georgetown University (J.D., 1970).

(For Biographical data on other Personnel, see New York, N.Y. Professional Biographies).

SLATER & ZEIEN, L.L.P.

1030 FIFTEENTH STREET, N.W.
SUITE 300
WASHINGTON, D.C. 20005
Telephone: 202-467-5900
Fax: 202-467-4045

Government Contracts, Government Procurement, International Government Contracts, Federal Contracts, Shipbuilding and Repair, Maritime Contracts, Shipyard Litigation, Complex Commercial Litigation, Maritime and Shipping Regulation Law, Ship Financing, Environmental Law, Transportation Law, Intellectual Property.

MARCUS B. SLATER, JR., born Kansas City, Missouri, 1939; admitted to bar, 1969, Maryland; 1972, District of Columbia. *Education:* Duke University (B.A., 1961); American University (J.D., 1969). Member, Editorial Board, American University Law Review, 1968-1969. Co-Author: "Contract Claims: Maximizing Interest and Protecting Appellate Jurisdiction," 3 Acquisition Issues 1 (Sept. 1993). *Member:* The District of Columbia Bar (Member, Section of Public Contracts Law); Maryland State Bar Association. ***PRACTICE AREAS:*** Government Contracts; Shipbuilding Contracts; Litigation; Complex Commercial Litigation; Maritime; Shipping; Regulation Law; Ship Financing. ***Email:*** s-z@ix.netcom.com

JENNIFER J. ZEIEN, born Bryn Mawr, Pennsylvania, 1957; admitted to bar, 1992, Pennsylvania; 1993, District of Columbia. *Education:* Tufts University (B.S.M.E., cum laude, 1979); Massachusetts Institute of Technology (S.M., 1980); George Washington University (J.D., with honors, 1992). Associate Editor, George Washington Journal of International Law & Economics. Author: "International Shipyard Subsidies: Can the United States Level The Playing Field?, George Washington Journal of International Law & Economics 25:2; "Revolution in International Liner Shipping; Implications for U.S. Ports," 106 Transactions 511 (1998); "Facing the Liner Shipping Revolution: Strategies for North American Ports," IAME Proceedings 221 (1999). Co-Author: "Reporting Spills and Accidental Releases," published in The Environmental Compliance Desk Reference, 1995 (Clark, Boardman, Callaghan); "The Economic Implications of Applying CERCLA to Ocean Shipping," Translaw (Fall 1996); "Contingent Valuation in Assessing Natural Resource Damages: an Analysis of U.S. Regulations under the Oil Pollution Act of 1990," 1996; "Sun Shipbuilding & Dry Dock Co.: Lessons for a 21st Century Shipyard?" 106 Transactions 363 (1998). Law Clerk to the Honorable Lawrence S. Margolis, United States Court of Federal Claims, 1992-1993. *Member:* District of Columbia Bar; Pennsylvania, Federal and American Bar Associations. Fellow, American Society of Naval Architects and Marine Engineers. (Also Of Counsel to Williams & Associates). ***LANGUAGES:*** French. ***PRACTICE AREAS:*** Maritime and Shipping Regulation Law; Transportation Law; Procurement Law; Government Contracts; Environmental Law; Intellectual Property; Litigation. ***Email:*** s-z@ix.netcom.com

OF COUNSEL

LEONARD EGAN, born Shreveport, Louisiana, 1941; admitted to bar, 1966, District of Columbia. *Education:* Harvard University (A.B., 1962; LL.B., 1965). Member, Board of Editors, Harvard Law Review, 1964-1965. *Member:* The District of Columbia Bar. ***PRACTICE AREAS:*** Antitrust Law; Litigation; Ship Financing. ***Email:*** s-z@ix.netcom.com

FREDERICK C. WILLIAMS (Also Member of Williams & Associates).

SLAVIT & GILL, P.C.

1025 THOMAS JEFFERSON STREET, N.W.
SUITE 425 WEST
WASHINGTON, D.C. 20007
Telephone: 202-342-1402
Telecopier: 202-342-8387
Email: OFFICE@SLAVITGILL.COM

Commercial Litigation and Arbitration, Corporate, Commercial Transactions, Distribution and Marketing, Technology, Media, Trademark and Copyright, Aviation, Real Estate, Government Contracts and Practice before the U.S. Departments of Transportation, Treasury and Commerce, Federal Aviation Administration, Patent and Trademark Office, Copyright Office, General Accounting Office and other departments and agencies.

FIRM PROFILE: For over a decade the Firm's attorneys have assisted business clients in the aviation, banking, beverage, computer, defense, finance, paper, real estate, sports and entertainment, video, film, and other media and other industries throughout the United States, Canada and overseas. Complex business litigation has been the cornerstone of the Firm's practice in such areas as commercial and government contracts, intellectual property, technology, fraud, financing and real estate. The Firm's attorneys have found that their years of experience as successful litigators give them an important edge in their other specialized practice areas. This has been true whether negotiating the terms of business transactions, drafting contracts and other transactional documents, or dealing with a variety of federal agencies and international tribunals. The Firm provides a complete package of services for clearing, registering, managing and monitoring trademarks and copyrights and represents clients in significant infringement and other "cutting-edge" cases. Its close working relationships with firms in New York, Miami, San Francisco, Montreal and other U.S. and international business centers assures that its clients are always well served. The Firm is the exclusive Washington, D.C. member of International Law Firms (ILF), an association of independent business law firms throughout the world.

HOWARD G. SLAVIT, born Fall River, Massachusetts, April 23, 1946; admitted to bar, 1973, Virginia and U.S. Claims Court; 1979, District of Columbia; 1984, New York and U.S. District Court, District of Columbia and Southern District of New York; 1985, U.S. District Court, Eastern District of New York; 1988, U.S. District Court, Eastern District of Virginia. *Education:* Tufts University (B.A., 1968); George Washington University (J.D., with honors, 1973). Author: "Airlines Battle Cocaine Traffickers," Airline Executive, March 1986. Co-Author: "When is a Distributorship a Franchise?," Beverage

(This Listing Continued)

Industry, Annual Manual 1995/1996. Law Clerk: GSA, Washington, D.C., 1972; to the Honorable Saul R. Gamer, Chief, Trial Division, U.S. Claims Court, Washington, D.C., 1973-1974. Trial Attorney, Court of Claims Section, Civil Division, U.S. Department of Justice, Washington, D.C., 1974-1978. Senior Trial Attorney, Enforcement Division, Office of General Counsel, U.S. Department of Energy, 1978-1979. Deputy Assistant General Counsel for Enforcement, U.S. Department of Energy, Washington, D.C., 1979-1984 (Recipient, Award for Superior Job Performance, 1983). Member, Panel of Commercial Arbitrators (since 1987), American Arbitration Association. Member, International Trademark Association, Computer Law Association. *Member:* The District of Columbia Bar (Member, Computer and Telecommunications Law, Intellectual Property, and Arts, Entertainment & Sports Sections); Virginia State Bar (Member, International Practice, Intellectual Property, and Business Law Sections); New York State Bar Association. ***Email:*** hslavit@slavitgill.com

ROBERT C. GILL, II, born Alhambra, California, August 24, 1960; admitted to bar, 1986, Virginia and U.S. District Court, Eastern District of Virginia; 1987, U.S. Court of Appeals, Fourth Circuit; 1988, District of Columbia; 1990, U.S. District Court for the District of Columbia. *Education:* Virginia Polytechnic Institute (B.A., 1983); George Mason University (J.D., 1986). Delta Theta Phi. Best Speaker, 1984 Moot Court Competition. Associate Justice, Moot Court Board, 1984-1985. National Moot Court Competitor, 1985. Chief Justice, Moot Court Board, 1985-1986. Member, Fairfax County, Virginia Consumer Arbitration Board. *Member:* Fairfax County and American (Member, Sections on: Business; Litigation; Real Property) Bar Associations; District of Columbia Bar (Member, Real Estate, Housing and Land Use Section); Virginia State Bar (Member, Sections on: Real Estate; Business). ***Email:*** rgill@slavitgill.com

---

JONATHAN M. KAYE, born Los Angeles, California, February 3, 1966; admitted to bar, 1994, Maryland; 1995, District of Columbia and U.S. District Court, District of Maryland. *Education:* University of Pennsylvania—Wharton School (B.S., magna cum laude, 1988); Georgetown University (J.D., cum laude, 1994). Recipient, American Jurisprudence Award in Civil Procedure. Associate Editor, American Criminal Law Review, 1993-1994. Co-Author: Note, "False Claims," 30 Am. Crim. L. Rev. 643 (1993); "When is a Distributorship a Franchise?," Beverage Industry, Annual Manual 1995/1996. *Member:* The District of Columbia Bar (Member, Arts, Entertainment & Sports Law Section); Maryland State Bar Association (Member, Business Law Section).

H. DAVID STARR, born Washington, D.C., June 1, 1972; admitted to bar, 1998, Maryland; 1999, District of Columbia. *Education:* University of Maryland at College Park (B.A., with honors, 1993); George Washington University (J.D., with honors, 1998). Phi Beta Kappa. Recipient, Second Prize, GWULS, American Society of Composers, Authors and Publishers Nathan Burkan Memorial Competition. Author: "Are the New Devices for Recording Music Off the Internet Legal?," The Copyright and New Media Law Newsletter, Vol. 3, Issue 3, 1999; "Where to Sue for Internet Actns," The Copyright and New Media Newsletter, Vol. 4, Issue 3, 2000. Panelist: Washington Area Music Association, Fall Seminar, Music Business and the Internet 107, October 21, 2000. Intern, Office of General Counsel, United States Copyright Office, 1997. *Member:* Maryland State Bar Association, Inc.; The District of Columbia Bar (Member, Intellectual Property Section); Washington Area Lawyers for the Arts; Washington Area Music Association; International Trademark Association; Copyright Society of United States of America (Washington, D.C. Chapter). ***Email:*** dstarr@slavitgill.com

MELISSA A. ZELLER, born New York, N.Y., September 27, 1970; admitted to bar, 1998, Virginia (Not admitted in District of Columbia). *Education:* University of New Hampshire (B.A., cum laude, 1992); George Mason University School of Law (J.D., 1998). Treasurer, George Mason Moot Court Board, 1997-1998. President, George Mason Criminal Law Association, 1997-1998. Member, George Mason Inn of Court, 1997—. *Member:* Virginia State Bar. ***Email:*** mzeller@slavitgill.com

KRISTIE G. HAYNES, born Richmond, Virginia, October 4, 1972; admitted to bar, 1997, Virginia; 1998, U.S. District Court, Eastern District of Virginia and U.S. Court of Federal Claims; 1999, District of Columbia, U.S. District Court, District of Columbia and U.S. Court of Appeals, Tenth Circuit. *Education:* University of Richmond (B.S., Biology, cum laude, with honors, 1993); George Mason University School of Law (J.D., 1997). Associate Editor, George Mason Civil Rights Law Journal, 1996-1997. *Member:* Virginia State and American Bar Associations. ***PRACTICE AREAS:*** Civil Litigation. ***Email:*** khaynes@slavitgill.com

SLEVIN & HART, P.C.

Established in 1991

1625 MASSACHUSETTS AVENUE, N.W., SUITE 450

WASHINGTON, D.C. 20036

Telephone: 202-797-8700

Fax: 202-234-8231

Email: slevinhart.com

Employee Benefits Law and Litigation.

FIRM PROFILE: Slevin & Hart, P.C. is a Washington, D.C.-based law firm specializing in all aspects of employee benefits law. Our attorneys provide a wide variety of counseling and advocacy services to clients. We have extensive experience in employee benefit plan design and implementation. In addition, our attorneys litigate before federal and state courts throughout the United States and also represent clients before various government agencies.

BARRY S. SLEVIN, born New York, New York, 1951; admitted to bar, 1975, California; 1976, New York and Florida; 1977, District of Columbia. *Education:* Syracuse University (A.B., cum laude, 1972); Brooklyn Law School (J.D., cum laude, 1975). Senior Editor, Brooklyn Law Review, 1974-1975. Author: "Internal Revenue Code Section 1231: Sale or Exchange of Involuntary Conversion," 40 Brooklyn Law Review, 1459, 1974; "Criminal Law: Entrapment," 40 Brooklyn Law Review 802, 1974; "Owner Participation in Multiemployer Plans," International Foundation of Employee Benefit Plans 1983, Annual Educational Conference Proceeding, 1984; "Defined Contribution Plans for Multiemployer Funds," Employee Benefits Journal, June 1996; "Service Providers and Other Professional Agreements," Employee Benefit Issues, The Multiemployer Perspective, International Foundation of Employee Benefit Plans, 1997 Annual Education Conference Proceedings, Vol. 39, Chapter 8; "Fiduciary Responsibility Under ERISA," Employee Benefit Issues, The Multiemployer Perspective, International Foundation on Employee Benefit Plans 1997 Annual Education Conference Proceedings, Vol. 39, Chapter 28; "Defined Contribution Plans: Obligations and Options," Employee Benefit Issues, The Multiemployer Perspective, 1998, Vol.40, International Foundation of Employee Benefit Plans, Chapter 54. Co-Author: "The Multiemployer Pension Plan Amendments Act of 1980: Explanation, Analysis, Recommendations and Suggested Amendments to Multiemployer Plans," 362 BNA Pension Reporter, October 5, 1981; "How Fiduciaries of Qualified Plans Can Avoid Liability to Themselves and the Plan," Taxation for Lawyers, January, 1983; Taxation for Accountants, February, 1983; "Asset Reversions Upon Plan Termination," Pension Briefings, Federal Publications, March, 1986; "1987 Employee Benefits Review," Pension Briefings, Federal Publications, 1988; "Plan Insurance and Plan Termination," Employee Benefits Law, American Bar Associations Section of Labor and Employment Law, 1991. Charter Fellow, American College of Employee Benefits Counsel. Advisory Board Member, National Conference of Unions and Employee Benefits Funds. Member, Association of Private Pension and Welfare Plans Termination Insurance Committee, 1981-1989; Working Committee, National Coordinating Committee for Multiemployer Plans, 1981-1989. Special Counsel, Pension Benefit Guaranty Corporation, 1975-1978. *Member:* The District of Columbia Bar; New York State and American (Co-Chair, Subcommittee on Pension Insurance and Termination, 1987-1991) Bar Associations; State Bar of California; The Florida Bar. ***PRACTICE AREAS:*** Employee Benefits.

THOMAS J. HART, born New York, New York, 1945; admitted to bar, 1971, Pennsylvania; 1972, District of Columbia. *Education:* Oberlin College (A.B., 1967); George Washington University (J.D., with honors, 1971). *Member:* Pennsylvania and American (Member, Labor Law Section, Employee Benefits Committee) Bar Associations; The District of Columbia Bar; International Foundation of Employee Benefit Plans. ***PRACTICE AREAS:*** Employee Benefits.

FREDRICK M. MARX, born Long Branch, New Jersey, 1955; admitted to bar, 1980, Pennsylvania; 1981, District of Columbia; 1988, Maryland. *Education:* Dickinson College (B.A., summa cum laude, 1977); University of Pennsylvania (J.D., magna cum laude, 1980). Phi Beta Kappa; Order of the Coif. Speaker, International Foundation of Employee Benefit Plans Trustees and Administrators Institute, 2000, 2001; National Conference of Union and Employer Benefit Funds. Co-Author: "Hurdles Mutual Funds Must Leap To Win Employee Benefit Market," The Journal of Mutual Fund Services, June, 1987; "International Business Transactions," Kluwer Publishing (1988). Staff Attorney, Office of Hearings and Appeals, U.S. Department of Energy, 1980-1981. *Member:* The District of Columbia Bar; Maryland State Bar; Pennsylvania Bar Association. ***PRACTICE AREAS:*** Employee Benefits.

JEFFREY S. ENDICK, born New York, New York, 1957; admitted to bar, 1982, New York; 1988, District of Columbia. *Education:* State University of New York at Stony Brook (B.A., magna cum laude, 1978); Cornell University (J.D., 1981). Phi Beta Kappa; Pi Sigma Alpha. Speaker, International Foundation of Employee Benefit Plans Annual Conference, 1995, 1997. Co-Author: "Asset Reversions Upon Plan Termination," Pension Briefings, Federal Publi-

(This Listing Continued)

SLEVIN & HART, P.C., Washington—Continued

cations, March 1986; "1987 Employee Benefits Review," Pension Briefings, Federal Publications, 1988. Contributing Author: "Employee Benefits Law," American Bar Association, Section of Labor and Employment Law, 1991; Attorney, Pension Benefit Guaranty Corporation, 1981-1984. *Member:* The District of Columbia Bar; New York State Bar Association. ***PRACTICE AREAS:*** Employee Benefits.

MARC H. RIFKIND, born Glasgow, Scotland, 1963; admitted to bar, 1987, Pennsylvania; 1988, District of Columbia. *Education:* Boston University (B.A., summa cum laude, with distinction in Political Science, 1984); University of Michigan (J. D., 1987). Contributing Author: "Employee Benefits Law," American Bar Association Section Labor and Employment Law, 1991. *Member:* The District of Columbia Bar. ***PRACTICE AREAS:*** Employee Benefits.

SHARON McNEILLY GOODMAN, born Yorktown, N.Y., 1963; admitted to bar, 1989, Maryland; 1990, District of Columbia. *Education:* The Johns Hopkins University (B.A., 1984); Northeastern University School of Law (J.D., 1988). Contributing Author: "Employee Benefits Law," American Bar Association, Section Labor and Employment Law, 1991. *Member:* The District of Columbia Bar; Maryland State and American Bar Associations.

ALLISON A. MADAN, born Bridgeport, Connecticut, 1962; admitted to bar, 1990, Pennsylvania; 1992, District of Columbia. *Education:* University of Scranton (B.S., 1984); Catholic University of America (J.D., 1990). Fanning Labor Law Scholar. Staff Member, Catholic University Law Review, Vol. 39, 1990. *Member:* The District of Columbia Bar; Pennsylvania and American Bar Associations. ***PRACTICE AREAS:*** Employee Benefits.

BETH A. BANGERT, born Green Bay, Wisconsin, October 9, 1970; admitted to bar, 2001, Maryland (Not admitted in District of Columbia). *Education:* Beloit College (B.A., 1992); American University (M.A., 1994); Catholic University of American (J.D., 2000). *Member:* Maryland State Bar Association, Inc. ***PRACTICE AREAS:*** ERISA; Employee Benefits.

LYNN A. BOWERS, born London, England, 1956; admitted to bar, 1994, Maryland; 1996, District of Columbia. *Education:* Antioch College (B.A., 1990); Georgetown University (J.D., magna cum laude, 1994). Order of the Coif. *Member:* Maryland State and Federal Bar Associations; District of Columbia Bar. ***PRACTICE AREAS:*** Employee Benefits.

RHEA A. LAGANO, born Huntington, New York, 1974; admitted to bar, 1999, North Carolina (Not admitted in District of Columbia). *Education:* State University of New York (B.A., 1996); University of North Carolina at Chapel Hill (J.D., 1999). Managing Editor, North Carolina Banking Institute Journal, 1998-1999. *Member:* North Carolina and American Bar Associations. ***PRACTICE AREAS:*** Employee Benefits. ***Email:*** rlagano@slevinhart.com

DEBRA L. PETCOVE, born Philadelphia, Pennsylvania, February 25, 1964; admitted to bar, 1989, Pennsylvania; 1991, District of Columbia; 1995, California. *Education:* University of Pennsylvania (B.A., magna cum laude, 1986); Georgetown University Law Center (J.D., 1989). *Member:* Pennsylvania Bar Association; District of Columbia Bar; State Bar of California. ***PRACTICE AREAS:*** Employee Benefits.

COLLEEN R. ROBERTSON, born Rochester, New York, 1967; admitted to bar, 1991, Virginia; 1992, District of Columbia. *Education:* Auburn University (B.A., with high honors, 1988); Columbia University (J.D., 1991). Stone Scholar. *Member:* The District of Columbia Bar; Virginia State and American Bar Associations. ***PRACTICE AREAS:*** Employee Benefits; Taxation.

MALCOLM C. SLEE, born Box Hill, Australia, 1972; admitted to bar, 1999, New York; 2000, District of Columbia. *Education:* Tufts University (B.A., 1994); Georgetown University (J.D., 1998). ***PRACTICE AREAS:*** Employee Benefits.

LAURA BARTON STACK, born New York, New York, 1968; admitted to bar, 1996, California; 1997, District of Columbia. *Education:* University of California, Santa Cruz (B.A., 1991); Hastings College of the Law, University of California (J.D., 1996). *Member:* The District of Columbia Bar; State Bar of California; American Bar Association. ***PRACTICE AREAS:*** Employee Benefits.

GLENN H. STEPHENS, III, born Lock Haven, Pennsylvania, March 12, 1958; (admission pending). *Education:* Millersville University of Pennsylvania (B.A., 1981); University of California, Los Angeles (M.A., 1987; Ph.D., 1992); University of California at Berkeley School of Law, (J.D., 2000). Honorary Lifetime Member, University of California, Los Angeles, Mortar Board, 1994. Member, American Political Science Association, 1987—. Editor-in-Chief, Berkeley Journal of Employment and Labor Law, 1998-1999. *Member:* The District of Columbia Bar. ***PRACTICE AREAS:*** ERISA; Labor Law; Medical Law; Employee Benefits.

SARAH E. SUHRE, born Silver Spring, Maryland, February 1, 1976; admitted to bar, 2000, Maryland; 2000, District of Columbia. *Education:* University of Maryland (B.A., 1997); Georgetown University (J.D., cum laude, 2000). Alpha Lambda Delta. *Member:* Montgomery County and Maryland State Bar Associations. ***PRACTICE AREAS:*** Employee Benefits.

MARC A. TENENBAUM, born Cleveland, Ohio, September 26, 1962; admitted to bar, 1989, Ohio; 1999, District of Columbia. *Education:* University of Michigan (A.B., 1984); The Ohio State University (J.D., 1989). ***PRACTICE AREAS:*** Employee Benefits Litigation.

JENNIFER C. WISEMAN, born Cheverly, Maryland, October 1, 1968; admitted to bar, 1993, Maryland; 1994, Virginia; 1996, District of Columbia. *Education:* Yale University (B.A., 1990); Washington & Lee University (J.D., 1993). *Member:* Maryland, Virginia and District of Columbia Bar Associations. ***PRACTICE AREAS:*** Employee Benefits.

SLOVER & LOFTUS

1224 SEVENTEENTH STREET, N.W.
WASHINGTON, D.C. 20036
Telephone: 202-347-7170
Telecopier: 202-347-3619
Email: info@sloverandloftus.com
URL: http://www.sloverandloftus.com

Administrative Law. Practice before Federal and State Courts, Commissions, Departments and Agencies. Commercial Arbitration, Transportation, Utility, Energy, Trade Regulation, Commercial Contracts, Government Contracts and Legislative Law.

WILLIAM L. SLOVER, born Washington, D.C., August 15, 1937; admitted to bar, 1962, District of Columbia. *Education:* Yale University (A.B., 1959); Columbia University (LL.B., 1962). *Member:* The District of Columbia Bar; Federal and American Bar Associations. ***Email:*** wls@sloverandloftus.com

C. MICHAEL LOFTUS, born Cheverly, Maryland, October 9, 1946; admitted to bar, 1973, Maryland; 1976, District of Columbia. *Education:* Wheeling College (B.S., 1968); Columbus School of Law, Catholic University of America (J.D., 1973). Editor-in-Chief, Catholic University of America Law Review, 1972-1973. Law Clerk to Judge Joseph H. Young, U.S. District Court, District of Maryland, 1973-1974. *Member:* The District of Columbia Bar; Maryland State, Federal and American Bar Associations. ***Email:*** cml@sloverandloftus.com

DONALD G. AVERY, born Elmhurst, Illinois, August 19, 1943; admitted to bar, 1969, District of Columbia; 1973, U.S. Supreme Court. *Education:* Princeton University (A.B., magna cum laude, 1965); Harvard University (J.D., 1968). Counsel and Assistant General Counsel, National Railroad Passenger Corporation (Amtrak), 1973-1979. *Member:* The District of Columbia Bar; American Bar Association (Member, Sections on: Public Utilities; Administrative Law). ***Email:*** dga@sloverandloftus.com

JOHN H. LESEUR, born Batavia, New York, October 30, 1952; admitted to bar, 1979, District of Columbia. *Education:* Dartmouth College (B.A., summa cum laude, 1974); Georgetown University (J.D., 1979). Phi Beta Kappa. *Member:* The District of Columbia Bar; American Bar Association (Chairman, Young Lawyers Division Transportation Law Committee, 1986-1987). ***Email:*** jhl@sloverandloftus.com

KELVIN J. DOWD, born Rochester, N.Y., September 24, 1956; admitted to bar, 1981, District of Columbia. *Education:* State University of New York at Albany (B.A., cum laude, 1978); Washington College of Law, American University (J.D., 1981). *Member:* The District of Columbia Bar. ***Email:*** kjd@sloverandloftus.com

ROBERT D. ROSENBERG, born Atlanta, Georgia, May 21, 1956; admitted to bar, 1982, District of Columbia and Georgia. *Education:* Brown University (A.B., magna cum laude, 1978); Harvard University (J.D., 1981). Phi Beta Kappa. Legislative Counsel, Congressman Thomas E. Petri, 1981-1982. *Member:* The District of Columbia Bar; State Bar of Georgia; American Bar Association. ***Email:*** rdr@sloverandloftus.com

CHRISTOPHER A. MILLS, born Chicago, Illinois, July 19, 1943; admitted to bar, 1968, Illinois; 1995, District of Columbia. *Education:* Amherst College (B.A., 1965); University of Michigan (J.D., 1968). ***Email:*** cam@sloverandloftus.com

FRANK J. PERGOLIZZI, born Brooklyn, New York, June 3, 1959; admitted to bar, 1984, North Carolina; 1985, Virginia; 1986, District of Columbia. *Education:* Villanova University (B.A., 1981); Wake Forest University (J.D., 1984). Recipient, North Carolina Academy of Trial Lawyers Award. Visiting Fellow, Catholic University of America, 1984-1985. *Member:* The District of Columbia Bar; North Carolina State Bar; Virginia State Bar; American Bar Association (Member, Litigation Section). ***Email:*** fjp@sloverandloftus.com

---

ANDREW B. KOLESAR III, born Pittsburgh, Pennsylvania, December 26, 1966; admitted to bar, 1991, Pennsylvania; 1992, District of Columbia.

(This Listing Continued)

Education: Cornell University (B.A., 1988); University of Notre Dame (J.D., 1991). *Member:* The District of Columbia Bar. **Email:** abk@sloverandloftus.com

PETER A. PFOHL, born Minneapolis, Minnesota, April 3, 1967; admitted to bar, 1997, District of Columbia. *Education:* University of Notre Dame (B.A., 1989); Columbus School of Law of the Catholic University of America (J.D., cum laude, 1997). Member, Catholic University of America Law Review, 1995-1997. Author: "Who Should Pay for Agency Adjudication?: A Study of $200,00 Filing Fees at the Surface Transportation Board," 25 Trans. L.J. 57 (1997); "Congressional Review of Agency Rulemaking: The 104th Congress and the Salvage Timber Directive," 14 J.L. Pol. 1 (1998). Legislative Assistant, Congressman George J. Hochbrueckner, 1989-1994. *Member:* The District of Columbia Bar. **Email:** pap@sloverandloftus.com

DANIEL M. JAFFE, born Cleveland, Ohio, June 7, 1970; admitted to bar, 1999, District of Columbia. *Education:* American University (B.A., cum laude, 1991); George Washington University (J.D., 1998). Moot Court Board. Trial Court Board. *Member:* The District of Columbia Bar. **Email:** dmj@sloverandloftus.com

KAREN HASSELL HERREN, born Redstone Arsenal, Alabama, September 8, 1971; admitted to bar, 1997, California; 2000, District of Columbia. *Education:* East Carolina University (B.A., 1993); Santa Clara University School of Law (J.D., 1997). Phi Alpha Delta. Member, Golden Key National Honor Society. *Member:* The District of Columbia Bar; The State Bar of California; American Bar Association.

GEOFFREY R. W. SMITH

1350 I STREET, NW, SUITE 900
WASHINGTON, D.C. 20005-7202
Telephone: 202-625-1224
Fax: 202-333-1637
Email: grwslawyer@aol.com
URL: http://www.lawyers.com/geoffreysmithlaw

Complex Litigation.

GEOFFREY R. W. SMITH, born San Francisco, California, May 26, 1945; admitted to bar, 1971, California and District of Columbia. *Education:* Stanford University (B.A., with honors, 1967; J.D., 1970). Editor, Stanford Law Review, 1969-1970. Member, Board of Editors, Food, Drug and Cosmetic Law Journal, 1987-1990. Member, Board of Directors, 1987— and Chairman, 1987-1988, American Tort Reform Association. Member, Regulatory Affairs Professional Society, 1987—. Associate General Counsel, Pharmaceutical Manufacturers Association, 1979-1987. Board Member and General Counsel, American Tort Reform Association, Food and Drug Law Institute. *Member:* American Bar Association (Member, Sections on: Business Law, 1970-1988; Antitrust, 1970—; Torts and Insurance Practice, 1978—; Administrative Law, 1975—; Member, Committees on: Food and Drug, 1972—; Ad Hoc Tort Reform, 1988; Chairman, Subcommittee on Punitive Damages, 1991; Health Forum). ***PRACTICE AREAS:*** Complex Litigation.

SMITH COOPER, LLP

1029 VERMONT AVENUE, N.W., SUITE 300
WASHINGTON, D.C. 20005-3517
Telephone: 202-789-8700
Fax: 202-789-8775
URL: http://www.lawyers.com/smithcooper

Complex-Multi District Litigation, Commercial Litigation, Business Law, Environmental Law, Products Liability, Toxic Torts, Civil Trials, Corporate Transactions, Finance, Taxation, Entertainment Law, Entertainment Acquisition, Development, Production and Distribution, Television and Motion Picture Programming and Development Legal Issues.

G. NELSON SMITH, III, born Detroit, Michigan, March 1, 1961; admitted to bar, 1986, Virginia (Not admitted in District of Columbia). *Education:* Howard University (B.A., magna cum laude, 1982); University of Virginia (J.D., 1986); University of Oslo, Oslo, Norway (Certificate of Achievement). Author: "Lawmaker As Lawbreaker: Enforcement Actions Against Municipalities For Failing to Comply With the Clean Water Act," 41 Cleveland State Law Review 685 (1994); "Trashing the Town and Making the Town Pay: What is Currently Wrong with Municipal Liability Scheme Under CERCLA," 26 Connecticut Law Review 585 (1994); "Waking the Sleeping Giant: The Use of Felony Sanctions Under CERCLA to Ensure Compliance with All Environmental Laws," 26 Creighton Law Review 49 (1993); "No Longer Just the Cost of Doing Business: Criminal Liability of Corporate Officials for Violations of the Clean Water Act and the Resource Conservation and Recovery Act," 53 Louisiana Law Review 119 (1992). *Member:* American Bar Association (Vice-Chair: Environmental Crimes Section; International Environmental Section; Section of Natural Resources. Member, Energy and Environmental Law Book Publishing Committee). ***PRACTICE AREAS:*** Environmental. **Email:** gnsmith@smithcooperllp.com

(This Listing Continued)

LAWRENCE N. COOPER, born Richmond, Virginia, March 11, 1961; admitted to bar, 1986, Virginia, 1988, District of Columbia. *Education:* Boston University (B.M., 1983); University of Virginia (J.D.., 1986). Phi Alpha Delta. Projects and Production Editor, Virginia Tax Review, 1985-1986. *Member:* The District of Columbia Bar; Virginia State Bar; American Bar Association (Member, Taxation Section). ***PRACTICE AREAS:*** Tax Law; Corporate and Transactional Law; Finance Law; Business Law. **Email:** incooper@smithcooperllp.com

---

KIMBERLY C. AYERS, admitted to bar, 1998, New York; 1999, District of Columbia. *Education:* Georgetown University (B.A., 1993); Tulane University of Louisiana (J.D., 1997). *Member:* The District of Columbia Bar. ***PRACTICE AREAS:*** Tax; Energy.

MARCUS ANTOINE CLIFTON, admitted to bar, 1998, New York (Not admitted in District of Columbia). *Education:* Virginia State University (B.S., 1993); Thomas M. Cooley Law School (J.D., 1998). ***PRACTICE AREAS:*** Entertainment Law.

DAMIEN V. ALEXANDER, born Washington, D.C., April 5, 1973; admitted to bar, 1998, Maryland; 1999, District of Columbia and West Virginia. *Education:* Catholic University (B.A., 1995); American University (J.D., 1998). *Member:* The District of Columbia Bar. ***PRACTICE AREAS:*** Legal Malpractice; Litigation; Business Planning; Intellectual Property.

OF COUNSEL

MICHAEL S. STEELE, born Camp Springs, Maryland, October 19, 1958; admitted to bar, 1992, Pennsylvania (Not admitted in District of Columbia). *Education:* Johns Hopkins University (B.A., 1981); Georgetown University (J.D., 1991). *Member:* Pennsylvania and American Bar Associations.

SMITH, GAMBRELL & RUSSELL, LLP

SUITE 800
1850 M STREET, N.W.
WASHINGTON, D.C. 20036
Telephone: 202-263-4300
Telecopier: 202-263-4329

Atlanta, Georgia Office: Suite 3100, Promenade II, 1230 Peachtree Street, N.E. Telephone: 404-815-3500. Fax: 404-815-3509.
Jacksonville, Florida Office: Bank of America Tower, 50 North Laura Street, Suite 2200. Telephone: 904-598-6100. Fax: 904-598-6300.

Patent, Trademark, Copyright, Antitrust, Unfair Competition and Trade Regulation Law. Practice before Federal Courts and Government Departments.

PARTNERS

ANDREW B. BEVERIDGE (1915-1972).
JOSEPH A. DEGRANDI (1927-1999).

DENNIS O. DOHERTY, born Boston, Massachusetts, 1952; admitted to bar, 1991, New Jersey and New York; 1994, Florida; 1995, Georgia (Not admitted in District of Columbia). *Education:* State University of New York at Albany (B.S., cum laude, 1975); New York University (M.B.A., 1987); Catholic University (J.D., 1990). Certified Public Accountant, New York, 1981. Note and Comment Editor, Catholic University Law Review. Co-Editor: Handbook on Professional Fees in Bankruptcy, Turnaround Management Association. *Member:* State Bar of Georgia; The Florida Bar; American Bar Association (Member, Business Law Section). (Also at Atlanta, Georgia Office). **Email:** ddoherty@sgrlaw.com

ROBERT G. WEILACHER, born New York, N.Y., December 11, 1934; admitted to bar, 1961, Virginia; 1962, District of Columbia; 1982, U.S. Supreme Court and U.S. Court of Appeals for the Federal Circuit; registered to practice before U.S. Patent and Trademark Office. *Education:* Columbia University (B.S., in Chem. Engr., 1957); George Washington University (LL.B., 1961). *Member:* The District of Columbia Bar; Bar Association of the District of Columbia; Virginia State Bar; American Bar Association; American Intellectual Property Law Association; German-American Lawyers Association. ***PRACTICE AREAS:*** Intellectual Property Law. **Email:** rweilacher@sgrlaw.com

FREDERICK F. CALVETTI, born February 20, 1945; admitted to bar, 1978, Virginia; 1980, U.S. Court of International Trade; 1981, U.S. Court of Federal Claims; 1982, U.S. Court of Appeals for the Federal Circuit and U.S. Supreme Court; 1984, District of Columbia and Michigan; 1985, New York; 1999, Illinois; registered to practice before U.S. Patent and Trademark Office, 1977. *Education:* Michigan Technological University (B.S.Ch.E., 1968;

(This Listing Continued)

SMITH, GAMBRELL & RUSSELL, LLP, Washington—Continued

M.S.Ch.E., 1971); University of Baltimore (J.D., 1975); George Washington University (LL.M., 1977). Adjunct Professor, George Washington University, 1978-1981. Law Clerk to Honorable Howard Markey, 1975-1977. Patent Examiner, 1969-1975. Engineer, G.M. Corp., 1968. Lectured and Published Worldwide. ***LANGUAGES:*** German and French. ***PRACTICE AREAS:*** Intellectual Property.

MICHAEL A. MAKUCH, born Akron, Ohio, February 4, 1958; admitted to bar, 1984, Ohio; 1985, District of Columbia; registered to practice before U.S. Patent and Trademark Office. *Education:* Yale University (B.S., 1980); Case Western Reserve University (J.D., 1984). *Member:* The District of Columbia Bar; Bar Association of the District of Columbia; American Bar Association; American Intellectual Property Law Association; International Trademark Association; Japan-America Society; Optical Society of America; Yale Engineering Association. ***PRACTICE AREAS:*** Intellectual Property Law.

DENNIS C. RODGERS, born Portland, Maine, August 2, 1962; admitted to bar, 1989, Virginia; 1990, District of Columbia; registered to practice before U.S. Patent and Trademark Office. *Education:* University of Maine at Orono (B.S. in Mech. Engr., with distinction, 1984); George Washington University (J.D., 1989). *Member:* The District of Columbia Bar; American Bar Association; American Intellectual Property Law Association. ***PRACTICE AREAS:*** Intellectual Property Law; Patent Prosecution; International Patent Prosecution. ***Email:*** drogers@sgrlaw.com

ASSOCIATES

MICHAEL K. CARRIER, born Cincinnati, Ohio, August 17, 1966; admitted to bar, 1996, Kentucky; 2000, District of Columbia; registered to practice before U.S. Patent and Trademark Office. *Education:* University of Cincinnati (B.S., 1990; J.D., 1996). Rho Chi Pharmaceutical Honor Society. Author: "Federal Preemption of Common Law Tort Awards by the Food, Drug and Cosmetic Act," 51 Food and Drug Law Journal 509 (1996). *Member:* American Intellectual Property Law Association; American Association for the Advancement of Science; American Chemical Society. ***PRACTICE AREAS:*** Patent Prosecution; Patent Counseling. ***Email:*** mcarrier@sgrlaw.com

BRANDON BOSS, born Baraboo, Wisconsin, July 22, 1973; admitted to bar, 1998, Louisiana; registered to practice before U.S. Patent and Trademark Office (Not admitted in District of Columbia). *Education:* University of Nebraska at Lincoln (B.A., 1994); Tulane University (J.D., 1998). Moot Court Board. ***PRACTICE AREAS:*** Patent; Trademarks. ***Email:*** bsboss@sgrlaw.com

SCOTT D. WOLDOW, born Teaneck, New Jersey, August 17, 1971; admitted to bar, 1997, Maryland; 1998, District of Columbia. *Education:* Hofstra University (B.A., 1993); American University (J.D., 1997; M.B.A., 1999). Phi Alpha Theta. Psi Chi. Order of Omega. *Member:* Bar Association of the District of Columbia (Member, Patent, Trademark and Copyright Section); American Bar Association; American Intellectual Property Law Association (Member, Intellectual Property Section); International Trademark Association. ***PRACTICE AREAS:*** Intellectual Property; Litigation; Antitrust. ***Email:*** sdwoldow@sgrlaw.com

PATRICK R. DELANEY, born Washington, D.C., September 12, 1963; admitted to bar, 2000, District of Columbia; registered to practice before U.S. Patent and Trademark Office. *Education:* University of Maryland (B.S., 1988); Catholic University of America (J.D., 1998); Johns Hopkins University (M.S., 1999). *Member:* American Intellectual Property Law Association (Member, Committees on: Biotechnology; Chemical Practice); Association of University of Technology Managers. ***Email:*** prdelaney@sgrlaw.com

MARY A. MONTEBELLO, born Jenkins, Kentucky, January 9, 1960; admitted to bar, 1985, Kentucky; 2000, District of Columbia; registered to practice before the U.S. Patent and Trademark Office. *Education:* University of Kentucky (B.A., Chemistry, 1982; J.D., 1985). *Member:* Kentucky and American Bar Associations; The District of Columbia Bar. ***PRACTICE AREAS:*** Patents. ***Email:*** mamontebello@sgrlaw.com

COUNSEL

JACOB S. FRENKEL, born San Francisco, CA, 1960; admitted to bar, 1985, Louisiana and U.S. Court of Appeals, Fifth Circuit; 1992, Maryland; 1998, U.S. Supreme Court (Not admitted in District of Columbia). *Education:* Tulane University (B.A., 1981; J.D., 1984). Co-Author: *Legal Ethics and the General Counsel of a Presidential Campaign.* Lecturer: Canadian Institute, 2001; Canadian Centre for Ethics and Corporate Policy 2001; Philadelphia Bar Association, 2000; SEC International Training Institute: Program of Securities Enforcement and Market Oversight, 1994-1999. Assistant District Attorney, 1985-1988. Senior Counsel, Division of Enforcement, Securities and Exchange Commission, Washington, D.C., 1988-1997. Associate Independent Counsel, 1995-1998, Counselor to the Independent Counsel, 1998-1999, In re Secretary of Agriculture Espy, Alexandria, VA. Special Counsel, Grant & Eisenhofer, Wilmington, DE, 1999-2000. (Also at Atlanta, Georgia Office). ***PRACTICE AREAS:*** Securities Litigation; SEC, NASD and State Enforcement; White Collar Crime; Internal Investigations; Securities Arbitration; Corporate Compliance; Campaign Finance; Health Care. ***Email:*** jsfrenkel@sgrlaw.com

PATENT AGENTS

BRETT L. NELSON, born Lemoore, California, January 15, 1970; (admission pending), registered to practice before U.S. Patent and Trademark Office. *Education:* Brigham Young University (B.S., 1994). ***Email:*** blnelson@sgrlaw.com

THOMAS L. WILLIS, JR., born Philadelphia, Pennsylvania, August 2, 1951; (admission pending). *Education:* Tufts University (B.S.E., Electrical, 1973); Rutgers University (M.S., Biomedical Engineering, 1984); Duquesne University (J.D., 1997); John Marshall Law School (LL.M., Intellectual Property, 1999). Member, IEEE, 1973-1984. *Member:* Michigan Intellectual Property Law Association; American Intellectual Property Law Association; Philadelphia Intellectual Property Lawyers Association. ***PRACTICE AREAS:*** Intellectual Property; Patents; Copyrights; Trademarks; Licensing. ***Email:*** tlwillis@sgrlaw.com

SMITH & METALITZ, L.L.P.

1747 PENNSYLVANIA AVENUE, N.W., SUITE 825
WASHINGTON, D.C. 20006-4604
Telephone: 202-833-4198
Fax: 202-872-0546
Email: info@smimetlaw.com
URL: http://www.smimetlaw.com

Copyrights, Trademarks, Entertainment Law, Electronic Commerce.

ERIC H. SMITH, born Los Angeles, California, January 7, 1943; admitted to bar, 1969, California and District of Columbia. *Education:* Stanford University (B.A., with honors, 1964); University of California at Berkeley (J.D., 1967); Johns Hopkins University (M.A., 1968). Senior Vice President and General Counsel, Public Broadcasting Service, 1980-1982. Chairman, U.S. Government Industry Functional Advisory Committee 3 on Intellectual Property, and Member, IFAC 4 on E-Commerce. President, International Intellectual Property Alliance (IIPA). *Member:* The District of Columbia Bar (Chairman, Committee on Copyright, 1983-1985); Computer Law Association; Copyright Society of the USA (Trustee, 1980-1983). ***PRACTICE AREAS:*** Copyrights; Entertainment and the Arts; Electronic Commerce; International Trade. ***Email:*** esmith@smimetlaw.com

STEVEN J. METALITZ, born Washington, D.C., February 4, 1951; admitted to bar, 1978, District of Columbia and South Carolina. *Education:* University of Chicago (A.B., 1972); Georgetown University (J.D., 1977). Counsel, US Senate Judiciary Committee, 1982-1989. *Member:* The District of Columbia Bar; South Carolina Bar. ***PRACTICE AREAS:*** Copyrights; Trademarks; Privacy Law; Electronic Commerce; Government. ***Email:*** metalitz@smimetlaw.com

ERIC J. SCHWARTZ, born New York, N.Y., April 25, 1957; admitted to bar, 1985, New York; 1986, District of Columbia. *Education:* Johns Hopkins University (B.A., 1979); Washington College of Law of American University (J.D., 1984). Adjunct Professor, Copyright Law, Georgetown University Law Center, 1998—. Author: U.S. Copyright Law Chapter in the treatise "International Copyright Law and Practice" edited by Paul Edward Geller, 1999—. Assistant Counsel, U.S. House of Representatives, Committee on Rules, 1985-1988. Policy Planning Advisor to the Register of Copyrights, U.S. Copyright Office, 1988-1994. Acting General Counsel, U.S. Copyright Office, 1994—. Member, Copyright Society of the U.S.A. (Trustee, 1996-1999). *Member:* The District of Columbia Bar; New York State Bar Association. ***PRACTICE AREAS:*** Copyrights; Trademarks; Electronic Commerce; Government. ***Email:*** schwartz@smimetlaw.com

MARIA S. STRONG, born California, 1963; admitted to bar, 1990, California; 1993, District of Columbia. *Education:* University of California at Los Angeles (B.A., 1985); University of Southern California (M.A., 1987); George Washington University (J.D., 1990). *Member:* State Bar of California; The District of Columbia Bar (Chairperson, Copyright Committee of Intellectual Property Law Section, 1999-2001). ***PRACTICE AREAS:*** Copyrights; International Trade. ***Email:*** mstrong@smimetlaw.com

---

MICHAEL N. SCHLESINGER, born New York, N.Y., 1967; admitted to bar, 1996, Virginia; 1997, District of Columbia. *Education:* Oberlin College (A.B., 1989); Columbia University (J.D., 1996). Author: "Exceptions and Limitations on the Prohibition of Circumvention of Technological Protection Measures" (ALAI 2001 Congress, June 2001); "Intellectual Property Law in China" (EAER, 1997). *Member:* Virginia State Bar; The District of Columbia Bar.

(This Listing Continued)

(This Listing Continued)

PRACTICE AREAS: Copyrights; Trademarks; International Trade. ***Email:*** mschlesinger@smimetlaw.com

SMITH, PACHTER, McWHORTER & ALLEN, P.L.C.

WASHINGTON, D.C.

(See Vienna, Virginia)

Government Contracts, Construction and Environmental Law.

SMITHWICK & BELENDIUK, P.C.

Established in 1988

5028 WISCONSIN AVENUE, N.W.
SUITE 301
WASHINGTON, D.C. 20016
Telephone: 202-363-4050
Telecopier: 202-363-4266
URL: http://www.lawyers.com/smithwick&belendiuk
Email: fcclaw@fccworld.com
URL: http://www.fccworld.com

Practice before the Federal Courts and Administrative Agencies. Communications, Radio, Television, Cable and Common Carrier.

GARY S. SMITHWICK, born High Point, North Carolina, May 5, 1946; admitted to bar, 1971, North Carolina; 1972, District of Columbia and U.S. Court of Appeals for the District of Columbia Circuit; 1974, U.S. Supreme Court; 1986, U.S. Court of Appeals, Fourth Circuit. *Education:* North Carolina State University (B. S., 1968); Wake Forest University (J.D., 1971). Phi Alpha Delta. Adjunct Professor, Administrative Law, Wake Forest University, 1977-1984. Attorney, Federal Communications Commission, Broadcast Bureau, 1971-1975. *Member:* The District of Columbia Bar; North Carolina State Bar; Federal Communications Bar Association. ***PRACTICE AREAS:*** Administrative; Communications; Radio and TV. ***Email:*** gsmithwick@fccworld.com

ARTHUR V. BELENDIUK, born New York, N.Y., October 4, 1955; admitted to bar, 1980, District of Columbia; 1985, U.S. Court of Appeals for the District of Columbia Circuit. *Education:* Rutgers University (B.A., 1977); Hofstra University (J.D., 1980). Attorney, Federal Communications Commission, Common Carrier Bureau, Tariff Division, 1981-1982. *Member:* The District of Columbia Bar; American Bar Association; Federal Communications Bar Association. ***PRACTICE AREAS:*** Administrative; Communications; Radio and TV; Cable; Common Carrier. ***Email:*** abelendiuk@fccworld.com

OF COUNSEL

JAMES K. EDMUNDSON, born Beckley, West Virginia, December 24, 1938; admitted to bar, 1963, West Virginia and U.S. District Court, Southern District of West Virginia; 1967, District of Columbia and U.S. District Court, District of Columbia; 1971, U.S. Court of Appeals, District of Columbia Circuit. *Education:* West Virginia University (B.A., 1960; J.D., 1963). Phi Delta Phi. Member, Board of Editors, West Virginia Law Review, 1962-1963. Author: Note, "Legislative Reapportionment: Baker v. Carr," 65 West Virginia Law Review 129, 1963. General and Trial Attorney, Federal Communications Commission, 1963-1966. *Member:* The District of Columbia Bar; Federal Communications Bar Association (Member, Mass Media Practice and Adjudicatory Practice Committees). ***PRACTICE AREAS:*** Telecommunications Law. ***Email:*** jkewva@aol.com

WILLIAM M. BARNARD, born Sioux City, Iowa, January 22, 1939; admitted to bar, 1966, District of Columbia; 1970, U.S. Supreme Court. *Education:* University of Denver (A.B., 1962); George Washington University (LL.B., 1966). Legal Counsel for Virginia Association of Broadcasters, 1982-1983. *Member:* The District of Columbia Bar; Bar Association of the District of Columbia; Federal Communications Bar Association. ***PRACTICE AREAS:*** Communication Law; Corporate Law. ***Email:*** Nevisbill@aol.com

ELLEN MANDELL EDMUNDSON, born Brooklyn, New York, November 20, 1952; admitted to bar, 1981, New York; 1982, District of Columbia. *Education:* Queens College of the City University of New York (B.A., cum laude, 1973); St. John's University (J.D., 1980). *Member:* New York State and Federal Bar Associations; The District of Columbia Bar; Federal Communications Bar Association; Womens Bar Association of the District of Columbia. ***PRACTICE AREAS:*** Telecommunications Law. ***Email:*** ellen@fccworld.com

SMOLEN PLEVY

WASHINGTON, D.C.

(See Vienna, Virginia)

General Corporate and Business, Tax, Real Estate, Wills and Estates, Family Law, Divorce and Custody, Litigation.

SNIDER & ASSOCIATES

Established in 1994

1054 31ST STREET, N.W., SUITE 400
WASHINGTON, D.C. 20007
Telephone: 202-347-2600
Fax: 202-347-7870
Email: sniderpatent@yahoo.com
URL: http://www.lawyers.com/snider&assoclaw

Intellectual Property Law, Patents, Trademarks, Copyrights, Government Contracts.

FIRM PROFILE: Snider & Associates specializes in intellectual property law, which includes patent, trademark, copyright, trade secret and unfair competition law and related areas of trade regulation, technology transfer and franchising. Practice is before the U.S. Patent and Trademark Office, the Food and Drug Administration, and the U.S. Court of Appeals for the Federal Circuit and the U.S. Court of Federal Claims. Patent practice covers all disciplines including chemical, biotechnological, pharmaceutical, mechanical, electrical, electronic, computer, semiconductor and metallurgical technologies. The firm also specializes in the counseling of individuals and entrepreneurs seeking and obtaining "small business innovation and research" contracts from the U.S. government.

RONALD R. SNIDER, born Lancaster, Ohio, May 22, 1937; admitted to bar, 1965, Michigan; 1967, District of Columbia; 1969, U.S. Claims Court; 1969-1982, U.S. Court of Customs and Patent Appeals; 1982, U.S. Court of Appeals for the Federal Circuit; registered to practice before U.S. Patent and Trademark Office. *Education:* Purdue University (B.S.E.E., 1960); University of Michigan (M.B.A., 1965; J.D., 1963); George Washington University (M.P.L., 1971). Author: "A Primer for Practice Before the United States Court of Claims," University of Maryland Law Forum, Trial Practice Issue, 1979; "Patent Accounting in the U.S. Court of Claims," Master of Law Thesis, George Washington University School of Law, 1971. Co-Author: J. Green and J.L. Harris, "Patent Policy Pertinent to Multi-National Cooperative Research," IDEA 13:575, Winter 1969-1970. Adjunct Professor of Law, Georgetown University Law Center, 1983-1987. Trial Attorney, Patent Section Civil Division, U.S. Department of Justice, 1969-1976. *Member:* The District of Columbia Bar; American Intellectual Property Law Association. ***PRACTICE AREAS:*** Litigation; Licensing Law; Intellectual Property Law. ***Email:*** sniderpatent@yahoo.com

SNYDER, SLUTKIN & LODOWSKI

WASHINGTON, D.C.

(See Baltimore, Maryland)

General Civil Trial and Appellate Practice before all State and Federal Courts. Business Fraud and Medical Malpractice.

SONENTHAL & OVERALL, PC

1120 19TH STREET N.W., SUITE 460
WASHINGTON, D.C. 20036
Telephone: 202-785-0227
Fax: 202-785-5904;
Email: rsonenthal@psiwash.org
Email: soverall@psiwash.org
URL: http://www.lawyers.com/soverall

Government Contracts, Federal Grants, Nonprofit Organizations Law, Corporate Governance; International Government Contracts, Renewable Energy, Civil Litigation.

SCOTT C. OVERALL, born Fort Benning, Georgia, June 30, 1956; admitted to bar, 1984, Tennessee; 1986, District of Columbia. *Education:* Brown University (A.B., magna cum laude, 1978); American University (J.D., 1983; LL.M., 1989). Recipient: Meritorious Honor Award, U.S. Agency for International Development, 1995; Samuel Lamport Prize in International Understanding, Brown University, for essay on Laos. Deputy Assistant General Counsel for Contracts and Commodity Management, Attorney Advisor, USAID, 1980-1995. Procurement Legislation Advisor, Asian Development Bank China Project, National Procurement Regulations for the Public Sector, 1998-2000. Co-Author: Website: USAID Sourcebook on Results-Oriented Grants and Cooperative Agreements, 1998. Articles: Towards Streamlining USAID Assistance Requirements for Foreign Awards, 8 Assistance Management Journal 73, Summer 1998 with Diana Esposito; Report Calls for Procurement Reform to Improve Collaboration Between NGOs and MDIs, InterAction Monday Developments, October 6, 1997; Partners or Hired Hands? Procurement Reform for Effective Collaboration Between NGOs and Multilateral Institutions (1997); Cost or Pricing Data under U.S. Government Contracts, USAID CONET Electronic Maga-

(This Listing Continued)

SONENTHAL & OVERALL, PC, Washington—Continued

zine, March and April, 1995. Speaker: Association of PVO Financial Managers Seminar on USAID Source/Origin, Fly American, Cargo Preference, and Related Rules, 1999; LAWASIA Conference on Combatting Corrupt Practices in Government Procurement: U.S. Law, Policy and Practice, Manila, 1997. Guest Instructor, International Development Law Institute, Development Lawyer's Course, 1992. Lecturer: International Project Procurement & Negotiation, International Law Institute, 1989-1992. Presenter: Procurement and Grants Law, USAID Conferences in Washington, 1994; Singapore and Bangkok, 1992; Baltimore, 1991. *Member:* American, Inter-Pacific and International Bar Associations; National Contract and Grant Management Associations. ***LANGUAGES:*** Mandarin Chinese. ***PRACTICE AREAS:*** Government Procurement; International Government Contracts; Federal Grants; International Construction Law; International Contracts; Foreign Corrupt Practices Act; International Nonprofit Organizations; NGO Law. ***Email:*** soverall@psiwash.org

ROBERT B. SONENTHAL, born New York, N.Y., January 30, 1949; admitted to bar, 1980, District of Columbia. *Education:* Harvard University (B.A., magna cum laude, 1970); Columbia University (M.A., 1972; M.Phil., 1973); University of Pennsylvania (J.D., cum laude, 1980). Co-Chairman, Moot Court Board, 1979-1980. Recipient: John H. Maurer Award, University of Pennsylvania Law School, 1980; Meritorious Service Award, U.S. Agency for International Development, 1992. Co-Author: "Section 301 and Exhaustion of Intra-Union Remedies: A Misbegotten Marriage" 128 University of Pennsylvania Law Review 989, 1980. Attorney Advisor, Bureau for Private Enterprise, 1985-1989, Bureau for Asia and Private Enterprise, 1989-1991; Assistant General Counsel, Litigation and Enforcement, U.S. Agency for International Development, 1991-1993. General Counsel: Population Services International, 1997—; Center for Conflict Prevention and Resolution in Africa, 1997—; Direct Fuel Cell Group, 1997—; National Hydrogen Association, 1997—; Solar Electric Power Association, 1998—; Partnership for African Environmental Sustainability, 1999—; International Research & Exchanges Board, 2000—. *Member:* District of Columbia Bar; American Bar Association. ***LANGUAGES:*** French. ***PRACTICE AREAS:*** Nonprofit Corporations; Corporate Governance; Government Contracts and Grants; Renewable Energy; Civil Litigation. ***Email:*** rsonenthal@psiwash.org

OF COUNSEL

RENEE R. MATALON, born Brooklyn, New York, November 13, 1956; admitted to bar, 1981, District of Columbia. *Education:* Harvard University (A.B., summa cum laude, 1978; J.D., 1981). Phi Beta Kappa. Associate: Donovan, Leisure, Newton & Irvine, 1981-1984; Wiley, Rein & Fielding, 1984-1985. Editor-in-Chief, Washington Jewish Week, 1985-1986. Attorney Advisor, U.S. Agency for International Development: Legislation and Policy, 1987-1989; USAID Central Programs and Bureau for Humanitarian Assistance, 1989-1994; Attorney Advisor, U.S. Department of Commerce: Legislative Counsel for Intellectual Property and Technology, 1997-1998. Newsletter Editor, National Lawyers' Committee for Civil Rights Under Law. ***LANGUAGES:*** French, Hebrew and Arabic. ***PRACTICE AREAS:*** Nonprofit Corporations; Litigation; Employment; Government Contracts; Federal Grants; International Contracts; Commercial Contracts; General Practice. ***Email:*** rmatalon@psiwash.org

NINA GLICKMAN NATHANI, born Haverford, Pennsylvania, September 8, 1960; admitted to bar, 1986, Pennsylvania; 1988, District of Columbia. *Education:* Yale University (B.A., 1982); University of Virginia (J.D., 1986). Member, Editorial Board, 1984-1986 and Executive Editor, 1985-1986, Virginia Journal of International Law. Associate: Akin, Gump, Strauss, Haver & Feld, 1986-1988; Steptoe & Johnson, 1988-1992; Attorney-Advisor, U.S. Agency for International Development, 1992-1998. Author: "Note, Keep Your Pollution to Yourself," 25 VA. J. Int'l. L. 693 (1985). *Member:* District of Columbia Bar. ***PRACTICE AREAS:*** Government Procurement; Non-Profit Organizations Law; Litigation; Intellectual Property. ***Email:*** nnathani@psiwash.org

TAMERA A. FILLINGER, born Portland, Oregon, December 22, 1959; admitted to bar, 1990, New York (Not admitted in District of Columbia). *Education:* University of California at Santa Barbara (B.A., 1982); University of California School of Law, Los Angeles (J.D., 1988). Recipient, U.S. Department of Education Fellowship in Language and Area Studies, Beijing, China, 1986-1987. Editor, UCLA Law Review, 1997-1998. Author, "Comment, The Anatomy of Protectionism: The Voluntary Restraint Agreements on Steel Imports," 35 UCLA Law Review 953 (1988). Associate and Member, China Practice Group, Paul, Weiss, Rifkind, Wharton & Garrison. Attorney Advisor, Africa Bureau, USAID 1992. Regional Legal Advisor: East and Southern Africa (Nairobi, Kenya), USAID; Indonesia and Sri Lanka (Jakarta, Indonesia), 1997-1999. ***LANGUAGES:*** Mandarin Chinese. ***PRACTICE AREAS:*** Nonprofit Organizations Law; Federal Grants; Government Contracts; Government Procurement; International Contracts; Corporate Governance. ***Email:*** tfillinger@psiwash.org

SONNENSCHEIN NATH & ROSENTHAL

1301 K STREET, N.W.
SUITE 600 EAST TOWER
WASHINGTON, D.C. 20005
Telephone: 202-408-6400
Fax: 202-408-6399
URL: http://www.sonnenschein.com

Chicago, Illinois Office: Suite 8000 Sears Tower, 233 South Wacker Drive. Telephone: 312-876-8000. Cable Address: "Sonberk". Telex: 25-3526. Facsimile: 312-876-7934.
New York, N.Y. Office: 1221 Avenue of the Americas. Telephone: 212-768-6700. Facsimile: 212-768-6800.
San Francisco, California Office: 685 Market Street, 6th Floor. Telephone: 415-882-5000. Facsimile: 415-543-5472.
Los Angeles, California Office: 601 South Figueroa Street, Suite 1500. Telephone: 213-623-9300. Facsimile: 213-623-9924.
St. Louis, Missouri Office: One Metropolitan Square, Suite 3000. Telephone: 314-241-1800. Facsimile: 314-259-5959.
Kansas City, Missouri Office: Suite 1100, 4520 Main Street, 64111. Telephone: 816-460-2400. Facsimile: 816-531-7545.
West Palm Beach, Florida Office: Phillips Point, West Tower, 777 South Flagler Drive, Suite 1102. Telephone: 561-833-2410. Facsimile: 561-833-8387.

General Practice.

RESIDENT PARTNERS

AMY L. BESS, born Bloomington, Illinois, March 3, 1960; admitted to bar, 1987, Illinois and U.S. District Court, Northern District of Illinois; 1989, District of Columbia and U.S. District Court, District of Columbia; 1993, U. S. Court of Appeals, Fourth Circuit; 1996, U.S. District Court, Central District of Illinois; 1998, U.S. Court of Appeals, Eighth Circuit; 2000, U.S. District Court, District of Maryland. *Education:* Illinois State University (B.S., summa cum laude, 1982); Northwestern University (J.D., 1987). Member, Mortar Board. Associate Note and Comment Editor, Journal of Criminal Law and Criminology, 1986-1987. *Member:* The District of Columbia Bar; American Bar Association; Women's Bar Association of the District of Columbia. ***PRACTICE AREAS:*** Employment Litigation; Employment Counseling. ***Email:*** alb@sonnenschein.com

JOHN J. CALKINS, born Holyoke, Massachusetts, June 2, 1968; admitted to bar, 1993, Maryland and Pennsylvania; 1994, U.S. District Court, District of Maryland; 1995, District of Columbia; 1996, U.S. Court of Appeals, Fourth Circuit. *Education:* Johns Hopkins University (B.A., 1990); American University (J.D., summa cum laude, 1993). Moot Court Board. Member, American University Law Review. *Member:* District of Columbia Bar; Maryland State and American (Intellectual Property Law Section) Bar Associations; American Intellectual Property Law Association. ***PRACTICE AREAS:*** Litigation; Intellectual Property; Technology. ***Email:*** jcalkins@sonnenschein.com

TODD R. ESKELSEN, born Brigham City, Utah, May 31, 1959; admitted to bar, 1985, Maryland; 1986, District of Columbia. *Education:* University of Utah (B.A., magna cum laude, 1982); Georgetown University (J.D., 1985). Phi Beta Kappa; Phi Kappa Phi. *Member:* The District of Columbia Bar; Maryland State Bar Association; National Council of Farmers Cooperatives (Chairman, Standing Subcommittee on Securities, Legal, Tax and Accounting Committee). ***LANGUAGES:*** Swedish. ***PRACTICE AREAS:*** Corporate Law; Real Estate; Cooperatives. ***Email:*** tre@sonnenschein.com

ELIZABETH A. FERRELL, born Morgantown, West Virginia, February 10, 1957; admitted to bar, 1982, South Carolina; 1985, District of Columbia. *Education:* University of South Carolina (B.A., 1979; J.D., 1982). Phi Beta Kappa; Order of the Coif. Member, National Moot Court Team. Articles Editor, South Carolina Law Review, 1981-1982. Author: "Torts, Annual Survey of South Carolina Law," 33 S.C.L. Rev. 159, 1981. Co-Author: Briefing Paper, "Motions Before Contract Appeals Boards," Federal Publications, Inc., 1986. Law Clerk to the Honorable Sol Blatt, Jr., U.S. District Court, District of South Carolina, 1982-1984. *Member:* South Carolina Bar; The District of Columbia Bar; American Bar Association. ***PRACTICE AREAS:*** Government Contract Law; Commercial Litigation. ***Email:*** eaf@sonnenschein.com

D. ANDREW FLOAM, born Baltimore, Maryland, November 9, 1965; admitted to bar, 1993, Maryland; 1999, Georgia; registered to practice before U.S. Patent and Trademark Office (Not admitted in District of Columbia). *Education:* University of Maryland at College Park (B.S.E.E., 1988); Catholic University of America (J.D., 1992). Adjunct Professor, Law, Shepard Board Law Center, NOVA Southeastern University, Spring 1996. *Member:* Maryland State Bar Association, Inc.; American Intellectual Property Law Association; Licensing Executive Society. ***PRACTICE AREAS:*** Electrical Intellectual Property; Electrical Patents; Information Technology; Computers and Software. ***Email:*** dfloam@sonnenschein.com

FRANCES J. HENDERSON, born Glasgow, Scotland, February 17, 1957; admitted to bar, 1985, District of Columbia. *Education:* University of Glasgow,

(This Listing Continued)

Scotland (LL.B., with honors, 1978); University of Virginia (LL.M., 1979); University of Minnesota (J.D., 1984). Associate Editor, Minnesota Law Review. Author: "Judicial Review Under the EAA: Section 13 & the Cost of Unreviewable Regulation," The Law & Policy of Export Controls," American Bar Association 1993; "British Deepsea Mining Legislation," 132 New L.J. 627 (1982). Lecturer, Public Law, University of Aberdeen, Scotland, 1980-1983. ***PRACTICE AREAS:*** International Trade. ***Email:*** fjh@sonnenschein.com

JOSEPH P. HORNYAK, born Silver Spring, Maryland, October 30, 1964; admitted to bar, 1990, Maryland; 1992, District of Columbia. *Education:* University of Maryland (B.S., 1986; J.D., 1990). Order of the Coif. Member, University of Maryland Law Review, 1989-1990. ***PRACTICE AREAS:*** Government Contracts Law; Commercial Litigation; Labor and Employment Litigation. ***Email:*** jzh@sonnenschein.com

MICHAEL L. KIKLIS, born Woburn, Massachusetts, December 15, 1962; admitted to bar, 1993, Washington; 1999, District of Columbia; registered to practice before U.S. Patent and Trademark Office. *Education:* University of Massachusetts at Lowell (B.S.C.S., 1985); Boston University (M.S.C.S., 1988); Syracuse Universit (J.D., 1993). Recipient, Rossman Award for Most Outstanding Article Published in the Journal of the Patent and Trademark Office Society, 1997. Member, Editorial Board, The Computer Lawyer. Author: "A Patent Saved Is a Patent Earned: A Word of Caution for Software Patent Practitioners," The Computer Lawyer, Volume 17, No. 1 (January 2000); "The Demise of the Mathematical Algorithm Rejection and the Emergence of the Utility-Based §101 Inquiry," The Computer Lawyer, Vol. 16, No. 8 (August 1999). Co-Author: "On-Line Copyright Issues, Recent Case Law and Legislative Changes Affecting Internet and Other On-Line Publishers," Journal of the Patent and Trademark Office Society, Vol. 79, Nos. 1-2 (January-February 1997); "A Patent Protection Strategy for Software Inventions," The Computer Lawyer, Vol. 14, No. 3 (March 1997). ***PRACTICE AREAS:*** Computer Technology; Patent Law. ***Email:*** m5k@sonnenschein.com

FRED L. LEVY, born Brooklyn, New York, June 18, 1953; admitted to bar, 1977, California; 1978, District of Columbia. *Education:* Cornell University (B.S., 1974); University of Southern California (J.D., 1977). *Member:* The District of Columbia Bar; State Bar of California. ***PRACTICE AREAS:*** Corporate Law. ***Email:*** fll@sonnenschein.com

LISA A. MACVITTIE, born Buffalo, New York, October 30, 1966; admitted to bar, 1993, Maryland; 1994, District of Columbia; 1996, U.S. District Court, District of Columbia. *Education:* College of William and Mary (B.A., 1988) Phi Beta Kappa; Georgetown University (J.D., cum laude, 1993). Senior Editor, Georgetown Law Journal. *Member:* The District of Columbia Bar (Member, Litigation Section); Maryland State and American (Member: Labor and Employment Law Section; Litigation Section) Bar Associations. ***PRACTICE AREAS:*** Litigation; Employment Law. ***Email:*** lam@sonnenschein.com

MICHAEL R. MARYN, born Washington, D.C., September 28, 1960; admitted to bar, 1989, District of Columbia. *Education:* The Ohio State University; University of Maryland (B.A., magna cum laude, 1983); Catholic University of American (J.D., 1989). Member, Catholic University Law Review. *Member:* The District of Columbia Bar (Member, Employee Benefits Committee, Section on Taxation); American Bar Association (Member, Employee Benefits Committee, Taxation Section). ***PRACTICE AREAS:*** Employee Benefits. ***Email:*** mrm@sonnenschein.com

KENNETH J. PFAEHLER, born Plainfield, New Jersey, May 3, 1961; admitted to bar, 1989, New York, U.S. District Court, Southern and Eastern Districts of New York; 1992, U.S. Court of Appeals, Tenth Circuit; 1999, District of Columbia; 2000, U.S. District Court for the District of Columbia. *Education:* University of Virginia (B.A., with distinction, 1983; M.A., 1985); Columbia University (J.D., 1988). Harlan Fiske Stone Scholar. Managing Editor, Columbia Human Rights Law Review, 1987-1988. Author: "The Writ of Habeas Corpus in the Philippines," Columbia Human Rights L. Rev., Vol. 19, No. 1. *Member:* The Association of the Bar of the City of New York; The District of Columbia Bar. ***PRACTICE AREAS:*** Litigation; Insurance. ***Email:*** kjp@sonnenschein.com

CARYL A. POTTER, III, born Norfolk, Virginia, April 4, 1947; admitted to bar, 1978, District of Columbia. *Education:* Stanford University (B.A., 1972); University of Missouri (J.D., 1973). Member, University of Missouri Law Review, 1972-1973. Co-Author: "The Environmental Liabilities of Government Contractors and Agencies," Federal Publications, Inc., 1990. ***PRACTICE AREAS:*** Government Contract Law; Commercial Litigation. ***Email:*** cap@sonnenschein.com

DOUGLAS E. ROSENTHAL, born New York, New York, February 12, 1940; admitted to bar, 1968, New York; 1976, U.S. Supreme Court; 1980, District of Columbia; U.S. District Court for the District of Columbia; U.S. Court of Appeals for the District of Columbia Circuit; U.S. District Court, Southern and Eastern Districts of New York; U.S. District Court, Eastern District of Michigan; U.S. District Court, Northern District of California; U.S. Court of Appeals, Second, Sixth and Eighth Circuits. *Education:* Yale College (B.A., 1961); Balliol College, Oxford; Columbia University (M.A., 1963); Yale Law School (LL.B., 1966); Yale University (Ph.D., 1970). Phi Beta Kappa.

(This Listing Continued)

Author: with Carl Green (Eds.), *Competition Regulation In The Pacific Rim,* Oceania Press, 1996; with William M. Knighton, *National Laws and International Commerce:* The Problem of Extraterritoriality, The Royal Institute of International Affairs, 1982; *Lawyer and Client:* Who's in Charge? Russell Sage Foundation, 1974. Assistant Chief, 1974-1977 and Chief, 1977-1980, Foreign Commerce Section, Antitrust Division, United States Department of Justice. Chairman, Committee on Extraterritoriality, Council Member, Section of International Law, American Bar Association, 1980-1985. Chairman, Board of Advisers, Eurowatch, Buraff, 1989. Member, Advisory Committee to reporters drafting the Restatement of Law Governing Lawyers. Member, Board of Advisers, Antitrust and Trade Regulation Report, BNA, since 1989—. Adjunct Professor of Competition Law, Tokyo University Law School, Winter, 1992. *Member:* American Bar Association; American Law Institute; Council on Foreign Relations. ***Email:*** der@sonnenschein.com

KIRK R. RUTHENBERG, born Blue Island, Illinois, December 31, 1952; admitted to bar, 1979, Illinois and U.S. District Court, Northern District of Illinois; 1989, District of Columbia and U.S. District Court, District of Columbia; 1991, Maryland; 1992, U.S. District Court, District of Maryland; 1993, U.S. Court of Appeals, Fourth Circuit. *Education:* University of Illinois (B.A., cum laude, 1975); Georgetown University (J.D., 1979). Phi Beta Kappa. Lead Articles Editor, Law and Policy in International Business, 1978-1979. Contributing Author, *Privacy and Security, International E-Commerce,* CCH 2001. Author: "Navigating the Net: Steering Clear of Legal Roadblocks on the Information Superhighway," Arthur Andersen Knowledge Network Serves, 1997; "Evidentiary Issues in Year 2000 Cases," Chapter 10 of Litigating Year 2000 Cases, West Group, June 1999; Note, "International Monetary Fund," Administrative Survey 1976-1977, 10 Law and Policy in International Business 253, 1978. ***PRACTICE AREAS:*** Commercial Litigation; Intellectual Property. ***Email:*** krr@sonnenschein.com

MICHAEL A. SCHLANGER, born New York, N.Y., December 9, 1943; admitted to bar, 1970, District of Columbia; 1974, U.S. Supreme Court; 1989, U.S. District Court, District of Maryland; 1994, U.S. Court of Appeals, Seventh Circuit; 1999, U.S. Court of Appeals, Fourth Circuit. *Education:* Columbia University (A.B., 1965); George Washington University (J.D., 1970). Order of the Coif. Notes Editor, George Washington Law Review, 1969-1970. Recipient, Federal Trade Commission's Outstanding Senior Executive Award for 1980; Neighborhood Legal Services Program's Meritorious Achievement Award, 1974. Instructor in Law, Washington College of Law, American University, 1973-1974. Assistant Director, Bureau of Competition, Federal Trade Commission, 1978-1981. Member, Executive Committee, Washington Lawyers Committee for Civil Rights and Urban Affairs, 1982—. Co-Author: "Priority Treatment in Bankruptcy of Tort Claims Resulting from the Negligence of a Receiver in a Prior Chapter XI Arrangement," 37 Geo. Wash. L. Rev. 674 (1969); "The Dispassionate and Efficient Prosecution, Defense and Settlement of Civil RICO Claims" (Iowa State Bar Association Corporate Counsel Section, 1992). ***PRACTICE AREAS:*** Litigation; RICO; Securities; Antitrust and Trade Regulation. ***Email:*** m2s@sonnenschein.com

ALBERT W. SHAY, born Cherry Hill, New Jersey, May 17, 1959; admitted to bar, 1987, Virginia; 1988, District of Columbia. *Education:* University of Maryland (B.A., 1982); Saint Louis University (M.H.A.; J.D., magna cum laude, 1987). *Member:* The District of Columbia Bar; Virginia State Bar; American Health Lawyers Assn. ***PRACTICE AREAS:*** Health Care; Administrative Law; Hospitals. ***Email:*** 4as@sonnenschein.com

JEFFREY L. SNYDER, born Los Angeles, California, September 9, 1957; admitted to bar, 1984, District of Columbia. *Education:* American University (B.A., cum laude, 1980; J.D., cum laude, 1983); Columbia University (LL.M., 1984). Note and Comment Editor, American University Law Review, 1982-1983. Author: *International Competition: Selected Compliance Management Issues for the last Half of the '90's and Beyond,* Corporate Counsel's International Quarterly (1996); *Iran-Libya Sanctions Act Perplexes Foreign Firms,* National Law Journal (1996); *U.S. Export Controls on Encryption Software,* Journal of World Intellectual Property (1998). Co-author: *International Litigation:* A Guide to Jurisdiction Practice and Strategy, Third Edition, 1998. *Member:* American Bar Association (Member, Section on International Law). ***PRACTICE AREAS:*** International Trade. ***Email:*** jsnyder@sonnenschein.com

RONALD E. STAUFFER, born Mitchell Air Force Base, New York, January 22, 1949; admitted to bar, 1973, District of Columbia; 1976, U.S. Court of Military Appeals; 1979, U.S. Tax Court; 1980, U.S. Court of Appeals, First Circuit. *Education:* Massachusetts Institute of Technology (S.B., 1970); Harvard University (J.D., magna cum laude, 1973). Tau Beta Pi; Sigma Gamma Tau. Editor, Harvard Law Review. Assistant to the General Counsel, Department of the Army, 1973-1977. *Member:* The District of Columbia Bar; American Bar Association (Chair, Employee Benefits Committee, Tort and Insurance Practice Section, 1992-1993; Chair, ERISA Litigation Subcommittee, Employee Benefits Committee, Taxation Section); American College of Employee Benefits Counsel (Charter Fellow). ***PRACTICE AREAS:*** Employee Benefits Law; Executive Compensation Law. ***Email:*** res@sonnenschein.com

EVELYN M. SUAREZ, born New York, N.Y., June 10, 1952; admitted to bar, 1979, District of Columbia. *Education:* Douglass College, Rutgers Univer-

(This Listing Continued)

SONNENSCHEIN NATH & ROSENTHAL, Washington—Continued

sity (B.A., cum laude, 1974); Georgetown University Law Center (J.D., 1979). Member, The American Criminal Law Review, 1978-1979. Legal Advisor to U.S. International Trade Commissioner Veronica Haggart, 1982-1984. Senior Attorney, Office of Regulations and Rulings, U.S. Customs Service, 1984-1988. Senior Attorney, Office of Chief Counsel, U.S. Customs Service, 1988-1989. *Member:* The District of Columbia Bar (Member, International Section); American Bar Association (Member, International Section). ***PRACTICE AREAS:*** Customs Law; International Trade.

LOUIS L.S. TAO, born November 11, 1942; admitted to bar, 1975, New York; 1983, District of Columbia. *Education:* National Taiwan University (B.A., 1963); Harvard University (LL.B., 1967); Cornell University (J.S.D., 1969; Ph.D., 1973). Research Associate in Law, Harvard University, 1969-1970. Andrew White Fellow. Ford Foundation Fellow, Cornell University, 1970-1973. Assistant Law Professor, National Taiwan University, 1967-1978. Associate Professor, S.U.N.Y. Associate Director, LEI, DOJ. General Counsel, AEPCO, Inc. Published Articles in Cornell Law Review, University of Pennsylvania Law Review, American Law Comp. L., International & Comp. L.O., Iona Law Review, Notre Dame Lawyer, Wayne Law Review, American Journal Asian Studies, American Political Science Review, other journals and five books in Chinese. Consultant to the Government of the Republic of China (Taiwan), 1971, 1976 and 1979. Nominated to Academia Sinica, 1979, 1981. ***Email:*** llt@sonnenschein.com

JEROME P. WEISS (Deceased, 1934-1996).

RESIDENT OF COUNSEL

L. JOHN OSBORN, born Waltham, Massachusetts, April 6, 1948; admitted to bar, 1974, Massachusetts; 1979, District of Columbia. *Education:* Boston College (A.B., 1970; J.D., 1974). Winner, National Moot Court Competition, 1973. Appellate Attorney, Office of General Counsel, Interstate Commerce Commission, 1974-1976. Appellate Attorney, Antitrust Division, U.S. Department of Justice, 1976-1977. Member, Association for Transportation Law, Logistics and Policy, 1979—. *Member:* The District of Columbia Bar; American Bar Association (Member, Antitrust and Public Law Sections). ***PRACTICE AREAS:*** Transportation; Economic Regulatory Law; Antitrust. ***Email:*** ljo@sonnenschein.com

JEAN C. EDWARDS, born St. Andrew, Jamaica, April 18, 1957; admitted to bar, 1995, Florida; 1997, District of Columbia; registered to practice before U.S. Patent and Trademark Office. *Education:* Emporia State University (B.A., with honors, 1977; B.S., 1977); University of Miami (B.S.M.E., 1979; J.D., cum laude, 1995). *Member:* The Florida Bar; The District of Columbia Bar. ***LANGUAGES:*** French. ***PRACTICE AREAS:*** Intellectual Property. ***Email:*** jedwards@sonnenschein.com

RESIDENT ASSOCIATES

DANIEL D. BARNOWSKI, born Royal Oak, Michigan, April 5, 1970; admitted to bar, 1995, Arizona; 1998, District of Columbia. *Education:* University of Michigan (B.A., with distinction, 1992; J.D., cum laude, 1995). ***PRACTICE AREAS:*** General Litigation. ***Email:*** ddb@sonnenschein.com

IMANTA M. BERGMANIS, born Minneapolis, Minnesota, October 18, 1968; admitted to bar, 1996, Minnesota; 1998, District of Columbia. *Education:* University of Minnesota (B.A.); William Mitchell College of Law (J.D., magna cum laude, 1996). Co-Author, with Daniel S. Kleinberger, Direct v. Derivative, or "What's a Lawsuit Between Friends in an 'Incorporated Partnership?'" 22 William Mitchell Law Review 1203, (1996). ***PRACTICE AREAS:*** Corporate Law. ***Email:*** imb@sonnenschein.com

ANNE M. BERTSCH, born San Antonio, Texas; admitted to bar, 1998, Maryland; 2000, District of Columbia. *Education:* University of Delaware (B.S., magna cum laude, 1993); Georgetown University (J.D., magna cum laude, 1998). Order of the Coif. Administrative Editor, Law and Policy in International Business. ***PRACTICE AREAS:*** Corporate Law. ***Email:*** amb@sonnenschein.com

WILLIAM E. COPLEY, III, born Middletown, Connecticut, September 23, 1974; admitted to bar, 1999, Virginia; 2000, District of Columbia. *Education:* Vanderbilt University (B.A., 1996); University of Chicago (J.D., 1999). *Member:* Virginia State Bar. ***PRACTICE AREAS:*** Litigation. ***Email:*** wxc@sonnenschein.com

HILARY DUKE, born N.Y., N.Y., December 18, 1963; admitted to bar, 1999, Virginia; 2000, District of Columbia; U.S. Court of Appeals, Fourth Circuit. *Education:* George Washington University (B.B.A., 1985); Georgetown Law Center (J.D., cum laude, 1999). Executive Editor, Journal of Legal Ethics. Certified Employee Benefits Specialist, 1994. *Member:* Virginia State Bar; The District of Columbia Bar; WEB Northern Virginia. ***PRACTICE AREAS:*** Employee Benefits; Executive Compensation. ***Email:*** hilary_duke@sonnenschein.com

KERRI B. GANNON, born 1974; admitted to bar, 2001, Massachusetts (Not admitted in District of Columbia). *Education:* Boston College (B.A., 1996); American University (J.D., 2000).

CATHERINE B. GARDNER, born December 22, 1969; admitted to bar, 1994, Maryland; 1996, District of Columbia. *Education:* Georgetown University (B.A., cum laude, 1991; J.D., cum laude, 1994). Member, Journal of Law and Policy in International Business. ***PRACTICE AREAS:*** Corporate. ***Email:*** cbg@sonnenschein.com

LORI E. GRAHAM, born February 8, 1972; admitted to bar, 1999, Maryland and District of Columbia. *Education:* University of Tulsa (B.A., 1994); London School of Economics, London, England (M.S.C., 1996); Georgetown University (J.D., 1998). ***PRACTICE AREAS:*** Corporate Transactions. ***Email:*** lgraham@sonnenschein.com

TRACI GREVER, born Waukegan, Illinois, August 16, 1971; (admission pending). *Education:* Illinois State University (B.A., 1993); De Paul University (J.D., 2001). Sullivan Fellow. Licensed U.S. Customs Broker, 1997. ***PRACTICE AREAS:*** International Trade; Customs Law. ***Email:*** tvg@sonnenschein.com

ALLYSON B. HANDLER, born Brooklyn, New York, May 18, 1971; admitted to bar, 1996, Maryland; 1998, District of Columbia. *Education:* University of Pennsylvania (B.A., 1993); Georgetown University (J.D., magna cum laude, 1996). Order of the Coif. ***PRACTICE AREAS:*** Litigation. ***Email:*** abh@sonnenschein.com

RAYMOND J. HO, born Taiwan, Republic of China, July 16, 1969; admitted to bar, 1994, Georgia; 1996, District of Columbia; registered to practice before U.S. Patent and Trademark Office. *Education:* Georgia Institute of Technology (B.S.E.E., 1991); Georgia State University (J.D., 1994); The John Marshall Law School (LL.M., Intellectual Property, 1995). Delta Theta Phi. Author: "International Legal Strategy," vol. IV-12. *Member:* American Bar Association; American Intellectual Property Law Association; Asian Pacific American Bar Association; Institute of Electrical and Electronics Engineers. ***LANGUAGES:*** Mandarin Chinese. ***PRACTICE AREAS:*** Patents; Trademarks; Copyrights; Trade Secrets. ***Email:*** rho@sonnenschein.com

LESLIE E. KLEIN, born Indianapolis, Indiana, December 8, 1970; admitted to bar, 1998, Maryland; 2000, District of Columbia. *Education:* Indiana University (B.A., with honors, 1992); American University, Washington College of Law (J.D., magna cum laude, 1998). Phi Beta Kappa. ***PRACTICE AREAS:*** Litigation. ***Email:*** lek@sonnenschein.com

LAURA A. LATTAL, born Morgantown, West Virginia, July 19, 1974; admitted to bar, 2001, New York (Not admitted in District of Columbia). *Education:* Miami University (B.A., 1996); Cornell Law School (J.D., 2000). Phi Beta Kappa. ***LANGUAGES:*** French. ***PRACTICE AREAS:*** Litigation. ***Email:*** lyl@sonnenschein.com

MARCI ROSE LEVINE, born Washington, D.C., October 7, 1970; admitted to bar, 1995, Maryland; 1996, District of Columbia. *Education:* Washington University (B.A., with honors, 1992); George Washington University (J.D., with high honors, 1995). Order of the Coif. Member, George Washington Law Review. *Member:* The District of Columbia Bar; American Health Lawyers Association. ***PRACTICE AREAS:*** Health Care. ***Email:*** M6L@sonnenschein.com

RENEE C. MACRI, born King of Prussia, Pennsylvania, January 19, 1976; admitted to bar, 2001, Virginia (Not admitted in District of Columbia). *Education:* James Madison University (B.A., 1998); Georgetown University Law Center (J.D., 2001). ***Email:*** rcm@sonnenschein.com

DREW W. MARROCCO, born New York, N.Y., December 31, 1968; admitted to bar, 1995, Virginia; 1996, District of Columbia. *Education:* University of Richmond (B.A., 1991); American University, Washington, D.C. (J.D., summa cum laude, 1995). Recipient: Don Monroe Cuslo Award for Excellence in Constitutional Law. ***PRACTICE AREAS:*** Government Contracts; Litigation. ***Email:*** dqm@sonnenschein.com

MICHELLE OCHS, born Livingston, New Jersey, June 30, 1973; admitted to bar, 1998, Illinois; 2000, District of Columbia. *Education:* Northwestern University (B.S., with highest distinction, 1995; J.D., cum laude, 1998). Order of the Coif. Coordinating Note and Comment Editor, Northwestern University Law Review. ***PRACTICE AREAS:*** Labor and Employment; Litigation. ***Email:*** mwo@sonnenschein.com

MEREDITH K. OLAFSON, born New Rockford, North Dakota, April 9, 1975; admitted to bar, 2000, California (Not admitted in District of Columbia). *Education:* Northwestern University (B.A., 1997); Georgetown University (J.D., 2000). Author, "The Concept of Limited Sovereignty & the Immigration Law Plenary Power Doctrine," 13 Geo. Immigr. L.J. 343, 433 (1999). *Member:* State Bar of California; American Bar Association; William B. Bryant American Inn of Court. ***LANGUAGES:*** Italian. ***PRACTICE AREAS:*** Litigation; Labor and Employment. ***Email:*** mko@sonnenschein.com

LISA P. PANDOHIE-JOHNSON, born Kingston, Jamaica, September 29, 1973; admitted to bar, 2000, Maryland (Not admitted in District of Columbia). *Education:* Yale University (B.A., 1995); Georgetown University Law Center

(This Listing Continued)

(J.D., 2000). Phi Delta Phi (Vice Magister, 1999-2000). Notes and Comments Editor, The Tax Lawyer. Assistant Editor, The Patent Journal. Chair, Alternative Dispute Resolution Society, 1999-2000. Honored Member, America's Registry of Outstanding Professionals, 2001-2002. *Member:* American Bar Association. ***PRACTICE AREAS:*** Patent Litigation; Litigation. ***Email:*** lpp@sonnenschein.com

JAMES W. REED, born Benton Harbor, Michigan, September 5, 1950; admitted to bar, 1999, Virginia; 2000, District of Columbia. *Education:* University of Michigan (A.B., with distinction, 1972); Fletcher School of Law and Diplomacy (M.A.L.D., 1981); Georgetown University Law Center (J.D., cum laude, 1999). Co-Author: "Developments in Encryption Export Controls," The Journal of World Intellectual Property, 1999. *Member:* American Bar Association (Member, Section on International Law). [Col., Inf., U.S. Army, 1972-1998.]. ***PRACTICE AREAS:*** International Trade Regulation. ***Email:*** j2r@sonnenschein.com

TRACI RITTENBERG, born Camden, New Jersey, February 24, 1973; admitted to bar, 2001, Virginia (Not admitted in District of Columbia). *Education:* Kenyon College (B.A., cum laude, with distinction, 1995); George Washington University Law Center (J.D., with honors, 2001). Member, George Washington University International Law Review. ***LANGUAGES:*** Japanese. ***PRACTICE AREAS:*** Corporate Law. ***Email:*** tar@sonnenschein.com

ALEXANDER H. SCHAEFER, born Nüremberg, Germany, September 18, 1973; admitted to bar, 1998, Virginia; 1999, U.S. Court of International Trade; 2000, District of Columbia. *Education:* Cornell University (B.A., 1995); George Mason University School of Law (J.D., 1998). *Member:* Virginia State Bar; U.S. Court of International Trade Bar. ***LANGUAGES:*** French and German. ***PRACTICE AREAS:*** International Trade; Customs. ***Email:*** a7s@sonnenschein.com

SAMEER UPADHYA, born Wheeling, West Virginia, September 2, 1975; admitted to bar, 2000, Maryland (Not admitted in District of Columbia). *Education:* Emory University (B.S., 1996); Georgetown University (J.D., 2000). ***PRACTICE AREAS:*** Corporate. ***Email:*** su@sonnenschein.com

ALISON B. WILSON, born Parkersburg, West Virginia, October 22, 1974; admitted to bar, 2000, Virginia (Not admitted in District of Columbia). *Education:* University of Virginia (B.A., 1997); George Washington University Law Center (J.D., with honors, 2000).

(For Complete Biographical Data on all Personnel, see Chicago, Illinois; Los Angeles, San Francisco, California; New York, N.Y.; Kansas City, St. Louis, Missouri and West Palm Beach, Florida Professional Biographies)

SONOSKY, CHAMBERS, SACHSE, ENDRESON & PERRY

Established in 1976

SUITE 1000, 1250 EYE STREET, N.W.
WASHINGTON, D.C. 20005
Telephone: 202-682-0240
Telecopier: 202-682-0249

Anchorage, Alaska Office: Sonosky, Chambers, Sachse, Miller & Munson. Suite 700, 900 West Fifth Avenue. Telephone: 907-258-6377. Telecopier: 907-272-8332.

Juneau, Alaska Office: Sonosky, Chambers, Sachse, Miller & Munson. 318 Fourth Street. Telephone 907-586-5880. Telecopier: 907-586-5883.

San Diego, California Office: Symphony Towers, 750 B Street, Suite 3300, 92101. Telephone: 619-595-8070. Fax: 619-595-8077.

Albuquerque, NM office: Sonosky, Chambers, Sachse, Endreson & Perry. 501 Tijeras Avenue, NW, Suite 200, 87102. Telephone: 505-247-0147.

General Trial, Administrative and Legislative Practice, Indian and Alaska Native Affairs, Public Land and Natural Resource Law, Energy, Constitutional Litigation, Election and Campaign Finance Law.

RESIDENT PARTNERS

MARVIN J. SONOSKY (1909-1997).

REID PEYTON CHAMBERS, born New York, New York, June 10, 1940; admitted to bar, 1968, District of Columbia. *Education:* Amherst College (B.A., magna cum laude, 1962); Balliol College, Oxford, England (B.A., 1964); Harvard University (LL.B., magna cum laude, 1967). Phi Beta Kappa. Member, Board of Editors, Harvard Law Review, 1965-1967. Acting Professor, UCLA School of Law, 1970-1973. Adjunct Professor, Georgetown University Law Center, 1978—. Chapman Distinguished Visiting Professor, University of Tulsa College of Law, 1988. Visiting Lecturer, Yale Law School, 1996—. Associate, Arnold & Porter, Washington, D.C., 1967-1970. Associate Solicitor, Department of the Interior, 1973-1976. *Member:* The District of Columbia Bar. ***Email:*** rchambers@sonosky.com

HARRY R. SACHSE, born Baton Rouge, Louisiana, April 1, 1934; admitted to bar, 1957, Louisiana; 1976, District of Columbia. *Education:* Louisiana State University (B.A., 1955; LL.B., 1957); University of Paris (Diplôme Droit Comparé, 1962). Editor-in-Chief, Louisiana Law Review, 1956-1957. Partner, Breazeale, Sachse and Wilson, Baton Rouge, Louisiana, 1958-1963. Assistant General Counsel, Agency for International Development, 1969-1971. Assistant to Solicitor General of the United States, 1971-1976. *Member:* The District of Columbia Bar; Louisiana State and American Bar Associations; American Law Institute. ***Email:*** hsachse@sonosky.com

DOUGLAS B. L. ENDRESON, born Roanoke, Virginia, August 18, 1953; admitted to bar, 1978, Wisconsin and U.S. District Court, Western District of Wisconsin; 1984, U.S. Court of Appeals, 7th Circuit; 1985, U.S. Court of Appeals, 6th Circuit; 1991, U.S. Court of Appeals, 2nd Circuit; 1995, U.S. Court of Appeals, 8th Circuit; 1999, District of Columbia. *Education:* Colby College (B.A., 1975); University of Wisconsin (J.D., with honors, 1978; LL.M., 1980). Law Clerk, The Honorable Shirley S. Abrahamson, Wisconsin Supreme Court, 1980-1981. Visiting Assistant Professor, University of New Mexico Law School, 1986-1987. Visiting Associate Professor, 1991 and Visiting Professor, 1997-1998, Arizona State University College of Law. *Member:* State Bar of Wisconsin; American Bar Association. ***Email:*** dendreson@sonosky.com

WILLIAM R. PERRY, born New York, New York, September 16, 1953; admitted to bar, 1978, District of Columbia. *Education:* Brown University (A.B., 1975); Georgetown University (J.D., magna cum laude, 1978). Staff Member, Georgetown Law Journal, 1977-1978. *Member:* The District of Columbia Bar. ***Email:*** wperry@sonosky.com

LLOYD BENTON MILLER, born New York, New York, December 14, 1953; admitted to bar, 1979, Alaska; 1980, District of Columbia. *Education:* Yale University (B.A., 1975); University of Virginia School of Law (J.D., 1978). Order of the Coif. Director, University of Virginia Post-Conviction Assistance Project, 1976-1977. Author: "Caught in a Crossfire: Conflict in the Courts, Alaska Tribes in the Balance," 1989 Harvard Indian Law Symposium (by the President and Fellows of Harvard College). Law Clerk to Judge James M. Fitzgerald, U.S. District Court for the District of Alaska, 1978-1979. Guest Lecturer, Alaska Native Law, Harvard University Law School, 1990 and 1991. Vice President, Board of Directors, 1985-1986 and President, 1986-1987, 1993-1994, Alaska Legal Services Corporation. *Member:* The District of Columbia Bar; Alaska (Founder and Chairman, Alaska Native Law Section, 1984-1994) and American Bar Association. (Resident, Anchorage, Alaska Office). ***Email:*** LLOYD@SONOSKY.COM

ANNE DORIS NOTO, born Hempstead, New York, May 17, 1958; admitted to bar, 1986, Maryland; 1998, District of Columbia. *Education:* Cornell University (B.A., 1980); George Washington University (J.D., magna cum laude, 1986). Order of the Coif. *Member:* Maryland State, Federal and American Bar Associations; The District of Columbia Bar. ***Email:*** anoto@sonosky.com

MARY J. PAVEL, born Shelton, Washington, November 3, 1965; admitted to bar, 1992, Washington; 1998, District of Columbia. *Education:* Dartmouth College (B.A., Sociology, 1988); University of Washington School of Law (J.D., 1992). *Member:* Washington State Bar Association; Native American Bar Association. ***Email:*** mpavel@sonosky.com

RESIDENT OF COUNSEL

ARTHUR LAZARUS, JR. (P.C.), born Brooklyn, New York, August 30, 1926; admitted to bar, 1951, New York; 1952, District of Columbia; 1954, U.S. Supreme Court. *Education:* Columbia University (B.A., cum laude, 1946); Yale University (J.D., 1949). Phi Beta Kappa. Visiting Lecturer on American Indian Law, Yale Law School, alternate years, 1971-1983. Associate, Fried, Frank, Harris, Shriver and Jacobson, Washington, D.C., 1950-1957; Partner, 1957-1991; Managing Partner, Washington Office, 1973-1986. *Member:* The District of Columbia Bar; American Bar Association. ***Email:*** alazarus@sonosky.com

MATTHEW S. JAFFE, born Sacramento, California, June 6, 1961; admitted to bar, 1986, Maryland; 1988, District of Columbia. *Education:* State University of New York at Binghamton (B.A., with honors, 1983); George Washington University (J.D., 1986). *Member:* The District of Columbia Bar; Maryland State Bar association. (Also, Member, Hobbs, Straus, Dean & Walker, Washington, D.C.). ***PRACTICE AREAS:*** Indians and Native Population. ***Email:*** mjaffe@hsdwdc.com

RESIDENT ASSOCIATES

JAMES T. MEGGESTO, born Syracuse, New York, July 12, 1971; admitted to bar, 1998, New York and District of Columbia. *Education:* State University of New York at Brockport (B.S., cum laude, 1993); Albany Law School of Union College (J.D., magna cum laude, 1997). Member, Justinian Society. Associate Editor, Albany Law Review. *Member:* New York State Bar Association; Native American Bar Association of the District of Columbia. ***Email:*** jmeggesto@sonosky.com

JAMES E. GLAZE, born Covina, California, September 27, 1961; admitted to bar, 1993, California and Alaska; 1994, U.S. District Court, District of Alaska; 1995, U.S. Court of Appeals for the District of Columbia Circuit; 1996,

(This Listing Continued)

SONOSKY, CHAMBERS, SACHSE, ENDRESON & PERRY, Washington—Continued

U.S. District Court, District of Oregon; 1999, U.S. Court of Appeals, Ninth Circuit (Not admitted in District of Columbia). *Education:* Humboldt State University (B.A., magna cum laude, 1984); University of California at San Diego (M.A., 1987); University of California School of Law at Davis (J.D., 1991). Recipient: Martin Luther King Service Award, 1991; Certificate of Appreciation for Outstanding Service awarded by Sacramento County Bar Association and Legal Services of Northern California. Law Clerk to the Honorable Edmond W. Burke, Alaska Supreme Court, 1991-1993. Member, Supreme Court Standing Advisory Committee on Civil Rules, 1996. Chair, Immigration Law Section, Alaska Bar Association, 1997-1998. *Member:* California Bar Association (inactive); American Immigration Lawyers Association. ***LANGUAGES:*** Spanish. ***PRACTICE AREAS:*** Native American Law; Employment Law; Immigration Law. ***Email:*** JGLAZE@SONOSKY.COM

DONALD J. SIMON, born Port Jervis, New York, October 21, 1953; admitted to bar, 1978, District of Columbia. *Education:* Harvard University (A.B., magna cum laude, 1975; J.D., cum laude, 1978). Phi Beta Kappa. Co-author: "Congressional Redistricting in the 1990's: The Impact of the 1982 Amendments to the Voting Right Act," George Mason University Civil Rights Law Journal, Winter, 1990. Author: "A Constitutional Rationale for the Independent Counsel Law," American Criminal Law Review, Fall, 1987; "The Constitutionality of the Special Prosecutor Law," University of Michigan Journal of Law and Reform, Fall, 1982. Associate General Counsel, Common Cause, 1981-1982. *Member:* The District of Columbia Bar; American Bar Association (Member, Election Law Committee, Administrative Law section, 1991).

(For Complete Biographical Data on all Personnel, See Professional Biographies, Anchorage and Juneau, Alaska)

ALAN B. SOSCHIN

400 SEVENTH STREET, N.W., SUITE 400
WASHINGTON, D.C. 20004
Telephone: 202-638-4264
Fax: 202-628-0249
Email: cardshp@aol.com

Family Law, Divorce, Custody, Visitations, Marital Property, Support, Pre-Nuptial Agreements, Family Mediation, Post-Divorce Modification, Criminal Defense, Traffic Violations, DWI, Drug Crimes, Business Fraud, White Collar Crimes, Homicide, Felonies, Misdemeanors, Automobile Accidents, Wrongful Death, Personal Injury.

FIRM PROFILE: Mr. Soschin is an experienced trial attorney well known throughout Washington, D.C. and Northern Virginia. For 28 years, his firm has represented individuals, families, juveniles, corrections officers, lawyers and other professionals from the Washington Metro region.

ALAN B. SOSCHIN, born Newark, New Jersey, February 26, 1947; admitted to bar, 1973, District of Columbia; 1979, Virginia. *Education:* Lehigh University (B.A., cum laude, 1969); Georgetown University (LL.B., 1972). ***PRACTICE AREAS:*** Family Law; Criminal Law; Personal Injury.

RICHARD HENRY SPEIDEL

1819 H STREET, N.W.
WASHINGTON, D.C. 20006
Telephone: 202-293-1455
Fax: 202-828-1057

Practice before the United States and Local Courts and Government Departments. Probate, Government Contract and International Law. Arbitration, Family Law and Trusts and Estates.

RICHARD HENRY SPEIDEL, born Louisville, Kentucky, June 18, 1920; admitted to bar, 1950, District of Columbia, U.S. Court of Appeals, for the District of Columbia Circuit; 1954-1982, U.S. Court of Claims; 1955, Court of Appeals, Maryland and U.S. Supreme Court; 1956, U.S. District Court, District of Maryland; 1982, U.S. Claims Court. *Education:* Harvard University (A.B., 1942); Columbia University (J.D., 1949). Phi Delta Phi. Editorial Consultant to the Federal Contracts Report, Bureau of National Affairs, 1967-1971. Member, Panel of Arbitrators, American Arbitration Association. *Member:* The District of Columbia Bar; Bar Association of the District of Columbia (Secretary, 1961-1962, Chairman, 1962-1963; 1967-1970; 1971-1972, Committee on International Law; Member, Claims Court Committee, 1967-1970); American Bar Association. ***LANGUAGES:*** French and Japanese.

REFERENCE: Riggs National Bank, Washington, D. C.

SPENCER & FRANK

WASHINGTON, D.C.

(See Venable, Attorneys at Law, Venable, Baetjer and Howard, LLP)

SPENCER, GRAHAM & HOLDERMAN

Established in 1947

2000 MASSACHUSETTS AVENUE, N.W.
WASHINGTON, D.C. 20036-1022
Telephone: 202-785-1220
Facsimile: 202-785-1807
Email: SGHLaw@aol.com

Probate, Trust, Estate Planning, Corporate and Tax Law and General Practice.

MEMBERS OF FIRM

SAMUEL SPENCER (1910-1997).

DONALD K. GRAHAM, born Shreveport, Louisiana, 1929; admitted to bar, 1955, Virginia; 1957, District of Columbia; 1959, U.S. Supreme Court. *Education:* University of Kentucky (B.S. in Commerce, 1951); University of Virginia Law School (J.D., 1955). Phi Delta Phi. *Member:* District of Columbia Bar; Bar Association of the District of Columbia; American Bar Association; Virginia State Bar. Fellow: American College of Trust and Estate Counsel.

RICHARD A. HOLDERMAN, born Oak Park, Illinois, 1938; admitted to bar, 1968, Virginia and District of Columbia. *Education:* University of Richmond (B.A., 1960); University of Virginia Law School (LL.B., 1968). Phi Beta Kappa. *Member:* The District of Columbia Bar; Virginia State Bar; American Bar Association.

PATRICK J. HOWLEY, born Silver Spring, Maryland, June 13, 1969; admitted to bar, 1995, Maryland; 1996, District of Columbia. *Education:* Boston College (B.A., 1991); Catholic University of America, Columbus School of Law (J.D., 1994). *Member:* Maryland State and American Bar Associations; The District of Columbia Bar.

R. SCOTT GARDNER, born Philadelphia, Pennsylvania, December 17, 1948; admitted to bar, 1973, Pennsylvania; 1977, District of Columbia; 1988, Virginia; 1991, Maryland. *Education:* University of Pennsylvania (B.A., 1970); Boston University (J.D., 1973). *Member:* The District of Columbia Bar; Virginia State Bar; Maryland State Bar Association.

THE SPERDUTO LAW FIRM, P.L.C.

2021 L STREET N.W.
SECOND FLOOR
WASHINGTON, D.C. 20036
Telephone: 202-408-8900
Fax: 202-408-8910
URL: http://www.sperdutolaw.com
Email: ksperduto@sperdutolaw.com
URL: http://www.lawyers.com/sperdutolawfirm

Complex Commercial Litigation including Financial Services, Shareholder, Real Estate, Environmental, Intellectual Property, Government Contracts, Employment, Insurance Coverage, Construction, and Sports Law.

FIRM PROFILE: The Sperduto Law Firm, P.L.C. was founded to provide clients with top-tier, complex commercial litigation expertise focusing on result-oriented and cost-effective services. The firm's success is based on its aggressive, service-based representation that is tailored to fit each client's specific needs and goals. The firm has substantial litigation experience in a number of areas, including financial services, real estate, shareholder litigation, litigation for corporate control, construction, sports, environmental, intellectual property, labor, government contracts, employment and insurance coverage, particularly D & O liability litigation and environmental coverage claims. Representative clients include a major oil company, a leading airline operating company, an aerospace research development firm, investment banks, venture capital firms, real estate developers, international investors, government contractors, technology companies, LCOR, Inc., JFK International Air Terminal, LLC, Swales Aerospace and the National Football League Players Association among others. The firm emphasizes its commitment to efficiency and client-responsiveness in the delivery of litigation services, and professional excellence in all its endeavors.

KIM HOYT SPERDUTO, born St. Joseph, Missouri, August 15, 1953; admitted to bar, 1980, New York and U.S. District Court, Southern and Eastern Districts of New York; 1983, U.S. Court of Appeals, Second Circuit and U.S. Supreme Court; 1987, District of Columbia; 1989, U.S. District Court for the District of Columbia, U.S. Court of Appeals for the District of Columbia Circuit and U.S. Court of Appeals, Fourth Circuit; 1993, Maryland; 1994, Virginia.

(This Listing Continued)

Education: Vanderbilt University (B.A., 1975); Duke University (M.P.P., 1978; J.D., 1979). Recipient, Annette Pinsky Award for Civil Rights, New York City, 1981. Law Clerk to the Hon. Thomas C. Platt, United States District Court, Eastern District of New York, 1979-1980. Author: "Medical Schools and the Entitlement Ethic," The Public Interest, Spring, 1980. *Member:* The District of Columbia Bar; Virginia State Bar; The Association of the Bar of the City of New York; American Bar Association; Construction Law Forum. ***REPORTED CASES:*** Reviewed at Andrews v. Koch, 554 F. Supp. 1099 and The New York Times, September 11, 1981 and November 19, 1981. ***PRACTICE AREAS:*** Financial Services Litigation; Real Estate Litigation; Insurance Coverage; Environmental Litigation; Intellectual Property; Employment Litigation; Ponce E.R.A. ***Email:*** ksperduto@sperdutolaw.com

---

MARIAN K. RIEDY, born Hope, Kansas, September 6, 1955; admitted to bar, 1982, District of Columbia and U.S. Court of Appeals, Fourth Circuit; 1992, U.S. District Court, District of Columbia. *Education:* University of Kansas (B.A., summa cum laude, 1977); Harvard University (J.D., 1981); Georgetown University Robert Emmett McDonough School of Business (M.B.A., 2000). Phi Beta Kappa. Law Clerk to Chief Judge Harrison L. Winter, U.S. Court of Appeals, Fourth Circuit, 1981-1982. Volunteer Mediator, Superior Court, District of Columbia. *Member:* The District of Columbia Bar; The Association of Trial Lawyers of America; Trial Lawyers Association of Metropolitan Washington, D.C. ***PRACTICE AREAS:*** Complex Commercial Litigation; High-Tech Business Litigation; Dispute Resolution; Intellectual Property.

JOHN E. HOWELL, born Pontiac, Michigan, June 29, 1940; admitted to bar, 1966, California, U.S. District Court, Northern and Eastern Districts of California and U.S. Court of Appeals, Ninth Circuit; 1970, U.S. Court of Appeals for the Armed Forces; 1991, District of Columbia; 1998, U.S. Court of Veterans Appeals. *Education:* University of Michigan (B.A., 1962; J.D., 1965). Former Chief Trial Judge, United States Air Force Trial Judiciary. Former Chief, Article III Judges Division, Administrative Office of the United States Courts. Master Secretary/Treasurer, Federal American Inn of Court. Treasurer, Judiciary Division, Federal Bar Association. *Member:* State Bar of California; The District of Columbia Bar; American Bar Association; Court of Appeals for the Armed Forces Bar; Court of Appeals for Veterans' Claims Bar; American Judges Association; ABA National Conference of Special Court Judges; American Judicature Society. ***PRACTICE AREAS:*** Litigation; Veterans Benefits. ***Email:*** jhowell@sperdutolaw.com

T. STEWART RAUCH, born Princeton, New Jersey, October 14, 1967; admitted to bar, 1995, Virginia; 1998, Georgia (Not admitted in District of Columbia). *Education:* Middlebury College (B.A., 1990); University of Virginia (J.D., 1995). *Member:* Virginia State Bar; State Bar of Georgia. ***PRACTICE AREAS:*** Complex Commercial Litigation; Litigation; Employment Law; Real Estate Litigation; Government Contracts; Sports Law; Construction Law; Licensing; Intellectual Property Law. ***Email:*** srauch@sperdutolaw.com

MICHAEL J. WADE, born Port Hueneme, California, September 23, 1968; admitted to bar, 2001, Virginia; U.S. Court of Appeals, Fourth Circuit (Not admitted in District of Columbia). *Education:* Washington & Lee University (B.A., 1990); George Mason University School of Law (J.D., 2001). *Member:* Virginia State Bar; Virginia Bar Association. ***PRACTICE AREAS:*** Complex Commercial Litigation; Bankruptcy; Construction Law; Environmental Litigation; Real Estate Litigation; Government Contracts. ***Email:*** mwade@sperdutolaw.com

---

SPIEGEL & McDIARMID

1350 NEW YORK AVENUE, N.W.
WASHINGTON, D.C. 20005-4798
Telephone: 202-879-4000
Facsimile: 202-393-2866
Email: info@spiegelmcd.com
URL: http://www.spiegelmcd.com

Energy, Administrative, Airports and Aviation, Antitrust, Appellate, Communications and Media, Environmental, Federal Legislative, Government Affairs, Hydroelectricity, Litigation, Municipal Infrastructure, Natural Resources, Public Utility, Qui Tam, Regulatory and Transportation Law before Federal and State Courts, Agencies and Congress.

FIRM PROFILE: Founded in Washington, DC, in 1967, Spiegel & McDiarmid is a mid-sized, national law firm that focuses on helping local and state governments and consumer groups develop and manage public infrastructure. Our firm is distinctive in that an abiding commitment to the public good permeates all areas of the practice. Clients include municipalities, cooperative utilities, public agencies, regional and national energy associations, airports, telecommunications service users and municipal providers of telecommunication services. The firm also assists local government clients in a range of federal legislative, appropriations and agency matters, and it manages the National Association of Local Environmental Professionals (NALGEP). Pro bono projects typically involve free speech/First Amendment issues, discrimination, gay rights, and local environmental matters.

(This Listing Continued)

MEMBERS OF FIRM

GEORGE SPIEGEL (1919-1997).

ROBERT C. McDIARMID, born New York, N.Y., July 13, 1937; admitted to bar, 1964, District of Columbia and Virginia, U.S. Court of Appeals for the District of Columbia; 1965, U.S. Court of Appeals, 4th, 6th and 9th Circuits; 1966, U.S. Court of Appeals, 3rd, 5th and 10th Circuits; 1967, U.S. Supreme Court, U.S. Court of Appeals, 7th and 8th Circuits and U.S. Court of Appeals for the Federal Circuit; 1970, U.S. Court of Appeals, 2nd Circuit; 1979, U.S. Court of Appeals, 1st Circuit; 1981, U.S. Court of Appeals, 11th Circuit. *Education:* Swarthmore College (B.S., with honors, 1958); Cornell University (M.S., 1960); Harvard University (LL.B., 1963). Recipient: McCabe Engineering Award. Co-Author: "The Shared Transmission System: A Model for Non-Discriminatory Access," 2 The Electricity Journal 12, 1989. Author: "Grand Bargain or Grand Larceny?" 8 The Electricity Journal 6, 1995. Attorney, Civil Division, Appellate Section, U.S. Department of Justice, 1964-1968. Assistant to the General Counsel, Federal Power Commission, 1968-1970. *Member:* The District of Columbia Bar; Bar Association of the District of Columbia; Energy (Member, Executive Committee, 1982-1983; Board of Directors, 1997-2000) and American Bar Associations; Virginia State Bar. ***PRACTICE AREAS:*** Energy; Antitrust; Litigation; Administrative Law; Utility Law. ***Email:*** robert.mcdiarmid@spiegelmcd.com

ROBERT A. JABLON, born New York, N.Y., October 6, 1939; admitted to bar, 1965, New York; U.S. Supreme Court, U.S. Court of Appeals, 1st, 4th, 5th, 6th, 9th, 11th, Federal and District of Columbia Circuits; 1969, District of Columbia. *Education:* Lehigh University (B.S., with honors, 1961); Harvard University (LL.B., 1964). Trial Attorney and Supervisory Trial Attorney, Federal Power Commission, 1965-1970. Assistant General Counsel, Administrative Proceedings, New York State Public Service Commission, 1970-1972. Member, Legal Subcommittee, National Association of Insurance Commissioners Task Force on Profitability and Investment Income, 1982-1983. Co-Author: Federal Power Commission Section, West's General Practice Manual, 1970; "Growth and Public Utilities," Bar Association of the City of New York Journal, 1972; "Possible Unintended Consequences of Florida's Havill Amendment," Bureau of Economic and Business Research, University of Florida, et al., October, 1983; Jablon, Wiegers, Bruner and Hempling, "The Legal Standard of Prudent Utility Practices in the Context of Joint Construction Projects," 20-21 NRECA-APPA Legal Reporting Service, 1984, 1985; Jablon, Trauger, Meiser, "Competitive Markets First, PUHCA 'Reform' Later," Electricity , Aug./Sept. (1991); American Public Power Association Legal Seminar, "Transmission Rulemaking and Cases Before FERC and the Federal Courts," 1993; Infocast: Power Transmission Access, Pricing and Policy, "Network Transmission Access, Wave of the Future?" 1994; "Network Transmission: A Sea of Change at FERC," Minnesota Municipal Utilities Association, 1994; "Some Observations on Strategic Consideration for Transmission Agreements and Kittens in the South," 1995; "Barriers to Municipalization," Competitive Utility (March 1996); "Welcome Back, Courts: The New Energy in Antitrust General Trends in Antitrust May Affect Competition," Competitive Utility (May 1996); Jablon and Blair, "Network Transmission Credits," Electricity Journal (June 1996); Jablon and Chadwick, "High-Cost Utilities: Stranded Costs and Stranded Profits," Competitive Utility (August 1996). *Member:* The District of Columbia Bar; New York State, Energy and American Bar Associations. ***PRACTICE AREAS:*** Antitrust; Energy; Municipal Utility Regulation; Complex Litigation; Regulatory Agency Practice; Deceptive Trade Practices; Price-Fixing; Property Law; Energy Competition. ***Email:*** robert.jablon@spiegelmcd.com

JAMES N. HORWOOD, born East Cleveland, Ohio, August 17, 1936; admitted to bar, 1961, Ohio; 1967, U.S. Supreme Court; 1973, District of Columbia and U.S. Court of Appeals for the District of Columbia Circuit; 1974, U.S. District Court for the District of Columbia; 1975, U.S. Court of Appeals, 9th Circuit; 1977, U.S. Court of Appeals, 4th Circuit; 1982, U.S. Court of Appeals, 2nd and 8th Circuits; 1983, U.S. Court of Appeals, 6th Circuit; 1996, U.S. Court of Appeals, 5th Circuit; 1998, U.S. Court of Appeals, 7th Circuit; 2000, U.S. Court of Appeals, 11th Circuit. *Education:* University of Pennsylvania (B.S. in Econ., 1958; LL.B., 1961). Attorney and Supervisory Trial Attorney: Federal Power Commission, 1962-1971; Postal Rate Commission, 1971-1972. Member, Board of Directors, Alliance for Community Media (Formerly National Federation of Local Cable Programmers), 1990—. *Member:* The District of Columbia Bar; Energy (Member, Executive Committee, 1984-1985; Member, Board of Directors, 1985-1987) and American Bar Associations; Federal Communications Bar Association (Co-Chair State and Local Practice Committee). ***PRACTICE AREAS:*** Communications Law; Contracts; Electric Power; Energy Regulation; Media and First Amendment; Public Utility; Telecommunications Competition; Telecommunications Law; Telecommunications Regulation; Energy; Cable Communications; Cable TV; Cable Franchising. ***Email:*** james.horwood@spiegelmcd.com

(This Listing Continued)

SPIEGEL & McDIARMID, Washington—Continued

ALAN J. ROTH, born Milwaukee, Wisconsin, November 26, 1933; admitted to bar, 1958, District of Columbia; 1960, U.S. Court of Appeals for the District of Columbia Circuit; 1968, U.S. Supreme Court; 1972, New York; 1977, U.S. Court of Appeals, 5th and 9th Circuits; 1981, U.S. Court of Appeals, 11th Circuit; 1983, U.S. Court of Appeals, 3rd and 10th Circuits. *Education:* Harvard University (A.B., cum laude, 1955; LL.B., 1958). Author: "The High Cost of Consolidated Edison Electricity," published by New York State Public Service Commission, 1975; "FERC Regulations on Right-sizing Pipeline Expansions and on No-notice Transportation Service," in Proceedings of the Eighth NARUC Biennial Regulatory Information Conference, 1992. Attorney and Supervisory Trial Attorney, Federal Power Commission, 1958-1969. Deputy Director for Compliance, Office of Foreign Direct Investments, U.S. Department of Commerce, 1969-1970. Executive Assistant to the Chairman, New York State Public Service Commission, 1970-1974. Commissioner, New York State Public Service Commission, 1974-1975. Member, Board of Directors, National Consumer Law Center, 1978—. *Member:* The District of Columbia Bar; Federal, Energy (Member, Board of Directors, 1992-1995) and American Bar Associations. ***PRACTICE AREAS:*** Administrative Law; Energy; Natural Gas; Natural Gas Regulation; Utility Law. ***Email:*** alan.roth@spiegelmcd.com

FRANCES E. FRANCIS, born Los Angeles, California, May 18, 1940; admitted to bar, 1965, New Jersey; 1974, District of Columbia and U.S. Court of Appeals for the District of Columbia Circuit; 1975, U.S. Court of Appeals, 9th Circuit; 1979, U.S. Court of Appeals, 1st and 8th Circuits; 1981, U.S. Supreme Court; 1982, U.S. Court of Appeals, 10th Circuit. *Education:* Dickinson College (B.A., 1962); Yale University (LL.B., 1965); Harvard University (M.P.A., 1969). Visiting Professor, National Law Center, George Washington University, 1980-1981. Assistant to Federal Power Commission Commissioner, 1965-1968. Attorney, Federal Power Commission, 1969-1970. Consultant: New England River Basin Commission, 1971-1972; Energy Policy Project, 1973-1974. *Member:* The District of Columbia Bar; New Jersey State, Energy and American Bar Associations. ***PRACTICE AREAS:*** Administrative Hearings and Appeals; Energy; Hydroelectricity; Energy Project Development; Utility Law; Hydroelectricity Licensing; Nuclear Power; Water Law. ***Email:*** frances.francis@spiegelmcd.com

DANIEL I. DAVIDSON, born Brooklyn, New York, September 19, 1936; admitted to bar, 1959, New York; 1960, U.S. Court of Appeals, 2nd Circuit; 1970, U.S. Court of Appeals for the District of Columbia Circuit; 1972, District of Columbia; 1975, U.S. Court of Appeals, 9th Circuit; 1980, U.S. Court of Appeals, 5th Circuit; 1981, U.S. Court of Appeals, 10th and 11th Circuits. *Education:* Columbia University (A.B., 1957; J.D., 1959). Phi Beta Kappa. Member, Columbia Law Review, 1958-1959. Kent Scholar. Author: "New Avenues to Antitrust Enforcement," 50 Public Power 28, November-December, 1992. Co-Author, "Market Power: Will We Know It When We See It?", a white paper on the California electric restructuring experience for the American Public Power Association. Law Clerk to Hon. Harold Medina and Hon. Learned Hand, U.S. Court of Appeals, 2nd Circuit, 1959-1960. Member, U.S. Delegation, Paris Peace Talks (Vietnam), 1969. Staff Member, National Security Council, 1968-1969. *Member:* The District of Columbia Bar; Energy and American Bar Associations. ***PRACTICE AREAS:*** Administrative Law; Antitrust; Energy; Hydroelectricity; Qui Tam; Utility Law; Regulatory Law; Utility Regulation. ***Email:*** daniel.davidson@spiegelmcd.com

THOMAS C. TRAUGER, born Oak Ridge, Tennessee, May 21, 1951; admitted to bar, 1977, District of Columbia; 1979, U.S. District Court for the District of Columbia; 1982, U.S. Court of Appeals for the District of Columbia Circuit; 1983, U.S. Court of Appeals, 6th Circuit; 1986, U.S. Court of Appeals, 9th Circuit. *Education:* Washington University (B.S.E.E. and A.B., 1972); University of Cologne, West Germany; Harvard University (J.D., 1977). Tau Beta Pi. Fulbright Scholar. *Member:* The District of Columbia Bar; Energy and American Bar Associations. ***PRACTICE AREAS:*** Energy; Alternative Dispute Resolution; Litigation; Antitrust; Agricultural Law. ***Email:*** tom.trauger@spiegelmcd.com

JOHN J. CORBETT, JR., born Lynn, Massachusetts, July 5, 1939; admitted to bar, 1968, District of Columbia, U.S. District Court for the District of Columbia and U.S. Court of Appeals for the District of Columbia Circuit; 1971, U.S. Supreme Court. *Education:* Catholic University of America (Ph.B., 1961); Georgetown University (J.D., 1965); George Washington University. *Member:* The District of Columbia Bar; American Bar Association (Member, Sections on: Urban, State and Local Government Law). ***PRACTICE AREAS:*** Transportation; Airport Law; Aviation and Aerospace; Legislative; Appellate Practice; Airport Finance and Development; Aviation Regulation. ***Email:*** jack.corbett@spiegelmcd.com

CYNTHIA SCHNEIDER BOGORAD, born New York, N.Y., January 5, 1953; admitted to bar, 1977, Massachusetts; 1978, U.S. District Court, District of Massachusetts and U.S. Court of Appeals, 4th Circuit; 1979, District of Columbia and U.S. Court of Appeals for the District of Columbia Circuit; 1980, U.S. District Court for the District of Columbia; 1985, U.S. Court of Appeals, 5th Circuit; 1988, U.S. Court of Appeals, 6th Circuit. *Education:* University of Pennsylvania (B.A., summa cum laude, 1974); Harvard University (J.D., magna cum laude, 1977). Phi Beta Kappa. Law Clerk for Hon. Walter Jay Skinner, District of Massachusetts, 1977-1978. Author: "Pulling the Plug on Market Power," Legal Times, Apr. 24, 2000; "How to Say 'Welcome' -- Market Power Barriers to Competition," Legal Times, Feb., 17, 1997; "False Start of PUHCA' --Standing Alone Repeal o the Public Utility Holding Company Act Will Impede Development of a Truly Competitive Electric Industry," *Legal Times,* Special Report, Supplement, Power Plays, Apr. 13, 1998, Vol XX, No. 46, pp. S30-S31, S34. *Member:* The District of Columbia Bar; Massachusetts, Energy and American Bar Associations. ***PRACTICE AREAS:*** Administrative Law; Antitrust; Energy; Litigation; Utility Law; Administrative Litigation. ***Email:*** cynthia.bogorad@spiegelmcd.com

GARY J. NEWELL, born Troy, New York, August 30, 1953; admitted to bar, 1978, District of Columbia and U.S. Court of Appeals for the District of Columbia Circuit; 1980, U.S. Court of Appeals, 7th Circuit; 1983, U.S. Court of Appeals, 3rd Circuit; 1999, U.S. Court of Appeals, 11th Circuit; 2001, U.S. Court of Appeals for the Federal Circuit. *Education:* Brown University (A.B., magna cum laude, 1975); University of Pennsylvania (J.D., 1978). Co-author: "Special Considerations Affecting the Use of Alternative Dispute Resolution Procedures in Regulatory Adjudications," Proceedings of the Eighth NARUC Biennial Regulatory Information Conference, 1992. *Member:* The District of Columbia Bar; Energy and American Bar Associations. ***PRACTICE AREAS:*** Energy; Utility Law; Alternative Dispute Resolution; Nuclear Power; Natural Gas. ***Email:*** gary.newell@spiegelmcd.com

SCOTT H. STRAUSS, born Brooklyn, New York, November 27, 1956; admitted to bar, 1981, District of Columbia; 1982, U.S. Court of Appeals for the District of Columbia Circuit; 1984, U.S. District Court, District of Columbia; 1987, U.S. Supreme Court. *Education:* Cornell University (B.S., 1978); University of Pennsylvania (J.D., cum laude, 1981). Order of the Coif. Editor, University of Pennsylvania Law Review, 1980-1981. Author: Comment, "Judicial Review and the Trend Toward More Stringent NLRB Standards on Arbitral Deferrals," University of Pennsylvania Law Review, Vol. 129, p. 738, 1981. *Member:* The District of Columbia Bar; Energy Bar Association. ***PRACTICE AREAS:*** Administrative Law; Energy; Telecommunications Law. ***Email:*** scott.strauss@spiegelmcd.com

BEN FINKELSTEIN, born Baltimore, Maryland, May 29, 1957; admitted to bar, 1982, District of Columbia; 1983, U.S. Court of Appeals, 8th and 10th Circuits; 1984, U.S. Court of Appeals for the District of Columbia and 6th Circuits and U.S. Claims Court; 1986, U.S. Supreme Court; U.S. District Court for the District of Columbia and Eastern and Western Districts of Arkansas; 1998, U.S. Court of Appeals, Fifth Circuit. *Education:* Haverford College (B.S., magna cum laude, 1979); Yale University (J.D., 1982). Phi Beta Kappa. *Member:* The District of Columbia Bar; American and Energy (Hydroelectric Regulation) Bar Associations. ***PRACTICE AREAS:*** Administrative Hearings and Appeals; Energy; Hydroelectricity; Federal Energy Regulation; Litigation; Hydroelectricity Licensing. ***Email:*** ben.finkelstein@spiegelmcd.com

LISA G. DOWDEN, born Lake Forest, Illinois, October 21, 1961; admitted to bar, 1986, District of Columbia; 1990, U.S. Court of Appeals, District of Columbia Circuit; 1994, U.S. Court of Appeals, Ninth Circuit; 1997, U.S. District Court for the District of Columbia. *Education:* Washington University (B.A., magna cum laude, 1983); Harvard University (J.D., 1986). Phi Beta Kappa. Publications: Co-authored *Market Power: Will We Know It When We See It?,* a white paper on the California electric restructuring experience for the American Public Power Association, with Robert C. McDiarmid and William S. Huang (December 2000); Co-authored *A modest Proposal, a discussion of the impact of the "second price" auction on bidding in the California markets,* with Robert C. McDiarmid and Daniel I. Davidson, Electricity Journal, January/February, 2001. *Member:* The District of Columbia Bar; Energy and American (Chair, Special Committee on Solid Waste, Energy and Environmental Section) Bar Associations. ***PRACTICE AREAS:*** Utility Law; Environmental Law; Energy. ***Email:*** lisa.dowden@spiegelmcd.com

RISE J. PETERS, born Roanoke, Virginia, April 14, 1961; admitted to bar, 1987, Virginia; 1989, District of Columbia; 1990, U.S. Court of Appeals, District of Columbia Circuit. *Education:* College of William and Mary (B.A. in Philosophy and Sociology with honors, 1983); Harvard University (J.D., 1987); Kennedy School of Government (M.P.P., 1987). Phi Beta Kappa. Author: Comment, "Northwest Airlines v. County of Kent, Michigan: More Than You Ever Wanted to Know about Airport Ratesetting," 22 Trans. L. J. 291, 1994. *Member:* The District of Columbia Bar; Virginia State Bar; American Bar Association; Aero Club of Washington. ***SPECIAL AGENCIES:*** DOT/FAA. ***PRACTICE AREAS:*** Aviation Law; Airport Law; Airport Regulation; International Aviation Law; Transportation. ***Email:*** rise.peters@spiegelmcd.com

PETER J. HOPKINS, born June 4, 1957; admitted to bar, 1987, District of Columbia; 1992, U.S. District Court for the District of Columbia. *Education:* Williams College (B.A. in History of Ideas, 1979); Georgetown University (J.D., cum laude, 1987). *Member:* The District of Columbia Bar. ***PRACTICE AREAS:*** Energy; Qui Tam Litigation; Telecommunications Law. ***Email:*** peter.hopkins@spiegelmcd.com

(This Listing Continued)

(This Listing Continued)

DAVID E. POMPER, born Queens, New York, August 10, 1962; admitted to bar, 1989, Pennsylvania; 1991, District of Columbia. *Education:* Swarthmore College (B.A., 1984); University of Pennsylvania (J.D., 1989). ***PRACTICE AREAS:*** Antitrust; Aviation Law; Energy; Environmental Law; Regulatory Law; Utility Law. ***Email:*** david.pomper@spiegelmcd.com

WILLIAM S. HUANG, born Urbana, Illinois, July 18, 1960; admitted to bar, 1987, New York; 1988, District of Columbia; 1995, California. *Education:* Harvard University (A.B., magna cum laude, 1981); Massachusetts Institute of Technology (Masters in City Planning, 1983); Yale University (J.D., 1986); University of California, Berkeley (Ph.D. in City and Regional Planning, 1998). *Member:* Energy Bar Association. ***PRACTICE AREAS:*** Energy; Hydroelectricity; Administrative Law; Contracts. ***Email:*** william.huang@spiegelmcd.com

OF COUNSEL

LEE C. WHITE, born Omaha, Nebraska, September 1, 1923; admitted to bar, 1950, Nebraska; 1958, District of Columbia; 1969, U.S. Supreme Court; 1970, U.S. Court of Appeals for the District of Columbia Circuit. *Education:* University of Nebraska at Lincoln (B.S. in E.E., 1948; LL.B., 1950). Editor-in-Chief, Nebraska Law Review, 1949-1950. Legislative Assistant to Senator John F. Kennedy, 1954-1957. Counsel, U.S. Senate Select Committee on Small Business, 1957-1958. Administrative Assistant to Senator John Sherman Cooper, 1958-1961. Assistant Special Counsel to President Kennedy, 1961-1963. Special Counsel to President Johnson, 1963-1966. Chairman, Federal Power Commission, 1966-1969. *Member:* The District of Columbia Bar (Member, Board of Governors, 1977-1980). ***PRACTICE AREAS:*** Environmental Law; Energy. ***Email:*** lee.white@spiegelmcd.com

SANDRA J. STREBEL, born Buffalo, New York, February 27, 1938; admitted to bar, 1962, District of Columbia; 1971, U.S. Court of Appeals for the District of Columbia Circuit; 1974, U.S. Supreme Court; 1977, U.S. Court of Appeals, 7th Circuit; 1982, U.S. Court of Appeals, 9th Circuit; 1989, Maryland; 1992, U.S. District Court, District of Maryland; 1995, U.S. Court of Appeals, 4th Circuit. *Education:* Cornell University (A.B., 1959); Duke University (LL.B., 1962). Member, Duke Law Review, 1960-1962. Attorney and Supervisory Trial Attorney, Federal Power Commission, 1962-1971. Adjunct Legal Writing Professor, University of Baltimore School of Law, 1997—. *Member:* The District of Columbia Bar; Maryland State, Federal, Energy and American Bar Associations. ***PRACTICE AREAS:*** Administrative Hearings and Appeals; Alternative Dispute Resolution; Environmental Law; Public Utility Law; Appellate Practice; Energy; Qui Tam. ***Email:*** sandra.strebel@spiegelmcd.com

MARGARET A. McGOLDRICK, born Fitchburg, Massachusetts, April 12, 1958; admitted to bar, 1984, District of Columbia; 1985, U.S. District Court for the District of Columbia and U.S. Court of Appeals for the District of Columbia Circuit. *Education:* Albion College (B.A., summa cum laude, 1980); Harvard University (J.D., cum laude, 1984). *Member:* The District of Columbia Bar; Energy and American Bar Associations. ***PRACTICE AREAS:*** Administrative Law; Arbitration; Contracts; Public Utility Law; Energy. ***Email:*** margaret.mcgoldrick@spiegelmcd.com

P. DANIEL BRUNER, born San Antonio, Texas, November 7, 1952; admitted to bar, 1981, District of Columbia; 1982, U.S. Court of Appeals for the District of Columbia, 4th and 10th Circuits; 1986, U.S. District Court, Eastern District of Arkansas; 1987, U.S. Court of Appeals, 6th Circuit; 1988, U.S. Court of Appeals,1st Circuit; 1990, U.S. District Court for the District of Columbia. *Education:* Rice University (B.A., summa cum laude, 1974); University of California at Berkeley (Graduate Studies, 1974-1975); University of Michigan (M.P.P., 1981; J.D., magna cum laude, 1981). Order of the Coif. Co-Author: Jablon, Wiegers, Bruner and Hempling, "The Legal Standard of 'Prudent Utility Practices' in the Context of Joint Construction Projects," 20-21 NRECA-APPA Legal Reporting Service, 1984-1985. Member, Whitman-Walker Clinic Legal Services Operating Committee, 1991-1994. Senior Litigation Attorney, Whitman-Walker Clinic, 1995—. *Member:* The District of Columbia Bar; Energy and American Bar Associations; National Association of Health Lawyers. ***PRACTICE AREAS:*** Energy; AIDS Litigation; Employment; Discrimination; Insurance; Disability. ***Email:*** spiegel@spiegelmcd.com

BARRY M. SMOLER, born Chicago, Illinois, March 25, 1940; admitted to bar, 1966, District of Columbia; 1969, U.S. Supreme Court. *Education:* Yale University (B.A., summa cum laude, 1962); Harvard University (J.D., 1965). Phi Beta Kappa. ***SPECIAL AGENCIES:*** Federal Energy Regulatory Commission: Deputy Assistant General Counsel for Pipeline Certificates, 1984-1989; Assistant General for Rulemaking and Environmental Law, 1990; Deputy Assistant General Counsel for Hydroelectric Licensing, 1991-2000. ***PRACTICE AREAS:*** Hydroelectricity Licensing. ***Email:*** barry.smoler@spiegelmcd.com

MARGARET A. MEISER, born Fort Yukon, Alaska, May 14, 1960; admitted to bar, 1990, Massachusetts; 1992, District of Columbia. *Education:* Yale University (B.A., cum laude, 1983); Harvard University (J.D., cum laude, 1989). Member, Harvard Legal Aid Bureau, 1987-1989. Georgetown Women's Law Fellow, U.S. Senate Subcommittee on Immigration and Refugee Affairs, 1989-1990. ***PRACTICE AREAS:*** Energy; Environmental Law; Public Interest Law. ***Email:*** meg.meiser@spiegelmcd.com

ASSOCIATES

MATTHEW W. WARD, born Sumter, South Carolina, July 23, 1969; admitted to bar, 1994, Virginia; 1997, District of Columbia and U.S. Court of Appeals, 11th Circuit. *Education:* American University (B.A., magna cum laude, 1991); University of Virginia (J.D., 1994). Author: "Profile of Business Leadership on Smart Growth: New Partnerships Demonstrate the Economic Benefits of Reducing Sprawl," Report of the National Association of Local Government Environmental Professional, 1999; "Project XL for Communities: An Alternate Path to Environmental Compliance," Municipal Lawyer, Nov./Dec. 1996, Vol. 37, No. 6; "Project XL: An Alternate Path for Environmental Leaders," in 1997 Wiley Environmental Law Update, ed. Stern & Volz (1997); "National Incentives for Smart Growth Communities," Natural Resources & Environment, Summer 1998, Vol. 13, No. 1; "Building a Brownfield Partnership from the Ground Up: Local Government Views on the Value and Promise of National Brownfields Initiatives," Report of the National Association of Local Government Environmental Professionals, 1997; "Clean Air on the Horizon? The Need for New Tools for Local Governments to Meet National Air Quality Objectives," Municipal Lawyer, March/April 1998, Vol. 39, No. 2; "Municipal Superfund Liability: How Industry is Trying to Dump Co-Disposal Landfill Liability on Localities through Litigation and Lobbying," paper presented at the International Municipal Lawyers Association 1998 Annual Meeting, November 9, 1998; "Getting the Dirt on Brownfields," Municipal Lawyer, July/August 1998; "HUD CDBG Brownfield Funding: A Building Block for Community Development," Report prepared for the Department of Housing and Urban Development by the National Association of Local Government Environmental Professionals, October 1998. Member: City of Charles Town, West Virginia City Council; Charles Town Planning Commission. Chairman, Board of Directors, Harper's Ferry Conservancy. Member, Jefferson County Planning Commission. *Member:* American Bar Association (Member, Environment and Energy Section); The District of Columbia Bar (Member, Environment, Energy and Natural Resources). ***PRACTICE AREAS:*** Environmental Law; Energy; Government Affairs; Regulatory Law; Clean Air; Smart Growth; Brownfields; Environmental Legislative Practice; Environmental Regulation. ***Email:*** matt.ward@spiegelmcd.com

JEFFREY A. SCHWARZ, born New York, N.Y., October 8, 1969; admitted to bar, 1994, Virginia; 1997, District of Columbia; 1998, Massachusetts. *Education:* University of Virginia (B.A., with distinction, 1991); Harvard University (J.D., cum laude, 1994). Phi Beta Kappa. ***PRACTICE AREAS:*** Litigation; Energy; Aviation Law. ***Email:*** jeffrey.schwarz@spiegelmcd.com

DAVID B. LIEB, born Washington, D.C., May 30, 1970; admitted to bar, 1997, Maryland; 1999, District of Columbia. *Education:* Virginia Polytechnic Institute and State University (B.A., magna cum laude, honors, 1992); University of Virginia (J.D., 1997). ***PRACTICE AREAS:*** Energy; Litigation; Utility Law. ***Email:*** david.lieb@spiegelmcd.com

PABLO O. NÜESCH, born Buenos Aires, Argentina, March 4, 1965; admitted to bar, 1997, South Carolina; 1999, District of Columbia. *Education:* Florida Institute of Technology (B.S. in Aviation Management, 1987); University of South Carolina (J.D., 1997). Chief Justice, Moot Court. Recipient, James Petigru Compleat Lawyer Award. *Member:* South Carolina Bar; District of Columbia Bar; American Bar Association (Member: Forum on Air and Space Law; International Law and Practice Section). ***PRACTICE AREAS:*** Aviation Law; Airport Law; Civil Litigation. ***Email:*** pablo.nuesch@spiegelmcd.com

ANDREA G. LONIAN, born Oklahoma City, Oklahoma, July 21, 1972; admitted to bar, 1998, Massachusetts; 1999, District of Columbia. *Education:* Georgetown University (A.B., 1995); Harvard University (J.D., 1998). ***PRACTICE AREAS:*** Energy; Litigation; Communications Law. ***Email:*** andrea.lonian@spiegelmcd.com

LARISSA A. SHAMRAJ, born Ann Arbor, Michigan, September 3, 1973; admitted to bar, 1999, Alaska; 2000, District of Columbia. *Education:* Wellesley College (B.A., summa cum laude, 1995); Harvard University (J.D., cum laude, 1998). Phi Beta Kappa. ***PRACTICE AREAS:*** Energy. ***Email:*** larissa.shamraj@spiegelmcd.com

TRACY E. CONNOR, born Raleigh, North Carolina, July 15, 1974; admitted to bar, 2000, Pennsylvania (Not admitted in District of Columbia). *Education:* Cornell University (B.A., 1996); University of Pennsylvania (J.D., 2000). ***PRACTICE AREAS:*** Energy; Litigation. ***Email:*** tracy.connor@spiegelmcd.com

LEGAL SUPPORT PERSONNEL

CAROL J. GLOSS, born Colorado Springs, Colorado, October 18, 1943. *Education:* University of Northern Colorado (B.A., 1965). Member, Association of Legal Administrators, 1982—. (Executive Director). ***Email:*** carol.gloss@spiegelmcd.com

(This Listing Continued)

SPIEGEL & McDIARMID, Washington—Continued

KENNETH A. BROWN, born Cincinnati, Ohio, March 18, 1957. *Education:* University of Michigan (B.A., 1980; Master of Public Policy, 1981). Instructor, U.S. Energy Policies and Politics, University of Michigan, 1981. Executive Director, Renew America, 1994. National Program Director, Clean Water Action, 1990-1992. Co-Founder and Director, New Jersey Environmental Federation, 1983-1989. Legislative Aide to Congressman Bill Gradison, 1977-1978. (Public Affairs Director). ***PRACTICE AREAS:*** Government Affairs; Government Relations. ***Email:*** kenneth.brown@spiegelmcd.com

SPIRER & GOLDBERG, P.C.

Established in 1982

927 FIFTEENTH STREET, N.W., THIRD FLOOR

WASHINGTON, D.C. 20005

Telephone: 202-628-2900

Telecopier: 202-628-4608

URL: http://www.spirerandgoldberg.com

Email: FGoldberg@spirerandGoldberg.com

URL: http://www.lawyers.com/spirergoldberglaw

Rockville, Maryland Office: 20 Courthouse Square, Suite 210, 20850. Telephone: 301-570-0343.

General Corporate, Non-Profit Organizations, Family Law, Personal Injury, Medical Malpractice, Professional Malpractice, International, Immigration, Estate Planning, Employment Law, Wrongful Death.

FIRM PROFILE: Spirer & Goldberg, P.C. was founded in 1982 and engages in a full-service general practice serving the needs of individuals, families and small businesses in the Washington, D.C. area. The firm provides expert advice and counsel in business transactions, domestic relations, employment law and general litigation, including personal injury, products liability, commercial disputes and professional negligence.

JULIAN H. SPIRER, born Brooklyn, New York, October 5, 1947; admitted to bar, 1972, New York; 1980, District of Columbia; 1981, U.S. Supreme Court; 1986, U.S. Court of International Trade; 1987, U.S. District Court for the District of Columbia; 1988, Maryland; 1989, U.S. District Court, District of Maryland. *Education:* Johns Hopkins University; Princeton University (A.B., summa cum laude, 1968); Harvard University (J.D., cum laude, 1971). Phi Beta Kappa. Burkan Copyright Prize. Editor, International Law Journal, 1970-1971. Author: "Ocean Dumping Deadline: Easing the Mandate Millstone," XI Fordham Urban Law Journal 1, 1982-1983; "In re Johannesburg Operatic and Dramatic Society v. Music Theatre International: Boycott of the South African State," 20 Copyright Law Symposium 154, 1972. Counsel, Congressman Benjamin S. Rosenthal, 1975-1978. Director, New York City Washington Office, 1978-1982. *Member:* The District of Columbia Bar. ***PRACTICE AREAS:*** Corporate; Tax Exempt Organizations; International Law; Civil Litigation; Immigration Law; Visas; Business Law. ***Email:*** JSpirer@spiererandgoldberg.com

FRED B. GOLDBERG, born Bronx, New York, June 4, 1951; admitted to bar, 1976, New York; 1979, District of Columbia; 1982, U.S. District Court, District of Columbia; 1983, U.S. Court of Appeals, District of Columbia Circuit; U.S. Supreme Court; 1990, U.S. District Court, District of Maryland; 1991, Maryland. *Education:* University of Maryland (B.A., 1972); John Marshall Law School (J.D., 1976). Adjunct Lecturer of Consumer and the Law, University of Maryland, 1979-1991. Research Director, National Consumer Information Center, 1976-1977. Attorney Advisor, U.S. Office of Consumer Affairs, 1977-1979. General Counsel, District of Columbia Office of Consumer Protection, 1979-1981. *Member:* The District of Columbia Bar; Maryland State Bar Association; District of Columbia Trial Lawyers Association (Member, Board of Governors); The Association of Trial Lawyers of America. ***LANGUAGES:*** Spanish. ***PRACTICE AREAS:*** Civil Litigation; Personal Injury; Products Liability; Medical Malpractice; Commercial Law; Automobile Accidents; Wrongful Death; Consumer Fraud. ***Email:*** FGoldberg@spirerandgoldberg.com

OF COUNSEL

HANS ULFSON ANDERSEN, born Falun, Sweden, April 10, 1953; admitted to bar, 1987, District of Columbia. *Education:* Uppsala University (J.D., 1980); George Washington Law Center (M.C.L., 1987; President, Foreign Attorneys in Master Studies). *Member:* District of Columbia Bar (Member, International Law Section). ***LANGUAGES:*** Swedish, Norwegian, Danish. ***PRACTICE AREAS:*** International Commercial Law. ***Email:*** spirgold@aol.com

SPRENGER & LANG, PLLC

Established in 1989

1614 TWENTIETH STREET, N.W.

WASHINGTON, D.C. 20009

Telephone: 202-265-8010

Fax: 202-332-6652

URL: http://www.sprengerlang.com

Minneapolis, Minnesota Office: Sprenger & Lang, PLLC, 325 Ridgewood Avenue. Telephone: 612-871-8910. Fax: 612-871-9270.

Employment Litigation, Professional and Trade Associations, Civil Rights, Complex Federal Litigation.

MEMBERS OF FIRM

JANE LANG, born New York, N.Y., March 16, 1947; admitted to bar, 1970, District of Columbia; 1974, U.S. Supreme Court. *Education:* Swarthmore College (B.A., with distinction, 1967); University of Pennsylvania (J.D., 1970). Phi Beta Kappa. Editor, University of Pennsylvania Law Review, 1969-1970. Partner, Steptoe & Johnson, 1977-1979, 1981-1986. General Counsel, U.S. Department of Housing and Urban Development, 1979-1981. Partner, Weissbrodt, Swiss & McGrew, 1986-1988 *Member:* The District of Columbia Bar. ***PRACTICE AREAS:*** Employment; Complex Federal Litigation; Professional and Trade Associations. ***Email:*** jlang@sprengerlang.com

PAUL C. SPRENGER, born Stillwater, Minnesota, September 8, 1940; admitted to bar, 1965, Minnesota; 1979, U.S. Supreme Court; 1987, District of Columbia. *Education:* University of Michigan (B.B.A., 1962; J.D., 1965). Special Counsel to Attorney General, Minnesota, 1975-1982 and Wisconsin, 1975-1981 and to Minister of Finance, Federal Republic of Germany, 1974-1983. Partner, Sprenger, Olson & Shutes, 1977-1988. *Member:* Minnesota State Bar Association; District of Columbia Bar. ***PRACTICE AREAS:*** Employment; Complex Federal Litigation. ***Email:*** psprenger@sprengerlang.com

MICHAEL D. LIEDER, born Washington, D.C., December 10, 1954; admitted to bar, 1984, District of Columbia. *Education:* Haverford College (B.A., 1977); Georgetown University (J.D., magna cum laude, 1984). Notes and Comments Editor, 1983-1984, Georgetown Law Journal. Associate, Foley & Lardner, 1984-1990. Co-Author: *Wild Justice: The People of Geronimo v. United States,*" Random House, 1997. Author: "Constructing a New Action for Negligent Infliction of Economic Loss: Building on Cardozo and Coase," 66 Washington L.R. 937, 1991. Co-Author with Jane Lang: "Beyond Political Rhetoric: The Civil Rights Act of 1991," Bench and Bar of Minnesota, March, 1992 at 16. Visiting Assistant Professor of Law, University of Toledo College of Law, 1990-1991. ***PRACTICE AREAS:*** Employment; Civil Rights; Complex Federal Litigation. ***Email:*** mlieder@sprengerlang.com

LAWRENCE P. SCHAEFER, born New York, N.Y., August 29, 1962; admitted to bar, 1988, Minnesota and U.S. District Court, District of Minnesota (Not admitted in District of Columbia). *Education:* University of Chicago (B.A., with honors in Political Science, 1984); University of Minnesota (J.D., magna cum laude, 1988). Order of the Coif; Phi Kappa Phi. Legal Writing Instructor, University of Minnesota Law School, 1986-1987. Member, Board of Directors, Minnesota Justice Foundation, 1988-1992. *Member:* Hennepin County, Minnesota State and American Bar Associations. (Resident, Minneapolis, Minnesota Office). ***PRACTICE AREAS:*** Employment; Civil Rights; Complex Federal Litigation. ***Email:*** lschaefer@sprengerlang.com

STEVEN M. SPRENGER, born Ann Arbor, Michigan, August 27, 1962; admitted to bar, 1988, Maryland; U.S. District Court, District of Maryland; 1989, District of Columbia; U.S. District Court, District of Columbia; 1993, Missouri and Kansas; U.S. District Court, Districts of Missouri and Kansas and U.S. Court of Appeals, Fourth and Tenth Circuits. *Education:* Grinnell College (B.A., 1985); University of Iowa (J.D., with high distinction, 1988). *Member:* The Association of Trial Lawyers of America; National Employment Lawyers Association (Kansas City Chapter). ***PRACTICE AREAS:*** Employment Law; Civil Rights; Complex Federal Litigation. ***Email:*** ssprenger@sprengerlang.com

DANIEL WOLF, born September 21, 1960; admitted to bar, 1987, Pennsylvania; 1990, District of Columbia. *Education:* Northwestern University (B.A., with highest distinction, 1982); University of Michigan (J.D., magna cum laude, 1986). Order of the Coif. Editor, Michigan Law Review, 1984-1985. Associate, Hughes Hubbard & Reed, 1989-1998 and Partner, 1998-2000. ***PRACTICE AREAS:*** Employment Law; Civil Rights; Human Rights; Complex Federal Litigation. ***Email:*** dwolf@sprengerlang.com

SUSAN E. STOKES, born Hibbing, Minnesota, May 20, 1962; admitted to bar, 1989, California; 1991, Minnesota, U.S. District Court, District of Minnesota and U.S. Court of Appeals, Third, Eighth and Ninth Circuits (Not admitted in District of Columbia). *Education:* St. Olaf College (B.A., cum laude, 1984); University of Minnesota (J.D., cum laude, 1989). Legal Writing Instructor, University of Minnesota Law School, 1988-1989. Associate, Pillsbury, Madison & Sutro, 1989-1994. *Member:* Hennepin County, Minnesota State (Governing Council, Labor and Employment Section) and American (Member, Litigation

(This Listing Continued)

Section) Bar Associations; State Bar of California; Minnesota Women Lawyers. (Resident, Minneapolis, Minnesota Office). ***PRACTICE AREAS:*** Employment Law; Civil Rights; Complex Federal Litigation. ***Email:*** sstokes@sprengerlang.com

SUSAN M. COLER, born St. Paul, Minnesota, April 22, 1948; admitted to bar, 1989, Illinois; 1991, Minnesota, U.S. District Court, District of Minnesota and U.S. Court of Appeals, Sixth and Eighth Circuits (Not admitted in District of Columbia). *Education:* Mundelein College (B.A., summa cum laude, 1971); University of Cincinnati College Conservatory of Music (M.M., 1977); Northwestern University School of Law (J.D., cum laude, 1989). Order of the Coif. Member, Northwestern Law Review, 1987-1989. Law Clerk to the Hon. Robert G. Renner, U.S. District Court, District of Minnesota, 1989-1991. (Resident, Minneapolis, Minnesota Office). ***PRACTICE AREAS:*** Employment Law; Civil Rights; Complex Federal Litigation. ***Email:*** scoler@sprengerlang.com

---

CYNTHIA J. TOTTEN, born Boston, Massachusetts, August 5, 1972; admitted to bar, 1998, California (Not admitted in District of Columbia). *Education:* Wellesley College (B.A., cum laude, 1994); Harvard University (J.D., 1997). ***LANGUAGES:*** Spanish. ***PRACTICE AREAS:*** Employment Law; Civil Rights; Complex Federal Litigation. ***Email:*** ctotten@sprengerlang.com

LISA C. STRATTON, born Boston, Massachusetts, January 17, 1964; admitted to bar, 1993, Minnesota; 1996, District of Columbia. *Education:* University of Virginia (B.A., 1986); University of Minnesota (J.D., magna cum laude, 1993). Order of the Coif. MacArthur Scholar. Associate Articles Editor, Minnesota Law Review, 1992-1993. Judicial Law Clerk to United States District Judge John R. Tunheim, 1996-1998. Judicial Law Clerk to Minnesota Supreme Court Justice Sandra S. Gardebring, 1993-1994. Author: "The Right to Have Rights: Gender Discrimination in Nationality Laws," 77 Minn. L. Rev. 195, 1992. Assistant Attorney General, Minnesota, 1994-1996. *Member:* Minnesota State and American Bar Associations; The District of Columbia Bar. (Resident, Minneapolis, Minnesota Office). ***LANGUAGES:*** Spanish. ***PRACTICE AREAS:*** Employment; Civil Rights; Complex Federal Litigation. ***Email:*** lstratton@sprengerlang.com

DAVID L. SHULMAN, born Norwalk, Connecticut, 1967; admitted to bar, 1995, Minnesota; U.S. District Court, District of Minnesota; U.S. Court of Appeals, Eighth Circuit (Not admitted in District of Columbia). *Education:* University of Minnesota (B.A., 1991; J.D., cum laude, 1995). Student Attorney, Legal Assistant to Minnesota Prisoners. Associate, Shulman Walcott & Shulman. Appeared in Eighth Circuit Court of Appeals, Federal District Court in Minnesota and Illinois, and Minnesota District Courts. ***LANGUAGES:*** French. ***PRACTICE AREAS:*** Civil Rights; Commercial Litigation; Antitrust; Class Actions; Employment Law; Personal Injury. ***Email:*** dshulman@sprengerlang.com

SARA MADSEN, born Cedar Falls, Iowa, September 21, 1953; admitted to bar, 1984, Minnesota; 1986, U.S. District Court, District of Minnesota; 1996, U.S. Court of Appeals, Ninth Circuit (Not admitted in District of Columbia). *Education:* Luther College (B.A., cum laude, 1975); William Mitchell College of Law (J.D., cum laude, 1983). *Member:* Hennepin County, Minnesota State, Federal and American Bar Associations. (Resident, Minneapolis, Minnesota Office). ***PRACTICE AREAS:*** Employment Law; Civil Rights; Complex Federal Litigation. ***Email:*** smadsen@sprengerlang.com

OF COUNSEL

MARA R. THOMPSON, born Yankton, South Dakota, October 7, 1963; admitted to bar, 1988, Minnesota and U.S. District Court, District of Minnesota; 1997, U.S. Court of Appeals, Eighth Circuit (Not admitted in District of Columbia). *Education:* University of Minnesota (B.A., magna cum laude, 1985); University of Minnesota Law School (J.D., cum laude, 1988). Recipient, Birkelow Scholarship Award, 1984. Associate: Harstad & Rainbow, 1988-1990; Gray, Plant, Mooty, Mooty & Bennett, 1991-1994. Member, State of Minnesota Harmful Substance Compensation Board, 1991-1994. *Member:* Hennepin County, Minnesota State and American Bar Associations. (Resident, Minneapolis, Minnesota Office). ***PRACTICE AREAS:*** Employment Litigation; Civil Rights. ***Email:*** mthompson@sprengerlang.com

TERESA K. PATTON, born Roseburg, Oregon, December 1, 1952; admitted to bar, 1988, California; 1989, Minnesota and U.S. District Court, District of Minnesota; 1992; Colorado (Not admitted in District of Columbia). *Education:* University of Minnesota (B.S., 1979); University of California (J.D., 1988). Member: Horizon 100 Professional Women's Group; Guatemalan Human Right Commission. Board Member, The Theater Space Project. *Member:* Hennepin County (Program Chair, 2000-2001 and Member, Labor and Employment Section) and Minnesota State Bar Associations; National Employment Lawyers Association (President, 1997-1998); Minnesota Women Lawyers. (Resident, Minneapolis, Minnesota Office). ***PRACTICE AREAS:*** Employment Law; Civil Rights; Complex Federal Litigation; Sexual Harassment; Sexual Abuse. ***Email:*** tpatton@sprengerlang.com

SPRIGGS & HOLLINGSWORTH

Established in 1982

1350 I STREET, N.W., SUITE 900
WASHINGTON, D.C. 20005
Telephone: 202-898-5800
Telecopier: 202-682-1639
Email: Postmaster@spriggs.com
URL: http://www.spriggs.com

Specializing in: Antitrust, Asbestos Defense, Banking Litigation, Civil Appeals, Complex Commercial Litigation, Construction Law, Drug and Medical Device Defense; Employment Law, Environmental Law, Federal Claims, Government Contracts, Government Procurement, Insurance Coverage, International Arbitration, Litigation, Products Liability, Toxic Torts and White Collar Crime.

MEMBERS OF FIRM

WILLIAM J. SPRIGGS, born Bloomington, Indiana, October 1, 1939; admitted to bar, 1964, Kansas; 1971, Colorado; 1972, District of Columbia; U.S. Supreme Court; U.S. Court of Appeals for the Federal Circuit; U.S. Court of Federal Claims. *Education:* Abilene Christian College (B.A., 1961); Washburn University (J.D., 1964). Sigma Tau Delta; Delta Theta Phi. Editor: Washburn Law Journal, 1963-1964; Author: "The False Claims Act," Government Contractor Briefing Papers No. 79-3, June 1979; "Stopping Work and Defective Specifications: Contradictory Duties From Inconsistent Cases," National Contract Management Journal, Vol. 13, Nos. 1 and 2, 1979; "Establishing the Government's Responsibility to Asbestos Victims," Mealey's Litigation Report, 1984. Co-author: "Government Contractors' Self-Governance Obligations and Employee Relations," Washington Legal Foundation, 1988. *Member:* District of Columbia Bar; American Bar Association (Member, Public Contract Law Section). [Captain, U.S. Marine Corps, 1964-1967]. ***PRACTICE AREAS:*** Government Contracts; Government Procurement; Litigation. ***Email:*** wspriggs@spriggs.com

JOE G. HOLLINGSWORTH, born Indianapolis, Indiana, March 3, 1949; admitted to bar, 1975, District of Columbia, U.S. Supreme Court and U.S Court of Appeals, First, Second, Third, Fourth, Sixth, Eighth, Ninth, Tenth, Eleventh Circuits; U.S. Court of Appeals for the District of Columbia Circuit; U.S. Court of Appeals for the Federal Circuit. *Education:* DePauw University (B.A., with distinction, 1971); Georgetown University (J.D., 1974). ***PRACTICE AREAS:*** Products Liability; Toxic Torts; Litigation; Drug and Medical Devices; Insurance Coverage; Federal Claims. ***Email:*** jhollingsworth@spriggs.com

CATHERINE R. BAUMER, born Butte, Montana, December 12, 1946; admitted to bar, 1978, District of Columbia; U.S. Court of Appeals for the District of Columbia Circuit; U.S. Court of Federal Claims. *Education:* George Washington University (B.A., 1969); Washington College of Law, American University (J.D., 1978). Editor-in-Chief, American University Law Review, 1977-1978. Co-Author: *Defusing The Asbestos Litigation Crisis: The Responsibility of the U.S. Government,* published by Washington Legal Foundation, 1986. *Member:* American Bar Association (Member, Public Contract Law and Litigation Sections). ***PRACTICE AREAS:*** Government Contracts; Banking Litigation; Litigation. ***Email:*** cbaumer@spriggs.com

EDWARD J. BEDER, JR., born Sonthofen, West Germany, March 29, 1948; admitted to bar, 1978, District of Columbia; U.S. Supreme Court. *Education:* United States Coast Guard Academy (B.S., with high honors, 1970); Stanford University (J.D., 1978). Order of the Coif. *Member:* American Bar Association (Member, Tort, Insurance and Antitrust Practice Sections); Defense Research Institute. [Lieutenant, U.S. Coast Guard, 1970-1975]. ***PRACTICE AREAS:*** Antitrust; International Arbitration; Complex Commercial Litigation; Insurance Coverage; Asbestos Defense. ***Email:*** ebeder@spriggs.com

BRUCE J. BERGER, born Passaic, New Jersey, August 14, 1950; admitted to bar, 1976, Massachusetts; 1980, District of Columbia; U.S. Supreme Court; U.S. Court of Appeals, Fourth, Sixth and Ninth Circuits; U.S. Court of Federal Claims. *Education:* University of Connecticut (B.A., with honors in Chemistry, 1972); Harvard University (J.D., cum laude, 1975). Phi Beta Kappa; Phi Kappa Phi; Phi Lambda Upsilon. Editor, Harvard Law Review, 1973-1975. Executive Editor, 1974-1975 and Editor, 1973-1974, Harvard Law Review. Law Clerk to Hon. John Minor Wisdom, Judge, U.S. Court of Appeals, Fifth Circuit, 1975-1976. Author: "The Prosecutor's Rebuttal Argument: The Proper Limits of the Doctrine of Invited Response," Criminal Law Bulletin, Jan.- Feb., 1983; "State and Federal Conflicts During Negotiations of Site Remedies in CERCLA Injunctive Actions," Toxics Law Reporter, July 8, 1987; "Practical Ideas for Superfund Settlements," Environmental Manager, January, 1990. Co-Author: "A Litigator's Introduction to Contaminant Fate and Transport Models," Toxics Law Reporter, January 1989; "Taking the Depositions of Plaintiffs' Experts in Toxic Tort Cases," Toxic Law Reporter, November, 1990; "Attacking an Expert's Opinion," Legal Guide to Working with Environmental Consultants, 1992; Conde v. Velsicol Chemical Corp.- Lessons for the Defense of Toxic Tort Cases," published in the Toxics Law Reporter, May 3, 1995; "Graduate Students' Injury Claims: Tort Liability or Workers' Compensation and the Impact

(This Listing Continued)

SPRIGGS & HOLLINGSWORTH, Washington—Continued

on Insurance Coverage," College Law Bulletin, April 18, 1996. Adjunct Professor of Trial Practice, Georgetown University Law Center, 1982-1985. Trial Attorney: Civil Rights Division, 1976-1980; Lands Division, 1983-1985, U.S. Department of Justice. *Member:* American Bar Association (Member, Litigation Law Section). ***PRACTICE AREAS:*** Toxic Torts; Litigation; Insurance Coverage; Environmental Law; Drug and Medical Device Defense. ***Email:*** bberger@spriggs.com

NEIL S. BROMBERG, born Queens, New York, June 28, 1966; admitted to bar, 1992, New York; 1993, District of Columbia and U.S. District Court, District of Columbia. *Education:* Brandeis University (B.A., magna cum laude, 1988); University of Pennsylvania School of Law (J.D., cum laude, 1991). Order of the Coif. Editor, University of Pennsylvania Law Review. Faculty presenter, "Internal Discovery on the Internet and other Electronic Databases," CLE Program on Electronic Discovery, District of Columbia Bar Winter Convention (March 2nd, 1999). *Member:* The District of Columbia Bar (Member, Litigation Section Steering Committee, 1998-2000; Chair, Nominating Committee, Litigation Section, 1999; Chair, Publications Committee, 1999); American Bar Association. ***PRACTICE AREAS:*** Products Liability; Toxic Torts; Litigation; Drug and Medical Device Defense. ***Email:*** nbromberg@spriggs.com

MARTIN C. CALHOUN, born Boston, Massachusetts, May 8, 1964; admitted to bar, 1989, District of Columbia; 1999, Maryland; U.S. Court of Appeals, Eleventh Circuit; U.S. Court of Appeals for the District of Columbia Circuit. *Education:* Yale University (B.A., magna cum laude, 1986); Georgetown University (J.D., magna cum laude, 1989). Order of the Coif. Leahy Prize, Moot Court Finalist. Executive Editor, Georgetown Law Journal, 1988-1989. Law Clerk, Hon. Charles R. Richey, U.S. District Court, District of Columbia, 1989-1991. Author, Note: "How to Thread the Needle: Toward a Checklist-Based Standard for Evaluating Ineffective Assistance of Counsel Claims," 77 Georgetown Law Journal 413 (1988). *Member:* The District of Columbia Bar; American Bar Association. ***LANGUAGES:*** German. ***PRACTICE AREAS:*** Products Liability; Toxic Torts; Litigation; Drug and Medical Device Defense; Insurance Coverage. ***Email:*** mcalhoun@spriggs.com

WILLIAM J. COPLE III, born Glen Cove, New York, May 13, 1955; admitted to bar, 1981, New York; 1984, District of Columbia; 1994, Virginia; U.S. Supreme Court; U.S. Court of Appeals, Fourth, Sixth and Eleventh Circuits; U.S. Court of Appeals for the District of Columbia Circuit; U.S. Court of Appeals for the Federal Circuit; U.S. Court of Federal Claims; U.S. District Court, Eastern District of Virginia; U.S. District Court, District of Columbia; U.S. District Court, Southern and Eastern Districts of New York; U.S. District Court, Northern District of Texas. *Education:* Washington & Lee University (B.A., 1977); St. John's University (J.D., 1980); Georgetown University (LL.M., International Law, 1986). Editor, St. John's Law Review, 1978-1980. Office of the Secretary of Defense, Office of General Counsel, 1980-1983. Chief Trial Counsel, U.S. Army Engineer Center, Fort Belvoir, Virginia, 1983-1984. Assistant U.S. Attorney, Eastern District of Virginia, 1984-1985. Executive Board and General Counsel, National Capital Area Council, Boy Scouts of America, 1994-1996. *Member:* American Bar Association. [Capt., U.S. Army, 1980-1985]. ***PRACTICE AREAS:*** Products Liability; Toxic Torts; Litigation; Drug and Medical Device Defense. ***Email:*** wcople@spriggs.com

DONALD W. FOWLER, born Greenville, South Carolina, June 4, 1951; admitted to bar, 1975, Maryland; 1984, District of Columbia; U.S. Supreme Court; U.S. Court of Appeals, Fourth, Sixth, Ninth and Eleventh Circuits; U.S. Court of Appeals for the District of Columbia Circuit; U.S. Court of Appeals for the Federal Circuit; U.S. Court of International Claims; U.S. Court of Federal Claims. *Education:* Cornell University (B.A., 1972); Yale University (J.D., 1975). *Member:* American Bar Association; Defense Research Institute. ***PRACTICE AREAS:*** Environmental Law; Litigation; Toxic Torts; Products Liability; Civil Appeals. ***Email:*** dfowler@spriggs.com

PATRICK R. HARKINS, born Bayonne, New Jersey, March 17, 1955; admitted to bar, 1982, District of Columbia; 1983, Virginia. *Education:* Augustana College-Illinois (B.A., 1977); American University (J.D., 1981). *Member:* American Bar Association. ***PRACTICE AREAS:*** Products Liability; Toxic Torts; Litigation; Asbestos Defense. ***Email:*** pharkins@spriggs.com

CYNTHIA KENDRICK, born Gulfport, Mississippi, March 16, 1966; admitted to bar, 1991, Maryland; 1993, District of Columbia; 1995, Florida and U.S. District Court, District of Maryland; 1996, U.S. District Court for the District of Columbia; 1998, U.S. District Court, Middle District of Florida. *Education:* Millsaps College (B.A., summa cum laude, 1988); Harvard Law School (J.D., cum laude, 1991). *Member:* American Bar Association (Litigation Section). ***PRACTICE AREAS:*** Products Liability; Toxic Torts; Litigation; Drug and Medical Device Defense. ***Email:*** ckendrick@spriggs.com

STEPHEN A. KLEIN, born New York, N.Y., March 18, 1965; admitted to bar, 1991, New York; 1992, District of Columbia. *Education:* University of Pennsylvania (B.A., magna cum laude, 1987); University of Michigan (J.D., cum laude, 1990). Member, University of Michigan Law Review. Author, "Insurance Recovery of Pre-notice Defense Costs," 34 Tort and Insurance Law

(This Listing Continued)

Journal 1103 (1999); Co-Author, "Pretrial Scheduling and Orders," Law and Practicing of Insurance Coverage Litigation (West 2000). ***PRACTICE AREAS:*** Insurance Coverage; Toxic Torts; Litigation. ***Email:*** sklein@spriggs.com

MICHAEL S. KOPLAN, born Washington, D.C., July 5, 1966; admitted to bar, 1991, Virginia; 1992, District of Columbia, U.S. District Court, Eastern District of Virginia and U.S. Court of Appeals, Fourth Circuit. *Education:* Rutgers College (B.A., 1988); The American University (J.D., 1991). Articles Editor, American University Administrative Law Journal, 1990-1991. ***PRACTICE AREAS:*** Construction Law; Litigation. ***Email:*** mkoplan@spriggs.com

ERIC G. LASKER, born Edison, New Jersey, May 28, 1965; admitted to bar, 1990, Pennsylvania (Inactive); 1991, District of Columbia. *Education:* University of Pennsylvania (B.A., summa cum laude, 1987); Yale University (J.D., 1990). ***PRACTICE AREAS:*** Products Liability; Toxic Torts; Litigation; Drug and Medical Device Defense; Insurance Coverage. ***Email:*** elasker@spriggs.com

KATHARINE R. LATIMER, born Lafayette, Louisiana, April 5, 1961; admitted to bar, 1986, District of Columbia, U. S. Supreme Court and U. S. Court of Appeals, Fourth, Sixth, Eighth, Ninth, Tenth and Eleventh Circuits. *Education:* University of Tennessee (B.A., magna cum laude, 1983); Georgetown University (J.D., cum laude, 1986). Member, Editorial Board, Mealey's Litigation Reports-Toxic Torts, 1992-1995. *Member:* American Bar Association (Member, Sections on: Litigation; Tort and Insurance Practice); Defense Research Institute. ***PRACTICE AREAS:*** Products Liability; Toxic Torts; Litigation; Drug and Medical Device Defense; Civil Appeals. ***Email:*** klatimer@spriggs.com

CHARLES S. LEEPER, born Pittsburgh, Pennsylvania, January 8, 1951; admitted to bar, 1976, New York; 1980, District of Columbia; U.S. Court of Appeals, Fourth, Fifth, Ninth and Eleventh Circuits; U.S. Court of Appeals for the District of Columbia Circuit. *Education:* Bucknell University (B.S., 1972); University of Pittsburgh (J.D., magna cum laude, 1975). Order of the Coif. Executive Note Editor, University of Pittsburgh School of Law, 1974-1975. Assistant U.S. Attorney for the District of Columbia, 1981-1988. *Member:* American Bar Association. ***PRACTICE AREAS:*** White Collar Crime; Litigation. ***Email:*** cleeper@spriggs.com

FRANK LEONE, JR., born Hong Kong, B.C.C., August 22, 1960; admitted to bar, 1985, Virginia; 1986, District of Columbia and U.S. Court of Appeals, Fourth and Ninth Circuits; U.S. District Court, District of Columbia; U.S. District Court, Eastern District of Virginia. *Education:* University of Virginia (B.A., with distinction, 1982; J.D., 1985). Omicron Delta Kappa. Author, "Environmental Compliance for the Construction Industry," Construction Briefings No. 2001-1 (Feb. 2001). Co-Author: "Opinion: Discovery in Superfund Cases," 11 Chemical Waste Litigation Reporter 654, 1986. *Member:* American Bar Association (Member, Sections on: Litigation; Environment). ***PRACTICE AREAS:*** Environmental Law; Litigation; Products Liability; Asbestos Defense. ***Email:*** fleone@spriggs.com

C. ROBERT MANOR, born Martinsburg, West Virginia, November 26, 1949; admitted to bar, 1987, Maryland; 1989, District of Columbia. *Education:* West Virginia University (B.A., Biology/Chemistry, 1971); University of Maryland (M.A., Environmental Science, 1979); Catholic University of America (J.D., 1987). Author: "Litigating DC to Daylight. Non-Ionizing Radiation: An Overview of the Physics and Biology," Medical Physics Publishing (1997); "The Science and Law of EMF in the United States," Australasian Insurance Forum (1995); "Electromagnetic Fields: What Are the Liability Risks?" 9 The John Liner Review - The Quarterly Review of Advanced Risk Management Strategies 36; "Front Doors, Backdoors, and Trapdoors To Acid Rain Control," 7 UCLA Journal of Environmental Law & Policy 97; "Living Organisms as Chemical Substances: The EPA's Biotechnology Policy Under the Toxic Substances Control Act," 13 Rutgers Computer & Technology Law Journal 409. *Member:* American Bar Association. ***PRACTICE AREAS:*** Products Liability; Toxic Torts; Litigation; Environmental Law; Drug and Medical Device Defense. ***Email:*** cmanor@spriggs.com

MARC S. MAYERSON, born Dayton, Ohio, April 11, 1961; admitted to bar, 1988, California; 1994, District of Columbia. *Education:* University of Michigan (A.B., with highest distinction, 1983); Harvard University (J.D., magna cum laude, 1986). Phi Beta Kappa. Editor, Harvard Law Review, 1984-1985. Law Clerk, Hon. Stephen R. Reinhardt, U.S. Court of Appeals, Ninth Circuit, 1986-1987. Author: "Affording Coverage for Gradual Property Damage Under Standard Liability Policies: A History." 8 Coverage (Sept./Oct. 1998) at 3; "Settlement of Complex Liability-Insurance Disputes," 33 Tort & Ins. L.J. 783 (1998); "Insurance Recovery for Year 2000 Losses," Andrews' Year 2000 Legal Bulletin (June 1998); "The Coverage Wars," Texas Lawyer, at 34 (Feb. 23, 1998); "Perfecting and Pursuing Liability Insurance Coverage," 32 Tort & Ins. L.J. (1997); "Watch for Exposures in Integration," Business Insurance, at 25 (Aug. 18, 1997); "Managing Complex Insurance Coverage Disputes," 32 Tort & Ins. L.J. 53 (1996); "Insurance Recovery of Litigation Costs: A Primer for Policyholders and Their Counsel," 30 Tort & Ins. L.J. 997 (1995). *Member:*

(This Listing Continued)

American Bar Association (Member, Sections on: Litigation; Tort and Insurance Practice). ***PRACTICE AREAS:*** Insurance Coverage; Litigation. ***Email:*** mmayerson@spriggs.com

DONALD R. McMINN, born Summit, New Jersey, July 26, 1964; admitted to bar, 1991, District of Columbia; U.S. Supreme Court; U.S. Court of Appeals for the District of Columbia Circuit. *Education:* Swarthmore College (B.A., with high honors, 1986); New York University School of Law (J.D., cum laude, 1990). Order of the Coif. Note Editor, N.Y.U.L. Rev., 1989-1990. Law Clerk for the Hon. Manuel Real, Chief Judges, U.S. District Court, Central California, 1990-1991. Author: "The Duty to Defend Following, Buss and Domtar: Restrictions on Insurance Carriers' Ability to Avoid Defense Costs Through Allocation," Mealey's Litigation Report: Insurance (October 21, 1997); "Latex Products Liability Litigation and Commercial General Liability Coverage," Mealey's Litigation Report: Latex (May 20, 1997); "ABA Formal Opinion 88-356: New Justification for Increased Use of Screening Devices to Avert Attorney Disqualification," 65 N.Y.U.L. Rev. 1231 (1990). ***PRACTICE AREAS:*** Insurance Coverage; Litigation. ***Email:*** dmcminn@spriggs.com

DOUGLAS L. PATIN, born Portsmouth, Virginia, August 8, 1954; admitted to bar, 1979, District of Columbia, 1980, Virginia; 1987, Maryland; U.S. Court of Appeals, Second, Third and Fourth Circuits; U.S. Court of Appeals for the District of Columbia Circuit; U.S. Court of Appeals for the Federal Circuit. *Education:* University of Wisconsin-River Falls (B.A., with highest honors, 1976); George Washington University (J.D., 1979). Co-Author: "Construction Insurance Coverages and Disputes," The Michie Company, September, 1994; "Construction Contracting," Government Contracts Program-National Law Center-George Washington University, Washington D.C., 1991. "Use of *Equal* Products," Construction Briefings, No. 80-4, Federal Publications, July, 1980; "'All' Risk Insurance," Construction Briefings, No. 81-6, Federal Publications, November, 1981; "Comprehensive General Liability Insurance," Construction Briefings, No. 82-2, Federal Publications, March, 1982; "UCC Problems in Construction," No. 83-6, Federal Publications, June, 1983; "Subcontract Incorporation By Reference Clauses," Construction Briefings, No. 85-7 Federal Publications, July, 1985; "Liability Insurance," Construction Briefings, No. 89-9, Federal Publications, August 1989; "Surety's Role in Default Terminations," Construction Briefings, No. 90-4, Federal Publications, March 1990. *Member:* American (Member, The Forum on the Construction Industry, Section of Public Contract Law) Bar Association. ***PRACTICE AREAS:*** Construction Law; Litigation. ***Email:*** dpatin@spriggs.com

GARY I. RUBIN, born Brooklyn, New York, October 22, 1946; admitted to bar, 1984, District of Columbia; U.S. Court of Appeals, Third Circuit; U.S. Court of Appeals for the District of Columbia Circuit; U.S. Court of Federal Claims; U.S. District Court for the District of Columbia. *Education:* Hofstra University (B.A., 1968); State University of New York at Binghamton (Ph.D., 1974); Catholic University (J.D., 1984). Associate Editor, Catholic University Law Review, 1983-1984. *Member:* American Bar Association (Member, Section on Natural Resources Law). ***PRACTICE AREAS:*** Toxic Torts; Litigation; Drug and Medical Device Defense; Environmental Law. ***Email:*** grubin@spriggs.com

BONNIE J. SEMILOF, born Kingston, New York, August 22, 1961; admitted to bar, 1986, Pennsylvania; 1988, District of Columbia. *Education:* George Washington University (B.A.P.I., 1983); Georgetown University (J.D., 1986). *Member:* American Bar Association. ***PRACTICE AREAS:*** Product Liability; Toxic Torts; Litigation; Drug and Medical Device Defense. ***Email:*** bsemilof@spriggs.com

ROBERT L. SHAPIRO, born Baltimore, Maryland, August 19, 1962; admitted to bar, 1987, Maryland; 1988, District of Columbia; U.S. Court of Appeals, Fifth Circuit; U.S. Court of Appeals for the District of Columbia Circuit; U.S. Court of Federal Claims; U.S. District Court for the District of Columbia. *Education:* University of Pennsylvania (B.S., cum laude, 1984); University of Chicago (J.D., 1987). Omicron Delta Epsilon. Law Clerk for the Hon. Edith H. Jones, U.S. Court of Appeals, Fifth Circuit, 1987-1988. Assistant U.S. Attorney, District of Columbia, 1991-1996. *Member:* American Bar Association. ***PRACTICE AREAS:*** Government Contracts; Banking Litigation; Litigation; Federal Claims. ***Email:*** rshapiro@spriggs.com

STEPHEN R. SPIVACK, born New York, N.Y., March 13, 1946; admitted to bar, 1972, Maryland; 1973, District of Columbia; 1975, U.S. Court of Appeals for the District of Columbia Circuit. *Education:* Temple University (B.A., 1968); George Washington University (J.D., with honors, 1972). Law Clerk to Honorable Leonard P. Walsh, U.S. District Court Judge for the District of Columbia, 1972-1973. Assistant U.S. Attorney, U.S. Attorney's Office, District of Columbia, 1974-1987. Chief, Special Prosecutions Section, 1983-1987. *Member:* American Bar Association (Member, White Collar Crime Committee of the Criminal Justice Section). ***PRACTICE AREAS:*** White Collar Crime; Litigation. ***Email:*** sspivack@spriggs.com

ROSEMARY STEWART, born Greenfield, Ohio, March 21, 1949; admitted to bar, 1975, District of Columbia; 1992, U.S. Supreme Court; U.S. Court of Appeals, Fifth and Tenth Circuits; U.S. District Court, Northern District of Texas; U.S. District Court for the District of Columbia. *Education:* Ohio Northern University (B.A., with distinction, 1971); Georgetown University (J.D., 1974). Pi Kappa Delta; Phi Kappa Phi; Mortar Board. Attorney, 1974-1990 and Director of Enforcement, 1982-1990, Federal Home Loan Bank Board and Office of Thrift Supervision. *Member:* American Bar Association. ***PRACTICE AREAS:*** Government Contracts; Banking Litigation; Civil Litigation. ***Email:*** rstewart@spriggs.com

JERRY STOUCK, born Washington, D.C., March 24, 1955; admitted to bar, 1981, District of Columbia; 1983, Maryland; U.S. Supreme Court; U.S. Court of Appeals for the District of Columbia Circuit; U.S. Court of Appeals for the Federal Circuit; U.S. Court of Federal Claims. *Education:* Wesleyan University (B.A., magna cum laude, 1977); New York University (J.D., 1980). Phi Beta Kappa. Law Clerk to the Hon. Raymond J. Pettine, Chief Judge, U.S. District Court, District of Rhode Island, 1980-1981. *Member:* American Bar Association. ***PRACTICE AREAS:*** Government Contracts; Banking Litigation; Complex Commercial Litigation; Federal Claims. ***Email:*** jstouck@spriggs.com

ROBERT J. SYMON, born Johnstown, Pennsylvania, January 8, 1966; admitted to bar, 1992, Pennsylvania,; 1993, District of Columbia; U.S. Court of Appeals for the Federal Circuit; U.S. Court of Federal Claims; U.S. District Court for the District of Columbia. *Education:* Washington & Jefferson College (B.A., 1988); University of Baltimore (J.D., 1992); George Washington University. *Member:* American Bar Association, (Member, Public Contract Law Section). ***PRACTICE AREAS:*** Government Contracts; Construction Law; Litigation. ***Email:*** rsymon@spriggs.com

PAUL V. WATERS, born Gettysburg, Pennsylvania, November 20, 1955; admitted to bar, 1983, District of Columbia and Maryland; U.S Supreme Court; U.S Court of Appeals, Fourth Circuit; U.S Court of Appeals for the District of Columbia Circuit; U.S Court of Appeals for the Federal Circuit; U.S. Court of Federal Claims; U.S. District Court, District of Maryland. *Education:* Catholic University of America (B.M.E., magna cum laude, 1977); Columbus School of Law (J.D., 1982). Tau Beta Pi. Author, "Design Build Contracting," George Washington University Government Contracts Program. Lecturer, In The Construction and Design Build Courses at George Washington University's National Law Center. Member, Associated Builders & Contractors, Inc. *Member:* American Bar Association. ***PRACTICE AREAS:*** Construction Law; Litigation. ***Email:*** pwaters@spriggs.com

REBECCA A. WOMELDORF, born Blacksburg, Virginia, July 15, 1966; admitted to bar, 1992, Georgia; 1994, Pennsylvania; 1996, District of Columbia; U.S Court of Appeals, Fourth, Fifth and Sixth Circuits; U.S Court of Appeals for the Federal District; U.S. Court of Federal Claims. *Education:* Rhodes College (B.A., cum laude, 1988); Washington & Lee School of Law (J.D., summa cum laude, 1991). Phi Beta Kappa; Order of the Coif. John Malone Honor Scholar. Recipient, John W. Davis Prize for Highest Academic Average in Graduating Class. Contributor and Lead Articles Editor, Washington & Lee Law Review. Clerk: Honorable Lewis F. Powell, Jr., Associate Judge of the United States Supreme Court (Ret.), 1992-1993; Honorable Anthony M. Kennedy, Associate Justice of the United States Supreme Court, 1992-1993; Honorable Robert R. Merhige, Jr., United States District Court for the Eastern District of Virginia, 1991-1992. ***PRACTICE AREAS:*** Litigation; Drug and Medical Device Defense; Complex Commercial Litigation; Civil Appeals; Employment Law. ***Email:*** rwomeldorf@spriggs.com

OF COUNSEL

JULIE A. BLUM, born Chicago, Illinois, June 29, 1960; admitted to bar, 1989, Illinois (inactive); 1990, District of Columbia. *Education:* San Diego State University (B.A., magna cum laude, with distinction in the major, 1982); Georgetown University Law Center (J.D., 1989). Phi Eta Sigma. Topics Editor, American Criminal Law Review, 1988-1989. Law Clerk to Honorable Mildred M. Edwards, Superior Court, District of Columbia, 1989-1990. Author: "Conspiracy" White Collar Crime Annual Survey of Law-Update, American Criminal Law Review, Volume 25, No. 3, Winter, 1988. *Member:* American Bar Association (Member, Sections on: Litigation; Torts and Insurance Practice). ***PRACTICE AREAS:*** Products Liability; Toxic Torts; Litigation; Drug and Medical Device Defense. ***Email:*** jblum@spriggs.com

CONRAD J. JACOBY, born Hadley, Massachusetts, January 4, 1968; admitted to bar, 1993, Maryland; 1996, District of Columbia. *Education:* Yale University (B.A., magna cum laude, with distinction in the major, 1990); Georgetown University Law Center (J.D., cum laude, 1993). Administrative Editor, The Tax Lawyer, 1992-1993. Author, "Partnership Profit Interests-Valuation and Taxability: The Aftermath of Campbell v. Commissioner," 45 Tax Law. 513 (1992). *Member:* American Bar Association. ***LANGUAGES:*** German. ***PRACTICE AREAS:*** Litigation; Information Technology. ***Email:*** cjacoby@spriggs.com

ASSOCIATES

SHAWN D. BRYANT, born Lewiston, Maine, April 9, 1971; admitted to bar, 1998, Maine and Massachusetts; 1999, District of Columbia. *Education:*

(This Listing Continued)

(This Listing Continued)

SPRIGGS & HOLLINGSWORTH, Washington—Continued

Colby College (B.A., cum laude, 1993); Duke University School of Law (J.D., 1998). ***PRACTICE AREAS:*** Litigation; Environmental Law; Toxic Torts. ***Email:*** sbryant@spriggs.com

WILLIAM S. D. CRAVENS, born Augusta, Georgia, October 15, 1972; admitted to bar, 1998, Massachusetts (Not admitted in District of Columbia). *Education:* Princeton University (A.B., summa cum laude, 1995); Washington & Lee University (J.D., magna cum laude, 1998). ***LANGUAGES:*** Arabic and French. ***PRACTICE AREAS:*** Products Liability; Toxic Torts; Litigation; Drug and Medical Device Defense.

JEAN M. CUNNINGHAM, born South Bend, Indiana, December 13, 1971; admitted to bar, 1997, New York and District of Columbia. *Education:* University of Notre Dame (B.A., with honors, 1993); George Washington University (J.D., with honors, 1996). ***PRACTICE AREAS:*** Products Liability; Toxic Torts; Litigation; Insurance Coverage; Asbestos Defense. ***Email:*** jcunningham@spriggs.com

CHRISTOPHER G. CWALINA, born Baltimore, Maryland, January 17, 1971; admitted to bar, 1997, Maryland; 1998, District of Columbia. *Education:* Gettysburg College (B.A., cum laude, 1993); University of Baltimore School of Law (J.D., 1997). *Member:* American Bar Association; Defense Research Institute. ***PRACTICE AREAS:*** Products Liability; Toxic Torts; Litigation; Drug and Medical Device Defense. ***Email:*** ccwalina@spriggs.com

MONICA A. FREAS, born Juarez, Chihuahua, Mexico, May 26, 1972; admitted to bar, 1998, Virginia; 1999, District of Columbia and U.S. Court of Federal Claims. *Education:* University of Central Florida (B.S., with honors, 1995); University of Washington (J.D., 1998). ***PRACTICE AREAS:*** Banking Litigation; Government Contracts; Complex Commercial Litigation. ***Email:*** mfreas@spriggs.com

ERIC A. FRECHTEL, born New York, New York, February 3, 1971; admitted to bar, 1996, Maryland; U.S Court of Appeals, Fourth Circuit; U.S. Court of Federal Claims; U.S. District Court, District of Maryland (Not admitted in District of Columbia). *Education:* Colgate University (B.A., 1993); University of Baltimore (J.D., magna cum laude, 1996). Law Clerk to the Honorable Joseph H.H. Kaplan, Circuit Court for Baltimore City, 1996-1997. *Member:* Baltimore City, Maryland State and American (Member, Fidelity and Surety Law Committee) Bar Associations. ***PRACTICE AREAS:*** Construction Law; Litigation.

GLENN S. GREENE, born Brooklyn, New York, April 15, 1965; admitted to bar, 1995, New York; 1996, District of Columbia; U.S. Court of Appeals, Ninth Circuit; U.S. Court of Federal Claims; U.S. Court of International Trade. *Education:* The Cooper Union (B.S., 1987; M.E., 1989); University of Texas (J.D., 1994). Order of Barristers. The American Journal of Criminal Law, 1992-1994 (Senior Editor, 1993-1994). *Member:* New York State and American Bar Associations; The District of Columbia Bar. ***PRACTICE AREAS:*** Government Contracts; Construction Law; Federal Claims; Litigation; Toxic Torts. ***Email:*** ggreene@spriggs.com

KIRBY T. GRIFFIS, born Bo, Sierra Leone, December 19, 1967; admitted to bar, 1995, Virginia; 1997, District of Columbia; U.S. Court of Appeals, Fourth and Tenth Circuits. *Education:* Emory University (B.A., 1990; M.A., summa cum laude, 1990); University of Virginia (J.D.). Phi Beta Kappa. Recipient, John Olin Prize in Law and Economics. Articles Editor, Virginia Law Review. Author, "Apportionment of Environmental Cleanup Costs Under the Owned-Property Exclusion in CGL Insurance Policies," 80 Va.L.Rev. 1351 (1996). Law Clerk for Hon. Glen M. Williams, Senior Judge, U.S. District Court, Western District of Virginia. *Member:* District of Columbia Bar; Virginia State Bar; American Bar Association (Member, Tort and Insurance Practice Section, 1995-1998). ***PRACTICE AREAS:*** Products Liability; Toxic Torts; Insurance Coverage; Drug and Medical Device Defense. ***Email:*** kgriffis@spriggs.com

VIVEK HATTI, born Mysore, Karnataka, India, September 18, 1971; admitted to bar, 1999, Ohio and U.S. District Court, Northern District of Ohio (Not admitted in District of Columbia). *Education:* College of William and Mary (A.B., high honors, Government, 1993); The George Washington University (J.D., 1999). Member: Moot Court Board of Directors, 1998-1999; George Washington University Journal of International Law & Economics, 1997-1999. Note, "India's Right to Reclaim Cultural and Art Treasures from Britain Under International Law, 32 George Washington Journal of International Law, 465 (2000). ***PRACTICE AREAS:*** Litigation; Banking Litigation. ***Email:*** vhatti@spriggs.com

ROBERT E. JOHNSTON, born Bethesda, Maryland, October 18, 1968; admitted to bar, 1994, Maryland; 1995, District of Columbia; 1996, U.S. Court of Appeals, Sixth Circuit; U.S. Court of Federal Claims; U.S. District Court, District of Columbia; U.S. District Court, District of Maryland. *Education:* Southern Methodist University (B.A. and B.B.A., with high honors, 1991); George Washington University National Law Center (J.D., with high honors, 1994). Pi Sigma Alpha; Order of the Coif. Member, The George Washington Law Review. Author, "1001 Attorneys General: Executive Employee Qui Tam Suits and the Constitution," 62 George Washington Law Review 608 (1994). *Member:* American Bar Association (Member, Sections on: Tort and Insurance Practice; Litigation). ***PRACTICE AREAS:*** Government Contracts; Banking Litigation; Complex Commercial Litigation; Insurance Coverage. ***Email:*** rjohnston@spriggs.com

CLAIRE E. KRESSE, born Buffalo, New York, June 13, 1969; admitted to bar, 1997, Virginia; 1998, District of Columbia. *Education:* Georgetown University (B.A., 1991); Duke University (J.D., 1996). Co-Author: "A State-By-State Guide to Construction & Design Law, Current Statutes and Practices," Chapter on District of Columbia Construction, Lien, and Bond Law, Section of Real Property, Probate and Trust Law, American Bar Association, Carl J. Circo and Christopher H. Little, Editors, 1998; "Public Assembly Facility Law, A Guide for Managers of Arenas, Auditoriums, Convention Centers, Performing Arts Centers, Race Tracks and Stadiums," Chapters on Government Contracts and the Procurement Process and Construction Disputes, Turner D. Madden, et al., The International Association of Assembly Managers, Inc., 1st ed., 1998. *Member:* Virginia State Bar; The District of Columbia Bar; American Bar Association; National Association of Women in Construction. ***PRACTICE AREAS:*** Construction Law; Government Contracts; Litigation. ***Email:*** ckresse@spriggs.com

CONRAD C. LEDOUX, born Bridgeport, Connecticut, December 16, 1964; admitted to bar, 1989, Connecticut; 1990, New York; 1995, District of Columbia and Maryland; 1997, Virginia; U.S. Court of Appeals, Third and Fourth Circuits; U.S. Court of Appeals for the Federal Circuit; U.S. Court of Federal Claims; U.S. Court of Appeals for the Armed Forces. *Education:* University of Bridgeport (B.S., 1986); Pace University School of Law (J.D., 1989). Tau Kappa Epsilon. National Marketing Honor Society. Charles A. Dana Scholar. Recipient: Blaine Sloan International Law Award; American Jurisprudence Award in Contracts. Editor-in-Chief, Pace International Law Review, 1988-1989. *Member:* Maryland State and American Bar Associations; Virginia State Bar. ***PRACTICE AREAS:*** Litigation; Government Contracts; Construction Law; Insurance Coverage. ***Email:*** cledoux@spriggs.com

MICHAEL R. MINER, born Bethesda, Maryland, November 7, 1973; admitted to bar, 1998, Maryland; 1999, District of Columbia, U.S. Court of Appeals for the Federal Circuit; U.S. Court of Federal Claims. *Education:* University of Michigan (B.A., 1995); George Washington University Law School (J.D., with honors, 1998). Author: "A Market-Based Solution to Ozone Nonattainment: New Jersey's Nitrogen Oxides Budget Program," 4 Environmental Lawyer 3, 1998. *Member:* Montgomery County and American Bar Associations; The District of Columbia Bar. ***PRACTICE AREAS:*** Government Contracts; Federal Claims; Litigation. ***Email:*** mminer@spriggs.com

ANDREA D. ROSE, born Washington, D.C., March 26, 1965; admitted to bar, 1996, Pennsylvania and New Jersey; 1997, District of Columbia and Virginia; U.S. Court of Appeals, Fourth Circuit; U.S. District Court, Eastern District of Pennsylvania; U.S. District Court, District of New Jersey; U.S. District Court, Eastern District of Virginia. *Education:* University of Pennsylvania (B.S.N., 1987; M.S.N., 1990); Temple University (J.D., cum laude, 1996). Recipient, American Jurisprudence Award for Excellence in Torts, 1993. Registered Nurse: Washington, D.C., 1987; Pennsylvania, 1987; New Jersey, 1990. *Member:* Pennsylvania and American (Member, Litigation Section) Bar Associations; The District of Columbia Bar; Virginia State Bar. ***PRACTICE AREAS:*** Products Liability; Toxic Torts; Drug and Medical Device Defense; Litigation. ***Email:*** arose@spriggs.com

PETER J. SKALABAN JR., born New Brunswick, New Jersey, February 8, 1969; admitted to bar, 1994, Pennsylvania; 1997, District of Columbia; U.S. Court of Appeals for the Federal Circuit; U.S. Court of Federal Claims. *Education:* University of Pennsylvania (B.A., cum laude, 1991); George Washington University National Law Center (J.D., highest honors, 1994). Order of the Coif. Associate Editor, The George Washington Law Review. Author, "Borak Breathes: Implying a Private Right of Action to Enforce SEC-Rule 14a-8," 61 George Washington Law Review 1514, 1993. Law Clerk to the: Hon. Wilson S. Cowen, Sr., Circuit Judge, U.S. Court of Appeals for the Federal Circuit, 1995-1996; Hon. Lawrence S. Margolis, Judge, U.S. Court of Federal Claims, 1994-1995. ***PRACTICE AREAS:*** Government Contracts; Construction Law; Litigation. ***Email:*** pskalaban@spriggs.com

SCOTT S. THOMAS, born Salt Lake City, Utah, January 12, 1967; admitted to bar, 1996, Utah; 1998, District of Columbia; U.S. Court of Appeals, Tenth and Eleventh Circuits; U.S. Court of Appeals for the District of Columbia Circuit. *Education:* Brigham Young University (B.A., magna cum laude with honors, 1991; J.D., cum laude, 1995). Phi Kappa Phi; Pi Sigma Alpha. Recipient, LeTourneau Award, American College of Legal Medicine, 1994. Executive Editor, B.Y.U. Journal of Public Law, 1993-1995. Author: "Beyond a Sour Lemon: A Look at *Grumet v. Board of Education of the Kiryas Joel Village School District,*" 8 B.Y.U. J. Pub. L. 531 (1994); "The Future of Religious Liberty in Argentina: Will a New Constitutional Mandate and Would Newly Proposed Laws Enhance Religious Liberty?" 1995 B.Y.U. L. Rev. 603; "An Insurer's Right to Settle Versus Its Duty to Defend Nonmeritorious Medical Malpractice Claims." 16 J. Legal Med. 545 (1995). Congressional Intern to

(This Listing Continued)

Hon. James A. McClure, U.S. Senate, Washington D.C., 1989. Judicial Clerk to Hon. Gregory S. Anderson, Idaho District Court, 1995-1996. *Member:* Utah State Bar; The District of Columbia Bar; American Bar Association (Member, Litigation and Young Lawyers Sections). ***LANGUAGES:*** Spanish. ***PRACTICE AREAS:*** Products Liability; Toxic Torts Litigation; Drug and Medical Device Defense. ***Email:*** sthomas@spriggs.com

SQUIRE, SANDERS & DEMPSEY L.L.P.

1201 PENNSYLVANIA AVENUE, N.W.
P.O. BOX 407
WASHINGTON, D.C. 20044-0407
Telephone: 202-626-6600
Fax: 202-626-6780
URL: http://www.ssd.com

U.S. Offices: Cincinnati, Cleveland, Columbus, Houston, Jacksonville, Los Angeles, Miami, New York, Palo Alto, Phoenix, San Francisco, Tampa, Tysons Corner.

European Offices: Bratislava, Brussels, Budapest, Kyiv, London, Madrid, Milan, Moscow, Prague.

Asian Offices: Almaty, Beijing, Hong Kong, Taipei, Tokyo.

General and International Practice.

PARTNERS

JOHN H. C. BARRON JR., born Washington, D.C., 1946; admitted to bar, 1971, District of Columbia; 1972, Maryland. *Education:* University of Maryland (A.B., 1968); Duke University (J.D., 1971). *Member:* The District of Columbia Bar; Economic Club of Washington. ***PRACTICE AREAS:*** Real Estate; Finance; Foreign Investment. ***Email:*** jbarron@ssd.com

TIMOTHY W. BERGIN, born Rochester, New York, 1951; admitted to bar, 1978, District of Columbia. *Education:* Georgetown University (B.S.F.S., magna cum laude, 1973); University of Bonn, West Germany; Tufts University (M.A., 1975); University of Pennsylvania (J.D., 1978). Phi Beta Kappa. *Member:* The District of Columbia Bar. ***PRACTICE AREAS:*** Litigation; Antitrust. ***Email:*** tbergin@ssd.com

SAM BLACK, born Oil City, Pennsylvania, 1943; admitted to bar, 1973, District of Columbia; 1974, U.S. Tax Court; 1981, U.S. Claims Court and U.S. Supreme Court. *Education:* Yale University (B.A., honors, 1965); Georgetown University (J.D., 1972). Legislative Assistant, U.S. House of Representatives, U.S. Senate, 1969-1972. Co-Counsel, Commission on Private Philanthropy and Public Needs, 1977. *Member:* District of Columbia Bar (Chair, Steering Committee, Taxation Division, 1974-1975); American Bar Association (Former Chair, Committee on VAT; Member, Committee on U.S. Activities of Foreigners and Tax Treaties; Member, Committee on Foreign Activities of U.S. Taxpayers). [Lt., U.S. Army, 1967-1969]. ***PRACTICE AREAS:*** Taxation; Corporate; Equipment Finance; International Acquisitions. ***Email:*** sblack@ssd.com

ANN R. BRASHEAR, born Los Angeles, California, 1956; admitted to bar, 1985, Virginia; 1986, District of Columbia. *Education:* University of Washington (B.S., magna cum laude, 1978); Georgetown University (J.D., magna cum laude, 1985). Phi Beta Kappa. *Member:* The District of Columbia Bar; Virginia State Bar; American Bar Association; National Association of Bond Lawyers. ***LANGUAGES:*** French. ***PRACTICE AREAS:*** Corporate; Public Finance. ***Email:*** abrashear@ssd.com

A. RANDOLPH BREGMAN, born Philadelphia, Pennsylvania, 1946; admitted to bar, 1985, District of Columbia; U.S. Court of Appeals for the District of Columbia Circuit. *Education:* Columbia University (B.A., 1968); Yale University (M.A., 1969); Georgetown University (J.D., cum laude, 1985). Adjunct Professor of Soviet Law, Georgetown University, 1986-1989. Former Chair and Founding Member of Board of Advisers for *Russian and Commonwealth of Independent States Business Law Reporter. Member:* The District of Columbia Bar; American Bar Association (Member, International Law Section); The Russian American Institute for Law and The Economy (Member, Board of Directors). ***LANGUAGES:*** Hebrew and Russian. ***PRACTICE AREAS:*** International Joint Ventures; International Business; Investment in Russia. ***Email:*** rbregman@ssd.com

ALAN L. BRIGGS, born Dayton, Ohio, 1942; admitted to bar, 1967, Ohio; 1970, California; 1989, Florida; 1995, District of Columbia, Virginia and Maryland. *Education:* Miami University (A.B., 1964); The Ohio State University (J.D., cum laude, 1967); George Washington University (LL.M., Patent and Intellectual Property Law, 1998). Phi Eta Sigma (Physics Honorary). Order of the Coif. Note Editor, Ohio State University Law Journal. *Member:* Columbus (President, 1984-1985), Ohio State (Member, Counsel of Delegates, 1980-1986) and American (Member, Litigation Section, Chairman, Banking and Financial Litigation Committee, 1980-1984; Chairman, National Institution on Trade Secrets, 1983-1984; Member: Intellectual Property Law Section and Litigation Section) Bar Associations; The District of Columbia Bar. Fellow,

(This Listing Continued)

American College of Trial Lawyers. (Managing Partner, Washington, D.C. Office). ***PRACTICE AREAS:*** Complex Business Litigation; Corporate Litigation; Securities; Intellectual Property. ***Email:*** abriggs@ssd.com

DONALD T. BUCKLIN, born Providence, Rhode Island, 1938; admitted to bar, 1968, Virginia and District of Columbia; 1971, U.S. Supreme Court; U.S. Court of Appeals, Federal, Fourth, Sixth and Third Circuits; U.S. Court of Federal Claims; U.S. District Court, District of Columbia, District of Maryland, Eastern District of Michigan and Eastern District of Virginia. *Education:* Providence College (B.S., 1960); The American University (J.D., cum laude, 1967). Phi Delta Phi. Editorial Board, American University Law Review, 1966-1967. Contributing Author: "Antitrust Counseling and Litigation Techniques," Matthew Bender, April, 1984. Law Clerk to The Honorable Judge Howard F. Corcoran, U.S. District Court, District of Columbia, 1967-1968. Assistant U.S. Attorney, 1968-1971. Appointed Independent Counsel Pursuant to Ethics in Government Act (under seal), 1991-1992; Senior Counsel, U.S. Senate Committee on Governmental Affairs, Special Investigation into Campaign Fundraising Practices, 1997. *Member:* The District of Columbia Bar (Treasurer, Board of Governors, 1985-1989; Member, 1982-1985 and Chairman, 1983-1984, Steering Committee, Litigation Section; Co-Chair, Task Force on Solo and Small Firm Practitioners; Member, U.S. District Court for District of Columbia Advisory Committee on Local Rules, 1989-1999; Member, District of Columbia Court of Appeals Committee on Unauthorized Practice of Law, 1989-1992; Voting Delegate, Judicial Conference for the District of Columbia Circuit, 1981—); Bar Association of the District of Columbia (Member, Board of Directors, 1990—; Secretary, 1993-1994; President-Elect, 1994-1995; President, 1995-1996; Co-Chairman: Executive Council, Criminal Practice Institute, 1973; Executive Council, Young Lawyers Section, 1972-1975); Virginia Bar Association; American Inn of Court (Master of Bench); Assistant U.S. Attorneys Association of the District of Columbia (President, 1974-1975); The Barristers; The Counselors—Washington, D.C. (Secretary, Executive Committee, 1999—); The Lawyers Club. Fellow, American College of Trial Lawyers (Chair, District of Columbia Committee). ***PRACTICE AREAS:*** Civil Litigation; White Collar Criminal Litigation. ***Email:*** dbucklin@ssd.com

JOHN A. BURLINGAME, born Havre de Grace, Maryland, 1965; admitted to bar, 1991, Virginia and U.S. Court of Appeals, Fourth Circuit; 1992, U.S. District Court, Eastern District of Virginia; 1993, U.S. Court of Appeals for the Federal Circuit; 1995, U.S. District Court, Western District of Virginia; 1996, U.S. District Court, District of Arizona; 1997, District of Columbia; 2001, U.S. District Court, Central District of Illinois. *Education:* Virginia Polytechnic Institute and State University (B.A., 1987); University of Richmond (J.D., 1991). Omicron Delta Kappa. Notes and Comments Editor, University of Richmond Law Review. *Member:* Alexandria and Virginia Bar Associations. ***Email:*** jburlingame@ssd.com

SARAH C. CAREY, born New York, N.Y., 1938; admitted to bar, 1966, District of Columbia; District of Columbia Superior Court; U.S. Court of Federal Claims; U.S. District Court, District of Columbia; U.S. Supreme Court. *Education:* Harvard University (B.A., magna cum laude, 1960); Georgetown University (LL.B., 1965). Member, Georgetown Law Journal, 1964-1965. Member, Board of Directors: Georgetown University Institute for Public Interest Representation, 1971-1984; American Arbitration Association, 1975-1984; Overseas Education Fund, 1982-1992; Institute for Soviet American Relations, 1982-1995; Council on Foreign Relations, 1990—; Eurasia Foundation (Member, 1993— and Chairman of Board, 1994—); Russian American Enterprise Fund, 1993-1995. Defense Enterprise Fund, 1994—; USDA Emerging Democracies Advisory Committee, 1995—. Board of Directors: Atlantic Council, The Russia Society, Women's Foreign Policy Group; International Women's Forum. ***LANGUAGES:*** Russian. ***PRACTICE AREAS:*** International Transactions; Privatization; Corporate Restructuring; International Investment Law. ***Email:*** scarey@ssd.com

JAMES V. DICK, born Boston, Massachusetts, 1947; admitted to bar, 1975, District of Columbia and U.S. Court of Appeals for the District of Columbia, Federal, Second and Sixth Circuits; 1976, U.S. District Court for the District of Columbia; 1985, U.S. Supreme Court; 1987, U.S. Court of Appeals, Eighth Circuit; 1987, U.S. Court of Appeals, Fifth Circuit; 1989, U.S. Court of Appeals, Third Circuit. *Education:* Amherst College (B.A., summa cum laude, 1969); Stanford University (J.D., 1974). Phi Beta Kappa. Note Editor, Stanford Law Review, 1973-1974. Attorney, Federal Trade Commission, 1974-1975. Counsel, U.S. Senate Select Committee on Intelligence Activities, 1975-1976. Trial Attorney, U.S. Department of Justice, Antitrust Division, 1976-1980. Counsel, Intelligence Oversight Board, White House Staff, 1980-1981. *Member:* The District of Columbia Bar; American Bar Association (Chair, Transportation Industry Committee, Antitrust Section). ***PRACTICE AREAS:*** Antitrust; Litigation; Regulatory. ***Email:*** jdick@ssd.com

CHARLES F. DONLEY II, born New York, New York, 1958; admitted to bar, 1988, District of Columbia; 1990, U.S. Court of Appeals for the District of Columbia Circuit. *Education:* Cornell University (A.B., 1982); Cambridge University (1986); University of Illinois (J.D., 1988). Phi Beta Kappa. Albert James Harno Fellow. Recipient: American Jurisprudence Award. *Member:* The District

(This Listing Continued)

SQUIRE, SANDERS & DEMPSEY L.L.P., Washington—Continued

of Columbia Bar. ***PRACTICE AREAS:*** International Aviation Law; Commercial Law; Contracts; Airline Regulation; Transportation Regulation. ***Email:*** cdonley@ssd.com

CHARLES FRIEDLANDER, born Moultrie, Georgia, 1953; admitted to bar, 1978, District of Columbia. *Education:* University of Georgia (B.A., summa cum laude, 1974); University of Virginia (J.D., 1978). Phi Beta Kappa. Member, National Moot Court. Author: "International Privatizations," Privatizing Governmental Functions, Law Journal Press, 2001. Member, Bretton Woods Committee, Energy Sector Advisory Group, 1996—. Member, International City Management Association, Public/Private Partnership Advisory Committee, 1990-1993. *Member:* District of Columbia Bar; American Bar Association. ***PRACTICE AREAS:*** Energy; Project Finance; Privatization; International Law; Corporate Law. ***Email:*** cfriedlander@ssd.com

EDWARD A. GELTMAN, born Newark, New Jersey, 1946; admitted to bar, 1971, District of Columbia and U.S. Court of Appeals, District of Columbia Circuit; 1972, U.S. District Court, District of Columbia; 1980, U.S. Supreme Court; 1998, U.S. Court of Appeals, Third Circuit. *Education:* Franklin and Marshall College (A.B., with honors, 1968); George Washington University (J.D., with honors, 1971). Order of the Coif. Member, George Washington Law Review, 1969-1971. Trial Attorney, Federal Trade Commission, 1971-1973. Recipient, Federal Trade Commission Certificate of Commendation. *Member:* The District of Columbia Bar (Antitrust and Trade Regulation Committee); American Bar Association (Member: Antitrust Law Section; Corporate Counseling, Internet and E-Commerce and Health Care Committees). ***PRACTICE AREAS:*** Antitrust and Trade Regulation; Advertising and Marketing Law; Complex Litigation; Grand Jury Practice; Medical Antitrust. ***Email:*** egeltman@ssd.com

CORALYN GOODE, born Edison, New Jersey, 1956; admitted to bar, 1981, District of Columbia; 1993, U.S. District Court, District of Columbia. *Education:* Georgetown University (A.B., 1978); College of William & Mary (J.D., 1981). Order of the Coif. Executive Editor, Research, *William and Mary Law Review,* 1980-81. ***PRACTICE AREAS:*** International Law; Project Finance; Construction Law; Public Contract Law. ***Email:*** cgoode@ssd.com

LISA G. HENNEBERRY, born Fairfax, Virginia, 1967; admitted to bar, 1992, Maryland; 1993, District of Columbia, U.S. Court of Federal Claims, U.S. Court of Appeals for the District of Columbia and Federal Circuits; U.S. District Court, District of Columbia. *Education:* Bryn Mawr College (B.A., cum laude, 1989); George Washington University (J.D., 1992). Notes and Projects Editor, George Washington Law Review. *Member:* District of Columbia Bar; American Bar Association. ***LANGUAGES:*** French and Spanish. ***PRACTICE AREAS:*** International Corporate Law; International Finance; Energy Law; Project Finance. ***Email:*** lhenneberry@ssd.com

JOHN C. HENRY JR., born Ashland, Kentucky, 1948; admitted to bar, 1981, District of Columbia. *Education:* Yale University (A.B., cum laude, 1970); Harvard University (J.D., cum laude, 1975). ***PRACTICE AREAS:*** Corporate; Financial Institutions; International Acquisitions; Joint Ventures. ***Email:*** jhenry@ssd.com

JOHN A. HOWELL, born Washington, D.C., 1950; admitted to bar, 1975, Virginia, U.S. District Court, Eastern District of Virginia and U.S. Court of Appeals, Fourth Circuit; 1976, U.S. Court of Appeals for the Armed Forces; 1977, District of Columbia; 1978, U.S. District Court for the District of Columbia and U.S. Court of Appeals for the District of Columbia Circuit; 1979, U.S. Supreme Court and U.S. Court of Federal Claims; 1987, U.S. Court of Appeals for the Federal Circuit. *Education:* Duke University (A.B., summa cum laude, 1972; J.D., 1975); George Washington University (LL.M., in Administrative Law, 1979). Phi Beta Kappa; Phi Alpha Delta. Member, 1973-1974 and Member, Editorial Board, 1974-1975, Duke Law Journal. Author: *Schedule Contracting: Selling Commercial Products and Services to the Government,* George Washington University, 1999; *Contracting for Commercial Products and Services,* George Washington University, 1999; "Governmentwide Agency Contracts: Vehicle Overcrowding on the Procurement Highway," 27 Public Contract Law Journal 395, 1998; Note: "X Corp. v. Doe and the New Material Clause: The New Frontier of Liability for Federal Supply Contractors," 24 Public Contract Law Journal, 343, 1995. Note, "Gifford-Hill & Co. v. FTC: Does NEPA Apply to Law Enforcement Adjudicatory Functions of an Agency?," Duke Law Journal 743, 1975. Faculty Member, The George Washington University Law School Government Contracts Program, 1992—. Faculty Member, Price Waterhouse Government Contracting Courses, 1989-1991. Associate Editor, Public Contract Law Journal. Charter Member, Board of Advisors, Coalition for Government Procurement. Attorney, Administrative Law Division, Office of the Judge Advocate General of the Navy, Washington, D.C., 1976-1979. President, Washington Duke Law Club, 1987-1990. *Member:* The District of Columbia Bar (Member, Government Contracts and Litigation Section); Virginia State Bar; Fairfax, Federal (Member, Government Contracts Section), Federal Circuit and American (Member, Forum on the Construction

(This Listing Continued)

Industry; Member, Sections on: Intellectual Property; Public Contract Law (Vice-Chair, Commercial Products and Services Committee, 1998—); Administrative Law and Regulatory Practice; Business Law) Bar Associations; Judge Advocates Association; National Contract Management Association. [Lt., JAGC, USNR]. ***PRACTICE AREAS:*** Government Contracts Law; Construction Law; National Security and Defense Procurement Law; Commercial Contracts. ***Email:*** jhowell@ssd.com

ROBERT B. KELLY, born Washington, D.C., 1956; admitted to bar, 1981, Virginia; 1992, District of Columbia. *Education:* Duke University (A.B., magna cum laude, 1978; J.D., 1981). Phi Beta Kappa. Co-Author: *Spectrum Regulation Handbook,* Thompson Publishing Group, 1994. *Member:* District of Columbia Bar; Virginia State Bar; Federal Communications Bar Association. ***Email:*** rkelly@ssd.com

GEORGE M. KNAPP, born Inglewood, CA, 1954; admitted to bar, 1978, CA; 1979, DC. *Education:* UCLA (B.A., 1975); George Washington University (J.D., 1978). Phi Beta Kappa; Pi Gamma Mu. Deputy Assistant General Counsel, Federal Energy Regulatory Commission, 1980. *Member:* State Bar of California; The District of Columbia Bar; American Bar Assn. (Chair, Alternate Energy Sources Committee, Section of Environment, Energy and Resources, 1985-1989; Section Chair, 1998-1999); Federal Energy Bar Assn. (Chair, International Energy Transactions Committee, 1995-1997). ***PRACTICE AREAS:*** Energy; Finance; International Law; Public Utilities; Privatization. ***Email:*** gknapp@ssd.com

SCOTT T. KRAGIE, born Chicago, Illinois, 1950; admitted to bar, 1975, District of Columbia; 1987, Ohio. *Education:* College of William & Mary (B.A., with honors, 1972); Indiana University (J.D., magna cum laude, 1975). Order of the Coif. Executive Editor, Indiana Law Journal, 1974-1975. Assistant U.S. Attorney, Office of the U.S. Attorney for the District of Columbia, 1979-1986. *Member:* The District of Columbia Bar; American Bar Association (Member, Sections of Litigation and Criminal Justice); National Health Lawyers' Association; National Association of College and University Attorneys. ***PRACTICE AREAS:*** Civil; Criminal and Administrative Litigation; Health Care. ***Email:*** skragie@ssd.com

HENRY W. LAVINE, born Philadelphia, Pennsylvania, 1936; admitted to bar, 1961, Ohio; 1976, District of Columbia. *Education:* University of Pennsylvania (B.A., 1957; J.D., 1961). *Member:* The Bar Association of the District of Columbia. ***PRACTICE AREAS:*** Corporate; Securities; Finance. ***Email:*** hlavine@ssd.com

GLENN W. LETHAM, born Arlington, Virginia, 1946; admitted to bar, 1972, Virginia; 1973, District of Columbia; 1978, U.S. Supreme Court; U.S. Court of Appeals, District of Columbia, Federal, Third, Fifth, Tenth and Eleventh Circuits; Supreme Court of Virginia. *Education:* College of William and Mary (A.B., 1968); Duke University (J.D., 1972). Phi Delta Phi. *Member:* The Bar Association of the District of Columbia; Federal Energy and American Bar Associations. ***PRACTICE AREAS:*** Energy Law; Federal Energy Regulatory Commission; Contracts; Utility Law; Antitrust. ***Email:*** gletham@ssd.com

JAMES J. MAIWURM, born Wooster, Ohio, 1948; admitted to bar, 1974, Ohio and U.S. District Court, Northern District of Ohio; 1975, U.S. Court of Appeals, Sixth Circuit; 1979, U.S. Supreme Court; 1986, District of Columbia and U.S. Court of Appeals for the District of Columbia Circuit; 1987, Maryland and New York. *Education:* College of Wooster (B.A., 1971); University of Michigan, Ann Arbor (J.D., 1974). Phi Beta Kappa. *Member:* District of Columbia Bar; New York State and American (Member, Communications Law and Business Law Sections) Bar Associations. ***PRACTICE AREAS:*** Business Law; Commercial Law; Joint Ventures; Mergers and Acquisitions; Securities Offerings. ***Email:*** jmaiwurm@ssd.com

JOSEPH P. MARKOSKI, born Floral Park, New York, 1948; admitted to bar, 1973, District of Columbia. *Education:* Georgetown University (B.S.F.S., magna cum laude, 1970; J.D., 1973). Phi Beta Kappa. Staff Member, 1971-1972 and Case and Notes Editor, 1972-1973, Georgetown Law Journal. Author: Note, "Bode v. National Democratic Party," 60 Georgetown Law Journal 1331, 1972; "Telecommunications Regulations as Barriers to the Transborder Flow of Information," 14 Cornell International Law Journal 284, 1981; "The Use of Telecommunications Facilities to Implement National Policies," 4 N.Y.L. Sch. J. Int'l and Comp. L. 55, 1984. Member, U.S. State Dept., Ad Hoc Strategic Planning Group of the CCITT National Committee, 1988-1992. *Member:* The District of Columbia Bar; American Bar Association; Federal Communications Bar Association; Computer Law Association; American Chamber of Commerce (U.K.); International Bar Association. ***PRACTICE AREAS:*** Telecommunications; Privatization. ***Email:*** jmarkoski@ssd.com

HERBERT E. MARKS, born Dayton, Ohio, 1935; admitted to bar, 1964, District of Columbia, U.S. Court of Appeals for the District of Columbia Circuit and U.S. Court of Federal Claims; 1971, U.S. Court of Appeals, Second Circuit; 1972, U.S. Court of Appeals, Fifth Circuit; U.S. Court of Military Appeals; U.S. District Court, District of Columbia; U.S. Supreme Court. *Education:* University of Michigan (A.B., with high distinction, 1957); Yale University (J.D., 1960). Phi Beta Kappa. Author: "Data Communications," Computers & The Law, American Bar Association, 1981; "The Structure of Telecommunications

(This Listing Continued)

Regulation and Markets: Regulation and Deregulation in the United States and Other Countries," 25 Jurimetrics 5, 1984; "A Computer Inquiry Trilogy: A Study of the Liberalization of Telecommunications Regulation in the U.S." Legal and Economic Aspects of Telecommunications, 593 (Elsevier Science Publisher, Amsterdam); "Telecommunications Act of 1996," 22 Computer Law & Tax Report 9 (1996). Associate General Counsel, Presidential Inaugural Committees, 1969, 1973 and 1981. Member, U.S. Delegation to the ITU European Regional Telecommunications Development Conference (Prague, 1991). Member, U.S. Delegation to I.T.U. Plenipotentiary Conference (Minneapolis, 1998). Chairman, U.S. Department of State Advisory Panel of International Telecommunications Law, 1987-1991. (International Coordinator of Firm Federal Regulatory Practice). *Member:* The District of Columbia Bar; American Bar Association (Member, Section of Science and Technology; Member of Council, 1985-1992, 1985 and Section Chair, 1990-1991); Computer Law Association (Director, 1971-1985; Member, Advisory Board, 1986—; President, 1975-1977); Federal Communications Bar Association. ***PRACTICE AREAS:*** Regulatory Affairs; Telecommunications. ***Email:*** hmarks@ssd.com

WILLIAM A. MOGEL, born New York, New York, 1942; admitted to bar, 1967, District of Columbia; 1970, U.S. Supreme Court; 1973, Maryland. *Education:* Hobart College (B.A., honors in English, cum laude, 1963); University of Pennsylvania (LL.B., 1966). Editor-in-Chief, Energy Law Journal, 1980—. Co-Editor, *Energy Law and Transactions* (five volumes, 1990). Author: *Transportation and Marketing of Natural Gas*, (1985); *Transportation and Marketing of Natural Gas: Update '86* (1986). Co-author: *Natural Gas: Current Federal and State Developments* (1987); Chapter, "Impact of FERC Order No. 436 on the Natural Gas Industry: Will It Affect Contracting Practices?" 32 Rocky Mt. Min L. Inst. (1986); "The Role of the Export Administration Act and the Foreign Corrupt Practices Act," 1 Tulsa J. of Comp. & Intl. Law 149 (1994); "Ratemaking for Oil Pipelines in the Outer Continental Shelf," 17 Tulsa L.J. 469 (1982); "Appropriateness of Imposing Common Carrier Status on Interstate Natural Gas Pipelines," 4 Energy L.J. 155 (1983); "Assessment of Section 311 of the Natural Gas Policy Act of 1978," 58 N. Dakota L. Rev. 575 (1982); "Assessment of Incremental Pricing Under the Natural Gas Policy Act," 29 Cath. U. L. Rev. 763 (1980); "Food, Fuel and Federal Curtailment Regulation," 56 Chi.-Kent L. Rev. 789 (1980); "The Effect of a Claim of Privilege Upon the Subpoena Power of an Administrative Law Judge," 28 Drake L. Rev. 67 (1978); "Res Judicata and Collateral Estoppel in Administrative Proceedings," 30 Baylor L. Rev. 463 (1978); "Award of Attorney's Feed in Administrative Proceedings: Is It in the Public Interest?" 49 Miss. L.J. 271 (1978); "Energy and the Environment: Must There Be a Choice?" 13 Cal. W. L. Rev. 1 (1976); "The Federal Power Commission's Authority to Set Area Rates by Rulemaking," 5 Seton Hall L. Rev. 31 (1973); "Bank Mergers and the Anti-Trust Laws," 17 Am. U. L. Rev. 57 (1967); "Looking for Markets? Try the Constitution," Public Utility Fortnightly 23 (1997); "GATT and the World Trade Organization," Export Today 11 (January 1995); "The 'Velvet Revolution' and Slovakia's Energy Industry," Public Utility Fortnightly 38 (December 1993); "Profile Slovakia," Export Today 57 (October 1993); "Will State Regulation Doom CNG Vehicles?" Natural Gas 6 (December 1990); "FERC's NOI: Is There a Problem That Requires a Solution?" Natural Gas 19 (February 1987); "Bankruptcy in a Regulated Industry," Natural Gas 12 (August 1986); "Will Natural Gas Curtailments Return? A Different Look at FERC's Order No. 436," Natural Gas 12 (February 1986); "By-Pass of Local Distribution Companies: A Concern for State Commissions," Natural Gas 11 (June 1985). Co-author: "OPIC: A Success Story for Business and Government," Export Today 28 (September 1991). Editor, *Natural Gas Yearbook* series (1988-1992). Professorial Lecturer, Law School, American University, 1980—. President, Foundation of the Energy Law Journal, 1989—. Trustee, Hobart College, 1980-1985. *Member:* Federal Energy Bar Association (Director, two terms). [Capt., U.S. Army, 1966-1969]. ***PRACTICE AREAS:*** Energy. ***Email:*** wmogel@ssd.com

JAMES P. MURPHY, born Jackson, Tennessee, 1944; admitted to bar, 1969, Ohio; 1970, U.S. District Court, Northern District of Ohio; 1972, U.S. Supreme Court and U.S. Court of Appeals, Sixth Circuit; 1984, District of Columbia, Maryland, U.S. District Court for the District of Columbia, U.S. District Court, District of Maryland and U.S. Court of Appeals for the District of Columbia and Fourth Circuits; 1993, U.S. Court of Federal Claims; 1996, U.S. District Court, District of Arizona; 1997, U.S. District Court, Central District of Illinois; U.S. Court of Appeals for the Federal Circuit. *Education:* University of Notre Dame (A.B., 1966); University of Michigan (J.D., cum laude, 1969). Associate Editor, Michigan Law Review. *Member:* The District of Columbia Bar; Cleveland, Ohio State and Maryland State Bar Associations. ***PRACTICE AREAS:*** Litigation. ***Email:*** jmurphy@ssd.com

JONATHAN JACOB NADLER, born East Rockaway, New York, 1956; admitted to bar, 1990, New York; 1991, District of Columbia; 1998, U.S. Supreme Court; U.S. Court of Appeals, District of Columbia, Fifth and Eighth Circuits. *Education:* Vassar College (A.B., 1978; Phi Beta Kappa); Columbia University (M.P.A., 1981; J.D., 1986). Notes and Comments Editor, Columbia Law Review. Harlan Fiske Stone Scholar. Clerk to Judge Joel M. Flaum, 7th Circuit. Visiting Lecturer (American Economic Law), China University of Political Science and Law (Beijing, PRC), 1992. Lecturer (Antitrust), American University, 1991—. *Member:* Federal Communications Bar Association; Computer Law Association. ***PRACTICE AREAS:*** Federal Regulatory; Telecommunications; Antitrust; Competition. ***Email:*** jnadler@ssd.com

DAVID A. NALL, born Oklahoma City, Oklahoma, 1951; admitted to bar, 1985, Maryland; U.S. Court of Appeals for the District of Columbia Circuit; 1989, District of Columbia. *Education:* University of Virginia (B.A., 1973); The Catholic University of America (J.D., 1985); Georgetown University (LL.M., 1987). Fellow, Institute for Public Representation, 1985-1987. *Member:* The District of Columbia Bar; Maryland State Bar Association; Federal Communications Bar Association. ***LANGUAGES:*** French. ***PRACTICE AREAS:*** Telecommunications; Regulatory Affairs. ***Email:*** dnall@ssd.com

PAUL A. O'HOP JR., born Camp Springs, Maryland, 1962; admitted to bar, 1989, California; 1990, District of Columbia; U.S. Court of Appeals, District of Columbia Circuit. *Education:* University of Notre Dame (B.A., with high honors, 1984; J.D., 1988); Universidad de Barcelona (Diploma de Estudios Hispanicos, 1985); Georgetown University (LL.M., International and Comparative Law, with distinction, 1994). Phi Beta Kappa. Recipient, Jessup International Moot Court Award, 1988. Exchange Associate, 1991-92, Loeff Claeys Verbeke, Amsterdam and Brussels. *Member:* State Bar of California; District of Columbia Bar; American Bar Association (International Law and Practice Section). ***LANGUAGES:*** Spanish. ***PRACTICE AREAS:*** International Corporate; International Finance. ***Email:*** pohop@ssd.com

ROBERT D. PAPKIN, born New Bedford, Massachusetts, 1933; admitted to bar, 1957, Massachusetts; 1964, District of Columbia; 1966, U.S. Supreme Court. *Education:* Harvard University (A.B., 1954; LL.B., 1957). Phi Beta Kappa. Legal Assistant, National Labor Relations Board, 1958-1961. Fulbright Fellowship, College of Europe, Bruges, Belgium, 1962-1963. *Member:* The Bar Association of the District of Columbia; American Bar Association; Federal Bar Association; Inter-American Bar Association; Latin American Air and Space Law Association. ***LANGUAGES:*** Spanish, French. ***PRACTICE AREAS:*** Regulatory Affairs; Aviation. ***Email:*** rpapkin@ssd.com

DOUGLAS L. POVICH, born Washington, D.C., 1960; admitted to bar, 1986, Pennsylvania; 1987, District of Columbia; 1996, U.S. Court of Appeals for the District of Columbia Circuit. *Education:* Union College (B.A., 1982); Georgetown University (J.D., 1985). Co-Author: *Spectrum Regulation Handbook,* Thompson Publishing Group, 1994. *Member:* The Bar Association of the District of Columbia; District of Columbia Bar; American Bar Association; Federal Communications Bar Association. ***PRACTICE AREAS:*** Technology Law; Telecommunications; Wireless Communications. ***Email:*** dpovich@ssd.com

BARRY A. PUPKIN, born Chicago, Illinois, 1950; admitted to bar, 1976, California and District of Columbia. *Education:* California State University at San Diego (A.B., with highest honors, 1972); Stanford University (J.D., 1975). Member, Stanford Law Review, 1974-1975. Trial Attorney, Federal Trade Commission, 1975-1976. Member, Advisory Committee, Management Center Europe, 1997-1999. *Member:* The District of Columbia Bar; The State Bar of California. ***PRACTICE AREAS:*** Regulatory Affairs; Antitrust and Trade Regulation. ***Email:*** bpupkin@ssd.com

EDWARD W. SAUER, born Morristown, New Jersey, 1949; admitted to bar, 1975, District of Columbia. *Education:* Georgetown University (B.S., 1971; J.D., 1974). Lead Articles Editor, Law & Policy in International Business, 1973-1974. *Member:* The District of Columbia Bar. ***LANGUAGES:*** French, German, Spanish (limited). ***PRACTICE AREAS:*** Aviation; Practice before U.S. Department of Transportation. ***Email:*** esauer@ssd.com

MARSHALL SANFORD SINICK, born Hartford, Connecticut, 1942; admitted to bar, 1968, Connecticut; 1972, District of Columbia. *Education:* Boston University (A.B., 1964); Indiana University (J.D., with honors, 1968). Order of the Coif. Member, Board of Editors, Indiana University Law Journal, 1967-1968. Trial Attorney, Bureau of Operating Rights, Civil Aeronautics Board, 1968-1971. Delegate and Speaker, International Bar Association Joint Conference, Bombay, India, 1984. *Member:* The District of Columbia Bar; Connecticut Bar Association. ***PRACTICE AREAS:*** Business Counseling; Litigation; Regulatory Affairs; Aviation. ***Email:*** msinick@ssd.com

RITCHIE T. THOMAS, born Cleveland, Ohio, 1936; admitted to bar, 1964, Ohio; 1971, District of Columbia; District of Columbia Superior Court; U.S. Court of Appeals, District of Columbia, Federal and Ninth Circuits; U.S. Court of Federal Claims; U.S. Court of International Trade; U.S. District Court, District of Columbia and Northern District of Ohio. *Education:* Cornell University (B.A., 1959); Case Western Reserve University (J.D., 1964). Order of the Coif. Associate Editor, Western Reserve Law Review, 1964. Associate Attorney, Office of General Counsel, U.S. Tariff Commission, 1964-1967. *Member:* The District of Columbia Bar; Federal Bar Association. ***LANGUAGES:*** German. ***PRACTICE AREAS:*** International Trade; International Transactions; Regulatory Affairs; Copyright. ***Email:*** rtthomas@ssd.com

NANCY A. WHITE, born Dubuque, Iowa, 1956; admitted to bar, 1981, Iowa; 1984, Colorado; 1988, District of Columbia; 1992, Virginia; U.S. Court of Appeals, District of Columbia, Eighth, Fifth, Sixth and Tenth Circuits. *Education:* University of Iowa (B.A., honors and with distinction, 1978); University of

(This Listing Continued)

SQUIRE, SANDERS & DEMPSEY L.L.P., Washington—Continued

Iowa (J.D., with distinction, 1981). Phi Beta Kappa. *Member:* Virginia and Colorado Bar Associations; Federal Energy Bar Association. ***PRACTICE AREAS:*** Energy. ***Email:*** nawhite@ssd.com

ROBERT I. WHITE, born Ventnor City, New Jersey, 1951; admitted to bar, 1977, District of Columbia. *Education:* Haverford College (B.A., with honors, 1974); George Washington University (J.D., with honors, 1977). Attorney, Office of General Counsel, Federal Trade Commission, 1977-1980. *Member:* American Bar Association; Federal Energy Bar Association. ***PRACTICE AREAS:*** Administrative Law; Appellate Practice; International Contracts; Energy Contracts; Federal Energy Law. ***Email:*** rwhite@ssd.com

GLENN M. YOUNG, born Landville, West Virginia, 1948; admitted to bar, 1975, Ohio; 1981, District of Columbia; U.S. Court of Appeals for the District of Columbia Circuit. *Education:* The Ohio State University (B.A., 1972); Harvard University (J.D., cum laude, 1975). *Member:* The District of Columbia Bar. ***PRACTICE AREAS:*** Litigation. ***Email:*** gyoung@ssd.com

OF COUNSEL

FRANCIS S. RATH, born New York, N.Y., 1955; admitted to bar, 1980, District of Columbia; 1988, Virginia. *Education:* Wesleyan University (B.A., cum laude, 1977); Georgetown University (J.D., cum laude, 1980). Editor, Law and Policy in International Business. ***LANGUAGES:*** Hungarian, German. ***PRACTICE AREAS:*** Eastern Europe; International Corporate. ***Email:*** frath@ssd.com

JUDITH J. SEMO, born Washington, D.C., 1952; admitted to bar, 1977, District of Columbia. *Education:* Brown University (B.A., magna cum laude, 1974); George Washington University (J.D., with honors, 1977). *Member:* The District of Columbia Bar (Health Law Section); American Bar Association (Health Law Section); American Society of Medical Association Counsel; AMA Doctors Advisory Network; American Health Lawyers Association; Anesthesia Administration Assembly; Medical Group Management Association. ***PRACTICE AREAS:*** Health Care; Professional Associations; Legislation. ***Email:*** jsemo@ssd.com

LOUIS STOKES, born Cleveland, Ohio, 1925; admitted to bar, 1953, Ohio; 1999, District of Columbia. *Education:* Cleveland College of Western Reserve University (1946-1949); Cleveland Marshall Law School (J.D., 1953). U.S. Representative, 11th District of Ohio, 1969-1999. [Technician 4th Grade, U.S. Army, 1943-1946]. ***Email:*** lstokes@ssd.com

ASSOCIATES

AMY L. BROWN, born Cleveland, Ohio, 1969; admitted to bar, 1994, Virginia; 1996, District of Columbia; U.S. District Court, Eastern District of Virginia; U.S. Court of Appeals, Eleventh Circuit; U.S. Supreme Court. *Education:* Stanford University (A.B., 1991); Duke University (J.D., 1994). ***Email:*** abrown@ssd.com

ELIZABETH C. COLLINS, born Washington, D.C., 1968; admitted to bar, 1996, New York and District of Columbia. *Education:* Colgate University (B.A., 1990); American University (J.D., 1995). ***LANGUAGES:*** Spanish. ***Email:*** ecollins@ssd.com

AMY L. EASTON, born Syracuse, New York, 1973; admitted to bar, 1998, Ohio; 1999, District of Columbia. *Education:* University of Michigan (B.A., cum laude, 1995); The Ohio State University (J.D., cum laude, 1998). ***Email:*** aeaston@ssd.com

AMY L. FRIEDMAN, born New York, New York, 1973; admitted to bar, 2001, New York and District of Columbia. *Education:* Yale University (B.A., with distinction, 1995); American University (J.D., magna cum laude, 2000). ***LANGUAGES:*** French. ***Email:*** afriedman@ssd.com

CHRISTOPHER H. GORDON, born Landstuhl, Germany, 1972; admitted to bar, 1998, Virginia; 1999, District of Columbia. *Education:* University of Virginia (B.A., 1995; J.D., 1998). ***Email:*** cgordon@ssd.com

MARK D. JOHNSON, born Cincinnati, Ohio, 1965; admitted to bar, 1993, Virginia; 1994, District of Columbia. *Education:* Bucknell University (B.A., cum laude, 1988); American University (J.D., cum laude, 1993). ***LANGUAGES:*** Spanish. ***Email:*** majohnson@ssd.com

DONNIE L. KIDD, JR., born Roanoke, Virginia, 1974; admitted to bar, 1999, District of Columbia, Virginia and U.S. Court of Appeals, Fourth Circuit; U.S. District Court for the District of Columbia. *Education:* University of Virginia (B.A., 1996); University of Richmond (J.D., magna cum laude, 1999). ***Email:*** dkidd@ssd.com

VLADIMIR V. KOUZNETSOV, born Moscow, Russia, 1971; admitted to bar, 1997, Ohio; 1999, District of Columbia. *Education:* Wittenberg University (B.A., 1993); Case Western Reserve University (J.D., 1997). ***LANGUAGES:*** Russian. ***Email:*** vkouznetsov@ssd.com

(This Listing Continued)

KEVIN S. LEVEY, born St. Louis, Missouri, 1971; admitted to bar, 1998, New York and District of Columbia. *Education:* American University (A.B., magna cum laude, 1993; J.D., cum laude, 1997). ***LANGUAGES:*** Spanish. ***Email:*** klevey@ssd.com

SUSAN L. MASLEN, born Brisbane, Australia, 1974; admitted to bar, 1999, New South Wales, Australia (Not admitted in the United States). *Education:* Griffith University (B.A., 1998; Bachelor of Laws, honors, 1998); Georgetown University (LL.M., 2001). ***LANGUAGES:*** German and Japanese. ***Email:*** smaslen@ssd.com

IAIN R. McPHIE, born Silver Spring, Maryland, 1970; admitted to bar, 2000, Virginia; 2001, District of Columbia. *Education:* Georgetown University (B.S.F.S., 1992); George Mason University (M.P.A., 1997); College of William & Mary (J.D., 2000). ***LANGUAGES:*** French. ***Email:*** imcphie@ssd.com

ALVARO J. MESTRE, born Haines City, Florida, 1970; admitted to bar, 1995, Maryland; 1996, District of Columbia and U.S. District Court, District of Maryland. *Education:* University of Florida at Gainesville (B.A., with honors, 1992); Georgetown University (J.D., 1995). ***LANGUAGES:*** Spanish. ***Email:*** amestre@ssd.com

BRUCE A. OLCOTT, born Fort Worth, Texas, 1961; admitted to bar, 1995, California (inactive); 1996, District of Columbia. *Education:* San Jose State University (B.A., with distinction, 1983); Columbia University (J.D., with honors, 1995). ***Email:*** bolcott@ssd.com

MARCELA VILLALTA SCOTT, born Bogota, Colombia, 1973; admitted to bar, 1993, Maryland; 2000, District of Columbia. *Education:* Indiana University (B.A., 1995); Georgetown University (J.D., 1999). ***LANGUAGES:*** Spanish, French. ***Email:*** mscott@ssd.com

ANNE K. SHUKIS, born Washington, D.C., 1973; admitted to bar, 2000, Virginia; 2001, Court of International Trade (Not admitted in District of Columbia). *Education:* Mary Washington College (B.A., cum laude, 1995); George Mason University (J.D., magna cum laude, 2000). ***LANGUAGES:*** Spanish. ***Email:*** ashukis@ssd.com

ANGELA M. SIMPSON, born Washington, D.C., 1972; admitted to bar, 2000, New York (Not admitted in District of Columbia). *Education:* University of Maryland (B.A., 1993); Vanderbilt University (J.D., 2000). ***Email:*** asimpson@ssd.com

THOMAS E. SKILTON, born Bronxville, New York, 1966; admitted to bar, 1993, New Jersey; 1994, New York; 1995, District of Columbia. *Education:* Dartmouth College (B.A., cum laude, 1989); Cornell University (J.D., 1993). ***LANGUAGES:*** Spanish. ***Email:*** tskilton@ssd.com

JAMES P. WEHNER, born St. Louis, Missouri, 1967; admitted to bar, 1995, Virginia; 1996, U.S. District Court, Eastern District of Virginia; 1997, District of Columbia; 2000, U.S. District Court for the District of Columbia, U.S. Court of Appeals, First Circuit. *Education:* Georgetown University (B.A., 1989; J.D., 1995). ***Email:*** jwehner@ssd.com

(For Biographical Data on Cincinnati, Cleveland and Columbus, Ohio, Los Angeles, Palo Alto and San Francisco, California, Miami, Jacksonville and Tampa, Florida, Houston, Texas, New York, New York, Phoenix, Arizona, Tysons Corner, Virginia, Almaty, Kazakhstan, Bratislava, Slovak Republic, Brussels, Belgium, Budapest, Hungary, Kyiv, Ukraine, London, England, Madrid, Spain, Moscow, Russian Federation, Prague, Czech Republic, Beijing and Hong Kong, China, Tokyo, Japan, Taipei, Taiwan and Milan, Italy Personnel, see Professional Biographies at those Points Respectively).

STAAS & HALSEY LLP

Established in 1971

700 ELEVENTH STREET, N.W., SUITE 500

WASHINGTON, D.C. 20001

Telephone: 202-434-1500
Facsimile: 202-434-1501
Email: info@s-n-h.com
URL: http://www.staasandhalsey.com

Patent, Trademark, Copyright, Unfair Competition and Computer Law. International Patent and Trademark Practice. Practice before Federal Courts and Administrative Agencies.

FIRM PROFILE: Since 1971, the law firm of Staas & Halsey LLP has assisted clients from every major nation in the world in protecting their intellectual and industrial property rights. We have represented clients in the courts of the United States, before various U.S. government agencies, and in arbitration hearings. By emphasizing innovative yet practical solutions, we provide our clients with efficient, personalized service. We are qualified to assist clients in technology-related matters, since every attorney in the firm has experience and expertise in a range of technical areas.

(This Listing Continued)

MEMBERS OF FIRM

H. J. STAAS, born Pittsburgh, Pennsylvania, July 6, 1938; admitted to bar, 1964, Virginia; 1965, New York; 1966, District of Columbia; 1967, U.S. Supreme Court; 1973-1982, U.S. Court of Customs and Patent Appeals; 1982, U.S. Court of Appeals for the Federal Circuit; registered to practice before U.S. Patent and Trademark Office. *Education:* Lehigh University (B.S., 1960; B.A., 1960); Georgetown University (LL.B., 1964). Phi Alpha Delta. *Member:* The District of Columbia Bar; Bar Association of the District of Columbia; Virginia State Bar; New York State and American Bar Associations; American Intellectual Property Law Association; Licensing Executives Society. ***PRACTICE AREAS:*** Intellectual Property Law; Patent, Trademark, Copyright and Unfair Competition. ***Email:*** hjstaas@s-n-h.com

JAMES D. HALSEY, JR., born Richmond, Virginia, December 1, 1935; admitted to bar, 1964, District of Columbia; 1974, U.S. Supreme Court and U.S. Claims Court; 1974-1982, U.S. Court of Customs and Patent Appeals; 1982, U.S. Court of Appeals for the Federal Circuit; registered to practice before U.S. Patent and Trademark Office. *Education:* University of Maryland (B.S.M.E., 1960); American University (J.D., 1963). *Member:* The District of Columbia Bar; Bar Association of the District of Columbia; American, Inter-American and International Bar Associations; American Judicature Society; American Intellectual Property Law Association; International Trademark Association; Union Internationale Des Avocats. ***PRACTICE AREAS:*** Intellectual Property Law; Patent, Trademark, Copyright and Unfair Competition. ***Email:*** jhalsey@s-n-h.com

DAVID M. PITCHER, born Ithaca, New York, April 3, 1945; admitted to bar, 1971, New York; 1973, U.S. Court of Appeals, District of Columbia Circuit; 1975, District of Columbia and U.S. District Court, District of Columbia; 1976-1982, U.S. Court of Customs and Patent Appeals; 1982, U.S. Court of Appeals for the Federal Circuit; registered to practice before U.S. Patent and Trademark Office. *Education:* University of Michigan (B.S.E., 1967); Syracuse University (J.D., 1970). Phi Delta Phi. *Member:* The District of Columbia Bar (Member, Section of Patent, Trademark and Copyright Law); Bar Association of the District of Columbia (Member, Section of Patent, Trademark and Copyright Law); Federal and American (Member, Section of Patent, Trademark and Copyright Law) Bar Associations; American Intellectual Property Law Association; Licensing Executives Society; International Association for the Protection of Intellectual Property (AIPPI). [Lt., JAGC, U.S. Navy, 1971-1974]. ***PRACTICE AREAS:*** Intellectual Property Law; Patent, Trademark, Copyright and Unfair Competition. ***Email:*** pitcher@s-n-h.com

JOHN C. GARVEY, born Washington, D.C., April 9, 1953; admitted to bar, 1979, District of Columbia; 1980-1982, U.S. Court of Customs and Patent Appeals; 1982, U.S. Court of Appeals for the Federal Circuit; 1980, U.S. Court of Appeals, District of Columbia Circuit; 1982, U.S. District Court, District of Columbia; registered to practice before U.S. Patent and Trademark Office. *Education:* Duke University (B.S.E., cum laude, 1975); George Washington University (J.D., with honors, 1979). Author, "Overview of an Infringement Analysis," Japan Intellectual Property Management Journal, Vol. 46, November 8, 1996. Co-Author: "Recent Trends in the Patentability of Computer Related Inventions: Is a Method of Doing Business Patentable?" International Legal Strategy, Vo. V-11, November 1996. *Member:* The District of Columbia Bar; American Bar Association (Member, Section of Patent, Trademark and Copyright Law); American Intellectual Property Law Association; Federal Circuit Bar Association. ***PRACTICE AREAS:*** Intellectual Property Law; Patent, Trademark, Copyright and Unfair Competition. ***Email:*** jgarvey@s-n-h.com

J. RANDALL BECKERS, born Birmingham, Alabama, March 12, 1952; admitted to bar, 1980, Alabama; 1982, District of Columbia and U.S. Court of Appeals for the Federal Circuit; 1984, U.S. District Court, District of Columbia; registered to practice before U.S. Patent and Trademark Office. *Education:* Auburn University (B.S.E.E., 1975); University of Alabama, Birmingham (M.S., Computer Science, 1977); Cumberland School of Law of Samford University (J.D., 1980). Phi Alpha Delta. Co-Author: "Throwing Out Baby Benson With the Bath Water: Proposing a New Test for Determining Statutory Subject Matter," The Computer Lawyer, Vol. 10, No. 1, January, 1993 and Jurimetrics Journal of Law, Science and Technology, Vol. 33, No. 1, Winter, 1993; "An Analysis of the Final U.S.P.T.O. Examination Guidelines for Computer-Related Inventions," International Legal Strategy," Vol. V-3, March 1996; "Recent Trends in the Patentability of Computer Related Inventions: Is a Method of Doing Business Patentable?" International Legal Strategy, Vol. V-11, November 1996; "Signature Financial Group as an Inventory Distributor: Would the Court View the Claim Differently?" Law Works, Intellectual Property Today, Vol. 4, No. 3, March 1997; "Best Mode and Software Related Inventions: Is Source Code Necessary?" Law Works, Intellectual Property Today, Vol. 4, No. 5, May 1997; "The Examination of Computer-Related Inventions by the U.S. Patent & Trademark Office," International Legal Strategy (ILS), IX-6, June 2000. *Member:* The District of Columbia Bar (Member, Sections of: Computer Law; Patent, Trademark and Copyright Law); Alabama State Bar; American Bar Association; American Intellectual Property Law Association. ***REPORTED CASES:*** In re Van Guens, 946 F.2d 845, 20 U.S.P.Q. 2d 1291 (Fed. Cir. 1991). ***PRACTICE AREAS:*** Intellectual Property Law; Patent, Trademark, Copyright and Unfair Competition. ***Email:*** jrbeckers@s-n-h.com

(This Listing Continued)

WILLIAM F. HERBERT, born Holyoke, Massachusetts, February 1, 1956; admitted to bar, 1981, Massachusetts; 1984, District of Columbia; 1991, U.S. Court of Appeals for the Federal Circuit; 1992, U.S. Supreme Court; registered to practice before U.S. Patent and Trademark Office. *Education:* Boston College (B.A., Biology and Psychology, 1978); Catholic University of America (J.D., 1981). Member, Catholic University Law Review, 1980-1981. Author: "'Failure to Disclose the Best Mode:' What the Public Doesn't Know Will Hurt Them," 64 J.P.O.S. 12, 1982; "Clearing Marks for U.S. Use and Registration," International Legal Strategy, Vol. VII-3, March 15,1998. *Member:* The District of Columbia Bar (Member: Intellectual Property Section Steering Committee, 1995-1999 (Co-Chairman, 1995-1998); Chairman, Patent Law Committee, 1993-1995; Lecturer, 1996-2001); Massachusetts (Member: Mentor Program; Business Law Section) and American Bar Associations; American Intellectual Property Law Association; The International Trade Commission Trial Lawyers Association; International Trademark Association; Prettyman-Leventhal American Inn of Court (1988-1991); Giles S. Rich American Inn of Court (Officer). ***REPORTED CASES:*** Luv & Care, Inc. v. Ansa Bottle Co., 2 U.S.P.Q. 2d, 1955 (SDNY 1987); The Loglan Institute Inc. v. The Logical Language Group Inc., 22 U.S.P.Q. 2d 1531 (Fed. Cir. 1992). ***PRACTICE AREAS:*** Intellectual Property Law; Patent, Trademark, Copyright and Unfair Competition. ***Email:*** wherbert@s-n-h.com

RICHARD A. GOLLHOFER, born Chicago, Illinois, January 3, 1955; admitted to bar, 1981, Illinois; 1985, District of Columbia; registered to practice before U.S. Patent and Trademark Office. *Education:* Rose-Hulman Institute of Technology (B.S., cum laude, 1977); IIT/Chicago-Kent College of Law (J.D., cum laude, 1981). Tau Beta Pi; Pi Mu Epsilon. Author: "Copyright Protection of Computer Software: What is it and how did we get it?" Software Law Journal, Vol. V, No. 4, 1992. Co-Author, "An Analysis of the Final U.S.P.T.O. Examination Guidelines for Computer Related Inventions," International Legal Strategy, Vol. V-3, March 1996. *Member:* The District of Columbia Bar (Member, Sections on: Computer and Telecommunications Law; Intellectual Property Law); American Bar Association; American Intellectual Property Law Association. ***PRACTICE AREAS:*** Intellectual Property Law; Patent, Trademark, Copyright and Unfair Competition. ***Email:*** ragollhofer@s-n-h.com

MARK J. HENRY, born Jeannette, Pennsylvania, April 15, 1967; admitted to bar, 1992, Virginia and New Jersey; 1994, District of Columbia; registered to practice before U.S. Patent and Trademark Office. *Education:* Pennsylvania State University (B.S.Chem.E., 1989); Widener University (J.D., 1992); Catholic University of America; George Washington University (M.S.E.E., 2000). Phi Alpha Delta. Recipient, American Jurisprudence Award in Family Law. Law Clerk, Westinghouse Electric Company Law Department, Intellectual Property Law Section, 1990. Author: "State Courts Hearing Patent Cases: A Cry for Help to the Federal Circuit," Dickinson Law Review, Vol. 101, 1996, reprinted in Intellectual Property Today, Vol. 4, Nos. 8 and 9 (1997); "The USPTO Reverses Policy on 'Bypass Continuation' Applications," Intellectual Property Today, Vol. 7, No. 5, (2000). Examiner, U.S. Patent and Trademark Office (Internship), 1991. *Member:* American Intellectual Property Law Association; American Institute of Chemical Engineers. ***PRACTICE AREAS:*** Intellectual Property Law; Patent, Trademark, Copyright and Unfair Competition. ***Email:*** mhenry@s-n-h.com

PAUL I. KRAVETZ, born Chicago, Illinois, April 11, 1963; admitted to bar, 1992, Illinois; 1994, District of Columbia; registered to practice before U.S. Patent and Trademark Office. *Education:* University of Iowa (B.S.E.E., 1986); De Paul University (J.D., 1992). Author: "Copyright Protection of Screen Displays After Lotus Development Corporation v. Paperback Software International," 4 DePaul Business Law Journal 485, 1992, reprinted 25 Intellectual Property Law Review 321, 1993; "' Idea/Expression Dichotomy' and ' Method of Operation': Determining Copyright Protection for Computer Programs," 8 DePaul Business Law Journal 75, 1995; "Copyright Protection of Computer Programs," 80 Journal of the Patent and Trademark Office Society (JPTOS) 41 (1998); "The Examination of Computer-Related Inventions by the U.S. Patent & Trademark Office," International Legal Strategy (ILS), IX-6, June 2000. *Member:* American Intellectual Property Law Association. ***PRACTICE AREAS:*** Patents; Copyrights; Trademarks. ***Email:*** pkravetz@s-n-h.com

GENE M. GARNER, II, born Washington, D.C., April 26, 1958; admitted to bar, 1988, Maryland and District of Columbia; 1995, U.S. Supreme Court; registered to practice before U.S. Patent and Trademark Office. *Education:* University of Maryland at College Park (B.S.E.E., 1980); Cornell University (M. Eng., 1981); University of Maryland at Baltimore (J.D., 1987); John Hopkins University (M.S., Biotech, 2001); Georgetown University Medical School. Tau Beta Pi; Eta Kappa Nu. *Member:* Prince Georges County, Maryland State and Federal Bar Associations; Bar Association of the District of Columbia; Institute of Electrical and Electronic Engineers; Institute of Electrical and Electronic Engineers Computer Society. ***PRACTICE AREAS:*** Intellectual Property Law; Patents; Trademarks; Copyright Law. ***Email:*** ggarner@s-n-h.com

(This Listing Continued)

STAAS & HALSEY LLP, Washington—Continued

MICHAEL D. STEIN, born New York, N.Y., May 24, 1965; admitted to bar, 1992, Maryland; 1994, District of Columbia; registered to practice before U.S. Patent and Trademark Office. *Education:* University of Pennsylvania (B.S.E.E., 1987); American University (J.D., cum laude, 1992). *Member:* Maryland State and American Bar Associations; District of Columbia Bar; American Intellectual Property Law Association; Licensing Executives Society; Asian-Pacific Lawyer's Association. ***PRACTICE AREAS:*** Intellectual Property Law; Patent, Trademark and Copyright Law. ***Email:*** mstein@s-n-h.com

ASSOCIATES

JONATHAN H. MUSKIN, born Long Island, New York, November 5, 1967; admitted to bar, 1996, New York, New Jersey and Georgia; 1997, U.S. District Court, Southern and Eastern Districts of New York; registered to practice before U.S. Patent and Trademark Office (Not admitted in District of Columbia). *Education:* Tulane University (B.S., Computer Science/Math, 1990); John Marshall Law School (J.D., 1995; L.L.M., with honors, 1998). *Member:* American Bar Association; American Intellectual Property Law Association; Computer Law Association. ***PRACTICE AREAS:*** Intellectual Property Law; Patents; Trademarks; Copyright Law. ***Email:*** jmuskin@s-n-h.com

STEPHEN T. BOUGHNER, born Canton, Ohio, September 2, 1971; admitted to bar, 1998, California and Ohio; 1999, New York; registered to practice before U.S. Patent and Trademark Office (Not admitted in District of Columbia). *Education:* University of Akron (B.S.E.E., 1994); University of Akron School of Law (J.D., 1997). *Member:* Ohio State, New York State and American Bar Associations; State Bar of California; American Intellectual Property Law Association. ***PRACTICE AREAS:*** Intellectual Property; Patents; Trademarks; Copyrights. ***Email:*** sboughner@s-n-h.com

CHRISTINE J. GILSDORF, born Richlands, Virginia, April 3, 1961; admitted to bar, 1998, Florida; 2000, District of Columbia; registered to practice before U.S. Patent and Trademark Office. *Education:* Virginia Polytechnic Institute and State University (B.S., Electrical Engineering, 1984); University of Dayton (M.S., Management Science, 1992; M.B.A., 1994); University of Cincinnati (J.D., 1998). Recipient, Ernest Karam Book Award. Member, University of Cincinnati Law Review. Author: Comment, "Trademark Protection for Trademarks Used as Internet Domain Names," University of Cincinnati Law Review, Vol. 65:4, Summer, 1997; Comment, "Copyright Liability of On-Line Service Providers," University of Cincinnati Law Review, Vol. 66:2, Winter, 1998. *Member:* American Bar Association; American Intellectual Property Law Association. [Capt., USAF, 1984-1988]. ***PRACTICE AREAS:*** Intellectual Property Law; Patents; Trademarks; Copyrights. ***Email:*** jgilsdorf@s-n-h.com

MEHDI D. SHEIKERZ, born Vienna, Austria, August 26, 1965; admitted to bar, 1996, Florida; registered to practice before U.S. Patent and Trademark Office (Not admitted in District of Columbia). *Education:* Virginia Polytechnic Institute and State University (B.S., Computer Science, 1988); Franklin Pierce Law Center (J.D., 1996; Master of Intellectual Property, 1996). Adjunct Professor, Florida Coastal School of Law, Fall, 1999. *Member:* The Florida Bar; American Bar Association. ***PRACTICE AREAS:*** Intellectual Property; Patents; Licensing; Trademarks; Copyrights. ***Email:*** msheikerz@s-n-h.com

JOHN H. STOWE, born Buford, Georgia, November 6, 1939; admitted to bar, 1971, Indiana; registered to practice before U.S. Patent and Trademark Office (Not admitted in District of Columbia). *Education:* Georgia Institute of Technology (B.E.E., 1964); Indiana University (J.D., 1971). *Member:* Intellectual Property Law Association. ***Email:*** jstowe@s-n-h.com

JAMES G. McEWEN, born Highland Park, Illinois, July 12, 1970; admitted to bar, 1996, Virginia; registered to practice before U.S. Patent and Trademark Office (Not admitted in District of Columbia). *Education:* University of Texas (B.S., 1993; A.S.E., 1993); George Washington University (J.D., with honors, 1996). *Member:* American Bar Association (Member, Sections on: Intellectual Property Law; Public Contract); American Intellectual Property Law Association; Government Patent Lawyers Association (Secretary, 1998-2000). ***PRACTICE AREAS:*** Patent Law; Trademark Law; Trade Secret; Licensing; Intellectual Property Law; Government Contracts; Technology Transfers. ***Email:*** jmcewen@s-n-h.com

MICHAEL JOHN BADAGLIACCA, born Suffern, New York, October 13, 1971; admitted to bar, 1997, New York; registered to practice before U.S. Patent and Trademark Office (Not admitted in District of Columbia). *Education:* Cornell University (B.S., 1993); Pepperdine University School of Law (J.D., cum laude, 1996). Associate Editor, Pepperdine University Law Review, 1995-1996. ***PRACTICE AREAS:*** Intellectual Property. ***Email:*** mbadagliacca@s-n-h.com

ALICIA M. CHOI, born San Salvador, El Salvador, January 19, 1966; admitted to bar, 1999, Ohio; registered to practice before U.S. Patent and Trademark Office (Not admitted in District of Columbia). *Education:* The Ohio State University (B.S.E.E., 1989); University of Akron (J.D., 1999). Alpha Lamda Delta; Phi Eta Sigma; Phi Alpha Delta. Member, Akron Law Review.

(This Listing Continued)

Member: American Intellectual Property Law Association; Intellectual Property and Technology Law Association. ***LANGUAGES:*** Spanish. ***PRACTICE AREAS:*** Patents. ***Email:*** achoi@s-n-h.com

HEATH E. WELLS, born Kettering, Ohio, March 12, 1969; admitted to bar, 1998, Virginia; U.S. Court of Appeals, Fourth Circuit; registered to practice before U.S. Patent and Trademark Office (Not admitted in District of Columbia). *Education:* Virginia Military Institute (B.S.C.E., 1991); Washington College of Law (J.D., 1998). *Member:* American Bar Association; American Intellectual Property Law Association. [Captain, U.S. Army Reserves, JAG Corps, 1987-2000.]. ***PRACTICE AREAS:*** Intellectual Property; Trademarks; Copyrights; Patents. ***Email:*** hwells@s-n-h.com

JAMES T. STROM, born Midland, Michigan, July 28, 1967; admitted to bar, 2000, Maryland; registered to practice before the U.S. Patent and Trademark Office (Not admitted in District of Columbia). *Education:* University of Maryland (B.S., Computer Science and Math, 1990); University of Memphis (J.D., 1998). *Member:* American Bar Association. ***PRACTICE AREAS:*** Intellectual Property. ***Email:*** jstrom@s-n-h.com

ERIC BERKOWITZ, born Philadelphia, Pennsylvania, November 6, 1965; admitted to bar, 1992, Pennsylvania (Not admitted in District of Columbia). *Education:* University of Pennsylvania (B.S.E.E., 1987); Rutgers University (J.D., 1992). ***PRACTICE AREAS:*** Intellectual Property; Patents; Trademarks; Copyright Law. ***Email:*** berkowitz@s-n-h.com

PATENT AGENT

PATRICK J. STANZIONE, born Yonkers, New York, March 31, 1964; (admission pending); admitted to bar, registered to practice before the U.S. Patent and Trademark Office. *Education:* Rensselaer Polytechnic Institute (B.S.E.E., 1990); Western New England College (J.D., 1999). Registered to practice before the U.S. Patent and Trademark Office. Primary Examiner, U.S. Patent and Trademark Office. *Member:* American Intellectual Property Law Association. (Patent Agent). ***PRACTICE AREAS:*** Intellectual Property; Patents; Trademarks. ***Email:*** pstanzione@s-n-h.com

---

STATLAND & BUCKLEY, P.C.

1828 L STREET, N.W.
SUITE 660
WASHINGTON, D.C. 20036-5112
Telephone: 202-296-0555
Fax: 202-296-9434
Email: lawyers@statbuck.com

General Civil, Litigation, Commercial, Corporate, Real Estate, Construction, Negligence, Family and Creditor's Rights.

EDWARD M. STATLAND, born Washington, D.C., August 20, 1932; admitted to bar, 1959, District of Columbia and Maryland; 1964, U.S. Supreme Court. *Education:* George Washington University (A.B., 1954; J.D., with honors, 1959). Member, Board of Editors, George Washington University Law Review, 1959. Assistant Corporation Counsel for the District of Columbia, 1960-1962. Member, Panel of Arbitrators: National Association of Securities Dealers, Inc.; American Arbitration Association; Maryland Health Claims Arbitration Panel. *Member:* The District of Columbia Bar; Bar Association of the District of Columbia; Montgomery County (Maryland), Maryland State and American Bar Associations; Association of Plaintiffs' Trial Attorneys; American Judicature Society. ***PRACTICE AREAS:*** Commercial Law; Broker-Dealer Arbitration; Arbitration; Estate Planning; Estate Administration. ***Email:*** estatland@statbuck.com

DAVID W. BUCKLEY, born Chicago, Illinois, September 26, 1945; admitted to bar, 1974, District of Columbia; 1975 Maryland; 2000, Virginia. *Education:* University of Notre Dame (A.B., 1967); University of Innsbruck, Austria; University of Michigan (M.A., 1968); George Washington University (J.D., with honors, 1974). Author: "Liens and Other Encumbrances Against Real Property," Realtor, September, 1982. Arbitrator, District of Columbia Superior Court. *Member:* The District of Columbia Bar; Bar Association of the District of Columbia (Chairman, Real Property Law Committee, 1980-1982); Maryland State Bar and American Bar Associations; Virginia State Bar; Maryland Trial Lawyers Association. ***PRACTICE AREAS:*** Commercial Litigation; Construction Law; Real Estate; Franchise Law. ***Email:*** dbuckley@statbuck.com

REPRESENTATIVE CLIENTS INCLUDE: Hitt Contracting, Inc.; Orndorff & Spaid, Inc.; HUD Federal Credit Union; Appalachian Spring.

LAW OFFICE OF ROBERT E. STEIN

4945 BRANDYWINE STREET, N.W.
WASHINGTON, D.C. 20016
Telephone: 202-686-9090
Fax: 202-686-9098
Email: resteinlaw@aol.com

Health Care Law, Mediation, Arbitration and Dispute Resolution, Employment and Disability Law.

ROBERT E. STEIN, born New York, N.Y., February 12, 1939; admitted to bar, 1964, New York; 1974, District of Columbia. *Education:* Brandeis University (B.A., 1960); Columbia Law School (LL.B., 1963); Hague Academy of International Law (Diploma, 1964). Author: "HIV Infected Health Care Workers: "Vaccine Liability and Participant Compensation Incentives in HIV Vaccine Trials," in Vol. 10, Aids Research and Human Retroviruses, 1994; "The Americans With Disabilities Act: New Rights, New Issues," The Arbitration Journal (June 1991). Adjunct Professor of Law, Georgetown Law Center, 1984—. *Member:* American Bar Association (Chair, 1997-2000 and Past Chair, 2000-2001, AIDS Coordinating Committee; Co-Chair, Health Rights Committee); American Law Institute; American Arbitration Association (Member, Panel of Arbitrators); National Health Lawyers Association (Panel Member, Alternative Dispute Resolution Service).

STEIN, MITCHELL & MEZINES

1100 CONNECTICUT AVENUE, N.W., SUITE 1100
WASHINGTON, D.C. 20036
Telephone: 202-737-7777
Email: jstein@steinmitchell.com
URL: http://www.steinmitchell.com

General, Civil, Criminal and Administrative Practice before Federal and Local Courts, Agencies and Departments.

MEMBERS OF FIRM

JACOB A. STEIN, born Washington, D.C., 1925; admitted to bar, 1948, District of Columbia; 1956, Maryland. *Education:* George Washington University (A.A.; LL.B., 1948; LL.D., Honorary, 1987). Recipient: Lawyer of the Year Award, Trial Lawyers Association of Metropolitan Washington, D.C., 1981; George Washington Law School's Distinguished Alumni Award, 1982. Honorary Doctor of Laws, Suffolk Law School, 1984. Recipient, Council for Court Excellence, Justice Potter Stewart Award, 1998. Author: "Closing Argument, The Art and The Law," Callaghan and Company, 1969; *Trial Handbook for Maryland Lawyers,* Lawyers Co-Operative Publishing Company, 1972-2001; *Personal Injury Damages,* 2nd Ed. 1991, Clark, Boardman Callaghan; "District of Columbia Tort Casefinder—An Analysis of all Appellate Tort Decisions for the District of Columbia," 3rd Ed.; *The Law of Law Firms,* Clark, Boardman, Callaghan, 1994. Adjunct Professor of Law: George Washington University Law School, 1984; Georgetown University Law School, 1985-2001; American University Law School, 1987. Visiting Lecturer, Harvard Law School, 1974-1991. Chairman, Admissions Committee of the District of Columbia Court of Appeals, 1974-1978. Chairman, United States District Court for the District of Columbia Committee on Local Court Rules, 1973-1987. Member: Judicial Conference, District of Columbia Circuit; Committee to Draft Maryland Civil Jury Instructions, 1977. Senior Editor, Litigation Journal, ABA Litigation Section. Selected by the Special Division of the United States Court of Appeals to serve as the Independent Counsel, 1984, re: Edwin Meese, III. *Member:* The District of Columbia Bar (President, 1982-1983); Bar Association of the District of Columbia (Vice President, 1967-1968; President, 1968-1969; Member, Committee on Grievances and Admissions, U.S. Court of Appeals, 1970-1974); Maryland State Bar Association; American Bar Association; The Association of Trial Lawyers of America; Trial Lawyers Association of Metropolitan Washington, D.C. (President, 1959-1960). Fellow, American College of Trial Lawyers.

GLENN A. MITCHELL, born Washington, D.C., March 28, 1936; admitted to bar, 1961, District of Columbia; 1967, Maryland. *Education:* University of Virginia (B.A., 1958); Georgetown University (J.D., 1961). Recipient, Lawyer of the Year Award, Trial Lawyers Association of Metropolitan Washington, D.C., 1973-1974. Co-author: *Administrative Law,* Matthew Bender Publishing Company, 1996. Trial Attorney, Federal Trade Commission, 1961-1964. Member, Judicial Conference, District of Columbia Circuit, 1975-1976. *Member:* The District of Columbia Bar; Bar Association of the District of Columbia (Member, Board of Directors, 1974-1976, 1996-1998); Chairman, Antitrust and Trade Association Committee, 1994-1996; Maryland State Bar Association, Inc.; American Bar Association (Member, Antitrust Section; Chairman, Labor Exemption Committee, 1987-1990); The Association of Trial Lawyers of America; Trial Lawyers Association of Metropolitan Washington, D.C. (Vice-President, 1971-1972; President, 1972-1973). Fellow, American College of Trial Lawyers. ***PRACTICE AREAS:*** Civil Litigation; Administrative Litigation; Antitrust; Trade Regulation. ***Email:*** gamitchell@steinmitchell.com

(This Listing Continued)

BASIL J. MEZINES, born Perth Amboy, New Jersey; admitted to bar, 1948, District of Columbia; 1963, Maryland. *Education:* George Washington University (B.A., 1946); George Washington University Law School (LL.B., 1948). Co-author: *Administrative Law,* Matthew Bender, 1991. Author: "Trade Associations and the Antitrust Laws," Bureau of National Affairs, 1983. Attorney, Federal Trade Commission, 1949-1959. Associate Executive Director, Federal Trade Commission, 1960. Senior Trial Attorney, Federal Trade Commission, 1961-1970. Executive Assistant to the Chairman, Federal Trade Commission, 1970. Director, Bureau of Competition, Federal Trade Commission, 1970. Executive Director, Federal Trade Commission, 1971-1973. Recipient, Outstanding and Superior Service Awards, from Federal Trade Commission in, 1960, 1963, 1968, 1970 and 1973. Member, Advisory Board, BNA Antitrust & Trade Regulation Report, 1973—. Member, Board of Trustees, Holton-Arms School, Washington, D.C., 1982-1985. Member, Board of Advisors, National Law Center, George Washington University, 1991-1997. *Member:* The District of Columbia Bar; Federal and American (Member, Section of Antitrust Law, Special Committee to Study the Role of the Federal Trade Commission, 1989) Bar Associations. ***PRACTICE AREAS:*** Antitrust; Trade Regulation.

GERARD E. MITCHELL, born Washington, D.C., December 30, 1944; admitted to bar, 1969, Maryland; 1970, District of Columbia. *Education:* Georgetown University (A.B., 1966); University of Virginia (LL.B., 1969). Recipient, Lawyer of the Year Award, Trial Lawyers Association of Metropolitan Washington, D.C., 1984. Member, Editorial Board, 1967-1968 and Notes and Decisions Editor, 1968-1969, Virginia Law Review. Adjunct Professor of Law, Washington College of Law, American University, 1973-1974. Instructor: D.C. Bar Continuing Legal Education Program, Civil Trial Practice, 1976-1979; Medical Malpractice, 1984, 1988. Faculty Member, Georgetown University Continuing Legal Education Program, 1990-1995. Law Clerk, Judge John P. Moore, Circuit Court for Montgomery County, Maryland, 1969-1970. Assistant State's Attorney, Montgomery County, Maryland, 1971-1972. Master, Charles Fahy American Inn of Court, 1987-1988. Member: D.C. Superior Court Advisory Committee on Civil Rules, 1978-2000; Judicial Conference of the District of Columbia, 1981-1992, 1998-1999; Member, Maryland Judicial Commission on Pro Bono, 1999-2000. *Member:* Montgomery County Bar Association; The District of Columbia Bar; Bar Association of the District of Columbia (Member, Board of Directors, 1984-1986); Maryland State Bar Association, Inc.; Trial Lawyers Association of Metropolitan Washington, D.C. (Vice President, 1977-1978; President, 1978-1979); Maryland Trial Lawyers Association; American Board of Trial Advocates (Advocate); The Counselors (President, 1989-1990); The Association of Trial Lawyers of America. Fellow, American College of Trial Lawyers. Certified as a Civil Trial Advocate by the National Board of Trial Advocacy. ***PRACTICE AREAS:*** Medical Malpractice; Personal Injury; Wrongful Death. ***Email:*** gemitchell@steinmitchell.com

ROBERT F. MUSE, born Boston, Massachusetts, July 24, 1947; admitted to bar, 1973, District of Columbia; 1982, Maryland; 1984, Massachusetts. *Education:* Boston College (B.S., 1969); Georgetown University (J.D., 1972). Law Clerk to Judge Frank J. Murray, U.S. District Court, Boston, Massachusetts, 1972-1973. Instructor, Trial Practice, Continuing Legal Education Program, District of Columbia Bar Association, 1978-1990. Adjunct Professor, Trial Practice and Congressional Investigations, Georgetown University Law Center, 1982-1985, 1997—. Instructor, Trial Advocacy, Harvard Law School, 1998—. Assistant Counsel, Select Committee on Presidential Campaign Activities, Senate Watergate Committee, U.S. Senate, 1973-1974. Staff Attorney, District of Columbia Public Defender Service, 1974-1979. Co-Chairperson, Criminal Practice Institute, District of Columbia Bar. Chairperson, Special Committee, Court Appointed Counsel Program in the Superior Court. Representative, Irish - Bloody Sunday Inquiry, International League of Human Rights. *Member:* Maryland State, Massachusetts and American Bar Associations; The District of Columbia Bar; The Association of Trial Lawyers of America. Fellow, American College of Trial Attorneys. ***Email:*** rmuse@steinmitchell.com

DAVID U. FIERST, born Washington, D.C., July 2, 1950; admitted to bar, 1975, District of Columbia; 1986, Maryland, U.S. District Court, District of Maryland including Trial Bar and U.S. District Court, District of Columbia. *Education:* University of Pennsylvania (B.A., 1972); George Washington University (J.D., 1975). Member, George Washington Law Review, 1973-1975. *Member:* The District of Columbia Bar; Maryland State Bar Association, Inc.; American Bar Association; The Association of Trial Lawyers of America; Maryland Trial Lawyers Association. ***REPORTED CASES:*** Midwest Radio Company v. Forum Publishing Company, 942 F.2d 1294 (8th cir. 1991); Moore v. Office of Personnel Management, 113 F.3d 216 (Fed. Cir. 1997); In the matter of Echlin Manufacturing Company, 105 F.T.C. 410 (1985); Anselmo v. King 902 F.Supp. 273 (D.D.C. 1995); Anselmo v. King, 942 F.Supp. 44 (D.D.C. 1996); Carpet Group International v. Oriental Rug Importers Assoc., 227 F.3d 62 (3d Cir. 2000); Pirshor v. DPM, 234 F.3d 1378 (3d. Cir. 2000); In re Detrois Auto Dedius Association, 955 F.2d 457 (6th Cir. 1992). ***PRACTICE AREAS:*** General Civil Litigation; Antitrust; Trade Regulation. ***Email:*** DFierst@Steinmitchell.com

RICHARD A. BUSSEY, born Cleveland, Ohio, December 16, 1950; admitted to bar, 1978, Georgia and District of Columbia; 1980, Virginia; 1981,

(This Listing Continued)

STEIN, MITCHELL & MEZINES, Washington—Continued

Maryland. *Education:* Ohio University (B.S.J., summa cum laude, 1972); Wake Forest University (J.D., cum laude, 1977). Phi Alpha Delta. *Member:* The District of Columbia Bar; State Bar of Georgia; Virginia State Bar; Maryland State Bar Association, Inc.; American Bar Association; The Association of Trial Lawyers of America. ***PRACTICE AREAS:*** Personal Injury; Civil Litigation.

PATRICK A. MALONE, born Lawrence, Kansas, December 12, 1951; admitted to bar, 1985, Maryland; 1986, District of Columbia and Virginia. *Education:* University of Kansas (B.A., summa cum laude, 1972); Yale University (J.D., 1984). Phi Beta Kappa; Harlan Fiske Stone Prize; C. LaRue Munson Prize; Potter Stewart Prize. Editor, Yale Law Journal, 1984. Law Clerk, Honorable Gerhard A. Gesell, U.S. District Court, District of Columbia, 1984-1985. Recipient, Lawyer of the Year, 1995, Trial Lawyers Association of Washington, D.C. Author: "You Have the Right to Remain Silent (Miranda After 20 Years)," The American Scholar, Summer 1986; "Failure to Diagnose Impending Heart Attack," 1 Am. Jur. Proof of Facts 3d. 691, 1988; "Discovery in Pharmaceutical Products Liability Cases," Trial, March 1996; "A Trial Lawyer Sings Psalms," Litigation, Summer 1997. Teaching Assistant, Legal Writing and Research, Yale Law School, 1983. *Member:* The District of Columbia Bar; Maryland State Bar Association, Inc.; Virginia State Bar; The Association of Trial Lawyers of America; Trial Lawyers Association of Metropolitan Washington, D. C. (Member, Board of Governors). ***REPORTED CASES:*** Benedi v. McNeil-PPC., Inc., 66 F.3d 1378 (4th Cir. 1995). ***PRACTICE AREAS:*** Civil Litigation; Medical Malpractice; Product Liability. ***Email:*** pmalone@steinmitchell.com

ROBERT L. BREDHOFF, born Washington, D.C., November 26, 1953; admitted to bar, 1981, District of Columbia; 1987, Maryland. *Education:* Princeton University (B.A., magna cum laude, 1975); Georgetown University (J.D., cum laude, 1980). Law Clerk to the Honorable James A. Belson, Associate Judge, District of Columbia Court of Appeals, 1980-1982; Assistant U.S. Attorney, U.S. Attorney's Office for the District of Columbia, 1982-1987. *Member:* The District of Columbia Bar; Maryland State Bar Association; The Association of Trial Lawyers of America. ***PRACTICE AREAS:*** Civil Litigation; Personal Injury; Criminal Law. ***Email:*** rbredhoff@steinmitchell.com

LAURIE A. AMELL, born Madison, Wisconsin, January 18, 1963; admitted to bar, 1992, Virginia; 1994, District of Columbia; 1998, Maryland. *Education:* Georgetown University (B.S.N., cum laude, 1986); George Mason University (J.D., 1991). Sigma Theta Tau; Phi Delta Phi. Registered Nurse, District of Columbia Board of Nursing, 1986. Author: "Medical Malpractice Review Panels- Time to Go," *The Journal,* VTLA, Summer 1991. Co-Author, With Robert T. Hall: "Review of the Virginia Birth-Related Neurological Injury Compensation Act," *The Journal,* VTLA, Winter 1991-1992. *Member:* Fairfax and American Bar Associations; Virginia State Bar; District of Columbia Bar; Maryland State Bar Association, Inc.; Trial Lawyers Association of District of Columbia (Member, Board of Governors, 1999); Virginia Trial Lawyers Association; Maryland Trial Lawyers Association; The Association of Trial Lawyers of America. ***PRACTICE AREAS:*** Medical Malpractice; Personal Injury; Tort Litigation. ***Email:*** lamell@steinmitchell.com

CHRISTOPHER H. MITCHELL, born Washington, D.C., February 13, 1962; admitted to bar, 1988, Pennsylvania and District of Columbia; 1992, Maryland. *Education:* Harvard University (B.A., 1984); Georgetown University (J.D., 1987). Law Clerk to the Honorable John H. Bayly, Jr., 1990-1991. *Member:* The District of Columbia Bar; Maryland Trial Lawyers Association; Maryland State Bar Association, Inc.; District of Columbia Trial Lawyers Association. ***Email:*** cmitchell@steinmitchell.com

ANDREW MICHAEL BEATO, born St. Louis, Missouri, June 18, 1969; admitted to bar, 1994, Maryland; 2000, District of Columbia. *Education:* Boston University (B.A., summa cum laude, 1991); American University (J.D., 1994). Phi Beta Kappa. Author: "Newly Independent and Separating States Succession to Treaties," 91 Am U. J. Int'l., L & Pol'y 525 (1994). *Member:* Maryland State and American Bar Associations; The District of Columbia Bar. ***PRACTICE AREAS:*** Antitrust; Trade Regulation. ***Email:*** abeato@steinmitchell.com

WILLIAM F. BURTON, born Detroit, Michigan, June 27, 1962; admitted to bar, 1991, Virginia, U.S. District Court, Eastern District of Virginia and U.S. Court of Appeals, Fourth Circuit; 1992, District of Columbia and U.S. District Court, District of Columbia; 1994, U.S. Court of Federal Claims; 1999, U.S. District Court, District of Maryland. *Education:* Miami University (B.A., 1984); Georgetown University (J.D., 1991). Adjunct Professor, Georgetown University Law Center, 2001—. *Member:* The District of Columbia Bar; Virginia State Bar; American Bar Association (Member, Sections on: Litigation; Tort and Insurance Practice); The Association of Trial Lawyers of America; Trial Lawyers Association of Metropolitan, Washington, D.C. ***PRACTICE AREAS:*** Civil Litigation; Business Litigation; Personal Injury Litigation. ***Email:*** wburton@steinmitchell.com

JOAN M. KIMMICH, born Washington, D.C., March 19, 1957; admitted to bar, 1991, Pennsylvania; 1992, Maryland and District of Columbia. *Education:* George Washington University (B.A., 1980); University of Maryland (M.Ed., 1983); George Washington University National Law Center (J.D., 1991). *Member:* The District of Columbia Bar; Maryland State, Pennsylvania State Bar and American Bar Associations. ***PRACTICE AREAS:*** Administrative Law; Antitrust; Trade Regulation; Civil Litigation.

OF COUNSEL

GEORGE A. FISHER, born Bronxville, New York, July 5, 1936; admitted to bar, 1961, District of Columbia. *Education:* Yale University (B.A., 1957); Georgetown University (LL.B., 1961). Co-author: Note, "The Insurable Interest of a Shareholder in his Corporation's Property and Key Men," 49 Georgetown L.J. 594. Court Law Clerk, U.S. Court of Appeals for the District of Columbia Circuit, 1961-1963. Clerk, U.S. Court of Appeals for the District of Columbia Circuit, 1976-1987. *Member:* The District of Columbia Bar; Bar Association of the District of Columbia; Federal and American Bar Associations; The Association of Trial Lawyers of America.

STEIN SHOSTAK SHOSTAK & O'HARA

A PROFESSIONAL CORPORATION

Established in 1933

SUITE 807, 1620 L STREET, N.W.
WASHINGTON, D.C. 20036-5605
Telephone: 202-223-6270
Telecopier: 202-659-4237
Email: tradelaw@steinshostak.com

Los Angeles, California Office: 515 South Figueroa Street, Suite 1200. Telephone: 213-486-0010. Fax: 213-486-0011.

San Diego, California Office: 2675 Customhouse Court, Suite B. Telephone: 619-661-6317. Fax: 619-661-1448.

Customs and International Trade Law. Practice before Federal Administrative Agencies. Trials and Appeals.

S. RICHARD SHOSTAK, born Omaha, Nebraska, July 16, 1931; admitted to bar, 1956, California, U.S. Circuit Court of Appeals, Ninth Circuit and U.S. District Court, Northern District of California; 1957, U.S. Customs Court; 1960, U.S. District Court, Central District of California, U.S. Court of Customs and Patent Appeals and U.S. Supreme Court; 1980, District of Columbia; 1980, U.S. Court of International Trade; 1982, U.S. Court of Appeals for the Federal Circuit. *Education:* Northwestern University and University of California at Berkeley (A.B., 1953); Boalt Hall School of Law, University of California (J.D., 1956). Phi Eta Sigma. Author: *Simplification of U.S. Customs Laws and Regulations,* Organizational Dynamics, Inc., 1979; "The Evolution of Item 807.00 of the Tariff Schedules of the United States and The Resulting Revolution of the Customs Laws," University of West Los Angeles Law Review, Vol. 12, 1980. Deputy District Attorney, Sonoma County, California, 1957-1959. Hearing Examiner, Civil Service Commission, City of Los Angeles, 1975-1982. Secretary, Committee for Production Sharing, 1976-1990. *Member:* Los Angeles County (Member, International Law Section, 1968—), Federal Circuit (Chair, Court of International Trade Appeals Committee, 1986-1987; Director, 1987-1990) and American (Member, International Law Section) Bar Associations; State Bar of California (Member, International Law Section); District of Columbia Bar; Wilshire Bar Association; Customs and International Trade Bar Association (Co-Chair, Special Committee on Trade Agreements, 1991-1993). ***PRACTICE AREAS:*** Customs Law; International Trade Law. ***Email:*** dshostak@steinshostak.com

JOSEPH P. COX, born Ellensburg, Washington, April 10, 1948; admitted to bar, 1977, California and U.S. District Court, Southern District of California; 1978, District of Columbia and U.S. Court of Customs and Patent Appeals; 1980, U.S. Customs Court and U.S. Court of International Trade; 1982, U.S. Court of Appeals for the Federal Circuit. *Education:* University of California at San Diego and University of California at Los Angeles (B.A., 1970); University of San Diego (J.D., 1977). Recipient: Marquardt Corporation Scholarship; Outstanding Achievement Award, U.S. Customs Service, Los Angeles, 1973. Air Security Officer, U.S. Customs Service, Los Angeles, 1970-1973. Inspector, U.S. Customs Service, San Ysidro, California, 1974-1977. Attorney: Penalties Branch, 1977, Commercial Fraud Penalties Branch, 1977-1979; Penalties Task Force, 1978 and Classification Branch, 1979, Office of Regulations and Rulings, U.S. Customs Service, Washington, D.C.; Office of Regional Counsel, U.S. Customs Service, Los Angeles, 1979-1980. *Member:* The District of Columbia Bar; Los Angeles County (Member, 1981—, Chair, 1984-1985 and 1992-1993, Customs Law Committee) and American (Member, Administrative Law Section; Vice-Chair, Customs and Tariffs Committee, 1985-1988) Bar Associations; State Bar of California (Member, International Law Section); Customs and International Trade Bar Association. ***PRACTICE AREAS:*** Customs Law; International Trade Law; Export Law. ***Email:*** jcox@steinshostak.com

BRUCE N. SHULMAN, born Washington, D.C., March 28, 1948; admitted to bar, 1975, District of Columbia; 1976, U.S. District Court for the District of Columbia and U.S. Court of Appeals, District of Columbia Circuit; 1977, U.S.

(This Listing Continued)

Court of Customs and Patent Appeals; 1977, U.S. Customs Court; 1982, U.S. Court of International Trade and U.S. Court of Appeals for the Federal Circuit. *Education:* George Washington University (B.A., 1970); Washington College of Law, American University (J.D., 1975). Attorney, Materials Classification Branch, 1976-1977, Freedom of Information and Privacy Branch, 1977-1978, Value Branch, 1978-1980 and 1983-1986, Commercial Fraud and Negligence Penalties Branch, 1978-1983 and Entry, Licensing and Restricted Merchandise Branch, 1987, Office of Regulations and Rulings, U.S. Customs Service, Washington, D.C. United States Delegate, Technical Committee on Customs Valuation, Customs Cooperation Council, 1983-1985. Advisor, U.S. Delegation, Committee on Customs Valuation, General Agreement on Tariffs and Trade, 1983-1986. Vice Chairman, Committee for Customs Automation Funding, 1998-2000. *Member:* The District of Columbia Bar; American Bar Association; Customs and International Trade Bar Association. [Staff Sergeant, USAR, 1971-1976]. (Resident). ***PRACTICE AREAS:*** Customs Law; International Trade Law; Export Licensing. ***Email:*** bshulman@dc.steinshostak.com

DAVID R. STEPP, born Statesville, North Carolina, September 8, 1961; admitted to bar, 1986, Georgia; 1987, California; 1988, U.S. Court of Appeals, Federal Circuit; 1989, U.S. Court of International Trade; 1990, District of Columbia. *Education:* Duke University (A.B., 1983); University of Georgia (J.D., 1986). Recipient, Dean Rusk Award for International law, 1985. Author: The 1984 "Country of Origin" Regulations for Textile Imports: Illegal Administration Action Under Domestic and International Law? 14 GA J. Int'l & Comp. L. 573 (1984). Co-author: "Criminal Customs Enforcement Among the U.S., Canada, and Mexico," 2 Indiana Int'l Comp. L. Rev. 337 (1992). *Member:* Los Angeles County Bar Association (Chair, Customs Law Committee, 1998-1999); State Bar of Georgia; State Bar of California; District of Columbia Bar; Washington Foreign Law Society (Member, Board of Directors, 1989-1997; President, 1996-1997). ***PRACTICE AREAS:*** Customs Law; International Trade Law. ***Email:*** dstepp@steinshostak.com

OF COUNSEL

SCOTT EDWARD ROSENOW, born Rochester, Minnesota, July 14, 1961; admitted to bar, 1988, Virginia; 1989, District of Columbia; 1991, U.S. Court of International Trade and U.S. Court of Appeals for the Federal Circuit. *Education:* University of Minnesota (B.A., 1984; J.D., 1988). Attorney, U.S. Customs Service, 1989-1992. *Member:* Virginia State Bar (Member, International Law Section); District of Columbia Bar; American Bar Association; Custom Lawyers Association. (Resident). ***PRACTICE AREAS:*** Customs Law; International Trade Law.

(For additional biographical data, see Professional Biographies at Los Angeles, California and San Diego, California)

STEPHENS LAW FIRM, PLLC

1029 VERMONT AVENUE, N.W., SUITE 400
WASHINGTON, D.C. 20005
Telephone: 202-331-8200

McLean, Virginia Office: 1800 Old Meadow Road. P.O. Box 1096. Telephone: 703-821-8700. Facsimile: 703-827-7761. Email: stelawfirm@aol.com

Nonprofit and Tax Exempt Organizations, Business, Corporate, Associations, Administrative and Federal Legislative Practice, Contracts, Commercial Law, General, Securities Law, Antitrust.

(For Complete Biographical Data on all Personnel, see Professional Biographies at McLean, Virginia)

STEPTOE & JOHNSON LLP

1330 CONNECTICUT AVENUE, N.W.
WASHINGTON, D.C. 20036
Telephone: 202-429-3000
Fax: 202-429-3902
Cable Address: "Stepjohn"
Email: kreddy@steptoe.com
URL: http://www.steptoe.com

Phoenix, Arizona Office: Collier Center, 201 East Washington Street, #1600, 85004. Telephone: 602-257-5200. Fax: 602-257-5299.

Los Angeles, California Office: 633 West Fifth Street, Suite 700, 90071. Telephone: 213-439-9400. Fax: 213-439-9599.

London, England Office: Steptoe & Johnson Rakisons, Clements House, 14/18 Gresham Street, EC2V 7JE. Telephone: +44 (0)20 7367 8000. Fax: +44 (0)20 7367 8001.

General Practice. Air and Surface Transportation, Alternative Dispute Resolution, Antitrust, Arbitration, Bankruptcy and Creditors Rights, Commercial Litigation, Corporate, Criminal Defense, Employment, Environment and Land Use, ERISA and Employee Benefits, Financial Services, Food and Drug, Government Contracts, Indian Affairs, Intellectual Property, Insurance Coverage Litigation, Insurance Law and Regulation, International Law, International Trade, Labor Standards, Legislative Advocacy, Oil Pipelines and Natural Gas Regulation, Products Liability, Real Estate, Reinsurance, Securities and SEC Enforcement, Space Commercialization, Tax, Technology and Electric Power, Telecommunications (domestic and international), Toxic Torts, Transactions, Trusts and Estates, Utility Finance.

The Firm of Steptoe & Johnson LLP, located in Washington, D.C., is no longer affiliated with the firm of Steptoe & Johnson with offices located in Clarksburg and Charleston, West Virginia.

MEMBERS

CALVIN H. COBB, JR., admitted to bar, 1950, District of Columbia and Maryland. *Education:* United States Naval Academy (B.S., with distinction, 1944); Georgetown University (LL.B., 1949). Leading Article Editor, Georgetown Law Journal, 1948-1949. ***PRACTICE AREAS:*** Corporate Planning, Transactions and Litigation; Securities. ***Email:*** ccobb@steptoe.com

MONROE LEIGH, admitted to bar, 1947, Virginia; 1948, District of Columbia. *Education:* Hampden-Sydney College (A.B., magna cum laude, 1940); University of Virginia (LL.B., 1947). Order of the Coif. Editor-in-Chief, Virginia Law Review, 1946-1947. ***PRACTICE AREAS:*** International Law; International Trade; Administrative Law; Arbitration. ***Email:*** mleigh@steptoe.com

RICHARD P. TAYLOR, admitted to bar, 1952, Virginia; 1956, District of Columbia. *Education:* Cornell University and University of Virginia (B.A., 1950); University of Virginia (LL.B., 1952). Order of the Coif. Book Review Editor, Virginia Law Review. Law Clerk to Judge Armistead M. Dobie, U.S. Court of Appeals, Fourth Circuit, 1952. ***PRACTICE AREAS:*** Administrative Law; Airport Law; Aviation Law; Transportation Law; Urban, State and Local Government Law; Legislative Advice. ***Email:*** rtaylor@steptoe.com

JOHN E. NOLAN, admitted to bar, 1955, District of Columbia; 1961, Maryland. *Education:* U.S. Naval Academy (B.S., 1950); Georgetown University (J.D., 1955). Associate Editor, Georgetown Law Journal, 1954-1955. Law Clerk to Justice Clark, U.S. Supreme Court, 1955-1956. ***Email:*** jnolan@steptoe.com

ROBERT D. WALLICK, admitted to bar, 1955, District of Columbia; 1961, Maryland. *Education:* Lehigh University (B.S., Elec. Eng., magna cum laude, 1948; B.S., Bus. Admin., magna cum laude, 1949); George Washington University (LL.B., 1955). Phi Beta Kappa; Order of the Coif. ***PRACTICE AREAS:*** Commercial Law; Construction Law; Contract Law; Government Contract Law; International Sales. ***Email:*** rwallick@steptoe.com

JAMES P. HOLDEN, admitted to bar, 1960, District of Columbia. *Education:* University of Colorado (B.S., 1953); Georgetown University (J.D., 1960). Member, Board of Editors, Georgetown University Law Journal, 1959-1960. ***PRACTICE AREAS:*** Tax Controversies. ***Email:*** jholden@steptoe.com

BETTY JO CHRISTIAN, admitted to bar, 1960, Texas; 1980, District of Columbia. *Education:* University of Texas (B.A., summa cum laude, 1957; LL.B., summa cum laude, 1960). Phi Beta Kappa; Order of the Coif; Chancellors. Articles Editor, Texas Law Review, 1959-1960. Law Clerk, Supreme Court of Texas, 1960-1961. ***PRACTICE AREAS:*** Transportation Law; Appellate Practice; Administrative Law; Railroad Law. ***Email:*** bchristi@steptoe.com

ROBERT E. JORDAN III, admitted to bar, 1962, District of Columbia; 1964, Virginia; 1998, California. *Education:* Massachusetts Institute of Technology (S.B., 1958); Harvard Law School (J.D., magna cum laude, 1961). Editor, Harvard Law Review, 1960-1961. ***PRACTICE AREAS:*** Antitrust; Energy Law; Litigation; Technology. ***Email:*** rjordan@steptoe.com

MATTHEW J. ZINN, admitted to bar, 1962, New York; 1963, District of Columbia. *Education:* University of Pennsylvania (B.S. in Econ. with honors, 1958); Harvard Law School (LL.B. magna cum laude, 1961). Beta Gamma Sigma; Beta Alpha Psi. Member, Harvard Law Review, 1959-1961. ***PRACTICE AREAS:*** Taxation Law, Federal Income Estate and Gift Taxation Law; Taxation of Individuals and Business Entities Law; Tax Controversies. ***Email:*** mzinn@steptoe.com

RICHARD H. WEISE, admitted to bar, 1962, Illinois; 1998, District of Columbia. *Education:* DePauw University (B.A., 1957); Northwestern/De Paul University (J.D., 1962). ***PRACTICE AREAS:*** Alternative Dispute Resolution; International; Litigation. ***Email:*** rweise@steptoe.com

ROBERT E. McLAUGHLIN, admitted to bar, 1965, District of Columbia; 1968, Virginia. *Education:* Iowa State University (B.S., 1960); Georgetown University (J.D., 1965). ***PRACTICE AREAS:*** Business Law; Corporate; Securities; Mergers and Acquisitions; Real Estate. ***Email:*** rmclaugh@steptoe.com

JAMES T. HALVERSON, admitted to bar, 1965, Minnesota; 1975, District of Columbia; 1976, New York; U.S. Supreme Court. *Education:* Harvard College (B.A., magna cum laude, 1962, Phi Beta Kappa); Harvard University (LL.B., cum laude, 1965). ***PRACTICE AREAS:*** Antitrust; Complex Litigation. ***Email:*** jhalvers@steptoe.com

MARTIN D. SCHNEIDERMAN, admitted to bar, 1967, District of Columbia. *Education:* Clark University (A.B., magna cum laude, 1963); Columbia Law School (LL.B., magna cum laude, 1966). Phi Beta Kappa. James Kent

(This Listing Continued)

STEPTOE & JOHNSON LLP, Washington—Continued

Scholar. Member, Columbia Law Review. ***PRACTICE AREAS:*** Labor and Employment; Government Contracts; Litigation; Transportation. ***Email:*** mschneid@steptoe.com

RICHARD O. CUNNINGHAM, admitted to bar, 1968, Maryland and District of Columbia. *Education:* George Washington University (A.B., with distinction, 1964; M.A., 1966; J.D., 1968). Phi Beta Kappa; Order of the Coif. Member, Editorial Board, George Washington Law Review, 1967-1968. ***PRACTICE AREAS:*** International Trade Law. ***Email:*** dhileman@steptoe.com

RICHARD H. PORTER, admitted to bar, 1968, District of Columbia. *Education:* Georgetown University (B.S.B.A., cum laude, 1964; J.D., cum laude, 1967). Member, Georgetown Law Review, 1966-1967. ***PRACTICE AREAS:*** Complex Civil Litigation; Reinsurance; Antitrust Law; Internal Corporate Investigations. ***Email:*** rporter@steptoe.com

SHELDON E. HOCHBERG, admitted to bar, 1968, New York; 1971, District of Columbia. *Education:* Columbia College (A.B., cum laude, 1964) Pulitzer Scholar; Harvard University (LL.B., cum laude, 1967). Member, Harvard Legal Aid Bureau, 1965-1966. ***PRACTICE AREAS:*** Administrative Law; International Law; Title Insurance Law. ***Email:*** shochber@steptoe.com

KENNETH I. JONSON, admitted to bar, 1968, Minnesota; 1975, District of Columbia. *Education:* University of Minnesota (B.A., 1965); University of Minnesota Law School (J.D., magna cum laude, 1968). Order of the Coif. Editor, Minnesota Law Review, 1967-1968. ***PRACTICE AREAS:*** Litigation. ***Email:*** kjonson@steptoe.com

J. A. BOUKNIGHT, JR., admitted to bar, 1968, North Carolina; 1973, District of Columbia. *Education:* Wofford College (A.B., 1965); Duke University (J.D., 1968). ***PRACTICE AREAS:*** Energy; Antitrust; Litigation. ***Email:*** jbouknig@steptoe.com

RONALD S. COOPER, admitted to bar, 1969, Georgia; 1972, District of Columbia. *Education:* University of Georgia (A.B., 1966); University of Georgia Law School (J.D., 1969). Phi Beta Kappa. Law Clerk to Judge Walter P. Gewin, U.S. Court of Appeals for the Fifth Circuit, 1969-1970. ***PRACTICE AREAS:*** Employment Discrimination Law; Employment Law; Age Discrimination; Wage and Hour Law; Defense Litigation. ***Email:*** rcooper@steptoe.com

TERENCE P. QUINN, admitted to bar, 1970, Virginia; 1972, District of Columbia; 1989, Arizona. *Education:* Iowa State University (B.S., 1961); American University (J.D., 1970). ***PRACTICE AREAS:*** Securities; Securities Offerings; Corporate Law; Acquisitions, Divestitures and Mergers Finance. ***Email:*** tquinn@steptoe.com

ROGER E. WARIN, born Des Moines, Iowa, June 14, 1945; admitted to bar, 1970, Nebraska; 1971, District of Columbia. *Education:* Creighton University (A.B., cum laude, 1967); Georgetown University (J.D., 1970). Law Clerk, Judge Oliver Gasch, U.S. District Court for the District of Columbia, 1970-1971. ***PRACTICE AREAS:*** Litigation; Legal Malpractice; Professional Liability; Federal Election Law; Intellectual Property Law; Insurance and Reinsurance. ***Email:*** rwarin@steptoe.com

F. MICHAEL KAIL, admitted to bar, 1972, Connecticut; 1973, District of Columbia. *Education:* Yale University (B.A., magna cum laude, 1967; Phi Beta Kappa); Oxford University, England (Certificate in Education, 1971); Yale Law School (LL.B., 1970). ***PRACTICE AREAS:*** Energy; Oil and Gas Pipelines; Litigation; Alternative Dispute Resolution. ***Email:*** mkail@steptoe.com

MARK J. SILVERMAN, admitted to bar, 1971, New York and District of Columbia. *Education:* Indiana University (B.S., 1967); Suffolk University (J.D., 1970); New York University (LL.M., in Taxation, 1971). Member, Suffolk University Law Review. Recipient, Harry J. Rudnick Memorial Award for Distinction in Taxation. ***PRACTICE AREAS:*** Taxation Law; Federal Income Estate and Gift Taxation Law; Taxation of Individuals and Business Entities Law. ***Email:*** msilverm@steptoe.com

WILLIAM KARAS, admitted to bar, 1972, Maryland; 1976, District of Columbia. *Education:* Columbia University (B.A., 1961); Harvard University and Rutgers University (J.D., 1970). ***PRACTICE AREAS:*** Aviation; Antitrust; Shipping; International Practice. ***Email:*** wkaras@steptoe.com

JOHN T. COLLINS, admitted to bar, 1972, Massachusetts; 1976, District of Columbia. *Education:* College of the Holy Cross (B.A., 1968); Georgetown University (J.D., 1971; LL.M., 1976). ***PRACTICE AREAS:*** Banking Law; Financial Institutions Law; Legislative Practice. ***Email:*** jcollins@steptoe.com

STEVEN H. BROSE, admitted to bar, 1973, District of Columbia. *Education:* Pennsylvania State University (B.A., 1969); Columbia University (J.D., 1972). Articles Editor, Columbia Law Review, 1971-1972. Law Clerk to Judge William H. Timbers, U.S. Court of Appeals, 2nd Circuit, 1972-1973. ***PRACTICE AREAS:*** Administrative Law; Energy Law; Oil and Gas Law; Public Utility Law; Pipeline Law. ***Email:*** sbrose@steptoe.com

ROBERT W. FLEISHMAN, admitted to bar, 1973, District of Columbia. *Education:* University of Kentucky (B.A., cum laude, 1967; Phi Beta Kappa); University of Michigan (J.D., cum laude, 1972). ***PRACTICE AREAS:*** Antitrust; Acquisitions, Divestitures, Mergers; Franchise Relations; International Business Law; Complex Litigation. ***Email:*** rfleishm@steptoe.com

HOWARD H. STAHL, admitted to bar, 1973, District of Columbia. *Education:* College of Charleston (B.S., 1969); Georgetown University (J.D., 1972). Law Clerk to Justice Samuel J. Roberts, Pennsylvania Supreme Court, 1972-1973. ***PRACTICE AREAS:*** Commercial Litigation. ***Email:*** hstahl@steptoe.com

W. GEORGE GRANDISON, admitted to bar, 1972, Connecticut; 1976, District of Columbia. *Education:* Tufts University and United States Military Academy (B.S., 1966); Yale Law School (J.D., 1972). [Capt., Office of the Judge Advocate General, International Affairs Division, U.S. Army, 1972-1976]. ***PRACTICE AREAS:*** International Trade Law. ***Email:*** wgrandis@steptoe.com

ARTHUR L. BAILEY, admitted to bar, 1972, District of Columbia. *Education:* Syracuse University (B.A., 1968); Washington College of Law of American University (J.D., 1972). ***PRACTICE AREAS:*** Insurance Taxation. ***Email:*** abailey@steptoe.com

HERBERT C. SHELLEY, admitted to bar, 1973, District of Columbia; 1985, Maryland. *Education:* Columbia College (B.A., 1969); Vanderbilt Law School (J.D., 1972); University of Brussels, Brussels, Belgium (LL.M., in International and Comparative Law, magna cum laude, 1973). Associate Articles and Research Editor, Vanderbilt Journal of Transnational Law, 1971-1972. ***PRACTICE AREAS:*** International Trade Law; Import and Export Law. ***Email:*** hshelley@steptoe.com

EDMUND W. BURKE, admitted to bar, 1973, District of Columbia; 1985, Texas. *Education:* Fordham University and Georgetown University (B.A., 1970); Georgetown University (J.D., 1973). ***Email:*** eburke@steptoe.com

MORGAN D. HODGSON, admitted to bar, 1973, District of Columbia. *Education:* Harvard University, Radcliffe College (A.B., cum laude, 1969); Stanford University (J.D., 1973). ***PRACTICE AREAS:*** Labor and Employment Law; Employee Benefits; Civil Litigation; Whistleblower Litigation. ***Email:*** mhodgson@steptoe.com

DOUGLAS G. GREEN, admitted to bar, 1973, District of Columbia. *Education:* Bowdoin College (B.A., cum laude, 1968); University of Virginia (M.A., 1969); Georgetown University (J.D., 1973). Editor, Georgetown University Law Journal, 1972-1973. ***PRACTICE AREAS:*** Energy; Antitrust; Litigation. ***Email:*** dgreen@steptoe.com

ELLEN D'ALELIO, admitted to bar, 1975, District of Columbia. *Education:* St. Mary's College (B.A., 1960); Universite de Caen, France and New York University (M.A., 1964); Harvard Law School (J.D., 1974). Fulbright Scholar. ***PRACTICE AREAS:*** Electronic Banking; Electronic Commerce; Banking; Banking Regulation; Corporate; Real Estate. ***Email:*** edalelio@steptoe.com

MARK F. HORNING, admitted to bar, 1975, District of Columbia. *Education:* Yale University (B.A., 1968); Yale Law School (J.D., 1974). ***PRACTICE AREAS:*** Antitrust; Insurance Regulatory Law; Class Actions; Constitutional and Appellate Litigation. ***Email:*** mhorning@steptoe.com

CHRISTOPHER T. LUTZ, admitted to bar, 1975, District of Columbia. *Education:* Princeton University (A.B., summa cum laude, 1971); Harvard University (J.D., cum laude, 1974). [Office of the Judge Advocate General of the Air Force, 1975]. ***PRACTICE AREAS:*** Litigation; Insurance Law; Employment Law. ***Email:*** clutz@steptoe.com

SAMUEL T. PERKINS, admitted to bar, 1975, District of Columbia. *Education:* Brown University (A.B., summa cum laude, 1967; Phi Beta Kappa); Yale University (J.D., 1974). Note and Comment Editor, Yale Law Journal, 1973-1974. ***PRACTICE AREAS:*** Oil and Gas Law; Energy Law; Environmental Regulation; Contract Law. ***Email:*** sperkins@steptoe.com

ELLEN M. McNAMARA, admitted to bar, 1975, Virginia; 1976, District of Columbia. *Education:* Douglass College (B.A., 1972, Phi Beta Kappa); University of Virginia (J.D., 1975). Order of the Coif. Member, 1973-1974 and Notes Editor, 1974-1975, Virginia Law Review. ***PRACTICE AREAS:*** Antitrust; Government Procurement. ***Email:*** emcnamara@steptoe.com

PAUL J. ONDRASIK, JR., admitted to bar, 1976, Pennsylvania; 1979, District of Columbia. *Education:* Princeton University (A.B., with distinction, 1972); University of Virginia (J.D., 1975). Order of the Coif. Member, 1973-1974 and Note Editor, 1974-1975, Virginia Law Review. Law Clerk to: Hon. Warren E. Burger, Chief Justice U.S. Supreme Court, 1976-1977; Hon. Collins J. Seitz, Chief Judge, U.S. Court of Appeals for the Third Circuit, 1975-1976. ***Email:*** pondrasi@steptoe.com

TOM COLLIER, admitted to bar, 1975, Mississippi; 1977, District of Columbia. *Education:* University of Virginia (B.A., 1972); University of Mississippi (J.D., with highest honors, 1975). Editor-in-chief, Miss. Law Journal. Law Clerk to Judge Charles Clark U.S. Court of Appeals for the Fifth Circuit, 1975-1976. ***PRACTICE AREAS:*** Settlement Advocacy; Risk Analysis; Natural Resources; Indian Law; Technology Law. ***Email:*** tcollier@steptoe.com

(This Listing Continued)

REID H. WEINGARTEN, admitted to bar, 1975, Pennsylvania; 1981, District of Columbia. *Education:* Cornell University (B.S., 1971); Hague Academy of International Law (1974) ; Dickinson Law School (J.D., 1975). ***PRACTICE AREAS:*** Criminal Law; Grand Jury Proceedings; Litigation; Professional Ethics and Discipline Law; Appellate Practice. ***Email:*** rweingar@steptoe.com

CHARLES C. READ, admitted to bar, 1975, California; 1983, District of Columbia; 1984, New York. *Education:* Harvard University (A.B., magna cum laude, 1971); University of California at Los Angeles (J.D., 1975). Member, UCLA Law Review, 1973-1975; Chief Comment Editor, 1974-1975. ***PRACTICE AREAS:*** Public Utility Law; Telecommunications Law; Energy Law; Business Litigation. ***Email:*** cread@steptoe.com

STEWART A. BAKER, admitted to bar, 1977, California; 1979, District of Columbia. *Education:* Brown University (A.B., 1970); University of California at Los Angeles (J.D., 1976). Recipient, Alumni Award for Academic Distinction. Chief Article Editor, UCLA Law, 1975-1976. Law Clerk to: Hon. Frank M. Coffin, Chief Judge, U.S. Court of Appeals, First Circuit, 1976-1977; Hon. John Paul Stevens, Associate Justice, Supreme Court of the United States, 1977-1978. ***PRACTICE AREAS:*** Technology Law; International Law. ***Email:*** sbaker@steptoe.com

CHARLES G. COLE, admitted to bar, 1976, District of Columbia. *Education:* Yale University (B.A., summa cum laude, 1973); Harvard University (J.D., magna cum laude, 1976). Recipient, Burton Award for Legal Writing, 2000. Law Clerk to: Justice Byron R. White, U.S. Supreme Court, 1977-1978; Judge Harold Leventhal, U.S. Court of Appeals for the District of Columbia, 1976-1977. ***PRACTICE AREAS:*** Pension and Profit Sharing Law; Administrative Law; Appellate Practice; Bankruptcy Law. ***Email:*** ccole@steptoe.com

SUSAN H. SERLING, admitted to bar, 1977, New York and District of Columbia. *Education:* Washington University (B.A., 1972); Columbia University (J.D., 1976); New York University (LL.M. in Taxation, 1979). Law Clerk to Judge Richard C. Wilbur, U.S. Tax Court, 1979. ***PRACTICE AREAS:*** Federal Income Taxation Law; Tax Controversies; Tax Procedure; Taxation of Individuals and Business Entities; Federal Tax Law. ***Email:*** sserling@steptoe.com

JOEL D. KAUFMAN, admitted to bar, 1976, Florida; 1977, District of Columbia. *Education:* Wharton School of Finance and Commerce, University of Pennsylvania (B.S., cum laude in Econ., 1972); Georgetown University Law Center (J.D., 1976). Staff Member, Law & Policy in International Business, Georgetown University Law Center, 1975-1976. ***PRACTICE AREAS:*** International Trade Law. ***Email:*** jkaufman@steptoe.com

FILIBERTO AGUSTI, admitted to bar, 1979, District of Columbia; 1991, New York. *Education:* University of Illinois (A.B., summa cum laude, 1974); Harvard University (J.D., 1977). Editor, Harvard Law Review, 1975-1977. Law Clerk to Judge William H. Timbers, U.S. Court of Appeals, Second Circuit, 1977-1978. ***Email:*** fagusti@steptoe.com

THOMAS P. BARLETTA, admitted to bar, 1977, California; 1979, District of Columbia. *Education:* Georgetown University (A.B., summa cum laude, 1973; Phi Beta Kappa); University of California at Berkeley (M.P.P., 1976; J.D., 1977). Order of the Coif. Member, University of California Law Review, 1976-1977. Law Clerk to Judge James R. Browning, Ninth Circuit Court of Appeals, 1977-1979. ***PRACTICE AREAS:*** Government Contracts. ***Email:*** tbarlett@steptoe.com

TIMOTHY M. WALSH, admitted to bar, 1977, Arizona; 1979, District of Columbia. *Education:* Stanford University (A.B., with distinction, 1974; Phi Beta Kappa); Yale University (J.D., 1977). ***Email:*** twalsh@steptoe.com

PETER L. WELLINGTON, admitted to bar, 1978, District of Columbia. *Education:* Harvard University (A.B., cum laude, 1971); University of Chicago (J.D., cum laude, 1977). Order of the Coif. Law Clerk to Hon. Frank A. Kaufman, U.S. District Judge, District of Maryland, 1977-1978. ***PRACTICE AREAS:*** Government Contract Law; Litigation. ***Email:*** pwelling@steptoe.com

OLIN L. WETHINGTON, admitted to bar, 1977, District of Columbia. *Education:* University of Pennsylvania (B.A., 1971; M.A., 1971); Harvard University (J.D., 1977). ***PRACTICE AREAS:*** International Business Law; Trade Regulation. ***Email:*** owething@steptoe.com

DARYL A. (SANDY) CHAMBLEE, admitted to bar, 1977, District of Columbia. *Education:* Georgetown University (B.S., cum laude, 1972); Catholic University of America (J.D., 1977). ***PRACTICE AREAS:*** Biotechnology; Health Care; Toxic Torts; Corporate Counseling; Civil Litigation. ***Email:*** schamble@steptoe.com

ANTHONY C. EPSTEIN, admitted to bar, 1978, District of Columbia; 1988, Maryland. *Education:* Yale College (B.A., summa cum laude, 1974); Yale Law School (J.D., 1977). Phi Beta Kappa. Law Clerk to Hon. Charles B. Renfrew, U.S. District Judge, Northern District of California, 1977-1978. ***PRACTICE AREAS:*** Antitrust; Telecommunications; Litigation. ***Email:*** aepstein@steptoe.com

STEPHEN A. FENNELL, admitted to bar, 1978, Pennsylvania; 1980, District of Columbia; 1987, Maryland. *Education:* University of Maryland (B.A., magna cum laude, 1974); Georgetown University (J.D., magna cum laude, 1978). Phi Beta Kappa. Editor, Georgetown Law Journal, 1977-1978. Law Clerk to Judge Edward S. Northrop, U.S. District Court for the District of Maryland, 1978-1979. ***PRACTICE AREAS:*** Litigation, Construction and Insurance Law. ***Email:*** sfennell@steptoe.com

SETH GOLDBERG, admitted to bar, 1978, District of Columbia; 1991, California. *Education:* State University of New York at Binghamton (B.A., 1975; Phi Beta Kappa); Stanford University (J.D., 1978). Editor, Stanford Law Review, 1977-1978. ***PRACTICE AREAS:*** Environmental Law; Pesticide Regulation; Administrative Law; Litigation. ***Email:*** sgoldberg@steptoe.com

SAMUEL M. SIPE, JR., admitted to bar, 1978, District of Columbia. *Education:* Princeton University (A.B., 1967); State University of New York at Buffalo (Ph.D., 1973); Yale University (J.D., 1978). ***PRACTICE AREAS:*** Antitrust Law; Railway/Railroad Law; Regulatory Law; Commercial Arbitration. ***Email:*** ssipe@steptoe.com

GARY A. MORGANS, admitted to bar, 1978, District of Columbia. *Education:* Trinity College (B.A., 1975); Georgetown University (J.D., 1978). ***PRACTICE AREAS:*** Energy Regulation; Electric Utility Law. ***Email:*** gmorgans@steptoe.com

ANNE E. MORAN, admitted to bar, 1978, District of Columbia; 1979, New York. *Education:* Wellesley College (B.A., 1975); Harvard University (J.D., 1978). Phi Beta Kappa. ***PRACTICE AREAS:*** Tax; Employee Benefits. ***Email:*** amoran@steptoe.com

J. WILLIAM KOEGEL, JR., admitted to bar, 1979, Ohio; 1980, District of Columbia; 1995, Virginia. *Education:* Northwestern University (B.A., cum laude, 1976); Boston College (J.D., cum laude, 1979). Articles Editor, Boston College Law Review, 1978-1979. Law Clerk to Hon. Anthony J. Celebrezze, U.S. Court of Appeals for the Sixth Circuit. 1979-1981. ***PRACTICE AREAS:*** Business Litigation; Commercial Litigation; Intellectual Property Litigation; Securities Litigation. ***Email:*** wkoegel@steptoe.com

STEVEN REED, admitted to bar, 1980, District of Columbia. *Education:* Harvard University (B.A., magna cum laude, 1974, Phi Beta Kappa; J.D., magna cum laude, 1979). Editor, Harvard Law Review. Law Clerk to Judge Levin H. Campbell, U.S. Court of Appeals for the First Circuit, 1979-1980. ***PRACTICE AREAS:*** Administrative Law; Energy Law; Natural Resources; Transportation; Oil and Gas Law. ***Email:*** sreed@steptoe.com

DANIEL C. SAULS, admitted to bar, 1980, District of Columbia and Georgia. *Education:* University of Virginia (B.A., with highest distinction, Phi Beta Kappa, 1976; J.D., 1979). Order of the Coif. Member, 1977-1978 and Articles Editor, 1978-1979, Virginia Law Review. Law Clerk to Hon. Collins J. Seitz, Chief Judge, U.S. Court of Appeals for the Third Circuit, 1979-1980. ***PRACTICE AREAS:*** Government Contracts; Health Care; Litigation; Construction Law; Insurance Coverage. ***Email:*** dsauls@steptoe.com

DAVID B. RASKIN, admitted to bar, 1979, District of Columbia. *Education:* University of Pennsylvania (B.A., 1976); Georgetown University (J.D., 1979). Topics Editor, American Criminal Law Review, 1978-1979. ***Email:*** draskin@steptoe.com

MELANIE F. NUSSDORF, admitted to bar, 1973, District of Columbia. *Education:* University of Pennsylvania (B.A., 1970); Georgetown University; New York University (J.D., 1973). ***PRACTICE AREAS:*** ERISA; Labor Law. ***Email:*** mnussdor@steptoe.com

PHILIP L. MALET, admitted to bar, 1979, Pennsylvania and District of Columbia. *Education:* University of Pennsylvania (B.S.E.E., cum laude, 1975); George Washington University (J.D., with honors, 1979). ***PRACTICE AREAS:*** Administrative Law; Communications Common Carrier; Cable T.V.; Consumer Fraud Law; Satellite Communications. ***Email:*** pmalet@steptoe.com

ANTONIA B. IANNIELLO, admitted to bar, 1980, District of Columbia. *Education:* Cornell University (B.A., 1975); Georgetown University (J.D., cum laude, 1980). Editor, Georgetown University Law Review. Law Clerk to Chief Judge James L. Latchum, U.S. District Court, District of Delaware, 1980-1982. ***PRACTICE AREAS:*** Insurance; Insurance Defense; Insurance Coverage; Malpractice Defense; RICO; Securities Litigation. ***Email:*** aianniel@steptoe.com

EDWARD J. KRAULAND, admitted to bar, 1980, District of Columbia. *Education:* Princeton University (A.B., cum laude, 1976); University of Michigan (J.D., cum laude, 1980). ***PRACTICE AREAS:*** Import Relief; Export Control; International Trade and Investment Regulatory Compliance; International Government Procurement; Immigration and Nationality Law; International Arbitration and Claims. ***Email:*** ekrauland@steptoe.com

J. WALKER JOHNSON, admitted to bar, 1978, Kansas; 1984, District of Columbia. *Education:* Cornell University (B.A., 1975); University of Kansas (J.D., 1978); Georgetown University (LL.M. in Taxation, 1984). Order of the Coif. Senior Articles Editor, Kansas Law Review, 1977-1978. ***PRACTICE AREAS:*** Federal Tax Law; Tax Controversies; Tax Procedure; Taxation; Taxation of Individuals and Business Entities. ***Email:*** wjohnson@steptoe.com

(This Listing Continued)

STEPTOE & JOHNSON LLP, Washington—Continued

ERIK L. KITCHEN, admitted to bar, 1979, District of Columbia. *Education:* Princeton University, Woodrow Wilson School of Public and International Affairs (B.A., magna cum laude, 1976; Phi Beta Kappa); Harvard University (J.D., cum laude, 1979). ***PRACTICE AREAS:*** Corporate Law; Government Investigations; Corporate Investigations; Foreign Corrupt Practices Act. ***Email:*** ekitchen@steptoe.com

MARK P. FITZSIMMONS, admitted to bar, 1980, Virginia; 1982, District of Columbia. *Education:* University of Vermont (B.A., magna cum laude, 1977); Northwestern University (J.D., cum laude, 1980). Articles Editor, Journal of Criminal Law and Criminology, 1979-1980. ***PRACTICE AREAS:*** Toxic Tort; Product Liability; Environmental; Civil Litigation. ***Email:*** mfitzsim@steptoe.com

SCOTT H. KATZMAN, admitted to bar, 1981, District of Columbia; 1993, New York. *Education:* Cornell University (B.S., 1978); Columbia University (J.D., 1981). ***PRACTICE AREAS:*** Business Law; Commercial Law; Corporate Transactions; Securities; Transactional Law. ***Email:*** skatzman@steptoe.com

KEVIN GOVER, admitted to bar, 1981, New Mexico; 1983, District of Columbia. *Education:* Princeton University (A.B., Public and International Affairs, 1978); University of New Mexico (J.D., cum laude, 1981). ***PRACTICE AREAS:*** American Indian Law; Administrative Law. ***Email:*** kgover@steptoe.com

STEVEN J. ROSS, admitted to bar, 1982, Texas; 1990, District of Columbia. *Education:* State University of New York at Binghamton (B.A., 1978); University of Houston (J.D., 1982). ***PRACTICE AREAS:*** Energy; Litigation. ***Email:*** sross@steptoe.com

JANE I. RYAN, admitted to bar, 1982, District of Columbia. *Education:* State University of New York at Geneseo (B.A., magna cum laude, 1974); George Washington University (J.D., with high honors, 1982). Order of the Coif. Articles Editor, George Washington Law Review, 1981-1982. ***PRACTICE AREAS:*** Energy; Litigation. ***Email:*** jryan@steptoe.com

JERALD S. HOWE JR., admitted to bar, 1983, District of Columbia. *Education:* Princeton University (A.B., magna cum laude, 1978; Phi Beta Kappa); Oxford University, Oxford, England (M.A., with honors, 1980); Harvard University (J.D., cum laude, 1983). Editor, Harvard Law Review, 1981-1983. Law Clerk to Judge George E. MacKinnon, U.S. Court of Appeals for the District of Columbia, 1983-1984. ***PRACTICE AREAS:*** Aerospace Law; Appellate Practice; Government Contract Law; Space Law. ***Email:*** jhowe@steptoe.com

VIRGINIA L. WHITE-MAHAFFEY, admitted to bar, 1983, District of Columbia. *Education:* Niagara University (B.A., summa cum laude, 1980; Delta Epsilon Sigma); Harvard University (J.D., 1983). ***PRACTICE AREAS:*** Appellate Practice; Environmental Insurance Coverage; Civil Litigation; Insurance Coverage. ***Email:*** vwhitema@steptoe.com

DAVID H. COBURN, admitted to bar, 1976, District of Columbia. *Education:* Brandeis University (B.A., magna cum laude, 1973); Georgetown University (J.D., 1976). Phi Beta Kappa. Member of Staff, 1974-1975 and Editor, 1975-1976, Law and Policy in International Business. ***PRACTICE AREAS:*** Administrative Law; Aviation Law; Transportation Law; Motor Carrier Law; Antitrust Law. ***Email:*** dcoburn@steptoe.com

ANTHONY J. LaROCCA, admitted to bar, 1984, District of Columbia. *Education:* University of Michigan (A.B., 1977); Harvard University (J.D., magna cum laude, 1984). ***PRACTICE AREAS:*** Antitrust Law; International Business Law; Economic Regulation. ***Email:*** alarocca@steptoe.com

ALFRED M. MAMLET, admitted to bar, 1984, California; 1985, District of Columbia. *Education:* Pomona College (B.A., 1981); Boalt Hall School of Law, University of California (J.D., 1984). Order of the Coif. Articles Editor, Industrial Relations Law Journal. ***PRACTICE AREAS:*** Communications Law; International Telecommunications; Computer Law. ***Email:*** amamlet@steptoe.com

STEVEN K. DAVIDSON, admitted to bar, 1985, Virginia; 1987, District of Columbia. *Education:* Boston University (B.A., summa cum laude, 1982; M.A., 1983); Northwestern University (J.D., 1985). Phi Beta Kappa; Mortar Board. ***PRACTICE AREAS:*** Civil Litigation; Commercial Litigation; White Collar Crime; Bankruptcy Law; Insurance Coverage. ***Email:*** sdavidso@steptoe.com

HARRY LEE, admitted to bar, 1986, Maryland; 1988, District of Columbia. *Education:* Georgia Institute of Technology (B.S., 1982); Catholic University of America (J.D., 1986). Member, Journal of Contemporary Health Law and Policy, 1985-1986. ***PRACTICE AREAS:*** Insurance Coverage; Complex Litigation; Professional Malpractice Law; Insurance Agents Errors and Omissions. ***Email:*** hlee@steptoe.com

MARK A. MORAN, admitted to bar, 1987, Michigan; 1988, District of Columbia. *Education:* University of Michigan (B.S., 1979; J.D., magna cum laude, 1986). Order of the Coif. ***PRACTICE AREAS:*** International Law; International Trade; International Arbitration. ***Email:*** mmoran@steptoe.com

THOMAS M. BARBA, admitted to bar, 1979, Pennsylvania; 1988, District of Columbia. *Education:* Temple University (B.A., 1976; J.D., 1979). ***PRACTICE AREAS:*** Litigation; Products Liability Law; Technology Law; Electronic Commerce. ***Email:*** tbarba@steptoe.com

WILLIAM T. HASSLER, admitted to bar, 1982, District of Columbia. *Education:* University of North Carolina-Chapel Hill (B.A., 1977); Yale University (J.D., 1980). Phi Beta Kappa. Law Clerk, Hon. Robert R. Merhige, Jr., 1980-1981. ***PRACTICE AREAS:*** Litigation; White Collar Criminal Matters; Environmental Law. ***Email:*** whassler@steptoe.com

LINDA S. STEIN, admitted to bar, 1983, District of Columbia. *Education:* Wellesley College (B.A., 1980; Phi Beta Kappa); Harvard University (J.D., cum laude, 1983). ***PRACTICE AREAS:*** Civil Litigation; Railroads; Energy; Environmental Litigation. ***Email:*** lstein@steptoe.com

CYNTHIA L. QUARTERMAN, admitted to bar, 1987, Missouri; 1989, District of Columbia. *Education:* Northwestern University (B.S., 1983); Columbia University (J.D., 1987). Charles Evans Hughes Scholar. Executive Editor, Columbia Journal of Environmental Law, 1986-1987. ***PRACTICE AREAS:*** Energy; Natural Resources; Environmental Law; Transportation; Administrative Law; Litigation. ***Email:*** cquarter@steptoe.com

RICHARD L. ROBERTS, admitted to bar, 1988, Maryland; 1991, District of Columbia. *Education:* Towson State University (B.S., 1984); University of Maryland (J.D., with honors, 1988). Member: Moot Court Board; National Moot Court Team. ***PRACTICE AREAS:*** Energy; Antitrust Law; Litigation. ***Email:*** rroberts@steptoe.com

MARK J. HULKOWER, admitted to bar, 1985, Pennsylvania; 1986, District of Columbia. *Education:* Cornell University (B.S., with honors, 1980); Georgetown University (J.D., magna cum laude, 1984). Editor, Georgetown Law Journal. Law Clerk, U.S. Court of Appeals, District of Columbia Circuit. ***PRACTICE AREAS:*** White Collar; Criminal Matters. ***Email:*** mhulkowe@steptoe.com

MARY ANN MANCINI, admitted to bar, 1984, Rhode Island; 1988, District of Columbia. *Education:* Washington College (B.A., 1980); Catholic University of America (J.D., 1984) ; Georgetown University (LL.M., Taxation, 1992). ***PRACTICE AREAS:*** Estate Planning; Estate & Trust Administration; Business Planning; Tax. ***Email:*** mmancini@steptoe.com

PANTELIS MICHALOPOULOS, admitted to bar, 1990, New York; 1996, District of Columbia. *Education:* The American College of Greece, Athens, Greece (B.S., highest distinction, 1987); The Law School of the National University of Athens, Greece (Diploma, 1988); University of Pennsylvania (LL.M., 1989). ***PRACTICE AREAS:*** Communications Law; Transportation Law; Regulatory Law; International Practice. ***Email:*** pmichalo@steptoe.com

STEVEN J. BARBER, admitted to bar, 1989, California; 1990, District of Columbia. *Education:* Brown University (B.A., magna cum laude, 1985); Harvard University (J.D., 1989). Executive Editor, Harvard Civil Rights-Civil Liberties Law Review, 1988-1989. ***PRACTICE AREAS:*** Commercial Litigation; Insurance; E-Commerce; Intellectual Property. ***Email:*** sbarber@steptoe.com

STUART T. F. HUANG, admitted to bar, 1989, Maryland; 1991, District of Columbia. *Education:* The Johns Hopkins University (B.E.S., 1978); University of Maryland (M.S.E.E., 1986); Washington College of Law of the American University (J.D., cum laude, 1989). ***PRACTICE AREAS:*** Intellectual Property. ***Email:*** shuang@steptoe.com

M. JEAN SCHLESINGER, admitted to bar, 1989, Virginia; 1991, District of Columbia. *Education:* American University (B.S., magna cum laude, 1986); Northwestern School of Law (J.D., 1989). ***PRACTICE AREAS:*** Surety Law; Litigation; Government Contracts. ***Email:*** jschlesi@steptoe.com

EDWARD R. MACKIEWICZ, admitted to bar, 1976, New Jersey; 1977, New York; 1978, District of Columbia; 1984, Maryland. *Education:* Yale University (B.A., magna cum laude, 1973); Columbia University (J.D., 1976). James Kent Scholar. Articles Editor, Columbia Journal of Transnational Law, 1975-1976. ***PRACTICE AREAS:*** Employee Benefits; Employment Law; Bankruptcy Law. ***Email:*** emackiew@steptoe.com

STEVEN B. TEPLINSKY, admitted to bar, 1983, Illinois; 1996, District of Columbia. *Education:* University of Michigan (A.B., highest honors, high distinction, 1980); University of Chicago (J.D., 1983). Associate Editor, University of Chicago Law Review, 1982-1983. Law Clerk to Hon. Charles L. Levin, Supreme Court of Michigan, 1983-1984. ***PRACTICE AREAS:*** Federal Income Tax. ***Email:*** steplins@steptoe.com

PETER LICHTENBAUM, admitted to bar, 1990, District of Columbia. *Education:* Princeton University (B.A., magna cum laude, 1986); Harvard University (J.D./M.P.P., cum laude, 1990). Phi Beta Kappa. ***LANGUAGES:*** French. ***PRACTICE AREAS:*** International Trade; International Law. ***Email:*** plichten@steptoe.com

CAROLINE GAUDET, admitted to bar, 1994, Virginia; 2000, District of Columbia. *Education:* London University (ext.; LL.B., 1975); College of Law,

(This Listing Continued)

Guildford, England; Georgetown University (LL.M., with distinction, 1993). Recipient, Annual Taxation Award, Research Institute of America. ***PRACTICE AREAS:*** Commercial Transactions; Commercial Real Estate. ***Email:*** cgaudet@steptoe.com

MATTHEW D. LERNER, admitted to bar, 1985, Maryland; 1986, District of Columbia. *Education:* Amherst College (A.B., 1982); Harvard University (J.D., magna cum laude, 1985). Phi Beta Kappa. Nelson Prize in Economics. Member, Harvard Law Review, 1983-1985. ***PRACTICE AREAS:*** Federal Tax Controversies; Tax Litigation; Criminal Taxation; Business Planning. ***Email:*** mlerner@steptoe.com

ERIC C. EMERSON, admitted to bar, 1991, Illinois; 1992, District of Columbia. *Education:* University of Iowa (B.A., 1986); University of Virginia (J.D., 1991). Phi Beta Kappa. ***PRACTICE AREAS:*** International Business Law; International Law. ***Email:*** eemerson@steptoe.com

SAVERY M. GRADOVILLE, admitted to bar, 1970, District of Columbia; 1971, Florida; 1981, Virginia. *Education:* Dunbarton College (B.A., summa cum laude, 1967); Georgetown University Law Center (J.D., 1970; LL.M., 1971). ***PRACTICE AREAS:*** Intellectual Property; Computer Law; Transactions; Licensing. ***Email:*** sgradoville@steptoe.com

KENNETH P. EWING, admitted to bar, 1991, Maryland; 1993, District of Columbia. *Education:* Yale University (B.A., cum laude, 1987); University of Michigan (J.D., cum laude, 1991). Associate and Contributing Editor, Michigan Law Review, 1989-1991. ***PRACTICE AREAS:*** Antitrust; International Law. ***Email:*** kewing@steptoe.com

CHRISTOPHER C. TAI, admitted to bar, 1987, California; 1989, District of Columbia. *Education:* University of California, Berkeley (A.B., 1982); Princeton University, Woodrow Wilson School of Public and International Affairs (M.P.A., 1987) Yale Law School (J.D., 1987). ***LANGUAGES:*** Mandarin Chinese. ***PRACTICE AREAS:*** Telecommunications; Commercial Transactions; Corporate; Corporate Finance; Joint Ventures; Strategic Alliances. ***Email:*** ctai@steptoe.com

RICHARD T. SAAS, admitted to bar, 1988, Tennessee; 1995, District of Columbia. *Education:* University of Tennessee (B.S., with highest honors, 1985; J.D., with high honors, 1988). Phi Kappa Phi. Articles Editor, Tennessee Law Review, 1986-1988. ***PRACTICE AREAS:*** Energy; Natural Resources; Utility Law. ***Email:*** rsaas@steptoe.com

STEVEN M. OSTER, admitted to bar, 1983, District of Columbia. *Education:* State University of New York at Albany (B.A., magna cum laude, 1980); Columbia University (J.D., 1983). Harlan Fiske Stone Scholar. ***PRACTICE AREAS:*** Administrative Law; Alternative Dispute Resolution; Business Transactions; Civil Litigation; Environmental, Natural Resources and Health and Safety; Toxic Tort Litigation. ***Email:*** soster@steptoe.com

OF COUNSEL

CECIL J. OLMSTEAD, admitted to bar, 1950, Georgia; 1978, District of Columbia. *Education:* University of Georgia (B.A., 1950; LL.B., 1951). Sterling Fellow, Yale Law School, 1951-1952. Recipient of LL.D. (Hon.) from Hull University, England, 1978. [1st Lt., USAF, 1943-1946]. ***PRACTICE AREAS:*** International Law; European Community Law; Law of the Sea; Economics Sanctions. ***Email:*** colmstea@steptoe.com

RICHARD DIAMOND, admitted to bar, 1974, District of Columbia. *Education:* Princeton University (A.B., magna cum laude, 1965); Yale University (M.A., 1971; LL.B., 1971). Law Clerk: Honorable Stanley A. Weigel, U.S. District Court, Northern District of California, 1971-1972; Honorable Warren E. Burger, Chief Justice of the United States, 1972-1973. ***Email:*** rdiamond@steptoe.com

KENNETH D. LUDWIG, admitted to bar, 1977, District of Columbia. *Education:* Haverford College (B.A., magna cum laude, 1972); Cambridge University, England (LL.B., 1975); Harvard University (J.D., 1976).

RICHARD A. WHITING, admitted to bar, 1950, District of Columbia. *Education:* Dartmouth College (A.B., cum laude, 1944); Yale University (LL.B., 1949). ***PRACTICE AREAS:*** Antitrust Law; Litigation; Trade Regulation Law. ***Email:*** whiting@srnet.com

STANLEY SMILACK, admitted to bar, 1974, New York; 1990, District of Columbia. *Education:* Massachusetts Institute of Technology (S.B., 1970); University of Michigan (J.D., cum laude, 1973). ***PRACTICE AREAS:*** Taxation. ***Email:*** ssmilack@steptoe.com

WILLIAM K. CONDRELL, admitted to bar, 1951, New York; 1964, District of Columbia. *Education:* Yale University (B.S., 1946); Massachusetts Institute of Technology (S.M., 1947); Harvard Law School (LL.B., 1950). ***PRACTICE AREAS:*** Public School Law; Individuals with Disabilities Education Act; Americans with Disabilities Act. ***Email:*** wkcondrell@condrell.org

SARA BETH WATSON, admitted to bar, 1985, Texas; 1988, District of Columbia. *Education:* Texas Christian University (B.S., magna cum laude, 1979); Southern Methodist University (J.D., cum laude, 1985). Order of the Coif. Notes and Comments Editor, Southwestern Law Journal, 1984-1985. Law Clerk to Hon. Will Garwood, U.S. Court of Appeals, Fifth Circuit, 1985-1986. ***PRACTICE AREAS:*** Chemical Regulation Law; Environmental Law; Food, Drug and Cosmetic Law; Hazardous Waste Law; OCC Safety and Health. ***Email:*** swatson@steptoe.com

CAROL A. MITCHELL, admitted to bar, 1983, District of Columbia. *Education:* Vassar College (A.B., with honors, 1979); Marshall-Wythe School of Law, College of William and Mary (J.D., 1982). Board of Editors, William & Mary Law Review. ***PRACTICE AREAS:*** International Trade and Customs Law. ***Email:*** cmitchel@steptoe.com

SCOTT A. HARMAN, admitted to bar, 1977, Vermont; 1978, District of Columbia; 1993, Maryland. *Education:* Middlebury College (B.A., 1973); University of Connecticut (J.D., 1977). ***PRACTICE AREAS:*** Energy; Business Transactions. ***Email:*** sharman@steptoe.com

JOSEPH E. STUBBS, admitted to bar, 1980, District of Columbia. *Education:* Michigan State University (B.S., with high honors, 1967, M.B.A., 1972); George Washington University (J.D., with high honors, 1979). Order of the Coif. ***PRACTICE AREAS:*** Energy Law; Regulatory Law. ***Email:*** jstubbs@steptoe.com

ERROL R. PATTERSON, admitted to bar, 1984, District of Columbia. *Education:* Purdue University (B.S.M.E., 1975); Georgetown University (J.D., 1984). Member, The District of Columbia Bar. ***Email:*** epatters@steptoe.com

ELLEN KOHN, admitted to bar, 1979, District of Columbia. *Education:* Brown University (B.A., 1976); University of Pennsylvania (J.D., cum laude, 1979). ***PRACTICE AREAS:*** Employee Benefits; ERISA. ***Email:*** ekohn@steptoe.com

JOHN J. DUFFY, admitted to bar, 1970, New York; 1973, District of Columbia. *Education:* Brown University (A.B., with honors, 1965); Cornell University (J.D., 1969). Notes and Comment Editor, Cornell Law Review, 1968-1969. ***PRACTICE AREAS:*** Natural Resources; Government Contract; Federal and State Election Law; Native American Law. ***Email:*** jduffy@steptoe.com

JAMES M. TALENS, admitted to bar, 1975, Pennsylvania; 1976, District of Columbia. *Education:* University of Pennsylvania (B.S.E.E., 1968); Temple University (M.B.A., 1972; J.D., 1975). ***LANGUAGES:*** Spanish. ***PRACTICE AREAS:*** Telecommunications; Communications; Wireless Communications; Satellite Communications. ***Email:*** jtalens@rcn.com

MARY WOODSON (MOLLY) POAG, admitted to bar, 1986, Texas; 1988, District of Columbia. *Education:* College of Charleston (B.A., magna cum laude, 1983); University of South Carolina (J.D., cum laude, 1986). Order of the Coif; Omicron Delta Kappa (Vice President); Sigma Alpha Phi; Pi Sigma Alpha. Articles Editor, University of South Carolina Law Review, 1985-1986. ***PRACTICE AREAS:*** Litigation; Environmental Insurance Litigation. ***Email:*** mpoag@steptoe.com

CAROLYN DOOZAN CLAYTON, admitted to bar, 1990, Virginia; 1991, District of Columbia. *Education:* University of Michigan (B.A., magna cum laude, 1970); George Mason University (J.D., with distinction, 1990). Phi Beta Kappa; Phi Kappa Phi. Notes Editor, George Mason Law Review, 1989-1990. ***LANGUAGES:*** French and Russian. ***PRACTICE AREAS:*** Transportation Law; Administrative Law. ***Email:*** cclayton@steptoe.com

ALICE ALEXANDRA KIPEL, admitted to bar, 1982, District of Columbia. *Education:* Princeton University (A.B., cum laude, 1979); Georgetown University Law Center (J.D., 1982). Staff Member, American Criminal Law Review, Georgetown University Law Center, 1981-1982. ***PRACTICE AREAS:*** International Trade Law; Customs Law; Import Law; Intellectual Property. ***Email:*** akipel@steptoe.com

THOMAS J. TRENDL, admitted to bar, 1988, Illinois; 1989, District of Columbia. *Education:* Illinois Wesleyan University (B.A., 1985); Georgetown University (LL.M. in International and Comparative Law, with distinction, 1989); University of Notre Dame, London Law Center, London, England; Southern Illinois University (J.D., 1988). Phi Alpha Delta. Associate Editor, Southern Illinois University Law Journal, 1987-1988. Jessup International Moot Court Team. ***PRACTICE AREAS:*** International Trade Law; Import and Export Law; Customs Law. ***Email:*** ttrendl@steptoe.com

JOHN L. JACOBUS, admitted to bar, 1989, New Jersey; 1990, District of Columbia; 1999, New York. *Education:* Harvard University (A.B., magna cum laude, 1986, Phi Beta Kappa; J.D., 1989). Senior Editor, Harvard Journal of Law and Public Policy, 1988-1989. Law Clerk, Hon. Maryanne Trump Barry, U.S.D.C., District of New Jersey, 1989-1991. ***REPORTED CASES:*** *Nixon v. United States, 978 F.2d 1269 (D.C. Cir. 1992); City of Benton v. NRC, 136 F.3d 824 (D.C. Cir. 1998); Szefczek v. Hillsborough Beacon, 286 N.J. Super. 242, 668A. 2d 1099 (Law Div. 1995).* ***PRACTICE AREAS:*** Civil Litigation; Antitrust. ***Email:*** jjacobus@steptoe.com

JENNIFER L. KEY, admitted to bar, 1991, Maryland; 1992, District of Columbia. *Education:* Dartmouth College (B.A., cum laude, 1986); George Washington University (J.D., with honors, 1991). ***PRACTICE AREAS:*** Energy Regulation. ***Email:*** jkey@steptoe.com

(This Listing Continued)

STEPTOE & JOHNSON LLP, Washington—Continued

DOUGLAS L. HILLEBOE, admitted to bar, 1983, California; 1985, District of Columbia; 1989, Texas. *Education:* Rice University (B.A., summa cum laude, 1980); University of Chicago (J.D., 1983). Phi Beta Kappa. ***PRACTICE AREAS:*** Antitrust; Litigation; International Trade. ***Email:*** dhilleboe@steptoe.com

JEFFREY F. PRYCE, admitted to bar, 1993, Pennsylvania; 1996, District of Columbia; 1999, U.S. Supreme Court. *Education:* Wesleyan University (B.A., 1982); Yale University (J.D., 1991); Cambridge University (M.Phil., 1986). Law Clerk to the Hon. Justice Byron R. White, 1991-1993. ***LANGUAGES:*** Spanish, French and German. ***PRACTICE AREAS:*** International Law; Electronic Commerce. ***Email:*** jpryce@steptoe.com

CAROL A. RHEES, admitted to bar, 1977, Virginia; 1980, District of Columbia. *Education:* Cornell University (A.B., 1973); University of Virginia (J.D., 1977). ***PRACTICE AREAS:*** Estate Planning. ***Email:*** crhees@steptoe.com

MAUREEN O'KEEFE WARD, admitted to bar, 1979, District of Columbia. *Education:* St. Louis University (B.A., summa cum laude, 1967); University of Chicago (J.D., cum laude, 1978). Order of the Coif. Comment Editor, University of Chicago Law Review, 1977-1978. Law Clerk to Judge Thomas Gibbs Gee, U.S. Court of Appeals, Fifth Circuit, 1978-1979. ***PRACTICE AREAS:*** Copyright; Computer Law; Technology Transfer; Trade Regulation Law; Trade Secrets Law; Trademarks. ***Email:*** mward@steptoe.com

DAVID L. ROLL, admitted to bar, 1965, Michigan; 1974, District of Columbia. *Education:* Amherst College (B.A., cum laude, Economics, 1962); University of Michigan (J.D., 1964). ***PRACTICE AREAS:*** Antitrust and Trade Regulation; Civil Trials; Complex Litigation; Energy Law; Government Regulation. ***Email:*** droll@steptoe.com

FREDERICK J. HORNE, admitted to bar, 1988, Massachusetts; 1989, District of Columbia. *Education:* Harvard University (A.B., cum laude, 1985); University of Michigan (J.D., cum laude, 1988). ***PRACTICE AREAS:*** Antitrust; Complex Litigation. ***Email:*** fjhorne@steptoe.com

ERIC G. SERRON, admitted to bar, 1985, Wisconsin and Minnesota; 1997, District of Columbia. *Education:* University of Wisconsin (B.A., 1979; M.A., 1983; J.D., 1984). Member, 1982-1983 and Note and Comment Editor, 1983-1984, Wisconsin Law Review. Law Clerk to the Hon. Barbara B. Crabb, U.S. District Court, Western District of Wisconsin, 1984-1985. ***PRACTICE AREAS:*** Employee Benefits. ***Email:*** eserron@steptoe.com

D. DOUGLAS PRICE, admitted to bar, 1968, District of Columbia. *Education:* University of Missouri (B.S. in Ch.E., 1965); George Washington University (J.D., with honors, 1968). Tau Beta Pi; Delta Theta Phi. ***PRACTICE AREAS:*** Intellectual Property Law; Chemical Patents; Mechanical Patents; Interference Law. ***Email:*** dprice@steptoe.com

SPECIAL COUNSEL

SUSAN G. BLUMENTHAL, admitted to bar, 1980, Virginia; 1988, District of Columbia; 1991, Maryland. *Education:* University of Michigan (B.A., with distinction, 1975); Case Western Reserve University (J.D., 1978). Member, Washington, D.C. Estate Planning Council, 1983—. ***PRACTICE AREAS:*** Estate Planning; Probate Administration; Trusts and Estates. ***Email:*** sblument@steptoe.com

DAVID A. CLARK, admitted to bar, 1991, Virginia (Not admitted in District of Columbia). *Education:* Virginia Polytechnic Institute and State University (B.A., 1988); Washington & Lee University (J.D., magna cum laude, 1991). ***PRACTICE AREAS:*** Litigation. ***Email:*** dclark@steptoe.com

JOHN FLYGER, admitted to bar, 1987, District of Columbia. *Education:* Macalester College (B.A., magna cum laude, 1983) Phi Beta Kappa; Duke University (J.D., 1987). Senior Editor, Law and Contemporary Problems, 1986-1987. ***PRACTICE AREAS:*** Litigation; Insurance Coverage. ***Email:*** jflyger@steptoe.com

HILDA A. MANUEL, admitted to bar, 1987, Arizona (Not admitted in District of Columbia). *Education:* University of California (B.A., 1972); University of New Mexico (J.D., 1976). ***PRACTICE AREAS:*** Natural Resources; Indian Law. ***Email:*** hmanuel@steptoe.com

MARCIA R. MITNICK, admitted to bar, 1982, District of Columbia. *Education:* University of Wisconsin (B.A., cum laude, 1974; M.A., 1976); Georgetown University (J.D., magna cum laude, 1982). Editor, Georgetown Law Journal. ***PRACTICE AREAS:*** Corporate; Securities; Technology Licensing. ***Email:*** mmitnick@steptoe.com

SHARON HYMAN SCHICK, admitted to bar, 1984, New York; 1987, District of Columbia. *Education:* State University of New York at Oneonta (B.A., 1980); Hofstra University (J.D., with distinction, 1983). Associate Editor, Hofstra Law Review, 1982-1983. ***PRACTICE AREAS:*** Intellectual Property. ***Email:*** sschick@steptoe.com

(This Listing Continued)

SCOTT D. WATKINS, admitted to bar, 1993, New York and U.S. District Court, Southern and Eastern Districts of New York; 1995, District of Columbia; registered to practice before U.S. Patent and Trademark Office. *Education:* Columbia University (B.S., Electrical Engineering, 1989); George Washington University (J.D., 1992). Eta Kappa Nu. (Public Service Counsel). ***PRACTICE AREAS:*** Intellectual Property. ***Email:*** swatkins@steptoe.com

BARBARA K. KAGAN, admitted to bar, 1978, District of Columbia. *Education:* Cornell University (B.A., 1975; J.D., 1978). (Public Service Counsel). ***Email:*** bkagan@steptoe.com

MATTHEW FRUMIN, admitted to bar, 1988, Maryland and District of Columbia. *Education:* University of Michigan (B.A., 1982); George Washington University, National Law Center (J.D., with high honors, 1988). Order of the Coif. Staff Member, George Washington University Law Review. ***PRACTICE AREAS:*** International Trade; International Arbitration; Litigation; Antitrust. ***Email:*** mfrumin@steptoe.co.n

ASSOCIATES

Benjamin R. Achenbach, Jr.
Aaron M. Altschuler
James C. Bailey
Robert A. Bailey (Not admitted in DC)
Alexandra E. P. Baj
Jean Male Baxley
Bruce C. Bishop
Michael A. Bishop
Mark A. Black (Not admitted in DC)
Amber Blaha
Rhonda M. Bolton
Yves Botteman
Stacey M. Brandenburg
Stephen C. Bullock
Jeffrey Scot Burk
George R. Calhoun, V
Stephanie Morris Carmody
Heather Doherty Clark
Gordon M. Clay
Carlynne S. Cockrum
Shannen W. Coffin
March Dolan Coleman (Not admitted in DC)
Thomas M. Contois
Troy Cribb (Trade Counsel)
Jody Allen Cummings (Not admitted in DC)
Evangeline de Gracia (Not admitted in DC)
Johnna Brooke Dumler
Elizabeth Johnson Dunaway (Not admitted in DC)
L. Benjamin Ederington
Jason H. Ehrenberg
James G. Ennis
Wm. Fletcher Fairey
Edward L. Froelich
Brooke L. Gaede
Kimberly A. Gates
Gary C. Geating
Susan Gihring
Tara R. Gingerich
Catherine M. Giovannoni
José Ramón González-Magaz
Carol R. Gosain
Kathleen M. Graber
Sean C. Griffin
Susan Harthill
Brian M. Heberlig
Andrew J. Hefty (Not admitted in DC)
Caroline J. Heller (Not admitted in DC)
Leslie R. Hoffman
Ryan Block Hotchkiss
Timothy K. Howard
Paul R. Hurst
Julie M. Jackson
Brian P. Kaufman (Not admitted in DC)
John J. Kavanagh, III (Not admitted in DC)
Tina Potuto Kimble
Jordan Lee Klingsberg
Galina V. Kolomietz
Stéphane Lagonico
Jessica B. Lang (Not admitted in DC)
Lindsey B. Lang
Todd Bradley Lantor
Margaret A. Lin
David S. Lorello (Not admitted in DC)
Alice E. Loughran
Shannon P. MacMichael
Gregory S. McCue
Patrick S. Menasco
Jacqueline Michaels (Not admitted in DC)
Scott Mirelson (admission pending)
Mary T. Mitchell
Kevin Brian Muhlendorf
Brian J. Newquist
Viet H. Ngo
Aaron P. Nocjar
Solomon J. Noh
John F. O'Connor Jr.
Marc A. Paul
Libretta A. Porta
Daniel J. Poynor
Gwendolyn Prothro
L. Matthew Quigley
Jennifer Quinn-Barabanov
Andrew William Racca
Timothy John Racicot
Gary E. Redente
James A. "Del" Renigar
Carrie Aleen Rhoads
David F. Rifkind
Luis R. Roselló
Melanie Jane Schneck
Andrew J. Sloniewsky
David D. Smyth, III (Not admitted in DC)
Mary J. R. Staley
Matthew L. Stennes
Ellen Hochstedler Steury
Lesley Stone
David N. Tanenbaum
Cynthia L. Taub
Stephanie A. Taylor
Brian J. Telpner
Shaun Leland Terrill
Lynn Ann Trujillo (Not admitted in DC)
Jamie D. Underwood
Richard R. Verma

(This Listing Continued)

ASSOCIATES (Continued)

Julie A. S. Vinyard
Richard M. Wartchow (Not admitted in DC)
Andrew J. Weinstein
Ripple L. Weistling
Gayle Weiswasser
Greg R. Yates
Matthew Yeo
Lisa M. Zarlenga

STERNE, KESSLER, GOLDSTEIN & FOX P.L.L.C.

Established in 1978

1100 NEW YORK AVENUE N.W.
WASHINGTON, D.C. 20005
Telephone: 202-371-2600
Fax: 202-371-2540
URL: http://www.skgf.com

Patent, Trademark, Copyright, Unfair Competition, Computer, Electronics, Biotechnology, Chemical, Interference, Alternative Dispute Resolution, Mechanical, Industrial Design, Internet, Related Litigation and Licensing.

FIRM PROFILE: Dedicated to the protection and enforcement of intellectual property rights, the law firm of Sterne, Kessler, Goldstein & Fox is recognized for its ability to meet the needs of clients working on the cutting edge of technology. The firm's professionals practice in a variety of areas, some of which are biotechnology, genomics and bioinformatics; information processing and e-commerce; medical device manufacturing and industrial design.

The firm's attorneys have experience in all aspects of domestic and foreign intellectual property law practice, including technology investigations and analyses (novelty, state-of-the-art, infringement, validity, registrability, clearance), procurement; enforcement (licensing, mediation, arbitration and litigation); and general client counseling relating to technology transfer, agreements, joint ventures, plant security and idea submission programs, corporation sponsored research contracts, university-industry relationships and government research funding.

Patent attorneys are registered to practice before the United States Patent and Trademark Office and the majority hold advanced degrees in engineering or science.

DIRECTORS OF FIRM

ROBERT GREENE STERNE, born Dallas, Texas, November 15, 1951; admitted to bar, 1977, Maryland; 1978, U.S. Claims Court; 1980, District of Columbia; 1982, U.S. District Court, District of Maryland; 1993, U.S. Court of Appeals for the Federal Circuit; registered to practice before U.S. Patent and Trademark Office. *Education:* Tufts University (B.S.E.E., 1973; M.S., 1975); University of Maryland (J.D., with honors, 1977); George Washington University. *Member:* Bar Association of Baltimore City; The District of Columbia Bar; Maryland State and American Bar Associations; American Intellectual Property Law Association (Member, Amicus Committee, 1994—; Co-Chairman, Institute on The Law of Computer Related Technology, 1984; Chairman, Institute on The Law of Computer Related Technology, 1988, 1992; Member, Legislative Initiatives Committee, 1988—; Member, The Ad Hoc Automation Advisory Committee to the PTO, 1984—; Member, Electronic and Computer Law Committee, 1977—); Computer Law Association; Maryland Patent Law Association. ***REPORTED CASES:*** In re Beauregard, 35 USPQ2d 1383 (Fed. Cir. 1995). ***PRACTICE AREAS:*** Intellectual Property Law.

EDWARD J. KESSLER, born Fall River, Massachusetts, June 3, 1943; admitted to bar, 1970, Virginia; 1970-1982, U.S. Court of Customs and Patent Appeals; 1978, District of Columbia; 1980, U.S. Supreme Court; 1982, Maryland and U.S Court of Appeals for the Federal Circuit; U.S. District Court for the District of Columbia, District of Maryland and Eastern District of Virginia; registered to practice before U.S. Patent and Trademark Office. *Education:* Washington University; George Washington University (B.S.E.E., with honors, 1967); George Washington University (J.D., 1970). Adjunct Professor of Law, George Mason University School of Law, 1996—. Member, Technical Advisory Committee on Computers in Education to the Maryland State Board of Education, 1985—. *Member:* The District of Columbia Bar; Virginia State Bar (Member, Patent, Trademark and Copyright Section); American Bar Association (Member: Section of Patent, Trademark and Copyright Law; Antitrust; Litigation; American Intellectual Property Law Association (Founding Co-Chair, Japanese Study Committee, 1989—); Maryland Patent Law Association; International Association for the Protection of Industrial Property. ***PRACTICE AREAS:*** Intellectual Property Law.

JORGE A. GOLDSTEIN, born Buenos Aires, Argentina, July 17, 1949; admitted to bar, 1983, District of Columbia, U.S. Claims Court and U.S. Court of Appeals for the Federal Circuit; registered to practice before U.S. Patent and Trademark Office. *Education:* Rensselaer Polytechnic Institute (B.S. in Chemistry, cum laude, 1971); Harvard University (Ph.D. in Chemistry, 1976); George Washington University (J.D., with high honors, 1982). Order of the Coif. *Member:* The District of Columbia Bar; American Bar Association (Member, Patent, Trademark and Copyright Section); American Intellectual Property Law Association (Member, Biotechnology Committee). ***LANGUAGES:*** Spanish, German and French. ***PRACTICE AREAS:*** Agrochemicals; Life Sciences; Technology Transfers; Biotechnology; Intellectual Property; Civil Litigation; Federal Litigation; International Litigation; Theft of Trade Secrets.

DAVID K.S. CORNWELL, born Portales, New Mexico, May 5, 1958; admitted to bar, 1983, New Mexico; 1988, U.S. Court of Appeals for the Federal Circuit; 1991, District of Columbia; registered to practice before U.S. Patent and Trademark Office. *Education:* University of New Mexico (B.S.M.E., 1980; J.D., 1983). Member, Advisory Board, University of New Mexico at Los Alamos, 1986-1987. *Member:* The District of Columbia Bar. ***PRACTICE AREAS:*** Litigation; Intellectual Property Law.

ROBERT W. ESMOND, born Baltimore City, Maryland, December 2, 1953; admitted to bar, 1989, District of Columbia; 1991, U.S. Court of Appeals for the Federal Circuit; registered to practice before U.S. Patent and Trademark Office. *Education:* University of Maryland (B.Sc., 1975); Northeastern University (Ph.D., 1981); University of Baltimore; George Washington University (J.D., 1989). *Member:* The District of Columbia Bar; Bar Association of the District of Columbia; The Court of Appeals for the Federal Circuit Bar; American Intellectual Property Law Association; American Chemical Society. ***PRACTICE AREAS:*** Intellectual Property Law.

TRACY-GENE GRAVELINE DURKIN, born Rhode Island, September 14, 1961; admitted to bar, 1989, District of Columbia; 1990, U.S. Court of Appeals, D.C. Circuit, U.S. Court of Appeals, Federal Circuit and U.S. District Court, District of Columbia; 1999, U.S. Supreme Court; registered to practice before U.S. Patent and Trademark Office. *Education:* Philadelphia College of Textiles and Science (B.S., 1983); George Washington University (J.D., 1989). *Member:* The District of Columbia Bar; AIPLA; Women's Bar Association of DC; National Association of Women Business Owners. ***PRACTICE AREAS:*** Intellectual Property Law; Mediation; Trademarks; Unfair Competition; Patents; Copyrights; Industrial Models and Designs; Medical Intellectual Property; Pharmaceutical Intellectual Property; Piracy; Protection of Personality.

MICHELE A. CIMBALA, born Pittsburgh, Pennsylvania, March 28, 1950; admitted to bar, 1991, Pennsylvania; 1992, District of Columbia; registered to practice before U.S. Patent and Trademark Office. *Education:* Pennsylvania State University (B.S., 1972); West Virginia University (Ph.D., 1977); George Washington University (J.D., 1991). Member: Professional Advisory Board, National Commission Entrepreneurship; American Association for the Advancement of Science; American Society of Biochemistry and Molecular Biology. *Member:* Pennsylvania, Federal Circuit and American Bar Associations; The District of Columbia Bar; American Intellectual Property Law Association. ***PRACTICE AREAS:*** Intellectual Property Law; Biotechnology Patents.

MICHAEL B. RAY, born Agana, Guam, March 15, 1964; admitted to bar, 1990, Maryland; 1992, District of Columbia; registered to practice before U.S. Patent and Trademark Office. *Education:* University of New Hampshire (B.S.E.E., 1986); Franklin Pierce Law Center (J.D., 1990). *Member:* The District of Columbia Bar; American Bar Association; American Intellectual Property Law Association. ***PRACTICE AREAS:*** Intellectual Property Law.

ROBERT E. SOKOHL, born Queens, New York, April 8, 1965; admitted to bar, 1991, District of Columbia and U.S. Court of Appeals for the Federal Circuit; registered to practice before U.S. Patent and Trademark Office. *Education:* Syracuse University (B.S.C.E., 1988); Washington College of Law of American University (J.D., 1991). *Member:* The District of Columbia Bar; American Intellectual Property Law Association. ***PRACTICE AREAS:*** Intellectual Property Law.

ERIC K. STEFFE, born Madison, Wisconsin, July 1, 1964; admitted to bar, 1994, District of Columbia; registered to practice before U.S. Patent and Trademark Office. *Education:* University of Georgia (B.S., Physics, 1986; M.S., Molecular Genetics, 1989); George Mason University School of Law, Patent Specialty Track (J.D., 1993). *Member:* The District of Columbia Bar (Member, Patent, Trademark and Copyright Section); American Intellectual Property Law Association. ***PRACTICE AREAS:*** Intellectual Property; Patent Licensing; Patent Infringement; Biochemical Patents; Biotechnology Patents; Molecular Biology Patents; Patent Litigation.

MICHAEL QUENTIN LEE, born Richmond, Virginia, January 8, 1962; admitted to bar, 1993, Pennsylvania and District of Columbia; registered to practice before U.S. Patent and Trademark Office. *Education:* University of Virginia (B.S.E.E., High Honors, 1984); University of Maryland (M.S.E.E., 1986); Georgetown University (J.D., cum laude, 1992). *Member:* The District of Columbia Bar; American Intellectual Property Law Association. ***PRACTICE AREAS:*** Intellectual Property Law.

STEVEN R. LUDWIG, born Reading, Pennsylvania, April 27, 1960; admitted to bar, 1995, District of Columbia; 1996, U.S. Court of Appeals for the Federal Circuit; 1999, U.S. Supreme Court; registered to practice before U.S. Patent and Trademark Office. *Education:* Pennsylvania State University (B.S.

(This Listing Continued)

STERNE, KESSLER, GOLDSTEIN & FOX P.L.L.C., Washington—Continued

Chemistry, 1982); University of Minnesota (M.S. Biochemistry, 1985; Ph.D. Biochemistry, 1987); George Washington University (J.D., 1995). *Member:* The District of Columbia Bar (Member, Intellectual Property Law Section); American Bar Association (Member, Sections on: Litigation; Intellectual Property Law); American Intellectual Property Law Association. ***PRACTICE AREAS:*** Intellectual Property Law; Interference Law; Litigation; Trade Secrets; Alternative Dispute Resolution; Licensing; Biotechnology; Chemistry; Pharmaceuticals; Food Science; Consumer Products; Plant Genetics.

LINDA E. ALCORN, born Washington, D.C., August 9, 1969; admitted to bar, 1994, District of Columbia; 1999, U.S. Court of Appeals for the Federal Circuit; 2000, U.S. Supreme Court; registered to practice before U.S. Patent and Trademark Office. *Education:* Cornell University (B.S., 1991); Boston University (J.D., 1994). *Member:* The District of Columbia Bar; American Bar Association; American Intellectual Property Law Association; Women's Bar Association. ***PRACTICE AREAS:*** Patent Litigation; Business Methods; Medical Devices; Consumer Products; Civil Appeals; Intellectual Property Litigation; Intellectual Property Portfolio Management; Intellectual Property Procurement; Mechanical Patents.

JOHN M. COVERT, born Philadelphia, Pennsylvania, July 24, 1963; admitted to bar, 1994, Pennsylvania; 2001, District of Columbia; registered to practice before U.S. Patent and Trademark Office. *Education:* St. Joseph's University (B.S., Chemistry, 1985); Lehigh University (M.S., Chemistry, 1987); George Mason University School of Law (J.D., with distinction, 1993). Patent Examiner, U.S. Patent and Trademark Office, 1988-1994. ***PRACTICE AREAS:*** Patent Law; Chemical Patent; Biotechnology.

SENIOR COUNSEL

SAMUEL L. FOX, born Salt Lake City, Utah, June 28, 1941; admitted to bar, 1967, District of Columbia; 1982, U.S. Claims Court; registered to practice before U.S. Patent and Trademark Office. *Education:* University of Maryland (B.S., 1963); George Washington University (LL.B., 1966). *Member:* The District of Columbia Bar; American Intellectual Property Law Association. ***PRACTICE AREAS:*** Intellectual Property Law.

ROBERT C. MILLONIG, born Perth Amboy, New Jersey, December 8, 1961; admitted to bar, 1994, District of Columbia; registered to practice before U.S. Patent and Trademark Office. *Education:* Manhattan College (B.S., cum laude, 1984); George Washington University National Law Center (J.D., with honors, 1994); Johns Hopkins University School of Medicine (Ph.D., 1990). Phi Beta Kappa; *Member:* The District of Columbia Bar; American Bar Association; American Intellectual Property Law Association. ***PRACTICE AREAS:*** Intellectual Property Law.

MICHAEL V. MESSINGER, born West Palm Beach, Florida, December 13, 1963; admitted to bar, 1995, District of Columbia. *Education:* Duke University (B.S., 1985); Georgetown University (J.D., 1995). *Member:* The District of Columbia Bar; American Intellectual Property Law Association; Giles S. Rich American Inns of Court. ***PRACTICE AREAS:*** Intellectual Property.

JUDITH U. KIM, born Seoul, South Korea; admitted to bar, 1995, Maryland; 1998, District of Columbia; registered to practice before U.S. Patent and Trademark Office. *Education:* University of Maryland (B.A., 1985; M.S., 1989; J.D., 1995). *Member:* American Bar Association; The District of Columbia Bar; American Intellectual Property Law Association; Women's Bar Association.. ***LANGUAGES:*** Korean. ***PRACTICE AREAS:*** Intellectual Property.

TIMOTHY J. SHEA, JR., born Washington, D.C., February 26, 1966; admitted to bar, 1995, Virginia; 1996, U.S. District Court, Eastern District of Virginia; 1997, District of Columbia; registered to practice before U.S. Patent and Trademark Office. *Education:* Washington and Lee University (B.S., Biology, 1988); Chicago-Kent College of Law (J.D., with high honors, 1995). Order of the Coif. *Member:* Virginia State Bar; The District of Columbia Bar. ***PRACTICE AREAS:*** Intellectual Property; Biotechnology; Patent Prosecution; Licensing.

PATRICK E. GARRETT, born New Jersey, December 15, 1962; admitted to bar, 1996, Maryland; 1998, District of Columbia; registered to practice before U.S. Patent and Trademark Office. *Education:* Widener University (B.S.E.E., 1985); University of Maryland (J.D., 1995). *Member:* Maryland State Bar Association, Inc.; District of Columbia Bar; American Intellectual Property Law Association. ***PRACTICE AREAS:*** Intellectual Property Law.

JEFFREY T. HELVEY, born Arlington, Virginia, March 22, 1965; admitted to bar, 1997, Texas (Not admitted in District of Columbia). *Education:* Pennsylvania State University (B.S.E.E., 1987); University of Texas at Arlington (M.S.E.E., 1993); University of Texas (J.D., 1996). *Member:* State Bar of Texas. ***PRACTICE AREAS:*** Patent Law. ***Email:*** jhelvey@skgf.com

(This Listing Continued)

HEIDI L. KRAUS, born Elkins Park, Pennsylvania, June 11, 1969; admitted to bar, 1997, Maryland; 1998, District of Columbia; registered to practice before U.S. Patent and Trademark Office. *Education:* Pennsylvania State University (B.S., 1991); George Washington University (J.D., 1997). Order of the Coif. *Member:* American Intellectual Property Law Association; Women's Bar Association. ***PRACTICE AREAS:*** Intellectual Property Law; Patent Prosecution; Life Sciences; Biomedical Technology; Pharmaceutical Intellectual Property; Intellectual Property Infringement; Chemical Intellectual Property. ***Email:*** hkraus@skgf.com

PATRICK D. O'BRIEN, born Columbus, Ohio, July 29, 1945; admitted to bar, 1997, Florida; 1998, Massachusetts, District of Columbia and U.S. Court of Appeals for the Federal Circuit; registered to practice before U.S. Patent and Trademark Office. *Education:* Virginia Military Institute (B.S., 1967); Air Force Institute of Technology (M.S., 1969); George Mason University School of Law (J.D., 1997). *Member:* The District of Columbia Bar; The Florida Bar; American Bar Association; American Intellectual Property Law Association; Armed Forces Communications and Electronics Association. [Col., Ret., USAF, 1967-1994]. ***PRACTICE AREAS:*** Intellectual Property Law. ***Email:*** pobrien@skgf.com

LAWRENCE B. BUGAISKY, born Chicago, Illinois, April 27, 1951; admitted to bar, 1998, District of Columbia; registered to practice before U.S. Patent and Trademark Office. *Education:* University of Illinois-Chicago (B.S., 1973; M.S., 1975); University of Chicago (Ph.D., 1980); American University, Washington College of Law (J.D., cum laude, 1997). Member: New York Academy of Sciences; American Society of Cell Biology. *Member:* The District of Columbia Bar; American Bar Association; American Intellectual Property Law Association. ***PRACTICE AREAS:*** Intellectual Property. ***Email:*** larryb@skgf.com

CRYSTAL D. SAYLES, born Washington, D.C., December 7, 1954; admitted to bar, 1998, Maryland; 2000, District of Columbia ; registered to practice before U.S. Patent and Trademark Office. *Education:* Boston University (B.S.E.E., 1978); Johns Hopkins University (M.S.E.E., 1983; M.S.C.S., 1985); American University, Washington College of Law (J.D., 1997). *Member:* Maryland State and American Bar Associations; The District of Columbia Bar; American Intellectual Property Law Association. ***PRACTICE AREAS:*** Intellectual Property. ***Email:*** csayles@skgf.com

EDWARD W. YEE, born Pittsburgh, Pennsylvania, October 18, 1957; admitted to bar, 1998, Maryland; 1999, District of Columbia; registered to practice before U.S. Patent and Trademark Office. *Education:* Yale University (B.A., 1980); Johns Hopkins University (M.S., 1988); University of Maryland (J.D., 1997). *Member:* Maryland State and American Bar Associations; The District of Columbia Bar; American Intellectual Property Law Association. ***PRACTICE AREAS:*** Patents. ***Email:*** eyee@skgf.com

ALBERT L. FERRO, born Baltimore, Maryland, February 9, 1966; admitted to bar, 1998, Maryland; registered to practice before U.S. Patent and Trademark Office (Not admitted in District of Columbia). *Education:* United States Naval Academy (B.S.A.E., with merit, 1988); University of Maryland (J.D., 1998). Tau Beta Pi; Order of the Coif. Professional Engineer, Connecticut, 1992-1994. [U.S. Navy, 1988-1993 (Active); 1993-1997 (Reserve) Lieutenant]. ***LANGUAGES:*** Spanish. ***PRACTICE AREAS:*** Patent Litigation; Patent Prosecution. ***Email:*** aferro@skgf.com

DONALD R. BANOWIT, born Washington, D.C., May 29, 1973; admitted to bar, 1998, Virginia, U.S. Court of Appeals, Fourth Circuit and U.S. District Court, Eastern District of Virginia; 1999, District of Columbia; registered to practice before U.S. Patent and Trademark Office. *Education:* University of Michigan (B.S.E., 1995); Georgetown University Law Center (J.D., 1998). *Member:* Virginia State Bar; The District of Columbia Bar. ***PRACTICE AREAS:*** Intellectual Property. ***Email:*** dbanowit@skgf.com

PETER A. JACKMAN, born Parma, Ohio, March 2, 1971; admitted to bar, 1998, Maryland; 1999, District of Columbia; registered to practice before U.S. Patent and Trademark Office. *Education:* Villanova University (B.S., 1993); Thomas Jefferson University (M.S., 1997); University of Baltimore (J.D., magna cum laude, 1998). Heuisler Honor Society. *Member:* Maryland State and American Bar Associations; The District of Columbia Bar; American Intellectual Property Law Association. ***PRACTICE AREAS:*** Intellectual Property Law. ***Email:*** pjackman@skgf.com

MOLLY A. McCALL, born Johnstown, Pennsylvania, April 10, 1963; admitted to bar, 1998, Pennsylvania; 1999, District of Columbia; registered to practice before U.S. Patent and Trademark Office. *Education:* University of Pittsburgh (B.S., magna cum laude, 1992; M.S., magna cum laude, 1994; J.D., 1998). *Member:* Pennsylvania State Bar; The District of Columbia Bar. ***PRACTICE AREAS:*** Intellectual Property Law. ***Email:*** mamcall@skgf.com

TERESA ULIVA MEDLER, born Rome, Italy, August 10, 1962; admitted to bar, 1998, Virginia and U.S. District Court, Eastern District of Virginia; 1999, District of Columbia and U.S. Court of Appeals for the District of Columbia Circuit; registered to practice before U.S. Patent and Trademark Office. *Education:* Clarkson University (B.S.M.E., 1984); George Washington University (J.D., 1998). *Member:* Virginia State Bar; The District of Columbia Bar; Ameri-

(This Listing Continued)

can Intellectual Property Law Association. ***PRACTICE AREAS:*** Patent Litigation; Patent Prosecution; Mechanical Patents; Design Patents; Coatings Technology; Medical Technology. ***Email:*** tmedler@skgf.com

JEFFREY S. WEAVER, born Alamogordo, New Mexico, July 6, 1966; admitted to bar, 1998, Maryland; 1999, District of Columbia; registered to practice before U.S. Patent and Trademark Office. *Education:* University of Illinois (B.S.E.E., 1988); University of Missouri, Rolla (M.S.E.E., 1991; M.S., Eng. Mgmt., 1992); University of Maryland (J.D., with honors, 1998). Phi Delta Phi. *Member:* Maryland State and American Bar Associations; The District of Columbia Bar; American Intellectual Property Law Association. ***PRACTICE AREAS:*** Intellectual Property. ***Email:*** jweaver@skgf.com

WILLIAM BRIAN EDGE, born Washington, D.C., August 28, 1970; admitted to bar, 1998, North Carolina (Not admitted in District of Columbia). *Education:* North Carolina Central University (B.S., Computer Science, 1993); Indiana University (J.D., 1998). *Member:* American Intellectual Property Law Association. ***PRACTICE AREAS:*** Intellectual Property. ***Email:*** bedge@skgf.com

KENDRICK PATTERSON, born Bainbridge, Georgia, June 5, 1966; admitted to bar, 1996, Maryland; 1999, District of Columbia; registered to practice before U.S. Patent and Trademark Office. *Education:* Georgia Institute of Technology (B.S.I.E., 1989); George Washington University (J.D., M.B.A., 1996). Phi Alpha Delta. Member, Institute of Industrial Engineers. *Member:* American Bar Association; American Intellectual Property Law Association. ***PRACTICE AREAS:*** Patent; Intellectual Property. ***Email:*** kpatters@skgf.com

DONALD J. FEATHERSTONE, born Lebanon, Pennsylvania, June 13, 1964; admitted to bar, 1999, District of Columbia; registered to practice before U.S. Patent and Trademark Office. *Education:* Lafayette College (B.S., Electrical Engineering); George Mason University (J.D.). *Member:* American Intellectual Property Law Association; Institute of Electrical and Electronics Engineers. ***PRACTICE AREAS:*** Intellectual Property Law. ***Email:*** donf@skgf.com

VINCENT L. CAPUANO, born Canton, Ohio, July 21, 1964; admitted to bar, 1999, District of Columbia; registered to practice before U.S. Patent and Trademark Office. *Education:* The Ohio State University (B.S., 1987); University of Texas (Ph.D., Organic Chemistry, 1991); University of Akron (J.D., 1999). *Member:* The District of Columbia Bar; American Intellectual Property Law Association. ***LANGUAGES:*** French. ***PRACTICE AREAS:*** Pharmaceutical Patent Procurement; Enforcement; FDA / ANDA. ***Email:*** vcapuano@skgf.com

JOHN A. HARROUN, born Baltimore, Maryland, April 24, 1969; admitted to bar, 1999, Maryland; registered to practice before U.S. Patent and Trademark Office (Not admitted in District of Columbia). *Education:* Clemson University (B.S.E.E., 1991; M.S.E.E., 1993); University of Maryland (J.D., 1999). ***PRACTICE AREAS:*** Intellectual Property. ***Email:*** jharroun@skgf.com

ALBERT J. FASULO, II, born Middlesex, England, June 12, 1962; admitted to bar, 1997, Maryland; registered to practice before U.S. Patent and Trademark Office (Not admitted in District of Columbia). *Education:* Imperial College, University of London (B.S., 1983); Johns Hopkins University (M.S., 1989); University of Baltimore School of Law (J.D., 1997). *Member:* Maryland State Bar Association, Inc.; American Bar Association. ***PRACTICE AREAS:*** Patent Law. ***Email:*** afasulo@skgf.com

ELDORA ELLISON FLOYD, born Pittsburgh, Pennsylvania, October 23, 1966; admitted to bar, 1999, Maryland; registered to practice before U.S. Patent and Trademark Office (Not admitted in District of Columbia). *Education:* Haverford College (B.S., 1988); Cornell University (Ph.D., 1993); Georgetown University (J.D., 1999). Phi Kappa Phi. ARCO Science Scholar. Fellow: Cornell University and State University of New York *Member:* American and Maryland State Bar Associations. ***PRACTICE AREAS:*** Patent Law. ***Email:*** efloyd@skgf.com

W. RUSSELL SWINDELL, born Toms River, New Jersey, October 5, 1970; (admission pending); admitted to bar, 2000, District of Columbia. *Education:* University of Virginia (B.S., Physics, 1993; M.A., Physics, 1995); University of Baltimore (J.D., 1999). ***PRACTICE AREAS:*** Computer Law; Internet Law; Electrical Intellectual Property; Industrial Property; Intellectual Property Portfolio Management; Intellectual Property Licensing. ***Email:*** swindell@skgf.com

THOMAS C. FIALA, born Carmel, New York, October 25, 1967; admitted to bar, 1998, New York and District of Columbia; registered to practice before U.S. Patent and Trademark Office. *Education:* Rensselaer Polytechnic Institute (B.S., 1989); University of Connecticut School of Law (J.D., with high honors, 1997). *Member:* District of Columbia Bar; New York State and American Bar Associations. ***PRACTICE AREAS:*** Patent Law; Intellectual Property Law. ***Email:*** tfiala@skgf.com

BRIAN J. DEL BUONO, born Fayetteville, North Carolina, April 18, 1961; admitted to bar, 2000, Virginia, U.S. Court of Appeals for the Federal Circuit, U.S. Court of Appeals, Fourth Circuit; 2001, U.S. District Court, Eastern District of Virginia (Not admitted in District of Columbia). *Education:* Juniata

(This Listing Continued)

College (B.S., 1982); The Pennsylvania State University (M.S., 1985; Ph.D., 1987); Georgetown University (J.D., cum laude, 2000). Beta Beta Beta. *Member:* American and Virginia Bar Associations; American Intellectual Property Association. ***PRACTICE AREAS:*** Intellectual Property Law; Civil Appeals; Biotechnology; Life Sciences; Medical Technology; Drug and Medical Device Regulation; Patents. ***Email:*** briand@skgf.com

VIRGIL LEE BEASTON, born Wilmington, Delaware, October 22, 1963; admitted to bar, 2000, Virginia; registered to Practice before U.S. Patent and Trademark Office (Not admitted in District of Columbia). *Education:* Pennsylvania State University (B.S.E.E., 1991); Shippensburg University (B.S., 1991); George Washington University (M.S.E.E., 1996); George Mason University School of Law (J.D., with honors, 2000). *Member:* Virginia State Bar. [Capt., U.S. Army Reserves, 1986—. SP4, U.S. Army, 1982-1986.]. ***PRACTICE AREAS:*** Patent Applications; Patent Prosecution; Patent Infringement; Patent Litigation. ***Email:*** vbeaston@skgf.com

RYAN J. STAMPER, born Seattle, Washington, February 9, 1975; admitted to bar, 2000, Virginia (Not admitted in District of Columbia). *Education:* University of Virginia (B.S., 1997); George Washington University (J.D., 2000). *Member:* American Intellectual Property Law Association. ***PRACTICE AREAS:*** Intellectual Property. ***Email:*** rstamper@skgf.com

REGINALD LUCAS, born Hampton, Virginia, January 24, 1970; admitted to bar, 2001, Virginia; registered to Practice before U.S. Patent and Trademark Office (Not admitted in District of Columbia). *Education:* Old Dominion University (B.S., 1993); College of William & Mary (J.D., 2000). *Member:* American Intellectual Property Law Association. ***PRACTICE AREAS:*** Electrical Intellectual Property.

THEODORE A. WOOD, born Fayetteville, North Carolina, March 21, 1959; admitted to bar, 1999, District of Columbia. *Education:* North Carolina A & T State University (B.S.E.E., 1981); Northrop University (M.S.E.E., 1984); University of Dayton (J.D., 1998). Recipient, CALI Award for Patent Law. [Major, Air Force, 1981-1995. Lt. Colonel, U.S. Air Force Reserves, 1995—.]. ***PRACTICE AREAS:*** Intellectual Property; Patents. ***Email:*** twood@skgf.com

ELIZABETH J. HAANES, born Pontiac, Michigan, October 14, 1956; admitted to bar, 2001, District of Columbia. *Education:* University of Michigan (B.S., 1980); University of Minnesota (Ph.D., 1989); University of Colorado at Boulder (J.D., 2000). ***PRACTICE AREAS:*** Biotechnology Patents; Biotechnology Patent Prosecution; Patent Applications; Intellectual Property. ***Email:*** bhaanes@skgf.com

KIMBERLY N. REDDICK, born Queens, New York; admitted to bar, 1996, New Jersey; 1997, New York (Not admitted in District of Columbia). *Education:* Dartmouth College (B.A., 1992); George Washington University (J.D., 1996). *Member:* New York State and American Bar Associations; American Intellectual Property Law Association. ***PRACTICE AREAS:*** Trademarks; Patents; Copyrights. ***Email:*** kreddick@skgf.com

BRUCE EDWARD CHALKER, born Warren, Ohio, February 3, 1948; admitted to bar, 2001, District of Columbia. *Education:* University of Miami (B.S., summa cum laude, 1970; Ph.D., 1975); George Washington University (J.D., with honors, 2000). ***PRACTICE AREAS:*** Intellectual Property. ***Email:*** bchalker@skgf.com

JOSEPH S. OSTROFF, born Summit, New Jersey, September 18, 1972; admitted to bar, 1997, Virginia; 1998, New Jersey and District of Columbia; registered to practice before U.S. Patent and Trademark Office. *Education:* Cornell University (B.S., with distinction, 1994); George Washington University (J.D., with honors, 1997). ***PRACTICE AREAS:*** Patents; Chemical Patents; Biotechnology Patents; Patent Interference Practice; Pharmaceutical Patents. ***Email:*** jostroff@skgf.com

STEVENS, DAVIS, MILLER & MOSHER, L.L.P.

Established in 1930

1615 L STREET, N.W.
SUITE 850
WASHINGTON, D.C. 20036
Telephone: 202-408-5100; 202-785-0100
Fax: 202-408-5200; 202-408-5088
Email: sdmm@stevensdavis.com
URL: http://www.stevensdavis.com

Domestic and International Practice in the field of Intellectual Property Law, concentrating on: Patents, Trademarks, Copyrights and Trade Secrets. Patent, Trademark, Copyright and Unfair Competition Litigation before Federal and State Courts. Specialized Practice in Patent Interference Proceedings before the Board of Appeals and Patent Interferences and Practice before the Trademark Trial and Appeal Board. Intellectual Property Licensing. Computer and High-Technology Law. Biotechnology Law. Food and Drug Administration Law. Anti-Counterfeiting Enforcement Efforts before the U.S. Customs Service and Federal Courts. Due

(This Listing Continued)

STEVENS, DAVIS, MILLER & MOSHER, L.L.P., Washington—Continued

Diligence Practice emphasizing Intellectual Property in the context of Corporate Acquisitions, Audits, Mergers, Corporate Financing and Initial Public Offerings.

MEMBERS OF FIRM

JAMES E. LEDBETTER, born Clearwater, Florida, October 6, 1950; admitted to bar, 1977, Georgia; 1978, Virginia; U.S. District Court, Eastern District of Virginia; U.S. Court of Appeals for the Federal Circuit; registered to practice before U.S. Patent and Trademark Office (Not admitted in District of Columbia). *Education:* University of Florida (B.E.S., with high honors, 1973; J.D., with honors, 1976). *Member:* Virginia State Bar. ***PRACTICE AREAS:*** Patent Law; Electrical Patents; Mechanical Patents; Trademarks; Copyrights; Trademark Licensing; Intellectual Property. ***Email:*** ledbetter@stevensdavis.com

THOMAS P. PAVELKO, born Bayonne, New Jersey, February 12, 1949; admitted to bar, 1980, Virginia; 1982, District of Columbia and U.S. Court of Appeals, Fourth Circuit, U.S. Court of Appeals for the Federal Circuit; registered to practice before U.S. Patent and Trademark Office. *Education:* Newark College of Engineering (B.S.ChE., 1970); George Mason University (J.D., with honors, 1980). Law Clerk, U.S. Patent Office Board of Appeals, 1976. Primary Examiner, U.S. Patent Office, 1977-1983. Assistant Solicitor, U.S. Patent and Trademark Office, 1983-1984. ***PRACTICE AREAS:*** Chemical Patents; Mechanical Patents; Biotechnology Patents. ***Email:*** pavelko@stevensdavis.com

ANTHONY P. VENTURINO, born New York, New York, October 5, 1956; admitted to bar, 1987, New Jersey 1988, New York and U.S. Court of Appeals for the Federal Circuit; 1997, District of Columbia; registered to practice before U.S. Patent and Trademark Office. *Education:* Manhattan College (B.Ch.E., magna cum laude, 1978; M.Ch.E., 1979); George Washington University (J.D., with honors, 1987). Professional Engineer, New Jersey, 1983. Board Member, National Association of Patent Practitioners, 1997-2001. Member, Licensing Executives Society. ***PRACTICE AREAS:*** Patent Law; Trademark Law; Licensing; Litigation. ***Email:*** venturino@stevensdavis.com

BARTH X. DE ROSA, born Washington, D.C., July 30, 1955; admitted to bar, 1982, Georgia; 1987, District of Columbia. *Education:* St. Francis College; George Washington University (B.A., 1977); University of Georgia School of Law (J.D., 1982). *Member:* The District of Columbia Bar; State Bar of Georgia; American Bar Association; International Trademark Association, TEC-The Executive Committee. ***PRACTICE AREAS:*** Intellectual Property; Trademarks; Copyrights; Litigation; Mergers and Acquisitions; Corporate Finance; Initial Public Offerings; Licensing. ***Email:*** derosa@stevensdavis.com

OF COUNSEL

PETER PECKARSKY, born Milwaukee, Wisconsin, April 16, 1947; admitted to bar, 1977, Wisconsin; 1979, District of Columbia; 1982, U.S. Court of Claims, U.S. Court of Appeals, Ninth Circuit and U.S. Court of Appeals for the Federal Circuit; 1984, California; 1987, U.S. Supreme Court; registered to practice before U.S. Patent and Trademark Office. *Education:* Massachusetts Institute of Technology (S.B., Elec. Eng./S.B., Pol. Sci, 1969); Case Western Reserve University (J.D., 1977). *Member:* The Association of Trial Lawyers of America; American Intellectual Property Law Association. ***PRACTICE AREAS:*** Intellectual Property; Complex Litigation; Antitrust; Corporate Law; Fraud; RICO; Securities. ***Email:*** peckarsky@stevensdavis.com

CHRISTOPHER M. COLLINS, born Wilmington, Delaware, December 7, 1960; admitted to bar, 1988, Virginia (Not admitted in District of Columbia). *Education:* University of Virginia (B.A., cum laude, 1983); George Washington University Law School (J.D., 1988). (Also Practicing Individually, McLean, Virginia). ***PRACTICE AREAS:*** Intellectual Property. ***Email:*** collins@stevensdavis.com

FRANK SEVER, JR., born Stowe Township, Pennsylvania, March 12, 1939; admitted to bar, 1981, Virginia; 1989, District of Columbia. *Education:* University of Pittsburgh (B.Ch.E., 1969); George Mason University (J.D., 1980). Former U.S. Patent Office Examiner. ***PRACTICE AREAS:*** Intellectual Property. ***Email:*** sever@stevensdavis.com

RUTH MAE FINCH, born Baltimore, Maryland, December 21, 1952; admitted to bar, 1978, Maryland and U.S. District Court, District of Maryland; 1991, U.S. Court of Appeals for the Federal Circuit; 1994, U.S. Court of Appeals, Fourth Circuit (Not admitted in District of Columbia). *Education:* University of Maryland (B.A., with honors, 1974; M.A., with honors, 1979); George Washington University; University of Baltimore (J.D., with honors, cum laude, 1978). Assistant State's Attorney, Baltimore City State's Attorney's Office, 1979-1990. *Member:* Maryland Trial Lawyers Association. ***PRACTICE AREAS:*** Intellectual Property; Litigation. ***Email:*** finch@stevensdavis.com

CLIFFORD L. TAGER, born Cleveland, Ohio; admitted to bar, 1987, Pennsylvania; 1989, Connecticut; U.S. Court of Appeals for the Federal Circuit; U.S. District Court, District of Connecticut; registered to practice before U.S. Patent and Trademark Office (Not admitted in District of Columbia). *Education:* Cleveland State University, Fenn College of Engineering (B.E.E., 1983); George Washington University (J.D., 1987). Tau Beta Pi; Eta Kappa Nu. Participant: Giles Sutherland Rich Moot Court Competition; Jessup Cup International Law Moot Court Competition. Patent Examiner, U.S. Patent and Trademark Office, Washington, D.C., 1983-1984. With Banner, Birch, McKie & Beckett, Washington, D.C., 1984-1988. Patent Attorney, Schlumberger-Doll Research and United Technologies Corporation, 1988-1991. *Member:* American Bar Association; American Intellectual Property Law Association; Connecticut Patent Law Association. ***PRACTICE AREAS:*** Intellectual Property (100%); Patents; Trademarks; Copyrights; Trade Secrets. ***Email:*** tager@stevensdavis.com

ERIC P. ROBINS, born Red Bank, New Jersey, April 12, 1974; admitted to bar, 1999, Virginia; registered to practise before the U.S. Patent and Trademark Office (Not admitted in District of Columbia). *Education:* University of Virginia (B.A., 1996); George Mason University School of Law (J.D., 1999). ***PRACTICE AREAS:*** Patents; Trademarks; Copyright. ***Email:*** robins@stevensdavis.com

DAVID E. HERRON II, born Kansas City, Missouri, July 11, 1966; admitted to bar, 1992, Missouri; 1993, Kansas; registered to practice before U.S. Patent and Trademark Office (Not admitted in District of Columbia). *Education:* Kansas State University (B.S.M.E., 1989); University of Missouri at Kansas City (J.D., 1992). Assistant Patent Examiner, U.S. Patent and Trademark Office, 1999-2000. ***PRACTICE AREAS:*** Patent Prosecution; Electro-Mechanical Patents; Patent Litigation. ***Email:*** herron@stevensdavis.com

ASSOCIATES

STEVEN D. LUSTIG, born New York, New York, April 19, 1968; admitted to bar, 1995, New York and Connecticut; 1998, District of Columbia. *Education:* Brandeis University (B.A., 1990); Syracuse University (M.A., 1991; J.D., 1994). *Member:* The District of Columbia Bar. ***Email:*** lustig@stevensdavis.com

NOREEN O'HARA WELCH, admitted to bar, 1999, Maryland (Not admitted in District of Columbia). *Education:* Brooklyn College of the City University of New York (B.S.); University of Maryland (M.S., 1974; J.D., 1998); George Washington University (M.S.A., 1981; Ph.D, 1990). Member: Association for Computing Machinery; IEEE Computer Society. *Member:* American Bar Association; American Intellectual Property Law Association. ***Email:*** welch@stevensdavis.com

SCOTT W. GOODE, born Manchester, New Hampshire, March 12, 1966; admitted to bar, 1994, Illinois and U.S. District Court, Northern District of Illinois; 1995, Florida; 1996, Wisconsin, U.S. District Court, Western District of Wisconsin and U.S. Court of Appeals, Seventh Circuit (Not admitted in District of Columbia). *Education:* Emory University (B.A., 1988); Nova Southeastern University Law Center (J.D., 1993); The John Marshall Law School, (LL.M., Intellectual Property, 1996). *Member:* The Florida Bar; American Bar Association. ***PRACTICE AREAS:*** Trademark; Trademark Litigation; Unfair Competition; Copyright. ***Email:*** sgoode@stevensdavis.com

KAREN ANN SEKOWSKI, born New Brunswick, New Jersey, August 12, 1975; admitted to bar, 2000, Maryland (Not admitted in District of Columbia). *Education:* Colgate University (B.A., 1997); Catholic University of America (J.D., 2000). ***PRACTICE AREAS:*** Intellectual Property; Trademark Litigation; Unfair Competition; Copyrights; Litigation. ***Email:*** sekowski@stevendavis.com

References will be provided upon request.

STEWART AND STEWART

Established in 1958

SUITE 200, 2100 M STREET, N.W.

WASHINGTON, D.C. 20037-1207

Telephone: 202-785-4185

Telecopier: 202-466-1286; 466-1287; 466-1288

Email: general@stewartlaw.com

URL: http://www.stewartlaw.com

Charleroi, Belgium Correspondent Office: Boulevard Dewandre 13, B6000 Charleroi. Telephone: 011-32-7-132-5131. Fax: 011-32-7-132-3526. Email: spinoit.wese@brutele.be

Moscow, Russia Representative Office: Leninskiy Prospect, Dom 42, Corpus 1, Suite 1562, Moscow 117119. Telephone: 011-7-095-938-7775. Fax: 011-7-095-938-7388. Email: stewart@pol.ru

Kiev, Ukraine Representative Office: 15/35 Kreshehatik Street, Kiev 252001 Ukraine. Telephone: 011-380-44-228-3857. Fax: 011-380-44-228-3113. Email: stewartlaw@mail.ru

International Trade Law and Policy, including Administrative and Judicial Proceedings and Dispute Settlement on Import and Export Activity. Advice and Lobbying on Multilateral, Plurilateral and Bilateral Trade Agreements and Negotia-

(This Listing Continued)

tions, International Dispute Settlement Proceedings on Trade Agreement Issues, Customs Law Representation and Advocacy, International Transaction Law, Investment Law, Competition Law and Corporate Law.

FIRM PROFILE: The Firm was founded in 1958 by Eugene L. Stewart as a general practice firm but has devoted most of its energies since its founding to international trade and customs issues. Today, in addition to helping industries, individual companies, workers and governments deal with import and export issues of concern in the U.S. (customs classification, valuation, audits, disputes, antidumping, countervailing duty, safeguard/escape clause, market access abroad, standards, rules of origin, sanitary and phytosanitary matters, government procurement, export controls, foreign corrupt practices matters, compliance with economic sanctions, dispute settlement within regional and multilateral agreements including NAFTA and the WTO, lobbying on legislation, monitoring and providing input on bilateral, regional and multilateral negotiations and agreements), we are also helping clients with similar issues in countries in other parts of the world (including Mexico, Canada, the E.U., Australia, F.T.A.A. region, the C.I.S. region, Asia, Africa). We have broadened our agenda to include transactional issues and electronic commerce. The firm has an associate law office in Belgium to represent client interests within the E.U. It has a representative office in Moscow to support client interest within the Russian Federation, and a representative office in Kiev to support client interests in Ukraine. The firm has worked with a wide variety of clients--e.g., agriculture, horticulture, consumer products including electronic products and components, chemicals, metals, transportation equipment, industrial equipment, rubber products, auto parts, antifriction bearings, glass, coatings, textiles, housewares, and various service sectors.

EUGENE L. STEWART Founder (1920-1998).

MEMBERS OF FIRM

TERENCE P. STEWART, born Washington, D.C., June 30, 1948; admitted to bar, 1979, District of Columbia; 1980, U.S. District Court for the District of Columbia; U.S. Court of Appeals for the District of Columbia; U.S. Court of International Trade; U.S. Customs Court; U.S. Court of Customs and Patent Appeals; 1982, U.S. Court of Appeals for the Federal Circuit; 1983, U.S. Supreme Court; 1985, U.S. Court of Appeals, Third Circuit; 1987, U.S. Court of Appeals, Ninth and Eleventh Circuits. *Education:* College of the Holy Cross (B.A., magna cum laude, 1970); Harvard University (M.B.A., 1972); Georgetown University (J.D., magna cum laude, 1979). Adjunct Professor, Georgetown University Law Center, 1995—. Honorary Doctorate: Ukrainian Academy of Foreign Trade, December 1999; Institute of Europe, Russian Academy of Sciences, October 2000. Editor: "Handbook on WTO Trade Remedy Disputes: The First Six Years (1995-2000)," Transnational Publishers, Inc., Spring 2001; *The GATT Uruguay Round: A Negotiating History (1986-1994),* Vol. IV: The End Game (Part I), Kluwer Law International, 1999; "WTO (The World Trade Organization)—The Multilateral Trade Framework for the 21st Century and U.S. Implementing Legislation," American Bar Association, 1996; "The States and the WTO: A Summary," Stewart and Stewart, Washington, D.C., March 1995; "Export Practice: Customs and International Trade Law," Practising Law Institute, Spring, 1994, Supplement 1998; *The GATT Uruguay Round: A Negotiating History (1986-1992),* Kluwer Law & Taxation Publishers, Volumes I, II & III, 1993; "The Cattle Industry in America: Portrait of an Industry in Crisis," A Report prepared for Ranchers-Cattlemen Action Legal Fund by Stewart and Stewart, February 2000; "The Cattle Industry in America: Portrait of an Industry in Crisis-The View from Elected Officials," February 2000; "The American Cattle Industry in Crisis: Restoring Hope and Fairness to Rural America, Proposals by R-Calf., February 2000. Author: "United States Japan Economic Disputes: The Role of Antidumping and Countervailing Duty Laws," 16(3) Arizona Journal of International & Comparative Law, Fall, 1999; "Dealing with the Fallout of Foreign Economic Dislocations Under the Antidumping and Countervailing Duty Laws," Georgetown University Law Center's 13th Annual International Trade Update, December 10, 1998; "Unfair Trade Practices and the Integration Process of the American Continent—A Perspective from a U.S. Practitioner," The Institute of Legal Research of the National Autonomous University of Mexico and the Unit of International Trade Practices of the Ministry of Commerce (SECOFI), Mexico City, Mexico, July 9, 1998; "Why Anti-Dumping Laws Need Not Be Cloned After Competition Laws Nor Replaced by Such Laws," Centre for Applied Studies in International Negotiations Anti-Dumping and Competition Policy, Geneva, Switzerland, July 11-12, 1996; Chapter 2, "The Uruguay Round Agreements Act: An Overview of Major Issues and Potential Trouble Spots," in *The World Trade Organization—The Multilateral Trade Framework for the 21st Century and U.S. Implementing Legislation*, ABA Section of International Law and Practice, 1996; "Overview of the Uruguay Round of Trade Negotiations," Russian Chamber of Commerce and Industry Conference on GATT/WTO, October 1995; "The GATT, the WTO and the Uruguay Round Agreements Act: The Countervailing Duty Law and the Subsidies Code: A Domestic Counsel's Perspective," Practicing Law Institute Seminar, September 1995; "Recent Developments in Administrative Practice: A Practitioner's Perspective on Anticircumvention, Protective Orders and Verification," in *The Commerce Department Speaks on International Trade and Investment 1994,* Vol. II at 365-504, Practicing Law Institute, October 1994; "The Development of U.S. Anti-Circumvention Law," The 1994 International Trade Update, GULC Continuing Legal Education Seminar, June 1994; "Overview of the Uruguay Round of Trade Negotiations," Before State Conference on Ukraine's Accession to GATT and the World Trade Organization, May 1994; "The Important Function of Antidumping Laws," *International Economic Insights,* Institute for International Economics, Vol. IV No. 6 at 46-48 (Nov.-Dec. 1993); "Introduction and Overview," chapter in *The GATT Uruguay Round: A Negotiating History (1986-1992),* Vol. I at 1 - 123, Kluwer Law & Taxation Publishers, 1993 (also available as an offprint); *U.S. International Trade Performance and Outlook: Competitive Position in the Automotive, Aerospace, and Chemical and Pharmaceutical Sectors: Hearings Before the Subcomm. on Trade of the House Common Ways and Means,* 102d Cong., 2d Sess., at 659-667, (March 11, 23, 30, 31 & April 7, 1992) (Serial 102-91), 1991; "Administration of the Antidumping Law: A Difference Perspective" in *Down in the Dumps—Administration of the Unfair Trade Laws,* Brookings Institution, 1991; "The Administration of Justice—the Responsibility of Bench and Bar: Evaluating the Fairness of Litigation: Preliminary Injunctions in Unfair Trade Cases: A Need for Reassessment of Existing Practice," Fifth Annual Judicial Conference of the U.S. Court of International Trade, 1988; "Computerized Data in Trade Cases: Legal Issues and Practical Questions for a Domestic Participant," Practicing Law Institute, 1987; "Judicial Oversight—Relations Between the Court and the Agencies: Judicial Review of Commerce Department Determinations in Antidumping and Countervailing Duty Cases, Finality and Exhaustion: Agency Interpretation Out of Step With Judicial Precedent," Third Annual Judicial Conference of the U.S. Court of International Trade, 1986; "Identifying and Measuring Domestic Subsidies: A Framework," International Trade Workshop ILI and ABA Section on International Law and Practice, 1986. Co-Author: A. Dwyer, "Handbook on WTO Trade Remedy Disputes: The First Six Years (1995-2000)," Transnational Publishers, Inc., 2001; P. McDonough and M. Prado, "Opportunities in the WTO for Increased Liberalization of Goods: Making Sure the Rules Work for all and that Special Needs are Addressed," 24 Fordham Int'l L.J., No.1, April 2001; R. Woodings, "Distribution Services and the General Agreement on Trade in Services," International Provision of Services and Sale of Goods Conference, Salzburg, Austria, October 26-29, 2000; J. R. Cannon, Jr., E. P. Salonen and D.R. Nuxoll, "Trade and Cattle: How the System is Failing an Industry in Crisis," 9 Minnesota Journal of Global Trade No. 2, Summer 2000 (also available as an offprint); A. Karpel, "Review of the Dispute Settlement Understanding: Operation of Panels," 31 Law & Pol'y Int'l Bus. (Georgetown Univ.) 593 (Spring 2000); A. Dwyer, "Sunset Reviews of Antidumping and Countervailing Duty Measures—US Implementation of Uruguay Round Commitments," 32 Journal of World Trade 101, October 1998; *WTO Antidumping and Subsidy Agreements: A Practitioner's Guide to Sunset Reviews in Australia, Canada, the European Union, and United States,* Kluwer Law International, July 1998; D. Johanson, "A Nexus of Trade and the Environment: The Relationship Between the Cartagena Protocol on Biosafety and the SPS Agreement of the World Trade Organization," Agricultural Sanitary & Phytosanitary and Standards Report, July 2000; "Policy in Flux: The European Union's Laws on Agricultural Biotechnology and Their Effects on International Trade," 19th Annual American Agricultural Law Association Conference, Columbus, Ohio, October 24, 1998, in Agricultural Sanitary & Phytosanitary and Standards Report, December 1998, reprinted in 4 Drake Journal of Agricultural Law 1 (1999); "The SPS Agreement of the World Trade Organization and the International Trade of Dairy Products," presented at the 25th International Dairy Congress, Aarhus, Denmark, September 21, 1998, printed in Agricultural Sanitary & Phytosanitary and Standards Report, October 1998, reprinted in 54 Food and Drug Law Journal 55 (1999); "Legal Comments on the Proposed Biosafety Protocol: Will the SPS Agreement of the World Trade Organization Permit Precautionary Risk Decisions?" presented at 2d Annual Roundtable of the American Bar Association's Section on Natural Resources, Energy and Environmental Law, Washington, D.C., June 24, 1998; "The WTO Beef Hormone Dispute: An Analysis of the Appellate Body Decision," March 1998, reprinted in Journal of International Law & Policy, University of California at Davis, Spring 1999; "The SPS Agreement and International Organizations: The Roles of the Codex Alimentarius Commission, the International Plant Protection Convention, and the International Office of Epizootics," January 1998, reprinted in 26 Syracuse Journal of International Law and Commerce 27, Fall 1998; "The WTO Beef Hormone Decisions," November 1997; "The U.S. and E.U. Veterinary Equivalency Agreement," Agricultural Sanitary & Phytosanitary and Standards Report, June 1997; "The SPS Agreement of the World Trade Organization and Plant Pest Infections: A Case Study of the 1997 Mediterranean Fruit Fly Outbreak in Florida," Agricultural Sanitary & Phytosanitary and Standards Report, August 1997, reprinted in 14 American University International Law Review 1107, 1999; Mara M. Burr, "Trade and Domestic Protection of Endangered Species: Peaceful Coexistence or Continued Conflict? The Shrimp Turtle Dispute and the World Trade Organization," 23 William and Mary Environmental Law and Policy Review, No. 1, Fall, 1998; Mara M. Burr, "The WTO's First Two and a Half Years of Dispute Resolution," 23 N.C. Int'l. L. & Com. Req. Issue 3 (June 1998); Mara M. Burr, "The WTO Panel Process:

(This Listing Continued)

(This Listing Continued)

STEWART AND STEWART, Washington—Continued

An Evaluation of the First Three Years," 32 Int'l. Lawyer 709 (Fall 1998); T.C. Brightbill, "Some Heretical Observations on the Interaction of U.S. Trade and Competition Laws: A Defense of U.S. Antidumping and Countervailing Duties," 4 United States-Mexico Law Journal, 1996; "Trade Law and Competition Policy in Regional Trade Arrangements," 27 Law & Pol'y Int'l & Bus., 1996; A.G. Stephens, "The History, Intent, and Potential of the WTO Trade Dispute Provisions," Resolving International Trade Disputes—National and Multinational Solutions, GULC Continuing Education Seminar, November 1995; A. Holmer & G. Horlick, "Enacted and Rejected Amendments to the Antidumping Law: In Implementation or Contravention of the Antidumping Agreement?," *The International Lawyer,* Vol. 29, No. 2, Summer, 1995; A. Mirtchev, G. Litman & K. Bland, "Foreign Investment in Bulgaria," *Foreign Investment in Central & East Europe,* Transnational Juris Publications, Inc., April/May 1994; C.J. Callahan, "Dispute Settlement Mechanisms," chapter in *The GATT Uruguay Round: A Negotiating History* (1986-1992), Vol. II at 2663-2875, Kluwer Law & Taxation Publishers, 1993 (also available as an offprint); S.G. Markel & M.T. Kerwin, "Antidumping," chapter in *The GATT Uruguay Round: A Negotiating History* (1986-1992), Vol. II at 1383-1710, Kluwer Law & Taxation Publishers, 1993 (also available as an offprint); M.A. Brilliant, "Safeguards," chapter in *The GATT Uruguay Round: A Negotiating History* (1986-1992), Vol. II at 1711-1820, Kluwer Law & Taxation Publishers, 1993; M. L. Png, "*The Growth of Singapore, Malaysia and Indonesia,*" Georgia Journal of International and Comparative Law Vol. 23, No. 1, Spring 1993; M.E. Edozien, "*Towards A Truly Global Marketing Strategy: A Need to Consider Trade and Investment Opportunities in West Africa,*" North Carolina Journal of International Law and Commercial Regulation, Vol. 1, Winter 1992; D. Abellard, "*Labor Laws and Social Policies in the European Community After 1992,*" *Law and Policy International Business,* Vol. 23, No. 3, Spring 1992; M.E. Edozien, "Regulating Investments In North Africa," April 1992; M.E. Edozien, "Regulation Of Investments In Sub-Saharan Africa," February 1992; A. Dwyer, "Measuring Domestic Subsidies: Preferential Provision of Goods or Services and Other Domestic Subsidies," GULC Continuing Legal Education Seminar, 1991; D. Abellard, "*Merger Control in the European Community: The EC Regulation On the Control of Concentrations Between Undertakings and Implementing Guidelines,*" *Northwestern Journal of International Law & Business,* Vol. 11, No. 2, Fall 1990. Listed in International Who's Who of Trade and Customs Lawyers, 1998—. Member, Board of Directors, Libbey, Inc., 1997—. Member, Board of Directors and Member, Nominating Committee, Refugee Voices, 1993-1995. Member, Council for Business Education of the Chamber of Commerce and Industry of the Russian Federation. Technical Advisor to the Governmental Commission on Ukraine's GATT Accession (Gov't of Ukraine). Member: Scientific Council, Foreign Trade, Ukraine Economic Journal; Russian American Chamber of Commerce; American Society of International Law, 1993—; U.S.-Africa Chamber of Commerce (Member, 1992-1995; Board of Directors, 1992-1995; Vice President, 1994-1995); International Trade Commission Trial Lawyers Association, 1979-1999; Federal Bar Association, 1987. *Member:* District of Columbia Bar (Member, U.S. Court of Appeals for the Federal Circuit Committee, 1983-1984); Federal Circuit (Member, Board of Directors, 2001— Chairman, 2000— Co-Chair, 1997-1999; Member, Council of Advisors, U.S. Court of Appeals for the Federal Circuit, 1999—; Co-Chair, Court of International Trade and International Trade Commission Appeals Committee, 1997— Member, 1994—) and American (Member: Task Force on International Trade and Antitrust, 1995—; Section of International Law and Practice, 1982—; International Trade Committee Steering Group, 1994—; AD/CVD Law Working Group, Central and East European Law Initiative (CEELI), 1994-1995) Bar Associations; Customs and International Trade Bar Association (Member, 1980—; President, 1998-2000; Vice President, 1996-1998; Member: Board of Directors, 1990—; Chairman, International Trade Committee, 1990-1996 (formerly known as the Unfair Trade and Trade Adjustment Committee); Member, Customs and Tariff Committee, 1990-1996); U.S. Court of International Trade (Member: Advisory Committee on Jurisdiction, 2000— Advisory Committee on Rules, 1989—; Ex Officio Member, 1998—; President, 1993-1998; Member, 1989-1998; Chairman, Planning Committee, Sixth Annual Judicial Conference, 1989). ***PRACTICE AREAS:*** Antidumping; Countervailing Duties; Safeguard/Escape Clause; International Trade Regulation; International Trade; World Trade Organization; North American Free Trade Agreement; Dispute Settlement; FTAA; Agriculture; Textiles; Government Procurement; Services; TRIPs; TRIMs; Import and Export Law; Sanitary and Phytosanitary Issues (SPS); Subsidies; Competition; Trade Regulation; Customs Law; Corporate Law. ***Email:*** tstewart@stewartlaw.com

WESLEY K. CAINE, born Chicago, Illinois, May 17, 1942; admitted to bar, 1972, Illinois; 1973, U.S. Court of International Trade; 1974, U.S. Court of Appeals for the Federal Circuit; 1978, District of Columbia and U.S. Court of Appeals for the District of Columbia; U.S. District Court for the District of Columbia. *Education:* University of Illinois (B.S., 1964); Northern Illinois University (M.A., 1969); De Paul University (J.D., 1972); New York University (LL.M., 1973). Author: *The GATT Uruguay Round:* A Negotiating History (1986-1994), Vol. IV: The End Game (Part I): Customs Valuation, Kluwer Law International, 1999; "A Case For Repealing the Antidumping Provisions of the Tariff Act of 1930," 13 Law & Pol. in Int'l Bus., No. 3, p. 1, 1981. Adjunct Professor, Customs Law, Georgetown University Law Center, 1998—. Trial Attorney, Customs Section, Civil Division, U.S. Department of Justice, 1973-1977. *Member:* The District of Columbia Bar; Bar Association of the District of Columbia; Illinois State and American (Member, Sections on: Antitrust and Administrative Law) Bar Associations; Customs and International Trade Bar Association. ***PRACTICE AREAS:*** Customs Law; International Trade; International Trade Regulation; Import and Export Law; Antidumping; Subsidies and Countervailing Duties; U.S. Foreign Trade Zones. ***Email:*** wcaine@stewartlaw.com

WILLIAM A. FENNELL, born Upper Darby, Pennsylvania, September 1, 1948; admitted to bar, 1977, Maryland; 1978, District of Columbia; 1988, U.S. Court of International Trade; 1989, U.S. Court of Appeals for the Federal Circuit and U.S. Claims Court. *Education:* Princeton University (A.B., 1970); Washington College of Law, American University (J.D., 1976). Author: "United States Trade Law Remedies: Our Defense Against the Visable Foot of Unfair Trade Practices," California International Practitioner (Vol. 11, No. 1, 2001). Co-Author: J.C. Ross and K.J. Thomson, *The GATT Negotiating History (1986-1992),* Vol. I, "Tropical Products," Kluwer Law & Taxation Publishers, 1993; J.W. Tyler, *The GATT Uruguay Round:* A Negotiating History (1986-1992), Vol. II, "Trade-Related Investment Measures ("TRIMs")," Kluwer Law & Taxation Publishers, 1993. Author: *The GATT Uruguay Round:* A Negotiating History (1986-1994), Vol. IV: The End Game (Part I), "Trade-Related Investment Measures ("TRIMs")," Kluwer Law International, 1999; "Practice Data Base Developers Plow New Ground," Legal Times, (March 12, 1986); "Data Base is Easily Tailored to Areas of Practice," Legal Times, (April 14, 1986); "Defining a Firm's Requirements," Of Counsel, (March 1986); "Graphically Speaking, Software Can Aid Litigator," Legal Times, (March 12, 1986); "Existing Wires May Serve Communications Needs," Legal Times, (February 10, 1986); "Amateurs Can Design Useful Legal Data Bases," Legal Times, (January 13, 1986); "Choosing a System: PC's or Mini?," Legal Times, (December 16, 1985); "Culture Shock: When Lawyers Hire Computer Folk," Legal Times, (November 18, 1985); "Future Holds Artificial Intelligence Uses in the Law," Legal Times, (October 21, 1985); "The Relational Data Base Management System," Of Counsel, (October 1985); "Rise of PC's Calls for Attention to Quality Control," Legal Times, (September 9, 1985), reprinted in Arthur Young International Newsletter for law firm consultants; "Computer Bids Help Avoid High-Tech Overload," Legal Times, (August 12, 1986), reprinted in Trial Magazine under title "An RFP Can Do Your Bidding," (December 1985); "Planning for Information Management," Of Counsel, (June 1985); "Lap-Top Computers Might Replace Yellow Pads," Legal Times, (April 8, 1985); "Data Processing: Major Automation Step for Firm," Legal Times, (March 11, 1985); "Semiconductor Laser Printers," Legal Times, (February 25, 1985); "Software Selection Varies With Attorneys' Needs," Legal Times, (January 14, 1985); "Linking Computers Is Easier Said Than Done," Legal Times, (December 17, 1984); "Computer Workstations Promise Diverse Uses," Legal Times, (November 12, 1984); "Automation Eases Substantive System Upkeep," Legal Times, (September 10, 1984); "Computer's Must Communicate—With Each Other," Legal Times, (July 2, 1984). Senior Research Computer Scientist, Federal Judicial Center, 1978, 1980-1982. *Member:* The District of Columbia Bar; Customs and International Trade Bar Association. ***PRACTICE AREAS:*** International Trade; International Trade Regulation; Import and Export Law; Antidumping; Export Regulation; North American Free Trade Agreement; Sanctions; Subsidies and Countervailing Duties; World Trade Organization (WTO); Computers and Software; Computer Law; Contracts; Information Technology; International; Software. ***Email:*** wfennell@stewartlaw.com

GEERT DE PREST, born Beernem, Belgium, May 28, 1954; admitted to bar, 1982, District of Columbia; 1990, U.S. Court of International Trade; 1993, U.S. Court of Appeals for the Federal Circuit. *Education:* Katholieke Universiteit, Leuven, Belgium (J.D., 1977); John Hopkins University, School for Advanced International Studies (M.A., 1979); George Washington University (M.C.L., 1981). Author: *The GATT Uruguay Round:* A Negotiating History (1986-1994), Vol. IV: The End Game, "GATT Articles," Kluwer Law International, 1999; *The GATT Uruguay Round:* A Negotiating History (1986-1992), Vol. II, GATT Articles, Kluwer Law & Taxation Publishers, 1993; "Exporting to the Countries of the European Communities; Special Issues," in Export Practice: Customs and International Trade Law, Practicing Law Institute, Spring 1994. *Member:* The District of Columbia Bar (Member, International Law Section); American Bar Association (International Law and Practice Section); Customs and International Trade Bar Association. ***LANGUAGES:*** Dutch and French. ***PRACTICE AREAS:*** International Trade; International Trade Regulation; Antidumping; European Union Law; Import and Export Law; Export Regulation; Countervailing Duty and Law. ***Email:*** gdeprest@stewartlaw.com

ALAN M. DUNN, born New Haven, Connecticut, February 16, 1953; admitted to bar, 1980, District of Columbia, U.S. Court of Appeals for the District of Columbia and U.S. Court of International Trade; 1981, U.S. District Court for the District of Columbia, U.S. Court of Appeals for the District of Columbia Circuit and U.S. Court of Appeals for the Federal Circuit; 1987, Virginia. *Education:* Washington & Lee University; George Mason University (B.S.,

(This Listing Continued)

1975); University of Virginia Law School (J.D., 1980); Academy of International Law, International Court of Justice, The Hague. Author: "Comparison and Analysis of Actions Under the Helms-Burton Act and D'Amato-Kennedy Act," Sanctions Unilaterales, Mondialisation du Commerce et Ordre Juridique International, University of Paris, Cedin-Paris X Naterre, Cahiers Internationaux, 1998; "Trading with Post Communist Societies: Strategic Issues With Non-Market Economies," Cold War Trade Laws: Responding to Revolution, ABA, Int'l Trade Committee, September 21, 1994. Contributing Author: "Strategic Guide to International Trade," Kogan Page, 1996; "Antidumping, in the World Trade Organization: Multilateral Trade Framework for the 21st Century and U.S. Implementing Legislation," American Bar Association, 1996; "Dumping, A Comparative Approach," Institute of International Business Law and Practice, 1995. Assistant Secretary, 1991-1993 and Deputy Assistant Secretary, 1989-1991, U.S. Department of Commerce. *Member:* District of Columbia Bar; Virginia and American (Member, Section on International Law) Bar Associations; Customs and International Trade Bar Association (Member, Judicial Selection Committee, 1997); Washington International Trade Association (Member, Council for Excellence in Government, 1993—). ***PRACTICE AREAS:*** International Trade. ***Email:*** adunn@stewartlaw.com

ASSOCIATES

DAVID S. JOHANSON, born Austin, Texas, February 25, 1964; admitted to bar, 1994, Pennsylvania; 1996, District of Columbia; 1997, U.S. Court of International Trade and U.S. Court of Appeals for the Federal Circuit. *Education:* Stanford University (B.A., 1987); Cambridge University (M.Phil., 1990); University of Texas (J.D., 1993). Co-Author: with William L. Bryant, "Eliminating Phytosanitary Trade Barriers: The Effects of the Uruguay Round Agreements on California Agricultural Exports," 6 San Joaquin Agricultural Law Review 1, 1996. Author: "Commentary on the Agreement on the Application of Sanitary and Phytosanitary Measures," in Law & Practice of the World Trade Organization, Oceana Publications, J. Dennin, ed., 1997. Co-Author: with Terence P. Stewart, "The U.S. and E.U. Veterinary Equivalency Agreement," Agricultural Sanitary & Phytosanitary and Standards Report, June 1997; with Terence P. Stewart, "The SPS Agreement of the World Trade Organization and Plant Pest Infestations: A Case Study of the 1997 Mediterranean Fruit Fly Outbreak in Florida," Agricultural Sanitary & Phytosanitary and Standards Report, August 1997, reprinted in 14 American University International Law Review 1107 (1999); with Terence P. Stewart, "The WTO Beef Hormone Decisions," Agricultural Sanitary & Phytosanitary and Standards Report, November 1997; with Terence P. Stewart, "The SPS Agreement of the World Trade Organization and International Organizations: The Roles of the Codex Alimentarius Commission, the International Plant Protection Convention, and the International Office of Epizootics," Agricultural Sanitary & Phytosanitary and Standards Report, January 1998, reprinted in 26 Syracuse Journal of International Law and Commerce 27 (1998); with Terence P. Stewart, "The WTO Beef Hormone Dispute: An Analysis of the Appellate Body Decision," Agricultural Sanitary & Phytosanitary and Standards Report, March 1998, reprinted in 5 Journal of International Law and Policy, University of California at Davis, 219 (1999); with Terence P. Stewart, "Legal Comments on the Proposed Biosafety Protocol: The SPS Agreement of the World Trade Organization Precautionary Risk Decisions" presented at 2nd Annual Roundtable on Biotechnology, Section on Natural Resources, Energy, and Environmental Law, American Bar Association, Washington, D.C., June 24, 1998; with Terence P. Stewart, "The SPS Agreement of the World Trade Organization and the International Trade of Dairy Products," presented by Terence P. Stewart at the 25th International Dairy Congress, Aarhus, Denmark, September 21, 1998, printed in Agricultural Sanitary & Phytosanitary and Standards Report, October 1998, reprinted in 54 Food and Drug Law Journal 55 (1999); with Terence P. Stewart, "Policy in Flux: The European Union's Laws on Agricultural Biotechnology and Their Effects on International Trade," Presented by Terence P. Stewart, 19th Annual American Agricultural Law Association Conference, Columbus, Ohio, October 24, 1998, in Agricultural Sanitary & Phytosanitary and Standards Report, December 1998, reprinted in 4 Drake Journal of Agricultural Law 243 (1999); with Thomas P. Redick, "The Biosafety Protocol: New International Biotechnology Agreement Provides Fodder for Legal Rumination," International Environmental Law Committee Newsletter, American Bar Association Section of Environment, Energy and Resources, March 2000, at 11; with Terence P. Stewart, "A Nexus of Trade and the Environment: The Relationship Between the Cartagena Protocol on Biosafety and the SPS Agreement of the World Trade Organization," Agricultural Sanitary & Phytosanitary and Standards Report, July 2000. Legislative Correspondent, Senator Phil Gramm (R-TX), 1988-1989; Legislative Assistant, Congressman Wally Herger (R-CA), 1993-1995; Legislative Director, Congressman George Radanovich (R-CA), 1995-1997. Member, Editorial Board, Agricultural Law Update. ***LANGUAGES:*** Spanish and French. ***PRACTICE AREAS:*** International Trade; International Agricultural and Food Regulation; International Environmental; World Trade Organization; Legislative. ***Email:*** djohanson@stewartlaw.com

DENNIS R. NUXOLL, born Wetzlar Hesse, Germany, June 13, 1973; admitted to bar, 1998, North Carolina; 1999, District of Columbia. *Education:* Duke University (B.A., 1995); University of North Carolina, Chapel Hill (J.D., 1998). Legislative Assistant, Office of Congressman Charlie Rose, 1993. Law Clerk, Cumberland County District Court, 1994. Special Assistant to the Deputy Director, North Carolina Department of Commerce, 1996. Legal Intern, Asia and the Pacific Section, Office of the U.S. Trade Representative, 1997; Civil Division, Commercial Litigation Branch, Department of Justice, 1997. Co-Author: with T. P. Stewart, Jr. R. Cannon, Jr. and E.P. Salonen, "Trade and Cattle: How the System is Failing an Industry in Crisis," 9 Minnesota Journal of Global Trade No. 2, Summer 2000. *Member:* North Carolina Bar Association; The District of Columbia Bar; Washington International Trade Association. ***LANGUAGES:*** German. ***PRACTICE AREAS:*** International Trade; Antidumping; Countervailing Duties; Administrative Law; Unfair Competition. ***Email:*** dnuxoll@stewartlaw.com

MARTA MARIA PRADO, born Miami, Florida, July 24, 1974; admitted to bar, 1999, Florida; 2000, U.S. Court of International Trade and U.S. Court of Appeals for the Circuit; 2001, District of Columbia. *Education:* Georgetown University (B.A., 1996; J.D., 1999). Co Author: T.P. Stewart and P.J. McDonough, "Opportunities In the WTO for Increased Liberalization of Goods: Making Sure the Rules Work for all and That Special Needs Are Addressed," 24 Fordham Int'l. L.J., No.1, April 2001. Member, Georgetown International Environmental Law Review, 1997-1999. *Member:* The Florida Bar; American Bar Association. ***LANGUAGES:*** Spanish. ***PRACTICE AREAS:*** International Trade; Antidumping; Countervailing Duties; World Trade Organization. ***Email:*** mprado@stewartlaw.com

AMY ANN KARPEL, born Springfield, Missouri, June 7, 1974; admitted to bar, 2000, New York and U.S. Court of International Trade, U.S. Court of Appeals for the Federal Circuit; 2001, District of Columbia. *Education:* University of Washington (B.A., cum laude, with honors, 1996); American University (J.D., cum laude, 1999). Phi Beta Kappa. Senior Articles Editor, American University Law Review, 1997-1999. Author: "The European Commission Decision on the Boeing-McDonnell Douglas Merger and the Need for Greater U.S.-EU Corporation in the Merger Field," 47 Am. U. L. Rev. 1029 (1998). Co-Author: T. Stewart, "Review of the Dispute Settlement Understanding: Operation of Panels," 31 Law & Pol'y Int'l Bus. (Georgetown Univ.) 593 (Spring 2000). *Member:* American Bar Association; Customs and International Trade Bar Association. ***LANGUAGES:*** German. ***PRACTICE AREAS:*** International Trade; Antidumping; Countervailing Duties; Unfair Trade; World Trade Organization. ***Email:*** akarpel@stewartlaw.com

OF COUNSEL

BERNARD SPINOIT, born Louvain, Belgium, February 8, 1954; admitted to bar, 1979, Belgium (Not admitted in the United States). *Education:* Université Catholique de Louvain (Ph.B., 1976; J.D., 1979; B.A., cum laude, Economics, 1980; M.A., cum laude, Economics, 1981); Georgetown University (LL.M., 1982); George Washington University (M.B.A., 1982). Phi Alpha Delta. Fulbright Scholar. Co-Authored with Alexis Jacquemin: "Economic and Legal Aspects of Cooperative Research: A European View," CEPS Working Document No. 16 (Economic) (Brussels: Centre for European Policy Studies, November 1985); Collaborated with Alexis Jacquemin, Compétition Européenne et Coopération entre Entreprises en Matiére de Recherche-Development (Luxembourg: Office des publications officielles des Communautés européennes, 1986), 124. *Member:* American Bar Association; International Bar Association; American Society of International Law. (Also practicing individually at Charleroi, Belgium). ***LANGUAGES:*** French, Dutch and German. ***PRACTICE AREAS:*** International Trade; Investment Law; International Transactions Law; International Customs Law; Civil Litigation; General Practice. ***Email:*** spinoit.wese@brutele.be

LANE STEVEN HUREWITZ, born Philadelphia, Pennsylvania, February 2, 1962; admitted to bar, 1987, Pennsylvania; 1988, District of Columbia; 1990, U.S. Court of International Trade; 1991, U.S. Court of Appeals for the Federal Circuit. *Education:* The American University (B.A., honors with distinction, 1984); George Washington University (J.D., 1987). Omicron Delta Epsilon; Pi Sigma Alpha. Author: The GATT Uruguay Round: A Negotiating History (1986-1992): Textiles, Kluwer Law and Taxation Publishers, 1993; "Informal and Indirect Incentives to United States Exports and United States Assistance in Opening Foreign Markets for United States Products and Services," in Export Practice: Customs and International Trade Law Institute, Spring 1994. Member, Board of Directors, Northwest Youth Alliance, Inc. *Member:* The District of Columbia Bar (Member, International Law Section); Bar Association of the District of Columbia; Pennsylvania and American Bar Associations; Customs and International Trade Bar Association. ***PRACTICE AREAS:*** International Trade; C.I.T.; CAFC; Administrative Law; ITA; ITC; International Trade Regulation; Import and Export Law; Antidumping; Countervailing Duty; Export Regulation; Investment Law; Customs Law; Unfair Competition Law. ***Email:*** lhurewitz@stewartlaw.com

PATRICK JOHN McDONOUGH, born Los Angeles, California, July 27, 1951; admitted to bar, 1989, Maryland; 1991, U.S. Court of International Trade; 1994, U.S. Court of Appeals for the Federal Circuit; 2001, District of Columbia. *Education:* University of Maryland (B.A., with high honors, 1973; J.D., with honors, 1988). Phi Kappa Phi. Author: *The GATT Uruguay Round:* A Negoti-

(This Listing Continued)

STEWART AND STEWART, Washington—Continued

ating History (1986-1994), Vol. IV: The End Game (Part I): Subsidies and Countervailing Measures, Kluwer Law International, 1999; *The GATT Uruguay Round:* A Negotiating History (1986-1992), "Subsidies and Countervailing Measures," Kluwer Law & Taxation publishers, 1993; "Industry—Specific and other Targeted Incentives," in Export Practice: Customs and International Trade Law Practising Law Institute, Spring 1994. Co-Author: T. Stewart and M. Prado, "Opportunities in the WTO for Increased Liberalization of Goods: Making Sure the Rules Work for all and That Special Needs Are Addressed," 24 Fordham Int'l. L.J., No.1, April 2001. *Member:* American Bar Association; Customs and International Trade Bar Association. ***PRACTICE AREAS:*** Civil Litigation: CIT, CAFC; Administrative Law; ITC; ITA; Customs Law; International Trade; International Trade Regulation; Import and Export Law; Antidumping; Export Regulation; Subsidies and Countervailing Duties; U.S. Foreign Trade Zones; Investment Law; Unfair Competition Law. ***Email:*** pmcdonough@stewartlaw.com

AMY S. DWYER, born Newton, Massachusetts, May 8, 1964; admitted to bar, 1991, Massachusetts and U.S. Court of International Trade; 1992, U.S. Court of Appeals for the Federal Circuit; 1993, District of Columbia; 2001, U.S. Supreme Court. *Education:* College of the Holy Cross (B.A., 1986); Loyola University of Chicago, Rome Center (1985); Boston College (J.D., 1990). Phi Delta Phi. Author: *The GATT Uruguay Round:* A Negotiating History (1986-1994), Vol. IV: The End Game (Part I): Trade-Related Aspects of Intellectual Property Rights, Kluwer Law International, 1999; "The Inter-American Court of Human Rights: Towards Establishing an Effective Regional Contentious Jurisdiction," 13 Boston College International and Comparative Law Review 127, 1990; "State Export Restrictions," in Export Practice: Customs and International Trade Law, Practising Law Institute, Spring 1994. Co-Author: T. Stewart, "Handbook on WTO Trade Remedy Disputes: The First Six Years (1995-2000)," Transnational Publishers, Inc.; T. Stewart, "Sunset Reviews of Antidumping and Countervailing Duty Measures—U.S. Implementation of Uruguay Round Commitments," 32(5) Journal of World Trade 101, October 1998; T. Stewart, "WTO Antidumping and Subsidy Agreements: A Practitioner's Guide to 'Sunset' Reviews in Australia, Canada, the European Union, and United States," Kluwer Law International, July 1998; "Measuring Domestic Subsidies: Preferential Provision of Goods or Services and Other Domestic Subsidies," GULC Continuing Legal Education Seminar, 1991. Executive Editor/European Economic Community, Boston College International and Comparative Law Review, 1988-1990. *Member:* Massachusetts and American Bar Associations; Customs and International Trade Bar Association. ***LANGUAGES:*** Italian. ***PRACTICE AREAS:*** International Trade; International Trade Regulation; Import and Export Law; Antidumping; North American Free Trade Agreement; World Trade Organization; Export Regulation; Subsidies and Countervailing Duties; Civil Litigation; CIT; CAFC; Administrative Law; ITA; ITC; Unfair Competition Law. ***Email:*** adwyer@stewartlaw.com

ERIC P. SALONEN, born Newark, New Jersey, January 23, 1959; admitted to bar, 1985, Pennsylvania; 1987, District of Columbia and U.S. District Court for the District of Columbia; 1989, U.S. Court of International Trade and U.S. Court of Appeals for the Federal Circuit. *Education:* Georgetown University School of Foreign Service (B.S.F.S., cum laude, 1981); University of Pennsylvania (J.D., 1985). Senior Articles Editor, Journal of Comparative Business and Capital Markets Law. Author: "One Tomato, Two Tomato...: Selection of Trade Remedy Laws in the Florida-Mexico Tomato Conflict," 11 Florida Journal of International Law, Spring, 1997; "Developments in WTO Dispute Settlement 1996," (part of International Legal Developments in Review: 1996), 31 The International Lawyer, 439-443, Summer 1997; Note, "Against the Current: Countervailing Duties, Upstream Subsidies and the Trade Remedies Reform Act of 1984," 7 Journal of Comparative Business and Capital Markets Law, 37-62, March 1985. Co-Author: with A. P. Victor, "The Application of U.S. Unfair Trade Laws to Energy Flows: Prospects and Risks," 11 University of Pennsylvania Journal of International Business Law, 301-337, Spring/Summer 1989; with T. P. Stewart, J.R. Cannon, Jr. and D. R. Nuxoll, "Trade and Cattle: How the System is Failing an Industry in Crisis," 9 Minnesota Journal of Global Trade, No.2, Summer 2000.. Attorney-Advisor to: Commissioner, 1991-1997 and Vice Chairman, 1994-1996, Janet A. Nuzum and Chairman, Marcia E. Miller, 1997, U.S. International Trade Commission. *Member:* District of Columbia Bar (Member, International Law Section, 1986—); American Bar Association (Member: Section on International Law and Practice, 1996—; Assistant Budget Officer, 1999—; International Trade Committee Steering Group, 1994—; International Trade Committee Vice Chair, 1999-2001; Co-Chair, 2001—); Member, U.S. Court of International Trade Advisory Committee, 1998—; Member, Customs and International Trade Bar Association, 1998—. ***LANGUAGES:*** Finnish. ***PRACTICE AREAS:*** International Trade; Antidumping; Countervailing Duty and Subsidy; Section 337 Unfair Import Investigations; Safeguards; Section 406 Market Disruption; Section 232 National Security Investigations; Section 332 Investigations; Generalized System of Preferences (GSP); NAFTA Chapter 19 Binational Panel Dispute Settlement; World Trade Organization (WTO). ***Email:*** esalonen@stewartlaw.com

(This Listing Continued)

JAMES R. HOLBEIN, born Toledo, Ohio, March 17, 1951; admitted to bar, 1979, Arkansas; 2000, District of Columbia. *Education:* University of California (B.A., 1975); University of Arkansas (J.D., 1979). Author: "The Mexico-European Community and Member States Economic Partnership, Political Coordination and Cooperation Agreement," with Juan Francisco Torres Landa and Omar Guerrero R., Submitted for publication, 35 International Lawyer Vol. 2, Summer 2001; "Is the WTO Dispute Resolution System Serving the Developing World's Interests?" submitted for publications as a chapter of , *The Future for Latin America in the Global Economy,* Patricia Rich, ed., Macmillan Press Ltd., pub., for publications Summer 2001; "Federal Government Careers in International Law," American Society of International Law Guide to Careers in International Law, 1999; "When Does State Regulation Become Expropriation?" For the North American Free Trade and Investment Report: *Survey of Federal Register Notices concerning NAFTA,* 6 issues 1999 and 2000; FTAA Update, May 15, 2000; North American Free Trade & Investment Report, July 1999; "A Survey of NAFTA ," Chapter 19, Panel Reviews, February 29, 2000; "FTAA Negotiations: Enhanced Importance After the Failure in Seattle?" January 24, 2000; "Telecommunications in a Free Trade Environment," September 30, 1999; "NAFTA Chapter 19, the U.S. Secretariat's Perspective," The Commerce Department Speaks on Trade and Investment, Practising Law Institute, 1998; "The Administration of Chapter 19 Binational Proceedings Under NAFTA," 5 United States-Mexico Law Journal 57, presented at Fifth Annual Conference of the U.S.-Mexico Law Institute, Inc., 1997; "NAFTA Organizations and Dispute Settlement," prepared for Georgetown University Law Center Conference, "Resolving International Trade Disputes," November 1995; "Evidentiary Issues Under the U.S.-Canada Free Trade Agreement and the Proposed North American Free Trade Agreement," American Bar Association Annual Meeting, April 1993; "The Case for Free Trade," Symposium on Free Trade and the Environment in Latin America, 15 Loyola of Los Angeles International and Comparative Law Journal 19, December 1992; "NAFTA Code of Conduct to Ensure Integrity of Dispute Settlement," Office of Government Ethics NEWSGRAM, Summer 1994; "An Analysis of Dispute Settlement under the U.S.-Canada Free Trade Agreement and the North American Free Trade Agreement," prepared for American Society of International Law, International Economic Law Forum, March 1993. Co-Author: with Laurinda Hicks, "Convergence of National Intellectual Property Norms in International Trading Agreements," 12 American University Journal of International Law and Policy 769, 1997; with Alicia Greenidge, "NAFTA Code of Conduct Provides International Guidelines for Ethical Behavior," 1 NAFTA: Law & Business Review of the Americas 50, Spring 1995; with Gary Carpentier and Ellen Grebasch, "Trade Agreements and Dispute Settlement Mechanisms in the Western Hemisphere," 25 Case Western Reserve Journal of International Law 531, Summer 1993; with Nick Ranieri, "Comparative Analysis of Specific Elements in U.S. and Canadian Unfair Trade Law," 26 International Lawyer 873, Winter 1992; Co-Editor: with Donald J. Musch, *North American Free Trade Agreements,* 6 volume looseleaf series, published by Oceana Publications, Inc. Attorney Advisor, U.S. Small Business Administration, 1979-1980. Foreign Service Officer, 1980-1987, Consular Officer, U.S. Embassy, Seoul, Korea, 1981-1982, International Economist, U.S. Embassy, Olso, Norway, 1983-1985, Staff Assistant for Assistant Secretary for Economic Affairs, 1985-1986 and Trade Negotiator, U.S.-Canada Free Trade Agreement, 1986-1987, U.S. Department of State. Mexico Division Director, 1988, Acting Director, Office of Latin America, 1991-1992, U. S. Department of Commerce, Secretary, FTA Binational Secretariat, 1989-1994, Secretary, NAFTA Secretariat, 1994-1999. Adjunct Assistant Professor of Law: Georgetown University Law Center, 1998; American University, Washington College of Law, 1993-2001; University of Maryland, 1993-1998. Member, Board of Advisors, U.S.-Mexico Conflict Resolution Center. *Member:* American Bar Association (Member, International Law and Practice Section; Vice Chair, Mexican Law Committee). ***LANGUAGES:*** Norwegian and Spanish. ***PRACTICE AREAS:*** International Trade; Alternative Dispute Resolution; Customs Law; Regional Trade Agreements. ***Email:*** jholbein@stewartlaw.com

EUGENE H. MOORE, born Waco, Texas, November 26, 1947; admitted to bar, 1972, Texas; 1993, New York (Not admitted in District of Columbia). *Education:* Baylor University (B.A., 1969; J.D., 1972). Phi Alpha Delta. Author and Speaker, "Doing Business in a Complex World," Seminar and Video, 1995. ***PRACTICE AREAS:*** Corporate (organization and governance); Commercial Transactions (U.S. and international); Mergers and Acquisitions; Litigation Management. ***Email:*** emoore9263@aol.com

STIER, ANDERSON & MALONE, LLC

2175 K STREET, NW, SUITE 320
WASHINGTON, D.C. 20037-1809
Telephone: 202-659-0303
Fax: 202-659-5968
Email: stierdc@aol.com
URL: http://www.stier.com

Skillman, New Jersey Office: 30 Vreeland Dr., 08558. Telephone: 609-597-6466. Fax: 609-497-2909.

(This Listing Continued)

Special Counsel Investigations, Corporate Compliance Monituring, Complex Litigation, Employment Relations, Sexual Harassment Investigations, Appellate and Administrative Practice.

FIRM PROFILE: Stier, Anderson & Malone conducts internal investigations for corporate and government clients nationwide. These investigations involve close coordination with corporate counsel, corporate boards of directors, and governmental regulatory agencies. The firm's practice also includes complex litigation in which extensive investigation is required, such as environmental law, employment relations, RICO cases, and white collar criminal defense.

RESIDENT PARTNERS

HOWARD T. ANDERSON, born San Antonio, Texas, April 2, 1946; admitted to bar, 1971, New Jersey; 1978, District of Columbia. *Education:* Dartmouth College (A.B., 1968); Harvard University (J.D., 1971). Phi Beta Kappa. Co-Author: "Conducting Internal Investigations in the Academic and Research Setting," Education Law Association, 1998; "Using Internal Investigations as an Alternative Strategy for Responding to a Crisis," Corporate Governance Advisor, September/October, 1997; "The Legal Landscape After Payton: Investigating Sexual Harassment Complaints," New Jersey Law Journal, April 28, 1997; "Employee Concerns Programs in the Nuclear Industry: Ten Guidelines for Utility Managers," American Nuclear Society, September, 1995; "What You Don't Know Can Hurt You: The Case For Special Counsel Investigations," California Management Review, Spring 1987; "Measuring the Disparate Impact of Employment Practices: The Wards Cove Decision and Congressional Attempts to Overturn It", ACCA Docket, Summer 1991; "Minimizing Government Intervention in Scientific Institutions, and Regulating Misconduct in the Government Research Organization," Sigma Xi Scientific Research Society, Forum Proceedings, Feb. 25-26, 1993. Deputy Attorney General, New Jersey, 1971-1977. Investigator, Investigation of Korean-American Relations, Subcommittee on International Organizations, U.S. House of Representatives, 1977-1978. Consultant, Senate Small Business Committee, 1978-1979. Attorney, Morgan Associates, 1979-1987. *Member:* District of Columbia Bar; American Bar Association. ***PRACTICE AREAS:*** Complex Litigation; Corporate Compliance; Civil RICO; Internal Corporate Investigations. ***Email:*** stierdcHTA@aol.com

PAUL F. COLARULLI, born Providence, Rhode Island, February 5, 1950; admitted to bar, 1977, Rhode Island; 1978, Massachusetts; 1979, District of Columbia; 1981, U.S. Supreme Court. *Education:* Hobart College (B.A., 1972); Columbia University (M.A., 1973); Harvard University (M.P.H., 1978); Boston University (J.D., 1977). Phi Beta Kappa. Editor, Boston University Law Review, 1976-1977. Co-Author: "Conducting Internal Investigations in the Academic and Research Setting," Education Law Association, 1998; "Employee Concerns Programs in the Nuclear Industry: Ten Guidelines for Utility Managers," American Nuclear Society, September, 1995. Author: "Treatment of Affiliated Transactions in Utility Rate Making: Western Electric Company and The Bell System," Public Utilities Law Anthology Vol. IV, 1977-1978; "The National Health Planning and Resources Development Act and State Action: A Reappraisal of the Role of Private Health Care Institutions," Boston University Law Review, Vol. 57 #3, 1977. Partner, Morgan Associates, 1978-1990. *Member:* The District of Columbia Bar; Rhode Island, Massachusetts and American Bar Associations. ***PRACTICE AREAS:*** Complex Litigation; Corporate Compliance; Civil RICO; Employment Law; Internal Corporate Investigations. ***Email:*** stierdcPFC@aol.com

ASSOCIATE

SUSAN J. CHAREN, born Princeton, New Jersey, September 28, 1965; admitted to bar, 1990, Pennsylvania and New Jersey; 2001, District of Columbia. *Education:* Rutgers College (B.A., 1987) Rutgers Law School, Newark (J.D., 1990). Staff Attorney, Office of the General Counsel, U.S. Dept. of Health and Human Services, 1996-2000. Law Clerk to the Hon. H. Jonathan Fox, 1990-1991. *Member:* New Jersey State (Member Young Lawyers Division) and American Bar Associations. ***PRACTICE AREAS:*** Complex Litigation; Internal Investigations; Corporate Compliance. ***Email:*** stierdcSJC@aol.com

OF COUNSEL

NANCY L. SINGER, born Brooklyn, New York, May 11, 1953; admitted to bar, 1977, New Jersey; 2001, District of Columbia. *Education:* Babson College (B.S.B.A., summa cum laude, 1974); Temple University School of Law (J.D., cum laude, 1977). Beta Gamma. Academic Achievement Award; Cardinal Key National Honor Society. Law Clerk: New Jersey Superior Court, 1978; Interstate Commerce Commission, 1978-1980. Assistant Attorney General, Chief, Fraud Prosecutions Bureau, New Jersey Division of Criminal Justice, 1980-1997. *Member:* Mercer County Bar Association, 1985-1990; and New Jersey State Bar Association, 1985-1990. ***PRACTICE AREAS:*** Internal Investigations; Complex Litigation. ***Email:*** stierdcNLS@aol.com

(For Complete Biographical Data on all Personnel, see Professional Biographies at Skillman, New Jersey)

STOEL RIVES LLP

SUITE 810, 1275 K STREET, N.W.
WASHINGTON, D.C. 20005-4006
Telephone: 202-347-7744
Facsimile: 202-347-7750
URL: http://www.stoel.com/

Portland, Oregon Office: Suite 2600, 900 S.W. Fifth Avenue. Telephone 503-224-3380.

Vancouver, Washington Office: Suite 725, 805 Broadway. Telephone: 360-699-5900.

Seattle, Washington Office: Suite 3600, One Union Square, 600 University. Telephone: 206-624-0900.

Boise, Idaho Office: Suite 1900, 101 S. Capitol Boulevard. Telephone: 208-389-9000.

Salt Lake City, Utah Office: Suite 1100, One Utah Center, 201 South Main Street. Telephone: 801-328-3131.

San Francisco California Office: 111 Sutter Street, Suite 700. Telephone: 415-617-8900.

Sacramento, California Office: 770 L Street, Suite 990. Telephone: 916-447-0700.

Tahoe City, California Office: 3000 N. Lake Boulevard, Suite 1, P.O. Box 7336. Telephone: 530-583-2116.

Administrative and Legislative Practice before Federal Agencies and U.S. Congress. Practice before Federal Energy Regulatory Commission. General Practice and Litigation in Oregon and Washington State Courts and Federal Courts. Energy Law, Public Utilities, Natural Resources and Environmental Law.

FIRM PROFILE: Stoel Rives is more than the sum of its 330 attorneys and 400-plus support professionals. We are a leading Northwest business-to-business law firm with both the technical expertise and know-how to provide creative solutions to help your company succeed. As one of the fastest growing law firms in the region, we are more equipped than ever to provide community leadership and the right connections. Stoel Rives understands how to foster companies at all stages of growth and can help you to succeed in today's dynamic marketplace.

With more "Best Lawyers in America" than any other Northwest-based law firm, Stoel Rives provides nationally recognized expertise in the following business-critical areas: corporate, securities and finance; commercial law and bankruptcy; construction and design; cyber law, eBusiness and telecom; energy and natural resources; environmental and land use; general business litigation and appellate law; health and hospital law; intellectual property; labor and employment, workers compensation and employee benefits; mergers and acquisitions; public law and finance; real estate; tax; wealth management.

RESIDENT PARTNER

ROBERT A. NELSON, JR., born Paterson, New Jersey, February 9, 1946; admitted to bar, 1973, Maryland; 1984, District of Columbia and U.S. Court of Appeals, Tenth Circuit; 1985, U.S. Court of Appeals, District of Columbia Circuit; 1986, U.S. Court of Appeals, Ninth Circuit; 1990, U.S. Court of Appeals, Fourth Circuit; 1993, U.S. Court of Appeals, Fifth Circuit. *Education:* Georgetown University (B.S., cum laude, 1968); University of Virginia (J.D., 1973). Attorney, Assistant to the Chairman, Attorney Advisor, Federal Energy Regulatory Commission, 1973-1983. ***PRACTICE AREAS:*** Energy Law; Energy Regulation; Energy Transactions; Litigation; Appellate. ***Email:*** ranelson@stoel.com

(For complete biographical data other personnel, see Professional Biographies at Portland, Oregon, Boise, Idaho, Salt Lake City, Utah and Vancouver & Seattle, Washington)

STORCH & BRENNER LLP

WASHINGTON, D.C.

(See Dilworth Paxson PLLC)

JOHN EDWARD STORMS, JR., P.A.

WASHINGTON, D.C.

(See Wheaton, Maryland)

Employment-Based Immigration Law.

STRASBURGER & PRICE, L.L.P.

A Partnership including Professional Corporations
1101 PENNSYLVANIA AVENUE N.W., 7TH FLOOR
WASHINGTON, D.C. 20004
Telephone: 202-756-2260
Fax: 202-756-7511
URL: http://www.strasburger.com

Dallas, Texas Office: 901 Main Street, Suite 4300. Telephone: 214-651-4300. Fax: 214-651-4330.

Austin, Texas Office: 600 Congress Avenue, Suite 2600. Telephone: 512-499-3600. Fax: 512-499-3660.

Houston, Texas Office: 1301 N. McKinney Street, Suite 3200. Telephone: 713-951-5600. Fax: 713-951-5660.

San Antonio, Texas Office: Bank of America Plaza, 300 Convent Street, Suite 900. Telephone: 210-250-6000. Fax: 210-250-6100.

Mexico City Office: Strasburger & Price, S.C., Montes Urales 632, Piso 3, Lomas de Chapultepec, 11000 Mexico D.F. Telephone: 525-202-7665. Fax: 525-202-2367.

Antitrust and Trade Regulation, Antitrust Class Actions, Appellate Practice, Bankruptcy, Workouts, Business Litigation, Commercial Litigation, Banking Litigation, Commercial Loans, Business Law, Commercial Law, Construction Law, Securities, Drug and Medical Device Defense, Environmental Law, Superfund, Toxic Torts, Nuclear Energy, Oil and Gas Law, Estate and Gift Taxation, Trusts and Estates Taxation, Wills, Fidelity and Surety, Finance, Franchises and Franchising, International Franchising, Franchise Law, Governmental Law, Local Government Law, County Government Law, Health Care, Health Law, Health Care Litigation, Managed Care, Medical Law, Nursing Home Litigation, Insurance, Insurance Defense, Commercial Insurance Defense, Insurance Bad Faith Defense, Insurance Coverage Defense, Insurance Reinsurance, Risk Management, Intellectual Property, Intellectual Property Licensing, Intellectual Property Litigation, New Media Law, Patent Litigation, Patent Licensing, Trademarks, Copyrights, International Law, International Trade, Labor and Employment, Employment Law, Personal Injury, Products Liability, Products Liability Defense, Mass Torts, Professional Liability, Real Estate, Zoning, Planning and Land Use, Taxation, International Taxation, Tax Controversies, Income Tax, White Collar Crime, Transportation, International Transportation Law.

FIRM PROFILE: For more than 60 years, Strasburger & Price, L.L.P. has been serving as trusted legal advisors to local, national and international corporations, privately-held companies, government entities and individuals. As one of the largest firms in the southwestern United States, and through our offices in Dallas, Austin, Houston, San Antonio and Mexico City, Strasburger & Price has the resources to handle just about any type of corporate legal matter.

Everyday our legal professionals strive to find innovative, effective, and practical solutions to our clients' legal and business issues. We pride ourselves on our ability to meet and exceed client expectations — differentiating ourselves from our competition based on our level of service and the value we provide to our clients. To learn more about Strasburger & Price, our areas of practice, and legal expertise, please visit our firm's website —www.strasburger.com— or contact any of our legal professionals at one of our five offices throughout Texas and in Mexico City.

MEMBER OF FIRM

MARK J. ANDREWS, admitted to bar, 1970, District of Columbia. *Education:* Harvard University (A.B., cum laude, 1966; J.D., 1969). Registered to practice before Federal Maritime Commission, Surface Transportation Board. *Member:* Transportation Lawyers Association (Chair, Legislative Committee, 1983-1986; Recipient of Distinguished Service Award, 1985; Member of Executive Committee, 1986-1999; President, 1992-1993); Canadian Transportation Lawyers' Association; Conference of Freight Counsel. ***PRACTICE AREAS:*** Cargo Claims; International Transportation Law; Logistics; Maritime Regulation; Motor Carrier Regulation; Transportation. ***Email:*** mark.andrews@strasburger.com

JANE WOODS LaFRANCHI, born October 19, 1956; admitted to bar, 1982, Texas (Not admitted in District of Columbia). *Education:* University of Texas (B.A., with highest honors and special honors in Spanish, 1979; J.D., with honors, 1982). Chancellor, Order of the Coif. Member, Texas Law Review, 1980-1982. ***LANGUAGES:*** English, Spanish and French. ***PRACTICE AREAS:*** International Business Law; International Franchising; Mexico Trade. ***Email:*** jane.lafranchi@strasburger.com

OF COUNSEL

KENNETH E. SIEGEL, admitted to bar, 1972, Pennsylvania (Not admitted in District of Columbia). *Education:* Duquesne University (B.S.B.A., 1969); Temple University (J.D., 1972). Trial Attorney, Interstate Commerce Commission, 1972-1976; Staff, Office of General Counsel, U.S. General Accounting Office, 1976-1977. Vice President and Deputy General Counsel, American Trucking Association, Inc. *Member:* Pennsylvania (Public Utilities Section) and American (Administrative Section, Transportation Committee) Bar Associations; Transportation Lawyers Association; Association for Transportation Law, Logistics and Policy. ***PRACTICE AREAS:*** Transportation; Federal Legislative Practice. ***Email:*** kenneth.siegel@strasburger.com

All Attorneys are Members of the State Bar of Texas

REPRESENTATIVE CLIENTS: Bank of America, N.A.; Chase Bank of Texas, National Association; Chevron U.S.A., Inc.; Columbia/HCA Healthcare Corp.; CompuCom Systems, Inc.; Coregis Group, Inc.; Dallas/Fort Worth International Airport; DDB Needham - Dallas; Dell Computer Corp.; 7-Eleven, Inc.; Fidelity and Deposit Insurance Corp.; Fossil, Inc.; Foster Grant Group, LP; General Motors Corp.; Global Industrial Technologies, Inc. (formerly INDRESCO Inc.); Horizon Health Corporation; HFS, Inc.; Houston Firefighter's Relief and Retirement Fund; International Business Machines Corp.; Maguire/Thomas Partners; Microsoft Corporation; Mitsubishi Motors Corp.; Mobil Land Development Corp.; Mobil Oil Corp.; Nissan Diesel America, Inc.; Oryx Energy Co.; PACCAR, Inc.; Royal Insurance Cos.; Saint-Gobain Corporation; Southern Foods Group, L.P.; Syndicates of Lloyd's of London; Tenet Healthcare Corp.; Texas Children's Hospital; Texas Industries, Inc.; Texas Medical Liability Trust; Texas Municipal League Intergovernmental Risk Pool; The Travelers Insurance Cos.

(For complete listing of other Personnel, see also Professional Biographies at Austin, Texas, Houston, Texas, San Antonio, Texas, Washington, D.C. and Mexico City, Mexico)

PAMELA B. STUART

Established in 1992
1101 CONNECTICUT AVENUE, N.W., SUITE 1000
WASHINGTON, D.C. 20036
Telephone: 202-835-2200
Facsimile: 202-835-2202
URL: http://www.stuart-law.com
Email: pamstuart@aol.com
URL: http://www.lawyers.com/pamelastuartlaw

Litigation, White Collar Criminal Defense, Labor and Employment, Employment Discrimination, Disability Discrimination, Commercial Law, International Law including Extradition and Immigration, Security Clearances, Congressional Investigations, Business Law, Health Law, Antitrust and Trade Regulation, Copyright and Trademark, Medical Malpractice, Wills, Trusts and Estates, Real Estate, Products Liability and Personal Injury, Estate Planning, Family Law.

PAMELA B. STUART, born New York, N.Y., February 13, 1949; admitted to bar, 1974, New York; 1975, District of Columbia; 1979, U.S. District Court,, District of Columbia; 1980, U.S. Court of Appeals, District of Columbia Circuit; U.S. Supreme Court; 1989, U.S. District Court, District of Maryland; 1992, Maryland; 1993, Virginia and U.S. Court of Appeals, 4th Circuit; 1994, Florida and U.S. District Court, Eastern District of Virginia; 1996, U.S. District Court, Northern District of New York; 1998, U.S. District Court, Southern District of Florida; 1999, U.S. District Court, Southern and Eastern Districts of New York; 2001, U.S. District Court, Middle District of Florida. *Education:* Mount Holyoke College (A.B., with distinction, 1970); University of Michigan (J.D., cum laude, 1973). Author: "The U.N. Convention on Contracts for the International Sale of Goods," Washington International Trade Association, Trade Trends, May/June 1988; "Keeping Your Workplace Drug Free," Business and Health, August 1989; "Prosecution, Not Warfare," The National Law Journal, December 10, 1990; "Treaty Traps: How To Get Your Client Through the Maze of Extradition," Criminal Justice, Winter 1992; "The Criminalization Theft: The Economic Espionage Act of 1996," 1 LSA Journal of International and Comparative Law, vol. 4, no2, Spring 1998. The Federal Trade Commission, Chelsea House, 1991; Contributor: The Department of Justice, Chelsea House, 1989. Instructor: Attorney General's Advocacy Institute, 1986-1987; Legal Education Institute, 1985-1986; National Institute for Trial Advocacy, 1978, 1990, 1992—. Member: Judicial Conference of the District of Columbia, 1985-1988, 1991—; Judicial Conference of the District of Columbia Circuit, 1994, 1996, 1998, 2000; Committee on Grievances, U.S. District Court for the District of Columbia, 1994—; Vice-Chair, 1996—; Board of Directors, Bar Association of the District of Columbia, 1996-1999 (Committee Chair of the Year, 1995); Board of Directors, Alumnae Association of Mount Holyoke College, 1986-1989, 1992-1995; Board of Governors, Federal City Club 1992—; Board of Directors, Anacostia Economic Development Corporation, 1993—. Trial Attorney and Deputy Assistant Director, Bureau of Consumer Protection Federal Trade Commission, Washington, D.C., 1973-1979. Assistant U.S. Attorney for the District of Columbia, 1979-1985. Senior Trial Attorney, Office of International Affairs, U.S. Dept. of Justice, Washington, D.C., 1985-1987. *Member:* Maryland State, Federal and American (Member, Sections of: Litigation, Criminal Justice, Labor and Employment Law, Torts and Insurance Practice, Business Law, International Law, Chair, International Criminal Law Committee of the Section of Criminal Justice, 1993-1996) Bar Associations; Assistant U.S. Attorneys Association of the District of Columbia (President, 1998-1999); The Women's Bar Association of the District of Columbia; The Association of Trial Lawyers of America; Trial Lawyers Association of the Washington Metropolitan Area; Washington Foreign

(This Listing Continued)

Law Society; Consular Corps of Washington (Executive Committee, 1995-1998); Master of the Bench, The Edward Bennett Williams Inn of Court. **LANGUAGES:** Spanish.

OF COUNSEL

KATHLEEN E. VOELKER, born Somerville, New Jersey, July 19, 1947; admitted to bar, 1977, Georgia; 1979, District of Columbia; U.S. District Court, District of Columbia. *Education:* Georgia State University (A.B., magna cum laude, 1974); University of Kentucky College of Law (J.D., 1977). Order of the Coif. Assistant U.S. Attorney, District of Columbia, 1979-1989; Trial Attorney, U.S. Department of Justice, Criminal Division, Public Integrity Section, Honors Program, 1977-1979. Chair, Planning Committee National Institute on Health Care Fraud, 1999. Member Board of Directors Robert A. Shuker Scholarship Fund. *Member:* Bar Association of the District of Columbia; The District of Columbia Bar (Member, Criminal Law and Individual Rights, Health Law and Litigation Sections); State Bar of Georgia (Member, Criminal, Health and Alternative Dispute Resolution Sections); American (Member, Criminal Justice, Health Law and Dispute Resolution Sections) Bar Association; American Health Lawyers Association; Assistant U.S. Attorneys Associaiton (President, 1993-1994). ***PRACTICE AREAS:*** Litigation; White Collar Criminal Defense; Health Law; Mediation; Employment Discrimination; Security Clearances. **Email:** kathleenvoelker@aol.com

SUGHRUE MION, PLLC

A Professional Limited Liability Company including Professional Corporations

Established in 1957

SUITE 800, 2100 PENNSYLVANIA AVENUE, N.W.
WASHINGTON, D.C. 20037-3213
Telephone: 202-293-7060
Facsimile: 202-293-7860
Email: sughrue@sughrue.com
URL: http://www.sughrue.com

Tokyo, Japan Office: Toei Nishi Shimbashi Building, Suite 4F, 13-5 Nishi Shimbashi 1-Chome 105. Telephone: (03) 3 503-3760.

Menlo Park, California Office: 1010 El Camino Real, Suite 360. Telephone: 650-325-5800. Facsimile: 650-325-6606.

Patent, Trademark, Copyright, Unfair Competition Law. Practice before the Federal Courts and Administrative Agencies. Antitrust, International Trade Regulation, International Patent and Trademark Law.

FIRM PROFILE: The firm of Sughrue Mion is engaged in the practice of law relating to intellectual property. The firm's diverse client base, encompasses a broad spectrum of multinational corporations, high technology growth companies and small start-up ventures. The firm represents its clients before the federal and state courts nationwide, as well as federal agencies having jurisdiction over matters that concern issues of international trade and intellectual property acquisition and protection. Moreover, the firm's proximity to the United States Patent and Trademark Office provides a unique opportunity to directly represent clients before that agency and, in particular, its Appellate Boards. The firm is well known for its representation of clients in connection with the development and exploitation of emerging technologies, such as superconductors, multiprocessors, biotechnology and robotics, as well as established technologies, such as data processing, nuclear engineering, chemicals, pharmaceuticals, photography, telecommunications and semiconductors. The firm has expanded over the years to its present complement of 37 partners and a comparable number of associates and clerks. The firm has spacious offices in Washington, D.C. and Menlo Park, California and an office in Tokyo, Japan that is staffed by partners and associates to provide services to a client base in the Pacific basin.

MEMBERS OF FIRM

RICHARD C. SUGHRUE (1921-2000).

JOHN H. MION, (P.C.), born Long Branch, New Jersey, February 18, 1931; admitted to bar, 1958, District of Columbia; 1960-1982, U.S. Court of Customs and Patent Appeals; 1965, U.S. Supreme Court; 1982, U.S. Court of Appeals for the Federal Circuit; registered to practice before U.S. Patent and Trademark Office. *Education:* Rutgers University (B.S.E.E., 1952); George Washington University (J.D., with Honors, 1958). Eta Kappa Nu. *Member:* The District of Columbia Bar; Bar Association of the District of Columbia (Chairman, Patent Office Affairs Committee, 1970, 1975-1977 and Member of Council, 1972-1975, Patent, Trademark and Copyright Law Section); American Bar Association; American Intellectual Property Law Association. ***PRACTICE AREAS:*** Intellectual Property Law. **Email:** jmion@sughrue.com

ROBERT J. SEAS, JR. (P.C.), born Cleveland, Ohio, November 1, 1932; admitted to bar, 1962, Virginia; 1963, District of Columbia; registered to practice before U.S. Patent and Trademark Office. *Education:* Carnegie Institute of Technology (B.S.E.E., 1954); George Washington University (LL.B., 1962). *Member:* The District of Columbia Bar; Bar Association of the District of Columbia; Virginia State Bar; American Bar Association; American Intellectual Property Law Association. ***PRACTICE AREAS:*** Intellectual Property Law. **Email:** jseas@sughrue.com

DARRYL MEXIC, (P.C.), born New Orleans, Louisiana, February 23, 1940; admitted to bar, 1966, District of Columbia and U.S. Court of Appeals for the District of Columbia Circuit; 1983, U.S. Court of Appeals for the Federal Circuit; registered to practice before U.S. Patent and Trademark Office. *Education:* Georgia Institute of Technology (B.E.E., 1961); Georgetown University (J.D., 1965). Phi Eta Sigma; Tau Beta Pi; Eta Kappa Nu. Author and Lecturer, "Patent Interference Practice," Patent Resources Group, 1974, 1976, 1979, 1981 and 1985. *Member:* The District of Columbia Bar: Bar Association of the District of Columbia; American Bar Association; American Intellectual Property Law Association. ***PRACTICE AREAS:*** Intellectual Property Law. **Email:** dmexic@sughrue.com

ROBERT V. SLOAN, (P.C.), born Syracuse, New York, September 30, 1933; admitted to bar, 1964, Maryland; 1969, U.S. Supreme Court; 1982, U.S. Court of Appeals for the Federal Circuit; registered to practice before U.S. Patent and Trademark Office (Not admitted in District of Columbia). *Education:* Le Moyne College, Syracuse, New York (B.S., Physics, 1955); University of Baltimore (LL.B., 1963). Delta Theta Phi. *Member:* Maryland State and American Bar Associations; American Intellectual Property Law Association; International Intellectual Property Association. ***PRACTICE AREAS:*** Intellectual Property Law. **Email:** rsloan@sughrue.com

PETER D. OLEXY, (P.C.), born Palmerton, Pennsylvania, June 9, 1943; admitted to bar, 1968, District of Columbia; 1969, U.S. Court of Appeals for the District of Columbia; 1978, U.S. Supreme Court; 1982, U.S. Court of Appeals for the Federal Circuit; registered to practice before U.S. Patent and Trademark Office. *Education:* Pennsylvania State University (B.S.Ch.E., 1965); George Washington University (J.D., with Honors, 1968). Delta Theta Phi: Order of the Coif. Lecturer: "Patent Interference Practice," Patent Resources Group, 1981 and 1986-1991; "Advanced Patent Application and Amendment Writing Workshop," Patent Resources Group, 1986-1991; "Patent Bar Review," Patent Resources Group, 1987-1988. Visiting Professor, Fudan University, Shanghai, PRC, Winter 1988 (U.S. Intellectual Property Law). Member, Editorial Advisory Board, Intellectual Property Law, 1987-1989. *Member:* The District of Columbia Bar; The Bar Association of the District of Columbia; American Bar Association; American Intellectual Property Law Association; International Association for the Protection of Industrial Property; Federation of Industrial Property Attorneys; International Trade Commission Trial Lawyers Association. ***PRACTICE AREAS:*** Intellectual Property Law. **Email:** polexy@sughrue.com

J. FRANK OSHA, born Boonville, Indiana, October 13, 1939; admitted to bar, 1967, District of Columbia and U.S. Court of Appeals for the District of Columbia Circuit; 1982, U.S. Court of Appeals for the Federal Circuit; registered to practice before U.S. Patent and Trademark Office. *Education:* Massachusetts Institute of Technology (B.S., 1962; M.S., 1963); Harvard University (LL.B., cum laude, 1966). Lecturer, "Patent Interference Practice," Patent Resources Group, 1974, 1976, 1979, 1981-1985, 1988, 1989. *Member:* The District of Columbia Bar; Bar Association of the District of Columbia; American Bar Association; American Intellectual Property Law Association; International Association for Protection of Industrial Property; International Trade Commission Trial Lawyers Association. ***PRACTICE AREAS:*** Intellectual Property Law. **Email:** fosha@sughrue.com

LOUIS GUBINSKY, (P.C.), born Baltimore, Maryland, April 25, 1941; admitted to bar, 1967, District of Columbia; 1968-1982, U.S. Court of Custom and Patent Appeals; 1982, U.S. Court of Appeals for the Federal Circuit; registered to practice before U.S. Patent and Trademark Office. *Education:* University of Maryland (B.S., in Pharmacy, 1962); Georgetown University (J.D., 1966). Lecturer, "Patent Interference Practice," Patent Resources Group, 1985-1988. *Member:* The District of Columbia Bar; American Bar Association; American Intellectual Property Law Association. ***PRACTICE AREAS:*** Intellectual Property Law; Biotechnology. **Email:** lgubinsky@sughrue.com

NEIL B. SIEGEL, born Chicago, Illinois, March 8, 1942; admitted to bar, 1967, District of Columbia; 1982, U.S. Court of Federal Claims and U.S. Court of Appeals for the Federal Circuit; registered to practice before U.S. Patent and Trademark Office. *Education:* University of Illinois (B.S.Aero.E., 1963); Northwestern University (J.D., 1966). Phi Delta Phi. Lecturer, "Federal Circuit Patent Law, Advanced Patent Prosecution," Patent Resources Group, 1984-1986. Special Legal Advisor, Commission on Government Procurement, 1971. Committee on Scientific and Technical Information, Federal Council on Science and Technology, 1971-1972. Chief, Patent Litigation and Claims Division, NASA Office of General Counsel, 1973-1974. *Member:* The District of Columbia Bar; American Bar Association (Chairman, PTC Committee 107, 1985-1987). ***PRACTICE AREAS:*** Intellectual Property Law; Litigation. **Email:** nsiegel@sughrue.com

(This Listing Continued)

SUGHRUE MION, PLLC, Washington—Continued

DAVID J. CUSHING, born Evanston, Illinois, May 13, 1952; admitted to bar, 1977, Maryland; 1978, District of Columbia; 1980, U.S. Court of Appeals for the District of Columbia Circuit; 1982, U.S. District Court for the District of Columbia; 1983, U.S. Court of Appeals for the Federal Circuit; registered to practice before U.S. Patent and Trademark Office. *Education:* University of Notre Dame (B.S.E.E., 1973); University of Maryland (J.D., 1976). *Member:* The District of Columbia Bar; American Bar Association; American Intellectual Property Law Association (Member, Programmable Machines and Processes Committee, 1982—); International Patent and Trademark Association; Computer Law Association. ***PRACTICE AREAS:*** Intellectual Property Law; Litigation. ***Email:*** dcushing@sughrue.com

CYNTHIA CLARKE WEBER, born Rochester, New York, May 1, 1951; admitted to bar, 1976, Maryland; 1977, District of Columbia and U.S. District Court for the District of Columbia; 1979, U.S. Court of Appeals for the District of Columbia Circuit; 1981, U.S. Court of Appeals, Second, Fourth and Seventh Circuits; 1981-1982, U.S. Court of Customs and Patent Appeals; 1982, U.S. Court of Appeals for the Federal Circuit; 1985, U.S. Supreme Court; registered to practice before U.S. Patent and Trademark Office. *Education:* Wellesley College (B.A., 1972); Catholic University (J.D., 1976). Wellesley Scholar. *Member:* The District of Columbia Bar; Bar Association of the District of Columbia; American Bar Association; U.S. Trademark Association. ***PRACTICE AREAS:*** Litigation; Trademark Law; Unfair Competition Law; Copyright Law. ***Email:*** cweber@sughrue.com

JOHN R. INGE, born Cumberland, Maryland, September 17, 1946; admitted to bar, 1974, Massachusetts; 1988, District of Columbia; registered to practice before U.S. Patent and Trademark Office. *Education:* Carnegie-Mellon University (B.S., with honors, 1968); Suffolk University (J.D., 1974). Eta Kappa Nu. Lecturer, "Basic U.S. Patent Practice," Japan, 1979-1988. *Member:* The District of Columbia Bar; Massachusetts and American Bar Associations; Licensing Executive Society; Foreign Lawyers Association of Japan; International Trade Commission Trial Lawyers Association. ***PRACTICE AREAS:*** Intellectual Property Law. ***Email:*** jinge@sughrue.com

JOSEPH J. RUCH, JR., born Philadelphia, Pennsylvania, March 3, 1948; admitted to bar, 1975, Pennsylvania; 1978, Virginia; 1983, U.S. Court of Appeals for the Federal Circuit; registered to practice before U.S. Patent and Trademark Office (Not admitted in District of Columbia). *Education:* Drexel University (B.S., 1971); George Washington University (J.D., 1975). *Member:* Virginia State Bar; Pennsylvania and American (Member, Sections on: Patent, Trademark and Copyright Law; Antitrust) Bar Associations; American Intellectual Property Law Association; Asian-Pacific Lawyers Association. ***PRACTICE AREAS:*** Intellectual Property Law. ***Email:*** jruch@sughrue.com

SHELDON I. LANDSMAN, (P.C.), born New York, New York, October 10, 1942; admitted to bar, 1968, New York; 1969, District of Columbia; 1969-1982, U.S. Court of Customs and Patent Appeals; 1970, U.S. Court of Appeals for the District of Columbia; 1980, U.S. Supreme Court; 1982, U.S. Court of Appeals for the Federal Circuit; registered to practice before U.S. Patent and Trademark Office. *Education:* City University of New York (B.E. in Ch.E., 1964); George Washington University (J.D., with honors, 1967). Order of the Coif. *Member:* The District of Columbia Bar; American Bar Association (Member, Section on Patent, Trademark and Copyright Law); American Intellectual Property Law Association; International Trade Commission Trial Lawyers Association. ***PRACTICE AREAS:*** Intellectual Property Law. ***Email:*** slandsman@sughrue.com

RICHARD C. TURNER, born Spartanburg, South Carolina, July 12, 1955; admitted to bar, 1981, District of Columbia and U.S. Court of Appeals for the District of Columbia Circuit; 1982, U.S. District Court for the District of Columbia; 1985, U.S. Court of Appeals for the Federal Circuit; 1989, Japan (Gaikokuho-Jimu Bengoshi); registered to practice before U.S. Patent and Trademark Office. *Education:* Rensselaer Polytechnic Institute (B.S., magna cum laude, 1976); George Washington University (J.D., with honors, 1981). Sigma Pi Sigma. Lecturer, U.S. Patent Academy, 1988. *Member:* The District of Columbia Bar (Member, Sections on: Patent, Trademark and Copyright Law; Antitrust; Trade Regulation); Bar Association of the District of Columbia; American Bar Association; Roppongi Bar Association; American Intellectual Property Law Association; The Association of Trial Lawyers of America; Asia-Pacific Lawyers Association; International Trade Commission Trial Lawyers Association; Association for the Advancement of Science. ***PRACTICE AREAS:*** Patent Law; Intellectual Property Law; Trade Regulation Law; Unfair Competition Law. ***Email:*** dturner@sughrue.com

HOWARD L. BERNSTEIN, (P.C.), born New York, New York, February 1, 1943; admitted to bar, 1969, New York and Virginia; 1971, District of Columbia, U.S. District Court, Eastern District of Virginia and U.S. District Court for the District of Columbia; 1972-1982, U.S. Court of Customs and Patent Appeals; 1975, U.S. Court of Appeals, Fourth Circuit; 1982, U.S. Court of Appeals for the Federal Circuit; registered to practice before U.S. Patent and Trademark Office. *Education:* City College of the City University of New York (B.S.E.E., 1964); Ohio State University; Brooklyn Law School (J.D., 1968). *Member:* The District of Columbia Bar; Fairfax County (Member, Continuing Legal Education Committee, 1980-1981), Federal and American (Member, Sections on: Litigation; Patent, Trademark and Copyright Law) Bar Associations; Virginia State Bar; American Intellectual Property Law Association. ***PRACTICE AREAS:*** Intellectual Property Law; Litigation. ***Email:*** hbernstein@sughrue.com

ALAN J. KASPER, born Buffalo, New York, April 9, 1943; admitted to bar, 1968, District of Columbia; 1969, U.S. Court of Appeals for the District of Columbia Circuit; 1975-1982, U.S. Court of Customs and Patent Appeals; 1985, U.S. Court of Appeals for the Federal Circuit; registered to practice before U.S. Patent and Trademark Office. *Education:* State University of New York at Buffalo (B.S.E.E., 1964); Georgetown University (J.D., 1968). Contributing Editor, "How to Keep Your Company Out of Court," Prentice Hall, 1984. *Member:* The District of Columbia Bar; American Bar Association; American Intellectual Property Law Association. ***PRACTICE AREAS:*** Intellectual Property Law; Litigation. ***Email:*** akasper@sughrue.com

KENNETH J. BURCHFIEL, born Muskogee, Oklahoma, April 21, 1951; admitted to bar, 1978, District of Columbia; registered to practice before U.S. Patent and Trademark Office. *Education:* Amherst College (A.B., cum laude, 1973); Cornell University (J.D., 1977). Fellow, Max Planck Institut Fuer Internationales und Auslaendisches Strafrecht, Freiburg im Breisgau, West Germany, 1979. Attorney, Equal Employment Opportunity Commission, 1979-1983. *Member:* The District of Columbia Bar; American Bar Association. ***LANGUAGES:*** Spanish and German. ***PRACTICE AREAS:*** Intellectual Property Law. ***Email:*** kburchfiel@sughrue.com

GORDON KIT, born Houston, Texas, May 7, 1954; admitted to bar, 1983, District of Columbia, U.S. District Court for the District of Columbia, U.S. Court of Appeals for the District of Columbia Circuit and U.S. Court of Appeals for the Federal Circuit; registered to practice before U.S. Patent and Trademark Office. *Education:* Columbia University (A.B., Biochemistry, 1976); University of California at Berkeley (M.A., Molecular Biology, 1978); American University (J.D., 1982). *Member:* The District of Columbia Bar; American Bar Association; American Intellectual Property Law Association. ***PRACTICE AREAS:*** Intellectual Property Law; Biotechnology. ***Email:*** gkit@sughrue.com

SUSAN J. MACK, born Manitowoc, Wisconsin, February 13, 1950; admitted to bar, 1983, District of Columbia; U.S. District Court of the District of Columbia; U.S. Court of Appeals for the District of Columbia and Federal Circuits; U.S. Supreme Court; registered to practice before U.S. Patent and Trademark Office. *Education:* University of Colorado at Boulder (B.A., 1972); University of Colorado Health Science Center (M.S., 1975); Denver University; American University (J.D., 1983). Phi Beta Kappa; Alpha Epsilon Delta. Recipient, American Jurisprudence Book Award for Property. *Member:* The District of Columbia Bar (Member, Steering Committee, 1989-1991, Section of Patent Trademark and Copyright); Bar Association of the District of Columbia (Chairperson, International Affairs Committee, 1986-1987; Treasurer, 1987-1988 and Council Member, 1988-1991, Patent, Trademark and Copyright Section); American Bar Association; American Intellectual Property Law Association; International Trade Commission Trial Lawyers Association; American Chemical Society. ***PRACTICE AREAS:*** Intellectual Property Law; Biotechnology. ***Email:*** smack@sughrue.com

FRANK L. BERNSTEIN, born Camden, New Jersey, November 21, 1959; admitted to bar, 1984, Wisconsin, District of Columbia and U.S. District Court, Western District of Wisconsin; 1997, California; registered to practice before U.S. Patent and Trademark Office. *Education:* California Institute of Technology (B.S., 1980); University of Wisconsin (M.B.A., 1984; J.D., 1984). Beta Gamma Sigma; Phi Delta Phi. *Member:* The District of Columbia Bar; State Bar of Wisconsin; State Bar of California; American Bar Association. ***PRACTICE AREAS:*** Intellectual Property Law; Litigation. ***Email:*** fbernstein@sughrue.com

MARK BOLAND, born Ottawa, Ontario, May 10, 1960; admitted to bar, 1985, Pennsylvania; 1994, District of Columbia; U.S. Court of Appeals for the Federal Circuit; registered to practice before U.S. Patent and Trademark Office. *Education:* College of the Holy Cross (B.A., Biol., 1982); Catholic University, Columbus School of Law (J.D., 1985). *Member:* Pennsylvania and American Bar Associations; District of Columbia Bar; American Intellectual Property Lawyers Association; International Trade Commission Trial Lawyers Association. ***PRACTICE AREAS:*** Intellectual Property Law; Litigation. ***Email:*** mboland@sughrue.com

WILLIAM H. MANDIR, born Brooklyn, New York, May 27, 1960; admitted to bar, 1987, Pennsylvania; 1989, District of Columbia; registered to practice before U.S. Patent and Trademark Office. *Education:* University of Maryland (B.S.E.E., 1983); Franklin Pierce Law Center (J.D., 1987). Eta Kappa Nu. *Member:* The District of Columbia Bar; American Bar Association; American Intellectual Property Law Association. ***PRACTICE AREAS:*** Intellectual Property Law; Litigation. ***Email:*** wmandir@sughrue.com

GARY D. KRUGMAN, born Brooklyn, New York, July 31, 1948; admitted to bar, 1974, District of Columbia and U.S. Court of Appeals for the District of

(This Listing Continued)

Columbia and Federal Circuits; 1976, U.S. District Court for the District of Columbia; 1978, U.S. Supreme Court; registered to practice before U.S. Patent and Trademark Office. *Education:* State University of New York at Albany (B.S., 1969); Case Western Reserve University (J.D., 1973). Author: Articles, 69 Trademark Reporter, May-June 1979, 70 Trademark Reporter, July-Aug. 1980; 73 Trademark Reporter, Jan.-Feb. 1983; 74 Trademark Reporter, July-Aug. 1984. *Member:* The District of Columbia Bar (Member, Section of Patent, Trademark and Copyright Law). ***PRACTICE AREAS:*** Trademark Law; Unfair Competition Law; Copyright Law. ***Email:*** gkrugman@sughrue.com

BRIAN W. HANNON, born Washington, D.C., April 10, 1957; admitted to bar, 1987, Pennsylvania and Maryland; 1989, District of Columbia; registered to practice before U.S. Patent and Trademark Office. *Education:* Villanova University (B.S.M.E., 1980); Catholic University (J.D., 1986). Pi Tau Sigma. *Member:* American Intellectual Property Lawyers Association. ***PRACTICE AREAS:*** Intellectual Property Law; Litigation. ***Email:*** bhannon@sughrue.com

ABRAHAM J. ROSNER, born New York, New York, February 26, 1956; admitted to bar, 1988, Virginia; 1989, District of Columbia; registered to practice before the U.S. Patent and Trademark Office. *Education:* Georgetown University (B.S., 1977); University of Maryland (M.S.Ch.E., 1979); George Mason University (J.D., 1988). Licensed Engineer, Virginia, 1988. *Member:* The District of Columbia Bar; Virginia State Bar. ***PRACTICE AREAS:*** Intellectual Property Law. ***Email:*** arosner@sughrue.com

BRUCE E. KRAMER, born Paterson, New Jersey, May 15, 1963; admitted to bar, 1989, District of Columbia; registered to practice before U.S. Patent and Trademark Office. *Education:* University of Virginia (B.S.Ch.E., 1985); University of Akron (J.D., 1989). Delta Theta Phi. Member, Akron Law Review, 1988-1989. *Member:* The District of Columbia Bar; American Bar Association. ***PRACTICE AREAS:*** Intellectual Property Law. ***Email:*** bkramer@sughrue.com

PAUL F. NEILS, born Allegan, Michigan, October 4, 1959; admitted to bar, 1989, District of Columbia; registered to practice before U.S. Patent and Trademark Office. *Education:* Michigan State University (B.S.M.E., 1982); Catholic University (J.D., 1989). *Member:* The District of Columbia Bar; American Bar Association; American Intellectual Property Law Association. ***PRACTICE AREAS:*** Intellectual Property Law. ***Email:*** pneils@sughrue.com

BRETT S. SYLVESTER, born Englewood, New Jersey, June 9, 1962; admitted to bar, 1987, Illinois; 1989, District of Columbia; registered to practice before U.S. Patent and Trademark Office. *Education:* Cornell University (B.S., 1984); John Marshall Law School (J.D., with distinction, 1987). Staff Member, John Marshall Law Review, 1986-1987. Law Clerk to the Honorable Giles S. Rich, U.S. Court of Appeals for the Federal Circuit, 1987-1989. *Member:* The District of Columbia Bar; American Bar Association (Member, Section of Patent, Trademark and Copyright Law); American Intellectual Property Law Association. ***PRACTICE AREAS:*** Intellectual Property Law. ***Email:*** bsylvester@sughrue.com

ROBERT M. MASTERS, born Rochester, Pennsylvania, March 25, 1963; admitted to bar, 1990, Maryland; 1992, District of Columbia; registered to practice before U.S. Patent and Trademark Office. *Education:* Pennsylvania State University (B.S.E.E., 1985); University of Baltimore (J.D., 1990). Eta Kappa Nu. ***PRACTICE AREAS:*** Intellectual Property Law; Litigation. ***Email:*** rmasters@sughrue.com

WILLIAM MACK WEBNER, born Columbus, Ohio, November 15, 1941; admitted to bar, 1968, Ohio; 1970, Illinois; 1972-1982, U.S. Court of Customs and Patent Appeals; 1975, New Jersey; 1976, District of Columbia; 1977, Virginia; 1980, U.S. District Court, Eastern District of Virginia, U.S. Court of Appeals, Fourth and Fifth Circuits; 1982, U.S. Court of Appeals for the Federal Circuit; 1983, U.S. Supreme Court, U.S. District Court, District of Columbia and U.S. Court of Appeals, Seventh Circuit; 1985, U.S. Court of Appeals, Sixth Circuit. *Education:* University of Akron (B.S., 1964; J.D., 1968); New York University (LL.M. in Trade Regulation, 1976). Phi Alpha Delta (President, Grant Chapter, 1967-1968). Chairman, Speakers Bureau, 1975-1976, Member, Board of Directors, 1985-1987, Chairman, Forum Committee, 1990-1992 and Member, Management Committee, International Trademark Association. *Member:* District of Columbia Bar (Member, Entertainment and Sports Law Section); Virginia, Ohio State, Illinois State and New Jersey State Bar Associations; International Trademark Association; American Intellectual Property Law Association. ***PRACTICE AREAS:*** Litigation; Trademark, Copyright and Unfair Competition Law; Trade Secret Law; Licensing. ***Email:*** mwebner@sughrue.com

GEORGE F. LEHNIGK, born Huntsville, Alabama, February 10, 1963; admitted to bar, 1991, Pennsylvania and New Jersey; 1995, District of Columbia; registered to practice before U.S. Patent and Trademark Office. *Education:* Duke University (B.S., magna cum laude, 1985); George Washington University (J.D., 1991). Member, Journal of International Law and Economics, 1990-1991. ***PRACTICE AREAS:*** Intellectual Property Law. ***Email:*** glehnigk@sughrue.com

JOHN T. CALLAHAN, born Hempstead, New York, October 3, 1963; admitted to bar, 1990, District of Columbia; registered to practice before the U.S. Patent and Trademark Office. *Education:* Catholic University (B.Ch.E., 1985); University of Baltimore (J.D., 1990). *Member:* District of Columbia Bar. ***PRACTICE AREAS:*** Intellectual Property Law. ***Email:*** jcallahan@sughrue.com

STEVEN M. GRUSKIN, born New London, Connecticut, September 12, 1966; admitted to bar, 1991, Florida and District of Columbia; 1993, U.S. District Court, Southern District of Florida and U.S. Court of Appeals for the Federal Circuit; registered to practice before U.S. Patent and Trademark Office. *Education:* University of Miami (B.S.M.E., 1988); George Washington University (J.D., 1991). Pi Tau Sigma; Tau Beta Pi. Recipient, Henry King Stanford Scholarship. Member, Student Intellectual Property Law Association, 1989-1991. *Member:* Broward County (Member, Patent, Trademark and Copyright Law Section) and American Bar Associations; The Florida Bar (Member, Patent, Trademark and Copyright Law Section); District of Columbia Bar (Member, Patent, Trademark and Copyright Law Section); Federal Circuit and Federal Bar Associations; Patent Law Association of South Florida; American Intellectual Property Law Association. ***PRACTICE AREAS:*** Intellectual Property Law. ***Email:*** sgruskin@sughrue.com

PETER A. McKENNA, born Bayonne, New Jersey, October 5, 1951; admitted to bar, 1994, New Jersey; 1996, District of Columbia; registered to practice before U.S. Patent and Trademark Office. *Education:* New Jersey Institute of Technology (B.S.E.E., 1988); Seton Hall University (J.D., cum laude, 1993). Phi Alpha Delta. Member: Federalist Society, 1989—; American Society of Hospital Engineers, 1989—. Author: "States May Not Impose Civil Penalties on the United States Government for Violations of State Statutes Promulgated Under the Authority of the Clean Water Act and the Resource Conservation and Recovery Act," 23 Seton Hall Law Review 762. *Member:* District of Columbia Bar. ***PRACTICE AREAS:*** Intellectual Property Law. ***Email:*** pmckenna@sughrue.com

EDWARD F. KENEHAN, JR., born Washington, D.C., December 27, 1950; admitted to bar, 1979, District of Columbia; registered to practice before U.S. Patent and Trademark Office. *Education:* Georgia Institute of Technology (B.S., 1972); American University (J.D., 1978). *Member:* District of Columbia Bar. ***PRACTICE AREAS:*** Intellectual Property. ***Email:*** ekenehan@sughrue.com

JOHN F. RABENA, born Camp Hill, Pennsylvania, April 18, 1965; admitted to bar, 1994, Maryland; 1995, District of Columbia; registered to practice before U.S. Patent and Trademark Office. *Education:* United States Military Academy (B.S.E.E., 1987); North Carolina State University (M.E.E., 1991); University of Baltimore (J.D., 1994). *Member:* Maryland State and American Bar Associations; District of Columbia Bar; American Intellectual Property Law Association. [Captain, U.S. Army, 1987-1990]. ***PRACTICE AREAS:*** Intellectual Property Law; Litigation. ***Email:*** jrabena@sughrue.com

GRANT K. ROWAN, born Baltimore, Maryland, June 20, 1968; admitted to bar, 1994, Maryland; 1995, District of Columbia. *Education:* University of Maryland (B.S.E.E., 1990); George Washington University (J.D., 1994). *Member:* The District of Columbia Bar. ***PRACTICE AREAS:*** Intellectual Property Law; Litigation. ***Email:*** growan@sughrue.com

SUSAN PERNG PAN, born Taipei, Taiwan, February 8, 1969; admitted to bar, 1995, Virginia; 1998, District of Columbia; registered to practice before U.S. Patent and Trademark Office. *Education:* University of Virginia (B.S.E.E., 1991); George Washington University (J.D., with honors, 1995). Editor, Journal of International Law & Economics, 1994-1995. *Member:* Virginia State Bar; American Intellectual Property Law Association. ***PRACTICE AREAS:*** Intellectual Property Law. ***Email:*** span@sughrue.com

KEVIN G. SMITH, born Washington, D.C., September 5, 1953; admitted to bar, 1980, Georgia and U.S. District Court, Northern District of Georgia; 1981, U.S. Claims Court and U.S. Court of Customs and Patent Appeals; 1982, U.S. Court of Appeals, Federal Circuit; 1988, District of Columbia and U.S. Court of Appeals, District of Columbia Circuit. *Education:* St. Mary's College of Maryland (B.A., 1976); Potomac School of Law (J.D., 1980). *Member:* Bar Association of the District of Columbia; District of Columbia Bar (Member, Section on Patents, Trademarks and Copyrights); State Bar of Georgia; American Bar Association; International Trademark Association. ***PRACTICE AREAS:*** Trademark Law. ***Email:*** ksmith@sughrue.com

JODY HALLER DRAKE, born Altoona, Pennsylvania, March 1, 1955; admitted to bar, 1981, Massachusetts; 1983, U.S. Court of Appeals for the Federal Circuit; 1992, District of Columbia. *Education:* Franklin and Marshall College (B.A., 1977); McGeorge School of Law, University of the Pacific; Western New England College (J.D., 1981). Senior Attorney, Department of Commerce, U.S. Patent and Trademark Office, 1983-1990. *Member:* District of Columbia Bar (Member, Section on Patents, Trademarks and Copyrights); American Bar Association (Co-Chair, Committee No. 203, Patent and Trademark Office Affairs, 1991-1992); INTA (Member, Patent and Trademark Office Committee, 1990-1994). ***PRACTICE AREAS:*** Trademark Law; Copyright Law. ***Email:*** jdrake@sughrue.com

(This Listing Continued)

(This Listing Continued)

SUGHRUE MION, PLLC, Washington—Continued

ASSOCIATES

LEE C. WRIGHT, born Elkhorn, Wisconsin, January 30, 1961; admitted to bar, 1996, Maryland; 1998, District of Columbia; registered to practice before U.S. Patent and Trademark Office. *Education:* University of Maryland (B.S., 1984); University of Maryland (M.S., 1987); George Mason University School of Law (J.D., 1996). ***PRACTICE AREAS:*** Intellectual Property. ***Email:*** lwright@sughrue.com

STANISLAV TORGOVITSKY, born Kiev, Ukraine, January 25, 1967; admitted to bar, 1996, Virginia; 2001, District of Columbia; registered to practice before U.S. Patent and Trademark Office. *Education:* George Washington University (B.A., 1988; J.D., 1996). *Member:* Virginia State Bar. ***LANGUAGES:*** Russian, Ukrainian and English. ***PRACTICE AREAS:*** Intellectual Property. ***Email:*** storgovitsky@sughrue.com

CARL J. PELLEGRINI, born Milwaukee, Wisconsin, September 16, 1960; admitted to bar, 1992, Wisconsin and U.S. District Court, Western and Eastern Districts of Wisconsin; 1998, District of Columbia; registered to practice before U.S. Patent and Trademark Office. *Education:* Marquette University (B.S.E.E., cum laude, 1982); George Washington University (M.B.A., 1989); University of Wisconsin-Madison (J.D., 1992). Tau Beta Pi. Author: "The European Economic Community's Council Directive Concerning General Product Safety," Wis. Int'l Law Journal, Vol. 10, No. 2, Spring 1992. *Member:* State Bar of Wisconsin; The District of Columbia Bar; American Bar Association. ***PRACTICE AREAS:*** Intellectual Property Prosecution; Intellectual Property Litigation. ***Email:*** cpellegrini@sughrue.com

KELLY G. HYNDMAN, born San Pierre, Indiana, November 29, 1960; admitted to bar, 1997, Virginia; 2000, District of Columbia; registered to practice before U.S. Patent and Trademark Office. *Education:* United States Military Academy (B.S., Computer Science concentration, 1982); Boston University (M.S., Computer Information Syst., 1989); Georgetown University (J.D., magna cum laude, 1997). Fraternal Order of the Coif. Commissioned Officer, Signal Corps, U.S. Army, 1982-1990. Systems Engineer and Software Engineer Lockheed-Martin Corporation, 1990-1995. *Member:* Virginia State Bar; American Bar Association; American Intellectual Property Association. ***Email:*** khyndman@sughrue.com

ELLEN RESNICK SMITH, born Pittsburgh, Pennsylvania, January 9, 1970; admitted to bar, 1997, Maryland; 2000, District of Columbia; registered to practice before U.S. Patent and Trademark Office. *Education:* Tufts University (B.S., Civil Engineering, 1992); George Mason University School of Law (J.D., 1997). Co-Author: with, D. Bhinge, L. Jones-Bateman, D. Mays, J. Patel, E. Resnick, "Environmental Readiness," The Military Engineer, Vol. 86, 1994; with D. Bhinge, L. Jones-Bateman, D. Mays, J. Patel, E. Resnick, "Baraboo Plant Provides Environmental Lessons," National Defense, Vol. LXXIX, July/August 1994; with D. Mays, D. Bhinge, L. Jones-Bateman, D. Mays, J. Patel, E. Resnick, "Environmental Readlines Pilot Study at the Badger Army Ammunition Plant, Baraboo, Wisconsin," American Defense Preparedness Association 20th Environmental Symposium Proceedings, San Antonio, TX, March 1994. Civil Engineer, Science Applications International Corporation, 1992-1997. *Member:* Maryland State Bar Association, Inc.;. ***Email:*** esmith@sughrue.com

RAJA N. SALIBA, born Fairfax, Virginia, December 14, 1966; admitted to bar, 1997, Maryland; 2000, District of Columbia; registered to practice before U.S. Patent and Trademark Office. *Education:* Virginia Tech University (B.S., Mechanical Engineering, 1987); College of William and Mary (M.B.A., Beta Gamma Sigma, 1992); George Washington University (J.D., with honors, 1997). Hydraulic Systems Engineer, Newport News Shipbuilding, 1988-1990. Manager of Business Operations, CTA Space Systems, 1992-1996. *Member:* Maryland State and American Bar Associations. ***LANGUAGES:*** Arabic and French. ***PRACTICE AREAS:*** Patent Litigation; Patent Prosecution. ***Email:*** rsaliba@sughrue.com

H. RAY HEFLIN, born Huntsville, Alabama, December 23, 1967; admitted to bar, 1997, Virginia; registered to practice before U.S. Patent and Trademark Office (Not admitted in District of Columbia). *Education:* Georgia Institute of Technology (B.S., Industrial Eng., 1990); Franklin Pierce Law Center (J.D., 1997). Moot Court Teaching Assistant, 1995-1996. *Member:* Virginia Bar Association; American Intellectual Property Association. ***Email:*** rheflin@sughrue.com

CHID SUBRAMANIAN, born Trivandrum, Kerala, India, August 10, 1961; admitted to bar, 1997, New York and New Jersey; 2000, District of Columbia; registered to practice before U.S. Patent and Trademark Office. *Education:* IIT, Bombay, India (B.Tech, Chemical Eng., 1984); University of Akron (M.S.Ch.E., 1986); University of Tennessee (M.S., Computer Science, 1988); Georgetown University Law Center (J.D., 1997). Sigma Xi; Upsilon Pi Epsilon. Author: "Acquisition of Expert Knowledge about Biological Treatment for CARTS," Proceedings, of EXPERSYS 91, Paris France, October 1991; "CARTS: A consistent methodology for Generating Treatment Trains," Proceedings of the National Research & Development Conference on the Control of Hazardous Materials, Anaheim, California, February 1991; "Detecting Abnormal Situations from Real Time Power Plant Data Using Machine Learning," Proceedings of the First International Conference on Industrial and Engineering Applications of Expert Systems, Tullahoma, Tennessee, July 1988. Research Assistant: University of Akron, 1984-1986; Space Institute, Utah, 1986-1988. Principal Project Manager, Roy F. Weston, Inc., 1986-1988. Senior Engineer, Automation Research Systems, Inc., 1993-1995. Technical Director, Ensys, Inc., 1991-1993, 1995-1996. Senior Technical Staff, Emplore Reasoning Systems, Inc., 1996-1997. *Member:* New York State and New Jersey State Bar Association. ***Email:*** csubramanian@sughrue.com

JEFFREY A. SCHMIDT, born Buffalo, New York, July 19, 1968; admitted to bar, 1997, Virginia, U.S. Supreme Court, and U.S. Court of Appeals, Federal Circuit; 1999, District of Columbia; registered to practice before U.S. Patent and Trademark Office. *Education:* University of Michigan (M.E., 1988); State University of New York at Buffalo (B.S., Mechanical Eng., cum laude, 1991); Catholic University of America, Columbus School of Law (J.D., cum laude, 1997). Tau Beta Pi; National Engineer Honor Society. Patent Examiner, U.S. Patent and Trademark Office. *Member:* Virginia and American Bar Associations; American Intellectual Property Law Association. ***Email:*** jschmidt@sughrue.com

PAUL J. WILSON, born Detroit, Michigan, November 2, 1961; admitted to bar, 1998, Maryland; 2001, District of Columbia; registered to practice before U.S. Patent and Trademark Office. *Education:* Michigan Technological University (B.S.E.E., 1983); University of Baltimore (J.D., 1998). ***PRACTICE AREAS:*** Electronics; Computers and Software; Intellectual Property. ***Email:*** pwilson@sughrue.com

ERIC P. HALBER, born Washington, D.C., September 9, 1963; admitted to bar, 1990, District of Columbia; 1992, Louisiana. *Education:* Lafayette College (B.S.M.E., 1985); New England School of Law (J.D., 1990); Tulane University (LL.M., Admiralty, 1992); University of New Orleans (Master's Program, 1997). Staff Member, 1988-1989, and Technical Editor, 1989, New England Journal on Criminal and Civil Confinement. Author, "Evolving Law and Rule 11," ABA Admiralty Litigation Newsletter (January 1997). Co-Author, "The U.S. Liability Regime for the Inland Leg of a Multimodal Transportation System by Road and Rail," with C. Davis, International Bar Association, New Orleans Conference (November 1993). *Member:* District of Columbia Bar; Louisiana State Bar Association. ***PRACTICE AREAS:*** Intellectual Property. ***Email:*** ehalber@sughrue.com

CHRISTOPHER R. LIPP, born Alexandria, Virginia, June 16, 1969; admitted to bar, 1998, Virginia; registered to practice before U.S. Patent and Trademark Office (Not admitted in District of Columbia). *Education:* Virginia Polytechnic Institute & State University (B.S., Electrical Engineering, 1991); George Mason University School of Law (J.D., 1998). Eta Kappa Nu; Gamma Beta Phi; Phi Eta Sigma. Member, Institute of Electrical and Electronics Engineers. *Member:* Virginia State Bar; Intellectual Property Law Society. ***PRACTICE AREAS:*** Intellectual Property. ***Email:*** clipp@sughrue.com

KEVIN M. BARNER, born Concord, California, April 5, 1965; admitted to bar, 1997, Maryland (Not admitted in District of Columbia). *Education:* University of Delaware (B.E.E., 1987); University of Baltimore (M.B.A., 1993; J.D., 1997). Sigma Delta Kappa. *Member:* Maryland State Bar Association. ***PRACTICE AREAS:*** Intellectual Property. ***Email:*** kbarner@sughrue.com

LEIGH ANN LINDQUIST, born Atlanta, Georgia; admitted to bar, 1998, Maryland; 2001, District of Columbia. *Education:* Smith College (A.B., History, 1993); George Washington University (J.D., with honors, 1998). Author, "An Examination of U.S. Failure to Comply with the Geographical Provisions of the TRIPS Agreement," 27 Ga. J. Int'l. & Comp. L. 309, 1999. *Member:* Maryland State Bar Association. ***PRACTICE AREAS:*** Intellectual Property. ***Email:*** llindquist@sughrue.com

JOHN W. BAIN, born Park Forest, Illinois, May 26, 1955; admitted to bar, 1998, District of Columbia; registered to practice before U.S. Patent and Trademark Office. *Education:* Purdue University (B.S., 1994); Indiana University School of Law (J.D., 1998). Licensed Commercial Pilot, Federal Aviation Administration. Member: Institute of Electrical and Electronics Engineers. *Member:* District of Columbia Bar; American Bar Association; American Intellectual Property Law Association. ***PRACTICE AREAS:*** Intellectual Property. ***Email:*** jbain@sughrue.com

DAVID A. KLEIN, born Miami, Florida, June 30, 1968; admitted to bar, 1999, Virginia; 2000, District of Columbia. *Education:* University of Florida (B.S.E.E., 1992; M.S., 1994); Georgetown University (J.D., 1999). *Member:* American Bar Association; American Intellectual Property Law Association. ***PRACTICE AREAS:*** Intellectual Property. ***Email:*** dklein@sughrue.com

L. RAUL TAMAYO, born Florence, South Carolina, January 31, 1973; admitted to bar, 1999, Virginia; 2001, District of Columbia. *Education:* University of Florida (B.S.Ch.E., 1995); Georgetown University (J.D., 1999). ***LANGUAGES:*** Spanish. ***PRACTICE AREAS:*** Intellectual Property Law. ***Email:*** rtamayo@sughrue.com

(This Listing Continued)

KEIKO K. TAKAGI, born Nashville, Tennessee, January 23, 1974; admitted to bar, 1999, Illinois (Not admitted in District of Columbia). *Education:* Vanderbilt University (B.S., 1996); Loyola University (J.D., 1999). ***LANGUAGES:*** Japanese. ***PRACTICE AREAS:*** Intellectual Property Law. ***Email:*** ktakagi@sughrue.com

DREW HISSONG, PH.D., born Canton, Ohio, February 20, 1967; admitted to bar, 1999, Ohio; 2000, District of Columbia; registered to practice before U.S. Patent and Trademark Office. *Education:* Kent State University (B.S., 1989); University of Illinois (M.S., 1991); University of North Carolina, Chapel Hill (Ph.D., 1998); Case Western Reserve University (J.D., 1999). *Member:* Ohio State Bar Association; American Intellectual Property Law Association. ***PRACTICE AREAS:*** Intellectual Property Law. ***Email:*** dhissong@sughrue.com

PAUL M. HIGGINS, born Fort Sill, Oklahoma, November 9, 1968; admitted to bar, 1996, Massachusetts; 1997, District of Columbia, U.S. District Court for the District of Columbia and U.S. Court of Appeals for the District of Columbia Circuit. *Education:* University of New Hampshire (B.A., 1991); Catholic University of America (J.D., 1995). Member, Moot Court, 1993-1995. Recipient, Plato Papps Scholarship. *Member:* The District of Columbia Bar; American Bar Association. ***PRACTICE AREAS:*** Trademark. ***Email:*** phiggins@sughrue.com

MAINAK HIMANSHU MEHTA, born Columbus, Ohio, June 19, 1970; admitted to bar, 1999, District of Columbia. *Education:* University of Virginia (B.S., 1993); George Mason University (J.D., 1998). *Member:* The District of Columbia Bar (Member, Intellectual Property Section), American Intellectual Property Law Association; Environmental Law Society. ***PRACTICE AREAS:*** Intellectual Property. ***Email:*** mmehta@sughrue.com

CRAIG W. SCHMOYER, born Danville, Illinois, August 1, 1945; admitted to bar, 2000, California (Not admitted in District of Columbia). *Education:* Purdue University (B.S.E.E., 1967); Southwestern University School of Law (J.D., 1999). ***Email:*** cschmoyer@sughrue.com

AMY E. SIMPSON, born Palo Alto, California, September 1, 1974; admitted to bar, 2000, Utah (Not admitted in District of Columbia). *Education:* University of Idaho (B.S., 1996); Franklin Pierce Law Center (J.D., 2000). ***PRACTICE AREAS:*** Patent Prosecution; Patent Litigation. ***Email:*** asimpson@sughrue.com

KEITH B. SCALA, born Grand Junction, Colorado, March 18, 1975; admitted to bar, 2000, Illinois; registered to practice before U.S. Patent and Trademark Office (Not admitted in District of Columbia). *Education:* Cornell University (B.S., 1997); John Marshall Law School (J.D., cum laude, 2000). ***PRACTICE AREAS:*** Patents. ***Email:*** kscala@sughrue.com

TERRANCE JAY WIKBERG, born Allentown, Pennsylvania, April 12, 1970; admitted to bar, 2000, Maryland; registered to practice before U.S. Patent and Trademark Office (Not admitted in District of Columbia). *Education:* Embry-Riddle Aerounautical University (B.S.A.E., 1992); University of Maryland (J.D., 2000). Order of the Coif. Author: Maryland Law Review, Vol.58, No. 3. ***PRACTICE AREAS:*** Patents. ***Email:*** twikberg@sughrue.com

MARK R. WOODALL, born Andover, Massachusetts, June 25, 1966; admitted to bar, 1999, District of Columbia; registered to practice before U.S. Patent and Trademark Office. *Education:* Virginia Polytechnic Institute and State University (B.S., 1990); George Mason University School of Law (J.D., 1998); George Mason University (B.S.E.E., 2000). *Member:* The District of Columbia Bar (Member, Intellectual Property Section, 1999—); Federal Circuit Bar Association; American Intellectual Property Law Association; The Rutherford Institute; The Christian Legal Society (Vice President, George Mason Chapter, 1995-1998). ***PRACTICE AREAS:*** Intellectual Property. ***Email:*** mwoodall@sughrue.com

RONALD L. KIMBLE, born Keyser, West Virginia, June 11, 1964; admitted to bar, 2001, Maryland; registered to practice before U.S. Patent and Trademark Office (Not admitted in District of Columbia). *Education:* University of Maryland, College Park (B.S., 1986); Johns Hopkins University (M.S., 1992); George Washington University (J.D., 2001). *Member:* Maryland State Bar Association. ***PRACTICE AREAS:*** Intellectual Property. ***Email:*** rkimble@sughrue.com

CAMERON W. BEDDARD, born Oak Park, Illinois, September 18, 1967; admitted to bar, 2001, Maryland; registered to practice before U.S. Patent and Trademark Office (Not admitted in District of Columbia). *Education:* Washington University (B.S.E.E., 1990); Georgetown University (J.D., 2000). ***PRACTICE AREAS:*** Patent Law. ***Email:*** cbeddard@sughrue.com

TIMOTHY P. CREMEN, born Royal Oak, Michigan, August 17, 1972; admitted to bar, 2000, Michigan (Not admitted in District of Columbia). *Education:* Michigan State University (B.S.M.E., 1995; J.D., 2000). ***PRACTICE AREAS:*** Intellectual Property. ***Email:*** tcremen@sughrue.com

MICHAEL J. WHITEHEAD, born Anderson, Indiana, January 19, 1974; admitted to bar, 2001, District of Columbia; registered to practice before U.S. Patent and Trademark Office. *Education:* The Ohio State University (B.S.E.E., 1997); Franklin Piece Law Center (J.D., 2000). Phi Alpha Delta. *Member:* The District of Columbia Bar; Institute of Electrical and Electronical Engineers. ***PRACTICE AREAS:*** Patent Law. ***Email:*** mjwhitehead@sughrue.com

(This Listing Continued)

DANIEL V. WILLIAMS, born Rochester, New York, August 18, 1971; admitted to bar, 2001, District of Columbia; registered to practice before U.S. Patent and Trademark Office. *Education:* Rochester Institute of Technology (B.S.M.E., 1996); Franklin Pierce Law Center (J.D., 2000). *Member:* The District of Columbia Bar; American Intellectual Property Law Association; American Society of Mechanical Engineers. ***PRACTICE AREAS:*** Intellectual Property. ***Email:*** dvwilliams@sughrue.com

JENNIFER M. HAYES, born Toledo, Ohio, November 30, 1968; admitted to bar, 1994, Maryland; 1996, District of Columbia; registered to practice before U.S. Patent and Trademark Office. *Education:* Howard University (B.S., 1991; J.D., 1994). Rho Chi Pharmacy Honor Society. Phi Alpha Delta. Registered Pharmacist, Maryland, 1991. *Member:* The District of Columbia Bar; American Intellectual Property Law Association (Member, Diversity in Intellectual Property Law Committee). ***PRACTICE AREAS:*** Patent Law. ***Email:*** jhayes@sughrue.com

WILLIAM K. YEE, born United Kingdom; admitted to bar, 2000, California (Not admitted in District of Columbia). *Education:* University of California at Davis (B.S., 1988); Santa Clara University (J.D., 2000). ***PRACTICE AREAS:*** Patent Law. ***Email:*** wyee@sughrue.com

JOHN M. SANDERS, born Chicago, Illinois, February 23, 1954; admitted to bar, 1980, Illinois; 1981, Michigan; 1986, Wisconsin (Not admitted in District of Columbia). *Education:* University of Illinois at Chicago (B.S., 1977); John Marshall Law School, Chicago (J.D., 1980; LL.M., 1993). ***PRACTICE AREAS:*** Intellectual Property. ***Email:*** jsanders@sughrue.com

YOSHINARI KISHIMOTO, born Hyogo, Japan, September 14, 1954; admitted to bar, 1991, Japan as Patent Attorney; 1999, New York and U.S. Court of Appeals for the Federal Circuit; registered to practice before U.S. Patent and Trademark Office (Not admitted in District of Columbia). *Education:* University of Tokyo (B.A., 1980); Keio University (LL.B., 1994); George Washington University (LL.M., 1998). Examiner, Japanese Government Patent Office, 1981-1991. Author: "A Comparative Study of Patent and Antitrust," Patent Journal, No. 6, 9, 10, Japan Patent Attorneys Association, 1995. Lecturer, Seminar For Foreign Examiners Assisted by WIPO, 1989. *Member:* New York State and American Bar Associations; American Intellectual Property Law Association; Japanese Patent Attorneys Association. ***LANGUAGES:*** Japanese. ***PRACTICE AREAS:*** Patent Application; Patent Prosecution; Litigation. ***Email:*** ykishimoto@sughrue.com

DAVID A. SUMY, born Pittsfield, Massachusetts, June 27, 1963; admitted to bar, 1998, Illlinois; 1999, District of Columbia. *Education:* Berklee College of Music (B.Mus., 1993); Harvard Extension School; John Marshall Law School (J.D., 1998; LL.M., 1999); Northwestern University College; University of Illinois. Recipient, Robert Bradford Newman Award. *Member:* The District of Columbia Bar; Illinois State Bar Association. [Lance Corporal, U.S. Marine Corps, 1981-1984]. ***PRACTICE AREAS:*** Patent Law. ***Email:*** dsumy@sughrue.com

JOHN M. BIRD, born Washington, D.C., March 9, 1973; admitted to bar, 2000, Maryland; registered to practice before U.S. Patent and Trademark Office (Not admitted in District of Columbia). *Education:* University of Maryland (B.S.M.E., 1995; J.D., 2000). ***PRACTICE AREAS:*** Patents. ***Email:*** jbird@sughrue.com

GEORGE BRIEGER, born Hungary, April 30, 1966; admitted to bar, 1994, New York; 1995, U.S. District Court, Eastern and Southern Districts of New York (Not admitted in District of Columbia). *Education:* Brooklyn College of the City University of New York (B.S., 1988); Benjamin N. Cardozo School of Law (J.D., 1993). George Washington University, Intellectual Property Program. Editor, New Europe Law Review. Member, Advisory Board, Budapest-New York Sister City Committee, 1996-2000. Instructor, Elte University School of Law, Budapest, Hungary, 1997-1998. *Member:* Association of the Bar of the City of New York; American Intellectual Property Law Association. ***Email:*** gbrieger@sughrue.com

SENIOR COUNSEL

ROBERT G. McMORROW, (P.C.), born Washington, D.C., January 18, 1930; admitted to bar, 1957, District of Columbia; registered to practice before U.S. Patent and Trademark Office. *Education:* Wilson Teacher's College (B.S., 1955); Georgetown University (LL.B., 1957; M.P.L., 1958). *Member:* The District of Columbia Bar; The Bar Association of the District of Columbia; American Bar Association (Member, Section on Patent, Trademark and Copyright Law); American Intellectual Property Law Association. ***PRACTICE AREAS:*** Intellectual Property Law; Trademark Law.

SULLIVAN & CROMWELL

1701 PENNSYLVANIA AVENUE, N.W.
WASHINGTON, D.C. 20006-5805
Telephone: 202-956-7500
Telecopier: 202-293-6330
URL: http://www.sullcrom.com

New York City Office: 125 Broad Street, 10004-2498. Telephone: 212-558-4000. Telex: 62694. Telecopier: 212-558-3588.

Los Angeles, California Office: 1888 Century Park East, 90067-1725. Telephone: 310-712-6600. Telecopier: 310-712-8800.

Palo Alto, California Office: 1870 Embarcadero Road, 94303-3308. Telephone: 650-461-5600. Telecopier: 650-461-5700.

Paris Office: 8, place Vendôme, 75001 Paris, France. Telephone: (011)(331) 44 50 60 00. Telecopier: (011)(331) 44 50 60 60.

London Office: St. Olave's House, 9a Ironmonger Lane, London EC2V 8EY, England. Telephone: (011)(44207) 710 6500. Telecopier: (011)(44207) 710 6565.

Melbourne Office: 101 Collins Street, Melbourne 3000, Australia. Telephone: (011)(613) 9635-1500. Telecopier: (011)(613) 9654-2422.

Tokyo Office: Otemachi First Square East Tower 16F, 5-1, Otemachi 1-chome, Chiyoda-ku, Tokyo 100-0004, Japan. Telephone: (011)(813) 3213-6140. Telecopier: (011)(813) 3213-6470.

Hong Kong Office: 28th Floor, Nine Queen's Road, Central, Hong Kong. Telephone: (011)(852) 2826-8688. Telecopier: (011)(852) 2522-2280.

Frankfurt Office: Neue Mainzer Strasse 52, 60311 Frankfurt am Main, Germany. Telephone: (011)(4969) 7191 26-0. Telecopier: (011)(4969) 7191 26-10.

Beijing Office: The Beijing Representative Office of Sullivan & Cromwell, Suite 501, China World Trade Center Tower 1, No. 1 Jianguo Menwai Avenue, Beijing 100004, P.R.C. Telephone: (011)(86) 10 6505 6120. Telecopier: (011)(86) 10 6505 6136.

Sydney Office: Level 34, The Chifley Tower, 2 Chifley Square, Sydney, NSW 2000, Australia. Telephone: (001) 61-2 8227-6700. Telecopier: (001) 61-2 8227-6750.

General Practice.

PARTNERS IN WASHINGTON, D.C.

H. RODGIN COHEN, born Charleston, WV, 1944; admitted to bar, 1971, New York (Not admitted in District of Columbia). *Education:* Harvard (B.A., 1965; LL.B., 1968). (Also at New York Office).

ROBERT H. CRAFT, JR., born New York, NY, 1939; admitted to bar, 1973, New York; 1977, District of Columbia. *Education:* Princeton (A.B., 1961); Oxford (B.A., 1963); Harvard (LL.B., 1966).

DARYL A. LIBOW, born White Plains, NY, 1959; admitted to bar, 1986, New York; 1995, District of Columbia. *Education:* Harvard (A.B., 1981); London School of Economics and Political Science (Graduate Diploma in International Law, 1982); Cornell (J.D., 1986). Co-chair, International Antitrust Committee, Section of International Law and Practice, 1997—, American Bar Association.

MARGARET K. PFEIFFER, born Elkin, NC, 1944; admitted to bar, 1976, New York; 1981, District of Columbia. *Education:* Duke (B.A., 1967); Rutgers (M.C.R.P.; J.D., 1974).

ROBERT SAMUEL RISOLEO, born Pittsburgh, PA, 1958; admitted to bar, 1988, New York (Not admitted in District of Columbia). *Education:* Yale (B.A., 1980; J.D., 1984); University of York (M.Sc., 1982).

KATHRYN E. RORER, born Port Jefferson, NY, 1967; admitted to bar, 1993, New York; 1994, District of Columbia. *Education:* Harvard (B.A., 1989; J.D., 1992).

DENNIS C. SULLIVAN, born Jersey City, NJ, 1959; admitted to bar, 1985, New York; 1991, District of Columbia. *Education:* Georgetown Univ. (B.S., 1981); Catholic Univ. of America (J.D., 1984).

EDWIN D. WILLIAMSON, born Florence, SC, 1939; admitted to bar, 1965, New York; 1988, District of Columbia. *Education:* Univ. of the South (B.A., 1961; D.C.L. (honorary), 1992); New York Univ. (J.D., 1964). The Legal Adviser, 1990-1993, U.S. Department of State.

OF COUNSEL IN WASHINGTON, D.C.

JANET THIELE GELDZAHLER, born Boston, MA, 1954; admitted to bar, 1980, New York; 1996, District of Columbia. *Education:* Univ. of Virginia (B.A., 1976; J.D., 1979).

SPECIAL COUNSEL IN WASHINGTON, D.C.

STEPHEN C. CONNOR, born Fairfax, VA, 1961; admitted to bar, 1990, New York (Not admitted in District of Columbia). *Education:* Duke (B.A., 1983; J.D., 1986).

(This Listing Continued)

THOMAS R. LEUBA, born Springfield, OH, 1964; admitted to bar, 1991, New York and District of Columbia. *Education:* Univ. of Colorado (B.A., 1986); George Washington Univ. (J.D., 1990).

PAUL J. McELROY, born Queens, NY, 1963; admitted to bar, 1990, New York and District of Columbia. *Education:* Univ. of Notre Dame (B.A., 1985); Catholic Univ. of America (J.D., 1988).

ASSOCIATES IN WASHINGTON, D.C.

CHRISTINE AYOTTE-BRENNAN, born Lowell, MA, 1974; admitted to bar, 2000, District of Columbia. *Education:* Boston College (B.A., 1996); Catholic Univ. of America (J.D., 1999).

TORYAH S. CAMERON, born Hattiesburg, MS, 1972; admitted to bar, 1998, New York; 2000, District of Columbia. *Education:* Harvard (A.B., 1994); Howard (J.D., 1997).

JOHN E. CAPPS, born Cookeville, TN, 1964; admitted to bar, 1995, New York (Not admitted in District of Columbia). *Education:* Vanderbilt (B.A., 1986; M.B.A., 1989); Univ. of Texas (J.D., 1994).

RITA M. CARRIER, born Luino, Italy, 1951; admitted to bar, 1984, District of Columbia; 1986, New York. *Education:* Manhattanville (B.A., 1974); Catholic Univ. of America (J.D., 1984).

ROBERT E. CHANDLER, born New York, NY, 1973; admitted to bar, 2000, New York (Not admitted in District of Columbia). *Education:* James Madison Univ. (B.S., 1994); College of William & Mary (J.D., 1999).

JENNIFER E. COOK, born Fall River, MA, 1971; admitted to bar, 2000, New York and District of Columbia. *Education:* Brown (B.S., 1993); American Univ., (J.D., 1999).

GEOFFREY P. EATON, born Urbana, IL, 1971; admitted to bar, 1999, New York (Not admitted in District of Columbia). *Education:* William & Mary (B.A., 1994); Univ. of Virginia (J.D., 1998).

BRUCE FEIN, born Washington, DC, 1976; admitted to bar, 2000, District of Columbia. *Education:* Univ. of Chicago (A.B., 1996; J.D., 1999).

ALEXANDER D. FINE, born Hartford, CT, 1972; admitted to bar, 2001, New York (Not admitted in District of Columbia). *Education:* Duke (A.B., 1994); Univ. of Virginia (J.D., 2000).

JACQUELINE SUZANNE HACKETT, born Queens, NY., 1974; admitted to bar, 2000, New York (Not admitted in District of Columbia). *Education:* Georgetown Univ. (B.S., 1996); Duke (J.D., 1998).

THOMAS F. HANCOCK, born Hamilton, OH, 1944; admitted to bar, 1980, District of Columbia. *Education:* Univ. of Illinois (M.A., 1972; J.D., 1977).

STEPHEN C. JACQUES, born Milford, MA, 1972; admitted to bar, 1999, New York and District of Columbia. *Education:* Boston College (B.A., 1994); American University (J.D., 1998).

ERIC J. KADEL, JR., born Port Jefferson, NY, 1970; admitted to bar, 2001, District of Columbia. *Education:* College of William & Mary (B.A., 1992); Univ. of Virginia (J.D., 1997).

ANNA M. KUZMIK, born Dearborn, MI, 1970; admitted to bar, 1995, New York and District of Columbia. *Education:* Wayne State Univ. (B.A., 1991); Harvard (J.D., 1994).

KATHERINE K. MARTIN, born Kiev, Ukraine, 1975; admitted to bar, 2000, New York (Not admitted in District of Columbia). *Education:* Syracuse (B.A., 1997; J.D., 1999).

JOSEPH JAMES MATELIS, II, born Silver Spring, MD, 1971; admitted to bar, 1997, New York; 1999, District of Columbia. *Education:* Univ. of North Carolina (B.A., 1993); Harvard (J.D., 1996).

LEE ANN ANDERSON McCALL, born Cincinnati, OH, 1966; admitted to bar, 1994, New York; 1995, District of Columbia. *Education:* Wellesley (B.A., 1988); Univ. of South Carolina (J.D., 1992).

ANN M. MILLER, born Badconstadd, West Germany, 1974; admitted to bar, 2000, New York and District of Columbia. *Education:* Smith College (B.A., 1996); Univ. of Arizona (J.D., 1999).

CHIDI J. OGENE, born Washington, DC, 1968; admitted to bar, 1999, New York (Not admitted in District of Columbia). *Education:* Univ. of Nigeria (LL.B., 1989); Georgetown Univ. (J.D./M.B.A., 1997).

BRADLEY P. SMITH, born Englewood, CO, 1970; admitted to bar, 1998, New York; 2000, District of Columbia. *Education:* Rice Univ. (B.A., 1993); Institut d'Etudes Politiques, Paris, France (Certificat d'Etudes Politiques, 1994); Yale (J.D., 1997).

MICHAEL K. SOPCHICK, born Honolulu, HI, 1961; admitted to bar, 1998, New York and District of Columbia. *Education:* Villanova (B.A., 1983); Catholic Univ. of America (J.D., 1997).

(This Listing Continued)

VERONIQUE K. WAITES, born Manchester, CT, 1973; admitted to bar, 2000, District of Columbia. *Education:* McGill Univ. (BA, 1995); Univ. of Virginia (JD, 1998).

JOY MARZILLI WILLING, born Providence, RI, 1964; admitted to bar, 1997, New York; 1998, District of Columbia. *Education.* Georgetown Univ. (B.S., 1986); American Univ. (J.D., 1996).

CHRISTOPHER M. ZOCHOWSKI, born New Brunswick, NJ, 1971; admitted to bar, 1999, District of Columbia. *Education:* Georgetown (B.A., 1993); George Washington Univ. (J.D., 1997).

(For Biographical Data on all Partners and Associates see Professional Biographies at New York, N.Y.)

SULLIVAN & WORCESTER LLP

Established in 1941

1025 CONNECTICUT AVENUE, N.W.

WASHINGTON, D.C. 20036

Telephone: 202-775-8190

Telecopier: 202-293-2275

URL: http://www.sandw.com

The firm also has offices at: One Post Office Square, Boston, Massachusetts, 02109. Telephone: 617-338-2800; 565 Fifth Avenue, New York, New York, 10017. Telephone: 212-486-8200; 292 Madison Avenue, New York, New York 10017-6307. Telephone: 212-213-8200.

Corporate and Administrative Law Practice before all Federal Departments and Agencies. Securities, Investment Companies, Banking, International Trade, Communications, High Technology, Municipal, Government Contracts and Federal Legislative Practice, ERISA, Real Estate Investment Trusts, Leasing, Mergers and Acquisitions, Closely-held Businesses, Debt/Equity Financing, Asset-Based Lending, Commercial Transactions, Private Placements, Public Offerings, Venture Capital Investments and SEC: Regulatory Compliance, Land Use and High Technology Law.

RESIDENT PARTNERS

JOHN A. DUDLEY, born 1932; admitted to bar, 1958, District of Columbia. *Education:* University of Pittsburgh (B.B.A., 1954); Georgetown University (J.D., 1958). Associate Director, Division of Investment Company/Advisor Division, Securities and Exchange Commission, 1958-1968. *Member:* The District of Columbia Bar; Federal Bar Association. ***PRACTICE AREAS:*** Mutual Funds; Investment Regulation. ***Email:*** jdudley@sandw.com

ROBERT N. HICKEY, born 1941; admitted to bar, 1966, New York; 1968, District of Columbia. *Education:* Canisius College (B.S., 1963); Georgetown University (J.D., 1966; LL.M., 1968). *Member:* Boston, Massachusetts and American Bar Associations. ***PRACTICE AREAS:*** Business Law; Securities. ***Email:*** rhickey@sandw.com

J. RANDOLPH MACPHERSON, born 1947; admitted to bar, 1972, California; 1981, District of Columbia;. *Education:* Santa Clara University (B.S., 1969; J.D.,1972); George Washington University (LL.M., 1976). Chairman, Litigation Section, 1994-1995; Law Firm Resources Project, 1980-1986, Boston Bar Association. Member, Board of Directors, Greater Boston Legal Services, 1987-1990. *Member:* Federal Communications Bar Association. ***PRACTICE AREAS:*** Government Contracts and Communications Law. ***Email:*** jmacpherson@sandw.com

DAVID M. LEAHY, born 1958; admitted to bar, 1985, New York; 1986, District of Columbia. *Education:* Columbia University (B.A., magna cum laude, 1980); Harvard University (J.D., cum laude, 1984). Phi Beta Kappa. ***PRACTICE AREAS:*** Investment Company Law; Investment Adviser Law; Securities Law. ***Email:*** dleahy@sandw.com

DAVID C. MAHAFFEY, born 1958; admitted to bar, 1982, District of Columbia; 1983, U.S. District Court for the District of Columbia and U.S. Court of Appeals, District of Columbia Circuit. *Education:* Princeton University (A.B., cum laude, 1979); Harvard University (J.D., 1982). Editor, Harvard Journal on Legislation, 1981-1982. Assistant General Counsel, Securities and Exchange Commission, 1986-1992; Counsel to the Commissioner, Securities and Exchange Commission, 1986. Author: "Pleading Reform, Plaintiff Qualification and Discovery Stays Under the Reform Act," 51 Business Lawyer 1101 (1996); "Full Disclosure, Market Discipline and Risk Taking: Rethinking Confidentiality in Bank Regulation," 69 Washington University Law Quarterly 1117 (1991). ***PRACTICE AREAS:*** Business Law; Investment Companies; Financing; Securities Law. ***Email:*** dmahaffey@sandw.com

RETIRED PARTNER

PAUL G. KIRK, JR., born 1938; admitted to bar, 1965, Massachusetts; 1975, District of Columbia; 1976, U.S. Supreme Court. *Education:* Harvard University (A.B., 1960; LL.B., 1964). Chairman, Democratic Party of the United States, 1985-1989. Co-Chair, Commission on Presidential Debates,

(This Listing Continued)

1987—. *Member:* The District of Columbia Bar; Massachusetts Bar Association. (Also at Boston, Massachusetts Office). ***PRACTICE AREAS:*** Business Law; Administrative Law; Corporate Law. ***Email:*** pkirk@sandw.com

ASSOCIATES

JANE B. MAXWELL, born 1952; admitted to bar, 1984, Pennsylvania; 1992, District of Columbia. *Education:* Brown University (B.A., 1974); American University (J.D., 1981). ***PRACTICE AREAS:*** Communications Law; Securities Law; Investment Companies. ***Email:*** jmaxwell@sandw.com

STACY H. OSTROWSKI, born 1970; admitted to bar, 1997, Virginia (Not admitted in District of Columbia). *Education:* University of North Carolina at Chapel Hill (B.A., 1992); Washington & Lee University (J.D., 1997). *Member:* Virginia State Bar. ***LANGUAGES:*** Spanish. ***PRACTICE AREAS:*** Securities Law; Investment Company Law; Government Contracts. ***Email:*** sostrowski@sandw.com

CHRISTINE S. BOEHM, born 1969; admitted to bar, 1996, Texas; 1998, District of Columbia. *Education:* Texas A & M University (B.B.A., 1992); University of Texas at Austin (J.D., 1995). Member, Board of Advocates, 1994-1995. *Member:* The District of Columbia Bar; State Bar of Texas. ***PRACTICE AREAS:*** Insurance Products; Mutual Funds. ***Email:*** cboehm@sandw.com

STAFF ATTORNEY

JOHN L. CHILTON, born 1974; admitted to bar, 2001, New York (Not admitted in District of Columbia). *Education:* Williams College (B.A., cum laude, 1997); George Washington University (J.D., 2001). *Member:* New York State Bar Association. ***PRACTICE AREAS:*** Government Contracts. ***Email:*** jchilton@sandw.com

(For Biographical Data on other Members of firm and Associates, see Professional Biographies at Boston, Massachusetts).

SUTHERLAND ASBILL & BRENNAN LLP

Established in 1924

1275 PENNSYLVANIA AVENUE, N.W.

WASHINGTON, D.C. 20004-2415

Telephone: 202-383-0100

Cable Address: "Sutab Wash"

Telex: 89-501

Facsimile: 202-637-3593

Email: info@sablaw.com

URL: http://www.sablaw.com

Atlanta, Georgia Office: 999 Peachtree Street, N.E., 30309-3996. Telephone: 404-853-8000.

New York, N.Y. Office: 350 Park Avenue, 25th Floor, 10022. Telephone: 212-655-3883.

Austin, Texas Office: 701 Brazos Street, Suite 1040, 78701-2559. Telephone: 512-478-1665.

Tallahassee, Florida Office: 2282 Killearn Center Boulevard, 32308-3561. Telephone: 850-894-0015.

General Practice. Trial and Appellate Practice in all Courts. Federal and State Tax, Antitrust and Trade Regulation, Securities, Arbitration, Energy, Environmental, Public Utility and Administrative Law, Corporate, Communications, Food and Drug Law, Financial Services, International, Employee Benefits, Estate Planning, Trusts, Probate, Government Contracts, Real Property, Patent, Copyright and Trademark Law, Legislative, Federal and State Insurance Company Practice, Construction Law.

MEMBERS OF THE FIRM IN WASHINGTON, D.C.

WILLIAM A. SUTHERLAND (1896-1987).

MAC ASBILL, SR. (1893-1992).

JOSEPH B. BRENNAN (1903-1991).

MAC ASBILL, JR. (1922-1992).

ERIC A. ARNOLD, born Philadelphia, Pennsylvania, June 27, 1964; admitted to bar, 1992, Michigan; 1993, District of Columbia. *Education:* Brown University (Sc.B., 1986); Vanderbilt University (J.D., 1991). Order of the Coif. Member, Vanderbilt Law Review, 1990-1991. ***PRACTICE AREAS:*** Broker-Dealer Regulation; Banking Law; Insurance Regulation; Corporate Law. ***Email:*** earnold@sablaw.com

FREDERICK R. BELLAMY, born Newark, New Jersey, January 28, 1954; admitted to bar, 1979, District of Columbia. *Education:* University of Virginia (B.A., 1976); Cornell University (J.D., magna cum laude, 1979). Order of the Coif. Business Manager, Cornell Law Review, 1978-1979. Law Clerk to Judge H. Emory Widener, Jr., U.S. Court of Appeals, Fourth Circuit, 1979-1980. ***PRACTICE AREAS:*** Insurance Products; Investment Company Law; Mutual Funds. ***Email:*** fbellamy@sablaw.com

(This Listing Continued)

SUTHERLAND ASBILL & BRENNAN LLP, Washington—Continued

HERBERT N. BELLER, born Illinois, 1943; admitted to bar, 1967, Illinois; 1969, District of Columbia. *Education:* Northwestern University (B.S.B.A., 1964; J.D., cum laude, 1967). Member, Editorial Board, Northwestern University Law Review, 1966-1967. Certified Public Accountant, Illinois, 1965. Law Clerk to Judge Theodore Tannenwald, Jr., United States Tax Court, 1967-1968. Adjunct Professor of Law, Georgetown University Law Center, 1972-1981. American Bar Association, Section of Taxation: Vice-Chair (Publications), 1993-1996; Chair-Elect (Publications), 2001-02; Editor-in-Chief, The Tax Lawyer, 1993-1996; Member of Council, 1989-1992; 1993-1996; Chair, Committee on Government Submissions, 1988-1989, and Committee on Closely Held Corporations, 1981-1983. *Member:* American College of Tax Counsel (Board of Regents); National Conference of Lawyers and CPAs. ***PRACTICE AREAS:*** Federal Tax Planning; Tax Controversies; Exempt Organizations. ***Email:*** hbeller@sablaw.com

STEVEN B. BOEHM, born New York, New York, May 22, 1954; admitted to bar, 1978, New Jersey; 1982, District of Columbia. *Education:* Rutgers College (B.A., 1975); Rutgers Law School (J.D., 1978). Phi Beta Kappa. Phillip J. Levin Scholar. Attorney, 1978-1982, and Counsel to Commissioner, 1982-1983, Securities and Exchange Commission. ***PRACTICE AREAS:*** Securities Offerings; Investment Company Law; Investment Regulation; Venture Capital; SEC Enforcement; Corporate Investigations. ***Email:*** sboehm@sablaw.com

GEORGE H. BOSTICK, born Birmingham, Alabama, December 9, 1944; admitted to bar, 1973, Virginia; 1975, District of Columbia. *Education:* Emory University (B.A., 1967); University of Virginia (J.D., 1973). Notes Editor, Virginia Law Review, 1972-1973. Law Clerk to Judge John C. Godbold, U.S. Court of Appeals, Fifth Circuit, 1973-1974. Adjunct Professor, Georgetown University Law Center, 1978-1980. *Member:* American Bar Association (Business Law Section Representative, 1983-1988, Chairman, 1988-1989, Joint Committee on Employee Benefits; Chairman, Business Law Section, Employee Benefits and Executive Compensation Committee, 1988-1992). ***PRACTICE AREAS:*** Employee Benefits; Executive Compensation; Taxation; ERISA. ***Email:*** gbostick@sablaw.com

JAMES RANDALL BUCHANAN, born Winston-Salem, North Carolina, August 27, 1963; admitted to bar, 1989, District of Columbia. *Education:* University of Virginia (B.A., 1985; J.D., 1989). Order of the Coif. Editor, Virginia Law Review, 1987-1989. ***PRACTICE AREAS:*** International Taxation; Federal Taxation; Tax Planning. ***Email:*** rbuchanan@sablaw.com

JAMES M. BUSHEE, born Melrose, Massachusetts, June 11, 1954; admitted to bar, 1982, District of Columbia, Michigan and Texas. *Education:* University of Texas at Austin (B.B.A., 1976); Catholic University of America (J.D., 1981). Vice Chair, Energy Committee, Administrative Law Section, 1987-1991. *Member:* American Bar Association (Vice Chair, Environmental Transactions, Section of Energy and Environment, 1992-1999); Energy Bar Association. [Captain, USMC, 1972-1976]. ***LANGUAGES:*** French. ***PRACTICE AREAS:*** Energy; Environmental; Telecommunications Law. ***Email:*** jbushee@sablaw.com

JAMES M. CAIN, born Danbury, Connecticut, April 14, 1955; admitted to bar, 1980, Nevada; 1981, California; 1986, District of Columbia. *Education:* University of Notre Dame (A.B., 1976); Georgetown University Law Center (J.D., 1979). Law Clerk to Honorable Edward C. Reed, Jr., United States District Judge for the District of Nevada, 1980-1981. ***PRACTICE AREAS:*** Corporate Law; Banks and Banking; Securities; Insurance; Commodities. ***Email:*** jcain@sablaw.com

NICHOLAS T. CHRISTAKOS, born Des Moines, Iowa, April 22, 1957; admitted to bar, 1982, District of Columbia, U.S. Court of Appeals, First and Fourth Circuits, U.S. Court of Federal Claims. *Education:* Harvard University (A.B., 1979); Georgetown University Law Center (J.D., 1982). Editor, American Criminal Law Review, 1981-1982. ***PRACTICE AREAS:*** Civil Litigation; Insurance Litigation; Reinsurance; Employment Litigation; Banking Litigation; ERISA Litigation. ***Email:*** nchristakos@sablaw.com

LOVIDA H. COLEMAN, JR., born Washington, D.C., May 21, 1949; admitted to bar, 1977, District of Columbia. *Education:* Radcliffe College, Harvard University (A.B., cum laude, 1972); Yale Law School (J.D., 1975). Law Clerk to Judge Wilfred Feinberg, U.S. Court of Appeals, Second Circuit, 1975-1976. Deputy General Counsel to Bush-Quale '92 Re-election Campaign and Deputy Director of Domestic Policy Issues, 1992. Deputy Independent Counsel to James C. McKay, 1978-1986. Special Assistant to Benjamin R. Civiletti in the Office of the Deputy Attorney General and the Attorney General of the United States, 1978-1980. Fellow, Institute of Politics, John F. Kennedy School of Government, Harvard University, 1986. Member, Board of Directors, Council for Excellence in Government. Member, Board of Washington Lawyers' Committee for Civil Rights and Urban Affairs. Member, Rand Board of Trustee, 1997—. Board Member, Drug Policy Research Center of Rand, 1990—. *Member:* American Law Institute. Fellow, American Bar Foundation. ***PRACTICE***

(This Listing Continued)

AREAS: Federal Practice; Business Litigation; Federal Criminal Law; Government Investigations; Discrimination; Unfair Trade. ***Email:*** lcoleman@sablaw.com

JAMES D. DARROW, born Evanston, Illinois, March 19, 1949; admitted to bar, 1976, New York; 1988, District of Columbia. *Education:* Bowdoin College (B.A., 1971); George Washington University National Law Center (J.D., with honors, 1975). Member, The George Washington University Law Review, 1973-1975. ***PRACTICE AREAS:*** Mergers and Acquisitions; Debt and Equity Finance; Securities; Commercial Contracts. ***Email:*** jdarrow@sablaw.com

WARREN N. DAVIS, born Denver, Colorado, May 2, 1947; admitted to bar, 1975, District of Columbia. *Education:* Georgetown University (B.S.F.S., 1969; J.D., 1974). Editor, Georgetown Law Journal, 1973-1974. Acting General Counsel, Federal Farm Credit Banks Funding Corporation, 1992. Assistant Professorial Lecturer in Law, George Washington University National Law Center, 1977-1986. ***PRACTICE AREAS:*** Derivative Products; Corporate Finance; Equipment Leasing; Corporate Fiduciary Law; Securities Disclosure. ***Email:*** wdavis@sablaw.com

JACOB DWECK, born Jerusalem, Israel, February 19, 1951; admitted to bar, 1976, District of Columbia; 1985, New York. *Education:* Brooklyn College of the City University of New York (B.A., magna cum laude, 1972); Georgetown University (J.D., 1976). Phi Beta Kappa. Member, Editorial Board, Law and Policy in International Business, 1975-1976. Student Editor, Federal Bar Journal, 1975-1976. . ***PRACTICE AREAS:*** Business Law; Business Regulation; Agency and Distributorships; Energy Regulation; Technology Law; Alternative Dispute Resolution. ***Email:*** jdweck@sablaw.com

PAUL F. FORSHAY, born Brooklyn, New York, April 9, 1959; admitted to bar, 1984, District of Columbia. *Education:* Haverford College (B.A., 1981); Washington College of Law, American University (J.D., 1984). Member, American University Law Review, 1982-1984. ***PRACTICE AREAS:*** Energy; Administrative Law; Regulatory Law; Utility Law; Transportation. ***Email:*** pforshay@sablaw.com

HAMILTON P. FOX, III, born Salisbury, Maryland, September 18, 1945; admitted to bar, 1971, Maine; 1972, District of Columbia. *Education:* University of Virginia (B.A., with honors, 1967); Yale University (LL.B., 1970). Phi Beta Kappa. Article and Book Review Editor, Yale Law Journal, 1969-1970. Instructor, University of Virginia School of Law, 1981-1984. Law Clerk to: Hon. Frank M. Coffin, U.S. Court of Appeals, First Circuit, 1970-1971; Hon. Stanley F. Reed and Hon. Lewis F. Powell, Jr., Supreme Court of the United States, 1971-1972. Assistant U.S. Attorney for the District of Columbia, 1972-1973, 1974-1977. Assistant Watergate Special Prosecutor, 1973-1974. Deputy Chief, Organized Crime and Racketeering Section, U.S. Department of Justice, 1977-1980. Associate Special Counsel, House Committee on Standards of Official Conduct, 1983-1984. President, Assistant U.S. Attorney's Association, 1988-1989. Member, 1989-1991, Vice-Chair, 1991-1993 and Chair, 1993-1996, District of Columbia Board on Professional Responsibility. Member, 1996-1997 and Chair, 1997—, D.C. Circuit Committee on Admissions and Grievances. ***PRACTICE AREAS:*** Litigation; White Collar Criminal Defense; Civil Litigation. ***Email:*** pfox@sablaw.com

THOMAS A. GICK, born New York, New York, July 22, 1956; admitted to bar, 1982, New York; 1988, District of Columbia. *Education:* The College of Insurance (B.B.A., 1978); State University of New York at Buffalo (J.D., cum laude, 1981). Trial Attorney, Tax Division, Department of Justice, 1981-1985. ***PRACTICE AREAS:*** Federal Taxation; Federal Tax Controversies; Insurance. ***Email:*** tgick@sablaw.com

DAVID S. GOLDSTEIN, born Boston, Massachusetts, March 21, 1955; admitted to bar, 1981, Massachusetts; 1982, Texas; 1989, District of Columbia. *Education:* Hampshire College (B.A., 1978); Boston University (J.D., 1981). Attorney-Adviser, 1986-1987, and Special Counsel, 1988-1989, Division of Investment Management, U.S. Securities and Exchange Commission. Assistant Vice President and Assistant General Counsel, The Variable Annuity Life Insurance Company, 1981-1985. ***PRACTICE AREAS:*** Securities Regulation; Investment Company Law; Investment Management; Insurance Regulation; Retirement Benefit Plans. ***Email:*** dgoldstein@sablaw.com

FRANCIS M. GREGORY, JR. (1941-1993).

EDWARD J. GRENIER, JR., born New York, New York, November 26, 1933; admitted to bar, 1959, District of Columbia; 1983, New York. *Education:* Manhattan College (B.A., summa cum laude, 1954); Harvard Law School (LL.B., magna cum laude, 1959). Epsilon Sigma Pi. Editor, Harvard Law Review, 1957-1959. Law Clerk to Chief Judge E. Barrett Prettyman, U.S. Court of Appeals, District of Columbia Circuit, 1959-1960. Instructor, 1964-1967 and Adjunct Professor, 1974-1979, Georgetown University Law Center. Director, 1973-1984, Secretary-Treasurer, 1975-1977 and Vice President, 1977-1978, Computer Law Association. *Member:* Bar Association of the District of Columbia (Chairman, Administrative Law Section, 1972-1973; Member, Board of Directors, 1973-1974); American Bar Association (Chair, 1986-1987, Chair-Elect, 1985-1986, Chairman: Committee on Environmental Quality Control, 1971-1976; Policies, By-Laws and Manual Committee, 1979-1984; Adjudica-

(This Listing Continued)

tion Committee, 1984-1985; Continuing Legal Education Committee, 1988-1991; Council Member, Section of Administrative Law and Regulatory Practice, 1975-1979; Section Delegate to the House of Delegates, 1991-1997); Prettyman-Leventhal American Inn of Court (Master of the Bench, 1988—; President, 1991-1992; Member, Executive Committee, 1989-1998), Federal Energy Bar Association (Vice-President, 1995-1996; President-Elect, 1996-1997; President, 1997-1998; Delegate to the ABA House of Delegates, 1999-2001; Member, Board of Directors, 1986-1989). Fellow, American Bar Foundation. ***PRACTICE AREAS:*** Federal Energy Regulation; Energy Regulation; Energy Contracts; Federal Administrative Law. ***Email:*** egrenier@sablaw.com

JAMES V. HEFFERNAN, born Washington, D.C., October 6, 1926; admitted to bar, 1953, District of Columbia; 1959, Maryland. *Education:* Cornell University (A.B., 1949; J.D., with distinction, 1952). Order of the Coif. Board of Editors, Cornell Law Quarterly, 1951-1952. Adjunct Professor, Georgetown University Law Center, 1978-1979. ***PRACTICE AREAS:*** Federal Income Tax; Federal Estate and Gift Tax; Federal Tax Controversies; Tax Planning; Tax Litigation. ***Email:*** jheffernan@sablaw.com

JAMES L. HENDERSON, III, born Griffin, Georgia, October 22, 1951; admitted to bar, 1976, Georgia (Not admitted in District of Columbia). *Education:* University of North Carolina (B.A., 1973) Morehead Scholar; University of Georgia (J.D., magna cum laude, 1976). Phi Beta Kappa; Order of the Coif. Research Editor, Georgia Law Review, 1975-1976. *Member:* State Bar of Georgia; American Bar Association; National Association of Bond Lawyers. ***PRACTICE AREAS:*** Finance; Government; Health Care; Non Profit and Charitable Organizations; Securities. ***Email:*** jlhenderson@sablaw.com

MARK D. HERLACH, born Milwaukee, Wisconsin, October 3, 1950; admitted to bar, 1975, District of Columbia. *Education:* Stanford University (B.A., with honors, 1972); University of Michigan (J.D., cum laude, 1975). Note Editor, Michigan Law Review, 1974-1975. Editor, "Joint Ventures in Eastern Europe," Euromoney Books, 1990. Chairman, Georgetown University Law Center Annual Conference on International Trade Law. Member, Advisory Board, North American Free Trade and Investment Report. *Member:* American Bar Association (Sections of Antitrust, International Law and Practice and Litigation); International Nuclear Law Association; American Society of International Law. ***PRACTICE AREAS:*** International Law; International Trade; Litigation; Communications and Media. ***Email:*** mherlach@sablaw.com

MARK D. JACKSON, born Miami, Florida, June 14, 1959; admitted to bar, 1985, Georgia; 1992, District of Columbia. *Education:* American University (B.S., cum laude, 1982); Emory University (J.D., 1985). *Member:* The District of Columbia Bar; State Bar of Georgia. ***PRACTICE AREAS:*** Real Estate; Secured Transactions Law; Debtor Creditor Law; Corporate Law. ***Email:*** mdjackson@sablaw.com

PAUL D. JACOKES, born Durham, North Carolina, February 10, 1953; admitted to bar, 1979, District of Columbia. *Education:* University of North Carolina, Chapel Hill (B.A., summa cum laude, 1975); Yale University (J.D., 1979); Georgetown University (LL.M., Taxation, 1987). Phi Beta Kappa. Legislation Attorney, Joint Committee on Taxation, U.S. Congress, 1984-1988. Adjunct Professor, Georgetown University Law Center, 1991-1993. *Member:* American Bar Association (Member, Taxation Section). ***PRACTICE AREAS:*** Federal Taxation. ***Email:*** pjacokes@sablaw.com

E. MICHAEL JOHNSON, born St. Paul, Minnesota, April 4, 1964; admitted to bar, 1991, Illinois; 1993, District of Columbia. *Education:* Morehouse College (B.S., summa cum laude, 1986); University of Minnesota (J.D., cum laude, 1991). Phi Beta Kappa. Walter J. Trogner Scholar. Articles Editor, Minnesota Law Review. Law Clerk to Hon. Nathaniel R. Jones, U.S. Court of Appeals, Sixth Circuit, 1991-1992. *Member:* American Bar Association (Subcommittee on Limited Liability Companies, Committee on Partnerships and Unincorporated Business Organizations, Section of Business Law). ***PRACTICE AREAS:*** Mergers and Acquisitions; Insurance Mergers and Acquisitions; Joint Ventures; International Joint Ventures; Corporate Commercial Law. ***Email:*** mjohnson@sablaw.com

PAUL W. KILLIAN, born Chicago, Illinois, June 1, 1947; admitted to bar, 1972, Virginia; 1973, District of Columbia. *Education:* Washington University (B.A., with honors, 1969); George Washington University National Law Center (J.D., with honors, 1972). Lecturer: "Recovery of Delay and Impact Costs," Brigham Young University, 1979, 1980. Member, National Panel of Construction Arbitrators, American Arbitration Association. ***PRACTICE AREAS:*** Construction Law; Commercial Law; Contracts; Government Contracts; Litigation. ***Email:*** pkillian@sablaw.com

SUSAN S. KRAWCZYK, born Warren, New Jersey, June 22, 1956; admitted to bar, 1984, Virginia; 1988, District of Columbia. *Education:* Indiana University of Pennsylvania (B.A., magna cum laude, 1978); George Washington National Law Center (J.D., with high honors, 1984). Order of the Coif. ***PRACTICE AREAS:*** Broker-Dealer Regulation; Investment Regulation; Financial Services Regulation; Insurance Regulation; Insurance Products. ***Email:*** skrawczyk@sablaw.com

CYNTHIA M. KRUS, born Chicago, Illinois, May 18, 1962; admitted to bar, 1989, Maryland; 1999, District of Columbia. *Education:* Emory University (B.A., 1984); Tulane University (J.D., cum laude, 1989). *Member:* The District of Columbia Bar; Maryland State and American Bar Associations. ***PRACTICE AREAS:*** Securities Offerings; Securities Regulation; Mergers and Acquisitions; Corporate Governance; Financial Institutions. ***Email:*** ckrus@sablaw.com

NEIL S. LANG, born New York, N.Y.; admitted to bar, 1968, New York; 1981, District of Columbia. *Education:* City College of New York (B.A., 1964); St. John's University (J.D., 1967). Associate Editor, Law Review, 1966-1967. Division of Enforcement, Securities and Exchange Commission, 1967-1968, 1972-1986, 1991-1995; Chief Trial Attorney, Division of Enforcement, 1980-1986. Adjunct Professor, Georgetown University Law Center. Co-author: "The Securities Enforcement Manual: Tactics and Strategies," Section of Business Law, American Bar Association, 1997; "The SEC's attempt to Impose a Regulatory Regime on Municipal Securities Issuers," Securities Regulation Law Journal, Fall 1996. ***PRACTICE AREAS:*** Securities; Litigation; Business Law; Legal Ethics; Professional Responsibility. ***Email:*** nlang@sablaw.com

ELISABETH A. LANGWORTHY, born Angleton, Texas, October 4, 1955; admitted to bar, 1984, Florida; 1986, District of Columbia. *Education:* Smith College (A.B., cum laude, 1977); George Washington University National Law Center (J.D., with honors, 1984). Member, George Washington Law Review, 1982-1984. ***PRACTICE AREAS:*** Trademarks; Copyrights; Intellectual Property Licensing; Intellectual Property Litigation. ***Email:*** llangworthy@sablaw.com

JEROME B. LIBIN, born Chicago, Illinois, October 27, 1936; admitted to bar, 1961, Illinois and District of Columbia. *Education:* Northwestern University (B.S., 1956); University of Michigan (J.D., 1959). Order of the Coif. Editor-in-Chief, Michigan Law Review, 1958-1959. Law Clerk to Associate Justice Charles E. Whittaker, U.S. Supreme Court, 1959-1960. Member: Committee of Visitors, University of Michigan Law School, 1968-1972; District of Columbia Tax Revision Commission, 1976-1978; Mayor's Revenue Policy Committee, 1980-1982. Master of the Bench, J. Edgar Murdock American Inn of Court. Consultant, American Law Institute International Tax Study Project, 1982-1986. Professorial Lecturer in Law, George Washington University, 1974-1980. *Member:* District of Columbia Bar (Chair, 1975-1977; Taxation Division); American Bar Association (Chair: Special Committee on Standing to Sue, 1973-1975; Special Committee on Integration, 1983-1986; Special Projects Committee, 1998-2000; Globalization Task Force, 1998-2000; Member of Council, Section of Taxation, 1992-1995); American Law Institute; International Fiscal Association (First Vice President and President-Elect, 2000-2001; Member, Central Executive Committee, 1995—) and Vice President, USA Branch, 1992—). Fellow: American College of Tax Counsel; American Bar Foundation. ***PRACTICE AREAS:*** Federal Taxation; International Taxation; Tax Litigation. ***Email:*** jlibin@sablaw.com

DAVID A. MASSEY, born Heidelberg, Germany, April 23, 1959; admitted to bar, 1984, District of Columbia. *Education:* University of Virginia (B.A., 1981; J.D., 1984). Phi Beta Kappa. ***PRACTICE AREAS:*** Mergers and Acquisitions; Insurance Mergers and Acquisitions; Securities Regulation; Corporate Organization; Mutual Funds. ***Email:*** dmassey@sablaw.com

KEITH R. McCREA, born Butler, Pennsylvania, August 4, 1947; admitted to bar, 1973, District of Columbia. *Education:* Lehigh University (B.S. in Chem.E., 1969); Georgetown University Law Center (J.D., 1973). *Member:* American Bar Association (Member of Council, Natural Resources Law Section, 1983-1986). ***PRACTICE AREAS:*** Electric Power; Energy Contracts; Energy Regulation; Federal Energy Regulation. ***Email:*** kmccrea@sablaw.com

MICHAEL R. MILES, born Salem, Ohio, December 11, 1950; admitted to bar, 1978, Ohio; 1983, District of Columbia. *Education:* Ohio University (B.S., 1972); Ohio State University (J.D., 1978); Georgetown University Law Center (LL.M., 1983). Order of the Coif. Attorney, Internal Revenue Service, Office of Chief Counsel, 1978-1982. ***PRACTICE AREAS:*** Corporate Taxation; Corporate Tax Planning; Federal Income Tax; Federal Tax Controversies; Leasing. ***Email:*** mmiles@sablaw.com

CLIFFORD E. MULLER, born Teaneck, New Jersey, March 30, 1956; admitted to bar, 1981, District of Columbia. *Education:* Bucknell University (B.S.B.A., magna cum laude, 1978); George Washington University National Law Center (J.D., with high honors, 1981). Order of the Coif; Delta Mu Delta. Professorial Lecturer in Law, George Washington University National Law Center, 1985-1990. *Member:* American Bar Association (Member, Financial Transactions Committee, 1990—; Subcommittee Chairman, International Financial Transactions Committee, 1991—). ***PRACTICE AREAS:*** International Taxation; Federal Taxation. ***Email:*** cmuller@sablaw.com

RICHARD G. MURPHY, JR., born Springfield, Illinois, August 31, 1948; admitted to bar, 1973, Georgia (Not admitted in District of Columbia). *Education:* Brown University (A.B., 1970); Vanderbilt University (J.D., 1973). Order of the Coif. *Member:* American Bar Association (Bankruptcy and Insolvency Committee, Section of Litigation; Banking Law Committee, Section of Business Law). ***PRACTICE AREAS:*** Bankruptcy; Commercial Litigation; Banks and Banking. ***Email:*** rgmurphy@sablaw.com

LLOYD LEVA PLAINE, born Washington, D.C., November 3, 1947; admitted to bar, 1975, District of Columbia. *Education:* University of Pennsylva-

(This Listing Continued)

SUTHERLAND ASBILL & BRENNAN LLP, Washington—Continued

nia (B.A., 1969); Harvard Law School; Georgetown University Law Center (J.D., 1975). Editor, Georgetown Law Journal, 1974-1975. Co-Author, Book, "Generation-Skipping Transfer Tax," Warren Gorham & Lamont/RIA, 1995, second edition 2001. Legislative Assistant to Representative Sidney Yates, 1971-1972. *Member:* The District of Columbia Bar (Member, Steering Committee, Estates, Trusts and Probate Law Section, 1987-1989); American Bar Association (Member, Sections on: Real Property, Probate and Trust Law; Chair, 1996-1997; Chair-Elect, 1995-1996, Vice Chair, 1993-1995; Secretary, 1991-1993; Member of Council, 1987-1998; Taxation: Chair, Estate and Gift Taxes Committee, 1991-1993, Vice-Chair, Estate and Gift Taxes Committee, 1989-1991; Chair, Generation—Skipping Transfer Tax Subcommittee, 1986-1991); District of Columbia Estate Planning Council (President, 1993-1994; Vice President, 1992-1993; Treasurer, 1991-1992). Fellow and Past Regent, American College of Trust and Estate Counsel. Fellow: American College of Tax Counsel; American Bar Foundation. Academician, The International Academy of Estate and Trust Law. ***PRACTICE AREAS:*** Estate and Gift Taxation; Trusts and Estates Taxation; Generation Skipping Tax; Transfer Tax; Business Estate Planning; Estate Administration; Trust Administration; Inheritance Tax. ***Email:*** lplaine@sablaw.com

PETER H. RODGERS, born New York, New York, July 2, 1948; admitted to bar, 1973, New York; 1975, District of Columbia. *Education:* Yale University (B.A., magna cum laude, 1969); Stanford University (J.D., 1972). Order of the Coif. Woodrow Wilson Scholar. ***PRACTICE AREAS:*** Energy; Environmental Law; Commodities; Commercial Law. ***Email:*** prodgers@sablaw.com

LISA ALPERT ROSEN, born Washington, D.C., August 25, 1958; admitted to bar, 1983, District of Columbia; 1990, Maryland. *Education:* Hofstra University (B.A., summa cum laude, 1980); Yale University (J.D., 1983). Phi Beta Kappa. Law Clerk to Chief Judge Frank A. Kaufman, U.S. District Court, Maryland. ***PRACTICE AREAS:*** Real Estate; Real Estate Finance; Real Estate Restructuring; Real Estate Bankruptcy; Real Estate Acquisitions. ***Email:*** lrosen@sablaw.com

STEPHEN E. ROTH, born Madison, Wisconsin, September 25, 1951; admitted to bar, 1978, District of Columbia. *Education:* University of Notre Dame (A.B., 1973); Yale Law School (J.D., 1976). Phi Beta Kappa. Editor, Yale Law Journal, 1975-1976. Law Clerk to Chief Judge Jesse E. Eschbach, U.S. District Court, Northern District of Indiana, 1976-1977. ***PRACTICE AREAS:*** Investment Management; Insurance Regulation; Securities Regulation; Mutual Funds; Insurance Products. ***Email:*** sroth@sablaw.com

BEVERLY J. RUDY, born Hartford, Connecticut, May 17, 1954; admitted to bar, 1981, District of Columbia. *Education:* Tufts University (B.A., magna cum laude, 1976); George Washington National Law Center (J.D., with high honors, 1981). Order of the Coif. Staff Member, Journal of International Law and Economics, 1979-1980. ***PRACTICE AREAS:*** Foreign Trade Sanctions; Petroleum Trading; Petroleum Contracts; Excise Tax; Energy. ***Email:*** brudy@sablaw.com

MICHAEL J. SHEA, born Scranton, Pennsylvania, December 31, 1931; admitted to bar, 1958, District of Columbia; 1959, Tennessee. *Education:* Georgetown University (A.B., summa cum laude, 1954; J.D., with honors, 1958). Attorney and Assistant Secretary, Tennessee Valley Authority, 1958-1961. *Member:* American Bar Association (Chairman, Committee on Contract Forms and Clauses, Section of Public Contract Law, 1981-1990). ***PRACTICE AREAS:*** Litigation; Government Contracts; Construction Law. ***Email:*** mshea@sablaw.com

DOUGLAS L. SIEGLER, born Washington, D. C., May 8, 1961; admitted to bar, 1986, Maryland; 1988, District of Columbia. *Education:* Princeton University (B.A., 1983); Duke University School of Law (J.D., with honors, 1986). *Member:* American Bar Association (Chair, Current Development Subcommittee, Estate and Gift Taxes Committee, 1995-1999; Vice-Chair, Estate and Gift Tax Committee, 1999—). Fellow, American College of Trust and Estate Counsel. ***PRACTICE AREAS:*** Estate and Gift Taxation; Fiduciary Income Tax; Generation Skipping Tax. ***Email:*** dsiegler@sablaw.com

KIMBERLY J. SMITH, born Cleveland, Ohio, August 21, 1962; admitted to bar, 1987, Virginia; 1988, District of Columbia. *Education:* College of William & Mary (B.A., 1984); Harvard Law School (J.D., cum laude, 1987). Phi Beta Kappa. Executive Editor, Harvard Journal on Legislation, 1986-1987. ***PRACTICE AREAS:*** Insurance Products; Mutual Funds; Securities Regulation. ***Email:*** ksmith@sablaw.com

W. MARK SMITH, born Kansas City, Missouri, May 7, 1955; admitted to bar, 1981, District of Columbia. *Education:* University of Kansas (B.A., 1977); Cornell University (J.D., magna cum laude, 1980). Order of the Coif; Phi Beta Kappa. Editor-in-Chief, Cornell Law Review, 1979-1980. Law Clerk to Chief Judge Clement F. Haynsworth, Jr., U.S. Court of Appeals, Fourth Circuit, 1980-1981. *Member:* American Bar Association (Chair, Employee Benefits Committee, Tort and Insurance Practice Section, 1991-1992). ***PRACTICE AREAS:*** Employee Benefits; Insurance; Taxation. ***Email:*** msmith@sablaw.com

(This Listing Continued)

GIOVANNA T. SPARAGNA, born Philadelphia, Pennsylvania, February 26, 1954; admitted to bar, 1980, New York; 1987, District of Columbia. *Education:* Richard Stockton State College (B.A., 1976); Syracuse University (J.D., 1979) Georgetown University Law Center (LL.M. in Taxation, 1987). Recipient, HEW Fellowship, 1977-1979. Notes and Comment Editor, Syracuse Journal of International Law and Commerce, 1977-1979. Attorney, Office of the Chief Counsel, Internal Revenue Service, 1979-1985. Adjunct Professor (LLM Program), Georgetown University Law Center. *Member:* American Bar Association (Chair, Subcommittee on International Mergers and Acquisitions Sections 338, 367). ***PRACTICE AREAS:*** Corporate Reorganization; International Corporate Taxation; International Mergers and Acquisitions; International Taxation; Tax Controversies. ***Email:*** gsparagna@sablaw.com

STEUART H. THOMSEN, born Baltimore, Maryland, March 2, 1954; admitted to bar, 1979, Maryland; 1980, District of Columbia. *Education:* Harvard University (A.B., magna cum laude, 1976); Harvard Law School (J.D., magna cum laude, 1979). Law Clerk to Judge Joseph H. Young, U.S. District Court, District of Maryland, 1979-1980. *Member:* American Bar Association (Chair, Employee Benefits Law Committee, Tort and Insurance Practice Section, 1997-1998). ***PRACTICE AREAS:*** Civil Litigation; ERISA; Insurance Litigation; Intellectual Property Litigation; Tax Litigation. ***Email:*** sthomsen@sablaw.com

F. BROOK VOGHT, born Jackson, Mississippi; admitted to bar, 1971, Florida; 1973, District of Columbia. *Education:* University of Alabama (B.S., 1967; M.A., 1968); University of Florida (J.D., 1971). Beta Gamma Sigma; Phi Kappa Phi; Phi Delta Phi; Order of the Coif. Executive Editor, Florida Law Review, 1970-1971. Attorney-Advisor to Judge William M. Drennen, U.S. Tax Court, 1971-1973. *Member:* The District of Columbia Bar; Bar Association of the District of Columbia; The Florida Bar; American Bar Association (Chair, Committee on Court Procedure, Section of Taxation, 1991-1993); Federal and Claims Court (Chair, Tax Section, 1988-1992) Bar Associations; American College of Tax Counsel; J. Edgar Murdock Inn of Court; American Bar Foundation. ***PRACTICE AREAS:*** Tax Litigation; Tax Appeals; Tax Audits; International Taxation; Taxation. ***Email:*** fvoght@sablaw.com

WILLIAM J. WALDERMAN, born Washington, D.C., July 17, 1946; admitted to bar, 1988, District of Columbia. *Education:* Harvard College (A.B., magna cum laude, 1968); University of Wisconsin Law School (J.D., cum laude, 1974); Georgetown University Law Center (LL.M. in Taxation, 1980). Phi Beta Kappa. Assistant Counsel, Office of the Solicitor, U.S. Department of Labor, 1985-1988. ***PRACTICE AREAS:*** ERISA Compliance; Insurance Products; Federal Income Tax. ***Email:*** bwalderman@sablaw.com

CAROL A. WEISER, born Elizabeth, New Jersey, November 7, 1952; admitted to bar, 1985, Pennsylvania; 1992, District of Columbia. *Education:* Hiram College (B.A., 1975); Temple University (J.D., magna cum laude, 1985). *Member:* American Bar Association (Chair: Committee on Employee Benefits and Executive Compensation, Section of Business Law, 1997-2001; Joint Committee on Employee Benefits, 2001-2002). ***PRACTICE AREAS:*** Qualified Retirement Plans; Non-Qualified Benefits; ERISA; Flexible Benefit Plans; Fringe Benefits. ***Email:*** cweiser@sablaw.com

DENA EVE WIGGINS, born Hobbsville, North Carolina, October 5, 1955; admitted to bar, 1988, District of Columbia; U.S. Court of Appeals, District of Columbia Circuit; U.S. Court of Appeals, Fourth and Fifth Circuits. *Education:* University of Richmond (B.A., magna cum laude, 1977); Georgetown University (J.D., 1988). *Member:* American and Federal Energy Bar Associations; The District of Columbia Bar. ***PRACTICE AREAS:*** Energy. ***Email:*** dwiggins@sablaw.com

MARY JANE WILSON-BILIK, born New York, New York, June 3, 1950; admitted to bar, 1990, Pennsylvania; 1992, District of Columbia. *Education:* College of New Rochelle (B.A., magna cum laude, 1971); Columbia University (Ph.D., 1980); Georgetown University (J.D., magna cum laude, 1990). Order of the Coif. Articles Editor, 1989-1990 and Staff Member, 1987-1989, Georgetown Law Journal. Clerk to Judge John M. Ferren, D.C. Court of Appeals, 1990-1991. ***PRACTICE AREAS:*** Investment Company Law; Insurance Products; Mutual Funds; Securities Regulation; Insurance Regulation; Life Insurance; Securities Registration. ***Email:*** mjwilsonbilik@sablaw.com

KATHERINE P. YARBROUGH, born Rochester, Minnesota, August 14, 1947; admitted to bar, 1987, Virginia; 1989, District of Columbia. *Education:* University of Illinois (B.S., 1969) Kappa Delta Pi; George Mason University School of Law (J.D. with distinction, 1987). Manuscripts Editor, George Mason Law Review, 1986-1987. ***PRACTICE AREAS:*** Energy; Federal Energy Regulation. ***Email:*** kyarbrough@sablaw.com

H. KARL ZESWITZ, JR., born Columbus, Georgia, May 6, 1953; admitted to bar, 1981, Pennsylvania and U.S. Tax Court; 1982, Louisiana; 1984, U.S. Court of Appeals, Fifth Circuit; 1986, U.S. Claims Court; 1987, District of Columbia and U.S. District Court for the District of Columbia; 1988, U.S. Supreme Court; 1990, California and U.S. Court of Appeals, Federal Circuit. *Education:* Pennsylvania State University (B.S., 1976); Dickinson School of Law (J.D., 1980); Georgetown University (LL.M. in Taxation, 1986). Beta Gamma Sigma. Recipient: Edward N. Polisher Award; Prentice-Hall Tax Award;

(This Listing Continued)

Thomas B. Chetwood Award. Adjunct Professor, Corporate Tax, Taxation of Partners and Partnerships, Income Tax Accounting, Consolidated Returns, Georgetown University Law Center, 1987—. *Member:* The District of Columbia Bar (Member, Section of Taxation); State Bar of California (Member, Tax Section), Louisiana State (Member, Tax Section) and American (Member, Sections of Taxation and Business) Bar Associations; J. Edgar Murdock American Inn of Court. ***PRACTICE AREAS:*** Tax Law; Federal Tax Planning; Corporate Taxation; Federal Tax Controversies; State Taxation; Tax Litigation; Tax Planning; Business Planning Law. ***Email:*** kzeswitz@sablaw.com

OF COUNSEL

JACK H. BLAINE, born Cleveland, Ohio, September 21, 1934; admitted to bar, 1961, Wisconsin; 1966, Illinois; 1979, District of Columbia. *Education:* University of Dayton (B.S., 1958); University of Wisconsin (LL.B., 1961). Member, Board of Journal of Insurance Regulation, 1989—. General Counsel, American Council Life Insurance, D.C., 1966-1989. *Member:* American Bar Association; Association of Life Insurance Counsel (Member, Board of Directors, 1987-1990). ***PRACTICE AREAS:*** Insurance Solvency; Insurance Mergers and Acquisitions; Insurance Products; Unfair Insurance Practices; Insurance Receiverships. ***Email:*** jblaine@sablaw.com

WILLIAM S. COREY, born Boston, Massachusetts, April 13, 1936; admitted to bar, 1962, Maryland; 1964, District of Columbia. *Education:* Dickinson College (A.B., 1958); George Washington University National Law Center (J.D., 1961). Order of the Coif; Omicron Delta Kappa. Staff Member, The George Washington Law Review, 1960-1961. Tax Law Specialist, Internal Revenue Service, 1959-1962. Attorney-Adviser to Judge Craig S. Atkins, United States Tax Court, 1962-1964. *Member:* The District of Columbia Bar (Steering Committee of Taxation Division, 1980-1982); American Bar Association (Chairman, Committee on Administrative Practice, 1974-1976; Special Committee on Confidentiality of Tax Returns, Section of Taxation, 1978-1981). ***PRACTICE AREAS:*** Federal Taxation; International Taxation; Tax Planning; Federal Tax Controversies. ***Email:*** wcorey@sablaw.com

JOEL E. HOFFMAN, born New York, N.Y., September 23, 1937; admitted to bar, 1960, New York; 1963, District of Columbia. *Education:* New York University (B.A., 1957); Yale University (LL.B., 1960). Phi Beta Kappa. Trial Attorney, Appellate Section, Antitrust Division, U.S. Department of Justice, 1960-1963. Member, Editorial Advisory Board, Food Drug Cosmetic Law Journal, 1981-1989. Adjunct Professor, Food and Drug Law: Franklin Pierce Law Center, 1996—; George Mason University Law School, 1998—. *Member:* The District of Columbia Bar (Member, Steering Committee, Division of Antitrust and Trade Regulation, 1977-1979); American Bar Association (Member of Council, Section of Administrative Law and Regulatory Practice, 1973-1976; Chairman, Food and Drug Committee, Section of Administrative Law and Regulatory Practice, 1976-1982, 1995-1999; Subcommittee on Regulations and Legislation, Food, Drug and Cosmetic Law Committee, Section of Business Law, 1975-1981; Vice-Chair, Consumer Products Regulation Committee, Section of Administrative Law and Regulatory Practice, 1982—; Vice Chair, Task Force on Integrated European Market, Section of Administrative Law and Regulatory Practice, 1989-1991). ***PRACTICE AREAS:*** Food, Drug and Cosmetic Law; Drug and Medical Device Regulation; Food and Drug Regulation; Product Safety; Deceptive Trade Practices; Trade Regulation. ***Email:*** jhoffman@sablaw.com

ROBERT G. LEVY, born Baltimore, Maryland, 1932; admitted to bar, 1960, Maryland (Not admitted in District of Columbia). *Education:* Dartmouth College (A.B., 1954); University of Virginia (LL.B., 1960). Order of the Coif. Member, Attorney General's Honor Law School Graduates' Program, 1960-1963. Attorney, Trial Section, Antitrust Division, U.S. Department of Justice, 1960-1963. Panelist, American Bar Association, Section on Antitrust Law, 1986. Panelist, Seminar on Distribution, New York Law Journal, 1984-1987. Lecturer: Antitrust and Economics, Department of Economics, Yale University, 1990-1994; Department of Economics, Johns Hopkins University, 1991—. Fellow, American College of Trial Lawyers. ***PRACTICE AREAS:*** Litigation; Civil Litigation; Intellectual Property; Trade Secrets; Antitrust. ***Email:*** rlevy@sablaw.com

WILLIAM H. PENNIMAN, born New Haven, Connecticut, June 4, 1948; admitted to bar, 1974, Maryland; 1975, District of Columbia. *Education:* Allegheny College (A.B., 1970); Georgetown University Law Center (J.D., 1974). Editor, Georgetown Law Journal, 1972-1974. Law Clerk to Judge C. Stanley Blair, U.S. District Court, District of Maryland, 1974-1975. Member, Board of Directors, Federal Energy Bar Association, 1994-1997. Member, Board of Directors, Energy Law Journal Foundation, 1997—. Treasurer, Energy Law Journal Foundation, 2000—. *Member:* American Bar Association (Vice Chair and Member of Gas Committee, Public Utility Law Section, 1996—). ***PRACTICE AREAS:*** Energy; Electric Power; Energy Contracts; Regulatory Law; Natural Resources; Natural Gas Pipelines; Natural Gas Contracts; Electric Utility Regulation. ***Email:*** wpenniman@sablaw.com

HOLLY H. SMITH, born Pittsburgh, Pennsylvania, January 16, 1957; admitted to bar, 1982, District of Columbia. *Education:* Georgetown University

(This Listing Continued)

(B.A., 1979); Catholic University (J.D., 1982). *Member:* District of Columbia Bar. ***PRACTICE AREAS:*** Securities; Broker-Dealer Regulation. ***Email:*** hsmith@sablaw.com

COUNSEL

THOMAS E. BISSET, born Upper Darby, Pennsylvania, January 19, 1962; admitted to bar, 1986, Pennsylvania; 1994, District of Columbia. *Education:* Villanova University (B.S., magna cum laude, 1983); Boston University School of Law (J.D., 1986); Georgetown University Law Center (LL.M., 1992). Attorney-Adviser, 1989-1991 and Senior Counsel, 1992-1993, Division of Investment Management, Attorney-Adviser, 1987-1989, Division of Market Regulation, U.S. Securities and Exchange Commission. ***PRACTICE AREAS:*** Insurance Products Regulation; Mutual Fund Regulation; Securities Regulation. ***Email:*** tbisset@sablaw.com

JAMES J. BRIODY, born Queens, New York, October 29, 1963; admitted to bar, 1990, Virginia; 1993, District of Columbia. *Education:* Georgetown University Law Center (B.A., 1985); University of Virginia (J.D., 1990). ***PRACTICE AREAS:*** Litigation; Construction Law; Contracts; Government Contracts; Commercial Law. ***Email:*** jbriody@sablaw.com

CHARLES M. FLICKINGER, born Indianapolis, Indiana, April 15, 1953; admitted to bar, 1983, Indiana; 1986, Georgia (Not admitted in District of Columbia). *Education:* University of Virginia (B.A., summa cum laude, 1976); Harvard University (M.A., 1977; J.D., cum laude, 1983). ***PRACTICE AREAS:*** Securities Regulation; Environmental Regulation; Mergers and Acquisitions; Corporate Law. ***Email:*** cmflickinger@sablaw.com

ANNE W. GELDON, born Washington, D. C., April 4, 1947; admitted to bar, 1975, District of Columbia; 1985, Maryland. *Education:* Cornell University (B.A., 1969); Harvard University (M.A., 1971; J.D., 1974). Phi Beta Kappa. ***PRACTICE AREAS:*** Estate Planning; Estate and Gift Taxation; Living Trusts; Estate Administration; Trust Administration. ***Email:*** ageldon@sablaw.com

NANCY L. HANKIN, born Washington, D.C., January 28, 1957; admitted to bar, 1983, Missouri; 1984, U.S. Court of Appeals for the Federal Circuit; 1998, District of Columbia. *Education:* University of North Carolina (B.A., cum laude, 1979); Washington University (J.D., 1983). *Member:* American Bar Association; American Intellectual Property Law Association. ***PRACTICE AREAS:*** Trademarks; Copyrights; Unfair Competition. ***Email:*** nhankin@sablaw.com

LORI E. HARWELL, born Baldwin, New York, June 7, 1962; admitted to bar, 1987, Florida; 1992, District of Columbia. *Education:* Florida State University (B.S., magna cum laude, 1984); University of Florida (J.D., with honors, 1987; LL.M., in Taxation, with high honors, 1990). Order of the Coif; Phi Kappa Phi. Member, University of Florida Law Review. Law Clerk to Hon. Julian I. Jacobs, U.S. Tax Court, 1990-1992. ***PRACTICE AREAS:*** Corporate Income Tax; Tax Planning; Tax Controversies. ***Email:*** lharwell@sablaw.com

IAN A. HERBERT, born Kansas City, Missouri, January 7, 1961; admitted to bar, 1985, Illinois; 1988, Pennsylvania (Not admitted in District of Columbia). *Education:* Washington University (B.A., 1982); The Wharton School, University of Pennsylvania (M.B.A., 1987); University of Illinois (J.D., 1985). ***PRACTICE AREAS:*** Employee Benefit Taxation; ERISA; Executive Compensation; Qualified Retirement Plans. ***Email:*** iherbert@sablaw.com

DOUGLAS J. LEARY, born Auburn, New York, August 15, 1963; admitted to bar, 1991, New York and District of Columbia. *Education:* Colgate University (B.A., 1985); Boston University (J.D., cum laude, 1990). G. Joseph Tauro Scholar; Paul J. Liacos Scholar; Edward F. Hennessey Scholar. Boston University Law Review (Staff, 1988-1989; Editor, 1989-1990). ***PRACTICE AREAS:*** Corporate Governance; Mergers and Acquisitions; Securities Offerings. ***Email:*** dleary@sablaw.com

ROXANE E. MAYWALT, born Auburn, New York, November 1, 1964; admitted to bar, 1992, New York and Massachusetts; 1999, District of Columbia. *Education:* Cornell University (B.S., 1986); Syracuse University (J.D., 1991). Member and Managing Editor, Syracuse Law Review, 1989-1991. Member, Syracuse University College of Law Moot Court Board, 1989-1991. Advisory Attorney, Federal Energy Regulatory Commission, 1991-1994. ***PRACTICE AREAS:*** Energy; Federal Energy Regulation; Gas Utilities; Electric Utilities. ***Email:*** rmaywalt@sablaw.com

CAROL T. McCLARNON, born Hammond, Indiana, December 24, 1960; admitted to bar, 1990, Ohio; 1999, District of Columbia. *Education:* Ball State University (B.S., 1983); Indiana University (J.D., cum laude, 1990). Managing Editor, Indiana Law Journal, 1989-1990. ***PRACTICE AREAS:*** Employee Benefits; ERISA Compliance. ***Email:*** cmcclarnon@sablaw.com

MARY PATRICIA MICHEL, born Milwaukee, Wisconsin, May 5, 1950; admitted to bar, 1982, District of Columbia; 1985, Illinois. *Education:* Georgetown University (B.S., 1972; J.D., 1982). Editorial Staff, American Criminal Law Review. Law Clerk to Judge Joseph V. Colaianni, U.S. Claims Court, 1982-1983. Member: National Law Alumni Board, Georgetown University Law

(This Listing Continued)

SUTHERLAND ASBILL & BRENNAN LLP, Washington—Continued

Center; Binational Panel Roster Chapter 19 of the North American Free Trade Agreement. ***PRACTICE AREAS:*** International Trade; International Law; Corporate; Litigation. ***Email:*** mmichel@sablaw.com

MARY E. MONAHAN, born Durham, North Carolina, August 10, 1964; admitted to bar, 1991, Maryland; 1992, District of Columbia. *Education:* Georgetown University (A.B., cum laude, 1986); George Washington University National Law Center (J.D., with high honors, 1991). Order of the Coif. Staff Member and Articles Editor, The George Washington Law Review, 1990-1991. ***PRACTICE AREAS:*** Federal Income Tax Litigation; Federal Income Tax Controversy. ***Email:*** mmonahan@sablaw.com

CHRISTER L. MOSSBERG, born Helsingborg, Sweden, March 30, 1945; admitted to bar, 1988, New York and District of Columbia. *Education:* Bates College (B.A., 1967); Indiana University (Ph.D., 1979); University of California at Berkeley (J.D., 1987). Mellon Fellow; Danforth Associate; Rector's Medal of Merit; William Riley Parker Memorial Prize. Fulbright Professor. ***PRACTICE AREAS:*** International Law; International Trade; Litigation; Corporate Law. ***Email:*** cmossberg@sablaw.com

SCOTT D. SILVERMAN, born Brooklyn, New York, December 30, 1958; admitted to bar, 1984, New York; 1992, North Carolina (Not admitted in District of Columbia). *Education:* Queens College of the City University of New York (B.A., 1980); Benjamin N. Cardozo School of Law (J.D., 1983). ***PRACTICE AREAS:*** Mergers and Acquisitions; Insurance Regulation. ***Email:*** ssilverman@sablaw.com

GREGORY STUART SMITH, born Wilmington, Delaware, February 24, 1959; admitted to bar, 1986, Georgia (Not admitted in District of Columbia). *Education:* Wake Forest University (B.A., cum laude, 1981); University of North Carolina at Chapel Hill (J.D., with honors, 1985). Phi Alpha Delta. Member and Research Editor, North Carolina Law Review, 1984-1985. Judicial Clerk to the Hon. Eugene A. Gordon, Senior United States District Judge for the Middle District of North Carolina. Author: Note, "Rutledge v. Tultex Corp./Kings Yarn," 62 North Carolina Law Review 573, 1984; Note, "Verlinden B.V. v. Central Bank of Nigeria," 9 North Carolina Journal of International Law & Comparative Regulation 187, 1984; Survey Note, "Henden v. North Carolina State Board of Elections," 62 North Carolina Law Review 1173, 1984; Note, "Federal & United States Jurisdiction Under the Foreign Sovereign Immunities Act," 9 N.C.J. Int'l L. 187, 1984; "An Insider's Guide: Creative Avenues for White Collar Clients," Fulton County Daily Report, White Collar Crime Supplement 10, July 1994; "A Little Off the Top: Accounting Firms Edge into the Legal Marketplace," cover story, reprint from Atlanta Lawyer, 4 Georgia Bar Journal 10, October 1998. Member, Leadership Georgia, 1993. Associate Counsel to the President of the United States, 2000-2001. *Member:* Atlanta (President, 1998-1999) and American (Member: House of Delegates, 1992—; Executive Council, Criminal Justice Section, 1996-1999) Bar Associations; State Bar of Georgia. ***REPORTED CASES:*** United States v. Granderson, 511 U.S. 39 (1994). ***PRACTICE AREAS:*** Litigation; White Collar Crime; Criminal Law; Appellate Practice. ***Email:*** gsmith@sablaw.com

LEWIS S. WIENER, born Brooklyn, New York, August 30, 1962; admitted to bar, 1988, New York and District of Columbia; 1993, Maryland; U.S. Claims Court; U.S. District Court for the District of Columbia; U.S. District Court, District of Maryland, Northern and Southern Districts of Texas and Southern and Eastern Districts of New York; U.S. Court of Appeals for the District of Columbia, Federal, Second, Fourth and Fifth Circuits; U.S. Court of International Trade. *Education:* State University of New York at Albany (B.A., cum laude, 1984); American University, Washington College of Law (J.D., 1987). Staff,, 1985-1986 and Managing Editor, 1986-1987, American University Journal of International Law & Policy. Author, Note: "Whither Implication- An analysis of the Implication Doctrine, Abrams v. Baylor College of Medicine," 1 American University Journal of International Law & Policy 331, 1986. Member: Environment and Natural Resources Division; General Litigation Section; Environmental Enforcement Section, U.S. Department of Justice, Washington, D.C., September, 1994 - February, 2000. Member, Advisory Council, United States Court of Federal Claims, 2000—. Member, U.S. Court of Federal Claims Governing Board, 1999-2001. *Member:* Montgomery County (Chair, Environmental Law Committee, 2000—), Federal Circuit and The United States Court of Federal Claims (President-Elect, 2001-2002) Bar Associations; District of Columbia Bar. ***PRACTICE AREAS:*** Litigation; Construction; Surety; Taking/Inverse Condemnation. ***Email:*** lwiener@sablaw.com

CATHERINE S. WOOLEDGE, born Oak Park, Illinois, June 1, 1942; admitted to bar, 1989, Pennsylvania, New Jersey and U.S. District Court, Eastern District of Pennsylvania and District of New Jersey; 1999, District of Columbia. *Education:* Purdue University (B.A., with honors, 1969; M.S. in Ed., 1973; Ph.D., 1975); College of William & Mary, Marshall-Wythe School of Law (J.D., 1989). *Member:* The District of Columbia Bar; Pennsylvania, New Jersey State and American Bar Associations. ***PRACTICE AREAS:*** Corporate; Securities; Investment Company Law; Investment Management; Securities Regulation. ***Email:*** cwooledge@sablaw.com

(This Listing Continued)

ASSOCIATES OF THE FIRM IN WASHINGTON, D.C.

JAMES A. BALDWIN, born McKeesport, Pennsylvania, April 25, 1968; admitted to bar, 1993, Pennsylvania (Not admitted in District of Columbia). *Education:* Villanova University (B.S., 1990); Georgetown University (J.D., 1993). ***LANGUAGES:*** French. ***PRACTICE AREAS:*** Corporate Finance; Mergers and Acquisitions; Financial Institutions Law. ***Email:*** jbaldwin@sablaw.com

LLOYD F. BERNARD, born Brooklyn, New York, January 8, 1962; admitted to bar, 1989, New York, Pennsylvania and New Jersey; 1990, District of Columbia. *Education:* State University of New York at Stony Brook (B.A., 1984); State University of New York at Stony Brook-W. Averell Harriman College (M.S., 1984); New York University School of Law (J.D., 1988). Note and Comment Editor, NYU Review of Law and Social Change, 1987-1988. ***PRACTICE AREAS:*** Investment Company Law; Mutual Funds; Insurance Products; Securities Regulation. ***Email:*** lbernard@sablaw.com

THOMAS ROBINSON BUNDY, III, born Landover, Maryland, March 5, 1973; admitted to bar, 2000, Maryland and New Jersey (Not admitted in District of Columbia). *Education:* Towson State University (B.S., Economics and Political Science, 1996); Howard University (J.D., 2000). Member: Charles Hamilton Houston Moot Court Team; Howard Law Journal. Recipient: Div. I Athletic Scholarship, Towson State University; Scholar-Athlete Awards, Towson State University; Merit Scholarship, Howard University; CALI Performance Awards, Howard University. *Member:* American Bar Association; The Association of Trial Lawyers of America. ***LANGUAGES:*** Spanish. ***PRACTICE AREAS:*** Litigation; Intellectual Property Litigation. ***Email:*** TBundy@sablaw.com

RONESHA A. BUTLER, born Philadelphia, Pennsylvania, January 9, 1973; admitted to bar, 2000, Pennsylvania and District of Columbia. *Education:* Pennsylvania State University (B.A., English and African-American Studies, 1994); Howard University (J.D., 1999). Member, Howard Law Journal, Howard University, 1997-1999. ***PRACTICE AREAS:*** Corporate Law. ***Email:*** rbutler@sablaw.com

ANN B. CAMMACK, born Englewood, New Jersey, July 30, 1963; admitted to bar, 1990, Virginia; 2000, District of Columbia. *Education:* Randolph Macon College (A.B., 1985); Washington and Lee University (J.D., 1990). ***PRACTICE AREAS:*** Taxation. ***Email:*** acammack@sablaw.com

ROBERT S. CHASE, II, born Salt Lake City, Utah, March 8, 1972; admitted to bar, 1997, Maryland; 1998, District of Columbia. *Education:* University of Utah (B.S., 1994); George Washington University (J.D., with honors, 1997). Member, George Washington University Law Review, 1995-1997. ***PRACTICE AREAS:*** Federal Income Tax; Tax Litigation; Corporate Taxation; Federal Tax Controversies. ***Email:*** rchase@sablaw.com

ERIC CICCORETTI, born Detroit, Michigan, September 18, 1967; admitted to bar, 1999, Michigan and U.S. District Court, Eastern District of Michigan (Not admitted in District of Columbia). *Education:* University of Michigan (A.B., 1989; J.D., 1998). *Member:* State Bar of Michigan. ***PRACTICE AREAS:*** Energy; Corporate Transactions. ***Email:*** eciccoretti@sablaw.com

ADAM COHEN, born Philadelphia, Pennsylvania, February 7, 1971; admitted to bar, 1996, Maryland; 1997, District of Columbia. *Education:* University of Virginia (B.A., with distinction, 1993); Harvard Law School (J.D., cum laude, 1996). Phi Beta Kappa. ***PRACTICE AREAS:*** Employee Benefit Taxation; ERISA; Executive Compensation; Qualified Retirement Plans. ***Email:*** acohen@sablaw.com

MARGARET M. CONNELL, born New York, N.Y., February 3, 1965; admitted to bar, 1997, Massachusetts (Not admitted in District of Columbia). *Education:* Tufts University (B.A., 1987); University of Kansas (J.D., 1996). ***PRACTICE AREAS:*** Corporate Law. ***Email:*** mconnell@sablaw.com

KATHLEEN M. DEVEREAUX, born Lansing, Michigan, March 2, 1976; admitted to bar, 2001, Maryland (Not admitted in District of Columbia). *Education:* University of Michigan (B.A., 1998); Northwestern University (J.D., 2001). ***PRACTICE AREAS:*** Litigation; Corporate Law. ***Email:*** kdevereaux@sablaw.com

MARSHALL O. DONLEY, III, born Washington, D.C., April 16, 1973; admitted to bar, 1998, Georgia (Not admitted in District of Columbia). *Education:* University of South Carolina (B.A., magna cum laude, 1995); Vanderbilt University (J.D., 1998). Phi Beta Kappa. Honors College. Managing Editor, Vanderbilt University Law Review. Law Clerk, U.S. District Court, Northern District of Florida. ***PRACTICE AREAS:*** Litigation; Securities. ***Email:*** modonley@sablaw.com

PAMELA K. ELLIS, born Pittsburgh, Pennsylvania, March 15, 1963; admitted to bar, 1988, Pennsylvania; 1989, District of Columbia. *Education:* Wellesley College (B.A., cum laude, with honors in Political Science, 1985); Vanderbilt University School of Law (J.D., 1988). Attorney, 1990-1994 and Senior Counsel, 1994-1997, Division of Investment Management, Securities and Exchange Commission. ***PRACTICE AREAS:*** Securities Regulation; Securities Registration; Securities Disclosure; Mutual Funds. ***Email:*** pellis@sablaw.com

(This Listing Continued)

JOHN J. FAHEY, born Jersey City, New Jersey, September 6, 1964; admitted to bar, 1999, New York; 2000, District of Columbia. *Education:* Lafayette College (B.A., 1986); Georgetown University (J.D., 1998). Order of the Coif. ***PRACTICE AREAS:*** Securities. ***Email:*** jfahey@sablaw.com

JOHN T. FITZGERALD, born Lake Forest, Illinois, July 28, 1975; (admission pending). *Education:* University of Michigan (B.A., History, 1997); George Washington University (J.D., 2000). ***PRACTICE AREAS:*** Securities. ***Email:*** jfitzgerald@sablaw.com

BLAIR E. FLYNN, born Falls Church, Virginia, January 29, 1974; admitted to bar, 1999, Alabama (Not admitted in District of Columbia). *Education:* University of Richmond (B.A., cum laude, 1996); University of Virginia (J.D., 1999). *Member:* American Bar Association. ***PRACTICE AREAS:*** Securities; Mergers and Acquisitions; Corporate Law. ***Email:*** bflynn@sablaw.com

DANIEL E. FRANK, born Seattle, Washington, January 26, 1967; admitted to bar, 1994, Virginia; 1995, District of Columbia. *Education:* University of Washington (B.A., magna cum laude, 1990) Phi Beta Kappa; The University of Chicago Law School (J.D., 1993). Senior Comment Editor, The University of Chicago Legal Forum. Law Clerk to Danny J. Boggs, U.S. Court of Appeals, Sixth Circuit, 1993-1994. ***PRACTICE AREAS:*** Energy Contracts; Energy Regulation; Electric Utilities; Electric Cooperatives Law; Public Utility Regulation. ***Email:*** dfrank@sablaw.com

DAPHNE G. FRYDMAN, born Washington, D.C., November 19, 1974; (admission pending). *Education:* Wesleyan University (B.A., 1996); Northwestern University (J.D., 2001). ***LANGUAGES:*** Spanish and Russian. ***PRACTICE AREAS:*** Corporate. ***Email:*** dfrydman@sablaw.com

KATHERINE E. GASPAREK, born Chula Vista, California, February 19, 1967; (admission pending). *Education:* George Mason University; George Mason University School of Law (J.D., magna cum laude, 2001). Author: George Mason Law Review, Vol. 7:3, Spring, 1999. ***PRACTICE AREAS:*** Corporate; Energy. ***Email:*** kgasparek@sablaw.com

KIRSTIN E. GIBBS, born Oswego, New York, August 8, 1968; admitted to bar, 1997, Maryland; 1999, District of Columbia. *Education:* LeMoyne College (B.A., 1990); Catholic University (J.D., 1997). *Member:* Bar Association of the District of Columbia; Maryland State Bar Association, Inc.; American Bar Association; Federal Energy Bar Association. ***PRACTICE AREAS:*** Energy and Commodities Division. ***Email:*** kgibbs@sablaw.com

DANIELLE GIROUX, born Worcester, Massachusetts, August 18, 1974; admitted to bar, 2000, District of Columbia. *Education:* James Madison University (B.A., 1996); George Mason University (J.D., cum laude, 2000). 8 Geo. Mason L. Rev. 355. Legal Writing Fellow. Dean's Scholar, George Madison University, 1999-2000. ***PRACTICE AREAS:*** Civil Litigation. ***Email:*** dgiroux@sablaw.com

MIRIAM E. GOLDSMITH, born Washington, D.C., May 25, 1976; (admission pending). *Education:* Wellesley College (B.A., 1998); Duke University (J.D., 2001). ***PRACTICE AREAS:*** Securities Regulation; Private Placement; Securities Registration. ***Email:*** mgoldsmith@sablaw.com

ELISABETH GRANO, born Poughkeepsie, New York, February 26, 1970; admitted to bar, 1996, Georgia; 2000, District of Columbia. *Education:* University of Delaware (B.S.B.A., 1992); Emory University (J.D., M.B.A., 1996). Fellow, Life Management Institute, 1998—. ***PRACTICE AREAS:*** Securities. ***Email:*** egrano@sablaw.com

BRYAN M. HAYNES, born Cleveland, Ohio, April 27, 1971; admitted to bar, 1998, Virginia; 1999, District of Columbia. *Education:* Virginia Polytechnic Institute and State University (B.A., 1993); George Mason University School of Law (J.D., magna cum laude, 1998). Associate Editor, George Mason Law Review, 1997-1998. Law Clerk to the Honorable Diane Gilbert Weinstein, U.S. Court of Federal Claims, 1998-1999. *Member:* American Bar Association. ***PRACTICE AREAS:*** Litigation. ***Email:*** bhaynes@sablaw.com

JOHN E. HINDING, born Saint Paul, Minnesota, August 1, 1972; admitted to bar, 1997, Virginia; 1998, District of Columbia. *Education:* University of Notre Dame (B.A., cum laude, 1994); Duke University (J.D., 1997). *Member:* Virginia State Bar; The District of Columbia Bar. ***PRACTICE AREAS:*** Tax; Federal Tax; Tax Controversies; International Tax. ***Email:*** jhinding@sablaw.com

REBECCA L. HIRSCH, born Pittsburgh, Pennsylvania, April 18, 1968; admitted to bar, 1994, Pennsylvania; 1999, District of Columbia. *Education:* Northwestern University (B.A., 1990); Tulane University School of Law (J.D., cum laude, 1993). Phi Beta Kappa. Notes and Comments Editor, Tulane Maritime Law Journal, 1992-1993. ***PRACTICE AREAS:*** Commercial Litigation; Business Litigation. ***Email:*** rhirsch@sablaw.com

JOHN L. HYNES, born Boulder, Colorado, October 17, 1967; admitted to bar, 2000, Virginia; 2001, District of Columbia. *Education:* Earlham College (B.A., 1990); Georgetown University (J.D., cum laude, 2000). Author: "Corporation Cannot Amortize Cost of Term Interests in Partnerships When Shareholders' Remainder Interests Are Funded By Extraordinary Distributions: CGF Industries v. Commissioner," 53 The Tax Lawyer 301 (1999). *Member:* Virginia State Bar; The District of Columbia Bar. ***PRACTICE AREAS:*** Federal Taxation. ***Email:*** jhynes@sablaw.com

RAWN M. JAMES, JR., born Miami, Florida, November 14, 1976; admitted to bar, 2001, District of Columbia. *Education:* Yale University (B.A., 1998); Duke University (J.D., 2001). ***PRACTICE AREAS:*** Litigation. ***Email:*** rjames@sablaw.com

GREGORY S. KAUFMAN, born Washington, D.C., August 16, 1973; admitted to bar, 1998, Maryland; 1999, District of Columbia. *Education:* Miami University (B.A., 1995); George Washington University (J.D., 1998). ***PRACTICE AREAS:*** Litigation. ***Email:*** gkaufman@sablaw.com

MARGARET ANNE KING, born Falls Church, Virginia, March 30, 1976; admitted to bar, 2001, Illinois (Not admitted in District of Columbia). *Education:* Emory University (B.A., magna cum laude, 1998); Harvard University (J.D., 2001). Phi Beta Kappa. ***PRACTICE AREAS:*** Tax Law. ***Email:*** mking@sablaw.com

BETH D. KNICKERBOCKER, born Greeley, Colorado, October 7, 1966; admitted to bar, 1992, Iowa (Not admitted in District of Columbia). *Education:* Cornell College (B.A., magna cum laude, 1989); University of Iowa (J.D., with high distinction, 1992). Phi Beta Kappa. Member, Mortar Board. Member, 1990-1991 and Senior Associate Editor, 1991-1992, Iowa Law Review. *Member:* Iowa State and American (Member, Administrative Law Section, 1998—) Bar Associations. ***PRACTICE AREAS:*** Insurance Regulation; Banking Law; Broker-Dealer Registration. ***Email:*** bknickerbocker@sablaw.com

MICHAEL KOFFLER, born New York, New York, May 12, 1971; admitted to bar, 1996, Maryland; 1998, District of Columbia. *Education:* State University of New York at Binghamton (B.A., summa cum laude, 1993); University of Pennsylvania (J.D., 1996). Phi Beta Kappa. *Member:* District of Columbia Bar; Maryland State and American Bar Associations. ***PRACTICE AREAS:*** Securities; Broker-Dealer Regulation; Investment Adviser Regulation; Distribution of Investment Products; Insurance Regulation; Investments; Investment Company Law. ***Email:*** mkoffler@sablaw.com

DAVID J. KRITZ, born Princeton, New Jersey, June 22, 1966; admitted to bar, 1992, New Jersey; 1993, New York; 1994, Pennsylvania; 1996, Texas; 1998, District of Columbia. *Education:* Northwestern University (B.A., 1989); University of Buffalo (J.D., 1992). Publications Editor, Buffalo Law Review. *Member:* American Bar Association (Member, Sections on: Tax; Business Law). ***PRACTICE AREAS:*** Employee Benefits; Tax Law. ***Email:*** dkritz@sablaw.com

RENE M. LAFORTE, born Chicago, Illinois, November 8, 1968; admitted to bar, 1993, Ohio (Not admitted in District of Columbia). *Education:* Pennsylvania State University (B.A., 1990); University of Dayton (J.D., 1993). Member, University of Dayton Law Review. Author, "The Constitutional Implications of Anti-Drug Loitering Ordinances in Ohio," U. Dayton L. Rev., Vol. 18:2, Spring 1993. ***PRACTICE AREAS:*** Trademarks; Copyrights; Unfair Competition. ***Email:*** rlaforte@sablaw.com

DAVID A. LAST, born August 16, 1973; admitted to bar, 2000, Maryland and New Jersey (Not admitted in District of Columbia). *Education:* Brandeis University (B.A., cum laude, 1995); Georgetown University (J.D., cum laude, 2000). Law Clerk to the Hon. Joan Feldon, Supreme Court of the District of Columbia. ***LANGUAGES:*** Spanish. ***PRACTICE AREAS:*** Litigation. ***Email:*** dlast@sablaw.com

MARIE KALAMARAS LEE, born Queens, New York, February 12, 1973; admitted to bar, 2000, Maryland (Not admitted in District of Columbia). *Education:* Boston University (B.A., magna cum laude, 1995); American University (J.D., magna cum laude, 2000). Golden Key National Honor Society. Executive Editor, American University Law Review, 1999-2000. *Member:* American Bar Association (Member, Tax Section). ***PRACTICE AREAS:*** Taxation; Employee Benefits. ***Email:*** mklee@sablaw.com

LING LING, born Shanghai, China, June 19, 1969; admitted to bar, 1998, New York and District of Columbia. *Education:* Shanghai International Studies University (B.A., 1991); University of North Carolina at Chapel Hill (J.D., with honors, 1997). Order of the Coif. Member, North Carolina Law Review. Author: Note, "Manuel v. United States: The Question of the Exclusivity Rule in Section 745 of the Suits in Admiralty Act," 75 N.C.L. Rev. 639, 1997. ***LANGUAGES:*** Chinese, English. ***PRACTICE AREAS:*** Corporate; Securities. ***Email:*** lling@sablaw.com

KURT E. LOPEZ, born Mexico City, D.F., Mexico, April 7, 1970; admitted to bar, 1998, Michigan (Not admitted in District of Columbia). *Education:* University of Michigan (B.A., 1994); Wayne State University (J.D., 1998). Recipient, G. Menendez Memorial Scholarship. *Member:* Hispanic Bar Association (D.C. Member, 1998). ***LANGUAGES:*** Spanish and French. ***PRACTICE AREAS:*** Corporate Law; Securities Law. ***Email:*** klopez@sablaw.com

RONALD R. MASSUMI, born Lorain, Ohio, December 30, 1953; admitted to bar, 1980, District of Columbia. *Education:* Vassar College (B.A., 1976); Georgetown University (J.D., 1980). Lead Articles Editor, The Tax Lawyer. Co-Author: "Civil RICO in the Public Interest: 'Everybody's Darling'," 19 Am.

(This Listing Continued)

SUTHERLAND ASBILL & BRENNAN LLP, Washington—Continued

Crim. L. Rev. 655. Attorney, Securities and Exchange Commission, General Counsel's Office, 1984-1986 and Division of Enforcement, 1986-1988. ***PRACTICE AREAS:*** Corporate Law; Securities; Business Litigation; White Collar Criminal Defense; Appellate Practice. ***Email:*** rmassumi@sablaw.com

CHANDRA McCLEARN, born Cheverly, Maryland, August 18, 1978; (admission pending). *Education:* Cornell University (B.A., 1998); Duke University (J.D., 2001). ***PRACTICE AREAS:*** Federal Income Taxation. ***Email:*** cmcclearn@sablaw.com

DONYELLE C. McCRAY, born Atlanta, Georgia, July 6, 1974; admitted to bar, 1999, Georgia; 2000, District of Columbia. *Education:* Spelman College (B.A., 1996); Harvard University (J.D., 1999). ***PRACTICE AREAS:*** Trusts and Estates. ***Email:*** dmccray@sablaw.com

JAY McDANELL, born Grand Forks, North Dakota, December 13, 1971; admitted to bar, 2000, Virginia (Not admitted in District of Columbia). *Education:* Tulane University of Louisiana (L.A., Economics, 1994); Georgetown University (J.D., 2000). Co-Author: "Computer Crimes," White Collar Crime Project, American Criminal Law Review. Member, American Criminal Law Review, 1998-2000. Technology Editor, Criminal Law Review, 1999-2000. ***PRACTICE AREAS:*** Civil Litigation. ***Email:*** jmcdannell@sablaw.com

MATTHEW G. McLAUGHLIN, born West Orange, New Jersey, April 23, 1972; admitted to bar, 1999, Maryland; 2000, District of Columbia. *Education:* Hamilton College (B.A., 1994); Catholic University of America (J.D., cum laude, 1999). Editor-in-Chief, Catholic University Law Review, 1998-1999. *Member:* Maryland State Bar Association; The District of Columbia Bar. ***PRACTICE AREAS:*** Tax Law. ***Email:*** mmclaughlin@sablaw.com

KATHERINE S. MILIN, born Chicago, Illinois, September 14, 1970; admitted to bar, 1999, Virginia; 2000, District of Columbia. *Education:* James Madison University (B.B.A., 1992); George Mason University (J.D., magna cum laude, 1999). Associate Editor, George Mason Law Review, 1997-1998. *Member:* American Bar Association. ***PRACTICE AREAS:*** Corporate Law; Securities. ***Email:*** kmilin@sablaw.com

SHEILA R. NOVAK, born Fairfax, Virginia, April 9, 1969; admitted to bar, 1996, Virginia; 1997, District of Columbia. *Education:* College of William & Mary (B.A., 1991; J.D., 1996). Member, William & Mary Law Review, 1995-1996. Author: "A Claim for Third Party Standing in Medical Malpractice Cases involving Repressed Memory Syndrome," Vol. 37, William & Mary Law Review, 1995. ***PRACTICE AREAS:*** Real Estate. ***Email:*** snovak@sablaw.com

VICTORIA A. O'CONNOR, born Huntington, West Virginia, November 3, 1972; admitted to bar, 1999, District of Columbia. *Education:* Georgetown University (B.A., magna cum laude, 1995; J.D., 1998). Pi Sigma Alpha. Staff, Law & Policy in International Business Journal, 1996-1998. ***PRACTICE AREAS:*** Corporate Taxation; International Taxation; Tax Controversies. ***Email:*** vo'connor@sablaw.com

HEATHER STACEY PARR, born Fort Lauderdale, Florida, November 19, 1973; admitted to bar, 1999, Delaware (Not admitted in District of Columbia). *Education:* University of Florida (B.A., with honors, 1996); College of William and Mary School of Law (J.D., 1999). Phi Delta Phi. Graduate Research Fellow, 1996-1999. Staff Member, William and Mary Environmental Law and Policy Review, 1997-1999. *Member:* Delaware State and American Bar Associations. ***PRACTICE AREAS:*** Corporate Litigation. ***Email:*** Stacey@sablaw.com

MICHAEL C. PAWLUK, born New York, N.Y., August 17, 1973; admitted to bar, 1999, Virginia; 2000, District of Columbia. *Education:* Georgetown University (B.S.F.S., 1994); University of Virginia (J.D., 1999). Phi Beta Kappa; Alpha Sigma Nu; Phi Alpha Theta. ***PRACTICE AREAS:*** Securities Regulation; Private Placement; Public Offerings; Securities Registration; Mergers and Acquisitions. ***Email:*** mpawluk@sablaw.com

SHANNAN STAMPER PETRILLA, born Ashland, Kentucky, March 14, 1972; admitted to bar, 1997, Ohio; 1998, Kentucky; 1999, District of Columbia. *Education:* Transylvania University (B.A., summa cum laude, 1994); Harvard University (J.D., 1997). Omicron Delta Kappa. *Member:* District of Columbia Bar; Kentucky and American Bar Associations. ***PRACTICE AREAS:*** International Taxation; Corporate Taxation; Partnership Taxation. ***Email:*** spetrilla@sablaw.com

PATRICE M. PITTS, born Washington, D.C., April 19, 1957; admitted to bar, 1985, District of Columbia. *Education:* Princeton University (A.B., cum laude, 1979); Yale University (J.D. and M.B.A., 1983). *Member:* The District of Columbia Bar (Member, Corporations, Finance and Securities Section); American Bar Association (Member, Business Law Section). ***PRACTICE AREAS:*** Insurance Products; Investment Company Act; Securities Regulation. ***Email:*** ppitts@sablaw.com

(This Listing Continued)

MICHAEL S. PONDER, born Anniston, Alabama, September 12, 1973; (admission pending). *Education:* Harvard University (A.B., 1996); University of Michigan (J.D., 2000). ***PRACTICE AREAS:*** Broker-Dealer Regulation. ***Email:*** mponder@sablaw.com

JENNIFER R. RAWERT, born Owensboro, Kentucky, November 22, 1967; admitted to bar, 1998, Kentucky; 1999, U.S. Tax Court (Not admitted in District of Columbia). *Education:* University of Notre Dame (B.B.A., 1989); Louis D. Brandeis School of Law, University of Louisville (J.D., 1997); Georgetown University (LL.M., 1999). Member, Louisville Law Review. *Member:* Kentucky Bar Association. ***PRACTICE AREAS:*** Business Law; Securities; Mergers and Acquisitions; Taxation. ***Email:*** jrawert@sablaw.com

THOMAS J. REYES, born Baton Rouge, Louisiana, November 9, 1962; admitted to bar, 1998, Massachusetts (Not admitted in District of Columbia). *Education:* University of Massachusetts (B.S., 1992); Boston University (J.D., 1997). Member, Journal of Science and Technology Law, 1995-1996. ***LANGUAGES:*** Spanish. ***PRACTICE AREAS:*** Corporate Law. ***Email:*** treyes@sablaw.com

THOMAS C. ROBERGE, JR., born Bridgeport, Connecticut, February 9, 1974; admitted to bar, 1999, Maryland; 2000, District of Columbia. *Education:* Georgetown University (A.B., magna cum laude, 1996; J.D., cum laude, 1999). Alpha Sigma Nu. *Member:* Maryland State (Member, Taxation and Young Lawyers Sections, 1999—) and American (Member, Taxation, Business Law and Young Lawyers Sections, 1999—) Bar Associations; The District of Columbia Bar (Member, Taxation Section, 2000—). ***PRACTICE AREAS:*** Tax Law. ***Email:*** troberge@sablaw.com

DAVID A. ROBY, JR., born Brookings, South Dakota, January 3, 1968; admitted to bar, 1993, Georgia; 1994, Florida; 1996, District of Columbia. *Education:* Florida State University (B.S., cum laude, 1990); University of Georgia (J.D., cum laude, 1993); University of Florida (LL.M. in Taxation, 1994). Order of the Coif. Notes Editor, Georgia Law Review, 1992-1993. Attorney-Adviser to Judge Carolyn P. Chiechi, U.S. Tax Court, 1994-1996. ***PRACTICE AREAS:*** Federal Income Tax; Corporate Income Tax; Partnership Taxation; Tax Planning; Federal Tax Controversies. ***Email:*** droby@sablaw.com

JELANI Y. ROPER, born Orange, New Jersey, November 9, 1973; (admission pending). *Education:* College of William & Mary (B.A., 1995); Georgetown University (J.D., 2001). ***Email:*** jroper@sablaw.com

AMISH M. SHAH, born Silver Spring, Maryland, October 10, 1971; admitted to bar, 1999, Maryland; 2000, District of Columbia. *Education:* University of Maryland (B.S.,1993); George Washington University (J.D.,with honors, 1999). Member, The Environmental Lawyer Law Journal, 1997-1999. Certified Public Accountant, 1996. Vice President, South Asian Bar Association at Washington, D.C., 2001. *Member:* Maryland State and American Bar Associations. ***PRACTICE AREAS:*** Federal Taxation; International Taxation; Tax Controversies. ***Email:*** ashah@sablaw.com

DANIEL R. SIMON, born Sangley Point, The Philippines, April 17, 1971; admitted to bar, 1999, North Carolina (Not admitted in District of Columbia). *Education:* Duke University (B.A., cum laude, with honors in Political Science, 1993); University of North Carolina, Chapel Hill (J.D., with honors, 1999). Notes Editor, North Carolina Law Review, 1998-1999. ***PRACTICE AREAS:*** Energy; Commodities. ***Email:*** dsimon@sablaw.com

STEVEN C. SPARLING, born Evanston, Illinois, October 27, 1968; (admission pending). *Education:* University of Pennsylvania (B.A., 1990); George Mason University (J.D., 2000). Mortar Board; Order of Omega. Recipient: Dean's Service Award; West Publishing Company "Hornbook" Award for Outstanding Scholastic Achievement, George Mason University. Finalist and Best Oralist, Spade Law Competition, 1999. Executive Editor, George Mason University Law Review. Author, George Mason Law Review, Volume 6, Issue 4. [Lt., U.S. Navy, 1991-1997]. ***PRACTICE AREAS:*** Energy; Commodities. ***Email:*** ssparling@sablaw.com

ALISA NAOMI STEIN, born Paris, France, November 1, 1975; admitted to bar, 2000, Virginia (Not admitted in District of Columbia). *Education:* University of Michigan (B.A., 1997); Georgetown University (J.D., 2000). ***PRACTICE AREAS:*** Energy; Commodities. ***Email:*** astein@sablaw.com

CHRISTOPHER F. TATE, born Washington, D.C., March 9, 1964; admitted to bar, 1997, Virginia; 1998, District of Columbia. *Education:* University of Virginia (B.A., 1985); George Mason University School of Law (J.D., 1997). Editor in Chief, George Mason Law Review, 1996-1997. ***PRACTICE AREAS:*** Tax Law; Estate and Gift Taxation. ***Email:*** ctate@sablaw.com

MARY E. THORNTON, born Dyersburg, Tennessee, November 28, 1969; admitted to bar, 1995, Virginia; 1998, District of Columbia. *Education:* University of Tennessee (B.S., summa cum laude, 1992); University of North Carolina School of Law (J.D., 1995). Order of the Coif. Member, North Carolina Law Review, 1993-1994. ***PRACTICE AREAS:*** Investment Company Law; Securities Regulation; Broker-Dealer Regulation; Insurance Products; Mutual Funds. ***Email:*** mthornton@sablaw.com

THOMAS M. TRACY, born Queens, New York, June 17, 1970; admitted to bar, 1996, New York; 1999, North Carolina (Not admitted in District of Colum-

(This Listing Continued)

bia). *Education:* State University of New York at Stony Brook (B.A., summa cum laude, 1992); University of Michigan (J.D., 1994). Phi Beta Kappa. *Member:* New York State Bar Association; North Carolina State Bar. ***PRACTICE AREAS:*** Real Estate; Litigation. ***Email:*** ttracy@sablaw.com

PAUL B. TURNER, born Richmond, Indiana, December 21, 1967; admitted to bar, 1996, Illinois; 1998, District of Columbia. *Education:* University of Chicago (A.B., with honors, 1990); University of Virginia (J.D., 1996). Order of the Coif; Phi Delta Phi; James C. Slaughter Award. Executive Editor, Virginia Law Review. *Member:* Seventh, Eleventh, Federal, DC Circuits and Illinois State Bar Associations. ***PRACTICE AREAS:*** Energy; Federal Energy Regulation; Sales and Use Tax; Energy Regulation. ***Email:*** pturner@sablaw.com

GAIL L. WESTOVER, born Hudson, New York, January 9, 1968; admitted to bar, 1997, Maryland; 1998, District of Columbia and U.S. District Court, District of Maryland. *Education:* Cornell University (B.S., 1990); Georgetown University (J.D., cum laude, 1997). Articles and Notes Editor, 1995-1996 and Staff Member, 1994-1995, American Criminal Law Review. *Member:* District of Columbia Bar; Maryland State and American Bar Associations. ***PRACTICE AREAS:*** Litigation. ***Email:*** gwestover@sablaw.com

WENDY ANN WILKENFELD, born Washington, D.C., May 1, 1974; admitted to bar, 1998, Virginia; 1999, District of Columbia. *Education:* Duke University (A.B., magna cum laude, 1995); Harvard University (J.D., 1998). ***PRACTICE AREAS:*** Estate and Gift Taxation; Trust and Estate; Federal Taxation. ***Email:*** wwilkenfeld@sablaw.com

CHARLES J. ZANGARA, born New Brunswick, New Jersey, May 4, 1965; admitted to bar, 2000, New York (Not admitted in District of Columbia). *Education:* Rutgers University (B.A., 1991); New York University (J.D., 1999). Author, "SEC v. Ad Claims," Business Law Today, March-April 2000. ***PRACTICE AREAS:*** Corporate Law. ***Email:*** czangara@sablaw.com

(For the Names and Biographical Data on the Firm's Atlanta, Georgia, New York, New York, Austin Texas and Tallahassee, Florida Personnel, See Professional Biographies at each of those cities).

SWARTZ & REED

Established in 1984

1825 JEFFERSON PLACE

WASHINGTON, D.C. 20036

Telephone: 202-429-0429

Email: swartzreed@earthlink.net

URL: http://www.lawyers.com/visas

Personal Injury, Product Liability and Medical Negligence Litigation.

FIRM PROFILE: Swartz & Reed represents catastrophically injured individuals and their families in civil actions, concentrating on injuries arising from medical negligence and dangerous products and medical devices. While most of our cases are from the Washington, D.C. metropolitan area, the firm has co-counseled cases nationwide. We have extensive experience handling claims against the United States under the Federal Tort Claims Act, as well as foreign claims under the Military Claims Act. The firm has a substantial background in cases involving many areas of medicine, including obstetrics & gynecology, surgery, cardiology, pediatrics, infectious disease, and emergency medicine.

MEMBERS OF FIRM

DEAN E. SWARTZ, born Hollywood, California, September 20, 1949; admitted to bar, 1974, Ohio; 1976, District of Columbia; 1978, U.S. Supreme Court; 1982, Virginia and Pennsylvania. *Education:* Stanford University (A.B., 1971); University of Toledo (J.D., 1974). Recipient, Chapin Award for Distinction in Forensics. Member, The Order of Barristers. Attorney, Office of the Judge Advocate General of the Navy, 1974-1978. Special Assistant General Counsel, U.S. Occupational Safety and Health Review Commission, 1978-1981. *Member:* Million Dollar Advocates Forum; The Association of Trial Lawyers of America (President's Club); Ohio Academy of Trial Lawyers; Virginia Trial Lawyers Association; National College of Advocacy (Advocate). [Major, U.S.M.C.R., 1971-1988]. (Certified as a Civil Trial Advocacy Specialist by the National Board of Trial Advocacy). ***Email:*** swartzreed@earthlink.net

BARRY S. REED, born Seattle, Washington, December 29, 1944; admitted to bar, 1981, Pennsylvania; 1983, District of Columbia. *Education:* University of Washington (B.A., 1967); George Washington University (M.D., 1971); Catholic University of America (J.D., 1980). *Member:* The District of Columbia Bar; American College of Legal Medicine. (On Leave of Absence).

ASSOCIATE

TIMOTHY A. WRAY, born Long Beach, California, March 27, 1949; admitted to bar, 2000, Virginia and District of Columbia. *Education:* United States Military Academy (B.S., 1971); Stanford University (A.M., 1979); George Mason University School of Law (J.D., magna cum laude, 1999). Fellow, Center for International Affairs, Harvard University, 1993-1994. Member, George Mason Law Review, 1997-1999. Recipient, Scott C. Whitney Writing Award, 2000. *Member:* The Association of Trial Lawyers of America; Virginia Trial Lawyers Association; Trial Lawyers Association of Metropolitan Washington, D.C. [Colonel, U.S. Army, 1971-1995.]. ***Email:*** swartzreed@earthlink.net

OF COUNSEL

ALLAN W. STEINHORN, born Baltimore, Maryland, April 29, 1955; admitted to bar, 1985, Maryland; 1987, District of Columbia; 1989, U.S. Supreme Court. *Education:* University of Maryland (B.G.S., 1978); University of Baltimore (J.D., 1985). Recipient, National Finalist in the National Student Trial Advocacy Competition, The Association of Trial Lawyers of America, 1985. Law Clerk to the Honorable Robert H. Mason, Associate Judge, Seventh Judicial Circuit of Maryland, 1985-1986. *Member:* The District of Columbia Bar; Prince George's County, Maryland State and American Bar Associations; The Association of Trial Lawyers of America; Trial Lawyers Association of Metropolitan Washington, D.C.; Maryland Trial Lawyers Association; J. Dudley Digges Inn; American Inns of Court.

JOHN A. BLAZER, born Cleveland, Ohio, December 19, 1948; admitted to bar, 1979, Virginia and District of Columbia; 1980, U.S. District Court for the District of Columbia and U.S. Court of Appeals for the District of Columbia Circuit; 1981, U.S. District Court, Eastern District of Virginia and U.S. Tax Court; 1984, U.S. Court of Appeals, Fourth Circuit; 1987, U.S. Supreme Court. *Education:* Georgetown University (A.B., 1971; J.D., 1979). Vice President, Student Bar Association, 1976-1978. *Member:* The District of Columbia Bar; Fairfax and American (Member, Section on: Litigation) Bar Associations; Virginia State Bar; Virginia Trial Lawyers Association; The Association of Trial Lawyers of America. ***Email:*** johnablazer@aol.com

(This Listing Continued)

SWIDLER BERLIN SHEREFF FRIEDMAN, LLP

3000 K STREET, N.W., SUITE 300

WASHINGTON, D.C. 20007

Telephone: 202-424-7500

Facsimile: 202-424-7643

URL: http://www.swidlaw.com

New York, N.Y. Office: The Chrysler Building, 405 Lexington Avenue. Telephone: 212-973-0111. Fax: 212-891-9598.

Litigation, Insurance Coverage, Employment Law, Telecommunications, Energy, Corporate, Bankruptcy, Creditor's Rights, Antitrust and Trade Regulation, Government Affairs, Environmental, Tax, ERISA, Real Estate, Structured Finance, Intellectual Property, International Trade.

STEVEN J. AGRESTA, born Paterson, New Jersey, September 4, 1948; admitted to bar, 1977, District of Columbia. *Education:* University of North Carolina at Chapel Hill (A.B., 1970); Massachusetts Institute of Technology (S.M., 1972); Harvard University (J.D., magna cum laude, 1975). Phi Beta Kappa. Woodrow Wilson Fellow, 1970. National Science Foundation Graduate Fellow, 1970-1972. Senior Editor, Harvard Law Review, 1974-1975. Law Clerk to Judge Joseph T. Sneed, U.S. Court of Appeals for the Ninth Circuit, 1975-1976. ***PRACTICE AREAS:*** Regulatory Law; Utility Law. ***Email:*** sjagresta@swidlaw.com

BERNARD P. BELL, born Philadelphia, Pennsylvania, October 5, 1959; admitted to bar, 1985, New York and U.S. District Court, Southern and Eastern Districts of New York; 1996, District of Columbia. *Education:* Colgate University (A.B., cum laude, 1981); Fordham University (J.D., 1984). Editor, Fordham Law Review, 1983-1984. Trial Attorney, Environmental Enforcement Section, Environment & Natural Resources Division, U.S. Department of Justice, 1989-1994. ***PRACTICE AREAS:*** Insurance Coverage; Insurance Litigation; Insurance Mediation; Environmental Litigation; Environmental Mediation. ***Email:*** bpbell@swidlaw.com

THOMAS A. BELLES, born Evansville, Indiana, April 14, 1956; admitted to bar, 1981, District of Columbia. *Education:* George Washington University (B.A., with distinction, 1978); Duke University (J.D., with distinction, 1981). Phi Beta Kappa. Member, Duke Law Journal, 1980-1981. Trial Attorney, Antitrust Division, Energy Section, U.S. Department of Justice, 1981-1984. Special Assistant U.S. Attorney, Superior Court of the District of Columbia, 1984. *Member:* The District of Columbia Bar. ***PRACTICE AREAS:*** Antitrust; Business Combinations; Regulated Industries; Telecommunications Competition; Utility Acquisitions. ***Email:*** tabelles@swidlaw.com

EDWARD BERLIN, born Bronx, New York, March 28, 1939; admitted to bar, 1961, New York; 1964, District of Columbia; 1966, U.S. Supreme Court. *Education:* City College of the City University of New York (B.B.A., 1958); Columbia University (LL.B., 1961); Georgetown University (LL.M., 1964). Harlan Fiske Stone Scholar, Columbia University. Visiting Professor, University

(This Listing Continued)

SWIDLER BERLIN SHEREFF FRIEDMAN, LLP,
Washington—Continued

of Denver School of Law, 1971, 1972 and 1974. Lecturer: Columbus School of Law, Catholic University, 1972; University of Wisconsin, 1974-1975. Commissioner and Deputy Chairman, New York State Public Service Commission, 1975-1977. Attorney, Civil Division, Appellate Section, U.S. Department of Justice, 1961-1966. Assistant General Counsel, Federal Power Commission, 1966-1969. *Member:* The District of Columbia Bar; New York State and American Bar Associations. ***PRACTICE AREAS:*** Regulatory Law; Utility Law. ***Email:*** eberlin@swidlaw.com

RUSSELL M. BLAU, born New York, N.Y., March 27, 1957; admitted to bar, 1982, District of Columbia; 1983, Maryland. *Education:* Harvard College (A.B., cum laude, 1978); Harvard Law School (J.D., magna cum laude, 1982). *Member:* The District of Columbia Bar; Federal Communications Bar Association. ***PRACTICE AREAS:*** Telecommunications Competition; Telecommunications Regulation; Communications Finance. ***Email:*** rmblau@swidlaw.com

ERIC J. BRANFMAN, born New York, N.Y., September 18, 1947; admitted to bar, 1973, District of Columbia; 1976, U.S. District Court for the District of Columbia; 1977, U.S. Court of Appeals, Eighth Circuit; 1984, U.S. Court of Appeals for the District of Columbia Circuit. *Education:* Columbia University (B.A., magna cum laude, 1969); Yale University (J.D., 1972). Phi Beta Kappa. Member, Board of Editors, Yale Law Journal, 1971-1972. Author: "Antitrust Consent Decrees - A Review and Evaluation of the First Seven Years Under The Antitrust Procedures and Penalties Act," 27 Antitrust Bulletin 303, 1982; "Measuring The Invisible Wall: Land Use Controls and the Residential Patterns of the Poor," 82 Yale Law Journal 483, 1973. Attorney-Advisor, Commissioner Elizabeth Hanford Dole, Federal Trade Commission, 1974-1975. *Member:* The District of Columbia Bar; American Bar Association (Member, Sections on: Litigation; Antitrust Law). ***PRACTICE AREAS:*** Telecommunications Competition; Telecommunications Regulation; Telecommunications Law; Telecommunications Contracts; Complex Litigation. ***Email:*** ejbranfman@swidlaw.com

DAVID J. BUTLER, born Pittsburgh, Pennsylvania, April 18, 1950; admitted to bar, 1975, District of Columbia; 1981, New York. *Education:* Yeshiva University (B.A., 1972); Georgetown University (J.D., 1975). Editor, Law & Policy in International Business, 1974-1975. Law Clerk to Hon. Abraham L. Marovitz, U.S. District Court, Northern District of Illinois, 1975-1977. *Member:* The District of Columbia Bar; American Bar Association. ***PRACTICE AREAS:*** Commercial Litigation; Mortgage Banking; Franchising; Employment Law. ***Email:*** djbutler@swidlaw.com

KEITH N. COLE, born Washington, D.C., September 23, 1958; admitted to bar, 1988, Washington; 1998, District of Columbia. *Education:* Duke University (B.S.E., magna cum laude, 1980); University of Virginia (J.D., 1987). Author: "The Small Business Regulatory Enforcement Fairness Act and the Regulatory Flexibility Act," 11 Tulane Environmental Law Journal, 281, 1998. Adjunct Professor, District of Columbia School of Law, 1992. Minority Counsel House, Energy and Commerce Committee, 1989-1995. Regulatory Affairs Counsel, U.S. Senate Small Business Committee, 1995-1997. *Member:* District of Columbia Bar. ***PRACTICE AREAS:*** Governmental Law; Legislative Practice; Environmental Law. ***Email:*** kncole@swidlaw.com

PAUL T. DENIS, born Rantoul, Illinois, August 18, 1958; admitted to bar, 1985, New York; 1993, District of Columbia. *Education:* Villanova University (B.A., summa cum laude, 1980); University of Michigan (M.A., 1983; J.D., cum laude, 1984). Author: *Current Law and Practice in Cross-Border Criminal Investigations*, in Competition Law for the 21st Century (J. Musgrove ed. 1998) (with Joel T. Kissack); *Antitrust Issues Will Arise in Electric Banking*, 15 no. 6 Bank Policy Report 4 (1996); *Antitrust Aspects of International Business Operations*, in The Law of Transnational Business Transactions (Nanda ed. 1993) (with Theodore L. Banks and Andrew I. Gavil); *Advances of the 1992 Horizontal Merger Guidelines in the Analysis of Competitive Effects*, 38 Antitrust Bull. 479 (1993); *Analysis of Uncommitted Entry Under the New Horizontal Merger Guidelines*, 17 Antitrust Litigator 6 (1992); *Practical Approaches:* An Insider's Look at the New Horizontal Merger Guidelines, 6 Antitrust 6 (1992); *Market Power in Antitrust Merger Analysis:* Refining the Collusion Hypothesis, 60 Antitrust L.J. 829 (1992); *European Community Merger Enforcement Under the New Merger Regulation:* A U.S. Enforcer's Perspective, in the Acquisitions Yearbook, 1992 (E. Shea ed.); *Focusing on the Characterization of Per Se Unlawful Horizontal Restraints*, 36 Antitrust Bull. 641 (1991); *Regulatory, Legislative and Administrative Changes Relating to Hart-Scott-Rodino Premerger Notification*, 56 Antitrust L.J. 817 (1987) (with Bruce J. Prager); *Importing Foreign Competition into American Antitrust—Is this the New "New Learning?"*, in Antitrust and Trade Policies in International Trade: Annual Proceedings of the Fordham Corporate Law Institute (B. Hawk ed. 1985) (with Stephen M. Axinn and Peter E. Greene). *Member:* District of Columbia Bar; American Bar Association (Member, Section of Antitrust Law; Chair, International Antitrust Committee, 1996-1997; Editorial Vice-Chair, Annual Review of Antitrust Law Developments, 1995-1996; Member, Editorial Board, Annual Review of Antitrust Developments, 1992-1993, 1993-1994 and 1994-1995;

(This Listing Continued)

Member, Editorial Board, Premerger Notification Practice Manual, 2d ed., 1988-1989). ***PRACTICE AREAS:*** Antitrust and Trade Regulation. ***Email:*** ptdenis@swidlaw.com

BARRY B. DIRENFELD, born Cleveland, Ohio, February 23, 1949; admitted to bar, 1976, Ohio and District of Columbia. *Education:* Kenyon College (B.A., 1971); Catholic University (J.D., 1975). Legislative Assistant, U.S. Senator Richard Stone, 1975-1976. Issues Director, Chief Speechwriter, Press Secretary, Metzenbaum for Senate Campaign, 1976. Chief Legislative Counsel, U.S. Senator Howard M. Metzenbaum, 1977-1978. Resident Fellow, Harvard University, John F. Kennedy Institute of Politics, 1978. Chief Counsel and Staff Director, Senate Subcommittee on Citizens & Shareholders Rights and Remedies, 1978. Chief Counsel and Staff Director, Senate Subcommittee on Antitrust, Monopoly and Business Rights, 1979. President and Director, New Energy Corporation of Indiana, 1979-1989. *Member:* Ohio State Bar Association; The District of Columbia Bar. ***PRACTICE AREAS:*** Legislative Lobbying; Governmental Affairs; Environmental Law. ***Email:*** bbdirenfeld@swidlaw.com

HELEN E. DISENHAUS, born Washington, D.C., November 2, 1948; admitted to bar, 1977, District of Columbia. *Education:* Mount Holyoke College (A.B., with honors and great distinction, 1970); Wesleyan University (M.A.T., 1972); Yale University (J.D., 1977). Phi Beta Kappa. Co-Author: "The Dynamically Changing Regulatory Climate for Foreign Investment in United States Telecommunications Companies," *Pacific Telecommunications Council Fourteenth Annual Conference* (1992); "In Search of Revenues: The Modification of Final Judgement's Impact on RBOC Activities Abroad," *Federal Communications Bar Association International Communications Practice Handbook* (1991). *Member:* The District of Columbia Bar; American Bar Association; Federal Communications Bar Association; Women's Bar Association of District of Columbia. ***PRACTICE AREAS:*** Regulatory Law; Telecommunications Law. ***Email:*** hedisenhaus@swidlaw.com

SUSAN E. DUVALL, born Pensacola, Florida, August 14, 1953; admitted to bar, 1978, District of Columbia. *Education:* Bucknell University (B.A., magna cum laude, with honors in Economics, 1975); University of Pennsylvania (J.D., cum laude, 1978). Phi Beta Kappa; Omicron Delta Epsilon. *Member:* The District of Columbia Bar; American Bar Association. ***REPORTED CASES:*** FANNIE MAE; HUD; FREDDIE MAC. ***PRACTICE AREAS:*** Real Estate Finance; Structured Finance; Mortgage-Backed Securities; Housing. ***Email:*** seduvall@swidlaw.com

LAURENCE J. EISENSTEIN, born Baltimore, Maryland, October 24, 1960; admitted to bar, 1985, Maryland; 1986, District of Columbia, U.S. Court of Appeals, 4th Circuit and U.S. District Court, District of Maryland; 1988, U.S. Court of Appeals, District of Columbia Circuit and U.S. District Court for the District of Columbia; 1991, U.S. Supreme Court. *Education:* Harvard University (B.A., magna cum laude, 1982); Harvard Law School (J.D., cum laude, 1985). Executive Editor, Harvard Environmental Law Review. Author: "Managing E-commerce Risks," 2 Mealey's Cyber Tech Litigation Report 25 (May 2000); "Cost Recovery for the Year 2000 Problem," Bank Accounting & Finance Journal (Winter 1998); "Insurance Coverage for the Year 2000," Tick, Tick, Tick (Fall 1997). Co-Author: "Abortion Clinic Protest and the First Amendment," 13 St. Louis U. Pub. L. Rev. 221 (1994) (with S. Semeraro); "Refuge Denied: Problems in the Protection of Vietnamese and Cambodians in Thailand and the Admission of Indochinese Refugees into the United States" (1989); "Forced Back and Forgotten: The Human Rights of Laotian Asylum Seekers in Thailand" (1989). Delegate, Democratic National Convention, 1980. Member: Presidential Transition Team, Civil Rights Division, Department of Justice, 1992; Governor's Commission on Developmental Disabilities, 1996—; Board, Pro Bono Resource Center, 1996—. Chairman of the Board, Maryland Disability Law Center, 1995—. *Member:* The District of Columbia Bar; Maryland State and American Bar Associations. ***PRACTICE AREAS:*** Insurance Coverage; Litigation. ***Email:*** ljeisenstein@swidlaw.com

JOHN R. FERGUSON, born Youngstown, Ohio, May 23, 1934; admitted to bar, 1963, Ohio; 1972, District of Columbia; 1977, U.S. Supreme Court. *Education:* The Ohio State University (B.A., 1957); Case Western Reserve University (J.D., 1963). Phi Delta Phi; Order of the Coif. Member, Editorial Board, Case Western Reserve Law Review, 1962-1963. Author: "The Case for Antitrust Suits Against Selected Industries," Part I, 7:4 Antitrust Law, 8 Econ. Review 25, 1975; Part II, 8:1 Antitrust Law, 8 Econ. Review 35, 1976. Lecturer, Executive Training Program, Louisiana State University, 1972-1987. Assistant to Director, Bureau of Competition, FTC, 1970-1971. Assistant General Counsel, FTC, 1971-1972. *Member:* District of Columbia Bar; Ohio State (Member, Antitrust Law Section) and American (Member, Antitrust Law Section) Bar Associations. ***PRACTICE AREAS:*** Litigation; Antitrust. ***Email:*** jrferguson@swidlaw.com

WARREN ANTHONY FITCH, born Jacksonville, Florida, January 29, 1944; admitted to bar, 1970, District of Columbia; 1971, U.S. Court of Appeals for the District of Columbia Circuit; 1973, U.S. Court of Appeals, 4th Circuit; 1984, Maryland; 1997, U.S. Court of Appeals, Fifth and Seventh Circuits. *Education:* Princeton University (A.B., cum laude, 1966); Harvard University (J.D., 1969). Instructor, Trial Practice, D.C. Bar Continuing Legal Education Program, 1981-1984. *Member:* The District of Columbia Bar (Member, Criminal Law and Individual Rights Section; Co-Chair, Steering Committee, 1975-

(This Listing Continued)

1979; Co-Chair, D.C. Criminal Practice Institute, 1977-1979; D.C. Superior Court Advisory Committee on Family Division Rules, 1977-1980; Chair, Juvenile Rules Subcommittee, 1978-1980; D.C. Superior Court Criminal Justice Act Committee, 1980-1983; D.C. Legal Ethics Committee, 1981-1987; Vice Chair, 1984-1986; Chair, 1986-1987; Member, Model Rules of Professional Conduct Committee, 1983-1989; D.C. New Rules Review Committee, 1991-1994; D.C. Court of Appeals Committee on Unauthorized Practice, 1992-1998). ***PRACTICE AREAS:*** Civil Litigation; Criminal Litigation; Professional Liability; Telecommunications Law. ***Email:*** wafitch@swidlaw.com

BRIAN W. FITZGERALD, born Baltimore, Maryland, November 1, 1954; admitted to bar, 1981, Maryland; 1982, District of Columbia; 1988, Virginia. *Education:* Indiana University (B.S., 1976); Antioch School of Law (J.D., 1981). Member, Antioch Law Journal, 1980-1981. Law Clerk, U.S. Senate Subcommittee on the Constitution, Committee on the Judiciary, 1979-1980. *Member:* The District of Columbia Bar; Maryland State and Virginia Bar Associations. ***PRACTICE AREAS:*** Government Affairs; Intellectual Property; Federal Election Law; Federal Practice. ***Email:*** bwfitzgerald@swidlaw.com

ROGER FRANKEL, born Washington, D.C., April 6, 1946; admitted to bar, 1971, District of Columbia; 1972, Maryland. *Education:* Brandeis University (B.A., 1968); George Washington University (J.D., with honors, 1971). Member, Maryland Merit Selection Panels, recommended appointment of two bankruptcy judges. Listed, "Best Lawyers in America," Naifeh and Smith, Under Bankruptcy Law. *Member:* The District of Columbia Bar. ***PRACTICE AREAS:*** Bankruptcy Law; Financial Restructuring; Creditors Rights; Workouts. ***Email:*** rfrankel@swidlaw.com

HAROLD P. GOLDFIELD, born Hartford, Connecticut, August 5, 1951; admitted to bar, 1977, Virginia; 1978, District of Columbia; 1980, New York. *Education:* Connecticut College (B.A., cum laude, 1973); Occidental College (M.A., 1975); Georgetown University (J.D., 1977). Member, National Advisory on Juvenile Justice and Delinquency Prevention, 1976-1980. Assistant Counsel, White House Staff, 1981-1982. Associate Counsel to the President, 1982-1983. Assistant Secretary of Commerce, 1984-1987. Member, Board of Directors: Overseas Private Investment Corporation, 1984-1987; National Chamber Foundation, 1998—. *Member:* The District of Columbia Bar; Virginia State Bar; New York State Bar Association. ***PRACTICE AREAS:*** International Practice; Trade Regulation Law; Government Affairs. ***Email:*** hpgoldfield@swidlaw.com

JAMES HAMILTON, born Chester, South Carolina, December 4, 1938; admitted to bar, 1963, North Carolina; 1967, District of Columbia; 1978, U.S. Supreme Court. *Education:* Davidson College (A.B., 1960); Yale University (LL.B., 1963); London University, London, England (LL.M., 1966). Phi Delta Phi. Recipient, Ford Foundation Travel and Study Grant, 1974-1975. Publications: *The Power to Probe: A Study of Congressional Investigations,* Random House, 1976 Vintage Books, 1977; "How to Put a Washer on a Faucet," The New York Times, March 13, 1976; "A McCarthy Era Tactic in the Assassination Committee," The New York Times, April 7, 1977; "Golden Fleece Decision Casts New Light on Congressional Informing Function," Legal Times, October 14, 1978; Book Review, Kurland, "Watergate and the Constitution," University of Chicago Law Review, 1978; "Congressmen Have a Right to Fair Trial Like Others," Legal Times, March 10, 1980; "Nixon's Weak Hold Over Haig Tapes," The National Law Journal, February 16, 1981; "Executive Privilege: A New Face-Off," The Los Angeles Times, December 8, 1981; "A Way Out of Executive-Privilege Dilemma," The Los Angeles Times, February 3, 1983; "E(lection) P(rotector) A(gency)?" The New York Times, March 29, 1983; "A Legislative Proposal For Resolving Executive Privilege Disputes Precipitated by Congressional Subpoenas," Harvard Journal on Legislation, Winter, 1984 (co-author); "Laws May Cover The Briefing Book Case," The Washington Post, June 1, 1984 (co-author); "The Carter Briefing Scandal," The Charlotte Observer, June 4, 1984; "Recalling Senator Sam's Passion," The Charlotte Observer, May 6, 1985; "A Suggested Compromise on Congressional Access to Grand Jury Material," The National Law Journal, January 27, 1986; "Can Congress Make Lawyers Talk?" The Washington Post, March 25, 1986; "Attorney-Client Privilege in Congress," Litigation, Winter 1986; "Legal Tools Limited to Enforce Subpoena," The National Law Journal, September 22, 1986; "Immunity Orders: No Need to Hesitate," The Washington Post, March 16, 1987; "Is There a Jury That Would Convict North?" The Charlotte Observer, September 13, 1987; "A Prosecutor's Shrewd Move," The National Law Journal, April 4, 1988; "In Congress, Rights Become Rites," Legal Times, May 9, 1988; "Iran-Contra Ruling: Immunity's Limits," Legal Times, November 14, 1988 (co-author); "Sleaze Factor Can Be Avoided," The National Law Journal, March 6, 1989; "No Time for Partisans," The New York Times, September 25, 1998 (co-author); "Ending the Clinton Crisis," Slate Magazine, (four articles) October 20 - December 2, 1998; "Attorney-Client Privilege: Does it Pertain to the Government?" The Washington Lawyer, January/February 1999 (contributor); "Swidler & Berlin v. United States: Strategic Choice in Supreme Court Litigation," Federal Discovery News, March 1999 (co-author); The Constitution and Its Amendments," MacMillan Reference USA, 1999 (contributor). Assistant Chief Counsel, Senate Select Committee on Presidential Campaign Activities (Watergate Committee), 1973-1974. Member: Judicial Conference for the District of Columbia Circuit, 1978, 1980; General Accounting Office Investigative Task

(This Listing Continued)

Force, 1985. Chief Counsel, Special Joint Committee on Referendum Review, Congress of Micronesia, 1978. Special Counsel, Human Resources Subcommittee, Post Office and Civil Service Committee, (for investigation of 1980 Reagan campaign), House of Representatives, 1983-1984. Deputy Chief Counsel, Alaska Senate Impeachment Inquiry, 1985. Clinton-Gore Transition Counsel for Nominations and Confirmations, 1992-1993. Member, Board of Directors, Council for Court Excellence, 1987-1992. Member, Panel of Arbitrators, American Arbitration Association. Member, President's Foreign Intelligence Advisory Board, 1996-1998. *Member:* The District of Columbia Bar (Member, Legal Ethics Committee, 1983-1989; Vice Chairman, 1987-1988; Chairman, 1988-1989; Chairman, Special Committee to Educate District of Columbia Bar on New Ethics Rules, 1990-1991); American Bar Association; American Bar Foundation. [1st Lt., U.S. Army, 1963-1965, Army Commendation Medal]. ***PRACTICE AREAS:*** Civil Litigation; White Collar Criminal Defense; Congressional Investigations; Government Investigations; Government Affairs. ***Email:*** jhamilton@swidlaw.com

GERALD S. HARTMAN, born New York, N.Y., November 26, 1944; admitted to bar, 1973, District of Columbia and U.S. District Court for the District of Columbia. *Education:* Columbia College (A.B., 1966); Columbia Graduate School of Business (M.B.A., 1968); George Washington University (J.D., with honors, 1972). Law Clerk to Judge James P. Coleman, U.S. Court of Appeals for the 5th Circuit, 1972-1973. Senior Trial Attorney, U.S. Department of Justice, Employment Section, Civil Rights Division, 1977-1980. Recipient, Special Commendation Award from the Attorney General. Adjunct Professor, George Washington University Law School, Equal Employment Law and Equal Employment Litigation, 1975-1983. Professor, Wake Forest University Law School, Equal Employment Law, Labor Law and Administrative Law, 1984-1986. Co-Author: *The Model Employer*, published by George Washington University Law School. *Member:* The District of Columbia Bar; North Carolina Bar Association. ***PRACTICE AREAS:*** Employment Law; Employment Litigation. ***Email:*** gshartman@swidlaw.com

JAMES J. HOECKER, born Rhinelander, Wisconsin; admitted to bar, 1978, Wisconsin; 1988, District of Columbia. *Education:* Northland College (B.A., cum laude, 1967); University of Kentucky (M.A., 1970; Ph.D., 1975); University of Wisconsin (J.D., 1978). Phi Delta Phi. Legal Writing Instructor, University of Wisconsin. Author: "The NEPA Mandate and Federal Regulation of the Natural Gas Industry," 13 Energy L. Il. 265, 1992; "FERC Changes the Rules of the Game," Petroleum Economist, July 1992; "New State Restrictions on Gas and Oil Production: A Domestic OPEC?" Natural Resources and Environment Magazine (ABA), Summer 1992; "Used and Useful: Autopsy of a Ratemaking Policy," 8 Energy L. Jl. 303, 1987; "Section INS 3.39, Wisconsin Administrative Code: The Origins and Development of a Medicare Supplement Insurance Regulation," The Insurance Law Journal, February 1979. Chairman, 1997-2001 and Commissioner, 1993-1997, Federal Energy Regulatory Commission. *Member:* American Bar Association; Energy Bar Association. ***PRACTICE AREAS:*** Energy; Administrative Law; Corporate. ***Email:*** jjhoecker@swidlaw.com

GREGORY W. HOMER, born Kansas City, Missouri, February 16, 1954; admitted to bar, 1979, District of Columbia, U.S. District Court, District of Columbia and U.S. Court of Appeals, District of Columbia Circuit; 1989, U.S. District Court, District of Maryland; 1991, Pennsylvania and U.S. District Court, Eastern District of Pennsylvania; 1992, U.S. Court of Appeals, Federal and Fourth Circuits; 1994, U.S. Court of Appeals, Ninth Circuit; 1996, U.S. Supreme Court; 1999, U.S. Court of Appeals, Seventh Circuit; 2000, U.S. Court of Appeals, Second and Eighth Circuits. *Education:* Yale University (B.A., cum laude, 1976); University of Virginia (J.D., 1979). Lecturer, Employment Law and Litigation, Wake Forest University School of Law, Continuing Legal Education Program. Co-Author: *The Model Employer*, The George Washington Law School, 1996. *Member:* The District of Columbia Bar; American Bar Association (Member, Labor and Employment Law Section). ***PRACTICE AREAS:*** Labor and Employment; Litigation. ***Email:*** gwhomer@swidlaw.com

ROBERT D. JACOBS, born Boston, Massachusetts, September 9, 1946; admitted to bar, 1971, District of Columbia. *Education:* University of Massachusetts (B.A., 1968); American University (J.D., with honors, 1971). Member, 1969-1971 and Editor, 1970-1971, American University Law Review. Trial Attorney, Federal Trade Commission, 1971-1976. *Member:* The District of Columbia Bar; American Bar Association. ***PRACTICE AREAS:*** Antitrust and Trade Regulation. ***Email:*** rdjacobs@swidlaw.com

KENNETH G. JAFFE, born Plainfield, New Jersey, June 5, 1957; admitted to bar, 1981, District of Columbia; 1990, U.S. Supreme Court. *Education:* State University of New York at Binghamton (B.A., 1978); Harvard University (J.D., cum laude, 1981). *Member:* The District of Columbia Bar. ***PRACTICE AREAS:*** Regulatory Law; Utility Law. ***Email:*** kgjaffe@swidlaw.com

J. PHILLIP JORDAN, born Dothan, Alabama, December 19, 1948; admitted to bar, 1974, Georgia; 1979, District of Columbia; 1984, Maryland. *Education:* Princeton University (A.B., magna cum laude, 1971); University of Virginia (J.D., 1974). Phi Beta Kappa; Order of the Coif. Editor, 1972-1973 and Editor-in-Chief, 1973-1974, University of Virginia Law Review. Law Clerk to: Judge J. Braxton Craven, Jr., U.S. Court of Appeals for the Fourth Circuit,

(This Listing Continued)

SWIDLER BERLIN SHEREFF FRIEDMAN, LLP, Washington—Continued

1974-1975; Justice Lewis F. Powell, Jr., U.S. Supreme Court, 1975-1976. Special Assistant to the Attorney General of the United States, 1977-1979. *Member:* The District of Columbia Bar; State Bar of Georgia; Maryland State Bar Association; Energy Bar Association. ***LANGUAGES:*** German. ***PRACTICE AREAS:*** Regulatory Law; Utility Law. ***Email:*** jpjordan@swidlaw.com

JEFFREY M. KARP, born Huntington, New York, August 22, 1952; admitted to bar, 1977, District of Columbia and U.S. Court of Appeals for the District of Columbia Circuit; 1978, U.S. District Court for the District of Columbia. *Education:* Brandeis University (B.A., magna cum laude with honors in politics, 1974); Antioch School of Law (J.D., 1977). Attorney: Environment and Natural Resources Division, United States Department of Justice, 1987-1990; Bureau of Consumer Protection, Federal Trade Commission, 1977-1987. *Member:* The District of Columbia Bar (Member: Computer and Telecommunications Law and Environment, Energy and Natural Resources Section). ***PRACTICE AREAS:*** Telecommunications; Right of Way Easements; Environmental; Hazardous Waste. ***Email:*** jmkarp@swidlaw.com

JEAN L. KIDDOO, born White Plains, New York, April 30, 1953; admitted to bar, 1980, District of Columbia; 1981, U.S. District Court for the District of Columbia and U.S. Court of Appeals for the District of Columbia Circuit; 1984, U.S. Supreme Court; 1995, U.S. Court of Appeals, Second Circuit; 1997, U.S. Court of Appeals, Fifth Circuit. *Education:* Colgate University (B.A., cum laude, 1975); Catholic University of America (J.D., magna cum laude, 1980). Member, Catholic University Law Review, 1979-1980. *Member:* The District of Columbia Bar; Federal Communications Bar Association (President, 1999-2000). ***PRACTICE AREAS:*** Telecommunications Law; Communications Common Carrier; FCC Regulation; Cable Communications; Wireless Communications. ***Email:*** jlkiddoo@swidlaw.com

KY E. KIRBY, born Pasadena, California, January 10, 1956; admitted to bar, 1985, Virginia; 1986, District of Columbia; U.S. Supreme Court; U.S. District Court, District of Columbia; U.S. District Court, Eastern District of Virginia; U.S. District Court, District of Maryland; U.S. District Court, District of Arizona; U.S. Court of Appeals, Fourth, Sixth, Eighth, Eleventh and District of Columbia Circuits. *Education:* George Mason University (B.S., summa cum laude, 1982); George Mason University School of Law (J.D., with honors, 1985). Production Editor, George Mason University Law Review, 1984-1985. ***PRACTICE AREAS:*** Civil Litigation; Telecommunications; False Advertising; Technology Litigation; Internet Law. ***Email:*** kekirby@swidlaw.com

DAVID F. KLEIN, born Brooklyn, New York, February 10, 1963; admitted to bar, 1989, New York; 1990, District of Columbia; U.S. Court of Appeals, District of Columbia, Fifth, Eleventh and Federal Circuits; U.S. District Court, District of Columbia. *Education:* Boston University (B.A., summa cum laude, 1985) Trustee Scholar and Phi Beta Kappa; Yale University (J.D., 1988). Executive Editor, Yale Journal on Regulation. Judicial Clerk, Hon. Julia Cooper Mack, District of Columbia Court of Appeals, 1988-1989. Assistant Counsel, National Treasury Employees Union, 1989-1996. Co-Chair, Committee of Federal Service Labor and Employment Law, American Bar Association, 1993-1996. ***LANGUAGES:*** Spanish, French and German. ***PRACTICE AREAS:*** Insurance Coverage Litigation. ***Email:*** dfklein@swidlaw.com

JOHN J. KLUSARITZ, born Allentown, Pennsylvania, December 18, 1957; admitted to bar, 1981, Massachusetts and District of Columbia. *Education:* Lehigh University (B.S., with highest honors, 1978); Harvard University Law School (J.D., with honors, 1981). Phi Beta Kappa; Beta Alpha Psi. Certified Public Accountant, Pennsylvania, 1978. Adjunct Professor, Georgetown Law School, Graduate School of Taxation, 1985-1996. *Member:* The District of Columbia Bar; American Bar Association; American Institute of Certified Public Accountants. ***PRACTICE AREAS:*** Corporate Law; Finance; Mergers and Acquisitions. ***Email:*** jjklusaritz@swidlaw.com

CHARLES H. KNAUSS, born Ann Arbor, Michigan, September 3, 1955; admitted to bar, 1982, District of Columbia. *Education:* Brown University (A.B., 1977); University of Michigan (J.D., 1981). Member, University of Michigan Journal of Law Reform, 1979-1980. Counsel, House Energy and Commerce Committee, United States Congress, 1987-1990. Associate, Hunton & Williams, 1982-1987. Co-Author: *The Clean Air Act Operating Permit Program:* A Handbook for Counsel, Environmental Managers, and Plant Managers, ABA 1993. Author, chapter entitled, "Agencies and Administrative Law," *Environmental Law in Michigan*, published by the University of Michigan Law School, 1983. *Member:* The District of Columbia Bar; American Bar Association (Member, Natural Resources, Energy and Environmental Law Section); Air & Waste Management Association. ***PRACTICE AREAS:*** Regulatory Law; Environmental Law; Legislative Counsel. ***Email:*** chknauss@swidlaw.com

MICHAEL N. LEVY, born 1963; admitted to bar, 1990, New York; 1991, District of Columbia. *Education:* Yale University (B.A., summa cum laude, 1985); Harvard Law School (J.D., magna cum laude, 1988). Phi Beta Kappa. Supreme Court Editor, Harvard Law Review. Author: "Civil RICO Is a Misnomer: The Need for Criminal Procedural Protections in Actions Under 18 U.S.C., §, 1964," Harvard Law Review, 1987. Co-Author, with Judge Louis F. Oberdofer, "On Clerkship Selection: A Reply to the Bad Apple," Yale Law Journal, 1992. Law Clerk to: Justice Lewis F. Powell, Jr, 1989-1990; Judge Louis F. Oberdorfer, 1988-1989. Assistant U.S. Attorney, District of Columbia, 1995-1999. Acting Deputy Assistant Secretary for Fair Housing and Equal Opportunity, U.S., Department of Housing and Urban Development, 1994-1995. White House Fellow, 1993-1994. ***PRACTICE AREAS:*** White Collar Criminal Defense; Corporate Compliance; Internal Investigations; Congressional Investigations; Governmental Investigations; Trial and Appellate Litigation. ***Email:*** mnlevy@swidlaw.com

MICHAEL J. LICHTENSTEIN, born Potchefstroom, South Africa, December 30, 1954; admitted to bar, 1988, Maryland; 1989, District of Columbia; U.S. District Court, District of Maryland; U.S. District Court, District of Columbia; U.S. District Court, District of Colorado and U.S. Court of Appeals, Fourth and Sixth Circuits. *Education:* Brandeis University (B.A., 1979); University of Pennsylvania (M.A., 1980; Ph.D., 1982); American University (J.D., 1988). Member, American University Law Review, 1986-1988. Member, Walter Chandler Inns of Court. Assistant Professor, Department of Criminal Justice, Temple University, 1983-1985. Adjunct and Assistant Professor, School of Justice, American University, 1985-1986. Author: "Who Is An Insider For Voting Purposes In A Single Asset Chapter 11," Journal of Bankruptcy Law and Practice, March/April 2001; "A Landlord's Options if a Tenant Files Chapter 11," *Real Estate Law Journal*, Winter 1992. *Member:* The District of Columbia Bar. ***PRACTICE AREAS:*** Commercial Litigation; Bankruptcy; Creditors Rights. ***Email:*** mjlichtenstein@swidlaw.com

ANDREW D. LIPMAN, born New Britain, Connecticut, October 20, 1951; admitted to bar, 1977, California; 1978, District of Columbia. *Education:* University of Rochester (B.A., summa cum laude, 1974); Stanford University (J.D., 1977). Phi Beta Kappa. Senior Articles Editor, Stanford Journal of International Law, 1976-1977. Vice Chairman of Firm, 1996—. Author: "Telecom Deregulation," Telephony Publishing, 1987. Co-Editor: "Commercial Real Estate Tenant's Handbook," John Wiley & Sons, 1987; "High Tech Real Estate," Dow Jones Irwin, 1985; "Teleports and the Intelligent City," Dow Jones Irwin, 1986; "Joint Ventures for Telecommunications Projects," *Construction Joint Ventures*, John Wiley & Sons (1992); "Guide to Monopoly, Competition and Regulation," 1996. Extern Law Clerk to: Justice Raymond Sullivan, Supreme Court of California, 1976-1977; U.S. Department of Transportation Legal Honors Program, 1977-1978. General Counsel: International Teleconferencing Association, 1983—; Satellite Operators and Users Technical Committee, 1986—. Member, Editorial Board, Telecommunications Regulatory Monitor, and Satellite Law Compendium, 1984—; X-Change Magazine, 1996. Senior Vice President, Legal and Regulatory Affairs, MFS Communications, 1988-1996. Member: Board of Directors, International Televent, 1990—; Pike and Fisher Internet Law and Regulation, 2001—. Co-Founder, Former Board of Directors, Alternative Local Telecommunications Association (ALTS). Member, Advisory Board, Stanford Law School Science, Technology and Law Program. *Member:* The District of Columbia Bar; State Bar of California; American Bar Association; Federal Communications Bar Association. ***PRACTICE AREAS:*** Regulatory Law; Telecommunications Law; Internet Law; Transportation Law. ***Email:*** adlipman@swidlaw.com

KENNETH G. LORE, born New York, N.Y., October 1, 1948; admitted to bar, 1973, Maryland; 1975, District of Columbia; 1980, New York. *Education:* American University (B.A., 1970); Washington College of Law (J.D., 1973). Associate Editor and Symposium Editor, American University Law Review, 1970-1973. Contributing Editor on Housing and Real Estate, *Legal Times*, 1978-1986. Author: *Mortgage-Backed Securities: Developments and Trends in the Secondary Mortgage Market,* West Publishing/Clark Boardman Co., Ltd., 1985 (Annual revised edition); *Real Estate Mortgage Investments Conduits—(REMICS),* Callahan/Clark Boardman Co., Ltd., 1988. Attorney-Advisor, Office of General Counsel, U.S. Department of Housing and Urban Development, 1973-1975. Vice Chairman, National Housing Conference, 1985-1989 and 1993-1998. Member: Advisory Board of the Federal National Mortgage Association, 1989-1990; Low and Moderate Income Housing Task Force; National Association of Homebuilders Multifamily Roundtable; Fannie Mae Housing Policy Advisory Committee; Fannie Mae Housing Impact Division Advisory Board; Center for Housing Policy Board. Chairman, Dean's Advisory Board, Washington College of Law at The American University. *Member:* The District of Columbia Bar; Maryland State, New York State and American Bar Associations. ***PRACTICE AREAS:*** Structured Finance; Real Estate; Housing; Securities. ***Email:*** kglore@swidlaw.com

THOMAS R. LOTTERMAN, born Worcester, Massachusetts, January 14, 1956; admitted to bar, 1983, District of Columbia. *Education:* Princeton University (A.B., 1977); University of Michigan (J.D., 1983). Trial Attorney, U.S. Department of Justice, Land and Natural Resources Division, 1987-1990. *Member:* The District of Columbia Bar; American Bar Association. ***PRACTICE AREAS:*** Environmental Law; Administrative Law; Litigation; Communications and Media; Commercial Law. ***Email:*** trlotterman@swidlaw.com

PERI N. MAHALEY, born Rangoon, Burma, December 20, 1955; admitted to bar, 1979, District of Columbia; 1980, U.S. District Court for the District

(This Listing Continued)

of Columbia; 1982, U.S. Court of Appeals, Fifth Circuit. *Education:* Georgetown University (B.S.F.S., summa cum laude, 1976); Georgetown University Law Center (J.D., magna cum laude, 1979). Articles Editor, The Georgetown Law Journal, 1978-1979. *Member:* The District of Columbia Bar. ***PRACTICE AREAS:*** Litigation; Insurance Coverage. ***Email:*** pnmahaley@swidlaw.com

BRUCE MARKOWITZ, born Buffalo, New York, March 22, 1954; admitted to bar, 1983, District of Columbia; 1984, Maryland. *Education:* University of Rochester (B.A., with high honors, 1976); State University of New York at Albany (M.P.A., with highest honors, 1977); Washington College of Law, American University (J.D., 1982). Editor, American University Law Review, 1981-1982. Presidential Fellow, Division of Research, Federal Deposit Insurance Corporation, Washington, D.C., 1978-1980. Co-Author: "D.C.'s New Settlement Law Drips with Consumer Protection," D.C. Bar Journal, Volume 1, Number 4, March, 1987. *Member:* The District of Columbia Bar (Member, Real Estate and Banking Section); Maryland State Bar Association (Member, Real Estate and Banking Section). ***PRACTICE AREAS:*** Corporate Transactions; Telecommunications; Banking Law; Real Estate; Bankruptcy; Restructuring. ***Email:*** bmarkowitz@swidlaw.com

THURGOOD MARSHALL, JR., born New York, N.Y.; admitted to bar, 1982, District of Columbia; U.S. District Court for the District of Columbia; U.S. Court of Appeals for the District of Columbia Circuit; U.S. Court of Appeals, Second Circuit; U.S. Supreme Court. *Education:* University of Virginia (B.A., 1978); University of Virginia School of Law (J.D., 1981). Law Clerk to Hon. Barrington D. Parker, U.S. District Court for the District of Columbia, 1981-1983. Counsel to Senator Al Gore, U.S. Senate Committee on Governmental Affairs, 1985-1987. Counsel to Senator Ernest F. Hollings and Senator Al Gore, U.S. Senate Committee on Commerce, Science and Transportation, 1987. Deputy Campaign Manager, Gore For President, 1987-1988. Counsel to Senator Edward M. Kennedy, U.S. Senate Committee on the Judiciary, 1988-1992. Director, Legislative Affairs, Office of the Vice President, 1993-1997. Assistant to the President and Cabinet Secretary, The White House, 1997-2001. Member: U.S. Supreme Court Historical Society, 1994—; Board of Directors, National Fish & Wildlife Foundation, 2001—. Vice Chair, U.S. Olympic Committee Ethics Oversight Committee, 2001—. *Member:* American Bar Association (Chair, Standing Committee Ethics Oversight Committee, 2001—). ***PRACTICE AREAS:*** Government Affairs. ***Email:*** tmarshall@swidlaw.com

SEAN P. McGUINNESS, born November 6, 1954; admitted to bar, 1981, District of Columbia; 1991, Maryland. *Education:* Tufts College (B.S., magna cum laude, 1976); Georgetown University (J.D., 1981). Executive Editor, Georgetown Law Journal, 1980-1981. *Member:* The District of Columbia Bar; Maryland State Bar Association. ***PRACTICE AREAS:*** Corporate Law; Securities; Project Finance. ***Email:*** spmcguinness@swidlaw.com

GLENN S. MILLER, born Philadelphia, Pennsylvania, April 27, 1967; admitted to bar, 1992, West Virginia; 1995, District of Columbia. *Education:* Louisiana State University (B.S., summa cum laude, 1988); Harvard Law School (J.D., cum laude, 1992). Book Review Editor, Harvard International Law Journal. Contributing Author, Export Handbook, Accounting Finance and Tax Guide. ***PRACTICE AREAS:*** Taxation. ***Email:*** gsmiller@swidlaw.com

LEONARD A. MILLER, born New York, N.Y., July 30, 1942; admitted to bar, 1967, Pennsylvania (Inactive); 1968, Massachusetts; 1970, District of Columbia; 1971, Washington (Inactive). *Education:* Brandeis University (B.A., cum laude, 1964); Harvard University (J.D., 1967). Co-Author: "Product Risk Reduction in the Chemical Industry," Executive Enterprises Publications Co., Inc., 1985; "NPDES Permit Handbook," (2nd ed.), Government Institutes, Inc., 1992; "Clean Water Handbook," (2nd ed.) Government Institutes, Inc., 1996. Branch Chief, National Air Pollution Control Administration, 1968-1970. Air Pollution Control Director, 1970-1972 and Enforcement Division Director, 1972-1976, U.S. Environmental Protection Agency-Region X (Seattle). Permit Division Director, 1976-1979 and Associate Deputy Assistant Administrator, 1979-1980, U.S. Environmental Protection Agency. ***PRACTICE AREAS:*** Environmental Law; Pesticide Regulation; Water Pollution; Insurance Coverage. ***Email:*** lamiller@swidlaw.com

JEROME C. MUYS, JR., born East Stroudsburg, Pennsylvania, August 20, 1954; admitted to bar, 1979, District of Columbia; 1981, U.S. District Court for the District of Columbia; 1985, U.S. District Court, District of Maryland; 1988, U.S. Supreme Court. *Education:* University of North Carolina at Chapel Hill (B.A., 1976); George Washington University (J.D., 1979; LL.M., 1985). *Member:* The District of Columbia Bar; American Bar Association. ***PRACTICE AREAS:*** Environmental Compliance; Groundwater Contamination; Hazardous Waste; Property Remediation; Superfund. ***Email:*** jcmuys@swidlaw.com

TIMOTHY A. NGAU, born Framingham, Massachusetts, March 25, 1953; admitted to bar, 1980, District of Columbia; 1982, New York; U.S. Supreme Court; U.S. District Court of the District of Columbia and U.S. Court of Appeals for the Ninth, Federal and District of Columbia Circuits. *Education:* Yale University (B.A., 1975); University of Chicago (M.A., 1977); Boston University (J.D., 1980). *Member:* Bar Association of the District of Columbia; American Bar Association (Member, Sections on: Antitrust Law; Litigation). ***PRACTICE AREAS:*** Commercial Litigation; Antitrust; Electric Utility; Regulated Industries. ***Email:*** tangau@swidlaw.com

JOSÉ A. PALMA, born Lima, Perú, February 7, 1968; admitted to bar, 1992, Mexico; 1994, New York; 2001, District of Columbia. *Education:* Universidad Iberoamericana in Mexico (J.D., 1990); Georgetown University (LL.M., 1992). *Member:* The District of Columbia Bar. ***LANGUAGES:*** Spanish. ***PRACTICE AREAS:*** Telecommunications; Transactional; International; Government Affairs. ***Email:*** japalma@swidlaw.com

STEPHEN C. PALMER, born Washington, D.C., July 13, 1949; admitted to bar, 1978, New York; 1989, District of Columbia. *Education:* Johns Hopkins University (B.A., 1971); School of Oriental and African Studies, University of London, London, England; Syracuse University College of Law (J.D., cum laude, 1977). Member, Board of Editors, Syracuse University Law Review, 1976-1977. Trial Attorney, Bureau of Competition, Federal Trade Commission, 1977-1987. *Member:* The District of Columbia Bar; New York State and American (Member, Sections on: Antitrust Law; Natural Resources, Energy and Environmental Law) Bar Associations. ***PRACTICE AREAS:*** Energy Law; Antitrust Law. ***Email:*** scpalmer@swidlaw.com

EDWARD A. PENNINGTON, born Annapolis, Maryland, May 14, 1956; admitted to bar, 1984, Virginia, U.S. Court of Appeals, Fourth Circuit and U.S. District Court, Eastern District of Virginia; 1988, U.S. Court of Appeals for the Federal Circuit; 1989, District of Columbia, U.S. District Court for the District of Columbia and U.S. Supreme Court; registered to practice before U.S. Patent and Trademark Office. *Education:* West Virginia University (B.S., 1978; M.A., 1980); George Mason University (J.D., 1983). Jessup International Moot Court Competition. *Member:* The District of Columbia Bar; Virginia State Bar (Board Member, Intellectual Property Section, 1997—); American Bar Association; American Intellectual Property Law Association. ***PRACTICE AREAS:*** Patent Litigation; Patent Prosecution; Trademark Litigation; Trademark Prosecution. ***Email:*** eapennington@swidlaw.com

MARK J. PLUMER, born Massapequa, New York, April 20, 1961; admitted to bar, 1987, Pennsylvania; 1987, District of Columbia. *Education:* Franklin & Marshall College (B.A., cum laude, 1983); George Washington University (J.D., cum laude, 1986). Phi Beta Kappa. Member, George Washington University Law Review. Author: Note, "Judicial Estoppel: The Refurbishing of a Judicial Shield," 55 Geo. Wash. L. Rev. 409 (1987). *Member:* The District of Columbia Bar. ***PRACTICE AREAS:*** Insurance Coverage. ***Email:*** mjplumer@swidlaw.com

RICHARD A. POPKIN, born Englewood, New Jersey, November 15, 1949; admitted to bar, 1975, Florida; 1976, District of Columbia and U.S. Court of Appeals for the District of Columbia Circuit. *Education:* George Washington University (B.A., with distinction, 1971; M.A., 1972); University of Miami (J.D., cum laude, 1975); Harvard University (LL.M., 1976). Phi Delta Phi. Member, Editorial Board, University of Miami Law Review, 1973-1975. Confidential Assistant to the Under Secretary of Commerce for International Trade, 1984-1985. Deputy for Policy to the Assistant Secretary of Commerce for Trade Administration, 1985-1987. *Member:* The District of Columbia Bar; The Florida Bar. ***LANGUAGES:*** Spanish. ***PRACTICE AREAS:*** International Law; Trade Regulation Law; Export Regulation; Foreign Trade Sanctions; World Trade Organization; Latin American Trade. ***Email:*** rapopkin@swidlaw.com

ANDREW M. RAY, born Buffalo, New York, June 13, 1966; admitted to bar, 1992, U.S. Court of Appeals, Fourth Circuit; 1993, District of Columbia. *Education:* Georgetown University (A.B., 1988); Duke University (M.A., Economics, 1991; J.D., with honors, 1991). Senior Editor, Law & Contemp. Problems, 1990-1991. Law Clerk, Hon. James M. Sprouse, U.S. Court of Appeals, Fourth Circuit, 1991-1992. Adjunct Professor, Insurance Theory and Regulation, George Mason University, 1994. *Member:* American Bar Association (Member, Business Law Section). ***PRACTICE AREAS:*** Corporate Law; Securities Law; Venture Capital; Information Technology; Telecommunications; Real Estate. ***Email:*** amray@swidlaw.com

RICHARD M. RINDLER, born Lowell, Massachusetts, September 23, 1944; admitted to bar, 1969, District of Columbia; 1974, U.S. Supreme Court, U.S. Court of Appeals for the District of Columbia, Fifth and Seventh Circuits. *Education:* McGill University, Montreal, Quebec (B.A., 1966); Georgetown University (J.D., 1969). Member, Georgetown University Law Review, 1967-1968. Assistant to General Counsel, Federal Trade Commission, 1972-1973. *Member:* The District of Columbia Bar. ***PRACTICE AREAS:*** Telecommunications; Regulated Industries; Antitrust. ***Email:*** rmrindler@swidlaw.com

KENNETH I. SCHANER, born Chicago, Illinois, April 9, 1941; admitted to bar, 1966, Illinois; 1970, District of Columbia. *Education:* University of Illinois (B.S., 1963; J.D., 1966). Phi Delta Phi. Editor, University of Illinois Law Review, 1965-1966. Attorney, Chief Counsel's Office, Internal Revenue Service, Legislation and Regulations Division, 1966-1970. *Member:* The District of Columbia Bar; American Bar Association (Member, Taxation Section). ***PRACTICE AREAS:*** Corporate Law; Tax Exempt Organizations; Taxation Law. ***Email:*** kischaner@swidlaw.com

(This Listing Continued)

SWIDLER BERLIN SHEREFF FRIEDMAN, LLP, Washington—Continued

JEFFREY S. SCHARFF, born Oceanside, California, October 9, 1957; admitted to bar, 1984, New York and Florida; 1990, Massachusetts; 1993, District of Columbia. *Education:* State University of New York at Binghamton (B.A., with honors, 1979); University of North Carolina at Chapel Hill (J.D., 1982). ***PRACTICE AREAS:*** Real Estate; Structured Finance. ***Email:*** jsscharff@swidlaw.com

GARY D. SLAIMAN, born Cardiff, Wales, September 2, 1956; admitted to bar, 1981, District of Columbia and U.S. Court of Appeals, District of Columbia Circuit. *Education:* University of Virginia (B.A., with high distinction, 1978; J.D., 1981). Notes Editor, Virginia Journal Natural Resources Law. Counsel, Senate Judiciary Subcommittee on Antitrust, Monopolies and Business Rights, 1989-1992. Chief Counsel and Staff Director, Senate Labor and Human Resources Subcommittee on Labor, 1992-1993. Council Member, American Bar Association General Practice Section, 1985-1989, Chairman, Committee on Federal Legislation, 1984-1989, 1992-1993. Chairman, Legislative Action Committee, American Bar Association Young Lawyers Division, 1983-1985. *Member:* The District of Columbia Bar; American Bar Association (Member, Sections on: Antitrust; General Practice). ***PRACTICE AREAS:*** Antitrust Law; Governmental Affairs; Communications and Media; Intellectual Property. ***Email:*** gdslaiman@swidlaw.com

MICHAEL L. SPAFFORD, born Syracuse, New York, 1958; admitted to bar, 1984, New York; 1992, District of Columbia; U.S. District Court, Southern District of New York; U.S. District Court, District of Columbia; U.S. Court of Appeals, District of Columbia and Federal Circuits; U.S. Court of Federal Claims. *Education:* State University of New York at Binghamton (B.A., 1980); Duke University (J.D., 1983). Author: "ADR and the Law Firm of the Future," ABA Dispute Resolution Magazine, 1996 Vol. 3, No. 2. *Member:* American Bar Association (Member, Center of Professional Responsibility). ***PRACTICE AREAS:*** Professional Liability; SEC Enforcement; Commercial Litigation; Government Investigations; White Collar Fraud. ***Email:*** mlspafford@swidlaw.com

NANCY KILLIEN SPOONER, born Guatemala City, Guatemala, September 11, 1966; admitted to bar, 1993, California and Virginia; 1996, District of Columbia. *Education:* College of William and Mary (B.A., 1988; J.D., 1992). Phi Alpha Theta; Pi Sigma Alpha. Member, ABA Administrative Law Review, 1991-1992. Clerk to the Honorable Glen M. Williams, Senior Judge for the Western District of Virginia, 1992-1993. *Member:* Federal Communications Bar Association. ***LANGUAGES:*** Spanish. ***PRACTICE AREAS:*** Telecommunications Law. ***Email:*** nkspooner@swidlaw.com

ROBERT N. STEINWURTZEL, born Newark, New Jersey, May 16, 1953; admitted to bar, 1978, District of Columbia. *Education:* Franklin & Marshall College (B.A., magna cum laude, 1975); George Washington University (J.D., 1978). Phi Beta Kappa; Pi Gamma Mu. Special Assistant, Assistant Secretary, Department of the Interior, 1975-1977. Attorney, Office of Enforcement, U.S. Environmental Protection Agency, 1978-1980. Board of Directors, *Hazardous Substances* 1985-1988. Participant, President's Private Sector Survey on Cost Control (Dept. of the Interior) 1982. *Member:* The District of Columbia Bar. ***PRACTICE AREAS:*** Environmental Law; Litigation; OSHA Law. ***Email:*** rnsteinwurtzel@swidlaw.com

MARY A. WALLACE, admitted to bar, 1989, District of Columbia. *Education:* Fairfield University (B.A., cum laude, 1986); George Washington University (J.D., with honors, 1989). Order of the Coif. Member, George Washington Law Review, 1988-1989. *Member:* The District of Columbia Bar. ***PRACTICE AREAS:*** Mergers, Acquisitions and Divestitures; Corporate Finance. ***Email:*** mawallace@swidlaw.com

CATHERINE WANG, born Buffalo, New York, December 8, 1959; admitted to bar, 1986, Maryland; 1992, District of Columbia. *Education:* State University of New York at Stony Brook (B.A., with honors, Phi Beta Kappa, 1982); Georgetown University Law Center (J.D., 1985). Notes and Comments Editor, The Tax Lawyer, 1984-1985. *Member:* Maryland State and Asian Pacific American Bar Associations; The District of Columbia Bar; Federal Communications Bar Association. ***PRACTICE AREAS:*** Regulatory Law; Telecommunications Law; Technology Law. ***Email:*** cwang@swidlaw.com

PRISCILLA ANNE WHITEHEAD, born New York, N.Y., April 15, 1960; admitted to bar, 1987, New York; 1988, U.S. Court of International Trade; 1989, Puerto Rico and U.S. District Court, District of Puerto Rico; U.S. Court of Appeals, First Circuit; 1991, U.S. Supreme Court; 1994, District of Columbia. *Education:* Georgetown University (B.S.L.A., 1982; J.D., 1986). Law Clerk to: Hon. José A. Fusté, U.S. District Judge, District of Puerto Rico, 1988-1989; Hon. Roberto Schmidt-Monge, U.S. Magistrate-Judge, District of Puerto Rico, 1987-1988. Assistant Counsel/Director, Intergovernmental Affairs, Puerto Rico Federal Affairs Administration, Puerto Rico Government, 1992. Elected to Board of Directors, Federal Bar Association, Puerto Rico Chapter. ***LANGUAGES:*** Spanish. ***PRACTICE AREAS:*** Telecommunication; International. ***Email:*** pawhitehead@swidlaw.com

(This Listing Continued)

MICHAEL B. WIGMORE, born Englewood, New Jersey, June 23, 1962; admitted to bar, 1991, Connecticut; 1993, District of Columbia; 1994, New York; 1998, U.S. Court of Appeals for the District of Columbia Circuit. *Education:* United States Merchant Marine Academy (B.S., with highest honors, 1984); George Washington University National Law Center (J.D., with high honors, Order of the Coif, 1990). *Member:* The District of Columbia Bar. ***PRACTICE AREAS:*** Environmental Law; Government Affairs. ***Email:*** mbwigmore@swidlaw.com

RICHARD H. WYRON, born Portsmouth, Virginia, September 10, 1954; admitted to bar, 1979, Virginia; 1981, District of Columbia; 1987, Maryland. *Education:* University of Virginia (B.A., 1976; J.D., 1979). Law Clerk to the Honorable Albert V. Bryan, Jr., U.S. District Court for the Eastern District of Virginia, 1979-1980. *Member:* The District of Columbia Bar; Maryland and American Bar Associations; American Bankruptcy Institute. ***PRACTICE AREAS:*** Bankruptcy Reorganization; Creditors Rights; Workouts; Commercial Transactions; Insurance Insolvency. ***Email:*** rhwyron@swidlaw.com

SENIOR OF COUNSEL

LESTER S. HYMAN, born Providence, Rhode Island, July 14, 1931; admitted to bar, 1955, Massachusetts; 1956, District of Columbia; 1961, U.S. Supreme Court. *Education:* Brown University (A.B., 1952); Columbia University (LL.B., 1955). Phi Alpha Delta. Lecturer, John F. Kennedy School of Government, Harvard University, 1968-1969. Attorney, U.S. Securities and Exchange Commission, 1955-1969. Assistant to Governor, Massachusetts, 1963-1964. Commissioner of Commerce, Massachusetts, 1964-1965. Chairman, Massachusetts Democratic State Committee, 1967-1968. Advisor, Board of International Legal Studies Program at The Washington College of Law at the American University. ***Email:*** lshyman@swidlaw.com

COUNSEL

SUZAN F. CHARLTON, born Takoma Park, Maryland, September 11, 1966; admitted to bar, 1991, Maryland; 1992, District of Columbia and U.S. District Court, District of Maryland; 1994, U.S. District Court, Northern District of California; 2001, U.S. Supreme Court. *Education:* Vassar College (B.A., cum laude, 1988); Georgetown University (J.D., 1991). Editor, The Georgetown Law Journal, 1991. *Member:* The District of Columbia Bar; American Bar Association. ***Email:*** sfcharlton@swidlaw.com

ROBIN F. COHN, born Brooklyn, New York, December 5, 1959; admitted to bar, 1985, Maryland; 1991, District of Columbia. *Education:* Brandeis University (B.A., 1981); Georgetown University Law Center (J.D., 1985). Attorney, General Counsel's Office, MCI Communications Corporation, 1988-1996. Contributing Author and Editor: *Commercial Damages: A Guide to Remedies in Business Litigation*, Matthew Bender & Company (1989-1996). *Member:* The District of Columbia Bar; Maryland Bar Association. ***PRACTICE AREAS:*** Telecommunications. ***Email:*** rfcohn@swidlaw.com

LYNN MONK GALLAGHER, born Miami, Florida, July 2, 1956; admitted to bar, 1985, Maryland and District of Columbia. *Education:* University of Florida (B.A., with high honors, 1979); Georgetown University (J.D., magna cum laude, 1984). Phi Beta Kappa. Co-Author: *The Clean Water Handbook* (2d ed. 1996); *NPDES Permit Handbook,* (2d ed. 1992). Author: "Clean Water Act," Chapter in *Environmental Law Handbook* (16th ed. 2001). *Member:* The District of Columbia Bar. ***PRACTICE AREAS:*** Water Pollution; Pesticides; Environmental Compliance; Environmental Enforcement. ***Email:*** lmgallagher@swidlaw.com

WILLIAM B. GLEW, JR., born Rochester, Minnesota, December 22, 1956; admitted to bar, 1984, Washington; 1985, U.S. District Court, Western District of Washington and U.S. Court of Appeals, Ninth Circuit; 1986, U.S. District Court, Eastern District of Washington; 1987, District of Columbia. *Education:* Yale University (B.A., 1979); University of Virginia (J.D., 1984). Articles Editor, Journal of Law and Politics, 1983-1984. *Member:* Washington State Bar Association (inactive); The District of Columbia Bar. ***PRACTICE AREAS:*** Federal Legislative Practice; Electric Utility Regulation. ***Email:*** wbglew@swidlaw.com

GEORGE I. GORDON, born New York, N.Y., December 12, 1930; admitted to bar, 1954, New York; 1995, District of Columbia. *Education:* Columbia College (A.B., 1952); Columbia Law School (J.D., 1954). Harlan Fiske Stone Scholar. Assistant U.S. Attorney, 1958-1961 and Chief Appellate Attorney, 1960-1961, Southern District of New York. Law Clerk to Hon. Edmund L. Palmieri, 1957 and Hon. Lawrence E. Walsh, 1957-1958, U.S. District Court, Southern District of New York. *Member:* Association of the Bar of the City of New York; New York State and American Bar Associations; The District of Columbia Bar. ***PRACTICE AREAS:*** Structured Finance; Real Estate. ***Email:*** gigordon@swidlaw.com

DAVID M. LUBITZ, born New York, N.Y., March 22, 1964; admitted to bar, 1991, Florida; 1993, New York; 1998, District of Columbia. *Education:* Harvard College (A.B., 1986); Columbia University (J.D., 1991). ***PRACTICE AREAS:*** Public Interest Law; Litigation. ***Email:*** dmlubitz@swidlaw.com

(This Listing Continued)

MILISSA A. MURRAY, born Syracuse, New York, July 15, 1958; admitted to bar, 1987, Maryland; 1988, District of Columbia and U.S. District Court, District of Maryland; 1990, U.S. District Court, District of Columbia. *Education:* Towson State University (B.S., 1980); University of Baltimore (J.D., 1986). Member, University of Baltimore Law Review, 1985-1986. *Member:* Anne Arundel County, Maryland State (Member, Environmental Law Section) and Federal Bar Associations; The District of Columbia Bar; Bankruptcy Bar Association of Maryland. ***PRACTICE AREAS:*** Environmental Litigation; Environmental Enforcement; Commercial Litigation; Bankruptcy; Business Reorganization. ***Email:*** mamurray@swidlaw.com

JAMIL E. NASIR, born Chicago, Illinois, December 18, 1955; admitted to bar, 1983, District of Columbia. *Education:* University of Michigan (B.G.S., with high distinction, 1978; J.D., magna cum laude, 1983). Award-winning science fiction writer. *Member:* The District of Columbia Bar. ***PRACTICE AREAS:*** Public Utilities; General Litigation; Environmental. ***Email:*** jenasir@swidlaw.com

WILLIAM T. O'NEIL, born Chicago, Illinois, August 2, 1963; admitted to bar, 1990, District of Columbia. *Education:* University of Notre Dame (B.A., 1985); Duke University School of Law (J.D., 1990). Editor, Law and Contemporary Problems, 1988-1990. *Member:* The District of Columbia Bar. ***PRACTICE AREAS:*** Litigation. ***Email:*** wtoneil@swidlaw.com

ALISA H. REFF, born New Brunswick, New Jersey, 1961; admitted to bar, 1988, Maryland; 1990, District of Columbia. *Education:* The American University (B.A., cum laude, 1983); Georgetown Law Center (J.D., 1988). Recipient, American Jurisprudence Award for Trial Practice. Staff Member, American Criminal Law Review, 1986-1988. Co-Author: "Maryland Handbook on Labor and Employment Law," Maryland Chamber of Commerce, 1989; "Sexual Harassment and Related Torts - The Employer's Perspective," American Bar Association, 1994; Revisions Editor, "Responding to Employment Discrimination Charges,"; "Avoiding Employment Discrimination Charges"; "Employer Discipline and Discharge," Matthew Bender & Co., Inc. *Member:* Maryland State (Member, Labor Law Section) and American (Member, Labor Law Section) Bar Associations; The District of Columbia Bar. ***PRACTICE AREAS:*** Employment Litigation; Equal Employment Opportunity Law; Fair Labor Standards; Family and Medical Leave Act; Sexual Harassment. ***Email:*** ahreff@swidlaw.com

DAVID B. RUBIN, born New York, N.Y., October 20, 1960; admitted to bar, 1985, Massachusetts; 1988, District of Columbia. *Education:* Brown University (A.B., 1982); Boston University School of Law (J.D., cum laude, 1985). *Member:* The District of Columbia Bar. ***PRACTICE AREAS:*** Energy Regulation; Federal Energy Regulation. ***Email:*** dbrubin@swidlaw.com

C. JOEL VAN OVER, born Boulder, Colorado, November 21, 1948; admitted to bar, 1983, Texas; 1984, District of Columbia. *Education:* University of Colorado (B.A., 1974); Boston College (J.D., magna cum laude, 1983). Author: Managed Care and Antitrust; Managed Care Contracting, Aspen Press (1997). Co-Author: Congressional Authority to Conduct Investigations and Subpoena Documents, Fraud in Government Contracting, Harcourt Brace Janovich (1985). *Member:* The District of Columbia Bar; State Bar of Texas; Federal and American (Member, Sections on: Antitrust; Intellectual Property) Bar Associations. ***PRACTICE AREAS:*** Intellectual Property; Commercial Litigation; Antitrust Counseling and Litigation; Government Contracting. ***Email:*** cjvanover@swidlaw.com

MICHAEL E. WARD, born Orange, New Jersey, December 22, 1946; admitted to bar, 1974, California; 1978, Massachusetts (inactive); 1990, U.S. Court of Appeals, District of Columbia Circuit; 1992, District of Columbia. *Education:* Dartmouth College (A.B., summa cum laude, 1969); Stanford University (J.D., 1974). Phi Beta Kappa. Member, Stanford University Law Review, 1973-1974. Deputy Public Defender, Orange County, California, 1974-1978. Assistant Counsel, Judiciary Committee, U.S. House of Representatives, 1979-1985. Co-Author: with Hon. R.F. Drinan and D.W. Beier, "The Federal Criminal Code: The Houses are Divided," 18 American Criminal Law Review 509, 1981. *Member:* State Bar of California; The District of Columbia Bar; Massachusetts Bar Association. ***Email:*** meward@swidlaw.com

TACIE H. YOON, born Pittsburgh, Pennsylvania, March 22, 1961; admitted to bar, 1987, Pennsylvania; 1989, District of Columbia. *Education:* Yale University (B.A., 1982); Boston College (J.D., 1987). *Member:* The District of Columbia Bar. ***PRACTICE AREAS:*** Civil Litigation; Complex Litigation. ***Email:*** thyoon@swidlaw.com

OF COUNSEL

PETER BARNES, born Cambridge, Massachusetts, April 13, 1940; admitted to bar, 1966, District of Columbia; 1984, Maryland. *Education:* Yale University (A.B., magna cum laude, 1962); Harvard University (LL.B., cum laude, 1965). *Member:* The District of Columbia Bar; Maryland State and American Bar Associations. ***PRACTICE AREAS:*** Real Estate; Civil Litigation; Complex Litigation. ***Email:*** pbarnes@swidlaw.com

(This Listing Continued)

DANIEL ERIC COHEN, born Louisville, Kentucky, March 16, 1961; admitted to bar, 1985, Kentucky; 1986, U.S. District Court, Western District of Kentucky; 1987, U.S. Court of Appeals, Sixth Circuit; 1988, District of Columbia and U.S. District Court for the District of Columbia; 1993, Virginia. *Education:* American University; University of Louisville (B.A., with honors, 1982); Kentucky, Chase College of Law (J.D., 1985). Member, Chase College of Law Law Review. Recipient, American Jurisprudence Award for Torts II. Author: Note, "No Defense for the Manufacturer—The Kentucky Supreme Court Restricts the 'Shifting Responsibility' Defense in Strict Products Liability Cases," 12 Northern Kentucky Law Review 347, 1985; "Minimizing Conflicts Between Contractors and Design Professionals," Fed Pubs. 1995; "Evidentiary Privileges—Sword or Shield," 2001. Law Clerk: Justice J. Calvin Aker, Supreme Court of Kentucky, 1985-1986; Judge John Lewis Smith, Jr., U.S. District Court, District of Columbia, 1987-1988. Assistant Attorney General for Commonwealth of Kentucky, 1986-1987. *Member:* Kentucky and American Bar Associations; The District of Columbia Bar. ***PRACTICE AREAS:*** Insurance; Intellectual Property; Environmental; Construction. ***Email:*** decohen@swidlaw.com

COLLEEN COVELL, born Upper Darby, Pennsylvania, May 18, 1964; admitted to bar, 1990, Massachusetts; 1991, District of Columbia; U.S. District Court, District of Columbia; U.S. Court of Appeals, District of Columbia Circuit. *Education:* University of Virginia (B.A., 1986); Boston College (J.D., 1990). Editor, Boston College Law Review. Assistant, United States Attorney for the District of Columbia, 1996-2000. ***PRACTICE AREAS:*** Employment Discrimination; White Collar Criminal; Trial Attorney. ***Email:*** ccovell@swidlaw.com

REBECCA P. DICK, born Columbus, Ohio, October 1, 1947; admitted to bar, 1978, New York; 2001, District of Columbia. *Education:* Denison University (B.A., cum laude, 1969); State University of New York at Buffalo (J.D., magna cum laude, 1977). Past Member, Department of Justice, Antitrust Division. *Member:* American Bar Association (Member, Antitrust Section). ***PRACTICE AREAS:*** Antitrust. ***Email:*** rpdick@swidlaw.com

L. ELISE DIETERICH, born Seattle, Washington, September 13, 1962; admitted to bar, 1988, District of Columbia; 1990, Washington (inactive). *Education:* Evergreen State College (B.A., 1982); Harvard Law School (J.D., cum laude, 1987). Clerkship, Judge John M. Ferren, District of Columbia Court of Appeals, 1987-1988. ***PRACTICE AREAS:*** Telecommunications. ***Email:*** ledieterich@swidlaw.com

PATRICK J. DONOVAN, born Washington, D.C., March 17, 1948; admitted to bar, 1976, Virginia; 1980, District of Columbia. *Education:* Brandeis University (A.B., 1971); Georgetown University Law Center (J.D., 1976). Deputy Chief, Competitive Pricing Division, Common Carrier Bureau, FCC, April 1996-March 1998. Associate Chief, Common Carrier Bureau, FCC, November 1994-February 1996. Acting Chief, Policy and Ruler Division, Cable Services Bureau, FCC, October 1984-May 1994. Special Counsel, Policy and Program Planning Division, Common Carrier Bureau, FCC, February 1993-June 1993. *Member:* Virginia State Bar; The District of Columbia Bar. ***PRACTICE AREAS:*** Telecommunications; Administrative Law. ***Email:*** pjdonovan@swidlaw.com

WILLIAM L. FISHMAN, born 1941; admitted to bar, 1966, District of Columbia. *Education:* Brown University (B.A., magna cum laude, 1962); Harvard Law School (J.D., 1965). Phi Beta Kappa. Author: "Property Rights, Reliance and Retroactivity Under the Communications Act of 1934," 50 Fed. Comm. L.J. (1997). Deputy Associate Administrator for Policy, 1974-1977, National Telecommunications and Information Administration, U.S. Department of Commerce. *Member:* The District of Columbia Bar. ***PRACTICE AREAS:*** Privacy Law; Communications Law. ***Email:*** wlfishman@swidlaw.com

ERIC J. FRANKLIN, born Columbus, Ohio, April 27, 1964; admitted to bar, 1991, Pennsylvania; 1993, District of Columbia; registered to practice before U.S. Patent and Trademark Office. *Education:* University of California at Davis (B.S., 1987); American University (J.D., 1991). Alpha Lambda Delta; Phi Delta Phi. Note and Comment Editor, American University Journal of International Law and Policy, 1990-1991. *Member:* The District of Columbia Bar; American Bar Association. ***Email:*** ejfranklin@swidlaw.com

ELIOT J. GREENWALD, born Brooklyn, New York, March 3, 1951; admitted to bar, 1977, New York; 1979, District of Columbia. *Education:* Cornell University (A.B., 1973); De Paul University (J.D., 1976). Editor, De Paul Law Review, 1975-1976. Attorney, Common Carrier Bureau, Federal Communications Commission, 1977-1981. *Member:* The District of Columbia Bar; Federal Communications Bar Association (Co-Chair, Land Mobile Practice Committee, 1990-1992). ***PRACTICE AREAS:*** Telecommunications Law; Wireless Communications; FCC Licensing; FCC Regulation; Cellular Telephone; Radio Common Carrier; Satellite Communications. ***Email:*** ejgreenwald@swidlaw.com

MARVIN T. GRIFF, born October 1, 1955; admitted to bar, 1981, Massachusetts; 1984, Louisiana; 1990, District of Columbia; 1993, Alabama. *Education:* Brandeis University (B.A., 1978); Tulane University School of Law (J.D.,

(This Listing Continued)

SWIDLER BERLIN SHEREFF FRIEDMAN, LLP, Washington—Continued

cum laude, 1981). Senior Trial Attorney, Office of General Counsel, Gas and Oil Litigation Section, Federal Energy Regulatory Commission, 1987-1989. Law Clerk, Office of Administrative Law Judges, Federal Energy Regulatory Commission, 1982-1983. Author: "What's New About The FERC's New Utility Merger Policy?" Public Utilities Fortnightly (Feb. 1, 1997); "Recent Federal Initiatives to Promote the Use of Natural Gas and Unconventional Gas: High Octane Delivery or Just Hot Air?" International Unconventional Gas Symposium Proceedings (1995). *Member:* Energy Bar Association. ***PRACTICE AREAS:*** Federal and State Regulated Energy and Pipeline Law; Utility Law. ***Email:*** mtgriff@swidlaw.com

HAROLD A. LEVY, born Atlantic City, New Jersey, May 22, 1950; admitted to bar, 1974, Pennsylvania; 1975, District of Columbia. *Education:* Kenyon College (B.A., cum laude, 1971); Georgetown University Law Center (J.D., 1974). Attorney-Advisor, U.S. Department of Housing and Urban Development, 1979-1990. Chief Attorney, U.S. Department of HUD, 1990-1992. *Member:* The District of Columbia Bar. ***PRACTICE AREAS:*** Real Estate; Finance; Housing Programs. ***Email:*** halevy@swidlaw.com

JOHN P. MORAN, born Trenton, New Jersey, August 18, 1952; admitted to bar, 1983, District of Columbia; 1984, U.S. District Court for the District of Columbia and U.S. Court of Appeals for the Federal Circuit; 1988, U.S. Supreme Court; 1996, U.S. District Court, District of Maryland. *Education:* Villanova University (B.E., cum laude, 1974); Rutgers University (M.S., 1980); Catholic University (J.D., 1983). Tau Beta Pi; Eta Kappa Nu. *Member:* The District of Columbia Bar (Member, Sections on: Patent, Trademark and Copyright Law; Litigation); American Intellectual Property Law Association. ***PRACTICE AREAS:*** Intellectual Property; Patents; Trademarks; Copyrights; Trade Secrets; International Trade Regulation. ***Email:*** jpmoran@swidlaw.com

DANIEL J. PERKA, born Pittsburgh, Pennsylvania, July 8, 1952; admitted to bar, 1978, Georgia; 1988, District of Columbia. *Education:* Princeton University (A.B., cum laude, 1974); Duke University (J.D., 1978). Member, Editorial Board, Duke Law Journal, 1978. Assistant General Counsel, Hotel Development, Marriott Corporation, 1981-1989. Chief Counsel, Network & Facilities, MCI Communications Corporation, 1989-1999. ***PRACTICE AREAS:*** Telecommunications; Cable Television; Real Estate. ***Email:*** djperka@swidlaw.com

CHARLES A. ROHE, born Los Angeles, California, November 22, 1948; admitted to bar, 1990, Illinois; 1999, District of Columbia. *Education:* University of Denver (B.A., 1970); Creighton University (J.D., 1989). *Member:* The District of Columbia Bar. ***PRACTICE AREAS:*** Telecommunications; Right of Way; Commercial Leasing. ***Email:*** carohe@swidlaw.com

MICHAEL L. SHOR, born Raleigh, North Carolina, December 1, 1950; admitted to bar, 1988, Virginia and U.S. Court of Appeals, Fourth Circuit; 1989, District of Columbia; 1993, U.S. District Court, District of Maryland; 1999, U.S. Court of Appeals, Fifth Circuit. *Education:* University of North Carolina (B.A., 1972); University of Maryland (M.S.W., 1979); New York Law School (J.D., cum laude, 1986). ***PRACTICE AREAS:*** Telecommunications; Litigation; Debtor-Creditor. ***Email:*** mlshor@swidlaw.com

TROY F. TANNER, born Inglewood, California, April 15, 1963; admitted to bar, 1988, Virginia; 1989, District of Columbia; 1990, U.S. Court of Appeals for the District of Columbia Circuit. *Education:* Brigham Young University (B.A., with honors, 1985); George Washington University (J.D., 1988). Attorney-Adviser, 1991-1996, Chief International Policy & Facilities Branch, 1996-1999, Federal Communications Commission. *Member:* The District of Columbia Bar (Co-Chair, Computer and Telecommunications Law Section, 1997-1999); Federal Communications Bar Association. ***PRACTICE AREAS:*** Telecommunications; International. ***Email:*** tftanner@swidlaw.com

JULIE A. WEISMAN, born New York, N.Y., June 28, 1953; admitted to bar, 1982, Connecticut; 1984, New York; 1996, District of Columbia. *Education:* Duke University (B.S., 1975); University of Georgia (M.F.R., 1979); Emory University (J.D., 1982). *Member:* The District of Columbia Bar. ***PRACTICE AREAS:*** Environmental Litigation. ***Email:*** jaweisman@swidlaw.com

PHYLLIS A. WHITTEN, born Plaquemine, Louisiana, March 21, 1955; admitted to bar, 1980, California; 1981, District of Columbia. *Education:* University of California, Berkeley (B.A., 1976); University of California, Hastings College of the Law (J.D., 1980). *Member:* State Bar of California; The District of Columbia Bar; Federal Communications Bar Association. ***PRACTICE AREAS:*** Telecommunications. ***Email:*** pawhitten@swidlaw.com

PATRICK J. WHITTLE, born Heidelberg, Germany, August 19, 1957; admitted to bar, 1981, District of Columbia. *Education:* Harvard College (A.B., cum laude, 1977); Vanderbilt University (J.D., 1981). Order of the Coif. Recipient, Five American Jurisprudence Awards. *Member:* The District of Columbia Bar; Federal Communications Bar Association. ***PRACTICE AREAS:*** Telecommunications. ***Email:*** pjwhittle@swidlaw.com

(This Listing Continued)

ROBERT V. ZENER, born St. Louis, Missouri, November 13, 1935; admitted to bar, 1959, New York; 1974, District of Columbia. *Education:* University of Chicago (A.B., 1954; J.D., 1958). Order of the Coif. Editor-in-Chief, University of Chicago Law Review, 1957-1958. Author: "Guide to Federal Environmental Law," Practising Law Institute 1981; Federal Environmental Law, chapter on "The Federal Law of Water Pollution Control" (West, 1974). Associate General Counsel (Water), 1971-1973, Deputy General Counsel, 1973-1975 and General Counsel, 1975-1976, U.S. Environmental Protection Agency. Assistant Chief, Appellate Section, Civil Division, U.S. Department of Justice, 1969-1971. Appellate Litigation Counsel, U.S. Department of Justice, 1990-1994. *Member:* The District of Columbia Bar. ***PRACTICE AREAS:*** Environment; Litigation. ***Email:*** rvzener@swidlaw.com

ASSOCIATES

DANIEL ABRAHAM, born Miami, Florida, June 15, 1972; admitted to bar, 2000, New York (Not admitted in District of Columbia). *Education:* University of Florida (B.A., 1994); New York Law School (J.D., magna cum laude, 1999). *Member:* New York State Bar Association. (practices under the supervision of principals of the firm). ***PRACTICE AREAS:*** Telecommunications. ***Email:*** dsabraham@swidlaw.com

SEAN A. ATKINS, born Windsor, Connecticut, July 22, 1969; admitted to bar, 1996, Virginia; 1999, District of Columbia. *Education:* University of Virginia (B.A., 1991; J.D., 1996). *Member:* The District of Columbia Bar; Federal Energy Bar Association. ***PRACTICE AREAS:*** Regulatory Law; Utility Law. ***Email:*** saatkins@swidlaw.com

HARISHA J. BASTIAMPILLAI, born Colombo, Sri Lanka, August 2, 1967; admitted to bar, 1992, Maryland; 1993, District of Columbia and U.S. District Court, District of Maryland; 1997 U.S. Supreme Court, U.S. Court of Appeals, Fourth, Fifth, Eighth and District of Columbia Circuits and U.S. District Court for the District of Columbia. *Education:* The Johns Hopkins University (B.A., 1989); Columbia University School of Law (J.D., 1992). Phi Beta Kappa. Harlan Fiske Stone Scholar. *Member:* Montgomery County and Maryland State Bar Associations; The District of Columbia Bar. ***REPORTED CASES:*** Allstate Insurance Company v. Campbell, 639 A.2d 652 (Md.1994); Campbell v. Allstate Insurance Company, 624 A.2d 1310 (Md.1993). ***PRACTICE AREAS:*** Telecommunications Regulatory; Telecommunications Litigation; Telecommunications Appellate Litigation. ***Email:*** hjbastiampillai@swidlaw.com

ROBERT C. BERTIN, born Albany, New York, October 27, 1968; admitted to bar, 1997, Virginia and U.S. Court of Appeals, Fourth Circuit; 1998, U.S. District Court, Eastern District of Virginia; registered to practice before U.S. Patent and Trademark Office (Not admitted in District of Columbia). *Education:* Virginia Polytechnic Institute and State University (B.S. Electrical Engineering, 1991); George Mason University School of Law (J.D., 1997). Recipient, Schlumberger Scholarship. *Member:* Virginia State Bar; American Bar Association; American Intellectual Property Law Association. ***PRACTICE AREAS:*** Patent Prosecution; Intellectual Property Litigation; Intellectual Property Licensing. ***Email:*** rcbertin@swidlaw.com

REBECCA A. BLACKMER, born Kansas City, Missouri, February 18, 1956; admitted to bar, 1996, Maryland; 1999, District of Columbia. *Education:* Kansas State University (B.S., 1978), Kappa Delta Pi; Pittsburg State University (M.S., 1980); The Catholic University of America (J.D., 1995). *Member:* American and Federal Energy Bar Associations. (practices under the supervision of principals of the firm). ***PRACTICE AREAS:*** Energy Law; Electric Power; Natural Gas; Utility Regulatory Law. ***Email:*** RABlackmer@swidlaw.com

JOSHUA M. BOBECK, born New York, N.Y., January 14, 1967; admitted to bar, 1992, New Jersey; 1993, New York; 1994, District of Columbia. *Education:* Rutgers University (B.A., 1989); Boston College (J.D., 1992). Legislative Counsel, Telecommunications U.S. General Services Administration, 1993-1999. *Member:* Federal Communications Bar Association. ***PRACTICE AREAS:*** Telecommunications. ***Email:*** jmbobeck@swidlaw.com

JESSICA Y. BREWSTER, born Meridian, Mississippi, July 20, 1973; admitted to bar, 1998, Maryland; 2000, District of Columbia. *Education:* Stanford University (B.A., departmental honors and with distinction, 1995), Phi Beta Kappa; Howard University School of Law (J.D., magna cum laude, 1998). Member, Howard Law Journal. Author: "Loyalty to the Profession: A Call for a Rule Prohibiting Sexual Relations Between Attorneys and Their Clients," Howard Law Journal, Volume 41. Clerk, Judge Alexander Williams, Jr., U.S. District Court, District of Maryland. ***PRACTICE AREAS:*** Litigation. ***Email:*** JYBrewster@swidlaw.com

REBECCA S. BRIGGS, born Wellsboro, Pennsylvania, September 17, 1973; admitted to bar, 2001, New York (Not admitted in District of Columbia). *Education:* University of Pittsburgh (B.A., 1996); Georgetown University (J.D., 2000). Administrative Editor, *Tax Lawyer*. ***PRACTICE AREAS:*** Telecommunications Law. ***Email:*** rsbriggs@swidlaw.com

CHRISTOPHER JAMES CARNEY, born Weehawken, New Jersey, July 14, 1973; admitted to bar, 1998, New Jersey; 1999, New York; U.S. District

(This Listing Continued)

Court, District of New Jersey; U.S. District Court, Southern District of New York; 2001 District of Columbia. *Education:* Connecticut College (B.A., 1995); American University (J.D., summa cum laude, 1998). Recipient, Don Monroe Casto Award in Constitutional Law. Member, American University Law Review, 1996-1998. *Member:* The District of Columbia Bar; American Bar Association; New York County Lawyer's Association. (practices under the supervision of principals of the firm). ***PRACTICE AREAS:*** Litigation. ***Email:*** cjcarney@swidlaw.com

AMY K. CARPENTER-HOLMES, born Albany, New York, March 19, 1972; admitted to bar, 1998, New York and District of Columbia. *Education:* Cornell University (B.S., 1994); American University, Washington College of Law (J.D., summa cum laude, 1997). Clerk, New York State Supreme Court, Appellate Division, Third Department, 1997-1998. *Member:* The District of Columbia Bar. ***PRACTICE AREAS:*** General Litigation. ***Email:*** akholmes@swidlaw.com

MELANIE K. CARR, born Waukesha, Wisconsin, April 4, 1974; admitted to bar, 2000, Maryland (Not admitted in District of Columbia). *Education:* University of Maryland at Baltimore County (B.A., 1996); University of Chicago Law School (J.D., 2000); University of Chicago, Irving B. Harris School of Public Policy Studies (M.A., distinguished scholar, 2000). Maryland Distinguished Scholar; Meyerhoff Scholar. President, Black Law Students' Association, 1997-1998. Finalist, National Achievement Award. (practices under the supervision of principals of the firm). ***PRACTICE AREAS:*** Government Affairs; Antitrust and Trade Regulation; Real Estate Finance. ***Email:*** mkcarr@swidlaw.com

MELISSA R. CASTRO, born Houston, Texas, December 15, 1971; admitted to bar, 1998, Missouri; 1999, District of Columbia. *Education:* University of Nebraska (B.A., cum laude, 1994); Georgetown University Law Center (J.D., 1998). Notes Editor, Georgetown Journal of Legal Ethics. ***PRACTICE AREAS:*** Antitrust; Consumer Protection; Litigation. ***Email:*** MRCastro@swidlaw.com

MARIA L. CATTAFESTA, born Summit, New Jersey, March 6, 1970; admitted to bar, 1996, Maryland and District of Columbia. *Education:* University of North Carolina at Chapel Hill (B.A., with highest distinction, 1992); Catholic University, Columbus School of Law (J.D., cum laude, 1995). Phi Beta Kappa; Phi Eta Sigma. Lead Articles Editor, Catholic University Law Review, 1994-1995. *Member:* The District of Columbia Bar; Maryland State and Federal Communications Bar Associations. ***PRACTICE AREAS:*** Telecommunications. ***Email:*** mlcattafesta@swidlaw.com

GRACE R. CHIU, born Seattle, Washington, August 18, 1955; admitted to bar, 1996, District of Columbia. *Education:* Brown University (A.B., 1977); American University (J.D., 1994). Brown University, Class of '77, Regional Class Secretary, 1977-1982. Member, American University Law Review, 1992-1994. *Member:* The District of Columbia Bar. ***PRACTICE AREAS:*** Telecommunications. ***Email:*** grchiu@swidlaw.com

ZENAS J. CHOI, born Alexandria, Virginia, June 25, 1972; admitted to bar, 1998, Virginia (Not admitted in District of Columbia). *Education:* Northeastern University (B.S., cum laude, 1994); Boston University School of Law (J.D., 1998). (practices under the supervision of principals of the firm). ***PRACTICE AREAS:*** Telecommunications. ***Email:*** ZJChoi@swidlaw.com

ARISTOTELIS A. CHRONIS, born Fairfax, Virginia, March 8, 1975; admitted to bar, 2000, Virginia (Not admitted in District of Columbia). *Education:* University of Virginia (B.A., 1997; J.D., 2000). (practices under the supervision of principals of the firm). ***PRACTICE AREAS:*** Telecommunications. ***Email:*** aachronis@swidlaw.com

KATHY L. COOPER, born Great Falls, Montana, March 10, 1964; admitted to bar, 1994, Pennsylvania; 1995, Maryland; 1996, District of Columbia. *Education:* University of Maryland (B.S., cum laude, 1988); Catholic University of America (J.D., cum laude, 1994). Who's Who Among University Students. Recipient: National Collegiate Business Merit Award; Certificate of Communications Law. Editor-in-Chief, CommLaw Conspectus: Journal of Communications Law and Policy. *Member:* The District of Columbia Bar; Federal Communications Bar Association. ***PRACTICE AREAS:*** Telecommunication. ***Email:*** klcooper@swidlaw.com

WENDY M. CREEDEN, born Des Moines, Iowa, March 8, 1970; admitted to bar, 1999, Virginia; 2000, District of Columbia. *Education:* George Washington University (B.A., 1992); George Mason University (J.D., 1999). Production Editor, Journal of International Legal Studies, 1996-1999. Legal Intern, Office of Commission Susan Ness, FCC, 1998. *Member:* Virginia State Bar; The District of Columbia Bar; American and Federal Communications Bar Associations. ***PRACTICE AREAS:*** Telecommunications. ***Email:*** wmcreeden@swidlaw.com

FRANK M. DALE, JR., born Morganton, North Carolina, September 25, 1967; admitted to bar, 1995, Pennsylvania; 1997, District of Columbia; 1998, U.S. District Court for the District of Columbia; 1999, U.S. Court of Appeals for the Federal Circuit. *Education:* University of North Carolina at Greensboro (B.A., summa cum laude, 1989); Ruhr-Universität Bochum, West Germany;

(This Listing Continued)

Duke University (A.M., 1994; J.D., 1994). Phi Beta Kappa; Fulbright Scholar. Member, Journal of Law and Contemporary Problems, 1992-1994. Law Clerk to Justice Maurice A. Hartnett III, Supreme Court of Delaware, 1994-1995. *Member:* The District of Columbia Bar. ***LANGUAGES:*** German. ***PRACTICE AREAS:*** Energy; Litigation. ***Email:*** fmdale@swidlaw.com

KRISTINE DEBRY, born Denver, Colorado, August 4, 1967; admitted to bar, 1997, Maryland (inactive); 1998, District of Columbia. *Education:* University of Utah (B.A., 1989); Georgetown University Law Center (J.D., 1997). Executive Editor, American Criminal Law Review. *Member:* The District of Columbia Bar. ***PRACTICE AREAS:*** Government Relations; Telecommunications. ***Email:*** kdebry@swidlaw.com

JAMES T. DELORENZO, born Passaic, New Jersey, January 3, 1974; admitted to bar, 1999, New Jersey; 2000, District of Columbia. *Education:* Duke University (A.B., cum laude, 1996): New York University (J.D., 1999). Associate Editor, New York University Journal of Law and Public Policy. ***PRACTICE AREAS:*** Government Affairs; Telecommunications; Internet Law. ***Email:*** jtdelorenzo@swidlaw.com

RONALD W. DEL SESTO JR., born Providence, Rhode Island, March 3, 1968; admitted to bar, 1998, Rhode Island and Maryland; 1999, District of Columbia. *Education:* Georgetown University (B.A., 1990); Catholic University (J.D., magna cum laude, 1998). Staff Member, 1996-1997 and Executive Editorial Board, Lead Articles Editor, 1997-1998, Catholic University Law Review. *Member:* Rhode Island, Maryland and American Bar Association; The District of Columbia Bar. ***Email:*** rwdelsesto@swidlaw.com

BENJAMIN D. DIAMOND, born Pittsburgh, Pennsylvania, May 6, 1952; admitted to bar, 1977, Pennsylvania, U.S. District Court, Western District of Pennsylvania and U.S. Court of Appeals, Third Circuit; 1981, New York; 1985, District of Columbia. *Education:* Harvard College (A.B., 1974); Duquesne University School of Law (J.D., 1977). *Member:* Allegheny County and American Bar Associations; The District of Columbia Bar. ***PRACTICE AREAS:*** Transactional; Real Estate; Finance. ***Email:*** bddiamond@swidlaw.com

MICHAEL P. DONAHUE, born Riverton, Wyoming, December 1, 1967; admitted to bar, 1996, Maryland; 1998, District of Columbia. *Education:* University of Southern California (B.A., 1990); Catholic University (J.D., cum laude, 1996). Staff Member, 1994-1995, and Production Editor, 1995-1996, ComLaw Conspectus, Journal of Communication Law and Policy. *Member:* The District of Columbia Bar; American Bar Association. ***PRACTICE AREAS:*** Telecommunications. ***Email:*** mpdonahue@swidlaw.com

OFER ELITZUR, born Pasadena, California, September 25, 1973; admitted to bar, 2000, California (Not admitted in District of Columbia). *Education:* University of California, Berkeley (B.A., with distinction, 1995); Harvard University Law School (J.D., cum laude, 2000). *Member:* State Bar of California; American Bar Association. ***PRACTICE AREAS:*** Corporate; Securities. ***Email:*** oelitzur@swidlaw.com

CHRISTINE F. ERICSON, born Chicago, Illinois; admitted to bar, 1992, Illinois; 1993, District of Columbia; 2000, U.S. Court of Appeals for the District of Columbia Circuit. *Education:* Duke University (A.B., 1987); University of Paris, Sorbonne, Paris, France (Adv. Diploma, 1988); Washington University (J.D., 1991). Regional Moot Court Team. Associate Editor, Washington University Journal of Urban and Contemporary Law. Staff Attorney, Office of the General Counsel, Federal Energy Regulatory Commission, 1991-1994. *Member:* The District of Columbia Bar; Energy and American Bar Associations. ***PRACTICE AREAS:*** Public Utilities; Energy; Environmental; Litigation. ***Email:*** cfericson@swidlaw.com

MICHAEL D. FARBER, born Morgantown, West Virginia, April 22, 1969; admitted to bar, 1995, Pennsylvania; 1996, District of Columbia. *Education:* Pennsylvania State University (B.S., 1991); George Washington University National Law Center (J.D. 1994). Order of the Coif. Senior Notes Editor, George Washington Law Review. Law Clerk, Judge Timothy K. Lewis, U.S. Court of Appeals, Third Circuit, 1995-1996. Trial Attorney, U.S. Department of Justice, Antitrust Division, 1997-1999. *Member:* American Bar Association (Member, Antitrust Law Section, 1994—). ***PRACTICE AREAS:*** Antitrust. ***Email:*** mdfarber@swidlaw.com

MICHAEL K. FEDERMAN, born New York, N.Y.; admitted to bar, 1996, Connecticut; 1997, New York; 2001, District of Columbia. *Education:* Cornell University (B.S., 1993), Gamma Sigma Delta Honors; George Washington University Law School (J.D., cum laude, 1996). Member, George Washington University Journal of International Law and Economics. *Member:* The Association of The Bar of The City of New York; New York State Bar Association (Member, Real Property Law Section). (practices under the supervision of principals of the firm). ***PRACTICE AREAS:*** Real Estate; Structured Finance; Construction. ***Email:*** MKFederman@swidlaw.com

BRETT P. FERENCHAK, born Hanover, New Hampshire, October 6, 1972; admitted to bar, 1997, Virginia; 1999, District of Columbia. *Education:* Duke University (A.B., 1994); University of Richmond, The T.C. Williams School of Law (J.D., 1997). Annual Survey Editor, University of Richmond Law Review. Author, Comment, "Regulating Indecent Broadcasting: Setting Sail

(This Listing Continued)

SWIDLER BERLIN SHEREFF FRIEDMAN, LLP, Washington—Continued

From Safe Harbors or Sunk by the V-Chip?," 30 U. Rich. L. Rev. 831, 1996. ***PRACTICE AREAS:*** Telecommunications. ***Email:*** BPFerenchak@swidlaw.com

JAMES FERGUSON, born New York, N.Y., May 24, 1960; admitted to bar, 1999, District of Columbia. *Education:* Park College (B.S., 1995); Howard University School of Law (J.D., 1999). ***PRACTICE AREAS:*** Telecommunications. ***Email:*** JWFerguson@swidler.com

TAMAR E. FINN, born Chicago, Illinois, May 14, 1969; admitted to bar, 1994, Pennsylvania; 1995, Maryland; 1996, District of Columbia. *Education:* Bucknell University (B.A., magna cum laude, with honors, 1991); Georgetown University (J.D., cum laude, 1994). Phi Beta Kappa. Mortar Board. *Member:* The District of Columbia Bar. ***PRACTICE AREAS:*** Telecommunications Regulation; Local Telecommunications Competition. ***Email:*** tefinn@swidlaw.com

MICHAEL W. FLEMING, born Ft. McClellan, Alabama, May 26, 1961; admitted to bar, 1994, Virginia; 1997, District of Columbia. *Education:* University of Virginia (B.A., 1983; J.D., 1994). Notes Editor, Virginia Environmental Law Journal. ***PRACTICE AREAS:*** Telecommunications Regulation; Local Telecommunications Competition. ***Email:*** mwfleming@swidlaw.com

LAURA A. FORD, born Baltimore, Maryland, November 8, 1973; admitted to bar, 1998, Maryland; 1999, District of Columbia. *Education:* Johns Hopkins University (B.A., with honors,1995); Duke University (M.A., Environmental Studies, 1998); Duke Law School (J.D., cum laude, 1998). ***PRACTICE AREAS:*** Environmental Law. ***Email:*** laford@swidlaw.com

SANDRA FRANCO, born Chicago, Illinois, October 19, 1971; admitted to bar, 1999, Maryland (Not admitted in District of Columbia). *Education:* University of Chicago (B.S., 1993); University of Florida (M.A., 1996); Georgetown University (J.D., magna cum laude, 1999). (practices under the supervision of principals of the firm). ***PRACTICE AREAS:*** Environmental Law. ***Email:*** spfranco@swidlaw.com

PAUL D. FRANGIE, born Cohoes, New York, June 23, 1972; admitted to bar, 1998, New York (Not admitted in District of Columbia). *Education:* State University of New York at Albany (B.A., 1994); Cornell University (J.D., 1997). Phi Beta Kappa. *Member:* New York State and American Bar Associations. ***PRACTICE AREAS:*** Antitrust. ***Email:*** pdfrangie@swidlaw.com

JONATHAN S. FRANKEL, born Cleveland, Ohio, June 11, 1970; admitted to bar, 1995, Maryland (inactive); 1997, Virginia and District of Columbia. *Education:* University of Michigan (B.A., 1992); George Mason University (J.D., 1995). Finalist, National Trial Advocacy Competition, 1995. *Member:* Maryland State Bar Association (Member, Young Lawyer's Public Service Committee, 1995—); American Inn of Court, George Mason Chapter, 1994. ***PRACTICE AREAS:*** Telecommunications. ***Email:*** jsfrankel@swidlaw.com

BRIAN G. FRIEL, born Newark, New Jersey, May 22, 1968; admitted to bar, 1994, New Jersey and U.S. District Court, District of New Jersey; 1996, District of Columbia; 2001, U.S. Court of Appeals for the District of Columbia Circuit and U.S. Court of Appeals, Eleventh Circuit. *Education:* Boston College (B.A., magna cum laude, 1990); St. John's University (J.D., cum laude, 1994). Member, 1992-1993 and Assistant Editor, 1993-1994, St. John's Law Review. Legal Counsel, Parents Initiative of the Washington Lawyers Committee for Civil Rights and Urban Affairs. ***PRACTICE AREAS:*** Insurance; Insurance Litigation; Litigation. ***Email:*** bgfriel@swidlaw.com

PAUL O. GAGNIER, JR., born Syracuse, New York, January 16, 1969; admitted to bar, 1994, Virginia; 1995, District of Columbia; U.S. Court of International Trade. *Education:* University of Rochester (B.A., magna cum laude, 1991); University of Pennsylvania (J.D., cum laude, 1994). Phi Beta Kappa. *Member:* Virginia State Bar; The District of Columbia Bar. ***LANGUAGES:*** Spanish and Portuguese. ***PRACTICE AREAS:*** Telecommunications. ***Email:*** pogagnier@swidlaw.com

GARY G. GALLANT, JR., born Camden, New Jersey, April 5, 1967; admitted to bar, 1992, New Jersey and Pennsylvania; 1994, District of Columbia; 2001, U.S. Supreme Court. *Education:* Rutgers University at Camden (B.A., 1989; J.D., 1992). Recipient: Political Science Student of the Year, 1989. ***PRACTICE AREAS:*** Legislative Practice. ***Email:*** gggallant@swidlaw.com

MARA GLASER, born Omaha, Nebraska, January 5, 1973; admitted to bar, 1998, Maryland; 1999, District of Columbia. *Education:* Creighton University (B.S.B.A., magna cum laude, 1995); Creighton University School of Law (J.D., magna cum laude, 1998). ***PRACTICE AREAS:*** Corporate. ***Email:*** maglaser@swidlaw.com

BROOKE DERATANY GOLDFARB, born Melbourne, Florida, October 9, 1969; admitted to bar, 1996, Florida; 1998, District of Columbia. *Education:* University of Virginia (B.A., with high distinction, 1991); Harvard University (J.D., 1996). Phi Beta Kappa. Echols Scholar. Rotary Scholar, Buenos Aires, Argentina, 1992. Fulbright Program Participant, Belo Horizon Brazil, 1992. Baker & McKenzie International Clerkship, Rio de Janeiro, Brazil, 1995. *Member:* The Florida Bar; The District of Columbia Bar; American Bar Association; Womens Bar Association of The District of Columbia. ***LANGUAGES:*** Spanish, Portuguese and French. ***PRACTICE AREAS:*** Corporate; Mergers and Acquisitions. ***Email:*** bmderatany@swidlaw.com

JEFFREY M. GOODMAN, born Palo Alto, California, February 15, 1973; admitted to bar, 1998, New Jersey (Not admitted in District of Columbia). *Education:* Connecticut College (B.A., 1995); American University (J.D., 1998). ***PRACTICE AREAS:*** Antitrust and Trade Regulation. ***Email:*** jmgoodman@swidlaw.com

KATHLEEN L. GREENAN, born Silver Spring, Maryland, October 9, 1969; admitted to bar, 1995, Maryland; 1997, District of Columbia. *Education:* University of Maryland (B.S., 1992); Catholic University, Columbus School of Law (J.D., 1995). ***Email:*** klgreenan@swidlaw.com

JONATHAN P. GUY, born Wolverhampton, United Kingdom, April 24, 1961; admitted to bar, 1994, New York; 1995, U.S. District Court, District of Maryland; 1996, District of Columbia; 1997, U.S. District Court, District of Columbia and U.S. Court of Appeals, Fourth Circuit. *Education:* London School of Economics (B.S., 1983); Stanford Law School (J.D., 1993). Member, 1991-1992 and Associate Editor, 1992-1993, Stanford Law Review. Editor, Stanford Environmental Law Review. ***PRACTICE AREAS:*** Litigation; Bankruptcy. ***Email:*** jpguy@swidlaw.com

PAUL B. HUDSON, born Columbia, South Carolina, October 2, 1972; admitted to bar, 1998, California; 1999, District of Columbia. *Education:* Duke University (B.A., 1994); Stanford Law School (J.D., 1997). Clerk, Hon. Rudi M. Brewster, U.S. District Court, Southern District of California, 1997-1998. ***PRACTICE AREAS:*** Telecommunications. ***Email:*** PBHudson@swidlaw.com

CHADWICK A. JACKSON, born Brooklyn, New York, May 3, 1970; admitted to bar, 1999, New York (Not admitted in District of Columbia). *Education:* Syracuse University (B.S., 1993; J.D., 1997). *Member:* New York State and American Bar Associations; American Intellectual Property Law Association. (practices under the supervision of principals of the firm). ***LANGUAGES:*** Spanish. ***PRACTICE AREAS:*** Intellectual Property; Licensing; Litigation. ***Email:*** cajackson@swidlaw.com

EDWARD W. KIRSCH, born Pittsburgh, Pennsylvania, July 8, 1959; admitted to bar, 1996, Maryland; 1998, District of Columbia. *Education:* United States Naval Academy (B.S., 1981); George Washington University (J.D., with honors, 1996). Author: "The Qui Tam Quagmire," Washington Legal Foundation, 1998. *Member:* The District of Columbia Bar; Maryland State Bar Association. [Lt., U.S. Navy, 1981-1986]. ***PRACTICE AREAS:*** Telecommunications Law; E-Commerce; Government Contracts. ***Email:*** ewkirsch@swidlaw.com

MICHAEL KUNSELMAN, born Buffalo, New York, September 5, 1974; admitted to bar, 2000, Maryland (Not admitted in District of Columbia). *Education:* University of Maryland (B.A., 1996; J.D., 2000). Order of the Coif. Member, University of Maryland Law Review, 1999-2000. *Member:* Energy Bar Association. ***PRACTICE AREAS:*** Energy. ***Email:*** mnkunselman@swidlaw.com

ALLISON F. LANDIS, born Brooklyn, New York, May 7, 1974; admitted to bar, 2000, New York and Massachusetts (Not admitted in District of Columbia). *Education:* University of Virginia (B.A., 1996); Boston University (J.D., 1999). Case and Note Editor, Boston University International Law Journal, 1998-1999. *Member:* New York State and Massachusetts Bar Associations. ***PRACTICE AREAS:*** Litigation. ***Email:*** aflandis@swidlaw.com

ALEXANDER J. LATHROP, born Morristown, New Jersey, September 1, 1968; admitted to bar, 1999, Virginia; 2001, District of Columbia. *Education:* University of California (B.A., with high honors, 1991); University of Virginia School of Law (J.D., 1999). Member, Virginia Tax Review. [Capt., USMC, 1991-1996]. ***PRACTICE AREAS:*** Litigation. ***Email:*** AJLathrop@swidlaw.com

TONY S. LEE, born Norman, Oklahoma, May 30, 1968; admitted to bar, 1994, Maryland; 1996, District of Columbia. *Education:* University of Maryland (B.S.E.E., 1991); American University (J.D., 1994). *Member:* Federal Communications Bar Association. ***PRACTICE AREAS:*** Communications Law. ***Email:*** tslee@swidlaw.com

AMY ELIZABETH LEHMAN, born San Diego, California, October 27, 1973; admitted to bar, 2000, California (Not admitted in District of Columbia). *Education:* Pomona College (B.A., 1995); University of Michigan at Ann Arbor (J.D., 2000). (practices under the supervision of principals of the firm). ***PRACTICE AREAS:*** Corporate Law. ***Email:*** aelehman@swidlaw.com

JOEL G. LEVI, born Biloxi, Mississippi, July 31, 1969; admitted to bar, 1996, New York and District of Columbia. *Education:* Vanderbilt University (B.A., cum laude, 1991); Cornell University (J.D., cum laude, 1995). Phi Delta Phi. *Member:* The District of Columbia Bar. ***LANGUAGES:*** French. ***PRACTICE AREAS:*** Litigation. ***Email:*** jglevi@swidlaw.com

(This Listing Continued)

SCOTT J. LEVITT, born Manhasset, New York, March 14, 1970; admitted to bar, 1995, New York; 1997, District of Columbia. *Education:* Cornell University (B.S., 1992); George Washington University (J.D., 1995). Member, George Washington Law Review. ***PRACTICE AREAS:*** Insurance Coverage Litigation; Employment Litigation. ***Email:*** sjlevitt@swidlaw.com

SUSAN DANIELLE LOYD, born Redwood City, California, June 3, 1970; admitted to bar, 1996, Massachusetts; 1998, U.S. District Court, District of Massachusetts; 2000, District of Columbia. *Education:* University of California at San Diego (B.A., 1991); Vermont Law School (J.D., cum laude, M.S.E.L., magna cum laude, 1995). Co-Author: "Sellers Can Transfer Environmental Liability," 25 Mass. L.W. 1591 (1997); "Real Estate Agreements: Protection Against Environmental Liability?" For the Defense (Defense Research Institute Publication) (March 1998). *Member:* Boston and American Bar Associations; The District of Columbia Bar. ***PRACTICE AREAS:*** Environmental Law. ***Email:*** sdloyd@swidlaw.com

PHILIP J. MACRES, born Palo Alto, California, November 23, 1966; admitted to bar, 1998, Florida; 1999, District of Columbia. *Education:* University of Florida (B.S.B.A., with high honors, 1988); Stetson University College of Law (J.D., cum laude, 1997). Moot Court Board; Phi Delta Phi; Federalist Society (Chapter President, 1996-1997). Recipient, Cecil C. Augusta Bailey Award. *Member:* American Bar Association. ***PRACTICE AREAS:*** Telecommunications. ***Email:*** pjmacres@swidlaw.com

HARRY N. MALONE III, born Havre de Grace, Maryland, October 14, 1952; admitted to bar, 1998, Maryland; 1999, District of Columbia. *Education:* Carnegie-Mellon University (B.S., 1974); University of Maryland School of Law (J.D., with honors, 1997). Recipient, Strahorn Prize for the Best Work in Evidence, 1995-1996. Articles Editor, Maryland Law Review. Author: Note, "Denying Trial Courts the Power to Grant Sua Sponte Transfers," 55 Maryland Law Review 75 (1996). *Member:* Federal Communications Bar Association. ***PRACTICE AREAS:*** Telecommunications. ***Email:*** hnmalone@swidlaw.com

DUKE K. McCALL, III, born Greenville, South Carolina, May 15, 1968; admitted to bar, 1993, South Carolina; 1997, District of Columbia; U.S. District Court, for the District of Columbia; U.S. District Court, District of South Carolina; U.S. Court of Appeals, Fourth Circuit; U.S. Supreme Court. *Education:* Furman University (B.A., cum laude, 1990); Vanderbilt University (J.D., 1993). Law Clerk: Honorable William W. Wilkins, Jr., U.S. Court of Appeals, Fourth Circuit, 1993-1994; Honorable William B. Traxler, Jr., U.S. District Court, District of South Carolina, 1994-1995. *Member:* American Bar Association. ***PRACTICE AREAS:*** Environmental; Litigation. ***Email:*** dkmccall@swidlaw.com

BRIAN M. McDERMOTT, born Huntington Valley, Pennsylvania, March 26, 1973; admitted to bar, 1998, Maryland; 1999, District of Columbia. *Education:* University of Florida (B.S., 1995); Catholic University of America (J.D., cum laude, 1998). ***PRACTICE AREAS:*** Telecommunications. ***Email:*** bmmcdermott@swidlaw.com

WENDY C. McGRAW, born July 1, 1970; admitted to bar, 1994, Virginia; 1997, District of Columbia; U.S. Court of Appeals, Fourth Circuit; U.S. District Court, Eastern District of Virginia. *Education:* Virginia Commonwealth University (B.A., magna cum laude, 1991); University of Virginia (J.D., 1994). *Member:* Virginia State Bar; The District of Columbia Bar. ***PRACTICE AREAS:*** Litigation. ***Email:*** wcmcgraw@swidlaw.com

ALICIA A. MEROS, born Silver Spring, Maryland, November 21, 1973; admitted to bar, 1998, Virginia and District of Columbia. *Education:* Vanderbilt University (B.E., Electrical Engineering, magna cum laude, 1995); George Washington Law School (J.D., 1998). Tau Beta Pi; Eta Kappa Nu. *Member:* Virginia and American Bar Associations; American Intellectual Property Law Association. ***PRACTICE AREAS:*** Intellectual Property; Patents; Trademarks; Copyrights; Trade Secrets; Unfair Practices. ***Email:*** aameros@swidlaw.com

KEVIN D. MINSKY, born Seattle, Washington, December 18, 1969; admitted to bar, 1998, Maryland and District of Columbia. *Education:* University of Washington (B.A., cum laude, 1993); Syracuse University College of Law (J.D., magna cum laude, 1997). Phi Beta Kappa. Justinian Honorary Law Society. Order of the Coif. Member, Syracuse Law Review. Author: "Constitutionality and Policy Ramifications of the Violent Programming Provisions in the Telecommunications Act of 1996," 47 Syracuse Law Review Vol. 4; "The Rights of Disabled Americans to Internet Access Under Federal Law," TDI National Directory and Resource Guide, The Blue Book, 2000. *Member:* American Bar Association; Communications Bar Association. ***PRACTICE AREAS:*** Telecommunications; Internet Law. ***Email:*** kdminsky@swidlaw.com

BRADLEY R. MILIAUSKAS, born Detroit, Michigan, August 6, 1970; admitted to bar, 1997, Virginia; 1999, District of Columbia. *Education:* College of William and Mary (B.A., 1992); University of Virginia School of Law (J.D., 1996). Member, Virginia Environmental Law Journal. ***PRACTICE AREAS:*** Energy. ***Email:*** brmiliauskas@swidlaw.com

JEFFREY A. MITCHELL, born Washington, D.C.; admitted to bar, 1997, Virginia; 1998, District of Columbia. *Education:* University of Washington

(This Listing Continued)

(B.A., 1993); Georgetown University Law Center (J.D., with honors, 1997). ***PRACTICE AREAS:*** Federal Civil Litigation; Administrative Litigation; Telecommunications. ***Email:*** jamitchell@swidlaw.com

JULIA M. MOORE, born Philadelphia, Pennsylvania, December 15, 1968; admitted to bar, 1996, New Jersey and Pennsylvania; 1998, District of Columbia. *Education:* American University (B.A., 1991); University of Virginia Law School (J.D., 1995). ***PRACTICE AREAS:*** Energy. ***Email:*** juliamoore@swidlaw.com

JAMES N. MOSKOWITZ, born Fairfax, Virginia, February 1, 1966; admitted to bar, 1996, Virginia; 1998, District of Columbia. *Education:* College of William & Mary (B.S., 1988); Georgetown University (J.D., 1996). ***PRACTICE AREAS:*** Telecommunications. ***Email:*** jnmoskowitz@swidlaw.com

SEAN P. O'HANLON, born Portsmouth, Virginia, April 30, 1971; admitted to bar, 2001, Virginia; registered to practice before U.S. Patent and Trademark Office (Not admitted in District of Columbia). *Education:* Georgia Institute of Technology (B.M.E., 1994); George Mason University School of Law (J.D., 2000). *Member:* Virginia and American Bar Associations; American Intellectual Property Law Association; Giles Sutherland Rich American Inn of Court; American Society of Mechanical Engineers. ***PRACTICE AREAS:*** Intellectual Property. ***Email:*** spohanlon@swidlaw.com

KELLY A. OLSON, born Waukesha, Wisconsin, October 20, 1973; admitted to bar, 1999, Wisconsin; 2001, Maryland (Not admitted in District of Columbia). *Education:* University of Wisconsin-La Crosse (B.S., summa cum laude, 1995); Syracuse University (J.D., cum laude, 1999). Member, Golden Key National Honor Society. Survey Editor, Journal of International Law and Commerce, 1998-1999. *Member:* State Bar of Wisconsin; Maryland State Bar Association. ***PRACTICE AREAS:*** Telecommunications Law. ***Email:*** kaolson@swidlaw.com

MELIKE S. ONCU, born Philadelphia, Pennsylvania, June 16, 1971; admitted to bar, 1996, New York; 1998, District of Columbia. *Education:* Lafayette College (B.A., 1993); George Washington University (J.D., 1996). ***LANGUAGES:*** Turkish. ***Email:*** msoncu@swidlaw.com

DOUGLAS D. ORVIS II, born Greensburg, Pennsylvania, August 7, 1971; admitted to bar, 1996, California; 1998, District of Columbia. *Education:* Indiana University (B.A. and B.A., 1993); University of California, Hastings College of the Law (J.D., 1996). Senior Articles Editor, Hastings Communications & Entertainment Law Journal. Member, Conference of California Public Utility Counsel, 1996—. *Member:* State Bar of California; The District of Columbia Bar. ***PRACTICE AREAS:*** Telecommunications; International. ***Email:*** ddorvis@swidlaw.com

THEODORE JOSEPH PARADISE, born Carson City, Nevada, July 15, 1974; admitted to bar, 2000, Virginia (Not admitted in District of Columbia). *Education:* University of Idaho (B.A., 1997); Georgetown University (J.D., 2000). Phi Alpha Delta. Member, Golden Key National Honor Society. Vice President, Mortar Board Honor Society. *Member:* American Bar Association; Energy Bar Association. (practices under the supervision of principals of the firm). ***PRACTICE AREAS:*** Energy Law. ***Email:*** tjparadise@swidlaw.com

MATTHEW A. PATER, born Long Branch, New Jersey, February 26, 1972; admitted to bar, 1997, Virginia; 2001, District of Columbia. *Education:* University of Richmond (B.S., 1994); University of Miami (J.D., 1997). *Member:* Virginia and American Bar Associations. ***PRACTICE AREAS:*** Intellectual Property. ***Email:*** mapater@swidlaw.com

RUTH PRITCHARD-KELLY, born Rome, Italy, March 15, 1961; admitted to bar, 1996, Maryland; 1997, District of Columbia. *Education:* University of Maryland (B.A., 1981; J.D., 1996); George Washington University (M.A., 1988). Senior Articles Editor, Maryland Journal of International Law and Trade. ***PRACTICE AREAS:*** Telecommunications. ***Email:*** rpkelly@swidlaw.com

DEIDRA NICOLE PROCTOR, born Washington, D.C., August 11, 1972; admitted to bar, 2000, Maryland (Not admitted in District of Columbia). *Education:* Morgan State University (B.A., 1994); Georgetown University Law School (J.D., 2000). *Member:* Maryland State and American Bar Associations. ***PRACTICE AREAS:*** Insurance Litigation; Litigation. ***Email:*** dnproctor@swidlaw.com

EDWARD S. QUILL, JR., born Portsmouth, Virginia, May 6, 1966; admitted to bar, 1995, Pennsylvania; 1997, District of Columbia. *Education:* University of Kent, Canterbury, England (Diploma, 1987); Bates College (B.A., 1988); University of Denver (J.D., with distinction, 1995); Georgetown University (M.B.A., Salutatorian, 1997). Order of St. Ives. Managing Editor, Journal of International Law and Policy. ***PRACTICE AREAS:*** Telecommunications; Transactional. ***Email:*** esquill@swidlaw.com

STEPHEN T. RAPTIS, born Huntington, West Virginia, October 13, 1969; admitted to bar, 1995, Pennsylvania; 1996, West Virginia; 1998, District of Columbia. *Education:* West Virginia University (B.A., 1992; J.D., 1995). ***Email:*** straptis@swidlaw.com

DAVID D. RINES, born New Haven, Connecticut, October 13, 1968; admitted to bar, 1999, Maryland (Not admitted in District of Columbia). *Educa-*

(This Listing Continued)

SWIDLER BERLIN SHEREFF FRIEDMAN, LLP, Washington—Continued

tion: University of Minnesota (B.F.A., 1990); Georgetown University (J.D., 1999). [Sgt., U.S. Army, 1990-1994]. ***LANGUAGES:*** Russian and French. ***PRACTICE AREAS:*** Telecommunications; International Law. ***Email:*** ddrines@swidlaw.com

KATHERINE A. ROLPH, born Alexandria, Virginia, March 13, 1965; admitted to bar, 1994, Virginia; 1996, District of Columbia. *Education:* University of Virginia (B.A., 1988); L'Institut d'études Politiques (C.E.P., 1990); University of Virginia School of Law (J.D., 1994). Phi Sigma Iota. Staff Member, Virginia Journal of Environmental Law, 1991-1993. Member: University of Virginia Environmental Law Forum, 1991-1994; J.B. Moore Society of International Law, 1991-1993. ***LANGUAGES:*** French and Italian. ***PRACTICE AREAS:*** Telecommunications. ***Email:*** karolph@swidlaw.com

W. RAY RUTNGAMLUG, born St. Louis, Missouri, January 29, 1973; admitted to bar, 2000, New York and District of Columbia. *Education:* Georgetown University (B.S.F.S., 1995); Cornell University (J.D., 1999). Symposium Editor, Cornell Law Review. *Member:* The District of Columbia Bar. (practices under the supervision of principals of the firm). ***PRACTICE AREAS:*** Telecommunications. ***Email:*** wrrutngamlug@swidlaw.com

BRENT T. SALMONS, born Long Branch, New Jersey, June 8, 1973; admitted to bar, 1999, Missouri (Not admitted in District of Columbia). *Education:* Southwest Missouri State University (B.S., magna cum laude, 1995); Georgetown University (J.D., cum laude, 1999). Gold Key. Author: "IOLTA's: Good Work or Good Riddance?" 11 Georgetown Journal of Legal Ethics 259, Winter, 1998. American Inns of Court, 1998-1999. (practices under the supervision of principals of the firm). ***PRACTICE AREAS:*** Corporate; Mergers and Acquisitions; Securities. ***Email:*** bsalmons@swidlaw.com

JASON R. SCHERR, born Baltimore, Maryland, November 16, 1972; admitted to bar, 1998, Maryland; 1999, U.S. District Court, District of Maryland; 2000, District of Columbia and U.S. Court of Appeals, Fourth Circuit. *Education:* University of Pennsylvania (B.A., 1994); University of Maryland (J.D., with honors, 1998). Phi Delta Phi. Member, University of Maryland Law Review, 1997-1998. Author: Note, "Pavel v. Johnson: A New Construction of Promissory Estoppel," 56 Maryland Law Review 711, 1997. *Member:* The Bar Association of Baltimore City; The District of Columbia Bar; Maryland State Bar Association. ***LANGUAGES:*** Spanish. ***PRACTICE AREAS:*** Commercial Litigation. ***Email:*** jrscherr@swidlaw.com

MICHAEL J. SCHUNCK, born Düsseldorf, Germany, June 15, 1967; admitted to bar, 2000, New York and District of Columbia. *Education:* Rhode Island College (B.A., 1988); New York University School of Law (J.D., 1999). ***LANGUAGES:*** German and Spanish. *Member: Federal Communications and American Bar Associations.* ***PRACTICE AREAS:*** Telecommunications; Internet; Antitrust; Privacy. ***Email:*** mjschunck@swidlaw.com

MICHAEL A. SCHWARTZ, born Ventura, California, June 26, 1956; admitted to bar, 1995, California; 1997, District of Columbia; registered to practice before U.S. Patent and Trademark Office. *Education:* California Institute of Technology (B.S.E.E., with honors, 1978); George Washington University (J.D., with high honors, 1994). Order of the Coif. *Member:* State Bar of California; The District of Columbia Bar; American Bar Association; American Intellectual Property Law Association; American Association for the Advancement of Science. ***PRACTICE AREAS:*** Patent; Intellectual Property. ***Email:*** maschwartz@swidlaw.com

MICHAEL C. SLOAN, born 1965; admitted to bar, 1995, Wisconsin; 1996, Illinois; 1998, District of Columbia. *Education:* Northwestern University (B.A., 1986); Indiana University (M.P.A., 1987); University of Wisconsin-Madison (J.D., cum laude, 1995). Law Clerk to the Hon. Juan M. Perez-Gimenez, U.S. District Court, District of Puerto Rico, 1995-1996. ***PRACTICE AREAS:*** Telecommunications Litigation. ***Email:*** msloan@swidlaw.com

RICHARD P. SPARLING, born Providence, Rhode Island, June 22, 1963; admitted to bar, 1991, Pennsylvania; 1992, District of Columbia. *Education:* Assumption College; George Washington University (B.A., 1985); Georgetown University (J.D., 1991). *Member:* American Bar Association; Federal Energy Bar Association. ***PRACTICE AREAS:*** Energy. ***Email:*** rpsparling@swidlaw.com

GREGG A. SPATH, born New Rochelle, New York, November 13, 1952; admitted to bar, 1978, New York; 1984, U.S. Supreme Court; 1990, Pennsylvania; 2001, District of Columbia. *Education:* University of Rochester (B.A., English, 1974); New England School of Law (J.D., 1977); New York University (LL.M., Trade Regulation, 1979). Phi Alpha Delta. Listed in *Who's Who in American Law*, 1986—. Member, Editorial Staff, 1975-1976 and Technical Editor, 1976-1977, New England Law Review. Author: Article, "Mone v. Greyhound Lines, Inc.: A Limited Advance in the Law of Prenatal Wrongful Death," 11 New England Law Review 669, 1976. Special Legal Consultant, Western Electric Company, 1978-1981. Attorney, St. Regis Paper Company, 1981-1982. Assistant General Counsel, United Merchants and Manufacturers, Inc., 1982-1987. General Counsel, Adidas USA, 1987-1988. Executive Vice President and General Counsel, Regency Manufacturing Company, Inc., 1988-1995. Corporate Counsel, Real Estate and Intellectual Property, Nextel Communications, Inc., 1996-2000. *Member:* The District of Columbia Bar; American Bar Association (Member, Communications and Intellectual Property Law Sections). ***PRACTICE AREAS:*** Telecommunications; E-Commerce; Software Licensing; Intellectual Property; Real Estate. ***Email:*** gaspath@swidlaw.com

JEANNE W. STOCKMAN, born Bethesda, Maryland, March 11, 1969; admitted to bar, 1994, Virginia; 1997, District of Columbia. *Education:* University of Virginia (B.S.E.E., 1991); University of Richmond (J.D., 1994). Member, Editorial Board and Manuscript Editor, University of Richmond Law Review, 1993-1994. ***PRACTICE AREAS:*** Telecommunications. ***Email:*** JWStockman@swidlaw.com

GREGG STRUMBERGER, born Englewood, New Jersey, November 13, 1970; admitted to bar, 1999, Massachusetts; 2001, District of Columbia. *Education:* Eastern Michigan University (B.S., magna cum laude, 1996); Boston University (J.D., 1999). *Member:* Federal Communications Bar Association. ***PRACTICE AREAS:*** Telecommunications; Antitrust. ***Email:*** gstrumberger@swidlaw.com

STEVEN J. TAVE, born Freehold, New Jersey, August 16, 1975; admitted to bar, 2000, Virginia; 2001, District of Columbia. *Education:* Northwestern University (B.A., 1997); University of Virginia (J.D., 2000). Editor, 1998-1999 and Articles Development Editor, 1999-2000, The Journal of Law and Politics. ***PRACTICE AREAS:*** Litigation. ***Email:*** sjtave@swidlaw.com

KATHRYN RAE TAYLOR, born Hampton, Virginia; admitted to bar, 1994, Virginia; 1995, District of Columbia. *Education:* University of Virginia (B.A., with high distinction, 1986); Harvard Law School (J.D., cum laude, 1994). Phi Beta Kappa. ***Email:*** krtaylor@swidlaw.com

DAVID TIGER, born Boston, Massachusetts, October 29, 1965; admitted to bar, 1992, Maryland; 1998, U.S. District Court, District of Maryland; 1999, District of Columbia. *Education:* University of Maryland (B.A., 1989; J.D., 1992). Member, Maryland Law Review, 1990-1991. Executive Editor - Articles, The Business Lawyer, 1991-1992. Author: "Impact Fees and Local Taxing Authority, Developments in Maryland Law, 1989-1990," 50 Md. L. Rev. 1214 (1991). ***PRACTICE AREAS:*** Real Estate; Structured Finance. ***Email:*** dtiger@swidlaw.com

ANDREW TOPPS, IV, born Washington, D.C., June 14, 1971; admitted to bar, 1997, Maryland (Not admitted in District of Columbia). *Education:* University of Virginia (B.A., 1993); Georgetown University (J.D., 1997). (practices under the supervision of principals of the firm). ***PRACTICE AREAS:*** Antitrust. ***Email:*** ajtopps@swidlaw.com

THOMAS SILVIO VALENTE, born Rutland, Vermont, February 10, 1976; admitted to bar, 2001, Vermont (Not admitted in District of Columbia). *Education:* Catholic University of America (B.A., 1998); University of Virginia (J.D., 2001). Intern, Senate Agriculture Committee, 1995, 1996. ***LANGUAGES:*** French and Italian. ***PRACTICE AREAS:*** Government Affairs. ***Email:*** tsvalente@swidlaw.com

MICHAEL A. VALERIO, born Mineola, New York, April 29, 1968; admitted to bar, 1993, Maryland; 1995, District of Columbia; U.S. District Court, District of Maryland; U.S. District Court, District of Columbia; U.S. Court of Federal Claims. *Education:* Johns Hopkins University (B.A., 1990); Catholic University (J.D., 1993). Recipient, American Jurisprudence Award in Criminal Law & Procedure, Commercial Transactions. Member, Catholic University Law Review, 1991-1993. Vernon X. Miller Scholar. ***PRACTICE AREAS:*** Litigation. ***Email:*** mavalerio@swidlaw.com

DAVID J. WALKER, born Olean, New York, February 6, 1961; admitted to bar, 1987, Maryland; 1990, District of Columbia. *Education:* Susquehanna University (B.A., magna cum laude, 1983); Washington College of Law (J.D., 1987). Pi Gamma Mu; Pi Sigma Alpha. ***PRACTICE AREAS:*** Telecommunications. ***Email:*** djwalker@swidlaw.com

EDIE WALTERS, born Livingston, Texas, November 20, 1973; admitted to bar, 1999, Texas; 2001, District of Columbia. *Education:* George Washington University (B.A., 1996); University of Houston (J.D., 1999). Awarded Honorable Mention, Editorial Board, Joseph Bernfeld Writing Competition for the California Bankruptcy Institute. Author: "An Ambiguous Answer: The Effect of Associations Communication Corporation v. Rash on Chapter 11 and Chapter 13 Collateral Valuation," 35 Houston Law Review 953, 1998. Member, Board of Directors, Houston Chapter of American Civil Liberties Union, 1998-1999. (practices under the supervision of principals of the firm). ***PRACTICE AREAS:*** Bankruptcy; Litigation. ***Email:*** ewalters@swidlaw.com

ERIC C. WANG, born Taipei, Taiwan, September 1, 1969; admitted to bar, 1993, Georgia; 1996, New York; 1999, District of Columbia. *Education:* Emory University (B.A., 1990); Emory University Law School (J.D., with distinction, 1993); New York University (LL.M., 1994). ***LANGUAGES:*** Mandarin Chinese. ***PRACTICE AREAS:*** Domestic Taxation; International Taxation. ***Email:*** ecwang@swidlaw.com

(This Listing Continued)

RANAN Z. WELL, born Chicago, Illinois, June 17, 1972; admitted to bar, 1999, District of Columbia and Maryland. *Education:* Yeshiva University (B.A., cum laude, 1994); Boston University (J.D., 1998). ***PRACTICE AREAS:*** Corporate; Securities; Bankruptcy. ***Email:*** rzwell@swidlaw.com

WILLIAM BANKS WILHELM, JR., born Pittsfield, Massachusetts, January 1, 1968; admitted to bar, 1993, Pennsylvania; 1994, District of Columbia. *Education:* College of the Holy Cross (A.B., 1989); Catholic University of America (J.D., 1993). Pi Sigma Alpha; Phi Alpha Delta. Associate Editor, Catholic University Law Review, 1992-1993. ***PRACTICE AREAS:*** Electronic Commerce; Telecommunications; Corporate Law. ***Email:*** wbwilhelm@swidlaw.com

JASON M. YANOWITZ, born July 2, 1969; admitted to bar, 2000, California, District of Columbia and Colorado. *Education:* University of Maryland (B.S., 1992); California Western School of Law (J.D., magna cum laude, 2000). *Member:* Colorado Bar Association; District of Columbia Bar; State Bar of California. ***PRACTICE AREAS:*** Telecommunications Law; Antitrust Law. ***Email:*** jmyanowitz@swidlaw.com

MARSHA E. SWISS

1735 20TH STREET, N.W.
WASHINGTON, D.C. 20009
Telephone: 202-986-5555
Fax: 202-462-0379
Email: betwixt@compuserve.com
URL: http://www.lawyers.com/swisslaw

Estate Planning, Probate, Fiduciary Law and General Civil Litigation.

MARSHA E. SWISS, born Pittsburgh, Pennsylvania, January 1, 1940; admitted to bar, 1966, District of Columbia. *Education:* Swarthmore College (B.A., 1962); Harvard University (LL.B., 1965). Trial Attorney, National Labor Relations Board, 1965-1967. Member: Staff, President's Commission on Campus Unrest, 1970; Advisory Committee on Superior Court Rules of Probate and Fiduciary Procedure, 1980-1994. *Member:* The District of Columbia Bar (Member: Alternative Dispute Resolution Committee, 1984-1987; Lawyers Malpractice Committee, 1984-1985; Washington, D.C. Estate Planning Council). ***LANGUAGES:*** French.

TIMOTHY J. SYLVIA

WASHINGTON, D.C.

(See Columbia, Maryland)

Civil Practice, Wills, Probate, Personal Bankruptcy, Personal Injury, Slip & Fall, Auto Accident, DWI, DUI, Assault, Misdemeanors, Traffic Violations, Felonies, Criminal.

ELLYN R. TANENBERG

1201 PENNSYLVANIA AVENUE NW, SUITE 300
WASHINGTON, D.C. 20004
Telephone: 202-387-7747
Fax: 301-649-5895
Email: tanenberg@taxlawyer-cpa.com
URL: http://www.lawyers.com/tanenberglaw

Bethesda, Maryland Office: 7272 Wisconsin Avenue, Suite 300. 20814. Telephone: 301-907-0019.

Taxation, Federal Estate and Gift Taxation, Federal Tax Controversies, Income Tax, Individual Taxation, International Income Tax, International Tax Controversies, International Taxation, Small Business Taxation, Divorce Taxation, Wills, Probate, Business Immigration Taxation.

FIRM PROFILE: Ms. Tanenberg is a CPA and a former tax executive with both Ernst & Young and Deloitte Touche. As a tax attorney, Ms. Tanenberg has focused her practice on careful attention to detail, prevention of IRS tax controversies and avoidance of criminal tax issues.

ELLYN R. TANENBERG, born Chicago, Illinois, January 21, 1949; admitted to bar, 1992, Pennsylvania; 1993, Maryland; 1994, District of Columbia. *Education:* University of Illinois (B.S., Accounting, with honors, 1970); Georgetown University (M.S., Taxation, 1987); Washington College of Law, American University (J.D., 1992). Recipient, James Scholar, University of Illinois. Law Clerk, U.S. Tax Court, 1993-1994. *Member:* Montgomery County (Member, Tax Section), Maryland State, Pennsylvania and American (Member, Tax Section) Bar Associations; District of Columbia Bar (Member, Tax Section); American Association Attorneys-CPA's; Maryland Association of Certified Public Accountants; American Institute of Certified Public Accountants (Member, Tax Section). ***PRACTICE AREAS:*** Taxation; Income Tax; Estate and Gift Taxation; Wills; Probate.

(This Listing Continued)

(For complete biographical data on all personnel, See Professional Biographies at Washington, D.C.)

JAMES J. TANSEY

2823 29TH STREET, N.W.
WASHINGTON, D.C. 20008
Telephone: 202-232-8557
Fax: 202-232-8549

Commercial Litigation. Construction Law, Government Contract, Surety Law, Mechanics Lien Law.

JAMES J. TANSEY, born Worcester, Massachusetts, July 26, 1944; admitted to bar, 1969, Massachusetts; 1973, Virginia; 1975, District of Columbia. *Education:* Williams College (A.B., 1966); Boston University (J.D., 1969). Author: "Differences Between Arbitration and Litigation," American Bar Association, 1990; "Drafting International Arbitration Provisions," Federal Publications, 1990; "Drafting Owner-Architect & Owner Contractor Agreements," Federal Publications, 1989; "Analyzing Contractor Claims," Federal Publications, 1988; "Calculation of Construction Damages: Engineering News Record, 1988. Attorney: U.S. Department of Justice, Washington, D.C., 1970-1974; White House Staff, 1974.

FREDERICK J. TANSILL & ASSOCIATES, LLC

WASHINGTON, D.C.

(See McLean, Virginia)

Trusts and Estates, Taxation, Corporate, Business, Estate Planning, Wills and Probate Administration.

TECHNOLOGY LAW GROUP, L.L.C.

5335 WISCONSIN AVENUE, N.W.
SUITE 440
WASHINGTON, D.C. 20015
Telephone: 202-895-1707
Fax: 202-244-8257
Email: mail@tlgdc.com
URL: http://www.tlgdc.com

Telecommunications, Litigation, Commercial Law, Regulatory Issues, Transactional Law.

NEIL S. ENDE, born Washington, D.C., March 11, 1956; admitted to bar, 1980, District of Columbia. *Education:* University of Rochester (B.A., cum laude, 1977); Boston College (J.D., cum laude, 1980). Editor, Uniform Commercial Code Reporter-Digest, 1979-1980. *Member:* The District of Columbia Bar; American Bar Association; Federal Communications Bar Association. ***PRACTICE AREAS:*** Communication Law; Civil Litigation. ***Email:*** nende@tlgdc.com

ASSOCIATE

ALEXANDRE B. BOUTON, born Brussels, Belgium, May 1, 1963; admitted to bar, 1990, Maryland; 1993, District of Columbia. *Education:* University of Maryland (B.A., Economics, 1987; B.A., Political Science, 1987); University of Maryland School of Law (J.D., 1990). *Member:* Maryland State and American Bar Associations; The District of Columbia Bar. ***LANGUAGES:*** French, Spanish.

TOM K. SINAI, born Tehran, Iran, January 24, 1971; admitted to bar, 2000, Maryland (Not admitted in District of Columbia). *Education:* Towson State University (B.S., cum laude, 1993); Gonzaga University (J.D., 1997). *Member:* Maryland State and American Bar Associations; Federal Communications Bar Association. ***Email:*** tsinai@tlgdc.com

GEORGE A. TEITELBAUM

Established in 1983

1629 K STREET N.W., SUITE 802

WASHINGTON, D.C. 20006

Telephone: 202-783-7177

Fax: 202-775-7465

Email: georget@clark.net

URL: http://www.arrowweb.com/gilt

URL: http://www.lawyers.com/lawyergeorge

Probate, Wills, Trusts and Estates, Estate Planning, Asset Protection, Conservatorship, Guardianship, Bankruptcy, Consumer Bankruptcy, Chapter 7 and 13, Business Law, Corporate Law, Divorce, Separation Agreements, Child Support, Child Custody, Adoption, Family Law, Landlord and Tenant Law, Civil Litigation, Negligence, Auto Accidents, Personal Injury.

FIRM PROFILE: George A. Teitelbaum has been in the sole practice of law for over sixteen years. He was selected as the Washington, D.C. attorney for several major legal service plans, including the Chase Manhattan, American Express and Montgomery Wards Legal Service Plans, to represent their members. In addition, he has done work for the Legal counsel for the elderly, as part of their outside attorney program.

GEORGE A. TEITELBAUM, born New York, N.Y., February 22, 1943; admitted to bar, 1983, District of Columbia and U.S. District Court for the District of Columbia; 1998, Maryland. *Education:* Polytechnic Institute of New York (B.S.E.E., 1965; M.S. Industrial Engineering, 1968); American University (J.D., 1980). Member, AARP Services Network. ***LANGUAGES:*** Hebrew.

TENENBAUM & SAAS, P.C.

WASHINGTON, D.C.

(See Bethesda, Maryland)

Business Law, Commercial Transactional Practice, Commercial Real Estate Law, Commercial Litigation, Corporate Legal Counseling, Commercial Landlord and Tenant Law, Leasing.

THACHER PROFFITT & WOOD

Established in 1913

1700 PENNSYLVANIA AVENUE, N.W.

WASHINGTON, D.C. 20006

Telephone: 202-347-8400

Facsimile: 202-626-1930

Email: firm@tpwlaw.com

URL: http://www.tpwlaw.com

Offices:

New York, N.Y.: 11 West 42nd Street. Telephone: 212-789-1200. Facsimile: 212-789-3500.

White Plains, N.Y.: 50 Main Street. Telephone: 914-421-4100. Facsimile: 914-421-4150/4151.

Jersey City, N.J.: One Exchange Place. Telephone: 201-369-3280. Facsimile: 201-369-3290/4151.

Affiliated Office:

México City, Mexico: Avenida Paseo de la Reforma No. 2620 - Piso 4, Colonia Lomas Altas, 11950 México, D.F. Telephone: +(52) (5) 257-2940. Facsimile: +(52) (5) 257-2950.

Admiralty and Maritime, Banking, Bankruptcy, Corporate, Employee Benefits, Insurance, Intellectual Property, Litigation, Mergers and Acquisitions, Real Estate, Securitization, Tax, Technology and Science, Transportation, Wills and Probate.

FIRM PROFILE: Thacher Proffitt & Wood provides high quality, client-oriented legal services. We are approximately 200 lawyers, located in New York City, Washington, D.C., Jersey City, N.J., White Plains, N.Y. and through a joint venture, Mexico City, Mexico. We believe that with our size and breadth of practice, we provide clients with quality, cost-efficient legal services with close personal contact at the partner level.

Thacher Proffitt & Wood was founded in 1848. We have a broad business and commercial practice organized by practice groups that cover the above mentioned areas of concentration. Our clients range from publicly held "Fortune 500" corporations to privately held companies and include commercial banks, thrift institutions, insurance companies, investment banks, securities brokerage firms, domestic and foreign manufacturing and trading companies and maritime companies. We also represent U.S. and foreign corporations, joint ventures and partnerships and governmental agencies and industry trade groups and associations.

(This Listing Continued)

MEMBERS OF FIRM

V. GERARD COMIZIO, born Yonkers, New York, January 10, 1955; admitted to bar, 1981, New York; 1996, District of Columbia. *Education:* Fordham University (B.A., 1977); Pace University (J.D., 1980); Georgetown University Law Center (LL.M., Securities Regulation, 1983). Case and Comment Editor, Pace Law Review. Adjunct Professor of Law, Banking and International Banking Law, Regulation of Financial Institutions, Washington College of Law, American University, Washington, D.C. Deputy Chief Counsel, Office of Thrift Supervision, U.S. Department of Treasury, 1989-1995. Deputy General Counsel and Director, Corporate Securities Division, 1986-1989; Deputy Director for Securities, 1984-1986, Federal Home Loan Bank Board. Attorney/Advisor, Securities and Exchange Commission, Corporate Finance Division, 1981-1984. Author: "Show Me The Money: Federal Banking Regulation of Executive Compensation and Benefit Matters," Boston University Law Review, Spring 2000; Contributing Author, Bank Founder's Guidebook, Guide to Instituting a Bank, SNL Securities, 1999; "The Role of Deposit Insurance: Financial System Stability and Moral Hazard," Vol. 4, Current Legal Issues Affecting Central Banks, International Monetary Fund (March 1997); "Third Party State Law Opinions in Bank and Thrifts Stock Offerings," New York Law Journal June 18, 1996; "Cross Industry Depository Institution Transactions: Current Regulatory Issues in Industry Consolidation," Consumer Finance Law Quarterly Report Vol. 45, No. 3 Summer 1991. Chairman, Subcommittee on Holding Companies, Savings Institutions Committee, American Bar Association. Member, Governing Committee, Conference on Consumer Finance Law. ***PRACTICE AREAS:*** Corporate and Financial Institutions; Securities. ***Email:*** gcomizio@tpwlaw.com

STEPHEN F. J. ORNSTEIN, born Washington, D.C., December 10, 1963; admitted to bar, 1989, Pennsylvania; 1990, District of Columbia. *Education:* Brown University (A.B., magna cum laude, 1986); Columbia University (J.D., 1989). Phi Beta Kappa. Harlan Fiske Stone Scholar. Author: "Examining the Effect of New Legislation on Consumer Protection for High Cost Mortgages," Real Estate Law journal, Vol. 25: 40, 1996; "National Flood Insurance - Analysis of the National Flood Insurance Reform Act of 1994 and Final Regulation Promulgated by the Federal Banking Agencies," Mortgage Bankers Association of America, 1996; "Recent High Cost Mortgage Litigation," The Review of Bankers and Financial Services, Vol. 16, No. 8, 2000. ***PRACTICE AREAS:*** Real Estate Law; Consumer Compliance Law. ***Email:*** sornstein@tpwlaw.com

RICHARD A. SCHABERG, born New Canaan, Connecticut, February 7, 1959; admitted to bar, 1985, District of Columbia; 1999, New York and Massachusetts. *Education:* Bucknell University (B.A., cum laude, 1981); George Washington University (J.D., 1985). *Member:* The District of Columbia Bar; American Bar Association. ***PRACTICE AREAS:*** Corporate and Financial Institutions; Securities; Mergers and Acquisitions. ***Email:*** rschaberg@tpwlaw.com

COUNSEL

JOSEPH A. SMITH, JR., born Charleston, West Virginia, November 9, 1949; admitted to bar, 1975, New York; 1989, North Carolina (Not admitted in District of Columbia). *Education:* Davidson College (A.B., 1971); University of Virginia (J.D., 1974). Author, "The Role of Outside Counsel in the Creation of Economic Value," 2 N.C. Banking Institute (1998). Co-author: "Strategic Alliances: Why, How and What to Watch Out For," 3 N.C. Banking Institute (1999); "Retail Delivery of Financial Services After the Gram-Leach-Bliley Act: How Will Public Policy Shape the 'Financial Services Supermark'?" 4 N.C. Banking Institute (2000). General Counsel, Centura Banks, Inc. (1992-2000). Member, Executive Committee, University of North Carolina Banking Institute. ***PRACTICE AREAS:*** Corporate Law; Financial Institutions Law. ***Email:*** jsmith@tpwlaw.com

ASSOCIATES

KARA L. BUE, born San Francisco, California, 1964; admitted to bar, 1993, California (Not admitted in District of Columbia). *Education:* Brown University (A.B., 1986); Loyola Law School, Los Angeles (J.D., 1993). Member, St. Thomas More Honor Society, 1991-1993. Author, "The Pitfalls of Financing Software Developers," The Secured Lender, November/December 1997. ***Email:*** kbue@tpwlaw.com

CHRISTIAN H. CHANDLER, born Akron, Ohio, June 9, 1972; admitted to bar, 1997, Illinois; 1999, New York; 2000, Massachusetts (Not admitted in District of Columbia). *Education:* Duke University (B.A., cum laude, 1994); Boston College (J.D., cum laude, 1997). ***PRACTICE AREAS:*** ERISA; Employee Benefits. ***Email:*** cchandler@tpwlaw.com

MATTHEW DYCKMAN, born Princeton, New Jersey, April 21, 1969; admitted to bar, 1994, Maryland; 1995, Virginia (Not admitted in District of Columbia). *Education:* University of Virginia (B.A., with high distinction, 1991); Duke University School of Law (J.D., 1994). Phi Beta Kappa. ***Email:*** mdyckman@tpwlaw.com

JEFFREY L. HARE, born Morgantown, West Virginia, February 8, 1972; admitted to bar, 1997, West Virginia and U.S. District Court, Southern District

(This Listing Continued)

of West Virginia (Not admitted in District of Columbia). *Education:* West Virginia University (B.A., cum laude, 1994; J.D., 1997). Honors Graduate and Presidential Scholar, West Virginia University. Recipient: B.F. Endsley Scholarship; Sam Angotti Law Scholarship. ***PRACTICE AREAS:*** Corporate; Banking; Securities; Limited Liability Company Law. ***Email:*** jhare@tpwlaw.com

SONG A. PAK, born Seoul, Korea, December 21, 1970; admitted to bar, 1999, New York, New Jersey and District of Columbia. *Education:* Pepperdine University (B.A., 1992; M.A., 1994); American University, Washington College of Law (J.D., M.B.A., 1998). Notes and Comment Editor, The American University International Law Review. Member, The American University National Trial Advocacy Team, 1996-1997. ***PRACTICE AREAS:*** Securities; Corporate Law; Financial Institutions Law. ***Email:*** spak@tpwlaw.com

SHEILA J. DOMBAL SWARTZ, born Montclair, New Jersey, August 19, 1970; admitted to bar, 1997, Maryland; 2000, District of Columbia. *Education:* University of Notre Dame (B.B.A., with honors, 1992); Washington College of Law - American University (J.D., magna cum laude, 1997). Managing Editor, American University Journal of International Law & Policy. Certified Public Accountant, New York, 1996. ***Email:*** sdombal@tpwlaw.com

MATTHEW S. YOON, born Seoul, South Korea, September 2, 1972; admitted to bar, 1999, New York (Not admitted in District of Columbia). *Education:* State University of New York at Albany (B.A., cum laude, 1994); Washington College of Law of American University (J.D., 1999). Articles Editor, American University Law Review. *Member:* American Bar Association (Member, Business Section). ***LANGUAGES:*** Hungarian, Korean. ***Email:*** myoon@tpwlaw.com

(For complete biographical data on all members of firm and counsel, see Professional Biographies at New York, New York)

THALER LIEBELER, LLP

Established in 1996

1919 PENNSYLVANIA AVENUE N.W., SUITE 200
WASHINGTON, D.C. 20006
Telephone: 202-466-4110
Fax: 202-466-2693
URL: http://www.lawyers.com/thaler&liebelerlaw

Chevy Chase, Maryland Office: 8555 Connecticut Avenue, Suite 201, 20815. Telephone: 301-941-8081. Fax: 301-941-8082.
Fairfax, Virginia Office: 9691-A Main Street. Telephone: 703-978-9883. Fax: 703-978-9055.

Civil Litigation, Labor and Employment, Business Law, Antitrust and Trade Regulation, Construction Law, Contracts, Alternative Dispute Resolution, Corporate.

PAUL S. THALER, born Washington, D.C., May 4, 1961; admitted to bar, 1987, Maryland; 1988, District of Columbia, U.S. District Court, District of Maryland, U.S. District Court, District of Columbia, U.S. Court of Appeals, 4th and District of Columbia Circuits, U.S. Court of International Trade and U.S. Supreme Court. *Education:* Vassar College (A.B., 1983); Georgetown University (J.D., 1987). Mediator, Superior Court of the District of Columbia, 1992—. Adjunct Professor, Business Ethics, Kogod School of Business, American University, 1999—. *Member:* The District of Columbia Bar; Montgomery County, Maryland State and American (Member, Dispute Resolution Section; Vice-Chair, Ethics Committee, 1994-1998) Bar Associations. ***REPORTED CASES:*** Kramer vs. Tri-County Community Development Corporation, Inc.; 581 A.2d 429 (Md. App. 1991). ***PRACTICE AREAS:*** Civil Litigation; Business Law; Employment Law; Family Law; Alternative Dispute Resolution. ***Email:*** PThaler@ThalerLiebeler.com

LARS H. LIEBELER, born New York, New York, January 7, 1962; admitted to bar, 1987, California; 1988, District of Columbia. *Education:* Middlebury College (B.A., with honors, 1984); Indiana University (J.D., cum laude, 1987). Administrative Editor, Indiana Law Journal, 1986-1987. Author, "Trademark Law, Economics and Grey-Market Policy," 62 Indiana Law Journal 753, 1987. Law Clerk to the Honorable Terrence W. Boyle, U.S. District Judge, Eastern District of North Carolina, 1987-1988. Associate, Akin, Gump, Strauss, Hauer & Feld, Litigation Group, 1988-1994. *Member:* State Bar of California; The District of Columbia Bar; Bar Association of the District of Columbia (Member, Litigation Committee). ***REPORTED CASES:*** American Cyanamid Co. vs. Fermenta Animal Health, 1994 WL 279826 (D.N.J. 1994), 54 F.3d 177 (3d Cir. 1995). ***PRACTICE AREAS:*** Civil Litigation; Employment Law; Antitrust and Trade Regulation; Construction Law. ***Email:*** LLiebeler@ThalerLiebeler.com

OF COUNSEL

LILLIAM MACHADO, born Miami, Florida, May 8, 1963; admitted to bar, 1991, Pennsylvania; 1994, District of Columbia. *Education:* Tulane University (B.A., 1985); University of California, Hastings College of Law (J.D., 1991); Georgetown University. Member, 1989-1990 and Senior Project Editor, 1990-1991, Hastings Constitutional Law Quarterly. Recipient, American Jurisprudence Award for Legal Writing and Research, 1990. Author, "Defining Public Policy After Foley In Cases of "Internal Whistleblowing": A Play in One Act", 8 California Labor & Employment Law Quarterly 14, 1991. Teaching Assistant, Legal Writing and Research, University of California, 1989-1990. Extern Law Clerk, Hon. Joseph T. Sneed, U.S. Court of Appeals, Ninth Circuit, 1990. (Resident, Chevy Chase, Maryland Office). ***Email:*** LLMachado@aol.com

JANE LEMLEY RASMUSSEN, born Washington, D.C. November 22, 1967; admitted to bar, 1993, Virginia; 1995, District of Columbia. *Education:* University of Virginia (B.A., with high distinction, 1990; J.D., 1993). *Member:* District of Columbia Bar (Member, Employment Law Section). ***PRACTICE AREAS:*** Litigation; Employment Law. ***Email:*** JaneLRasmussen@aol.com

CATHLEEN SCHMIDT GORMLEY, born Norfolk, Virginia, April 20, 1961; admitted to bar, 1986, Virginia. *Education:* James Madison University (B.B.A., 1983); George Mason University (J.D., 1986). *Member:* Fairfax Bar Association; Virginia State Bar; National Association of Elder Law Attorneys. (Resident, Fairfax, VA Office). ***PRACTICE AREAS:*** Estate Planning; Estate Administration; Asset Protection; Tax Law; Business Formation; Civil Litigation. ***Email:*** gormlaw@erols.com

LAUREN A. GREENBERG, born Charlottesville, Virginia, April 3, 1971; admitted to bar, 1999, New York and Maryland; 2000, District of Columbia and U.S. Court of Appeals, 4th Circuit. *Education:* Dartmouth College (A.B., 1993); Catholic University-Columbus School of Law (J.D., 1998). Recipient, Miriam Rooney Memorial Scholarship. Editor-in-Chief, Journal of Contemporary Health Law and Policy, 1997-1998. Law Clerk, The Honorable Peter B. Krauser, Maryland Court of Special Appeals, 2000-2001. Author, "In God We Trust-Faith Healing Subject To Liability," 14 J. Contemp. Health Law and Policy, 1998. ***LANGUAGES:*** Spanish and French. ***PRACTICE AREAS:*** Litigation. ***Email:*** LGreenberg@ThalerLiebeler.com

REPRESENTATIVE CLIENTS: Marketing & Research Resources, Inc.; Tuckahoe Recreation Club, Inc.; ServiceMaster, L.P.; Computing Technology Industry Association; U.S. Seedless, L.L.C.; Medical Software Solutions, Inc.; Information Strategies, Inc.; IAMS; Pet Imaging, LLC; Oehme, van Sweden & Associates, Inc.

THELEN REID & PRIEST LLP

MARKET SQUARE
701 PENNSYLVANIA AVENUE, N.W.
WASHINGTON, D.C. 20004-2608
Telephone: 202-508-4000
Facsimile: 202-508-4321
URL: http://www.thelenreid.com

San Francisco, California Office: 101 Second Street, Suite 1800. Telephone: 415-371-1200. Fax: 415-371-1211.
Los Angeles, California Office: 34th Floor, 333 South Grand Avenue. Telephone: 213-621-9800. Fax: 213-623-4742.
Silicon Valley/San Jose, California Office: 17th Floor, 333 West San Carlos Street. Telephone: 408-292-5800. Fax: 408-287-8040.
New York, New York Office: 40 West 57th Street. Telephone: 212-603-2000. Fax: 212-603-2001.
Morristown, New Jersey Office: 65 Madison Avenue, Suite 100. Telephone: 973-644-3400. Fax: 973-644-3159.

General and International Practice. Antitrust and Trade Regulations, Bankruptcy, Business Litigation, Commercial Finance, Construction, Corporate, Environmental, Equipment Leasing, Franchising, Government Contracts, Insurance, Intellectual Property, Labor and Employment Relations, Mining, Project Finance, Real Estate and Land Use, Securities, Tax Benefits, Trusts and Estates, Technology Law, Tort Law, Energy, Utility, Entertainment, International, Internet, Telecommunications and Year 2000 Law.

FIRM PROFILE: Thelen Reid & Priest LLP is the result of the largest bicoastal law firm merger in history. The 400-attorney full-service firm, created on July1, 1998, combines the power and resources of California's Thelen, Marrin, Johnson & Bridges and New York-based Reid & Priest. Both predecessor firms had rich histories, with more than 130 years of combined service to a broad range of clients - from the industries that built this country to those that drive today's global information technology revolution. Thelen Reid & Priest LLP offers its clients the complementary strengths of two of the most respected law firms in the country and an unprecedented array of national and international legal sources.

DANIEL M. BERMAN, born Washington, D. C., October 2, 1957; admitted to bar, 1983, District of Columbia; 1984, U.S. Tax Court; 1997, U.S. Court of Federal Claims, U.S. Court of Appeals for the Federal Circuit and U.S. Supreme Court. *Education:* Harvard College (A.B., magna cum laude, 1979); Harvard Law School (J.D., cum laude, 1983). Phi Beta Kappa. Recipient, Endicott Peabody Saltonstall Prize. Member, Washington International Tax Study Group. Adjunct Professor of Law, Georgetown University Law Center, 1998—.

(This Listing Continued)

THELEN REID & PRIEST LLP, Washington—Continued

Deputy International Tax Counsel, U.S. Department of the Treasury, 1995-1997. Legislation Counsel, Joint Committee on Taxation of the U.S. Congress, 1989-1995. *American Bar Association (Member, Tax Section); International Fiscal Association.* ***PRACTICE AREAS:*** International Taxation; Tax Planning; International Law; Federal Legislative Practice; International Government Relations. ***Email:*** dberman@thelenreid.com

HOWARD A. COOPER, born Savannah, Georgia, July 12, 1955; admitted to bar, 1987, District of Columbia. *Education:* University of North Carolina (B.S., 1977); University of Virginia School of Law (J.D., 1980); Georgetown University Law Center (LL.M. in Taxation, 1987). Phi Beta Kappa. *Member:* American Bar Association (Section on Taxation); The District of Columbia Bar (Section on Taxation; Member, Committee on Regulated Public Utilities; Member, Committee on Capital Recovery and Leasing); National Association of Bond Lawyers. ***PRACTICE AREAS:*** Tax. ***Email:*** hcooper@thelenreid.com

BENJAMIN I. DELANCY, born Minneapolis, Minnesota, November 21, 1951; admitted to bar, 1979, California (Not admitted in District of Columbia). *Education:* Dartmouth College (A.B., 1973); University of Georgia (J.D., 1977). Order of the Coif. Law Clerk to Judge Lewis R. Morgan, U.S. Court of Appeals, Fifth Circuit, 1977-1978. ***PRACTICE AREAS:*** Employee Benefits; Executive Compensation. ***Email:*** bdelancy@thelenreid.com

DEBORAH A. DEMASI, born Newark, New Jersey, October 29, 1956; admitted to bar, 1980, New York; 1982, U.S. District Court, Southern and Eastern Districts of New York; 1986, District of Columbia. *Education:* Seton Hall University (B.A., summa cum laude, 1977); Fordham University (J.D., 1980). Member, Fordham Law Review, 1979-1980. *Member:* American Bar Association; Bar Association of The District of Columbia Bar; International Bar Association. ***PRACTICE AREAS:*** Infrastructure Development; Project Finance. ***Email:*** ddemasi@thelenreid.com

CHARLES M. ENGLISH, JR., born Alexandria, Virginia, March 30, 1959; admitted to bar, 1984, Virginia; 1985, District of Columbia; 1990, Maryland. *Education:* University of Virginia (B.S., 1981; J.D., 1984). *Member:* American Bar Association; Agricultural Law Association. ***REPORTED CASES:*** United States v. Hawkins, Nos. 87-5535, 87-5536, 87-5546, United States Court of Appeals for the Fourth Circuit, 836 F.2d 547; 1987 U.S. App. Lexis 16851, December 30, 1987, Decided, Rules of the Fourth Circuit Court of Appeals may Limit Citation to Unpublished Opinions. Please refer to the rules of the United States Court of Appeals for this Circuit; Also reported in the Bound Volume at: 836 F.2d 548; Northwestern Mut. Life Ins. Co. v. Atlantic Research Corp., Civil No. 93-1347-A, United States District Court for the Eastern District of Virginia, Alexandria Division, 847 F. Supp. 389; 1994 U.S. Dist. Lexis 3794; 38 ERC (BNA) 1811; 24 ELR 21165, March 29, 1994, Decided; Hillside Dairy, Inc. v. Veneman, No. 97-16571, United States Court of Appeals for the Ninth Circuit, 1998, U.S. App. Lexis 2783, February 9, 1998, Submitted, The Panel finds this case suitable for decision without oral argument. See Fed. R. App. P. 34(a); 9th Cir. R. 34-4., February 19, 1998, Filed Rules of the Ninth Circuit Court of Appeals may Limit Citation to Unpublished Opinions. Please refer to the of the United States Court of Appeals for this Circuit. Reported in Table Case Format at: 1998 U.S. App. Lexis 11449; Hillside Dairy, Inc. v. Lyonws, 259 F.3d 1148 (9th Cir. 2001). ***PRACTICE AREAS:*** Government Affairs. ***Email:*** cenglish@thelenreid.com

MARK FOX EVENS, born Richmond, Virginia, November 13, 1949; admitted to bar, 1975, Virginia; 1980, District of Columbia. *Education:* University of North Carolina at Chapel Hill (A.B., 1971); University of Virginia (J.D., 1975). Order of the Grail. Department of Justice, Trial Attorney, 1976-1982. *Member:* District of Columbia Bar; Virginia State Bar; American Bar Association (Section on Litigation, Government Contracts, Environmental Law). ***PRACTICE AREAS:*** Litigation. ***Email:*** mevens@thelenreid.com

LEE M. GOODWIN, born Baltimore, Maryland, September 6, 1950; admitted to bar, 1975, District of Columbia; 1980, U.S. Court of Claims and U.S. Tax Court. *Education:* Dartmouth College (A.B., cum laude, 1972); University of Michigan (J.D., cum laude, 1975). *Member:* Federal Energy Bar Association (Chairman, Committee on Non-Utility Generation, 1991-1992; Chairman, 1985-1986, 1990-1991, Vice Chairman, 1984-1985, 1989-1990, Committee on Taxation). ***SPECIAL AGENCIES:*** Federal Energy Regulatory Commission. ***PRACTICE AREAS:*** Electric Power and Infrastructure Project Acquisition; Development and Finance; Electric Power Regulation. ***Email:*** lgoodwin@thelenreid.com

ROBERT T. HALL, III, born Norfolk, Virginia, August 25, 1945; admitted to bar, 1971, District of Columbia; 1977, New York. *Education:* Washington & Lee University (B.S., 1967); Georgetown University (J.D., 1971). *Member:* The District of Columbia Bar; Federal Energy and American Bar Associations. ***PRACTICE AREAS:*** Infrastructure Development; Project Finance. ***Email:*** rhall@thelenreid.com

DAVID E. JACOBSON, born Port Chester, New York, 1949; admitted to bar, 1975, New York; 1976, District of Columbia. *Education:* University of Rochester (B.A., with distinction, 1971); State University of New York at Buffalo (J.D., cum laude, 1974); Georgetown University (LL.M. in Taxation, 1977). Attorney Advisor, Office of Chief Counsel, Internal Revenue Service, 1974-1979. Tax Counsel, Committee on Finance, United States Senate, 1979-1981. *Member:* The District of Columbia Bar; New York State (Section on Taxation) and American (Vice-Chair, 1988-1990 and Chair, 1990-1992, Regulated Public Utilities Committee, Tax Section) Bar Associations. ***PRACTICE AREAS:*** Tax. ***Email:*** djacobson@thelenreid.com

WILLIAM A. KIRK, JR., born Bryan, Texas, August 5, 1952; admitted to bar, 1983, District of Columbia. *Education:* Swarthmore College (B.A., 1974); Georgetown University (J.D., 1981). *Member:* The District of Columbia Bar; American Bar Association. ***PRACTICE AREAS:*** Government Affairs. ***Email:*** wkirk@thelenreid.com

RICHARD J. LEIDL, born Elmhurst, New York, 1951; admitted to bar, 1977, New York; 1979, District of Columbia. *Education:* Boston College (B.A., summa cum laude, 1973); University of Virginia (J.D., 1976). Phi Beta Kappa. *Member:* The District of Columbia Bar; New York State and American Bar Associations. ***PRACTICE AREAS:*** Government Affairs. ***Email:*** rleidl@thelenreid.com

PHILLIP G. LOOKADOO, born Hot Springs, Arkansas, July 28, 1953; admitted to bar, 1980, Georgia and District of Columbia. *Education:* West Virginia University (B.S., 1975); University of Virginia (M.S., 1977); Emory University (J.D., 1980). *Member:* The District of Columbia Bar; State Bar of Georgia; Energy Bar Association. ***PRACTICE AREAS:*** Infrastructure Development; Energy Marketing Transactions; Energy Regulation; Project Finance; International Transactions. ***Email:*** plookadoo@thelenreid.com

ANDREW F. MACDONALD, born Medina, New York, March 16, 1948; admitted to bar, 1973, District of Columbia; 1982, Ohio; 1993, Georgia. *Education:* University of Rochester (B.A., 1970); George Washington University (J.D., 1973); Georgetown University (LL.M., 1976). Attorney, Advisor, 1973-1976 and Special Counsel, 1976-1981, U.S. Securities and Exchange Commission. Attorney: American Electric Power Company, Inc., 1981-1984; Prudential Capital Corp. and Prudential Power Funding Associates, 1986-1990. Special Project Finance Counsel, U.S. Synthetic Fuels Corporation, 1984-1986. *Member:* The District of Columbia Bar; Federal Energy Bar Association. ***PRACTICE AREAS:*** Business; Finance. ***Email:*** amacdonald@thelenreid.com

STEPHAN M. MINIKES, born Berlin, Germany, 1938; admitted to bar, 1965, New York; 1977, District of Columbia. *Education:* Cornell University (B.S., 1961); Yale University (J.D., 1964). Member, Executive Committee, Yale Law School Association, 1981-1983, 1986-1989, 1994—. Senior Vice-President, Export-Import Bank of the United States, 1974-1977. Counsel to the Special Consultant to the President of the United States for Energy, 1973. Counsel and Special Assistant to the Chief of Naval Operations, 1972-1974. Member, Board of Directors, American Council on Germany, 1991—. *Member:* The District of Columbia Bar; Bar Association of the District of Columbia; The Association of the Bar of the City of New York; Federal and American Bar Associations; American Society of International Law. ***PRACTICE AREAS:*** Administrative Law; Government Contract Law; International Trade Law; Legislative Practice. ***Email:*** sminikes@thelenreid.com

JAMES K. MITCHELL, born Buffalo, New York, May 2, 1943; admitted to bar, 1971, New York; 1972, District of Columbia; U.S. Supreme Court, U.S. Court of Appeals for the District of Columbia Circuits and for the Fifth, Sixth, Eighth, Ninth and Eleventh Circuits; U.S. District Court for the District of Columbia. *Education:* Cornell University (B.S., 1964); New York University (M.B.A., 1970); University of Idaho (J.D., 1970). Member, Idaho Law Review, 1968-1970. *Member:* District of Columbia Bar; American Bar Association (Section of Administrative Law and Regulatory Practice); Federal Energy Bar Association, Edison Electric Institute Legal Committee. ***PRACTICE AREAS:*** Business; Finance. ***Email:*** jmitchell@thelenreid.com

ANDREW DAVID NESS, born San Francisco, California, October 29, 1952; admitted to bar, 1977, California; 1980, District of Columbia; 1986, Virginia. *Education:* Stanford University (B.S., 1974); Harvard University (J.D., magna cum laude, 1977). Tau Beta Pi. ***PRACTICE AREAS:*** Construction Law; Government Contracts. ***Email:*** adness@thelenreid.com

KEVIN O'BRIEN, born Washington, D.C., March 20, 1954; admitted to bar, 1984, California (Not admitted in District of Columbia). *Education:* Georgetown University (B.A., 1976); University of San Francisco (J.D., cum laude, 1984). Member, McAuliffe Honor Society. Articles Editor, University of San Francisco Law Review. *Member:* Bar Association of San Francisco; American Bar Association. ***PRACTICE AREAS:*** Construction Law; Environmental Litigation; General Commercial Litigation. ***Email:*** kobrien@thelenreid.com

MARK J. RIEDY, born Detroit, Michigan, April 1, 1953; admitted to bar, 1980, District of Columbia; U.S. District Court, District of Columbia; U.S. Court of Appeals, Federal and D.C. Circuits; U.S. Court of Claims; U.S. Tax Court; U.S. Court of International Trade. *Education:* University of Michigan (B.A., summa cum laude, Phi Beta Kappa; Phi Eta Sigma, 1975); Georgetown University Law Center (J.D., 1979). Board of Directors of the U.S.-India Business Council (General Counsel, 1994—), U.S.-India Subcommission (U.S. State Department appointed, 1995—), International Private Energy Association

(This Listing Continued)

(This Listing Continued)

(Chairman, India Energy Council, 1994—), Clean Fuels Development Coalition (General Counsel, 1995); Board of Advisors of American Council for Renewable Energy (General Counsel, 2001—), Indian American Republican Council (General Counsel, 2001—), Unit Trust of India Ventures Ltd. (2001—), Trade Builders Inc. (2001—), Long Beach-Calcutta Sister Cities Program (Chairman, 1997—); Member of U.S.-Bangladesh Business Council (General Counsel, 2000—), South Asia Regional Energy Coalition (General Counsel, 2001—), National Hydropower Association (Chairman, International Policy Committee (1997—), U.S.-India Commercial Alliance (Chairman, Energy Regulatory Committee, 1995—), Northern Virginia Technology Council (2000—), The Indus Entrepreneurs Association (2000—) and Indian CEO Council. ***LANGUAGES:*** Spanish. ***PRACTICE AREAS:*** Energy; Communications Law; Information Technology; International Trade; Project Finance. ***Email:*** mriedy@thelenreid.com

RICHARD Y. ROBERTS, born Birmingham, Alabama, July 3, 1951; admitted to bar, 1976, Alabama; 1981, District of Columbia. *Education:* Auburn University (B.E.E., 1973); University of Alabama School of Law (J.D., 1976); George Washington University National Law Center (LL.M., 1981). Commissioner, United States Securities and Exchange Commission, 1990-1995. Administrative Assistant and Legislative Director, United States Senator Richard Shelby, 1987-1990, and United States Representative Richard Shelby, 1979-1982. Author: "Leveling the Playing Field: The Need for Investor Protection for Bank Sales of Loan Participations," 63 Fordham Law Review 2115 (May 1995) (co-authored with Randall W. Quinn); "Environmental Liability Disclosure and Staff Accounting, Bulletin No. 95," 50 Business Lawyer 1 (November 1994) (co-authored with Kurt R. Hohl). ***PRACTICE AREAS:*** Business; Finance. ***Email:*** rroberts@thelenreid.com

KENNETH B. WEINER, born New York, N.Y., October 13, 1954; admitted to bar, 1986, New York; 1997, District of Columbia. *Education:* Case Western Reserve University (B.S.C.E., 1976); New York Law School (J.D., summa cum laude, 1986). Research Editor and Book Review Editor, New York Law School Law Review, 1985-1986. Professional Engineer, New Jersey, 1981. ***PRACTICE AREAS:*** Project Finance; Asset Based Finance; Franchise Law. ***Email:*** kweiner@thelenreid.com

OF COUNSEL

RAYMOND F. DACEK, born Cleveland, Ohio, September 25, 1930; admitted to bar, 1956, Ohio; 1975, District of Columbia. *Education:* University of Pennsylvania (B.S. in Econ., 1952); Harvard University (LL.B., 1956). Edison Electric Institute (Tax Consultant). Co-Author: "Federal Taxation of Energy," *Energy Law and Transactions,* 1990. *Member:* The District of Columbia Bar. ***PRACTICE AREAS:*** Tax. ***Email:*** rdacek@thelenreid.com

WILLIAM A. DEVAN, born Wilmington, Delaware, August 13, 1964; admitted to bar, 1993, Virginia (Not admitted in District of Columbia). *Education:* College of William & Mary (A.B., 1986; J.D., 1992); Queen Mary Westfield College, University of London, London, England (LL.M., 1993). *Member:* Virginia State Bar (Board of Governors, Construction Section). ***REPORTED CASES:*** Food Lion, Inc. v. S.L. Nusbaum Inc., 202 F.3d 223 (4th Cir. 2000); Spence - Parker v. Maryland Ins. Group, 937 F. Supp. 551 (E.D. Va 1998); Harrison & Bates, Inc. v. Featherstone Assocs., L.P., 484 S.E. 2d 883 (Va. 1997). ***PRACTICE AREAS:*** Construction; International Law; Commercial Law. ***Email:*** wdevan@thelenreid.com

KEITH S. FISCHLER, born New York, N.Y., September 20, 1957; admitted to bar, 1983, New York; 1984, District of Columbia; 1995, Virginia. *Education:* Cornell University (B.S., 1979); Georgetown University (J.D., cum laude, 1982). ***PRACTICE AREAS:*** Employment Law; Labor Law. ***Email:*** kfischler@thelenreid.com

STEVEN S. HONIGMAN, born Brooklyn, N.Y., May 14, 1948; admitted to bar, 1973, New York; 1974, District of Columbia; 1976, U.S. Supreme Court; U.S. Court of Appeals, Second and District of Columbia Circuits and U.S. Court of Military Appeals; U.S. District Court for the District of Columbia and Southern and Eastern Districts of New York. *Education:* New York University (B.A., 1969); Yale University (J.D., 1972). Phi Beta Kappa. Author: "Navy Blue Goes Green," *Proceedings* of the United States Naval Institute, August 1998. Recipient: Department of the Navy Distinguished Public Service Award, 1998; Aegis Excellence Award, 1995; Navy Achievement Medal, 1977. General Counsel of the Navy, 1993-1998. Public Member, Military Justice Act of 1983 Advisory Commission. Member, Executive Committee, Yale Law School Association. Member, United States Naval Institute. Director, DRS Technologies, Inc. (Chair, Ethics Committee and Member, Executive Compensation Committee) and The Wornick Company. Member, Finnish-American Chamber of Commerce. *Member:* The Association of the Bar of the City of New York; District of Columbia Bar; New York State and American (Chairman, Standing Committee on Military Law, 1986-1989) Bar Associations. Fellow, American Bar Foundation. ***PRACTICE AREAS:*** Commercial Litigation; Securities Litigation; Environmental Law; Nuclear Regulation; Government Contracts; International Defense Industry Business; Reinsurance. ***Email:*** shonigman@thelenreid.com

(This Listing Continued)

EDWARD L. PITTMAN, born Tampa, Florida, July 8, 1956; admitted to bar, 1984, Florida; 1992, District of Columbia. *Education:* University of Florida (B.A., 1978; J.D., 1984); Georgetown University (LL.M., 1988). Executive Editor, University of Florida Law Review. Chief Executive Officer and President, Quantitative Group of Funds, 1992-1998. Attorney, Brown & Wood, 1992. Staff Attorney, Special Counsel, Assistant Chief Counsel, Counsel to Commissioner Roberts, U.S. Securities & Exchange Commission, 1984-1992. Economics Assistant, Research Division, Commodity Futures Trading Commission, 1979-1980, 1981. *Member:* The Florida Bar; District of Columbia Bar. ***PRACTICE AREAS:*** Business; Finance. ***Email:*** epittman@thelenreid.com

JOHN R. SCHAEFGEN, JR., born Akron, Ohio, November 11, 1948; admitted to bar, 1978, District of Columbia. *Education:* Georgetown University (B.S., 1970; J.D., 1978). *Member:* The District of Columbia Bar; Federal Energy Bar Association. ***PRACTICE AREAS:*** Infrastructure Development; Project Finance. ***Email:*** jschaefgen@thelenreid.com

JOHANNES W. WILLIAMS, born Monroe, Michigan, May 22, 1957; admitted to bar, 1985, Wisconsin; 1986, U.S. Court of Appeals for the District of Columbia; 1987, District of Columbia; 1997, U.S. Supreme Court. *Education:* Ball State University (B.A., 1979); University of Wisconsin (M.A., 1981); Georgetown University (J.D., 1985). Contributing Author and Editor, *Criminal Practice Trial Manual,* published by D.C. Public Defender Service and the Bar Association of the District of Columbia, 1983-1990. Author: "Another Perspective: Supreme Support," *Electric Perspectives* (September/October 1999); "Free At Last: How the Powell Fugitive Slave Family Became and Stayed Free," with Judge Allen Sharp, XVII *Supreme Court Historical Society,* Quarterly, No. 1 (1996); "Open Transmission Access," 16 *IEEE Power Engineering Review,* No. 5 (May 1996). Instructor: Georgetown University Law Center, Legal Research and Writing, 1983-1985; Washington College of Law, The American University, Legal Methods, 1987-1988. [U.S. Navy, 1982]. (Director, Industry Legal Affairs). ***LANGUAGES:*** German. ***PRACTICE AREAS:*** Energy; Electric Industry Structure; Federal and State Regulation; Electric Utilities. ***Email:*** jwwilliams@thelenreid.com

RESIDENT ASSOCIATES

AMY B. COMER, born Belleville, Illinois, March 5, 1971; admitted to bar, 2000, New York (Not admitted in District of Columbia). *Education:* Utah State University (B.A., 1993); Tulane University of Louisiana (J.D., 1998). ***PRACTICE AREAS:*** Energy. ***Email:*** acomer@thelenreid.com

MICHELLE R. DEPUY, born LaGrande, Oregon, March 24, 1968; admitted to bar, 2000, Virginia and District of Columbia, U.S. District Court, Eastern and Western Districts of Virginia, U.S. District Court for the District of Columbia, U.S. Court of Federal Claims, U.S. Court of Appeals for the Federal Circuit. *Education:* Portland State University (B.A., with honors, 1996); George Washington University Law School (J.D., 1999). ***PRACTICE AREAS:*** Construction; Government Contracts; International. ***Email:*** mdepuy@thelenreid.com

JEFFREY R. GANS, born Elizabeth, New Jersey, September 30, 1966; admitted to bar, 1995, Virginia; 1996, District of Columbia. *Education:* University of Florida (B.A., 1989); Catholic University of America (J.D., magna cum laude, 1995). ***PRACTICE AREAS:*** Commercial Litigation; Construction Litigation; White Collar Criminal Defense. ***Email:*** jgans@thelenreid.com

NICHOLAS C. GEALE, born Santa Monica, California, December 18, 1974; admitted to bar, 1999, California; 2001, District of Columbia. *Education:* Claremont McKenna College (B.A., cum laude, 1996); Georgetown University (J.D., 1999). ***LANGUAGES:*** French. ***PRACTICE AREAS:*** Labor and Employment; Litigation. ***Email:*** ngeale@thelenreid.com

ANDREA LACHENMAYR, admitted to bar, 2000, New York; 2001, District of Columbia. *Education:* Wesleyan University (B.A., 1992); Georgetown University (J.D., 1999). ***PRACTICE AREAS:*** Business and Finance; Project and Asset Finance; General Corporate; Securities. ***Email:*** alachenmayr@thelenreid.com

SIMONE R. MCBEAN, born June, 1972; admitted to bar, 2000, New York (Not admitted in District of Columbia). *Education:* Northwestern University (B.S., 1994); Fordham University (J.D., 1999). ***PRACTICE AREAS:*** Mergers and Acquisitions; General Corporate; Long Term Financing/Indenture. ***Email:*** smcbean@thelenreid.com

CHRISTINE O'CONNOR, admitted to bar, 1989, Massachusetts; 1993, California; 1997, District of Columbia. *Education:* Georgetown University (B.A., 1984); University of Notre Dame (J.D., 1989). ***PRACTICE AREAS:*** Construction. ***Email:*** ocon7413@mlb.com

AMBARI PRAKASH, born Gorakhpur, U.P., India, February 8, 1970; admitted to bar, 1997, Connecticut; 1998, New York; 1999, District of Columbia. *Education:* University of Vermont (B.A., 1992); Georgetown University Law Center (J.D., 1997). ***LANGUAGES:*** Hindi, Spanish. ***PRACTICE AREAS:*** Corporate Law; Project and Asset Finance. ***Email:*** aprakash@thelenreid.com

SUSAN TAHERNIA, born Shiraz, Iran, September 3, 1964; admitted to bar, 1990, Maryland; 1991, District of Columbia; 1993, Virginia; 1994, Colorado and Minnesota; 1996, Pennsylvania; 1997, California. *Education:* Univer-

(This Listing Continued)

THELEN REID & PRIEST LLP, Washington—Continued

sity of Tulsa (B.A., summa cum laude, 1986); Georgetown University Law Center (J.D., 1989). (Resident, McLean, Virginia Office). ***PRACTICE AREAS:*** Labor and Employment. ***Email:*** stahernia@thelenreid.com

MARY MARGARET UTTERBACK, born Chestertown, Maryland, January 15, 1963; admitted to bar, 1991, Maryland; 1993, District of Columbia; 1996, Virginia; U.S. District Court, District of Maryland, the District of Columbia and Eastern District of Virginia; U.S. Court of Appeals for the District of Columbia, Fourth, Fifth and Sixth Circuits. *Education:* McGill University, Montreal, Quebec, Canada (B.A., with honors, 1985); University of Maryland School of Law (J.D., with honors, 1991). ***LANGUAGES:*** French and Chinese. ***REPORTED CASES:*** Breda Transp. v. Wash. Metro. Area Transit Auth., Civil Action No. PJM 01-551, United States Districts Court for the District of Maryland, 2001 U.S. Dist. Lexis 15400, August 30, 2001, Decided, August 30, 2001, Opinion Filed; Logan v. Burgers Ozark Country Cured Hams, Inc., No. 00-30652, United States Court of Appeals for the Fifth Circuit, 263 F.3d 447; 2001 U.S. App. Lexis 20309, September 12, 2001, Decided; Medical Mut. v. Denise DeSoto, Nos. 99-3988, 00-3571, United States Court of Appeals for the Sixth Circuit, 245 F.3d 561; 2001 U.S. App. Lexis 4895; 2001 Fed. App. 0083A (6th Cir.), September 21, 2000, Argued, March 27, 2001, Decided, March 27, 2001, Filed, Rehearing Denied May 25, 2001, Reported at: 2001 U.S. App. Lexis 11222; Reetz v. Jackson, Civil Action No. 96-1541 (PLF), United States District Court for the District of Columbia, 176 F.R.D. 412; 1997 U.S. Dist. Lexis 20644, November 20, 1997, Decided, November 21, 1997, Filed; Harris v. Otis Elevator Co., No. 1422, September Term, 1991, Court of Special Appeals of Maryland, 92 Md. App. 49; 606 A.2d 305; 1992 Md. App. Lexis 108, May 11, 1992, Filed. ***PRACTICE AREAS:*** Commercial Litigation; Intellectual Property; Health Care; Trade Regulation. ***Email:*** mutterback@thelenreid.com

TODD JASON WAGNON, born Wichita, Kansas, July 31, 1973; admitted to bar, 1998, Virginia; 1999, District of Columbia. *Education:* Georgetown University (B.S.F.S., 1994); George Washington University National Law Center (J.D., 1998). ***PRACTICE AREAS:*** Construction. ***Email:*** wagn7954@mlb.com

ALIYA WONG, born New York, N.Y., September 5, 1972; admitted to bar, 1998, New York (Not admitted in District of Columbia). *Education:* Yale University (B.A., 1994); New York University (J.D., 1997). ***PRACTICE AREAS:*** Employee Benefits; Taxation. ***Email:*** awong@thelenreid.com

WENDY M. YOVIENE, born Baltimore, Maryland, April 1, 1970; admitted to bar, 1998, Florida and District of Columbia; 1999, Virginia. *Education:* University of Virginia (B.A., 1992; J.D., 1997). ***PRACTICE AREAS:*** Government Affairs. ***Email:*** wyoviene@thelenreid.com

SPECIALISTS AND ADVISORS

Barry I. Berkoff (Legislative Representative)
Sharon Hardie (Legislative Representative)
Nancy K. West (Legislative Representative)

(For biographical data of firm's other attorneys, please see Professional Biographies at Los Angeles, San Francisco and San Jose, California and New York, New York).

THOMAS & LIBOWITZ, P.A.

WASHINGTON, D.C.

(See Baltimore, Maryland)

A full service law firm: Litigation in all Courts and Administrative Agencies. Business and Commercial Law (Corporate and Securities, Communications and Media Law, Construction Law. Mergers and Acquisitions, Financing (Public and Private Debt, Public and Private Equity and Conventional Commercial Financing Arrangements and Business Reorganizations) Tax Law, Franchising Regulation and Enforcement, Employment Law (Contracts, Compensation Plans, Harassment/ Discrimination Issues). International Law (representation of U.S. business in foreign jurisdictions and of foreign businesses in U.S). Banking, Bankruptcy, and Creditors' Rights (Banking/Bankruptcy workouts). Estate Planning and Charitable Trust and Foundations. Family Law, Product Liability, Insurance Defense, Real Estate, and Zoning.

THOMASON AND HESSMER, LLC

WASHINGTON, D.C.

(See Bethesda, Maryland)

Estate Planning, Estate Administration, Trust Administration, Elder Law, Trust Law, Probate, Guardianship, Federal Estate and Gift Taxation, Trusts and Estates Taxation, Business Estate Planning and International Estate Planning.

THOMPSON COBURN LLP

1909 K STREET, N.W., 6TH FLOOR
WASHINGTON, D.C. 20006-1101
Telephone: 202-585-6900
Telecopier: 202-585-6969
for attorney email use: first initial of first name, last name@thompsoncoburn.com e.g. aallred@thompsoncoburn.com
Email: info@thompsoncoburn.com
URL: http://www.thompsoncoburn.com

St. Louis, Missouri Office: One Firstar Plaza. Telephone: 314-552-6000. Telecopier: 314-552-7000.
Belleville, Illinois Office: 525 West Main Street. Telephone: 618-277-4700. Telecopier: 618-236-3434.

Admiralty, Antitrust, Business Immigration, Commercial Finance, Corporate, Government Contracts, International Trade and Transactions, Litigation, Maritime, Mass Transit, Postal, Transportation, Utilities.

MEMBERS OF FIRM

ANTHONY A. ANDERSON, admitted to bar, 1979, District of Columbia. *Education:* Johns Hopkins University (B.A., 1976); University of Virginia (J.D., 1979). ***PRACTICE AREAS:*** Mass Transit Federal Compliance; Americans with Disabilities Act; Administrative Law.

RICHARD K. BANK, admitted to bar, 1966, District of Columbia and Connecticut. *Education:* Cornell University (B.S., 1963; J.D., 1966). ***PRACTICE AREAS:*** International Trade; Maritime Law; Legislative Law.

MURRAY J. BELMAN, admitted to bar, 1960, District of Columbia. *Education:* Cornell University (A.B., 1957); Harvard University (J.D., cum laude, 1960). Attorney Adviser, 1961-1965, Assistant Legal Adviser for Economic Affairs, 1965-1967 and Deputy Legal Adviser, 1967-1969, Department of State. ***PRACTICE AREAS:*** International Trade; International Business; General Corporate.

BONNIE S. BLAIR, admitted to bar, 1976, District of Columbia. *Education:* Penn Morton College; Wesleyan University (B.A., summa cum laude, 1972); Harvard University (J.D., 1976). ***PRACTICE AREAS:*** Energy; Complex Litigation; Utilities.

R. LAWRENCE COUGHLIN, admitted to bar, 1959, Pennsylvania and District of Columbia; 1999, Montana. *Education:* Yale University (A.B., 1950); Harvard Graduate School of Business Administration (M.B.A., 1954); Temple University (J.D., 1958). ***PRACTICE AREAS:*** Government Relations; Transportation; International Commerce.

WARREN L. DEAN, JR., admitted to bar, 1975, Maryland; 1980, District of Columbia. *Education:* University of Maryland (B.A., 1972); University of Maryland School of Law (J.D., 1975); Georgetown University Law Center (LL.M., in Tax, 1979). Attorney: Office of the General Counsel, U.S. International Trade Commission, 1975-1977; Office of the Assistant General Counsel for International Law, Department of Transportation, 1978-1980; Office of International Tax Counsel, Department of the Treasury, 1982. Deputy Assistant General Counsel for International Law, Department of Transportation, 1981-1983. Assistant General Counsel for International Law, U.S. Department of Transportation, 1983-1988. ***PRACTICE AREAS:*** Antitrust and Trade Regulation; Transportation; Aviation and Aerospace.

EDWARD J. GILL, JR., admitted to bar, 1974, District of Columbia. *Education:* Georgetown University (A.B., 1968; LL.M., 1977); Columbus School of Law of the Catholic University of America (J.D., 1973). ***PRACTICE AREAS:*** Administrative Law; Construction Law; Legislative Law.

MICHAEL A. GREENSPAN, admitted to bar, 1965, New York; 1968, District of Columbia. *Education:* Cornell University (B.A., 1962); Columbia University (LL.B., 1965). Senior Attorney, 1969-1972 and Assistant Secretary, 1972-1973, Board of Governors of the Federal Reserve System. ***PRACTICE AREAS:*** Financial Institutions; Mergers and Acquisitions; Administrative.

MARJORIE F. KRUMHOLZ, admitted to bar, 1981, District of Columbia. *Education:* University of Rochester (B.A., magna cum laude, 1978); George Washington University (J.D., with honors, 1981). ***PRACTICE AREAS:*** Maritime Finance; Corporate Finance; General Corporate.

KATHERINE S. NUCCI, admitted to bar, 1981, District of Columbia. *Education:* University of Virginia (B.A., 1972); Catholic University of America (J.D., 1981). ***PRACTICE AREAS:*** Government Contract Law.

MICHAEL G. ROBERTS, admitted to bar, 1983, District of Columbia; 1994, Florida. *Education:* Michigan State University (B.A., 1977); American University (J.D., 1982). ***PRACTICE AREAS:*** Admiralty and Maritime Law; Legislative Practice; Transportation.

DAVID M. SCHWARTZ, admitted to bar, 1992, Texas; 1993, District of Columbia. *Education:* University of Texas at Austin (B.A., 1984); Fletcher

(This Listing Continued)

School of Law and Diplomacy (M.A.L.D., 1987); Harvard Law School (J.D., 1991). ***PRACTICE AREAS:*** International Trade; Commercial Litigation; Immigration.

EDWARD J. SHEPPARD, IV, admitted to bar, 1969, District of Columbia and Virginia. *Education:* Princeton University (A.B., cum laude, 1963); University of Virginia (LL.B., 1969). ***PRACTICE AREAS:*** Maritime Law; Transportation Law; International.

PATRICIA N. SNYDER, admitted to bar, 1978, Missouri; 1979, District of Columbia. *Education:* Lehigh University (B.A., 1974); Washington University (J.D., 1978). Attorney, Office of the General Counsel, Civil Aeronautics Board, 1979-1984; Office of the General Counsel, International Law, 1985-1995. ***PRACTICE AREAS:*** Aviation and Aerospace; Transportation; Environmental.

JANE SUTTER STARKE, admitted to bar, 1982, New York; 1988, District of Columbia. *Education:* Connecticut College (B.A., 1978); Hofstra University (J.D., 1981). ***PRACTICE AREAS:*** Transportation; Legislative Law.

GERALD D. STOLTZ, admitted to bar, 1974, Massachusetts; 1975, District of Columbia; 2000, New York. *Education:* Williams College (B.A., 1970); George Washington University (J.D., with honors, 1974). Law Clerk to Judge Frank H. Freedman, U.S. District Court, Boston, 1974-1975. ***PRACTICE AREAS:*** Maritime Finance; International Finance Law; Project Finance.

MARCELA B. STRAS, admitted to bar, 1980, District of Columbia. *Education:* University of Wisconsin (B.A., 1973); University of Miami (J.D., 1978); Georgetown University Law Center (LL.M., 1981). ***PRACTICE AREAS:*** International Trade Law; Immigration Law; Customs Law.

DAVID R. STRAUS, admitted to bar, 1970, District of Columbia. *Education:* Dartmouth College (A.B., 1967); University of Pennsylvania (J.D., 1970). Attorney, United States Postal Service, 1970-1973. ***PRACTICE AREAS:*** Administrative; Postal; Utility.

TIMOTHY SULLIVAN, admitted to bar, 1975, Virginia; 1976, District of Columbia. *Education:* University of Michigan (B.A., 1970); Georgetown University Law Center (J.D., 1975). ***PRACTICE AREAS:*** Government Contract Law.

G. KENT WOODMAN, admitted to bar, 1974, Oklahoma; 1976, District of Columbia. *Education:* Oklahoma State University (B.A., 1971); Vanderbilt University School of Law (J.D., 1974). ***PRACTICE AREAS:*** Transportation.

OF COUNSEL

MILTON D. ANDREWS, admitted to bar, 1963, Oklahoma; 1968, New York, District of Columbia and U.S. Supreme Court. *Education:* Phillips University (B.S., 1959); University of Oklahoma (J.D., 1963); George Washington University (LL.M., Foreign Trade and Investment Law, 1966); University of Paris, France. Trial Attorney, Civil Division and Civil Rights Division, U.S. Department of Justice (Honor Graduates Program), 1963-1966. ***PRACTICE AREAS:*** International Trade; Business Law; Immigration Law.

ASSOCIATES

EILEEN P. BROWN, admitted to bar, 1993, Pennsylvania; 1994, New York; 1999, District of Columbia. *Education:* Villanova University (B.A., 1990); Catholic University of America (J.D., 1993). ***PRACTICE AREAS:*** Maritime Finance; Corporate Finance; Maritime Law.

GABRIELA CARÍAS-TROCONIS, admitted to bar, 1992, Caracas, Venezuela; 2001, New York (Not admitted in District of Columbia). *Education:* Universidad Católica Andrés Bello (Abogado, 1992); American University (LL.M., 2000). ***PRACTICE AREAS:*** International Trade; Commercial Transactions; Tobacco Litigation.

JACQUELINE T. COLCLOUGH, admitted to bar, 1991, Maryland; 1992, District of Columbia; 1994, New York. *Education:* St. Anselm College (B.S.N., magna cum laude, 1988); Catholic University of America (J.D., 1991). ***PRACTICE AREAS:*** General Corporate; Transportation; Commercial Finance.

MATTHEW H. KAISER, admitted to bar, 1999, New York; 2000, District of Columbia. *Education:* American University (B.A., 1993); College of William and Mary (J.D., 1998). ***PRACTICE AREAS:*** Maritime Finance; International Finance; Admiralty and Maritime.

CARLA MILLER, admitted to bar, 1999, Maryland; 2001, District of Columbia. *Education:* University of Pennsylvania (B.S., 1995); Emory University School of Law (J.D., 1998). ***PRACTICE AREAS:*** Litigation; Transportation; International Trade.

MARK L. PARSONS, admitted to bar, 2001, New York (Not admitted in District of Columbia). *Education:* Ohio Wesleyan University (B.A., 1991); George Washington University (J.D., 2000). Phi Beta Kappa. ***PRACTICE AREAS:*** International Trade; Utility Law; Postal Law.

(This Listing Continued)

DAVID SEIDMAN, admitted to bar, 1997, Illinois; 2001, District of Columbia. *Education:* University of Pennsylvania (B.A., 1994); Washington University (J.D., 1997). ***PRACTICE AREAS:*** Transportation; Aviation; Maritime Law.

REPRESENTATIVE CLIENTS: *Financial:* Banc One Leasing Corp.; Bank of America; Bankers Trust Company; Banque Nationale de Paris; GATX Capital Corp.; General Electric Capital Corp.; Key Global Finance; Lazard Freres Co., LLC.; Senstar Capital Corp.; State Street Bank and Trust Company. *Transportation:* Air Transportation Association of America; Broward County, Florida; American Commercial Lines, LLC.; Cargill, Incorporated; Crowley Maritime Corp.; Federal Express Corporation; The Great Lakes Towing Company; Lake Charles Harbor and Terminal District; Oglebay Norton Company; Port of Palm Beach; Shell Bermuda (Overseas) Limited; South Carolina State Ports Authority. *Utilities:* American Municipal Power-Ohio, Inc.; Cities of Anaheim, Azusa, Banning, Colton and Riverside, Calif. *General:* American Business Press; Apasco, S.A. de C.V.; Appleton Papers, Inc.; Cold Finished Steel Bar Institute; Ispat Inland, Inc.; Kentucky Electric Steel, Inc.; Lukens, Inc.; Rapistan Demag Corporation; Riso, Inc.; Tecumseh Products Company; Urethane Products Corporation; Venepal, S.A.C.A.; World Bank. *Mass Transit:* Los Angeles Metropolitan Transportation Authority; Massachusetts Bay Transportation Authority; Regional Transportation Commission of Southern Nevada.

THOMPSON HINE LLP

1920 N STREET, N.W., SUITE 800
WASHINGTON, D.C. 20036-1600
Telephone: 202-331-8800
Fax: 202-331-8330
Telex: 904173
Cable Address: "Caglaw"
Email: Attorneys@ThompsonHine.com
URL: http://www.ThompsonHine.com

Cleveland, Ohio Office: 3900 Key Center, 127 Public Square, 44114-1216. Telephone: 216-566-5500. Fax: 216-566-5800. Email: Attorneys@ThompsonHine.com.

Cincinnati, Ohio Office: 312 Walnut Street, 14th Floor, 45202-4029. Telephone: 513-352-6700. Fax: 513-241-4771. Email: Attorneys@ThompsonHine.com.

Columbus, Ohio Office: One Columbus, 10 West Broad Street, 43215-3435. Telephone: 614-469-3200. Fax: 614-469-3361. Email: Attorneys@ThompsonHine.com.

Dayton, Ohio Office: 2000 Courthouse Plaza, N.E., 10 West Second Street, 45402-1706. Telephone: 937-443-6600. Fax: 937-443-6637, 937-443-6635. Email: Attorneys@ThompsonHine.com.

Brussels, Belgium Office: Place J. Jacobs 5, 1000 Brussels, Belgium, Telephone: 011 (32-2) 514-5400. Fax: 011 (32-2) 514-2932. Email: Attorneys@ThompsonHine.com.

Administrative Law, Admiralty and Maritime Law, Agency and Distributorships, Antitrust and Trade Regulation, Aviation and Aerospace, Bankruptcy, Banks and Banking, Biotechnology, Business Law, Business Litigation, Business Regulation, Business Transactions, Closely Held Business Law, Joint Ventures, Class Actions, Commercial Law, Commercial Real Estate, Communications and Media, FCC Regulation, Computers and Software, Construction Law, Contracts, Copyrights, Corporate Law, Corporate Finance, Corporate Litigation, Corporate Tax Controversies, Debtor and Creditor, Employee Benefits, ERISA, Energy, Energy Regulation, Environmental Law, Finance, Commercial Finance, Franchises and Franchising, General Practice, Government, False Claims Act, Qui Tam Litigation, Government Contracts, Health Care, Insurance Coverage, Insurance Regulation, Intellectual Property, International Law, International Trade, Internet Law, Labor and Employment, Litigation, Complex Litigation, Medicare Fraud and Abuse, Mergers, Acquisitions and Divestitures, Natural Resources, Nonprofit and Charitable Organizations, Occupational Safety and Health, OSHA, Partnership Law, Patents, Probate, Products Liability, Product Safety, Professional Liability, Public Finance, Railroad Law, Real Estate, Regulatory Law, Drug and Medical Device Regulation, Food and Drug Regulation, International Regulatory Law, Regulated Industries, Securities, Initial Public Offerings, Public Offerings, Taxation, Tax Controversies, Toxic Torts, Trade Secrets, Trademarks, Transportation, Trusts and Estates, Unfair Competition, Utility Law, White Collar Crime, Zoning, Planning and Land Use.

FIRM PROFILE: Established in 1911, Thompson Hine today is among the nation's largest corporate law firms and was recently selected as one of the Best Corporate Law Firms in America (in a survey of 32,000 corporate directors conducted by Corporate Board Member magazine). Thompson Hine attorneys serve some of the premier businesses in the world, including:

Alltel, Anthem Blue Cross/Blue Shield, Avery Dennison, BIC Corporation, Chiquita Brands International, Eaton Corporation, Evenflo Company, Eveready (Energizer), Ford Motor Company, Ford Motor Credit, Formica Corp., Goodrich Corporation, Goodyear Tire and Rubber Co., Hartford Insurance, Intimate Brands, Inc. (Victoria's Secret, Bath & Body Works), Jo-Ann Stores, Inc., Kelly Services, Inc., KeyCorp/KeyBank, Lexis-Nexis, The Mead Corporation, Medical Mutual of Ohio, Milacron Inc., Newell Rubbermaid, Nordson Corporation, Oglebay Norton Company, Ohio Bankers Association, Omnicare, Inc., Parker Hannifin, Polyone

(This Listing Continued)

THOMPSON HINE LLP, Washington—Continued

Corporation, Procter & Gamble, S.C. Johnson & Son, Inc., Sherwin-Williams, Smythe Cramer Co., SuperValu, Time Warner Cable, Toro Company, Verizon Wireless, and Whirlpool Corporation.

Thompson Hine attorneys provide a wide range of corporate legal services, represented by the following practice groups:

BANKRUPTCY - We represent major secured and unsecured lenders, creditors' committees, credit enhancement providers, debtors and various other parties of interest in finance transactions, workouts and bankruptcy matters.

BUSINESS LITIGATION - We represent corporate clients in a wide variety of business litigation - from corporate control contests and insurance disputes, to class actions, securities fraud, and tax controversies.

BUSINESS REGULATION & GOVERNMENT AFFAIRS - We regularly represent clients before state, federal and local agencies, including DOT, International Trade Commission, Consumer Product Safety Commission, Federal Reserve Board, FDIC, FCC, FAA, FDA, Federal Highway Administration, Federal Railroad Administration, FERC, PUCO, State Department of Insurance, Surface Transportation Board, Federal Motor Carrier Safety Administration and the Federal Maritime Commission.

COMMERCIAL & PUBLIC FINANCE - We handle complex commercial finance transactions (including senior debt, subordinated debt and mezzanine financing transactions and private debt placements), public finance, asset securitizations and general bank regulatory law.

COMPETITION, ANTITRUST & WHITE-COLLAR CRIME - We represent clients in antitrust and competition matters, trade restraint and price discrimination issues, franchising and distribution, misappropriation of trade secrets, false advertising, enforcement of noncompetition covenants and interference with business relationships.

CONSTRUCTION - We represent owners, design professionals, construction managers, contractors and sureties in connection with all facets of the building industry and have served in the role of Project Counsel for billions of dollars of construction at sites across the United States.

CORPORATE, M&A AND SECURITIES - We represent both emerging and established businesses in their most important business transactions, from start-up through IPOs, joint ventures, mergers, acquisitions and beyond.

eBUSINESS & EMERGING TECHNOLOGIES - This group unites experienced counsel from various disciplines around one central goal: helping business realize the opportunities and manage the risks of electronic and technological commerce.

EMPLOYEE BENEFITS - We advise clients regarding qualified, non-qualified and welfare benefit plans; resolution of controversies with the IRS, DOL, PBGC and other agencies; incentive and equity-based compensation arrangements; statutory and regulatory compliance; ERISA fiduciary duties; ESOPs; multi-employer plans; and ERSIA litigation.

ENVIRONMENTAL - We help clients understand the environmental aspects of their business transactions, craft methods of allocating risk and counsel them on their compliance obligations under local, state and federal laws.

HEALTH CARE - We represent physician groups, hospitals, clinical laboratories, diagnostic service providers, pharmaceutical manufacturers, medical device manufacturers and health insurance providers.

INTELLECTUAL PROPERTY - We assist clients with patents, trademarks, copyrights, trade secrets, computer software, internet related issues, employment relationships and intellectual property litigation.

INTERNATIONAL - We advise clients on trade regulation issues, customs and duty matters, foreign investment and joint ventures, NAFTA matters, importing and exporting issues, intellectual property protection, and immigration matters.

LABOR & EMPLOYMENT - We represent clients in employment litigation, workers' compensation proceedings, immigration matters, collective bargaining, administrative proceedings before the Department of Labor, OSHA, EEOC, NLRB and various state agencies.

PERSONAL & SUCCESSION PLANNING - We assist clients in the management and transmission of wealth, the succession to the control of businesses and other personal and family concerns.

PRODUCT LIABILITY - We have handled thousands of product liability matters involving mechanical, chemical, electrical, medical, aerospace, automotive and other products.

(This Listing Continued)

REAL ESTATE - We represent clients in Real Estate Development; Corporate Real Estate; Zoning and Land Use; Real Estate Investment and Financing; and Real Estate Investment Trusts.

TAXATION - We counsel clients in business transactions and financings, tax controversy, litigation, legislative and regulatory activities, executive compensation and tax planning, international taxation, state and local taxation and foundation and exempt organization matters.

AMOS BURT THOMPSON (1871-1965).
CHARLES P. HINE (1877-1942).
WALTER L. FLORY (1880-1951).
DAVID J. HOOKER (Managing Partner).
PATRICIA MANN SMITSON (Partner-in-Charge, Cincinnati).
PAUL N. HARRIS (Partner-in-Charge, Cleveland).
THOMAS J. BONASERA (Partner-in-Charge, Columbus).
JOSEPH M. RIGOT (Partner-in-Charge, Dayton).
DAVID H. BAKER (Partner-in-Charge, Washington, D.C.).

MEMBERS OF FIRM

DAVID H. BAKER, born Rome, New York, August 27, 1955; admitted to bar, 1979, District of Columbia. *Education:* Hamilton College (B.A., with honors, 1976), Sorbonne University and L' Institut d'Etudes Politiques, Paris, France; George Washington University (J.D., 1979). Member, Journal of International Law and Economics. Author: "Section 214 of the Staggers Rail Act: Is it Working as Congress Intended," 14 University of Denver Transportation Law Journal 205, 1986; "Third Time's The Charm: The Exemption for Ferry Service," Vol. 41, No. 3, *Your Letter of the Law,* 1991. Instructor, Transportation Regulation, University of Maryland and the Department of Defense (Military Traffic Management Command). Board Member, International Consumer Product Safety and Health Organization, 2001—. Member, American Society of Association Executives, 1997—. Co-Chair, CPSC Committee, American Bar Association, 1991—. Director, Bar Association of D.C., 1987-1990, 1991-1992. President, Association of Transportation Law, Logistics and Policy, 1997. (Partner-in-Charge, Washington, D.C.). ***LANGUAGES:*** French. ***PRACTICE AREAS:*** Transportation Law; Government Affairs; Regulatory Law; Product Safety Law. **Email:** David.Baker@ThompsonHine.com

KARYN A. BOOTH, born Niagara Falls, New York, July 7, 1967; admitted to bar, 1993, New York, District of Columbia; 1994, U.S. Court of Appeals, District of Columbia Circuit; 1995, U.S. District Court for the District of Columbia; 1997, U.S. Court of Appeals, Eighth Circuit; 1999, U.S. Supreme Court and U.S. Court of International Trade; 2001, U.S. District Court, District of Maryland. *Education:* Ithaca College (B.S., cum laude, 1989); Syracuse University (J.D., cum laude, 1992). Associate Editor, International Law Journal, Syracuse University, 1991-1992. Featured Columnist in *Ask the Attorney,* Joc Online, www.joc.com. Author: *Reform of the Carriage of Goods by Sea Act*, 33rd Transportation Law Institute Papers and Proceedings, Oct. 2000; *Service Contracts Under the Ocean Shipping Reform Act of 1998: Contracting From the Shipper*, Survey of Maritime Administrative Law, Vol. 8, 1999; *What Will the Future Hold for Railroad Customers?*, Survey of Maritime Administrative Law, Vol. 7, 1998; *Featured columnist for Ask the Attorney*, JOC Online, www.joc-.com. Participant in seminars and panels throughout the United States on the Ocean Shipping Reform Act of 1998 and proposed legislative reform of the Carriage of Goods By Sea Act. *Member:* New York State and American Bar Associations; District of Columbia Bar; Association of Transportation Law, Logistics and Policy (President, D.C. Chapter, 1999-2000); Maritime Administration Bar Association. ***PRACTICE AREAS:*** Transportation; Maritime Law; Administrative Law; Legislative. **Email:** Karyn.Booth@ThompsonHine.com

IRVING P. COHEN, born Port Chester, New York, February 22, 1941; admitted to bar, 1970, Maryland; 1971, District of Columbia; 1973, U.S. District Court, District of Maryland; 1974, U.S. Supreme Court. *Education:* New York University (B.S., 1963); Georgetown University (J.D., 1970). Certified Public Accountant, New York, 1967. Formerly of Semmes, Bowen & Semmes. *Member:* The District of Columbia Bar. (Resident). ***PRACTICE AREAS:*** Tax Law; Estate Planning; Business Law; Personal Planning; Successions. ***Email:*** Irv.Cohen@ThompsonHine.com

NICHOLAS J. DiMICHAEL, born Washington, D.C., January 10, 1948; admitted to bar, 1978, District of Columbia. *Education:* Marquette University (B.A., 1969); Queens College of the City University of New York (M.A., 1971); Georgetown University (J.D., magna cum laude, 1978). *Member:* The District of Columbia Bar; Federal Energy and American Bar Associations; Association for Transportation Law, Logistics and Policy. ***PRACTICE AREAS:*** Transportation; Energy; Administrative Law; Litigation. **Email:** Nick.Dmichael@ThompsonHine.com

CHARLES L. FREED, born Canton, Ohio, September 23, 1949; admitted to bar, 1974, Ohio; 1979, District of Columbia; 1980, U.S. Supreme Court.

(This Listing Continued)

Education: Miami University (B.A., cum laude, 1971); Northwestern University (J.D., cum laude, 1974). Associate Editor of Antitrust Magazine published by the Antitrust Section of the American Bar Association. Author: "Antitrust and the Duty to License Intellectual Property - Can Manufacturers Be Compelled to Deal with ISO's?" Antitrust; Fall, 1999; "Current Status of the Keogh Doctrine," ICC Practitioners' Journal, 1984; "Reconsidering the Per Se Approach to Tying Agreements," University of Toledo Law Review, 1982. Lecturer: "Product Launches - Distribution Alternatives and Issues," Ohio State Bar Association Corporate Counsel Section Seminar, 1999; "Planning and Negotiating an Acquisition to Minimize Risk," Ohio State Bar Association 32nd Annual Antitrust Institute, 1998; "The Antitrust and Intellectual Property Interface," American Bar Association, Intellectual Property Section, 1997. *Member:* American Bar Association (Member, Antitrust Section; Chair of the Private Antitrust Litigation Committee, 1995-1998; Associate Editor of Antitrust); District of Columbia Bar (Member, Antitrust and Trade Regulation Section); American Bar Association Forum on Franchising. ***TRANSACTIONS:*** Representation of numerous clients in mergers investigations, including PVC version, circuit board laminates hydraulic components, aerospace components, hospital equipment, children's car seats, retail fabrics and crafts, radio stations, aluminum sheet and foil, and machine tools. Representation of clients in antitrust and unfair competition suits involving supermarkets, ATM Networks, long distance telephone service, industrial fittings, and industrial valves. Representation of clients of franchise and distribution issues, including litigation crisis, out of franchise and distributor terminations and preparation of franchise disclosure materials. ***PRACTICE AREAS:*** Antitrust and Trade Regulation; Franchising; Competition; Health Care. ***Email:*** Chuck.Freed@ThompsonHine.com

BARRY A. FRIEDMAN, born New York, N.Y., June 15, 1951; admitted to bar, 1976, New York; 1977, District of Columbia; 1983, Maryland. *Education:* State University of New York at Buffalo (B.A., 1972); Boston University (J.D., 1975). Phi Beta Kappa. Formerly of Semmes, Bowen & Semmes. Author: "The Effect of Petroleum Divestiture on Price and Supply," The Future of American Oil, 1976. Co-Author, "Consumer Redress Through the Small Claims Court: A Model Consumer of Justice Act," Industry & Communications Law Review, 1977. Book Review, "Ling: The Rise, Fall and Return of a Texas Titan," 1973. *Member:* The District of Columbia Bar; American Bar Association (Member, Telecommunications Committee; Business Law Section)Federal Communications Bar Association; Maryland Lawyers for the Arts. (Resident). ***PRACTICE AREAS:*** Communications Law; Commercial Law; Administrative Law; Corporate Law; Securities; Government Affairs; Regulatory Law; Taxation. ***Email:*** Barry.Friedman@ThompsonHine.com

FREDERICK B. GIBBON, born Boston, Massachusetts, January 1, 1945; admitted to bar, 1972, Ohio; 1983, District of Columbia. *Education:* Yale University (B.A., 1967); University of Virginia (J.D., 1972). ***PRACTICE AREAS:*** Employee Benefits Law. ***Email:*** Fritz.Gibbon@ThompsonHine.com

PETER A. GREENE, born Brooklyn, New York, March 28, 1937; admitted to bar, 1966, District of Columbia; 1970, U.S. Supreme Court. *Education:* St. John's University (B.B.A., 1958); Georgetown University (J.D., 1966). Author: "Restrictions on Off-Bill Discounting: Saying No to the Marketplace," Papers and Proceedings, 65th Annual Meeting, Association of Transportation Law, Logistics and Policy; 1994; "Federal Preemption of Motor Carrier Acquisitions," Papers and Proceedings, 23rd Annual Transportation Law Institute, 1990; Motor Carrier Section, Annual Report of Section of Public Utilities, Communication and Transportation Law, American Bar Association, 1987-1995; "Impact of Staggers Act on Legal Remedies Available to Shippers," Papers and Proceedings, Western Transportation Law Institute, 1981. President, Association of Transportation Law, Logistics and Policy, 1989-1990. *Member:* District of Columbia Bar; American (Member, Public Utilities Section; Communications and Transportation Law; Council Member, 1992-1994; Administrative Law and Regulatory Practice Section) and Federal Bar Associations; Transportation Lawyers Association. ***PRACTICE AREAS:*** Transportation Law; Government Affairs; Regulatory Agency Practice; Administrative and Regulatory Law. ***Email:*** Peter.Greene@ThompsonHine.com

JEFFREY O. MORENO, born Palatka, Florida, May 5, 1966; admitted to bar, 1991, Virginia; U.S. Court of Appeals, Fourth Circuit; 1992, U.S. Court of Appeals, District of Columbia Circuit; 1993, District of Columbia; 2001, U.S. District Court for the District of Columbia. *Education:* Eckerd College (B.A., with Honors, 1988); Georgetown University (J.D., 1991). Co-author: "Preemption of Local Regulation of Radio Antennas," Federal Communications Law Journal, Vol. 46, No. 3, June, 1994; "Transportation," *Fourth Edition of the Kirk-Othmer Encyclopedia of Chemical Technology*. *Member:* District of Columbia Bar; Virginia State Bar; Federal Communications and American Bar Associations; Association of Transportation Law (Logistics and Policy); National Association of Telecommunications Officers and Advisors. ***PRACTICE AREAS:*** Communications; Transportation; Administrative Law. ***Email:*** Jeff.Moreno@ThompsonHine.com

MARK ROY SANDSTROM, born Buffalo, New York, September 30, 1942; admitted to bar, 1969, Michigan; 1972, District of Columbia; 1975, U.S. Court of International Trade; 1976, U.S. Supreme Court. *Education:* University of Tubingen, Germany (1962-1963); University of Michigan (B.A., 1964; J.D., 1968); University of Munich, Germany (1968-1969). Attorney-Advisor, Office of Assistant General Counsel for International Affairs, U.S. Treasury Department, 1969-1973. Professional Staff Member, U.S. Senate Committee on Finance, 1973-1975. Former Co-Chair, International Trade Committee, Council Member, Section of International Law and Practice, American Bar Association; Life Member, American Society of International Law. Author: "Summary of the U.S. Antidumping Statute," International Quarterly, Business Laws, Inc., 1997; "Market Access: Overview of Tariffs and Other Border Measures Affecting Access to Foreign Markets," The World Trade Organization, Multilateral Trade Framework for the 21st Century and U.S. Implementing Legislation, American Bar Association, 1996. ***LANGUAGES:*** German, French and Spanish. ***PRACTICE AREAS:*** International Trade Law; Customs Law; International Business Law; Government Affairs; Regulatory Law. ***Email:*** Mark.Sandstrom@ThompsonHine.com

DANIEL E. TOOMEY, born Brooklyn, New York; admitted to bar, 1968, District of Columbia; 1973, U.S. Supreme Court; 1977, Maryland; 1990, Virginia. *Education:* St. Peter's College (B.A., 1964); Georgetown University (J.D., 1967). Fellow, American College of Trial Lawyers. Author: "The Scheduling Expert: A Primer on Selection and Preparing Direct and Cross," The Construction Lawyer, April 1995; "The Indemnity Clause and Insurance," Forum on the Construction Industry, 10th Annual Meeting, American Bar Association, April 1994; "Surety, Insurance, Construction and Hazardous Waste: A Toxic Mix?" The Construction Lawyer, January, 1994; "Good Faith and Fair Dealing: The Well-Nigh Irrefragable Need for a New Standard in Public Contract Law," 20 Pub.C.L.J.87 (1990); "What Every Construction Executive Should Know About Criminal Law and Ethics When Considering Contracting with the U.S. Government," Associated Builders and Contractors of Virginia, 1994. Co-Author: "Too Many Hats? Representing Sureties Principals, Indemnitory Insure & Insurers in Construction Contracts," Forum on the Construction Industry, 12th Annual Meeting, American Bar Association, May 1996; "Who Do You Trust: What Fiduciary Responsibility Does the Surety Have to it Principal," National Bond Claims Association Seminar Surety Have to its Principal, October 1998; "Express Warranties and Sick Building Syndrome," Mealy's Sick Building Litigation Conference, November 1999; "Debarment and Suspension"; Construction Briefings, Federal Publications, Inc., Edition III, March 1989; "Chapter 6 - Proving & Pricing Construction Claims," Disruption Claims, NY, John Wiley & Sons, 1996; "Disruption Claims," Proving and Pricing Construction Claims, Chapter 6, pp. 141-166, *New York:* John Wiley & Sons; 1990; "Civil and Criminal Liability for Improperly Obtained Information - The Continued Drift of Ill Wind," Public Contract Law Committee, Spring Meeting, 1989. Lecturer: Forum on the Construction Industry and Torts and Insurance Practice Section Joint Program, American Bar Association, January 1995; IADC Program, Committee on Fidelity and Surety Law, American Bar Association, Demonstrator, Jan 1995/Jan 1996; Torts and Insurance Practice Section, American Bar Association National Convention, Moderator; August 1995; Forum on the Construction Industry, Tenth Annual Meeting, Panelist, April 1994; "Ethics in Government Contracting," Judicial Conference of the U.S. Court of Federal Claims Presenter, 1999; Forum on the Construction Industry, 12th Annual Meeting, Moderator; 1996; The National Institute: Shaping the Future of Public Construction and Suretyship, 1992; Procurement Integrity and Compliance, sponsored by the American Bar Association's Section of Public Contract Law, entitled "Civil and Criminal Liability for Improperly Obtained Information - The Continued Drift of Ill Wind," 1989. Adjunct Professor of Law: Construction Contracts; Criminal Trial Practice (Graduate Program), Georgetown University Law Center, 1978—; Intensive Session on Trial Advocacy Skills, Washington, D.C. Team Leader, Georgetown University Law Center, 1978—; National Institute of Trial Advocacy (NITA) Faculty at Harvard Law School Teacher's Program and Boulder, Colorado National Basic and Advanced courses, 1977—. Law Clerk, D.C. Court of Appeals. Member, Advisory Committee to U.S. Court of Federal Claims. Assistant U.S. Attorney for the District of Columbia. Mediation Panel, U.S. District Court for the District of Columbia, 1998—. *Member:* American Bar Association (Public Contract Law Section: Surety Bonds Committee, Former Vice-Chair, Construction Law Committee; Litigation Section; Forum Committee on the Construction Industry, Division 7 Chair, 1995-1997; Torts and Insurance Practice Section, Fidelity and Surety Committee); District of Columbia Bar; Assistant U.S. Attorneys' Association of the District of Columbia (Former President); Washington Building Congress; Surety Claims Institute; National Bond Claims Association; The Barristers; The Counsellors. ***LANGUAGES:*** Spanish. ***PRACTICE AREAS:*** Construction; Surety; Competition; Government Contracts; Commercial Litigation; White Collar Crime; Mediation Services. ***Email:*** Dan.Toomey@ThompsonHine.com

THOMAS W. WILCOX, born Washington, D.C., March 25, 1958; admitted to bar, 1987, Virginia and U.S. Court of Appeals, Fourth Circuit; 1988, District of Columbia. *Education:* Utah State University (B.S., 1980); George Mason University School of Law (J.D., 1987). Associate Editor, George Mason University Law Review, 1987. *Member:* Virginia State Bar, American and Federal Energy Bar Associations; District of Columbia Bar; Association for Transportation Law, Logistics and Policy. ***PRACTICE AREAS:*** Transportation; Electric Utility Regulation; Environmental Law; Natural Resources; Government Affairs and Regulations. ***Email:*** Tom.Wilcox@ThompsonHine.com

(This Listing Continued)

(This Listing Continued)

THOMPSON HINE LLP, Washington—Continued

FREDERIC L. WOOD, born Altoona, Pennsylvania, November 7, 1945; admitted to bar, 1970, District of Columbia; 1974, U.S. Supreme Court; 1992, Maryland. *Education:* University of Pennsylvania (A.B., 1967); George Washington University (J.D., with honors, 1970). *Member:* District of Columbia Bar; American Bar Association; Association for Transportation Law, Logistics and Policy. ***PRACTICE AREAS:*** Appellate Practice; Administrative Law; Transportation; Taxation and Employee Benefits; Estate Planning Law; Antitrust; Trade Regulation. ***Email:*** Rick.Wood@ThompsonHine.com

ASSOCIATES

FRANK S. BALDINO, born Hackensack, New Jersey, April 5, 1962; admitted to bar, 1987, New Jersey and U.S. District Court, District of New Jersey; 1988, U.S. Tax Court; 1990, New York and District of Columbia. *Education:* Muhlenberg College (B.A., 1984); Seton Hall University (J.D., 1987); New York University (LL.M. in Taxation, 1990). Attorney, Advisory to Judge Perry Shields, United States Tax Court, 1990-1992. *Member:* District of Columbia Bar (Member, Tax Section, Committee on Estate Planning; Estates, Trusts and Probate Section); American Bar Association (Member, Real Property, Probate and Trust Section) Financial Planning. ***PRACTICE AREAS:*** Taxation; Corporate Law; Business Planning; Personal Planning; Successions; Estate Planning; Estate Administration; Charitable Giving. ***Email:*** Frank.Baldino@ThompsonHine.com

DAVID M. CHURCH, born Anchorage, Alaska, January 25, 1974; (admission pending). *Education:* Northwest Nazarene College (B.A., 1996); George Fox University (M.A., 1997); Washington & Lee University (J.D., 2001). Oregon Teaching License, 1997. *Member:* American Bar Association. ***PRACTICE AREAS:*** Business Litigation; Personal Succession Planning. ***Email:*** David.Church@ThompsonHine.com

CAROLINA COLL, born Buenos Aires, Argentina, February 11, 1970; admitted to bar, 2000, Virginia (Not admitted in District of Columbia). *Education:* United States Military Academy (B.S., 1992); Georgetown University Law Center (J.D., cum laude, 2000). Studies of Latin America. Distinguished Cadet. Member, West Point Society of D.C. [Captain (Military Intelligence), U.S. Army, 1992-1997]. ***LANGUAGES:*** Spanish. ***PRACTICE AREAS:*** Customs Law; International Trade; Antitrust; FCC Regulation. ***Email:*** Carol.Coll@ThompsonHine.com

SCOTT A. HARVEY, born Washington, D.C., June 15, 1966; admitted to bar, 1991, Pennsylvania; 1993, Virginia; 1994, District of Columbia; 1996, U.S. District Court, Eastern District of Virginia; U.S. Bankruptcy Court, Eastern District of Virginia; 1997, U.S. District Court, Western District of Virginia. *Education:* University of Virginia (B.A., with honors, 1988; J.D., 1991). Phi Beta Kappa. Co-Author: "Hazardous Chemicals and the Right to Know: A Guide to Compliance with SARA Title III," Executive Enterprises, Inc. (1992). Contributing Author: "Environmental Crimes," Shepards-McGraw Hill Publishing Co. (1992). ***PRACTICE AREAS:*** Environmental; Administrative Law; Litigation. ***Email:*** Scott.Harvey@ThompsonHine.com

MICHAEL H. HIGGINS, born Washington, D.C., February 14, 1972; admitted to bar, 2000, Maryland. *Education:* Swarthmore College (B.A., 1995); American University (J.D., 2000). ***PRACTICE AREAS:*** Transportation. ***Email:*** Mike.Higgins@ThompsonHine.com

KARL M. LASKAS, born Pittsburgh, Pennsylvania, April 7, 1970; admitted to bar, 1999, Ohio (Not admitted in District of Columbia). *Education:* University of Pittsburgh (B.A., magna cum laude, 1990); Yale University (M.A., magna cum laude, 1993); University of Virginia School of Law (J.D., 1999). ***PRACTICE AREAS:*** Intellectual Property; Government Affairs; Regulations. ***Email:*** Karl.Laskas@ThompsonHine.com

STEPHEN T. LOVELADY, born Ithaca, New York, November 2, 1957; admitted to bar, 1990, Texas; 1997, Maryland; 1998, District of Columbia. *Education:* Florida Atlantic University (B.S.M.E., 1978); University of Houston Law Center (J.D., cum laude, 1990). Order of the Coif. Associate Editor, Houston Law Review, 1989-1990. Co-Author, with J. Lanier Yeates, Indemnification and Anti-Indemnity Statutes - Part II, 38th Annual Mineral Law Institute (Louisiana State University), 1991. *Member:* State Bar of Texas; District of Columbia Bar (Member, Corporate, Finance and Securities Law Section; Computer and Telecommunications Law Section); Federal Communications Bar Association. ***PRACTICE AREAS:*** Commercial Transactions; Corporate; Securities; Real Estate; Banking; General Business Matters. ***Email:*** Steve.Lovelady@ThompsonHine.com

JULIA M. MCCALMON, born Los Angeles, California, July 2, 1969; admitted to bar, 1996, Virginia; 1998, District of Columbia. *Education:* California State University (B.A., Political Science and American Studies, magna cum laude, 1992); Georgetown University (J.D., 1995). Senior Notes Editor, American Criminal Law Review. Law Fellow, Legal Research and Writing. Co-Author: "Market Access," The World Trade Organization, Multilateral Trade Framework for the 21st Century and U.S. Implementing Legislation, 1996; "Summary of the U.S. Antidumping Statute," Laws of International Trade, March 1998; "Controls on Foreign Investments in the United States," Doing Business in and With the United States, 1999; "White Collar Crime," American Criminal Law Review, 1993. *Member:* District of Columbia Bar (Member, International Law Section); American Bar Association (Member, International Law and Practice Section; ILEX Committee Vice Chair). ***LANGUAGES:*** Chinese (Mandarin and Cantonese). ***TRANSACTIONS:*** Representation of clients in the agriculture, paper, textile, chemical and defense industries. ***PRACTICE AREAS:*** Customs Law; Export Licensing; International Trade Law. ***Email:*** Julia.Mccalmon@ThompsonHine.com

TAMARA M. MCNULTY, born Wauwatosa, Wisconsin, 1967; admitted to bar, 1995, Wisconsin and U.S. District Court, Western District of Wisconsin; 1996, Virginia and U.S. Court of Appeals, Fourth Circuit; 1997, U.S. District Court, Eastern District of Virginia; 1999, District of Columbia, U.S. District Court, District of Columbia, U.S. Bankruptcy Court, Eastern District of Virginia and U.S. Court of Appeals, District of Columbia Circuit; 2000, U.S. District Court, District of Maryland; 2001, U.S. District Court, Western District of Virginia. *Education:* University of Wisconsin (B.A., 1991; J.D., 1995). Phi Alpha Delta. Author, Publications: "The Telecommunications Decency Act: A First Amendment Analysis," New Tech News, November 1995; "The Communications Decency Act: The Saga Continues," New Tech News, May 1997. Lecturer: "Cinderella's Shoes are Too Small: The Surety's Limited Right to Assert the Pay-When-Paid Clause Defense of Its Principal," National Bond Claims Association Annual Meeting, October 2000. Speaker, "Performance and Payment Bond Surities and Their Roles," Lohrman Conference on Construction Law, June 2001. *Member:* The District of Columbia Bar; Virginia State Bar (Member, Construction and Litigation Section); State Bar of Wisconsin (Member, Young Lawyer's Division; Non-Resident Lawyers Division); American Bar Association (Member, Litigation, Tort and Insurance Practice Section and Environment Section), National Bond Claims Association; Washington Building Congress; National Institute of Trial Advocacy;. ***PRACTICE AREAS:*** Construction Litigation; Commercial Litigation. ***Email:*** Tamara.Mcnulty@ThompsonHine.com

JENNIFER L. NOAH, born Buffalo, New York, June 1, 1973; admitted to bar, 1999, New York and U.S. District Court, Western District of New York; 2001, District of Columbia. *Education:* State University of New York at Geneseo (B.S., 1995); State University of New York at Buffalo (J.D., 1998). Member, Delta Mu Delta, National Business Honor Society. Member, Moot Court Board. *Member:* New York State and American Bar Associations. ***PRACTICE AREAS:*** Government Affairs; Regulations. ***Email:*** Jennifer.Noah@ThompsonHine.com

BARBARA E. PARISI, born October 21, 1972; admitted to bar, 1997, Virginia; 1999, District of Columbia. *Education:* University of Virginia (B.A., 1994; J.D., 1997). ***PRACTICE AREAS:*** Consumer Product Safety. ***Email:*** Barbara.Paris@ThompsonHine.com

CHRISTOPHER D. PERRY, born Charleston, West Virginia, November 6, 1965; admitted to bar, 1997, Virginia and U.S. District Court, Eastern District of Virginia; 1998, District of Columbia. *Education:* Virginia Polytechnic Institute and State University (B.S., 1989); Case Western Reserve University (J.D., magna cum laude, 1997). Order of the Coif. *Member:* Virginia State Bar (Member, International Law Section) and American Bar Association (Member, International Law and Practice Section). ***PRACTICE AREAS:*** Customs Law; Import and Export Law; International Trade; Transportation; Construction; Government Affairs; Regulatory Law. ***Email:*** Chris.Perry@ThompsonHine.com

ANGELA M. VARNER, born Southfield, Michigan; admitted to bar, 1999, District of Columbia; 2000, Michigan. *Education:* University of Michigan (B.A., 1994); Howard University School of Law (J.D., 1999). Judicial Law Clerk, Michigan Supreme Court. ***PRACTICE AREAS:*** Personal and Succession Planning; Corporate Law; Securities. ***Email:*** Angela.Varner@ThompsonHine.com

SENIOR ATTORNEY

AMY G. DAVIES, born San Francisco, California, April 26, 1956; admitted to bar, 1985, District of Columbia. *Education:* Oberlin College (B.A., 1979); University of Wisconsin (J.D., 1984). ***PRACTICE AREAS:*** Employee Benefits Law; ERISA. ***Email:*** Amy.Davies@ThompsonHine.com

OF COUNSEL

GILBERT B. LESSENCO, born Baltimore, Maryland, June 19, 1929; admitted to bar, 1953, District of Columbia; 1955, Maryland. *Education:* Johns Hopkins University (B.S., 1950); Harvard University (LL.B., 1953). Omicron Delta Kappa. Named Outstanding Young Lawyer of the Year by the Junior Bar Section of the Bar Association of the District of Columbia, 1965. Listed in: *Who's Who in America; Who's Who in the Law.* Commissioner, 1987-1992, Chairman, 1989-1990, Washington Suburban Sanitary Commission. Formerly of Semmes, Bowen & Semmes. Professor, Johns Hopkins University Graduate School of Professional Studies in Business and Education, Teaching Marketing and Business Law, 1997—. *Member:* The District of Columbia Bar. [First

(This Listing Continued)

Lieut., U.S.A.F., 1953-1955]. (Resident). ***PRACTICE AREAS:*** Consumer Product Safety Commission; Lobbying; Administration Law; Estate; Government Affairs; Regulatory Law. ***Email:*** Gil.Lessenco@ThompsonHine.com

JOHN K. MASER III, born New Holland, Pennsylvania, February 12, 1945; admitted to bar, 1973, District of Columbia, U.S. Court of Appeals for the District of Columbia, Third, Fourth, Fifth, Sixth, Seventh and Tenth Circuits; U.S. Bankruptcy Courts. *Education:* Pennsylvania State University (A.B., 1967); Georgetown University (J.D., 1972). Rail Editor, Journal of Transportation Law, Logistics and Policy, 1989—. President, National Association of Transportation Law, Logistics and Policy, 1983-1984. *Member:* District of Columbia Bar; American Bar Association; Association for Transportation Law, Logistics and Policy. ***PRACTICE AREAS:*** Administrative Law; Transportation Law. ***Email:*** Jack.Maser@ThompsonHine.com

STAFF ATTORNEY

PATRICIA W. S. DOUGLAS, born Bridgeport, Connecticut, November 6, 1950; admitted to bar, 1981, Kansas; 1992, District of Columbia. *Education:* Southern Connecticut State College (B.A., 1977); Washburn University of Topeka (J.D., 1981). Compliance Manager, Segal Co., 1988-1992 and 1992-1995; Associate, Slevin & Hart, D.C., 1995-1998. *Member:* District of Columbia Bar. ***PRACTICE AREAS:*** Employee Benefits; ERISA. ***Email:*** Patricia.Douglas@ThompsonHine.com

(For complete biographical data on Lawyers in Offices other than Washington, D.C., see Professional Biographies at the Respective Office Location)

THOMPSON, O'DONNELL, MARKHAM, NORTON & HANNON

Established in 1946

THE SOUTHERN BUILDING
805 FIFTEENTH STREET, N.W., SUITE 705
WASHINGTON, D.C. 20005
Telephone: 202-289-1133
Facsimile: 202-289-0275

Torts, Surety and Fidelity Law. Insurance, Government Contract Claims in Courts and Departments. Trials and Appeals, Federal, District of Columbia, Maryland and Virginia Courts. Estate Planning, Wills, Trusts, Probate and Taxation, Criminal Defense.

FIRM PROFILE: During its 50-year history this firm has prided itself in providing effective and responsive service to its clients in trials and litigation; wills, trusts and estates; personal injury; insurance coverage; products and professional liability; construction litigation; grand jury and white collar criminal matters; alternative dispute resolution; and general legal matters.

JOHN JUDE O'DONNELL, born Washington, D.C., January 29, 1932; admitted to bar, 1956, District of Columbia and U.S. Court of Appeals, District of Columbia Circuit; 1960, U.S. Court of Military Appeals; 1961, U.S. Claims Court; 1962, Maryland and U.S. Supreme Court. *Education:* Villanova University (A.B., 1953); Georgetown University (J.D., 1956; LL.M., 1957). Phi Alpha Delta. Law Clerk to Chief Judge Matthew F. McGuire, United States District Court for the District of Columbia, 1957-58. Assistant U.S. Attorney, District of Columbia, 1958-61. Member, D.C. Court of Appeals Committee on Unauthorized Practice, 1979-1986. Mediator-Arbitrator, Superior Court for District of Columbia. Mediator, United States District Court for District of Columbia. Arbitrator: American Arbitration Association; Health Claims Arbitration Panel of Maryland. *Member:* Bar Association of the District of Columbia (President, 1980-81; Member, Board of Directors, 1976-82; Lawyers of The Year, 1990); The District of Columbia Bar (Member, Board of Governors, 1981-1984); Montgomery County, Maryland State and American (Member, House of Delegates, 1980-81) Bar Associations; The Barristers (President, 1987); The Counselors; D.C. Defense Lawyer Association (Recipient, Lawyer of the Year, 1995). Fellow, American College of Trial Lawyers (State Chairperson, 1991-1993. (Office also at 27 Wood Lane, Rockville, Maryland). ***PRACTICE AREAS:*** General Practice; Alternative Dispute Resolution; Medical Malpractice; Professional Liability; Estate Litigation. ***Email:*** jjo@tomnh.com

JULIAN E. MARKHAM, JR., born Eustis, Florida, January 27, 1942; admitted to bar, 1967, Florida; 1970, District of Columbia and Virginia; 1978, Maryland. *Education:* Washington & Lee University (B.A., 1964); University of Florida (J.D., 1967). Phi Delta Phi. *Member:* The District of Columbia Bar (Member, Steering Committee of Estate, Trust and Probate Division, 1985-1987; Chair, 1986-1987); Bar Association of the District of Columbia (Chair, Probate and Trust Law Committee, 1982-1983); Maryland State and American Bar Associations; The Florida Bar; Virginia State Bar; The Barristers. Fellow, American College of Trust and Estate Counsel. (Offices also at 27 Wood Lane, Rockville, Maryland and 4113 Lee Highway, Arlington, Virginia). ***PRACTICE AREAS:*** Trusts and Estates; Estate Planning; Estate Administration; Trust Administration; Fiduciary Litigation. ***Email:*** jem@tomnh.com

(This Listing Continued)

RANDELL HUNT NORTON, born Newport, Rhode Island, November 21, 1948; admitted to bar, 1973, Virginia; 1974, District of Columbia; 1984, Maryland. *Education:* University of Virginia (B.A., 1970; J.D., 1973). Law Clerk to Judge Joseph M. Hannon, Superior Court of the District of Columbia, 1973-1974. "Lawyer of the Year," 1987; President, 1988-1989; Newsletter Editor, 1986-1999, D.C. Defense Lawyers Association. Barrister, Charles Fahy American Inn of Court (VI), 1983-1986. Member, Advisory Committee, National Center for State Courts Civil Discovery Project, 1990-1991. *Member:* The District of Columbia Bar (Co-Chair, Section IV Steering Committee, 1989-1992; Member, Nominating Committee, 1999-2000); Bar Association of the District of Columbia (Chair, Federal Courts Committee, 1990-1991); Maryland State and American Bar Associations; Virginia State Bar; Defense Research Institute; Virginia Association of Defense Attorneys; Northern Virginia Defense Lawyers Association; The Barristers. (Offices also at 27 Wood Lane, Rockville, Maryland and 4113 Lee Highway, Arlington, Virginia). ***PRACTICE AREAS:*** Insurance Coverage; Construction Liability; Arbitration; Personal Injury; Products Liability; Professional Liability. ***Email:*** rhn@tomnh.com

JAMES W. GREENE, born Buffalo, New York, May 15, 1940; admitted to bar, 1964, New York; 1980, District of Columbia, U.S. Supreme Court, U.S. Court of Appeals for the District of Columbia Third and Fourth Circuits, U.S. District Court for the District of Columbia and U.S. District Court, District of Maryland. *Education:* Amherst College (B.A., 1961); University of Michigan (J.D., 1964). Counsel, New York State Legislature, Select Committee to Study Revision of Corporation Laws, 1972-1974. *Member:* Erie County, New York State and American (Member, Sections of: Litigation; Tort and Insurance Practice) Bar Associations; District of Columbia Bar; International Association of Defense Counsel; Association of Defense Trial Attorneys; District of Columbia Defense Lawyers Association (President, 1991-1992; Recipient, Lawyer of The Year, 1999); The Counsellors. ***PRACTICE AREAS:*** Litigation; Insurance Coverage; Environmental Law; Arbitration. ***Email:*** jwg@tomnh.com

J. MICHAEL HANNON, born Washington, D.C., September 9, 1950; admitted to bar, 1981, District of Columbia and Maryland; 1982, U.S. Court of Appeals for the District of Columbia Circuit; 1984, U.S. District Court for the District of Columbia; 1991, U.S. Court of Veterans Appeals; 1992, U.S. Court of Appeals for the Federal Circuit and U.S. Supreme Court; 1995, U.S. Court of Appeals, Ninth Circuit; 1996, U.S. District Court, District of Maryland; 1998, U.S. Court of Appeals, Fourth Circuit. *Education:* Princeton University (A.B., 1972); University of Michigan (M.A., 1976); Columbus School of Law of the Catholic University of America (J.D., 1980). Barrister: Charles Fahy American Inn of Court; George Washington American Inn of Court. Master, Thurgood Marshall American Inn of Court. Law Clerk to the Honorable Frank Q. Nebeker of the District of Columbia Court of Appeals, 1980-1981. Assistant U.S. Attorney, District of Columbia, 1981-1988. Chairman, Rules Advisory Committee, U.S. Court of Veterans Appeals, 1992-2000. *Member:* The District of Columbia Bar; Bar Association of the District of Columbia; Maryland State and American (Member, Grand Jury Committee of the Criminal Justice Section) Bar Associations; Defense Research Institute (State Representative); District of Columbia Defense Lawyers Association; The Barristers; The Counselors; The Lawyers' Club. ***REPORTED CASES:*** Brown v. Gardner, 130 L.Ed.2d 462 (S.Ct., 1994). ***PRACTICE AREAS:*** Premises Liability; Grand Jury Practice; ERISA; Professional Liability; White Collar Crime. ***Email:*** jmh@tomnh.com

KENNETH G. STALLARD, born Wise, Virginia, May 1, 1963; admitted to bar, 1988, West Virginia and U.S. District Court, Southern District of West Virginia; 1989, Virginia, District of Columbia, U.S. District Court, Western District of Virginia, U.S. Court of Appeals, Fourth Circuit and U.S. Tax Court; 1990, U.S. District Court, Eastern District of Virginia and U.S. District Court, District of Columbia; 1991, U.S. Court of Appeals, District of Columbia Circuit; 1996, U.S. District Court, District of Maryland. *Education:* Virginia Polytechnic Institute and State University (B.A., 1985); Washington & Lee University (J.D., 1988). *Member:* Raleigh County (Secretary/Treasurer, 1988-1989) and West Virginia Bar Associations; The District of Columbia Bar; Virginia State Bar; West Virginia State Bar (Member, Employment Law Committee, 1989-1990); Defense Research Institute; District of Columbia Defense Lawyers Association; Virginia Association of Defense Attorneys; Northern Virginia Defense Lawyers Association; The Barristers. (Office also at 4113 Lee Highway, Arlington, Virginia). ***PRACTICE AREAS:*** Small Corporations; Construction Defects; Commercial Leasing; Contract Litigation; Personal Injury. ***Email:*** kgs@tomnh.com

BROOKE A. PINKERTON, born Pittsburgh, Pennsylvania, November 5, 1963; admitted to bar, 1991, Maryland; 1992, District of Columbia and U.S. District Court for the District of Columbia; 1995, U.S. Courts of Appeals for the Fourth and District of Columbia Circuits; 1995, U.S. Court of Veterans Appeals; 1996, U.S. Supreme Court; 1998, U.S. District Court, District of Maryland. *Education:* University of California at Los Angeles (B.A., 1985); Catholic University of America (J.D., 1991). Barrister, Thurgood Marshall American Inn of Court. *Member:* The District of Columbia Bar; Bar Association of the District of Columbia; Maryland State and American Bar Associations; District of Columbia Defense Lawyers Association (Secretary, 1999-2001); Women's Bar Association; Defense Research Institute; The Barristers. (Office also at 27

(This Listing Continued)

THOMPSON, O'DONNELL, MARKHAM, NORTON & HANNON, Washington—Continued

Wood Lane, Rockville, Maryland). ***PRACTICE AREAS:*** Employment; Premises Liability; Insurance Defense; Personal Injury; Nursing Home Litigation. ***Email:*** bap@tomnh.com

ASSOCIATES

MATTHEW W. CARLSON, born Takoma Park, Maryland, May 18, 1969; admitted to bar, 1994, Maryland; 1996, District of Columbia; 1997, Virginia; 1998, U.S. District Court, Eastern District of Virginia, U.S. District Court, District of Maryland and U.S. District Court for the District of Columbia. *Education:* University of Maryland (B.S., 1991); Catholic University of America (J.D., 1994). Member, Catholic University National Moot Court Team, Philip C. Jessup International Law Moot Court Competition, 1993. *Member:* Maryland State (Member, Sections on: Labor and Employment Law, 1994—; Negligence, Insurance and Workers' Compensation, 1998—) and American (Member, Sections on: Labor and Employment Law, 1994—; Injury to Persons and Property, 1997—; Tort and Insurance Practice, 1999—) Bar Associations; District of Columbia Bar (Section of Labor Relations, 1996—); Virginia State Bar (Section of Litigation, 1997—); District of Columbia Defense Lawyers Association; The Barristers. ***PRACTICE AREAS:*** Tort Defense; General Litigation; Workers' Compensation; Labor and Employment Law. ***Email:*** mwc@tomnh.com

MICHELE L. BULGER, born Baltimore, Maryland, October 3, 1961; admitted to bar, 1991, Pennsylvania; 1998, District of Columbia and U.S. District Court for the District of Columbia. *Education:* Franklin and Marshall College (B.A., 1983); Georgetown University (J.D.). *Member:* The District of Columbia Bar; American Bar Association; District of Columbia Defense Lawyers Association. ***PRACTICE AREAS:*** General Practice; Personal Injury; Premise Liability; Products Liability; Insurance Coverage; Professional Liability; Estate Litigation.

TAMIKA L. TAYLOR, born Charlotte, North Carolina, March 21, 1973; admitted to bar, 2000, Maryland (Not admitted in District of Columbia). *Education:* University of South Carolina (B.A., 1995); Howard University School of Law (J.D., 2000). Delta Sigma Theta. Recipient, American Jurisprudence Award, Insurance Law and Debtors & Creditors Rights. *Member:* Maryland, American and National Bar Associations. ***PRACTICE AREAS:*** Employment Law; Insurance Defense; Personal Injury; Civil Litigation; Insurance Coverage. ***Email:*** TLT@TOMNH.COM

OF COUNSEL

JAMES F. BROMLEY, born Denver, Colorado, June 26, 1935; admitted to bar, 1960, District of Columbia. *Education:* University of Colorado and Hamilton College (B.A., 1957); University of Colorado and Harvard University (LL.B., 1960). Phi Beta Kappa; Delta Sigma Rho; Phi Delta Phi. Editor in Chief, Journal of Transportation Law, Logistics and Policy, 1974—. Mediation Multidoor Program, D.C. Superior Court. *Member:* District of Columbia Bar; American Bar Association. ***PRACTICE AREAS:*** Life Insurance; Mediation and Arbitration; Trademark Law; Copyright Law; Transportation Law; Appellate Practice. ***Email:*** jfb@tomnh.com

REPRESENTATIVE CLIENTS: Royal Insurance Co.; Selective Insurance Co.; Sumitomo Marine Management (U.S.A.), Inc.; Tokio Marine Management, Inc.; American Re-insurance Co.; Jefferson Insurance Group; Monticello Insurance Group; General Reinsurance Corporation; PMA Insurance Company; Paradigm Insurance Company; Pekin Insurance Company; CNA Insurance; Fireman's Fund American Insurance Cos., San Francisco, Calif.; The Hartford; Liberty Mutual Insurance Co.; Chubb Group; Bernard F. Locraft, Civil Engineers, Washington, D.C.; Washington Mutual Investors Fund (General Counsel); The Tax-Exempt Fund of Maryland (General Counsel); The Tax-Exempt Fund of Virginia (General Counsel); The Growth Fund of Washington (General Counsel); Brown Investigative Group, Inc.; Allfirst Trust Company, N.A.; Allfirst Bank; Gordon-Maizel Construction Company, Inc.; Penn-America Group, Inc; Xerox Corporation; Gallagher-Bassett Services, Inc.

THOMPSON & WALDRON

WASHINGTON, D.C.

(See Alexandria, Virginia)

General Civil Practice, Government Contract, Construction and Contract Law, Suretyship, Federal Administrative and Legislative Practice.

THOMSEN AND BURKE, LLP

SUITE 500, 1225 EYE STREET, N.W.
WASHINGTON, D.C. 20005
Telephone: 202-682-4741
Fax: 202-547-3713
URL: http://www.t-b.com

Baltimore, Maryland Office: Suite 400, One North Charles Street, 21201. Telephone: 410-539-2595. FAX: 410-783-0710.

(This Listing Continued)

Federal Taxation and Estate Planning. Corporation, Probate and Trust Law, International Trade Law and Government Contracts.

ROSZEL C. THOMSEN, II, born Baltimore, Maryland, 1958; admitted to bar, 1985, Maryland and District of Columbia. *Education:* Harvard University (B.A., with honors, 1980); American University, Washington College of Law (J.D., 1984); American University, School of International Service (M.A., 1987). *Member:* The District of Columbia Bar; Maryland State and American (Member, Sections on: International Law and Practice; Real Property, Probate and Trust Law) Bar Associations. ***LANGUAGES:*** Arabic. ***PRACTICE AREAS:*** Corporate Law; International Trade; Export Regulation; Business Law; Government Contracts. ***Email:*** roz@t-b.com

ANTOINETTE D. PAYTAS, born Idaho Falls, Idaho, January 7, 1959; admitted to bar, 1997, Maryland; 1998, District of Columbia. *Education:* University of Maryland (B.S., 1981); Florida Institute of Technology (M.S., 1993); University of Maryland (J.D., 1997). *Member:* Baltimore City, Maryland State and American Bar Associations; The District of Columbia Bar; National Contract Management Association. ***PRACTICE AREAS:*** Corporate Law; International Trade; Export Regulation; Business Law. ***Email:*** tpaytas@t-b.com

(For Complete Biographical Data on all Personnel, see Professional Biographies at Baltimore, Maryland)

LAW OFFICES OF JUSTIN THORNTON

1615 L STREET, N.W., SUITE 1200
WASHINGTON, D.C. 20036
Telephone: 202-778-0559
Telecopier: 202-530-0625
Email: jat@thorntonlaw.com
URL: http://www.lawyers.com/thorntonlaw

White Collar Crime with emphasis on Tax Fraud, Financial Crimes, Health Care Fraud and Abuse, and Corporate Compliance.

FIRM PROFILE: A former federal prosecutor, Justin Thornton engages in a broad-ranging white collar criminal defense practice which is national in scope. His clientele includes individuals and corporations, both foreign and domestic. An experienced negotiator and a skilled trial lawyer, Justin Thornton frequently works closely with attorneys and accountants whose clients require his white collar expertise in such diverse areas as tax fraud, health care fraud and abuse, government procurement fraud, and related financial crimes and investigations. Mr. Thornton also advises clients on matters of corporate compliance and issues arising under federal sentencing guidelines.

JUSTIN ALLEN THORNTON, born North Carolina, 1950; admitted to bar, 1977, South Carolina; 1979, District of Columbia; 1988, North Carolina. *Education:* University of North Carolina at Chapel Hill (B.A., 1971); University of Exeter School of Law, Exeter, England; University of South Carolina (J.D., 1977). Recipient, Outstanding Attorney Award, U.S. Department of Justice, Tax Division, 1984; IRS Assistant Commissioner's Award and Designation as Honorary IRS Special Agent, 1987. Publications: "Money Laundering, Fraud, and the Three Dimensions of Chapter 3(D) of the Federal Sentencing Guidelines," Ninth Annual National Federal Sentencing Guidelines Seminar (2000); "Conundrum in the Caymans: How Substantial Assistance May Conflict with Principles of International Law and Constitutional Due Process," ABA National Institute on White Collar Crime (2000); "Guideline Sentencing in Tax Fraud Cases: Recent Developments in Calculating Tax Loss," ABA National Institute on White Collar Crime (1999); "Obtaining Evidence from the United States of America," International Association of Prosecutors, 1998 Annual Conference, Dublin Ireland; "Lawyer Under Attack: The Expanding Assertion of the Crime-Fraud Privilege," Institute for Continuing Legal Education Seminar on White Collar Crime (1998); "Representing a Taxpayer before the Criminal Investigation Division Arrives," ABA National Institute on Criminal Tax Fraud (1997); "May a Foreign National Successfully Assert a Fifth Amendment Claim for Fear of Foreign Prosecution," International Enforcement Law Reporter, Vol. 10, Issue 9, September 1994; "Crime Doesn't Pay - But Counsel May: Criminal Exposure in the Everyday Practice of Law," Criminal Justice, Vol. 8, No.3 Fall 1993 and republished in Corporate Counsel's Quarterly, Vol 10, No. 1, January 1994; "Corporate Punishment: The New Federal Sentencing Guidelines for Organizations," South Carolina Lawyer, Vol. 4, No. 2, September/October 1992; "Legal Briefs: the Case of the Non-Filer," CPA Report, August, 1993. Senior Trial Attorney, Tax Division, 1979-1987 and Criminal Division, 1978-1979, U.S. Department of Justice, Washington, D.C. Permanent Member, Judicial Conference of the U.S. Court of Appeals for the Fourth Circuit. Charter Member, United States Sentencing Commission, Practitioners Advisory Group, 1989—. *Member:* American (Member: Section on Litigation, Committees on Criminal and Tax Litigation; Section on Criminal Justice, Committee on White Collar Crime; Chairman/Co-Chairman, Tax Enforcement Subcommittee,

(This Listing Continued)

1992—; Section on Taxation, Committee on Civil and Criminal Penalties) and International (Member, Business Crime Committee) Bar Associations; National Association of Criminal Defense Lawyers.

TIGHE PATTON ARMSTRONG TEASDALE, P.L.L.C.

A Professional Limited Liability Company

Established in 1994

1747 PENNSYLVANIA AVENUE, N.W.
SUITE 300
WASHINGTON, D.C. 20006-4604
Telephone: 202-454-2800
Facsimile: 202-454-2805
URL: http://www.tighepatton.com

Complex Civil and Criminal Litigation, Government Contracts, Congressional and Federal Agency Representation, International Representation, Administrative and Trade Association Law, Antitrust, Tax and Securities Enforcement, Business Law, Construction Law.

KEVIN P. TIGHE, (P.C.), born Salem, Massachusetts, May 24, 1944; admitted to bar, 1969, Massachusetts; 1980, District of Columbia; U.S. District Court, District of Columbia; U.S. Court of Appeals, District of Columbia Circuit. *Education:* St. Anselm's College (B.A., 1966); Catholic University of America Law School (J.D., 1969). Co-Author: "Antitrust Consent Degrees—An Analysis and History by Industry of Justice Department Consent Decrees from 1906-1974," Lawyers Cooperative Publishing Co., 1974; "Trade Regulation by Negotiation—An Analysis of Federal Trade Commission Consent Decrees," Bureau of National Affairs, 1974. Chief Legislative Counsel, National Automobile Dealers Association, 1969-1978. Washington Counsel, Governmental Affairs, American Motors Corporation, 1978-1984. Washington Counsel, Chrysler Corporation for Regulatory Affairs, 1984-1988. *Member:* The District of Columbia Bar; Massachusetts and American Bar Associations. ***PRACTICE AREAS:*** Administrative Law; Regulatory Law; Commercial Law; Corporate Law; Business Law; Trade and Professional Associations; Legislative Practice. ***Email:*** ktighe@tighepatton.com

THOMAS EARL PATTON, born Indianapolis, Indiana, November 25, 1940; admitted to bar, 1966, District of Columbia; New York; 1970, U.S. Supreme Court; 1982, Virginia; U.S. District Court, Eastern District of Virginia and District of Maryland; U.S. Court of Appeals, District of Columbia, Second, Fourth, Fifth, Sixth, Seventh, Ninth, Tenth and Federal Circuits; U.S. Court of Federal Claims. *Education:* The Catholic University of America (B.A., cum laude, 1962; J.D., summa cum laude, 1965). Editor-in-Chief, Catholic University Law Review, 1965. Author, *Securities Fraud,* Michie, 1989. Co-Author: "The Purchase or Sale Restriction of SEC Rule 10b-5," 14 Catholic University Law Review, 1969; "Cases and Materials in Federal Practice and Procedure," Catholic University, 1984. Distinguished Lecturer: Federal Practice and Procedure, 1981-1992; White Collar Crimes, 1995—, Catholic University. Associate, Sullivan & Cromwell, 1965-1969. Counsel, U.S. Senate Special Committee on Aging, 1970. Member, Williams & Connolly, 1970-1975. Assistant General Counsel for Regulatory Litigation, U.S. Department of Energy, 1977-1978. Partner, Schnader, Harrison, Segal & Lewis, 1979-1994. Board of Regents, Catholic University, 1992-1997. *Member:* District of Columbia Bar (Founder and Chair, Litigation Section, 1981-1983; Chair, Lawyer Counseling Committee, 1981-1984); American Bar Association (Vice Chair, Complex Crimes Committee, 1987; Member: Section of Litigation). ***PRACTICE AREAS:*** Corporate Law; Finance; Securities; Complex Civil and Criminal Litigation. ***Email:*** tpatton@tighepatton.com

PAUL N. MURPHY, born Governor's Island, New York, May 29, 1944; admitted to bar, 1973, Virginia, Maryland, District of Columbia and all Federal Courts, U.S. Tax Court. *Education:* Washington & Lee University (A.B., magna cum laude, 1966); University of Virginia (J.D., 1973). Assistant United States Attorney, District of Columbia, 1974-1981. Senior Trial Attorney, Tax Division, Criminal Section, U.S. Department of Justice, 1981-1988. [Cdr., USNR, 1966-1970]. ***PRACTICE AREAS:*** Tax and Securities Enforcement; Complex Civil and Criminal Litigation. ***Email:*** pmurphy@tighepatton.com

WALTER G. BIRKEL, born New York, N.Y., June 22, 1947; admitted to bar, 1973, District of Columbia, U.S. District Court, District of Columbia, U.S. District Court, District of Maryland and U.S. Court of Appeals, Fifth Circuit; 1987, U.S. Court of Federal Claims and U.S. Tax Court. *Education:* University of Virginia (B.A., with high distinction, 1969); Harvard University (J.D., cum laude, 1973). Phi Beta Kappa; Phi Eta Sigma. Comment Editor, Harvard Civil Rights-Civil Liberties Law Review, 1972-1973. *Member:* District of Columbia Bar (Chair, Lawyer Counseling Committee, 1991-1992); Bar Association of the District of Columbia. ***PRACTICE AREAS:*** Complex Civil Litigation; False Claims Act; Products Liability; Personal Injury Litigation; Government Contracts. ***Email:*** wbirkel@tighepatton.com

(This Listing Continued)

BRENT S. FRANZEL, born St. Louis, Missouri, June 29, 1961; admitted to bar, 1988, Missouri and District of Columbia. *Education:* University of Missouri (B.J., 1983); Duke University (J.D., 1986). Staff Director, Senate International Finance Subcommittee, 1995-1996. Legislative Counsel to Senator Christopher S. Bond, 1987-1995. Research and Policy Development Director for Missourians for Kit Bond, 1986. Legislative Assistant to Governor Bond, 1981-1982 and 1984. *Member:* District of Columbia Bar; The Missouri Bar. ***PRACTICE AREAS:*** International Business Transactions; International Government Relations; Legislation. ***Email:*** bfranzel@tighepatton.com

CAROL ELDER BRUCE, born East Orange, New Jersey, June 7, 1949; admitted to bar, 1975, District of Columbia. *Education:* George Washington University (B.A., 1971; J.D., 1974). Recipient: Department of Justice Outstanding Service Award, 1981. Instructor: National Institute for Trial Advocacy, Georgetown Law Center, 1997; Mandatory D.C. Court of Appeals Legal Ethics Course for new D.C. Bar admittees, 1997—. Assistant U.S. Attorney, District of Columbia, 1975-1985. Deputy Independent Counsel in the Independent Counsel investigation of Attorney General Edwin Meese, 1988; Independent Counsel, Investigation of Secretary of the Interior Bruce Babbitt, 1998—. International Criminal Law Specialist, Bosnian War Crimes Tribunal, Coalition for International Justice, 1996. *Member:* The District of Columbia Bar (Board of Governors, 1995-2000; D.C. Bar Legal Ethics Committee, 1993-1995; American Bar Association (Member: White Collar Crime Committee, Criminal Justice Section, 1988—; Presidents Working Group on Lawyers' Representation of Regulated Clients, 1992; CEELI Russian Criminal Jury Trial Initiative Working Group, 1993-1994); Edward Bennett Williams American Inn of Court. ***PRACTICE AREAS:*** White Collar Crime; Civil Litigation. ***Email:*** cbruce@tighepatton.com

KERMIT A. ROSENBERG, born Wheeling, West Virginia, September 24, 1945; admitted to bar, 1974, Virginia; 1975, District of Columbia; 1992, Maryland and U.S. District Court, District of Maryland. *Education:* Ohio State University (B.S., 1967); Georgetown University (J.D., 1974). Member, Panel of Bankruptcy Trustees, Eastern District of Virginia. *Member:* Arlington County Bar Association; Virginia State Bar (Member, Bankruptcy Law Section); District of Columbia Bar (Member, Corporation, Finance & Securities Law Section, Business Bankruptcy Committee). ***PRACTICE AREAS:*** Bankruptcy; Insolvency. ***Email:*** krosenberg@tighepatton.com

JOHN B. MONTGOMERY, born Bethesda, Maryland, June 13, 1948; admitted to bar, 1973, Missouri; 1986, U.S. Supreme Court; 1998, District of Columbia. *Education:* United States Naval Academy (B.S., 1970); University of Missouri, Columbia (J.D., 1973); Georgetown University (LL.M., Labor Law, 1982). Director of Legislation, Office of Secretary of the Navy, 1990-1993. Special Counsel to Navy General Counsel, 1993-1996. Special Assistant to Secretary of Defense, 1997-1998. Special Assistant to Undersecretary of Defense, Acquisition and Technology, 1998-1999. [Captain, Judge Advocate General's Corps, U.S. Navy, 1974-1999]. ***PRACTICE AREAS:*** Business Acquisitions and Technology Law; Government Relations; Legislation; Military Base Closures & Development. ***Email:*** jmontgomery@tighepatton.com

RICHARD H. GORDIN, born Washington, D.C., May 11, 1948; admitted to bar, 1974, Illinois; 1977, District of Columbia; 1995, Maryland. *Education:* Purdue University (B.S., with highest distinction, with honors in Mathematics, 1970); Northwestern University (M.A., 1974; J.D., magna cum laude, 1974). Order of the Coif. Instructor, Pretrial Substantive and Procedural Motions, D.C. Bar. Assistant U.S. Attorney for the District of Columbia, 1980-1984. ***PRACTICE AREAS:*** Complex Litigation; Criminal Law. ***Email:*** rgordin@tighepatton.com

PATRICK B. FAZZONE, born Fairfield, Connecticut, December 12, 1953; admitted to bar, 1982, District of Columbia. *Education:* University of Connecticut (B.A., magna cum laude, Phi Beta Kappa, with distinction in Pol. Sc. and French, 1975); Duke University (J.D., 1981). Member, Moot Court Board. Note and Comment Editor, Duke Law Journal. Fulbright Scholar in International Trade and Business Law, Geneva, Switzerland, 1981. Fulbright Scholar in International Trade Law, Sydney, Australia, 1989. Author: numerous articles on international trade and business. Co-Author: "Doing Business Internationally," ABA Pub., 1996. Lecturer in Law, University of Sydney, 1989-1991. Guest Lecturer, Duke University School of Law International Program, 1994-1996. Chairman, International Trade Committee, American Chamber of Commerce in Australia. *Member:* The District of Columbia Bar (International Section), American Intellectual Property Association. ***LANGUAGES:*** English, French, Italian. ***PRACTICE AREAS:*** Commercial Law; Commercial Transactions; Corporate Law; Intellectual Property; International Trade. ***Email:*** pfazzone@tighepatton.com

DAVID J. TAYLOR, born Ft. Worth, Texas, December 21, 1943; admitted to bar, 1969, District of Columbia; 1973, U.S. Supreme Court. *Education:* Institute for American Universities, Aix-en-Provence, France (Certificate of European Studies, 1964); Austin College (B.A., 1965); Georgetown University (J.D., 1969). Phi Delta Phi, Legal Fraternity. Member, Board of Editors, Law and Policy in International Business, Vol.1, No.1. Law Clerk to Honorable Edward A. Tamm, U.S. Court of Appeals for the District of Columbia Circuit,

(This Listing Continued)

TIGHE PATTON ARMSTRONG TEASDALE, P.L.L.C., Washington—Continued

1969-1970. ***LANGUAGES:*** French. ***PRACTICE AREAS:*** Complex Civil Litigation; Government Contracts; Nonprofit Organizations Law. ***Email:*** dtaylor@tighepatton.com

---

BRIAN C. QUINN, born Manhasset, New York, February 11, 1965; admitted to bar, 1998, Maryland (Not admitted in District of Columbia). *Education:* Catholic University of America (B.A., Business Administration, M.A., Financial Mgmt., 1993; J.D., 1997). *Member:* Maryland State and American Bar Associations. ***PRACTICE AREAS:*** Corporate Law; Securities; Complex Civil and Criminal Litigation; Computer and Software; Information Technology; Trademarks. ***Email:*** bquinn@tighepatton.com

JOSEPH G. COSBY, born Bogota, Columbia, June 24, 1960; admitted to bar, 1989, Massachusetts and U.S. District Court, District of Massachusetts; 2001, District of Columbia. *Education:* University of Chicago (A.B., 1982); University of Michigan (J.D., cum laude, 1988). Law Clerk to the Hon. Jerry E. Smith, U.S. Court of Appeals, Fifth Circuit. ***PRACTICE AREAS:*** Complex Commercial Litigation; Criminal Litigation; Bankruptcy Litigation. ***Email:*** jcosby@tighepatton.com

DENNIS A. SOMECH, born Isla Verde, Puerto Rico, November 24, 1974; admitted to bar, 2000, Virginia (Not admitted in District of Columbia). *Education:* Emory University (B.A., 1992); George Washington University (J.D., 1999). Member, Moot Court Board. Law Clerk, Office of Independent Counsel, 1998-1999. ***LANGUAGES:*** Spanish and French. ***PRACTICE AREAS:*** Complex Litigation; Civil Litigation; White Collar Crime; Government Contracts; Internet Law. ***Email:*** dsomech@tighepatton.com

OF COUNSEL

ALAN H. KENT, born 1946; admitted to bar, 1969, New York; 1973, District of Columbia; 1974, Maryland, 1975, Pennsylvania. *Education:* Boston Univ. (B.S. in B.A., 1967; J.D., 1969); L'Academie de Droit International, The Hague, The Netherlands (Certificat d'Application, 1969); George Washington Univ. (LL.M., 1979). Phi Alpha Delta. Member and Counsel, District of Columbia Court of Appeals Committee on Admissions to the Bar, 2000—. Member, District of Columbia Judicial Conference, 2000—. Member, District of Columbia Bar Attorney/Client Arbitration Board, 2001—. Author: "The Architect's Duty: Owner-Contractor Disputes Involving Allegations of Architect Fault," 46 Ins. Csl. J. 31 (1979), "Recovering Indirect Costs," Construction Briefings 80-6, Federal Publications, Inc., Nov., 1980; "Litigation Against the Federal Government and Its Officials," Pennsylvania Bar Institute, 1982; "Audit of Contract Costs," Construction Briefings No. 85-5, Federal Publications, Inc., May, 1985; "Construction Claims Under Maryland Law," The Cambridge Institute, 1991; "Wrongful Discharge," 27 Md. Bar. J. 40, Jan/Feb, 1994. Member, National Construction and Commercial Panels, Large/Complex Case Designee, American Arbitration Association. Trial Counsel, U.S. General Services Administration, 1971-1973. *Member:* The District of Columbia Bar; Maryland State, Federal (Chairman, Committee on Government Construction Contracting, 1985-1993) and American Bar Associations. ***PRACTICE AREAS:*** Construction Law; Government Contracts; Commercial Litigation; Alternative Dispute Resolution. ***Email:*** akent@tighepatton.com

---

TOBIN, O'CONNOR & EWING

A Partnership of Professional Corporations

Established in 1993

5335 WISCONSIN AVENUE, N.W., SUITE 700

WASHINGTON, D.C. 20015

Telephone: 202-362-5900

Fax: 202-362-5901

URL: http://www.dstlaw.com

Alexandria, Virginia Office: 908 King Street, Suite 200. Telephone: 703-836-7071. Fax: 703-836-7099.

Litigation, Trial Practice, Criminal Defense, Tax, Business, Transactional Matters, Corporate, Exempt Securities, Environmental, Government Contracts, Computer, Estate Planning, Probate Law, Real Estate.

MEMBERS OF FIRM

DAVID C. TOBIN, (P.C.), born New Castle, Pennsylvania, March 3, 1959; admitted to bar, 1984, Pennsylvania; 1985, U.S. Court of Appeals, Fifth Circuit; 1986, District of Columbia; 1993, Maryland. *Education:* Westminster College (B.A., magna cum laude, 1981); George Washington University (J.D., with high honors, 1984). Order of the Coif. Notes Editor, George Washington Law Review, 1983-1984. Law Clerk to the Honorable John R. Brown, U.S. Court of Appeals for the Fifth Circuit, 1984-1985. *Member:* The District of Columbia Bar; Pennsylvania and American Bar Associations. ***PRACTICE AREAS:*** Civil Litigation; Criminal Litigation; Administrative Law; White Collar Crime. ***Email:*** dctobin@dstlaw.com

STEPHEN J. O'CONNOR, (P.C.), born Kensington, Maryland, October 9, 1959; admitted to bar, 1985, Maryland, District of Columbia and Virginia. *Education:* James Madison University (B.B.A., magna cum laude, 1981); George Washington University (J.D., with honors, 1984). Managing Editor, George Washington Journal of International Law and Economics, 1983-1984. *Member:* The District of Columbia Bar; Maryland State Bar Association; Virginia State Bar. ***PRACTICE AREAS:*** Transaction; Tax; Business; Corporate; Exempt Securities; Real Estate; Environmental; Government Contract; Computer; Estate Planning; Probate Law. ***Email:*** sjoconnor@dstlaw.com

TODD EWING, (P.C.), born Leon, Iowa, January 20, 1965; admitted to bar, 1992, District of Columbia. *Education:* University of Stirling; Iowa State University (B.S., 1987); Drake Universit y (J.D., 1991). C. Edwin Moore Moot Court Finalist. Legal Intern, Office of Commissioner Seeley Lodwick, Summer 1990. Author: "The Treaty with Poland Concerning Business and Economic Relations: Does it Provide More Incentive To The American Investor?" 11 Nw. J. Int'l. L. & Bus. 352, (1990). *Member:* The District of Columbia Bar; Maryland and Virginia Land Title Associations. ***PRACTICE AREAS:*** Real Estate; Transaction; Business; Corporate; Wills; Probate. ***Email:*** tbewing@dstlaw.com

ASSOCIATES

JOHN M. TRAN, born Saigon, South Vietnam, January 30, 1960; admitted to bar, 1984, Virginia, Maryland and U.S. District Court, Eastern District of Virginia, U.S. Court of Appeals, Fourth Circuit, U.S. Supreme Court (Not admitted in District of Columbia). *Education:* George Washington University (B.A., 1981; J.D., 1984). Assistant Commonwealth's Attorney for the City of Alexandria, 1988-1993. Special Assistant U.S. Attorney for the Eastern District of Virginia, 1991-1993. *Member:* Alexandria, Arlington, Fairfax and Federal Bar Associations; Virginia State Bar Council (18th Judicial Circuit); Asian American Bar Association. (Resident, Alexandria, Virginia Office). ***REPORTED CASES:*** Thompson v. Commonwealth, (1992), Bankruptcy. ***PRACTICE AREAS:*** Criminal Defense; Corporate Law; Business Law; Commercial Litigation. ***Email:*** jmtran@dstlaw.com

DAVID A. CONFORTI, born Poughkeepsie, New York, August 14, 1964; admitted to bar, 1990, New York; 1991, U.S. District Court, Southern and Eastern Districts of New York; 1998, District of Columbia. *Education:* Colgate University (B.S., 1986); St. John's University (J.D., 1989). Member, St. John's Law Review. *Member:* New York State and American Bar Associations; The District of Columbia Bar. ***PRACTICE AREAS:*** Corporate; Business; Commercial Litigation. ***Email:*** daconforti@dstlaw.com

DONNA R. S. PEERY, born Midland, Texas, September 20, 1963; admitted to bar, 1994, Texas; 1996, U.S. District Court, Northern District of Texas; 1998, U.S. District Court, Southern District of Texas and U.S. Court of Appeals, Fifth Circuit; 2001, District of Columbia. *Education:* Abilene Christian University (B.B.A., cum laude, 1985); Texas Tech University (J.D., cum laude, 1994). Treasurer, 1992-1993 and Justice, 1993-1994, Phi Alpha Delta. Law Clerk to the Honorable Jorge A. Solis, U.S. District Judge, Northern District of Texas, Dallas Division, 1995. Co-Author: "Litigation Involving HMOs," U.T. School of Law Managed Care Litigation Conference, Fall 1996; "Suing and Defending Managed Health Care Providers," U.T. School of Law Seminar, Fall 1997; "New and Evolving Issues in Managed Care Liability," State Bar of Texas Advanced Medical Malpractice Seminar, Spring 1998; "Managed Care Liability in Texas," 1999. *Member:* State Bar of Texas. ***PRACTICE AREAS:*** Federal Litigation; Commercial Litigation; Civil Litigation. ***Email:*** drspeery@dstlaw.com

CATHERINE E. SCHMITT, born South Ruislip, England, October 9, 1964; admitted to bar, 1999, Iowa; 2001, District of Columbia. *Education:* University of Maryland (B.S., Dietetics, 1988; B.S., Paralegal Studies, 1994); Drake University Law School (J.D., 1999). *Member:* Iowa State and American Bar Associations. ***PRACTICE AREAS:*** Real Estate. ***Email:*** ceschmitt@dstlaw.com

ANTHONY M. BLACK, born Shenandoah, Iowa, July 10, 1962; admitted to bar, 1991, Virginia; 1992, District of Columbia. *Education:* University of Iowa (B.A., 1985); University of Virginia (J.D., 1991). Legislative Assistant, U.S. Representative Jim Lighfoot, 1985-1988. ***PRACTICE AREAS:*** Telecommunications; Electronic Commerce. ***Email:*** amblack@dstlaw.com

OF COUNSEL

KERRY McLAIN RICHARD, born Berwyn, Illinois, July 10, 1965; admitted to bar, 1990, Massachusetts and U.S. District Court, District of Massachusetts; 1992, District of Columbia and U.S. Court of Appeals, First Circuit; 1994, Maryland and U.S. District Court, District of Columbia; 1995, U.S. District Court, District of Maryland and D.C. Circuit Court of Appeals. *Education:* University of Denver (B.A., summa cum laude, 1987); Boston University (J.D., cum laude, 1990). Phi Beta Kappa; Mortar Board. Editor-in-Chief,

(This Listing Continued)

Boston University Legislative Services, 1989-1990. Author: "Your Legal Rights Before, During and After An Inspection By OSHA", JAVMA, June 1, 1994, Vol. 204, No. 11. *Member:* Maryland State and American Bar Associations (Member, Employment Law Section); The District of Columbia Bar; American Veterinary Medical Law Association. (Also Member, Jarrard & Richard, Bethesda, Maryland). ***REPORTED CASES:*** Allan, et al. v. Adage, Inc., 967 F.2d 695 (1st Cir. 1992); Grunseth v. Marriott Corp., 872 F. Supp. 1069 (D.D.C. 1995), aff'd, 79 F.3d 169 (D.C. Cir. 1996). ***PRACTICE AREAS:*** Management Labor Law; Employment Law; Business Immigration; Corporate Law; Commercial Litigation. ***Email:*** kmrichard@dstlaw.com

PAUL M. TOULOUSE

Established in 1977

503 D STREET, N.W.

WASHINGTON, D.C. 20001

Telephone: 202-347-4020

Telecopier: 202-347-1942

Email: PMToulouse@aol.com

URL: http://www.lawyers.com/toulouselaw

Civil Litigation with Special Emphasis in the Areas of Personal Injury including Professional Negligence, Medical Malpractice, Vehicular Liability, General Personal Injury Claims and Worker's Compensation, District of Columbia Consumer Protection Procedures Act Law, Probate Litigation, Real Estate Litigation, Bankruptcy Litigation, Divorce and Separation, Estate Planning and Administration.

FIRM PROFILE: Since 1977, Paul M. Toulouse has offered clients in the district and surrounding states of Maryland and Virginia an aggressive civil trial practice in state and federal courts. Concentrating on personal injury cases, Mr. Toulouse handles medical malpractice, professional negligence, vehicular liability and workers compensation, as well as litigating bankruptcy, divorce, probate and real estate matters. He is an active member of state and national trial lawyer associations.

PAUL M. TOULOUSE, born Palmer, Massachusetts, December 27, 1949; admitted to bar, 1975, District of Columbia, U.S. District Court for the District of Columbia and U.S. Court of Appeals for the District of Columbia Circuit; 1985, Virginia, U.S. District Court, Eastern District of Virginia and U.S. Court of Appeals for the Fourth Circuit; 1995, Maryland and U.S. District Court, District of Maryland. *Education:* Fairfield University (B.A., 1971); Georgetown University (J.D., 1974). *Member:* District of Columbia Bar; Virginia Bar Association; Maryland State Bar Association, Inc.; Association of Trial Lawyers of America; Trial Lawyers Association of Washington, D.C. ***PRACTICE AREAS:*** Personal Injury; Professional Malpractice; Probate; Family Law; Real Estate.

DAVID P. TOWEY

1914 SUNDERLAND PLACE, N.W.

WASHINGTON, D.C. 20036

Telephone: 202-452-9886

Facsimile: 202-452-9896

Email: dpt@sprynet.com

URL: http://www.lawyers.com/davidtowey

White Collar Criminal Defense and Civil Litigation with emphasis on Federal Criminal Law, Grand Jury Practice, Corporate Investigations, Trial Practice, Criminal Appeals, Government Contract Fraud, Criminal Antitrust, RICO, Federal Civil Litigation, Securities Fraud, Governments Contracts, False Claims Act, Qui Tam Litigation, Civil Fraud, Libel, Slander and Defamation and Gaming Law.

FIRM PROFILE: After experience working with larger Washington, D.C. firms, David Towey now engages in his own broad-based criminal defense and civil litigation practice on a national scale. He has represented corporations and individuals in white collar criminal defense matters in a wide range of substantive areas including government contracts fraud, criminal antitrust, Food and Drug Administration cases, international export and customs investigations, covert government operations, bribery and gratuity prosecutions, obstruction of justice charges, federal racketeering allegations, independent counsel investigations and criminal tax fraud. Mr. Towey is a skilled trial lawyer, has successfully resolved countless matters through negotiation and has prevailed in criminal defense appeals. He is also broadly experienced in federal and state civil and regulatory practice including government contracts litigation, antitrust and securities cases, class action matters, internal corporate and special litigation committee investigations, qui tam false claim act cases and libel litigation. Mr. Towey works closely with law firms and other professionals whose corporate clients and employees require experienced assistance in these sensitive areas.

(This Listing Continued)

DAVID P. TOWEY, born New York, N.Y., September 6, 1949; admitted to bar, 1975, District of Columbia, U.S. District Court for the District of Columbia and U.S. Court of Appeals for the District of Columbia and Second Circuits; 1980, U.S. Supreme Court and U.S. Temporary Emergency Court of Appeals; 1986, U.S. Court of Appeals, Fourth Circuit. *Education:* C.W. Post College (B.A., summa cum laude, 1971); Harvard University (J.D., cum laude, 1974). Winner and Best Oralist, Final Round, Ames Moot Court Competition. *Member:* The District of Columbia Bar. ***REPORTED CASES:*** U.S. v. White, 887 F.2d 287 (D.C. Cir. 1997).

TRAINUM, SNOWDON & DEANE, P.C.

Established in 1988

1317 F STREET, NW, SUITE 350

WASHINGTON, D.C. 20004

Telephone: 202-783-5488

Facsimile: 202-783-5502

URL: http://www.lawyers.com/trainumsnowdon&deane

General Practice before all U.S. Courts, Departments and Agencies, Real Estate, Taxation, Corporate Law, Legislative Practice, Estate Planning, Litigation, Environmental and Energy Law.

FIRM PROFILE: The firm of Trainum, Snowdon & Deane, P.C. has over 150 years of combined legal experience in areas ranging from Corporate and Administrative Law to Probate, Trusts and Estate Planning. The firm has achieved and maintained Martindale-Hubbell's highest rating for legal ability and ethical conduct, and this is reflected in the high-quality legal representation the firm provides for their clients.

JOHN RUSSELL DEANE III, born Baltimore, Maryland, December 27, 1943; admitted to bar, 1972, Virginia; 1973, District of Columbia. *Education:* American University (B.A., 1968); Georgetown University (J.D., 1972). Member, Georgetown Law Journal, 1970-1972. Staff Assistant to the President of the United States, 1971-1972. Deputy Assistant General Counsel, Federal Energy Administration, 1974-1975. *Member:* The District of Columbia Bar; Virginia State Bar; American Bar Association. ***PRACTICE AREAS:*** Corporate Law; Administrative Law; Nonprofit and Charitable Organizations.

RICHARD W. SNOWDON III, born Plainfield, New Jersey, February 7, 1943; admitted to bar, 1968, District of Columbia; 1970, U.S. Tax Court; 1974, U.S. Claims Court. *Education:* Syracuse University (B.S., 1965); George Washington University (J.D., with honors, 1968). Member, Washington, D.C. Estate Planning Council, 1978. *Member:* The District of Columbia Bar. [Capt., U.S. Army Infantry Branch, 1968-1970]. ***PRACTICE AREAS:*** Trusts and Estates; Nonprofit and Charitable Organizations; Taxation; Probate.

CHARLES A. TRAINUM, JR., born Washington, D.C., October 1, 1941; admitted to bar, 1966, Virginia; 1969, District of Columbia. *Education:* Virginia Polytechnic Institute (B.S., 1963); University of Virginia (LL.B., 1966). *Member:* The District of Columbia Bar; Virginia State Bar Association. ***PRACTICE AREAS:*** Real Estate; Corporate Laws; Alcoholic Beverages; Trusts and Estates.

OF COUNSEL

THOMAS A. FRAZIER, JR., born Clarksdale, Mississippi, January 3, 1934; admitted to bar, 1959, Virginia; 1962, District of Columbia and U.S. Tax Court; 1965, U.S. Supreme Court and U.S. Claims Court; 1973, U.S. Court of Appeals, District of Columbia Circuit. *Education:* University of Virginia (B.A., 1954; LL.B., 1959). Phi Beta Kappa; Phi Delta Phi; Order of the Coif; Raven Society. Member, Editorial Board, 1957-1959, Comments and Projects Editor, 1958-1959, University of Virginia Law Review. Trial Attorney, Tax Division, Department of Justice, Washington D.C., 1959-1962. Instructor in Corporate Taxation and Reorganizations, George Washington University Masters in Taxation Program, 1964-1967. *Member:* The District of Columbia Bar (Member, Tax Section); The Virginia State Bar (Member, Section on Taxation); American Bar Association (Member, Tax Section). [Captain, USAFR, 1954-1962]. ***PRACTICE AREAS:*** Federal and State Taxation; Probate; Trusts and Estates.

RONALD D. LARSON, born Chicago, Illinois, June 1, 1935; admitted to bar, 1962, Illinois; 1972, District of Columbia. *Education:* Knox College (B.A., 1957); Northwestern University (J.D., 1962). Adjunct Professor, Estate Planning, Georgetown University School of Law, 1975-1982. Certified Financial Planner, Maryland, 1983. *Member:* The District of Columbia Bar; Illinois State Bar Association; D.C. Estate Planning Council. ***PRACTICE AREAS:*** Estate Planning; Probate.

RAYBURN HANZLIK, born Los Angeles, California June 7, 1938; admitted to bar, 1975, Virginia and District of Columbia. *Education:* The Principia College (B.S., 1973); University of Virginia (M.A., 1968; J.D., 1975). Staff Assistant to the President, 1971-1973. Associate Director, White House Domestid Policy. Director, White House Conference on Youth, 1970-1971. Associate Director, White House Domestic Council, 1975-1977. Administrator, Economic

(This Listing Continued)

TRAINUM, SNOWDON & DEANE, P.C., Washington—Continued

Regulatory Administration, U.S. Department of Energy, 1981-1985. ***PRACTICE AREAS:*** Corporate Law; Business Law; Energy; Environmental Law. ***Email:*** rdhanzlik@aol.com

MICHAEL J. TREVELLINE

601 PENNSYLVANIA AVENUE, N.W.
SUITE 900 SOUTH
WASHINGTON, D.C. 20004-2601
Telephone: 202-737-1139
Outside D.C. Metropolitan Area: 1-800-587-1700
Fax: 202-783-3423
Email: MJTrevelline@cs.com

Business Law and Commercial Litigation with special emphasis in the areas of Small Business Formation and Venture Capital, Investor Responsibility, International Trade, Securities Arbitration, Political Asylum.

FIRM PROFILE: The firm emphasizes providing advice to and representation of businesses with the total business climate in mind—especially an understanding of how to keep the business competitive.

MICHAEL J. TREVELLINE, born Las Vegas, Nevada, March 22, 1961; admitted to bar, 1987, Louisiana and New York; 1993, District of Columbia. *Education:* Southern Illinois University (B.A., 1983); Louisiana State University (J.D., 1986); Georgetown University Law Center (LL.M., 1992). Certified Translator, Paris, 1988 by Chambre of Commerce et D'Industrie de Paris. Author: "European Communities Standardization Policy: A New Means to Regulate Foodstuffs," European Competition Law Review, Vol. 14, Issue 2. *Member:* Bar Association of the District of Columbia; Louisiana and American Bar Associations; Alliance Française de Washington. [Captain, JAG, US Air Force, 1987-1991; US Air Force Reserve, 1995—]. ***LANGUAGES:*** French. ***PRACTICE AREAS:*** Small Business; General Practice; Securities Arbitration; Political Asylum; Trade Regulation; Litigation; Insurance Claims.

LAW OFFICES OF TRONCONE & ASSOCIATES

666 ELEVENTH STREET, NW, SUITE 315
WASHINGTON, D.C. 20001
Telephone: 202-232-5100
Telecopier: 202-232-6140
URL: http://www.us-visas.net
Email: frtusa@starpower.net
URL: http://www.lawyers.com/usvisalaw

Business Immigration, Investment-Based Visas, Consular Law, and Visas.

FIRM PROFILE: Troncone & Associates provides US Visa and Immigration counseling and services to businesses and individuals located in the US and throughout the globe. With considerable experience in counseling and representing foreign entrepreneurs, investors, and businesses seeking to establish and staff start-up and/or newly acquired facilities in the US, Troncone & Associates works closely with our clients to structure their investments to facilitate the acquisition of appropriate visa status for themselves and/or their foreign executives, managers, professional employees and specialized workers. Troncone & Associates regularly represents clients in immigration related matters filed with the US Immigration and Naturalization Service and the Department of Labor throughout the United States. Troncone & Associates also maintains an active visa law practice, appearing before US Consular Missions overseas, especially at the US Embassies and Consulates in Japan and Canada, where we service our clients through our affiliate offices in Tokyo and Toronto.

FREDERICK R. TRONCONE, born Erie, Pennsylvania, March 24, 1957; admitted to bar, 1982, Pennsylvania and U.S. District Court, Western District of Pennsylvania; 1985, District of Columbia; 1986, U.S. Court of Appeals for the Federal Circuit; 1988, Hawaii and U.S. District Court, District of Hawaii; 1990, U.S. Court of Appeals, District of Columbia Circuit. *Education:* Pennsylvania State University (B.A., 1979); University of Toledo (J.D., 1982). Student Articles Editor, University of Toledo Law Review. Speaker, Business Investments and Immigration Programs, Honolulu, Hawaii and Japan. Attorney Consultant, American Life and Business Services, Tokyo, Japan. Former Attorney Advisor to the General Counsel of the National Labor Relations Board in Washington, D.C. *Member:* Pennsylvania and Hawaii State Bar Associations; The District of Columbia Bar; American Immigration Lawyers Association (Former Chair, Hawaii Chapter). (Also Of Counsel, Aitken, Irvin, Berlin & Vrooman, Washington,

(This Listing Continued)

D.C.). ***PRACTICE AREAS:*** Business Immigration; Consular Law; Visas; Investor Visas; Family Immigration Law. ***Email:*** frtusa@starpower.net

TROUT & RICHARDS, P.L.L.C.

1100 CONNECTICUT AVENUE, N.W., SUITE 730
WASHINGTON, D.C. 20036
Telephone: 202-463-1920
Fax: 202-463-1925
Email: trlaw@troutrichards.com
URL: http://www.troutrichards.com

Alexandria, Virginia Office: 301 North Pitt Street, 22314. Telephone: 703-519-8840.

Trial and appellate practice, with particular emphasis on complex commercial litigation, white collar criminal defense and the defense of agency enforcement actions.

ROBERT P. TROUT, born Roanoke, Virginia, July 17, 1948; admitted to bar, 1973, Virginia; 1975, District of Columbia; 1977, U.S. Supreme Court; 1980, Maryland; U.S. Court of Appeals for the District of Columbia and Fourth Circuits. *Education:* Washington & Lee University (B.A., 1970); University of Virginia (J.D., 1973). Note Editor, Virginia Journal of International Law. Trial Attorney, Criminal Division, U.S. Department of Justice, 1973-1975. Assistant U.S. Attorney, Maryland, 1975-1979. Instructor, Trial Advocacy, Georgetown University; DC Bar CLE, 1990. Associate Deputy Independent Counsel, 1995-1996. *Member:* The District of Columbia Bar (Member, Steering Committee, Litigation Section, 1982-1986; Chair, 1984-1985; Member, District of Columbia Bar Standing Committee on Alternate Dispute Resolution); Maryland State and American Bar Associations; Virginia State Bar. ***PRACTICE AREAS:*** Commercial Litigation; White Collar Criminal Defense and Enforcement. ***Email:*** rtrout@troutrichards.com

JOHN THORPE RICHARDS, JR., born Washington, D.C., February 9, 1960; admitted to bar, 1987, Virginia and U.S. District Court, Eastern District of Virginia; 1988, District of Columbia; 1996, Maryland; U.S. Court of Appeals for the District of Columbia and Fourth Circuit. *Education:* St. Lawrence University (B.A., 1984); University of Virginia (J.D., 1987). Phi Beta Kappa; Omicron Delta Kappa. Executive Editor, Virginia Journal of International Law, 1986-1987. Law Clerk to Honorable Albert V. Bryan, Jr., Chief Judge, U.S. District Court, Eastern District of Virginia, 1987-1988. *Member:* Alexandria, Maryland State and American Bar Associations; District of Columbia Bar; Virginia State Bar. ***PRACTICE AREAS:*** Commercial Litigation; Criminal Litigation. ***Email:*** jtr@troutrichards.com

AMY BERMAN JACKSON, born Baltimore, Maryland, July 22, 1954; admitted to bar, 1979, District of Columbia; 1986, Virginia. *Education:* Harvard College (A.B., cum laude, 1976); Harvard Law School (J.D., cum laude, 1979). Law Clerk to Judge Harrison L. Winter, U.S. Court of Appeals, Fourth Circuit, 1979-1980. Assistant U.S. Attorney, District of Columbia, 1980-1986. Instructor: National Institute for Trial Advocacy, 1985-1990; Harvard Law School, Trial Advocacy Workshop, 1984-1992; Georgetown University Law Center CLE Intensive Session in Trial Advocacy Skills, 1985-1990; Team Leader, 1991-1993; Emory Law School Trial Workshop, 1990. *Member:* The District of Columbia Bar (Delegate to ABA House of Delegates, 1986-1989, Chair, Judicial Evaluation Committee, 1992-1994); American Bar Association (Co-Chair: Training the Advocate Committee, Section of Litigation, 1989-1990; Co-Director, Division IV, 1991-1992; Member: Task Force on Jury Initiatives, 1996-1997; White Collar Crime Committee, Criminal Justice Section); Women's Bar Association. ***PRACTICE AREAS:*** Complex Litigation; Criminal Investigations and Defense; Criminal Trials; Civil Trials; Appeals. ***Email:*** abj@troutrichards.com

PATRICIA E. CONNELLY, born Schenectady, New York, October 31, 1956; admitted to bar, 1982, District of Columbia and Maryland; U.S. District Court, District of Columbia; U.S. District Court, District of Maryland; U.S. Court of Appeals, Fourth Circuit. *Education:* State University of New York at Albany (B.A., 1977); Syracuse University (J.D., 1981). Law Clerk to Honorable Richard J. Clark, Charles County Circuit Court, Maryland, 1981-1983. President, Women's Law Caucus, 1979-1980. *Member:* Maryland State Bar Association; The District of Columbia Bar. ***PRACTICE AREAS:*** Commercial Litigation; Civil Litigation; Civil Practice. ***Email:*** patricia@troutrichards.com

TROUTMAN SANDERS LLP

A Partnership including Professional Corporations

401 NINTH STREET, N.W., SUITE 1000

WASHINGTON, D.C. 20004-2134

Telephone: 202-274-2950

Fax: 202-274-2994

URL: http://www.troutmansanders.com

Atlanta, Georgia Office: Bank of America Plaza, 600 Peachtree Street, N.W., Suite 5200. Telephone: 404-885-3000. Facsimile: 404-885-3900.

Other Atlanta Offices at: 999 Peachtree Street, Suite 750, 30309. Telephone: 404-885-3651, Facsimile: 404-885-3652.

Hong Kong Office: Suite 3503A Two Exchange Square, 8 Connaught Place, Central, Hong Kong. Telephone: 852-2533-7888. Facsimile: 852-2533-7898.

London, England Office: 10th Floor, Dashwood House, 69 Old Broad Street, EC2N1QS. Phone: (207) 065-2600. Fax: (207) 065-2777.

Richmond, Virginia Office: Troutman Sanders Mays & Valentine, 1111 East Main Street, P.O. Box 1122, 23218-1122. Telephone: 804-697-1200. Facsimile: 804-697-1339.

West End Office: Troutman Sanders Mays & Valentine, 500 Libbie Avenue, Suite 2A, Richmond, 23226. Telephone: 804-697-1200. Facsimile: 804-288-8366.

Norfolk, Virginia Office: Troutman Sanders Mays & Valentine, 999 Waterside Drive, P.O. Box 3670, 23514-3670. Telephone: 757-687-7700. Facsimile: 757-687-7701.

Tysons Corner, Virginia Office: Troutman Sanders Mays & Valentine, 1660 International Drive, Suite 600, McLean, 22102. Telephone: 703-734-4334. Facsimile: 703-734-4340.

Virginia Beach, Virginia Office: Troutman Sanders Mays & Valentine, 4425 Corporation Lane, Suite 420, P.O. Box 61185, 23466-1185. Telephone: 757-687-7500. Facsimile: 757-687-7510.

Communications, Corporate, Energy, Environment, Federal Regulatory, Intellectual Property, Legislation, Litigation, Transportation.

FIRM PROFILE: Tracing its origin to 1897, Troutman Sanders is one of Atlanta's oldest and largest law firms, with nearly 500 lawyers. Troutman Sanders is a full-service law firm engaged in virtually every aspect of civil and commercial law. Our reputation and stability are evidenced by long-standing relationships with many major business organizations, including multinational corporation and banking institution, regional companies, start-up enterprises, foreign governments, federal and state agencies, non-profit organizations, individuals, and entrepreneurs.

Troutman Sanders' clients are active in a broad range of industries, such as telecommunications, banking and financial services, computer hardware and software, energy services, transportation, food service, health care, entertainment and sports, lodging, and real estate, with offices in Atlanta, Richmond, Washington, D.C., Tyson's Corner, Norfolk, Virginia Beach, London and Hong Kong. Our lawyers have represented clients in transactions around the world and our firm's practice reflects the broad reach and complex concerns of businesses operating in a global economy.

MEMBERS OF FIRM

C. JONATHAN BENNER, born 1948; admitted to bar, 1973, District of Columbia; 1976, U.S. Court of Appeals for the District of Columbia Circuit; 1977, U.S. Supreme Court; 1980, U.S. Court of Appeals, Ninth Circuit; 2000, U.S. Court of Appeals, Fourth Circuit. *Education:* American University, School of International Service (B.A., 1970); Georgetown University Law Center (J.D., 1973). General Counsel, Public Service, Federal Maritime Commission, 1981-1986. *Member:* District of Columbia Bar; Maritime Administrative Bar Association. ***LANGUAGES:*** French. ***PRACTICE AREAS:*** Transportation; Administrative Law; Federal Regulation of Maritime Transportation; Litigation; Legislative and Governmental Affairs Representation. ***Email:*** jonathan.benner@troutmansanders.com

TODD R. COLES, born Evergreen Park, Illinois, May 1, 1964; admitted to bar, 1991, Illinois and District of Columbia. *Education:* University of Illinois (B.A., History, Political Science and Economics, cum laude, 1987); Washington College of Law of American University (J.D., magna cum laude, 1991). Phi Beta Kappa. Dean's Fellow. Member, The American University Law Review. Author: "Does the Privacy Act of 1974 Protect Your Right to Privacy? An Examination of the Routine Use Exemption," 40 Am. U. L. Rev., 1990. *Member:* The District of Columbia Bar; American Bar Association. ***PRACTICE AREAS:*** Energy; Project Finance; Project Development. ***Email:*** todd.coles@troutmansanders.com

M. LISANNE CROWLEY, born Boston, Massachusetts, October 21, 1959; admitted to bar, 1985, Massachusetts and District of Columbia. *Education:* Wellesley College (B.A., 1981); Northwestern University (J.D., 1984). Articles Editor, Journal of Criminal Law and Criminology, 1983-1984. *Member:* Energy Bar Association (Member, Board of Directors). ***PRACTICE AREAS:*** Energy Law; Federal Regulation. ***Email:*** lisanne.crowley@troutmansanders.com

KEVIN C. FITZGERALD, born Redlands, California, October 15, 1962; admitted to bar, 1991, Massachusetts; 1994, District of Columbia. *Education:* George Washington University (B.A., 1985; M.I.A., 1988; J.D., 1991). *Member:* Federal Energy and American Bar Associations. ***PRACTICE AREAS:*** Energy; Legislative Corporate Reorganization; Regulatory Law. ***Email:*** kevin.fitzgerald@troutmansanders.com

BENJAMIN LEE ISRAEL, born New York, N.Y., September 4, 1962; admitted to bar, 1987, Maryland; 1988, District of Columbia; 1994, U.S. District Court, District of Maryland; 1996, U.S. Court of Appeals, District of Columbia Circuit. *Education:* Syracuse University (B.A., magna cum laude, 1984); George Washington University (J.D., with honors, 1987). *Member:* The District of Columbia Bar; Maryland State and Federal Energy Bar Associations. ***PRACTICE AREAS:*** Electric, Natural Gas and Independent Power Development and Regulation; Federal and State Election Law; Energy; Real Estate; Finance; Public Finance. ***Email:*** benjamin.israel@troutmansanders.com

THOMAS C. JENSEN, born Pasadena, California, October 16, 1958; admitted to bar, 1984, Oregon; 1998, District of Columbia. *Education:* University of Southern California (B.A., History, 1980); Northwestern School of Law of Lewis & Clark College (J.D., 1983). ***PRACTICE AREAS:*** Natural Resources; Energy; Environmental Law; Federal Regulatory Policy; Public Policy Legislation; Property Takings. ***Email:*** thomas.jensen@troutmansanders.com

JOHN R. MOLM, born Dubuque, Iowa, October 25, 1947; admitted to bar, 1973, North Carolina; 1976, Georgia; 1998, District of Columbia. *Education:* North Dakota State University (B.A., 1970); Georgetown University Law Center (J.D., 1973). Blue Key. *Member:* The North Carolina State Bar; State Bar of Georgia; American Bar Association. ***PRACTICE AREAS:*** Energy Law and Hydropower Compliance and Licensing; Environmental Law; Railroad Transportation; Water Rights; Transportation; Public Finance; Finance; Real Estate. ***Email:*** john.molm@troutmansanders.com

WILLIAM A. MULLINS, born La Junta, Colorado, October 7, 1961; admitted to bar, 1988, Colorado and District of Columbia. *Education:* University of Colorado (B.A., summa cum laude, in general honors, magna cum laude in Political Science, 1984; J.D., 1987). Phi Beta Kappa. Rothgerber Moot Court. Chief Counsel to Commissioners Andre, Emmett, Walden, Interstate Commerce Commission, Surface Transportation Board, 1987-1993. *Member:* Colorado Bar Association; The District of Columbia Bar; Association for Transportation Law, Logistics, Policy. ***PRACTICE AREAS:*** Transportation; Administrative Law; Government Relations; Antitrust. ***Email:*** william.mullins@troutmansanders.com

STUART F. PIERSON, born Washington, D.C., June 25, 1943; admitted to bar, 1969, District of Columbia; 1984, New York. *Education:* Hobart College (B.A., cum laude, 1965); Duke University Law School (J.D., 1968). U.S. Department of Justice, Civil Rights Division, 1968-1971. Assistant U.S. Attorney, Western District of Washington, 1971-1973. Special Assistant U.S. Attorney, Western District of Washington, 1973-1974. Verner, Liipfert, Bernhard, McPherson & Hand, 1977-1988; Davis Wright Tremaine, 1988-1996; Levine Pierson Sullivan & Kock, L.L.P., 1997-1998. Chair, D.C. Court of Appeals Committee on Unauthorized Practice, 1992—. *Member:* District of Columbia Bar; Bar Association of the District of Columbia; American Bar Association (Member, Forum on Communications Law; Chair, TIPS Committee on Defamation Torts, 1994-1995); National Association of Criminal Defense Lawyers; The Association of Trial Lawyers of America. ***PRACTICE AREAS:*** Qui Tam Litigation; Grand Jury Practice; White Collar Crime; Insurance Defense. ***Email:*** stuart.pierson@troutmansanders.com

RONALD R. ROSS, born Washington, D.C., February 10, 1960; admitted to bar, 1986, District of Columbia. *Education:* Yale University (B.A., Political Science, cum laude, 1982); Harvard University (J.D., 1985). Instructor, Legal Methods program, Harvard Law School, 1983, 1984. Member: Yale Club of New York City; Yale Club of Washington, D.C.; Capital Society. *Member:* The District of Columbia Bar; Bar Association of the District of Columbia; National and American Bar Associations. ***PRACTICE AREAS:*** Project Finance; Privatizations; Acquisitions; Corporate; Public Finance; Finance; Real Estate. ***Email:*** ronald.ross@troutmansanders.com

DONALD F. SANTA, JR., born New Haven, Connecticut, October 16, 1958; admitted to bar, 1983, District of Columbia. *Education:* Duke University (A.B., magna cum laude, 1980); Columbia University (J.D., 1983). Stone Scholar, 1981-1982. *Member:* The District of Columbia Bar; Federal Energy and American (Member, Sections on: Public Utility Law; Administrative Law) Bar Associations. ***PRACTICE AREAS:*** Energy Marketing; Regulatory; Public Policy Legislation. ***Email:*** donald.santa@troutmansanders.com

CLIFFORD S. SIKORA, born Harrisburg, Pennsylvania, May 14, 1962; admitted to bar, 1989, Pennsylvania (Not admitted in District of Columbia). *Education:* Cornell University (B.S., 1984); University of Delaware (M.P.A., 1986); University of Dayton (J.D., 1989). Executive Editor, 1988-1989 and Staff Member, 1987-1988, Dayton L.Rev. Author: "Engineering Exotic Blends in

(This Listing Continued)

(This Listing Continued)

TROUTMAN SANDERS LLP, Washington—Continued

Utility Mergers," Mergers and Acquisitions, September, 1997; "The Changing Electricity Supply Market: New Challenges, Opportunities for Hydro," *Hydro Review,* Vol. XV, No. 1, Feb. 1996; "FERC's New Approach to Economic Analysis: Putting it in Perspective," *Hydro Review,* Vol. XIV, No. 7, Dec. 1995. Counsel, U.S. Senate Committee on Energy and Natural Resources (1995-1996). Legal Advisor, Commissioner, Donald F. Santa, Jr., FERC (1993-1995). *Member:* Bar of the Commonwealth of Pennsylvania. ***PRACTICE AREAS:*** Electric Utility Regulation; Independent Power Production; Public Policy; Legislation; Regulatory Policy; Regulatory Law. ***Email:*** clifford.sikora@troutmansanders.com

ROGER D. WILLIAMS, born Smyrna, Tennessee, August 11, 1957; admitted to bar, 1991, Alabama; 1992, District of Columbia. *Education:* Vanderbilt University (B.E., Chem. Engr., cum laude, 1979); Tulane University (M.S., Petroleum Engr., 1988); University of Alabama (J.D., summa cum laude, 1991). Tau Beta Pi; Order of the Coif. Member, Alabama Law Review, 1989-1991. Recipient, Dean M. Leigh Harrison Award. Registered Professional Engineer, Florida, 1983 and Alabama, 1986. *Member:* Federal Energy Bar Association. ***PRACTICE AREAS:*** Project Development; Project Finance; Oil and Gas. ***Email:*** rogerd.williams@troutmansanders.com

ASSOCIATES

ELIZABETH ANNE BELL, born Columbus, Ohio, August 26, 1971; admitted to bar, 1999, California (Not admitted in District of Columbia). *Education:* University of Vermont; Georgetown University (J.D., 1999). *Member:* State Bar of California. ***PRACTICE AREAS:*** Indian Law; Environmental Law. ***Email:*** elizabeth.bell@troutmansanders.com

SANDRA L. BROWN, born Cleveland, Ohio, June 10, 1968; admitted to bar, 1993, Ohio; 1995, Maryland; 1996, District of Columbia and U.S. District Court, District of Maryland; 1997, U.S. District Court, District of Columbia. *Education:* Goshen College (B.A., 1990); Ohio Northern University (J.D., 1993). National Order of Barristers. ***PRACTICE AREAS:*** Transportation Regulation; Litigation; Government Relations; Transportation. ***Email:*** sandra.brown@troutmansanders.com

VIRGINIA A. BRUNELLI, born Piracicaba, São Paulo, Brazil, March 21, 1974; admitted to bar, 2000, New York (Not admitted in District of Columbia). *Education:* Duke University School of Law (LL.M., 2000). *Member:* Brazilian Bar Association (Member, São Paulo Section). ***LANGUAGES:*** English, Portuguese, Spanish, Italian and French. ***PRACTICE AREAS:*** Project Finance; International Transactions. ***Email:*** virginia.brunelli@troutsanders.com

ANTOINE P. COBB, born Fort Bragg, North Carolina, May 21, 1970; admitted to bar, 1996, Virginia; 1998, District of Columbia. *Education:* Norfolk State University (B.A., cum laude, 1992); George Mason University School of Law (J.D., 1995). *Member:* Energy Bar and American Bar Associations. ***PRACTICE AREAS:*** Government Affairs; Utility Regulation; Regulatory Law. ***Email:*** antoine.cobb@troutmansanders.com

AMIE V. COLBY, born St. Louis, Missouri, January 11, 1972; admitted to bar, 1999, Maryland; 2000, District of Columbia. *Education:* Vanderbilt University (B.A., 1994); Georgetown University Law Center (J.D., 1999). ***PRACTICE AREAS:*** Administrative Law; Energy; Environmental Law; Regulatory Law. ***Email:*** amie.colby@troutmansanders.com

WILLIAM R. DERASMO, born Suffern, New York, February 12, 1969; admitted to bar, 1994, New Jersey; 1995, New York (Not admitted in District of Columbia). *Education:* Colgate University (B.A., 1991); Wake Forest University (J.D., 1994). *Member:* New York State Bar Association; Energy Bar Association. ***REPORTED CASES:*** 657 N.Y.S.2d 254; 657 N.Y.S.2d 498; 656 N.Y.S.2d 570; 657 N.Y.S.2d 216; 656 N.Y.S.2d 703; 657 N.Y.S.2d 233; 655 N.Y.S.2d 677; 655 N.Y.S.2d 681; 656 N.Y.S.2d 972; 654 N.Y.S.2d 203; 653 N.Y.S.2d 732; 653 N.Y.S.2d 831; 653 N.Y.S.2d 44; 653 N.Y.S.2d 175; 650 N.Y.S.2d 53; 649 N.Y.S.2d 953; 649 N.Y.S.2d 735; 649 N.Y.S.2d 744; 648 N.Y.S.2d 748; 648 N.Y.S.2d 758; 648 N.Y.S.2d 50; 648 N.Y.S.2d 58; 647 N.Y.S.2d 58; 647 N.Y.S.2d 126; 646 N.Y.S.2d 730; 646 N.Y.S.2d 736; 644 N.Y.S.2d 94; 643 N.Y.S.2d 779; 642 N.Y.S.2d 380; 640 N.Y.S.2d 658; 640 N.Y.S.2d 302; 657 N.Y.S.2d 370; 655 N.Y.S.2d 680; 655 N.Y.S.2d 682; 656 N.Y.S.2d 970; 654 N.Y.S.2d 208; 653 N.Y.S.2d 443; 653 N.Y.S.2d 165; 653 N.Y.S.2d 170; 653 N.Y.S.2d 46; 650 N.Y.S.2d 360; 650 N.Y.S.2d 1015; 649 N.Y.S.2d 742; 649 N.Y.S.2d 75; 648 N.Y.S.2d 751; 648 N.Y.S.2d 179; 648 N.Y.S.2d 479; 647 N.Y.S.2d 1019; 647 N.Y.S.2d 580; 646 N.Y.S.2d 729; 646 N.Y.S.2d 908; 644 N.Y.S.2d 359; 644 N.Y.S.2d 99; 642 N.Y.S.2d 101; 640 N.Y.S.2d 655; 640 N.Y.S.2d 686; 638 N.Y.S.2d 228. ***PRACTICE AREAS:*** Energy; Administrative Law; Regulatory Law; Utility Law. ***Email:*** william.derasmo@troutmansanders.com

ILANA R. FISHER, born Los Angeles, California, September 24, 1972; admitted to bar, 1998, Massachusetts; 1999, District of Columbia and U.S. District Court, District of Massachusetts; 2001, U.S. District Court for the District of Columbia. *Education:* University of California, Irvine (B.A., 1994); Hebrew University, Jerusalem, Israel (1992-1993); Cornell University (J.D., 1998). Co-Author: with William F. Causey, "Personnel Handbooks Incite Suits," Nat'l L.J., Nov. 20, 2000, at B13. *Member:* American Bar Association. ***PRACTICE AREAS:*** Complex and Multi-District Litigation; Labor and Employment. ***Email:*** ilana.fisher@troutmansanders.com

JEFFREY M. JAKUBIAK, born Princeton, New Jersey, October 4, 1971; admitted to bar, 1998, New York; 1999, District of Columbia. *Education:* Stanford University (A.B., with honors, 1993); Cornell University (J.D., 1997). Note Editor, Cornell Journal of Law and Public Policy. *Member:* District of Columbia Bar. ***LANGUAGES:*** French. ***PRACTICE AREAS:*** Regulated Industries; Regulatory Law. ***Email:*** jeffrey.jakubiak@troutmansanders.com

DANIEL M. MALABONGA, born Manila, Philippines, May 29, 1958; admitted to bar, 1984, Philippines; 1993, New York; 1999, District of Columbia. *Education:* University of the Philippines (A.B., cum laude, Philosophy, 1979; LL.B., cum laude, 1983). Phi Kappa Phi; Order of the Purple Feather. Member, Society of Law Students, 1980-1982. Member, UP-Flag Paralegal Volunteer Corps. *Member:* New York State Bar Association; District of Columbia Bar; Integrated Bar of the Philippines. ***LANGUAGES:*** English and Tagalog. ***PRACTICE AREAS:*** International Arbitration; International Litigation; General Practice; Philippine Law. ***Email:*** daniel.malabonga@troutmansanders.com

WILLIAM P. MARSAN, born Oakland, California, June 1, 1963; admitted to bar, 1989, Massachusetts; 1996, District of Columbia. *Education:* Boston College (B.A., 1986); George Washington University (J.D., 1989). Legislative Director, U.S. Rep. Charles T. Canady (R-FL), 1995-1996. Certified Arbitrator, National Association of Securities Dealers. [Lt., JAGC, U.S. Navy, 1989-1993]. ***PRACTICE AREAS:*** Government Affairs; Utility Regulation; Electronic Commerce; Regulatory Law. ***Email:*** william.marsan@troutmansanders.com

EILEEN M. MOORHEAD, born Tucson, Arizona; admitted to bar, 1995, California; 1999, District of Columbia. *Education:* Wellesley College (B.A., 1986); University of Miami (J.D., 1995). *Member:* Bar Association of the District of Columbia. ***PRACTICE AREAS:*** Federal Regulatory Policy; Environmental Law; Natural Resources. ***Email:*** eileen.moorhead@troutmansanders.com

MELISSA L. PIGNATELLI, born San Diego, California, May 3, 1974; admitted to bar, 1999, Maryland; 2000, District of Columbia. *Education:* University of Virginia (B.A., Foreign Affairs, 1996); Washington & Lee University (J.D., 1999). Women's Law Student Organization. *Member:* Maryland State and American Bar Associations; The District of Columbia Bar; Energy Bar Association. ***PRACTICE AREAS:*** Energy; Administrative Law; Legislative Practice; Environmental Law; Regulatory Law. ***Email:*** melissa.pignatelli@troutmansanders.com

DAVID C. REEVES, born Seattle, Washington, March 25, 1955; admitted to bar, 1980, Virginia; 1999, District of Columbia. *Education:* University of North Carolina (B.A., with honors in Political Science, 1977); Duke University School of Law (J.D., 1980). Phi Beta Kappa; Phi Eta Sigma. ***PRACTICE AREAS:*** Transportation Regulation; Transportation; Corporate Law. ***Email:*** david.reeves@troutmansanders.com

R. MICHAEL SWEENEY, born Kingston, New York, December 2, 1965; admitted to bar, 1992, Connecticut; 1993, New York, Massachusetts and U.S. District Court, Northern and Southern Districts of New York (Not admitted in District of Columbia). *Education:* St. Lawrence University (B.A., 1988); University of Notre Dame; Capital University (J.D., 1992); George Washington University (LL.M., 1996). (Resident). ***PRACTICE AREAS:*** Federal Regulatory; Project Finance; Project Development; Public Utilities Law; Environmental; Electronic Commerce; Mergers and Acquisitions; Regulatory Law. ***Email:*** michael.sweeney@troutmansanders.com

DIONNE THOMPSON, born Port Gibson, Mississippi, January 8, 1967; admitted to bar, 1994, Pennsylvania (Not admitted in District of Columbia). *Education:* Harvard University (B.A., 1989); University of Virginia (J.D., 1993). ***LANGUAGES:*** French. ***PRACTICE AREAS:*** Federal Regulatory; Public Law; Regulatory Law. ***Email:*** dionne.thompson@troutmansanders.com

SIF THORGEIRSSON, born London, England, August 13, 1971; admitted to bar, 1998, Maryland; 1999, District of Columbia. *Education:* McGill University (B.A., 1993); George Washington University (J.D., 1998). Articles Editor, The George Washington Journal of International Law and Economics, 1997-1998. ***LANGUAGES:*** Icelandic, French. ***PRACTICE AREAS:*** Project Development; Project Finance; International Law; Corporate Law; Finance; Public Finance; Real Estate. ***Email:*** sif.thorgeirsson@troutmansanders.com

CHARLES A. ZDEBSKI, born New York, New York, November 12, 1966; admitted to bar, 1994, Virginia and U.S. Court of Appeals, Fourth Circuit; 1995, Maryland and U.S. District Court, Eastern District of Virginia; 1996, District of Columbia, U.S. Bankruptcy Court, Eastern District of Virginia, U.S. District Court for the District of Columbia, U.S. Court of Appeals for the District of Columbia Circuit; 1998, U.S. District Court, District of Maryland; 1999, U.S. District Court, Eastern District of Wisconsin. *Education:* Harvard University (A.B., with honors, 1988); George Washington University (J.D., with honors, 1994). Member, Moot Court Board, 1992-1994. Member, Journal of Interna-

(This Listing Continued)

(This Listing Continued)

tional Law and Economics, 1992-1994. *Member:* Virginia and American (Member, Litigation Section) Bar Associations. ***LANGUAGES:*** Spanish. ***PRACTICE AREAS:*** Business Litigation; Complex Litigation; Employment Litigation; Litigation; Complex and Multi-District Litigation. ***Email:*** charles.zdebski@troutmansanders.com

OF COUNSEL

JAMES C. BEH, born Des Moines, Iowa, November 2, 1958; admitted to bar, 1985, District of Columbia; 1986, U.S. District Court, District of Columbia and U.S. Court of Appeals, District of Columbia Circuit; 1988, U.S. Supreme Court; 1992, U.S. Court of Federal Claims; 1993, U.S. Court of Appeals, Eleventh Circuit; 1997, U.S. Court of Appeals, First Circuit. *Education:* Georgetown University (A.B., 1981; J.D., 1984). Articles Editor, Georgetown Law Journal, 1983-1984. Co-Author: "FERC Fails To Resolve Aspects of Rolled-in-Versus Incremental Debate," 12 Natural Gas 18 (August 1995); "What? Me Worry? FERC looks at the Wave of New Pipeline Proposals," 1CCH Power and Telecom Law 3, January/February 1998. *Member:* The District of Columbia Bar; Federal Energy and American Bar Associations; Federal Electric Bar Association. Fellow, American Inns of Court, 1983-1984. (Resident). ***PRACTICE AREAS:*** Energy Law; Public Utility Law; Administrative Law; Regulatory Law. ***Email:*** james.beh@troutmansanders.com

SEAN T. CONNAUGHTON, born Brooklyn, New York, February 25, 1961; admitted to bar, 1992, Virginia; 1993, District of Columbia and Court of Veterans Appeals. *Education:* U.S. Merchant Marine Academy (B.S., 1983); Georgetown University (M.A., 1988); George Mason University (J.D., 1992). Chairman, Prince William Board of County Supervisors, 2000—. [U.S. Coast Guard, 1983-1986; U.S. Naval Reserves, 1986—; Third Mate, Merchant Marines, 1998]. ***PRACTICE AREAS:*** Marine Transportation; Government Affairs; Environmental. ***Email:*** sean.connaughton@troutmansanders.com

ROBERT G. DREHER, born Bath, New York, December 17, 1951; admitted to bar, 1981, Massachusetts; 1982, California; 1986, District of Columbia. *Education:* Harvard College (A.B., 1973); Brown University (M.A., 1979); Yale University (J.D., 1981). Adjunct Professor, George Washington University Law School, 1991mmdash;. Deputy General Counsel, U.S. Environmental Protection Agency, 1996-2000. ***PRACTICE AREAS:*** Environmental Law; Litigation. ***Email:*** robert.dreher@troutmansanders.com

MARY CLARE FITZGERALD, born January 18, 1946; admitted to bar, 1994, Pennsylvania; 2000, District of Columbia. *Education:* College of William & Mary (B.A., 1968); Johns Hopkins University, School of Advanced International Studies (M.A. International Relations); George Mason University School of Law (J.D., 1994). ***PRACTICE AREAS:*** Electronic Commerce; Banking; Government Relations; Communications and Media. ***Email:*** mc.fitzgerald@troutmansanders.com

LEONARD L. FLEISIG, born New York, N.Y., June 9, 1953; admitted to bar, 1991, New York; 1992, U.S. District Court, Southern and Eastern Districts of New York and U.S. Court of International Trade; 1993, District of Columbia and U.S. District Court for the District of Columbia. *Education:* Victoria University, Manchester, England (B.A., with honors, 1975); New York University (J.D., 1990). *Member:* Maritime Law Association; Maritime Administrative Bar Association (Vice-President, 2000-2001). ***PRACTICE AREAS:*** Transportation; Trade; Customs. ***Email:*** leonard.fleisig@troutmansanders.com

THOMAS J. HEALEY, JR., born Evergreen Park, Illinois, March 6, 1963; admitted to bar, 1998, Illinois; 1996, Georgia (Not admitted in District of Columbia). *Education:* John Carroll University (B.S./B.A., 1985); University of Illinois (J.D., 1988). ***PRACTICE AREAS:*** Railroad Regulatory; Labor and Employment; Litigation; Commercial Law; Contracts; Personal Injury Law; Transportation. ***Email:*** thomas.healey@troutmansanders.com

MICHAEL L. KESSLER, born Malden, Massachusetts, October 24, 1953; admitted to bar, 1980, Massachusetts; 1984, District of Columbia. *Education:* Brown University (B.A., 1975); Vermont Law School (J.D., cum laude, 1980). *Member:* Federal Energy and American Bar Associations. ***PRACTICE AREAS:*** Energy Law; Regulatory; Finance; Real Estate; Public Finance. ***Email:*** michael.kessler@troutmansanders.com

SOTIRIS A. (TED) PLANZOS, born Brooklyn, New York, July 25, 1957; admitted to bar, 1983, New York and U.S. District Court, Southern and Eastern Districts of New York; 1989, District of Columbia. *Education:* John Jay College of Criminal Justice of the City University of New York (B.A., 1979); California Western University (J.D., 1982). Recipient, American Jurisprudence Award, Trusts and Estates. Assistant District Attorney, Bronx County, 1983-1989. Special Assistant U.S. Attorney, Southern District of New York, 1986-1988. Senior Counsel Division, Enforcement Securities & Exchange Commission, 1989-1992. Deputy Chief of Organized Crime and Racketeering Section, Department of Justice, 1992-2000. ***LANGUAGES:*** Greek. ***PRACTICE AREAS:*** Complex Litigation; White Collar Criminal Defense; Securities; White Collar Crime. ***Email:*** ted.planzos@troutmansanders.com

BONNIE A. SUCHMAN, born Lakewood, New Jersey, May 7, 1958; admitted to bar, 1983, District of Columbia; 1985, U.S. District Court for the

(This Listing Continued)

District of Columbia; 1992, Maryland. *Education:* Bard College (B.A., 1980); George Washington University (J.D., 1983). Senior Attorney, Edison Electric Institute, 1988-1989. *Member:* The District of Columbia Bar; Women's Bar Association. ***PRACTICE AREAS:*** Energy; Utility Law; Regulatory Law. ***Email:*** bonnie.suchman@troutmansanders.com

(For Biographical data on all Personnel, see Professional Biographies at Atlanta, Georgia)

TROW & KEARNEY, P.C.

Established in 1993

SUITE 440
5335 WISCONSIN AVENUE, N.W.
WASHINGTON, D.C. 20015-2003
Telephone: 202-537-4830
Fax: 202-537-4831
Email: mailbox@tk-law.com

Immigration and Nationality Law.

FIRM PROFILE: Trow & Kearney, P.C. specializes in U.S. immigration and nationality law, and within this field it concentrates on immigration matters involving employment, trade, investment, and other business activities. The firm assists clients in obtaining temporary work visas, permanent resident status, and U.S. citizenship, and in integrating their immigration objectives with business and tax objectives. The firm also counsels U.S. employers on compliance with federal requirements for verification of employees' work authorization. The firm represents clients throughout the United States and around the world before the U.S. Immigration and Naturalization Service, the U.S. Department of State, the U.S. Department of Labor, state employment agencies and U.S. embassies and consulates abroad.

STEPHEN C. TROW, born Ann Arbor, Michigan, September 28, 1951; admitted to bar, 1978, District of Columbia. *Education:* State University of New York at Binghamton; University of Colorado at Colorado Springs (B.A., cum laude, 1975); Cornell University (J.D., cum laude, 1978). Member, Board of Editors, Cornell Law Review, 1977-1978. Author: "Visa Classifications For Foreign Investors and Business Personnel," Manual of Foreign Investment in the United States, Shepard's/McGraw Hill, 1984. *Member:* American Bar Association; American Immigration Lawyers Association. ***PRACTICE AREAS:*** Immigration and Nationality Law. ***Email:*** s.trow@tk-law.com

MARY M. KEARNEY, born Johnstown, Pennsylvania, February 16, 1954; admitted to bar, 1979, District of Columbia; 1980, U.S. Court of Appeals for the District of Columbia Circuit and U.S. District Court for the District of Columbia; 1983, U.S. Supreme Court and U.S. Court of Appeals, Ninth Circuit; 1987, Maryland. *Education:* University of Virginia (B.A., with distinction, 1976; J.D., 1979). Member, Editorial Board, 1977-1978 and Notes Editor, 1978-1979, Virginia Journal of International Law. Author: Comment, 17 Virginia Journal of International Law 567, 1977; "Immunities of International Organizations," 22 Virginia Journal of International Law 247, 1982. *Member:* American Immigration Lawyers Association. ***PRACTICE AREAS:*** Immigration and Nationality Law. ***Email:*** m.kearney@tk-law.com

LINDA A. RAHAL, born Massachusetts, March 7, 1964; admitted to bar, 1993, Maryland; 1995, District of Columbia. *Education:* Tufts University (B.A., cum laude, 1986); The American University, Washington College of Law (J.D., magna cum laude, 1992). *Member:* American Immigration Lawyers Association (Department of Labor committee, 1999-2001; Vermont Service Center Committee, 2000-2001). ***PRACTICE AREAS:*** Immigration and Nationality Law. ***Email:*** l.rahal@tk-law.com

---

CYNTHIA B. HEMPHILL, born San Francisco, California, June 7, 1961; admitted to bar, 1995, New York; 1996, District of Columbia. *Education:* Yale University (B.A., 1983); Howard University (J.D., 1993). *Member:* American Immigration Lawyers Association; Women's Bar Association. ***PRACTICE AREAS:*** Immigration and Nationality Law. ***Email:*** c.hemphill@tk-law.com

JOAN J. KARAGANIS, born Silver Spring, Maryland, February 16, 1969; admitted to bar, 1995, Maryland; 2001, District of Columbia. *Education:* Catholic University of America (B.A., magna cum laude, 1990; J.D., with Certificate in International Law and Comparative Studies, 1993). Phi Beta Kappa. *Member:* American Immigration Lawyers Association. ***PRACTICE AREAS:*** Immigration and Nationality Law. ***Email:*** j.karaganis@tk-law.com

NORMA BRISCOE HOFFPAUIR, born Delhi, India, 1964; admitted to bar, 1994, Pennsylvania, Maryland and District of Columbia; U.S. District Court, District of Maryland. *Education:* University of Maryland, University College (B.S., 1987); Howard University (J.D., 1993). *Member:* American Bar

(This Listing Continued)

TROW & KEARNEY, P.C., Washington—Continued

Association; American Immigration Lawyers Association. ***LANGUAGES:*** Hindi. ***PRACTICE AREAS:*** Immigration and Nationality Law. ***Email:*** n. hoffpauir@tk-law.com

OF COUNSEL

DONALD L. MOOERS, born Bangor, Maine, April 12, 1960; admitted to bar, 1987, Maryland; 2000, District of Columbia. *Education:* Duke University (B.A., magna cum laude, 1981); George Washington University (J.D., 1986). *Member:* Montgomery County Bar Association; American Immigration Lawyers Association; Biotechnology Industry Organization; Montgomery County Chamber of Commerce; Maryland Chamber of Commerce. ***PRACTICE AREAS:*** Immigration and Naturalization. ***Email:*** d.mooers@tk-law.com

TUCKER, FLYER

WASHINGTON, D.C.

(See Venable, Attorneys at Law, Venable, Baetjer and Howard, LLP)

TYLER, BARTL, BURKE & GORMAN, P.L.C.

WASHINGTON, D.C.

(See Alexandria, Virginia)

Appellate Practice, Bankruptcy, Insolvency, Reorganization, Workouts, Real Estate, Corporate Law, Commercial Law, Debtor and Creditor, Business Law, Contracts, Wills and Probate, Criminal, Personal Injury, Domestic Relations Law, Estate Planning, Litigation, General Practice and Trials.

UNGARETTI & HARRIS

1500 K STREET, N.W., SUITE 250

WASHINGTON, D.C. 20005-1714

Telephone: 202-639-7500

Fax: 202-639-7505

Email: info@uhlaw.com

URL: http://www.uhlaw.com

Chicago, Illinois Office: 3500 Three First National Plaza. Telephone: 312-977-4400. FAX: 312-977-4405.

General Practice, including Business and Corporate, Financial Services and Securities, Litigation and Appeals, Real Estate, Health Care, Information Technology, Public Finance, Legislative and Regulatory Affairs, Labor and Employment, Employee Benefits, Taxation, Affordable Housing, Environmental, Bankruptcy and Creditors' Rights, Estates and Trusts, Gaming Law, Intellectual Property and Patent Litigation, Class Actions and Securities Arbitration.

PARTNERS

JOSEPH A. CARI, JR., admitted to bar, 1978, Illinois; 1984, U.S. Supreme Court (Not admitted in District of Columbia). Appointed by President Clinton to the Board of Trustees of the Woodrow Wilson Center, 1995 and as Chairman of the Board in 1999. ***PRACTICE AREAS:*** Business Law; Legislative Practice; Regulatory Law. ***Email:*** jacari@uhlaw.com

EDWARD P. FABERMAN, admitted to bar, 1970, New York; 1975, District of Columbia. *Education:* The American University (B.S., 1967); St. John's University School of Law (J.D., 1970). ***PRACTICE AREAS:*** Administrative Agency Practice; Airline Regulation; Airport Regulation; Aviation Law; Environmental Law. ***Email:*** epfaberman@uhlaw.com

CHARLES S. KONIGSBERG, admitted to bar, 1983, Ohio, District of Columbia and U.S. Supreme Court. *Education:* Kenyon College (A.B., magna cum laude, 1980); Case Western Reserve University (J.D., 1983). (Resident). ***PRACTICE AREAS:*** Legislative, Regulatory and Public Policy. ***Email:*** cskonigsberg@uhlaw.com

ASSOCIATES

PAGE C. FAULK, admitted to bar, 1997, Maryland (Not admitted in District of Columbia). *Education:* Southern Methodist University (B.A., 1992); Dickinson School of Law of the Pennsylvania State University (J.D., 1997). (Resident). ***Email:*** pcfaulk@uhlaw.com

MICHELLE M. FAUST, admitted to bar, 1998, New York (Not admitted in District of Columbia). *Education:* Syracuse University (B.A., cum laude, 1992); American University (J.D., 1997). (Resident). ***Email:*** mmfaust@uhlaw.com

(For complete biographical data on all personnel, see Professional Biographies at Chicago, Illinois)

VAN CLEVE & EDER

Established in 1995

1155 CONNECTICUT AVENUE, N.W., SUITE 300

WASHINGTON, D.C. 20036

Telephone: 202-467-8022

Fax: 202-887-9144

Email: gvclaw@erols.com

Civil Litigation, including Patent Licensing, Copyright and Trademark Licensing, Contract, Fraud, Antitrust, Class Action, Civil Rights, Employment and other Complex Litigation and Appeals; Specialty Risk Insurance Matters. Environmental Law, Corporate Investigations, Government Contracts, Intellectual Property.

FIRM PROFILE: Our attorneys have represented clients in civil litigation matters in courts in fifteen states and the District of Columbia, and five federal courts of appeal.

GEORGE VAN CLEVE, born New Brunswick, New Jersey, October 6, 1952; admitted to bar, 1977, Illinois; 1979, District of Columbia. *Education:* University of Chicago (B.A., with honors, 1973, Phi Beta Kappa); Harvard University (J.D., cum laude, 1977). Deputy Assistant Attorney General, Environment and Natural Resources Division, U.S. Department of Justice, 1989-1991. Special Counsel to Secretary of Defense, 1989. Chief Minority Counsel, House Select Committee to Investigate Covert Arms Transactions with Iran, 1986-1987. *Member:* The District of Columbia Bar. ***REPORTED CASES:*** Reardon v. United States, 947 F.2d 1509 (1st Cir. 1991); United States v. 313.34 Acres, 923 F.2d 698 (9th Cir. 1991); Upper Snake River Chptr. of Trout Unlimited v. Hodel, 921 F.2d 232 (9th Cir. 1990); Devils Lake Sioux Tribe v. North Dakota, 917 F.2d 1049 (8th Cir. 1990); Aulston v. United States, 915 F.2d 584 (10th Cir. 1990); Nevada v. Burford, 918 F.2d 854 (9th Cir. 1990); Portsmouth Redev. & Hous. Auth. v. BMI Apts. Assocs., 847 F. Supp. 380 (E.D. Va. 1994); United States v. Exxon Corp. and Exxon Shipping Co., Crim. No. A90-015 CR, 1990 U.S. Dist. Lexis 1821 (D. Alaska 1990). ***Email:*** gvclaw@erols.com

ELLIOT D. EDER, born St. Louis, Missouri, May 6, 1958; admitted to bar, 1986, Massachusetts; 1987, District of Columbia. *Education:* Harvard University (A.B., cum laude, 1981); Boston University (J.D., 1986). Trial Attorney, Environmental and Nat. Resources Div., U.S. Department of Justice, 1989-1995. Successively an Associate, Of Counsel and Partner, Jones, Day, Ravis & Pogue, 1995-2000. USLaw.com, Inc., Gen. Counsel, Law Ops, 2000-2001. Co-Vice Chair, ABA/SEER Special Committee on Science and Technology, 2001. Author, "The Standards of Admissibility of Scientific and Technical Evidence," Lead chapter in Scientific Evidence and Experts Handbook (Aspen Law & Business, 2001). *Member:* American Bar Association (Litigation and Intellectual Property Sections). ***REPORTED CASES:*** U.S. v. Ekco Housewares, 853 F. Supp. 975 (S.D. Ohio 1994), affirmed in part, 62 F.3d 806 (6th Cir. 1995); U.S. v. Prod. Plated Plastics, 762 F.Supp. 722 (W.D. Mich. 1991), affirmed, 955 F.2d 45 (6th Cir. 1992), cert. denied, 506 U.S. 820 (1992). ***Email:*** eevcalaw@erols.com

VAN NESS FELDMAN

A PROFESSIONAL CORPORATION

Established in 1977

SEVENTH FLOOR, 1050 THOMAS JEFFERSON STREET, N.W.

WASHINGTON, D.C. 20007-3877

Telephone: 202-298-1800

Fax: 202-338-2416

Email: vnf@vnf.com

URL: http://www.vnf.com

Seattle, Washington Office: 821 Second Avenue, Suite 2000. Telephone: 206-623-9372. Fax: 206-623-4986.

Energy, Environmental Law, Natural Resources, Federal Legislative Practice, Natural Gas, Electric Power, Electric Utilities, Energy Regulation, Hydroelectricity, International Energy Law, Public Land Law, Land Reclamation, Oil and Gas Law, Water Law, Endangered Species Act, Clean Water Act, Clean Air Act, Alaska Native Law, Indian Law, Taxation, Transportation, Administrative Law, Administrative Litigation.

FIRM PROFILE: Van Ness Feldman is a Washington, D.C.-based law firm concentrating on government policy and regulatory issues in the areas of energy, environmental, natural resource and transportation law. The firm prides itself on its creativity and success in representing a broad range of clients on "cutting edge" issues that are considered by the legislative, executive and judicial branches of the Federal government.

HOWARD J. FELDMAN, born Milwaukee, Wisconsin, March 6, 1939; admitted to bar, 1964, Wisconsin; 1965, U.S. Tax Court; 1967, U.S. Supreme Court; 1969, District of Columbia. *Education:* University of Wisconsin (B.B.A., cum laude, 1960; LL.B., 1964). Certified Public Accountant, Wisconsin, 1965.

(This Listing Continued)

Attorney, Appellate Section, Tax Division, Department of Justice, Washington, D.C., 1964-1968. Chief Counsel, U.S. Senate Permanent Subcommittee on Investigations of the Committee on Government Operations, 1973-1977. *Member:* The District of Columbia Bar; State Bar of Wisconsin; Federal and American Bar Associations. [Capt., JAGC, U.S. Army, 1961-1969]. ***PRACTICE AREAS:*** Taxation; Public Lands; Federal Legislative Practice. ***Email:*** hjf@vnf.com

WILLIAM J. VAN NESS, JR., born Wolf Point, Montana, January 20, 1938; admitted to bar, 1966, Washington; 1976, District of Columbia and U.S. Supreme Court; 1986, Alaska. *Education:* Western Washington State College (B.A., 1962); University of Washington (LL.B., 1966). Special Counsel, 1966-1969 and Chief Counsel, 1970-1976, U.S. Senate Interior and Insular Affairs Committee. *Member:* Alaska Bar Association; The District of Columbia Bar; Washington State Bar. (Resident, Seattle, Washington Office). ***PRACTICE AREAS:*** Energy; Environment; Public Lands; Land Reclamation; Federal Legislative Practice. ***Email:*** bvn@vnf.com

BEN YAMAGATA, born Rexburg, Idaho, April 12, 1947; admitted to bar, 1973, Idaho; 1979, District of Columbia. *Education:* Harvard University (B.A., 1969); George Washington University Law Center (J.D., 1972). Professional Staff Member, Senate Special Committee on Aging, 1973-1974. Legislative Counsel, U.S. Senator Frank Church, 1974-1975. Counsel and Staff Director, U.S. Senate Subcommittee on Energy Research and Development, 1975-1977. *Member:* The District of Columbia Bar; Idaho State Bar; American Bar Association. ***PRACTICE AREAS:*** Energy; Government Relations; Federal Legislative Practice; Technology Transfers; Transportation. ***Email:*** bny@vnf.com

ROBERT G. SZABO, born Monroe, Louisiana, February 24, 1947; admitted to bar, 1972, Louisiana; 1978, U.S. Supreme Court and District of Columbia. *Education:* Louisiana State University (B.S., 1970; J.D., 1972). Law Clerk, Justice John A. Dixon, Jr., Supreme Court of Louisiana, 1972-1973. Legislative Assistant, U.S. Senator J. Bennett Johnston, 1975-1978. *Member:* The District of Columbia Bar; Louisiana State Bar Association. ***PRACTICE AREAS:*** Environmental Law; Natural Resources; Government. ***Email:*** rgs@vnf.com

ALAN L. MINTZ, born Norwalk, Connecticut, April 5, 1949; admitted to bar, 1974, Connecticut; 1976, District of Columbia. *Education:* University of Michigan (B.A., 1970); Yale Law School (J.D., 1974). Attorney, Office of Exceptions and Appeals, Federal Energy Administration, 1974-1977. *Member:* The District of Columbia Bar (Member: Executive Committee; Environment, Energy and Natural Resources Committee, 1982-1984); Connecticut and American Bar Associations. ***PRACTICE AREAS:*** Public Lands; Alaska Natives; Energy; Natural Resources. ***Email:*** alm@vnf.com

ROBERT R. NORDHAUS, born Albuquerque, New Mexico, March 27, 1937; admitted to bar, 1963, New Mexico; 1981, District of Columbia. *Education:* Stanford University (B.A., 1960); Yale University (LL.B., 1963). Assistant Counsel, Office of House Legislative Counsel, 1963-1974. Counsel, Interstate and Foreign Commerce Committee, U.S. House of Representatives, 1975-1976. General Counsel, Federal Energy Regulatory Commission, 1977-1980. General Counsel, U.S. Department of Energy, 1993-1997. *Member:* The District of Columbia Bar; State Bar of New Mexico; Federal Energy and American Bar Associations. ***PRACTICE AREAS:*** Energy; Environment. ***Email:*** rrn@vnf.com

GARY D. BACHMAN, born Butler, Pennsylvania, March 17, 1953; admitted to bar, 1978, District of Columbia; 1979, U.S. Court of Appeals, District of Columbia Circuit; 1980, U.S. Court of International Trade; 1983, U.S. Supreme Court. *Education:* Bucknell University (B.A., 1975); Washington College of Law of The American University (J.D., cum laude, 1978). Member, Board of Directors, National Hydropower Association, 1987-1988. *Member:* The District of Columbia Bar; Federal Energy and American Bar Associations. ***PRACTICE AREAS:*** Energy; Environment; Hydroelectricity; Electric Utilities; Public Lands; Water. ***Email:*** gdb@vnf.com

MARGARET A. MOORE, born Orange, New Jersey, October 17, 1955; admitted to bar, 1980, District of Columbia. *Education:* Dickinson College (B.A., magna cum laude, 1977); George Washington University (J.D., 1980). Phi Beta Kappa. Attorney Advisor, 1982-1983 and Staff Attorney, 1983-1985, Federal Energy Regulatory Commission. *Member:* The District of Columbia Bar; Federal Energy and American Bar Associations. ***PRACTICE AREAS:*** Electric Power; Federal Energy Regulation; Energy Contracts; Utility Acquisitions. ***Email:*** mam@vnf.com

J. CURTIS MOFFATT, born North Wilkesboro, North Carolina, January 22, 1951; admitted to bar, 1976, North Carolina; 1979, District of Columbia. *Education:* Duke University (B.A., cum laude, 1973); University of North Carolina at Chapel Hill (J.D., 1975). Legal Assistant to the Chairman of the Federal Energy Regulatory Commission, 1977-1979. *Member:* North Carolina and American Bar Associations; The District of Columbia Bar; Federal Energy Bar Association. ***PRACTICE AREAS:*** Administrative Law; Energy; Natural Gas; Petroleum. ***Email:*** jcm@vnf.com

RICHARD A. AGNEW, born New Bern, North Carolina, October 8, 1951; admitted to bar, 1979, Washington; 1984, Alaska. *Education:* University of Washington (B.A., 1973); Seattle University School of Law (J.D., 1979). Staff

(This Listing Continued)

Counsel, Office of Congressman Don Young, 1980-1983; Minority Counsel, U.S. house of Representatives, Subcommittee on Public Lands and National Parks, 1983-1985; Chief Minority Counsel and Staff Director, U.S. House Interior and Insular Affairs Committee, 1985-1991. *Member:* Alaska, Washington State and American Bar Associations. (Resident, Seattle, Washington Office). ***PRACTICE AREAS:*** Natural Resources; Energy; Public Lands; Indians and Native Populations; Federal Legislative Practice; Utilities. ***Email:*** raa@vnf.com

HOWARD E. SHAPIRO, born Chicago, Illinois, December 18, 1926; admitted to bar, 1955, District of Columbia; 1960, U.S. Supreme Court. *Education:* University of Illinois (B.Sc., with honors, 1952); Columbia University (LL.B., 1955). *Member:* The District of Columbia Bar; American Bar Association. [U.S. Maritime Service, 1945-1946; U.S. Army, 1946-1949]. ***LANGUAGES:*** Spanish, French and Italian. ***PRACTICE AREAS:*** Appellate Practice; Energy; Antitrust; Regulated Industries; Federal Administrative Law. ***Email:*** hes@vnf.com

MICHAEL A. SWIGER, born Hawthorne, Nevada, June 24, 1955; admitted to bar, 1982, District of Columbia; 1990, U.S. Supreme Court; U.S. Court of Appeals for the District of Columbia and Ninth Circuits. *Education:* Kenyon College (A.B., summa cum laude, with high honors in Political Science, 1977); Yale University (M.A., 1982; M.Phil., 1982; J.D., 1982). Phi Beta Kappa. *Member:* The District of Columbia Bar (Member, Section on Environment, Energy and Natural Resources Law); Federal Energy Bar Association (Chair, Hydroelectric Regulation Committee, 1994-1995, 1997-1998). ***PRACTICE AREAS:*** Energy; Natural Resources; Administrative Law; Hydroelectricity; Environmental Law. ***Email:*** mas@vnf.com

DANIEL S. PRESS, born New York, N.Y., September 19, 1943; admitted to bar, 1969, Arizona; 1974, District of Columbia and U.S. Claims Court; 1981, U.S. Court of Appeals for the District of Columbia Circuit; 1982, U.S. Court of Appeals, Ninth Circuit; U.S. Supreme Court. *Education:* Columbia University (A.B., 1964); Yale Law School (LL.B., 1968). Reginald Heber Smith Community Lawyer Fellow, 1968-1970. ***PRACTICE AREAS:*** Indian Law; Indian Economic Development. ***Email:*** dsp@vnf.com

JULIA R. RICHARDSON, born Columbus, Ohio, September 21, 1946; admitted to bar, 1971, Michigan; 1975, District of Columbia; 1980, U.S. Court of Appeals for the District of Columbia Circuit. *Education:* University of Michigan (A.B., 1968; J.D., 1971). Office of General Counsel, Litigation Division, Federal Energy Administration, 1975-1976 and Executive Office of the President, Office of Energy Policy and Planning, 1977. *Member:* The District of Columbia Bar; State Bar of Michigan; Federal Energy and American Bar Associations; Energy Law Journal Foundation (Member, Board of Directors). ***PRACTICE AREAS:*** Energy; Natural Gas; Electric Power; International Energy. ***Email:*** jrr@vnf.com

RICHARD A. PENNA, born 1946; admitted to bar, 1971, District of Columbia; 1977, U.S. Court of Appeals, Tenth Circuit; 1978, U.S. Supreme Court. *Education:* St. Bonaventure University (B.S., 1968); Catholic University of America (J.D., 1971). Attorney, Office of Enforcement, Environmental Protection Agency, 1971-1977. Assistant Director, National Commission on Air Quality, 1978-1981. *Member:* The District of Columbia Bar. ***PRACTICE AREAS:*** Clean Air Act; Environmental. ***Email:*** rap@vnf.com

MITCHELL H. BERNSTEIN, born New York, N.Y., 1949; admitted to bar, 1974, New York; 1981, District of Columbia. *Education:* University of Pennsylvania (A.B., summa cum laude, 1970); Yale Law School (J.D., 1973). Phi Beta Kappa. *Member:* The District of Columbia Bar; American Bar Association. ***PRACTICE AREAS:*** Environment; Clean Air Act; Hazardous Waste; Superfund. ***Email:*** mhb@vnf.com

JOHN H. BURNES, JR., born New Haven, Connecticut, February 27, 1947; admitted to bar, 1972, Connecticut; 1980, District of Columbia. *Education:* Trinity College (B.A., 1969); University of Connecticut (J.D., cum laude, 1972). Staff Attorney: Federal Power Commission, Office of the Solicitor, 1972-1976; U.S. Department of Justice, Criminal Division, Appellate Section, 1976-1978. *Member:* The District of Columbia Bar; Connecticut, Federal Energy and American Bar Associations. ***PRACTICE AREAS:*** Natural Gas; Energy; Administrative Law; Federal Energy Regulation. ***Email:*** jhb@vnf.com

STEPHEN C. FOTIS, born Washington, D.C., March 22, 1955; admitted to bar, 1986, Maryland; 1988, District of Columbia. *Education:* Dartmouth College (B.A., 1977); Washington College of Law of the American University (J.D., 1986). *Member:* The District of Columbia Bar; The Bar Association of Baltimore City; Maryland State Bar Association. ***PRACTICE AREAS:*** Environment; Clean Air Act; Natural Resources; Air Pollution; Air Quality. ***Email:*** scf@vnf.com

THOMAS C. ROBERTS, born Aberdeen, South Dakota, June 28, 1954; admitted to bar, 1979, Alaska (Not admitted in District of Columbia). *Education:* South Dakota State University (B.S., 1976); University of Utah (J.D., 1979; LL.M., 1987). *Member:* Alaska Bar Association. ***PRACTICE AREAS:*** Environment; Energy; Natural Resources; Alaska Natives; Public Policy. ***Email:*** tcr@vnf.com

(This Listing Continued)

VAN NESS FELDMAN, A PROFESSIONAL CORPORATION, Washington—Continued

JOHN J. BUCHOVECKY, born Pittsburgh, Pennsylvania, April 29, 1960; admitted to bar, 1988, Pennsylvania; 1989, District of Columbia. *Education:* University of Southern California (A.B., 1984); Washington College of Law of the American University (J.D., 1988). *Member:* The District of Columbia Bar; Pennsylvania and Federal Energy Bar Associations. ***PRACTICE AREAS:*** Electric Power; Energy. ***Email:*** jjb@vnf.com

DAVID P. YAFFE, born Waukegan, Illinois, 1952; admitted to bar, 1977, Virginia; 1978, District of Columbia. *Education:* Johns Hopkins University (B.A., 1974); George Washington University (J.D., with honors, 1977). *Member:* The District of Columbia Bar; Virginia State Bar; American (Vice Chair, Electric Power Committee and Public Utility Law) and Federal Energy Bar Associations. ***LANGUAGES:*** Dutch. ***PRACTICE AREAS:*** Energy; Contracts; Administrative Law; Electric Utilities; Public Utilities. ***Email:*** dpy@vnf.com

CHERYL FEIK RYAN, born Denver, Colorado, May 26, 1962; admitted to bar, 1988, New York; 1992, District of Columbia. *Education:* Mount Holyoke College (A.B., 1984); Duke University (J.D., M.A., in Economics, 1987). *Member:* New York State, Federal Energy and American Bar Associations; District of Columbia Bar. ***PRACTICE AREAS:*** Energy; Electric Utilities; Administrative Litigation. ***Email:*** cfr@vnf.com

THERESA I. ZOLET, born Stevens Point, Wisconsin, January 27, 1962; admitted to bar, 1988, Maryland; 1989, District of Columbia. *Education:* Goucher College (B.A., with honors in Economics, 1984); University of Maryland (J.D., 1987). *Member:* The District of Columbia Bar; Maryland State, Federal Energy and American Bar Associations. ***PRACTICE AREAS:*** Natural Gas; Federal Energy Regulation; Administrative Law; Energy. ***Email:*** tiz@vnf.com

PAUL KORMAN, born Brooklyn, New York, December 9, 1948; admitted to bar, 1976, New York; 1978, District of Columbia. *Education:* Brooklyn College of the City University of New York (B.A., 1972); New York Law School (J.D., 1975). Special Assistant, Federal Power Commission, 1975-1977; Assistant to Commissioner George Hall, Federal Energy Regulatory Commission, 1977-1979. *Member:* Federal Energy and American Bar Associations. ***PRACTICE AREAS:*** Administrative Litigation; Natural Gas; Energy; Federal Energy Regulation. ***Email:*** pik@vnf.com

PATRICIA FRY GODLEY, born Chicago, Illinois, April 2, 1948; admitted to bar, 1979, District of Columbia; 1987, Texas. *Education:* Trinity University (B.A., 1970); Memphis State University (M.A., 1973); University of Texas (J.D., 1979). Special Assistant to the Deputy Secretary, U.S. Department of Energy, 1993-1994. Assistant Secretary for Fossil Energy, U.S. Department of Energy, 1994-1998. *Member:* Federal Energy and American Bar Associations. ***PRACTICE AREAS:*** Energy; Government; Natural Resources. ***Email:*** pfg@vnf.com

PAMELA J. ANDERSON, born Akron, Colorado, August 1, 1960; admitted to bar, 1990, Colorado; 1992, District of Columbia. *Education:* Colorado School of Mines; University of Northern Colorado (B.S., 1982); University of Denver (J.D., 1989). Certified Public Accountant, March, 1986. *Member:* Colorado Bar Association; Federal Energy Bar Association. ***PRACTICE AREAS:*** Natural Gas Regulation; Taxation; Government Contracts. ***Email:*** pja@vnf.com

STEVEN RICHARDSON, born Franklin, Indiana, August 18, 1948; admitted to bar, 1973, Indiana (Not admitted in District of Columbia). *Education:* Indiana University (B.A., 1970); Indiana University School of Law (J.D., 1973). Chief of Staff, Bureau of Reclamation, 1995-2000. ***PRACTICE AREAS:*** Natural Resources; Energy; Native American. ***Email:*** rsr@vnf.com

DOUGLAS W. SMITH, born Mineola, New York, February 18, 1959; admitted to bar, 1987, Massachusetts; 1988, District of Columbia. *Education:* Massachusetts Institute of Technology (S.B., 1981); Yale University (J.D., 1986). *Member:* The District of Columbia Bar; Federal Energy and American Bar Associations. ***Email:*** dws@vnf.com

OF COUNSEL

HOWARD S. BLEICHFELD, born Buffalo, New York, May 31, 1959; admitted to bar, 1991, District of Columbia. *Education:* Cornell University (B.S., 1979); George Mason University School of Law (J.D., 1991). *Member:* The District of Columbia Bar; American Bar Association. ***PRACTICE AREAS:*** Environment; Clean Water Act; Wetlands Regulation; Clean Air Act. ***Email:*** hsb@vnf.com

SHIPPEN HOWE, born Washington, D. C., November 14, 1955; admitted to bar, 1982, District of Columbia. *Education:* Boston University (B.A., cum laude, 1978); Case Western Reserve University (J.D., 1981). *Member:* The District of Columbia Bar; Federal Energy and American Bar Associations. ***PRACTICE AREAS:*** Energy; Natural Gas. ***Email:*** sxh@vnf.com

(This Listing Continued)

RICHARD G. KOZLOWSKI, born Baltimore, Maryland, December 22, 1938; admitted to bar, 1972, Maryland; 1993, U.S. Supreme Court; 1996, District of Columbia. *Education:* Johns Hopkins University (B.E.S., 1961); Catholic University of America (J.D., 1972). U.S. Environmental Protection Agency: Branch Chief, 1972-1976; Director of the Noise Enforcement Division, 1976-1979; Director of the Field Operations Enforcement Division, Office of Mobile Sources, 1979-1988; Director of the Water Enforcement Program, 1988-1994. *Member:* Maryland State and Federal Bar Associations. ***PRACTICE AREAS:*** Environment; Clean Water Act. ***Email:*** rgk@vnf.com

SAM KALEN, born Abington, Pennsylvania, July 30, 1958; admitted to bar, 1984, Missouri; 1985, Illinois; 1986, District of Columbia. *Education:* Clark University (B.A., cum laude, with high honors in History, 1980); Washington University (J.D., 1984). Law Clerk, Hon. Warren D. Welliver of Missouri Supreme Court, 1984-1986. Department of Interior, Office of the Solicitor, 1994-1996. *Member:* The District of Columbia Bar; Illinois State and American Bar Associations. ***PRACTICE AREAS:*** Natural Resources; Environment; Energy; Administrative Law; Constitutional Law. ***Email:*** smk@vnf.com

MALCOLM C. McLELLAN, born Seattle, Washington, November 16, 1966; admitted to bar, 1993, Washington; U.S. District Court, Eastern and Western Districts of Washington; U.S. Bankruptcy Court, Eastern District of Washington; U.S. court of Appeals, Ninth Circuit. *Education:* University of Washington (B.A., 1989); Gonzaga University (J.D., cum laude, 1993). *Member:* Chelan-Douglas County, Washington State, Federal and American Bar Associations. (Resident, Seattle, Washington Office). ***PRACTICE AREAS:*** Energy; Environment; Municipal; Commercial. ***Email:*** mcm@vnf.com

J. CURTIS RICH, born St. Paul, Minnesota, April 7, 1964; admitted to bar, 1995, Montana (Not admitted in District of Columbia). *Education:* Whitman College (B.A., 1986); University of Montana School of Law (J.D., 1992). Natural Resource and Energy Policy Counsel, Office of Senator Max Baucus, U.S. Senate Environment and Public Works Committee, 1992-1996. *Member:* State Bar of Montana. ***PRACTICE AREAS:*** Energy; Natural Resources; Environment; Public Lands; Taxation. ***Email:*** jcr@vnf.com

JOSEPH B. NELSON, born Gooding, Idaho, December 7, 1965; admitted to bar, 1992, California; 1994, District of Columbia. *Education:* University of Idaho (B.A., with honors, 1988); Catholic University of America (J.D., 1992). Phi Beta Kappa. Staff Assistant, U.S. Sen. James A. McClure, 1988-1990; Legislative Assistant, U.S. Rep. Larry E. Craig, 1990-1991. ***PRACTICE AREAS:*** Natural Resources; Water; Energy. ***Email:*** jbn@vnf.com

JAY T. RYAN, born Norwalk, Connecticut, May 13, 1966; admitted to bar, 1991, Illinois; 1992, District of Columbia. *Education:* University of Rochester (B.A., 1988); De Paul University (J.D., 1991); American University (LL.M., International Trade, 1993); George Washington University (LL.M., Environmental Law, 1997). *Member:* District of Columbia Bar; Federal Energy and American Bar Associations; Republican National Lawyers Association. ***PRACTICE AREAS:*** Energy; Environment; Government Relations. ***Email:*** jtr@vnf.com

---

SUSAN A. MOORE, born Flint, Michigan, March 28, 1962; admitted to bar, 1997, Virginia (Not admitted in District of Columbia). *Education:* University of Michigan (B.A., 1984); Catholic University of America (J.D., cum laude, 1997). *Member:* Federal Energy Bar Association. ***PRACTICE AREAS:*** Natural Gas; Hydroelectricity; Indian Law. ***Email:*** sam@vnf.com

BRITT S. FLEMING, born Pittsburgh, Pennsylvania, March 27, 1972; admitted to bar, 1997, Maryland and District of Columbia. *Education:* Dartmouth College (B.A., magna cum laude, 1994); Washington College of Law of the American University (J.D., cum laude, 1997). Phi Beta Kappa. ***PRACTICE AREAS:*** Energy; Environment. ***Email:*** bss@vnf.com

JAELEEN KOOKESH ARAUJO, born Juneau, Alaska, February 16, 1973; admitted to bar, 1998, Alaska; 1999, District of Columbia. *Education:* Stanford University (B.A., 1995); University of New Mexico (J.D., 1998). *Member:* Federal and American Bar Associations; Native American Bar Association. ***PRACTICE AREAS:*** Federal Indian Law; Alaska Native Law; Legislative Practice. ***Email:*** jka@vnf.com

JONATHAN D. SIMON, born Englewood, New Jersey, April 10, 1970; admitted to bar, 1998, Virginia; 1999, District of Columbia. *Education:* Cornell University (B.A., 1992); George Washington University (J.D., 1998). Office of U.S. Senator Frank Lautenberg, 1993-1995 (Legislative Correspondent, 1993-1994; Special Research Assistant, 1994; Special Projects Assistant/Legislative Assistant, 1995). *Member:* Federal Energy and American Bar Associations. ***PRACTICE AREAS:*** Natural Resources; Energy; Environment. ***Email:*** jxs@vnf.com

ANGELA M. ADDISON, born Los Angeles, California, April 25, 1964; admitted to bar, 1998, Louisiana (Not admitted in District of Columbia). *Education:* Southern University (B.S.E.E., 1991); Loyola University School of Law (J.D., 1997). *Member:* Louisiana State, Federal Energy and American Bar As-

(This Listing Continued)

sociations; American Association for Blacks in Energy. ***PRACTICE AREAS:*** Natural Gas Pipelines; Electric Energy; Public Utility Regulation. ***Email:*** ama@vnf.com

JANET L. WOODKA, born Washington, D.C., December 16, 1964; admitted to bar, 1992, Louisiana; 1995, Maryland (Not admitted in District of Columbia). *Education:* Boston College (B.A., 1987); Tulane University School of Law (J.D., 1992); The National Law Center, George Washington University (LL.M., 1999). ***PRACTICE AREAS:*** Environmental Compliance; Permitting; Litigation. ***Email:*** jlw@vnf.com

ANDREW B. ART, born New Haven, Connecticut, August 16, 1969; admitted to bar, 1999, Massachusetts; 2000 District of Columbia. *Education:* Kenyon College (B.A., 1991); American University, Washington College of Law (J.D., cum laude, 1999). *Member:* Massachusetts, American and Energy Bar Associations. ***PRACTICE AREAS:*** Energy; Electric Power; Administrative Law; Litigation; Adjudication. ***Email:*** aba@vnf.com

CHARLES R. SENSIBA, born Flagstaff, Arizona, July 31, 1971; admitted to bar, 1999, Colorado (Not admitted in District of Columbia). *Education:* University of Utah (B.S., 1995); University of Colorado School of Law (J.D., 1999). *Member:* Colorado, American and Energy Bar Associations. ***PRACTICE AREAS:*** Energy; Natural Resources; Environmental. ***Email:*** crs@vnf.com

KYLE W. DANISH, born Lansing, Michigan, December 18, 1967; admitted to bar, 1997, New Jersey; 1999, District of Columbia. *Education:* Haverford College (B.A., 1989); Princeton University Woodrow Wilson School of Public and International Affairs (M.P.A., 1996); Temple University (J.D., 1997). *Member:* District of Columbia Bar; New Jersey State and American (Vice Chair, Committee on Climate Change and Sustainable Development) Bar Associations; American Society of International Law. ***PRACTICE AREAS:*** Environment; International Environment. ***Email:*** kwd@vnf.com

BRIAN M. ZIMMET, born Washington, D.C., May 13, 1969; admitted to bar, 1995, Maryland (Not admitted in District of Columbia). *Education:* University of Rochester (B.A., 1991); University of Virginia (J.D., 1995). Law Clerk, Judge John Bishop, Court of Special Appeals of Maryland, 1995-1996. Staff Attorney, Court of Special Appeals of Maryland, 1997-1999. Legislative Counsel, Councilmember Sharon Ambrose, Council of the District of Columbia, 1999-2000. ***PRACTICE AREAS:*** Energy; Electric Power. ***Email:*** bmz@vnf.com

KEVIN W. FLYNN, born Baltimore, Maryland, 1969; admitted to bar, 2000, Maryland (Not admitted in District of Columbia). *Education:* Colby College (B.A., 1993); University of Maryland (J.D., 2000). Staff Assistant, Senator Patrick Leahy (D-VT), U.S. Senate, 1993-1995. Legislative Staff Assistant, Committee on Agriculture, Nutrition & Forestry, 1995-1996 and Committee on Judiciary, 1997, U.S. Senate. ***PRACTICE AREAS:*** Electric Power; Natural Gas. ***Email:*** kwf@vnf.com

NICK GOLDSTEIN, born New Bedford, Massachusetts, 1973; admitted to bar, 2001, Massachusetts (Not admitted in District of Columbia). *Education:* Hobart College (B.A., 1995); Vermont Law School (J.D., 2000; M.S.E.L., magna cum laude, 2000). ***PRACTICE AREAS:*** Energy; Environment. ***Email:*** nxg@vnf.com

RICARDO NOGUEIRA, born Newark, New Jersey, April 20, 1970; admitted to bar, 1996, New Jersey (Not admitted in District of Columbia). *Education:* Lafayette College (B.A., 1992); Seton Hall University (J.D., 1995). ***LANGUAGES:*** Portuguese and Spanish. ***PRACTICE AREAS:*** International Transactions; Energy; Climate Change; Mergers and Acquisitions. ***Email:*** rpn@vnf.com

EVAN REESE, born East Stroudsburg, Pennsylvania, October 31, 1971; admitted to bar, 2000, Virginia; 2001, District of Columbia. *Education:* Colgate University (B.A., 1995); Tulane University of Louisiana (J.D., cum laude, 2000). Member, Moot Court Board. *Member:* Virginia State Bar; The District of Columbia Bar; Federal Energy and American Bar Associations. ***LANGUAGES:*** Russian. ***PRACTICE AREAS:*** Energy; Oil and Gas Law; Oil and Gas Pipelines. ***Email:*** ecr@vnf.com

VINCENZO FRANCO, born Faenza, Italy, May 4, 1970; admitted to bar, 2001, New York and District of Columbia. *Education:* University of Bologna (LL.B., summa cum laude, 1996); Syracuse University (M.A., 2000); University of Wisconsin Law School (M.L.I., 2001). *Member:* American Bar Association. ***LANGUAGES:*** Italian. ***PRACTICE AREAS:*** International Trade; International Environment; Energy. ***Email:*** vbf@vnf.com

ROBERT GLENN VARNER, JR.

901 15TH STREET, N.W., SUITE 700
WASHINGTON, D.C. 20005-2327
Telephone: 202-371-6273
Fax: 202-371-6279
Email: rgv74@aol.com
URL: http://www.lawyers.com/varnerlaw

Local Government, Environmental, International, Telecommunications, Project Finance.

ROBERT GLENN VARNER, JR., born Alexandria, Virginia, June 27, 1947; admitted to bar, 1974, Florida; 1982, District of Columbia and U.S. Tax Court. *Education:* United States Air Force Academy; University of Florida (B.A., 1969); Stetson University (J.D., 1974). Chief Assistant County Attorney, Pinellas County, Florida, 1976-1980. ***PRACTICE AREAS:*** Local Government Law; Environmental Law; International Law.

LAW OFFICE OF EDWARD G. VARRONE

910 17TH STREET, N.W.
SUITE 800
WASHINGTON, D.C. 20006
Telephone: 202-861-3150
Fax: 202-861-3152
URL: http://www.lawyers.com/varronelaw

Wills, Trusts and Estates, Elder Law, Family Law, Civil Litigation.

EDWARD G. VARRONE, born Dover, New Jersey, June 29, 1953; admitted to bar, 1978, District of Columbia; 1979, Maryland, U.S. Court of Appeals for the District of Columbia Circuit and U.S. District Court for the District of Columbia; 1984, U.S. District Court, District of Maryland. *Education:* American University (B.A., cum laude, 1975); George Washington University (J.D., 1978). Omicron Delta Kappa; Pi Sigma Alpha; Pi Gamma Mu. Law Clerk, The Honorable H. Carl Moultrie I, Chief Judge, Superior Court of the District of Columbia, 1978-1980. Vice President, American University Alumni Association. D.C. Superior Court Probate Rules Advisory Committee, 1994—. *Member:* District of Columbia Bar (Family Law and Probate Sections); Bar Association of the District of Columbia; Montgomery County and American Bar Associations; District of Columbia Judicial Conference. ***REPORTED CASES:*** Ellis v. James V. Huron Assoc., District of Columbia App., 565 A.2d 615 (1989).

A.H. VELARDE & ASSOCIATES, P.C.

WASHINGTON, D.C.
(See McLean, Virginia)

International Fiduciary, Trustee and Banking Services, Business Negotiations, Due Diligence, Contracts, Trade, Financing and Taxation.

VENABLE ATTORNEYS AT LAW

VENABLE, BAETJER, HOWARD & CIVILETTI, LLP
A Partnership including Professional Corporations
Established in 1900
SUITE 1000, 1201 NEW YORK AVENUE, N.W.
WASHINGTON, D.C. 20005
Telephone: 202-962-4800
Fax: 202-962-8300
URL: http://www.venable.com
REVISERS OF THE MARYLAND LAW DIGEST FOR THIS DIRECTORY.

Baltimore, Maryland Office: Venable, Baetjer and Howard LLP, 1800 Mercantile Bank & Trust Building, 2 Hopkins Plaza. Telephone: 410-244-7400. Fax: 410-244-7742.
McLean, Virginia Office: Venable, Baetjer and Howard LLP, Suite 400, 2010 Corporate Ridge. Telephone: 703-760-1600. Fax: 703-821-8949.
Rockville, Maryland Office: Venable, Baetjer and Howard LLP, Suite 500, One Church Street, P. O. Box 1906. Telephone: 301-217-5600. Fax: 301-217-5617.
Towson, Maryland Office: Venable, Baetjer and Howard LLP, 210 Allegheny Avenue, P. O. Box 5517. Telephone: 410-494-6200. Fax: 410-821-0147.

General Practice. Administrative; Antitrusts; Appellate; Banking; Bankruptcy and Creditor's Rights; Communications; Consumer Financial Services; Construction Litigation; Corporate; Corporate Finance and Securities; Electronic Marketing and Distribution; Employee Benefits; Environmental; Estates and Trusts; Govern-

(This Listing Continued)

VENABLE ATTORNEYS AT LAW, VENABLE, BAETJER, HOWARD & CIVILETTI, LLP, Washington—Continued

ment Contracts; Health Care; Immigration; Information Law; Insurance Defense and Coverage; Intellectual Property; International; Labor and Employment; Legislative and Regulatory; Litigation; Civil, Commercial and Criminal; Products Liability Litigation; Public Finance; Real Estate Development and Financing; Taxation; Tax Controversies Litigation; Technology.

MEMBERS OF FIRM

A. HOPE ADAMS, born Rocky Mount, North Carolina, July 23, 1965; admitted to bar, 1992, North Carolina; 1998, District of Columbia. *Education:* North Carolina School of the Arts (B.M., 1987); Campbell University (J.D., cum laude, 1992); University of Florida (LL.M., Taxation, 1993). Staff Member, Campbell Law Review; Staff Member, Florida Tax Review. *Member:* North Carolina State Bar; The District of Columbia Bar; American Bar Association. ***PRACTICE AREAS:*** Corporate Transactions. ***Email:*** ahadams@venable.com

DAVID G. ADAMS, born Monroe, Louisiana, January 30, 1953; admitted to bar, 1977, Georgia; 1995, District of Columbia. *Education:* University of Southwestern Louisiana (B.A., 1974); New York University School of Law (J.D., 1977). Law Clerk to Judge Winston E. Arnow, U.S. District Court for the Northern District of Florida, 1977-1978. Director, Policy Development and Coordination Staff/Associate Chief Counsel for Drugs/Attorney, U.S. Food and Drug Administration, 1978-1994. Editor: "Fundamentals of Law and Regulations," the FDA Modernization Act, Foli, 1998; "Fundamentals of Law and Regulations," Vol. II, Therapeutic Products, Foli, 1997. Author: "FDA's Final Regulations on Generic Drug Approval: Marketing Exclusivity," Legal Mind, Vol. 131, 1995; "FDA's Final Regulation on Generic Drug Approval: Patent Protections, Patent Challenges," Legal Mind, Vol. 128, 1994; "FDA Regulation of Communications on Pharmaceutical Products," Seton Hall Law Review, Vol. 24, 1994; "FDA Policy on Industry-Supported Scientific and Educational Activities," Food and Drug Law Journal, Vol. 47, 1993; "Pharmaceutical Advertising: Education vs. Promotion," J. of Pharmaceutical Marketing and Management, Vol. 7, 1992, reprinted in *Promotion of Pharmaceuticals,* D. Pathak Ed., 1992. Co-Author: "USPTO and FDA Rulings Limit Uruguay Round Agreements Act Benefits and Protections for Certain Patents on FDA-Regulated Products," Legal Mind Vol. 136, 1995. Adjunct Professor, The George Washington University Law School. Chairman, Food and Drug Committee, Section of Business Law, American Bar Association, 1994-1999. *Member:* The District of Columbia Bar. ***SPECIAL AGENCIES:*** Food and Drug Administration; Federal Trade Commission. ***PRACTICE AREAS:*** Food and Drug Law; Advertising Law. ***Email:*** dgadams@venable.com

ANDREW C. AITKEN, born Washington, D.C., May 24, 1961; admitted to bar, 1988, Maryland; 1989, U.S. District Court, District of Maryland; 1991, U.S. Court of Appeals for the Federal Circuit; 2000, District of Columbia; registered to practice before U.S. Patent and Trademark Office. *Education:* Loyola College (B.S., Biology, 1983); Catholic University of America (J.D., 1988). Law Clerk to the Honorable L. Leonard Ruben, Circuit Court of Montgomery County Maryland, 1988-1989. *Member:* Maryland State and American Bar Associations. ***PRACTICE AREAS:*** Patent Litigation; Patent Prosecution; Medical Patents; Mechanical Patents; Intellectual Property Litigation; Trademark Prosecution; Trademark Litigation. ***Email:*** acaitken@venable.com

RICHARD L. AITKEN, born St. Louis, Missouri, May 30, 1930; admitted to bar, 1956, District of Columbia; 1983, U.S. Court of Appeals for the Federal Circuit; 1989, Maryland; registered to practice before U.S. Patent and Trademark Office. *Education:* Cornell University (B.E.E., 1953); George Washington University (J.D., 1956). Delta Theta Phi. Patent Editor, George Washington University Law Review, 1955-1956. Patent Examiner, U.S. Patent and Trademark Office, 1953-1956. *Member:* The District of Columbia Bar; Maryland State Bar Association, Inc.; American Bar Association; American Intellectual Property Law Association. ***PRACTICE AREAS:*** Intellectual Property; Patents; Trademarks; Computers and Software; Electronic Patents. ***Email:*** rlaitken@venable.com

ROBERT G. AMES, born Buffalo, New York, February 24, 1949; admitted to bar, 1973, Georgia; 1976, District of Columbia; 1980, Maryland. *Education:* Temple University (B.B.A., 1970); George Washington University (J.D., with honors, 1973). Order of the Coif. *Member:* Bar Association of Baltimore City; Maryland State, Federal and American Bar Associations; District of Columbia Bar; State Bar of Georgia. (Also at Baltimore, Maryland Office). ***PRACTICE AREAS:*** Labor Law (Management); Employment Discrimination; Wrongful Discharge; Employee Relations; Personnel Management Law; Union Avoidance; Collective Bargaining; Arbitration Law; Federal and State Wage and Hour Compliance. ***Email:*** rgames@venable.com

JAMES K. ARCHIBALD, born Greenfield, Massachusetts, March 29, 1949; admitted to bar, 1975, Maryland; 1985, District of Columbia; 1998, Maine. *Education:* Johns Hopkins University (B.A., 1971); University of Maryland (J.D., 1975). Omicron Delta Kappa. Co-Chairman, Moot Court Board, 1974-1975. Co-author: *Pleading Cases of Action in Maryland* (MICPEL, 1991; Second Edition, 1998); *Pattern Examinations of Witnesses for the Maryland Lawyer* (3rd Edition, 1995); *Model Witness Examinations,* (ABA, 1997). Aide to Congressman Paul S. Sarbanes, 1971-1972. Member, Board of Trustees, 1978-1986, Chairman, 1984-1986, Maryland State Universities and Colleges. Member, Board of Trustees, The Johns Hopkins University, 1997-2000. *Member:* Bar Association of Baltimore City; Maryland State and American (Section of Litigation) Bar Associations; Defense Research Institute, Inc. (Former Maryland State Chairman); Maryland Association of Defense Trial Counsel (President, 1988-1989); International Association of Defense Counsel; Product Liability Advisory Council, Inc.; The American Law Institute. (Also at Baltimore, Maryland Office). ***PRACTICE AREAS:*** Civil Practice and Litigation; Products Liability Law; Professional Malpractice Law. ***Email:*** jkarchibald@venable.com

MAURICE BASKIN, born Miami, Florida, June 25, 1954; admitted to bar, 1978, District of Columbia; 1979, Florida; 1988, Maryland. *Education:* Harvard University (B.A., magna cum laude, 1975); University of Florida (J.D., 1978). Senior Editor, University of Florida Law Review, 1977-1978. Winner, Florida Bar Moot Court Competition, 1978. Adjunct Professor, Labor Law, Georgetown University Law Center, 1981-1987. Member: Labor Relations Committee, U.S. Chamber of Commerce; Legal Section, American Society of Association Executives. *Member:* Bar Association of the District of Columbia; The Florida Bar; Maryland State and American (Member: Section of Labor and Employment Law, RICO, Antitrust and Labor Law Committee; Public Contract Section; Forum Committee on the Construction Industry) Bar Associations. ***SPECIAL AGENCIES:*** NLRB; EEOC; U.S. Department of Labor. ***PRACTICE AREAS:*** Labor (Management) Law; Wrongful Discharge Law; Civil Rights Law; Litigation; Appellate Practice. ***Email:*** mnbaskin@venable.com

KENNETH C. BASS, III, born Richmond, Virginia, February 11, 1944; admitted to bar, 1970, Virginia; 1971, District of Columbia. *Education:* Duke University (A.B., summa cum laude, 1965); Yale University (LL.B., 1969). Phi Beta Kappa; Order of the Coif. Member, Board of Editors, Yale Law Journal, 1967-1969. Law Clerk to Justice Hugo L. Black, U.S. Supreme Court, 1969-1970. Counsel for Intelligence Policy, U.S. Department of Justice, 1979-1981. Adjunct Professor, Georgetown Law Center. *Member:* The District of Columbia Bar; Virginia State Bar; American Bar Association; The American Academy of Appellate Lawyers (President-Elect); Edward Coke Appellate Inns of Court. (Also at McLean, Virginia Office). ***PRACTICE AREAS:*** Appellate Practice; Intellectual Property Litigation; Constitutional Litigation; Civil Practice; Litigation. ***Email:*** kbass@venable.com

JOHN B. BEATY, born Middletown, New York, June 8, 1953; admitted to bar, 1978, District of Columbia; 1985, Maryland. *Education:* Michigan State University (B.S. with highest honors, 1975); University of Chicago (J.D., 1978). Deputy General Counsel, First American Bankshares, Inc., 1992-1993. General Counsel, First American Bank, 1992-1993. Assistant General Counsel, Professional Liability Section, Resolution Trust Corporation, 1989-1992. Branch Chief, Litigation and Special Projects Division, Federal Home Loan Bank Board, 1986-1989. *Member:* The District of Columbia Bar; Maryland State Bar Association; Virginia State Bar. ***PRACTICE AREAS:*** Financial Institutions; Business; Corporate. ***Email:*** jbeaty@venable.com

LAWRENCE B. BERNARD, born Rockville Centre, New York, June 13, 1948; admitted to bar, 1973, District of Columbia; 1979, U.S. District Court for the District of Columbia; 1987, U.S. Court of Appeals, Second Circuit; 1989, U.S. Supreme Court; 1991, Maryland; 1992, U.S. Court of Appeals for the Federal Circuit and U.S. District Court, District of Maryland; 1994, U.S. Court of Appeals, Fourth Circuit; 1996, Virginia; 1997, U.S. District Court, Eastern District of Virginia. *Education:* Cornell University (B.A., 1970); Harvard Law School (J.D., 1973). Trial Attorney, Federal Trade Commission, 1974-1987. Instructor, FTC-NITA Trial Advocacy and Deposition Program, 1980-1987. Associate Professorial Lecturer-in-Law, The George Washington University, 1989-1991. *Member:* Maryland State and American Bar Associations; The District of Columbia Bar. ***PRACTICE AREAS:*** Litigation; Antitrust; Advertising Law. ***Email:*** lbbernard@venable.com

CONNIE N. BERTRAM, born Yorktown, Virginia, September 19, 1965; admitted to bar, 1990, Virginia and U.S. District Court, Eastern District of Virginia; 1992, District of Columbia; 1999, Maryland; U.S. District Court, District of Maryland; U.S. District Court for the District of Columbia; U.S. Court of Appeals, Fourth Circuit. *Education:* College of William & Mary (B.B.A., 1987); George Washington University National Law Center (J.D., with honors, 1990). Omicron Delta Kappa; Phi Delta Phi (Vice-President, 1988-1989). Dean's Fellow. Member: Moot Court Board (Executive Committee, 1988-1990); National Moot Court Team. Editor, George Washington Journal of International Law and Economics, 1989-1990. Instructor: NITA Deposition Program, 1996—; NITA Trial Skills Program, 2001—. Adjunct Professor, Legal Writing, George Washington University Law School, 1995-1997. *Member:* Virginia State Bar; The District of Columbia Bar (Co-Chair and Member, Steering Committee, Labor and Employment Section, 1999—). ***PRACTICE AREAS:*** Labor and Employment. ***Email:*** cnbertram@venable.com

JOSEPH G. BLOCK, born Johnstown, Pennsylvania, November 11, 1947; admitted to bar, 1972, Pennsylvania; 1977, District of Columbia; 1981, Cali-

(This Listing Continued)

fornia. *Education:* University of Michigan (B.A., with high honors, high distinction in History, 1969), Phi Beta Kappa; Harvard University (J.D., 1972). Trial Attorney, Defender Association of Philadelphia, 1972-1976. General Counsel to the Minority, Permanent Subcommittee on Investigations of the Governmental Affairs Committee, U.S. Senate, 1977-1979. Chief Counsel to the Minority, Permanent Subcommittee on Investigations of the Governmental Affairs Committee, U.S. Senate, 1979-1981. Attorney, Law Offices Of Barry Tarlow, Los Angeles, California, 1981-1984. U.S. Department of Justice, 1985-1991. Chief, Environmental Crimes Section, Environment and Natural Resources Division, 1988-1991 (Assistant Chief, 1987-1988 and Trial Attorney, 1985-1987). U.S. Environmental Protection Agency, 1991. Special Assistant for Criminal Enforcement Office of Enforcement, May/August, 1991. Principal, Trade and Environment Policy Advisory Committee (provide policy advice to United States Trade Representative and EPA), November, 1994—. *Member:* American Bar Association (Vice Chair, Environmental Crimes Committee, Section of Natural Resources, Energy and Environmental Law, 1988—; Co-Chair, Environmental Crimes Subcommittee, International Criminal Law Committee, Criminal Justice Section, 1991); Master, Edward Bennett Williams Inn of Court, 1989. ***PRACTICE AREAS:*** Environmental Crimes; White Collar Crime; Internal Investigations; Environmental Auditing and Preventive Counseling; International Environmental Law. ***Email:*** jgblock@venable.com

ROBERT J. BOLGER, JR., born Philadelphia, Pennsylvania, April 25, 1955; admitted to bar, 1982, Maryland; 1998, District of Columbia. *Education:* University of Virginia (B.A., with highest distinction, 1977; J.D., 1982). Phi Beta Kappa. *Member:* The District of Columbia Bar; The Bar Association of Baltimore City; Maryland State and American Bar Associations; Federal Communications Bar Association. (Also at Baltimore, Maryland Office). ***PRACTICE AREAS:*** Business Law; Tax Law; Corporate Law; Technology Development; Emerging Businesses; Venture Capital. ***Email:*** rjbolger@venable.com

NEAL D. BORDEN, born Baltimore, Maryland, November 3, 1941; admitted to bar, 1966, Maryland, U.S. District Court, District of Maryland and U.S. Tax Court (Not admitted in District of Columbia). *Education:* Harvard University (A.B., 1963); University of Maryland (LL.B., 1966). Gamma Eta Gamma. Editor-in-Chief, Maryland Law Review, 1965-1966. Law Clerk to Judge Edward S. Northrop, U.S. District Court, District of Maryland, 1966-1967. Executive Vice President, Jiffy Lube International, Inc., 1986-1988. *Member:* The Bar Association of Baltimore City; Maryland State and American Bar Associations; International Franchise Association. (Also at Baltimore, Maryland Office). ***PRACTICE AREAS:*** Franchise and Distribution Law; Corporate Law; Federal Taxation; State Taxation. ***Email:*** ndborden@venable.com

JAMES R. BURDETT, born Taylor, Pennsylvania, September 29, 1951; admitted to bar, 1984, Pennsylvania; 1985, New Jersey and U.S. District Court, District of New Jersey; 1991, Texas; 1998, District of Columbia; registered to practice before U.S. Patent and Trademark Office. *Education:* U.S. Naval Academy (B.S., 1973); George Washington University (M.S.A., 1981); Delaware Law School of Widener University (J.D., 1984). *Member:* Pennsylvania and American (Member, Section on Patent, Trademark and Copyright Law) Bar Associations; Philadelphia Patent Law Association; American Intellectual Property Law Association (Co-Chair, Multimedia Law Subcommittee). [LCDR, U.S. Navy, 1969-1979]. ***PRACTICE AREAS:*** Intellectual Property. ***Email:*** jrburdett@venable.com

ANTHONY M. CAREY, born Baltimore, Maryland, May 31, 1935; admitted to bar, 1963, Maryland (Not admitted in District of Columbia). *Education:* Princeton University (A.B., 1957); Harvard University (LL.B., 1963); Johns Hopkins University (M.L.A., 1970). Assistant Attorney General, State of Maryland, 1967-1969. Executive Secretary, Maryland State Board of Ethics, 1970-1978. Special Assistant for Energy Matters, U.S. Department of Housing and Urban Development, 1979-1981. *Member:* The Bar Association of Baltimore City; Maryland State and American Bar Associations. (Also at Baltimore, Maryland Office). ***PRACTICE AREAS:*** Environmental and Energy Law. ***Email:*** acarey@venable.com

WALLACE E. CHRISTNER, born Dayton, Ohio, April 7, 1959; admitted to bar, 1985, Virginia; 1995, Maryland and District of Columbia. *Education:* Duke University (B.A., cum laude, 1982); College of William & Mary (J.D., 1985); Georgetown University (LL.M., 1991). *Member:* The District of Columbia Bar; Virginia, Maryland State (Member, Section on Taxation) and American (Member, Section on Business Law and Taxation) Bar Associations. ***Email:*** wechristner@venable.com

ARTHUR E. CIRULNICK, born Brooklyn, New York, June 20, 1954; admitted to bar, 1979, District of Columbia. *Education:* University of California at Santa Barbara (B.A., 1975); University of San Francisco (J.D., magna cum laude, 1979). Professorial Lecturer in Law, George Washington University Law School, 1985—. *Member:* The District of Columbia Bar. ***PRACTICE AREAS:*** Corporate Law; Mergers and Acquisitions; Year 2000 Computer Conversion. ***Email:*** aecirulnick@venable.com

BENJAMIN R. CIVILETTI (P.C.), born Peekskill, New York, July 17, 1935; admitted to bar, 1961, Maryland; 1981, District of Columbia. *Education:* Johns Hopkins University (A.B., 1957); Columbia University and University of Maryland (LL.B., 1961). Law Clerk to Judge W. Calvin Chestnut, U.S. District Court, District of Maryland, 1961-1962. Assistant U.S. Attorney, 1962-1964. Assistant Attorney General, Criminal Division, U.S. Department of Justice, 1977-1978. Deputy Attorney General of the United States, 1978-1979. Attorney General of the United States, 1979-1981. Trustee, Johns Hopkins University, 1980-1998. Chairman, The Maryland Legal Services Corporation, 1982-1986. Member, Martindale-Hubbell Legal Advisory Board, 1990—. *Member:* District of Columbia Bar; The Bar Association of Baltimore City; Maryland State and American (Chairman, Litigation Section Council, 1986-1988; Member, House of Delegates, 1990—) Bar Associations; American Law Institute. Fellow: Maryland Bar Foundation; American Bar Foundation; American College of Trial Lawyers. (Also at Baltimore and Towson, Maryland Offices). ***PRACTICE AREAS:*** Litigation; Government Investigations and Special Investigations; Antitrust Law; Corporate Governance. ***Email:*** brciviletti@venable.com

ROGER A. COLAIZZI, born Rochester, Pennsylvania, June 16, 1958; admitted to bar, 1983, Pennsylvania; 1984, Maryland; 1988, District of Columbia; 1991, New York, Virginia and U.S. District Court, Eastern District of Virginia; 1992, U.S. District Court for the District of Columbia. *Education:* Dickinson College (B.A., 1980); Delaware Law School of Widener University (J.D., 1983). Recipient: Anthony Mach Memorial Scholarship, Economics; Delaware Law Forum Award. Editor-in-Chief, Delaware Law Forum, 1982-1983. Trial Attorney, U.S. Department of Justice, Civil Rights Division, Employment Litigation Section, 1983-1987. Special Assistant, U.S. Attorney, District of Columbia, 1986-1987. *Member:* The District of Columbia Bar (Member, Litigation Section, 1987—); Virginia State Bar (Member, Litigation Section, 1991—); Maryland State, New York State and Pennsylvania Bar Associations. ***PRACTICE AREAS:*** Litigation; Technology; Intellectual Property; Electronic Commerce; Commercial Law; 2000 Computer Conversion; Finance Law. ***Email:*** racolaizzi@venable.com

KEVIN B. COLLINS, born Silver Spring, Maryland, November 9, 1965; admitted to bar, 1992, Maryland; 1994, District of Columbia; 1997, U.S. District Court, District of Maryland, U.S. Court of Appeals, Fourth Circuit and U.S. Supreme Court. *Education:* Worcester Polytechnic Institute (B.S., Mechanical Engineering, 1987); University of Baltimore (J.D., magna cum laude, 1992). Member, Heuisler Honor Society. Associate Editor, University of Baltimore Law Review, Vol. 21. Law Clerk to the Honorable Robert L. Karwacki, Court of Appeals of Maryland, 1992-1993. ***PRACTICE AREAS:*** Intellectual Property Litigation; Commercial Litigation; Civil Litigation. ***Email:*** kbcollins@venable.com

BRYSON L. COOK (P.C.), born Baltimore, Maryland, April 17, 1948; admitted to bar, 1974, Maryland (Not admitted in District of Columbia). *Education:* Princeton University (A.B., magna cum laude, 1970); Wharton School of Finance and Commerce (M.B.A., 1973); University of Pennsylvania (J.D., cum laude, 1973). Order of the Coif. Recipient, Gordon A. Block Award. Adjunct Professor, University of Maryland Law School, 1981. *Member:* Bar Association of Baltimore City; Maryland State and American Bar Associations; International Fiscal Association. (Also at Baltimore, Maryland Office). ***PRACTICE AREAS:*** Corporate Law; Mergers and Acquisitions; Taxation Law; Estate Planning Law. ***Email:*** blcook@venable.com

WILLIAM P. COOK, born Brooklyn, New York, June 16, 1952; admitted to bar, 1979, California; 1991, Maryland; 1999, District of Columbia. *Education:* George Washington University (B.A., 1974); Southwestern University Law School (J.D., 1978). General Counsel, U.S. Immigration and Naturalization Service, 1989-1991. [U.S. Navy, 1980-1984; CDR, USNR, 1984—Veteran, Operation Desert Storm]. ***PRACTICE AREAS:*** Legislative Practice; Public Policy; Corporate; Securities. ***Email:*** wpcook@venable.com

JOHN F. COONEY, born Worcester, Massachusetts, January 1, 1949; admitted to bar, 1973, Massachusetts; 1977, District of Columbia; 1978, U.S. District Court for the District of Columbia, U.S. District Court, District of Massachusetts and U.S. Supreme Court; U.S. Court of Appeals for the District of Columbia Circuit, U.S. Court of Appeals, First, Third, Fourth and Ninth Circuits and U.S. Court of Appeals for the Federal Circuit. *Education:* Brown University (A.B., magna cum laude, 1970); University of Chicago (J.D., 1973). Phi Beta Kappa; Order of the Coif. Associate Editor, University of Chicago Law Review, 1972-1973. Lead Author: "Environmental Crimes Deskbook," Environmental Law Institute, 1995. Author: "Legal and Political History of Wine," University of California Book of Wine, 1983; "Who Will Pay for the Year 2000?" The Computer Lawyer, Fall, 1997. Deputy General Counsel, Office of Management and Budget, 1982-1987. Assistant to the Solicitor General, Department of Justice, 1975-1976. *Member:* The District of Columbia Bar; American Bar Association (Member, Council Section, Administrative Law and Regulatory Policy, 2000—). ***PRACTICE AREAS:*** Regulatory, Environmental; Appellate; Constitutional. ***Email:*** jcooney@venable.com

THOMAS J. COOPER, born Cambridge, Massachusetts, December 8, 1943; admitted to bar, 1975, District of Columbia. *Education:* George Washington University (B.A., 1966; M.A., in International Affairs, 1971); Tulane University (J.D., 1974). Phi Delta Phi. Minority Counsel to U.S. House Administration Committee, 1976-1977. Administrative Assistant to Congressman Matthew J. Rinaldo, 1979-1982. Executive Assistant to Assistant Secretary of Com-

(This Listing Continued)

VENABLE ATTORNEYS AT LAW, VENABLE, BAETJER, HOWARD & CIVILETTI, LLP, Washington—Continued

merce for Trade Administration, 1983. Assistant to Deputy Assistant Secretary of Commerce for Export Administration, 1983-1986. *Member:* The District of Columbia Bar. ***PRACTICE AREAS:*** Exports Control Law; International Trade Law; Election Law; Legislation Representation (Federal and District of Columbia). ***Email:*** tjcooper@venable.com

WILLIAM D. COSTON, born Ann Arbor, Michigan, October 9, 1950; admitted to bar, 1976, Massachusetts; 1977, U.S. Court of Appeals, 9th Circuit; 1978, U.S. Court of Appeals, 10th Circuit; 1979, District of Columbia and U.S. Supreme Court; 1983, U.S. Court of Appeals, 3rd Circuit; 1990, U.S. Court of Appeals, 6th Circuit; 1992, U.S. Court of Appeals, 4th Circuit. *Education:* University of Michigan (B.A., with highest honors, 1972); Harvard University (J.D., cum laude, 1975). Phi Beta Kappa. Law Clerk to Chief Judge T. John Lesinski and Hon. Dorothy C. Riley, State of Michigan, Court of Appeals, 1975-1976. Attorney, Appellate Section, Antitrust Division, Department of Justice, 1976-1979. Special Assistant United States Attorney, Alexandria, Virginia, 1978-1979. ***PRACTICE AREAS:*** Litigation; Antitrust Law and Trade Regulation Law; Intellectual Property. ***Email:*** wdcoston@venable.com

CARLA DRALUCK CRAFT, born Atlanta, Georgia, June 11, 1966; admitted to bar, 1991, Maryland; 1993, District of Columbia. *Education:* University of Pennsylvania (B.A., cum laude, 1988); Emory University (J.D., with distinction, 1991). *Member:* Maryland State and American (Member, Section of Public Contract Law) Bar Associations; District of Columbia Bar. ***PRACTICE AREAS:*** Government Contracts. ***Email:*** ccraft@venable.com

DONALD P. CRESTON, born Bronxville, New York, July 27, 1965; admitted to bar, 1991, Connecticut; 1992, New York; 1994, District of Columbia. *Education:* Boston College (B.A., 1987); University of Pittsburgh (J.D., cum laude, 1991). Note and Comment Editor, University of Pittsburgh Law Review. *Member:* Connecticut and New York State Bar Associations; District of Columbia Bar. ***PRACTICE AREAS:*** Securities Regulation; Corporate Finance. ***Email:*** dpcreston@venable.com

PETER J. CURTIN, born Cincinnati, Ohio, September 18, 1967; admitted to bar, 1991, District of Columbia; 1992, U.S. Army Court of Military Review; 1993, U.S. Court of Appeals, Fourth Circuit; 1998, U.S. District Court, District of Maryland. *Education:* University of Cincinnati (B.A., summa cum laude, 1988); Georgetown University (J.D., magna cum laude, 1991). Phi Beta Kappa; Delta Theta Phi; Order of the Coif. *Member:* The District of Columbia Bar; American Bar Association (Member, Sections on: Litigation; Intellectual Property; Criminal Justice). [Capt., U.S. Army, 1992-1995]. ***PRACTICE AREAS:*** Intellectual Property Litigation; General Litigation. ***Email:*** pjcurtin@venable.com

PAUL A. DEBOLT, born Lorain, Ohio, September 16, 1963; admitted to bar, 1989, Ohio; 1997, District of Columbia. *Education:* John Carroll University (B.A., 1986); Ohio State University (J.D., 1989). *Member:* American Bar Association (Member, Section of Public Contract Law); NCMA. [Captain, U.S. Army, 1990-1995]. ***PRACTICE AREAS:*** Government Contracts; Complex Litigation. ***Email:*** pado3@venable.com

JEFFREY A. DUNN, born East Orange, New Jersey, July 26, 1951; admitted to bar, 1976, Missouri; 1984, Maryland and District of Columbia. *Education:* University of Kansas (B.A., cum laude, 1973); Georgetown University (J.D., 1976). Beta Gamma Sigma. *Member:* The District of Columbia Bar; Bar Association of Baltimore City; Maryland State and American Bar Associations; Maryland Association of Defense Trial Counsel. (Also at Baltimore, Maryland Office). ***PRACTICE AREAS:*** Intellectual Property; Commercial Litigation; Public Contract Law. ***Email:*** jadunn@venable.com

SUSAN T. EDLAVITCH, born Washington, D.C., September 29, 1948; admitted to bar, 1976, Indiana; 1979, District of Columbia and Maryland; 1991, U.S. Tax Court. *Education:* Washington University (B.A., 1970); Indiana University (J.D., 1976);George Washington University (LL.M., highest honors, Taxation, 1990). Phi Beta Kappa. Author: "The Disguised Sale Question under the Service's Final Regulations," 20 Journal of Real Estate Taxation 211 (Spring 1993); "Corporate Items on 1998 Business Plan -- Status Update and Summary of Year-End Published Guidance," 40 Tax Management Memorandum S-69, March 1999. Law Clerk, Hon. V. Sue Shields and Hon. Patrick D. Sullivan, Indiana Court of Appeals (1976-1979). Attorney Advisor, IRS Offices of Assistant Chief Counsel, Corporate and Passthroughs and Special Industries (1988-1996). *Member:* The District of Columbia Bar; Maryland State Bar Association Inc.; American Bar Association. ***PRACTICE AREAS:*** Federal Taxation Law. ***Email:*** stedlavitch@venable.com

CRAIG A. EMDEN, born Cincinnati, Ohio, April 10, 1955; admitted to bar, 1980, District of Columbia. *Education:* Miami University (B.S., magna cum laude, 1977); George Washington University (J.D., with honors, 1980); Georgetown University (M.L.T., 1984). Beta Gamma Sigma; Order of the Coif. Member, George Washington University Law Review, 1979-1980. Author: "Current Decision, Redding v. Commissioner," George Washington University Law Review, November 1979. Co-Author: "The Low-Income Housing Credit Provides Shelter from the Cold and Taxes," Journal of Taxation of Investments, Winter 1995. *Member:* District of Columbia Bar; American Bar Association (Member: Taxation Section; Affordable Housing Forum). ***PRACTICE AREAS:*** Taxation Law; Affordable Housing; Real Estate. ***Email:*** caemden@venable.com

MICHAEL J. FERRELL, born Detroit, Michigan, March 27, 1951; (admission pending). *Education:* Mercy College of Detroit (B.A., 1973); George Mason University (J.D., 1980). ***Email:*** mjferrell@venable.com

ANITA J. FINKELSTEIN, born Cleveland, Ohio, January 2, 1957; admitted to bar, 1982, District of Columbia. *Education:* Wittenberg University (B.A. in Economics and Business Administration, summa cum laude, 1979); Yale University (J.D., 1982). Member, Mortar Board. *Member:* The District of Columbia Bar; American Bar Association (Member, Section of Business Law). ***PRACTICE AREAS:*** Securities Regulation; Corporate; Corporate Finance. ***Email:*** ajfinkelstein@venable.com

MICHAEL R. FLYER, born Brooklyn, N.Y., November 13, 1937; admitted to bar, 1963, District of Columbia. *Education:* University of Michigan (B.A., 1959); University of Michigan Law School (J.D., 1962). Attorney, National Office, 1962-1969 and Section Chief, Corporate Reorganization Branch, 1968-1969, Internal Revenue Service. Associate Professor, George Washington University Law School, 1972—. Co-Chair, Refreshing the Growing Business, American Law Institute/American Bar Association. Trustee, Massachusetts School of Law. *Member:* The District of Columbia Bar (Member, Steering Committee, Division of Taxation, 1978); American Bar Association (Member, Corporate Tax Committee). ***PRACTICE AREAS:*** Business Law; Tax Law. ***Email:*** mrflyer@venable.com

ROBERT J. FRANK, born New York, N.Y., July 27, 1924; admitted to bar, 1960, New York; 1968, U.S. District Court, Southern and Eastern Districts of New York; 1972, Virginia; 1974-1982, U.S. Court of Customs and Patent Appeals; 1978, District of Columbia; 1979, U.S. District Court for the District of Columbia; 1982, U.S Court of Appeals for the Federal Circuit; 1984, U.S. Supreme Court and U.S. Court of Appeals for the District of Columbia Circuit; registered to practice before the U.S. Patent and Trademark Office. *Education:* Cornell University (B.E.E., 1949); Polytechnic Institute of New York (M.E.E., 1955); Brooklyn Law School (LL.B., 1959). Professional Engineer, New York, 1954. *Member:* The District of Columbia Bar; Virginia State Bar; American Bar Association; American Intellectual Property Law Association; Institute of Electrical and Electronics Engineers. ***PRACTICE AREAS:*** Patent Law; Trademark Law. ***Email:*** rjfrank@venable.com

RONALD R. GLANCZ, born Bay City, Michigan, January 29, 1943; admitted to bar, 1968, Michigan; 1969, U.S. Court of Appeals for the District of Columbia Circuit; 1972, U.S. Supreme Court; 1974, District of Columbia. *Education:* University of Michigan (B.A., 1964; J.D., cum laude, 1968). Order of the Coif. Assistant Editor, Michigan Law Review, 1967-1968. Author: "Reform Law Expands Bank's Options," American Banker, March 17, 2000; "Why Insurers Are Buying Thrifts Now," *National Underwriter,* March 2, 1998; "Bank Insurance Sales Spark Regulatory Rumblings," National Law Journal, September 8, 1997; "Insurance? It's in the Bank," National Law Journal, August 26, 1996; "Comparing Proposals For Glass-Steagall Reform," Bank Investment Representative, May, 1995; "Courts Tearing Down The Barriers to Branching," American Banker, July 27, 1993. Co-author: "Current Issues In Officer/Director Liability, Indemnification And Insurance Coverage," BNA's Banking Report, November 7, 1988. Assistant General Counsel, Federal Deposit Insurance Corporation, 1984-1988. Director, Litigation Division, Office of the Comptroller of the Currency, 1979-1984. Assistant Director, 1975-1979, Honors Attorney, 1965-1975, Civil Division, Appellate Section, United States Department of Justice (represented Federal Reserve). Member, Exchequer Club of Washington. Member: National Association of Corporate Directors Best Practices Council; Women in Housing and Finance (WHF). *Member:* Federal and American (Chair, Subcommittee on Insurance; Former Vice Chair, Audit, Examination and Compliance, Banking Law Committee) Bar Associations; The District of Columbia Bar. ***SPECIAL AGENCIES:*** FED; OCC; OTS; FDIC; NCUA. ***PRACTICE AREAS:*** Banking Regulation; Thrift Institution Regulation; Bank Mergers and Acquisitions; Electronic Banking; Fair Lending; Financial Holding Company Regulation; Bank Directors and Officers Liability; New Products and Services; Credit Union Law; Bank Litigation; Alternative Dispute Resolution; Corporate Investigations. ***Email:*** rglancz@venable.com

EDWARD F. GLYNN, JR., born Boston, Massachusetts, May 5, 1947; admitted to bar, 1972, New York; 1975, District of Columbia; 1981, Maryland. *Education:* McGill University (B.A., 1968); Cornell Law School (J.D., 1971). Moot Court Board. Assistant Director (International Antitrust), Associate Director, Bureau of Competition Federal Trade Commission, 1981-1990. *Member:* Association of the Bar of the City of New York; American Bar Association (Member, Sections on: Antitrust Law; Litigation; Member, Council of the Antitrust Section). ***LANGUAGES:*** French. ***PRACTICE AREAS:*** Antitrust, Consumer Protection and Trade Regulation. ***Email:*** efglynn@venable.com

DAVID W. GOEWEY, born Andrews AFB, Maryland, August 22, 1962; admitted to bar, 1987, Virginia; 1988, District of Columbia; 2000, Maryland;

(This Listing Continued)

U.S. Court of Appeals for the Federal Circuit; U.S. Court of Appeals for the District of Columbia Circuit; U.S. Court of Appeals, Fourth Circuit. *Education:* University of Virginia (B.A., 1984); College of William & Mary (J.D., 1987). Executive Editor, Research, William & Mary Law Review, 1986-1987. ***PRACTICE AREAS:*** Litigation. ***Email:*** dwgoewey@venable.com

MICHAEL A. GOLLIN, born Rochester, New York, July 3, 1957; admitted to bar, 1985, New York and Massachusetts; 1991, District of Columbia and Maryland; registered to practice before U.S. Patent and Trademark Office. *Education:* Princeton University (A.B., 1978); University of Zurich, Switzerland (M.S., 1981); Boston University (J.D., 1984). Author: "New Rules for Natural Products Research," Nature Biotechnology 17:921, 1999; "Patent Strategies in China," Managing Intellectual Property, November, 1997; "Introduction," International Protection of Intellectual Property Rights, FT Law & Tax, 1997; "At the Crossroads: Intellectual Property Rights and Agricultural Biotechnology," Proceedings of the Third Asia-Pacific Conference on Agricultural Biotechnology, 1996; "Protecting Intellectual Property," Inventors' Digest, March and May, 1996; "Provisional Patent Applications: File Early, File Often," The Law Works, August, 1995; "Biological Materials Transfer Agreements," Bio/Technology 13:243, 1995; "Patenting Recipes From Nature's Kitchen," Bio/Technology 12:406, 1994; "Using Intellectual Property to Improve Environmental Protection," 4 Harvard Journal of Law and Technology 193, 1991; "Patent Law and the Environment/Technology Paradox," 20 Environmental Law Reporter 10171, 1990. Co-Author: "Innovations in Ground Water and Soil Cleanup: From Concept to Commercialization," National Academy Press, 1997 (as member of Committee on Innovative Remediation Technologies, National Research Council); "Global Policies, Local Actions: The Role of National Legislation in Sustainable Biodiversity Prospecting," 2 Boston University Journal of Science and Technology Law 16, May, 1996; "Biodiversity Prospecting," World Resources Institute, 1993; "Discovery in Patent Cases," in Intellectual Property Counseling and Litigation, Matthew Bender, 1993. Adjunct Professor, Georgetown University, McDonough School of Business, 2001. Trustee, Rene Dubos Center for Human Environments, Inc., 1994—. *Member:* American Bar Association (Vice Chair, Section on Natural Resources, Energy and Environmental Law Committee on Emerging Environmental Technologies, 1992—). ***LANGUAGES:*** German and French. ***PRACTICE AREAS:*** Intellectual Property; Patent Law; Biotechnology; Trademarks; Environmental Law. ***Email:*** magollin@venable.com

ROBERT GENE GOTTLIEB, born Newark, N.J., May 13, 1951; admitted to bar, 1976, Virginia; 1978, District of Columbia. *Education:* Pennsylvania State University (B.A., cum laude, 1973); George Washington University (J.D., with honors, 1976). Professorial Lecturer in Law: George Washington University Law School, 1985-1995; Georgetown University Law School, 1990—. *Member:* The District of Columbia Bar; Virginia State Bar. ***PRACTICE AREAS:*** Real Estate; Tax Law; Business Law. ***Email:*** rggottlieb@venable.com

JAN K. GUBEN, born Baltimore, Maryland, November 11, 1942; admitted to bar, 1967, Maryland (Not admitted in District of Columbia). *Education:* Tusculum College (B.A., 1964); University of Baltimore School of Law (LL.B., 1967). Lecturer, Real Estate, Johns Hopkins University, 1986-1995. Member: American College of Real Estate Lawyers; Real Estate Advisory Board, Johns Hopkins University, 1985-1995. *Member:* The Bar Association of Baltimore City; Maryland State and American Bar Associations. (Also at Baltimore, Maryland Office). ***PRACTICE AREAS:*** Real Estate Law; Corporate Law; Partnership Law; Tax Law. ***Email:*** jkguben@venable.com

GARY D. HAILEY, born Joplin, Missouri, May 30, 1952; admitted to bar, 1978, Texas; 1996, District of Columbia. *Education:* Rice University (B.A., cum laude, 1974); Harvard University (J.D., cum laude, 1977). Vice-President and General Counsel for Regulatory Affairs, National Media Corporation, 1992-1995. Attorney Advisor, Federal Trade Commissioner Mary L. Azcuenaga, 1985-1991. Staff Attorney and Program Advisor, FTC Bureau of Consumer Protection, 1977-1985. *Member:* The District of Columbia Bar. ***PRACTICE AREAS:*** Advertising; Trade Regulation; Direct Marketing. ***Email:*** ghailey@venable.com

MARK B. HARRISON, born Bronx, New York, February 20, 1953; admitted to bar, 1977, Pennsylvania; 1977-1982, U.S. Court of Customs and Patent Appeals; 1982, District of Columbia, U.S. District Court for the District of Columbia and U.S. Court of Appeals for the Federal Circuit; registered to practice before U.S. Patent and Trademark Office. *Education:* State University of New York (B.A., 1973); Rutgers University (J.D., 1977). Author: "How to Maintain a United States Trademark Registration Without Use in Commerce: Section 8 and Registrations Under Section 44," 74 Trademark Reporter 254, 1984. Trademark Examiner, U.S. Patent and Trademark Office, 1977-1981. *Member:* The District of Columbia Bar; Pennsylvania Bar Association. ***PRACTICE AREAS:*** Trademark Law; Copyright Law; Computer Law. ***Email:*** mbharrison@venable.com

GREGORY B. HAUPTMAN, born Washington, D.C., April 5, 1951; admitted to bar, 1976, Maryland; 1977, District of Columbia. *Education:* Washington University (A.B., 1973); George Washington University (J.D., with high honors, 1976). Order of the Coif. *Member:* The District of Columbia Bar; Maryland State Bar Association. ***PRACTICE AREAS:*** Real Estate-Commercial Law; Finance Law. ***Email:*** gbhauptman@venable.com

PETER E. HEYWARD, born New York, N.Y., June 23, 1953; admitted to bar, 1980, New York; 1991, District of Columbia. *Education:* Wesleyan University (B.A., 1974); Columbia University (J.D., 1979). Harlan Fiske Stone Scholar. *Member:* Association of the Bar of the City of New York (Member, Banking Law Committee, 1999-2001); American Bar Association (Member, Banking Law Committee, 1990—; Vice Chair, International Banking Subcommittee, 1998-2000; Chair, Financial Holding Companies Subcommittee, 2000—). ***LANGUAGES:*** French and Russian. ***PRACTICE AREAS:*** Financial Institutions; Corporate. ***Email:*** peheyward@venable.com

GARY M. HNATH, born Buffalo, New York, January 13, 1958; admitted to bar, 1985, Maryland, District of Columbia and U.S. District Court, District of Columbia; 1987, U.S. District Court, District of Maryland and U.S. Court of Appeals, District of Columbia; 1988, U.S. Supreme Court; 1991, Federal Circuit; 1993, Virginia and U.S. District Court, Eastern District of Virginia. *Education:* Michigan State University (B.A., with high honors, 1980); Harvard University (J.D., cum laude, 1983). Phi Beta Kappa; Tau Sigma. Law Clerk to Judge Walter E. Black, Jr., U.S. District Court, District of Maryland, 1983-1984. Senior Attorney, Office of Unfair Import Investigations, U.S. International Trade Commission, 1988-1991. Author: "Litigating Trade Secret Cases at the International Trade Commission," 19 AIPLA Quarterly Journal No. 2 (1991). Co-Author: "Changes in Section 337 As A Result of the GATT-Implementing Legislation," 22 AIPLA Quarterly Journal Nos. 3 and 4 (1995). *Member:* The District of Columbia Bar; Maryland State and American (Member, Sections on: Intellectual Property and Litigation) Bar Associations; American Intellectual Property Law Association (Chair, ITC Committee, 1993-1995); ITC Trial Lawyers Association (President, 1996-1997). ***PRACTICE AREAS:*** Intellectual Property and Complex Civil Litigation. ***Email:*** ghnath@venable.com

KENNETH R. HOFFMAN, born Washington, D.C., August 1, 1952; admitted to bar, 1977, Maryland; 1998, District of Columbia. *Education:* Frostburg State College (B.S., cum laude, 1974); University of Maryland (J.D., with honors, 1977). Order of the Coif. Adjunct Professor, University of Baltimore Graduate Tax Program. Contributing Author: *The 403(b) Answer Book,* 2nd Ed., Aspen Publishers, Inc. (Annuities and Other Forms of Investments). Member, Comptroller's Task Force on Tax Reform, 1985-1986. Law Clerk to Judge C. Awdry Thompson, Court of Special Appeals of Maryland, 1977-1978. *Member:* Maryland State (Chair: Section of Taxation, 1991-1992; Special Committee on Pro Bono, 1995-1997; President, Pro Bono Resource Center of Maryland, Inc., 1997-1999) and American (Member, Committee on Employee Benefits) Bar Associations. (Also at Baltimore, Maryland Office). ***PRACTICE AREAS:*** Taxation Law; Employee Benefits Law. ***Email:*** krhoffman@venable.com

KENNETH G. HURWITZ, born Brooklyn, New York, February 22, 1952; admitted to bar, 1976, District of Columbia and U.S. Court of Appeals, District of Columbia Circuit and U.S. District Court, District of Columbia; 1980, New York; 1987, Maryland and U.S. District Court, District of Maryland. *Education:* Columbia University (B.A., 1972); Wharton School of Finance and Commerce, University of Pennsylvania (M.B.A., 1976); University of Pennsylvania (J.D., 1976). Phi Beta Kappa. Notes Editor, Energy Law Journal. Executive Director, Maryland Public Service Commission, 1983-1987. *Member:* The District of Columbia Bar; Association of the Bar of the City of New York; Federal Energy and American (Member: Sections on: Public Utility Law; Administrative Law, Chair Energy Committee) Bar Associations. (Also at Baltimore, Maryland Office). ***PRACTICE AREAS:*** Energy; Telecommunications. ***Email:*** kghurwitz@venable.com

GREGORY F. JENNER, born Portland, Oregon, August 8, 1953; admitted to bar, 1979, Oregon; 1992, District of Columbia. *Education:* Portland State University (B.S., with high honors, 1975); New York University (J.D., cum laude, 1979). Order of the Coif. Recipient, George P. Foulk Award. Note and Comment Editor, New York University Law Review, 1978-1979. Tax Counsel, U.S. Senate Finance Committee, 1985-1989. Special Assistant to the Assistant Secretary of the Treasury for Tax Policy, U.S. Treasury Department, 1989-1992. *Member:* American Bar Association (Chair, Committee on Government Relations, Taxation Section, 1997-1999; Council Member, 2000— and Chair, 2001—, Tax Shelter Task Force; Member: Estate and Gift Taxes Committee; Formation of Tax Policy Committee). Fellow, American College of Tax Counsel. ***PRACTICE AREAS:*** Tax Law; Legislative Practice; Estate Planning. ***Email:*** gfjenner@venable.com

PAUL T. KAPLUN, born Glen Cove, New York, January 20, 1956; admitted to bar, 1985, Maryland; 1986, District of Columbia. *Education:* Georgetown University (B.S.B.A., magna cum laude, 1978; J.D., 1984). Certified Public Accountant, Virginia, 1980. Adjunct Faculty, Georgetown University Law Center, 1992—. *Member:* The District of Columbia Bar (Member, Section on Taxation); Maryland State and American (Member, Sections on: Business Law; Taxation) Bar Associations. ***PRACTICE AREAS:*** Corporate Law; Taxation Law; Business Law. ***Email:*** ptkaplun@venable.com

(This Listing Continued)

VENABLE ATTORNEYS AT LAW, VENABLE, BAETJER, HOWARD & CIVILETTI, LLP, Washington—Continued

LAWRENCE A. KATZ, born Queens, New York, October 1, 1953; admitted to bar, 1978, District of Columbia; 1984, U.S. Supreme Court; 1985, Maryland. *Education:* State University of New York at Buffalo (B.A., magna cum laude, 1975); Georgetown University (J.D., 1978). Phi Beta Kappa. Member, American Bankruptcy Institute. *Member:* The District of Columbia Bar (Member, Sections of: Litigation; Corporation, Finance and Securities Law); Bar Association of the District of Columbia; Maryland State (Member, Section of Litigation) Bar Association; Bankruptcy Bar Association for the District of Maryland; The Association of Trial Lawyers of America. (Resident). ***PRACTICE AREAS:*** Bankruptcy Law; Litigation; Commercial Law. ***Email:*** lakatz@venable.com

JOSHUA J. KAUFMAN, born New York, N.Y., October 31, 1950; admitted to bar, 1977, Maryland; 1978, District of Columbia, U.S. District Court for the District of Columbia, U.S. District Court, District of Maryland and U.S. District Court, Southern District of New York; 1981, U.S. Tax Court and U.S. Claims Court; 1983, New York; 1985, U.S. Court of Appeals, Second and Fourth Circuits; U.S. Supreme Court. *Education:* University of Maryland (B.A. 1972); George Washington University (J.D., with honors, 1975). Adjunct Professor, Washington College of Law, 1989—. Founder and Executive Director, Volunteer Lawyers for the Arts, D.C., 1977-1999. Director, Society To Prevent Trade in Stolen Art (S.T.O.P.) 1995-2000. *Author, Regular Columns:* "Cyberlaw," Legal Times; "ArtLaw," Art Business News; "Strictly Business," The Artist Magazine; "Computers for Lawyers," Washington Lawyer, 1985-1998. *Member:* District of Columbia Bar; American Bar Association; Copyright Society U.S.A. ***LANGUAGES:*** Hebrew and French. ***REPORTED CASES:*** CCNV v. Reid, 109 S. Ct. 2166; Kank v. Weschler, 561 A.2d 1003 (D.C. App. 1989); Barry v. Donnelly, 781 F.2d 1041 (4th Cir. 1986); Zitelman v. Metropolitan Insurance Agency, 482 A.2d 426 (D.C. App. 1984); Davis v. Davis, 417 A.2d 1008 (D.C. App. 1984); Spackman v. D.C. Dept. of Empl. Services et al 590 A2d 515 (D.C. App 1991); Agence France-Press v. Dept. of Defense et al 762 F.Supp. 1558 (S Dist. NY 1991); National Catholic Reporter v. Federal Bureau of Investigation (D.C. D.C., 1981); Weissmann v. Freeman, 684 F.Supp. 1248 (S.D. N.Y. 1988) rev'd 868 F2d 1313 (2d Cir. 1989) as Amicus; Graffman v. Doe, U.S. Dist. Lexis 1399 (DCSDNY-1) Affirm 2nd Cir. Ct. App. 1999. ***PRACTICE AREAS:*** Copyright Law; Trademark Law; Art Law; Entertainment Law; Computer Law; Electronic Commerce; Media Law; Civil Litigation; Defamation; Right of Publicity; Intellectual Property; International Licensing; Copyright Litigation. ***Email:*** jjkaufman@venable.com

MICHAEL E. KAUFMANN, born Indianapolis, Indiana, March 17, 1960; admitted to bar, 1986, New York; 1989, District of Columbia. *Education:* University of Maryland at College Park (B.A., summa cum laude, 1982); Georgetown University (J.D., 1985). Member, The Tax Lawyer, Georgetown University, 1984-1985. Assistant District Attorney, New York County, 1985-1988. *Member:* Association of the Bar of the City of New York; New York State and Energy Bar Associations; District Attorney's Association of the State of New York. ***PRACTICE AREAS:*** Energy; Public Utility; Regulatory Litigation; Contracts. ***Email:*** mekaufmann@venable.com

GABOR J. KELEMEN, born Budapest, Hungary, February 10, 1930; admitted to bar, 1972, Virginia; registered to practice before U.S. Patent and Trademark Office (Not admitted in District of Columbia). *Education:* Polytechnic University, Hungary and American University (B.A., 1966); Washington College of Law of American University (J.D., 1969). *Member:* Virginia State Bar. ***LANGUAGES:*** German, French and Hungarian. ***PRACTICE AREAS:*** Patent Law. ***Email:*** gjkelemen@venable.com

THOMAS J. KELLY, JR., born Williamsport, Pennsylvania, July 18, 1953; admitted to bar, 1981, District of Columbia. *Education:* LaSalle College (B.S., 1976); Catholic University of America (J.D., 1980). Law Clerk to the Honorable H. Carl Moultrie, Chief Judge, Superior Court, Washington, D.C., 1980-1982. Assistant United States Attorney, Washington, D.C., 1986-1989. *Member:* The Bar Association of the District of Columbia (Chairman, Young Lawyers Section Pro Bono Committee, 1990; Recipient of Young Lawyer of the Year Award, 1991); American Bar Association. ***PRACTICE AREAS:*** Environmental Crimes Law; White Collar Criminal Law. ***Email:*** tjkelly@venable.com

CAMPBELL KILLEFER, born Hermosa Beach, California, March 14, 1950; admitted to bar, 1977, California; 1979, District of Columbia. *Education:* Stanford University (B.A., 1972); Hastings College of the Law, University of California (J.D., 1977). Editor-in-Chief, Hastings Constitutional Law Quarterly, 1976-1977. Author: "Emergency Evidence," *Litigation* Magazine, Vol. 19, No. 1, American Bar Association; "Some Disputes Still Deserve Their Day in Court," *Wall Street Journal,* pages A-10, October 12, 1992; *Securities & Exchange Commission v. Drexel Burnham Lambert, Inc.,* 88 Civ. 6209 (MP) (S.D.N.Y.), 1991-2000. Appointed by Senior District Judge Pollack as Trustee of the Drexel Civil Disgorgement Fund. Serves on Center for Public Resources Institute of Dispute Resolution, Panels on Technology, Construction, Trademarks and Copyrights Disputes. *Member:* American Bar Association (Member,

(This Listing Continued)

Sections on: Litigation; Intellectual Property; Dispute Resolution, 1977-2001). ***PRACTICE AREAS:*** Litigation; Intellectual Property; Arbitration; Alternative Dispute Resolution. ***Email:*** ckillefer@venable.com

ROBERT KINBERG, born St. Louis, Missouri, February 24, 1948; admitted to bar, 1975, Virginia; 1976, U.S. Claims Court; 1977-1982, U.S. Court of Customs and Patent Appeals; 1982, District of Columbia, U.S. District Court, Eastern District of Virginia and U.S. Court of Appeals for the Federal Circuit; registered to practice before U.S. Patent and Trademark Office. *Education:* Washington University (B.S.E.E., 1970); George Washington University (J.D., with honors, 1975). Tau Beta Pi; Eta Kappa Nu. Treasurer, Government Patent Lawyers Association, 1979. Partner, Spencer & Frank, 1982-1987 and 1989-1998; Venable, 1998—. Vice President, Power International, Inc., 1987-1989. Member, Office of General Counsel, National Aeronautics and Space Administration, 1975-1982. Patent Advisor: Office of the Judge Advocate General, Department of Air Force, 1973-1975; Department of the Navy, 1972-1973. Patent Examiner, 1970-1972. *Member:* The District of Columbia Bar; Virginia State Bar; American Intellectual Property Law Association; International Association for the Protection of Industrial Property. ***PRACTICE AREAS:*** Patent Law; Trademark Law. ***Email:*** rkinberg@venable.com

JEFFREY D. KNOWLES, born Washington, D.C., April 22, 1949; admitted to bar, 1976, New York; 1977, District of Columbia. *Education:* Columbia University (B.A., 1971); New York Law School (J.D., 1975). General Counsel, Electronic Retailing Association (Formerly the National Informercial Marketing Association. *Member:* The District of Columbia Bar; The Association of the Bar of the City of New York; American Bar Association. ***SPECIAL AGENCIES:*** Consumer Product Safety Commission; Federal Communications Commission; Federal Trade Commission; Food and Drug Administration; U.S. Postal Service. ***PRACTICE AREAS:*** Administrative Law; Advertising; Direct Marketing; Licensing; Contracts; Trade Regulation Law. ***Email:*** jdknowles@venable.com

NORMAN N. KUNITZ, born Philadelphia Pennsylvania, July 18, 1935; admitted to bar, 1961, District of Columbia; 1962, U.S. Court of Appeals for the District of Columbia Circuit; 1962-1982, U.S. Court of Customs and Patent Appeals; 1970, California and U.S. Supreme Court; 1982, U.S. Court of Appeals for the Federal Circuit; registered to practice before U.S. Patent and Trademark Office. *Education:* Drexel University (B.S.E.E., 1957); George Washington University (J.D., 1961). Phi Alpha Delta; Eta Kappa Nu. Patent Examiner, U.S. Patent Office, 1957-1962. *Member:* The District of Columbia Bar; Bar Association of the District of Columbia; The State Bar of California; American Bar Association; American Intellectual Property Law Association; International Trade Commission Trial Lawyers Association. ***PRACTICE AREAS:*** Patent Law; Trademark Law. ***Email:*** nnkunitz@venable.com

BROCK R. LANDRY, born Detroit, Michigan, September 15, 1947; admitted to bar, 1974, Illinois; 1982, District of Columbia. *Education:* Yale University (B.A., cum laude, 1970); University of Michigan (J.D., 1974). [Lt., U.S.A.R., 1970-1976]. ***PRACTICE AREAS:*** Association Law; International Trade; Environmental Law; Administrative Law. ***Email:*** brlandry@venable.com

FERNAND A. LAVALLEE, born Arlington, Virginia, October 10, 1963; admitted to bar, 1989, Virginia; 1990, U.S. Court of International Trade and U.S. Court of Appeals for the Federal Circuit; 1991, District of Columbia. *Education:* Georgetown University (A.B., 1985); College of William & Mary (J.D., 1988). Delta Theta Phi (Dean, Tucker Senate, 1987-1988). Member, William & Mary Law Review, 1986-1988. Faculty, George Washington University Law School, Government Contracts Program, 1995-1999. Course Director, Federal Publications, Seminars, Cooperative Agreements and other Transactions, 1995—. Representative, Student Bar Association, 1985-1986. *Member:* District of Columbia Bar; Virginia State Bar; American Bar Association. [Infantry, 1984 CPT., Company Commander, Maryland Army National Guard]. ***PRACTICE AREAS:*** Government Contracts, International Commercial Transactions. ***Email:*** lavallee@venable.com

SHMUEL (SANDY) LIVNAT, born Detroit, Michigan, December 4, 1948; admitted to bar, 1992, Pennsylvania; 1993, District of Columbia; registered to practice before U.S. Patent and Trademark Office. *Education:* Hebrew University, Jerusalem, Israel (B.S., summa cum laude, 1971); University of Michigan (M.S., Genetics, 1972); Weizmann Institute of Science, Israel (Ph.D., Cell Biol./Immunology, 1976); George Washington University (J.D., 1992). Post doctoral fellow, research instructor, medical research associate and professor, 1976-1988, Fred Hutchinson Cancer Research Center; University of Washington; Duke University Medical School; University of South Florida College of Medicine; University of Rochester School of Medicine and Dentistry. *Member:* The District of Columbia Bar; The Bar Association of the District of Columbia; American Bar Association (Member, Patent, Trademark and Copyright Section); American Intellectual Property Law Association; Association of University Technology Managers; American Association of Immunologists; American Association for the Advancement of Science. ***LANGUAGES:*** Hebrew. ***Email:*** slivnat@venable.com

THOMAS J. MADDEN, born Trenton, New Jersey, September 13, 1941; admitted to bar, 1968, New Jersey and District of Columbia; registered to

(This Listing Continued)

practice before U.S. Patent and Trademark Office. *Education:* Villanova University (B.S., Electrical Engineering, 1964); Columbus School of Law, Catholic University (J.D., cum laude, 1968). Member, Editorial Staff, Catholic University Law Review, 1967-1968. Author: "Procurement Reforms of the FY 1996 Defense Authorization Act," (Federal Publications Briefing Papers, 1996); "Strict Scrutiny and the Future of Federal Procurement Set-Aside Programs in the Wake of *Adarand:* Does 'Strict in Theory' Mean 'Fatal in Fact'?" (Federal Contracts Report, 1995); "Best Value Procurement Manual (Federal Publications, 1995); "Organizational Conflicts of Interest," (Federal Publications Briefing Paper, 1994); "Knowing the Ropes in Buying U.S. Contractors," (Mergers and Acquisitions, 1990); "The Government and Trade Secrets," (Practising Law Institute, 1985); "Government Consulting Contracts," (Federal Publications Briefing Papers, 1983); "Bedtime for Bivens - Substituting the United States as Defendant in Constitutional Tort Suits," (Harvard Journal on Legislation, 1983). Adjunct Professor of Contract Law, American University, 1980-1984. General Counsel: U.S. Department of Justice, Law Enforcement Assistance Administration, 1972-1979; U.S. Department of Justice, Office of Justice Assistance, Research and Statistics, 1980. Director, National Advisory Commission on Criminal Justice Standards and Goals, 1971-1973. Advisor to U.S. Office of Management and Budget on Federal Assistance Programs, 1979-1980. Member, U.S. Department of Defense, Advisory Panel on Stream-Lining and Codifying Acquisition Laws, 1991-1993. President, Court of Federal Claims Bar Association, 1999-2000. *Member:* American Bar Association (Chairman, Public Contract Law Section, 1988-1989; President, Fellows of the Public Contract Law Section, 1992-1993; Fellow, Public Contract Law Section). Life Fellow, American Bar Foundation. ***PRACTICE AREAS:*** Government Contract Law; Intellectual Property; Legislative Practice. ***Email:*** tmadden@venable.com

VICKI MARGOLIS, born Cleveland, Ohio, December 9, 1964; admitted to bar, 1989, Maryland; 1990, U.S. Court of Appeals, Fourth, Sixth and Federal Circuits, U.S. Tax Court and U.S. District Court, District of Maryland; 1991, District of Columbia; 1997, California and U.S. District Court, District of Colorado. *Education:* Miami University (B.S., 1986); University of Maryland School of Law (J.D., with honors, 1989). Order of the Coif. *Member:* Bar Association of Baltimore City; Maryland State and American (Member: Section on Litigation; Section on Intellectual Property) Bar Associations; The District of Columbia Bar; State Bar of California; Women's Bar Association of Maryland; American Intellectual Property Law Association. (Also at Baltimore, Maryland Office). ***PRACTICE AREAS:*** Intellectual Property Litigation; Commercial Litigation. ***Email:*** vmargolis@venable.com

CHARLES R. "ROD" MARVIN, JR., born Elizabeth, New Jersey, February 26, 1953; admitted to bar, 1982, New Jersey;1983, U.S. Court of Military Review; 1994, U.S. Court of Appeals, Federal Circuit; 1996, District of Columbia and U.S. Court of Federal Claims. *Education:* Michigan State University (B.A., with honors, 1975); Boston University (J.D., 1978); Judge Advocate General's School Army, (LL.M., 1988); George Washington University (LL.M., with highest honors, Government Procurement Law, 1995). Listed in Who's Who in American Law, 1995—. Co-Author: "Commercial Practices in Federal Government IT Procurements - Is 'Full and Open Competition' Already Dead?" *Acquisition Issues,* with Thomas J. Madden, Vol. 5., No. 4, 1995; "The Pre-Sentence Report: Preparing for the Second Half of the Case," The Army Lawyer, February, 1989. Lecturer, *Negotiated Procurements and Socioeconomic Policies,* ABA Fundamentals of Federal Procurement Law Course, December, 1995. Chief, Trial Team 5 and Protest Branch, U.S. Army Contract Appeals Division, 1991-1994. *Member:* Federal and American (Member, Public Contract Law Section and Bid Protest Committee; Member, Sections on: Litigation; Natural Resources, Energy and Environmental Law) Bar Associations; Federal Circuit Bar Association (Member, Government Contract Committee); Boards of Contract Appeals Bar Association (Member, Board of Governors, 1993-1996); National Contract Management Association. [Judge Advocate General's Corps. 1983-1994; Major, U.S. Army, 1979-1994]. ***PRACTICE AREAS:*** Government Contract Law; Commercial Litigation; Computer. ***Email:*** crmarvin@venable.com

CLIFTON E. McCANN, born Des Moines, Iowa, July 11, 1950; admitted to bar, 1978, Virginia, U.S. District Court, Eastern District of Virginia and U.S. Court of Appeals, Fourth Circuit; 1982, U.S. Court of Appeals for the Federal Circuit; 1983, U.S. Supreme Court; 1984, District of Columbia, U.S. District Court for the District of Columbia and U.S. Court of Appeals for the District of Columbia Circuit; registered to practice before U.S. Patent and Trademark Office. *Education:* Northern Illinois University (B.S., 1972); Columbus School of Law, Catholic University of America (J.D., 1977); George Washington University (LL.M., Patent and Trade Regulation Law, 1985). Delta Theta Phi. Intellectual Property Counsel to American Mensa, Ltd, Fort Worth, Texas, 1984—. *Member:* Bar Association of the District of Columbia (Executive Council Member, Patent, Trademark and Copyright Law Section, 1985—; Chair, 1996-1997; Section Representative to National Council of Intellectual Property Law Associations, 1998-1999); The District of Columbia Bar (Chair, Trademark Committee, Patent, Trademark and Copyright Section, 1985-1989); American Bar Association (Member, Intellectual Property Law Section, Chair, Subcommittee on Patent Claim Interpretation Procedures in Federal Litigation, 1996-1998 and Chair, Committee on Federal Intellectual Property Litigation Practice

(This Listing Continued)

and Procedure, 1999—); American Intellectual Property Law Association; Patent Lawyers Club of Washington, D.C. ***PRACTICE AREAS:*** Patent Litigation; Patents; Trademarks; Copyrights; New Media Law; Unfair Competition. ***Email:*** cemccann@venable.com

HEATHER L. McDOWELL, born Pittsburgh, Pennsylvania, April 12, 1965; admitted to bar, 1990, Maryland; 1991, Virginia; 1993, District of Columbia and U.S. District Court, District of Maryland; 1996, U.S. District Court, District of Columbia. *Education:* Pennsylvania State University (B.S., with honors and distinction, 1987); George Washington University (J.D., 1990). Member, University Scholars Program. Member: Federal Trade Commission, 1991-1994; Federal Communications Commission, 1994-1996. ***PRACTICE AREAS:*** Communications Law; Advertising; Electronic Commerce. ***Email:*** hlmcdowell@venable.com

LINDSAY BEARDSWORTH MEYER, born Bridgeport, Connecticut, April 11, 1961; admitted to bar, 1987, Virginia; 1988, District of Columbia; 1990, U.S. Court of Appeals for the District of Columbia Circuit, U.S. Court of Appeals for the Federal Circuit and U.S. Court of International Trade. *Education:* Universite de Rouen, France; University of Connecticut (B.S., cum laude, 1983); The National Law Center, George Washington University (J.D., 1987). Licensed U.S. Customs Service Broker. *Member:* Virginia State Bar; The District of Columbia Bar; American Bar Association. ***PRACTICE AREAS:*** International Trade; International Transactional Law. ***Email:*** lbmeyer@venable.com

DANIEL L. MORGAN, born Newark, New Jersey, October 17, 1952; admitted to bar, 1977, Connecticut; 1979, District of Columbia. *Education:* Tufts University (B.A., magna cum laude, 1974); University of Connecticut School of Law (J.D., with honors, 1977); Georgetown University (LL.M., Taxation, 1981). Lecturer, Catholic University School of Law, 1984-1996; Professional Lecturer in Law, George Washington University Law School, 1997—. Member, Advisory Board, Journal of Taxation of Employee Benefits. Member, Board of Editors, Employee Benefits for Nonprofits. Attorney, Office of Chief Counsel, Internal Revenue Service, 1977-1981. *Member:* The District of Columbia Bar; Connecticut Bar Association. Charter Fellow, American College of Employee Benefits Counsel. ***PRACTICE AREAS:*** Employee Benefits Law; Employment Law; Corporate Law. ***Email:*** dlmorgan@venable.com

ANDREA I. O'BRIEN, born New York, N.Y., December 30, 1960; admitted to bar, 1985, Maryland; 1986, District of Columbia. *Education:* University of Notre Dame (B.A., magna cum laude, 1982); Georgetown University (J.D., 1985). Phi Beta Kappa. *Member:* The District of Columbia Bar; Maryland State Bar Association. ***PRACTICE AREAS:*** Employee Benefits; Employment Law; Corporate Law. ***Email:*** aiobrien@venable.com

JERRY R. O'CONOR, born Washington, D.C., February 3, 1951; admitted to bar, 1977, Maryland; 1978, District of Columbia. *Education:* University of Maryland (B.A., 1974; J.D., with honors, 1977); George Washington University (L.L.M., Environmental Law, with highest honors, 1978); New York University (L.L.M., Taxation, 1981). *Member:* The District of Columbia Bar; Maryland State Bar Association. ***PRACTICE AREAS:*** Commercial; Real Estate; Environmental Law. ***Email:*** JROC@venable.com

PATRICK E. O'DONNELL, born New York, N.Y., 1937; admitted to bar, 1962, District of Columbia, U.S. District Court, District of Columbia and U.S. Court of Appeals, District of Columbia Circuit. *Education:* Georgetown University (B.A., 1959); Washington College of Law, American University (LL.B., 1962). Phi Alpha Delta. Assistant Corporation Counsel, District of Columbia, 1962-1970. Legal Assistant to the Chairman, FCC, 1970-1972. Special Assistant to President Nixon (Legislative Affairs), 1970-1973. Deputy Assistant Attorney General (Legislative Affairs), 1973-1974. Special Assistant for Legislative Affairs to: President Nixon, 1973-1974; President Ford 1974-1976. Washington Counsel, General Electric Corporation, 1976-1978. Washington Counsel, J.C. Penney Co., 1978-1980. Director, Legislative Affairs and Regional Political Director, Senator Howard Baker For President Campaign, 1980. Deputy Director for Legislative Affairs, Reagan For President Campaign and the Reagan Transition Team, 1980-1981. Vice Chairman, Finance Committee, Washington, D.C. Bush for President Campaign, 1992. Member, Congress Relations Private Sector Advisory Committee, Bush for President Campaign, 1992. Member, Board, United Services Organization (USO), 1976-1995. Member, President's Commission on Broadcasting to Cuba (Radio Marti), 1981-1985. Member: O'Connor & Hannon, 1981-2001; Venable, Baetjer, Howard & Civiletti, LLP, 2001—. *Member:* The District of Columbia Bar. ***Email:*** po'donnell@venable.com

GEORGE F. PAPPAS, born Washington, D.C., October 5, 1950; admitted to bar, 1976, Maryland, U.S. District Court, District of Maryland and U.S. Court of Appeals, Fourth Circuit; 1984, U.S. Supreme Court and U.S. Court of Appeals, District of Columbia Circuit; 1986, U.S. District Court, District of Columbia; 1991, District of Columbia and U.S. Court of Appeals, Federal Circuit; 1993, U.S. Court of Appeals, Second Circuit and U.S. District Court, Western District of Texas; 1994, U.S. Court of Appeals, Sixth and Seventh Circuits; 1995, U.S. Court of Federal Claims. *Education:* University of Maryland (B.A., with highest honors, 1972; J.D., 1975). Phi Beta Kappa; Omicron Delta Kappa.

(This Listing Continued)

VENABLE ATTORNEYS AT LAW, VENABLE, BAETJER, HOWARD & CIVILETTI, LLP, Washington—Continued

Founding Editor-in-Chief, International Trade Law Journal, 1974-1975. Member, Moot Court Board, 1974-1975. Master of the Bench, American Inns of Court, Inn XVIII, 1989-1993. Lecturer, Washington College of Law, The American University, 1980-1983. Author: "Law of Patent Damages," ALI-ABA Course of Study Materials, September, 1994; "Remedies for Patent, Trademark and Copyright Infringement," Federal Judicial Center Intellectual Property Seminar for Federal Judges, June, 1996; "Patent Litigation in the Eastern District of Virginia," IDEA: The Journal of Law and Technology, Volume 35 No. 4 (Co-Author, with Robert G. Sterne), May, 1995; (Translated into Japanese) "Intellectual Property Management," Japan Intellectual Property Association, Vol. 47, No. 2, February, 1997; (Translated into German) "Mitteilungen Der Deutschen," Patentanwalte, Summer, 1997; "The Architecture of Modern Federal Intellectual Property," Federal Judicial Center's Travelling Intellectual Property Seminar for Federal Judges of 1997 Ninth Circuit Judicial Conference. *Member:* Maryland State and American Bar Associations; The District of Columbia Bar; American Intellectual Property Law Association; United States Trademark Association; International Association of Defense Counsel. (Also at Baltimore, Maryland Office). ***PRACTICE AREAS:*** Intellectual Property and Technology Related Litigation and Counseling; Litigation. ***Email:*** gfpappas@venable.com

JOHN J. PAVLICK, JR., born Wurzburg, Germany, March 30, 1948; admitted to bar, 1978, Pennsylvania; 1982, U.S. Supreme Court; 1989, U.S. Court of Federal Claims; 1991, District of Columbia. *Education:* U.S. Military Academy (B.A., 1970); University of Pennsylvania Law School (J.D., 1978). Author or Co-Author: "Release of Unit Prices after McDonnell Douglas Corp. v. NASA," 35 Procurement Law, Co-Author, Winter 2000; "Healthcare Exclusions: A Comprehensive Guide," Contributor, American Bar Association, 1997; "Preventing Data Fraud," Environmental Test & Analysis, 1997; "Suspension and Debarment: The Government's Ultimate Sanction," Environmental Laboratory Washington Report, 1997; "Best Value Procurement: The Best Ways to Obtain Environmental Testing," Environmental Laboratory Washington Report, 1997; "New GAO Protest Make Significant Changes," Environmental Laboratory Washington Report, 1996; "Procurement Reforms of the FY 1996 Defense Authorization Act," Co-Author, Federal Publications Briefing Papers, 1996; "Responding to Criminal and Life in a Fishbowl—Environmental Labs in 90s," Environmental Testing & Analysis, 1996; *The Practitioner's Guide to Suspension and Debarment,* Second Edition, Contributing Author, American Bar Association, 1996; "Organizational Conflicts of Interest Issues in Environmental Contract and Collateral Consequences of an Environmental Criminal Conviction," Hazardous Materials Control Resources Institute, 1995; "Organization Conflicts of Interest/Edition II," Federal Publications Briefing Papers, 1994; "Contracting for Environmental Services," National Contract Management Association, National Education Seminar, 1994. *Member:* Federal (Member, Government Contracts Section; Co-Chair, Commercial Products Committee) and American (Member, Public Contract Law Section; Co-Chair, Debarment and Suspension Committee) Bar Associations; National Contract Management Association. [U.S. Army, 1970-1990; Lieut. Col. Retired]. ***PRACTICE AREAS:*** Government Contracts; Regulatory Law and Compliance; Internal Investigations; Freedom of Information Act; Civil Fraud; Collateral Consequences of Criminal Convictions. ***Email:*** jpavlick@venable.com

JULIE A. PETRUZZELLI, born Glenn Ridge, New Jersey, April 18, 1957; admitted to bar, 1983, New York; 1989, District of Columbia; 1997, U.S. Supreme Court and U.S. Court of Appeals for the Federal Circuit; U.S. District Court, Southern and Eastern Districts of New York and U.S. District Court for the District of Columbia; registered to practice before U.S. Patent and Trademark Office. *Education:* Brown University (Sc.B., 1979); University of Virginia (J.D., 1982). *Member:* The District of Columbia Bar; New York State and American (Member, Sections on: Litigation; Intellectual Property) Bar Associations; New York Patent, Trademark and Copyright Law Association; American Intellectual Property Law Association. ***PRACTICE AREAS:*** Intellectual Property; Complex Civil Litigation. ***Email:*** japetruzzelli@venable.com

THOMAS H. QUINN, born Pawtucket, Rhode Island, 1937; admitted to bar, 1963, Rhode Island; 1964, District of Columbia. *Education:* Providence College (A.B., 1959); Georgetown University (LL.B., 1963). Attorney and Legislative Counsel, Office of the Comptroller of the Currency, U.S. Treasury Department, 1963-1966. Member, U.S. Government Board for International Broadcasting, appointed, 1974-1976; reappointed, 1976-1979 and 1979-1982. Alternate U.S. Observer, International Fund for Ireland, appointed, 1993. *Member:* The District of Columbia Bar; Bar Association of the District of Columbia; Rhode Island and American Bar Associations. ***Email:*** thquinn@venable.com

TODD H. REUBEN, born Washington, D.C., June 30, 1961; admitted to bar, 1989, District of Columbia. *Education:* Emory University (B.B.A., 1983); George Washington University (J.D., 1989). Certified Public Accountant, Maryland, 1984. *Member:* The District of Columbia Bar. ***PRACTICE AREAS:*** Tax Law; Business Planning Law; Partnership Law; Business Transaction Law. ***Email:*** threuben@venable.com

(This Listing Continued)

TAMARA SCHIEBEL RICKMAN, born Seattle, Washington, September 18, 1958; admitted to bar, 1987, Maryland; 1989, District of Columbia. *Education:* Georgetown University (B.S.F.S., 1981); Catholic University (J.D., 1987). ***PRACTICE AREAS:*** Real Estate; Commercial Transactions. ***Email:*** tsrickman@venable.com

JAMES E. ROGAN, born San Francisco, California, August 21, 1957; admitted to bar, 1984, California (Not admitted in District of Columbia). *Education:* University of California at Berkeley (B.A., Political Science, 1979); University of California School of Law, Los Angeles (J.D., 1983). Member, University of California at Los Angeles Law Review, 1982-1983. Adjunct Professor: Criminal Law, Glendale University College of the Law, 1987-1995; Trial Advocacy, Southwestern University College of Law, 1988-1995. Member, Selective Service System, 1981—. Deputy District Attorney, County of Los Angeles, 1985-1990. Judge, 1990-1994 and Presiding Judge, 1993-1994, Los Angeles County Court. Member, 1994-1996 and Majority Leader, California State Assembly. Assistant Majority Whip, 1997-2001, Member, Speaker's "Kitchen Cabinet" and Majority Leader's "Kitchen Cabinet" Advisory Groups, Member, House Commerce Committee, 1997-2001 and Member, House Judiciary Committee, 1998-2001, United States House of Representatives. *Member:* Los Angeles County and American Bar Associations; State Bar of California. ***Email:*** jerogan@venable.com

JANET F. SATTERTHWAITE, born Washington, D.C., April 29, 1960; admitted to bar, 1986, Virginia; 1988, District of Columbia; 1993, Washington. *Education:* Yale University (B.A., 1982); Christ's College, Cambridge University, England; University of Virginia (J.D., 1986). ***LANGUAGES:*** French. ***PRACTICE AREAS:*** Trademark Prosecution; Trademark Counseling; Trademark Litigation; Licensing; Internet Law. ***Email:*** jfsatterthwaite@venable.com

MARY JANE SAUNDERS, born Waltham, Massachusetts, October 15, 1956; admitted to bar, 1982, Virginia; 1992, U.S. Supreme Court; 1993, District of Columbia. *Education:* Virginia Polytechnic Institute & State University (B.A., 1978); Mercer University (J.D., 1981). Author: "Criminal Copyright Infringement and the Copyright Felony Act," 71 Denver University Law Review 671 (1994). ***PRACTICE AREAS:*** Intellectual Property; Technology; Employment; Litigation. ***Email:*** mjsaunders@venable.com

MICHAEL SCHATZOW, born Washington, D.C., April 22, 1949; admitted to bar, 1973, District of Columbia; 1984, Maryland. *Education:* Case Western Reserve University (A.B., cum laude, 1970); University of Chicago (J.D., 1973); Georgetown University (LL.M., 1978). Member, Advisory Board, BNA Criminal Practice Manual, 1988-1996. Member, Faculty, Tulane University Clinical Advocacy Program, 1979-1980. Instructor, U.S. Attorney General's Advocacy Institute, 1979-1982. Assistant Federal Public Defender, District of Maryland, 1975-1978; Assistant U.S. Attorney, Eastern District of Louisiana, 1978-1981 (Chief of Trials, 1980-1981). Assistant U.S. Attorney, District of Maryland, 1982-1985 (Chief of Fraud Cases, 1983-1985). Special Assistant U.S. Attorney, District of Hawaii, 1983. *Member:* The District of Columbia Bar; Maryland State (Member, Sections on: Criminal Law; Litigation) and American Bar Associations. (Also at Baltimore, Maryland Office). ***PRACTICE AREAS:*** Criminal Law; Litigation; Professional Discipline. ***Email:*** mschatzow@venable.com

MICHAEL A. SCHLESINGER, born Great Neck, New York, December 8, 1958; admitted to bar, 1985, New York; 1986, U.S. Tax Court; 1988, District of Columbia. *Education:* Lehigh University (B.S., 1980); Boston University School of Law (J.D., cum laude, 1984), J. Joseph Tauro Distinguished Scholar; Georgetown University Law Center (M.L.T., 1989). Note and Case Editor, Boston University Law Review, 1983-1984. Adjunct Professor, Business Planning, Georgetown University Law Center, 1995-1997. Co-Chairman, American University Family Business Forum, 1997-1998. *Member:* The District of Columbia Bar; New York State Bar Association. ***PRACTICE AREAS:*** Business Law; Mergers and Acquisitions; Real Estate. ***Email:*** maschlesinger@venable.com

RICHARD D. SCHMIDT, born Evansville, Indiana, March 7, 1951; admitted to bar, 1985, New York (Not admitted in District of Columbia). *Education:* Milton College (B.A., 1975); Franklin Pierce Law Center (J.D., 1984). *Member:* American Bar Association; American Intellectual Property Law Association. ***PRACTICE AREAS:*** Intellectual Property. ***Email:*** rdschmidt@venable.com

MARINA V. SCHNELLER, born Portland, Maine, February 24, 1943; admitted to bar, 1972, Virginia, District of Columbia and U.S. Court of Appeals for the District of Columbia Circuit; 1976, U.S. Supreme Court; 1982, U.S. Court of Appeals for the Federal Circuit; registered to practice before U.S. Patent and Trademark Office. *Education:* Smith College (A.B., 1965); University of Vermont (M.S. in Chemistry, 1968); American University (J.D., 1972). Sigma Xi. Recipient, American Chemists Medal (A.C.S.), 1965. Law Clerk to Judge Helen Nies, U.S. Court of Appeals for the Federal Circuit, 1982-1984. Candidate, Who's Who in Science and Technology, 1997. Author: "History Purpose and Sanction of 35USC 102(d)," *International Review of Industrial Property and Copyright Law,* Vol. II, p. 324, 1980. Author and Lecturer: "1979 BNA Patent Law Conference"; "Advanced Application and Amendment Writ-

(This Listing Continued)

ing," 1976—. Lecturer, George Mason University School of Law, 1993. Member, Advisory Board, U.S. Patents Quarterly, BNA, 1985—. Attorney, Cushman, Darby & Cushman, 1974-1980. Counsel, Intellectual Property, Mobil Oil Corp., 1984-1998. *Member:* Virginia State Bar; American Intellectual Property Lawyers Association (Secretary, Trademark Section, 1973-1974; Chairman, Subcommittee on Recent Court Decisions, 1979-1980); American Hellenic Lawyers Association of Washington, D.C. (Chairperson, 1979-1980); American Chemical Society. ***PRACTICE AREAS:*** Intellectual Property. ***Email:*** mvschneller@venable.com

JAMES E. SCOTT, born Santa Cruz, California, April 17, 1947; admitted to bar, 1973, Michigan; 1978, Pennsylvania; 1984, U.S. Court of Appeals, Second Circuit; 1986, U.S. Court of Appeals for the District of Columbia Circuit and U.S. Court of Appeals, Tenth Circuit; 1988, California; 2000, District of Columbia. *Education:* Georgetown University (B.S.F.S., 1969); University of Michigan (J.D., 1972). Author: *Federal Law of Banking & Insurance,* 1989. Adjunct Professor: Catholic University, 1985-1986; University of California Boalt Hall School of Law, 1995-1996. *Member:* American Bar Association (Secretary, 1992-1995 and Vice, Chair, 2000—, Banking Law Committee; Vice-Chair, Subcommittee on Legislation, 1996). ***PRACTICE AREAS:*** Banking; Finance; Regulatory Law. ***Email:*** jescott@venable.com

A. CHRISTOPHER SEGA, born Frankfurt, Germany, October 12, 1954; admitted to bar, 1991, Maryland; 1992, District of Columbia. *Education:* Dartmouth College (A.B., 1976); George Washington University (M.B.A., 1982); Catholic University of America (J.D., 1991). S.P. Tuck Scholar; Faculty Award, Vernon Miller Scholar; Francis S. Gallagher Scholar. Author: "Beware the Risks of Family Limited Partnerships," *Legal Times,* September, 1998; "Issues Relating to the Change of Trust Situs," D.C. Bar Publication, November, 1999; "Current Developments in Income, Gift, Estate and Generation Skipping Transfer Tax," American Bar Association *Tax Lawyer,* Summer, 2000. Lecturer, International Taxation, Catholic University of America, Columbus School of Law, 1992-1995. *Member:* The District of Columbia Bar; American Bar Association (Member, Sections on: Real Property, Probate and Trust Law; Tax Law; Co-Chair, Important Developments and Publications Subcommittee); U.S. Tax Court Bar; Washington, D.C. Estate Planning Council. (Also at Rockville, Maryland Office). ***LANGUAGES:*** German. ***PRACTICE AREAS:*** Trusts and Estates; Tax Law; Business Planning. ***Email:*** acsega@venable.com

DAVID E. SELLINGER, born February 28, 1949; admitted to bar, 1977, New York; 1979, District of Columbia; 1988, Maryland. *Education:* Harvard University (B.A., cum laude, 1972); New York University (J.D., 1976). Articles Editor, New York University Law Review, 1975-1976. Assistant United States Attorney for the District of Columbia, 1980-1984; Co-Author: "The Self-Evaluative Privilege: Preserving Confidentiality of Compliance Information," Working Paper Series No. 66, published by Washington Legal Foundation, 1996. Law Clerk, Hon. Robert J. Ainsworth, Jr., U.S. Court of Appeals for the Fifth Circuit, 1976-1977. Member, Board of Directors, Washington Council of Lawyers, 1979-1982. Member, Board of Directors, Council for Court Excellence, 1989-1994. Chair, Court Improvements Committee, Council for Court Excellence, 1995-1998. Member, Executive Committee, Council for Court Excellence, 1995—. Member, Steering Committee, Litigation Section of The District of Columbia Bar, 1995—. Co-Chair, Litigation Section, The District of Columbia Bar, 1997. Chair, Litigation Section, District of Columbia Bar, 1997-1998. *Member:* The District of Columbia Bar; Maryland State and New York State Bar Associations. ***PRACTICE AREAS:*** Complex Civil Litigation; Commercial Litigation; White Collar Criminal Defense. ***Email:*** desellinger@venable.com

GARY L. SHAFFER, born Pittsburgh, Pennsylvania, 1949; admitted to bar, 1979, Pennsylvania, U.S. District Court, Western District of Pennsylvania and U.S. Court of Appeals for the Federal Circuit; U.S. Supreme Court; 1999, District of Columbia; registered to practice before U.S. Patent and Trademark Office. *Education:* University of Pittsburgh (B.S., Chemistry, 1971; J.D., 1979); University of Pittsburgh School of Medicine (1971-1972); Johns Hopkins University (Masters in Biotechnology, 2000). President, Omicron Delta Kappa, 1970-1971. Recipient, United States Law Week Award. Author: "Moore Defines the Issues But Only Legislation Will Settle the Controversy," Vol. 9, No. 4, Biotechnology Law Report, 1990. *Member:* District of Columbia Bar; Pennsylvania and American Bar Associations; Lawyer-Pilots Bar Association; American Intellectual Property Law Association; International Trademark Association; Licensing Executives Society. ***PRACTICE AREAS:*** Patent Litigation; Patent Prosecution; Biotechnology; Pharmaceuticals; Medical Devices; Chemistry; Patent Licensing; Trademark Licensing; Trademark Prosecution; Trademark Litigation. ***Email:*** glshaffer@venable.com

JOHN P. SHANNON, JR., born Buffalo, New York, June 26, 1946; admitted to bar, 1975, Virginia; 1980, U.S. Supreme Court; 1982, U.S. Court of Appeals for the Federal Circuit; 1991, District of Columbia; registered to practice before U.S. Patent and Trademark Office. *Education:* University of Detroit (B.M.E., 1969); George Washington University (J.D., 1974). Patent Examiner, U.S. Patent and Trademark Office, 1970-1979. *Member:* Virginia State Bar (Member, Patent, Trademark and Copyright Law Section). ***PRACTICE AREAS:*** Intellectual Property; Patents; Mechanical Patents; International Patents; Trademarks; International Trademarks. ***Email:*** jpshannon@venable.com

(This Listing Continued)

JAMES L. SHEA, born Baltimore, Maryland, June 19, 1952; admitted to bar, 1977, Maryland; 1998, District of Columbia. *Education:* Princeton University (A.B., cum laude, 1974); University of Virginia (J.D., 1977). Order of the Coif. Law Clerk to Judge Joseph H. Young, U.S. District Court, District of Maryland, 1977-1978. Assistant Attorney General, State of Maryland, 1981-1983. *Member:* The Bar Association of Baltimore City; Maryland State and American Bar Associations. (Also at Baltimore, Maryland Office). ***PRACTICE AREAS:*** Federal Civil Practice; Products Liability; Litigation; Banking and Commercial Litigation; Construction Litigation. ***Email:*** jlshea@venable.com

JULIAN L. SHEPARD, admitted to bar, 1984, Indiana; 1985, Pennsylvania; 1987, U.S. Supreme Court; 1988, District of Columbia. *Education:* Indiana University (B.S., 1980; J.D., 1983); Georgetown University. Phi Delta Phi. Senior Policy Advisor, Mass Media, National Telecommunications and Information Administration, 1988-1990. Vice President and General Counsel, Association for Maximum Service Television, Inc., 1990-1995. *Member:* Federal Communications Bar Association (Co-Chair, Law Journal Committee, 1992-1994). ***PRACTICE AREAS:*** Telecommunications Law; Communications; Mergers and Acquisitions; Information Technology; Internet Law; Business Law; Privacy Law; High Technology; Wireless Communications; Satellite Communications. ***Email:*** jlshepard@venable.com

JOE A. SHULL, born Houston, Texas, September 8, 1945; admitted to bar, 1969, Texas; 1973, District of Columbia; 1976, Virginia; 1993, Maryland. *Education:* University of Texas (B.B.A., 1967; J.D., 1969); George Washington University (LL.M. in Taxation, 1976). Law Clerk to Trial Judges of the U.S. Court of Claims, 1972-1973. *Member:* The District of Columbia Bar; Virginia State Bar; Maryland State and American Bar Associations. ***PRACTICE AREAS:*** Corporate; Securities; Commercial; Creditors' Rights; Partnership Law. ***Email:*** jashull@venable.com

KENNETH S. SLAUGHTER, born Washington, D.C., July 5, 1951; admitted to bar, 1976, District of Columbia. *Education:* Brown University (A.B., 1973); Georgetown Law Center (J.D., 1976). Attorney Adviser, U.S. Department of Treasury, 1976-1979. Assistant General Counsel, 1979-1983, National Cooperative Bank and Corporate Vice President, General Counsel and Secretary, 1983-1987. *Member:* The District of Columbia Bar. ***PRACTICE AREAS:*** State Government Law; Local Government Law; Corporate Law; Health Care; Hospital Law; Gaming Law; Municipal Labor Law. ***Email:*** ksslaughter@venable.com

HERBERT G. SMITH, II, born Newport News, Virginia, March 15, 1958; admitted to bar, 1984, Virginia; 1996, District of Columbia. *Education:* Washington & Lee University (B.A., cum laude, 1980; J.D., 1983). *Member:* Virginia State Bar (Member, Sections on Litigation and Construction Law); The District of Columbia Bar. ***PRACTICE AREAS:*** Commercial Litigation; Construction Litigation; Product Liability Litigation. ***Email:*** hgsmith@venable.com

GEORGE H. SPENCER, born Vienna, Austria, June 21, 1928; admitted to bar, 1952, New York; 1953-1982, U.S. Court of Customs and Patent Appeals; 1953, U.S. Court of Military Appeals; 1957, U.S. District Court, Southern District of New York; 1958, U.S. Supreme Court; 1958-1982, U.S. Court of Claims; 1959, District of Columbia and U.S. Court of Appeals for the District of Columbia Circuit; 1973, U.S. Court of Appeals, Fourth Circuit; 1977, U.S. Court of International Trade; 1982, U.S. Court of Appeals for the Federal Circuit; registered to practice before U.S. Patent and Trademark Office. *Education:* Cheshire Academy; Yale University (B.E., 1948); Cornell University (J.D., 1952). Patent Examiner, U.S. Patent Office, 1952-1954. Member, National Panel of Arbitrators, American Arbitration Association. *Member:* The District of Columbia Bar; Bar Association of the District of Columbia; American Bar Association; American Intellectual Property Law Association; German American Law Association; Judge Advocates Association; Lawyer-Pilots Bar Association; International Trade Commission Trial Lawyers Association; Intellectual Property Institute of Canada (Foreign Associate); American Inn of Court (Master of the Bench, The Prettyman-Leventhal). [U.S. Army Reserve, Signal Corps, 1948-1956, Judge Advocate General's Corps, 1956-1962]. ***LANGUAGES:*** German and French. ***PRACTICE AREAS:*** Intellectual Property Law; Patent Law; Trademark Law; Litigation. ***Email:*** ghspencer@venable.com

DAVID E. SPRINGER, born Anniston, Alabama, June 30, 1953; admitted to bar, 1979, District of Columbia. *Education:* Duke University (A.B., magna cum laude, 1975); Washington College of Law, American University (J.D., 1979). ***PRACTICE AREAS:*** Legislative. ***Email:*** despringer@venable.com

JUDSON W. STARR, born Boulder, Colorado, July 18, 1945; admitted to bar, 1975, District of Columbia; 1978, Virginia. *Education:* Washington and Jefferson College (B.A., 1968); Georgetown University (J.D., 1975). Editor, Georgetown Review of Law and Public Interest, 1974-1975. Fellow, Trial Advocacy Program, Georgetown University. Director, Environmental Crimes Unit, 1982-1987. Chief, Environmental Crimes Section, Land and Natural Resources Division, U.S. Department of Justice, 1987-1988. Co-Author: *Environmental Crimes Deskbook,* (Environmental Law Institute), 1995; *Environmental Criminal Liability:* Avoiding and Defending Enforcement Actions, (BNA Books), 1995; "Criminal Liability for Environmental Matters," Environmental Aspects

(This Listing Continued)

VENABLE ATTORNEYS AT LAW, VENABLE, BAETJER, HOWARD & CIVILETTI, LLP, Washington—Continued

of Real Estate Transactions, American Bar Association, 1995. Author: "Countering Environmental Crimes," 13 Boston College Environmental Affairs Law Review 379 (1986); "Turbulent Times at Justice and EPA: The Origins of Environmental Criminal Prosecutions and the Work That Remains," 59 George Washington Law Review 900 (1991); "Toward an Environmental Voluntary Disclosure Program," 16 Columbia Journal of Environmental Law 2 (1991); "The Knock on the Door: Preparing for and Responding to a Criminal Investigation," Chemical Manufacturers Association, 1991, second edition 1999. Member, Environmental Crimes Advisory Group, U.S. Sentencing Commission. *Member:* American (Co-Chairman, Subcommittees on Environmental Crimes, Business Law Section and Criminal Law Section, 1989—) and International Bar Associations; Environmental Crimes Advisory Group; U.S. Sentencing Commission. [Capt., U.S. Army, Intelligence Branch, 1968-1971]. (Also at Baltimore, Maryland Office). ***PRACTICE AREAS:*** Environmental Law; Environmental Crimes; Litigation; Government and Special Investigations Law; Criminal Law. ***Email:*** jwstarr@venable.com

GERARD TREANOR, born Medford, Massachusetts, July 1, 1943; admitted to bar, 1969, District of Columbia; 1977, Virginia. *Education:* College of the Holy Cross (A.B., 1965); Catholic University of America (J.D., 1968). Member, Catholic University Law Review, 1966-1967. Law Clerk to Chief Judge Edward M. Curran, U.S. District Court, District of Columbia, 1968-1969. Assistant U.S. Attorney for the District of Columbia, 1973-1977. *Member:* The District of Columbia Bar; Virginia State Bar; American Bar Association (Member, Sections on: Litigation; Criminal Law); National Association of Criminal Defense Lawyers; Assistant U.S. Attorneys Association of the District of Columbia (President, 1980-1981); National College for Criminal Defense (Member, Board of Regents, 1981-1986); Virginia College of Criminal Defense Attorneys (President, 1983-1984); The Barristers; The Counsellors; The Lawyers Club of Washington, D.C. Fellow: American Bar Foundation; American College of Trial Lawyers. [LCDR, JAGC, U.S. Navy, 1969-1972]. ***PRACTICE AREAS:*** Criminal Litigation; Commercial Litigation; Appeals. ***Email:*** gtreanor@venable.com

STEFAN F. TUCKER, born Detroit, Michigan, December 31, 1938; admitted to bar, 1964, District of Columbia. *Education:* University of Michigan (B.B.A., 1960); University of Michigan (J.D., 1963). Order of the Coif. Assistant Editor, Michigan Law Review, 1962-1963. Member: Editorial Board, *Practical Tax Strategies* 1972—; Editorial Advisory Board, The Journal of Real Estate Taxation, 1975—; Editorial Advisory Board, The Practical Real Estate Lawyer, 1984—. Author: *Tax Planning for Real Estate Transactions,* West Group, 1989—. Professorial Lecturer in Law: George Washington University Law School, 1970-1990; Georgetown University Law School, 1990—; University of Miami Law School, 1976-1978. Board of Trustees, Massachusetts School of Law, Andover, Massachusetts, 1989—. Life Member, American Law Institute. Member: American College of Real Estate Lawyers, 1981—; American College of Tax Counsel, 1995—; Board of Directors, American Tax Policy Institute, 2000—. *Member:* The District of Columbia Bar; American Bar Association (Chair, Taxation Section, 1998-1999). ***PRACTICE AREAS:*** Tax Law; Business Law; Real Estate; Partnerships; Estate Planning. ***Email:*** sftucker@venable.com

IAN D. VOLNER, born New York, N.Y., June 2, 1940; admitted to bar, 1967, New York; 1970, District of Columbia. *Education:* Colgate University (B.A., 1962); Columbia University (LL.B., 1965). Phi Beta Kappa. Member, Board of Editors, Columbia University Law Review. Adjunct Professor of Law, New York Law School, 1981-1988. Staff Attorney, Federal Communications Commission, Review Board, 1968-1970. *Member:* District of Columbia Bar Association; Federal Communications Bar Association; American Bar Association. ***SPECIAL AGENCIES:*** FCC, FTC, Postal Rate Commission, U.S. Postal Service. ***PRACTICE AREAS:*** Mass Media; Direct Marketing; Telecommunications; Legislative Practice. ***Email:*** idvolner@venable.com

MARTHA JO WAGNER, born April 6, 1951; admitted to bar, 1982, District of Columbia; 1985, Pennsylvania; 1997, Georgia. *Education:* University of Maryland (B.A., summa cum laude, 1979); Georgetown University (J.D., cum laude, 1982). Phi Beta Kappa; Phi Kappa Phi; Phi Alpha Theta. Member, Student Editorial Board, The Tax Lawyer, 1981-1982. *Member:* State Bar of Georgia; The District of Columbia Bar; American Bar Association (Member, Section on Labor and Employment Law; Management Co-Chair, Subcommittee on Fiduciary Responsibility). ***PRACTICE AREAS:*** Employee Benefits; ERISA Litigation. ***Email:*** mjwagner@venable.com

BARBARA L. WAITE, born Columbus, Mississippi, July 7, 1952; admitted to bar, 1984, District of Columbia; 1985, U.S. District Court for the District of Columbia, U.S. Court of International Trade, U.S. Court of Appeals for the District of Columbia Circuit and U.S. Court of Appeals for the Federal Circuit; 1989, U.S. Supreme Court; 1998, U.S. District Court, District of Arizona. *Education:* Memphis State University (B.A., summa cum laude, 1980); Georgetown University (J.D., 1984). Managing Editor, American Criminal Law Review, 1983-1984. *Member:* American Bar Association (Chairman, International Communications Committee, Section of International Law & Practice, 1986-1989); Federal Communications Bar Association; Copyright Society of the U.S.A.. ***PRACTICE AREAS:*** Intellectual Property Law. ***Email:*** pwaite@venable.com

ASHLEY J. WELLS, born Buffalo, New York, February 18, 1943; admitted to bar, 1980, California and U.S. Court of Appeals, Ninth Circuit; 1984, District of Columbia; registered to practice before U.S. Patent and Trademark Office. *Education:* Erie County Technical Institute (A.A.S., 1962); University of Santa Clara (B.S. in Chemistry, 1969; M.B.A., 1976; J.D., 1979). Gamma Pi Epsilon; Beta Gamma Sigma; Phi Alpha Delta (Edmonds Chapter, Secretary, 1977, President, 1978). Author: Casenote, "Parker v. Flook," Patentability of Computer Programs, 19 Santa Clara Law Review 483, 1979. *Member:* The District of Columbia Bar; State Bar of California; American Intellectual Property Law Association. ***PRACTICE AREAS:*** Intellectual Property Law; Patents. ***Email:*** ajwells@venable.com

JUDITH L. WHEAT, born East Orange, New Jersey, September 14, 1961; admitted to bar, 1989, Virginia; 1991, District of Columbia, U.S. District Court, Eastern District of Virginia, U.S. District Court, District of Columbia and U.S. Court of Appeals, Fourth and Federal Circuits; 1996, U.S. Court of Appeals for the District of Columbia Circuit. *Education:* Georgetown University (B.S.F.S., 1983; J.D., magna cum laude, 1989). Member, Order of the Coif. International Championship Team, Jessup Moot Court Competition, 1987. Law Clerk to the Honorable Barbara M. Keenan, Court of Appeals of Virginia, 1989-1991; Supreme Court of Virginia, 1991. *Member:* Virginia State Bar; The District of Columbia Bar (Member, Steering Committee, Criminal Law and Individual Rights Section); American Bar Association; Women's Bar Association of D.C. (Former Co-Chair, Mentoring Committee, Litigation Forum). ***LANGUAGES:*** Spanish. ***PRACTICE AREAS:*** Criminal Litigation; Civil Litigation. ***Email:*** jlwheat@venable.com

N. FRANK WIGGINS, born Santa Monica, California, July 22, 1947; admitted to bar, 1974, District of Columbia. *Education:* Iowa State University (B.S., 1969); University of Michigan (J.D., magna cum laude, 1972). Order of the Coif. Associate Editor, University of Michigan Law Review, 1971-1972. Associate Professor, Northwestern Law School, 1975-1978. *Member:* Bar Association of the District of Columbia. ***SPECIAL AGENCIES:*** Federal Communications Commission; Federal Trade Commission; Postal Rate Commission; U.S. Postal Service. ***PRACTICE AREAS:*** Litigation; Administrative Law. ***Email:*** fwiggins@venable.com

THOMAS G. WISEMAN, born Brooklyn, New York, September 8, 1947; admitted to bar, 1984, Virginia; 1998, District of Columbia; registered to practice before U.S. Patent and Trademark Office. *Education:* Long Island University (B.S., Chemistry, 1969); Pennsylvania State University (M.S., Organic Chemistry, 1971); University of Baltimore School of Law (J.D., 1982). Author: "Biotechnology Patent Practice—A Primer," AIPLA Quarterly Journal, Vol. 16, Nos. 3 & 4, 1988-1989, pp. 394-417; "The Reversible Hydration of Formaldehyde Thermodynamic Parameters," J. of Physical Chem., Vol. 74, 1970, p. 2746; "A Study of the Coupling Reaction Between Ethyl Thiophosphate and the Sulfhydryl Group of BSA," Master's Thesis, Pennsylvania State University, 1971. Acting Patent Branch Chief, National Institutes of Health, Office of Technology Transfer, 1991-1993. Examiner-in-Chief, 1990-1991, Supervisory Patent Examiner, 1983-1990 and Primary Patent Examiner, 1972-1983, U.S. Patent and Trademark Office. Associate Lecturer, Chemistry Department, Long Island University, 1972. *Member:* District of Columbia Bar; Virginia and American Bar Associations; American Intellectual Property Law Association; American Chemical Society; American Association for the Advancement of Science; Government Patent Lawyers Association. ***PRACTICE AREAS:*** Patent Prosecution. ***Email:*** tgwiseman@venable.com

ALLEN WOOD, born Helena, Arkansas, December 14, 1945; admitted to bar, 1975, Virginia; 1978, District of Columbia; 1983, U.S. District Court for the District of Columbia; registered to practice before U.S. Patent and Trademark Office. *Education:* Austin College (B.A., 1968); Texas Christian University (M.A., 1972); American University (J.D., 1975). *Member:* The District of Columbia Bar; Virginia State Bar (inactive). ***PRACTICE AREAS:*** Intellectual Property Law; Patent Law. ***Email:*** awood@venable.com

OF COUNSEL

RALPH P. ALBRECHT, born Watertown, New York, August 23, 1965; admitted to bar, 1997, District of Columbia; 1999, U.S. Court of Appeals for the Federal Circuit; registered to practice before U.S. Patent and Trademark Office. *Education:* Virginia Polytechnic Institute (B.S.E.E., cum laude, 1989); George Mason University (J.D., 1997). *Member:* Bar Association of the District of Columbia (Member, Patent, Trademark and Copyright Section Council); District of Columbia Bar; American Bar Association; American Intellectual Property Lawyers' Association; Capitol Telecommunications Professionals. ***PRACTICE AREAS:*** Intellectual Property; Patents; Trademarks; Copyrights; Computers and Software; Electronic Patents. ***Email:*** rpalbrecht@venable.com

ROBERT S. BABAYI, born Tehran, Iran, January 18, 1959; admitted to bar, 1992, Florida; 2000, District of Columbia; registered to practice before U.S. Patent and Trademark Office. *Education:* Florida International University

(This Listing Continued)

(B.S.E.E., 1981); University of Miami (J.D., 1992). *Member:* The Florida Bar; American Bar Association; American Intellectual Property Law Association. ***LANGUAGES:*** Farsi. ***PRACTICE AREAS:*** Intellectual Property; Patent Prosecution; Technology Licensing. ***Email:*** rsbabayi@venable.com

FEI-FEI CHAO, born Hong Kong, September 20, 1955; admitted to bar, 1997, Maryland; 1998, District of Columbia. *Education:* National Chung-Hsing University, Taichung, Taiwan (B.S., Botany, 1977; M.S., Microbiology & Molecular Biology, 1979); University of Oklahoma (Ph.D., Biochemistry, 1985); University of Maryland (J.D., 1996). Member: NIH Alumni Association, 1988; Mid-Atlantic Lipid Society, 1989; American Chemical Society, 1993. *Member:* American Bar Association; American Intellectual Property Law Association. ***LANGUAGES:*** Chinese. ***PRACTICE AREAS:*** Patent Applications; Patent Prosecution; Patent Infringement; Technology Transfers; Technology Licensing; Trademark Prosecution; Copyrights; Intellectual Property Litigation. ***Email:*** fchao@venable.com

PAUL F. DAEBELER, born Ridley Park, Pennsylvania, August 27, 1966; admitted to bar, 1991, Pennsylvania, New Jersey and U.S. District Court, District of New Jersey and Eastern District of Pennsylvania; 1992, U.S. Court of Appeals, 3rd and Federal Circuits; 1993, District of Columbia; 1995, U.S. Supreme Court; 1998, New York; registered to practice before U.S. Patent and Trademark Office. *Education:* Lehigh University (B.S.E.E., 1988); Widener University (J.D., 1991). *Member:* American Intellectual Property Law Association; Rochester Intellectual Property Law Association (Corresponding Secretary, 1999-2000; Recording Secretary, 2000-2001). ***PRACTICE AREAS:*** Intellectual Property.

DAVID G. DICKMAN, born Lake Charles, Louisiana, March 26, 1952; admitted to bar, 1986, Missouri; 1990, Florida; 1999, District of Columbia. *Education:* U.S. Coast Guard Academy (B.S., 1974); St. Louis University (J.D., 1986). Managing Editor, 1985-1986 and Outstanding Student Article, 1985, St. Louis University Law Journal. Author: "Criminal Law Issues Associated With Enforcement of Environmental Laws by the United States Coast Guard," ALI-ABA Seminar on Criminal Enforcement of Environmental Law, 1997; "Recent Developments in the Criminal Enforcement of Maritime Environmental Law," Tulane Maritime Law Journal, Winter 1999; "Defending Against the Criminal Enforcement of Maritime Environmental Law," ALI-ABA Business Law Course Materials Journal, 2000; "Environmental Criminal Liability in the United States—A Handbook for the Marine Industry," Chamber of Shipping of America, 2000. Deputy Head of U.S. Delegation, Marine Environment Protection Committee, International Maritime Organization, 1998. *Member:* Maritime Law Association of the United States. [Cmdr., U.S. Coast Guard, 1974-1998]. ***PRACTICE AREAS:*** Environmental Law; Environmental Criminal Defense; Maritime International Law; Administrative; Regulatory Law. ***Email:*** dgdickman@venable.com

ROBERT C. HARMALA, born Montebello, California, January 27, 1969; admitted to bar, 1995, California; 1996, District of Columbia. *Education:* University of California, Berkeley (A.B., 1991); University of Southern California (J.D., 1994). ***PRACTICE AREAS:*** Legislative Practice.

FRANK HORTON, born Cuero, Texas, December 12, 1919; admitted to bar, 1947, New York; 1978, District of Columbia. *Education:* Louisiana State University, Baton Rouge, Louisiana (B.A., 1941); Cornell University, Ithaca, New York (LL.B., 1947). Phi Kappa Phi; Order of the Coif. Member, of Congress, United States House of Representatives (Member, 1963-1993; Chairman, Bipartisan Commission on Federal Paperwork, 1975-1977; Ranking Minority Member, Government Operations Committee, 1973-1993; Ranking Minority Member, Legislation and National Security Subcommittee, 1973-1993; Member, Post Office and Civil Service Committee, Ranking Minority Member, Subcommittee on Postal Operations and Services; Member, Subcommittee on Human Resources; Ranking Minority Member, Commission on Congressional Mailing Standards - Franking Commission, 1980-1993; Member, House Senate Joint Committee Atomic Energy. Member, Commission on Federal Procurement, 1969-1973. Co-Founder and Co-Chairman, Northeast-Midwest Congressional Coalition, 1977-1993. Dean, New York Republican Delegation and Chairman, New York Bipartisan Congressional Delegation, 1991-1993. Past President, Federation of Bar Associations of Western New York. *Member:* Monroe County, New York State and American Bar Associations; Bar Association of District of Columbia; Veterans of Foreign Wars, American Legion (Member, National Advisory Group). [Lt., Col., US Army, 1941-1946]. ***PRACTICE AREAS:*** Government Contracts. ***Email:*** fhorton@venable.com

ERIK V. HUEY, born Uniontown, Pennsylvania, July 8, 1967; admitted to bar, 1993, Georgia; 2000, District of Columbia. *Education:* University of Miami (B.B.A., 1989); University of Notre Dame (J.D., 1992). Beta Gamma Sigma; Omicron Delta Kappa; Pi Sigma Alpha. Mortar Board, University of Miami President's 100. *Member:* Atlanta and American Bar Associations; State Bar of Georgia. ***PRACTICE AREAS:*** Telecommunications; Government Relations; Legislative Practice; Regulatory. ***Email:*** evhuey@venable.com

REBECCA E. PEARSON, born Baltimore, Maryland, January 14, 1964; admitted to bar, 1989, Florida; 2000, District of Columbia. *Education:* Duke University (A.B., 1985); University of North Carolina at Chapel Hill (J.D., 1989); George Washington University (LL.M. in Government Procurement, with highest honors, 1996). Articles Editor, North Carolina Journal of International Law and Commercial Regulation, 1988-1989. Student Editor-in-Chief, 1995-1996 and Member, Editorial Board, 1996—, American Bar Association Public Contract Law Journal. Author: "The Air Force's Experience with the Expanded Bid Protest Jurisdiction in the Court of Federal Claims," 34 Procurement Lawyer 3, Fall, 1998; "Should Congress Squeeze the Sharman?" 28 Public Contract Law Journal 597, Summer, 1999. Co-Author, "Release of Unit Prices After McDonnell Douglas Corp. v. NASA," 35 Procurement Lawyer 9, Winter, 2000. Co-Taught Seminar, "Expanded Bid Protest Jurisdiction at the Court of Federal Claims," 98th Government Contract Law Symposium, The Judge Advocate General's School, U.S. Army, December 9, 1998. Taught Seminar, "Contract Interpretation," NCMA Boston Chapter 39th Annual March Workshop, March 15, 2000. *Member:* American Bar Association. [USAF, 1989-1999]. ***PRACTICE AREAS:*** Public Contract Law. ***Email:*** repearson@venable.com

DAVID W. RUTSTEIN, born New York, N.Y.; admitted to bar, 1969, Pennsylvania; 1970, District of Columbia. *Education:* University of Pennsylvania (B.A., 1966); George Washington University (J.D., with honors, 1969). Deputy Attorney General, Pennsylvania, 1969-1970. Associate, 1970-1975 and Partner, 1975-1978, Danzansky, Dickey, Tydings, Quint & Gordon, Washington, D.C. Chairman of the Board, 2000 and Treasurer, Greater Washington Board of Trade. Board of Directors (Member of Executive Committee), Federal City Council. President, Washington Hebrew Home for the Aged, 1989-1991. Treasurer, Vice Chairman and Chairman of the Board, 1995-1999, Eugene and Agnes E. Foundation. *Member:* Bar Association of the District of Columbia; Washington Metropolitan Area Corporate Counsel Association (Chairman of Board, 1985). ***Email:*** dwrutstein@venable.com

MICHAEL A. SARTORI, born St. Louis, Missouri; admitted to bar, 1998, Virginia; 1999, District of Columbia; registered to practice before U.S. Patent and Trademark Office. *Education:* University of Notre Dame (B.S.E.E., 1987; M.S.E.E., 1981; Ph.D., 1991); Georgetown University (J.D., cum laude, 1998). Author: "Tax Ramifications of the Recent Changes in the Patent Laws," The Tax Lawyer, Vol. 40, No. 4, Summer 1996, pp. 981-989; "A Proposal for the Registration of Domain Names," The Trademark Reporter, Vol. 87, no. 5, September-October, 1997; "An Economic Incentive Analysis of the Jury's Role in Patent Litigation," pp. 638-659, Journal of the Patent and Trademark Office Society, Vol. 79, no. 5, May, 1997, pp. 331-361. Lecturer, Catholic University of America, Department of Mechanical Engineering, 1991. Post-Doctorate Research Associate, University of Notre Dame, Department of Electrical Engineering, 1991. Patent Examiner, U.S. Patent and Trademark Office, 1994-1996. Senior Project Manager, U.S. Navy, Naval Surface Warfare Center, 1991-1994. ***PRACTICE AREAS:*** Intellectual Property. ***Email:*** masartori@venable.com

CHARLES E. SLITER, born Detroit, Michigan, August 25, 1949; admitted to bar, 1974, Ohio; 1977, District of Columbia. *Education:* University of Notre Dame (B.A., cum laude, 1971); Georgetown University Law Center (J.D., 1974). *Member:* The District of Columbia Bar. ***LANGUAGES:*** French. ***PRACTICE AREAS:*** Hotel and Resort Law; Corporate Transactions; Commercial Finance; Financial Institution Regulation. ***Email:*** cesliter@venable.com

JEFFREY S. TENENBAUM, born Boston, Massachusetts, October 29, 1968; admitted to bar, 1996, District of Columbia. *Education:* University of Pennsylvania (B.A., 1990); Catholic University of America (J.D., 1995). Author of Association Tax Compliance Guide, ASAE, 2000. Frequent lecturer and Author on Association Legal topics for American Society of Association Executives, Greater Washington Society of Association Executives, Legal Times, Association Law and Policy, Association Management, Executive Update, Association Trends, The Exempt Organization Tax Review, National Center for Nonprofit Law, and other industry organizations and publications. Editorial Advisory Boards, 1996— and Chairman, 2000—, Association Law and Policy and Nonprofit Tax and Financial Strategies. Recipient, Greater Washington Society of Association Executives Chairman's Award, 1997. *Member:* Bar Association of the District of Columbia; American Bar Association (Tax Section, 1994—); American Society of Association Executives (Legal Section Council, 1998—; Legal, Finance and Administration Sections, 1995—); Greater Washington Society of Association Executives (Government and Public Affairs Advisory Council, 1995—; Foundation Board of Trustees, 1997—). ***PRACTICE AREAS:*** Trade and Professional Association Law. ***Email:*** jstenenbaum@venable.com

ARIEL VANNIER, born Paris, France, March 15, 1960; admitted to bar, 1984, Maryland; 1998, District of Columbia. *Education:* The Johns Hopkins University (B.A., 1981); Washington & Lee University School of Law (J.D., 1984). Order of the Coif. *Member:* The Bar Association of Baltimore City; Maryland State and American Bar Associations. (Also at Baltimore, Maryland Office). ***LANGUAGES:*** French. ***PRACTICE AREAS:*** Corporate; Securities Regulation; Corporate Finance. ***Email:*** avannier@venable.com

CATHERINE M. VOORHEES, born Ridley Park, Pennsylvania, December 16, 1960; admitted to bar, 1988, Virginia and Supreme Court of Virginia; 1991, District of Columbia; 1990, U.S. Court of Appeals, Federal Circuit; registered to practice before U.S. Patent and Trademark Office. *Education:*

(This Listing Continued)

VENABLE ATTORNEYS AT LAW, VENABLE, BAETJER, HOWARD & CIVILETTI, LLP, Washington—Continued

Lafayette College (B.S.E.E., 1982); George Mason University School of Law (J.D., 1988). Examiner, United States Patent and Trademark Office, 1982-1988. *Member:* Federal Circuit and American Bar Associations; Virginia State Bar; The District of Columbia Bar; American Intellectual Property Law Association. ***PRACTICE AREAS:*** Patents; Trademarks; Copyrights. ***Email:*** cmvoorhees@venable.com

ASSOCIATES

CHAD C. ANDERSON, born July 8, 1975; admitted to bar, 2000, Virginia; registered to practice before U.S. Patent and Trademark Office (Not admitted in District of Columbia). *Education:* North Carolina State University (B.S.E., 1997); University of Richmond (J.D., 2000). ***PRACTICE AREAS:*** Patent Prosecution; Intellectual Property Litigation. ***Email:*** canderson@venable.com

THEODORE W. ATKINSON, born Portsmouth, Ohio, May 8, 1970; admitted to bar, 1995, Virginia; 1998, District of Columbia. *Education:* Old Dominion University (B.S., 1992); College of William & Mary (J.D., 1995). Order of the Barristers. Chief Justice, Moot Court Board, 1991-1992. Law Clerk to Hon. Robert J. Wooldridge, Jr., Nineteenth Judicial Circuit, Fairfax, Virginia. Chief Prosecutor, Office of Judicial Prosecutors, Judicial Council, 1991-1992. *Member:* Virginia State Bar (Chair, Professionalism Committee, Young Lawyers' Conference, 1997-1999); Northern Virginia Technology Council, American Intellectual Property Law Association. ***PRACTICE AREAS:*** Intellectual Property Litigation. ***Email:*** twatkinson@venable.com

HARRY I. ATLAS, born Indianapolis, Indiana, July 22, 1971; admitted to bar, 1997, Maryland; 1999, District of Columbia. *Education:* New Israel Rabbinical College (B.T.L., 1994); University of Maryland School of Law (J.D., 1997). (Also at Baltimore, Maryland Office). ***Email:*** hiatlas@venable.com

MARCIA A. AUBERGER, born Rochester, New York, November 8, 1963; admitted to bar, 1989, Texas; 1998, District of Columbia. *Education:* State University of New York at Buffalo (B.A., 1985); South Texas College of Law (J.D., 1989). *Member:* District of Columbia Bar; State Bar of Texas; American Bar Association; Women's Bar Association of the District of Columbia; International Trademark Association. ***PRACTICE AREAS:*** Trademark Prosecution; Trademarks; Trademark Litigation. ***Email:*** maauberger@venable.com

PURVI BADIANI, born India, December 8, 1974; admitted to bar, 1998, New Jersey; 2000, District of Columbia. *Education:* Rutgers University (B.A., cum laude, 1995); Georgetown University (J.D., 1998). *Member:* American Bar Association. ***LANGUAGES:*** Hindi and Gujarati. ***Email:*** pbadiani@venable.com

GREGORY S. BRAKER, born Beaver Dam, Wisconsin, June 9, 1962; admitted to bar, 1992, Maryland; 1994, District of Columbia. *Education:* Evangel College (B.A., magna cum laude, 1984); University of Maryland (M.A., with honors, 1987); Georgetown University Law Center (J.D., 1992). *Member:* Maryland State and American Bar Associations; Bar Association of the District of Columbia; Environmental Law Institute. ***PRACTICE AREAS:*** Environmental Law; Environmental Compliance; Internal Investigations; Criminal Defense. ***Email:*** gsbraker@venable.com

RITA L. BRICKMAN, born New York, N.Y., November 23, 1965; admitted to bar, 1994, Maryland; 1996, District of Columbia. *Education:* University of Pennsylvania (B.S., B.A., 1987); Boston University (J.D., cum laude, 1994). Articles Editor, Boston University Public Interest Law Journal, 1993-1994. *Member:* American and Energy Bar Associations. ***PRACTICE AREAS:*** Energy; Public Utility; Energy Project Development; Administrative Law. ***Email:*** rlbrickman@venable.com

JENNIFER J. BRUTON, born Wilmington, North Carolina, January 16, 1971; admitted to bar, 1997, North Carolina; 2000, District of Columbia. *Education:* University of North Carolina (B.A., 1993); Wake Forest University (J.D., 1997). ***PRACTICE AREAS:*** Real Estate. ***Email:*** jjbruton@venable.com

FRANK A. CIATTO, born Jersey City, New Jersey, July 25, 1966; admitted to bar, 1994, New Jersey; 1995, New York and District of Columbia. *Education:* Georgetown University (B.S.B.A., cum laude, 1988; J.D., 1994). Certified Public Accountant, New York, 1991. ***PRACTICE AREAS:*** Corporate Law; Business Transactions. ***Email:*** faciatto@venable.com

ROSEMARY E. DAILEY, born Washington, D.C., February 26, 1972; admitted to bar, 1997, Maryland; 1998, District of Columbia. *Education:* Miami University (B.A., 1993); Catholic University of America (J.D., cum laude, 1997). Member, Catholic University Journal of Contemporary Health Law and Policy. *Member:* Maryland State and Federal Bar Associations; The District of Columbia Bar. ***LANGUAGES:*** Spanish. ***PRACTICE AREAS:*** Labor and Employment; Immigration. ***Email:*** redailey@venable.com

MOLLY A. DELEA, born Baltimore, Maryland, May 2, 1971; admitted to bar, 2000, Virginia (Not admitted in District of Columbia). *Education:* University of Richmond (B.S.B.A., 1993; J.D., 2000). Member, 1998-1999 and Executive Editor, 1999-2000, University of Richmond Law Review. Member, Moot Court Board. Member, Client Counseling and Negotiations Board, 1998-2000. Certified Public Accountant, Virginia, 1995. *Member:* Virginia Bar Association. ***PRACTICE AREAS:*** Trusts and Estates. ***Email:*** madelea@venable.com

W. PATRICK DOHERTY, born St. Louis, Missouri, September 17, 1973; admitted to bar, 2000, Maryland (Not admitted in District of Columbia). *Education:* Georgetown University (B.S.F.S., 1995); George Washington University (J.D., with honors, 2000). *Member:* Maryland State and American (Member, International Law Section) Bar Associations. ***LANGUAGES:*** Japanese. ***PRACTICE AREAS:*** Government Contracts; Litigation. ***Email:*** wpdoherty@venable.com

KATHLEEN S. DOLAN, born Arlington, Virginia, September 9, 1972; admitted to bar, 1998, Virginia and U.S. District Court, Eastern District of Virginia; 1999, U.S. District Court, Western District of Virginia; 2000, District of Columbia. *Education:* Marquette University (B.A., cum laude, 1995); Catholic University of America (J.D., cum laude, 1998). Certificate in International and Comparative Studies, Catholic University of America. Member, Catholic University of America Law Review, 1996-1998. Moot Court Associate. Member, Environmental Law National Team. Executive Board Member, Student Bar Association. *Member:* Virginia State Bar; The District of Columbia Bar; American Bar Association. ***LANGUAGES:*** Spanish. ***PRACTICE AREAS:*** Environmental; White Collar Crime. ***Email:*** ksdolan@venable.com

RICHARD F. ENSOR, born Washington, D.C., October 28, 1972; admitted to bar, 1998, Virginia and U.S. District Court, Eastern District of Virginia; 1999, Maryland and U.S. District Court, District of Maryland (Not admitted in District of Columbia). *Education:* George Mason University (B.S., 1995); College of William and Mary (J.D., 1998). ***PRACTICE AREAS:*** Government Contracts; Construction Law; Commercial Litigation. ***Email:*** rfensor@venable.com

PATRICIA A. EXPOSITO, born Hackensack, New Jersey, March 16, 1966; admitted to bar, 1996, Maryland; 1998, District of Columbia. *Education:* University of Virginia (B.A., 1988); Catholic University of America (J.D., magna cum laude, 1996). Editorial Assistant, The Catholic University Law Review. Law Clerk to the Hon. Howard S. Chasanow, Court of Appeals of Maryland, 1996-1997. *Member:* The District of Columbia Bar. ***PRACTICE AREAS:*** Labor; Litigation. ***Email:*** paexposito@venable.com

DANIELLE FAGRE, born Minneapolis, Minnesota, May 4, 1972; admitted to bar, 1999, Maryland; 2000, Minnesota (Not admitted in District of Columbia). *Education:* University of Puget Sound (B.A., 1994); Washington College of Law, American University (J.D., cum laude, 1999). *Member:* Maryland State, Minnesota State and American Bar Associations. ***PRACTICE AREAS:*** Legislative Practice; Election Law; Privacy Law. ***Email:*** dfagre@venable.com

DAVID M. FARNUM, born Rockford, Illinois, October 14, 1969; admitted to bar, 2000, Connecticut (Not admitted in District of Columbia). *Education:* University of Chicago (A.B., with honors, 1992); University of Iowa (M.A., 1995); Yale University (J.D., 1998). Law Clerk to the Hon. Alan H. Nevas, U.S. District Court, District of Connecticut, 1998-1999. *Member:* Connecticut Bar Association. ***Email:*** dfarnum@venable.com

RACHEL L. FINKLE, born Providence, Rhode Island, May 27, 1973; admitted to bar, 2000, Maryland (Not admitted in District of Columbia). *Education:* Boston College (B.A., 1995); Boston College Law School (J.D., 2000). ***PRACTICE AREAS:*** Legislative Practice; Regulatory. ***Email:*** rlfinkle@venable.com

BRIAN L. FLACK, born Marlborough, Massachusetts, November 7, 1972; admitted to bar, 1999, New York; 2001, District of Columbia. *Education:* Pennsylvania State University (B.S., 1994); Pace University (J.D., 1998). *Member:* New York State (Member, Environmental Section) and American (Member, Environmental, Energy and Resources Section) Bar Associations. ***PRACTICE AREAS:*** Environmental; Energy; White Collar Crime. ***Email:*** blflack@venable.com

DARRYL L. FRANKLIN, born Pascagoula, Mississippi, July 19, 1974; admitted to bar, 1999, Virginia; 2000, District of Columbia. *Education:* American University (B.A., 1996); College of William & Mary (J.D., 1999). *Member:* Virginia State Bar; National Bar Association. ***PRACTICE AREAS:*** Commercial Litigation; Labor and Employment. ***Email:*** dfranklin@venable.com

CHRISTOPHER E. GATEWOOD, born Charlotte, North Carolina, September 16, 1972; admitted to bar, 2000, Virginia (Not admitted in District of Columbia). *Education:* Wake Forest University (B.A., magna cum laude, 1995); University of Virginia (J.D., 2000). ***PRACTICE AREAS:*** Litigation; Intellectual Property; Antitrust Law; Trade Regulation Law. ***Email:*** cegatewood@venable.com

JASON L. GOLDBLATT, born Philadelphia, Pennsylvania, May 23, 1970; admitted to bar, 1996, Maryland; 1997, District of Columbia. *Education:* Duke University (A.B., 1992); George Washington University (J.D., 1996). *Member:* District of Columbia Bar; Maryland State Bar Association. ***PRACTICE AREAS:*** Business Law; Partnership Law. ***Email:*** jgoldblatt@venable.com

(This Listing Continued)

REBECCA L. GOLDSMITH, born New Haven, Connecticut, September 25, 1971; admitted to bar, 1997, Maryland; 1999, District of Columbia. *Education:* Brandeis University (B.A., cum laude, 1993); Washington College of Law of American University (J.D., cum laude, 1997). Note and Comment Editor, American Bar Association Administrative Law Review, 1996-1997. Author: Note, "Babbitt v. Sweet Home Chapter of Communities for a Great Oregon: A Legislative Challenge Between Private Landowners and the Endangered Species Act," 49 Administrative Law Review 1, 1997. *Member:* Maryland State and American Bar Associations. ***PRACTICE AREAS:*** Intellectual Property; Patent Litigation. ***Email:*** rgoldsmith@venable.com

KEITH G. HADDAWAY, born Baltimore, Maryland, April 15, 1958; admitted to bar, 1997, Maryland; 1998, District of Columbia; registered to practice before U.S. Patent and Trademark Office. *Education:* St. Mary's College of Maryland (B.S., with high honors, 1980); University of Maryland (Ph.D. in Organic Chemistry, 1987); George Washington University (J.D., with honors, 1997). Member, Moot Court Board, 1994-1997. Member, 1995-1997 and Articles Editor, 1996, The Environmental Lawyer. *Member:* Maryland State and American Bar Associations; American Intellectual Property Law Association. ***PRACTICE AREAS:*** Intellectual Property. ***Email:*** kghaddaway@venable.com

JOHN F. HENAULT, JR., born Weymouth, Massachusetts, October 9, 1970; admitted to bar, 2000, Virginia (Not admitted in District of Columbia). *Education:* St. Louis University (B.A., 1996); George Mason University School of Law (J.D., magna cum laude, 2000). Executive Editor, George Mason Law Review. [Cpl., E4, U.S. Marine Corps, 1988-1992]. ***PRACTICE AREAS:*** Commercial Litigation; White Collar Crime. ***Email:*** jhenault@venable.com

LINDA A. HILDRETH, born Washington, D.C., July 4, 1957; admitted to bar, 1988, Virginia; 1990, District of Columbia. *Education:* Vassar College (A.B., 1979); College of William and Mary (M.A., 1988); University of Virginia (J.D., 1988). Maguire Fellow; Dillard Fellow. *Member:* Virginia State Bar; District of Columbia Bar. ***PRACTICE AREAS:*** Real Estate; Commercial Transactions. ***Email:*** lahildreth@venable.com

TONYA D. HORTON, born Fayetteville, North Carolina, August 11, 1975; admitted to bar, 2000, Maryland (Not admitted in District of Columbia). *Education:* Howard University (B.A., magna cum laude, 1997); University of North Carolina (J.D., 2000). Phi Beta Kappa; Pi Sigma Alpha. Author: "An Introduction to the Euro," 3 NC Banking Institute, 435 1999. ***PRACTICE AREAS:*** Trademark Prosecution; Intellectual Property Litigation. ***Email:*** tdhorton@venable.com

BRIAN M. HUDSON, born Sawyer AFB, Michigan, January 2, 1971; admitted to bar, 1999, Virginia; 2001, District of Columbia. *Education:* University of North Carolina, Chapel Hill (B.A., 1993); Georgetown University (J.D., 1999). ***PRACTICE AREAS:*** Labor Law; Employment Litigation; Employee Benefits. ***Email:*** bmhudson@venable.com

BARIS H. IPEKER, born Silver Spring, Maryland, June 2, 1969; admitted to bar, 1994, Georgia; 1996, Maryland; 1997, District of Columbia. *Education:* University of Virginia (B.S., 1991); Emory University (J.D., 1994). ***LANGUAGES:*** Turkish. ***PRACTICE AREAS:*** Real Estate; Business Transactions; Telecommunications. ***Email:*** bhipeker@venable.com

DAVIDA H. ISAACS, born New York, N.Y.; admitted to bar, 1996, New York; 1998, District of Columbia. *Education:* Brandeis University (B.A., magna cum laude, 1992); New York University (J.D., 1995). Staff Editor, 1993-1994 and Associate Editor, 1994-1995, Review of Law and Social Change. Author: "It's Nothing Personal - But Should It Be? Finding Agent Liability for Violations of the Federal Employment Discrimination Statutes," N.Y.U. Review of Law and Social Change, Vol. XXII, No. 3. Member, Committee on Military Affairs and Justice, Co-Chair, Subcommittee on Gender Issues in the Military, The Association of the Bar of the City of New York. *Member:* The District of Columbia Bar. ***PRACTICE AREAS:*** Intellectual Property Litigation; Patent Litigation; Trademark Litigation; Trademark Prosecution. ***Email:*** dhisaacs@venable.com

JEFFRI A. KAMINSKI, born Pittsburgh, Pennsylvania, August 13, 1968; admitted to bar, 1997, Pennsylvania; 1999, District of Columbia; registered to practice before U.S. Patent and Trademark Office. *Education:* University of Pittsburgh (B.S.E.E., 1992); Ohio Northern University (J.D., with distinction, 1996). Phi Kappa Phi. Moot Court. Member, Law Review. *Member:* American Bar Association; American Intellectual Property Law Association. ***PRACTICE AREAS:*** Intellectual Property; Electrical Patent Prosecution; Technology Licensing. ***Email:*** jakaminski@venable.com

HOYUN KIM, born Seoul, Korea, April 24, 1960; admitted to bar, 1987, District of Columbia; 1989, Virginia; 1999, Maryland. *Education:* George Washington University (B.A., with honors, 1983; J.D., 1987). Phi Beta Kappa. *Member:* Virginia State Bar; Asian Pacific American Bar Association of the Greater Washington Area; Women's Bar Association; Washington Area Lawyers for the Arts. ***PRACTICE AREAS:*** Bankruptcy; Creditors Rights. ***Email:*** hkim@venable.com

(This Listing Continued)

MARY ANN KNOECKEL, born Warwick, Rhode Island, January 3, 1959; admitted to bar, 1991, Hawaii; 1998, District of Columbia. *Education:* University of Hawaii (B.B.A., with distinction, 1988); University of Texas (J.D., 1991). Beta Gamma Sigma; Phi Kappa Phi; Outstanding Senior in International Business, University of Hawaii. *Member:* Hawaii State and American Bar Associations; The District of Columbia Bar. ***PRACTICE AREAS:*** Real Estate; Commercial Law. ***Email:*** maknoeckel@venable.com

JEANNY K. LEE, born Los Angeles, California, December 8, 1970; admitted to bar, 1998, New York, Maryland and District of Columbia. *Education:* Harvard University (B.A., 1993); Georgetown University (J.D., 1997). *Member:* Maryland State and New York State Bar Associations; The District of Columbia Bar. ***PRACTICE AREAS:*** Corporate; Business Transactions. ***Email:*** jklee@venable.com

MARK A. MACHI, born San Francisco, California, March 29, 1967; admitted to bar, 1995, Maryland; 1996, U.S. District Court, District of Maryland and U.S. Court of Appeals, Fourth Circuit; 1998, District of Columbia; 2000, U.S. District Court, District of Columbia. *Education:* University of California, Santa Cruz (B.A., 1990); University of Maryland (J.D., 1995). Order of the Coif; Moot Court Board. Law Clerk to Magistrate Judge Susan K. Gauvey and Magistrate Judge Paul W. Grimm, U.S. District Court for the District of Maryland.

KAREN E. MASON, born Monahans, Texas, February 23, 1965; admitted to bar, 1994, Pennsylvania; 2000, District of Columbia. *Education:* Bowdoin College (A.B., cum laude, 1987); Case Western Reserve University (J.D., 1993). Staff Member, 1990-1992; Editor, 1992-1993, Case Western Reserve University School of Law Journal of International Law. ***PRACTICE AREAS:*** Real Estate; Commercial Law; Telecommunications Law. ***Email:*** kemason@venable.com

JOHN W. McGLYNN, born Glen Cove, New York, November 19, 1973; admitted to bar, 1998, Maryland (Not admitted in District of Columbia). *Education:* Loyola College (B.A., 1995); Catholic University of America (J.D., 1998). ***PRACTICE AREAS:*** Intellectual Property. ***Email:*** jwmcglynn@venable.com

CHARLOTTE M. McGUINNESS, born Orange, New Jersey, January 6, 1949; admitted to bar, 1999, Maryland; 2000, District of Columbia. *Education:* Shimer College (A.B., 1972); Rutgers University (Ph.D., 1984); Georgetown University (J.D., 1999). *Member:* Maryland State and American Bar Associations. ***PRACTICE AREAS:*** Patent Prosecution. ***Email:*** cmmcguinness@venable.com

JEANNETTE C. MEACHAM, born California, November 28, 1972; admitted to bar, 1998, Virginia; 2000, District of Columbia. *Education:* Boston College (B.A., cum laude, 1995); College of William & Mary (J.D., 1998). Phi Delta Phi. Articles Editor, The William & Mary Environmental Law and Policy Review. ***PRACTICE AREAS:*** Corporate Finance; Securities; Corporate. ***Email:*** jcmeacham@venable.com

JOHN P. MOY, born Chicago Heights, Illinois, August 24, 1972; admitted to bar, 1999, New York; 2000, District of Columbia. *Education:* University of California at Berkeley (B.S., 1994); New York University School of Law (J.D., 1998). Online Editor, 1997-1998 and Staff Editor, 1996-1997, New York University Journal of International Law and Politics. *Member:* American Bar Association. ***PRACTICE AREAS:*** Intellectual Property Litigation. ***Email:*** jpmoy@venable.com

ERIC S. NAMROW, born Washington, D.C., August 16, 1967; admitted to bar, 1996, Maryland; 2000, District of Columbia. *Education:* Bucknell University (B.A., 1989); Oxford University (M.Phil., 1993); University of Maryland (J.D., 1996). ***PRACTICE AREAS:*** Intellectual Property Litigation. ***Email:*** esnamrow@venable.com

CHELLIS E. NEAL, born Munich, Germany, 1957; admitted to bar, 1990, Maryland; 1996, District of Columbia; registered to practice before U.S. Patent and Trademark Office. *Education:* Frederick Community College (A.A., 1978); University of Maryland (B.A., 1992); University of Baltimore School of Law (J.D., magna cum laude, 1990). Registered Nurse, Maryland, 1978. Law Clerk for the Honorable Lawrence Rodowsky, Maryland Court of Appeals. Staff Attorney, Branch of Enforcement, Securities and Exchange Commission, 1992-1994. Author: Casenote, Levit v. Ingersoll Rand Financial Corp., 874 F.2d 1186 (7th Cir. 1989) 18 U.B. Law Review 589 (1989). *Member:* American Bar Association (Member, Section on Intellectual Property); American Intellectual Property Law Association. ***Email:*** ceneal@venable.com

JEANNE LOUISE NEWLON, born Sarasota, Florida, July 9, 1970; admitted to bar, 1996, Maryland; 1997, District of Columbia and Florida. *Education:* University of Florida (B.S.B.A., 1992); The George Washington University (J.D., with high honors, 1996); Georgetown University (LL.M., Taxation, with honors, 1999). Phi Kappa Phi; Omicron Delta Epsilon. Editor, The Environmental Lawyer. Author: "New Requirements for Alternative-Fueled Automobiles: Fuel Economy and the CAFE Program," 1 Envtl. Law. 891 (1995). ***PRACTICE AREAS:*** Estate Planning; Tax. ***Email:*** jlnewlon@venable.com

(This Listing Continued)

VENABLE ATTORNEYS AT LAW, VENABLE, BAETJER, HOWARD & CIVILETTI, LLP, Washington—Continued

CRISTINA G. NICCOLINI, born Grosse Pointe, Michigan, March 18, 1972; admitted to bar, 1998, Michigan (Not admitted in District of Columbia). *Education:* Cornell University (B.A., 1995); University of Michigan (J.D., 1997). ***PRACTICE AREAS:*** Litigation. ***Email:*** cgniccolini@venable.com

SAMUEL ADAM OZECK, born 1974; admitted to bar, 1999, Virginia; 2000, District of Columbia. *Education:* College of William & Mary (B.A., magna cum laude, 1995); Harvard University (J.D., 1999). Pi Sigma Alpha. *Member:* Virginia State Bar; Federal and American (Member, Business Law Section, Banking Law Committee) Bar Associations; Women in Housing and Finance. ***PRACTICE AREAS:*** Banking Law; Corporate Finance. ***Email:*** saozeck@venable.com

JEFFREY R. PANKRATZ, born Midland, Michigan, April 7, 1960; admitted to bar, 1991, Indiana; 2000, Maryland and District of Columbia. *Education:* Albion College; California Polytechnic State University (B.S., Business Administration, with honors, 1983); Indiana University School of Law (J.D., cum laude, 1991). Member, Moot Court. Co-Author: "IRS Rulings May Significantly Reduce Eligible Basis in Tax Credit Transactions," American Bar Association Journal on Affordable Housing and Community Development Law, Winter 2001. Author: "Meeting the Legal Needs of Community-Based Development Organizations," American Bar Association, Division for Public Service Monograph Services, 1992; "Neutral Principles and the Right to Neutral Access to the Courts," 67 Indiana Law Journal 1091, 1991. Adjunct Faculty, Indiana University School of Law, Fall, 1998. *Member:* The District of Columbia Bar; American Bar Association (Member: Business Section; Affordable Housing Forum). ***PRACTICE AREAS:*** Affordable Housing; Community Development; Business Law; Tax Law; Real Estate; Tax Exempt Organizations. ***Email:*** jrpankratz@venable.com

MONICA CHARISSE PARCHMENT, born Baltimore, Maryland, May 8, 1970; admitted to bar, 1996, Virginia; 1998, District of Columbia. *Education:* Mount St. Mary's College (B.A., 1993); George Washington University (J.D., 1996). ***PRACTICE AREAS:*** Government Contracts; Technology Law; Civil Litigation. ***Email:*** mcparchment@venable.com

JACQUELINE LEVASSEUR PATT, born El Paso, Texas, September 12, 1971; admitted to bar, 1999, Maryland; 2000, District of Columbia. *Education:* University of Maryland (B.S., with honors, 1990; J.D., 1999). Recipient: William P. Cunningham Award; Corpus Juris Secundum Award; Margaret E. Coonan Memorial Prize. Notes and Comments Editor, The Business Lawyer. ***PRACTICE AREAS:*** Trademark Prosecution; Intellectual Property Litigation. ***Email:*** jlpatt@venable.com

ANDREW DOUGLAS PRICE, born Alexandria, Virginia, January 31, 1969; admitted to bar, 1996, Virginia; 1998, District of Columbia. *Education:* Vanderbilt University (B.A., 1991); Southern Methodist University (J.D., 1996). *Member:* American Bar Association. ***PRACTICE AREAS:*** Trademarks. ***Email:*** adprice@venable.com

JOHANA A. REED, born Paris, France, July 30, 1959; admitted to bar, 1997, Virginia and Maryland; 1998, District of Columbia. *Education:* Virginia Commonwealth University (B.S., 1981); American University (M.S., 1985); Florida Institute of Technology (M.S., 1991); Georgetown University Law Center (J.D., 1997). Member, Inns of Court, 1996-1997. Co-Author: "'The Christian Doctrine'-Hey, I Didn't Agree To That!" National Contract Management Journal, U. 28, I. 2, 1997; "Year 2000 Legal Issues-An Analytical Frame Work," http://www.venable.com/tools/y2k/legalissues.html. *Member:* American Bar Association; Women's Bar Association; National Contract Management Association. ***PRACTICE AREAS:*** Government Contracts; Corporate. ***Email:*** jareed@venable.com

MARTIN L. SAAD, born Detroit, Michigan, March 21, 1970; admitted to bar, 1996, Maryland; 1999, District of Columbia and U.S. Court of Appeals for the Federal Circuit; 2000, U.S. Supreme Court. *Education:* University of Michigan (B.A., 1992; J.D., 1996). Associate Editor, Michigan Journal of International Law, 1994-1995. *Member:* The District of Columbia Bar. ***LANGUAGES:*** French. ***PRACTICE AREAS:*** Internet Law; Advertising Law; Sweepstakes; Intellectual Property; Litigation; Regulatory Law; Antitrust. ***Email:*** mlsaad@venable.com

CHANTEL SHEAKS, born South Bend, Indiana, May 5, 1971; admitted to bar, 1996, Virginia; 1997, Georgia; 2000, District of Columbia. *Education:* Randolph-Macon Woman's College (B.A., 1991); Northeastern University (J.D., 1996). ***LANGUAGES:*** Spanish. ***PRACTICE AREAS:*** Employee Benefits. ***Email:*** csheaks@venable.com

JAGPREET SINGH, born Washington, D.C., November 16, 1970; admitted to bar, 1995, New Jersey; 1996, Virginia; 1998, District of Columbia. *Education:* University of Richmond (B.S., cum laude, 1992); Villanova University (J.D., 1995). Business Editor, 1994-1995 and Staff Editor, 1993-1994, Villanova Environmental Law Journal. *Member:* The District of Columbia Bar; Virginia State Bar (Member, Sections on: Business; Corporate; Member, Young Lawyers Conference); American Bar Association (Member, Sections on: Business; Corporate). ***PRACTICE AREAS:*** Corporate; Securities; Corporate Finance. ***Email:*** jsingh@venable.com

MELISSA LANDAU STEINMAN, born Boston, Massachusetts, December 27, 1968; admitted to bar, 1993, Maryland; 1994, U.S. Court of Appeals, Third Circuit; 1995, District of Columbia; 1996, U.S. District Court for the District of Columbia; 1997, U.S. Supreme Court and U.S. District Court, District of Maryland; 1998, U.S. Court of Appeals, Fourth Circuit. *Education:* Columbia University (A.B., cum laude, 1990); Harvard University (J.D., 1993). *Member:* American Bar Association (Member, Antitrust and Litigation Sections). ***PRACTICE AREAS:*** Antitrust and Distribution; Regulatory; Technology Law; Electronic Commerce; Litigation. ***Email:*** mlsteinman@venable.com

LISA ANN TAVARES, born Bridgeport, Connecticut, November 30, 1968; admitted to bar, 1996, Massachusetts (Not admitted in District of Columbia). *Education:* Spelman College (B.A., 1990); Boston College (J.D., 1995). ***PRACTICE AREAS:*** Employee Benefits; ERISA; Tax. ***Email:*** latavares@venable.com

F. ALVIN TAYLOR, born Columbia, South Carolina,; admitted to bar, 1999, Maryland; 2000, District of Columbia. *Education:* Auburn University (B.S.C.E., cum laude, 1991); Georgetown University (J.D., cum laude, 1999). Member: National Moot Court Competition Team; National Civil Rights Moot Court Competition Team. Senior Articles and Note Editor, American Criminal Law Review. Co-Author: "Procedural Issues," Twelfth Annual White Collar Crime Survey, 34 Amer. Crim. L. Rev. 883, 1997. *Member:* Maryland State, American and Energy Bar Associations; District of Columbia Bar. ***PRACTICE AREAS:*** Energy; Environmental Law. ***Email:*** fataylor@venable.com

ERIC E. TUCKER, born Baltimore, Maryland, October 23, 1969; admitted to bar, 1995, Maryland; 1999, District of Columbia. *Education:* Gettysburg College (B.A., 1991); University of Maryland School of Law (J.D., 1995). ***PRACTICE AREAS:*** Corporate; Securities. ***Email:*** eetucker@venable.com

DALE C. VAN DEMARK, born Taipei, Taiwan, May 24, 1970; admitted to bar, 1997, Connecticut; 1998, New York; 2000, District of Columbia. *Education:* State University of New York at Purchase (B.A., cum laude, 1994); Pace University (J.D., cum laude, 1997). Articles Editor, Pace Law Review. Contributing Author: Management of An Accounting Practice Handbook, AICPA; Author, "Grubart v. Great Lakes Dredge and Dock Company: A Reasonable Conclusion to the Debate on Admiralty Tort Jurisdiction," 17 Pace Law Review 553. *Member:* New York State and American (Member, Business Law Section) Bar Associations. ***PRACTICE AREAS:*** Business Law; Corporate Law; Taxation. ***Email:*** dcvandemark@venable.com

RUSSELL J. E. VERBY, born Huntington, New York, March 18, 1968; admitted to bar, 1994, Pennsylvania (Not admitted in District of Columbia). *Education:* University of Maine (B.S., 1990); Western New England School of Law (J.D., 1993). [Lt. Comr., JAG Corps, U.S. Navy, 1994—]. ***PRACTICE AREAS:*** Civil Litigation; Criminal Litigation. ***Email:*** rjverby@venable.com

GREGORY L. WADDOUPS, born Oklahoma City, Oklahoma, January 20, 1967; admitted to bar, 1994, Utah; 1997, U.S. Court of Federal Claims; 1999, U.S. Court of Appeals, Federal Circuit; 2000, District of Columbia. *Education:* Utah State University (B.A., magna cum laude, 1991); University of Utah (J.D., 1994). Phi Kappa Phi. Leary Scholar. Editor-in-Chief, Journal of Contemporary Law, 1993-1994. *Member:* American Bar Association (Member, Litigation and Public Contract Law Section); The Association of Trial Lawyers of America. [Capt., JAGC, USAF, 1994-1999]. ***LANGUAGES:*** Danish. ***PRACTICE AREAS:*** Commercial Litigation; Arbitration; Products Liability. ***Email:*** glwaddoups@venable.com

WILLIAM C. WALLER, born Huntington, New York, February 22, 1969; admitted to bar, 1995, New York; 1996, District of Columbia and California. *Education:* Colgate University (A.B., summa cum laude, 1991); Harvard University Law School (J.D., cum laude, 1994). Majority Counsel, U.S. House Government Reform Subcommittee on Regulatory Affairs, 2000-2001. Chair, Administrative Law Regulatory Reform Subcommittee, Federalist Society. Adjunct Professor, George Mason University School of Law, 1997-1999. ***PRACTICE AREAS:*** Food and Drug; Advertising; Government; Legislative Practice; Regulatory. ***Email:*** wcwaller@venable.com

MARGARET T. WATKINS, born Pittsburgh, Pennsylvania, May 25, 1967; admitted to bar, 1998, Maryland; 1999, District of Columbia; 2000, U.S. District Court for the District of Columbia. *Education:* Johns Hopkins University (B.A., 1989); Harvard Graduate School (M.Ed., 1991); Georgetown University (J.D., 1997). Law Clerk, Hon. Henry H. Kennedy, Jr., U.S. District Court, District of Columbia. ***PRACTICE AREAS:*** Litigation. ***Email:*** mtwatkins@venable.com

ROBIN WAUGH-FARRETTA, born Saint Andrew, Jamaica; admitted to bar, 1999, New Jersey and New York; 2000, District of Columbia. *Education:* St. John's University (B.A., 1984); Fordham University (J.D., 1999). Recipient, Corpus Juris Secundum Award. ***PRACTICE AREAS:*** Corporate. ***Email:*** rwfarretta@venable.com

(This Listing Continued)

ERIC J. WEIERSTALL, born San Francisco, California; admitted to bar, 1999, New York; 2000, District of Columbia; registered to practice before U.S. Patent and Trademark Office. *Education:* Syracuse University (B.S., 1994; B.A., 1994; J.D., cum laude, 1997; M.S., 1998). Member, Justinian Society. Member, Syracuse Law Review. *Member:* New York State and American Bar Associations; District of Columbia Bar; American Intellectual Property Law Association. ***PRACTICE AREAS:*** Patents. ***Email:*** ejweierstall@venable.com

ALAN D. WILBUR, born Traverse City, Michigan, May 20, 1974; admitted to bar, 2000, Virginia; 2001, U.S. District Court, Eastern District of Virginia (Not admitted in District of Columbia). *Education:* Michigan State University (B.A., 1996); College of William & Mary (J.D., 2000). ***PRACTICE AREAS:*** Commercial Litigation. ***Email:*** adwilbur@venable.com

YVETTE D. WILLIAMS, born Washington, D.C., February 15, 1968; admitted to bar, 2000, Maryland (Not admitted in District of Columbia). *Education:* Princeton University (A.B., 1989); University of Maryland School of Law (J.D., with honors, 2000). Phi Delta Phi. *Member:* Maryland State Bar Association. ***PRACTICE AREAS:*** Environmental Law; Energy; State Government; Local Government Law; Administrative Law. ***Email:*** ydwilliams@venable.com

KRISTIN K. WOODY, born Washington, D.C., April 23, 1971; admitted to bar, 1997, Virginia; 1998, District of Columbia. *Education:* Duke University (B.A., 1993); Georgetown University (J.D., 1997). Author: "The World Trade Organization's Committee on Trade and the Environment," 8 Georgetown International Environmental Law Review 459, 1996. Co-Author: "The Food and Drug Modernization Act of 1997: Impact and Implementation," with Geoff Levitt, Journal of Biolaw and Business, 1998. *Member:* Virginia State Bar; American Bar Association (Member, International Section). ***LANGUAGES:*** French. ***PRACTICE AREAS:*** International; Food and Drug Regulation. ***Email:*** kkwoody@venable.com

DAMON W. D. WRIGHT, born Richmond, Virginia, December 9, 1971; admitted to bar, 1996, Virginia; 1997, U.S. District Court, Eastern District of Virginia; 1998, U.S. Bankruptcy Court, Eastern District of Virginia; 1999, District of Columbia, U.S. Court of Appeals, Fourth Circuit; 2000, U.S. District Court, District of Maryland and U.S. District Court, District of Columbia. *Education:* James Madison University (B.S. in Political Science and Psychology, 1993); George Mason University School of Law (J.D., 1996). Howard Fellow, Office of the Public Defender, Alexandria, Virginia, 1994-1995. Member, George Mason University Civil Rights Law Journal, 1994-1996. Co-Author: "Virginia's Discriminatory Treatment of Criminal Appeals: Some Constitutional and Policy Consideration," 6 George Mason University Civil Rights Law Journal 1, 1996. Law Clerk to the Hon. Barry R. Poretz, U.S. Magistrate Judge, U.S. District Court, Eastern District of Virginia, 1996-1997. ***PRACTICE AREAS:*** Complex Commercial Litigation; Criminal Litigation; Constitutional Litigation. ***Email:*** dwdwright@venable.com

GILDA M. ZIMMET, born Baltimore, Maryland, March 23, 1971; admitted to bar, 1997, Maryland; 2001, District of Columbia. *Education:* University of Pennsylvania (B.A., magna cum laude, 1993); Georgetown University (J.D., 1997). Phi Beta Kappa. Clerk to Judge Alan Wilner, Court of Appeals of Maryland, 1997-1998. *Member:* Maryland State Bar Association; District of Columbia Bar. (Also at Baltimore, Maryland Office). ***LANGUAGES:*** French. ***PRACTICE AREAS:*** Trusts and Estates. ***Email:*** gmzimmet@venable.com

LINDA J. ZIRKELBACH, born Munich, Germany, August 17, 1973; admitted to bar, 1999, Maryland; 2000, District of Columbia and U.S. District Court, District of Maryland. *Education:* University of Michigan (B.A., 1995), Phi Sigma Pi; American University (J.D., cum laude, 1999). Phi Sigma Pi. Articles Editor, The American University Journal of Gender, Social Policy & the Law. Member, Giles S. Rich American Inn of Court. *Member:* American Bar Association; Women's Bar Association of Washington, D.C. ***PRACTICE AREAS:*** Intellectual Property Litigation; Trademarks; Copyrights; Patents; Internet Law. ***Email:*** lzirkelbach@venable.com

REVISERS OF THE MARYLAND LAW DIGEST FOR THIS DIRECTORY.

(For Complete Biographical Data on Personnel at Baltimore, Rockville and Towson, Maryland and McLean, Virginia see Professional Biographies at those locations).

VERNER, LIIPFERT, BERNHARD, McPHERSON AND HAND

CHARTERED

Established in 1960

901 15TH STREET, N.W.

WASHINGTON, D.C. 20005-2301

Telephone: 202-371-6000

Cable Address: "Verlip"

Fax: 202-371-6279

Email: verner.com

URL: http://www.verner.com

Las Vegas, Nevada Affiliate Office: Gary C. Moss, Hughes Center, 3960 Howard Hughes Parkway, Suite 400, 89109. Telephone: 702-737-3433. Facsimile: 702-737-1612.

Administrative Law, Alternative Dispute Resolution, Antitrust and Trade Regulation, Aviation and Aerospace, Bankruptcy, Business Law, Casinos and Gambling, Civil Practice, Civil Rights, Class Actions, Commercial Law, Communications and Media, Constitutional Law, Contracts, Corporate Law, Criminal Law, Debtor and Creditor, Election, Campaign and Political Law, Energy, Entertainment and the Arts, Environmental Law, Federal Practice, Finance, Financial Restructuring, General Practice, Government, Government Contracts, Health Care, Hospital Law, Indians and Native Populations, Insurance, International Law, International Trade, Investments, Internet Ventures, Labor and Employment, Legal Ethics and Professional Responsibility, Legislative Practice, Litigation, Media Law, Mergers, Acquisitions and Divestitures, Municipal Law, Natural Resources, Nonprofit and Charitable Organizations, Privatizations, Public Finance, Railroad Law, Real Estate, Regulatory Law, Resorts and Leisure, Securities, Sports Law, Taxation, Technology and Science, Trademarks, Transportation, Urban Development, Utility Law, White Collar Crime, Workouts.

FIRM PROFILE: Verner Liipfert is a firm of over 200 attorneys and consultants, representing clients in virtually all areas of the law. Our attorneys work hard to maintain the firm's original commitment to excellence and to provide cost-efficient legal services to their clients.

MICHAEL D. BERG, admitted to bar, 1974, District of Columbia and Hawaii. *Education:* Syracuse University (B.A., cum laude, 1969); Georgetown University (J.D., 1973). Federal Communications Commission, 1976-1977. Sr. Associate General Counsel, National Association of Broadcasters, 1981-1986; Partner: Miller & Holbrooke, Washington, D.C., 1986-1992; Akin, Gump, Straus, Hauer & Feld, Washington, D.C., 1992-1994. ***PRACTICE AREAS:*** Communications Law; International Law. ***Email:*** mdberg@verner.com

BERL BERNHARD, admitted to bar, 1954, District of Columbia; 1958, U.S. Supreme Court. *Education:* Dartmouth College (B.A., magna cum laude, with highest distinction in Government, 1951; A.M., 1974); Yale University (J.D., 1954). Phi Delta Phi; Phi Beta Kappa. Staff Director, U.S. Commission on Civil Rights, 1961-1963. Consultant to the Secretary of State, 1963-1965. Senior Advisor to the Secretary of State, 1980-1981. Special Counsel for the Democratic National Committee, 1965-1971. General Counsel, Democratic Senatorial Campaign Committee, 1965-1971. National Presidential Campaign Manager for Senator Edmund Muskie, 1971-1972. ***PRACTICE AREAS:*** Corporate Law; Regulatory; Legislation; Transportation Law. ***Email:*** bbernhard@verner.com

MATTHEW C. BERNSTEIN, admitted to bar, 1992, Pennsylvania; 1994, District of Columbia. *Education:* Columbia University (A.B., 1987); London School of Economics, London, England; Georgetown University Law Center (J.D., 1992). Managing Editor, American Criminal Law Review, 1991-1992. ***PRACTICE AREAS:*** Legislative and Federal Affairs; Environmental. ***Email:*** mcbernstein@verner.com

JAMES J. BLANCHARD, admitted to bar, 1968, Michigan; U.S. District Court, Eastern and Western Districts of Michigan; U.S. Supreme Court; 2000, District of Columbia. *Education:* Michigan State University (B.A., 1964; M.B.A., 1965); University of Minnesota (J.D., 1968). U.S. Ambassador to Canada, 1993-1996. Governor, State of Michigan, 1983-1991. U.S. Congressman, 1975-1983. *Member:* State Bar of Michigan; National Governor's Association (Chairman, Legal Affairs Committee, 1987); Democratic Governor's Association (Chairman, 1988). ***PRACTICE AREAS:*** International Trade; Federal Affairs; Energy; Communications; Environmental. ***Email:*** jjblanchard@verner.com

R. STUART BROOM, admitted to bar, 1974, Tennessee 1977, U.S. Supreme Court; 1981, District of Columbia. *Education:* Marion Institute (A.A., 1968); University of Alabama (B.A., 1970); University of Tennessee at Knoxville (J.D., 1973); George Washington University (LL.M., 1983). Phi Alpha Delta. [Capt., JAGC, U.S. Army, 1974-1978]. ***PRACTICE AREAS:*** Municipal Solid Waste Resource Recovery Law; Environmental Law; Co-generation Law. ***Email:*** rsbroom@verner.com

(This Listing Continued)

VERNER, LIIPFERT, BERNHARD, McPHERSON AND HAND, CHARTERED, Washington—Continued

HOPEWELL H. DARNEILLE, III, admitted to bar, 1974, Maryland; 1975, District of Columbia. *Education:* Yale University (A.B., 1968); Georgetown University (J.D., 1974). Lead Articles Editor, American Criminal Law Review, 1973-1974. Law Clerk to the Hon. Edward S. Northrop, Chief Judge, U.S. District Court for the District of Maryland, 1974-1975. [With U.S. Army, 1968-1971]. ***PRACTICE AREAS:*** Government Contracts Law; Litigation; Maritime Law. ***Email:*** hhdarneille@verner.com

ANDREW D. ESKIN, admitted to bar, 1985, New York and New Jersey; 1986, District of Columbia. *Education:* Stanford University (B.A., 1979); University of California at Berkeley (M.B.A., 1984); University of California, Hastings College of Law (J.D., 1984). Member, Hastings International and Comparative Law Review. Attorney, Federal Trade Commission, Bureau of Competition, 1985-1986. Legislative Director, Senator Richard Bryan (D-NV), 1989-1990. ***PRACTICE AREAS:*** Federal Practice; Antitrust and Trade Regulation; Transportation; Financial Services; Tax Law; Health; Political Law. ***Email:*** adeskin@verner.com

WILLIAM C. EVANS, admitted to bar, 1966, District of Columbia; 1970, U.S. Supreme Court. *Education:* University of North Carolina (B.S., 1962; LL.B., 1965). ***PRACTICE AREAS:*** Aviation Law; Surface Transportation; Administrative. ***Email:*** wcevans@verner.com

J. CATHY FOGEL, admitted to bar, 1977, District of Columbia. *Education:* University of Wisconsin-Madison (B.S., 1964); Catholic University of America (J.D., 1977). Member, Catholic University Law Review, 1976-1977. *Member:* Federal Energy Bar Association (Former Chairperson, Committees on Power Marketing Agencies and Federal Power Act, Parts II & III). ***PRACTICE AREAS:*** Energy Law. ***Email:*** jcfogel@verner.com

HAROLD I. FREILICH, admitted to bar, 1977, Pennsylvania; 1979, District of Columbia. *Education:* Muhlenberg College (B.A., summa cum laude, 1974); Duke University (J.D., 1977). Phi Beta Kappa. ***PRACTICE AREAS:*** International Finance; Project Finance; Corporate Law; Security Law. ***Email:*** hifreilich@verner.com

ANDREA JILL GRANT, admitted to bar, 1975, District of Columbia. *Education:* Washington University (B.A., magna cum laude, 1971; J.D., 1974); Georgetown University. Phi Beta Kappa. *Member:* American Bar Association (Member, Section of Natural Resources Law). ***PRACTICE AREAS:*** Legislative Law; Energy Law. ***Email:*** ajgrant@verner.com

MARLA GROSSMAN, admitted to bar, 1993, Maryland; 1994, District of Columbia. *Education:* Yale University (B.A., summa cum laude, 1990); Harvard University (J.D., cum laude, 1993). Phi Beta Kappa. Counsel to Senate Judiciary Committee, 1997-1999. (Member and Director of Internet Ventures Group). ***PRACTICE AREAS:*** Internet Ventures; Federal Affairs; Entertainment Law. ***Email:*** mgrossman@verner.com

DOUGLAS W. HALL, admitted to bar, 1989, Ohio; 1991, District of Columbia; 1994, U.S. Supreme Court. *Education:* University of Pittsburgh (B.A., summa cum laude, 1985); Georgetown University (J.D., magna cum laude, 1989). Order of the Coif. ***PRACTICE AREAS:*** Labor and Employment Law; Litigation. ***Email:*** dwhall@verner.com

LLOYD N. HAND, admitted to bar, 1957, Texas; 1970, District of Columbia. *Education:* University of Texas (B.A., 1952; J.D., 1957). Phi Alpha Delta. Assistant to Senate Majority Leader and Vice President Lyndon Johnson, 1957-1961. U.S. Chief of Protocol with rank of Ambassador, 1965-1966. Member, Board of Governors, Georgetown University School of Foreign Service, 1977. Member of the Board, Blair House Restoration Fund. [Lt., U.S. Navy, 1951-1955]. ***LANGUAGES:*** Spanish. ***PRACTICE AREAS:*** Corporate; Legislative; Trade. ***Email:*** lnhand@verner.com

ALAN N. HERNANDEZ, admitted to bar, 1990, Massachusetts and U.S. District Court, District of Massachusetts; 1999, District of Columbia. *Education:* Wesleyan University (B.A., 1985); Harvard University (J.D., 1990). Member, Harvard Legal Aid Bureau, 1988-1990. ***LANGUAGES:*** Spanish. ***PRACTICE AREAS:*** Corporate; Transactional; Securities; International Business. ***Email:*** anhernandez@verner.com

THOMAS M. INGOLDSBY, admitted to bar, 1970, Iowa; 1978, District of Columbia. *Education:* Brown University (B.A., 1967); Duke University (J.D., 1970). Member, Office of Chief Counsel, Internal Revenue Service, 1970-1977. ***PRACTICE AREAS:*** Project Finance; Public Finance; International Finance. ***Email:*** tmingoldsby@verner.com

THOMAS J. KELLER, admitted to bar, 1971, District of Columbia; 1972, Maryland; 1977, U.S. Supreme Court. *Education:* University of Akron (B.A., 1966); American University (J.D., 1971). General Counsel, Executive Office of the President, Office of Telecommunications Policy, 1975-1976. ***PRACTICE AREAS:*** Communications Law; Intellectual Property Law. ***Email:*** tjkeller@verner.com

(This Listing Continued)

GARY J. KLEIN, admitted to bar, 1971, District of Columbia; 1977, U.S. Supreme Court. *Education:* Cornell University (B.S., 1968); Columbia University (J.D., 1971). Managing Editor, Columbia Law Review, 1970-1971. Associate, Covington & Burling, 1971-1973. Legislative Assistant to Senator Jacob K. Javits, 1973-1975. Minority Counsel, Senate Government Affairs Subcommittee on Energy, 1975-1977. ***PRACTICE AREAS:*** Legislative Law; Energy Law; Environmental Law; Infrastructure Development; Privatization Law. ***Email:*** gklein@verner.com

WILLIAM D. KRAMER, admitted to bar, 1969, Massachusetts; 1974, District of Columbia. *Education:* Oberlin College (A.B., magna cum laude, 1965); Kennedy School of Government, Harvard University (M.P.A., 1969); Harvard Law School (J.D., 1969). Phi Beta Kappa. *Member:* The District of Columbia Bar. ***Email:*** wdkramer@verner.com

ERWIN G. KRASNOW, admitted to bar, 1961, Massachusetts; 1963, District of Columbia; 1965, U.S. Supreme Court. *Education:* Boston University (A.B., summa cum laude, 1958); Harvard University (J.D., 1961); Georgetown University (LL.M., 1965). Phi Beta Kappa. Adjunct Professor: Georgetown University Graduate School of Arts and Science, 1997, 1998; Georgetown University Law Center, 1984; Professorial Lecturer: Catholic University of American School of Law, 1982. General Counsel, National Association of Broadcasters, Washington, D.C., 1976-1984. *Member:* Federal Communications Bar Association (Member: Board of Editors, Federal Communications Bar Journal, 1973-1975; Executive Committee, 1976-1979; Treasurer, 1984-1985). ***PRACTICE AREAS:*** Communications Law. ***Email:*** egkrasnow@verner.com

LAWRENCE E. LEVINSON, admitted to bar, 1957, New York; 1958, U.S. Supreme Court (Not admitted in District of Columbia). *Education:* Syracuse University (B.S., 1952); Harvard University (LL.B., 1955). Phi Beta Kappa. Deputy Counsel to President of the United States, 1965-1968. Senior Vice President, Paramount Communications, 1969-1995. [Judge Advocate Division, U.S. Army, 1955-1957]. ***PRACTICE AREAS:*** Media; Communications; Military Base Reconversion. ***Email:*** lelevinson@verner.com

DON CHARLES LEWIS, admitted to bar, 1985, Texas; 1986, District of Columbia. *Education:* University of Texas at Austin (B.A., with high honors, 1979; J.D., with honors, 1984). Law Clerk to Hon. Jack Roberts and Hon. James R. Nowlin, U.S. District Court, Western District of Texas, 1984-1985. ***PRACTICE AREAS:*** Antitrust Law; Healthcare Law; Litigation. ***Email:*** dclewis@verner.com

HARRIET LIPKIN, admitted to bar, 1978, Indiana; 1982, U.S. Supreme Court; 1992, District of Columbia. *Education:* Washington University (A.B., cum laude, 1975); Antioch School of Law (J.D., 1978). Editor, Abortion Law Reporter, 1978. Partner: Pantaleo, Lipkin & Moss, P.C., 1992-1998; Akin, Gump, Strauss, Hauer & Feld, LLP, 1987-1992. Member, Board of Directors, Indiana Municipal Lawyers Association, 1983-1987. ***PRACTICE AREAS:*** Labor Law; Employment Law; Civil Rights Law. ***Email:*** hlipkin@verner.com

MARTIN T. LUTZ, admitted to bar, 1989, Texas; 1991, District of Columbia. *Education:* University of Notre Dame (B.A., with honors, 1984); University of Texas (J.D., with honors, 1989). Editor-in-Chief, Texas International Law Journal. *Member:* State Bar of Texas; The District of Columbia Bar; American Society of International Law. ***Email:*** mtlutz@verner.com

JOSEPH L. MANSON, III, admitted to bar, 1974, Georgia; 1975, District of Columbia. *Education:* University of Virginia (B.S., 1970); Emory University (J.D., 1974). Phi Delta Phi. Member, Board of Editors, Emory Law Journal, 1973-1974. Senior Editor, *The Railway Labor Act*, BNA Books, 1995. *Member:* American Bar Association (Member, Section of Labor and Employment Law, Management Co-Chairman, Railway and Airline Labor Law Committee, 1993-1996). ***PRACTICE AREAS:*** Aviation Law; International Transactions; Labor Law; Litigation. ***Email:*** jlmanson@verner.com

HARRY McPHERSON, admitted to bar, 1956, Texas; 1969, District of Columbia. *Education:* University of the South (B.A., 1949); Columbia University; University of Texas (LL.B., 1956). Deputy Under Secretary of the Army for International Affairs, 1963-1964. Assistant Secretary of State for Educational and Cultural Affairs, 1964-1965. Counsel, then Special Counsel to the President, White House, 1965-1969. Member, President's Commission on the Accident at Three Mile Island, 1979. President, Federal City Council, Washington, 1983-1988. President, Economic Club of Washington, 1992-1999. Vice Chairman, United States International Cultural and Trade Center Commission, 1988-1992. Member, Defense Base Closure and Realignment Commission, 1993. ***PRACTICE AREAS:*** Legislative Law; Regulatory Law. ***Email:*** hcmcpherson@verner.com

KAREN TURNER McWILLIAMS, admitted to bar, 1992, Virginia; 1993, District of Columbia. *Education:* University of Virginia (B.S., 1988); George Mason University (J.D., 1992). Notes Editor, 1991-1992, George Mason University Law Review. *Member:* Virginia Association of Black Women Attorneys (President). ***PRACTICE AREAS:*** Employment Law; Labor Law. ***Email:*** kmcwilliams@verner.com

BRENDA G. MEISTER, admitted to bar, 1988, Pennsylvania (Not admitted in District of Columbia). *Education:* George Mason University School of

(This Listing Continued)

Business (M.A., 1983); George Mason University School of Law (J.D., 1987). Served President George Bush at the White House, 1989. Appointed Director of Congressional and Federal Relations, National Transportation Safety Board, 1989-1991. Appointed Deputy Director and Acting Director, Office for Victims of Crimes, U.S. Justice Department, 1991-1993. ***PRACTICE AREAS:*** Legislative Practice; International Tax Policy. ***Email:*** bgmeister@verner.com

MARTIN MENDELSOHN, admitted to bar, 1967, District of Columbia; 1970, U.S. Supreme Court; 1973, Illinois. *Education:* Brooklyn College (A.B., 1963); George Washington University (LL.B., 1966). Phi Delta Phi. Chief Counsel, Subcommittee on Immigration Refugees and International Law, Judiciary Committee, U.S. House of Representatives, 1980. Administrative Assistant, U.S. House of Representatives, 1976-1977. Chief, Special Litigation Unit, Immigration and Naturalization Service, U.S. Department of Justice, 1977-1979. Deputy Director, Litigation, Office of Special Investigations, U.S. Department of Justice, 1979-1980. ***PRACTICE AREAS:*** International Law; Legislative Law. ***Email:*** mmendelsohn@verner.com

JOHN A. MERRIGAN, admitted to bar, 1973, District of Columbia. *Education:* Georgetown University (A.B., 1970); Loyola University (J.D., cum laude, 1973). Alpha Sigma Nu. Member, National Council for Political Management, The George Washington University. Chair, Democratic National Committee, Democratic Business Council, 1998-2001. *Member:* District of Columbia Bar; American Bar Association. ***PRACTICE AREAS:*** Regulatory and Legislative Law.

JOHN R. MIETUS, JR., admitted to bar, 1990, Maryland; 1991, District of Columbia. *Education:* Cornell University; University of Maryland (B.A., cum laude, 1987); Georgetown University (J.D., cum laude, 1990). Phi Beta Kappa. ***PRACTICE AREAS:*** Aviation Law; Transportation Law. ***Email:*** jrmietus@verner.com

EVAN M. MIGDAIL, admitted to bar, 1979, Maryland; 1981, District of Columbia. *Education:* University of Pennsylvania (B.A./M.A., 1976); Villanova University (J.D., 1979). *Member:* The District of Columbia Bar; American Bar Assn. ***LANGUAGES:*** Spanish. ***PRACTICE AREAS:*** Federal Tax; Nonprofit and Charitable Organizations; Legislative; Political Law. ***Email:*** emigdail@verner.com

GARY C. MOSS (See listing for Las Vegas, Nevada Office).

RONALD B. NATALIE, admitted to bar, 1962, District of Columbia. *Education:* Tufts University (A.B., 1957); George Washington University (J.D., with highest honors, 1962). Order of the Coif; Phi Alpha Delta. Member, Board of Editors, George Washington Law Review, 1961-1962. Office of General Counsel, U.S. Commission on Civil Rights, 1962-1964. Vice Chairman, 1971-1988, Chairman, 1988—, Close-Up Foundation. Chief Counsel, President's Commission on the Accident at Three Mile Island, 1979. [Lt., U.S. Navy, 1957-1962]. ***PRACTICE AREAS:*** Labor Law; Employment Law. ***Email:*** rbnatalie@verner.com

PAUL E. NORDSTROM, admitted to bar, 1982, District of Columbia. *Education:* Middlebury College (B.A., cum laude, 1978); New York University (J.D., 1981). President, Federal Energy Regulatory Commission, 2000—. *Member:* Federal Energy (Vice President, Treasurer and Board Member, 1987-1990, 1996—) and American (Chairman, Energy Committee, Section on Administrative Law, 1996-1999) Bar Associations. ***PRACTICE AREAS:*** Public Utility Law; Administrative Law. ***Email:*** penordstrom@verner.com

PETER S. PANTALEO, admitted to bar, 1976, Pennsylvania; 1977, North Dakota; 1989, District of Columbia. *Education:* University of Wisconsin (B.S., 1971); University of North Dakota (J.D., with honors, 1976). Editor-in-Chief, North Dakota Law Review. ***PRACTICE AREAS:*** Labor Law; Employment Law; Civil Rights. ***Email:*** pspantaleo@verner.com

STEVEN R. PHILLIPS, admitted to bar, 1988, North Carolina; 1998, District of Columbia. *Education:* Campbell University (B.B.A., 1984, J.D., 1987). Member, Board of Editors, Campbell University Law Review. Legislative Counsel and Director, Senator Jesse Helms, 1987-1997. *Member:* North Carolina State Bar. ***LANGUAGES:*** French. ***PRACTICE AREAS:*** Legislative; International Trade; Communications. ***Email:*** srphillips@verner.com

B. DONOVAN PICARD, admitted to bar, 1976, Virginia; 1977, District of Columbia. *Education:* University of Virginia (B.A., with high honors, 1965; M.A., 1966; J.D., 1976). Phi Beta Kappa; Omicron Delta Kappa. U.S. Foreign Service Officer, Vietnam, Japan, Korea and Washington, D.C., 1966-1976. *Member:* The District of Columbia Bar. ***Email:*** bdpicard@verner.com

NEIL T. PROTO, admitted to bar, 1973, District of Columbia; 1976, U.S. Supreme Court; 1983, Connecticut. *Education:* Southern Connecticut State University (B.A., 1967); George Washington University (M.A., Intl. Affairs, 1969; J.D., with honors, 1972). Adjunct Professor, Georgetown University Graduate School, 1990-2000. General Counsel, President's Nuclear Safety Oversight Committee, 1980-1981. Attorney, Environment and Natural Resources Division, U.S. Department of Justice, 1972-1979. ***PRACTICE AREAS:*** Environmental; Administrative; Urban Development; Litigation. ***Email:*** ntproto@verner.com

(This Listing Continued)

SHERRY A. QUIRK, admitted to bar, 1982, District of Columbia. *Education:* Mount Holyoke College (A.B., 1976); L'Universite de Paris, Paris, France; Washington College of Law of American University (J.D., 1982). Law Clerk to Administrative Law Judges, Federal Energy Regulatory Commission, 1982-1983. Attorney-Advisor, Office of Opinions and Review, Federal Energy Regulatory Commission, 1983-1984. ***PRACTICE AREAS:*** Energy Law; Legislative Law. ***Email:*** saquirk@verner.com

MICHAEL J. ROBERTS, admitted to bar, 1966, District of Columbia and Maryland; 1970, U.S. Supreme Court. *Education:* Duke University (A.B., 1958); Washington College of Law, American University (J.D., 1965). Phi Alpha Delta. Editor-in-Chief, American University Law Review, 1964-1965. Aviation Editor, Association for Transportation Law, Logistics and Policy, 1987—. [Lt. U.S. Navy, 1958-1962]. ***PRACTICE AREAS:*** Aviation Law; Administrative Law; Legislative Law. ***Email:*** mjroberts@verner.com

DAVID R. SIDDALL, admitted to bar, 1977, District of Columbia; 1984, U.S. Supreme Court. *Education:* Lindenwood College (B.A., 1972); George Washington University (J.D., 1977). Legal Advisor, Federal Communications Commissioner, Susan Ness, 1994-1998. Chief, Spectrum Management, 1991-1994. *Member:* Federal Communications Bar Association. ***PRACTICE AREAS:*** Communications; High Technology. ***Email:*** drsiddall@verner.com

LAWRENCE R. SIDMAN, admitted to bar, 1973, Massachusetts; 1975, District of Columbia; 1981, U.S. Supreme Court. *Education:* Amherst College (A.B., magna cum laude, 1970); Boston College Law School (J.D., magna cum laude, 1973). Phi Beta Kappa; Order of the Coif. Editor, Annual Survey of Massachusetts Law, 1972-1973. Law Clerk to the Hon. Christopher J. Armstrong, Massachusetts Appeals Court, 1973-1974. Chief Counsel and Staff Director: House Subcommittee on Energy, Conservation and Power, 1985-1987; House Subcommittee on Telecommunications and Finance, 1987-1989. ***LANGUAGES:*** French and Hebrew. ***PRACTICE AREAS:*** Legislative Law; Communications Law; Government Contracts Law. ***Email:*** lrsidman@verner.com

CYNTHIA M. SURRISI, admitted to bar, 1982, Minnesota (Not admitted in District of Columbia). *Education:* University of North Dakota (B.A., 1971); William Mitchell College of Law (J.D., cum laude, 1982). Commissioner, City of Mendota Heights Airport Relations Commission, 1994-1996. ***PRACTICE AREAS:*** Labor and Employment; Aviation Law; Administrative Law; Contracts.

DEBORAH A. SWANSTROM, admitted to bar, 1988, Maryland; 1989, District of Columbia. *Education:* St. Cloud State University (B.A., summa cum laude, 1985, Phi Kappa Phi); George Washington University (J.D., with honors, 1988). *Member:* Energy Bar Association (Secretary); Women's International Network of Utility Professionals (Chair, Legislative Issues Committee); Womens Council on Energy and the Environment. ***PRACTICE AREAS:*** Energy Law; Administrative and Appellate Litigation. ***Email:*** daswanstrom@verner.com

SUSAN O'HEARN TEMKIN, admitted to bar, 1979, Connecticut; 1985, District of Columbia. *Education:* University of Connecticut (B.A., 1976); Western New England College (J.D., cum laude, 1979); New York University (LL.M. in Taxation, 1980). Law Clerk, Honorable Meade Whitaker, U.S. Tax Court, 1983-1985. Attorney-Advisor, Interpretative Division, Office of Chief Counsel, Internal Revenue Service, Washington, D.C., 1981-1983. ***PRACTICE AREAS:*** Tax Law; Transactional Law. ***Email:*** sotemkin@verner.com

JAMES M. VERNER, admitted to bar, 1937, North Carolina; 1947, Tennessee; 1950, District of Columbia; 1958, U.S. Supreme Court. *Education:* Biltmore Junior College and University of North Carolina (A.B., 1936); University of North Carolina (LL.B., 1938). Associate Editor, North Carolina Law Review, 1937-1938. Executive Director, Civil Aeronautics Board, 1950-1953. Assistant to Attorney General, North Carolina, 1938-1940. (Emeritus). ***PRACTICE AREAS:*** Aviation Law.

CLINTON A. VINCE, admitted to bar, 1975, New York; 1976, District of Columbia; 1979, U.S. Supreme Court. *Education:* Trinity College (A.B., 1971); Georgetown University (J.D., 1974). Chair, Board of Directors, Foundation of Energy Law Journal, 1995-1998. Member: Keystone Center Board of Trustees, 1992—; Advisory Committee, Program on Energy, the Environment and the Economy, Aspen Institute; Roundtable Center for Strategic & International Studies. ***PRACTICE AREAS:*** Energy Law; International Commercial Law; General Litigation. ***Email:*** cavince@verner.com

LINDA M. WEINBERG, admitted to bar, 1987, Florida; 1988, U.S. Court of International Trade; 1989, District of Columbia; 1990, Maryland. *Education:* University of California at Irvine (B.A., 1983); Université de Montpellier, France; Tel Aviv University, Israel; Loyola Law School, Los Angeles, California (J.D., 1987). Staff Member, Loyola of Los Angeles Law Review, 1985-1986. ***LANGUAGES:*** French and Hebrew. ***PRACTICE AREAS:*** Customs; Export Control; International Trade. ***Email:*** lmweinberg@verner.com

ERIC T. WERNER, admitted to bar, 1990, Ohio; 1992, District of Columbia. *Education:* Miami University (B.S., 1985); Catholic University of America (J.D., 1990). Associate Editor, Catholic University Law Review, 1989-1990.

(This Listing Continued)

VERNER, LIIPFERT, BERNHARD, McPHERSON AND HAND, CHARTERED, Washington—Continued

Clerk to Hon. Anthony J. Celebrezze, U.S. Court of Appeals, Sixth Circuit, 1990-1991. ***PRACTICE AREAS:*** Mass Media; Telecommunications; Litigation. ***Email:*** etwerner@verner.com

WILLIAM A. ZEITLER, admitted to bar, 1969, Virginia; 1974, District of Columbia; 1986, New York. *Education:* Georgetown University (B.S.F.S., 1965); University of Virginia School of Law (J.D., 1968). Attorney Advisor, U.S. Tariff Commission, 1973-1975. Attorney Advisor, U.S. International Trade Commission, 1975-1978. Supervisory Attorney Advisor, U.S. International Trade Commission, 1979-1986. ***LANGUAGES:*** German and Persian. ***PRACTICE AREAS:*** International Trade Law; Customs Law. ***Email:*** wazeitler@verner.com

JOHN H. ZENTAY, admitted to bar, 1958, Missouri; 1962, U.S. Supreme Court; 1966, District of Columbia. *Education:* Harvard University (A.B., cum laude, 1953; LL.B., 1958). Legislative Assistant to Senator Stuart Symington, 1958-1962. Member, Legislative Presentation Staff, Agency for International Development, Department of State, 1963-1966. [With U.S. Army, 1953-1955]. ***PRACTICE AREAS:*** Legislative Law; Energy Law. ***Email:*** jhzentay@verner.com

SPECIAL COUNSEL

ROBERT J. DOLE, admitted to bar, 1952, Kansas (Not admitted in District of Columbia). *Education:* Washburn University (A.B., LL.B., 1952). Member, U.S. Congress, 1961-1969. U.S. Senator, Kansas, 1969-1996. Chairman, Republican National Committee, 1971-1974. Senate Republican Leader, 1985-1996. Republican Nominee for President of the United States, 1996. Presidential Medal of Freedom, 1997. ***Email:*** rjdole@verner.com

GEORGE J. MITCHELL, admitted to bar, 1960, Maine and District of Columbia. *Education:* Bowdoin College (B.A., 1954); Georgetown University Law Center (LL.B., 1960). Trial Attorney, U.S. Department of Justice, 1960-1962. Assistant County Attorney, Cumberland County, Maine, 1971. U.S. Attorney, Maine, 1977-1979. U.S. District Judge, 1979-1980. U.S. Senator, Maine, 1980-1995. Majority Leader, U.S. Senate, 1988-1995. Chairman, Northern Ireland Peace Talks. [With U.S. Army, 1954-1956]. (Also Senior Counsel, Preti, Flaherty, Beliveau & Pachios, Portland, Maine). ***Email:*** gjmitchell@verner.com

W. DeVIER PIERSON, admitted to bar, 1957, Oklahoma; 1966, U.S. Supreme Court; 1969, District of Columbia. *Education:* University of Oklahoma (A.B., magna cum laude, 1953; LL.B., magna cum laude, 1957). Phi Beta Kappa; Order of the Coif. Managing Editor, University of Oklahoma Law Review, 1956-57. National Championship Moot Court Team, 1956. Chief Counsel, Joint Committee on the Organization of the Congress, 1965-67. Associate Special Counsel to the President of the United States and Counselor of the White House Office, 1967-68. Special Counsel to the President of the United States, 1968-69. *Member:* The District of Columbia Bar; Oklahoma, Federal and American Bar Associations. (Also Member, Pierson Semmes and Bemis). ***Email:*** wdpierson@verner.com

SENIOR COUNSEL

ALVARO CIFUENTES DE CASTRO, admitted to bar, 1975, Puerto Rico; 1984, New York; 1999, District of Columbia. *Education:* University of Puerto Rico (B.B.A., magna cum laude, 1972; J.D., magna cum laude, 1975). *Member:* Colegio de Abogados de Puerto Rico. ***LANGUAGES:*** Spanish. ***PRACTICE AREAS:*** Corporate Law; Commercial Law. ***Email:*** acifuentes@verner.com

SENIOR ADVISOR

DR. RICHARD GARON. *Education:* New York University (Ph.D., 1983). Listed in Who's Who in America. ***Email:*** rgaron@verner.com

DANA M. MARSHALL. *Education:* Case Western Reserve University (B.S., 1969); Ohio State University (M.B.A., 1972). Chair, International Policy Committee, North Virginia Technology Council. ***LANGUAGES:*** Spanish and French. ***PRACTICE AREAS:*** International Business Consulting. ***Email:*** dmmarshall@verner.com

OF COUNSEL

GREGG S. AVITABILE, admitted to bar, 1989, Maryland; 1990, District of Columbia. *Education:* Trinity College (B.A., 1986); George Washington University (J.D., magna cum laude, 1989). Order of the Coif. Author: Religious Dissemination and Scheduling for Sabbath, NATO News, 2/99; Sexual Harassment Policy Imperative, Textile Rental, 1/99. *Member:* Maryland State and American (Member, Sections on: Labor, Litigation and Employment) Bar Associations; The District of Columbia Bar. ***PRACTICE AREAS:*** Labor Law; Employment Law; Litigation; Commercial. ***Email:*** gsavitabile@verner.com

(This Listing Continued)

HOWELL E. BEGLE, JR., admitted to bar, 1969, New York and U.S. Court of Military Appeals; 1974, District of Columbia. *Education:* University of the South (B.A., cum laude, 1965); Institute for American Universities, Aix-en-Provence, France; University of Michigan (J.D., cum laude, 1968). Order of the Coif; Pi Sigma Alpha. *Member:* The District of Columbia Bar; American Bar Association. [JAGC, USA, 1969-1973]. ***PRACTICE AREAS:*** Corporate Law; Entertainment Law. ***Email:*** hebegle@verner.com

DOUGLAS KNOX BEMIS, JR., admitted to bar, 1963, Arkansas; 1965, U.S. Court of Federal Claims; 1968, U.S. Supreme Court; 1969, U.S. Tax Court; 1970, District of Columbia. *Education:* Yale University (B.A., magna cum laude, 1960); Harvard University (J.D., cum laude, 1963); Magdalen College, Oxford University, England. Attorney, Tax Division, U.S. Department of Justice, 1965-1969. *Member:* The District of Columbia Bar; Arkansas Bar Association; Federal Energy Bar Association. ***PRACTICE AREAS:*** Litigation; Energy. ***Email:*** kbemis@verner.com

LEONARD GARMENT, admitted to bar, 1949, New York; 1966, U.S. Supreme Court; 1967, District of Columbia. *Education:* Brooklyn College; Brooklyn Law School (LL.B., summa cum laude, 1949). Special Consultant, Assistant and Counsel to President Nixon, 1969-1974. Assistant to President Ford, 1974. U.S. Representative, Commission on Human Rights of the United Nations Economic and Social Council and Counselor, U.S. Delegation to the United Nations, 1975-1977. Chairman, Commission on the Federal Judiciary of Senator Daniel P. Moynihan, 1976-1988. ***PRACTICE AREAS:*** Litigation; Government Relations. ***Email:*** lgarment@verner.com

PHILIP R. HOCHBERG, admitted to bar, 1966, District of Columbia. *Education:* Syracuse University (B.S., 1961); American University (M.A., 1974); George Washington University (LL.B., 1965). Order of the Coif; Phi Delta Phi. Managing Editor, George Washington Law Review, Vol. 33, 1964-1965. Special Counsel, Communications Subcommittee, United States House of Representatives, 1977. ***PRACTICE AREAS:*** Sports Law; Entertainment Law; Communications Law. ***Email:*** prhochberg@verner.com

JAMES K. JACKSON, admitted to bar, 1966, Texas; 1970, District of Columbia. *Education:* Wake Forest College; Southern Methodist University (B.B.A., 1963); University of Texas (LL.B., 1966). Attorney, Office of the Chief Counsel, Internal Revenue Service, 1966-1970. ***PRACTICE AREAS:*** Taxation; Business Entities Law; Tax Controversies. ***Email:*** jkjackson@verner.com

DAVID B. JACOBSOHN, admitted to bar, 1968, New York; 1980, District of Columbia. *Education:* Cornell University (B.A., 1965; J.D., 1968). Attorney, U.S. Securities and Exchange Commission, 1969-1972. Director, Securities Disclosure Division, Comptroller of the Currency, 1972-1978. Special Assistant to Director, Federal Deposit Insurance Corporation, 1978-1979. Co-Chair, Legal Problems of Bank Regulations, 1978-1990. ***PRACTICE AREAS:*** Financial Institutions; Federal Legislative and Administrative Matters; Securities Law. ***Email:*** dbjacobsohn@verner.com

JOANNA S. KISHNER (See listing for Las Vegas, Nevada Office).

STANLEY W. LEGRO, admitted to bar, 1967, California; 1971, U.S. Supreme Court; 1977, District of Columbia. *Education:* U.S. Naval Academy (B.S., with distinction, 1959); Harvard University (J.D., cum laude, 1966). Member, San Diego City Planning Commission, 1971-1973. Assistant Administrator for Enforcement, U.S. Environmental Protection Agency, 1975-1977. Board of Advisors, Harvard Environmental Law Review, 1975-1988; National Advisory Committee on Oceans and Atmosphere, 1985-1988. ***PRACTICE AREAS:*** Environmental Law. ***Email:*** swlegro@verner.com

PAUL T. LUTHER, admitted to bar, 1992, Texas; 1994, District of Columbia. *Education:* Rice University (B.A., summa cum laude, 1987); University of Texas, Austin (J.D., with honors, 1992). Phi Beta Kappa; Sigma Delta Pi. *Member:* State Bar of Texas; The District of Columbia Bar; American Bar Association. ***LANGUAGES:*** Spanish, Portuguese. ***Email:*** ptluther@verner.com

FREDERICK J. McCONVILLE, admitted to bar, 1985, District of Columbia. *Education:* United States Military Academy (B.S., 1959); Harvard University (M.P.A., 1966; J.D., cum laude, 1985). [Col., U.S. Army, 1959-1982]. ***PRACTICE AREAS:*** Corporate Transactions; Securities Transactions. ***Email:*** fjmcconville@verner.com

MIKOL S. B. NEILSON, admitted to bar, 1978, California; 1979, District of Columbia. *Education:* University of Santa Clara (B.S., summa cum laude, 1974; J.D., summa cum laude, 1977); New York University (LL.M. in Taxation, 1978). Clerk, U.S. Tax Court, 1978-1980. Legislation Attorney, Joint Committee on Taxation, U.S. Congress, 1981-1984. ***PRACTICE AREAS:*** Federal and State Taxation. ***Email:*** msneilson@verner.com

MARILYN A. PEARSON, admitted to bar, 1976, Minnesota; 1979, District of Columbia. *Education:* University of Minnesota (B.A., Sociology, 1973; J.D., 1976). ***PRACTICE AREAS:*** Labor and Employment. ***Email:*** mapearson@verner.com

MARTIN SCHAEFERMEIER, admitted to bar, 1990, District of Columbia. *Education:* Albert-Ludwigs University, Freiburg, Germany (J.D., 1989); Duke University (LL.M., 1990). *Member:* The District of Columbia Bar. ***LAN-***

(This Listing Continued)

GUAGES: German, French. ***REPORTED CASES:*** AIMCOR v. United States, United States Court of Appeals for the Federal Circuit, Court No. 97-1266; AIMCOR v. United States, United States Court of Appeals, for the Federal Circuit, Court No. 97-1009; AIMCOR v. United States, United States Court of Appeals for the Federal Circuit, Court No. 96-1502; AIMCOR v. United States, United States Court of Appeals for the Federal Circuit, Court No. 95-130. ***Email:*** mschaefermeier@verner.com

REGINA Y. SPEED-BOST, admitted to bar, 1990, Maryland and U. S. District Court, District of Maryland; 2000, U.S. Supreme Court (Not admitted in District of Columbia). *Education:* Dartmouth College (A.B., 1987); Georgetown University (J.D., 1990). Legal Advisor, Federal Energy Regulatory Commission, William L. Massey, 1997-1998. *Member:* American Bar Association; Maryland State Energy Bar Association. ***PRACTICE AREAS:*** Energy Regulatory Law; Administrative Law. ***Email:*** ryspeed-bost@verner.com

CLIFFORD E. STEVENS, JR., admitted to bar, 1991, Maryland; 1999, District of Columbia. *Education:* University of Notre Dame (B.A., summa cum laude, 1988); Columbia University (J.D., 1991). Stone Scholar. ***PRACTICE AREAS:*** International Commerce; Litigation. ***Email:*** cestevens@verner.com

MICHAEL A. TAYLOR, admitted to bar, 1965, District of Columbia. *Education:* Dickinson College (B.A., 1961); American University (J.D., 1964). Assistant General Counsel, 1972-1974, Regional Attorney, 1974-1976 and Regional Director, 1976-1979, National Labor Relations Board. ***PRACTICE AREAS:*** Labor Law; Employment Law. ***Email:*** mataylor@verner.com

CELESTE M. WASIELEWSKI, admitted to bar, 1988, Illinois; 1989, District of Columbia. *Education:* University of Michigan (B.A., 1985); George Washington University (J.D., 1988). Phi Alpha Delta. *Member:* Illinois State and American Bar Associations; District of Columbia Bar. ***PRACTICE AREAS:*** Labor and Employment Law. ***Email:*** cmwasielewski@verner.com

---

KELLI A. ANDREWS, admitted to bar, 1995, Florida; 1997, District of Columbia. *Education:* Bucknell University (B.A., magna cum laude, 1992); Cornell University (J.D., 1995). Associate, Dickstein Shapiro Morin & Oshinsky, Washington, D.C., 1998-2000. *Member:* The Florida Bar; District of Columbia Bar. ***PRACTICE AREAS:*** White Collar Crime; Litigation; Criminal Law. ***Email:*** kaandrews@verner.com

HEVER M. BASCON, JR., admitted to bar, 1989, Philippines; 1995, New York (Not admitted in District of Columbia). *Education:* University of the Philippines (B.S.B.M., 1984); Ateneo de Manila University (LL.B., Second Honors, 1988); Georgetown University Law Center. ***PRACTICE AREAS:*** Mergers and Acquisitions; Corporate Law. ***Email:*** hbascon@verner.com

VIRGINIA R. BOGGS, admitted to bar, 1995, Maryland; 1997, District of Columbia. *Education:* Georgetown University B.A. (Govt., magna cum laude, 1991); George Washington National Law Center (J.D., 1995). ***LANGUAGES:*** Spanish. ***PRACTICE AREAS:*** Legislative Practice; Federal Practice. ***Email:*** vrboggs@verner.com

JESSIE MARIE BROOKS, admitted to bar, 1988, New York; 1990, District of Columbia. *Education:* Marymount Manhattan College (B.S., 1985); Brooklyn Law School (J.D., 1988). Certified Public Accountant, Virginia, 1985. ***PRACTICE AREAS:*** International Commerce; Litigation. ***Email:*** jmbrooks@verner.com

JAMIE E. BROWN, admitted to bar, 1994, Connecticut; 1999, District of Columbia. *Education:* University of South Florida (B.A., 1990); Georgetown University Law Center (J.D., 1994). Member, Georgetown Journal of Legal Ethics. Legislative Counsel to Senator Connie Mack, 1995-1998. ***PRACTICE AREAS:*** Legislative. ***Email:*** jebrown@verner.com

JUSTIN M. CAWLEY, admitted to bar, 1999, Virginia; 2000, District of Columbia. *Education:* University of Richmond (B.A., 1993); Georgetown University Law Center (J.D., cum laude, 1999). ***PRACTICE AREAS:*** International Law. ***Email:*** jmcawley@verner.com

DYLAN CORS, admitted to bar, 1997, Wisconsin; 1999, District of Columbia. *Education:* Massachusetts Institute of Technology (S.B., Physics, 1991); Duke University School of Law (J.D., magna cum laude/LL.M., 1997). Editor-in-Chief, Duke Journal of Comparative and International Law, 1996-1997. ***LANGUAGES:*** German, Russian. ***Email:*** dcors@verner.com

VIRGINIA C. DAILEY, admitted to bar, 2000, Florida; 2001, U.S. Court of International Trade (Not admitted in District of Columbia). *Education:* Florida State University (B.S., 1996; J.D., summa cum laude, 1999). Order of the Coif. Member: Moot Court; Florida State University Law Review. ***LANGUAGES:*** French. ***PRACTICE AREAS:*** International Trade; International Dispute Resolution. ***Email:*** vdailey@verner.com

PATRICIA A. DEEM, admitted to bar, 1997, Maryland; 1998, District of Columbia; 1999, Washington. *Education:* University of Oregon (B.A., 1990); University of Maryland (J.D., 1997). Alpha Lambda Delta. ***PRACTICE AREAS:*** Environmental. ***Email:*** padeem@verner.com

(This Listing Continued)

LAWRENCE DUNCAN, III, admitted to bar, 1994, Pennsylvania; 1995, District of Columbia. *Education:* Harvard University (B.A., 1990); University of Virginia School of Law (J.D., 1994). Editorial Board Member, Virginia Journal of Law and Politics. ***PRACTICE AREAS:*** Legislative; Federal Affairs; Communications. ***Email:*** lduncan@verner.com

DAVID A. FITZGERALD, admitted to bar, 1995, Colorado; 1997, District of Columbia. *Education:* Colorado College (B.A., 1988); Catholic University of America (J.D., 1995). ***PRACTICE AREAS:*** Energy. ***Email:*** dafitzgerald@verner.com

NEIL FRIED, admitted to bar, 1996, New York; 1997, District of Columbia. *Education:* Northwestern University (B.S.J., 1991); Washington University (J.D., 1994). Member, Washington University Law Review. Author: "Dodging the Communications Decency Act When Analyzing Libel Liability of on-line Services," Columbia Science and Technology Law Review, Nov. 29, 1999. ***PRACTICE AREAS:*** Telecommunications; Media. ***Email:*** nfried@verner.com

CARMODY ANN GABA, admitted to bar, 2000, Virginia (Not admitted in District of Columbia). *Education:* Virginia Polytechnic Institute and State University (B.A., 1996); Washington College of Law of American University (J.D., 2000). Phi Alpha Delta (Treasurer, 1998-1999; Member, 1998-2000; Clerk, 1999-2000). Member, Federalist Society, 1998-2000. *Member:* Virginia State Bar. ***PRACTICE AREAS:*** Labor and Employment; Transportation. ***Email:*** cagaba@verner.com

EMMA F. HAND, admitted to bar, 2001, Virginia (Not admitted in District of Columbia). *Education:* University of Virginia (B.A., with high distinction, 1997); Georgetown University Law Center (J.D., 2001). Golden Key Honor Society. Member, Georgetown Immigration Law Journal. ***PRACTICE AREAS:*** Energy. ***Email:*** ehand@verner.com

NOELLE MONTANO HAWLEY, admitted to bar, 1997, Virginia; 1999, District of Columbia. *Education:* Duke University (B.A., 1991); George Mason University (J.D., 1997). ***PRACTICE AREAS:*** Legislative. ***Email:*** nmhawley@verner.com

STEVEN R. JOHNSON, admitted to bar, 1993, Maryland; 1995, District of Columbia. *Education:* University of Michigan (B.A., 1986); Georgetown University Law Center (J.D., cum laude, 1993). Member, American Criminal Law Review, 1991-1993. ***PRACTICE AREAS:*** Environmental; Administrative. ***Email:*** srjohnson@verner.com

BRIAN P. KALMAER (See listing for Las Vegas, Nevada Office).

JOHN M. R. KNEUER, admitted to bar, 1994, New Jersey; 2000, District of Columbia. *Education:* Catholic University of America (B.A., 1990; J.D., 1994). Attorney-Advisor, Federal Communications Commission, 1996-1997. ***PRACTICE AREAS:*** Communications. ***Email:*** jmkneuer@verner.com

KAREN M. LUTJEN, admitted to bar, 1996, Virginia; 1997, District of Columbia. *Education:* Boston University (B.S., summa cum laude, 1993); University of Notre Damė (J.D., cum laude, 1996). ***PRACTICE AREAS:*** Taxation; Corporate; International Taxation. ***Email:*** kmlutjen@verner.com

JENIFER J. MARTIN, admitted to bar, 1997, Michigan; 1999, District of Columbia. *Education:* University of Michigan (B.A., honors in Spanish, 1989); Georgetown University (J.D., 1996). Notes Editor, Journal of Law and Policy in International Business. ***PRACTICE AREAS:*** Legislative. ***Email:*** jjmartin@verner.com

KERIM P. MAY, admitted to bar, 1999, Maryland; 2001, District of Columbia. *Education:* Wesleyan University (B.A., 1993); Washington College of Law, American University (J.D., cum laude, 1999). Executive Editor, Administrative Law Review, 1998-1999. *Member:* American Bar Association; Energy Bar Association. ***PRACTICE AREAS:*** Energy. ***Email:*** kpm@verner.com

WILLIAM H. MINOR, admitted to bar, 1995, Maryland; 1996, District of Columbia. *Education:* Tufts University (B.A., magna cum laude, 1989); Columbia University (J.D., 1995). Editor in Chief, Columbia Journal of Law & Social Problems, 1994-1995. Legislative Asst. Rep. Edward J. Markey, 1989-1992. Author, "Corporate Lobbying: Federal & State Regulation, BNA Corp. Practice Series, 1999. ***PRACTICE AREAS:*** Legislative; Federal Matters; Political Law. ***Email:*** whminor@verner.com

NKEMDILIM OKEKE, (admission pending). *Education:* Georgia State University (B.S., 1996); Tulane Law School (J.D., 2000). Member: Business Law Society, 1998; Black Law Student Association, 1998-2000. *Member:* State Bar of Texas; American Bar Association. ***PRACTICE AREAS:*** Energy; Corporate; International. ***Email:*** nokeke@verner.com

JAMES A. PICKUP, admitted to bar, 1997, Maryland; 2000, District of Columbia. *Education:* University of St. Andrews, Scotland (M.A., hons., 1989); Columbia University (M.I.A., 1991); Georgetown University Law Center (J.D., magna cum laude, 1997). Order of the Coif. Legislative Assistant and Budget Associate, The Hon. Anthony C. Beilenson, 1992-1997. ***PRACTICE AREAS:*** Legislative Practice; Federal Practice. ***Email:*** jpickup@verner.com

LORRAINE QUIROGA, admitted to bar, 2000, Florida; 2001, District of Columbia. *Education:* Florida State University (B.S., 1992); Washington Col-

(This Listing Continued)

VERNER, LIIPFERT, BERNHARD, McPHERSON AND HAND, CHARTERED, Washington—Continued

lege of Law, American University (J.D., 2000). Dean's List; Phi Alpha Alpha. *Member:* American Bar Association. ***LANGUAGES:*** Spanish. ***PRACTICE AREAS:*** Legislative; Trade. ***Email:*** lq@verner.com

KAREN ANNE REGAN, admitted to bar, 1999, North Carolina; 2001, District of Columbia. *Education:* Trinity College (B.A., Philosophy, with honors, 1993); University of North Carolina (J.D., with honors, 1999). Executive Editor, North Carolina Journal of International Law & Commercial Regulation, 1998-1999. Author: "Chow v. Immigration and Naturalization Services," 23 N.C.J. of International Law & Commercial Regulation. ***PRACTICE AREAS:*** Legislative. ***Email:*** karegan@verner.com

SARA A. ROBINSON, admitted to bar, 2000, Illinois (Not admitted in District of Columbia). *Education:* University of Notre Dame (B.A., 1997); University of Chicago (J.D., 2000). Phi Beta Kappa. *Member:* Illinois State Bar Association. ***PRACTICE AREAS:*** International. ***Email:*** sarobinson@verner.com

JOYCE A. ROGERS, admitted to bar, 2000, Maryland (Not admitted in District of Columbia). *Education:* Williams College (B.A., 1988); University of Pennsylvania (J.D., 2000). Legislative Assistant, Representative Stacy Hager, 1989-1991. Legislative Director, Representative Corrine Brown, 1994-1997. ***PRACTICE AREAS:*** Federal Affairs. ***Email:*** jarogers@verner.com

TIMOTHY M. RUTTEN, admitted to bar, 1992, Oregon; 1999, District of Columbia. *Education:* Oregon State University (B.S., 1987); Willamette University College of Law (J.D., 1992). ***PRACTICE AREAS:*** Legislative; Federal Affairs. ***Email:*** tmrutten@verner.com

RACHEL SCHOTTLAND, admitted to bar, 2001, New York (Not admitted in District of Columbia). *Education:* Cornell University, School of Industrial and Labor Relations (B.S., with honors, 1997); Vanderbilt University School of Law (J.D., 2000). ***PRACTICE AREAS:*** Labor and Employment Law. ***Email:*** reschottland@verner.com

LELA R. SCOTT, admitted to bar, 2000, Maryland; 2001, District of Columbia. *Education:* Georgetown University (B.S.F.S., 1995); University of Virginia (J.D., 2000). ***PRACTICE AREAS:*** International Law; Export Controls. ***Email:*** lrscott@verner.com

SUSANNAH SHAKOW, admitted to bar, 1998, Virginia; 1999, District of Columbia. *Education:* Davidson College (B.A., 1990); University of Virginia (J.D., 1998). ***PRACTICE AREAS:*** Legislative; Health Care Law. ***Email:*** swshakow@verner.com

ROBIN REMIS SHICHMAN, admitted to bar, 1996, Massachusetts; 1998, New York and District of Columbia. *Education:* Union College (B.A., 1991); Columbus School of Law, Catholic University of America (J.D., cum laude, 1996). ***LANGUAGES:*** Hebrew and French. ***PRACTICE AREAS:*** Energy Law. ***Email:*** rrshichman@verner.com

THOMAS R. SNIDER, admitted to bar, 2001, Massachusetts (Not admitted in District of Columbia). *Education:* University of Notre Dame (B.A., 1997); Harvard Law School (J.D., 2000). ***PRACTICE AREAS:*** International Commerce; Litigation; Legislative Practice. ***Email:*** trsnider@verner.com

GOPAL SWAMINATHAN, admitted to bar, 1995, New York; 1997, District of Columbia. *Education:* Wesleyan University (B.A., 1985); Owen Graduate School of Management, Vanderbilt University (M.B.A., 1988); Brooklyn Law School (J.D., 1994). ***LANGUAGES:*** Tamil. ***PRACTICE AREAS:*** Energy Law; Corporate Law. ***Email:*** gswaminathan@verner.com

JENNIFER H. TRIBULSKI, admitted to bar, 1993, Connecticut; 1994, New York (Not admitted in District of Columbia). *Education:* Clark University (B.A., Economics, 1990); Quinnipiac College School of Law (J.D., 1993). Phi Alpha Delta. *Member:* Connecticut Bar Association (Chair, Young Lawyers Division, 1993-1995). ***PRACTICE AREAS:*** Energy; Environmental. ***Email:*** jhtribulski@verner.com

LYNN M. VAN BUREN, admitted to bar, 1997, Wisconsin; 2001, District of Columbia. *Education:* St. Norbert College (B.A., with honors, 1992); University of Wisconsin-Madison (J.D., 1997). Order of the Coif. Senior Note and Comment Editor, Wisconsin International Law Journal, 1996-1997. ***LANGUAGES:*** Spanish. ***Email:*** lmvanburen@verner.com

ORLANDO E. VIDAL, admitted to bar, 1991, Pennsylvania; 1998, District of Columbia. *Education:* Haverford College (B.A., 1988); Boston University (J.D., 1991). Executive Editor, Boston University Public Interest Law Journal. Assistant U.S. Attorney, Eastern District of Pennsylvania, 1994-1998. ***LANGUAGES:*** Spanish and French. ***PRACTICE AREAS:*** Civil Litigation; White Collar Criminal Defense; International. ***Email:*** oevidal@verner.com

JANET BAKER WALKER, admitted to bar, 1997, New York and New Jersey; 1998, District of Columbia. *Education:* Williams College (B.A., 1990); Exeter College, Oxford University (1988-1989); Syracuse University (M.P.A., 1991); University of Virginia (J.D., 1996). Recipient: Award for Scholastic Excellence in International Business Transactions; Superior Achievement

(This Listing Continued)

Award, U.S. Department of Justice. Budget/Policy Analyst, U.S. Department of Justice, 1991-1993. ***PRACTICE AREAS:*** Corporate; Finance; Technology. ***Email:*** jbwalker@verner.com

LINDA J. WILLARD, admitted to bar, 1994, Texas; 1996, District of Columbia. *Education:* Georgetown University (A.B., magna cum laude, 1991); Georgetown University Law Center (J.D., 1994). Phi Beta Kappa. Topics Editor, Law and Policy in International Business. Counsel, U.S. Senate Committee on Environment and Public Works, 1995-1998. ***Email:*** ljwillard@verner.com

PRINCIPALS

SUZANNE D. CARTWRIGHT. *Education:* University of California at Davis (B.A., Pol. Sci., summa cum laude, 1979); University of Maryland at College Park (M.A., Public Management, 1984). (Director of Urban Development). ***PRACTICE AREAS:*** Urban Development Policy; Transportation Policy; Legislative Strategies. ***Email:*** sdcartwright@verner.com

DENIS J. DWYER. *Education:* Gettysburg College (B.A., 1978). Former Member: National Committee on Uniform Traffic Control Devices (Member, Technical Committee); Transportation Research Board (Former Committee Member). (Director of Legislative and Federal Affairs). ***Email:*** djdwyer@verner.com

ROSEMARY B. FREEMAN. *Education:* Wayne State University. Former Deputy Director, State of Michigan, Washington, D.C. Office. Executive Director, Democratic National Platform Committee, 1988. (Director of Public Affairs). ***PRACTICE AREAS:*** Legislative Law. ***Email:*** rfreeman@verner.com

VICKI HART. *Education:* Fairfield University (B.S., with honors, 1986); Yale University (M.P.H., 1990). Registered Nurse, 1986. (Director of Legislative and Federal Affairs). ***Email:*** vhart@verner.com

DAVID A. WEISS. *Education:* Hamilton College (B.A., 1975); Georgetown University (M.S.F.S., 1978). Foreign Service Officer, 1980-1990. Assistant U.S. Trade Representative, Executive Office of the President, 1987-1997. (Director of Trade Policy). ***LANGUAGES:*** French. ***PRACTICE AREAS:*** International Trade; International Transactions. ***Email:*** daweiss@verner.com

LEGAL SUPPORT PERSONNEL

SARA W. MORRIS. *Education:* Dickinson College (B.A., 1985). Senior Administrator, Subcommittee on Telecommunications and Finance, U.S. House of Representatives, 1987-1994. (Telecommunications Consultant). ***PRACTICE AREAS:*** Communications. ***Email:*** swmorris@verner.com

NANCY A. SHELIGA. *Education:* Georgetown University (B.S., magna cum laude, 1988). Phi Beta Kappa. (Legislative Consultant). ***PRACTICE AREAS:*** Legislative Law. ***Email:*** nsheliga@verner.com

---

VINSON & ELKINS L.L.P.

A Registered Limited Liability Partnership

THE WILLARD OFFICE BUILDING
1455 PENNSYLVANIA AVENUE, N.W.
WASHINGTON, D.C. 20004-1008
Telephone: 202-639-6500
Fax: 202-639-6604
URL: http://www.velaw.com

Austin, Texas Office: One American Center Suite 2700, 600 Congress Avenue, Austin, Texas, 78701-3200. Telephone: 512-542-8400. Fax: 512-542-8612.

Beijing, China Office: 20/F, Beijing Silver Tower, No. 2, Dong San Huan Bei Lu, Chaoyang District, 100027. Telephone: +86-10-6410-6300. Fax: +86-10-6410-6360.

Dallas, Texas Office: 3700 Trammell Crow Center, 2001 Ross Avenue, Dallas, Texas, 75201-2975. Telephone: 214-220-7700. Fax: 214-220-7716.

Houston, Texas Office: 2300 First City Tower, 1001 Fannin, Houston, Texas, 77002-6760. Telephone: 713-758-2222. Fax: 713-758-2346.

London, England Office: City Point, 33rd Floor, 1 Ropemaker Street, London EC2Y 9UE, England. Telephone: (44-20) 7065-6000. Fax: (44-20) 7065-6001.

Moscow, Russia Office: 16 Ulitsa Spiridonovka, Second Floor, 103001 Moscow, Russia. Telephone: (7-095) 956-1995. Local Fax: (7-095) 956-1996. U.S. Satellite Fax: (212) 803-0142.

New York, N.Y. Office: 666 Fifth Avenue, 26th Floor, New York, N.Y., 10103-0040. Telephone: 917-206-8000. Fax: 917-206-8100.

Singapore Office: 6 Battery Road, #39-01, Singapore, 049909. Telephone: (65) 536-8300. Fax: (65) 536-8311. Avenue, N.W., Washington, D.C., 20004-1008.

General Civil and Trial Practice. Admiralty, Antitrust, Aviation, Banking, Corporation, Environmental, Insurance, International, Labor, Municipal, Oil and Gas, Patent, Real Estate, Taxation, Trademark and Copyright, Trust and Utility Law.

(This Listing Continued)

RESIDENT PARTNERS

MICHAEL A. ANDREWS, born Houston, Texas, February 7, 1944; admitted to bar, 1971, Texas; 1995, District of Columbia. *Education:* University of Texas (B.A., 1967); Southern Methodist University (J.D., 1970). Phi Alpha Delta. Law Clerk to U.S. District Judge, Southern District of Texas, 1971-1972. Assistant District Attorney, Harris County, Texas, 1972-1976. U.S. Representative, 25th Congressional District of Texas, 1983-1994. ***PRACTICE AREAS:*** Public Policy.

DAVID T. ANDRIL, born Elizabeth, New Jersey, August 5, 1956; admitted to bar, 1980, District of Columbia. *Education:* Georgetown University (B.S., 1977); University of Virginia (J.D., 1980). ***PRACTICE AREAS:*** Energy; Federal Energy Regulation; Contracts; Natural Gas Regulation; International Business Transactions.

STEPHEN ANGLE, born Evansville, Indiana, March 8, 1949; admitted to bar, 1975, District of Columbia. *Education:* Texas Christian University (B.A., magna cum laude, 1971); University of Texas (J.D., magna cum laude, 1974). Phi Beta Kappa; Order of the Coif. ***PRACTICE AREAS:*** Electric Industry Restructuring; Public Utility Regulation; Hydroelectricity.

ALDEN L. ATKINS, born Charleston, Illinois, October 14, 1959; admitted to bar, 1985, New York and District of Columbia. *Education:* University of Virginia (B.A., 1981; J.D., 1984). Order of the Coif; Phi Beta Kappa. ***PRACTICE AREAS:*** Litigation; Complex and Multi-District Litigation; Antitrust and Trade Regulation; Trade Secrets; White Collar Crime.

DENNIS M. BARRY, born Washington, D.C., January 16, 1951; admitted to bar, 1976, Texas; 1983, District of Columbia. *Education:* Ohio Wesleyan University (B.A., 1972); University of Virginia (J.D., 1975). Phi Beta Kappa. Listed 1993 in The Best Lawyers in America, in Health Care Law. ***PRACTICE AREAS:*** Health Law; Medicare and Medicaid; Hospital Law.

C. MICHAEL BUXTON, born Chicago, Illinois, November 8, 1946; admitted to bar, 1971, Kentucky; 1974, District of Columbia. *Education:* Rice University (B.A., 1968); University of Kentucky (J.D., 1971). Kentucky Law Journal, 1969-1971 (Comments Editor, 1970-1971). Order of the Coif. Attorney-Advisor, Office of Legal Counsel, United States Department of Justice, 1971-1973. Special Assistant United States Attorney, District of Columbia, 1972. Law Clerk to the Hon. William H. Rehnquist, U.S. Supreme Court, 1973-1974. ***PRACTICE AREAS:*** White Collar Crime; Litigation; Antitrust and Trade Regulation.

MICHAEL R. CHARNESS, born May 25, 1954; admitted to bar, 1979, District of Columbia. *Education:* University of Pennsylvania (B.A., magna cum laude, 1976); Georgetown University (J.D., 1979). *Member:* Association of Small Research Engineering and Technical Services Companies; Professional Services Council; Contract Services Association; National Council of Public-Private Partnerships. ***PRACTICE AREAS:*** Litigation.

DAVID B. COHEN, born Glen Ridge, New Jersey, March 27, 1958; admitted to bar, 1983, Texas; 1989, District of Columbia. *Education:* University of Texas (B.A., 1980; J.D., 1983). Phi Beta Kappa. ***PRACTICE AREAS:*** Natural Resources Law; Business Law; Telecommunications Law; Project Financing Law.

CHRISTOPHER P. B. ERCKERT, born New York, N.Y.; admitted to bar, 1992, New Jersey; 1994, New York; 2000, District of Columbia. *Education:* Oglethorpe University (B.A., magna cum laude, 1986); Columbia University (J.D., 1989). Harlan Fiske Stone Scholar. ***LANGUAGES:*** Spanish and Portuguese. ***PRACTICE AREAS:*** Project Finance; International Business Law; Energy; Capital Markets.

KY P. EWING, JR., born Victoria, Texas, January 7, 1935; admitted to bar, 1959, District of Columbia. *Education:* Baylor University (B.A., 1956); Harvard University (LL.B., 1959). Alpha Chi. Deputy Assistant Attorney General, Antitrust Division, U.S. Department of Justice, 1978-1980. ***PRACTICE AREAS:*** Litigation; Antitrust and Trade Regulation.

TEGAN M. FLYNN, born Queens, New York, June 28, 1963; admitted to bar, 1988, California; 1989, District of Columbia. *Education:* Smith College (A.B., 1985); Harvard University (J.D., 1988). Phi Beta Kappa. ***PRACTICE AREAS:*** Litigation.

CATHERINE S. GALLAGHER, born Washington, D.C., July 20, 1960; admitted to bar, 1986, New York; 1988, Arizona; 1990, District of Columbia. *Education:* Yale University (B.A., cum laude, 1982); Georgetown University Law Center (J.D., 1985). ***PRACTICE AREAS:*** Securities; Corporate Law; Structured Finance; Business Law; Mergers, Acquisitions and Divestitures.

KEVIN A. GAYNOR, born Cambridge, Massachusetts, October 5, 1948; admitted to bar, 1973, Connecticut; 1978, District of Columbia; 1991, Maryland. *Education:* University of Connecticut (B.A., 1970); University of Virginia (J.D., 1973). Attorney, Environmental Protection Agency, 1975-1976. Trial Attorney, Environmental Enforcement Section, Department of Justice, 1983-1984. Assistant United States Attorney, District of Maine, 1985. Assistant Section Chief Environmental Enforcement Section, Department of Justice, 1986-1987. ***PRACTICE AREAS:*** Alternative Dispute Resolution; Environmental Law; White Collar Crime; Litigation.

JAY H. HEBERT, born Lake Charles, Louisiana, January 31, 1961; admitted to bar, 1986, Texas (Not admitted in District of Columbia). *Education:* Rice University (B.A., summa cum laude, 1983); Harvard University (J.D., magna cum laude, 1986). Phi Beta Kappa; Omicron Delta Epsilon. Law Clerk to Hon. Patrick E. Higginbotham, U.S. Court of Appeals for the 5th Circuit, 1986-1987. *Member:* American Law Institute. ***PRACTICE AREAS:*** Securities; Corporate Law; Telecommunications Law; Mergers, Acquisitions and Divestitures; Partnership Law.

MICHAEL J. HENKE, born Evansville, Indiana, August 3, 1940; admitted to bar, 1965, Texas; 1967, District of Columbia. *Education:* Baylor University (B.A., summa cum laude, 1962; LL.B., 1965); New York University (LL.M., 1966). Baylor Law Review, 1964-1965. Phi Delta Phi; Alpha Chi; Omicron Delta Kappa. Adjunct Professor, University of Virginia Law School, 1988—. Listed since 1987 in The Best Lawyers in America, in Business Litigation. ***PRACTICE AREAS:*** Litigation; Antitrust and Trade Regulation; Administrative Law; Federal Energy Regulation; Alternative Dispute Resolution.

GEORGE C. HOPKINS, born Rockville Centre, New York, May 21, 1959; admitted to bar, 1985, Pennsylvania; 1986, New Jersey; 1993, District of Columbia. *Education:* Tufts University (B.A., cum laude, 1981); Boston College (J.D., 1985). ***LANGUAGES:*** French, Russian. ***PRACTICE AREAS:*** Administrative Law; Environmental Law.

NEIL W. IMUS, born Washington, D.C., March 16, 1953; admitted to bar, 1985, District of Columbia. *Education:* Davidson College (B.S., 1975); George Washington University (M.B.A., 1981); Georgetown University (J.D., 1985). Georgetown Law Journal, 1983-1985 (Editor, 1984-1985). ***PRACTICE AREAS:*** Litigation; Antitrust and Trade Regulation.

DAVID R. JOHNSON, born Honolulu, Hawaii, March 3, 1964; admitted to bar, 1989, Virginia; 1990, District of Columbia. *Education:* University of Virginia (B.A., Economics and Philosophy, 1986); Marshall-Wythe School of Law, College of William & Mary (J.D., 1989). ***PRACTICE AREAS:*** Litigation.

GARY M. KOTARA, born San Antonio, Texas, June 28, 1955; admitted to bar, 1983, Texas; 1996, District of Columbia. *Education:* Texas A&M University (B.S.E.E., 1977); South Texas (J.D., 1982). Order of the Lytae; Eta Kappa Nu; Phi Eta Sigma; Phi Kappa Phi; Tau Beta Pi. ***PRACTICE AREAS:*** International Business Transactions; Energy; Business Law.

MARK S. LAUFMAN, born Houston, Texas, July 22, 1954; admitted to bar, 1981, District of Columbia. *Education:* University of Texas (B.A., magna cum laude, 1976); George Washington University (J.D., magna cum laude, 1981). ***PRACTICE AREAS:*** Energy; Project Finance and Development; Mergers, Acquisitions and Divestitures; Outsourcing; Computer Services.

WILLIAM E. LAWLER, III, born Washington, D.C., May 21, 1960; admitted to bar, 1985, Maryland; 1986, District of Columbia. *Education:* University of Notre Dame (B.A., cum laude, 1982); Georgetown University (J.D., cum laude, 1985). ***PRACTICE AREAS:*** Litigation.

CATHY A. LEWIS, born Clarksville, Tennessee, November 13, 1946; admitted to bar, 1978, District of Columbia; 1979, Virginia. *Education:* Miami University, Ohio (B.S., cum laude, 1968); Georgetown University (J.D., 1978). Phi Beta Kappa; Kappa Delta Pi; Pi Sigma Alpha. Georgetown Law Journal, 1975-1978. Assistant to Counsel to Chairman, 1974-1978 and Attorney, 1978-1979, Board of Governors of the Federal Reserve System. ***PRACTICE AREAS:*** Litigation; Antitrust and Trade Regulation; Finance.

KATHLEEN C. LITTLE, born January 6, 1953; admitted to bar, 1980, District of Columbia. *Education:* University of Maryland (B.S., magna cum laude, 1977); George Washington University (J.D., cum laude, 1980). ***PRACTICE AREAS:*** Litigation.

PAUL S. MACO, born Allentown, Pennsylvania, May 14, 1952; admitted to bar, 1978, New York; 1986, Massachusetts; 2001, District of Columbia. *Education:* Lehigh University (B.A., 1974); New York University (J.D., 1977). Omicron Delta Kappa. Director, Office of Municipal Securities, U.S. Securities and Exchange Commission, 1995-2000. Director, National Association of Bond Lawyers, 1989-1992. ***PRACTICE AREAS:*** Public Finance Law; Securities.

ROBERT A. MAZER, born Baltimore, Maryland, August 20, 1951; admitted to bar, 1978, District of Columbia. *Education:* University of Maryland (B.S., 1973); Catholic University of America (M.A., 1975); American University (J.D., 1978). ***PRACTICE AREAS:*** Communications Law.

LARRY A. ODAY, born Chillicothe, Ohio, November 27, 1947; admitted to bar, 1973, Illinois; 1980, District of Columbia. *Education:* Case Western Reserve University (B.A., 1969); Cleveland State University; Illinois Institute of Technology (J.D., 1973). ***PRACTICE AREAS:*** Health Law; Legislative Practice; Medicare and Medicaid; Hospital Law.

MARK R. SPIVAK, born New York, N.Y., November 5, 1958; admitted to bar, 1983, New Jersey (inactive); 1984, District of Columbia. *Education:* Mu-

(This Listing Continued)

VINSON & ELKINS L.L.P., Washington—Continued

hlenberg College (B.A., magna cum laude, 1980); Georgetown University (J.D., 1983). Associate Editor, The Tax Lawyer, 1982-1983. ***PRACTICE AREAS:*** Project Finance; Energy.

GREGORY C. STAPLE, born London, England, May 23, 1953; admitted to bar, 1978, New York; 1979, District of Columbia. *Education:* University of Rochester (B.A., summa cum laude, 1974); University of Michigan (J.D., cum laude, 1977). Phi Beta Kappa. Member, Editorial Board, Telecommunications Policy. Founder, TeleGeography. ***PRACTICE AREAS:*** Telecommunications Law; Communications and Media; Commercial Law.

JOHN D. TAURMAN, born Charleston, West Virginia, May 22, 1946; admitted to bar, 1971, District of Columbia; 1984, Texas. *Education:* Duke University (B.A., magna cum laude, 1968); Harvard University (J.D., cum laude, 1971). Harvard Law Review (Editor, 1969-1971). Phi Beta Kappa. ***PRACTICE AREAS:*** Litigation; Complex and Multi-District Litigation; International Arbitration; Contracts; Antitrust and Trade Regulation.

CHARLES D. TETRAULT, born South Hadley, Massachusetts, December 16, 1950; admitted to bar, 1975, Massachusetts; 1977, District of Columbia. *Education:* Cornell University (B.S., 1972); George Washington University (J.D., 1975). Order of the Coif. Law Clerk to the Hon. Allan M. Hale, Chief Justice, Massachusetts Appeals Court, 1975-1976. ***PRACTICE AREAS:*** Litigation; Energy; White Collar Crime.

MARK H. TUOHEY, III, born Rochester, N.Y., September 27, 1946; admitted to bar, 1973, District of Columbia; 1981, New York. *Education:* St. Bonaventure University (B.A., 1968); Fordham University (J.D., 1973). Barristers. Fordham Urban Law Journal, 1972-1973 (Writing and Research Editor, 1973). Special Counsel to the District of Columbia for the Investigation of Police Misconduct and Mismanagement, 1998. Deputy Independent Counsel, Whitewater Investigation, 1994-1995. Special Trial Counsel, Department of Justice, Criminal Division, 1977-1979. Assistant U. S. Attorney, District of Columbia, 1973-1977. Adjunct Professor: Georgetown University Law Center, 1978-1982; Catholic University School of Law, 1980-1981. Fellow: American College of Trial Lawyers; American Bar Foundation; American Law Institute. Member, The District of Columbia Bar (President, 1993-1994). ***PRACTICE AREAS:*** Litigation; White Collar Crime; Complex and Multi-District Litigation; Alternative Dispute Resolution.

CHRISTINE L. VAUGHN, born Camden, New Jersey, December 20, 1949; admitted to bar, 1975, District of Columbia. *Education:* Douglass College, Rutgers University (B.A., 1972); Georgetown University (J.D., 1975; LL.M., 1981). Phi Beta Kappa. Special Assistant to Assistant Secretary for Tax Policy, U.S. Treasury Department, 1981-1984. *Member:* The District of Columbia Bar (Co-Chair, Steering Committee, Taxation Section, 1999-2001). ***PRACTICE AREAS:*** Taxation; Legislative Practice.

ADAM WENNER, born Washington, D.C., May 7, 1950; admitted to bar, 1976, Florida; 1977, District of Columbia. *Education:* Carleton College (B.A., 1972); University of Miami (LL.B., 1976). Order of the Coif. Deputy Assistant General Counsel, Federal Energy Regulatory Commission, 1980-1981. ***PRACTICE AREAS:*** Administrative Law; Federal Energy Regulation.

ANITA RUTKOWSKI WILSON, born Kingston, Jamaica, May 27, 1965; admitted to bar, 1991, District of Columbia. *Education:* College of William & Mary (B.S., 1986); University of Virginia (J.D., 1990). Phi Beta Kappa; Phi Eta Sigma; Alpha Lambda Delta. ***PRACTICE AREAS:*** Administrative Law; Federal Energy Regulation.

PAUL L. YDE, born Madison, Wisconsin, May 20, 1959; admitted to bar, 1985, Ohio; 1996, District of Columbia. *Education:* University of Wisconsin (B.S., 1982); University of Kansas (M.A. in Economics, 1985; J.D., 1985). Member, Federal Trade Commission, 1988-1990, 1993-1995. *Member:* American Bar Association (Assistant Editor, Antitrust, 2000—; Chairman, Economics Committee, Antitrust Section, 1997-2000; Editorial Vice Chair, Antitrust Law Journal, 1993-1997); American Economics Association. ***PRACTICE AREAS:*** Litigation; Antitrust and Trade Regulation; Unfair Competition.

RESIDENT OF COUNSEL

DONNA J. BOBBISH, born Dearborn, Michigan, January 4, 1957; admitted to bar, 1983, District of Columbia. *Education:* Mount Holyoke College (A.B., summa cum laude, 1979); Georgetown University (J.D., 1982). Phi Beta Kappa. Law Clerk, Office of Administrative Law Judges, 1982-1984. Attorney Adviser, Electric Rates and Corporate Regulation, 1984-1987; Trial Attorney, Gas and Oil Litigation, 1987, Federal Energy Regulatory Commission. *Member:* Federal Energy Bar Association. ***PRACTICE AREAS:*** Energy Law; Energy Regulation.

BECKY M. BRUNER, born Cleburne, Texas, August 28, 1959; admitted to bar, 1985, Texas; 1998, District of Columbia. *Education:* University of Texas (B.A., 1981; M.P.A., 1985; J.D., 1985). ***PRACTICE AREAS:*** Energy.

(This Listing Continued)

DEBRA J. DUNCAN, born Teaneck, New Jersey, July 3, 1956; admitted to bar, 1986, Virginia; 1987, District of Columbia. *Education:* College of William and Mary (B.A., 1978); George Washington University (J.D., 1986). Order of the Coif. ***PRACTICE AREAS:*** Federal Taxation; Tax Controversies; Tax Litigation; International Taxation.

GRETA L.H. LICHTENBAUM, born Philadelphia, Pennsylvania, June 16, 1965; admitted to bar, 1990, Pennsylvania; 1991, District of Columbia. *Education:* Haverford College (B.A., 1986); Harvard University (J.D., 1990). Phi Beta Kappa. ***PRACTICE AREAS:*** International Trade; International Law.

JOSEPH E. LYNCH, born Ithaca, New York, February 12, 1956; admitted to bar, 1985, Virginia; 1986, District of Columbia. *Education:* Cornell University (B.A., 1978); University of Virginia (J.D., 1984). Judicial Law Clerk to Hon. James H. Michael, Jr., U.S. District Court for the Western District of Virginia, 1984-1985. ***PRACTICE AREAS:*** Health Law.

SAMUEL B. STERRETT, born Washington, D.C., December 17, 1922; admitted to bar, 1950, Virginia; 1951, District of Columbia. *Education:* Amherst College (B.A., 1947); University of Virginia (LL.B., 1950); New York University (LL.M. in Taxation, 1959). Office of Regional Counsel, New York IRS, 1956-1960. Judge, 1968-1988 and Chief Judge, 1985-1988, U.S. Tax Court. Member, J. Edger Murdock American Inn of Court. Fellow: American College of Tax Counsel; American Bar Foundation. ***PRACTICE AREAS:*** Litigation; Taxation; International Taxation.

ROBERT D. VANDER LUGT, born December 16, 1965; admitted to bar, 1992, Virginia; 1994, District of Columbia. *Education:* Oral Roberts Univ. (B.A., summa cum laude, 1987); Univ. of Virginia (J.D., 1991). Adjunct Professor of International Institutions, Georgetown University Law Center, 1997—. *Member:* American Society of International Law; Naval Institute. [LCDR., Special Duty , Intelligence, USNR, Current Top Secret Clearance based on an SBI, 1990—]. ***PRACTICE AREAS:*** Litigation; International Trade; Government Contracts; International Law; Aviation and Aerospace.

RESIDENT ASSOCIATES

Virginia Navarrete Brooks; Melissa K. Cantrell; Christopher K. Carr; Mikeal M. Clayton; Christopher M. Dawe (Not admitted in DC); ***John S. Decker; Benjamin Erulkar; Alexander M. Evans*** (Not admitted in DC); ***James R. Farnsworth; John M. Faust; Judith M. Feldt*** (Not admitted in DC); ***E. Malia Godfrey; David K. Godschalk; Jennifer Monday Goldman*** (Not admitted in DC); ***Melissa R.H. Hall; Karl Kiffin Hennessee*** (Not admitted in DC); ***Helen M. Hight*** (Not admitted in DC); ***Joseph E. Hunsader*** (Not admitted in DC); ***Mark Reid Klupt; Douglas J. Lanzo; Mary N. Lehner; Benjamin S. Lippard*** (Not admitted in DC); ***Dionne C. Lomax; Mark Alan Lowry*** (Not admitted in DC); ***Stacey Kyle Luck*** (Not admitted in DC); ***Bruce C. McCulloch; Leah E. Medway; J. Todd Metcalf*** (Not admitted in DC); ***Andrew J. Miller*** (Not admitted in DC); ***Alexander Paul Okuliar*** (Not admitted in DC); ***Daniel A. Petalas; R. Edward Price; Suzanne D. Reifman; Amanda Lynn Riedel*** (Not admitted in DC); ***Robert J. Rothwell*** (Not admitted in DC); ***Andrew Ruskin*** (Not admitted in DC); ***Gail D. Sausser*** (Not admitted in DC); ***Justin M. Shellaway*** (Not admitted in DC); ***Meghan S. Skelton*** (Not admitted in DC); ***David P. Steinberger; Charles Alan Stormont*** (Not admitted in DC); ***Sara C. Weinberg; James M. Wilson*** (Not admitted in DC).

(For Complete Biographical data on all Personnel, see Professional Biographies at Houston, Texas)

VOGEL & SLADE, L.L.P.

1225 NINETEENTH STREET, N.W.
SUITE 300
WASHINGTON, D.C. 20036
Telephone: 202-223-4711
Fax: 202-223-4714
URL: http://www.lawyers.com/vogel&slade
Email: robvogel@wizard.net
Email: ssladeesq@aol.com
URL: http://www.fraudbuster.com

Qui Tam Litigation, False Claims Act, Complex Multi-District Litigation, Trial Practice, White Collar Crimes, Health Care Fraud.

FIRM PROFILE: Vogel & Slade, L.L.P. is engaged in a general litigation practice at both the trial and appellate level, with specialties in health care and qui tam cases under the False Claims Act.

ROBERT L. VOGEL, born New York, N.Y., August 12, 1958; admitted to bar, 1986, New Jersey; 1987, New York; 1988, District of Columbia; 1990, Maryland. *Education:* Amherst College (B.A., summa cum laude, 1981); Stanford Law School (J.D., 1985). Phi Beta Kappa. Author: "The Public Disclosure Bar Against Qui Tam Suits," Public Contract Law Journal, Vol. 24, No. 4, Summer 1995. Instructor, Department of Justice Conferences on: Affirmative

(This Listing Continued)

Civil Enforcement, 1999; Health Care Fraud, 1995; Defense Procurement Fraud, 1990. Law Clerk to Hon. Frank M. Johnson, Jr., U.S. Court of Appeals, Eleventh Circuit, 1985-1986. Trial Attorney, Department of Justice, Civil Division, Commercial Litigation Branch, 1987-1990. *Member:* American Bar Association. ***REPORTED CASES:*** U.S. ex rel. Aflatooni v. KPS, 163 F.3d 516 (9th Cir. 1999); U.S. ex rel. Trim v. McKean, 31 F. Supp. 2d 1308 (W.D. Okla. 1998); U.S. ex rel. Semtner v. Medical Consultants, Inc., 170 F.R.D. 490 (W.D. Okla. 1997); U.S. ex rel. Siller v. Becton Dickinson, 21 F.3d 1339 (4th Cir.), cert. denied, 513 U.S. 928 (1994); U.S. v. O'Connell, 890 F.2d 563 (1st Cir. 1989); Avco Corp. v. DOJ, 884 F.2d 621 (D.C. Cir. 1989). ***PRACTICE AREAS:*** False Claims Act; Qui Tam Litigation; Health Care Fraud; Health Care Litigation. ***Email:*** robvogel@wizard.net

SHELLEY R. SLADE, born New York, N.Y., September 18, 1958; admitted to bar, 1985, California; 1987, District of Columbia. *Education:* Princeton University (B.A., magna cum laude, 1980); Stanford University (J.D., 1984). Author: "Truth and its Consequences: Should You Voluntarily Disclose Overbillings to Law Enforcement," The Health Lawyer, Vol. 12, No. 5, June 2000; "False Claims Act Civil Investigative Demands," The Civil False Claims Act and Qui Tam Enforcement, American Bar Association Center for Continuing Legal Education, 1998. Lecturer: "The Civil False Claims Act and Qui Tam Enforcement, ABA Conference, 1998; Conferences on Health Care Fraud, Department of Justice and Federal Bureau of Investigation, 1998 and 1999. Awarded: D.C. Bar Association, Pro Bono Lawyer of the Year 1989; General Services Administration, Public Service Award, 1992; Department of Health & Human Services, Office of Inspector General's Integrity Award, 1995; Department of Justice, Meritorious Award, 1997. Associate, Arnold & Porter, 1984-1989. Trial Attorney, Department of Justice, Civil Division, Commercial Litigation Branch, 1990-1998. Civil Division Senior Counsel, Health Care Fraud, Department of Justice, 1998-1999. *Member:* American Bar Association. ***PRACTICE AREAS:*** False Claims Act; Litigation; Health Care Fraud; Health Care Compliance. ***Email:*** ssladeesq@aol.com

WILLIAM R. VOLTZ

2120 L STREET, N.W., SUITE 700
WASHINGTON, D.C. 20037
Telephone: 202-293-2131
Fax: 202-293-0947

General and Administrative Practice including Trials in all Courts, Medical Malpractice, Legal Malpractice, Corporate Law, Business Law, Probate Law, Trusts and Estates, Financial Planning, Wealth Preservation.

WILLIAM R. VOLTZ, born Syracuse, New York, May 12, 1936; admitted to bar, 1962, New York and District of Columbia; 1974, Maryland. *Education:* Le Moyne College (B.S., 1958); Georgetown University (LL.B., 1961). *Member:* District of Columbia Bar; Bar Association of the District of Columbia; Maryland State and American Bar Associations; The Association of Trial Lawyers of America. ***PRACTICE AREAS:*** Civil Litigation; Medical Malpractice; Legal Malpractice; Personal Injury; Trusts and Estates; Family Law.

VORYS, SATER, SEYMOUR AND PEASE LLP

Established in 1909
11TH FLOOR, 1828 L STREET, N.W.
WASHINGTON, D.C. 20036-5109
Telephone: 202-467-8800
Telex: 440693
Telecopier: 202-467-8900
URL: http://www.vssp.com

Columbus, Ohio Office: 52 East Gay Street, P.O. Box 1008, 43216-1008. Telephone: 614-464-6400. Telex: 241348. Telecopier: 614-464-6350.
Cleveland, Ohio Office: 2100 One Cleveland Center, 1375 East Ninth Street, 44114-1724. Telephone: 216-479-6100. Telecopier: 216-479-6060.
Cincinnati, Ohio Office: Suite 2100, 221 East Fourth Street, P.O. Box 0236, 45201-0236. Telephone: 513-723-4000. Telecopier: 513-723-4056.
Alexandria, Virginia Office: 277 South Washington Street, Suite 310, 22314. Telephone: 703-837-6999. Facsimile: 703-549-4492.

Commercial Litigation, Copyright/Patent/Trademark, Federal Legislative, Government Contracts, Intellectual Property, Customs, International Trade, Export Control, International, Congressional Investigations, White Collar Defense.

JOSEPH D. LONARDO, born Cleveland, Ohio, October 15, 1947; admitted to bar, 1972, Ohio; 1973, U.S. District Court, Northern District of Ohio; 1974, U.S. District Court, Southern District of Ohio; 1979, U.S. Court of Appeals, Fourth Circuit; 1983; U.S. Court of Appeals, Sixth Circuit; 1986, U.S. District Court, Northern District of California; 1989, U.S. District Court, Eastern District of Michigan; 1990, U.S. Court of Appeals, Tenth Circuit; 1997, U.S. Supreme Court; 1998, District of Columbia. *Education:* Georgetown University (A.B., 1969); University of Michigan (J.D., cum laude, 1972). *Member:* American Bar Association (Member: Section of Natural Resources, Energy and Environmental Law; Litigation Section); Defense Research and Trial Lawyers Association; International Association of Defense Counsel (Member, Toxic/Hazardous Substances Litigation Committee). ***PRACTICE AREAS:*** Litigation; Environmental Law. ***Email:*** jdlonardo@vssp.com

JAMES K. ALFORD, born Summit, New Jersey, September 3, 1949; admitted to bar, 1974, Connecticut; 1975, U.S. Tax Court; 1977, District of Columbia; 1978, U.S. Supreme Court. *Education:* Ohio Wesleyan University (B.A. Econ., 1971); New England School of Law (J.D., 1974). Editor, New England School of Law Prison Law Journal, 1974. *Member:* The District of Columbia Bar (Member, Sections on: International Law; Taxation); American Bar Association (Member, Sections on: Taxation; International Law); International Trade Association of Northern Virginia (President, 1989—); Washington International Trade Association; Washington Foreign Law Society; World Affairs Council; Foreign Policy Association. ***PRACTICE AREAS:*** International Taxation; Corporate Taxation. ***Email:*** jkalford@vssp.com

CORY M. AMRON, born New York, New York; admitted to bar, 1977, District of Columbia. *Education:* University of Rochester (B.A., with distinction, 1974); Harvard Law School (J.D., 1977). Phi Beta Kappa. *Member:* The District of Columbia Bar (Chair, Commercial Real Estate Committee, 1986-1989; Member, Steering Committee, Real Estate Housing and Land Use Section, 1989-1994; Editor, D.C. Practice Manual, 1985-1987; Member, Reproductive Cancer Task Force, 1994-1996); Bar Association of the District of Columbia (Chair, Young Lawyers Section, 1983-1984; Member, Board of Directors, 1985-1987); American Bar Association (Chair, Commission on Women in the Profession, 1991-1994; Member, Commission on Domestic Violence, 1998—; Member, Task Force on Law Schools and the Profession: Narrowing the Gap, 1988-1992. Young Lawyers Division: Director, 1986-1989; Member, Executive Council, 1985-1988); Women's Bar Association of the District of Columbia (Member, Board of Directors, 1994-1997; Treasurer, 1982-1983); Commercial Real Estate Women. ***PRACTICE AREAS:*** Real Estate; Commercial Law; Trademark Law; Copyright Law; Licensing; Infringement. ***Email:*** cmamron@vssp.com

STEVEN R. BECKER, born Endicott, New York, 1962; admitted to bar, 1987, Virginia; 1987, U.S. Court of Appeals, Fourth Circuit; 1988, District of Columbia and Maryland; 1990, U.S. Court of Appeals, District of Columbia; 1999, U.S. Court of Appeals, Sixth Circuit. *Education:* Lafayette College (A.B., 1984); George Washington University (J.D., 1987). Phi Delta Phi. Recipient, Van Vleck Moot Court Award. *Member:* American Bar Association. ***PRACTICE AREAS:*** Professional Liability; Employment Law. ***Email:*** srbecker@vssp.com

THOMAS H. BENTZ, JR., born Ludington, Michigan, March 21, 1973; admitted to bar, 1998, Illinois and U.S. District Court, Northern District of Illinois; 2000, District of Columbia. *Education:* University of Michigan (B.A., 1995); Loyola University (J.D., with honors, 1998). Phi Alpha Delta. Author: "Internet Filters in Public Libraries," Illinois Library Association; "Privacy Rights: May Schools Monitor Use of E-mail and the Internet?" and "Some Suggestions for Surviving Y2K," Klein, Thorpe and Jenkins, Annual School Law Conference. Author and Co-Editor, Chapter Supplements: "Lane's Goldstein Trial Practice Guide" and "Lane's Medical Litigation Guide". *Member:* Chicago and Illinois State Bar Associations. ***PRACTICE AREAS:*** Litigation. ***Email:*** thbentz@vssp.com

THOMAS R. BOLAND, born Archbald, Pennsylvania, August 15, 1936; admitted to bar, 1966, District of Columbia, U.S. Claims Court and U.S. Supreme Court; 1974, U.S. Court of Appeals for the Federal Circuit; U.S. District Court, Southern District of Ohio; registered to practice before U.S. Patent and Trademark Office. *Education:* University of Scranton (B.S., Philosophy and B.S., Chemistry, 1960); Georgetown University (J.D., 1965). Delta Theta Phi. *Member:* The District of Columbia Bar (Co-Chairman, Institute on Copyrights, 1978; Chairman: Continuing Legal Education Committee, 1979-1980; Steering Committee, 1981-1983); American Bar Association (Member: Antitrust Section Committee on Trade Secrets and Interference with Contracts, Patent, Trademark and Copyright Section, 1978-1981; Committee on Access to Government Information, 1979-1981; Administrative Law Section; Vice Chairman, Committee on Patents, 1980-1981); American Chemical Society; American Intellectual Property Law Association (Chairman, Committee on Elections, 1978-1980; Member: Committee on Unfair Competition-Trade Secrets, 1979-1980; Licensing Committee, Subcommittee on Licensing Genetic Materials, 1980—; Trade Secrets, 1979-1983; Chairman, Subcommittee on University Patent Policy, 1983-1984); National Association of College and University Attorneys (Co-Chairman, Section on Intellectual Property, 1981-1984); International Trademark Association; Licensing Executive Society. ***PRACTICE AREAS:*** Intellectual Properties Law; Licensing Law; Trade Secret Law; Litigation. ***Email:*** trboland@vssp.com

CATHY A. BRAXTON, born Washington, D.C., April 26, 1966; admitted to bar, 1991, Pennsylvania; 1994, District of Columbia; 1998, Illinois. *Education:* George Washington University (B.A., 1988); Temple University (J.D., 1991). *Member:* The District of Columbia Bar; Pennsylvania, Illinois State and National Bar Associations, Women in International Trade (Chicago Chapter,

(This Listing Continued)

VORYS, SATER, SEYMOUR AND PEASE LLP, Washington—Continued

Board Member, 1998—); International Trade Club (Chicago Chapter). ***PRACTICE AREAS:*** Customs; International Trade. ***Email:*** cabraxton@vssp.com

PAMELA A. BRESNAHAN, born Washington, D.C., November 21, 1954; admitted to bar, 1980, Maryland and U.S. District Court, District of Maryland; 1981, U.S. Court of Appeals, Fourth Circuit; 1982, District of Columbia; 1984, U.S. District Court for the District of Columbia and U.S. Supreme Court; 1987, U.S. District Court, Eastern District of Pennsylvania; 1988, New York and U.S. Court of Appeals, Third Circuit; 1989, U.S. Court of Appeals, Second Circuit; 1993, U.S. District Court, Southern District of New York. *Education:* University of Maryland (B.A., magna cum laude with general honors, 1976; J.D., with honors, 1980). Phi Beta Kappa; Phi Kappa Phi. Member, Paca-Brent Inn of Court, 1994—. Member, Professional Liability Underwriting Society, 1995—. Author: "Malpractice Makes Malperfect," The ALI Restatement, National Conference on Professional Responsibility, May 1995; "Conflicts of Interest," National Legal Malpractice Conference, May 1994; "Who's the Client?" ABA Journal, May 1994; "What to Do if You're Sued: A Primer for the Lawyer/Defendant," Insurance Liability Reporter, 1991; "Breaking Up is Hard to Do," ABA Journal, November 1995. Instructor, National College of Advocacy, 1984-1986. Visiting Professor, University of Maryland Honors Program, 1981-1985. *Member:* The District of Columbia Bar; Maryland State (Chair, Young Lawyers Section, 1986-1987; Member, Committee on Judicial Appointments, 1991-1992) and American (House of Delegates: Chair, Teller's Committee, 1994—; Assembly Delegate, 1991—; Young Lawyers' Division Delegate, 1998-1999; Chair and Member, Standing Committee on Lawyers' Professional Liability, 1993—; Program Chair, National Legal Malpractice Conference, October 1994) Bar Associations; Women's Bar Association of Maryland (President, 1987-1988). Fellow: American Bar Foundation; Maryland Bar Foundation. ***PRACTICE AREAS:*** Professional Liability; Intellectual Property; Employment; Lawyer Discipline; Commercial Litigation. ***Email:*** pabresnahan@vssp.com

JEAN-MARC BRUN, born Haiti, February 3, 1959; admitted to bar, 1991, New York; 1993, District of Columbia. *Education:* State University of New York at Buffalo (B.A., 1981); Benjamin Cardozo School of Law (J.D., 1991). *Member:* District of Columbia Bar (Member, Intellectual Property Law Section). ***LANGUAGES:*** French. ***PRACTICE AREAS:*** Trademarks; Licensing; Unfair Competition. ***Email:*** jmbrun@vssp.com

JAMES M. BURNS, born New York, New York, November 12, 1961; admitted to bar, 1986, California; 1987, District of Columbia; 1994, U.S. Supreme Court; 1999, U.S. Court of Federal Claims and U.S. Tax Court. *Education:* Colgate University (A.B., cum laude, 1983); University of California at Los Angeles (J.D., 1986). Order of the Barristers. Recipient: Best Brief Award, Moot Court Competition, UCLA; Simon Scholarship. UCLA National Moot Court Team Representative, Western Regional Champions. *Member:* American Bar Association (Vice Chair, Antitrust Section, Insurance Subcommittee, 1999—). ***PRACTICE AREAS:*** Antitrust; Commercial Litigation; Trademarks. ***Email:*** jmburns@vssp.com

KAREN E. CHRISTIAN, born Columbus, Ohio, December 14, 1973; admitted to bar, 2001, Virginia (Not admitted in District of Columbia). *Education:* Ohio University (B.A., 1996); The Ohio State University (J.D., with honors, 2001). Phi Beta Kappa; Order of the Coif. ***Email:*** kechristian@vssp.com

WARREN W. GLICK, born Baltimore, Maryland, July 14, 1927; admitted to bar, 1952, District of Columbia and Maryland. *Education:* Johns Hopkins University (B.A., 1949); Harvard University (J.D., 1952). Phi Beta Kappa. Vice President and Senior Vice President for Financing, 1969-1973; Acting Executive Vice President, 1973-1975; General Counsel, 1975-1984, Export-Import Bank of the United States, 1975-1984. ***PRACTICE AREAS:*** International Law; Finance; Commercial Law. ***Email:*** wwglick@vssp.com

ELIZABETH TONI GUARINO, born Oceanside, N.Y., February 4, 1947; admitted to bar, 1977, Virginia; 1980, District of Columbia. *Education:* State University of New York at Plattsburgh (B.A., 1971); State University of New York at Binghamton; Washington & Lee University (J.D., 1977). Author: Article, "U.S. Tobacco Regulation-Review and Outlook," Zeitschrift für das gesamte Lebensmittelrecht (ZLR), January 1999; "The U.S. Food Safety Initiative: Recent Development in Food Safety Regulation to Address Present Day Issues and Prepare for the Future," European Food Law Review, Vol. 8 (Mar. 18, 1998); Chapter in Antitrust & Trade Associations--How Trade Regulation Laws Apply to Trade and Professional Associations, Handbook published by the Section of Antitrust Law, American Bar Association (1996); "Nutrient Descriptor and Disease Claims for Food," 48 Food and Drug L.J. No. 4 (1993). Attorney, including Vice President, General Counsel; Vice President, Government Affairs Counsel; Senior Counsel, Regulatory Affairs, Grocery Manufacturers of America, 1990-1995; Attorney, Kraft General Foods, Inc., 1986-1990; Federal Trade Commission, 1980-1986; Federal Labor Relations Authority, 1979-1980; Equal Employment Opportunity Commission, 1978-1979; U.S. Department of Labor, 1977-1978. Past Chairman (1996), Editorial Advisory Board, Food and Drug Law Journal. *Member:* International Bar Association (Secretary, Products

(This Listing Continued)

Liability, Advertising, Unfair Competition and Consumer Affairs Committee); Salvation Army Leadership Council. ***PRACTICE AREAS:*** Food and Drug; Advertising. ***Email:*** etguarino@vssp.com

RICHARD J. LEON, born South Natick, Massachusetts, December 3, 1949; admitted to bar, 1975, Rhode Island; 1976, U.S. District Court, District of Rhode Island; 1977, U.S. Court of Appeals, Second Circuit; 1986, U.S. Supreme Court; 1990, U.S. Court of Appeals, Fourth Circuit; 1991, District of Columbia, U.S. District Court, District of Columbia and U.S. Court of Appeals, District of Columbia Circuit. *Education:* College of the Holy Cross (A.B., 1971); Suffolk University (J.D., cum laude, 1974); Harvard University (LL.M., 1981). Order of Barristers. Author: "Environmental Criminal Enforcement: A Mushrooming Cloud," 63 St. John's Law Rev. 679, 1989; Chapter 16, Environmental Criminal Law, "Lawyers' Desk Book on White-Collar Crime," 1991. Assistant Professor of Law, St. John's University Law School, 1979-1983. Instructor and Lecturer, Trial Advocacy, The Attorney General's Advocacy Institute, U.S. Department of Justice, 1987. Adjunct Professor, Congressional Investigations, Georgetown University Law Center, 1997—. Trustee, Suffolk University, 1990-1998. Past President, Suffolk Law School Alumni Association, 1987-1988. Past President, Suffolk Law School Associations of Metropolitan New York, 1983-1985 and Metropolitan Washington, 1986-1988. Law Clerk to: Chief Justice McLaughlin and the Justice of Superior Court of Massachusetts, 1974-1975; Justice Thomas F. Kelleher, Supreme Court of Rhode Island, 1975-1976. Special Assistant, U.S. Attorney, Southern District of New York, 1977-1978. Senior Trial Attorney, Criminal Section, Tax Division, U.S. Department of Justice, 1983-1987. Recipient, Tax Division Outstanding Attorney Award, 1985. Deputy Chief Minority Counsel, U.S. House Select Iran-Contra Committee, 1987-1988. Deputy Assistant Attorney General, Environmental Enforcement, Environment & Natural Resources Division, U.S. Department of Justice, 1988-1989. Chief Minority Counsel to Cong. Hyde and Republican Members of the U.S. House Foreign Affairs Committee "October Surprise" Task Force, 1992. Special Counsel to Cong. Leach and the Republican Members of the U.S. House Banking, Finance and Urban Affairs Committee (Whitewater Hearings), 1994. Special Counsel to Co-Chairmen Livingston and Cardin and the Members of the U.S. House Ethics Reform Task Force, 1997. Commissioner, The President's Commission on White House Fellowships, 1990-1993. Member, Federal Bar Council, Second Circuit, 1978—. Member, Admissions and Grievance Committee, U.S. Court of Appeals, District of Columbia Circuit, 1994—. *Member:* Rhode Island and American (Member, Sections of: Natural Resources, Energy and Environmental Law; Criminal Justice-White Collar Crime Subcommittee; Taxation) Bar Associations; Edward Bennett Williams American Inn of Court (Washington, D.C.). ***PRACTICE AREAS:*** White-Collar Criminal Defense; Congressional Investigations; Civil Trial Litigation; Environmental Litigation. ***Email:*** rjleon@vssp.com

PETER A. MARTIN, born Bristol, Pennsylvania, July 9, 1960; admitted to bar, 1986, New Jersey and U.S. District Court, District of New Jersey; 1988, District of Columbia, U.S. Court of International Trade and U.S. Court of Appeals, Federal Circuit. *Education:* Vassar College (A.B., cum laude, 1983); Temple University (J.D., 1986). Law Secretary to the Assignment Judge, Superior Court, Mercer County, New Jersey, 1986-1987. Attorney-Advisor, U.S. Customs Service, Office of Regulations and Rulings, 1987-1988. *Member:* American Bar Association; International Trade Commission Trial Lawyers; Customs and International Trade Bar Association. ***PRACTICE AREAS:*** Antidumping; Customs Law; Export Regulation; Foreign Trade Sanctions; Import and Export Law; U.S. Foreign Trade Zones. ***Email:*** pamartin@vssp.com

NIHAR R. MOHANTY, born Riverdale, Maryland, March 27, 1967; admitted to bar, 1992, Maryland; 1995, District of Columbia; U.S. District Court, District of Maryland and U.S. Court of Appeals, Fourth Circuit. *Education:* University of Maryland (B.A., magna cum laude, 1989); Phi Beta Kappa; University of Illinois College of Law (J.D., magna cum laude, 1992). ***Email:*** nrmohanty@vssp.com

MICHAEL SEAN PURCELL, born Wilkes-Barre, Pennsylvania, January 10, 1967; admitted to bar, 1992, Virginia and U.S. District Court, Eastern District of Virginia; 1999, District of Columbia and U.S. Court of Appeals, Fourth Circuit. *Education:* American University (B.A., 1989); Catholic University of America (J.D., 1992). Recipient, American Jurisprudence Award, Constitutional Law and Conflicts of Law. *Member:* Virginia State Bar; District of Columbia Bar; American Bar Association (Member, Business and International Sections). ***PRACTICE AREAS:*** Corporate Law; International Law. ***Email:*** mspurcell@vssp.com

RONALD E. SHAPIRO, born Washington, D.C., September 23, 1953; admitted to bar, 1978, Maryland; 1979, U.S. Tax Court and U.S. District Court, District of Maryland; 1984, U.S. Court of Appeals for the Federal Circuit, U.S. Supreme Court and District of Columbia; 1990, Virginia. *Education:* Johns Hopkins University (B.A., with honors, 1975); University of Maryland (J.D., with honors, 1978); George Washington University (LL.M., in Patent and Trade Regulation Law, 1983). Editor-in-Chief, The Maryland Law Forum, 1977-1978. Recipient, William P. Cunningham Award for Exceptional Achievement, University of Maryland School of Law, 1978. *Member:* The District of Columbia

(This Listing Continued)

Bar; Virginia State Bar; American Bar Association; International Trademark Association; International Association for the Protection of Industrial Property; Licensing Executives Society. ***Email:*** reshapiro@vssp.com

ELIZABETH TREUBERT SIMON, born Port Jefferson, New York, December 22, 1968; admitted to bar, 1999, New York and U.S. District Court, Eastern and Southern Districts of New York; 2000, District of Columbia, Maryland and U.S. District Court, District of Maryland. *Education:* University of Pennsylvania (B.A., 1990; M.S., 1993); Albany Law School (J.D., cum laude, 1998). Member: Justinian Society; Albany Law School Inns of Court, 1997-1998. Co-Author: with C. Biblow, "The Reemergence of Market-Share Liability for Industrywide Claims for the Defense," Defense Research Institute, August 1999. *Member:* New York State and American Bar Associations. ***PRACTICE AREAS:*** Litigation; Professional Liability. ***Email:*** entreubert@vssp.com

MICHAEL S. SNARR, born Washington, D.C.; admitted to bar, 2001, New York (Not admitted in District of Columbia). *Education:* University of Utah (B.A., Political Science, 1996); Georgetown University (M.S.F.S., International Finance, 2000; J.D., 2000). ***LANGUAGES:*** Hungarian and French. ***Email:*** mssnarr@vssp.com

GEORGE W. SWENSON, JR., born Minneapolis, Minnesota, 1933; admitted to bar, 1992, Pennsylvania; 1995, District of Columbia and Minnesota; registered to practice before U.S. Patent and Trademark Office. *Education:* Spring Hill College (B.S., Chem. 1958); Loyola University (M.S., 1960; Ph.D., 1963); George Washington University (J.D., 1991). ***Email:*** gwswenson@vssp.com

RANDAL C. TEAGUE, born Durham, North Carolina, May 19, 1944; admitted to bar, 1972, Florida and District of Columbia; 1975, U.S. Supreme Court; 1979, Massachusetts. *Education:* American University (B.A., 1967); George Washington University (J.D., 1971; LL.M., summa cum laude, 1972); Honorary, Allen University (LL.D., 1973). Pi Sigma Alpha. Policy Development Coordinator, 1971-1973 and Acting Assistant Director for Operations, 1973, Office of Economic Opportunity, Executive Office of the President of the United States. Administrative Assistant and Legislative Counsel, U.S. Representative Jack F. Kemp, 1973-1979. Corporate Attorney, 1979-1980 and Division Counsel, 1980-1981, Cabot Corporation, Boston, Massachusetts. Chairman, U.S. Agency for International Development Advisory Committee on Voluntary Foreign Aid, 1987-1991. ***PRACTICE AREAS:*** International Business; Legislative Practice; Taxation; International Taxation; Federal Taxation. ***Email:*** rcteague@vssp.com

JOHN W. WILMER, JR., born Baltimore, Maryland, December 4, 1948; admitted to bar, 1975, Florida; 1976, District of Columbia. *Education:* Princeton University (A.B., cum laude, 1970); Georgetown University Law Center (J.D., 1975). Law Clerk to Chief Judge Pierce Lively, U.S. Court of Appeals for the Sixth Circuit, 1975-1976. ***PRACTICE AREAS:*** Federal Civil Litigation; Environmental Law; Appellate Practice; Occupational Safety and Health Law. ***Email:*** jwwilmer@vssp.com

REID M. WILSON, born Madison, Wisconsin, February 24, 1970; admitted to bar, 1997, Virginia; 1999, Maryland and Pennsylvania (Not admitted in District of Columbia). *Education:* University of South Carolina (B.A., 1993); The George Washington University Law School (J.D., 1997). ***PRACTICE AREAS:*** Trademarks; Licensing; Unfair Competition. ***Email:*** rmwilson@vssp.com

(For Biographical Data of all Partners and Associates see Professional Biographies at Columbus, Ohio).

WAGNER & ASSOCIATES

733 FIFTEENTH STREET, N.W., SUITE 908
WASHINGTON, D.C. 20005-2112
Telephone: 202-638-2222
Fax: 202-638-1838
Email: attywagner@msn.com
URL: http://www.lawyers.com/wagnerlaw

Trusts and Estates, Estate Litigation, Financial Planning, Family Wealth Transfer, Retirement Planning, Contested Wills, Inheritance, Probate, Missing Heir Searches, Wills, Small Business Law, Family Business Successions, Business Organization, Business Planning, Minority Business Law, Asset Protection, Bankruptcy Chapter 7, Bankruptcy Chapter 11, Bankruptcy Chapter 13, Civil Practice, Administrative Law, Regulatory Law.

FIRM PROFILE: Wagner & Associates is a woman and minority owned law firm that has provided quality legal counsel for clients throughout the Washington, D.C. community including Montgomery and Prince Georges counties in Maryland. Ms. Brenda C. Wagner is an experienced litigator and for over 22 years she has represented individuals, families and small businesses.

BRENDA CAROL WAGNER, born Fayetteville, North Carolina, April 18, 1951; admitted to bar, 1977, North Carolina and U.S. District Court, Middle District of North Carolina; 1979, District of Columbia; 1983, U.S. Court of

(This Listing Continued)

Appeals, Fourth Circuit; 1987, Maryland; 1991, U.S. District Court, District of Maryland. *Education:* North Carolina Central University (B.S., 1973; J.D., 1976). Hearing Officer: North Carolina ABC Board, 1978-1979; District of Columbia Department of Public Housing, 1991-1997. Research Director, North Carolina Department of Administration, 1979-1980. Assistant Public Defender, NOrth Carolina Public Defender, 27A Judicial District, 1980-1981. Assistant Corporate Counsel, District of Columbia Government, 1986-1987. Commissioner, North Carolina Property Tax Study Commission, 1981-1982. Board Member: Legal Services Board, Raleigh, North Carolina, 1978-1980; United Way Board, 1980-1981; Planning Board, Rocky Mount, 1983-1986. Member, League of Women Voters, 1996—. Life Member, Urban League, Washington, DC, 1996—. *Member:* American and National Bar Associations; Women's Bar Association of DC; American Trial Lawyers Association. ***PRACTICE AREAS:*** Probate; Real Estate; Bankruptcy. ***Email:*** attywagner@emailmsn.com

ROBERT B. WALKER

WASHINGTON, D.C.

(See Herndon, Virginia)

Transportation Law, Litigation, General Business and Corporate legal matters, Bankruptcy, Administrative Law Practice, Estate Planning and Administration.

WALLACE KING MARRARO & BRANSON, PLLC

1050 THOMAS JEFFERSON STREET, N.W.
WASHINGTON, D.C. 20007
Telephone: 202-204-1000
Fax: 202-204-1001
URL: http://www.wallaceking.com

Complex Commercial Litigation, Alternative Dispute Resolution, International Arbitration, Environmental Law and Litigation, Insurance Coverage.

RICHARD E. WALLACE, JR., born Boston, Massachusetts, November 24, 1954; admitted to bar, 1982, District of Columbia and U.S. District Court, District of Columbia; 1988, Maryland and U.S. District Court, District of Maryland; 1994, U.S. Court of Appeals for the District of Columbia and 4th Circuits; 1996, U.S. District Court, Southern District of Texas; 1997, U.S. Supreme Court. *Education:* University of Massachusetts (B.A., 1978); Harvard University (J.D., 1982). Author: "Consolidated Arbitration in the United States," 10 J. Int'l Arbitration 5, 1993. Co-Author: Branson and Wallace, "Arbitrator Immunity Under United States Law," in Immunity of Arbitrators, England, J. Lew ed. 1990; Branson and Wallace, "Developments in International Commercial Arbitration in the United States," in Jahrbuch fur die Praxis der Schiedsgerichtsbarkeit Band 3, 1989, O. Glossner ed. 1990; Branson and Wallace, "Awarding Interest in International Commercial Arbitration: Establishing a Uniform Approach," 28 Virginia Journal of International Law 919, 1988; Branson and Wallace, "Court-Ordered Consolidated Arbitrations in the United States," 5 J. Int'l Arbitration 89, 1988; Branson and Wallace, "Choosing the Substantive Law to Apply in International Commercial Arbitration," 27 Virginia Journal of International Law 39, 1986. Arbitration Faculty, International Law Institute, 1987—. *Member:* District of Columbia Bar; Maryland State and American Bar Associations. Fellow, Chartered Institute of Arbitrators, England, 1995—. ***PRACTICE AREAS:*** Litigation; Arbitration. ***Email:*** rwallace@wallaceking.com

ANTHONY F. KING, born Indianapolis, Indiana, June 29, 1963; admitted to bar, 1989, Michigan, U.S. District Court, Eastern District of Michigan and U.S Court of Appeals, Sixth Circuit; 1991, U.S. Court of Appeals for the District of Columbia Circuit; 1992, District of Columbia and U.S. District Court, District of Columbia; 1994, U.S. Court of Appeals, Fourth Circuit; 1995, U.S. Supreme Court; 1996, U.S. District Court, Southern District of Texas; 1999, U.S. Court of Appeals, Third Circuit. *Education:* Wabash College (A.B., 1984); Harvard University (J.D., cum laude, 1987). Law Clerk, The Honorable Damon J. Keith, United States Court of Appeals for the Sixth Circuit, 1987-1989. *Member:* The District of Columbia Bar; State Bar of Michigan; American Bar Association. ***PRACTICE AREAS:*** Litigation; Environmental Law. ***Email:*** aking@wallaceking.com

CHRISTOPHER H. MARRARO, born New York, N.Y., March 3, 1952; admitted to bar, 1983, New Jersey and U.S. District Court, District of New Jersey; 1984, District of Columbia; 1990, U.S. Court of Appeals for the District of Columbia Circuit; U.S. Court of Appeals, Fifth Circuit. *Education:* Gettysburg College (B.A., 1974); University of Alberta (M.Sc., 1978); Franklin Pierce Law Center (J.D., 1981). Author: "Revising The Ozone Standard In Quantitative Risk Assessment In Regulation," Brookings Institution, 1982; "Environmental & Occupational Health and the New Federation," IDEA The Journal of Law and Technology, Vol. 23, No. 3, 1983. *Member:* The District of Columbia Bar; American Bar Association (Member, Section on Natural Resources, Energy and

(This Listing Continued)

WALLACE KING MARRARO & BRANSON, PLLC, Washington—Continued

Environmental Law; Chairman, Planning Committee of the Annual Conference on Environmental Law). ***LANGUAGES:*** Spanish. ***PRACTICE AREAS:*** Environmental Law; Litigation. ***Email:*** cmarraro@wallaceking.com

DAVID J. BRANSON, admitted to bar, 1973, Illinois; 1976, New York; 1979, District of Columbia; 1985, U.S. Supreme Court. *Education:* Catholic University of America (A.B., 1966); Georgetown University (J.D., 1973); St. John's College, Cambridge University, Cambridge, England (LL.M., 1975). Author: "Selecting an Arbitral Forum: A Guide to Cost-Effective International Arbitration," Virginia Journal of International Law, 1984. Co-Author: Branson and Wallace, "Choosing the Substantive Law to Apply in International Commercial Arbitration," 27 Virginia Journal of International Law 39, 1986; "Annulments of 'Final' ICSID Awards Raise Questions About the Process," The National Law Journal, 1986; "Ethics for International Arbitrators," 3 Arbitration International 72, 1987; "Continuous Ownership of a Claim," Journal of International Arbitration, 1987; Branson and Wallace, "Awarding Interest in International Commercial Arbitrations: Establishing a Uniform Approach," 28 Virginia Journal of International Law, 919, 1988; Branson and Wallace, "Court Ordered Consolidated Arbitrations in the United States," 5 Journal of International Arbitration 89, 1988; Branson and Wallace, "Developments in International Arbitration in the United States," Jahrbuch fur die Prais der Schiedsgerichtsbarkeit, Band 2, 1988, O. Glossner ed.; Band 3, 1989; Branson and Wallace, "Arbitrator Immunity Under United States Law," Immunity of Arbitrators, England, J. Lew, 1990; "The Ken-Ren Case," 10 Arbitration International, No. 3, 1994; "Arbitrability and Pre-emption," 12 Arbitration International 2, 1996. Adjunct Professor, Georgetown University Law Center, 1979-1985. Partner, White & Case, 1982-1985. Partner, Kaye, Scholer, Fierman, Hays & Handler, 1985-1995. *Member:* District of Columbia Bar; American (Vice Chairman, International Commercial Arbitration Committee, Section of International Law and Practice, 1984-1985) and International (Vice Chairman, Committee D, Procedures for Settling Disputes, 1986-1990) Bar Associations. [Capt., USAF, 1966-1970]. (Of Counsel to Stewart and Stewart, Washington, D.C.). ***LANGUAGES:*** German. ***PRACTICE AREAS:*** International Arbitration. ***Email:*** dbranson@wallaceking.com

JULIE RONDER DOMIKE, born St. Paul, Minnesota, December 29, 1954; admitted to bar, 1986, Maryland; 1988, District of Columbia. *Education:* Mt. Holyoke College (B.A., cum laude, 1976); Georgetown University (J.D., 1986). Attorney-Advisor and Branch Chief, Air Enforcement Division, USEPA, 1987-1996. *Member:* The District of Columbia Bar; Maryland State and American (Member, Section of Environment, Energy and Resources Law; Vice Chairman, Air Quality Committee, 1999-2002). ***LANGUAGES:*** Spanish (Fluent) and Portuguese. ***PRACTICE AREAS:*** Environmental. ***Email:*** jdomike@wallaceking.com

COUNSEL

PETER C. CONDRON, born Oceanside, New York, January 19, 1962; admitted to bar, 1988, New York and U.S. District Court, Southern and Eastern Districts of New York; 1989, District of Columbia; 1991, U.S. District Court for the District of Columbia; 1992, U.S. Court of Appeals, District of Columbia Circuit; 1997, U.S. Court of Appeals, Seventh Circuit. *Education:* St. John's University (B.S., 1984); College of William & Mary (J.D., 1987). Member, William & Mary Law Review, 1985-1987. Articles Editor, The Colonial Lawyer, 1987. *Member:* The District of Columbia Bar. ***PRACTICE AREAS:*** Litigation. ***Email:*** pcondron@wallaceking.com

DAVID M. DORSEN, born New York, N.Y., October 10, 1935; admitted to bar, 1960, District of Columbia and New York State; 1979, U.S. Supreme Court. *Education:* Harvard University (A.B., 1956; J.D., 1959). Editor, Harvard Law Review, 1957-1959. Assistant U.S. Attorney, Southern District of New York, 1964-1969. Assistant Chief Counsel, Senate Select Committee on Presidential Campaign Activities, 1973-1974. Chairman, District of Columbia Bar Fee Arbitration Board, 1982-1984. Visiting Lectures, Terry Sanford Institute of Public Policy, Duke University, 1995—. Adjunct Professor, Georgetown University Law Center, 2000—. ***PRACTICE AREAS:*** Civil Litigation; Libel and Slander Law.

WILLIAM F. HUGHES, born Olean, New York, March 14, 1964; admitted to bar, 1991, Pennsylvania; 1992, U.S. Court of Appeals, District of Columbia and Tenth Circuits; 1993, District of Columbia. *Education:* Georgetown University (B.A., 1987; J.D., cum laude, 1990). Contributing Author: *Environmental Crimes*, Shepard's, 1992; "Used Oil: Disposal Options, Management Practices and Potential Liability," Government Institutes, 1991. *Member:* American Bar Association. ***PRACTICE AREAS:*** Environmental Law; Litigation. ***Email:*** bhughes@wallaceking.com

JOHN W. KAMPMAN, born Hammond, Indiana, May 18, 1947; admitted to bar, 1986, Connecticut; 1989, District of Columbia. *Education:* California State University-Northridge (B.S., 1970; M.S., 1978); University of Bridgeport (J.D., magna cum laude, 1985). *Member:* The District of Columbia Bar. [Captain, U.S. Air Force, 1971-1976]. ***PRACTICE AREAS:*** Environmental Law; Litigation. ***Email:*** jkampman@wallaceking.com

RICKARD F. PFIZENMAYER, born Hattiesburg, Mississippi, December 4, 1944; admitted to bar, 1969, Ohio; 1972, District of Columbia; 1987, South Carolina; 1989, Tennessee. *Education:* Duke University (A.B., magna cum laude, 1966); University of Michigan (J.D., cum laude, 1969). Phi Beta Kappa. Member, Editorial Board, Michigan Law Review. Assistant General Counsel, Texaco Inc., 1990-2000. General Counsel, Bridgestone (U.S.A.), Inc., 1988-1990. Partner, 1979-1986 and Associate, 1973-1979 and 1969-1972, Squire, Sanders & Dempsey. Staff Attorney, Executive Office of The President, Pay Board Office of General Counsel, 1972-1973 (Chief, Resolutions and Decisions and Orders Section). *Member:* District of Columbia Bar; South Carolina Bar. ***PRACTICE AREAS:*** Corporate Law; Employment Law; Antitrust; Environmental Law. ***Email:*** rpfizenmayer@wallaceking.com

---

STEVEN C. DUBUC, born New York, N.Y., May 15, 1968; admitted to bar, 1994, Virginia; 1996, District of Columbia. *Education:* Cornell University (B.A., cum laude, 1990); Georgetown University (J.D., magna cum laude, 1994). Phi Beta Kappa. *Member:* American Bar Association. ***PRACTICE AREAS:*** Environmental Law; Litigation; Education; Environmental Regulation. ***Email:*** sdubuc@wallaceking.com

LETTA F. SNEED, born Savannah, Georgia, March 24, 1971; admitted to bar, 1997, New York; 2000, District of Columbia. *Education:* Princeton University (A.B., 1993); New York University (J.D., 1996). ***PRACTICE AREAS:*** Commercial Litigation. ***Email:*** lsneed@wallaceking.com

ANGELA M. PELLETIER, admitted to bar, 1998, New York and District of Columbia. *Education:* University of Oklahoma (B.A., 1994); University of Pennsylvania (J.D., summa cum laude, 1997). University of Pennsylvania Law Review. *Member:* The District of Columbia Bar; New York State Bar Association. ***PRACTICE AREAS:*** Litigation; Environmental Law; Intellectual Property. ***Email:*** apelletier@wallaceking.com

TAMARA R. PARKER, born June 6, 1958; admitted to bar, 1993, New York; 1994, District of Columbia; 1996, U.S. Court of Appeals, Fourth and Eleventh Circuits. *Education:* Ohio State University (1975-1978); Wright State University (B.A., 1981); University of Dayton Law School; Yale University (J.D., 1992). Recipient, American Jurisprudence Award in Legal Research and Writing. Editor, Yale Law and Policy Review. *Member:* The District of Columbia Bar. ***PRACTICE AREAS:*** Civil Litigation; Products Liability; Toxic Torts. ***Email:*** tparker@wallaceking.com

RUBEN F. REYNA, born Warsaw, Indiana, August 2, 1972; admitted to bar, 1997, Maryland (Not admitted in District of Columbia). *Education:* Georgetown University (B.A., 1994); University of Michigan (J.D., 1997). ***PRACTICE AREAS:*** Litigation. ***Email:*** rreyna@wallaceking.com

SUSAN V. WATSON, born Baltimore, Maryland, April 11, 1968; admitted to bar, 1997, Maryland; 1998, District of Columbia. *Education:* University of Maryland (B.S., 1993); Georgetown University (J.D., 1997). ***Email:*** svwatson@wallaceking.com

ALEC ZACAROLI, born La Crosse, Wisconsin, June 16, 1969; admitted to bar, 1999, Virginia; 2000, District of Columbia. *Education:* George Washington University (B.A., 1991); American University at Washington (J.D., cum laude, 1998). *Member:* District of Columbia Bar; Virginia State Bar. ***PRACTICE AREAS:*** Environmental Law; Litigation. ***Email:*** azacaroli@wallaceking.com

SEAN R. WARD, born Bethesda, Maryland, January 11, 1971; admitted to bar, 1998, Virginia (Not admitted in District of Columbia). *Education:* University of Virginia (B.A., 1993); Columbus School of Law (J.D., 1997). ***PRACTICE AREAS:*** Environmental Litigation. ***Email:*** sward@wallaceking.com

LAWRENCE D. WASKO

SUITE 900
1150 CONNECTICUT AVENUE, N.W.
WASHINGTON, D.C. 20036
Telephone: 202-862-4370
Fax: 202-331-0599
Email: ldwasko@erols.com
URL: http://www.lawyers.com/waskolaw

Aviation Law, Aircraft Finance and Leasing, Contracts, Letters of Credit, Aviation Insurance, Aeronautical Regulation, Aircraft Sales, Airport Finance and Development, International Aviation Law.

FIRM PROFILE: Offering over 30 years experience, the law firm of Lawrence D. Wasko represents a broad array of both international and domestic aviation clients. They include aircraft sales and leasing companies, charter carriers, cargo carri-

(This Listing Continued)

ers, pilot training facilities, foreign air carriers, aircraft parts companies, freight forwarders, travel agency and tour operators, airline entrepreneurs, airline certificators and aviation management and consulting firms.

LAWRENCE D. WASKO, born Yonkers, New York, October 27, 1932; admitted to bar, 1964, District of Columbia. *Education:* Pratt Institute and Harpur College (A.B., 1958); Georgetown University (J.D., 1963). Air Transport Examiner, Civil Aeronautics Board, 1958-1962. Adjunct Professor of International Business Diplomacy, Georgetown University, 1970-1989. *Member:* District of Columbia Bar; Bar Association of the District of Columbia. ***PRACTICE AREAS:*** Aviation Law; International Trade.

ASSOCIATE

JACQUELYN N. GLUCK, born Cleveland, Ohio, August 29, 1961; admitted to bar, 1991, New York (Not admitted in District of Columbia). *Education:* Miami University (B.A., 1983); American University (J.D., 1990). Phi Delta Phi. Member, American Geophysical Union. *Member:* New York State and American Bar Associations. ***LANGUAGES:*** French, German and Italian. ***PRACTICE AREAS:*** Aviation Law; International Aviation Law; Aeronautical Regulation; Contracts; Litigation.

MICHAEL F. WASSERMAN

800 SEVENTH STREET, N.W., SUITE 201
WASHINGTON, D.C. 20001-3718
Telephone: 202-842-3290
Facsimile: 202-842-2385
Email: mfw@law.com

Trial Practice, Appellate Practice, Complex and Multi-District Litigation, Contract Litigation, Corporate Law, Business Litigation, Employment Litigation, Libel, Slander and Defamation, Real Estate Litigation, U.S. Supreme Court Litigation, Legal Ethics, Landlord and Tenant Law, Leasing, Small Business Law, Products Liability Defense.

FIRM PROFILE: Michael F. Wasserman has focused is practice on civil litigation with a special emphasis on the historical perspective surrounding the adjacent legal issues. His firm's clients have included specialty manufacturers, universities, educational facilities, corporations, landlords, small businesses and individuals from the Washington, D.C. area as well as Maryland and Virginia.

MICHAEL F. WASSERMAN, born Poughkeepsie, New York, March 24, 1965; admitted to bar, 1993, Virginia; 1994, Maryland and District of Columbia. *Education:* Wesleyan University (B.A., 1990); University of Minnesota (J.D., magna cum laude, 1993). Law Clerk to the Hon. Vanessa Ruiz for the District of Columbia Court of Appeals, 1994-1996.

WASSERMAN, MANCINI & CHANG

1915 EYE STREET, N.W., SUITE 400
WASHINGTON, D.C. 20006
Telephone: 202-783-8905
Fax: 202-333-1688
URL: http://www.lawyers.com/wassermanmancini&chang

Immigration and Nationality and International Law. Practice before Government Agencies. Trial, Appellate and Supreme Court Practice. Business Immigration.

MEMBERS OF FIRM

JACK WASSERMAN (1913-1980).

MARK A. MANCINI, born Erie, Pennsylvania, April 3, 1948; admitted to bar, 1973, Pennsylvania; 1974, District of Columbia. *Education:* University of Pennsylvania (A.B., 1970); Temple University (J.D., 1973). Author: "Excludability for Lack of a Valid Labor Certificate as a Species of Fraud," Immigration and Nationality Law Review, Vol. II, 1979; "Fraud under the Immigration and Nationality Act," Vol. 56, Notre Dame Lawyer No. 4, page 668, April 1981. Adjunct Professor, Immigration Law: George Washington University, 1975-1980; Catholic University, 1988-1992. Instructor, Foreign Service Institute, Department of State, 1980—. *Member:* The District of Columbia Bar; The Bar Association of the District of Columbia (Chairman, Naturalization Committee, 1985—); Pennsylvania Bar Association; American Immigration Lawyers Association (Chairman, District of Columbia Chapter, 1974-1976 and 1985-1986); Union Internationale Des Avocats. ***PRACTICE AREAS:*** Immigration and Nationality Law.

SAM HSIEN-CHENG CHANG, born Nanking, China, September 6, 1946; admitted to bar, 1981, District of Columbia. *Education:* Taiwan University, Taipei, Taiwan (LL.B., 1968); Howard University (M.C.L., 1975). Principal, Gaithersburg Chinese School, 1983-1984. Secretary, Taiwan University Alumni Association, Washington D.C. Chapter, 1982-1983. General Counsel,

(This Listing Continued)

Asian American Voters' Coalition, 1986-1987. Vice President of Chinese American Chamber of Commerce, 1988—. General Counsel, Metro Washington Chinese Restaurant Association, 1988—. Host, Free Legal Affairs Program, Channel 56, Fairfax, Virginia, 1989-1992. Free Immigration Law Program, Channel 16, World Today Cable TV, Montgomary County, Maryland, 1997—. *Member:* The District of Columbia Bar; Bar Association of the District of Columbia; American Bar Association; American Immigration Lawyers Association. ***LANGUAGES:*** Chinese and Taiwanese. ***PRACTICE AREAS:*** Immigration and Nationality Law.

ASSOCIATES

RICHARD W. CHANG, born Tainan, Taiwan, February 14, 1972; admitted to bar, 1997, New Jersey and U.S. District Court, District of New Jersey; 1998, Maryland, District of Columbia, U.S. Court of Appeals, District of Columbia Circuit and Fourth Circuit. *Education:* University of Illinois (B.A., 1994); Catholic University of America, Columbus School of Law (J.D., 1997). Delta Theta Phi. Recipient: Catholic University of America Law Extra Mile Leadership Award, 1996; Catholic University of America Law Asian Pacific American Law Students Association Leadership Award, 1996. Vice President, Asian-Pacific American Law Students Association, 1995-1996. Fourth Circuit Representative, 1995-1996 and Conference Co-Chair, 1996, National Asian Pacific American Law Students Association. Who's Who in American Law Students, 1997-1998. *Member:* Asian Pacific American Bar Association (Member and Chairperson, Advanced Communications Board). ***LANGUAGES:*** Mandarin. ***PRACTICE AREAS:*** Immigration Law; Trademarks; Copyrights; Small Business Law. ***Email:*** dizz@msn.com

ROBIN L. WILLIAMSON, born Falls Church, Virginia, October 13, 1973; admitted to bar, 1999, Virginia (Not admitted in District of Columbia). *Education:* Washington & Lee University (B.A., 1995); Samford University, Cumberland School of Law (J.D., 1998). *Member:* American Immigration Lawyers Association. ***LANGUAGES:*** Spanish. ***PRACTICE AREAS:*** Immigration and Naturalization.

TAMARA Y. DOWTON, born Brooklyn, New York, 1969; admitted to bar, 1997, Maryland (Not admitted in District of Columbia). *Education:* University of Virginia (B.A., with highest distinction, 1993); California Western School of Law, San Diego (J.D., 1996); Georgetown University Law Center (LL.M., with honors, 1997). Phi Beta Kappa; Phi Sigma Pi. Deans List. Member: Golden Key National Honor Society; International Foreign Language Honor Society; National Spanish Honorary Society. Recipient: T. Braxton Woody Scholarship for Best Foreign Language Student; Best Appellate Brief Award; Wiley Manuel Pro Bono Award. ***LANGUAGES:*** French, Spanish, German and Italian. ***PRACTICE AREAS:*** Immigration and Naturalization.

REFERENCE: First American Bank, Washington, D.C.

BRADLEY S. WATERMAN

SUITE 1040, EAST TOWER
1301 K STREET, N.W.
WASHINGTON, D.C. 20005
Telephone: 202-682-1616
Fax: 202-682-2232
Email: BSW1040@aol.com

Civil and Criminal Tax Controversies, Federal Income Tax Planning.

BRADLEY S. WATERMAN, born Cambridge, Massachusetts, May 24, 1949; admitted to bar, 1977, Massachusetts and District of Columbia. *Education:* Johns Hopkins University (B.A., 1971); University of Richmond (J.D., 1976); New York University (LL.M. in Taxation, 1977). Master, J. Edgar Murdock American Inn of Court. Chair, Tax Audits and Litigation Committee, Taxation Section, The District of Columbia Bar, 1993-1996.

WATSON COLE GRINDLE WATSON, P.L.L.C.

WASHINGTON, D.C.

(See Dykema Gossett PLLC)

WATSON & RENNER

1919 M STREET, N.W., SUITE 400
WASHINGTON, D.C. 20036-3307
Telephone: 202-737-6300
Fax: 202-737-7611
Email: WR@W-R.com
URL: http://www.lawyers.com/watson&rennerlaw

State and Federal Court Trials, Regulatory Trials, Proceedings, Small Business, General Counselling, Personal Injury Claims, Medical Causation, Cancer Causation, Toxic Torts, Electric and Magnetic Fields, Chemical and Physical Exposures, Microwave Communication, Transmission Line Siting, Surgeons' Liability, Products Liability, Intellectual Property Litigation.

(This Listing Continued)

WATSON & RENNER, Washington—Continued

FIRM PROFILE: The law firm of Watson & Renner represents electric utilities, manufacturers, telecommunications companies and other industries in cancer claims, toxic torts and environmental exposure claims. The firm has an international practice with special emphasis on medical and cancer causation.

Watson & Renner also provides general business counselling for both small and large companies.

THOMAS C. WATSON, born Poplar Bluff, Missouri, February 26, 1945; admitted to bar, 1972, Missouri; 1973, District of Columbia and U.S. Court of Appeals for the District of Columbia Circuit; 1974, U.S. Court of Appeals, Second, Eighth and Tenth Circuits; 1975, U.S. District Court for the District of Columbia and U.S. Supreme Court; 1978, U.S. Court of Appeals, Fourth, Fifth, Seventh and Ninth Circuits; 1993, U.S. District Court, District of Maryland. *Education:* University of Memphis (B.S., 1967; M.Ed., 1968); Washington University (J.D., 1972). Chief Comments Editor, Washington University Law Review, 1971-1972. Law Clerk to Judge Webster, U.S. District Court, Eastern District of Missouri, 1972-1973. Listed in: Who's Who in America; Who's Who in American Law. *Member:* The District of Columbia Bar; American Bar Association; The Association of Trial Lawyers of America; Bioelectromagnetics Society. ***PRACTICE AREAS:*** Trials; Medical and Cancer Causation; Technology and Science Law.

CURTIS S. RENNER, born Paris, France, June 24, 1958; admitted to bar, 1988, Massachusetts; 1995, District of Columbia; 2000, U.S. District Court, District of Columbia; 2001, U.S. District Court, District of Maryland. *Education:* Wesleyan University (B.A., 1981); Harvard University (J.D., cum laude, 1988). Phi Beta Kappa. Author: *The Scientific & Legal Bases for Litigating EMF Property Claims,* American Bar Association, 1994. *Member:* The District of Columbia Bar; American Bar Association; Defense Research Institute. ***LANGUAGES:*** French. ***PRACTICE AREAS:*** Trials and Litigation; Scientific Trials; Medical Causation; Cancer & Carcinogenesis; Toxic Torts; Environmental Health Claims.

NICHOLAS WYCKOFF WOODFIELD, born Port Chester, New York, March 12, 1968; admitted to bar, 1995, Alabama; 2001, District of Columbia. *Education:* Washington & Lee University (B.A., 1990); Cumberland School of Law of Samford University (J.D., 1995); University of Oxford, Oxford, England (2000). Phi Delta Phi. Co-author: "A Practitioner's Guide to Alabama's Tort of Bad Faith," 57 Ala. Law 277 (1996). Author: "The Policy/Operational Dichotomy in Intra-State Tort Liability: An example of the Ever-continuing Transformation of the Common Law," 29 Denv. J. L. & Pol'y 27, 2001. *Member:* Alabama State Bar; The District of Columbia Bar. ***PRACTICE AREAS:*** Trial Practice; Litigation; Medical Causation; Cancer and Carcinogenesis; Toxic Torts; Environmental Health Claims. ***Email:*** Nwoodfield@W-R.com

LEGAL SUPPORT PERSONNEL

RONALD L. HANSON (Firm Administrator).

REPRESENTATIVE CLIENTS: Utility Health Sciences Group; Cable & Wireless; American Electric Power (AEP); Cingular.

WATT, TIEDER, HOFFAR & FITZGERALD, L.L.P.

601 PENNSYLVANIA AVENUE, N.W., SUITE 900
WASHINGTON, D.C. 20004
Telephone: 703-749-1000
Telecopier: 703-893-8029
Email: contactus@wthf.com
URL: http://www.wthf.com

McLean Virginia Office: 7929 Westpark Drive, Suite 400, Telephone: 703-749-1000. Telecopier: 703-893-8029.
Irvine California Office: 3 Park Plaza, Suite 1500. Telephone: 949-852-6700.
Affiliated Frankfurt, Germany Office: Heiermann Franke Knipp, Kettenhofweg 126, D-603325 Frankfurt, Germany. Telephone: 011 49 69 975 82 20.
Affiliated Florence, Italy Office: Roberto Tassi & Associates: Via Dei Della Robbia n. 68, 50132, Florence, Italy. Telephone: 011 39 55 500 1448.

Construction, Government Contracts, Suretyship, International Business, Admiralty/Maritime and Real Estate Law.

FIRM PROFILE: Watt, Tieder, Hoffar & Fitzgerald, L.L.P. is at the forefront of developments in the legal industry. On a typical day, our attorneys are at work for clients throughout the United States, Canada, Europe, the Middle East, South America, Australia and Africa. With more than 70 attorneys devoted to serving government and civil construction, government supply and service contracting, marine engineering and shipbuilding, and real estate industry clients, we bring to bear the high level of skill that develops only in an intensely focused practice.

FIRM MEMBER

JOHN B. TIEDER, JR., born 1946; admitted to bar, 1971, Virginia; 1972, District of Columbia and U.S. Court of Federal Claims. *Education:* Johns Hopkins University (A.B., 1968); Syracuse University and American University (J.D., 1971). Lecturer in Law, Marshall-Wythe School of Law, College of William & Mary, 1977—. *Member:* The District of Columbia Bar; Virginia, Federal, American and Inter-Pacific Bar Associations; Virginia State Bar; American College of Construction Lawyers (Charter Member). ***PRACTICE AREAS:*** International Construction; Construction; Government Contracts. ***Email:*** jtieder@wthf.com

REPRESENTATIVE CLIENTS: Bechtel; Clark Construction; Construction Pioneers; D B Riley, Inc.; Deutsche-Babcock, Ltd.; Dillingham Corp.; Donohoe Construction Company; Ebasco Constructors, Inc.; Essex Electro Engineers, Inc.; Fidelity and Deposit Co. of Maryland; First Union National Bank; Guarantee Company of North America; S.A. Healy Co.; ICI Canada, Inc.; Impreglio; Insurance Company of North America; Kiewit; Kimmins Environmental Services; Kingston Associates; MCI Constructors, Inc.; Mitsui Babcock Energy; Mobil Oil Corporation; Morrison Knudsen; Ohio Casualty Insurance Co.; Preussag/Noell; Raytheon Engineers and Constructors, Inc.; Sunrise Retirement Homes; Trinity Industries, Inc.; USF&G; Westinghouse; H.B. Zachary; Zell Industries.

(For Complete Biographical data on all Personnel, see Professional Biographies at McLean, Virginia).

WEADON & ASSOCIATES

3338 N STREET, N.W.
WASHINGTON, D.C. 20007
Telephone: 202-965-4100
Fax: 202-965-4252
Email: weadonassociates@aol.com

International Trade, International Transactions, International Trade Regulation, High Technology Law, Export Control, Customs, Intellectual Property, Ethical Business Practices, Logistics and Dispute Resolution.

FIRM PROFILE: Weadon & Associates has for over twenty-five years represented small to large high technology enterprises (both domestic and foreign) engaged in the global marketplace.

Mr. Weadon continues to teach graduate students at George Mason University and is an internationally recognized authority on technology transfer, international cyber law and international trade regulation. His firm provides hands-on experience in the critical regulatory areas surrounding civilian and military technology ventures and e-commerce enterprise world-wide. This includes export controls (including encryption), customs, logistics, intellectual property, ethical business practices, business structure contracting and regulatory compliance (including enforcement defense).

DONALD ALFORD WEADON, JR., born Brisbane, Australia, September 15, 1945; admitted to bar, 1976, California; 1988, District of Columbia; 1992, U.S. Court of International Trade. *Education:* Cornell University (B.A., 1968); State Department Sabbatical, 1966; Hastings College of Law, University of California (J.D., 1975); Harvard Business School adjunct program at the Iran Center for Management Studies (M.B.A., 1976). Recipient, Snodgrass Moot Court Competition Award, 1974. Adjunct Professor: International Business Law, Golden Gate University School of Law, 1978-1979; Export Administration and Customs Law, Graduate Program in International Transactions, George Mason University Institute of Public Policy, 1991—. Member, U.S. Department of State Defense Trade Advisory Group, 1992—. *Member:* Bar Association of San Francisco; The District of Columbia Bar (Member, International Law Section); State Bar of California (Member, International Law Section); American Bar Association (Chairman, Subcommittees on: China Trade Law, Section of International Law & Practice, 1982-1984; Software and Technical Data Exports, Section on Corporation, Banking and Business Law, 1983-1984). [CDR, USNR, 1968-1972]. ***LANGUAGES:*** French, Farsi, Japanese. ***PRACTICE AREAS:*** Export Compliance; Export Regulation; Foreign Trade Sanctions; Foreign Asset Control; Customs Compliance; International Trade and Transactions; Government Contracts; Administrative Law; Intellectual Property. ***Email:*** dweadon@aol.com

COUNSEL

THOMAS P. SCOTT, III, born Atlanta, Georgia, September 23, 1958; admitted to bar, 1983, Georgia; 1987, District of Columbia. *Education:* Davidson College (B.A., 1980); University of Georgia School of Law (J.D., 1 983). Special Projects Editor, Georgia Journal of International and Comparative Law. *Member:* The District of Columbia Bar; American Bar Association (Member, International Law Section). ***LANGUAGES:*** German. ***PRACTICE AREAS:*** International Trade and Transactions; Customs Law; Export Compliance; Ex-

(This Listing Continued)

port Regulation; Foreign Trade Sanctions; Foreign Asset Control. ***Email:*** tpscott@erols.com

WEBER & ASSOCIATES, P.C.

Established in 1987

1730 K STREET, N.W., SUITE 304

WASHINGTON, D.C. 20006

Telephone: 202-628-0200

Fax: 202-628-0021

Email: glweber44@aol.com

Energy, Environmental and Appellate Practice. Energy Regulatory, Litigation Practice before the F.E.R.C. and the E.P.A.

FIRM PROFILE: For more than 25 years George L. Weber has conducted a National Energy and Environmental Litigation Practice. The firm primarily represents natural gas pipe line companies in rate cases and controversies in certificate and compliance proceedings and in general business counselling. Mr. Weber is readily available to advise other law firms on issues centered around energy & environmental regulations.

GEORGE L. WEBER, born Pipestone, Minnesota, July 16, 1944; admitted to bar, 1971, Virginia; 1972, U.S. Tax Court, U.S. Court of Appeals for the District of Columbia Circuit and U.S. Claims Court; 1981, U.S. Court of Appeals, Fifth Circuit; 1985, District of Columbia. *Education:* University of South Dakota (B.A., 1966); George Washington University (M.A., 1970; J.D., 1971). Phi Delta Phi. Student Association (President, 1965). *Member:* The District of Columbia Bar; Virginia State Bar; Federal Energy and American Bar Associations.

RONALD L. WEBNE

1701 Q STREET, N.W.

WASHINGTON, D.C. 20009

Telephone: 202-518-0418

Fax: 202-518-0318

Email: RWebne@aol.com

URL: http://www.lawyers.com/webnelaw

General Litigation, specializing in Commercial, Tort, Landlord and Tenant, and other Real Estate Related Matters; General Corporate and Business Law.

FIRM PROFILE: Mr. Webne's practice is primarily centered around civil trial work in Maryland and the District of Columbia.

RONALD L. WEBNE, born Toledo, Ohio, May 14, 1947; admitted to bar, 1972, District of Columbia; 1978, Illinois, 1988, Maryland. *Education:* Miami University (B.A., 1969); George Washington University (J.D., 1972). ***REPORTED CASES:*** Frank Emmet Real Estate Inc. v. Monroe, 562 A.2d 134 (D.C.App. 1989). ***PRACTICE AREAS:*** General Practice; General Civil Litigation; Corporate Litigation; Landlord and Tenant Law; Corporate Law.

WEBSTER, CHAMBERLAIN & BEAN

Established in 1973

SUITE 1000, 1747 PENNSYLVANIA AVENUE, N.W.

WASHINGTON, D.C. 20006

Telephone: 202-785-9500

Fax: 202-835-0243

General and Administrative Practice before all Federal Courts, Departments and Agencies. Corporation, Tax, Antitrust, Trade Regulation, Labor, Environmental, Intellectual Property, Contract and Non-Profit Organization Law.

FIRM PROFILE: Webster, Chamberlain & Bean is a general practice law firm specializing in the representation of tax-exempt organizations, including trade associations, professional societies, charities and advocacy groups. In addition to legal concerns of particular relevance to nonprofit organizations, the firm provides counsel on general corporate matters, as well as taxation, antitrust, regulatory, election law, employment and intellectual property issues. Webster, Chamberlain & Bean also has a strong legislative practice and represents its clients before state and federal courts and federal administrative agencies. The firm is listed in the Bar Register of Preeminent Lawyers.

MEMBERS OF FIRM

ARTHUR L. HEROLD, born Shreveport, Louisiana, January 24, 1941; admitted to bar, 1966, Louisiana; 1969, District of Columbia. *Education:* Tulane University (B.A., 1963; LL.B., 1966). Trial Attorney, Federal Trade Commission, 1967-1970. *Member:* The District of Columbia Bar; Bar Association of the District of Columbia (Chairman, Antitrust Law Committee, 1974-1976,

(This Listing Continued)

1982-1984, 1992, 1997), Louisiana State and American (Chairman, Trade Association Committee, Antitrust Law Section, 1975-1977) Bar Associations. Fellow, American Bar Foundation. ***PRACTICE AREAS:*** Association Law; Antitrust and Trade Regulation; General Corporate; Employment; Election Law. ***Email:*** aherold@wc-b.com

ALAN P. DYE, born Eustis, Florida, April 4, 1946; admitted to bar, 1971, Florida; 1973, U.S. Tax Court; 1974, U.S. Claims Court; 1975, District of Columbia; 1982, U.S. Court of Appeals for the Federal Circuit. *Education:* Duke University (A.B., 1968); University of Florida (J.D., 1971); New York University (LL.M. in Taxation, 1973). Phi Delta Phi. Attorney-Advisor to Judge Austin Hoyt, U.S. Tax Court, 1973-1975. *Member:* The District of Columbia Bar; The Florida Bar; American Bar Association (Member, Exempt Organizations Committee of the Taxation Section, 1977—). Fellow, American College of Tax Counsel. ***PRACTICE AREAS:*** Exempt Organizations; Taxation; Election Law; General Corporate; Association Law. ***Email:*** adye@wc-b.com

EDWARD D. COLEMAN, born Washington, D.C., May 21, 1934; admitted to bar, 1963, Maryland; 1981, U.S. Supreme Court; 1990, District of Columbia; 1992, U.S. Tax Court. *Education:* Georgetown University (A.B., 1956; J.D., 1959). Guest Lecturer, Master Tax Program, Georgetown University Law Center, 1984—. Member, Exempt Organizations Division, 1963-1989 and Division Director, 1986-1989, Internal Revenue Service. *Member:* The District of Columbia Bar; Maryland State Bar Association, Inc.; American Bar Association (Member, Exempt Organizations Committee, Taxation Section). Fellow, American College of Tax Counsel. ***PRACTICE AREAS:*** Taxation; Exempt Organizations. ***Email:*** ecoleman@wc-b.com

FRANK M. NORTHAM, born Indianapolis, Indiana, October 22, 1946; admitted to bar, 1974, Indiana; 1975, District of Columbia and Virginia; 1978, U.S. Supreme Court. *Education:* Yale University (B.A., 1969); Indiana University School of Law (J.D., magna cum laude, 1974). Articles Editor, Indiana Law Review, 1973-1974. Delegate to Judicial Conference of the District of Columbia, 1978-1979. *Member:* The District of Columbia Bar; Virginia and American (Member, Section on Litigation) Bar Associations; Virginia State Bar. ***PRACTICE AREAS:*** Taxation; Trade and Professional Associations; Nonprofit and Charitable Organizations; Antitrust and Trade Regulation; Litigation; Election Law.

JOHN W. HAZARD, JR., born Washington, D.C., March 17, 1953; admitted to bar, 1980, Virginia; 1983, District of Columbia. *Education:* Virginia Polytechnic Institute and State University (B.A., 1976); Ohio Northern University (J.D., 1979). Phi Alpha Delta. Member, Ohio Northern University Law Review, 1978-1979. Recipient, Guy Award for Excellence in Legal Journalism. Author: *Copyright Law In Business and Practice,* West Group Publishing. *Member:* The District of Columbia Bar; Virginia State Bar. ***PRACTICE AREAS:*** Trademark and Copyright Law; Publishing Law; Artist Rights; Entertainment Law.

HUGH K. WEBSTER, born Washington, D.C., November 25, 1961; admitted to bar, 1986, Maryland; 1987, District of Columbia. *Education:* Middlebury College (B.A., 1983); Duke University Law School (J.D., 1986). Author: "The Law of Associations," Matthew Bender, supp. 1997—; "Trade Associations," BNA, 1997; "Fiduciary Duties of Nonprofit Officers and Directors, BNA, 2001. *Member:* The District of Columbia Bar; Maryland State Bar Association, Inc.; International Association of Association Management Companies; American Society of Association Executives (Member, Legal Council Section). ***PRACTICE AREAS:*** Trade and Professional Associations; Nonprofit and Charitable Organizations. ***Email:*** hwebster@wc-b.com

DAVID P. GOCH, born Trenton, New Jersey, July 19, 1966; admitted to bar, 1991, Maryland; 1994, District of Columbia. *Education:* University of Michigan (B.G.S., 1988); University of Maryland (J.D., 1991). Order of the Coif. Phi Delta Phi. *Member:* District of Columbia Bar; Maryland State Bar Association, Inc.; American Bar Association (Member, Section of Business Law). ***PRACTICE AREAS:*** Trade and Professional Associations; Nonprofit and Charitable Organizations; Government Relations. ***Email:*** dgoch@wc-b.com

ASSOCIATES

CHARLES M. WATKINS, born Newport News, Virginia, September 12, 1954; admitted to bar, 1981, District of Columbia; 1983, U.S. Claims Court. *Education:* Franklin and Marshall College (A.B., 1976); Dickinson School of Law (J.D., 1981). Phi Alpha Delta. *Member:* The District of Columbia Bar; American Bar Association (Member, Section of Taxation). ***PRACTICE AREAS:*** Trade and Professional Associations; Tax Exempt Organizations; Employee Benefits; Employment Taxation. ***Email:*** CWatkins@wc-b.com

DOUGLAS W. MACDONALD, born Boston, Massachusetts, September 11, 1969; admitted to bar, 1997, Massachusetts; 1999, District of Columbia. *Education:* University of New Hampshire (B.A., 1991); Western New England School of Law (J.D., 1997). *Member:* Massachusetts and American Bar Associations; District of Columbia Bar; American Society of Association Executives.

(This Listing Continued)

WEBSTER, CHAMBERLAIN & BEAN, Washington—Continued

PRACTICE AREAS: Corporate Law; Business Law; Intellectual Property Law; Trade and Professional Associations; Nonprofit Corporations. ***Email:*** dmacdonald@wc-b.com

HEIDI K. ABEGG, born St. Louis, Missouri, April 29, 1971; admitted to bar, 1996, Indiana and U.S. District Court, Northern and Southern Districts of Indiana; 1997, Florida; 1999, U.S. Court of Appeals, District of Columbia Circuit; 1999, District of Columbia; 2000, U.S. Supreme Court. *Education:* Valparaiso University (B.A., cum laude, 1993; J.D., 1996). Delta Theta Phi. Treasurer, Republican Victory Committee, 1999-2001. Member, Federalist Society. *Member:* Terre Haute, Indiana State and American Bar Associations; The Florida Bar; District of Columbia Bar. ***PRACTICE AREAS:*** Nonprofit Organizations Law; Charitable Organizations Law; Trade and Professional Associations; Constitutional Law; Election and Campaign Finance Law; Civil Litigation; Appellate Practice; Administrative Agency Practice. ***Email:*** habegg@wc-b.com

OF COUNSEL

J. COLEMAN BEAN, born Lexington, Virginia, August 9, 1928; admitted to bar, 1957, Virginia; 1962, District of Columbia; 1983, Maryland. *Education:* Washington & Lee University and United States Military Academy (B.S., 1950); University of Virginia (LL.B., 1957); Georgetown University (LL.M. in Taxation, 1963). Member, Small Business Administration National Advisory Council, 1972-1973. Order of the Coif. *Member:* The District of Columbia Bar; Bar Association of the District of Columbia; Maryland State Bar Association; Virginia State and American Bar Associations; American Judicature Society. (Retired). ***PRACTICE AREAS:*** Corporate Law.

CHARLES E. CHAMBERLAIN, born Locke Township, Ingham County, Michigan, July 22, 1917; admitted to bar, 1949, Virginia and Michigan; 1958, U.S. Supreme Court; 1961, District of Columbia. *Education:* University of Virginia (B.S., 1941; LL.B., 1949). Delta Theta Phi. Prosecuting Attorney of Ingham County, Michigan, 1955-1956. Member, U.S. House of Representatives, Sixth District, Michigan, 1957-1974 (House Ways and Means Committee, 1969-1974). *Member:* The District of Columbia Bar; Virginia State Bar; State Bar of Michigan. ***PRACTICE AREAS:*** Corporate Law.

KENT MASTERSON BROWN, born Lexington, Kentucky, February 5, 1949; admitted to bar, 1974, Kentucky; 1975, U.S. Court of Appeals, Sixth Circuit; 1977, U.S. District Court, Eastern District of Kentucky; 1978, U.S. Supreme Court; 1985, U.S. Court of Appeals, Eleventh Circuit and U.S. District Court, Central District of Illinois; 1989, U.S. Court of Appeals, Fifth Circuit (Not admitted in District of Columbia). *Education:* Centre College of Kentucky (B.A., 1971); Washington & Lee University School of Law (J.D., 1974). Delta Theta Phi. *Member:* Fayette County and Kentucky Bar Associations; National Health Lawyers Association; American Society of Law & Medicine. (Also Practicing Individually in Danville, Kentucky). ***PRACTICE AREAS:*** Constitutional Law; Administrative Law; Civil Rights; Litigation; Health Care and Hospital Law; Medical Legal Law.

JAMES BOPP, JR., born Terre Haute, Indiana, February 8, 1948; admitted to bar, 1973, Indiana and U.S. Supreme Court (Not admitted in District of Columbia). *Education:* Indiana University (B.A., 1970); University of Florida (J.D., 1973). Instructor, Commercial Law, Indiana University, 1977-1978. Deputy Attorney General, 1973-1975. Deputy Prosecutor, Vigo County, 1979-1987. General Counsel, National Right to Life Committee, 1978—. *Member:* Terre Haute and Indiana State Bar Associations; The Federalist Society. (Also Member, Bopp, Coleson & Bostrom, Terre Haute, Indiana). ***PRACTICE AREAS:*** Constitutional Law; Civil Litigation; Non-Profit Corporations Law; Election Law; Appeals.

WEBSTER, FREDRICKSON & BRACKSHAW

Established in 1982

SUITE 300, 1819 H STREET, N.W.
WASHINGTON, D.C. 20006
Telephone: 202-659-8510
Telecopier: 202-659-4082
Email: firm@wf82.com

General Civil, Appellate and Administrative Practice. Public Utility, Business, Taxation, Real Estate, Bankruptcy, Commercial Litigation, Labor, Employment and Personal Injury Law.

MEMBERS OF FIRM

WENDELL W. WEBSTER, born Washington, D.C., July 7, 1950; admitted to bar, 1976, District of Columbia. *Education:* Boston University (B.S., 1972); Howard University (J.D., cum laude, 1975); Harvard University (LL.M., 1978). Recipient, American Jurisprudence Award for Property, 1972. Editor-in-Chief: Howard Law Journal, 1974-1975; Federal Bar Journal, 1979-1981. Author: "Tenant's Remedy When Landlord Has Breached Warranty of Habitability," 18 Howard Law Journal 468, 1975; "Tax Aspects of Bankruptcy Reform Act of 1978," Tax Adviser, April, 1979; "Impact of the Bankruptcy Act of 1978 on Consumers," National Bar Bulletin, April, 1979. Instructor: Federal Taxation, Catholic University Law School, 1981-1982; Taxation, Howard University Law School, 1989-1992. Law Clerk to Hon. John Garrett Penn, Superior Court of the District of Columbia, 1975-1977. Member, 1984-1990 and Chairman, 1988-1990, Board of Equalization and Review, District of Columbia. *Member:* The District of Columbia Bar; Washington Bar Association (Chairman, Law Day Committee, 1980-1981; Member, Board of Directors, 1983—; President, 1990-1991. Bankruptcy Trustee, 1994—. [Capt., ADG, USAR, 1980-1981]. ***PRACTICE AREAS:*** Public Utilities; Bankruptcy; Commercial Law. ***Email:*** wwebster@wf82.com

BRUCE A. FREDRICKSON, born Washington, D.C., June 12, 1951; admitted to bar, 1976, Virginia; 1977, District of Columbia, U.S. District Court for the District of Columbia and U.S. Court of Appeals for the District of Columbia Circuit; 1980, U.S. Supreme Court; 1983, U.S. Court of Appeals for the Federal Circuit; 1988, U.S. Court of Appeals, 4th Circuit. *Education:* Dartmouth College (B.A., summa cum laude, 1973); George Washington University (J.D., with high honors, 1976). Phi Beta Kappa. Recipient: Trial Lawyer Of The Year, Trial Lawyers For Public Justice, 2000; Lawyer Of The Year, Metropolitan Washington Employment Lawyers Association, 2001. Adjunct Professor, Trial Practice, Washington College of Law of The American University, 1986—. *Member:* The District of Columbia Bar; Virginia State Bar; Dartmouth Lawyers Association; The Association of Trial Lawyers of America; National Employment Lawyers Association; Metropolitan Washington Employment Lawyers Association (President, 1991-1993; Member, Board of Directors, 1991—); Trial Lawyers For Public Justice; Fellow, College Of Labor and Employment Lawyers. ***PRACTICE AREAS:*** Employment Law; Labor Law; Personal Injury; Litigation. ***Email:*** bfredrickson@wf82.com

SUSAN L. BRACKSHAW, born Arlington, Massachusetts, December 5, 1949; admitted to bar, 1982, District of Columbia; 1983, U.S. District Court for the District of Columbia, U.S. Court of Appeals for the District of Columbia Circuit, U.S. Court of Appeals for the Federal Circuit and U.S. Court of Military Appeals; 1988, U.S. Court of Appeals, 4th Circuit; 1997, U.S. Supreme Court. *Education:* University of Massachusetts (B.A., 1972); Smith College; Washington College of Law of The American University (J.D., 1982). Recipient: Trial Lawyer Of The Year, Trial Lawyers For Public Justice, 2000; Trial Lawyer Of The Year, Metropolitan Washington Employment Lawyers Association, 2001; Mooer's Trophy, 1982. Author: "Health Care of Children Over Objections of the Parents: Clash of Rights," 2 Medicine and Law 221, 1983. Adjunct Professor, Trial Practice, Washington College of Law of The American University, 1986—. *Member:* The District of Columbia Bar; Metropolitan Washington Employment Lawyers Association; National Employment Lawyers Association; Trial Lawyers For Public Justice. ***PRACTICE AREAS:*** Employment Law; Labor Law; Personal Injury; Litigation. ***Email:*** sbracksh@wf82.com

LINDA M. CORREIA, born Taunton, Massachusetts, March 17, 1963; admitted to bar, 1991, Massachusetts; 1992, District of Columbia and U.S. District Court for the District of Columbia; 1995, U.S. Court of Appeals for the District of Columbia Circuit; 2000, U.S. District Court, District of Maryland. *Education:* Boston University (B.A., 1985); Washington College of Law, American University (J.D., 1991). Recipient: Trial Lawyer Of The Year, Trial Lawyers For Public Justice, 2000. Author, "'A' Is For Alar: EPA's Persistent Failure to Remove Hazardous Pesticides from the Food Supply," 16 Chem. Reg. Rep. (BNA) 868, August 14, 1992. *Member:* The District of Columbia Bar; National Employment Lawyers Association; Metropolitan Washington Employment Lawyers Association; Trial Lawyers For Public Justice. ***PRACTICE AREAS:*** Administrative Law; Labor and Employment; Commercial Litigation; Bankruptcy. ***Email:*** lcorreia@wf82.com

ASSOCIATES

JONATHAN C. PUTH, born Morristown, New Jersey, April 15, 1958; admitted to bar, 1992, Pennsylvania; 1993, District of Columbia; 1994, U.S. District Court for the District of Columbia; 1999, U.S. Court of Appeals for the District of Columbia Circuit. *Education:* University of Colorado (B.A., 1981); Georgetown University (J.D., 1992). Recipient: Trial Lawyer Of The Year, Trial Lawyers For Public Justice, 2000. *Member:* The District of Columbia Bar (Member, Labor & Employment Section); National Employment Lawyers Association; Metropolitan Washington Employment Lawyers Association (Member, Board of Directors, 1999—); Trial Lawyers For Public Justice. ***PRACTICE AREAS:*** Employment Law; Labor Law; Personal Injury; Litigation. ***Email:*** jputh@wf82.com

JEFFREY E. FALLON, born Reading, Pennsylvania, September 23, 1971; admitted to bar, 1996, Virginia and U.S. Court of Appeals, 4th Circuit; 1997, District of Columbia; 1999, U.S. District Court for District of Columbia. *Education:* Georgetown University (B.A., cum laude, 1993); George Washington University (J.D., 1996). Recipient: Trial Lawyer Of The Year, Trial Lawyers For Public Justice, 2000. *Member:* Metropolitan Washington Employment Lawyers

(This Listing Continued)

Association; National Employment Lawyers Association; Trial Lawyers for Public Justice. ***PRACTICE AREAS:*** Litigation; Employment and Labor; Public Utilities; Personal Injury. ***Email:*** jfallon@wf82.com

SCOTT MARTIN, born Des Moines, Iowa, July 9, 1974; admitted to bar, 2000, Maryland (Not admitted in District of Columbia). *Education:* University of Iowa (B.A., 1997); George Washington University (J.D., 2000). *Member:* Maryland State Bar Association, Inc. ***PRACTICE AREAS:*** Bankruptcy; Employment Law.

R. KENLY WEBSTER, P.C.

1201 CONNECTICUT AVENUE N.W., SIXTH FLOOR
WASHINGTON, D.C. 20036
Telephone: 202-822-3628
Fax: 202-659-0084
Email: kenlywebster@usa.net
URL: http://www.lawyers.com/rkenlywebster

Litigation, Criminal Law and Business Law.

FIRM PROFILE: Formerly an assistant United States attorney and a partner in Shaw Pittman, Mr. Webster provides counsel in matters involving criminal defense, general litigation, government investigations, alternative dispute resolution and corporate problem solving.

R. KENLY WEBSTER, born New York, N.Y., May 16, 1933; admitted to bar, 1961, New York (inactive); 1965, District of Columbia. *Education:* Princeton University (A.B., 1955); University of Virginia (LL.B., 1960). Assistant U.S. Attorney, 1965-1968. Principal Deputy General Counsel, Department of Army, 1968-1973. Recipient of the Department of Army Award for Distinguished Civilian Service, 1973. *Member:* The District of Columbia Bar. [Lt. (j.g.), U.S. Navy, 1955-1957]. ***PRACTICE AREAS:*** Litigation; Criminal Law; Business Law.

WECHSLER, SELZER & GURVITCH

CHARTERED

WASHINGTON, D.C.

(See Bethesda, Maryland)

Corporate and Individual Income Tax Planning, Taxation, Estate and Gift Tax Planning, Estate and Trust Administration, Pension and Profit Sharing Plans, Employee Benefits, Business and Real Property Acquisitions, Dispositions and Financings, Bankruptcy, Banking, Health Care, Technology Law, Creditors' Rights, Collections, Civil, Tax and Domestic Law Litigation before all Federal and State Courts in Maryland, District of Columbia and Virginia.

WEHNER & YORK

Established in 1993
1029 VERMONT AVENUE, N.W.
SUITE 300
WASHINGTON, D.C. 20005
Telephone: 202-543-2700
Facsimile: 202-543-2023
Email: mmyork@worldnet.att.net
URL: http://www.lawyers.com/w&ylaw

Reston, Virginia Office: 11860 Sunrise Valley Drive, Suite 100, 20191. Telephone: 703-476-8300. Fax: 703-476-8300.

Litigation including Commercial, White Collar, Media Law with special emphasis in the areas of Libel, Slander, First Amendment and Copyright Infringement.

FIRM PROFILE: The Wehner & York firm has both a National and Mid Atlantic Regional practice in Defense Litigation and Media Law.

MEMBERS OF FIRM

STEPHEN V. WEHNER (1954-2000).

MICHAEL M. YORK, born High Point, North Carolina, April 10, 1953; admitted to bar, 1979, North Carolina and Kentucky; 1993, District of Columbia, U.S. Supreme Court, U.S. Court of Appeals, District of Columbia, Fourth, Sixth and Federal Circuits and U.S. District Court, District of Columbia and Eastern and Western Districts of Kentucky. *Education:* University of Kentucky (B.A., 1974); University of North Carolina (J.D., 1978). Co-Author: "Ocean and Coastal Law," U.S. Department of Commerce, 1977. Staff Attorney, Kentucky Legislative Research Commission, 1978-1979. Reporter and Washington Correspondent, The Lexington Herald-Leader, 1979-1987. Investigative Reporter and Federal Courts Correspondent, The Washington Post, 1987-1993. Winner of the Pulitzer Prize for Investigative Reporting, 1986. *Member:* The District of

(This Listing Continued)

Columbia Bar; North Carolina State Bar; Kentucky Bar Association. ***PRACTICE AREAS:*** Media Law; Civil Litigation; Criminal Defense. ***Email:*** myork@worldnet.att.net

WEIL, GOTSHAL & MANGES LLP

A Limited Liability Partnership including Professional Corporations
1615 L STREET, N.W.
SUITE 700
WASHINGTON, D.C. 20036
Telephone: 202-682-7000
Telecopier: 202-857-0939; 857-0940
Telex: 440045
URL: http://www.weil.com

New York, N.Y. Office: 767 Fifth Avenue. Telephone: 212-310-8000. Cable Address: "Wegoma". Telex: 424281; 423144. Telecopier: 212-310-8007.
Dallas, Texas Office: 100 Crescent Court, Suite 1300. Telephone: 214-746-7700. Fax: 214-746-7777.
Houston, Texas Office: 700 Louisiana Street, Suite 1600. Telephone: 713-546-5000. Telecopier: 713-224-9511.
Redwood Shores, California Silicon Valley Office: 201 Redwood Shores Parkway, Telephone: 650-802-3000. Telecopier: 650-802-3100.
Miami, Florida Office: 701 Brickell Avenue, Suite 2100. Telephone: 305-577-3100. Telecopier: 305-374-7159.
Brussels, Belgium Office: 81 avenue Louise, Box 9-10, 1050 Brussels. Telephone: 011-32-2-543-7460. Telecopier: 011-32-2-543-7489.
Budapest, Hungary Office: Bank Center, Granite Tower, H-1944 Budapest. Telephone: 011-36-1-302-9100. Fax: 011-36-1-302-9110.
London, England Office: The Helicon, One South Place, London EC2M 2WG. Telephone: 011-44-207-903-1000. Telecopier: 011-44-207-903-0990.
Prague, Czech Republic Office: Charles Bridge Center, Krizovnicke nam. 1, 110 00 Prague 1, Czech Republic. Telephone: 011-420-2-2140-7300. Telecopier: 011-420-2-2140-7310.
Warsaw, Poland Office: Warsaw Financial Center, ul.Emilii Plater 53 00-113 Warsaw. Telephone: 011-48-22-520-4000. Telecopier: 011-48-22-520-4001.
Frankfurt am Main, Germany Office: Main Tower, Box 19, 31st Floor, Neue Mainzer Strasse 52-58, 60311 Frankfurt am Main. Telephone: 49 69 21659 600. Facsimile: 49 69 21659 699.

Advertising, Antitrust/Competition Law, Art, Auditing and Accounting Litigation, Aviation, Banking and Financial Services, Bankruptcy, Biotechnology, Business and Securities, Business Finance and Restructuring, Capital Markets, Civil RICO, Class Actions, Consumer Finance, Corporate, Corporate Governance, Criminal (white collar crime), Crisis Management, Cross-Border Transactions, Debt and Equity Offerings, Derivatives, Emerging Companies, Employee Benefits, Energy, Entertainment, Environmental, Executive Compensation, Financial Services, First Amendment, Franchising, Fringe Benefits, Government Investigations, Health Care, Insurance, Intellectual Property, International, International Dispute Resolution, International Trade, Internet, Joint Ventures, Labor and Employment, Lending, Litigation, Media and Communications, Mergers and Acquisitions, Oil and Gas, Patent, Pension Funds, Private Equity, Pro Bono, Product Liability, Project Finance, Property and Finance, Public Finance, Public Policy, Real Estate, Restructurings, RICO, SEC Enforcement, Securities Offerings, Sports, Structured Alliances, Structured Finance, Tax, Technology, Telecommunications, Toxic Torts, Trade Practices and Regulatory Law, Trade Secret Litigation, Trusts and Estates, Venture Capital, Workouts.

FIRM PROFILE: Weil, Gotshal & Manges LLP, now in its seventh decade, is a widely respected law firm, now one of the largest in the U.S. The firm has approximately 875 lawyers in 11 offices, including U.S. Offices in Dallas, Houston, Miami, New York, Silicon Valley and Washington, D.C., and international offices in Brussels, Budapest, London, Prague and Warsaw. We serve a remarkably diverse client base, including many of the leading companies in their fields, both in the United States and internationally. Weil, Gotshal & Manges has the breadth of a full-service law practice, with vast experience in virtually all areas of the law. The firm's departments are Business Finance and Restructuring, Business and Securities Litigation, Corporate, Litigation, Real Estate, Tax, Trade Practices and Regulatory Law, and Trusts and Estates. However, its many targeted interdisciplinary practice groups range from energy to project finance to high technology. Weil, Gotshal & Manges has experienced steady growth, from 150 lawyers in 1976 to its current size of approximately 875. Our strength is derived from our diversity, and we expect to continue to grow as we anticipate and respond to the changing needs of our dynamic client base.

PARTNERS

M. JEAN ANDERSON, born Casper, Wyoming, September 27, 1943; admitted to bar, 1975, District of Columbia and U.S. Court of Appeals for the District of Columbia Circuit; 1976, U.S. District Court for the District of

(This Listing Continued)

WEIL, GOTSHAL & MANGES LLP, Washington—Continued

Columbia; 1987, U.S. Court of International Trade; 1995, U.S. Court of Appeals for the Federal Circuit. *Education:* l' Institut d'Etudes Politiques, Universite de Paris, France (Certificat, 1964); Northwestern University (B.A., 1965); Georgetown University (J.D., 1975). Member, Mortar Board. Executive Editor, *Georgetown University Law Review*. Adjunct Professor, International Trade Law, American University, Washington College of Law, 1982-1986. Adjunct Professor, The GATT and U.S. Trade Agreements, Georgetown University Law Center, 1989-1992. Chief Counsel for International Trade, 1986-1988, Senior Trade Advisor and Special Counsel to the Under Secretary for International Trade, 1982-1986, U.S. Department of Commerce. *Member:* The District of Columbia Bar (Chairman, International Law Section, 1985-1986; Member, Steering Committee, 1984-1985); American Bar Association (Member, Section of International Law and Practice; Council Member, Section of International Law and Practice, 1995—; Chair, International Trade Committee, 1992-1993; Working Group on GATT Panel Review, 1993; Co-Chair: Canadian Law Committee, 1989-1990; Trade Law Working Group, EC 1992 Task Force, 1990; International Trade Committee, 1990-1992; North American Free Trade Agreement Task Force, 1991-1993; Member: Working Group on Multilateral Trade Agreements, 1993; Task Force on Antitrust and Market Access, 1994-1995; Trade and Antitrust Task Force, 1995—). ***PRACTICE AREAS:*** International Trade Policy; Litigation; International Trade Negotiations; GATT; NAFTA; Lobbying; Dispute Settlement. ***Email:*** jean.anderson@weil.com

RICHARD BEN-VENISTE, born New York, N.Y., 1943; admitted to bar, 1968, New York; 1975, District of Columbia. *Education:* Muhlenberg College (A.B., magna cum laude, 1964); Columbia University (LL.B., 1967) Harlan Fiske Stone Scholar; Northwestern University (LL.M., 1968). Awarded LL.D., honorary by Muhlenberg College, 1975. Co-Author: *Stonewall:* The Real Story of the Watergate Prosecution, Simon & Schuster, 1977. Assistant U.S. Attorney, Southern District, New York, 1968-1973 and Chief, Special Prosecution Section, 1971-1973. Chief, Watergate Task Force, Watergate Special Prosecution Force, U.S. Department of Justice, 1973-1975. Special Outside Counsel, Senate Subcommittee on Governmental Operations, 1976-1977. Special Counsel, (Minority) Senate Whitewater Committee, May, 1995-June, 1996. Co-founder, Trial Lawyers for Public Justice, 1981. Chairman, D.C. Advisory Committee on Prison Education Reform, 1984-1986. ***PRACTICE AREAS:*** Commercial Litigation; Securities Fraud; RICO; Tax Evasion; Antitrust; Bribery; Special Prosecution.

DAVID R. BERZ, born Chicago, Illinois, May 21, 1948; admitted to bar, 1973, District of Columbia; 1977, U.S. Supreme Court; 1985, New York. *Education:* George Washington University (B.A., 1970; J.D., with honors, 1973). Member, National Moot Court Team. Editor, *George Washington University Journal of International Law and Economics*, 1972-1973. Co-Author: *Environmental Law in Real Estate and Business Transactions*, Matthew Bender 1992; "Environmental Crimes," Obermaier and Morvillo, eds. *White Collar Crime*, Law Journal Seminars Press (1994). Author: "Keep Risk Reduction Decisions in the Boardroom-The Valdez Principles," *The Environmental Forum*, March/April, 1990. Co-Author: "Lender Liability Under CERCLA: Coping with the Eleventh Circuit's Ruling in Fleet Factors," *Banking Law Journal*, November/December, 1990, *Environmental Audit Handbook*, Executive Enterprises, 1987. Member, Board of Editors, *Chemical Waste Litigation Reporter*, 1986—. Environmental Editor, *Inside Litigation*, 1991—. *Member:* The District of Columbia Bar; Federal and American (Member, Environmental Controls Committee, Corporation, Banking and Business Law Section; Vice Chairman, Environmental Quality Control Committee, Section of Administrative Law, 1978-1981) Bar Associations; U.S. Chamber of Commerce (Member, Environment Committee, 1993—); Defense Research Institute (Member, Environmental Law Committee). ***PRACTICE AREAS:*** Environmental Law and Litigation; Product Liability; Insurance Coverage Litigation. ***Email:*** david.berz@weil.com

W. MICHAEL BOND, born Seneca, South Carolina, February 5, 1956; admitted to bar, 1980, Texas; 1991, District of Columbia. *Education:* University of South Carolina (B.S. in Accounting, magna cum laude, 1977); University of Virginia (J.D., 1980). ***PRACTICE AREAS:*** Real Estate; Securitization; Lending; Finance; Workouts and Restructurings; Leasing; Development. ***Email:*** michael.bond@weil.com

DAVID I. BOWER, born Wilkes-Barre, Pennsylvania, October 13, 1954; admitted to bar, 1979, Connecticut; 1988, District of Columbia. *Education:* University of Delaware (B.A., 1976); University of Pennsylvania (J.D., 1979); New York University Law School (LL.M., Taxation, 1984). ***Email:*** david.bower@weil.com

ANNEMARGARET CONNOLLY, born Methuen, Massachusetts, March 9, 1963; admitted to bar, 1988, Massachusetts; 1996, District of Columbia. *Education:* Syracuse University (A.B., B.S., 1984); George Washington University (J.D., 1988). ***Email:*** annemargaret.connolly@weil.com

CAROLYN M. DUPUY, born New Haven, Connecticut, June 4, 1950; admitted to bar, 1983, District of Columbia. *Education:* Mount Holyoke (B.A., 1972); University of Illinois (M.A., 1975); Georgetown University (J.D., 1983; M.L.T., 1988). Co-Author: "Taxation of Financial Instruments Equity Derivatives: Principles and Practice," with D. Kevin Dolan, 15 Va. Tax Review 161 (1996); "Final Conduit Regulations," with D. Kevin Dolan and Michael Walsh, 24 T.M.I.J. 522 (1995); "Foreign Losses," with D. Kevin Dolan, 71 TAXES 935 (1993); "The Foreign Tax Credit - Overview and Creditability Issues," with D. Kevin Dolan, 901 T.M. Portfolio (1993); "Revised and Final Proposed Section 904(d) Regulations," 21 T.M.I.J. 415 (1992); "The Cost Sharing Alternative and the Proposed Regulations," with D. Kevin Dolan, 21 T.M.I.J. 359 (1992); "Intercompany Pricing: Section 482," with D. Kevin Dolan, No. 301 Practicing Law Institute, Foreign Investment in the United States: A Practical Approach for the 1990s, 183 (1990); "The Future of the Foreign Tax Credit — Some Preliminary Observations for Reform," with D. Kevin Dolan, 18 T.M.I.J. 487 (1989). ***Email:*** carolyn.dupuy@weil.com

E. MICHAEL FLANAGAN, born Philadelphia, Pennsylvania, July 12, 1949; admitted to bar, 1979, District of Columbia and U.S. District Court for the District of Columbia. *Education:* United States Naval Academy (B.S., 1971); George Washington University (J.D., with high honors, 1978). Author: "Liability and Risk Management Issues," in *Discharge Planning: An Interdisciplinary Approach to Continuity of Care,* ed., Patricia J. Volland, National Health Publishing, 1988; "Certificate of Need and Licensure," in *Home Health Administration,* ed. Marilyn D. Harris, National Health Publishing, 1988; "Stark Reality," Health Progress, April, 1990. *Member:* Bar Association of the District of Columbia; American Bar Association; American Health Lawyers Association; National Association for Home Care; District of Columbia Health Care Association. [LT, U.S. Navy, 1971-1979]. ***PRACTICE AREAS:*** Health Law; Regulatory Law; Corporate Law. ***Email:*** michael.flanagan@weil.com

DAVID A. HICKERSON, born Hartselle, Alabama, April 20, 1961; admitted to bar, 1987, Virginia; 1988, District of Columbia. *Education:* Vanderbilt University (B.A., magna cum laude, 1983); University of Michigan (J.D., magna cum laude, 1987). Phi Beta Kappa. Order of the Coif. Member, Michigan Law Review, 1985-1987. ***PRACTICE AREAS:*** Tax Litigation; Contract Disputes; Business and Partnership Disputes; Patent, Copyright and Trademark Litigation; White Collar Criminal Litigation. ***Email:*** david.hickerson@weil.com

DAVID B. HIRD, born New York, N.Y., January 31, 1950; admitted to bar, 1977, District of Columbia; 1978, U.S. District Court, District of Columbia and U.S. Court of Appeals, District of Columbia Circuit; 1981, U.S. Supreme Court; 1990, U.S. District Court, District of Arizona; 1997, U.S. Court of Appeals, Fifth and Eleventh Circuits. *Education:* Cornell University (A.B., 1972); University of Michigan (A.M., 1973); New York University (J.D., 1977). Order of the Coif. Associate Editor, *New York University Law Review*, 1976-1977. ***PRACTICE AREAS:*** Litigation; Environmental Law; Insurance Law; Superfund; RCRA; TSCA; Toxic Torts; Environmental Compliance.

PETER D. ISAKOFF, born New York, N.Y., February 4, 1951; admitted to bar, 1979, New York; 1982, District of Columbia. *Education:* Columbia University (B.A., cum laude, 1973; J.D., 1978). James Kent Scholar. Editor, *Columbia Law Review*, 1977-1978. Co-Author: "Environmental Crimes," Obermaier and Morvillo, eds. *White Collar Crime*, Law Journal Seminars Press; "Strategic Discovery in the Complex Case," Richard A. Rothman, ed., *Litigating Complex Cases: From the Inside Out*, Glasser Legal Works. Author: "Unconstitutional Discrimination in Choice of Law," 77 *Columbia Law Review* 272, 1977. Law Clerk to: Chief Judge Wilfred Feinberg, U.S. Court of Appeals for the Second Circuit, 1978-1979; Associate Justice John Paul Stevens, U.S. Supreme Court, 1979-1980. Trial Attorney, Criminal Division, U.S. Department of Justice, 1980-1983. *Member:* The District of Columbia Bar. ***PRACTICE AREAS:*** Civil, Criminal and Tax Litigation; Government Contracts Fraud; Securities Fraud; Antitrust; Trade Secret Litigation; Reinsurance; Food and Drug Litigation; RICO.

ROBERT C. ODLE, JR., born Port Huron, Michigan, February 15, 1944; admitted to bar, 1969, Michigan; 1985, District of Columbia and U.S. Supreme Court. *Education:* Wayne State University (B.A., 1966); Detroit College of Law (J.D., with honors, 1969; Doctor of Laws, Honoris Causa, 1992). Delta Theta Phi. Assistant Secretary, U.S. Department of Energy, 1981-1985. Deputy Assistant Secretary, U.S. Department of Housing and Urban Development, 1973-1976. Staff Assistant to the President of the United States, 1969-1971. *Member:* The District of Columbia Bar; State Bar of Michigan. ***PRACTICE AREAS:*** Administrative Law; Energy Law; Environmental Law; Government Law; International Law; Legislative Practice.

CHARLES E. ROH, JR., born New York, N.Y., April 18, 1947; admitted to bar, 1973, District of Columbia. *Education:* Princeton University (B.A., cum laude, 1969); Harvard Law School (J.D., 1973). Deputy Chief Negotiator, NAFTA, 1991-1993. United States Trade Representative, Associate General Counsel, 1983-1989. Legal Counsel, USTR Mission to GATT, 1980-1983. Member: Senate Finance Staff, 1979-1980; Department of State, Office of Legal Affairs, 1973-1979. Assistant United States Trade Representative, 1989-1994. *Member:* The District of Columbia Bar; American Bar Association. ***LANGUAGES:*** French, Spanish. ***PRACTICE AREAS:*** International Trade and Investment; Public Policy. ***Email:*** chip.roh@weil.com

(This Listing Continued)

STANLEY SPORKIN, born 1932; admitted to bar, 1958, District of Columbia. *Education:* Pennsylvania State University (B.A.); Yale University (LL.B.). ***Email:*** stanley.sporkin@weil.com

STANLEY M. SPRACKER, born Milwaukee, Wisconsin, December 17, 1952; admitted to bar, 1980, District of Columbia; 1981, U.S. District Court for the District of Columbia; 1985, U.S. Court of Appeals for the District of Columbia Circuit; 1986, U.S. Supreme Court. *Education:* University of Wisconsin (B.A., with highest honors, 1973); Jewish Theological Seminary (M.A., 1977); University of Chicago (J.D., 1980). Phi Beta Kappa, Phi Kappa Phi. Co-Author: *Environmental Issues in Real Estate and Business Transactions*, Matthew Bender, October 1992; "The Treatment of Environmental Matters in Bankruptcy Cases," *Bankruptcy Developments Journal*, 1995; "A Trial Lawyer's Perspective on the Pollution Exclusion," *The Environmental Law Reporter*, February 1995; "Sovereignty and the Regulation of International Business in the Environmental Area: An American Viewpoint," *Canada-United States Law Journal*, 1994; "Environmental Protection and International Trade: NAFTA As A Means of Eliminating Environmental Contamination as a Competitive Advantage," *Georgetown International Environmental Law Review* (Summer 1993); "Dolphins and Tuna: Renewed Attention on the Future of Free Trade and Protection of the Environment," *Columbia Journal of Environmental Law* (Spring 1993); "Lender Liability Under CERCLA," *Columbia Business Law Review* (Winter 1991). Co-Chair: "Annual Environmental Litigation Institute," (Prentice-Hall) 1992, 1993, 1994, 1995; "Environmental Issues in Business Transactions," (Prentice-Hall), 1988, 1989, 1990. *Member:* The District of Columbia Bar (Member, Section on Natural Resources, Energy and Environmental Law); American Bar Association. ***PRACTICE AREAS:*** Environmental Law; Health and Safety Law; EPA; OSHA. ***Email:*** stanley.spracker@weil.com

BRUCE H. TURNBULL, born Iowa City, Iowa, May 19, 1951; admitted to bar, 1976, District of Columbia; 1984, U.S. District Court for the District of Columbia. *Education:* Cornell University (B.A., 1973); George Washington University (J.D., with honors, 1976). *Member:* The District of Columbia Bar; American Bar Association. ***PRACTICE AREAS:*** International Trade; Intellectual Property Policy; Telecommunications. ***Email:*** bruce.turnbull@weil.com

KARL T. WALLI, born Almont, Michigan, January 28, 1956; admitted to bar, 1982, Virginia (Not admitted in District of Columbia). *Education:* University of Tennessee (B.A., 1979); University of North Carolina (J.D., 1982). ***Email:*** karl.walli@weil.com

WALTER E. ZALENSKI, admitted to bar, 1984, District of Columbia and Maryland. *Education:* George Washington University (B.A., with distinction and special honors, 1981; J.D., 1984). ***PRACTICE AREAS:*** Banking. ***Email:*** walter.zalenski@weil.com

COUNSEL

GREGORY HUSISIAN, born Elmira, New York, December 29, 1964; admitted to bar, 1992, New York; 1993, District of Columbia. *Education:* Cornell University (B.A., 1987; J.D., magna cum laude, 1990).

MICHAEL LYLE, born Rochester, New York, October 11, 1963; admitted to bar, 1988, Illinois (Not admitted in District of Columbia). *Education:* University of Rochester (B.A., 1985); Case Western Reserve University (J.D., cum laude, 1988). ***PRACTICE AREAS:*** Litigation.

LORETTA JO ROBY, born Moorehead, Minnesota, November 2, 1963; admitted to bar, 1990, New York; 1998, District of Columbia. *Education:* St. Mary's University (B.B.A., 1986); University of Texas at Austin (J.D., 1989); New York University (LL.M., 1990). Certified Public Accountant, Texas, 1992. *Member:* American Bar Association (Member, Tax Section); National Association of Bond Lawyers. ***PRACTICE AREAS:*** Tax Law.

RESIDENT ASSOCIATES

SANDRA M. AISTARS, born Syracuse, New York, September 22, 1968; admitted to bar, 1996, Maryland (Not admitted in District of Columbia). *Education:* Bard College (B.A., 1990); University of Baltimore (J.D., summa cum laude, 1996).

TODD W. BETKE, born Evanston, Illinois, August 27, 1967; admitted to bar, 1994, Illinois; 1997, District of Columbia. *Education:* Colgate University (B.A., 1989); ITT/Chicago-Kent College of Law (J.D., 1994).

GREGG S. BUKSBAUM, born Huntington, New York, August 6, 1971; admitted to bar, 1997, New York and U.S. District Court, Southern and Eastern Districts of New York; 1998, District of Columbia. *Education:* University of Michigan (B.A., 1993); Brooklyn Law School (J.D., 1996). *Member:* New York State and American Bar Associations. ***PRACTICE AREAS:*** Corporate Law; Private Equity. ***Email:*** gregg.buksbaum@weil.com

CHRISTOPHER T. CARDINALE, born Kingston, New York, April 5, 1971; admitted to bar, 1999, New York (Not admitted in District of Columbia). *Education:* Providence College (B.A., 1993); University at Albany (M.A., 1995); American University (J.D., cum laude, 1998). ***LANGUAGES:*** Spanish. ***PRACTICE AREAS:*** International Trade; Corporate Law. ***Email:*** christopher.cardinale@weil.com

JEFFREY L. CIMBALO, born Seal Beach, California, September 11, 1967; admitted to bar, 1999, New York (Not admitted in District of Columbia). *Education:* Georgetown University (B.S.F.S., 1989); John F. Kennedy School of Government, Harvard University (M.P.A., 1993); University of Virginia (J.D., 1998). ***PRACTICE AREAS:*** Litigation. ***Email:*** jeffrey.cimbalo@weil.com

AMY T. DIXON, born Columbus, Ohio, September 26, 1972; admitted to bar, 1997, Virginia; 2000, District of Columbia. *Education:* University of North Carolina at Chapel Hill (B.A., 1994); University of Notre Dame (J.D., 1997).

CONNIE M. ERICSON, born Kansas City, Missouri, August 24, 1950; admitted to bar, 1999, Texas (Not admitted in District of Columbia). *Education:* Gustavus Adolphus College (B.A., 1970); University of Houston Law Center (J.D., 1999). Order of the Coif. ***PRACTICE AREAS:*** Environmental Law. ***Email:*** connie.ericson@weil.com

LISA R. FINE, born Buffalo, New York, December 11, 1970; admitted to bar, 1999, New York (Not admitted in District of Columbia). *Education:* Tufts University (B.A., 1993); Georgetown University Law Center (J.D., 1998). ***Email:*** lisa.fine@weil.com

MELANIE A. FRANK, born Philadelphia, Pennsylvania, April 29, 1972; admitted to bar, 1998, Maryland (Not admitted in District of Columbia). *Education:* University of Florida (B.A., 1994); Catholic University of America (J.D., 1998). U.S. Department of Commerce. ***LANGUAGES:*** French. ***PRACTICE AREAS:*** International Trade. ***Email:*** melanie.frank@weil.com

PETER M. FRIEDMAN, born New York, N.Y., August 2, 1972; admitted to bar, 1998, Illinois; 1999, U.S. Court of Appeals, Seventh Circuit (Not admitted in District of Columbia). *Education:* Trinity College (B.A., 1994); Northwestern University (J.D., cum laude, 1998). Order of the Coif. Author, 88 Journal of Criminal Law and Criminology 683, 1998. Law Clerk, U.S. Court of Appeals Hon. Joel M. Flaum, 1998-1999. Federal Communications Commission, 1999-2000. Acting Legal Advisor, Cable Services Bureau. ***PRACTICE AREAS:*** Litigation; Public Policy. ***Email:*** peter.m.friedman@weil.com

JACQUELINE M. GORDON, born Washington, D.C., December 10, 1956; admitted to bar, 1982, Texas; 1985, District of Columbia; 1987, Virginia. *Education:* University of Florida (B.A., with high honors, 1979); University of Virginia (J.D., 1982). Phi Beta Kappa. *Member:* American Corporate Counsel Association. ***LANGUAGES:*** Spanish. ***PRACTICE AREAS:*** Real Estate; Real Estate Finance; Corporate Transactions; Secondary Financing; Health Care.

JOANNE M. GUERRERA, born New York, N.Y., April 9, 1969; admitted to bar, 1994, Virginia; 1996, District of Columbia. *Education:* Boston College (B.A., 1991); George Washington University (J.D., 1994).

JAHNA M. HARTWIG, born San Diego, California, October 4, 1971; admitted to bar, 2000, California (Not admitted in District of Columbia). *Education:* George Washington University (B.A., 1993; J.D., 1999). Law Clerk to the Honorable, Thomas J. Aquilino, Jr., 1999-2001. ***PRACTICE AREAS:*** International Trade. ***Email:*** jahna.hartwig@weil.com

GEORGE J. HAZEL, born Queens, New York, March 19, 1975; admitted to bar, 1999, Virginia and U.S. District Court, Eastern District of Virginia; 2000, District of Columbia and U.S. District Court, Western District of Virginia. *Education:* Morehouse College (B.A., 1996); Georgetown University Law Center (J.D., 1999). ***PRACTICE AREAS:*** Litigation. ***Email:*** george.hazel@weil.com

P.J. HIMELFARB, born Flushing, New York, May 18, 1965; admitted to bar, 1991, Maryland and District of Columbia. *Education:* University of Maryland (B.S., magna cum laude, 1986; J.D., 1991). Member, 1989-1990, Notes and Comments Editor, 1990-1991, Maryland Law Review.

TIMOTHY HRUBY, born Ithaca, New York, May 28, 1968; admitted to bar, 1995, New York; 1997, District of Columbia. *Education:* University of Arizona (B.A., 1990); Georgetown University (J.D./M.S.F.S., 1994). ***LANGUAGES:*** French. ***PRACTICE AREAS:*** International Trade. ***Email:*** timothy.hruby@weil.com

CHRISTINE P. HSU, born Philadelphia, Pennsylvania, February 27, 1971; admitted to bar, 1996, Maryland; 1997, District of Columbia. *Education:* Harvard-Radcliffe Colleges (A.B., cum laude, 1993); Georgetown University Law Center (J.D., 1996).

KRISTIN G. KING, born Washington, D.C., September 21, 1968; admitted to bar, 1998, Virginia; 2000, District of Columbia. *Education:* Virginia Tech (B.A., 1990); George Mason University (J.D., 1997). ***PRACTICE AREAS:*** Technology Law; Public Policy. ***Email:*** kristin.king@weil.com

HOLLY E. WASHINGTON LOISEAU, born Charlotte Amalie, St. Thomas, U.S.V.I., March 1, 1970; admitted to bar, 1995, Pennsylvania and Maryland; 1996, District of Columbia. *Education:* University of Virginia (B.A., 1991); George Washington University (J.D., 1994).

(This Listing Continued)

WEIL, GOTSHAL & MANGES LLP, Washington—Continued

JOSEPH D. LOONEY, born Washington, D.C., July 31, 1971; admitted to bar, 1996, Maryland; 1997, Virginia; 1998, District of Columbia. *Education:* Lee University (B.A., 1992); University of Maryland (J.D., with honors, 1996). ***PRACTICE AREAS:*** Consumer Finance; Banking. ***Email:*** joseph.looney@weil.com

SCOTT MABERRY, born Wheat Ridge, Colorado, April 12, 1964; admitted to bar, 1994, New York; 1996, District of Columbia. *Education:* Northwestern University (B.S., 1988); Georgetown University (M.S., 1994); Georgetown University Law Center (J.D., 1994).

TERRI T. MALLETT, born Washington, D.C.; admitted to bar, 1994, Georgia; 1995, District of Columbia. *Education:* Howard University (B.S., 1984); Georgia State University (J.D., 1994). *Member:* District of Columbia Bar; State Bar of Georgia. ***Email:*** terri.mallett@weil.com

JOSEPH F. MILLER, born Westwood, New Jersey, January 25, 1960; admitted to bar, 1990, New Jersey; 1994, New York and Maryland (Not admitted in District of Columbia). *Education:* State University of New York Maritime College (B.S., 1982); New York Law School (J.D., 1990). *Member:* Maryland State and American Bar Associations. ***PRACTICE AREAS:*** Real Estate. ***Email:*** joseph.miller@weil.com

JOHN B. O'LOUGHLIN, JR., born Camden, New Jersey, October 21, 1961; admitted to bar, 1996, Maryland; 1998, District of Columbia. *Education:* Towson University (B.S., 1983); University of Maryland School of Law (J.D., 1996). Associate Editor, Maryland Law Review. *Member:* District of Columbia Bar; American Bar Association. ***PRACTICE AREAS:*** Environmental Law; OSHA; Product Safety. ***Email:*** john.o'loughlin@weil.com

THERESA M. REGAN, born Kansas City, Missouri, February 9, 1967; admitted to bar, 1997, Missouri (Not admitted in District of Columbia). *Education:* University of Kansas (B.A., 1990); Washington University (J.D., 1997). ***PRACTICE AREAS:*** Securities; Corporate Law. ***Email:*** theresa.regan@weil.com

JOHN M. RYAN, born Harvey, Illinois, August 10, 1961; admitted to bar, 1993, Maryland; 1994, District of Columbia. *Education:* University of Wisconsin-Madison (B.A., with distinction, 1982); George Washington University (M.A., 1986); Georgetown University Law Center (J.D., cum laude, 1993).

ROGER N. SIMON, born Washington, D.C., October 6, 1965; admitted to bar, 1993, Maryland; 1994, District of Columbia. *Education:* Tufts University (B.A., cum laude, 1987); George Washington University (J.D., with honors, 1993). *Member:* American Bar Association. ***PRACTICE AREAS:*** Real Estate Finance; Mortgage Securitization; Loans. ***Email:*** roger.simon@weil.com

DAVID N. SOUTHARD, born Rochester, Michigan, February 6, 1970; admitted to bar, 1999, Virginia and U.S. District Court, Eastern District of Virginia; 2000, U.S. District Court, Western District of Virginia; 2001, District of Columbia. *Education:* James Madison University (B.S., 1992); American University (J.D., 1999). International Law Review. ***PRACTICE AREAS:*** Litigation; Regulatory Law. ***Email:*** david.southard@weil.com

J. SLOANE STRICKLER, born New Orleans, January 14, 1969; admitted to bar, 2001, New York (Not admitted in District of Columbia). *Education:* University of California, Santa Barbara (B.A., 1993); George Washington University (J.D., 2001). ***PRACTICE AREAS:*** International Trade. ***Email:*** sloane.strickler@weil.com

ADAM P. STROCHAK, born Philadelphia, Pennsylvania, September 20, 1965; admitted to bar, 1993, Maryland; 1994, U.S. District Court for the District of Maryland and U.S. District Court for the District of Arizona; 1996, District of Columbia. *Education:* University of Vermont (B.A., cum laude, 1987); George Washington University National Law Center (J.D., with honors, 1993).

MAUREEN TESTONI, born Oak Park, Illinois; admitted to bar, 1997, Virginia; 1998, District of Columbia. *Education:* University of Chicago (B.A., 1988); George Washington University (J.D., 1997).

HELLE R. WEEKE, born Copenhagen, Denmark, October 16, 1964; admitted to bar, 1992, New York and North Carolina; 1995, Virginia; 1998, District of Columbia. *Education:* University of Copenhagen, Copenhagen, Denmark (Candidata Juris, 1990); Duke University (LL.M., 1991); John Hopkins University, Paul H. Nitze School of Advanced International Studies (Master of International Public Policy, 2000). ***PRACTICE AREAS:*** International Trade.

LARRY I. WILLIS, born Chicago, Illinois, January 7, 1967; admitted to bar, 1996, Illinois; 1998, District of Columbia. *Education:* University of Iowa (B.A., 1990); John Marshall Law School (J.D., 1995). Transportation Trades Department, AFL-CIO. ***PRACTICE AREAS:*** Public Policy; Transportation; Communications Law; Technology Law; E-Commerce. ***Email:*** larry.willis@weil.com

VINCENT S. WONG, born Rangoon, Burma, October 30, 1970; admitted to bar, 1997, New York and New Jersey (Not admitted in District of Columbia). *Education:* Bernard M. Baruch College of the City University of New York (B.B.A., magna cum laude, 1992); Brooklyn Law School (J.D., 1996). *Member:* New York State Bar Association; New York County Lawyers Association; Asian American Bar Association of New York. ***LANGUAGES:*** Burmese, Chinese. ***PRACTICE AREAS:*** Corporate Law. ***Email:*** vincent.wong@weil.com

(For complete biographical data on New York, New York, Dallas, Texas, Houston, Texas, Menlo Park, California, Miami, Florida, Brussels, Belgium, Budapest, Hungary, London, England, Prague, Czech Republic, Warsaw, Poland and Frankfurt am Main, Germany, see Professional Biographies at those locations)

WEINER BRODSKY SIDMAN KIDER PC

1300 NINETEENTH STREET, N.W., FIFTH FLOOR
WASHINGTON, D.C. 20036
Telephone: 202-628-2000
Telecopier: 202-628-2011
Email: info@wbsk.com
URL: http://www.wbsk.com

General Administrative, Corporate, Legislative and Litigation Practice. Finance, Housing, Mortgage Banking, Consumer Credit and Regulatory Compliance, Real Estate, Transportation, Mergers and Acquisitions and Financial Institutions.

FIRM PROFILE: Weiner Brodsky Sidman Kider PC has a national practice specializing in providing legal counsel to the mortgage finance and transportation industries. The firm represents clients in complex commercial transactions and private litigation, including the defense of class action lawsuits, and advises clients on a broad range of regulatory and governmental matters.

Weiner Brodsky Sidman Kider PC attorneys have been involved in the real estate and mortgage finance industry for over two decades, and our firm is one of the leading law firms in the country practicing in this area. A number of the firm's members have served as senior officials with the U.S. Department of Housing and Urban Development and are experts in housing finance matters. Weiner Brodsky Sidman Kider PC assists clients with various real estate and mortgage banking related transactions, including purchases and sales of portfolios of mortgage assets, the acquisition and sale of mortgage companies, the structuring of new business opportunities, consumer credit compliance issues, manufactured housing, reverse mortgages, home improvement loans, the defense of complex class action litigation, and state law licensing and other requirements.

The firm's transportation group specializes in representation of short line and regional railroads. In addition to assisting clients to acquire and finance railroad properties, Weiner Brodsky Sidman Kider PC has an active practice before all federal regulators of railroads. The firm has extensive expertise in matters arising under the Railway Labor Act, including the negotiation of collective bargaining agreements. The transportation group also represents companies that manufacture trucks and truck equipment on a broad range of issues, including compliance with federal regulations and federal excise tax matters.

RICHARD J. ANDREANO, JR., born El Paso, Texas, October 28, 1958; admitted to bar, 1983, District of Columbia; 1984, Virginia. *Education:* State University of New York, Oneonta (B.A., with high honors, 1980); George Washington University (J.D., with honors, 1983). Editor: RESPA-Escrow Issues, 1995. Co-author: "Capital Rules Cast New Light on Purchased Servicing," Savings Institutions, May 1990; "Purchased Servicing Faces Stricter Limits," Savings Institutions, June 1991. *Member:* The District of Columbia Bar; Virginia State Bar; American Bar Association. ***PRACTICE AREAS:*** Mortgage Banking; Financial Institutions; Consumer Credit; Regulatory Compliance; Mergers and Acquisitions. ***Email:*** andreano@wbsk.com

JAMES A. BRODSKY, born New York, N.Y., May 7, 1945; admitted to bar, 1973, District of Columbia. *Education:* Cornell University (B.S., 1967); Columbia University (M.S., 1968); Georgetown University (J.D., 1972). Editor, Georgetown Law Journal, 1970-1972. Law Clerk to Hon. Thomas Flannery, U.S. District Court for District of Columbia, 1971-1972. Court Law Clerk, U.S. Court of Appeals for the District of Columbia Circuit, 1972-1973. Deputy Assistant Secretary, U.S. Department of Housing and Urban Development, 1976-1977. Commissioner, 1982-1991, and Chairman, Housing Opportunities Commission of Montgomery County, Maryland. Chairman, Washington Area Housing Partnership, 1991-1996; Director and Chairman, Montgomery Housing Partnership, Inc., 1999—. ***PRACTICE AREAS:*** Mortgages; Real Estate Finance; Mortgage Banking; Mergers and Acquisitions; Asset Sales; Regulatory Compliance; Federal Agency Proceedings. ***Email:*** brodsky@wbsk.com

JO A. DEROCHE, born Marquette, Michigan, August 14,1949; admitted to bar, 1991, Michigan; 1993, District of Columbia. *Education:* University of Michigan (B.A., 1971); Detroit College of Law (J.D., cum laude, 1991). Labor Attorney/Manager Labor Relations, CN North America, Detroit, Michigan, 1985-1992. Labor Relations Officer, National Railroad Passenger Corporation, 1982-1985. Chief Labor Cost and Productivity Analysis, U.S. Railway Association, 1980-1982. Member, Association for Transportation Law, Logistics and Policy. *Member:* State Bar of Michigan; The District of Columbia Bar; Ameri-

(This Listing Continued)

can Bar Association (Member, Railway and Airline Labor Law Committee). ***PRACTICE AREAS:*** Railway Labor Act; Collective Bargaining Agreement; Negotiation and Arbitration; Transportation; Regulatory Compliance. ***Email:*** deroche@wbsk.com

CYNTHIA L. GILMAN, born Dayton, Ohio, January 20, 1960; admitted to bar, 1985, California; 1996, District of Columbia. *Education:* Emory University (B.A., with honors, 1982); University of San Diego (J.D., cum laude, 1985). University of San Diego School of Law Law Review, 1983-1985. *Member:* State Bar of California; The District of Columbia Bar. ***PRACTICE AREAS:*** Mortgage Banking Law; Financial Institutions; Corporate Litigation. ***Email:*** gilman@wbsk.com

DON J. HALPERN, born Bronx, New York, May 2, 1962; admitted to bar, 1988, Pennsylvania; 1990, District of Columbia; 1992, Virginia, U.S. Court of Appeals, Fourth Circuit and U.S. District Court, Eastern District of Virginia. *Education:* University of Pennsylvania (B.A., 1984); Rutgers University (J.D., 1987); New York University School of Law (LL.M., 1991). Associate Editor, Rutgers Law Journal, 1985-1987. *Member:* The District of Columbia Bar; Virginia State Bar; Pennsylvania State and American Bar Associations. ***PRACTICE AREAS:*** Mortgage and Real Estate Finance; Mortgage Banking; Mergers and Acquisitions; Asset Sales; Corporate Law; Regulatory Compliance; Federal Agency Proceedings. ***Email:*** halpern@wbsk.com

MITCHEL H. KIDER, born New York, N.Y., November 24, 1956; admitted to bar, 1981, District of Columbia; 1982, U.S. District Court for the District of Columbia; 1983, U.S. Court of Appeals for the District of Columbia Circuit; 1984, New York and California; 1987, U.S. District Court, Central District of California; 1991, U.S. Court of Appeals, Seventh Circuit; 1995, U.S. Court of Appeals, Tenth Circuit and U.S. District Court, Eastern District of New York; 1998, U.S. District Court, District of Maryland; 1999, U.S. District Court, Northern District of California and U.S. District Court, Western District of Michigan; 2000, U.S. Court of Appeals, Fourth Circuit; 2001, U.S. District Court, Central District of Illinois and U.S. District Court, Northern District of Illinois. *Education:* University of Wisconsin (B.A., 1978); Washington University (J.D., 1981). Recipient, Milton F. Napier Trial Award, 1981. Staff Member, 1979-1980 and Recent Developments Editor, 1980-1981, Urban Law Annual. Columnist, "The Mortgage Counselor," Secondary Marketing Executive. Author: *RESPA Escrow Issues,* Mortgage Bankers Association of America, 1995; *Quality Control for Mortgage Servicers,* Mortgage Bankers Association of America, 1991; "RESPA: The Forgotten Issues," Mortgage Banking, January 1991. Co-Author: *Handbook of Quality Control,* Mortgage Bankers Association of America, 1993; "Another December Surprise," Mortgage Banking, December 1992; "Recent Developments in Urban Redevelopment," 21 Urban Law Annual 317, 1981. Faculty Fellow, Mortgage Bankers Association of America. Faculty Member and Lecturer, School of Mortgage Banking, 1991. Lecturer, Learning Center for Real Estate Finance, 1991. Trial Attorney, Office of General Counsel, U.S. Department of Housing and Urban Development, 1981-1986. *Member:* The District of Columbia Bar; State Bar of California; New York State and American (Member, Litigation Division) Bar Associations. ***PRACTICE AREAS:*** Litigation; Mortgages; Real Estate Finance; Mortgage Banking; Mergers and Acquisitions; Asset Sales; Regulatory Compliance; Federal Agency Proceedings; Financial Institutions. ***Email:*** kider@wbsk.com

MARK H. SIDMAN, born Brooklyn, New York, February 4, 1956; admitted to bar, 1980, Pennsylvania; 1982, District of Columbia. *Education:* Hobart College (B.A., 1977); University of Pittsburgh (J.D., 1980). Staff Member, University of Pittsburgh Law Review, 1978-1980. Special Assistant to the Executive Vice President, United States Railway Association, 1981-1982. *Member:* The District of Columbia Bar; Pennsylvania Bar Association (inactive). ***PRACTICE AREAS:*** Transportation; Mergers and Acquisitions; Asset Sales; Regulatory Compliance; Federal Taxation. ***Email:*** sidman@wbsk.com

HARVEY E. WEINER, born New York, N.Y., December 30, 1944; admitted to bar, 1969, New York; 1972, District of Columbia. *Education:* Queens College of the City University of New York (B.A., 1966); New York University (J.D., cum laude, 1969). Co-Author: "Federal Legislation Affecting Mortgage Credit," 38 The Business Lawyer, 1311, May, 1983; "Capital Rules Cast New Light on Purchased Servicing," Savings Institutions, May 1990; "Purchased Servicing Faces Stricter Limits," Savings Institutions, June 1991. Attorney Advisor, Office of the General Counsel, 1969-1974, Special Assistant to the Assistant Secretary for Housing Production and Mortgage Credit FHA Commissioner, 1974-1976 and Deputy Assistant Secretary for Regulatory Programs—Interstate Land Sales Administrator, 1976-1977, U.S. Department of Housing and Urban Development. *Member:* The District of Columbia Bar; Federal and American Bar Associations. ***PRACTICE AREAS:*** Mortgages; Real Estate Finance; Mortgage Banking; Mergers and Acquisitions; Asset Sales; Regulatory Compliance; Federal Agency Proceedings; Financial Institutions. ***Email:*** weiner@wbsk.com

OF COUNSEL

DONALD C. BROWN JR., born Odessa, Texas, November 16, 1949; admitted to bar, 1989, Virginia; 1992, District of Columbia. *Education:* Southern Methodist University (B.F.A., 1971); University of Connecticut (J.D., summa cum laude, 1989). Editor-in-Chief, University of Connecticut Law Review, 1988-1989. *Member:* Virginia State Bar; The District of Columbia and American Bar Associations. ***PRACTICE AREAS:*** Litigation. ***Email:*** brown@wbsk.com

SUSAN L. KORYTKOWSKI, born Buffalo, New York, January 10, 1953; admitted to bar, 1981, District of Columbia. *Education:* D'Youville College (B.A., 1974); University of North Carolina (J.D., 1981). Counsel, Federal Deposit Insurance Corporation (1993-1995). Trial Attorney, Civil Division, U.S. Department of Justice (1986-1993). Attorney-Advisor, Office of Administrative Proceedings and Program Enforcement, U.S. Department of Housing and Urban Development (1984-1986). ***PRACTICE AREAS:*** Litigation. ***Email:*** korytkowski@wbsk.com

SHERRI L. LEDNER, born Denville, New Jersey, September 28, 1964; admitted to bar, 1989, Maryland; 1990, District of Columbia; 1992, Virginia and U.S. District Court, District of Maryland. *Education:* University of Maryland (B.A., 1986); George Washington University (J.D., with honors, 1989). *Member:* Maryland State and American Bar Associations; Virginia State Bar; The District of Columbia Bar; Women in Housing and Finance. ***PRACTICE AREAS:*** Mortgage Banking Law; Consumer Finance; Regulatory Compliance. ***Email:*** ledner@wbsk.com

JAMES M. MILANO, born Baton Rouge, Louisiana, August 20, 1960; admitted to bar, 1989, Louisiana; 1992, Georgia; 1996, Virginia; 2000, Maryland; 2001, District of Columbia. *Education:* Louisiana State University (B.A., 1983; J.D., 1989); Emory University (LL.M., 1991). Member, Consumer Financial Services Subcommittee; Manufactured Housing Institute Finance Lawyers Committee. Staff Attorney, State of Louisiana First Circuit Court of Appeals. Corporate Counsel, Fleet Finance, Inc.; Legal Counsel, Approved Financial, Inc.; Vice-President, Legal Counsel, Dynex Financial, Inc. *Member:* Louisiana State and American Bar Associations; State Bar of Georgia; Virginia State Bar. ***PRACTICE AREAS:*** Mortgage Banking Law; Consumer Credit; Regulatory Compliance; Real Estate; Financial Institutions. ***Email:*** milano@wbsk.com

DAVID M. SOUDERS, born St. Louis, Missouri, April 29, 1955; admitted to bar, 1985, Missouri; 1993, District of Columbia; 1996, U.S. Court of Federal Claims. *Education:* Holy Cross College (B.A., 1977); Washington University (J.D., 1985). Order of the Coif, Law Review, Washington University. Law Clerk to Judge Nangle, Chief Judge, U.S. District Court, Eastern District of Missouri, 1985-1986. Civil Division, U.S. Department of Justice, 1986-2000. *Member:* The Missouri Bar; District of Columbia Bar Association. [Nuclear Power Program, U.S. Navy, 1977-1982.]. ***PRACTICE AREAS:*** Litigation; Regulatory Compliance; Administrative Law. ***Email:*** souders@wbsk.com

---

ANDREW N. CLINE, born Syracuse, New York, January 26, 1972; admitted to bar, 1998, Louisiana (Not admitted in District of Columbia). *Education:* George Washington University (B.A., 1994); Tulane University of Louisiana (J.D., cum laude, 1997). *Member:* Louisiana State Bar Association. ***PRACTICE AREAS:*** Mortgage Banking Law; Consumer Finance. ***Email:*** cline@wbsk.com

TROY W. GARRIS, born Corpus Christi, Texas, March 7, 1966; admitted to bar, 1998, New York and Texas; 2001, District of Columbia. *Education:* University of Houston (B.A., 1990); American University Washington College of Law (J.D., magna cum laude, 1997). Taiheiyou Law Office, Osaka, Japan, 1998-1999. U.S. Surface Transportation Board, Office of General Counsel, 1999-2000. ***LANGUAGES:*** Japanese. ***PRACTICE AREAS:*** Transportation; Corporate Law; Mergers and Acquisitions; Railway Labor Law; Surface Transportation; Highways; Regulatory Law. ***Email:*** garris@wbsk.com

KAREN RUTH GUSTAVSON, born Suffern, New York, October 26, 1966; admitted to bar, 1994, Maryland; 2000, District of Columbia. *Education:* University of Maryland (B.A., 1988); Loyola University (J.D., 1994). *Member:* Maryland State (Member, Business Law Section), District of Columbia and American (Member, Business Law Section) Bar Associations. ***PRACTICE AREAS:*** Mortgage Banking; Real Estate Finance; Financial Institutions Law; Regulatory Compliance. ***Email:*** gustavson@wbsk.com

SUZANNE DE ARMOND MUCCHETTI, born Dallas Texas, February 15, 1969; admitted to bar, 2000, Maryland; 2001, District of Columbia. *Education:* Smith College (B.A., 1991); American University Washington College of Law (J.D., 2000). Managing Editor, Administrative Law Review, 1999-2000. *Member:* Maryland State Bar Association. ***PRACTICE AREAS:*** Mortgage Banking Law; Real Estate Finance; Regulatory Compliance. ***Email:*** mucchetti@wbsk.com

LEAH SCHMULEWITZ-GETLAN, born Livingston, New Jersey, February 2, 1971; admitted to bar, 1996, New Jersey; 1997, New York and U.S. District Court, District of New Jersey; 1999, District of Columbia. *Education:* Johns Hopkins University (B.A., 1993); University of Pittsburgh (J.D., 1996). *Member:* District of Columbia and American (Member, Litigation Section) Bar Associations. ***PRACTICE AREAS:*** Litigation. ***Email:*** getlan@wbsk.com

(This Listing Continued)

WEINER BRODSKY SIDMAN KIDER PC, Washington—Continued

JOHN D. SOCKNAT, born Ames, Iowa, September 16, 1968; admitted to bar, 1995, Virginia; 1998, District of Columbia. *Education:* James Madison University (B.A., cum laude, 1990); Catholic University of America (J.D., 1995). ***PRACTICE AREAS:*** Mortgage Banking; Consumer Credit; Regulatory Compliance; Financial Institutions. ***Email:*** socknat@wbsk.com

DIAN PATRICIA STEVENS, born Charlotte Amalie, St. Thomas, U.S. Virgin Islands, July 25, 1972; admitted to bar, 2000, Maryland (Not admitted in District of Columbia). *Education:* Seton Hill College (B.A., 1994); George Washington University Law School (J.D., 1999). *Member:* Maryland State Bar Association. ***PRACTICE AREAS:*** Corporate Law.

CYNTHIA G. SWANN, born Canandaigua, New York, December 14, 1961; admitted to bar, 1992, Virginia; 1994, District of Columbia. *Education:* State University of New York at Buffalo (B.S., summa cum laude, 1984); University of Maryland (M.A., 1989); Georgetown University Law Center (J.D., cum laude, 1992). Georgetown Law Review. *Member:* American Bar Association. ***PRACTICE AREAS:*** Litigation. ***Email:*** swann@wbsk.com

MICHAEL S. WALDRON, born Trenton, New Jersey, January 17, 1970; admitted to bar, 1995, Maryland; 1998, District of Columbia. *Education:* Lafayette College (B.A., 1992); Catholic University of America Columbus School of Law (J.D., 1995). ***PRACTICE AREAS:*** Mortgage Banking; Real Estate Finance; Regulatory Compliance. ***Email:*** waldron@wbsk.com

ROSE-MICHELE WEINRYB, born Princeton, New Jersey, October 16, 1971; admitted to bar, 1996, Maryland; 1998, District of Columbia. *Education:* Lafayette College (B.A., magna cum laude, 1993); American University, Washington College of Law (J.D., summa cum laude, 1996). *Member:* Maryland State Bar Association. ***PRACTICE AREAS:*** Transportation; Regulatory Compliance; Mergers and Acquisitions; Asset Sales; Federal Taxation. ***Email:*** weinryb@wbsk.com

LEGAL SUPPORT PERSONNEL

GOVERNMENT RELATIONS SPECIALIST

ANN B. SHEARER, born Easton, Maryland, May 11, 1951. *Education:* Syracuse University (1969-1971); University of Maryland (B.A., 1973). Editor: *Land Use and Construction Regulations - A Builder's View,* Washington, D.C., National Association of Home Builders, 1982; *Builder's Reference Manual - Guidelines for Affordable Housing,* Washington, D.C., National Association of Home Builders, 1981. Author: "Community Infrastructure: Who Should Pay?," Builder Magazine, September 1982, Hanley-Wood, Inc. for the National Association of Home Builders; "Massachusetts' Governor Says 'No' to Advocates of No Housing," NAHB News, June 14, 1982, Washington, D.C., National Association of Home Builders. Member, Women in Housing and Finance, 1984—. ***PRACTICE AREAS:*** Mortgage and Real Estate Finance; Mortgage Banking; Regulatory Compliance; Government Relations. ***Email:*** shearer@wbsk.com

COMPLIANCE SPECIALIST

ANDREW E. ZIRNEKLIS, born Riga, Latvia, February 22, 1941. *Education:* Western Michigan University. Recipient, Vice Presidential Hammer Award for Assistance in Government Streamlining, 1996. ***Email:*** zirneklis@wbsk.com

---

THE WEISBAUM LAW FIRM

1850 M STREET, N.W., SUITE 250
WASHINGTON, D.C. 20036
Telephone: 202-293-2299
Toll free: 1-866-293-5351
Fax: 202-293-1788
Email: weisbaum@earthlink.net
URL: http://www.lawyers.com/weisbaumlawfirm

FIRM PROFILE: The Weisbaum Law Firm is committed to providing excellent, cost-effective legal representation to individuals and businesses in the D.C. Metropolitan area. Founded with a strong background in civil litigation, we understand the personal and financial risks associated with any lawsuit. We place a premium on candor in our contacts with clients, and understand the importance of prompt, efficient problem solving. We would welcome the opportunity to serve you.

STEVEN M. WEISBAUM, born Baltimore, Maryland, February 10, 1964; admitted to bar, 1991, Maryland; 1993, District of Columbia. *Education:* Hobart College (B.S., Chemistry, 1986); Boston University (J.D., 1991). *Member:* Montgomery County and Maryland State Bar Associations; District of Columbia Bar; The Association of Trial Lawyers of America. ***REPORTED CASES:*** Goldman v. Bequai, et al., 19 F.3d 666 (D.C. Cir. 1994); Atchison, T. & S.F. Ry. v. Pena, 44 F.3d 437 (7th Cir. 1994); Goebel v. Denver & Rio Grande Grande Western R.R., 215 F.3d 1083 (10th Cir. 2000). ***PRACTICE AREAS:*** Railroad Safety Law; Federal Employers Liability Act (FELA); Trade Association Law; Commercial Contacts; Labor and Employment Law; Personal Injury; Civil Litigation; Trusts and Estates. ***Email:*** weisbaum@earthlink.net

(This Listing Continued)

JONATHAN M. WEISGALL

CHARTERED
Established in 1983
1200 NEW HAMPSHIRE AVENUE, NW
SUITE 300
WASHINGTON, D.C. 20036
Telephone: 202-828-1378
Facsimile: 202-828-1380
Email: JWeisgall@aol.com

General Federal and Legislative Practice. Administrative, Energy and Natural Resources Law, Electric Power, Energy Power, Energy Project Development, Energy Regulation, Independent Power. Federal and U.S. Claims Court Litigation.

JONATHAN M. WEISGALL, born Baltimore, Maryland, March 17, 1949; admitted to bar, 1974, District of Columbia and New York; 1981, U.S. Claims Court; 1982, U.S. Supreme Court; 1983, Supreme Court of the Republic of the Marshall Islands. *Education:* Columbia College (B.A., magna cum laude, 1970); Stanford University (J.D., 1973). Phi Beta Kappa. Member, Board of Editors, Stanford Law Review, 1972-1973. Author, *Operation Crossroads: The Atomic Tests at Bikini Atoll,* 1994. Executive Producer, Documentary, "Radio Bikini," 1988. Adjunct Professor of Law, Georgetown University Law Center. Law Clerk, Hon. Ben. C. Duniway, U.S. Court of Appeals, Ninth Circuit, 1973-1974. Vice President, Legislative/Regulatory Affairs, MidAmerican Energy Holdings Co., Inc. , 1995—. Chairman, Board of Directors: Center for Energy Efficiency and Renewable Technologies, 1996—; President, Geothermal Energy Association, 2000—. *Member:* The District of Columbia Bar. ***Email:*** jweisgall@aol.com

---

LAW OFFICES
JAY S. WEISS, P.C.

Established in 1968
1828 L STREET, N.W., SUITE 902
WASHINGTON, D.C. 20036
Telephone: 202-872-1545
Fax: 202-296-0568
URL: http://www.lawyers.com/jaysweiss

Rockville, Maryland Office: One Central Plaza, Suite 802, 11300 Rockville Pike 20852. Telephone: 301-770-9440. FAX: 301-770-5217

Civil Trial Practice in District of Columbia and Maryland, Personal Injury, Automobile Injuries, Premises Liability, Security Liability, Commercial Transactions, General Trial Litigation.

JAY S. WEISS, born Washington, D.C., August 11, 1940; admitted to bar, 1967, District of Columbia; 1969, U.S. Court of Military Appeals and U.S. Claims Court; 1971, U.S. Supreme Court. *Education:* University of Maryland (A.B., 1963); Howard University (J.D., 1966). Law Clerk, Judge Austin Fickling, District of Columbia Court of General Sessions and District of Columbia Court of Appeals, 1966-1967. Member, Panel of Arbitrators, American Arbitration Association. *Member:* The District of Columbia Bar; Bar Association of the District of Columbia; Federal and American Bar Associations; Trial Lawyers Association of Metropolitan Washington D.C.; The Association of Trial Lawyers of America. ***PRACTICE AREAS:*** Personal Injury; Commercial Litigation; General Trial Litigation.

BARRY S. KOPIT, born Washington, D.C., May 29, 1955; admitted to bar, 1985, Maryland; 1989, District of Columbia, U.S. Supreme Court, U.S. Court of Military Appeals and U.S. District Court for the District of Columbia. *Education:* Hiram College (B.A., 1977); Southwestern University School of Law; American University, Washington College of Law (J.D., 1985). *Member:* The District of Columbia Bar; Bar Association of the District of Columbia; Montgomery County, Maryland State and American Bar Associations; The Association of Trial Lawyers of America; Maryland Trial Lawyers Association; Trial Lawyers Association of Metropolitan Washington, D.C. ***PRACTICE AREAS:*** Personal Injury; Commercial Litigation; General Trial Litigation.

WEISSBRODT & RACIN

1721 LAMONT STREET
WASHINGTON, D.C. 20010
Telephone: 202-265-2516
Fax: 202-483-7895
Email: awjrlaw@erols.com
URL: http://www.lawyers.com/weissbrodt&racin

Representing American Tribes, Civil Rights Litigation and Corporate Law.

MEMBERS OF FIRM

ABE W. WEISSBRODT, born New York, N.Y., April 18, 1913; admitted to bar, 1940, New York; 1951, District of Columbia; 1955, U.S. Claims Court; 1968, U.S. Supreme Court. *Education:* College of the City of New York (A.B., 1934); Columbia University (LL.B., 1938). Attorney with Treasury Department, 1942-1946. With North African Economic Board and Office of Military Government, U.S. in Sicily, Italy and Germany, 1943-1945. Trial Attorney with Justice Department, 1946-1951. *Member:* The District of Columbia Bar. ***PRACTICE AREAS:*** Civil Rights; Fair Employment Law; Federal Indian Law.

JOHN P. RACIN, born Cleveland, Ohio, August 4, 1948; admitted to bar, 1977, District of Columbia; 1985, Maryland. *Education:* West Virginia University (B.A., 1970); Antioch School of Law (J.D., 1977). *Member:* The District of Columbia Bar; Maryland State Bar Association. ***PRACTICE AREAS:*** Litigation; Civil Rights Law; Fair Employment Law.

BRYANT L. WELCH & ASSOCIATES

WASHINGTON, D.C.

(See Potomac, MD)

HMO/Managed Care Liability, Health Care Liability, Medical Malpractice, Personal Injury, ERISA, Mental Health Law, Psychology Malpractice, Psychiatric Malpractice, Psychotherapy Malpractice, Insurance Law, FEHBA Preemption.

GREGORY K. WELLS & ASSOCIATES, P.A.

WASHINGTON, D.C.

(See Largo, Maryland)

Civil Trial Practice in all Maryland and Washington, D.C. Courts. Emphasizing Plaintiffs Medical Malpractice, Wrongful Death and Serious Personal Injury, Entertainment Law.

WELSH & KATZ, LTD.

WASHINGTON, D.C.

(See Chicago, Illinois)

Technology and Intellectual Property Law including Patent, Trademark, Copyright, Trade Secret, Unfair Competition and Related Antitrust Law, and Trials and Appeals.

WELSH & KATZ, LTD.

WASHINGTON, D.C.

(See Arlington, Virginia)

Technology and Intellectual Property Law including Patent, Trademark, Copyright, Trade Secret, Unfair Competition and Related Antitrust Law, and Trials and Appeals.

WENDEROTH, LIND & PONACK, L.L.P.

Established in 1921

2033 K STREET, N.W., SUITE 800
WASHINGTON, D.C. 20006-1021
Telephone: 202-721-8200
Fax: 202-721-8250 (G-III)
202-833-3015 (G-IV)
Email: wlp@wenderoth.com
URL: http://www.wenderoth.com

Patent, Trademark, Copyright and Unfair Competition Law. International Patent and Trademark Practice.

FIRM PROFILE: Since its founding in 1921, Wenderoth, Lind & Ponack has been engaged in an international and domestic patent, trademark and copyright practice, securing intellectual property protection for both domestic and foreign corporations and associates. The firm's extensive client list ranges from small high-technology firms to large multinational corporations, many of which it has represented for more than fifty years.

The firm is listed in the Bar Register of Preeminent Lawyers.

MEMBERS OF FIRM

E. F. WENDEROTH (1886-1974).

JOHN E. LIND (1892-1983).

A. PONACK (1900-1969).

MICHAEL R. DAVIS, born Rochester, New York, January 28, 1942; admitted to bar, 1970, District of Columbia and U.S. Court of Appeals, District of Columbia Circuit; 1988, U.S. Court of Appeals for the Federal Circuit; registered to practice before U.S. Patent and Trademark Office. *Education:* Rochester Institute of Technology (B.S., Chem., 1965); Syracuse University (M.B.A., 1966); George Washington University (J.D., 1969). *Member:* The District of Columbia Bar; American Bar Association; American Intellectual Property Law Association; International Association for the Protection of Industrial Property. ***PRACTICE AREAS:*** Chemicals; Pharmaceuticals; Metallurgy; Biochemicals.

MATTHEW M. JACOB, born Brooklyn, New York, December 29, 1939; admitted to bar, 1970, Virginia; 1971, District of Columbia; 1971-1982, U.S. Court of Customs and Patent Appeals; 1982, U.S. Court of Appeals for the Federal Circuit; registered to practice before U.S. Patent and Trademark Office. *Education:* Brooklyn College (B.S., Chem., 1960); New York University (M.S., Organic Chemistry, 1964); American University (J.D., 1969). Delta Theta Phi. Author: "Patentability of Natural Products," 52 J.P.O.S. 473, 1970. *Member:* The District of Columbia Bar; Virginia State Bar; American Bar Association; American Chemical Society; American Intellectual Property Law Association; International Association for the Protection of Industrial Property. ***PRACTICE AREAS:*** Chemical Patent Prosecution; Patent Interference Practice; Patent Licensing.

WARREN M. CHEEK, JR., born New York, N.Y., October 28, 1955; admitted to bar, 1983, Florida; 1986, U.S. District Court, Middle District of Florida; 1989, District of Columbia; U.S. District Court for the District of Columbia; U.S. Court of Appeals for the Federal Circuit; U.S. Supreme Court; registered to practice before the U.S. Patent and Trademark Office. *Education:* Wake Forest University; University of Florida (B.S., 1979; J.D., 1983); University of Florida College of Medicine (1979-1980, post graduate research in Pharmacology); Johns Hopkins University (M.S., in Biotechnology). Phi Alpha Delta (Justice, 1982). *Member:* The District of Columbia Bar; The Florida Bar; American Bar Association (Member, Section of Patent, Trademark and Copyright Law); American Intellectual Property Law Association; International Association for the Protection of Industrial Property. ***PRACTICE AREAS:*** Chemical Patents; Biotechnology and Pharmaceutical Patents.

NILS E. PEDERSEN, born Copenhagen, Denmark, March 28, 1960; admitted to bar, 1989, Virginia; 1991, District of Columbia; registered to practice before U.S. Patent and Trademark Office; 1992, U.S. Court of Appeals for the Federal Circuit. *Education:* University of Maryland (B.S.M.E., 1983); George Mason University (J.D., 1989). *Member:* American Bar Association; American Intellectual Property Law Association. ***LANGUAGES:*** Danish. ***PRACTICE AREAS:*** Mechanical Patents; Electrical Patents; Prosecution; Licensing.

CHARLES R. WATTS, born Wilmington, Delaware, June 16, 1962; admitted to bar, 1990, Virginia; 1991, District of Columbia; 1998, U.S. Court of Appeals for the Federal Circuit; U.S. Supreme Court; registered to practice before U.S. Patent and Trademark Office. *Education:* University of Delaware (B.S.M.E., 1984); George Mason University School of Law (J.D., 1990). *Member:* Virginia State Bar; District of Columbia Bar; American Bar Association; American Intellectual Property Law Association. ***PRACTICE AREAS:*** Mechanical Patents; Electrical Patents; Patent Applications; Prosecution; Licensing.

MICHAEL S. HUPPERT, born Livingston, Montana, September 7, 1958; admitted to bar, 1990, Virginia; 1996, District of Columbia; registered to practice before U.S. Patent and Trademark Office. *Education:* Montana State University (B.S.C.E., 1982); George Mason University (J.D., 1990). Patent Examiner Initial Training Instructor, 1991. *Member:* The District of Columbia Bar; Virginia State Bar; American Bar Association; American Intellectual Property Law Association. ***PRACTICE AREAS:*** Patent Law; Mechanical Patents; Patent Prosecution.

OF COUNSEL

JOHN T. MILLER, born Johnson City, Tennessee, May 14, 1935; admitted to bar, 1965, Virginia; 1965-1982, U.S. Court of Customs and Patent Appeals; 1966, District of Columbia and Florida; 1982, U.S. Court of Appeals for the Federal Circuit; registered to practice before U.S. Patent and Trademark Office. *Education:* East Tennessee State University (B.A., Chem., 1957); George Washington University (J.D., 1964). Delta Theta Phi. *Member:* The District of Columbia Bar; Virginia State Bar; The Florida Bar; American and Federal Circuit

(This Listing Continued)

WENDEROTH, LIND & PONACK, L.L.P., Washington—Continued

Bar Associations; American Intellectual Property Law Association; Patent and Trademark Institute of Canada; International Association for the Protection of Industrial Property. ***PRACTICE AREAS:*** Patents; Chemical Patents; Pharmaceutical Patents; Interference Practice.

JOHN T. FEDIGAN, born Auburn, New York, December 21, 1932; admitted to bar, 1967, Virginia; 1968, District of Columbia; 1975-1982, U.S. Court of Customs and Patent Appeals; 1982, U.S Court of Appeals for the Federal Circuit; registered to practice before U.S. Patent and Trademark Office. *Education:* Le Moyne College (B.S., Chem., 1955); Catholic University of America (LL.B., 1966). *Member:* The District of Columbia Bar; Virginia and American Bar Associations; American Intellectual Property Law Association; International Association for the Protection of Industrial Property. ***PRACTICE AREAS:*** Patents; Chemical Patents; Prosecution; Interference Practice.

ASSOCIATES

LEE CHENG, born Tainan, Taiwan, ROC, September 3, 1966; admitted to bar, 1996, Maryland; 1997, District of Columbia; registered to practice before U.S. Patent and Trademark Office. *Education:* University of Michigan at Ann Arbor (B.S., Cellular Molecular Biology, 1989); Franklin Pierce Law Center (Master of Intellectual Property, magna cum laude, 1994); Syracuse University (J.D., cum laude, 1995); Johns Hopkins University (M.S., Biotechnology, with honors, 1997). Member: Trademark Moot Court Team, Franklin Pierce Law Center; Journal of International Law and Commerce, Syracuse University. *Member:* Maryland State and American Bar Associations; The District of Columbia Bar; American Intellectual Property Law Association; Licensing Executive Society, Chinese Biopharmaceutical Association. ***LANGUAGES:*** Mandarin Chinese. ***PRACTICE AREAS:*** Biotechnology Patents; Pharmaceutical Patents; Chemical Patents; Patent Prosecution.

KAUSHAL R. ODEDRA, born December 24, 1969; admitted to bar, 1995, Wisconsin; 1996, Florida; 2001, District of Columbia; U.S. District Court, Eastern and Western Districts of Wisconsin; U.S. District Court, Middle District of Florida; U.S. Court of Appeals for the Federal Circuit; registered to practice before U.S. Patent and Trademark Office. *Education:* University of Minnesota Institute of Technology (B.S., Mech. Engr., 1992); Marquette University Law School (J.D., 1995); Franklin Pierce Law Center (Master of Intellectual Property, 1995). Member, Saul Lefkowitz National Moot Court Team. *Member:* The Florida Bar; State Bar of Wisconsin; American Bar Association; American Intellectual Property Law Association; International Trademark Association. ***PRACTICE AREAS:*** Trademark and Copyright Law.

DHIREN R. ODEDRA, born June 22, 1971; admitted to bar, 1998, Minnesota; 2001, District of Columbia; registered to Practice before U.S. Patent and Trademark Office. *Education:* University of Wisconsin-Milwaukee (B.S., Electrical Engineering, 1993); Temple University School of Law (J.D., 1997). Patent Examiner, U.S. Patent and Trademark Office, 1995-1996. *Member:* Minnesota State Bar and American Intellectual Property Lawyers Associations. ***PRACTICE AREAS:*** Patent Law; Electrical Patents; Computer and Software Patents; Patent Prosecution.

DAVID M. OVEDOVITZ, admitted to bar, 1999, Virginia; registered to practice before U.S. Patent and Trademark Office (Not admitted in District of Columbia). *Education:* Union College (B.S., Electrical Engineering, 1995); George Mason University School of Law (J.D., 1998). *Member:* Virginia and American Bar Associations; American Intellectual Property Law Association. ***PRACTICE AREAS:*** Patents.

JOSEPH M. GORSKI, born Detroit, Michigan, October 12, 1961; admitted to bar, 1996, Virginia; registered to Practice before U.S. Patent and Trademark Office (Not admitted in District of Columbia). *Education:* Michigan State University (B.S.M.E., 1983); George Mason University School of Law (J.D., 1995). *Member:* Virginia Bar Association. ***PRACTICE AREAS:*** Mechanical Patent Prosecution; Electrical Patent Prosecution.

W. DOUGLAS HAHM, born Plainfield, New Jersey, March 9, 1968; admitted to bar, 2000, Virginia; registered to practice before U.S. Patent and Trademark Office (Not admitted in District of Columbia). *Education:* Pennsylvania State University (B.S.M.E., 1990); George Mason University (J.D., cum laude, 2000). *Member:* Virginia State Bar; American Intellectual Property Law Association; GSR American Inn of Court. ***PRACTICE AREAS:*** Patent Prosecution; Mechanical Patents.

JEFFREY R. FILIPEK, born Hazleton, Pennsylvania, July 28, 1970; admitted to bar, 2000, Pennsylvania; 2001, District of Columbia; registered to practice before U.S. Patent and Trademark Office. *Education:* Pennsylvania State University (B.S.E.E., 1992); Columbus School of Law of The Catholic University of America (J.D., 2000). ***PRACTICE AREAS:*** Patents.

JOHN J. FIGUEROA, born New York, New York, May 10, 1959; admitted to bar, 1999, New York (Not admitted in District of Columbia). *Education:* Iowa State University (B.S., 1983); University of Iowa (B.S., 1991); Fordham University Law School (J.D., 1998); SUNY - Stony Brook (M.S., 1998). Turner Fellow, SUNY-Stony Brook, 1991-1995. *Member:* New York State and American Bar Associations; American Chemical Society. ***LANGUAGES:*** Spanish. ***PRACTICE AREAS:*** Patent Prosecution; Chemical Patents.

THOMAS D. ROBBINS, born Ft. Meade, Maryland, December 26, 1970; admitted to bar, 2000, Maryland; registered to practice before U.S. Patent and Trademark Office (Not admitted in District of Columbia). *Education:* University of Maryland (B.S.E.E., 1993); Catholic University of America (J.D., 2000). ***PRACTICE AREAS:*** Mechanical Patent Prosecution; Electrical Patent Prosecution.

RALPH WERNER

HAMILTON SQUARE
600 FOURTEENTH STREET, N.W.
SIXTH FLOOR
WASHINGTON, D.C. 20005
Telephone: 202-628-6550
Fax: 202-628-6554
Email: rwlegal@aol.com
URL: http://www.lawyers.com/ralphwerner

Commercial Real Estate, Commercial Law, Landlord and Tenant Law, Leasing, Corporate Law, Securities, Complex Commercial Litigation, Commercial Bankruptcy.

FIRM PROFILE: For over 25 years, attorney Ralph Werner has provided expert business counsel in commercial real estate transactions. Clients to the firm have included commercial office and retail developers, building owners and investors, commercial landlords and tenants, commercial real estate buyers and sellers, property service and suppliers and real estate management companies. Mr. Werner regularly advises and counsels in matters involving financing, security offerings and regulation of initial public offerings. The firm also continues to focus strongly in matters requiring complex commercial litigation.

RALPH WERNER, born New York, N.Y., August 26, 1935; admitted to bar, 1960, New York; 1962, U.S. District Court, Southern District of New York; 1967, District of Columbia; 1968, U.S. Supreme Court; 1971, U.S. Court of Appeals, District of Columbia; 1980, U.S. District Court, District of Maryland; 1984, Maryland; 1985, U.S. Court of Appeals, Fourth Circuit. *Education:* New York University (B.A., cum laude, 1956); Harvard Law School (LL.B., 1959). Phi Beta Kappa. Staff Executive, Advisory Commission on Reapportionment to New York State Legislature, 1965-1966. General Counsel, District of Columbia Redevelopment Land Agency, 1967-1975. Consultant, Office of Rail Public Counsel, 1978. *Member:* The District of Columbia Bar (Member, Sections of: Real Estate, Housing and Community Development; Litigation). ***PRACTICE AREAS:*** Real Estate; Corporate Law; Litigation.

WEST & FEINBERG, P.C.

WASHINGTON, D.C.

(See Bethesda, Maryland)

Corporate, Estate Planning, Business, Health, Taxation, Probate, Estate Administration, Pension Planning and Employee Benefits, Commercial, Newsletter Sales, Mergers and Acquisitions.

WHARTON LEVIN EHRMANTRAUT KLEIN & NASH

A PROFESSIONAL ASSOCIATION

WASHINGTON, D.C.

(See Annapolis, Maryland)

General Trial and Appellate Practice in all State and Federal Courts. With Emphasis on Defense of Product Liability, Toxic Tort, Asbestos, Aviation, Medical Malpractice and Professional Malpractice Litigation. Commercial Litigation.

WHITE & CASE

Limited Liability Partnership
601 THIRTEENTH STREET, NW, SUITE 600 SOUTH
WASHINGTON, D.C. 20005-3807
Telephone: 202-626-3600
Facsimile: 202-639-9355
URL: http://www.whitecase.com

Los Angeles, California: Telephone: 213-620-7700. Facsimile: 213-687-0758; 213-452-2330; 213-452-2331.

(This Listing Continued)

Palo Alto, California: Telephone: 650-213-0300. Facsimile: 650-213-8158.
San Francisco, California: Telephone: 415-544-1100. Facsimile: 415-544-0202.
Miami, Florida: Telephone: 305-371-2700. Facsimile: 305-358-5744; 305-358-5766.
New York, New York: Telephone: 212-819-8200. Facsimile: 212-354-8113.
Berlin, Germany: White & Case, Feddersen. Telephone: (49-30) 880 911-0. Facsimile: (49-30) 880 911-297.
Bratislava, Slovakia: White & Case, Feddersen. Telephone: (421-7) 5441-5100. Facsimile: (421-7) 5441-6100.
Brussels, Belgium: Telephone: (32-2) 219-16-20. Facsimile: (32-2) 219-16-26.
Budapest, Hungary: Réczicza Law Firm White & Case. Telephone: (36-1) 488-5200. Facsimile: (36-1) 488-5299.
Dresden, Germany: White & Case, Feddersen. Telephone: (49-351) 8 02 02 77. Facsimile: (49-351) 8 02 02 79.
Dusseldorf, Germany: White & Case, Feddersen. Telephone: (49-211) 4 91 95-0. Facsimile: (49-211) 49 19 51 00.
Frankfurt, Germany: White & Case, Feddersen. Telephone: (49-69) 2 99 94-0. Facsimile: (49-69) 28 26 15.
Hamburg, Germany: White & Case, Feddersen. Telephone: (49-40) 3 50 05-0. Facsimile: (49-40) 35 00 51 11.
Helsinki, Finland: Asianajotoimisto White & Case Oy. Telephone: (358-9) 228-641. Facsimile: (358-9) 228-64228.
Istanbul, Turkey: White & Case Müşavirlik Ltd. Şti. Telephone: (90-212) 275-75-33. Facsimile: (90-212) 275-75-43.
London, England: Telephone: (44-20) 7600-7300. Facsimile: (44-20) 7600-7030.
Milan, Italy: White & Case, Varrenti e Associati. Telephone: (39-02) 7600-2930. Facsimile: (39-02) 7600-2936.
Moscow, Russia: Telephone: (7-095) 787-3000. Facsimile: (7-095) 787-3001.
Paris, France: Telephone: (33-1) 55-04-15-15. Facsimile: (33-1) 55-04-15-16.
Prague, Czech Republic: White & Case, Feddersen. Telephone: (420-2) 24 81-08 08; 24 81-17 96; 24 10 80 00. Facsimile: (420-2) 24 81-03 30; 24 81-02 52; 24 10 81 00.
Rome, Italy: White & Case, Varrenti e Associati. Telephone: (39-06) 420-0871. Facsimile: (39-06) 4200-8758.
Stockholm, Sweden: White & Case Advokat AB. Telephone: (46-8) 506-323-00. Facsimile: (46-8) 611-21-22.
Warsaw, Poland: White & Case, Warsaw. Telephone: (48-22) 625-33-33; (48-22) 622-67-67; (43-89) 12-19-06. Facsimile: (48-22) 628-22-28.
Johannesburg, Republic of South Africa: Telephone: 27 (11) 884-7689. Facsimile: 27 (11) 884-7229.
Almaty, Kazakhstan: Telephone: (7-3272) 50-74-91. Facsimile: (7-3272) 50-74-93.
Ankara, Turkey: White & Case Müşavirlik Ltd. Şti. Telephone: (90-312) 442-5680. Facsimile: (90-312) 442-5691/4.
Bangkok, Thailand: White & Case (Thailand) Limited. Telephone: (662) 656-1721 to 32. Facsimile: (662) 656-1733/34.
Beijing, China: Colin Ng & Partners, Beijing China. Telephone: (86-10) 6539-1230. Facsimile: (86-10) 6539-1280.
Bombay/Mumbai, India: Liaison Office, (91-22) 282-6300/01/02/03. Facsimile: (91-22) 282-6305.
Hanoi, Vietnam: Telephone: (84-4) 934-5410/5411. Facsimile: (84-4) 934-5412.
Ho Chi Minh City, Vietnam: Telephone: (84-8) 821-0888. Facsimile: (84-8) 823-6902.
Hong Kong: White & Case, Solicitors. Telephone: (852) 2822-8700. Facsimile: (852) 2845-9070.
Shanghai, China: Telephone: (86-21) 6321-2200. Facsimile: (86-21) 6323-9252.
Singapore, Republic of Singapore: White & Case, Colin Ng & Partners. Telephone: (65) 225-6000. Facsimile: (65) 225-6009.
Tokyo, Japan: White & Case, LLP - Kandabashi Law Offices (Registered Association). Telephone: (81-3) 3259-0200. Facsimile: (81-3) 3259-0150.
Manama, Bahrain: Telephone: (973) 538-600. Facsimile: (973) 532-342.
Jeddah, Saudi Arabia: Law Office of Hassan Mahassni, Telephone: (966-2) 665-4353. Facsimile: (966-2) 669-2996.
Riyadh, Saudi Arabia: Law Office of Hassan Mahassni, Telephone: (966-1) 464-4006. Facsimile: (966-1) 465-1348.
Mexico City, Mexico: White & Case, S.C. Telephone: (52) 5-540-9600. Facsimile: (52) 5-540-9699.
São Paulo, SP, Brazil: Telephone: (55-11) 3171-0011. Facsimile: (55-11) 3171-0041.
Associated Law Firm(s):
Bombay/Mumbai, India: India Law Services (ILS). Telephones: (91-22) 284-1995; (91-22) 284-1847. Facsimile: (91-22) 285-0824.
New Delhi, India: India Law Services (ILS). Telephone: (91-11) 607-1602/3/4. Facsimile: (91-11) 608-8860.
Jakarta, Indonesia: Ali Budiardjo, Nugroho, Reksodiputro, Counsellors at Law. Telephone: (62-21) 250-5125. Facsimile: (62-21) 250-5392; 250-5646.

General Practice.

(This Listing Continued)

PARTNERS

DAVID A. BALTO, born Minneapolis, Minnesota, August 1, 1952; admitted to bar, 1987, District of Columbia. *Education:* Northeastern University School of Law (M.P.A., 1978; J.D., 1983). ***Email:*** dbalto@whitecase.com

LINDA E. CARLISLE, born San Antonio, Texas, December 17, 1948; admitted to bar, 1980, District of Columbia; 1990, New York. *Education:* University of Texas (B.A., 1970); Catholic University of America (J.D., 1980); Georgetown University (M.L.T., 1984). *Member:* The District of Columbia Bar; New York State, Federal and American Bar Associations; Wall Street Tax Association; American Law Institute Tax Advisory Group; International Fiscal Association; Tax Coalition. ***PRACTICE AREAS:*** Federal Income Tax; Federal Taxation; International Taxation. ***Email:*** lcarlisle@whitecase.com

WILLIAM J. CLINTON, born St. Louis, Missouri, September 21, 1953; admitted to bar, 1982, District of Columbia; 1983, Court of International Trade; 1984, U.S. Court of Appeals for the Federal Circuit. *Education:* Georgetown University (B.S., 1976; J.D., 1982). *Member:* The District of Columbia Bar. ***Email:*** wclinton@whitecase.com

CHRISTOPHER F. CORR, born Philadelphia, Pennsylvania, September 24, 1961; admitted to bar, 1986, Pennsylvania; 1988, District of Columbia. *Education:* Pennsylvania State University (B.A., 1983); Tyler University, Rome, Italy; Tel Aviv University, Ramat Aviv, Israel; George Washington University (J.D., 1986). *Member:* The District of Columbia Bar. ***PRACTICE AREAS:*** International Trade Law; International Communications Law; International Business Law. ***Email:*** ccorr@whitecase.com

CHRISTOPHER M. CURRAN, born New York, New York, December 12, 1960; admitted to bar, 1986, New York; 1987, District of Columbia. *Education:* University of Virginia (B.A., with distinction, 1982); University of Pennsylvania (J.D., 1985). ***PRACTICE AREAS:*** Corporate Litigation; International Litigation; Foreign Corrupt Practices Act. ***Email:*** ccurran@whitecase.com

BRUCE N. DAVIS, born New Orleans, Louisiana, December 18, 1957; admitted to bar, 1984, Texas; 1994, District of Columbia. *Education:* University of Virginia (B.A., 1980); Harvard University (J.D., 1983); Southern Methodist University (LL.M., 1987). ***PRACTICE AREAS:*** Taxation; International Income Tax; International Taxation. ***Email:*** bdavis@whitecase.com

VICTOR J. DeSANTIS, born Baltimore, Maryland, March 8, 1960; admitted to bar, 1986, New York; 1987, District of Columbia. *Education:* Yale University (B.A., 1982); Harvard University (J.D., 1985). ***PRACTICE AREAS:*** Infrastructure Development; Project Finance; International Investment. ***Email:*** vdesantis@whitecase.com

J. MARK GIDLEY, born Houston, Texas, April 22, 1961; admitted to bar, 1987, New York; 1989, District of Columbia and Texas. *Education:* University of Kansas (B.S., B.G.S., 1983); Columbia University (J.D., 1986). *Member:* The Association of the Bar of the City of New York; District of Columbia Bar; American Bar Association. ***PRACTICE AREAS:*** Antitrust; Mergers and Acquisitions; Commercial Litigation. ***Email:*** mgidley@whitecase.com

DAVID A. HILDEBRANDT, born Milwaukee, Wisconsin, October 21, 1943; admitted to bar, 1970, Wisconsin; 1977, District of Columbia. *Education:* Brigham Young University (B.S., 1967); University of Wisconsin (J.D., 1970). *Member:* American Bar Association. ***PRACTICE AREAS:*** International Compensation; International Benefits. ***Email:*** dhildebrandt@whitecase.com

DAVID P. HOULIHAN, born Youngstown, Ohio, May 14, 1937; admitted to bar, 1965, District of Columbia. *Education:* Youngstown State University (B.S., 1959); Georgetown University (LL.B., 1964). *Member:* The District of Columbia Bar; American Bar Association. ***PRACTICE AREAS:*** International Trade. ***Email:*** dhoulihan@whitecase.com

DAVID W. HUNT, born Washington, D.C., September 27, 1952; admitted to bar, 1977, Georgia; 1981, District of Columbia. *Education:* University of Virginia (B.A., 1974; J.D., 1977). *Member:* District of Columbia Bar; State Bar of Georgia; Energy Bar Association. ***PRACTICE AREAS:*** Corporate Transactions; Project Finance; Public Utilities; Utility Acquisitions. ***Email:*** dhunt@whitecase.com

CAROLYN B. LAMM, born Buffalo, New York, August 22, 1948; admitted to bar, 1973, Florida; 1975, District of Columbia; 1983, New York. *Education:* State University of New York College at Buffalo (B.S., 1970); University of Miami (J.D., 1973). *Member:* The District of Columbia Bar (President, 1997-1998); The Florida Bar; Federal, American and International Bar Associations; American Society of International Law. Council, American Law Institute. ***PRACTICE AREAS:*** International Arbitration; International Trade; Litigation. ***Email:*** clamm@whitecase.com

J. ROGER MENTZ, born New York, N.Y., March 10, 1942; admitted to bar, 1967, New York; 1976, District of Columbia. *Education:* Princeton University (B.S.E., 1963); University of Virginia (LL.B., 1966). *Member:* The District of Columbia Bar; New York State and American Bar Associations; European-American Tax Institute (Board of Advisors); International Fiscal Association. ***PRACTICE AREAS:*** Taxation. ***Email:*** rmentz@whitecase.com

(This Listing Continued)

WHITE & CASE, Washington—Continued

EDWARD R. NEAHER, JR., born Rockville Centre, New York, March 20, 1958; admitted to bar, 1985, New York; 1989, District of Columbia; 1997, Hong Kong. *Education:* Williams College (B.A., 1980); Cornell University (J.D., 1983). ***PRACTICE AREAS:*** Project Finance; International Private Equity; Capital Markets; Venture Capital. ***Email:*** eneaher@whitecase.com

ROBERT D. PAUL, born Worcester, Massachusetts, June 29, 1941; admitted to bar, 1968, District of Columbia; 1970, Massachusetts. *Education:* Boston College (B.A., 1963); Harvard Law School (LL.B., 1966); New York University School of Law (LL.M., 1967). *Member:* The District of Columbia Bar; Bar Association of the District of Columbia, Massachusetts, Federal and American Bar Associations. ***PRACTICE AREAS:*** Antitrust; Litigation. ***Email:*** rpaul@whitecase.com

ABBY COHEN SMUTNY, born New York, New York, May 6, 1964; admitted to bar, 1991, New York; 1993, District of Columbia. *Education:* London School of Economics (Certificate, 1985); Vassar College (A.B., 1986); Université des Langues et Lettres de Grenoble (Certificate, 1986); University of Chicago (J.D., 1990). *Member:* The District of Columbia Bar; American and International Bar Associations; American Society of International Law. ***PRACTICE AREAS:*** International Arbitration; International Dispute Resolution; International Investment. ***Email:*** asmutny@whitecase.com

GREGORY J. SPAK, born New Kensington, Pennsylvania, July 10, 1962; admitted to bar, 1987, Pennsylvania; 1989, District of Columbia. *Education:* Georgetown University (B.S.F.S., 1984; J.D., 1987). *Member:* American Bar Association; Inter-American Bar Association. ***Email:*** gspak@whitecase.com

WALTER J. SPAK, born New Kensington, Pennsylvania, July 23, 1951; admitted to bar, 1978, Pennsylvania; 1979, District of Columbia. *Education:* Sophia University, Tokyo, Japan; University of Notre Dame (B.A., 1973); Georgetown University Law Center (J.D., 1977); Center for International Legal Studies, Salzburg, Austria. *Member:* The District of Columbia Bar. ***PRACTICE AREAS:*** International Trade Regulation. ***Email:*** wspak@whitecase.com

GEORGE J. TERWILLIGER III, born New Brunswick, New Jersey, June 5, 1950; admitted to bar, 1978, District of Columbia; 1982, Vermont. *Education:* Seton Hall University (B.A., 1973); Antioch School of Law (J.D., 1978). ***PRACTICE AREAS:*** Government Investigations; Complex Litigation; Health Care Fraud; Election Law; Voting Rights; First Amendment Litigation. ***Email:*** gterwilliger@whitecase.com

PARTNER OF COUNSEL

WILLIAM P. McCLURE, born Washington, D.C., May 25, 1925; admitted to bar, 1951, District of Columbia. *Education:* Wharton School of Commerce and Finance, University of Pennsylvania (B.S., 1949); George Washington University (J.D., 1951; LL.M., 1954); The Hague Academy of International Law at The Hague, Holland, 1952. *Member:* The District of Columbia Bar; Bar Association of the District of Columbia; Maryland State and American Bar Associations. ***PRACTICE AREAS:*** Taxation. ***Email:*** wmcclure@whitecase.com

SPECIAL COUNSEL

CHARLES N. BROWER, born Plainfield, New Jersey, June 5, 1935; admitted to bar, 1962, New York; 1970, District of Columbia. *Education:* Harvard University (B.A., 1957; J.D., 1961). *Member:* The District of Columbia Bar; The Association of the Bar of the City of New York; New York State, American and International Bar Associations; American Law Institute; American Society of International Law; International Law Association. ***PRACTICE AREAS:*** International Arbitration; International Dispute Resolution; International Investment. ***Email:*** cbrower@whitecase.com

HORACIO A. GRIGERA NAON, born Buenos Aires, Argentina, July 1, 1947; admitted to bar, 1972, Buenos Aires Federal Courts; 1986, New York; 1989, U.S. Supreme Court (Not admitted in District of Columbia). *Education:* Nacional Sarmiento (Bachiller, 1965); University of Buenos Aires (J.D., 1972; Ph.D., 1983); Harvard Law School (LL.M., 1984; S.J.D., 1985). *Member:* American and International Bar Associations; American Law Institute. ***PRACTICE AREAS:*** International Commercial Arbitration; Project Finance; Oil and Gas Law; Corporate; International Sales. ***Email:*** hgrigeranaon@whitecase.com

COUNSEL

ROBERT J. BITTMAN, born Chicago, Illinois, May 9, 1962; admitted to bar, 1988, Maryland; 1990, Virginia; 1997, Florida; 1999, District of Columbia. *Education:* University of Maryland (B.A., 1984); Catholic University, Columbus School of Law (J.D., 1987). ***PRACTICE AREAS:*** Litigation; Criminal Law; Civil Litigation. ***Email:*** bbittman@whitecase.com

ELLEN M. JAKOVIC, born Albany, New York, November 14, 1960; admitted to bar, 1985, Massachusetts; 1986, New York and District of Columbia. *Education:* Harvard University (A.B., 1982; J.D., 1985). *Member:* The District of Columbia Bar; American Bar Association (Antitrust and Litigation Sections); Women's Bar Association. ***PRACTICE AREAS:*** Antitrust. ***Email:*** ejakovic@whitecase.com

DAOUD L. KHAIRALLAH, born Bhahdoun, Lebanon; admitted to bar, 1965, Lebanon; 1982, Virginia; 1994, District of Columbia. *Education:* Lebanese University Law School (Lic.En.Dr., 1965); University of Michigan (MC.L., 1970; LL.M., 1971; S.J.D., 1973). *Member:* Virginia State Bar; District of Columbia Bar; Beirut Bar Association. ***PRACTICE AREAS:*** Project Finance; Privatization; International Settlement of Disputes; International Investment. ***Email:*** dkhairallah@whitecase.com

ANNE D. SMITH, born Syracuse, New York, May 19, 1950; admitted to bar, 1976, Virginia; 1977, District of Columbia; 1983, New York. *Education:* Syracuse University (B.A., 1972); Georgetown University (J.D., 1976). *Member:* Virginia State Bar; The District of Columbia Bar; New York State Bar Association. ***PRACTICE AREAS:*** Federal Administrative Law; Civil Litigation; Foreign Sovereign Immunities Act; International Arbitration. ***Email:*** asmith@whitecase.com

LAURA M. WILSON, born Athens, Ohio, November 1, 1959; admitted to bar, 1986, Wisconsin; 1987, District of Columbia. *Education:* University of Wisconsin (B.A., 1982; J.D., 1986). *Member:* The District of Columbia Bar; Federal Energy and American Bar Associations. ***Email:*** lwilson@whitecase.com

ASSOCIATES

ARIANA ALMAJAN, born La Jolla, California, March 17, 1974; admitted to bar, 1999, California; 2000, District of Columbia. *Education:* Yale University (B.A., 1996); University of Chicago (J.D., 1999). ***Email:*** aalmajan@whitecase.com

JOCELYN A. AQUA, born New York, N.Y., September 2, 1968; admitted to bar, 1995, Pennsylvania; 1997, District of Columbia. *Education:* Pennsylvania State University (B.A., 1990); George Washington University (M.A., 1995; J.D., 1995). *Member:* Pennsylvania Bar Association; The District of Columbia Bar. ***Email:*** jaqua@whitecase.com

KARIE J. BARWIND, born Ithaca, New York, October 6, 1972; admitted to bar, 1998, Illinois; 2001, District of Columbia. *Education:* Syracuse University (B.A./ B.F.A., 1995); Cornell Law School (J.D., 1998). ***Email:*** kbarwind@whitecase.com

VINCENT BOWEN, born Takoma Park, Maryland, April 7, 1961; admitted to bar, 1986, Maryland; 1988, District of Columbia. *Education:* Boston College (B.A., 1983); George Washington University (J.D., 1986). ***Email:*** vbowen@whitecase.com

PATRICK J. BROWNE, JR., born New Orleans, Louisiana, October 1, 1969; admitted to bar, 1996, Louisiana; 1999, District of Columbia. *Education:* Tulane University of Louisiana (B.S.M., 1992; J.D., 1995); Georgetown University Law Center (LL.M., 1999). ***Email:*** pbrowne@whitecase.com

RICHARD J. BURKE, born Augsburg, Germany, February 8, 1963; admitted to bar, 1990, New York; 1993, District of Columbia. *Education:* Harvard University (A.B., 1985); Georgetown University (M.S.F.S., 1990; J.D., 1990). ***Email:*** rburke@whitecase.com

PETER J. CARNEY, born Boston, Massachusetts, July 2, 1970; admitted to bar, 1996, Virginia; 1998, District of Columbia. *Education:* Colby College (B.A., 1992); Washington College of Law, American University (J.D., 1996). ***Email:*** pcarney@whitecase.com

DANIEL S. CHEN, born Taiwan, Republic of China, October 5, 1953; admitted to bar, 1990, Virginia (Not admitted in District of Columbia). *Education:* National Chengchi University (LL.B., 1977); Soochow University School of Law (LL.M., 1985); University of Virginia School of Law (LL.M., 1986; S.J.D., 1993). ***Email:*** trri627@ibm.net

ELIZABETH L. CHENEY, born Madison, Wisconsin, July 28, 1966; admitted to bar, 1996, Virginia; 1997, District of Columbia. *Education:* The Colorado College (B.A., 1988); University of Chicago (J.D., 1996). ***Email:*** echeney@whitecase.com

GUSTAV CHIARELLO, born Cooperstown, New York, July, 1968; admitted to bar, 1999, Virginia; 2000, District of Columbia. *Education:* Catholic University of America (B.A., 1991); Georgetown University (M.P.P., 1996); George Mason University School of Law (J.D., 1999). ***Email:*** gchiarello@whitecase.com

EILEEN M. COLE, born Fairfax County, Virginia, October 20, 1972; admitted to bar, 1998, New York; 2001, District of Columbia. *Education:* University of Virginia (B.A., 1994; J.D., 1997). *Member:* Bar Association of the District of Columbia; New York State Bar Association. ***PRACTICE AREAS:*** Litigation. ***Email:*** ecole@whitecase.com

JAIME M. CROWE, born Seville, Spain, January 17, 1969; admitted to bar, 1994, Virginia; 1995, District of Columbia. *Education:* George Mason

(This Listing Continued)

University (B.A., 1991); George Washington University (J.D., 1994). *Member:* Virginia State Bar; The District of Columbia Bar. ***Email:*** jcrowe@whitecase.com

NICOLE ERB, born New York, N.Y., July 9, 1967; admitted to bar, 1999, New York; 2000, District of Columbia. *Education:* Reed College (B.A., 1991); Columbia University School of Law (J.D., 1998). *Member:* New York State Bar Association. ***Email:*** nerb@whitecase.com

ROBERT G. GOSSELINK, born Damascus, Syria, August 8, 1964; admitted to bar, 1995, New York; 1998, District of Columbia; 1998, U.S. Court of International Trade. *Education:* Oberlin College (B.A., 1986); Boston College (J.D., 1994); Fletcher School of Law and Diplomacy, Tufts University (M.A.L.D., 1994). ***Email:*** rgosselink@whitecase.com

ERIC GRANNON, born Brooklyn, New York, March 3, 1972; admitted to bar, 1999, Maryland; 2001, District of Columbia. *Education:* Brooklyn College of the City University of New York (B.A., 1995); Howard University School of Law (J.D., 1998). ***PRACTICE AREAS:*** Trial and Appellate Litigation; Antitrust Litigation; Foreign Corrupt Practices Act. ***Email:*** egrannon@whitecase.com

YUE GUAN, born China, January 21, 1966; admitted to bar, 1999, New York (Not admitted in District of Columbia). *Education:* Peking University (B.A., 1988); American University (LL.M., 1996). ***Email:*** yguan@whitecase.com

R. SHAWN GUNNARSON, born Ogden, Utah, September 24, 1965; admitted to bar, 1995, Utah; 1999, U.S. Supreme Court (Not admitted in District of Columbia). *Education:* Brigham Young University (B.A., 1991); J. Reuben Clark Law School (J.D., 1994). ***PRACTICE AREAS:*** Government Investigations; Complex Litigation; Appellate Litigation. ***Email:*** rgunnarson@whitecase.com

GREGG A. HAND, born Los Angeles, California, July 16, 1962; admitted to bar, 1988, New York and District of Columbia; 1994, U.S. Supreme Court and U.S. District Court for the District of Columbia. *Education:* Franklin and Marshall College (B.A., 1984); Boston University (J.D., 1987). *Member:* Bar Association of The District of Columbia; New York State and American Bar Associations. ***Email:*** ghand@whitecase.com

KAREN HANRAHAN, born Indianapolis, Indiana, October 22, 1969; admitted to bar, 2000, Maryland and District of Columbia. *Education:* Indiana University (B.A., 1992); American University (M.A., 1995); University of Washington (J.D., 2000). ***Email:*** khanrahan@whitecase.com

LAURIE A. HARTMAN, admitted to bar, 1994, Massachusetts; 1995, Pennsylvania; 1999, District of Columbia. *Education:* Boston University (B.A., 1990); College of William & Mary (J.D., 1994). ***Email:*** lhartman@whitecase.com

PAUL G. HEGLAND, born Fargo, North Dakota, May 27, 1943; admitted to bar, 1971, Minnesota; 2000, District of Columbia and U.S. Court of International Trade. *Education:* University of Minnesota (B.A., 1968; J.D., 1971). ***PRACTICE AREAS:*** Customs; International Trade. ***Email:*** phegland@whitecase.com

ECKHARD R. HELLBECK, admitted to bar, 1996, New York; 2000, Frankfurt am Main, Germany; 2001, District of Columbia. *Education:* Freie Universitat Berlin (State Exam, 1986); American University, Washington College of Law (LL.M., 1987). *Member:* Bar Association of the District of Columbia; New York State, American and International Bar Associations; German-American Law Association; American Society of International Law; International Law Association. ***Email:*** ehellbeck@whitecase.com

DOUGLAS M. JASINSKI, born Lexington, Kentucky, March 28, 1968; admitted to bar, 1994, Maryland; 1997, District of Columbia. *Education:* Catholic University of America (B.A., 1990; J.D., 1994). *Member:* American Bar Association (Section of Antitrust Law). ***Email:*** djasinski@whitecase.com

GEOFFREY B. LANNING, born New York, N.Y., February 8, 1946; admitted to bar, 1976, California (Not admitted in District of Columbia). *Education:* Harvard University (B.A., 1970); University of San Diego (J.D., 1976). ***Email:*** glanning@whitecase.com

ADAMS C. LEE, born Columbus, Ohio, May 25, 1967; admitted to bar, 1994, New York; 1995, District of Columbia. *Education:* Harvard University (A.B., 1989); New York University (J.D., 1993). ***Email:*** alee@whitecase.com

ALBERT LO, born February 15, 1966; admitted to bar, 1997, Illinois; 1998, District of Columbia. *Education:* Louisiana State University (B.S., 1994); Chicago-Kent College of Law (J.D., 1997). ***Email:*** alo@whitecase.com

RAJEEV K. MALIK, born Akron, Ohio, July 17, 1973; admitted to bar, 1998, Ohio; 2000, District of Columbia. *Education:* Miami University (B.A., 1995); The Ohio State University (J.D., 1998). ***Email:*** rmalik@whitecase.com

WILLIAM J. MORAN, admitted to bar, 1999, Virginia (Not admitted in District of Columbia). *Education:* University of Notre Dame (B.A., 1992); University of Virginia (J.D., 1999). ***Email:*** wmoran@whitecase.com

(This Listing Continued)

FRANK H. MORGAN, born Lower Merion, Pennsylvania, May 9, 1973; admitted to bar, 1998, Virginia; 2000, District of Columbia. *Education:* Villanova University (B.A., 1995); Columbus School of Law, Catholic University of America (J.D., 1998). ***Email:*** fmorgan@whitecase.com

EMIL NEMEC, born Bratislava, Slovak Republic, March 15, 1967; admitted to bar, 1994, Czech Republic; 1997, New York; 1998, Slovak Republic (Not admitted in District of Columbia). *Education:* Comenius University, Slovak Republic (J.D., 1989); George Washington University, USA (LL.M., 1992); Comenius University (Ph.D., 1995). ***Email:*** enemec@whitecase.com

JOHN W. OWCZARSKI, born Waterbury, Connecticut, October 26, 1962; admitted to bar, 1988, Massachusetts; 1990, New York; 1996, District of Columbia. *Education:* University of Pennsylvania (B.S., 1985); Columbia University (J.D., 1988). ***Email:*** jowczarski@whitecase.com

FRANK PANOPOULOS, born New York, N.Y., December 15, 1957; admitted to bar, 1992, New York; 1998, District of Columbia. *Education:* Manhattan College (B.A., 1980); Columbia University (J.D., 1991). *Member:* The District of Columbia Bar; New York State Bar Association. ***Email:*** fpanopoulos@whitecase.com

GEORGE L. PAUL, born Huntsville, Alabama, July 12, 1967; admitted to bar, 1993, New York; 1995, District of Columbia. *Education:* Mississippi State University (B.A., 1989); Harvard University (J.D., 1992). ***Email:*** gpaul@whitecase.com

STEPHEN R. PAYNE, born Summit, New Jersey, November 16, 1959; admitted to bar, 1988, New York (Not admitted in District of Columbia). *Education:* Middlebury College (B.A., 1982); Cornell Law School (J.D., 1987). ***Email:*** spayne@whitecase.com

JOHN ERIC PODGORE, born San Antonio, Texas, December 7, 1970; admitted to bar, 1998, New York (Not admitted in District of Columbia). *Education:* Princeton University (A.B., 1993); Duke University School of Law (J.D., 1997). ***PRACTICE AREAS:*** Corporate Law. ***Email:*** jpodgore@whitecase.com

AMA B. ROMAINE, born Toronto, Ontario, Canada, May 27, 1972; admitted to bar, 2000, New York; 2001, District of Columbia. *Education:* York University (B.A., 1994); Howard University (J.D., 1999). ***Email:*** aromaine@whitecase.com

FRANK J. SCHWEITZER, born Bridgeport, Connecticut, September 14, 1968; admitted to bar, 1994, New York; 1996, District of Columbia; 1997, U.S. Court of Appeals for the Federal Circuit and U.S. Court of International Trade. *Education:* Fairfield University (B.A., 1990); Capital University Law School (J.D., 1993); Georgetown University Law Center (LL.M., 1996). ***Email:*** fschweitzer@whitecase.com

JONATHAN SEIGER, born New York, N.Y., January 11, 1957; admitted to bar, 2000, Rhode Island (Not admitted in District of Columbia). *Education:* University of Wisconsin-Madison (B.A., 1978); Georgetown University Law Center (J.D., 1999). *Member:* Rhode Island and American Bar Associations. ***PRACTICE AREAS:*** International Trade Law; Corporate Law. ***Email:*** jseiger@whitecase.com

MARK A. SHALABY, born San Jose, California, May 13, 1973; admitted to bar, 1999, New York and District of Columbia. *Education:* Stanford University (B.A., 1994); Georgetown Law Center (J.D./M.S.F.S., 1998). ***Email:*** mshalaby@whitecase.com

RUTA KALVAITIS SKUCAS, born St. John's, Newfoundland, Canada, July 1, 1971; admitted to bar, 1998, Maryland; 2001, District of Columbia. *Education:* Boston College (B.A., M.A., 1993); Boston University (J.D., 1998). ***Email:*** rskucas@whitecase.com

ERIC P. SPOONER, born New York, N.Y., September 22, 1965; admitted to bar, 1992, Georgia; 1995, District of Columbia. *Education:* Brown University (A.B., 1987); Harvard Law School (J.D., 1992). ***Email:*** espooner@whitecase.com

LEE A. STEVEN, born Mexico City, Mexico, April 12, 1962; admitted to bar, 1998, Virginia; 2000, District of Columbia. *Education:* Wheaton College (B.S., 1985); University of Texas at Arlington (M.A., 1991); University of Virginia (J.D., 1998). ***Email:*** lsteven@whitecase.com

PAUL F. STONE, born Santa Barbara, California, July 29, 1971; admitted to bar, 2000, California; 2001, District of Columbia. *Education:* University of California at San Diego (B.A., 1994); Cambridge University (M.Phil., 1996); University of Pennsylvania (J.D., 1999). ***Email:*** pstone@whitecase.com

CALEB W. SULLIVAN, born Harvard, Massachusetts, June 16, 1958; admitted to bar, 1985, California; 2001, District of Columbia. *Education:* Grinnell College (A.B.., 1980); Golden Gate University (J.D., 1985); Columbia Law School (LL.M., 2001); School of International and Public Affairs (M.I.A., 2001). *Member:* State Bar of California; American Bar Association; American Society of International Law. ***Email:*** csullivan@whitecase.com

(This Listing Continued)

WHITE & CASE, Washington—Continued

JEFFREY D. TALBERT, born Goldsboro, North Carolina, February 9, 1975; admitted to bar, 2000, Hawaii and District of Columbia. *Education:* Kalamazoo College (B.A., 1997); University of Michigan (J.D., 2000). ***Email:*** jtalbert@whitecase.com

PETER P. THIEMAN, born Washington D.C., January 17, 1968; admitted to bar, 1994, Virginia; 1998, District of Columbia. *Education:* University of Virginia (B.A., 1990); Chicago-Kent College of Law (J.D., 1993). *Member:* District of Columbia Bar; Virginia and American Bar Associations; Energy Bar Association. ***Email:*** pthieman@whitecase.com

MARA E. R. TOPPING, born Washington, D.C., December 8, 1959; admitted to bar, 1999, New York; 2000, District of Columbia. *Education:* Cornell University (B.A., 1980); Institute of Archaeology, University of London (M.A., 1981); University of Chicago (Ph.D., 1995); Georgetown University Law Center (J.D., 1998). *Member:* The District of Columbia Bar; New York State and American Bar Associations. ***Email:*** mtopping@whitecase.com

LYLE B. VANDER SCHAAF, born Sioux Center, Iowa, July 14, 1962; admitted to bar, 1988, Maryland; 1989, District of Columbia. *Education:* University of Iowa (B.A., 1985); Washington College of Law of American University (J.D., 1988). Office of General Counsel, U.S. International Trade Commission, 1991-1996. *Member:* American Bar Association (International Trade Section); American Society of International Law (Secretary and Newsletter Editor). ***Email:*** lvanderschaaf@whitecase.com

HEATHER J. VAN SLOOTEN, born Bethesda, Maryland, October 22, 1972; admitted to bar, 2001, New York (Not admitted in District of Columbia). *Education:* American University (B.A., 1995); University of Virginia (J.D., 2000). *Member:* New York State and American Bar Associations. ***Email:*** hvanslooten@whitecase.com

FRANCIS A. VASQUEZ, JR., born Topeka, Kansas, October 11, 1964; admitted to bar, 1992, New York; 1994, District of Columbia. *Education:* California Institute of Technology (B.S., 1988); Georgetown University Law Center (J.D., 1991). *Member:* The District of Columbia Bar; New York State and American Bar Associations. ***Email:*** fvasquez@whitecase.com

DONNA VETRANO, admitted to bar, 2001, New York (Not admitted in District of Columbia). *Education:* Hofstra University (B.A., 1992); Tulane Law School (J.D., 2000). *Member:* New York State Bar Association. ***PRACTICE AREAS:*** Litigation; Intellectual Property. ***Email:*** dvetrano@whitecase.com

KRISTIN D. WELLS, born Washington, D.C., December 27, 1966; admitted to bar, 1999, Maryland (Not admitted in District of Columbia). *Education:* Brown University (A.B., 1989); American University (M.A., 1994); Columbia Law School (J.D., 1996). ***Email:*** kwells@whitecase.com

KRISTINA ZISSIS, born San Francisco, California, April 17, 1966; admitted to bar, 1994, Pennsylvania; 1996, District of Columbia. *Education:* Johns Hopkins University (B.A., 1988; M.A., 1989); American University (J.D., 1994). ***Email:*** kzissis@whitecase.com

(For biographical data as to other locations, see Professional Biographies at New York, New York; Los Angeles and Palo Alto, California; Miami, Florida; Berlin, Dresden, Düsseldorf, Frankfurt and Hamburg, Germany; Bratislava, Slovakia; Brussels, Belgium; Budapest, Hungary; Helsinki, Finland; Istanbul and Ankara, Turkey; London, England; Milan and Rome, Italy; Moscow, Russia; Paris, France; Prague, Czech Republic; Stockholm, Sweden; Warsaw, Poland; Jeddah and Riyadh, Saudi Arabia; Manama, Bahrain; Almaty, Kazakhstan; Bangkok, Thailand; Bombay, India; Hanoi and Ho Chi Minh City, Vietnam; Hong Kong and Shanghai, China; Jakarta, Indonesia; Singapore, Republic of Singapore; Tokyo, Japan; Johannesburg, Republic of South Africa; Mexico City, Mexico; São Paulo, Brazil).

WHITEFORD, TAYLOR & PRESTON L.L.P.

Established in 1933

1025 CONNECTICUT AVENUE, N.W.
WASHINGTON, D.C. 20036-5405
Telephone: 202-659-6800
Fax: 202-331-0573
Email: wt&pllp@wtplaw.com
URL: http://www.wtplaw.com

Baltimore, Maryland Office: 7 Saint Paul Street. Telephone: 410-347-8700. Fax: 410-752-7092.
Towson, Maryland Office: 210 West Pennsylvania Avenue. Telephone: 410-832-2000. Fax: 410-832-2015.
Columbia, Maryland Office: 10440 Little Patuxent Parkway. Telephone: 410-884-0700. Fax: 410-884-0719.
Alexandria, Virginia Office: 1317 King Street. Telephone: 703-836-5742. Fax: 703-836-0265.

(This Listing Continued)

Administrative Law, Admiralty and Maritime Law, Advertising and Marketing, Aged and Aging, Agency and Distributorships, Antitrust and Trade Regulation, Appellate Practice, Bankruptcy, Banking and Finance, Biotechnology, Business Law, Chancery and Equity, Civil Practice, Civil Rights, Class Action Defense, Collections, Commercial Law, Commercial Real Estate, Communications and Media, Computers and Software, Constitutional Law, Construction Law, Consumer Law, Contracts, Copyrights, Corporate Law, Debtor and Creditor, Disabilities, Education Law, Election, Campaign and Political Law, Eminent Domain, Employee Benefits, Energy, Environmental Law, Equipment Finance and Leasing, Fidelity and Surety, Finance, Franchises and Franchising, General Practice, Government, Government Contracts, Guardianship and Conservatorship, Health and Hospital, Housing Law, Immigration and Naturalization, Insurance, Insurance Defense, Intellectual Property, International Law, International Trade, Investments, Labor and Employment, Law Enforcement, Leases and Leasing, Legal Ethics and Professional Responsibility, Libel, Slander and Defamation, Litigation, Media Law, Medical Malpractice, Medicare and Medicaid, Mergers, Acquisition and Divestitures, Mortgages, Municipal Law, Natural Resources, Negligence, Nonprofit and Charitable Organizations, Occupational Safety and Health, Partnership Law, Patents, Personal Injury, Premise Liability, Privacy Law, Probate, Products Liability, Professional Liability, Property Law, Public Finance, Railroad Law, Real Estate, Regulatory Law, RICO, Securities, Taxation, Technology and Science, Torts, Toxic Torts, Trade Secrets, Trademarks, Transportation, Trusts and Estates, Unfair Competition, White Collar Crime, Wills, Workers Compensation, Zoning, Planning and Land Use.

FIRM PROFILE: Whiteford, Taylor & Preston L.L.P. is a full service law firm providing representation in the Mid-Atlantic Region for local, national and multinational clients. All offices offer the full resources of the firm with practice concentrations that reflect the special needs of groups of clients and industries. Our diverse client base includes businesses of all sizes and types including banks and financial institutions, manufacturers, distributors, health care institutions and providers, retailers, contractors, service businesses, insurers and non-profit organizations. For more information about Whiteford, Taylor & Preston, and greater detail about our attorneys, please visit our website: www.wtplaw.com.

PARTNERS

GLENN R. BONARD, born Nice, France, 1943; admitted to bar, 1968, Virginia; 1969, U.S. Court of Military Appeals; 1972, District of Columbia. *Education:* Lehigh University (B.A., 1965); Georgetown University (J.D., 1968); George Washington University (LL.M., 1973). *Member:* District of Columbia Bar; Virginia State Bar; American Bar Association. ***PRACTICE AREAS:*** Business Law; Trusts and Estates; Taxation; Real Estate. ***Email:*** gbonard@wtplaw.com

JOSEPH D. DOUGLASS, born Little Rock, Arkansas, 1952; admitted to bar, 1978, Maryland; 1984, District of Columbia. *Education:* University of Michigan (A.B., 1974); University of Pennsylvania (J.D., 1977). *Member:* District of Columbia Bar; Montgomery County, Maryland State and American Bar Associations. ***PRACTICE AREAS:*** Community Association Law; Condominium Association Law; Cooperative Housing Law; Homeowners Association Law. ***Email:*** jdouglass@wtplaw.com

JULIANNE ERIN DYMOWSKI, born Cleveland, Ohio, 1967; admitted to bar, 1992, Maryland; 1993, District of Columbia. *Education:* George Washington University (B.A., 1989); Washington College of Law, American University (J.D., 1992). *Member:* Montgomery County and Maryland State Bar Associations; District of Columbia Bar. (Also at Columbia, MD). ***PRACTICE AREAS:*** Community Association Law; Cooperative Association Law; Real Estate Collections; Contracts; Accreditation Law. ***Email:*** jdymowski@wtplaw.com

JOHN J. HATHWAY, born Norfolk, Virginia, 1955; admitted to bar, 1985, Maryland; 1988, District of Columbia. *Education:* Catholic University (B.A., 1977); University of Baltimore (J.D., 1985). Law Clerk, Honorable Joseph H.H. Kaplan, Circuit Court for Baltimore City, 1985-1986. *Member:* Maryland State Bar Association; District of Columbia Bar. (Also at Columbia, MD). ***PRACTICE AREAS:*** Insurance Litigation; Business Litigation. ***Email:*** jhathway@wtplaw.com

KENNETH J. INGRAM, born Jersey City, New Jersey, 1945; admitted to bar, 1970, Missouri; 1972, District of Columbia; 1973, U.S. Claims Court; 1982, Virginia. *Education:* Amherst College (B.A., 1967); Washington University (J.D., 1970). *Member:* District of Columbia Bar; Virginia State Bar; U.S. Claims Court; American Bar Association. ***PRACTICE AREAS:*** Government Contracts; Community Association Law; Civil Practice. ***Email:*** kingram@wtplaw.com

ARTHUR P. ROGERS, born Lowell, Massachusetts, 1935; admitted to bar, 1960, Massachusetts and New Hampshire; 1985, District of Columbia. *Education:* Merrimack College (B.S., 1957); Suffolk University Law School (LL.B., 1960; J.D., 1964). *Member:* New Hampshire, Massachusetts and American Bar

(This Listing Continued)

Associations; District of Columbia Bar. ***PRACTICE AREAS:*** Corporate Law; Labor and Employment; Alternative Dispute Resolution; Mediation. ***Email:*** arogers@wtplaw.com

ANDREW J. TERRELL, born Abington, Pennsylvania, 1962; admitted to bar, 1989, Virginia; 1991, District of Columbia, U.S. Bankruptcy Court for the Eastern District of Virginia and U.S. District Court, Eastern District of Virginia; 1992, U.S. District Court, District of Columbia, U.S. Court of Appeals, District of Columbia and 4th Circuits. *Education:* St. Michael's College (B.A., 1984); George Mason University (J.D., 1989). *Member:* Alexandria and American Bar Associations; Virginia State Bar; District of Columbia Bar. ***PRACTICE AREAS:*** Litigation; Construction Law; Insurance Defense; Condominium Law. ***Email:*** aterrell@wtplaw.com

RESIDENT OF COUNSEL

CATHERINE D. BERTRAM, born Minneapolis, Minnesota, 1964; admitted to bar, 1989, Maryland; 1990, District of Columbia; 1995, Texas; U.S. District Court, District of Maryland; U.S. District Court for the District of Columbia; U.S. District Court, Eastern and Northern Districts of Texas. *Education:* University of Wisconsin, Madison (B.A., 1986); Catholic University of America (J.D., 1989). Federal Appointee to National Advisory Research Resources Council, 2000-2004. Civil Mediator, District of Columbia Superior Court. *Member:* Maryland State Bar Association, Inc.; The District of Columbia Bar; State Bar of Texas; District of Columbia Women's Bar Association; District of Columbia Hospital Association; District of Columbia Defense Lawyers Association; Maryland Society of Risk Managers; Defense Research Institute. ***PRACTICE AREAS:*** Medical Malpractice; General Insurance Defense. ***Email:*** cbertram@wtplaw.com

EDWARD S. COGEN, born New York, N.Y., 1935; admitted to bar, 1960, New York; 1961, District of Columbia; 1969, U.S. Supreme Court. *Education:* Cornell University (B.A., 1956; J.D., with distinction, 1960). Editor-in-Chief, Cornell Law Quarterly (1959-1960). *Member:* District of Columbia Bar; American Bar Association. ***PRACTICE AREAS:*** Corporate Law; Business Law. ***Email:*** ecogen@wtplaw.com

LEE A. SATTERFIELD, born Chowan County, North Carolina, 1933; admitted to bar, 1963, District of Columbia. *Education:* Howard University (A.B., 1962; LL.B., 1962). *Member:* District of Columbia Bar; Bar Association of the District of Columbia; American and National Bar Associations; Federal Communications Bar Association. ***PRACTICE AREAS:*** Communications Law; Regulatory Law; Government Affairs; Corporate Law. ***Email:*** wt&pllp@wtplaw.com

C. WILLIAM TAYLER, born Buffalo, New York, 1923; admitted to bar, 1949, New York; 1952, District of Columbia; 1954, U.S. Supreme Court. *Education:* University of Rochester (A.B., 1947); Edinburgh University, Edinburgh, Scotland; Harvard University (J.D., 1949). President, Washington Metropolitan Chapter, Community Associations Institute, 1986, Chair, D.C. Legislative Committee, 1998—. *Member:* District of Columbia Bar; Bar Association of the District of Columbia; American Bar Association. Fellow, American Bar Foundation. ***PRACTICE AREAS:*** Condominium Law; Cooperative Association Law; Education Law; Litigation. ***Email:*** wtayler@wtplaw.com

ASSOCIATES

CRYSTAL S. DEESE, born Charlotte, North Carolina, 1969; admitted to bar, 1996, South Carolina and Maryland; 1997, District of Columbia and Virginia. *Education:* Winthrop College (B.A., summa cum laude, 1993); American University (J.D., cum laude, 1996). *Member:* The District of Columbia Bar; South Carolina Bar; Virginia State Bar; Maryland State Bar Association, Inc. ***PRACTICE AREAS:*** Litigation; Medical Malpractice. ***Email:*** cdeese@wtplaw.com

JANE SAINDON DUDLEY, born Plainfield, New Jersey, 1949; admitted to bar, 1997, Virginia; 1998, Maryland and District of Columbia. *Education:* American University (B.A., 1971); George Mason University School of Law (J.D., 1997). ***PRACTICE AREAS:*** Business Law; Estate Planning; Community Association Law. ***Email:*** jdudley@wtplaw.com

JENNIFER S. JACKMAN, born Maryland, 1973; admitted to bar, 1998, Maryland; 2000, District of Columbia; 2001, Virginia. *Education:* University of Delaware (B.A., 1995); University of Baltimore (J.D., cum laude, 1998); The George Washington University School of Law (LL.M., 2000). *Member:* Frederick County, Maryland State and American Bar Associations; The District of Columbia Bar; District of Columbia Defense Bar. ***PRACTICE AREAS:*** Insurance Defense Litigation; Litigation; Medical Malpractice Defense. ***Email:*** jjackman@wtplaw.com

BRIAN J. McCABE, born Washington, D.C., 1969; admitted to bar, 1995, Maryland; 1996, District of Columbia, U.S. District Court, District of Maryland and U.S. District Court for the District of Columbia; 1997, Virginia; 1998, U.S. District Court, Eastern District of Virginia. *Education:* Boston College (B.A., cum laude, 1991); George Washington University National Law Center (J.D., 1995). *Member:* Montgomery County, Maryland State and Virginia Bar Associations; District of Columbia Bar. ***PRACTICE AREAS:*** Litigation; Community Association Law. ***Email:*** bmccabe@wplaw.com

SONJA A. MISHALANIE, born Calgary, Alberta, 1972; admitted to bar, 2000, Virginia (Not admitted in District of Columbia). *Education:* Cornell University (B.S., 1994); University of Maryland (J.D., 2000). *Member:* Virginia and American Bar Associations. ***PRACTICE AREAS:*** Civil Litigation; Condominium Association Law; Environmental Law. ***Email:*** smishalanie@wtplaw.com

VALERIE L. TETRO, born Manhattan, New York, 1960; admitted to bar, 1986, Maryland; 1994, U.S. Court of Appeals, 4th Circuit; 1998, U.S. District Court, District of Maryland; 1999, District of Columbia. *Education:* Connecticut College (B.A., 1982); The Washington College of Law, American University (J.D., 1985); Georgetown University Law Center (LL.M., 1986). *Member:* Maryland State and American Bar Associations; The District of Columbia Bar. ***PRACTICE AREAS:*** Insurance Defense Litigation; Medical Malpractice; Appellate Practice; Insurance Coverage. ***Email:*** vtetro@wtplaw.com

ERIC A. VENDT, born Washington, D.C., 1969; admitted to bar, 1995, Virginia; 1996, Maryland; 1998, District of Columbia. *Education:* Bucknell University (B.S., 1991); The American University (J.D., 1995). *Member:* American Bar Association; Northern Virginia Society of Certified Public Accountants. ***PRACTICE AREAS:*** Business Law; Taxation and Estate Planning; Technology; Copyright Law. ***Email:*** evendt@wtplaw.com

(For complete biographical data on personnel at Baltimore, Columbia and Towson, Maryland, see Professional Biographies at those locations)

WHITNEY & BOGRIS, LLP

WASHINGTON, D.C.

(See Towson, Maryland)

Trial and Appellate Practice in all State and Federal Courts, Products Liability, Medical Malpractice, Toxic Torts, Employment Law, Insurance Coverage, Business Litigation.

THE WICKS GROUP, PLLC

Established in 1999

1101 17TH STREET, SUITE 604
WASHINGTON, D.C. 20036
Telephone: 202-457-7790
Fax: 202-457-7799
Email: TheWicksGroup@aol.com

Aviation, International, Commercial Transportation and Regulatory Law.

FIRM PROFILE: The firm is a multidisciplinary practice ("MPD") who represents a number of foreign and domestic aviation interests in regulatory and commercial matters, including U.S., Canadian, British and companies based in the former Soviet Union. We represent a major U.S. passenger airline on regulatory matters in Washington DC and act as General Counsel, North America, for one of our largest clients - a foreign cargo airline. We also represent a major British ports and airport management company in commercial and regulatory matters in the United States. We secure various types of governmental approvals and handle other regulatory activities involving the Federal Aviation Administration, the Department of State, the Department of Transportation, the Treasury Department, the Immigration and Naturalization Service, and relevant foreign governmental counterparts. We also assist in various business matters in the United States and Europe. We provide Washington regulatory support on behalf of our clients including FAA-related certification issues and enforcement actions. We handle a variety of general corporate tasks including drafting, analyzing and negotiating purchase agreements, lease agreements, financing arrangements, joint venture agreements, and agency agreements. The firm also consults Russian clients in a variety of "doing Business" issues in the United States, as well as U.S. clients in "doing Business" issues in Russia/RIS, and assists clients in establishing and facilitating their business relationships in the U.S. and Russian/RIS markets.

GLENN P. WICKS, born Litchfield, Connecticut, April 8, 1966; admitted to bar, 1991, Virginia; 1992, District of Columbia. *Education:* George Washington University (B.A., magna cum laude, 1988; J.D., with honors, 1991). Editor, George Washington Journal of International Law and Economics, 1990-1991. Attorney: Ginsburg, Feldman & Bress, Chartered, 1990-1992; Hogan & Hartson L.L.P., 1992-1999. *Member:* Virginia State Bar; The District of Columbia Bar; American Bar Association; International Aviation Club. ***PRACTICE AREAS:*** Aviation; International; Transportation; Regulatory. ***Email:*** gpwicks@aol.com

EKATERINA A. GRIMES, born Moscow, Russia, December 7, 1954. *Education:* Moscow State Linguistic University (graduate degree in Linguistics,

(This Listing Continued)

THE WICKS GROUP, PLLC, Washington—Continued

with honors, 1997; Candidate of Sciences/Ph.D. Linguistics, 1986). Department of English Stylistics, Moscow State Linguistic University, 1977-1987; Department of English and Foreign Economic Relations, Academy of Foreign Trade, Moscow, Russia, 1987-1992; Russian Specialist, Hogan & Hartson, L.L.P. from 1993-2000. (Consultant). ***Email:*** ekagrimes@aol.com

WICKWIRE GAVIN, P.C.

TWO LAFAYETTE CENTRE
SUITE 450, 1133-21ST STREET, N.W.
WASHINGTON, D.C. 20036-3002
Telephone: 202-887-5200
Telecopier: 202-223-0120
URL: http://www.wickwire.com

Vienna, Virginia Office: Wickwire Gavin, P.C., International Gateway, 8100 Boone Boulevard, Suite 700. Telephone: 703-790-8750. Fax: 703-448-1801.
Madison, Wisconsin Office: Wickwire Gavin, P.C., Suite 800, 22 East Mifflin Street, P.O. Box 1683. Telephone: 608-257-2029. Telecopier: 608-257-2029.
Los Angeles, California, Office: Wickwire Gavin LLP, 38th Floor, 725 South Figueroa Street. Telephone: 213-688-9500. Telecopier: 213-627-6342.

Construction, Government and Public Contracts, Fidelity and Surety, Federal Grant, Environmental, Bankruptcy, Corporate, and Commercial Law.

FIRM PROFILE: Since its founding in 1974, Wickwire Gavin, P.C. has been recognized as a prominent force in the areas of construction and government contracts. We have extensive experience in construction scheduling, the selection and creation of project delivery systems, risk allocation, design professional malpractice, privatization, ADR, claims, and litigation. In the government contracts area, we regularly assist clients with bid protests, contract administration, and federal assistance audits. We provide advice on postal procurement, suspension, debarment, the False Claims Act, and claims and actions before the Boards of Contract Appeals and the U.S. Court of Federal Claims. Our experience in these areas, combined with the technical backgrounds of our attorneys, enables us to provide domestic and international clients with practical business advice, legal counsel, and representation in our specific practice areas. The nearly 40 Wickwire Gavin attorneys practice from offices in Virginia, Washington, DC, Wisconsin, and California.

Jon M. Wickwire (See Vienna, Virginia Listing)
Donald G. Gavin (See Vienna, Virginia Listing)
Robert J. Smith (See Madison, Wisconsin Listing)
Michael C. Loulakis (See Vienna, Virginia Listing)
Stanley M. Salus (See Vienna, Virginia Listing)
Brian W. Mullins (See Madison, Wisconsin Listing)
Jeffrey G. Gilmore (See Vienna, Virginia Listing)
Owen J. Shean (See Vienna, Virginia Listing)
Stephen B. Hurlbut (See Vienna, Virginia Listing)
Hugh N. Anderson (See Madison, Wisconsin Listing)
David P. Hendel (See Vienna, Virginia Listing)
David P. Dapper (See Los Angeles, California Listing)
Edward G. Gallagher (See Vienna, Virginia Listing)
William B. Fisher (See Vienna, Virginia Listing)
Shannon J. Briglia (See Vienna, Virginia Listing)
Carl A. Sinderbrand (See Madison, Wisconsin Listing)
Michael A. Gatje (See Vienna, Virginia Listing)
Stephen J. Densmore (See Los Angeles, California Office)
Mark R. Berry (See Vienna, Virginia Listing)
Mark J. Groff (See Vienna, Virginia Listing)
Daniel J. Donohue (See Vienna, Virginia Listing)
Roger P. Heyman (See Los Angeles, California Listing)
Jodi M. Lewis (See Los Angeles, California Listing)
Claude P. Goddard, Jr. (See Vienna, Virginia Listing)

Brian P. Waagner (See Vienna, Virginia Listing)
Elizabeth M. Lascheid (See Los Angeles, California Listing)
Simon J. Santiago (See Vienna, Virginia Listing)
Samuel K. Robison (See Vienna, Virginia Listing)
Kayhan M. Fatemi (See Los Angeles, California Listing)
Hal J. Perloff (See Vienna, Virginia Listing)
Robert H. Shaffer, Jr. (See Los Angeles, California Listing)
Mary K. Monville (Not admitted in DC; See Madison, Wisconsin Listing)
Louis J. Dennis (See Los Angeles, California Listing)
Lauren P. McLaughlin (See Vienna, Virginia Listing)

(This Listing Continued)

Julia Ann Bitner (See Vienna, Virginia Listing)
Scott B. Hillman (See Vienna, Virginia Listing)

OF COUNSEL

J. Kent Holland, Jr. (See Vienna, Virginia Listing)

(For biographical data on other personnel, see Vienna, Virginia, Madison, Wisconsin and Los Angeles, California Professional Biographies)

WILEY REIN & FIELDING LLP

1776 K STREET, N.W.
WASHINGTON, D.C. 20006-2304
Telephone: 202-719-7000
Facsimile: 202-719-7049
URL: http://www.wrf.com

McLean, Virginia Office: 7925 Jones Branch Drive, Suite 6200. Telephone: 703-905-2800. URL: http://www.wrf.com.

General Practice, Advertising, Antitrust, Appellate, Aviation, Broadcasting, Business and Finance, Communications, Copyright, E-Commerce, Education, Election Law and Government Ethics, Employment and Labor, Energy, Food and Drug, Franchise, Government Affairs, Government Contracts, Health Care, Insurance, Intellectual Property, International Trade, Internet and E-Commerce, Legislative, Litigation, Mass Media, Patent, Privacy, Public Policy, Regulatory, Technology, Telecommunications, Trademark, White Collar Defense, Wireless.

MEMBERS OF FIRM

RICHARD E. WILEY, born Peoria, Illinois, July 20, 1934; admitted to bar, 1958, Illinois; 1972, District of Columbia. *Education:* Northwestern University (B.S., 1955; J.D., 1958); Georgetown University (LL.M., 1962). General Counsel, 1970-1972, Commissioner, 1972-1974 and Chairman, 1974-1977, Federal Communications Commission. *Member:* Federal (President, 1976-1977) and American (Chairman, Administrative Law and Regulatory Practice Section, 1994; Chairman, Young Lawyers Section, 1969; Chairman, Board of Editors, ABA Journal, 1983-1988; Chairman, Forum Committee on Communications, 1985-1987; Chairman, Committee on Scope and Correlation, 1988-1989; Chairman, Committee on Governmental Affairs, 1997-2000) Bar Associations; Federal Communications Bar Association (President, 1986-1987); American Bar Foundation (Life Fellow). ***PRACTICE AREAS:*** Communications. ***Email:*** rwiley@wrf.com

BERT W. REIN, born Brooklyn, New York, February 7, 1941; admitted to bar, 1964, District of Columbia. *Education:* Amherst College (B.A., summa cum laude, 1961); Harvard Law School (LL.B., summa cum laude, 1964). Law Clerk to Justice John M. Harlan, U.S. Supreme Court, 1966-1967. Deputy Assistant Secretary of State, Economic and Business Affairs, 1970-1973. Director, U.S. Chamber of Commerce, 1990-1994. Director, National Chamber Litigation Center, 1990. Author: "Whither Daubert? Reliable Resolution of Scientifically-Based Causality Issues in Toxic Tort Cases," Rutgers Law Review, Winter 1998. *Member:* International Trade Commission Trial Lawyers Association (President 1990-1991). ***PRACTICE AREAS:*** Litigation; Antitrust; International. ***Email:*** brein@wrf.com

FRED F. FIELDING, born Philadelphia, Pennsylvania, March 21, 1939; admitted to bar, 1965, Pennsylvania; 1974, District of Columbia. *Education:* Gettysburg College (A.B., 1961); University of Virginia (J.D., 1964). Member, Editorial Board, University of Virginia Law Review, 1962-1964. Assistant Counsel, 1970-1972, Deputy Counsel, 1972-1974 and Counsel, 1981-1986, to the President of the United States. U.S. Designated Arbitrator, Arbitration Tribunal on U.S.-U.K. Air Dispute, 1989-1994. Member, Board of Directors, U.S. Air Shuttle, 1992-1997. Member: Panel of Arbitrators of the International Centre for Settlement of Investment Disputes, 1987-1995 (Presidential Appointment); President's Commission on Federal Ethics Law Reform, 1989 (Presidential Appointment); Secretary of Transportation's Task Force on Aviation Disasters, 1997-1998 (Secretarial Appointment); American Bar Association, Standing Committee on Federal Judiciary, 1996—, Life Fellow. Reagan-Bush Transition: Conflict of Interest Counsel; Bush-Quayle Campaign, 1988: Republican National Convention Advisor; Campaign Counsel - Senator Quayle. Bush-Quayle Transition: Deputy Director. Bush-Quayle Campaign, 1992: Senior Legal Advisor. Bush-Cheney Transition, Clearance Counsel, 2001. Center for Democracy: Member, Board of Directors, 1995-1998, Acting Chairman, 1996-1998; Board of Trustees, Gettysburg College, 1998—; The University of Virginia Miller Center, Commission of the Selection of Federal Judges, 1994-1997; Arlington Health Foundation, Board of Directors, 1997—. *Member:* Bar Association of the District of Columbia (Director, 1996-1998). ***PRACTICE AREAS:*** Government Affairs; Business Law; Crisis Management; White Collar Litigation. ***Email:*** ffielding@wrf.com

THOMAS W. BRUNNER, born New York, N.Y., September 9, 1945; admitted to bar, 1970, Connecticut; 1973, District of Columbia. *Education:* Co-

(This Listing Continued)

lumbia University (A.B., cum laude, 1966); Yale University (J.D., 1970). ***PRACTICE AREAS:*** Insurance; Privacy Law; Health Care; Litigation. ***Email:*** tbrunner@wrf.com

JAMES H. WALLACE, JR., born Atlanta, Georgia, February 8, 1941; admitted to bar, 1967, District of Columbia; registered to practice before U.S. Patent and Trademark Office. *Education:* University of South Carolina (B.S.E.E., 1963); Georgetown University Law Center (J.D., 1966). Tau Beta Pi; Eta Kappa Nu; Pi Mu Epsilon. Associate Editor, Georgetown Law Journal, 1965-1966. ***PRACTICE AREAS:*** Litigation; Intellectual Property; Patents. ***Email:*** jwallace@wrf.com

CHARLES OWEN VERRILL, JR., born Biddeford, Maine, September 30, 1937; admitted to bar, 1962, District of Columbia; 1966, U.S. Supreme Court. *Education:* Tufts University (A.B., 1959); Duke University (J.D., 1962). Order of the Coif. Adjunct Professor, International Trade Law and Regulation, Georgetown University Law Center, 1978—. Charles Fahy Distinguished Adjunct Professor, Georgetown University Law Center, 1993. Adjunct Professor, International Trade Law and Business Transactions, Duke University Law School, 1998—. Member, Board of Visitors, Duke University Law School. Trustee, International Law Institute, 1981—. ***PRACTICE AREAS:*** International Trade; Mediation; Arbitration. ***Email:*** cverrill@wrf.com

RAND L. ALLEN, born Huntington, West Virginia, May 13, 1946; admitted to bar, 1976, Virginia; 1977, District of Columbia; 1984, U.S. Court of Federal Claims. *Education:* United States Military Academy (B.S., 1968); Georgetown University (J.D., 1976). *Member:* American Bar Association, Section on Public Contract Law (Secretary, 1996-1997; Vice-Chairman, 1997-1998; Chair-Elect, 1998-1999; Chair, 1999-2000). (Resident, McLean, Virginia Office). ***PRACTICE AREAS:*** Government Contracts; Litigation. ***Email:*** rallen@wrf.com

R. MICHAEL SENKOWSKI, born Vicksburg, Michigan, September 12, 1946; admitted to bar, 1971, Virginia; 1976, District of Columbia. *Education:* Yale University (B.A., 1968); George Washington University (J.D., with honors, 1971). Trial Attorney, Litigation Division, Federal Communications Commission, 1971-1974. Assistant to Chairman, Federal Communications Commission, 1974-1977. (Resident, McLean, Virginia Office). ***PRACTICE AREAS:*** Telecommunications; Internet; Electronic Commerce; International. ***Email:*** mike_senkowski@wrf.com

ANDREW S. KRULWICH, born New York, N.Y., July 7, 1941; admitted to bar, 1966, New York; 1968, District of Columbia; 1970, U.S. Supreme Court; 1973, U.S. Court of Appeals, 5th Circuit. *Education:* Columbia University (B.A., 1962; LL.B., 1965); Institute of Criminology, Cambridge University, England. Founder and Editor-in-Chief, Columbia Journal of Law and Social Problems, 1964-1965. Author: "Evolving Constitutional Privacy Doctrines Affecting Healthcare Enterprise," 55 Food and Drug Law Journal 491, 2000. General Counsel, United States Consumer Product Safety Commission, 1979-1981. Chairman, OECD Working Party on Product Safety, 1980-1981. ***PRACTICE AREAS:*** Food and Drug; Advertising Law; Product Safety; Litigation. ***Email:*** akrulwic@wrf.com

LAWRENCE W. SECREST, III, born Alexandria, Virginia, November 24, 1942; admitted to bar, 1968, Virginia; 1972, District of Columbia. *Education:* American University (B.A., 1965); George Washington University (J.D., 1968). Legal Assistant to Chairman, 1974-1975, Administrative Assistant to Chairman, 1975-1976 and Deputy General Counsel, 1976-1977, Federal Communications Commission. ***PRACTICE AREAS:*** Communications. ***Email:*** lsecrest@wrf.com

RICHARD J. BODORFF, born Rockford, Illinois, February 25, 1949; admitted to bar, 1974, Tennessee; 1975, District of Columbia. *Education:* Denison University (B.A., cum laude, 1971); Vanderbilt University (J.D., 1974). Attorney: Legislation Division, 1974-1976; Litigation Division, 1976-1977, Office of General Counsel, Federal Communications Commission. Member, Board of Directors, Commonwealth Public Broadcasting Corporation, 1985—; Vice Chairman, 1994—. Trustee, Association of America's Public Television Stations, 1995-2001; Vice Chairman, 2000-2001. ***PRACTICE AREAS:*** Communications. ***Email:*** rbodorff@wrf.com

LAURA A. FOGGAN, born Lake Forest, Illinois, September 21, 1958; admitted to bar, 1983, District of Columbia. *Education:* University of Pennsylvania (B.A., magna cum laude, 1980; M.S.Ed., 1980); George Washington University (J.D., with high honors, 1983). Order of the Coif. Author: "The File on Trial: Bad Faith," Journal of Insurance Coverage, 2001. ***PRACTICE AREAS:*** Appellate; Insurance; Litigation. ***Email:*** lfoggan@wrf.com

JEFFREY S. LINDER, born Manhasset, New York, May 13, 1958; admitted to bar, 1983, District of Columbia. *Education:* Duke University (A.B., 1980); Stanford University (J.D., 1983). Phi Beta Kappa. ***PRACTICE AREAS:*** Communications. ***Email:*** jlinder@wrf.com

JAN WITOLD BARAN, born Ingolstadt, Germany, May 14, 1948; admitted to bar, 1973, Tennessee; 1976, District of Columbia; 1980, U.S. Supreme Court. *Education:* Ohio Wesleyan University (B.A., 1970); Vanderbilt University (J.D., 1973). Author: The Election Law Primer For Corporations, 1984, 1988, 1992, 2000; "Political Parties and Spending Limits," Harvard Journal of Law & Public Policy 83, 2000. Executive Assistant to the Chairman, Federal Election Commission, 1977-1979. General Counsel, George Bush for President, Inc., 1987-1988. General Counsel, Bush-Quayle 88, Inc., 1988. General Counsel, American Bicentennial Presidential Inaugural, Inc., 1988. General Counsel, Republican National Committee, 1989-1992. Member, President's Commission on Federal Ethics Law Reform, 1989. Ambassador and Chairman, U.S. Delegation, World Administrative Radio Conference (WARC), Spain (1991-1992). General Counsel, Business-Industry Political Action Committee (BIPAC), 1996—. *Member:* American Bar Association (Chairman, Standing Committee on Election Law, 1990-1993; Chairman, Advisory Commission on Election Law, 1993-2000; Member, Commission on Public Financing of Judicial Campaigns). ***PRACTICE AREAS:*** Election Law. ***Email:*** jbaran@wrf.com

WILLIAM A. ROBERTS, III, born Cape Girardeau, Missouri, November 5, 1947; admitted to bar, 1976, Iowa; 1978, District of Columbia; 1997, U.S. Court of Federal Claims. *Education:* Black Hills State College (B.A., 1973); University of Iowa (J.D., 1976); George Washington University (LL.M., with honors, 1980). Assistant to the General Counsel, U.S. Navy, 1979-1982. Chief Counsel, Wang Laboratories, Inc., Federal System Division, 1982-1985. Member, Task Force on E-Commerce, Defense Science Board. ***PRACTICE AREAS:*** Government Contracts. ***Email:*** wroberts@wrf.com

JOHN B. WYSS, born Evanston, Illinois, November 23, 1947; admitted to bar, 1972, California; 1974, District of Columbia. *Education:* Stanford University (B.S., summa cum laude, 1969); Yale University (J.D., 1972). Phi Beta Kappa. Attorney, Antitrust Division, Department of Justice, 1972-1974. ***PRACTICE AREAS:*** Antitrust; Litigation; Insurance; Intellectual Property. ***Email:*** jwyss@wrf.com

RICHARD L. McCONNELL, born Johnson City, Tennessee, March 15, 1952; admitted to bar, 1978, District of Columbia. *Education:* University of Tennessee (B.A., with highest honors, 1974); University of Virginia (J.D., 1977). Phi Beta Kappa. Order of the Coif. Member, Virginia Law Review. Law Clerk to Hon. Bailey Brown, U.S. District Court, Western District of Tennessee, 1977-1978. ***PRACTICE AREAS:*** Litigation; Insurance; Reinsurance; Environmental Law. ***Email:*** rmcconne@wrf.com

BRUCE L. McDONALD, born Chicago, Illinois, June 11, 1941; admitted to bar, 1967, District of Columbia. *Education:* Harvard College (A.B., 1963); Harvard Law School (LL.B., 1966); George Washington University (LL.M., 1970). ***PRACTICE AREAS:*** Litigation; Privacy. ***Email:*** bmcdonal@wrf.com

PETER J. KLARFELD, born Holyoke, Massachusetts, August 19, 1947; admitted to bar, 1973, Virginia; 1975, District of Columbia. *Education:* University of Virginia (B.A., 1969; J.D., 1973); University of Chicago (M.A., 1971). Order of the Coif. Member, Editorial Board, Virginia Law Review, 1972-1973. Law Clerk to Hon. Robert R. Merhige, Jr., U.S. District Court, Eastern District of Virginia, 1973-1974. Attorney-Advisor, Office of Legal Counsel, U.S. Department of Justice, 1974-1976. ***PRACTICE AREAS:*** Franchise; Litigation. ***Email:*** pklarfel@wrf.com

MATTHEW S. SIMCHAK, born Washington, D.C., September 29, 1947; admitted to bar, 1973, District of Columbia and U.S. Court of Federal Claims; 1985, Massachusetts. *Education:* Trinity College (B.A., 1969); University of Virginia (J.D., 1972). Member, Board of Advisors, Federal Contracts Report, 1984-1993. Member, Advisory Board of the Government Contractor, 1998—. Co-Author: "Licensing Software and Technology to the U.S. Government" (2000). Member, Government Operations Cluster, Clinton/Gore Transition, 1992. ***PRACTICE AREAS:*** Government Contracts. ***Email:*** msimchak@wrf.com

CARL R. RAMEY, born Binghamton, New York, February 15, 1941; admitted to bar, 1968, District of Columbia; 1999, Maryland. *Education:* Marietta College (A.B., 1962); Michigan State University (M.A., 1964); George Washington University (J.D., 1967). Member, Editorial Staff, George Washington Law Review, 1965-1967. Co-Chair, Editorial Advisory Board, Federal Communications Law Journal, 1993-1996. ***PRACTICE AREAS:*** Communications. ***Email:*** cramey@wrf.com

PHILIP J. DAVIS, born Urbana, Illinois, February 26, 1948; admitted to bar, 1973, Illinois; 1974, District of Columbia. *Education:* Trinity College, Connecticut (B.A., 1970); George Washington University (J.D., 1973). Order of the Coif. Notes Editor, The George Washington University Law Review. Law Clerk to Judge Bernard M. Decker, U.S. District Court, Northern District of Illinois, 1973-1974. ***PRACTICE AREAS:*** Government Contracts; Litigation. ***Email:*** pdavis@wrf.com

JAMES R. W. BAYES, born Washington, D.C., October 9, 1950; admitted to bar, 1976, Virginia; 1977, District of Columbia. *Education:* Duke University (B.A., magna cum laude, 1973); University of Virginia (J.D., 1976). Order of the Coif. Member, Editorial Board, Virginia Law Review, 1974-1976. ***PRACTICE AREAS:*** Communications. ***Email:*** jbayes@wrf.com

ROBERT J. BUTLER, born Niagara Falls, New York, May 10, 1954; admitted to bar, 1979, District of Columbia. *Education:* Michigan State University (B.A., with high honors, 1976); Harvard Law School (J.D., magna cum laude, 1979). Phi Kappa Phi. Member, Advisory Committee, Congressional

(This Listing Continued)

WILEY REIN & FIELDING LLP, Washington—Continued

Internet Caucus. *Member:* American Bar Association (Chair: Committee on Domestic Telecommunications and Information Services, 1990-1992; Chair, Communications Law Division, 1992-1998; Council Member and Budget Officer, 1998—; Section of Science and Technology: Governing Board, Forum Committee on Communications Law, 1993-1996: Chair, Subcommittee on Information Infrastructure, Committee on the Law of Commerce in Cyberspace; Section of Business Law, 1996-1999); U.S. Chamber of Commerce (Chair, Telecommunications Task Force, 1996-1998; Member, Steering Committee, Global Telecommunications and Information Task Force, 1998-2000). ***PRACTICE AREAS:*** Telecommunications; Internet; E-Commerce; Privacy Law. ***Email:*** rbutler@wrf.com

BRUCE G. JOSEPH, born Philadelphia, Pennsylvania, July 7, 1954; admitted to bar, 1979, Pennsylvania; 1981, District of Columbia. *Education:* University of Pennsylvania (B.S., B.A., summa cum laude, 1976); Harvard Law School (J.D., magna cum laude, 1979). Phi Beta Kappa. Editor and Case Editor, Harvard Law Review, 1977-1979. Law Clerk to Hon. James Hunter, III, U.S. Court of Appeals, Third Circuit, 1979-1980. ***PRACTICE AREAS:*** Intellectual Property; Internet; Electronic Commerce; Food and Drug; Litigation. ***Email:*** bjoseph@wrf.com

THOMAS W. KIRBY, born Lake Charles, Louisiana, July 25, 1950; admitted to bar, 1975, District of Columbia; 1988, Maryland. *Education:* Louisiana State University (B.A., 1972); Georgetown University Law Center (J.D., 1975). Editor, Georgetown Law Journal, 1974-1975. Law Clerk to Judge Myron Bright, U.S. Court of Appeals, Eighth Circuit, 1975-1976. ***PRACTICE AREAS:*** Litigation; Intellectual Property; Election Law. ***Email:*** tkirby@wrf.com

J. TIMOTHY HOBBS, born Yakima, Washington, September 23, 1941; admitted to bar, 1969, District of Columbia. *Education:* Université de Paris, France and University of Washington (B.A., 1964); Washington College of Law of American University (J.D., 1968). Phi Alpha Delta. ***PRACTICE AREAS:*** Trademarks; Copyrights; Unfair Competition. ***Email:*** thobbs@wrf.com

ROBERT L. PETTIT, born Springfield, Missouri, August 14, 1952; admitted to bar, 1977, District of Columbia. *Education:* University of Missouri (B.A., summa cum laude, 1974); Duke University (J.D., 1977). Phi Beta Kappa. Senior Legal Advisor to Commissioner Dawson (1982-1986) and General Counsel (1989-1992), Federal Communications Commission. Associate Deputy Secretary of Transportation, 1988-1989. Transition Team for Independent Agencies, Office of the President-Elect, 1988-1989. Trustee, Federal Communications Bar Association Foundation, 1991-1992. *Member:* Federal Communications Association (Executive Committee, 1992-1995). ***PRACTICE AREAS:*** Communications. ***Email:*** rpettit@wrf.com

JIM SLATTERY, born Atchison, Kansas, August 4, 1948; admitted to bar, 1975, Kansas; 1997, District of Columbia. *Education:* Washburn University (B.S., 1971; J.D., 1975). Member: Kansas State House of Representatives, 1973-1979; U.S. House of Representatives (D-KS), 1983-1995. Member, The House Energy and Commerce Committee, 1983-1995, The Veterans' Affairs Committee, 1983-1995, The House Budget Committee, 1985-1991, and The House Banking Committee, 1990-1992. Chair, Childhood Disability Commission, Department of Health and Human Services. Former Member of Congress. ***PRACTICE AREAS:*** Government Affairs; International Trade; Energy. ***Email:*** jslatter@wrf.com

KEITH S. WATSON, born Philadelphia, Pennsylvania, July 25, 1942; admitted to bar, 1968, District of Columbia. *Education:* Trinity College (B.A., 1964); Harvard University (J.D., 1967); Connecticut College (M.A., 1970). ***PRACTICE AREAS:*** Insurance; Litigation. ***Email:*** kwatson@wrf.com

ARTHUR I. CANTOR, born Brooklyn, New York, September 1, 1938; admitted to bar, 1963, District of Columbia. *Education:* Columbia University (A.B., 1959); Harvard Law School (LL.B., 1962). Member, Special Trial Section, 1962-1967 and Appellate Section, 1968, Antitrust Division, Department of Justice. Special Assistant to the Assistant Attorney General, Antitrust Division, 1969-1972. Author: "Tying, Exclusive Dealing, and Franchising Issues," Practicing Law Institute, 2000; "Franchising as a Turnaround Technique," Turnaround Management Association, 2000. *Member:* American Bar Association. ***PRACTICE AREAS:*** Franchise; Antitrust. ***Email:*** acantor@wrf.com

ROBERT A. SMITH, born Edison, New Jersey, May 11, 1954; admitted to bar, 1979, District of Columbia. *Education:* Catholic University of America (B.A., 1976; J.D., 1979). Phi Beta Kappa. Commercial Arbitrator, American Arbitration Association. ***PRACTICE AREAS:*** Franchise, Licensing and Distribution. ***Email:*** rsmith@wrf.com

SAMUEL D. WALKER, born Madison, Wisconsin, June 21, 1958; admitted to bar, 1984, North Carolina; 1993, District of Columbia. *Education:* Duke University (A.B., magna cum laude, 1980); Harvard Law School (J.D., cum laude, 1984). Phi Beta Kappa. Law Clerk to Judge John D. Butzner, Jr., U.S. Court of Appeals, Fourth Circuit. Special Assistant to the Assistant Secretary for Employment Standards, 1989, Deputy Wage and Hour Administrator and Acting Wage and Hour Administrator, 1990, Acting Assistant Secretary for Employment Standards, 1990-1991, and Deputy Assistant Secretary for Employment Standards, 1991, U.S. Department of Labor. Acting Assistant Secretary for Intergovernmental and Interagency Affairs and Deputy Assistant Secretary for Intergovernmental and Interagency Affairs, 1992, U.S. Department of Education, 2001. Assistant Clearance Counsel, Bush-Cheney Presidential Transition. Core Editor, "The Fair Labor Standards Act," BNA 2000. *Member:* American Bar Association (Chair, Sub-Committee on Fair Labor Standards). ***PRACTICE AREAS:*** Employment; Education; Litigation. ***Email:*** swalker@wrf.com

PETER D. ROSS, born Boston, Massachusetts, December 3, 1961; admitted to bar, 1986, California; 1988, District of Columbia. *Education:* Stanford University (A.B., with honors and distinction, 1983); Harvard Law School (J.D., cum laude, 1986). Mass Media Advisor, 1989-1991 and Senior Legal Advisor, 1992-1993 to Commissioner, Federal Communications Commission. *Member:* American Bar Association (Former Chair, Communications Committee, Section of Administrative Law and Regulatory Practice); Federal Communications Bar Association (Chair, FCBA Foundation; Former Co-Chair, Cable Practice Committee). ***PRACTICE AREAS:*** Internet; Electronic Commerce; Communications. ***Email:*** pross@wrf.com

L. KAY TATUM, born Houston, Texas, February 2, 1951; admitted to bar, 1980, Texas; 1983, District of Columbia. *Education:* Tulane University (B.A., summa cum laude, 1972); Rice University (M.A., 1976; Ph.D., 1978); University of Houston (J.D., cum laude, 1980). Phi Beta Kappa. ***PRACTICE AREAS:*** Business Law; Finance. ***Email:*** ktatum@wrf.com

THOMAS W. QUEEN, born Piqua, Ohio, December 19, 1949; admitted to bar, 1976, District of Columbia. *Education:* Yale College (B.A., cum laude, 1972); Harvard Law School (J.D., cum laude, 1976). ***PRACTICE AREAS:*** Intellectual Property; Franchise; Litigation; Antitrust. ***Email:*** tqueen@wrf.com

PETER D. SHIELDS, born Rochester, New York, January 29, 1962; admitted to bar, 1988, New York and District of Columbia; U.S. Supreme Court and U.S. Court of Appeals for the District of Columbia Circuit. *Education:* State University of New York at Cortland (B.A., with honors, 1984); Syracuse University (J.D., 1987). Pro Bono Attorney of the Year, District of Columbia Bar, 1993-1994. President-Elect, Federal Communications Bar Association, 2001—. ***PRACTICE AREAS:*** Communications. ***Email:*** pshields@wrf.com

ANDREW G. McBRIDE, born Paterson, New Jersey, June 26, 1960; admitted to bar, 1990, New York; 1991, District of Columbia. *Education:* College of the Holy Cross (B.A., magna cum laude, 1982); Stanford University (J.D., with distinction, 1987). Phi Beta Kappa. Member, Order of the Coif, 1987. Rotary Fellow, 1983. Law Clerk to: Judge Robert Bork, U.S. Court of Appeals, District of Columbia Circuit, 1987-1988; Justice Sandra Day O'Connor, U.S. Supreme Court, 1988-1989. Adjunct Professor, Stanford University, Stanford-in-Washington, 1990-1992. U.S. Department of Justice, 1989-1992. Assistant U.S. Attorney, Alexandria, Virginia, 1992-1998. ***PRACTICE AREAS:*** Communications; Appellate Practice; Litigation. ***Email:*** amcbride@wrf.com

WILLIAM B. BAKER, born Richmond, Virginia, September 3, 1957; admitted to bar, 1983, New York; 1985, District of Columbia. *Education:* University of Virginia (B.A., 1979; J.D., 1982). *Member:* American Bar Association (Chair, Communications Law Division, Section on Science and Technology, 1998-2001 and Chair, Postal Matters Committee, 1998-2000 and Vice Chair, 1993-1998). ***PRACTICE AREAS:*** Communications; Internet; Privacy; Postal. ***Email:*** wbaker@wrf.com

ALAN H. PRICE, born New York, N. Y., September 29, 1959; admitted to bar, 1984, District of Columbia. *Education:* State University of New York at Stony Brook (B.A., 1980); George Washington University (J.D., with honors, 1983). Editor, George Washington Journal of International Law and Economics. Law Clerk to Hon. Louis Spector, Senior Judge, U.S. Claims Court, 1983-1984. ***PRACTICE AREAS:*** International Trade. ***Email:*** aprice@wrf.com

GREGORY J. VOGT, born Newton, Kansas, July 28, 1954; admitted to bar, 1979, District of Columbia. *Education:* University of Kansas (B.A., summa cum laude, 1976); Northwestern University School of Law (J.D., cum laude, 1979). Phi Beta Kappa. Executive Editor, Northwestern University Law Review. Chief, Enforcement Division, 1985-1989, Chief, Mobile Services Division, 1989-1992 and Chief, Tariff Division, 1992-1994, Common Carrier Bureau, Federal Communications Commission. Deputy Chief, 1994-1996, Cable Services Bureau, Federal Communications Commission. Author: "Cap-Sized: How the Promise of the Price Cap Voyage to Competition Was Lost in a Sea of Good Intentions," Federal Communications Law Journal (March 1999). ***PRACTICE AREAS:*** Communications. ***Email:*** gvogt@wrf.com

EDWIN O. BAILEY, born San Jose, California, May 19, 1940; admitted to bar, 1966, Missouri; 1975, District of Columbia. *Education:* Princeton University (A.B., 1962); Washington University (J.D., 1965); McGill University, Montreal, Canada (LL.M., 1968). ***PRACTICE AREAS:*** Litigation; Aviation. ***Email:*** ebailey@wrf.com

DAVID E. HILLIARD, born Mayfield, Kentucky, May 9, 1950; admitted to bar, 1975, Kentucky; 1977, District of Columbia. *Education:* University of

(This Listing Continued)

Kentucky (B.B.A., 1972); University of Virginia (J.D., 1975). Beta Gamma Sigma; Phi Eta Sigma. General Attorney, Cable Television Bureau, Federal Communications Commission, 1975-1976. ***PRACTICE AREAS:*** Communications. ***Email:*** dhilliard@wrf.com

JOHN B. REYNOLDS, III, born Wilmington, Delaware, October 1, 1956; admitted to bar, 1982, District of Columbia; 1990, New York. *Education:* Williams College (B.A., 1978); Yale University (J.D., 1981). Phi Beta Kappa. Law Clerk to Judge Caleb M. Wright, U.S. District Judge, District of Delaware, 1981-1982. Attorney-Adviser, Office of the Legal Adviser, U.S. Department of State, 1982-1988. *Member:* American Bar Association (Member, Committee on National Security and International Law, Chair, 1992-1993, Co-Chair, 1994-1996; Vice-Chair, Committee on Export Controls and Economic Sanctions, 1998—). ***PRACTICE AREAS:*** International Trade; Internet; Electronic Commerce. ***Email:*** jreynold@wrf.com

DANIEL J. STANDISH, born Denver, Colorado, January 15, 1960; admitted to bar, 1986, Colorado (inactive); 1988, District of Columbia. *Education:* Bowdoin College (A.B., magna cum laude, 1983); University of Chicago (J.D., 1986). Phi Beta Kappa. Assistant U.S. Attorney, District of Columbia, 1989-1993. ***PRACTICE AREAS:*** Insurance; Litigation. ***Email:*** dstandish@wrf.com

JAMES T. BRUCE, III, born Richmond, Virginia, March 27, 1947; admitted to bar, 1975, District of Columbia; registered to practice before U.S. Patent and Trademark Office. *Education:* Princeton University (B.S.E., cum laude, 1969; M.S.E., 1973); George Washington University (J.D., with honors, 1974). Senior Counsel, Senate Committee on Energy and Natural Resources, 1977-1990. ***PRACTICE AREAS:*** Government Affairs; Internet; Electronic Commerce; Energy. ***Email:*** jbruce@wrf.com

JOHN A. HODGES, born Pittsburgh, Pennsylvania, November 18, 1940; admitted to bar, 1968, District of Columbia. *Education:* Harvard College (A.B., 1962); Columbia University (LL.B., with honors, 1968). ***PRACTICE AREAS:*** International Trade; Product Liability; Energy; Environmental. ***Email:*** jhodges@wrf.com

JERRY V. HAINES, born Braham, Minnesota, August 12, 1944; admitted to bar, 1981, Pennsylvania; 1985, District of Columbia. *Education:* University of Minnesota (B.S., 1965; M.A., 1970); Duquesne University (J.D., summa cum laude, 1981). Editor-in-Chief, Duquesne Law Review, 1980-1981. Law Clerk to Hon. Ruggero J. Aldisert, U.S. Court of Appeals, Third Circuit, 1981-1983. ***PRACTICE AREAS:*** Communications. ***Email:*** jhaines@wrf.com

JOHN L. BARTLETT, born Los Angeles, California, June 9, 1942; admitted to bar, 1967, District of Columbia. *Education:* University of California, Los Angeles (A.B., 1963); Stanford University (LL.B., 1967). Order of the Coif. ***PRACTICE AREAS:*** Communications. ***Email:*** jbartlett@wrf.com

RICHARD C. LOWERY, born Washington, D.C., October 23, 1941; admitted to bar, 1967, Virginia; 1968, District of Columbia. *Education:* Davidson College (B.A., 1964); University of Virginia (LL.B., 1967). Order of the Coif. ***PRACTICE AREAS:*** Antitrust; Litigation. ***Email:*** rlowery@wrf.com

BARBARA VAN GELDER, born Winchester, Massachusetts, July 24, 1950; admitted to bar, 1977, District of Columbia. *Education:* Boston University (B.A., 1972); Emory University (J.D., 1976). Former Assistant U.S. Attorney, District of Columbia, 1983-1997. Deputy Chief, Civil Division, 1994-1997. Staff Attorney, 1977-1997, Executive Assistant to the Commissioners, 1980-1983, Federal Election Commission. ***PRACTICE AREAS:*** Litigation; White Collar Crime; Government Contracts; Telecommunications; Labor and Employment. ***Email:*** bvangeld@wrf.com

HUGH LATIMER, born New York, N.Y., March 23, 1933; admitted to bar, 1958, District of Columbia. *Education:* Harvard University (A.B., 1955; J.D., 1958). ***PRACTICE AREAS:*** Advertising; Internet; Electronic Commerce; Intellectual Property. ***Email:*** hlatimer@wrf.com

JOHN E. FIORINI, III, born Sayre, Pennsylvania, October 3, 1946; admitted to bar, 1971, District of Columbia. *Education:* Georgetown University (B.S., magna cum laude, 1968); University of Pennsylvania (J.D., 1971). Phi Beta Kappa. *Member:* The District of Columbia Bar; Federal Communications Bar Association. ***PRACTICE AREAS:*** Communications Law. ***Email:*** jfiorini@wrf.com

JAMES C. RUBINGER, born New York, New York, October 1, 1955; admitted to bar, 1980, Virginia; 1982, New York; 1984, District of Columbia. *Education:* Brown University (B.A., 1977); George Washington University (J.D., 1980). Member, Order of the Coif. Editor-in-Chief, The George Washington Law Review. Law Clerk to Judge J. Clifford Wallace, U.S. Court of Appeals for the Ninth Circuit, 1980-1981. ***PRACTICE AREAS:*** Franchise; Litigation; Intellectual Property; Antitrust. ***Email:*** jrubinge@wrf.com

DONNA COLEMAN GREGG, born Port Clinton, Ohio, November 1, 1948; admitted to bar, 1975, District of Columbia. *Education:* University of Michigan (B.A., 1971); Duke University (J.D., 1974). Phi Beta Kappa. Attorney, Federal Communications Commission, 1975. ***PRACTICE AREAS:*** Communications; Internet; Electronic Commerce. ***Email:*** dgregg@wrf.com

(This Listing Continued)

PAUL F. KHOURY, born Philadelphia, Pennsylvania, August 29, 1961; admitted to bar, 1986, District of Columbia; U.S. Court of Federal Claims. *Education:* Dartmouth College (B.A., magna cum laude, 1983); George Washington University (J.D., 1986). Order of the Coif. *Member:* American Bar Association (Member, Public Law Section, Co-Chair, Contract Claims and Disputes Resolution Committee, 2000—). ***PRACTICE AREAS:*** Government Contracts; Litigation. ***Email:*** pkhoury@wrf.com

CAROL A. LAHAM, born Boston, Massachusetts, December 17, 1959; admitted to bar, 1985, Massachusetts; 1988, District of Columbia. *Education:* Wellesley College (B.A., 1981); New York University School of Law (J.D., 1984). Phi Beta Kappa. Appellate Litigation Team, Federal Election Commission, 1984-1987. *Member:* American Bar Association (Member, Standing Committee on Election Law; Co-Chair, Committee of Election Law, Section on Administrative Law, 1997—; Vice Chair: Committee of Election Law, Section of Administrative Law, 1993-1997; Committee on International and Comparative Administrative Law, 1994-1997). ***PRACTICE AREAS:*** Election Law. ***Email:*** claham@wrf.com

EILEEN P. BRADNER, born Toledo, Ohio, May 29, 1959; admitted to bar, 1987, Ohio; 1988, U.S. Court of International Trade; 1989, District of Columbia. *Education:* University of Toledo (B.A., magna cum laude, 1980); Georgetown University (J.D., magna cum laude, 1987). *Member:* The District of Columbia Bar (Co-Chairman, International Trade Committee). ***PRACTICE AREAS:*** International Trade; Government Affairs. ***Email:*** ebradner@wrf.com

KIRK J. NAHRA, born Cleveland, Ohio, July 13, 1962; admitted to bar, 1987, Ohio; 1988, District of Columbia. *Education:* Georgetown University (B.A., magna cum laude, 1984); Harvard University (J.D., cum laude, 1987). Author: "The Top Twelve HIPAA Privacy Issues for Health Plans," BNA's Health Plan & Provider Report, March 2001; "What Every Insurer Needs to Know About Privacy," Mealey's Emerging Insurance Disputes, November 2000. General Counsel, National Health Care Anti-Fraud Association. ***PRACTICE AREAS:*** Insurance Fraud; Privacy; Compliance Programs. ***Email:*** knahra@wrf.com

MICHAEL L. STURM, born Dallas, Texas, May 20, 1962; admitted to bar, 1987, Virginia; 1990, District of Columbia. *Education:* College of William & Mary (B.A., 1984) Phi Beta Kappa; Harvard Law School (J.D., cum laude, 1987). ***PRACTICE AREAS:*** Litigation; Intellectual Property; Franchise. ***Email:*** msturm@wrf.com

DOMINIC T. BODENSTEINER, born Cedar Rapids, Iowa, July 14, 1960; admitted to bar, 1986, Nevada; 1987, District of Columbia. *Education:* University of Nevada (B.S., 1983); George Washington University (J.D., with honors, 1986). ***PRACTICE AREAS:*** Business Law; Finance. ***Email:*** doc@wrf.com

KATHRYN BUCHER, born Bloomington, Illinois, March 19, 1958; admitted to bar, 1983, District of Columbia; 1984, U.S. Court of Federal Claims. *Education:* University of Vermont (B.A., cum laude, 1980); Cornell University (J.D., 1983). Senior Editor, Cornell International Law Journal, 1982-1983. *Member:* The District of Columbia Bar; American Bar Association; American Health Lawyers Association. ***PRACTICE AREAS:*** Health Care Regulation; Health Care Litigation; Insurance; Government Contracts; Privacy. ***Email:*** kbucher@wrf.com

DORTHULA H. POWELL-WOODSON, born Richmond, Virginia, September 6, 1956; admitted to bar, 1982, Virginia; 1998, District of Columbia. *Education:* Virginia Union University (B.A., magna cum laude, 1978); University of Richmond (J.D., 1981). Author: "The HIPAA Standards for Electronic Transactions — Analysis of Routine Health Plan Transmissions," HMOs and Health Plans Digest, American Health Lawyers Association, Winter, 2000. Director, Commonwealth of Virginia, Department of Personnel and Training, 1990-1994. Vice-President, National Public Programs and Vice President and Legal Counsel, Options Health Care, 1994-1996. Vice President, Legal Affairs, Value Behavioral Health, 1996-1998. *Member:* American Bar Association (Member, Public Contract and Health Law Sections, 1998—); Virginia State Bar (Board of Governors, Health Law Section, 1998—); American Health Lawyers Association. ***PRACTICE AREAS:*** Health Care; Government Contracts; Privacy Law. ***Email:*** dpowell-woodson@wrf.com

THEODORE A. HOWARD, born Bronx, New York, November 26, 1956; admitted to bar, 1982, District of Columbia; U.S. Court of Federal Claims. *Education:* University of Notre Dame (B.A., 1978); Harvard University (J.D., 1981). Co-Author: with J. Oshinsky, *Practitioner's Guide To Litigating Insurance Coverage Actions,* Aspen Law & Business, Second Edition, 1998 and Supplement, 2001. Adjunct Professor, Insurance Theory and Regulation, George Mason School of Law, Summer, 1994. President and Chairman, Board of Directors, District of Columbia Prisoners' Legal Services Project, Inc., 1995—. *Member:* The District of Columbia Bar. ***PRACTICE AREAS:*** Insurance. ***Email:*** thoward@wrf.com

RICHARD A. IFFT, born Fort Belvoir, Virginia, September 1, 1959; admitted to bar, 1985, Maryland and District of Columbia. *Education:* College of William & Mary (B.A., with honors, 1981); Georgetown University (J.D., magna cum laude, 1984). Phi Beta Kappa. *Member:* The District of Columbia Bar. ***PRACTICE AREAS:*** Insurance. ***Email:*** rifft@wrf.com

(This Listing Continued)

WILEY REIN & FIELDING LLP, Washington—Continued

GREGORY P. CIRILLO, born New York, New York, March 22, 1961; admitted to bar, 1987, New York; 1988, District of Columbia; 2001, Virginia. *Education:* Georgetown University (B.A., 1983; J.D., cum laude, 1987). Staff Member, Journal of Law and Policy in International Business, 1986-1987. Co-Chair, Advisory Board, Georgetown University Technology Law Project, 1996—. *Member:* The District of Columbia Bar; Computer Law Association. (Resident, McLean, Virginia Office). ***PRACTICE AREAS:*** Business Law; Internet Law; Electronic Commerce; Aviation Law; Aerospace Law. ***Email:*** gcirillo@wrf.com

DANIEL B. HASSETT, born Rockville Centre, New York, April 6, 1962; admitted to bar, 1989, Massachusetts; 1991, District of Columbia; 1999, Virginia. *Education:* Providence College (B.S., cum laude, 1984); University of Texas at Austin (J.D., 1989). *Member:* The District of Columbia Bar; Massachusetts Bar Association; Computer Law Association. (Resident, McLean, Virginia Office). ***PRACTICE AREAS:*** Business Law; Internet Law; Electronic Commerce. ***Email:*** dhassett@wrf.com

JOHN R. SHANE, born Muncie, Indiana, March 13, 1962; admitted to bar, 1988, Maryland; 1989, District of Columbia. *Education:* Bucknell University (B.A., magna cum laude, 1984); Georgetown University (J.D., magna cum laude, 1988). Order of the Coif. ***PRACTICE AREAS:*** International Trade. ***Email:*** jshane@wrf.com

ERIC W. DESILVA, born Silver Spring, Maryland, January 1, 1965; admitted to bar, 1991, District of Columbia. *Education:* University of Maryland (B.S., 1986); University of Michigan (J.D., cum laude, 1989). ***PRACTICE AREAS:*** Communications. ***Email:*** edesilva@wrf.com

WAYNE D. JOHNSEN, born Staten Island, New York, January 20, 1959; admitted to bar, 1988, Virginia; 1991, District of Columbia. *Education:* State University College at Buffalo (B.A., 1980); Syracuse University (M.S., 1982); Georgetown University (J.D., magna cum laude, 1988). Order of the Coif. ***PRACTICE AREAS:*** Communications; Business Law; Finance; Internet Law; Electronic Commerce. ***Email:*** wjohnsen@wrf.com

FLOYD B. CHAPMAN, born Ft. Bragg, North Carolina, June 23, 1963; admitted to bar, 1993, Florida; U.S. District Court, Southern District of Florida; U.S. Court of Appeals, Eleventh and Federal Circuits; 1999, District of Columbia; registered to practice before U.S. Patent and Trademark Office. *Education:* Georgia Institute of Technology (B.E.E., with high honors, 1986); Florida International University (M.B.A., 1990); University of Miami (J.D., magna cum laude, 1993). Eta Kappa Nu; The Order of the Coif. Associate Editor, 1991-1992 and Executive Editor, 1992-1993, Inter-American Law Review. *Member:* The Florida Bar. ***PRACTICE AREAS:*** Intellectual Property. ***Email:*** fchapman@wrf.com

PATRICIA J. PAOLETTA, born Evanston, Illinois, May 12, 1962; admitted to bar, 1988, Virginia; 1989, District of Columbia. *Education:* Manchester College, Oxford, England; Boston College (B.A., summa cum laude, 1984); Georgetown University (J.D., 1988). Phi Beta Kappa. Topics Editor, Georgetown Criminal Law Journal. Author: "Survey of White Collar Crime: Sentencing," 24 American Criminal Law Review, 1987. Chair: Telecommunications and Infrastructure Subcommittee; High-Tech Committee, U.S. Chamber, May, 2001. Counsel, Telecommunications, U.S. House of Representatives, 1996-1999. Director, Telecommunications Trade Policy, 1995-1996. Senior Legal Advisor, International Bureau, 1994-1995. *Member:* District of Columbia Bar; Virginia State Bar; Federal Communications Bar Association (Chair, International Practice Committee, 2001-2002). ***PRACTICE AREAS:*** International Telecommunications Law; Trade Policy; Government Relations. ***Email:*** tpaoletta@wrf.com

DALE E. HAUSMAN, born Saratoga Springs, New York, March 21, 1961; admitted to bar, 1989, District of Columbia. *Education:* Cornell University (B.A., 1983); Georgetown University Law Center (J.D., magna cum laude, 1989). Order of the Coif. ***PRACTICE AREAS:*** Insurance; Litigation. ***Email:*** dhausman@wrf.com

TODD M. STANSBURY, born Port Arthur, Texas, March 8, 1962; admitted to bar, 1990, Maryland; 1992, District of Columbia. *Education:* Texas A & M University (B.S., 1984); American University (J.D., summa cum laude, 1990). ***PRACTICE AREAS:*** Communications; Business Law; Finance. ***Email:*** tstansbu@wrf.com

GREGORY L. MASTERS, born Hagerstown, Maryland, March 20, 1964; admitted to bar, 1989, Virginia; 1997, District of Columbia. *Education:* Southern Illinois University (B.A., 1986); Catholic University of America (J.D., 1989). ***PRACTICE AREAS:*** Communications; Business Law; Finance. ***Email:*** gmasters@wrf.com

DAVID W. KOCH, born Moline, Illinois, January 14, 1960; admitted to bar, 1985, Michigan; 1993, District of Columbia. *Education:* University of Iowa (B.S., with high honors, 1981); University of Michigan (J.D., cum laude, 1984). Co-Author: "The Election Franchise Agreement," Franchising World, Parts I and II, September/October and November/December 2000; "Online Privacy

(This Listing Continued)

101: A Franchiser Survival Guide," Franchise Law Journal, American Bar Association, Volume 19, Number 2, Fall, 1999. Attorney-Advisor to the Chairman, Federal Trade Commission, 1987-1989. ***PRACTICE AREAS:*** Franchise; Antitrust. ***Email:*** dkoch@wrf.com

BRUCE A. McDONALD, born Detroit, Michigan, June 12, 1953; admitted to bar, 1980, District of Columbia. *Education:* University of California (B.A., 1976); Leningrad State University (1976); American University, Washington College of Law (J.D., 1979). ***PRACTICE AREAS:*** Intellectual Property Law; Trademarks; International Law. ***Email:*** mcdonaldb@wrf.com

ROSEMARY C. HAROLD, born Des Moines, Iowa, April 9, 1958; admitted to bar, 1991, Pennsylvania; 1993, District of Columbia. *Education:* College of William and Mary (B.A., 1980); University of Missouri (M.A., 1985); Georgetown University (J.D., magna cum laude, 1991). Order of the Coif. Author: "Cable Open Access: Exorcising the Ghosts of 'Legacy' Regulations," Cyberlaw Symposium, Northern Kentucky Law Review, Spring, 2001. ***PRACTICE AREAS:*** Communications; Internet; Electronic Commerce. ***Email:*** rharold@wrf.com

GREGORY LYONS, born Tehran, Iran, July 28, 1963; admitted to bar, 1991, Maryland; 1993, District of Columbia; admitted to practice before U.S. Patent and Trademark Office. *Education:* University of Maryland (B.S.E.E., summa cum laude, 1986; M.S.E.E., 1988); Harvard University (J.D., cum laude, 1991). ***PRACTICE AREAS:*** Intellectual Property; Litigation. ***Email:*** glyons@wrf.com

WILLIAM A. McGRATH, born Brooklyn, New York, April 13, 1961; admitted to bar, 1991, Virginia; 1993, District of Columbia. *Education:* Southern Methodist University (B.F.A., 1982); College of William & Mary (J.D., 1991). Project Editor, Administrative Law Review. Law Clerk to Hon. William T. Prince, U.S. Magistrate Judge, Eastern District of Virginia, 1991-1992. District of Columbia Bar Pro Bono Lawyer of the Year, 1997-1998. ***PRACTICE AREAS:*** Advertising; Food and Drug; Internet; Electronic Commerce; Litigation. ***Email:*** wmcgrath@wrf.com

JOHN C. YANG, born Taipei, Taiwan, December 17, 1968; admitted to bar, 1992, Illinois; 1993, District of Columbia. *Education:* Washington University (A.B., 1989); The George Washington University Law School (J.D., with honors, 1992). Book Review and Articles Editor, The George Washington University Law Review. Associate Professorial Lecturer in Law, George Washington University Law School. Editorial Advisory Board, Environmental Claims Journal (1996—). General Counsel, 2000— and Member, Organization of Chinese Americans. *Member:* The District of Columbia Bar (Secretary, 1998-1999; General Counsel, 2000—); National Asian Pacific American Bar Association (General Counsel, 2000—; Southeast Regional Governor, 1999—; President, D.C. Chapter, 1997-1998). ***Email:*** jyang@wrf.com

MARY E. BORJA, born Oklahoma City, Oklahoma, May 11, 1969; admitted to bar, 1994, District of Columbia. *Education:* The Johns Hopkins University (B.A., 1990); University of Miami (J.D., magna cum laude, 1993). Order of the Coif. Senior Articles Editor, University of Miami Law Review. Author: "Appointment of Damages; Options for Insurers," Coverage, January/February 2001. Co-Chair, Insurance Coverage Connection Subcommittee, Litigation Section. ***PRACTICE AREAS:*** Litigation; Insurance. ***Email:*** mborja@wrf.com

JOHN M. BURGETT, born Las Cruces, New Mexico, December 8, 1967; admitted to bar, 1992, New Mexico; 1994, District of Columbia. *Education:* New Mexico State University (B.A. in Journalism, with honors, 1989); Syracuse University, S.I. Newhouse School of Public Communications (M.S. in Television-Radio-Film, 1992); Syracuse University College of Law (J.D., magna cum laude, 1992). Phi Kappa Phi; Order of the Coif. Notes and Comments Editor, Syracuse Law Review. ***PRACTICE AREAS:*** Communications Law. ***Email:*** jburgett@wrf.com

TANJA E. HENS, born Eugene, Oregon, February 4, 1969; admitted to bar, 1993, Illinois (inactive); 1995, District of Columbia. *Education:* Georgetown University (B.S., magna cum laude, 1990); University of Chicago (J.D., 1993). ***PRACTICE AREAS:*** Franchise Law; Litigation. ***Email:*** thens@wrf.com

SCOTT M. McCALEB, born Silver Spring, Maryland, May 10, 1966; admitted to bar, 1991, Maryland; 1993, District of Columbia. *Education:* Brown University (A.B., 1988); Georgetown University Law Center (J.D., 1991). U.S. Army Corps of Engineers Honors Program, 1992-1995. Instructor: U.S. Army Judge Advocate General's School, 1996—; George Mason University School of Law, 1996—. Law Clerk to Hon. Haldane Robert Mayer, U.S. Court of Appeals for the Federal Circuit, 1995-1997. Member: Advisory Committee to the U.S. Court of Appeals for the Federal Circuit; Editorial Board: Federal Circuit Bar Journal (1988—); Procurement Law Advisor (1997—). *Member:* American Bar Association. [Capt., U.S. Army, 1992-1995]. ***Email:*** smccaleb@wrf.com

SUZANNE YELEN, born Bethesda, Maryland, July 22, 1968; admitted to bar, 1993, Florida; 1994, District of Columbia. *Education:* Yale University (B.A., summa cum laude, 1990; J.D., 1993). Phi Beta Kappa. ***Email:*** syelen@wrf.com

(This Listing Continued)

OF COUNSEL

ROBERT E. BOONE, JR., born Tuscaloosa, Alabama, May 4, 1940; admitted to bar, 1965, Alabama; 1975, New York; 1976, District of Columbia. *Education:* University of Alabama (B.S., 1962; J.D., 1965). ***Email:*** bboone@wrf.com

TYRONE BROWN, born Norfolk, Virginia, November 5, 1942; admitted to bar, 1968, New York; 1970, District of Columbia. *Education:* Hamilton College (A.B., 1964); Cornell University (LL.B., with distinction, 1967). Managing Editor, Cornell Law Review. Law Clerk to Chief Justice Earl Warren, U.S. Supreme Court, 1967-1968. ***PRACTICE AREAS:*** Communications Law. ***Email:*** tbrown@wrf.com

STUART F. CARWILE, born Lynchburg, Virginia, August 26, 1942; admitted to bar, 1967, Virginia; 1968, U.S. Tax Court; 1994, District of Columbia. *Education:* University of Virginia (B.S., 1964; LL.B., 1967). ***PRACTICE AREAS:*** Corporate. ***Email:*** scarwile@wrf.com

CHRISTINE E. CONNELLY, born Washington, D.C., January 7, 1963; admitted to bar, 1988, Maryland; 1991, District of Columbia. *Education:* University of Maryland (B.S., magna cum laude, 1985) Phi Beta Kappa; Georgetown University (J.D., cum laude, 1988). ***PRACTICE AREAS:*** Franchise Law. ***Email:*** cconnell@wrf.com

KURT E. DeSOTO, born Moses Lake, Washington, July 19, 1956; admitted to bar, 1984, Virginia; 1988, District of Columbia. *Education:* Georgetown University (A.B., 1980); Columbia School of Law (J.D., 1984). Editor, Columbia Human Rights Law Review, 1983-1984. General Attorney, Common Carrier Bureau, Federal Communications Commission, 1984-1987. ***PRACTICE AREAS:*** Communications Law. ***Email:*** kdesoto@wrf.com

ELIZABETH ANN EASTWOOD, born San Juan, Puerto Rico, February 11, 1966; admitted to bar, 1990, Virginia; 1991, District of Columbia. *Education:* College of William and Mary (B.A., 1987); University of Virginia (J.D., 1990). ***PRACTICE AREAS:*** Insurance. ***Email:*** eastwood@wrf.com

CARL R. FRANK, born Los Angeles, California, September 19, 1959; admitted to bar, 1983, District of Columbia. *Education:* Syracuse University (B.S., cum laude, 1980); American University (J.D., cum laude, 1983). Adjunct Professor of Law, American University, 1988-1990. ***PRACTICE AREAS:*** Communications Law. ***Email:*** cfrank@wrf.com

JOHN F. KAMP, born Rock Rapids, Iowa, February 26, 1946; admitted to bar, 1980, District of Columbia. *Education:* University of Notre Dame (B.A., 1968); University of Iowa (Ph.D., 1973); University of Tulsa (J.D., 1980). Assistant Professor, University of Tulsa, 1974-1980. Director, Office of Congressional and Public Affairs, Federal Communications Commission, 1985-1989. *Member:* District of Columbia Bar; Federal Communications Bar Association. ***PRACTICE AREAS:*** Internet Law; Electronic Commerce; Privacy Law; Advertising Law. ***Email:*** jkamp@wrf.com

STEPHEN D. HALLIDAY, born Newport News, Virginia, October 18, 1948; admitted to bar, 1974, Virginia; 1998, District of Columbia. *Education:* Duke University (B.A., 1970); College of William & Mary, Marshall-Wythe School of Law (J.D., 1974); Georgetown University (M.L.T., 1978). ***Email:*** shallida@wrf.com

PHILLIP H. HARRINGTON, born Coco Solo, Panama Canal Zone, February 13, 1940; admitted to bar, 1991, Virginia and District of Columbia. *Education:* U.S. Naval Academy (B.S., 1962); University of Michigan (M.B.A., with distinction, 1972); George Mason University (J.D., with distinction, 1990). *Member:* American Bar Association (Past Chair, Federal Contract Forms, Clauses and Regulations Committee, Co-Chair, Commercial Products and Services Committee; Public Contracts Section, 1994-1995). [Capt., S.C. U.S. Navy, Ret., 1962-1991; Commanding Officer, NRCC Long Beach and DCASMA, San Diego]. ***PRACTICE AREAS:*** Government Contracts. ***Email:*** pharring@wrf.com

BRIAN A. JOHNSON, born Orange, California, July 28, 1940; admitted to bar, 1967, District of Columbia; 1972, Florida. *Education:* Duke University (A.B., 1963); George Washington University (J.D., with honors, 1966). Co-Chair, Transactional Practice Committee of the Federal Communications Bar Association (1995-1997). ***PRACTICE AREAS:*** Business Law; Finance; Communications. ***Email:*** bjohnson@wrf.com

CHRISTOPHER KELLY, born Wilmington, Delaware, January 6, 1961; admitted to bar, 1989, Delaware, Pennsylvania and District of Columbia. *Education:* The University of Delaware (B.A., 1983); The Delaware Law School (J.D., 1988). Attorney-Advisor, Trademark Examining Operations, U.S. Patent and Trademark Office, 1990-1994. *Member:* Delaware State Bar Association (Member, Intellectual Property Section). ***Email:*** ckelly@dwrf.com

KATHLEEN A. KIRBY, born Woodside, New York, June 25, 1959; admitted to bar, 1991, Pennsylvania; 1992, District of Columbia. *Education:* University of Virginia (B.S., 1981); Catholic University of America (J.D., 1991). Executive Editor, Catholic University Law Review, 1990-1991. ***PRACTICE AREAS:*** Communications Law. ***Email:*** kkirby@wrf.com

(This Listing Continued)

DAVID J. KULIK, admitted to bar, 1994, California; 1996, District of Columbia; registered to practice before U.S. Patent and Trademark Office. *Education:* University of California at San Diego (B.A., Chemistry/Biochemistry, 1984); George Washington University (J.D., 1994). *Member:* State Bar of California (Member, Intellectual Property Section); American Bar Association (Member, Intellectual Property Section); American Intellectual Property Law Association; American Association for the Advancement of Science. ***PRACTICE AREAS:*** Intellectual Property. ***Email:*** dkulik@wrf.com

MARY JO MANNING, born Philadelphia, Pennsylvania, August 6, 1942; admitted to bar, 1967, South Carolina; 1969, District of Columbia. *Education:* Hood College (B.A., 1964); University of South Carolina (J.D., cum laude, 1967). Chief Communications Counsel, Senate Commerce Science and Transportation Committee, 1976-1981. ***PRACTICE AREAS:*** Government Affairs; Communications Law. ***Email:*** mmanning@wrf.com

PETER D. O'CONNELL, born Oceanport, N.J., December 12, 1933; admitted to bar, 1959, District of Columbia. *Education:* Georgetown University (B.S., 1956); Georgetown University Law Center (J.D., 1959). ***PRACTICE AREAS:*** Communications Law. ***Email:*** poconnel@wrf.com

MARNIE K. SARVER, born Spokane, Washington, August 24, 1946; admitted to bar, 1980, District of Columbia. *Education:* Denison University (B.A., 1968); Duquesne University (J.D., 1979). Phi Beta Kappa. ***PRACTICE AREAS:*** Communications Law. ***Email:*** msarver@wrf.com

DAVID M. SOUTHALL, born Hartford, Connecticut, December 21, 1942; admitted to bar, 1980, Maryland and District of Columbia. *Education:* Florida State University (B.A., 1966); Harvard University (M.B.A., 1970); University of Maryland (J.D., with honors, 1980). Phi Kappa Phi. [Major, USAF, 1960-1980]. ***PRACTICE AREAS:*** Government Contracts; Business Law. ***Email:*** dsouthal@wrf.com

ASSOCIATES

KARYN K. ABLIN, born Ames, Iowa, June 22, 1966; admitted to bar, 1995, Virginia; 1997, District of Columbia. *Education:* Oral Roberts University (B.S.,B.A., summa cum laude, 1988); University of Virginia (J.D., 1995). Order of the Coif. Executive Editor and Editor, Virginia Law Review. Editorial Board Member, Virginia Journal of International Law. ***Email:*** kablin@wrf.com

ROBIN C. ADAMS, born St. Petersburg, Florida, June 29, 1973; admitted to bar, 2000, Colorado (Not admitted in District of Columbia). *Education:* Florida State University (B.S., 1994); William & Mary School of Law (J.D., 1998). William & Mary Law Review. ***Email:*** radams@wrf.com

THOMAS W. ANTONUCCI, born Chicago, Illinois, August 18, 1972; admitted to bar, 1999, District of Columbia. *Education:* Grand Valley State University (B.B.A., magna cum laude, 1995); Emory University School of Law (J.D., with distinction, 1998). Order of the Coif. ***Email:*** tantonuc@wrf.com

SCOTT E. BAIN, born Windom, Minnesota, April 12, 1971; admitted to bar, 1997, Minnesota; 2000, District of Columbia; registered to practice before U.S. Patent and Trademark Office. *Education:* University of Minnesota (B.E.E., summa cum laude, 1994); Boalt Hall School of Law, University of California (J.D., 1997). Managing Editor, Berkeley Technology Law Journal. Former Law Clerk, Hon. Randall R. Rader, U.S. Court of Appeals for the Federal Circuit. ***Email:*** sbain@wrf.com

DANIELLE E. BERRY, born St. Joseph, Missouri, June 10, 1973; admitted to bar, 1998, Virginia; 1999, Maryland and District of Columbia. *Education:* Middlebury College (B.A., magna cum laude, 1995); College of William & Mary (J.D., 1998). Phi Delta Phi. ***Email:*** dberry@wrf.com

ERIKA C. BIRG, born Chicago, Illinois; admitted to bar, 1995, Georgia (Not admitted in District of Columbia). *Education:* University of North Carolina at Chapel Hill (B.A., with distinction, 1988); Emory University School of Law (J.D., with distinction, 1994). Order of the Coif. Recipient: Harry L. and Elenore Raoul Greene Scholarship; American Jurisprudence Awards in Contracts, Real Estate Sales and Finance, Condominium Law and Insurance Law. Associate Editor, Emory Law Journal, 1993-1994. Law Clerk: Honorable Stanley F. Birch, Jr., United States Court of Appeals for the Eleventh Circuit, 1994-1995; Honorable Willis B. Hunt, Jr., United States District Court for the Northern District of Georgia, 1995-1997. Author: "Application of the 'Inevitable Disclosure ' Doctrine in Georgia," Ga. B.J., 58, April, 1999; Comment, "Redefining 'Owner or Operator ' Under CERCLA to Preserve Traditional Notions of Corporate Law," 43 Emory L.J. 771, 1994. *Member:* State Bar of Georgia. ***PRACTICE AREAS:*** Litigation. ***Email:*** ebirg@wrf.com

SETH J. BLONDER, born Los Angeles, California, October 4, 1975; admitted to bar, 2001, California (Not admitted in District of Columbia). *Education:* University of California, Berkeley (B.A., magna cum laude, 1997); Harvard University (J.D., 2000). Phi Beta Kappa. ***Email:*** sblonder@wrf.com

MICHELLE E. BOARDMAN, admitted to bar, 1999, Virginia; 2000, District of Columbia. *Education:* Brown University (B.A., 1994); University of Chicago (J.D., 1998). Chicago Law Review. Clerk, Judge Frank H. Easterbrook, Seventh Circuit Court of Appeals, 1998-1999. ***Email:*** mboardma@wrf.com

(This Listing Continued)

WILEY REIN & FIELDING LLP, Washington—Continued

TIMOTHY C. BRIGHTBILL, born Denver, Colorado, April 25, 1965; admitted to bar, 1994, Maryland; 1996, District of Columbia. *Education:* Medill School of Journalism, Northwestern University (B.S., with honors, 1987); Georgetown University Law Center (J.D., 1994). *Member:* American Bar Association (Vice Chair, International Law and Practice International Trade Committee). ***Email:*** tbrightbill@wrf.com

DORANN BUNKIN, born Panorama City, California, December 23, 1968; admitted to bar, 1996, California; 1999, District of Columbia. *Education:* University of California, Los Angeles (B.A., magna cum laude, 1991); Yale Law School (J.D., 1994). Executive Editor, Yale Law and Policy Review. Former Attorney Advisor, Video Services Division, Federal Communications Commission. ***Email:*** dbunkin@wrf.com

CALEB P. BURNS, born Philadelphia, Pennsylvania, February 6, 1974; admitted to bar, 2001, New York and District of Columbia. *Education:* Duke University (B.A., cum laude, 1996); New York University (J.D., 2000). Member: Outstanding Scholar Program, Antitrust Division, United States Department of Justice, 1996-1997; Moot Court Board. ***Email:*** cburns@wrf.com

JENNIFER E. CHUNG, born Seoul, Korea, January 12, 1968; admitted to bar, 1999, New York; 2000, District of Columbia. *Education:* Brown University (B.A., 1989); George Washington University Law School (J.D., cum laude, 1998). Articles Editor, George Washington Law Review. ***Email:*** jchung@wrf.com

DONALD E. CLARK, JR., born Jacksonville, North Carolina, September 23, 1960; admitted to bar, 1996, North Carolina and South Carolina; 1998, District of Columbia. *Education:* Duke University (B.S., Business, 1982); Wake Forest University (M.B.A., 1996; J.D., 1996). Certified Public Accountant, North Carolina, 1986. ***Email:*** dclark@wrf.eom

WILLIAM J. COLWELL, born Norwich, New York, December 3, 1969; admitted to bar, 1999, District of Columbia. *Education:* Northwestern University (B.A., 1991); Duke University School of Law (J.D., cum laude, 1999). ***Email:*** wcolwell@wrf.com

M. EVAN CORCORAN, admitted to bar, 1991, Virginia; 1993, District of Columbia. *Education:* Princeton University (A.B., cum laude, 1986); Georgetown University Law Center (J.D., 1991). ***Email:*** ecorcora@wrf.com

JASON P. CRONIC, born Atlanta, Georgia, September 12, 1968; admitted to bar, 1993, Illinois; 1994, District of Columbia; 1998, New York. *Education:* Tulane University of Louisiana (B.A., cum laude, 1990); University of Chicago (J.D., 1993). ***Email:*** jcronic@wrf.com

MARJORIE J. DICKMAN, born Baltimore, Maryland, May 10, 1971; admitted to bar, 1997, Maryland; 1998, District of Columbia. *Education:* Duke University (A.B., cum laude, 1993); Georgetown University Law Center (J.D., cum laude, 1997). Member, Editorial Board, The Georgetown Law Journal. ***Email:*** mdickman@wrf.com

HEATHER O. DIXON, born Youngstown, Ohio, November 4, 1974; admitted to bar, 1999, Virginia; 2000, District of Columbia. *Education:* Virginia Polytechnic Institute and State University (B.S., summa cum laude, 1996); University of Virginia (J.D., 1999). Phi Beta Kappa. ***Email:*** hdixon@wrf.com

SUSAN D. DRAKE, born Dunedin, Florida, April 30, 1970; admitted to bar, 1997, Virginia; 2000, District of Columbia. *Education:* American University (B.S., cum laude, 1992); Catholic University of America (J.D., 1997). ***Email:*** sdrake@wrf.com

BROOK A. EDINGER, born St. Louis, Missouri, June 16, 1968; admitted to bar, 1995, Virginia; 1997, District of Columbia. *Education:* College of William & Mary (B.A., with highest honors, 1991; J.D., 1994). Law Clerk to Chief Judge Ross W. Krumm, U.S. Bankruptcy Court, Western District of Virginia, 1994-1995. ***Email:*** bedinger@wrf.com

JANET L. EICHERS, born Washington, D.C., July 25, 1966; (admission pending). *Education:* University of Miami (B.B.A., 1988); George Washington University (M.B.A., 1991); George Mason University (J.D., 2000). *Member:* Virginia Bar Association; District of Columbia Bar. ***Email:*** jeichers@wrf.com

MARISA GALLEHR FAUNCE, born Washington, D.C., July 4, 1970; admitted to bar, 1994, Virginia; 1995, District of Columbia. *Education:* University of Virginia (B.A., 1991); College of William & Mary, Marshall-Wythe School of Law (J.D., 1994). Order of the Coif. Member, William and Mary Law Review. ***Email:*** mfaunce@wrf.com

LESLIE D. FETTER, born Windber, Pennsylvania, October 31, 1974; admitted to bar, 1999, District of Columbia. *Education:* Elizabethtown College (B.A., 1996); University of Pittsburgh (J.D., 1999). Research Editor, University of Pittsburgh Law Review. Order of the Coif. ***Email:*** lfetter@wrf.com

MEREDITH FUCHS, born New York, N.Y., March 28, 1966; admitted to bar, 1994, New York; 1996, District of Columbia. *Education:* London School of Economics (B.S., 1988); New York University (J.D., cum laude, 1993). Law Clerk to the: Hon. Patricia M. Wald, U.S. Court of Appeals for the District of Columbia Circuit, 1996-1997; Hon. Paul L. Friedman, U.S. District Court for the District of Columbia, 1994-1996. ***Email:*** mfuchs@wrf.com

THOMAS S. GARRETT, born Bedford, Virginia, June 18, 1968; admitted to bar, 1999, District of Columbia. *Education:* University of Richmond (B.A., 1990); University of Virginia (J.D., 1998). ***Email:*** tgarrett@wrf.com

BRADLEY K. GILLEN, born Annapolis, Maryland, September 10, 1976; admitted to bar, 2000, Virginia (Not admitted in District of Columbia). *Education:* Hampden-Sydney College (B.A., 1997); University of Virginia (J.D., 2000). Phi Beta Kappa. ***Email:*** bgillen@wrf.com

ELIZABETH E. GOLDIN, born Washington, D.C., December 23, 1969; admitted to bar, 1999, District of Columbia. *Education:* University of Wisconsin-Madison (B.A., 1991); Drake University Law School (J.D., 1998); Drake University School of Journalism and Mass Communications (M.A., 1998). Phi Alpha Delta. ***Email:*** egoldin@wrf.com

REBECCA P. GOODHEART, born Hartford, Connecticut, December 31, 1974; admitted to bar, 2000, Virginia; 2001, District of Columbia. *Education:* Georgetown University (B.S.F.S., cum laude, 1996); University of Virginia (J.D., 2000). Articles Editor, Virginia Journal of International Law, 1998-2000. ***Email:*** rgoodhea@wrf.com

CHRISTOPHER HALE, born Mobile, Alabama, September 18, 1973; admitted to bar, 2000, Florida; 2001, District of Columbia. *Education:* University of Miami (B.A., H.P.I.S., cum laude, 1995); Duke University (J.D., with honors, 2000; M.E.M., 2000). ***Email:*** chale@wrf.com

MARTHA E. HELLER, born Albany, New York, February 16, 1970; admitted to bar, 1998, Maryland and District of Columbia. *Education:* Cornell University (B.A., with distinction, 1992), Phi Beta Kappa; University of Virginia (J.D., 1997). ***Email:*** mheller@wrf.com

EVAN S. HENSCHEL, born Washington, D.C., October 19, 1969; admitted to bar, 2001, New York (Not admitted in District of Columbia). *Education:* University of Pennsylvania (B.A., 1991); George Washington University (J.D., 2000). Articles Editor, The George Washington Law Review. ***Email:*** ehensche@wrf.com

JENNIFER D. HINDIN, born Hollis, New York, April 6, 1971; admitted to bar, 1997, New York; 1998, District of Columbia. *Education:* Georgetown University (B.S.F.S., 1993); New York University (J.D., cum laude, 1996). Junior Fellow, Center for International Studies. *Member:* Women's Bar Association of D.C. (Co-Chair, Communications Forum). ***Email:*** jhindin@wrf.com

KIMBERLY HRABOSKY, born Anaheim, California, December 9, 1975; admitted to bar, 2000, Virginia; 2001, District of Columbia. *Education:* Mary Washington College (B.A., 1997); George Mason University School of Law (J.D., 2000). ***Email:*** khrabosk@wrf.com

JENNIFER S. HUBER, born Sanford, Maine, November 16, 1968; admitted to bar, 1996, California; 1998, District of Columbia. *Education:* Georgetown University (B.A., 1990); University of San Francisco Law School (J.D., 1996). Member, Board of Directors, Moot Court. Comments Editor, University of San Francisco Law Review. *Member:* The District of Columbia Bar; State Bar of California; American Bar Association. ***Email:*** jhuber@wrf.com

ERICA R. JACOBSON, born St. Charles, Illinois, 1972; admitted to bar, 2000, Maryland; 2001, District of Columbia. *Education:* University of Maryland (B.A., magna cum laude, 1994); Columbus School of Law of The Catholic University of America (J.D., cum laude). Phi Beta Kappa. Phi Kappa Phi. ***Email:*** ejacobso@wrf.com

MEL R. JIGANTI, born Chicago, Illinois, March 13, 1970; admitted to bar, 1998, Illinois; 2001, District of Columbia. *Education:* University of Notre Dame (B.A., 1992; J.D., 1998). (Resident, McLean, Virginia Office). ***Email:*** mjiganti@wrf.com

JEFFREY L. JOHNSON, born Columbus, Ohio, January 31, 1974; admitted to bar, 2001, Utah (Not admitted in District of Columbia). *Education:* Brigham Young University (B.Acc., 1999; M.Acc., 2001; J.D., 2001). Certified Public Accountant, Florida, 2001. ***LANGUAGES:*** Portuguese. ***PRACTICE AREAS:*** Corporate Law.

NICHOLAS A. KESSLER, born Cincinnati, Ohio, June 2, 1974; admitted to bar, 1999, District of Columbia. *Education:* Yale University (B.A., with distinction, Economics, 1996); University of Virginia (J.D., 1999). Technology and Production Editor, Virginia Environmental Law Journal, 1998-1999. ***Email:*** nkessler@wrf.com

KATHLEEN S. KIM, born Seoul, Korea, April 15, 1974; admitted to bar, 2000, New York; 2001, District of Columbia. *Education:* University of Virginia (B.A., 1996); Harvard Law School (J.D., 1999). Phi Beta Kappa. *Member:* New York State and American Bar Associations; District of Columbia Bar; Asian Pacific American Bar Association. ***LANGUAGES:*** Korean. ***PRACTICE AREAS:*** Directors and Officers Liability; Litigation. ***Email:*** kkim@wrf.com

EVE KLINDERA, born New York, New York, July 23, 1974; admitted to bar, 1999, Maryland; 2000, District of Columbia. *Education:* University of

(This Listing Continued)

(This Listing Continued)

Maryland (B.A., Journalism, 1996); George Washington University Law School (J.D., 1999). Member, Order of the Coif. Former Law Clerk to the Honorable Marvin J. Garbis, U.S. District Court, District of Maryland. ***Email:*** eklinder@wrf.com

DIANE L. KRAWCZUN, born Hamilton, New Jersey, November 15, 1967; admitted to bar, 1994, New Jersey; 1997, District of Columbia. *Education:* St. Joseph's University (B.A., 1989); St. Louis University School of Law (J.D., cum laude, 1994); Georgetown University Law Center (LL.M., 1995). Notes and Comments Editor, Public Law Review. ***Email:*** dkrawczu@wrf.com

ERIC W. LEONARD, born Englewood, New Jersey, August 6, 1972; admitted to bar, 1997, Maryland; 1998, District of Columbia; 2001, Virginia. *Education:* Johns Hopkins University (B.A., 1994); George Washington University Law School (J.D., with honors, 1997). (Resident, McLean, Virginia Office). ***Email:*** eleonard@wrf.com

WILLIAM LIETH, born Brooklyn, New York, November 3, 1947; admitted to bar, 1980, District of Columbia; 1983, U.S. Court of Federal Claims. *Education:* C.W. Post Campus of Long Island University (B.A., cum laude, 1969); George Washington University (J.D., with honors, 1980). Executive Editor, The Advocate. ***Email:*** wlieth@wrf.com

ANDREW K. LONG, born Cleveland, Ohio, September 7, 1970; admitted to bar, 1999, District of Columbia. *Education:* University of Delaware (B.A., 1992); University of Pennsylvania (J.D., 1998). ***Email:*** along@wrf.com

MARCUS E. MAHER, born Muscatine, Iowa, November 6, 1973; admitted to bar, 1999, District of Columbia. *Education:* University of Iowa (B.S., 1996); Harvard Law School (J.D., 1999). ***Email:*** mmaher@wrf.com

KEVIN J. MAYNARD, born Providence, Rhode Island, May 26, 1969; admitted to bar, 1996, Maryland; 1998, District of Columbia. *Education:* Cornell University (B.A., 1991); George Washington University (J.D., with high honors, 1996). Order of the Coif. Member, George Washington University Law Review. Law Clerk to the Hon. Lawrence S. Margolis, U.S. Court of Federal Claims, 1996-1997. ***Email:*** kmaynard@wrf.com

JOHN A. McCULLOUGH, born Washington, D.C., October 27, 1945; admitted to bar, 1971, District of Columbia. *Education:* Princeton University (B.A., magna cum laude, 1967); Yale University (J.D., 1970). Phi Beta Kappa. *Member:* The District of Columbia Bar; American Bar Association; Computer Law Association. ***Email:*** jmccullo@wrf.com

NICOLE M. McGINNIS, born Annapolis, Maryland, November 1, 1973; admitted to bar, 1998, Virginia; 1999, District of Columbia. *Education:* Dartmouth College (A.B., magna cum laude, 1995); University of Chicago (J.D., 1998). ***Email:*** nmcginni@wrf.com

CHRISTOPHER M. MILLS, born Washington, D.C., July 2, 1968; admitted to bar, 1999, Virginia. *Education:* Catholic University of America (B.A., 1991); George Washington University (J.D., with honors, 1999). Member, The George Washington University Law Review. (Resident, McLean, Virginia Office). ***Email:*** cmills@wrf.com

KARALEE C. MORELL, born Stratford, Connecticut, December 4, 1973; admitted to bar, 1999, District of Columbia. *Education:* University of Connecticut (B.A., summa cum laude, 1995), Phi Beta Kappa; Cornell University (J.D., 1998). Order of the Coif. ***Email:*** kmorell@wrf.com

BRIAN NUTERANGELO, admitted to bar, 1993, Pennsylvania; 1994, District of Columbia. *Education:* Boston University (B.S.B.A., 1990); The American University (J.D., 1993). Law Clerk to the Hon. Ricardo M. Urbina, U.S. District Court, District of Columbia, 1994-1996. ***Email:*** bnuteran@wrf.com

KRISTINA R. OSTERHAUS, born Miami, Florida, March 21, 1973; admitted to bar, 1998, Virginia, District of Columbia. *Education:* Wake Forest University (B.A., magna cum laude, 1994); University of Chicago (J.D., 1997). Law Clerk to the Hon. Kenneth L. Ryskamp, U.S. District Court, Southern District of Florida. ***Email:*** kosterha@wrrf.com

MARK A. PACELLA, born Brockton, Massachusetts, June 15, 1965; admitted to bar, 1995, Massachusetts; 2000, District of Columbia; registered to practice before U.S. Patent and Trademark Office. *Education:* Rensselaer Polytechnic Institute (B.S., Chemistry, 1987); George Washington University (J.D., with highest honors, 1994). Order of the Coif. Member, The George Washington Law Review. ***Email:*** mpacella@wrf.com

JOHN F. PAPANDREA, born Meriden, Connecticut, December 29, 1972; admitted to bar, 1998, Connecticut; 1999, District of Columbia and New York. *Education:* Yale University (B.A., magna cum laude, with distinction, 1995); University of Chicago (J.D., 1998). ***Email:*** jpapandr@wrf.com

MATTHEW S. PETERSEN, admitted to bar, 1999, Utah; 2000, District of Columbia. *Education:* Brigham Young University (B.A., 1996); University of Virginia (J.D., 1999). ***Email:*** mpeterse@wrf.com

(This Listing Continued)

JAMES D. PHIPPS, born Oakland, California, October 31, 1964; admitted to bar, 1996, California; 2000, District of Columbia. *Education:* Brigham Young University (B.A., 1992; J.D., 1996); Fulbright Fellow (Saudi Arabia-Islamic Law, 1994-1995). ***Email:*** jphipps@wrf.com

DANIEL B. PICKARD, born Huntingdon Valley, Pennsylvania, August 11, 1967; admitted to bar, 1995, California (inactive); 1997, District of Columbia. *Education:* Pennsylvania State University (B.A., 1989); Golden Gate University School of Law (J.D., with honors, 1995); Georgetown University Law Center (LL.M., with distinction, 1998). ***Email:*** dpickard@wrf.com

LESLIE A. PLATT, born Midland, Michigan, October 19, 1967; admitted to bar, 1995, District of Columbia and New York. *Education:* Albion College (B.A., cum laude, 1989); College of William & Mary, Marshall-Wythe School of Law (J.D., 1994). Board Editor, William and Mary Law Review. ***Email:*** lplatt@wrf.com

LESLIE JOHNSON PUJO, born Omaha, Nebraska, December 28, 1965; admitted to bar, 1997, Maryland and District of Columbia. *Education:* Trinity University, San Antonio, Texas (B.A., 1988); The George Washington University National Law Center (J.D., with highest honors, 1995); University of Toulouse (D.E.S.S., with honors, 1996). Order of the Coif. Senior Notes Editor, The George Washington University Law Review. ***Email:*** lpujo@wrf.com

BENJAMIN B. REED, born Columbia, South Carolina, September 22, 1973; admitted to bar, 1999, District of Columbia. *Education:* University of South Carolina (B.A.S., magna cum laude, 1995), Phi Beta Kappa; University of Virginia (J.D., 1998). ***Email:*** breed@wrf.com

D. MARK RENAUD, born Sikeston, Missouri, March 15, 1972; admitted to bar, 2000, Virginia; 2001, District of Columbia. *Education:* Yale University (B.A., 1994); University of Virginia (J.D., 2000). ***Email:*** mrenaud@wrf.com

RONALD J. RINALDI, born Concord, Massachusetts, January 26, 1961; (admission pending). *Education:* Brigham Young University (B.A., 1985); Columbia University School of Law (J.D., 1991); Oxford University (Rhodes Scholar, 1985-1988). Harlon Fiske Stone Scholar. Articles Editor, Columbia Law Review. Judicial Clerk, Chambers of Judge Patricia M. Wald, U.S. Court of Appeals, D.C. Circuit, 1991-1992. Assistant Professor of Law, University of Arizona College of Law, 1992-1996. ***Email:*** rrinaldi@wrf.com

CHRISTOPHER L. ROBBINS, born Smithville, Missouri, March 22, 1972; admitted to bar, 1997, Virginia; 1998, District of Columbia. *Education:* Princeton University (A.B., cum laude, 1994); Vanderbilt University (J.D., 1997). Managing Editor, Vanderbilt Law Review. Member, Vanderbilt Moot Court Board. ***Email:*** crobbins@wrf.com

PAUL G. ROCHE, born Hartford, Connecticut, March 20, 1960; admitted to bar, 1989, District of Columbia. *Education:* University of Connecticut (B.A., magna cum laude, 1982); Georgetown University (J.D., 1989). ***Email:*** proche@wrf.com

JESSICA N. ROSENTHAL, born Fort Benning, Georgia, July 15, 1974; admitted to bar, 1999, Virginia and Maryland; 2000, District of Columbia. *Education:* Tufts University (B.A., 1996); George Washington University Law School (J.D., 1999). Order of the Coif. ***Email:*** jrosenth@wrf.com

OREN ROSENTHAL, born Miami, Florida, February 18, 1971; admitted to bar, 1996, Florida; 1998, District of Columbia. *Education:* Northwestern University (B.S.& M.A., 1993); University of Michigan (J.D., 1996). Law Clerk to the Hon. Lenore C. Nesbitt, U.S. District Court, Southern District of Florida, 1996-1998. Intern to Honorable Phyllis A. Kruvitch, U.S. Court of Appeals, Eleventh Circuit, 1994. ***Email:*** orosenth@wrf.com

RANDALL D. ROTH, admitted to bar, 1996, New York (Not admitted in District of Columbia). *Education:* State University of New York at Albany (B.A., 1986); University of Pennsylvania Law School (J.D., 1993). ***PRACTICE AREAS:*** Litigation; Insurance Law. ***Email:*** rroth@wrf.com

MATTHEW J. SCHNEIDER, born Ann Arbor, Michigan, December 16, 1973; admitted to bar, 2000, Michigan; 2001, District of Columbia. *Education:* Cambridge University (Certificate in International Affairs, cum laude, 1995); Michigan State University (B.A., cum laude, 1996); University of Michigan (J.D., 2000). Assistant to the Governor, Governor John Engler, Michigan, 1996-1997. ***Email:*** mschneid@wrf.com

TIMOTHY W. STALEY, born Annapolis, Maryland, 1972; admitted to bar, 1997, Maryland; 1998, District of Columbia. *Education:* John Carroll University (B.A., cum laude, 1994); Catholic University of America, Columbus School of Law (J.D., cum laude, with honors, 1997). Member, Law Review, 1995-1997. Moot Court Member, 1994-1997. ATLA National Trial Moot Court Team Member, CUA, 1997. Dean's Cup, CUA Moot Court Finalist, 1997. CUA, Law School Scholarship, 1996-1997. Co-Author: "The Impact of ADR and the Civil False Claims Act on the Contract Disputes Process," *2001 ABA Federal Procurement Institute,* Annapolis, Maryland; "Third Year of COFC Postaward Bid Protest Jurisdiction: A Work in Progress." *The Government Contractor,* Vol. 42, No. 15, April 12, 2000. Monthly contributor, Fried Frank's *Government Contracts Alert* (TM) Internet publication, 1998-2000. Contributing writer, "The *Spearin* Doctrine: It Isn't What It Used To Be," *The Construction Lawyer,*

(This Listing Continued)

WILEY REIN & FIELDING LLP, Washington—Continued

Vol. 16, No. 4, October 1996. Judicial Clerk to The Honorable Robert J. Yock, U.S. Court of Federal Claims, 1997-1998. *Member:* American Bar Association (Member: Public Contracts Committee; Bid Protest Committee). ***PRACTICE AREAS:*** Government Contracts; Litigation; Business Counseling. ***Email:*** tstaley@wrf.com

E. KENNETH STEGEBY, born Sundsvall, Sweden, May 24, 1966; admitted to bar, 2000, Utah; 2001, District of Columbia. *Education:* Florida International University (B.A., summa cum laude, 1996); Brigham Young University (J.D., cum laude, 1999). Omicron Delta Kappa. Teaching Fellow, Brigham Young University Law School, 1998-1999. Editor, BYU Law Review. Law Clerk to Chief Judge Dee V. Benson, Federal District Court of Utah, 2000-2001. ***Email:*** kstegeby@wrf.com

GERARD M. STEGMAIER, born Fairfax, Virginia, September 12, 1970; admitted to bar, 2000, Virginia; 2001, District of Columbia. *Education:* George Mason University (B.A., with distinction, 1992; J.D., magna cum laude, 2000). Recipient: Fairfax Bar Association Scholarship; Dean Engle Award. Joint Commission on Technology and Science-Privacy Advisory Committee. *Member:* Virginia and Federal Circuit Bar Associations. ***PRACTICE AREAS:*** Internet Law; E-Commerce; Business Law; Finance; Intellectual Property; Privacy Law. ***Email:*** gstegmai@wrf.com

SANDRA TVARIAN STEVENS, born Chicago, Illinois, August 5, 1973; admitted to bar, 1997, Illinois; 1998, District of Columbia. *Education:* American University (B.A., cum laude, 1994); Washington College of Law, American University (J.D., summa cum laude, 1997). ***Email:*** sstevens@wrf.com

ALEXANDER K. SUN, born Fort Wayne, Indiana, May 4, 1969; admitted to bar, 1996, Florida, Massachusetts and New York; 2000, District of Columbia. *Education:* Georgetown University (B.S., 1991; J.D., 1995). *Member:* Asian Pacific Bar Association of the Greater Washington, D.C. Area (Board Member). ***Email:*** asun@wrf.com

STEPHEN C. TOSINI, admitted to bar, 2000, District of Columbia. *Education:* University of Maryland (B.S., 1988); Johns Hopkins University (M.S., 1990); University of Miami (J.D., magna cum laude, 2000). Member, Order of the Coif. Member, University of Miami Law Review. ***Email:*** stosini@wrf.com

JOSHUA S. TURNER, born Detroit, Michigan, January 3, 1973; admitted to bar, 1999, District of Columbia. *Education:* University of Michigan (B.A., Political Science, 1995; J.D., 1999). ***Email:*** jturner@wrf.com

DANIEL J. WADLEY, born American Fork, Utah, September 22, 1973; admitted to bar, 2000, Virginia; 2001, District of Columbia. *Education:* Brigham Young University (B.S., cum laude, 1997); Georgetown University (J.D., cum laude, 2000). ***Email:*** dwadley@wrf.com

ALYSA BETH WAKIN, born Bridgeport, Connecticut, July 12, 1968; admitted to bar, 1995, Connecticut; 1996, New York (Not admitted in District of Columbia). *Education:* New York University (B.A., 1990); Villanova University (J.D., 1995). ***Email:*** awakin@wrf.com

C. HEATHER WALKER, born Great Lakes, Illinois, September 13, 1974; admitted to bar, 2000, District of Columbia. *Education:* University of Florida (B.A., 1996); Georgetown University (J.D., 2000). ***Email:*** hwalker@wrf.com

MARY OATES WALKER, born Cadiz, Kentucky, December 20, 1967; admitted to bar, 1996, Pennsylvania and District of Columbia; 1998, U.S. District Court, Eastern District of Pennsylvania and U.S. Tax Court. *Education:* Howard University (B.A., cum laude, 1989; J.D., 1994). Co-Captain, National Moot Court Team. Merit Fellow, Howard University School of Law. *Member:* American Bar Association. ***Email:*** mwalker@wrf.com

CHRISTINE QUICKENDEN WASHINGTON, born Bozeman, MT, May 13, 1969; admitted to bar, 1999, New York; 2000, District of Columbia. *Education:* Georgetown University (B.S.F.S., 1991); American University (J.D., cum laude, 1998). ***Email:*** cwashing@wrf.com

DINEEN PASHOUKOS WASYLIK, born Austin, Texas, July 17, 1972; admitted to bar, 1999, New York and District of Columbia; 2000, Florida. *Education:* Cornell University (B.S., 1994); Georgetown University (J.D., 1998). *Member:* The District of Columbia Bar; The Florida Bar. ***Email:*** dwasylik@wrf.com

ELIZABETH A. WHALLEY BUONO, born Carmel, New York, October 18, 1966; admitted to bar, 2000, Virginia (Not admitted in District of Columbia). *Education:* Boston College School of Nursing (B.S.N., cum laude, 1988); St. John's University College of Business Administration (M.B.A., 1993); George Mason University School of Law (J.D., 2000). Registered Nurse: Virginia, 1988; Massachusetts, 1995. *Member:* Virginia (Member, Health Law Group) and American (Member, Health Law Group) Bar Associations. ***PRACTICE AREAS:*** Health Care; FDA; Insurance; HIPAA Privacy and Fraud; Government Contracts. ***Email:*** ebuono@wrf.com

(This Listing Continued)

AMY E. WORLTON, born Portland, Oregon, August 6, 1971; admitted to bar, 2000, District of Columbia. *Education:* Brigham Young University (B.A., 1993); New York University (J.D., 2000); Princeton University (M.P.A.). ***Email:*** aworlton@wrf.com

DEREK A. YEO, born Sunbury-upon-Thames, England, January 9, 1966; admitted to bar, 1998, Virginia; 2000, District of Columbia. *Education:* Cambridge University, England (B.A., M.A., 1988); College of William & Mary (J.D., 1998). Order of the Coif. Assistant Articles Editor, William & Mary Law Review. Articles Editor, William & Mary Environmental Law and Policy Review. ***Email:*** dyeo@wrf.com

WILKES ARTIS

CHARTERED

(Formerly Wilkes, Artis, Hederick & Lane)

SUITE 400, 1150 18TH STREET, N.W.
WASHINGTON, D.C. 20036-3841
Telephone: 202-457-7800
URL: http://www.wilkesartis.com

Real Estate Tax, Assessment and Condemnation, Transactional Real Estate.

FIRM PROFILE: Wilkes Artis, Chartered was founded in 1926 and has a long history of participation in the growth and development of the Washington Metropolitan and Suburban region. The firm is well known for its experience and expertise in all aspects of federal and state eminent domain matters and real property tax assessment litigation. Representing regional, national and international clients, Wilkes Artis offers its services in the District of Columbia, Maryland and Virginia.

JAMES C. WILKES (1899-1968).

JAMES E. ARTIS (1907-1978).

CHARLES A. CAMALIER, III, born Washington, D.C., November 2, 1951; admitted to bar, 1977, Maryland; 1978, District of Columbia. *Education:* University of Notre Dame (B.B.A., 1974); Georgetown University (J.D., 1977). Co-Author: "Commercial Property Tax Assessments: An Appealing Process," Realtor, March, 1982; "Commercial Property Tax Assessments: New Developments and Insights," Realtor, March, 1983. *Member:* The District of Columbia Bar; Montgomery County, Maryland State and American Bar Associations. ***PRACTICE AREAS:*** Real Property Tax and Assessment Law; Condemnation; Litigation. ***Email:*** ccamalier@wilkesartis.com

ILENE BAXT BOORMAN, born Los Angeles, California, October 22, 1960; admitted to bar, 1989, Virginia; 1992, District of Columbia. *Education:* George Washington University (B.B.A., 1986); Georgetown University (J.D., 1989). Co-Author: "Virginia State Real Property," Chapter in The Propety Tax Deskbook, American Bar Association (2001). *Member:* Fairfax and American Bar Associations; Virginia State Bar; Virginia Trial Lawyers Association; American Property Tax Council; Urban Land Institute; National Association of Industrial and Office Properties (Member, Programs Committee); American Inns of Court; Appraisal Institute (Affiliate Member). ***PRACTICE AREAS:*** Real Property Tax Assessment Law; Condemnation; Construction Law. ***Email:*** iboorman@wilkesartis.com

STANLEY J. FINEMAN, born Brooklyn, New York, May 3, 1939; admitted to bar, 1964, New York; 1976, District of Columbia. *Education:* University of Michigan (B.A., 1960); Columbia University (LL.B., 1963). Assistant Chief, Land Acquisition Section, U.S. Department of Justice, 1975. Legal Columnist, The Appraisal Journal, 1981-1989. ABA Speaker, Eminent Domain, 1987, 1988 and 1989. Member, Tax Rules Committee, D.C. Superior Court. *Member:* The District of Columbia Bar. Founding Member, American Property Tax Counsel. ***PRACTICE AREAS:*** Real Property Tax and Assessment Law; Condemnation; Litigation. ***Email:*** sfineman@wilkesartis.com

DAVID A. FUSS, born Washington, D.C., January 23, 1958; admitted to bar, 1987, Maryland; 1988, District of Columbia; U.S. Court of Appeals for the District of Columbia Circuit and U.S. Tax Court. *Education:* University of Michigan (A.B., 1982); Catholic University (J.D., 1987). Member, Journal of Contemporary Health Law and Policy, 1986-1987. Law Clerk to Chief Judge Fred B. Ugast, District of Columbia Superior Court, 1987-1988. *Member:* The District of Columbia Bar; Maryland State and American Bar Associations; American Inns of Court; Association of Former Intelligence Officers. ***PRACTICE AREAS:*** Real Property Tax Litigation; Federal and State Condemnation; Federal and State Tax Controversy; Administrative Law. ***Email:*** dfuss@wilkesartis.com

ERIC S. KASSOFF, born New York, New York, October 9, 1960; admitted to bar, 1986, Maryland; 1987, Pennsylvania; 1988, District of Columbia. *Education:* Boston University (B.S., magna cum laude, Finance and Accounting, 1982; J.D., 1986). Author: "Alternative Infrastructure Financing: Development Districts Pave the Way," Land Use Law and Zoning Digest, January 1991. Law Clerk, Massachusetts Inspector General, 1985-1986. Director and General Counsel, Jewish Community Center of Greater Washington, 1996— Director,

(This Listing Continued)

1998—, President, 1997-1999, Maryland/D.C. Chapter, National Association of Industrial and Office Properties. Director, 1994-2000, Chairman, Multi-Family Housing Conference; Chairman, Legal Action Committee, 1994 and Chairman, Finance Committee, 1995, Suburban Maryland Building Industry Association. *Member:* The District of Columbia Bar; Maryland State, Pennsylvania and American Bar Associations. ***PRACTICE AREAS:*** Real Property Valuation Litigation; Real Property Tax Law; Public Finance; Zoning; Real Estate Transactions. ***Email:*** ekassoff@wilkesartis.com

KENNETH A. MAX, born May 20, 1947; admitted to bar, 1977, Maryland; 1978, District of Columbia. *Education:* Temple University (B.A., 1969; M.B.A., 1972); Georgetown University (J.D., 1977). Certified Public Accountant, 1972. *Member:* Maryland State and American Bar Associations; The District of Columbia Bar. ***PRACTICE AREAS:*** Real Estate Tax Appeals; Transactional Real Estate; Estate Planning. ***Email:*** kmax@wilkesartis.com

STUART A. TUROW, born Washington, D.C., February 21, 1960; admitted to bar, 1986, Maryland; 1987, District of Columbia. *Education:* University of Delaware (B.S., 1982); University of Bridgeport (J.D., 1986). Recipient, Outstanding Legal Scholarship Award, Bridgeport Law School. Author: Comment, "Oklahoma Routes NCAA 7-2 in the 'Television Bowl': NCAA v. Board of Regents of the University of Oklahoma," 6 Univ. of Bridge. L. Rev. 333, 1985; "Maryland Real Property Tax," Chapter of Bar Association of D.C. Real Estate Practice Book. *Member:* District of Columbia Bar; Maryland State Bar Association; District of Columbia Building Industry Association (Tax and Impositions Subcommittee); American Property Tax Counsel. ***PRACTICE AREAS:*** Real Property Tax and Assessment Law; Condemnation and Zoning Law. ***Email:*** sturow@wilkesartis.com

MATTHEW G. AHRENS, born Columbus, Nebraska, November 9, 1965; admitted to bar, 1993, Virginia; 1994, Maryland; 1996, District of Columbia. *Education:* Rice University (B.A., 1987); George Washington University (J.D., 1993). Honors in Moot Court and Trial Advocacy. Member, George Washington Journal of International Law and Economics, 1991-1993. *Member:* The District of Columbia Bar; Virginia State Bar; Maryland State and American Bar Associations. ***PRACTICE AREAS:*** Real Property Tax and Assessment Law. ***Email:*** mahrens@wilkesartis.com

LEGAL SUPPORT PERSONNEL

LEGAL ASSISTANTS

CAROL R. ALBERT, born Winston-Salem, North Carolina, November 10, 1961. *Education:* Vanderbilt University (B.A., 1984). ***PRACTICE AREAS:*** Commercial Real Estate Tax and Assessment Appeals. ***Email:*** calbert@wilkesartis.com

SHARON L. HOPKINS, born Newfoundland, New Jersey, April 27, 1967. *Education:* University of Maryland (B.A., Political Science/Economics, 1992). *Member:* National Association of Legal Assistants (NALA). ***PRACTICE AREAS:*** Commercial Real Estate Tax and Assessment Appeals. ***Email:*** shopkins@wilkesartis.com

LINDSEY A. DENDY, born Washington, D.C., August 19, 1979. *Education:* George Mason University (B.A., 2001). ***PRACTICE AREAS:*** Commercial Real Estate Tax and Assessment; Appeals. ***Email:*** ldendy@wilkesartis.com

MARC R. BOLADO, born Wilmington, Delaware, October 30, 1969. *Education:* Idaho State University (B.Sc., 1998). ***PRACTICE AREAS:*** Commercial Real Estate Tax and Assessment; Appeals. ***Email:*** mbolado@wilkesartis.com

WILKES, ARTIS, HEDRICK & LANE

WASHINGTON, D.C.

(See Wilkes Artis, Chartered)

WILKINSON BARKER KNAUER, LLP

Established in 1982

2300 N STREET, N.W., SUITE 700
WASHINGTON, D.C. 20037
Telephone: 202-783-4141
Fax: 202-833-2360; 783-5851
Email: info@wbklaw.com
URL: http://www.wbklaw.com

Administrative and Regulatory Practice before Federal Agencies, Legislative Practice before Congress, and Trial and Appellate Practice before Federal Courts. Practice sectors include: Communications and Telecommunications, Corporate and Commercial Transactions, Information Technology, Intellectual Property, International Telecommunications, Trade and Investment, Legislation and Litigation.

(This Listing Continued)

FIRM PROFILE: The Firm provides a wide range of legal services to clients in the communications, information technology, internet, e-commerce and related fields. WBK also specializes in legislation, litigation, corporate and international commercial transactions, joint ventures, mergers, acquisitions, and Latin American and Caribbean law, international telecommunications, trade and investments. In the telecommunications field the Firm has special emphasis on wireless and advanced technologies, including PCS, cellular, third generation mobile, messaging, video services (broadcast, wireless cable, fiber optic and cable) wireless local loop and broadband services, MDS, MMDS, LMDS, 39 GHz and satellite.

Wilkinson Barker Knauer's domestic and international clients include Fortune 500 Companies, small and mid-sized corporations. Internet service providers, utilities, municipalities, universities, trade associations, foreign governments and foundations.

MEMBERS OF FIRM

GLEN A. WILKINSON (1911-1985).

ROBERT W. BARKER (1919-1987).

ROSEL H. HYDE (1900-1992).

LEON T. KNAUER, born New York, N.Y., July 16, 1932; admitted to bar, 1961, Connecticut; 1962, District of Columbia; 1965, U.S. Supreme Court. *Education:* Fordham University (B.S. in Math, 1954); Georgetown University (J.D., 1961). Staff Member, Georgetown University Law Journal, 1960-1961. Law Clerk to Judge Charles F. McLaughlin, U.S. District Court for the District of Columbia, 1961-1962. Instructor, Georgetown University Law Center, 1965-1966. Editor: *Telecommunications Act Handbook, A Complete Reference for Business* (Government Institute, 1996); *Beyond the Telecommunications Act, A Domestic and International Prospective for Business* (Government Institute, 1998). Author: "El Entorno Mundial de las Telecomunicaciones, " Derecho de las Telecomunicaciones (Ministerio de Fomento, Spain, 1997). Associate, 1962-1968 and Partner, 1968-1982 Wilkinson, Cragun & Barker. *Member:* District of Columbia Bar; State Bar Association of Connecticut; The Bar Association of the District of Columbia; American Bar Association; Federal Communications Bar Association (Treasurer, 1981-1982; Member, Executive Committee, 1982-1983). [Capt., U.S. Marine Corps, 1954-1957]. ***PRACTICE AREAS:*** Telecommunications Law; International Commercial Transactions. ***Email:*** lknauer@wbklaw.com

L. ANDREW TOLLIN, born Wilmington, Delaware, November 28, 1950; admitted to bar, 1976, New York; 1978, District of Columbia; U.S. Supreme Court. *Education:* George Washington University (B.A., 1972; J.D., 1975). Member: George Washington Law Review, 1973-1975. Attorney, Litigation Division, General Counsel's Office, Federal Communications Commission, 1979-1983. Former Adjunct Faculty Member, George Washington University. Legislative Assistant, U.S. Senator J. Caleb Boggs. Associate, Mudge Rose Guthrie & Alexander, New York, N.Y. Author: "The Battle for Portland, Maine," 52 Fed. Comm. L.J._, 1999; *Beyond the Telecommunications Act - A Domestic and International Perspective for Business,* 1998; *The Comparative Renewal Process: A New Approach Based on Old Law,* 1 Communications Law Conspectus, 1993; "Who Will Regulate Utility-Owned Fiber-Optic Networks? The States or The FCC?" Public Utilities Fortnightly, 1988; "The RKO Case: Unique Facts with Extraordinary Consequences," 35 Federal Communications Law Journal 275, 1983. Chairman, Advisory Council of the First Amendment Center, 1988-1991. *Member:* American Bar Association; Federal Communications Bar Association. (Managing Partner). ***PRACTICE AREAS:*** Communications; Telecommunications Law; Administrative Litigation; Appellate Practice. ***Email:*** latollin@wbklaw.com

KENNETH E. SATTEN, born Queens, New York, June 15, 1955; admitted to bar, 1979, District of Columbia. *Education:* State University of New York at Buffalo (B.A., summa cum laude, 1976); George Washington University (J.D., with high honors, 1979). Order of the Coif; Phi Beta Kappa. Member, George Washington Law Review, 1978-1979. Author: Note, "Pretrial Suppression Hearings Presumptively Closed to Public when Adverse Publicity Threatens Impaneling of Impartial Jury in County of Venue," 47 George Washington Law Review 319, 1978. Associate, Wilkinson, Cragun & Barker, 1979-1982. *Member:* The District of Columbia Bar; The Federal Communications Bar Association. ***PRACTICE AREAS:*** Communications Law; Administrative Law; Corporate Law; Commercial Transactions. ***Email:*** ksatten@wbklaw.com

MICHAEL DEUEL SULLIVAN, born New York, N.Y., February 14, 1952; admitted to bar, 1978, District of Columbia; 1981, U.S. Court of Appeals for the District of Columbia Circuit; 1982, U.S. Court of Appeals, Second Circuit; 1995, U.S. Court of Appeals, Sixth Circuit; 1996, U.S. Court of Appeals, Eleventh and Fifth Circuits; 1997, U.S. Court of Appeals, Ninth Circuit; 1998, U.S. Court of Appeals, Eighth Circuit. *Education:* Washington University (A.B., 1975); Catholic University (J.D., 1978). Appellate Attorney, Office of General Counsel, FCC, 1980-1983. Chief, Mobile Services Division, Common Carrier Bureau, FCC, 1983-1986. *Member:* The District of Columbia Bar; American Bar Association; Federal Communications Bar Association. ***PRAC-***

(This Listing Continued)

WILKINSON BARKER KNAUER, LLP, Washington— Continued

TICE AREAS: Administrative Litigation; Appellate Practice; Communications; Telecommunications Law; Information Technology; Internet law. ***Email:*** msullivan@wbklaw.com

KATHRYN A. ZACHEM, born Freedom, Pennsylvania, April 16, 1958; admitted to bar, 1985, Virginia; 1987, District of Columbia. *Education:* George Washington University (B.A., 1980); George Mason University School of Law (J.D., 1985). Delta Theta Phi. *Member:* The District of Columbia Bar; Virginia State Bar; Federal Communications Bar Association (Member, Executive Committee, 1997-1998; Co-Chair, Land Mobile Practice Committee, 1989-1991); Women's Bar Association; Federal Communications Bar Association Foundation (Member, Executive Committee, 1997, 1998; Co-Chair, Charitable Distributions Committee, 1991-1992). ***PRACTICE AREAS:*** Communications; Telecommunications Law; Administrative Law. ***Email:*** kzachem@wbklaw.com

F. THOMAS MORAN, born Cortland, New York, June 13, 1945; admitted to bar, 1973, District of Columbia; 1990, Maryland. *Education:* Brown University (A.B., 1968); Wharton School of Finance, University of Pennsylvania (M.B.A., 1970); American University (J.D., 1973); Georgetown University (LL.M., in Taxation, 1976). Associate Editor, American University Law Review, 1972-1973. Attorney, Interpretative Division, Office of the Chief Counsel for the Internal Revenue Service, 1973-1977. *Member:* The District of Columbia Bar; American Bar Association. ***PRACTICE AREAS:*** Communications; Commercial Transactions; Telecommunications Law; Tax Law. ***Email:*** ftmoran@wbklaw.com

PAUL J. SINDERBRAND, born New York, N.Y., November 21, 1953; admitted to bar, 1979, New York; 1981, District of Columbia. *Education:* Columbia University (B.A., 1975); Georgetown University (J.D., magna cum laude, 1978). Member, Moot Court. Member, 1976-1977 and Editor, 1977-1978, Law & Policy in International Business. Co-author: "1976-1977 Administration Survey: Civil Aeronautics Board," 9 Law & Policy in International Business 141, 1977. *Member:* District of Columbia Bar; New York State Bar Association; Federal Communications Bar Association. ***PRACTICE AREAS:*** Communications; Telecommunications Law; Corporate; Commercial Transactions; Appellate Practice; Administrative Litigation; Trial Practice; International Telecommunications. ***Email:*** psinderbrand@wbklaw.com

KENNETH D. PATRICH, born New York, N.Y., March 12, 1951; admitted to bar, 1981, District of Columbia; 1983, U.S. District Court for the District of Columbia and U.S. Court of Appeals for the District of Columbia Circuit; 1990, U.S. Supreme Court. *Education:* Buffalo State College (B.A., 1972); Georgetown University (J.D., 1981). Member, American Criminal Law Review, 1980-1981. Associate, Wilkinson, Cragun & Barker, 1981-1982. *Member:* The District of Columbia Bar; Federal Communications Bar Association. ***PRACTICE AREAS:*** Telecommunications Law; Administrative Law. ***Email:*** kpatrich@wbklaw.com

LAWRENCE J. MOVSHIN, born Newark, New Jersey, January 5, 1949; admitted to bar, 1974, Georgia; 1978, District of Columbia. *Education:* Rutgers University (B.A., 1971); George Washington University (J.D., with honors, 1974). Co-Author: "The FCC's Computing Devices Rules--A Case Study," Emory Law Journal, Spring, 1981. Author: "Developments In Wireless Communications--Navigating The Regulatory Morass," Proceedings of the Wireless Informations Forum, 1991. *Member:* The District of Columbia Bar; Federal Communications Bar Association (Treasurer, 1985-1986; Member, Executive Committee, 1985-1989; Chair, Wireless Telecommunications Practice Committee, 1993-1995; Chair, Professional Responsibility Committee, 1995-1996). ***PRACTICE AREAS:*** Communications; Telecommunications Law; Corporate; Commercial Transactions; International Telecommunications. ***Email:*** lmovshin@wbklaw.com

LINDA M. WELLSTEIN, born Milwaukee, Wisconsin, December 5, 1956; admitted to bar, 1984, District of Columbia. *Education:* Marquette University (B.A., cum laude, with honors, 1979); Georgetown University Law Center (J.D., 1983). Member, *American Criminal Law Review,* 1980-1983. Co-Author: *The Changing Regulatory Terrain of Cable Television,* 35 Catholic University Law Review 705, Spring, 1986. Author: *Complying with EEO,* Telecater, May 1987. Contributor, Labor and Employment Law Committee Report of the ABA, 1982. Adjunct Professor: International Telecommunications Regulation, Georgetown University Law Center, 1989-1997; International Telecommunications Regulation, The Columbus School of Law, Catholic University, 1989-1994. Director, Maryland Board, National Women's Political Caucus, 1992—. Director, 1993-1997, Vice President, 1994-1995 and President, 1995-1996, Satellite Federal Credit Union. Associate: Cole, Raywid & Braverman, 1983-1985; Schnader, Harrison, Segal, Lewis (Washington, D.C.), 1985-1987. Compa ñia Anonima National Telefonos de Venezuela (CANTV), Caras, Venezuela, 1997—, International Legal Advisor for Commercial & Telecommunication for Regulatory Matters; COMSAT International, Senior Division Counsel, 1993-1997, COMSAT Corporation, World Systems Division General Attorney, 1987-1993. *Member:* The District of Columbia Bar; American Bar Association; Federal Communications Bar Association; Women's Bar Association of the District of Columbia (Co-Chair, Communications Forum, 1985-1988 and 1991-1992); International Bar Association; Venezuelan American Chamber of Commerce. (Resident, Caracas, Venezuela Office). ***LANGUAGES:*** English and Spanish. ***PRACTICE AREAS:*** International Commercial Transactions; Information Technology; Information Technology Outsourcing; Electronic Commerce; Joint Ventures; Corporate Law; Mergers and Acquisitions. ***Email:*** lwellstein@wbklaw.com

WILLIAM J. SILL, born Rochester, New York, May 11, 1953; admitted to bar, 1978, Pennsylvania; 1985, District of Columbia. *Education:* George Washington University; Temple University School of Communications & Theatre (B.A., in Communications, 1975); Temple University School of Law (J.D. 1978). Recipient, Presidential Scholar. Attorney: International Conference Staff—Common Carrier Bureau, Federal Communications Commission, 1983; International Facilities Division, Common Carrier Bureau, 1982-1983; Federal Communications Broadcasting Bureau, 1979-1982; United States Railway Association, 1978-1979. *Member:* The District of Columbia Bar; Pennsylvania and American Bar Associations; Federal Communications Bar Association (Co-Chair, Wireless Telecommunications Practice Committee, 1996-1998). ***TRANSACTIONS:*** Global Crossing Ltd.-Frontier Corp.; Frontier Corp.-BAMS; GTE-Contel Merger (FCC). ***PRACTICE AREAS:*** Telecommunications Law; Commercial Transactions. ***Email:*** wsill@wbklaw.com

JONATHAN V. COHEN, born Washington, D.C., November 25, 1956; admitted to bar, 1983, District of Columbia. *Education:* University of Pennsylvania-Wharton School (B.S. in Economics, 1978); Georgetown University (J.D., 1982). Assistant Counsel to the President, Office of Presidential Personnel, The White House, 1993. Federal Communications Commission, 1993-1998: Special Assistant to the Chairman, 1993; Senior Counsel, Office of Plans and Policy, 1993-1995; Assistant Chief for Law, Mass Media Bureau, 1995-1997; Associate Chief, Wireless Telecommunications Bureau, 1997-1998. *Member:* The District of Columbia Bar; Federal Communications Bar Association (Co-Chair, Committee on Global Telecommunications Development). ***PRACTICE AREAS:*** Telecommunications Law; Administrative Law. ***Email:*** joncohen@wbklaw.com

ROBERT D. PRIMOSCH, born New York, N.Y., July 22, 1961; admitted to bar, 1987, New York; 1988, District of Columbia. *Education:* Georgetown University (B.A., magna cum laude, 1983; J.D., 1986). Co-Chair, Ad Hoc Committee on Alternative Multichannel Practice, 1997. *Member:* District of Columbia Bar; Federal Communications Bar Association. ***PRACTICE AREAS:*** Communications; Telecommunications Law; Corporate; Commercial Transactions; Appellate Practice. ***Email:*** primosch@wbklaw.com

TIMOTHY J. COONEY, born Glenview, Illinois, June 20, 1953; admitted to bar, 1979, Illinois; 1980, District of Columbia. *Education:* Georgetown University (A.B., 1975); Georgetown University Law Center (J.D., 1979). Trial Attorney, Federal Energy Regulatory Commission, 1979-1983. ***PRACTICE AREAS:*** Communications Law; Administrative Law; Federal Regulatory Law. ***Email:*** tcooney@wbklaw.com

ROBERT G. KIRK, born Arlington, Massachusetts, August 2, 1966; admitted to bar, 1992, Massachusetts; 1994, District of Columbia and U.S. Court of Appeals for the District of Columbia Circuit; 1995, U.S. Court of Appeals, Sixth Circuit; 1996, U.S. Court of Appeals, Fifth and Eleventh Circuits; 1997, U.S. Court of Appeals, Ninth Circuit; 1998, U.S. Court of Appeals, Eighth Circuit. *Education:* Merrimack College (B.A., 1988); George Washington University National Law Center (J.D., 1991). Editor-in-Chief, George Washington Journal of International Law and Economics, 1990-1991. Co-Author: "The Comparative Renewal Process: A New Approach Based on Old Law," 1 Communications Law Conspectus, 1993. Author: "Wireless Mobile Communications," Telecommunications Act Handbook: A Complete Reference for Business, Chapter 5, 1996. *Member:* American Bar Association; Federal Communications Bar Association. ***PRACTICE AREAS:*** Communications; Telecommunications Law; Appellate Practice; Administrative Litigation; Internet Law. ***Email:*** rkirk@wbklaw.com

J. WADE LINDSAY, born Heidelberg, Germany, April 29, 1961; admitted to bar, 1988, District of Columbia. *Education:* Haverford College (A.B., 1983); Emory University (J.D., 1988). *Member:* The District of Columbia Bar. ***PRACTICE AREAS:*** Communications; Telecommunications Law; Energy; Natural Resources; Administrative Litigation; Appellate Practice. ***Email:*** jlindsay@wbklaw.com

CAROLYN W. GROVES, born Fairfield, Connecticut, December 17, 1967; admitted to bar, 1992, Pennsylvania; 1994, District of Columbia. *Education:* University of Scranton (B.A., cum laude, 1989); Catholic University of America, Columbus School of Law (J.D., 1992). Editor, Catholic University Law Review, Vol. 41. Author: "California v. Federal Communications Commission: Continuing the Struggle Between Sections 151 and 152 of the Communications Act," 40 Cath. U. L. Rev. 893, 1991. Member: National Jesuit Honor Society; Communications Law Institute, Columbus School of Law. *Member:* Pennsylvania Bar Association; The District of Columbia Bar; Federal Communications Bar Association. ***PRACTICE AREAS:*** Communications; Telecommunications Law; Administrative Law. ***Email:*** cgroves@wbklaw.com

(This Listing Continued)

BARRY P. MILLER, born Grimsby, England, June 13, 1961; admitted to bar, 1987, Mississippi; 1990, District of Columbia; 1993, Virginia; 1996, Maryland. *Education:* University of Alabama (B.S., 1983; M.B.A., 1984; J.D., 1987). Gamma Beta Phi; Gamma Iota Sigma. Recipient: American Jurisprudence Award for Trade Regulations. Author: "Trademark Counterfeiting Handbook (Chapter 3)," Aspen Law and Business 1999; "New Risks to Imports of Gray Market Goods," Trademark America, 1993. Adjunct Professor of Law, George Mason University Law School, 1994-1995. ***PRACTICE AREAS:*** Intellectual Property Law; Privacy Law; Computer and Internet Law; Broadcasting Law; Telecommunications Law; Corporate Transactions; Intellectual Property Litigation. ***Email:*** bmiller@wbklaw.com

CRAIG EDWARD GILMORE, born Cleveland, Ohio, February 21, 1968; admitted to bar, 1993, Virginia; 1995, District of Columbia; U.S. Court of Appeals, Fourth, Fifth, Sixth, Ninth and Eleventh Circuits and U.S. Court of Appeals for the District of Columbia Circuit. *Education:* Boston University (B.A., magna cum laude, 1990); Catholic University (J.D., 1993). Associate Editor, Catholic University Law Review, Vol. 42. Author: "Payne v. Tennessee: Rejection of Precedent, Recognition of Victim Impact Worth," 41 Catholic University Law Review 469 (1992). *Member:* American Bar Association; The District of Columbia Bar; Federal Communications Bar Association. ***PRACTICE AREAS:*** Communications; Telecommunications Law; Administrative Law; Appellate Practice. ***Email:*** cgilmore@wbklaw.com

L. CHARLES KELLER, born San Jose, California, February 20, 1967; admitted to bar, 1994, California; 1996, District of Columbia. *Education:* University of California (B.A., cum laude, 1990); University of San Francisco (J.D., 1993). Member, McAuliffe Honor Society. Recipient, American Jurisprudence Awards for Legal Research and Writing, and Evidence. Articles Editor, University of San Francisco Law Review, 1992-1993. Intern, Hon. Joyce L. Kennard, California Supreme Court. Chief, Network Services Division, Common Carrier Bureau, FCC, 1999-2001. Deputy Chief, Accounting Policy Division, Common Carrier Bureau, FCC, 1999. *Member:* State Bar of California; The District of Columbia Bar; Federal Communications Bar Association. ***LANGUAGES:*** French and Dutch. ***SPECIAL AGENCIES:*** FCC. ***PRACTICE AREAS:*** Telecommunications Law. ***Email:*** ckeller@wbklaw.com

OF COUNSEL

PIERRE J. LaFORCE, born Berlin, New Hampshire, March 29, 1936; admitted to bar, 1960, District of Columbia. *Education:* St. Anselm College (A.B., magna cum laude, 1957); Georgetown University (J.D., 1960). Editor, Georgetown Law Journal, 1959-1960. *Member:* The District of Columbia Bar; The Bar Association of the District of Columbia; American Bar Association; Barristers. ***PRACTICE AREAS:*** Appellate Practice; Trial Practice; Corporate; Commercial Transactions; Administrative Litigation. ***Email:*** plaforce@wbklaw.com

ASSOCIATES

GEORGINA L.O. FEIGEN, born New York, N.Y., January 28, 1966; admitted to bar, 1993, Maryland (Not admitted in District of Columbia). *Education:* Boston University (B.S., 1988); Catholic University of America (J.D., 1993). Lead Article Editor, CommLaw Conspectus, Vol. 1, No. 1. *Member:* Maryland State and American Bar Associations; Federal Communications Bar Association. ***LANGUAGES:*** Spanish. ***PRACTICE AREAS:*** Communications; Telecommunications Law; International Telecommunications. ***Email:*** gfeigen@wbklaw.com

JOSÉ ANDRÉS ROMERO ANGRISANO, born Caracas, Venezuela, November 2, 1970; admitted to bar, 1993, Venezuela. *Education:* Universidad Católica Andrés Bello (Abogado, 1993); Cornell University (LL.M., 1995). *Member:* Caracas and International Bar Associations; Federal Communications Bar Association; Colegio de Abogados del Distrito Federal. (Resident, Caracas, Venezuela Office). ***LANGUAGES:*** Spanish and English. ***PRACTICE AREAS:*** Telecommunications Law; Information Technology; Commercial Transactions; Corporate Law; Tax Law; Foreign Investment. ***Email:*** jromero@wbklaw.com

DAVID KENT JUDELSOHN, born New York, New York, September 18, 1968; admitted to bar, 1994, New York; 2000, District of Columbia. *Education:* Union College (B.A., 1990); Suffolk Law School (J.D., 1993). *Member:* Federal Communications Bar Association. ***PRACTICE AREAS:*** Communications Law. ***Email:*** djudelsohn@wbklaw.com

LYNN H. JOHANSON, born Ponca City, Oklahoma, March 18, 1969; admitted to bar, 1994, Texas; 1996, District of Columbia; 1998, U.S. Court of Appeals, District of Columbia Circuit. *Education:* Vanderbilt University (B.S., cum laude, 1991); University of Texas at Austin (J.D., 1994). Notes Editor, The Review of Litigation, 1993-1994. *Member:* Federal Communications Bar Association. ***PRACTICE AREAS:*** Communications; Telecommunications Law; Energy; Administrative Law; Appellate Practice. ***Email:*** ljohanson@wbklaw.com

(This Listing Continued)

JEFFREY SCOTT COHEN, born Brooklyn, New York, May 23, 1966; admitted to bar, 1995, New York; 1996, District of Columbia; 1997, U.S. Court of Appeals for the District of Columbia Circuit; 1998, U.S. Supreme Court. *Education:* George Washington University (B.S.E.E., 1988; J.D., with honors, 1994). *Member:* American Bar Association; Federal Communications Bar Association. ***PRACTICE AREAS:*** Internet Technology; Telecommunications; Administrative Litigation; Appellate Practice. ***Email:*** jcohen@wbklaw.com

CAMILLE HANSEN, born Alexandria, Virginia, March 3, 1969; admitted to bar, 1995, Utah; 1997, District of Columbia. *Education:* Brigham Young University (B.A., 1990; J.D., 1995). Order of the Barristers. *Member:* Utah State Bar; The District of Columbia Bar; Federal Communications Bar Association; American Bar Association. ***LANGUAGES:*** German. ***PRACTICE AREAS:*** Communications Law; Administrative Law. ***Email:*** chansen@wbklaw.com

PAIGE K. FRONABARGER, born New Orleans, Louisiana, January 9, 1970; admitted to bar, 1995, Louisiana; 1999, District of Columbia. *Education:* Louisiana State University and A. and M. College (B.A., 1992); Loyola University (J.D., 1995); Georgetown University (Masters of Law in Securities Regulation). ***PRACTICE AREAS:*** Corporate; Commercial Transactions; Finance. ***Email:*** pfronabarger@wbklaw.com

ARTHUR THOMAS LECHTMAN, born Izmir, Turkey, September 17, 1969; admitted to bar, 1995, California; 1998, District of Columbia. *Education:* University of California at Los Angeles (B.A., 1991); University of Southern California (M.A., 1992); Pepperdine University (J.D., 1995). *Member:* Federal Communications Bar Association. ***Email:*** alechtma@wbklaw.com

VLADIMIR J. FALCÓN, born Caracas, Venezuela, January 5, 1971; admitted to bar, 1995, Venezuela. *Education:* Universidad Católica Andrés Bello (Lawyer, 1993); Cornell University (LL.M., 1996); University of Paris II, Panthéon-Assas (D.S.U.(LL.M.), 1997). Law Clerk, Sixth and Seventh Courts of First Instance in Civil, Commercial and Traffic Matters of Caracas, 1991-1994. *Member:* Caracas and International Bar Associations; Federal Communications Bar Association. (Resident, Caracas, Venezuela Office). ***LANGUAGES:*** Spanish, English, French. ***PRACTICE AREAS:*** Telecommunications Law; Information Technology; Commercial Law; Corporate Law; Mergers and Acquisitions; Joint Ventures; Foreign Investment. ***Email:*** vfalcon@wbklaw.com

ROBERT G. MORSE, born Havre de Grace, Maryland, May 5, 1968; admitted to bar, 1996, Maryland; 1998, District of Columbia. *Education:* Stanford University (A.B., 1990); George Washington University Law School (J.D., with honors, 1996). Member, George Washington Journal of International Law and Economics, 1994-1996. Author: "European Union Mobile Telecommunications Policy and the Communications Act of 1934; Can Congress Avoid a Collision on the Information Superhighway," 29 Geo. Wash. J. Int'l L. & Econ. 197 (1995). *Member:* American Bar Association; Federal Communications Bar Association. ***PRACTICE AREAS:*** Telecommunications Law; Administrative Law. ***Email:*** rmorse@wbklaw.com

BRIAN W. HIGGINS, born Reno, Nevada, December 21, 1964; admitted to bar, 1996, Nevada; 1998, District of Columbia. *Education:* Williamette University (B.A., 1985); College of William and Mary (M.A., 1995); George Washington University (J.D., 1996). Articles Editor, The American Intellectual Property Law Association Quarterly Journal, 1995-1996. ***PRACTICE AREAS:*** Communications; Telecommunications Law. ***Email:*** bhiggins@wbklaw.com

CATHERINE CURRAN BUTCHER, born New York, New York, November 20, 1969; admitted to bar, 1996, Maryland; 1998, District of Columbia. *Education:* University of Richmond (B.A., cum laude, 1991); College of William & Mary (J.D., 1996). Author: "Privatization of Telecommunications in the European Union," William & Mary Administrative Law Review, Summer 1996. *Member:* Federal Communications Bar Association. ***LANGUAGES:*** Spanish. ***PRACTICE AREAS:*** Communications.

KEVIN M. JORDAN, born Scranton, Pennsylvania, April 20, 1970; admitted to bar, 1996, Virginia (Not admitted in District of Columbia). *Education:* University of Scranton (B.S., 1992); University of Tulsa College of Law (J.D., 1996); Georgetown University Law Center (LL.M., 1997). Phi Delta Phi. Member, Tulsa Journal of Comparative and International Law, 1994-1995. Author: "Qualitex Co. v. Jacobsen Products Co., the Unanswered Question— Can Color Ever Be Inherently Distinctive?" 85 Trademark Reporter 371, 1995. ***PRACTICE AREAS:*** Corporate Law; Commercial Transactions; Taxation. ***Email:*** kjordan@wbklaw.com

WILLIAM R. LAYTON, born Miami, Oklahoma, February 13, 1969; admitted to bar, 1998, Maryland; 1999, District of Columbia. *Education:* Oklahoma State University (B.A., 1991); George Washington University (J.D., 1997). Articles Editor, American Intellectual Property Law Association Quarterly Journal, 1996-1997. *Member:* Maryland State Bar Association; Federal Communications Bar Association (Member, Young Lawyers Committee). ***PRACTICE AREAS:*** Telecommunications Law. ***Email:*** wlayton@wbklaw.com

TIMOTHY A. KRUYER, born Flint, Michigan, July 10, 1973; admitted to bar, 1998, Colorado; 2001, District of Columbia. *Education:* Michigan State University (B.A., 1995); University of Denver (J.D., 1998). Articles Editor,

(This Listing Continued)

WILKINSON BARKER KNAUER, LLP, Washington—Continued

Denver Journal of International Law and Policy, 1997-1998. ***LANGUAGES:*** French. ***PRACTICE AREAS:*** Telecommunications Law; Communications Law; Administrative Litigation. ***Email:*** tkruyer@wbklaw.com

PAUL J. NAGLE, born Washington, D.C., January 4, 1974; admitted to bar, 1999, Maryland (Not admitted in District of Columbia). *Education:* University of Maryland, College Park (B.A., 1996); Catholic University (J.D., 1999). Member, Institute for Communications Law Studies. *Member:* Maryland State Bar Association, Inc.; Federal Communications Bar Association. ***PRACTICE AREAS:*** Telecommunications Law; Internet Law. ***Email:*** pnagle@wbklaw.com

LAURA A. SCHINK, born Lakeland, Florida, December 13, 1972; admitted to bar, 1999, District of Columbia. *Education:* Indiana University (B.A., 1995); Newhouse School of Communications (M.A., 1998); Syracuse University (J.D., 1998). *Member:* Federal Communications Bar Association. ***PRACTICE AREAS:*** Telecommunications. ***Email:*** lschink@wklaw.com

ANNE H. SULLIVAN, born Gaithersburg, Maryland, April 30, 1974; admitted to bar, 1999, Maryland; 2001, District of Columbia. *Education:* Guilford College (B.S., 1996); University of Baltimore (J.D., cum laude, 1999). Associate, Montgomery County, Maryland Inns of Court, 2000—. Certified Mediator, Maryland, 1999. *Member:* American Bar Association; Federal Communications Bar Association. ***PRACTICE AREAS:*** Telecommunications Law. ***Email:*** asullivan@wbklaw.com

CHRISTOPHER G. ERNST, born Bryn Mawr, Pennsylvania, December 2, 1966; admitted to bar, 2000, Maryland (Not admitted in District of Columbia). *Education:* Hartwick College (B.A., 1989); Catholic University of America, Columbus School of Law (J.D., 1999). *Member:* Federal Communications Bar Association. ***PRACTICE AREAS:*** Telecommunications Law; Wireless Communications. ***Email:*** cernst@wbklaw.com

KEITH R. MURPHY, born Philadelphia, Pennsylvania; admitted to bar, 2000, Virginia (Not admitted in District of Columbia). *Education:* Pennsylvania State University (B.S., 1996); George Washington University Law School (J.D., 2000). Member, Moot Court Honors Board, 1999-2000. Recipient, Judge Albert H. Grenadier Award for Oral Advocacy, 2000. Managing Editor, George Washington International Law Review, 1998-2000. *Member:* Federal Communications Bar Association. ***PRACTICE AREAS:*** Communications Law. ***Email:*** kmurphy@wbklaw.com

KATHRYN P. WILDRICK, born Summit, New Jersey, January 10, 1974; admitted to bar, 2000, New York (Not admitted in District of Columbia). *Education:* Princeton University (A.B., 1996); George Washington University Law Center (J.D., 1999). ***LANGUAGES:*** French. ***PRACTICE AREAS:*** Telecommunications. ***Email:*** kwildrick@wbklaw.com

ZACHARY ANDREWS ZEHNER, born San Clemente, California, June 14, 1973; admitted to bar, 2000, Virginia (Not admitted in District of Columbia). *Education:* Trinity College (B.A., 1995); Washington College of Law of American University (J.D., cum laude, 2000). Author: "Lutheran Church-Missouri Synod v. FCC: The End of Judicial Deference to FCC Policymaking in the Affirmative Action Debate," American University Administrative Law Review, Vol. 51 (Spring, 1999). ***PRACTICE AREAS:*** Telecommunications Law. ***Email:*** zzehner@wbklaw.com

CHRISTOPHER D. ORNELAS, born South Haven, Michigan, August 11, 1968; admitted to bar, 2001, District of Columbia. *Education:* University of Virginia (B.A., Rhetoric and Communications, 1992); Washington College of Law (J.D., 2000). ***PRACTICE AREAS:*** Mass Media Law; Telecommunications Law; Trademarks; Corporate Transactions; Commercial Transactions. ***Email:*** cornelas@wbklaw.com

SANDRA G. WILKOF

WASHINGTON, D.C.

(See Bethesda, Maryland)

Family Law, Divorce, Custody, Visitation, Marital Property, Child Support, Separation Agreements.

DANIEL S. WILLARD, P.C.

WASHINGTON, D.C.

(See Rockville)

Business Law, Corporate Law, Small Business Law, Incorporations, Partnerships, New Businesses, Buy/Sell Agreements, Business/Corporation Sales, Business Acquisitions, Business Debt, Collections, Contracts, Leases, Business Bankruptcy, Commercial Litigation, Mechanics Liens, Construction Law, Real Property, Family Businesses.

WILLEY AND CROOKS

Established in 1950

1616 H STREET, N.W.
WASHINGTON, D.C. 20006-4985
Telephone: 202-628-2477
Fax: 202-347-3422
Email: esqjcb@aol.com

General Civil Practice. Probate, Thrift Institutions.

JAMES A. CROOKS (1911-1982).

JAMES A. WILLEY (Retired).

JAMES C. BEADLES, born Silver Spring, Maryland, June 22, 1947; admitted to bar, 1972, Maryland; 1974, District of Columbia; 1977, U.S. Supreme Court. *Education:* George Washington University (B.A., 1969; J.D., 1972). *Member:* The District of Columbia Bar; Bar Association of the District of Columbia (Chairman, Real Property Committee, 1978-1980); Maryland State and American Bar Associations. ***PRACTICE AREAS:*** Probate Administration; Estates; Wills; Thrift Institutions Law. ***Email:*** ESQJCB@aol.com

WILLIAMS & ASSOCIATES

1030 FIFTEENTH STREET., N.W.
SUITE 300
WASHINGTON, D.C. 20005-1501
Telephone: 202-842-0431
Fax: 202-467-4045
Email: fcw@bellatlantic.net
URL: http://www.lawyers.com/dc-patentlaw

Patent Prosecution, Patent Portfolio and Infringement Analysis, with special emphasis in the areas of Medical and Surgical Devices and Digital Signal Processing; Government Contract Claim Preparation and Prosecution.

FIRM PROFILE: The firm emphasizes, with respect to patent and other intellectual property problems, analytical depth and the ability to select crucial facts and considerations from clutter. It specializes in sorting through and simplifying patent matters having highly judgmental aspects and those that are dauntingly complicated or fluid, especially those in respect to which others have despaired or floundered and given up. The firm also serves as counsel to investors and investment consortia evaluating start-up companies for potential investment. In this capacity it evaluates, in a due-diligence context, patent positions of target companies.

FREDERICK C. WILLIAMS, born Medford, Massachusetts; admitted to bar, 1974, Virginia; 1975, Massachusetts; 1981, District of Columbia; 1984, Maryland; registered to practice before U.S. Patent and Trademark Office. *Education:* Boston College (B.S.); University of North Carolina (M.S.; Ph.D.); University of Michigan (J.D., magna cum laude, 1974). Author: "The United States Congress and Nonproliferation," International Security, Fall 1978, p. 45; "Nuclear Nonproliferation: The Spent Fuel Problem," Frederick C. Williams and David A. Deese (eds), Pergamon Press, New York, 1979; "Intellectual Property Protection for Multimedia Signal Processing Applications," presented at the 1998 NATO Advanced Study Institute, Signal Processing. Research Associate, University of Rochester Nuclear Structure Research Laboratory, 1969-1971. Research Fellow, Center for Science and International Affairs, Kennedy School of Government, Harvard University, 1977-1978. Attorney-Advisor, U.S. Arms Control and Disarmament Agency, 1978-1980. Acting Assistant General Counsel, 1987-1989, Deputy Assistant General Counsel, 1990-1992 and Patent Attorney, 1991-1994, U.S. Department of Energy. *Member:* The District of Columbia Bar; Virginia State Bar; American Bar Association; American Physical Society. (Also Of Counsel to Slater & Zeien, L.L.P.).

OF COUNSEL

JENNIFER J. ZEIEN (Also Member, Slater & Zeien, Washington, D.C.).

JAMES L. LEWIS (Also, Associate Levy & Grandinetti, Washington, D.C.).

PATENT AGENT

YAN LAN, born China, 1974. *Education:* Light Industry University, Beijing, China (B.S., Chemical Engineering, 1996); Franklin Pierce Law Center (Master of Intellectual Property, 1999). ***LANGUAGES:*** Chinese. ***PRACTICE AREAS:*** Patents.

WILLIAMS & CONNOLLY LLP

725 TWELFTH STREET, N.W.
WASHINGTON, D.C. 20005-5901
Telephone: 202-434-5000
Fax: 202-434-5029

Practice in Federal Courts and before Federal Departments and Agencies.

MEMBERS OF FIRM

EDWARD BENNETT WILLIAMS (1920-1988).

PAUL R. CONNOLLY (1922-1978).

DAVID POVICH, born Washington, D.C., June 8, 1935; admitted to bar, 1962, District of Columbia; 1978, U.S. Court of Appeals, Fourth Circuit; 1980, U.S. Tax Court; 1981, U.S. Court of Appeals, Fifth and Eleventh Circuits; 1984, U.S. District Court, District of Maryland including Trial Bar; 1997, U.S. Court of Appeals, Third Circuit. *Education:* Yale University (B.A., 1958); Columbia University (LL.B., 1962). Law Clerk to Judge Thomas D. Quinn, District of Columbia Court of Appeals, 1962-1963. *Member:* The District of Columbia Bar; The Bar Association of the District of Columbia; American Bar Association; The Barristers; The Lawyers' Club. ***Email:*** dpovich@wc.com

STEVEN M. UMIN, born New York, N.Y., January 28, 1939; admitted to bar, 1965, California; 1967, District of Columbia. *Education:* Yale University (B.A., 1959; LL.B., 1964); Oxford University, Rhodes Scholar, England (1st B.M., 1961). Phi Beta Kappa; Order of the Coif. Law Clerk to: Chief Justice Roger Traynor, California Supreme Court, 1964-1965; Associate Justice Potter Stewart, U.S. Supreme Court, 1965 Term. Public Member, United States Delegation to the Conference on Security and Cooperation in Europe. Member, Board of Directors, National Multiple Sclerosis Society. *Member:* The District of Columbia Bar; The Bar Association of the District of Columbia; The State Bar of California. ***PRACTICE AREAS:*** Administrative Agency Practice; Administrative Hearings and Appeals; Appellate Practice; Arbitration; Art Fraud; Banking Litigation; Civil Appeals; Civil Litigation; Commercial Litigation; Contract Litigation; Corporate Investigation; Corporate Litigation; Criminal Appeals; Criminal Defense; Criminal Investigation; Health Care Litigation; International Arbitration; International Dispute Resolution; Mediation; U.S. Supreme Court Litigation. ***Email:*** sumin@wc.com

JOHN W. VARDAMAN, born Montgomery, Alabama, April 22, 1940; admitted to bar, 1967, District of Columbia. *Education:* Washington & Lee University (A.B., 1962); Harvard University (LL.B., 1965). Law Clerk to Associate Justice Hugo L. Black, U.S. Supreme Court, 1965-1966. Member, D.C. Circuit Advisory Committee on Procedures, 1990-1992. District of Columbia Bar Task Force on Civility in the Profession. Member, ABA Long Range Planning Group on Civil Justice System Improvements, 1993-1994. *Member:* The District of Columbia Bar; American College of Trial Lawyers. ***PRACTICE AREAS:*** Complex Litigation; Mass Torts; Products Liability Defense. ***Email:*** jvardaman@wc.com

PAUL MARTIN WOLFF, born Kansas City, Missouri, July 22, 1941; admitted to bar, 1968, District of Columbia. *Education:* University of Wisconsin (B.A., 1963); Harvard University (LL.B., 1966). Phi Kappa Phi; Phi Beta Kappa. Author: "Demonstrative Evidence," Forensic Sciences, 1982. Lecturer, Catholic University Law School, 1970-1973. Law Clerk to Judge James R. Durfee, U.S. Court of Claims, 1966-1967. Member, Executive Committee, Washington, D.C. Chapter, Lawyers Committee for Civil Rights Under Law, 1980-1990. Member, Board of Directors, The Stuart Stiller Foundation, 1980-1997. Member, Board of Directors, Washington Legal Clinic for the Homeless, 1988-1999. Member, Board of Directors, Opportunities for Older Americans Foundation, 1988-1993. Member: Board of Directors, Emeritus Foundation, 1993-1999; Board of Directors, Executive Committee, Washington Performing Arts Society, 1990—; District of Columbia Sports Commission, 1995-1999. Member, Board of Directors, Economic Club of Washington, 1996—. Trustee, Federal City Council (Executive Committee, 1994—). Member, Board of Visitors, Kogod College of Business, American University, 1993—. Member, Board of Trustees, American University, 1995—. Member: Board of Directors, Committee on Public Education, 1996-1999; Board of Overseers, Corcoran Gallery of Art, 1996—; Vice Chairman, District of Columbia Public Charter School Resource Center, 1999—. *Member:* The District of Columbia Bar; American Bar Association; Washington Council of Lawyers (Co-Founder, Board of Directors, 1971-1974); American Law Institute. Fellow, American Bar Foundation. ***PRACTICE AREAS:*** Arbitration; Banking Litigation; Business Litigation; Business Mediation; Civil Practice; Civil Litigation; Commercial Litigation; Commercial Real Estate Litigation; Complex Litigation; Construction Litigation; Contract Litigation; Copyright Litigation; Corporate Litigation; Federal Civil Litigation; Insurance Litigation; Intellectual Property Litigation; Libel Defense; Media and First Amendment; Mediation; Real Estate Litigation; Securities Litigation. ***Email:*** pwolff@wc.com

J. ALAN GALBRAITH, born Washington, D.C., July 3, 1941; admitted to bar, 1966, Massachusetts; 1967, California; 1969, District of Columbia; 1982, Maryland. *Education:* Harvard University (B.A., 1963); University of Michigan

(This Listing Continued)

(J.D., 1966). Order of the Coif. Author: "Linkletter, Shott, and the Retroactivity Problem in Escobedo," 64 Michigan Law Review 832, 1966. Associate-in-Law, Boalt Hall School of Law, University of California, 1966-1967. Staff Attorney for Hon. Stanley Mosk, California Supreme Court, 1967-1968. *Member:* The District of Columbia Bar; State Bar of California; Maryland State, Massachusetts and American (Member, Section of Litigation) Bar Associations. ***PRACTICE AREAS:*** Civil Practice; Commercial Litigation; ERISA Litigation; Federal Civil Practice; Legal Malpractice Defense; Patent Litigation; Commercial Arbitration. ***Email:*** agalbraith@wc.com

JOHN G. KESTER, born Oshkosh, Wisconsin, June 18, 1938; admitted to bar, 1964, District of Columbia; 1968, U.S. Supreme Court. *Education:* University of Wisconsin (B.A., 1959); Université d'Aix-Marseille, France (Fulbright Scholar); Harvard University (LL.B., magna cum laude, 1963). Phi Beta Kappa; Phi Kappa Phi. Member, 1961-1963 and President, 1962-1963, Harvard Law Review. Author: "Soldiers Who Insult the President," Harvard Law Review, June 1968; "Constitutional Restrictions on Political Parties," Virginia Law Review, May, 1974; "The Law Clerk Explosion," Litigation, Spring, 1983; "The Future of the Joint Chiefs of Staff," AEI Foreign Policy and Defense Review, March 1980; "Do We Need the Service Secretary?" Washington Quarterly, Winter, 1981; "Designing a U.S. Defense General Staff," Strategic Review, Summer, 1981; "Some Myths of U.S. Extradition Law," Georgetown Law Journal, April 1988; "State Governors and the Federal National Guard," Harvard Journal of Law & Public Policy, winter 1988. Visiting Lecturer in Law, Duke University, 1968; Assistant Professor of Law, University of Michigan, 1968-1969. Law Clerk to Mr. Justice Black, U.S. Supreme Court, 1963-1965. Deputy Assistant Secretary of the Army, 1969-1972. The Special Assistant to the Secretary and Deputy Secretary of Defense, 1977-1978. Awarded Decoration for Distinguished Civilian Service, Department of the Army, 1971; Department of Defense Medal For Distinguished Public Service, 1979. Member: Board of Visitors, U.S. Air Force Academy, 1979-1981; Chemical Warfare Review Commission, 1985; Academic Advisory Board, U.S. Naval Academy, 1978-1982; Board of Zoning Appeals, Alexandria, Virginia, 1975-1977; Regional Selection Panel for White House Fellows, 1985-1990; Advisory Committee of Nancy Reagan Drug Abuse Fund, 1986-1990; Program Committee, Supreme Court Historical Society, 1988-1991; Board of Directors, Historical Society of The District of Columbia Circuit, 1990—. Vice Chairman, Defense Science Board Task Force on MX Missile Environmental Impact, 1980-1982. Contributing Editor, Washingtonian Magazine, 1980—; Military Logistics Forum, 1984-1988. Member, Army Science Board, 1995-1998. *Member:* The District of Columbia Bar (Member, Legal Ethics Committee, 1982-1988); American Bar Association (Member, Sections on: Litigation; Criminal Law; International Law); American Society of International Law. Fellow, American Bar Foundation. [Capt., JAGC, U.S. Army, 1965-1968]. ***Email:*** jkester@wc.com

WILLIAM E. McDANIELS, born Needham, Massachusetts, July 1, 1941; admitted to bar, 1967, District of Columbia; 1983, Maryland. *Education:* Williams College (B.A., 1963); Georgetown University (J.D., 1966). Graduate Fellow in Criminal Law and Litigation, University of Pennsylvania, 1966-1968. Public Defender, Philadelphia Public Defender's Office, 1966-1968. Adjunct Professor, Evidence, Criminal Law and Advanced Criminal Procedure, Georgetown University Law Center, 1970-1987. Instructor, National Institute for Trial Advocacy, 1975—. *Member:* The District of Columbia Bar; Maryland State and American Bar Associations. Fellow, American College of Trial Lawyers. ***PRACTICE AREAS:*** Administrative Law; Complex and Multi-District Litigation; Criminal Law; Intellectual Property; Libel, Slander and Defamation; Litigation; Products Liability; Torts; Trade Secrets; White Collar Crime. ***Email:*** wmcdaniels@wc.com

BRENDAN V. SULLIVAN, JR., born Providence, Rhode Island, March 11, 1942; admitted to bar, 1967, Rhode Island; 1970, District of Columbia, U.S. District Court for the District of Columbia and U.S. Court of Appeals for the District of Columbia Circuit; 1972, U.S. Supreme Court; 1974, U.S. District Court for the District of Maryland; 1979, U.S. Court of Appeals, Third Circuit; 1981, U.S. Court of Appeals, Fourth Circuit; 1991, U.S. Court of Appeals, Sixth Circuit; 1996, U.S. Court of Appeals, Ninth Circuit; 1998, U.S. Court of Federal Claims. *Education:* Georgetown University (A.B., 1964; J.D., 1967). Author: "Grand Jury Proceedings," Litigation and Administrative Practice—Series—Criminal Law Course Handbook Series No. 121, 1981; "Techniques for Dealing with Pending Criminal Charges or Criminal Investigations," Litigation and Administrative Practice Series—Criminal Law Course Handbook Series No. 130, 1983; "White Collar Criminal Practice Grand Jury," Litigation and Administrative Practice Series—Criminal Law Course Handbook No. 137, 1985. Lecturer, Trial Practice and Criminal Law: Practicing Law Institute (PLI), 1981—; The Maryland Institute for Continuing Professional Education of Lawyers, Inc. (MICPEL), 1979—; District of Columbia Criminal Practice Institute (CPI), 1975-1981. *Member:* The District of Columbia Bar; Rhode Island and American Bar Associations. Fellow: American College of Trial Lawyers. ***Email:*** bsullivan@wc.com

AUBREY M. DANIEL, III, born Monks Corner, South Carolina, May 16, 1941; admitted to bar, 1966, Virginia; 1969, U.S. Court of Military Appeals; 1971, District of Columbia and U.S. District Court for the District of Columbia;

(This Listing Continued)

WILLIAMS & CONNOLLY LLP, Washington—Continued

1972, U.S. Court of Appeals for the District of Columbia Circuit, U.S. Court of Appeals for the Fourth Circuit and U.S. District Court, Eastern District of Virginia; 1973, U.S. Supreme Court; 1975, U.S. Court of Appeals for the Fifth Circuit and U.S. District Court, Northern District of Texas; 1988, Maryland. *Education:* University of Virginia (B.A., 1963); University of Richmond (LL.B., 1966). Phi Delta Phi. Member, McNeil Law Society. Awarded, National District Attorneys Association Outstanding Service, 1971. Author: "The Defense of Superior Orders," University of Richmond Law Review, 1973. Member, Board of Directors: University of Richmond Law School Association, 1972-1975 and 1990-1993. Member, Continuing Legal Education Advisory Committee, Georgetown University Law Center, 1986-1988. *Member:* The District of Columbia Bar; The Bar Association of the District of Columbia; Maryland State and American Bar Associations. Fellow: American College of Trial Lawyers. [Capt., U.S. Army, JAGC, 1967-1971]. ***Email:*** adaniel@wc.com

RICHARD M. COOPER, born Philadelphia, Pennsylvania, November 13, 1942; admitted to bar, 1970, District of Columbia; 1973, U.S. Supreme Court. *Education:* Haverford College (B.A., summa cum laude, 1964); Oxford University, Oxford, England (B.A., 1st Class, 1966; M.A., 1970); Harvard University (J.D., summa cum laude, 1969). Phi Beta Kappa. Rhodes Scholar. President, Harvard Law Review, 1968-1969, Volume 82. Author: "Drug Labeling and Products Liability: The Role of the Food and Drug Administration," 41 Food Drug Cosmetic L.J. 233 (1986); "Regulation Through Private Litigation", 47 Food and Drug L.J. 437 (1992); "Problems of Outcomes Studies: Data Access, Conflicts of Interest, and Peer Review," J. Ass'n of Food & Drug Officials, Mar. 1994 at 36; "Unapproved Uses of Drugs: An Analysis and Some Proposals," 49 Food and Drug L.J. 4 (1994); "Corporate Regulatory Crimes and the Sentencing Revolution," Business Crimes Bull., Apr. 1994, 8; "Taking Steps Against Corporate Crime: An Approach After *Caremark,*" Bus. Crimes Bull., Jan., 1997; The WLF Case Thus Far: Not With a Bang But a Whimper, 55 Food & Drug L.J. 477 (2000); Co-Editor, "Fundamentals of Law and Regulation," (FDLI 1997). Adjunct Professor, Georgetown University Law Center, 1987-1992; 1995-1996. Law Clerk to Justice Brennan, U.S. Supreme Court, 1969-1970. Senior Lecturer, Law Development Center, Kampala, Uganda, 1970-1971. Senior Member, Office of Energy Policy and Planning, Executive Office of the President, 1977. Chief Counsel, U.S. Food and Drug Administration, 1977-1979. Member, Committee on Priority Mechanisms, National Academy of Sciences, 1980-1983. Member, Committee on Contraceptive Development, Institute of Medicine, 1987-1990. Member, Advisory Panel on Strategies for Medical Technology Assessment, U.S. Congressional Office of Technology Assessment, 1980-1981. Chairman, Editorial Advisory Board, Food and Drug L.J., 1985-1986; Member, 1981-1988, 1992-1996. Chairman, Board of Editors, Business Crimes Bulletin, 1996—. Columnist on Business Crime, National Law Journal, 1998—. Member, Board of Managers, Haverford College, 1997—. *Member:* The District of Columbia Bar; American Bar Association (Member, Section of Corporation, Banking and Business Law). ***PRACTICE AREAS:*** Administrative Law; Constitutional Law; Criminal Law; Litigation; Drug and Medical Device Regulation. ***Email:*** rcooper@wc.com

GERALD A. FEFFER, born Washington, D.C., April 24, 1942; admitted to bar, 1968, New York; 1980, District of Columbia. *Education:* Lehigh University (B.A., 1964); University of Virginia (J.D., 1967). Deputy Assistant Attorney General, Tax Division, Department of Justice, 1979-1981. Assistant U.S. Attorney, Southern District of New York, 1971-1976. Assistant Chief, Criminal Division, 1976. Editorial Board, "Business Crimes Bulletin: Compliance & Litigation." Chairman, ABA Annual National Institute on Criminal Tax Fraud. *Member:* The District of Columbia Bar; American Bar Association (Member, Sections on: Criminal Justice, Litigation and Taxation; Past Chairman, Committee on Civil and Criminal Tax Penalties, 1985-1987); National Association of Criminal Defense Lawyers; Wong Sun Society. Fellow: American College of Trial Lawyers; American College of Tax Counsel. ***PRACTICE AREAS:*** Criminal Defense; Criminal Law; Criminal Taxation. ***Email:*** gfeffer@wc.com

ROBERT P. WATKINS, born Boston, Massachusetts, July 6, 1937; admitted to bar, 1966, District of Columbia. *Education:* Harvard University (A.B., 1959); Columbia University (LL.B., 1965); Cambridge University, Institute of Criminology, England (Diploma, 1969). Phi Delta Phi. With U.S. Department of Justice, Civil Rights Division, 1965-1966. Hearing Counsel, Federal Maritime Commission, 1967. Law Clerk to Judge William B. Bryant, U.S. District Court for the District of Columbia, 1968. Assistant United States Attorney, Washington, D.C., 1968-1972. Williams & Connolly, 1972—; Partner, 1976—. United States Circuit Judge Nominating Panel for the District of Columbia, 1977-1980; Board of Trustees, Public Defender Service for the District of Columbia, 1977-1983; Chairman, 1979-1981; Citizen's Gambling Study Commission for the District of Columbia, 1977-1978. Board of Directors, Associated Harvard Alumni, 1978-1981. Member: Board of Trustees, Sidwell Friends School, 1986-1994; Circuit Advisory Committee on Procedures for U.S. Court of Appeals for the District of Columbia Circuit, 1985-1987. Member: District of Columbia Financial Responsibility and Management Assistance Authority, 1998-2001. *Member:* The District of Columbia Bar (Member, Hearing Committee of Disciplinary Board, 1974-1977; Board of Governors, 1980-1983); The Bar Association of the District of Columbia; American Bar Association (Standing Committee on Federal Judiciary, 1991-1993; Chair, 1993-1994); National Bar Association. Fellow, American College of Trial Lawyers. ***PRACTICE AREAS:*** Bid Protests; Civil Rights; Civil Litigation; Class Actions; Class Action Defense; Collective Bargaining; Criminal Law; Employment Discrimination; Federal Litigation; Government Contracts; Labor and Employment; Litigation; Medical Malpractice; Personal Injury; Race Discrimination; Sex Discrimination; Sexual Harassment; Title VII Discrimination. ***Email:*** bwatkins@wc.com

JERRY L. SHULMAN, born Columbia, South Carolina, October 23, 1946; admitted to bar, 1972, District of Columbia; 1975, U.S. Court of Appeals, Fifth Circuit; 1978, U.S. Court of Appeals for the District of Columbia Circuit; 1997, U.S. Court of Appeals for the Federal Circuit. *Education:* Yale University (B.A., summa cum laude, 1968); Harvard University (J.D., magna cum laude, 1971). Phi Beta Kappa. Articles and Book Review Editor, Harvard Law Review, 1970-1971. Adjunct Professor, Georgetown Law School, 1982. *Member:* The District of Columbia Bar. ***Email:*** jshulman@wc.com

LEWIS H. FERGUSON, III, born Abilene, Texas, October 22, 1944; admitted to bar, 1971, Massachusetts; 1973, District of Columbia; 1975, U.S. Claims Court and U.S. Tax Court. *Education:* Yale University (B.A., 1966); Kings College, Cambridge University, Cambridge, England (B.A., 1968; M.A., 1973); Harvard University (J.D., 1971). Member, Board of Editors, Harvard Law Review, 1969-1971. Adjunct Professor, Georgetown University Law Center, 1980-1982, 1984-1990. *Member:* The District of Columbia Bar; American Bar Association (Member, Sections on Taxation; Litigation). ***PRACTICE AREAS:*** Asset Sales; Biomedical Technology; Biotechnology Licensing; Business Dissolutions; Business Formation; Business Planning; Business Reorganization; Business Start-Ups; Business Succession Planning; Business Successions; Business Transactions; Business Transfers; Buying and Selling of Businesses; Debt Finance; Emerging Growth Companies; Entrepreneurial Business Law; Equity Finance; Joint Ventures; Private Placement; SEC Enforcement; Secured Finance; Securities Fraud; Securities Regulation; Shareholder Agreements; Shareholder Disputes; Shareholder Rights; Shareholder Law; Strategic Alliances; Unsecured Finance. ***Email:*** lferguson@wc.com

ROBERT B. BARNETT, born Waukegan, Illinois, August 26, 1946; admitted to bar, 1971, District of Columbia; 1972, U.S. Court of Appeals for the Fifth Circuit; 1975, U.S. Supreme Court; 1976, U.S. Court of Appeals for the District of Columbia Circuit. *Education:* University of Wisconsin (B.A., with honors, 1968); University of Chicago (J.D., cum laude, 1971). Phi Beta Kappa; Phi Kappa Phi; Phi Eta Sigma; Order of the Coif. Staff Member, 1969-1970 and Comments Editor, 1970-1971, University of Chicago Law Review. Adjunct Professor of Constitutional Law, Georgetown University Law School, 1973-1980. Law Clerk to: Judge John Minor Wisdom, U.S. Court of Appeals for the Fifth Circuit, 1971-1972; Mr. Justice Byron R. White, U.S. Supreme Court, 1972-1973. Legislative Assistant to Senator Walter F. Mondale, U.S. Senate, 1973-1975. Chairman, Committee for Public Advocacy, Washington, D.C., 1977-1979. Member: Board of Trustees, John F. Kennedy Center for the Performing Arts, 1994—; Board of Visitors, Sanford Institute of Public Policy, Duke University, 1998—; Board of Visitors, University of Chicago Law School, 2001—. *Member:* The District of Columbia Bar; American Bar Association; American Law Institute. ***PRACTICE AREAS:*** Administrative Agency Practice; Commercial Law; Communications and Media; Contracts; Corporate Law; Employment Contracts; Entertainment Law; General Practice; Government Agency Practice; Government Relations; Intellectual Property; Literary Property; Litigation; Privacy Law. ***Email:*** rbarnett@wc.com

DAVID E. KENDALL, born Camp Atterbury, Indiana, May 2, 1944; admitted to bar, 1974, New York; 1977, U.S. Supreme Court; 1978, District of Columbia; 1993, Maryland. *Education:* Wabash College (B.A., 1966); Oxford University, England, Rhodes Scholar (M.A., 1968); Yale University (J.D., 1971). Phi Beta Kappa. Note and Comment Editor, Yale Law Journal, 1970-1971. Author: "Constitutional Vandalism," 30 U. New Mexico Law Review 155 (2000); "Opinion Is Protected Expression Under the Constitution," 2 Communications Lawyer 5, 1984. "How to Keep Your Client Alive," 3 Criminal Defense 9, 1976; "The Affirmative Duty to Integrate in Higher Education," 79 Yale Law Journal 666, 1970. Co-Author: "The Lottery and The Draft," with Leonard Ross, Harper & Row, 1970. Adjunct Professor: Columbia University Law School, 1977-1978; Georgetown University Law Center, 1985-1995. Law Clerk to Mr. Justice Byron R. White, U.S. Supreme Court, 1971-1972. *Member:* The District of Columbia Bar; New York State and Maryland State Bar Associations. ***Email:*** dkendall@wc.com

GREGORY B. CRAIG, born Norfolk, Virginia, March 4, 1945; admitted to bar, 1973, District of Columbia; 1977, U.S. Supreme Court. *Education:* Harvard University (B.A., magna cum laude, 1967); Cambridge University, Cambridge, England (Diploma in Historical Studies, 1968); Yale University (J.D., 1972). Phi Beta Kappa. The John Harvard Scholar, the Lionel DeJersey Harvard Fellow, 1967-1968. Teacher: Trial Practice, Yale Law School, 1975-1976; Trial Advocacy Institute, Harvard Law School, 1982-1986. Assistant Federal Public Defender, District of Connecticut, 1974-1976. Senior Advisor on Foreign Policy and Defense, Office of Senator Edward M. Kennedy, 1984-1988. Member,

(This Listing Continued)

Board of Directors: Carnegie Endowment for International Peace, 1989— (Vice Chairman); Robert F. Kennedy Memorial, 1989—; International Human Rights Law Group, 1989-1996; Foreign Student Service Council, 1990-1996; Overseas Development Council, 1993-1996; Mexican American Legal Defense and Education Fund (MALDEF), 1995-1997. *Member:* The District of Columbia Bar. ***PRACTICE AREAS:*** Federal Administrative Law; Congressional Investigations; Criminal Law; Immigration Law; International Law; Litigation; Labor and Employment. ***Email:*** gcraig@wc.com

JOHN J. BUCKLEY, JR., born New York, N.Y., May 18, 1947; admitted to bar, 1973, New York; 1977, District of Columbia. *Education:* Georgetown University (A.B., magna cum laude, 1969); The University of Chicago (J.D., cum laude, 1972). Phi Beta Kappa; Pi Sigma Alpha; Order of the Coif. Editor-in-Chief, The University of Chicago Law Review, 1971-1972. Law Clerk to Judge John Minor Wisdom, U.S. Court of Appeals for the Fifth Circuit, 1972-1973. Law Clerk to Justice Lewis F. Powell, Jr., U.S. Supreme Court, 1973-1974. Special Assistant to Hon. Edward H. Levi, Attorney General of the United States, U.S Department of Justice, 1975-1977. *Member:* The District of Columbia Bar; New York State and American Bar Associations. ***Email:*** jbuckley@wc.com

TERRENCE O'DONNELL, born New York, N.Y., March 3, 1944; admitted to bar, 1971, District of Columbia; 1977, U.S. Court of Appeals for the District of Columbia Circuit; 1985, U.S. District Court, District of Maryland; 1987, U.S. Court of Appeals, Fourth Circuit; 1990, U.S. Court of Appeals for the Armed Forces; 1993, U.S. Court of Federal Claims; 1996, U.S. Supreme Court and U.S. Court of Appeals for the Federal Circuit. *Education:* United States Air Force Academy (B.S., 1966); Georgetown University (J.D., 1971). Recipient: Department of Defense Medal for Distinguished Public Service, 1992; Attorney General's Distinguished Service Award, 1992. Office of the General Counsel, The Price Commission, 1971-1972. Deputy Special Assistant to the President, The White House, 1973-1974. Special Assistant to the President and Appointments Secretary, The White House, 1974-1977. U.S. Representative, United Nations Program for the Prevention of Crime and the Treatment of Offenders, 1977-1980. Member, Board of Visitors, 1981-1984 and Chairman, Board of Visitors, 1985-1987, U.S. Air Force Academy. Williams & Connolly, 1977-1989 and 1992—. General Counsel, Department of Defense, 1989-1992. Executive Vice President and General Counsel, Textron, 2000—. Member, U.S. Court of Federal Claims Advisory Council, 1990—. Member, United States Administrative Conference, 1990-1992. Member, U.S. Court of Appeals for the Armed Forces Code Committee, 1993-1995. Director: Gerald R. Ford Foundation, 1987—; A.F. Academy Falcon Foundation, 1989—. *Member:* The District of Columbia Bar; The Bar Association of the District of Columbia; American Bar Association. [Capt. U.S.A.F., 1966-1971]. ***PRACTICE AREAS:*** Administrative Law; Business Law; Government Contracts; Litigation; Products Liability. ***Email:*** todonnell@wc.com

JOHN K. VILLA, born Ypsilanti, Michigan, June 9, 1948; admitted to bar, 1973, Michigan; 1975, District of Columbia. *Education:* Duke University (A.B., 1970); University of Michigan Law School (J.D., 1973). Associate Editor, Michigan Law Review, 1971-1973. In National Law Journal's List of 100 Most Influential Lawyers in America. Author: Corporate Counsel Guidelines (2 vol.), West and American Corporate Counsel Association (ACCA), 1999; *Bank Directors', Officers' and Lawyers' Civil Liabilities,* Aspen Publishing 1992; *Banking Crimes: Fraud, Money Laundering and Embezzlement,* (2 vol.) West, 1987; "The Criminal Sanction," Banking Law Report 2: 71, August, 1985; "Currency Transaction Reporting Failures," Banking Law Report 2:165, March 1986; Note: 70 Michigan Law Review, 171; Note: 71 Michigan Law Review, 372; "A Critical View of Bank Secrecy Act Enforcement and the Money Laundering Status," 37 Catholic University Law Review, 489. Trial Attorney, United States Department of Justice, (Honors Program), 1973-1977. Attorney General's Special Commendation Award for Outstanding Service, 1975. Special Assistant United States Attorney, United States Attorney's Office for the District of Columbia, 1976. Member, Advisory Board, Georgetown Corporate Counsel Institute. Co-Chairman, Bank and Savings and Loan Supervision, Enforcement and Compliance Conference, 1984-1995. Chairman, ALI-ABA Program "Failing Financial Institutions," 1987-1992. Editor-in-Chief, *Money Laundering Law Report,* 1990-1998. Member: Advisory Board, *Banking Attorney,* 1989-1993; Editorial Advisory Board, *Banking Policy Report,* 1989-1996; Editorial Board, *Bank/Thrift Litigation Enforcement News,* 1989-1996; Editorial Advisory Board, *DOJ Alert,* 1991-1998; Board of Advisors, *Bank Bailout Litigation News,* 1991-1998; Board of Editors, *Law Firm Partnership Benefits Report,* 1994-1998. Adjunct Professor, Georgetown Law School "Counseling the Corporation in Crises". *Member:* The District of Columbia Bar; American Bar Association (Member, Sections on: Litigation; Business Law); American Law Institute. ***PRACTICE AREAS:*** Administrative Litigation; Bank Fraud; Corporate Investigations; Corporate Litigation; Directors and Officers Insurance Coverage; Directors and Officers Liability; Legal Malpractice Defense; Securities Litigation; White Collar Criminal Defense. ***Email:*** jvilla@wc.com

BARRY S. SIMON, born New Haven, Connecticut, November 13, 1949; admitted to bar, 1976, District of Columbia. *Education:* Harvard University (B.A., magna cum laude, 1971; J.D., magna cum laude, 1974). Phi Beta Kappa.

(This Listing Continued)

President, Harvard Law Review, 1973-1974. Visiting Lecturer in Law, University of Michigan Law School, 1979. Adjunct Professor, Criminal Procedure, Georgetown University Law Center, 1981-1984. Law Clerk to: Honorable J. Skelly Wright, U.S. Court of Appeals for the District of Columbia Circuit, 1974-1975; Justice William J. Brennan, Jr., U.S. Supreme Court, 1975-1976. *Member:* The District of Columbia Bar. ***PRACTICE AREAS:*** Appellate Practice; Criminal Law; Litigation; Qui Tam Litigation; White Collar Crime. ***Email:*** bsimon@wc.com

KEVIN T. BAINE, born New York, N.Y., August 18, 1949; admitted to bar, 1975, New York; 1977, District of Columbia; 1985, Maryland. *Education:* Princeton University (A.B., cum laude, 1971); University of Pennsylvania (J.D., magna cum laude, 1974). Order of the Coif. Comment Editor, University of Pennsylvania Law Review, 1973-1974. Law Clerk to: Judge Edward Weinfeld, U.S. District Court for the Southern District of New York, 1974-1975; Associate Justice Thurgood Marshall, U.S. Supreme Court, 1975-1976. *Member:* The District of Columbia Bar; American Bar Association (Co-Chair, First Amendment and Media Litigation Committee, Section of Litigation, 1989-1992; Co-Chair, Resource Development Committee, Section of Litigation, 1995-1996). ***Email:*** kbaine@wc.com

STEPHEN L. URBANCZYK, born Buffalo, New York, May 9, 1949; admitted to bar, 1974, California; 1978, U.S. Supreme Court and District of Columbia; 1985, Maryland. *Education:* Holy Cross College (A.B., cum laude, 1971); Stanford University (J.D., 1974). Managing Editor, Stanford Law Review, 1973-1974. Law Clerk, Judge Irving Hill, Central District of California, 1974-1975. Assistant to the Solicitor General, U.S. Department of Justice, 1975-1978. *Member:* The District of Columbia Bar; American Bar Association. ***PRACTICE AREAS:*** Civil Practice; Litigation; Mass Torts; Medical Malpractice; Products Liability; Trial Practice. ***Email:*** surbanczyk@wc.com

PHILIP J. WARD, born New York, N.Y., December 11, 1949; admitted to bar, 1975, California; 1977, Wisconsin; 1979, District of Columbia. *Education:* Stanford University (A.B., with distinction, 1971); Harvard University (J.D., magna cum laude, 1974). Phi Beta Kappa. Member, Board of Editors, 1972-1973 and Developments and Note Editor, 1973-1974, Harvard Law Review. Law Clerk to Hon. Marvin E. Frankel, U.S. District Court, Southern District of New York, 1974-1975. *Member:* The District of Columbia Bar; State Bar of Wisconsin (inactive); State Bar of California. ***Email:*** pward@wc.com

F. WHITTEN PETERS, born Omaha, Nebraska, August 20, 1946; admitted to bar, 1978, District of Columbia. *Education:* Harvard College (B.A., magna cum laude, 1968); Harvard Law School (J.D., magna cum laude, 1976). President, Harvard Law Review. Lecturer, Columbus School of Law, 1988-1990. Adjunct Professor, Georgetown Law Center, 1990-1995. Secretary of the Air Force, 1999-2001. Under Secretary of the Air Force, 1997-1999. Principal Deputy General Counsel, Department of Defense, 1995-1997. *Member:* The District of Columbia Bar (Chair, Rules of Professional Conduct Committee, 1991-1996); American Bar Association. Fellow, American Bar Foundation. [Lt., U.S. Navy, 1969-1973]. ***PRACTICE AREAS:*** Aviation and Aerospace; Civil Practice; Computers and Software; Criminal Law; Government; Government Contracts; Military Base Closures; National Security. ***Email:*** wpeters@wc.com

JAMES A. BRUTON, III, born Ottawa, Illinois, September 3, 1949; admitted to bar, 1975, Pennsylvania; 1978, U.S. Supreme Court; 1982, District of Columbia; 1985, U.S. Tax Court and U.S. District Court for the District of Columbia; 1992, U.S. Court of Federal Claims; U.S. Court of Appeals, First, Second, Third, Fourth, Fifth, Sixth, Seventh, Eighth, Ninth, Tenth and Eleventh Circuits; 1993, U.S. Court of Appeals for the Federal Circuit. *Education:* University of North Carolina at Chapel Hill (A.B., 1971); Temple University (J.D., 1975); Georgetown University (LL.M., Taxation, 1978). Associate Editor, Temple Law Quarterly, 1974-1975. Author: New York University Forty-seventh Annual Institute on Federal Taxation, Chapter 53, "Correcting (or Not Correcting) Erroneous Tax Returns," Matthew Bender & Co., Inc., N.Y., N.Y. 1989. Attorney, Office of Chief Counsel, Internal Revenue Service, 1975-1977. Tax Division, U.S. Department of Justice: Trial Attorney, Appellate Section, 1977-1981; Deputy Assistant Attorney General, 1989-1992; Acting Assistant Attorney General, 1992-1993. *Member:* The District of Columbia Bar (Member, Section of Taxation); Federal and American (Member, Sections on: Criminal Justice; Litigation; Taxation; Co-Chair: Tax Litigation Committee, Litigation Section, 2000—) Bar Associations. Fellow, American College of Tax Counsel. ***Email:*** jbruton@wc.com

PETER J. KAHN, born Hartford, Connecticut, June 13, 1951; admitted to bar, 1976, Connecticut; 1977, District of Columbia, U.S. District Court for the District of Columbia and U.S. Court of Appeals for the District of Columbia Circuit; 1979, U.S. Court of Appeals for the Ninth Circuit; 1980, U.S. Supreme Court; 1981, U.S. Court of Appeals for the Fifth and Eleventh Circuits; 1984, U.S. District Courts for Maryland, Connecticut, Southern District of New York and the Eastern District of Michigan; 1985, U.S. Court of Appeals for the Fourth Circuit; 1989, U.S. Court of Appeals for the Second Circuit; 1998, U.S. Court of Appeals for the Third Circuit. *Education:* Yale University (B.A., cum laude, 1973); Duke University (J.D., 1976). Article Editor, Duke University Law Journal, 1975-1976. Author: "*Brennan v. Buckeye Industries, Inc.:* The Constitutionality of an OSHA Warrantless Search," 1975 Duke Law Journal 406.

(This Listing Continued)

WILLIAMS & CONNOLLY LLP, Washington—Continued

Member, Board of Visitors, Duke University School of Law, 1996-2001, Chairman, Board of Visitors, Duke University School of Law, 2001—. *Member:* The District of Columbia Bar; Connecticut, American and International Bar Associations. ***Email:*** pkahn@wc.com

JUDITH A. MILLER, born Dayton, Ohio, August 3, 1950; admitted to bar, 1977, District of Columbia; 1979, U.S. Court of Appeals for the District of Columbia; 1985, U.S. Supreme Court. *Education:* Beloit College (B.A., summa cum laude, 1972); Yale University (J.D., 1975). Phi Beta Kappa. Editor, Yale University Law Journal, 1974-1975. Law Clerk to Judge Harold Leventhal, U.S. Court of Appeals for the District of Columbia Circuit, 1975-1976; Law Clerk to Associate Justice Potter Stewart, U.S. Supreme Court, 1976-1977; General Counsel, U.S. Department of Defense, The Pentagon, Washington, D.C., 1994-1999. Recipient: Department of Defense Medal for Distinguished Public Service, 1997; Bronze Palm to the Department of Defense Medal for Distinguished Public Service, 1999; Department of the Army Decoration for Distinguished Public Service, 1999; Beloit College Distinguished Service Citation, 1997; National Association of Attorneys General (NAAG) Volunteer Recognition Award for sustained assistance to the states in preparation for arguments before the Supreme Court of the United States. Recognized by National Law Journal as one of "50 Most Influential Women Lawyers in America," 1998. Author: "Implementing Change" in Carter & White, *Keeping the Edge: Managing Defense for the Future* (M.I.T., 2000); "The Psychiatrist as Expert Witness, " in Rossi, *Expert Witnesses* (ABA 1991). Assistant to the Secretary and Deputy Secretary of Defense, 1977-1979. Member, Beloit College Board of Trustees, 1978—. Associate, 1979-1984, Partner, 1985-1994, 2000—, Williams & Connolly LLP, Washington, D.C.; Member, Defense Science Board; Executive Council, American Society of International Law; ABA Standing Committee on Law and National Security; District of Columbia Civil Justice Reform Act Advisory Group, 1992-1995; Advisory Board on the Investigative Capability of the Department of Defense, 1994. *Member:* The District of Columbia Bar; American Bar Association (Co-Chair, Federal Practice Task Force; Co-Chair, Litigation Section Annual Meeting); American Law Institute. Fellow, American Bar Foundation. ***PRACTICE AREAS:*** Aerospace Technology; Antitrust; Complex Business Litigation; Computer Security; Constitutional Law; Electronic Commerce; Executive Employment Law; Export Compliance; Government Contracts; International Law; National Security; Satellite Communications; White Collar Crime. ***Email:*** jmiller@wc.com

LON S. BABBY, born Brooklyn, New York, February 21, 1951; admitted to bar, 1976, Connecticut; 1977, District of Columbia; 1981, U.S. Supreme Court; 1986, U.S. Claims Court. *Education:* Lehigh University (B.A., 1973); Yale University (J.D., 1976). Phi Beta Kappa; Omicron Delta Kappa. Editor, Yale Law Journal, 1974-1976. Author: "Aliens' Right to Teach - Political Socialization and the Public Schools," 85 Yale Law Journal 90, 1976. Adjunct Faculty, George Washington University Law School, 1991, 1992, 1993. Law Clerk to Hon. M. Joseph Blumenfeld, U.S. District Judge, District of Connecticut, 1976-1977. *Member:* The District of Columbia Bar; Connecticut and American Bar Associations; Sports Lawyers Association. ***PRACTICE AREAS:*** Contracts; Employment Contracts; Entertainment Contracts; Executive Employment Law; Executive Severance Contracts; Labor and Employment; Professional Sports Law; Sports Contracts; Sports Law; Sports Licensing; Sports Marketing Law. ***Email:*** lbabby@wc.com

MICHAEL S. SUNDERMEYER, born Kansas City, Missouri, February 8, 1951; admitted to bar, 1976, Virginia; 1977, District of Columbia; 1982, Maryland. *Education:* University of Kansas (B.A., 1973); University of Virginia (J.D., 1976). Phi Beta Kappa; Omicron Delta Kappa; Order of the Coif. Editor-in-Chief, Virginia Law Review, 1975-1976. Author: "Filthy Words, The FCC and the First Amendment: Regulating Broadcast Obscenity," 61 Virginia Law Review 579, 1975. Law Clerk to: The Hon. Harry A. Blackmun, U.S. Supreme Court, 1977-1978; The Hon. John Minor Wisdom, U.S. Court of Appeals, Fifth Circuit, 1976-1977. *Member:* The District of Columbia Bar; Maryland State Bar Association; Virginia State Bar; American Bar Association. ***PRACTICE AREAS:*** Commercial Litigation; Complex Litigation; Federal Administrative Law; Judicial Review; Legal Ethics; Legal Malpractice Defense; Products Liability Defense; Trial Practice. ***Email:*** msundermeyer@wc.com

JAMES T. FULLER, III, born Selma, Alabama, February 27, 1946; admitted to bar, 1971, Virginia; 1972, Washington; 1981, District of Columbia. *Education:* Auburn University (B.S., 1968); University of Virginia (J.D., 1971). Phi Eta Sigma; Omicron Delta Kappa. Adjunct Professor of Law, American University Law School, 1973-1975. Attorney, Interpretative Division, Chief Counsel's Office, 1972-1975, Staff Assistant to Deputy Chief Counsel, 1975-1977 and Staff Assistant to Chief Counsel, 1977-1980, Internal Revenue Service. *Member:* The District of Columbia Bar; American Bar Association (Member, Taxation Section). ***PRACTICE AREAS:*** Taxation; Business Law; Nonprofit and Charitable Organizations. ***Email:*** jfuller@wc.com

DOUGLAS R. MARVIN, born East Stroudsburg, Pennsylvania, August 20, 1947; admitted to bar, 1972, Virginia and Pennsylvania; 1976, U.S. Supreme Court; 1977, District of Columbia. *Education:* Lafayette College, (A.B., 1969); University of Virginia (J.D., 1972). Order of the Coif. Member, University of Virginia Law Review, 1972. Attorney-Advisor, Office of Legal Counsel, U.S. Department of Justice, 1972-1974. Counsel, U.S. Senate Judiciary Committee, 1974. Counselor to the Attorney General, U.S. Department of Justice, 1975-1977. *Member:* The District of Columbia Bar; Pennsylvania, Virginia and American Bar Associations; American Law Institute.

BRUCE R. GENDERSON, born Washington, D.C., July 30, 1952; admitted to bar, 1977, Pennsylvania (inactive); 1978, District of Columbia; 1989, Maryland. *Education:* Duke University (B.A., summa cum laude, 1974); University of Pennsylvania (J.D., magna cum laude, 1977). Phi Beta Kappa; Order of the Coif. Article Editor, University of Pennsylvania Law Review, 1976-1977. Author: "The Constitutionality of the New York Municipal Wage Freeze and Debt Moratorium: Resurrection of the Contract Clause," 125 University of Pennsylvania Law Review 167, 1976. Law Clerk to: Judge Irving L. Goldberg, Fifth Circuit Court of Appeals, Dallas, Texas, 1977-1978. *Member:* The District of Columbia Bar. ***PRACTICE AREAS:*** Civil Litigation; Complex Litigation; Government Contracts; Intellectual Property; Patent Litigation; Pharmaceutical Intellectual Property; Professional Liability; Trial Practice; White Collar Criminal Defense. ***Email:*** bgenderson@wc.com

CAROLYN H. WILLIAMS, born Oshkosh, Wisconsin, October 5, 1950; admitted to bar, 1978, District of Columbia; 1979, U.S. District Court for the District of Columbia and U.S. Court of Appeals for the District of Columbia Circuit; 1984, U.S. District Court, District of Maryland including Trial Bar; 1988, Maryland; 1992, U.S. District Court, Northern District of California; 1996, U.S. Court of Appeals, Fourth Circuit; 1997, U.S. Court of Appeals, Eleventh Circuit; 2000, U.S. Court of Appeals, Third Circuit. *Education:* Lawrence University and Smith College (B.A., summa cum laude, 1972); Girton College, Cambridge University, Cambridge, England (B.A., with honors, 1975; M.A., 1979); Yale University (J.D., 1978). Phi Beta Kappa. Lecturer, Seventh Annual Toxic Tort Institute, Emerging Areas of Litigation, 1993. Lecturer, Complex Civil Procedure, Yale Law School, 1995 and 1998. Member, The American Law Institute. *Member:* The District of Columbia Bar; Maryland State and American Bar Associations. ***PRACTICE AREAS:*** Commercial Litigation; Complex and Multi-District Litigation; Complex Litigation; Environmental Litigation; Federal Civil Practice; Legal Malpractice Defense; Libel Defense; Medical Malpractice; Products Liability; Professional Liability. ***Email:*** cwilliams@wc.com

FRANK LANE HEARD III, born Houston, Texas, December 29, 1950; admitted to bar, 1979, District of Columbia. *Education:* Yale University (B.A., summa cum laude, 1973; J.D., 1978); Trinity College, Cambridge University (Honours B.A., 1975; M.A., 1979). Phi Beta Kappa. Law Clerk to Hon. Frank M. Johnson, Jr., U.S. District Court, Middle District of Alabama, 1978-1979. *Member:* The District of Columbia Bar. ***PRACTICE AREAS:*** Appellate Practice; Civil Practice; Class Actions; Complex and Multi-District Litigation; Litigation; Products Liability; Mass Torts. ***Email:*** lheard@wc.com

STEVEN R. KUNEY, born Arlington, Virginia, April 10, 1948; admitted to bar, 1978, District of Columbia. *Education:* Wesleyan University (B.A., 1970); University of Pennsylvania (M.A., 1978; J.D., 1978). Phi Beta Kappa; Order of the Coif. Member, University of Pennsylvania Law Review, 1975-1978. Author: Note, "Guidelines for Extending Implied Warranties to Service Markets," 125 University of Pennsylvania Law Review 365, 1976. Adjunct Professor of Law, Georgetown University Law Center, 1995—. Adjunct Lecturer, Antitrust Law, Columbus School of Law, The Catholic University of America, 1989-1994. *Member:* The District of Columbia Bar. ***Email:*** skuney@wc.com

GERSON A. ZWEIFACH, born New York, N.Y., March 26, 1953; admitted to bar, 1980, New York; 1981, District of Columbia. *Education:* Brown University (A.B., 1975); Yale University (J.D., 1979). Phi Beta Kappa. Officer, Yale Law Journal, Vol. 88, 1978-1979. Law Clerk to: Hon. Pierre N. Leval, U.S. District Court, Southern District of New York, 1979-1980; Hon. David L. Bazelon, U.S. Court of Appeals, District of Columbia Circuit, 1980-1981. *Member:* The District of Columbia Bar; New York State Bar Association. ***Email:*** gzweifach@wc.com

PAUL MOGIN, born Neptune, New Jersey, July 19, 1956; admitted to bar, 1981, District of Columbia; 1982, U.S. Court of Appeals, Fourth Circuit; 1983, U.S. Court of Appeals, for the District of Columbia Circuit; 1987, U.S. Court of Appeals, Ninth Circuit; 1988, U.S. Supreme Court; 1990, U.S. Tax Court and U.S. Court of Appeals for the Federal Circuit; 1991, U.S. Court of Appeals, Third Circuit; 1994, U.S. District Court, Central District of Illinois; 1997, U.S. Court of Appeals, Fifth Circuit; 1999, U.S. Court of Appeals, Seventh Circuit; 2000, U.S. Court of Appeals, Eleventh Circuit. *Education:* Princeton University (B.A., summa cum laude, 1977); Harvard Law School (J.D., magna cum laude, 1980). Recipient: John G. Buchanan Prize in Politics, 1977; Sears Prize, 1978. Editor, Harvard Law Review, 1978-1980. Law Clerk: Judge Henry J. Friendly, U.S. Court of Appeals, Second Circuit, 1980-1981; Justice Thurgood Marshall, U.S. Supreme Court, 1982-1983. Author: "Justices Limit Scope of Mail Fraud Statute," Bus. Crimes Bull., Dec. 2000; "Why Judges, Not Juries, Should Set Punitive Damages," 65 U. Chi. L. Rev. 179 (1998); "Constitutional Limits on the Use of Deadly Force," 18 American Crim. L. Rev. 533 (1981). Seminar: "Practice in the United States Supreme Court," Suffolk & Nassau County Bar

(This Listing Continued)

Associations, May 16, 1999. *Member:* The District of Columbia Bar; American Bar Association (Member: Section on Litigation; Section on Criminal Justice). ***PRACTICE AREAS:*** Appellate Practice; Civil Litigation; Class Actions; Criminal Appeals; U.S. Supreme Court Litigation; White Collar Criminal Defense. ***Email:*** pmogin@wc.com

HOWARD W. GUTMAN, born Bronx, New York, July 8, 1956; admitted to bar, 1982, New York; 1983, District of Columbia. *Education:* Columbia University (B.A., summa cum laude, 1977); Harvard University (J.D., magna cum laude, 1980). Phi Beta Kappa. Author: "Academic Determinism: The Division of the Bill of Rights," 54 Southern California Law Review 295, January, 1981. Co-Author: "The Honorable Irving L. Goldberg: A Place In History," 49 SMU Law Review 1, 1995. Associate Editor, Litigation Magazine, 1984—. Law Clerk to: Hon. Irving L. Goldberg, U.S. Court of Appeals, 5th Circuit, 1980-1981; Hon. Potter Stewart, Associate Justice U.S. Supreme Court, 1981-1982 (Retired). Special Assistant to the Honorable William H. Webster, Director, Federal Bureau of Investigation, 1985-1986. *Member:* The District of Columbia Bar; New York State Bar Association. ***PRACTICE AREAS:*** Commercial Litigation; Federal Civil Practice; Legal Malpractice; Litigation; Real Estate Litigation; White Collar Crime. ***Email:*** hgutman@wc.com

STEVEN A. STEINBACH, born San Diego, California, October 7, 1956; admitted to bar, 1982, District of Columbia; 1996, U.S. Supreme Court; U.S. Court of Appeals for the District of Columbia, Second and Fourth Circuits; U.S. District Court for the District of Columbia. *Education:* Harvard University (A.B., magna cum laude, 1978); Yale University (J.D., 1981). Phi Beta Kappa. Editor, Yale Law Journal, 1980-1981. Author: Note, "A Procedural Framework for the Disclosure of Business Records Under the Freedom of Information Act," 90 Yale Law Journal 400, 1980. Law Clerk to Honorable Arlin M. Adams, U.S. Court of Appeals for the Third Circuit, 1981-1982. *Member:* The District of Columbia Bar; American Bar Association. ***PRACTICE AREAS:*** Appellate Practice; Computers and Software; Criminal Law; Litigation; White Collar Crimes. ***Email:*** ssteinbach@wc.com

MARK S. LEVINSTEIN, born Pittsburgh, Pennsylvania, June 17, 1958; admitted to bar, 1983, District of Columbia, Maryland, New Jersey, U.S. District Court, District of New Jersey; 1985, Virginia, U.S. District Court for the District of Columbia and U.S. District Court, Eastern District of Virginia; 1986, U.S. District Court, District of Maryland, U.S. Court of Appeals, Fourth Circuit and U.S. Court of Appeals for the District of Columbia Circuit; 1987, U.S. Court of Appeals, Second Circuit; 1989, U.S. Court of Appeals, Ninth Circuit; 1991, U.S. Supreme Court. *Education:* University of Virginia (B.A., with honors, 1979); Harvard University (J.D., cum laude, 1982). Phi Beta Kappa; Omicron Delta Kappa. Raven Society. Echols Scholar. Instructor, Legal Methods, 1980-1982 and Coordinator, Legal Methods Program, 1981-1982, Harvard Law School. Executive Editor, Harvard Journal of Law and Public Policy, 1981-1982. Co-Author: "Sports Law: Cases and Materials," Carolina Academic Press, 1997. Chairman, Annual Law Journal Seminars-Press Sports Law Program, N.Y.C., 1996-2000. Adjunct Professor of Law, Catholic University of America, 1985-1992. Adjunct Professor of Law, George Washington University School of Law, 1991-1993. Adjunct Professor of Law, Georgetown University Law Center, 1993—. Law Clerk, Honorable W. Arthur Garrity, Jr., U.S. District Court, District of Massachusetts, 1982-1983. *Member:* The District of Columbia Bar; Maryland State, New Jersey State and American Bar Associations; Virginia State Bar; The Association of Trial Lawyers of America; Sports Lawyer Association. ***Email:*** mlevinstein@wc.com

MARY GREER CLARK, born Santa Monica, California, December 4, 1945; admitted to bar, 1982, District of Columbia. *Education:* Stanford University (A.B., magna cum laude, 1967); University of Pittsburgh (M.A., 1971); Yale University (J.D., 1982). Phi Beta Kappa. *Member:* The District of Columbia Bar; American Bar Association (Member, Sections on: Litigation; Business Law; Criminal Justice). ***PRACTICE AREAS:*** Administrative Litigation; Banking Litigation; Financial Institution Failures; Legal Ethics; Legal Malpractice Defense; Directors and Officers Insurance Coverage; Directors and Officers Liability; Securities Litigation. ***Email:*** mclark@wc.com

VICTORIA RADD ROLLINS, born Indianapolis, Indiana, February 28, 1957; admitted to bar, 1985, District of Columbia. *Education:* Harvard University (A.B., summa cum laude, 1978); London School of Economics (M.Sc., with distinction, 1979); Harvard University (J.D., magna cum laude, 1982). Phi Beta Kappa. Editor, 1980-1981 and Articles Editor, 1981-1982, Harvard Law Review. Law Clerk to: Judge J. Skelly Wright, U.S. Court of Appeals for the District of Columbia Circuit, 1982-1983; Justice Sandra Day O'Connor, U.S. Supreme Court, 1983-1984. Associate Counsel to the President, 1993-1995; Deputy Assistant to the President and Deputy Communications Director, 1995-1996; Assistant to the President and Chief of Staff to the Chief of Staff, 1996-1998. *Member:* The District of Columbia Bar; American Bar Association. ***PRACTICE AREAS:*** Complex Litigation; Federal Civil Litigation; Media and First Amendment; Media Libel. ***Email:*** vrollins@wc.com

DANIEL FRANKLIN KATZ, born New Haven, Connecticut, May 14, 1957; admitted to bar, 1984, Missouri, District of Columbia and U.S. Court of Appeals, Tenth Circuit; 1985, U.S. Court of Appeals, Fourth Circuit; 1986, U.S. Court of Appeals, Eleventh Circuit; 1989, U.S. District Court, District of Maryland; 1995, U.S. Court of Appeals, Fifth Circuit; 1997, U.S. Court of Appeals, Ninth Circuit; 1998, U.S. District Court, District of Arizona, U.S. District Court, District of Colorado and U.S. District Court, Northern District of Georgia. *Education:* Williams College (B.A., magna cum laude, 1979); Duke University (J.D., 1983). Phi Beta Kappa. Senior Editor, Law and Contemporary Problems, 1982-1983. Co-Author: "From Wanderers to Workers: A Survey of Federal and State Employment Rights of the Mentally Ill," Volume 45, Law and Contemporary Problems, Summer, 1982; "Transferable Development Rights," Lincoln Institute of Land Policy, 1981. Author: "Extra - Territorial Civil RICO Jurisdiction," ALI-ABA Transnational & Commercial Trade Litigation Study Materials, 23-50, 1986. *Member:* The District of Columbia Bar; The Missouri Bar; American Bar Association. ***PRACTICE AREAS:*** Complex Litigation. ***Email:*** dkatz@wc.com

ROBERT M. KRASNE, born Audubon, Iowa, 1955; admitted to bar, 1983, District of Columbia. *Education:* Georgetown University (A.B., 1978; J.D., 1983). Principal Author: Chapter 3 "Administrative Enforcement" of *Bank Directors', Officers' and Lawyers' Civil Liabilities,* Prentice-Hall Law and Business, Inc., 1992. Member, Office of the Comptroller of the Currency, 1978-1980; 1983-1986 (Examiner, 1978-1980, Enforcement and Compliance Division, 1983-1984 and Legal Advisory Services Division, 1984-1986). Special Assistant United States Attorney, United States Attorney's Office for the Western District of Louisiana, 1985-1986. Lecturer, Federal Financial Institutions Examination Council, 1987-1990. *Member:* The District of Columbia Bar; Federal and American Bar Associations. ***Email:*** rkrasne@wc.com

KATHLEEN L. BEGGS, born Baltimore, Maryland, March 6, 1957; admitted to bar, 1983, New York and U.S. District Court, Southern and Eastern Districts of New York; 1988, District of Columbia; 1990, U.S. District Court for the District of Columbia; 1992, U.S. Supreme Court and U.S. Court of Appeals for the District of Columbia Circuit. *Education:* Wellesley College (B.A., 1979); Harvard University (J.D., 1982). Phi Beta Kappa. *Member:* The District of Columbia Bar; New York State and American Bar Associations; The Barristers. ***Email:*** kbeggs@wc.com

WILLIAM R. MURRAY, JR., born Philadelphia, Pennsylvania, June 12, 1959; admitted to bar, 1984, District of Columbia; 1985, U.S. Court of Appeals for the District of Columbia Circuit and U.S. Court of International Trade; 1989, U.S. District Court for the District of Columbia. *Education:* Siena College (B.A., summa cum laude, 1981); Georgetown University (J.D., summa cum laude, 1984). Articles Editor, Georgetown Law Journal, 1983-1984. Author: Case Comment, "Requiring Omniscience: The Duty to Warn of Scientifically Undiscoverable Product Defects, Beshada v. Johns-Manville Products Corp., 90 N.J. 191, 447 A.2d 539 (1982)," 71 Georgetown Law Journal 1635-1660 (1983). Court Law Clerk, United States Court of Appeals for the District of Columbia Circuit, 1984-1985. *Member:* The District of Columbia Bar; American Bar Association. ***Email:*** bmurray@wc.com

EVA PETKO ESBER, born Philadelphia, Pennsylvania, November 3, 1959; admitted to bar, 1984, Pennsylvania; 1986, District of Columbia and U.S. District Court for the District of Columbia; 1987, Virginia, U.S. District Court, Eastern District of Virginia and U.S. Court of Appeals, Fourth Circuit. *Education:* Saint Joseph's University (B.A., summa cum laude, 1981); Georgetown University (J.D., magna cum laude, 1984). Alpha Sigma Nu; Pi Sigma Alpha. Executive Editor, Georgetown Law Journal, 1983-1984. Law Clerk, the Honorable Thomas F. Hogan, United States District Court for the District of Columbia, 1984-1985. *Member:* The District of Columbia Bar; Virginia State Bar; Pennsylvania and American Bar Associations. ***PRACTICE AREAS:*** Banking Litigation; Check Fraud; Fraud and Deceit; Hospital Liability Defense; Employment Discrimination; Fiduciary Liability; Fiduciary Litigation; White Collar Criminal Defense. ***Email:*** eesber@wc.com

STEPHEN D. RABER, born Santa Barbara, California, March 23, 1959; admitted to bar, 1985, California; 1986, District of Columbia and Virginia; 1996, U.S. Supreme Court. *Education:* University of California at Los Angeles (A.B., magna cum laude, 1982); University of Virginia (J.D., 1985). Phi Beta Kappa; Mortar Board. *Member:* The District of Columbia Bar; State Bar of California; Virginia State Bar; American Bar Association; The Association of Trial Lawyers of America; Virginia Trial Lawyers Association; The Barristers. ***Email:*** sraber@wc.com

DAVID C. KIERNAN, born Red Bank, New Jersey, April 7, 1958; admitted to bar, 1987, Virginia; 1988, District of Columbia; 1993, Maryland. *Education:* Duke University (B.A., magna cum laude, 1980; M.D., 1985; J.D., 1985). Licensed Physician, District of Columbia, 1989. Adjunct Professor, Georgetown University Law Center, 1992-1996; U.S. Patent and Trademark Office. *Member:* The District of Columbia Bar; Virginia State Bar; Maryland State Bar Association. Fellow, American College of Legal Medicine. ***PRACTICE AREAS:*** Civil Practice; Commercial Litigation; Complex Litigation; Intellectual Property Litigation; Medical Malpractice; Patent Litigation; Personal Injury; Products Liability; Torts. ***Email:*** dkiernan@wc.com

LON E. MUSSLEWHITE, born Los Angeles, California, August 14, 1950; admitted to bar, 1984, Pennsylvania; 1985, District of Columbia; 1992, Maryland; U.S. Court of Federal Claims and U.S. Tax Court. *Education:* West Ches-

(This Listing Continued)

WILLIAMS & CONNOLLY LLP, Washington—Continued

ter University (B.S., summa cum laude, 1975); American University (J.D., 1984); New York University (LL.M., in Taxation, 1986). Law Clerk to the Honorable Mastin G. White, U.S. Claims Court, 1984-1985. Member, 1982-1983; Note and Comment Editor, 1983-1984, American University Law Review. Certified Public Accountant, Pennsylvania, 1977. Revenue Agent, Examination Division, Internal Revenue Service, 1981-1984. *Member:* The District of Columbia Bar; Maryland State, Pennsylvania, Federal and American (Member, Sections of: Taxation (Exempt Organizations and Estate and Gift Taxes Committee); Real Property, Probate and Trust Law; Chair, Estate and Gift Taxes Committee's Task Force on Simplification, 1995-1998; Co-Chair, Estate and Gift Taxes Committee's Subcommittee on Employee Benefit Plans, 1999—) Bar Associations; District of Columbia Estate Planning Council; National Capital Gift Planning Council. ***Email:*** lmusslewhite@wc.com

HEIDI K. HUBBARD, born Seattle, Washington, September 8, 1961; admitted to bar, 1986, Utah; 1987, District of Columbia; 1988, U.S. District Court for the District of Columbia; 1990, U.S. Court of Appeals for the District of Columbia; 1996, U.S. Supreme Court and U.S. Court of Appeals, Eleventh Circuit. *Education:* Brigham Young University (B.A., summa cum laude, 1983); Stanford University (J.D., 1986). Member, 1984-1986 and Managing Editor, 1985-1986, Stanford Law Review. Author: "Separation of Powers Within the United Nations: A Revised Role for the International Court of Justice," 38 Stan. L. Rev. 165, 1985. Visiting Assistant Professor of Law, Brigham Young University, 1992-1993. *Member:* The District of Columbia Bar; Utah State Bar; American Bar Association (Member, Litigation Section). ***PRACTICE AREAS:*** Complex Litigation; Litigation; Mass Torts; Products Liability. ***Email:*** hhubbard@wc.com

GLENN J. PFADENHAUER, born Reading, Pennsylvania, July 23, 1959; admitted to bar, 1987, Virginia; 1988, District of Columbia, Maryland, U.S. District Court for the District of Columbia and U.S. District Court, Eastern District of Virginia; 1989, U.S. District Court, District of Maryland. *Education:* College of William and Mary (B.B.A., 1981); Georgetown University (J.D., magna cum laude, 1987). Beta Gamma Sigma; Order of the Coif. Member, 1985-1986 and Associate Editor, 1986-1987, Georgetown Law Journal. *Member:* The District of Columbia Bar; Virginia State Bar; Maryland State and American Bar Associations. ***PRACTICE AREAS:*** Commercial Litigation; Criminal Law; Patent Litigation. ***Email:*** gpfadenhauer@wc.com

GEORGE A. BORDEN, born Philadelphia, Pennsylvania, November 12, 1961; admitted to bar, 1988, Massachusetts; 1989, New York, District of Columbia and U.S. District Court, District of Maryland; 1990, U.S. District Court for the District of Columbia; 1991, U.S. District Court, Southern District of New York; U.S. Court of Appeals, District of Columbia Circuit; 1993, U.S. Supreme Court; 1996, U.S. District Court, Central District of Illinois; U.S. Court of Appeals, Seventh Circuit. *Education:* Princeton University (A.B., 1984); Harvard University (J.D., magna cum laude, 1987). Member, 1985-1987 and Executive Editor, 1986-1987, Harvard Law Review. Author: "The Prosecutor's Duty to Disclose to Defendants Pleading Guilty," 99 Harvard L. Rev. 1004, 1986; Case Comment, 100 Harvard L. Rev. 295, 1986. Law Clerk to Hon. Amalya L. Kearse, U.S. Court of Appeals, Second Circuit, 1987-1988. *Member:* The District of Columbia Bar; American Bar Association (Member: Committee on Securities Litigation; Committee on Class Actions and Derivative Suits). ***PRACTICE AREAS:*** Appellate Practice; Civil Practice; Class Action Defense; Commercial Litigation; Intellectual Property Litigation. ***Email:*** gborden@wc.com

ROBERT J. SHAUGHNESSY, born Chicago, Illinois, August 18, 1961; admitted to bar, 1988, Virginia; 1989, District of Columbia. *Education:* Princeton University (A.B., cum laude, 1983); University of Virginia (J.D., 1987). Order of the Coif. Executive Editor, Virginia Law Review, 1986-1987. Author: "Trademark Parody: A Fair Use and First Amendment Analysis," 72 Virginia L. Rev. 1079, 1986. Law Clerk to Hon. Collins J. Seitz, U.S. Court of Appeals, Third Circuit, 1987-1988. *Member:* The District of Columbia Bar; Virginia State Bar. ***Email:*** bshaughnessy@wc.com

JONATHAN P. GRAHAM, born São Paulo, Brazil, April 2, 1960; admitted to bar, 1988, California; 1989, District of Columbia; 1990, U.S. District Court for the District of Columbia; 1991, U.S. Court of Appeals, Fourth Circuit and U.S. District Court, Western District of Texas; 1995, U.S. Court of Appeals, District of Columbia Circuit; 1996, U.S. Court of Appeals, Fifth Circuit; 1997, U.S. Supreme Court and U.S. Court of Appeals, Second Circuit; 2000, U.S. Court of Appeals, First Circuit. *Education:* Pitzer College (B.A., with honors, 1982); University of Texas (J.D., with honors, 1987). Editor-in-Chief, Texas Law Review, 1986-1987. Author: "Privacy, Computers and the Commercial Dissemination of Personal Information," 65 Texas L. Rev. 1395 (1987); "Grappling with Vicarious Criminal Liability for Corporations," Business Crimes Bulletin, Oct., 1996. Law Clerk to Hon. Joseph T. Sneed, U.S. Court of Appeals, 9th Circuit, 1987-1988. Member, Board of Trustees, Pitzer College, 1997—. *Member:* The District of Columbia Bar; State Bar of California. ***LANGUAGES:*** Portuguese. ***PRACTICE AREAS:*** Civil Appeals; Commercial Litigation; Complex Litigation; Employment Discrimination; Environmental Criminal Defense; Fraudulent Conveyance; Health Care Fraud; Intellectual Property Litigation; International Litigation; Foreign Sovereign Immunities Act; White Collar Criminal Defense. ***Email:*** jgraham@wc.com

ALLEN P. WAXMAN, born Flushing, New York, March 7, 1962; admitted to bar, 1987, Massachusetts; 1989, District of Columbia. *Education:* Dartmouth College (B.A., magna cum laude, 1984); Harvard University (J.D., magna cum laude, 1987). Phi Beta Kappa. Judicial Clerk with the Honorable Thomas P. Jackson, U.S. District Court for the District of Columbia, 1987-1988. Presentations: "The Use of Technology in the Courtroom," Defense Research Institute; "Analysis of the Third Restatement," State Bar of Texas, Advanced Medical Malpractice Course; "The Intersection Between FDA Regulations and Products Liability Law," American Conference Institute; Adjunct Professor of Law, Georgetown University, 1996—; Board Member, Thurgood Marshall Academy, 2001—. *Member:* The District of Columbia Bar; Massachusetts Bar Association. ***PRACTICE AREAS:*** Litigation; Medical Malpractice; Personal Injury; Products Liability; Torts. ***Email:*** awaxman@wc.com

DAVID S. BLATT, born New Haven, Connecticut, September 27, 1963; admitted to bar, 1990, Pennsylvania; 1991, U.S. Court of Federal Claims; 1992, District of Columbia; 1994, U.S. Court of Appeals for the Federal Circuit; 1996, U.S. Court of Appeals, Fifth Circuit and U.S. Supreme Court; 1997, U.S. Court of Appeals, First Circuit. *Education:* Yale University (B.A., summa cum laude, 1985; J.D., 1988). Author: "The Development of the Hero: Sigmund Freud and the Reformation of the Jewish Tradition," 11:4 Psychoanalysis and Contemporary Thought, 639-703 (1988). Law Clerk to Judge Alvin B. Rubin, 5th Circuit Court of Appeals, Baton Rouge, Louisiana, 1988-1989. *Member:* The District of Columbia Bar. ***PRACTICE AREAS:*** Banking Litigation; Commercial Litigation; Federal Civil Practice; Intellectual Property Litigation; Legal Professional Liability; Products Liability Defense; Professional Liability; Tort Liability. ***Email:*** dblatt@wc.com

ARI S. ZYMELMAN, born Boston, Massachusetts, March 4, 1963; admitted to bar, 1989, District of Columbia, Illinois, U.S. Supreme Court, U.S. Tax Court and U.S. Court of Federal Claims. *Education:* Yale University (B.A., cum laude, distinction in Economics, 1984); University of Chicago (J.D., with honors, 1988). Order of the Coif. Law Clerk to Honorable Frank H. Easterbrook, U.S. Court of Appeals, 7th Circuit, 1988-1989. *Member:* The District of Columbia Bar; Illinois State Bar Association; Federal Circuit Bar Association. ***Email:*** azymelman@wc.com

REGINA G. MALONEY, born New York, New York, May 14, 1962; admitted to bar, 1992, New York and District of Columbia. *Education:* University of Pennsylvania (B.A., cum laude, 1984); Georgetown University (J.D., magna cum laude, 1988). Order of the Coif. Senior Editor, Criminal Procedure Project, Georgetown Law Journal, 1987-1988. Law Clerk: Hon. William J. Brennan, Jr., Assoc. Justice of U.S., 1989-1990; Hon. Thomas A. Clark, U.S. Court of Appeals, Eleventh Circuit, 1988-1989. Adjunct Professor, Georgetown University Law Center, 1994. *Member:* The District of Columbia Bar. ***Email:*** rmaloney@wc.com

DANE H. BUTSWINKAS, born Norfolk, Virginia, March 9, 1961; admitted to bar, 1989, Virginia, U.S. District Court, Eastern District of Virginia and U.S. Court of Appeals, Fourth Circuit; 1990, District of Columbia. *Education:* James Madison University (B.S., 1983); George Mason University (M.A., 1986); University of Virginia (J.D., 1989). Omicron Delta Kappa; Order of the Coif. First Place, William Minor Lile Moot Court Competition, 1989. Member: Mortar Board Society; Raven Society. Member, Virginia Law Review, 1987-1989. Recipient, Eppa Hunton Memorial Book Award; Stephen Pierre Traynor Award. *Member:* The District of Columbia Bar; Virginia State Bar. ***PRACTICE AREAS:*** Commercial Litigation; Electronic Commerce Litigation; Employment Litigation; White Collar Litigation. ***Email:*** dbutswinkas@wc.com

LAURIE S. FULTON, born Sioux Falls, South Dakota, July 2, 1949; admitted to bar, 1989, Virginia, U.S. Court of Appeals, Fourth Circuit and U.S. District Court, Eastern District of Virginia; 1990, District of Columbia and U.S. Court of Appeals for the District of Columbia Circuit; 1992, U.S. District Court, Western District of Virginia; 1996, U.S. Supreme Court and U.S. District Court, Central District of Illinois; 2000, U.S. Court of Appeals, Eleventh Circuit and U.S. District Court, District of Columbia. *Education:* University of Nebraska, Omaha (B.A., magna cum laude, 1971); Georgetown University (J.D., magna cum laude, 1989). Order of the Coif. Managing Editor, American Criminal Law Review Vol. 26, 1988-1989. Author: "The Right to Counsel Clause of the Sixth Amendment," American Criminal Law Review, Vol. 26, No. 4, spring 1989; "Environmental Crimes," White Collar Crime: Survey of Law, American Criminal Law Review, Vol. 25, No. 3, winter 1988. *Member:* The District of Columbia Bar; Virginia State Bar. ***Email:*** lfulton@wc.com

DENNIS M. BLACK, born New York, New York, April 23, 1964; admitted to bar, 1990, Maryland; 1992, District of Columbia; U.S. Court of Appeals for the District of Columbia Circuit and U.S. Court of Appeals, 11th Circuit. *Education:* Texas A & M University (B.S., 1986); University of Chicago (J.D., 1989). Order of the Coif. National Merit Scholar. President's Endowed Scholar. Managing Editor, University of Chicago Law Review, 1988-1989. Author:

(This Listing Continued)

"Section 29(b) of the Securities Exchange Act: A Structural Analysis," 56 U. Chi. L. Rev. Judicial Clerk, Judge Richard A. Posner, U.S. Court of Appeals, 7th Circuit. *Member:* The District of Columbia Bar. ***Email:*** dblack@wc.com

PHILIP A. SECHLER, born Chicago, Illinois, March 2, 1963; admitted to bar, 1990, Pennsylvania, District of Columbia, U.S. Court of Appeals, Fourth Circuit, U.S. Court of Appeals, Seventh Circuit, U.S. District Court for the District of Columbia, U.S. District Court for the District of Maryland and U.S. Court of Appeals for the District of Columbia Circuit. *Education:* Pennsylvania State University (B.S., with high distinction, 1985); Georgetown University (J.D., summa cum laude, 1989). Order of the Coif. Editor-in-Chief, Georgetown Law Journal, 1988-1989. Law Clerk to Circuit Judge Francis D. Murnaghan, Jr., U.S. Court of Appeals, Fourth Circuit, 1989-1990. Adjunct Professor at Georgetown University Law Center, 1999—. *Member:* The District of Columbia Bar; American Bar Association; International Association of Defense Counsel. ***PRACTICE AREAS:*** Administrative Law; Commercial Law; Constitutional Law; Consumer Law; Food, Drug and Cosmetic Law; Health Care Litigation; Insurance; Intellectual Property; Litigation; Medical Malpractice. ***Email:*** psechler@wc.com

LYNDA SCHULER, born Aurora, Illinois, July 8, 1962; admitted to bar, 1989, Maryland; 1990, District of Columbia. *Education:* Rice University (B.A., summa cum laude, 1984); University of Michigan (J.D., magna cum laude, 1989). Order of the Coif. Associate and Contributing Editor, Michigan Law Review, 1987-1989. *Member:* Bar Association of the District of Columbia; American Bar Association. ***PRACTICE AREAS:*** Civil Practice; Estate Litigation; Fiduciary Litigation; Legal Malpractice; Litigation; Trust Litigation. ***Email:*** lschuler@wc.com

PAUL K. DUEFFERT, born Waconia, Minnesota, May 20, 1963; admitted to bar, 1988, Minnesota; 1989, Missouri; 1991, Pennsylvania; 1992, District of Columbia; U.S. Court of Appeals, Eighth and Ninth Circuits, U.S. District Court for the District of Columbia, U.S. District Court, Eastern District of Missouri, U.S. District Court, Northern District of New York and U.S. District Court, District of Arizona. *Education:* University of Minnesota (B.A., magna cum laude, 1985); Harvard Law School (J.D., cum laude, 1988). Phi Beta Kappa. Managing Editor, Harvard Journal on Legislation, 1987-1988. Instructor, Legal Methods Program on Pretrial Advocacy, Harvard Law School, 1987-1988. Author: "The Role of Regulatory Compliance in Tort Actions," 26 Harv. J. on Legis. 175, 1989. Law Clerk to the Hon. John R. Gibson, U.S. Court of Appeals for the Eighth Circuit, 1988-1989. *Member:* Minnesota State and American Bar Associations; The Missouri Bar; The District of Columbia Bar. ***PRACTICE AREAS:*** Administrative Law; Civil Litigation; Copyright Litigation; First Amendment; Food and Drug Regulation; Privacy and Publicity; Trademark Litigation; Trial Practice. ***Email:*** pdueffert@wc.com

R. HACKNEY WIEGMANN, born Charlotte, North Carolina, June 21, 1964; admitted to bar, 1989, Virginia; 1991, District of Columbia. *Education:* Duke University (B.A., magna cum laude, 1986); Harvard University (J.D., magna cum laude, 1989). Phi Beta Kappa. Editor, Harvard Law Review, 1987-1989. Law Clerk to Judge J. Harvie Wilkinson, III, U.S. Court of Appeals, Fourth Circuit, 1989-1990. Special Counsel to the General Counsel, United States Department of Defense, 1994-1996. *Member:* Virginia State Bar; The District of Columbia Bar; American Bar Association. ***Email:*** hwiegmann@wc.com

ROBERT M. CARY, born Evanston, Illinois, May 10, 1964; admitted to bar, 1990, Virginia; 1991, Maryland; 1992, District of Columbia; 1997, U.S. Supreme Court. *Education:* Dartmouth College (A.B., 1986); University of Virginia (J.D., 1990). Order of the Coif. Virginia Law Review. Law Clerk, Honorable Eugene F. Lynch, U.S. District Judge, Northern District of California, 1990-1991. *Member:* Maryland State and American Bar Associations; The District of Columbia Bar; Virginia State Bar. ***PRACTICE AREAS:*** Commercial Litigation; Criminal Defense; Professional Liability Defense; Securities Litigation; Trial Practice. ***Email:*** rcary@wc.com

KEVIN M. HODGES, born Baltimore, Maryland, April 18, 1965; admitted to bar, 1990, Maryland; 1991, District of Columbia; 1992, U.S. District Court, District of Maryland; 1993, U.S. District Court, District of Columbia; 1996, U.S. Court of Appeals, District of Columbia Circuit; 1997, U.S. Court of Appeals, Fourth Circuit; 2001, U.S. Court of Federal Claims. *Education:* Brown University (Sc.B., 1986); Georgetown University (J.D., magna cum laude, 1990). Order of the Coif. Notes and Comments Editor, Georgetown Law Journal, 1990. Law Clerk, Hon. Thomas A. Flannery, U.S. District Court, District of Columbia, 1990-1991. *Member:* Maryland State and American Bar Associations; The District of Columbia Bar. ***PRACTICE AREAS:*** Commercial Litigation; False Claims Act; Government Contracts; Litigation; Professional Liability; Qui Tam Litigation. ***Email:*** khodges@wc.com

DAVID M. ZINN, born Washington, D.C., April 29, 1964; admitted to bar, 1990, California; 1992, District of Columbia. *Education:* Brown University (A.B., magna cum laude, 1986); Harvard University (J.D., cum laude, 1990). Law Clerk to the Honorable Mariana R. Pfaelzer, U.S. District Court, Central District of California, 1990-1991. Attorney and Special Assistant to the General Counsel, Central Intelligence Agency, 1991-1993. *Member:* The District of Columbia Bar. ***LANGUAGES:*** French. ***Email:*** dzinn@wc.com

(This Listing Continued)

JOSEPH G. PETROSINELLI, born Providence, Rhode Island, September 28, 1966; admitted to bar, 1991, Maryland; 1992, District of Columbia; 1993, U.S. District Court for the District of Columbia and U.S. District Court, Northern District of New York; 2000, U.S. Supreme Court. *Education:* Brown University (A.B., 1988); Georgetown University (J.D., magna cum laude, 1991). Order of the Coif. Associate Editor, Georgetown Law Journal, 1989-1991. Author: "The Admissibility of DNA Typing: A New Methodology," 79 Geo. L. J. 313 (1990). Certified Agent, National Basketball Players Association. *Member:* The District of Columbia Bar; American Bar Association. ***PRACTICE AREAS:*** Criminal Defense; Grand Jury Practice; Litigation; Products Liability. ***Email:*** jpetrosinelli@wc.com

STEVEN M. FARINA, born Stamford, Connecticut, May 26, 1966; admitted to bar, 1992, Illinois; 1993, District of Columbia. *Education:* Duke University (A.B., 1988); University of Michigan (J.D., magna cum laude, 1991). Order of the Coif. Book Review Editor, Law Review. Law Clerk, Hon. Amalya L. Kearse, U.S. Court of Appeals, Second Circuit. *Member:* The District of Columbia Bar. ***PRACTICE AREAS:*** Class Action Defense; Complex and Multi-District Litigation; Libel and Slander; Defamation; Products Liability Defense; Securities Class Actions. ***Email:*** sfarina@wc.com

KEVIN M. DOWNEY, born Pittsburgh, Pennsylvania, January 27, 1967; admitted to bar, 1991, Pennsylvania; 1993, District of Columbia. *Education:* Dartmouth College (A.B., magna cum laude, 1988); Harvard University (J.D., magna cum laude, 1991). Phi Beta Kappa. Editor, Harvard Law Review. Author: "Prisoners of Foreign Policy: An Argument for Ideological Neutrality in Asylum", 104 Harv. L. Rev. 1878 (1991); "Holmes: A Legend in Search of Demystification", 103 Harv. L. Rev. 800 (1990). Law Clerk, Hon. Edward Becker, U.S. Court of Appeals, Third Circuit, 1991-1992. Adjunct Professor of Law, George Washington University Law School, 1998—; Adjunct Professor of Law, Georgetown University Law Center, 1999—. ***Email:*** kdowney@wc.com

THOMAS G. HENTOFF, born New York, New York, June 2, 1964; admitted to bar, 1992, Pennsylvania; 1993, District of Columbia. *Education:* Wesleyan University (B.A., with honors, 1985); Columbia University (J.D., 1991). Harlan Fiske Stone Scholar. Senior Editor, Columbia Law Review. Law Clerk, Hon. Phyllis A. Kravitch, U.S. Court of Appeals, 11th Circuit. Author: "Speech, Harm and Self-Government: Understanding the Ambit of the Clear and Present Danger Test," 91 Columbia Law Review 1453 (1991). *Member:* Pennsylvania Bar Association; The District of Columbia Bar. ***PRACTICE AREAS:*** Copyrights; Complex Litigation; Intellectual Property; Media and First Amendment; Media Libel; Trademarks. ***Email:*** thentoff@wc.com

KUMIKI GIBSON, born Buffalo, New York, May 24, 1959; admitted to bar, 1988, Massachusetts; 1989, New York; 1990, District of Columbia. *Education:* Harvard University (A.B., cum laude, 1985); Northeastern University (J.D., 1988). Law Clerk to the Honorable Clifford S. Green, U.S. District Court, Eastern District of Pennsylvania, 1988-1989. Associate, Arnold & Porter, Washington, D.C., 1989-1992. Trial Attorney, U.S. Department of Justice, Civil Rights Division/Criminal Section, 1992-1993. Associate Counsel, 1993-1995 and Counsel, 1995-1997, to the Vice President of the United States. Member, Administrative Council of the United States, 1995-1996; Current Member, District of Columbia Commission on Judicial Disabilities and Tenure; and District of Columbia Court of Appeals Board of Professional Responsibility. ***PRACTICE AREAS:*** Civil Litigation; Criminal Defense; Employment Discrimination. ***Email:*** kgibson@wc.com

PAUL B. GAFFNEY, born New York, New York, May 8, 1964; admitted to bar, 1992, Texas; 1993, District of Columbia; 1995, U.S. District for the District of Columbia; 1996, U.S. Court of Appeals, Third Circuit and U.S. District Court, District of Maryland; 1997, U.S. Court of Appeals, Ninth Circuit. *Education:* Duke University (A.B., 1986); University of Chicago (J.D., with honors, 1991). Comment Editor, University of Chicago Legal Forum, 1990-1991. Co-Author: "Dealing With the Resurgent Prior Restraint," with Richard S. Hoffman, Communications Lawyer, Fall, 1996. Law Clerk, Hon. James B. Loken, U.S. Court of Appeals, Eighth Circuit, 1991-1992. ***Email:*** pgaffney@wc.com

EMMET T. FLOOD, born Chicago, Illinois, June 6, 1956; admitted to bar, 1992, Connecticut and U.S. District Court, District of Connecticut; 1995, District of Columbia; 1996, U.S. Supreme Court; 1998, U.S. Court of Appeals, Eighth Circuit; 1999, U.S. Court of Appeals, Second, Third and Sixth Circuits. *Education:* University of Dallas (B.A., magna cum laude, 1978); University of Texas (M.A., 1981; Ph.D., 1986); Yale Law School (J.D., 1991). John Fletcher Caskey Prize, 1989. Executive Committee Coordinator, Volume 100, Yale Law Journal, 1990-1991. Law Clerk to the Honorable Ralph K. Winter, U.S. Court of Appeals, Second Circuit, 1991-1992. Law Clerk to Associate Justice Antonin Scalia, U.S. Supreme Court, 1993-1994. Author, "Fact Construction and Judgment in Constitutional Adjudication," 100 Yale Law Journal 1795 (1991). ***Email:*** eflood@wc.com

ROBERT A. VAN KIRK, born Edina, Minnesota, February 13, 1965; admitted to bar, 1991, District of Columbia; 1993, U.S. Court of Appeals for the District of Columbia Circuit; 1994, U.S. Court of Appeals, 10th Circuit; 1995, U.S. Supreme Court; 1997, U.S. Court of Appeals, 4th Circuit; U.S. Court of Federal Claims. *Education:* University of Notre Dame (B.A., summa cum

(This Listing Continued)

WILLIAMS & CONNOLLY LLP, Washington—Continued

laude, 1987) Phi Beta Kappa, Omicron Delta Epsilon; Duke University School of Law (J.D., with high honors, 1990). Order of the Coif. Note Editor, Duke Law Journal, 1989-1990. Author: "The Evolution of Useful Life Statutes in the Products Liability Reform Effort," Duke Law Journal 1689, 1989. Law Clerk, The Honorable Paul H. Roney, U.S. Court of Appeals, Eleventh Circuit, 1990-1991. Trial Attorney, U.S. Department of Justice, Civil Division, Federal Programs Branch (Honors Program), 1991-1995. Office of Counsel to the President, 1995-1996. Acting Deputy Assistant Attorney General, U.S. Department of Justice, Office of Policy Development, 1996-1997. *Member:* The District of Columbia Bar; American Bar Association (Member: Litigation Section; Administrative Section). ***PRACTICE AREAS:*** Administrative Law; Commercial Law; Federal Government Law; First Amendment Law. ***Email:*** rvankirk@wc.com

MARCIE R. ZIEGLER, born Newark, New Jersey, May 29, 1967; admitted to bar, 1992, Maryland; 1993, U.S. District Court, District of Maryland and U.S. Court of Appeals, Fourth Circuit; 1995, District of Columbia; 1996, U.S. Court of Appeals, Federal Circuit; 1997, U.S. District Court, District of Columbia; 1998, U.S. Court of Appeals, Sixth and District of Columbia Circuits. *Education:* Princeton University (A.B., cum laude, 1989); Yale University (J.D., 1992). Phi Beta Kappa. Law Clerk, Hon. Benson Everett Legg, U.S. District Court, District of Maryland, 1992-1993. *Member:* District of Columbia Bar; American Bar Association (Member, Criminal Justice, Litigation Sections). ***PRACTICE AREAS:*** Civil Appeals; Criminal Appeals; Federal Civil Practice; Legal Malpractice; Medical Malpractice; White Collar Criminal Defense. ***Email:*** mziegler@wc.com

KENNETH C. SMURZYNSKI, born Winchester, Massachusetts, August 25, 1966; admitted to bar, 1992, Maryland; 1993, U.S. District Court, District of Maryland and U.S. Court of Appeals, Fourth Circuit; 1994, District of Columbia; 1995, U.S. District Court, District of Columbia; 1996, U.S. Supreme Court. *Education:* Brown University (A.B., magna cum laude, 1988); Georgetown University Law Center (J.D., magna cum laude, 1992). Phi Beta Kappa; Order of the Coif. Articles Editor, Georgetown Law Journal, 1991-1992. Law Clerk, Hon. Marvin J. Garbis, U.S. District Court, District of Maryland, 1992-1993. Author: Note, "Modeling Campaign Contributions: The Market for Access and its Implications for Regulation," 80 Georgetown Law Journal 1891 (1991). ***PRACTICE AREAS:*** Commercial Litigation; Litigation; Real Estate Litigation. ***Email:*** ksmurzynski@wc.com

JOHN E. SCHMIDTLEIN, born Washington, D.C., March 12, 1966; admitted to bar, 1993, California, U.S. District Court, District of Maryland and U.S. Court of Appeals, Fourth Circuit; 1994, District of Columbia; 1995, U.S. Court of Appeals, District of Columbia Circuit. *Education:* Brown University (A.B., 1988); Georgetown University Law Center (J.D., magna cum laude, 1992). Order of the Coif. Associate Editor, Georgetown Law Review. Adjunct Professor of Law, Georgetown University Law Center, The George Washington University Law School. Law Clerk, Hon. J. Frederick Motz, U.S. District Court, District of Maryland, 1992-1993. ***PRACTICE AREAS:*** Antitrust and Trade Regulation; Class Actions; Complex and Multi-District Litigation; General Practice; Litigation; Sports Law; Unfair Competition; White Collar Crime. ***Email:*** jschmidtlein@wc.com

---

ERIC A. KUHL, born Baltimore, Maryland, August 4, 1959; admitted to bar, 1990, Maryland; 1991, U.S. Court of Appeals, Fourth Circuit and U.S. District Court, District of Maryland; 1992, District of Columbia; 1998, U.S. Supreme Court. *Education:* St. Mary's College of Maryland (B.A., 1982); University of Baltimore (J.D., magna cum laude, 1990). Managing Editor, University of Baltimore Law Review, 1989-1990. Judicial Clerk, Honorable Marvin J. Garbis, U.S. District Court, District of Maryland, 1990-1991. *Member:* Maryland State and American Bar Associations; The District of Columbia Bar. ***Email:*** ekuhl@wc.com

SHARON L. DAVIS, born Huntsville, Alabama, July 3, 1967; admitted to bar, 1991, Texas; 1993, District of Columbia. *Education:* Birmingham-Southern College (B.S., 1988); University of Chicago (J.D., with high honors, 1991). Law Clerk to Hon. Patrick E. Higginbotham, U.S. Court of Appeals, Fifth Circuit, 1991-1992. *Member:* State Bar of Texas; The District of Columbia Bar. ***Email:*** sdavis@wc.com

MATTHEW J. HERRINGTON, born Syracuse, New York, October 3, 1967; admitted to bar, 1994, Maine; 1996, District of Columbia. *Education:* Syracuse University (B.A., 1989); Yale Law School (J.D., 1993). 1989 Syracuse Scholar. Managing Editor, Yale Law Journal, Vol. 102. Author: "Popular Sovereignty in Pennsylvania: 1776-1791," 67 Temple Law Review 575 (1994). Clerkship, Hon. Conrad K. Cyr, U.S. Court of Appeals, First Circuit, Ellsworth, Maine, 1993-1994. Majority Counsel, U.S. Senate Campaign Finance Investigation, 1997. ***PRACTICE AREAS:*** Commercial Litigation; Constitutional Law; International Criminal Law; Congressional Investigations; Media Libel; Trade Secrets. ***Email:*** mherrington@wc.com

(This Listing Continued)

SUZANNE H. WOODS, born Charlottesville, Virginia, June 20, 1966; admitted to bar, 1995, California; 1997, District of Columbia. *Education:* Yale University (B.A., cum laude, 1988); Stanford Law School (J.D., with distinction, 1993). Order of the Coif. Senior Note Editor, Stanford Law Review, 1992-1993. Law Clerk to: Honorable William H. Orrick, Jr., U.S. District Court, Northern District of California, 1993-1994; Honorable Bruce M. Selya, U.S. Court of Appeals, First Circuit, 1994-1995. ***Email:*** swoods@wc.com

CRAIG D. SINGER, born Washington, D.C., May 10, 1967; admitted to bar, 1994, Pennsylvania; 1995, District of Columbia. *Education:* Wesleyan University (B.A., 1990); University of Chicago (J.D., with highest honors, 1993). Member, Order of the Coif. Articles Editor, University of Chicago Law Review, 1992-1993. Author: "Conduct and Belief: Public Employees' First Amendment Rights to Free Expression and Political Affiliation," 59 University of Chicago Law Review 897, 1992. Law Clerk to: Hon. John Paul Stevens, Associate Justice, U.S. Supreme Court, 1994-1995; Hon. Abner J. Mikva, Chief Judge, U.S. Court of Appeals for the District of Columbia Circuit, 1993-1994. *Member:* American Bar Association. ***PRACTICE AREAS:*** Appellate Practice; Civil Practice; Constitutional Law; Criminal Law; Litigation. ***Email:*** csinger@wc.com

JAMES L. TANNER, JR., born Greensboro, North Carolina, October 13, 1968; admitted to bar, 1993, Illinois and District of Columbia. *Education:* University of North Carolina at Chapel Hill (B.A., 1990); University of Chicago (J.D., 1993). *Member:* Bar Association of the District of Columbia. ***PRACTICE AREAS:*** Corporate Law; Securities; Sports Law. ***Email:*** jtanner@wc.com

KATHLEEN QUIMBY GARCIA, born Norwich, Connecticut, November 17, 1967; admitted to bar, 1994, Virginia; 1995, District of Columbia; registered to practice before U.S. Patent and Trademark Office. *Education:* Dartmouth College (B.A., 1989); University of Virginia (J.D., 1994). Phi Beta Kappa. Virginia Chapter of the Order of the Coif. Member, University of Virginia Law Review, 1992-1994. ***Email:*** kgarcia@wc.com

J. ANDREW KEYES, born Washington, D.C., November 17, 1969; admitted to bar, 1994, Virginia; 1995, U.S. Court of Appeals, District of Columbia Circuit; 1996, District of Columbia. *Education:* University of Virginia (B.A., 1991; J.D., 1994). Managing Board, Virginia Law Review. Clerkship, Hon. Karen LeCraft Henderson, U.S. Court of Appeals for the District of Columbia Circuit, 1994-1995. ***PRACTICE AREAS:*** Civil Practice; Complex Commercial Litigation; Complex Litigation; Contract Litigation; Criminal Defense; Federal Civil Practice. ***Email:*** akeyes@wc.com

NICOLE CHAPIN DUKE, born Morristown, New Jersey, 1968; admitted to bar, 1994, New Jersey, Maryland and U.S. District Court, District of New Jersey; 1996, District of Columbia; 1998, U.S. District Court, District of Columbia. *Education:* Yale University (B.A., 1990); Georgetown University Law Center (J.D., 1994). Order of the Coif. Editor-in-Chief, Georgetown Journal of Legal Ethics, 1993-1994. Note, Regulation of Public Interest Law Firms By the IRS and the Bar: Making It Hard To Serve the Public Good, 7 Georgetown Journal of Legal Ethics 437 (1993). Law Clerk to Hon. Harold H. Greene, U.S. District Court, District of Columbia, 1994-1995. ***Email:*** nchapinduke@wc.com

JULIA B. SHELTON, born Boynton Beach, Florida, July 16, 1968; admitted to bar, 1997, Virginia; 1999, District of Columbia. *Education:* Rhodes College (B.A., summa cum laude, 1990); Vanderbilt University (J.D., 1994). Phi Beta Kappa; Order of the Coif. Law Clerk to: Hon. J. Harvie Wilkinson, Jr., Chief Judge, U.S. Court of Appeals, Fourth Circuit, 1994-1995; Hon. Sandra Day O'Connor, Associate Justice, U.S. Supreme Court, 1995-1996. ***Email:*** jshelton@wc.com

GILBERT O. GREENMAN, born Pittsfield, Massachusetts, July 22, 1967; admitted to bar, 1994, Washington; 1995, U.S. District Court, District of Hawaii; 1996, U.S. Court of Appeals, Ninth Circuit; 1997, Maryland; 1998, District of Columbia. *Education:* Columbia University (B.A., cum laude, 1989); Harvard University (J.D., magna cum laude, 1994). Author: "Son of *Simon & Schuster:* A 'True Crime' Story of Motive, Opportunity and the First Amendment," 18 University of Hawaii Law Review 201 (Winter/Spring, 1996). Law Clerk to: The Hon. Robert R. Beezer, Ninth Circuit Court of Appeals, Seattle, Washington, 1995-1996; The Hon. David Alan Ezra, U.S. District Court, Honolulu, Hawaii, 1994-1995. ***PRACTICE AREAS:*** Civil Fraud; Civil RICO; Federal Criminal Law; Grand Jury Practice; Professional Liability Defense; Tort Defense; White Collar Criminal Defense. ***Email:*** ggreenman@wc.com

MAURITA ELAINE HORN, born Topeka, Kansas, November 24, 1968; admitted to bar, 1997, New York; 1998, District of Columbia. *Education:* Texas A & M University (B.A./B.A., 1991); University of Chicago (J.D., cum laude, 1994). Comment Editor, University of Chicago Law Review, 1993-1994. Author: "Confessional Stipulations: Preventing Waiver of Constitutional Rights," 60 University of Chicago Law Review, 1993. Judicial Law Clerk: Hon. Stephen Reinhardt, U.S. Court of Appeals, Ninth Circuit, 1994-1995; Office of the Appellate Defender, 1995-1996. ***PRACTICE AREAS:*** Labor and Employment; Litigation. ***Email:*** mehorn@wc.com

(This Listing Continued)

ENU A. MAINIGI, born New Delhi, India, April 9, 1970; admitted to bar, 1994, Maryland; 1997, District of Columbia and U.S. District Court, District of Columbia. *Education:* American University (B.S., summa cum laude, 1991); Harvard University (J.D., 1994). Law Clerk to the Hon. Franklin S. VanAntwerpen, Eastern District of Pennsylvania, 1994-1995. *Member:* The District of Columbia Bar; Maryland State Bar Association. ***Email:*** emainigi@wc.com

MICHAEL F. O'CONNOR, born Torrington, Connecticut, May 31, 1964; admitted to bar, 1994, Virginia; 1995, District of Columbia. *Education:* University of Virginia (B.A., cum laude, 1986); Harvard University (J.D., cum laude, 1994). *Member:* The District of Columbia Bar; Virginia State Bar. ***PRACTICE AREAS:*** Business Law; Corporate Law; Mergers, Acquisitions and Divestitures. ***Email:*** moconnor@wc.com

THOMAS C. VILES, admitted to bar, 1988, New York; 1991, District of Columbia, Massachusetts. *Education:* Harvard University (A.B., 1980); New York University (J.D., 1987); Cambridge University, England (LL.M., 1993; Ph.D., Law, 2000). Arthur Garfield Hays Fellow. Articles Editor, Annual Survey of American Law. American Friends of Cambridge University and Sidney Sussex North American Foundation Scholarships. Law Clerk to Hon. William Wayne Justice, Chief Judge, U.S. District Court, Eastern District of Texas, 1987-1988. Lecturer, Supervisor and Assessor in Law: Cambridge University, 1994-2000. John Thornely Law Fellow and Research Fellow: Sidney Sussex College, Cambridge University, 1997-2000. Research Fellow: Lauterpacht Research Centre for International Law, Cambridge University, 1999-2000. Teacher: Foreign and Commonwealth Office International Law Course, England, 1999. Visiting Assistant Professor: University of Texas, 1988. Fellow of the Society of Advanced Legal Studies, 2000—. Royal Institute of International Affairs, 1999—. European Criminal Bar Association, 1998—. *Member:* National Association of Criminal Defense Lawyers (Vice Chair, International Law Committee, 1998—); American Society of International Law. ***Email:*** tviles@wc.com

OLIVER GARCIA, born Buffalo, New York, May 25, 1970; admitted to bar, 1995, Texas; 1997, District of Columbia; 1998, U.S. District Court for the District of Columbia; 1999, U.S. District Court, District of Maryland; 2000, U.S. Court of Appeals, Eleventh Circuit. *Education:* Columbia University (A.B., 1992); University of Texas (J.D., with honors, 1995). ***LANGUAGES:*** Spanish. ***Email:*** ogarcia@wc.com

PAUL T. HOURIHAN, born February 6, 1967; admitted to bar, 1995, Virginia; 1996, District of Columbia. *Education:* University of Virginia (B.A., 1988; J.D., 1995). Order of the Coif. Raven Society. Book Reviews and Essays Editor, Virginia Law Review, 1994-1995. Author: "Earl Washington's Confession: Mental Retardation and the Law of Confessions," 81 Va. L. Rev. 1471 (1995). *Member:* The District of Columbia Bar; Virginia State Bar; American Bar Association. ***Email:*** phourihan@wc.com

PAUL C. RAUSER, admitted to bar, 1998, New York; 1999, District of Columbia. *Education:* Wesleyan University (B.A., 1991); Yale University (J.D., 1995). ***PRACTICE AREAS:*** White Collar Criminal Law; Civil Litigation.

WILLIAM J. BACHMAN, born Perth Amboy, New Jersey, January 17, 1961; admitted to bar, 1995, Virginia; 1998, District of Columbia. *Education:* West Chester University (B.S., 1982); Georgetown University (J.D., cum laude, 1995). Editor, Criminal Procedure Project, Georgetown Law Journal, 1993-1994. Law Clerk to the Hon. Thomas F. Hogan, U.S. District Court for the District of Columbia, 1995-1996. *Member:* The District of Columbia Bar. ***Email:*** wbachman@wc.com

MARGARET A. KEELEY, born Yuba City, California, November 29, 1968; admitted to bar, 1995, California; 1997, District of Columbia. *Education:* Georgetown University (B.A., 1991); University of Chicago (J.D., with high honors, 1995). Order of the Coif. Law Clerk to the Hon. Alfred T. Goodwin, U.S. Court of Appeals, Ninth Circuit, 1995-1996. *Member:* State Bar of California; The District of Columbia Bar. ***PRACTICE AREAS:*** Civil Litigation; Commercial Litigation; Criminal Defense; Election and Campaign Finance; First Amendment Law. ***Email:*** mkeeley@wc.com

ANN H. RAKESTRAW, born Roanoke, Virginia, May 25, 1970; admitted to bar, 1995, Texas; 1996, U.S. Court of Appeals, Ninth Circuit; 1997, District of Columbia. *Education:* University of Virginia (B.A., 1992; J.D., 1995). Order of the Coif. Notes Editor, Virginia Law Review, 1994-1995. Law Clerk, Hon. Robert R. Beezer, U.S. Court of Appeals, Ninth Circuit, 1995-1996. ***Email:*** arakestraw@wc.com

JAMES GIBSON, born Summit, New Jersey, October 23, 1968; admitted to bar, 1997, Virginia; 1999, District of Columbia. *Education:* Yale University (B.A., 1991); University of Virginia (J.D., 1995). *Member:* The District of Columbia Bar; American Bar Association. ***PRACTICE AREAS:*** Copyrights; Criminal Defense; Federal Civil Practice; Legal Ethics and Professional Responsibility. ***Email:*** jgibson@wc.com

MARY-ROSE PAPANDREA, born Meriden, Connecticut, May 5, 1970; admitted to bar, 1995, Connecticut; 1996, New York; 1997, District of Columbia. *Education:* Yale University (B.A., 1992); University of Chicago (J.D., 1995). Order of the Coif; Phi Beta Kappa. Law Clerk to: Associate Justice David H. Souter, U.S. Supreme Court, 1997-1998; Judge Douglas Ginsburg, U.S. Court of Appeals for the District of Columbia Circuit, 1996-1997; Judge John G. Koeltl, U.S. District Court, Southern District of New York, 1995-1996. *Member:* The District of Columbia Bar. ***LANGUAGES:*** Italian. ***Email:*** mpapandrea@wc.com

GABRIEL E. GORE, born Detroit, Michigan, February 10, 1969; admitted to bar, 1994, Missouri; 1995, U.S. District Court, Eastern District of Missouri (Not admitted in District of Columbia). *Education:* Southwest Missouri State University (B.A., cum laude, 1991); University of Chicago (J.D., 1994). Law Clerk to the Hon. John R. Gibson, 8th Circuit Court of Appeals, 1994-1995. Assistant U.S. Attorney, Eastern District of Missouri, 1995-1999. Assistant Special Counsel for the John C. Danforth Office of Special Counsel, Waco Investigation, 1999-2000. *Member:* The Missouri Bar. ***REPORTED CASES:*** United States v. Clyde Beason, 220 F.3d 964 (8th Cir. 2000); United States v. Denise Due, 205 F.3d 1030 (8th Cir. 1999); United States v. Williams, 194 F.3d 886 (8th Cir. 1999); United States v. Waller, 168 F.3d 496 (8th Cir. 1998); United States v. Regans, 125 F.3d 685 (8th Cir. 1997); United States v. Jones, 121 F.3d 369 (8th Cir. 1997); Malady v. United States, 120 F.3d 119 (8th Cir. 1997); United States v. Cody, 114 F.3d 772 (8th Cir. 1997); United States v. Moore, 108 F.3d 878 (8th Cir. 1997); United States v. Blake, 107 F.3d 651 (8th Cir. 1997); United States v. Williams, 104 F.3d 213 (8th Cir. 1997). ***PRACTICE AREAS:*** White Collar Criminal Defense; Complex Commercial Litigation; Manufacturers Liability. ***Email:*** ggore@wc.com

EDWARD J. BENNETT, born San Francisco, California, October 29, 1964; admitted to bar, 1996, Virginia; U.S. District Court, Eastern District of Virginia and U.S. Court of Appeals, 4th Circuit; 1998, District of Columbia. *Education:* University of Notre Dame (B.A., 1986); Duke University (J.D., with high honors, 1996). Order of the Coif. Editor-in-Chief, Law and Contemporary Problems. Law Clerk to the Hon. James C. Cacheris, Chief Judge, Eastern District of Virginia. [Lieut., U.S. Navy, 1986-1993]. ***Email:*** ebennett@wc.com

KATHLEEN M. RYAN, born New York, N.Y., December 1, 1971; admitted to bar, 1996, Virginia; 1997, U.S. District Court, District of Maryland; 1998, District of Columbia. *Education:* Harvard University (A.B., cum laude, 1993; J.D., cum laude, 1996). Member, 1993-1995; Executive Editor, 1995-1996, Harvard Women's Law Journal. Clerk to the Hon. Frederic N. Smalkin, U.S. District Court, District of Maryland, 1996-1997. *Member:* American Bar Association. ***PRACTICE AREAS:*** Corporate Law; Media Law; Publishing Law. ***Email:*** kryan@wc.com

MARA WALKER MURPHY, born Washington, D.C., December 29, 1970; admitted to bar, 1996, California; 1997, District of Columbia; 1998, U.S. District Court for the District of Columbia; 2000, U.S. District Court, Central District of California. *Education:* Colorado College (B.A., 1991); University of Virginia (J.D., 1996). Member, Editorial Board, 1994-1995 and Book Reviews Editor, 1995-1996, Virginia Law Review. Law Clerk to the Hon. Thomas Penfield Jackson, U.S. District Court for the District of Columbia, 1996-1997. Extern to the Hon. Malcolm F. Marsh, U.S. District Court for the District of Oregon, Summer, 1994. *Member:* State Bar of California; The District of Columbia Bar; American Bar Association. ***LANGUAGES:*** Italian. ***Email:*** mmurphy@wc.com

TOBIN J. ROMERO, born Minneapolis, Minnesota, February 17, 1971; admitted to bar, 1998, New York; 1999, District of Columbia; 2000, U.S. District Court, District of Columbia. *Education:* Georgetown University (B.A., magna cum laude, 1993; J.D., magna cum laude, 1996). Phi Beta Kappa; Alpha Sigma Nu; Order of the Coif. Member, 1994-1995 and Primary Editor, 1995-1996, Criminal Procedure Project, Georgetown Law Journal. Author: Note, "Liberal Discovery on Selective Prosecution Claims: Fulfilling the Promise of Equal Justice," 84 Georgetown Law Journal 2043, 1996. Law Clerk, Hon. Peter K. Leisure, U.S. District Court, Southern District of New York. Associate Member, Edward Bennett Williams American Inn of Court; Instructor of Mock Trial Advocacy, Georgetown University Law Center, 2000-2001. ***PRACTICE AREAS:*** Criminal Law; Litigation; White Collar Crime. ***Email:*** tromero@wc.com

BETH A. LEVENE, born New Brunswick, New Jersey, October 20, 1970; admitted to bar, 1997, Maryland; 1998, District of Columbia. *Education:* Dartmouth College (B.A., magna cum laude, 1992); University of Chicago (J.D., with honors, 1996). Order of the Coif. Clerkship, Judge Jesse E. Eschbach of the Seventh Circuit Court of Appeals. ***Email:*** blevene@wc.com

GLEN DONATH, born New York, N.Y., March 25, 1970; admitted to bar, 1998, New York and District of Columbia. *Education:* Yale University (B.A., magna cum laude, with distinction in the major, 1992); University of Chicago Law School (J.D., with high honors, 1996). Member, Order of the Coif. Staff Member, 1994-1995 and Comment Editor, 1995-1996, University of Chicago Law Review. Author: "Curing Cancerphobia Phobia: Reasonableness Redefined," 62 University of Chicago Law Review 1113 (1995), reprinted in 45 Defense Law Journal 337 (1996). Law Clerk, Hon. A. Raymond Randolph, U.S. Court of Appeals for the District of Columbia Circuit, 1996-1997. ***PRACTICE AREAS:*** Litigation. ***Email:*** gdonath@wc.com

(This Listing Continued)

WILLIAMS & CONNOLLY LLP, Washington—Continued

LISA M. DUGGAN, born Madison, Wisconsin, November 21, 1969; admitted to bar, 1996, Maryland; 1997, U.S. District Court, District of Maryland and U.S. Court of Appeals, Fourth Circuit; 1998, District of Columbia. *Education:* University of Virginia (B.A., 1991); University of Pennsylvania (J.D., 1996). Law Clerk to Hon. Frank A. Kaufman, U.S. District Court, District of Maryland, 1996-1997. ***PRACTICE AREAS:*** Civil Litigation. ***Email:*** lduggan@wc.com

THOMAS G. WARD, born Denville, New Jersey, April 16, 1971; admitted to bar, 1997, New York and Massachusetts; 1999, District of Columbia. *Education:* Drew University (B.A., summa cum laude, 1993) Pi Sigma Alpha; Columbia University School of Law (J.D., 1996). Harlan Fiske Stone Scholar, 1993-1996. Managing Editor, Columbia Journal of Transnational Law, 1994-1996. Law Clerk to the Hon. Diarmuid F. O'Scannlain, U.S. Court of Appeals, Ninth Circuit, 1997-1998. Judicial Extern to the Hon. John G. Koeltl, U.S. District Court, Southern District of New York, 1995-1996. Associate (Corporate Finance, Mergers & Acquisitions), Sullivan & Cromwell, 1996-1997. *Member:* New York State and Massachusetts Bar Associations; The District of Columbia Bar. ***PRACTICE AREAS:*** Intellectual Property; Litigation. ***Email:*** tward@wc.com

WILLIAM T. BURKE, born San Antonio, Texas, October 15, 1969; admitted to bar, 1995, Virginia; 2001, District of Columbia. *Education:* Princeton University (B.A., 1991); University of Virginia (J.D., 1995). [U.S. Air Force, 1995-2000; Capt., Judge Advocate General's Department]. ***PRACTICE AREAS:*** Litigation; White Collar Criminal Defense. ***Email:*** wburke@wc.com

LAURA HAAS PARSKY, born New York, N.Y., March 20, 1969; admitted to bar, 1995, California; 1998, District of Columbia. *Education:* Yale University (B.A., magna cum laude, 1991); University of California, Boalt Hall School of Law (J.D., 1995). U.S. Department of Justice, Criminal Division, Narcotic and Dangerous Drug Section, 1996-2000. ***Email:*** lparsky@wc.com

JOHN E. JOINER, born Midwest City, Oklahoma, January 27, 1970; admitted to bar, 1996, Colorado; 1999, District of Columbia. *Education:* University of Oklahoma (B.B.A. in Economics & Bachelor of Accountancy, 1993); University of Denver (J.D., 1996). Articles Editor, University of Denver Law Review, 1998-1999. Law Clerk: The Honorable Mary Beck Briscoe, U.S. Court of Appeals, Tenth Circuit, 1997-1998; The Honorable Clarence A. Brimmer, U.S. District Court, District of Wyoming, 1996-1997; The Honorable Steve C. Briggs, Colorado Court of Appeals. *Member:* Colorado and American Bar Associations; The District of Columbia Bar. ***PRACTICE AREAS:*** Appellate Practice; Civil Litigation; Class Action Litigation; Complex and Multi-District Litigation; Complex Commercial Litigation; Environmental and Toxic Torts; Franchises and Franchising; Fraud and Deceit. ***Email:*** jjoiner@wc.com

DAVID S. ARDIA, admitted to bar, 1997, New York; 1998, District of Columbia. *Education:* Clarkson University (B.S., 1989); State University of New York (M.S., 1995); Syracuse University (J.D., summa cum laude, 1996). Order of the Coif. Articles Editor, Syracuse Law Review. Member, Moot Court Board. Law clerk to the Honorable Conrad Cyr, U.S. Court of Appeals for the First Circuit, 1998-1999; Law Clerk to the Honorable Thomas McAvoy, U.S. District Court for the Northern District of New York, 1996-1998. Author: "Does the Emperor Have No Clothes? Enforcement of International Laws Protecting the Marine Environment," 19 Mich. J. Int'l L. 497 (1998), "Takings Doctrine Moves Onto Unpaved Ground," 24 REAL ESTATE L.J. 195 (1996). *Member:* New York State and American Bar Associations; District of Columbia Bar. ***PRACTICE AREAS:*** Constitutional Law; Criminal Law; Environmental Law; Intellectual Property Litigation; Defamation; Litigation. ***Email:*** dardia@wc.com

LUBA SHUR, born St. Petersburg, Russia, June 26, 1971; admitted to bar, 1997, Massachusetts; 1998, District of Columbia; 1999, U.S. Court of Appeals, Fifth Circuit; 2000, U.S. Court of Appeals, Third Circuit. *Education:* University of Virginia (B.A., 1993; J.D., 1996). Order of the Coif. Member, 1994-1995 and Articles Editor, 1995-1996, Virginia Law Review. Law Clerk: The Honorable Henry A. Politz, U.S. Court of Appeals, Fifth Circuit; The Honorable James H. Michael, Jr., U.S. District Court, Western District of Virginia. Author: Student Note, "Content-Based Distinctions in a University Funding System and the Irrelevance of the Establishment Clause: Putting Wide Awake to Rest," 81 Virginia Law Review 1665 (1995). ***LANGUAGES:*** Russian. ***PRACTICE AREAS:*** Litigation. ***Email:*** lshur@wc.com

HELEN I. DOOLEY, born Long Branch, New Jersey, June 12, 1971; admitted to bar, 1995, North Carolina and U.S. Court of Appeals, Tenth Circuit; 1997, U.S. District Court, Northern, Eastern and Western Districts of Oklahoma and District of Columbia. *Education:* Duke University (B.A., 1992; J.D., 1995). Phi Beta Kappa. Article Editor, Duke Law Journal, 1994-1995. Clerkships: Judge Deanell Reece Tacha, Tenth Circuit Court of Appeals, 1995-1996; Judge Sven Erik Holmes, Northern District of Oklahoma, 1996-1997. *Member:* The District of Columbia Bar; North Carolina State Bar; American Bar Association. ***PRACTICE AREAS:*** Business Law; Corporate Law. ***Email:*** hdooley@wc.com

(This Listing Continued)

NICHOLAS J. BOYLE, born Glasgow, Scotland, December 22, 1972; admitted to bar, 1997, New York (Not admitted in District of Columbia); 2001, U.S. District Court, Central District of Illinois, U.S. Court of Federal Claims, U.S. Court of International Trade and U.S. Court of Appeals for the District of Columbia and Federal Circuits (Not admitted in District of Columbia). *Education:* London University, King's College (LL.B., First Class Honors, 1994); University of Cambridge, Emmanuel College (LL.M., 1995); Harvard Law School (LL.M., 1996). Fulbright Scholar. Author: With D.V.Smalley, "The European Union," *International Survey of Investment Adviser Regulation,* (M.Macharge and B. Clark, Eds., 2nd Ed.). Lecturer: "Civil Liberties and Constitutional Law," University of London, 1994-1995. ***PRACTICE AREAS:*** Practice Limited to Federal Litigation; Media and First Amendment; Antitrust. ***Email:*** nboyle@wc.com

BONNIE DUNNINGER NATHAN, born Newark, New Jersey, March 5, 1968; admitted to bar, 1997, Maryland; 1998, New Jersey; 1999, District of Columbia. *Education:* University of Michigan (B.A., with high honors, 1989); Georgetown University (M.P.P., 1994; J.D., magna cum laude, 1997). Order of the Coif. Member, Georgetown Law Journal, 1995-1997. Law Clerk to the Hon. Timothy K. Lewis, U.S. Court of Appeals, Third Circuit, 1997-1998. ***PRACTICE AREAS:*** Employment Discrimination; Litigation. ***Email:*** bnathan@wc.com

CHARLES T. KIMMETT, JR., born Elizabeth, New Jersey, February 20, 1972; admitted to bar, 1998, New Jersey; 1999, District of Columbia. *Education:* Rutgers University (B.A., with highest honors, 1994); Yale University (J.D., 1997). Phi Beta Kappa. Notes Editor, Yale Law Journal, 1996-1997. Author: "Permanent Replacements, Presidential Power, and Politics: Judicial Overreaching in Chamber of Commerce v. Reich," 106 Yale Law Journal, 1996; "The Undeniable Politics of Labor Law," 106 Yale Law Journal, 1996; "Rethinking Mass Tort Law, 105 Yale Law Journal, 1996. Law Clerk to the Hon. Stewart G. Pollock, New Jersey Supreme Court, 1997-1998. ***PRACTICE AREAS:*** Civil Appeals; Civil Litigation; Civil Practice; Class Actions; Commercial Real Estate Litigation; Contract Litigation; Libel and Slander; Defamation; Media and First Amendment. ***Email:*** ckimmett@wc.com

ADAM L. PERLMAN, born Washington, D.C., October 14, 1972; admitted to bar, 1997, Maryland; 1998, District of Columbia; U.S. District Court, District of Maryland; U.S. Court of Appeals, Fourth Circuit; U.S. District Court, District of Columbia; U.S. Court of Appeals, District of Columbia Circuit; U.S. Supreme Court. *Education:* Tufts University (B.A., magna cum laude, 1994); University of Pennsylvania (J.D., summa cum laude, 1997). Law Clerk to the Honorable Marvin J. Garbis, U.S. District Court for the District of Maryland, 1997-1998. *Member:* The District of Columbia Bar; Maryland State Bar Association. ***PRACTICE AREAS:*** Civil Practice; Commercial Litigation; Libel and Slander; Litigation; Media and First Amendment; Patent Litigation. ***Email:*** aperlman@wc.com

MICHAEL J. LEOTTA, born Washington, D.C., May 4, 1972; admitted to bar, 1997, Maryland; 1998, U.S. Court of Appeals, Fourth Circuit and U.S. District Court, District of Maryland; 1999, District of Columbia; 2000, Seneca Nation of Indians. *Education:* University of Maryland (B.A., 1994); Harvard Law School (J.D., 1997). Member, Harvard Law Review, 1995-1997. Author: Note, *Keeping Secrets in Cyberspace: Establishing Fourth Amendment Protection for Internet Communication,* 110 Harv. L. Rev. 1591 (1997). Co-Author: "The Fifth Amendment Privilege Against Cross Examination," Geo. Law Journal, Vol. 85, 1997. Clerk, 1997-1998, Judge Francis D. Murnaghan, Jr., U.S. Court of Appeals for the Fourth Circuit. *Member:* Maryland State Bar Association; District of Columbia Bar; Federal Bar Association. ***PRACTICE AREAS:*** Computer Law; Media and First Amendment; Litigation. ***Email:*** mleotta@wc.com

RUSSELL D. COVEY, born Salem, Oregon, June 19, 1965; admitted to bar, 1998, New York; 1999, District of Columbia. *Education:* Amherst College (B.A. in Political Science, 1987); Princeton University (M.A. in Politics, 1991); Yale University (J.D., 1997). Author: Note, "Adventures in the Zone of Twilight, Separation of Powers and National Security in the Mexican Bailout," 105 Yale Law Journal 1311, 1996; "Beating The Prisoner at Prisoner's Dilemma: The Evidentiary Significance of a Witness's Refusal to Testify," 47 American University Law Review 105, 1997. ***PRACTICE AREAS:*** General Civil; Criminal Litigation. ***Email:*** rcovey@wc.com

ANDREW W. RUDGE, born New York, N.Y, June 7, 1972; admitted to bar, 1998, New York; 1999, District of Columbia. *Education:* Duke University (A.B., 1994); University of Virginia (J.D., 1997). Order of the Coif. ***Email:*** arudge@wc.com

DENEEN C. HOWELL, born Philadelphia, Pennsylvania, June 21, 1971; admitted to bar, 1997, California; 1999, District of Columbia. *Education:* Yale University (B.A., cum laude, 1993); Stanford University (J.D., 1997). Member, 1995-1997 and President, 1996-1997, Stanford Law Review. Corporate Counsel, The Times Mirror Company, 1997-1998. *Member:* District of Columbia Bar (Sections on: Arts, Entertainment and Sports Law; Corporations, Finance and Securities Law; and Labor and Employment Law); State Bar of California; American and National Bar Associations. ***LANGUAGES:*** Spanish. ***PRAC-***

(This Listing Continued)

TICE AREAS: Business Formation; Business Transactions; Copyright Licensing; Copyright Registration; Entertainment Law; Executive Compensation; Executive Severance Contracts; Marketing Law; Mergers and Acquisitions; Music Law; Publishing Contracts; Sports Law. ***Email:*** dhowell@wc.com

MATTHEW S. AMATRUDA, born Baltimore, Maryland, October 27, 1970; admitted to bar, 1999, New York and District of Columbia. *Education:* Wesleyan University (B.A., 1993); Columbia University (J.D., 1997). Kent Scholar, 1994-1995, 1996-1997. Stone Scholar, 1995-1996. Law Clerk to Judge Diana E. Murphy, U.S. Court of Appeals, Eighth Circuit, 1997-1998. ***PRACTICE AREAS:*** Litigation. ***Email:*** mamatruda@wc.com

JASON M. LEVIEN, born New York, N.Y., May 17, 1971; admitted to bar, 1999, New Jersey (Not admitted in District of Columbia). *Education:* Pomona College (B.A., 1993); University of Michigan (M.P.P., 1997; J.D., 1997). Clarence Darrow Scholar. Staebler Fellow. Co-Author: "Cleaning Up Judicial Elections: Examining the First Amendment Limitations on Judicial Campaign Expenditures," Michigan Law & Policy Review, 1997; "Protecting the Right to Petition: Why a Lobbying Contingency Fee Prohibition Violates the Constitution," Harvard Journal on Legislation, 1998; "A New Horizon for Campaign Finance Reform," Harvard Journal on Legislation, 2000. Law Clerk to the Hon. Diana Gribbon Motz, U.S. Court of Appeals, Fourth Circuit, 1997-1998. ***PRACTICE AREAS:*** Sports Law; Litigation. ***Email:*** jlevien@wc.com

DAVID H. ANGELI, born Pittsfield, Massachusetts, August 9, 1967; admitted to bar, 1997, Maryland; 1998, U.S. District Court, District of Maryland and District of Columbia. *Education:* Boston University (B.S., summa cum laude, 1989); Georgetown University (J.D., magna cum laude, 1997). Order of the Coif. White Collar Crime Senior Project Editor, The American Criminal Law Review, 1996-1997. Author: "A 'Second Look' at Crack Cocaine Sentencing Policies: One More Try for Federal Equal Protection," 34 The American Criminal Law Review 1211, 1997. Co-Author: "Federal Criminal Conflict of Interest, Project, Eleventh Survey of White Collar Crime," The American Criminal Law Review, 1996. Law Clerk to the Hon. Thomas Penfield Jackson, U.S. District Court for the District of Columbia, 1997-1999. *Member:* Maryland State and American Bar Associations; The District of Columbia Bar. [Lieut., U.S. Navy, 1989-1994]. ***PRACTICE AREAS:*** Criminal Litigation; Civil Litigation. ***Email:*** dangeli@wc.com

DAVID C. RIEVESCHL, born New Haven, Connecticut, September 30, 1968; admitted to bar, 1998, New York and District of Columbia. *Education:* Duke University (B.A., 1991); A.B. Freeman School of Business (M.B.A., 1997); Tulane Law School (J.D., magna cum laude, 1997). Order of the Coif. Recipient: George Dewey Nelson Memorial Award; Morton A. Aldrich Scholarship; Levy-Rosenblum Institute for Entrepreneurship TABA Community Service Award. Member, 1995-1996, and Managing Editor, 1996-1997, Tulane Law Review. *Member:* New York State and American Bar Associations; Bar Association of the District of Columbia. ***PRACTICE AREAS:*** Business Law; Corporate Law; Finance; Mergers, Acquisitions and Divestitures; Securities. ***Email:*** drieveschl@wc.com

ALEX G. ROMAIN, born Boston, Massachusetts, June 27, 1970; admitted to bar, 1997, Massachusetts; 2000, District of Columbia. *Education:* Yale University (B.A., 1992); University of Michigan (J.D., 1997). Law Clerk to Judge Reginald C. Lindsay, U.S. District Court for the District of Massachusetts, 1997-1998; Judge Sandra L. Lynch, U.S. Court of Appeals for the First Circuit, 1998-1999. ***LANGUAGES:*** French, Spanish. ***Email:*** aromain@wc.com

DAVID A. FORKNER, born Ft. Collins, Colorado, May 24, 1971; admitted to bar, 1997, Colorado; 1999, District of Columbia. *Education:* University of Denver (B.A., 1993; J.D., 1997). Phi Delta Kappa. Order of St. Ives. Law Clerk: The Honorable Thomas M. Shanahan, U.S. District Court for the District of Nebraska, 1997-1999; The Honorable Jesse E. Eschbach, Seventh Circuit U.S. Court of Appeals, 1999-2000. Author: "U.S. Sentencing Guidelines," 73 Denv. L. Rev. 963; "Essential Facilities," 13 Berkeley Tech. J. 565; "Weaving a Tangled Web," 36 Harv. J. on Legis. 161. Instructor, Creighton University School of Law, 1998-1999. ***Email:*** forkner@worldnet.att.net

FRANCIS M. HAMILTON III, born Birmingham, Alabama, April 11, 1972; admitted to bar, 1998, Tennessee and Georgia; 2001, District of Columbia. *Education:* Rhodes College (B.A., magna cum laude, 1994); Washington & Lee University (J.D., summa cum laude, 1997). Phi Beta Kappa; Order of the Coif. Clerk, Honorable Jerome Turner, United States District Court for the Western District of Tennessee, 1997-1998. ***Email:*** fhamilton@wc.com

ELIZABETH A. O'BRIEN, born Chicago, Illinois, November 6, 1970; admitted to bar, 1998, Georgia; 2000, District of Columbia. *Education:* University of Michigan (B.A., 1992; J.D., 1997). Clerk for the Hon. Orinda D. Evans, Northern District of Georgia, 1998-1999. *Member:* American Bar Association. ***PRACTICE AREAS:*** Civil Litigation; Criminal Defense; General Practice; Trial Practice. ***Email:*** eobrien@wc.com

LAURA P. STOUT, born Plainfield, New Jersey, March 3, 1970; admitted to bar, 1999, Virginia and District of Columbia. *Education:* Princeton University (B.A., magna cum laude, 1992); Harvard University (J.D., magna cum laude, 1998). ***Email:*** lstout@wc.com

(This Listing Continued)

STEPHEN A. BECK, born Andrews Air Force Base, Maryland, July 5, 1973; admitted to bar, 1998, Texas; 2000, District of Columbia. *Education:* University of Texas at Austin (B.B.A., with high honors, 1995; J.D., with honors, 1998); Georgetown University (LL.M. in Taxation, with distinction, 2000). ***PRACTICE AREAS:*** Taxation. ***Email:*** sbeck@wc.com

JONATHAN M. LANDY, born Philadelphia, Pennsylvania, November 6, 1973; admitted to bar, 1999, Maryland; 2000, District of Columbia. *Education:* Dartmouth College (B.A., magna cum laude, 1995); Yale University (J.D., 1998). Senior Editor, Yale Law Journal. Law Clerk, Hon. Louis F. Oberdorfer, U.S. District Court for the District of Columbia, 1998-1999. *Member:* Maryland State Bar Association, Inc. ***PRACTICE AREAS:*** Appellate Practice; Intellectual Property. ***Email:*** jlandy@wc.com

CHRISTOPHER N. MANNING, born Washington, D.C., July 2, 1973; admitted to bar, 1999, District of Columbia, Maryland, Massachusetts and New York. *Education:* Duke University (A.B., magna cum laude, 1995); Harvard University (J.D., magna cum laude, 1998). Phi Beta Kappa. Editor-in-Chief, Harvard Journal of Law & Technology, 1997-1998. Law Clerk to the Hon. Dennis Jacobs, U.S. Court of Appeals for the Second Circuit, 1998-1999. Author: Note, "Live and Let Die?: Physician-Assisted Suicide and the Right to Die," 9 Harv. J.L. & Tech. 513 (1996). *Member:* Maryland State and American Bar Associations; The District of Columbia Bar; The Association of Trial Lawyers of America. ***PRACTICE AREAS:*** Civil Litigation; Criminal Defense; General Practice; Media and First Amendment; Trial Practice. ***Email:*** cmanning@wc.com

JEFFREY M. SMITH, born New York, N.Y., August 8, 1972; admitted to bar, 1999, Maryland; 2000, District of Columbia. *Education:* University of Pennsylvania, Wharton School (B.S., magna cum laude, 1994); Duke University (J.D., high honors, 1998). Order of the Coif. Note Editor, Duke Law Journal, 1997-1998. Author: The Role of the Attorney In Protecting (And Impairing) Shareholder Interests," 47 Duke L.J. 161. *Member:* The District of Columbia Bar. ***PRACTICE AREAS:*** Litigation. ***Email:*** jsmith@wc.com

STACEY DANSKY, born New Haven, Connecticut, September 17, 1973; admitted to bar, 1998, Texas; 1999, District of Columbia. *Education:* Vanderbilt University (B.A., magna cum laude, 1995); University of Texas (J.D., with honors, 1998). Phi Beta Kappa; Order of the Coif; Chancellors. Chief Notes Editor, Texas Law Review. Author: "Eliminating Strict Employer Liability in Quid Pro Quo Sexual Harassment Cases," 76 Texas L. Rev. 435 (1997). Law Clerk to the Honorable Lee H. Rosenthal, United States District Court, Southern District of Texas, 1998-1999. ***PRACTICE AREAS:*** Litigation. ***Email:*** sdansky@wc.com

THOMAS E. SHAKOW, born Washington, D.C., November 15, 1972; admitted to bar, 1998, California; 2001, District of Columbia. *Education:* Yale University (B.A., 1994; J.D., 1998). Essays Editor, Yale Law Journal, 1997-1998. Law Clerk, The Honorable Robert L. Eastaugh, Alaska Supreme Court, 1998-1999. ***Email:*** tshakow@wc.com

GREGORY M. GILCHRIST, admitted to bar, 2000, California; 2001, District of Columbia. *Education:* Stanford University (A.B., 1994); Columbia University (J.D., 1998). ***Email:*** ggilchrist@wc.com

RYAN T. SCARBOROUGH, born Austin, Texas, September 27, 1971; admitted to bar, 1998, Virginia; 2000, District of Columbia. *Education:* Duke University (A.B., summa cum laude, 1994); Harvard Law School (J.D., cum laude, 1998). Phi Beta Kappa. Fulbright Scholar to Japan. Law Clerk to Honorable Alan C. Kay, U.S. District Court, District of Hawaii. Author: "Will Health Care Economic Information Lead to Therapeutic-Class Warfare or Welfare?" 111 Harvard Law Review 2384 (1998). ***LANGUAGES:*** Japanese. ***PRACTICE AREAS:*** Litigation. ***Email:*** rscarborough@wc.com

WILLIAM G. CHILDS, born Bartlesville, Oklahoma, July 1, 1971; admitted to bar, 1998, Minnesota; 2001, District of Columbia. *Education:* Macalester College (B.A., 1994); University of Texas at Austin (J.D., with high honors, 1998). Chief Articles Editor, Texas Law Review, 1997-1998. Author: "The Intersection of Peremptory Challenges, Challenges for Cause, and Harmless Error," 27 Am. J. Crim. L. 49 (1999). *Member:* Minnesota State Bar Association. ***PRACTICE AREAS:*** Business Crimes; Business Litigation; Civil Practice; Commercial Crimes; Commercial Litigation; Contract Litigation; Corporate Investigations; Corporate Litigation; Criminal Defense; Criminal Fraud; Federal Criminal Law; Intellectual Property; Litigation; Patent Infringement; Patent Litigation; White Collar Crime. ***Email:*** wchilds@wc.com

JENNIFER G. WICHT, born Ithaca, New York, April 24, 1970; admitted to bar, 1999, Massachusetts; 2001, District of Columbia. *Education:* Haverford College (B.A., 1992); Georgetown University (J.D., 1998). ***Email:*** jwicht@wc.com

ZOE S. POULSON, born New York, N.Y., September 10, 1974; admitted to bar, 1998, Virginia and U.S. Court of Appeals, Fourth Circuit; 1999, District of Columbia and U.S. District Court, District of Columbia. *Education:* Wake Forest University (B.A., magna cum laude, 1995); Harvard Law School (J.D., cum laude, 1998). ***PRACTICE AREAS:*** Litigation. ***Email:*** zpoulson@wc.com

(This Listing Continued)

WILLIAMS & CONNOLLY LLP, Washington—Continued

STEPHEN D. ANDREWS, born Charlotte, North Carolina, March 11, 1973; admitted to bar, 2000, California; 2001, District of Columbia. *Education:* Harvard University (A.B., magna cum laude, 1995); University of Chicago (J.D., with high honors, 1998). Order of the Coif. Law Clerk to the Honorable Stephen V. Wilson, U.S. District Court for the Central District of California, 1998-1999; Law Clerk to the Honorable Susan H. Black, U.S. Court of Appeals for the Eleventh Circuit, 1999-2000. ***Email:*** sandrews@wc.com

JONATHAN S. JEFFRESS, born Washington, D.C., November 22, 1971; admitted to bar, 1998, Virginia (Not admitted in District of Columbia). *Education:* Williams College (B.A., 1994); University of Virginia (J.D., 1998). Notes Development Editor, Virginia Law Review. Law Clerk, The Honorable Thomas F. Hogan, U.S. District Court for the District of Columbia, 1998-2000. ***Email:*** jjeffress@wc.com

MARY BETH LONG, born Clearfield, Pennsylvania, August 20, 1963; admitted to bar, 1998, Virginia; 2000, District of Columbia; 2001, U.S. District Court, District of Columbia. *Education:* Pennsylvania State University (B.A., 1985); Washington & Lee University (J.D., 1998). Phi Beta Kappa; Omicron Delta Kappa. Employment: Central Intelligence Agency, 1986-1999. *Member:* Virginia Bar Association. ***LANGUAGES:*** Spanish. ***PRACTICE AREAS:*** Litigation. ***Email:*** mlong@wc.com

BRADLEY J. BONDI, born Tampa, Florida, January 29, 1974; admitted to bar, 1999, District of Columbia, Florida, U.S. District Court, Northern, Middle and Southern Districts of Florida and U.S. Court of Appeals, Eleventh and Fourth Circuits. *Education:* University of Florida (B.S., with highest honors, 1995; M.B.A., 1998; J.D., with high honors, 1998). Beta Gamma Sigma. Order of the Coif. Awarded: The Outstanding Male Graduate, 1995; University of Florida Hall of Fame. Member, 1996-1998 and Best Advocate, 1998, Trial Competition Team. Law Clerk to the Hon. Edward E. Carnes, U.S. Court of Appeals, Eleventh Circuit, 1999-2000. Co-Author: "Revising Latent Defects: A Painful Walk Down Memory Lane," 1999 Southern Surety and Fidelity Claims Conference. ***PRACTICE AREAS:*** Litigation. ***Email:*** bbondi@wc.com

JANET C. FISHER, born Abington, Pennsylvania, May 13, 1973; admitted to bar, 1998, Maryland; 1999, Pennsylvania, District of Columbia, U.S. District Court, District of Maryland and U.S. District Court for the District of Columbia. *Education:* Cornell University (B.S., with honors, 1995); Harvard University (J.D., 1998). Supervising Editor, 1996-1997 and Articles Editor, 1998, Harvard Journal on Legislation. Law Clerk, Judge Richard W. Roberts, U.S. District Court for the District of Columbia, 2000-2001. Author, "Reinventing a Livelihood: How United States Labor Laws, Labor-Management Cooperation Initiatives and Privatization Affect Public Sector Labor Markets," 34 Harvard Journal on Legislation 557 (Summer 1997). *Member:* Pennsylvania and American Bar Associations; The District of Columbia Bar. ***PRACTICE AREAS:*** Litigation; Constitutional Law. ***Email:*** jfisher@wc.com

JULI ANN LUND, born Sao Paulo, Brazil, April 17, 1972; admitted to bar, 1998, Minnesota; 1999, U.S. District Court, District of Minnesota (Not admitted in District of Columbia). *Education:* Southern Methodist University (B.A., 1994); University of Wisconsin-Madison (M.A., 1995); Yale University (J.D., 1998). Phi Beta Kappa. ***Email:*** jlund@wc.com

KATHERINE P. CHIARELLO, born Dallas, Texas, November 30, 1972; admitted to bar, 1998, Texas (Not admitted in District of Columbia). *Education:* Trinity University (B.A., 1995); University of Texas School of Law (J.D., 1998). Order of the Coif. Articles Editor, Texas Law Review, 1997-1998. Author: "Successive Prosecutions and Compound Criminal Statutes: A Functional Test," 77 Texas L. Rev. 333 (1998)(With Susan R. Klein). ***Email:*** kchiarello@wc.com

THOMAS H. L. SELBY, born Austin, Texas, September 27, 1967; admitted to bar, 1999, Texas; 2000, District of Columbia. *Education:* University of Chicago (B.A., 1990); University of Texas, Austin (J.D., 1999). Order of the Coif. Member, Texas Law Review, 1997-1999. ***PRACTICE AREAS:*** Litigation; Criminal; Civil. ***Email:*** tselby@wc.com

LEONARD D. BROWN, JR., born Philadelphia, Pennsylvania, July 7, 1967; admitted to bar, 2000, New York; 2001, District of Columbia. *Education:* Pennsylvania State University (B.A., 1988; M.B.A., summa cum laude, 1994); University of Pennsylvania (J.D., 1999). Toll Fellow; Maxwell Scholar. Law Clerk, The Honorable James T. Giles, Chief Judge, U.S. District Court, Eastern District of Pennsylvania. *Member:* American Bar Association; National Black MBA Association. ***PRACTICE AREAS:*** Corporate Law; Sports Law. ***Email:*** lbrown@wc.com

BRIAN A. McLACHLAN, born Kirkland, Washington, July 16, 1963; admitted to bar, 2000, Washington and Virginia; 2001, District of Columbia. *Education:* University of Washington (B.A., 1995; J.D., with high honors, 1999). Order of the Coif. Recipient: Knauss-SeaGrant Congressional Fellowship. *Member:* Washington State and American Bar Association; Virginia State Bar; District of Columbia Bar. ***PRACTICE AREAS:*** Litigation. ***Email:*** bmclachlan@wc.com

(This Listing Continued)

KEVIN HARDY, born Philadelphia, Pennsylvania, July 30, 1974; admitted to bar, 2000, Maryland; 2001, District of Columbia. *Education:* Cornell University (A.B., 1996); Columbia University School of Law (J.D., 1999). Harlan Fiske Stone Scholar; Elkins Prize. Special Issue Chair and Senior Editor, Columbia Law Review. Law Clerk, Judge Walter K. Stapleton, U.S. Court of Appeals for the Third Circuit, 1999-2000. ***Email:*** khardy@wc.com

RILEY HENDERSON ROSS III, born Virginia Beach, Virginia, June 6, 1971; admitted to bar, 1999, Virginia; 2001, District of Columbia. *Education:* Longwood College (B.S., 1993); Western Kentucky University (M.A., 1995); University of Virginia (J.D., 1999). Law Clerk, The Honorable James C. Cacheris, U.S. District Court, Eastern District of Virginia, 1999-2000. *Member:* Virginia Bar Association; Virginia Trial Lawyers Association. ***PRACTICE AREAS:*** Litigation. ***Email:*** rross@wc.com

GABRIEL FELDMAN, born New York, N.Y., October 9, 1973; admitted to bar, 2000, New York (Not admitted in District of Columbia). *Education:* Duke University (B.A., 1995; M.A., 1999; J.D., with honors, 1999). ***Email:*** gfeldman@wc.com

EDWARD COLEMAN BARNIDGE, III, born St. Louis, Missouri, June 30, 1971; admitted to bar, 1999, Virginia; 2001, District of Columbia. *Education:* University of Notre Dame (B.A., 1993); University of Virginia (J.D., 1999). Phi Beta Kappa; Order of the Coif. ***PRACTICE AREAS:*** Litigation; Criminal Law. ***Email:*** ebarnidge@wc.com

JANA D. JOBES, born Norwalk, California, August 7, 1973; admitted to bar, 1999, Alabama and U.S. District Court, Middle and Northern Districts of Alabama; 2001, District of Columbia; registered before U.S. Patent and Trademark Office. *Education:* University of Alabama in Huntsville (B.S.E., 1996); Tulane University (J.D., 1999). Order of the Coif. *Member:* Birmingham and American Bar Associations; Alabama State Bar. ***PRACTICE AREAS:*** Litigation; Intellectual Property. ***Email:*** jjobes@wc.com

JOSEPH M. TERRY, born Santa Barbara, California, March 2, 1974; admitted to bar, 2001, District of Columbia. *Education:* Northwestern University (B.A., with honors, 1996); University of Chicago (J.D., with honors, 1999). Law Clerk to the Honorable W. Eugene Davis, U.S. Court of Appeals for the Fifth Circuit, 1999-2000.

CHRISTINE M. CABEZAS-GANSLER, born Sacramento, California, March 11, 1973; admitted to bar, 1999, Maryland; 2000, District of Columbia. *Education:* Yale University (B.A., 1995); University of Virginia Law School (J.D., 1999). ***LANGUAGES:*** Spanish and French. ***PRACTICE AREAS:*** Litigation. ***Email:*** ccabezas-ganzler@wc.com

BRIAN S. MORRISON, born Augusta, Maine, October 6, 1974; admitted to bar, 1999, Massachusetts (Not admitted in District of Columbia). *Education:* Brandeis University (B.A., 1996); Harvard Law School (J.D., 1999). ***Email:*** bmorrison@wc.com

KATHERINE R. TROMBLE, born Baltimore, Maryland, August 3, 1972; admitted to bar, 1999, Virginia; 2000, District of Columbia. *Education:* Georgetown University (B.A., 1994); Vanderbilt University (J.D., 1999). Phi Beta Kappa; Alpha Sigma Nu. Order of the Coif. Law Clerk, The Honorable Gerald B. Tjoflat, U.S. Court of Appeals for the Eleventh Circuit, 1999-2000. ***Email:*** ktromble@wc.com

DANIEL A. RESTREPO, born Washington, D.C., January 9, 1971; admitted to bar, 1999, Virginia; 2001, District of Columbia. *Education:* University of Virginia (B.A., 1993); University of Pennsylvania (J.D., magna cum laude, 1999). Order of the Coif. Law Clerk, Hon. Anthony J. Scirica, U.S. Court of Appeals for the Third Circuit, 1999-2000. ***LANGUAGES:*** Spanish. ***PRACTICE AREAS:*** Litigation. ***Email:*** drestrepo@wc.com

WILLIS N. SAUTTER, born Georgetown, Kentucky, April 1, 1970; admitted to bar, 2001, New York and U.S. District Court, Southern District of New York (Not admitted in District of Columbia). *Education:* Yale University (B.A., cum laude, with distinction in major, 1993); University of Chicago Law School (J.D., with honors, 1999). Staff Member, University of Chicago Law Review, 1997-1999. Law Clerk to the Hon. Edith H. Jones, U.S. Court of Appeals, Fifth Circuit, 1999-2000. ***Email:*** wsauter@wc.com

CHRISTINA P. GIFFIN, born Silver Spring, Maryland, May 3, 1967; admitted to bar, 1999, Virginia and U.S. Court of Appeals, Fourth Circuit (Not admitted in District of Columbia). *Education:* Reed College (B.A., 1990); George Washington University Law School (J.D., summa cum laude, 1999). Order of the Coif; Moot Court; Dean's Fellow. Recipient: Maurice Shapiro Public Interest Fellowship; Charles Glover Award. Member, George Washington Law Review, 1998-2000. Law Clerk to The Honorable Richard W. Roberts, 1999-2000. *Member:* Virginia State Bar.

BRIAN J. BUCKELEW, born Berkeley, California, January 16, 1973; admitted to bar, 1999, California; 2000, District of Columbia. *Education:* University of Arizona (B.A., 1995); Boalt Hall School of Law, University of California (J.D., 1999). Law Clerk to the Hon. Pasco M. Bowman, II, U.S. Court of Appeals, Eighth Circuit, 2000-2001. *Member:* State Bar of California; The District of Columbia Bar. ***PRACTICE AREAS:*** Litigation. ***Email:*** bbuckelew@wc.com

(This Listing Continued)

MICHAELA ALLBEE, born Burlington, Vermont, April 29, 1972; admitted to bar, 1999, Massachusetts (Not admitted in District of Columbia). *Education:* Brown University (B.A., 1994); Georgetown University Law Center (J.D., 1999). ***PRACTICE AREAS:*** Corporate Law.

AARON P. MAURER, born September 14, 1973; admitted to bar, 1999, North Carolina; registered to practice before U.S. Patent and Trademark Office (Not admitted in District of Columbia). *Education:* North Carolina State University (B.S., 1996); Harvard Law School (J.D., 1999). *Member:* North Carolina State Bar; American Bar Association.

BRAD M. SNYDER, born Oak Park, Illinois, June 28, 1972; admitted to bar, 2001, Maryland (Not admitted in District of Columbia). *Education:* Duke University (A.B., 1994); Yale University (J.D., 1999). ***Email:*** bsnyder@wc.com

MANISH K. MITAL, born Auburn, New York; July 20, 1976; admitted to bar, 2000, Virginia; 2001, District of Columbia. *Education:* Massachusetts Institute of Technology (S.B., 1997); Harvard Law School (J.D., magna cum laude, 2000). ***PRACTICE AREAS:*** Litigation. ***Email:*** mmital@wc.com

NATHAN P. SUTTON, born Astoria, Oregon, June 22, 1973; admitted to bar, 2001, California (Not admitted in District of Columbia). *Education:* North Carolina State University (B.S., 1996); University of Chicago (J.D., 2000). *Member:* State Bar of California. ***PRACTICE AREAS:*** Intellectual Property; Antitrust; Litigation.

DANIEL D. WILLIAMS, born Philadelphia, Pennsylvania, October 27, 1969; (admission pending). *Education:* University of Rochester (B.S., 1991); Georgetown University (J.D., 2000).

ANA L. REYES, born Uruguay, February 8, 1974; admitted to bar, 2001, New York (Not admitted in District of Columbia). *Education:* Transylvania University (B.A., 1996); Harvard University (J.D., 2000).

HEIDI E. MURDY, born Pittsburgh, Pennsylvania, April 7, 1975; admitted to bar, 2001, New York and District of Columbia. *Education:* Duquesne University (B.A., 1996); Yale Law School (J.D., 2000). Adjunct Professor of Constitutional Law, University of Tulsa Law School, 2001. *Member:* New York State Bar Association. ***PRACTICE AREAS:*** Litigation. ***Email:*** hmurdy@wc.com

JONATHAN B. PITT, born Washington, D.C., June 21, 1972; (admission pending). *Education:* University of Pennsylvania (B.A., 1994); Yale Law School (J.D., 2000). ***LANGUAGES:*** Spanish. ***Email:*** jpitt@wc.com

JOSH A. COHEN, born Boston, Massachusetts, August 26, 1974; (admission pending). *Education:* Williams College (B.A., 1996); Yale Law School (J.D., 2001). ***Email:*** jcohen@wc.com

TODD F. BRAUNSTEIN, born New Hyde Park, New York, August 31, 1975; (admission pending). *Education:* Harvard University (A.B., 1997; J.D., 2001). Member, Harvard Law Review, 2000-2001. ***Email:*** tbraunstein@wc.com

SHANA LAVERNE FULTON, born Indianapolis, Indiana, September 3, 1976; admitted to bar, 2001, North Carolina and U.S. District Court, Eastern District of Carolina (Not admitted in District of Columbia). *Education:* University of North Carolina at Chapel Hill (B.A., 1998); Columbia University (J.D., 2001). Author, "Religion in Prisons, Jailhouse Lawyers Manual," Human Rights Law Review. *Member:* North Carolina State Bar. ***PRACTICE AREAS:*** Litigation.

ERIN E. BROPHY, born Chicago, Illinois, September 21, 1976; (admission pending). *Education:* University of Notre Dame (B.A., summa cum laude, 1998); Georgetown University Law Center (J.D., cum laude, 2001). Phi Beta Kappa; Alpha Kappa Delta. ***Email:*** ebrophy@wc.com

OF COUNSEL

VINCENT J. FULLER, born Ossining, New York, June 21, 1931; admitted to bar, 1956, District of Columbia and U.S. Court of Appeals for the District of Columbia; 1957, New York; 1962, U.S. Supreme Court; 1964, U.S. District Court, Southern District of New York; 1965, U.S. Court of Appeals, Second Circuit; 1967, U.S. Court of Appeals, Fifth Circuit; 1969, U.S. Court of Appeals, Sixth Circuit; 1976, U.S. Court of Appeals, Ninth Circuit; 1977, U.S. Court of Appeals, Seventh Circuit. *Education:* Williams College (B.A., 1952); Georgetown University (LL.B., 1956; awarded LL.D., 1988). *Member:* The District of Columbia Bar; Bar Association of the District of Columbia; New York State and American Bar Associations; The Barristers; American Board of Criminal Lawyers. Fellow, American College of Trial Lawyers. ***Email:*** vinful81@msn.com

RAYMOND W. BERGAN, born Pittsburgh, Pennsylvania, May 28, 1930; admitted to bar, 1954, District of Columbia. admitted to bar, 1954, District of Columbia; 1955, U.S. Court of Military Appeals and U.S. Court of Appeals for the District of Columbia Circuit; 1960, U.S. Supreme Court; 1962, U.S. Court of Appeals, Fourth Circuit and U.S. District Court, Northern District of Alabama; 1964, U.S. Court of Appeals, Third Circuit; 1965, U.S. Courts of Appeals, Fifth, Eighth and Ninth Circuits; 1969, U.S. Court of Appeals, Second Circuit; 1971, U.S. Court of Appeals, Sixth Circuit; 1979, U.S. Court of Appeals, Seventh Circuit; 1970, U.S. Tax Court; 1984, U.S. Court of Appeals for the Federal Circuit; 1985, U.S. Court of Appeals, Eleventh Circuit; 1986, U.S. District Court, District of Maryland including Trial Bar; 1990, U.S. District Court, Southern District of Alabama. *Education:* College of the Holy Cross (B.S., 1952); Georgetown Law School (LL.B., 1954). Phi Alpha Delta. Author: The Durham Case, "Mental Cause," as a Criminal Defense, 43 Georgetown Law Journal 58, 1955; "Defending Cases Under the Hobbs and Travel Acts," 2 Criminal Defense Techniques §3500, 1979; "Federal Complicity and Conspiracy Statutes," 6th Annual (Fordham Law School) Corporate Law Institute, 187, 1981; "Thoughts About Closing Argument," 12 Litigation 36, Summer 1986. Member, Board of Trustees, Marymount University, 1988-1997. Member, Board of Directors, Opera Theatre of Northern Virginia, 1999-2001; Member, Board of Directors, Cripple Creek Golf & Country Club, 1997—, Club Secretary, 2000—. Panelist, Commercial Arbitration Panel, American Arbitration Association, 1998-2000. *Member:* The District of Columbia Bar; The Bar Association of the District of Columbia; American Bar Association (Member, Criminal Justice, Labor and Employment Law, Antitrust Law and Litigation Sections); American Judicature Society; Association of Trial Lawyers of America. Fellow, American College of Trial Lawyers. [1st Lt., JAGC, USAR, 1955-1958]. ***PRACTICE AREAS:*** Administrative Litigation; Antitrust and Trade Regulation; Civil Practice; Criminal Law; Automotive Franchises and Dealerships; Franchise Litigation; White Collar Criminal Defense. ***Email:*** rbergan@wc.com

JEREMIAH C. COLLINS, born Newark, New York, August 12, 1929; admitted to bar, 1954, District of Columbia; 1957, New York; 1971, U.S. Supreme Court. *Education:* Georgetown University (B.S., 1951; J.D., 1954). Alpha Sigma Nu; Phi Delta Phi. Adjunct Professor, Georgetown University Law Center: Trial Practice, 1964-1975; Damages and Remedies, 2002—. *Member:* The District of Columbia Bar (Member, Board of Professional Responsibility, 1973-1976); The Bar Association of the District of Columbia; The Lawyers Club (President, 2000); International Association of Insurance Counsel; Practising Law Institute (Member, National Advisory Board, 1969-1973); The Barristers (President, 1977, 1978); The Counsellors. Fellow, American College of Trial Lawyers. ***Email:*** jcollins@wc.com

LYMAN G. FRIEDMAN, born Chicago, Illinois, May 13, 1918; admitted to bar, 1943, Missouri; 1958, District of Columbia. *Education:* Brown University and Washburn University of Topeka (B.A., 1941); Washburn University of Topeka (LL.B., 1943). Office of Regional Counsel, Internal Revenue Service, Cincinnati, Ohio, Attorney, 1950-1958. Acting Assistant Regional Counsel (Appellate), 1957-1958. *Member:* The District of Columbia Bar; Bar Association of the District of Columbia; Federal and American Bar Associations.

COUNSEL

DANIEL J. HURSON, born Boston, Massachusetts, July 14, 1947; admitted to bar, 1972, Maryland; 1973, District of Columbia, U.S. Court of Appeals, Fourth Circuit and U.S. District Court, District of Maryland; 1980, U.S. Supreme Court; 1981, U.S. Court of Appeals, Second Circuit; 1982, U.S. Court of Appeals, Eleventh Circuit; 1992, Texas. *Education:* Georgetown University (A.B., cum laude, 1969); Harvard University (J.D., 1972). Pi Sigma Alpha. Law Clerk, Hon. Harrison L. Winter, U.S. Court of Appeals, Fourth Circuit, 1972. Special Commendation for Outstanding Service, U.S. Department of Justice, 1978; Author: "The Trial of A Highly Publicized Case—A Prosecutor's View," 16 American Criminal Law Review 473, 1979; "Limiting the Mail Fraud Statute—A Legislative Approach," 20 American Criminal Law Review 423, 1983. Adjunct Professor, American University, 1983. Assistant Chief Litigation Counsel, U.S. Securities and Exchange Commission, 1997-2000. Assistant U.S. Attorney, Maryland, 1974-1980. *Member:* Maryland State Bar Association; District of Columbia Bar. ***PRACTICE AREAS:*** SEC Enforcement; White Collar Criminal Defense. ***Email:*** dhurson@wc.com

WILLIAMS & JENSEN

A PROFESSIONAL CORPORATION

Established in 1972

1155 - 21ST STREET, N.W., SUITE 300
3 LAFAYETTE CENTRE
WASHINGTON, D.C. 20036
Telephone: 202-659-8201
Facsimile: 202-659-5249
Email: fd@wms-jen.com

Federal Policy Practice. Congressional, Executive Branch and Administrative Representation, Constitutional and Statutory Construction and Contract Litigation, General Commercial Representation.

FIRM PROFILE: Williams & Jensen, a professional legal corporation, was organized by Messrs. J.D. Williams and Robert E. Jensen in May, 1970. Williams & Jensen currently employs twenty attorneys; eleven are shareholders. Williams & Jensen engages primarily in a federal policy practice which consists principally of representing its clients' interests before the Congress and related administrative agencies. The firm also specializes in federal court litigation relating to constitu-

(This Listing Continued)

WILLIAMS & JENSEN, A PROFESSIONAL CORPORATION, Washington—Continued

tional and statutory construction issues. Williams & Jensen's areas of concentration include securities, antitrust, corporate finance, pension and tax, financial services, pharmaceuticals, biotechnology, health, energy, international trade, agriculture, transportation, environmental, communications and federal election law.

In one capacity or another, Williams & Jensen has appeared before or worked with virtually all federal government agencies and executive branch departments. Williams & Jensen has extensive legislative experience with the Congress.

GEORGE D. BAKER, born New York, N.Y., September 10, 1952; admitted to bar, 1978, New York; 1979, District of Columbia. *Education:* Hamilton College (B.A., 1974); Catholic University (J.D., 1977). Associate Editor, Catholic University Law Review, 1976-1977. Author, "The Entitlements Program," 25 Catholic University Law Review, 1976. Teaching Assistant, Legal Research and Writing, Catholic University Law School, 1976-1977. *Member:* The District of Columbia Bar; American Bar Association (Member, Section on Energy and National Resources). ***PRACTICE AREAS:*** Energy and Environment Law; Agriculture Law; Trade Litigation. ***Email:*** gdbaker@wms-jen.com

PHILIP E. BECHTEL, born Baltimore, Maryland, July 30, 1950; admitted to bar, 1975, Maryland; 1980, District of Columbia. *Education:* Franklin & Marshall College (A.B., 1971); Georgetown University (J.D., 1975). Phi Beta Kappa. Chief Counsel, Senate Banking Committee, 1997-1999; Deputy Staff Director, Senate Banking Committee, 1995-1997; Legislative Director and General Counsel, Senator Alfonse M. D'Amato (R-NY), 1990-1995; Supervisory Trial Attorney, Enforcement, Federal Energy Regulatory Commission, 1987-1990; Director, Administrative Litigation, U.S. Consumer Product Safety Commission, 1982-1987; Attorney, Office of the General Counsel, U.S. Consumer Product Safety Commission, 1975-1982. *Member:* The District of Columbia Bar; Maryland State Bar Association. ***PRACTICE AREAS:*** Financial Institutions; Banking. ***Email:*** pebechtel@wms-jen.com

BARBARA WIXON BONFIGLIO, born Washington, D.C., June 2, 1961; admitted to bar, 1988, Pennsylvania; 1989, District of Columbia and U.S. Supreme Court. *Education:* Frostburg State College; University of Maryland (B.S., 1983); University of Baltimore (J.D., 1987). Deputy Editor-in-Chief, Federal Bar News and Journal, 1992—. *Member:* The District of Columbia Bar (Member, Government Contracts Section); American Bar Association; Boards of Contract Appeals Bar Association (President, 1999-2000; Member, Board of Governors; Chair, Annual Meeting Committee, 1992-1993). ***PRACTICE AREAS:*** Government Contract Law; Administrative Law; Judicial Litigation; Construction Law; Federal and State Election Law. ***Email:*** bwbonfiglio@wms-jen.com

WILLIAM B. CANFIELD, III, born Detroit, Michigan, May 22, 1946; admitted to bar, 1973, Michigan and U.S. District Court, Eastern District of Michigan; 1979, District of Columbia. *Education:* Denison University (B.A., 1968); Michigan State University-Detroit College of Law (J.D., 1973). Counsel, Committee on House Administration, U.S. House of Representatives, 1975-1976. Counsel to the Librarian of Congress, 1976-1978. Counsel, Committee on Ethics, U.S. Senate, 1978-1986. Republican Chief Counsel, Committee on Rules, U.S. Senate, 1987-1989. Chief Counsel, National Republican Senatorial (Campaign) Committee, 1989-1991. Staff Director and Counsel, Republican Conference Secretary, U.S. Senate, 1991-1993. General Counsel, Lugar For President Committee, 1995-1998. General Counsel, Hatch for President Committee, 1999-2000. Co-Author: "Ethics In Government: A View From The Senate," Hofstra Law Review, Vol. 16, No. 2 (Winter, 1988). Member, The Committee for the Study of the American Electorate. *Member:* The District of Columbia Bar; State Bar of Michigan; American Bar Association (Standing Committee on Election Law). [U.S. Army, 1968-1970, Vietnam, 1969-1970, E-5]. ***PRACTICE AREAS:*** Election, Campaign and Political Law; Legislative Practice; Congressional Investigations. ***Email:*** wbcanfield@wms-jen.com

BERTRAM W. CARP, born Los Angeles, California, December 18, 1944; admitted to bar, 1969, California; 1977, District of Columbia; 1984, Massachusetts. *Education:* Stanford University (B.A., 1966; J.D., 1968). Attorney, Office of General Counsel, U.S. Department of Health, Education and Welfare, 1969-1970. Legislative Counsel to U.S. Senator Walter F. Mondale, 1970-1977. Deputy Assistant to the President of the United States for Domestic Affairs and Policy, 1977-1981. *Member:* The District of Columbia Bar; State Bar of California; Massachusetts Bar Association; Federal Communications and American Bar Associations. ***PRACTICE AREAS:*** Communications Law; Federal Legislative Practice. ***Email:*** bwcarp@wms-jen.com

DAVID E. FRANASIAK, born Batavia, New York, August 1, 1951; admitted to bar, 1978, New York and District of Columbia. *Education:* State University of New York at Buffalo (B.A., 1973; M.B.A., J.D., 1978). Former Staff Director, House Small Business Tax Subcommittee, 1979-1981. *Member:* District of Columbia Bar; New York State and American Bar Associations. ***PRACTICE AREAS:*** Federal Tax Policy; Tax Law; Environmental; Energy; Securities Law; Financial Institutions and Banking. ***Email:*** defranasiak@wms-jen.com

ROBERT E. GLENNON, JR., born Decatur, Illinois, April 23, 1948; admitted to bar, 1974, Florida; 1975, U.S. Tax Court; 1977, District of Columbia. *Education:* University of Illinois (B.S., 1971); University of Florida (J.D., 1974; LL.M. in Taxation, 1975). Instructor of Law, University of Florida College of Law, 1975-1976. *Member:* The District of Columbia Bar; The Florida Bar; American Bar Association. [Capt., USAR, 1971-1979]. ***PRACTICE AREAS:*** Federal Tax Policy; Tax Law; Financial Institutions and Banking. ***Email:*** reglennon@wms-jen.com

J. STEVEN HART, born Quantico, Virginia, November 29, 1953; admitted to bar, 1979, District of Columbia. *Education:* Oklahoma University (B.B.A., magna cum laude, 1976); Georgetown University (J.D., magna cum laude, 1979). Beta Gamma Sigma; Phi Delta Phi. Certified Public Accountant, Oklahoma, 1976. Assistant to the Chairman of the President's Task Force on ERISA Reorganization, Office of Management and Budget, 1978-1979. Special Assistant to the Assistant Attorney General for Legal Policy, Department of Justice, 1981-1983. 1999 Arthur Bartelo Fellow in Business Administration at the Michael C. Price School of Business Administration. *Member:* The District of Columbia Bar; American Bar Association. ***PRACTICE AREAS:*** Transportation Law; Labor & Employee Benefits; Communications.

CAROLE L. KUEBLER (1948-1979).

KAREN JUDD LEWIS, born Palo Alto, California, November 28, 1957; admitted to bar, 1989, Oregon; 1990, District of Columbia. *Education:* Mills College (B.A., 1980); Northwestern School of Law, Lewis & Clark College (J.D., 1988). Associate Editor, Environmental Law Review, 1987-1988. *Member:* The District of Columbia Bar; Oregon State Bar. ***PRACTICE AREAS:*** Transportation Law; Health Law. ***Email:*** kjlewis@wms-jen.com

ROBERT J. MARTINEZ, born Albuquerque, New Mexico, August 7, 1953; admitted to bar, 1979, District of Columbia; 1981, U.S. Claims Court; 1982, U.S. Court of Appeals for the Federal Circuit. *Education:* Princeton University (B.S.E., Civil Engineering, 1975); Georgetown University (J.D., 1979). Phi Delta Phi (Exchequer, 1978-1979). *Member:* The District of Columbia Bar; Federal and American (Member, Sections on: Administrative Law; Public Contract Law Section) Bar Associations. ***Email:*** rjmartinez@wms-jen.com

JOHN J. McMACKIN, JR., born Brockway, Pennsylvania, January 10, 1952; admitted to bar, 1977, Pennsylvania; 1979, District of Columbia. *Education:* University of Notre Dame (B.A., 1974); Yale University (J.D., 1977). Phi Beta Kappa. *Member:* The District of Columbia Bar. ***Email:*** jjmcmackin@wms-jen.com

GEORGE G. OLSEN, born Springfield, Massachusetts, September 10, 1950; admitted to bar, 1975, District of Columbia, U.S. Supreme Court, U.S. Court of Appeals for the District of Columbia, Fourth, Fifth and Federal Circuits, U.S. Claims Court, U.S. Temporary Emergency Court of Appeals and U.S. Court of Veterans Appeals. *Education:* Saint Anselm College (B.A., magna cum laude, 1972); George Washington University (J.D., with honors, 1975). Former Member, Rules Advisory Committee of the United States Court of Veterans Appeals. *Member:* The District of Columbia Bar; The Bar Association of the District of Columbia; American Bar Association (Member, Section on Antitrust Law); National Health Lawyers Association; Association of Hospital Attorneys. ***PRACTICE AREAS:*** Health Care; Pharmaceuticals; Managed Care; Medicare and Medicaid; Administrative Litigation; Antitrust and Trade Regulation; Biotechnology; Genetics. ***Email:*** ggolsen@wms-jen.com

ANTHONY J. RODA, born Stamford, Connecticut, March 31, 1961; admitted to bar, 1990, Virginia; 1991, District of Columbia. *Education:* University of London, London, England; University of Maryland (B.A., 1983); Catholic University of America (J.D., 1989); Georgetown University Law Center (LL.M., Tax, 1995). Legislative Assistant, 1983-1984, Legislative Director, 1985-1986, U.S. Representative Stewart McKinney. Legislative Director, U.S. Representative Steve Gunderson, 1987-1988. Director of Legislative Strategy, House Republican Whip Newt Gingrich, 1989-1992. *Member:* Virginia State Bar; District of Columbia Bar; U.S. Supreme Court Bar. ***PRACTICE AREAS:*** Intellectual Property; Bankruptcy; Antitrust; Trade; Taxation; Labor. ***Email:*** ajroda@wms-jen.com

DAVID A. STARR, born Flemington, New Jersey, June 16, 1958; admitted to bar, 1981, District of Columbia. *Education:* Miami University (A.B., 1978); Washington University (J.D., 1981). Order of the Coif. Senior Editor, Washington University Law Review, 1980-1981. Legislative Director to Senator Howard Metzenbaum, 1981-1988. Instructor, National Institute on Employee Benefits in Bankruptcy, 1988-1989. *Member:* The District of Columbia Bar; American Bar Association. ***Email:*** dastarr@wms-jen.com

JEFFREY A. TASSEY, born Annapolis, Maryland, July 1, 1953; admitted to bar, 1980, District of Columbia. *Education:* College of Wooster (B.A., 1974); Washington University School of Law (J.D., 1978). Member, The Urban Law Annual Law Review. Staff Counsel, Hon. Doug Barnard, Jr., (D-GA) 1985-

(This Listing Continued)

1990. Counsel, Subcommittee on Commerce, Consumer and Monetary Affairs, House Committee on Government Operations, 1990-1992. Executive Vice President, Legal and Government Affairs, The American Financial Services Association, 1993-2000. ***PRACTICE AREAS:*** Legislative Practice; Financial Services Law; Bankruptcy. ***Email:*** jatassey@wms-jen.com

J. D. WILLIAMS, born Cooke County, Texas, December 2, 1937; admitted to bar, 1962, Oklahoma and District of Columbia. *Education:* University of Oklahoma (B.B.A., 1959); George Washington University (J.D., 1962); Georgetown University (LL.M., in Taxation, 1965). Order of the Coif; Beta Gamma Sigma; Omicron Delta Kappa; Phi Alpha Delta. Member, Board of Student Editors, George Washington Law Review, 1960-1961. Assistant to Senator Robert S. Kerr, 1959-1961. Managing Editor, Federal Bar Journal, 1963-1964. *Member:* The District of Columbia Bar; The Bar Association of the District of Columbia; American Bar Association. [Capt., JAGC, USAR, active duty, 1962-1965]. ***PRACTICE AREAS:*** Federal Legislative and Policy Matters.

TRACY DOHERTY TAYLOR, born Richmond, California, July 7, 1963; admitted to bar, 1996, California; 1998, District of Columbia. *Education:* University of California at Berkeley (B.A., 1985): George Washington University (J.D., 1996). *Member:* State Bar of California; The District of Columbia Bar. ***PRACTICE AREAS:*** Telecommunications Law; Technology Law. ***Email:*** tdtaylor@wms-jen.com

DAVID MICHAEL LANDERS, born Ann Arbor, Michigan, February 23, 1962; admitted to bar, 1995, Maryland; 1997, District of Columbia. *Education:* Duke University (B.A., 1988); George Mason University School of Law (J.D., 1993). Associate Member, George Mason University Civil Rights Law Journal, 1992-1993. Legislative Assistant, Representative Elton Gallegly (R-CA), 1994. Banking Counsel, Representative Fred Heineman (R-NC), 1995-1996. Legislative Counsel, Senator Launch Faircloth (R-NC), 1997-1998. *Member:* The District of Columbia Bar; Maryland State Bar Association. ***Email:*** dmlanders@wms-jen.com

KARINA V. LYNCH, born Manhasset, New York, June 15, 1973; admitted to bar, 1999, Connecticut and New York (Not admitted in District of Columbia). *Education:* Hofstra University (B.A., 1995); Washington College of Law of American University (J.D., 1998). Member, Labor Law Journal. Research Assistant, 1996-1997 and Investigative Counsel, 1997-1999, U.S. Senate Special Committee on Aging. Counsel, U.S. Senate Committee on Governmental Affairs, Permanent Subcommittee on Investigations, 1999-2000. ***PRACTICE AREAS:*** Health Care; Pharmacy Law; Administrative Law; Antitrust. ***Email:*** kvlynch@wms-jen.com

ARSHI SIDDIQUI, born Sacramento, California, July 22, 1972; (admission pending). *Education:* University of California, Davis (B.A., 1994); Georgetown University Law Center (J.D., 1997). Ways and Means Counsel, Congressman Xavier Becerra, 1998-2001. Legislative Assistant, Congresswoman Eva Clayton, 1997-1998. ***PRACTICE AREAS:*** Legislative Practice; Taxation; Trade; Communications Law. ***Email:*** asiddiqui@wms-jen.com

FRANK C. VLOSSAK, born Lewiston, New York, August 14, 1967; admitted to bar, 1999, Virginia (Not admitted in District of Columbia). *Education:* Hamilton College (B.A., 1989); George Mason University (J.D., 1999). Legislative Assistant, Representative Merrill Cook (R-UT), 1997-1998. ***PRACTICE AREAS:*** Legislative Practice; Energy; Environmental Law; Transportation. ***Email:*** fcvlossak@wms-jen.com

OF COUNSEL

ROBERT E. JENSEN, born South Bend, Indiana, January 23, 1938; admitted to bar, 1966, Virginia and District of Columbia; 1974, U.S. Supreme Court. *Education:* Miami University, Oxford, Ohio (B.S., 1960); George Washington University (LL.B., 1966). Omicron Delta Kappa; Order of the Coif. Associate Editor, George Washington Law Review, 1965-1966. *Member:* The District of Columbia Bar; The Bar Association of the District of Columbia; Virginia State Bar; American Bar Association.

WILLIAMS MULLEN

Established in 1909

1666 K STREET, NW

SUITE 1200

WASHINGTON, D.C. 20006

Telephone: 202-833-9200

Fax: 202-293-5939

URL: http://www.williamsmullen.com

Richmond Office: Two James Center, 1021 East Cary Street. P.O. Box 1320, 23218-1320. Telephone: 804-643-1991. Fax: 804-783-6507.

Charlottesville, Virginia Office: Enterprise Center, 401 East Market Street, Suite 101, 22902-5264. Telephone: 434-851-5700. Fax: 434-783-6507. Fax within area: 434-817-0977.

(This Listing Continued)

London, England Office: 2 Old Garden House, The Lanterns, Bridge Lane, London SW 11 3AD. Telephone: (011-44-71) 223-2765. Fax: (011-44-71) 350-0156.

Newport News Office: Harbor Bank Center, Suite 210, One Old Oyster Point Road, 23602-7119. Telephone: 757-249-5100. Fax: 757-249-5109.

Northern Virginia Office: 8270 Greensboro Drive, Suite 700, McLean, Virginia, 22102. Telephone: 703-760-5200. Fax: 804-783-6568. Fax within area: 703-748-0244.

Virginia Beach Office: One Columbus Center, Suite 900, 23462-6762. Telephone: 757-499-8800. Fax: 757-473-0395.

Detroit, Michigan Office: 11th Floor Buhl Building, 535 Griswold Street, 48226-3681. Telephone: 313-962-0643. Fax: 313-962-0688.

Ann Arbor, Michigan Office: 300 North Fifth Avenue, Suite 230, 48104. Telephone: 734-213-2700. Fax: 734-213-6832.

Bloomfield Hills, Michigan Office: 33 Bloomfield Hills Parkway, Suite 100, 48304. Telephone: 248-642-4345. Fax: 248-642-2005.

Antitrust, Business Law, Commercial Banking and Finance, Communications, Creditor's Rights and Bankruptcy, E-Commerce, Employee Benefits, Energy, Environmental, Estate Planning and Administration, Franchise, Government Contracts, Governmental Affairs, Health Care, Immigration, International, Labor and Employment, Litigation, Maritime, Mergers and Acquisitions, Mortgage Banking, Real Estate, Securities, Tax, and Technology and Intellectual Property.

FIRM PROFILE: Williams Mullen provides comprehensive legal services to regional, national and international business clients. With 230 attorneys and offices in Virginia, Washington, D.C., Michigan and London, we deliver innovative solutions to support our clients' diverse business activities. Attention to clients' individualized needs and an extensive application of new technology and legal information services have been the foundation of Williams Mullen's progressive approach to law practice since the firm was founded more than 90 years ago.

LEWIS C. WILLIAMS (1875-1959).

JAMES MULLEN

JAMES R. CANNON, JR., born Newport, Rhode Island, October 8, 1957; admitted to bar, 1982, District of Columbia; 1983, U.S. Court of International Trade; 1985, U.S. Court of Appeals for the Federal Circuit. *Education:* University of Virginia (B.A., 1979); American University (J.D., 1982). Echols Scholar. Author: "Binational Panel Dispute Settlement Under Article 1904 of the United States-Canada Free Trade Agreement: A Procedural Comparison with the United States Court of International Trade," 22 Law & Pol'y Int'l Bus. 689, 1991; "Material Injury and the Business Cycle in Antidumping and Countervailing Duty Cases," 14 B.C. Int'l & Comp. L. Rev. 53, 1991; "Should the Federal Circuit Take a 'Hard Look ' at International Trade Cases in the 1990's?" 40 Am. U.L. Rev. 1093, 1991; Simplification of Antidumping Actions: Efficiency at What Price?" Vol. 25, Law & Pol'y Int'l Bus., 1993; "Resolving Disputes Under NAFTA Chapter 19," Shepard's/McGraw-Hill, Inc., 1994; "NAFTA Dispute Resolution Provisions Applicable to Environmental Disputes in Agricultural Trade," presented at the 16th Annual Educational Conf., Am. Ag. Law Assn. (Nov. 3-4, 1995); "Dispute Settlement in Antidumping and Countervailing Duty Cases," The World Trade Organizations Multilateral Framework for the 21st Century and U.S. Implementing Legislation, ABA, 1996. Co-Author: with T. P. Stewart, E. P. Salonen and D. R. Nuxoll, "Trade and Cattle: How the System is Failing an Industry in Crisis," 9 Minnesota Journal of Gloval Trade, No.2, Summer 2000; "GATT Panels Need Restraining Principles," 26 Law & Pol'y Intl. Bus., 1993; "Forum: Binational Dispute Resolution Procedures Under the Canada-United States Free Trade Agreement—Experiences to Date and Portents for the Future," Washington, D.C., April 23, 1991, 24 N.Y.U. J. Intl. L. & Pol. 341, 1991; "Trade and Cattle: How the System is Failing an Industry in Crisis," 9 Minn. J. Global Trade 449, 2000. *Member:* The District of Columbia Bar; American Bar Association (Member, Sections on: International and Administrative Law; Committee on International Trade Regulation); Federal Circuit Bar Association; Customs and International Trade Bar Association (Board of Directors, 2000). ***PRACTICE AREAS:*** Civil Litigation; Administrative; Trade Regulation; Antidumping; Customs Law; International Trade; International Trade Regulation; Import and Export Law; Export Regulation; North American Free Trade Agreement; Sanctions; Subsidies and Countervailing Duties; World Trade Organization (WTO). ***Email:*** jcannon@williamsmullen.com

STUART G. CHRISTIAN (1883-1967).

FRANCIS T. COLEMAN, born Washington, D.C., April 26, 1939; admitted to bar, 1965, District of Columbia; 1968, Maryland. *Education:* Georgetown University (A.B., 1961; J.D., 1964; LL.M., 1970). Member, Georgetown University Law Journal, 1963-1964. Recipient: J.F.K. Labor Law Award. Instructor, Labor Law, Georgetown Law Center, 1971-1980. Chairman, CUE Labor Lawyers Advisory Committee, 1984-1985; Chairman, ASAE Legal Section, 1993-1994. Member, American Employment Lawyers Council, 1992-1999. Member, College of Employment and Labor Lawyers, 1998-1999. *Member:* The District of Columbia Bar; Maryland State and American Bar Associations. [JAG, USMC, 1964-1967]. ***PRACTICE AREAS:*** Arbitration; Collective Bargaining;

(This Listing Continued)

WILLIAMS MULLEN, Washington—Continued

Discrimination; Employer Liability; Employment at Will; Employment Rights; Employment Termination; EEO; Executive Employment; Labor Relations; Management Labor Law; Sexual Harassment; Union Labor Law; Wage and Hour Law; Wrongful Terminations. ***Email:*** tcoleman@williamsmullen.com

MICHAEL R. GEROE, born Los Angeles, California, April 12, 1968; admitted to bar, 1994, California, District of Columbia, New York, U.S. Court of Appeals, Federal Circuit and U.S. Court of International Trade; 2000, U.S. Supreme Court. *Education:* University of California at Berkeley; Georgetown University (B.S.F.S., summa cum laude, 1990); Columbia University (J.D., 1993). Phi Beta Kappa; Alpha Epsilon Pi. Foreign Language Area Studies Fellow. Articles Editor, Columbia Journal of Transnational Law, 1992-1993. Author: "CVD Law from the General to the Specific: Some of the Significant Issues and Developments," Georgetown U. Law Center CLE Annual Int'l Trade Update, 1994; "Hungary and a New Paradigm for the Protection of Ethnic Minorities in Central and Eastern Europe," 32 Columbia Journal of Transnational Law 673 (1995); "The Uruguay Round and the Weakening of U.S. Countervailing Duty Law," Amer. Conf. Institute, 1995; "NATO Should Look East Before It Leaps," 24 ABA Int'l Law News 1 (Summer 1995); "Preparing for '96: A Guide to Federal Election Campaign Law Compliance for Corporations and Individuals," December 1995; "The Lobbying Disclosure Act of 1995: Pre- and Post-Employment Restrictions on the USTR and DUSTR," 25 ABA Int'l Law News 1 (Summer 1996); "Complying with U.S. Antibribery Laws," 31 Int'l Lawyer 1037 (Winter 1997); "Document Retention and Destruction: Recent Developments," ALI/ABA Course of Study: Litigation Techniques in Federal and State Courts, Phil. December 1999. Organizer and Moderator: Panel on the Partnership for Peace, American Bar Association, 1994; Panel on Representing Foreign Clients in the U.S., American Bar Association, 1997. Associate Councillor and Councillor, The Atlantic Council of the United States, 1994-2001. Commissioner, Advisory Neighborhood Commission of the District of Columbia, 1995-1997. Member, Board of Advisors, Axsysnet, Inc., 1997-2001. *Member:* New York State and American (Member, International Law Section, 1994-2001) Bar Associations; State Bar of California; The District of Columbia Bar; Bar Association of the District of Columbia (Member, Board of Directors, Young Lawyers Section, 1996-2001; Member, Steering Committee, 1996-2001 and Treasurer, 1999, Operation Crackdown; Vice-Chairman, Corporate Law Committee, 2000-2001). ***LANGUAGES:*** Hungarian. ***PRACTICE AREAS:*** International Business Law; Corporate Law; Export Regulation; Antitrust. ***Email:*** mgeroe@williamsmullen.com

THOMAS B. McVEY, born Queens, New York, July 28, 1954; admitted to bar, 1980, New York and U.S. District Court, Southern and Eastern Districts of New York; 1981, District of Columbia; 1987, U.S. Supreme Court and U.S. Court of International Trade. *Education:* Columbia University (B.A., 1976); Georgetown University (J.D., 1979). Recipient, Caroline Phelps Stokes Award from Columbia College. Member, U.S. Delegation to the United Nations Commission on International Trade (UNCITRAL), 23rd Plenary Session, 1990-1992. Author: "Countertrade: Business Practices, Legal Issues and Policy Dilemmas," 16 Law and Policy in International Business p.1, 1984; "Exxon-Florio-Regulation of Foreign Investment In The United States"; "Washington Watch," and "World Watch," for International Executive, published by the American Management Association. Co-author: "An Overview of the U.S. Export Control Laws," The Lawyers Brief, 1985. Editor: International Trade Reference Handbook, published by International Trade Association of Northern Virginia, 1983; The International Executive's Guidebook to Washington. Lecturer: International Law Institute of Georgetown University, 1985; American Management Association; World Trade Institute; American Association of Exporters and Importers. Member, Board of Directors (Ex Oficio), Virginia State Bar International Practice Section. Member, Board of Directors, Washington International Trade Association, 1983-1986. Consulting Expert to the Group of Thirty on the Group's Study on Countertrade and Contributing Author to Group's Report "Countertrade in the World Economy," 1985. Founding Director, Washington International Trade Association, 1982. *Member:* The District of Columbia Bar; American Bar Association (Member, Section on International Law and Practice) Bar Associations. ***PRACTICE AREAS:*** International Business; Corporate Law; Finance Law; Banking Law. ***Email:*** tmcvey@williamsmullen.com

WARREN E. NOWLIN, born Lynchburg, Virginia, February 18, 1956; admitted to bar, 1984, Virginia; 1988, District of Columbia; 1994, Maryland. *Education:* University of Virginia (B.S., 1978); Washington & Lee University (J.D., magna cum laude, 1984). Order of the Coif; Phi Delta Phi. Recipient, Prentice Hall, Inc., Taxation Award, Washington & Lee University, 1984. *Member:* The District of Columbia Bar (Member: Business Law Section; Corporation, Finance and Securities Law Section); Virginia State Bar (Member, Business Law Section); Maryland State and American (Member, Section on Business Law) Bar Associations. ***LANGUAGES:*** German. ***PRACTICE AREAS:*** Corporate; Securities; Mergers and Acquisitions; Banking; Venture Capital. ***Email:*** wnowlin@williamsmullen.com

(This Listing Continued)

JIMMIE V. REYNA, born Tucumcari, New Mexico, November 11, 1952; admitted to bar, 1979, New Mexico; 1980, U.S. District Court, District of New Mexico; 1983, U.S. Court of Appeals, Tenth Circuit; 1987, U.S. Court of International Trade; 1989, U.S. Court of Appeals for the Federal Circuit; 1994, District of Columbia. *Education:* University of Rochester (B.A., 1975); University of New Mexico (J.D., 1978). Recipient: Lifetime Honorary Membership, Society of Hispanic Professional Engineers, New Mexico Chapter, 1982; Spirit of Excellence Award, Albuquerque Hispano Chamber of Commerce, 1985; Distinguished Citizen Award, Military Airlift Command, United States Air Force, 1986. Author: *The Role of Certain Consultative and Bilateral Arrangements Between The U.S. and Mexico As A Foundation For Free Trade Negotiations,* (United States and Mexico Business Conference, 1990); *NAFTA Safeguards:* Providing Temporary Relief from Increased Imports, in "The North American Free Trade Agreement: Issues, Options and Implications," 94 (Baker and Bialos, ed. 1992, ABA); *Developing International Markets:* Expanding Production to Other Countries, in "Helping Your Virginia Client Go International," IVB 1 (Fourth Annual International Law Seminar, Virginia CLE, Virginia Law Foundation), 1992; *A Preliminary Review of the NAFTA Rules of Origin,* 1 U.S.-Mex. L.J. 127, 1993; *Trade Treaties; Regulation of Trade Through Trade Agreements*, in Export Practice, Customs and International Trade Law, Practising Law Institute (1994); "The GATT Uruguay Round: A Negotiating History (1986-1992) Services," Kluwer Law & Taxation Publishers, 1993; "Passport to North American Trade: Rules of Origin and Customs Procedure Under NAFTA," Shepard's/McGraw-Hill Inc., 1995; *NAFTA Chapter 19 Binational Panel Reviews in Mexico:* A Marriage of Two Distinct Legal Systems, U.S. Mexico Law Journal, Vol. 5, 1997; WTO Negotiations on Maritime Transport Services: A Survey of Issues and Implications (Admiralty and Trade Issues in the New Millenium, Maritime Law: International Trade Society, Regent University, April 2000). President, Albuquerque Hispano Chamber of Commerce, 1984; National Security Forum, Maxwell Air Force Base, 1986; Delegate: ABA ILEX Briefing Delegation, "Mexico's New Foreign Investment Regulations," 1990. Board of Directors, Community Services for Autistic Adults and Children, 1988—. Board of Directors, U.S. Mexico Law Institute, 1993—. Member, U.S. roster of panelists for NAFTA Chapter 19 trade disputes; (U.S.) Member of World Trade Organization indicative list of non-governmental panel candidates for dispute settlement, trade in goods and trade in services. (WTO, GATT, GATS), 1994—. Member: National Hispanic Bar Association, 1998—; Customs and International Trade Bar Association, 1998—. *Member:* State Bar of New Mexico; American Bar Association (Chairman, 1993-1994; Vice-Chairman, 1991-1993, Mexican Law Committee, International Law and Practice Section; Chairman, Subcommittee on U.S.- Mexico Foreign Trade, 1994—. Co-Chair, MERCOSUR Subcommittee, International Committee, ABA Section on Dispute Resolution. ***LANGUAGES:*** Spanish. ***PRACTICE AREAS:*** International Trade; International Trade Regulations; International Trade Agreements; Import and Export Law; Antidumping; Export Regulation; World Trade Organization (WTO); North American Free Trade Agreement; Latin America Trade; Pacific Rim Trade; Investment; Customs Law. ***Email:*** jreyna@williamsmullen.com

ROBERT F. RILEY, born Cleveland, Ohio, October 4, 1957; admitted to bar, 1985, Ohio; 1987, District of Columbia, U.S. Court of Appeals for the District of Columbia Circuit and U.S. Court of Appeals, Fifth Circuit; 1991, Virginia. *Education:* Saint Louis University (B.A., 1979); Case Western Reserve University (J.D., 1985). Recipient, International Academy of Trial Lawyers Advocacy Award. Trial Attorney, Federal Energy Regulatory Commission 1985-1986. *Member:* Energy Bar Association (Chair, Generation and Power Marketing Committee). ***PRACTICE AREAS:*** Energy; Legislative Practice; Regulatory Law. ***Email:*** rriley@williamsmullen.com

ROBERT D. ROSEMAN, born Boston, Massachusetts, December 9, 1947; admitted to bar, 1972, Maryland; 1975, U.S. District Court, District of Maryland; 1977, U.S. Court of Appeals, Fourth Circuit Court and U.S. Supreme Court; 1980, District of Columbia. *Education:* Boston University (B.A., 1969); George Washington University (J.D., 1972). *Member:* Montgomery County and Maryland State Bar Associations; District of Columbia Bar. ***PRACTICE AREAS:*** Real Estate; Finance; Business; Corporate Transactional. ***Email:*** broseman@williamsmullen.com

---

JULIA K. BAILEY, born Oklahoma City, Oklahoma, February 17, 1964; admitted to bar, 1996, Maryland; 2000, District of Columbia. *Education:* Southern Methodist University (B.A., Business, 1986); University of Arkansas (J.D., 1993); Georgetown University (M.B.A., 1995). *Member:* American Bar Association (Member, International Law Section). ***LANGUAGES:*** Spanish. ***PRACTICE AREAS:*** International Business Transactions; International Trade; Customs Law; Export Regulation; International Anti-Corruption; International Government Relations. ***Email:*** jbailey@williamsmullen.com

KAREN A. DONER, born Montreal, Canada, 1971; admitted to bar, 1997, Virginia, U.S. District Court, Eastern District of Virginia, U.S. District Court, District of Columbia and U.S. Court of Appeals, Fourth Circuit; 1998, District of Columbia; 1999, Maryland. *Education:* University of Delaware (B.A., 1993);

(This Listing Continued)

Loyola University, Chicago (J.D., 1996). *Member:* Virginia State Bar. ***PRACTICE AREAS:*** Labor and Employment; Commercial Litigation. ***Email:*** kdoner@williamsmullen.com

JOELLE KAY OGG, born Lakeland, Florida, September 12, 1972; admitted to bar, 1997, Maryland; 2000, District of Columbia. *Education:* Wellesley College (B.A., cum laude, 1994); George Washington University (J.D., with honors, 1997). *Member:* The District of Columbia Bar; Maryland State and American (Member, Executive Committee, Public Utilities, Transportation and Telecommunications Committee, Young Lawyers Division) Bar Associations. ***PRACTICE AREAS:*** Energy Law. ***Email:*** jogg@williamsmullen.com

WILLIAM E. POMERANZ, born San Francisco, California, U.S.A., January 19, 1960; admitted to bar, 1998, Maryland; 2001, District of Columbia. *Education:* Haverford College (B.A., 1982); University of London (Ph.D., 1990); American University (J.D., 1998). Author: "The Russian Constitutional Courts Interpretation of Federalism," Parker School Journal of East European Law, No. 4, 1997. ***LANGUAGES:*** Russian. ***PRACTICE AREAS:*** International Law; Commercial Law; E-Commerce; Corporate; Russian Law. ***Email:*** wpomeranz@williamsmullen.com

(For Biographical data on all Personnel, see Professional Biographies at Richmond, Virginia)

PETER C. WILLIAMS

WASHINGTON, D.C.

(See Alexandria, Virginia)

Banking, Electronic Banking, Mortgage Banking, Electronic Commerce, Commercial Transactions, Creditor's Rights and Real Estate. Commercial Mediation.

WILLKIE FARR & GALLAGHER

THREE LAFAYETTE CENTRE
1155 21ST STREET, N.W.
WASHINGTON, D.C. 20036-3384
Telephone: 202-328-8000
Fax: 202-887-8979

New York, N.Y. Office: Willkie Farr & Gallagher, The Equitable Center, 787 Seventh Avenue, 10019-6099. Telephone: 212-728-8000. Fax: 212-728-8111.

Washington, D.C. Office: Willkie Farr & Gallagher, Three Lafayette Centre, 1155 21st Street, N.W., 20036-3384. Telephone: 202-328-8000. Fax: 202-887-8979; 202-331-8187.

Paris, France Office: Willkie Farr & Gallagher, 21-23 rue de la Ville l'Evêque, 75008. Telephone: 011-33-1-53-43-45-00. Fax: 011-33-1-40-06-96-06.

London, England Office: Willkie Farr & Gallagher, 35 Wilson Street, EC2M 2SJ. Telephone: 011-44-171-696-9060. Fax: 011-44-171-417-9191.

Frankfurt, Germany Office: Willkie Farr & Gallagher, Senckenberganlage 16, D-60325, Frankfurt am Main. Telephone: +49 69 79302 0. Fax: +49 69 79302 222.

Milan, Italy Office: Studio Legale Delfino & Associati - Willkie Farr & Gallagher, Via Michele Barozzi, 2, 20122. Telephone: 001 39 02 76363 1. Fax: 011 39 02 76363 636.

Rome, Italy Office: Studio Legale Delfino & Associati - Willkie Farr & Gallagher, Via di Ripetta, 142, 00186. Telephone: +39 06 68 63 64 03. Fax: +39 06 68 63 63 63.

General Practice.

RESIDENT MEMBERS

WILLIAM H. BARRINGER, born Washington, D.C., December 3, 1948; admitted to bar, 1973, District of Columbia. *Education:* Brown University (A.B., 1970); Georgetown University (J.D., 1973; LL.M., 1976). Author: "Section 337: A Case For Repeal Or Change," 8 Georgia Journal of International and Comparative Law, 1978; "Legal Aspects of Foreign Direct Investment In Developing Countries," A Lawyers Guide To International Business Transactions, ALI/ABA, 1980; "Antidumping and Countervailing Duty Investigations Under the Trade Agreements Act of 1979," 14 Journal of International Law and Economics, 1980; "The Defense of Antidumping and Countervailing Duty Investigations Under the Trade Agreements Act of 1979," 6 North Carolina Journal of International Law & Commercial Regulation, 1981; "Out Of Focus: The Use Of Section 301 To Address Anticompetitive Practices In Foreign Markets," UCLA Journal of International Law and Foreign Affairs, 1996; "Competition Policy and Cross Border Dispute Resolution: Lessons Learned from the U.S.-Japan Film Dispute," 6 George Mason Law Review, 1998; "Paying the Price for Big Steel: 100 Billion in Trade Restraints and Corporate Welfare," American Institute for Imported Steel 2000. Schulte Zur Hausen Fellow, Institute for International and Foreign Trade Law, Georgetown University and Frankfurt University, Germany, 1973-1975. Executive Director, Investment Negotiation Center, Institute for International and Foreign Trade Law, Georgetown University Law Center, 1975-1976. *Member:* The District of Columbia Bar; Bar Association of the District of Columbia; American Bar Association. ***Email:*** wbarringer@willkie.com

STEPHEN R. BELL, born Menominee, Michigan, 1942; admitted to bar, 1967, Wisconsin and Minnesota; 1971, District of Columbia. *Education:* Georgetown University (A.B., 1964); University of Wisconsin (J.D., 1967). Order of the Coif; Phi Delta Phi. Member, 1965-1967 and Note Editor, 1966-1967, Wisconsin Law Review. *Member:* The District of Columbia Bar; State Bar of Wisconsin; American Bar Association; Federal Communications Bar Association; Computer Law Association. ***Email:*** sbell@willkie.com

SUE D. BLUMENFELD, born New York, N.Y., November 5, 1952; admitted to bar, 1977, New Jersey; 1981, District of Columbia. *Education:* State University of New York at Binghamton (B.A., 1974); Rutgers University at Camden (J.D., with high honors, 1977). Member, 1975-1976 and Notes and Comment Editor, 1976-1977, Rutgers-Camden Law Journal. Attorney, Bureau of Competition, Federal Trade Commission, 1977-1979. Special Assistant to the Chief, Common Carrier Bureau, Federal Communications Commission, 1979-1981. *Member:* The District of Columbia Bar; Federal Communications Bar Association. ***Email:*** sblumenfeld@willkie.com

FRANCIS M. BUONO, born Flushing, New York, March 31, 1965; admitted to bar, 1992, Virginia; 1993, District of Columbia. *Education:* Georgetown University (B.A., summa cum laude, 1987; J.D., magna cum laude, 1992). Phi Beta Kappa. Author: "The Hype Over Hyperlinked Terms of Service -- They Are Likely Unenforceable," E-Commerce Law Report, January 2001. Co-Author: "Maximizing the Enforceability of Click-Wrap Agreements," E-Commerce Law Report November 1999, and also published in the Journal of Technology Law and Policy, Spring 2000; "Limiting Tort Liability for Online Third-Party Content Under Section 230 of the Communications Act," Federal Communications Law Journal, May 2000; "Using the Digital Millennium Copyright Act to Limit Potential Copyright Liability Online," Richmond Journal of Law & Technology, Winter 1999-2000; "Emerging Issues in Internet Law," WFG September 1999. Board Member, Executive Committee, United Way of the National Capital Area, Law Firms Division, 1995-1998. *Member:* Virginia and American Bar Associations; Federal Communications Bar Association. ***PRACTICE AREAS:*** Telecommunications Law; Internet Law; Intellectual Property Licensing. ***Email:*** fbuono@willkie.com

KEVIN B. CLARK, born Warren, Pennsylvania, October 20, 1954; admitted to bar, 1979, District of Columbia; 1988, New York. *Education:* Georgetown University (B.A., magna cum laude, 1976; J.D., 1979). Phi Beta Kappa; Alpha Sigma Nu. Lambert Spronck Medalist. Articles Editor, American Criminal Law Review, 1978-1979. *Member:* The District of Columbia Bar; New York State and American Bar Associations. ***Email:*** kclark@willkie.com

CHRISTOPHER A. DUNN, born Maracaibo, Venezuela, June 1, 1951; admitted to bar, 1975, District of Columbia. *Education:* Brown University (A.B., 1972); Georgetown University (J.D., 1975). Student Editor-in-Chief, The Tax Lawyer 1974-1975. Co-Author: "Trade Agreement Program of the United States," A Lawyer's Guide to International Business Transactions, 1977; "The Buy American Act and Other Buy National Programs," A Lawyer's Guide to International Business Transactions, 1977; "Antidumping and Countervailing Duty Investigations Under the Trade Agreements Act of 1979," 14 George Washington Journal of Law and Economics, 1979; "Revocation of Antidumping Duty Orders," International Trade Policy: The Lawyer's Perspective, 1985; "International Trade Practice," International Business & Law. Law Clerk: Trial Division, U.S. Court of Claims, 1975-1976; Chief Judge Wilson Cowen, U.S. Court of Appeals for the Federal Circuit, 1976-1977. *Member:* Bar Association of the District of Columbia. ***Email:*** cdunn@willkie.com

JAMES P. DURLING, born Norwalk, Connecticut, October 30, 1958; admitted to bar, 1984, District of Columbia. *Education:* Haverford College (B.A., 1980); Princeton University (M.P.A., 1984); New York University (J.D., 1984). Phi Beta Kappa. Articles Editor, NYU Law Review, 1983-1984. National Finalist, Craven Moot Court Competition. Author: "International Trade Issues Affecting Japanese Investment in the Newly Industrializing Countries of Asia," 18 Kokusai Shooji Hoomu 975, 1990; "Out Of Focus: The Use Of Section 301 To Address Anticompetitive Practices In Foreign Markets," UCLA Journal of International Law and Foreign Affairs, 1996; "Transfer Pricing Quadrangulation," The Metropolitan Corporate Counsel, 1996. *Member:* The District of Columbia Bar; American Bar Association; American Economic Association. ***Email:*** jdurling@willkie.com

MICHAEL H. HAMMER, born Beaufort, South Carolina, March 28, 1954; admitted to bar, 1980, District of Columbia. *Education:* Rutgers University (B.A., 1976); George Washington University (J.D., 1980). *Member:* The District of Columbia Bar; Federal Communications Bar Association. ***Email:*** mhammer@willkie.com

THOMAS JONES, born Huntington, New York, November 5, 1965; admitted to bar, 1993, New York; 1995, District of Columbia. *Education:* Georgetown University (B.A., magna cum laude, 1988; J.D., 1992).

DAVID P. MURRAY, born Kankakee, Illinois, 1960; admitted to bar, 1985, Ohio; 1986, District of Columbia. *Education:* Malone College (B.A., summa

(This Listing Continued)

WILLKIE FARR & GALLAGHER, Washington—Continued

cum laude, 1982); Georgetown University Law Center (J.D., magna cum laude, 1985). Editor, Georgetown Law Journal, 1984-1985. *Member:* District of Columbia Bar; American Bar Association. **Email:** dmurray@willkie.com

KENNETH J. PIERCE, born Cherry Hill, New Jersey, March 28, 1956; admitted to bar, 1984, District of Columbia. *Education:* University of Vermont (B.A., magna cum laude, 1978; Phi Beta Kappa); Cornell University (J.D., cum laude, 1984). Lead Note Editor, Cornell International Law Journal, Earl Warren Prize. Legislative Assistant to U.S. Senator Patrick Leahy, 1979-1981. Author: "A History of the Abenaki People," University of Vermont (1977); "Public Cryptography, Arms Export Controls and the First Amendment: A Need for Legislation," 17 Cornell International Law Journal 197 (1984); "Sanctions to Control Party Misbehavior in International Arbitration," 26 Virginia Journal of International Law 291 (1986); "Transfer Pricing Quadrangulation," The Metropolitan Corporate Counsel, 1996. Co-Author: "Thailand's Application of Post-Uruguay Round Antidumping Procedures," Trade Balance, a Law Journal of the Royal Thai Government, Ministry of Justice (April-June 1997); "Revocation of Antidumping Orders Under the New U.S. Sunset Review Procedures," Trade Laws, a Journal of the Republic of Korea, Ministry of Justice (August 1998); "Paying the Price for Big Steel," June 2000. *Member:* The District of Columbia Bar; American Bar Association. **Email:** kpierce@willkie.com

DANIEL L. PORTER, born Boston, Massachusetts, September 6, 1960; admitted to bar, 1985, Maryland; 1986, District of Columbia. *Education:* Columbia University (B.A., 1982); Cornell Law School (J.D., with Specialization in Intl. Legal Affairs, 1985). Articles Editor, Cornell International Law Journal, 1984-1985. *Member:* Federal and American Bar Associations. **Email:** dporter@willkie.com

PHILIP L. VERVEER, born Corvallis, Oregon, January 19, 1944; admitted to bar, 1969, District of Columbia. *Education:* Georgetown University (B.S.F.S., 1966); University of Chicago (J.D., 1969). Trial Attorney, Antitrust Division, U.S. Department of Justice, 1969-1977. Supervisory Attorney, Bureau of Competition, Federal Trade Commission, 1977-1978. Chief, Cable Television Bureau, Broadcast Bureau, Common Carrier Bureau, Federal Communications Commission, 1978-1981. *Member:* The District of Columbia Bar. **Email:** pverveer@willkie.com

THEODORE C. WHITEHOUSE, born Washington, D.C., October 16, 1954; admitted to bar, 1979, District of Columbia. *Education:* University of Virginia (B.A., with distinction, 1976); Georgetown University (J.D., cum laude, 1979). Law Clerk to Hon. George H. Revercomb, Superior Court of the District of Columbia, 1979-1980. Trial Attorney, Antitrust Division, U.S. Department of Justice, 1980-1982. *Member:* The District of Columbia Bar. **Email:** twhitehouse@willkie.com

RESIDENT COUNSEL

RUSSELL L. SMITH, born Atlanta, Georgia, September 9, 1946; admitted to bar, 1972, District of Columbia. *Education:* Vanderbilt University (B.A., 1968); University of Georgia (J.D., cum laude, 1972). Phi Kappa Phi. Minority Counsel, Committee on Energy and Commerce, U.S. House of Representatives, 1984-1988. Special Advisor, International Trade Administration, U.S. Department of Commerce, 1982-1984. Washington Counsel, Conrail, 1976-1982. Attorney-Advisor, U.S. Treasury Dept., 1972-1976. **Email:** rsmith@willkie.com

RETIRED COUNSEL

BRIAN CONBOY, born New York, N.Y., June 3, 1938; admitted to bar, 1963, New York; 1967, District of Columbia. *Education:* Fordham University (B.S., 1960; LL.B., 1963). *Member:* Bar Association of the District of Columbia; American Bar Association; Federal Communications Bar Association. **Email:** bconboy@willkie.com

NOEL HEMMENDINGER, born Bernardsville, New Jersey, December 25, 1913; admitted to bar, 1937, District of Columbia; 1938, New York. *Education:* Princeton University (A.B., 1934); Harvard Law School (LL.B., 1937). Editor, Harvard Law Review, 1935-1937. Secretary to U.S. Circuit Court Judge Julian W. Mack, 1937-1938. Assistant U.S. Attorney, SDNY, 1939-1940. Special Assistant to U.S. Attorney General, Claims Division, 1941-1942. Military Service, 1942-1946. Department of State, 1946-1956. Acting Director, Office of Northeast Asian Affairs, 1956. Deputy Director and Director, United States-Japan Trade Council, Washington, D.C., 1957-1977. *Member:* The District of Columbia Bar; American Bar Association. **Email:** nhemmendinger@willkie.com

RESIDENT ASSOCIATES

James M. Assey, Jr.; Miriam A. Bishop; Randy Branitsky; A. Renée Callahan; Lucy G. Carlson; Kasey Chappelle (Not admitted in DC); ***Carolyn W. Conkling; Gregory K. Conway; Joseph G. Davis; David M. Don; Demetrios Eleftheriou; Julia K. Eppard; Jonathan A. Friedman; Jeneba Jalloh Ghatt; Kurt Hague*** (Not admitted in DC); ***D. Gunnar Halley; Michael G. Jones; Sophie J. Keefer; Angie W. Kronenberg; Robert L. LaFrankie; Jennifer D. McCarthy; Kelly N. McCollian*** (Not admitted in DC); ***John L. McGrew; Kevin M. Miller; Matthew R. Nicely; Carrie Lee Owens; Stephen C. Robertson; Gabriel R. Sanz-Rexach; Christi Shewman; Pamela S. Strauss; Raymond F. Sullivan, Jr.; Andrew E. Thomas; Sean M. Thornton; Karl von Schriltz; Richard F. Waddington; Ryan G. Wallach*** (Not admitted in DC); ***Teresa S. Werner*** (Not admitted in DC).

(For complete biographical data on all personnel, see Professional Biographies at New York, N.Y.).

WILMER, CUTLER & PICKERING

2445 M STREET, N.W.
WASHINGTON, D.C. 20037-1420
Telephone: 202-663-6000
Fax: 202-663-6363
Email: Law@Wilmer.Com
URL: http://www.wilmer.com

Baltimore, Maryland Office: 100 Light Street, 21202. Telephone: 410-986-2800. Fax: 410-986-2828.

New York, New York Office: 520 Madison Avenue, 10022. Telephone: 212-230-8800. Fax: 212-230-8888.

Northern Virginia Office: 1600 Tysons Boulevard, 10th Floor, Tysons Corner, VA 22102. Telephone: 703-251-9700. Fax: 703-251-9797.

European Offices:

4 Carlton Gardens, London, SW1Y 5AA, England. Telephone: +44 (20) 7872 1000. Fax: +44 (20) 7839 3537.

Rue de la Loi 15#, B-1040 Brussels, Belgium. Telephone: +32 (2) 285 49 00. Fax: +32 (2) 285 49 49.

Friedrichstrasse 95, D-10117 Berlin, Germany. Telephone: +49 (30) 20 22 64 00. Fax: +49 (30) 20 22 65 00.

Administrative Law, Alternative Dispute Resolution, Antitrust and Trade Regulation, Appellate Practice, Aviation and Aerospace, Bankruptcy, Banks and Banking, Broker-Dealer Regulation, Business Law, Civil Practice, Communications and Media, Computer and Software, Constitutional Law, Consumer Law, Corporate Investigations, Corporate Law, Criminal Law, Election, Campaign and Political Law, Electronic Commerce, Employee Benefits, Energy, Environmental Law, EU Competition, Finance, Financial Institutions Law, General Practice, Government Contracts, Government, Insurance, Intellectual Property, International Dispute Resolution, International Trade, International Law, Investments, Latin America Trade, Litigation, Mass Media Law, Mergers, Acquisitions and Divestitures, Natural Resources, Occupational Safety and Health, Products Liability, Regulatory Law, RICO, Securities, Taxation, Telecommunications Law, Toxic Torts, Transportation and White Collar Crime.

FIRM PROFILE: Wilmer, Cutler & Pickering has a diverse national and international regulatory, commercial, legislative, and civil and criminal litigation practice. With offices in Washington, New York, Baltimore, Northern Virginia, London, Brussels, and Berlin, the firm is able to meet the needs of its clients in matters involving issues of state, federal, international, or European Union law.

The firm handles: general civil and criminal practice in U.S. state and federal courts; trials and appeals; rulemaking and adjudicative proceedings; international and national litigation and arbitration; legislation; and corporate transactions.

The firm's substantive areas of expertise include: antitrust, appellate litigation, arbitration, aviation, banking, bankruptcy, broker-dealer compliance, capital markets transactions, civil rights, class action litigation, communications, computer, congressional investigations, consumer protection, corporate transactions, employee benefits, energy regulation, environmental, federal election law, financial institutions regulation, food and drug, German law, government contracts, high-technology transactions, insurance, intellectual property, international aviation, defense, and aerospace, international dispute resolution, international transactions, international trade, investment management, mergers and acquisitions, occupational health and safety, products liability, professional conduct and liability, privatization and project financing, real estate, securities enforcement, litigation and regulation, sports law, tax, telecommunications, U.S. and EU legislative matters, venture capital transactions, and white collar criminal law.

The firm devotes a significant portion of its practice to pro bono representation. Its lawyers also are active in various projects to improve the administration of justice and in organized bar activities at the local, national, and international level.

RICHARD H. WILMER (1892-1976).

J. ROGER WOLLENBERG (1919-2000).

PARTNERS

LOUIS R. COHEN, born November 28, 1940; admitted to bar, 1967, District of Columbia. *Education:* Harvard University (A.B., 1962; LL.B., 1966);

(This Listing Continued)

Wadham College, Oxford, England. Note Editor, Harvard Law Review. Clerk to Justice John M. Harlan, U.S. Supreme Court, October Term, 1967; Chief Judge Bailey Aldrich, 1st Circuit. Visiting Professor of Law, Stanford University, 1981 (Corporate Finance). Lecturer on Law, Harvard University, 1985 (Corporate Finance). Deputy Solicitor General of the United States, 1986-1988. *Member:* American Law Institute; American Academy of Appellate Lawyers. ***PRACTICE AREAS:*** Appellate Practice; Federal Litigation; Corporate Law. ***Email:*** lcohen@wilmer.com

MICHAEL R. KLEIN, born April 10, 1942; admitted to bar, 1966, Florida; 1969, District of Columbia. *Education:* University of Miami (B.B.A., 1963; J.D., 1966); Harvard University (LL.M., 1967). Editor-in-Chief, University of Miami Law Review. Adjunct Professor of Law (Securities Regulation), George Washington University, 1971-1974; University of Virginia, 1969-1971. Assistant Professor of Law, Louisiana State University, 1967-1969. Chairman of the Board: CoStar Group, Inc., 1987—; Precept Corporation, 1999—. Vice Chairman of the Board, Perini Corporation, 1997—. Member of the Board: SRA International, Inc., 1998—; First Home Financial LLC, 2000—. *Member:* American Law Institute. ***PRACTICE AREAS:*** Securities; Corporate Law; Mergers, Acquisitions and Divestitures; Civil Practice. ***Email:*** mklein@wilmer.com

F. DAVID LAKE, JR., born February 8, 1943; admitted to bar, 1967, Virginia and District of Columbia. *Education:* Amherst College (B.A., 1964); University of Virginia (LL.B., 1967). Notes Editor, Virginia Law Review. Steering Committee, District of Columbia Bar Tax Section, 1992-1998. Adjunct Professor (Taxation), Georgetown University, 1970-1976. Office of Tax Legislative Counsel and Special Assistant to the Assistant Secretary for Tax Policy, Department of the Treasury, 1969-1971. ***PRACTICE AREAS:*** Taxation. ***Email:*** dlake@wilmer.com

JEFFREY M. LANG, born June 23, 1942; admitted to bar, 1967, Virginia; 1970, District of Columbia. *Education:* Bowdoin College (B.A., 1964); University of Virginia (LL.B., 1967). Research Editor, Virginia Journal of International Law. Associate, Bridgeman, Long & Pyeatt, 1970-1975. Deputy General Counsel, U.S. International Trade Commission, 1975-1979; Professional Staff Member, U.S. Senate Committee on Finance, 1979-1986; Chief International Trade Counsel, U.S. Senate Committee on Finance, 1986-1990; Counsel, Winthrop, Stimson, Putnam & Roberts, 1990-1994; Partner, Winthrop & Stimson, 1994-1995; Deputy United States Trade Representative, 1995-1998. [With U.S. Army, 1968-1970]. ***PRACTICE AREAS:*** International Regulatory Law; International Trade; Legislation; European Community Law. ***Email:*** jlang@wilmer.com

PAUL J. MODE, JR., born February 23, 1938; admitted to bar, 1968, District of Columbia. *Education:* Cornell University (B.M.E., 1961); Harvard University (LL.B., 1967). Board of Editors, Harvard Law Review. Author, *Before the Dispute Arises: Planning and Drafting for ADR*, Alternative Dispute Resolution in the Americas (1997). Co-Author, *The Litigation Partner and the Settlement Partner*, 12 Litigation 33 (1986). Chief Counsel, Senate Subcommittee on Constitutional Amendments, 1970-1973. Editorial Board, Alternatives to the High Cost of Litigation, 1992—. Executive Committee, 1999— and Commission on the Future of Arbitration, 1998-2000, CPR Institute for Dispute Resolution. ***PRACTICE AREAS:*** Civil Practice. ***Email:*** pjmode@wilmer.com

STEPHEN F. BLACK, born November 28, 1944; admitted to bar, 1969, District of Columbia. *Education:* Harvard University (A.B., magna cum laude, 1965); University of Michigan (J.D., magna cum laude, 1968); Balliol College, Oxford, England (M.Litt., 1970). Administrative and Book Review Editor, University of Michigan Law Review. Marshall Scholar, 1968-1970. Adjunct Professor (Securities Regulation), George Washington University, 1980-1982. Author: *Private Securities Litigation Reform Act: A Preliminary Analysis,* 24 Sec. Reg. L.J.117 (1996); *Complying with the Foreign Corrupt Practices Act* (Matthew Bender, 1997—); *Civil Litigation in the United States: A Practical Guide for German Companies* (1985) (published in Germany, 1987); *Internal Corporate Investigations* (Matthew Bender, 1985—). ***PRACTICE AREAS:*** Securities; Civil Practice. ***Email:*** sblack@wilmer.com

C. BOYDEN GRAY, born February 6, 1943; admitted to bar, 1969, North Carolina; 1970, District of Columbia. *Education:* Harvard University (A.B., 1964); University of North Carolina (J.D., 1968). Editor-in-Chief, North Carolina Law Review. Clerk to Chief Justice Earl Warren, U.S. Supreme Court, October Term, 1968. Council Member, Administrative Conference of the United States, 1993-1996. Counsel to the President of the United States, 1989-1993; Counsel to the Vice-President of the United States, 1981-1989. ***PRACTICE AREAS:*** International Law; Environmental Law. ***Email:*** bgray@wilmer.com

RONALD J. GREENE, born November 29, 1942; admitted to bar, 1968, District of Columbia. *Education:* Harvard University (A.B., 1964; LL.B., 1968). Supreme Court and Note Editor, Harvard Law Review. Clerk to Justice Thurgood Marshall, U.S. Supreme Court, October Term, 1968. ***PRACTICE AREAS:*** Antitrust and Trade Regulation; Banks and Banking; Consumer Credit. ***Email:*** rgreene@wilmer.com

(This Listing Continued)

CHARLES S. STARK, born 1944; admitted to bar, 1968, Illinois; 2001, District of Columbia. *Education:* Princeton University (A.B., 1965); Yale University (LL.B., 1968). Trial Lawyer, General Litigation Section, 1970-1978, Assistant Chief, Special Litigation Section, 1978-1980 and Chief, Foreign Commerce Section, Antitrust Division, 1980-2001, U.S. Department of Justice. (Resident, European Office, Brussels, Belgium). ***PRACTICE AREAS:*** Antitrust; Competition. ***Email:*** cstark@wilmer.com

GARY D. WILSON, born June 7, 1943; admitted to bar, 1970, District of Columbia. *Education:* Stanford University (B.A., 1965; LL.B., 1968). Articles Editor, Stanford Law Review. Clerk to Justice Thurgood Marshall, U.S. Supreme Court, October Term, 1969; Judge Wilfred Feinberg, 2d Circuit. Visiting Professor of Law (Antitrust Law and Antitrust Litigation), Stanford University, 1981-1982. ***PRACTICE AREAS:*** Civil Practice; Patents; Antitrust and Trade Regulation; Natural Resources. ***Email:*** gwilson@wilmer.com

C. LORING JETTON, JR., born February 10, 1943; admitted to bar, 1969, New York; 1970, District of Columbia. *Education:* Harvard University (A.B., 1964); Columbia University (J.D., 1969). Writing and Research Editor, Columbia Law Review. Clerk to Judge Wilfred Feinberg, 2d Circuit. ***PRACTICE AREAS:*** Antitrust and Trade Regulation; Civil Practice. ***Email:*** ljetton@wilmer.com

WILLIAM T. LAKE, born November 13, 1943; admitted to bar, 1969, California; 1972, District of Columbia. *Education:* Yale University (B.A., 1965); Stanford University (LL.B., 1968). President, Stanford Law Review. Clerk to Justice John M. Harlan, U.S. Supreme Court, October Term, 1969; Judge Henry J. Friendly, 2d Circuit. Co-author, *A Question of Access,* The Daily Deal.com (August 2000); *Open Cables Looming, But Several Paths Can Take Us There,* Legal Times (July 2000); *Competition in International Telecommunications Services,* 97 Columbia Law Review 874 (May 1997); *Interconnection and Other Key Issues for the Liberalization of Telecommunications Markets: The U.S. Experience,* in Telecommunication: Vom Monopol zum Wettbewerb (Ulrich Imenga, Natalie Lübben, Hans-Peter Schwintowski eds. 1998); *The FCC's Quid Pro Quo: Open Entry for Foreign Carriers Conditioned on Reduced Accounting Rates,* Global Telecoms Business (May 1998); *Regulating Telecommunications: Ten Recommendations for Latin American Authorities,* Connect-World Latin America (First Quarter 1997); *WTO Accord Creates US Opportunities for Foreign Investors and Operators,* Global Telecoms Business (Apr./May 1997); *Competition in International Telecommunications Services,* 97 Colum. L.Rev. 701 (Apr. 1997); *Local Telephone Interconnection -- U.S. and Europe Can Learn Together,* Global Telecoms Business (Feb./Mar. 1997); *Can We Talk? Round Two in the Fight Over the FCC's Interconnection Order,* Legal Times (Feb. 1997); *How to Set Up a Telecommunications Regulator,* Global Telecoms Business (Dec. 1996/Jan. 1997); *The Telecommunications Act of 1996 -- A New Charter for Competition in the United States*, Global Telecoms Business (Apr./May 1996); *Supercarriers Compete in Global Arena*, National Law Journal (Apr. 1996); *New PCS Regulations Enacted in Chile*, Global Telecoms Business (Dec. 1995/Jan. 1996). Author, *Monopoly or Competition: The Legal Framework in the European Communities,* Legal and Economic Aspects of Telecommunications (S. Schaff ed., 1990). Member, Council on Foreign Relations. Counselor to the Administrator, Environmental Protection Agency, in connection with the United Nations Conference on Environment and Development, 1992. Deputy Legal Adviser, Department of State, 1980-1981. Counsel, Council on Environmental Quality, Executive Office of the President, 1970-1973. *Member:* American Law Institute. ***PRACTICE AREAS:*** Communications and Media; International Law. ***Email:*** wlake@wilmer.com

JEFFREY A. MANLEY, born 1941; admitted to bar, 1968, Ohio (inactive); 1972, District of Columbia. *Education:* Harvard University (A.B., 1963; A.M., 1968; LL.B., 1968). Foreign Service Officer, U.S. Department of State, 1968. Attorney, Civil Aeronautics Board, 1969-1971. Attorney, Postal Rate Commission, 1971-1972. ***PRACTICE AREAS:*** Aviation Law; Administrative Law. ***Email:*** jmanley@wilmer.com

C. THOMAS HICKS, III, born 1945; admitted to bar, 1970, Georgia; 1972, Virginia; 1981, District of Columbia. *Education:* Virginia Polytechnic Institute and State University (B.S.C.E., 1967); University of Georgia (J.D., 1970); Georgetown University (LL.M., 1975). (Resident, Northern Virginia Office). ***PRACTICE AREAS:*** Business Transactions; Corporate Finance; Taxation. ***Email:*** thicks@wilmer.com

NEIL J. KING, born February 3, 1945; admitted to bar, 1971, New York and District of Columbia. *Education:* Harvard University (B.A., 1966; J.D., 1970). Editor, Harvard Law Review. Clerk to Judge Henry J. Friendly, 2d Circuit. Author, *RCRA Relationship to Other Laws*, ABA RCRA Manual (1993); *Questions Still Loom Over Land Ban*, Environmental Manager 9 (July 1990). Member, EPA Advisory Committee on Trade and Environment, 1992-1993. ***PRACTICE AREAS:*** Appellate Litigation; Environmental Law; Occupational Safety and Health Law; Civil Practice; International Trade. ***Email:*** nking@wilmer.com

DIETER G. F. LANGE, born January 6, 1943; admitted to bar, 1974, Germany (Not admitted in District of Columbia). *Education:* Universities of Heidelberg, Bonn and Oxford. First State Examination (1968); Second State

(This Listing Continued)

WILMER, CUTLER & PICKERING, Washington—Continued

Examination (1974). Co-author, Civil Litigation in the United States: A Practical Guide for German Companies (1985) (published in Germany, 1987). (Resident, European Office, London, England). ***PRACTICE AREAS:*** International Law; Aviation. ***Email:*** dlange@wilmer.com

CHARLES S. LEVY, born July 26, 1945; admitted to bar, 1971, District of Columbia. *Education:* Boston University (B.A., 1967); George Washington University (J.D., 1970). Member, Investment Policy Advisory Committee, Office of U.S. Trade Representative, 1982-1994. Member, Investment and Services Advisory Committee, Office of U.S. Trade Representative, 1994-1996. Member, Advisory Committee on International Investment, Department of State, 1989-1992. Member, Advisory Committee on International Economic Policy, Department of State, 1996—; Member of Standing Committee on Extortion and Bribery, International Chamber of Commerce, 1996—. Vice President, Emergency Committee for American Trade (ECAT), 1980-1981. Legal Adviser, International Trade Commission, 1979-1980. Legislative Assistant, Senator Adlai E. Stevenson, 1973-1975. Legislative Assistant, Congressman John C. Culver, 1971. Counsel, House Foreign Affairs Subcommittee on Foreign Economic Policy, 1971-1973. ***PRACTICE AREAS:*** International Law. ***Email:*** clevy@wilmer.com

ROBERT B. McCAW, born December 24, 1943; admitted to bar, 1970, Virginia; 1971, District of Columbia; 2000, New York. *Education:* Georgetown University (B.S., 1965); University of Virginia (J.D., 1970). Editor-in-Chief, Virginia Law Review. Clerk to Justice Hugo L. Black, U.S. Supreme Court, October Term, 1970. Author, Outline on Some Current U.S. Criminal Issues Affecting Domestic and International Securities Transactions, ABA Section on International Law and Practice and Criminal Justice (Annual Meetings 1988-1989); Practice Before the Judicial Panel on Multidistrict Litigation, 5 Securities Law Techniques: Transactions Litigation 108 (1987—). Professional Lecturer in Law (Securities Regulation), George Washington University, 1980-1983. (Resident, New York Office). ***PRACTICE AREAS:*** Securities Enforcement; Civil Practice; Criminal Practice. ***Email:*** rmccaw@wilmer.com

A. DOUGLAS MELAMED, born 1945; admitted to bar, 1970, District of Columbia. *Education:* Yale University (B.A., magna cum laude, 1967); Harvard University (J.D., cum laude, 1970). Editor, Harvard Law Review. Clerk to Judge Charles M. Merrill, Ninth Circuit. Co-author, with Guido Calabresi, *Property Rules, Liability Rules and Inalienability --One View of the Cathedral,* 85 Harvard Law Review 1089 (1972). Contributing Editor: *Antitrust Law Journal.* Acting Assistant Attorney General, U.S. Department of Justice, Antitrust Division, 2000-2001. Principal Deputy Assistant Attorney General, U.S. Department of Justice, Antitrust Division, 1996-2000. ***PRACTICE AREAS:*** Antitrust. ***Email:*** dmelamed@wilmer.com

RICHARD W. CASS, born January 13, 1946; admitted to bar, 1971, Connecticut; 1972, District of Columbia. *Education:* Princeton University (A.B., 1968); Yale University (J.D., 1971). Clerk to Judge William H. Timbers, 2d Circuit. Adjunct Professor of Law (Corporation Finance), Georgetown University, 1985. ***PRACTICE AREAS:*** Corporate Law; Securities Law; Finance; Mergers, Acquisitions & Divestitures; Sports Law; Biotechnology. ***Email:*** rcass@wilmer.com

BRUCE H. RABINOVITZ, born 1945; admitted to bar, 1971, Virginia; 1977, District of Columbia; 1982, California. *Education:* Washington University (B.A., 1967); George Washington University (J.D., with honors, 1971). Order of the Coif. ***PRACTICE AREAS:*** Transportation Law; Asset Based Financing Law; Administrative Law. ***Email:*** brabinovitz@wilmer.com

A. STEPHEN HUT, JR., born December 6, 1946; admitted to bar, 1974, District of Columbia. *Education:* University of Pennsylvania (B.A., 1968); Harvard University (J.D., 1972). Note Editor, Harvard Law Review. Clerk to Judge Wilfred Feinberg, 2d Circuit. Executive Committee Council for Court Excellence, 1994-1998, 2001—. Board of Trustees, Council for Court Excellence, 1991—. Acting Special Assistant to the General Counsel, Department of Defense, 1977. ***PRACTICE AREAS:*** Appellate Litigation; Civil Practice; Insurance. ***Email:*** shut@wilmer.com

DAVID R. JOHNSON, born August 8, 1945; admitted to bar, 1973, District of Columbia. *Education:* Yale University (B.A., 1967; J.D., 1972); University College, Oxford, England. Clerk to Judge Malcolm R. Wilkey, D.C. Circuit. Co-author, *Law and Borders — The Rise of Law in Cyberspace*, 48 Stanford Law Review 1367 (May 1996) (1997 McGannon Award); *And How Shall the Net Be Governed?; The New Civic Virtue of the Internet.* ***PRACTICE AREAS:*** Electronic Commerce. ***Email:*** djohnson@wilmer.com

MARK POLLAK, born July 16, 1947; admitted to bar, 1972, Maryland (Not admitted in District of Columbia). *Education:* Brooklyn College of the City University of New York (B.A., cum laude, 1968); University of Pennsylvania (M.C.P., 1972; J.D., 1972). (Resident, Baltimore, Maryland Office). ***PRACTICE AREAS:*** Real Estate. ***Email:*** mpollak@wilmer.com

JOHN ROUNSAVILLE, JR., born January 19, 1944; admitted to bar, 1973, District of Columbia. *Education:* University of Texas (A.B., 1966); Columbia University, School of International and Public Affairs; Harvard University (J.D., 1972). Editor-in-Chief, Columbia Journal of International Affairs. ***PRACTICE AREAS:*** Civil Practice; Criminal Practice; International Law; Antitrust and Trade Regulation. ***Email:*** jrounsaville@wilmer.com

ROGER M. WITTEN, born November 13, 1946; admitted to bar, 1973, District of Columbia. *Education:* Dartmouth College (A.B., 1968); Harvard University (J.D., 1972). Clerk to Judge Harrison L. Winter, 4th Circuit. Co-author, *Complying with the Foreign Corrupt Practices Act* (Matthew Bender, 1998, 1999); *Buckley Stops Here — Loosening the Judicial Stranglehold on Campaign Finance Reform,* Report of the Twentieth Century Fund Working Group on Campaign Finance Litigation (Chairman of the Working Group), 1998. Co-editor, *Regulating Campaign Finance*, Annals of the American Academy of Political and Social Science (1986). Chair, Committee on Election Law, ABA Administrative Law Section, 1988-1990. Assistant Special Prosecutor, Watergate Special Prosecution Force, 1973-1974. Member, WCP Management Committee. ***PRACTICE AREAS:*** Civil Litigation; Foreign Corrupt Practices Act; International Dispute Resolution; Internal Corporate Investigations; White Collar Crime. ***Email:*** rwitten@wilmer.com

ROBERT C. CASSIDY, JR., born May 16, 1946; admitted to bar, 1973, Pennsylvania; 1975, District of Columbia. *Education:* Johns Hopkins University (B.A., 1968); University of Pennsylvania (J.D., 1973); Georgetown University (LL.M., 1977). General Counsel, Office of the U.S. Trade Representative, Executive Office of the President, 1979-1981; International Trade Counsel, Senate Finance Committee, 1975-1979. Co-chair, International Trade Committee (1986-1990), Counsellor (1996-1998) and Government Affairs Officer (1998-2001), ABA Section of International Law and Practice. ***PRACTICE AREAS:*** International Aviation Law; Aviation Defense; Aerospace Law; International Trade; Legislative Practice. ***Email:*** rcassidy@wilmer.com

JOHN D. GREENWALD, born July 27, 1945; admitted to bar, 1973, New York (Not admitted in District of Columbia). *Education:* University of North Carolina (B.A., 1967); Columbia University (J.D., 1972). Editor-in-Chief, Columbia Journal of Transnational Law. Adjunct Professor (International Trade Law), Georgetown University, 1984—. Deputy Assistant Secretary for Import Administration, Department of Commerce, 1980-1981. Deputy General Counsel, Office of U.S. Trade Representative, Executive Office of the President, 1978-1979. ***PRACTICE AREAS:*** International Trade. ***Email:*** jgreenwald@wilmer.com

JOHN H. HARWOOD II, born September 20, 1945; admitted to bar, 1973, District of Columbia. *Education:* Harvard University (A.B., 1967); Columbia University (J.D., 1973); Georgetown University (LL.M., 1974). Adjunct Professor (Professional Responsibility), Georgetown University, 1978. Author: *Regulators may drive a hard bargain before approving SBC/Ameritech*, Global Telecoms Business (June 1998); *Regulating the Converged Voice-Data Marketplace*, Global Telecoms Business (April 1998); *The FCC's unbundling and pricing rules: effects on incentives for facilities-based entry,* Global Telecoms Business (June/July 1997); *Telecommunications and Competition in the European Union: Is the North American and British Experience a Guide?* (presented at American Institute for Contemporary German Studies, Berlin, Germany, 15-16 May 1997); *Competition in International Telecommunications Services*, Columbia Law Review, Volume 97, No. 4 (May 1997); *Regulating Telecommunications: Ten Recommendations for Latin American Authorities*, Connect-World Latin America (First Quarter 1997); *ADR Under the Telecom Act of 1996: A Model for the Telecom Industry in Latin America?* (presented at World Research Group Seminar, Miami, Florida, 7-8 April 1997); *Local telephone interconnection -- U.S. and Europe can learn together*, Global Telecoms Business (Feb./March 1997); *Entry Barriers Fall, Opening the Way to Expanded Services*, Global Telecoms Business -- Americas Yearbook 1996; *German Telecommunications Act of 1996 Implements New Regulatory Structure*, Global Telecoms Business (Oct./Nov. 1996); *Competition in International Telecommunications Services* (presented at Conference on Telecommunications Law, Columbia Law School, 8 Nov. 1996); *Competition in Local Telephone Markets: U.S. Developments* (presented in Paris, May 1995); *Satellites and Data Services: Indispensable Components of PCS* (presented Santiago, Apr. 1995); *The Emerging Strategic Alliances in International Telecommunications*, Global Telecoms Business (Oct./Nov. 1994). ***PRACTICE AREAS:*** Communications and Media; Electronic Commerce; International Law. ***Email:*** jharwood@wilmer.com

MARY CAROLYN COX, born June 10, 1949; admitted to bar, 1975, Alabama; 1976, District of Columbia. *Education:* Agnes Scott College (B.A., 1971); Yale University (J.D., 1974). Clerk to Judge Frank M. Johnson, Jr., M.D. Alabama. ***PRACTICE AREAS:*** Employment Law; Ethics; Litigation. ***Email:*** mcox@wilmer.com

CHRISTOPHER R. LIPSETT, born February 21, 1949; admitted to bar, 1977, District of Columbia; 2000, New York. *Education:* Princeton University (A.B., 1971); University of Pennsylvania (J.D., 1974). Articles Editor, University of Pennsylvania Law Review. Clerk, U.S. Supreme Court, October Term, 1975; Judge Irving L. Goldberg, Fifth Circuit. (Resident, New York Office). ***PRACTICE AREAS:*** Banks and Banking; Civil Practice. ***Email:*** clipsett@wilmer.com

(This Listing Continued)

WILLIAM J. PERLSTEIN, born February 7, 1950; admitted to bar, 1974, Connecticut; 1976, District of Columbia; 2000, New York. *Education:* London School of Economics; Union College (B.A., 1971); Yale University (J.D., 1974). Managing Editor, Yale Law Journal. Clerk to Judge Marvin E. Frankel, S.D. New York. Author, *The EPIC Saga: A Case Study in Syndication and Bankruptcy,* The Workout Game (Bloch ed., 1987). Director, American Bankruptcy Institute, 1989-1993, 1997—. Chairman, Management Committee, Wilmer, Cutler & Pickering. Vice Chair, Bankruptcy Courts Subcommittee, ABA Business Bankruptcy Committee, 1991-1996. Chair, Legislation Subcommittee, ABA Business Bankruptcy Committee, 1996—. Director, Neighborhood Legal Services Program (D.C.). Member: American Law Institute. Fellow: American College of Bankruptcy; American Bar Foundation. ***PRACTICE AREAS:*** Bankruptcy; Civil Practice. ***Email:*** bperlstein@wilmer.com

MARIANNE K. SMYTHE, born June 10, 1942; admitted to bar, 1975, District of Columbia. *Education:* Bucknell University (B.S., 1963); University of North Carolina (J.D., 1974). Articles Editor, North Carolina Law Review. Author, *Government Supervised Self-Regulation in the Securities Industry and the Antitrust Laws; Suggestions for an Accommodation*, 62 North Carolina Law Review 475 (1984). Professor of Law and Assistant Provost (Administrative Law, Environmental Law, and Contracts), University of North Carolina, 1981-1987. Director, Division of Investment Management, Securities and Exchange Commission, 1990-1993. Executive Assistant to Chairman, Securities and Exchange Commission, 1990. Associate Director, Division of Investment Management, Securities and Exchange Commission, 1988-1990. ***PRACTICE AREAS:*** Securities Law; Corporate Law; Investments. ***Email:*** msmythe@wilmer.com

ANDREW B. WEISSMAN, born May 26, 1949; admitted to bar, 1974, California; 1976, District of Columbia. *Education:* University of Rochester (A.B., 1970); Harvard University (J.D., M.P.P., 1974). Co-author, Civil RICO Litigation (2d ed. 1992). Executive Assistant to the Secretary of Housing and Urban Development, 1977-1979. ***PRACTICE AREAS:*** Securities; White Collar Crime; RICO; Civil Practice; Criminal Practice. ***Email:*** aweissman@wilmer.com

AMBASSADOR CHARLENE BARSHEFSKY, born August 11, 1950; admitted to bar, 1975, District of Columbia. *Education:* University of Wisconsin-Madison (B.A., 1972); Catholic University of America (J.D., 1975). U.S. Trade Representative, 1996-2001. Deputy U.S. Trade Representative and Acting U.S. Trade Representative, 1993-1996. Partner, 1983-1993 and Associate, 1975-1983, Steptoe & Johnson. (Senior International Partner). ***PRACTICE AREAS:*** International Trade; International Business Law; Investments; Regulatory Law; Negotiable Instruments. ***Email:*** cbarshefsky@wilmer.com

LYNN BREGMAN, born March 14, 1949; admitted to bar, 1975, District of Columbia. *Education:* Beaver College (B.A., 1971); George Washington University (J.D., 1975). Clerk to Chief Judge David L. Bazelon, D.C. Circuit. ***PRACTICE AREAS:*** Insurance; Civil Practice; Litigation. ***Email:*** lbregman@wilmer.com

WILLIAM R. McLUCAS, born August 12, 1950; admitted to bar, 1975, Pennsylvania; 1998, District of Columbia; 1999, New York. *Education:* Pennsylvania State University (B.A., 1972); Temple University (J.D., 1975). Phi Beta Kappa. Research Editor, Temple Law Quarterly. Various staff positions, 1977-1989; Director, Division of Enforcement, 1989-1998, Securities and Exchange Commission. Recipient: President's Award for Distinguished Service, 1989; National Public Service Award, National Society of Public Administration, 1996; Justice Tom C. Clark Outstanding Lawyer, Federal Bar Association, 1997. ***PRACTICE AREAS:*** Securities; Regulatory; Litigation. ***Email:*** wmclucas@wilmer.com

STEPHEN P. DOYLE, born December 25, 1950; admitted to bar, 1977, District of Columbia. *Education:* Harvard University (A.B., 1972); University of Texas (J.D., 1976). Editor-in-Chief, Texas Law Review. Clerk to Judge Wilfred Feinberg, 2d Circuit. ***PRACTICE AREAS:*** International Law; Corporate Law; Aviation. ***Email:*** sdoyle@wilmer.com

WILLIAM R. RICHARDSON, JR., born October 6, 1952; admitted to bar, 1977, Virginia and District of Columbia. *Education:* Princeton University (A.B., 1973); University of Virginia (J.D., 1976). Executive Editor, Virginia Law Review. Clerk to Judge John C. Godbold, 5th Circuit. *Member:* Federal Communications Bar Association. ***PRACTICE AREAS:*** Communications and Media. ***Email:*** wrichardson@wilmer.com

KURT L. SCHMOKE, born December 1, 1949; admitted to bar, 1976, Maryland; 2000, District of Columbia. *Education:* Yale University (B.A., 1971); Harvard University (J.D., 1976). Rhodes Scholar, Oxford University. Mayor, City of Baltimore, 1987-1999. State's Attorney, Baltimore, 1982-1987. Assistant United States Attorney, 1978-1981. Member, White House Domestic Policy Staff, 1977. (Resident, Baltimore, Maryland Office). ***Email:*** klschmoke@wilmer.com

HARRY J. WEISS, born January 4, 1952; admitted to bar, 1977, Massachusetts; 1993, District of Columbia. *Education:* Johns Hopkins University (A.B., 1973); Boston University (J.D., 1976). Co-Author, *Preventing Insider Trading*, 19 Rev. Sec & Commodities Reg. 233 (1986). Office of the General

(This Listing Continued)

Counsel (Special Trial Counsel), 1982-1985 and Division of Enforcement (Branch Chief, Assistant Director, Associate Director), 1985-1993, Securities and Exchange Commission. General Counsel and Senior Vice President, PaineWebber, Inc., 1993-1995. Co-Chair, SEC Enforcement Subcommittee of the Securities Litigation Committee of the Section of Litigation, American Bar Association, 1998-2001. ***PRACTICE AREAS:*** Securities; Regulatory Law; Litigation. ***Email:*** hweiss@wilmer.com

BRANDON BECKER, born March 19, 1954; admitted to bar, 1978, California and District of Columbia. *Education:* University of Minnesota (B.A., summa cum laude, 1974); University of San Diego (J.D., magna cum laude, 1977); Columbia University (LL.M., 1979). Articles Editor, San Diego Law Review. Co-Author: with Francois-Ihor Mazar, *Risk Management of Financial Derivative Products: Who's Responsible for What?* 21 J. Corp. L. 177 (1995); with David A. Westbrook and Soo J. Yim, *OnLine Trading: Issuers, Broker-Dealers and SROs,* in Securities in the Electronic Age: A Practical Guide (J. Olson & H. Pitt, eds., 1998). Director, Division of Market Regulation, Securities and Exchange Commission, 1993-1995. ***PRACTICE AREAS:*** Finance; Securities; Regulatory. ***Email:*** bbecker@wilmer.com

RUSSELL J. BRUEMMER, born April 23, 1952; admitted to bar, 1978, Minnesota; 1980, District of Columbia; 2001, New York. *Education:* Luther College (B.A., 1974); University of Michigan (J.D., 1977). Editor-in-Chief, University of Michigan Journal of Law Reform. Clerk to Judge William H. Webster, 8th Circuit. Author, *Intelligence Community Reorganization: Declining the Invitation to Struggle*, 101 Yale Law Journal 867 (1992). Co-author, *Unfriendly Takeovers of Depository Institutions: The Federal Banking Law Considerations*, 33 American University Law Review 309 (1984). General Counsel, Central Intelligence Agency, 1988-1990. Special Counsel to the Director of Central Intelligence, 1987-1988. Chief Counsel-Congressional Affairs, Federal Bureau of Investigation, 1980-1981. Member, Council on Foreign Relations; Member, American Law Institute. Chair, Subcommittee on Bank Holding Companies, Banking Law Committee, ABA Business Law Section, 1985-1988. Vice Chair and Chair, Subcommittee on Securities, Banking Law Committee, ABA Business Law Section, 1993-1995, 1998-1999. ***PRACTICE AREAS:*** Corporate Law; Finance; Banks and Banking. ***Email:*** rbruemmer@wilmer.com

BRUCE E. COOLIDGE, born August 29, 1947; admitted to bar, 1978, California (inactive); 1979, District of Columbia. *Education:* Yale University (B.A., 1974); University of California at Berkeley (J.D., 1977). ***PRACTICE AREAS:*** Securities; Civil Practice; Criminal Practice. ***Email:*** bcoolidge@wilmer.com

JUANITA A. CROWLEY, born January 11, 1953; admitted to bar, 1977, District of Columbia. *Education:* Trinity College (B.A., 1974); Georgetown University (J.D., 1977). Executive Editor, Georgetown Law Journal. Clerk to Judge Herbert F. Murray, D. Maryland. ***PRACTICE AREAS:*** Civil Practice; Employment Law; Complex Litigation. ***Email:*** jcrowley@wilmer.com

JOHN PAYTON, born December 27, 1946; admitted to bar, 1977, California; 1979, District of Columbia. *Education:* Pomona College (B.A., 1973); Harvard University (J.D., 1977). Comments Editor, Harvard Civil Rights - Civil Liberties Law Review. Clerk to Judge Cecil F. Poole, N.D. California. Corporation Counsel for the District of Columbia, 1991-1994. President, District of Columbia Bar, 2001. ***PRACTICE AREAS:*** Civil Practice; Civil Rights. ***Email:*** jpayton@wilmer.com

TODD D. STERN, born 1951; admitted to bar, 1977, New York; 2000, District of Columbia. *Education:* Dartmouth College (B.A., summa cum laude, 1973); Harvard University (J.D., cum laude, 1977). Phi Beta Kappa. Counselor to the Secretary, Treasurer Department, 1999-2001. Assistant to the President for Special Projects, 1998-1999, Assistant to the President and Staff Secretary, 1995-1998 and Deputy Assistant to the President and Deputy Staff Secretary, 1993-1995, The White House. Senior Counsel to Senator Patrick Leahy, Senate Judiciary Committee, 1990-1993. Member, Council on Foreign Relations. Trustee, Washington Institute for Near East Policy. Senior Advisor to German Marshall Fund of the United States. ***LANGUAGES:*** French. ***PRACTICE AREAS:*** Strategic Alliances; Congressional Investigations; Government Relations. ***Email:*** tstern@wilmer.com

SETH P. WAXMAN, born November 28, 1951; admitted to bar, 1977, District of Columbia; 1982, U.S. Supreme Court. *Education:* Harvard University (A.B., summa cum laude, 1973); Yale University (J.D., 1977). Phi Beta Kappa. Rockefeller Fellow, 1973-1974. Master, Edward Coke Appellate Inn of Court. Recipient: Edmund J. Randolph Award, United States Department of Justice, 2001; ABA Pro Bono Public Award, 1988; Anti-Defamation League Benjamin J. Cardozo Certificate of Merit, 1987. Editor, 1975-1976 and Managing Editor, 1976-1977, Yale Law Journal. Law Clerk to Judge Gerhard A. Gesell, U.S. District Court, District of Columbia, 1977-1978. Director, Legal Affairs Magazine. Author: "Does the Solicitor General Matter?" 52 Stan. L. Rev. 1115 (May 2001); "Defending Congress," 79 N.C. L. Rev. 1073 (May 2001); "In the Shadow of Daniel Webster: Arguing Appeals in the Twenty-First Century," The Federal Lawyer, Vol. 47, No. 10 (November-December 2000); "Twins at Birth: Civil Rights and the Role of the Solicitor General," 75 Ind. L.J.

(This Listing Continued)

WILMER, CUTLER & PICKERING, Washington—Continued

1297 (2000); "The Physics of Persuasion: Arguing the New Deal," 88 Geo. L.J. 2399 (2000); "'Presenting the Case of the United States As It Should Be': The Solicitor General in Historical Context," J.S. Ct. Hist., Vol. II, at 3 (1998); "Balancing the See-Saw: The Religion Clauses in the Clinton Era," 99 The Jewish Lawyer, Vol. II, No. 2 (1996); "Enforcing a Congressional Mandate," 85 Yale L.J. 721 (1976). Instructor, National Institute of Trial Advocacy, 1988-1994. Distinguished Visitor from Practice and Visiting Professor of Law, 2001, Georgetown University Law Center. Visiting Fellow, John F. Kennedy School of Government, Institute of Politics, Harvard University, 2001. Solicitor General of the United States, 1997-2001. Acting Deputy Attorney General of the United States, 1997. Deputy Solicitor General, 1996-1997. Associate Deputy Attorney General, 1994-1996. Formerly with Miller, Cassidy, Larroca & Lewin, 1978-1994. Principal, Council for Excellence in Government. Director: Supreme Court Institute; Harvard University Alumni Association; National Foundation for Jewish Culture. Member, Harvard University Committee To Visit Harvard College. Honorary Special Agent, Federal Bureau of Investigation, 2001. *Member:* The District of Columbia Bar; American Bar Association (Chair, Task Force on Habeas Corpus, Litigation Section, 1989-1994; Liaison, to Administrative Office of U.S. Courts Project on Cameras in Federal Courts; Liaison, Death Penalty Post-Conviction Representation Project, 1986-1994). Fellow: American Bar Foundation; American Academy of Appellate Attorneys. ***PRACTICE AREAS:*** Supreme Court Litigation; Appellate Practice; Complex Litigation; Criminal Law; Constitutional Law; Administrative Law. ***Email:*** swaxman@wilmer.com

WILLIAM J. WILKINS, born October 4, 1952; admitted to bar, 1977, Georgia; 1983, District of Columbia. *Education:* Yale University (B.A., 1974); Harvard University (J.D., 1977). Senate Finance Committee Staff, 1981-1988; Staff Director and Chief Counsel (1987-1988). Chair, Government Relations Committee, 1994-1996 and Member, ABA Section of Taxation; Vice Chair, Committee on Government Submissions, 1996-1998; Vice Chair, Communications, 1999-2001; Vice Chair, Government Relations, 2001—. Fellow, American College of Tax Counsel. ***PRACTICE AREAS:*** Taxation. ***Email:*** bwilkins@wilmer.com

ANDREW N. VOLLMER, born August 14, 1953; admitted to bar, 1978, District of Columbia. *Education:* Miami University (B.A., 1975); University of Virginia (J.D., 1978). Notes and Virginia Survey Editor, Virginia Law Review. Lecturer (International Civil Litigation in U.S. Courts), Stanford University, 1993. Adjunct Professor (International Civil Litigation in U.S. Courts), Georgetown University, 1992. ***PRACTICE AREAS:*** International Law; Securities. ***Email:*** avollmer@wilmer.com

THOMAS W. WHITE, born October 25, 1952; admitted to bar, 1978, District of Columbia; 1999, New York; 2001, Virginia. *Education:* Harvard University (A.B., 1975); Columbia University (J.D., 1978). Articles and Book Review Editor, Columbia Law Review. Clerk to Judge Harold Leventhal, D.C. Circuit. (Resident, Northern Virginia Office). ***PRACTICE AREAS:*** Corporate Law; Bankruptcy. ***Email:*** twhite@wilmer.com

MATTHIAS WISSMANN, born April 15, 1949; admitted to bar, 1980, Germany (Not admitted in District of Columbia). *Education:* University of Bonn; University of Tübingen; First State Examination (1974); Second State Examination (1978). Federal Minister of Transport, German Government, 1993-1998. *Member:* German Bundestag. (Resident, European Office, Berlin, Germany). ***PRACTICE AREAS:*** European Union Law; German Public Law; Corporate Law; Environmental Law. ***Email:*** mwissman@wilmer.com

BRUCE M. BERMAN, born August 9, 1954; admitted to bar, 1980, District of Columbia. *Education:* Williams College (B.A., 1976); Yale University (J.D., 1979). Clerk to Judge Walter K. Stapleton, D. Delaware. Member, Federal Practice Task Force, ABA Litigation Section, 1998—. ***PRACTICE AREAS:*** Civil Practice; Educational Testing Law; Criminal Practice; Food, Drug and Cosmetic Regulation. ***Email:*** bberman@wilmer.com

THOMAS F. CONNELL, born October 22, 1949; admitted to bar, 1979, District of Columbia. *Education:* Princeton University (A.B., summa cum laude, 1971); University of Pennsylvania (J.D., cum laude, 1979). Articles Editor, University of Pennsylvania Law Review. Clerk to Judge Edward Weinfeld, S.D. New York. Lecturer (Legal Ethics), University of Pennsylvania, 1983. Vice Chair, Committee on Adjudication, ABA Administrative Law Section, 1989-1990. ***PRACTICE AREAS:*** Civil Practice; Trial Practice; Insurance. ***Email:*** tconnell@wilmer.com

CHARLES E. DAVIDOW, born July 25, 1954; admitted to bar, 1980, District of Columbia; 2000, New York. *Education:* Amherst College (B.A., 1976); Harvard University (J.D., 1979). Treasurer, Harvard Law Review. Clerk to Judge Walter R. Mansfield, 2d Circuit. Adjunct Professor (Corporations), Georgetown University, 1991. ***PRACTICE AREAS:*** Securities; Civil Practice. ***Email:*** cdavidow@wilmer.com

TERRILL A. HYDE, born September 3, 1947; admitted to bar, 1979, District of Columbia. *Education:* Dakota State College (B.S., 1973); South Dakota State University (M.A., 1976); University of Nebraska (J.D., 1979). Editor-in-Chief, Nebraska Law Review. Co-Author: Hyde, Dubroff, Rose, *The Use of Partnerships and LLCs in Structuring Consolidated Groups,* N.Y.U. Fed. Tax Inst. 56 (1998). Adjunct Professor, Tax, Georgetown University Law Center. Tax Legislative Counsel, Department of the Treasury, 1991-1992. Deputy Tax Legislative Counsel (Regulatory Affairs), Department of the Treasury, 1989-1991. Former Council Director, Corporate Tax and Affiliated and Related Corporations Committees, ABA Section of Taxation. Former Member of the Council of the ABA Section of Taxation; Former Chair, Committee on Affiliated and Related Corporations, ABA Section of Taxation. Former Vice Chair, District of Columbia Bar Taxation Section's Exempt Organizations Committee. Fellow of the American College of Tax Counsel and the American Bar Foundation. ***PRACTICE AREAS:*** Taxation. ***Email:*** thyde@wilmer.com

DUANE D. MORSE, born September 19, 1950; admitted to bar, 1980, District of Columbia. *Education:* Northwestern University (B.A., 1972); University of Michigan (J.D., 1979). Note Editor, Michigan Law Review. Clerk to Judge Harry Phillips, 6th Circuit. (Resident, Northern Virginia Office). ***PRACTICE AREAS:*** Bankruptcy; Corporate Law; Real Estate. ***Email:*** dmorse@wilmer.com

DR. ANDREAS WEITBRECHT, born November 14, 1947; admitted to bar, 1986, Germany (1996, Landgericht and Kammergericht Berlin) (Not admitted in District of Columbia). *Education:* University of Bonn. First State Examination (1974); Second State Examination Bavaria (1979). University of California at Berkeley (LL.M., 1984); University of Augsburg (Dr. jur., 1986). Assistant Professor (European Community Law, International Competition Law, and Administrative Regulation of Business), Augsburg University, 1980-1985. Author: *The Prohibition of Transnational Mergers,* 1986; The European Merger Control Regulation - The First Three Years (EuZW 1993); The Leniency Notice in European Antitrust Law (EuZW 1997); regular reports on the development of EU competition law in EuZW; numerous articles on EU and German competition law. (Resident, European Offices, Berlin, Germany and Brussels, Belgium). ***PRACTICE AREAS:*** EU Competition. ***Email:*** aweitbrecht@wilmer.com

ROBERT B. BELL, born August 31, 1953; admitted to bar, 1981, District of Columbia; 1987, New York. *Education:* Dartmouth College (B.A., summa cum laude, 1975); Cambridge University (M.A., 1977); Stanford Law School (J.D., 1980). Phi Beta Kappa. Order of the Coif. Articles Editor, Stanford Journal of International Law. Law Clerk to: Judge Thomas A. Flannery, U.S. District Court, District of Columbia, 1980-1981; Justice Byron R. White, U.S. Supreme Court, 1981-1982. ***PRACTICE AREAS:*** Antitrust; EU Competition; Litigation. ***Email:*** rbell@wilmer.com

KATHRYN C. BROWN, born June 22, 1952; admitted to bar, 1981, New York (Not admitted in District of Columbia). *Education:* Marist College (B.A., magna cum laude, 1974); Syracuse University (J.D., summa cum laude, 1980). Order of the Coif. Lead Articles Editor, Syracuse Law Review, 1979-1980. Chief, Common Carrier Bureau, 1998 and Chief of Staff, 1998-2001, Federal Communications Commission. Associate Administrator, Office of Policy Analysis and Development, National Telecommunications & Information Administration, U.S. Department of Commerce, 1995-1998. *Member:* American Bar Association; Federal Communications Bar Association. ***PRACTICE AREAS:*** Communications Law; Telecommunications Law; Electronic Commerce; Public Utility Law; Consumer Protection Law. ***Email:*** kbrown@wilmer.com

JOHN H. RATLIFF, born January 13, 1957; admitted to bar, 1980, Middle Temple, England and Wales (Not admitted in District of Columbia). *Education:* University College, Oxford (B.A. Hons., 1979); European Commission Internship (1981, Hon. Sir Peter Bristow Award Holder); Young Lawyers' Programme to Germany (1981-1982); Europa Institute, University of Amsterdam (Diploma in European Integration Law, 1983). Co-Author: "Organizing EC Competition Compliance, Competition Fair or Foul (Book/Video) 1995. *Member:* International Bar Association; British Association for Sport and the Law. (Resident, European Office, Brussels, Belgium). ***PRACTICE AREAS:*** EC Competition Law; Merger Control; EC Agricultural Law; EC Litigation. ***Email:*** jratliff@wilmer.com

DANIEL H. SQUIRE, born April 14, 1954; admitted to bar, 1980, District of Columbia. *Education:* Yale University (B.A., 1976); Harvard University (J.D., 1980). Author: *The Economic Growth and Regulatory Paperwork Reduction Act of 1996* (with M. Indick, R. Greene), 114 The Banking Law Journal 298, April 1997; *Environmental Liabilities in Bankruptcy Cases,* Bankruptcy Litigation Manual (rev. ed. 2000-2001); *Corporate Successor Liability Under CERCLA: Who's Next?* (with W. Ingram, D. Frost), 43 Southwestern Law Journal 887 (1990). ***PRACTICE AREAS:*** Civil Practice; Environmental Law; Financial Institutions; Litigation. ***Email:*** dsquire@wilmer.com

CHARLES D. TOY, born 1955; admitted to bar, 1981, New York (Not admitted in District of Columbia). *Education:* Harvard College (B.A., cum laude, 1977; J.D., 1980). Phi Beta Kappa. Adjunct Professor of Law, Foreign Direct Investment, the George Washington University National Law Center, 1994-1995. Vice President and General Counsel, 1993-2001, Vice President for Investment Funds, 1998-1999, Vice President for Finance, 1995-1996, Overseas

(This Listing Continued)

Private Investment Corporation. ***LANGUAGES:*** Chinese (Toisan, Cantonese, Mandarin), Spanish, German. ***PRACTICE AREAS:*** Business Transactions; Corporate Finance; Project Finance. ***Email:*** ctoy@wilmer.com

PETER K. VIGELAND, born 1955; admitted to bar, 1981, New York. *Education:* Dartmouth College (B.A., magna cum laude, 1977); Columbia University (J.D., 1980). Stone Scholar. Counsel and Partner, LeBoeuf, Lamb, Greene & MacRae, L.L.P., 1996-2000. Assistant U.S. Attorney and Chief of Major Crimes. Attorney's Office, Southern District of New York, 1989-1996. Curtis, Mallet-Prevost, Colt & Mosle Association, 1984-1989. Attorney's Office, Southern District of New York, 1989-1996. Assistant District Attorney, New York County District Attorney's Office, 1980-1984. (Resident, New York Office). ***PRACTICE AREAS:*** Litigation. ***Email:*** pvigeland@wilmer.com

GARY B. BORN, born September 14, 1955; admitted to bar, 1984, District of Columbia. *Education:* Haverford College (B.A., 1978); University of Pennsylvania (J.D., summa cum laude, 1981). Phi Beta Kappa. Articles Editor, University of Pennsylvania Law Review. Clerk to Justice William H. Rehnquist, U.S. Supreme Court, October Term, 1982; Judge Henry J. Friendly, 2d Circuit. Author, *International Civil Litigation in United States* Courts (3d ed. 1996); *International Arbitration Agreements and Forum Selection Clauses: Planning, Drafting and Enforcing* (1999); *International Commercial Arbitration International and U.S. Aspects* (2000); *A Reappraisal of the Extraterritorial Reach of U.S. Law*, 24 Law and Policy in International Business 1 (1992). Visiting Lecturer (International Business Transactions), University College, London, 1991—. Adjunct Professor of Law (International Civil Litigation), University of Virginia, 1991 (International Civil Litigation), Georgetown University, 1987-1992. Associate Professor of Law (International and Constitutional Law), University of Arizona, 1985-1986. Co-chair, Committee on International Aspects of Litigation, ABA International Section, 1988-1992. *Member:* American Law Institute. (European Office, London, England). ***PRACTICE AREAS:*** International Arbitration; International Litigation; International Law; Alternative Dispute Resolution. ***Email:*** gborn@wilmer.com

VERONICA G. KAYNE, admitted to bar, 1981, District of Columbia. *Education:* University of Pennsylvania (B.A., 1976); University of California (M.A., 1978); Villanova University (J.D., cum laude, 1981). Order of the Coif. Member, Editorial Board, Villanova Law Review. Deputy Assistant Director, 1997-1998 and Assistant Director, 1998-2000, Anticompetitive Practices Division, Federal Trade Commission, Bureau of Competition. ***PRACTICE AREAS:*** Antitrust. ***Email:*** vkayne@wilmer.com

DAVID W. OGDEN, born November 12, 1953; admitted to bar, 1983, District of Columbia; 1986, Virginia. *Education:* Grinnell College; University of Pennsylvania (B.A., summa cum laude, 1976); Harvard University (J.D., magna cum laude, 1981). Phi Beta Kappa. Recipient: J. Edmund Randolph Award, U.S. Department of Justice, 2001; Attorney General's Medallion, 1999; Department of Defense Medal for Distinguished Public Service, 1995. Editor, Harvard Law Review, 1979-1981. Law Clerk to: Hon. Abraham D. Sofaer, U.S. District Court, Southern District of New York, 1981-1982; Justice Harry A. Blackmun, U.S. Supreme Court, 1982-1983. Co-Author: "Carriers, Insurers, and the United States in International Air Carrier Litigation: Nothing in Common?" Lawyer-Pilots Bar Assoc. Journal, Vol. XXII, No. 3, at 23 (Fall 200); "The Federal Government's Perspective on Post-Lexecon Multidistrict Litigation," Aviation Lit. Quarterly, at 10 (Fall/Winter 2000); with J. Jacobs, "Legal Risk Management for Associations: A Legal Compliance Guide for Volunteers and Employees of Trade and Professional Associations," 1st ed. (1995); "Is There a First Amendment "Right to Remain Silent"?" Federal Bar News & Journal, Vol. 40, No. 6, at 368 (July 1993); "In Appreciation of Justice Blackmun," 1990 Annual Survey of American Law xxxiii. Adjunct Professor, Constitutional Law, Georgetown University Law Center, 1991-1995. Member and Governmental Representative, Advisory Committee on the Civil Rules, Judicial Conference of the United States, 1999-2000. Assistant Attorney General over the Civil Division, 2000-2001, Acting Assistant Attorney General, 1999-2000, Chief of Staff to the Attorney General, 1998-1999, Counselor to the Attorney General, 1997-1998 and Associate Deputy Attorney General, 1995-1997, United States Department of Justice. Deputy General Counsel & Legal Counsel, United States Department of Defense, 1994-1995. Partner: Jenner & Block, Washington, D.C., 1988-1994. Partner, 1986-1988 and Associate, 1983-1985, Ennis Friedman & Bersoff, Washington, D.C. *Member:* The District of Columbia Bar; Virginia State Bar, American Bar Association. ***PRACTICE AREAS:*** Civil and Appellate Litigation; Administrative and Constitutional Law; Media and First Amendment Law; Association Law. ***Email:*** dogden@wilmer.com

JOHN B. WATKINS V, born February 4, 1956; admitted to bar, 1981, Maryland; 1998, District of Columbia. *Education:* Johns Hopkins University (B.A., 1977); University of Michigan (J.D., 1981). *Member:* Maryland State and American (Member, Business Law Section; Federal Regulation of Securities and Partnerships and Unincorporated Business Organizations Committees) Bar Associations. (Also at Baltimore, Maryland Office). ***PRACTICE AREAS:*** Corporate Law; Securities Law. ***Email:*** jwatkins@wilmer.com

PHILIP D. ANKER, born November 15, 1957; admitted to bar, 1983, District of Columbia. *Education:* University of Pennsylvania (B.A., magna cum laude, 1978); George Washington University (J.D., with highest honors, 1982). Order of the Coif. Editor-in-Chief, George Washington Law Review. Clerk to Judge Paul H. Roney, 11th Circuit. Former Co-chair, Debtor's Practice Subcommittee, Bankruptcy and Insolvency Committee, ABA Litigation Section. ***PRACTICE AREAS:*** Bankruptcy; Bankruptcy Litigation; Civil Practice. ***Email:*** panker@wilmer.com

JOSEPH K. BRENNER, born December 23, 1956; admitted to bar, 1982, District of Columbia. *Education:* Cornell University (A.B., 1979); Georgetown University (J.D., 1982). Managing Editor, Georgetown Law Journal. Clerk to the Court, D.C. Circuit. ***PRACTICE AREAS:*** Securities; Civil Practice; Criminal Practice. ***Email:*** jbrenner@wilmer.com

CAROL CLAYTON, born August 11, 1958; admitted to bar, 1982, District of Columbia. *Education:* University of Utah (B.A., 1979); University of Virginia (J.D., 1982). Articles Editor, Virginia Environmental Law Journal. Co-author, *Law of Environmental Protection*; *Environmental Auditing Handbook*. Member, Management Committee, Wilmer, Cutler & Pickering. ***PRACTICE AREAS:*** Environmental Law; Civil Practice; Complex Litigation. ***Email:*** cclayton@wilmer.com

MEREDITH B. CROSS, born October 14, 1957; admitted to bar, 1983, Georgia; 1998, District of Columbia. *Education:* Duke University (B.A., cum laude, 1979); Vanderbilt University (J.D., 1982). Order of the Coif. Member, Vanderbilt Law Review, 1980-1982. Clerk to Judge Albert J. Henderson, 11th Circuit. Securities and Exchange Commission, Division of Corporation Finance: Attorney Fellow, Office of Chief Counsel, 1990-1992; Deputy Chief Counsel, 1992; Chief Counsel, 1992-1994; Associate Director, International and Small Business, 1994; Deputy Director, 1994-1998. ***PRACTICE AREAS:*** Corporate Law; Securities. ***Email:*** mcross@wilmer.com

THOMAS P. OLSON, born March 31, 1953; admitted to bar, 1984, New York; 1985, District of Columbia. *Education:* University of Michigan (B.A., 1975); Harvard University (J.D., 1982). Treasurer, Harvard Law Review. Clerk to Judge Walter R. Mansfield, 2d Circuit. Author: *The Iron Law of Consensus: Congressional Responses to Proposed Copyright Reforms Since the 1909 Act*, 36 Journal of the Copyright Society 109 (1989). Adjunct Professor of Copyright Law, Georgetown Law Center, 1996-1997. Staff Counsel to the Senate Judiciary Committee's Subcommittee on Patents, Copyrights and Trademarks, 1983-1984. ***PRACTICE AREAS:*** Civil Practice; Intellectual Property. ***Email:*** tolson@wilmer.com

PATRICK J. CAROME, born November 20, 1957; admitted to bar, 1984, Massachusetts; 1985, District of Columbia. *Education:* Boston College (B.A., 1980); Harvard University (J.D., 1983). Editor, Harvard Civil Rights-Civil Liberties Law Review. Clerk to Judge Milton Pollack, S.D. New York. Staff Counsel, House Select Committee to Investigate Covert Arms Transactions with Iran, 1987-1988. Chair, Government Information and Right to Privacy Committee, ABA Administrative Law Section, 1990-1994; Vice Chair, 1989-1990. Co-chair, Steering Committee of the Administrative Law and Agency Practice Section of the Bar of the District of Columbia, 1997-1998. ***PRACTICE AREAS:*** Communications and Media; Civil Practice. ***Email:*** pcarome@wilmer.com

ANDREW D. KAIZER, born May 7, 1956; admitted to bar, 1983, Massachusetts; 1987, New York (Not admitted in District of Columbia). *Education:* Boston University (B.A., 1978); Harvard University (J.D., 1983). Member: Complaint Mediation Panel, New York Supreme Court, Appellate Division, 1st Department, 1995—. *Member:* The Association of the Bar of the City of New York (Member, Securities Regulation Committee, Securities Litigation Subcommittee, 2001—). (Resident, New York Office). ***PRACTICE AREAS:*** Litigation; SEC Enforcement; Securities Regulation; Commodities Enforcement and Regulation; White Collar Crime. ***Email:*** akaizer@wilmer.com

ROBERT T. NOVICK, born October 6, 1958; admitted to bar, 1984, District of Columbia; U.S. Court of International Trade. *Education:* Bucknell University (B.A., 1980); American University (J.D., cum laude, 1983). Executive Editor, American University Law Review, 1982-1983. Partner, 1991-1997 and Associate, 1983-1990, Steptoe & Johnson LLP. ***LANGUAGES:*** German. ***PRACTICE AREAS:*** International Trade and Business Law; International Investments Law; International Law; Customs. ***Email:*** rnovick@wilmer.com

STEPHEN W. PRESTON, born May 30, 1957; admitted to bar, 1983, District of Columbia. *Education:* Yale University (B.A., 1979); Trinity College, University of Dublin (Diploma, 1980); Harvard University (J.D., 1983). Clerk to Judge Phyllis A. Kravitch, Eleventh Circuit. Visiting Fellow, Center for Law in the Public Interest, Washington, D.C., 1984-1985. Associate then Partner, Wilmer, Cutler & Pickering, Washington, D.C., 1986-1993. Principal Deputy General Counsel, Department of Defense, 1993-1995. Acting General Counsel, 1994. Deputy Assistant Attorney General, U.S. Department of Justice, 1995-1998. General Counsel, Department of the Navy, 1998-2000. Recipient: Distinguished Public Service Medal, Department of Defense, 1995, 2000; Distinguished Public Service Award, Department of the Navy, 2000. ***PRACTICE AREAS:*** Appellate Litigation; Civil Litigation; Defense and Aerospace; False Claims Act and Qui Tam; Foreign Corrupt Practices Act; Government Contracts; Internal Corporate Investigations. ***Email:*** spreston@wilmer.com

(This Listing Continued)

WILMER, CUTLER & PICKERING, Washington—Continued

DR. ROLAND STEINMEYER, born December 17, 1954; admitted to bar, 1983, Munich; Notary Public, 1996, Berlin (Not admitted in District of Columbia). *Education:* University of Augsburg; First State Examination (1980); Second State Examination (1983); University of Cape Town (LL.M., 1980); University of Würzburg (Dr. jur., 1985). Assistant Lecturer, Civil Law, University of Augsburg, 1981-1983. (Resident, European Office, Berlin, Germany). ***PRACTICE AREAS:*** Corporate Law; Civil Practice; Mergers and Acquisitions; Real Estate. ***Email:*** rsteinmeyer@wilmer.com

WILLIAM A. WILSON III, born 1956; admitted to bar, 1983, Connecticut; 1985, New York; 1997, Hong Kong (Not admitted in District of Columbia). *Education:* Yale University (B.A., 1978); New York University (J.D., 1983; M.A., 1983). ***LANGUAGES:*** French, German and Chinese (Mandarin and Cantonese). ***PRACTICE AREAS:*** Finance; Corporate Law; International Law; Venture Capital. ***Email:*** wwilson@wilmer.com

SHEILA C. CHESTON, born November 5, 1958; admitted to bar, 1986, New York and District of Columbia. *Education:* Dartmouth College (B.A., 1980); Columbia University (J.D., 1984). Clerk to Judge W.A. Norris, Ninth Circuit. Adjunct Professor, Georgetown University, 1991—. General Counsel, Defense Base Closure and Realignment Commission, 1993; Special Associate Counsel to the President of the United States, 1994; Department of the Air Force: Deputy General Counsel, 1993-1994, General Counsel, 1995-1998, Acting Under Secretary, 1997. ***PRACTICE AREAS:*** Congressional Investigations; Government Contracts; International Aviation Law; Aviation Defense; Aerospace Law; International Dispute Resolution; International Arbitration; International Litigation; Import and Export Law. ***Email:*** scheston@wilmer.com

DAVID P. DONOVAN, born June 26, 1958; admitted to bar, 1984, District of Columbia. *Education:* Iowa State University (B.S., 1980); Georgetown University (J.D., 1984). Editor-in-Chief, Georgetown Law Journal. Clerk to Judge Thomas A. Flannery, D. District of Columbia. (Resident, Northern Virginia Office). ***PRACTICE AREAS:*** Civil Practice; Products Liability. ***Email:*** ddonovan@wilmer.com

PAUL A. VON HEHN, born January 16, 1950; admitted to bar, 1981, Germany (Not admitted in District of Columbia). *Education:* University of Tübingen. First State Examination (1978); Second State Examination (1981). Columbia University (LL.M., 1983); University of East Asia, Macau (Diploma in Chinese Law, 1989). Assistant Professor (German contract and commercial law), University of Tübingen, 1979-1981. (Resident, European Office, Brussels, Belgium). ***PRACTICE AREAS:*** International Transactions; Aviation; Telecommunications. ***Email:*** pvonhehn@wilmer.com

MARC C. HANSEN, born January 2, 1960; admitted to bar, 1985, New York; 1990, Denmark (Not admitted in District of Columbia). *Education:* University of Nice (Faculty of Law, 1978-1979); University of Copenhagen (Cand. Jur., 1983); University of Michigan (LL.M., 1984). Co-author, "The EU Copyright Directive: Why It Matters," *Global Counsel* (June 2001); "Legal Recognition for Copy Control Systems," *European Counsel* (November 1999); "European State Aid Control as a Business Tool," *The European Antitrust Review* (1999); *Border Controls Applied to Counterfeit Pirated, or Patented Products CIPIC Journal,* Vol. 89 (Tokyo 1999); *The New European Union Antidumping Regulation,* International Business Law Journal, No. 4, pp. 465-492 (1995); *Collective Dominance Under the EC Merger Regulation,* 30 Common Market Law Review 787 (1993); *The GATT Protocol of Provisional Application: A Dying Grandfather?* 27 Columbia Journal of Transnational Law 263 (1989). (Resident, European Offices, Brussels, Belgium and London, England). ***PRACTICE AREAS:*** Antitrust; Competition and State Aid Law; Information Technology Law; Intellectual Property; International Trade. ***Email:*** mhansen@wilmer.com

ANDREW K. PARNELL, born August 19, 1953; admitted as Solicitor, 1979, England and Wales. *Education:* Cambridge University (B.A., 1975). Author, *Enforcing United States Judgments Abroad - England,* Enforcing Foreign Judgments in the United States and United States Judgments Abroad (Ronald A. Brand, Jr., ed., 1992). (Resident, European Office, London, England). ***PRACTICE AREAS:*** International Transactions; Corporate Law. ***Email:*** aparnell@wilmer.com

JOHN W. RYAN, born 1957; admitted to bar, 1986, Pennsylvania; 1987, District of Columbia; 1991, New York; 1993, U.S. Supreme Court; registered to practice before U.S. Patent and Trademark Office. *Education:* College of the Holy Cross; Bucknell University (B.A., Chem., 1981); Syracuse University (J.D., 1985); George Washington University (LL.M., 1988); Albany Medical College (Trustee's tuition scholarship for graduate studies in biochemistry, 1990-1991). Author: "The Sliding Scale of Personal Jurisdiction Via the Internet," Stanford Technology Law Review, Winter, 2000; "International Licensing Agreements," Bio/Pharmaceutical Outsourcing Report, March, 2000; "The Treatment of Territorial Restrainats under Patent and Know-How Licenses," Albany Law Journal of Science and Technology, Vol. 3, 1993. Adjunct Professor of Law, Licensing of Indust. Prop. II, Albany Law School, 1990-1992. *Member:* The District of Columbia Bar; American Intellectual Property Law Association; Licensing Executives Society. ***PRACTICE AREAS:*** Intellectual Property Licensing; Patent Infringement Opinions; Patent Litigation. ***Email:*** jryan@wilmer.com

HOWARD M. SHAPIRO, born May 8, 1960; admitted to bar, 1986, New York; 1997, District of Columbia. *Education:* Williams College (B.A., 1982); Yale University (J.D., 1985). Articles and Book Review Editor, Yale Law Journal. Clerk to Judge Pierre N. Leval, S.D. New York. Assistant U.S. Attorney for the Southern District of New York, 1987-1992. Associate Professor of Law, Cornell Law School, 1993. General Counsel of the Federal Bureau of Investigation, 1993-1997. ***PRACTICE AREAS:*** Criminal Law; Internal Investigations; White Collar Crime; Civil Practice. ***Email:*** hshapiro@wilmer.com

ROGER W. YOERGES, born November 28, 1958; admitted to bar, 1986, Florida; 1993, District of Columbia. *Education:* University of Florida (B.A., 1980); Stetson University (J.D., 1985). Articles and Symposia Editor, Stetson Law Review. Clerk to Judge C. Roger Vinson, N.D. Florida. ***PRACTICE AREAS:*** Products Liability; Civil Practice; Food, Drug and Cosmetics Regulation. ***Email:*** ryoerges@wilmer.com

MARK D. CAHN, born August 21, 1961; admitted to bar, 1987, New York; 1988, District of Columbia. *Education:* Tufts University (B.A., 1983); Yale University (J.D., 1986). Editor, Yale Journal on Regulation. Clerk to Judge John J. Gibbons, 3d Circuit; Judge Herbert J. Stern, D. New Jersey. ***PRACTICE AREAS:*** Civil Practice; Securities; Antitrust; Criminal Law. ***Email:*** mcahn@wilmer.com

ERIC R. MARKUS, born May 13, 1960; admitted to bar, 1987, New York; 1988, District of Columbia. *Education:* Yale University (B.A., 1982; J.D., 1986); Princeton University, Woodrow Wilson School (M.P.A., 1986). Executive Editor, Yale Journal on Regulation. Clerk to Judge Marvin Katz, E.D. Pennsylvania. ***PRACTICE AREAS:*** Corporate Law; Securities; Bankruptcy. ***Email:*** emarkus@wilmer.com

RANDOLPH D. MOSS, born 1961; admitted to bar, 1987, New York; 1989, District of Columbia. *Education:* Hamilton College (A.B., summa cum laude, 1983); Yale University (J.D., 1986). Phi Beta Kappa. Editor, Yale Law Journal. Clerk to: Judge Pierre N. Leval, Southern District of New York; Associate Justice John Paul Stevens, U.S. Supreme Court, October Terms, 1987 and 1988. Assistant Attorney General, U.S. Department of Justice, Office of Legal Counsel, 2000-2001. Acting Assistant Attorney General, U.S. Department of Justice, Office of Legal Counsel, 1998-2000. Deputy Assistant Attorney General, U.S. Department of Justice, Office of Legal Counsel, 1996-1998. ***PRACTICE AREAS:*** Constitutional Law; Administrative Law; Complex Civil Litigation. ***Email:*** rmoss@wilmer.com

JORGE E. ALERS, born December 8, 1959; admitted to bar, 1986, Florida; 1990, Colorado; 1995, District of Columbia. *Education:* Colorado State University (B.A., with highest distinction, 1982); Harvard University (J.D., 1986). Phi Beta Kappa. *Member:* District of Columbia Bar. ***LANGUAGES:*** Spanish and French. ***PRACTICE AREAS:*** International Mergers and Acquisitions; Cross-Border Finance; Project Finance. ***Email:*** jalers@wilmer.com

J. BECKWITH BURR, admitted to bar, 1995, District of Columbia. *Education:* Yale University (B.A., cum laude, 1977); Georgetown University (J.D., magna cum laude, 1987). Order of the Coif. Editor, Georgetown Law Journal. Administrative Assistant, U.S. Representative Fortney H. Stark, Jr., 1978-1981. Attorney-Advisor, Federal Trade Commission, 1995-1997. Senior Internet Policy Advisor, Associate Administrator and Director of International Affairs, National Telecommunications & Information Administration, 1997-2000. ***PRACTICE AREAS:*** Electronic Commerce; Privacy Law; Security Clearances; Data Protection; Corporate Transactions; Technology Transactions; Communications Law; Technology Law. ***Email:*** bburr@wilmer.com

MARK A. DEWIRE, admitted to bar, 1987, Maryland; 1988, Massachusetts; 1998, District of Columbia. *Education:* Georgetown University (B.S., 1981); Boston University (J.D., 1987). *Member:* Maryland State and American (Member, Business Law Section) Bar Associations. (Also at Baltimore, Maryland Office). ***PRACTICE AREAS:*** Corporate Law; Securities Law. ***Email:*** mdewire@wilmer.com

PAUL A. ENGELMAYER, born April 12, 1961; admitted to bar, 1988, New York; 1990, District of Columbia. *Education:* Harvard University (B.A., summa cum laude, 1983; J.D., magna cum laude, 1987). Treasurer, Harvard Law Review. Clerk to: Justice Thurgood Marshall, U.S. Supreme Court, 1988-1989; Chief Judge Patricia M. Wald, U.S. Court of Appeals, District of Columbia Circuit. Author: "The Modification of Consent Decrees in Institutional Reform Litigation," 99 Harvard Law Review 1020 (1986). Chief, Major Crimes Unit, U.S. Attorney's Office, Southern District of New York, 1996-1999. Assistant to U.S. Solicitor General, 1994-1996. Assistant U.S. Attorney and Deputy Chief Appellate Attorney, Southern District of New York, 1989-1994. (Resident, New York Office). ***PRACTICE AREAS:*** Appellate Practice; U.S. Supreme Court Litigation; General Litigation; Securities Litigation; White Collar Crime. ***Email:*** pengelmayer@wilmer.com

SIMON FIRTH, born April 10, 1962; admitted as Solicitor, 1987, England and Wales (Not admitted in the United States). *Education:* Girton College,

(This Listing Continued)

Cambridge, England (B.A., Hons., 1983; M.A., Hons., 1987). Author, "Marketing Hedge Funds in Europe: Legal, Regulatory and Tax Issues," chapter in "Hedge Funds: A Special Report," Sweet and Maxwell. ***PRACTICE AREAS:*** Securities Regulation; Financial Services; Investment Management. ***Email:*** sfirth@wilmer.com

ERIC J. MOGILNICKI, born September 5, 1960; admitted to bar, 1986, Massachusetts; 1994, District of Columbia; 1996, U.S. Supreme Court. *Education:* Yale University (B.A., summa cum laude, 1982; J.D., 1986). Phi Beta Kappa. Editor, Yale Law and Policy Review. Chief Elections Counsel, Massachusetts Attorney General's Office, 1989-1991. Assistant Attorney General, Massachusetts Attorney General's Office, 1987-1991. ***PRACTICE AREAS:*** Civil Practice; Securities; Litigation; Banking. ***Email:*** emogilnicki@wilmer.com

ROBERT B. STACK, born February 9, 1955; admitted to bar, 1987, New York; 1988, District of Columbia. *Education:* State University of New York at Albany (B.A., 1976); New York University (M.A., 1980); Georgetown University (J.D./M.S.F.S., 1984). Editor-in-Chief, Georgetown Law Journal. Clerk to Justice Potter Stewart (Ret.), U.S. Supreme Court, October Term, 1985; Judge Thomas A. Flannery, D. District of Columbia. ***PRACTICE AREAS:*** Taxation; Civil Practice. ***Email:*** rstack@wilmer.com

LEWIS J. LIMAN, born December 3, 1960; admitted to bar, 1988, New York (Not admitted in District of Columbia). *Education:* Harvard College (A.B., magna cum laude, 1983); London School of Economics (M.Sc., Economics, with distinction, 1984); Yale Law School (J.D., 1987). Articles Editor, Yale Law Journal. Editor, Yale Journal of International Law. Clerk to Justice John Paul Stevens, U.S. Supreme Court, 1989-1990 terms. Clerk to Judge Pierre N. Leval, S.D. New York. Associate, Cravath, Swaine & Moore, 1991-1995. Deputy Chief Appellate Attorney, Assistant United States Attorney, S.D. New York, 1995-1999. (Resident, New York Office). ***PRACTICE AREAS:*** Antitrust; Commercial Litigation; Securities and Class Action Litigation; Securities Regulation; White Collar Crime. ***Email:*** lliman@wilmer.com

R. SCOTT KILGORE, born March 25, 1960; admitted to bar, 1985, Virginia; 1987, District of Columbia. *Education:* Virginia Polytechnic Institute and State University (B.A., 1982); University of Virginia (J.D., 1985). Member, Senior Editorial Board, Virginia Law Review. Moderator, Executive Compensation and Employee Benefits Forum on Counsel Connect, 1994-1998; National Association of Stock Plan Professionals. (Also at Northern Virginia Office). ***PRACTICE AREAS:*** Executive Compensation; Employment Law; Corporate Transactions; Employee Benefits. ***Email:*** skilgore@wilmer.com

THOMAS E.D. MILLSPAUGH, born November 13, 1960; admitted to bar, 1987, Maryland (Not admitted in District of Columbia). *Education:* University of North Carolina (B.A., with highest honors, 1983); University of Virginia (J.D., 1987). Phi Beta Kappa. Morehead Scholar. (Resident, Baltimore, Maryland Office). ***PRACTICE AREAS:*** Business Law; Corporate Law; Finance; Real Estate. ***Email:*** tmillspaugh@wilmer.com

YOON-YOUNG LEE, born April 17, 1963; admitted to bar, 1988, Virginia; 1989, District of Columbia. *Education:* Johns Hopkins University (B.A., 1985); Harvard University (J.D., 1988). ***PRACTICE AREAS:*** Securities; SEC Enforcement. ***Email:*** ylee@wilmer.com

JAMES R. WRATHALL, born September 14, 1962; admitted to bar, 1987, Maryland; 1990, District of Columbia. *Education:* Tulane University (B.S.M., 1984); Georgetown University (J.D., 1987). Associate Editor, Georgetown Law Journal. ***PRACTICE AREAS:*** Civil Practice; Appellate Practice; Information and Privacy; Bankruptcy; Environmental Law. ***Email:*** jwrathall@wilmer.com

GAIL C. BERNSTEIN, born August 27, 1960; admitted to bar, 1988, Massachusetts; 1990, District of Columbia. *Education:* Hebrew University of Jerusalem (B.A., 1981); Harvard University (J.D., 1988). Clerk to Judge Douglas P. Woodlock, D. Massachusetts. ***Email:*** gbernstein@wilmer.com

STEVEN F. CHERRY, born June 5, 1962; admitted to bar, 1991, Illinois; 1992, District of Columbia. *Education:* Indiana State University (B.S., 1983); Indiana University (M.P.A., 1986); University of Michigan (J.D., 1989). Note Editor, Michigan Law Review. Clerk to Judge Robert R. Beezer, 9th Circuit. (Resident, Northern Virginia Office). ***Email:*** scherry@wilmer.com

SUSAN P. CRAWFORD, born February 27, 1963; admitted to bar, 1991, California; 1992, District of Columbia. *Education:* Yale University (B.A., 1984; J.D., 1989). Clerk to Judge Raymond J. Dearie, E.D. New York. ***PRACTICE AREAS:*** Electronic Commerce. ***Email:*** scrawford@wilmer.com

ROBERT F. HOYT, born September 8, 1964; admitted to bar, 1990, Pennsylvania; 1991, District of Columbia. *Education:* Cornell University (B.S., 1986); University of Pennsylvania (J.D., M.A., 1989). Comment Editor, University of Pennsylvania Law Review. Clerk to Justice Herbert P. Wilkins, Supreme Judicial Court of Massachusetts. ***PRACTICE AREAS:*** Securities; Corporate; Litigation. ***Email:*** bhoyt@wilmer.com

DR. NATALIE LÜBBEN, born December 21, 1961; admitted to bar, 1990, Germany (Not admitted in District of Columbia). *Education:* Free University of Berlin; University of Geneva; First State Examination (1987); Second State Examination (1990); Free University of Berlin (Dr. jur. s.c.l., 1992). Author,

(This Listing Continued)

The Freedom to Use the Airspace (1993); *German Efforts to Regulate E-Commerce* (2000); *Telecommunications, Multimedia and Internet Regulation in Germany* (2000). Co-author: *Access to Airports Close to National Boundaries* (2001); *Telecommunications: Key Market of the Future -- From Monopoly to Competition* (1996); *The Regulation of Ground Handling at European Airports* (1994); *Legal Instruments for the Allocation of Traffic in the Airport System Berlin-Brandenburg* (1993). Assistant Professor, Administrative and Constitutional Law, Free University of Berlin, 1990-1992. *Member:* Berlin and German Bar Associations; German Female Lawyers Association. (Resident, European Office, Berlin, Germany). ***LANGUAGES:*** German and French. ***PRACTICE AREAS:*** Aviation Law; Telecommunications Law; Data Protection; Electronic Commerce; Multimedia Law; Public Procurement Law. ***Email:*** nluebben@wilmer.com

LYNN R. CHARYTAN, born October 29, 1965; admitted to bar, 1991, New York and District of Columbia. *Education:* Columbia University (B.A., summa cum laude, 1987); Harvard University (J.D., magna cum laude, 1990). Clerk to Judge Stanley Sporkin, D. District of Columbia. ***PRACTICE AREAS:*** Communications; Electronic Commerce. ***Email:*** lcharytan@wilmer.com

MICHAEL R. HOLTER, born September 11, 1965; admitted to bar, 1988, Solicitor of the Supreme Court; 1998, England and Wales (Not admitted in District of Columbia). *Education:* Trinity Hall, Cambridge University, U.K. (B.A., 1987). Tutor, Inns of Court School of Law, 1988-1989. (Resident, European Office, London, England). ***PRACTICE AREAS:*** Aviation Law; Corporate Transactions; Telecommunications Law. ***Email:*** mholter@wilmer.com

THOMAS MUELLER, born September 22, 1965; admitted to bar, 1990, Massachusetts; 1991, New York; 1992, District of Columbia. *Education:* Williams College (B.A., magna cum laude, 1987); Harvard University (J.D., cum laude, 1990). Clerk to Judge Walter Jay Skinner, D. Massachusetts. Fellow, Max Planck Institute for Foreign and International Patent, Copyright and Competition Law (Munich), 1991-1992. (Also at European Office, Brussels, Belgium). ***PRACTICE AREAS:*** EU Competition; Antitrust. ***Email:*** tmueller@wilmer.com

JONATHAN NUECHTERLEIN, born 1964; admitted to bar, 1994, District of Columbia. *Education:* Yale University (B.A., summa cum laude, 1986; J.D., 1990). Phi Beta Kappa. Articles Editor, Yale Law Journal. Clerk to: Judge Stephen F. Williams, D.C. Circuit; Justice David H. Souter, U.S. Supreme Court, October Term, 1991. Deputy General Counsel, Federal Communications Commission, 2000-2001. Assistant to the Solicitor General, U.S. Department of Justice, 1996-2000. Special Counsel, Federal Communications Commission, 1995-1996. ***PRACTICE AREAS:*** Telecommunications Law; Appellate Practice. ***Email:*** jnuechterlein@wilmer.com

CATHERINE KANE RONIS, born 1964; admitted to bar, 1991, Florida; 1992, District of Columbia. *Education:* College of the Holy Cross (B.A., 1986); Syracuse University (J.D., magna cum laude, 1990). Order of the Coif. Senior Editor, Syracuse Law Review, 1989-1990. *Member:* American Bar Association (Member, Communications Law Committee). ***PRACTICE AREAS:*** Communications Law; Telecommunications Law. ***Email:*** cronis@wilmer.com

CHRISTIAN L. DUVERNOY, born October 3, 1962; admitted to bar, 1989, New York; 1990, District of Columbia. *Education:* Harvard University (A.B., 1984); Free University of Berlin (DAAD Fellow); University of Michigan (J.D., 1988). Order of the Coif. Stagiaire, Court of Justice of the European Communities. (Resident, European Office, Brussels, Belgium). ***PRACTICE AREAS:*** Communications Law; Competition; Information Technology. ***Email:*** cduvernoy@wilmer.com

JAMES W. LOWE, born August 7, 1963; admitted to bar, 1990, New York and 1991, District of Columbia; 1993, U.S. Supreme Court. *Education:* Yale University (B.A., summa cum laude, 1985); Harvard University (J.D., magna cum laude, 1989). Phi Beta Kappa. National Merit Scholar. Managing Editor, Harvard Journal on Legislation. Urban Fellow, Mayor's Office of Transportation Policy, City of New York, 1985-1986. Clerk to Judge Peter K. Leisure, S.D. New York. Trial Attorney, U.S. Department of Justice, Antitrust Division, 1990-1994. ABA Section of Antitrust Law, Internet Committee Chair, 1996-1999; Vice-Chair, Section One Committee, 1999—. Fellow, British-American Project. ***PRACTICE AREAS:*** Antitrust; EU Competition; Aviation Law; Aviation Defense; Telecommunications Law. ***Email:*** jlowe@wilmer.com

ALI M. STOEPPELWERTH, born March 30, 1963; admitted to bar, 1990, California; 1996, District of Columbia. *Education:* Stanford University (B.A., 1985; J.D., 1989); Princeton University (M.P.A., 1989); University of Amsterdam (LL.M., 1993). Associate Editor, Stanford University Law Review. Clerk to Chief Judge Alfred T. Goodwin, 9th Circuit. ***PRACTICE AREAS:*** Antitrust; EU Competition; Media Law; Electronic Commerce. ***Email:*** astoeppelwerth@wilmer.com

JAMES E. ANDERSON, born January 31, 1965; admitted to bar, 1992, Utah; 1995, District of Columbia. *Education:* Ricks College (A.S., 1986); University of Utah (B.A., 1988); Brigham Young University (J.D., 1992). Leader Articles Editor, Brigham Young University Law Review. ***PRACTICE AREAS:*** Investment Management; Securities. ***Email:*** janderson@wilmer.com

(This Listing Continued)

WILMER, CUTLER & PICKERING, Washington—Continued

GREGORIO B. CATER, born June 27, 1965; admitted to bar, 1993, Connecticut; 1995, District of Columbia. *Education:* University of Oklahoma (B.A., with highest honors, 1987); Yale University (J.D., 1992). Essays Editor, Yale Law Journal. Clerk to Judge Jose A. Cabranes, D. Connecticut. (Also Resident, European Office, London, England). ***PRACTICE AREAS:*** Corporate Finance; Corporate Transactions; Electronic Commerce; International Aviation Law; Aviation Defense; Aerospace Law; Technology Law; Venture Capital. ***Email:*** gcater@wilmer.com

ERIK H. CORWIN, born August 9, 1963; admitted to bar, 1993, Massachusetts; 1994, District of Columbia. *Education:* Harvard University (A.B., 1985; A.M., 1988; J.D., 1992). Editor, Harvard Law Review; Harvard Journal on Legislation. Clerk to Judge James L. Buckley, D.C. Circuit. ***PRACTICE AREAS:*** Taxation. ***Email:*** ecorwin@wilmer.com

DENISE ESPOSITO, born February 8, 1967; admitted to bar, 1992, Maryland; 1995, District of Columbia. *Education:* Rutgers University (B.A., 1988); University of Michigan (J.D., magna cum laude, 1992). Order of the Coif. Editor, Michigan Law Review. ***PRACTICE AREAS:*** Biotechnology; Complex Contract Disputes; Litigation; Products Liability; Product Safety. ***Email:*** desposito@wilmer.com

ANDREW N. GOLDMAN, born February 7, 1967; admitted to bar, 1993, New York and New Jersey. *Education:* The Wharton School, University of Pennsylvania (B.S., 1989); Brooklyn Law School (J.D., 1992). Member, Moot Court Honor Society. Notes and Comments Editor, Brooklyn Journal of International Law. Clerk to Chief U.S. Bankruptcy Judge Tina L. Brozman, Southern District of New York. Author: "In re Burger Boys: Are Landlords Being Grilled in the Second Circuit," 63 B'klyn L. Rev. 437 (1997); "The Effect of Diplomatic Immunity on Divorce Judgments," 18 B'klyn J. Int'l L. 281 (1992). Lecturer, "Investing in Distressed Internet Companies," Institute for International Research, Spring 2000; Lecturer, "The E-Bankruptcy Estate," Brooklyn Law School Zaretsky Roundtable Seminar, Spring 2000. Associate: Weil Gotshal & Manges LLP, 1994-1998; Schulte, Roth & Zabel LLP, 1998-2001. (Resident, New York Office). ***PRACTICE AREAS:*** Bankruptcy; Corporate Restructuring. ***Email:*** agoldman@wilmer.com

SOO J. YIM, born August 15, 1966; admitted to bar, 1993, California; 1994, District of Columbia. *Education:* Harvard University (A.B., magna cum laude, 1989; J.D., magna cum laude, 1992). Fellow, Olin Fellowship for Law & Economics, 1991-1992. Fellow, Ford Fellowship for Public International Law at the World Bank, 1992-1993. ***PRACTICE AREAS:*** Broker-Dealer Regulation; Electronic Commerce; Financial Institutions Law; Investment Management; SEC Enforcement. ***Email:*** syim@wilmer.com

BRIGIDA BENITEZ, born November 11, 1968; admitted to bar, 1993, Massachusetts; 1995, District of Columbia. *Education:* University of Florida (B.S., with high honors, 1990); Boston College (J.D., 1993). Editor-in-Chief, Boston College Law Review. ***PRACTICE AREAS:*** Appellate Practice; Trial Practice; Internal Investigations; Alternative Dispute Resolution. ***Email:*** bbenitez@wilmer.com

STUART F. DELERY, born November 8, 1968; admitted to bar, 1993, Virginia; 1996, District of Columbia. *Education:* University of Virginia (B.A., with highest distinction, 1990); Yale University (J.D., 1993). Articles Editor, Yale Law Journal. Clerk to Judge Gerald B. Tjoflat, 11th Circuit; Justice Byron R. White, U.S. Supreme Court, October term 1994. ***PRACTICE AREAS:*** Litigation; Securities Law. ***Email:*** sdelery@wilmer.com

JENNIFER M. DROGULA, born August 15, 1964; admitted to bar, 1992, New York; 1993, District of Columbia. *Education:* University of Texas at Austin (B.A., 1987); Duke University (J.D., LL.M., 1991). Phi Beta Kappa. ***PRACTICE AREAS:*** Latin America; Corporate. ***Email:*** jdrogula@wilmer.com

CRAIG T. GOLDBLATT, born September 9, 1968; admitted to bar, 1994, Pennsylvania and New Jersey; 1996, District of Columbia. *Education:* Georgetown University (B.A., magna cum laude, 1990); University of Chicago (J.D., honors, 1993). Comment Editor, University of Chicago Law Review. Clerk to: Justice David H. Souter, U.S. Supreme Court, October Term, 1995; Judge Richard D. Cudahy, 7th Circuit. ***PRACTICE AREAS:*** Bankruptcy; Litigation. ***Email:*** cgoldblatt@wilmer.com

JOHN J. KALLAUGHER, born February 5, 1952; admitted to bar, 1978, New York; admitted to practice, 1997, England and Wales (Not admitted in District of Columbia). *Education:* Harvard University (A.B., 1973); Cornell University (J.D., 1977). Research Editor, Cornell Law Review. Visiting Professor, University College London (EC Competition Law, and Comparative Antitrust Law -- US/EC). (Resident, European Office, London, England). ***PRACTICE AREAS:*** International Law; Antitrust and Trade Regulation. ***Email:*** jkallaugher@wilmer.com

GLYNN D. KEY, born February 8, 1964; admitted to bar, 1989, District of Columbia. *Education:* University of Virginia (B.A., 1986; J.D., 1989). President, Board of Managers, University of Virginia, 2001-2002. Counselor to Secretary Bruce Babbitt and Associate Solicitor of the U.S. Department of the Interior, 1995-1996. Special Assistant to the Secretary of the Interior, 1993-1995. ***PRACTICE AREAS:*** Corporate Law. ***Email:*** gkey@wilmer.com

SATISH M. KINI, born March 28, 1965; admitted to bar, 1993, New York; 1994, District of Columbia. *Education:* Colgate University (B.A., magna cum laude, 1985); Columbia Law School (J.D., 1992). Phi Beta Kappa. Managing Editor, Columbia Law Review. Clerk to Judge Richard J. Cardamone, 2nd Circuit. Author: "The New SEC Privacy Rules," Insights: The Corporate and Securities Law Advisor, August 2000; "Impact of the 1999 Financial Modernization Act on Investment Advisers and Investment Companies," Securities & Commodities Regulation, April 11, 2000; "Fed Letter Eases Limits on Using Affiliate Securities as Loan Collateral," Banking Policy Report, May 17, 1999. Co-Author: "Subordinated Debt: A Capital Markets Approach to Bank Regulation," 61 Boston College Law Rev. 195, 2000; "The Interstate Banking and Branching Efficiency Act: New Options, New Problems," 112 Banking Law J. 100, 1995. Counsel, Legal Division, Federal Reserve Board, 1996-1998. ***PRACTICE AREAS:*** Financial Institutions; Investment Management. ***Email:*** skini@wilmer.com

MARK S. SHELTON, born April 5, 1967; admitted to bar, 1992, Kansas; 1994, District of Columbia. *Education:* University of Kansas (B.A., 1989); University of Virginia (J.D., 1992). Order of the Coif. Articles Review Board, Virginia Law Review. Clerk to Judge C. Arlen Beam, 8th Circuit. Adjunct Professor, The Regulation of Securities Markets and Professionals, Georgetown University Law Center, 1999—. ***PRACTICE AREAS:*** Securities Law; Broker-Dealer Regulation. ***Email:*** mshelton@wilmer.com

SENIOR COUNSEL

LLOYD N. CUTLER, born November 10, 1917; admitted to bar, 1940, New York; 1946, District of Columbia. *Education:* Yale University (B.A., 1936; LL.B., 1939). Honorary LL.D., Yale University, 1983; Princeton University, 1994; Jefferson Medal in Law, University of Virginia, 1995; Trinity College, 2000. Editor-in-Chief, Yale Law Journal. Clerk to Judge Charles Clark, 2d Circuit. Member, Council on Foreign Relations. Counsel to the President of the United States, 1979-1980, 1994. Chair, ABA Section of Individual Rights and Responsibilities, 1969. Member, ABA House of Delegates, 1970. Member, United States Group, Permanent Court of Arbitration, 1984-1993. Honorary Bencher, Middle Temple, London. *Member:* American Law Institute (Member of Council, 1974—). ***PRACTICE AREAS:*** Alternative Dispute Resolution; Business Law; Constitutional Law; International Law; Regulatory Law. ***Email:*** lcutler@wilmer.com

JOHN H. PICKERING, born February 27, 1916; admitted to bar, 1941, New York; 1947, District of Columbia. *Education:* University of Michigan (A.B., 1938; J.D., 1940). Honorary LL.D., University of the District of Columbia, 1995; Honorary LL.D., University of Michigan, 1996. Board of Editors, Michigan Law Review. Recipient: American Bar Foundation 50 Year Award, 1993; American Bar Association ABA Medal, 1999. Clerk to Justice Frank Murphy, U.S. Supreme Court, October Terms, 1941-1942. Board of Directors, National Center for State Courts, 1987-1993. President, District of Columbia Bar, 1979-1980. State Delegate to American Bar Association, 1984-1993. D.C. Bar Delegate, 1993-1997; Senior Lawyer Division Delegate, 1997—. Chair, ABA Commission on Legal Problems of the Elderly, 1985-1993; Senior Advisor, 1993-1995; Chair 1995-1996; Chair, ABA Senior Lawyers Division, 1996-1997. Chair, Advisory Committee on Procedures, D.C. Circuit, 1976-1982. Chair of Mediators, D.C. Circuit, 1987—. Life Fellow, American Bar Foundation. *Life Member:* American Law Institute. ***PRACTICE AREAS:*** Civil Practice; Energy; Business Law; Natural Resources. ***Email:*** jpickering@wilmer.com

COUNSEL

LESTER NURICK, born December 2, 1914; admitted to bar, 1937, New York; 1981, District of Columbia. *Education:* College of the City of New York (B.S.S., 1934); Brooklyn Law School (LL.B., 1937). Author, *Costs in International Arbitration*, 7 International Center for the Settlement of Investment Disputes Review-Financial International Law Journal 57 (1992); *Negotiation of Transnational Bank Loan Agreements Entered Into by Developing Country Borrowers: Legal and Other Issues*, United Nations Centre on Transnational Corporations (1983). Adjunct Professor (Structure and Financing of International Projects), Georgetown University, 1981-1999. Professorial-Lecturer (Structure and Financing of International Projects), George Washington University, 1961-1980. Counsel, World Bank, 1946-1980, retiring as Vice-President. Co-chair, ABA National Institute on Negotiating and Drafting International Commercial Contracts, 1986-1987. *Member:* American Society of International Law. ***PRACTICE AREAS:*** International Law; Arbitration; Project Finance. ***Email:*** lnurick@wilmer.com

LEONARD M. SHAMBON, born March 22, 1945; admitted to bar, 1973, New York; 1974, District of Columbia. *Education:* Yale University (B.A., 1967); University of Pennsylvania (J.D., 1972). Member, Editorial Board, University of Pennsylvania Law Review. Clerk to Judge Oscar H. Davis, U.S. Court

(This Listing Continued)

of Claims. Director, Office of Compliance, Import Administration, U.S. Department of Commerce, 1980-1986. Antitrust Counsel, House Judiciary Committee, 1975-1979. Chair, Committee on International Trade Regulation, ABA Section of Administrative Law and Regulatory Practice, 1990-1993. Vice-Chair, Predecessor Committee on Customs, Tariffs and Trade, 1988-1990. Member, Steering Committee on International Trade, ABA Section of International Law and Practice, 1994—. ***PRACTICE AREAS:*** International Trade. ***Email:*** lshambon@wilmer.com

VICTORIA E. SCHONFELD, born December 9, 1950; admitted to bar, 1976, New York. *Education:* University of Pennsylvania (B.A., summa cum laude, 1972); Columbia University (J.D., 1975). Phi Beta Kappa. Stone Scholar. Co-author, textbook, "Mutual Funds Activities of Banks," Prentice Hall (1994), with Melanie Fein and David Freeman. (Resident, New York Office). ***PRACTICE AREAS:*** Securities Law; Investment Management; Business Transactions. ***Email:*** vschonfeld@wilmer.com

WILLIAM J. FLANAGAN, born August 20, 1952; admitted to bar, 1977, Virginia; 1980, District of Columbia. *Education:* Georgetown University (B.S.F.S., summa cum laude, 1974; J.D., 1977). Phi Beta Kappa. Articles Editor, American Criminal Law Review. Clerk to Judge Thomas A. Flannery, U.S. District Court for the District of Columbia. Assistant Counsel for Regulation, Office of the Solicitor, Plan Benefits Security Division, U.S. Department of Labor, 1978-1986. ***PRACTICE AREAS:*** Employee Benefits. ***Email:*** bflanagan@wilmer.com

CAROL H. FISHMAN, born September 6, 1941; admitted to bar, 1978, District of Columbia. *Education:* Wellesley College (B.A., 1963); George Washington University (J.D., 1978). Editor-in-Chief, George Washington Law Review. ***PRACTICE AREAS:*** Insurance; Civil Practice. ***Email:*** cfishman@wilmer.com

JOSEPH E. KILLORY, JR., born August 17, 1954; admitted to bar, 1979, District of Columbia. *Education:* Harvard University (A.B., 1976; J.D., 1979). (Resident, Northern Virginia Office). ***PRACTICE AREAS:*** Trial and Appellate Litigation; Arbitration; Alternative Dispute Resolution; E-Commerce; Intellectual Property; Securities; Employment Law; Energy; Insurance. ***Email:*** tkillory@wilmer.com

CHRISTOPHER J. HERRLING, born November 11, 1954; admitted to bar, 1981, New York and District of Columbia. *Education:* University of Rochester (B.A., 1976); Catholic University of America (J.D., 1980). *Member:* The District of Columbia Bar; The Legal Aid Society of the District of Columbia (Trustee). ***Email:*** cherrling@wilmer.com

ROGER J. PATTERSON, born July 11, 1956; admitted to bar, 1983, District of Columbia. *Education:* University of Minnesota (B.E.S., 1978); University of Chicago (J.D., 1981). Associate Editor, University of Chicago Law Review. Clerk to Judge Dorothy W. Nelson, 9th Circuit. ***PRACTICE AREAS:*** Corporate Law; Securities. ***Email:*** rpatterson@wilmer.com

DANIEL B. PHYTHYON, born August 11, 1956; admitted to bar, 1981, District of Columbia. *Education:* Westminster College (B.A., magna cum laude, 1978); Cornell University (J.D., 1981). Majority Staff Counsel, Senate Committee on Commerce, Science and Transportation, 1981-1986. Vice President, Congressional Liaison, National Association of Broadcasters, 1986-1994. Director, Office of Legislative and Intergovernmental Affairs, Federal Communications Commission, 1996-1997. Deputy Chief, Wireless Telecommunications Bureau, Federal Communications Commission, 1997. Chief, Wireless Telecommunications Bureau, Federal Communications Commission, 1997-1998. ***PRACTICE AREAS:*** Communications and Media; Electronic Commerce; Legislative Practice. ***Email:*** dphythyon@wilmer.com

MATTHEW A. CHAMBERS, born Jacksonville, Florida, November 15, 1957; admitted to bar, 1982, Washington; 1995, District of Columbia. *Education:* Duke University (A.B., 1979); University of Michigan (J.D., 1982). Phi Beta Kappa; Order of the Coif. Associate Director, Division of Investment Management, Securities and Exchange Commission, 1991-1995. ***PRACTICE AREAS:*** Securities Regulation; Mutual Funds; Investment Partnerships; Investment Company Law; Derivative Products.

ENRIQUE GOMEZ-PINZON, admitted to bar, 1983, Colombia; 1987, New York; 2000, District of Columbia. *Education:* Universidad de los Andes, Bogota, Colombia (Law Degree, 1983); Georgetown University; Harvard University (LL.M., 1985). Professor, International Public Law, Universidad de los Andes, Bogota, Colombia, 1988-1990. Director, Colombian Government Trade Bureau, Washington, D.C., 1998-2000. Founder and Managing Partner, Gomez Pinzon & Asociados, Bogotá, Colombia, 1992-1998. Counsel to the President, Banco de Bogotá, 1987-1989. *Member:* The Association of the Bar of the City of New York; American and International Bar Associations; ICSID Roster of Arbitrators; American Society of International Law. ***LANGUAGES:*** Spanish. ***PRACTICE AREAS:*** Mergers and Acquisitions; International Arbitration; International Trade; Project Finance; Privatization. ***Email:*** egomezpinzon@wilmer.com

JOANNE F. CATANESE, admitted to bar, 1984, New York; 1987, Maryland (Not admitted in District of Columbia). *Education:* City University of New York, Queens College (B.A., 1974); St. John's University (M.B.A., 1981; J.D., 1983). Research Editor, Law Review. (Resident, Baltimore, Maryland Office). ***PRACTICE AREAS:*** Corporate Law; Securities; Mergers and Acquisitions; Venture Capital. ***Email:*** jcatanese@wilmer.com

ROBERT G. BAGNALL, born August 7, 1956; admitted to bar, 1986, New York and District of Columbia. *Education:* Yale University (B.A., 1977); Harvard Law School (J.D., 1985). Editor, Harvard Civil Rights - Civil Liberties Law Review. Co-Author, with Kimble C. Cannon, *The National Securities Markets Improvement Act of 1996: Summary and Discussion,* 25 Securities Regulation L.J.3 (1997). Adjunct Professor, Georgetown University, 2000—. Securities and Exchange Commission, Division of Investment Management, Senior Special Counsel (Office of Chief Counsel), 1995-1996, Assistant Chief of Office (Office of Regulatory Policy) 1993-1995. ***PRACTICE AREAS:*** Securities Law. ***Email:*** rbagnall@wilmer.com

JEAN-MICHEL COUMES, born January 15, 1964; admitted to bar, 1994, Paris (Not admitted in District of Columbia). *Education:* College of Europe (Diplôme des Hautes Etudes Européennes, 1989); Law University Toulouse (Master in Law, 1985; D.E.S.S., 1987). (Resident, European Office, Brussels, Belgium). ***Email:*** jcoumes@wilmer.com

BRENT J. GURNEY, admitted to bar, 1985, Illinois; 1987, District of Columbia. *Education:* Kalamazoo College (B.A., magna cum laude, 1981); Harvard Law School (J.D., cum laude, 1985). Phi Beta Kappa. Comments Editor, Harvard International Law Journal. Clerk to Justice Warren Matthews, Supreme Court of Alaska. Assistant United States Attorney, 1991-1999 and Deputy Chief, Southern Division, 1996-1999, United States Attorney's Office for the District of Maryland. ***PRACTICE AREAS:*** Complex Litigation; White Collar Crime. ***Email:*** bgurney@wilmer.com

JAMES H. MANN, born February 14, 1960; admitted to bar, 1986, District of Columbia. *Education:* Harvard University (B.A., summa cum laude, 1982); Columbia University (J.D., 1986). Stone Scholar, Schlesinger Prize. (Resident, New York Office). ***LANGUAGES:*** Russian. ***PRACTICE AREAS:*** Consumer Banking; Banking Regulation. ***Email:*** jmann@wilmer.com

NANCY L. MANZER, born July 27, 1961; admitted to bar, 1989, New York and District of Columbia. *Education:* Harvard University (A.B., 1983); Cornell University (J.D., 1988). Articles Editor, Cornell Law Review. Clerk to the Senior Judges, D.C. Court of Appeals. ***PRACTICE AREAS:*** Civil Litigation; Insurance. ***Email:*** nmanzer@wilmer.com

JUTTA VON FALKENHAUSEN, born March 18, 1963; admitted to bar, 1993, Berlin (Not admitted in District of Columbia). *Education:* Free University of Berlin; University of Geneva; First State Examination (1988); Harvard University (M.P.A., 1990); Second State Examination (1993). (Resident, European Office, Berlin, Germany). ***PRACTICE AREAS:*** German Law; International Transactions; Civil Litigation. ***Email:*** jvonfalkenhausen@wilmer.com

LEON B. GREENFIELD, born October 16, 1964; admitted to bar, 1990, Pennsylvania; 1994, District of Columbia. *Education:* Pennsylvania State University (B.S., 1986); University of Chicago (J.D., 1989). Associate Editor, University of Chicago Law Review. Clerk to Judge Stanley Marcus, S.D. Florida. ***PRACTICE AREAS:*** Antitrust; Corporate Investigations; Securities Law. ***Email:*** lgreenfield@wilmer.com

RONALD I. MELTZER, born August 12, 1948; admitted to bar, 1990, New York and District of Columbia. *Education:* Ohio University (B.A., 1970); Columbia University (Ph.D., 1975); State University of New York at Buffalo (J.D., 1989). Assistant Professor of Political Science, State University of New York at Buffalo, 1975-1983; Associate Professor, 1983-1989. Adjunct Professor, School of International Service, American University, 1993-1996. Author, *The U.S. Renewal of the GSP: Implications for North-South Trade*, 20 Journal of World Trade Law 507 (1986); *The Deterioration of the GATT Framework in International Trade Relations*, Politics in the United Nations System (Finkelstein ed., 1988); *Foreign Agents Regulation Act*, The Lobbying Manual: A Compliance Guide for Lawyers and Lobbyist (American Bar Association, 1998). ***PRACTICE AREAS:*** International Trade; International Aviation. ***Email:*** rmeltzer@wilmer.com

MARTIN SEYFARTH, born December 22, 1961; admitted to bar, 1999, Germany (Not admitted in District of Columbia). *Education:* Rheinische Friedrich-Wilhelms University; First State Examination (1989); Cologne Higher Regional Court; Second State Examination (1993). Chief of Staff, German Federal Ministry of Transport, 1993-1998. (Resident, European Office, Berlin, Germany). ***PRACTICE AREAS:*** European Union Law; German Democratic Republic Law. ***Email:*** mseyfarth@wilmer.com

ERIC J. MAHR, born May 25, 1965; admitted to bar, 1990, Pennsylvania; 1998, District of Columbia. *Education:* Bucknell University (B.A., 1987); Salford University, Manchester, England; University of Pittsburgh (J.D., magna cum laude, 1990). Order of the Coif. Executive Editor, University of Pittsburgh Law Review. Clerk to Judge Raymond J. Broderick, U.S. District Court, Eastern District of Pennsylvania. Trial Attorney, Civil Division, Federal Programs

(This Listing Continued)

WILMER, CUTLER & PICKERING, Washington—Continued

Branch, U.S. Department of Justice, 1992-1997. (Resident, European Office, Brussels, Belgium). ***PRACTICE AREAS:*** Antitrust; EU Competition; Civil Litigation. ***Email:*** emahr@wilmer.com

JEFFREY E. McFADDEN, born May 6, 1957; admitted to bar, 1990, Maryland; 1992, District of Columbia. *Education:* U.S. Naval Academy (B.S., with distinction, 1979); Georgetown University (J.D., magna cum laude, 1990). Clerk to Judge Francis D. Murnaghan, Jr., 4th Circuit. ***PRACTICE AREAS:*** Securities Enforcement; Securities Litigation; White Collar Crime. ***Email:*** jmcfadden@wilmer.com

BRIAN J. MENKES, born November 18, 1962; admitted to bar, 1990, Massachusetts; 1991, District of Columbia. *Education:* Central Connecticut State University (B.S., 1985); Western New England College (J.D., magna cum laude, 1990); New York University (LL.M., 1991). ***PRACTICE AREAS:*** Tax; Corporate Transactions; Venture Capital. ***Email:*** bmenkes@wilmer.com

NELSON R. OLIVEIRA, born May 31, 1962; admitted to bar, 1992, New York (Not admitted in District of Columbia). *Education:* Bowdoin College (B.A., 1984); Boston College (J.D., cum laude, 1990). Senior Commercial Counsel, Overseas Private Investment Corporation, 1996-2001. ***LANGUAGES:*** Portuguese. ***PRACTICE AREAS:*** Business Transactions; Corporate Finance; Project Finance. ***Email:*** noliveira@wilmer.com

JILL REYNOLDS SEIDMAN, born March 27, 1965; admitted to bar, 1990, Maryland. *Education:* University of Maryland (B.A., magna cum laude, 1987; J.D., cum laude, 1990). Phi Beta Kappa. Articles Editor, Maryland Law Review. (Resident, Baltimore, Maryland Office). ***LANGUAGES:*** Spanish. ***PRACTICE AREAS:*** Real Estate; Electronic Commerce; Corporate Law. ***Email:*** jseidman@wilmer.com

DAVID R. LURIE, born July 8, 1962; admitted to bar, 1992, New York (Not admitted in District of Columbia). *Education:* Swarthmore College (B.A., with high honors, 1984); Fordham University (J.D., cum laude, 1991). Articles Editor, Fordham Law Review, 1990-1991. Clerk to Judge John M. Walker, Jr., U.S. Court of Appeals, Second Circuit, 1992-1993. Author: "Sixth Amendment Implications of Informant Participation in Defense Meetings," 58 Fordham Law Review, 1990. Co-Author: with Norman Redlich, "First Amendment Issues Presented by the Information Super Highway," 24 Seton Hall Law Review 101, 1995; with Norman Redlich, "Federalism: A Surrogate for What Really Matters," 23 Ohio Northern University Law Review 1273, 1997; with Lawrence Pedowitz and Carol Miller, "Amendments to the FCPA for More Honest Competition Overseas," Business Crimes, March 1999. (Resident, New York Office). ***PRACTICE AREAS:*** Litigation; Securities. ***Email:*** dlurie@wilmer.com

BRUCE H. NEWMAN, born Bronx, New York, March 29, 1965; admitted to bar, 1991, New Jersey; 1992, New York. *Education:* Rutgers College (B.A., 1987); Yeshiva University (J.D., 1991). *Member:* American Bar Association. (Resident, New York Office). ***PRACTICE AREAS:*** Securities.

CATHLEEN P. PETERSON, born 1964; admitted to bar, 1991, Pennsylvania; 1994, District of Columbia. *Education:* University of Utah (B.A., 1987); University of Pennsylvania (J.D., 1991). ***PRACTICE AREAS:*** Aviation Defense; Government Contracts; Administrative Law. ***Email:*** cpeterson@wilmer.com

WILLIAM E. WHITE, born August 3, 1966; admitted to bar, 1991, California (Not admitted in District of Columbia). *Education:* Boston College (B.A., 1988); Pepperdine University (J.D., cum laude, 1991). Clerk to Judge James M. Ideman, Central District of California. Securities and Exchange Commission, Division of Enforcement, Los Angeles Regional Office; Staff Attorney, 1991-1994; Branch Chief, 1994-1997; Senior Trial Counsel, 1997-1999. ***PRACTICE AREAS:*** Securities Law. ***Email:*** wwhite@wilmer.com

CRISTINA MENDOZA BOURELLY, born June 12, 1966; admitted to bar, 1992, Maryland; 1994, District of Columbia. *Education:* Duke University (B.A., 1988); Northwestern University School of Law (J.D., 1992). Counsel to International Finance Corporation, 1997-2000. ***LANGUAGES:*** Spanish, French, Italian. ***PRACTICE AREAS:*** Corporate Transactions; Project Finance; Privatization; Technology Law; Venture Capital. ***Email:*** cmendozabourelly@wilmer.com

STEVEN P. FINIZIO, born April 27, 1966; admitted to bar, 1993, California; 1995, District of Columbia. *Education:* Georgetown University (A.B., 1988); University of Chicago (J.D., 1992). Associate Articles Editor, University of Chicago Law Review. Clerk to Judge Diarmuid F. O'Scannlain, 9th Circuit. (Resident, European Office, London, England). ***PRACTICE AREAS:*** International Dispute Resolution; Litigation; Securities Law. ***Email:*** sfinizio@wilmer.com

FRASER L. HUNTER, JR., born 1966; admitted to bar, 1993, New York. *Education:* Brown University (A.B., 1988); Columbia University (J.D., 1992). Clerk to the Hon. Martin L.C. Feldman, U.S.D.J., Eastern District of Louisiana. (Resident, New York Office). ***PRACTICE AREAS:*** Securities; Litigation. ***Email:*** fhunter@wilmer.com

(This Listing Continued)

KAREN M. MINCAVAGE, born March 9, 1967; admitted to bar, 1992, North Carolina; 1999, District of Columbia. *Education:* University of Michigan (B.S., with high honors, 1989); University of North Carolina (J.D., with honors, 1992). Order of the Coif. Member, North Carolina Journal of International Law and Commerce Regulation. Branch Chief, 1997-1998 and Senior Counsel, Staff Attorney, 1992-1997, U.S. Securities and Exchange Commission, Division of Enforcement. ***PRACTICE AREAS:*** Securities Law. ***Email:*** kmincavage@wilmer.com

JEAN PAUL M. POITRAS, born February 18, 1968; admitted to bar, 1995, Ontario; 1996, New York (Not admitted in District of Columbia). *Education:* Carleton University (B.A., 1988); McGill University (LL.B./B.C.L., 1992); University of Paris (D.E.A., 1993). Executive Editor, McGill Law Journal. Clerk to Supreme Court of Canada. (Resident, European Office, Brussels, Belgium). ***Email:*** jppoitras@wilmer.com

JEFFREY A. ROTH, born July 30, 1967; admitted to bar, 1992, Illinois; 1999, District of Columbia; 2001, New York. *Education:* University of Michigan (A.B., with high distinction, 1989; J.D., cum laude, 1992). Note Editor, University of Michigan Journal of Law Reform. (Resident, New York Office). ***PRACTICE AREAS:*** Securities Law; Broker-Dealer Regulation. ***Email:*** jroth@wilmer.com

BETH A. STEKLER, born December 30, 1967; admitted to bar, 1992, Maryland; 1994, District of Columbia. *Education:* Cornell University (B.A., with distinction, 1989); Yale University (J.D., 1992). Editor, Yale Law and Policy Review. ***PRACTICE AREAS:*** Broker-Dealer Compliance; Investment Management; Securities Law. ***Email:*** bstekler@wilmer.com

MANLEY WILLIAMS, born September 7, 1964; admitted to bar, 1993, New York (not active); 1998, District of Columbia. *Education:* Stanford University (B.A., with distinction and honors, 1987); Columbia University (M.A., 1989); Harvard University (J.D., magna cum laude, 1992). Firestone Medal; Columbia University Fellow. ***PRACTICE AREAS:*** Financial Institutions. ***Email:*** mlwilliams@wilmer.com

J. BARCLAY COLLINS, III, born June 4, 1967; admitted to bar, 1994, New York; 1995, District of Columbia. *Education:* Brown University (A.B., magna cum laude, 1989); Columbia University (J.D., 1993). Editor-in-Chief, Columbia Journal of Environmental Law. Harlan Fiske Stone Scholar, 1992, 1993. ***PRACTICE AREAS:*** Tax Law. ***Email:*** jbcollins@wilmer.com

DOUGLAS J. DAVISON, born August 29, 1968; admitted to bar, 1993, Pennsylvania; 2001, District of Columbia. *Education:* The Pennsylvania State University (B.S., 1990; J.D., cum laude, 1993). Adjunct Professor, Securities Regulation, The George Washington University School of Law, 2001. Counsel to the Chairman, U.S. Securities & Exchange Commission, 2000-2001. Branch Chief, SEC Division of Enforcement, 1999-2000. Senior Counsel, Staff Attorney, SEC Division of Enforcement, 1997-1999. ***PRACTICE AREAS:*** Securities Law. ***Email:*** ddavison@wilmer.com

JEFFREY A. ROTH, born July 30, 1967; admitted to bar, 1992, Illinois; 1999, District of Columbia; 2001, New York. *Education:* University of Michigan (A.B., with high distinction, 1989; J.D., cum laude, 1992). Note Editor, University of Michigan Journal of Law Reform. (Resident, New York Office). ***PRACTICE AREAS:*** Securities Law; Broker-Dealer Regulation. ***Email:*** jroth@wilmer.com

COLLEEN DOHERTY-MINICOZZI, born August 13, 1968; admitted to bar, 1994, New York; 1996, District of Columbia. *Education:* Princeton University (A.B., cum laude, 1990); Stanford University (J.D., 1993). Phi Beta Kappa. Clerk to: Judge Stanley Sporkin, D. District of Columbia; Judge William Cahill, San Francisco Superior Court. ***PRACTICE AREAS:*** Securities Law. ***Email:*** cdoherty-minicozzi@wilmer.com

SARA E. EMLEY, born November 12, 1967; admitted to bar, 1993, Ohio; 1995, District of Columbia. *Education:* University of Michigan (B.A., 1990); Duke University (J.D., 1993; LL.M., 1993). Note Editor, Duke Law Journal. Clerk to Judge Stephanie Seymour, 10th Circuit. ***PRACTICE AREAS:*** Securities Law; Investment Management; Broker-Dealer Regulation. ***Email:*** semley@wilmer.com

AUGUSTO REPETTO, born March 25, 1964; admitted to bar, 1988, Buenos Aires, Argentina; 1995, New York; 2001, District of Columbia. *Education:* Pontificia Universidad Catolica Argentina, Santa Maria de los Buenos Aires (Abogado, 1988); Southern Methodist University (LL.M., 1993). ***Email:*** arepetto@wilmer.com

JOLIE F. ZIMMERMAN, born May 28, 1967; admitted to bar, 1993, California; 1999, District of Columbia. *Education:* Stanford University (A.B., 1989); Georgetown University (J.D., cum laude, 1993). Member, The Tax Lawyer. ***PRACTICE AREAS:*** Securities Law. ***Email:*** jzimmerman@wilmer.com

VAN W. ELLIS, born March 15, 1969; admitted to bar, 1994, North Carolina; 1996, District of Columbia. *Education:* Duke University (A.B., summa cum laude, 1991; J.D., with high honors, 1994). Order of the Coif. Note Editor, Duke Law Journal. Clerk to Judge John D. Butzner, Jr., 4th Circuit. ***Email:*** vwellis@wilmer.com

(This Listing Continued)

GREGORY J. EWALD, born February 10, 1966; admitted to bar, 1994, Pennsylvania; 1995, Colorado; 1997, District of Columbia; 2001, Virginia. *Education:* The Colorado College (B.A., cum laude, 1988); University of Denver (J.D., 1994). Phi Beta Kappa; Order of St. Ives. International Trade Editor, Denver Journal of International Law & Policy. Clerk to Justice George E. Lohr, Supreme Court of Colorado; Judge C. Arlen Beam, 8th Circuit. (Resident, Northern Virginia Office). ***PRACTICE AREAS:*** Corporate Transactions; Corporate Finance; E-Commerce; Technology Transactions; Venture Capital Transactions; Asia Practice; Latin American Practice. ***Email:*** gewald@wilmer.com

JONATHAN J. FRANKEL, born May 13, 1969; admitted to bar, 1995, New Jersey; 1996, District of Columbia. *Education:* Harvard University (A.B., summa cum laude, 1991); Yale University (J.D., 1994). Phi Beta Kappa. Recipient, Harlan Fiske Stone Prize. Articles Editor, Yale Law Review. Clerk to Judge Stephen F. Williams, D.C. Circuit. Law Intern, Office of the Solicitor General, U.S. Department of Justice, 1994. ***Email:*** jfrankel@wilmer.com

SAMIR JAIN, born March 26, 1969; admitted to bar, 1995, California; 1997, District of Columbia. *Education:* Stanford University (B.S., with honors, 1991); Harvard University (J.D., magna cum laude, 1994). Phi Beta Kappa. Editor, Harvard Law Review. Articles Editor, Harvard Journal of Law and Technology. Clerk to Judge James R. Browning, 9th Circuit. ***PRACTICE AREAS:*** Telecommunications Law; Electronic Commerce; Internet Law; Appellate Practice. ***Email:*** sjain@wilmer.com

ANDREW J. LORENTZ, born February 22, 1962; admitted to bar, 1994, Virginia; 1995, District of Columbia. *Education:* University of Pennsylvania (B.A., 1985); Boston University (M.A., 1990); Georgetown University (J.D., cum laude, 1994). Recipient, American Jurisprudence Award in Constitutional Law. Georgetown University Journal of Law and Policy and International Business. (Resident, European Office, Brussels, Belgium). ***PRACTICE AREAS:*** International Transactions; EU Competition. ***Email:*** alorentz@wilmer.com

RONALD C. MACHEN, born May 6, 1969; admitted to bar, 1994, Illinois; 1995, District of Columbia. *Education:* Stanford University (A.B., 1991); Harvard University (J.D., 1994). Clerk to Judge Damon J. Keith, Sixth Circuit. Lecturer, Trial Advocacy, Howard University School of Law, 1998. Assistant U.S. Attorney, U.S. Department of Justice, Office of the U.S. Attorney for the District of Columbia, 1997-2001. ***PRACTICE AREAS:*** White Collar Crime; Internal Investigations; Civil Litigation; Complex Litigation. ***Email:*** rmachen@wilmer.com

GORDON PEARSON, born December 29, 1961; admitted to bar, 1995, Massachusetts; 1996, District of Columbia. *Education:* Rice University (B.S., 1984); Columbia University (J.D., 1994). Harlan Fiske Stone Scholar, 1992-1993 and 1993-1994. Articles Editor, Columbia Human Rights Law Review. Clerk to Judge Norman H. Stahl, 1st Circuit. ***Email:*** gpearson@wilmer.com

JANET DURHOLZ RIDGE, born February 8, 1960; admitted to bar, 1996, New York; 1997, District of Columbia. *Education:* St. John's College (B.A., 1982); Cornell University (M.A., 1988; J.D., 1994). Articles Editor, Cornell Law Review. Clerk to Judge Richard J. Cardmone, 2nd Circuit. Kerr Memorial Prize, A.D. White Fellow. ***Email:*** jridge@wilmer.com

ERIKA L. ROBINSON, born November 26, 1967; admitted to bar, 1995, New York; 1996, District of Columbia. *Education:* Harvard-Radcliffe College (A.B., 1989); Georgetown University (J.D., magna cum laude, 1994). Order of the Coif. Executive Editor, The Tax Lawyer. ***Email:*** erobinson@wilmer.com

SVEN B. VÖLCKER, born November 11, 1966; admitted to bar, 1996, Berlin, Germany; 2000, New York (Not admitted in District of Columbia). *Education:* Universities of Kiel and Bonn, Harvard University (LL.M., 1996). Stagiaire, Directorate General for Competition, European Commission, 1994. (Resident, European Office, Brussels, Belgium). ***Email:*** svoelcker@wilmer.com

ADAM M. ABENSOHN, born October 29, 1969; admitted to bar, 1995, New York and District of Columbia. *Education:* University of Michigan (B.A., with high honors, 1991); Georgetown University (J.D., magna cum laude, 1994). Order of the Coif. Member, American Criminal Law Review. Clerk to Judge Sonia Sotomayor, U.S. Court of Appeals, Second Circuit, 1998-1999 and U.S. District Court, Southern District of New York, 1996-1997. (Resident, New York Office). ***Email:*** aabensohn@wilmer.com

FRANCA HARRIS GUTIERREZ, born December 16, 1968; admitted to bar, 1995, New York; 1999, District of Columbia. *Education:* Columbia University (B.A., 1990; M.B.A., 1994; J.D., 1994). Co-Editor-in-Chief, Columbia Journal of Gender and Law. ***Email:*** fharris@wilmer.com

KEVIN P. McENERY, born August 8, 1951; admitted to bar, 1977, District of Columbia. *Education:* Brown University (A.B., 1973); University of Virginia (J.D., 1976). Notes Editor, Virginia Journal of International Law. Clerk to Judge George R. Gallagher, D.C. Court of Appeals. Attorney: President's Commission on Organized Crime, 1985-1986; U.S. Securities and Exchange Commission, 1987-2000. ***Email:*** kmcenery@wilmer.com

JOSEPH R. PROFAIZER, born October 5, 1967; admitted to bar, 1993, Texas; admitted as a Solicitor, 1998, England and Wales; 2001, District of Columbia. *Education:* University of Texas (B.A., magna cum laude and special honors, 1990; J.D., 1993); London School of Economics (LL.M., with merit, 1999). Phi Beta Kappa. Research and Submissions Editor, Texas International Law Journal, 1992-1993. Clerk to Judge George P. Kazen, U.S. District Court, Southern District of Texas. ***PRACTICE AREAS:*** Litigation; Arbitration; International Law. ***Email:*** jprofaizer@wilmer.com

CATHERINE M. SAADEH, born April 20, 1969; admitted to bar, 1994, Maryland; 1995, District of Columbia. *Education:* George Washington University (B.A., summa cum laude, 1991), Phi Beta Kappa; Harvard Law School (J.D., 1994). Articles Editor, Harvard International Law Journal. Attorney, Division of Investment Management, U.S. Securities and Exchange Commission, 1996-1999. ***PRACTICE AREAS:*** Securities. ***Email:*** csaadeh@wilmer.com

JEREMY S. SIMON, born July 15, 1969; admitted to bar, 1994, Maryland; 1995, District of Columbia. *Education:* Duke University (B.A., summa cum laude, 1991), Phi Beta Kappa; Duke University School of Law (J.D., high honors, 1994). Order of the Coif. Executive Editor, Alaska Law Review. ***Email:*** jsimon@wilmer.com

ERIKA K. SINGER, born May 6, 1970; admitted to bar, 1994, Pennsylvania; 1997, District of Columbia. *Education:* Michigan State University (B.A., with high honors, 1991); University of Chicago (J.D., with honors, 1994). Phi Beta Kappa. Articles Editor, University of Chicago Law Review. Clerk to Chief Judge Richard A. Posner, Seventh Circuit. Adjunct Professor, American University, Washington College of Law, 2001. Attorney, Securities and Exchange Commission, Office of the General Counsel, 1997-1999. ***Email:*** esinger@wilmer.com

JOERN BECKER, born November 1, 1965; admitted to bar, 1997, Berlin, Germany. *Education:* Universities of Freiburg and Trier (First State Examation, 1992, Second State Examination 1995; Dr. jur. 1997). (Resident European Office, Berlin, Germany). ***PRACTICE AREAS:*** Corporate Law. ***Email:*** jbecker@wilmer.com

OF COUNSEL

JAMES S. CAMPBELL, born September 19, 1938; admitted to bar, 1966, District of Columbia. *Education:* Yale University (B.A., 1960); Stanford University (LL.B., 1964). Member, Editorial Board, Stanford Law Review. Clerk to Justice William O. Douglas, U.S. Supreme Court, October Term, 1964. ***PRACTICE AREAS:*** Antitrust and Trade Regulation; Aviation; International Law. ***Email:*** jcampbell@wilmer.com

MICHAEL L. BURACK, born October 10, 1942; admitted to bar, 1971, California; 1972, District of Columbia. *Education:* Wesleyan University (B.A., 1964); California Institute of Technology (1965); Stanford University (M.S., 1967; J.D., 1970). Managing Editor, Stanford Law Review. Clerk to Judge Ben C. Duniway, 9th Circuit. Co-author, *An Introduction to the Use of Risk Analysis Methodology in Accident Litigation*, 42 Journal of Air Law and Commerce 133 (1976). Associate Editor, Public Contract Law Journal, ABA Public Contract Law Section, 1988-1994. Member, Judicial Evaluation Committee, District of Columbia Bar, 1992-1994. ***PRACTICE AREAS:*** Litigation; Civil Practice; Government Contracts; Computers and Software; Commercial Law; Antitrust. ***Email:*** mburack@wilmer.com

JOEL ROSENBLOOM, born September 25, 1930; admitted to bar, 1954, Indiana; 1965, District of Columbia. *Education:* University of Illinois (B.A., 1951); Indiana University (J.D., 1954). Note Editor, Indiana Law Journal, 1953-1954. Clerk to Judge James A. Emmert, Indiana Supreme Court. Author: "Authority of the Federal Communications Commission," in "Freedom and Responsibility," Coons Ed. NWU Press (1961); "On the Sixtieth Anniversary of the Communications Act," 47 Fed.Comm. L.J. 365 (1994); "Cable Television Amendments," in "The Communications Act: A Legislative History of the Major Amendments 1934-1996," Paglin Ed., Pike & Fischer (1999). Special Assistant to Chairman, 1963-1965 and Legal Assistant to Chairman, 1961-1963, Federal Communications Commission. ***PRACTICE AREAS:*** Communications Law; Mass Media Law. ***Email:*** jrosenbloom@wilmer.com

DANIEL K. MAYERS, born July 10, 1934; admitted to bar, 1960, District of Columbia. *Education:* Harvard University (A.B., 1955; LL.B., 1960). Articles Editor, Harvard Law Review, 1959-1960. Clerk to Justice Felix Frankfurter, U.S. Supreme Court, October Term, 1960. Executive Assistant to Undersecretary of State, 1965-1967. ***PRACTICE AREAS:*** Antitrust; Trade Regulation. ***Email:*** dmayers@wilmer.com

STEPHEN H. SACHS, born January 31, 1934; admitted to bar, 1960, Maryland; 1988, District of Columbia. *Education:* Haverford College (B.A., 1954); New College, Oxford, England; Yale University (LL.B., 1960). Clerk to Judge Henry Edgerton, D.C. Circuit. Author, "The Exclusionary Rule: A Prosecutor's Defense," 1 Criminal Justice Ethics 28 (1982). Attorney General of Maryland, 1979-1987. U.S. Attorney, 1967-1970 and Assistant U.S. Attorney, 1961-1964, District of Maryland. Fellow, American College of Trial Lawyers. ***PRACTICE AREAS:*** Civil Practice; Criminal Law; White Collar Crime. ***Email:*** ssachs@wilmer.com

DENNIS M. FLANNERY, born February 10, 1939; admitted to bar, 1964, New York; 1968, District of Columbia. *Education:* Fordham University (A.B.,

(This Listing Continued)

WILMER, CUTLER & PICKERING, Washington—Continued

1961); University of Pennsylvania (LL.B., 1964). Editor-in-Chief, University of Pennsylvania Law Review, 1963-1964. Clerk to Chief Justice Earl Warren, U.S. Supreme Court, October Term, 1964. ***PRACTICE AREAS:*** Civil Practice. ***Email:*** dflannery@wilmer.com

ASSOCIATES

CATHY HAESANG AHN, born December 1, 1974; admitted to bar, 1999, Massachusetts (Not admitted in District of Columbia). *Education:* Harvard University (A.B., summa cum laude, 1996; J.D., cum laude, 1999). Phi Beta Kappa. ***Email:*** cahn@wilmer.com

MAYA ALEXANDRI, born May 7, 1975; admitted to bar, 1999, California (inactive) and Louisiana; 2000, District of Columbia. *Education:* Rutgers University (B.A., with high honors, 1994); University of California at Los Angeles (J.D., 1998). Member, Order of the Coif. Managing Editor: UCLA Law Review; UCLA Women's Law Journal. Law Clerk to: Judge Fortunato Pedro Benavides, Fifth Circuit; Chief Judge F.A. Little, Jr., Western District of Louisiana. Teaching Fellow, Progressive Social Movements and Free Speech, UCLA, 1998. ***Email:*** malexandri@wilmer.com

FIONA HUANG ANDERSON, born May 18, 1971; admitted to bar, 1998, California; 1999, District of Columbia. *Education:* University of California at Berkeley (B.A., summa cum laude, 1993); Harvard University (J.D., cum laude, 1997). Phi Beta Kappa. Teaching Fellow, Economics, Harvard College, 1994-1997. ***Email:*** fanderson@wilmer.com

YLENIA ARIANO, born March 31, 1971; admitted to bar, 1998, Naples, Italy. *Education:* University of Study Federico II, Italy (Law Degree, cum laude, 1994); College of Europe, Belgium (LL.M., 1998). Stagiaire, European Commission, 1998-1999. (Resident, Brussels, Belgium Office). ***LANGUAGES:*** Italian and French. ***Email:*** yariano@wilmer.com

TIMOTHY B. ATKINS, born August 27, 1962; admitted to bar, 2000, Maryland; 2001, District of Columbia. *Education:* Messiah College (B.A., cum laude, 1986); Georgetown University Law Center (J.D., cum laude, 1999). Special Agent, 1989-2000 and Supervisory Special Agent, 1996-2000, Federal Bureau of Investigation. ***Email:*** tatkins@wilmer.com

STEPHANIE AVAKIAN, born April 15, 1970; admitted to bar, 1996, New York and New Jersey. *Education:* The College of New Jersey (B.A., magna cum laude, 1992); Temple University (J.D., magna cum laude, 1995). Counsel to Commissioner Paul Carey, 1998-1999. Branch Chief, Division of Enforcement, 1997-1998. Staff Attorney, Securities and Exchange Commission, 1995-1997. (Resident, New York Office). ***Email:*** savakian@wilmer.com

DAVID J. AVENI, born December 30, 1971; admitted to bar, 1999, Maryland; 2000, District of Columbia. *Education:* Georgetown University (B.S., magna cum laude, 1993); Duke University (J.D., high honors, 1998). Phi Beta Kappa. Order of the Coif. Senior Note Editor, Duke Law Journal, 1997-1998. Clerk to Judge Gerald B. Tjoflat, U.S. Court of Appeals, Eleventh Circuit. ***Email:*** daveni@wilmer.com

JEFFREY D. AYER, born April 23, 1969; admitted to bar, 1996, Arizona; 1997, District of Columbia. *Education:* Rice University (B.A., 1991); University of Arizona (J.D., summa cum laude, 1995). Order of the Coif. Managing Editor, Arizona Law Review. Law Clerk to Judge Stephen Trott, 9th Circuit. ***Email:*** jayer@wilmer.com

R. KEVIN BAILEY, born February 9, 1969; admitted to bar, 1999, Massachusetts; 2001, District of Columbia. *Education:* Duke University (B.A., cum laude, 1991; J.D., 1998); Northwestern University (M.A., 1992). Note Editor, Duke Law Journal; Managing Editor, Duke Journal of Gender Law & Policy, 1997-1998. Clerk to Judge Carl E. Stewart, U.S. Court of Appeals, Fifth Circuit. ***Email:*** kbailey@wilmer.com

CAROL J. BANTA, born January 31, 1971; admitted to bar, 1997, Maryland; 1998, District of Columbia. *Education:* Swarthmore College (B.A., 1993); University of Michigan Law School (J.D., cum laude, 1996). Contributing Editor, Michigan Law Review. Clerk to Judge Karen Nelson Moore, U.S. Court of Appeals, Sixth Circuit. ***Email:*** cbanta@wilmer.com

CYNTHIA BARABAN, born November 19, 1968; admitted to bar, 1999, Ohio; 2001, District of Columbia. *Education:* DePauw University (B.A., cum laude, 1991); Indiana University (J.D., magna cum laude, 1998). Order of the Coif. Executive Articles Editor, Indiana Law Journal, 1997-1998. Clerk to Senior Judge S. Arthur Spiegel, Southern District of Ohio. ***LANGUAGES:*** Russian. ***Email:*** cbaraban@wilmer.com

URSULA C. BASS, born November 6, 1968; admitted to bar, 1997, Virginia; 2000, District of Columbia. *Education:* Columbia University; Barnard College (B.A., magna cum laude, 1991); The American University, Washington College of Law (J.D., cum laude, 1996). Articles Editor, American University Journal of International Law & Policy, 1995-1996. Clerk to Thomas S. Kenny, 19th Judicial Circuit of Virginia, Fairfax County. ***LANGUAGES:*** German. ***Email:*** ubass@wilmer.com

(This Listing Continued)

LAURALYN ELIZABETH BEATTIE, born February 8, 1972; admitted to bar, 1998, Texas; 2000, District of Columbia. *Education:* Arizona State University (B.A., summa cum laude, 1994); Trinity College, University of Dublin (1994-1995); Duke University (J.D., magna cum laude, 1998). Rotary Ambassadorial Scholar. Notes Editor, Alaska Law Review. Clerk to Judge Julia Gibbons, Western District of Tennessee. ***Email:*** lbeattie@wilmer.com

BETH BIEDRONSKI, born March 1, 1970; admitted to bar, 2000, Maryland; 2001, District of Columbia. *Education:* Dickinson College (B.A., magna cum laude, 1992); Washington & Lee University (J.D., 2000). Phi Beta Kappa. ***LANGUAGES:*** Spanish. ***Email:*** bbiedronski@wilmer.com

MARK BIETER, born August 16, 1967; admitted to bar, 2001, Maryland (Not admitted in District of Columbia). *Education:* Gonzaga University (B.A., cum laude, 1990); Duke University (J.D., 2000). Legislative Assistant and Assistant Press Secretary to U.S. Congressman Larry Larocco, 1993-1994. ***LANGUAGES:*** Basque and Spanish. ***Email:*** mbieter@wilmer.com

LAURA BLOOD, born January 29, 1971; admitted to bar, 1997, Texas; 1998, District of Columbia. *Education:* Wake Forest University (B.A., 1992), Phi Beta Kappa; University of Texas at Austin (J.D., with high honors, 1997). Texas Law Review. ***Email:*** lblood@wilmer.com

CHRISTOPHER P. BOWERS, born February 19, 1972; admitted to bar, 1999, Maryland; 2000, District of Columbia. *Education:* Fordham College (B.A., summa cum laude, 1994); Phi Beta Kappa; University of Chicago (J.D., high honors, 1997). Order of the Coif. Patnio Fellow. Articles Editor, University of Chicago Law Review. Clerk to: Chief Justice William H. Rehnquist, U.S. Supreme Court, October Term, 1998; Judge Pamela Ann Rymer, U.S. Court of Appeals, Ninth Circuit. ***Email:*** cbowers@wilmer.com

DAVID K. BOWSHER, born July 10, 1973; admitted to bar, 2000, Georgia; 2001, District of Columbia. *Education:* Brown University (A.B., with honors, 1995); Duke University (J.D., cum laude, 1999). Member, Order of the Coif. Article Editor, Duke Law Journal. Teacher, English, Culver Academies, Culver, Indiana, 1995-1996. Law Clerk to Judge William H. Yohn, Jr., Eastern District of Pennsylvania. Legal Intern, Department of Justice, Antitrust Division, Litigation 1 Section, 1997. ***LANGUAGES:*** French. ***Email:*** dbowsher@wilmer.com

JOSHUA T. BRADY, born September 27, 1972; admitted to bar, 1999, Maryland; 2000, District of Columbia. *Education:* Georgetown University (A.B., magna cum laude, 1994); Phi Beta Kappa; Yale University (J.D., 1999). Editor, Yale Law Journal. ***Email:*** jbrady@wilmer.com

CLIFTON L. BRINSON, born April 13, 1972; admitted to bar, 2000, District of Columbia. *Education:* Duke University (B.A., cum laude, 1993); Yale University (J.D., 1998). Notes Editor, Yale Law Journal, 1997-1998. Clerk to Judge Gerald B. Tjoflat, Eleventh Circuit. ***Email:*** cbrinson@wilmer.com

JÉRÔME BROCHE, born July 21, 1972; admitted to bar, 2000, Paris (Not admitted in District of Columbia). *Education:* College Stanislas; Ecole Supérieure des Sciences Economiques & Commerciales (ESSEC, 1995); Cergy-Pontoise University (M.A., 1996). (Resident, European Office, Brussels, Belgium). ***Email:*** jbroche@wilmer.com

SAM BRODERICK-SOKOL, born December 7, 1967; admitted to bar, 2001, District of Columbia. *Education:* University of Pennsylvania (B.A., cum laude, 1990); University of California at Los Angeles (J.D., 1998). Order of the Coif. Chief Articles Editor, UCLA Law Review, 1997-1998. Clerk to: Judge Susan Graber, Ninth Circuit; Judge Robert Timlin, Central District of California. Legal Intern, Office of the White House Counsel, 1997. ***Email:*** sbroderick-sokol@wilmer.com

REED MICHAEL BRODSKY, born November 24, 1969; admitted to bar, 1997, New Jersey; 1998, District of Columbia and New York. *Education:* Duke University (B.A., 1991); Vanderbilt University (J.D., 1995). Authorities Editor, Vanderbilt Journal of Transnational Law. Clerk to Judge Hector M. Laffitte, District of Puerto Rico. ***Email:*** rbrodsky@wilmer.com

BRANT K. BROWN, born March 4, 1975; admitted to bar, 2000, Virginia; 2001, District of Columbia. *Education:* Vanderbilt University (B.A., magna cum laude, 1997; J.D., 2000). Managing Editor, Vanderbilt Law Review. ***Email:*** bbrown@wilmer.com

CHRISTOPHER T. BRUNEAU, born January 30, 1969; admitted to bar, 1995, New York; 1997, District of Columbia. *Education:* Georgetown University (B.A., cum laude, 1991; J.D., 1995); Johns Hopkins University School of Advanced International Studies (M.A., 1995). Articles Editor, The Tax Lawyer. ***Email:*** cbruneau@wilmer.com

PATRICIA M. BYRNE, born June 21, 1971; admitted to bar, 1999, California; 2000, District of Columbia. *Education:* University of Otago (B.A., with first class honors, 1994; LL.B., 1995); Institute of Professional Legal Studies, University of Victoria (Diploma, 1996); University of California at Berkeley (J.D., 1999). Managing Editor, Ecology Law Quarterly. ***Email:*** pbyrne@wilmer.com

ANTONIO CAPOBIANCO, born December 9, 1969; admitted to bar, 1996, Rome, Italy (Not admitted in the United States). *Education:* Roskilde

(This Listing Continued)

Univesitet Center, Denmark (Diploma in European Social Law, with distinction, 1991); LUISS University, Rome (J.D., 1993); Free University of Brussels, Belgium (LL.M., European Law, with distinction, 1994); New York University (LL.M., International Trade, 2000). Attorney, Italian Competition Authority, 1997-1999. Intern, Office of the Attorney General , State of New York, Antitrust Bureau, 1999-2000. (Resident, European Office, Brussels, Belgium). ***LANGUAGES:*** Italian, English and French. ***Email:*** acapobianco@wilmer.com

MEGAN L. CARLYLE, born November 21, 1970; admitted to bar, 1998, Illinois; 2001, District of Columbia. *Education:* Emory University (B.A., 1993); Duke University (J.D., 1998). ***Email:*** mcarlyle@wilmer.com

KEVIN M. CARROLL, born September 24, 1966; admitted to bar, 1996, Maryland; 1997, District of Columbia. *Education:* United States Military Academy (B.S., 1988); University of Maryland (J.D., with honors, 1996). Order of the Coif. Associate Editor, Maryland Law Review, 1995-1996. ***Email:*** kcarroll@wilmer.com

LINDA BRAY CHANOW, born May 31, 1970; admitted to bar, 1999, Maryland; 2000, District of Columbia. *Education:* Bethany College (B.A., 1992); American University (J.D., magna cum laude, 1999). Member, American University Law Review. Clerk to Senator Edward M. Kennedy, Committee on Health, Education, Labor & Pensions. ***Email:*** lchanow@wilmer.com

STEVE CHARNOVITZ, born September 15, 1953; admitted to bar, 1999, New York and District of Columbia. *Education:* Yale University (B.A., 1975; J.D., 1998); Kennedy School of Government (M.P.P., 1983). Policy Director, U.S. Competitiveness Policy Council, 1991-1995. Legislative Assistant, Steering and Policy Committee, U.S. House of Representatives, 1987-1991. ***Email:*** scharnovitz@wilmer.com

ANDERSON CHEN, born March 25, 1966; admitted to bar, 2001, New Jersey and District of Columbia. *Education:* Duke University (B.S.E.E., 1988); Virginia Polytechnic Institute & State University (M.S.E.E., 1995); George Washington University (J.D., 2000). Assistant Patent Examiner, U.S. Patent and Trademark Office, 1995-1998. [Electronic Engineer, U.S. Navy, 1991-1995]. ***Email:*** achen@wilmer.com

MARK CHENOWETH, born November 24, 1972; admitted to bar, 2001, Kansas (Not admitted in District of Columbia). *Education:* Yale University (B.A., 1995); University of Chicago (J.D., 1999). Associate Editor, University of Chicago Legal Forum, 1998-1999. Advisory Board Member, Chicago Journal of International Law. Clerk to Judge Danny J. Boggs, Sixth Circuit. ***Email:*** mchenoweth@wilmer.com

GREGORY SCOTT CHERNACK, born February 17, 1971; admitted to bar, 1998, New Jersey; 1999, New York; 2001, District of Columbia. *Education:* Harvard University (B.A., magna cum laude, 1993); University of Oxford (B.A., 1995); Yale University (J.D., 1998); University of Oxford (M.A., 2000). Articles Editor, Yale Law Journal. Clerk to: Judge Ralph Winter, Second Circuit; Judge Jack Weinstein, Eastern District of New York. ***Email:*** gchernack@wilmer.com

CYNTHIA H. CLARK, born January 9, 1972; admitted to bar, 1998, Maryland; 1999, District of Columbia. *Education:* Howard University (B.A., summa cum laude, 1994); Yale University (J.D., 1997). Phi Beta Kappa. Editor, Yale Journal of Law & Humanities. ***LANGUAGES:*** Spanish. ***Email:*** cclark@wilmer.com

C. RUSSELL CLAUSE, born August 19, 1969; admitted to bar, 1997, District of Columbia. *Education:* Duke University (A.B., cum laude, 1991); Oxford University; Northwestern University (J.D., 1994); Georgetown University (LL.M., with distinction, 1998). Note and Comment Editor, Journal of International Law & Business. ***Email:*** rclause@wilmer.com

MELANIE D. COATES, born May 16, 1970; admitted to bar, 1995, Virginia; 1996, Maryland; 1997, District of Columbia. *Education:* Duke University (A.B., cum laude, 1991); University of Richmond (J.D., magna cum laude, 1995). Associate Editor, University of Richmond Law Review. Intern to Justice Elizabeth B. Lacy, Supreme Court of Virginia. ***Email:*** mcoates@wilmer.com

LINDA COFFIN, admitted to bar, 1998, Missouri and District of Columbia. *Education:* University of Missouri (B.A.B.J., magna cum laude, 1993); University of Michigan (J.D., 1997). Clerk to Missouri Supreme Court. ***Email:*** lcoffin@wilmer.com

GILES T. COHEN, born July 11, 1970; admitted to bar, 1998, New York; 2001, District of Columbia. *Education:* Cornell University (B.A., with distinction, 1992); University of Pennsylvania (J.D., cum laude, 1997). Comments Editor, University of Pennsylvania Law Review, 1996-1997. ***Email:*** gcohen@wilmer.com

PAUL W. CONNELL, born March 6, 1972; admitted to bar, 1998, Wisconsin and Illinois; 2001, District of Columbia. *Education:* University of Wisconsin-Parkside (B.A., cum laude, 1994); Marquette University (J.D., magna cum laude, 1998). Executive Editor, Marquette Law Review. Clerk to Chief Judge J.P. Stadtmueller, Eastern District of Wisconsin. ***Email:*** pconnell@wilmer.com

(This Listing Continued)

BRYAN N. CORBETT, born November 28, 1972; admitted to bar, 1999, New York; 2000, District of Columbia. *Education:* University of Notre Dame (B.A., magna cum laude, 1995); George Washington University (J.D., 1998). Order of the Coif. Recipient: Corpus Juris Secundum Award for Contracts; John Orandaux Award. Editor-in-Chief, George Washington University Law Review, 1997-1998). Clerk to Judge Emory Widener, Jr., Fourth Circuit. ***Email:*** bcorbett@wilmer.com

LOWRY A. CROOK, born December 15, 1970; admitted to bar, 1999, Texas; 2000, District of Columbia. *Education:* University of Texas (B.A., 1993; J.D., high honors, 1999); LBJ School of Public Affairs (M.P.Aff., 1999). Order of the Coif. Chancellors Honorary Society. Notes Editor, Texas Law Review, 1998-1999. Clerk to Judge Greg Abbott, Supreme Court of Texas. ***Email:*** lcrook@wilmer.com

ANDREW J. CURRIE, born November 30, 1969; admitted to bar, 1996, Michigan; 2000, District of Columbia. *Education:* University of Michigan (B.A., 1992); Michigan State University (J.D., magna cum laude, 1996). Recipient: Jurisprudence Award in Taxation; Stephen T. Roumell Award. Note and Comment Editor, 1994-1995 and Managing Editor of Casenotes, Michigan State University Law Review. ***Email:*** acurrie@wilmer.com

CHRISTOPHER R.L. DAVIES, born October 1, 1970; admitted to bar, 1998, New York; 1999, District of Columbia. *Education:* Wesleyan University (B.A., high honors, 1993); Beijing Normal University (1988-1989); Inter-University Program for Chinese Studies (1991-1992); Stanford University (J.D., with distinction, 1996). Phi Beta Kappa. Senior Article Editor, Stanford Law Review; Lead Editor, Stanford Journal of International Law; Editor, Stanford Journal of Law and Policy. Clerk to: Judge James L. Buckley, District of Columbia Circuit; Judge William W Schwarzer, Northern District of California. ***Email:*** cdavies@wilmer.com

MELISSA HALL DAVIS, born December 15, 1973; admitted to bar, 2001, Virginia (Not admitted in District of Columbia). *Education:* Cornell University (B.A., with distinction, 1996); University of Virginia (J.D., 2001). Member, Editorial Board, Virginia Law Review, 2000-2001. Intern, Public Integrity Section, U.S. Department of Justice. ***Email:*** mdavis@wilmer.com

JOSHUA C. DELANEY, born Belleville, Illinois, October 10, 1964; admitted to bar, 1996, Maryland; 2000, District of Columbia. *Education:* Georgetown University (B.A., 1993); University of Baltimore (J.D., 1996). ***Email:*** jdelaney@wilmer.com

RICARDO R. DELFIN, born August 21, 1974; admitted to bar, 2000, Florida; 2001, District of Columbia. *Education:* Cornell University (B.A., 1996); Katholieke Universiteit, Leuven, Belgium; Northwestern University (J.D., 2000). ***Email:*** rdelfin@wilmer.com

YOLANDA M. DEMIANCZUK, born April 21, 1971; admitted to bar, 1998, New Jersey; 1999, District of Columbia; 2001, New York. *Education:* Yale University (B.A., 1993); Columbia University School of Law (J.D., 1997). Member, Editorial Board, Columbia Journal of Transnational Law. Clerk to Judge Robert Kugler, District of New Jersey. ***LANGUAGES:*** French and Polish. ***Email:*** ydemianczuk@wilmer.com

ELIZABETH K. DERBES, born October 30, 1970; admitted to bar, 1999, California; 2000, District of Columbia. *Education:* Harvard University (B.A., 1992); University of Chicago (J.D., 1998). Member, Editorial Board, University of Chicago Law Review, 1998-1999. Clerk to Judge Martin L.C. Feldman, U.S. District Court, Eastern District of Louisiana. Intern, Office of Special Investigations, U.S. Department of Justice. ***LANGUAGES:*** German and French. ***Email:*** ederbes@wilmer.com

ARLO DEVLIN-BROWN, admitted to bar, 2000, New York (Not admitted in District of Columbia). *Education:* Columbia University (B.A., summa cum laude, 1995); Harvard University (J.D., magna cum laude, 1999). Phi Beta Kappa. Clerk to Judge Kermit Lipez, First Circuit. ***Email:*** adevlin-brown@wilmer.com

KYLE DE YOUNG, born October 6, 1972; admitted to bar, 1999, Illinois; 2001, District of Columbia. *Education:* University of Michigan (B.A., 1995; J.D., cum laude, 1999). Law Clerk to Judge Suzanne B. Conlon, Northern District of Illinois. Intern, Department of Justice, Federal Programs Branch, Summer, 1999. ***Email:*** kdeyoung@wilmer.com

FLAVIA DISTEFANO, born December 20, 1967; admitted to bar, 1994, Rome, Italy (Not admitted in District of Columbia). *Education:* Free University of Brussels (ERASMUS Scholar, 1993); University of Catania (Dr.Jur., summa cum laude, 1994); Institute of European Studies, Free University of Brussels (Certificate in European Law, 1995; LL.M., with distinction, 2001). Internship, Council of the European Union, 1994. (Resident, European Office, Brussels, Belgium). ***Email:*** fdistefano@wilmer.com

ALLISON DRIMMER, born August 7, 1969; admitted to bar, 1999, Maryland (Not admitted in District of Columbia). *Education:* Stanford University (B.A., 1991); Georgetown University (J.D., 1998; M.B.A., 1998). Clerk to Associate Judge John M. Steadman, D.C. Court of Appeals. ***Email:*** adrimmer@wilmer.com

(This Listing Continued)

WILMER, CUTLER & PICKERING, Washington—Continued

DANIEL F. DUCHOVNY, born May 29, 1969; admitted to bar, 1998, Maryland; 1999, District of Columbia. *Education:* University of Maryland (B.S., cum laude, 1992); Georgetown University Law Center (J.D., cum laude, 1997). ***Email:*** dduchovny@wilmer.com

N. JEREMI DURU, born June 11, 1973; admitted to bar, 1999, Maryland; 2001, District of Columbia. *Education:* Brown University (B.A., 1995); Harvard University (J.D., 1999; M.P.P., 1999). Line Editor, Journal on Legislation. Law Clerk to Judge Damon J. Keith, Sixth Circuit. ***Email:*** jduru@wilmer.com

PAUL R. ECKERT, born May 1, 1967; admitted to bar, 1997, New York; 1998, District of Columbia; 1999, Virginia. *Education:* Tulane University (B.A., 1989); College of William & Mary (J.D., 1996). Order of the Coif. Editor-in-Chief, William & Mary Law Review, 1995-1996. Clerk to Judge William Garwood, U.S. Court of Appeals, Fifth Circuit, 1996-1997. [Lieut., U.S. Navy, 1989-1993]. ***Email:*** peckert@wilmer.com

KNIGHT ELSBERRY, admitted to bar, 1997, Illinois; 2001, District of Columbia. *Education:* University of Chicago (B.A., 1994); University of Michigan (J.D., 1997). ***Email:*** kelsberry@wilmer.com

LARA A. ENGLUND, born January 21, 1970; admitted to bar, 1996, Virginia; 1998, District of Columbia. *Education:* College of William & Mary (B.A., cum laude, 1991); University of Chicago (J.D., high honors, 1995). Order of the Coif. Comment Editor, University of Chicago Law Review. Clerk to Judge A. Raymond Randolph, D.C. Circuit. ***Email:*** lenglund@wilmer.com

GAIL SUSAN ENNIS, born October 21, 1962; admitted to bar, 1998, Maryland; 2000, District of Columbia. *Education:* University of North Carolina at Chapel Hill (B.S., 1985); Brooklyn Law School (J.D., magna cum laude, 1998). Senior Associate, Journal of Law & Policy. ***Email:*** gennis@wilmer.com

DR. BJÖRN FASTERLING, born April 12, 1972; admitted to bar, 2001, Berlin, Germany. *Education:* University of Osnabrück (First State Examination, 1997; Dr. iur., 2001); University of Stockholm (LL.M., 1998); Supreme Court of Schleswig-Holstein (Second State Examination, 2001). (Resident, European Office, Berlin, Germany). ***Email:*** bfasterling@wilmer.com

LAURA E. FEIN, born May 2, 1969; admitted to bar, 1996, New Jersey; 1998, New York and District of Columbia. *Education:* Harvard College (A.B., magna cum laude, 1992); Hebrew University; Columbia University (J.D., 1996). Harlan Fiske Stone Scholar. Book Review Editor, Columbia Journal of Gender and Law. Writing and Research Editor, Columbia Journal of Law and Social Problems. ***Email:*** lfein@wilmer.com

DEBORAH M. FIELD, born May 21, 1969; admitted to bar, 1996, District of Columbia and New York. *Education:* Syracuse University (B.A., magna cum laude, 1991); George Washington University (J.D., with high honors, 1995). Phi Beta Kappa; Order of the Coif. Member, George Washington Law Review. Staff Attorney, Division of Enforcement, U.S. Securities and Exchange Commission, 1998-2000. *Member:* The District of Columbia Bar. ***Email:*** dfield@wilmer.com

LUIS A. FELDSTEIN-SOTO, born July 26, 1960; admitted to bar, 1996, California; 1998, District of Columbia. *Education:* Haverford College, PA (B.A., 1982); Columbia University (M.S., 1983); Stanford University (J.D., 1996). ***Email:*** lfeldstein@wilmer.com

LYNN M. FISCHER, admitted to bar, 1999, Maryland; 2001, District of Columbia. *Education:* The American University (B.A., 1989); Stanford University (J.D., 1999). Member, Executive Board, Stanford Journal of International Law. Clerk to Judge Paul R. Michel, Federal Circuit. Project Manager and Policy Officer, North American Commission for Environmental Cooperation, 1995-1996. ***LANGUAGES:*** Spanish. ***Email:*** lfischer@wilmer.com

JOHN C. FORD, born September 1971; admitted to bar, 1997, Michigan; 1998, Illinois (Not admitted in District of Columbia). *Education:* Stanford University (B.A., 1993); University of Michigan (J.D., cum laude, 1997). Book Review Editor, Michigan Law Review. Clerk to Judge Deanell Reece Tacha, U.S. Court of Appeals, Tenth Circuit, 1997-1998. ***Email:*** jford@wilmer.com

SUSAN D. FRANCK, born July 16, 1973; admitted to bar, 1998, Minnesota; 2000, District of Columbia. *Education:* Simon's Rock College of Bard (A.A., with distinction, 1991); Macalester College (B.A., summa cum laude, 1993); Phi Beta Kappa; University of Minnesota (J.D., magna cum laude, 1998); Order of the Coif; University of London (LL.M., with merit, 1999). Recipient, Polk Foundation Scholarship, Macalester College. U.S.-U.K. Fulbright Scholar to the United Kingdom, 1998-1999. Associate Articles Editor, Minnesota Law Review. ***Email:*** sfranck@wilmer.com

JAMES W. FROST, born July 11, 1967; admitted to bar, 1995, Maryland; 2001, District of Columbia. *Education:* Oberlin College (B.A., 1989); American University (J.D., 1995). Attorney, Federal Trade Commission, Bureau of Competition, Anticompetitive Practices Division, 1995-2000. ***Email:*** jfrost@wilmer.com

ELLEN K. FULTON, born November 30, 1971; admitted to bar, 2000, Illinois; 2001, District of Columbia. *Education:* Southern Methodist University

(This Listing Continued)

(B.S., magna cum laude, 1992); University of Chicago (J.D., 2000). Phi Beta Kappa. Symposium Editor, The University of Chicago Law School Roundtable, 1999-2000. ***Email:*** efulton@wilmer.com

DANIEL M. GALLAGHER, JR., born May 31, 1972; admitted to bar, 1999, Maryland; 2000, District of Columbia. *Education:* Georgetown University (B.A., 1994); Columbus School of Law, Catholic University (J.D., magna cum laude, 1999). Vernon X. Miller Scholar. Staff Member, Catholic University Law Review. ***Email:*** dgallagher@wilmer.com

ERIC S. GALLER, born June 29, 1964; admitted to bar, 1995, Maryland; 1997, District of Columbia. *Education:* Reed College (B.A., 1987); American University (J.D., summa cum laude, 1994). Senior Staff, American University Law Review. Clerk to Judge Irma S. Raker, Maryland Court of Appeals. (Also at Baltimore, Maryland Office). ***Email:*** egaller@wilmer.com

PARAMITA GHOSH, born August 16, 1967; admitted to bar, 1999, California; 2001, District of Columbia; registered to practice before U.S. Patent and Trademark Office. *Education:* University of Pennsylvania (B.S.E.E., 1989); Georgetown University (J.D., 1999). Article Editor, Georgetown International Environmental Law Review, 1998-1999. Patent Examiner, U.S. Patent and Trademark Office, 1990-1992, 1994-1997. ***Email:*** pghosh@wilmer.com

JOSHUA S. GOLDWERT, born December 18, 1973; admitted to bar, 2000, New York; 2001, District of Columbia. *Education:* University of Pennsylvania (B.A., magna cum laude, 1995); New York University (J.D., cum laude, 1998). Senior Articles Editor, Annual Survey of American Law. Law Clerk to: Judge Ronald Lee Gilman, Sixth Circuit; Judge Jay C. Waldman, Eastern District of Pennsylvania. ***Email:*** jgoldwert@wilmer.com

GAYTON P. GOMEZ, born June 30, 1965; admitted to bar, 1996, New York (Not admitted in District of Columbia). *Education:* State University of New York at Brockport (B.A., summa cum laude, 1988); Yale Law School (J.D., 1995). Executive Editor, Yale Journal of International Law. (Resident, New York Office). ***Email:*** ggomez@wilmer.com

MICHAEL E. GORDON, born April 6, 1969; admitted to bar, 1997, Illinois; 1999, District of Columbia. *Education:* Harvard University (A.B., 1991); University of Michigan (J.D., 1997). Clerk to Judge Susan J. Dlott, Southern District of Ohio. ***Email:*** mgordon@wilmer.com

TERRY GRAY, born September 20, 1973; admitted to bar, 2001, District of Columbia. *Education:* University of Virginia (B.A., 1995); Stanford University (J.D., 1999). Editor: Stanford Law Review, 1998-1999; Stanford Law and Policy Review, 1998-1999. Clerk to Senior Judge Thelton E. Henderson, Northern District of California. ***Email:*** tgray@wilmer.com

MAURA E. GRIFFIN, born November 19, 1967; admitted to bar, 1996, Massachusetts; 1999, District of Columbia. *Education:* College of the Holy Cross (B.A., 1989); Tulane University of Louisiana (J.D., magna cum laude, 1996); Georgetown University (LL.M., with distinction, 1998). Order of the Coif. Recipient, Forgotston Scholarship. Articles Editor, Tulane Law Review. ***Email:*** mgriffin@wilmer.com

JENNIFER E. GRISHKIN, born August 11, 1972; admitted to bar, 1998, New Jersey; 1999, District of Columbia. *Education:* Wake Forest University (B.A., summa cum laude, 1994); Yale University (J.D., 1997). Phi Beta Kappa. Senior Editor, Yale Law Journal; Member, Yale Journal of Law and Feminism. Law Clerk to the Honorable Walter K. Stapleton, Third Circuit. ***Email:*** jgrishkin@wilmer.com

PETER GRUNDBERG, born May 28, 1975; admitted as solicitor, 2001, England and Wales. *Education:* Corpus Christi College, Cambridge University (B.A., 1996); College of Law, London (L.P.C., 1998); Folksuniversitetet (Legal Diploma, Jöken, 1999). (Resident, European Office, London, England). ***LANGUAGES:*** Swedish, French and Italian. ***Email:*** pgrundberg@wilmer.com

GERD AXEL GUTERMUTH, born March 10, 1971. (Not admitted in District of Columbia). *Education:* University of Passau (1990-1992); University of Aix-en-Provence (Certificate of Political Studies, 1993); Ruprecht-Karls-University (First State Examination, 1996); Karlsruhe Court of Appeals, Second State Examination (1998); New York University (LL.M., 1999). (Resident, European Office, Brussels, Belgium). ***Email:*** agutermuth@wilmer.com

PATRICK GUTIERREZ, born August 1, 1972; admitted to bar, 2000, Virginia; 2001, District of Columbia. *Education:* University of Virginia (B.A., 1994); University of Pennsylvania (J.D., 2000). Associate Editor and Senior Editor, Journal of International and Economic Law, 1999-2000. ***Email:*** pgutierrez@wilmer.com

CORA TUNG HAN, born November 12, 1970; admitted to bar, 1996, Massachusetts; 1997, New York; 1998, District of Columbia; 2000, California. *Education:* Harvard University (B.A., 1992); University of Chicago (J.D., 1996). Comment Editor, University of Chicago Law Review, 1995-1996. Clerk to Judge Morton A. Brody, District of Maine. ***Email:*** chan@wilmer.com

RUSSELL P. HANSER, born April 2, 1972; admitted to bar, 1997, Massachusetts; 2001, District of Columbia. *Education:* Amherst College (B.A.,

(This Listing Continued)

magna cum laude, 1994); Harvard University (J.D., cum laude, 1997). John M. Olin Fellow in Law and Economics. Primary Editor, Harvard Law Review. Clerk to Judge Norman Stahl, First Circuit. ***Email:*** rhanser@wilmer.com

ANNE HARKAVY, born May 18, 1973; admitted to bar, 1999, Maryland; 2000, District of Columbia. *Education:* Harvard University (A.B., magna cum laude, 1995; J.D., cum laude, 1998). Harvard National Scholar. Clerk to Judge Paul V. Niemeyer, U.S. Court of Appeals, Fourth Circuit. ***Email:*** aharkavy@wilmer.com

WILHELM M.A. HARTUNG, born January 27, 1966; admitted to bar, 1997, Germany (Landgericht Berlin) (Not admitted in District of Columbia). *Education:* University of Bonn. First State Examination (1993); Second State Examination (1996); University of Bonn (Dr.jur., 2000). (Resident, European Office, London, England; also at Berlin, Germany Office). ***Email:*** whartung@wilmer.com

DAVID HEFFERNAN, born November 17, 1963; admitted to bar, 1996, Virginia; 1997, District of Columbia. *Education:* Trinity College, Dublin, Ireland (B.A., honors, 1985); University College, Dublin, Ireland (M.B.S., 1988); Catholic University of America, Columbus School of Law (J.D., summa cum laude, 1996). Senior Lead Articles Editor, Catholic University Law Review, 1995-1996. ***Email:*** dheffernan@wilmer.com

STEPHEN R. HEIFETZ, born January 17, 1971; admitted to bar, 1996, Maryland; 1998, District of Columbia. *Education:* Stanford University (A.B., with distinction, 1993); Oxford University, Oxford, England; Georgetown University (J.D., magna cum laude, 1996). Order of the Coif. Olin Fellow in Law & Economics. Senior Articles Editor, The Georgetown Law Journal. Adjunct Professor, Constitutional Issues, Georgetown University Law Center, 1999. Staff Attorney: Office of General Counsel, Central Intelligence Agency, 1996-1998; Asset Forfeiture and Money Laundering Section, Criminal Division, Department of Justice, 1998-2000. ***Email:*** sheifetz@wilmer.com

JAN C. HEITHECKER, born October 14, 1968; admitted to bar, 2000, Berlin, Germany. *Education:* Universities of Bonn and Munich (First State Exam, 1994); Berlin Court of Appeals (Second State Exam, 1997). Editor, Wirtchaft und Wettbewerb, 1997-1999. Instructor, European and German Public Law, University of Jena, 1998-1999. (Resident, European Office, Brussels, Belgium). ***LANGUAGES:*** German and Spanish. ***Email:*** jheithecker@wilmer.com

ANDREW M. HERMAN, born September 30, 1969; admitted to bar, 1995, Georgia; 1996, District of Columbia. *Education:* University of North Carolina at Chapel Hill (B.S.B.A., with distinction, 1992; MAC, 1992); Columbia University (J.D., 1995). Phi Beta Kappa. Harlan Fiske Stone Scholar. Submissions Editor, Journal of Transnational Law. ***Email:*** aherman@wilmer.com

RACHAEL HILL, born March 31, 1974; admitted to bar, 2001, District of Columbia. *Education:* University of Chicago (B.A., with honors, 1995; J.D., with high honors, 1999). Order of the Coif. Comment Editor, University of Chicago Law Review, 1998-1999. Clerk to Judge Mary Schroeder, Ninth Circuit. ***Email:*** rhill@wilmer.com

DARRIN HOSTETLER, born March 10, 1967; admitted to bar, 1998, California; 2001, District of Columbia. *Education:* Arizona State University (B.S., 1990); Stanford University (J.D., with distinction, 1997). Member, Stanford Law Review. Clerk to Judge Joseph T. Sneed, Ninth Circuit. ***Email:*** dhostetler@wilmer.com

ERIC J. HOUGEN, born July 4, 1971; admitted to bar, 1998, Maryland; 1999, District of Columbia. *Education:* Luther College (B.A., 1993); University of Iowa (J.D., 1998). Phi Beta Kappa. Order of the Coif. ***Email:*** ehougen@wilmer.com

SABRINA HOULTON, admitted to bar, 1998, Maryland; 2000, District of Columbia. *Education:* Wesleyan University (B.A., 1993); Stanford University (J.D., 1998). Clerk to Judge Stephen M. Orlofsky, District of New Jersey. ***Email:*** shoulton@wilmer.com

MATTHEW HUGGINS, born February 6, 1964; admitted to bar, 1997, Massachusetts and New York; 1998, District of Columbia. *Education:* Dartmouth College (B.A., summa cum laude, 1986); Harvard Law School (J.D., cum laude, 1996). Clerk to Judge Theodore Tannenwald Jr., U.S. Tax Court. ***Email:*** mhuggins@wilmer.com

STEVEN E. HUGIE, born October 3, 1969; admitted to bar, 1997, Utah; 2000, District of Columbia. *Education:* Brigham Young University (B.A., summa cum laude, 1993); Yale Law School (J.D., 1996). Editor, Yale Law Journal. Clerk to Judge J. Daniel Mahoney, Second Circuit. ***Email:*** shugie@wilmer.com

KATE HUTCHINS, born September 22, 1975; admitted to bar, 2001, New York (Not admitted in District of Columbia). *Education:* University of Michigan (B.A., with highest distinction, 1997); Yale University (J.D., 2000). Articles Editor, Yale Journal of International Law, 1999-2000. Clerk to Judge Richard D. Cudahy, Seventh Circuit. ***Email:*** khutchins@wilmer.com

(This Listing Continued)

JEFFREY S. HYDRICK, born July 31, 1971; admitted to bar, 1996, Wisconsin; 1998, District of Columbia. *Education:* University of Miami (B.B.A., magna cum laude, 1993); Harvard University (J.D., 1996). ***Email:*** jhydrick@wilmer.com

T. ANTHONY "TODD" JAYE, born March 27, 1970; admitted to bar, 2000, Virginia and Wisconsin; 2001, District of Columbia. *Education:* University of Wisconsin-Madison (B.B.A., 1992); Marquette University Law School (J.D., magna cum laude, 2000). Staff Member, Marquette University Law Review, 1998-1999. Recipient, CALI Awards in: Criminal Law; Unfair Trade Practices; Legal Ethics; Legal Communication. Thomas J. Crowley Scholar. ***Email:*** tjaye@wilmer.com

HEATHER A. JONES, born March 5, 1972; admitted to bar, 1999, Kansas; 2001, District of Columbia. *Education:* Dartmouth College (A.B., 1994); University of Kansas (J.D., 1999). Order of the Coif. Member, Kansas Law Review. Clerk to Judge Arlen Beam, Eighth Circuit. Corpsmember, 1994-1995 and Team Leader, 1995-1996, Americorps National Civilian Community Corps. ***Email:*** hjones@wilmer.com

TIMOTHY KANG, born October 2, 1971; admitted to bar, 2000, Virginia; 2001, District of Columbia. *Education:* Drexel University (B.S., 1994); American University (J.D., 2000). Patent Examiner, U.S. Patent and Trademark Office, 1994-2000. ***LANGUAGES:*** Korean. ***Email:*** tkang@wilmer.com

DR. JÖRG KARENFORT, born June 8, 1969; admitted to bar, 1999, Munich, Germany (Not admitted in District of Columbia). *Education:* Philipps-University Marburg (First State Examination, 1994; Dr. iur., 1998); London School of Economics and Political Science (LL.M., 1996); Institute d'Études Politique de Paris (Half Course, 1997); Supreme Court of Berlin (Second State Examination, 1999). Assistant Lecturer, Case Studies in European and Public International Law, Johannes-Gutenberg University, Mainz, 1995. (Resident, European Office, Berlin, Germany). ***Email:*** jkarenfort@wilmer.com

MANIJEH NAN KARGAHI, born January 22, 1969; admitted to bar, 1998, Illinois; 2000, District of Columbia. *Education:* University of Illinois (B.A., 1991); Chicago-Kent College of Law, Illinois Institute of Technology (J.D., with honors, 1997). Chicago-Kent Law Review. Clerk to Judge S. Martin Teel, Jr., U.S. Bankruptcy Court for the District of Columbia. ***Email:*** mkargahi@wilmer.com

JASON KEARNS, born March 19, 1971; admitted to bar, 1996, Illinois; 2001, District of Columbia. *Education:* University of Denver (B.A., summa cum laude, 1993); University of Pennsylvania (J.D., cum laude, 1996); Harvard University (M.P.P., 2000). Phi Beta Kappa. Member, Moot Court Board. Intern: Office of U.S. Trade Representative, 1999; Appellate Body, World Trade Organization, 2000. ***LANGUAGES:*** Russian. ***Email:*** jkearns@wilmer.com

RACHAEL D. KENT, born April 17, 1974; admitted to bar, 1998, Maryland; 1999, District of Columbia. *Education:* Georgetown University (B.A., cum laude, 1995); Duke University (J.D., magna cum laude, 1998). Order of the Coif. Member, Duke Law Journal, 1997-1998. (Resident, European Office, London, England). ***Email:*** rakent@wilmer.com

GREGORY S. KNELL, born October 4, 1969; admitted to bar, 1997, New York; 1999, District of Columbia. *Education:* Duke University (A.B., summa cum laude, Phi Beta Kappa, 1991); Columbia University (J.D., 1996). Harlan Fiske Stone Scholar. Editor, Journal of Transnational Law. Clerk to: Judge Leonard I. Garth, 3rd Circuit; Judge Anita B. Brody, E.D. Pennsylvania. ***Email:*** gknell@wilmer.com

NATALIE H. KOSSAK, born February 10, 1972; admitted to bar, 1998, New York and New Jersey; 1999, District of Columbia and Virginia. *Education:* Binghamton University (B.A, 1994); Hofstra University School of Law (J.D., with distinction, 1997). Associate Editor, Hofstra Law Review. (Also at Northern Virginia Office). ***Email:*** nkossak@wilmer.com

MARY E. KOSTEL, born March 22, 1964; admitted to bar, 1994, Virginia; 2000, District of Columbia. *Education:* Princeton University (A.B., 1986); University of Virginia (J.D., 1993). Margaret G. Hyde Award. Editor-in-Chief, Virginia Law Review. Clerk to: Judge Sam C. Pointer, N.D. Alabama; Judge James R. Browning, 9th Circuit. ***Email:*** mkostel@wilmer.com

LAURA B. KOTANCHIK, born July 7, 1971; admitted to bar, 2000, Illinois and District of Columbia. *Education:* Wellesley College (B.A., magna cum laude, 1993); Phi Beta Kappa; University of Oxford (M.Phil., 1995); University of Chicago (J.D., 1999). Articles Editor, University of Chicago Legal Forum. ***Email:*** lkotanchik@wilmer.com

HEIDI E. KRANZ, born November 10, 1972; admitted to bar, 2000, New York and District of Columbia. *Education:* Georgetown University (B.S., magna cum laude, 1994; J.D., magna cum laude, 1999). Phi Beta Kappa. Order of the Coif. Articles Editor, Georgetown Law Journal. ***LANGUAGES:*** Spanish, Italian and Portuguese. ***Email:*** hkranz@wilmer.com

DAVID M. KREEGER, born February 9, 1972; admitted to bar, 1998, Florida; 1999, District of Columbia. *Education:* Columbia College (B.A.,

(This Listing Continued)

WILMER, CUTLER & PICKERING, Washington—Continued

1993); University of Miami (J.D., summa cum laude, 1998). Articles and Comments Editor, The University of Miami Law Review. ***Email:*** dkreeger@wilmer.com

AMY T. KREIGER, born June 22, 1970; admitted to bar, 1996, Massachusetts and District of Columbia. *Education:* University of Massachusetts, Amherst (B.A., 1992); Harvard University (J.D., magna cum laude, 1995). Phi Beta Kappa. ***Email:*** akreiger@wilmer.com

SOPHIE JANE LAMB, born August 14, 1974; admitted to bar, 1998, England and Wales (Barrister) (Not admitted in District of Columbia). *Education:* University of Manchester, U.K. and Université de Bourgogne, France (LL.B., first class honors, 1996); London School of Economics (LL.M., Banking Law, 1997); Inns of Court School of Law, London (Bar Vocational Course, 1998). Prince of Wales Scholar. Lecturer, London School of Economics, LL.M. Banking Law. (Resident, European Office, London, England). ***LANGUAGES:*** French. ***Email:*** slamb@wilmer.com

HITE COLBY LANE, born March 4, 1974; admitted to bar, 1999, Mississippi; 2001, District of Columbia. *Education:* Millsaps College (B.S., magna cum laude, 1996); Harvard Law School (J.D., 1999). ***Email:*** clane@wilmer.com

J. WELBY LEAMAN, born November 28, 1970; admitted to bar, 2000, New York; 2001, District of Columbia. *Education:* Messiah College (B.S., summa cum laude, 1993); Yale Law School (J.D., 1996). Advisor, Government of Peru, 1997-2000. ***Email:*** wleaman@wilmer.com

CHRISTIAN LEATHLEY, born May 7, 1973; admitted as Solicitor, 1999, England and Wales. *Education:* University College, Durham University (B.A., Hons. Law, 1995); College of Law, Guildford (1996). Recipient: Superior Diploma in Business Spanish, Madrid Chamber of Commerce; Training Contract, Bruckhaus Deringer (London/Madrid). (Resident, European Office, London, England). ***LANGUAGES:*** English, Spanish and Portuguese. ***Email:*** cleathley@wilmer.com

PETER M. LEE, born November 3, 1971; admitted to bar, 1998, Maryland; 1999, District of Columbia. *Education:* Colgate University (B.A., magna cum laude, 1994); Duke University (J.D., high honors, 1998). Year-in-Review Editor, Alaska Law Review. Clerk to Judge Jon. P. McCalla, Western District of Tennessee. ***Email:*** plee@wilmer.com

MICHAEL LEFFEL, born July 26, 1967; admitted to bar, 1998, Wisconsin; 1999, District of Columbia. *Education:* Concordia College (B.A., magna cum laude, 1989); University of Michigan (J.D., cum laude, 1997). Managing Editor, Michigan Law Review. Clerk to Judge Karen Nelson Moore, 6th Circuit. ***Email:*** mleffel@wilmer.com

JEFFREY A. LEHTMAN, born August 12, 1975; admitted to bar, 2000, Florida; 2001, District of Columbia. *Education:* Vanderbilt University (B.A., summa cum laude, 1997); University of Michigan (J.D., cum laude, 2000). Intern, Office of General Counsel, U.S. Trade Representative, 1999. ***Email:*** jlehtman@wilmer.com

ROBIN A. LENHARDT, born October 3, 1967; admitted to bar, 1995, Massachusetts; 1997, New York; 1998, District of Columbia. *Education:* Brown University (A.B., honors, 1989); Harvard Law School (J.D., cum laude, 1995); J.F.K. School of Government, Harvard University (M.P.A., 1995). Skadden Fellow, Lawyers' Committee for Civil Rights Under Law, 1997-1998. Harvard Civil Rights Civil Liberties Law Review. Clerk to: Judge Hugh H. Brownes, First Circuit; Justice Stephen G. Breyer, U.S. Supreme Court, October Term, 1996. Attorney Advisor, Office of Legal Counsel, U.S. Department of Justice, 1998-2000. Adjunct Professor, Appellate Advocacy, Howard University Law School, 1999. ***Email:*** rlenhardt@wilmer.com

JACK ALAN LEVY, born October 2, 1971; admitted to bar, 1999, District of Columbia and New York. *Education:* Johns Hopkins University (B.A., 1993); Fulbright Scholar, Paraguay (1993-1994); Georgetown University (M.S.F.S., 1998; J.D., 1998). Phi Beta Kappa. Weintal Scholar. Order of the Coif. Senior Articles Editor, The Georgetown Law Journal. Law Clerk to Judge Sonia Sotomayor, Second Circuit. ***LANGUAGES:*** Spanish and Guarani. ***Email:*** jlevy@wilmer.com

NATAN J. LEYVA, born July 16, 1965; admitted to bar, 2000, New York; 2001, District of Columbia. *Education:* Harvard College (A.B., summa cum laude, 1996); Yale Law School (J.D., 1999). Phi Beta Kappa. ***LANGUAGES:*** Spanish. ***Email:*** nleyva@wilmer.com

SCOTT LLEWELLYN, born September 10, 1968; admitted to bar, 1998, California; 2000, District of Columbia. *Education:* Yale University (B.A., cum laude, 1990); University of Michigan (J.D., cum laude, 1997). Executive Article Editor, Michigan Telecommunications & Technology Law Review. Clerk to Judge Clarence A. Brimmer, U.S. District Court, District of Wyoming, 1997-1998; Judge Diarmuid F. O'Scannlain, U.S. Court of Appeals, Ninth Circuit, 1998-1999. ***Email:*** sllewellyn@wilmer.com

(This Listing Continued)

DAVID A. LUIGS, born February 18, 1966; admitted to bar, 1996, Maryland; 1997, District of Columbia. *Education:* College of William & Mary (B.A., 1988); University of Michigan (J.D., magna cum laude, 1995). Phi Sigma Alpha. Order of the Coif. Notes Editor, Michigan Law Review. Clerk to Judge J. Edward Lumbard, 2nd Circuit. ***Email:*** dluigs@wilmer.com

DAVID LYNN, born October 3, 1967; admitted to bar, 1995, Maryland. *Education:* Loyola College (B.B.A., magna cum laude, 1989; M.S., 1991); University of Maryland (J.D., with honors, 1995). Articles Editor, The Business Lawyer. Special Counsel, Division of Corporation Finance, U.S. Securities and Exchange Commission. (Resident, Baltimore, Maryland Office). ***Email:*** dlynn@wilmer.com

CHERIE L. MACAULEY, born August 18, 1970; admitted to bar, 1996, Massachusetts; 1997, District of Columbia. *Education:* Williams College (B.A., magna cum laude, 1992); Yale University (J.D., 1995). Phi Beta Kappa. Member, Yale Journal of Law and Humanities. ***Email:*** cmacauley@wilmer.com

JEANINE L. MAGURSHAK, born April 16, 1970; admitted to bar, 1999, New York; 2000, District of Columbia. *Education:* Wesleyan University (B.A., 1992); Georgetown University (J.D., magna cum laude, 1998). Order of the Coif. ***Email:*** jmagurshak@wilmer.com

ASHOK MANNAVA, born August 2, 1969; admitted to bar, 1999, Virginia (Not admitted in District of Columbia). *Education:* Northeastern University (B.S.E.E., 1992); Catholic University of America (J.D., 1999). Former Patent Examiner, U.S. Patent & Trademark Office. ***Email:*** amannava@wilmer.com

TERRY A. MARONEY, born July 6, 1967; admitted to bar, 1999, New York (Not admitted in District of Columbia). *Education:* Oberlin College (B.A., 1989); New York University (J.D., summa cum laude, 1998). Order of the Coif. Notes Editor, New York University Law Review, 1997-1998. Clerk to Judge Amalya L. Kearse, Second Circuit. Adjunct Faculty Member, New York University, 1999-2001. ***LANGUAGES:*** Spanish. ***Email:*** tmaroney@wilmer.com

MORIS MASHALI, born September 21, 1973; admitted to bar, 1997, New York; admitted as solicitor, 2000, England and Wales. *Education:* King's College, London (LL.B., 1995); Cornell University (LL.M., 1996); College of Law, Guildford (L.P.C., 1997). (Resident, European Office, London, England). ***LANGUAGES:*** French and Spanish. ***Email:*** mmashali@wilmer.com

JONATHAN M. MASTRANGELO, born May 7, 1971; admitted to bar, 1996, Maryland; 1997, District of Columbia. *Education:* State University of New York, Albany (B.A., summa cum laude, 1993); University of Pennsylvania (J.D., magna cum laude, 1996). Phi Beta Kappa; Order of the Coif. ***Email:*** jmastrangelo@wilmer.com

MAREN LEE MATAL, born December 5, 1969; admitted to bar, 1997, District of Columbia. *Education:* Arizona State University (B.S., summa cum laude, 1992); University of Chicago (J.D., 1996). Phi Beta Kappa. Symposium Editor, The University of Chicago Legal Forum Journal. ***Email:*** mmatal@wilmer.com

ANN PERRY MAYO, born January 30, 1970; admitted to bar, 1996, Illinois; 1998, District of Columbia. *Education:* College of the Holy Cross (B.A., magna cum laude, 1992); Chicago-Kent College of Law (J.D., with high honors, 1996). Editor-in-Chief, Chicago-Kent Law Review. Clerk to Judge Harry D. Leinenweber, N.D. Illinois. ***Email:*** aperry@wilmer.com

SEAN P. McCANN, born March 21, 1972; admitted to bar, 1998, Georgia; 2001, District of Columbia. *Education:* Vanderbilt University (B.A., cum laude, 1994); Cornell University (J.D., magna cum laude, 1998). Member, Order of the Coif. General Editor, Cornell Law Review. Law Clerk to Judge William T. Moore, Jr., Southern District of Georgia. ***Email:*** smccann@wilmer.com

JEREMY K. McKOWN, born 1971; admitted to bar, 1999, New York; 2000, District of Columbia; registered to practice before U.S. Patent and Trademark Office. *Education:* Ithaca College (B.S., 1993); Bucknell University (M.S., 1996); Syracuse University (J.D., 1998). ***Email:*** jmckown@wilmer.com

CHRISTOPHER McWHINNEY, admitted to bar, 2000, Florida; 2001, District of Columbia; registered to practice before U.S. Patent and Trademark Office. *Education:* College of William and Mary (B.S., 1994); University of Miami (J.D., cum laude, 1999). Member, University of Miami International and Comparative Law Review. ***Email:*** cmcwhinney@wilmer.com

CHRISTOPHER J. MEADE, born October 29, 1968; admitted to bar, 1997, New York; 2001, U.S. Supreme Court (Not admitted in District of Columbia). *Education:* Princeton University (A.B., magna cum laude, 1990); New York University (J.D., magna cum laude, 1996). Order of the Coif. Editor-in-Chief, New York University Law Review, 1995-1996. Clerk to: Justice John Paul Stevens, U.S. Supreme Court, October Term, 1997; Judge Harry T. Edwards, D.C. Circuit. ***Email:*** cmeade@wilmer.com

WENDY MEHARG, born April 5, 1975; admitted to bar, 1999, England and Wales (Not admitted in District of Columbia). *Education:* Magdalene College, Cambridge University (B.A., law, 1996); College of Law, England (Post Graduate Diploma in Legal Practice, 1997). (Resident, European Office, London, England). ***Email:*** wmeharg@wilmer.com

(This Listing Continued)

DAVID S. MENDEL, born January 19, 1969; admitted to bar, 1998, Massachusetts (inactive); 1999, New York; 2001, District of Columbia. *Education:* Brown University (A.B., magna cum laude, 1991); University of Michigan (J.D., magna cum laude, 1997). Phi Beta Kappa; Order of the Coif. Article Editor, Michigan Law Review. Clerk to Judge Harry T. Edwards, D.C. Circuit. Trial Attorney, Federal Programs Branch, Civil Division, U.S. Department of Justice, 1998-2001. ***Email:*** dmendel@wilmer.com

WENDY JANE MILES, born October 21, 1970; admitted to bar, 1994, New Zealand; 2000, England and Wales (Not admitted in District of Columbia). *Education:* University of Canterbury (B.A., 1993; LL.B., 1993; LL.M., with first class honors, 1998). Tutor, Law of Evidence, University of Canterbury Law School, 1994-1997. (Resident, European Office, London, England). ***Email:*** wmiles@wilmer.com

JOEL MILLAR, born May 17, 1971; admitted to bar, 1999, New York; 2001, District of Columbia. *Education:* University of Florida (B.A., 1993); University of Pennsylvania (J.D., cum laude, 1996). Phi Beta Kappa. Executive Editor, University of Pennsylvania Law Review. Clerk to Judge Anita B. Brody, Eastern District of Pennsylvania. ***Email:*** jmillar@wilmer.com

ANJA MILLER, born September 29, 1974; admitted to bar, 2001, New York (Not admitted in District of Columbia). *Education:* Stanford University (B.A., 1996; M.A., with distinction, 1996); Harvard University (J.D., cum laude, 2000). Editor, Harvard Human Rights Law Journal, 1999-2000. Adjunct Teaching Staff Member, Tutorial on Emerging National Security Affairs, Georgetown School of Foreign Service, 2001. Co-Founder and President, Harvard Colloquium on International Affairs. ***LANGUAGES:*** German and Spanish. ***Email:*** amiller@wilmer.com

JOSEPH C. MINKO, born December 21, 1972; admitted to bar, 2000, Maryland. *Education:* Wake Forest University (B.S., magna cum laude, 1995); University of Maryland (J.D., 2000). Phi Beta Kappa.. Order of the Coif. (Resident, Baltimore, Maryland Office). ***Email:*** jminko@wilmer.com

ELIZABETH L. MITCHELL, born 1971; admitted to bar, 1999, Massachusetts; 2001, New York (Not admitted in District of Columbia). *Education:* University of North Carolina at Chapel Hill (B.S., with highest distinction, 1993); Harvard University (J.D., cum laude, 1998). Phi Beta Kappa. Executive Articles Editor, Harvard Women's Law Journal, 1997-1998. Clerk to Judge Walter K. Stapleton, Third Circuit. Teaching Fellow, Constitutional Interpretation, Harvard University, 1997-1998. Trial Attorney, Torts Branch, Civil Division, U.S. Department of Justice, 1999-2001. ***Email:*** emitchell@wilmer.com

DAVID S. MOLOT, born June 6, 1969; admitted to bar, 1998, Massachusetts; 2000, District of Columbia. *Education:* Yale University (B.A., cum laude, 1991); George Washington University (J.D., with highest honors, 1997). Order of the Coif. Notes Editor, The George Washington University Law Review, 1996-1997. Clerk to Judge Stewart Dalzell, U.S. District Court, Eastern District, Pennsylvania. ***Email:*** dmolot@wilmer.com

SOPHIE MOONEN, born November 6, 1971; admitted to bar, 1996, Brussels; 1999, New York (Not admitted in District of Columbia). *Education:* University of Liège (Licence en droit, with honors, 1993); University of Michigan (LL.M., 1995). Stagiaire, Directorate-General for Competition, European Commission, 1993-1994. (Resident, European Office, Brussels, Belgium). ***Email:*** smoonen@wilmer.com

MARK S. MORELLI, born March 4, 1969; admitted to bar, 1996, Illinois (Not admitted in District of Columbia). *Education:* Brown University (B.A., 1991); Phi Beta Kappa; Western Illinois University; Yale Law School (J.D., 1996). Clerk to Judge Joan B. Gottschall, U.S. District Court, Northern District of Illinois. ***Email:*** mmorelli@wilmer.com

AMBER MORRELL, born May 9, 1975; admitted to bar, 2001, New York and District of Columbia. *Education:* Georgetown University (B.S.F.S., 1997); Duke University (J.D., 2000). ***LANGUAGES:*** Spanish. ***Email:*** amorrell@wilmer.com

TREVOR MORRISON, born May 16, 1971; admitted to bar, 2001, Maryland (Not admitted in District of Columbia). *Education:* University of British Columbia, Vancouver, British Columbia, Canada (B.A., honours, 1994); Columbia University (J.D., 1998). Book Review Editor, Columbia Journal of Transnational Law, 1997-1998. Clerk to Judge Betty Fletcher, Ninth Circuit. Attorney-Advisor, Office of Legal Counsel, U.S. Department of Justice, 2000-2001. Bristow Fellow, Office of the Solicitor General, U.S. Department of Justice, 1999-2000. ***Email:*** tmorrison@wilmer.com

PEIRCE R. MOSER, born March 9, 1967; admitted to bar, 2001, California (Not admitted in District of Columbia). *Education:* California State University (B.S., 1996); University of Virginia (J.D., 1999). Order of the Coif. Essays Editor, Virginia Law Review, 1998-1999. Clerk to Chief Judge Carolyn Dineen King, Fifth Circuit. ***Email:*** pmoser@wilmer.com

PETER J. MUCCHETTI, born June 5, 1968; admitted to bar, 1997, Texas; 1999, District of Columbia. *Education:* Yale University (B.A., cum laude, 1989); Harvard Law School (J.D., cum laude, 1995). Editor-in-Chief, Harvard Latino Law Review. Line Editor, Harvard Journal on Legislation. Clerk to Judge Lee H. Rosenthal, Southern District of Texas. ***Email:*** pmucchetti@wilmer.com

(This Listing Continued)

SEAN MULCAHY, born 1970; admitted to bar, 2000, Maryland. *Education:* University of Maryland (B.A., 1996); University of Baltimore (J.D., summa cum laude, 2000). Member, University of Baltimore Law Review. Clerk to Judge Susan K. Gauvey, District of Maryland. (Resident, Baltimore, Maryland Office). ***Email:*** smulcahy@wilmer.com

JOHN C. NAGEL, born April 19, 1970; admitted to bar, 1997, District of Columbia. *Education:* Dartmouth College (B.A., magna cum laude, 1992); Duke University (J.D., with high honors, 1995). Order of the Coif. Senior Note Editor, Duke Law Journal. Clerk to Judge Walter K. Stapleton, 3rd Circuit. ***Email:*** jnagel@wilmer.com

JOEL A. NICHOLS, born September 5, 1972; admitted to bar, 2000, Texas; 2001, District of Columbia. *Education:* Abilene Christian University (B.A., summa cum laude, 1995); Emory University (J.D., with high honors, 2000; M.Div., 2000). Order of the Coif. Articles Editor, Emory Law Journal, 1999-2000. Clerk to Judge Gerald B. Tjoflat, Eleventh Circuit. ***Email:*** jnichols@wilmer.com

STEPHANIE NICOLAS, born 1972; admitted to bar, 2000, Massachusetts, New York and District of Columbia. *Education:* Brown University (B.A., 1994); Georgetown University (J.D., magna cum laude, 1999). Order of the Coif. Notes and Articles Editor, Law and Policy in International Business, 1998-1999. ***Email:*** snicolas@wilmer.com

WILLIAM R. NIFONG, born November 14, 1966; admitted to bar, 2001, District of Columbia. *Education:* Duke University (B.A., magna cum laude, 1989; J.D., 2000; LL.M., cum laude, 2000); University of Michigan (M.A., 1992); Northwestern University (M.S., 1993). Phi Beta Kappa. Executive Editor, Duke Law Journal, 1999-2000. ***LANGUAGES:*** French, German and Latin. ***Email:*** wnifong@wilmer.com

JUSTIN OCHS, born December 29, 1972; admitted to bar, 2000, New York (Not admitted in District of Columbia). *Education:* Cornell University (B.A., 1995); University of Virginia (J.D., 1999). Member, Virginia Journal of International Law. ***Email:*** jochs@wilmer.com

JENNIE O'FLANAGAN, born July 8, 1971; admitted to bar, 1999, Florida; 2000, District of Columbia. *Education:* Eckerd College (B.A., highest honors, 1993); Yale University (J.D., 1998). Clerk to Judge Donald M. Middlebrooks, Southern District of Florida. ***Email:*** joflanagan@wilmer.com

STEFAN OHLHOFF, born April 18, 1968; admitted to bar, 1999, Germany (Not admitted in District of Columbia). *Education:* University of Geneva; Ruprecht-Karls-Universität, Heidelberg (First State Examination, 1994); School of Oriental and African Studies, University of London (LL.M., 1995); University of Kiel (Graduiertenkolleg of National and International Environmental Law); Supreme Court of Berlin (Second State Examination, 1999). Recipient: Research Fellowship, 1995-1996; Francis Deàk Award, American Society of International Law, 2000. ***Email:*** sohlhoff@wilmer.com

DENNIS W. O'NEILL, born October 26, 1973; admitted to bar, 1998, District of Columbia; 2000, Delaware. *Education:* Villanova University (B.A., 1995); Catholic University of America, Columbus School of Law (J.D., cum laude, 1998). Lead Articles Editor, The Journal of Contemporary Health Law and Policy. (Resident, Northern Virginia Office). ***Email:*** do'neill@wilmer.com

JAMES FRANCIS O'REILLY, born November 23, 1970; admitted to bar, 1997, Massachusetts; 1998, District of Columbia. *Education:* Yale University (B.A., magna cum laude, 1992); Harvard University (J.D., magna cum laude, 1996). ***Email:*** jo'reilly@wilmer.com

JONATHAN E. PAIKIN, born June 7, 1971; admitted to bar, 1997, New York; 2000, District of Columbia. *Education:* The Johns Hopkins University (B.A., 1993); University of Pennsylvania (J.D., cum laude, 1996). Phi Beta Kappa. ***Email:*** jpaikin@wilmer.com

IJAY PALANSKY, born August 17, 1972; admitted to bar, 1996, California; 1998, District of Columbia. *Education:* University of Western Ontario (B.A., 1993); Harvard University (J.D., cum laude, 1996). ***Email:*** ipalansky@wilmer.com

E. STUART PARKER, born July 9, 1973; admitted to bar, 2000, District of Columbia. *Education:* University of Alabama (B.A., 1995); Georgetown University Law Center (J.D., cum laude, 2000). ***Email:*** sparker@wilmer.com

KIMBERLY PARKER, born May 28, 1970; admitted to bar, 1998, New York; 1999, District of Columbia. *Education:* Princeton university (A.B., magna cum laude, 1992); Harvard Law School (J.D., magna cum laude, 1996). Articles Editor, Harvard Law Review. Clerk to Judge Alfred T. Goodwin, 9th Circuit. ***Email:*** kparker@wilmer.com

A. KRISAN PATTERSON, born August 8, 1973; admitted to bar, 2001, Alaska (Not admitted in District of Columbia). *Education:* Universidad de Cordoba, Spain; Smith College (B.A., cum laude, 1995); University of Texas at Austin (J.D., 2000). Fulbright Scholar. Articles Editor, Texas Law Review, 1999-2000. Clerk to Judge Royce Lamberth, D.C. District Court. ***LANGUAGES:*** Spanish. ***Email:*** kpatterson@wilmer.com

(This Listing Continued)

WILMER, CUTLER & PICKERING, Washington—Continued

NANCY E. FURMAN PAUL, born February 16, 1969; admitted to bar, 1996, New York; 1999, District of Columbia. *Education:* Yale University (B.A., magna cum laude, 1991); Harvard University (J.D., cum laude, 1995). Articles Editor, Harvard Civil Rights-Civil Liberties Law Review. Clerk to Chief Judge Charles P. Sifton, E.D. New York. ***Email:*** nfurman@wilmer.com

CHRISTIAN C.D. PETERSEN, born April 2, 1969; admitted to bar, 1998, Massachusetts and District of Columbia. *Education:* University of California, Santa Barbara (B.A., magna cum laude, 1991); University of California, Los Angeles (M.A., 1994); Boston University (J.D., cum laude, 1997). Editor-in-Chief, Boston University International Law Journal. ***Email:*** cpetersen@wilmer.com

JOHN V. H. PIERCE, born December 19, 1969; admitted to bar, 1997, New York (Not admitted in District of Columbia). *Education:* Institut d'Etudes Politiques (Certificate d'Etudes Politiques, 1991); Georgetown University, School of Foreign Service (B.S.F.S., magna cum laude, 1992); Georgetown University Law Center (J.D., cum laude, 1996). Associate Editor, Law and Policy in International Business. Clerk to Judge M. Margaret McKeown, U.S. Court of Appeals, Ninth Circuit, 1998-1999. (Resident, New York Office). ***Email:*** jpierce@wilmer.com

MICHAEL PLOTNICK, born February 29, 1972; admitted to bar, 1997, Maryland; 1998, District of Columbia. *Education:* Tufts University (B.A., cum laude, 1994); George Washington University (J.D., with highest honors, 1997). Order of the Coif. Associate, George Washington Law Review. ***Email:*** mplotnick@wilmer.com

GWENDOLYN K. PONDER, born July 19, 1972; admitted to bar, 2001, Massachusetts, New York and District of Columbia. *Education:* University of California at Berkeley (B.A., 1995); Georgetown University Law Center (J.D., cum laude, 2000). Editor-in-Chief, Law and Policy in International Business. ***Email:*** gponder@wilmer.com

JAY V. PRABHU, born October 7, 1970; admitted to bar, 1996, Maryland; 1998, District of Columbia. *Education:* Boston College (B.A., magna cum laude, 1992); Harvard University (J.D. and M.P.P., 1996). Boykin C. Wright Prize. Managing Editor, Harvard Journal on Legislation. Ames Moot Court Competition, Finals Oralist, Championship Team, Team Captain. Clerkships: Summer Clerk, U.S. Justice Department, Civil Fraud; U.S. Attorney's Office, Boston, MA. ***Email:*** jprabhu@wilmer.com

MATTHEW P. PREVIN, born February 26, 1970; admitted to bar, 1997, New York; 1998, District of Columbia. *Education:* Yale University (B.A., 1992); Georgetown University (J.D., cum laude, 1996). Senior Book Review and Essays Editor, Georgetown Law Journal. Clerk to Judge Cornelia Kennedy, 6th Circuit. (Resident, New York Office). ***Email:*** mprevin@wilmer.com

LORI HAMILTON PRICE, born July 18, 1962; admitted to bar, 1993, Maryland; 2001, District of Columbia. *Education:* University of Maryland (B.A., with high honors, 1984; J.D., 1993). Order of the Coif. Economist, Analyst and Staff Attorney, U.S. Securities and Exchange Commission, 1987-2000. ***Email:*** lprice@wilmer.com

ELOISE QUARLES, admitted to bar, 1995, Maryland; 2000, District of Columbia. *Education:* Loyola College (B.A., 1992); University of Maryland (J.D., 1995). Staff Attorney, 1995-1998 and Special Counsel, 1998-2000, Division of Corporate Finance, U.S. Securities and Exchange Commission. ***Email:*** equarles@wilmer.com

MARTIN F. RAMIREZ, admitted to bar, 1997, New Jersey; 2000, District of Columbia and New York. *Education:* Stanford University (B.A., 1989); Columbia University (J.D., 1996). ***Email:*** mramirez@wilmer.com

DAVID ALFRED JOHN RAMM, born August 15, 1969; admitted to bar, 1998, United Kingdom (Solicitor). *Education:* University of Birmingham (B.Eng., Hons., 1990); Girton College, Cambridge University (Ph.D, 1994); College of Law, Guildford (Diploma, 1996); University of Bristol (Diploma, 1999). (Resident, European Office, London, England). ***Email:*** dramm@wilmer.com

ARUN RATTAN, born November 19, 1971; admitted to bar, 1998, England and Wales (Not admitted in District of Columbia). *Education:* Durham University (1990-1993); Northumbria Law School (Common Professional Examination, 1994; Legal Practice Course, 1995); University of Eastern England (LL.M., 1996). Trainee Solicitor (Salans Hertzfeld & Heibronn, London Office, 1998); Stagiaire, Merger Task Force, DG Competition, European Commission, 1999. (Resident, European Office, Brussels, Belgium). ***Email:*** arattan@wilmer.com

MATTHEW McDAVID REED, born June 27, 1970; admitted to bar, 1996, Maryland; 1998, North Carolina; 2000, District of Columbia. *Education:* Princeton University (A.B., 1992); George Washington University (J.D., 1996). Law Clerk, Department of the Interior, Bureau of Land Management, 1994-1996. (Resident, Baltimore, Maryland Office). ***Email:*** mreed@wilmer.com

(This Listing Continued)

NEIL MICHAEL RICHARDS, born October 31, 1972; admitted to bar, 1997, Virginia; 1998, U.S. Court of Appeals, Fourth Circuit (Not admitted in District of Columbia). *Education:* George Washington University (B.A., summa cum laude, 1994); University of Virginia (M.A., 1997; J.D., 1997). Phi Beta Kappa. Member, Order of the Coif. Executive Editor, University of Virginia Law Review. Member, Virginia Journal of International Law. Law Clerk to: Judge Paul Niemeyer, Fourth Circuit; Chief Justice Rehnquist, U.S. Supreme Court, 1998-1999. Hugo Black Faculty Fellow (Property, Regligion and the Constitution), University of Alabama School of Law, 1999-2000. ***Email:*** nrichards@wilmer.com

JULIE M. RIEWE, born September 26, 1970; admitted to bar, 2000, California; 2001, District of Columbia. *Education:* Duke University (A.B., 1993; M.P.P., 1999; J.D., 1999). Editor-in-Chief and Articles Editor, Duke Journal of Gender Law and Policy. Member, Editorial Board, Duke Law Journal. Law Clerk to Judge Diana E. Murphy, Eighth Circuit. ***LANGUAGES:*** Spanish. ***Email:*** jriewe@wilmer.com

JEROME J. ROCHE, born April 10, 1970; admitted to bar, 1997, Illinois; 2001, District of Columbia. *Education:* Purdue University (B.S., 1992); University of Michigan (J.D., 1997). Staff Attorney, Division of Market Regulation, U.S. Securities and Exchange Commission, 1997-2000. ***Email:*** jroche@wilmer.com

JENNIFER M. ROCKOFF, born January 3, 1973; admitted to bar, 2001, Virginia and District of Columbia. *Education:* Princeton University (B.A., 1995); University of Virginia (J.D., 2000). Member, Editorial Board, Virginia Journal of International Law, 1999-2000. Clerk to Senior Judge Albert V. Bryan, Eastern District of Virginia. Vice Consul to U.S. Consulate General, St. Petersburg, Russia, 1996-1997. ***LANGUAGES:*** Russian and Spanish. ***Email:*** jrockoff@wilmer.com

JOSH L. ROLAND, born November 8, 1969; admitted to bar, 1996, New York; 1997, District of Columbia. *Education:* Brown University (B.A., 1991); George Washington University (J.D., with honors, 1995). Attorney Advisor, Federal Communications Commission, Wireless Telecommunications Bureau, Actions and Industry Analysis Division, 1996-1998. Legal Advisor to the Bureau Chief, Federal Communications Commission, Wireless Telecommunications Bureau, 1998-1999. ***Email:*** jroland@wilmer.com

JOHN-ALEX ROMANO, born January 29, 1973; admitted to bar, 2000, Maryland; 2001, District of Columbia. *Education:* Georgetown University (B.S.F.S., summa cum laude, 1995; J.D., summa cum laude, 1999). Member, Order of the Coif. Articles Editor, Georgetown Law Journal. Law Clerk to Judge Stanley S. Harris, District Court for the District of Columbia. ***Email:*** jromano@wilmer.com

JORIAN ROSE, born December 17, 1969; admitted to bar, 1998, New York. *Education:* Hobart College (B.A., 1992); St. John's University (J.D., 1997). Associate Managing Editor, American Bankruptcy Institute Law Review. Clerk to Judge Burton R. Lifland, U.S. Bankruptcy Court, Southern District of New York. (Resident, New York Office). ***Email:*** jrose@wilmer.com

STEVEN ROSEN, born November 25, 1970; admitted to bar, 1998, New York; 1999, District of Columbia. *Education:* Georgetown University (B.A., 1992); George Washington University (J.D., 1997). Member, George Washington Law Review. Clerk to Judge Samuel G. Wilson, Western District of Virginia. ***Email:*** srosen@wilmer.com

CHARLES COLIN RUSHING, born October 26, 1972; admitted to bar, 1999, Virginia; 2001, District of Columbia. *Education:* James Madison University (B.A., with honors, 1995); University of Virginia (J.D., 1999). Member, Order of the Coif. Executive Editor, Virginia Law Review. Law Clerk to Judge T.S. Ellis, III, Eastern District of Virginia. ***Email:*** crushing@wilmer.com

PETER B. RUTLEDGE, born September 13, 1970; admitted to bar, 2000, Maryland (Not admitted in District of Columbia). *Education:* Harvard University (B.A., magna cum laude, 1992); University of Aberdeen (M.Litt., 1994); University of Chicago (J.D., with high honors, 1997). Order of the Coif. Executive Editor, The University of Chicago Law Review, 1996-1997. Clerk to: Chief Judge J. Harvie Wilkinson, III, Fourth Circuit; Associate Justice Clarence Thomas, U.S. Supreme Court, October Term, 1998. Teaching Assistant, Introduction to Philosophy, University of Aberdeen, 1994. Executive Fellow, California Health & Welfare Agency, 1992-1993. ***LANGUAGES:*** German. ***Email:*** prutledge@wilmer.com

MICHAEL RYAN, born August 11, 1971; admitted to bar, 2000, Virginia; 2001, District of Columbia. *Education:* University of Pennsylvania (B.A., cum laude, 1993); University of Notre Dame (M.A., 1997); University of Virginia (J.D., 2000). Teaching Assistant, Introduction to Philosophy, University of Notre Dame, 1995-1997. ***Email:*** mryan@wilmer.com

ROBERT-PAUL SAGNER, born November 29, 1972; admitted to bar, 2001, New York (Not admitted in District of Columbia). *Education:* Columbia University (B.A., 1994; J.D., 2000). Executive Editor, Columbia-VLA Journal of Law and the Arts, 1999-2000. ***Email:*** rpsagner@wilmer.com

SAMUEL J. SALARIO, JR., born Tampa, Florida, October 15, 1970; admitted to bar, 1996, Florida; 1999, District of Columbia. *Education:* Ameri-

(This Listing Continued)

can University (B.A., 1992); University of Florida (J.D., with high honors, 1995). Order of the Coif. Board Member, University of Florida Law Review. Law Clerk to Judge Wm. Terrell Hodges, U.S. District Court, Middle District of Florida, 1996-1998. ***Email:*** ssalario@wilmer.com

JOSEPH J. SAMARIAS, born July 6, 1971; admitted to bar, 1997, Virginia; 1998, District of Columbia and U.S. District Court, Eastern District of Virginia. *Education:* Vanderbilt University (B.A., magna cum laude, 1993); Washington University (J.D., 1997). Managing Editor, Washington University Law Quarterly. ***Email:*** jsamarias@wilmer.com

ALEC J. SCHEINER, born March 7, 1970; admitted to bar, 1997, Maryland; 1998, District of Columbia. *Education:* Georgetown University (B.S.F.S., cum laude, 1992; J.D., cum laude, 1997). (Resident, New York Office). ***LANGUAGES:*** Spanish. ***Email:*** ascheiner@wilmer.com

KRISANNE SCHLACHTER, born January 8, 1975; admitted to bar, 2000, Georgia; 2001, District of Columbia. *Education:* University of Notre Dame (B.B.A., summa cum laude, 1997); University of Virginia (J.D., 2000). Beta Gamma Sigma. Editor-in-Chief, Virginia Tax Review. ***Email:*** kschlachter@wilmer.com

HARTMUT SCHNEIDER, born May 3, 1969; admitted to bar, 2000, Berlin, Germany. *Education:* Universite de Paris X (License en droit, 1993); Universities of Frankfurt/M. and Freiburg (First State Exam, 1996; Dr. jur., 1997); Berlin Court of Appeals (Second State Exam, 1999); University of Michigan (LL.M., 2000). Research Assistant in EC Law, University of Freiburg, 1996-1997. (Resident, European Office, Berlin, Germany). ***Email:*** hschneider@wilmer.com

RUEDIGER SCHUETT, born April 18, 1971; admitted to bar, 1999, Berlin, Germany. *Education:* Free University Berlin (First State Exam, 1995); Berlin Court of Appeals (Second State Exam, 1998); King's College, London, England (LL.M., 2000). Clerk, Federal Cartel Office, Berlin, Germany, 1995. (Resident, European Office, Berlin, Germany). ***LANGUAGES:*** German and Russian. ***Email:*** rschuett@wilmer.com

ADAM J. SCHWARTZ, born 1973; admitted to bar, 1999, Maryland; 2000, District of Columbia. *Education:* Vassar College (B.A., with honors, 1995); George Washington University (J.D., with high honors, 1999). Order of the Coif. Notes Editor, The George Washington Law Review, 1998-1999. ***Email:*** aschwartz@wilmer.com

FRANZ T. SCHWARZ, born May 31, 1973; admitted to bar, 1997, Austria (Rechtsanwaltsanwaerter) (Not admitted in District of Columbia). *Education:* University of Vienna (M. iur., 1991); London School of Economics (LL.M., with merits, 1999). Military Lawyer, Parliamentary Complaints Commission, Austria, 1996. (Resident, European Office, London, England). ***Email:*** fschwarz@wilmer.com

RACHEL SHACHTER, admitted to bar, 2001, Virginia (Not admitted in District of Columbia). *Education:* College of William & Mary (B.A., cum laude, 1994); University of Virginia (J.D., 2001). Member, Editorial Board, Virginia Law Review, 2000-2001. ***Email:*** rshachter@wilmer.com

OMAR SHAH, born August 1, 1972; admitted to bar, 1999, England and Wales. *Education:* Worcester College, Oxford University (B.A., Hons., 1995); Free University of Brussels (Masters of Law, with distinction, 1996); BPP Law School, London, England (Legal Practice Course, 1997). Stagiaire, Telecommunications Unit, DG Competition, European Commission, 2000. (Resident, European Office, London, England). ***LANGUAGES:*** French and German. ***Email:*** oshah@wilmer.com

THOMAS E. SHARP, born January 3, 1972; admitted to bar, 1998, New York; 2000, District of Columbia. *Education:* State University of New York at Buffalo (B.A., 1994); Yale University (J.D., 1997). Clerk to Judge Myron H. Thompson, U.S. District Court, Middle District, Alabama. ***Email:*** tsharp@wilmer.com

SCOTT A. SHEPARD, born April 6, 1973; admitted to bar, 2000, Georgia; 2001, District of Columbia. *Education:* University of Richmond (B.A., summa cum laude, 1995); Vanderbilt University (M.A., 1996); University of Virginia (J.D., 1999). Order of the Coif. Member, Editorial Board, University of Virginia Law Review, 1998-1999. Clerk to Judge Jerry E. Smith, Fifth Circuit. ***Email:*** sshepard@wilmer.com

JAMES A. SHEPHERD, born December 14, 1961; admitted to bar, 1995, Virginia; 1997, Michigan (Not admitted in District of Columbia). *Education:* Western Maryland College (B.A., 1985); Indiana University (J.D., cum laude, 1995). Articles Editor, Indiana Journal of Global Legal Studies, 1994-1995. Clerk to Judge Jo Ann C. Stevenson, Bankruptcy Court, Western District of Michigan. ***Email:*** jshepherd@wilmer.com

JONATHAN H. SIEGELBAUM, born August 1, 1973; admitted to bar, 2000, Virginia (Not admitted in District of Columbia). *Education:* Williams College (B.A., cum laude, 1995); University of Virginia (J.D., 2000). Order of the Coif. Notes Editor, Virginia Law Review, 1999-2000. Clerk to Judge Norman H. Stahl, First Circuit. ***Email:*** jsiegelbaum@wilmer.com

(This Listing Continued)

CHRISTOPHER P. SIMKINS, born September 15, 1970; admitted to bar, 1997, Illinois; 1999, District of Columbia. *Education:* Brigham Young University (B.A., magna cum laude, 1993); J. Reuben Clark Law School, Brigham Young University (J.D., magna cum laude, 1997). Order of the Coif. Managing Editor, Brigham Young University Law Review. ***Email:*** csimkins@wilmer.com

OMARI S. SIMMONS, born February 4, 1974; admitted to bar, 1999, Maryland (Not admitted in District of Columbia). *Education:* Wake Forest University (B.A., magna cum laude, 1996); University of Pennsylvania (J.D., 1999); Pembroke College, University of Cambridge, United Kingdom (LL.M., 2001). Senior Editor, University of Pennsylvania Journal of Constitutional Law, 1998-1999. Clerk to Chief Justice E. Norman Veasey, Supreme Court of Delaware. ***Email:*** osimmons@wilmer.com

POLLY B. SMOTHERGILL, born May 11, 1975; admitted to bar, 2001, New York and District of Columbia. *Education:* University of Michigan (B.A., highest honors, 1997); Harvard University (J.D., 2000). Phi Beta Kappa. Executive Editor, Harvard Women's Law Journal. ***Email:*** psmothergill@wilmer.com

O. CARTER SNEAD, IV, born December 23, 1972; admitted to bar, 1999, Maryland; 2001, District of Columbia. *Education:* St. John's College (B.A., 1996); Georgetown University (J.D., magna cum laude, 1999). Order of the Coif. Associate Editor, American Criminal Law Review. Clerk to Judge Paul J. Kelly, Tenth Circuit. ***LANGUAGES:*** Spanish. ***Email:*** csnead@wilmer.com

HYUNG SOHN, born November 1, 1962; admitted to bar, 2000, Virginia; 2001, District of Columbia; registered to practice before U.S. Patent and Trademark Office. *Education:* Carnegie Mellon University (B.S.E.E., 1985); George Washington University (M.S., 1996); George Mason University (J.D., 2000). Computer Analyst, U.S. Department of Commerce. ***LANGUAGES:*** Korean. ***Email:*** hsohn@wilmer.com

JOSHUA R. STEBBINS, born October 5, 1970; admitted to bar, 1998, Massachusetts; 2000, District of Columbia; 2001, New York. *Education:* The Johns Hopkins University (B.A., 1992); New York University School of Law (J.D., magna cum laude, 1997). Order of the Coif. Senior Editor, The Environmental Law Journal. Clerk to Judge Joseph A. DiClerico, Jr., District of New Hampshire. ***Email:*** jstebbins@wilmer.com

TODD R. STEGGERDA, born April 14, 1965; admitted to bar, 1998, Pennsylvania; 2001, District of Columbia. *Education:* United States Naval Academy (B.S., with merit, 1987); University of Iowa (J.D., with high distinction, 1997). Order of the Coif. Editor-in-Chief, Journal of Corporation Law. Adjunct Assistant Professor, Aviation Law, Embry-Riddle Aeronautical University, 1999-2000. ***Email:*** tsteggerda@wilmer.com

NATACHA D. STEIMER, born September 22, 1970; admitted to bar, 1995, Maryland; 2001, District of Columbia. *Education:* American University (B.A., magna cum laude, 1992); George Washington University (J.D., with highest honors, 1995). George Washington Law Review. ***Email:*** nsteimer@wilmer.com

LESLIE ANNE STURTEVANT, admitted to bar, 1999, New York; 2001, District of Columbia. *Education:* Brown University (A.B., magna cum laude, 1991); University of Michigan (J.D., with honors, 1997). Managing Editor, Michigan Journal of International Law, 1996-1997. ***Email:*** lsturtevant@wilmer.com

AMANDA L. TANTUM, born December 27, 1975; admitted to bar, 2000, Virginia (Not admitted in District of Columbia). *Education:* Stetson University (B.S., B.A., summa cum laude, 1997); University of Virginia (J.D., 2000). Research & Projects Editor, Virginia Journal of International Law, 1999-2000. Clerk to Senior District Judge Kenneth L. Ryskamp, Southern District of Florida. ***LANGUAGES:*** Spanish. ***Email:*** atantum@wilmer.com

DAVID TAYLOR, born May 8, 1971; admitted as Solicitor, 1997, England and Wales. *Education:* New College, Oxford University (B.A., First Class, 1992); College of Law, Guildford, England (C.P.E., 1993; L.P.C., 1994). (Resident, European Office, London, England). ***Email:*** dtaylor@wilmer.com

NICOLE TELECKI, born June 23, 1971; admitted to bar, 1997, New York and District of Columbia. *Education:* Princeton University (B.A., 1993); Boston University (J.D., cum laude, 1996). Note Editor, Boston University International Law Journal. ***Email:*** ntelecki@wilmer.com

PAUL M. TIAO, admitted to bar, 1996, New York; 2000, District of Columbia. *Education:* Massachusetts Institute of Technology (S.B., 1989); Columbia University School of Law (J.D., 1995); Woodrow Wilson School Public and International Affairs, Princeton University (M.P.A., 1995). Articles Editor, Columbia Human Rights Law Review. Law Clerk to Judge Mary Schroeder, Ninth Circuit. Trial Attorney, U.S. Department of Justice, Civil Rights Division, 1996-2000. ***Email:*** ptiao@wilmer.com

JOHN A. TRENOR, born April 24, 1969; admitted to bar, 1996, New York; 1997, District of Columbia. *Education:* Cornell University (B.A., 1991); Woodrow Wilson School of Public and International Affairs, Princeton University (M.P.A., 1995); University of Chicago (J.D., with honors, 1995). Member, University of Chicago Law Review. ***Email:*** jtrenor@wilmer.com

(This Listing Continued)

WILMER, CUTLER & PICKERING, Washington—Continued

JOHN A. VALENTINE, born November 24, 1970; admitted to bar, 1998, Pennsylvania; 2001, District of Columbia. *Education:* Bowdoin College (A.B., magna cum laude, 1993); University of Pennsylvania (J.D., cum laude, 1997). Law Clerk to Judge Joseph L. McGlynn, Jr., U.S. District Court, Eastern District of Pennsylvania, 1997-1998. ***Email:*** jvalentine@wilmer.com

DARCY LYNN VAN KIRK, born August 17, 1971; admitted to bar, 1998, Florida; 2001, District of Columbia. *Education:* Washington and Lee University (B.A., 1993); Duke University (J.D., with honors, 1998). Member, Law and Contemporary Problems. ***PRACTICE AREAS:*** Corporate Securities. ***Email:*** dvankirk@wilmer.com

ESMÉE GRÄFIN VON DER GROEBEN, born May 31, 1971; admitted to bar, 1998, Berlin, Germany (Not admitted in District of Columbia). *Education:* Free University of Berlin. First State Examination (1995); Second State Examination (1997); Stagiaire Bundeskartellamt, Germany (1996). (Resident, European Office, Berlin, Germany). ***Email:*** evdgroeben@wilmer.com

DIERDRE VON DORNUM, born May 21, 1969; admitted to bar, 2001, New York. *Education:* University of California at Los Angeles (B.A., magna cum laude, 1991); Columbia University (J.D., 1997); Princeton University (M.A., 1997). Review and Essay Editor, Columbia Law Review, 1996-1997. Clerk to: Judge Anita B. Brody, Eastern District of Pennsylvania; Judge Stephen Reinhardt, Ninth Circuit; Justice Ruth Bader Ginsburg, U.S. Supreme Court, October Term, 2000. (Resident, New York Office). ***LANGUAGES:*** French, German, Latin and Ancient Greek. ***Email:*** dvondornum@wilmer.com

PHILIPP FREIHERR VON HOYENBERG, born August 27, 1969; admitted to bar, 1998, Berlin, Germany (Not admitted in District of Columbia). *Education:* Universities of Freiburg and Heidelberg (First State Examination, 1994; Dr.jur., 1996); Georgetown University (LL.M., with distinction, 1996); Berlin Supreme Court (Second State Examination, 1998). (Resident European Office, Berlin, Germany). ***LANGUAGES:*** German and English. ***Email:*** pvonhoyenberg@wilmer.com

KERRIE A. WALSH, born November 29, 1962; admitted to bar, 1993, California (Not admitted in District of Columbia). *Education:* San Francisco State University (B.S., 1985); University of San Francisco (J.D., cum laude, 1992). Certified Public Accountant, California. (Resident, European Office, London, England). ***Email:*** kwalsh@wilmer.com

NICOLE R. WALTER, born September 30, 1974; admitted to bar, 2000, Maryland; 2001, District of Columbia. *Education:* University of North Carolina (B.S.P.H., cum laude, 1996); George Washington University (J.D., magna cum laude, 2000). Order of the Coif. Member, The Environmental Lawyer. ***Email:*** nwalter@wilmer.com

DEIRDRE WATERS, born January 7, 1975; admitted to bar, 1998, Ireland (Not admitted in District of Columbia). *Education:* University College Cork (B.C.L., honours, 1995); University College Dublin (LL.M., distinction, 1996). (Resident, European Office, Brussels, Belgium). ***Email:*** dwaters@wilmer.com

JOSHUA D. WEINBERG, born May 26, 1972; admitted to bar, 1998, New York; 1999, District of Columbia. *Education:* University of Pennsylvania (B.A., magna cum laude, 1994); Columbia Law School (J.D., 1997). Harlan Fiske Stone Scholar. Managing Editor, Columbia Law Review. Notes Editor, Columbia Journal of Transnational Law. Clerk to Judge Edward E. Carnes, 11th Circuit. ***Email:*** jweinberg@wilmer.com

TODD E. WIENCH, born September 5, 1973; admitted to bar, 1998, Illinois; 1999, District of Columbia. *Education:* Marquette University (B.A., 1995); Drake University Law School (J.D., with highest honors, 1998); Georgetown University (LL.M., with distinction, 1999). Order of the Coif. Senior Staff Member, Drake Law Review. ***Email:*** twiench@wilmer.com

CHRISTOPHER A. WILBER, born October 23, 1972; admitted to bar, 1999, District of Columbia. *Education:* Miami University (B.S., 1995); Georgetown University (J.D., cum laude, 1998). Member, Law & Policy in International Business. ***Email:*** cwilber@wilmer.com

ROGER S. WISE, born September 27, 1969; admitted to bar, 1997, New York; 2001, District of Columbia. *Education:* Yale University (B.A., magna cum laude, distinction in major, 1992); Harvard University (J.D., cum laude, 1996). Phi Beta Kappa. Articles Editor, International Law Journal. ***LANGUAGES:*** Chinese (Mandarin). ***Email:*** rwise@wilmer.com

ISHA RAUCHLE YOUHAS, born July 4, 1975; admitted to bar, 2000, Virginia and New Jersey (Not admitted in District of Columbia). *Education:* University of Michigan (B.S., 1993); Duke University (J.D., with honors, 2000; LL.M., 2000). Executive Editor, Law & Contemporary Problems, 1999-2000. Law Clerk to Judge Andrew J. Kleinfeld, Ninth Circuit. ***LANGUAGES:*** Spanish. ***Email:*** iyouhas@wilmer.com

TAMARA ZIESCHANG, born August 21, 1970; admitted to bar, 2000, Berlin, Germany (Not admitted in the United States). *Education:* Julius-Maximilians-Universitat Wurzburg, Rheinische Friedrich-Wilhelms-Universitat Bonn, Germany (First State Exam, 1996); District Court of Cologne (Second State Exam, 2000). German. (Resident, European Office, Berlin, Germany). ***Email:*** tzieschang@wilmer.com

(This Listing Continued)

DÖRTE ZIMMERMANN, born January 8, 1968; admitted to bar, 1998, Germany (Not admitted in District of Columbia). *Education:* University of Bonn (1989-1992); University of Geneva (1991-1992); University of Regensburg, First State Examination (1994); King's College, London (LL.M., 1995); Second State Examination (1997). Clerk to Kammergericht, Berlin. (Resident, European Office, Berlin, Germany). ***Email:*** dzimmermann@wilmer.com

TODD ZUBLER, born July 19, 1970; admitted to bar, 1996, Indiana; 1998, District of Columbia. *Education:* Washington University (A.B., summa cum laude, 1992); University of Oxford (M.Sc., with distinction, 1994); Harvard University (J.D., magna cum laude, 1996). Senior Editor, Harvard Journal of Law and Public Policy. Clerk to Judge Michael S. Kanne, Seventh Circuit. Teaching Fellow, Social Analysis 10, Harvard College, 1995-1996. Deputy General Counsel, McCain 2000, Inc. ***Email:*** tzubler@wilmer.com

WILSON, ELSER, MOSKOWITZ, EDELMAN & DICKER LLP

THE COLORADO BUILDING, FIFTH FLOOR
1341 "G" STREET, N.W.
WASHINGTON, D.C. 20005
Telephone: 202-626-7660
Telex: 89453.
Facsimile: 202-628-3606
URL: HTTP://WWW.WEMED.COM

New York, N.Y., Los Angeles, California, San Diego, California, San Francisco, California, Newark, New Jersey, Philadelphia, Pennsylvania, Baltimore, Maryland, Miami, Florida, Chicago, Illinois, White Plains, New York, Dallas, Texas, Houston, Texas, Albany, New York, Garden City, New York, Boston, Massachusetts, London, England.

Affiliates: Paris, France: HPMBC, Munich, Germany: Bach, Langheid Dallmayr, Cologne, Germany: Bach, Langheid Dallmayr, Frankfurt/Main, Germany: Bach, Langheid Dallmayr, Berlin, Germany: Bach, Langheid Dallmayr.

FIRM PROFILE: Wilson, Elser, Moskowitz, Edelman & Dicker LLP is a full service international law firm with a network of offices throughout the United States. We handle General Insurance and Reinsurance Litigation including Commercial, Corporate and Securities Law, Domestic and International Property and Casualty Insurance and Reinsurance, Products and Professional Liability, Toxic Tort Defense, Environmental Impairment Liability, Medical and Hospital Malpractice, Municipal and Public Officials Liability, Trusts and Estates. Aviation, Marine and Inland Marine, Fiduciary Liability, General Subrogation, Labor/Employment Liability and Governmental Relations.

RESIDENT PARTNERS

PAUL D. KRAUSE, born Teaneck, New Jersey, April 28, 1946; admitted to bar, 1972, Virginia; 1975, District of Columbia and U.S. Supreme Court. *Education:* University of Virginia and Fairleigh Dickinson University (B.A., 1969); University of Richmond (J.D., 1972). Phi Delta Phi. *Member:* The District of Columbia Bar; Bar Association of the District of Columbia; Fairfax, Federal and American Bar Associations; Virginia State Bar; Virginia Trial Lawyers Association; Northern Virginia Defense Lawyers Association; Virginia Association of Defense Attorneys; District of Columbia Defense Lawyers Association; The Counselors; The Barristers; The Federation of Insurance and Corporate Counsel. ***PRACTICE AREAS:*** Health Care; Medical Malpractice. ***Email:*** krausep@wemed.com

CAROL ANN PETREN, born Boston, Massachusetts, May 2, 1952; admitted to bar, 1977, Missouri (Not admitted in District of Columbia). *Education:* Boston College (B.A., magna cum laude, 1974); Valparaiso University School of Law; University of Missouri (J.D., 1977; LL.M., 1978). ***PRACTICE AREAS:*** Health Care; Medical Malpractice. ***Email:*** petrenc@wemed.com

ROBERT B. WALLACE, born Washington, D.C., April 23, 1944; admitted to bar, 1970, Virginia; 1973, District of Columbia. *Education:* George Washington University (B.A., 1966; J.D., 1970). ***PRACTICE AREAS:*** Insurance; Litigation; Construction Law; Corporate Law; Securities. ***Email:*** wallacer@wemed.com

LAURA NACHOWITZ STEEL, born New York, N.Y., October 5, 1956; admitted to bar, 1982, District of Columbia; 1989, Maryland. *Education:* Johns Hopkins University; Barnard College of Columbia University (B.A., magna cum laude, with honors in Anthropology, 1978); George Washington University (J.D., with honors, 1982). ***PRACTICE AREAS:*** Insurance Defense Law; Professional Malpractice Law; Psychotherapy Law; Fire Litigation; Police Civil Liability. ***Email:*** steell@wemed.com

WINSTEAD SECHREST & MINICK P.C.

SUITE 1200
1666 K STREET, NW
WASHINGTON, D.C. 20006
Telephone: 202-293-8130
Fax: 202-872-1431
URL: http://www.winstead.com

Dallas, Texas Office: 5400 Renaissance Tower, 1201 Elm Street. Telephone: 214-745-5400. Telex: 73-0051. Fax: 214-745-5390.

Houston, Texas Office: 2400 Bank One Center, 910 Travis Street. Telephone: 713-650-8400. Telex: 73-0051. Fax: 713-650-2400.

Austin, Texas Office: Suite 800, 100 Congress Avenue. Telephone: 512-474-4330. Telex: 73-0051. Fax: 512-370-2850.

Fort Worth, Texas Office: Suite 1100, 777 Main Street. Telephone: 817-420-8200. Fax: 817-420-8201.

The Woodlands, Texas Office: 10077 Grogan's Mill Road, Suite 475. Telephone: 281-367-2222. Fax: 281-363-0660.

Mexico, D.F., Mexico Office: Winstead y Rivera, S.C., Av. Insurgentes Sur 1685, Piso 13-04, Torre Diamante, Colonia Guadalupe Inn, Delegacion Alvaro Obregon, 01020, Mexico, D.F., Mexico. Telephone: (011-525) 5661-3025. Fax: (011-525) 5661-3033.

General Business Practice: Aviation, Bankruptcy and Reorganization, Cable and Communications, Construction, Corporate, Emerging Business, Eminent Domain, Employee Benefits, Energy, Environmental, Estate Planning, Financial Institutions, Government Relations, Healthcare, Insurance, Intellectual Property, International, Labor and Employment, Legislative Relations, Litigation, Mergers and Acquisitions, Probate, Public Finance, Public Law, Public/Administrative, Real Estate, Securities, Sports and Entertainment, Surety, Taxation, Transportation and Zoning.

DANIEL H. BRANCH, born Montreal, Quebec, March 5, 1958; admitted to bar, 1983, Texas; 1986, New York; 1989, District of Columbia; U.S. District Court, Northern District of Texas. *Education:* Oklahoma Christian University (B.A., summa cum laude, B.S., summa cum laude, 1980); Southern Methodist University (J.D., 1983). Phi Delta Phi; Order of Barristers. Editor, Journal of Air Law and Commerce, Southern Methodist University Law Review, 1982-1983. Law Clerk to the Hon. Jack Pope, Chief Justice, Supreme Court of Texas, 1983-1984. Appointed by Governor George W. Bush to the Board of Directors of the Texas Public Finance Authority, 1995-2001, Secretary, 1995-1997, Vice Chairman, 1997—. Chairman, United States Executive Committee, British-American Project, Johns Hopkins University, Paul H. Nitze School of Advanced International Studies. Board of Directors, John G. Tower Center for Political Studies. Member: The Dallas Breakfast Group; The Dallas Assembly; Dallas Committee on Foreign Relations. Author and Speaker: "One Person's Property is Another Person's Collateral: Negotiating Rights to Casualty Insurance Proceeds and Condemnation Awards in Mortgages," ABA Annual Meeting, Chicago, Illinois, 1995; "The Practical Real Estate Lawyer," Vol. 13, No. 1, January 1997. *Member:* The Association of the Bar of the City of New York; Dallas (Real Property Law Section) and American (Member, Sections on: Business Law and Real Property, Probate and Trust Law; Member, Committees on: Mortgages; Debt Financing; Design and Construction, including the Americans with Disabilities Act) Bar Associations; State Bar of Texas (Real Estate, Probate and Trust Law Section); The District of Columbia Bar; Dallas Real Estate Council; International Council of Shopping Centers. Fellow, Dallas Bar Foundation. (Also at Dallas, Texas Office). ***Email:*** dbranch@winstead.com

---

WINSTON & STRAWN

Established in 1853
1400 L STREET, N.W.
WASHINGTON, D.C. 20005-3502
Telephone: 202-371-5700
Telecopier: 202-371-5950
Email: postmaster@winston.com
URL: http://www.winston.com

Chicago, Illinois Office: 35 West Wacker Drive, 60601. Telephone: 315-558-5600. Facsimile: 312-558-5700.

New York, N.Y. Office: 200 Park Avenue, 10166-4193. Telephone: 212-294-6700. Telecopier: 212-294-4700.

Los Angeles, California Office: 444 South Flower, 10th Floor, 90071-2911. Telephone: 213-615-1700.

Geneva, Switzerland Office: 43 Rue du Rhone, 1204. Telephone: +41-22 317 75 75. Fax: +41-22 317 75 00

Paris, France Office: 21 Avenue Victor Hugo. 75116. Telephone: 331-5364-8282. Fax: 331-5364-8220.

Alternative Dispute Resolution, Antitrust, Asset Securitization, Banking, Bankruptcy, Workouts and Financial Restructurings, Commercial Lending, Contracts, Corporate, Corporate Finance, E-Commerce, Employee Benefits and Executive Compensation, Energy, Environmental Law, Healthcare, Immigration, Intellectual Property, International, Labor and Employment Relations, Lease Finance, Litigation, Maritime, Mergers and Acquisitions, Product Liability, Project Finance, Public Finance, Real Estate, Securities, State and Federal Governmental Relations and Regulatory Affairs, Tax, Technology, Transportation, Trusts and Estates and White Collar Criminal Defense.

FIRM PROFILE: Winston & Strawn, founded in 1853, is one of the nation's oldest and largest law firms. With nearly 825 attorneys in offices in Chicago, New York, Washington, DC, Los Angeles, Geneva, Switzerland and Paris, France, the firm provides a full range of legal services to clients throughout the United States and abroad, including Fortune 500 companies, major commercial and financial institutions, governments and governmental entities, as well as small and midsize companies, individuals and entrepreneurs from virtually every industry.

MEMBERS OF FIRM

NORMAN R. VANDER CLUTE (1932-2001).

J. MICHAEL McGARRY, III, born Sacramento, California, July 30, 1943; admitted to bar, 1969, District of Columbia; 1972, Maryland. *Education:* University of Pennsylvania (B.S., 1965); University of Virginia (LL.B., 1969). Law Clerk to Judge Matthew F. McGuire, U.S. District Court, District of Columbia, 1969-1970. Assistant U.S. Attorney, 1970-1973. *Member:* The District of Columbia Bar. (Resident). ***PRACTICE AREAS:*** Energy Law; Administrative Law; Natural Resources Law. ***Email:*** jmcgarry@winston.com

NICHOLAS S. REYNOLDS, born Grosse Pointe, Michigan, June 16, 1944; admitted to bar, 1971, Virginia; 1973, District of Columbia. *Education:* Wilkes College (B.S., 1968); College of William & Mary and George Washington University (J.D., with honors, 1971). Member, William & Mary Law Review, 1969-1970. *Member:* The District of Columbia Bar; Virginia and American (Chairman, Atomic Energy Committee, Section on Public Utility, Communications and Transportation Law, 1980-1995) Bar Associations. (Resident). ***PRACTICE AREAS:*** Energy Law; Public Utility Law; Nuclear Energy; Electric Power; Energy Acquisitions; Energy Regulation; Federal Energy Regulation; International Energy Law. ***Email:*** nreynold@winston.com

DEAN L. OVERMAN, born Chicago, Illinois, October 9, 1943; admitted to bar, 1969, Illinois; 1977, District of Columbia. *Education:* Hope College (A.B., 1965); University of California at Berkeley (J.D., 1969). Reginald Heber Smith Fellow, 1969-1970. *Member:* The District of Columbia Bar; Chicago, Illinois State and American Bar Associations. (Resident). ***PRACTICE AREAS:*** General Corporate. ***Email:*** doverman@winston.com

DONALD K. DANKNER, born Buffalo, New York, October 3, 1947; admitted to bar, 1973, District of Columbia. *Education:* University of Wisconsin (B.A., 1969); George Washington University (J.D., with honors, 1973). Member, Law Review, 1971-1973. Law Clerk to the Honorable Austin L. Fickling, Associate Judge, District of Columbia Court of Appeals, 1973-1974. *Member:* The District of Columbia Bar; Energy Bar Association. (Resident). ***PRACTICE AREAS:*** Energy Law; Litigation. ***Email:*** ddankner@winston.com

WILLIAM J. MADDEN, JR., born Washington, D.C., 1939; admitted to bar, 1965, District of Columbia; 1973, U.S. Supreme Court. *Education:* College of the Holy Cross (A.B., 1961); University of Michigan (J.D., 1964). Trial Attorney, Federal Power Commission, 1965-1968. *Member:* The District of Columbia Bar; Federal Energy Bar Association (Member, Board of Directors, 1992-1994). (Resident). ***PRACTICE AREAS:*** Energy Law; Environmental Law; Public Utility Law. ***Email:*** wmadden@winston.com

JOHN P. PROCTOR, born Kewaunee, Wisconsin, 1942; admitted to bar, 1968, District of Columbia; 1970, U.S. Court of Military Appeals; 1975, U.S. Court of Appeals for the District of Columbia Circuit; 1984, New York. *Education:* Princeton University (B.A., 1964); University of Pennsylvania (LL.B., 1967). Recipient, Bernard B. Payton Award, 1964. *Member:* The District of Columbia Bar; Federal and American (Vice-Chairman, Air Quality Committee, Natural Resources Law Section, 1984—) Bar Associations. (Resident). ***PRACTICE AREAS:*** Environmental Law; Energy Law. ***Email:*** jproctor@winston.com

EDWARD F. GERWIN, JR., born Waldwick, New Jersey, February 14, 1955; admitted to bar, 1980, District of Columbia; 1981, U.S. District Court, District of Columbia, U.S. Court of Appeals, District of Columbia and U.S. Court of International Trade. *Education:* Villanova University (B.A., summa cum laude, 1977); Georgetown University (J.D., cum laude, 1980). Phi Kappa Phi. St. Thomas More Medal. Case and Notes Editor, Law and Policy in International Business, 1979-1980. Author: "The Special Prosecutor Provisions of the Ethics in Government Act of 1978," 36 Record of the Association of the Bar of the City of New York 420, 1981; "An Introduction to U.S. Export Control Laws," 32 The Practical Lawyer 25, 1986; "The Exxon-Florio Statute and Final Regulations," 7-8/1992 Der Schweizer Treuhänder 471. Teaching Fellowship in Legal Writing and Research, Georgetown University, 1978-1979. *Member:* The District of Columbia Bar. (Resident). ***PRACTICE AREAS:*** International Trade; Administrative Law; Government. ***Email:*** egerwin@winston.com

(This Listing Continued)

WINSTON & STRAWN, Washington—Continued

JOHN R. KEYS, JR., born Cincinnati, Ohio, June 10, 1948; admitted to bar, 1975, District of Columbia; 1981, U.S. Supreme Court. *Education:* Denison University and University of Notre Dame (A.B., 1970); Georgetown University (J.D., 1974). Phi Beta Kappa; Alpha Kappa Delta. Member, Executive Board, Law and Policy in International Business, 1973-1974. Member, National Panel of Arbitrators, American Arbitration Association; Arbitration Roster, D.C. Superior Court. *Member:* The District of Columbia Bar; American Bar Association. (Resident). ***PRACTICE AREAS:*** Litigation; Antitrust Law; International Law; Government Contracts/Grants.

LEONARD W. BELTER, born Queens, New York, January 23, 1943; admitted to bar, 1968, New York and U.S. Court of Military Appeals; 1970, District of Columbia; 1973, U.S. Claims Court; 1974, U.S. Supreme Court. *Education:* St. Bonaventure University (B.A., 1964); Columbia University (LL.B., cum laude, 1967). Harlan Fisk Stone Scholar, Columbia University, 1966 and 1967. Assistant U.S. Attorney, 1970-1973. *Member:* The District of Columbia Bar. (Resident). ***PRACTICE AREAS:*** Federal Energy Regulatory Law; Public Utility Law; Litigation. ***Email:*** lbelter@winston.com

THOMAS M. BUCHANAN, born Washington, D.C., December 28, 1953; admitted to bar, 1980, District of Columbia; 1981, U.S. Court of Appeals for the District of Columbia Circuit; 1982, Virginia, U.S. Court of Appeals, Fourth Circuit and U.S. District Court, Eastern District of Virginia; 1984, U.S. Supreme Court and Supreme Court of Virginia. *Education:* St. Louis University (B.A., magna cum laude, 1976); Georgetown Law Center (J.D., 1980). Author: "The Classified Information Procedures Act: A Shield Against Disclosure of Classified Information or Another Sword in Arsenal of the Prosecutor," ABA Complex Crimes Journal, 1989 and Corporate Criminal Liability Reporter, Vol. 3, No. 3, 1989. Assistant U.S. Attorney, Alexandria, Virginia, 1981-1984. *Member:* The District of Columbia Bar; Virginia State Bar; Maryland State Bar Association. (Resident). ***PRACTICE AREAS:*** White Collar Crime; Complex Litigation; Civil Litigation; Banking Litigation. ***Email:*** tbuchana@winston.com

PETER N. HIEBERT, born Bakersfield, California, July 31, 1949; admitted to bar, 1981, District of Columbia. *Education:* Columbia University (B.A., 1972); Georgetown University (J.D., 1981). Member, 1979-1980 and Editor, 1980-1981, Georgetown Law Journal. *Member:* The District of Columbia Bar. (Resident). ***PRACTICE AREAS:*** International Trade Law; Administrative Law; Legislative Practice. ***Email:*** phiebert@winston.com

ERIC L. HIRSCHHORN, born New York, N.Y., April 28, 1946; admitted to bar, 1968, New York; 1972, U.S. Supreme Court; 1973, District of Columbia. *Education:* University of Chicago (B.A., 1965); Columbia University (J.D., cum laude, 1968). Harlan Fiske Stone Scholar. Author, "The Export Control and Embargo Handbook (Oceana 2000). Reginald Heber Smith Community Lawyer Fellow (MFY Legal Services, Inc.), 1968-1971. Counsel, Democratic Study Group, New York State Assembly, 1971. Legislative Assistant to Rep. Bella Abzug, U.S. House of Representatives, 1971-1973. Chief Counsel, Subcommittee on Government Information and Individual Rights, U.S. House of Representatives, 1975-1977. Deputy Associate Director for International Affairs and Trade, U.S. Office of Management and Budget (President's Reorganization Project), 1977-1980. Deputy Assistant Secretary for Export Administration, U.S. Department of Commerce, 1980-1981. Executive Secretary, Industry Coalition on Technology Transfer, 1986—. *Member:* The District of Columbia Bar (Member, Legal Ethics Committee, 1997-1998, 1999-2001; Vice Chair, 2001—); The Association of the Bar of the City of New York; American Bar Association Center on Professional Responsibility; Computer Law Association; Thurgood Marshall American Inn of Court. (Resident). ***PRACTICE AREAS:*** Export Regulation; Customs Law; Legal Ethics and Professional Responsibility; Federal Litigation; Foreign Asset Control; Foreign Corrupt Practices Act; Foreign Sovereign Immunities Act; Food, Drug and Cosmetic Law; Legislative Practice. ***Email:*** ehirschh@winston.com

FREDERICK J. KILLION, born Wichita, Kansas, November 10, 1953; admitted to bar, 1979, District of Columbia; 1981, California. *Education:* Saint Mary's College (B.A., 1976); Northwestern University School of Law (J.D., cum laude, 1979). *Member:* The District of Columbia Bar. (Resident). ***PRACTICE AREAS:*** Energy Law; Litigation. ***Email:*** fkillion@winston.com

JOHN C. KIRTLAND, born Salina, Kansas, April 29, 1939; admitted to bar, 1971, District of Columbia; 1974, U.S. Supreme Court; 1977, U.S. Court of Appeals for the District of Columbia Circuit. *Education:* U.S. Naval Academy (B.S., 1961); George Washington University (J.D., 1971). Member, Order of the Coif. Counsel, U.S. Senate Committee on Commerce, Science and Transportation, 1971-1977. *Member:* The District of Columbia Bar. (Resident). ***PRACTICE AREAS:*** Legislative Practice; International Trade Law. ***Email:*** jkirtlan@winston.com

MICHAEL R. LEMOV, born New York, N.Y., January 21, 1935; admitted to bar, 1960, New York; 1971, District of Columbia; 1995, Maryland. *Education:* Colgate University (B.A., magna cum laude, 1956); Harvard University (LL.B., 1959). Phi Beta Kappa. Author: "State and Local Control Over Nuclear Reactors Under the Atomic Energy Act," New York University Law Review, 1964; "Administrative Agency News Releases," George Washington Law Review, 1968; "Underreporting Defects Is Risky," National Law Journal, 1992; "Consumer Product Safety Commission-Regulatory Manual," Sheppards-McGraw Hill Publishing Company, 1981; "How to Manage Product Recalls Successfully," Handbook of Business Strategy, 1999; "Products Liability: Federal Reporting Confusion," National Law Journal, 1998; "Can You Risk A Recall?," Business Law Today (American Bar Association), September 1999. Chief Counsel, Subcommittee on Oversight and Investigations, House Commerce Committee, 1975-1977. Special Counsel, Subcommittee on Commerce and Finance, House Commerce Committee, 1971-1975. Counsel, House Banking and Currency Committee. General Counsel, National Commission on Product Safety, Washington, D.C., 1968-1970. Trial Attorney, Department of Justice, Washington, D.C., 1966-1968. *Member:* The District of Columbia Bar. (Resident). ***PRACTICE AREAS:*** Product Safety; Product Recall; Warranty Law; Advertising and Marketing; Product Packaging and Labeling; Federal Regulatory; Legislative Practice.

ROBERT M. RADER, born Camden, New Jersey, September 9, 1946; admitted to bar, 1972, New Jersey; 1977, District of Columbia; 1982, U.S. Supreme Court. *Education:* Lafayette College (A.B., cum laude, 1968); Cornell University (J.D., 1971). Phi Beta Kappa. Editor, Cornell Law Review. Author: "Offsite Emergency Planning For Nuclear Power Plants: A Case of Governmental Gridlock," Washington Legal Foundation, 1986; "Demise of the Neighborhood School Plan," 55 Cornell Law Review 594, 1970; "Alien Crewmen: United States Asylum Policy," 4 Cornell International Law Journal 167, 1971. Law Clerk to Hon. James A. Coolahan, U.S. District Judge, District of New Jersey, 1971-1973. Trial Attorney, Civil Division, U.S. Department of Justice, 1973-1978. *Member:* The District of Columbia Bar. (Resident). ***PRACTICE AREAS:*** Commercial Litigation; Energy Litigation; Environmental Litigation. ***Email:*** rrader@winston.com

MARK J. WETTERHAHN, born New York, N.Y., June 13, 1944; admitted to bar, 1972, Maryland; 1973, District of Columbia; 1976, U.S. Supreme Court. *Education:* Queens College of the City University of New York (B.A., 1966); Columbia University (B.S., 1966; M.S., 1968); American University (J.D., 1972). Phi Beta Kappa. *Member:* The District of Columbia Bar; American Society of Mechanical Engineers; American Nuclear Society. (Resident). ***PRACTICE AREAS:*** Atomic (Nuclear) Law; Energy Law; Nuclear Waste. ***Email:*** mwetterh@winston.com

DAVID A. REPKA, born Wilmington, Delaware, May 21, 1957; admitted to bar, 1981, District of Columbia. *Education:* Northwestern University (B.A., 1978); Georgetown University (J.D., cum laude, 1981). Phi Beta Kappa. Attorney, U.S. Nuclear Regulatory Commission, 1981-1984. *Member:* The District of Columbia Bar. (Resident). ***PRACTICE AREAS:*** Nuclear Energy; Nuclear Waste; Administrative Agency Practice; Administrative Hearings and Appeals. ***Email:*** drepka@winston.com

JOHN A. WAITS, II, born Greenville, Mississippi, June 6, 1947; admitted to bar, 1978, New York and U.S. District Court, Eastern and Southern Districts of New York; 1988, District of Columbia; 1989, U.S. Supreme Court. *Education:* University of Mississippi (B.A., summa cum laude, 1969); University of Virginia (M.A., with honors, 1972); New York University (J.D., 1977). Fulbright Scholar, University of Hamburg. Administrative Assistant to Congressman David R. Bowen, 1980-1982. Counsel to House Agriculture Subcommittee, 1979-1980. *Member:* The District of Columbia Bar. (Resident). ***PRACTICE AREAS:*** Legislative Practice; Administrative/Regulatory Law; Agriculture; Economic Development; Trade; Government Election; Campaign Ethics; Political Law. ***Email:*** jwaits@winston.com

JAMES H. BURNLEY IV, born High Point, North Carolina, July 30, 1948; admitted to bar, 1973, North Carolina; 1989, District of Columbia. *Education:* Yale University (B.A., magna cum laude, 1970); Harvard University (J.D., 1973). Secretary, 1987-1989, Deputy Secretary, 1983-1987, General Counsel, 1983, U.S. Department of Transportation. Associate Deputy Attorney General, Department of Justice, 1982-1983. Public Member, Administrative Conference of U.S., 1987-1993. Vice-Chairman, Virginia Port Authority, 1997—. *Member:* The District of Columbia Bar. (Resident). ***PRACTICE AREAS:*** Administrative Law; Regulatory Law; Transportation Law; Government Relations. ***Email:*** jburnley@winston.com

BENJAMIN P. FISHBURNE, III, born South Bend, Indiana, November 14, 1943; admitted to bar, 1971, District of Columbia. *Education:* University of Notre Dame (B.A., 1965); University of Virginia (LL.B., 1968). Order of the Coif. Professorial Lecturer, American University School of Law, 1973-1975. *Member:* The District of Columbia Bar; American Bar Association (Chairman, Committee on Middle Eastern Law, 1978-1981). (Resident). ***PRACTICE AREAS:*** International Commercial Transactions; Corporate Finance; High Technology; International Dispute Resolution. ***Email:*** bfishbur@winston.com

BARRY J. HART, born Philadelphia, Pennsylvania, February 26, 1948; admitted to bar, 1973, Pennsylvania; 1977, District of Columbia. *Education:* Dartmouth College (B.A., 1970); George Washington University (J.D., 1973); New York University (LL.M., 1976). *Member:* The District of Columbia Bar.

(This Listing Continued)

(Resident). ***PRACTICE AREAS:*** International Taxation; Tax Exempt Organizations; Nonprofit Corporations; International Corporate Law; International Corporate Transactions. ***Email:*** bjhart@winston.com

CHARLES L. KINNEY, born Parkersburg, West Virginia, May 31, 1952; admitted to bar, 1979, District of Columbia and U.S. District Court for the District of Columbia; 1986, U.S. Supreme Court. *Education:* Georgetown University (B.S.F.S., 1974; J.D., 1979). Chief Floor Counsel, U.S. Senate. *Member:* The District of Columbia Bar. (Resident). ***PRACTICE AREAS:*** Federal Governmental Relations; Regulatory Affairs.

JAMES R. CURTISS, born Lincoln, Nebraska, December 20, 1953; admitted to bar, 1979, Nebraska and U.S. District Court, District of Nebraska; 1985, District of Columbia; 1992, U.S. Supreme Court. *Education:* University of Nebraska (B.A., 1976; J.D., 1979). Director: Baltimore Gas & Electric; Cameco Corporation. *Member:* The District of Columbia Bar; Federal Energy Bar Association. (Resident). ***PRACTICE AREAS:*** Energy Law; Electric Power; Nuclear Energy Law. ***Email:*** jcurtiss@winston.com

ROBERT A. MANGRUM, born Shelbyville, Tennessee, July 16, 1941; admitted to bar, 1966, Tennessee; 1969, U.S. Court of Federal Claims; 1970, District of Columbia, U.S. District Court for the District of Columbia and U.S. Supreme Court; 1983, U.S. Court of Appeals for the Federal Circuit. *Education:* University of Tennessee (B.S., 1964; J.D., 1966); George Washington University (LL.M., 1971). Phi Delta Phi. *Member:* The District of Columbia Bar; Bar Association of the District of Columbia; Tennessee, Federal and American (Member, Public Contract Law Section) Bar Associations; National Contract Management Association. [Capt., U.S. Army, JAGC, 1966-1970]. (Resident). ***PRACTICE AREAS:*** Government Contract Law. ***Email:*** rmangrum@winston.com

WILLIAM G. MIOSSI, born Evanston, Illinois, June 22, 1959; admitted to bar, 1985, Illinois; 1987, U.S. District Court, Northern District of Illinois; 1994, District of Columbia. *Education:* Georgetown University (B.S., 1981; M.A., 1983; J.D., 1985). Theta Phi Alpha. Law Clerk to Honorable June L. Green, U.S. District Judge, District of Columbia, 1985-1987. *Member:* Chicago and American Bar Associations; The District of Columbia Bar. ***LANGUAGES:*** French. ***PRACTICE AREAS:*** Labor and Employment. ***Email:*** wmiossi@winston.com

JAMES T. PITTS, born Hot Springs, Arkansas, March 21, 1949; admitted to bar, 1973, Arkansas; 1986, District of Columbia. *Education:* Hendrix College (B.A., 1970); University of Arkansas (J.D., 1973); Georgetown University (LL.M., 1984). Comments Editor, Arkansas Law Review, 1973. Chief Counsel, Arkansas Securities Department, 1976-1980. Acting Securities Commissioner, Arkansas, 1980. Assistant Director, Securities and Corporate Practices Division, Office of the Comptroller of the Currency, 1982-1987. LEGIS Fellow, Staff of House Subcommittee on Commerce, Consumer and Monetary Affairs, 1986. First General Counsel, District of Columbia Office of Banking and Financial Institutions, 1987. *Member:* The District of Columbia Bar. (Resident). ***PRACTICE AREAS:*** Transportation Law; Banking Law; Securities Regulation Law; Litigation.

JOHN ALBERT WHITTAKER, IV, born Everett, Washington, December 5, 1950; admitted to bar, 1976, Washington; 1980, District of Columbia. *Education:* University of Washington (B.A., in Economics, with honors, 1973); University of Santa Clara (J.D., cum laude, 1976). *Member:* The District of Columbia Bar; Washington State Bar Association (inactive). (Resident). ***PRACTICE AREAS:*** Federal Energy Regulation; Hydroelectricity Licensing; Hydroelectricity; Environmental Administrative Law; Administrative Agency Practice. ***Email:*** jwhittak@winston.com

TIMOTHY M. BROAS, born Detroit, Michigan, March 21, 1954; admitted to bar, 1979, New Jersey; 1980, New York; 1981, U.S. District Court, Southern District of New York and U.S. Court of Appeals, First and Second Circuits; 1985, District of Columbia and U.S. District Court for the District of Columbia; 1986, U.S. Court of Appeals, Ninth Circuit; 1990, U.S. Court of Appeals, Sixth and Fourth Circuits. *Education:* Boston College (B.A., magna cum laude, 1976); College of William & Mary (J.D., 1979). Law Clerk to Justice Mark A. Sullivan, New Jersey Supreme Court, 1979-1980. Director, Council for Court Excellence, Washington, D.C. *Member:* The Association of the Bar of the City of New York; The District of Columbia Bar; American Bar Association. (Resident). ***PRACTICE AREAS:*** Criminal Litigation; Civil Litigation. ***Email:*** tbroas@winston.com

GORDON ALAN COFFEE, born Dallas, Texas, September 9, 1958; admitted to bar, 1984, District of Columbia; 1986, Virginia. *Education:* University of Virginia (B.A., with distinction, 1981); University of Texas (J.D., 1984). *Member:* The District of Columbia Bar; Virginia State Bar. (Resident). ***PRACTICE AREAS:*** Commercial Litigation; Health Care Litigation; Legal Malpractice; Criminal Defense. ***Email:*** gcoffee@winston.com

RICHARD A. HIBEY, born Utica, New York, June 20, 1941; admitted to bar, 1965, District of Columbia; 1966, U.S. Court of the Armed Forces; 1970, U.S. Supreme Court. *Education:* Le Moyne College (A.B., cum laude, 1962); Georgetown University (J.D., 1965; LL.M., 1966). The Barristers. Author: "The Trial of a Rape Case: An Advocate's Analysis of Corroboration, Consent and Character," II American Criminal Law Review 309, 1973; "Application of the Mail and Wire Fraud Statutes to International Bribery: Questionable Prosecutions of Questionable Payments," 9 Ga. J. Int'l. and Comp. L. 49, Winter, 1979; "The Practical Necessity for Amendment of the Foreign Corrupt Practices Act: S. 708—The Current Legislative Initiative," 10 Hofstra Law Review, 1982; "Defense Perspectives on Recurring Issues in National Security Litigation," Center For Law and National Security, University of Virginia, 1986; "The Alien Tort Statute: A Defense Perspective On Its Dubious Resurrection," Copyright 1989 American Bar Association; "Practical Considerations Attending Negotiations With the Justice Department During The Investigative/Grand Jury Phase Of A White Collar Case," Georgetown University Law Center CLE Federal Enforcement, 1989; "Voir Dire In Federal White Collar Crime Trials—A Traditional Approach to Jury Selection," Georgetown University Law Center CLE Federal Enforcement, 1992; "Reliance On the Advice of Counsel Defense in Medicare and Medicaid Anti-Kickback Cases," ABA National Institute - Health Care Fraud, 1995. Adjunct Professor, Washington College of Law, American University, 1972-1986. Staff Attorney, Legal Aid Agency for District of Columbia, 1966-1968. Assistant U.S. Attorney for District of Columbia, 1968-1971. *Member:* The District of Columbia Bar; American Bar Association; The Barristers; The Lawyers Club. Fellow, American College of Trial Lawyers. (Resident). ***PRACTICE AREAS:*** Litigation.

CHRISTOPHER C. McISAAC, born Rochester, New York, 1959; admitted to bar, 1985, Virginia; 1986, District of Columbia. *Education:* University of North Carolina (B.A., with highest honors, 1982), Morehead Scholar; University of Virginia (J.D., 1985). Phi Beta Kappa. Adjunct Professor of Law, Georgetown University Law Center. Member, Bretton Woods Committee. *Member:* The District of Columbia Bar; Virginia State Bar. (Resident). ***PRACTICE AREAS:*** Project Finance; Corporate Finance; Banking.

ERIC W. BLOOM, born Philadelphia, Pennsylvania, April 19, 1962; admitted to bar, 1988, Pennsylvania; 1989, District of Columbia. *Education:* George Washington University (B.A., magna cum laude, 1984; J.D., with honors, 1987). Co-Author: "FDIC/RTC Suits Against Bank and Thrift Officers and Directors—Why Now, What's Left?" Fordham L. Review, May 1995. *Member:* The District of Columbia Bar. (Resident). ***PRACTICE AREAS:*** Commercial Litigation; Criminal Litigation; Financial Institutions Litigation.

MICHAEL L. SIBARIUM, born Queens, New York, September 22, 1959; admitted to bar, 1985, Maryland and District of Columbia. *Education:* University of Connecticut (B.A., summa cum laude, 1981); George Washington University (J.D., with honors, 1984). Phi Beta Kappa. Member, The George Washington Journal of International Law and Economics, 1982-1984. *Member:* The District of Columbia Bar; American Bar Association. (Resident). ***PRACTICE AREAS:*** Litigation; Antitrust Law; E-Commerce; Trade Regulation Law; Trade and Professional Associations. ***Email:*** msibariu@winston.com

THOMAS L. MILLS, born Elmira, New York, January 4, 1948; admitted to bar, 1975, District of Columbia. *Education:* United States Coast Guard Academy (B.S., 1970); George Washington University (J.D., with honors, 1975). Order of the Coif. Member, George Washington University Law Review, 1973-1975. *Member:* The District of Columbia Bar. [Lieut., U.S. Coast Guard, 1970-1975]. (Resident). ***PRACTICE AREAS:*** Health Care; Maritime Law. ***Email:*** tmills@winston.com

CONSTANTINE G. PAPAVIZAS, born St. Paul, Minnesota, June 19, 1957; admitted to bar, 1984, Virginia; 1985, District of Columbia. *Education:* Georgetown University (B.A., 1978); Columbia University (M.I.A., 1981); George Washington University (J.D., with honors, 1984); University of Thessaloniki, Greece, International Public Law Institute. Pi Sigma Alpha. Author: "New Developments in U.S.-Flag Vessel Financing and Citizenship Requirements," 24 Tulane Maritime Law Journal, 1999; "Penalty Enacted for Vessels Detained Under U.S. Port State Control Program," The International Journal of Shipping Law, March 1999; "Build and Charter Makes a Comeback," Marine Log, February 1998; "Foreign Crew Members Exempted from U.S. Tax," The International Journal of Shipping Law, December 1997; "Prevention of Biological Pollution — The U.S. National Invasive Species Act of 1996," The International Journal of Shipping Law, March 1997; "1995-1996 U.S. Maritime Legislative Developments," 28 Journal of Maritime Law and Commerce, January 1997; "The OECD Shipbuilding Agreement and its Effects on U.S. Law," 26 Journal of Maritime Law and Commerce, July 1995. Co-Author: "1997-98 U.S. Maritime Legislative Developments," 30 Journal of Maritime Law and Commerce, July 1999; "Compliance Tide Leaves Issues Open," The National Law Journal, July 6, 1998; "HMO Legislation Is Aimed at Protecting Patients," The National Law Journal, April 7, 1997; "Veering Off Course," Legal Times, March 20, 1995. *Member:* The District of Columbia Bar. (Resident). ***LANGUAGES:*** Greek. ***PRACTICE AREAS:*** Health Care; Maritime Law; Securities. ***Email:*** cpapaviz@winston.com

JEFFREY G. BERMAN, born New York, N.Y., May 29, 1957; admitted to bar, 1982, District of Columbia; 1983, Florida. *Education:* Brown University (B.A., magna cum laude, 1979); Harvard University (J.D., 1982). Director, Harvard Legislative Research Bureau, 1980-1981. *Member:* The District of Columbia Bar; The Florida Bar. (Resident). ***PRACTICE AREAS:*** Energy Law; Communications Law; Government Relations; Corporate Law.

(This Listing Continued)

WINSTON & STRAWN, Washington—Continued

EDMUND D. COOKE, JR., born Springfield, Ohio, December 4, 1942; admitted to bar, 1973, Michigan; 1979, District of Columbia. *Education:* Howard University; Kent State University (B.A., 1965); University of Michigan (J.D., 1973). Adjunct Professor, Syracuse University School of Law, 1988-1992. *Member:* The District of Columbia Bar; State Bar of Michigan. [Capt., USAF, 1966-1970]. (Resident). ***PRACTICE AREAS:*** Employment Relations; Labor Relations; Government Relations.

PETER M. KIRBY, born Washington, D.C., June 30, 1945; admitted to bar, 1979, District of Columbia, U.S. District Court for the District of Columbia and U.S. Court of Appeals, District of Columbia Circuit. *Education:* Fordham University (B.A., 1967); Georgetown University (J.D., 1979). *Member:* The District of Columbia Bar; American Bar Association. (Resident). ***PRACTICE AREAS:*** Energy; Corporate. ***Email:*** pkirby@winston.com

JOHN FEHRENBACH, born Newark, New Jersey, November 7, 1952; admitted to bar, 1978, District of Columbia; 1979, U.S. District Court, District of Columbia and U.S. Court of Appeals, District of Columbia Circuit; 1994, U.S. Court of Appeals, Fifth Circuit; 1995, U.S. District Court, Northern District of Indiana. *Education:* University of Delaware (B.A., 1974); Catholic University of America (J.D., 1978). Co-Author: "EPA Development of Revised Drinking Water Standards for Radionuclides," presented at Waste Management '99, Tuscon, AZ (March 1999); "The Waste Isolation Pilot Plant-A Paradigm for Meeting the Challenge of External Regulation," presented at Waste Management '98, Tuscon, AZ (March 1998); "Environmental Risks in Purchasing Properties from the RTC," in Journal of RTC Real Estate (May/June 1992). Contributor: "EPA's Final Rule on Lender Liability under Superfund," in Environmental Management Review (1992). Member: Environmental Law Institute; American Nuclear Society (Public Policy Committee); and Vice-Chair, Environmental Policy Commission, 1996-1998; Waste to Energy Task Force, Recycling Study Subcommittee, 1996-1998; Alternative Fuels Task Force, 1997-1998 and 1000 Friends of Alexandria, 1999—, City of Alexandria, VA. *Member:* The District of Columbia Bar (Member, Section on Environment, Energy and Natural Resources). (Resident). ***REPORTED CASES:*** U.S. v. G.E. and Town of Moreau, N.D.N.Y. (1988) (BNA, Toxic Law Reporter); Active Products Corp. v. A.H. Choitz & Co., 33 Chem. Waste Litig. Reporter 381 (N.D. IN., Ft. Wayne Div., Oct. 17, 1996). ***PRACTICE AREAS:*** Environmental Law; Regulatory Law; Energy Law; Government; Administrative Law. ***Email:*** jfehrenb@winston.com

WILLIAM N. HALL, born Stockholm, Sweden, January 5, 1953; admitted to bar, 1978, District of Columbia, U.S. Court of Appeals, Fifth, Ninth and District of Columbia Circuits, U.S. District Court, District of Columbia and U.S. District Court, Northern District of Indiana. *Education:* Bucknell University (B.A., cum laude, 1975); Georgetown University Law Center (J.D., 1978). Case and Note Editor, The Georgetown Law Journal, 1977-1978. Co-Author: "EPA's Final Rule on Lender Liability Under Superfund," Environmental Management Review, 3rd Quarter, 1992; "Environmental Risks in Purchasing Properties from the RTC," Journal of RTC Real Estate, May/June 1992. Author: "Environmental Audits—A Corporate Response to Bhopal," Environmental Forum, August, 1985. Co-Author: "Complying with EPA's Premanufacture Notification Requirements," Environmental Analyst, March and April, 1984; "Due Process at Sentencing: An Empirical and Legal Analysis of the Disclosure of Presentence Reports in Federal Courts," 93 Harvard Law Review 1613, June 1980. Member, Board of Directors: District of Columbia Sports and Entertainment Commission, 1995-1999; Federal City Council; National Capital Development Corp., 1994-1995. *Member:* Bar Association of The District of Columbia (Co-Chair, Environmental Law Committee, 1993-1995); The District of Columbia Bar (Member, Environmental Law Section); American Bar Association (Member, Section on Natural Resources, Energy and Environmental Law). (Resident). ***PRACTICE AREAS:*** Environmental Law; Sports Law. ***Email:*** whall@winston.com

WILLIAM A. ANDERSON, II, born Richmond, Virginia, January 9, 1947; admitted to bar, 1974, Virginia and U.S. Court of Appeals, Fourth, Fifth, Tenth and District of Columbia Circuits. *Education:* United States Air Force Academy; University of North Carolina (A.B., 1968); John F. Kennedy School of Government, Harvard University (M.P.P., 1973); Harvard Law School (J. D., cum laude, 1973). Phi Beta Kappa. *Member:* The Virginia and American (Council, Section on Natural Resources, Energy and Environmental Law, 1981-1983; Liaison to Standing Committee on Environmental Law, 1983-1986; Chairman, Water Quality Committee, 1978-1980; Alternate, Coordinating Group on Regulatory Reform, 1981-1985; Liaison to Central and Eastern European Legal Initiative, 1990-1991; Co-Chair, Subcommittee on International Environmental Controls Committee, Section of Business Law, 1990—; Member, Section on Administrative Law) Bar Associations; The District of Columbia Bar; Virginia State Bar. (Resident). ***PRACTICE AREAS:*** Environmental. ***Email:*** wanderso@winston.com

PATRICK L. SCHMIDT, born Sturgis, Michigan, May 19, 1956; admitted to bar, 1986, Maryland; 1987, District of Columbia. *Education:* Harvard University (B.A., magna cum laude, 1978); Georgetown University Law Center

(This Listing Continued)

(J.D., 1984); University of Madrid (Complutense) Law School, Madrid, Spain (Doctoral Program in International Law, 1984-1985). Recipient, Rotary Foundation Graduate Fellowship, 1984-1985. Senior Lead Articles Editor, Law and Policy in International Business, 1983-1984. Author: "Foreign Investment in Cuba: A Preliminary Analysis of Cuba's New Joint Venture Law," 15 Law and Policy in International Business 689, 1983; "Exon-Florio: A Primer for Foreign Investors and Foreign Lenders Doing Business in the USA," 20 International Business Lawyer 485, 1992; "The Exon-Florio Statute: How It Affects Foreign Investors and Lenders in the United States," 27 The International Lawyer 795, 1993. Co-Author: "DBS Under FCC and International Regulation," 37 Vanderbilt Law Review 67, 1984; "The Exon-Florio Statute and Final Regulations," 7-8 Der Schweizer Treuhander/L'expert-Comptable Suisse 471, 1992. Instructor, Legal Research and Writing, Georgetown University Law Center, 1984-1985. *Member:* The District of Columbia Bar (Member, Section on International Law). (Resident). ***LANGUAGES:*** Spanish. ***PRACTICE AREAS:*** Federal Legislative; International. ***Email:*** pschmidt@winston.com

GUY A. MORLEY, born Poughkeepsie, New York, November 22, 1959; admitted to bar, 1988, New York; 1996, District of Columbia. *Education:* State University of New York, College at Cortland (B.A., summa cum laude, 1982); Beijing Teachers College, Peoples Republic of China; University of Virginia (J.D., 1987). Pi Sigma Alpha; Phi Alpha Theta; Phi Delta Phi (Magister, 1985-1986). *Member:* The District of Columbia Bar; New York State Bar Association. (Resident). ***PRACTICE AREAS:*** Project Finance; Corporate Law; Energy Law. ***Email:*** gmorley@winston.com

JOAN B. TUCKER FIFE, born Knoxville, Tennessee, September 2, 1961; admitted to bar, 1986, Virginia; 1987, District of Columbia; 1989, California, U.S. Court of Appeals, Fourth and Eleventh Circuits, U.S. Court of Appeals for the District of Columbia Circuit, U.S. District Court, Eastern and Western Districts of Virginia and U.S. District Court, Central District of California, U.S. Supreme Court. *Education:* Northwestern University (B.A., 1983); Vanderbilt University (J.D., 1986). *Member:* State Bar of California; Virginia State Bar; The District of Columbia Bar. (Resident). ***PRACTICE AREAS:*** Employment Litigation; Employment Law; Title VII Discrimination; Sexual Harassment; Employment Disability Discrimination; Americans with Disabilities Act; Age Discrimination in Employment; Race Discrimination; Sexual Discrimination; ERISA Class Actions; Whistleblower Litigation; Class Action Defense.

KATHRYN M. SUTTON, born New Haven, Connecticut, January 19, 1964; admitted to bar, 1988, District of Columbia; 1989, U.S. District Court for the District of Columbia; 1990, U.S. Court of Appeals for the District of Columbia Circuit. *Education:* Pennsylvania State University (B.A., summa cum laude, 1985); Georgetown University (J.D., cum laude, 1988). Phi Beta Kappa. *Member:* The District of Columbia Bar. (Resident). ***PRACTICE AREAS:*** Nuclear Energy Law. ***Email:*** ksutton@winston.com

CAROL A. JOFFE, born Roslyn, New York, October 19, 1950; admitted to bar, 1979, Massachusetts; 1980, Maryland; 1981, District of Columbia. *Education:* Wheaton College (A.B., with honors, 1972); Northeastern University (J.D., 1979). Mediator, Civil Division, Superior Court, District of Columbia. *Member:* The District of Columbia Bar. (Resident). ***PRACTICE AREAS:*** Civil Litigation. ***Email:*** cjoffe@winston.com

CHARLES B. MOLSTER, III, born Richmond, Virginia, March 11, 1956; admitted to bar, 1984, Virginia; 1985, District of Columbia. *Education:* University of Virginia (B.A., 1979); University of Richmond (J.D., 1983). Law Clerk, Hon. James C. Cacheris, U.S. District Court, Eastern District of Virginia, Alexandria Division, 1983-1984. *Member:* The District of Columbia Bar; Virginia State Bar; American Bar Association; Virginia Trial Lawyers Association. (Resident). ***REPORTED CASES:*** Hadeed v. Medic 24, 237 Va. 277, 377 S.E. 2d 589 (1989); Unlimited Screw Products v. MALM, et al., 781 F.Supp. 1121 (E.D. Va. 1991); Smith v. Allstate, 241 Va. 477, 403 S.E. 2d 696 (1991); Crowley v. NATA, 691 A.2d 1169 (D.C. App. 1997). ***PRACTICE AREAS:*** Commercial Litigation; Business Litigation; Employment Defense; Antitrust Litigation; Patent Litigation. ***Email:*** cmolster@winston.com

ERIC J. MARCOTTE, born Pawtucket, Rhode Island, November 11, 1957; admitted to bar, 1988, Texas; 1993, U.S. Court of Appeals for the Federal Circuit; 1995, District of Columbia; 1997, U.S. District Court for the District of Columbia. *Education:* Park College (B.S., magna cum laude, 1982); University of Texas (J.D., with honors, 1987). *Member:* State Bar of Texas; The District of Columbia Bar; American Bar Association (Member, Public Contract Law Section, 1991—). [with U.S.A.F., 1979-1993; Major, Air National Guard, 1993—]. ***PRACTICE AREAS:*** Government Contracts; Commercial Law. ***Email:*** emarcott@winston.com

DONN C. MEINDERTSMA, born Grand Haven, Michigan, March 11, 1962; admitted to bar, 1987, Michigan; 1988, District of Columbia, U.S. District Court for the District of Columbia and U.S. District Court, Western District of Michigan; 1991, U.S. Court of Appeals for the District of Columbia Circuit; 1992, U.S. Court of Appeals, Fifth Circuit; 1994, U.S. Supreme Court; 1997, U.S. Court of Appeals, Fourth Circuit; 1998, U.S. Court of Appeals, Eleventh Circuit; 2000, U.S. Court of Appeals, Seventh Circuit. *Education:* Calvin College (B.A., 1984); University of Michigan (J.D., 1987). Author: "State Job

(This Listing Continued)

Reference Immunity Statues," Legal Aspects of Employee Handbooks and Policies, 1998. Member, 1985-1986 and Executive Editor, 1986-1987, University of Michigan Journal of Law Reform. *Member:* The District of Columbia Bar; State Bar of Michigan. (Resident). ***PRACTICE AREAS:*** Labor and Employment Law; Employment Litigation; Whistleblower Litigation. ***Email:*** dmeinder@winston.com

THOMAS C. POINDEXTER, born Indianapolis, Indiana, September 19, 1955; admitted to bar, 1990, Virginia and U.S. Court of Appeals, Fourth Circuit; 1991, District of Columbia. *Education:* Purdue University (B.S., Nuclear Engr., 1977); George Mason University (J.D., 1990). Managing Editor, Civil Rights Law Journal, 1990. Mediator, District of Columbia Superior Court, 1990-1997. *Member:* The District of Columbia Bar; Virginia State Bar; American Bar Association; American Nuclear Society. (Resident). ***SPECIAL AGENCIES:*** Department of Energy; Nuclear Regulatory Commission. ***PRACTICE AREAS:*** Administrative Law; Nuclear Energy Law. ***Email:*** tpoindex@winston.com

VINCENT D. SALVATORE, JR., born Jakarta, Indonesia, June 29, 1954; admitted to bar, 1980, New York and U.S. District Court, Southern and Eastern Districts of New York; 1997, District of Columbia. *Education:* Dartmouth College (B.A., summa cum laude, 1976); Harvard University (J.D., 1979). Phi Beta Kappa. *Member:* Bar Association of the District of Columbia; American Bar Association; Washington Foreign Law Society. (Resident). ***LANGUAGES:*** French and Italian. ***PRACTICE AREAS:*** International Project Finance; Infrastructure Development; Asset Based Finance; Foreign Corrupt Practices Act. ***Email:*** vsalvato@winston.com

ROBERT LINN DRAPER, born Utica, New York, August 9, 1964; admitted to bar, 1990, Texas; 1993, District of Columbia. *Education:* Williams College (B.A., 1987); Southern Methodist University School of Law (J.D., 1990). *Member:* American Bar Association (Vice Chairman, Corporate Finance Committee, Section of Public Utility, Communications and Transportation Law). (Resident). ***PRACTICE AREAS:*** Corporate Law; Project Finance; Energy Project Development; Cogeneration; Electric Power; Electric Power Joint Ventures; Energy Contracts; Energy Finance; Independent Power; International Project Finance. ***Email:*** rdraper@winston.com

MARY E. WALL, born Boston, Massachusetts, May 18, 1954; admitted to bar, 1986, Virginia and U.S. Court of Appeals, Fourth, Fifth and District of Columbia Circuits. *Education:* University of Massachusetts (B.S., cum laude, 1977); George Washington University (J.D., 1986). *Member:* The Virginia State Bar; American Bar Association; Women's Council on Energy and the Environment. (Resident). ***PRACTICE AREAS:*** Environmental Law; Environmental Compliance; Environmental Due Diligence; Environmental Insurance; Environmental Lender Liability; Environmental Permitting; Environmental Risk Management. ***Email:*** mwall@winston.com

DAVID C. ROMM, born Washington, D.C., April 20, 1948; admitted to bar, 1977, Ohio; 1978, District of Columbia; 1990, Virginia. *Education:* University of Maryland (B.A., with high honors, 1973); The Ohio State University (J.D., 1977). Best Advocate, Moot Court Competition, 1977. Author: "Surety Bad Faith Claims-How to Avoid Them and How to Defend Them," Oct. 1993; "When Does the Owner Waive Its Right to Terminate the Principal for Default--How to Recognize a Waiver Against the Owner for the Non-Performing Principal, Or, How to Get Back Those Progress Payments," Northeast Surety & Fidelity Claims Conference, 1991; "Surety Recourse Against the Owner for the Non-Performance Principal, or, How to Get Back Those Progress Payments, Northeast Surety & Fidelity Claims Conference, 1991. Co-Author: "Construction Litigation Superconference," Andrews Publications, 1986-1989; "Owner Damages," American Construction Owners Association: Construction Owners Monograph Series, March 1986; "Recent Decisions Affecting Recovery of Home Office Overhead During Extended Performance Periods," Construction Claims Monthly, August 1983. Speaker: National Association of Independent Sureties, West Palm Beach, 1999; Northeast Surety and Fidelity Claims Conference, 1991-1992; Construction Litigation, Super Conference 1986, Laguna Nigel, California and 1986 New York, New York; Seminar, University of Maryland "Successful Construction Claims Management," June and September 1982. *Member:* Ohio State and American (Member, Sections of: Surety and Fidelity; Public Contract Law; Litigation) Bar Associations; The District of Columbia Bar; Virginia State Bar. (Resident). ***PRACTICE AREAS:*** Surety; Construction; Government Contracts; Civil Litigation. ***Email:*** dromm@winston.com

GARRY R. BOEHLERT, born Flushing, New York, January 30, 1956; admitted to bar, 1981, Virginia (Not admitted in District of Columbia). *Education:* University of Virginia (B.A., with distinction, 1978); Marshall-Wythe School of Law, College of William and Mary (J.D., 1981). Law Clerk, Armed Services Board of Contract Appeals, 1980. Co-Author and Lecturer: "Public and Private Infrastructure Development," Federal Publications, 1996; Panelist, "The Future of Privatization," Federal Publications, 1996, Construction Contracts Year-in-Review. Author: "Building for the Government at a Profit: Public-Private Partnering," Virginia Business Law Journal, 1996. *Member:* Virginia

(This Listing Continued)

State Bar. (Resident). ***PRACTICE AREAS:*** Construction; Government Contracts; Litigation; Public-Private Development. ***Email:*** gboehler@winston.com

MICHAEL K. ATKINSON, born Pulaski, New York, May 16, 1964; admitted to bar, 1991, District of Columbia. *Education:* Syracuse University (B.A., 1986); Cornell University (J.D., 1991). *Member:* The District of Columbia Bar. (Resident). ***PRACTICE AREAS:*** Trial Practice. ***Email:*** matkinso@winston.com

FATON A. BACAJ, born Perugia, Italy, August 14, 1957; admitted to bar, 1991, Virginia; 1993, District of Columbia. *Education:* St. John's College (B.A., 1979); Catholic University of America (J.D., 1991). *Member:* The District of Columbia Bar; Virginia State Bar. (Resident). ***PRACTICE AREAS:*** Business Law; Computers and Software; Corporate Law; Mergers, Acquisitions and Divestitures; Securities; Technology and Science. ***Email:*** fbacaj@winston.com

F. STANLEY ECHOLS, born Miami, Florida, January 10, 1945; admitted to bar, 1979, Florida and District of Columbia. *Education:* University of Florida (B.S., 1969; M.B.A., 1970; Ph.D., 1973); Georgetown University (J.D., 1978). *Member:* The District of Columbia Bar; The Florida Bar. (Resident). ***PRACTICE AREAS:*** Energy Law; Environmental Law; Regulatory Law; Administrative Law.

SANDRA L. PEARLMAN, born Framingham, Massachusetts, October, 29, 1963; admitted to bar, 1991, Pennsylvania; 1997, District of Columbia. *Education:* Bryant College (B.S., 1987); Washington College of Law of American University (J.D., 1989); School of International Service of American University (M.A., 1991). *Member:* The District of Columbia Bar; American Bar Association. (Resident). ***PRACTICE AREAS:*** Labor and Employment; Affirmative Action; Employment Discrimination; Equal Employment Opportunity Law; Fair Employment Practices; Personnel Policies; Wage and Hour Law; Business Immigration; Disability Law. ***Email:*** spearlma@winston.com

RAYMOND B. WUSLICH, born Hochwaldhausen, Germany, October 9, 1959; admitted to bar, 1988, Pennsylvania; 1989, District of Columbia. *Education:* University of Pittsburgh (B.A., 1981; M.P.I.A., 1986); American University, Washington College of Law (J.D., 1988). Senior Note and Comment Editor, The American University Law Review, 1987-1988. Law Clerk, Honorable Malcolm Muir, U.S. District Court, Middle District of Pennsylvania, 1988-1989. *Member:* The District of Columbia Bar; Pennsylvania and Energy Bar Associations. (Resident). ***PRACTICE AREAS:*** Energy Law; Litigation. ***Email:*** rwuslich@winston.com

RICHARD F. WILLIAMSON, born Oakland, California, March 18, 1950; admitted to bar, 1975, Georgia (inactive); 1977, Virginia; 1996, District of Columbia. *Education:* University of Virginia (B.A., with high distinction, 1972; J.D., 1975). Phi Beta Kappa. *Member:* The District of Columbia Bar; Virginia and American Bar Associations; State Bar of Georgia; Virginia State Bar. (Resident). ***PRACTICE AREAS:*** Commercial Real Estate; Corporate Finance.

SUSAN CANNON LONGSTREET, born Washington, D.C., July 18, 1944; admitted to bar, 1984, Virginia and U.S. Court of Appeals, Fourth Circuit; 1985, District of Columbia. *Education:* Duke University; George Washington University (B.A., 1967); Marshall Wythe School of Law, College of William & Mary (J.D., 1984). Phi Alpha Delta. Member, Board of Directors: Housing Opportunities for Women; Fractured Atlas Productions. *Member:* The District of Columbia Bar (Member, Real Estate Section); Bar Association of the District of Columbia; Virginia State Bar; American Bar Association (Member: Real Property, Probate and Trust Law Section; Forum on Affordable Housing and Community Development Law; Real Estate Committee); Women's Bar Association of the District of Columbia; National Association of Real Estate Investment Trusts. (Resident). ***PRACTICE AREAS:*** Real Estate Finance; Commercial Real Estate; Real Estate Acquisitions; Real Estate Investment Trusts; Real Property; Affordable Housing. ***Email:*** slongstr@winston.com

WILLIAM A. HORIN, born Springfield, Illinois, August 21, 1954; admitted to bar, 1979, District of Columbia; 1980, U.S. District Court, District of Columbia; 1981, U.S. Court of Appeals, District of Columbia Circuit. *Education:* Northwestern University (B.S.Ch.E., 1976; M.S.Ch.E., 1976); Georgetown University (J.D., 1979). Tau Beta Pi. *Member:* The District of Columbia Bar (Member, Sections on: Administrative Law; Energy Law); American Institute of Chemical Engineers. ***PRACTICE AREAS:*** Administrative Law; Administrative Agency Practice; Federal Administrative Law; Energy; Energy Regulation; Nuclear Energy. ***Email:*** whorin@winston.com

ROBERT A. BERGER, born Shelby, Ohio, October 12, 1966; admitted to bar, 1992, District of Columbia; 1995, Virginia. *Education:* Evangel College (B.A., 1989); Boston University (J.D., magna cum laude, 1992). (Resident).

GERALD P. FARANO, born New York, N.Y., September 10, 1966; admitted to bar, 1992, Pennsylvania; 1993, District of Columbia. *Education:* Bucknell University (B.A., 1988); George Washington University (J.D., 1991); Georgetown University (LL.M., with distinction, 1992). (Resident). ***Email:*** gfarano@winston.com

ANDREAS H. LESKOVSEK, born Silver Spring, Maryland, March 25, 1965; admitted to bar, 1990, Maryland; 1991, District of Columbia. *Education:* University of Maryland (B.A., summa cum laude, 1987); Georgetown Univer-

(This Listing Continued)

WINSTON & STRAWN, Washington—Continued

sity Law Center (J.D., magna cum laude, 1990). Phi Beta Kappa; Pi Sigma Alpha. Member, Law and Policy in International Business, 1988-1989. Author: "U.S.-Romanian Trade: Foreign Debt, Tariff and Future Prospects or Problems?" Law and Policy in International Business, Vol. 21, No. 1 (Fall, 1989). (Resident). ***PRACTICE AREAS:*** Environmental Law.

JAY L. LEVINE, born Van Nuys, California, March 20, 1965; admitted to bar, 1991, New York; 1998, District of Columbia. *Education:* University of Maryland (B.A., 1987); Fordham University School of Law (J.D., cum laude, 1990). *Member:* The District of Columbia Bar. (Resident).

PETER M. D'AMBROSIO, born Hartford, Connecticut, September 2, 1950; admitted to bar, 1976, Virginia and U.S. Court of Federal Claims (Not admitted in District of Columbia). *Education:* Georgetown University (B.A., 1972; J.D., 1976). Editor, Law and Policy in International Business, International Law Review, 1975-1976. Co-Author: Chapter, "Claims Against the Government," in *Proving and Pricing Construction Claims,* 2d Edition (John Wiley & Sons, Inc.), 1996; "Dealing With International Contracting Risks," 86-5 Construction Briefings, Federal Publications, Inc., 1986; *The Electrical Contractor's Handbook of Claims Avoidance and Management,* Reston Publishing Company, 1984; "Project Scheduling and Construction Claims," Construction Consultants International Corp., 1978. Author: "Effective Procedures For Risk Management In International Construction," Engineering News-Record, 1984-1985; "Resolving International Construction Claims and Disputes," World Construction, 1983; "Construction Claims For The Owner," Practicing Law Institute, 1983-1984; The Project Schedule And The Claim," Engineering News-Record, 1978-1985. *Member:* Virginia State Bar; American Bar Association (Member: Litigation Section; Forum Committee on the Construction Industry); National and International Panels of Arbitrators; American Arbitration Association. (Resident). ***REPORTED CASES:*** SAE/American Mid-Atlantic, Inc. GS-BACA12294 et al., Lexis 390, October 23, 1998; G&M Electrical Contractors Co., GSBCA No. 4683, 79-1 BCA § 13,571 (1978); Daniel International Corp. v. Better Construction, Inc., 593 So. 2d 524 (1991); Premier Electrical Construction Co. v. Morse Diesel, et al., 628 N.E. 2d 1090 (1993). ***PRACTICE AREAS:*** Construction Claims; Construction and Surety Law; Public Construction Law. ***Email:*** pdambros@winston.com

THOMAS GALLI, born Vineland, New Jersey, 1962; admitted to bar, 1988, California; 1991, District of Columbia. *Education:* Wharton School, University of Pennsylvania (B.S., magna cum laude, 1985); Stanford University (J.D., 1988). *Member:* District of Columbia Bar; State Bar of California; American Bar Association. ***PRACTICE AREAS:*** Commercial Real Estate. ***Email:*** thomas.galli@piperrudnick.com

HOWARD R. MAJEV, born New York, N.Y., December 10, 1952; admitted to bar, 1978, Maryland; 1995, District of Columbia. *Education:* The Johns Hopkins University (B.A., 1973); University of Maryland (J.D., 1976). Omicron Delta Kappa. Articles Editor, Maryland Law Review, 1975-1976. Executive Assistant to the President of the Baltimore City Council, 1976-1979. *Member:* Maryland State and American Bar Associations; District of Columbia Bar. ***LANGUAGES:*** Polish. ***PRACTICE AREAS:*** Real Estate.

ALLAN A. FANUCCI, born Scranton, Pennsylvania, January 25, 1953; admitted to bar, 1982, New Jersey and U.S. District Court, District of New Jersey; 1983, New York and U.S. District Court, Southern and Eastern Districts of New York; 1990, U.S. Court of Appeals for the Federal Circuit; 1996, District of Columbia; registered to practice before U.S. Patent and Trademark Office. *Education:* Wilkes College (B.S., Materials Engineering, 1974); Stevens Institute of Technology (M.S., Metallurgy, 1979); St. John's University (J.D., 1982). *Member:* American and Federal Circuit Bar Associations; New York Intellectual Property Law Association; American Intellectual Property Law Association. (Also at New York, New York). ***PRACTICE AREAS:*** Intellectual Property; Patents.

OF COUNSEL

JOHN L. NAPIER, born Bennettsville, South Carolina, May 16, 1947; admitted to bar, 1972, South Carolina; 1975, U.S. Supreme Court; 1978, U.S. Tax Court and U.S. Court of Appeals, Fourth Circuit; 1983, District of Columbia; 1987, U.S. Court of Federal Claims. *Education:* Davidson College (A.B., 1969); University of South Carolina (J.D., 1972). Legislative Assistant to Senator Strom Thurmond, 1972-1973. Minority Counsel: U.S. Senate Judiciary Committee, Subcommittee on Administrative Practice and Procedure, 1972-1973; Antitrust and Monopoly Subcommittee, 1976-1978. Chief Counsel to the Minority, U.S. Senate Special Committee on Official Conduct, 1977. Professional Staff Member and Minority Counsel, U.S. Senate Veterans Affairs Committee, 1973-1976. Chief Legislative Assistant and Counsel to Senator Strom Thurmond, 1976-1978. United States Congressman, Sixth District of South Carolina, 1981-1983. Judge, U.S. Court of Federal Claims, 1986-1989. Member, National Advisory Council, 1989—. Member, Board of Commissioners on Grievances and Discipline, South Carolina Supreme Court, 1984-1986. Private Judge, The Private Adjudication Center, Inc., Duke University, 1990. Outside

(This Listing Continued)

Counsel, U.S. House of Representatives, Committee on House Administration Task Force to Investigate the Operation and Management of the Office of the Postmaster, 1992. *Member:* South Carolina Bar; The District of Columbia Bar; American Bar Association. (Resident). ***PRACTICE AREAS:*** Federal Legislative; Regulatory; Governmental Law; Government Affairs; Lobbying; Federal Legislative Practice; Congressional Investigations. ***Email:*** jnapier@winston.com

JOSEPH B. KNOTTS, JR., born Baltimore, Maryland, July 21, 1938; admitted to bar, 1964, District of Columbia; 1976, U.S. Supreme Court. *Education:* Princeton University (A.B., 1960); Harvard University (LL.B., 1963). Attorney, Office of General Counsel, Atomic Energy Commission, 1963-1966 and 1970-1972. *Member:* The District of Columbia Bar. (Resident). ***PRACTICE AREAS:*** Nuclear Energy Law; Energy Law; Public Utility Law. ***Email:*** jknotts@winston.com

LAWRENCE I. KIERN, born New Orleans, Louisiana, December 29, 1952; admitted to bar, 1986, Michigan; 1994, District of Columbia. *Education:* United States Coast Guard Academy (B.S., 1974); Wesleyan University (M.A., 1979); University of Michigan (J.D., 1985); University of Connecticut (Ph.D., 1996). Phi Kappa Phi; Phi Alpha Theta. Author: "Liability, Compensation, and Financial Responsibility Under the Oil Pollution Act of 1990: A Review of the First Decade," Tulane Maritime Law Journal, Summer 2000. "Environmental Damages Under Federal Law," Tulane Law Review, Dec. 1997. Deputy Chief and Legislative Counsel, Coast Guard Congressional Affairs, 1994-1998. *Member:* State Bar of Michigan; Maritime Law Association. [U.S. Coast Guard, 1970-1998]. (Resident). ***PRACTICE AREAS:*** Admiralty and Maritime Law; Environmental; Federal Legislative Practice; Oil Pollution; Regulatory; Litigation. ***Email:*** lkiern@winston.com

FRANCISCO J. PAVIA, born San Juan, Puerto Rico, June 4, 1964; admitted to bar, 1991, Massachusetts and District of Columbia. *Education:* Princeton University (A.B., 1986); Harvard Law School (J.D., 1990). (Resident).

KRISTA L. PAGES, born Ridgewood, New Jersey, September 12, 1963; admitted to bar, 1989, Virginia and District of Columbia. *Education:* St. Lawrence University (B.A., cum laude, 1985); American University Washington College of Law (J.D., 1988). Pi Sigma Alpha. Co-Author: "The Civil False Claims Act-Legislation in Turmoil," The Construction Lawyer, Vol. 19, No. 1, Jan., 1999; "Admissibility of Expert Testimony under the Daubert Standard," 97-7 Construction Briefings 2d, Federal Publications, June 1997; "Industrial Security Clearances: Heightened Importance in a World of Corporate Acquisitions, Takeovers and Foreign Investment," Public Contract Law Journal, Vol. 18, No. 2, March 1989. *Member:* Virginia State Bar; District of Columbia Bar; American Bar Association (Member, Sections on: Public Contract Law; Forum Committee on the Construction Industry and Litigation); National Association of Women in Construction; American Institute of Constructors. (Resident). ***Email:*** kpages@winston.com

BERYL F. ANTHONY, JR., born El Dorado, Arkansas, 1938; admitted to bar, 1963, Arkansas; 1992, U.S. Supreme Court (Not admitted in District of Columbia). *Education:* University of Arkansas (B.S.,B.A., 1961; J.D., 1963). Assistant Attorney General, Arkansas, 1963-1965. Prosecuting Attorney, 13th Judicial Circuit, 1971-1976. Member, U.S. House of Representatives, D. Ark., 4th Dist., 1979-1992. (Resident). ***PRACTICE AREAS:*** Legislative Law. ***Email:*** banthony@winston.com

SENIOR ATTORNEYS

ANNE W. COTTINGHAM, born Thomasville, Georgia, December 3, 1951; admitted to bar, 1979, District of Columbia; 1980, U.S. Court of Appeals, Eighth Circuit; 1982, U.S. Court of Appeals, District of Columbia Circuit; 1984, U.S. Court of Appeals, Fourth Circuit. *Education:* University of North Carolina (A.B., with highest honors, 1973; M.A., 1976); Duke University (J.D., 1979). Phi Beta Kappa. *Member:* The District of Columbia Bar. ***PRACTICE AREAS:*** Nuclear Energy; Energy Regulation; Nuclear Waste; Administrative Agency Practice. ***Email:*** acotting@winston.com

ASSOCIATES

John R. Ates; Timothy Ayers (Not admitted in DC); ***Lori A. Bean; Dennis W. Bishop*** (Not admitted in DC); ***H. Allen Black III*** (Not admitted in DC); ***Matthew A. Campbell*** (admission pending); ***Patricia L. Campbell; Laura E. Chenoweth*** (Not admitted in DC); ***M. Carter DeLorme; Jeanne M. Dennis; Michael Thomas Dyson; Paul S. Ebert; Seannon M. Fallon*** (admission pending); ***Donald P. Ferraro; Carey W. Fleming; Erika M. Fleming*** (Not admitted in DC); ***Bryant E. Gardner; Marion Kristal Goldberg; Douglas N. Greenburg; Robert T. Hall*** (Not admitted in DC); ***Cynthia L. Hansen*** (Not admitted in DC); ***Sunshine Hernandez*** (Not admitted in DC); ***Roger A. Keller, Jr.*** (Not admitted in DC); ***Charles B. Klein; Susan A. MacIntyre; David J. Mandl*** (Not admitted in DC); ***Jeffrey W. Mayes; Donald W. McLaughlin, Jr.; Michael J. McLaughlin*** (Not admitted in DC); ***John McMickle*** (Not admitted in DC); ***Marc Zaki Michael*** (Not admitted in DC); ***Daniel J. Michaels*** (admission pending); ***Angela M. Moore*** (Not admitted in DC); ***Gina M. Petro; Lanelle K. Polen*** (admission pending); ***Brooke D. Poole***

(This Listing Continued)

(Not admitted in DC); ***Sean G. Saxon*** (Not admitted in DC); ***Scott A. Schipma; Gregory K. Smith*** (Not admitted in DC); ***William B. Fenning Steinman; Thomas M. Stimson; Anne W. Stukes*** (Not admitted in DC); ***Zach Wilks*** (Not admitted in DC); ***Jeffrey A. Wolfson.***

STAFF ATTORNEYS

Pamela A. Rons.

(For Complete Biographical Data on all Personnel, see Chicago, Illinois Professional Biographies).

JOHN F. WITHERSPOON

SUITE 500
815 CONNECTICUT AVENUE, N.W.
WASHINGTON, D.C. 20006-4004
Telephone: 202-835-3700
Facsimile: 202-293-2902
Email: jfw@witherspoonlaw.com

Patent, Trademark and Copyright Law.

JOHN F. WITHERSPOON, born Danville, Illinois, March 26, 1933; admitted to bar, 1965, District of Columbia; 1965-1982, U.S. Court of Customs and Patent Appeals; 1968, U.S. Supreme Court; 1982, U.S. Court of Appeals for the Federal Circuit; registered to practice before U.S. Patent and Trademark Office. *Education:* Eastern Illinois University; United States Military Academy; University of Illinois (B.S., 1955; M.Ed., 1958; M.S., 1960); Georgetown University (J.D., 1964). Delta Theta Phi. Author: "So-Called Common Assignee Double Patenting—An Issue in Search for a Home," APLA Quarterly Journal, Vol. IV, No. 4, p. 329, 1976; "The Board of Appeals of the United States Patent and Trademark Office," Annual of Industrial Property, Warden Ed., 1976, Common Law Reports Ltd., London, England; "Ex Parte Patent Developments," 81 F.R.D. 164, 1978; "The Standard of Patentability in the United States," AIPLA Selected Legal Papers, Vol. IV, No. 1, p.F-1, 1986; "Wilson Sporting Goods: Clarification or Confusion?" 140 F.R.D. 125, 1991; "Turning the Corner: A Tribute to Judge Giles Sutherland Rich," 76 J.Pat. & Trademark Off. Soc'y, 332, 1994. Co-Author: "U.S. Patent Law and Practice," Seminar Services International, Brussels, Belgium, 1976. Editor: "Nonobviousness—the Ultimate Condition of Patentability," The Bureau of National Affairs, Inc., Washington, D.C., 1980. Distinguished Professor of Intellectual Property Law and Coordinator of specialty track in Intellectual Property Law, George Mason University School of Law, 1992—. Adjunct Professor of Law, Georgetown University Law Center, 1998-2000. Lecturer: John Marshall Law School Symposia, 1967, 1975, 1979; The Practising Law Institute, 1968, 1972, 1975, 1980; The Institute for International Learning, 1975-1980, 1984; The Bureau of National Affairs, 1982. Program Director, The Bureau of National Affairs' Patent Law Conferences, Washington, D.C., 1977-1980. Member, Advisory Board, BNA's Patent, Trademark and Copyright Journal, 1979—. Examiner-in-Chief and Member, Board of Appeals, U.S. Patent and Trademark Office, 1971-1978. Law Clerk to Judge Giles S. Rich, U.S. Court of Customs and Patent Appeals, 1964-1966. *Member:* District of Columbia Bar (Chair, Patent, Trademark and Copyright Law Division, 1980-1981); Bar Association of the District of Columbia (Member: Patent, Trademark and Copyright Law Section; Council, 1971-1974, 1980-1983); American Bar Association (Member, Intellectual Property Law Section); Federal Circuit Bar Association (Chair, Committee on Continuing Legal Education, 1989-1992); American Intellectual Property Law Association (Chair, Committee on Continuing Legal Education, 1981-1983); International Intellectual Property Association; New York Intellectual Property Law Association; Licensing Executives Society; American Judicature Society; The Giles Sutherland Rich American Inn of Court (Emeritus); American Chemical Society; Patent and Trademark Office Society; American Association for the Advancement of Science; New York Academy of Sciences. ***PRACTICE AREAS:*** Patent Law.

WITT & NOLAN LLP

Established in 1988

SUITE 600
1140 CONNECTICUT AVENUE, N.W.
WASHINGTON, D.C. 20036
Telephone: 202-296-3333
Telecopier: 202-296-0416

Chevy Chase, Maryland Office: Suite 801, 5530 Wisconsin Avenue. Telephone: 202-296-3333.

Family Law, General Litigation.

MEMBERS OF FIRM

HAL WITT, born Washington, D.C., May 15, 1936; admitted to bar, 1959, New York; 1962, District of Columbia and U.S. Supreme Court; 1975, Maryland. *Education:* University of Chicago (B.A., 1954; J.D., 1958); University of Paris, Paris, France. Law Clerk to Judge J. Warren Madden, U.S. Court of Claims, 1959-1961. General Counsel, 1965-1966, Deputy Executive Director, 1966-1968, United Planning Organization of the National Capital Area. *Member:* The District of Columbia Bar (Member, Steering Committee, Family Law Division, 1974-1977); Montgomery County and Maryland State Bar Associations. ***PRACTICE AREAS:*** Family Law.

JAMES G. NOLAN, born Washington, D.C., January 11, 1943; admitted to bar, 1972, Maryland and District of Columbia. *Education:* Georgetown University (A.B., 1965); George Washington University (J.D., with honors, 1971). Phi Delta Phi. Law Clerk to: Judge John P. Moore, Circuit Court for Montgomery County, Maryland, 1971; Judge William H. McCullough, Circuit Court for Prince George's County, Maryland, 1971-1972. *Member:* The District of Columbia Bar; Montgomery County, Maryland State and American Bar Associations; American Academy of Matrimonial Lawyers. ***PRACTICE AREAS:*** Family Law.

ASSOCIATE

MARJORIE JUST, born Norwood, Massachusetts, June 2, 1968; admitted to bar, 1994, Maryland; 1995, District of Columbia. *Education:* Duke University (A.B., cum laude, 1990); George Washington University (J.D., 1994). Member, George Washington Journal of International Law and Economics. *Member:* The District of Columbia Bar; Montgomery County, Maryland State and American Bar Associations. ***PRACTICE AREAS:*** Family Law.

WOLF, ARNOLD & CARDOSO, P.C.

Established in 1977

1801 K STREET, N.W.
SUITE 203L
WASHINGTON, D.C. 20006
Telephone: 202-857-0585
Facsimile: 202-293-2068
Email: wac@interlawyers.com
URL: http://www.interlawyers.com

New York, N.Y. Office: Wolf, Arnold & Knoll, P.C., 590 Madison Avenue. Telephone: 212-521-4410. Fax: 212-465-9104.
Rio de Janeiro, Brazil Office: Cardoso, Rocha, Trindale & Lara Resende.
Bogota, Colombia Office: Arango, Nieto, Calderon & Asociados.
Caribbean Office: Dunn, Cox, Orett and Ashenheim, Kingston, Jamaica.
Other Associated offices also throughout Latin America, the Caribbean, Asia and the South Pacific.

International Business, Joint Ventures and other Trans-National Transactions, International Telecommunications, International Investments, International Arbitration, Representation before the World Bank, IFC, Inter-American Development Bank, EXIM Bank, OPIC, other U.S. and Foreign Governmental Agencies, North America Free Trade Agreement, GATT and World Trade Organization, U.S.T.R. Advisors on Laws of Europe, the Middle East, Argentina, Brazil, Colombia and other Latin American and Caribbean Countries. Foreign Investment Law, International Commercial Contracts, International Corporate Finance. Latin America Trade and Finance. Privatization, International Intellectual Property, Internet Law.

FIRM PROFILE: The firm, which was started in 1977, specializes in facilitating foreign and cross-border investments, joint ventures, other international business and investment oriented activities and resolving problems arising out of such transactions, both in the United States and overseas, particularly in Latin America, the Caribbean, Australia, Asia, the Pacific, Europe and the Middle East, utilizing where necessary our network of associated local law firms in more than 25 countries.

The firm also represents clients from outside the United States in business transactions in and with business entities in the United States, including investments, import financing, loans, establishing business operations and other financial transactions, strategic and other relationships with U.S. companies and sales and commercial transactions.

The firm advises clients on NAFTA, WTO and other international trade issues, customs law and related matters, international trade litigation and arbitration as well as USTR, ITC internet, domain name arbitration and ITA issues.

The firm advises on privatizations, particularly in telecommunications, participates in arbitrations and other dispute resolutions and work-outs. We also advise governments on market oriented activities such as appropriate investment codes, incentive laws, and other investment inducing projects.

Associated with law firms in more than 25 countries.

ELTING ARNOLD (1912-1988).

(This Listing Continued)

WOLF, ARNOLD & CARDOSO, P.C., Washington—Continued

MAURICE WOLF, born London, England, October 15, 1931; admitted to bar, 1962, New York; 1964, District of Columbia; 1980, U.S. Supreme Court. *Education:* Universidad Nacional Autonoma de Mexico (Certificate, 1957); University of California at Los Angeles (B.A., with honors, 1959); Columbia University (LL.B., 1962). Harlan Fiske Stone Scholar, 1962. Co-Author: "Doing Business with the International Financing Organizations in Washington," BNA, 1982; "Regional or Multilateral Free Trade Arrangements," Free Trade in the Americas (UNAM, 1997). Co-Director, American University Law School International Law Program, Santiago, Chile, Summer, 1997. Visiting Professor of International Law, Washington College of Law, American University, 1996-1997. Visiting Professor, University of Georgia Law School, 1998. Attorney-Advisor, Office of Satellite Communications, Federal Communications Commission, 1962-1966. Attorney, 1966-1974 and Senior Counsel, 1974-1977. Legal Department, Inter-American Development Bank. President, Columbia Society of International Law, 1961-1962. Advisory Director, Institute for Transnational Arbitration. *Member:* The District of Columbia Bar (Chairman, Banking and Finance Subcommittee, Committee on International Investment and Finance, 1975-1976); American Society of International Law; Inter-American Bar Foundation (Director, Committee on International Trade in the Americas; Member, Editorial Advisory Committee, International Legal Materials, 1997-2000). Arbitrator Member, American Arbitration Center of International Arbitration. ***LANGUAGES:*** Spanish and Portuguese. ***SPECIAL AGENCIES:*** Inter-American Development Bank; International Finance Corporation; World Bank; I.I.C.; MIGA; ICSID; EX-IM Bank; OPIC; A.A.A.; I.C.C.; NAFTA, WTO. ***PRACTICE AREAS:*** International Business Transactions; International Joint Ventures; International Telecommunications; Latin American and Caribbean Transactions; Foreign Investment Law; Export Investment in Finance; International Commercial Arbitration; International Conflicts of Laws; International Trade Law; Latin American Trade and Finance; Loans. ***Email:*** mwolf@interlawyers.com

DENNIS A. FOSTER, born Iron Station, North Carolina, August 24, 1949; admitted to bar, 1988, Maryland; 2001, District of Columbia. *Education:* University of North Carolina, Chapel Hill (B.A., summa cum laude, 1971); University of Florence, Institute of Comparative Law (externship, 1976); Stanford University (J.D., 1977); University of London, School of Oriental and African Studies (M.A., Development Economics/Middle East Studies, 1981). Member, Board of Editors of the "Stanford International Law Journal," 1975-1976. Author, "Internet Domain Names and Trademark Right Enforcement," Summer 2000, Maryland Bar Newsletter. Instructor, Comparative Law, University of Genoa, 1985-1986. Adjunct Professor, Business Law, St. Xavier Chicago/Milan, M.B.A. Program. United States Diplomatic Corps (Foreign Service), 1981-1991. Specialist, political and economic/commercial affairs. Postings included Beirut, Genoa, Washington, D.C. and Abu Dhabi. Member: Professional Affiliations with Organizations dedicted to methods of Alternate Dispute Resolution; The World Intellectual Property Organization; The International Chamber of Commerce. *Member:* Maryland Bar Association. [United States Army, 1971-1974; Russian Linguist/Intelligence specialist]. (Also of Counsel, Studio Legale Mondini-Rusconi). ***LANGUAGES:*** English, French, Italian, Arabic, Russian, German and Spanish. ***PRACTICE AREAS:*** International Business Law; International Arbitration; International Mediation; International Copyright Law; International Trademarks; Internet Law. ***Email:*** dafoster@interlawyers.com

CARLOS E. CARDOSO, admitted to bar, 1959, Brazil (Not admitted in the United States). *Education:* Catholic University, Rio de Janeiro (LL.B.); Tulane Law School (M.C.L.). ***LANGUAGES:*** Portuguese, English, French and Spanish. ***PRACTICE AREAS:*** Brazilian Business and Litigation; International Business Transactions, Arbitration; MERCOSUR.

LAWRENCE I. KNOLL, admitted to bar, 1989, New York, U.S. District Court, Southern and Eastern Districts of New York and U.S. Court of International Trade (Not admitted in District of Columbia). *Education:* State University of New York at Stony Brook (B.A., 1985); University of Pennsylvania Law School (J.D., 1988). Internship, Judge Jane Restani, U.S. Court of International Trade, Summer, 1987. (Also with Wolf, Arnold & Knoll, P.C., New York, New York). ***LANGUAGES:*** Hebrew. ***PRACTICE AREAS:*** International Contracts; International Commercial Law; International Commercial Arbitration; Import and Export Law; International Licensing; International Joint Ventures; Customs Law; International Trade Regulation. ***Email:*** ariknoll@interlawyers.com

GILBERTO ARANGO, admitted to bar, 1948, Columbia (Not admitted in the United States). *Education:* Universidad Nacional, Facultad de Derecho y Ciencias Políticas. Counsel to the President of Colombia, 1952-1953. Governor, State (Departamento) of Caldas, 1959-1960. Professor of International Commercial Law: Universidad de los Andes, 1954-1957. Senator, State of Caldas, 1958-1966. President, Asociación de Exportadores de Cafe, 1975—. ***LANGUAGES:*** Spanish and English. ***PRACTICE AREAS:*** Colombian and Latin American Business; Government Representation; Foreign Transactions; Arbitration.

(This Listing Continued)

OF COUNSEL

EDWARD RAMOS SOUSA, admitted to bar, 1987, New Jersey and U.S. Court of International Trade (Not admitted in District of Columbia). *Education:* University of Paris, Sorbonne-Paris IV (Language Certificate, 1977); Brandeis University (B.A., 1978); University of Pennsylvania (J.D., 1981). *Member:* The Association of the Bar of The City of New York; New Jersey State Bar Association (Member, Committee on International Law, 1987—). ***LANGUAGES:*** French, Spanish, Portuguese. ***PRACTICE AREAS:*** International Business Law; International Investment; International Banking Law; International Economic Development; Artistic Property; International Arbitration. ***Email:*** ers@interlawyers.com

---

WOLF & WOLF

Established in 1892

SUITE 1210, 1001 CONNECTICUT AVENUE, N.W.

WASHINGTON, D.C. 20036

Telephone: 202-296-3300
Fax: 202-296-3303
Email: BigBad@AYA.Yale.edu

General Practice.

MEMBERS OF FIRM

ALEXANDER WOLF (1866-1930).

WILLIAM B. WOLF, SR. (1905-1992).

WILLIAM B. WOLF, JR., born Washington, D.C., 1927; admitted to bar, 1951, District of Columbia; 1954, U.S. Supreme Court; 1963, Maryland. *Education:* Princeton University (A.B., 1948); Oxford University, graduate study; Yale University (LL.B., 1951). Phi Alpha Delta. *Member:* The District of Columbia Bar; Bar Association of the District of Columbia; American Bar Association. ***Email:*** BigBad@Alumni.Princeton.edu

---

WOMBLE CARLYLE SANDRIDGE & RICE

Established in 1977

SUITE 700, 1401 EYE STREET

WASHINGTON, D.C. 20005

Telephone: 202-857-4400
Telecopier: 202-467-6910
Email: lawyers@wcsr.com
URL: http://www.wcsr.com

Winston-Salem, North Carolina Office: 200 West Second Street, P.O. Drawer 84. Telephone: 336-721-3600. Fax: 336-721-3660. New Address Effective March, 2002: One West Fourth Street, 27101.

Charlotte, North Carolina Office: 3300 One First Union Center, 301 South College Street. Telephone: 704-331-4900. Fax: 704-331-4955.

Raleigh, North Carolina Office: 2100 First Union Capitol Center, 150 Fayetteville Street Mall, P.O. Box 831. Telephone: 919-755-2100. Fax: 919-755-2150.

Research Triangle Park, North Carolina Office: 2530 Meridian Parkway, Suite 400 (Durham), 27713. Telephone: 919-484-2300. Fax: 919-484-2340.

Greensboro, North Carolina Office: 300 North Greene Street. Telephone: 336-574-8030. Fax: 336-574-4520.

Atlanta, Georgia Office: One Atlantic Center, 1201 West Peachtree Street, Suite 3500. Telephone: 404-872-7000. Fax: 404-888-7490.

Other Atlanta, Georgia Office: Suite 404, 2296 Henderson Mill Road, N.E. Telephone: 770-492-9030. Fax: 770-492-9609.

Greenville, South Carolina Office: 700 Poinsett Plaza, 104 South Main Street, P.O. Box 10208. Telephone: 864-255-5400. Fax: 864-255-5440.

McLean, Virginia Office: 6862 Elm Street, Eighth Floor. Telephone: 703-790-3310. Facsimile: 703-790-2623 (7th Floor); 703-394-2205 (3rd Floor); 703-288-0622 (8th Floor).

General Civil Practice, Trial and Appellate Litigation. Administrative, Antitrust, Aviation, Banking, Bankruptcy and Creditor's Rights, Bond Financing, Civil Rights, Commercial, Construction, Consumer Lending, Corporate, E-Commerce, Employee Benefits, Environmental, Estate Planning, Family, Government Relations, Health Care, Insurance, Intellectual Property, International, Labor and Employment, Municipal, Negligence, Probate, Product Liability, Real Estate, Retirement Plans, Securities, Taxation, Toxic Tort, Wills and Trusts Law.

FIRM PROFILE: Womble Carlyle Sandridge & Rice, PLLC, which traces its history to 1876, is a full-service law firm that delivers sophisticated and innovative legal services to a wide spectrum of business clients in industries that include information technology, health care, manufacturing, telecommunications and financial services. The Firm also represents a variety of governmental units and agencies.

(This Listing Continued)

Womble Carlyle's mission is to provide value to clients by combining professional skill, technology and a thorough understanding of clients' needs to deliver high quality, cost-effective and responsive service. The firm is comprised of approximately 430 lawyers and 838 staff members operating from offices in Atlanta, GA; Greenville, SC; Charlotte, Winston-Salem, Research Triangle Park, Raleigh and Greensboro, NC; McLean, VA and Washington, DC.

The Firm considers technology and the benefits it offers an integral part of the legal services it provides. All of the Firm's offices are linked for full communications by telephone, fax, electronic mail and video conference over a wide area network. The Firm takes full advantage of its sophisticated computer technology for support in large-case litigation, as well as management of complex transactions. The Director of Technology is responsible for implementing existing systems, and in some instances, developing new software applications to meet specific client needs. The firm-wide communications and computer network permit the Firm to allocate resources from all offices, as needed, as well as to establish direct, secure links with clients and their legal departments, thus enhancing the responsiveness and efficiency of the Firm's lawyers.

The lawyers of Womble Carlyle have traditionally been active in community affairs, in Bar and other professional activities, and in state government. Many lawyers assume leading roles in civic and professional organizations, and several have served the government in elected or appointed positions.

LAW FIRM ALLIANCES/ASSOCIATIONS: ***TOLEDO CONFERENCE GROUP LEX MUNDI***

RESIDENT MEMBERS

ERIK D. BOLOG, born New York, New York, April 13, 1965; admitted to bar, 1991, Maryland and Virginia; 1992, District of Columbia; 1994, Colorado. *Education:* State University of New York at Binghamton (B.A., 1987); Washington College of Law, American University (J.D., 1990). Member, The Walter Chandler Inn of Court, Washington, D.C. *Member:* Montgomery County and American Bar Associations; District of Columbia Bar; Virginia State Bar; The Association of Trial Lawyers of America; The Trial Lawyers Association of Washington, D.C. ***PRACTICE AREAS:*** Business Litigation; Professional Negligence; Civil Rights Litigation; Bankruptcy Litigation. ***Email:*** ebolog@wcsr.com

DESMOND D. CONNALL, JR., born Portland, Oregon, September 16, 1954; admitted to bar, 1981, Maryland; 1983, District of Columbia. *Education:* Princeton University (A.B., 1976); Stanford University (J.D., 1981). Author: "A History of the Arizona Ground Water Management Act," Arizona State Law Journal 313, 1982. *Member:* District of Columbia Bar; Maryland State and American Bar Associations; International Council of Shopping Centers. ***PRACTICE AREAS:*** Leasing; Workouts; Real Estate; Bankruptcy. ***Email:*** dconnall@wcsr.com

W. ANDREW COPENHAVER, born Roanoke, Virginia, November 10, 1946; admitted to bar, 1972, North Carolina; 1980, U.S. Supreme Court (Not admitted in District of Columbia). *Education:* Duke University (A.B., 1969); University of North Carolina (J.D., 1972). Listed in Best Lawyers in America, Business Litigation and First Amendment Rights. *Member:* Forsyth County, North Carolina and American Bar Associations; North Carolina Federal Bar Advisory Council. (Also at Winston-Salem, North Carolina Office). ***PRACTICE AREAS:*** Antitrust Law; Unfair Trade Practices; Defamation; Intellectual Property Litigation. ***Email:*** acopenhaver@wcsr.com

RICHARD G. DAVID, born Washington, D.C., November 22, 1941; admitted to bar, 1967, District of Columbia. *Education:* University of Pennsylvania (B.S., cum laude, 1963); Harvard University (J.D., cum laude, 1966). Law Clerk, U.S. Claims Court, 1966-1968. *Member:* District of Columbia Bar; American Bar Association. ***PRACTICE AREAS:*** Commercial Real Estate Transactions; Contracts; Leasing; Business Formation and Planning; Taxation. ***Email:*** rdavid@wcsr.com

TAINA E. M. EDLUND, born Pâlkâne, Finland, September 9, 1958; admitted to bar, 1985, District of Columbia; 1991, New York. *Education:* Yale University (B.A., cum laude, 1980); Georgetown University (J.D., 1985). Associate Editor, The Tax Lawyer, 1984-1985. *Member:* The District of Columbia Bar; American Bar Association (Tax Section, Employee Benefits Committee). ***LANGUAGES:*** Finnish, French. ***Email:*** tedlund@wcsr.com

DIANE J. FUCHS, born New Rochelle, New York, May 15, 1947; admitted to bar, 1974, New Jersey; 1978, District of Columbia; 1979, U.S. Supreme Court. *Education:* Douglass College, Rutgers University (B.A., 1969); London School of Economics, London, England; Rutgers University (J.D., 1973). Phi Beta Kappa. Adjunct Professor: Washington School of Law, American University, 1979; Antioch School of Law, 1981. Executive Editor, Compensation Planning Journal, 1983-1999. Board of Governors of American College of Employee Benefits Counsel. American Society of Association Executives Legal Section (Council Member, 1998—); Tax Management Advisory Board, Tax Management, Inc., 1990—; Board of Directors, Washington Chamber Symphony, 1992-1997. Pro Bono Counsel to: District of Columbia Women's Bar Association Foundation, 1998—; American Youth Understanding Diabetes Abroad, Inc., 1996—. Honors: Charter Fellow, American College of Employee Benefits Counsel; Board of Fellows, July 2000. *Member:* American Bar Association (Chair, Employee Benefits Committee, Section of Taxation, 2000-2001, Vice Chair, 1997-1999; Health Care Task Force, Section of Taxation, 1994—; Joint Committee on Employee Benefits); District of Columbia Bar. ***PRACTICE AREAS:*** Taxation; Employee Benefits; Executive Compensation; Employment Law; Exempt Organizations. ***Email:*** dfuchs@wcsr.com

JOHN D. HAGNER, born Cincinnati, Ohio, April 12, 1945; admitted to bar, 1973, District of Columbia and Maryland. *Education:* University of Cincinnati (B.S.M.E., 1968); Georgetown University (J.D., 1973). Omicron Delta Kappa; Pi Tau Sigma. Member, Board of Editors, Georgetown Law Journal, 1971-1973. Adjunct Professor for Real Estate Finance, Georgetown University Law Center, 1995—. Best International Real Estate Lawyers, 2000, by Business Law Research, Ltd., London, England. *Member:* District of Columbia Bar; Maryland State and American Bar Associations; American College of Real Estate Lawyers. [U.S. Public Health Service, 1968-1971; Sanitary Engineer (Lieutenant)]. ***PRACTICE AREAS:*** Commercial Real Estate; Corporate; Business; Insurance Law. ***Email:*** jhagner@wcsr.com

PAUL A. KAPLAN, born Jersey City, New Jersey, November 28, 1951; admitted to bar, 1976, District of Columbia; 1982, Maryland. *Education:* Boston University (B.A., magna cum laude, 1973); University of Pennsylvania (J.D., cum laude, 1976). Order of the Coif. Member, University of Pennsylvania Law Review, 1974-76. *Member:* District of Columbia Bar; Maryland State and American Bar Associations. (Managing Member, District of Columbia Office). ***PRACTICE AREAS:*** Civil Litigation. ***Email:*** pkaplan@wcsr.com

N. PETER KOSTOPULOS, born Norfolk, Virginia, April 12, 1953; admitted to bar, 1978, District of Columbia; 1988, Florida; 1992, Virginia. *Education:* Georgetown University (B.A., 1974); Georgetown University Law Center (J.D., 1978). Author: Editor, "Legal Environment for Foreign Direct Investment in the United States," Institute for International and Foreign Trade Law, Georgetown University Law Center, 1981. Assistant U.S. Attorney, U.S. Department of Justice, Southern District of Florida, 1982-1987. Trial Attorney: Bureau of Competition, Federal Trade Commission, 1978-1982; Fraud Section, Criminal Division, U.S. Department of Justice, 1987-1990. Co-Chair, Strategic Alliance Committee, U.S.A. and Canada, Licensing Executive Society, 1992-2000. *Member:* The District of Columbia Bar (Member, Litigation Section); American Bar Association (Member, Intellectual Property Section). ***LANGUAGES:*** French. ***PRACTICE AREAS:*** Technology Law; International Trade; Litigation; Intellectual Property Licensing; Intellectual Property Litigation; Commercial Litigation. ***Email:*** pkostopulos@wcsr.com

STUART A. KRUGER, born Norfolk, Virginia, October 30, 1954; admitted to bar, 1982, Virginia and District of Columbia. *Education:* University of Virginia (B.S., with honors, 1977; J.D., 1982). *Member:* District of Columbia Bar: Virginia State Bar; American Bar Association; American College of Mortgage Attorneys. ***PRACTICE AREAS:*** Real Estate. ***Email:*** skruger@wcsr.com

ELIZABETH C. LEE, born New Haven, Connecticut, June 22, 1959; admitted to bar, 1985, Pennsylvania; 1986, New Jersey; 1991, District of Columbia. *Education:* Oberlin College (B.A., with honors, 1981); Georgetown University Law Center (J.D., 1985). Lead Articles Editor, Journal of Law and Policy in International Business, 1984-1985. Author: "Bauxite for Butter-The U.S. Jamaican Agreement and the Future of Barter in U.S. Trade Policy," Journal of Law and Policy in International Business, Vol. 16, 1984; "Celebrity Look-Alikes: Re-Thinking the Right of Privacy and Right of Publicity," Entertainment and Sports Law Journal, Vol. 2, 1985. *Member:* District of Columbia Bar; Pennsylvania State and American (Member, Sections of Real Property, Probate and Trust Law, Business and International Law) Bar Associations. ***PRACTICE AREAS:*** Business Formation and Planning; Commercial and Real Estate Transactions; Contracts; Corporate and Real Estate Finance. ***Email:*** elee@wcsr.com

KENNETH W. LOGWOOD, born Lynchburg, Virginia, October 3, 1948; admitted to bar, 1978, District of Columbia. *Education:* University of Massachusetts (B.A., summa cum laude, 1975); Yale University (J.D., 1978). Member: Urban Land Institute; National Association of Industrial and Office Properties; Northern Virginia Building Industry Association; National Association of Homebuilders. *Member:* District of Columbia Bar; American Bar Association. ***PRACTICE AREAS:*** Real Estate. ***Email:*** klogwood@wcsr.com

PAMELA V. ROTHENBERG, born Fort Knox, Kentucky, December 11, 1958; admitted to bar, 1984, Illinois; 1985, District of Columbia. *Education:* Tufts University (B.A., summa cum laude, 1981); Northwestern University (J.D., 1984). Phi Beta Kappa. Member, Editorial Board, Northwestern Journal of International Law and Business, 1983-1984. Author, "Exit Strategies," The National Law Journal, September 7, 1998. *Member:* District of Columbia Bar; American Bar Association. ***PRACTICE AREAS:*** Business Formation and Planning; Commercial and Real Estate Transactions; Real Estate and Technology; Contracts; Leasing. ***Email:*** prothenberg@wcsr.com

(This Listing Continued)

WOMBLE CARLYLE SANDRIDGE & RICE, Washington—Continued

HOWARD N. SOLODKY, born Buffalo, New York, June 28, 1951; admitted to bar, 1977, New York; 1980, District of Columbia. *Education:* Clark University (B.A., cum laude, 1973); State University of New York at Buffalo (J.D., cum laude, 1976); George Washington University (L.L.M., Taxation, with highest honors, 1980). Phi Beta Kappa. Comments Editor, Buffalo Law Review, 1975-1976. Law Clerk to Appellate Division, 3rd Department of New York State Supreme Court, 1976-1977. Attorney, Interpretative Division, Office of the Chief Counsel, Internal Revenue Service, 1977-1981. *Member:* American Bar Association (Member, Section of Tax Law); The National Association of Bond Lawyers. ***PRACTICE AREAS:*** Taxation; Municipal Finance; Corporate Law. ***Email:*** hsolodky@wcsr.com

JEFFREY L. TARKENTON, born Portsmouth, Virginia, June 28, 1956; admitted to bar, 1981, Virginia; 1984, District of Columbia. *Education:* College of William & Mary (B.A., with highest honors, 1978; J.D., 1981). Phi Eta Sigma. Member, Mortar Board. Law Clerk to Honorable Blackwell N. Shelley, U.S. Bankruptcy Court, Eastern District of Virginia, 1981-1983. Editor, Bankruptcy Law News, Virginia State Bar. Author, "Proceeds in Bankruptcy; United Virginia Bank v. SLAB Fork Coal Company," 89 West Virginia Law Review, 783, Spring 1987. *Member:* District of Columbia Bar; Virginia State Bar (Board of Governors, Bankruptcy Section); Maryland Federal Bar Association; American Bar Association. Master, Chandler Inn of Court. ***PRACTICE AREAS:*** Bankruptcy; Civil Litigation. ***Email:*** jtarkenton@wcsr.com

STANLEY J. WROBEL, born Chicago, Illinois, March 18, 1951; admitted to bar, 1975, Illinois; 1976, District of Columbia; 1979, Virginia and U.S. Supreme Court. *Education:* University of Chicago (B.S., 1972; J.D., 1975). Administrative Attorney, Judicial Panel on Multi District Litigation, 1976-1979. Member, Editorial Staff, Manual for Complex Litigation, 1976-1979. *Member:* District of Columbia Bar; Virginia State Bar; American Bar Association. ***PRACTICE AREAS:*** Real Estate; Corporate Law. ***Email:*** swrobel@wcsr.com

ASSOCIATES

CHRISTOPHER D. BELL, born Fort Dix, New Jersey, July 30, 1967; admitted to bar, 1996, Virginia; 1999, District of Columbia. *Education:* University of Texas (B.A., 1990; J.D., 1996); Harvard University (M.P.A., 1992). Member, Texas Environmental Law Journal, 1994-1996. Member, Urban Land Institute, 1998—. *Member:* The District of Columbia Bar; Virginia State Bar. ***PRACTICE AREAS:*** Real Estate; Commercial Leasing. ***Email:*** chbell@wcsr.com

GINA M. BOSCARINO, born Greensburg, Pennsylvania, February 6, 1974; admitted to bar, 1997, Pennsylvania; 1999, District of Columbia. *Education:* University of Pittsburgh (B.A., summa cum laude, 1994); The George Washington University (M.P.H., 1997; J.D., 1997). Phi Beta Kappa. *Member:* Pennsylvania and American Bar Associations. ***PRACTICE AREAS:*** Employee Benefits; Pensions; Executive Compensation; Health Care; Exempt Organizations. ***Email:*** gboscarino@wcsr.com

GRACE CAVELLI, born Flushing, New York, August 28, 1963; admitted to bar, 1995, Virginia; 1996, District of Columbia and Maryland. *Education:* State University of New York at Binghamton (B.A., 1987); University of Maryland (M.A., 1991); Catholic University (J.D., cum laude, 1995). Member, Catholic University Law Review. *Member:* American Bar Association. ***PRACTICE AREAS:*** Real Estate; Litigation; Corporate. ***Email:*** gcavelli@wcsr.com

SABRINA CICCARELLO, born Washington, D.C., July 20, 1976; admitted to bar, 2001, Virginia, U.S. District Court, Eastern and Western Districts of Virginia and U.S. Court of Appeals, Fourth Circuit (Not admitted in District of Columbia). *Education:* University of Maryland (B.S. and B.A., English, 1998); Washington & Lee University (J.D., 2001). Phi Beta Kappa; Omicron Delta Kappa; Moot Court Executive Board. ***LANGUAGES:*** Italian. ***PRACTICE AREAS:*** Taxation; Banking Law; Finance; Property Law. ***Email:*** sciccarello@wcsr.com

J. DAVID FOLDS, born Augusta, Georgia, December 24, 1966; admitted to bar, 1993, North Carolina; 1996, District of Columbia; 1999, Virginia. *Education:* University of the South (B.A., 1989); London School of Economics (M.S., 1991); University of North Carolina (J.D., 1993). Omicron Delta Kappa. Member, North Carolina Journal of International law and Commercial Regulation. Law Clerk, Honorable William L. Stocks, Chief Judge, U.S. Bankruptcy Court, Middle District of North Carolina, 1994-1995. *Member:* American Bar Association. ***PRACTICE AREAS:*** Commercial Litigation; Bankruptcy. ***Email:*** dfolds@wcsr.com

JAMES W. GLADSTONE, born Cincinnati, Ohio, October 26, 1960; admitted to bar, 1984, Texas; 1986, District of Columbia. *Education:* University of Texas (B.A., cum laude, 1981; J.D., 1984). Law clerk to the Hon. Harry Lee Hudspeth, U.S. District Court, Western District of Texas. *Member:* The District of Columbia Bar (Member, Litigation Section). ***PRACTICE AREAS:*** Civil Litigation. ***Email:*** jgladstone@wcsr.com

(This Listing Continued)

JACQUELINE P. PUENTES, born Pasadena, California, April 26, 1974; admitted to bar, 2001, Virginia (Not admitted in District of Columbia). *Education:* Amherst College (B.A., magna cum laude, 1996); Vanderbilt University (J.D., 2000). Administrative Editor, Journal of Transnational Law. ***LANGUAGES:*** Spanish. ***PRACTICE AREAS:*** Banking, Finance and Property. ***Email:*** jpuentes@wcsr.com

RAQUEL CHEATHAM SKINNER, born Brooklyn, New York, November 15, 1971; admitted to bar, 1998, New Jersey and New York; 1999, District of Columbia. *Education:* Spelman College (B.A., summa cum laude, 1993); University of Pennsylvania Law School (J.D., 1997). *Member:* The District of Columbia Bar. ***PRACTICE AREAS:*** Real Estate. ***Email:*** rskinner@wcsr.com

OF COUNSEL

PHILIP J. BERKOWITZ, born Bronx, New York, November 25, 1965; admitted to bar, 1989, New York; 1995, District of Columbia; 1998, U.S. District Court, Northern District of New York and U.S. Supreme Court; U.S. Tax Court. *Education:* Columbia University (A.B., 1988; J.D., 1988). Harlan Fiske Stone Scholar. Recipient, Milton P. Kupfer Scholarship. Co-Author: with Colleen P. Mahoney, "Recent Enforcement Cases," Georgetown University Law Center, CLE on Federal Enforcement, October 1994, updated and republished as "Recent Enforcement Cases," with William R. McLucas, 26th Annual Institute on Securities Regulation, PLI Corporate Law and Practice Handbook Series No. 868, November 1994; with Colleen P. Mahoney, "Enforcement Issues," PLI Corporate Law and Practice Course Handbook 881, March 1995; with Colleen P. Mahoney, "Recent S.E.C. Enforcement Cases," PLI Corporate Law and Practice Course Handbook 885, April 1995. Formerly with: Paul, Weiss, Rifkind, Wharton & Garrison, New York, N.Y., 1988-1991; Kutak Rock, LLP, Washington, D.C., 1999-2001. Senior Counsel, Enforcement Division, U.S. Securities & Exchange Commission, 1991-1995. Trial Attorney, Tax Division, U.S. Department of Justice, Washington, D.C., 1995-1999. Member, Legal & Compliance Division, Securities Industry Association, 2001—. *Member:* The District of Columbia Bar (Member, Litigation Section, 1995—); American Bar Association (Member, Pretrial Practice and Discovery Committee, 2000— and Member, 1995—, Litigation Sectionl; Member, Securities Litigation Subcommittee, Business and Corporate Litigation Committee, Business Law Section, 2000—); Charles Fahy American Inn of Court (Barrister, 2000-2001). ***REPORTED CASES:*** Mobile Med Support Servs. v. United States, 2000-2 U.S. Tax Cas. (CCH) ¶50,775 (D. Conn. 2000); JB Oxford Holdings, Inc. v. Net Trade, Inc., 76 F. Supp. 2d 1363 (S.D. Fla. 1999) (brief only); Elieff v. United States, 1999 U.S. Dist. LEXIS 12205 (N.D.N.Y. 1999); Rosano v. United States, 67 F. Supp. 2d 113 (E.D.N.Y. 1999); Warshay v. United States, 83 A.F.T.R.2d (RIA) 1675 (E.D.N.Y. 1999); United States v. Alfano, 34 F. Supp. 2d 827 (E.D.N.Y. 1999); McCorkill v. United States, 32 F. Supp. 2d 46 (D. Conn. 1999); Dubay v. Scott, 98-2 U.S. Tax Cas. (CCH) ¶P50,810, 82 A.F.T.R.2d (RIA) 6770 (D. Conn. 1998); Bellovin v. United States, 1998 U.S. Dist. LEXIS 5918 (E.D.N.Y. 1998); United States v. Bednarcyk, 80 A.F.T.R.2d (RIA) 8352 (W.D.N.Y. 1997); Bellovin v. United States, 983 F. Supp. 344 (E.D.N.Y. 1997); United States v. Nirelli, 97-2 U.S. Tax Cas. (CCH) ¶50,751, 80 A.F.T.R.2d (RIA) 6856 (W.D.N.Y. 1997); Ertman v. United States, 972 F. Supp. 706 (D. Conn. 1997); Andrew v. Department of Treasury, IRS, 1997 U.S. Dist. LEXIS 11462 (E.D.N.Y. 1997); Elpi v. United States, 968 F. Supp. 54 (D. Conn. 1997); Aguilar v. United States, 79 A.F.T.R.2d (RIA) 2557 (D. Conn. 1997); Dubay v. IRS, 79 A.F.T.R.2d (RIA) 1238 (D. Conn. 1997); Leining v. United States, 97-1 U.S. Tax Cas. (CCH) ¶50,254, 79 A.F.T.R.2d (RIA) 831, Unemployment Ins. Rep. (CCH) P15,684B (D. Conn. 1996); Robinson-Adams v. IRS, 96-2 U.S. Tax Cas. (CCH) ¶50,425, 78 A.F.T.R.2d (RIA) 5760 (E.D.N.Y. 1996); Chandon v. United States, 77 A.F.T.R.2d (RIA) 2186 (D. Conn. 1996); United States v. Nirelli, 77 A.F.T.R.2d (RIA) 850 (W.D.N.Y. 1996); Pomper v. United States, 1995 U.S. Dist. LEXIS 10803 (D.N.H. 1995); SEC v. Parkersburg Wirelss Ltd. Liab. Co., 156 F.R.D. 529, 30 Fed. R. Serv. 3d (Callaghan) 91, Fed. Sec. L. Rep. (CCH) P98,383, (D.D.C. 1994); Cook v. IRS (In re Cook), 230 B.R. 475 (Bankr. D. Conn. 1999). ***PRACTICE AREAS:*** Commercial Litigation; Securities Litigation; Securities Arbitration; SEC Enforcement; Tax Litigation; Tax Controversies. ***Email:*** pberkowitz@wcsr.com

P. TERRENCE GAFFNEY, born Evanston, Illinois, June 29, 1958; admitted to bar, 1991, Ohio; 1996, Maryland and District of Columbia. *Education:* John Carroll University (B.A., 1984); Cleveland State University (J.D., 1989). Author: "Medical Waste Disposal," Environment, Cleveland, May, 1999; "The United States Supreme Court Rules on the Issue of Whether Beneficiaries of a Group Health Plan can File a Claim under RICO Against the Insurer," The Health Lawyer: ABA Health Law Section, April, 1999, with David Finucane. *Member:* Defense Research Institute. ***Email:*** tgaffney@wcsr.com

KEVIN D. JONES, born New Bern, North Carolina, March 31, 1962; admitted to bar, 1989, Pennsylvania (Not admitted in District of Columbia). *Education:* University of North Carolina at Chapel Hill (B.A., Political Science, 1984); University of Michigan Law School (J.D., 1987). Order of the Grail; Order of the Old Well. Recipient: Ernest L. Mackie Award; Ferebee Taylor Award. Legislative Assistant, Senator Lloyd M. Bentsen, Jr., 1991-1993. Member, Federal Task Force on Assistance to Families in Aviation Disasters. Board

(This Listing Continued)

of Directors, University of North Carolina General Alumni Association. Board of Directors, Video Action Fund. *Member:* American Bar Association (Member: Public Utility, Communications and Transportation Law Section; Communications Law Forum Committee, Entertainment and Sports Industries Forum Committee). ***PRACTICE AREAS:*** Public Policy; Legislation; Aviation Law; Surface Transportation Law; Communications Law. ***Email:*** kejones@wcsr.com

LEGAL SUPPORT PERSONNEL

DONNA M. ERAT. *Education:* The American University. Certificate of Accommodation from U.S. Department of Transportation, 1999. Executive Producer fo Public Awareness Video on Flood Hazard Mitigation that won honorable mention in Communicator Awards. FEMA's Meritorious Service Award. Author: The 1993 and 1995 Midwest Floods: Hazard Mitigation Through Property Acquisition and Relocation (FEMA, 1995). (Associate Director of Federal Government Relations). ***Email:*** derat@wcsr.com

DEBRA M. BRYANT. *Education:* Meredith College (B.A., Psychology and Political Studies, 1978); North Carolina State University (M.P.A., 1980). Distinguished Service Award, North Carolina Democratic Club of Washington, D.C., July 1999; American Association of Women Emergency Physicians, Meritorious Service Award, October 1993. Tar Heel Circle, 1986—, Chair, 1994-1999; Women in Government Relations, 1985—; Health, State Affairs, PACs & Politics, and Grassroots Task Force, 1988-1998; Washington Area State Relations Group, 1988-1990, Board of Directors, 1989-1990; North Carolina Society of Washington, D.C., 1983—, President, 1988-1990, Board of Governors, 1985-1987, 1995—; North Carolina Democratic Club of Washington, D.C., 1983—, President, 1985-1986. (Director of Federal Government Relations). ***Email:*** debryant@wcsr.com

(For Biographical Data of other Personnel, see Professional Biographies at Charlotte, Raleigh, Research Triangle Park, Winston-Salem, North Carolina, Atlanta, Georgia, Greenville, South Carolina and McLean, Virginia)

WOOD, DAWSON & HELLMAN

WASHINGTON, D.C.

(See Hawkins, Delafield & Wood, New York, New York)

WOOD, MAINES & BROWN

CHARTERED

1827 JEFFERSON PLACE, N.W.
WASHINGTON, D.C. 20036
Telephone: 202-293-5333
Fax: 202-293-9811
Email: wmb@wmblaw.org

Telecommunications Law emphasizing FCC Issues.

BARRY D. WOOD, born Richland, Washington, April 1, 1948; admitted to bar, 1977, Washington; 1980, District of Columbia; 1987, U.S. Supreme Court. *Education:* Brigham Young University (B.S., magna cum laude, 1972; J.D., cum laude, 1976). Attorney, Federal Communications Commission, 1977-1979. *Member:* The District of Columbia Bar; Federal Communications Bar Association. ***LANGUAGES:*** French. ***PRACTICE AREAS:*** Contracts; Communications Law. ***Email:*** bwood@wmblaw.org

RONALD D. MAINES, born Binghamton, New York, May 2, 1956; admitted to bar, 1984, District of Columbia; 1985, U.S. Court of Appeals for the District of Columbia Circuit; 1989, U.S. Supreme Court; 1995, U.S. Court of Appeals, Fifth Circuit; 1998, U.S. Court of Appeals, Fourth and Tenth Circuits. *Education:* Davidson College (B.A., 1978); University of Notre Dame (M.A., 1980); Wake Forest University (J.D., 1983). Director, Institute for Supreme Court Studies. Adjunct Professor of Philosophy, Georgetown University, Constitutional Litigation. (Also Member, Maines & Loeb). ***Email:*** rmaines@wmblaw.org

PAUL H. BROWN, born Seattle, Washington, July 11, 1948; admitted to bar, 1974, Utah; 1979, District of Columbia; 1985, Michigan. *Education:* University of Utah (B.S., 1972; J.D., 1974). Attorney, Federal Trade Commission, 1974-1977. Consultant, U.S. Department of Energy, 1989-1997. *Member:* District of Columbia Bar; Federal Communication Bar Association. ***PRACTICE AREAS:*** Communications Law; Environmental Law. ***Email:*** pbrown@wmblaw.org

STUART W. NOLAN, JR., born Altoona, Pennsylvania, December 25, 1968; admitted to bar, 1999, Virginia and U.S. Court of Appeals, Fourth Circuit (Not admitted in District of Columbia). *Education:* American University (B.A., 1992); Catholic University of America (J.D., with Certificates of Law & Public Policy Program and Institute for Communications Law Studies, 1998). Research Associate, 1992-1994, Visiting Fellow, 1995, Capital Research Center. *Member:* Virginia State Bar; District of Columbia Bar; Federal Communications Bar

(This Listing Continued)

Association. ***PRACTICE AREAS:*** Communications Law. ***Email:*** snolan@wmblaw.org

WOODLEY, GENSER & McGILLIVARY

Established in 1946

SUITE 400, 1125 15TH STREET, N.W.
WASHINGTON, D.C. 20005
Telephone: 202-833-8855
Fax: 202-452-1090
Email: info@wgm.laborlaw.com
URL: http://www.wgmlaborlaw.com

Labor and Administrative Law. Practice before all Federal Courts, Departments and Agencies.

MEMBERS OF FIRM

THOMAS A. WOODLEY, born San Francisco, California, March 16, 1947; admitted to bar, 1972, California; 1973, District of Columbia and U.S. District Court for the District of Columbia; 1977, U.S. Supreme Court. *Education:* Gonzaga University (A.B., magna cum laude, 1969); Georgetown University (J.D., 1972). Member, Executive Editorial Board, Georgetown Law Journal, 1971-1972. Author: "Emergency Labor Disputes and The Public Interest: The Proposals For Legislative Reform," 17 St. Louis Law Journal 47, 1972; "Landlord's Duty to Protect Tenants From Criminal Acts of Third Parties: The View From 1500 Massachusetts Avenue," 59 Georgetown Law Journal 1153, 1971. Law Clerk to The Hon. Oliver Gasch, U.S., District Court for the District of Columbia, 1972-1973. Trial Attorney, National Labor Relations Board, Appellate Court Branch, 1974-1976. *Member:* The District of Columbia Bar; Bar Association of the District of Columbia; American Bar Association. [1st Lt., U.S. Army Infantry, 1973-1974]. ***PRACTICE AREAS:*** Public Sector Labor Relations Law; Railway Labor Act Law; Fair Labor Standards Law; Constitutional Law; Employment Discrimination Law.

ERICK J. GENSER, born Providence, Rhode Island, August 8, 1953; admitted to bar, 1979, Illinois; 1982, District of Columbia and U.S. Supreme Court; 1983, U.S. District Court for the District of Columbia. *Education:* American University (B.S.B.A., cum laude, 1975); Boston University (J.D., 1979). Phi Kappa Phi.; Omicron Delta Kappa; Pi Sigma Alpha. Attorney, Federal Labor Relations Authority, Washington Regional Office, 1979-1982. *Member:* The District of Columbia Bar. ***PRACTICE AREAS:*** Collective Bargaining; Employment Discrimination Law; Public Sector Labor Relations Law; Railway Labor Act Law; Employee Benefit Plans Law.

GREGORY K. McGILLIVARY, born Eugene, Oregon, April 4, 1957; admitted to bar, 1983, Washington; 1986, Virginia; 1987, District of Columbia. *Education:* Northwestern University (B.A., 1979); University of Oregon (J.D., 1983). Articles Editor, University of Oregon Law Review, 1982-1983. Attorney, Federal Labor Relations Authority, Washington Regional Office, 1983-1985. Union Chair, Committee of Federal Labor Standards of Legislation. *Member:* The District of Columbia Bar; American Bar Association; The Association of Trial Lawyers of America. ***PRACTICE AREAS:*** Public Sector Labor Relations Law; Employment Discrimination Law; Fair Labor Standards Law.

DOUGLAS L. STEELE, born Auburn, New York, May 4, 1964; admitted to bar, 1990, New York and U.S. District Court, Northern and Western Districts of New York; 1993, U.S. Court of Appeals, Second Circuit; 1994, Virginia and U.S. Court of Federal Claims; 1995, District of Columbia; 1999, U.S. Court of Appeals, Eighth and Eleventh Circuits. *Education:* Syracuse University (B.S., cum laude, 1986; J.D., summa cum laude, 1989). Order of the Coif. Member, Justinian Society. Recipient, Scribes Award. National Appellate Team. Lead Articles Editor, Syracuse Law Review, 1988-1989. Author: "Covert Action and the War Powers Resolution: Preserving the Constitutional Balance," Syracuse Law Review, Vol. 39, 1988; "The Current State of Affirmative Action," Labor and Employment Law Section Newsletter, Vol. 15, No. 3 (NYS Bar Association, 1990). *Member:* New York State (Member, Labor and Employment Law Section) and American (Member: Sections on: Labor and Employment Law; Litigation; Individual Rights and Responsibilities; Young Lawyers Division) Bar Associations. ***PRACTICE AREAS:*** Labor and Employment Law; Fair Labor Standards Law.

KURT T. RUMSFELD, born Dallas, Texas, February 25, 1963; admitted to bar, 1993, Maryland; 1996, District of Columbia and U.S. Supreme Court; U.S. Court of Appeals, Third and Eighth Circuits; U.S. Court of Appeals for the Federal Circuit; U.S. District Court for the District of Columbia; U.S. District Court for the District of Maryland. *Education:* Williams College (B.A., 1985); Northeastern University Law School (J.D., 1993); Georgetown University Law Center (LL.M., with distinction, Labor and Employment Law, 2000). Law Clerk, District of Columbia Court of Appeals, 1993-1994. Attorney-Adviser, U.S. Department of Labor, Washington, D.C., 1995-1996. *Member:* Maryland State (Member, Labor and Employment Law Section) and American Bar Associations; The District of Columbia Bar; The Association of Trial Lawyers of

(This Listing Continued)

WOODLEY, GENSER & McGILLIVARY, Washington—Continued

America; National Employment Lawyers Association. ***PRACTICE AREAS:*** Labor and Employment Law; Fair Labor Standards Law; Public Sector Labor Relations Law.

MOLLY ANN ELKIN, born St. Louis, Missouri, April 27, 1968; admitted to bar, 1993, Maryland; 1996, District of Columbia; 1997, Virginia. *Education:* University of Wisconsin at Madison (B.A., 1990); George Washington University (J.D., with honors, 1993). Phi Beta Kappa. Assistant Counsel, National Treasury Employees Union, 1993-1996. *Member:* Maryland State and American Bar Associations. ***PRACTICE AREAS:*** Public Sector Labor Relations; Employment Discrimination; Fair Labor Standards Law.

MANAR SWEILLAM MORALES, born Albany, New York, March 22, 1971; admitted to bar, 1997, Maryland; 1999, District of Columbia, U.S. Court of Federal Claims and U.S. District Court, District of Maryland. *Education:* Cornell University, School of Industrial Labor Relations (B.S., 1993); Catholic University, Columbus school of Law (J.D., 1997). *Member:* Maryland State and American Bar Associations; District of Columbia Bar. ***LANGUAGES:*** Arabic. ***PRACTICE AREAS:*** Labor and Employment Law; Fair Labor Standards Law; Public Sector Labor Relations.

DENISE M. DUNKIN, born Manhasset, New York, July 16, 1971; admitted to bar, 1997, New York; 1999, District of Columbia. *Education:* State University of New York at Binghamton (B.A., 1993); Fordham University (J.D., 1996); Georgetown University (LL.M., Labor and Employment Law, 2000). Articles and Notes Editor, Fordham Urban Law Journal, 1995-1996. ***PRACTICE AREAS:*** Labor and Employment Law; Fair Labor Standards Law; Public Sector Labor Relations Law. ***Email:*** denise.dunkin@mulholland-hickey.com

GENERAL COUNSEL FOR: International Association of Fire Fighters; International Brotherhood of Firemen & Oilers and Fund Counsel for its National Pension, Staff Union Pension and Health and Welfare Plans.
REPRESENTATIVE CLIENTS: American Federation of Government Employees; National Border Patrol Council; Fire Fighter Associations.

DANIEL J. WRIGHT

WASHINGTON, D.C.

(See Rockville, Maryland)

Banking, Capital Markets. Litigation, General Civil and Trial Practice in all Courts.

WRIGHT, ROBINSON, OSTHIMER & TATUM

SUITE 920
5335 WISCONSIN AVENUE, N.W.
WASHINGTON, D.C. 20015
Telephone: 202-244-4668
Telefax: 202-244-5135
URL: http://www.wrightrobinson.com

Richmond, Virginia Office: Suite 400, 411 East Franklin Street. Telephone: 804-783-1100.
Los Angeles, California Office: Suite 1800, 888 South Figueroa Street. Telephone: 213-488-0503. Telex: 213-624-3755.
San Francisco, California Office: Suite 1800, 44 Montgomery Street. Telephone: 415-391-7111.

General Civil and Trial Practice. Products Liability, Construction, Corporate, Insurance and Environmental Law.

PRINCIPALS

WILLIAM H. ROBINSON, JR., born Abingdon, Virginia, December 21, 1943; admitted to bar, 1974, Virginia (Not admitted in District of Columbia). *Education:* Vanderbilt University (B.A., 1966; J.D., 1974); University of Colorado (M.A., 1967). Order of the Coif. Student Writing Editor, Vanderbilt Law Review, 1973-1974. *Member:* Richmond, Virginia and American Bar Associations; Virginia State Bar; Defense Research and Trial Lawyers Association; Virginia Association of Defense Attorneys. (Also at Richmond, Virginia Office). ***PRACTICE AREAS:*** Trials; Product Liability Defense Litigation; Complex and Multi-District Defense Litigation. ***Email:*** wrobinson@wrightrobinson.com

THOMAS S. SCHAUFELBERGER, born Quantico, Virginia, January 28, 1955; admitted to bar, 1981, Virginia; 1983, District of Columbia. *Education:* Virginia Polytechnic Institute and State University (B.S., 1977); Georgetown University Law Center (J.D., 1981). *Member:* Virginia and American Bar Associations; District of Columbia Bar; Virginia State Bar. ***PRACTICE AREAS:*** Insurance Coverage; Commercial and Environmental Litigation. ***Email:*** tschauf@wrightrobinson.com

(This Listing Continued)

PAUL A. FITZSIMMONS, born Royal Oak, Michigan, October 3, 1958; admitted to bar, 1985, Illinois; 1986, U.S. District Court, Northern District of Illinois; 1994, District of Columbia. *Education:* University of Michigan (A.B., with distinction, 1980; J.D., cum laude, 1984); The Queens University of Belfast, Belfast, Northern Ireland. *Member:* Chicago Bar Association. ***PRACTICE AREAS:*** Insurance Coverage Litigation; Insurance Defense Litigation; Commercial Litigation; Libel Litigation. ***Email:*** pfitzsim@wrightrobinson.com

TERRENCE M.R. ZIC, born Brooklyn, New York, April 24, 1961; admitted to bar, 1989, Maryland; 1991, U.S. District Court, District of Maryland; 1992, District of Columbia. *Education:* Loyola College in Maryland (B.A., 1983); Georgetown University Law Center (J.D., 1989). Member, Georgetown Journal of Legal Ethics, 1987-1988. Law Clerk to Chief Judge Robert C. Murphy, Court of Appeals of Maryland, 1989-1990. *Member:* District of Columbia Bar; Maryland State and American Bar Associations. ***PRACTICE AREAS:*** Product Liability Defense; General Civil Litigation. ***Email:*** tzic@wrightrobinson.com

ASSOCIATES

DANIEL G. KRASNEGOR, born Washington, D.C., March 17, 1969; admitted to bar, 1993, Georgia; 1995, District of Columbia. *Education:* Washington University (A.B., 1990); Emory University (J.D., 1993). *Member:* Federal Bar Association; National Organization of Veterans Advocates. ***REPORTED CASES:*** Dunn v. West 11 Vet. App 462 (1998); Stegall v. West 11 Vet. App 268 (1998). ***PRACTICE AREAS:*** Veteran's Benefits; Appellate Practice; Litigation; Federal Tort Claims. ***Email:*** dkrasnegor@wrightrobinson.com

KATHLEEN S. PIRRI, born Sutton, West Virginia, May 9, 1958; admitted to bar, 1986, District of Columbia; 1996, Maryland. *Education:* Marshall University (B.S., 1982); University of Toledo (J.D., 1985). Member, 1984 and Coordinator, 1985, National Mock Trial Team. Member, National Order of the Barristers. *Member:* Bar Association of the District of Columbia. ***PRACTICE AREAS:*** Commercial Litigation; Employment Litigation. ***Email:*** kpirri@wrightrobinson.com

CHRISTOPHER A. GLASER, born Sylva, North Carolina, February 28, 1973; admitted to bar, 1998, Maryland; 1999, Virginia and District of Columbia. *Education:* University of Maryland (B.A., 1995); Pace University (J.D., 1998). Member, Pace University Environmental Law Review. *Member:* Virginia State Bar; The District of Columbia Bar. ***PRACTICE AREAS:*** Civil Litigation. ***Email:*** cglaser@wrightrobinson.com

JEREMY C. CHOU, born Seoul, Korea, February 13, 1970; admitted to bar, 1997, New York and Idaho; 2001, District of Columbia. *Education:* Baylor University (B.A., 1992); American University (J.D., 1996). *Member:* Idaho State Bar; The District of Columbia Bar; American Bar Association. ***LANGUAGES:*** Chinese. ***PRACTICE AREAS:*** Litigation; Employment. ***Email:*** jchou@wrightrobinson.com

(For Complete Biographical Data on Personnel at Los Angeles, California, San Francisco, California and Richmond, Virginia see Professional Biographies at those locations)

WRIGHT & TALISMAN, P.C.

Established in 1948

1200 G STREET, N.W., SUITE 600
WASHINGTON, D.C. 20005-3802
Telephone: 202-393-1200
Fax: 202-393-1240
Email: mail@wrightlaw.com
URL: http://www.wrightlaw.com

Practice before Federal and State Regulatory Agencies, Departments, Legislatures and Courts. Energy, Communications, Environmental, Construction, Project Finance, International, Labor, Corporate and Insurance Law, Commercial Litigation and Government Relations.

FIRM PROFILE: Since the late 1940's, Wright & Talisman has been a leader in the practice of law in the field of regulated industries--counseling and representing clients in complex administrative trials, rulemakings, legislative proceedings, negotiations, project financings and related court matters. As the relationship between government and commercial enterprise has changed over the years, so too has the Firm's range of legal services grown to meet the changing needs of its clients. With a broad range of clients spread nationally and internationally, the Firm's energy, communications, environmental, government relations, project financing and various commercial practice areas concentrate upon some of the more consequential issues affecting its clients.

HARRY S. LITTMAN (1906-1982).

DALE A. WRIGHT (1927-1989).

GREGORY GRADY, born Takoma Park, Maryland, October 10, 1945; admitted to bar, 1973, District of Columbia and U.S. Court of Appeals, District

(This Listing Continued)

of Columbia Circuit; 1975, U.S. Court of Appeals, Fourth Circuit; 1976, U.S. Supreme Court; 1979, U.S. Court of Appeals, Tenth and Fifth Circuits; 1981, U.S. Court of Appeals, Eleventh Circuit; 1982, U.S. Court of Appeals, Sixth Circuit; 1988, U.S. District Court for the District of Columbia. *Education:* University of Virginia (B.A., 1969); Tulane University (J.D., 1972). Attorney, Federal Power Commission, 1973-1974. *Member:* The District of Columbia Bar; Energy Bar Association. ***PRACTICE AREAS:*** Energy Regulation. ***Email:*** grady@wrightlaw.com

JAMES T. McMANUS, born Beaumont, Texas, December 7, 1947; admitted to bar, 1975, District of Columbia; 1981, U.S. Court of Appeals, Fifth and Eleventh Circuits; 1982, U.S. Supreme Court and U.S. Court of Appeals, Sixth Circuit; 1984, U.S. Court of Appeals, Ninth and District of Columbia Circuits; 1993, U.S. Court of Appeals, Tenth Circuit; 2000, U.S. District Court, District of Columbia. *Education:* University of Southwestern Louisiana (B.S.E.E., 1971); George Washington University (J.D., with honors, 1975). Tau Beta Pi; Eta Kappa Nu. Contributing Author, "Energy Law and Transactions," Matthew Bender & Co., 1995. Staff Witness and Engineer, Federal Power Commission, 1971-1975. Attorney, Federal Power Commission, 1975-1977. Assistant Corporation Counsel, District of Columbia, 1977-1978. *Member:* The District of Columbia Bar; Energy and American (Law Practice Management, Public Utility and Natural Resources Sections) Bar Associations. ***PRACTICE AREAS:*** Energy; Regulatory Law. ***Email:*** mcmanus@wrightlaw.com

ALAN J. STATMAN, born Glen Ridge, New Jersey, June 30, 1953; admitted to bar, 1978, Florida; 1979, U.S. District Court, District of Columbia and U.S. Court of Appeals, District of Columbia Circuit; 1980, District of Columbia and U.S. District Court, Southern District of Florida; 1981, U.S. Court of Appeals, Fifth and Tenth Circuits; 1983, U.S. Supreme Court. *Education:* University of Tennessee; Oregon State University (B.S., with high honors, 1975); Syracuse University (J.D., 1978). Phi Kappa Phi; Phi Delta Phi. Notes Editor, Syracuse Law Review, 1977-1978. Law Clerk to: C. Clyde Atkins, Chief U.S. District Judge, 1978-1979 and Eugene P. Spellman, U.S. District Judge, 1979-1980, U.S. District Court, Southern District of Florida. *Member:* The District of Columbia Bar; The Florida Bar; Energy and American (Antitrust, Natural Resources, Public Utility Sections) Bar Associations. ***PRACTICE AREAS:*** Energy. ***Email:*** statman@wrightlaw.com

DOUGLAS O. WAIKART, born Washington, D.C., October 25, 1953; admitted to bar, 1978, District of Columbia; 1979, U.S. Court of Appeals, District of Columbia and Fifth Circuits and U.S. District Court, District of Columbia; 1981, U.S. Court of Appeals, Eleventh Circuit; 1983, U.S. Supreme Court; 1985, U.S. Court of Appeals, Tenth Circuit. *Education:* University of Maryland (B.A., with high honors, 1975); George Washington University (J.D., with honors, 1978). Phi Kappa Phi; Omicron Delta Kappa. *Member:* The District of Columbia Bar; Energy Bar Association (Chair, Environment Committee, 1997-1998). ***PRACTICE AREAS:*** Energy. ***Email:*** waikart@wrightlaw.com

MICHAEL E. SMALL, born Washington, D.C., June 24, 1954; admitted to bar, 1979, District of Columbia; 1980, U.S. Court of Appeals, District of Columbia Circuit; 1984, U.S. Court of Appeals, Ninth Circuit; 1985, U.S. Court of Appeals, Fifth and Tenth Circuits and U.S. Supreme Court; 1988, U.S. Court of Appeals, Third, Sixth and Seventh Circuits. *Education:* University of Virginia (B.S. in Nuclear Engineering, 1976); Antioch University (J.D., 1979). Author: "A Guide to FERC Regulation and Ratemaking of Electric Utilities and other Power Suppliers," Edison Electric Institute, 1994; "Guide to Electric Utility Ratemaking at the Federal Energy Regulatory Commission," Atlantic Information Services, Inc., 1989; "Federal Pricing at Wellhead - Disputes Remain," Natural Gas Monthly, October 1989; "FERC Electric Rate Primer," 5 Energy Law Journal 1, 1984; "Indian Protection Under the National Environmental Policy Act," 5 American Indian Journal 6, 1979. Attorney, Electric Rate Section, 1979-1981, Special Assistant for Gas Pipeline and Electric Rates to Deputy General Counsel for Litigation, 1982-1984 and Attorney, Solicitor's Office, 1984-1985, Federal Energy Regulatory Commission. *Member:* The District of Columbia Bar; Energy and American (Member, Sections on: Administrative Law; Antitrust; Natural Resources; Public Utility) Bar Associations. ***PRACTICE AREAS:*** Energy. ***Email:*** small@wrightlaw.com

MICHAEL J. THOMPSON, born Canton, Ohio, September 9, 1955; admitted to bar, 1981, District of Columbia; 1983, Virginia and U.S. Court of Appeals, Fourth Circuit; 1984, U.S. Court of Appeals, Tenth and Federal Circuits; 1985, U.S. Supreme Court and U.S. Court of Appeals, District of Columbia Circuit; 1990, U.S. Court of Appeals, Eleventh Circuit; 1992, U.S. Court of Appeals, Fifth Circuit. *Education:* The Ohio State University (B.S.B.A., cum laude, 1977); George Washington University (J.D., with honors, 1981). Phi Kappa Phi; Beta Gamma Sigma. Author: "NUG Prospects: Dream or Nightmare?" Electricity Journal, April 1996. Law Clerk and Attorney, Chemical Control Division, Office of Toxic Substances, U.S. Environmental Protection Agency, 1980-1981. Member, California Conference of Public Utility Counsel. *Member:* The District of Columbia Bar; Virginia State Bar; Energy and American (Member, Sections on: Natural Resources; Public Utility; Antitrust; Litigation) Bar Associations. ***PRACTICE AREAS:*** Energy Regulation; Communications; Common Carrier Law. ***Email:*** thompson@wrightlaw.com

(This Listing Continued)

JOSEPH S. KOURY, born Syracuse, New York, March 24, 1953; admitted to bar, 1981, New York and District of Columbia; 2000, U.S. District Court, District of Columbia. *Education:* State University of New York at Albany (B.A., 1975); Albany Law School of Union University (J.D., 1980); George Washington University (LL.M., with highest honors, 1985). Phi Beta Kappa; Psi Chi. Editor, Albany Law Review, 1980. Attorney, Federal Energy Regulatory Commission, 1980-1984. *Member:* The District of Columbia Bar; Energy Bar Association. ***PRACTICE AREAS:*** Energy. ***Email:*** koury@wrightlaw.com

JEFFREY G. DiSCIULLO, born Brooklyn, New York, August 10, 1954; admitted to bar, 1984, District of Columbia; U.S. Court of Appeals, District of Columbia Circuit and U.S. Court of Appeals, Eleventh Circuit. *Education:* University of Florida (B.A., 1976); Catholic University (J.D., 1984). Recipient, American Jurisprudence Awards in Contracts, 1981 and Creditors Rights, 1983. *Member:* The District of Columbia Bar; Energy Bar Association. ***PRACTICE AREAS:*** Energy. ***Email:*** disciullo@wrightlaw.com

ARNOLD B. PODGORSKY, born Glen Cove, New York, February 8, 1951; admitted to bar, 1975, District of Columbia; 1977, U.S. Court of Appeals, Seventh and Eighth Circuits; 1978, U.S. Court of Appeals, Second, Fourth and Ninth Circuits; 1979, U.S. Supreme Court; 1980, U.S. Court of Appeals, Fifth Circuit and U.S. District Court for the District of Columbia; 1981, U.S. Court of International Trade; 1984, U.S. Court of Appeals for the District of Columbia Circuit; 1985, U.S. Court of Federal Claims. *Education:* Alfred University (B.A., with honors, 1972); Syracuse University (J.D., 1975). Pi Gamma Mu. Justinian Society. Associate Editor, Syracuse Law Review. Author, Comment, "Recent Developments in Labor Law Successorship," 26 Syracuse Law Review 798 (1975). Attorney, National Labor Relations Board, Advice Branch, 1975-1976, Appellate Court Branch, 1977-1978. *Member:* The District of Columbia Bar; Bar Association of the District of Columbia; American Bar Association (Member, Litigation Section). ***PRACTICE AREAS:*** Litigation; Energy Contracts. ***Email:*** podgorsky@wrightlaw.com

BARRY S. SPECTOR, born New Rochelle, New York, January 2, 1951; admitted to bar, 1976, Virginia; 1979, District of Columbia and U.S. Court of Appeals for the District of Columbia Circuit; 1981, U.S. District Court for the District of Columbia; 1983, U.S. Supreme Court; 1985, U.S. Court of Appeals, Fourth Circuit; 1992, U.S. Court of Appeals, Fifth Circuit. *Education:* University of Rochester (B.A., with distinction, 1973); George Washington University (J.D., with high honors, 1976). Order of the Coif. *Member:* The District of Columbia Bar; Virginia State Bar; Energy and American Bar Associations. ***PRACTICE AREAS:*** Energy; Electric Utilities. ***Email:*** spector@wrightlaw.com

ROBERT H. LAMB, born Richmond, Virginia, March 5, 1943; admitted to bar, 1974, Mississippi; 1975, Virginia (Not admitted in District of Columbia). *Education:* University of Virginia (B.A., 1967); University of Mississippi (J.D., 1974). Chief Legislative Assistant, U.S. Representative D.E. Satterfield, III, 1974-1976. Professional Staff Member, U.S. House of Representatives Committee on Energy and Commerce, 1976-1981. Washington Representative, American Petroleum Institute, 1981-1986. [1st Lt, USMCR, 1st BN., 1st Marines, 1st MARDIV, Vietnam, 1968-1970]. ***PRACTICE AREAS:*** Legislative Lobbying; Regulated Industries. ***Email:*** lamb@wrightlaw.com

PAUL M. FLYNN, born St. Louis, Missouri, March 16, 1960; admitted to bar, 1985, Maryland; 1986, District of Columbia; 1990, U.S. Court of Appeals, Tenth and District of Columbia Circuits. *Education:* St. Louis University (B.A., magna cum laude, 1982); George Washington University (J.D., 1985). Contributing Author, "Regulation of the Gas Industry," Matthew Bender & Co., 1991. *Member:* The District of Columbia Bar; Maryland State, Energy (Chair, Committee on Natural Gas Regulation, 1996-1997) and American Bar Associations. ***PRACTICE AREAS:*** Energy Regulation; Hydroelectricity Licensing. ***Email:*** flynn@wrightlaw.com

SCOTT M. DuBOFF, born Chicago, Illinois, June 19, 1947; admitted to bar, 1973, Wisconsin; 1975, District of Columbia. *Education:* University of Wisconsin (B.A., 1969; J.D., cum laude, 1973). Author: "U.S. EPA's New Source Performance Standards and Emissions Guidelines for Municipal Waste Combustion Facilities--Revised Regulations Become Final--'Finally'," Air & Waste Management Association, June 1996; "The 1990 Amendments and Section 304: The Specter of Increased Citizen Suit Enforcement," Natural Resources & Environment, American Bar Association, November 1992; "EPA's 'Ben' Model: Challenging Excessive Penalty Calculations," Toxics Law Reporter (BNA), May 1992; "Difficult Hurdles Ahead for Municipal Solid Waste Management--An Analysis of Carbone," The Municipal Lawyer, August 1994. Contributing Author: "Regulation of the Gas Industry," Matthew Bender & Co., 1991. Attorney: Federal Power Commission, Office of the General Counsel, 1973-1975; Office of the Solicitor, 1975-1977. *Member:* The District of Columbia Bar (Member, Environment, Energy and Natural Resources Division, 1983—); American Bar Association (Member, Sections on: Natural Resources; Energy; Environmental Law). ***PRACTICE AREAS:*** Environmental Regulation; Appellate Practice. ***Email:*** duboff@wrightlaw.com

CARRIE L. BUMGARNER, born West Palm Beach, Florida, March 6, 1959; admitted to bar, 1984, Missouri; 1985, Illinois; 1990, District of Colum-

(This Listing Continued)

WRIGHT & TALISMAN, P.C., Washington—Continued

bia; 1994, U.S. District Court, District of Columbia; 1992, U.S. Court of Appeals, Fifth Circuit. *Education:* Washington University (A.B., 1981); St. Louis University (J.D., 1984). Staff Member, Public Law Review, 1983-1984. Law Clerk, Missouri Court of Appeals, St. Louis, Missouri, 1984-1986. Attorney/Advisor, General Services Administration, Washington, D.C., 1988-1989. ***PRACTICE AREAS:*** Litigation; Energy. ***Email:*** bumgarner@wrightlaw.com

WENDY N. REED, born Richmond, Virginia, February 18, 1967; admitted to bar, 1992, Virginia and U.S. Court of Appeals, Fourth Circuit (Not admitted in District of Columbia). *Education:* University of Virginia (B.A., with distinction, 1989); Marshall-Wythe School of Law, College of William & Mary (J.D., 1992). Phi Beta Kappa. Editor-in-Chief, William & Mary Journal of Environmental Law. *Member:* Energy and American Bar Associations. ***PRACTICE AREAS:*** Energy. ***Email:*** reed@wrightlaw.com

---

DAVID S. BERMAN, born Stamford, Connecticut, November 3, 1959; admitted to bar, 1993, Maryland; 1994, District of Columbia and U.S. Court of Appeals, District of Columbia and Fifth Circuits. *Education:* Washington University (B.A., 1982); Catholic University of America (J.D., 1993). Editorial Assistant, Catholic University Law Review, 1992-1993. *Member:* Energy Bar Association. ***PRACTICE AREAS:*** Energy. ***Email:*** berman@wrightlaw.com

DEBORAH C. BRENTANI, born São Paulo, Brazil, March 1, 1972; admitted to bar, 1998, Massachusetts; 2001, District of Columbia. *Education:* University of Pennsylvania (B.A., 1994); Cornell Law School (J.D., 1998). *Member:* American Bar Association. ***PRACTICE AREAS:*** Energy. ***Email:*** brentani@wrightlaw.com

OF COUNSEL

HAROLD L. TALISMAN, born Akron, Ohio, May 11, 1928; admitted to bar, 1953, Ohio; 1957, U.S. District Court, District of Columbia and U.S. Court of Appeals, District of Columbia, Fifth, Seventh, Tenth and Eleventh Circuits; 1961, U.S. Supreme Court. *Education:* The Ohio State University (B.S.B.A., 1950; J.D., 1953). Member, Board of Editors, Ohio State University Law Review, 1952-1953. Contributing Author, "Regulation of the Gas Industry," Matthew Bender & Co., 1991. *Member:* The District of Columbia Bar; Bar Association of the District of Columbia; Energy and American Bar Associations; American Inns of Court. ***PRACTICE AREAS:*** Energy. ***Email:*** talisman@wrightlaw.com

ROBERT H. BENNA, born New York, N.Y., October 24, 1946; admitted to bar, 1982, District of Columbia; 1983, Maryland; 1985, U.S. Court of Appeals District of Columbia Circuit; 1987, U.S., Court of Appeals, Fourth and Fifth Circuits; 1988, U.S. Court of Appeals, Sixth Circuit; 1989, U.S. Court of Appeals, Third Circuit; 1990, U.S. Supreme Court; 1993, U.S. Court of Appeals, Eleventh Circuit; 1995, North Carolina. *Education:* City College of the City University of New York (B.M.E., 1968); George Washington University (J.D., with honors, 1982). Pi Tau Sigma. Staff Witness and Engineer, Bureau of Natural Gas, Federal Power Commission, 1971-1976. Technical Assistant, Office of Administrative Law Judges, Federal Energy Regulatory Commission, 1976-1983. *Member:* The District of Columbia Bar; Maryland State, North Carolina, Energy and American (Member, Alternative Dispute Resolution Section) Bar Associations; American Society of Mechanical Engineers. ***PRACTICE AREAS:*** Alternative Dispute Resolution; Energy. ***Email:*** benna@wrightlaw.com

KENNETH S. KAUFMAN, born Perth Amboy, New Jersey, November 3, 1957; admitted to bar, 1985, Maryland; 1986, District of Columbia; 1988, U.S. District Court for the District of Columbia; 1989, U.S. Court of Appeals, Fifth and Ninth Circuits and U.S. Court of Appeals for the District of Columbia Circuit; 1993, U.S. Court of Appeals for the Federal Circuit; 1996, U.S. District Court, District of Connecticut; 1997, U.S. District Court, Southern District of Indiana; 1999, U.S. Supreme Court; 2000, U.S. Court of Appeals, Fourth Circuit. *Education:* Cornell University (A.B., with distinction, 1980); Georgetown University (J.D., 1985). Editor, American Criminal Law Review, 1984-1985. *Member:* The District of Columbia Bar (Member, Environment, Energy and Natural Resources Division); Maryland State and American Bar Associations. ***PRACTICE AREAS:*** Litigation; Environmental Law; Insurance Coverage. ***Email:*** kaufman@wrightlaw.com

PALMA R. YANNI

Established in 1990

2612 P STREET, N.W.
WASHINGTON, D.C. 20007
Telephone: 202-338-1995
Fax: 202-338-1994
URL: http://www.palma-yanni.com
Email: palma-yanni@mindspring.com
URL: http://www.lawyers.com/yannilaw

Immigration Law and International Business Matters.

PALMA R. YANNI, born Philadelphia, Pennsylvania, May 18, 1955; admitted to bar, 1979, Illinois; 1980, District of Columbia, U.S. District Court for the District of Columbia and U.S. Court of Appeals for the District of Columbia; 1983, U.S. Supreme Court; 1986, Maryland. *Education:* Mount Holyoke College (B.A., magna cum laude, 1976); Northwestern University School of Law (J.D., 1979). Editor-in-Chief, The Consular Practice Toolbox: Samples, Charts and Applications, AILA, 1994. Associate Editor: "Immigration Options for Professors and Researchers, Robert P. Deasy, Editor in Chief, AILA, 1994. Author: "Rerailing the Train: The True Meaning of 'National Interest,' " 1998-1999, *Immigration & Nationality Law Handbook* (AILA 1998); "Business Investors: E-2 Nonimmigrants and EB-5 Immigrants," 92-8 Immigration Briefings, August, 1992. Co-Author: "Exchange Visitors (J Visa Holders)," *1993-94 Immigration & Nationality Law Handbook,* with G. Endelman, ATLA, 1993. *Member:* The District of Columbia Bar; American Bar Association; American Immigration Lawyers Association (Member, Executive Committee, 1998—; Chair, Annual Conference Program, 1995); Women's Bar Association of D.C. (Co-Chair, Executive Endorsement Committee, 1986-1988); American Immigration Law Foundation (Board of Trustees, 1992-1998). ***PRACTICE AREAS:*** Immigration and Nationality Law.

YOUNG, GOLDMAN & VAN BEEK

A PROFESSIONAL CORPORATION

SUITE 800, 2000 L STREET N.W.
WASHINGTON, D.C. 20036
Telephone: 703-684-3260

Alexandria, Virginia Office: 510 King Street, Suite 416. Telephone: 703-684-3260. Facsimile: 703-548-4742.

Civil Litigation, Commercial Leasing, Commercial Loans, Telecommunications, Creditor's Rights, Bankruptcy, Real Estate Development, Business Law, Employment, Non-Profit Corporations, and Motor Sports Law.

(For Complete Biographical Data on all Personnel see Professional Biographies at Alexandria, Virginia)

YOUNG & VALKENET, L.L.C.

WASHINGTON, D.C.

(See Baltimore, Maryland)

General Civil Trial and Appellate Practice. Negligence, Commercial and Construction Litigation, Surety, Life and Health Insurance Claims, Admiralty and Maritime Law. Small Corporation and Business Law.

BARNABY W. ZALL

WASHINGTON, D.C.

(See Rockville, Maryland)

Nonprofit and Charitable Organizations, Constitutional Law, Appellate and Trial Litigation, Public Policy, Legislative Practice, Lobbying, First Amendment Law, Fourteenth Amendment Law, Public Charities, Nonprofit Tax Law.

CARL E. ZENTZ, P.A.

WASHINGTON, D.C.

(See Fort Washington, Maryland)

Real Estate Settlements, Personal Injury, Automobile Accidents.

ZEVNIK HORTON LLP

THE WARNER BUILDING
1299 PENNSYLVANIA AVENUE, N.W.
NINTH FLOOR
WASHINGTON, D.C. 20004
Telephone: 202-824-0950
Facsimile: 202-824-0955
Email: law@zevnik.com
URL: http://www.zevnik.com

Boston, Massachusetts Office: One International Place, Fourteenth Floor. Telephone: 617-790-2970. Facsimile: 617-790-2910.
San Francisco, California Office: 225 Bush Street, Seventeenth Floor. Telephone: 415-364-6300. Facsimile: 415-364-6333.
Los Angeles, California Office: 333 South Grand Avenue, Twenty First Floor. Telephone: 213-437-5200. Facsimile: 213-437-5222.
Chicago, Illinois Office: Zevnik Horton, 77 West Wacker Drive, Thirty Third Floor. Telephone: 312-977-2500. Facsimile: 312-977-2560.
London, England Office: 4 Kings Bench Walk, Temple, London EC4Y 7DL. Telephone: 207-822-8822. Facsimile: 207-822-8844.
Roseland, New Jersey: 103 Eisenhower Parkway, First Floor. Telephone: 973-618-5300. Facsimile: 973-618-5333.
Philadelphia, Pennsylvania Office: 620 Chestnut Street, Tenth Floor. Telephone: 215-440-8450. Facsimile: 215-440-8459.

Commercial Litigation, Environmental Law, Insurance Coverage, Toxic Tort Litigation, International Law, Transactions involving corporate tax, securities, media and broadcasting, broker-dealer and real estate advice and representation. Practice before State and Federal Courts and Administrative Tribunals, including the National Association of Securities Dealers, Inc., the New York Stock Exchange and the Securities Exchange Commission.

PAUL ANTON ZEVNIK, born Ashland, Wisconsin, November 2, 1950; admitted to bar, 1977, California; 1978, District of Columbia, U.S. District Court for the District of Columbia, U.S. Court of Appeals for the District of Columbia Circuit and U.S. District Court, Northern District of California; 1980, U.S. Court of Appeals, Ninth Circuit and U.S. Tax Court; 1981, U.S. Supreme Court and U.S. Claims Court; 1984, U.S. Court of Appeals for the Federal Circuit; 1985, Pennsylvania. *Education:* Harvard University (A.B., magna cum laude, 1972; A.M., 1972; J.D., cum laude, 1976). Author: "Federal Product Liability Legislation," American Bar Association, 1986; "When an Underlying Carrier Goes Broke: Recent Trends in 'Drop Down' Coverage," Coverage, ABA Committee on Insurance Coverage Litigation, Vol. 1, 1989. Faculty, Management of Mass Tort Litigation, Practising Law Institute, 1983. Fellow, Joint Center for Urban Studies, Harvard University and Massachusetts Institute of Technology, 1976. *Member:* The District of Columbia Bar; State Bar of California; Pennsylvania and Federal Communications Bar Associations. ***PRACTICE AREAS:*** Insurance Coverage; Environmental Law; Toxic Tort Litigation; Broadcasting and Media Transactions. ***Email:*** PZEVNIK@ZEVNIK.COM

MICHEL YVES HORTON, born Washington, D.C., October 22, 1951; admitted to bar, 1984, California and District of Columbia. *Education:* Virginia Commonwealth University (B.S., cum laude, 1978); College of William & Mary (J.D., 1981). Kappa Tau Alpha. Author: "Bad Faith Insurance Litigation and Insurance Broker Liability," Practising Law Institute, Vol. 231; "The Impact of Antitrust and RICO Treble Damage Theories on the Insurance Industry," ABA National Institute, 1986; "When an Underlying Carrier Goes Broke: Recent Trends in 'Drop Down' Coverage," Coverage, ABA Committee on Insurance Coverage Litigation, Vol. 1, 1989. *Member:* The District of Columbia Bar; State Bar of California. (Resident, Los Angeles, California Office). ***PRACTICE AREAS:*** Insurance Coverage; Commercial Litigation. ***Email:*** MHORTON@ZEVNIK.COM

JOHN D. SHUGRUE, born Phoenix, Arizona, August 30, 1962; admitted to bar, 1987, Illinois (Not admitted in District of Columbia). *Education:* University of Denver (B.A., Honors, 1984); University of North Carolina (J.D., Honors, 1987). Member, University of North Carolina Law Review. Articles Editor, North Carolina Journal of International Law and Commercial Regulation. Author: "Insurance Coverage Disputes," Law Journal Seminars-Press (co-author); "Illinois Environmental Insurance Coverage Law, " 11 *Env'tal Claims Journal* 113 (Winter 1999) (co-author); "Tips to Help Preserve Insurance Coverage, " The Corporate Counsellor (May and June 1999) (co-author); "Parol Evidence Myths in Insurance Coverage Litigation, " 1 *Journal Insurance Coverage* 1 (Summer 1998) (co-author); "Lloyd's Names Litigation in the United States: Is the Glass Half Empty of Half Full? " 4 *Int'l Insurance Law Review* 91 (March 1996). *Member:* American Bar Association (Past Co-Chair, Insurance Coverage Litigation Committee, Litigation Section; Federal Practice Task Force, Litigation Section). (Resident, Chicago, Illinois Office). ***PRACTICE AREAS:*** Insurance Coverage; Commercial Litigation. ***Email:*** JSHUGRUE@ZEVNIK.COM

CHARLES J. MALARET, born San Francisco, California, April 17, 1964; admitted to bar, 1989, California (Not admitted in District of Columbia). *Education:* University of San Francisco (B.A., 1986); University of California at Davis (J.D., 1989). Member, Moot Court Board. Recipient, American Jurisprudence Award. *Member:* State Bar of California. (Resident, Los Angeles, California Office). ***PRACTICE AREAS:*** Commercial Litigation; Insurance; Environmental Law; Litigation. ***Email:*** CMALARET@ZEVNIK.COM

MICHAEL JOHN MIGUEL, born Gridley, California, March 15, 1962; admitted to bar, 1989, California, U.S. District Court, Central District of California and U.S. Court of Appeals, Ninth Circuit; 1991, U.S. District Court, Southern District of California; 1994, Massachusetts, U.S. District Court, District of Massachusetts; 1995, U.S. Court of Appeals, First Circuit; 1998, District of Columbia. *Education:* University of California at Los Angeles (B.A., English, 1986); University of Southern California (J.D., 1989). Phi Delta Phi. Recipient, American Jurisprudence Award in Pretrial Advocacy. Staff Editor, U.S.C. Journal of Law & Environment, 1987-1988. Author: Commentary, "Landlord Has Right to Inspect for Hazardous Waste: Sachs v. Exxon" California Environmental Law Reporter (Bender), November 1992; Commentary, "Purchaser of Contaminated Property May State Tort Claims Against Prior Owners: Newhall Land and Farming Co. v. Superior Court" California Environmental Law Reporter, November 1993; "Use of Experts, Admissibility Issues and Fingerprinting Techniques in L.U.S.T. Litigation," printed in Leaking Underground Storage Tanks, Massachusetts Continuing Legal Education, October 1996. Lectures: Keynote Speaker, "A Legal Perspective on Dating and Fingerprinting Petroleum Hydrocarbons," sponsored by the Groundwater Resources Association of California (September 1993); Lecturer, "Use of Expert Witnesses" sponsored by California Continuing Education of the Bar (October 2000); Lecturer, "Fundamentals of Insurance Litigation" sponsored by California Continuing Education of the Bar (April 2001); Lecturer, "Proving the Technical Case: Soil and Groundwater Contamination with an Emphasis on Hydrocarbons" sponsored by the University of Wisconsin-Madison (May 1994); Panelist, "Leaking Underground Storage Tanks: Sources of Liability; Strategies to Establish Causation and Recover Costs," sponsored by Massachusetts Continuing Legal Education (October 1996). *Member:* State Bar of California; Massachusetts Bar Association; District of Columbia Bar. (Resident, Boston, Massachusetts Office). ***PRACTICE AREAS:*** Environmental Litigation; General Civil Litigation; Environmental Insurance Recovery Litigation; Toxic Tort Defense. ***Email:*** MMIGUEL@ZEVNIK.COM

PATRICK MICHAEL McGOVERN, born Yeovil, Somerset, England, June 9, 1955; admitted to bar, 1982, England and Wales (Solicitor of the Supreme Court); 1986, New York; 1987, U.S. District Court, Southern District of New York; 1991, U.S. District Court, Eastern District of New York; 1996, U.S. Court of Appeals, Second Circuit; 1999, District of Columbia; 2000, California. *Education:* University of Sheffield, England (LL.B., with Honors, 1976; M.A., 1978); College of Law, Guildford, England (Solicitors Final Qualifying Exam, 1979). *Member:* Law Society of England and Wales. (Resident, Los Angeles, California Office). ***LANGUAGES:*** French. ***PRACTICE AREAS:*** International Law; Insurance Coverage; Commercial Litigation. ***Email:*** PMCGOVERN@ZEVNIK.COM

SPECIAL PARTNERS

LEON G. KRASINSKI, born Natrona, Pennsylvania, April 18, 1944; admitted to bar, 1971, Pennsylvania; U.S. Supreme Court (Not admitted in District of Columbia). *Education:* Fordham University (A.B., 1966); Georgetown University Law Center (J.D., 1970). (Resident, Roseland, New Jersey Office). ***PRACTICE AREAS:*** Corporate Transactions; Mergers and Acquisitions; Joint Ventures; Litigation. ***Email:*** LKRASINSKI@ZEVNIK.COM

THOMAS JAMES WINGARD, born Pittsburgh, Pennsylvania, June 29, 1962; admitted to bar, 1987, Pennsylvania; 1988, California (Not admitted in District of Columbia). *Education:* Wabash College (A.B., cum laude, 1984); Hastings College of the Law, University of California (J.D., 1987). *Member:* Beverly Hills, Los Angeles County (Member, Business Law Section), and Pennsylvania Bar Associations; State Bar of California (Member, Business Section). (Resident, Los Angeles, California Office). ***PRACTICE AREAS:*** Mergers and Acquisitions; Securities; Corporate Finance; Health Care. ***Email:*** TWINGARD@ZEVNIK.COM

MICHAEL J. WILSON, born Springfield, Ohio, May 30, 1964; admitted to bar, 1989, District of Columbia, New Jersey and U.S. District Court, District of New Jersey; 1990, Maryland and U.S. District Court, District of Columbia; 1991, U.S. District Court, District of Maryland and U.S. Court of Appeals, Fourth Circuit; 1992, U.S. Court of Appeals, Seventh Circuit. *Education:* Miami University (B.A., 1986); Catholic University of America (J.D., 1989). ***PRACTICE AREAS:*** Litigation; Insurance; Environmental. ***Email:*** MWILSON@ZEVNIK.COM

GREGORY M. CORK, born Sacramento, California, September 27, 1965; admitted to bar, 1993, California, U.S. District Court, Northern, Central, Southern and Eastern Districts of California and U.S. Court of Appeals, Ninth Circuit; 1998, U.S. Court of Appeals, Eighth Circuit; 2000, District of Columbia. *Edu-*

(This Listing Continued)

ZEVNIK HORTON LLP, Washington—Continued

cation: University of Virginia (B.A., 1987; J.D., 1992). *Member:* American Bar Association. ***PRACTICE AREAS:*** Commercial Litigation; Insurance Coverage. ***Email:*** GCORK@ZEVNIK.COM

YOLANDA C. GRIFFIN, born Springfield, Massachusetts, July 28, 1970; admitted to bar, 1996, New Jersey; 1997, District of Columbia. *Education:* University of Delaware (B.A., magna cum laude, 1992); Harvard University (J.D., 1995). Technical Editor, Harvard Environmental Law Review. *Member:* American Bar Association; Environmental Law Institute; American Trial Lawyers Association. ***PRACTICE AREAS:*** Environmental; Insurance Coverage; Litigation. ***Email:*** YGRIFFIN@ZEVNIK.COM

ZUCKERMAN SPAEDER LLP

Established in 1975

1201 CONNECTICUT AVENUE, N.W., SUITE 1200

WASHINGTON, D.C. 20036-2638

Telephone: 202-778-1800

Fax: 202-822-8106

Email: counsel@zuckerman.com

Miami, Florida Office: 201 South Biscayne Boulevard, Suite 900. Telephones: 305-358-5000; Broward County: 305-523-0277. Fax: 305-579-9749.

Ft. Lauderdale, Florida Office: One East Broward Boulevard, Suite 700. Telephone: 954-356-0463. Fax: 954-356-0406.

Baltimore, Maryland Office: Suite 2440, 100 East Pratt Street. Telephone: 410-332-0444. Fax: 410-659-0436.

Tampa, Florida Office: 401 East Jackson Street, Suite 2525. Telephone: 813-221-1010. Fax: 813-223-7961.

New York, N.Y. Office: 1114 Avenue of the Americas, 27th Floor, Grace Building. Telephone: 212-479-6500. Fax: 212-479-6512.

Wilmington, Delaware Office: One Commerce Center, 1201 Orange Street, Suite 650, Post Office Box 1028. Telephone: 302-427-0400. Fax: 302-427-8242.

Litigation (Civil, White Collar Criminal), Bankruptcy and Workouts, Taxation, Real Estate, Partnership, Corporate, Commercial and Health Care law.

FIRM PROFILE: Handling matters throughout the country and abroad, before federal and state courts and federal agencies and departments, Zuckerman Spaeder LLP has more than 70 lawyers in offices in Baltimore, Miami, New York, Tampa, Washington and Wilmington. The firm litigates white collar criminal defense and federal enforcement actions, and prosecutes and defends complex civil actions, including commercial litigation, securities fraud class actions, malpractice litigation, antitrust, tax, and Native American land claims. Zuckerman Spaeder's health care lawyers handle regulatory, fraud and abuse, antitrust, compliance, and licensing issues, as well as litigation. The firm's creditor-debtor rights practice counsels troubled companies and manages major bankruptcy reorganizations and out-of-court workouts. The business and tax attorneys at the firm focus on corporate transactions including the formation, sale, and merger of business entities; real estate transactions; tax counseling; and estate planning.

MEMBERS OF FIRM

ROGER E. ZUCKERMAN, born Washington, D.C., November 3, 1942; admitted to bar, 1968, District of Columbia and U.S. Court of Appeals for the District of Columbia; 1975, U.S. Court of Appeals for the Fourth, Fifth, Ninth and Eleventh Circuits and U.S. Tax Court; 1996, U.S. Court of Federal Claims. *Education:* University of Wisconsin (B.S., 1964); Harvard University (LL.B., 1967). Phi Beta Kappa. Assistant United States Attorney, District of Columbia, 1968-1972. Recipient: Assistant United States Attorney's Award for Superior Performance, 1971; Assistant United States Attorney's Association Distinguished Alumnus Award, 2000. Co-Author: "Family Ties: When Prosecutors Overreach," ABA Criminal Justice Magazine, Vol. 7, Number 1, Spring 1992; "The Gloves Are Off," ABA Criminal Justice Magazine, Vol. 2, No. 4, Winter 1988; "Negotiating Effectively With the Government in Corporate Criminal Investigations," Corporate Criminal Liability Reporter," Vol. 1, No. 3, Summer 1987; "Confronting Investigations for Procurement Fraud," 8 The National Law Journal, No. 28, p. 26, 1986; "New Attention to Procurement Fraud," 8 The National Law Journal, No. 27, P.20, 1986; *Strategy and Tactics in the Prosecution and Defense of Complex Wire—Interception Cases,* 1976 NWC Commission Studies 26 (GPO). *Member:* The District of Columbia Bar; American Bar Association (Member, Sections of Litigation and Criminal Justice). Fellow, American College of Trial Lawyers. ***PRACTICE AREAS:*** Complex Civil and Criminal Litigation. ***Email:*** rzuckerman@zuckerman.com

MARK W. FOSTER, born Bryn Mawr, Pennsylvania, December 10, 1942; admitted to bar, 1971, Connecticut; 1972, District of Columbia; 1975, U.S. Supreme Court; 1977, U.S. Claims Court; 1981, U.S. Tax Court; 1985, Maryland. *Education:* Yale University (B.A., cum laude, 1965); Harvard University (J.D., cum laude, 1971). Lecturer, George Washington University National Law

(This Listing Continued)

Center, Trial Techniques, 1974-1982. Attorney, 1971-1975 and Chief, Trial Section, 1974-1975, Public Defender Service, Washington, D.C. Associate, Bierbower & Rockefeller, Washington, D.C., 1975-1976. *Member:* The District of Columbia Bar (Member, Committees on Judicial Selection and Tenure, 1974-1979; Member, Re-evaluation of Court Reorganization, 1977-1981; Co-Chairperson, Division V Steering Committee, Criminal Law and Individual Rights, 1975-1977; Member, Hearing Committee, Board on Professional Responsibility, 1980-1982; Member, Board on Professional Responsibility, 1982-1988; Vice Chairman, 1983-1984; Chairman, 1984-1988; Member, Committee to Review the Disciplinary System, 1992-1993; Member, Committee to Review the New Disciplinary Rules, 1992-1994; Member, Ethics Committee, 1993-1999; Vice Chair, 1997-1999). ***LANGUAGES:*** French. ***PRACTICE AREAS:*** Complex Commercial Transactions; Civil Litigation; Business Organization; Legal Ethics and Lawyer Discipline; Partnership Law. ***Email:*** mwfoster@zuckerman.com

ROGER C. SPAEDER, born Cleveland, Ohio, December 20, 1943; admitted to bar, 1971, District of Columbia, U.S. District Court for the District of Columbia and U.S. Court of Appeals for the District of Columbia Circuit; 1976, U.S. Supreme Court; 1979, U.S. Court of Federal Claims; 1984, U.S. District Court for the District of Maryland including Trial Bar; 1985, U.S. Court of Appeals, Second and Fourth Circuits. *Education:* Bowling Green University (B.S., 1965); George Washington University (J.D., with honors, 1970). Omicron Delta Kappa. Special Counsel to Executive Office of President of the United States, 2000-2001. Cardozo Prize Judge, Yale Law School, 1992. Master, Edward Bennett Williams Inn of Court, 1996—. Author: "Special Litigation Committees Can Ease Court Battles," CLII American Banker, No. 42, p. 5, 1987; "Subpoenaed Documents: Organizational Records, The Fifth Amendment and Related Issues in Corporate Investigations," Corporate Counsel's Guide to Handling Government Investigations, p. 1235, Business Laws, Inc. 1988. Co-Author: "Gratuities and The Government Contractor," 2 Corporate Criminal Liability Reporter, No. 2, p. 14, 1988; "Negotiating Effectively With the Government in Corporate Criminal Investigations," 1 Corporate Criminal Liability Reporter, No. 3. p. 20, 1987; "New Attention to Procurement Fraud," 8 The National Law Journal, No. 27, p. 20, 1986; "Confronting Investigations for Procurement Fraud," 8 The National Law Journal, No. 28, p. 26, 1986; "Immunity Negotiations: Law and Tactics," 7 Criminal Justice, No. 2, ABA, Summer, 1992; "Effective Withdrawal from a Business Conspiracy," 9 Criminal Justice, No. 1, ABA, Spring, 1994; "Immunity Negotiations: Law and Practice," Department of Justice Manual, §9-23.800A, Prentice Hall Law & Business, 1994 ed.; "Voluntary Disclosure Blues: Meeting Corporation's Disparate Goals," 3 Business Crimes Bulletin, No. 1, p. 1, February 1996. Lecturer: Criminal Practice Institute, Bar Association of the District of Columbia, 1977-1980; Continuing Legal Education, District of Columbia Unified Bar, 1979-1989. Program Chair, Annual National Institute, "Federal Enforcement," Georgetown University Law Center Continuing Legal Education Division and Criminal Litigation Committee, Section of Litigation, American Bar Association, 1987—. Faculty Member, National Institute for Trial Advocacy, 1978-1979. Adjunct Faculty Member: Georgetown University Law Center, 1979-1980; American University Center for Administration of Justice, 1976-1979. Assistant United States Attorney, District of Columbia, 1971-1976. Member, D.C. Circuit Judicial Conference, 1991. *Member:* The District of Columbia Bar; Federal and American (Member, Sections of Litigation, Criminal Justice, and Antitrust Law; Co-Chair, Complex Crimes Committee, Litigation Section, 1989-1992) Bar Associations; The Association of Trial Lawyers of America; National Association of Criminal Defense Lawyers; Defense Research Institute. ***PRACTICE AREAS:*** Complex Criminal and Civil Litigation. ***Email:*** spaeder@zuckerman.com

BRUCE GOLDSTEIN, born Charleston, South Carolina, July 10, 1944; admitted to bar, 1969, Virginia and District of Columbia. *Education:* University of South Carolina and University of North Carolina (A.B., 1966); George Washington University (J.D., with honors, 1969). Phi Delta Phi. *Member:* The District of Columbia Bar (Member: Committee on Bankruptcy, Reorganization and Secured Transactions, Division III, 1978; Committee of the District Court, 1978); Bar Association of the District of Columbia; Virginia State Bar. ***PRACTICE AREAS:*** Bankruptcy. ***Email:*** bgoldstein@zuckerman.com

WILLIAM W. TAYLOR, III, born Richmond, Virginia, July 30, 1944; admitted to bar, 1969, North Carolina; 1970, District of Columbia. *Education:* University of North Carolina (A.B., 1966); Yale University (LL.B., 1969). Phi Beta Kappa. Law Clerk to Hon. Caleb M. Wright, Chief Judge, U.S. District Court for the District of Delaware, 1969-1970. Staff Attorney and Special Assistant for Staff Training and Supervision, District of Columbia Public Defender Service, 1970-1975. Adjunct Professor, Columbus School of Law, Catholic University of America, 1973-1976. Visiting Professor, University of North Carolina School of Law, Fall, 1991. Faculty Member, National Institute for Trial Advocacy. Member, 1977-1984 and Chairman, 1978-1984, District of Columbia Commission on Judicial Disabilities and Tenure. Member, Board of Trustees, D.C. Public Defender Service; Member, Board of Trustees, See Forever Foundation. Chairperson, D.C. Public Defender Service Association, 1985-1990. Council Member, ABA Criminal Justice Section, Vice-Chair, Governmental Relations, 1989-1992, Chair, 1996-1997. Fellow: American College of

(This Listing Continued)

Trial Lawyers. ***PRACTICE AREAS:*** Criminal and Civil Litigation; Commercial Litigation; Native American Civil Rights; Election Law. **Email:** wwtaylor@zuckerman.com

PETER R. KOLKER, born New York, N.Y., May 4, 1942; admitted to bar, 1966, Illinois and U.S. District Court, Northern District of Illinois; 1968, District of Columbia and U.S. Court of Appeals for the District of Columbia Circuit; 1971, U.S. Supreme Court; 1982, Maryland and U.S. Court of Appeals, Fourth Circuit; 1989, U.S. Court of Appeals, Eleventh Circuit; 1996, Florida and U.S. District Court, Southern District of Florida. *Education:* Cornell University (B.A., 1963); University of Chicago (J.D., 1966). Attorney: Office of Deputy Attorney General, U.S. Department of Justice, 1968-1969; D.C. Public Defender Service, 1969-1973. Co-Director, Judicial Conference Staff Report, 1973. Partner, Zuckerman Spaeder LLP, 1979—. *Member:* The District of Columbia Bar; Maryland State Bar Association; The Florida Bar. ***LANGUAGES:*** French. ***PRACTICE AREAS:*** Financial Litigation; White Collar Crime; Contested Trust and Estate Litigation; Domestic Relations Litigation. **Email:** prkolker@zuckerman.com

JOHN F. EVANS (1941-1988).

MICHAEL R. SMITH, born Camden, Arkansas, November 5, 1953; admitted to bar, 1980, District of Columbia, 1985, Louisiana; 1990, Maryland. *Education:* Tulane University (B.A., summa cum laude, 1976); Stanford University (J.D., 1979). Phi Beta Kappa. Member, 1977-1978 and Associate Editor, 1978-1979, Stanford Law Review. Law Clerk to: Judge Albert Tate, Jr., U.S. Court of Appeals, Fifth Circuit, 1984-1985; Chief Judge William Wayne Justice, U.S. District Court, Eastern District of Texas, 1979-1980. *Member:* The District of Columbia Bar; Louisiana, Maryland State and American Bar Associations. ***PRACTICE AREAS:*** Civil Trial; Criminal Trial; Litigation; Trial Practice. **Email:** msmith@zuckerman.com

HERBERT BETTER, born Baltimore, Maryland, April 10, 1944; admitted to bar, 1968, Maryland and U.S. District Court, District of Maryland; 1972, U.S. Court of Appeals, Fourth Circuit. *Education:* John Hopkins University (B.A., 1965); University of Pennsylvania; University of Maryland (LL.B., 1968). Phi Beta Kappa. Member, Maryland Law Review, 1967-1968. Associate, Weinberg and Green, Baltimore, Maryland, 1968-1972. Legislative Analyst, Maryland State Legislature, 1969. Assistant U.S. Attorney, 1972-1987, First Assistant U.S. Attorney, 1978-1983, Court Appointed U.S. Attorney, 1981 and Senior Litigation Counsel, 1985-1987, U.S. Attorneys Office, Maryland. Member, Maryland ADR Services, Inc., 1994—. *Member:* Maryland State (Member: Federal Court Committee; Section of Litigation) and Federal (Chairman, Board of Governors, Maryland Chapter, 1993-1994; President, 1997-1998) Bar Associations. (Resident, Baltimore, Maryland Office). ***PRACTICE AREAS:*** Complex Criminal and Civil Litigation and Mediation. **Email:** hbetter@zuckerman.com

RONALD B. RAVIKOFF, born New York, N.Y., April 1, 1948; admitted to bar, 1977, Florida (Approved areas of Practice under Florida State Bar Designation Plan; Antitrust and Trade Regulation Law); 1978, District of Columbia, U.S. District Court, Southern District of Florida including Trial Bar, U.S. Court of Appeals, Fifth Circuit and U.S. Court of Appeals for the District of Columbia Circuit; 1981, U.S. Court of Appeals, Eleventh Circuit; 1982, U.S. Supreme Court; 1988, U.S. District Court, Middle District of Florida; 1992, New York. *Education:* Cornell University (B.S., 1970; M.R.P., 1972); University of Miami (J.D., cum laude, 1977). Editor-in-Chief, University of Miami Law Review, 1976-1977. Author: "Social Responsibility in Investment Policy and the Prudent Man Rule," 68 California Law Review 518, 1980; "Establishing An Antitrust Compliance Program," 57 Florida Bar Journal 254, 1983; "ABA The Antitrust Health Care Handbook," 1988; "Using Experts in Business Valuation Cases," Florida Bar Quarterly, 1989; "Litigating Claims Against Failed Financial Institutions," (Fla. Bar 1991); "Attorney-Client and Work-Product Privilege Issues in Failed Financial Institution Litigation," (ABA 1991); "Attorney-Client and Work-Product Issues in Financial Institutions," (USLSI 1991); "Making Claims Against Failed Financial Institutions," 66 Florida Bar Journal 40, 1992. Special Counsel to Metropolitan Dade County, 1981-1982. President, University of Miami Law Alumni Association, 1994-1995. *Member:* The District of Columbia Bar; Dade County and American (Member, Commercial Litigation and Banking Committee) Bar Associations; The Florida Bar (Member, Trial Lawyers Section, Business Litigation Committee, Chair, 1992-1993, Grievance Committee 11 "H", 1985-1988); The Association of Trial Lawyers of America; The Academy of Florida Trial Lawyers. (Resident, Miami, Florida Office). ***PRACTICE AREAS:*** Civil Trial; Antitrust Law; Deceptive Trade Practices; Securities Litigation; Unfair Competition Law. **Email:** rravikoff@zuckerman.com

MICHAEL S. PASANO, born Kansas City, Missouri, March 10, 1951; admitted to bar, 1976, Missouri; 1977, District of Columbia; 1978, U.S. District Court for the District of Columbia and U.S. Court of Appeals for the District of Columbia Circuit; 1985, Florida; 1986, U.S. Supreme Court and U.S. Court of Appeals, Eleventh Circuit; 1989, U.S. Court of Appeals, Fifth Circuit; 1991, U.S. District Court, Southern District of Florida; 1993, U.S. District Court, Middle District of Florida; 1999, U.S. Court of Appeals, First, Second and Sixth Circuits. *Education:* Georgetown University (A.B., 1973); Yale University (J.D., 1976). Phi Beta Kappa. Law Clerk to Honorable Aubrey Robinson, U.S. District

(This Listing Continued)

Court, Washington, D.C., 1976-1977. Assistant U.S. Attorney, 1978-1985. Chief, Fraud Unit, 1983 and Chief, Northern Division Offices, 1983-1985, U.S. Attorney's Office for Southern District of Florida. Frequent Lecturer and Contributor to ABA Criminal Justice Magazine. *Member:* The District of Columbia Bar; The Missouri Bar; The Florida Bar; American Bar Association (Vice Chair, CLE, 2000—; Vice Chair, Government Affairs, 1999-2000; Council Member, Criminal Justice Section, 1995-1998; Chairman, Defense Function Committee, 1992-1995 and Vice Chair, White Collar Crime Committee, 1993—, Criminal Justice Section; Chairman, Florida Regional White Collar Crime Subcommittee, 1991—; Eleventh Circuit Federal Public Defender Committee, 1994—; Eleventh Circuit Attorney Discipline Committee, 1993—; Southern District Criminal Justice Act Committee, 1995—). (Miami and Ft. Lauderdale, Florida Offices). ***PRACTICE AREAS:*** Criminal Trial Practice; Asset Forfeitures; Business Crimes Law; Criminal Tax Investigation; White Collar Criminal Defense. **Email:** mpasano@zuckerman.com

ANTHONY THOMPSON, born Boston, Massachusetts, March 18, 1949; admitted to bar, 1976, Massachusetts; 1977, District of Columbia; 1981, U.S. Supreme Court; 1983, Maryland. *Education:* Harvard University (A.B., cum laude, 1971); Antioch School of Law (J.D., 1976). Trial Attorney, U.S. Department of Justice, Civil Division, 1976-1979. Author: "Piercing the Veil of State Action: The Revisionist Theory and a Mythical Application to Self-Help Repossession," Wisconsin Law Review 1, 1977. *Member:* The District of Columbia Bar; Maryland State and American Bar Associations. ***PRACTICE AREAS:*** Business Law; International Transactions; Real Estate; Corporate Law; Finance; Design Professionals; Native American Law. **Email:** athompson@zuckerman.com

NELSON C. COHEN, born Harrisburg, Pennsylvania, November 8, 1947; admitted to bar, 1973, Maryland; 1974, District of Columbia, U.S. District Court, District of Maryland and U.S. District Court for the District of Columbia. *Education:* Pennsylvania State University (B.S., 1969); George Washington University (J.D., with honors, 1973). *Member:* The District of Columbia Bar; Bar Association of the District of Columbia; Montgomery County (Member, 1982— and Chairman, 1982, Section of Bankruptcy), Maryland State and American Bar Associations; Bankruptcy Bar Association of Maryland (Member, Board of Directors, 1988-1990; Chairman, Rockville Division, 1989-1990). ***PRACTICE AREAS:*** Commercial Litigation; Bankruptcy and Creditor Rights. **Email:** ncohen@zuckerman.com

STEVEN M. SALKY, born Memphis, Tennessee, March 20, 1954; admitted to bar, 1982, District of Columbia. *Education:* Trinity College (B.A., with highest honors, 1976) Phi Beta Kappa; London School of Economics, London, England; Yale University (J.D., 1981). Recipient, Thurmond Arnold Appellate Competition Prize, 1981. Stuart Stiller Teaching Fellowship, Georgetown University Law Center Criminal Justice Clinic, 1983-1984. Law Clerk to Hon. Theodore Newman, District of Columbia Court of Appeals, 1981-1982. *Member:* The District of Columbia Bar. ***PRACTICE AREAS:*** Criminal and Civil Litigation; Complex Litigation; Criminal Law; Grand Jury Proceedings. **Email:** ssalky@zuckerman.com

MARSHALL S. WOLFF, born Worthington, Minnesota, November 30, 1948; admitted to bar, 1976, California; 1982, District of Columbia. *Education:* Harvard College (A.B., magna cum laude, 1970); Yale University (J.D., 1974). Phi Beta Kappa. Law Clerk to Judge Robert C. Zampano Jr., U.S. District Court, District of Connecticut, 1974-1975. *Member:* The District of Columbia Bar; State Bar of California; American Bar Association. ***PRACTICE AREAS:*** Business Law; Real Estate; Finance; Workouts; Bankruptcy. **Email:** mwolff@zuckerman.com

MORRIS WEINBERG, JR., born Chattanooga, Tennessee, 1950; admitted to bar, 1975, Georgia; 1979, District of Columbia; 1985, Florida. *Education:* Princeton University, Woodrow Wilson School of Urban and International Affairs (B.A., 1972); Vanderbilt University (J.D., 1975). Assistant U.S. Attorney, Southern District of New York, 1979-1985. *Member:* The District of Columbia Bar; The Florida Bar; State Bar of Georgia; American Bar Association (Member, White Collar Crime Committee, Criminal Law Section, 1987—). (Resident, Tampa, Florida Office). ***PRACTICE AREAS:*** Complex, Criminal and Civil Litigation; White Collar Criminal Defense; Healthcare Fraud; Grand Jury Proceedings; State and Federal Administrative Proceedings; RICO. **Email:** sweinberg@zuckerman.com

BLAIR G. BROWN, born New Orleans, Louisiana, February 17, 1957; admitted to bar, 1982, New York; 1983, District of Columbia and U.S. District Court, Eastern, Southern and Northern Districts of New York; 1984, U.S. District Court for the District of Columbia and U.S. Court of Appeals for the District of Columbia Circuit; 1988, U.S. Court of Appeals, Eleventh Circuit and U.S. Supreme Court; 1989, Maryland, Virginia, U.S. District Court, Eastern District of Virginia and U.S. Court of Appeals, Fourth Circuit. *Education:* Tulane University (B.A., magna cum laude, 1978); New York University (J.D., 1981). Root-Tilden Scholar. Pro Se Law Clerk, U.S. Court of Appeals for the Second Circuit, 1981-1983. Law Clerk, Honorable Leonard P. Moore, U.S. Court of Appeals for the Second Circuit, 1982-1983. Staff Attorney and Deputy Chief, Trial Division, Public Defender Service for the District of Columbia, 1983-1988. Lecturer, Criminal Practice Institute, 1986-1990. Instructor, Har-

(This Listing Continued)

ZUCKERMAN SPAEDER LLP, Washington—Continued

vard Law School Trial Advocacy Workshop, 1991. Author: "Improving Immunity Agreements," Corporate Counsel's Guide to Handling Government Investigations (1995); "Access to Information During the Investigation of a Procurement Fraud Case," Federal Procurement Fraud 1992; "The Preponderance of Evidence Standard at Sentencing," 29 American Criminal Law Review 907 (1992). *Member:* The District of Columbia Bar (Co-Chair, Steering Committee, Section on Criminal Law and Individual Rights, 1990-1992); American Bar Association (Member, Sections on: Litigation; Criminal Justice); National Association of Criminal Defense Lawyers. ***PRACTICE AREAS:*** Criminal and Civil Litigation. ***Email:*** bgbrown@zuckerman.com

MARTIN S. HIMELES, JR., born Baltimore, Maryland, March 13, 1956; admitted to bar, 1982, New York, U.S. Court of Appeals, Fourth Circuit and U.S. District Court, Southern and Eastern Districts of New York and District of Maryland; 1990, Maryland. *Education:* Yale College (B.A., summa cum laude, 1978); Harvard Law School (J.D., magna cum laude, 1981). Phi Beta Kappa. Editor, Harvard Civil Rights-Civil Liberties Law Review, 1980-1981. Law Clerk to Judge Francis D. Murnaghan, Jr., U.S. Court of Appeals, Fourth Circuit. Assistant U.S. Attorney, Baltimore, MD., 1986-1990. Co-Author: "Private Actions for Securities Fraud," Dealing with Damages, N.J. Itzkoff, ed., 1983. Vice President, Maryland Chapter, American Jewish Committee. Delegate, Baltimore Jewish Council, 1989—. Member, Board of Governors, Leevindale Hebrew Geriatric Center and Hospital, 1999—. *Member:* Maryland State (Federal District Court Liaison, Joint Committee, Litigation Section, 2001—) and Federal (President, Maryland Chapter) Bar Associations. (Resident, Baltimore, Maryland Office). ***LANGUAGES:*** French. ***PRACTICE AREAS:*** Complex Litigation; White Collar Criminal Defense. ***Email:*** mhimeles@zuckerman.com

EDWARD J. M. LITTLE, born Boston, Massachusetts, January 6, 1949; admitted to bar, 1975, New York, U.S. District Court, Southern and Eastern Districts of New York and U.S. Court of Appeals, Second Circuit. *Education:* Boston College (A.B., magna cum laude, 1970; J.D., 1974). Presidential Scholar. Executive Editor, Boston College Law Review, 1973-1974. Assistant U.S. Attorney, U.S. Attorney's Office, Southern District of New York, 1982-1989. Deputy Chief of Criminal Division, 1988-1989. *Member:* Association of the Bar of the City of New York; American Bar Association (Member, Criminal Law Section). (Resident, New York, N.Y. Office). ***PRACTICE AREAS:*** Criminal Defense; Securities Litigation; General Corporate Litigation. ***Email:*** elittle@zuckerman.com

THOMAS J. MEEKS, born Tampa, Florida, February 23, 1953; admitted to bar, 1980, Florida; 1981, Georgia, U.S. District Court, Southern District of Florida including Trial Bar, U.S. District Court, Northern District of Georgia and U.S. Court of Appeals, Fifth and Eleventh Circuits. *Education:* University of Florida (B.A., with high honors, 1975; J.D., 1979). Member, Moot Court Team. Senior Editor, University of Florida Law Review, 1979. Law Clerk to U.S. District Judge Horace T. Ward, Northern District of Georgia, Atlanta Division, 1980-1981. Vice-Chairperson, Ad Hoc Committee on Rules and Procedures and Ad Hoc Committee on Attorney Admissions, Peer Review and Judicial Grievance, United States District Court, Southern District of Florida. *Member:* Dade County and American Bar Associations; The Florida Bar (Co-Chairman, Civil Procedure Rules Committee, 1984-1987); State Bar of Georgia. Fellow, American Bar Foundation. (Resident, Miami, Florida Office). ***PRACTICE AREAS:*** Business Litigation; Trade Secrets Litigation; Broker Litigation; Construction Litigation; Civil Fraud Litigation. ***Email:*** tmeeks@zuckerman.com

GRAEME W. BUSH, born Washington, D.C., March 23, 1950; admitted to bar, 1976, Maryland; 1977, District of Columbia; 1986, New York. *Education:* Wesleyan University (B.A., 1971); University of Maryland (J.D., 1976). Order of the Coif. Author: "Piercing the Corporate Veil," US Litigation: A Guide for Asian Corporations (AsiaLaw & Practice, April 1996); "The Impact of RICO Forfeiture on Legitimate Business," 65 Notre Dame L. Rev. 996 (1990). ***PRACTICE AREAS:*** Civil; Securities; ERISA; Legal Malpractice; Criminal Litigation; Corporate. ***Email:*** gbush@zuckerman.com

CARL S. KRAVITZ, born Boston, Massachusetts, October 12, 1955; admitted to bar, 1981, District of Columbia and Massachusetts; 1993, New York. *Education:* Harvard University (A.B., 1977); Columbia University (J.D., 1980). Harlan Fiske Stone Scholar. Law Clerk, Hon. Stephen Reinhardt, Ninth Circuit Court of Appeals, 1980-1981. Faculty, National Institute of Trial Advocacy. ***PRACTICE AREAS:*** Civil and Criminal Litigation; Trial Practice. ***Email:*** ckravitz@zuckerman.com

DEBORAH J. JEFFREY, born Baltimore, Maryland, March 28, 1962; admitted to bar, 1986, Maryland and U.S. Court of Appeals, Fourth Circuit; 1988, District of Columbia and U.S. District Court, District of Maryland; 1989, U.S. District Court for the District of Columbia and U.S. Court of Appeals for the District of Columbia Circuit; 1991, U.S. Supreme Court. *Education:* The Johns Hopkins University (B.A., with General and Departmental Honors, 1982); Harvard Law School (J.D., cum laude, 1985). Phi Beta Kappa; Omicron Delta Kappa; Pi Sigma Alpha. Editor in Chief, Harvard Civil Rights-Civil

(This Listing Continued)

Liberties Law Review, 1984-1985. Deputy Director, Massachusetts Legislative Commission on Violence Against Children, 1984. Law Clerk to Hon. Harrison L. Winter, Chief Judge, U.S. Court of Appeals, Fourth Circuit, 1985-1986. *Member:* The District of Columbia Bar. ***PRACTICE AREAS:*** Complex Civil, Enforcement and Criminal Litigation; Securities Litigation; Suspension and Debarment; Legal Ethics; Lawyer Discipline; Professional Liability. ***Email:*** djeffrey@zuckerman.com

THOMAS B. MASON, born Washington, D.C., September 27, 1956; admitted to bar, 1985, Maryland and U.S. District Court, District of Maryland; 1986, U.S. Court of Appeals, Fourth Circuit; 1988, District of Columbia and U.S. District Court for the District of Columbia; 1992, U.S. Court of Appeals, Fifth Circuit; 1995, U.S. Court of Appeals, District of Columbia Circuit. *Education:* Yale University (B.A., 1979); Columbia University (J.D., 1983). Harlan Fiske Stone Scholar. Adjunct Professor, Catholic University School of Law, 1986-1991. ***LANGUAGES:*** French. ***PRACTICE AREAS:*** White Collar Criminal Defense; Extradition; Asset Forfeitures; Attorney Discipline; Wineries and Vineyards. ***Email:*** tmason@zuckerman.com

LESLIE BERGER KIERNAN, born New York, N.Y., February 26, 1959; admitted to bar, 1986, Maryland; 1987, District of Columbia. *Education:* Brown University (A.B., 1981); Georgetown University (J.D., cum laude, 1986). Member, 1984-1985 and Senior Articles Editor, 1985-1986, Georgetown Law Journal. ***PRACTICE AREAS:*** Criminal Litigation; Civil Litigation; Congressional Investigations; Government Ethics; Election Law. ***Email:*** lbkiernan@zuckerman.com

CYRIL V. SMITH, born Boston, Massachusetts, August 4, 1960; admitted to bar, 1986, Virginia; 1988, District of Columbia; 1990, Maryland. *Education:* Dartmouth College (B.A., 1981); University of Virginia (J.D., 1986). Author: with Frank B. Cross, "The Reagan Administration's Non-Proliferation Non-Policy," Catholic University Law Review, 1984; "Borrowers Use Obscure (ECOA) Law for Protection from Creditors," The Daily Record, Sept., 18, 1993. Lecturer: "Claims Against the Federal Government Under the Federal Tort Claims Act," MTLA Seminar, March 12, 1993; "Key Procedural Aspects of Federal Death Penalty Practice," MCDAA Annual Meeting, June 6, 1998. *Member:* Bar Association of Baltimore City; Maryland Federal (Member, Board of Governors, 1996— and Treasurer, 1999—), Maryland State and Virginia Bar Associations; Bar Association of the District of Columbia; Serjeant's Inn of Court. (Resident, Baltimore, Maryland Office). ***LANGUAGES:*** French. ***REPORTED CASES:*** Gardner v. Mayor and City Council of Baltimore, 969 F.2d 63 (4th Cir. 1992); Chevy Chase Bank, FSB v. Claires, 71S A.2d 199 (Md. 1998); Bredehoft v. Alexander, 686 A.2d 586 (D.C. App. 1996); Rushford v. The New Yorker Magazine, 14 Media L. Rep. (BNA) 1025 (1987). ***PRACTICE AREAS:*** Complex Civil and Criminal Litigation; White Collar Criminal Defense. ***Email:*** csmith@zuckerman.com

STEPHEN J. BRONIS, born Miami, Florida, February 23, 1947; admitted to bar, 1972, Florida and U.S. District Court, Southern District of Florida; 1973, District of Columbia; 1977, U.S. Court of Appeals, Fifth Circuit; 1978, U.S. Supreme Court; 1981, U.S. Court of Appeals, Eleventh Circuit; 1986, U.S. District Court, Middle District of Florida; 1994, Colorado; 1996, U.S. District Court, District of Colorado and U.S. Court of Appeals, Tenth Circuit; 1998, U.S. Tax Court. *Education:* University of Florida (B.S.B.A., 1969); Duke University (J.D., 1972). Faculty: NITA and Trial Advocacy, Cardozo Law School, 1985; University of North Carolina Law School, 1985; Nova University Law School, 1990. Nominated for appointment to the Florida Supreme Court, 1998. Elected as Florida Bar's Representative to the ABA House of Delegates, 1999-2001. Appointed Member, Commission on Professionalism, Florida Supreme Court, 2000-2003. *Member:* Dade County (Member, Board of Directors, 1989) and American Bar Associations; The Florida Bar (Member, Judicial Nominating Procedures Committee, 1989; Appointed Representative to U.S. 11th Circuit Judicial Conference, 2001-2004); Florida Association of Criminal Defense Lawyers (President, 1980-1981; Board of Directors, 1986); American Board of Criminal Lawyers (Vice President, 1981); National Association of Criminal Defense Lawyers; California Attorneys for Criminal Justice. (Resident, Miami, Florida Office). ***PRACTICE AREAS:*** Criminal Trial and Complex Litigation; Health Care Fraud. ***Email:*** sbronis@zuckerman.com

RONALD H. WEICH, born New York, N.Y., November 19, 1959; admitted to bar, 1984, New York; 1997, District of Columbia. *Education:* Columbia University (B.A., magna cum laude, 1980); Yale University (J.D., 1983). Adjunct Professor of Law, Emory Law School, 1995. Assistant District Attorney, Office of the New York County District Attorney, 1983-1987. Special Counsel, U.S. Sentencing Commission, 1987-1989. Counsel to Senator Specter, Committee on the Judiciary, 1989 and Chief Counsel for Drug Control Policy, Committee on Labor and Human Resources, 1990-1994, U.S. Senate. General Counsel, 1992-1994 and Minority General Counsel, 1995, Committee on Labor and Human Resources and Chief Counsel to Senator Kennedy, Committee on the Judiciary, 1995-1997, U.S. Senate. ***PRACTICE AREAS:*** Government Relations; Congressional Investigations; Criminal and Civil Litigation. ***Email:*** rweich@zuckerman.com

ELEANOR H. SMITH, born Greensboro, North Carolina, April 17, 1960; admitted to bar, 1988, New York and District of Columbia; 1989, U.S. District

(This Listing Continued)

Court, District of Columbia and U.S. Court of Appeals, District of Columbia Circuit; 1999, U.S. Supreme Court. *Education:* University of North Carolina (B.A., 1982); Columbia University School of Law (J.D., 1987). Phi Beta Kappa. Harlan Fiske Stone Scholar. Recipient, Jane Marks Murphy Prize for Effective Advocacy. Law Clerk to U.S. District Judge Harold Greene, 1987-1988. *Member:* The District of Columbia Bar (Co-Chairperson, Steering Committee, Administrative Law and Agency Practice Section, 1991-1994); American Bar Association. ***PRACTICE AREAS:*** Civil and Criminal Litigation; Administrative Law; Freedom of Information; Privacy Law; Native American Law. ***Email:*** esmith@zuckerman.com

LISA A. CAHILL, born New York, New York, January 9, 1963; admitted to bar, 1990, Connecticut; 1991, New York; 1992, U.S. District Court, Southern and Eastern Districts of New York; 1993, U.S. District Court, District of Connecticut. *Education:* Georgetown University (B.A., 1985); College of William & Mary (J.D., 1990). Executive Editor, William & Mary Law Review, 1990. Co-Author: "Nondelegation After Mistretta: Phoenix or Phaëthon," William & Mary Law Review, Vol. 31, No. 4. Law Clerk to the Honorable T.F. Gilroy Daly, U.S. District Judge, District of Connecticut, 1990-1992. (Resident, New York, N.Y. Office). ***PRACTICE AREAS:*** Litigation; Criminal Law. ***Email:*** lcahill@zuckerman.com

JENNIFER RAE COBERLY, born Lawrence, Kansas, May 19, 1962; admitted to bar, 1990, Texas; 1992, Florida; U.S. District Court, Southern and Middle Districts of Florida, U.S. District Court, Western District of Texas and U.S. Court of Appeals, Fifth Circuit. *Education:* Florida State University (B.A., summa cum laude, 1984); Yale University (J.D., 1990). President, Florida Association for Women Lawyers, 1990. Member, Board of Directors, Pace School for Girls, 1995-1998. *Member:* The Florida Bar (Member, Board of Governors; Chair, Evaluation Committee, 1990). (Resident, Miami, Florida Office). ***PRACTICE AREAS:*** Employment Litigation; Commercial Law; International Litigation. ***Email:*** jcoberly@zuckerman.com

NORMAN L. EISEN, born Los Angeles, California, November 11, 1960; admitted to bar, 1991, Maryland; 1992, District of Columbia and U.S. District Court, District of Maryland; 1993, U.S. District Court, District of Columbia and U.S. Court of Appeals, District of Columbia Circuit. *Education:* Brown University (A.B., magna cum laude, 1985); Harvard Law School (J.D., cum laude, 1991). ***PRACTICE AREAS:*** Civil (General Civil) Practice; White Collar Criminal Defense. ***Email:*** nleisen@zuckerman.com

DAVID H. BRODY, born Queens, New York, October 16, 1963; admitted to bar, 1989, Virginia; 1990, District of Columbia; 1991, Alabama. *Education:* Duke University (B.A., with distinction in History, 1986); Vanderbilt University (J.D., 1989). Senior Managing Editor, Vanderbilt Law Review, 1988-1989. Recipient, Johnson & Swanson Appellate Advocacy Award, 1987. ***PRACTICE AREAS:*** Real Estate; Corporate; Business. ***Email:*** dhbrody@zuckerman.com

WILLIAM B. FLEMING, born Greenwich, Connecticut, August 18, 1962; admitted to bar, 1992, Connecticut and New York; 1993, U.S. District Court, Southern and Eastern Districts of New York. *Education:* Princeton University (A.B., 1985); Fordham University (J.D., 1991). Law Clerk to the Honorable John E. Sprizzo, U.S. District Judge, Southern District of New York, 1991-1993. Member, American Corporate Counsel Association, 1993-1995. (Resident, New York, N.Y. Office). ***PRACTICE AREAS:*** General Commercial and Securities Litigation; Criminal Law; Accountants Liability. ***Email:*** wfleming@zuckerman.com

THOMAS G. MACAULEY, born Bridgeport, Connecticut, August 25, 1966; admitted to bar, 1995, Delaware. *Education:* University of Virginia (B.A., 1988); Tulane Law School (J.D., magna cum laude, 1994). Editor-in-Chief, Tulane Law Review, 1993-1994. Law Clerk to Judge John M. Duhé, Jr., U.S. Court of Appeals for the Fifth Circuit, 1994-1995. Associate, Skadden, Arps, Slate, Meagher & Flom LLP, 1995-2000. *Member:* Delaware State and American Bar Associations; American Bankruptcy Institute. (Resident, Wilmington, Delaware Office). ***PRACTICE AREAS:*** Business Reorganization; Creditors Rights; Complex Civil Litigation; Corporate Governance. ***Email:*** tmacauley@zuckerman.com

WILLIAM B. SCHULTZ, born Bloomington, Indiana, March 16, 1948; admitted to bar, 1975, Virginia and District of Columbia. *Education:* Yale University (B.A., 1970); University of Virginia (J.D., 1974). Adjunct Professor, Georgetown University, 1983-1993, 1996. Deputy Assistant Attorney General, Civil Division, 1990-2000. *Member:* Virginia State Bar. ***PRACTICE AREAS:*** Food and Drug Regulation; Appellate Practice; Civil Litigation. ***Email:*** wschultz@zuckerman.com

COUNSEL

ELIZABETH G. TAYLOR, born Durham, North Carolina, January 13, 1954; admitted to bar, 1984, District of Columbia, U.S. District Court, District of Columbia, U.S. Court of Appeals, District of Columbia Circuit and U.S. Supreme Court. *Education:* University of North Carolina (B.A., summa cum laude, 1976); Yale Divinity School (M.A.R., 1979); University of Virginia School of Law (J.D., 1982). Order of the Coif. Articles Editor, Virginia Law Review. Recipient, Margaret G. Hyde Award. Law Clerk to the Honorable Frank M. Coffin, U.S. Circuit Judge for the First Circuit, 1982-1983. Law Clerk to the Honorable Harry A. Blackmun, Associate Justice, U.S. Supreme Court, 1983-1984. Member: District of Columbia Public Defender Service, 1984-1992; Office of Independent Counsel, 1994-1995. Adjunct Professor, Georgetown University Law Center, 1993-1996. The District of Columbia Bar Board on Professional Responsibility (Member, 1996— and Member, Hearing Committee, 1988-1994). ***PRACTICE AREAS:*** Criminal Litigation. ***Email:*** etaylor@zuckerman.com

LEE FUGATE, born St. Petersburg, Florida, January 10, 1947; admitted to bar, 1974, Florida; 1981, U.S. District Court, Middle District of Florida; 1985, 11th Circuit Court of Appeals. *Education:* University of South Florida (B.A., 1969); Cumberland School of Law of Samford University (J.D., 1973). Assistant State Attorney, Clearwater, 1974-1981. Assistant State Attorney, 1st & 3rd Grand Jury for Prosecution of Organized Crime, 1975-1979. Appointed Assistant Special Prosecutor, Governors Council for Prosecution of Organized Crime, 1979-1981. Member, Mentor Panel, Middle District of Florida, Tampa Division. *Member:* The Florida Bar; Federal and American Bar Associations; National Association of Criminal Defense Lawyers; Florida Association of Criminal Defense Lawyers; Pinellas County and Hillsborough County Criminal Defense Lawyers Associations. (Resident, Tampa, Florida Office). ***Email:*** lfugate@zuckerman.com

MARTIN I. KALISH, born New York, N.Y., October 25, 1944; admitted to bar, 1986, Florida and U.S. District Court, Southern District of Florida. *Education:* Brandeis University (B.A., magna cum laude, 1966); Albert Einstein College of Medicine (M.D., 1970); University of Miami (J.D., cum laude, 1986). Alpha Omega Alpha. Louis D. Brandeis Scholar. Assistant in Medicine, Johns Hopkins University School of Medicine, 1972-1974. Clinical Associate, National Institutes of Health (Biochemistry and Endocrinology), 1972-1974. Clinical and Research Fellow, Massachusetts General Hospital and Research Fellow in Medicine, Harvard Medical School, 1975-1977. Assistant Professor of Medicine, Albert Einstein College of Medicine, 1977-1978. Clinical Instructor in Medicine, 1979-1982, Clinical Assistant Professor of Medicine, 1982-1989, and Clinical Associate Professor of Medicine, 1989—, University of Miami School of Medicine. Registered Physician: New York, Maryland, Massachusetts and California (Inactive); Florida (Active), 1978—. Surgeon, U.S. Public Health Service, 1972-1974. *Member:* The Florida Bar; American Bar Association; American Health Lawyers Association. Diplomate, American Board of Internal Medicine and Subspecialty of Rheumatology. (Miami and Ft. Lauderdale, Florida Offices). ***PRACTICE AREAS:*** Health Care; Hospital Law; Pharmaceutical; Biotechnology Law; Administrative Law; Litigation; Product Liability Law. ***Email:*** mkalish@zuckerman.com

SALLY J. McKEE, born Peoria, Illinois, May 19, 1957; admitted to bar, 1982, Missouri; 1983, Illinois; 1997, Florida. *Education:* University of Illinois at Urbana/Champaign (B.S., high honors, 1979); Washington University (J.D., 1982; LL.M., Taxation, 1985). (Miami and Ft. Lauderdale, Florida Offices). ***PRACTICE AREAS:*** Health Care. ***Email:*** smckee@zuckerman.com

DAVID A. REISER, born New York, N.Y., September 21, 1956; admitted to bar, 1982, District of Columbia; 1983, U.S. District Court, District of Columbia and U.S. Court of Appeals, District of Columbia Circuit; 1984, Ohio (inactive), U.S. District Court, Southern District of Ohio and U.S. Court of Appeals, Sixth Circuit; 1985, Connecticut (retired); 1986, U.S. Court of Appeals, Eleventh Circuit and U.S. Supreme Court; 1992, U.S. Court of Appeals, Fourth Circuit. *Education:* Yale University (B.A., summa cum laude, with distinction in History, 1977; J.D., 1981). Phi Beta Kappa. E. Barrett Prettyman Fellow, Georgetown University Law Center, 1982-1984. Visiting Assistant Professor, University of Cincinnati College of Law, 1984-1985. Visiting Professor of Clinical Law, George Washington University Law School, 1995-1996. Staff Attorney, 1986-1991, Special Litigation Counsel, 1991-1998 and General Counsel, 1998-1999, Public Defender Service for the District of Columbia. Special Assistant to the General Counsel, Department of Housing and Urban Development, 1999-2001. *Member:* The District of Columbia Bar (Member, Steering Committee, Section on Courts, Lawyers and the Administration of Justice, 1990-1994); American Bar Association (Member: Task Force on Guilty Plea Standards, Criminal Justice Standards Committee, 1996-1998; Criminal Justice Standing Committee, 1998—). ***Email:*** dreiser@zuckerman.com

ASSOCIATES

VIRGINIA WHITEHILL GULDI, born Erie, Pennsylvania, June 28, 1963; admitted to bar, 1989, Delaware; 1990, U.S. District Court, District of Delaware; 1991, U.S. Court of Appeals, Third Circuit; 1992, Virginia and U.S. District Court, District of Maryland; 1995, U.S. Court of Appeals, Fourth Circuit and U.S. District Court, Eastern District of Virginia; 1996, District of Columbia and U.S. District Court, District of Columbia. *Education:* University of Pennsylvania (B.S.E. Chemical Engineering, 1986; B.S.E. Finance, 1986); Delaware Law School of Widener University (J.D., magna cum laude, 1989). Phi Delta Phi. Schaffer Scholar. Note and Comment Editor, Delaware Journal of Corporate Law, 1988-1989. Law Clerk to Chief Justice Andrew D. Christie, Delaware Supreme Court. *Member:* Delaware State Bar Association. ***PRACTICE AREAS:*** Bankruptcy. ***Email:*** vguldi@zuckerman.com

(This Listing Continued)

ZUCKERMAN SPAEDER LLP, Washington—Continued

LYNN F. KAUFMANN, born Hartford, Connecticut, September 16, 1951; admitted to bar, 1990, California, U.S. District Court, Northern District of California and U.S. Court of Appeals, Ninth Circuit; 1992, District of Columbia, U.S. District Court for the District of Columbia and U.S. Court of Appeals for the District of Columbia Circuit; 1996, Maryland. *Education:* University of Pennsylvania (A.B., 1971; A.M., 1975; Ph.D., 1979); Boalt Hall School of Law, University of California (J.D., 1990). Order of the Coif. *Member:* State Bar of California (Inactive); District of Columbia Bar; Maryland State Bar Association. ***PRACTICE AREAS:*** Litigation. ***Email:*** lfkaufmann@zuckerman.com

DEBORAH S. RICHARDSON, born New York, N.Y., July 25, 1970; admitted to bar, 1995, Maryland; 1996, U.S. District Court, District of Maryland and U.S. Court of Appeals, Fourth Circuit. *Education:* University of Maryland (B.A., 1992); University of Baltimore (J.D., summa cum laude, 1995). Heuisler Honor Society. Associate Articles Editor, University of Baltimore Law Review, 1994-1995. Law Clerk to Judge Deborah K. Chasanow, U.S. District Court, District of Maryland, 1995-1997. *Member:* Maryland State and Federal Bar Associations. (Resident, Baltimore, Maryland Office). ***PRACTICE AREAS:*** White Collar Criminal Defense; Complex Civil Litigation. ***Email:*** drichardson@zuckerman.com

PATRICE A. SHELBURNE, born Boston, Massachusetts, March 10, 1965; admitted to bar, 1998, Virginia; 1999, District of Columbia and Maryland. *Education:* Wellesley College (B.A., 1988); Georgetown University Law Center (J.D., 1998). ***PRACTICE AREAS:*** Litigation. ***Email:*** pshelburne@zuckerman.com

KRISTEN M. FLYNN, born Washington, D.C., February 16, 1968; admitted to bar, 1998, Maryland; 1999, District of Columbia. *Education:* Amherst College (B.A., 1990); University of Michigan (J.D., cum laude, 1997). Law Clerk to the Honorable Rosemary Barkett, U.S. Court of Appeals, Eleventh Circuit, 1997-1998. ***PRACTICE AREAS:*** Civil Litigation; Criminal Litigation. ***Email:*** kflynn@zuckerman.com

CARLOS T. ANGULO, born New York, New York, April 18, 1964; admitted to bar, 1990, New York; 2000, District of Columbia. *Education:* Haverford College (B.A., magna cum laude, 1986); Yale University (J.D., 1989). Phi Beta Kappa. ***PRACTICE AREAS:*** Litigation; Legislative Practice. ***Email:*** ctangulo@zuckerman.com

JOEL D. SCHWARTZ, born Orange, New Jersey, November 25, 1962; admitted to bar, 1990, Texas; 1994, Pennsylvania; 2000, District of Columbia. *Education:* Franklin and Marshall College (A.B., 1984); Eagleton Institute of Politics; Rutgers University at New Brunswick (M.A., 1985); New York University (J.D., 1990). Staff Attorney, Defender Association of Philadelphia, 1994-1999; Texas Resource Center, 1992-1994; Texas Rural Legal Aid, Inc., 1990-1992. *Member:* National Association of Criminal Defense Lawyers. Fellow, Skadden Foundation. ***PRACTICE AREAS:*** Criminal Litigation; Civil Litigation. ***Email:*** jdschwartz@zuckerman.com

AMIT P. MEHTA, born Patan Gujarat, India, December 27, 1971; admitted to bar, 1997, California (inactive); 2000, District of Columbia. *Education:* Georgetown University (B.A., magna cum laude, 1993); University of Virginia (J.D., 1997). Phi Beta Kappa; Order of the Coif; Alpha Sigma Nu. Law Clerk to the Honorable Susan P. Graber, U.S. Court of Appeals, Ninth Circuit, 1998-1999. ***PRACTICE AREAS:*** Litigation. ***Email:*** amehta@zuckerman.com

CAROLINE ALICE JUDGE, born Littleton, Massachusetts, August 11, 1971; admitted to bar, 1999, Massachusetts; 2001, District of Columbia. *Education:* University of Vermont (B.A., summa cum laude, 1993); Harvard Law School (J.D., magna cum laude, 1999). ***PRACTICE AREAS:*** Litigation. ***Email:*** cjudge@zuckerman.com

ALEXANDRA FOSTER, born Rabat, Morocco, May 2, 1972; admitted to bar, 1999, Texas; 2000, District of Columbia. *Education:* Harvard University (B.A., 1993); University of Texas at Austin (J.D., 1999). Strauss Fellowship; Baron and Budd Fellowship. *Member:* State Bar of Texas; The District of Columbia Bar. ***LANGUAGES:*** French. ***PRACTICE AREAS:*** Litigation. ***Email:*** afoster@zuckerman.com

MARY I. PETERS, born Cincinnati, Ohio, June 10, 1969; admitted to bar, 1998, Maryland; 2000, District of Columbia. *Education:* University of Michigan (A.B., with distinction, 1991); University of Virginia (J.D., 1998). Law Clerk to the Honorable Ellen Segal Huvelle, District of Columbia Superior Court. ***PRACTICE AREAS:*** Civil Litigation; Criminal Law. ***Email:*** mpeters@zuckerman.com

DAVID W. HOTES, born Wilmington, Delaware, March 29, 1965; admitted to bar, 1995, Maryland; 1999, District of Columbia. *Education:* Lehigh University (B.S., Accounting, 1988); University of Maryland (J.D., with honors, 1995). Certified Public Accountant, Maryland, 1988. *Member:* Maryland State and American Bar Associations; District of Columbia Bar. ***PRACTICE AREAS:*** Business Law; Corporate Law; Real Estate; Taxation. ***Email:*** dhotes@zuckerman.com

(This Listing Continued)

CYNTHIA L. TIPPETT, born Baltimore, Maryland, July 16, 1973; admitted to bar, 2000, Maryland; 2001, U.S. District Court, District of Maryland. *Education:* Georgia Southern College (B.A., 1995); University of Maryland (M.S., 1997; J.D., with honors, concentrations in Environmental Law and Health Care Law, 2000). Member, Moot Court. Executive Editor, Journal of Health Care Law & Policy, University of Maryland, 1999-2000. *Member:* Maryland State Bar Association. (Resident, Baltimore, Maryland Office). ***PRACTICE AREAS:*** White Collar Criminal Defense; Complex Litigation. ***Email:*** ctippett@zuckerman.com

REFERENCE: District of Columbia National Bank/Sovran.

(For complete biographical data on other personnel, see Professional Biographies in Baltimore, Maryland, New York, N.Y., Miami, Fort Lauderdale and Tampa, Florida and Wilmington, Delaware Offices).

ZUCKERT, SCOUTT & RASENBERGER, L.L.P.

Established in 1964

888 SEVENTEENTH STREET, N.W.

WASHINGTON, D.C. 20006-3309

Telephone: 202-298-8660

Telecopier: 202-342-0683

URL: http://www.zsrlaw.com

Civil and Administrative Litigation Practice. General Practice with emphasis on International Business, Domestic and International Aviation, Surface Transportation, Antitrust, Taxation, Government Contracts, Asset-based Transactions, Labor and Employee Benefits, Bankruptcy, Immigration. Legislative Practice.

MEMBERS OF FIRM

EUGENE M. ZUCKERT (1911-2000).

RICHARD A. ALLEN, born Washington, D.C., July 27, 1945; admitted to bar, 1971, District of Columbia; 1976, U.S. Court of Appeals, District of Columbia Circuit; 1977, U.S. Supreme Court. *Education:* Harvard University (B.A., cum laude, 1967); Columbia University (J.D., 1970). Note and Comment Editor, Columbia Law Review, 1969-1970. Law Clerk to Judge Carl McGowan, U.S. Court of Appeals, District of Columbia Circuit, 1971. Assistant to the Solicitor General of the United States, 1976-1979. General Counsel, Interstate Commerce Commission, 1979-1982. *Member:* The District of Columbia Bar. ***PRACTICE AREAS:*** U.S. Supreme Court Litigation; Transportation Regulation; Motor Carrier Regulation; Civil Litigation; Railroad Labor Law. ***Email:*** raallen@zsrlaw.com

MALCOLM L. BENGE, born Wilmington, Delaware, September 13, 1955; admitted to bar, 1983, District of Columbia. *Education:* Wesleyan University (B.A., cum laude, 1977); University of Pennsylvania (J.D., 1983). *Member:* The District of Columbia Bar. ***PRACTICE AREAS:*** Administrative Law; Aviation and Aerospace; Equipment Finance and Leasing; Transportation. ***Email:*** mlbenge@zsrlaw.com

JAMES A. CALDERWOOD, born Washington, D.C., December 4, 1941; admitted to bar, 1970, Maryland; 1972, U.S. Claims Court; 1973, District of Columbia; 1974, U.S. Supreme Court; 1976, U.S. District Court for the District of Columbia and U.S. Court of Appeals, District of Columbia Circuit. *Education:* University of Maryland (B.S., 1964); George Washington University (J.D., with honors, 1970). Chairman, Editorial Board, Antitrust Transportation Reports, 1983-1989. Member, General Council, Society of Government Economists, 1972-1975, 1978-1983. Special Assistant U.S. Attorney for the District of Columbia, 1973. With U.S. Department of Justice, Antitrust Division, 1970-1980. *Member:* The District of Columbia Bar; Maryland State, Federal, Federal Energy and American Bar Associations; Transportation Lawyers Association (Co-Chairman, Antitrust Committee, 1998—); Association of Transportation Law, Logistics and Policy (Past President, D.C. Chapter). ***PRACTICE AREAS:*** Administrative Law; Antitrust and Trade Regulation; Energy; Government Contracts; Transportation. ***Email:*** jacalderwood@zsrlaw.com

WILLIAM H. CALLAWAY, JR., born Washington, D.C., April 26, 1951; admitted to bar, 1976, Virginia; 1977, District of Columbia. *Education:* Duke University (B.A., magna cum laude, 1973); University of Virginia (J.D., 1976). Phi Beta Kappa. Author: "Commercial Aircraft Transactions," CCH Incorporated. *Member:* The District of Columbia Bar; Virginia State Bar. ***PRACTICE AREAS:*** International Aviation Law; Aircraft Finance and Leasing; Asset-Based Finance; International Commercial Finance. ***Email:*** whcallaway@zsrlaw.com

FRANK J. COSTELLO, born Syracuse, New York, March 22, 1944; admitted to bar, 1970, District of Columbia. *Education:* Dartmouth College (A.B., 1965); Georgetown University (J.D., 1970). *Member:* The District of Columbia Bar; American Bar Association (Chair, Aviation Committee, Section of Public Utility, Communications and Transportation Law); Maritime Law Association; The Association of Trial Lawyers of America. ***PRACTICE AREAS:*** Federal Administrative Law; Maritime Commercial Law; Aviation; Commercial Litigation. ***Email:*** fjcostello@zsrlaw.com

(This Listing Continued)

JAMES A. HARRIS, born Pocatello, Idaho, November 19, 1957; admitted to bar, 1982, Washington (inactive); 1985, U.S. Tax Court; 1986, District of Columbia; 1994, Maryland. *Education:* Idaho State University (B.A. with high honors, 1979); University of Washington (J.D., with honors, 1982); Georgetown University (LL.M., 1985). Law Clerk to Judge Edna G. Parker, U.S. Tax Court, 1982-1985. *Member:* The District of Columbia Bar; Washington State and American Bar Associations. ***PRACTICE AREAS:*** Tax Exempt Organizations; Nonprofit Tax Law; Charitable Giving; Tax Controversies; Estate Planning. ***Email:*** jaharris@zsrlaw.com

RALPH L. KISSICK, born Washington, D.C., September 6, 1940; admitted to bar, 1969, District of Columbia; 1970, U.S. Claims Court; 1980, U.S. Supreme Court. *Education:* Yale University (B.A., 1962); University of Michigan (J.D., 1969). Law Clerk, U.S. Court of Claims, 1969-1970. *Member:* The District of Columbia Bar; American Bar Association; National Contract Management Association. ***PRACTICE AREAS:*** International Government Contracts; Federal Contracts; Aerospace Contracts; Aircraft Finance and Leasing. ***Email:*** rlkissick@zsrlaw.com

RICHARD D. MATHIAS, born Shorewood, Wisconsin, August 17, 1940; admitted to bar, 1966, District of Columbia and U.S. Supreme Court. *Education:* College of the Holy Cross (B.S., 1962); Harvard University (LL.B., cum laude, 1965). *Member:* The District of Columbia Bar. ***PRACTICE AREAS:*** Airline Regulation; International Aviation. ***Email:*** rdmathias@zsrlaw.com

LONNIE ANNE PERA, born Bethlehem, Pennsylvania, December 18, 1959; admitted to bar, 1990, Maryland; 1991, Pennsylvania and District of Columbia. *Education:* Bucknell University (B.A., 1982); Catholic University of America (J.D., 1990). Associate Editor, Catholic University Law Review, 1989-1990. *Member:* Maryland State, Pennsylvania and American Bar Associations; The District of Columbia Bar. ***PRACTICE AREAS:*** Airline Regulation; Aviation Law; International Aviation Law; International Trade. ***Email:*** lapera@zsrlaw.com

RONALD S. PERLMAN, born Miami, Florida, March 8, 1948; admitted to bar, 1972, Massachusetts; 1973, U.S. Court of Military Appeals; 1975, Florida; 1976, U.S. Supreme Court; 1979, U.S. Court of Federal Claims; 1981, District of Columbia; 1983, U.S. Court of Appeals for the Federal Circuit. *Education:* Brooklyn College (B.A., 1969); Boston College Law School (J.D., 1972); George Washington University (LL.M., in Federal Procurement Law, 1980). Adjunct Professor, Federal Procurement Law, American University, 1980-1989. Judge Advocate, U.S. Air Force (1973-1977). Trial Counsel, U.S. General Services Administration, 1977-1980. *Member:* The District of Columbia Bar; Massachusetts, Federal and American Bar Associations; The Florida Bar; National Contract Management Association (Fellow, 1990). ***PRACTICE AREAS:*** Government Contracts. ***Email:*** rsperlman@zsrlaw.com

ANDREW R. PLUMP, born New York, N.Y., December, 19, 1953; admitted to bar, 1978, New York; 1984, U.S. Supreme Court; 1988, District of Columbia. *Education:* State University of New York at Binghamton (B.A., 1974); University of Pennsylvania (J.D., 1977). Assistant District Attorney, Kings County, New York, 1977-1987. *Member:* The District of Columbia Bar. ***PRACTICE AREAS:*** Commercial Litigation; Civil Litigation; Employment Litigation; Federal Contracts; Transportation Regulation. ***Email:*** arplump@zsrlaw.com

RICHARD P. SCHWEITZER, born Louisville, Kentucky, April 4, 1957; admitted to bar, 1981, Kentucky; 1982, District of Columbia. *Education:* University of Kentucky (B.A., 1977; J.D., 1981). Legislative Counsel, Private Truck Council of America, 1983-1988. *Member:* The District of Columbia Bar; Kentucky Bar Association. ***PRACTICE AREAS:*** Regulated Industries; Interstate Tax; State Taxation; Interstate Commerce; Motor Carrier Law. ***Email:*** rpschweitzer@zsrlaw.com

CHARLES J. SIMPSON, JR., born Washington, D.C., September 16, 1951; admitted to bar, 1979, District of Columbia; 1980, U.S. Court of Appeals for the District of Columbia Circuit; 1986, U.S. Supreme Court. *Education:* Tufts University (B.A., magna cum laude, 1974); Georgetown University (J.D., 1979). Lead Articles Editor, Law and Policy in International Business, 1978-1979. *Member:* The District of Columbia Bar. ***PRACTICE AREAS:*** Antitrust; Aviation Law; Commercial Litigation; International Law. ***Email:*** cjsimpson@zsrlaw.com

RACHEL B. TRINDER, born Ibadan, Nigeria, February 21, 1955; admitted to bar, 1979, District of Columbia; 1980, U.S. Court of Appeals, District of Columbia Circuit; 1986, U.S. Supreme Court. *Education:* Oxford University (M.A., jurisprudence, 1977); University of Virginia (LL.M., 1978). Board Member/Executive Committee, International Institute of Air and Space Law, Leiden University, 1992—. President: Aero Club of Washington, 2000; International Aviation Club, 1986. *Member:* The District of Columbia Bar; Federal (Chair: International Law Section, 1994-1996; Space Law Committee, 1990-1994); International Bar Association; American Institute of Aeronautics and Astronautics; Middle Temple. ***PRACTICE AREAS:*** Aviation Law; Airport Regulation; Employment Claims; Aerospace Law; Commercial Litigation. ***Email:*** rbtrinder@zsrlaw.com

(This Listing Continued)

MONIQUE E. YINGLING, born Pittsfield, Massachusetts, October 28, 1951; admitted to bar, 1977, California and U.S. Court of Appeals, Ninth Circuit; 1982, U.S. Claims Court; 1983, U.S. Tax Court; 1984, District of Columbia; 1989, U.S. Supreme Court. *Education:* Vassar College (A.B., cum laude, 1973); University of Tennessee (J.D., 1977); Georgetown University (LL.M., in Taxation, 1984). Order of the Coif. Assistant Editor, University of Tennessee Law Review, 1975-1976. Trial Attorney, Tax Division, Department of Justice, 1978-1983. *Member:* The District of Columbia Bar; State Bar of California; American Bar Association. ***PRACTICE AREAS:*** Federal Tax Controversies; Federal Taxation; Income Tax; Tax Controversies; Tax Exempt Organizations. ***Email:*** meyingling@zsr.com

SCOTT M. ZIMMERMAN, born Cleveland, Ohio, June 27, 1962; admitted to bar, 1992, Virginia; 1993, District of Columbia; 1998, U.S. District Court, Eastern District of Virginia. *Education:* Cornell University (B.A., 1985); College of William & Mary (J.D., 1992). Staff Member, William & Mary Law Review, 1990-1992. *Member:* The District of Columbia Bar. ***Email:*** smzimmerman@zsrlaw.com

OF COUNSEL

DENISE A. DANIELS, born Washington, D.C., July 18, 1956; admitted to bar, 1985, Maryland; 1986, District of Columbia and Virginia; 1988, U.S. Court of Appeals, Fourth Circuit; 1995, U.S. Supreme Court. *Education:* University of Maryland (B.S., 1978; J.D., 1984). Special Counsel to the Vice Chairman, National Transportation Safety Board, 1996-2000; Special Counsel to the Chief Counsel, Federal Aviation Administration, 1989-1991. Attorney, Federal Aviation Administration, 1987-1991. *Member:* The District of Columbia Bar; Virginia State Bar. ***PRACTICE AREAS:*** Aviation Law; Aviation Regulation; Airport Law; Aviation Accidents; Transportation Safety. ***Email:*** dadaniels@zsrlaw.com

JAMES L. DEVALL, born Kansas City, Kansas, August 22, 1941; admitted to bar, 1968, District of Columbia; 1973, U.S. Court of Appeals, District of Columbia and Ninth Circuits and U.S. Supreme Court. *Education:* Kansas University (B.A., 1963); Fletcher School of Law and Diplomacy (M.A., 1964); University of California at Berkeley (J.D., 1967). Phi Beta Kappa. *Member:* The District of Columbia Bar; Federal, American and International Bar Associations. ***PRACTICE AREAS:*** Airline Regulation; Aviation Law; International Aviation Law. ***Email:*** jldevall@zsrlaw.com

PAMELA L. MEREDITH, born Montreal, Canada, August 27, 1956; admitted to bar, 1989, New York (Not admitted in District of Columbia). *Education:* Tersbraaten Gymnasium (Artium, 1975); University of Oslo School of Law (J.D. equivalent, 1981); McGill University, Air & Space Law Institute (LL.M., 1983). Adjunct Professor of Satellite Communications and Space Law, American University, Washington College of Law, 1989—. *Member:* Federal Bar Association. ***PRACTICE AREAS:*** Aerospace Law; Aerospace Contracts; Space Law. ***Email:*** plmspace@erols.com

RAYMOND J. RASENBERGER, born New York, N.Y., September 30, 1927; admitted to bar, 1957, District of Columbia and U.S. Court of Appeals, District of Columbia Circuit; 1961, U.S. Supreme Court. *Education:* Dartmouth College (A.B., with distinction, 1949); Syracuse University (A.M., 1957); George Washington University (J.D., 1957). Order of the Coif. *Member:* The District of Columbia Bar. ***PRACTICE AREAS:*** Mediation; Arbitration. ***Email:*** rjrasenberger@zsrlaw.com

JERROLD SCOUTT, JR., born Hastings, Nebraska, January 19, 1922; admitted to bar, 1949, Pennsylvania and District of Columbia; 1950, U.S. Court of Appeals, District of Columbia Circuit; 1955, U.S. Supreme Court. *Education:* Carleton College (A.B., 1943); Fletcher School of Law and Diplomacy (M.A., 1944); Harvard University (LL.B., 1948). Phi Beta Kappa. *Member:* The District of Columbia Bar; American Bar Association. Fellow, American College of Trial Lawyers.

GERALD L. WAID, born Gadsden, Alabama, January 25, 1955; admitted to bar, 1990, New York; 2000, District of Columbia. *Education:* Auburn University (B.A., with high honor, 1977); University of Texas at Austin (M.A., Government, 1983; J.D., with high honor, 1989). Order of the Coif. Counsel and Senior Counsel, Export-Import Bank of the United States, 1991-1999. ***PRACTICE AREAS:*** Aircraft Finance and Leasing; International Finance. ***Email:*** glwaid@zsrlaw.com

SENIOR POLICY ADVISOR

ROBERT T. FRANCIS II, born Springfield, Massachusetts, February 5, 1938. *Education:* Williams College (A.B., 1960). Congressional Relations Officer, DOT/FAA, 1977-1979. Special Assistant to Director, European FAA Office, 1979-1982; Chief, Policy and International Staff, FAA Southern Region, 1982-1986; Senior Representative, FAA Western Europe, 1986-1995; Vice-Chairman, National Transportation Safety Board, 1995-2000. ***PRACTICE AREAS:*** Aviation Regulation; Transportation Safety; Aviation Accidents; International Government Relations; Maritime Accidents. ***Email:*** rtfrancis@farragutintl.com

(This Listing Continued)

ZUCKERT, SCOUTT & RASENBERGER, L.L.P., Washington—Continued

JONATHAN HOWE, born New Haven, Connecticut, December 8, 1937; (admission pending). *Education:* Yale University (B.A., cum laude, 1960); (Yale Law School, LL.B, 1963). Deputy Chief Counsel, FAA, 1978-1980; Regional Administrator, FAA, 1981-1986; President, National Business Aircraft Association, 1986-1992; Zuckert, Scoutt & Rasenberger, L.L.P., 1992-1997; Director General, Airports Council International, Geneva, 1997-2001. ***PRACTICE AREAS:*** Aeronautical Regulation; Airport Regulation; Aviation; Federal Aviation Regulation; International Aviation. ***Email:*** jhowe@farragutintl.com

DIRECTOR OF GOVERNMENT AFFAIRS

PAUL E. SCHOELLHAMER, born Pomona, California, July 26, 1947. *Education:* University of California at Santa Cruz (B.A., 1970). Staff to Aviation Subcommittee, U.S. House of Representatives, 1981-1984. Vice President, Government Affairs, Republic Airlines, 1984-1985; Vice President, Government Affairs, Northwest Airlines, 1985-1990. Chief of Staff, Public Works and Transportation Committee, U.S. House of Representatives, 1993-1995. Vice-President, Planning and Development, Lockheed Martin IMS, 1995-1997. ***PRACTICE AREAS:*** Government Affairs; Transportation. ***Email:*** peschoellhamer@zsrlaw.com

ASSOCIATES

PATRICIA E. BRUCE, born Far Rockaway, New York, May 21, 1955; admitted to bar, 1993, Florida; 1995, District of Columbia. *Education:* St. John's University (B.A., summa cum laude, 1977); University of Miami (J.D., cum laude, 1993). Staff Member, University of Miami Law Review, 1991-1993. Articles and Comments Editor, University of Miami Law Review, 1992-1993. *Member:* The District of Columbia Bar; The Florida Bar; American Bar Association; Women's Bar Association of the District of Columbia. ***Email:*** pebruce@zsrlaw.com

ROBERT A. DeHAAN, born Peoria, Illinois, January 10, 1969; admitted to bar, 1994, Illinois; 1996, District of Columbia. *Education:* University of Illinois (A.B., 1991; J.D., 1994). Notes and Comments Editor, University of Illinois Law Review, 1993-1994. ***Email:*** radehaan@zsrlaw.com

JEFFREY A. MORSE, born Milwaukee, Wisconsin, November 17, 1962; admitted to bar, 1999, Wisconsin, U.S. Tax Court, U.S. Court of Appeals, Seventh and Federal Circuits; 2001, District of Columbia; U.S. District Court, Eastern District of Wisconsin. *Education:* University of Wisconsin (B.A., cum laude, 1995); Marquette University (J.D., 1998); University of Missouri (LL.M., Taxation, 1999). Staff Member, Marquette University Law Review, 1996-1998. *Member:* State Bar of Wisconsin; The District of Columbia Bar; American Bar Association. ***PRACTICE AREAS:*** Taxation; Employee Benefits. ***Email:*** jamorse@zsrlaw.com

SHANNON M. MOYER, born Honolulu, Hawaii, August 13, 1975; admitted to bar, 2000, Virginia; 2001, District of Columbia. *Education:* Syracuse University (B.A., summa cum laude, 1997); George Washington University (J.D., 2000). Staff Member, 1998-1999, and Note Editor, 1999-2000, American Intellectual Property Law Association Quarterly Journal. *Member:* Virginia State Bar; The District of Columbia Bar. ***Email:*** smmoyer@zsrlaw.com

NISHA SAXENA, born Luton, England, August 29, 1975; admitted to bar, 2001, New York and District of Columbia. *Education:* University of Minnesota (B.S., with distinction, 1997); George Washington University (J.D., with honors, 2000). Member, The Public Contract Law Journal, 1998-2000. *Member:* The District of Columbia Bar. ***Email:*** nsaxena@zsrlaw.com

JOL A. SILVERSMITH, born Morristown, New Jersey, November 26, 1972; admitted to bar, 1998, Maryland and Massachusetts; 1999, District of Columbia. *Education:* Harvard University (A.B., cum laude, 1994; J.D., cum laude, 1998); London School of Economics (M.Sc., 1995). Senior Editor, Harvard Civil Rights-Civil Liberties Law Review, 1997-1998. Law Clerk to the Justices of the Superior Court of Massachusetts, 1998-1999. *Member:* Massachusetts, Maryland State, Federal and American Bar Associations; The District of Columbia Bar. ***Email:*** jasilversmith@zsrlaw.com

LEGISLATIVE PROFESSIONAL

KENNETH C. HINES, born Fresno, California, December 24, 1960. *Education:* California State University (B.A., 1984); California State University (M.A., 1989). ***Email:*** kchines@zsrlaw.com

Languages: English, French, Norwegian and Spanish.

LYNNE K. ZUSMAN & ASSOCIATES, P.C.

1818 N STREET, NW
SUITE 701

WASHINGTON, D.C. 20036

Telephone: 202-659-1971

Fax: 202-659-0454

URL: http://www.lawyers.com/lynnezusmanlaw

Federal Regulatory Law, Administrative Litigation, Governmental Law, Whistle-blower Litigation, Employment Law, White Collar Criminal Defense, Inspector General Investigations, Business Fraud, Contract Disputes, Executive Compensation, Wrongful Termination, Corporate Investigations, Congressional Investigations.

FIRM PROFILE: Lynne K. Zusman is a former trial attorney for the U.S. Department of Justice. For more than 17 years, Ms. Zusman has conducted a practice serving clients across the country in a variety of cases and for purposes of representation in general litigation.

LYNNE K. ZUSMAN, born New York, N.Y., March 27, 1939; admitted to bar, 1964, California; 1974, U.S. Supreme Court; 1977, U.S. Court of Appeals for the District of Columbia Circuit; 1979, District of Columbia; 1984, Virginia, U.S. District Court, Eastern District of Virginia and U.S. Court of Appeals, Fourth Circuit; 1987, U.S. Court of Appeals for the Federal Circuit; 1990, Maryland and U.S. District Court, District of Maryland. *Education:* Bryn Mawr College (A.B., cum laude with honors in Political Science, 1959); Yale University (LL.B., 1962). Research Assistant, Assistant to the Dean, Stanford Law School, 1962-1967. Trial Attorney, U.S. Department of Justice: Criminal Division, Appellate Section, 1974-1976, Civil Division; Freedom of Information and Privacy Section, 1976-1977; Chief, 1977-1979, Special Litigation Counsel, 1979. Special Assistant U.S. Attorney, U.S. Attorney's Office, District of Columbia, 1979-1981. Deputy General Counsel for Litigation, U.S. Department of Health and Human Services, 1981-1983. Vice President and General Counsel, Allegheny Beverage Corporation, 1983-1984. Treasurer, Yale Law School Washington Club, 1989-1990. Member, Board of Directors, American Jewish Congress (National Capital Region), 1992-1994. Counsel for the Commission of Democracies, Washington, D.C., 2001—. *Member:* The District of Columbia Bar; Montgomery County, Maryland State, Federal and American (Member, Administrative Law and Regulatory Practice Section; 2002, Council; Vice Chair, Government Information and Right to Privacy; Co-Chair, Government Personnel; A.B.A. Advisory Committee to Standing Committee on Law and National Security, 1986-1996) Bar Associations; Virginia State Bar; State Bar of California.

OF COUNSEL

RICHARD D. GLOVSKY, born Boston, Massachusetts, August 27, 1947; admitted to bar, 1972, Massachusetts; 1975, District of Columbia. *Education:* Dartmouth College (A.B., 1969); Boston College (J.D., 1972). Editor, Boston College Law Review, 1971-1972. Assistant United States Attorney, 1975-1980 and Chief, Civil Division, 1978-1980, District of Massachusetts. Attorney/Advisor, Office of Legal Counsel, Department of Justice, 1973-1975. (Also Member, Glovsky & Associates, Boston, Massachusetts and Washington, D.C.).

ZWERLING & KEMLER, P.C.

WASHINGTON, D.C.

(See Alexandria, Virginia)

Civil and Criminal Trials and Appeals in all State and Federal Courts.

LAW SCHOOL SECTION

This Section features academic and professional profile information on law schools and full time faculty and provides an alphabetical roster of schools offering first professional degree programs. Schools that are ABA-accredited and provisionally-accredited are denoted by a tagline which includes the year of ABA approval.

Consult this Section when seeking information about law schools in general or when more detailed information about the academic character, programs and teaching staff of a particular school is needed.

The Law School Section offers a forum for legal educators and practitioners to communicate, identify and share common interests and expertise.

Institutions presenting detailed profile information in this edition are listed on the following pages.

2002 EDITION PARTICIPATING LAW SCHOOLS

Albany Law School, Union University .... Albany, New York
American University Washington College of Law .... Washington, District of Columbia
Arizona State University College of Law .... Tempe, Arizona
Ave Maria School of Law .... Ann Arbor, Michigan
Benjamin N. Cardozo School of Law, Yeshiva University .... New York, New York
Boston University School of Law .... Boston, Massachusetts
Brigham Young University, J. Reuben Clark Law School .... Provo, Utah
Brooklyn Law School .... Brooklyn, New York
California Western School of Law .... San Diego, California
Campbell University, Norman Adrian Wiggins School of Law .... Buies Creek, North Carolina
Capital University Law School .... Columbus, Ohio
Case Western Reserve University School of Law .... Cleveland, Ohio
Catholic University of America Columbus School of Law, The .... Washington, D.C.
Chapman University School of Law .... Anaheim, California
Chicago-Kent College of Law, Illinois Institute of Technology .... Chicago, Illinois
City University of New York, School of Law at Queens College .... Flushing, New York
Cleveland State University - Cleveland-Marshall College of Law .... Cleveland, Ohio
College of William and Mary School of Law .... Williamsburg, Virginia
Columbia University School of Law .... New York, New York
Cornell University Law School .... Ithaca, New York
Cumberland School of Law at Samford University .... Birmingham, Alabama
Dickinson School of Law of The Pennsylvania State University, The .... Carlisle, Pennsylvania
Drake University Law School .... Des Moines, Iowa
Duke University School of Law .... Durham, North Carolina
Duquesne University School of Law .... Pittsburgh, Pennsylvania
Emory University School of Law .... Atlanta, Georgia
Fordham University School of Law .... New York, New York
Franklin Pierce Law Center .... Concord, New Hampshire
George Mason University School of Law .... Arlington, Virginia
George Washington University Law School, The .... Washington, D.C.
Golden Gate University School of Law .... San Francisco, California
Gonzaga University School of Law .... Spokane, Washington
Harvard Law School .... Cambridge, Massachusetts
Hofstra University School of Law .... Hempstead, Long Island, New York
Howard University School of Law .... Washington, D.C.
Indiana University School of Law-Bloomington .... Bloomington, Indiana
Indiana University School of Law-Indianapolis .... Indianapolis, Indiana
Inter-American University of Puerto Rico-School of Law .... San Juan, Puerto Rico
John Marshall Law School .... Atlanta, Georgia
John Marshall Law School, The .... Chicago, Illinois
Louis D. Brandeis School of Law - University of Louisville .... Louisville, Kentucky
Loyola University - New Orleans School of Law .... New Orleans, Louisiana
Marquette University Law School .... Milwaukee, Wisconsin
Mercer University Walter F. George School of Law .... Macon, Georgia
Michigan State University - Detroit College of Law .... East Lansing, Michigan
Mississippi College School of Law .... Jackson, Mississippi
Nashville School of Law .... Nashville, Tennessee
New England School of Law .... Boston, Massachusetts

2002 EDITION PARTICIPATING LAW SCHOOLS – continued

New York Law School	New York, New York
New York University School of Law	New York, New York
Northeastern University School of Law	Boston, Massachusetts
Northern Illinois University College of Law	DeKalb, Illinois
Northwestern School of Law of Lewis and Clark College	Portland, Oregon
Northwestern University School of Law	Chicago, Illinois
Notre Dame Law School	Notre Dame, Indiana
Nova Southeastern University Shepard Broad Law Center	Fort Lauderdale, Florida
Ohio Northern University Claude W. Pettit College of Law	Ada, Ohio
Ohio State Michael E. Ortiz University College of Law, The	Columbus, Ohio
Oklahoma City University School of Law	Oklahoma City, Oklahoma
Pace University School of Law	White Plains, New York
Pepperdine University School of Law	Malibu, California
Regent University School of Law	Virginia Beach, Virginia
Roger Williams University, Ralph R. Papitto School of Law	Bristol, Rhode Island
Rutgers, The State University of New Jersey School of Law, Camden	Camden, New Jersey
Rutgers, The State University of New Jersey School of Law, Newark	Newark, New Jersey
St. John's University School of Law	Jamaica, New York
Saint Louis University School of Law	St. Louis, Missouri
St. Thomas University School of Law	Miami, Florida
Seattle University School of Law	Seattle, Washington
Seton Hall University School of Law	Newark, New Jersey
South Texas College of Law	Houston, Texas
Southern Illinois University School of Law	Carbondale, Illinois
Southern Methodist University School of Law	Dallas, Texas
Southern University Law Center	Baton Rouge, Louisiana
Stetson University College of Law	St. Petersburg, Florida
Suffolk University Law School	Boston, Massachusetts
Syracuse University College of Law	Syracuse, New York
Temple University Beasley School of Law	Philadelphia, Pennsylvania
Texas Southern University, Thurgood Marshall School of Law	Houston, Texas
Texas Tech University School of Law	Lubbock, Texas
Thomas Jefferson School of Law	San Diego, California
Thomas M. Cooley Law School	Lansing, Michigan
Touro College Jacob D. Fuchsberg Law Center	Huntington, New York
University of Akron School of Law, The	Akron, Ohio
University of Alabama School of Law	Tuscaloosa, Alabama
University of Arizona, James E. Rogers College of Law, The	Tucson, Arizona
University of Arkansas at Fayetteville School of Law	Fayetteville, Arkansas
University of Baltimore School of Law	Baltimore, Maryland
University of Chicago Law School	Chicago, Illinois
University of Colorado School of Law	Boulder, Colorado
University of Connecticut School of Law	Hartford, Connecticut
University of Denver College of Law	Denver, Colorado
University of Detroit Mercy School of Law	Detroit, Michigan
University of Florida Fredric G. Levin College of Law	Gainesville, Florida
University of Houston Law Center	Houston, Texas
University of Idaho College of Law	Moscow, Idaho

2002 EDITION PARTICIPATING LAW SCHOOLS – continued

University of Illinois College of Law .... Champaign, Illinois
University of Iowa College of Law .... Iowa City, Iowa
University of Kentucky College of Law .... Lexington, Kentucky
University of Maine School of Law .... Portland, Maine
University of Maryland School of Law .... Baltimore, Maryland
University of Miami School of Law .... Coral Gables, Florida
University of Mississippi School of Law .... University, Mississippi
University of Missouri - Kansas City School of Law .... Kansas City, Missouri
University of Nebraska College of Law .... Lincoln, Nebraska
University of Pennsylvania Law School .... Philadelphia, Pennsylvania
University of Pittsburgh School of Law .... Pittsburgh, Pennsylvania
University of Richmond School of Law .... Richmond, Virginia
University of San Francisco School of Law .... San Francisco, California
University of Texas School of Law .... Austin, Texas
University of Toledo College of Law, The .... Toledo, Ohio
University of Tulsa College of Law, The .... Tulsa, Oklahoma
University of Virginia School of Law .... Charlottesville, Virginia
University of Washington School of Law .... Seattle, Washington
University of Wisconsin Law School .... Madison, Wisconsin
Valparaiso University School of Law .... Valparaiso, Indiana
Villanova University School of Law .... Villanova, Pennsylvania
Washington and Lee University School of Law .... Lexington, Virginia
Washington University School of Law .... St. Louis, Missouri
Western New England College School of Law .... Springfield, Massachusetts
Western State University College of Law .... Fullerton, California
Willamette University College of Law .... Salem, Oregon

ALBANY LAW SCHOOL, UNION UNIVERSITY

80 NEW SCOTLAND AVENUE
ALBANY, NEW YORK 12208
Telephone: (518) 445-2311
Fax: (518) 445-2315
http://www.als.edu

ABA Approved Since 1930

Founded in 1851, Albany Law School is the oldest independent law school in North America and the oldest law school in New York state. Located in the heart of New York's Capital Region, the private institution of 700 students equips each student with the analytical skills required to be an attorney, the practical skills necessary to meet clients' needs, and the intellectual tools and supportive resources to distinguish themselves in their chosen field. The Law School's dedicated, accessible faculty, active alumni/ae involvement, and myriad opportunities for developing and practicing professional skills create an environment where students can immerse themselves in the experience of lawyering.

Albany Law School offers three- and four-year programs leading to a Juris Doctor degree, joint degree programs in business, public administration, social welfare, urban planning, and a new master of science in legal studies degree for professionals in other fields. The traditional course of study acquaints students with sources of law while giving them a thorough knowledge and understanding of legal rules and principles, both in their historical context and their contemporary application. Students develop legal reasoning and other analytical skills while learning ethical principles and professional standards. Graduates are well equipped for work in private practice, the judiciary, government service, public interest law, business, or any career that draws on legal skills. Albany Law School graduates are highly successful in securing employment; 96 percent of recent graduates were employed within nine months of graduation.

The School has 48 full-time faculty and 33 adjunct faculty. The relatively small size of the student body and intimate campus fosters a close-knit, supportive atmosphere. The collegial environment encourages frequent contact between students and faculty and friendship among students, leading to bonds that sustain them while at law school, and often continue throughout their lifetime. Albany Law School alumni/ae provide mentoring support to current students as well as employment opportunities and networking contacts to fellow graduates through the Career Advisory Network. The School has produced a long line of outstanding legal practitioners, scholars and jurists, as well as distinguished leaders in business and government. These include Hon. Victoria A. Graffeo, associate judge, New York State Court of Appeals; Mary O. Donohue, New York State lieutenant governor; William McKinley, 25th president of the United States; Kate Stoneman, first female member of the New York State Bar; Hon. Lawrence H. Cooke, former chief judge of New York; and Richard Parsons, co-chief operating officer of AOL Time Warner, Inc.

Albany is a superb location for the study of law. Home to one of the world's largest government structures, the city provides a rich environment for students interested in the workings of government and the judicial system. The close proximity of the New York State Legislature, Court of Appeals (New York's highest court), federal courts, and numerous state agencies provide students with excellent opportunities to study and actively participate in the development, implementation, and judicial review of legislation, public policy, and regulation oversight. The School's Government Law Center conducts interdisciplinary study and research on government and the problems facing governments, and introduces law students to policy analysis and public service through research programs, externships, public conferences, and legislative seminars. The Science and Technology Law Center allows students to get hands-on experience dealing with high-tech legal issues. Supervised by staff and volunteer attorneys, students help provide affordable legal assistance for start-up and early-stage companies through the Entrepreneurial Legal Assistance Program.

Journals produced by students include the *Albany Law Review*, *Albany Law Journal of Science and Technology*, and *Albany Law Environmental Outlook*. The Schaffer Law Library, built in1986, provides an inviting study environment with seating for hundreds of students. The book and microfilm collections number more than half a million volumes and equivalents. The library computer lab provides access to the Internet and online legal research systems such as LEXIS-NEXIS, WESTLAW, and DIALOG.

The Admissions Committee, in making decisions on individual applications, focuses on two broad classifications of criteria. The first is "objective academic criteria," including LSAT. undergraduate grade-point average, the academic strength of the undergraduate institution, and the rigor of the undergraduate program. The second, of equal importance, is "uniqueness of life experience and background," including employment experience; life experience that suggests an ability and commitment to the accomplishment of difficult goals and overcoming of substantial obstacles; and racial, ethnic, religious, gender, sexual orientation, cultural, and national affiliations that themselves are indicators of uniqueness. The goal of the Admissions Committee, by considering all of these factors, is to enroll a highly qualified, diverse student body.

Albany Law School is part of an exciting new entity in Albany - the University Heights Association, a consortium of four neighboring institutions. The unique, 30-acre campus serves the students at the Law School, Albany Medical College, Albany College of Pharmacy, and The Sage Colleges. Plans for the shared space include a hotel and conference center, a bookstore and cafe, and landscaped common areas. The Capital Region is the home of 17 colleges and universities, and abounds with cultural and recreational opportunities, including exceptional halls and theaters for the performing arts and the Pepsi Arena for major entertainment and sporting events. The nearby Adirondack, Berkshire, Catskill, and Green mountain ranges offer the best skiing, hiking, and backpacking opportunities in the Northeast.

(This Listing Continued)

ALBANY LAW SCHOOL, UNION UNIVERSITY—Continued

President and Dean: Thomas H. Sponsler (518) 445-2380
Admissions and Financial Aid: Dawn Chamberlaine (518) 445-2326
Government Law Center: Patricia Salkin (518) 445-2351
Science & Technology Law Center: Frederick Provorny (518) 283-8890
Academic Affairs: Dale Moore (518) 445-2343
Library: Robert Begg (518) 445-2340
Career Planning: Sandra Mans (518) 445-2332
Alumni Affairs: Helen Adams-Keane (518) 445-3216
Registrar: Nancy J. Kelsey (518) 445-2324
Institutional Advancement: Christian Kersten (518) 445-3231
Student Affairs: Connie Mayer (518) 445-2393

FULL TIME FACULTY

THOMAS H. SPONSLER*, (President and Dean; Professor of Law)**, born Toledo, Ohio, October 14, 1942; admitted to bar, 1967, Ohio; 1973, Louisiana; 1988, California; 1997, New York. *Education:* University of Toledo (B.A., 1964; J.D., 1967); Yale Law School (LL.M., 1968). ***COURSES: Introduction to Procedure, Evidence. ***Email:*** tspon@mail.als.edu

---

PENELOPE F. ANDREWS*, (Kate Stoneman Endowed Visiting Professor of Law and Democracy)**, admitted to bar, 1989, South Africa. *Education:* University of Natal (B.A., 1980; LL.B., 1982); Columbia University (LL.M., 1984). ***COURSES: International Protection of Human Rights.

PAMELA J. ARMSTRONG*, (Director of Lawyering Program and Lawyering Professor)**, born Utah; admitted to bar, 1986, Massachusetts; 1987, New York. *Education:* Tufts University (B.A., 1977); State University of New York at Albany (M.A., 1980); Albany Law School (J.D., 1986). ***COURSES: Lawyering, Drafting, Pre-Trial Practice I and II, Introduction to Civil Procedure, Client Interviewing and Counseling. ***Email:*** parms@mail.als.edu

JOHN T. BAKER*, (Professor of Law)**, born Louisville, Kentucky, March 15, 1940; admitted to bar, 1966, New York.. *Education:* Fisk University (A.B., 1962); Howard University (L.L.B., 1965). ***COURSES: Business Organizations, Corporate Governance and Finance, Non-Profit Organizations, Political and Civil Rights.. ***Email:*** jbake@mail.als.edu

JOSEPH T. BAUM*, (Assistant Clinical Professor and Director, Litigation Project)**, born Amsterdam, New York, May 25, 1944; admitted to bar, 1973, New York. *Education:* Siena College (B.A., 1966); Albany Law School (J.D., 1972). ***COURSES: Litigation Project.

ROBERT THOMAS BEGG*, (Director, Law Library; Professor of Law, and Associate Dean)**, born Pittsburgh, Pennsylvania, August 14, 1947; admitted to bar, 1976, Ohio. *Education:* Slippery Rock College (B.S., 1969); Rutgers University (M.L.S., 1974); University of Oregon (J.D., 1973). ***COURSES: The Legal Profession. ***Email:*** rbegg@mail.als.edu

IRA MARK BLOOM*, (Professor of Law)**, born New York, New York, November 10, 1944; admitted to bar, 1970, New York. *Education:* City College of New York (B.B.A., 1966); Syracuse University College of Law (J.D., 1969). ***COURSES: Introduction to Taxation, Federal Taxation of Estates, Property I, Trusts and Estates, Estate Planning.

VINCENT MARTIN BONVENTRE*, (Professor of Law)**, born Brooklyn, New York, November 11, 1948; admitted to bar, 1977, New York. *Education:* Union College (B.S., 1972); Brooklyn Law School (J.D., 1976); University of Virginia (M.A.P.A., 1981). ***COURSES: Criminal Law, Criminal Procedure, Professional Responsibility (Ethics), State Constitutional Adjudication, Judicial Process.

ROBERT HENRY BOWMAR*, (Professor of Law)**, born Norwood, Massachusetts, August 7, 1937; admitted to bar, 1970, Massachusetts. *Education:* Boston University (A.B., 1960; M.A., 1962); Northwestern University (J.D., 1966). ***COURSES: Mortgages and Liens, Secured Transactions.

BRIDGIT M. BURKE*, (Assistant Clinical Professor and Director, Civil Rights and Disabilities Law Project)**, admitted to bar, 1990, New York. *Education:* Southampton College, Long Island University (B.S., 1986); Albany Law School (J.D., 1989). ***COURSES: Civil Rights and Disabilities Law Project. ***Email:*** bburk@mail.als.edu

J. STEPHEN CLARK*, (Assistant Professor of Law)**, admitted to bar, 1995, Illinois. *Education:* University of Tennessee (B.A., 1991); Yale Law School (J.D., 1995). ***COURSES: Constitutional Law, Human Sexuality and the Law, Labor Law. ***Email:*** sclar@mail.als.edu

JOSEPH M. CONNORS*, (Assistant Clinical Professor and Director, AIDS Law Project)**, admitted to bar, 1989, New York. *Education:* State University of New York at Buffalo (B.A., 1985); Albany Law School (J.D., 1988). ***COURSES: AIDS Law Project.

PATRICK M. CONNORS*, (Assistant Professor of Law)**, admitted to bar, 1989, New York. *Education:* Georgetown University (B.A., 1985); St. John's University School of Law (J.D., 1988). ***COURSES: The Legal Profession, New York Practice, Professional Responsibility Seminar. ***Email:*** pconn@mail.als.edu

NORMAN T. DEUTSCH*, (Professor of Law)**, born Baltimore, Maryland, December 27, 1944; admitted to bar, 1973, Maryland (inactive); 1985, New York. *Education:* University of Maryland (B.A., 1973; J.D., 1973). ***COURSES: Contracts, Constitutional Law I and II, First Amendment, Political and Civil Rights, Secured Transactions.

HAROLD DUBROFF*, (Professor of Law)**, born Brooklyn, New York, January 1, 1943; admitted to bar, 1966, New York. *Education:* Case Western Reserve University (B.A., 1964); New York University (LL.B., 1966; LL.M., 1968). ***COURSES: Contracts, Corporate Tax I, Federal Taxation of Estates, Introduction to Taxation, Low-Income Taxpayer Project, Taxation of Business Entities I, Trusts and Estates.

JAMES THUO GATHII*, (Assistant Professor of Law)**, *Education:* University of Nairobi (LL.B., 1992); Kenya School of Law (Post-Graduate Diploma in Legal Practice, 1994); Harvard Law School (LL.M., 1995; S.J.D., 1999). ***COURSES: Business Organizations, Criminal Law, International Law.

STEPHEN E. GOTTLIEB*, (Professor of Law)**, born New York, New York, June 2, 1941; admitted to bar, 1967, New York; 1970, Missouri; 1977, West Virginia. *Education:* Princeton University (B.A., 1962); Yale Law School (LL.B., 1965). ***COURSES: Comparative Constitutional Law, Jurisprudence, U.S. Supreme Court Watch, Internet Law, Scientific Evidence, Technology and Privacy. ***Email:*** sgott@mail.als.edu

(This Listing Continued)

ALBANY LAW SCHOOL, UNION UNIVERSITY—Continued

PETER HAINES HALEWOOD,* (Professor of Law)**, born Portland, Oregon; admitted to bar, 1994, New York. *Education:* University of Toronto (B.A., 1985); McGill University (M.A., 1987); University of British Columbia (LL.B., 1990); Columbia University (LL.M., 1994). ***COURSES: Property I, International Law, International Human Rights Law, International Intellectual Property Law, Foreign Relations and National Security Law, Contemporary Perspectives on Law. ***Email:*** phale@mail.als.edu

ANN HOROWITZ,* (Assistant Lawyering Professor; Adjunct Clinical Professor)**, born New York, New York, July 19, 1953; admitted to bar, 1980, New York. *Education:* Yale University (B.A., 1975); New York University (J.D., 1979). ***COURSES: Introduction to Lawyering, Summary Judgement Clinic. ***Email:*** ahoro@mail.als.edu

MICHAEL JOHN HUTTER,* (Professor of Law)**, born Camp Lejune, North Carolina, September 25, 1945; admitted to bar, 1971, New York. *Education:* Brown University (A.B., 1967); Boston College (J.D., 1970). ***COURSES: Antitrust: Market Structure, Evidence, Advanced Evidence, Expert Testimony, Unfair Trade Practices. ***Email:*** mhutt@mail.als.edu

KATHERYN D. KATZ,* (Professor of Law)**, born Chicago, Illinois, September 3, 1933; admitted to bar, 1971, New York and U.S. District Court, Northern District of New York. *Education:* University of California, Berkeley (A.B., 1955); University of New Mexico; Albany Law School (J.D., 1970). ***COURSES: Family Law, Children and the Law, Human Reproduction: Legal and Moral Issues Seminar, Women and the Law. ***Email:*** kkatz@mail.als.edu

MARY A. LYNCH,* (Director, Clinical Legal Studies Program; Clinical Professor of Law)**, born Bronx, New York, September 25, 1960; admitted to bar, 1986, New York. *Education:* New York University (B.A., 1982); Harvard University (J.D., 1985). ***COURSES: Domestic Violence, Domestic Violence Prosecution Project. ***Email:*** mlync@mail.als.edu

TIMOTHY D. LYTTON,* (Associate Professor of Law)**, *Education:* Yale University (B.A., 1987); Yale Law School (J.D., 1991). ***COURSES: Advanced Torts, Alternative Dispute Resolution, Jurisprudence: An Introduction to the Philosophy of Law, Torts. ***Email:*** tlytt@mail.als.edu

GREGORY N. MANDEL,* (Assistant Professor of Law)**, admitted to bar, 1997, California. *Education:* Wesleyan University (B.A., 1991); Stanford University Law School (J.D., 1996). ***COURSES: Industrial Property I, Industrial Property II.

DAVID L. MARKELL,* (Professor of Law)**, born Denver, Colorado, October 23, 1953; admitted to bar, 1979, District of Columbia and New York. *Education:* Brandeis University (B.A., 1975); University of Virginia School of Law (J.D., 1979). ***COURSES: Environmental Law, Administrative Law, Environmental Practice and Procedure, Environmental Regulation, Hazardous Waste Law, International Environmental Law, Land Use. ***Email:*** dmark@mail.als.edu

JOAN LEARY MATTHEWS,* (Assistant Lawyering Professor and Adjunct Professor of Law)**, admitted to bar, 1984, New York. *Education:* University of Maryland (B.A., 1978); Albany Law School (J.D., 1983). ***COURSES: Introduction to Lawyering, Environmental Regulation, Legislation Drafting. ***Email:*** jmatt@mail.als.edu

NANCY M. MAURER,* (Clinical Professor of Law)**, born New York, New York, March 7, 1953; admitted to bar, 1979, New York and South Carolina. *Education:* Middlebury College (B.A., 1975); George Washington University (J.D., 1978). ***COURSES: Disability Law Seminar, Civil Rights and Disabilities Law Project, Fact Investigation. ***Email:*** nmaur@mail.als.edu

CONNIE MAYER,* (Clinical Professor of Law, Associate Dean for Student Affairs)**, born Springfield, Illinois, June 29, 1952; admitted to bar, 1977, Texas; 1986, New York. *Education:* Eastern Illinois University (B.A., 1974); University of Houston (J.D., 1977). ***COURSES: Pre-Trial and Trial Practice, AIDS Law Project, AIDS Law Seminar. ***Email:*** cmaye@mail.als.edu

DALE L. MOORE,* (Associate Dean for Academic Affairs, Professor of Law)**, born Philadelphia, Pennsylvania, August 10, 1950; admitted to bar, 1987, New York. *Education:* University of Pennsylvania (B.A., 1979; J.D., 1982). ***COURSES: Torts, Health Law, Introduction to Civil Procedure, Bioethics Seminar, Legal Issues in Medicine. ***Email:*** dmoor@mail.als.edu

DANIEL GARY MORIARTY,* (Professor of Law)**, born Burlington, Vermont, December 1, 1941; admitted to bar, 1968, New York. *Education:* Georgetown University (B.S., F.S., 1964; J.D., 1967). ***COURSES: Criminal Law, White Collar Crimes, Legal History, Remedies. ***Email:*** dmori@mail.als.edu

NANCY K. OTA,* (Professor of Law)**, *Education:* University of California, Berkeley (B.S., 1977); Tulane University (M.B.A., 1983); Stanford University (J.D., 1992); Georgetown University Law Center. ***COURSES: Commercial Law Survey, Business Organizations, Issues in Law and Society, Sales, Lease, and Payment Law, Immigration Law and Policy. ***Email:*** nota@mail.als.edu

DAVID ANTHONY PRATT,* (Professor of Law)**, born Liverpool, England, January 11, 1949; admitted to bar, 1975, England and Wales; 1978, New York. *Education:* Hartford College, Oxford University (B.A., 1970). ***COURSES: Deferred Compensation and Employee Benefits, Introduction to Taxation, Elder Law. ***Email:*** dprat@mail.als.edu

PETER PREISER,* (Professor of Law)**, born New York, New York, April 27, 1931; admitted to bar, 1957, New York. *Education:* New York University (B.S., 1954; LL.B., 1957). ***COURSES: Constitutional Law, Criminal Procedure: Adjudication, Criminal Procedure Under the 4th, 5th, and 6th Amendments, Advanced Criminal Law.

FREDERICK A. PROVORNY,* (Harold Tyler Professor of Law and Technology and Director, Science and Technology Law Center)**, born Brooklyn, New York, September 7, 1946; admitted to bar, 1970, New York; 1975, District of Columbia; 1977, Missouri; 1987, Maryland; 1989, California. *Education:* New York University (B.S., 1966); Columbia University (J.D., 1969). ***COURSES: Technology Transfer, Law and Science, Science and Technology Field Placement. ***Email:*** fprov@mail.als.edu

JAMES DOWNING REDWOOD,* (Professor of Law)**, born Baltimore, Maryland, January 14, 1949; admitted to bar, 1984, California. *Education:* Oberlin College (B.A., 1971); Loyola Law School (J.D., 1983). ***COURSES: Constitutional Law, Business Organizations, Securities Regulation, Torts.

PATRICIA YOUNGBLOOD REYHAN,* (Professor of Law)**, born Seattle, Washington, June 15, 1952; admitted to bar, 1978, Washington. *Education:* Washington State University (B.A., 1975); Willamette University College of Law (J.D., 1978); Harvard Law School (LL.M., 1980). ***COURSES: Property, Conflicts of Laws, Transnational Litigation in U.S. Courts, International Commercial Arbitration. ***Email:*** preyh@mail.als.edu

PATRICIA SALKIN,* (Associate Dean, Director of the Government Law Center, Professor of Government Law)**, born Suffern, New York, August 18, 1964; admitted to bar, 1989, New York. *Education:* State University of New York, Albany (B.A., 1985); Albany Law School (J.D., 1988). ***COURSES: Land Use Planning, Housing Law and Policy, Government Ethics. ***Email:*** psalk@mail.als.edu

(This Listing Continued)

ALBANY LAW SCHOOL, UNION UNIVERSITY—Continued

ALEX Y. SEITA*, (Professor of Law)**, admitted to bar, 1976, California; 1980, New York. *Education:* California Institute of Technology (B.S., 1973); Stanford Law School (M.B.A., J.D., 1976). ***COURSES: International Business Transactions, Introduction to Intellectual Property, Antitrust: Bankruptcy, Bankruptcy Reorganizations, International Finance, Japanese Law and Trade. ***Email:*** aseit@mail.als.edu

LAURIE SHANKS*, (Assistant Clinical Professor and Director, Field Placement Program)**, born Phoenix, Arizona, December 24, 1952; admitted to bar, 1977, Arizona; 1989, Indiana and New York. *Education:* Arizona State University (B.S., 1974; J.D., 1977). ***COURSES: Field Placement Project, Trial Tactics, Semester in Practice Project. ***Email:*** lshan@mail.als.edu

DAVID D. SIEGEL*, (Distinguished Professor of Law)**, born Brooklyn, New York, October 18, 1931; admitted to bar, 1958, New York. *Education:* Brooklyn College (B.A., 1958); St. John's University (J.D., 1958); New York University (LL.M., 1964). ***COURSES: Federal Jurisdiction and Practice, Conflicts of Laws, New York Practice I and II, Introduction to Procedure.

NANCY JOANN SOONPAA*, (Associate Lawyering Professor and Associate Director, Lawyering Program)**, born Minneapolis, Minnesota, July 28, 1961; admitted to bar, 1988, North Dakota. *Education:* University of North Dakota (B.A., 1983; M.A., 1990; J.D., 1987). ***COURSES: Lawyering, Advanced Legal Writing, Negotiating for Lawyers. ***Email:*** nsoon@mail.als.edu

SANDRA M. STEVENSON*, (Professor of Law)**, born Orlando, Florida, June 22, 1943; admitted to bar, 1972, New York. *Education:* Houghton College (B.A., 1968); Albany Law School (J.D., 1971). ***COURSES: State Constitutional Law, Torts, Copyright Law, State and Local Government. ***Email:*** sstev@mail.als.edu

JENEAN M. TARANTO*, (Assistant Lawyering Professor)**, admitted to bar, 1989, New York. *Education:* Kenyon College (B.A., 1984); Case Western Reserve University School of Law (J.D., 1988). ***COURSES: Introduction to Lawyering. ***Email:*** jtara@mail.als.edu

ROBERT J. TYMANN*, (Professor of Law)**, born Queens, New York, December 13, 1941; admitted to bar, 1967, New York. *Education:* St. John's University (B.A., 1963; J.D., 1966). ***COURSES: Selected Problems in Torts, Torts, Contracts. ***Email:*** rtyma@mail.als.edu

JOHN C. WELSH*, (Professor of Law)**, born Catskill, New York, May 28, 1931; admitted to bar, 1955, New York. *Education:* University of Notre Dame (B.S., 1952); Albany Law School (LL.B., 1955). ***COURSES: Trusts and Estates, Property I and II.

DONNA E. YOUNG*, (Professor of Law)**, born Toronto, Canada; admitted to bar, 1993, New York. *Education:* University of Toronto (B.S.C., 1987); Osgoode Hall Law School, York University (LL.B., 1991); Columbia Law School (LL.M., 1996). ***COURSES: Employment Discrimination Law, Employment Regulation, Introduction to Civil Procedure, Political and Civil Rights, Women and Work. ***Email:*** dyoun@mail.als.edu

---

AMERICAN UNIVERSITY WASHINGTON COLLEGE OF LAW

4801 MASSACHUSETTS AVENUE, N.W.
WASHINGTON, D.C. 20016-8181
Telephone: (202) 274-4000
Fax: (202) 274-4107

ABA Approved Since 1940.

American University Law School was originally established as the independent Washington College of Law in 1896. Its founders were two early women lawyers, Ellen Spenser Mussey and Emma M. Gillett, who began their co-educational school so that women as well as men would have the opportunity to study law in an academic setting in the Nation's capital. Known since its merger with the University in 1947 as American University Washington College of Law, the school is located in upper northwest Washington in an area of magnificent residences, many of which are occupied by high federal government officials, ambassadors from other countries and members of the city's professional elite. The school offers both full and part time programs leading to the J.D., LL.M. and S.J.D. degrees and is fully accredited by the American Bar Association and the Association of American Law Schools. The school moved into a new facility in January 1996.

Our Dean, Claudio Grossman, has described American University Washington College of Law as "an exciting educational institution with a rich curriculum, a multitude of teaching methods and styles, a supportive and cooperative student body, and wonderful opportunities for learning both within and outside the classroom." Legal education at American University Washington College of Law is centered on a commitment to excellence in teaching, scholarship and service. It is this dedication that has persuaded many of our faculty members to come to the law school from distinguished careers with leading law firms, in public service, or at other law schools.

This dedication is evident in the small classes, even in the first year, which foster close faculty-student and student-student interaction of a type not found in many law schools. First year sections total no more than ninety-five, and these are divided into small classes for research and writing classes. Each first year section has at least one substantive class of no more than 45 students. The average upper division course includes only forty students. Seminars average fourteen. Though appropriately very competitive, the school still operates with an ambience based on real collegiality.

American University Washington College of Law offers programs that lead to the J.D. degree as well as joint programs with other colleges of the University that lead to the J.D. and a masters degree. These include law and international affairs, law and business administration and law and justice. The law school also offers programs leading to two LL.M. degrees; one in international legal studies, with specialization in the following areas: international business law, international organizations, international environmental law, international protection of human rights, and gender and the law, and another in law and government, with specialization in administrative law and regulatory policy. The school is home to one of the oldest and highest regarded clinical programs in the nation. There are four student-edited scholarly journals and several specialized moot court competitions, including the Inter-American Moot Court Competition, the only one in the U.S. conducted in both English and Spanish.

Washington is without par as a law student's city. It is the center of the nation's legal institutions with federal and state agencies, courts, trade associations, public interest groups, corporations and hundreds of private law firms, including most of the nation's largest. Washington College of Law students thus have innumerable and unmatched opportunities for hands-on lawyering experiences including externships, clinics and other independent study. The city also offers opportunities in the international sector due to the presence of official delegations

(This Listing Continued)

AMERICAN UNIVERSITY WASHINGTON COLLEGE OF LAW—Continued

from around the world as well as many private trade and human rights organizations.

Students doing legal research have access to the school's state-of-the-art Law Library with its own collections, which now total almost 500,000 volumes including books, microforms and electronic materials. Included are official depositories for the United States Government Printing Office and the European Union. Washington also is home to many other libraries that are open to students of the American University Washington College of Law on a reciprocal basis. These include those of at least six other law schools and eight universities. Our students also have the use of various government agencies' libraries and those of international and other organizations.

Dean: Claudio Grossman (202) 274-4004
Associate Dean for Academic Affairs: Robert D. Dinerstein (202) 274-4141
Associate Dean for Academic Affairs: Andrew D. Pike (202) 274-4231
Associate Dean for Student Affairs: David Jaffe (202) 274-4052
Assistant Dean for Academic Services and Registrar: Rebecca Davis (202) 274-4081
Director of Library: Patrick E. Kehoe (202) 274-4374
Director of the Clinical Program: Richard J. Wilson (202) 274-4246
Director, International Legal Studies Program: Daniel Bradlow (202) 274-4110

FULL TIME FACULTY

CLAUDIO GROSSMAN*, (Dean and Raymond I. Geraldson Scholar in International and Human Rights Law)**, born Valparaiso, Chile, November 26, 1947. *Education:* University of Chile (Licenciado en Ciencias Juridicas, 1973); G.U. Amsterdam (Dr. in de Rechtsgeleerdheid, 1980). ***COURSES: Comparative Law, Human Rights, International Law, International Organizations, Regional International Organizations. ***Email:*** GROSSMAN@wcl.american.edu

DAVID E. AARONSON*, (Professor of Law and B.J. Tennery Scholar)**, born Washington, D.C., September 19, 1940; admitted to bar, 1965, District of Columbia; 1975, Maryland. *Education:* George Washington University (B.A., 1961; M.A., 1964; Ph.D., 1970); Harvard University Law School (LL.B., 1964); Georgetown University Law Center (LL.M., 1965). ***COURSES: Criminal Procedure, Evidence, Trial Practice. ***Email:*** DAARONS@wcl.american.edu

EVELYN GINSBERG ABRAVANEL*, (Professor of Law)**, born New York, N.Y., September 25, 1951; admitted to bar, 1975, Ohio; 1976, District of Columbia. *Education:* Case Western Reserve University (A.B., 1972; J.D., 1975). ***COURSES: Future Interests, Personal Property, Real Property, Wills, Trusts and Estates. ***Email:*** ABRAVAN@wcl.american.edu

***MUNEER AHMAD*, (Assistant Professor of Law)**, admitted to bar, 1997, New York, California. *Education:* Harvard University (A.B., 1993; J.D., 1996).

PADIDEH ALA'I*, (Associate Professor of Law)**, born Teheran, Iran, June 13, 1964; admitted to bar, 1989, Pennsylvania; 1990, District of Columbia. *Education:* University of Oregon, Robert D. Clark Honor's College (B.A., 1985); Harvard Law School (J.D., 1988). ***COURSES: International Trade, GATT/WTO, International Business Transactions, Law and Development. ***Email:*** palai@wcl.americam.edu

KENNETH ANDERSON*, (Professor of Law)**, born 1956; admitted to bar, 1989, New York. *Education:* UCLA (B.A., 1983); Harvard (J.D., 1986). ***COURSES: Business Associations, Corporate Finance, International Business Transactions, Nonprofit Law. ***Email:*** kanderson@wcl.american.edu

ISAIAH BAKER*, (Associate Professor of Law)**, born Chicago, Illinois, June 19, 1939; admitted to bar, 1972, New York; 1978, District of Columbia; 1987, Maryland. *Education:* Yale University (B.A., 1961); Columbia University (M.B.A., 1970; J.D., 1970); Harvard University Law School (LL.M., 1971); DePaul University (M.A., 1972). ***COURSES: Commercial Law, Commercial Paper, Consumer Law, Contracts, Unfair Trade Practices (Trademarks). ***Email:*** BAKER@wcl.american.edu

JONATHAN BAKER*, (Associate Professor of Law)**, born 1955; admitted to bar, 1982, District of Columbia. *Education:* Harvard University (A.B., 1977; J.D., 1982); Stanford University (M.A., 1978; Ph.D., 1986). ***COURSES: Antitrust, Economic Regulation, Law and Economics. ***Email:*** jbaker@wcl.american.edu

SUSAN D. BENNETT*, (Professor of Law)**, born Boston, Massachusetts, August 3, 1952; admitted to bar, 1980, Maryland; 1989, District of Columbia. *Education:* Yale University (B.A., 1973; M.A., 1975); Columbia University (J.D., 1979). ***COURSES: Clinical Teaching, Community Economic Development, Poverty Law. ***Email:*** SBENNET@wcl.american.edu

DANIEL D. BRADLOW*, (Professor of Law)**, born Johannesburg, South Africa, October 23, 1955; admitted to bar, 1983, District of Columbia and New York. *Education:* University of Witwaterand (B.A., 1977); Northeastern University School of Law (J.D., 1982); Georgetown University Law Center (LL.M., 1985). ***COURSES: International Financial Law, International Financial Institutions, International Economic Law. ***Email:*** BRADLOW@wcl.american.edu

PAMELA BRIDGEWATER*, (Associate Professor of Law)**, *Education:* Florida Agricultural & Mechanical University (B.S.); Florida State University (J.D.); University of Wisconsin (LL.M.). ***COURSES: Property, Trusts & Estates, Reproductive Rights.

BARLOW BURKE*, (Professor of Law and John S. Myers and Alvina Reckman Myers Scholar)**, born Philadelphia, Pennsylvania, July 29, 1941; admitted to bar, 1967, Pennsylvania. *Education:* Harvard University (A.B., 1963); University of Pennsylvania (LL.B., 1966; M.C.P., 1968); Yale Law School (LL.M., 1970; S.J.D., 1977). ***COURSES: Land Use and Planning, Natural Resources, Real Estate Transactions, Real Property. ***Email:*** BBURKE@wcl.american.edu

SUSAN D. CARLE*, (Associate Professor of Law)**, born Dacca, East Pakistan, February 15, 1960; admitted to bar, 1989, Pennsylvania; 1993, District of Columbia. *Education:* Bryn Mawr College (A.B., 1982); Yale Law School (J.D., 1988). ***COURSES: Legal Ethics, Legal Profession, Labor Law, Employment Law, Torts. ***Email:*** SCARLE@wcl.american.edu

DAVID F. CHAVKIN*, (Professor of Law)**, born Mineola, New York, October 9, 1946; admitted to bar, 1973, California; 1974, Utah; 1981, Maryland; 1991, District of Columbia. *Education:* Michigan State University (B.S., 1968); University of California at Berkeley (J.D., 1973). ***COURSES: Civil Practice Clinic, Health Law, Civil Procedure, Supervised Externship Seminar. ***Email:*** DCHAVKIN@wcl.american.edu

(This Listing Continued)

AMERICAN UNIVERSITY WASHINGTON COLLEGE OF LAW—Continued

JOHN BERNARD CORR*, (Professor of Law)**, born Montreal, Canada, May 8, 1942; admitted to bar, 1979, District of Columbia; 1980, New York. *Education:* John Carroll University (B.A., 1963; M.A., 1964); Kent State University (Ph.D., 1971); Georgetown University Law Center (J.D., 1978). ***COURSES: Civil Procedure, Conflict of Laws, Corporate Bankruptcy, Creditors' and Debtors' Rights, International Conflict of Laws. ***Email:*** corr@wcl.american.edu

PATRICK CRAWFORD*, (Assistant Professor of Law)**, born Mount Kisco, New York, September 4, 1964; admitted to bar, 1994, California. *Education:* Columbia University (B.A., 1988); University of Virginia (M.A., 1993; J.D., 1993). ***COURSES: Tax, Banking, Corporations, Business Planning. ***Email:*** pcrawfo@wcl.american.edu

ANGELA J. DAVIS*, (Professor of Law)**, born Fort Benning, Georgia, July 2, 1956; admitted to bar, 1982, District of Columbia. *Education:* Howard University (B.A., 1978); Harvard Law School (J.D., 1981). ***COURSES: Criminal Law, Criminal Procedure, Race and Crime. ***Email:*** angelad@wcl.american.edu

ROBERT D. DINERSTEIN*, (Professor of Law and Associate Dean for Academic Affairs)**, born New York, N.Y., May 3, 1953; admitted to bar, 1978, New York; 1983, District of Columbia; 1984, Maryland. *Education:* Cornell University (A.B., 1974); Yale Law School (J.D., 1977). ***COURSES: Civil Rights, Clinical Teaching, Criminal Justice Clinic, Disability and the Law, Interviewing/Counseling/Negotiation, Law and Psychiatry, Rights of Civilly Institutionalized Persons. ***Email:*** RDINERS@wcl.american.edu

WALTER A. EFFROSS*, (Professor of Law and Director E-Commerce Program)**, born New Brunswick, New Jersey, August 7, 1963; admitted to bar, 1987, New Jersey; 1990, District of Columbia. *Education:* Princeton University (A.B., 1984); Harvard Law School (J.D., 1987). ***COURSES: Negotiable Instruments, Sales and Secured Transactions, E-Commerce, Business Associations. ***Email:*** EFFROSS@wcl.american.edu

CHRISTINE HAIGHT FARLEY*, (Assistant Professor of Law)**, born New York, July 5, 1966; admitted to bar, 1994, New York. *Education:* State University of New York at Binghamton (B.A., 1989); SUNY Buffalo School of Law (J.D., 1994); Columbia Law School (LL.M., 1997; J.S.D., Candidate). ***COURSES: Trademarks, Intellectual Property, International Trademarks, Art Law. ***Email:*** cfarley@wcl.american.edu

ROBERT KOGOD GOLDMAN*, (Professor of Law and Louis C. James Scholar)**, born Washington, D.C., November 26, 1944; admitted to bar, 1971, Virginia; 1972, District of Columbia. *Education:* University of Pennsylvania (B.A., 1967); University of Virginia (J.D., 1971). ***COURSES: Human Rights Law, International Humanitarian Law, International Law.

LEWIS A. GROSSMAN*, (Associate Professor of Law)**, born New York, N.Y., June 3, 1964; admitted to bar, 1990, Connecticut; 1992, New York; 1994, Pennsylvania, District of Columbia. *Education:* Yale University (B.A., 1986; M.A., 1991; M.Phil, 1992); Harvard University (J.D.1990). ***COURSES: American Legal History, Civil Procedure, Food and Drug Law. ***Email:*** LEWISG@wcl.american.edu

EGON GUTTMAN*, (Professor of Law and Louis P. Levitt Memorial Trust Scholar)**, born Neuruppin, Netherlands, January 27, 1927; admitted to bar, 1952, Middle Temple, England. *Education:* University of Cambridge; University of London (LL.B., 1950; LL.M., 1952). ***COURSES: Commercial Law, Comparative Law, Corporate Finance, International Capital Raising, Letters of Credit, Negotiable Instruments, Regulation of Commodities Trading, Regulation of Securities Markets, Sales and Secured Transactions, Securities Regulation. ***Email:*** GUTTMAN@wcl.american.edu

MARK M. HAGER*, (Professor of Law)**, born Evanston, Illinois, November 5, 1955; admitted to bar, 1984, Massachusetts; 1989, District of Columbia. *Education:* Amherst College (B.A., 1977); Harvard University (M.A., 1982; Ph.D., 1990); Harvard University Law School (J.D., 1983). ***COURSES: Constitutional Law, Jurisprudence, International Labor Law, Labor and Employment Law, Torts. ***Email:*** MHAGER@wcl.american.edu

PETER A. JASZI*, (Professor of Law)**, born Washington, D.C., December 20, 1946; admitted to bar, 1972, District of Columbia. *Education:* Harvard University (B.A., 1968); Harvard University Law School (J.D., 1971). ***COURSES: Property, Copyright, Endangered Species and Animal Rights, English Legal History, International Copyright, Law and Literature. ***Email:*** PJASZI@wcl.american.edu

PATRICK E. KEHOE*, (Professor of Law)**, born Olympia, Washington, November 12, 1941; admitted to bar, 1966, Washington. *Education:* Seattle University (B.C.S., 1963); University of Washington (J.D., 1966; M.L.Libr., 1968). ***COURSES: Agency and Partnership, Employer-Employee Relations, Admiralty, Legal Research and Writing. ***Email:*** PKEHOE@wcl.american.edu

NICHOLAS N. KITTRIE*, (University Professor)**, born United Kingdom, March 26, 1930; admitted to bar, 1957, Kansas; 1959, District of Columbia. *Education:* University of Kansas (LL.B., 1950; M.A., 1951); Georgetown University Law Center (LL.M., 1963; S.J.D., 1968). ***COURSES: Criminal Law, Criminal Procedure, International Criminal Law, International Law, Political Crime and Terrorism.

CANDACE SAARI KOVACIC-FLEISCHER*, (Professor of Law)**, born Washington, D.C., March 19, 1947; admitted to bar, 1974, Massachusetts; 1976, District of Columbia. *Education:* Wellesley College (A.B., 1969); Northeastern University School of Law (J.D., 1974). ***COURSES: Contracts, Employment Discrimination, Injunctions and Advanced Remedies, Remedies, Remedies for Constitutional and Complex Cases, Sex-based Discrimination, Work and Parenting. ***Email:*** KOVACIC@wcl.american.edu

JEFFREY S. LUBBERS*, (Fellow In Law and Government)**, born Madison, Wisconsin, January 26, 1949; admitted to bar, 1975, Maryland; 1976, Washington, D.C.. *Education:* Cornell University (A.B., 1971); University of Chicago (J.D., 1974). ***COURSES: Administrative Law, Alternative Dispute Resolution. ***Email:*** isl26@aol.com

ROBERT BENNETT LUBIC*, (Professor of Law Emeritus)**, born Pittsburgh, Pennsylvania, March 9, 1929; admitted to bar, 1953, Pennsylvania; 1965, District of Columbia. *Education:* University of Pittsburgh (A.B., 1950; J.D., 1953); Georgetown University (M.P.L., 1959). ***Email: RLUBIC@wcl.american.edu

JAMES P. MAY*, (Professor of Law)**, born Washington, D.C., June 26, 1951; admitted to bar, 1976, District of Columbia. *Education:* Carleton University (B.A., 1973); Harvard University Law School (J.D., 1976). ***COURSES: Antitrust, Contracts, Law and Economics, Legal History. ***Email:*** may@wcl.american.edu

BINNY MILLER*, (Professor of Law)**, born Boston, Massachusetts, February 26, 1956; admitted to bar, 1985, Minnesota; 1988, District of Columbia; 1991, Maryland. *Education:* Carleton University (B.A., 1978); University of Chicago (J.D., 1983). ***COURSES: Clinical Teaching, Interviewing and Counseling. ***Email:*** BMILLER@wcl.american.edu

ELLIOTT S. MILSTEIN*, (Professor of Law)**, born Hartford, Connecticut, October 19, 1944; admitted to bar, 1969, Connecticut, 1973, District of Columbia. *Education:* University of Hartford (B.A., 1966); University of Connecticut School of Law (J.D., 1969); Yale Law School (LL.M., 1971). ***COURSES: Alternate Dispute Resolution,

(This Listing Continued)

AMERICAN UNIVERSITY WASHINGTON COLLEGE OF LAW—Continued

Clinical Teaching, Criminal Law, Lawyer Bargaining, Legal Profession, Office Practice. ***Email:*** ELLIOTT@wcl.american.edu

ANTHONY C. MORELLA*, (Professor of Law and University General Counsel (1969-1994))**, born Malden, Massachusetts, August 31, 1930; admitted to bar, 1959, District of Columbia; 1976, Maryland. *Education:* Boston University (A.B., 1952); American University Washington College of Law (J.D., 1958). ***COURSES: Trial Practice, Pre-Trial Litigation.

***MARK NILES*, (Associate Professor of Law)**

DIANE F. ORENTLICHER*, (Professor of Law)**, born May 2,1955; admitted to bar, 1981, District of Columbia. *Education:* Yale University (B.A., 1977); Columbia University (J.D., 1981). ***COURSES: International Law, Ethnic Identity and International Law, International Organizations and International Business and Human Rights. ***Email:*** ORENTLIC@wcl.american.edu

PENELOPE JANE PETHER*, (Associate Professor of Law and Director of Legal Rhetoric & Writing Program)**, born Griffith, New South Wales Australia, October 3, 1957; admitted to bar, 1982, New South Wales, Australia and High Court of Australia. *Education:* University of Sydney (B.A., 1980; LL.B., 1982; Ph.D., 1997); University of New England (M.Litt., 1985). ***COURSES: Legal Method, Criminal Law, Law and Literature, Legal Theory, Lawyering Skills, Legal Research & Writing. ***Email:*** ppether@wcl.american.edu

ANDREW D. PIKE*, (Professor of Law and Associate Dean for Academic Affairs)**, born New York, N.Y., July 30, 1950; admitted to bar, 1976, Pennsylvania; 1977, District of Columbia. *Education:* Swarthmore College (B.A., 1972); University of Pennsylvania (J.D., 1976). ***COURSES: Corporate Income Taxation, Federal Personal Income Taxation, Estate and Gift Taxation, Pension Law, Tax Policy. ***Email:*** PIKE@wcl.american.edu

NANCY D. POLIKOFF*, (Professor of Law)**, born February 25, 1952; admitted to bar, 1975, District of Columbia; 1976, Maryland. *Education:* University of Pennsylvania (B.A., 1972); Georgetown University Law Center (J.D., 1975); George Washington University (M.A., 1980). ***COURSES: Family Law, Civil Procedure. ***Email:*** NPOLIKO@wcl.american.edu

ANDREW F. POPPER*, (Professor of Law)**, born New York, N.Y., March 3, 1948; admitted to bar, 1973, Illinois; 1975, District of Columbia. *Education:* Baldwin-Wallace College (B.A., 1970); DePaul University (J.D., 1973); George Washington University National Law Center (LL.M., 1976). ***COURSES: Administrative Law, Federal Regulatory Process, Torts, Product Liability. ***Email:*** APOPPER@wcl.american.edu

JAMIN BEN RASKIN*, (Professor of Law)**, born Washington, D.C., December 13, 1962; admitted to bar, 1987, Massachusetts. *Education:* Harvard University (B.A., 1983); Harvard University Law School (J.D., 1987). ***COURSES: Constitutional Law, First Amendment, Criminal Law, Criminal Procedure, Law of the American Political Process, Local Government. ***Email:*** RASKIN@wcl.american.edu

PAUL R. RICE*, (Professor of Law)**, born Huntington, West Virginia, July 28, 1943; admitted to bar, 1968, West Virginia; 1969, Connecticut. *Education:* Marshall University (B.B.A., 1965); West Virginia University (J.D., 1968); Yale Law School (LL.M., 1972). ***COURSES: Evidence. ***Email:*** PRICE@wcl.american.edu

IRA P. ROBBINS*, (Professor of Law and Justice and Barnard T. Welsh Scholar)**, born Brooklyn, New York, January 2, 1949; admitted to bar, 1974, New York; 1984, District of Columbia. *Education:* University of Pennsylvania (A.B., 1970); Harvard University Law School (J.D., 1973). ***COURSES: Conflict of Laws, Criminal Law, Judicial Process, Post-Conviction Remedies, Prisoners' Rights. ***Email:*** ROBBINS@wcl.american.edu

SEYMOUR J. RUBIN*, (Professor of Law Emeritus in Residence)**, born Chicago, Illinois, April 6, 1914; admitted to bar, 1939, Illinois; 1943, District of Columbia. *Education:* Harvard University Law School (LL.B., 1938; LL.M., 1939). ***COURSES: Corporations, International Organizations, International Transactions, Transnational Corporations.

TEEMU RUSKOLA*, (Assistant Professor)**, born Oulu, Finland, March 1, 1965; admitted to bar, 1996, New York. *Education:* Stanford University (B.A., 1990; M.A., 1999); Yale Law School (J.D., 1995). ***COURSES: Contracts, Commercial Law, Comparative Law. ***Email:*** truskola@wcl.american.edu

JAMES E. SALZMAN*, (Professor of Law)**, born 1963. *Education:* Yale University (B.A., 1985); Harvard University (J.D., 1989; M.S., 1990). ***COURSES: Contracts, Administrative Law, International Environmental Law, Environmental Law. ***Email:*** SALZMAN@wcl.american.edu

THOMAS O. SARGENTICH*, (Professor of Law)**, born Los Angeles, California, May 9, 1950; admitted to bar, 1978, District of Columbia. *Education:* Harvard University (B.A., 1972); Magdalen College, Oxford University (M.Phil., 1974); Harvard University Law School (J.D., 1977). ***COURSES: Administrative Law, Administrative Reform, Constitutional Law, Constitutional Theory, Presidential Power, The Separation of Powers. ***Email:*** TSARGEN@wcl.american.edu

HERMAN SCHWARTZ*, (Professor of Law)**, born New York, N.Y., December 19, 1931; admitted to bar, 1957, New York; 1962, District of Columbia. *Education:* Harvard University A.B., 1953); Harvard University Law School (J.D., 1956). ***COURSES: Civil Rights, Constitutional Law, Criminal Procedure, Regulated Industries. ***Email:*** HSCHWAR@wcl.american.edu

ANN C. SHALLECK*, (Professor of Law and Director, Women & the Law Program)**, born New York, N.Y., August 10, 1949; admitted to bar, 1978, Pennsylvania; 1984, District of Columbia. *Education:* Bryn Mawr College (A.B., 1971); Harvard University Law School (J.D., 1978). ***COURSES: Clinical Teaching, Family Law, Women and the Law, Theories of Pedagogy. ***Email:*** Shalleck@wcl.american.edu

MARY SIEGEL*, (Professor of Law)**, born May 3, 1951; admitted to bar, 1975, District of Columbia; 1976, Ohio. *Education:* Vassar College (A.B., 1972); Yale Law School (J.D., 1975). ***COURSES: Advanced Corporate Law, Business Associations, Business Planning, Corporations, Financial Institutions, Securities Regulation, Advanced Securities Law. ***Email:*** MSIEGEL@wcl.american.edu

RITA SIMON*, (University Professor)**, born November 26, 1931. *Education:* University of Chicago (Ph.D., 1957). ***COURSES: Law and the Behavioral Sciences, Law and the Social Sciences, Research in Law and Society, Sociology of Law. ***Email:*** RSIMON@american.edu

BRENDA V. SMITH*, (Associate Professor)**, born June 6, 1959; admitted to bar, 1985, Pennsylvania, District of Columbia, Maryland. *Education:* Spelman College (B.A., 1980); Georgetown University (J.D., 1984). ***COURSES: Clinical Teaching, Professional Responsibility, Litigation, Economic Development. ***Email:*** bvsmith@wcl.american.edu

JANET R. ALTMAN SPRAGENS*, (Professor of Law)**, born Washington, D.C., March 31, 1943; admitted to bar, 1968, District of Columbia. *Education:* Wellesley College (B.A., 1964); George Washington National Law Center (J.D., 1968). ***COURSES: Corporate Income Tax, Federal Partnership Income Tax, Federal Personal Income Tax, Tax Clinic, Tax Policy. ***Email:*** SPRAGENS@wcl.american.edu

(This Listing Continued)

AMERICAN UNIVERSITY WASHINGTON COLLEGE OF LAW—Continued

MICHAEL E. TIGAR*, (Professor of Law and Edwin A. Mooers, Sr., Scholar)**, born Glendale, California, January 18, 1941; admitted to bar, 1967, District of Columbia; 1993, New York. *Education:* University of California, Berkeley (B.A., 1962, J.D., 1966). ***COURSES: Federal Courts, Criminal Law, International Human Rights, Trial Advocacy, Appellate Jurisdiction and Advocacy. ***Email:*** metigar@tigarlaw.com

ROBERT G. VAUGHN*, (Professor of Law and A. Allen King Scholar)**, born March 10, 1944; admitted to bar, 1969, Oklahoma; 1971, District of Columbia. *Education:* University of Oklahoma (B.A., 1966; J.D., 1969); Harvard University Law School (LL.M., 1970). ***COURSES: Civil Procedure, Legislation, Public Employment Law, Public Information Law and Policy, Torts. ***Email:*** Vaughn@wcl.american.edu

LETI VOLPP*, (Associate Professor of Law)**, born 1965; admitted to bar, 1993, California. *Education:* Princeton University (B.A., 1986); Harvard University (M.S.P.H., 1988); University of Edinburgh (M.S., 1989); Columbia University (J.D., 1993). ***COURSES: Property, Critical Race Theory, Immigration, Feminist Theory, Labor and Employment. ***Email:*** lvolpp@wcl.american.edu

PERRY E. WALLACE, JR.*, (Professor of Law)**, born Nashville, Tennessee, February 19, 1948; admitted to bar, 1978, District of Columbia. ***COURSES: Accounting, Business Associations, Corporate Finance, Corporations, Environmental Law. ***Email:*** WALLACE@wcl.american.edu

BURTON D. WECHSLER*, (Professor of Law Emeritus)**, born Gary, Indiana, August 22, 1924; admitted to bar, 1949, Illinois; 1951, Indiana. *Education:* Michigan University (B.A., 1947); Harvard University Law School (J.D., 1949). ***Email: WECHSLER@wcl.american.edu

***STEPHEN WERMIEL*, (Associate Professor of Law)**, born 1950; admitted to bar, 1984, District of Columbia. *Education:* Tufts University (B.A., 1972); American University (J.D., 1982).

JOAN CHALMERS WILLIAMS*, (Professor of Law)**, born January 5, 1952; admitted to bar, 1980, District of Columbia. *Education:* Yale University (B.A., 1974); Harvard University Law School (J.D., 1980). ***COURSES: Employment Discrimination Law, Family Law, Feminist Jurisprudence, Property, Redistribution in American Law and Politics, Women's Legal History. ***Email:*** WILLIAMS@wcl.american.edu

PAUL ROBERT WILLIAMS*, (Assistant Professor, Director of the M.A./J.D. Joint Degree Program)**, born 1965; admitted to bar, 1991, California; 1998, District of Columbia. *Education:* University of California at Davis (A.B., 1987); University of Cambridge (Ph.D., 1998); Stanford Law School (J.D., 1990). ***COURSES: International Law & Foreign Affairs, Law of the Sea, Advanced Issues of Public International Law and State Succession. ***Email:*** pwilliams@wcl.american.edu

RICHARD J. WILSON*, (Professor of Law and Director of the Clinical Program)**, born 1943; admitted to bar, 1972, Illinois; 1990, District of Columbia. *Education:* DePaul University (B.A., 1965); University of Illinois (J.D., 1972). ***COURSES: Clinical Teaching, Comparative Criminal Procedure, Criminal Procedure, Human Rights. ***Email:*** RWILSON@WCL.american.edu

---

APPALACHIAN SCHOOL OF LAW

P.O. BOX 2825
GRUNDY, VIRGINIA 24614

ARIZONA STATE UNIVERSITY COLLEGE OF LAW

P.O. BOX 877906
TEMPE, ARIZONA 85287-7906
Telephone: (480) 965-6188
Fax: (480) 965-6521
http://www.asu.edu/law

ABA Approved Since 1969

Founded in 1967, the College of Law at Arizona State University boasts a strong general law curriculum supported by three lead programs and an outstanding teaching faculty.

Located in the Phoenix metropolitan area, ASU is a Research I institution serving one of the most dynamic and diverse communities in the country. The College of Law student body typically represents over 100 educational institutions. The students are attracted by the quality of legal education available at ASU, its commitment to innovative teaching and scholarship, very reasonable tuition and low student/faculty ratio. A busy calendar of distinguished scholars, jurists and public officials enriches the student experience and fosters a strong sense of community among the faculty.

The entering class is typically 150 students per year, equally divided between the sexes, with an average age of 27. Minority representation is 30%. The ASU College of Law combines the best traditions of American legal education with innovative programs supported by strong community partnerships.

Founded in 1985, the Center for the Study of Law, Science, and Technology contributes, through research and education, to the informed development of law on issues generated by scientific advances and their technological applications. Center Faculty fellows, an extraordinary group of science trained law professors, include nationally recognized scholars in intellectual property and computer law, scientific evidence, environmental law, biotechnology, risk management, communications law, bioethics and health care law. Recent Center projects include: defining the proper scope of copyright protection for computer software; law reform to govern the explosion of information and medical application in human genetics; the forensic use of DNA identification technologies; the Internet's impact on legal concepts of jurisdiction, free expression, and privacy; and the implications of biological perspectives on human sexual aggression. Center faculty and students edit and co-publish, with the American Bar Association, the prestigious, peer refereed *Jurimetrics: The Journal of Law, Science and Technology*, the oldest and most widely circulated journal in the field of law and science.

The Clinical Program has been an integral part of the College of Law since its earliest days and is one of the most comprehensive in the nation. Most ASU law students participate in at least one of ASU's four "live client" clinics: Criminal Practice, the Public Defender, the Civil Practice, and the Lodestar Mediation Clinic. The Civil Practice Clinic

(This Listing Continued)

ARIZONA STATE UNIVERSITY COLLEGE OF LAW —Continued

operates as a law firm within the law school and focuses on civil cases. Students work with faculty members to handle their own cases and represent their clients at administrative hearings and civil trials. The Lodestar Mediation Clinic offers students the opportunity to understand the problem-solving dimension of lawyering. Students work with faculty and professional mediators on a broad range of disputes in the metro Phoenix area, and participate in seminars exploring mediation as a valuable alternative to litigation. Simulation courses in trial advocacy, negotiation and mediation, and pre-trial discovery practice are also available. In addition, there is a rich externship program, offering over 50 hands-on learning opportunities for students.

The Indian Legal Program enjoys a position of national leadership. The student body currently includes 35 Native Americans, and alumni include many outstanding Indian attorneys who are pursuing distinguished careers in both public and private practice. The Indian Legal Program Coordinates a Certificate Program that offers several courses in Indian Law, including Federal Indian Law, Advanced Indian Law, Cultural Resources, Tribal Law, and Tribal Environmental Policy. Students in the Certificate Program also complete coursework in areas such as natural resources and environmental law, employment law, administrative law and tax law designed to augment the more specialized coursework and provide the necessary foundation for practice in Indian Law. An outstanding faculty and long-term partnerships with tribal governments contribute to the strength and reputation of ASU in this critical area.

Among the resources available at Arizona State University to both students and the legal community is the award-winning Ross-Blakley Law Library, a visually stunning, state-of-the-art facility housing one of the finest collections in the Rocky Mountain West. The library includes over 351,000 volumes and microform equivalents. The entire catalog is accessible through on-line terminals and the resources include a 30-station computer lab and two 10-station research facilities for LEXIS and WESTLAW.

Dean and Professor of Law & Affiliate Prof. of Philosophy: Patricia D. White (480) 965-6188
Prof. of Law & Assoc. Dean of Academic Affairs & Research: Patrick McKinley Brennan (480) 965-6134
Associate Dean and Director of Ross-Blakley Law Library: Victoria Trotta (480) 965-2521
Assistant Dean and Director of Admissions: Brenda Brock (480) 965-1474
Assistant Dean, Student Services: Leslie Mamaghani (480) 965-1302
Assistant Dean, Administrative and Business Services: Rhonda Sandler (480) 965-6925
Director, Indian Legal Programs: Kate Rosier (480) 965-6204
Director, Lodestar Mediation Clinic: Ann E. Woodley (480) 965-3109
Dir., Center for the Study of Law, Science & Technology: Andrew Askland (480) 965-2465
Dir., Legal Method & Writing & Academic Success Program: Judith M. Stinson (480) 965-8512
W.P. Carey Director of Career Services: Ilona DeRemer (480) 965-5808
Director of Communications: Jodi Weisberg (480) 965-1689
Director of Development: Tom Stevick (480) 965-3096
Director, Financial Aid & Student Development: Michael Bossone (480) 727-7429

FULL TIME FACULTY

PATRICIA D. WHITE*, (Dean and Professor of Law and Affiliate Professor of Philosophy)**, born Syracuse, New York, July 8, 1949; admitted to bar, 1975, District of Columbia; 1988, Michigan, 1995, Utah. *Education:* University of Michigan (B.A., 1971; M.A., 1974; J.D., 1974). ***COURSES: Taxation, Trust & Estates, Legal Philosophy, Torts, Legal Profession. ***Email:*** patricia.white@asu.edu

HANNAH R. ARTERIAN*, (Professor of Law)**, born New York, New York, September 9, 1949; admitted to bar, 1974, New York. *Education:* Elmira College (B.A., 1970); University of Iowa College of Law (J.D., 1973). ***COURSES: Constitutional Law, Employment Law, Employment Discrimination, Labor Relations I and II, Title VII; Theory and Proof. ***Email:*** hannah.arterian@asu.edu

JENNIFER R. BARNES*, (Visiting Clinical Professor of Law)**, born Colorado Springs, Colorado, 1956; admitted to bar, 1987, Arizona. *Education:* University of Wisconsin (B.S., 1978); Arizona State University College of Law (J.D., 1987). ***COURSES: Lawyering, Theory & Practice. ***Email:*** jennifer.barnes@asu.edu

ROBERT D. BARTELS*, (Charles M. Brewer Professor of Trial Advocacy)**, born Ft. Bragg, North Carolina, December 16, 1944; admitted to bar, 1970, California and Michigan; 1971, Iowa. *Education:* University of Michigan (B.A., 1966); Stanford Law School (J.D., 1969). ***COURSES: Evidence, Civil Procedure, Trial Practice, Welfare Law. ***Email:*** robert.bartels@asu.edu

PAUL BENDER*, (Professor of Law)**, born Brooklyn, New York, May 31, 1933; admitted to bar, 1958, District of Columbia. *Education:* Harvard (A.B., 1954; LL.B., 1957). ***COURSES: Constitutional, Civil Rights, Copyright, Unfair Competition, Criminal and Civil Procedures.

MICHAEL A. BERCH*, (Professor of Law)**, born San Francisco, California, April 1, 1935; admitted to bar, 1959, New York; 1971, Arizona. *Education:* Columbia College (B.A., 1956); Columbia Law School (J.D., 1959). ***COURSES: Civil Procedure, Federal Courts, Ethics, Civil Rights, Complex Litigation. ***Email:*** michael.berch@asu.edu

PATRICK MCKINLEY BRENNAN*, (Professor of Law and Associate Dean of Academic Affairs and Research)**, born San Diego, California, June 27, 1966; admitted to bar, 1996, California. *Education:* Yale (B.A., 1988); University of Toronto (M.A., 1989); University of California, Boalt Hall School of Law (J.D., 1993). ***COURSES: Federal Courts, Criminal Law, Administrative Law, Jurisprudence. ***Email:*** patrick.brennan@asu.edu

CHARLES R. CALLEROS*, (Professor of Law)**, born Sacramento, California, June 10, 1953; admitted to bar, 1978, California; 1981, Arizona. *Education:* University of California at Santa Cruz (B.A., 1975); University of California at Davis (J.D., 1978). ***COURSES: Contracts, Torts, Legal Clinic, Advanced Writing, Civil Rights. ***Email:*** charles.calleros@asu.edu

ROBERT N. CLINTON*, (Professor of Law and Barry Goldwater Chair of American Institutions)**, born Detroit, Michigan, August 1, 1946; admitted to bar, 1971, Illinois; 1973, Iowa. *Education:* University of Michigan (B.A., 1968); University of Chicago (J.D., 1971). ***COURSES: American Indian Law, Constitutional Law, Copyrights, Federal Jurisdiction. ***Email:*** robert.clinton@asu.edu

***SELWYN L. DALLYN*, (Clinical Professor)**, born Baton Rouge, Louisiana, 1951; admitted to bar, 1978, Iowa; 1983, Arizona. *Education:* Cornell University; Graceland College (B.A.,1975);

(This Listing Continued)

ARIZONA STATE UNIVERSITY COLLEGE OF LAW —Continued

University of Iowa College of Law (J.D., 1978). ***COURSES:*** Lawyering Skills Seminar, Criminal Law, Criminal Procedure, Evidence and Trial Advocacy. ***Email:*** chuck.dallyn@asu.edu

MARK ROBERT DAUBER, **(Clinical Professor)**, born Phoenix, Arizona, April 1, 1955; admitted to bar, 1983, Arizona; 1986, California. *Education:* University of California (A.B., 1977); Arizona State University (J.D., 1983). ***COURSES:*** Alternative Dispute Resolution, Civil Clinic. ***Email:*** bob.dauber@asu.edu

KIRSTEN K. DAVIS, **(Legal Writing Professor)**, born Wheeling, West Virginia, 1970; admitted to bar, 1995, Ohio; 1996, West Virginia; 2000, Arizona. *Education:* The Ohio State University (B.A., 1992); The Ohio State University College of Law (J.D., 1995). ***COURSES:*** Legal Research and Writing. ***Email:*** kirsten.davis@asu.edu

THOMAS JOSEPH DAVIS, **(Professor of History and Visiting Professor of Law)**, born New York, New York, 1946; admitted to bar, 1996, Arizona. *Education:* Fordham University (A.B., 1967); Columbia University (M.A., 1968; Ph.D., 1974); State University of New York at Buffalo (J.D., 1973); Ball State University (M.A., 1976). ***COURSES:*** Civil Rights, Employment Law, Labor Law, Property Law, Race and the Law, U.S. Constitutional, U.S. Legal History. ***Email:*** tjdavis@asu.edu

IRA MARK ELLMAN, **(Professor)**, born New York, New York, July 30, 1945; admitted to bar, 1975, California. *Education:* Reed College (B.A., 1967); University of Illinois (M.A., 1969); University of California at Berkeley, Boalt Hall School of Law (J.D., 1973). ***COURSES:*** Family Law, Property, Gender. ***Email:*** ira.ellman@asu.edu

JOSEPH M. FELLER, **(Professor of Law)**, born Washington, D.C., August 9, 1953; admitted to bar, 1985, California. *Education:* Harvard (B.A., 1975); University of California at Berkeley (Ph.D., 1979); Harvard (J.D., 1984). ***COURSES:*** Environmental/Natural Resources Law, Public Lands Management, Water Law. ***Email:*** joseph.feller@asu.edu

DALE BECK FURNISH, **(Professor of Law)**, born Iowa City, Iowa, February 11, 1940; admitted to bar, 1965, Iowa; 1973, Arizona. *Education:* Grinnell College (B.A., 1962); University of Iowa (J.D., 1965); University of Michigan (LL.M., 1970). ***COURSES:*** Commercial Law, Contracts, Creditor-Debtor, International Trade, Comparative Law. ***Email:*** dale.furnish@asu.edu

ROBERT A. GORMAN, **(Professor of Law)**, born New York, New York, April 22, 1937; admitted to bar, 1962, New York. *Education:* Harvard University (A.B., 1958; LL.B., 1962); University College, Oxford, Fulbright Scholarship, 1958-59. ***COURSES:*** Copyright, Intellectual Property, Labor Law. ***Email:*** robert.gorman@asu.edu

BETSY N. GREY, **(Professor of Law)**, born New York, New York; admitted to bar, 1981, District of Columbia. *Education:* Barnard College (B.A., 1975); Georgetown University (J.D., 1979). ***COURSES:*** Torts, Civil Procedure, Products Liability, Mass Torts. ***Email:*** betsy.grey@asu.edu

SANFORD M. GUERIN, **(Professor of Law)**, born Tacoma Park, Maryland, February 7, 1950; admitted to bar, 1974, California. *Education:* Boston University (B.S., 1971); University of San Francisco School of Law (J.D., 1974); New York University School of Law (LL.M., 1975). ***COURSES:*** Federal Income Taxation, Real Estate Planning, Estate Planning.

TAMARA S. HERRERA, **(Professor Legal Writing)**, born Syracuse, New York, September 19, 1969; admitted to bar, 1996, Arizona. *Education:* Grinnell College (B.A., 1991); University of Nebraska (J.D., 1996). ***COURSES:*** Legal Writing. ***Email:*** tamara.herrera@asu.edu

ANDREW D. HURWITZ, **(Distinguished Visitor from Practice)**, born New York, New York, October 1, 1947; admitted to bar, 1973, Connecticut; 1974, Arizona. *Education:* Princeton University (A.B., 1968); Yale University (J.D., 1972). ***COURSES:*** Civil Procedure, Ethics, Legislative Process, Supreme Court Litigation. ***Email:*** adhurwitz@omlaw.com

OWEN DONALD JONES, **(Professor of Law)**, born Glen Ridge, New Jersey, May 29, 1963; admitted to bar, 1991, Pennsylvania; 1992, District of Columbia. *Education:* Amherst College (B.A., 1985); Yale (J.D., 1991). ***COURSES:*** Contracts, Biology, Evolution and Law. ***Email:*** owen.jones@asu.edu

DAVID KADER, **(Professor of Law)**, born Germany, April 9, 1947; admitted to bar, 1972, Washington and California. *Education:* California State University at Fresno (B.A., 1969); University of Washington (J.D., 1972); University London (LL.M., 1974). ***COURSES:*** Criminal Procedure, Torts, Religion and the Constitution, Constitutional Law. ***Email:*** david.kader@asu.edu

DENNIS S. KARJALA, **(Professor of Law)**, born New York, New York, December 19, 1939; admitted to bar, 1972, California. *Education:* Princeton University (B.S.E., 1961); University of Illinois (Ph.D., 1965); University of California at Berkeley (J.D., 1972). ***COURSES:*** Copyright, Computer Law, Corporations, Securities Law, Income Taxation. ***Email:*** dennis.karjala@asu.edu

DAVID H. KAYE, **(Regents' Professor of Law)**, born Ft. Lauderdale, Florida, March 22, 1947; admitted to bar, 1973, Oregon. *Education:* Massachusetts Institute of Technology (B.S., 1968); Harvard (M.A., 1969); Yale (J.D., 1972). ***COURSES:*** Evidence, Employment Discrimination, Genetics and Law, Law and Science, Law and Social Science. ***Email:*** k@asu.edu

JOHN D. LESHY, **(Professor of Law)**, born Winchester, Ohio, October 7, 1944; admitted to bar, 1969, Ohio; 1972, California; 1977, District of Columbia; 1991, Arizona. *Education:* Harvard (A.B., 1966; J.D., 1969). ***COURSES:*** Constitutional, Environmental, Indian, Water Law, Public Land/Resources.

GARY TOBIAS LOWENTHAL, **(Professor of Law)**, born New York, New York, May 21, 1944; admitted to bar, 1970, California; 1990, Arizona. *Education:* Harvard University (A.B., 1966); University of Chicago Law School (J.D., 1969). ***COURSES:*** Criminal Law, Criminal Procedure, Negotiations, Clinical Legal Education. ***Email:*** gary.lowenthal@asu.edu

MYLES V. LYNK, **(Kiewit Foundation Professor of the Legal Profession)**, born New York, New York, November 15, 1948; admitted to bar, 1977, New York; 1979, Massachusetts; 1982, District of Columbia. *Education:* Harvard University (A.B., 1971; J.D., 1976). ***COURSES:*** Administrative Law, Corporations, Civil Procedure. ***Email:*** myles.lynk@asu.edu

GARY E. MARCHANT, **(Associate Professor and Director, Center for the Study of Law, Science and Technology)**, born Squamish, British Columbia, Canada, July 5, 1958; admitted to bar, 1991, Massachusetts; 1993, District of Columbia. *Education:* University of British Columbia (B.Sc., 1980; Ph.D., 1986); Harvard Law School (J.D., 1990); Kennedy School of Government (M.P.P., 1990). ***COURSES:*** Environmental Law, Law Science & Technology. ***Email:*** gary.marchant@asu.edu

ALAN ADAMS MATHESON, **(Professor of Law)**, born Cedar City, Utah, February 2, 1932; admitted to bar, 1960, Utah; 1975, Arizona. *Education:* University of Utah (B.A., 1953; M.S., 1957; J.D., 1959); Columbia University. ***COURSES:*** Constitutional Law, Administrative Law, Education Law, Community Property. ***Email:*** alan.matheson@asu.edu

(This Listing Continued)

ARIZONA STATE UNIVERSITY COLLEGE OF LAW —Continued

SAMANTHA A. MOPPETT*, (Legal Writing Professor)**, born Boston, Massachusetts, 1969; admitted to bar, 1995, Massachusetts. *Education:* Bucknell University (B.A., 1991); Suffolk University (J.D., 1995). ***COURSES: Legal Practice Skills, Legal Research & Writing. ***Email:*** samantha.moppet@asu.edu

JEFFRIE G. MURPHY*, (Regents' Professor of Law and Philosophy)**, born Woodruff, South Carolina, November 26, 1940. *Education:* Johns Hopkins University (B.A., 1962); University of Rochester (Ph.D., 1966); University of California at Los Angeles (Post-Doctoral N.D.E.A. Fellow). ***COURSES: Jurisprudence. ***Email:*** jeffrie.murphy@asu.edu

CHAD L. NOREUIL*, (Legal Writing Professor)**, born Taylorville, Illinois, May 18, 1969; admitted to bar, 1995, Illinois. *Education:* University of Illinois at Urbana-Champaign (B.A., 1991; J.D., 1995). ***COURSES: Business Law, Legal Research and Writing. ***Email:*** chad.noreuil@asu.edu

CATHERINE GAGE O'GRADY*, (Professor of Law & Director of Clinical Programs)**, born Hamilton, New York, June 1, 1959; admitted to bar, 1987, Arizona. *Education:* University of Michigan (B.B.A, 1981); Arizona State University (J.D., 1987). ***COURSES: Civil Procedure, Clinical Education, Trial and Appellate Advocacy. ***Email:*** catherine.ogrady@asu.edu

SIGMUND G. POPKO*, (Legal Writing Professor)**, born Fitchburg, Massachusetts, May 30, 1962; admitted to bar, 1988, Arizona Supreme Court; U.S. District Court, Arizona; 1992, U.S. Court of Appeals for the Ninth Circuit. *Education:* University of Arizona (B.A., 1984); University of Arizona College of Law (J.D., 1987). ***COURSES: Legal Research and Writing. ***Email:*** sigmund.popko@asu.edu

CHARLES A. PULASKI, JR.*, (Visiting Professor)**, born Flushing, New York, October 22, 1941; admitted to bar, 1967, Connecticut; 1969, U.S. Tax Court; 1970, U.S. Supreme Court; 1973, Iowa; U.S. District Court, Southern and Northern Districts of Arizona; 1986, Arizona. *Education:* Yale University (B.A., 1964); Yale University Law School (LL.B., 1967). ***COURSES: Tax. ***Email:*** pulaskc@swlaw.com

JONATHAN ROSE*, (Professor of Law)**, born St. Paul, Minnesota, December 25, 1938; admitted to bar, 1963, Minnesota; 1974, Arizona. *Education:* University of Pennsylvania (B.A., 1960); University of Minnesota (LL.B., 1963). ***COURSES: Legal Ethics, Contracts, Antitrust, Regulation of Business. ***Email:*** jonathan.rose@asu.edu

MICHAEL J. SAKS*, (Professor of Law and Psychology)**, born Philadelphia, Pennsylvania, March, 1947. *Education:* Penn State University (B.A. and B.S., 1969); Ohio State University (M.A., 1972; Ph.D., 1975); Yale University (M.S.L., 1983). ***COURSES: Criminal Law, Evidence, Law and Science, Law and Social Science.

GEORGE SCHATZKI*, (Professor of Law)**, born 1933; admitted to bar, 1958, Massachusetts; 1961, Texas. *Education:* Harvard University (A.B., 1955; LL.B., 1958; LL.M., 1965). ***COURSES: Civil Procedure, Employment Discrimination, Labor and Employment Law, Legal Profession. ***Email:*** george.schatzki@asu.edu

MILTON R. SCHROEDER*, (Professor of Law)**, born Philadelphia, Pennsylvania, July 24, 1940; admitted to bar, 1966, District of Columbia; 1967, Illinois; 1972, Arizona. *Education:* Wesleyan University (B.A., 1962); University of Chicago (J.D., 1965). ***COURSES: Commercial Law, Banking Law and Regulation. ***Email:*** milton.schroeder@asu.edu

RALPH SPRITZER*, (Professor of Law)**, born New York, New York, April 27, 1917; admitted to bar, 1941, New York. *Education:* Columbia University (B.S., 1937; LL.B., 1940). ***COURSES: Criminal Procedure, Antitrust.

ANN MARIE STANTON*, (Professor of Law)**, born Minneapolis, Minnesota, April 10, 1949; admitted to bar, 1977, California and Minnesota. *Education:* University of Minnesota (B.A., 1971); Stanford University (J.D., 1975; Ph.D., 1977). ***COURSES: Family Law, Juvenile Law, Law and Social Science. ***Email:*** ann.stanton@asu.edu

JUDITH MARIE STINSON*, (Director Legal Method & Writing & ASP)**, born Okinawa, Japan, August 24, 1964; admitted to bar, 1988, Arizona; 1988, U.S. Court of Appeals, Ninth Circuit; 1988, U.S. District Court, District of Arizona. *Education:* University of Arizona (B.S., 1985; J.D., 1988). ***COURSES: Legal Writing. ***Email:*** judith.stinson@asu.edu

DANIEL STANTON STROUSE, born Los Angeles, California, October 8, 1949; admitted to bar, 1980, Wisconsin; 1987, Ohio. *Education:* Harvard College (A.B., 1971); Harvard School of Public Health (S.M., 1977); University of Wisconsin (J.D., 1980). ***COURSES:*** Health Law; Law, Science and Technology. ***Email:*** daniel.strouse@asu.edu

SAMUEL SUTTON*, (Visiting Professor of Law)**, born Chicago, Illinois, 1941; admitted to bar, 1968, United States Patent Office; 1969, District of Columbia and Arizona. *Education:* University of Arizona (B.A., 1964; B.S.E.E., 1967); George Washington University (J.D., 1969). ***COURSES: Copyright Practice, Commercial Torts, Intellectual Property, International Business Transactions, Patent Law. ***Email:*** sam.sutton@asu.edu

FERNANDO R. TESON*, (Professor of Law and Affiliate Professor of Philosophy)**, born Buenos Aires, Argentina, August 3, 1950; admitted to bar, Argentina. *Education:* Universidad De Buenos Aires (J.D., 1975); Northwestern University (S.J.D., 1987). ***COURSES: International, Jurisprudence, Comparative Constitutional, International Human Rights. ***Email:*** fernando.teson@asu.edu

REBECCA TSOSIE*, (Lincoln Professor of Native American Law and Ethics, and Executive Director, Indian Legal Programs)**, born Los Angeles, California, August 8, 1961; admitted to bar, 1991, California and Arizona. *Education:* University of California at Los Angeles (B.A., 1987; J.D., 1990). ***COURSES: Property, Indian Law. ***Email:*** rebecca.tsosie@asu.edu

BONNIE POITRAS TUCKER*, (Professor of Law)**, born New York, New York, August 4, 1939; admitted to bar, 1980, Colorado; 1981, Arizona; 1984, California. *Education:* Syracuse University (B.S., 1961); University of Colorado (J.D., 1980). ***COURSES: Disability Law, Judicial Remedies, Criminal Law, Wills and Trusts. ***Email:*** bonnie.tucker@asu.edu

JAMES WEINSTEIN*, (Amelia D. Lewis Professor of Constitutional Law)**, born Chicago, Illinois, February 15, 1953; admitted to bar, 1979, California. *Education:* University of Pennsylvania (B.A., 1975; J.D., 1978). ***COURSES: Constitutional Law, Free Speech, Federal Courts, Civil Procedure, Legal History. ***Email:*** james.weinstein@asu.edu

LAURENCE H. WINER*, (Professor of Law)**, born Lynn, Massachusetts, October 30, 1946; admitted to bar, 1977, Massachusetts. *Education:* Boston University (B.A., 1967; Ph.D., 1973); Yale Law School (J.D., 1977). ***COURSES: Media Law, Constitutional Law, Professional Ethics/Responsibility, Defamation, Torts. ***Email:*** lhwiner@asu.edu

AVE MARIA SCHOOL OF LAW

3475, PLYMOUTH ROAD
ANN ARBOR, MICHIGAN 48105
Telephone: (734) 827-8043
Fax: (734) 622-0123
www.avemarialaw.edu

Ave Maria School of Law, a Catholic law school dedicated to education lawyers with the finest professional skills, opened in August 2000. Inspired by Pope John Paul II's encyclical *fides et Ratio*, Ave Maria School of Law offers a distinctive legal education- an education characterized by the harmony of faith and reason. Formed by outstanding professional training and distinctive educational philosophy, the Law School's graduates will be equipped for leading positions in law firms, corporate legal offices, the judiciary, and national, state, and local government.

The Law School's curriculum reflects its mission- to provide its students a superior legal education enhanced by instruction in the teachings of the Catholic Church and natural law as they relate to the practice of law and the development of professional men and women. The curriculum is structured to ensure a rigorous intellectual environment in which all students receive the legal and moral foundation to become outstanding professional lawyers. The Law School's curriculum grounds students in the fundamentals of the law, developing both their knowledge and the skills critical to the intelligent practice of the profession. The Law School's curriculum also develops in its students an informed and mature judgment through which they will analyze and approach those issues and problems that the practice of law presents.

Ave Maria School of Law's inaugural class included seventy-one men and women from thirty states and Canada, representing thirty-six undergraduate institutions. The students possess a median LSAT of 158 and an average undergraduate GPA of 3.3. Many students come to Ave Maria School of Law after receiving graduate degrees, or enjoying successful careers as accountants, engineers, salespersons, social workers, educators, or military officers.

Ave Maria School of Law's faculty consists of a talented group of well-published legal scholars, including former United States Court of Appeals for the District of Columbia Judge and United States Supreme Court nominee Robert Bork. Faculty members have taught at prestigious law Schools throughout the country, worked at major law firms and state and federal government agencies, served in the Judge Advocate General's Corps, and clerked for Judges on the United States Court of Appeals for the District of Columbia, and the Fourth, Sixth, and Ninth Circuits.

The Law School is dedicated to ensuring that students gain a clear, practical, and comprehensive understanding of the law. To achieve this goal, Law School faculty use a variety of teaching methods, including the Socratic method, lectures, group discussions, and writing assignments. To optimize the benefits associated with these teaching methods, the Law School intends to maintain a low faculty-to-student ratio.

The Legal Research, Writing and Advocacy Program at Ave Maria School of Law on an innovative three-semester program designed to teach the fundamentals of legal practice. Although an emphasis on effective and persuasive legal writing is at the heart of the program, each semester has a different focus. The first semester focuses on analysis and research where students learn the role of lawyer as counselor and gain experience in traditional methods of legal research. The second semester focus is advocacy, when students, through the St. Thomas More Moot Court competition, write an appellate brief and argue it before a panel of faculty and practicing lawyers. The third semester, taken in the second year of law school, aims at preparing students for the actual practice of law, in conditions that simulate those of a law office. The finalists for the inaugural St Thomas More Moot Court competition argued before a three-judge panel of Sixth Circuit judges.

Located in Ann Arbor, Michigan, Ave Maria School of Law is housed in an eighty-four thousand square foot building that sits on an 11-acre campus. A twelve-million-dollar renovation transformed a former corporate headquarters into a world-class teaching facility. All seats in the classrooms are networked allowing students to access Library, Internet, and other resources from their desktops. Faculty and guest lecturers can utilize multimedia tools to display Web sites or other media. Faculty are encouraged to use technology in their courses and the classroom technology resources facilitate this use of technology.

The Law Library's collection is rich and full and is designed to meet the research needs of the Law School's students, satisfy the demands of the Law School curriculum, and facilitate the education of its students. It also supports the teaching, research, and service interests of the faculty, and serves the school's special teaching, research, and service objectives. The collection is comprised of over 225,000 volumes and volume equivalents and is particularly strong in American federal and state materials, Michigan law, Canon law and Catholic social thought, and non-law social science and humanities titles. Emphasis is also given to emerging areas of the law, such as cyber law and e-commerce, bioethics and the law, and elder law. Students have access to many Web-based databases, both law and non-law, through the Law School network.

The Law Library has seating for 281 students, which includes seating for 120 students in a spacious reading room, six group study rooms, and seating in three discreet areas of the main stacks. Two computer labs are also available, one instructional and one general-purpose lab. In addition, all the student carrels and study tables seating in the library are wired for direct network access.

Ave Maria School of Law offers a distinctive legal education- an education characterized by harmony of faith and reason. The Law School's rigorous intellectual environment and focus on the broader issues of legal philosophy equip graduates to serve as shapers of the culture and leaders in society. Ave Maria's approach to the study of law provides a rewarding education for law and life.

(This Listing Continued)

AVE MARIA SCHOOL OF LAW—Continued

Dean: Bernard Dobranski (734) 827-8043
Associate Dean for Academic Affairs: Joseph L. Falvey, Jr. (734) 827-8071
Director of Administrative Services: Mark Chesney (734) 827-8069
Assistant Dean for Admissions: Michael Kenney (734) 827-8064
Director of Career Services: William Peper (734) 827-8066
Chaplain: Fr. Michael Orsi (734) 827-8068
Director of Development: Fr. Liam Barr (734) 827-8077
Financial Aid Officer: Jennifer Sutch (734) 827-8051
Director of the Library and Information Technology: Mitchell Counts (734) 827-8038
Associate Dean/Registrar: Kaye Castro (734) 827-8050

FULL TIME FACULTY

JANE ADOLPHE*, (Assistant Professor of Law)**, admitted to bar, 1995, New York. *Education:* University of Calgary (B.A., 1985); University of McGill (L.L.Bl.; B.C.L., 1990); Pontificia Universita della Santa Croce (Licentiate in Canon Law, 1997). ***COURSES: International Law, Canon Law, Family Law, International Human Rights.

HOWARD BROMBERG*, (Associate Professor of Law)**, born New York, New York, September 22, 1958; admitted to bar, 1984, New York. *Education:* Harvard (B.A., 1980; J.D., 1983); Stanford (J.S.M., 1991). ***COURSES: Property, Legal Writing.

LEO L. CLARKE*, (Professor)**, born Ontario, Canada, April 26, 1950; admitted to bar, 1975, California; 1980, District of Columbia; 1990, Washington. *Education:* Stanford University (B.A., 1972); Harvard University (B.A., 1972); UCLA (J.D., 1975). ***COURSES: Commercial Law, Corporate Law.

MITCHELL EUGENE COUNTS*, (Director of the Library and Info. Tech. and Associate Professor of Law)**, born Detroit, Michigan, May, 9, 1947. *Education:* Central Michigan University (B.S., 1970); South Texas College of Law (J.D., 1984); Indiana University (M.L.S., 1990). ***COURSES: Advanced Legal Research.

BERNARD DOBRANSKI*, (President and Dean)**, born Pittsburgh, Pennslyvania, September 3, 1939; admitted to bar, 1964, Virginia. *Education:* University of Notre Dame (B.B.A., 1961); University of Virginia (J.D., 1964). ***COURSES: Jurisprudence, Labor Law, Federal Courts.

JOSEPH L. FALVEY, JR.*, (Associate Dean and Professor of Law)**, born Dayton, Ohio, March 18, 1959; admitted to bar, 1994, Michigan. *Education:* University of Notre Dame (B.A., 1981; J.D., 1987); Judge Advocate General's School (L.L.M., 1991). ***COURSES: Criminal Law, Criminal Procedure, Evidence, Trial Advocacy.

BRUCE PATRICK FROHNEN*, (Assistant Professor of Law)**, born Salt Lake City, Utah, December 18, 1962; admitted to bar, 1994, Georgia. *Education:* California State University (B.A., 1984); University of California at Davis (M.A., 1985); Cornell University (M.A., 1987; Ph.D., 1988); Emory University School of Law (J.D., 1993). ***COURSES: Property Professional Responsibility, Legal History, Jurisprudence, Constitutional Law.

MICHAEL O. KENNEY*, (Dean of Admissions)**, born Toledo, Ohio, December 27, 1958; admitted to bar, 1986, Ohio. *Education:* University of Notre Dame (B.A., 1980; J.D., 1983); George Washington University (L.L.M., 1993). ***COURSES: Trial Practice, Environmental Law, Appellate Advocate.

EDWARD CHARLES LYONS*, (Assistant Professor of Law)**, born Los Angeles, California, December 30, 1960; admitted to bar, 1998, California. *Education:* University of San Francisco (B.A., 1983); University of St. Thomas (M.A., 1987; Ph.D., 1998); Notre Dame Law School (J.D., 1994). ***COURSES: Torts, Products Liability, Jurisprudence, Federal Taxation.

EUGENE R. MILHIZER*, (Associate Professor of Law)**, born Detroit, Michigan, February 4, 1954; admitted to bar, 1979, Michigan. *Education:* University of Michigan (B.A., 1976); University of Michigan School of Law (J.D., 1979); Judge Advocate Generals School (L.L.M., 1988). ***COURSES: Criminal Law, Criminal Procedure, Evidence Advocacy.

MOLLIE ANN MURPHY*, (Associate Professor of Law)**, born Marion, Ohio, August 12, 1955; admitted to bar, 1982, District of Columbia. *Education:* St Mary's College (B.A., 1977); Notre Dame Law School (J.D., 1980). ***COURSES: Torts, Complex Litigation, Advanced Torts, Mass Torts.

RICHARD S. MYERS*, (Professor of Law)**, born Philadelphia, Pennsylvania, August 26, 1955; admitted to bar, 1981, Ohio; 1982, District of Columbia. *Education:* Kenyon College (B.A., 1977); Notre Dame Law School (J.D., 1980). ***COURSES: Civil Procedure, Conflict of Laws, Constitutional Law.

PHILIP ANTHONY PUCILLO*, (Assistant Professor of Law)**, born Orange, New Jersey, June 20, 1970; admitted to bar, 1996, New Jersey; 2001, District of Columbia. *Education:* Lafayette College (A.B., 1992); Tulane Law School (J.D., 1996). ***COURSES: Appellate Procedure, Federal Courts, Administrative Law.

STEPHEN JOSEPH SAFRANEK*, (Professor)**, born Omaha, Nebraska, June 30, 1960; admitted to bar, 1988, Illinois. *Education:* University of San Francisco (B.A., 1981); University of Dallas (M.A., 1983); Notre Dame (J.D., 1988). ***COURSES: Contracts, Sales, Professional Responsibility, State and Local Governments.

JAMES ANDREW SONNE*, (Assistant Professor of Law)**, born Philadelphia, Pennsylvania, March 7, 1972; admitted to bar, 1997, Virginia. *Education:* Duke University (B.A., 1994); Harvard Law School (J.D., 1997). ***COURSES: Civil Procedure, Labor Law, Employment Law.

BAYLOR UNIVERSITY SCHOOL OF LAW

SOUTH 5th STREET
P.O. BOX 97288
WACO, TEXAS 76798-7288

BENJAMIN N. CARDOZO SCHOOL OF LAW YESHIVA UNIVERSITY

55 FIFTH AVENUE
NEW YORK, NEW YORK 10003
Telephone: (212) 790-0200
Fax: (212) 790-0345
http://www.cardozo.yu.edu

ABA Approved Since 1978.

The Benjamin N. Cardozo School of Law is a dynamic institution that provides a challenging and stimulating intellectual experience, a rigorous foundation in fundamental legal concepts, exposure to the knotty and concrete problems encountered by practicing lawyers, and an opportunity for students with widely different substantive and professional interests to pursue studies they consider important.

Cardozo's outstanding faculty is drawn from the leading ranks of America's legal scholars and practitioners. Many hold advanced degrees in areas other than law, bringing added dimensions to the quality of learning. Cardozo is ranked as having the 15th most prolific faculty in the country and one of the top ten programs in both Intellectual Property, and Dispute Resolution.

Cardozo's student body numbers approximately 950, with roughly the same number of men and women. They come from a broad distribution of undergraduate schools, disciplines, and interests. Approximately 20% of the students come from minority groups and nearly 20% are returning to school after a hiatus.

Cardozo offers a unique approach to the study of law: a balance of a scholarly exploration of the philosophical underpinnings of legal, social, and economic structures and professional training in the doctrinal knowledge and practice skills needed to effectively practice law. The *Jacob Burns Institute for Advanced Legal Studies* supports advanced academic research, major symposia, and student scholarships. *The Samuel and Ronnie Heyman Center on Corporate Governance* sponsors major conferences and research in the area of corporate and business law, and the role of corporations and corporate managers in our society. *The Floersheimer Center for Constitutional Democracy* focuses on comparative constitutionalism and new democracies.

In the *Appellate Externship Program,* students work in the Appeals Unit of the New York City Department of Law under the supervision of an appellate attorney and an instructor. Under the *Alexander Judicial Fellows Program,* students have the opportunity to clerk full-time for one semester for a federal judge. In the full-time US Attorney's Office, Southern District New York externship, students work closely with assistant US Attorneys in the criminal division who are engaged primarily in white-collar crime prosecutions. The *Summer Institute for Placement and Career Development* offers intensive seminars linked to related field placements in the areas of Bankruptcy, Environmental Law, Family Law Practice, Labor, Alternative Dispute Resolution, Urban Law and Government, Judicial Process and Ethics, International Trade Law, Entertainment Law, and Civil and Criminal Litigation. Cardozo offers summer programs in Israel at The Hebrew University of Jerusalem, at Central European University in Budapest, and Oxford University in Great Britain.

Cardozo's clinics provide students with substantive practical experience to augment the theoretical training that occurs in the classroom. In the area of criminal law, students may participate in the *Criminal Law Clinic,* the *Criminal Appeals Clinic, The Innocence Project,* or the *Prosecutor Practicum.* Students selected for the *Criminal Law Clinic* do field work in the Brooklyn Criminal Court, representing the criminally accused. The *Criminal Appeals Clinic* allows students to represent indigent appellants before the First Department of the Appellate Division of the New York State Supreme Court. Students in *The Innocence Project* help wrongfully-convicted persons to gain freedom through DNA evidence. *Prosecutor Practicum* participants work in the Manhattan District Attorney's Office, performing many of the functions of an assistant district attorney, under the supervision of an instructor and a senior assistant district attorney. The *Intensive Trial Advocacy Program* brings to the campus 175 trial lawyers and judges from around the US for a two-week program of hands-on trial practice.

Cardozo's *Bet Tzedek Legal Services Clinic* advocates on behalf of poor, homebound elderly and people with disabilities. The *Mediation Clinic* provides arbitration and mediation experience in situations involving personal and social conflict. The *Tax Clinic* is an innovative program that provides students with practical experience in tax law by representing taxpayers in cases pending before the United States Tax Court. There is also an *Immigration Clinic* and *Holocaust Claims Restitution Clinic.*

Cardozo sponsors a Moot Court Honor Society, one faculty journal, and five student publications. The *Law Review, Arts and Entertainment Law Journal, Journal of International and Comparative Law, The Online Journal of Conflict Resolution,* and the *Women's Law Journal* (formerly the *Women's Annotated Legal Bibliography,* the first annotated bibliography of legal commentary on women's issues) select students on the basis of scholarship and writing ability. *Cardozo Studies in Law and Literature* is a professional journal, edited by a senior member of the faculty and guided by a distinguished board of editors. Students have the opportunity also to work on two faculty newsletters, *The New York Real Estate Reporter* and the *Communications in Transition Newsletter.*

The J.D. program, requiring 84 credits, consists of six full-time semesters of study. First-year students take a series of basic, prescribed courses; second- and third-year programs are elective, with the exception of distribution requirements and required courses in professional responsibility, upper level legal writing, and advanced legal research. An LL.M. degree is offered in Intellectual Property and in General Studies.

Cardozo offers the Accelerated Entry Plan (AEP), which allows students to begin their studies in either January or May and complete the six semesters in two-and-one-half years. Students beginning in January complete two semesters by the end of the summer; students beginning in May complete one semester during the summer and then have the option of continuing in the fall or returning the following summer to complete the second semester. AEP classes are small and provide the same depth of legal training as the traditional program.

Cardozo is on 11 floors of the Brookdale Center located in Greenwich Village. The Dr. Lillian and Dr. Rebecca Chutick Law Library occupies three floors containing over 450,000 volumes and is fully equipped with computers, microfiche and microfilm readers and reader printers. A residence hall is located one block away.

Established in 1976, Cardozo is accredited by both the ABA and AALS. It holds a charter from the Order of the Coif.

(This Listing Continued)

BENJAMIN N. CARDOZO SCHOOL OF LAW YESHIVA UNIVERSITY—Continued

Dean: David Rudenstine (212) 790-0310
Senior Associate Dean: Laura Cunningham (212) 790-0307
Assistant Dean for Admissions: Robert L. Schwartz (212) 790-0329
Financial Aid Assistant Director: Tom Curtain (212) 790-0392
Director of Law Library: Lynn Wishart (212) 790-0222
Assistant Dean for Placement: Jacquelyn L. Burt (212) 790-0374
Assistant Dean for Student Affairs: Judith Mender (212) 790-0313

FULL TIME FACULTY

DAVID RUDENSTINE*, (Dean and Dr. Herman George & Kate Kaiser Professor of Constitutional Law)**, born Danbury, Connecticut, February 26, 1942; admitted to bar, 1970, New York. *Education:* Yale University (B.A., 1963; M.A.T., 1965); New York University (J.D.,1969). ***COURSES: Constitutional Law, First Amendment, Federal Courts, Labor Arbitration, Civil Procedure, Cultural Property. ***Email:*** rudenstn@ymail.yu.edu

PARIS R. BALDACCI*, (Clinical Professor of Law and Supervising Attorney)**, born Scranton, Pennsylvania, October 13, 1943; admitted to bar, 1988, New York. *Education:* University of Scranton (B.A., 1965); Marquette University (Ph.D., 1974); City University of New York Law School at Queens College (J.D., 1987). ***COURSES: Civil Litigation Clinic, Lawyering, Elder Law, Sexual Orientation & The Law, Social Welfare Law. ***Email:*** baldacci@ymail.yu.edu

J. DAVID BLEICH*, (Herbert & Florence Tenzer Professor of Jewish Law and Ethics)**, born 1936. *Education:* Brooklyn College (B.A., 1960; M.A., 1968); Columbia University (Ph.D., 1974). ***COURSES: Advanced Jewish Law, Jewish Law and Contemporary Legal Issues, Property, Religion and Law in the United States, Bioethics and the Law. ***Email:*** bleich@ymail.yu.edu

LESTER BRICKMAN*, (Professor of Law)**, born New York, New York, September 4, 1940; admitted to bar, 1965, Florida; 1977, New York. *Education:* Carnegie Institute of Technology (B.S., 1961); University of Florida (J.D., 1964); Yale University (LL.M., 1965). ***COURSES: Professional Responsibility, Contracts, Land Use. ***Email:*** brickman@ymail.yu.edu

DAVID GRAY CARLSON*, (Professor of Law)**, born 1952; admitted to bar, 1978, New York. *Education:* University of California at Santa Barbara (B.A., 1974); University of California, Hastings College of Law (J.D., 1977). ***COURSES: Commercial Law, Creditors Rights, Hegel's Science of Logic, Property, Real Estate Transactions. ***Email:*** dcarlson@ymail.yu.edu

LAURA E. CUNNINGHAM*, (Senior Associate Dean and Professor of Law)**, admitted to bar, 1980, California; 1988, New York. *Education:* University of California, Davis (B.S., 1977); University of California, Hastings College of Law (J.D., 1980); New York University (LL.M., 1988). ***COURSES: Federal Income Taxation, Taxation of Partnerships, Estate and Gift Taxation, Tax Policy, Estate Planning. ***Email:*** cunningh@ymail.yu.edu

LAWRENCE A. CUNNINGHAM*, (Professor of Law and Director, Samuel and Ronnie Heyman Center on Corporate Governance)**, born Wilmington, Delaware, July 10, 1962; admitted to bar, 1989, New York. *Education:* University of Delaware (B.A., 1985); Benjamin N. Cardozo School of Law, Yeshiva University (J.D., 1988). ***COURSES: Accounting, Contracts, Corporations, Corporate Finance. ***Email:*** cunning@ymail.yu.edu

EDWARD DE GRAZIA*, (Professor of Law)**, born Chicago, Illinois, February 5, 1927; admitted to bar, 1952, District of Columbia. *Education:* University of Chicago (B.A., 1948; J.D., 1951); Yale University (Post-Doctoral Fellow, 1972-1974). ***COURSES: Criminal Law, First Amendment, Prosecutive Function, Supreme Court. ***Email:*** degrazia@ymail.yu.edu

MITCHELL LAWRENCE ENGLER*, (Associate Professor)**, born New York, New York; admitted to bar, 1991, New York and Connecticut. *Education:* New York University (B.A., 1987; J.D., 1990; LL.M., 1991). ***COURSES: Taxation, Corporations.

E. NATHANIEL GATES*, (Professor of Law)**, born Red River, New Mexico, November 14, 1954; admitted to bar, 1988, New York. *Education:* Yale University (B.A., 1977; J.D., 1987). ***COURSES: Constitutional Law, Critical Race Theory, Employment Discrimination, Legal History, Criminal Law. ***Email:*** monchan@aol.com

MYRIAM E. GILLES*, (Assistant Professor of Law)**, born Brooklyn, New York, March 7, 1971; admitted to bar, 1997, New York. *Education:* Harvard College (B.A., 1993); Yale Law School (J.D., 1996). ***COURSES: Civil Rights, Torts, Health Law.

TOBY GOLICK*, (Clinical Professor of Law and Director of Bet Tzedek Legal Services Clinic)**, born Boston, Massachusetts, April 9, 1945; admitted to bar, 1969, New York. *Education:* Barnard College (A.B., 1966); Columbia University (J.D., 1969). ***COURSES: Civil Litigation, Social Welfare Law, Elder Law. ***Email:*** tgolick@ymail.yu.edu

PETER GOODRICH*, (Professor of Law)**, born England, September 13, 1954. *Education:* University of Sheffield Law School (LL.B., 1975); Faculty of Law, University of Edinburgh (Ph.D., 1984). ***COURSES: Contracts, Remedies, Rhetoric History. ***Email:*** goodrich@ymail.yu.edu

MINASSE HAILE*, (Professor of Law)**, born Harrer, Ethiopia. *Education:* University of Wisconsin (B.A., 1950); Columbia University (J.D., 1954; M.A., 1957; Ph.D., 1961). ***COURSES: Comparative Law, International Law, International Organizations, Human Rights. ***Email:*** haile@ymail.yu.edu

MALVINA HALBERSTAM*, (Professor of Law)**, born 1937; admitted to bar, 1962, New York; 1968, California. *Education:* Brooklyn College (B.A., 1957); Columbia University (J.D., 1961; M.I.A., 1964). ***COURSES: Criminal Procedure, Human Rights, International Law, International Criminal Law, U.S. Foreign Relations Law. ***Email:*** halbrstm@ymail.yu.edu

MARCI A. HAMILTON*, (Paul R. Verkuil Professor of Public Law and Director, Intellectual Property Law Program)**, born Dallas, Texas, July 22, 1957; admitted to bar, 1989, Pennsylvania and District of Columbia. *Education:* Vanderbilt University (B.A., 1979); Pennsylvania State University (M.A., Philosophy, 1982; M.A., English, 1984); University of Pennsylvania (J.D., 1988). ***COURSES: Constitutional Law, Domestic and International Law, Intellectual Property Law, Copyright Law, Trademark Law, Law of Cyberspace. ***Email:*** hamilton02@aol.com

EVA H. HANKS*, (Dr. Samuel Belkin Professor of Law and Society)**, born 1929. *Education:* Freie Universitat (Referendar, 1951); University of California at Los Angeles (LL.B., 1960); Columbia University (LL.M., 1962; J.S.D., 1969). ***COURSES: Property, Legal Method, Environmental Law, Torts, Animal Rights. ***Email:*** hanks@ymail.yu.edu

***JOHN LAWRENCE HANKS*, (Professor of Law)**, born 1939;

(This Listing Continued)

BENJAMIN N. CARDOZO SCHOOL OF LAW YESHIVA UNIVERSITY—Continued

admitted to bar, 1996, New York. *Education:* Rutgers University, Newark (B.S., 1966; J.D., 1968); Columbia University (LL.M., 1972; M.A., Economics, 1972). ***COURSES:*** Contracts, Torts, Business Torts, Franchise Law, Organized Crime, Governance of New York City. ***Email:*** jhanks@ymail.yu.edu

MICHAEL ERIC HERZ, **(Professor of Law)**, born 1957; admitted to bar, 1986, New York. *Education:* Swarthmore College (B.A., 1979); University of Chicago (J.D., 1982). ***COURSES:*** Administrative Law, Constitutional Law, Elements of Law, Environmental Law, Legislation. ***Email:*** herz@ymail.yu.edu

KYRON JAMES HUIGENS, **(Associate Professor of Law)**, born Rapid City, South Dakota, August 17, 1959; admitted to bar, 1984, Washington. *Education:* Washington University (A.B., 1981); Cornell Law School (J.D., 1984). ***COURSES:*** Criminal Law, Criminal Procedure, Death Penalty and Habeas Corpus. ***Email:*** khuigens@ymail.yu.edu

ARTHUR JOHN JACOBSON, **(Max Freund Professor of Litigation & Advocacy)**, born 1948; admitted to bar, 1974, New York; 1975, Massachusetts. *Education:* Harvard University (B.A., 1969; J.D., 1974; Ph.D., 1978). ***COURSES:*** Civil Procedure, Contracts, Jurisprudence. ***Email:*** ajacobsn@ymail.yu.edu

MELANIE B. LESLIE, **(Associate Professor of Law)**, born Las Vegas, Nevada, March 17, 1961; admitted to bar, 1991, New Jersey; 1992, New York. *Education:* University of Oregon (B.A., 1983); Benjamin N. Cardozo School of Law (J.D., 1991). ***COURSES:*** Property, Trusts & Estates, Evidence. ***Email:*** leslie@ymail.yu.edu

LELA PORTER LOVE, **(Professor of Law)**, born Washington, D.C., December 19, 1950; admitted to bar, 1979, District of Columbia; 1981, New York; 1983, New Hampshire. *Education:* Harvard University (A.B., 1973); Georgetown University Law Center (J.D., 1979). ***COURSES:*** Mediation, Conflict Resolution Processes and Skills. ***Email:*** love@ymail.yu.edu

PETER LUSHING, **(Professor of Law)**, born 1941; admitted to bar, 1965, New York; 1983, New Jersey. *Education:* Columbia University (B.A., 1962; LL.B., 1965). ***COURSES:*** Civil Procedure, Criminal Law, Criminal Procedure, Evidence. ***Email:*** petelush@att.net

JOHN OLDHAM MCGINNIS, **(Professor of Law)**, born New York, New York, March 21, 1957; admitted to bar, 1984, New York. *Education:* Harvard University (B.A., 1978; J.D., 1983); Balliol College, Oxford (M.A., 1980). ***COURSES:*** Constitutional Law, Administrative Law, Antitrust, International Trade and Investment, Law and Economics, Law and Biology. ***Email:*** mcginnis@ymail.yu.edu

LESLIE S. NEWMAN, **(Associate Professor and Director of Legal Writing)**, born New York, New York, February 9, 1953; admitted to bar, 1979, Massachusetts; 1986, New York. *Education:* Brown University (A.B., 1975; M.A., 1975); Boston University (J.D., 1978). ***COURSES:*** Legal Writing, Research and Lawyering Skills, Moot Court, Advanced Writing and Editing, Appellate Advocacy and Drafting, Elements of Law. ***Email:*** newman@ymail.yu.edu

JONATHAN OBERMAN, **(Associate Clinical Professor of Law)**, born New York, New York, May 23, 1953; admitted to bar, 1983, New Jersey; New York. *Education:* Columbia University (B.A., 1974; M.A., 1976; M.Phil., 1979); Northeastern University (J.D., 1982). ***COURSES:*** Criminal Law Clinic, Criminal Law. ***Email:*** oberman@ymail.yu.edu

MONROE E. PRICE, **(Joseph & Sadie Danciger Prof. of Law; Dir., Howard M. Squadron Program in Media, Law and Society)**, born Vienna, Austria, August 18, 1938; admitted to bar, 1967, California; 1983, New York. *Education:* Yale University (B.A., 1960; LL.B., 1964). ***COURSES:*** Administrative Law, Copyright, Law and the American Indian, Law and the Arts, Regulation of Electronic Media, Family Law. ***Email:*** price@ymail.yu.edu

MICHEL ROSENFELD, **(Justice Sydney L. Robins Professor of International Law and Human Rights)**, born 1948; admitted to bar, 1976, New York. *Education:* Columbia University (B.A., 1969; M.A., 1971; M.Phil., 1978; Ph.D., 1991); Northwestern University (J.D., 1974). ***COURSES:*** Constitutional Law, Comparative Constitutional Law, Jurisprudence, Legal Profession, Philosophy of Human Rights. ***Email:*** mrosnfld@ymail.yu.edu

LESLIE SALZMAN, **(Clinical Professor of Law & Supervising Attorney)**, admitted to bar, 1982, New York. *Education:* Tufts University (B.A., 1978); New York University (J.D., 1981). ***COURSES:*** Social Welfare Litigation, Clinical Education, Elder Law. ***Email:*** salzman@ymail.yu.edu

BARRY SCHECK, **(Professor of Law and Director of Clinical Education; Co-Director for the Innocence Project)**, born New York, New York, September 19, 1949; admitted to bar, 1974, California; 1975, New York. *Education:* Yale University (B.A., 1971); University of California, Berkeley (J.D., 1974). ***COURSES:*** Criminal Law Clinic, Criminal Law, Professional Responsibility, Trial Advocacy. ***Email:*** scheck@ymail.yu.edu

JEANNE L. SCHROEDER, **(Professor of Law)**, born New York, New York, June 7, 1954; admitted to bar, 1979, New York. *Education:* Williams College (A.B., 1975); Stanford University (J.D., 1978). ***COURSES:*** Commercial Law, Securities Law, Corporations. ***Email:*** schroedr@ymail.yu.edu

WILLIAM SCHWARTZ, **(University Professor)**, born Providence, Rhode Island, May 6, 1933; admitted to bar, 1956, District of Columbia; 1962, Massachusetts; 1989, New York. *Education:* Boston University (A.A., 1952; J.D., 1955); Boston University Graduate School (A.M., 1960); Harvard Law School Graduate Program (Graduate Studies, 1995); Honorary Degrees: LHD (Hebrew College, 1996); LHD (Yeshiva University, 1998). ***COURSES:*** Torts, Property, Estate Planning, Trusts & Estates.

SCOTT JONATHAN SHAPIRO, **(Professor of Law)**, born New York, New York, November 23, 1964; admitted to bar, 1992, New York. *Education:* Columbia College (B.A., 1987); Yale Law School (J.D., 1990); Columbia University (Ph.D., 1996). ***COURSES:*** Jurisprudence, Family Law, Criminal Law, Elements of Law, Constitutional Law. ***Email:*** sshapiro@ymail.yu.edu

PAUL M. SHUPACK, **(Professor of Law)**, born Brooklyn, New York, May 20, 1940; admitted to bar, 1971, New York. *Education:* Columbia University (A.B., 1961); University of Chicago (J.D., 1970). ***COURSES:*** Commercial Law, Contracts. ***Email:*** shupack@ymail.yu.edu

JONATHAN L.F. SILVER, **(Professor of Law)**, born 1948; admitted to bar, 1973, Pennsylvania. *Education:* Yale University (B.A., 1969); University of Pennsylvania (J.D., 1973). ***COURSES:*** Elements of Law, Federal Jurisdiction, Jurisprudence, Labor Law, Torts, Constitutional Law.

EDWARD STEIN, **(Associate Professor of Law)**, born Washington, DC, November 11, 1965. *Education:* Williams College (B.A., 1987); MIT (Ph.D., 1992); Yale (J.D., 2000). ***COURSES:*** Family Law, Evidence, Sexual Orientation & the Law, Statutory Interpretation. ***Email:*** ed@edstein.com

STEWART E. STERK, **(H. Bert & Ruth Mack Professor of Real Estate Law)**, born New York, New York, November 29, 1952; admitted to bar, 1977, New York. *Education:* Columbia University (A.B., 1973; J.D., 1976). ***COURSES:*** Property, Conflict of Laws, Land

(This Listing Continued)

BENJAMIN N. CARDOZO SCHOOL OF LAW YESHIVA UNIVERSITY—Continued

Use Regulation, Trusts and Estates, Copyright. ***Email:*** sterk@ymail.yu.edu

SUZANNE LAST STONE*, (Professor of Law)**, born 1952; admitted to bar, 1980, New York. *Education:* Princeton University (A.B., 1974); Columbia University (J.D., 1978). ***COURSES: Civil Procedure, Criminal Law, Federal Jurisdiction, Law and Religion. ***Email:*** sstone@ymail.yu.edu

PETER TILLERS*, (Professor of Law)**, born Riga, Latvia, 1943; admitted to bar, 1970, California. *Education:* Yale University (B.A., 1966); Harvard University (J.D., 1969; LL.M., 1972). ***COURSES: Civil Procedure, Evidence, Advanced Evidence, Theories of Evidence, Fact Investigation. ***Email:*** tillers@ymail.yu.edu

PAUL R. VERKUIL*, (Professor of Law)**, born Staten Island, New York, December 4, 1939; admitted to bar, 1968, New York; 1990, District of Columbia; 1991, Virginia. *Education:* William and Mary (A.B., 1961); University of Virginia (J.D., 1967); New York University (J.S.D., 1972). ***COURSES: Administrative Law; Regulation and Deregulation. ***Email:*** verkuil@ymail.yu.edu

RICHARD H. WEISBERG*, (Walter H. Floersheimer Professor of Constitutional Law)**, born 1944; admitted to bar, 1976, New York. *Education:* Brandeis University (B.A., 1965); Columbia University (J.D., 1974); Cornell University (M.A., 1967; Ph.D., 1970). ***COURSES: Constitutional Law, Law and Literature, Torts, Trusts and Estates, First Amendment, Legal Systems during the Holocaust. ***Email:*** rhweisbg@ymail.yu.edu

LYNN WISHART*, (Director of Law Library and Professor of Legal Research)**, born 1948; admitted to bar, 1984, District of Columbia. *Education:* West Virginia University (A.B., 1969); University of Michigan (A.M.L.S., 1971); Washington University (J.D., 1977). ***COURSES: Advanced Legal Research. ***Email:*** wishart@ymail.yu.edu

CHARLES M. YABLON*, (Professor of Law)**, born 1951; admitted to bar, 1976, New York. *Education:* Columbia University (B.A., 1972); Yale University (J.D., 1975). ***COURSES: Civil Procedure, Corporations, Injunctions, Settlement of Litigation. ***Email:*** yablon@ymail.yu.edu

ELLEN YAROSHEFSKY*, (Clinical Professor of Law)**, born Brooklyn, New York, April 17, 1948; admitted to bar, 1976, Washington; 1984, New York. *Education:* Douglass College, Rutgers University (B.A., 1969); Rutgers University - Newark (J.D., 1975). ***COURSES: Criminal Law Clinic, Professional Responsibility. ***Email:*** yaroshef@ymail.yu.edu

EDWARD A. ZELINSKY*, (Professor of Law)**, born 1950; admitted to bar, 1975, Connecticut. *Education:* Yale University (B.A., 1972; M.A., 1975; J.D., 1975; M. Phil., 1978). ***COURSES: Federal Taxation, Corporate Taxation, International Taxation, Pensions and Benefits. ***Email:*** zelinsky@ymail.yu.edu

BOSTON COLLEGE LAW SCHOOL

885 CENTRE STREET
NEWTON, MASSACHUSETTS 02159

BOSTON UNIVERSITY SCHOOL OF LAW

765 COMMONWEALTH AVENUE
BOSTON, MASSACHUSETTS 02215
Telephone: (617) 353-3112
Fax: (617) 353-7400
http://www.bu.edu/LAW

ABA Approved Since 1925

Boston University School of Law provides a strong curriculum and a rich array of opportunities for students interested in law. Located on the main campus of Boston University along the Charles River, the School of Law recently celebrated its 125th anniversary. The School is accredited by the American Bar Association and is a charter member of the Association of American Law Schools.

Sixty full-time faculty members provide the large majority of classroom teaching. In addition, more than fifty part-time faculty provide specialized instruction, and eighteen teaching fellows offer instruction in the First Year Writing Program. The faculty carries on a long-standing tradition at the School of Law of excellence in classroom instruction, while building an international reputation for research and writing that addresses the most difficult legal issues faced by our society.

The School of Law annually considers over 5,000 applications for the approximately 275 places in the entering J.D. class. The School also offers programs for LL.M. degrees in Taxation (established in 1959), Banking and Financial Law (1984), and American Law for Foreign Lawyers (1995). Students come from a wide range of backgrounds and schools, and with experiences and perspectives that continually enrich the School. From its founding in 1872, the School of Law has had a policy of opening its doors to women and minorities.

The curriculum consists of an extremely diverse selection of courses, seminars and clinical programs. After the first year, students have free choice of courses, except for a required course in Professional Responsibility and fulfillment of an upperclass writing requirement. The School's objective is to equip the student with sufficient knowledge and understanding of law and legal systems to enable use of this knowledge in any form of legal practice or in any other service or career. The School has developed concentrations in the curriculum for those students wishing to specialize in particular areas of the law, including Business Organizations and Finance Law, Environmental Law, Health Care Law, Intellectual Property Law , International Law and Litigation and Dispute Resolution.

The School of Law offers eight dual-degree programs with other graduate divisions of Boston University, including a J.D./M.B.A. and a J.D./M.B.A with Concentration in Health Care Management (with the Graduate School of Management), a J.D./M.S. in Mass Communication (with the College of Communication), a J.D./M.P.H. (with the School of Public Health), a J.D./M.A. in Preservation Studies, a J.D./LL.M. in taxation, a J.D./M.A. in International Relations and a J.D./M.A. in Philosophy and the Law (with the Graduate School of Arts and Sciences), a J.D./M.S.W. (with the School of Social Work), and a J.D./L.L.M. in Banking and Financial Law.

The School of Law is a national leader in developing semester-abroad programs. It offers students the opportunity to study abroad at one of

(This Listing Continued)

BOSTON UNIVERSITY SCHOOL OF LAW—Continued

eight locations-Buenos Aires, Argentina; Lyon, France; Paris, France; Oxford, England; Leiden, The Netherlands; Tel Aviv, Israel; Florence, Italy; and Hong Kong, China.

Students at the School publish six law journals. Students also participate in a broad range of organizations dedicated to community service and to social activities. A majority of students participates in extracurricular moot court, negotiation or client counseling competitions.

The School sponsors four research centers and institutes: The Morin Center for Banking and Financial Law, The Norman Neal Pike Center on Law and Disability, The Center for Law and Technology, and The Institute of Jewish Law. The American Society of Law, Medicine & Ethics, an independent professional association is housed at the School of Law.

The School of Law library contains more than 550,000 volumes, more than 5,500 serial subscriptions, and extensive facilities for computer research.

The Career Development Office provides a wide variety of programs and employer contacts to assist students in planning their careers and securing challenging positions. Graduates of the School of Law work in a broad range of legal and non-legal jobs throughout the country and the world. More than 16,000 living alumni have achieved great distinction in the private practice of law on the bench, in politics and other public service, in academia, and in business. Many alumni continue to support the school by acting as advisors and mentors to current students and recent graduates.

Dean: Ronald A. Cass (617) 353-3112
Director of Admissions/Financial Aid: Joan Horgan (617) 353-3100
Library Director: Dan J. Freehling (617) 353-2309
Career Development Director: Elizabeth Armour (617) 353-3141

FULL TIME FACULTY

SUSAN MUSARRAT AKRAM, **(Clinical Associate Professor)**, born 1956; admitted to bar, 1983, California; 1989, Massachusetts. *Education:* Michigan (B.A., 1979); Georgetown (J.D., 1982); Institute International des Droits de L'Homme (Diplomate, 1996). ***COURSES:*** Clinical Teaching, Comparative Refugee/Asylum Law, Immigration/Asylum Law, Trial Advocacy.

GEORGE J. ANNAS, **(Professor of Law)**, born 1945; admitted to bar, 1970 Massachusetts and Minnesota. *Education:* Harvard, Cambridge (A.B., 1967; J.D., 1970; M.P.H., 1972). ***COURSES:*** Bioethics Health and Human Rights, Law and Literature.

JOHN S. BAERST, **(Prof., Banking Law & Dir., Morin Center for Banking Law Studies & Grad. Banking Law)**, born 1944; admitted to bar, 1973, New York. *Education:* St. Anselm College (B.A., 1965); College International di Sant Anselmo (S.T.B., 1968); Union Theological Seminary, NYC (S.T.M., 1970); Columbia (J.D., 1972). ***COURSES:*** Banking, International Banking, International Securities Transactions, Resolution of Transactional Disputes.

MICHAEL BARAM, **(Professor & Director, Law & Tech. Center)**, born 1935; admitted to bar, 1962, Massachusetts. *Education:* Tufts University (B.S., 1957); Columbia (LL.B., 1960). ***COURSES:*** Administrative Law; Advanced Environmental Law, Corporate Risk Management, Environmental Law, Law & Science, Products Liability.

RANDY E. BARNETT, **(Austin B. Fletcher Professor)**, born 1952; admitted to bar, 1977, Illinois. *Education:* Northwestern (B.A., 1974); Harvard (J.D., 1977). ***COURSES:*** Agency & Partnership; Constitutional Theory, Contracts, Criminal Law, Cyber Law.

HUGH W. BAXTER, **(Associate Professor)**, born 1958. *Education:* Stanford (A.B., 1980); Yale (Ph.D., 1985); Stanford (J.D., 1990). ***COURSES:*** Federal Courts (Supreme Court), Jurisprudence, Torts.

JACK MICHAEL BEERMANN, **(Professor)**, born 1958; admitted to bar, 1983, Illinois; 1985, Massachusetts. *Education:* Wisconsin (B.A., 1980); University of Chicago (J.D., 1983). ***COURSES:*** Administrative Law, Allocation of Government Power, Civil Rights, Contracts, Federal Jurisdiction, Supreme Court Decision-making.

ROBERT G. BONE, **(Professor & Harry Elwood Warren Scholar)**, born 1951; admitted to bar, 1978, Massachusetts. *Education:* Stanford University (B.A., 1973); Harvard (J.D., 1978). ***COURSES:*** Civil Procedure, Complex Litigation, Game Theory & Litigation. Intellectual Property, Jurisprudence.

JOSEPH F. BRODLEY, **(Hon. Frank R. Kenison Scholar-in-Law, Prof., Law & Econ & Sr. Assoc. Dean)**, born 1926; admitted to bar, 1953, California; 1956, New York. *Education:* U.C.L.A., (B.A., 1949); Yale (LL.B., 1952); Harvard (LL.M., 1953). ***COURSES:*** Antitrust, Corporate Finance, Corporations, Law & Technology, Regulated Industries.

CONSTANCE A. BROWN, **(Clinical Associate Professor)**, born 1949; admitted to bar, 1981, Massachusetts; 1987, Maine. *Education:* Boston College (J.D., 1981). ***COURSES:*** Clinical Teaching.

ROBERT G. BURDICK, **(Dir., Legal Aid Prog. & Clin. Assoc. Professor)**, born 1946; admitted to bar, 1972, Massachusetts. *Education:* Boston University (J.D., 1972). ***COURSES:*** Advanced Federal Litigation, Interviewing, Counseling, Negotiating, Lawyering Process, Professional Responsibility, Trial Advocacy.

FRANCES M. BURNS, **(Clinical Associate Professor)**, born 1949; admitted to bar, 1973, Massachusetts. *Education:* Boston College (J.D., 1973). ***COURSES:*** Clinical Teaching, Trial Advocacy.

DANIELA CARUSO, **(Associate Professor)**, born 1964. *Education:* University of Bari, Italy (LL.B., 1987); Harvard (LL.M. 1990); University of Italy (Doc. in Law, 1992). ***COURSES:*** Comparative Law, European Union Law, Contracts.

RONALD A. CASS, **(Dean and Bigelow Professor of Law)**, born 1949; admitted to bar, 1973, Maryland; 1974, District of Columbia; 1979, Virginia. *Education:* University of Virginia (B.A., 1970; J.D., 1973). ***COURSES:*** Administrative Law, International Trade Law, Antitrust Law, Communications Law.

JANE MASLOW COHEN, **(Professor)**, born 1945; admitted to bar, 1971, Massachusetts. *Education:* Wellesley College (B.A., 1967); Yale (J.D., 1971). ***COURSES:*** Domestic Relations, Jurisprudence (Law & Literature), Legal Profession, Life & Death, Property Law.

MARY CARMEL CONNAUGHTON, **(Clinical Associate Professor)**, born 1952; admitted to bar, 1985, Massachusetts. *Education:* Brandeis University (B.A., 1974); Smith College (M.S.W., 1978); New York University (J.D., 1985). ***COURSES:*** Clinical Teaching, Trial Advocacy.

JUDITH E. DIAMOND, **(Clinical Associate Professor)**, admitted to

(This Listing Continued)

BOSTON UNIVERSITY SCHOOL OF LAW—Continued

bar, 1974, Massachusetts. *Education:* Michigan (B.A., 1966); Wisconsin (M.A., 1968); Boston University (J.D., 1974). ***COURSES:*** Clinical, Interviewing, Counseling & Negotiation, Trial Practice (Advocacy).

WARD FARNSWORTH*, (Associate Professor)**, born 1967. *Education:* Wesleyan University (B.A., 1989); University of Chicago (J.D., 1994). ***COURSES: Civil Procedure, Torts.

ALAN L. FELD*, (Professor)**, born 1940; admitted to bar, 1963, New York; 1974, Massachusetts. *Education:* Columbia (A.B., 1960); Harvard (LL.B., 1963). ***COURSES: Corporation Finance, Law and the Arts, Legislative Process, Tax Exempt Organizations, Tax Policy, Taxation, Federal.

STANLEY Z. FISHER*, (Professor)**, born 1936; admitted to bar, 1963, District of Columbia; 1970, Massachusetts. *Education:* Oberlin College (B.A., 1957); Yale (LL.B., 1963). ***COURSES: Clinical Teaching, Criminal Law, Criminal Procedure, Juvenile Law, Legal Profession.

TAMAR FRANKEL*, (Professor)**, born 1925; admitted to bar, 1949, Israel; 1972, Massachusetts. *Education:* Harvard (LL.M., 1964; S.J.D., 1972). ***COURSES: Corporations, Employee Profit Sharing & Benefit Plans, Partnerships, Regulation of Investment Management, Securitization of Debt.

DAN J. FREEHLING*, (Associate Dean, Technology, Professor & Librarian)**, born 1950; admitted to bar, 1977, Florida. *Education:* Huntingdon College (B.S., 1972); Alabama (J.D., 1975; M.L.S., 1977). ***COURSES: Advanced Legal Research, Legal Research & Writing.

LEONARD H. GLANTZ*, (Professor of Law)**, born 1948; admitted to bar, 1973, Massachusetts. *Education:* Boston University (B.A., 1970; J.D., 1973). ***COURSES: Children and The Law, Tobacco and The Law.

WENDY JANE GORDON*, (Professor & Paul J. Liacos Scholar in Law)**, born 1949; admitted to bar, 1975, Connecticut, 1976, District of Columbia. *Education:* Cornell University, College of Arts & Sciences (B.A., 1971); Pennsylvania (J.D., 1975). ***COURSES: Copyright, Intellectual Property Theory, Intellectual Property, Jurisprudence, Law & Economics.

ERIC D. GREEN*, (Professor)**, born 1946; admitted to bar, 1973, California; 1979, Massachusetts. *Education:* Brown University (A.B., 1968); Harvard (J.D., 1972). ***COURSES: Constitutional Law, Evidence, Legal Method, Varieties of Dispute Resolution.

MICHAEL C. HARPER*, (Professor & Barreca Labor Relations Scholar)**, born 1948; admitted to bar, 1973, Indiana; 1976, District of Columbia. *Education:* Harvard (A.B., 1970; J.D., 1973). ***COURSES: Administrative Law, Employment Discrimination, Labor Law, Sports Law.

OONA ANNE HATHAWAY*, (Associate Professor)**, born Portland, Oregon, September 20, 1972; admitted to bar, 1998, New York; 1999, District of Columbia. *Education:* Harvard University (B.A., 1994); Yale Law School (J.D., 1997). ***COURSES: Civil Procedure, International Law. ***Email:*** ohathawa@bu.edu

NEIL S. HECHT*, (Professor & Director, The Institute of Jewish Law)**, born 1934; admitted to bar, 1959, New York; 1973, Massachusetts. *Education:* Rabbinic (B.A., 1954); Yeshiva (1954); Yale (J.D., 1959); Columbia (LL.M., 1964). ***COURSES: Agency, Evidence, Historic Preservation Law, Jewish Law, Real Property.

KEITH NORMAN HYLTON*, (Professor & Law Alumni Scholar)**, born 1960. *Education:* Harvard (A.B., 1982; J.D., 1989); M.I.T. (Ph.D., 1986). ***COURSES: Antitrust, Labor Law, Law & Economics, Torts.

MARIA O'BRIEN HYLTON*, (Professor)**, born 1960; admitted to bar, 1987, Massachusetts; 1988, District of Columbia. *Education:* Harvard (A.B., 19820; Yale (J.D., 1985). ***COURSES: Criminal Law, Employee Benefits, Insurance Law, Legislation, Problems in Labor & Employment, Public Sector Labor Law.

WENDY J. KAPLAN*, (Clinical Professor)**, born 1949; admitted to bar, 1974, Massachusetts. *Education:* Mount Holyoke College (A.B., 1971); Boston College (J.D., 1974). ***COURSES: Clinical Teaching, Criminal Justice, Juvenile Law.

VIKRAMADITYA S. KHANNA*, (Associate Professor of Law)**, *Education:* Victoria University of Wellington, New Zealand (B.C.A., LL.B.); Harvard Law School (LL.M., S.J.D.). ***COURSES: White Collar Crime, Corporations, Securities.

LOIS H. KNIGHT*, (Clin. Professor & Director, Clin. & Advocacy Programs)**, born 1948; admitted to bar, 1973, Massachusetts. *Education:* Tufts University (B.S., 1970); Georgetown (J.D., 1973). ***COURSES: ADR, Clinical Teaching, Legal Externship, Trial Advocacy.

SUSAN PARIS KONIAK*, (Professor)**, born 1954; admitted to bar, 1979, District of Columbia. *Education:* New York University (B.A., 1975); Yale (J.D., 1978). ***COURSES: Business Ethics, Constitutional Law, Criminal Law, Legal Profession.

PNINA LAHAV*, (Professor)**, born 1945. *Education:* Hebrew University (LL.B., 1968); Yale (LL.M., 1971; J.S.D., 1973)DISPLAY. ***COURSES: Civil Liberties, Comparative Constitutional Law, First Amendment.

FREDERICK M. LAWRENCE*, (Professor & Law Alumni Scholar)**, born 1955; admitted to bar, 1981, New York. *Education:* Williams College (B.A., 1977); Yale (J.D., 1980). ***COURSES: Civil Procedure, Civil Rights Crimes, Civil Rights Enforcement, Criminal Law.

GARY STEVEN LAWSON*, (Professor and Abraham & Lillian Benton Scholar)**, born Seattle, Washington, October 14, 1958; admitted to bar, 1983, Washington. *Education:* Claremont Men's College (B.A., 1980); Yale Law School (J.D., 1983). ***COURSES: Administrative Law, Property, Advanced Administrative Law, Future Interests, Securities Regulation. ***Email:*** glawson@bu.edu

GERALD LEONARD*, (Associate Professor)**, born 1960. *Education:* Michigan (Ph.D., 1992; J.D., 1995). ***COURSES: Criminal Law, Legal History.

JULIUS BYRON LEVINE*, (Professor)**, born 1939; admitted to bar, 1963, Maine; 1964, Massachusetts. *Education:* Harvard (B.A., 1960; J.D., 1964); Oxford University (Ph.D., 1969). ***COURSES: Administrative Law, Civil Procedure, Estates, Judicial Administration, Pleading, Practice & Procedure, Practice Court, Trial & Appellate Advocacy, Trusts.

DAVID BARRY LYONS*, (Professor & Law Alumni Scholar)**, born 1935. *Education:* Brooklyn College (B.A., 1960); Harvard (M.A., 1963; Ph.D., 1963). ***COURSES: Constitutional Theory, Jurisprudence, Legal Process.

TRACEY MACLIN*, (Professor)**, born 1958; admitted to bar, 1984, New Jersey; 1985, New York. *Education:* Tufts University (B.A., 1980); Columbia (J.D., 1983). ***COURSES: Civil Rights, Constitutional Law, Criminal Justice, Criminal Procedure.

WENDY K. MARINER*, (Professor of Law)**, born 1946; admitted to bar, 1972, New York; 1980, Massachussets. *Education:* Wellesley College (B.A., 1968); Columbia University (J.D., 1971); Harvard School of Public Health (M.P.H., 1979); New York University (L.L.M., 1979). ***COURSES: Managed Care and The Law.

(This Listing Continued)

BOSTON UNIVERSITY SCHOOL OF LAW—Continued

STEPHEN G. MARKS*, (Associate Dean & Professor)**, born 1952. *Education:* Cal., Irvine (B.A., 1974); Cal., Berkeley (M.A., 1977; J.D., 1978; Ph.D., 1981). ***COURSES: Corporations, Finance, Law & Economics, Managerial Economics, Securities Regulation.

MICHAEL JAMES MEURER*, (Associate Professor)**, born Mankato, Minnesota, February 1, 1958. *Education:* MIT (S.B., 1980); University of Minnesota (J.D., 1985; Ph.D., 1986). ***COURSES: Intellectual Property, Law & Economics, Patent Law, Copyright Law. ***Email:*** meurer@bu.edu

FRANCES H. MILLER*, (Professor)**, born 1938; admitted to bar, 1966, Massachusetts. *Education:* Mount Holyoke College (A.B., 1960); Boston University (J.D., 1965). ***COURSES: Antitrust Issues in Health Care, Domestic Relations, Estate Planning, Future Interest & Estate Planning, Law & Medicine, Trusts & Estates.

WALTER W. MILLER, JR.*, (Professor)**, born 1932; admitted to bar, 1964, New York; 1979, Massachusetts. *Education:* Harvard (A.B., 1954); Luth. Theo. Seminary at Philadelphia (B.D., 1957); Buffalo (J.D., 1964); Harvard (LL.M., 1965). ***COURSES: Commercial Law, Commercial Paper, Conflict of Laws, Contracts, Creditors' Rights.

NANCY J. MOORE*, (Professor)**, born 1949; admitted to bar, 1974, New York; Pennsylvania. *Education:* Smith College (A.B., 1970); Columbia (J.D., 1973). ***COURSES: Evidence, Law & Medical Ethics, Legal Profession, Torts.

EVA NILSEN*, (Clinical Associate Professor)**, born 1944; admitted to bar, 1977, District of Columbia, Virginia; 1978, Maryland; 1980, Massachusetts. *Education:* Yale College (B.A., 1974); University of Virginia (J.D., 1977); Georgetown (LL.M., 1980). ***COURSES: Criminal Justice, Criminal Law Clinic, Prisoners Rights Clinic, Sentencing Theory & Process.

MAUREEN ANNE O'ROURKE*, (Professor & Associate Dean, Administration and Graduate Programs)**, born 1963; admitted to bar, 1991, New York. *Education:* Marist College (B.S., 1985); Yale (J.D., 1990). ***COURSES: Commercial Law, Intellectual Property, Sales & Secured Transactions.

WILLIAM W. PARK*, (Professor)**, born 1947; admitted to bar, 1972, Massachusetts; 1980, District of Columbia. *Education:* Yale (B.A., 1969); Columbia (J.D., 1972); Cambridge (M.A., 1975). ***COURSES: International Banking, International Commercial Arbitration, International Transactions, Law & Religion, Taxation, Federal.

DANIEL G. PARTAN*, (R. Gordon Butler Scholar-in-Law & Professor)**, born 1933; admitted to bar, 1959, Massachusetts. *Education:* Harvard (LL.B., 1958; LL.M., 1961). ***COURSES: Admiralty, International Law, International Organizations, International Transactions.

MARK PETTIT, JR.*, (Professor)**, born 1946; admitted to bar, 1972, New York; 1974, Illinois. *Education:* Bowdoin College (A.B., 1968); University of Chicago (J.D., 1971). ***COURSES: Commercial Law, Consumer Law, Contracts, Evidence.

DAVID ROSSMAN*, (Professor & Director, Clinical Programs in Criminal Law)**, born 1947; admitted to bar, 1972, Massachusetts. *Education:* Dartmouth College (A.B., 1968); Harvard (J.D., 1971). ***COURSES: Clinical Teaching, Criminal Procedure, Law & Social Science.

WILLIAM E. RYCKMAN, JR.*, (Professor)**, born 1934; admitted to bar, 1958, Indiana; 1972, Massachusetts. *Education:* Indiana University (B.S., 1956) Indiana, Bloomington (LL.B., 1958). ***COURSES: Equity, Land Use, Real Property.

ROBERT B. SEIDMAN*, (Professor Emeritus)**, born 1920; admitted to bar, 1948, New York; 1951, Connecticut. *Education:* Harvard University (B.A., 1941); Columbia University (L.L.B., 1948). ***COURSES: Legislation, Legal Process.

DAVID J. SEIPP*, (Professor)**, born 1955; admitted to bar, 1983, Massachusetts. *Education:* Harvard (A.B., 1977; J.D., 1982); Oxford University (B.A., 1979); Cambridge University (LL.B., 1980);. ***COURSES: Copyright, Intellectual Property, Legal History, Property.

KATHARINE BAIRD SILBAUGH*, (Professor)**, born 1963; admitted to bar, 1993, Illinois. *Education:* Amherst College (B.A., 1985); University of Chicago (J.D., 1992). ***COURSES: Family Law, Torts, Women & the Law, Employment Law.

KENNETH W. SIMONS*, (Professor & M.L. Sykes Scholar)**, born 1952; admitted to bar, 1979, Massachusetts. *Education:* Yale College (B.A., 1975); Michigan (J.D., 1978). ***COURSES: Constitutional Law, Criminal Law, Rights & Justice, Supreme Court Decision Making, Torts.

THEODORE S. SIMS*, (Professor)**, born 1944; admitted to bar, 1970, District of Columbia. *Education:* Columbia (A.B., 1967); University of Chicago (J.D., 1970); M.I.T. (Ph.D., 1995). ***COURSES: Federal Income Taxation, Federal Tax Policy, Law & Economics, Quantitative Methods, Trusts & Estates.

MANUEL A. UTSET*, (Associate Professor)**, born 1962; admitted to bar, 1988, New York. *Education:* Georgetown (B.S.F.S., 1984); Michigan (J.D., 1967). ***COURSES: Commercial Law, Corporate Finance, Corporations.

ROBERT VOLK*, (Associate Professor Legal Writing & Director, 1st Year Writing Program)**, born 1951; admitted to bar, 1978, Massachusetts. *Education:* Boston University (J.D., 1978). ***COURSES: Gay & Lesbian Rights, Legal Research & Writing.

JAY DOUGLAS WEXLER*, (Associate Professor)**, born Lynn, Massachusetts, April 12, 1969; admitted to bar, 1999, Illinois. *Education:* Harvard University (B.A., 1991); University of Chicago (M.A., 1993); Stanford Law School (J.D., 1997). ***COURSES: Administrative Law, Law & Religion.

LARRY W. YACKLE*, (Professor)**, born 1946; admitted to bar, 1973, Kansas. *Education:* Kansas (A.B., 1968; J.D., 1973); Harvard (LL.M., 1974). ***COURSES: Constitutional Law, Federal Jurisdiction.

BRIGHAM YOUNG UNIVERSITY
J. REUBEN CLARK LAW SCHOOL

PROVO, UTAH 84602
Telephone: (801) 378-4274
Fax: (801) 378-3595
www.law.byu.edu

ABA Approved Since 1974

Brigham Young University, surrounded by the majestic Rocky Mountains, was founded in 1875 by The Church of Jesus Christ of Latter-day Saints in Provo, Utah. Today, after more than a century of steady growth, it has become the largest privately owned, church-related university in the United States.

Intensive learning in a stimulated setting -- nurturing the mind, body, and spirit -- is central to the mission of Brigham Young University. The J. Reuben Clark Law School was founded in 1973 to continue this tradition while providing an excellent legal education and offering diverse opportunities for legal scholarship. Since its creation, the Law School has added a unique dimension to the ongoing activities of the university. Its students and faculty engage in wide-ranging academic pursuits, and its alumni have become successful legal professionals in cities across the country and around the world. The Law School enjoys respect among its peer institutions, and its history is often pointed to as an example of how a young law school can succeed. The eight Law School alumni who have served as U.S. Supreme Court clerks since the first class graduated 24 years ago are an unprecedented testament to the success of the Law School in training legal professionals.

As a member of the Association of American Law Schools (AALS), the J. Reuben Clark Law School provides equal opportunity in legal education for all persons without discrimination on the grounds of race, color, religion, national origin, sex, sexual orientation, age, handicap, or disability (AALS Bylaw 64 (a)]. Because of the Law School's religious affiliation and purpose, AALS regulations as applied to the Law School require equal opportunity on the basis of sexual orientation but not on the basis of conduct. All members of the Law School community are required to comply with the Brigham Young University Honor Code, which requires chastity outside -of marriage and fidelity in marriage. High standards of honor, integrity, and morality; graciousness in personal behavior; application of Christian ideals to everyday living; and abstinence from tobacco, alcohol, and other harmful drugs are required of every student.

The law faculty, which comes from a large diversity of law schools and professional experience, is widely recognized for its outstanding scholarship and classroom teaching.

The specific objective of the curriculum is to maximize the students' mastery of legal reasoning and legal method - in addition to teaching the core of the basic substantive rules of the law and imparting an appreciation for its institutions and traditions.

Students are taught to analyze complex factual situations; to separate the relevant from the irrelevant; and to reason inductively, deductively, and by analogy. They learn to recognize the potential inapplicability of established rules to situations materially different from those in which the rules were developed.

Students are also schooled in the arts of written and oral advocacy, draftsmanship, mediation, and negotiation. In addition, they learn to recognize the deficiencies in existing rules and to contribute to the creation of new rules, advocating positions with clarity, persuasion, and honor. The development of these skills must embrace the great variety of activities in which lawyers engage. Lawyers are probably best known for their work in the private sector, representing clients in and out of the courtroom in the prevention and resolution of conflicts. In addition, lawyers have traditionally occupied key roles in forming and executing policy at all levels of government. The Law School prepares its graduate to function as responsible, well-informed participants in the public and private affairs of a society in which the law plays a vital role in regulating and setting standards.

Through the career services offered at the Law School, students are assisted in their employment search. Year in and year out, this assistance, combined with the students' best efforts, results in Brigham Young University law students securing excellent positions with judges, in law firms, and in public work.

Legal education at this school does not include the sponsorship of particular political objectives, except as may flow from loyalty to the Constitution and from a commitment to the highest ideals of personal character and individual liberty as the foundation upon which an enduring legal system must rest.

Legal training involves the learning of skills by practice. The student must be an active participant in that process. Because a variety of legal skills must be developed, several methods are used, such as Socratic or inductive teaching, problem solving, seminars, individual research and clinical experience.

The J. Reuben Clark Law School is located on the east side of a beautiful planned mall in the eastern section-of the Brigham Young University campus. The building's five floors contain eleven classrooms, three seminar rooms, a student commons area, a student lunchroom, ample spaces for student organizations and activities, a large computer lab as well as a computer training room, and the Howard W. Hunter Law Library.

The newly enlarged Howard W. Hunter Law Library takes up the north half of the law building. For many years the law library has been one of the most technological advanced in the world. The remodeled facility provides even better electronic access to legal materials. Besides the wide array of resources available in electronic format, the library houses a paper and microform m collection nearing 400,000 volumes and volume equivalents. Via interlibrary loan, students have access to many more titles found in the catalogs and collections of over 150 other institutions that, like the Hunter Library, subscribe to the Research Library Information Network.

In addition to individual private study carrels, the enlarged library features 26 group study rooms, spacious casual seating, and three classrooms where professional library faculty teach classes to familiarize students with specific types of legal research and library holdings. Computer training for general and specific databases, often in conjunction with the legal research classes, will be taught in the classrooms as well. Other specialized rooms will be dedicated to video viewing, interactive video, microforms, and audio hookups to specific classes for parents who must occasionally bring young children to school.

The library faculty are highly regarded for their scholarship and willingness to be of service to both the Law School community and the larger community. All faculty members have graduate professional degrees in library science and most have law degrees. All are active in law library associations, publishing, and research.

(This Listing Continued)

BRIGHAM YOUNG UNIVERSITY, J. REUBEN CLARK LAW SCHOOL—Continued

Dean: H. Reese Hansen (801) 378-6383
Associate Dean: J. Clifton Fleming (801) 378-2485
Associate Dean: Constance K. Lundberg (801) 378-6385
Associate Dean: Kathy D. Pullins (801) 378-5576
Associate Dean: Kevin J. Worthen (801) 378-2619
Assistant Dean: Carl Hernandez (801) 378-6386
Assistant Dean and Career Services Director: Mary Hoagland (801) 378-7831
Admissions Director: Lola Wilcock (801) 378-4277

FULL TIME FACULTY

H. REESE HANSEN*, (Dean & Professor)**, born April 8, 1942; admitted to bar, 1972, Utah. *Education:* Utah State University (B.S., 1964); University of Utah (J.D., 1972). ***COURSES: Civil Procedure, Commercial Law, Contracts, Estate and Gift Taxation, Estate Planning, Estates, Trusts. ***Email:*** HansenR@lawgate.byu.edu

KIF AUGUSTINE-ADAMS*, (Associate Professor)**, born June 14, 1964; admitted to bar, 1992, December. *Education:* Brigham Young University (B.A., 1988); Harvard (J.D., 1992). ***COURSES: International Law, Torts. ***Email:*** AdamsK@lawgate.byu.edu

STEVEN ELMO AVERETT*, (Assistant Director of Externships)**, born Richfield, Utah, July 24, 1954; admitted to bar, 1989, Utah and Idaho. *Education:* Brigham Young University (B.S., 1978; M.L.S., 1985; J.D., 1988). ***COURSES: Externships and Legal Research. ***Email:*** averetts@lawgate.byu.edu

JAMES H. BACKMAN*, (Professor)**, born December 31, 1943; admitted to bar, 1972, Utah. *Education:* Harvard (B.A., 1969); University of Utah (J.D., 1972. ***COURSES: Clinical Teaching, Natural Resources, Real Estate Transactions, Real Property. ***Email:*** BackmanJ@lawgate.byu.edu

JEAN W. BURNS*, (Professor)**, born February 7, 1948; admitted to bar, 1973, Illinois; 1975, Pennsylvania; 1987, Utah. *Education:* Vanderbilt (B.A., 1970); University of Chicago (J.D., 1973). ***COURSES: Antitrust, Civil Procedure, Commercial Law, Commercial Paper, Trade Regulation. ***Email:*** BurnsJ@lawgate.byu.edu

SCOTT W. CAMERON*, (Associate Dean)**, born July 16, 1946; admitted to bar, 1976, Utah. *Education:* Stanford (B.A., 1970; M.A., 1971); Brigham Young University (J.D., 1976). ***COURSES: Education Law. ***Email:*** CameronS@Lawgate.byu.edu

ELIZABETH ANNE CLARK*, (Professor and Associate Director)**, born Washington, D.C., June 10, 1970; admitted to bar, 1999, Utah; 2000, District of Columbia. *Education:* Brigham Young University (B.A., 1994); J. Reuben Clark Law School (J.D., 1997). ***COURSES: Comparative & Church-State Law. ***Email:*** clarke@lawgate.byu.edu

DAVID DOMINGUEZ*, (Professor)**, born March 15, 1954; admitted to bar, 1980, California. *Education:* Yale (B.A., 1977); California, Berkeley (J.D., 1980). ***COURSES: Alternate Dispute, Criminal Justice, Labor Law. ***Email:*** DominguezD@lawgate.byu.edu

MARGUERITE A. DRIESSEN*, (Associate Professor)**, born September 30, 1963. *Education:* Brigham Young University (B.A., 1985); Stanford (J.D., 1989). ***COURSES: Criminal Law, Evidence. ***Email:*** DriessenM@lawgate.byu.edu

W. COLE DURHAM, JR.*, (Professor)**, born February 26, 1948; admitted to bar, 1975, Utah. *Education:* Harvard (A.B., 1972; J.D., 1975). ***COURSES: Comparative Law, Constitutional Law, Criminal Law, International Law, Jurisprudence, International Organizations, Legal History. ***Email:*** DurhamC@lawgate.byu.edu

LARRY ECHOHAWK*, (Professor)**, born August 2, 1948; admitted to bar, 1973, Utah; 1974, California; 1979, Idaho. *Education:* Brigham Young University (B.S., 1970); University of Utah (J.D., 1973). ***COURSES: Criminal Law, Criminal Trial Practice, Federal Indian Law, Professional Responsibility, Public Lands and Natural Resources. ***Email:*** EchohawkL@lawgate.byu.edu

LARRY C. FARMER*, (Professor)**, born February 20, 1942. *Education:* Washington (B.S., 1968); Brigham Young University (Ph.D., 1975). ***COURSES: Computer-based Expert Systems in Law Practice, Law and Behavioral Science, Legal Interviewing and Counseling. ***Email:*** FarmerL@lawgate.byu.edu

JOHN E. FEE*, (Assistant Professor)**, born Provo, Utah, July 3, 1968; admitted to bar, 1995, Utah; 1998, District of Columbia. *Education:* Brigham Young University (B.A., 1992); University of Chicago (J.D., 1995). ***COURSES: Property, Environmental Law, Landuse. ***Email:*** feej@lawgate.byu.edu

J. CLIFTON FLEMING*, (Ernest L. Wilkinson Professor and Associate Dean)**, born July 24, 1942; admitted to bar, 1967, Washington; 1979, Utah. *Education:* Brigham Young (B.S., 1964); George Washington (J.D., 1967). ***COURSES: Business Planning, Corporate Finance, Estate Planning, International Transactions, Taxation, Federal. ***Email:*** FlemingC@lawgate.byu.edu

GALEN L. FLETCHER*, (Government Documents/Microforms Librarian)**, born Ogden, Utah, September 20, 1961. *Education:* Goldenwest College (A.A., 1984); Brigham Young University (B.A., 1987; J.D./M.L.I.S., 1993). ***COURSES: Legal Research, Legal History. ***Email:*** fletcherg@lawgate.byu.edu

CHESNEY DOUGLAS FLOYD*, (Professor)**, born September 10, 1942; admitted to bar, 1967, California. *Education:* MIT (B.S., 1964); Stanford (J.D., 1967). ***COURSES: Administrative Law, Antitrust, Civil Procedure, Civil Rights, Federal Courts. ***Email:*** FloydD@lawgate.byu.edu

FREDERICK M. GEDICKS*, (Professor)**, born May 17, 1953; admitted to bar, 1980, Arizona. *Education:* Brigham Young University (B.A., 1977); Southern California (J.D., 1980). ***COURSES: Constitutional Law, Corporations, Law and Religion, Poverty Law, Securities Regulation. ***Email:*** GedicksF@lawgate.byu.edu

KRISTIN BETH GERDY*, (Director, Advocacy Program)**, born Boulder, Colorado, November 18, 1969; admitted to bar, 1995, Utah. *Education:* Brigham Young University (B.A., 1992); J. Reuben Clark Law School (J.D., 1995). ***COURSES: Legal Research & Writing. ***Email:*** gerdyk@lawgate.byu.edu

MICHAEL GOLDSMITH*, (Professor)**, born March 6, 1951; admitted to bar, 1976, Vermont; 1976, New York; 1987, Utah. *Education:* Cornell (B.A., 1972; J.D., 1975). ***COURSES: Criminal Law, Criminal Procedure, Evidence, Human Rights Law, RICO, Principles of Evidence. ***Email:*** GoldsmithM@lawgate.byu.edu

JAMES D. GORDON, III*, (Professor)**, born February 9, 1954; admitted to bar, 1980, California; 1981, Utah. *Education:* Brigham Young (B.A., 1977); California, Berkeley (J.D., 1980). ***COURSES: Contracts, Issues in Legal Education, Legal Writing, Professional Seminar, Securities. ***Email:*** GordonJ@lawgate.byu.edu

(This Listing Continued)

BRIGHAM YOUNG UNIVERSITY, J. REUBEN CLARK LAW SCHOOL—Continued

CARL HERNANDEZ III*, (Assistant Dean)**, born Fresno, California, December 28, 1962; admitted to bar, 1993, California. *Education:* Brigham Young University (B.A., 1988); Brigham Young University Marriot School of Management (M.P.A., 1992); Brigham Young University J. Reuben Clark Law School (J.D., 1992). ***COURSES: Municipal Land Use. ***Email:*** hernandezc@lawgate.byu.edu

GARY LOREN HILL*, (Deputy Director of the Law Library)**, born Salt Lake City, Utah, December 19, 1948; admitted to bar, 1977, Utah. *Education:* Brigham Young University (B.A., 1972); Samford University (J.D., 1976); Denver University (M.L.L., 1981). ***COURSES: Legal Research. ***Email:*** hillg@lawgate.byu.edu

MARY H. HOAGLAND*, (Assistant Dean)**, born Provo, Utah, August 3, 1948; admitted to bar, 1994, Utah. *Education:* Brigham Young University (B.A., 1972); San Diego State University (M.A., 1978); San Joaquin College of Law (J.D., 1985). ***COURSES: Professional Development. ***Email:*** hoaglandm@lawgate.byu.edu

THOMAS REX LEE*, (Associate Professor)**, born December 28, 1964; admitted to bar, 1992, Utah; 1994, District of Columbia. *Education:* Brigham Young University (B.A., 1988); University of Chicago (J.D., 1991). ***COURSES: Civil Procedure, Remedies. ***Email:*** leet@lawgate.byu.edu

A. SCOTT LOVELESS*, (Executive Director, World Family Policy Center)**, born Ely, Nevada, October 13, 1951; admitted to bar, 1979, District of Columbia. *Education:* Brigham Young University (B.A., 1975; PhD, 2000); J. Reuben Clark Law School (J.D., 1978). ***COURSES: Oil & Gas, Public Lands. ***Email:*** lovelessas@lawgate.byu.edu

CONSTANCE K. LUNDBERG*, (Professor, Associate Dean, Director of Law Library)**, born July 1, 1947; admitted to bar, 1972, Utah. *Education:* Arizona State (B.A., 1968); Utah (J.D., 1972); Brigham Young (M.Lis., 1993). ***COURSES: Clinical Teaching, Environmental Law, Federal Courts, Law and Social Science, Poverty Law, Real Property, Natural Resources. ***Email:*** LundbergC@lawgate.byu.edu

STANLEY D. NEELEMAN*, (Professor)**, born April 16, 1943; admitted to bar, 1972, Colorado. *Education:* Westminster College (B.A., 1967); George Washington (M.A., 1969); Denver (J.D., 1972). ***COURSES: Business Associations, Estate Planning, Taxation, Federal. ***Email:*** NeelemanS@lawgate.byu.edu

ROBERT SPENCER PAYNE*, (Assistant Law Librarian)**, born Albuquerque, New Mexico, August 19, 1970; admitted to bar, 1999, Utah. *Education:* University of New Mexico (B.A., 1993); J. Reuben Clark School of Law (J.D., 1999). ***COURSES: Legal Research. ***Email:*** payner@lawgate.byu.edu

CHERYL B. PRESTON*, (Professor)**, born November 23, 1952; admitted to bar, 1980, California; 1983, Utah. *Education:* Brigham Young University (B.A., 1975; J.D., 1979). ***COURSES: Bankruptcy, Commercial Paper, Creditor Rights, Lender Liability, Social Policy and Feminist Legal Thought, Planning, Drafting and Negotiation, Secured Transactions. ***Email:*** PrestonC@lawgate.byu.edu

KATHY D. PULLINS*, (Associate Dean)**, born March 15, 1952. *Education:* Brigham Young University (B.A., 1985; J.D., 1988). ***COURSES: Alternative Dispute Resolution. ***Email:*** PullinsK@lawgate.byu.edu

JAMES R. RASBAND*, (Associate Professor)**, born March 20, 1963; admitted to bar, 1991, Washington. *Education:* Brigham Young University (B.A., 1986); Harvard (J.D., 1989). ***COURSES: Torts. ***Email:*** RasbandJ@lawgate.byu.edu

BRETT GILBERT SCHARFFS*, (Associate Professor)**, born Salt Lake City, Utah, March 22, 1963; admitted to bar, 1994, New York. *Education:* Georgetown University (B.S.B.A., 1986; M.A., 1987); Oxford University (B.Phil., 1989); Yale Law School (J.D., 1992). ***COURSES: Corporate, International, Jurisprudence. ***Email:*** scharffsb@lawgate.byu.edu

DENNIS STAHLE SEARS*, (Associate Director for Legal Research & Reference)**, born Salt Lake City, Utah, July 02, 1951; admitted to bar, 1985, Utah. *Education:* Brigham Young University (B.S./B.A., 1975; M.A., 1981; M.L.I.S., 1993); J. Reuben Clark (J.D./M.B.A., 1985). ***COURSES: First Year Legal Research, Advanced Legal Research. ***Email:*** searsd@lawgate.byu.edu

DAVID A. THOMAS*, (Professor)**, born February 4, 1944; admitted to bar, 1972, Utah. *Education:* Brigham Young (B.A., 1967; M.L.S., 1977); Duke (J.D., 1972). ***COURSES: Civil Procedure, Legal History, Legal Research and Writing, Property. ***Email:*** ThomasD@lawgate.byu.edu

LYNN D. WARDLE*, (Professor)**, born November 15, 1947; admitted to bar, 1975, District of Columbia; 1976, Arizona; 1981, Utah. *Education:* Brigham Young University (B.A., 1971); Duke (J.D., 1974). ***COURSES: Biomedical Ethics and Law, Children and the Law, Civil Procedure, Community Property, Family Law, Origins of the Constitution, Conflict of Laws. ***Email:*** WardleL@lawgate.byu.edu

JOHN (JACK) W. WELCH*, (Professor)**, born October 15, 1946; admitted to bar, 1975, California; 1981, Utah. *Education:* Brigham Young University (B.A., 1970; M.A., 1970); Duke (J.D., 1975). ***COURSES: Agency and Partnerships, Corporations, Federal Taxation, Legal History, Legal Profession. ***Email:*** WelchJ@lawgate.byu.edu

RICHARD G. WILKINS*, (Professor)**, born December 12, 1952; admitted to bar, 1980, California; 1981, District of Columbia; 1985, Utah. *Education:* Brigham Young University (B.A., 1976; J.D., 1979). ***COURSES: Civil Procedure, Civil Rights, Constitutional Law, Federal Courts. ***Email:*** WilkinsR@lawgate.byu.edu

GERALD R. WILLIAMS*, (Professor)**, born February 7, 1942; admitted to bar, 1969, Utah. *Education:* Brigham Young University (B.A., 1966); Utah (J.D., 1969). ***COURSES: Alternative Dispute Resolution, Remedies. ***Email:*** WilliamsG@lawgate.byu.edu

STEPHEN G. WOOD*, (Professor)**, born March 19, 1941; admitted to bar, 1972, District of Columbia; 1977, Utah. *Education:* Utah (B.A., 1966; J.D., 1969); Columbia (J.S.D., 1980). ***COURSES: Administrative Law, Comparative Law, Employment Law, Entertainment Law, Labor Law, Sports Law, International Transactions. ***Email:*** WoodS@lawgate.byu.edu

KEVIN J. WORTHEN*, (Professor and Associate Dean)**, born April 15, 1956; admitted to bar, 1984, Arizona. *Education:* College of Eastern Utah (A.S., 1978); Brigham Young University (B.A., 1979; J.D., 1982). ***COURSES: Legislation, Native American Law, State and Local Government. ***Email:*** WorthenK@lawgate.byu.edu

BROOKLYN LAW SCHOOL

250 JORALEMON STREET
BROOKLYN, NEW YORK 11201
Telephone: (718) 625-2200
Fax: (718) 780-0395
http://www.brooklaw.edu

ABA Approved Since 1937.

ACCREDITATION

Brooklyn Law School is a nationally renowned private, independent law school which since 1937 has been fully approved by the American Bar Association. It is also a member of the Association of American Law Schools.

ENVIRONMENT FOR LEARNING

The School is headquartered at the intersection of Brooklyn Heights, the Brooklyn Civic Center, and Downtown Brooklyn. On one side of the School is Brooklyn Heights. Designated a National Historic District in 1965, the Heights presents a veritable history of American residential architecture, with fine examples of almost every style popular since the 1820s. Stately houses, lush gardens, and tree-lined back streets make the Heights one of the most tranquil and beautiful neighborhoods of New York City. Stretching out directly in front of the School is the Civic Center. Situated within the Center are the New York State Supreme and Family Courts, the Kings County District Attorney's Office, and Borough Hall, which houses the offices of the Borough President. Inside a radius of several blocks are the U.S. District Court and U.S. Attorney's Office for the Eastern District of New York, the U.S. Bankruptcy Court, the State Appellate Division Court, the Kings County Surrogate's Court, City Civil and Criminal Courts, the Legal Aid Society, numerous city, state and federal governmental agencies, and a concentration of law firms. On the other side of the School is Downtown Brooklyn, which is now in the midst of an urban renaissance. The investment firm of Morgan Stanley & Co. has built a major office tower around the corner from the School. A high technology educational and business center, MetroTech, has risen three blocks away. Just a few minutes away is Wall Street with its array of law firms, financial institutions, and stock and commodity exchanges, as well as the headquarters for many international corporations and for the broadcasting, publishing, and garment industries. Only twenty minutes away, in midtown Manhattan, is the exciting Broadway theater district.

ENROLLMENT OPTIONS & STUDENT BODY

Students may enroll in either the full-time or part-time division. The full-time Juris Doctor degree program requires three years of full-time attendance during the day. The part-time program normally requires four years of study. Part-time students may elect either a day or an evening or a combined day and evening program. The School's overall J.D. enrollment was 1,499 for the 2000-2001 academic year: 1,029 students in the full-time division and 470 in the part-time division. Women constituted 50% of the enrollment, while minority students accounted for approximately 22.1%. Our students came to us from 39 states, the District of Columbia, Puerto Rico, and 37 countries. Collectively, they were graduated from 308 colleges and universities.

FACULTY

Brooklyn Law School has long been recognized as a superb "teaching school" -- its faculty composed of innovative classroom instructors who are genuinely accessible for their students. The School boasts several faculty who are nationally distinguished experts in their field, and whose texts and casebooks are used in law schools across the country. Moreover, the faculty is replete with respected scholars who are actively engaged in influencing legal and public policy in the world at large. For the 2000-2001 academic year, the faculty was composed of 68 full-time members and 98 adjunct members. The student/faculty ratio was 19.3/1. Women constituted nearly 37% of our tenured and tenure-track faculty, a proportion which surpasses most other law schools.

PHYSICAL FACILITIES & LIBRARY

The School's principal academic facilities are housed in two interconnected buildings: a 10-story building that opened in 1968, and a new 11-story addition to the main building that was designed by world-renowned architect Robert A.M. Stern. The new building features a major library expansion, a student center and dining hall with full food service, seminar and skills training classrooms, a conference and reception center, and increased office space for faculty and student organizations. Equipped with state-of-the-art media and computer-assisted legal research and instruction facilities, including four computer labs, the building is expected to meet the Law School's needs well into this century. The School's new, technologically advanced library has one of the largest collections of legal materials in New York, containing more than 492,000 volumes of hardcopy, microforms, computer programs and cassettes. OCLC terminals provide rapid on-line bibliographic access to the holdings of hundreds of libraries nationwide. Spread throughout the Library are wired carrels and tables to accommodate laptop computers. Through the LAN, students have access to word processing, LEXIS/NEXIS, WESTLAW, INTERNET, DIALOG, WILSONLINE, LAWDESK, Dow Jones News/Retrieval and other global information resources. Its 20,000 square feet of new space includes seating for 700, three beautiful reading rooms, 25 group-study rooms, six conference rooms, several student lounges, and space to allow for a 50% expansion of our current collection.

CURRICULUM

The curriculum consists essentially of 13 clusters of courses in business and financial law, civil practice and litigation, commercial law, criminal law, estate and family law, intellectual property, media, and information law, international and comparative law, international business law, law and economic regulation, legal history and jurisprudence, public interest law, taxation, and urban law. The emphasis in all courses is on legal principles applicable throughout the American legal system; accordingly, our graduates are prepared to practice across the United States. The core of the first-year curriculum is a Seminar Section Program that provides groups of approximately 35-40 students with a small-class experience in a substantive, required course during the first semester. This program is augmented by our First-Year Legal Writing Program which focuses on developing each student's writing ability and research skills. Nine full-time and eleven adjunct writing instructors work with students on a one-to-one basis. By choosing from over 160 elective courses, upperclass students may pursue either a general program of study or one that focuses on a specialized area of the law.

PROFESSIONAL SKILLS PROGRAM & JOINT DEGREE PROGRAMS

Our Professional Skills Program consists of an extensive array of in-house and extern clinics and simulation courses. By graduation, almost all full-time students take advantage of one or more of these offerings. In-house clinics include our Children's Law Center Clinic, Consumer Counseling and Bankruptcy Clinic, Corporate and Real Estate Clinic, Elderlaw Clinic, Federal Litigation Clinic, Prosecutors Clinic, Safe Harbor Clinic, Securities Arbitration Clinic. Externships

(This Listing Continued)

BROOKLYN LAW SCHOOL—Continued

include the Capital Defender Clinic, Criminal Appeals Clinic-Legal Aid Society, Criminal Appeals Clinic-Manhattan District Attorney's Office, and the Mediation Clinic. Law-In-Practice Internships include our Civil Practice Internship, Criminal Practice Internship, and Judicial Clerkship Internship. The School, in conjunction with other prominent universities in New York City, sponsors six interdisciplinary programs leading to the joint degrees of Juris Doctor and Master in: Public Administration; Urban Planning; Law and Political Science; City and Regional Planning and Law; Business Administration; and Library and Information Science.

ADDITIONAL CURRICULAR AND CO-CURRICULAR ACTIVITIES

An effective approach to maximizing our students' learning potential is a comprehensive Academic Success Program offered in the first year. The Program consists of an early-start summer legal process course, a remedial support program for the legal writing and research course, and a series of practical, participatory workshops dealing with topics such as grammar, case briefing, exam skills, and writing for scholarly journals. Outside the classroom, students study complex legal issues on their own, by writing for scholarly publications and competing in moot court arguments. For example, our students publish three journals: the *Brooklyn Law Review,* the *Brooklyn Journal of International Law,* and the *Journal of Law and Policy.* The Moot Court Honor Society sponsors a number of intramural moot court teams which participate, with an impressive record of success, in national competitions.

FELLOWSHIP PROGRAMS

The School's Center for the Study of International Business Law trains lawyers to function in a global environment, shaping international law and business policy. Our curriculum offers more than 30 courses in international law. The Center sponsors a Fellowship Program and hosts symposia on international business issues. In 1985, Brooklyn Law School established the Edward V. Sparer Public Interest Law Fellowship Program which has provided stipends to 220 students who have served as legal interns in nearly 88 public interest law offices nationwide and around the world. It also sponsors forums that bring prominent scholars, lawyers, and public policy advocates to the School to discuss current issues in public interest law.

ADMISSION, FINANCIAL AID & HOUSING

The first-year class is admitted only in the fall semester. Conferment of a baccalaureate degree prior to matriculation at the School is required. All applicants must take the Law School Admission Test and subscribe to the Law School Data Assembly Service. Although there is no actual filing deadline, we suggest that completed applications be filed between October 1 and February 1. The School offers a broad program of financial assistance. Need is met through a combination of scholarships, grants, loans and work-study assistance. A merit scholarship program offers scholarships in varying amounts to candidates whose quantifiable admission qualifications place them in the highest part of the entering class. The School owns seven residence halls in Brooklyn Heights, offering affordable housing only a few blocks from the School for a limited number of students.

BAR PASSAGE, PLACEMENT & ALUMNI

Since 1990, Brooklyn Law School graduates have achieved an average 84% pass rate on the New York State Bar Examination, as compared to a statewide pass rate of 79%. The Career Center, with six attorney-counselors and four career services assistants, comprising one of the largest law school placement offices in New York, is able to offer unusually comprehensive services to students and alumni. The Center emphasizes individualized career counseling, including assistance with resume and cover letter writing, interviewing skills, and networking techniques, as well as career planning generally. Individual counseling is supplemented with skills workshops and panel discussions. An active public service program, encompassing both traditional public interest as well as government service, is led by an attorney-counselor with several years of public interest practice. Of equal priority is an aggressive job development program which supplements a substantial on-campus interviewing program and a web-based job listings service. Since its founding in 1901, Brooklyn Law School has served as a training ground for distinguished members of the bar and bench. Our graduates practice in many of the nation's leading law firms, corporations and public interest organizations. Our alumni now number over 15,300. Spread throughout 46 states, the District of Columbia, two U.S. territories, and 14 foreign countries -- and active in all aspects of the legal profession -- our alumni form a crucial component of the School's job placement strategy.

Dean and Professor of Law: Joan G. Wexler (718) 780-7900
Dean of Admissions and Financial Aid: Henry W. Haverstick III (718) 780-7906
Director of Financial Aid: Gerard N. Anderson (718) 780-7915
Law Librarian and Professor of Law: Sara Robbins (718) 780-7980
Director of the Career Center: Joan A. King (718) 780-7963
Director of Institutional Advancement: Diane Nardone (718) 780-7564
Associate Dean for Academic Affairs and Professor of Law: Victor Zonana (718) 780-7902
Associate Dean for Development and Professor of Law: Michael A. Gerber (718) 780-7923
Associate Dean for Student Affairs and Professor of Law: Carol L. Ziegler (718) 780-7904

FULL TIME FACULTY

JOAN G. WEXLER,* (Joseph Crea Dean & Professor of Law)**, born 1946; admitted to bar, 1976, New York. *Education:* Cornell (B.S., 1968); Harvard (M.A.T., 1970); Yale (J.D., 1974). ***COURSES: Estate & Gift Taxation, Estates, Family Law, Trusts.

RICHARD ALLAN,* (Professor of Law)**, born 1931; admitted to bar, 1962, New York. *Education:* Washington Square College (B.A., 1953); New York University (LL.B., 1962). ***COURSES: Civil Procedure, Entertainment Law, Family Law.

MICHAEL J. BAZYLER,* (Visiting Professor of Law)**, born 1952; admitted to bar, 1978. *Education:* University of California - Los Angeles (B.A., 1974); University of Southern California Law School (J.D., 1978). ***COURSES: Torts.

URSULA BENTELE,* (Professor of Law)**, born 1943; admitted to bar, 1970, New York. *Education:* Swarthmore College (B.A., 1965); University of Chicago (J.D., 1969). ***COURSES: Capital Defender Clinic & Seminar, Criminal Law, Safe Harbor Clinic.

MARGARET A. BERGER,* (Susanne J. and Norman Miles Professor of Law)**, born 1932; admitted to bar, 1956, New York. *Education:* Radcliffe College (A.B., 1953); Columbia (J.D., 1956). ***COURSES: Civil Procedure, Evidence, Individual Justice & Mass Torts, Science & Law.

(This Listing Continued)

BROOKLYN LAW SCHOOL—Continued

NATHANIEL A. BERMAN,* (Visiting Professor of Law)**, born 1957; admitted to bar, 1987. *Education:* Yale College (B.A., 1980); Harvard Law School (J.D., 1985). ***COURSES: International Law, Regional Human Rights, International Trade Law, European Union Law.

STACY CAPLOW,* (Professor of Law & Director, Clinical Education)**, born 1948; admitted to bar, 1973, New York. *Education:* Smith College (B.A., 1969); New York University (J.D., 1972; LL.M., 1982). ***COURSES: Advanced Criminal Law, Clinical Education, Criminal Law, Criminal Procedure, Safe Harbor Clinic.

EVE CARY,* (Associate Professor of Legal Writing)**, born 1943; admitted to bar, 1972, New York. *Education:* Sarah Lawrence College (B.A., 1965); New York University (J.D., 1971). ***COURSES: Appellate Advocacy, Criminal Law, Legal Writing.

NEIL B. COHEN,* (Professor of Law)**, born 1952; admitted to bar, 1977, Massachusetts; 1979, New Jersey. *Education:* M.I.T. (S.B., 1974); New York University (J.D., 1977). ***COURSES: Advanced Commercial Law, Commercial Law, Commercial Paper, Constitutional Law, International Commercial Transactions.

BRIAN E. COMERFORD,* (Professor of Law)**, born 1941; admitted to bar, 1967, New York. *Education:* Fordham University (A.B., 1963; J.D., 1966); New York University (LL.M., 1973). ***COURSES: Estate Planning, Corporate Taxation, Federal Estate and Gift Taxation, Federal Income Taxation.

JOSEPH CREA,* (Professor Emeritus)**, born 1915; admitted to bar, 1947, New York. *Education:* Brooklyn (J.D., 1947; B.A., 1948; LL.M., 1968; LL.D., 1992). ***COURSES: Commercial Paper, Corporations.

MARY JO EYSTER,* (Associate Clinical Professor of Law & Director, Civil Clinic, Bankruptcy Clinic)**, born 1951; admitted to bar, 1979, New York. *Education:* New York University (B.A., 1975; J.D., 1978). ***COURSES: Bankruptcy Clinic, Judicial Clinic.

ELIZABETH FAJANS,* (Associate Professor of Legal Writing)**, born 1950. *Education:* Sarah Lawrence College (B.A., 1972); Rutgers University (M.A., 1976; Ph.D., 1979). ***COURSES: Advanced Legal Writing.

MARY R. FALK,* (Associate Professor of Legal Writing)**, born 1942; admitted to bar, 1981, New York. *Education:* New York University (J.D., 1980). ***COURSES: Advanced Legal Writing, Appellate Advocacy, Legal Writing.

JAMES A. FANTO,* (Professor of Law)**, born 1951; admitted to bar, 1986, Pennsylvania; 1988, District of Columbia. *Education:* Notre Dame (B.A., 1973); Michigan (M.A., 1975); Pennsylvania (J.D., 1985); Michigan (Ph.D., 1988). ***COURSES: Banking, Corporate Finance, Corporations, Securities Regulation.

RICHARD T. FARRELL,* (Professor of Law)**, born 1937; admitted to bar, 1964, New York. *Education:* St. John's University (B.A., 1959); Brooklyn Law School (LL.B., 1964). ***COURSES: Evidence, New York Civil Practice.

ROGER W. FINDLEY,* (Visiting Professor of Law)**, born 1935; admitted to bar, 1961. *Education:* DePauw University (A.B., 1957); University of Michigan Law School (J.D., 1960). ***COURSES: Property, International Environmental Law.

NANCY H. FINK,* (Professor of Law)**, born 1942; admitted to bar, 1971, New York. *Education:* City College of New York (B.A., 1965); Brooklyn Law School (J.D., 1970); Harvard (LL.M., 1976). ***COURSES: Criminal Law, Family Law.

MARYELLEN FULLERTON,* (Professor of Law)**, born 1946; admitted to bar, 1978, District of Columbia; 1986, New York. *Education:* Duke University (B.A., 1968); Antioch College (J.D., 1978). ***COURSES: Asylum Under International & U.S. Law, Civil Procedure, Federal Courts, International Human Rights, International Law, International Litigation.

MARSHA GARRISON,* (Professor of Law)**, born 1949; admitted to bar, 1977, New York. *Education:* Utah (B.A., 1970); Harvard (J.D., 1975). ***COURSES: Bioethical Decision Making (Health Law), Children & the Law, Family Law, Trusts & Estates.

MICHAEL A. GERBER,* (Associate Dean for Development and Professor of Law)**, born 1950; admitted to bar, 1978, New York. *Education:* New York University (B.A., 1972; J.D., 1977). ***COURSES: Business Reorganization, Debtor and Creditor Rights.

JOEL M. GORA,* (Professor of Law)**, born 1942; admitted to bar, 1967, New York. *Education:* Pomona College (B.A., 1963); Columbia University (LL.B., 1967). ***COURSES: Civil Liberties, Civil Procedure, Constitutional Law, Federal Jurisdiction.

ROBERT H. HABL,* (Professor of Law)**, born 1936; admitted to bar, 1962, New York. *Education:* St. John's University (A.B., 1958); New York University (LL.B., 1961; LL.M., 1968). ***COURSES: Contracts, Property, Insurance.

MARGARET HAHN-DUPONT,* (Instructor of Law)**, born New York, New York, October 30, 1965; admitted to bar, 1992, New York and District of Columbia. *Education:* University of Pennsylvania (B.A, 1987); Georgetown University Law Center (J.D., 1991). ***COURSES: Legal Research & Writing.

MARTIN R. HAUPTMAN,* (Professor of Law)**, born 1939; admitted to bar, 1965, New York. *Education:* Hofstra (B.B.A., 1962); Brooklyn Law School (LL.B., 1965); New York University (LL.M., 1967). ***COURSES: Legal Accounting, Federal Estate and Gift Taxation, Federal Income Taxation.

WILLIAM E. HELLERSTEIN,* (Professor of Law)**, born 1939; admitted to bar, 1962, District of Columbia; 1964, New York. *Education:* Brooklyn College (B.A., 1959); Harvard (J.D., 1962). ***COURSES: Civil Rights Law, Constitutional Law, Criminal Procedure, Evidence.

SUSAN N. HERMAN,* (Professor of Law)**, born 1947; admitted to bar, 1975, New York. *Education:* Barnard College (A.B., 1968); New York University (J.D., 1974). ***COURSES: Constitutional Law, Criminal Law, Criminal Procedure, Law & Literature.

NAN D. HUNTER,* (Professor of Law)**, born 1949; admitted to bar, 1975, District of Columbia; 1982, New York. *Education:* Northwestern (B.A., 1971); Georgetown (J.D., 1975). ***COURSES: Civil Procedure, Gender, Sexuality & the Law, Health Law.

EDWARD J. JANGER,* (Associate Professor of Law)**, born 1961; admitted to bar, 1988, Connecticut; 1990, District of Columbia. *Education:* Yale College (B.A., 1983); University of Chicago Law School (J.D., 1987). ***COURSES: Business Reorganizations, Commercial Paper, Debtor and Creditor Rights, Public Choice and Regulation of Business.

GEORGE W. JOHNSON, III,* (Professor of Law)**, born 1939; admitted to bar, 1967, Florida. *Education:* Davidson College (A.B., 1961); University of Florida (J.D., 1967); New York University (LL.M., 1971). ***COURSES: Environmental Law, Land Use, Legal Process, Real Property.

***BERYL R. JONES,* (Professor of Law)**, born 1950; admitted to bar, 1978, Pennsylvania; 1984, New York. *Education:* Oberlin College

(This Listing Continued)

BROOKLYN LAW SCHOOL—Continued

(B.A., 1971); New York University (J.D., 1978). ***COURSES:*** Copyright, Professional Responsibility, Property, The Arts & the Law.

ROBERT ANDREW KAHN*, (Instructor of Law)**, born Brookline, Massachusetts, July 3, 1963; admitted to bar, 1990, New York; 1991, Maryland; 1992, District of Columbia. *Education:* Columbia University (B.A., 1985); New York University Law School (J.D., 1989); Johns Hopkins University (Ph.D., 2000). ***COURSES: Legal Writing. ***Email:*** rak3765@hotmail.com

ROBERTA S. KARMEL*, (Professor of Law and Co-Director, Center for the Study of International Business Law)**, born 1937; admitted to bar, 1962, New York. *Education:* Radcliffe (B.A., 1959); New York University (LL.B., 1962). ***COURSES: Administrative Law, Corporations, Securities Regulation.

CLAIRE KELLY*, (Visiting Assistant Professor of Law)**, born 1965; admitted to bar, 1994, New York. *Education:* Barnard (B.A., 1987); Brooklyn Law School (J.D., 1993). ***COURSES: Administrative Law, Civil Procedure, International Trade Law.

MINNA J. KOTKIN*, (Professor of Law)**, born 1951; admitted to bar, 1975, Pennsylvania; 1976, New York. *Education:* Barnard College (B.A., 1972); Rutgers Law School, Camden (J.D., 1975). ***COURSES: Civil Rights, Clinical Teaching, Federal Litigation, Interviewing and Counseling.

BAILEY H. KUKLIN*, (Professor of Law)**, born 1941; admitted to bar, 1967, California; 1970, New York. *Education:* Nebraska (B.S., 1963); Michigan (J.D., 1966). ***COURSES: Contracts, Legal Process, Torts.

JEROME M. LEITNER*, (Professor of Law)**, born 1926; admitted to bar, 1949, New York. *Education:* Brooklyn College (B.A., 1947); New York University (LL.B., 1949). ***COURSES: Estates, Torts, Trial Advocacy.

MICHAEL P. MADOW*, (Professor of Law)**, born 1949; admitted to bar, 1983, New York; 1984, District of Columbia. *Education:* Amherst College (B.A., 1971); Harvard (M.A., 1978); Columbia (J.D., 1982). ***COURSES: Civil Liberties, Constitutional Law: Death Penalty, Criminal Law, Mass Communications Law.

***DANIEL S. MEDWED*, (Instructor of Law)**, born 1968; admitted to bar, 1995, Massachusetts; 1998, New York. *Education:* Yale University (B.A., 1991); Harvard Law School (J.D., 1995).

JOHN J. MEEHAN*, (Professor Emeritus)**, born 1923; admitted to bar, 1950, New York. *Education:* Brooklyn (LL.B., 1950). ***COURSES: Estates & Trusts.

GARY MINDA*, (Professor of Law)**, born 1946; admitted to bar, 1976, Michigan; 1986, New York. *Education:* Michigan State University (B.A., 1972); Wayne State (J.D., 1975; M.A., 1977). ***COURSES: Administrative Law, Antitrust, Advanced Labor Problems, Employment Law, Labor Law, Legal Process.

SAMUEL K. MURUMBA*, (Professor of Law)**, born 1950. *Education:* Makerere University, Kampala, Uganda (LL.B., 1975); Monash University, Australia (LL.M., 1980; Ph.D., 1986). ***COURSES: Copyright Law, Intellectual Property, International Human Rights, Jurisprudence, Property, Trademarks.

ARTHUR R. PINTO*, (Professor of Law and Co-Director, Center for the Study of International Business Law)**, born 1947; admitted to bar, 1973, New York. *Education:* Colgate (A.B., 1969); New York University (J.D., 1972). ***COURSES: Contracts, Corporate Finance, Corporations, Securities Regulation.

ROBERT M. PITLER*, (Professor of Law)**, born 1941; admitted to bar, 1967, New York. *Education:* City College of New York (B.B.A., 1963); Brooklyn Law School (LL.B., 1966; LL.M., 1967); Michigan (S.J.D., 1968). ***COURSES: Criminal Law, Criminal Procedure, Evidence, Evidence Workshop.

NORMAN S. POSER*, (Professor of Law)**, born 1928; admitted to bar, 1958, New York. *Education:* Harvard (A.B., 1948; LL.B., 1958). ***COURSES: Contracts, Corporate Finance, Corporations, Securities Regulation.

RADHIKA RAO*, (Visiting Professor of Law)**, admitted to bar, 1995. *Education:* Harvard College (A.B., 1986); Harvard Law School (J.D., 1990). ***COURSES: Property, Reproductive Rights.

LEO RASKIND*, (Visiting Professor of Law)**, born 1919. *Education:* London School of Economics (Ph.D., 1952); Yale (LL.B., 1955). ***COURSES: Copyright Law, Antitrust Law, Trademarks.

DANA BRAKMAN REISER*, (Assistant Professor of Law)**, born Huntington, New York, 1973; admitted to bar, 1999, Massachusetts. *Education:* University of Pennsylvania (B.A., 1995); Harvard Law School (J.D., 1998). ***COURSES: Nonprofit Organizations, Property.

JAYNE STEFANIE RESSLER*, (Instructor of Law)**, born New York, New York, 1967; admitted to bar, 1994, Pennsylvania; 1996, New Jersey; 1998, New York. *Education:* University of Pennsylvania The Wharton School (B.S., B.A., 1989); University of Pennsylvania Law School (J.D., 1994). ***COURSES: Legal Research and Writing, Legal Drafting. ***Email:*** jressler@brooklaw.edu

WILLIAM L. REYNOLDS*, (Visiting Professor of Law)**, born 1945; admitted to bar, 1972. *Education:* Dartmouth College (A.B., 1967); Harvard Law School (J.D., 1970). ***COURSES: Antitrust, International Business Transactions.

SARA ROBBINS*, (Librarian & Professor of Law)**, born 1952; admitted to bar, 1985, Ohio. *Education:* Cincinnati (B.A., 1974); Pratt Institute (M.S.L.S., 1977); Ohio State University (J.D., 1985). ***COURSES: Advanced Legal Research.

JOHN A. RONAYNE*, (Professor Emeritus)**, born 1916; admitted to bar, 1948, New York. *Education:* Fordham (B.S., 1937; J.D., 1948); New York University (M.P.A., 1957; LL.M., 1960). ***COURSES: Agency & Partnership.

JENNIFER L. ROSATO*, (Professor of Law)**, born 1961; admitted to bar, 1987, Pennsylvania. *Education:* Cornell (B.S., 1983); Pennsylvania (J.D., 1987). ***COURSES: Children & the Law, Civil Procedure, Family Law, Legal Profession.

ELIZABETH M. SCHNEIDER*, (Professor of Law)**, born 1948; admitted to bar, 1974, New York. *Education:* Bryn Mawr College (B.A., 1968); The London School of Economics & Political Science (M.Sc., 1969); New York University (J.D., 1973). ***COURSES: Battered Women & the Law, Civil Procedure, Women and the Law.

PAUL M. SCHWARTZ*, (Professor of Law)**, born 1959; admitted to bar, 1989, Arkansas. *Education:* Brown University (B.A., 1981); Yale Law School (J.D., 1985). ***COURSES: Computer Law, Family Law, Health Law, Information Privacy Law, Telecommunications Regulation.

ANTHONY J. SEBOK*, (Professor of Law)**, born 1963; admitted to bar, 1994, New York. *Education:* Cornell (B.A., 1984); Oxford University (M.Phil., 1986); Yale (J.D., 1991); Princeton (Ph.D., 1993). ***COURSES: Jurisprudence, Torts.

***AMOS SHAPIRA*, (Visiting Professor of Law)**, born 1937; admitted to bar, 1961, Israel. *Education:* Hebrew University (Master of Law, 1962); Columbia University (Master of Comparative Law, 1963); Yale

(This Listing Continued)

BROOKLYN LAW SCHOOL—Continued

University (Doctor of Science of Law, 1968). ***COURSES:*** Comparative Constitutional Law, Conflict of Laws.

LISA C. SMITH*, (Assistant Clinical Professor of Law)**, born 1954; admitted to bar, 1979, New York. *Education:* Franklin & Marshall College (B.A., 1975); Brooklyn Law School (J.D., 1978). ***COURSES: Criminal Law Clinic, Prosecutor's Clinic and Seminar.

LAWRENCE M. SOLAN*, (Professor of Law)**, born 1952; admitted to bar, 1982, New Jersey; 1984, New York. *Education:* Brandeis University (B.A.); University of Massachusetts (Ph.D.,); Harvard Law School (J.D.). ***COURSES: Legislation and Statutory Interpretation, Property, Remedies.

SUSAN D. SUSMAN*, (Assistant Professor of Legal Writing)**, born 1947; admitted to bar, 1976, New York. *Education:* Oberlin College (A.B.); Harvard Graduate School of Education (M.A.T.); New York University School of Law (J.D.). ***COURSES: Fundamentals of Legal Drafting, Legal Writing.

CARRIE W. TEITCHER*, (Assistant Professor of Legal Writing)**, born 1956; admitted to bar, 1982, New York. *Education:* Brooklyn College (B.A., 1978); Brooklyn Law School (J.D., 1981). ***COURSES: Legal Writing.

AARON D. TWERSKI*, (Newell De Valpine Professor of Law)**, born 1939; admitted to bar, 1965, Wisconsin; 1971, Pennsylvania; 1974, New York. *Education:* Beth Medrash Elyon (A.B., 1960); Marquette University (J.D., 1965); University of Wisconsin (B.S., 1970). ***COURSES: Products Liability, Torts.

MARILYN R. WALTER*, (Professor of Law & Director, Legal Writing Program)**, born 1943; admitted to bar, 1973, New York. *Education:* Toronto (B.A., 1965); Northeastern (J.D., 1972). ***COURSES: Advanced Legal Writing, Civil Rights (Employment Discrimination), Legal Writing.

STEVEN L. WINTER*, (Professor of Law)**, born 1953; admitted to bar, 1978, New York. *Education:* Yeshiva (B.A., 1974); Columbia University (J.D., 1977). ***COURSES: Civil Procedure, Constitutional Law, Jurisprudence, Federal Courts and the Federal System.

DAVID YASSKY*, (Assistant Professor of Law)**, born 1964; admitted to bar, 1992, New York; 1993, District of Columbia. *Education:* Princeton University (A.B., 1986); Yale Law School (J.D., 1990). ***COURSES: Administrative Law, Criminal Law, Federalism.

JONATHAN YOVEL*, (Visiting Assistant Professor of Law)**, admitted to bar, 1993, Israel. *Education:* Tel Aviv University (LL.B. and B.A., 1992); Northwestern University School of Law (LL.M., 1995; S.J.D., 1997). ***COURSES: Contracts, Commercial Transactions: Commercial Paper/Banking, International Sales.

CAROL L. ZIEGLER*, (Associate Dean for Student Affairs & Associate Professor of Legal Writing)**, born 1947; admitted to bar, 1974, New York. *Education:* Cornell (B.A., 1968); New York University (J.D., 1973). ***COURSES: Legal Process, Legal Profession.

VICTOR ZONANA*, (Associate Dean for Academic Affairs & Professor of Law)**, born 1940; admitted to bar, 1965, New York. *Education:* Hofstra College (B.S.); New York University (LL.B. and LL.M.). ***COURSES: Federal Income Taxation, Corporate Taxation, International Taxation, Taxation: Partnership.

CALIFORNIA WESTERN SCHOOL OF LAW

225 CEDAR STREET
SAN DIEGO, CALIFORNIA 92101
Telephone: (619) 239-0391
Fax: (619) 685-2916
http://www.californiawestern.edu

ABA Approved Since 1962.

California Western School of Law, located in downtown San Diego, is among the few independent, nonprofit law schools in the country. California Western is accredited by the American Bar Association (1962) and is a member of the Association of American Law Schools (1967).

Chartered in 1924, California Western attained independent status in 1975. This independence allows students and faculty to focus specifically on the teaching, research, and study of Law. Learning is not limited to classroom discussion, but flows into the hallways, en route to the Law Library, or at lunch in the Castetter Courtyard. Rare at other institutions, but common at California Western, the collegiality among faculty and students is second only to the teaching of law.

California Western's mission is to "Educate Creative Problem Solvers", and the law school is committed to offering students a contemporary approach to legal education-coupled with a vigorous traditional curriculum that produces compassionate, ethical, and effective members of the legal profession. The law is a noble profession, a calling of a select few members of society who see the true meaning of being a lawyer-to counsel, help, resolve, and prevent legal confrontation.

California Western's distinguished faculty of scholars and practitioners challenges students to find answers, apply facts, research what the law is and should be, and understand how law influences the lives of individuals, organizations, and societies. Creative Solutions emerge in classroom discussions, internship experiences, moot court problems, *Law Review* participation, and informal dialogue between students and faculty and with lawyers in San Diego's dynamic bar.

In addition to a well-balanced Juris Doctor curriculum, which includes a strong emphasis in Creative Problem Solving and Trial Advocacy Skills, California Western offers impressive opportunities in interdisciplinary training. Specialized programs, developed collaboratively with the University of California , San Diego (UCSD) and San Diego State University (SDSU), include the J.D./M.S.W. Program Welfare and J.D./M.B.A. with SDSU and J.D./Ph.D. programs in both Political Science and History with UCSD. Areas of concentration, which provide students with advanced study in select areas of law, include International Law; Creative Problem Solving; Labor and Employment Law; Child, Family, and Elder Law; and Criminal Prosecution and Defense Practice.

Among the advantages at California Western is the trimester academic calendar, which allows for three complete terms each year and the opportunity for students to earn their J.D. in two years.

The McGill Center for Creative Problem Solving is a legal education institute working with legal educators, students, lawyers, judges, and society in exploring collaborative approaches to conflict resolution and problem solving. The development of a casebook in Creative Problem Solving-for use in legal education curriculum and in training seminars

(This Listing Continued)

CALIFORNIA WESTERN SCHOOL OF LAW—Continued

for practitioners-is among its most challenging objectives. The center is also a leader in the Latin American judicial reform and rule of law movement.

The Institute for Criminal Defense Advocacy is dedicated to improving the quality of criminal defense representation. The institute hosts an acclaimed national Trial Skills Academy for attorneys from across the country. Within the institute is the California Innocence Project, a California Western program that investigates convictions and assists in representing clients who are incarcerated despite strong evidence of innocence.

Through the National Center for Preventive Law and the Louis M. Brown Program in Preventive Law, faculty and students collaborate in research, courses, public lectures, and community projects regarding techniques of forecasting and preventing potential legal confrontations.

Students, alumni, faculty, and San Diego bench and bar study and conduct research in California Western's new Law Library, a four-story, 50,000-square-foot resource center with more than 150,000 hardbound volumes; 129,000 microform equivalent volumes; and 3,750 serial subscriptions. Dedicated September 11, 2000 by U.S. Supreme Court Justice Anthony Kennedy, the state-of-art Law Library contains the essential resources required for legal research.

Dean: Steven Ray Smith (619) 525-1405
Associate Dean, Academic Affairs: Janet M. Bowermaster (619) 525-1413
Associate Dean, Administration: Mark I. Weinstein (619) 525-1410
Chief Financial Officer, Business Office: Lenore L. Fraga (619) 525-7097
Director, Law Library: Phyllis C. Marion (619) 525-1489
Assistant Dean, Career Services: Louis W. Helmuth (619) 525-7093
Assistant Dean, Mission Initiatives: James M. Cooper (619) 525-1430
Assistant Dean, Student & Diversity Services: Linda N. Dews (619) 525-7642
Director, Admissions: Traci Howard (619) 525-1401
Executive Director, Financial Aid: Kyle C. Poston (619) 525-7061
Interim Director, Alumni Relations: Martha P. Shumaker (619) 525-7643
Dir., Inst. for Crim. Def. Advoc. & CA. Innocence Project: Justin P. Brooks (619) 525-7079
Director, McGill Center for Creative Problem Solving: James M. Cooper (619) 525-1430
Director, National Center for Preventive Law: Thomas D. Barton (619) 525-1687

FULL TIME FACULTY

STEVEN RAY SMITH*, (President, Dean & Professor)**, born 1946; admitted to bar, 1971, Iowa; 1987, Kentucky; 1993, Ohio. *Education:* Buena Vista College (B.A., 1968); Iowa (J.D. and M.A., 1971). ***COURSES: Law & Medicine, Law & Psychology, Torts.

WILLIAM JOSEPH ACEVES*, (Professor)**, born 1964; admitted to bar, 1990, California. *Education:* Claremont Mckenna College (B.A., 1986); University of Southern California (J.D.; M.A., 1990); UCLA School of Law (LL.M., 1996). ***COURSES: Human Rights, Comparative Law, International Law.

THOMAS D. BARTON*, (Professor and Director, Louis M. Brown Program in Preventive Law)**, born 1949; admitted to bar, 1975, New York; 1990, California. *Education:* Tulane (B.A., 1971); Cornell (J.D.,1974); Cambridge University (Ph.D., 1982). ***COURSES: Contracts, Energy Policy, Jurisprudence, Law & Social Science, Professional Responsibility, Taxation, Federal.

MICHAL R. BELKNAP*, (Professor and Director, J.D./Ph.D. Dual-Degree Program in History)**, born 1943; admitted to bar, 1983, Georgia. *Education:* U.C.L.A. (B.A., 1965); Wisconsin (M.A., 1967, Ph.D., 1973); University of Texas (J.D., 1981). ***COURSES: Constitutional Law, Criminal Law, Legal History, Legal Method, Torts, Warren Court.

LAURENCE A. BENNER*, (Professor)**, born 1945; admitted to bar, 1971, Illinois; 1975, Michigan; 1979, District of Columbia. *Education:* Michigan State University (B.A., 1967); University of Chicago (J.D., 1970). ***COURSES: Clinical Teaching, Constitutional Law, Criminal Law, Criminal Procedure, Evidence, Legal Method.

ROBERT A. BOHRER*, (Professor)**, born 1949; admitted to bar, 1974, Illinois. *Education:* Haverford College (B.A., 1971); Illinois (J.D., 1974); Harvard (LL.M., 1979). ***COURSES: Administrative Law, Biotechnology Law, Environmental Law, Property, Torts.

JANET MARIE FRAHM BOWERMASTER*, (Associate Dean, Academic Affairs & Professor)**, born 1948; admitted to bar, 1984, Illinois; Indiana. *Education:* Huntington College (B.S., 1971); Illinois (M.S., 1976; J.D., 1984). ***COURSES: Community Property, Family Law, Juvenile Law.

ARTHUR W. CAMPBELL*, (Professor)**, born 1944; admitted to bar, 1971, District of Columbia; 1971, West Virginia; 1974, California. *Education:* Harvard (A.B., 1966); West Virginia University (J.D., 1971); Georgetown University (LL.M., 1974). ***COURSES: Copyright, Criminal Law, Criminal Procedure, Entertainment Law, Federal Courts.

SUSAN A. CHANNICK*, (Professor)**, admitted to bar, 1980, California. *Education:* Cornell (B.A., 1965); California Western School of Law (J.D., 1980). ***COURSES: Aging, Law & Public Policy, Community Property, Contracts, Family Law, Remedies, Trusts & Estates.

BARBARA J. COX*, (Professor)**, born 1956; admitted to bar, 1982, Wisconsin. *Education:* Wisconsin (J.D., 1982). ***COURSES: Civil Procedure, Property, Sexual Orientation & the Law, Women & the Law.

ELLEN J. DANNIN*, (Professor)**, born 1951; admitted to bar, 1978, Michigan. *Education:* Michigan (B.A., 1975; J.D., 1978). ***COURSES: Civil Procedure, Collective Bargaining Issues, Employment Law, Evidence, Labor Relations.

ROBERT R. DEKOVEN*, (Legal Writing Professor)**, born Chicago, Illinois, September 24, 1958; admitted to bar, 1984, California. *Education:* San Diego State University (B.A., 1980); California Western School of Law (J.D., 1983). ***COURSES: Legal Writing, Appellate Advocacy. ***Email:*** rdekoven@cwsl.edu

***MICHAEL H. DESSENT*, (Professor & Dean Emeritus)**, born 1942; admitted to bar, 1967, California. *Education:* Northwestern (B.S., 1964; J.D., 1967).

SCOTT B. EHRLICH*, (Professor)**, born 1952; admitted to bar, 1977, New York; 1978, California. *Education:* SUNY, Stonebrook (B.A., 1973); New York University (J.D., 1976); Harvard (LL.M., 1980). ***COURSES: Bankruptcy, Business Planning, Legal Analysis, Legal Method, Property, Secured Transactions.

(This Listing Continued)

CALIFORNIA WESTERN SCHOOL OF LAW—Continued

FLORALYNN EINESMAN*, (Professor)**, born 1955; admitted to bar, 1980, California. *Education:* McGill (B.A., 1977); Boston University (J.D., 1980). ***COURSES: Clinical Teaching, Criminal Justice, Criminal Procedure, Juvenile Justice, Trial Advocacy.

RICHARD J. FINK*, (Professor)**, born 1948; admitted to bar, 1974, California; 1976, Washington. *Education:* Stanford (J.D., 1974). ***COURSES: Environmental Law, Natural Resources, Property.

PAUL J. GUDEL*, (Professor)**, born 1948; admitted to bar, 1984, Illinois. *Education:* University of Chicago (B.A., 1970; M.A., 1973); North Western (J.D., 1984). ***COURSES: Contracts, Employment Discrimination, Employment Law, Jurisprudence, Law & Literature, Philosophy of Law.

CHRISTINE B. HICKMAN*, (Associate Professor)**, born 1949; admitted to bar, 1975, California; 1977, District of Columbia. *Education:* Yale (B.A., 1971); Harvard (J.D., 1974). ***COURSES: California Civil Procedure, Civil Procedure, Pre-Trial Procedure.

MARILYN J. IRELAND*, (Professor)**, born 1943; admitted to bar, 1969, Illinois; 1976, Missouri. *Education:* Miami University, Oxford (B.A., 1966); University of Chicago (J.D., 1969). ***COURSES: Antitrust, Civil Procedure, Constitutional Law, Evidence, Torts, Women & the Law.

ANDREA L. JOHNSON*, (Professor & Director, Center for Telecommunications Law)**, born 1956; admitted to bar, 1982, District of Columbia. *Education:* Harvard (J.D., 1981). ***COURSES: Administration Law, Business Organizations, Land Use, Local Government, Real Property, Telecommunications Law.

JANEEN KERPER*, (Professor & Latin American Programs Coordinator, McGill Center for Creative Problem Solving)**, born 1946; admitted to bar, 1973, California. *Education:* Stanford (B.A., 1967); Harvard (M.A., 1968; J.D., 1973). ***COURSES: Contracts Evidence, Pretrial Practice, Professional Responsibility, Remedies, Torts, Trial Practice.

WILLIAM C. LYNCH*, (Professor)**, born 1932; admitted to bar, 1956, Massachusetts; 1975, California. *Education:* Boston College (B.A., 1953; J.D., 1956); George Washington (LL.M.). ***COURSES: Conflict of Laws, Evidence, Law of the Sea, Legal Research & Writing, Remedies, Torts.

F. PHILIP MANNS, JR.*, (Professor and Director, J.D./M.B.A. Dual-Degree Program)**, born 1960; admitted to bar, 1987, Maryland; 1988, Georgia. *Education:* University of Virginia (B.S.Ch.E., 1982); Maryland (J.D., 1987). ***COURSES: Commercial Paper, Estates & Trusts, Taxation, Federal.

PHYLLIS CASTLE MARION*, (Director, Law Library & Professor)**, born 1944; admitted to bar, 1990, Minnesota. *Education:* Michigan State University (B.A., 1966); University of Chicago (M.A., 1968); William Mitchell (J.D., 1990). ***COURSES: Legal Research & Writing.

IRWIN D. MILLER*, (Professor & Director, Clinical Internship Program)**, born 1950; admitted to bar, 1977, Texas. *Education:* University of Texas (B.B.A., 1973); Houston (J.D., 1977). ***COURSES: Clinical Teaching, Interviewing, Counseling & Negotiation, Legal Research & Writing.

LINDA H. MORTON*, (Professor)**, born 1953; admitted to bar, 1982, Massachusetts; 1989, California. *Education:* Princeton (A.B., 1977); Northeastern (J.D., 1981). ***COURSES: Alternative Dispute Resolution, Clinical Teaching, Legal Drafting, Trial & Appellate Advocacy.

JOHN E. NOYES*, (Professor & Director, International Legal Studies Program)**, born 1951; admitted to bar, 1977, Connecticut. *Education:* Amherst College (B.A., 1973); University of Virginia (J.D., 1977). ***COURSES: Conflict of Laws, International Business Transactions, International Law, Remedies, Torts.

LAURA MARIE PADILLA*, (Professor)**, born 1962; admitted to bar, 1988, California; District of Columbia. *Education:* Stanford (B.A., 1983; J.D., 1987). ***COURSES: Community Property, Estates & Trusts, Gender, Property & Law, Property.

MATTHEW ARNOLD RITTER*, (Legal Skills Professor)**, born 1956. *Education:* Rice University (B.A., 1978); Boston University (M.Div, 1981); Yale University (Ph.D., 1988); California Western School of Law (J.D., 1997). ***COURSES: Legal Skills.

ROBERTA S. ROBINSON*, (Legal Writing Professor)**, born New York City, August 13, 1957; admitted to bar, 1981, California. *Education:* State University (B.A., 1978); University of Michigan (J.D., 1981). ***COURSES: Legal Research, Legal Writing, Appellate Advocacy. ***Email:*** rrobinson@cwsl.edu

KATHARINE ROSENBERRY*, (Professor and Academic Director, McGill Center for Creative Problem Solving)**, born 1943; admitted to bar, 1975, California. *Education:* Northwestern (B.A., 1965); Illinois (M.Ed., 1966); San Diego (J.D., 1975). ***COURSES: Common Interest Real Estate Developments, Condominiums, Co-ops & Planned Communities, Land Use, Legal Research, Property, Remedies.

GLORIA L. SANDRINO*, (Associate Professor)**, born 1958; admitted to bar, 1987, New York; 1990, Florida. *Education:* Rutgers College (B.A., 1981); Harvard (J.D., 1984). ***COURSES: Business Organizations, International Business Transactions, Mexican Law.

JAQUELYN HERSH SLOTKIN*, (Director, M.C.L./L.L.M. Program for Foreign Lawyers; Legal Writing Professor)**, born 1942; admitted to bar, 1982, California. *Education:* Pittsburgh (B.A., 1963); West Virginia (M.A., 1965); University of Arizona (Ph.D., 1976); San Diego (J.D., 1982). ***COURSES: Clinical Teaching, Legal Analysis, Legal Research & Writing.

GLENN C. SMITH*, (Professor and Director, J.D./Ph.D. Program in Political Science)**, born 1953; admitted to bar, 1978, District of Columbia. *Education:* George Washington (B.A., 1975); New York University (J.D., 1978); Georgetown (LL.M., 1979). ***COURSES: Administrative Law, Constitutional Law, Legal Method, Legislation, Supreme Court, Decision Making.

DONALD J. SMYTHE*, (Assistant Professor of Law)**, born Fort Erie, Canada, March 30, 1959. *Education:* Carleton University (B.A.; 1983; M.A., 1986); Yale University (M.Phil., 1989; Ph.D., 1992); University of Virginia (J.D., 1999). ***COURSES: Law & Economics, Property, Sales, Secured Transactions. ***Email:*** dsmythe@cwsl.edu

JAN STIGLITZ*, (Professor)**, born 1947; admitted to bar, 1975, New York; 1982, California. *Education:* Buffalo (B.A., 1970); Albany (J.D., 1975); Harvard (LL.M.; 1980). ***COURSES: Civil Procedure, Criminal Appellate Advocacy, Employment Law, Sports Law, Torts.

ROBERTA K. THYFAULT*, (Legal Writing Professor)**, born Denver, Colorado, November 7, 1952; admitted to bar, 1984, California; 1985, Colorado. *Education:* Metropolitan State College (B.A., 1980); California Western School of Law (J.D., 1984). ***COURSES: Legal Research, Legal Writing, Appellate Advocacy. ***Email:*** rthyfault@cwsl.edu

JANET WEINSTEIN*, (Professor & Director J.D./M.S.W. Dual Degree Program)**, born 1946; admitted to bar, 1974, California. *Education:* U.C.L.A. (B.A., 1968); San Diego (J.D., 1974). ***COURSES: Child Abuse & Neglect, Clinical Teaching, Interviewing & Counseling, Legal Analysis, Mediation.

(This Listing Continued)

CALIFORNIA WESTERN SCHOOL OF LAW—Continued

MARK I. WEINSTEIN*, (Associate Dean, Administration & Professor)**, born 1948; admitted to bar, 1972, Pennsylvania; 1978, Missouri. *Education:* Rutgers (B.A., 1969); George Washington (J.D., 1972). ***COURSES: Clinical Teaching, Interviewing, Counseling & Negotiation.

DANIEL BRIAN YEAGER*, (Professor)**, born 1959; admitted to bar, 1991, California. *Education:* Kenyon College (A.B., 1979); University of Florida (J.D., 1989); Illinois (LL.M., 1991). ***COURSES: Criminal Law Theory, Criminal Law, Criminal Procedure, Law & Literature.

CAMPBELL UNIVERSITY NORMAN ADRIAN WIGGINS SCHOOL OF LAW

P. O. BOX 158
BUIES CREEK, NORTH CAROLINA 27506
Telephone: (910) 893-1750
Fax: (910) 893-1829
culaw@webster.campbell.edu

ABA Approved Since 1979

The Norman Adrian Wiggins School of Law at Campbell University was established in 1976. From its inception, the School of Law was envisioned as a unique and different law school. It is a small, highly personal, academically and professionally demanding, and innovative law school located within commuting distance of the dynamic and rapidly growing Raleigh/Research Triangle area.

The School of Law concentrates on the integration of the practical with the theoretical in a highly structured curriculum. The members of the law faculty recognize their responsibility to help law students acquire foundation skills and knowledge, to develop advocacy skills and to become fully integrated legal professionals. Graduates are thus more fully prepared to engage in the practice of law upon their completion of Campbell's program. Campbell law students have a tradition of success in Moot Court, Client Counseling and Trial Competitions. In addition, Campbell law graduates consistently perform at the highest level on bar examinations.

The School of Law identifies itself as a distinctly Christian institution whose character and programs reflect the Judeo-Christian tradition. This theological commitment is viewed as an expansion, not a confining or limiting, of the concept of academic freedom in its purest form. As part of this tradition, the School of Law seeks to instill within its students a sense of vocation which combines principles of excellence in the calling of law, the identification of gifts and interests, the employment of one's skills in service to God and the community, and the shaping of one's profession in accord with ultimate values.

In addition to taking into account traditional indicators of academic and professional success in its applicants, the School of Law requires a personal visit to campus and applicant interview by a member of the law faculty as a prerequisite to admission. The applicant is evaluated during this interview and also has the opportunity to evaluate the School of Law. The School of Law sponsors a Performance Based Admissions Program during each summer session.

The School of Law seeks students who view the practice of law as a privilege to engage in a professional life of service to others. The heritage and finest traditions of the legal profession must include leadership in their communities and an overriding concern that justice be served in all matters.

Dean: Willis P. Whichard (910) 893-1751
Admissions: Alan Dale Woodlief, Jr. (910) 893-1754
Library: Karen C. Sorvari (910) 893-1791
Career Services: T. Brandon Wright (910) 893-1784
Alumni Affairs: T. Brandon Wright (910) 893-1784

FULL TIME FACULTY

WILLIS P. WHICHARD*, (Dean and Professor of Law)**, born Durham, North Carolina, May 24, 1940; admitted to bar, 1965, North Carolina. *Education:* University of North Carolina at Chapel Hill (A.B.; J.D.); University of Virginia (LL.M.; S.J.D.). ***COURSES: Judicial Process, Professional Responsibility/Ethics. ***Email:*** whichard@webster.campbell.edu

THOMAS PERRIN ANDERSON*, (Professor of Law)**, born Anniston, Alabama, April 15, 1948; admitted to bar, 1975, Alabama. *Education:* University of Alabama (B.A., 1970); Cumberland School of Law of Samford University (J.D., 1975); Temple University School of Law (LL.M., 1984). ***COURSES: Trial Advocacy, Pretrial Litigation, Civil Procedure, Evidence, Mediation. ***Email:*** anderson@webster.campbell.edu

ANTHONY V. BAKER*, (Associate Professor of Law)**, admitted to bar, 1981, North Carolina. *Education:* Duke University (B.A., 1977); University of North Carolina at Chapel Hill (J.D., 1981); University of Wisconsin (LL.M., 1998). ***COURSES: Criminal Law, Criminal Procedure, Constitutional Law, Legal History.

RICHARD THOMAS BOWSER*, (Associate Professor of Law)**, born Grove City, Pennsylvania, January 19, 1961; admitted to bar, 1991, Pennsylvania. *Education:* Grove City College (B.A., 1984); Westminster Theological Seminary (M.A., 1986); Campbell University (J.D., 1991). ***COURSES: Constitutional Law, Estate Gift Taxation, Estate Planning, Jurisprudence. ***Email:*** bowser@webster.campbell.edu

ALAN L. BUTTON*, (Professor of Law)**, born Bellefonte, Pennsylvania, June 23, 1954; admitted to bar, 1982, New York. *Education:* Cornell University (A.B., 1976); Washington & Lee University (J.D., 1981); University of Cambridge (LL.M., 1989). ***COURSES: Torts, Debtor-Creditor Law, Environmental Law, Media Law. ***Email:*** button@webster.campbell.edu

LYNN ROBERT BUZZARD*, (Professor of Law)**, born Ohio, January 15, 1940; admitted to bar, 1984, Illinois. *Education:* Duke University (B.A., 1963; M.A.T., 1966; M.Div., 1968); DePaul University (J.D., 1984). ***COURSES: Alternative Dispute Resolution, Constitutional Law, International Law, Immigration, Non-Profit Organizations, Remedies, Church-State. ***Email:*** buzzard@webster.campbell.edu

(This Listing Continued)

CAMPELL UNIVERSITY NORMAN ADRIAN WIGGINS SCHOOL OF LAW—Continued

JEAN MARIE CARY*, (Professor of Law)**, born Louisville, Kentucky, March 6, 1949; admitted to bar, 1975, North Carolina. *Education:* Duke University (B.A., 1971); Georgetown University Law Center (J.D., 1975). ***COURSES: Family Law, Trial Advocacy, Evidence, Introduction to Trial Advocacy, Advanced Trial Advocacy. ***Email:*** cary@webster.campbell.edu

JOHNNY C. CHRISCOE, JR.*, (Associate Professor of Law)**, born Troy, North Carolina, August 19, 1957; admitted to bar, 1990, North Carolina. *Education:* Pembroke State University (B.A., 1980); Campbell University, Norman Adrian Wiggins School of Law (J.D., 1990). ***COURSES: Insurance Law, Trial Advocacy. ***Email:*** chriscoe@webster.campbell.edu

MARGARET PERSON CURRIN*, (Associate Dean and Professor of Law)**, born Oxford, North Carolina, June 17, 1950; admitted to bar, 1979, North Carolina. *Education:* Meredith College (A.B., 1972); Campbell University School of Law (J.D., 1979); Georgetown University Law Center (1980). ***COURSES: Administrative Law, Federal Crimes, Legislative Representation, Externship Program. ***Email:*** currin@webster.campbell.edu

F. LEARY DAVIS, JR.*, (Professor of Law and Director, IS-POL-SED)**, born Zebulon, North Carolina, December 4, 1941; admitted to bar, 1967, North Carolina. *Education:* Wake Forest University (B.A., 1964; J.D., 1967); Columbia University (LL.M., 1984). ***COURSES: Basic Small Business Drafting, Business Associations, Law Firm Planning, Community and Organizational Leadership, Introduction to Leadership, Professionalism Lecture Series, Corporations, Strategic Practice and Law Firm Planning.. ***Email:*** davis@webster.campbell.edu

CATHERINE ROSS DUNHAM*, (Assistant Professor of Law)**, admitted to bar, 1996, North Carolina. *Education:* University of North Carolina at Chapel Hill (B.A., 1987); Campbell University (J.D., 1996). ***COURSES: Legal Research and Writing. ***Email:*** dunham@webster.campbell.edu

PATRICK KIRK HETRICK*, (Professor of Law)**, born Milwaukee, Wisconsin, March 11, 1945; admitted to bar, 1971, Wisconsin. *Education:* University of Wisconsin-Milwaukee (B.S., 1967); Marquette University Law School (J.D., 1971). ***COURSES: Real Estate Law, Education Law, Property. ***Email:*** hetrick@webster.campbell.edu

WILLIAM O. KING*, (Visiting Professor of Law)**, born Louisburg, North Carolina, July 29, 1937; admitted to bar, 1964, North Carolina. *Education:* University of North Carolina (A.B., 1959); Wake Forest University (LL.B., 1964). ***COURSES: Professional Ethics & Responsibilities, Trial Advocacy. ***Email:*** king@webster.campbell.edu

CHARLES CORLING LEWIS*, (Professor of Law)**, born Richmond, Virginia, March 23, 1946; admitted to bar, 1971, Virginia. *Education:* Washington & Lee University (B.A., 1968; J.D., 1971). ***COURSES: Commercial Law, Code Pleading, Contract Planning. ***Email:*** lewis@webster.campbell.edu

ROBERT O. LOFTIS, JR.*, (Professor of Law)**, born Birmingham, Alabama, August 5, 1942; admitted to bar, 1973, Tennessee; 1974, Georgia. *Education:* Florida Atlantic University (B.S., 1969); Emory University (J.D., 1972). ***COURSES: Income Taxation, Taxation of Business Entities, Business Planning, Law & Accounting. ***Email:*** loftis@webster.campbell.edu

RICHARD A. LORD*, (Professor of Law)**, born New York, New York, January 8, 1951; admitted to bar, 1975, Tennessee. *Education:* Ashland College; Alfred University (B.A., 1971); Memphis State University School of Law (J.D., 1975); Yale Law School (LL.M., 1976). ***COURSES: Contracts, Commercial Law. ***Email:*** lord@webster.campbell.edu

JAMES B. MCLAUGHLIN, JR.*, (Professor of Law)**, born Grand Rapids, Michigan, May 4, 1946; admitted to bar, 1973, Georgia. *Education:* Georgia Southern University (B.S.Ed., 1968); Mercer University (J.D., 1973). ***COURSES: Property, Estate Administration, Wills & Trusts. ***Email:*** mclaugh@webster.campbell.edu

JAMES STANLEY MCQUADE*, (Lynch Professor of the Philosophy of Law)**, born Bangor, North Ireland, October 7, 1929. *Education:* Queen's University, Belfast, Ireland (B.D.; B.A.; Ph.D; LL.B.; M.D.). ***COURSES: Jurisprudence, Products Liability, Legal History Law and Medicine.

RICHARD T. RODGERS*, (Professor of Law)**, born Pittsburgh, Pennsylvania, November 15, 1946; admitted to bar, 1971, Florida and North Carolina. *Education:* University of North Carolina (A.B., 1968; J.D., 1971). ***COURSES: Law Office Operation & Management, Start Your Own Law Firm, Real Estate Transactions, Advanced Real Property Law, Local Government. ***Email:*** rodgers@webster.campbell.edu

KAREN C. SORVARI*, (Associate Professor of Law and Law Librarian)**, born New York, New York, September 3, 1943; admitted to bar, 1985, North Carolina. *Education:* Florida Atlantic University (B.A., 1967); University of Rochester (M.A., 1969); State University College of Arts and Sciences, Geneseo (M.L.S., 1972); Campbell University School of Law (J.D., 1985). ***COURSES: Advanced Legal Writing. ***Email:*** sorvari@webster.campbell.edu

E. GREGORY WALLACE*, (Associate Professor of Law)**, born Little Rock, Arkansas, May 20, 1953; admitted to bar, 1990, Arkansas. *Education:* University of Arkansas (B.A., 1975); Dallas Theological Seminary (M.A., 1982); University of Arkansas, Little Rock (J.D., 1990); University of Virginia (LL.M., 1993); Candidate for S.J.D. Degree at University of Virginia School of Law. ***COURSES: Civil Rights Litigation, Federal Courts, Contracts, Land Use, Environmental Law, First Amendment, Social Security Disability Law. ***Email:*** wallace@webster.campbell.edu

OLIVIA LEIGH WEEKS*, (Associate Librarian and Assistant Professor of Law)**, born Raleigh, North Carolina, October 17, 1947; admitted to bar, 1991, North Carolina. *Education:* Meredith College (B.A., 1969); East Carolina University (M.L.S., 1980); Campbell University (J.D., 1990). ***COURSES: Legal Research. ***Email:*** weeks@webster.campbell.edu

ALAN DALE WOODLIEF, JR.*, (Associate Dean for Admissions and Assistant Professor of Law)**, born Oxford, North Carolina, January 5, 1969; admitted to bar, 1994, North Carolina. *Education:* University of North Carolina (B.A., 1991); Campbell University (J.D., 1994). ***Email: woodlief@webster.campbell.edu

WILLIAM ALLEN WOODRUFF*, (Professor of Law)**, born Montgomery, Alabama, July 29, 1948; admitted to bar, 1978, South Carolina; 1979, Alabama; 1992, District of Columbia. *Education:* University of Alabama (B.A., 1970); University of South Carolina (J.D., 1978). ***COURSES: Evidence, Government Litigation, Military Law, Trial and Health Law. ***Email:*** woodruff@webster.campbell.edu

CAPITAL UNIVERSITY LAW SCHOOL

303 E. BROAD STREET
COLUMBUS, OHIO 43215-3200
Telephone: (614) 236-6500
Fax: (614) 236-6972
www.law.capital.edu

ABA Approved Since 1950.

Capital University provides personalized quality liberal arts education that is coupled with professional training. It was founded in 1830, making it one of the oldest colleges in the Midwest. Capital University is comprised of these undergraduate colleges: the College of Arts and Sciences, the Conservatory of Music, the School of Nursing, the School of Management and the Law School. Capital offers six undergraduate degrees, five graduate degrees and more then 40 majors and 28 minors. Capital is coeducational and has a total student body of about 4,000 and a faculty of approximately 175.

Capital University Law School traces its origin to 1903. The Law School, then known as Columbus Law School, was distinctive because of its commitment to provide working class people the opportunity to join the legal profession. The American Bar Association accredited the school, then called Franklin Law School, in 1954. The Law School became affiliated with Capital University in 1966. In 1982, Capital University Law School became a member of the Association of American Law Schools.

Since 1966, the Law School has experienced tremendous growth. The school's full-time faculty has grown in numbers from 5 to 31. In 1997, the school moved to a state-of-the-art facility in downtown Columbus. The school's new location places it in the heart of Ohio's business and legal communities. The new location is within blocks of The Supreme Court of Ohio, Ohio's State Capitol, numerous state agencies, including the Ohio Attorney General's Office, the Franklin County Courts and the City of Columbus' judicial complex. The Law School is near a federal district court and most of Central Ohio's largest law firms, insurance companies and banks. Student life is enhanced due to the Law School's close proximity to the cultural heart of Ohio, including the Columbus Art Museum, Columbus' major theaters, and its renowned museum of science and industry (COSI).

The new law building includes ample study space, attractive classrooms, a courtroom, computer training facilities, and an outstanding law library.

Capital Law School and the College of Management offer a joint Juris Doctor/Master of Business Administration degree. The Law School and the School of Nursing offer a joint Juris Doctor/Master of Science in Nursing degree. The law school, along with Ohio University, offers a joint Juris Doctor/Master of Sports Administration. In addition, the Graduate Tax Program offers graduate studies in business and taxation for lawyers and accountants. A combined J.D./LL.M. allows law students to focus their electives in the area of taxation and to obtain a Master of Law in Taxation or Master of Laws in Business with one additional full-time semester after completion of the Juris Doctorate degree. A special area of strength is the wide range of legal skills courses offered at Capital Law School. The Center for Dispute Resolution, the Institute for Citizen Education, and the Institute for International Legal Education provide innovative legal education programs. The Dave Thomas Center for Adoptive Law is the premier center for the study of adoption law and policy in the United States. Lawyering skills are developed at Capital through a combination of coursework and special programs such as Law Review, Moot Court, Trial Advocacy, the Law Clinics, Externships, and the Night Prosecutors' Program.

Capital's law library, one of the largest law libraries in Ohio and a federal depository, contains 250,000 volumes and microfilm equivalents. The law library subscribes to both WESTLAW and LEXIS for its students and faculty. The library staff includes four lawyer-librarians who hold both Juris Doctor and Master of Library Science degrees.

Each fall approximately 250 new students in the day and evening programs begin their legal studies at Capital. This year, our students come to Capital from 37 states, the District of Columbia, Canada, and a number of other foreign countries. The student body represents a broad range of social, ethnic, religious and economic segments of our diverse society.

Capital University Law School is committed to preparing students for important roles in society. This preparation begins in the classroom, where Capital's faculty prides itself on excellent classroom instruction, demanding from itself and its students the very best in preparation, research, scholarly writing, and participation in professional associations to remain current and knowledgeable in the law and law-related issues.

Students have the opportunity to participate in more than 25 student organizations. The Law School's moot court team has advanced from the regional competition to the national competition for five of the last ten years in the ABA National Moot Court Competition. The Capital University Law Review provides students the opportunity to edit a major legal journal.

To meet the needs of our students, the Career Services Office offers career counseling, career education, and workshops on resume writing, interviewing, and job search strategies. This office provides information on employers and employer contact through the campus interview program.

Capital University Law School is particularly proud of the accomplishments of its graduates. Presidents of the Ohio State Bar Association, Presidents of the Columbus Bar Association, a member of Congress from Columbus, leaders in the business community and many judges and state legislators are numbered among the 5,000 Capital Law graduates throughout the country.

Dean: Steven Bahls (614) 236-6383
Graduate Tax and Business Programs: Mary K. Ming (614) 236-6402
Paralegal Programs: Mary K. Ming (614) 236-6402
Center for Dispute Resolution: Roberta Mitchell (614) 236-6516
Center for Adoption: Kent Markus (614) 236-6545
Library: Donald Hughes (614) 236-6464
Career Services: Amy DeLong (614) 236-6888
Development and Alumni Affairs: James Richardson (614) 236-6601
Registrar: Leslie Gardner (614) 236-6442

(This Listing Continued)

CAPITAL UNIVERSITY LAW SCHOOL—Continued

FULL TIME FACULTY

STEVEN C. BAHLS, **(Dean and Professor of Law),** born Des Moines, Iowa, September 4, 1954; admitted to bar, 1979, Wisconsin; 1989, Montana. *Education:* University of Iowa (B.B.A., 1976); Northwestern University (J.D., 1979). ***COURSES:*** Business Associations, Agricultural Law, Entrepreneurship Law, Transnational Practice of Law. ***Email:*** sbahls@law.capital.edu

JAMES RICHARD BEATTIE, **(Assistant Professor),** born Glenridge, New Jersey, February 23, 1952; admitted to bar, 1993, New York. *Education:* Muskingum College (B.A., 1974); Tulane University (M.A., 1981); Vanderbilt University School of Law (J.D., 1991); Columbia University School of Law (LL.M., 2000). ***COURSES:*** Civil Procedure, Law and Religion, Modern Legal Philosophy. ***Email:*** jbeattie@law.capital.edu

CAROLE BERRY, **(Professor of Law),** born Lansing, Michigan, May 30, 1943; admitted to bar, 1970, Ohio; 1971, Michigan. *Education:* Michigan State University (B.S., 1967); Ohio State University (J.D., 1970; Ph.D., 1990). ***COURSES:*** Taxation, Legal Research and Writing, Oral Advocacy. ***Email:*** cberry@law.capital.edu

JOSIAH H. BLACKMORE, **(Professor and President Emeritus, Capital University),** born Marietta, Ohio, November 26, 1934; admitted to bar, 1962, Ohio. *Education:* Miami University (B.A., 1956); The Ohio State University College of Law (J.D., 1962). ***COURSES:*** Evidence, Civil Procedure, Legal Systems, Constitutional Law. ***Email:*** jblackmore@law.capital.edu

JANET GEORGE BLOCHER, **(Director, Legal Research & Writing Program),** born Ohio, August 29, 1958; admitted to bar, 1985, Georgia; 1990, Ohio. *Education:* Ohio Northern University (B.A., 1980); Capital University Law School (J.D., 1985). ***COURSES:*** Legal Research & Writing, Externships. ***Email:*** jblocher@law.capital.edu

WILLIAM H. BLUTH, **(Professor of Law),** born New York, New York, October 31, 1945; admitted to bar, 1969, New York; 1970, Ohio. *Education:* City College of the City University of New York (B.A., 1966); Boston College (J.D., 1969). ***COURSES:*** Criminal Law, Criminal Procedure, Family Law, Remedies. ***Email:*** wbluth@law.capital.edu

MARGARET CORDRAY, **(Professor of Law),** born Los Angeles, California, October 18, 1961; admitted to bar, 1987, California; 1990, Ohio. *Education:* University of the Pacific (B.A., 1983); University of California at Berkeley, Boalt Hall School of Law (J.D., 1986); Oxford University (B.C.L., 1988). ***COURSES:*** Evidence, Remedies. ***Email:*** mcordray@law.capital.edu

STANTON G. DARLING II, **(Professor of Law),** born Camp Blanding, Florida, May 11, 1944; admitted to bar, 1968, District of Columbia; 1972, California; 1984, Ohio. *Education:* Ohio State University (B.A., summa cum laude, 1965); Georgetown University (J.D., 1968). ***COURSES:*** Torts, Civil Procedure, Product Liability. ***Email:*** sdarling@law.capital.edu

MICHAEL DISTELHORST, **(Professor of Law),** born Columbus, Ohio, February 11, 1949; admitted to bar, 1976, Ohio. *Education:* Capital University (B.A., 1971; J.D., 1976). ***COURSES:*** Contracts, Commercial Law, Professional Responsibility, Jurisprudence. ***Email:*** mdistelh@law.capital.edu

JEFFREY T. FERRIELL, **(Professor of Law),** born Columbus, Ohio, November 27, 1953; admitted to bar, 1978, California. *Education:* Ohio State University (B.S., 1975); Santa Clara University (J.D., 1978); University of Illinois (LL.M., 1983). ***COURSES:*** Bankruptcy, Commercial Law, Federal Courts, Contracts. ***Email:*** jferriel@law.capital.edu

BRIAN A. FREEMAN, **(Professor of Law),** born Erie, Pennsylvania, October 30, 1940; admitted to bar, 1965, Ohio. *Education:* Oberlin College (A.B., 1962); Ohio State University (J.D., 1965). ***COURSES:*** Constitutional Law, Trusts. ***Email:*** bfreema@law.capital.edu

SUSAN M. GILLES, **(Professor of Law),** born Glasgow, Scotland, February 3, 1960; admitted to bar, 1985, Ohio. *Education:* University of Glasgow (LL.B., 1981); Harvard University (LL.M., 1982). ***COURSES:*** Civil Procedure, First Amendment, Administrative Law, Torts, and Comparative Law. ***Email:*** sgilles@law.capital.edu

MYRON C. GRAUER, **(Professor of Law),** born Pittsburgh, Pennsylvania, December 28, 1948; admitted to bar, 1975, Pennsylvania; 1976, District of Columbia; 1985, Ohio. *Education:* University of Vermont (B.A., 1971); University of Pittsburgh (J.D., 1975); Yale University (LL.M., 1980). ***COURSES:*** Federal Taxation, Estates and Trusts. ***Email:*** mgrauer@law.capital.edu

DENNIS DANIEL HIRSCH, **(Assistant Professor of Law),** born New York, New York, May 22, 1962; admitted to bar, 1994, New York; 1995, District of Columbia. *Education:* Columbia University (B.A., 1985); Yale Law School (J.D., 1991). ***COURSES:*** Environmental Law, Property. ***Email:*** dhirsch@law.capital.edu

DONALD A. HUGHES, JR., **(Director of the Law Library and Professor of Law),** born Norwalk, Connecticut, April 6, 1952; admitted to bar, 1982, North Dakota. *Education:* Hamilton College (B.A., 1974); University of Connecticut (M.A., 1978; J.D., 1981); Southern Connecticut State College (M.L.S., 1981). ***COURSES:*** Legal Writing, Copyright, Law and Literature. ***Email:*** dhughes@law.capital.edu

DANIEL T. KOBIL, **(Professor of Law),** born Toledo, Ohio, August 26, 1956; admitted to bar, 1983, Ohio. *Education:* University of Toledo (B.A., 1978; J.D., 1983). ***COURSES:*** Constitutional Law, Commercial Law, Appellate Practice and Procedure, Legal Research and Writing. ***Email:*** dkobil@law.capital.edu

MAX KRAVITZ, **(Professor of Law),** born Cleveland, Ohio, November 2, 1946; admitted to bar, 1973, Ohio. *Education:* Ohio State University (B.A., 1969); Capital University Law School (J.D., 1973). ***COURSES:*** Criminal Law, Criminal Procedure, Clinical Education. ***Email:*** mkravitz@law.capital.edu

SUSAN E. LOOPER-FRIEDMAN, **(Professor of Law),** born Oxford, United Kingdom, January 9, 1955; admitted to bar, 1981, California; 1982, Massachusetts. *Education:* Universite de Grenoble (Degree, 1974); University of Wisconsin (B.A., 1977); University of Santa Clara (J.D., 1981); Harvard University (LL.M., 1984). ***COURSES:*** Property, Jurisprudence, Legal History, Comparative Law. ***Email:*** slooper@law.capital.edu

KENT R. MARKUS, **(Director, Dave Thomas Center for Adoption Law and Professor of Law),** born Cleveland, Ohio, February 1, 1959; admitted to bar, 1984, Ohio. *Education:* Northwestern University (B.S., 1981); Harvard Law School (J.D., 1984). ***COURSES:*** Prosecutional Issues, Remedies, Administrative Law, Ethics of Government Lawyers. ***Email:*** kmarkus@law.capital.edu

DAVID N. MAYER, **(Professor of Law),** born Flint, Michigan, December 1, 1955; admitted to bar, 1984, District of Columbia. *Education:* University of Michigan (A.B., 1977; J.D., 1980); University of Virginia (M.A., History, 1982; Ph.D., History, 1988). ***COURSES:*** Constitutional History, Legal History, Intellectual Property, Copyright, and Unfair Trade Practices. ***Email:*** dmayer@law.capital.edu

(This Listing Continued)

CAPITAL UNIVERSITY LAW SCHOOL—Continued

SHIRLEY L. MAYS*, (Associate Professor of Law)**, born Springfield, Ohio, November 21, 1954; admitted to bar, 1988, Ohio. *Education:* Central State University (B.A., 1976); Harvard University (J.D., 1987). ***COURSES: Business Associations, Agency/Partnership, Corporations, Sex-Based Discrimination, Local Government Law. ***Email:*** smays@law.capital.edu

KEN MEISSNER*, (Visiting Assistant Professor)**, born Brooklyn, New York, September 9, 1943; admitted to bar, 1976, California. *Education:* Santa Clara University (J.D., 1975); University of Washington (LL.M., 1996). ***COURSES: Tax. ***Email:*** kmeissner@law.capital.edu

ROBERTA S. MITCHELL*, (Professor of Law and Director, Center for Dispute Resolution)**, born Mansfield, Ohio, March 28, 1943; admitted to bar, 1972, Ohio. *Education:* West Virginia University (B.A., 1965); Capital University Law School (J.D., 1972). ***COURSES: Clinical, Dispute Resolution, Negotiation, Mediation, Interviewing and Counseling. ***Email:*** rmitchel@law.capital.edu

JEAN A. MORTLAND*, (Professor of Law)**, born Galion, Ohio, November 19, 1931; admitted to bar, 1964, Ohio. *Education:* Ohio State University (B.S., 1952); Capital University Law School (J.D., 1964); New York University School of Law (LL.M., 1969). ***COURSES: Property, Insurance, Conflict of Laws. ***Email:*** jmortlan@law.capital.edu

HAYWARD REYNOLDS*, (Professor of Law)**, born Hammond, Indiana, December 27, 1930; admitted to bar, 1966, Florida; 1978, Ohio. *Education:* Indiana University (A.B., 1953; J.D., 1965). ***COURSES: Jurisprudence, Comparative Law, Conflicts of Law. ***Email:*** hreynolds@law.capital.edu

ATHORNIA STEELE*, (Professor of Law)**, born Dayton, Ohio, November 10, 1951; admitted to bar, 1977, Ohio. *Education:* Capital University (B.A., 1974; J.D., 1977). ***COURSES: Agency, Partnership, Corporations, Securities Regulations, Corporate Finance. ***Email:*** asteele@law.capital.edu

MARK STRASSER*, (Professor of Law)**, born Bridgeport, Connecticut, June 15, 1955; admitted to bar, 1993, California. *Education:* Harvard University (B.A., 1977); University of Chicago (Ph.D., 1984); Stanford University (J.D., 1993). ***COURSES: Family Law, Jurisprudence, Professional Responsibility. ***Email:*** mstrasse@law.capital.edu

LANCE TIBBLES*, (Professor of Law)**, born Heppner, Oregon, September 29, 1938; admitted to bar, 1964, Oregon. *Education:* University of Oregon (B.S., with honors, 1960; LL.B., 1963). ***COURSES: Law and Medicine, Bioethics, Professional Responsibility. ***Email:*** ltibbles@law.capital.edu

DANIEL C. TURACK*, (Professor of Law)**, born Toronto, Ontario, Canada, October 5, 1934; admitted to bar, 1965, Ontario. *Education:* University of Toronto (B.A., 1957); Osgoode Hall (LL.B., 1960); University of Michigan (LL.M., 1961; S.J.D., 1969). ***COURSES: Contracts, Public International Law, Admiralty, Human Rights, Comparative Law, International Business Transactions. ***Email:*** dturack@law.capital.edu

ROBERT J. WADE*, (Professor of Law)**, born Martinsville, Indiana, October 24, 1938; admitted to bar, 1964, Indiana; 1972, Ohio. *Education:* Indiana University (B.S., 1960); University of Michigan (J.D., 1963); Southern Methodist University (LL.M., 1968). ***COURSES: Taxation. ***Email:*** rwade@law.capital.edu

FLOYD D. WEATHERSPOON*, (Professor of Law)**, admitted to bar, 1985, Ohio. *Education:* North Carolina A&T State University (B.S., 1971); Howard University (J.D., 1977). ***COURSES: Labor Law, Labor Relations, Employment Discrimination, Labor Arbitration. ***Email:*** fweatherspoon@law.capital.edu

N. DOUGLAS WELLS*, (Professor of Law)**, born Orangeburg, South Carolina, February 23, 1952; admitted to bar, 1981, Missouri; 1983, Tennessee. *Education:* Morehouse College (A.B., 1974); University of Tennessee (J.D., 1980); University of Illinois College of Law. ***COURSES: Property, Administrative Law, Family Law. ***Email:*** dwells@law.capital.edu

RICHARD J. WOOD*, (Professor of Law)**, born Binghamton, New York, December 3, 1951; admitted to bar, 1977, California. *Education:* University of Kentucky (B.A., 1974); Ohio State University (J.D., 1977); Georgetown University (LL.M., 1985). ***COURSES: Federal Tax, Agency, Partnership, Corporations. ***Email:*** rwood@law.capital.edu

---

CASE WESTERN RESERVE UNIVERSITY SCHOOL OF LAW

11075 EAST BOULEVARD
CLEVELAND, OHIO 44106
Telephone: (216) 368-3283
Fax: (216) 368-6144
Web: http://www.law.cwru.edu

ABA Approved Since 1923.

Case Western Reserve University School of Law traces its origins to 1892, when the Western Reserve University School of Law opened its doors. At a time when Cleveland was becoming a major industrial center, and consequently an important center for the practice of law, the local bar felt that the city should have its own university-affiliated law school. The law school received its current name in 1967 when Western Reserve University merged with the Case Institute of Technology.

From the beginning, the school has been a leader in legal education. The school always has required a three-year course of study, although in the late 1800's there were only half a dozen law schools requiring more than two years. Even more unusual was this school's requirement, instituted in 1911, that entering students have college degrees. At the time, only the Harvard and Columbia law schools had such a rule. The school was a pioneer in educating African-Americans and women for the bar; it admitted its first black student in 1892 and graduated its first woman in 1921. The school was fully accredited by the American Bar Association in 1924 and is a charter member of the Association of American Law Schools and the Order of the Coif.

The award-winning law school building is located in the heart of University Circle, a 500-acre area encompassing Case Western Reserve University and 70 other educational and cultural institutions. The building itself is a modern self-contained complex built in 1971 and expanded in 1994 to provide offices for the law journals and student organizations, a number of common areas, and small seminar rooms designed to accommodate upper-level courses, 70 percent of which have fewer than 40 students.

The library is a spacious one, containing more than 365,000 books and volume-equivalents. In addition, the school is distinguished as an electronic learning environment. Case Western Reserve University has

(This Listing Continued)

CASE WESTERN RESERVE UNIVERSITY SCHOOL OF LAW—Continued

installed a campus-wide fiber-optic cable network that has attracted national attention. The law school itself has computer facilities on every floor of the library, providing access to more than 700 electronic services and library catalogs, 75 CD-ROM applications, and a wide range of software services.

Case Western Reserve University School of Law offers the degrees of J.D., LL.M. in Taxation, and LL.M. in United States Legal Studies, as well as eight dual degrees: J.D./M.B.A., J.D./M.D., J.D./M.A. (legal history), J.D./M.A. (bioethics), J.D./M.S.S.A. (social work), J.D./M.P.H. (public health), J.D./M.S.M.-I.S. (Information Systems), and J.D./M.N.O. (nonprofit organizations). The school's J.D. enrollment is around 630, nearly all of them full-time students. They come from every area of the country, from more than 300 colleges and universities, and from dozens of different majors. Women make up nearly half the class, and students of color make up approximately 13 percent. More than 57 percent worked between college and law school. Many had prior careers in health care, business, science and engineering, government and nonprofit management, and more than 15 percent have advanced degrees.

The first-year curriculum consists of required courses - as well as one elective, including the Research, Analysis, and Writing (RAW) program, which is staffed by full-time instructors, all experienced lawyers. Each RAW section meets in a small group. After the first year every student must take Professional Responsibility and a course with a substantial writing requirement. Students may elect to pursue a concentration in one of four areas: Litigation, International Law, Health Law, Business Organizations, Public Law Concentration with tracks in Public and Regulatory Institutions, and Individual Rights and Social Reform.

In addition to traditional classes in substantive law, Case Western Reserve offers numerous professional skills courses. The school also offers a simulation course, The Lawyering Process, in which students conduct mock interviews and client counseling sessions, and practice negotiation skills. In the Milton A. Kramer Law Clinic Center, students represent actual clients in a law office setting. They keep time sheets, manage files, lead case conferences, draft documents, negotiate settlements and pleas, and represent clients in court, all under the supervision of full-time faculty who are experienced practitioners.

The school sponsors three student-edited journals: Case Western Reserve Law Review, the Journal of International Law, and Health Matrix: The Journal of Law-Medicine. Students also have the opportunity to participate in moot court and mock trial programs, as well as the Student Bar Association and more than 40 other organizations designed to further the goals of the school and the legal community.

The Law-Medicine Center focuses on the whole range of legal, social, economic, scientific, and ethical issues in which law and medicine are interrelated. The Center also sponsors lectures, major conferences, and smaller forums. The Health Matrix journal further contributes to the center's goal of immersing students in a broad range of health law issues.

The law school also prepares students for a global practice. Frederick K. Cox International Law Center has enabled the school to strengthen even further the international law curriculum, sponsor visiting scholars from around the world, and provide study and work opportunities for students. The Canada-U.S. Law Institute, sponsored with the law school of the University of Western Ontario, offers courses, co-curricular programs, and student exchanges.

Currently, the Case Western Reserve law school's full-time faculty numbers 49. As a result, the student-teacher ratio is about 13 to 1. In addition, there is a cadre of more than 80 adjunct faculty: judges and practitioners who teach a skills course or a substantive course in a specialized area such as admiralty law or juvenile law.

Alumni of the law school work in traditional and nontraditional legal careers throughout the world. The 8,200 living alumni are lawyers in firms of all sizes from solo practice to the world's largest law firms, corporate legal departments, government, and private enterprise. They are also well represented in the judiciary, politics, education, and cultural and philanthropic institutions. Graduates of CWRU include federal judges; all levels of local and state judges; members of Congress; officers at Fortune 500 corporations; faculty members at law schools throughout the country; and a best-selling novelist.

Dean: Gerald Korngold (216) 368-3283
Associate Dean for Academic Affairs: Andrew P. Morriss (216) 368-2085
Associate Dean for Development and Public Affairs: Sonia M. Winner (216) 368-4495
Assoc. Dean, Student Srvs Enrollment Plan., & Spec. Projects: Barbara Andelman (216) 368-3600
Director of the Law Library: Kathleen Carrick (216) 368-6357
Assistant Dean for Career Services: Susan Seliga (216) 368-6353

FULL TIME FACULTY

GERALD KORNGOLD*, (Dean and Everett D. and Eugenia S. McCurdy Professor)**, born Philadelphia, Pennsylvania, August 20, 1952; admitted to bar, 1977, Pennsylvania; 1979, District of Columbia; 1995, Ohio. *Education:* University of Pennsylvania (B.A., 1974; J.D., 1977). ***COURSES: Property, Real Estate, Wills, Trusts, and Future Interests. ***Email:*** gxk2@po.cwru.edu

BRYAN LAMAR ADAMSON*, (Associate Professor)**, born Warren, Ohio, June 7, 1963; admitted to bar, 1990, Ohio. *Education:* Miami University (B.S./ B.Phil., 1983); Purdue University (M.A., 1987); Case Western Reserve University (J.D., 1990). ***COURSES: Clinical Program. ***Email:*** bla@po.cwru.edu

JONATHAN H. ADLER*, (Assistant Professor)**, born Philadelphia, Pennsylvania, November 3, 1969; admitted to bar, 2000, Virginia. *Education:* Yale University (B.A., 1991); George Mason University (J.D., 2000). ***COURSES: Environmental Law, International Environmental Law Seminar, Constitutional Law. ***Email:*** jha5@po.cwru.edu

ARTHUR D. AUSTIN II*, (Edgar A. Hahn Professor)**, born Stanton, Virginia, December 2, 1932; admitted to bar, 1964, Virginia; 1970, District of Columbia. *Education:* University of Virginia (B.S., 1958); Tulane University (J.D., 1963). ***COURSES: Antitrust, Intellectual Property, Trends and Tensions in Legal Education, Contracts. ***Email:*** ada@po.cwru.edu

JESSICA WILEN BERG*, (Assistant Professor of Law and Biomedical Ethics)**, born January 31, 1970; admitted to bar, 1994, Massachusetts. *Education:* Cornell University (B.A., 1991); Cornell Law School (J.D., 1994). ***COURSES: Law and Bioethics. ***Email:*** jwb14@po.cwru.edu

DAVID J. CARNEY*, (Instructor)**, born Syracuse, New York, May 2, 1964; admitted to bar, 1989, Ohio. *Education:* Hiram College (B.A., 1986); University of Michigan (J.D., 1989). ***COURSES: Legal Writing, Appellate Advocacy. ***Email:*** djc5po.cwru.edu

(This Listing Continued)

CASE WESTERN RESERVE UNIVERSITY SCHOOL OF LAW—Continued

KATHLEEN MICHELE CARRICK*, (Associate Professor and Director of the Law Library)**, born Cleveland, Ohio, June 11, 1950; admitted to bar, 1977, Ohio. *Education:* Duquesne University (B.A., 1972); University of Pittsburgh (M.L.S., 1973); Cleveland State University (J.D., 1977). ***COURSES: Advanced Legal Information Systems. ***Email:*** kxc4@po.cwru.edu

WILLIAM M. CARTER*, (Assistant Professor)**, born Youngstown, Ohio, May 9, 1971; admitted to bar, 1998, Ohio; 2000, District of Columbia; 4th Circuit; 2001, U.S. District Court for the District of Columbia. *Education:* Bowling Green State University (B.S., 1994); Case Western Reserve University (J.D., 1998). ***COURSES: Civil Procedure, Civil Rights, International Human Rights. ***Email:*** wmc@po.cwru.edu

LAURA BROWN CHISOLM*, (Professor)**, born Washington, D.C., January 3, 1948; admitted to bar, 1981, Ohio. *Education:* University of Maryland; Case Western Reserve University (B.A., 1977; J.D., 1981). ***COURSES: Property, Wills & Trusts, and Future Interests, Law of Nonprofit Organizations, Legislation. ***Email:*** lbc@po.cwru.edu

HIRAM ELIAS CHODOSH*, (Professor and Director of the Frederick K. Cox International Law Center)**, born New Jersey, September 27, 1962; admitted to bar, 1992, New York. *Education:* Wesleyan University (B.A., 1985); Yale University (J.D., 1990). ***COURSES: Comparative and International Dispute Resolution Seminar, Comparisons of Laws, Conflict of Laws, Global Perspectives. ***Email:*** hxc22@po.cwru.edu

RONALD JOHN COFFEY*, (Professor)**, born Cincinnati, Ohio, September 27, 1936; admitted to bar, 1961, Ohio. *Education:* Xavier University (A.B., 1958); University of Cincinnati (LL.B., 1961); Harvard University (LL.M., 1966). ***COURSES: Business Associations, Securities Regulation, Advanced Securities Regulation. ***Email:*** rjc4@po.cwru.edu

GEORGE W. DENT, JR.*, (Schott - van den Eynden Professor of Business Organizations Law)**, born Danbury, Connecticut, July 7, 1947; admitted to bar, 1974, New York. *Education:* Columbia University (B.A., 1969; J.D., 1973); New York University (LL.M., 1981). ***COURSES: Business Associations, Mergers & Acquisitions, Business Planning. ***Email:*** gwd@po.cwru.edu

MELVYN R. DURCHSLAG*, (Professor)**, born Chicago, Illinois, September 26, 1940; admitted to bar, 1965, Illinois; 1967, Ohio. *Education:* Northwestern University (B.S., 1962; J.D., 1965). ***COURSES: Constitutional Law, State and Local Government. ***Email:*** mrd@po.cwru.edu

JONATHAN L. ENTIN*, (Professor of Law and Political Science)**, born Quincy, Massachusetts, August 24, 1947; admitted to bar, 1982, District of Columbia. *Education:* Brown University (A.B., 1969); Northwestern University (J.D., 1981). ***COURSES: Constitutional Law, Administrative Law, Social Science & Law, Supreme Court Seminar. ***Email:*** jle@po.cwru.edu

PETER BEN FRIEDMAN*, (Instructor and Director of Research, Analysis, and Writing Program)**, born Cleveland, Ohio, October 1, 1959; admitted to bar, 1985, New York. *Education:* Brown University (A.B., 1981); University of Michigan (J.D., 1984). ***COURSES: Legal Writing, Pretrial Practice, Contracts. ***Email:*** pbf2@po.cwru.edu

LEON GABINET*, (Professor and Executive Director of the Graduate Tax Program)**, born Ostrow, Poland, June 1, 1927; admitted to bar, 1955, Oregon; 1970, Ohio. *Education:* University of Chicago (Ph.B., 1950; J.D., 1953). ***COURSES: Corporate Tax Programs, Estate Planning and Taxation , Federal Income Tax, Tax Policy Seminar. ***Email:*** lxg5@po.cwru.edu

PETER MILTON GERHART*, (Professor)**, born Milwaukee, Wisconsin, July 4, 1945; admitted to bar, 1971, New York. *Education:* Northwestern University (B.A., 1967); Columbia University (J.D., 1971). ***COURSES: Antitrust, Intellectual Property, International Business Transactions, International Trade and Developments. ***Email:*** pmg2@po.cwru.edu

PAUL CHARLES GIANNELLI*, (Albert J. Weatherhead III and Richard J. Weatherhead Professor)**, born New York, New York, May 21, 1945; admitted to bar, 1970, Virginia; 1987, Ohio. *Education:* Providence College (B.A., 1967); George Washington University (M.S.F.S., 1973); University of Virginia (J.D., 1970; LL.M., 1975). ***COURSES: Criminal Procedure, Evidence , Scientific Evidence Seminar. ***Email:*** pcg@po.cwru.edu

JONATHAN CHARLES GORDON*, (Instructor)**, born Cleveland, Ohio, February 14, 1959; admitted to bar, 1986, Ohio. *Education:* Columbia College (B.A., 1981); Columbia University School of Law (J.D., 1985). ***COURSES: Legal Writing. ***Email:*** jcg4@po.cwru.edu

THOMAS I. HAUSMAN*, (Adjunct Professor and Administrative Director of LL.M. in Taxation Program)**, born Toledo, Ohio, August 12, 1948; admitted to bar, 1973, Ohio; 1974, Florida. *Education:* University of Colorado (B.A., 1970); Ohio State University (J.D., 1973); New York University (LL.M., 1976). ***COURSES: Business Planning, Corporate Tax Problems, Federal Income Taxation. ***Email:*** tih@po.cwru.edu

MICHAEL R. HEISE*, (Professor)**, born Chicago, Illinois, March 30, 1960; admitted to bar, 1987, Illinois. *Education:* Stanford University (A.B., 1983); University of Chicago (J.D., 1987); Northwestern University (Ph.D., 1990). ***COURSES: Constitutional Law, Business Torts, Education and Law Seminar and Law and Public Policy. ***Email:*** mxh94@po.cwru.edu

KATHERINE M. HESSLER*, (Associate Professor)**, born Rockville Center, New York, October 21, 1963; admitted to bar, 1989, Virginia; 1989, District of Columbia; 1996, Ohio. *Education:* George Washington University (B.A., 1985); William & Mary (J.D., 1987); Georgetown (L.L.M., 1997). ***COURSES: Clinical Program. ***Email:*** kmh25@po.cwru.edu

SHARONA HOFFMAN*, (Assistant Professor)**, born San Rafael, California, July 23, 1964; admitted to bar, 1988, California; 1989, District of Columbia; 1996, Texas. *Education:* Wellesley College (B.A., 1985); Harvard Law School (J.D., 1988); University of Houston (L.L.M., 1999). ***COURSES: Health Law and the Constitution, Employment Discrimination, Civil Procedure. ***Email:*** sxh90@po.cwru.edu

ERIK MICHAEL JENSEN*, (David L. Brennan Professor of Law)**, born Washington, D.C., August 26, 1945; admitted to bar, 1980, New York. *Education:* MIT (S.B., 1967); University of Chicago (M.A., 1972); Cornell University (J.D., 1979). ***COURSES: Taxation, American Indian Law, Business Planning. ***Email:*** emj@po.cwru.edu

D.R. JONES*, (Adjunct Instructor and Deputy Director of the Law Library)**, *Education:* Mercer University (B.A., 1979; J.D., 1982); Washington University (M.L.S., 1991);. ***Email: drj5@po.cwru.edu

LEWIS R. KATZ*, (John C. Hutchins Professor & Director, LL.M. in U.S. Legal Studies)**, born New York, November 15, 1938; admitted to bar, 1963, Indiana; 1973, Ohio. *Education:* Queens College (A.B., 1959); Indiana University (J.D., 1963). ***COURSES: Criminal Law, Criminal Procedure, Foreign Graduate Seminar. ***Email:*** lrk@cwru.edu

***HENRY THOMAS KING, JR.*, (Professor and U.S. Director of the Canada-U.S. Law Institute)**, born Meriden, Connecticut, May 27, 1919; admitted to bar, 1943, Connecticut; 1946, New York; 1960,

(This Listing Continued)

CASE WESTERN RESERVE UNIVERSITY SCHOOL OF LAW—Continued

District of Columbia; 1963, Ohio. *Education:* Yale University (B.A., 1941; LL.B., 1943). ***COURSES:*** International Arbitration.

JULIET P. KOSTRITSKY, **(John Homer Kapp Professor)**, born Eugene, Oregon, June 10, 1954; admitted to bar, 1981, New York. *Education:* Harvard University (A.B., 1976); University of Wisconsin (J.D., 1980). ***COURSES:*** Contracts, Property, Commercial Paper. ***Email:*** jpk3@po.cwru.edu

ROBERT P. LAWRY, **(Professor and Director of the Center for Professional Ethics)**, born Pittsburgh, Pennsylvania, March 19, 1941; admitted to bar, 1967, Pennsylvania. *Education:* Fordham University (B.A., 1963); University of Pennsylvania (J.D., 1966); Oxford University (Dip. in Law, 1967). ***COURSES:*** Professional Responsibility, Jurisprudence, Criminal Law, International Organization, Ethics in the Profession. ***Email:*** rpl2@po.cwru.edu

WILBUR CHARLES LEATHERBERRY, **(Professor and Director of Skills Courses and Advocacy Programs)**, born Canton, Ohio, June 18, 1943; admitted to bar, 1968, Ohio. *Education:* Case Western Reserve University (A.B., 1965; J.D., 1968). ***COURSES:*** Contracts, Insurance, Sales. ***Email:*** wcl@po.cwru.edu

KENNETH F. LEDFORD, **(Associate Professor of History and Law)**, born Gulfport, Mississippi, August 17, 1953; admitted to bar, 1978, Virginia. *Education:* University of North Carolina (B.A., 1975; J.D., 1978); Johns Hopkins University (Ph.D., 1989). ***COURSES:*** European Legal Professions, European Union Law. ***Email:*** kx115@po.cwru.edu

JACQUELINE D. LIPTON, **(Assistant Professor)**, born Cleveland, Ohio, January 6, 1967; admitted to bar, 1993, State of Victoria, Australia and High Court of Australia. *Education:* University of Melbourne (B.A., 1989); La Trobe University (B.A., 1991); Monash University (LL.M., 1995); Cambridge University (LL.M., 1998); University of Melbourne (LL.B., 1992); Griffith University (Ph.D., 2001). ***COURSES:*** Commercial Information and the Law, Cyberlaw, International Business Transactions. ***Email:*** jdl14@po.cwru.edu

JUDITH P. LIPTON, **(Professor and Co-director of Milton A. Kramer Law Clinic Center)**, born Connecticut, April 7, 1949; admitted to bar, 1979, Connecticut; 1980, Ohio. *Education:* University of Wisconsin (B.S., 1971; M.S.S.W., 1972); University of Connecticut (J.D., 1979). ***COURSES:*** Clinical Program. ***Email:*** jpl@po.cwru.edu

KENNETH R. MARGOLIS, **(Professor and Co-director of Milton A. Kramer Law Clinic Center)**, born Cleveland, Ohio, September 25, 1950; admitted to bar, 1976, California; 1978, Ohio. *Education:* University of California (B.A., 1972); Case Western Reserve University (J.D., 1976). ***COURSES:*** Clinical Program, Federal Judicial Externship. ***Email:*** krm@po.cwru.edu

JAMES WILSON MCELHANEY, **(Joseph C. Hostetler Professor)**, born New York, New York, December 10, 1937; admitted to bar, 1962, Wisconsin. *Education:* Duke University (A.B., 1960; LL.B., 1962). ***COURSES:*** Trial Tactics, Evidence, Civil Procedure.

LOUISE WENNER MCKINNEY, **(Professor)**, born Philadelphia, Pennsylvania, June 2, 1942; admitted to bar, 1978, Ohio. *Education:* Heidelberg College (B.A., 1963); Case Western Reserve University (J.D., 1978). ***COURSES:*** Clinical Program. ***Email:*** lem4@po.cwru.edu

KEVIN C. MCMUNIGAL, **(Judge Ben C. Green Professor of Law)**, born Chester, Pennsylvania, December 23, 1950; admitted to bar, 1979, California. *Education:* Stanford (B.A., 1973); University of California, Berkeley (J.D., 1979). ***COURSES:*** Professional Responsibility, Federal Criminal Law, Evidence, Criminal Law. ***Email:*** kcm@po.cwru.edu

MAXWELL JONATHAN MEHLMAN, **(Arthur E. Petersilge Professor of Law, Professor of Biomedical Ethics, Director, Law-Medicine Center)**, born Washington, D.C., November 4, 1948; admitted to bar, 1975, District of Columbia; 1988, Ohio. *Education:* Reed (B.A., 1970); Oxford University (B.A., 1972); Yale (J.D., 1975). ***COURSES:*** Health Law, Torts. ***Email:*** mjm@po.cwru.edu

KATHRYN SORDS MERCER, **(Instructor)**, born Cleveland, Ohio, January 25, 1956; admitted to bar, 1983, Ohio. *Education:* Duke University (A.B., 1977); Case Western Reserve (M.S.S.A., 1983; J.D., 1983; Ph.D, 1997). ***COURSES:*** Legal Writing, Lawyering Process, Alternative Dispute Resolution, Family Law. ***Email:*** klm7@po.cwru.edu

ANDREW PETTIT MORRISS, **(Assoc. Dean, Academic Affairs, Gallen J. Roush Prof. of Business Law and Regulation, Assoc. Prof., Economics)**, born Philadelphia, Pennsylvania, July 16, 1960; admitted to bar, 1985, Texas. *Education:* Princeton University (A.B., 1981); University of Texas (J.D., 1984); MIT (Ph.D., 1994). ***COURSES:*** Employment Law, Law & Economics, Administrative Law, Property, International Economic Integration. ***Email:*** apm5@po.cwru.edu

CRAIG ALLEN NARD, **(Professor and Director of Center for Law, Technology and the Arts)**, born Charleroi, Pennsylvania, August 16, 1965; admitted to bar, 1990, Texas; 1997, Patent Bar. *Education:* Washington & Jefferson College (B.A., 1987); Capital University (J.D., 1990); Columbia University (LL.M.,1995; J.S.D., 1999). ***COURSES:*** Patent Law, Intellectual Property, Intellectual Property Theory.

SPENCER NETH, **(Professor)**, born Piqua, Ohio, August 14, 1939; admitted to bar, 1964, Ohio; 1966, Massachusetts. *Education:* Miami University (A.B., 1961); Harvard University (J.D., 1964; LL.M., 1966). ***COURSES:*** Contracts, Consumer Protection, Products Liability, Commercial Law. ***Email:*** sxn6@po.cwru.edu

SIDNEY I. PICKER, JR., **(Professor)**, born New York, New York, July 7, 1934; admitted to bar, 1960, California; 1973, Ohio. *Education:* Dartmouth College (A.B., 1956); Stanford University (LL.B., 1959); Yale University (LL.M., 1960). ***COURSES:*** International Law, International Trade, International Negotiation. ***Email:*** sxps@po.cwru.edu

MORRIS G. SHANKER, **(Professor)**, born Cleveland, Ohio, August 23, 1926; admitted to bar, 1952, Ohio. *Education:* Purdue University (B.S.Eng., 1948); University of Michigan (M.B.A., 1952; J.D., 1952). ***COURSES:*** Sales, Property Security, Debtor-Creditor Law. ***Email:*** mxs15@po.cwru.edu

CALVIN WILLIAM SHARPE, **(John Deaver Drinko-Baker & Hostetler Professor)**, born Greensboro, North Carolina, February 22, 1945. *Education:* Clark College (B.A., 1967); Northwestern University (J.D., 1974); Chicago Theological Seminary (M.A., 1996). ***COURSES:*** Employment Law, Evidence, Labor Arbitration and Collective Bargaining, Labor Law, Alternative Dispute Resolution. ***Email:*** cws2@po.cwru.edu

ANN SOUTHWORTH, **(Professor)**, born Corning, New York, July 6, 1960; admitted to bar, 1986, California; 1987, District of Columbia. *Education:* Princeton University; Stanford University (B.A., 1982; J.D., 1985). ***COURSES:*** American Legal Profession, Professional Responsibility, Civil Procedure. ***Email:*** axs76@po.cwru.edu

THEODORE L. STEINBERG, **(Professor of History and Law)**, born Brooklyn, New York, April 25, 1961. *Education:* Tufts University (B.A., 1983); Brandeis University (Ph.D., 1989). ***COURSES:*** Environmental History and Law Seminar, Social History and Law Seminar. ***Email:*** txs18@po.cwru.edu

ROBERT N. STRASSFELD, **(Professor)**, born Boston, Massachusetts, July 1, 1954; admitted to bar, 1985, Maryland; 1988, District of

(This Listing Continued)

CASE WESTERN RESERVE UNIVERSITY SCHOOL OF LAW—Continued

Columbia. *Education:* Wesleyan University (B.A., 1976); University of Rochester (M.A., 1980); University of Virginia (J.D., 1984). ***COURSES:*** Labor Law, Legal History, Torts, Vietnam War and the Law. ***Email:*** rns3@po.cwru.edu

CAROL A. TUROWSKI,* (Assistant Professor)**, born 1961; admitted to bar, 1988, New York. *Education:* City University of New York (B.A., 1982; J.D., 1987); Columbia (M.A., 1997). ***COURSES: Clinical Program. ***Email:*** cat8@po.cwru.edu

THE CATHOLIC UNIVERSITY OF AMERICA COLUMBUS SCHOOL OF LAW

WASHINGTON, D.C. 20064
Telephone: (202) 319-5144
Fax: (202) 319-4498
www.law.edu

ABA Approved Since 1925.

The School of Law at The Catholic University of America is committed to excellence in legal education within the profound intellectual tradition of the Church. Giving priority to the sacred dignity and uniqueness of each human person, the law school program is a standing invitation for men and women to pursue a professional calling fully informed by faith, moral inquiry and respect for the rule of law. The rigorous course of study embodies, in the words of the university's first rector, "the harmony between reason and revelation... and the genius of America."

Founded by Pope Leo XIII in the late 19th Century, The Catholic University of America maintains a singular charter and standing both within the Church in America and around the world. Welcoming students and faculty of all faiths ever since its inception in 1897, the School of Law understands legal training as a form of servant-leadership enabling lawyers to take up the burdens of others and make possible a civil and peaceful life in accord with God's creative design. Often referenced as the Columbus School of Law because of its alliance with an early program of legal education supported by the Knights of Columbus, the 1.6 million "strong right arm" of the lay Church, the CUA law school has been accredited by the Association of American Law Schools since 1921 and the American Bar Association since 1925.

The CUA law faculty are well-recognized for their teaching and scholarly distinction throughout a comprehensive and well-structured curriculum. The law school takes full advantage of its strategic location just minutes from the Congress and the Supreme Court by enlivening required study with presentations by national and international decision-makers, either as adjunct faculty or distinguished lecturers. The highly regarded Institutes in Law and Religion as well as Law and Public Policy introduce students to the jurisprudential sources and legislative, administrative and empirical methods necessary to make law both just and effective. Another Institute dealing with Comparative and International Law prepares law students for global legal work and is attractively augmented by a sought-after summer program. Conducted at The 14th Century Jagiellonian University, one of Europe's most prestigious universities, CUA students study, not as insulated sightseers, but collaboratively with their international peers. And long before other law schools incorporated a few classes discussing the Internet and advanced technology, CUA's Communications Law Institute has been inviting talented students to address the multi-faceted legal problems of new and established forms of media in courses and integrated fieldwork with the FCC, Congress and the telecommunications industry, itself. Guided by the Church's preferential option for the poor and believing that the measure of any society is how it treats its most vulnerable citizens, CUA law school is the acknowledged pioneer in clinical legal instruction in Washington, D.C. The school's Columbus Community Legal Services translates faith into action by meeting the needs of the elderly, the oppressed, and the least advantaged with compassion and dedication.

The CUA School of Law occupies a state-of-the-art facility completed in 1994 and situated amidst the university's venerable stone structures and spacious tree-lined quadrangles. The 170,000 square foot law building with ample library, classroom, student activity, and office space is built around a magnificent atrium. Our alumni are privileged to serve in both high elective and appointed office and as principals in law firms and businesses across the nation. In the profession, the families they nourish, and the communities they build or sustain, are the living testament to CUA's commitment to excellence shaped by faith.

The law school's enrollment of more than 900 students in day and evening divisions is an ideal size for a broad educational experience in a small school setting. The first-year day class of approximately 230 and the evening class of approximately 70 students are sectioned so that individual courses have 32 to 65 students. Upperclass course size ranges from 10 to 80 students. The law school typically receives about eight applications for each space in the entering class. The student body is diverse with 28 percent minority students, 50 percent women, and about 225 undergraduate schools, 50 states and about eight foreign countries represented. Fewer than 50 percent of the students enter directly from college.

Co-curricular activities include three student-edited scholarly journals -- *Catholic University Law Review, COMMLAW Conspectus: Journal of Communications Law and Policy,* and the *Journal of Contemporary Health Law and Policy*; the Thurgood Marshall American Inn of Court; and the Moot Court Association, which sponsors interschool and intraschool competitions throughout the academic year.

Dean: Douglas W. Kmiec
Associate Dean for Academic Affairs: William F. Fox, Jr.
Associate Dean for External and Student Affairs: Mara R. Duffy
Associate Dean for Administration: Michael A. Kanne
Associate Dean for Institutional Advancement: Margaret A. King
Assistant Dean for External and Student Affairs: Frank A. Grosso
Assistant Dean for Academic Affairs: Georgia Niedzielko
Assistant Dean for Academic Services: Natividad V. Garcia
Director of Admissions: Eric J. Eden
Director of Legal Career Services: Kristen McManus

(This Listing Continued)

THE CATHOLIC UNIVERSITY OF AMERICA COLUMBUS SCHOOL OF LAW—Continued

FULL TIME FACULTY

DOUGLAS W. KMIEC*, (Dean and Saint Thomas More Professor of Law)**, born Chicago, Illinois, September 24, 1951; admitted to bar, 1976, Illinois; 1980, California. *Education:* Northwestern University (B.A., with honors, 1973); University of Southern California (J.D., 1976). ***COURSES: Constitutional Law, Property, Catholic Social Teaching, Jurisprudence and the Law.

HELEN M. ALVARE*, (Associate Professor)**, born Lansdowne, Pennsylvania, October 8, 1960; admitted to bar, 1984, Pennsylvania; District of Columbia, 1987. *Education:* Villanova University (B.S., 1981); Catholic University of America (M.A., 1989); Cornell University (J.D., 1984). ***COURSES: Property. ***Email:*** alvare@law.edu

***HON. SYLVIA BACON*, (Judge-in-Residence)**

LOUIS J. BARRACATO*, (Associate Professor)**, born 1941; admitted to bar, 1966, District of Columbia. *Education:* Fairfield University (B.S.S., 1962); Catholic University of America Columbus School of Law (J.D., 1965). ***COURSES: Evidence, Trial Advocacy, Professional Responsibility.

MARGARET M. BARRY*, (Associate Professor)**, born 1953; admitted to bar, 1981, Virgin Islands; 1985, Maryland and District of Columbia. *Education:* Luther College (B.A., 1975); University of Minnesota (J.D., 1980). ***COURSES: Families and the Law Clinic.

MAXWELL H. BLOOMFIELD, III*, (Professor Emeritus of Law, Professor Emeritus of History)**, born 1931; admitted to bar, 1957, Texas. *Education:* Rice University (B.A., 1952); Harvard Law School (LL.B., 1957); Tulane University (Ph.D., 1962). ***COURSES: History of Early American Law, History of Modern American Law, Law and Literature.

MARSHALL J. BREGER*, (Professor and Director, Health Law Institute)**, born 1946; admitted to bar, 1974, New York; 1989, District of Columbia. *Education:* University of Pennsylvania (B.A., M.A., 1967); Oriel College, Oxford University (B.Phil., 1970); University of Pennsylvania Law School (J.D., 1973). ***COURSES: Administrative Law, Advanced Administrative Law, Introduction to International Arbitration and Mediation, Alternative Dispute Resolution, Separation of Power.

STACY L. BRUSTIN*, (Assistant Professor)**, born 1963; admitted to bar, 1989, Illinois; 1990, District of Columbia. *Education:* Tufts University (B.A., 1985); Harvard Law School (J.D., 1989). ***COURSES: The General Practice Clinic.

LEROY D. CLARK*, (Professor)**, born 1934; admitted to bar, 1961, New York. *Education:* City College of New York (B.A., 1956); Columbia University (LL.B., 1961). ***COURSES: Criminal Law, Criminal Procedure, Fair Employment Law, Labor Law.

ROBERT A. DESTRO*, (Professor)**, born 1950; admitted to bar, 1975, California; 1976, Ohio. *Education:* Miami University (B.A., 1972); University of California at Berkeley (J.D., 1975). ***COURSES: Constitutional Law, Professional Responsibility, Conflict of Laws, First Amendment Seminar, Religious Liberty, The Law of Church/State Relations.

SARAH HELENE DUGGIN*, (Visiting Associate Professor)**, born Philadelphia, Pennsylvania, June 22, 1954; admitted to bar, 1980, Pennsylvania. *Education:* Smith College (A.B., 1976); University of Pennsylvania (J.D., 1979). ***COURSES: Constitutional Law, Corporations.

SUSANNA FREDERICK FISHER*, (Assistant Professor)**, *Education:* Princeton University (A.B., 1987); University of Oxford (Merion College) (B.A., Jurisprudence, 1987); University of Virginia (LL.M., 1995). ***COURSES: Civil Procedure, Copywrite, Cyberlaw.

CLIFFORD S. FISHMAN*, (Professor)**, born 1945; admitted to bar, 1969, New York; 1979, District of Columbia; 1980, Maryland. *Education:* University of Rochester (B.A., 1966); Columbia University School of Law (J.D., 1969). ***COURSES: Criminal Law, Criminal Procedure, Administration of Criminal Justice, Advanced Criminal Procedure, Evidence.

WILLIAM F. FOX, JR.*, (Associate Dean for Academic Affairs and Professor)**, born 1942; admitted to bar, 1973, New Mexico; 1977, District of Columbia. *Education:* George Washington University (B.G.S., 1970); Catholic University of America Columbus School of Law (J.D., 1972); Harvard Law School (LL.M., 1974). ***COURSES: Civil Procedure, Administrative Law, Alternative Dispute Resolution Techniques, Federal Courts, International Business Transactions, Natural Resources Law and Policy.

GEORGE E. GARVEY*, (Professor)**, born 1942; admitted to bar, 1972, Wisconsin. *Education:* University of Illinois (B.A., 1969); University of Wisconsin (J.D., 1972). ***COURSES: Constitutional Law, Corporations, Antitrust, Advanced Antitrust, International Economic Regulations, Property, Regulated Industries, Unfair Trade Practices.

JOHN L. GARVEY*, (Professor Emeritus)**, born 1927; admitted to bar, 1948, District of Columbia and Kentucky. *Education:* Xavier University, Cincinnati (A.B., 1945; LL.D., 1978); The Catholic University of America Columbus School of Law (J.D., 1948); University of Michigan (S.J.D., 1967). ***COURSES: Trusts and Estates, Federal Taxation of Wealth Transfers, Remedies.

***REV. DAVID J.K. GRANFIELD, O.S.B.*, (Professor Emeritus)**, *Education:* College of the Holy Cross (A.B., 1944); Harvard University Law School (LL.B., 1947); The Catholic University of America (M.A., 1953; S.T.D., 1962), Columbus School of Law Since 1960.

ROGER C. HARTLEY*, (Professor)**, born 1943; admitted to bar, 1970, Pennsylvania; 1973, District of Columbia. *Education:* Cornell University (B.S., 1965); University of Pittsburgh (J.D., 1970); George Washington University National Law Center (LL.M., 1972). ***COURSES: Constitutional Law; Federal Courts; Labor Law, Labor Law, Seminars: Collective Bargaining and Labor Arbitration and Rights of Individuals with Disabilities, Appellate Advocacy; *Law Review* Advisor.

REGINA T. JEFFERSON*, (Professor)**, born 1958; admitted to bar, 1987, Maryland; 1988, District of Columbia. *Education:* Howard University (B.S., 1981); George Washington University National Law Center (J.D., 1987); Georgetown University Law Center (LL.M., 1991). ***COURSES: Federal Income Taxation, Partnership Taxation, ERISA: Pensions (Tax Policy).

WILLIAM A. KAPLIN*, (Professor)**, born 1942; admitted to bar, 1968, District of Columbia. *Education:* University of Rochester (A.B., 1964); Cornell University (J.D., 1967). ***COURSES: Comparative Constitutional Law, Advanced Constitutional Law: First Amendment, Civil Rights Law, Education Law, Education Law Practice: A Simulated Lawyering Experience, Health Law Journal I and II.

KATHRYN KELLY*, (Associate Professor)**, born 1953; admitted to bar, 1978, District of Columbia; 1984, Maryland. *Education:* Butler University (B.A., 1975); University of Notre Dame Law School (J.D., 1978). ***COURSES: Torts, Evidence, Civil Procedure, Complex Litigation, Seminar, Interviewing, Counseling and Negotiation Skills.

***CATHERINE F. KLEIN*, (Associate Professor)**, born 1952; admitted

(This Listing Continued)

THE CATHOLIC UNIVERSITY OF AMERICA COLUMBUS SCHOOL OF LAW—Continued

to bar, 1978, Ohio; 1979, District of Columbia. *Education:* Northwestern University (B.A., 1974); University of Cincinnati (J.D., 1978). ***COURSES:*** Families and the Law Clinic.

LISA G. LERMAN*, (Professor and Director, Law and Public Policy Program)**, born 1955; admitted to bar, 1979, District of Columbia. *Education:* Barnard College, Columbia University (B.A., 1976); New York University School of Law (J.D., 1979); Georgetown University Law Center (LL.M., 1984). ***COURSES: Contracts, Professional Responsibility, Legal Externship: Becoming a Lawyer, Public Policy Practicum.

URBAN A. LESTER*, (Associate Professor)**, born 1929; admitted to bar, 1962, District of Columbia. *Education:* The Catholic University of America (B.A., 1954); Catholic University of America Columbus School of Law (1959). ***COURSES: Civil Procedure, Professional Responsibility, Corporations, Federal Litigation, Federal Practice and Procedure, Remedies, Trial Advocacy.

DAVID A. LIPTON*, (Professor)**, born 1945; admitted to bar, 1973, New York; 1982, District of Columbia. *Education:* Cornell University (B.A., 1966); Columbia University (M.A., 1968); University of Michigan Law School (J.D., 1972). ***COURSES: Corporate Finance Seminar, Corporations, Securities Markets Regulation Seminar, Securities Regulation: Issuance, Securities Regulations: Trading, SEC Student Training Program.

RETT R. LUDWIKOWSKI*, (Professor and Director, Comparative and International Law Institute)**, born 1943; admitted to bar, 1973, Poland. *Education:* Jagiellonian University (M.A.Law, 1966; Ph.D.Law, 1971; Ph.D., 1976). ***COURSES: Comparative Law, Comparative and International Trade, Law of the European Union, Public International Law, Post-Socialist Legal Systems.

RAYMOND B. MARCIN*, (Professor)**, born 1938; admitted to bar, 1964, Connecticut; 1974, District of Columbia. *Education:* St. John's Seminary (A.B., 1959); Fairfield University (A.B., 1961); Fordham University School of Law (J.D., 1964); Catholic University of America (M.S.L.S., 1984). ***COURSES: Civil Procedure, Constitutional Law, Family Law, Legisprudence, Remedies, Catholic Natural Law Tradition.

***STEPHEN G. MARGETON*, (Director of Law Library and Professor)**, born 1945. *Education:* Mt. St. Mary's College (A.B., 1967); George Washington University National Law Center (J.D., 1970); Catholic University of America (M.S.L.S., 1973).

VERYL V. MILES*, (Professor)**, born 1955; admitted to bar, 1980, District of Columbia; 1986, Virginia. *Education:* Wells College (B.A., 1977); Catholic University of America Columbus School of Law (J.D., 1980). ***COURSES: Bankruptcy, Commercial Transaction, Creditors' and Debtors' Rights, Sales.

BENJAMIN W. MINTZ*, (Professor)**, born 1927; admitted to bar, 1954, New York. *Education:* Brooklyn College (A.B., 1948); Columbia University (LL.B., 1952); Yeshiva University (Ord., 1954). ***COURSES: Administrative Law, Advanced Administrative Law, Appellate Advocacy, Contemporary Social Issues Under Jewish Law, Professional Responsibility, Law and Public Policy, Employment Law, Legislation.

MICHAEL F. NOONE, JR.*, (Professor)**, born 1934; admitted to bar, 1957, California and District of Columbia. *Education:* Georgetown University (B.S., 1955; LL.B., 1957; LL.M., 1962); George Washington National Law Center (S.J.D., 1965). ***COURSES: Torts, Federal Litigation, Products Liability, Seminar, Remedies, Comparative Law Seminar: Political Violence.

REV. RAYMOND C. O'BRIEN*, (Professor)**, born 1944; admitted to bar, 1969, Virginia; 1978, District of Columbia. *Education:* La Salle College (A.B., 1966); University of Virginia (J.D., 1969); Catholic University of America (M.Ch.A., 1975; D.Min., 1985). ***COURSES: Trusts & Estates, Family Law.

J.P. OGILVY*, (Associate Professor & Coordinator of Clinical Programs)**, born 1945; admitted to bar, 1973, Oregon; 1977, Ohio; 1980, New York; 1981, District of Columbia; 1985, Texas. *Education:* Portland State University (B.A., 1968); Northwestern School of Law of Lewis and Clark College (J.D., 1973); Georgetown University Law Center (LL.M., 1982). ***COURSES: Civil Procedure; Interviewing, Counseling ; Mediation and Negotiation, Legal Internship; Becoming a Law: D.C. Law Students in Courts.

KENNETH JAMES PENNINGTON*, (Professor)**, born Salem, New Jersey, October 06, 1941. *Education:* University of Wisconsin (B.A., 1965; M.A., 1967); Cornell University (Ph.D., 1972). ***COURSES: Legal History.

ANTONIO F. PEREZ*, (Associate Professor)**, born 1958; admitted to bar, 1986, New York; 1987, District of Columbia. *Education:* Harvard University (A.B., 1982); Columbia University School of Law (J.D., 1985). ***COURSES: Contracts, Public International Law, International Economic Regulation, Anti-Trust, International Regulation of Telecommunications, *Law Review* Advisor.

RALPH J. ROHNER*, (Professor)**, born 1938; admitted to bar, 1964, Maryland. *Education:* The Catholic University of America (A.B., 1960); Catholic University of America, Columbus School of Law (J.D., 1963). ***COURSES: Commercial Transactions, Consumer Transactions, Sales and Leases, Consumer Law Seminar.

SILVIA GONZALEZ ROMAN*, (Visiting Associate Professor)**, born Havana, Cuba, December 18, 1959; admitted to bar, 1983, District of Columbia. *Education:* Adelphi University (B.A., 1980); George Washington University, The National Law Center (J.D., 1983). ***COURSES: Criminal Law and Criminal Procedure.

HEIDI M. SCHOONER*, (Associate Professor)**, born 1960; admitted to bar, 1985, Virginia; 1987, District of Columbia. *Education:* Duke University (A.B., 1982); Georgetown University Law Center (J.D., 1985). ***COURSES: Contracts, Commercial Transactions, Banking Law, Corporations.

ELLEN M. SCULLY*, (Clinical Assistant Professor and Director of Columbus Community Legal Services)**, born 1942; admitted to bar, 1967, Massachusetts; 1971, District of Columbia. *Education:* Salve Regina University (A.B., 1964); Catholic University of America Columbus School of Law (J.D., 1967). ***COURSES: Advocacy for the Elderly, General Practice Clinic, The Families and Law Clinic.

LUCIA ANN SILECCHIA*, (Associate Professor)**, born 1967; admitted to bar, 1990, Connecticut; 1991, District of Columbia and New York. *Education:* Queens College, City University of New York (B.A., 1987); Yale Law School (J.D., 1990). ***COURSES: Corporations, Environmental Law, Property, Advanced Legal Writing and Research, Environmental Crimes.

KARLA W. SIMON*, (Professor)**, born 1947; admitted to bar, 1972, North Carolina. *Education:* Western College (B.A., 1969); Duke University School of Law (J.D., 1972); New York University School of Law (LL.M., 1976). ***COURSES: Administrative Law, Corporate Taxation, Federal Income Taxation, International and Comparative Taxation, Not-for-Profit Organization Law.

GEORGE P. SMITH, II*, (Professor)**, born 1939; admitted to bar, 1964, Indiana; 1969, District of Columbia. *Education:* Indiana University, Bloomington (B.S., 1961; J.D., 1964); Columbia University (LL.M., 1975); Indiana University (L.L.D., 1998). ***COURSES: Property; Environmental Law; Health Law; *Health Law Journal* I and II; Law, Science and Medicine; Public International Law; Land Use.

(This Listing Continued)

THE CATHOLIC UNIVERSITY OF AMERICA COLUMBUS SCHOOL OF LAW—Continued

HON. FRED B. UGAST, **(Judge-in-Residence)**

WILLIAM J. WAGNER, **(Professor and Director, The Interdisciplinary Program in Law and Religion)**, born 1951; admitted to bar, 1979, New York; 1986, District of Columbia. *Education:* University of California, Los Angeles (B.A., 1975); Yale Law School (J.D., 1978); Catholic University of America (M.A., 1983). ***COURSES:*** Constitutional Law, Contracts, Family Law, Jurisprudence, Law and Literature, Sources of Christian Jurisprudence.

G. GRAHAM WAITE, **(Professor Emeritus)**, *Education:* University of Wisconsin (B.S., 1947; LL.B., 1950; S.J.D., 1958).

GEOFFREY R. WATSON, **(Professor)**, born 1960; admitted to bar, 1987, Massachusetts. *Education:* Yale College (B.A., 1982); Harvard Law School (J.D., 1986). ***COURSES:*** Contracts, Comparative Law, Conflicts of Law, Criminal Law, Public International Law, History of Early American law, History of Modern American Law.

LEAH WORTHAM, **(Associate Professor)**, born 1948; admitted to bar, 1973, Georgia; 1981, District of Columbia. *Education:* Macalester College (B.A., 1970); Harvard Law School (J.D., 1973). ***COURSES:*** Professional Responsibility, Becoming a Lawyer, Criminal Law.

HARVEY L. ZUCKMAN, **(Professor and Director, Institute for Communications Law Studies)**, born 1934; admitted to bar, 1960, California; 1971, District of Columbia. *Education:* University of Southern California (A.B., 1956); New York University School of Law (LL.B., 1959). ***COURSES:*** Torts, Family Law, First Amendment Problems of the Media, *CommLaw Conspectus I and II.*

CHAPMAN UNIVERSITY LAW SCHOOL

1 UNIVERSITY DRIVE
ORANGE, CALIFORNIA 92866
Telephone: (714) 628-2500
Fax: (714) 628-2501
http://www.chapman.edu/law/index.html

ABA Approved Since 1998 (Provisional)

Chapman University is a 138-year old, independent institution of liberal arts and professional training dedicated to providing a solid foundation of knowledge that enables its graduates to become fully educated members of society. Chapman University began formal study on the feasibility of establishing a School of Law in May 1993. Based on the findings and recommendation of the committee, the university announced the establishment of a new law school in September 1994. The first class commenced in August 1995 in temporary quarters. Construction began in 1997 on a new state-of-the-art building to house the School of Law. The building is located on the Orange campus. It was completed the spring of 1999 and now houses the Law School.

The American Bar Association (ABA) granted provisional approval to Chapman University School of Law in February 1998.

The law school library collection consists of more than 244,000 volumes and equivalents. The Library utilizes the INNOPAC system for its on-line public access catalog, including other modules used for various library functions.

The law school student body numbers approximately 325, with a recent entering class of 135 for the fall 2001 term. The faculty numbers 24, 10 of whom are women.

Admission to the law school is gained by committee approval, based on applicant's credentials. Although the LSAT and GPA are the most important factors in the admissions process, other considerations are: professional experience, volunteer and community service, letters of recommendation, unusual achievement, special circumstances, honors, class diversity, economic hardship, trend of grades, completion of graduate level work, previous attendance at another law school and a record on integrity and law compliance.

The school graduated its first class in May 1998.

Vice President and Dean: Parham Williams (714) 628-2555
Associate Dean for Academic Affairs: Scott Howe (714) 628-2516
Associate Dean for Student Services: Joanne Punu (714) 628-2550
Director of the Law Library: Sheryl Summers Kramer (714) 628-2537
Director of Development: Susan Jenkins (714) 628-2518
Director of Financial Aid: Peggy Crawford (714) 628-2510
Assistant Dean of Career Services/Externship: Vicki M. Huebner (714) 628-2517
Registrar: Maryam Isles (714) 628-2513

FULL TIME FACULTY

PARHAM H. WILLIAMS, **(Vice President and Dean)**, born Lexington, Mississippi, June 8, 1931; admitted to bar, 1954, Mississippi. *Education:* University of Mississippi (B.A., 1953; LL.B., 1954); Yale Law School (LL.M., 1965). ***Email:*** wilham@chapman.edu

---

CRAIG ANTHONY ARNOLD, **(Associate Professor of Law)**, born Montreal, Canada, May 22, 1965; admitted to bar, 1990, Missouri; 1992, Texas. *Education:* University of Kansas (B.A., 1987); Stanford Law School (J.D., 1990). ***COURSES:*** Property, Land Use, Environmental Law, Land Development & the Environment. ***Email:*** caarnold@chapman.edu

TOM W. BELL, **(Associate Professor)**, admitted to bar, 1993, California. *Education:* University of Kansas/University de Nice (B.A., 1987); University of Southern California (M.A., 1989); University of Chicago School of Law (J.D., 1993). ***COURSES:*** Intellectual Property, Contracts, Agency, Partnerships, & Unincorporated Bus. Assoc. ***Email:*** tbell@chapman.edu

DENIS BINDER, **(Professor of Law)**, born San Francisco, California, May 14, 1946; admitted to bar, 1971, California. *Education:* University of San Francisco (A.B., 1967; J.D., 1970); University of Michigan (S.J.D., 1973). ***COURSES:*** Antitrust, Torts, Toxic Torts. ***Email:*** dbinder@chapman.edu

DANIEL B. BOGART, **(Professor of Law)**, born Atlanta, Georgia,

(This Listing Continued)

CHAPMAN UNIVERSITY LAW SCHOOL—Continued

August 14, 1960; admitted to bar, 1986, Georgia. *Education:* Duke University (B.A., 1982; M.A., 1986; J.D., 1986). ***COURSES:*** Bankruptcy, Property, Real Estate, Commercial Leasing, Economics. ***Email:*** bogart@chapman.edu

MARY KATHERINE DARMER, **(Visiting Assistant Professor of Law)**, born Atlanta, Georgia, October 31, 1964; admitted to bar, 1989, Connecticut; 1990, New York. *Education:* Princeton University (A.B., 1986); Columbia University (J.D., 1989). ***COURSES:*** Torts, Civil Procedure. ***Email:*** kbaird@chapman.edu

FRANK J. DOTI, **(Professor of Law)**, born Chicago, Illinois, May 24, 1943; admitted to bar, 1969, Illinois; 1985, California; 1990, California Bar, Certified Tax Specialist; 1992, Colorado. *Education:* University of Illinois (B.S., 1966; C.P.A., 1966); Chicago-Kent (J.D., 1969). ***COURSES:*** Taxation. ***Email:*** fdoti@chapman.edu

JOHN C. EASTMAN, **(Associate Professor of Law)**, born Lincoln, Nebraska, April 21, 1960; admitted to bar, 1997, California. *Education:* University of Dallas (B.A., 1982); Claremont Graduate School (Ph.D., 1993; M.A., 1989); University of Chicago (J.D., 1995). ***COURSES:*** Constitutional Law, Legal History. ***Email:*** jeastman@chapman.edu

KURT FREDERICK EGGERT, **(Assistant Professor and Director of Clinical Education)**, born Hays, Kansas, February, 21, 1959; admitted to bar, 1984, California. *Education:* Rice University (B.A., 1981); University of California at Berkeley School of Law (Boalt Hall) (J.D., 1984). ***COURSES:*** Clinical Education/Elder Law, Remedies. ***Email:*** keggert@chapman.edu

GREGORY H. FOX, **(Visiting Assistant Professor of Law)**, born Boston, Massachusetts, April 3, 1961; admitted to bar, 1987, Massachusetts; 1988, District of Massachusetts, First Circuit. *Education:* Bates College (B.A., 1982); New York University (J.D., 1986). ***COURSES:*** International Law, International Business Transactions, Legal Writing. ***Email:*** gfox@chapman.edu

HUGH HEWITT, **(Associate Professor of Law)**, born Warren, Ohio, February 22, 1956; admitted to bar, 1983, District of Columbia; 1989, California. *Education:* Harvard College (A.B., 1978); University of Michigan (J.D., 1983). ***COURSES:*** Constitutional Law, Administrative Law.

SCOTT W. HOWE, **(Associate Dean for Academic Affairs and Professor of Law)**, born Knobnoster, Missouri, November 28, 1956; admitted to bar, 1981, District of Columbia; 1990, Massachusetts. *Education:* University of Missouri (A.B., 1977); University of Michigan (J.D., 1981). ***COURSES:*** Criminal, Criminal Procedure, Capital Punishment, Evidence. ***Email:*** swhowe@chapman.edu

VICKI M. HUEBNER, **(Assistant Dean of Career Services/Externship)**, born Redondo Beach, California, January 3, 1966; admitted to bar, 1992, California. *Education:* Brigham Young University (B.A., 1987; J.D., 1992). ***COURSES:*** Professional Development. ***Email:*** vhuebner@chapman.edu

SUSAN SMITH JENKINS, **(Director of Development)**, born Rochester, NY. *Education:* University of California, Berkeley (B.A). ***COURSES:*** Responsible Fund Raising and Development. ***Email:*** sjenkins@chapman.edu

SUSANNA M. KIM, **(Associate Professor of Law)**, admitted to bar, 1994, California. *Education:* Stanford University (B.A., 1991); UCLA School of Law (J.D., 1994). ***COURSES:*** Corporations, Legal Ethics. ***Email:*** sukim@chapman.edu

SHERYL HEATHER SUMMERS KRAMER, **(Library Director and Associate Professor of Law)**, born Detroit, Michigan, September 21, 1954. *Education:* Wayne State University (B.S., 1977; M.S.L.S, 1978); Detroit College of Law (J.D., 1989). ***COURSES:*** Advanced Legal Research, Computer Assisted Legal Research. ***Email:*** skramer@chapman.edu

LISA LITWILLER, **(Assistant Professor of Law)**, born Los Angeles, California, October 20, 1962; admitted to bar, 1991, California. *Education:* University of Southern California (B.A., 1985; J.D., 1991). ***COURSES:*** Contracts, Legal Research & Writing. ***Email:*** llitwill@chapman.edu

CELESTINE RICHARDS MCCONVILLE, **(Associate Professor of Law)**, born Cleveland, Ohio, October 16, 1965; admitted to bar, 1991, Illinois; 1993 District of Columbia. *Education:* Boston University (B.A., 1988); Georgetown University Law Center (J.D., 1991). ***COURSES:*** Constitutional Law, Criminal Law, Wills & Trusts. ***Email:*** mcconvil@chapman.edu

JEREMY M. MILLER, **(Professor of Law and Dean Emeritus Tenured)**, born Boston, Massachusetts, April 2, 1954; admitted to bar, 1980, Massachusetts. *Education:* Yale (B.A., 1976); Meru (B.S., 1977); Tulane (J.D., 1980); University of Pennsylvania (LL.M., 1981). ***COURSES:*** Criminal Law & Procedure, Legal Ethics. ***Email:*** kayshva@aol.com

SHARON C. NANTELL, **(Professor of Law)**, born Cleveland, Ohio, February 2, 1951; admitted to bar, 1977, Ohio; 1979, Colorado. *Education:* Cleveland State University (B.A., 1973); Cleveland-Marshall College of Law (J.D., 1976); Georgetown University Law Center (LL.M., 1979). ***COURSES:*** Taxation, Wills & Trusts, Corporations, Estate & Gift Taxation. ***Email:*** nantell@chapman.edu

NANCY LYNN SCHULTZ, **(Professor of Law)**, born Detroit, Michigan, April 24, 1957; admitted to bar, 1981, Pennsylvania. *Education:* University of Wisconsin (B.A., 1978); University of Pennsylvania (J.D., 1981). ***COURSES:*** Negotiations, Client Interviewing, Legal Writing, Advocacy. ***Email:*** nschultz@chapman.edu

WILLIAM LEE STALLWORTH, **(Salvatori Professor of Law)**, born Cleveland, Ohio, June 11, 1948; admitted to bar, 1983, Ohio; 1983, Sixth Circuit Court of Appeals. *Education:* Cornell University (B.A., 1970); Stanford University (Ph.D., 1982); Harvard Law School (J.D., 1979). ***COURSES:*** Contracts, UCC-Sales, UCC-Secured Transactions, Remedies. ***Email:*** stallwor@aol.com

NHAN THIEN VU, **(Assistant Professor of Law)**, born Saigon, Vietnam, March 13, 1971; admitted to bar, 1997, California. *Education:* Harvard University (A.B., 1992); Yale Law School (J.D., 1995). ***COURSES:*** Civil Procedure, Civil Rights, Corporations, International Business Transactions. ***Email:*** vu@chapman.edu

ROBIN S. WELLFORD, **(Associate Professor)**, born Portland, Maine, April 12, 1953; admitted to bar, 1982, Illinois; 1983, Missouri. *Education:* Northwestern University (B.A., 1975); Washington University (J.D., 1982). ***COURSES:*** Legal Writing, ADR, Legal Ethics. ***Email:*** wellford@chapman.edu

---

CHICAGO-KENT COLLEGE OF LAW, ILLINOIS INSTITUTE OF TECHNOLOGY

565 WEST ADAMS STREET
CHICAGO, ILLINOIS 60661
Telephone: (312) 906-5000
Fax: (312) 906-5280
http://www.kentlaw.edu

ABA Approved Since 1936.

Chicago-Kent College of Law, Illinois Institute of Technology, is a national leader in legal education, recognized for its scholarly excellence and for its commitment to being the "Law School Ahead of the Times." Its faculty -- one of the most productive groups of legal scholars in the country, publishing leading texts and articles across a wide array of subjects -- bring their scholarship to the classroom, where students explore topical issues that enliven discussions and enrich learning. Each year, a select group of outstanding prospective law students is admitted to the Honors Scholars Program, which provides enrichment opportunities to broaden students' perspectives on law and the legal profession and to cultivate their leadership skills.

Chicago-Kent is renowned for its curricular innovation. Its acclaimed Legal Research and Writing Program is the most comprehensive legal writing curriculum in the nation. The law school is committed to providing interdisciplinary opportunities for legal education through its specialized programs in environmental and energy law, intellectual property law, international and comparative law, labor and employment law, and litigation and alternative dispute resolution as well as through formal Interprofessional Projects with other academic units of IIT.

Chicago-Kent is also a leader in practical skills training. The Law Offices of Chicago-Kent pioneered the development of a sequential clinical curriculum and was the first fee-generating law clinic operated by an American law school. Chicago-Kent provides practical skills training through internships with the Law Offices and externships with law firms, corporate law departments, government, public interest agencies and federal judges. The law school's other practical skills programs also successfully prepare Chicago-Kent graduates for the practice of law and bring nationwide attention to Chicago-Kent. Students in its championship-winning Trial Advocacy and Moot Court programs regularly win local, regional and national competitions.

Chicago-Kent was the first law school in the country to make the use of computers an integral component of legal education. Chicago-Kent's Center for Law and Computers provides national and international leadership in exploring the use of technology in law practice and legal education and is located within one of the most technologically advanced law schools in the world. This foremost research and teaching center develops computer course materials to improve legal education by transforming the law school classroom into an electronic learning environment. Its extensive distance learning initiatives evaluate and experiment with legal education applications of distance learning technologies, including e-mail, discussion groups, chat rooms, streaming video and audio, video conferencing, and computer whiteboard tools.

To address globalization of the law and other global considerations, Chicago-Kent's Global Law and Policy Initiative provides a framework for policy-orientated inquiry, backed-up by information resources and the highest-powered legal analysis. It serves as a forum for discussion and development of scholarship and global policy analysis among academics, law students, business executives, government officials, labor leaders and public interest advocates.

Chicago-Kent is a key component of the Institute for Science, Law and Technology, a multidisciplinary policy and research institute that brings together skilled researchers from various academic units of IIT with expertise in such areas as biological and physical sciences, energy, engineering, the environment, ethics, biomedicine, information technology, law and psychology. The institute's focus is to anticipate social needs and push science, technology and policy into new frontiers to create solutions that solve societal problems and meet commercial interests.

Chicago-Kent's Institute for Law and the Workplace is a national center for research, training, dialogue and reflection on the law that governs the workplace. The institute pools the resources of leading scholars and the practicing professional community to train students and professionals, monitor policies and trends, and address major issues in a neutral setting.

Chicago-Kent offers a number of dual degree programs that reflect the law school's philosophy that tomorrow's legal professionals will require the broadest possible range of interprofessional skills to achieve success. The law school offers dual J.D./master's degree programs in business administration, environmental management, financial markets and regulation, financial markets and trading, financial services law, public administration, public health, and taxation.

Chicago-Kent offers an LL.M. degree in taxation and conducts an LL.M. program in international and comparative law that teaches attorneys about American legal practices and traditions. An LL.M. degree in financial services law is offered through IIT's Center for Law & Financial Markets.

Chicago-Kent College of Law is the second oldest law school in Illinois. It was founded in 1888 by two judges who believed that legal education should be available to working men and women. Soon after its founding, the College of Law graduated its first female and minority students. It was accredited by the American Bar Association in 1936, became a member of the Association of American Law Schools in 1951, and was elected unanimously to the Order of the Coif law school honor society in 1988.

From an initial gathering of several law clerks studying in judges' chambers, Chicago-Kent has grown to a current enrollment of more than one thousand students, with more than 60 resident faculty members and an adjunct faculty of respected practicing attorneys and judges. Chicago-Kent is a national law school. Its students come from 45 states and several foreign countries and from more than 100 colleges and universities. Forty-nine percent are women and 13 percent are minorities.

Chicago-Kent is housed in a modern, ten-story building located in downtown Chicago. The home of the "law school of the future" is nationally emulated as a model in law school design and features the latest in education and information technology. The IIT Downtown Campus Libraries are located here in a large facility that includes the library of Chicago-Kent College of Law, one of the 25 largest law school libraries in the country; the library of Stuart Graduate School of Business, a distinguished collection of business-related materials; and the Library of International Relations, a large and comprehensive international law collection that serves as a unique resource in the Midwest. The Downtown Campus Libraries have extensive electronic resources, in addition to the print collections, to support the institution's programs.

Chicago-Kent offers nine annual continuing legal education programs, including a conference on Section 1983 Civil Rights Liability, a conference on Not-For-Profit organizations, the Federal Tax Institute, and the Federal Sector Labor Relations and Labor Law Program. It also presents annual endowed lectures on labor law, law and technology, and international and comparative law.

(This Listing Continued)

CHICAGO-KENT COLLEGE OF LAW, ILLINOIS INSTITUTE OF TECHNOLOGY—Continued

Dean: Henry H. Perritt, Jr. (312) 906-5010
Office of Admissions and Financial Aid: (312) 906-5020
Office of Career Services: (312) 906-5200
Office of Continuing Legal Education: (312) 906-5090
Office of Development and Alumnae/i Relations: (312) 906-5240
Office of Public Affairs: (312) 906-5250
Law Library: (312) 906-5600

FULL TIME FACULTY

HENRY H. PERRITT, JR.*, (Dean, Professor of Law, and Vice President for the Downtown Campus)** , born Little Rock, Arkansas, December 30, 1944; admitted to bar, 1976, Virginia; 1977, Pennsylvania; 1980, District of Columbia; 1993, Maryland; 1998, Illinois; U.S. Supreme Court. *Education:* Massachusetts Institute of Technology (S.B., 1966; S.M., 1970); Georgetown University Law Center (J.D., 1975). ***COURSES: Administrative Law, Conflict of Laws.

SUSAN J. ADAMS*, (Assoc. Prof., Legal Research & Writing; Dep. Dir., Legal Research & Writing Prog.;Dir., of Writing Srvs.)** , born Connecticut, October 23, 1947; admitted to bar, 1990, Illinois and Indiana. *Education:* University of Wisconsin-Madison (B.A., 1969; M.A., 1970); Valparaiso University (J.D., 1990). ***COURSES: School Law, Immigration Law, Legal Law.

LORI B. ANDREWS*, (Distinguished Prof. of Law; Assoc. V.P., Downtown Campus; Dir., Institute for Science, Law and Tech.)** , born Chicago, Illinois, September 26, 1953; admitted to bar, 1978, California; 1979, Illinois. *Education:* Yale University (B.A., 1975; J.D., 1978). ***COURSES: Genetics and Law, Reproductive Technology Law, Health Care Law.

KATHARINE K. BAKER*, (Associate Professor of Law)** , born Boston, Massachusetts, November 8, 1962; admitted to bar, 1990, Pennsylvania. *Education:* Harvard-Radcliffe College (B.A., 1984); University of Chicago Law School (J.D., 1989). ***COURSES: Environmental Law, Family Law.

MARK D. BAUER*, (Visiting Assistant Professor of Law)** , born New York City, February 19, 1962; admitted to bar, 1988, Pennsylvania; 1994, Illinois. *Education:* The University of Chicago (B.A., 1983); Emory University School of Law (J.D., 1988). ***COURSES: Legal Writing.

FRED P. BOSSELMAN*, (Professor of Law)** , born Oak Park, Illinois, June 14, 1934; admitted to bar, 1959, Illinois; 1984, Florida. *Education:* University of Colorado (A.B., 1956); Harvard University Law School (J.D., 1959). ***COURSES: Environmental Law, Land Use, Property.

RALPH L. BRILL*, (Professor of Law)** , born Chicago, Illinois, December 19, 1935; admitted to bar, 1960, Illinois. *Education:* University of Illinois (B.A., 1957; J.D., 1960). ***COURSES: Torts.

EVELYN BRODY*, (Professor of Law)** , born New Jersey, June 29, 1955; admitted to bar, 1981, District of Columbia; 1985, Wisconsin. *Education:* Massachusetts Institute of Technology; Yale University (B.A., 1976); Georgetown University Law Center (J.D., 1981). ***COURSES: Tax.

BARTRAM S. BROWN*, (Associate Professor of Law, and Co-Director of the Program in International and Comparative Law)** , born Indianapolis, Indiana, October 14, 1952; admitted to bar, 1977, California. *Education:* Harvard University (B.A., 1974); Columbia University (J.D., 1977). ***COURSES: International Law, International Human Rights Law, Contracts.

GERALD BROWN*, (Clinical Associate Professor of Law and Director of the Graduate Program in Taxation)** , born Chicago, Illinois, February 8, 1936; admitted to bar, 1961, Illinois. *Education:* De Paul University (B.S.C., 1958); University of Chicago (J.D., 1961). ***COURSES: Taxation, Accounting and Business Law, Tax Clinic.

HOWARD S. CHAPMAN*, (Professor of Law)** , born Chicago, Illinois, October 16, 1941; admitted to bar, 1968, Illinois. *Education:* University of Illinois (B.S., 1963; J.D., 1967). ***COURSES: Tax.

LEWIS COLLENS*, (President and Professor of Law)** , born 1938; admitted to bar, 1966, Illinois. *Education:* University of Illinois (B.S., 1960; M.A., 1963); University of Chicago (J.D., 1966). ***COURSES: Corporations, Professional Responsibility.

RICHARD J. CONVISER*, (Professor of Law)** , born 1938; admitted to bar, 1963, California; 1965, Illinois. *Education:* University of California at Berkeley (B.S., 1959); University of California at Berkeley, Boalt Hall School of Law (J.D., 1962); University of Cologne, Germany (Dr. Jur., 1964). ***COURSES: Business Organizations, Antitrust, Conflict of Laws, Torts.

MOLLY D. CURRENT*, (Visiting Assistant Professorof Law)** , born Alexandria, Louisiana, July 22, 1960; admitted to bar, 1986, Washington; 1988, District of Columbia. *Education:* University of North Carolina (B.A., 1982); Georgetown University Law Center (J.D., 1985). ***COURSES: Legal Writing, Administrative Law.

JONATHAN DECATORSMITH*, (Assistant Professor of Clinical Practice)**, born Philadelphia, Pennsylvania, December 18, 1961; admitted to bar, 1986, Illinois, 1999, Minnesota. *Education:* University of Illinois (B.A., 1983); University of Colorado (J.D., 1986). ***COURSES: Tax Clinic, Federal Tax Procedures.

GRAEME DINWOODIE*, (Professor of Law)** , born Glasgow, Scotland, 1966; admitted to bar, 1989, New York. *Education:* University of Glasgow (LL.B., 1987); Harvard Law School (LL.M., 1988); Columbia Law School (J.S.D., 2000). ***COURSES: Conflict of Laws, Trademark Law, International Intellectual Property.

HOWARD C. EGLIT*, (Professor of Law)** , born Chicago, Illinois, September 20, 1942; admitted to bar, 1967, Illinois; 1973, District of Columbia and U.S. Supreme Court. *Education:* University of Michigan (B.A., 1963); University of Chicago (J.D., 1967). ***COURSES: Constitutional Law, Employment Discrimination, Law and Aging (Elder Law).

DAVID J. GERBER*, (Distinguished Professor of Law and Co-Director of the Program in International and Comparative Law)**, born St. Louis, Missouri, August 14, 1945; admitted to bar, 1973, New York. *Education:* Trinity College (B.A., 1967); Yale University (M.A., 1969); University of Chicago (J.D., 1972). ***COURSES: Comparative Law, International Business Transactions, European Community Law.

DOUGLAS WM. GODFREY*, (Visiting Assistant Professor ofLaw)** , born District of Columbia, December 27, 1958; admitted to bar, 1987, New York; 1990, Illinois. *Education:* University of Illinois at Urbana-Champaign (B.A, 1981; M.A., 1986); University of Michigan (J.D., 1986). ***COURSES: Legal Research and Writing, Criminal Procedure.

(This Listing Continued)

CHICAGO-KENT COLLEGE OF LAW, ILLINOIS INSTITUTE OF TECHNOLOGY—Continued

RICHARD J. GONZALEZ*, (Clinical Professor of Law)**, born Canton, Ohio, March 11, 1953; admitted to bar, 1978, Illinois. *Education:* Northwestern University (B.A., 1975); Ohio State University College of Law (J.D., 1978). ***COURSES: Clinical Employment Discrimination, Negotiation, Alternative Dispute Resolution.

SANFORD N. GREENBERG*, (Assoc. Professor of Appellate Advocacy; Director of the Appellate Advocacy Program)**, born Newark, New Jersey, April 27, 1948. *Education:* Princeton University (A.B., 1970); University of California Berkeley (M.A., 1971; Ph.D., 1978); George Washington University (J.D., 1990). ***COURSES: Appellate Advocacy, Administrative Law.

SUZANNE S. GREENE*, (Assistant Professor of Legal Research and Writing)**, born Buffalo, New York, January 18, 1943; admitted to bar, 1985, Illinois. *Education:* Barnard College (B.A., 1968); Columbia University (M.A., 1969; Ph.D.; 1977); University of Chicago (J.D.). ***COURSES: Legal Research and Writing.

VIVIEN C. GROSS*, (Clinical Professor of Law; Director of the Judicial Externship Program & Internship Program)**, born Chicago, Illinois; admitted to bar, 1973, Illinois. *Education:* Northwestern University (B.A., 1967); University of Illinois (M.A., 1969); Indiana University (J.D., 1973). ***COURSES: All Clinical Externship Programs, Professional Responsibility.

PHILIP N. HABLUTZEL*, (Professor of Law)**, born Flagstaff, Arizona, August 23, 1935; admitted to bar, 1967, Illinois. *Education:* Louisiana State University (B.A., 1958); The University of Chicago (M.A., 1960; J.D., 1967). ***COURSES: Corporations, Securities Regulation, Banking Law, International Securities Regulation, Financial Services Products.

SARAH K. HARDING*, (Associate Professor of Law)**, born London, Ontario, Canada, February 11, 1965. *Education:* McGill University (B.A., 1985); Dalhousie University (LL.B., 1989); Oxford University (B.C.L., 1991); Yale Law School (LL.M., 1993). ***COURSES: Property, Torts, Feminist Jurisprudence.

STEVEN L. HARRIS*, (Professor of Law)**, born New York City, New York, July 20, 1949; admitted to bar, 1973, Illinois; 1974, California; 1978, Michigan. *Education:* University of Chicago (B.A., 1970; J.D., 1973). ***COURSES: Secured Transactions, Bankruptcy, Commercial Paper.

STEPHEN E. HENDERSON*, (Visiting Assistant Professor of Law)**, admitted to bar, 1999, Texas. *Education:* University of California (B.S., 1995). ***COURSES: Cybercrime, Cyberlaw, Criminal Law.

BETH ANNE HENNING*, (Visiting Assistant Professor)**, born Hammond, Indiana, February 4, 1964; admitted to bar, 1989, Indiana; 1991, Illinois. *Education:* University of Illinois (B.A., 1986); Valparaiso University School of Law (J.D., 1989); The John Marshall Law School (L.L.M., 2000). ***COURSES: Legal Research and Writing, Environmental Law, Environmental Litigation.

STEVEN J. HEYMAN*, (Associate Professor of Law)**, born Washington, D.C., August 15, 1959; admitted to bar, 1986, Pennsylvania. *Education:* Harvard University (A.B., 1979; J.D., 1984). ***COURSES: Torts, Constitutional Law, First Amendment, Jurisprudence.

CLAIRE ARIANE HILL*, (Associate Professor of Law)**, born New York, New York, 1958; admitted to bar, 1984, New York; 1988, District of Columbia. *Education:* University of Chicago (B.A., 1977; M.A., 1980); American University (J.D., 1983); Columbia (J.S.D., 1998). ***COURSES: Comparative Corporate Governance, Contracts (Law & Economics of Contracting), Partnership Tax.

TIMOTHY R. HOLBROOK*, (Assistant Professor of Law)**, born Canton, Ohio, August 23, 1971; admitted to bar, 1997, New York; 1998, District of Columbia. *Education:* North Carolina State University (B.S., 1993); Yale Law School (J.D., 1996). ***COURSES: Patent Law, Property.

PAMELA A. KENTRA*, (Visiting Assistant Clinical Professor of Law)**, born Oak Park, Illinois, October 27, 1967; admitted to bar, 1992, Illinois. *Education:* University of Illinois at Urbana-Champaign (B.A., 1989); Chicago-Kent College of Law (J.D., 1992). ***COURSES: Mediation, Alternative Dispute Resolution, Clinical Practice Skills.

RICHARD KLING*, (Clinical Professor of Law)**, born Chicago, Illinois, December 15, 1945; admitted to bar, 1971, Illinois. *Education:* University of Illinois (B.A., 1967); Northwestern University School of Law (J.D., 1971). ***COURSES: Evidence, Criminal Law, Forensic Science.

EDWARD M. KRAUS*, (Assistant Professor of Clinical Practice)**, born Granville, Ohio, November 29, 1966; admitted to bar, 1993, Wisconsin; 1994, Illinois. *Education:* University of Michigan (B.A., 1988); Georgetown University (J.D., 1993). ***COURSES: Health. ***Email:*** ekraus@kentlaw.edu

HAROLD J. KRENT*, (Professor of Law and Associate Dean)**, born Cleveland, Ohio, February 28, 1956; admitted to bar, 1983, District of Columbia. *Education:* Princeton University (A.B., 1977); New York University School of Law (J.D., 1982). ***COURSES: Administrative Law, Constitutional Law, Criminal Law.

GARY S. LASER*, (Associate Professor of Law and Director of Clinical Education)**, born Chicago, Illinois, May 22, 1937; admitted to bar, 1965, Florida and Illinois. *Education:* University of Miami (B.B.A., 1959; J.D., 1965). ***COURSES: Civil Procedure, Clinical Legal Education.

JEROLD R. LAVIN*, (Visiting Associate Professor of Law and Managing Director of Graduate Studies in Financial Services Law)**, born Chicago, 1960; admitted to bar, 1986, Illinois. *Education:* University of Illinois at Urbana-Champaign (B.A., 1982); Harvard University (J.D., 1985). ***COURSES: International Business Transactions, International Law, Legal Research and Writing, Real Estate Transactions.

LAURIE E. LEADER*, (Associate Professor of Clinical Practice)**, born Chicago, Illinois, October 23, 1951; admitted to bar, 1978, Illinois. *Education:* Washington University (A.B., 1973); Cleveland-Marshall College (J.D., 1977). ***COURSES: Employment Relationship, Illinois Civil Procedure.

CHRISTOPHER R. LESLIE*, (Assistant Professor of Law)**, born California, October 24, 1964; admitted to bar, 1994, California. *Education:* University of California Los Angeles (B.A., 1986); Kennedy School, Harvard University (M.P.P., 1988); Boalt Hall, University of California Berkeley (J.D., 1993). ***COURSES: Antitrust, Corporation, Contracts.

MARTIN H. MALIN*, (Professor of Law and Director of the Institute for Law and the Workplace)**, born New York, N.Y., May 2, 1953; admitted to bar, 1976, Michigan; 1992, Illinois. *Education:* Michigan State University (B.A., 1973); George Washington University National Law Center (J.D., 1976). ***COURSES: Labor Law, Employment Law, Employment Discrimination, Jurisprudence.

NANCY S. MARDER*, (Associate Professor of Law)**, born 1958; admitted to bar, 1989, Connecticut. *Education:* Yale University (B.A., 1980; J.D., 1987); University of Cambridge (M. of Phil., 1982). ***COURSES: Civil Procedure; Juries, Judges & Trials; Law, Literature & Feminism.

(This Listing Continued)

CHICAGO-KENT COLLEGE OF LAW, ILLINOIS INSTITUTE OF TECHNOLOGY—Continued

MARCIA L. MCCORMICK*, (Visiting Assistant Professor of Law)**, born Fort Dodge, Iowa, May 16, 1967; admitted to bar, 1993, Iowa; 1994, Illinois. *Education:* University of Iowa College of Law (J.D., 1993). ***COURSES: Legal Writing.

JOSEPH F. MORRISSEY*, (Visiting Assistant Professor of Law)**, born Chicago, Illinois, March 9, 1967; admitted to bar, 1993, Illinois. *Education:* Princeton University (A.B., 1989). ***COURSES: Legal Research and Writing.

SHELDON H. NAHMOD*, (Distinguished Professor of Law)**, born Chicago, Illinois, December 21, 1940; admitted to bar, 1965, Illinois; 1971, Pennsylvania. *Education:* University of Chicago (B.A., 1962); Harvard University Law School (J.D., 1965; LL.M., 1971). ***COURSES: Constitutional Law, Civil Rights, Jurisprudence.

DALE A. NANCE*, (Professor of Law)**, born Dallas, Texas, March 9, 1952; admitted to bar, 1977, California. *Education:* Rice University (B.A., 1974); Stanford University Law School (J.D., 1977); University of California at Berkeley (M.A., 1982). ***COURSES: Evidence, Property, Jurisprudence.

TERRANCE A. NORTON*, (Clinical Professor of Law)**, born Oak Park, Illinois, January 3, 1945; admitted to bar, 1970, Illinois. *Education:* University of Notre Dame (B.A., 1967); De Paul University College of Law (J.D., 1970). ***COURSES: Clinic, Dispute Resolution, Legal Negotiation.

MICKIE VOGES PIATT*, (Associate Professor of Law and Co-Director of the Program in Intellectual Property Law)**, admitted to bar, 1979, Texas. *Education:* University of Texas (B.A., 1975; M.L.S., 1976; J.D., 1979). ***COURSES: Privacy, Computers and the Law, Wills, Emerging Technologies and the Law.

GREGORY C. PINGREE*, (Visiting Assistant Professor of Law)**, born Salt Lake City, Utah, September 7, 1960. *Education:* Brigham Young University (B.A., 1984); Brown University (M.A., 1987; Ph.D., 2001); Boalt Hall School of Law (J.D., 1995). ***COURSES: Legal Research and Writing.

MARK D. ROSEN*, (Assistant Professor of Law)**, born New York, New York, May 5, 1964; admitted to bar, 1986, Illinois; 1999, Minnesota. *Education:* University of Illinois (B.A, 1983); University of Colorado (J.D., 1986). ***COURSES: Constitutional Law, State and Local Government, Contracts.

DAVID S. RUDSTEIN*, (Professor of Law)**, born Leeds, England, September 27, 1946; admitted to bar, 1971, Illinois. *Education:* University of Illinois (B.S., 1968; LL.M., 1975); Northwestern University School of Law (J.D., 1971);. ***COURSES: Criminal Law and Procedure.

JULIE S. SCHRAGER*, (Visiting Assistant Professor of Law)**, born Evanston, Illinois, June 2, 1965; admitted to bar, 1989, Illinois; 1991, District of Columbia; 1995, Massachusetts. *Education:* Harvard/Radcliffe College (A.B., 1986); University of Chicago Law School (J.D., 1989). ***COURSES: Legal Research and Writing.

JEFFREY G. SHERMAN*, (Professor of Law and Senior Advisor to the Graduate Program in Taxation)**, born New York, N.Y., July 25, 1946; admitted to bar, 1972, Minnesota. *Education:* Harvard University (A.B., 1968); Harvard University Law School (J.D., 1972). ***COURSES: Estates and Trusts, Taxation, Employee Benefits.

PEGGY SMITH*, (Assistant Professor of Law)**, *Education:* Yale University (B.A., 1987); Harvard Law School (J.D., 1993). ***COURSES: Employment Relationships, Contracts.

MICHAEL I. SPAK*, (Professor of Law)**, born Chicago, Illinois, December 20, 1936; admitted to bar, 1961, Illinois and Michigan. *Education:* De Paul University (B.S., 1958); De Paul University College of Law (J.D., 1961); Northwestern University School of Law (LL.M., 1962). ***COURSES: Uniform Commercial Code, Uniform Code of Military Justice.

RONALD W. STAUDT*, (Professor of Law and Associate Vice President for Law, Business and Technology)**, born Lorain, Ohio, September 21, 1946; admitted to bar, 1970, Illinois; 1973, Arizona. *Education:* St. Joseph's College (B.A., 1967; B.S., 1967); University of Chicago (J.D., 1970). ***COURSES: Computer Law, Copyright.

JOAN E. STEINMAN*, (Distinguished Professor of Law)**, born Brooklyn, New York, June 19, 1947; admitted to bar, 1973, Illinois. *Education:* University of Rochester (A.B., with high distinction, 1969); University of Birmingham; Harvard University Law School (J.D., cum laude, 1973). ***COURSES: Civil Procedure, Complex Litigation, Federal Courts.

MARGARET G. STEWART*, (Professor of Law)**, born Chicago, Illinois, March 1, 1947; admitted to bar, 1972, New York. *Education:* Kalamazoo College (B.A., 1968); Northwestern University School of Law (J.D., 1971). ***COURSES: Constitutional Law, Federal Courts, Civil Procedure.

MARY ROSE STRUBBE*, (Assoc. Prof., Legal Res. & Writ.; Dir., Legal Res. & Writ. Prog.; Assist. Dir., Inst. for Law & the Workplace)**, born Illinois, July 19, 1948; admitted to bar, 1981, Illinois. *Education:* Mundelein College (B.A., 1970); Chicago-Kent College of Law (J.D., 1981). ***COURSES: Legal Writing, Estates and Trusts.

A. DAN TARLOCK*, (Distinguished Professor of Law and Director of the Program in Environmental and Energy Law)**, born Oakland, California, June 2, 1940; admitted to bar, 1965, California. *Education:* Stanford University (A.B., 1962); Stanford University Law School (LL.B., 1965). ***COURSES: Environmental Law, Water Law, Natural Resources Law, Property.

DAVID C. THOMAS*, (Clinical Professor of Law)**, born Pittsburgh, Pennsylvania, October 28, 1943; admitted to bar, 1968, Illinois; 1990, California. *Education:* Kenyon College (A.B., 1965); University of Michigan Law School (J.D., 1968). ***COURSES: Criminal Procedure, Clinical Education.

RICHARD WARNER*, (Associate Professor of Law)**, born San Diego, California, June 13, 1946. *Education:* Stanford University (B.A., 1968); University of California at Berkeley (Ph.D., 1976); University of Southern California (J.D., 1989). ***COURSES: Contracts, Jurisprudence.

LANCE WILLIAMS*, (Visiting Assistant Professor of Clinical Practice)**, born Arlington, Texas; admitted to bar, 1994, Louisiana; 1997, Illinois. *Education:* Tulane University (B.A., 1991); Louisiana State University (J.D., 1994). ***COURSES: Information Technology, Entrepreneurship Clinic.

RICHARD W. WRIGHT*, (Professor of Law)**, born St. Louis, Missouri, November 10, 1946; admitted to bar, 1974, California. *Education:* California Institute of Technology (B.S., 1968); Loyola University (J.D., 1973); Harvard University Law School (LL.M., 1975). ***COURSES: Torts, Jurisprudence.

CITY UNIVERSITY OF NEW YORK SCHOOL OF LAW AT QUEENS COLLEGE

65-21 MAIN STREET
FLUSHING, NEW YORK 11367
Telephone: (718) 340-4200
Fax: (718) 340-4482
website: www.law.cuny.edu

ABA Approved Since 1985

Opened in 1983, the City University of New York School of Law at Queens College (CUNY School of Law) is the only law school which, from its inception, has defined its mission as training law students for public service. "Law in the Service of Human Needs" is the Law School's motto and, accordingly, its goal is to teach students to be lawyers who will use their skills to serve the public interest. To this end, the Law School has developed a unique and comprehensive curriculum which integrates lawyering skills with legal doctrine at every level, making it a national leader in progressive legal education. It has a distinguished and diverse faculty of both scholars and educators, many of whom have extensive backgrounds as public interest practitioners. Fifty-eight percent of its faculty are women and thirty-six percent are members of minority groups.

Cognizant of the profession's criticism that legal education fails to prepare law graduates for effective law practice, the curriculum of the CUNY School of Law is rich in classroom courses and clinical programs which emphasize practice as well as doctrine and theory. Unlike most law schools where lawyering, writing and clinical courses are grafted onto, and are secondary to, the traditional curriculum, these courses are an integral part of the School's curriculum. In the first year, students learn legal reasoning, professional responsibility, legal writing and other lawyering skills in a year-long Lawyering Seminar where clinical methodology is integrated with doctrinal material. In the second year, students are required to take a one-semester Lawyering Seminar in an area of public interest law.

In the third year, students select either an elective concentration in housing and community economic development, equality or health law, or a live-client clinical program. For the past nine years, leading legal educators have placed the School's clinical program among the top ten in the country. Serving as an umbrella to several different clinics, the School's "in-house law firm," Main Street Legal Services, Inc., houses an Immigrant and Refugee Rights Clinic, a Defender Clinic, an Elder Law Clinic, a Battered Women's Rights Clinic, an International Women's Human Rights Clinic, and a Mediation Clinic.

CUNY's student body of close to 450 is impressively diverse. A majority of the students are women and approximately thirty-nine percent are minority group members, a number of whom are first generation immigrants. The median age of all students is now 29; median age of this year's entering class is 29 and many come to the School after successful prior careers or with advanced degrees. Roughly sixty-five percent of the students are New York State residents with the remaining thirty-five percent from at least seventeen states and seven countries. About twenty percent are graduates of the CUNY system and over 180 colleges and universities are represented among its graduates. Recognizing that many of its students are parents, the Law School has one of the few on-site child-care centers for children of law students in the country.

CUNY is successful in its mission to train law students to be socially conscious and caring attorneys with a commitment to public service and public interest law. Of its class of 2000 graduates, fifty-two percent went to work as attorneys in the Public sector, nearly double the 28% average reported for entire class of 2000 throughout the country. Many CUNY law students come from communities that are currently underserved by the legal profession and, upon graduation, many return to practice law with or within those communities.

In 1998, the Student Division of the American Bar Association named CUNY the Public Interest School of the Year, and the National Association for Public Interest Law gave Dean Kristin Booth Glen its Law School Dean of the Year Award.

Employers of CUNY law graduates include public interest organizations such as the Legal Aid Society of New York City, American Civil Liberties Union, Coalition for an International Criminal Court, Asian American Legal Defense and Education Fund Sanctuary for Families, District Council 37, In Motion, Center for Disability Rights, Southeast Asian Resource Center, Defenders Association of Philadelphia, Prisoners Legal Services, South Brooklyn Legal Services, Connecticut Legal Services, Lawyers Committee for Human Rights, New York Immigration Coalition, Chicago Legal Assistance, and the Dade County Public Defenders Office. Many CUNY graduates work in government institutions such as the New York City Law Department, the District Attorneys' offices in Manhattan, Brooklyn, Queens and the Bronx; the United States Attorneys Office for the Southern District of Florida; the Office of the New York State Attorney General; the United States Environmental Protection Agency; the New York State Legislature; National Labor Relations Board; the United States Congress, and the New York State Legislature. In addition, many graduates serve as judicial clerks in federal and state, trial and appellate courts.

As part of the largest urban, and third largest, university system in the country, CUNY law students have access to vast resources and a world-class faculty which includes Nobel laureates, Pulitzer Prize winners, and MacArthur Fellows. Additionally, CUNY School of Law is working with CUNY's other senior colleges, including the Hunter College School of Social Work, the MBA program at Baruch College, the School of Public Health at Hunter College, the graduate program in criminal justice at the John Jay College of Criminal Justice, and the CUNY Graduate School and University Center. Together they are working to develop joint-degree programs, cross-listing courses, team-teaching, and developing a seriously integrated interdisciplinary approach to such areas as welfare, health law and immigration and immigrant's law. The Law School's Community Legal Resource Network (CLRN), funded by the Open Society Institute and other foundations, is now in its successful third year of supporting and resourcing law graduates who work in underserved areas in solo or small-firm practices. Three graduates who work with the CLRN program received the 2001 ABA Pro Bono Publico Award.

(This Listing Continued)

CITY UNIVERSITY OF NEW YORK, SCHOOL OF LAW AT QUEENS COLLEGE—Continued

Dean: Kristin Booth Glen (718) 340-4202
Associate Dean for Academic Affairs: Mary Lu Bilek (718) 340-4340
Associate Dean for Administration and Finance: Dave Fields (718) 340-4220
Assist. Dean for Enrollment Management & Dir. of Admissions: Yvonne Cherena-Pacheco (718) 340-4210
Assistant Dean of Students: Frank Shih (718) 340-4207
Director of Library: Gregory Koster (718) 340-4260
Director of Development and External Relations: Andrea Shapiro Davis (718) 340-4386
Director of Institutional Advancement and Publications: Dorothy M. Zellner (718) 340-4441
Director of Career Planning: Sam M. Sue (718) 340-4233
Director of Financial Aid: Angela Joseph (718) 340-4284
Executive Assistant to the Dean: Anne Taylor (718) 340-4425

FULL TIME FACULTY

KRISTIN BOOTH GLEN*, (Dean and Professor of Law)**, born New York, August 16, 1942; admitted to bar, 1967, New York. *Education:* Stanford University (B.A., 1963); Columbia University School of Law (LL.B., 1966). ***COURSES: Family Law, Elder Law, Evidence, Bioethics, Feminist Jurisprudence. ***Email:*** glen@mail.law.cuny.edu

PENELOPE ANDREWS*, (Associate Professor of Law)**, born South Africa, September 18, 1954; admitted to bar, 1989, South Africa. *Education:* University of Natal (B.A., 1980; LL.B., 1982); Columbia University (LL.M., 1984). ***COURSES: International Human Rights, Torts. ***Email:*** andrews@mail.law.cuny.edu

MARIA ARIAS*, (Assistant Professor of Law)**, born Dominican Republic, December 25, 1957; admitted to bar, 1986, New York. *Education:* University of Rochester (B.A., 1979); New York University (J.D., 1984). ***COURSES: Battered Women's Rights Clinic. ***Email:*** arias@mail.law.cuny.edu

PAULA ELLEN BERG*, (Associate Professor of Law)**, born Minneapolis, Minnesota, February 15, 1955; admitted to bar, 1983, New York. *Education:* Hampshire College (B.A., 1977); Rutgers University (J.D., 1982). ***COURSES: Health Law, Torts, AIDS & the Law. ***Email:*** berg@mail.law.cuny.edu

MARY LU BILEK*, (Associate Dean for Academic Affairs & Assistant Professor of Law)**, born Chicago, Illinois, November 3, 1955; admitted to bar, 1981, New York. *Education:* St. Mary's College (B.A., 1977); Harvard Law School (J.D., 1980). ***COURSES: Civil Procedure, Professional Responsibility, Contracts, Professional Skills. ***Email:*** bilek@mail.law.cuny.edu

BERYL S. BLAUSTONE*, (Professor of Law)**, born Minneapolis, Minnesota, 1949; admitted to bar, 1975, District of Columbia. *Education:* University of Minnesota (B.A., 1972); Antioch Law School (J.D., 1975). ***COURSES: Evidence, Mediation & Alternative Dispute Resolution, Mediation Clinic. ***Email:*** blaustone@mail.law.cuny.edu

SUSAN BRYANT*, (Associate Dean for Academic Affairs)**, born Washington, June 24, 1948; admitted to bar, 1973, Pennsylvania; 1975, District of Columbia; 1977, New York. *Education:* Xavier College (B.A., 1970); Georgetown (J.D., 1973; LL.M., 1980). ***COURSES: Evidence, Family, Clinical. ***Email:*** bryant@mail.law.cuny.edu

JANET M. CALVO*, (Associate Professor of Law)**, born 1947; admitted to bar, 1974, New York. *Education:* New York University School of Law (J.D., 1973). ***COURSES: Health Law, Lawyering, Civil Clinic, Civil Procedure, Immigration & Nationality Law. ***Email:*** calvo@mail.law.cuny.edu

JOHN CICERO*, (Associate Professor of Law)**; born 1949; admitted to bar, 1977, New York. *Education:* New England School of Law (J.D., 1975); New York University School of Law (LL.M., 1977). ***COURSES: Evidence, Labor Law, Lawyering, Pre-Trial Litigation. ***Email:*** cicero@mail.law.cuny.edu

RHONDA COPELON*, (Professor of Law & Director, International Women's Human Rights Clinic)**, born New Haven, Connecticut, September 15, 1944; admitted to bar, 1971, New York. *Education:* Bryn Mawr (B.A., 1966); Institut d'etudes Politiques (C.E.P., 1965); Yale (LL.B., 1970). ***COURSES: International Women's Human Rights Law Clinic, International Human Rights, Constitutional Law, Family Law, Gender & Law. ***Email:*** copelon@mail.law.cuny.edu

LUIS J. DEGRAFFE*, (Associate Professor)**, born 1949; admitted to bar, 1976, New York. *Education:* St. John's University (B.A., 1971); Antioch School of Law (J.D., 1975). ***COURSES: Housing, Evidence, Civil Procedure, Landlord/Tenant, Professional Responsibility, Trial Practice, New York Practice. ***Email:*** degraffe@mail.law.cuny.edu

FRANK E. DEALE*, (Associate Professor of Law)**, born Tallahassee, Florida, April 1, 1952; admitted to bar, 1979, Pennsylvania. *Education:* Antioch College (B.A., 1976); University of Pennsylvania (J.D., 1979). ***COURSES: Civil Procedure, Federal Courts, Civil Rights. ***Email:*** deale@mail.law.cuny.edu

JOHN DELANEY*, (Associate Professor of Law)**, born 1932; admitted to bar, 1960, New York. *Education:* Fordham College (B.B.S. 1954); New School for Social Research (M.A.L,S., 1972); New York Law School (J.D., 1959) New York University Law School (LL.M., 1965). ***COURSES: Criminal Law, First Amendment, Jurisprudence, Comparative Criminal Law. ***Email:*** delaney@mail.law.cuny.edu

PAMELA EDWARDS*, (Assistant Professor of Law)**, born New York, New York, December 14, 1959; admitted to bar, 1992, New York. *Education:* New York University (B.S., 1980; M.B.A., 1983; J.D., 1991). ***COURSES: Commercial Law. ***Email:*** edwardsp@mail.law.cuny.edu

JOHN M. FARAGO*, (Associate Professor of Law)**, born 1951. *Education:* Harvard University (B.A. and M.A.T., 1972); New York University (Ph.D. Candidate, Higher Education, 1975-1978); New York University School of Law (J.D., 1978). ***COURSES: Contracts, Family Law, Education Law, Civil Procedure. ***Email:*** farago@mail.law.cuny.edu

DAVE FIELDS*, (Associate Dean)**, born New York, January 3, 1949; admitted to bar, 1980, New York. *Education:* Queens College (B.A., 1972; M.A., 1973); St. John's University (J.D., 1979). ***Email: fields@mail.law.cuny.edu

PAMELA GOLDBERG*, (Associate Professor of Law)**, born San Antonio, Texas, February 24, 1953; admitted to bar, 1983, New York. *Education:* University of Texas (B.A., 1978); New York Law School (J.D., 1983). ***COURSES: Immigration, Human Rights, Refugees. ***Email:*** goldberg@mail.law.cuny.edu

VICTOR M. GOODE*, (Associate Professor of Law)**, born Monroe, Louisiana, November 7, 1947; admitted to bar, 1974, New Jersey. *Education:* Northwestern University (B.A., 1970); Rutgers University, Newark (J.D., 1973). ***COURSES: Civil Rights, Trial Practice, Clinic, Ethics. ***Email:*** goode@mail.law.cuny.edu

(This Listing Continued)

CITY UNIVERSITY OF NEW YORK, SCHOOL OF LAW AT QUEENS COLLEGE—Continued

SIDNEY L. HARRING,* (Professor of Law)**, born 1947; admitted to bar, 1972, Wisconsin; 1990, New York. *Education:* Macalester College (B.A., 1968); University of Wisconsin (M.S., 1970; J.D., 1972; Ph.D., 1976). ***COURSES: Criminal Law, Criminal Procedure, Legal History, Legal Profession, Native American Rights. ***Email:*** harring@mail.law.cuny.edu

SHARON HOM,* (Professor of Law)**, born Hong Kong, 1951; admitted to bar, 1981, New York. *Education:* Sarah Lawrence College (B.A., 1974); New York University School of Law (J.D., 1980). ***COURSES: Contracts, International Human Rights, Feminist Jurisprudence, Immigration, Comparative Law, Administrative Law. ***Email:*** hom@mail.law.cuny.edu

DINESH KHOSLA,* (Professor of Law)**, born India, March 30, 1949; admitted to bar, 1972, India. *Education:* Delhi University (B.Com., 1969; LL.B., 1972); Yale (LL.M., 1977; J.S.D., 1981). ***COURSES: International Law, Law in a Market Economy, International Trade, Civil Disobedience.

JUDITH KIMERLING,* (Assistant Professor-Joint Appointment with Queens College CUNY.)**, admitted to bar, 1983, New York. *Education:* University of Michigan (B.A., 1978); Yale Law School (J.D., 1982); Visiting Scholar-Yale Law School 1995-1996. ***COURSES: Environmental Law. ***Email:*** kimerling@mail.law.cuny.edu

JEFFREY L. KIRCHMEIER,* (Associate Professor of Law)**, born Columbus, Ohio, May 17, 1962; admitted to bar, 1989, Ohio; 1991, District of Columbia; 1992, Arizona. *Education:* Case Western Reserve University Law School (B.A., 1984; J.D., 1989). ***COURSES: Criminal Law, Criminal Procedure, Death Penalty and Habeas Corpus. ***Email:*** kirchmeier@mail.law.cuny.edu

GREGORY E. KOSTER,* (Director of the Law Library and Professor of Law)**, admitted to bar, 1982, New York. *Education:* Stanford University (B.A., 1969); Columbia University (M.L.S., 1970; M.I.A., 1974); Pace University (J.D., 1981). ***COURSES: Legal Research. ***Email:*** koster@mail.law.cuny.edu

JULIE LIM,* (Library Associate Professor)**, *Education:* Queens College (B.A.); University of Washington (M.L.S.); Seattle University School of Law (J.D.). ***COURSES: Legal Research. ***Email:*** lim@mail.law.cuny.edu

STEPHEN JAMES LOFFREDO,* (Associate Professor of Law)**, born Bronx, New York, January 30, 1955; admitted to bar, 1982, New York. *Education:* Yale College (B.A., 1977); Harvard Law School (J.D., 1981). ***COURSES: Constitutional Law, Poverty Law, Health Law, Administrative Law, Immigration, Clinical Law. ***Email:*** loffredo@mail.law.cuny.edu

SHIRLEY LUNG,* (Adjunct Assistant Professor of Law)**, born Hong Kong, October 26, 1960. *Education:* Cornell University (B.A., 1981); New York University School of Law (J.D., 1985). ***COURSES: Torts, Academic Support, Lawyering. ***Email:*** lung@mail.law.cuny.edu

ANDREA LORETTA MCARDLE,* (Associate Professor, Director of Legal Writing)**, born Bronxville, New York, June 7, 1953; admitted to bar, 1979, New York. *Education:* Fordham University (B.A., 1975); New York University (J.D., 1978); Columbia School of Law (LL.M., 1988); Columbia University (M.A., 1995). ***COURSES: Lawyering Seminar, Legal Writing. ***Email:*** mcardle@mail.law.cuny.edu

CHERYL MEYER,* (Adjunct Assistant Professor of Law)**, born Brooklyn, New York, March 6, 1949; admitted to bar, 1987, New York. *Education:* Queens College (B.A., 1968); Hunter College (M.S., 1970); CUNY Law School (J.D., 1986). ***COURSES: UCC: Sales, Secured Transactions, Commercial Paper, Contracts, Wills, Business Associations, Writing, Analysis. ***Email:*** meyer@mail.law.cuny.edu

JENNY RIVERA,* (Associate Professor of Law)**, admitted to bar, 1986, New York. *Education:* Princeton University (B.A., 1982); New York University School of Law (J.D., 1985); Columbia University School of Law (LL.M., 1993). ***COURSES: Civil Procedure, Property, Administrative Law, Constitutional Law, State & Local Government Law. ***Email:*** rivera@mail.law.cuny.edu

RUTHANN ROBSON,* (Professor of Law)**, born 1956; admitted to bar, 1980, Florida. *Education:* Stetson University School of Law (J.D., 1979); University of California at Berkeley (LL.M., 1990). ***COURSES: Constitutional Structures, Criminal Procedure, Feminist Jurisprudence, Law & Sexuality, Law & Family Relations, Public Institutions. ***Email:*** robson@mail.law.cuny.edu

JOSEPH A. ROSENBERG,* (Associate Professor of Law)**, born New York, March 14, 1958; admitted to bar, 1987, New York. *Education:* Northwestern University (B.S.Ed., 1980); City University of New York (J.D., 1986). ***COURSES: Clinic, Elder Law, Wills, Trusts and Estates. ***Email:*** rosenberg@mail.law.cuny.edu

MERRICK T. ROSSEIN,* (Professor of Law)**, born 1945; admitted to bar, 1976, New York. *Education:* Alfred University (B.A., 1967); New York University (M.P.A., 1972); Antioch Law School (J.D., 1975). ***COURSES: Administrative Law, Employment Discrimination, Civil Rights, Trial Practice, Constitutional Law. ***Email:*** rossein@mail.law.cuny.edu

JONATHAN KENT SAXON,* (Associate Law Library Professor of Law)**, born New York, New York, March 29, 1961; admitted to bar, 1994, New York. *Education:* University of Bridgeport (B.S., 1984); Pratt Institute (M.S.L.S., 1993); Brooklyn Law School (J.D., 1993). ***COURSES: Legal Research. ***Email:*** saxon@mail.law.cuny.edu

BETTIE H. SCOTT,* (Law School Library Associate Professor of Law)**, born Raleigh, North Carolina, March 26, 1938. *Education:* University of North Carolina (B.A., 1959); University of Hawaii (M.L.S., 1975); McGeorge School of Law (J.D., 1981). ***COURSES: Legal Research. ***Email:*** scott@mail.law.cuny.edu

ROBERT F. SEIBEL,* (Associate Professor)**, admitted to bar, 1971, Massachusetts; 1979, Illinois; 1980, Iowa; 1981, Maine; 1988, New York. *Education:* Bowdoin College (B.A., 1968); Northeastern University School of Law (J.D., 1971). ***COURSES: Elderlaw Clinic, Women and The Law Clinic, Judicial Ext., and Estate Planning Clinic. ***Email:*** seibel@mail.law.cuny.edu

PATRICIA ANNE TAYLOR,* (Executive Asst. to the Dean and Higher Educ. Officer)**, born Weems, Virginia, March 8, 1945; admitted to bar, 1988, New York. *Education:* Hampton University (B.A., 1965); Drexel University (M.S.L.S., 1970); New York Law School (J.D., 1987). ***COURSES: Torts, Administrative Law, Legal Research. ***Email:*** taylor@mail.law.cuny.edu

ROSARIA S. VIGORITO,* (Library Associate Professor)**, born 1959; admitted to bar, 1986, New York. *Education:* New York University (B.A., 1981); Rutgers University (M.L.S., 1995); Brooklyn Law School (J.D., 1985); New York University School of Law (LL.M., 1987). ***COURSES: Legal Research. ***Email:*** vigorito@mail.law.cuny.edu

DEBORAH ZALESNE,* (Associate Professor)**, born Philadelphia, Pennsylvania, March 27, 1966; admitted to bar, 1992, Colorado. *Education:* Williams College (B.A., 1988); University of Denver College of Law (J.D., 1992); Temple University School of Law (LL.M., 1997). ***COURSES: Contracts, Sales, Corporations. ***Email:*** zalesne@mail.law.cuny.edu

***JEAN G. ZORN,* (Professor of Law)**, born Massachusetts, January 2, 1942; admitted to bar, 1976, Massachusetts; 1978, New York. *Education:* University of California at Berkeley (B.A., 1965);

(This Listing Continued)

CITY UNIVERSITY OF NEW YORK, SCHOOL OF LAW AT QUEENS COLLEGE—Continued

University of Wisconsin at Madison (M.A., 1968; J.D., 1973). ***COURSES:*** Lawyering, Property, Corporations, Law & Anthropology. ***Email:*** zorn@mail.law.cuny.edu

---

CLEVELAND STATE UNIVERSITY
CLEVELAND-MARSHALL COLLEGE OF LAW

1801 EUCLID AVENUE
CLEVELAND, OHIO 44115
Telephone: (216) 687-2344
Fax: (216) 687-6881
http://www.law.csuohio.edu

ABA Approved Since 1957.

Cleveland State University's 104 year-old Cleveland-Marshall College of Law is the direct descendant of two night law schools: the Cleveland Law School, founded in 1897, and the John Marshall School of Law, founded in 1916. The Cleveland Law School was the first law school in the state to admit women and one of the first to admit minorities. In 1946 the two schools merged to become the Cleveland-Marshall Law School; in 1969 the law school joined the city's new public university and was renamed the Cleveland-Marshall College of Law of Cleveland State University. Today, the College of Law, with both day and evening divisions, is the city's only public law school.

Cleveland-Marshall grants the J.D., the L.L.M., the J.D./M.B.A., the J.D./M.E.S., the J.D./M.P.A. and the J.D./M.U.P.D.D. The College of Law is accredited by the American Bar Association and the Association of American Law Schools.

The College's library, classrooms, offices, and student social center are contained in one centrally located building, adjacent to the city's thriving theater district and in proximity to the city's major corporate, non-profit, legal and judicial centers. Thus students studying law at Cleveland-Marshall have abundant recreational and employment opportunities.

A new multi-million dollar law library opened in the fall of 1997. This 85,000 net-square-feet research and learning facility is among the largest academic law libraries in the country, housing the second largest academic law collection in Ohio. Students preparing for legal practice in the 21st century have access to all on-line research services, a 50-seat computer lab, 17 group study rooms, a bibliographic instruction room, a state-of-the-art media center, and 206 student carrels with built-in power and network ports for portable computers. The Cleveland-Marshall Law Library has been a selective federal depository since 1979.

The College of Law provides a comprehensive program of legal instruction. In addition to traditional courses, the College's two student-edited journals, Moot Court Program, five legal clinics, externships, advocacy program, and legal writing courses comprise a professional skills-building curriculum. The *Journal of Law and Health* and the *CSU Law Review* refine students' writing, research and editing skills; the Moot Court Program provides them with experience in the appellate process. The Employment Law Clinic offers free legal counsel to clients on a variety of employment-related issues, while the Housing Law Clinic seeks to assist needy clients with landlord/tenant and other housing problems. Students in the Law & Public Policy Clinic serve governmental and non-profit agencies in need of legal services. In the College's Environmental Law Clinic, students study and propose legal solutions to environmental problems. In the Community Advocacy Clinic students provide legal assistance on a variety of projects to community and non-profit agencies active in restoring the area's endangered neighborhoods. The Judicial Externship Program places upper-level students in the offices of federal and state judges. Students may also elect externships in the U.S. Attorney's office, the office of the Federal Public Defender, and University Hospitals. The advocacy curriculum offers courses in trial and pre-trial practice, alternative dispute resolution, arbitration, and mediation, while the writing and research curriculum develops these important lawyering skills in future lawyers. Finally, students interested in careers in international law may choose to participate in the College's Summer Institute for Law Students in St. Petersburg, Russia.

The College's curriculum is complemented by these lecture series: the Cleveland-Marshall Visiting Scholar Lectures; the Baker & Hostetler Lectures; the Forrest B. Weinberg Memorial Lectures; and the Distinguished Jurist Lectures.

The law school also has a very active Pro Bono Program. In 2000-2001 students volunteered over 8,300 hours to community service programs and organizations such as Habitat for Humanity, the Cleveland Food Bank, and the Homeless Legal Assistance Project.

Cleveland-Marshall's 45 faculty members are outstanding teachers and scholars. A number are Fulbright Scholars, and many have lectured abroad. Several of the College's faculty have argued ground-breaking cases before the United States Supreme Court. Cleveland-Marshall faculty members publish in the country's most prestigious journals and are the authors of casebooks, treatises and scores of other publications on a broad range of subjects. These research interests are often translated into elective course offerings that expose students to contemporary trends in legal practice and scholarship. Many of the faculty practiced law extensively before assuming their careers as educators, and many have come from backgrounds of distinguished public service.

Approximately 800 students from over 100 colleges and universities throughout the country study law at Cleveland-Marshall. They include recent college graduates as well as others who are changing or beginning new careers after years of teaching, business, or other professional experience. Approximately 48 percent of the student body are women and approximately one third are evening students, earning their J.D. in four-or five-year programs. The student body is notable for its diversity in life experience and ethnic backgrounds. This diversity enriches the educational program and makes the law school community exciting and dynamic.

Cleveland-Marshall has an aggressive Office of Career Planning. 96% of the class of 2000 are employed or are enrolled in full-time degree programs. Other student services include an Office of Financial Aid. Approximately 75 percent of the student body receive financial assistance.

Cleveland-Marshall graduates include a number of the state's outstanding jurists. Several judges serving on the U.S. District Court for the Northern District of Ohio, Eastern Division, are graduates. The first woman to serve as a U.S. Magistrate Judge in the Northern District of Ohio is a Cleveland-Marshall graduate. In addition to a large representation of municipal and county judges, the former Chief Justice of the Ohio Supreme Court and several current Ohio Court of Appeals judges are alumni of Cleveland-Marshall. Cleveland-Marshall has two judges on the 16-member U.S. Court of Federal Claims in Washington D.C.

(This Listing Continued)

CLEVELAND STATE UNIVERSITY, CLEVELAND-MARSHALL COLLEGE OF LAW—Continued

Among Cleveland-Marshall alumni are an Ohio Governor, an Ohio Attorney General, three former Cleveland Mayors, numerous County Commissioners, a U.S. Senator, many U.S. Representatives and numerous Ohio Legislators and Cleveland City Council representatives. Presently, the U.S. Attorney for the Northern District of Ohio is a graduate of the school, as is a Cuyahoga County Commissioner and the Lieutenant Governor of the State of Ohio. Cleveland-Marshall graduates are prominent in the state legislature as well.

Cleveland-Marshall alumni and alumnae number among the city's most distinguished attorneys: Currently, the managing partners of several of the city's leading law firms are graduates. Alumni are leaders and members of non-profit community organizations and public interest law firms, including the Executive Director of Cleveland Works, Inc., and the Director of the Cleveland Legal Aid Society. Graduates are leaders in business and industry as well. Cleveland Marshall ranks top among the top 22 law schools with the greatest number of graduates serving as corporate counsel.

Finally, several well-regarded journalists received law degrees from Cleveland-Marshall, including the Chief of the NBC Washington News Bureau, the former Director of Public Affairs for the U.S. Department of Justice, the editor and publisher of the *ABA Journal*, and many Cleveland columnists and feature writers.

Dean: Steven H. Steinglass (216) 687-2300
Associate Dean: Jack Guttenberg (216) 687-3852
Admissions: Margaret McNally (216) 687-2304
Financial Aid: Catherine Buzanski (216) 687-6887
Associate Dean, Law Library Director and Professor of Law: Michael J. Slinger (216) 687-3547
Placement: M. Jayne Hurst Geneva (216) 687-6871
Alumni Affairs: Mary McKenna (216) 687-2368
External Affairs: Louise P. Dempsey (216) 687-2536
Academic Affairs: Jean Lifter (216) 687-4557

FULL TIME FACULTY

STEVEN H. STEINGLASS*, (Professor of Law and Dean)**, born 1942; admitted to bar, 1968, Wisconsin; 1981, Ohio. *Education:* University of Pennsylvania (B.S., 1964); Columbia Law School (LL.B., 1967). ***COURSES: Federal Jurisdiction, Civil Procedure, Section 1983 Litigation, State Constitutional Law.

LINDA L. AMMONS*, (Associate Professor of Law)**, born 1953; admitted to bar, 1987, Ohio. *Education:* Oakwood College (B.A., 1974); Ohio State University (M.A., 1980; J.D., 1987). ***COURSES: Administrative Law, Legislation, Women and the Law.

DAVID R. BARNHIZER*, (Professor of Law)**, born 1944; admitted to bar, 1969, Colorado; 1973, Ohio. *Education:* Muskingum College (A.B., 1966); Ohio State University (J.D., 1969); Harvard University (LL.M., 1972). ***COURSES: Trial Advocacy, Lawyers' Strategies, Jurisprudence, Environmental Law, Environmental Law Clinic.

SUSAN J. BECKER*, (Associate Professor of Law)**, born 1955; admitted to bar, 1984, Ohio. *Education:* Eastern Kentucky University (B.A., 1977); Cleveland State University (J.D., 1983). ***COURSES: Contracts, Civil Procedure, Pretrial Practice, Externships, Fair Employment Practices Clinic, Remedies.

***GORDON J. BEGGS*, (Staff Attorney for Employment Law Clinic)**, born 1947; admitted to bar, 1974, Ohio. *Education:* University of Pennsylvania (B.A., 1970; J.D., 1973).

BEVERLY BLAIR*, (Legal Writing Lecturer)**, born 1949; admitted to bar, 1985, Ohio. *Education:* Hiram College (B.A., 1971); Cleveland State University (M.S., 1975); Case Western Reserve University (M.S., 1979); Cleveland-Marshall College of Law (J.D., 1985). ***COURSES: Legal Writing, Research and Advocacy.

AMY E. BLENKHORN*, (Visiting Assistant Professor of Law)**, born 1959; admitted to bar, 1984, Ohio. *Education:* Cleveland State University (B.A., 1981); Cleveland-Marshall College of Law (J.D., 1984). ***COURSES: Estates and Trusts, Property. ***Email:*** amy.blenkhorn@law.csuohio.edu

CAROLYN BROERING-JACOBS*, (Legal Writing Lecturer)**, born 1969; admitted to bar, 1994, Ohio. *Education:* University of Notre Dame (B.A., 1991); Ohio State University School of Law (J.D., 1994). ***COURSES: Legal Writing, Research and Advocacy. ***Email:*** carolyn.broering@law.csuohio.edu

THOMAS D. BUCKLEY*, (Professor of Law)**, born 1937; admitted to bar, 1965, North Dakota; 1971, Illinois. *Education:* Fordham University (A.B., 1958); Yale Law School (LL.B., 1961). ***COURSES: Commercial Law, Bankruptcy, Civil Liberties, Secured Transactions.

APRIL CHERRY*, (Associate Professor of Law)**, born 1964; admitted to bar, 1990, Connecticut. *Education:* Vassar College (A.B., 1986); Yale Law School (J.D., 1990). ***COURSES: Property, Women and the Law, Parents, Children and the State.

***SCHUYLER M. COOK*, (Reference Librarian)**, born 1959; admitted to bar, 1988, Ohio. *Education:* Kent State University (M.L.S., 1991); Cleveland-Marshall College of Law (J.D., 1987).

PHYLLIS L. CROCKER*, (Associate Professor of Law)**, born 1956; admitted to bar, 1987, Illinois; 1992, Texas. *Education:* Yale University (B.A., 1978); Northeastern University School of Law (M.A., 1985; J.D., 1985). ***COURSES: Capital Punishment, Civil Procedure, Criminal Trial Process.

***PAMELA DAIKER-MIDDAUGH*, (Staff Attorney for Law and Public Policy Clinic and Administrator of the Pro Bono Program)**, born 1962; admitted to bar, 1989, Ohio. *Education:* Emory University (B.A., 1985); Cleveland-Marshall College of Law (J.D., 1998).

DENA S. DAVIS*, (Professor of Law)**, born 1947. *Education:* Marlboro College (B.A., 1972); University of Iowa (Ph.D., 1986); University of Virginia (J.D., 1990). ***COURSES: Biomedical Ethics, Church and State, Torts, AIDS and the Law.

MICHAEL H. DAVIS*, (Professor of Law)**, born 1946; admitted to bar, 1975, Colorado; 1977, Massachusetts and New York; 1981, Tennessee. *Education:* Occidental College (B.A., 1967); Hofstra Law School (J.D., 1975); Harvard Law School (LL.M., 1979). ***COURSES: Torts, Intellectual Property, Comparative Law.

***LOUISE P. DEMPSEY*, (Assistant Dean of External Affairs)**, born 1944; admitted to bar, 1982, Ohio. *Education:* McGill University (B.A., 1966); Cleveland-Marshall College of Law (J.D., 1981).

***VERONICA M. DOUGHERTY*, (Associate Professor of Law)**, born

(This Listing Continued)

CLEVELAND STATE UNIVERSITY, CLEVELAND-MARSHALL COLLEGE OF LAW—Continued

1955. *Education:* Bethany College (B.A., 1977); Kent State University (M.A., 1981); Harvard University (M.P.P., 1987); Harvard Law School (J.D., 1987). ***COURSES:*** Antitrust, Corporations.

KATHLEEN C. ENGEL, **(Assistant Professor)**, born 1959; admitted to bar, 1990, Massachusetts. *Education:* Smith College (A.B., 1982); University of Texas Law School (J.D., 1988). ***COURSES:*** Torts, Fair Employment Practices Law.

PATRICIA J. FALK, **(Associate Professor of Law)**, born 1957; admitted to bar, 1986, Nebraska. *Education:* Union College (B.A., 1979); University of Nebraska-Lincoln (J.D., 1983; Ph.D., 1988). ***COURSES:*** Criminal Law, Family Law, Social Science and the Law, White Collar Crime.

JOEL J. FINER, **(Professor of Law)**, born 1938; admitted to bar, 1964, District of Columbia. *Education:* City College of New York (B.B.A., 1959); Yale University (M.A., 1963; LL.B., 1963). ***COURSES:*** Criminal Law, Criminal Procedure, Law and Medicine, Biomedical Ethics, Family Law.

JOAN FLYNN, **(Associate Professor of Law)**, born 1959; admitted to bar, 1989, Illinois. *Education:* Grinnel College (B.A., 1982); New York University School of Law (J.D., 1987). ***COURSES:*** Civil Procedure, Labor Law, Administrative Law.

DAVID F. FORTE, **(Professor of Law)**, born 1941; admitted to bar, 1986, Ohio. *Education:* Harvard College (A.B., 1963); University of Manchester (M.A., 1965); University of Toronto (Ph.D., 1974); Columbia University (J.D., 1976). ***COURSES:*** Constitutional Law, International Law, Comparative Law, Islamic Law, Jurisprudence, International Human Rights.

STEPHEN W. GARD, **(Professor of Law)**, born 1947; admitted to bar, 1973, Indiana; 1980, Ohio. *Education:* DePauw University (B.A., 1969); Indiana University (J.D., 1973); University of Chicago (LL.M., 1975). ***COURSES:*** Constitutional Law, Remedies, Torts, First Amendment Rights.

PETER D. GARLOCK, **(Associate Professor of Law)**, born 1939; admitted to bar, 1974, New York. *Education:* Yale University (B.A., 1960; LL.B., 1966; Ph.D., 1972). ***COURSES:*** Criminal Law, Torts, American Legal History, Juvenile Law, Child, Family, and State.

DEBORAH A. GEIER, **(Professor of Law)**, born 1957; admitted to bar, 1987, New York. *Education:* Baldwin-Wallace College (A.B., 1983); Case Western Reserve University (J.D., 1986). ***COURSES:*** Federal Income Taxation, Corporate Taxation, Federal Income Taxation of International Transactions, Partnership Tax, Federal Indian Law.

SHELDON GELMAN, **(Professor of Law)**, born 1946; admitted to bar, 1973, New Jersey. *Education:* Rutgers College (A.B., 1967); Rutgers School of Law-Newark (J.D., 1973); Harvard Law School (LL.M., 1980). ***COURSES:*** Civil Procedure, Psychiatry and Law, Contracts, Evidence, Constitutional Law, Jurisprudence.

LOUIS B. GENEVA, **(Associate Professor of Law)**, born 1947; admitted to bar, 1973, Ohio; 1977, Connecticut. *Education:* Miami University (B.A., 1969); Suffolk University (J.D., 1973); New York University (LL.M., 1974). ***COURSES:*** Corporate Taxation, Estate Planning, Federal Income Taxation, Wealth Transfer Tax, Partnership Tax.

M. JAYNE HURST GENEVA, **(Director of Career Planning)**, born 1945; admitted to bar, 1988, Ohio. *Education:* Hiram College (B.A., 1967); The Ohio State University (M.A., 1969); Cleveland-Marshall College of Law (J.D., 1987).

BRIAN A. GLASSMAN, **(Legal Writing Lecturer)**, born 1955; admitted to bar, 1981, Ohio. *Education:* Connecticut College (B.A., 1977); Boston University School of Law (J.D., 1981). ***COURSES:*** Legal Writing, Research and Advocacy.

DAVID B. GOSHIEN, **(Professor of Law)**, born 1937; admitted to bar, 1962, North Carolina; 1976, Ohio. *Education:* Brown University (A.B., 1959); University of Chicago (J.D., 1962). ***COURSES:*** Contracts, Federal Income Taxation, Tax Policy, Wealth Transfer Taxation.

JACK A. GUTTENBERG, **(Professor of Law and Associate Dean)**, born 1951; admitted to bar, 1976, Georgia and Michigan; 1982, Ohio. *Education:* University of Michigan (B.A., 1973); Wayne State University (J.D., 1976). ***COURSES:*** Criminal Law, Criminal Procedure, Trial Advocacy, Pretrial Practice, Externships, Professional Responsibility.

S. CANDICE HOKE, **(Associate Professor of Law)**, born 1955; admitted to bar, 1984, Massachusetts. *Education:* Hollins College (B.A., 1977); Yale Law School (J.D., 1983). ***COURSES:*** Federal Jurisdiction, Civil Procedure, Jurisprudence Seminar, Constitutional Law.

LOLITA K. BUCKNER INNISS, **(Assistant Professor of Law)**, born 1961; admitted to bar, 1988, New Jersey; 1997 Michigan. *Education:* Princeton University (A.B., 1983); University of California at Los Angeles School of Law (J.D., 1986). ***COURSES:*** Criminal Law, Property, Administrative Law, Immigration Law.

W. DENNIS KEATING, **(Professor of Urban Affairs and Law)**, born 1943; admitted to bar, 1968, District of Columbia. *Education:* Loyola College-Baltimore (A.B., 1965); University of Pennsylvania (J.D., 1968); University of California-Berkeley (M.C.P., 1971; Ph.D., 1979). ***COURSES:*** Housing Law, Planning Law.

SANDRA J. KERBER, **(Legal Writing Lecturer)**, born 1943; admitted to bar, 1982, Ohio. *Education:* Baldwin-Wallace College (B.A., 1965); Cleveland-Marshall College of Law (J.D., 1981). ***COURSES:*** Legal Writing, Research and Advocacy.

DEBORAH J. KLEIN, **(Legal Writing Lecturer)**, born 1951; admitted to bar, 1978, Ohio. *Education:* Kent State University (B.A., 1975); Cleveland-Marshall College of Law (J.D., 1978). ***COURSES:*** Legal Writing, Research and Advocacy.

KENNETH J. KOWALSKI, **(Assistant Director of Employment Law Clinic)**, born 1949; admitted to bar, 1981, Ohio. *Education:* Case Western Reserve University (B.A., 1971); Cleveland State University (M.Ed., 1974); Ohio State University (J.D., 1981).

ARTHUR R. LANDEVER, **(Professor of Law)**, born 1936; admitted to bar, 1961, New York; 1981, Ohio. *Education:* New York University (A.B., 1957; J.D., 1960; Ph.D., 1969). ***COURSES:*** Constitutional Law, Legal Skills and Analysis, Interviewing, Counseling and Negotiating, Social Science and Law, Legal Profession.

STEPHEN R. LAZARUS, **(Associate Professor of Law)**, born 1939; admitted to bar, 1965, New York; 1972, District of Columbia; 1974, Ohio. *Education:* Williams College (A.B., 1961); Harvard Law School (LL.B., 1964). ***COURSES:*** Civil Procedure, Evidence, Constitutional Law, Ethics and Professional Responsibility, Immigration and Nationality Law, Property.

JEAN B. LIFTER, **(Assistant Dean of Academic Affairs)**, born 1947; admitted to bar, 1975, Pennsylvania; 1985, Ohio. *Education:* Wellesley College (B.A., 1969); Harvard University (J.D., 1975).

KERMIT J. LIND, **(Staff Attorney for Law and Public Policy Clinic)**, born 1941; admitted to bar, 1985, Ohio. *Education:* Goshien College (B.A., 1964); University of Chicago (M.A., 1966); Cleveland-Marshall College of Law (J.D., 1984).

(This Listing Continued)

CLEVELAND STATE UNIVERSITY, CLEVELAND-MARSHALL COLLEGE OF LAW—Continued

TAYYAB MAHMUD*, (Professor of Law)**, born 1954; admitted to bar, 1987, California; 1990, Pakistan. *Education:* University of Punjab (B.A., 1975); University of Hawaii (M.A., 1977; Ph.D., 1981); Hastings College of the Law, University of California (J.D., 1987). ***COURSES: Contracts, Torts, International Law, International Business Transactions, Jurisprudence.

CLAIRE C. ROBINSON MAY*, (Legal Writing Instructor)**, born 1971; admitted to bar, 1996, Ohio; 1999, U.S. Court of Appeals 10th Circuit; 2000, U.S. District Court, District of Columbia; 2001, U.S. District Court Northern District of Ohio. *Education:* Harvard University (A.B., 1993); Case Western Reserve (J.D., 1996). ***COURSES: Legal Writing and Research, Advocacy.

PATRICIA A. MCCOY*, (Professor of Law)**, born 1954; admitted to bar, 1984, District of Columbia. *Education:* Oberlin College (B.A., 1976); University of California-Berkeley (J.D., 1983). ***COURSES: Banking Regulation, Securities Regulation, Property, Civil Procedure.

KARIN MIKA*, (Assistant Director of Legal Writing Program and Director of the Moot Court Program)**, born 1962; admitted to bar, 1990, Ohio. *Education:* Baldwin-Wallace College (B.A., 1986); Cleveland-Marshall College of Law (J.D., 1989). ***COURSES: Legal Writing, Research and Advocacy Program.

KEVIN F. O'NEILL*, (Assistant Professor of Law and Director of Law Alumni Continuing Legal Education Program)**, born 1955; admitted to bar, 1985, Ohio. *Education:* San Francisco State University (B.A., 1977); Case Western Reserve University Law School (J.D., 1984). ***COURSES: Contracts, Evidence, Externships.

KUNAL M. PARKER*, (Associate Professor of Law)**, born 1968; admitted to bar, 1995, New York. *Education:* Harvard University (B.A., 1990); Harvard Law School (J.D., 1994). ***COURSES: Property, Bankruptcy.

JANE M. PICKER*, (Professor of Law)**, born 1935; admitted to bar, 1961, Connecticut; 1971, Ohio. *Education:* Swarthmore College (A.B., 1957); Yale University (LL.B., 1960). ***COURSES: International Law, Fair Employment Practice, International Law and Human Rights, Class Actions, Employment Law Clinic, International Law Seminar.

***ELLEN QUINN*, (Assistant Director of Public Services for Law Library)**, born 1954; admitted to bar, 1966, Ohio. *Education:* University of Akron (B.A., 1979); Kent State University (M.L.S. 1977); Cleveland-Marshall College of Law (J.D., 1995).

HEIDI GOROVITZ ROBERTSON*, (Associate Professor of Law)**, born 1964; admitted to bar, 1990, Wisconsin and California; 1992, District of Columbia. *Education:* Tufts University (B.A., 1985); University of Wisconsin Law School (J.D., 1990); Columbia University School of Law (LL.M., 1995; presently J.S.D. candidate). ***COURSES: Property, Environmental Law.

ALAN MILES RUBEN*, (Professor of Law)**, born 1931; admitted to bar, 1957, Pennsylvania; 1972, Ohio. *Education:* University of Pennsylvania (B.A., 1953; M.A., 1956; J.D., 1956). ***COURSES: Securities Regulation, Corporations, Agency and Partnership, Jurisprudence, Ethics and Professional Responsibility.

***MICHAEL J. SLINGER*, (Director of the Law Library, Professor of Law and Associate Dean)**, born 1956. *Education:* University of Pittsburgh (B.A., 1978); University of South Carolina (M.L.S., 1979); Duquesne University School of Law (J.D., 1984).

DAVID SNYDER*, (Assistant Professor of Law)**, born 1966; admitted to bar, 1993, District of Columbia; 1991, Louisiana; 1992, Maryland. *Education:* Yale University (B.A., 1988); Tulane Law School (J.D., 1991). ***COURSES: Contracts, Commercial Law.

LLOYD B. SNYDER*, (Professor of Law)**, born 1944; admitted to bar, 1970, Ohio. *Education:* University of Pennsylvania (B.S., 1966; J.D., 1969). ***COURSES: Evidence, Legal Profession, Pretrial Practice, Externship Seminars.

WILLIAM L. TABAC*, (Professor of Law)**, born 1940; admitted to bar, 1967, Virginia; 1975, Ohio. *Education:* Case Western Reserve University (B.A., 1962); George Washington University (J.D., 1966). ***COURSES: Contracts, Commercial Law, Consumer Remedies, Secured Transactions.

ADAM THURSCHWELL*, (Assistant Professor of Law)**, born 1958; admitted to bar, 1991, New York. *Education:* Yale University (B.A., 1980); University of Pennsylvania Law School (J.D., 1984). ***COURSES: Criminal Law, Criminal Procedure, Evidence, Jurisprudence.

***BARBARA J. TYLER*, (Legal Writing Lecturer)**, born 1943; admitted to bar, 1989, Ohio. *Education:* Baldwin-Wallace College (B.A., 1986); Cleveland-Marshall College of Law (J.D., 1989).

***KATHERINE A. VAN TASSEL*, (Assistant Visiting Professor of Law)**, born 1957; admitted to bar, 1986, Ohio; 1996, Georgia. *Education:* Case Western Reserve University, Frances Payne Bolton School of Nursing (R.N., B.S.N., 1980); Case Western Reserve University School of Law (J.D., 1986).

ALAN WEINSTEIN*, (Associate Professor of Law and Director of the JD/MPA and Law & Public Policy Programs)**, born 1944; admitted to bar, 1978, Massachusetts; 1981, Wisconsin. *Education:* University of Pennsylvania (B.A., 1967); University of California-Berkeley (J.D., 1977); Massachusetts Institute of Technology (M.C.P., 1979). ***COURSES: Land Use Planning, Environmental Law, Alternate Dispute Resolution, Law and Public Policy, Administrative Law, Legislation.

STEPHEN J. WERBER*, (Professor of Law, Director of Law Alumni Continuing Legal Education Programs)**, born 1940; admitted to bar, 1965, District of Columbia and New York; 1980, Ohio. *Education:* Adelphi University (B.A., 1961); Cornell University (J.D., 1964); New York University (LL.M., 1970). ***COURSES: Contracts, Products Liability, Evidence, Appellate Advocacy, Advanced Brief Writing.

FREDERIC WHITE*, (Professor of Law and Associate Dean)**, born 1948; admitted to bar, 1973, Ohio. *Education:* Columbia College (B.A., 1970); Columbia University (J.D., 1973). ***COURSES: Administrative Law, Property, Land Use Control, Local Government Law, Estates and Trusts.

JAMES G. WILSON*, (Professor of Law)**, born 1947; admitted to bar, 1974, Kentucky; 1978, Michigan; 1981, Ohio. *Education:* Princeton University (B.A., 1969); University of Chicago Law School (J.D., 1974). ***COURSES: Constitutional Law, Administrative Law, Legal History, Jurisprudence.

COLLEGE OF WILLIAM AND MARY SCHOOL OF LAW

P.O. BOX 8795
WILLIAMSBURG, VIRGINIA 23187-8795
Telephone: (757) 221-3800
Fax: (757) 221-3261
http://www.wm.edu/law

ABA Approved Since 1932.

At the direction of Governor Thomas Jefferson, the first academic chair of law in the United States was created at the College of William & Mary in 1779. George Wythe, Jefferson's tutor at William and Mary and a signer of the Declaration of Independence, was awarded the chair. The College conferred its first Bachelor of Laws Degree in 1793.

The William & Mary School of Law now is different in many ways, but continues to be one of the country's most highly regarded small public law schools. We also continue to adhere to Jefferson and Wythe's ideal -- that the school exists to train outstanding lawyers who are also exemplary citizens.

The Law School is home to the Institute of Bill of Rights Law, which sponsors programs on emerging constitutional issues each year. The Annual Supreme Court Preview, held each fall, typically includes nationally-known journalists such as Linda Greenhouse of the *New York Times,* Tony Mauro of *USA Today* and Joan Biskupic of the *Washington Post.* The Institute also sponsors an academic symposium each year as well as a student-initiated symposium and has sponsored an impressive series of publications.

The Law School is also the home of the McGlothlin Moot Courtroom, the most technologically-advanced courtroom in the country, and the nationally-recognized Legal Skills Program, a two-year required sequence of courses focusing on basic lawyering skills including interviewing and fact-gathering, research and writing, negotiating, drafting, and trial and appellate advocacy. This program is also the vehicle for teaching professional ethics at the law school, and was recently awarded the ABA Gambrell Award for Professionalism.

William & Mary's students produce four law journals: The *William & Mary Law Review,* the *William & Mary Bill of Rights Journal,* the *William & Mary Environmental Law & Policy Review* and the *William & Mary Journal of Women & the Law.* They also conduct the William B. Spong Moot Court Tournament every Spring.

Dean: W. Taylor Reveley, III (757) 221-3790
Vice Dean: Lynda L. Butler (757) 221-3843
Associate Dean, Administration: Lizbeth Jackson (757) 221-3782
Library Director: James S. Heller (757) 221-3252
Associate Dean, Career Services: Robert E. Kaplan (757) 221-3805
Associate Dean, Development and Alumni Affairs: Sally Kellam (757) 221-3795
Associate Dean, Office of Admission: Faye F. Shealy (757) 221-3784

FULL TIME FACULTY

W. TAYLOR REVELEY, III,* (Dean and Professor of Law)**, born Churchville, Virginia, January 6, 1943; admitted to bar, 1970, Virginia; 1977, District of Columbia. *Education:* Princeton University (A.B., 1965); University of Virginia (J.D., 1968). ***COURSES: Citizen Lawyers.

PETER A. ALCES,* (Rita Anne Rollins Professor of Law)**, born Brooklyn, New York, January 9, 1956; admitted to bar, 1980, Illinois. *Education:* Lafayette University (B.A., 1977); University of Illinois (J.D., 1980). ***COURSES: Sales, Contracts, Payment Systems, Bankruptcy, Products Liability.

JAYNE W. BARNARD,* (Cutler Professor of Law)**, born Cleveland, Ohio, July 26, 1947; admitted to bar, 1975, Illinois; 1988, Virginia. *Education:* University of Illinois (B.S., 1970); University of Chicago (J.D., 1975). ***COURSES: Corporations, Securities Regulation, Food and Drug Law, Agency and Partnership.

LYNDA L. BUTLER,* (Vice Dean and Professor of Law)**, born Frankfurt, Germany, September 14, 1951; admitted to bar, 1978, District of Columbia; 1982, Virginia. *Education:* William and Mary (B.S., 1973); University of Virginia (J.D., 1978). ***COURSES: Property, Land Use, Toxic Torts, Law and Public Policy.

LAN CAO,* (Professor of Law)**, born Vietnam, August 11, 1961; admitted to bar, 1989, New York. *Education:* Mount Holyoke College (B.A., 1983); Yale Law School (J.D., 1987). ***COURSES: International Business, International Trade, Public International Trade.

GLENN E. COVEN, JR.,* (Mills E. Godwin Professor of Law)**, born Leesburg, Virginia, May 8, 1942; admitted to bar, 1966, New York. *Education:* Swarthmore College (B.A., 1963); Columbia University (LL.B., 1966). ***COURSES: Corporate Taxation, Federal Income Tax, International Business Planning, International Intellectual Property, Torts.

NEAL E. DEVINS,* (Goodrich Prof. of Law & Lecturer in Government & Research Fellow, Institute of Bill of Rights Law)**, born Brooklyn, New York, November 18, 1957; admitted to bar, 1983, Tennessee; 1987, District of Columbia. *Education:* Georgetown (A.B., 1978); Vanderbilt (J.D., 1982). ***COURSES: Constitutional Law, Family and the State, Administrative Law, Law & Public Policy.

A. MECHELE DICKERSON,* (Professor of Law)**, born Memphis, Tennessee, September 8, 1962; admitted to bar, 1990, Pennsylvania; 1991, District of Columbia; 1992, Virginia. *Education:* Harvard-Radcliffe (B.A., 1984); Harvard (J.D., 1988). ***COURSES: Bankruptcy, Civil Procedure, Business Reorganization and Bankruptcy.

DAVISON M. DOUGLAS,* (Hanson Professor of Law and Director, Institute of Bill of Rights Law)**, born Charlotte, North Carolina, September 16, 1956; admitted to bar, 1984, North Carolina. *Education:* Princeton (A.B., 1978); Yale Divinity School (M.A.R., 1983); Yale University (J.D., 1983; Ph.D., 1992). ***COURSES: Employment Law, Constitutional Law, American Legal History, Contracts, Evidence, Labor Law.

JOHN DUFFY,* (Associate Professor of Law)**, born Pittsfield, Massachusetts, November 22, 1963; admitted to bar, 1991, Pennsylvania; 1994, District of Columbia; 1996, PTO. *Education:* Harvard College (A.B., 1985); University of Chicago Law School (J.D., 1989). ***COURSES: Administrative Law, Patent Law, Torts, Telecommunications.

(This Listing Continued)

COLLEGE OF WILLIAM AND MARY SCHOOL OF LAW —Continued

JAMES DWYER*, (Assistant Professor of Law)**, born Albany, New York, September 27, 1961; admitted to bar, 1988, District of Columbia; 1988, New York. *Education:* Boston College (B.A., 1984); Yale Law School (J.D., 1987); Stanford University (Ph.D., 1995). ***COURSES: Property, Family Law, Children's Rights, Trusts and Estates.

WALTER S. FELTON*, (Assistant Professor of Law and Counselor to the Governor & Director of Policy)**, born Suffolk, Virginia, July 28, 1944; admitted to bar, 1969, Virginia. *Education:* Richmond (B.A., 1966; J.D., 1969). ***COURSES: Trial Advocacy, Criminal Procedure II.

MICHAEL J. GERHARDT*, (Hanson Professor of Law)**, born Madison, Wisconsin, April 6, 1956; admitted to bar, 1985, District of Columbia, Georgia. *Education:* Yale (B.A., 1978); London School of Economics (M.Sc., 1979); University of Chicago (J.D., 1982). ***COURSES: Congress & the Presidency, Constitutional Law, Federal Courts, Health Law, Legal History, Legislation, Telecommunications, Constitutional Theory, Arguments & Perspectives.

SUSAN GROVER*, (Associate Professor of Law)**, born Philadelphia, Pennsylvania, February 11, 1951; admitted to bar, 1984, District of Columbia. *Education:* Hollins College (A.B., 1973); Georgetown (J.D., 1983). ***COURSES: Civil Procedure, Employment Discrimination, Women and the Law.

I. TROTTER HARDY*, (Associate Dean for Technology, Professor of Law)**, born Newport News, Virginia, April 10, 1946. *Education:* University of Virginia (B.A., 1968); American (M.S., 1974); Duke (J.D., 1981). ***COURSES: Torts, Intellectual Property, Copyright and New Technology.

JAMES S. HELLER*, (Director of the Law Library and Professor of Law)**, born Detroit, Michigan, April 11, 1950; admitted to bar, 1976, California; 1978, District of Columbia. *Education:* Michigan (B.A., 1971); San Diego (J.D., 1976); California-Berkeley (M.L.S., 1977). ***COURSES: Advanced Research Techniques, Law and Literature.

RICHARD M. HYNES*, (Assistant Professor of Law)**, born Santa Monica, California, August 30, 1968; admitted to bar, 1997, California. *Education:* Georgetown University (B.S.F.S., 1990); University of Chicago (J.D., 1997); University of Pennsylvania (Ph.D., 1998). ***COURSES: Contracts, Corporate Law Seminar.

CHARLES H. KOCH*, (Dudley Warner Woodbridge Professor of Law)**, born Cheverly, Maryland, July 30, 1944; admitted to bar, 1969, District of Columbia and Maryland. *Education:* Maryland (B.A., 1966); George Washington (J.D., 1969); University of Chicago (LL.M., 1975). ***COURSES: Administrative Law, Federal Courts, Energy Law, Comparative Constitutional Systems.

FREDRIC I. LEDERER*, (Chancellor Professor of Law and Director, Courtroom 21)**, born San Diego, California, October 18, 1946; admitted to bar, 1972, New York. *Education:* Polytechnic University (B.S., 1968); Columbia (J.D., 1971); University of Virginia (LL.M., 1976). ***COURSES: Evidence, Legal Skills, Legal Technology.

JOHN W. LEE*, (Professor of Law)**, born Chicago, Illinois, April 1, 1943; admitted to bar, 1968, North Carolina; 1970, Virginia. *Education:* University of North Carolina (B.A., 1965); University of Virginia (LL.B., 1968); Georgetown (LL.M., 1970). ***COURSES: Federal Income Tax, Real Estate Taxation, Small Business Planning, Taxation of Small Business.

JOHN M. LEVY*, (Director, Graduate Program in the American Legal System and Professor of Law)**, born Washington, D.C., October 16, 1939; admitted to bar, 1969, Virginia. *Education:* New York University (B.A., 1962); Syracuse (J.D., 1968). ***COURSES: Legal Skills, Clinical Externships.

LINDA A. MALONE*, (Marshall-Wythe Foundation Professor of Law)**, born Chattanooga, Tennessee, June 16, 1954; admitted to bar, 1978, Georgia; 1979, Illinois. *Education:* Vassar College (B.A., 1975); Duke (J.D., 1978); Illinois (LL.M., 1984). ***COURSES: Environmental Law, Public International Law, Womens' Rights in International Law and Society.

PAUL MARCUS*, (Haynes Professor of Law)**, born New York City, New York, December 8, 1946; admitted to bar, 1972, California. *Education:* U.C.L.A. (A.B., 1968; J.D., 1971). ***COURSES: Criminal Law, Criminal Procedure, Copyright, Law and Literature, Entertainment Law Litigation.

ALAN J. MEESE*, (Cabell Research Professor of Law)**, born Sacramento, California, December 25, 1964; admitted to bar, 1989, Virginia. *Education:* William & Mary (A.B., 1986); University of Chicago (J.D., 1989). ***COURSES: Antitrust Theory, Corporations, Economic Analysis of Law.

JAMES E. MOLITERNO*, (Professor of Law)**, born Youngstown, Ohio, August 21, 1953; admitted to bar, 1980, Ohio and West Virginia. *Education:* Youngstown State University (B.S., 1977); Akron (J.D., 1980). ***COURSES: Legal Skills, Professional Responsibility, Evidence.

MITCHELL B. REISS*, (Director of the Reeves Center for International Studies and Professor of Law)**, born Dayton, Ohio, June 12, 1957; admitted to bar, 1990, District of Columbia. *Education:* Williams College (B.A., 1979); Tufts University (M.A.L.D., 1982); Oxford University (D.Phil., 1985); Columbia University (J.D., 1988). ***COURSES: National Security Law.

RONALD H. ROSENBERG*, (Professor of Law)**, born New York City, New York, February 8, 1949; admitted to bar, 1975, District of Columbia. *Education:* Columbia (B.A., 1971; M.R.P., 1974); University of North Carolina (J.D., 1975). ***COURSES: Environmental Law, Land Use, Property, Local Government, Real Estate Transactions.

ELMER J. SCHAEFER*, (Professor of Law)**, born Elmhurst, Illinois, June 4, 1942; admitted to bar, 1968, Illinois. *Education:* Northwestern (B.A., 1961; M.A., 1965); Harvard (J.D., 1968). ***COURSES: Corporate Finance, Corporations, Freshman Seminar, Remedies, Antitrust.

ALEMANTE G. SELASSIE*, (Associate Professor of Law)**, born Gondar, Ethiopia, July 26, 1944; admitted to bar, 1985, Wisconsin. *Education:* Haile Selassie I University (LL.B., 1969; M.L.I., 1972); Wisconsin (J.D., 1984). ***COURSES: Contracts, Law and Development, Secured Transactions.

MICHAEL STEIN*, (Assistant Professor of Law)**, born New York, New York, July 10, 1963; admitted to bar, 1989, New York. *Education:* New York University (B.A., 1985); Harvard Law School (J.D., 1988); University of Cambridge (Ph.D., 1998). ***COURSES: Civil Procedure, Disability Law, English Legal History.

KATHRYN R. URBONYA*, (Professor of Law)**, born Beloit, Wisconsin, January 27, 1953; admitted to bar, 1983, North Dakota; 1984, Minnesota. *Education:* Beloit College (B.A., 1975); North Dakota (M.A., 1980; J.D., 1983). ***COURSES: Constitutional Law, Constitutional Tort Litigation, Fourth Amendment Seminar.

CYNTHIA WARD*, (Professor of Law)**, born Boston, Massachusetts, May 9, 1958.. *Education:* Wellesley (B.A., 1980); Yale (J.D., 1991). ***COURSES: Property, Feminist Jurisprudence, Criminal Law.

RICHARD A. WILLIAMSON*, (Chancellor Professor of Law)**, born Columbus, Ohio, September 9, 1943; admitted to bar, 1968, Ohio; 1973, Virginia. *Education:* Ohio University (B.B.A., 1965); Ohio State (J.D., 1968). ***COURSES: Criminal Law, Criminal Procedure Survey, White Collar Crime.

COLUMBIA UNIVERSITY SCHOOL OF LAW

435 WEST 116 STREET
NEW YORK, NEW YORK 10027
Telephone: (212) 854-2680
Fax: (212) 854-7946
http://www.columbia.edu/cu/law

ABA Approved Since 1923.

Columbia Law School has a long and distinctive history. In the late eighteenth century, as the study of law was emerging as a university discipline, James Kent was named Professor of Law at Columbia College. His second course of lectures became the classic *Commentaries on American Law*. The Law School was officially founded in 1858. Over the years, the Law School's high standards of excellence have attracted exceptional students who have gone on to become respected lawyers, professors and judges.

The distinguished faculty maintains a vigorous academic environment. The full-time faculty, which is responsible for the vast bulk of the teaching, consists of nationally known lawyers and scholars. Columbia professors publish widely in academic journals and their comments on the law appear regularly in the nation's media. Many of the faculty participate in public interest activities and are active in legal education organizations. Columbia's location in New York City enables it to draw on outstanding legal practitioners to teach advanced seminars in cutting-edge practice areas.

At the heart of the Columbia Law School education is the foundation curriculum, revised by the faculty in 1989. The teaching of the rules of law, which change rapidly in our constantly evolving society, is secondary to providing students with the intellectual tools and practical skills necessary to practice law in the 21st century. The predominant teaching method for foundation courses is the discussion method.

The elective curriculum is rich and varied. In the Clinical Education Program, for example, students gain real-life legal experience by working on actual cases. Students interview, investigate, develop a strategy, counsel and negotiate for their clients in a variety of legal forums including administrative agencies and the courts. Classroom courses include everything from corporate mergers and acquisitions to feminist jurisprudence.

To help students understand the ethical problems they may face as practicing attorneys, the Law School has created The Profession of Law course. Held for third-year students before the formal start of school, the obligatory class encourages students to consider difficult ethical questions that are part of the careers of all attorneys. Videos, role-playing and alumni lectures are utilized in this revolutionary course, among the first of its kind in the nation.

The library, with its 348,330 titles in 1,003,032 volumes, 210,431 microforms and 792,601 manuscript items, is a tremendous resource for students. The materials can be used to trace worldwide development of law from ancient China and the Roman Empire through medieval canon and secular law to modern civil and common law. A staff of specially-trained librarians assists researchers and instructs students on the use of research tools. All of the Law Library's holdings are electronically cataloged and searchable by dedicated terminals in the library - as well as through the Law School's network, or through the Internet. Databases include, LEXIS/NEXIS, WESTLAW and a growing number of titles on CD-ROM. There is also an extraordinary rare book collection. Columbia's location in New York City provides unparalleled opportunities for research and the Law School maintains connections with many institutions. Additionally, student computer access and support is maintained by the Law School's Information Technology Department, one of the largest and most sophisticated law school IT units in the country.

This tradition of excellence continues in the present. Last year, the school received more than 6,500 applications competing for 356 places. Our students come from a rich variety of backgrounds: 130 undergraduate colleges and universities; 41 states and 16 foreign countries were represented in the upcoming class of 2004; 35% were members of ethnic minorities; and 65% came to law school with prior life and professional experience. Columbia is committed to the principle that admission decisions are made without regard to financial need. The financial aid program helps fulfill that commitment.

The Office of Career Services provides a full range of counseling services to both students and graduates. The office assists with interviews, maintains a comprehensive database on major employers and provides extensive group and individual counseling. It also brings to campus employers in whom students have expressed an interest. More than 800 employers (90% of which are law firms) visit the school yearly. 97.4% of the Class of 2000 were employed by graduation. The median overall starting salary for the Class of 2000, for all types of employment, was $125,000.

Columbia is dedicated to the proposition that law is a profession that serves the public interest. The Center for Public Interest Law helps students develop their interest in public service law, presents lectures and panels on public interest issues and promotes the placement of students in public service and public interest jobs. The office also implements the school's mandatory pro bono service program (40 hours). The Human Rights Internship Program gives students the opportunity to be of service in support of human rights in this country and around the world. In the past, student interns have worked in areas such as voting rights, school segregation and employment discrimination in settings from San Francisco to South Africa, from Appalachia to Bangladesh.

There are 14 student-edited journals published, which include the *Columbia Law Review, Human Rights Law Review, American Journal of International Arbitration, Journal of Asian Law, Columbia Journal of Transnational Law, Columbia Journal of Law and Social Problems, Columbia Journal of Gender and Law*, the *Columbia Journal of Business Law, The National Black Law Journal* and *Columbia Science and Technology Law Review*. And the Dean of Students Office is responsible for the numerous extracurricular activities at the Law School. Organizations devoted to social, political and intellectual interests, include, among many others, the Black Law Students Association, Christian Legal Fellowship, The Federalist Society, Environmental Law Society, the Older and Wiser Law Students Association (OWLS), Asian Pacific American Law Students Association, Latin American Law Students Association, Native American Law Students Association, South Asian law Students Association, Arab Law Students Association, Jewish Law Students Association, Entertainment Sports Law Society, Public Interest Law Foundation, and Domestic Violence Project.

The Law School provides very sophisticated computer services, with all users - including students, as well as faculty and administrators - connected by a network. Network connections for student use are also provided in the dorm rooms, and in public areas within the law library for lap top users. Users have access to word-processing, database, spreadsheet and graphic software, electronic mail and a variety of

(This Listing Continued)

COLUMBIA UNIVERSITY SCHOOL OF LAW—Continued

Internet-based services - such as library catalogs at other institutions, on-line career services and many other resources. The Library houses two computer labs, one for general student use and one for training purposes. In addition, a fully networked and computer supported journal production facility is provided for the law journals in an adjacent building.

Dean: David Leebron (212) 854-2675
Admissions: James Milligan (212) 854-2674
Financial Aid: Alice Rigas (212) 854-7603
Library: Kent McKeever (212) 854-4228
Career Services: Ellen Wayne (212) 854-1664
Development & Alumni/ae Relations: Linda Nelson (212) 854-1387

FULL TIME FACULTY

DAVID W. LEEBRON*, (Dean and Lucy G. Moses Professor of Law)**, born Philadelphia, Pennsylvania; admitted to bar, 1980, Hawaii; 1981, Pennsylvania; 1982, New York. *Education:* Harvard University (B.A., 1976); Harvard Law School (J.D., 1979). ***COURSES: International Economic Law, Torts, International Law, Human Rights.

JOSE ALVAREZ*, (Professor of Law)**, born 1955; admitted to bar, 1983, District of Columbia. *Education:* Harvard (B.A., 1977; J.D., 1981); Oxford (M.A., 1979);. ***COURSES: Evidence, International Law, International Legal Theory, Foreign Investment, International Organizations, Problems in International Law.

MARK BARENBERG*, (Professor of Law)**, born 1955; admitted to bar, 1985, New York. *Education:* Harvard University (B.A., 1977); London School of Economics (M.Sc., 1978); Harvard Law School (J.D., 1982). ***COURSES: Democratic Theory and Law, Employment Discrimination, Labor Law, Legal Theory.

VIVIAN BERGER*, (Nash Professor Emerita of Law)**, born New York, N.Y., July 22, 1944; admitted to bar, 1974, New York. *Education:* Radcliffe College (B.A., 1966); Columbia University School of Law (J.D., 1973). ***COURSES: Criminal Law, Criminal Process (Specialties: Death Penalty, Habeas Corpus).

GEORGE BERMANN*, (Charles Keller Beekman Professor of Law)**, born Fall River, Massachusetts, December 2, 1945; admitted to bar, 1972, New York. *Education:* Yale University (B.A., 1967); Yale Law School (J.D., 1971); Columbia University School of Law (LL.M., 1975). ***COURSES: European Law, European Community Law, Comparative Law, Transnational Litigation.

BARBARA ARONSTEIN BLACK*, (George Welwood Murray Professor of Legal History)**, born Brooklyn, New York, May 6, 1933; admitted to bar, 1955, New York; 1958, Connecticut. *Education:* Brooklyn College (B.A., 1953); Columbia University School of Law (LL.B., 1955); Yale University (Ph.D., 1975). ***COURSES: Commercial Law, Contracts, Legal History.

VINCENT A. BLASI*, (Corliss Lamont Professor of Civil Liberties)**, born 1943; admitted to bar, 1968, Texas. *Education:* Northwestern University (B.A., 1964); University of Chicago (J.D., 1967). ***COURSES: Constitutional Law, Torts, First Amendment.

RICHARD BRIFFAULT*, (Joseph Chamberlain Professor of Legislation)**, born New York, March 15, 1954; admitted to bar, 1979, New York. *Education:* Columbia University (B.A., 1974); Harvard Law School (J.D., 1977). ***COURSES: State and Local Government Law, Property, Law of Politics and Elections, Foundations of the Regulatory State.

MARVIN A. CHIRELSTEIN*, (Professor of Law)**, born Chicago, Illinois, October 8, 1928; admitted to bar, 1955, New York. *Education:* University of California at Berkeley (A.B., 1950); University of Chicago (J.D., 1953). ***COURSES: Contracts, Taxation.

JOHN C. COFFEE, JR.*, (Adolf A. Berle Professor of Law)**, born Albany, New York, November 15, 1944; admitted to bar, 1970, New York; 1978, District of Columbia. *Education:* Amherst College (B.A., 1966); Yale Law School (LL.B., 1969); New York University School of Law (LL.M., 1976). ***COURSES: Corporations, Securities Law, Criminal Law, White Collar Crime Seminar.

KIMBERLE WILLIAMS CRENSHAW*, (Professor of Law)**, admitted to bar, . *Education:* Harvard Law School (J.D., 1984); University of Wisconsin (LL.M., 1985). ***COURSES: Civil Rights Law, Advanced Con Law, Equal Protection, Intersectionalities.

LORI FISLER DAMROSCH*, (Henry L. Moses Professor of Law and International Organization)**, born Santa Monica, California, November 4, 1953; admitted to bar, 1976, Connecticut; 1980, District of Columbia; 1982, New York. *Education:* Yale University (B.A., 1973); Yale Law School (J.D., 1976). ***COURSES: International Law, Constitutional Law of U.S. Foreign Relations.

MICHAEL C. DORF*, (Professor of Law; Vice Dean)**, *Education:* Harvard (A.B., 1986); Harvard Law School (J.D., 1990). ***COURSES: Civil Procedures, Constitutional Law, Theories of Constitutional Interpretation, Federal Courts.

HAROLD EDGAR*, (Julius Silver Professor in Law, Science and Technology)**, born New York, November 19, 1942; admitted to bar, 1968, New York. *Education:* Harvard University (A.B., 1964); Columbia University School of Law (LL.B., 1967). ***COURSES: Medical Law, Food and Drug Law, Patents, Criminal Law.

R. RANDLE EDWARDS*, (Walter Gellhorn Professor of Law; Director of the Center for Chinese Legal Studies)**, born 1934. *Education:* Harvard University (A.B., 1956); Harvard Law School (J.D., 1964). ***COURSES: Chinese Law, Chinese Legal History, Comparative Law, Comparative Socialist Law, International Law.

CYNTHIA L. ESTLUND*, (Professor of Law)**, born 1957; admitted to bar, 1984, Pennsylvania; 1985, District of Columbia; 1992, Texas. *Education:* Lawrence University (B.A.); Yale University Law School (J.D., 1983). ***COURSES: Labor Law, Property.

JEFFREY FAGAN*, (Professor of Law and Public Health)**, born New York, New York, December 17, 1946. *Education:* New York University (B.Eng., 1968); University of Buffalo (M.Eng., 1971; Ph.D., 1975). ***COURSES: Criminology, Empirical Legal Studies, Law and Social Sciences. ***Email:*** fagan@law.columbia.edu

E. ALLAN FARNSWORTH*, (Alfred McCormack Professor of Law)**, born Providence, Rhode Island, June 30, 1928; admitted to bar, 1952, District of Columbia; 1956, New York. *Education:* University of Michigan (B.S., 1948); Yale University (M.A., 1949); Columbia University School of Law (J.D., 1952). ***COURSES: Contracts, Commercial Law, International Trade.

***ROBERT A. FERGUSON*, (George Edward Woodberry Professor**

(This Listing Continued)

COLUMBIA UNIVERSITY SCHOOL OF LAW—Continued

in Law, Literature and Criticism), born 1942. *Education:* Harvard University (A.B., 1964; Ph.D., 1974); Harvard Law School (J.D., 1968). ***COURSES:*** Law and Literature, Trial in American Life, Law and Letters in American Culture.

GEORGE P. FLETCHER*, (Cardozo Professor of Jurisprudence)**, born Chicago, Illinois, March 5, 1939; admitted to bar, 1970, California. *Education:* Cornell University; University of California at Berkeley (B.A., 1960); University of Chicago (J.D., 1963; M.C.L., 1965). ***COURSES: Torts, Criminal Law, Legal Philosophy.

KATHERINE M. FRANKE*, (Professor of Law; Co-Director, Center for the Study of Law and Culture)**, born Illinois, February 21, 1959; admitted to bar, 1986, California; 1987, New York. *Education:* Barnard College (B.A., 1981); Northeastern University Law School (J.D., 1986); Yale Law School (LL.M., 1993; J.S.D., 1998). ***COURSES: Civil Rights, Torts, Feminism, Queer Theory. ***Email:*** kfranke@law.columbia.edu

RICHARD GARDNER*, (Professor of Law and International Organization)**, born July 9, 1927; admitted to bar, 1952, New York. *Education:* Harvard University (B.A., 1948); Oxford University (Ph.D., 1954); Yale University (LL.B., 1951). ***COURSES: International Law.

ALEJANDRO M. GARRO*, (Adjunct Professor of Law and Senior Research Scholar)**, born La Plata, Argentina, April 8, 1950; admitted to bar, 1975, Argentina; 1982, New York; 1984, Madrid. *Education:* National University La Plata (J.D., 1975); Columbia University (J.S.D., 1990). ***COURSES: Comparative & Latin American Law, Inter-American System for Protection of Human Rights.

PHILIP M. GENTY*, (Clinical Professor of Law)**, born Pueblo, Colorado, July 12, 1955; admitted to bar, 1981, New York; 1982, U.S. District Court, Southern District of New York; 1984, U.S. District Court, Eastern District of New York. *Education:* Colorado College (B.A., 1977); New York University School of Law (J.D., 1980). ***COURSES: Clinical Teaching, Prisoners' Rights, Family Law.

RONALD J. GILSON*, (Marc and Eva Stern Professor of Law & Business)**, born Chicago, Illinois, September 14, 1946; admitted to bar, 1972, California. *Education:* Washington University (A.B., summa cum laude, 1968); Yale Law School (J.D., 1971). ***COURSES: Corporations, Corporate Acquisitions, Legal Profession.

JANE C. GINSBURG*, (Morton L. Janklow Prof. of Literary and Artistic Property Law; Dir., Kernochan Center for Law, Media/Arts)**, born Freeport, New York, July 21, 1955; admitted to bar, 1982, New York. *Education:* University of Chicago (B.A., 1976; M.A., 1977); Harvard Law School (J.D., 1980); University of Paris II (D.E.A., 1985). ***COURSES: Copyright, Trademarks, International Intellectual Property, Legal Methods.

VICTOR P. GOLDBERG*, (Thomas Macioce Professor of Law; Co-Director, Center for Law & Economic Studies)**, born Washington, D.C., November 26, 1941. *Education:* Oberlin College (B.A., 1963); Yale University (Ph.D., 1970). ***COURSES: Law and Economics, Antitrust, Contracts.

HARVEY J. GOLDSCHMID*, (Dwight Professor of Law)**, born New York, May 6, 1940; admitted to bar, 1965, New York. *Education:* Columbia University (B.A., 1962); Columbia University School of Law (J.D., 1965). ***COURSES: Corporation Law, Securities Law, Antitrust (Trade Regulation) Law, Non-profit Institutions Law.

JEFFREY N. GORDON*, (Alfred W. Bressler Professor of Law; Co-Director, Center for Law & Economic Studies)**, born Richmond, Virginia, June 18, 1949; admitted to bar, 1977, New York; 1981, District of Columbia. *Education:* Yale University (B.A., 1971); Harvard Law School (J.D., 1975). ***COURSES: Corporations, Mergers and Acquisitions, Regulation.

FRANK P. GRAD*, (Joseph Chamberlain Professor Emeritus of Legislation)**, born Vienna, Austria, May 2, 1924; admitted to bar, 1949, New York. *Education:* Brooklyn College (B.A., 1947); Columbia University School of Law (LL.B., 1949). ***COURSES: Environmental Law, Public Health Law, Legislation and Legislative Drafting.

R. KENT GREENAWALT*, (University Professor)**, born Brooklyn, New York, June 25, 1936; admitted to bar, 1963, New York. *Education:* Swarthmore College (A.B., 1958); Oxford University (B.Phil., 1960); Columbia University School of Law (LL.B., 1963). ***COURSES: Constitutional Law, Criminal Law, Legal Philosophy.

JACK GREENBERG*, (Professor of Law)**, born 1924; admitted to bar, 1949, New York. *Education:* Columbia University (B.A., 1945; LL.B., 1948). ***COURSES: Civil Procedure, Civil Rights, Post Apartheid Constitution in South Africa.

LOUIS HENKIN*, (University Professor Emeritus; Special Service Professor)**, born Smolyan, Russia, November 11, 1917; admitted to bar, 1941, New York; 1947, U.S. Supreme Court. *Education:* Yeshiva University (A.B., 1937); Harvard Law School (LL.B., 1940). ***COURSES: Constitutional Law, International Law, Human Rights.

ALFRED HILL*, (Simon H. Rifkind Professor Emeritus of Law)**, admitted to bar, 1943, New York. *Education:* College of the City of New York (B.S., 1937); Brooklyn Law School (LL.B., 1941); Harvard (S.J.D., 1957). ***COURSES: Conflict of Laws, Corporations, Federal Jurisdiction and Torts.

JAMES L. HOOVER*, (Professor of Law and Vice Dean for Administration)**, born Oklahoma City, Oklahoma, June 15, 1945; admitted to bar, 1975, Missouri. *Education:* University of Oklahoma (B.A., 1967; J.D., 1973); University of Washington (M.L., 1974). ***COURSES: Legal Research.

SAMUEL ISSACHAROFF*, (Harold R. Medina Professor in Procedural Jurisprudence and Professor of Law)**, born 1954; admitted to bar, 1984, Pennsylvania; 1993, Texas. *Education:* Binghamton University (B.A., 1975); Yale (J.D., 1983). ***COURSES: Civil Procedure, Constitutional Law II, The Political Process, Election & Voting Rights Law; Employment Law, Legal Process.

CONRAD JOHNSON*, (Clinical Professor of Law)**, born New York, N.Y., January 27, 1953; admitted to bar, 1980, New York. *Education:* Columbia University (B.A., 1975); Brooklyn Law School (J.D., 1978). ***COURSES: Civil Rights, Civil Procedure, Evidence, Housing Law, Trial Practice.

WILLIAM K. JONES*, (Charles Evans Hughes Professor Emeritus of Law)**, born New York, N.Y., September 1, 1930; admitted to bar, 1955, New York; 1957, Ohio. *Education:* Columbia University (A.B., 1952); Columbia University School of Law (LL.B., 1954). ***COURSES: Torts, Property, Contracts.

BRADLEY C. KARKKAINEN*, (Associate Professor of Law)**, *Education:* University of Michigan (B.A., 1974); Yale Law School (J.D., 1994). ***COURSES: Land Use Controls, Environmental Law.

AVERY WEINER KATZ*, (Professor of Law)**, born 1958; admitted to bar, 1986, Michigan. *Education:* Michigan (B.A., 1980); Harvard (A.M., 1983; J.D., 1985; Ph.D., 1986). ***COURSES: Commercial Law, Contracts, Law & Economics, Sales, Strategic Behavior & the Law, Foundations of the Economic Approach to Law.

***JOHN M. KERNOCHAN*, (Nash Professor Emeritus of Law; Founding Director, Kernochan Center for Law, Media and the Arts)**, *Education:* Harvard (B.A., 1942); Columbia University School

(This Listing Continued)

COLUMBIA UNIVERSITY SCHOOL OF LAW—Continued

of Law (LL.B., 1948). ***COURSES:*** Intellectual Property, Law and The Arts.

CAROL B. LIEBMAN*, (Clinical Professor of Law)**, born Louisville, Kentucky, November 4, 1940; admitted to bar, 1975, Massachusetts; 1992, District of Columbia; 1993, New York. *Education:* Wellesley College (B.A., 1962); Rutgers University (M.A., 1963); Boston University (J.D., 1975). ***COURSES: Clinical, Alternative Dispute Resolution, Professional Responsibility.

JAMES S. LIEBMAN*, (Simon H. Rifkind Professor of Law)**, born Albuquerque, New Mexico, December 30, 1952; admitted to bar, 1979, California; 1988, New York. *Education:* Yale University (B.A., 1974); Stanford University Law School (J.D., 1977). ***COURSES: Evidence, Criminal Law, Civil Rights.

LANCE LIEBMAN*, (William S. Beinecke Professor of Law; Director, Parker School)**, born Newark, New Jersey, September 11, 1941. *Education:* Yale University (B.A., 1962); Cambridge University (M.A., 1964); Harvard Law School (LL.B., 1967). ***COURSES: Employment Law.

DEBRA LIVINGSTON*, (Professor of Law)**, born Waycross, Georgia, April 15, 1959; admitted to bar, 1985, New York. *Education:* Princeton University (B.A., 1980); Harvard University (J.D., 1984). ***COURSES: Criminal Procedure, Evidence, Criminal Law.

EDWARD LLOYD*, (Evan M. Frankel Clinical Professor in Environmental Law)**, born Princeton, New Jersey, August 14, 1948; admitted to bar, 1974, New Jersey. *Education:* Princeton University (A.B. Chemistry, 1970); University of Wisconsin Law School (J.D., 1973). ***COURSES: Environmental Law, Clinic. ***Email:*** elloyd@law.columbia.edu

LOUIS LOWENSTEIN*, (Simon H. Rifkind Professor Emeritus of Finance and Law)**, born New York, June 13, 1925; admitted to bar, 1953, New York. *Education:* Columbia University (B.S., 1947); University of Maryland (M.F.S., 1951); Columbia University School of Law (LL.B., 1953). ***COURSES: Corporate Finance, Accounting, Corporations.

GERARD E. LYNCH*, (Paul J. Kellner Professor of Law)**, born New York, N.Y., September 4, 1951; admitted to bar, 1976, New York. *Education:* Columbia University (B.A., 1972); Columbia University School of Law (J.D., 1975). ***COURSES: Criminal Law, Criminal Procedure, Constitutional Law, Professional Responsibility.

JOHN F. MANNING*, (Michael I. Sovern Professor of Law)**, born Los Angeles, April 11, 1961; admitted to bar, 1986, Pennsylvania; 1990, California. *Education:* Harvard University (A.B., 1982; J.D., 1985). ***COURSES: Administrative Law, Federal Courts, Legislation.

GILLIAN METZGER*, (Associate Professor of Law)**, born New York, October 2, 1965; admitted to bar, 1997, New York. *Education:* Yale University (B.A., 1987); Oxford University (B.Phil., 1990); Columbia University School of Law (J.D., 1995). ***COURSES: Constitutional Law. ***Email:*** gmetzger@law.columbia.edu

CURTIS J. MILHAUPT*, (Fuyo Professor of Japanese Law & Legal Institutions; Director, Center for Japanese Legal Studies)**, born 1962; admitted to bar, 1990, New York; 1992, District of Columbia. *Education:* Notre Dame (B.A., 1984); Columbia (J.D., 1989). ***COURSES: Business Planning, Comparative Law, Japanese Law, Corporations, Financial Institutions.

EBEN MOGLEN*, (Professor of Law)**, born New Haven, Connecticut, July 13, 1959; admitted to bar, 1988, New York. *Education:* Swarthmore College (A.B., 1980); Yale Law School (J.D., 1985); Yale University (Ph.D., 1993). ***COURSES: Legal History, Property, Jurisprudence.

HENRY PAUL MONAGHAN*, (Harlan Fiske Stone Professor of Constitutional Law)**, born 1934; admitted to bar, 1958, Massachusetts. *Education:* University of Massachusetts (B.A., 1955); Yale Law School (LL.B., 1958); Harvard Law School (LL.M., 1960). ***COURSES: Constitutional Law, Federal Jurisdiction.

ARTHUR W. MURPHY*, (Joseph Solomon Prof. Emer. in Wills Trusts & Estates)**, born Boston, Massachusetts, January 25, 1922; admitted to bar, 1949, New York. *Education:* Harvard (B.A., 1943); Columbia (LL.B., 1948). ***COURSES: Legal Method, Trusts & Estates, Administrative Law.

SUBHA NARASIMHAN*, (Professor of Law)**, born Delhi, India, May 1948; admitted to bar, 1981, New York. *Education:* Imperial University (B.A., 1970); Stanford University (Ph.D., 1975); Columbia University School of Law (J.D., 1980). ***COURSES: Contracts, Torts, Feminist Theory, Consumer Law.

GERALD L. NEUMAN*, (Herbert Wechsler Professor of Federal Jurisprudence)**, born Mineola, New York, May 22, 1952; admitted to bar, 1982, Massachusetts. *Education:* Harvard University (A.B., 1973); Massachusetts Institute of Technology (Ph.D., 1977); Harvard Law School (J.D., 1980). ***COURSES: Constitutional Law, Comparative Law, Immigration Law, Administrative Law.

LAWRENCE NEWMAN*, (Everett B. Birch Adjunct Professor in Wills, Trusts & Estates)**, born 1931; admitted to bar, 1956, New York. *Education:* Dartmouth (A.B., 1952); Yale (LL.B., 1955); New York (S.J.D., 1963); Yeshiva (L.S.; M.S., 1990). ***COURSES: Estate & Gift Taxation, Estate Planning, Estates & Trusts, Postmortem Estate Planning.

KATHARINA PISTOR*, (Associate Professor of Law)**, born Freiburg, Germany, May 23, 1963. *Education:* University of Freiburg - Germany (J.D., 1988); University of London (LL.M., 1989); University of Munich (Dr. Jur., 1998). ***COURSES: Comparative Law, Corporate Law, European Business Law, Law and Development. ***Email:*** kpisto@law.columbia.edu

CATHERINE POWELL*, (Associate Clinical Professor of Law; Executive Director, Human Rights Institute)**, born 1965; admitted to bar, 1994, New York. *Education:* Yale College (B.A., 1987; J.D., 1992); Princeton (M.A., 1991). ***COURSES: Human Rights Clinic.

ANDRZEJ RAPACZYNSKI*, (Professor of Law)**, born Poland, November 26, 1947; admitted to bar, 1984, New York. *Education:* Warsaw University (B.A., 1968); Columbia University School of Law (Ph.D., 1974); Yale Law School (J.D., 1982). ***COURSES: Constitutional Law, Torts, Property, Comparative Law, Political Theory.

JOSEPH RAZ*, (Visiting Professor of Jurisprudence)**, admitted to bar, . *Education:* The Hebrew University (Magister Juris, 1963); Oxford University (D.Phil., 1967). ***COURSES: Moral, Political and Legal Philosophy.

ALBERT J. ROSENTHAL*, (Maurice T. Moore Professor Emeritus of Law; Dean Emeritus of the Faculty of Law)**, *Education:* Pennsylvania (B.A., 1938); Harvard (L.L.B., 1941). ***COURSES: Constitutional Law, Contracts, Commercial Transactions, Environmental Law, Employment Discrimination.

CHARLES F. SABEL*, (Professor of Law and Social Science)**, *Education:* Harvard (A.B., 1969); Harvard University (Ph.D., 1978). ***COURSES: Foundations of the Regulatory State.

***WILLIAM M. SAGE*, (Professor of Law)**, *Education:* Harvard (A.B.,

(This Listing Continued)

1982); Stanford University School of Medicine (M.D.); Stanford Law School (J.D., 1988). ***COURSES:*** Foundations, Health Law.

CAROL SANGER*, (Professor of Law)**, born Nurnberg, Germany, December 30, 1948; admitted to bar, 1976, California. *Education:* Wellesley College (B.A., 1970); Michigan Law School (J.D., 1976). ***COURSES: Contracts, Family Law, Children & Law, Gender, Law and Equality. ***Email:*** csanger@law.columbia.edu

OSCAR SCHACHTER*, (Hamilton Fish Professor Emeritus of International Law and Diplomacy)**, *Education:* College of The City of New York (B.S.S., 1936); Columbia University School of Law (J.D., 1939). ***COURSES: Human Rights and Economic Development, Theory & Practice in International Law.

BARBARA A. SCHATZ*, (Clinical Professor of Law; Director of Clinical Programs)**, born Philadelphia, Pennsylvania, December 23, 1948; admitted to bar, 1974, New York. *Education:* University of Pennsylvania (B.A., 1969); Harvard Law School (J.D., 1973). ***COURSES: Clinical Subjects (Mediation, Community Development, Art Law).

DAVID M. SCHIZER*, (Associate Professor of Law)**, born 1968; admitted to bar, 1996, New York. *Education:* Yale College (B.A., 1990); Yale University (M.A., 1990; J.D., 1993). ***COURSES: Financial Institutions, Taxation, Federal.

HANS SMIT*, (Stanley H. Fuld Professor of Law)**, born Amsterdam, The Netherlands, August 13, 1927; admitted to bar, 1949, The Netherlands; 1974, New York. *Education:* University of Amsterdam (LL.B., highest honors, 1946; J.D., highest honors, 1949); Columbia University School of Law (LL.B., 1958); University of Paris I (J.S.D., honoris causa, 1991). ***COURSES: Civil Procedure, International Arbitration, International Business Transactions.

MICHAEL SOVERN*, (Chancellor Kent Professor of Law; President Emeritus of the University)**, born New York, N.Y., December 1, 1931; admitted to bar, 1956, New York. *Education:* Columbia University (B.A., 1953); Columbia University School of Law (LL.B., 1955). ***COURSES: Conflict Resolution, Legal Method.

JANE SPINAK*, (Edward Ross Aranow Clinical Professor of Law)**, born 1952; admitted to bar, 1980, New York. *Education:* Smith College (B.A., 1974); New York University (J.D., 1979). ***COURSES: Family Advocacy Clinic, Children and the Law (on leave).

RICHARD BERENSON STONE*, (Wilbur H. Friedman Professor of Tax Law)**, born 1943; admitted to bar, 1967, Louisiana. *Education:* Harvard University (B.A., 1963); Harvard Law School (LL.B., 1967). ***COURSES: Business Planning, Contracts, Corporate Tax, Taxation.

PETER L. STRAUSS*, (Betts Professor of Law and Vice Dean)**, born New York, N.Y., February 26, 1940; admitted to bar, 1965, District of Columbia. *Education:* Harvard University (A.B., 1961); Yale Law School (LL.B., 1964). ***COURSES: Administrative Law, Legal Methods, Constitutional Law, Legal Education.

SUSAN STURM*, (Professor of Law)**, born Glen Cove, New York, December 23, 1954; admitted to bar, 1980, New York; 1982, Massachusetts. *Education:* Brown University (B.A., 1976); Yale Law School (J.D., 1979). ***COURSES: Civil Procedure, Employment Discrimination, Workplace Regulation, Public Law Remedies. ***Email:*** ssturm@law.columbia.edu

KENDALL THOMAS*, (Professor of Law; Co-Director, Center for the Study of Law and Culture)**, born East Chicago, Indiana, February 22, 1957. *Education:* Yale University (B.A., 1978); Yale Law School (J.D., 1982). ***COURSES: Torts, Communications Law, Constitutional Law, Law and Sexuality, Critical Race Theory.

H. RICHARD UVILLER*, (Arthur Levitt Professor of Law)**, born New York, N.Y., July 3, 1929; admitted to bar, 1953, New York; 1954, District of Columbia. *Education:* Harvard University (B.A., 1951); Yale Law School (LL.B., 1953). ***COURSES: Criminal Procedure (Constitutional); Evidence, Legal Writing.

JEREMY J. WALDRON*, (Maurice & Hilda Friedman Professor of Law; Director, Center for Law & Philosophy)**, born New Zealand, October 13, 1953; admitted to bar, 1978, New Zealand. *Education:* University of Otago (B.A., 1974; LL.B., 1978); University of Oxford (D.Phil., 1986). ***COURSES: Jurisprudence. ***Email:*** jwaldron@law.columbia.edu

PATRICIA J. WILLIAMS*, (Professor of Law)**, *Education:* Wellesley College; Harvard University. ***COURSES: Contracts, Jurisprudence.

JOHN WITT*, (Associate Professor of Law)**, born Philadelphia, February 9, 1972; admitted to bar, 2000, New York. *Education:* Yale University (B.A., 1994; Ph.D., 2000); Yale University Law School (J.D., 1999). ***COURSES: American Legal History, Torts. ***Email:*** jwitt@law.columbia.edu

WILLIAM F. YOUNG*, (James L. Dohr Professor Emeritus of Law)**, born Marshall, Texas, May 2, 1925; admitted to bar, 1949, Texas. *Education:* University of Texas (B.A., 1948; LL.B., 1949); Harvard Law School. ***COURSES: Contracts, Bankruptcy, Commercial Law.

LAWRENCE ZELENAK*, (Professor of Law)**, born Tacoma, Washington, July 11, 1955; admitted to bar, 1979, Washington. *Education:* Santa Clara University (B.A., 1976); Harvard Law School (J.D., 1979). ***COURSES: Taxation, Torts. ***Email:*** lzelen@law.columbia.edu

MARY MARSH ZULACK*, (Clinical Professor of Law)**, born Denver, Colorado, December 28, 1942; admitted to bar, 1970, New York. *Education:* Smith College (B.A., 1965); University of Michigan (J.D., 1969). ***COURSES: Housing Discrimination, Community Development.

CORNELL UNIVERSITY LAW SCHOOL

MYRON TAYLOR HALL
ITHACA, NEW YORK 14853
Telephone: (607) 255-0565
Fax: (607) 255-7193
http://www.law.cornell.edu

ABA Approved Since 1923.

Since its founding in 1887, Cornell Law School has sought to exemplify the ideal stated by then-University President Andrew D. White:

"Our aim should be to keep its instruction strong, its standards high, and so to send out not swarms of hastily prepared pettifoggers, but a fair number of well-trained, large-minded, morally based lawyers in the best sense, who as they gain experience may be classed as jurists and become

(This Listing Continued)

CORNELL UNIVERSITY LAW SCHOOL—Continued

a blessing to the country, at the bar, on the bench, and in various public bodies."

Today, Cornell Law School is a major center of research and a leader in legal education. Its state-of-the-art facilities, in Ithaca, New York, are among the most beautiful in the nation. Its faculty are known as both prolific scholars and top-flight teachers. Its students are among the most talented, and heavily recruited, in the country. Its graduates are leaders here and abroad.

The Law School's relatively small size assures that students are able to sample widely from the richness of the curriculum and to interact effectively with the faculty. The school also benefits from its close connection with the other twelve graduate and undergraduate colleges that make up Cornell University, the largest of the Ivy League universities. A variety of joint degree and other more informal programs provide students with a wide range of options in shaping their studies to suit their particular interests and strengths.

In keeping with the traditions of Cornell University, the Law School has a strong international focus, and is at the forefront of technological developments that are in the process of revolutionizing legal education and legal practice. The Berger International Legal Studies program consists of a set of courses and activities that allow students to integrate substantive legal principles with practical, cross-cultural experiences. The recently established Paris Institute of International and Comparative Law combines the Law School's resources with those of the University of Paris I (Pantheon-Sorbonne), one of the world's oldest and most respected universities. The Law School's Legal Information Institute has been a pioneer in the application of Internet and CD-ROM technology to legal education and law practice. Commentators consider LII's site on the world-wide-web to be one of the most influential and important sites in the Internet legal world.

Over half of the Law School's students participate in various clinical programs offered as part of the curriculum. They also benefit from a strong writing and research emphasis in the first year and later, in writing-intensive seminars. In addition, students publish three scholarly journals: the *Cornell Law Review,* the *Cornell International Law Journal,* and the *Cornell Journal of Law and Public Policy.* The result is graduates who have not only a strong theoretical background, but also the practical skills necessary to feel comfortable in the world of law practice.

The Law School is located in the Finger Lakes region of central New York, an area known for its scenic beauty, its recreational and cultural opportunities, and the many wineries in the surrounding hills. Ithaca is a small city distinguished by an unexpected range of diversions and enlivened by its large university community. The Fall recruiting season makes a perfect time for law firms, government agencies and other employers to interview students, visit the area, and take in the colors, the harvest, and the clear air that characterize our annual change of seasons. Visiting employers can be sure of an interesting slate of interviews and, when not talking to students, may take advantage of the amenities of the on-campus Statler Hotel (run under the auspices of Cornell's world-renowned Hotel School).

Dean: Russell K. Osgood (607) 255-3527
Associate Dean for Academic Affairs: John A. Siliciano (607) 255-9093
Associate Dean and Dean of Students/Career Services: Anne Lukingbeal (607) 255-5839
Assistant Dean and Dean of Admissions and Financial Aid: Richard Geiger (607) 255-5141
Assistant Dean for Development: Harry B. Ash (607) 255-3370
Assistant Dean for Alumni and International Affairs: Charles D. Cramton (607) 255-5251
Assistant Dean for Administration and Finance: Richard F. Robinson (607) 255-4299
Law Librarian: Claire Germain (607) 255-5857

FULL TIME FACULTY

RUSSELL K. OSGOOD*, (Allan R. Tessler Dean & Professor of Law)**, born Fairfield, Ohio, October 25, 1947; admitted to bar, 1974, Massachusetts. *Education:* Yale (B.A., 1969; J.D., 1974). ***COURSES: Constitutional Law, Taxation, Jurisprudence.

KATHRYN ABRAMS*, (Professor of Law)**, born Ann Arbor, Michigan, June 23, 1958. *Education:* Harvard-Radcliffe College (B.A., 1980); Yale Law School (J.D., 1984). ***COURSES: Constitutional Law, Feminist Jurisprudence, Voting Rights, Local Government, Feminism and Gender Discrimination, Voting and Political Participation.

GREGORY S. ALEXANDER*, (Professor of Law)**, born Chicago, Illinois, November 3, 1948. *Education:* University of Illinois (B.A., 1970); Northwestern University (J.D., 1973). ***COURSES: Trusts and Estates, Property.

JOHN J. BARCELO III*, (William Nelson Cromwell Professor of Law)**, born New Orleans, Louisiana, September 23, 1940; admitted to bar, 1967, Louisiana; 1974, District of Columbia; 1975, New York. *Education:* Tulane (B.A., 1962; J.D., 1966); Harvard (S.J.D., 1977). ***COURSES: International Business Transactions, European Union, International Commercial Arbitration, Torts, Admiralty.

KEVIN M. CLERMONT*, (Flanagan Professor of Law)**, born New York, New York, October 25, 1945; admitted to bar, 1971, Massachusetts; 1974, New York. *Education:* Princeton (A.B., 1967); Harvard (J.D., 1971). ***COURSES: Civil Procedure, International Litigation.

STEVEN D. CLYMER*, (Assistant Professor)**, born White Plains, New York, May 16, 1958; admitted to bar, 1983, Pennsylvania; 1987, California; 1996, New York. *Education:* Cornell (B.A., 1980; J.D., 1983). ***COURSES: Criminal Law & Procedure, Evidence, Trial Advocacy.

NANCY L. COOK*, (Senior Lecturer/Staff Attorney)**, born February 23, 1951; admitted to bar, 1977, Maryland; 1988, District of Columbia. *Education:* Ohio State (B.A., 1972); Georgetown (J.D., 1977). ***COURSES: Clinical, Criminal.

ROGER C. CRAMTON*, (Stevens Professor of Law)**, born Pittsfield, Massachusetts, May 18, 1929; admitted to bar, 1956, Vermont, Michigan and New York. *Education:* Harvard (B.A., 1950); University of Chicago (J.D., 1955). ***COURSES: Legal Ethics, Torts, Conflict of Laws.

THEODORE EISENBERG*, (Henry Allen Mark Professor of Law)**, born Brooklyn, New York, October 26, 1947; admitted to bar, 1972, Pennsylvania; 1974, New York; 1977, California. *Education:* Swarthmore (B.A., 1969); University of Pennsylvania (J.D., 1972). ***COURSES: Bankruptcy, Civil Rights, Tax, Empirical Studies.

CYNTHIA R. FARINA*, (Professor of Law)**, born Pennsylvania, June 25, 1954; admitted to bar, 1980, District of Columbia; 1981, Massachusetts. *Education:* Ursinus (B.A., 1976); Boston University (J.D., 1980). ***COURSES: Administrative Law, Federal Courts, Injunctions, Separation of Powers.

(This Listing Continued)

CORNELL UNIVERSITY LAW SCHOOL—Continued

GLENN G. GALBREATH*, (Senior Lecturer/Staff Attorney)**, born Pittsburgh, Pennsylvania, December 25, 1946; admitted to bar, 1974, Ohio; 1986, New York. *Education:* Westminster College (B.A., 1971); Case Western Reserve (J.D., 1974). ***COURSES: Clinics, Trial Advocacy.

STEPHEN P. GARVEY*, (Associate Professor)**, born Cortland, New York, September 24, 1965; admitted to bar, 1993, New York and District of Columbia. *Education:* Colgate (B.A., 1987); Oxford (M.Phil., 1989); Yale (J.D., 1992). ***COURSES: Criminal Procedure, Legal Process, Capital Sentencing.

CLAIRE M. GERMAIN*, (Edward Cornell Law Librarian & Professor of Law)**, born Chaumont, France. *Education:* Paris III-Sorbonne (Lic., 1971); Paris XII (LL.B., 1974); Louisiana State (M.C.L., 1975); University of Denver (M.L.L., 1977). ***COURSES: Comparative Law, Legal Research, Information Technology, French Law.

ROBERT A. GREEN*, (Associate Professor)**, born Washington, D.C., October 8, 1949; admitted to bar, 1983, District of Columbia. *Education:* University of Chicago (B.A., 1971); California Institute of Technology (M.S., 1973); Georgetown (J.D., 1983). ***COURSES: Taxation, International Trade.

GEORGE A. HAY*, (Edward Cornell Professor of Law and Professor of Economics)**, born 1942. *Education:* LeMoyne (B.S., 1963; M.A., 1967); Northwestern (Ph.D., 1969). ***COURSES: Advanced Antitrust Law & Policy, Antitrust & Health Care.

JAMES A. HENDERSON, JR.*, (Frank B. Ingersoll Professor of Law)**, born Miami, Florida, February 6, 1938; admitted to bar, 1962, Florida; 1965, Massachusetts. *Education:* Princeton (A.B., 1959); Harvard (LL.B., 1962; LL.M., 1964). ***COURSES: Torts, Products Liability, Insurance, Environmental Law, Legal Process.

ROBERT A. HILLMAN*, (Edwin H. Woodruff Professor of Law)**, born New York, New York, December 23, 1946; admitted to bar, 1973, New York; 1976, Iowa. *Education:* University of Rochester (B.A., 1969); Cornell (J.D., 1972). ***COURSES: Contracts, Commercial Law.

BARBARA J. HOLDEN-SMITH*, (Associate Professor)**, born Washington, D.C., November 2, 1950; admitted to bar, 1984, Illinois; 1987, District of Columbia. *Education:* Lake Forest (B.S., 1973); University of Chicago (J.D., 1984). ***COURSES: Civil Procedure, Federal Courts, Legal History.

SHERI LYNN JOHNSON*, (Professor of Law)**, born Minnesota, September 12, 1954; admitted to bar, 1980, New York. *Education:* University of Minnesota (B.A., 1975); Yale (J.D., 1979). ***COURSES: Constitutional Law, Criminal Procedure, Death Penalty.

LILY KAHNG*, (Associate Professor)**, born Plainfield, New Jersey, April 13, 1960; admitted to bar, 1986, New York. *Education:* Princeton (A.B., 1980); Columbia (J.D., 1984); New York University Law School (LL.M., 1991). ***COURSES: Federal Income Tax, Federal Estate and Gift Tax.

LYNN M. LOPUCKI*, (A. Robert Noll Professor of Law)**, born Detroit, Michigan, December 22, 1944; admitted to bar, 1968, Florida; 1970, California. *Education:* University of Michigan (A.B., 1965; J.D., 1967); Harvard (LL.M., 1970). ***COURSES: Secured Transactions, Bankruptcy, Intellectual Property.

JONATHAN R. MACEY*, (J. DuPratt White Professor of Law)**, born May 8, 1955; admitted to bar, 1986, Georgia. *Education:* Harvard (A.B., 1977); Yale (J.D., 1982). ***COURSES: Banking Regulation, Corporate Finance, Securities Regulation.

PETER W. MARTIN*, (Jane M. G. Foster Professor of Law)**, born Ohio, April 11, 1939; admitted to bar, 1964, Ohio. *Education:* Cornell (B.A., 1961); Harvard (LL.B., 1964). ***COURSES: Intellectual Property, Property, Legal Informatics.

FRED S. MCCHESNEY*, (Professor of Law)**, born Washington, D.C., November 19, 1948. *Education:* Holy Cross College (A.B., 1970); University of Miami (J.D., 1978); University of Virginia (Ph.D., 1982). ***COURSES: Antitrust, Corporate Finance, Corporations, Statistics and the Law.

JOANNE M. MINER*, (Director, Cornell Legal Aid, Senior Lecturer)**, born Oswego, New York, July 31, 1946; admitted to bar, 1975, Connecticut; 1986, New York. *Education:* Elmira College (B.A., 1968); International Christian University, Mitaka, Tokyo, Japan; University of Connecticut (J.D., 1975). ***COURSES: Civil Clinic, Women & Law Clinic, Law Guardian Externship.

LARRY I. PALMER*, (Professor of Law)**, born St. Louis, Missouri, June 17, 1944; admitted to bar, 1970, California. *Education:* Harvard (B.A., 1966); Yale (LL.B., 1969). ***COURSES: Law and Medicine, Legislation.

JEFFREY J. RACHLINSKI*, (Associate Professor)**, born Buffalo, New York, June 22, 1966; admitted to bar, 1994, California. *Education:* Johns Hopkins (B.A.M.A., 1988); Stanford (Ph.D., 1994). ***COURSES: Environmental Law, Administrative Law, Civil Procedure.

FAUST F. ROSSI*, (Samuel S. Leibowitz Professor of Trial Techniques)**, born Rochester, New York, August 9, 1932; admitted to bar, 1960, New York. *Education:* University of Toronto (B.A., 1953); Cornell (LL.B., 1960). ***COURSES: Evidence, Civil Procedure, Trial Advocacy.

STEWART J. SCHWAB*, (Professor of Law)**, born Chapel Hill, North Carolina; admitted to bar, 1982, District of Columbia. *Education:* Swarthmore (B.A., 1975); University of Michigan (J.D., 1980; Ph.D., 1981). ***COURSES: Law & Economics, Torts, Employment Law, Corporations.

ROBERT F. SEIBEL*, (Senior Lecturer/Staff Attorney)**, born New York, New York, September 26, 1946; admitted to bar, 1971, Massachusetts; 1979, Illinois; 1980, Iowa; 1981, Maine; 1986, New York. *Education:* Bowdoin (A.B., 1968); Morehouse (I.S.E.M.); Northeastern (J.D., 1971). ***COURSES: Clinic, Women and the Law, Estate Planning, Judicial Externship.

STEVEN H. SHIFFRIN*, (Professor of Law)**, born Los Angeles, California, May 3, 1941; admitted to bar, 1975, California. *Education:* Loyola University of Los Angeles (B.A., 1963; J.D., 1975); San Fernando Valley State College (M.A., 1964). ***COURSES: Constitutional Law, Jurisprudence, Defamation & Privacy.

JOHN A. SILICIANO*, (Associate Dean for Acad. Affairs, Professor of Law)**, born 1953; admitted to bar, 1981, District of Columbia. *Education:* Cornell (B.A., 1975); Princeton (M.P.A., 1979); Columbia (J.D., 1979). ***COURSES: Torts, Criminal Law, Law & Psychology.

GARY J. SIMSON*, (Associate Dean for Faculty Development, Professor of Law)**, born Newark, New Jersey, March 18, 1950; admitted to bar, 1974, Connecticut; 1980, New York. *Education:* Yale (B.A., 1971; J.D., 1974). ***COURSES: Constitutional Law, Conflict of Laws.

KATHERINE VAN WEZEL STONE*, (Professor of Law)**, born 1948; admitted to bar, 1980, New York. *Education:* Harvard (B.A., 1970; J.D., 1979). ***COURSES: Labor Law, Contracts, Advanced Labor Law, Arbitration & Alternative Dispute Resolution.

(This Listing Continued)

CORNELL UNIVERSITY LAW SCHOOL—Continued

BARRYSTROM*, (Senior Lecturer/Staff Attorney)**, born Bronx, New York, March 4, 1947; admitted to bar, 1997, New York. *Education:* Rochester Institute of Technology (B.S., 1970); Cornell (J.D., 1974). ***COURSES: Governmental Benefits, Poverty Law.

ROBERT S. SUMMERS*, (William G. McRoberts Professor in the Administration of Law)**, born Halfway, Oregon, September 19, 1933; admitted to bar, 1959, Oregon; 1974, New York. *Education:* University of Oregon (B.S., 1955); Harvard (LL.B., 1959). ***COURSES: Contracts, Legal Philosophy.

WINNIE F. TAYLOR*, (Professor of Law)**, born 1951; admitted to bar, 1976, New York. *Education:* Grambling State University (B.A., 1972); Buffalo (J.D., 1975); University of Wisconsin - Madison (LL.M., 1979). ***COURSES: Consumer Law, Contracts, Credit Discrimination, Commercial Law, Employment Discrimination.

DAVID WIPPMAN*, (Associate Professor)**, born Minneapolis, Minnesota, December 15, 1954; admitted to bar, 1982, District of Columbia. *Education:* Princeton (B.A., 1976); Yale (M.A., 1978; J.D., 1982). ***COURSES: Public International Law, Human Rights.

CHARLES W. WOLFRAM*, (Charles Frank Reavis Sr. Professor of Law)**, born Cleveland, Ohio, February 28, 1937; admitted to bar, 1962, District of Columbia; 1974, Minnesota. *Education:* Notre Dame (B.A., 1959); University of Texas (LL.B., 1962). ***COURSES: Legal Ethics.

CREIGHTON UNIVERSITY SCHOOL OF LAW

24th AND CALIFORNIA
OMAHA, NEBRASKA 68178

CUMBERLAND SCHOOL OF LAW AT SAMFORD UNIVERSITY

800 LAKESHORE DRIVE
BIRMINGHAM, ALABAMA 35229
Telephone: (205) 726-2400
Fax: (205) 726-2673
http://cumberland.samford.edu

ABA Approved Since 1949

Founded 1847 in Lebanon, Tenn., Cumberland School of Law at Samford University is one of the oldest law schools in the United States. In its 154 years, Cumberland has produced a long list of distinguished graduates, including two Supreme Court justices, numerous judges and outstanding lawyers, and a U.S. Secretary of State known as the father of the United Nations.

In 1961, the law school was purchased by Samford University in Birmingham, Ala., a city of more than one million residents. The move to Birmingham established for Cumberland students a keen advantage: close proximity to a full range of federal courts, state courts, administrative agencies and nationally recognized law firms, where many Cumberland lawyers have found rewarding work before and after graduation.

Cumberland School of Law has attracted a faculty of 32 full-time professors, including a Rhodes Scholar, a former governor, a former U.S. attorney, numerous former federal law clerks and prominent legal historians. Although the faculty produces an impressive amount of quality legal scholarship, Cumberland remains committed to its original purpose: training people to be lawyers.

That commitment helps Cumberland recruit an outstanding and diverse student body from the Southeast and beyond who consistently are ahead of the pack in their summer clerkships and first year of practice. Cumberland requires students to know how to conduct proper legal research, write concise and compelling briefs, and argue persuasively in court. Their classroom studies are enhanced by participating in Cumberland's nationally recognized moot court teams; two academic journals, the *Cumberland Law Review* and the *American Journal of Trial Advocacy*; and a trial advocacy program that has won a reputation for success against the best teams in the nation. Courses ranging from the technical and practical to the highly theoretical, and a rich set of extracurricular activities, help prepare students for productive and satisfying careers in the legal profession. Mindful of the need for a global view of the law, Cumberland offers programs in international and comparative law at the University of Durham, England, and at the University of Sao Paulo, Brazil, and another in international environmental law in Victoria, British Columbia.

A gift from one of Samford University's most generous friends has provided an inspiring sanctuary for law students, legal scholars and practicing attorneys: The Lucille Stewart Beeson Law Library, a state-of-the-art center for research and study, which opened in 1995. With a comprehensive collection of books and materials, 12 conference rooms, 474 study spaces, the latest online legal research tools, and a staff of seven professional librarians-three with law degrees-the four-story Beeson library is both visually stunning and superbly functional.

Dean and Professor of Law: John L. Carroll (205) 726-2704
Associate Dean for Academic Affairs: Henry C. Strickland III (205) 726-8411
Assistant Dean for Admissions/Alumni: Mitzi S. Davis (205) 726-2936
Assistant Dean for Continuing Legal Education and Asst. Prof: LaVone R. Warren (205) 726-2779
Vice Dean, Financial Aid/Development: James N. Lewis (205) 726-2887
Law Librarian and Professor of Law: Larurel R. Clapp (205) 726-2714
Director, Career Services: Jeanette Rader (205) 726-2797
Director, Communications/External Relations: Virginia Gilbert Loftin (205) 726-2158

(This Listing Continued)

CUMBERLAND SCHOOL OF LAW AT SAMFORD UNIVERSITY—Continued

FULL TIME FACULTY

JOHN L. CARROLL*, (Dean and Professor of Law)**, born Washington, D.C., October 19, 1943; admitted to bar, 1974, Alabama. *Education:* Tufts University (B.A., 1965); Samford University Cumberland School of Law (J.D., 1974); Harvard University (LL.M., 1975). ***COURSES: Complex Litigation, Federal Jurisdiction, Civil Procedure, Lawyering Skills and Legal Reasoning. ***Email:*** carroll@samford.edu

THOMAS CHARLES BERG*, (Professor of Law)**, born Chicago, Illinois, August 18, 1960; admitted to bar, 1989, Illinois. *Education:* Northwestern University (B.S.J., 1982); Oxford University (B.A., 1984); University of Chicago (J.D., 1987). ***COURSES: Constitutional Law, Torts. ***Email:*** tcberg@samford.edu

THOMAS BRAD BISHOP*, (Professor of Law)**, born Roanoke, Alabama, January 7, 1940; admitted to bar, 1971, Alabama. *Education:* Samford University (B.A., 1961); University of Alabama (M.A., 1962); Cumberland School of Law at Samford University (J.D., 1971). ***COURSES: Contracts, Uniform Commercial Code, Municipal Courts. ***Email:*** tbbishop@samford.edu

JOSEPH W. BLACKBURN*, (Palmer Professor of Law)**, born Mayfield, Kentucky, February 24, 1947; admitted to bar, 1974, Alabama. *Education:* University of Kentucky (B.S., 1969); University of Virginia (J.D., 1974). ***COURSES: Federal Income Tax, Estate and Gift Tax, Law and Accounting, Business Planning, Corporate Tax, International Tax. ***Email:*** jwblackb@samford.edu

ALEXANDER J. BOLLA, JR.*, (Professor of Law)**, born Hazelton, Pennsylvania, September 3, 1942; admitted to bar, 1971, Colorado; 1972, Ohio; 1974, United States Supreme Court; 1980, Alabama. *Education:* Ohio State University (B.A., 1968; B.S., 1968; J.D., 1970). ***COURSES: Contracts, Business Law, Law, Computers, Lawyering Skills and Legal Reasoning. ***Email:*** ajbolla@samford.edu

KARON OWEN BOWDRE*, (Professor of Law)**, born Montgomery, Alabama, April 25, 1955; admitted to bar, 1981, Alabama. *Education:* Samford University (B.A., 1977); Cumberland School of Law at Samford University (J.D., 1981). ***COURSES: Insurance and Professional Responsibility. ***Email:*** kobowdre@samford.edu

ALBERT PRESTON BREWER*, (Professor of Law)**, born Bethel Springs, Tennessee, October 26, 1928; admitted to bar, 1952, Alabama. *Education:* University of Alabama (A.B., 1952; J.D., 1952). ***COURSES: Professional Responsibility, Law Office Practice and Management, State Constitutional Law.

LAUREL R. CLAPP*, (Law Librarian and Professor of Law)**, born Montgomery, Alabama; admitted to bar, 1975, Texas; 1979, Alabama. *Education:* David Lipscomb College (B.A., 1966); Mercer University (J.D., 1969); University of Washington (M.L.Lib., 1970). ***COURSES: Legal Research and Writing. ***Email:*** lrclapp@samford.edu

CHARLES D. COLE*, (Berson Professor of Law)**, born Monroeville, Alabama, May 14, 1938; admitted to bar, 1966, Alabama. *Education:* Auburn University (B.S., 1966); Cumberland School of Law at Samford University (J.D., 1966); New York University (LL.M., 1971). ***COURSES: Constitutional Law, Civil Procedure and Legal Process. ***Email:*** cdcole@samford.edu

MICHAEL E. DEBOW*, (Professor of Law)**, born Tupelo, Mississippi, May 3, 1956; admitted to bar, 1981, District of Columbia. *Education:* University of Alabama (B.A., 1977; M.A., 1978); Yale University (J.D., 1980). ***COURSES: Antitrust, Administrative Law, Corporate Finance. ***Email:*** medebow@samford.edu

W. JAMES ELLISON*, (Professor of Law)**, born Rock Hill, South Carolina, January 28, 1947; admitted to bar, 1978, Tennessee; 1981, United States Supreme Court; 1988, Alabama. *Education:* Rutgers University (B.A., with high honors, 1974); University of Michigan (J.D., 1977). ***COURSES: Criminal Law, Corporate and White Collar Crimes, Constitutional Criminal Procedure. ***Email:*** wjelliso@samford.edu

JILL E. EVANS*, (Associate Professor of Law)**, born Cleveland, Ohio, October 29, 1957; admitted to bar, 1984, California; 1985, Illinois. *Education:* Pamona College; University of California, Irvine (B.S., 1979); Northwestern University (J.D./M.M., 1983). ***COURSES: Contracts, Environmental Law. ***Email:*** jeevans@samford.edu

CAROLYN BURGESS FEATHERINGILL*, (Professor of Law)**, born Huntsville, Alabama, January 6, 1947; admitted to bar, 1972, Alabama. *Education:* Randolph-Macon Woman's College (A.B., 1969); University of Virginia (J.D., 1972). ***COURSES: Wills and Trusts, Estate Tax.

MICHAEL D. FLOYD*, (Professor of Law)**, born Atlanta, Georgia, July 24, 1953; admitted to bar, 1987, Georgia. *Education:* Princeton University (A.B., 1975); New York University (M.S., 1977); Emory University (J.D., 1987). ***COURSES: Secured Transactions, Negotiable Instruments, Consumer Protection, Federal Income Tax. ***Email:*** mdfloyd@samford.edu

JOHN C. GODBOLD*, (Leslie S. Wright Professor of Law)**, born Coy, Alabama, March 24, 1920; admitted to bar, 1948, Alabama. *Education:* Auburn University (B.S., 1940); Harvard University (J.D., 1943). ***COURSES: Federal Practice and Procedure.

ROBERT J. GOODWIN*, (Professor of Law)**, born St. Louis, Missouri, February 18, 1949; admitted to bar, 1974, Missouri; 1988, Alabama. *Education:* University of Missouri (A.B., 1971); Washington University (J.D., 1974). ***COURSES: Criminal Law, Evidence, Trial Practice, Public School Law. ***Email:*** rjgoodwi@samford.edu

PAUL KURUK*, (Professor of Law)**, born Bawku, Ghana, December 8, 1957; admitted to bar, 1986, New York; 1989, California. *Education:* University of Ghana (LL.B., 1981); Ghana Law School (B.L., 1983); Temple University School of Law (LL.M., 1985); Stanford Law School (J.S.D., 1989). ***COURSES: Commercial Transactions. ***Email:*** pkuruk@samford.edu

DAVID J. LANGUM*, (Professor of Law)**, born Oakland, California, October 24, 1940; admitted to bar, 1966, California; 1972, United States Supreme Court; 1981, Michigan. *Education:* Dartmouth College (A.B., 1962); San Jose State University (M.A., 1976); Stanford University (J.D., 1965); University of Michigan (LL.M., 1981; S.J.D., 1985). ***COURSES: Evidence, Legal History, Property. ***Email:*** djlangum@samford.edu

EDWARD C. MARTIN*, (Professor of Law)**, born Nashville, Tennessee, October 24, 1948; admitted to bar, 1976, Tennessee. *Education:* University of Tennessee (B.S., 1970; J.D., 1975). ***COURSES: Torts, Products Liability, Damages, Professional Responsibility. ***Email:*** ecmartin@samford.edu

LEONARD J. NELSON, III*, (Professor of Law and Director, Lawyering Skills and Legal Reasoning Program)**, born Spokane, Washington, July 31, 1949; admitted to bar, 1974, Washington; 1979, Oklahoma. *Education:* Whitman College; University of Washington (B.A., 1970); Gonzaga University (J.D., 1974); Yale University (LL.M., 1984). ***COURSES: Torts, Health Law, International Law, Lawyering Skills and Legal Reasoning. ***Email:*** ljnelson@samford.edu

***TRISHA C. OLSON*, (Associate Professor)**, born September 28, 1954.

(This Listing Continued)

CUMBERLAND SCHOOL OF LAW AT SAMFORD UNIVERSITY—Continued

Education: University of California, Berkeley (B.S., 1988); Boalt Hall School of Law, University of California, Berkeley; Yale University (J.D., 1991). ***COURSES:*** Evidence, Professional Responsibility. ***Email:*** tcolson@samford.edu

WILLIAM G. ROSS, **(Professor of Law)**, born Orlando, Florida, December 22, 1954; admitted to bar, 1980, New York. *Education:* Stanford University (A.B., 1976); Harvard University (J.D., 1979). ***COURSES:*** Civil Procedure, Torts, Constitutional Law. ***Email:*** wgross@samford.edu

DAVID MARK SMOLIN, **(Professor of Law)**, born New York, New York, December 12, 1958; admitted to bar, 1986, Ohio. *Education:* New College of the University of South Florida (B.A., 1980); University of Cincinnati (J.D., 1986). ***COURSES:*** Criminal Law, Family Law, Constitutional Law, Criminal Justice, International Law, Juvenile Law, Law and Religion. ***Email:*** davdes@juno.com

JOSEPH A. SNOE, **(Professor of Law)**, born Conroe, Texas, February 7, 1949; admitted to bar, 1981, Texas. *Education:* University of Texas (B.B.A., 1971; J.D., 1981). ***COURSES:*** Federal Income Taxation, Property. ***Email:*** jasnoe@samford.edu

R. THOMAS STONE, **(Professor of Law)**, born April 5, 1945; admitted to bar, 1971, Florida. *Education:* Virginia Polytechnic Institute and State University (B.S., 1965); Emory University (J.D., 1969); University of Tennessee (Ph.D., 1975); University of Illinois (LL.M., 1978). ***COURSES:*** Contracts, Business Organizations, Government Regulations. ***Email:*** rtstone@samford.edu

HENRY C. STRICKLAND, III, **(Associate Dean and Professor of Law)**, born Atlanta, Georgia, October 4, 1958; admitted to bar, 1984, Georgia; 1985, North Carolina. *Education:* Presbyterian College (B.A., 1980); Vanderbilt University (J.D., 1983). ***COURSES:*** Civil Procedure, Remedies, Alternative Dispute Resolution, Conflict of Law. ***Email:*** hcstrick@samford.edu

PATSY W. THOMLEY, **(Professor of Law)**, born Petrey, Alabama, June 30, 1939; admitted to bar, 1980, Alabama. *Education:* Auburn University (B.S., 1960); Samford University (M.A., 1969); Cumberland School of Law at Samford University (J.D., 1980). ***COURSES:*** Property. ***Email:*** pwthomle@samford.edu

HOWARD PHILIP WALTHALL, **(Professor of Law)**, born Birmingham, Alabama, November 11, 1941; admitted to bar, 1967, Alabama. *Education:* Harvard University (A.B., 1964; LL.B., 1967). ***COURSES:*** Uniform Commercial Code, Bankruptcy and Creditors' Remedies, Corporations. ***Email:*** hpwaltha@samford.edu

STEPHEN J. WARE, **(Professor of Law)**, born Bronxville, New York, October 11, 1965; admitted to bar, 1991, New York; 1992, U.S. District Court, Southern and Eastern Districts of New York. *Education:* University of Chicago (B.A., 1987; J.D., 1990). ***COURSES:*** Commercial Transactions. ***Email:*** sjware@samford.edu

LAVONE RICKMAN WARREN, **(Assistant Dean for Continuing Legal Education and Assistant Professor)**, born Tokyo, Japan, August 14, 1951; admitted to bar, 1981, Mississippi. *Education:* Enterprise State Junior College (A.A., 1971); University of Alabama (B.A., 1973); University of Mississippi (J.D., 1981). ***COURSES:*** Business Organizations, Lawyering Skills and Legal Reasoning, Securities Regulation. ***Email:*** lrwarren@samford.edu

DEBORAH YOUNG, **(Professor of Law)**, born Louisville, Kentucky, May 18, 1956; admitted to bar, 1983, Kentucky; 1986, District of Columbia. *Education:* University of Kentucky (B.A., 1978); University of Michigan (J.D., 1982). ***COURSES:*** Evidence, Trial Practice. ***Email:*** dyoung@samford.edu

---

DEPAUL UNIVERSITY COLLEGE OF LAW

25 EAST JACKSON BOULEVARD
CHICAGO, ILLINOIS 60604

THE DICKINSON SCHOOL OF LAW OF THE PENNSYLVANIA STATE UNIVERSITY

150 SOUTH COLLEGE STREET
CARLISLE, PENNSYLVANIA 17013
Telephone: (717) 240-5000
Fax: (717) 240-5213
Web Site: www.dsl.psu.edu

ABA Approved Since 1931

Founded in 1834, The Dickinson School of Law is the oldest law school in Pennsylvania and the fifth oldest in the nation. On July 1, 1997, the Law School affiliated with Penn State, becoming The Dickinson School of Law of The Pennsylvania State University. On July 1, 2000 the two institutions were fully merged. As part of Penn State, the Law School has enhanced technological capabilities and is now offering its students opportunities for combined degree programs in a number of fields, including public administration, business administration, environmental management and information systems. The Law School and the University's College of Agricultural Sciences have collaborated on an Agricultural Law Research and Education Center, located at the Law School.

Over the years, Dickinson has stressed the importance of providing a balance between the theoretical and practical aspects of legal education in a curriculum that prepares our graduates to practice in any jurisdiction and in a variety of fields of law. Thirty-six professors and professor-administrators work with some 50 adjunct professors to teach more than 100 courses in the Juris Doctor (J.D.) and Master of Laws curricula. Dickinson's summer overseas programs, its master's program for foreign lawyers, its new London Semester program, and its co-sponsorship of an international symposium on economic crime are enhancing its reputation both in the United States and abroad while enabling its students to gain a unique international perspective.

Known for educating skilled advocates, Dickinson has been the recipient of the prestigious Emil Gumpert Award for Excellence in the Teaching of Trial Advocacy from the American College of Trial Lawyers and Professor Gary Gildin received the 1999 Richard S. Jacobson Award for Excellence in Teaching Trial Advocacy from the Roscoe Pound Foundation. Recognizing that advocacy skills are indispensable throughout the profession, the School places great emphasis on developing these skills through classroom work, clinical experience, and moot court competition. Dickinson teams participate in

(This Listing Continued)

THE DICKINSON SCHOOL OF LAW OF THE PENNSYLVANIA STATE UNIVERSITY—Continued

as many as ten interscholastic moot court programs each year. Dickinson's fine reputation for teaching advocacy has spawned a popular Trial Advocacy Seminar and Workshop and Prosecutors' Trial Advocacy Seminar and Workshop for young practitioners conducted at the Law School each year. In honor of an Alumnus, his children and their spouses have donated funds to create the Honorable G. Thomas and Anne G. Miller Chair in Advocacy and the new Miller Center for Public Interest Advocacy.

Long before the ABA's MacCrate Commission report emphasized the importance of teaching lawyering skills, Dickinson was in the forefront of providing opportunities for students to gain real-life, hands-on experience. Dickinson students begin their law school careers with an integrated, two-semester course in lawyering skills, with particular focus on research and writing. Other courses help students to develop essential interviewing, counseling, negotiation, and mediation skills. Dickinson students have many different kinds of clinical experiences available to them, including clinics in Elder Law; Family Law; Disability Law; and Art, Sports, and Entertainment Law, as well as field placements in state government, legal services, public defender and prosecutors' offices, and courts. The Law School's close proximity to Harrisburg, the state capital, facilitates opportunities for work in state government agencies and private law firms during the school year and in the summer.

Dickinson has three scholarly student journals, including the *Dickinson Law Review,* one of the oldest law reviews in the country, the *Dickinson Journal of International Law,* and the *Dickinson Environmental Law Review.*

In the early 1980s, Dickinson became one of the first law schools to establish a summer overseas comparative law program for American students. Today, law students from throughout the United States enroll for the opportunity to visit the legal and cultural centers of Florence, Italy; Strasbourg, France; Vienna, Austria; Brussels, Belgium, Oxford, England, and the Hague to learn from renowned scholars and practitioners.

Dickinson also was an innovator in providing comparative law programs for foreign lawyers. In 1968, the School initiated a master's degree program in comparative law for foreign lawyers whose degrees are not based substantially on the English Common Law system. Since that time, students from almost four dozen different nations have earned their LL.M. in comparative law degree from Dickinson. Dickinson's foreign students make significant contributions to their nations and the world and forge friendships with faculty, fellow students, and others that will last a lifetime. They also enhance the educational atmosphere for American students who learn from them the customs, culture, and legal traditions of other nations.

Dickinson's extensive library houses more than 400,000 volumes and equivalents and offers student access to computerized legal instructional programs, LEXIS and Westlaw computer research terminals, and a computer lab with IBM personal computers, software, and printers. Students also have on-line access to Penn State University's four-million-volume catalog and access to a variety of research data bases in the Penn State system, as well as access to the libraries of the Big Ten Universities.

Perhaps the most valuable aspect of a Dickinson education is its intimate learning environment fostered by ready accessibility of faculty. Unlike many larger law schools, Dickinson's academic atmosphere, while competitive, is friendly and cooperative. Students and faculty truly get to know each other and often interact on a social level.

Student enrollment is approximately 540, with students from 31 states and seven foreign countries and about 200 undergraduate schools. Nearly 10 percent come to us with degrees beyond the bachelor's. Almost half have worked full time before enrolling in law school. Dickinson's 6,200 alumni practice from coast to coast and in major metropolitan areas throughout the United States, as well as in several U.S. territories and many foreign countries. Recent placement statistics show that more than 90 percent of graduates who report their job status are employed within six months after graduation. Most recent graduates work in private practice, although a rather high percentage begin their careers as judicial clerks.

Dean: Peter G. Glenn
Vice Dean: Michael J. Navin
Associate Dean for Academic Affairs: Harvey A. Feldman
Associate Dean for Student Affairs: Michael A. Mogill
Director of the Library: James R. Fox
Director of Law Admissions: Barbara W. Guillaume (717) 240-5207
Director of Graduate Law Admissions: Dianne I. Nichols (717) 240-5207
Director of Financial Aid: Joyce James (717) 241-3524
Director of Alumni Relations: Deborah Fulham-Winston (717) 240-5250
Director of Career Services: Gicine P. Brignola (717) 240-5201
Director, Law School Relations: Beth Esler (717) 240-5247
Director of Development and External Affairs: Robert S. Arp (717) 240-5252

FULL TIME FACULTY

PETER G. GLENN*, (Dean and Donald J. Farage Professor)**, born Stamford, Connecticut, July 20, 1943; admitted to bar, 1970, Ohio. *Education:* Middlebury College (A.B., 1965); University of Pennsylvania (J.D., 1968). ***COURSES: Professional Responsibility.

ROBERT M. ACKERMAN*, (Professor of Law and Director, Center for Dispute Resolution)**, born Yonkers, New York, March 26, 1951; admitted to bar, 1976, Colorado; 1984, Pennsylvania. *Education:* Colgate University (B.A, 1973); Harvard Law School (J.D., 1976). ***COURSES: Torts, Advocacy, Dispute Resolution, Legislative & Administrative Process & Interpretation.

PETER CHRISTOPHER ALEXANDER*, (Professor of Law)**, born Suffern, New York, October 10, 1958; admitted to bar, 1983, Illinois. *Education:* Southern Illinois University (B.A., 1979); Northeastern University (J.D., 1983). ***COURSES: Debtor and Creditor, Advanced Debtor and Creditor Law, Evidence.

LARRY CATA BACKER*, (Professor of Law)**, born Miami Beach, Florida, February 1, 1955; admitted to bar, 1982, California. *Education:* Brandeis University (B.A., 1977); Harvard University (M.P.P., 1979); Columbia University (J.D., 1982). ***COURSES: Civil Procedure, Constitutional Law, Comparative Corporate Law.

***WILLIAM B. BARKER*, (Professor of Law)**, born McKeesport, Pennsylvania, March 20, 1950; admitted to bar, 1978, New York; 1979, District of Columbia. *Education:* Columbia University and State University of New York at Buffalo (B.A., 1974; J.D., 1977); On-Site

(This Listing Continued)

THE DICKINSON SCHOOL OF LAW OF THE PENNSYLVANIA STATE UNIVERSITY—Continued

Program Co-Director and Academic Director of the 2002 Land Semester Program. ***COURSES:*** Partnership Taxation, Basic Federal Tax, Taxation, International Taxation, Comparative Taxation, European Tax Law, Tax Policy.

LANCE COLE, **(Assistant Professor of Law)**, born July 24, 1959; admitted to bar, 1984, District of Columbia. *Education:* University of Arkansas (B.S.P.A., 1981); Harvard Law School (J.D., 1984). ***COURSES:*** Agency and Partnership, Legislative and Administrative Process and Interpretation, Enterprise Organization, Assisting in Advocacy Program.

LOUIS F. DEL DUCA, **(A. Robert Noll Professor of Law, Associate Dean and Director, Center for International and Comparative Law)**, born Italy, July 2, 1926; admitted to bar, 1955, Pennsylvania. *Education:* Temple University (B.A., 1950); Harvard University (J.D., 1952); University of Rome (Dott. diGiur, 1954). ***COURSES:*** Secured Transactions, Comparative Law, Introduction to U.S. Legal System.

SUSAN BETH FARMER, **(Professor)**, born Elyria, Ohio, 1952; admitted to bar, 1977, Alabama; 1988, District of Columbia and New York. *Education:* Wellesley College (B.A., 1974); Vanderbilt Law School (J.D., 1977). ***COURSES:*** Field Placement Clinics, Criminal Law, White Collar Crime.

STEPHANIE FARRIOR, **(Professor)**, born Bangkok, Thailand, February 26, 1954; admitted to bar, 1983, District of Columbia. *Education:* Macalester College (B.A., 1974); University of Pennsylvania (M.A., 1976); American University (J.D., 1982); Harvard University (LL.M., 1990).

HARVEY A. FELDMAN, **(Professor, Associate Dean for Academic Affairs)**, born Philadelphia, Pennsylvania, February 23, 1945; admitted to bar, 1969, Pennsylvania. *Education:* University of Pennsylvania (B.A., 1966); Dickinson School of Law (J.D., 1969); George Washington University (LL.M., 1974). ***COURSES:*** Property, Appellate Practice, Real Estate Transactions.

JAMES R. FOX, **(Professor and Director, Law Library)**, born Dayton, Ohio, June 30, 1950; admitted to bar, 1976, Pennsylvania. *Education:* Otterbein College (B.A., 1972); Ohio State University (J.D., 1974); Drexel University (M.S., 1978). ***COURSES:*** Air and Space Law, Advanced Legal Research.

ROBERT A. GATTER, **(Assistant Professor of Law)**, born Philadelphia, Pennsylvania, February 14, 1964; admitted to bar, 1990, Colorado; 1995, Wisconsin. *Education:* Johns Hopkins University (B.A., 1986); University of Pennsylvania (J.D., 1990). ***COURSES:*** Contracts, Healthcare Law.

GARY S. GILDIN, **(Prof./Holder of The Hon. G. Thomas & Anne G. Miller Chair in Advoc./Dir., Miller Ctr. for Pub. Interest Advoc.)**, born Chicago, Illinois, March 22, 1952; admitted to bar, 1976, Illinois; 1982, Pennsylvania. *Education:* University of Wisconsin (B.A., 1973); Stanford University (J.D., 1976). ***COURSES:*** Trial Advocacy, Criminal Procedure.

EDWARD W. HAUGHNEY, **(Professor)**, born Brooklyn, New York, December 8, 1917; admitted to bar, 1949, New York. *Education:* Brooklyn College; St. John's University (LL.B., 1949); George Washington University (M.S., 1966). ***COURSES:*** Federal Practice.

EILEEN M. KANE, **(Assistant Professor)**, born New York, New York; admitted to bar, 2000, New York. *Education:* Hunter College (B.A., 1985); Cornell University (Ph.D., 1993); Fordham University School of Law (J.D., 1998). ***COURSES:*** Patents, Internet Law, Science & Law.

WILLIAM J. KEATING, **(Professor)**, born Buffalo, New York, December 26, 1924; admitted to bar, 1954, District of Columbia; 1979, Pennsylvania. *Education:* Canisius College (B.S., 1947); Georgetown University (J.D., 1954). ***COURSES:*** Law of Franchising.

CHRISTINE H. KELLETT, **(Professor, Director The Agricultural Law Research and Education Center)**, born February 10, 1942; admitted to bar, 1975, Pennsylvania. *Education:* University of New Mexico (B.A., 1964); The Dickinson School of Law (J.D., 1975). ***COURSES:*** Constitutional Law, Supreme Court, State and Local Government Law.

JOHN H. KNOX, **(Assistant Professor of Law)**, born Chapel Hill, North Carolina, February 6, 1963; admitted to bar, 1988, Pennsylvania; 1994, Texas. *Education:* Rice University (B.A., 1984); Stanford Law School (J.D., 1987). ***COURSES:*** Property I & II, Environmental Law, International Trade & the Environment.

JOHN A. MAHER, **(H. Laddie and F. Montagne Professor)**, born Brooklyn, New York, December 3, 1930; admitted to bar, 1957, New York; 1960, District of Columbia; 1986, Pennsylvania. *Education:* University of Notre Dame (A.B., 1951); New York University (LL.B., 1956, LL.M., Trade Regulation, 1957). ***COURSES:*** Maritime Law.

CAMILLE C. MARION, **(Joseph B. Kelly Lawyering Skills Professor, Director, Lawyering Skills Program)**, born Scranton, Pennsylvania, June 22, 1954; admitted to bar, 1989, Pennsylvania. *Education:* University of Scranton (B.S., 1976); The Dickinson School of Law (J.D., 1989). ***COURSES:*** Lawyering Skills.

MICHAEL MOGILL, **(Professor, Associate Dean for Student Affairs)**, born Chicago, Illinois, November 5, 1950; admitted to bar, 1976, Georgia. *Education:* University of Illinois (B.A., 1972); Northeastern University (J.D., 1976); Temple University (LL.M., 1989). ***COURSES:*** Torts, Products Liability, Evidence, Remedies.

FRANCIS J. MOOTZ III, **(Professor of Law)**, born Long Beach, California, June 3, 1961; admitted to bar, 1986, Connecticut. *Education:* University of Notre Dame (B.A., 1983); Duke University Graduate School (A.M., 1986); Duke University Law School (J.D., 1986). ***COURSES:*** Contracts, Sales, Negotiable Instruments, Payment Systems, Legislative and Administrative Process and Interpretation.

JANE MULLER-PETERSON, **(Joseph B. Kelly Lawyering Skills Professor)**, born New Haven, Connecticut, December 27, 1947; admitted to bar, 1979, Wisconsin; 1982, Pennsylvania. *Education:* Macalester College (B.A., 1970); University of Wisconsin (M.A., 1976; J.D., 1979). ***COURSES:*** Lawyering Skills.

PERRIE H. NAIDES, **(Joseph B. Kelly Lawyering Skills Professor)**, born New York, New York, November 15, 1952; admitted to bar, 1989, Iowa; 2001 Pennsylvania. *Education:* University of California - Berkeley (A.B., 1974); University of California - San Francisco (Ph.D., 1981); University of Iowa (J.D., 1989). ***COURSES:*** Lawyering Skills.

ROSS NANKIVELL, **(Joseph B. Kelly Lawyering Skills Professor)**, born Melbourne, Australia, October 20, 1943; admitted to bar, 1970, Supreme Court of Victoria (Australia); 1977, Federal Courts of Australia. *Education:* University of Melbourne (LL.B., 1969); Monash University (D.I.P. (Diploma in Family Law), 1996). ***COURSES:*** Lawyering Skills.

MICHAEL J. NAVIN, **(Professor, Vice Dean, Chair, Admissions)**, born Waterbury, Connecticut, March 14, 1943; admitted to bar, 1969, Washington. *Education:* University of Connecticut (B.S., 1965; J.D., 1969). ***COURSES:*** Insurance Law, Contracts.

KATHERINE C. PEARSON, **(Professor of Law)**, born Phoenix, Arizona, September 20, 1953; admitted to bar, 1979, Florida; 1981, New Mexico. *Education:* University of Arizona (B.A., 1974);

(This Listing Continued)

THE DICKINSON SCHOOL OF LAW OF THE PENNSYLVANIA STATE UNIVERSITY—Continued

University of Miami (J.D., 1979). ***COURSES:*** Conflict of Laws, Elder Law, Elder Law Clinic, Evidence.

THOMAS M. PLACE,* (Professor of Law)**, born Duluth, Minnesota, October 4, 1945; admitted to bar, 1969, Wisconsin; 1971, Kentucky; 1975, Pennsylvania. *Education:* Marquette University (B.A., 1966; J.D., 1969). ***COURSES: Criminal Procedure, First Amendment, Post-Conviction Process, Legal Clinics, Advanced Criminal Procedure, Assisting in Advocacy Program.

MARY KATHLEEN EADS POLACHECK,* (Writing Specialist)**, born Philadelphia, Pennsylvania, December 10, 1955; admitted to bar, 1982, Pennsylvania. *Education:* Villanova University (B.S.B.A., 1977; M.A., 1979; J.D., 1982). ***COURSES: Writing Workshop, Writing and Editing for Lawyers.

CARLA D. PRATT,* (Assistant Professor of Law)**, born Oklahoma City, Oklahoma, October 3, 1968; admitted to bar, 1993, Pennsylvania and New Jersey. *Education:* East Texas State University (B.A., 1989); Howard University (J.D., 1992). ***COURSES: Contracts, Professional Responsibility, Race, Racism and American Law Seminar.

ROBERT E. RAINS,* (Professor of Law)**, born Washington, D.C., January 21, 1949; admitted to bar, 1974, Pennsylvania; 1975, Massachusetts; 1977, District of Columbia. *Education:* Michigan State University (B.A., 1970); Harvard University (J.D., 1974). ***COURSES: Legal Clinics, Law and Individuals with Disabilities, Education Law, Juvenile Law, Family Law.

JANE RIGLER,* (Professor of Law)**, born New Hampton, Iowa, February 22, 1950; admitted to bar, 1975, Florida; 1986, District of Columbia. *Education:* University of Iowa (B.A., 1972); Florida State University (J.D., 1975); New York University (LL.M., 1978). ***COURSES: Labor Law, Criminal Law, Employment Legislation, Fair Employment Law.

VICTOR C. ROMERO,* (Professor of Law)**, born Manila, Philippines, January 28, 1965; admitted to bar, 1992, California. *Education:* Swarthmore College (B.A., 1987); University of Southern California Law Center (J.D., 1992). ***COURSES: Torts, Immigration Law, Race, Racism and American Law, Constitutional Law, Equal Protection Law.

GEOFFREY R. SCOTT,* (Professor of Law)**, born Fort Lewis, Washington, September 3, 1946; admitted to bar, 1971, Indiana; 1980, Pennsylvania. *Education:* Valparaiso University (B.A., 1968; J.D., 1971); Yale University (LL.M., 1973). ***COURSES: Jurisprudence, Artistic Persons and Property, Estate Planning, Law, Science and Policy, Art, Sports and Entertainment Law Clinics, The Right To, Copyrights.

LAUREL S. TERRY,* (Professor of Law)**, born Los Angeles, California, July 31, 1955; admitted to bar, 1981, California and Oregon; 1983, Washington. *Education:* University of California at San Diego (B.A., 1977); University of California at Los Angeles (J.D., 1980). ***COURSES: Professional Responsibility, Trial Advocacy, Civil Procedure.

NANCY A. WELSH,* (Assistant Professor of Law, Associate Director, Center for Dispute Resolution)**, born Erie, Pennsylvania, June 30, 1957; admitted to bar, 1982, Minnesota. *Education:* Allegheny College (B.A., 1979); Harvard Law School (J.D., 1982). ***COURSES: Civil Procedure I & II, Client Counseling, Negotiation and Mediation, Dispute Resolution.

DRAKE UNIVERSITY LAW SCHOOL

2507 UNIVERSITY AVENUE
DES MOINES, IOWA 50311
Telephone: (515) 271-2824
Fax: (515) 271-4118

ABA Approved Since 1923

Drake University Law School, one of the twenty-five oldest law schools in the nation, traces its history to 1865. It is a Charter Member of the Association of American Law Schools, has been accredited by the American Bar Association since 1923, and is one of only seventy-five ABA approved law schools to have a Chapter of Order of the Coif. Admission is selective, and the student body is diverse. For 1999-00 the Law School included students from 133 undergraduate institutions, 36 states and 3 foreign countries. Women comprised 45 percent and persons of color 12 percent of the overall student body of approximately 360 full-time students.

The size of the Law School facilitates the offering of a modern education of high quality in a personalized setting. Twenty-eight full-time faculty have extensive experience in private practice and government service, outstanding academic credentials, and a commitment to excellence in the classroom. They produce research and scholarly publications reflecting practical and theoretical orientations and have designed a curriculum that is diverse and national in scope. A solid curriculum is enhanced by advanced courses and instruction in an array of subjects, including constitutional, agricultural, corporate, taxation, health and environmental law. Instruction in the use of computers is a central feature of legal education at Drake. The curriculum is planned to include not only basic and advanced substantive courses but also to emphasize professional skills development through simulation courses, extensive internships, and nationally recognized Clinical opportunities. All students observe and discuss a real trial in the unique Trial Practicum experience. Drake faculty and students also participate with judges and practicing attorneys in two chapters of the American Inns of Court Foundation.

Drake offers a widely varied curriculum on constitutional law. Drake is also home to the Constitutional Law Resource Center, which sponsors a lecture series and an annual symposium that attract nationally recognized constitutional scholars. A distinguished lectureship, the Dwight D. Opperman Lecture in Constitutional Law, emphasizes the significance of constitutional study at Drake. To date, the lecture has been delivered by nine United States Supreme Court justices.

Drake has one of the few programs in the nation addressing important issues in national and international agricultural law and policy. The Agricultural Law Center offers students the opportunity to help conduct research, publish the *Drake Journal of Agricultural Law* , and write articles and monographs on a wide range of subjects.

Cartwright Hall, Opperman Hall, and the Neal and Bea Smith Law Center constitute the Law School's physical facilities. Built in 1976, Cartwright is the main law school facility. The Dwight D. Opperman Hall and Law Library, dedicated in April, 1993, houses the Law Library, a computer classroom and other seminar rooms, more than 200 study carrels, 18 small study rooms and specialized centers devoted to Constitutional Law and Agricultural Law.

Extensive clinical opportunities, including client representation, a prosecutor internship, and judicial clerkship programs, enable students

(This Listing Continued)

DRAKE UNIVERSITY LAW SCHOOL—Continued

to gain practical experience, develop good lawyering skills and render public service as a part of their legal education. As part of the clinical program, students serve clients in all phases of client representation, ranging from client interviewing to negotiations with opposing counsel to trial itself. Clients include Drake students and staff, low income persons, senior citizens, victims of domestic violence and defendants accused of serious misdemeanors. These programs are housed in the Neal and Bea Smith Law Center, a fully computerized law office and educational facility built in 1987. Drake's clinical programs are supported by federal endowment appropriations totaling $4.5 million. Drake was one of two law schools in the country to receive such awards. In 1994 a $1.8 million addition to the Center was completed and dedicated. It includes a spacious courtroom, five classrooms accommodating classes of 18-20 students, and the Center for Public Service Attorneys.

Students engage in a wide range of co-curricular and extra-curricular activities. These include the *Drake Law Review*, which is published four times a year. Drake also has a strong moot court program. Drake's nationally-recognized moot court program takes students out of the classroom and further sharpens their skills in critical thinking, legal research, mock trials, negotiations, client counseling, brief writing, and oral advocacy through simulated litigation competitions. Students participate in nine national and three intramural moot court competitions. They have enjoyed success in the national competitions, including first place in the regional tournament of the National Moot Court Competition in seven out of the last ten years. In 1998, Drake finished second out of more than 160 law schools in the National Competition, largest moot court competition in the country. The climax of the moot court year comes on Supreme Court Day, an annual spring competition that the Law School has conducted for over sixty years. Second and third year law students brief and argue an appellate case, with the final four contestants presenting their arguments to a special session of Iowa Supreme Court. Drake students have regularly occupied leadership positions in the Law Student Division of the American Bar Association in the Eighth Circuit and served as liaisons to sections of the ABA. The Drake chapter of VITA, a project sponsored jointly by the Internal Revenue Service and the Law Student Division of the ABA, provides free income tax counseling and assistance to low income, elderly, and non-English speaking persons as well as persons with disabilities. The 1994-95 National Black Law Students Association President was a Drake student.

Drake graduates are practicing in each of the 50 states and the District of Columbia, and the school's alumni include leaders of the Bar; state governors; United States Congressmen; state Supreme Court Justices; other state and federal judges; legal educators; and business leaders.

Dean: C. Peter Goplerud III (515) 271-3985
Admission and Financial Aid Director: J. Kara Blanchard (515) 271-2782
Library Director: John D. Edwards (515) 271-2141
Career Services Director: Rick Sheriff (515) 271-4119

FULL TIME FACULTY

C. PETER GOPLERUD III*, (Dean and Professor of Law)**, born Cincinnati, Ohio, January 4, 1949; admitted to bar, 1974, Kansas; 1992, Colorado. *Education:* University of Kansas (B.A. 1971; J.D. 1974). ***COURSES: Sports Law, Environmental Law, Land Use Law, Administrative Law.

JAMES ALBERT ADAMS*, (Richard and Anita Calkins Distinguished Professor of Law)**, born Englewood, New Jersey, November 15, 1942; admitted to bar, 1967, New York; 1971, District of Columbia; 1977, Iowa. *Education:* Duke University (A.B., 1964; J.D., 1967). ***COURSES: Criminal Procedure, Evidence, Trial Advocacy.

JAMES A. ALBERT*, (Professor of Law)**, born Cedar Rapids, Iowa, July 2, 1947; admitted to bar, 1976, Iowa. *Education:* Drake University (B.F.A., 1971); University of Notre Dame (J.D., 1976). ***COURSES: Administrative Law, Torts, Media Law.

JERRY L. ANDERSON*, (Professor)**, born McPherson, Kansas, October 17, 1959; admitted to bar, 1984, Missouri. *Education:* University of Kansas (B.S., 1981); Stanford University (J.D., 1984). ***COURSES: Environmental Law, Environmental Litigation, Property, Natural Resources Law.

THOMAS E. BAKER*, (James Madison Professor and Chair of the Constitutional Law Resource Center)**, born February 25, 1953; admitted to bar, 1977, Florida. *Education:* Florida State (B.S., 1974); University of Florida (J.D., 1977). ***COURSES: Constitutional Law, Federal Courts, Civil Procedure.

TANYA K. BARTHOLOMEW*, (Associate Director, Center for Legislative Practice and Legal Writing Instructor)**, born December 8, 1958; admitted to bar, 1992, Iowa. *Education:* University of Oregon (B.S., 1981); Drake University (J.D., 1992). ***COURSES: Legal Writing Research & Writing.

MARTIN D. BEGLEITER*, (Professor of Law)**, born Middletown, Connecticut, October 31, 1945; admitted to bar, 1971, New York. *Education:* University of Rochester (B.A., 1967); Cornell University (J.D., 1970). ***COURSES: Estate Planning, Wills, Trusts, Federal Income Taxation, Federal Estate and Gift Taxation.

ANDREA S. CHARLOW*, (Professor of Law)**, born New York, October 3, 1952; admitted to bar, 1979, New York. *Education:* Vassar College (A.B., 1973); Albany Law School of Union University (J.D., 1978); Columbia University (LL.M., 1982). ***COURSES: Family Law, Public International Law, International Trade, Comparative Law, Negotiations.

HUNTER CLARK*, (Professor of Law)**, born Washington, D.C., September 1, 1955; admitted to bar, 1980, District of Columbia. *Education:* Harvard College (A.B., 1976); Harvard Law School (J.D., 1979). ***COURSES: Constitutional Law, Public International Law, International Trade, State and Local Government, U.S. Supreme Court Seminar.

LAURIE KRATKY DORE*, (Professor of Law)**, born Carmel, California, November 8, 1958; admitted to bar, 1984, Texas; 1996 Iowa. *Education:* Creighton University (B.A., 1981); Southern Methodist University (J.D., 1984). ***COURSES: Civil Procedure, Criminal Law, Conflict of Laws, Complex Litigation, Pretrial Advocacy.

MATTHEW G. DORE*, (Professor of Law)**, born Port Arthur, Texas, November 4, 1958; admitted to bar, 1984, Texas. *Education:* Rice University (B.A., 1981); University of Texas (J.D., 1984). ***COURSES: Business Associations, Securities, Commercial Law.

***JOHN D. EDWARDS*, (Director of the Law Library and Professor of Law)**, born Louisiana, Missouri, September 15, 1953; admitted to bar, 1978, Missouri. *Education:* Southeast Missouri State University (B.A., 1975); University of Missouri at Columbia (M.A.L.S., 1979);

(This Listing Continued)

DRAKE UNIVERSITY LAW SCHOOL—Continued

University of Missouri at Kansas City (J.D., 1977). ***COURSES:*** Legal Research and Writing, Computers and the Law, Computer-Assisted Legal Research.

SALLY BELINKOFF FRANK*, (Professor of Law)**, born Jersey City, New Jersey, February 24, 1959; admitted to bar, 1983, New Jersey; 1984, New York; 1985, District of Columbia; 1990, Iowa. *Education:* Princeton University (A.B., 1980); Antioch University (M.A.T., 1988); New York University (J.D., 1983). ***COURSES: Clinic, Trial Advocacy, Women and the Law.

NEIL D. HAMILTON*, (Ellis and Nelle Levitt Distinguished Professor of Law)**, born Creston, Iowa, January 22, 1954; admitted to bar, 1979, Iowa. *Education:* Iowa State University (B.S., 1976); University of Iowa (J.D., 1979). ***COURSES: Agricultural Law, Legislation, Negotiations, Land Use, Environmental Law.

***DAVID B. HANSON*, (Information Technology/Reference Librarian and Instructor)**, born West Point, New York, October 6, 1969. *Education:* Luther College (B.A., 1992); University of Missouri at Columbia (M.A.L.S., 1993).

ROBERT C. HUNTER*, (Professor of Law)**, born Pittsburgh, Pennsylvania, October 28, 1940; admitted to bar, 1967, Ohio. *Education:* University of Pittsburgh (B.A., 1963); Duke University (J.D., 1967). ***COURSES: Civil Procedure, Federal Jurisdiction, Constitutional Law, Education Law.

***SUZANNE J. LEVITT*, (Director of the Drake Legal Clinic and Professor of Law)**, born 1960; admitted to bar, 1986, New York, Illinois, S.D.N.Y., 7th Circuit, U.S. Supreme Court. *Education:* Barnard College (A.B.); New York Law School (J.D., 1985); Yale Law School (LL.M.).

RUSSELL E. LOVELL II*, (Professor of Law)**, born Springfield, Missouri, May 6, 1944; admitted to bar, 1969, Nebraska and Missouri; 1971, Indiana; 1977, Iowa. *Education:* University of Notre Dame (B.B.A., 1966); University of Nebraska (J.D., 1969); University of Missouri at Kansas City (LL.M., 1971). ***COURSES: Constitutional Law, Employment Discrimination, Civil Rights, Administrative Law.

CATHY LESSER MANSFIELD*, (Professor of Law)**, born Cleveland, Ohio, March 21, 1960; admitted to bar, 1987, Arizona. *Education:* New York University (B.A., 1982); University of Virginia (J.D., 1987). ***COURSES: Consumer Law, Contracts, Payment Systems.

J. KARNALE MANUEL*, (Visiting Associate Professor of Law)**, born Des Moines, Iowa, April 02, 1950; admitted to bar, 1978, Iowa. *Education:* Drake University (B.S., B.A., 1973; J.D., 1978). ***COURSES: Legal Clinical Education.

DAVID MCCORD*, (Associate Dean and Professor of Law)**, born Vincennes, Indiana, November 23, 1953; admitted to bar, 1978, Arizona. *Education:* Illinois Wesleyan University (B.A., 1975); Harvard University (J.D., 1978). ***COURSES: Criminal Law, Civil Procedure, Evidence, Trial Advocacy, Post-Conviction Remedies.

KEITH C. MILLER*, (Ellis and Nelle Levitt Distinguished Professor)**, born Des Moines, Iowa, June 14, 1951; admitted to bar, 1976, Missouri. *Education:* University of Missouri at Kansas City (B.A., 1973; J.D., 1976); University of Michigan (LL.M., 1979). ***COURSES: Torts, Products Liability, Workers' Compensation.

JAMES R. MONROE*, (Professor of Law)**, born Uvalde, Texas, May 19, 1943; admitted to bar, 1973, Iowa and Florida. *Education:* University of Northern Iowa (B.A., 1966); Denver University (M.B.A., 1967); University of Iowa (J.D., 1973); New York University (LL.M., 1977). ***COURSES: Federal Income Tax, Corporate Tax, Tax Procedure, State and Local Tax.

LAWRENCE E. POPE*, (Director, Center for Legislative Practice and Professor of Law)**, born February 28, 1940; admitted to bar, 1967, Iowa. *Education:* Drake University (B.A., 1964; J.D., 1967); New York University (LL.M., 1969). ***COURSES: Administrative Law, Constitutional Law, Labor Law, Problems in Labor Law.

DANIEL L. POWER*, (Professor of Law)**, born Cedar Rapids, Iowa, January 7, 1934; admitted to bar, 1960, Iowa and Missouri. *Education:* St. Louis University (B.S., 1957; J.D., 1960); Georgetown University (LL.M., 1964). ***COURSES: Client Representation, Litigation, Judicial Clerkships, Evidence, Federal Income Tax, Trial Advocacy, Director for Public Service Attorneys Professional Development.

ELIZABETH E. QUINLAN*, (Legal Writing Instructor)**, born Des Moines, Iowa, September 27, 1957; admitted to bar, 1991, Iowa. *Education:* University of Iowa (B.A., 1981); Drake University (J.D., 1990). ***COURSES: Legal Research & Writing.

ROBERT R. RIGG*, (Director, Criminal Defense Program and Visiting Associate Professor)**, born Springfield, Illinois, March 13, 1954; admitted to bar, 1978, Iowa. *Education:* Drake University (B.A., 1975; J.D., 1977). ***COURSES: Criminal Law and Procedure, Clinic-Adv. Representation in Criminal Cases.

GREGORY C. SISK*, (Richard and Anita Calkins Distinguished Professor of Law)**, born Des Moines, Iowa, May 29, 1960; admitted to bar, 1985, Washington (inactive); 1992, Iowa. *Education:* Montana State University (B.A., 1981); University of Washington (J.D., 1984). ***COURSES: Civil Procedure, Litigation with the Federal Government, Ethics, Law and Religion.

MAURA IRENE STRASSBERG*, (Associate Professor of Law)**, born Grand Junction, Colorado, May 14, 1956; admitted to bar, 1985, Massachusetts; 1986, New York. *Education:* Swarthmore College (B.A., 1977); Boston University (M.A., 1981); Columbia University (J.D., 1984). ***COURSES: Ethics, Pretrial Advocacy, Civil Procedure, Contracts.

***DEBORAH E. SULZBACH*, (Acquisitions/Reference Librarian and Instructor)**, born Burlington, Iowa, February 9, 1954. *Education:* Finch College (B.A., 1975); Indiana University (M.L.S., 1977).

JULIE A. THOMAS*, (Technical Services Librarian and Assistant Professor)**, born Ames, Iowa, June 7, 1957. *Education:* Iowa State University (B.A., 1979); University of Iowa (M.A., 1984). ***COURSES: Computer-Assisted Legal Research.

DAVID S. WALKER*, (Dwight D. Opperman Distinguished Professor of Law)**, born Akron, Ohio, July 9, 1944; admitted to bar, 1970, Ohio; 1972, Indiana. *Education:* Yale University (B.A., 1966); University of Virginia (LL.B., 1969). ***COURSES: Civil Procedure, Business Associations, Advanced Problems in Corporate Law.

***KAREN L. WALLACE*, (Circulation/Reference Librarian and Instructor)**, born Omaha, Nebraska, February 02, 1971. *Education:* University of Iowa (B.A., 1993; M.A., 1994).

MELISSA HEAMES WERESH*, (Legal Writing Instructor)**, born Pittsburgh, Pennsylvania, February 16, 1967; admitted to bar, 1992, Ohio. *Education:* Wake Forest University (B.A., 1989); University of Iowa (J.D., 1992). ***COURSES: Legal Research and Writing.

DUKE UNIVERSITY SCHOOL OF LAW

BOX 90362, SCIENCE DRIVE & TOWERVIEW ROAD
DURHAM, NORTH CAROLINA 27708
Telephone: (919) 613-7002
Fax: (919) 613-7158
http://www.law.duke.edu

ABA Approved Since 1931

Established as a graduate professional school in 1930, Duke University School of Law has created a unique academic community. Its mission is to prepare students for responsible, ethical and productive lives in the legal profession. Recognizing that its graduates will face unprecedented challenge and change within society and the field of law, Duke Law School strives to develop within each student a capacity for legal reasoning, intellectual discipline and critical analysis, equipping its graduates with tools which can be adapted and applied across the spectrum of legal practices.

Unlike many schools, Duke is committed to remaining relatively small, limiting entering classes to about 200 students. With a total enrollment of close to 650, the majority of whom are enrolled in the three-year JD program, students are selected from a strong applicant pool and are among the most capable law students in the United States and abroad. Students come from almost every state and more than 25 different countries. International students are highly qualified foreign law graduates participating in the LL.M. and S.J.D. programs.

The faculty make an important contribution to the community atmosphere at Duke Law School. Renowned for their excellence and productivity, faculty members have made a commitment to teaching and take a strong personal interest in their students. With the basic law courses, students select courses from an extensive list of electives that vary in format, pedagogy and content. Visiting and adjunct professors from the legal profession and other national and international law schools bring new perspectives to students.

Duke University is composed of undergraduate programs and graduate and professional schools that have earned an international reputation for quality and innovation and offer an extensive network of interdisciplinary collaborations. Law students benefit from Duke's offering of innovative joint-degree programs.

The Law School gives students an opportunity to contribute to one of its seven journals - all of which are accessible online - and to further develop writing and oral advocacy skills in Moot Court competitions. Students are encouraged to attend the visiting lecture series, and student leaders have hosted several significant conferences. Members of the Law School's 31 student organizations participate in a wide variety of campus and community programs and projects.

In addition, students can participate in a variety of Law School programs, such as the Program in Public Law, the Center for Global Capital Markets, the Center on Law, Ethics and National Security, the Aids Legal Assistance Project, the Center for Sports Law and Policy, the Children's Law Clinic, the Death Penalty Clinic, and the Public Interest and Pro Bono Programs. There is also a strong international focus: the Law School offers two Summer Institutes in Transnational Law, one in Geneva and one in Hong Kong.

The recent renovation and expansion of the Law School's physical plant gives the School flexibility to bring state-of-the-art technology to the study of law. The library is one of the best law libraries in the United States. The print collection is supplemented and enhanced by a superior electronic network with global capabilities.

The strength of Duke's faculty, the distinction achieved by alumni, the attainments and creativity of the students, and the outstanding facility combine to create a world-class law school. Duke University School of Law is recognized nationally and internationally for leadership in research, education, and public service, equipping its students for legal careers that uphold the highest tradition of excellence.

Duke Law School is fully accredited by the American Bar Association and is a member of the Association of American Law Schools.

Dean: Katharine T. Bartlett (919) 613-7001
Academic Affairs: James E. Coleman Jr. (919) 613-7057
Academic Affairs: Theresa A. Newman (919) 613-7133
Admissions/Financial Aid: Dennis J. Shields (919) 613-7200
Library: Richard A. Danner (919) 613-7115
Placement: Robert Smith (919) 613-7028
External Relations/Communications: Linda Steckley (919) 613-7256
Student Affairs: Elizabeth Gustafson (919) 613-7007
Public Interest Activities and Special Projects: E. Carol Spruill (919) 613-7130

FULL TIME FACULTY

KATHARINE T. BARTLETT*, (Dean and A. Kenneth Pye Professor of Law)**, born 1947; admitted to bar, 1975, California; 1980, North Carolina. *Education:* Wheaton College (B.A., 1968); Harvard University (M.A., 1969); University of California (J.D., 1975). ***COURSES: Family Law, Gender Law, Contracts. ***Email:*** bartlett@law.duke.edu

SARA SUN BEALE*, (Charles L.B. Lowndes Professor)**, born 1949; admitted to bar, 1974, Michigan. *Education:* University of Michigan (B.A., 1971); University of Michigan Law School (J.D., 1974). ***COURSES: Criminal Law, Criminal Procedure. ***Email:*** beale@law.duke.edu

FRANCESCA E. BIGNAMI*, (Assistant Professor)**, born 1970; admitted to bar, 1998, Massachusetts; 1999, District of Columbia. *Education:* Harvard University (A.B., 1991); University of Oxford Balliol College (M.S.C., 1992); Yale University Law School (J.D., 1996). ***COURSES: International Law, Administrative Law, Comparative Law, Law of the European Union. ***Email:*** bignami@law.duke.edu

JAMES D.A. BOYLE*, (Professor of Law)**, born 1959. *Education:* Glasgow University (L.L.B., 1980); Harvard Law School (S.J.D., 1986). ***COURSES: Intellectual Property, Torts, Legal Theory, Law and Literature, Cyberlaw. ***Email:*** boyle@law.duke.edu

***MICHAEL H. BRADLEY*, (F.W. Kirby Professor of Investment Banking and Professor of Law)**, born 1947. *Education:* University of

(This Listing Continued)

DUKE UNIVERSITY SCHOOL OF LAW—Continued

Idaho (A.B., 1969); Syracuse University (M.B.A., 1974); University of Chicago (Ph.D., 1979). ***COURSES:*** Corporate Finance, Law & Economics.

***H. KEITH H. BRODIE*, (James B. Duke Professor of Psychiatry and Professor of Law)**, born 1939. *Education:* Princeton University (A.B., 1961); Columbia University (M.D., 1965); University of Richmond (LL.D., 1987); High Point University (L.H.D., 1992).

MICHAEL BYERS*, (Associate Professor of Law)**, *Education:* University of Saskatchewan (B.A., 1988); McGill University Law School (LL.B., B.C.L., 1992); Cambridge University (Ph.D., 1996). ***COURSES: International Law, International Dispute Resolution, International Relations. ***Email:*** byers@law.duke.edu

PAUL D. CARRINGTON*, (Harry R. Chadwick Senior Emeritus Professor of Law)**, born 1931; admitted to bar, 1955, Texas; 1964, Ohio; 1970, Michigan. *Education:* University of Texas (B.A., 1952); Harvard Law School (LL.B., 1955). ***COURSES: Civil Procedure, International Civil Litigation, Lawyers in American History, Legal Profession. ***Email:*** pdc@law.duke.edu

GEORGE C. CHRISTIE*, (James B. Duke Professor)**, born 1934; admitted to bar, 1957, New York; 1958, District of Columbia. *Education:* Columbia University (A.B., 1955; J.D., 1957); Cambridge University (Dipl. Law, 1962); Harvard Law School (S.J.D., 1966). ***COURSES: Jurisprudence, Torts. ***Email:*** gcc@law.duke.edu

CHARLES T. CLOTFELTER*, (Z. Smith Reynolds Professor of Public Policy Studies, Professor of Economics and Professor of Law)**, born 1947. *Education:* Duke University (B.A., 1969); Harvard Law School (M.A., 1972; Ph.D., 1974). ***COURSES: Public Finance, Education Policy.

JAMES E. COLEMAN, JR.*, (Professor of the Practice)**, born 1946; admitted to bar, 1975, New York. *Education:* Harvard University (A.B., 1970); Columbia University School of Law (J.D., 1974). ***COURSES: Criminal Law, Death Penalty Clinic, Ethics, Negotiation and Mediation. ***Email:*** jcoleman@law.duke.edu

JAMES D. COX*, (Brainerd Currie Professor)**, born 1943; admitted to bar, 1970, California. *Education:* University of California, Hastings College of Law (J.D., 1969); Harvard Law School (LL.M., 1971). ***COURSES: Commercial Law, Corporate Finance, Corporate Governance, Corporations, Securities Regulation. ***Email:*** james.cox@duke.edu

JEROME MCCRISTAL CULP, JR.*, (Professor)**, born 1950. *Education:* University of Chicago (B.A., 1972; M.A., 1974); Harvard Law School (J.D., 1978). ***COURSES: Black Jurisprudence, Employment Discrimination, Labor Law. ***Email:*** culp@law.duke.edu

RICHARD A. DANNER*, (Associate Dean, Library & Computing Services & Research Professor)**, born 1947; admitted to bar, 1979, Wisconsin. *Education:* University of Wisconsin (B.A., 1969; M.S., 1975); University of Wisconsin Law School (J.D., 1979). ***COURSES: Legislation. ***Email:*** danner@law.duke.edu

WALTER E. DELLINGER, III*, (Douglas B. Maggs Professor of Law)**, born 1941; admitted to bar, 1970, North Carolina; 1972, California. *Education:* University of North Carolina (A.B., 1963); Yale University Law School (LL.B., 1966). ***COURSES: Constitutional History, Constitutional Law. ***Email:*** wed@law.duke.edu

DEBORAH A. DEMOTT*, (David F. Cavers Professor)**, born 1948; admitted to bar, 1974, New York. *Education:* Swarthmore College (B.A., 1970); New York University School of Law (J.D., 1973). ***COURSES: Agency & Partnership, Corporate Finance, Corporations, Fiduciary Obligations. ***Email:*** demott@law.duke.edu

DIANE DIMOND*, (Clinical Professor of Law and Director of Writing)**, born Kalamazoo, Michigan, November 22, 1951; admitted to bar, 1978, New York; 1983, North Carolina. *Education:* University of Iowa (B.A., 1973); Harvard Law School (J.D., 1977). ***COURSES: Negotiation and Mediation, Legal Analysis, Research and Writing. ***Email:*** dimond@law.duke.edu

ROBINSON O. EVERETT*, (Professor)**, born 1928; admitted to bar, 1950, North Carolina; 1954, District of Columbia. *Education:* Harvard University (A.B., 1947); Harvard Law School (J.D., 1950); Duke University (LL.M., 1959). ***COURSES: Criminal Law, Criminal Procedure, Law & National Defense, Military Law. ***Email:*** everett@law.duke.edu

PETER G. FISH*, (Professor, Political Science & Law)**, born 1937. *Education:* Princeton University (A.B., 1960; A.M., 1965); Johns Hopkins University (Ph.D., 1968). ***COURSES: American Constitutional Interpretation, Judicial Administration, Judicial Process.

JOEL L. FLEISHMAN*, (Professor of Law and Public Policy Sciences)**, born 1934; admitted to bar, 1959, North Carolina. *Education:* University of North Carolina (A.B., 1955; M.A., 1959); University of North Carolina School of Law (J.D., 1959); Yale University (LL.M., 1960). ***COURSES: Legal Regulation, Political Ethics.

KOICHIRO FUJIKURA*, (Adjunct Professor)**, born 1934. *Education:* Dashiva University, Japan (Bach. of Law, 1957); Amherst College (B.A., 1961); Northwestern University (LL.M., 1962); Harvard Law School (LL.M., 1963). ***COURSES: Comparative Law, Environmental Law, Torts.

XI-QING GAO*, (Adjunct Professor)**, *Education:* University of International Business & Economics (B.A., 1978); Duke University School of Law (J.D., 1986). ***COURSES: International Business Transactions with China, Chinese Securities Law.

MARTIN P. GOLDING*, (Professor, Philosophy & Law)**, born 1930. *Education:* Columbia University, College of Physicians & Surgeons (Ph.D., 1959). ***COURSES: Jewish Law, Jurisprudence, Philosophy of Law, Responsibility in Law & Morals.

PAUL H. HAAGEN*, (Professor)**, born 1950; admitted to bar, 1983, Pennsylvania. *Education:* Haverford College (B.A., 1972); Oxford University (B.A., 1974); Princeton University (M.A., 1976); Yale University Law School (J.D., 1982; Ph.D., 1986). ***COURSES: Contracts, Legal History, Sports Law. ***Email:*** haagen@law.duke.edu

STANLEY HAUERWAS*, (Gilbert T. Rowe Professor of Legal Ethics, Professor of Law)**, *Education:* Southwestern University (B.A., 1962); Yale University Law School (B.D., 1965; M.A., M.Phil., Ph.D., 1968). ***COURSES: Ethics.

CLARK C. HAVIGHURST*, (William Neal Reynolds Professor of Law)**, born 1933; admitted to bar, 1958, Illinois; 1962, New York. *Education:* Princeton University (A.B., 1955); Northwestern University School of Law (J.D., 1958). ***COURSES: Antitrust, Health Care Financing & Competition, Health Care Law & Policy, Regulated Industries. ***Email:*** hav@law.duke.edu

CYNTHIA B. HERRUP*, (Professor of History & Law)**, born 1950. *Education:* Northwestern University (B.S.J., 1972; Ph.D., 1982). ***COURSES: History of English Criminal Law.

DONALD L. HOROWITZ*, (James B. Duke Professor & Charles S. Murphy Professor)**, born 1939; admitted to bar, 1962, New York; 1979, District of Columbia. *Education:* Syracuse University (A.B., 1959; LL.B., 1961); Harvard University (LL.M., 1962; A.M., 1965; Ph.D., 1967). ***COURSES: Comparative Law & Policy, Ethnic Group Relations, Labor Law. ***Email:*** dhorowitz@law.duke.edu

(This Listing Continued)

DUKE UNIVERSITY SCHOOL OF LAW—Continued

TRINA JONES,* (Professor)**, born 1966; admitted to bar, 1992, District of Columbia. *Education:* Cornell University (B.A., 1988); University of Michigan Law School (J.D., 1991). ***COURSES: Civil Procedure, Employment Discrimination, Race and the Law. ***Email:*** tjones@law.duke.edu

DAVID L. LANGE,* (Professor)**, born 1938; admitted to bar, 1964, Illinois; 1988, North Carolina. *Education:* University of Illinois (B.S., 1960); University of Illinois College of Law (J.D., 1964). ***COURSES: Communications, Entertainment Law, Intellectual Property, Patents, Trademarks. ***Email:*** lange@law.duke.edu

CAROLYN MCALLASTER,* (Clinical Professor of Law)**, born New York, July 22, 1949; admitted to bar, 1976, North Carolina. *Education:* University of North Carolina (B.A., 1972); University of North Carolina School of Law (J.D., 1976). ***COURSES: Lawyering Skills, Aids Law. ***Email:*** mcallaster@law.duke.edu

FRANCIS E. MCGOVERN,* (Professor)**, born 1945; admitted to bar, 1973, Virginia; 1974, District of Columbia and Texas; 1982, Alabama. *Education:* Yale University (B.A., 1967); University of Virginia School of Law (J.D., 1973). ***COURSES: Alternative Dispute Resolution, Conflict Resolution, Products Liability, Mass Torts. ***Email:*** mcgovern@law.duke.edu

THOMAS B. METZLOFF,* (Professor)**, born 1954; admitted to bar, 1982, Georgia. *Education:* Yale University (B.A., 1976); Harvard Law School (J.D., 1979). ***COURSES: Alternative Dispute Resolution, Civil Procedure, Distinctive Aspects of U.S. Law, Ethics in the Legal Profession, Mass Torts. ***Email:*** metzloff@law.duke.edu

MADELINE H. MORRIS,* (Professor)**, born 1957. *Education:* Yale University (B.A., 1986); Yale University Law School (J.D., 1989). ***COURSES: Criminal Law, International Criminal Law. ***Email:*** madeline.morris@duke.edu

ROBERT P. MOSTELLER,* (Harry R. Chadwick Sr., Professor)**, born 1948; admitted to bar, 1975, North Carolina; 1976, District of Columbia. *Education:* University of North Carolina (B.A., 1970); Harvard University (M.P.P., 1975); Yale University Law School (J.D., 1975). ***COURSES: Criminal Procedure, Evidence. ***Email:*** rpm@law.duke.edu

JONATHAN K. OCKO,* (Adjunct Professor of Legal History)**, born 1946. *Education:* Trinity College (B.A., 1966); Yale University (M.A., M.Phil., 1970); Yale University Law School (Ph.D., 1975). ***COURSES: Chinese Civil Law, Chinese Legal History. ***Email:*** ocko@law.duke.edu

H. JEFFERSON POWELL,* (Professor of Law and Divinity)**, born 1954. *Education:* University of Wales (B.A., 1975); Duke University (A.M., 1977; Ph.D., 1991); Yale University Law School (M.Div., 1979; J.D., 1982). ***COURSES: Constitutional History, Constitutional Law, Contracts. ***Email:*** powell@law.duke.edu

JEROME H. REICHMAN,* (Bunyan S. Womble Professor of Law)**, born 1936. *Education:* University of Chicago (B.A., 1955); Yale University Law School (J.D., 1979). ***COURSES: Contracts, Copyright, Intellectual Property in International Trade, Patents, Trademarks and Unfair Competition Law. ***Email:*** reichman@law.duke.edu

WILLIAM A. REPPY, JR.,* (Charles L. B. Lowndes Emeritus Professor of Law)**, born 1941; admitted to bar, 1966, California; 1971, North Carolina. *Education:* Stanford University (A.B., 1963); Stanford University Law School (J.D., 1966). ***COURSES: Animal Law, Appellate Practice, Community Property, Conflict of Laws, Estates, Federal Courts, Real Property. ***Email:*** war@law.duke.edu

THOMAS D. ROWE, JR.,* (Elvin R. Latty Professor of Law)**, born 1942; admitted to bar, 1971, District of Columbia; 1976, North Carolina. *Education:* Yale University (B.A., 1964); Oxford University (M.Phil., 1967); Harvard Law School (J.D., 1970). ***COURSES: Civil Procedure, Complex Litigation, Constitutional Law, Federal Court, Remedies. ***Email:*** trowe@law.duke.edu

RICHARD L. SCHMALBECK,* (Professor)**, born 1947; admitted to bar, 1975, Ohio; 1977, District of Columbia. *Education:* University of Chicago (B.A., 1970; J.D., 1975). ***COURSES: Estate and Gift Tax, Exempt Organizations, Federal Income Tax. ***Email:*** schmalbeck@law.duke.edu

CHRISTOPHER H. SCHROEDER,* (Charles S. Murphy Professor of Law and Public Policy)**, born 1948; admitted to bar, 1974, California. *Education:* Princeton University (B.A., 1968); Yale University (M.Div., 1971); University of California, Berkeley School of Law (Boalt Hall) (J.D., 1974). ***COURSES: Administrative Law, Environmental Law, Land Use Planning, Property, The Congress. ***Email:*** schroeder@law.duke.edu

STEVEN L. SCHWARCZ,* (Professor)**, born 1949; admitted to bar, 1975, New York. *Education:* New York University School of Engineering & Science (B.S., summa cum laude, 1971); Columbia University (J.D., 1974). ***COURSES: Commercial Law, Bankruptcy, Corporate Reorganization, Corporate Finance, Capital Markets. ***Email:*** schwarcz@law.duke.edu

MARTIN J. STONE,* (Professor of Law and Philosophy)**, born 1961. *Education:* Brandeis University (B.A., 1982); Yale University Law School (J.D., 1985); Balliol College, Oxford (B.Phil., 1988). ***COURSES: Jurisprudence, Social Philosophy, Tort Law. ***Email:*** stone@law.duke.edu

LAURA S. UNDERKUFFLER,* (Professor)**, admitted to bar, 1978, Minnesota. *Education:* Carlton College (B.A., 1974); William Mitchell College of Law (J.D., 1978); Yale University Law School (LL.M., 1987; J.S.D., 1994). ***COURSES: Advanced Topics in Property, Criminal Justice, Federal Courts, Property. ***Email:*** underkuffler@law.duke.edu

WILLIAM W. VAN ALSTYNE,* (William R. Perkins & Thomas C. Perkins Professor of Law)**, admitted to bar, 1958, California. *Education:* University of Southern California (B.A., 1955); Stanford University Law School (J.D., 1958). ***COURSES: Civil Rights, Constitutional Law, First Amendment Law. ***Email:*** wva@law.duke.edu

NEIL VIDMAR,* (Russell M. Robinson, II Professor of Law and Professor of Psychology: Social & Health Sciences)**, born 1940. *Education:* MacMurray College (A.B., 1962); University of Illinois (M.A., 1965; Ph.D., 1967). ***COURSES: Negotiation & Mediation, Psychology of Litigation Process, Social Science Evidence. ***Email:*** vidmar@law.duke.edu

JOHN C. WEISTART,* (Professor)**, born 1943; admitted to bar, 1968, Illinois; 1970, North Carolina. *Education:* Illinois Wesleyan University (A.B., 1965); Duke University School of Law (J.D., 1968). ***COURSES: Athletics and the Legal Process, Commercial Law, Contracts, Creditors Rights, Labor Law. ***Email:*** weistart@law.duke.edu

JONATHAN B. WIENER,* (Professor of Law & Environmental Policy)**, born 1962; admitted to bar, 1988, Massachusetts; 1991, District of Columbia. *Education:* Harvard University (A.B., 1984); Harvard Law School (J.D., 1987). ***COURSES: Environmental Law, Property, Risk Assessment & Management. ***Email:*** wiener@law.duke.edu

DUQUESNE UNIVERSITY SCHOOL OF LAW

HANLEY HALL, 900 LOCUST STREET
PITTSBURGH, PENNSYLVANIA 15282-0702
Telephone: (412) 396-6300
Fax: (412) 396-6283
http://www.duq.edu/law/law.html

ABA Approved Since 1960

The Duquesne University School of Law received its first class in 1911 and is the only multi-division law school in Western Pennsylvania. Duquesne University, founded in 1878, is a Catholic university administered by the Congregation of the Holy Ghost. Admission requirements, instruction, and the nature and scope of the work required of students are identical for the three-year day division, the four-year evening division and the four year part-time day division. The Law School program focuses on the importance of basic intellectual ability in the training of a lawyer, while at the same time illustrating the vital roles of justice, common sense, prudent judgment, sensitivity to and concern for people, self-motivation and an appetite and capacity for sustained, hard work. Accredited by the American Bar Association and a member of the Association of American Law Schools, Duquesne Law School is proud of its outstanding reputation for academic excellence as well as its long-standing tradition of community service.

Located overlooking Pittsburgh's "Golden Triangle," Duquesne's 39-acre campus is uniquely situated. This location affords opportunities for scholarly pursuits in an academic environment and access, within walking distance, to the downtown legal, business and government communities, and state and federal courts.

In 1982, the Law School moved into the newly completed Edward J. Hanley Hall. This modern facility houses all classrooms, faculty offices and study rooms for the Law School, including the James P. McArdle Moot Court Room and the John E. Laughlin Memorial Library. The library has more than 197,711 volumes and microform equivalents, to which substantial additions are constantly being made. The library contains group-study rooms, individual study carrels, the Robert Broughton Learning Center, the Law School's computer lab, and the ALCOA Audio Visual Center. The A/V Center, which consists of 6 semi-private workstations, each equipped with a VCR/TV unit, an audiocassette player/recorder and headphones, allows our students to take increased advantage of the video revolution in instructional technology. Law School clinics are located in the nearby Fisher Hall, adjoining the downtown Pittsburgh legal community. In 2001, the John E. Murray Jr., Pavilion was added to Hanley Hall. The Murray Pavilion includes faculty offices, two new classrooms, an expanded student lounge and a second courtroom classroom.

The School of Law is operated on the two semester system. The Juris Doctor degree is awarded upon successful completion of the required program of study.

The curriculum, designed to give the student a well-rounded legal education, contains a core of required courses plus a variety of electives. The foundation for advanced courses is provided by the mandatory first-year subjects: legal process and procedure; contracts; criminal law; civil procedure; property; torts; and legal research and writing. Electives are offered after the first year of study in such developing areas as litigation skills, international trade law, health care law, environmental law, law and technology, patent law, law and academic administration, and law and human resources. These elective courses provide an opportunity to explore the more contemporary problems of law and society. The course of study, fully conforming to ABA and AALS accreditation standards, is sufficiently broad to prepare students for practice in all states. In addition, three joint degree programs are currently offered, J.D./M.B.A., J.D./M.S. in Environmental Science and Management, and J.D./M.Div.

Duquesne offers students an opportunity to participate in numerous educational and professional activities. Moot Court Boards conduct programs in which students compete on the local, regional and national levels. Clinical programs offered at the Law School include the Economic Development Clinic, Criminal Justice (Public Defenders) Clinic and the newly-established Family Rights Clinic. In addition to these three in-house clinics internships are available with the Pennsylvania Supreme Court, Pennsylvania Superior Court, Commonwealth Court of Pennsylvania, United States Court of Appeals for the Third Circuit, the United States District Court for the Western District of Pennsylvania, the Court of Common Pleas of Allegheny County and certain neighboring counties, and the United States Bankruptcy Court. Students may choose to intern with a local government office such as the Allegheny County Solicitor, the Allegheny County District Attorney, the Office of the United States Attorney for the Western District of Pennsylvania, the Pittsburgh regional office of the Department of Environmental Resources or the Pennsylvania Attorney General's office.

The Law School operates a summer program for American law students in Beijing, China in collaboration with the China University of Political Science and Law; a summer program for American law students in Dublin, Ireland in collaboration with the law faculty of University College Dublin; a summer program for American law students in Moscow, Russia in collaboration with the law faculty of the Moscow Institute of International Business; and co-produces an Internet Web Site on Russian commercial law together with the law faculties of Moscow State University and the Moscow Institute of International Business.

Duquesne's *Law Review,* the school's award-winning newsmagazine, *Juris,* and the Duquesne Business Law Journal along with the Student Bar Association, are the largest student groups. Additionally, our students may serve in organizations such as Black Law Student Association, Sports and Entertainment Law Society, International Law Society, Phi Alpha Delta Legal Fraternity, Association of Trial Lawyers, Women's Law Association, Public Interest Law Association, Corporate Law Society, Environmental Law Society, the Federalist Society, or the Health Care Law Association.

Dean: Nicholas P. Cafardi (412) 396-6280
Admissions: Ronald J. Ricci (412) 396-6313
Financial Aid: Ronald J. Ricci (412) 396-6313
Financial Aid: Joseph P. Campion (412) 396-4299
Library: Frank Y. Liu (412) 396-5018
Career Services Placement: Ella Kwisnek (412) 396-6279
Alumni Affairs: Amy Eozzo Black (412) 396-5215

(This Listing Continued)

DUQUESNE UNIVERSITY SCHOOL OF LAW—Continued

FULL TIME FACULTY

NICHOLAS P. CAFARDI*, (Dean and Professor of Law)**, born Pittsburgh, Pennsylvania, November 18, 1948; admitted to bar, 1975, Pennsylvania. *Education:* Gregorian University, Rome, Italy (Ph.B., 1970); Duquesne University (M.A., 1972); University of Pittsburgh (J.D., 1975); University of St. Thomas Aquinas, Rome, Italy (J.C.L., 1987). ***COURSES: Tax Exempt Organizations, European Community Law, Legal Process & Procedure, Canon Law.

SAMUEL J. ASTORINO*, (Professor of Law)**, born Carnegie, Pennsylvania, June 6, 1932; admitted to bar, 1983, Pennsylvania. *Education:* University of Pittsburgh (A.B., 1956; M.A., 1957; Ph.D., 1962); Duquesne University School of Law (J.D., 1982). ***COURSES: American Legal History, Criminal Law, Professional Responsibility, International Law, Torts.

ROBERT S. BARKER*, (Professor of Law)**, born Pittsburgh, Pennsylvania, June 1, 1941; admitted to bar, 1966, Pennsylvania. *Education:* Duquesne University (B.A., 1963; M.A., 1974; J.D., 1966). ***COURSES: Constitutional Law, Civil Procedure, Comparative Law, Legal Process & Procedure.

PATRICK J. BASIAL*, (Associate Dean and Professor of Law)**, born Pittsburgh, Pennsylvania, May 24, 1938; admitted to bar, 1963, Pennsylvania. *Education:* Duquesne University (B.A., 1960; J.D., 1963). ***COURSES: Labor Relations Law, Collective Bargaining and Labor Arbitration.

VANESSA S. BROWNE-BARBOUR*, (Assistant Professor)**, born Dover, Delaware, June 7, 1955; admitted to bar, 1993, Pennsylvania. *Education:* Carnegie-Melllon University (B.A., 1978); Duquesne University School of Law (J.D., 1993). ***COURSES: Torts, Family Law, Civil and Family Justice Clinic. ***Email:*** browne@duq.edu

NICK S. FISFIS*, (Professor of Law)**, born Pennsylvania, July 7, 1937; admitted to bar, 1963, Pennsylvania. *Education:* University of Pennsylvania (A.B., 1959; J.D., 1962). ***COURSES: Commercial Transactions, Constitutional Criminal Procedures, Professional Responsibility, Agency, Contracts, Secured Transactions.

KENNETH G. GORMLEY*, (Professor of Law)**, born Pittsburgh, Pennsylvania, March 19, 1955; admitted to bar, 1980, Pennsylvania. *Education:* University of Pittsburgh (B.A., 1977); Harvard University (J.D., 1980). ***COURSES: Constitutional Law, State Constitutional Law, Civil Rights Litigation, Legal Writing, Political & Civil Rights.

KENNETH E. GRAY*, (Professor of Law)**, born Yonkers, New York, June 25, 1944; admitted to bar, 1970, Illinois; 1978, Pennsylvania. *Education:* Iona College (B.A., 1966); Harvard University (J.D., 1969; M.P.A., 1970). ***COURSES: Property, Real Estate Planning, Political and Civil Rights, Administrative Law, Civil Procedure, Law & Psychology.

KENNETH HIRSCH*, (Professor of Law)**, born Riverside, California, October 21, 1943; admitted to bar, 1968, Illinois; 1970, California; 1979, Pennsylvania. *Education:* University of Illinois (B.A., 1965); University of Illinois College of Law (J.D., 1968); Harvard University Law School (LL.M., 1971). ***COURSES: Property, Criminal Law, Corporate Taxation, Negotiable Instruments.

MARTHA JORDAN*, (Associate Professor)**, born San Bernadino, California, January 26, 1957; admitted to bar, 1982, Tennessee; 1988, Colorado. *Education:* Memphis State University (B.S., 1978); University of Arizona (J.D., 1981); University of Denver (LL.M., 1988). ***COURSES: Income Tax, Taxation of Corporations and Shareholders, Estate Planning, Federal Income Tax, Taxation of Partners & Partnerships.

MARGARET K. KRASIK*, (Associate Professor)**, born Johnstown, Pennsylvania, December 13, 1947; admitted to bar, 1976, Pennsylvania. *Education:* Barnard College (A.B., 1969); University of Pittsburgh (M.L.S., 1973); Duquesne University School of Law (J.D., 1976). ***COURSES: Employment Law, Legal Writing, Administrative Law, Legal Rights of the Elderly, Employment Rights of the Individual Worker, Fiduciary Administration, Civil Procedure.

ELLA ANN KWISNEK*, (Assistant Dean and Professor)**, born Latrobe, Pennsylvania, June 18, 1965; admitted to bar, 1991, Pennsylvania. *Education:* Saint Vincent College (B.A., 1987); Duquesne (J.D., 1991). ***COURSES: Legal Research & Writing.

BRUCE LEDEWITZ*, (Professor of Law)**, born New Haven, Connecticut, March 1, 1952; admitted to bar, 1977, Connecticut; 1979, Pennsylvania. *Education:* Georgetown University (B.S., F.S., 1974); Yale University (J.D., 1977). ***COURSES: Constitutional Law, Criminal Law, Federal Jurisdiction, Presidential Power, Criminal Law & Procedure, Federal Courts & the Federal System, Pennsylvania State Constitutional Law.

FRANK YINING LIU*, (Director of the Law Library and Professor of Law)**, born Wu-Ning, China, February 7, 1943. *Education:* University of Texas (M.C.J., 1970; M.L.S., 1971); Taiwan University (LL.B., 1965); Yale University (Graduate Fellowship, 1966). ***COURSES: Legal Research and Writing, Comparative Law (Chinese).

KELLEN MCCLENDON*, (Associate Professor)**, born New Castle, Pennsylvania, May 7, 1944; admitted to bar, 1974, Pennsylvania. *Education:* Westminster College (B.A., 1966); Duquesne University (J.D., 1974). ***COURSES: Administrative Law, Agency, Legal Research and Writing, Local Government Law, Torts, Advanced Legal Writing.

JOSEPH SABINO MISTICK*, (Director of Clinical Legal Education and Professor)**, born Braddock, Pennsylvania, March 3, 1949; admitted to bar, 1979, Pennsylvania. *Education:* University of Pittsburgh (B.A., 1971); Duquesne University School of Law (J.D., 1979). ***COURSES: Torts, Land Use Planning, Remedies and Damages, Economic Community Development Clinic (Director).

JOHN E. MURRAY, JR.*, (President, Duquesne University and Professor of Law)**, born Philadelphia, Pennsylvania, December 20, 1932; admitted to bar, 1959, Wisconsin; 1986, Pennsylvania. *Education:* LaSalle University (B.S., 1955); Catholic University of America (J.D., 1958); University of Wisconsin (S.J.D., 1959). ***COURSES: Contracts, Commercial Transactions (Sales, Commercial Paper, Secured Transactions).

ALFRED S. PELAEZ*, (Professor of Law)**, born Avella, Pennsylvania, October 19, 1935; admitted to bar, 1961, Pennsylvania. *Education:* University of Pittsburgh (A.B., 1957; LL.B., 1960); Yale University (LL.M., 1966). ***COURSES: Contracts, Admiralty, Federal Courts and the Federal System, Sentencing and Criminal Sanctions.

JOHN THOMAS RAGO*, (Associate Dean and Assistant Professor of Law)**, born Pittsburgh, Pennsylvania, May 11, 1955; admitted to bar, 1987, Pennsylvania. *Education:* Duquesne University (B.A., History/English, 1979; J.D., 1987). ***COURSES: Legal Research and Writing.

RONALD J. RICCI*, (Dean of Admissions and Professor of Law)**, born Pittsburgh, Pennsylvania, June 6, 1951; admitted to bar, 1976, Pennsylvania. *Education:* Duquesne University (B.S. in B.A., 1973; J.D., 1976). ***COURSES: Corporate Law, Securities Regulation, Law and Accounting.

***RAYMOND F. SEKULA*, (Associate Dean and Professor of Law)**,

(This Listing Continued)

DUQUESNE UNIVERSITY SCHOOL OF LAW—Continued

born Pittsburgh, Pennsylvania, May 5, 1940; admitted to bar, 1966, Pennsylvania and U.S. Supreme Court. *Education:* Duquesne University (B.S.B.A., 1962); Duquesne University School of Law (J.D., 1965); University of Virginia (LL.M., 1966). ***COURSES:*** Evidence, Conflict of Laws, Taxation, Corporations, Agency, Law and Accounting.

NANCY PERKINS SPYKE, **(Associate Professor of Law)**, born Boston, Massachusetts, September 14, 1953; admitted to bar, 1986, Florida. *Education:* Mt. Holyoke College (B.A., 1975); Nova Law Center (J.D., 1986). ***COURSES:*** Environmental Law, Art and the Law, Legal Writing, Property, Legal Research & Writing (Director).

S. MICHAEL STREIB, **(Professor of Law)**, born Philadelphia, Pennsylvania, September 17, 1949; admitted to bar, 1979, Pennsylvania. *Education:* Ursinus College (B.A., 1971); University of Pittsburgh (M.B.A., 1973); Duquesne University School of Law (J.D., 1979). ***COURSES:*** Torts, Federal Income Taxation, Constitutional Criminal Procedure, Remedies and Damages, Product Liability, Accounting for Lawyers, Trial Advocacy.

ALISON MCMORRAN SULENTIC, **(Assistant Professor of Law)**, born South Ruislip, England, May 10, 1962; admitted to bar, 1989, Texas. *Education:* Harvard/Radcliffe (A.B., 1984); University of the Witwatersrand, South Africa (M.A., 1987); Harvard Law School (J.D., 1989). ***COURSES:*** Health Care Law, Employee Benefits, UCC Sales.

ROBERT D. TAYLOR, **(Professor of Law)**, born Pittsburgh, Pennsylvania, October 23, 1938; admitted to bar, 1979, Pennsylvania. *Education:* University of Pittsburgh (B.S., 1960); Pittsburgh Theological Seminary (M.Div., 1963); Duquesne University School of Law (J.D., 1979). ***COURSES:*** Federal Civil Procedure, Philosophy of Law, Comparative Law (Europe), Law and Religion, Civil Procedure, Comparative Law (Chinese).

MARK D. YOCHUM, **(Associate Professor)**, born Pittsburgh, Pennsylvania, November 12, 1952; admitted to bar, 1977, Pennsylvania. *Education:* Carnegie Mellon University (B.A., 1974); Georgetown University (J.D., 1977). ***COURSES:*** Bankruptcy, Federal Income and Estate Tax, Legal Writing, Taxation, Professional Responsibility, Tax Practice and Procedure.

EMORY UNIVERSITY SCHOOL OF LAW

GAMBRELL HALL
ATLANTA, GEORGIA 30322-2770
Telephone: (404) 727-6816
Fax: (404) 727-6820
www.law.emory.edu

ABA Approved Since 1923.

The Emory University School of Law was founded in 1916 and has grown from a strong regional law school to one that is nationally recognized for an outstanding faculty, rigorous curriculum, and highly qualified student body. Emory is a member of the Association of American Law Schools, and has a chapter of The Order of the Coif.

The faculty of the School of Law comprises 51 full-time members plus several international scholars who divide their time between Emory and institutions in other countries. They publish extensively, and are active in numerous professional organizations, including the American Bar Association, Association of American Law Schools, American Law Institute, American Law and Economics Association, American Judicature Society, American Comparative Law Association, Centre for the Reform of International Courts, Law of the Sea Institute, American Society of International Law, and Free Enterprise Advisory Council.

Emory publishes three student-edited journals, offers an extensive Moot Court program that has resulted in victories in several regional and national competitions in recent years, and has more than twenty other student organizations through which Emory students round out their academic experiences and professional aspirations.

The Emory Law Library collection includes more than 300,000 volumes and more than 5,000 serial subscriptions. The library has taken advantage of resource technology as it has become available in recent years; thus, the collection is supplemented by access to the major research databases. Emory students are trained on both Lexis and Westlaw, and also have access to the university's own research database and to the Internet through the Law School's server and web site. In 1995, the library moved into its newly-completed, state-of-the-art facility, the Hugh F. MacMillan Law Library. As a result, the library's space has nearly doubled.

The curriculum at Emory is broad and includes a strong theoretical component as well as practical training opportunities. In addition to numerous clinical field placements, students may earn academic credit while providing legal assistance through Emory's Turner Environmental Law Clinic and the Barton Child Law and Policy Clinic. In recent years, Emory has established relationships with several foreign countries, which result in regular visits to the faculty by faculty from Russia, Germany and Hungary.

Emory's Kessler Eidson Trial Techniques Program (KETTP) has received national recognition as the most outstanding litigation training program for law students in the U.S. The KETTP draws on the combined expertise of more than 200 trial lawyers, judges, and district attorneys who serve as visiting faculty. Emory's students learn how to prepare a case for trial as well as how to present themselves before judge and jury.

Emory strives to imbue its students with a sense of professional responsibility as lawyers who are servants of democracy. Consequently, the curriculum includes an increasing number of courses in public law. Moreover, because of the strong commitment among Emory students to serving the public interest, in 1989 students formed the Emory Public Interest Committee (EPIC) for the purpose of supporting *pro bono* work. As a result of EPIC's work, students have been able to spend their summers in public interest employment that otherwise would have been impossible for them. Emory Law School recently received the American Bar Association's E. Smythe Gambrell Award for innovative teaching of ethics and professionalism.

The Emory Law School's Office of Career Services works closely with students, graduates, and employers in the placement process. The Career Services Office coordinates an extensive on-campus interviewing program each fall as well as off-campus interviewing programs in key cities; participates in the Southeastern Law Placement Consortium and the South Atlantic Recruiting Conference; coordinates numerous job fairs; and provides extensive individual career counseling to Emory students and alumni. The staff of the Office of Career Services also includes a public interest coordinator who advises students on careers in the public interest.

The Emory University School of Law has a proud history of training

(This Listing Continued)

EMORY UNIVERSITY SCHOOL OF LAW—Continued

competent and principled lawyers. Its graduates serve on the bench and bar and in a variety of public interest positions. Emory is committed to continuing its record of providing high quality training to committed individuals.

Interim Dean: Peter Hay (404) 712-8815
Dean of Faculty: Richard D. Freer (404) 727-6838
Associate Dean for Academic Affairs: Polly J. Price (404) 727-7869
Associate Dean for Library and Information Technology: Robin Mills Schreiber (404) 727-6983
Director of Finance and Administration: Brent Conway (404) 727-6793
Assistant Dean for Admission: Lynell A. Cadray (404) 727-6801
Assistant Dean for Career Services: Naomi McLaurin (404) 727-6513
Assistant Dean for Development: Rosanne Patton (404) 727-5582
Assistant Dean for Student Affairs: Elizabeth N. Antonakakis (404) 727-6809

FULL TIME FACULTY

PETER HAY,* (Interim Dean and L.Q.C. Lamar Professor of Law)**, born Germany, September 17, 1935. *Education:* University of Michigan (B.A., 1958; J.D., 1958). ***COURSES: Comparative Law, Contracts, Conflicts of Laws, Jurisprudence, European Community Law, International Organizations. ***Email:*** phay@law.emory.edu

HOWARD E. ABRAMS,* (Professor of Law)**, born California, May 5, 1955; admitted to bar, 1980, California. *Education:* University of California at Irvine (B.A., 1976); Harvard University (J.D., 1980). ***COURSES: Contracts, Federal Income Taxation, Partnership Taxation. ***Email:*** habrams@law.emory.edu

ROBERT AHDIEH,* (Assistant Professor of Law)**, admitted to bar, 1997. *Education:* Princeton University (A.B., 1994); Yale Law School (J.D., 1997). ***COURSES: Comparative Law. ***Email:*** rahdieh@law.emory.edu

FRANK SPRUILL ALEXANDER,* (Professor of Law; Fellow, Law & Religion Program)**, born North Carolina, October 15, 1952; admitted to bar, 1978, Georgia. *Education:* University of North Carolina (B.A., 1973); Harvard Law School (J.D., 1978); Harvard Divinity School (M.T.S., 1978). ***COURSES: Real Estate, Property, Law & Theology, State and Local Government Law. ***Email:*** lawfsa@law.emory.edu

ABDULLAHI AHMED AN-NA'IM,* (Charles Howard Candler Prof. of Law; Dir., Religion and Human Rights Project & Law and Religion Program)**, born Sudan, November 19, 1946; admitted to bar, 1977, Sudan. *Education:* University of Khartoum, Sudan (LL.B., 1970); University of Cambridge (LL.M., 1973; Dip. Crim., 1973); University of Edinburgh (Ph.D., in Law, 1976). ***Email: aannaim@law.emory.edu

THOMAS C. ARTHUR,* (Professor of Law & Interim Vice Provost for International Affairs)**, born Virginia, July 11, 1946; admitted to bar, 1972, Virginia and District of Columbia. *Education:* Duke University (A.B., 1968); Yale University (J.D., 1971). ***COURSES: Administrative Law, Antitrust, Civil Procedure, Federal Courts, Legal Method. ***Email:*** lawtca@law.emory.edu

MARGO ANDREA BAGLEY,* (Assistant Professor of Law)**, born Nashville, Tennessee, October 6, 1963; admitted to bar, 1996, Georgia. *Education:* University of Wisconsin-Madison (B.S.CLE., 1986); Emory University (J.D., 1996). ***COURSES: Contracts, Patent Law. ***Email:*** mbagley@law.emory.edu

DAVID J. BEDERMAN,* (Professor of Law)**, born Atlanta, July 26, 1961; admitted to bar, 1987, Georgia; 1988, District of Columbia. *Education:* Princeton University (A.B., 1983); London School of Economics (M.Sc., 1984); University of Virginia (J.D., 1987); University of London (Ph.D., 1996). ***COURSES: Public International Law, Torts, International Institutions, Law of International Common Spaces, Customary Law, Legal Methods, Admiralty. ***Email:*** lawdjb@law.emory.edu

HAROLD J. BERMAN,* (Robert W. Woodruff Professor of Law and Fellow, Carter Center of Emory University)**, born Connecticut, February 13, 1918. *Education:* Dartmouth College (B.A., 1938); London School of Economics (Certificate, 1939); Yale University (M.A., 1942; LL.B., 1947); James Barr Ames Professor Emeritus (Harvard). ***COURSES: Russian Law, Jurisprudence, International Trade Law, Comparative Legal History. ***Email:*** hberman@law.emory.edu

ANITA BERNSTEIN,* (Sam Nunn Professor of Law)**, born New York, January 17, 1961; admitted to bar, 1986, New York. *Education:* Queens College (B.A., 1981); Yale (J.D., 1985). ***COURSES: Torts, Products Liability, Feminist Theory, Legal Ethics, Jurisprudence. ***Email:*** abernste@law.emory.edu

MICHAEL J. BROYDE,* (Associate Professor of Law; Associate Director, Law and Religion Program)**, born New York, May 12, 1964; admitted to bar, 1989, New York. *Education:* Yeshiva University (B.A., 1984; Ordination, 1989); New York University (J.D., 1988). ***COURSES: Jewish Law, Law & Religion, Arbitration, Alternate Dispute Resolution, Federal Courts, Secured Credit. ***Email:*** mbroyde@law.emory.edu

RALPH BRUBAKER,* (Associate Professor of Law)**, born Indiana, October 31, 1962; admitted to bar, 1990, Ohio. *Education:* University of Illinois (B.S., with highest honors, 1985; M.B.A., 1989; J.D., summa cum laude, 1989). ***COURSES: Contracts, Business Associations, Bankruptcy, Bankruptcy Procedure. ***Email:*** rbrubake@law.emory.edu

WILLIAM WADE BUZBEE,* (Professor of Law)**, born New York, May 20, 1960; admitted to bar, 1986, Massachusetts; 1987, New York; 1990, District of Columbia. *Education:* Amherst College (B.A., magna cum laude, 1983); Columbia University (J.D., 1986). ***COURSES: Environmental Law, Administrative Law, Property, Land Use, Advanced Environmental Law. ***Email:*** wbuzbee@law.emory.edu

WILLIAM J. CARNEY,* (Charles Howard Candler Professor of Law)**, born Illinois, May 10, 1937; admitted to bar, 1962, Colorado; 1975, Wyoming; 1986, Georgia. *Education:* Yale University (B.A., 1959; LL.B., 1962). ***COURSES: Corporate Law. ***Email:*** lawwjc@law.emory.edu

KATHLEEN CLEAVER,* (Senior Lecturer)**, born New York, May 13, 1945; admitted to bar, 1990, New York. *Education:* Yale University (B.A., 1984; J.D., 1989). ***COURSES: Legal History, Legal Ethics, Torts, Litigation. ***Email:*** kcleaver@law.emory.edu

A. MORGAN CLOUD, III,* (Charles Howard Candler Professor of Law)**, born Washington, D.C., March 5, 1947; admitted to bar, 1977, Florida; 1981, California. *Education:* Grinnell College (B.A., 1969); University of Iowa (M.A., 1972); Cornell University (J.D., 1977). ***COURSES: Criminal Law, Criminal Procedure, Corporate Crime, Comparative Constitutional Law, Evidence. ***Email:*** mcloud@law.emory.edu

(This Listing Continued)

EMORY UNIVERSITY SCHOOL OF LAW—Continued

NANCY R. DASPIT*, (Instructor)**, born Louisiana, September 4, 1951; admitted to bar, 1995, Georgia. *Education:* University of Southwestern Louisiana (B.S., 1973); Emory University School of Law (J.D., 1995). ***COURSES: Legal Writing, Research and Advocacy Program. ***Email:*** ndaspit@law.emory.edu

RICHARD L. DOERNBERG*, (K.H. Gyr Professor of International Legal Studies)**, born New York, July 10, 1948; admitted to bar, 1977, New York. *Education:* Yale University (B.A., 1970); Wesleyan University (M.A.T., 1972); University of Connecticut (J.D., 1976); New York University (LL.M., 1980). ***COURSES: International Taxation. ***Email:*** doernberg@law.emory.edu

MARTHA GRACE DUNCAN*, (Professor of Law)**, admitted to bar, 1985, Pennsylvania and District of Columbia. *Education:* Occidental College (B.A.); Columbia University (Ph.D., 1976; M.A.); Yale University (J.D., 1983). ***COURSES: Criminal Law, Law and Psychoanalysis, Juvenile Law, Law and Literature. ***Email:*** mdunc01@law.emory.edu

A. JAMES ELLIOTT*, (Associate Dean for External Affairs & Adjunct Professor of Law)**, born Georgia, October 30, 1941; admitted to bar, 1966, Georgia. *Education:* Emory University (B.A., 1963; J.D., 1966); Kennesaw State University (M.B.A., 1997). ***COURSES: Legal Profession, Real Estate Finance. ***Email:*** jelliott@law.emory.edu

RICHARD D. FREER*, (Dean of Faculty and Robert Howell Hall Professor of Civil Procedure)**, born New Jersey, April 3, 1953; admitted to bar, 1978, California. *Education:* University of California at San Diego (B.A., 1975); University of California at Los Angeles (J.D., 1978). ***COURSES: Civil Procedure, Federal Jurisdiction. ***Email:*** rfreer@law.emory.edu

DAVID J. GARROW*, (Presidential Distinguished Professor)**, born New Bedford, Massachusetts, May 11, 1953. *Education:* Wesleyan University (B.A., 1975); Duke University (Ph.D., 1981). ***COURSES: Legal History, Civil Rights, Supreme Court, U.S. Reproductive Rights. ***Email:*** garrow@emory.edu

NATHANIEL E. GOZANSKY*, (Professor of Law)**, born Illinois, January 12, 1940; admitted to bar, 1964, Florida; 1971, District of Columbia and Georgia. *Education:* Florida State University (B.S., 1961); University of Miami (J.D., 1964); Yale University (LL.M., 1965). ***COURSES: Contracts and Family Law. ***Email:*** gozo@law.emory.edu

MELVIN GUTTERMAN*, (Professor of Law)**, born New York, September 14, 1937; admitted to bar, 1963, New York; 1975, Georgia. *Education:* University of Michigan (B.A., 1959); Brooklyn Law School (J.D., 1962); Northwestern University (LL.M., 1967). ***COURSES: Criminal Law, Criminal Procedure, Prisoners' Rights, Post Conviction Remedies, Criminal Justice Film Workshop. ***Email:*** mgutter@law.emory.edu

JAMES B. HUGHES, JR.*, (Associate Professor of Law)**, born Georgia, February 14, 1954; admitted to bar, 1979, Georgia. *Education:* University of Connecticut (B.S., 1976); Yale University (J.D., 1979). ***COURSES: Property, Legal Profession, Real Estate. ***Email:*** jhugh01@law.emory.edu

HOWARD OWEN HUNTER*, (Interim Provost and Executive Vice President for Academic Affairs and Professor of Law)**, born Brunswick, Georgia, October 14, 1946; admitted to bar, 1971, Georgia. *Education:* Yale University (A.B., 1968; J.D., 1971). ***COURSES: Contracts, Remedies, Constitutional Law. ***Email:*** hunter@law.emory.edu

BARBARA KATZ*, (Instructor)**, born New York, December 11, 1958; admitted to bar, 1992, Georgia. *Education:* State University of New York, Stony Brook (B.A., 1983); The City University of New York at Queens (J.D., 1992). ***COURSES: Legal Writing, Research and Advocacy Program. ***Email:*** bekatz@law.emory.edu

HARRIET M. KING*, (Associate Professor of Law & Senior Vice Provost, Academic Affairs)**, born South Carolina, March 25, 1943; admitted to bar, 1967, Wisconsin. *Education:* Agnes Scott College (B.A., 1964); Vanderbilt University (LL.B., 1967); Harvard University (LL.M., 1973). ***COURSES: Insurance, Contracts, Family Law. ***Email:*** provhmk@emory.edu

ANDREW KULL*, (Robert Thompson Professor of Law)**, born Washington, D.C., July 18, 1947; admitted to bar, 1978, New York. *Education:* University of California at Berkeley (B.A., 1969); Oxford University (B.A./M.A., 1973); University of Chicago (J.D., 1977). ***COURSES: Contracts, Negotiable Instruments, Sales, Restitution. ***Email:*** akull@law.emory.edu

JENNIFER MATHEWS*, (Instructor)**, born California, October 21, 1969; admitted to bar, 1997, New York, New Jersey; 1999, Georgia. *Education:* Amherst College (B.S., 1991); Rutgers University (J.D., 1997). ***COURSES: Legal Writing, Research and Advocacy Program. ***Email:*** jennifer_mathews@lawlink.law.emory.edu

JULIE MAYFIELD*, (Turner Fellow, Turner Environmental Law Clinic)**, born Georgia, April 5, 1967; admitted to bar, 1996, Georgia. *Education:* Davidson College (B.A., 1989); Emory University (J.D., 1996). ***COURSES: Turner Fellow in Environmental Law, Environmental Advocacy. ***Email:*** jmayfie@law.emory.edu

WILLIAM TY MAYTON*, (Thomas J. Simmons Professor of Law)**, born Tennessee, May 1, 1941; admitted to bar, 1972, District of Columbia; 1974, California. *Education:* University of South Carolina (B.S., 1963); Columbia University (J.D., 1972). ***COURSES: Constitutional Law, Administrative Law. ***Email:*** lawwtm@law.emory.edu

MARC L. MILLER*, (Professor of Law)**, born Illinois, July 28, 1959; admitted to bar, 1984, California; 1988, District of Columbia. *Education:* Pomona College (B.A., 1981); University of Chicago (J.D., 1984). ***COURSES: Crime in America, Criminal Law, Criminal Procedure, Legal Aspects of Biodiversity, Torts. ***Email:*** mmiller@law.emory.edu

JEFFREY N. PENNELL*, (Richard H. Clark Professor of Law)**, born Illinois, September 5, 1949; admitted to bar, 1975, Illinois. *Education:* Northwestern University (B.A., 1971; J.D., 1975). ***COURSES: Wealth Transfer Tax, Trusts & Estates, Estate Planning, Federal Income Taxation.

JANETTE B. PRATT*, (Administrative Professor for Field Placements)**, born England, June 7, 1947. *Education:* London School of Economics (LL.B., 1968); New York University (LL.M., 1969). ***COURSES: Clinical Supervision. ***Email:*** jprat01@law.emory.edu

POLLY J. PRICE*, (Associate Dean for Academic Affairs and Associate Professor of Law)**, born Arkansas, April 7, 1964; admitted to bar, 1989, Georgia. *Education:* Emory University (B.A./M.A., 1986); Harvard University (J.D., 1989). ***COURSES: Legal History, Torts, Legal Methods. ***Email:*** pprice@law.emory.edu

DAVID RAY*, (Instructor)**, born 1971; admitted to bar, 1994, Florida; 1997, Georgia. *Education:* Davidson College (B.A., 1989); University of Georgia (J.D., 1994). ***COURSES: Legal Writing, Research and Advocacy Program. ***Email:*** dray@law.emory.edu

***ANNE M. RECTOR*, (Administrative Professor for Legal Writing and Academic Assistance Programs)**, born Missouri, January 9, 1953; admitted to bar, 1987, Georgia. *Education:* University of Missouri

(This Listing Continued)

EMORY UNIVERSITY SCHOOL OF LAW—Continued

(B.Mus., 1975; M.Mus., 1977); Emory University School of Law (J.D., 1987). ***COURSES:*** Legal Research, Writing and Advocacy. ***Email:*** arector@law.emory.edu

JENNIFER MURPHY ROMIG, **(Instructor)**, born Missouri, December 23, 1972; admitted to bar, 1998, Georgia. *Education:* University of Missouri (A.B., 1995; B.J., 1995); University of Virginia (J.D., 1998). ***COURSES:*** Legal Writing, Research, and Advocacy. ***Email:*** jromig@law.emory.edu

PAUL H. RUBIN, **(Professor of Law and Economics)**, born Boston, Massachusetts, August 9, 1942. *Education:* University of Cincinnati (B.A., 1963); Purdue (Ph.D., 1970). ***COURSES:*** Law & Economics. ***Email:*** prubin@emory.edu

ROBERT A. SCHAPIRO, **(Associate Professor of Law)**, born New York, September 6, 1962; admitted to bar, 1990, Connecticut; 1992, New York and District of Columbia. *Education:* Yale University (B.A., 1984; J.D., 1990); Stanford University (M.A., 1986). ***COURSES:*** Civil Procedure, Constitutional Law, Legal Profession, Remedies. ***Email:*** rschapir@law.emory.edu

ROBIN MILLS SCHREIBER, **(Associate Dean for Library and Information Technology and Professor of Law)**, born Illinois, January 10, 1947; admitted to bar, 1976, South Carolina. *Education:* Indiana University (A.B., 1969; M.L.S., 1970); University of South Carolina (J.D., 1976). ***Email:*** rmills@law.emory.edu

JULIE SEAMAN, **(Instructor)**, born New York, July 10, 1964. *Education:* University of Pennsylvania (B.A., 1986); Harvard Law School (J.D., 1989). ***COURSES:*** Legal Writing, Research and Advocacy Program.

CHARLES A. SHANOR, **(Professor of Law)**, born North Carolina, September 17, 1946; admitted to bar, 1973, Georgia; 1991, District of Columbia. *Education:* Rice University (B.A., 1968); Oxford University (B.Juris., 1972); University of Virginia (J.D., 1973). ***COURSES:*** Labor Law, Constitutional Law, Employment Discrimination, Employment Law. ***Email:*** cshanor@law.emory.edu

GEORGE B. SHEPHERD, **(Associate Professor of Law)**, born Connecticut, September 15, 1960; admitted to bar, 1987, California. *Education:* Yale University (B.A., 1982); Harvard Law School (J.D., 1986). ***COURSES:*** Civil Procedure, Evidence, Law & Economics. ***Email:*** gshep@law.emory.edu

GARY RANDALL SMITH, **(Professor of Law)**, born Arkansas, October 16, 1944; admitted to bar, 1969, Kentucky; 1970, Florida and Georgia. *Education:* University of Kentucky (B.A., 1967; J.D., 1969); New York University (LL.M., 1970). ***COURSES:*** Torts, Evidence, Workers' Compensation, Health Law. ***Email:*** lawgrs@law.emory.edu

TIMOTHY P. TERRELL, **(Professor of Law)**, born Japan, October 2, 1949; admitted to bar, 1974, Georgia. *Education:* University of Maryland (B.A., 1971); Yale University (J.D., 1974); Oxford University (Dipl. in Law, 1980). ***COURSES:*** Legal Ethics, Jurisprudence, Property, Constitutional Theory, Estates. ***Email:*** tterrell@law.emory.edu

JOHAN D. VAN DER VYVER, **(I.T. Cohen Professor of International Law and Human Rights)**, born South Africa, February 21, 1934. *Education:* Potchefstroom University (B.Com., 1954; LL.B., 1956; Honn., B.A., 1965); University of Pretoria (LL.D., 1973); Zululand (LL.D. honoris causa, 1993). ***COURSES:*** International Human Rights, International Criminal Law. ***Email:*** jvyver@law.emory.edu

FRANK J. VANDALL, **(Professor of Law)**, born Pennsylvania, January 7, 1942; admitted to bar, 1967, Tennessee. *Education:* Washington & Jefferson College (B.A., 1964); Vanderbilt University (J.D., 1967); University of Wisconsin-Madison (LL.M., 1968; S.J.D., 1979). ***COURSES:*** Torts, Products Liability, Relational Torts. ***Email:*** fvandall@law.emory.edu

TIBOR VARADY, **(Professor of Law; Director for the Interdiscipliary Study of Religion)**, born May 25, 1939; admitted to bar, 1962, Yugoslavia. *Education:* Belgrade Law School (J.D., 1962; LL.M., 1962); Harvard University (LL.M., 1970; S.J.D., 1970). ***COURSES:*** International Commercial Arbitration, International Trade & Commercial Transactions. ***Email:*** tvarady@law.emory.edu

JOHN WITTE JR., **(Jonas Robitscher Prof.; Dir., Ctr. for the Interdisciplinary Study of Religion; Dir. of Law & Religion Program)**, born Ontario, August 14, 1959; admitted to bar, 1986, Georgia. *Education:* Calvin College (B.A., 1982); Harvard University (J.D., 1985). ***COURSES:*** American Constitutional Law, Church and State, Criminal Law, American Legal History. ***Email:*** jwitte@law.emory.edu

KAREN WORTHINGTON, **(Barton Fellow in Child Law and Policy)**, born Ft. Benning, Georgia, April 9, 1968; admitted to bar, 1994, Georgia. *Education:* Eckerd College (B.A., 1990); Emory University School of Law (J.D., 1994). ***COURSES:*** Child Advocacy, Policy Development. ***Email:*** worthing@law.emory.edu

---

FLORIDA STATE UNIVERSITY COLLEGE OF LAW

425 WEST JEFFERSON STREET
TALLAHASSEE, FLORIDA 32306-1600

FORDHAM UNIVERSITY SCHOOL OF LAW

140 WEST 62ND STREET
NEW YORK, NEW YORK 10023
Telephone: (212) 636-6810
Fax: (212) 636-6921

ABA Approved Since 1936

Fordham Law School, founded in 1905, offers the Doctor of Law (J.D.) degree to approximately 1,400 students in its day and evening divisions. Approximately 250 law students live in school housing at the Lincoln Center campus. Housing preference is given to first-year students. Over 300 American and foreign colleges are represented in the student body. The faculty is composed of approximately sixty full-time professors and over 200 adjunct professors. The adjunct faculty is drawn from leading jurists, practicing attorneys, and government officials.

The Law School also offers the Master of Laws (LL.M.) degree in two areas: Banking, Corporate and Finance Law and International Business

(This Listing Continued)

FORDHAM UNIVERSITY SCHOOL OF LAW—Continued

and Trade Law. In addition, it offers the joint Doctor of Law/Master of Business Administration degree in conjunction with the Fordham University Graduate School of Business Administration, the joint Doctor of Law/Master of Social Work degree in conjunction with the Fordham University Graduate School of Social Work and the joint Doctor of Law/Master of Arts degree in conjunction with the Fordham University Graduate School of Arts and Sciences.

The course of study for the degree of Doctor of Law (J.D.) covers three academic years in the day division and four academic years in the evening division. The Master of Laws degrees can be obtained either on a full or part-time basis.

Fordham Law School is a member of the Association of American Law Schools and is approved by the American Bar Association. Its degree is recognized in every jurisdiction of the United States, and its graduates are eligible to sit for all state bar examinations provided residency and filing requirements are met. The Law School is a chapter of The Order of the Coif.

Admission standards at Fordham Law School are among the most competitive in the United States, and annually receives approximately 5000 applications were received for the 450 seats available in the fall entering class. This highly selective process is reflected in the student body which is comprised of individuals representing a wide range of interests, skills, abilities, and accomplishments.

Instruction at Fordham Law School is given by a full-time faculty of distinguished scholars and a part-time specialized faculty. First year classes are sectioned so that each student has one class in a major subject with an enrollment of about thirty-five. Other first year classes vary in size but range from approximately 40 to 115 students. Most first year classes are under 80 students. Legal writing is taught in groups of about 20 students.

The Law School is located in the heart of New York City. It is next door to Lincoln Center for the Performing Arts, whose constituent institutions include the New York State Theatre, featuring the New York City Ballet and the New York City Opera; Avery Fisher Hall, home of the New York Philharmonic; and the Metropolitan Opera House. It is also minutes away from the world's leading legal and financial centers. New York's Central Park lies two blocks to the east. This fortunate location affords Fordham law students an opportunity for personal and professional growth which is rare in American legal education.

Dean: John D. Feerick (212) 636-6875
Admissions Dean: William J. Moore (212) 636-6810
Financial Aid Director: James A. McGough (212) 636-6815
Professor of Research and Library Services: Janet R. Tracy (212) 636-6906
Placement Director: Michael Schiumo (212) 636-6930
Alumni Affairs Assistant Dean: Robert J. Reilly (212) 636-6806

FULL TIME FACULTY

JOHN D. FEERICK*, (Dean and Professor of Law)**, born 1936; admitted to bar, 1961, New York. *Education:* Fordham University (B.S., 1958; LL.B., 1961). ***COURSES: Employment Discrimination, Constitutional History.

ABRAHAM ABRAMOVSKY*, (Professor of Law; Director, International Criminal Law Center)**, born 1946; admitted to bar, 1971, New York. *Education:* Queens College of the City University of New York (B.A., 1967); State University of New York at Buffalo (J.D., 1970); Columbia University (LL.M., 1971; J.S.D., 1976). ***COURSES: Criminal Law, Complex Criminal Litigation, International Criminal Law, Drug Law.

MARC M. ARKIN*, (Professor of Law)**, born 1951; admitted to bar, 1984, New York. *Education:* Oberlin College (A.B., 1973); Yale University (M.A., 1975; M. Phil., 1976; J.D., 1982; Ph.D., 1983). ***COURSES: Criminal Law, Civil Procedure, Conflict of Laws.

CHERYL G. BADER*, (Associate Clinical Professor of Law)**, *Education:* State University of New York at Stony Brook (B.A., 1983); Hofstra University (J.D., 1986); Columbia University (LL.M., 1997). ***COURSES: Criminal Defense.

HELEN HADJIYANNAKIS BENDER*, (Associate Professor of Law)**, born 1945; admitted to bar, 1984, New York. *Education:* Vassar College (B.A., 1969); Fordham University (J.D., 1978). ***COURSES: Contracts, Remedies.

SUSAN BLOCK-LIEB*, (Professor of Law)**, *Education:* University of Michigan (B.A., 1979; J.D., 1982). ***COURSES: Contracts.

ROBERT BYRN*, (Professor of Law Emeritus)**, *Education:* Fordham (B.S., 1953; J.D., 1959). ***COURSES: Torts.

DANIEL J. CAPRA*, (Philip D. Reed Professor of Law)**, born 1953; admitted to bar, 1978, New York. *Education:* Rockhurst College (A.B., 1974); University of California (J.D., 1977). ***COURSES: Constitutional Criminal Law, Evidence, Professional Responsibility, Criminal Procedure: Investigation.

RICHARD S. CARNELL*, (Associate Professor of Law)**, admitted to bar, 1982, California. *Education:* Yale University (B.A., 1975), Harvard University (J.D., 1982). ***COURSES: Banking Law, Corporations.

YUNG FRANK CHIANG*, (Professor of Law)**, born 1936; admitted to bar, 1960, Taiwan; 1974, New York. *Education:* National Taiwan University (LL.B., 1958); Northwestern University (LL.M., 1962); University of Chicago (J.D., 1965). ***COURSES: Commercial Transactions, Commercial Finance, Commercial Paper, Civil Law System, Comparative Law, Far Eastern Contract and Commercial Law, Trade with Asian Nations.

JAMES A. COHEN*, (Associate Professor of Law and Director of Clinical Education)**, born 1948; admitted to bar, 1976, New York. *Education:* Long Island University (B.A., 1972); Syracuse University (J.D., 1975). ***COURSES: Criminal Defense Clinic.

JEFFREY M. COLON*, (Associate Professor of Law)**, born 1961; admitted to bar, 1989, New York; 1990, District of Columbia. *Education:* Yale University (B.A., 1983; J.D., 1987); Georgetown University (M.L.T., 1993). ***COURSES: Income Tax, International Taxation, Taxation of Financial Products.

ELIZABETH B. COOPER*, (Associate Professor of Law)**, born 1961; admitted to bar, 1988, New Jersey; 1989, New York. *Education:* University of Pennsylvania (B.A., 1983); New York University (J.D., 1988). ***COURSES: Civil Rights and Employment Discrimination Clinic; AIDS and the Law.

***MARY C. DALY*, (James H. Quinn Professor of Law; Director of**

(This Listing Continued)

FORDHAM UNIVERSITY SCHOOL OF LAW—Continued

The Stein Institute of Law and Ethics), born 1947; admitted to bar, 1973, New York. *Education:* Fordham University (B.A., 1969; J.D., 1972); New York University (LL.M., 1978); University of Paris (Zichkla Fellow, 1972-1973). ***COURSES:*** Professional Responsibility.

DEBORAH W. DENNO, **(Professor of Law)**, born 1952; admitted to bar, 1990, Pennsylvania. *Education:* University of Virginia (B.A., 1974); University of Toronto (M.A., 1975); University of Pennsylvania (Ph.D., 1982; J.D., 1989). ***COURSES:*** Criminal Law, Law and Science, Topics in Advanced Criminal Law, Torts.

MATTHEW DILLER, **(Professor of Law)**, admitted to bar, 1987, New York. *Education:* Harvard University (A.B., 1981); Harvard University Law School (J.D., 1987). ***COURSES:*** Civil Procedure, Social Welfare Law,, Administrative Law.

CARL FELSENFELD, **(Professor of Law)**, born 1927; admitted to bar, 1954, New York. *Education:* Dartmouth College (A.B., 1948); Columbia University (M.S., 1950; J.D.,1954). ***COURSES:*** Banking Law, International Banking, Bankruptcy, Commercial Paper.

JILL E. FISCH, **(Professor of Law)**, born 1960; admitted to bar, 1985, Connecticut; 1986, New York. *Education:* Cornell University (B.A., 1982); Yale University (J.D., 1985). ***COURSES:*** Corporations, Securities Law, Advanced Corporate Law, Federal Courts.

MARTIN S. FLAHERTY, **(Professor of Law & Co-Director, Joseph R. Crowley Program in International Human Rights)**, born 1958; admitted to bar, 1992, New Jersey; 1993, New York. *Education:* Princeton University (B.A., 1981); Yale University (M.A., 1982; M. Phil, 1987); Columbia University (J.D., 1988). ***COURSES:*** Constitutional Law, Constitutional History, International Human Rights.

JAMES E. FLEMING, **(Professor of Law)**, born 1954; admitted to bar, 1987, New York. *Education:* University of Missouri (B.A., 1977); Princeton University (A.M., 1981; Ph.D., 1988); Harvard University (J.D., 1985). ***COURSES:*** Constitutional Law, Constitutional Theory, Remedies.

MARTIN FOGELMAN, **(McGivney Professor of Law)**, born 1928; admitted to bar, 1950, New York. *Education:* Syracuse University (B.A., 1948; J.D., 1950). ***COURSES:*** Corporations.

ROGER J. GOEBEL, **(Professor of Law; Director of the Center on European Union Law)**, born 1935; admitted to bar, 1961, New York. *Education:* Manhattan College (B.A., 1957); New York University (LL.B., 1960; LL.M., 1961). ***COURSES:*** Agency, European Union Law, EEC Corporate and Trade Law.

BRUCE A. GREEN, **(Louis Stein Professor of Law; Director of the Stein Center for Ethics and Public Interest Law)**, born 1955; admitted to bar, 1982, New York. *Education:* Princeton University (A.B., 1978); Columbia University (J.D., 1981). ***COURSES:*** Criminal Procedure: Investigation, Professional Responsibility, Ethics in Criminal Advocacy.

ABNER S. GREENE, **(Professor of Law)**, born 1960; admitted to bar, 1987, Pennsylvania; 1988, District of Columbia. *Education:* Yale University (B.A., 1982); University of Michigan (J.D., 1986). ***COURSES:*** Criminal Law, Law and Religion, Family Law, Administrative Law, Freedom of Speech.

HUGH C. HANSEN, **(Professor of Law)**, born 1946; admitted to bar, 1973, New York; 1973, Florida. *Education:* Rutgers University (A.B., 1968); Georgetown University (J.D., 1972); Yale University (LL.M., 1977). ***COURSES:*** Constitutional Law, Copyright Law, Trademark Law, EEC Intellectual Property Licensing, Advanced Copyright, Advanced Trademarks.

TRACY E. HIGGINS, **(Associate Professor of Law & Co-Director, Joseph R. Crowley Program in International Human Rights)**, born 1964; admitted to bar, 1992, Massachusetts; 1992, New York. *Education:* Princeton University (B.A., 1986); Harvard University (J.D., 1990). ***COURSES:*** Civil Procedure, Federal Courts, Feminist Legal Theory, International Human Rights.

LEAH A. HILL, **(Associate Clinical Professor of Law)**, born 1959; admitted to bar, 1987, New York. *Education:* City University of New York, Brooklyn College (B.A., 1982); Rutgers University (J.D., 1985). ***COURSES:*** Clinical Legal Education, Battered Women's Rights Clinic.

GAIL D. HOLLISTER, **(Professor of Law)**, born 1945; admitted to bar, 1971, New York. *Education:* University of Wisconsin (B.S., 1967); Fordham University (J.D., 1970). ***COURSES:*** Torts, Legal Writing, Legal Process.

NICHOLAS J. JOHNSON, **(Associate Professor of Law)**, born 1959; admitted to bar, 1984, Georgia; 1986, Pennsylvania. *Education:* West Virginia University (B.S., 1981; B.A., 1981); Harvard University Law School (J.D., 1984). ***COURSES:*** Contracts, Environmental Law, Legal Process.

ROBERT J. KACZOROWSKI, **(Professor of Law)**, born 1938; admitted to bar, 1983, New York. *Education:* Loyola University (B.S.C., 1960); DePaul University (M.A., 1967); New York University (J.D., 1982); University of Minnesota (Ph.D., 1971). ***COURSES:*** Constitutional Law, American Legal History-Seminar, American Legal History-Survey.

JAMES L. KAINEN, **(Associate Professor of Law)**, born 1953; admitted to bar, 1979, New York. *Education:* Brown University (A.B., 1975); Harvard University (J.D., 1978). ***COURSES:*** Property, Evidence, Trusts, Legal Process.

CONSTANTINE N. KATSORIS, **(Wilkinson Professor of Law)**, born 1932; admitted to bar, 1957, New York. *Education:* Fordham University (B.S., 1953; J.D., 1957); New York University (LL.M., 1963). ***COURSES:*** Estate Planning, Federal and Local Taxation, Securities Arbitration, Accounting for Lawyers.

MICHAEL R. LANZARONE, **(Professor of Law)**, born 1936; admitted to bar, 1963, New York. *Education:* Fordham University (B.A., 1958; LL.B., 1961); New York University (LL.M., 1973). ***COURSES:*** Civil Procedure, Labor Law, SEC Regulations.

MICHAEL T. MADISON, **(Professor of Law)**, born 1941; admitted to bar, 1967, New York; 1975, Virginia. *Education:* George Washington University (A.B., 1963); Harvard University (J.D., 1966); New York University (LL.M., 1971). ***COURSES:*** Property, Real Estate Finance.

DONALD L. MAGNETTI, **(Associate Professor of Law)**, born 1940; admitted to bar, 1980, New York and New Jersey; 1981, Florida. *Education:* Fordham University (A.B., 1963; J.D., 1979); Woodstock College (Ph.L., 1964); Johns Hopkins University (Ph.D., 1969). ***COURSES:*** Torts, Trusts, Legal Process.

MARIA L. MARCUS, **(Joseph M. McLaughlin Professor of Law)**, born 1933; admitted to bar, 1961, New York. *Education:* Oberlin College (B.A., 1954); Yale University (J.D., 1957). ***COURSES:*** Criminal Justice, Discovery, Corporate and White Collar Crime.

MICHAEL M. MARTIN, **(Associate Dean and Alpin J. Cameron Professor of Law)**, born 1943; admitted to bar, 1966, Iowa; 1970, Washington; 1975, New York. *Education:* University of Iowa (B.A., 1964; J.D., 1966); Oxford University (B.Litt., 1968). ***COURSES:*** Evidence, Torts.

(This Listing Continued)

FORDHAM UNIVERSITY SCHOOL OF LAW—Continued

MICHAEL W. MARTIN*, (Associate Professor of Law)**, *Education:* University of Virginia (B.A., 1987); Fordham (J.D., 1992). ***COURSES: Welfare Rights Clinic.

EDWARD F.C. MCGONAGLE*, (Professor of Law)**, admitted to bar, 1957, Massachusetts; 1979, New York. *Education:* Princeton University (A.B., 1947); Yale University (M.A., 1951); Boston College (LL.B., 1957); Harvard University (LL.M., 1964). ***COURSES: Administrative Law, Decedents' Estates, Land Use Planning, Trusts and Estates.

ANN MOYNIHAN*, (Associate Clinical Professor of Law)**, admitted to bar, New York. *Education:* City University of New York (B.A., 1973); New York University (J.D., 1977). ***COURSES: Child Abuse and Neglect, Family and Child Protection Clinic.

JACQUELINE M. NOLAN-HALEY*, (Associate Professor of Law)**, born 1949; admitted to bar, 1975, Massachusetts; 1977, New York; 1978, District of Columbia. *Education:* Emmanuel College (A.B., 1971); Suffolk University (J.D., 1975); New York University (LL.M., 1981). ***COURSES: Alternate Dispute Resolution, Advanced Negotiation, Mediation Clinic Seminar.

GIDEON PARCHOMOVSKY*, (Associate Professor of Law)**, *Education:* Hebrew University (LL.B., 1993); University of California, Berkeley (LL.M., 1995); Yale University (J.S.D., 1998). ***COURSES: Property, Copyright Law.

MARK R. PATTERSON*, (Associate Professor of Law)**, born 1956; admitted to bar, 1992, Massachusetts. *Education:* Ohio State (B.S.E.E., 1978; M.S., 1980); Stanford (J.D., 1991). ***COURSES: Antitrust, Corporations, Law and Science.

RUSSELL G. PEARCE*, (Professor of Law)**, born 1956; admitted to bar, 1982, New York. *Education:* Yale University (B.A. 1978; J.D., 1981). ***COURSES: Remedies, Professional Responsibility, Legal Process.

JOSEPH M. PERILLO*, (Distinguished Professor of Law)**, born 1933; admitted to bar, 1955, New York. *Education:* Cornell University (A.B., 1953; J.D., 1955). ***COURSES: Contracts, Legal Process.

ERNEST EARL PHILLIPS*, (Professor of Law)**, born 1929; admitted to bar, 1955, Texas; 1955, District of Columbia; 1969, New York. *Education:* Spring Hill College (B.A., 1951); Georgetown University (LL.B., 1954; LL.M., 1958). ***COURSES: Property, Domestic Relations.

THOMAS M. QUINN*, (Sidney C. Norris Professor of Law)**, born 1924; admitted to bar, 1950, New York. *Education:* College of the Holy Cross (B.A., 1947); Bellarmine College (Ph.L., 1955); Harvard University (J.D., 1950; LL.M., 1956); Woodstock College (S.T.L., 1961). ***COURSES: Commercial Finance, Commercial Transactions, Child Abuse & Neglect.

JOEL R. REIDENBERG*, (Professor of Law; Director of Graduate Program)**, born 1961; admitted to bar, 1986, New York; 1988, District of Columbia. *Education:* Dartmouth College (A.B., 1983); Columbia University (J.D., 1986); University De Paris I (Pantheon-Sorbonne) (D.E.A., dr. int'l. eco. 1987). ***COURSES: International Trade Law, Contracts, Comparative Law, Information Technology Law.

DANIEL CHARLES RICHMAN*, (Professor of Law)**, born 1958; admitted to bar, 1986, New York. *Education:* Harvard University (A.B., 1980); Oxford University (1980-1981); Yale University (J.D., 1984). ***COURSES: Criminal Procedure: Adjudication, Evidence, Federal Criminal Law.

DAVID A. SCHMUDDE*, (Associate Professor of Law)**, born 1945; admitted to bar, 1973, Florida; 1978, New York. *Education:* Marquette University (B.S., 1968); North Carolina State (M.A., 1970); University of Florida (J.D., 1972). ***COURSES: Corporate Tax, Income Tax, Partnership Tax, Federal Tax Procedure, Real Estate Finance, Property.

BETH G. SCHWARTZ*, (Associate Clinical Professor of Law)**, born 1952; admitted to bar, 1979, New York. *Education:* State University of New York at Buffalo (B.A., 1973); St. John's University (J.D., 1978). ***COURSES: Foundation Skills, Children's Disability and Special Education Clinic.

DONALD L. SHARPE*, (Professor of Law)**, born 1934; admitted to bar, 1963, Pennsylvania; 1968, New York. *Education:* Oberlin College (B.A., 1956); Harvard University (M.A., 1960); Boston College (LL.B., 1962); New York University (LL.M., 1966). ***COURSES: Income Tax, Business Tax, Advanced Business Tax, Taxation of Estates and Trusts.

MARCELLA SILVERMAN*, (Associate Clinical Professor of Law)**, born 1954; admitted to bar, 1983, New York. *Education:* Cornell University College of Arts & Sciences (B.A., 1976); New York University School of Law (J.D., 1982). ***COURSES: Community Lawyering Clinic.

ANDREW B. SIMS*, (Professor of Law)**, born 1948; admitted to bar, 1974, New York. *Education:* Amherst College (A.B., 1970); Harvard University (J.D., 1973). ***COURSES: Constitutional Law, Mass Media Law, Entertainment Law.

TERRY SMITH*, (Associate Professor of Law)**, born 1964; admitted to bar, 1991, District of Columbia, New Jersey and Pennsylvania. *Education:* Brown University (A.B., 1986); New York University School of Law (J.D., 1989). ***COURSES: Civil Procedure, Labor and Employment Law, Voting Rights.

GEMMA SOLIMENE*, (Associate Professor of Law)**, *Education:* State University of New York at Stony Brook (B.A, 1984); New York University (J.D., 1987). ***COURSES: Civil Employment and Disability Rights Clinic.

LINDA SUGIN*, (Associate Professor of Law)**, born 1962; admitted to bar, 1989, New York. *Education:* Harvard University (B.A., 1985); New York University (J.D., 1988). ***COURSES: Income Tax, Corporations, Federal Tax Policy.

JOSEPH C. SWEENEY*, (John D. Calamari Distinguished Professor of Law)**, born 1933; admitted to bar, 1957, Massachusetts. *Education:* Harvard University (A.B., 1954); Boston University (J.D., 1957); Columbia (LL.M., 1963). ***COURSES: Admiralty, Air Law, International Business Transactions.

DR. LUDWIK TECLAFF*, (Professor of Law Emeritus)**, *Education:* Oxford (Mag. Jur., 1944); Columbia (M.L.S., 1955); New York University (LL.M., 1961; J.S.D., 1965). ***COURSES: International Law, Law of the Sea, International Environmental Law, Jurisprudence.

STEVE THEL*, (Professor of Law)**, born 1954; admitted to bar, 1979, Georgia. *Education:* North Texas State University (B.A., 1976); Harvard University (J.D., 1979). ***COURSES: Contracts, Corporate Finance, Securities Regulation.

CHANTAL THOMAS*, (Associate Professor of Law)**, born 1970; admitted to bar, 1996, New York. *Education:* McGill University (B.A., 1992); Harvard (J.D., 1995). ***COURSES: International Trade Law, Law & Economic Development, Contracts.

JANET R. TRACY*, (Professor of Research and Library Services)**, born 1941; admitted to bar, 1970, New York. *Education:* University of Oregon (B.A., 1963); University of Washington (M.L., 1964); Harvard University (J.D., 1969). ***COURSES: Legal Bibliography, Legal Writing.

(This Listing Continued)

WILLIAM MICHAEL TREANOR*, (Professor of Law (on leave))**, born 1957; admitted to bar, 1987, New Jersey. *Education:* Yale (B.A., 1979; J.D., 1985); Harvard (A.M., 1982). ***COURSES: Criminal Law, Legal History, Property.

RACHEL VORSPAN*, (Director of Legal Writing; Associate Professor of Law)**, born 1945; admitted to bar, 1980, New York. *Education:* University of California (A.B., 1967); Columbia University (M.A., 1968; Ph.D., 1975); Harvard University (J.D., 1979). ***COURSES: Legal Writing, English Legal History.

IAN S. WEINSTEIN*, (Associate Professor of Law)**, born 1959; admitted to bar, 1986, District of Columbia; 1988, New York. *Education:* Reed College (B.A., 1981); New York University (J.D., 1986); Georgetown University (LL.M., 1990). ***COURSES: Foundation Skills, Children's Disability and Special Education.

CHARLES M. WHELAN, S.J.*, (Professor of Law)**, born 1926; admitted to bar, 1954, District of Columbia. *Education:* Woodstock College (A.B., 1950; Ph.L., 1951; S.T.L., 1958); Georgetown University (LL.B., 1954; LL.M., 1955). ***COURSES: Constitutional Law, Legal Writing, Supreme Court Seminar, First Amendment.

BENJAMIN C. ZIPURSKY*, (Associate Professor of Law)**, born 1960; admitted to bar, 1992, New York. *Education:* Swarthmore College (B.A., 1982); University of Pittsburgh (M.A., 1985; Ph.D., 1987); New York University (J.D., 1991). ***COURSES: Torts, Law & Philosophy, Advanced Torts - Defamation & Privacy, Tort Theory.

FRANKLIN PIERCE LAW CENTER

2 WHITE STREET
CONCORD, NEW HAMPSHIRE 03301
Telephone: (603) 228-1541
Fax: (603) 228-1074

ABA Approved Since 1974

Founded in 1973, Franklin Pierce Law Center is a private, independent, ABA-accredited law school located in Concord, NH, with an enrollment of approximately 450 students. The Law Center remains, by choice, one of the smallest independent law schools in the United States. Our small size enables us to focus on students as individuals. Students learn in a close, cooperative, informal environment, and enjoy frequent contact with professionally active faculty.

Pierce Law offers professional programs leading to a juris doctor (JD), a master of intellectual property (MIP), diploma in intellectual property (DIP), a master of laws in intellectual property (LLM), a master of education law (MEL), and certificate of advanced graduate study degree in education law (CAGS). The MEL and CAGS degree programs are designed for primary and secondary school administrators, superintendents, and teachers. The MIP program is a unique one-year program that draws intellectual property practitioners and administrators from around the world. For a decade, *U.S. News and World Report* has consistently ranked Franklin Pierce Law Center among the nation's top five law schools for the study of intellectual property.

Franklin Pierce Law Center integrates traditional courses with the practical skills necessary for practicing law in a profound way. Students gain a thorough academic grounding and have an opportunity to develop and use newly learned hands-on skills. Pierce Law offers concentrations -opportunities for students to shape their education and gain experience in one or more areas of the law. Concentrations are flexible guides for the second half of law school enables students to shape their education to prepare for the real needs of legal practice. Each concentration involves survey and specialty courses, an array of simulations, clinics, or externships to develop skills, and a culminating experience such as a seminar or advanced practice opportunity that pulls all the elements together. Concentrations include:

Business and e-commerce Law
A concentration in business and e-commerce law prepares students for traditional corporate or nonprofit practice in private firms or corporate legal departments, as well as tax practice, estate planning, or work with business start-ups in fields ranging from technology to real estate.

Social Justice
At Pierce Law, students become a force for change, advocating for social justice in cutting-edge practice areas such as elder and disability law, family and children's law, and criminal law. Students work in legal clinics, representing real clients and learning what it takes to run a practice efficiently, ethically and profitably, while remaining accessible to the under-represented in our communities. Opportunities to participate in externships set up in courts, law firms, agencies and businesses nationwide.

Criminal Law
The criminal law concentration not only prepares graduates for a career in the familiar roles of defender or prosecutor, it allows students to explore other areas, such as the burgeoning field of white collar crime resulting from new technologies.

Education Law
The education law curriculum focuses on providing a comprehensive understanding of the law and legal systems to allow you to work confidently in the education arena.

Elder and Disability Law
A background in health law prepares students for work in patient advocacy organizations, private law firms and governmental agencies.

General Practice
Students who choose to concentrate in general practice emerge from their legal education at the Law Center as independent practitioners competent to counsel and represent clients.

Pierce Law's Devine, Millimet & Branch Courtroom provides students with opportunities to gain experience in a high-tech facility equipped with the state-of-art hardware and software programs that will be used by one-third of all federal district courts by the year 2003. Trough a variety of courses held in a courtroom, students expand their knowledge of visual persuasion beyond the traditional bounds of demonstrative evidence. Workshops on building electronic briefs are offered on regular basis. Working in concert with our interactive multi-media curriculum, the combination results in unequalled opportunities to explore advocacy, education and the delivery of legal services. In addition, the school's new smart classroom is equipped with the latest electronic presentation technology.

Comprised of 26 full-time members and 48 adjuncts, the faculty is dedicated to teaching and to providing students the best possible legal education. All are experienced practitioners, many national and international experts in their respective fields. They are committed to academic excellence and scholarship and to inspiring graduates to seek rewarding and successful careers.

Pierce Law produces three publications: *IDEA: The Journal of Law and*

(This Listing Continued)

FRANKLIN PIERCE LAW CENTER—Continued

Technology, Risk: Health, Safety and Environmental and *the Annual Survey of New Hampshire Law.* Institutes at the Germeshausen Center for the Law of Innovation and Entrepreneurship, the Greenberg Trademark Institute and the Intellectual Property Summer Institute.

Dean: John D. Hutson (603) 228-1541(1100)
Vice Dean: Keith M. Harrison (603) 228-1541(1146)
Director of Admissions: Lory Attalla (603) 228-9217
Director of Financial Aid: Clinton Hanson (603) 228-1541(1104)
Library Director: Judy Gire (603) 228-1541(1129)
Assistant Dean for Career Services: Mary B. Sheffer (603) 228-1541(1175)
Registrar: Dianna Powers (603) 228-1541(1103)
Vice-President for Business: Jeannie MacKay (603) 228-1541(1125)
Director of Intellectual Property Graduate Programs: William O. Hennessey (603) 228-1541(1172)
Dir., Germeshausen Ctr. for the Law of Innov. and Entrepre.: Karl F. Jorda (603) 228-1541(1109)
Dir. of Children's Advocacy Clinic: Mary Pilkington Casey (603) 228-1541(1166)
Director of Education Law Institute: Sarah Redfield (603) 228-1541(1152)
Director of Institute for Health, Law and Ethics: David Frydman (603) 228-1541(1180)
Director of Social Justice Institute: Brigitte Holmes (603) 228-1541

FULL TIME FACULTY

***JOHN D. HUTSON*, (Dean)**

KEITH F. BARNABY*, (Director, Criminal Practice Clinic, Professor Law)**, born October 09, 1956; admitted to bar, 1985, New Hampshire; 1992, California. *Education:* Colgate University (B.A., 1978); University of Denver College of Law (J.D., 1985). ***COURSES: Criminal Practice Clinic Classroom Component. ***Email:*** kbarnaby@fplc.edu

JON L. CAVICCHI, born Plymouth, Massachusetts, April 15, 1959; admitted to bar, 1985, Massachusetts; 1986, California. *Education:* Stonehill College (B.A., 1981); Franklin Pierce Law Center (J.D., 1984). ***COURSES:*** Intellectual Property Research Tools, MIP Research. ***Email:*** jcavicchi@fplc.edu

JOSEPH A. DICKINSON*, (Professor of Law)**, born Ridgeway, Pennsylvania, April 30, 1947; admitted to bar, 1974, Pennsylvania; 1977, Tennessee; 1982, New Hampshire. *Education:* Haverford College (B.A., 1970); New York University (J.D., 1973). ***COURSES: Introduction to UCC, Employment Law, Contracts, Moot Court. ***Email:*** jdickinson@fplc.edu

THOMAS G. FIELD, JR.*, (Professor of Law)**, born Morgantown, West Virginia, June 8, 1942; admitted to bar, 1969, West Virginia; 1974, Ohio; 1975, New Hampshire. *Education:* West Virginia University (A.B., 1964; J.D., 1969); New York University (LL.M., Trade Regulation, 1970). ***COURSES: Administrative and Related Process in Intellectual Property, Administrative Process, Introduction to Intellectual Property, Moot Court, LLM Thesis Seminar. ***Email:*** tfield@fplc.edu

JON M. GARON*, (Professor of Law)**, born 1963; admitted to bar, 1988, California. *Education:* University of Minnesota (B.A., 1985); Columbia University School of Law (J.D., 1988). ***COURSES: Entertainment, Business, IP Copyright and Entertainment, Corporations, Contracts. ***Email:*** jgaron@fplc.edu

HUGH GIBBONS*, (Professor of Law)**, born Boston, Massachusetts, September 14, 1939; admitted to bar, 1964, Illinois. *Education:* Northwestern University (B.A., 1961); University of Chicago (M.B.A., 1968); Northwestern University (J.D., 1964). ***COURSES: Torts, Information Torts, Legal Philosophy, Law and Economics, Moot Court, Remedies. ***Email:*** hgibbons@fplc.edu

JUDITH A. GIRE*, (Library Director and Professor of Law)**, born Scranton, Pennsylvania, March 23, 1947. *Education:* Wilson College (B.A., 1969); University of Michigan (A.M.L.S., 1970); Franklin Pierce Law Center (J.D., 1983). ***COURSES: Legal Research, Advanced Legal Research, Moot Court. ***Email:*** jgire@fplc.edu

WILLIAM O. HENNESSEY*, (Professor of Law and Director of Graduate Programs)**, born Providence, Rhode Island, September 20, 1946; admitted to bar, 1987, New Hampshire. *Education:* Brown University (A.B., 1968); University of Michigan (Ph.D., 1980); Franklin Pierce Law Center (J.D., 1986). ***COURSES: Intellectual Property, International Economic Regulation, MIC Research & Writing, Public International Law, Moot Court. ***Email:*** bhennessey@fplc.edu

RICHARD A. HESSE*, (Professor Emeritus of Law)**, born Johnstown, Pennsylvania, October 2, 1934; admitted to bar, 1968, District of Columbia. *Education:* Indiana University of Pennsylvania (B.S., 1958); Temple University (M.A., 1964); Northwestern University; Georgetown University Law Center (J.D., 1968). ***COURSES: Civil Rights & Liberties, Constitutional Law, Supreme Court Seminar, Professional Responsibility, Moot Court. ***Email:*** dhesse@fplc.edu

***BRIGITTE HOLMES*, (Director of Social Justice Institute)**, born Harrisburg, Virginia, March 25, 1957; admitted to bar, 1984, Alaska; 1988, New Hampshire. *Education:* Golden State University School of Law (B.A., 1978; J.D., 1983).

MARCUS HURN*, (Professor of Law)**, born Neosho, Missouri, October 27, 1952; admitted to bar, 1977, Missouri; 1983, New Hampshire. *Education:* Southwest Missouri State (B.S., 1974); University of Missouri, Kansas City (J.D., 1977); Sterling Fellow, Yale Law School. ***COURSES: Business Problems & Strategy, Conflicts of Law, Debtor/Creditor Relations, Property, Moot Court. ***Email:*** mhurn@fplc.edu

CRAIG S. JEPSON*, (Professor of Law)**, born Los Angeles, California, July 15, 1958; admitted to bar, 1987, California; 1975, District of Columbia; 1981, Commonwealth of Virginia. *Education:* University of Southern California (B.S., 1979; J.D., 1987); Pepperdine University (M.B.A., 1982). ***COURSES: Biotechnology Patent Practice. ***Email:*** cjepson@fplc.edu

CHRISTOPHER MALLATRATT JOHNSON, born Washington, DC, June 16, 1967; admitted to bar, 1994, California; 1995, Georgia; 1996, Alabama. *Education:* Carleton College (B.A., 1989); Harvard Law School (J.D., 1994). ***COURSES:*** Criminal Law and Procedure. ***Email:*** cjohnson@fplc.edu

***KARL F. JORDA*, (David Rines Professor of Intellectual Property Law)**, born Germany, April 29, 1929; admitted to bar, 1957, Illinois and Indiana; 1961, New York. *Education:* Johann Wolfgang Goethe University, Frankfurt, Germany; College of Great Falls (B.A., 1953);

(This Listing Continued)

FRANKLIN PIERCE LAW CENTER—Continued

Notre Dame University (M.A., 1954; J.D., 1957). Adjunct Professor, The Fletcher School of Law and Diplomacy, Tufts University, Medford, MA. ***COURSES:*** Licensing/Technology Transfer, Intellectual Property Management. ***Email:*** kjorda@fplc.edu

KIMBERLY KIRKLAND*, (Professor of Law)**, born 1961; admitted to bar, 1990, Massachusetts; 1994, New Hampshire. *Education:* Williams College (B.A., 1983); Northeastern University School of Law (J.D., 1990). ***COURSES: Civil Procedure, Employment Law. ***Email:*** kkirkland@fplc.edu

CYNTHIA R. LANDAU*, (Assistant Law Librarian and Professor of Law)**, born Independence, Missouri, July 18, 1949. *Education:* Park College (B.A., 1971); University of Missouri, Columbia (M.L.S., 1972); Franklin Pierce Law Center (J.D., 1980). ***COURSES: Legal Research. ***Email:*** clandau@fplc.edu

WILLIAM D. MURPHY*, (Professor of Law)**, born Washington, D.C., January 31, 1949; admitted to bar, 1974, Pennsylvania; 1976, District of Columbia; 1980, Massachusetts; 1993, New York. *Education:* Denison University (B.A., 1971); Harvard University (M.B.A., 1981; D.B.A., 1987); Dickinson School of Law (J.D., 1974). ***COURSES: Antitrust Law, Business Associations, Essential Business Concepts, Information Technologies, Moot Court. Of counsel: Devine, Millimet & Branch, Manchester, NH. ***Email:*** bmurphy@fplc.edu

ELLEN J. MUSINSKY*, (Professor of Law)**, born Brookline, Massachusetts, June 17, 1950; admitted to bar, 1975, New Hampshire. *Education:* University of Vermont (B.A., 1972); Northeastern University (J.D., 1975). ***COURSES: Administrative Law and Advocacy, Family Law, Non Profit Corporations, Moot Court. ***Email:*** emusinsky@fplc.dedu

JOHN LAWRENCE ORCUTT*, (Professor of Law)**, born California, November 01, 1967; admitted to bar, 1994, New York. *Education:* University of California, Berkeley (B.A., 1990; J.D., 1993). ***COURSES: Business Associations, Mergers and Acquisitions, Securities Regulation, Start-ups. ***Email:*** jorcutt@fplc.edu

MARY T. PILKINGTON-CASEY*, (Assistant Clinical Professor; Director, Childrens' Advocacy Clinic)**, born Connecticut, August 13, 1948; admitted to bar, 1986, New Hampshire. *Education:* Central Connecticut State University (B.A., 1973); University of Hartford; Franklin Pierce Law Center (J.D., 1986); Boston College (M.S.W., 1975). ***COURSES: Children's Advocacy, Civil Practice Clinic, Advanced Civil Practice Clinic, Moot Court. ***Email:*** mpcasey@fplc.edu

SARAH E. REDFIELD*, (Professor of Law)**, born Portland, Maine, October 18, 1948; admitted to bar, 1974, Maine. *Education:* Mount Holyoke College (B.A., 1970); Northeastern Law School (J.D., 1974); Harvard Law School (LL.M., 1983). ***COURSES: Administrative Process, Environmental Law, Education Law, Moot Court. ***Email:*** sredfield@fplc.edu

SUSAN M. RICHEY*, (Professor of Law)**, born Waynesboro, Pennsylvania, July 24, 1950; admitted to bar, 1982, California. *Education:* College of William and Mary (B.S., 1973); University of Baltimore (B.A., 1977); University of Maryland School of Law (J.D., 1980). ***COURSES: Trademarks and Deceptive Practices, Copyright Law, Information Technologies, Moot Court. ***Email:*** srichey@fplc.edu

ALBERT SCHERR*, (Professor of Law)**, born Bennington, Vermont, September 6, 1952; admitted to bar, 1982, New Hampshire. *Education:* Yale University (B.A., 1974); Vermont Law School (J.D., 1981). ***COURSES: Evidence, Trial Advocacy, Expert Witnesses & Scientific Evidence, Intellectual Property Litigation. ***Email:*** bscherr@fplc.edu

MITCHELL M. SIMON*, (Professor of Law)**, born New York, N.Y., December 28, 1951; admitted to bar, 1977, New Hampshire. *Education:* Hofstra University (B.S., 1973); Boston University (J.D., 1977). ***COURSES: Health Law I, Professional Responsibility, Community Lawyering. ***Email:*** msimon@fplc.edu

SOPHIE SPARROW*, (Professor of Law)**, born 1958; admitted to bar, 1986, New Hampshire. *Education:* Harvard College (A.B., 1982); Harvard Law School (J.D., 1986). ***COURSES: Legal Writing and Analysis, Legal Research. ***Email:*** ssparrow@fplc.edu

PETER WRIGHT*, (Director of Clinical Programs)**, born Bay Shore, New York, June 26, 1950; admitted to bar, 1980, New Hampshire. *Education:* Pennsylvania State University (B.A., 1976); Franklin Pierce Law Center (J.D., 1980). ***COURSES: Civil Practice Clinic, Mediation Clinic. ***Email:*** pwright@fplc.edu

---

GEORGE MASON UNIVERSITY SCHOOL OF LAW

3301 NORTH FAIRFAX DRIVE
ARLINGTON, VIRGINIA 22201-4426
Telephone: (703) 993-8000
Fax: (703) 993-8088
http://www.law.gmu.edu

ABA Approved Since 1980.

The George Mason University School of Law, the state university law school in Northern Virginia, is located in Arlington, Virginia, across the Potomac River from Washington, D.C. It is nationally known for its law and economics curriculum, and pioneered the concept of specialized J.D. programs, in which it offers eight areas of concentration: Intellectual Property Law; Regulatory Law; Corporate and Securities Law; International Business; Litigation Law; Personal Law; Criminal Law; and Legal and Economic Theory. George Mason is a center of legal scholarship and academic excellence, particularly in law and economics. Although George Mason is among the nation's youngest law schools, *U.S. News and World Report* ranks it in the first tier of American law schools.

Many George Mason graduates are selected for clerkships with federal and state judges, and are recruited and hired by the U.S. Department of Justice and other government agencies, as well as the most prominent law firms in the nation. The law faculty is dedicated to research, publication, and teaching and ranks in the top 25 of all law faculties in terms of scholarly productivity and influence according to an influential recent study that appeared in the *Journal of Legal Studies.*

George Mason puts special emphasis on teaching clear and succinct legal writing skills because these skills are essential to success in the legal profession. In many courses, students receive a writing grade separate from and in addition to the usual grade for substantive knowledge. A separate "writing GPA" appears on each student's transcript.

George Mason's specialty programs foster skills that are directly applicable to the area of law in which a student plans to practice or is particularly interested. The new Technology Law Program combines course work in the fields of technology law, intellectual property law,

(This Listing Continued)

GEORGE MASON UNIVERSITY SCHOOL OF LAW
—Continued

and business law. It provides J.D. students with the skills necessary to succeed in today's rapidly changing legal environment. The Corporate and Securities Law Track is designed to give students a well-rounded education coupled with specialized preparation for practice in law firms or corporate counsel offices in fields relating to corporations, corporate finance, and financial markets. The Regulatory Law Track prepares students to work in or practice before federal and/or state regulatory agencies. The Intellectual Property Law Track is designed for students with scientific or engineering backgrounds who plan to enter the growing field of intellectual property law. The International Business Track prepares students for practice in the rapidly changing global business community. The Litigation Law Track provides an academic program meant to develop a sound understanding of the theory and institutions underlying dispute resolution.

In addition, students can pursue a specialty sequence from within the General Law Program, the traditional curriculum for students who choose not to enter one of the specialty tracks. Each specialty sequence provides a basic understanding of one of seven subject matter areas and requires 14-16 credit hours, leaving about one-third of the 84-credit-hour total to the student's own choosing. Specialty sequences include the following: Corporate and Securities Law; Intellectual Property Law; International Business; Legal and Economic Theory; Litigation Law; Personal Law; Criminal Law; Regulatory Law; and Tax Law.

George Mason has approximately 750 students in its day and evening programs. The median LSAT score of the fall 2001 entering class was 160; the median GPA was 3.40.

The Law Library's collection consists of almost 400,000 volumes. The law and economics, intellectual property, financial services, international law, litigation, and corporate portions of the collection are of special distinction. LEXIS and WESTLAW provide each student with individualized accounts, which allow access to these research databases both at home and at school. Computer technology resources of George Mason University, including computer-assisted instruction, are widely used by law students.

George Mason School of Law has been home to the Law & Economics Center since 1986. The Law & Economics Center is best known for its teaching institutes in economics for federal judges and law professors from all over the nation. In 2001 the LEC offers six one-week programs and two two-day programs on subjects ranging from law and economics, evolutionary biology and political philosophy. It will also sponsor an academic conference on the rule of law. Law & Economics Center programs foster understanding among judges and professors of the application of economic analysis to legal issues.

George Mason provides many services to enhance students' law school experiences. The Career Development and Alumni Services Office, for example, offers individual counseling, career planning, and job placement sessions and maintains a resource file on firms, corporations, government agencies, courts, and graduate programs. The law school is an active member of the National Association for Law Placement. At least 30 student organizations provide students with the opportunity to become involved in activities of special interest.

In November 1999, Governor Gilmore officially dedicated the National Center for Technology & Law - The Tech Center - at a ceremony held in the law school's atrium. The Tech Center is an in-house think tank that examines the relationship of existing legal framework to the rapidly evolving information-based economy. A solution-oriented organization, The Tech Center works with business and government leaders to remove legal barriers to innovation, streamline the regulatory process, and ensure that the law evolves to keep pace with changes in technology.

The Tech Center is a forum in which federal legislators and regulators from Washington, D.C., can meet with high technology business leaders from Northern Virginia to debate the application of laws to specific technology issues and to develop policy proposals aimed to encouraging technological progress and economic growth. The Tech Center uses its location - only three and one-half miles from Reagan Washington National Airport -- to attract business leaders from around the world to participate in its programs along with government officials and scholars. The Tech Center's programs include the Global Internet Summit, a distinguished speaker series, conferences on current issues in information technology and biotechnology policy, and the sponsorship of academic research.

Dean: Mark F. Grady
Associate Dean for Academic Affairs: Daniel Polsby
Associate Dean for Student Academic Affairs: Winston S. Moore
Assoc. Dean, Research & Technology & Dir. of the Law Library: Deborah Keene
Director of Admissions and Assistant Dean: Anne Richard
Dir. of Career Development & Alumni Services & Assist. Dean: Victoria Huber
Director of Academic Records and Registrar: Patricia Hupalo
Director, Law & Economics Center & Professor of Law: F.H. Buckley
Chairman, National Center for Technology & Law: Bradford C. Brown

---

FULL TIME FACULTY

MARK F. GRADY*, (Dean)**, born Minneapolis, Minnesota, August 16, 1948; admitted to bar, 1975, Pennsylvania. *Education:* University of California, Los Angeles (A.B., 1970; J.D., 1973). ***COURSES: Torts.

MICHAEL ABRAMOWICZ*, (Assistant Professor of Law)**, admitted to bar, 1998, Texas. *Education:* Amherst College (B.A., 1994); Yale Law School (J.D., 1998). ***COURSES: Administrative Law, Civil Procedure.

ROBERT A. ANTHONY*, (George Mason University Foundation Professor of Law)**, born Washington, D.C., December 28, 1931; admitted to bar, 1957, California; 1971, New York; 1972, District of Columbia. *Education:* Yale University (B.A., 1953); Oxford University (B.A., Juris, 1955); Stanford Law School (J.D., 1957). ***COURSES: Administrative Law, Federal Courts.

PETER BERKOWITZ*, (Associate Professor of Law)**, born Chicago, Illinois, August 5, 1959. *Education:* Swarthmore College (B.A., 1981); Hebrew University of Jerusalem (M.A., 1985); Yale University (Ph.D., 1987); Yale Law School (J.D., 1990). ***COURSES: Advanced Constitutional Law, Legal & Economic Concepts, Moral & Political Foundations of Law.

DAVID E. BERNSTEIN*, (Associate Professor of Law)**, born New York, New York, July 4, 1967; admitted to bar, 1992, Pennsylvania and District of Columbia. *Education:* Brandeis University (B.A., 1988); Yale Law School (J.D., 1991). ***COURSES: Products Liability, Torts, Advanced Evidence.

***KAROL BOUDREAUX*, (Assistant Dean and Director Juris Master Program)**, born Pueblo, Colorado, October 7, 1960. *Education:*

(This Listing Continued)

GEORGE MASON UNIVERSITY SCHOOL OF LAW —Continued

Butler's University/Douglas College (B.A., 1983); University of Virginia (J.D., 1992). ***COURSES:*** International Trade, Environmental Law, International Law.

***BRADFORD C. BROWN*, (Chairman of the National Center for Technology & Law)**, born Waterbury, Connecticut, February 17, 1958; admitted to bar, Illinois. *Education:* Providence College (B.A., 1980); Harvard University (M.A., 1982); Catholic University (J.D., 1986).

F.H. BUCKLEY*, (Professor of Law)**, born Canada, 1948; admitted to bar, 1982, Ontario. *Education:* McGill University (B.A., 1969; LL.B., 1974); Harvard University (M.A., 1975). ***COURSES: Bankruptcy, Corporate Law, Jurisprudence.

JAMES E. BYRNE*, (Associate Professor of Law)**, born Detroit, Michigan, December 6, 1945; admitted to bar, 1977, Florida; 1983, Maryland. *Education:* University of Notre Dame (B.A., 1968); Stetson University (J.D., 1977); University of Pennsylvania (LL.M., 1978). ***COURSES: Commercial Paper, Electronic Commerce, Contracts.

TERRENCE CHORVAT*, (Assistant Professor of Law)**, born Chicago, Illinois, November 20, 1964. *Education:* Northwestern University (B.A., 1986); University of Chicago, School of Law (J.D., 1989); New York University (LL.M., 1992). ***COURSES: Income Tax, International Tax, Partnership Tax.

LLOYD R. COHEN*, (Professor of Law)**, born New York, New York, February 12, 1947; admitted to bar, 1983, Georgia. *Education:* Harvard University (B.A., 1968); State University of New York at Binghamton (M.A., 1973; Ph.D., 1976); Emory University (J.D., 1983). ***COURSES: Quantitative Methods for Lawyers, Trusts & Estates, International Economics.

JOHN L. COSTELLO*, (Professor of Law)**, born Carlisle, Pennsylvania, June 13, 1930; admitted to bar, 1956, Pennsylvania; 1978, Virginia. *Education:* Dickinson College (A.B., 1952); Dickinson School of Law (J.D., 1955); Fletcher School of Law and Diplomacy (M.A., 1964); University of Virginia (LL.M., 1975). ***COURSES: Professional Responsibility, Practice, Criminal Law.

JOANMARIE I. DAVOLI*, (Clinical Professor of Law & Director of Law & Mental Illness Clinic)**, born Fairfax, Virginia, June 12, 1963; admitted to bar, 1989, South Carolina, District of Columbia; 1993, Virginia. *Education:* University of Virginia (B.A., 1985); Georgetown University (J.D., 1988). ***COURSES: Trial Advocacy, Mental Illness Clinic.

ERNEST WILLIAM DUBESTER*, (Professor and Chairman Dispute Resolution Program)**, born Passaic, New Jersey, September 4, 1950; admitted to bar, 1976, New Jersey, Florida; 1980, District of Columbia. *Education:* Boston College (A.B., 1972); Columbus School of Law Catholic University (J.D., 1978); Georgetown University Law Center (L.L.M.:,1980). ***COURSES: Alternative Dispute Resolution, Mediation Negotiation Arbitration.

STEVEN J. EAGLE*, (Professor of Law)**, born New York, N.Y., February 20, 1945; admitted to bar, 1976, Ohio. *Education:* City College of the City University of New York (B.B.A., 1965); Yale Law School (LL.B., 1970). ***COURSES: Property, Constitutional Law, Land Use Planning.

RONALD M. ETTERS*, (Visiting Clinical Professor of Law)**, born San Antonio, Texas, November 6, 1948; admitted to bar, 1976, Virginia; 1980, District of Columbia. *Education:* American University (B.A., 1971; J.D., 1976). ***COURSES: Alternative Dispute Resolution.

ERNEST GELLHORN*, (George Mason University Foundation Professor of Law)**, born Oak Park, Illinois, March 30, 1935; admitted to bar, 1962, Ohio; 1975, Virginia; 1976, Arizona; 1986, District of Columbia; 1990, California. *Education:* University of Minnesota (B.A., 1956; LL.B., 1962). ***COURSES: Antitrust, Advanced Administrative Law.

NORMAN C. GILLESPIE*, (Visiting Associate Professor of Law)**, born Philadelphia, Pennsylvania, January 23, 1943; admitted to bar, 1991, New York. *Education:* Bates College (B.A., 1964); University of Wisconsin (Ph.D., 1970); Stanford Law School (J.D., 1990). ***COURSES: Professional Responsibility, Insurance Law.

MICHAEL S. GREEN*, (Assistant Professor of Law)**, born Berkeley, California, November 12, 1960. *Education:* University of California, Berkeley (B.A., 1982); Yale University (Ph.D., 1990); Yale Law School (J.D., 1996). ***COURSES: Civil Procedure, Jurisprudence.

JOHN HASNAS*, (Associate Professor of Law)**, born New York, New York, January 1, 1953; admitted to bar, 1978, North Carolina. *Education:* Lafayette College (B.A., 1974); Duke University (J.D., 1978; Ph.D., 1988); Temple University (LL.M., 1992). ***COURSES: Torts, White Collar Crime, Bioethics.

***VICTORIA M. HUBER*, (Assistant Dean and Director of Career and Alumni Services)**, born Baltimore, Maryland, October 17, 1967; admitted to bar, 1993, Maryland; 1994, Washington, D.C.. *Education:* Dartmouth College (B.A., 1990); University of Virginia (J.D., 1992).

RICHARD IPPOLITO*, (Professor of Law)**, born Fitchburg, Massachusetts, October 25, 1948. *Education:* Lowell Technological Institute (B.S., 1970); University of Chicago (Ph.D., 1974). ***COURSES: Legal & Economic Concepts, Statistics.

D. BRUCE JOHNSEN*, (Professor of Law)**, born Oakland, California, November 3, 1954. *Education:* University of Washington (B.A., Economics, 1977; M.S., Economics, 1980; Ph.D., Economics, 1987); Emory University (J.D., 1985). ***COURSES: Securities Regulation, Business Associations, Law of Investment Management.

PAUL D. KAMENAR*, (Clinical Professor of Law)**, born Ohio, April 5, 1948; admitted to bar, 1975, District of Columbia. *Education:* Rutgers College (B.A., 1970); Georgetown University (J.D., 1975). ***COURSES: Appellate Advocacy, Public Interest Clinic.

***DEBORAH M. KEENE*, (Associate Dean & Director of Law Library)**, born Nashville, Tennessee, September 29, 1952. *Education:* Vanderbilt University (B.A., 1974; M.L.S., 1975); University of Tennessee (J.D., 1980).

BRUCE H. KOBAYASHI*, (Professor of Law)**, born Los Angeles, California, May 24, 1959. *Education:* University of California at Los Angeles (B.S., 1981; M.A., 1982; Ph.D., 1986). ***COURSES: Intellectual Property, Law & Economics, Evidence.

MICHAEL I. KRAUSS*, (Professor of Law)**, born New York, New York, April 21, 1951; admitted to bar, 1978, Quebec; 1991, Virginia. *Education:* Carleton University (B.A., cum laude, 1973); Sherbrooke University (LL.L., 1976); Yale Law School (LL.M., 1977); Columbia University. ***COURSES: Torts, Products Liability, Jurisprudence, Legal Ethics.

WILLIAM H. LASH, III*, (Professor of Law)**, born Jersey City, New Jersey, January 21, 1961; admitted to bar, 1986, New Jersey; 1988, District of Columbia. *Education:* Yale University (B.A., 1982); Harvard University (J.D., 1985). ***COURSES: International Business and Trade, Business Associations, Securities Regulation, Corporate Finance.

LEANDRA LEDERMAN*, (Associate Professor)**, born New York, New York, June 1, 1966; admitted to bar, 1991, New York; 1993, U.S. Tax Court. *Education:* Bryn Mawr College (A.B., 1987); New York University (J.D., 1990; LL.M., 1993). ***COURSES: Income Tax, Corporate Tax, Tax Procedure.

(This Listing Continued)

GEORGE MASON UNIVERSITY SCHOOL OF LAW —Continued

CRAIG S. LERNER*, (Assistant Professor of Law)**, born New York, New York, March 29, 1966; admitted to bar, 1995, Massachusetts; 1996, New York; 1997, District of Columbia. *Education:* Harvard University (A.B., 1987; J.D., 1994); University of Chicago (M.A., 1990). ***COURSES: Criminal Procedure, Conflicts of Law.

WESLEY J. LIEBELER*, (Professor of Law)**, born 1931; admitted to bar, 1958, New York. *Education:* Macalester College (B.A., 1953); University of Chicago (J.D., 1957). ***COURSES: Antitrust.

NELSON LUND*, (Professor of Law and Co-Editor, Supreme Court Economic Review)**, born Chicago, Illinois, September 2, 1951; admitted to bar, 1986, Texas. *Education:* St. John's College (B.A., 1974); Catholic University of America (M.A., 1978); Harvard University (Ph.D., 1981); University of Chicago (J.D., 1985). ***COURSES: Legislation, Constitutional Law, Second Amendment.

KIMBERLY A. MOORE*, (Associate Professor of Law)**, born Baltimore, Maryland, June 15, 1968; admitted to bar, 1995, Maryland; 1996, District of Columbia. *Education:* Massachusetts Institute of Technology (B.S.E.E., 1990; M.S., 1991); Georgetown University (J.D., 1994). ***COURSES: Intellectual Property, Patents.

***WINSTON S. MOORE*, (Associate Dean)**, born Durham, North Carolina, February 13, 1942; admitted to bar, 1970, District of Columbia. *Education:* Davidson College (A.B., 1964); University of Michigan (J.D., 1970).

TIMOTHY J. MURIS*, (George Mason University Foundation Professor of Law)**, born Massillion, Ohio, November 18, 1949; admitted to bar, 1974, California; 1983, U.S. Supreme Court. *Education:* San Diego State University (B.A., 1971); University of California at Los Angeles (J.D., 1974). ***COURSES: International Trade, Antitrust, Administrative and Regulatory Law, Contracts.

MICHAEL O'NEILL*, (Assistant Professor of Law)**, born Baldwin, Wisconsin, March 5, 1962; admitted to bar, District of Columbia, Wisconsin. *Education:* Brigham Young University (B.A., 1987); Yale Law School (J.D., 1990). ***COURSES: Criminal Law, Criminal Procedure.

FRANCESCO PARISI*, (Professor of Law)**, born Rome, Italy, May 31, 1962; admitted to bar, 1985, Italy. *Education:* University of Rome (D.Jur., 1985); University of California at Berkeley, Boalt Hall School of Law (LL.M., 1988; J.S.D., 1990; M.A., Economics, 1995). ***COURSES: Comparative Law, International Law, European Common Law.

JEFFREY S. PARKER*, (Professor of Law)**, born Alexandria, Virginia, September 6, 1952; admitted to bar, 1979, New York. *Education:* Georgia Institute of Technology (B.I.E., 1975); University of Virginia (J.D., 1978). ***COURSES: Litigation Theory, Civil Procedure, Evidence, Criminal Law.

***STEPHEN T. PARR*, (Assistant Dean)**, born Atlanta, Georgia, October 11, 1968. *Education:* Georgia Institute of Technology (B.S., 1990; M.S., 1992); Princeton University (M.A. Economics, 1994); Yale Law School (J.D., 1999).

DANIEL D. POLSBY*, (Professor of Law and Associate Dean)**, born Norwich, Connecticut, March 14, 1945; admitted to bar, 1971, Minnesota; 1972, District of Columbia; 1976, Illinois; 1981, New York. *Education:* Oakland University (B.A., 1964); University of Minnesota (J.D., 1971). ***COURSES: Criminal Law.

ALISON HUBER PRICE*, (Director Legal Writting Program)**, born Baltimore, Maryland, July 26, 1964; admitted to bar, 1989, Georgia. *Education:* Dickinson College (B.A., 1986); University of Georgia (J.D., 1989). ***COURSES: Legal Research, Writing and Analysis.

LARRY E. RIBSTEIN*, (George Mason University Foundation Professor of Law)**, born Chicago, Illinois, April 23, 1946; admitted to bar, 1972, Illinois. *Education:* Johns Hopkins University (B.A., 1968); University of Chicago (J.D., 1972). ***COURSES: Corporation, Partnership, Conflict of Laws.

ANNE MARIE RICHARD*, (Assistant Dean and Director of Admissions)**, born Gardner, Massachusetts, January 31, 1959; admitted to bar, 1984, Virginia; 1985, District of Columbia; 1993, Florida. *Education:* Boston College (A.B. and M.A., 1981); Yale Law School (J.D., 1984). ***Email: arichar5@gmu.edu

CHARLES S. ROBB*, (Distinguished Visiting Professor of Law and Public Policy)**, born 1939; admitted to bar, 1973, Virginia; 1973, District of Columbia. *Education:* University of Virginia (J.D., 1973). ***COURSES: National Security, State-Federal Relations, Anti-Discrimination Policy, Fiscal Policy.

DAVID A. SCHUM*, (Professor of Law & Professor of Information Technology & Engineering)**, born Chicago, Illinois, February 20, 1932. *Education:* Southern Methodist University (B.A., 1956; M.A., 1960); Ohio State University (Ph.D., 1964). ***COURSES: Evidence.

LINDA A. SCHWARTZSTEIN*, (Vice Provost for Academic Affairs and Professor of Law)**, born Orange, New Jersey, June 27, 1952; admitted to bar, 1976, New Jersey; 1977, New York and District of Columbia; 1981, Maryland. *Education:* Brandeis University (A.B., 1973); University of Michigan (J.D., 1976); New York University School of Law (LL.M., Taxation, 1977); George Mason University (M.A., Economics, 1992; Ph.D., 1994). ***COURSES: Income Tax, Corporate Tax, Tax Policy, International Taxation, Business Associations.

LOREN SMITH*, (Distinguished Visiting Professor)**, born 1944; admitted to bar, Illinois. *Education:* Northwestern University (B.A., 1966; J.D., 1969). ***COURSES: Federal Election Law, Government Contracts, Appellate Practice.

KENNETH W. STARR*, (Distinguished Visiting Professor of Law)**, born Vernon, Texas, July 21, 1946; admitted to bar, 1973, California; 1979, Virginia and District of Columbia. *Education:* George Washington University (A.B., 1968); Brown University (A.M., 1969); Duke Law School (J.D., 1973). ***COURSES: Constitutional Law Seminar.

PAUL F. STAVIS*, (Associate Clinical Professor of Law & Director of Law & Psychiatry Center)**, born Ossining, New York, May 19, 1947; admitted to bar, 1973, New York. *Education:* Syracuse University (B.A., 1969); State University of New York at Buffalo (J.D., 1972). ***COURSES: Mental Illness and Law.

MAXWELL L. STEARNS*, (Professor of Law)**, born Bangor, Maine, December 2, 1960; admitted to bar, 1987, Massachusetts; 1991, Pennsylvania. *Education:* University of Pennsylvania (B.A., 1983); University of Virginia (J.D., 1987). ***COURSES: Constitutional Law, Public Choice and Public Law, First Amendment, Contracts.

***ALISON TANNER*, (Assistant Dean)**, born Chicago, Illinois, October 10, 1966; admitted to bar, 1993, Illinois; 1994, District of Columbia. *Education:* University of Illinois (B.S., 1988); University of Chicago (M.B.A., 1993; J.D., 1993).

ALBERT G. TRAMPOSCH*, (Co-Director, Intellectual Property Program)**, born New York City, New York, February 5, 1955; admitted to bar, 1986, Washington; 1989, District of Columbia. *Education:* Johns Hopkins University (A.B., 1976); University of Washington (J.D. ,1986). ***COURSES: Intellectual Property.

***GORDON TULLOCK*, (Professor of Law)**, born Rockford, Illinois,

(This Listing Continued)

GEORGE MASON UNIVERSITY SCHOOL OF LAW —Continued

February 13, 1922. *Education:* Yale University (Chinese, 1951); Cornell University (Chinese, 1952); University of Chicago (J.D., 1947). ***COURSES:*** Public Choice, Law & Economics.

DEBORAH WEISS*, (Associate Professor of Law)**, born New York, New York, September 2, 1958; admitted to bar, 1966, District of Columbia. *Education:* Yale University (B.A., 1980); Columbia University (J.D., 1983); Harvard University (M.A., 1988). ***COURSES: Corporate Finance.

***JACK WERTZBERGER*, (Assistant Dean and Director of Development)**, born Debuque, Iowa, June 12, 1953; admitted to bar, 1984, Iowa. *Education:* University of Notre Dame (A.B., 1976); University of Iowa (J.D., 1984).

TODD ZYWICKI*, (Associate Professor of Law)**, born 1966; admitted to bar, 1994, Georgia. *Education:* Clemson University (M.A., 1990); University of Virginia (J.D., 1993). ***COURSES: Contracts, Creditors' & Debtors' Rights, Law & Economics.

THE GEORGE WASHINGTON UNIVERSITY LAW SCHOOL

2000 H STREET, N.W.
WASHINGTON, D.C. 20052
Telephone: (202) 994-6288
Fax: (202) 994-5157
www.law.gwu.edu

ABA Approved Since 1923

The George Washington University Law School is the oldest law school in the District of Columbia. It was founded in 1865 and has grown to become one of the largest schools in the country. Its total student population numbers approximately 1,700. This figure includes over 1,200 full-time Juris Doctor (J.D.) students, 200 part-time J.D. students and over 200 graduate law students.

The Law School is one of the eight academic units of The George Washington University, which was originally established by charter of Congress in 1821 as The Columbian College. The University also includes the Columbian School of Arts and Sciences, the School of Medicine and Health Sciences, the School of Engineering and Applied Science, the Graduate School of Education and Human Development, the School of Business and Public Management, the Elliott School of International Affairs and the School of Public Health and Health Services.

Situated on the GW campus in downtown Washington, D.C., the Law School is ideally located in the heart of the nation's capital. It is four blocks from the White House and only minutes away from the Capitol, the Supreme Court and most federal departments and agencies. This location offers students of the Law School a special opportunity to study and observe first-hand the institutions of government at work.

The purpose of the Law School is to prepare men and women to meet the needs of society in many fields of law and to encourage scholarly research and writing in law. As a national school, the Law School does not emphasize any particular geographic area in its instruction; therefore, it prepares students to practice law in any part of the country. The Law School seeks to fulfill these objectives through a rich and varied curriculum taught by eminent professors and highly qualified specialized instructors; an extensive clinical law program in which students learn legal skills by actual practice; five law journals that specialize in public law, international law, environmental law, government contracts law, and intellectual property law; trial practice; participation in moot court competitions; a series of student professional co-curricular activities; studies on an advanced level for foreign as well as for U.S. students; a continuing legal education program for members of the bar, providing them with opportunities for course work within the curriculum; and scholarly research and writing in the law.

The faculty of the Law School is one of its greatest strengths. Many faculty members have written leading textbooks in their fields, in areas as diverse as civil procedure, admiralty, professional ethics, taxation, evidence, consumer law and international human rights. In addition to scholarly work, many faculty are involved in developing public policy for government agencies and Congress. Classroom teaching is very much valued by the faculty and student evaluations indicate high regard for the caliber of teaching provided by both full and part-time faculty.

The Law School is fully accredited by the American Bar Association and is a charter member of the Association of American Law Schools.

Dean: Michael Kent Young (202) 994-6288
Associate Dean of Admissions: Robert Stanek (202) 739-0648
Associate Dean of Financial Aid: Robert Stanek (202) 739-0641
Library: Scott Pagel (202) 994-7337
Placement: Fred Thrasher (202) 994-7340
Alumni Affairs: Marsha Shinkman (202) 496-2232

FULL TIME FACULTY

MICHAEL K. YOUNG*, (Dean and Professor of Law)**, born 1949; admitted to bar, 1976, California; 1985, New York. *Education:* Brigham Young University (B.A., 1973); Harvard University (J.D., 1976). ***COURSES: Japanese Law, International Trade Law, International Commercial Transactions, International Environmental Law.

MARTIN J. ADELMAN*, (Professor of Law; Director of the Intellectual Property Law Program)**, born 1937; admitted to bar, 1963, Michigan. *Education:* University of Michigan (B.A., 1958; M.S., 1959; J.D., 1962). ***COURSES: Patent Law, International and Comparative Patent Law, Intellectual Property Law.

JOHN F. BANZHAF*, (Professor of Law)**, born 1940; admitted to bar, 1965, New York; 1966, District of Columbia. *Education:* Massachusetts Institute of Technology (B.S.E.E., 1962); Columbia University (J.D., 1965). ***COURSES: Administrative Law, Law and the Disabled, Legal Activism, Torts.

***JEROME A. BARRON*, (Harold Green Professor of Law)**, born 1933; admitted to bar, 1959, Massachusetts; 1960, District of Columbia. *Education:* Tufts University (A.B., 1955); Yale University (J.D., 1958);

(This Listing Continued)

THE GEORGE WASHINGTON UNIVERSITY LAW SCHOOL —Continued

The George Washington University (LL.M., 1960). ***COURSES:*** Administrative Law, Civil Procedure, Constitutional Law, Federal Courts, Broadcast and Cable Regulation.

ALBERTO M. BENITEZ*, (Associate Professor of Clinical Law)**, born June 4, 1960; admitted to bar, 1987, Illinois. *Education:* State University of New York at Buffalo (J.D., 1986). ***COURSES: Immigration Clinic, Immigration Law. ***Email:*** abenitez@main.nlc.gwu.edu

RAJ K. BHALA*, (Associate Dean, Int'l and Compar. Legal Studies and Patricia Roberts Harris Research Professor of Law)**, born 1962; admitted to bar, 1990, New York, District of Columbia, Colorado; 1991, Minnesota. *Education:* Duke University (B.A., 1984); London School of Economics (M.Sc., 1985); Oxford University (M.Sc., 1986); Harvard University (J.D., 1989). ***COURSES: International Trade Law, International Business Transactions.

CHERYL D. BLOCK*, (Professor of Law)**, born 1955; admitted to bar, 1980, New York. *Education:* Hofstra University (B.A., 1976); University of Buffalo (J.D., 1979). ***COURSES: Corporations, Legislation, Partnership Law and Taxation, Taxation, Federal.

WILLIAM W. BRATTON*, (Professor of Law; Samuel Tayler Research Professor of Law)**, born 1951; admitted to bar, 1977, New York. *Education:* Columbia University (B.A., 1973; J.D., 1976). ***COURSES: Contracts, Corporations.

ROBERT BRAUNEIS*, (Associate Professor of Law)**, admitted to bar, 1989, Illinois. *Education:* University of California (B.A., 1982); Harvard Law School (J.D., 1989). ***COURSES: Property Law, Real Estate Transactions, Land Use Regulation, Local Government Law.

MARY CLARK BRITTINGHAM*, (Associate Professor of Clinical Law; Director Outside Placement Program)**, born July 15, 1952; admitted to bar, 1982, District of Columbia. *Education:* Bard College (B.A., 1974); Antioch School of Law (J.D., 1980). ***COURSES: Clinical Externship. ***Email:*** mbritt@clinic.gwu.edu

KAREN B. BROWN*, (Professor of Law; Donald Phillip Rothschild Research Professor of Law)**, born September 19, 1954; admitted to bar, 1980, New York; 1984, District of Columbia. *Education:* Princeton University (A.B., 1976); NY University School of Law (J.D., 1979); NY University School of Law (LL.M. 1987). ***COURSES: Tax, Corporate Tax, International Tax, Business Planning. ***Email:*** kbrown@main.nlc.gwu.edu

PAUL D. BUTLER*, (Professor of Law)**, admitted to bar, 1987, New York; 1989, District of Columbia. *Education:* Yale University (B.A., 1982); Harvard Law School (J.D., 1986). ***COURSES: Criminal Law, Criminal Procedure.

NAOMI CAHN*, (Professor of Law)**, born 1957; admitted to bar, 1984, New York; 1985, District of Columbia. *Education:* Princeton University (B.A., 1979); Columbia University (J.D., 1983); Georgetown University Law Center (LL.M., 1989). ***COURSES: Employer Discrimination, Domestic Violence, Family Law, International Women's Rights, Housing, Trusts & Estates.

W. BURLETTE CARTER*, (Professor of Law)**, born 1961; admitted to bar, 1986, New York; 1990, District of Columbia. *Education:* Agnes Scott College (B.A., 1982); Harvard Law School (J.D., 1985). ***COURSES: Civil Procedure, Evidence, Sports Law.

MARY CHEH*, (Professor of Law; Elyce Zenoff Research Professor of Law)**, born 1950; admitted to bar, 1975, New Jersey; 1977, District of Columbia and Massachusetts. *Education:* Rutgers University (B.A., 1972; J.D., 1975); Harvard Law School (LL.M., 1977). ***COURSES: Constitutional Law, Corporations, Civil Procedure, Creditors Rights, Jurisprudence, Criminal Procedure.

BRADFORD CLARK*, (Professor of Law)**, born 1963; admitted to bar, 1988, Pennsylvania; 1990, District of Columbia. *Education:* Florida State University (B.A., 1981); Columbia University (J.D., 1985). ***COURSES: Civil Procedure, Constitutional Law, Federal Courts.

ROBERT JAMES COTTROL*, (Professor of Law and History; Harold Paul Green Research Professor of Law)**, born 1949; admitted to bar, 1984, Pennsylvania; 1985, District of Columbia. *Education:* Yale University (A.B., 1971; Ph.D., 1978); Georgetown University Law Center (J.D., 1984). ***COURSES: Civil Rights, Constitutional Law, Criminal Law, Legal History, Law and Social Economic History.

CHARLES B. CRAVER*, (Professor of Law; Leroy Sorenson Merrifield Research Professor of Law)**, born 1944; admitted to bar, 1973, California. *Education:* Cornell University (B.S., 1967; M.I.L.R., 1968); University of Michigan (J.D., 1971). ***COURSES: Comparative Industrial Relations, Criminal Law, Employment Discrimination, Labor Arbitration and Collective Bargaining, Labor Law, Legal Negotiating, Public Sector Labor Relations.

LYNN E. CUNNINGHAM*, (Professor of Clinical Law)**, born June 28, 1944; admitted to bar, 1973, New York; 1975, District of Columbia. *Education:* Cornell University (A.B., 1966); Union Theological Seminary (B.D., 1969); Columbia University (J.D., 1972). ***COURSES: Administrative Advocacy Clinic, Housing Rights Law. ***Email:*** lynn@clinic.lc.gwu.edu

LISA DE SANCTIS*, (Associate Professor of Clinical Law)**, born 1971; admitted to bar, 1996, California. *Education:* University of California, Berkeley (B.A., 1993; J.D., 1996). ***COURSES: Domestic Violence Clinic.

RENEE DEVIGNE*, (Associate Dean for Student Affairs and Professorial Lecturer in Law)**, born 1957; admitted to bar, 1984, Maryland. *Education:* Georgetown University (B.S.F.S., 1979; J.D., 1982). ***COURSES: Government Lawyering Seminar.

C. THOMAS DIENES*, (Lyle T. Alverson Professor of Law)**, born 1940; admitted to bar, 1964, Illinois; 1989, District of Columbia. *Education:* Loyola University (B.S., 1961); Northwestern University (J.D., 1964; Ph.D., 1968);. ***COURSES: Civil Rights, Constitutional Law, Torts, Print Media Law.

JACK H. FRIEDENTHAL*, (Freda H. Alverson Professor of Law)**, born 1931; admitted to bar, 1959, California; 1990, District of Columbia. *Education:* Stanford University (A.B., 1953); Harvard University (J.D., 1958). ***COURSES: Civil Procedure, Conflict of Laws, Evidence, Law and Poverty.

THERESA A. GABALDON*, (Professor of Law; Carville Dickinson Benson Research Professor of Law)**, born 1954; admitted to bar, 1978, Arizona; 1990, District of Columbia. *Education:* University of Arizona (B.S., 1975); Harvard University (J.D., 1978). ***COURSES: Contracts, Corporations, Securities Regulation, Professional Responsibility.

MIRIAM GALSTON*, (Associate Professor of Law)**, born 1946; admitted to bar, 1982, District of Columbia. *Education:* Cornell University (B.A., 1967); University of Chicago (Ph.D., 1973); Yale University (J.D., 1982). ***COURSES: Bankruptcy, Corporations and Jurisprudence.

JEFFREY S. GUTMAN*, (Assistant Dean for Academic Affairs and Professor of Clinical Law)**, admitted to bar, 1986, District of Columbia. *Education:* Stanford University (B.A., 1983); Harvard University (J.D., 1986). ***COURSES: Administrative Advocacy Clinic, Civil Procedure.

(This Listing Continued)

THE GEORGE WASHINGTON UNIVERSITY LAW SCHOOL —Continued

MATTHEW P. HARRINGTON*, (Assistant Dean for Administration)**, born 1959; admitted to bar, 1990, Pennsylvania. *Education:* McGill University (B.TH., 1987); Boston University (J.D., 1990); Unviversity of Pennsylvania (S.J.D., 2000). ***COURSES: Commercial Law, Corporations, Legal History.

LAURENT R. HOURCLE*, (Professor of Environmental Law; Co-Director of the Environmental Law Program)**, born 1946; admitted to bar, 1971, North Carolina. *Education:* Boston University (B.S., 1968); Central Michigan University (M.A., 1980); Duke University (J.D., 1971); The George Washington University (LL.M., 1982). ***COURSES: Environmental Law.

SHI-LING HSU*, (Associate Professor of Law)**, born 1961; admitted to bar, 1987, California. *Education:* Columbia University (B.S., 1983; J.D., 1987); University of California, Davis (M.S., 1994, Ph.D., 1998). ***COURSES: Environmental Law, Law and Economics.

CAROL L. IZUMI*, (Professor of Clinical Law, Assistant Dean for Clinical Affairs)**, born 1954; admitted to bar, 1980, District of Columbia; 1982, Virginia. *Education:* Oberlin College (B.A., 1976); Georgetown University (J.D., 1980). ***COURSES: Consumer Mediation Clinic, Mediation.

DAVID MARIO JOHNSON*, (Assistant Dean for Student Affairs)**, born April 13, 1964; admitted to bar, 1990, Ohio; 1991, District of Columbia; 1996, Supreme Court of the United States. *Education:* Georgetown University (B.A., 1986 and J.D., 1990). ***COURSES: Legal Rhetoric, Uniform Commercial Code, Debtor-Creditor. ***Email:*** djohnson@main.nlc.gwu.edu

GERALD P. JOHNSTON*, (Professor of Law)**, born 1937; admitted to bar, 1963, California; 1964, District of Columbia. *Education:* Wesleyan University (B.A., 1959); Duke University (LL.B., 1962). ***COURSES: Estate Planning, Professional Responsibility, Trusts and Estates, Real Property Taxation, Federal.

SUSAN R. JONES*, (Professor of Clinical Law)**, born 1957; admitted to bar, 1984, District of Columbia. *Education:* Brandeis University (B.A., 1978); Antioch College (M.A., 1985); Antioch School of Law (J.D., 1980). ***COURSES: Small Business Clinic, Business Planning.

SUSAN LOUISE KARAMANIAN*, (Assistant Dean, International and Comparative)**, born 1958; admitted to bar, 1985, Texas. *Education:* Auburn University (B.S., 1979); Oxford University (B.A., 1982); University of Texas (J.D., 1985). ***COURSES: U.S. Law.

ORIN S. KERR*, (Associate Professor of Law)**, born 1971; admitted to bar, 1997, New Jersey. *Education:* Princeton University (B.S.E., 1993); Stanford University (M.S., 1994); Harvard University (J.D., 1997). ***COURSES: Criminal Law and Procedure, Internet Law, Intellectual Property.

WILLIAM E. KOVACIC*, (Professor of Law)**, born 1952; admitted to bar, 1979, New York. *Education:* Princeton University (A.B., 1974); Columbia University (J.D., 1978). ***COURSES: Contracts, Antitrust Law, Government Contracts.

CYNTHIA LEE*, (Professor of Law)**, admitted to bar, 1989, California. *Education:* Stanford University (B.A., 1983); Boalt Hall School of Law (J.D., 1989). ***COURSES: Criminal Law and Procedure.

FREDERICK J. LEES*, (Gubin Professor of Government Contract Law; Co-Director of the Government Procurement Law Program)**, born 1930; admitted to bar, 1962, Virginia. *Education:* University of Virginia (B.A., 1952); American University (J.D., 1961). ***COURSES: Government Contracts.

RENEE B. LETTOW LERNER*, (Associate Professor of Law)**, born 1968; admitted to bar, 1995, Virginia; 1997, District of Columbia. *Education:* Princeton University (A.B., 1990); Yale University (J.D., 1995). ***COURSES: Criminal Procedure, Conflict of Laws, Legal History Seminar. ***Email:*** rlettow@main.nlc.gwu.edu

IRA C. LUPU*, (Professor of Law; Louis Harkey Mayo Research Professor of Law)**, born 1946; admitted to bar, 1971, Massachusetts. *Education:* Cornell University (A.B., 1968); Harvard University (J.D., 1971). ***COURSES: Administrative Law, Constitutional Law, Religion and the Constitution.

JENNIFER P. LYMAN*, (Professor of Clinical Law)**, born 1950; admitted to bar, 1978, California; 1979, District of Columbia. *Education:* Yale University (A.B., 1972); Stanford University (J.D., 1978). ***COURSES: Appellate Advocacy Clinic (Field Work), Appellate Advocacy Clinic (Lawyering Process), Criminal Procedure, Evidence.

GREGORY E. MAGGS*, (Professor of Law)**, born 1964; admitted to bar, 1989, District of Columbia; 1989, New York; 1990, Massachusetts. *Education:* Harvard University (A.B., 1985; J.D., 1989). ***COURSES: Creditors and Debtors Rights, Contracts, Commercial Paper.

JOAN S. MEIER*, (Professor of Clinical Law)**, born 1957; admitted to bar, 1983, Illinois; 1986, District of Columbia. *Education:* Harvard University (A.B., 1980); University of Chicago (J.D., 1983). ***COURSES: Family Law, Domestic Violence Clinic.

PETER H. MEYERS*, (Professor of Clinical Law)**, born 1946; admitted to bar, 1971, District of Columbia. *Education:* Marietta College (B.A., 1968); George Washington University National Law Center (J.D., 1971). ***COURSES: Drugs and the Law, Vaccine Injury Clinic.

LAWRENCE E. MITCHELL*, (Professor of Law; John Theodore Fey Research Professor of Law)**, born 1956; admitted to bar, 1982, New York. *Education:* Williams College (B.A., 1978); Columbia University (J.D., 1981). ***COURSES: Administrative Law, Corporate Finance, Corporations, Jurisprudence, Securities Regulation.

JONATHAN T. MOLOT*, (Associate Professor of Oppenheim/Antitrust and Trade Regulation Law)**, admitted to bar, Massachusetts, New York, District of Columbia. *Education:* Yale University (B.S., 1988); Harvard University (J.D., 1992). ***COURSES: Civil Procedure, Federal Courts.

THOMAS D. MORGAN*, (Oppenheim Professor of Antitrust and Trade Regulation Law)**, born 1942; admitted to bar, 1965, Illinois. *Education:* Northwestern University (B.A., 1962); University of Chicago (J.D., 1965). ***COURSES: Antitrust, Professional Responsibility, Antitrust and Trade Regulation Law.

***THOMAS A. MORRISON*, (Associate Dean of the Law School for Administrative Affairs)**, born 1947; admitted to bar, 1977, Wisconsin. *Education:* Marquette University (B.A., 1969, J.D., 1977); The George Washington University (LL.M., 1984).

SEAN D. MURPHY*, (Associate Professor of Law)**, admitted to bar, Maryland. *Education:* Catholic University of America (B.A., 1982); Columbia University (J.D., 1985); Cambridge University (LL.M., 1987); University of Virginia (S.J.D., 1995). ***COURSES: International Law, International Business Transactions.

DAWN C. NUNZIATO*, (Associate Professor Law)**, born 1965; admitted to bar, 1994, Maryland; 1995, U.S. District Court, District of Maryland; 1996, District of Columbia. *Education:* University of Virginia (B.A., 1987; M.A., 1988; J.D., 1994). ***COURSES: Property, Law in Cyberspace.

***SCOTT B. PAGEL*, (Associate Dean for Information Services;**

(This Listing Continued)

THE GEORGE WASHINGTON UNIVERSITY LAW SCHOOL —Continued

Professor of Law; Director for the Law Library), born 1950. *Education:* Michigan State University (B.A., 1972); University of California, Berkeley (J.D., 1985); University of Michigan (M.A.L.S., 1988). ***COURSES:*** Legal Research, Legal Bibliography.

ROBERT E. PARK*, (Professor of Law)**, born 1952. *Education:* University of Florida (B.S. 1952; B.A., 1957; J.D., 1961); Yale University (LL.M., 1965). ***COURSES: Administrative Law, Constitutional Law, Jurisprudence, Privacy.

ROBERT J. PERONI*, (Professor of Law; Robert Kramer Research Professor of Law)**, born 1953; admitted to bar, 1976, Illinois; 1979, California. *Education:* DePaul University (B.S.C., 1973); Northwestern University (J.D., 1976); New York University (LL.M., 1980). ***COURSES: Corporations, International Taxations, Partnership and Corporate Taxation, Tax Policy, Taxation, Federal.

TODD PETERSON*, (Professor of Law)**, born 1951; admitted to bar, 1976, District of Columbia. *Education:* Brown University (B.A., 1973); University of Michigan (J.D., 1976). ***COURSES: Civil Procedure, Constitutional Law, Federal Courts.

RICHARD J. PIERCE, JR.*, (Lyle T. Alverson Professor of Law)**, born 1943; admitted to bar, 1972, District of Columbia. *Education:* Lehigh University (B.S., 1965); University of Virginia (J.D., 1972). ***COURSES: Evidence, Torts, Conflict of Laws, Regulated Industry, Antitrust.

PETER RAVEN-HANSEN*, (Professor of Law; Glen Earl Weston Research Professor of Law)**, born 1946; admitted to bar, 1974, Massachusetts; 1975, District of Columbia. *Education:* Harvard University (B.A., 1968; J.D., 1974). ***COURSES: Administrative Law, Civil Procedure, Federal Courts, Local Government, National Security Law.

ARNOLD W. REITZE*, (J.B. and Maurice C. Shapiro Professor of Environmental Law; Co-Director of the Environmental Law Prog.)**, born 1938; admitted to bar, 1962, New Jersey; 1969, Ohio; 1971, District of Columbia; 1980, Virginia. *Education:* Fairleigh Dickinson University (B.A., 1960); Rutgers University (J.D., 1962); John Hopkins College (M.P.H., 1985). ***COURSES: Environmental Law, Natural Resources, Water Rights, Air Pollution Control.

ALFREDA ROBINSON*, (Assoc. Dean, for Strat. Planning & Skills Training; Assoc. Dir., Litigation & Dispute Res. Prog.)**, admitted to bar, 1978, District of Columbia. *Education:* University of Chicago (B.A., 1973; M.A., 1976); The George Washington University (J.D., 1978). ***COURSES: Pre-Trial Advocacy.

DAVID ROBINSON, JR.*, (Professor of Law)**, born 1928; admitted to bar, 1956, Oregon; 1971, District of Columbia. *Education:* Reed College (B.A., 1950); Columbia University (J.D., 1956); Harvard University (LL.M., 1965). ***COURSES: Criminal Law, Criminal Procedure, Evidence.

JEFFREY ROSEN*, (Associate Professor of Law)**, born 1964; admitted to bar, 1992, Pennsylvania; 1992, District of Columbia. *Education:* Harvard (A.B., 1986); Yale University (J.D., 1991). ***COURSES: Constitutional Law, Criminal Procedure, Privacy. ***Email:*** jrosen@main.nlc.gwu.edu

CATHERINE J. ROSS*, (Associate Professor of Law)**, born 1949; admitted to bar, 1987, Connecticut; 1988, New York. *Education:* Yale (B.A., 1971; Ph.D., 1977; J.D., 1987). ***COURSES: Family Law, Evidence. ***Email:*** cross@main.nlc.gwu.edu

STEPHEN A. SALTZBURG*, (Howrey Prof. of Trial Advoc., Litigation and Prof. Responsibility; Dir., Litigation & Dispute Res. Prog.)**, born 1945; admitted to bar, 1971, California; 1972, District of Columbia; 1977, Virginia. *Education:* Dickinson College (B.A., 1967); University of Pennsylvania (J.D., 1977). ***COURSES: Civil Procedure, Constitutional Law, Corrections Law, Criminal Law, Criminal Procedure, Evidence, Trial Advocacy.

JOAN E. SCHAFFNER*, (Associate Professor of Law)**, born 1957; admitted to bar, 1990, California; 1992, District of Columbia. *Education:* University of Southern California (B.S.M.E., 1979; J.D., 1990); Massachusetts Institute of Technology (M.S.M.E., 1981). ***COURSES: Civil Procedure, Intellectual Property, Sexuality and the Law, Gender Discrimination.

ROGER E. SCHECHTER*, (Professor of Law; William Thomas Fryer Research Professor of Law)**, born 1953; admitted to bar, 1977, New York. *Education:* George Washington University (B.A., 1973); Harvard University (J.D., 1976). ***COURSES: Antitrust, Evidence, Intellectual Property, Torts, Trade Regulation.

STEVEN L. SCHOONER*, (Associate Professor of Law)**, admitted to bar, Virginia, District of Columbia. *Education:* Rice University (B.A., 1982); College of William and Mary (J.D., 1985); The George Washington University (LL.M., 1989). ***COURSES: Government Contract Law.

JOSHUA I. SCHWARTZ*, (Professor of Law; Co-Director of the Government Procurement Law Program)**, born 1951; admitted to bar, 1977, New York; 1978, District of Columbia. *Education:* Harvard University (B.A., 1973); Cornell Law School (J.D., 1976; M.P.R., 1977). ***COURSES: Administrative Law, Civil Procedure, Legislation, Real Property, Government Contracts Law.

MICHAEL SELMI*, (Professor of Law)**, born 1961; admitted to bar, 1987, California. *Education:* Stanford University (A.B., 1983); Harvard University (J.D., 1987). ***COURSES: Employment Law, Criminal Law, Constitutional Law.

JONATHAN R. SIEGEL*, (Professor of Law)**, born 1962; admitted to bar, 1990, Connecticut and New York; 1992, District of Columbia. *Education:* Harvard University (A.B., 1984); Yale University (J.D., 1989). ***COURSES: Legislation, Civil Procedure, Federal Courts and Federalism.

ERIC S. SIRULNIK*, (Professor of Law; Assoc. Dean for Clinical Affairs and Research Development)**, born 1944; admitted to bar, 1968, Massachusetts; 1972, District of Columbia. *Education:* Franklin & Marshall College (B.A., 1965); Boston University (J.D., 1968); The George Washington University, (LL.M., 1970). ***COURSES: Administration of Criminal Law, Clinical Studies in Urban Law, Clinical Teaching (Community Organizations), Criminal Law, Drugs and the Law, Torts, Trial Advocacy, Trial Practice Court.

PETER JEREMY SMITH*, (Associate Professor of Law)**, born 1970; admitted to bar, 1998, Massachusetts. *Education:* Yale University (B.A., 1992); Harvard Law School (J.D., 1997). ***COURSES: Administrative Law, Civil Procedure, Constitutional Law.

LOUIS B. SOHN*, (Distinguished Research Professor of Law)**, born 1914. *Education:* John Casimir University (Sc.M., 1935; LL.M., 1935); Harvard University (LL.M., 1940; S.J.D., 1958). ***COURSES: International Law, International Organizations, International Protection of Human Rights, Law of the Sea, United Nations Law.

LEWIS D. SOLOMON*, (Theodore Rinehart Professor of Business Law)**, born 1941; admitted to bar, 1969, New York. *Education:* Cornell University (B.A., 1963); Yale University (J.D., 1966). ***COURSES: Corporation Finance, Corporations, Estate Planning, Estates, Law and Social Science, Taxation, Federal.

***JOHN A. SPANOGLE*, (Professor of Law; William Wallace**

(This Listing Continued)

THE GEORGE WASHINGTON UNIVERSITY LAW SCHOOL —Continued

Kirkpatrick Research Professor of Law), born 1934; admitted to bar, 1960, Tennessee; 1961, California; 1970, District of Columbia; 1974, Maine. *Education:* Princeton University (B.S.E. in E.E., 1957); University of Chicago (J.D., 1960). ***COURSES:*** Antitrust, Banking Regulation, Commercial Law, Consumer Law, International Commercial Law, International Transactions, Payment Systems, E-Commerce.

***ROBERT V. STANEK*, (Associate Dean for Admissions and Financial Aid)**, born 1944; admitted to bar, 1979, District of Columbia. *Education:* Pennsylvania State University (B.A., 1966); The George Washington University (J.D., 1979).

JAMES E. STARRS*, (Professor of Law and of Forensic Sciences)**, born 1930; admitted to bar, 1958, New York; 1966, District of Columbia. *Education:* St. John's University (B.A., 1958; LL.B., 1958); New York University (LL.M., 1959). ***COURSES: Criminal Law, Criminal Procedure, Forensic Science and Criminal Law.

RALPH G. STEINHARDT*, (Professor of Law & International Affairs.; Arthur Selwyn Miller Research Professor of Law)**, born 1954; admitted to bar, 1980, District of Columbia. *Education:* Bowdoin College (B.A., 1976); Harvard University (J.D., 1980). ***COURSES: Aviation and Space Law, Conflict of Laws, International Civil Litigation, International Law, International Transactions, Jurisprudence.

JOAN H. STRAND*, (Professor of Clinical Law, Assistant Dean for Career Development and Alumni Affairs)**, born 1950; admitted to bar, 1976, District of Columbia. *Education:* George Washington University (B.A., 1972; J.D., 1975);. ***COURSES: Clinical Teaching, Trial Practice.

SONIA M. SUTER*, (Associate Professor of Law)**, born 1963. *Education:* Michigan State University (B.A., 1985); University of Michigan (M.S., 1987; J.D., 1994). ***COURSES: Torts, Genetics and the Law, Law and Medicine.

JOHN R. THOMAS*, (Associate Professor of Law)**, born 1967; admitted to bar, 1992, Maryland; 1997 United Patent and Trademark Office. *Education:* Carnegie Mellon University (B.S., 1989); University of Michigan University (J.D. 1992); George Washington University (LL.M., 1994). ***COURSES: Patent Law, Contracts. ***Email:*** jthomas@main.nlc.gwu.edu

ROGER H. TRANGSRUD*, (Prof. of Law; Oswald Symister Colclough Research Prof. of Law, Senior Assoc. Dean for Academic Affairs)**, born 1950; admitted to bar, 1975, Minnesota; 1977, District of Columbia. *Education:* Carleton College (B.A., 1972); University of Chicago (J.D., 1975). ***COURSES: Complex Litigation, Civil Procedure, Federal Courts, Remedies.

JONATHAN TURLEY*, (J.B. and Maurice C. Shapiro Professor of Public Interest Law)**, born 1961; admitted to bar, 1987, Illinois; 1988, District of Columbia. *Education:* University of Chicago (B.A., 1983); Northwestern University (J.D., 1987). ***COURSES: Clinical Teaching, Environmental Law, Legislation, Prisoner Project, Torts.

ROBERT W. TUTTLE*, (Associate Professor of Law)**, born 1963; admitted to bar, 1991, Virginia. *Education:* College of William and Mary (B.A., 1985); Lutheran School of Theology (M.A., 1989); George Washington University (J.D., 1991); University of Virginia (Ph.D., 1994). ***COURSES: Property, Professional Responsibility, Jurisprudence, Trusts & Estates.

LORRI SHEALY UNUMB*, (Associate Professor of Legal Research & Writing; Director of Legal Research & Writing Program)**, born Columbia, South Carolina, June 27, 1968; admitted to bar, 1993, South Carolina; 1995, District of Columbia. *Education:* University of South Carolina (B.A., 1990; J.D., 1993). ***COURSES: Legal Research & Writing, Appellate Practice.

ARTHUR E. WILMARTH, JR*, (Professor of Law)**, born 1951; admitted to bar, 1975, Florida; 1976, District of Columbia; 1992, Pennsylvania. *Education:* Yale University (B.A., 1972); Harvard University (J.D., 1975). ***COURSES: Banking Law, Contracts, Corporations. ***Email:*** awilmarth@main.nlc.gwu.edu

LUIZE E. ZUBROW*, (Professor of Law)**, born 1947; admitted to bar, 1972, Wisconsin; 1974, District of Columbia. *Education:* University of Colorado (B.A., 1969; J.D., 1972). ***COURSES: Commercial Law, Commercial Paper, Creditor's Rights.

GEORGETOWN UNIVERSITY LAW CENTER

600 NEW JERSEY AVENUE, N.W.
WASHINGTON, D.C. 20001

GEORGIA STATE UNIVERSITY COLLEGE OF LAW

UNIVERSITY PLAZA
ATLANTA, GEORGIA 30303

GOLDEN GATE UNIVERSITY SCHOOL OF LAW

536 MISSION STREET
SAN FRANCISCO, CALIFORNIA 94105
Telephone: (415) 442-6600
Fax: (415) 442-6609

ABA Approved Since 1956.

Since its inception in 1901, Golden Gate University School of Law has integrated the teaching of practical skills and traditional legal theory. Having both top academic credentials and extensive practice experience, the Law School's faculty brings to the classroom a practical dimension often lacking in legal education. Faculty members have influenced the development of the law in health care, real estate development, rent control and low-income housing, artists' rights, alternative dispute resolution, and international law. A distinguished adjunct faculty also brings special practical expertise to the Law School curriculum.

The Law School offers both full-time day and part-time evening programs. Students may begin in either the fall or spring. IPAC (Integrated Professional Apprenticeship Curriculum) is a special honors

(This Listing Continued)

GOLDEN GATE UNIVERSITY SCHOOL OF LAW —Continued

program in which students receive intensive skills training and spend two semesters working full-time in law offices or government agencies.

The Law School offers an extensive practice-oriented curriculum which emphasizes clinical training. The Law School houses three clinics as well as having an extensive outside placement program. In the Women's Employment Rights Clinic, students represent low-income women with employment-related problems. The Environmental Law and Justice Clinic focuses on student representation of environmental organizations and community groups in low-income and minority communities. The Constitutional Law Clinic, established in 1976 as part of the Western Center for Constitutional Rights, has developed a national reputation for innovative and successful work on cases.

Through Golden Gate's field placement clinics, students work closely with attorneys practicing in the areas of criminal prosecution and defense, family law, immigration law, real estate development, environmental regulation, landlord-tenant law, and public interest law. Golden Gate students also obtain judicial externships with the California Supreme Court, the federal district court, and California state appellate and superior courts.

The Law School's highly-regarded litigation program trains students in every aspect of litigation, from the pre-trial thinking and planning stages, to the techniques of a trial, to the appellate review of a case. Teams representing the Law School have recently won four regional championships in trial competitions and were semi-finalists in six others. Additionally, Golden Gate students have won honors at the regional level in appellate competitions. Besides learning courtroom tactics, Golden Gate students learn techniques of mediation and arbitration in Alternative Dispute Resolution, and the Lawyering Skills course teaches students the skills involved in counseling, interviewing and negotiation.

Because writing is the lawyer's basic tool, the Law School emphasizes the development of writing skills. Students take a writing course every year to master the skills needed to draft a wide array of legal documents. Top students may write for the three issues of the *Golden Gate University Law Review* published annually by the Law School. The Law School also publishes the *Annual Summary of International and Comparative Law.*

The Law School offers concentrations in International Law and Environmental Law. As part of the International Law program, students may attend an overseas summer program focusing on Pacific Rim issues in Bangkok, Thailand, in cooperation with Chulalongkorn University. Golden Gate participates in a student and faculty exchange program with the University of Paris at Nanterre. The Law School also offers an LL.M. and S.J.D. in International Legal Studies.

The Environmental Law program, in addition to offering such basic courses as Environmental Law, Natural Resources Protection, and Land Use Regulation, offers advanced seminars in Hazardous Waste Law and Policy, International Environmental Law and California Environmental Law. The Law School also offers an LL.M. in Environmental Law.

Golden Gate awards Specialization Certificates in the areas of International Law, Public Interest Law, Litigation, Real Estate, Business Law, Criminal Law, Labor and Employment Law, and Environmental Law. Each Specialization Certificate evidences completion of core courses and electives and significant clinical experience in the specialty area. The Law School also offers combined degrees with other graduate programs. Students may earn a combined J.D./M.B.A. degree in just 3 years.

The Law School also houses the Graduate Program in Taxation. Established in 1978, the Graduate Program is the major tax center on the West Coast. The program offers an LL.M. in Taxation. The program is offered both in San Francisco and Los Angeles.

The Law School offers an LL.M. in United States Legal Studies, serving law graduates and attorneys from the U.S. and abroad.

Approximately 3200 students apply each year for admission to a fall entering class of 170 and a spring entering class of 30. Applicants are chosen from over 100 undergraduate schools and come from all over the United States and from many foreign countries as well. Students have diverse backgrounds, from recent college graduates to working professionals.

Dean: Peter G. Keane (415) 442-6610
Associate Dean of Academic Affairs: David B. Oppenheimer (415) 442-6673
Associate Dean of Student Services: Susan Schechter (415) 442-6614
Associate Dean of Budget & Administration: Greg A. Egertson (415) 442-6616
Assistant Dean of Admissions: Cheryl Barnes (415) 442-6635
Financial Aid Director: Cheryl Barnes (415) 442-6635
Director, Law Library: Sarah Hooke Lee (415) 442-6685
Director of Career Services: Susanne Aronowitz (415) 442-6626
Marketing and Events Director: Lorri Ungaretti (415) 442-6636

FULL TIME FACULTY

PETER G. KEANE*, (Dean and Professor of Law)**, born Brooklyn, New York, February 8, 1943; admitted to bar, 1968, Texas; 1970, California. *Education:* City College of New York (B.A., 1965); Southern Methodist University Law School (J.D., 1968). ***COURSES: Evidence, Criminal Procedure, Professional Responsibility, Ethics.

M. MICHELE ANGLADE*, (Director, Academic Assistance Program)**, born New York, New York, December 8, 1965; admitted to bar, 1993, California. *Education:* Wellesley College (B.A., 1987); Harvard Law School (J.D., 1992). ***COURSES: Legal Analysis. ***Email:*** manglade@ggu.edu

BARBARA ANSCHER*, (Professor of Law)**, born Detroit, Michigan, March 12, 1957; admitted to bar, 1986, California. *Education:* Stanford University (B.A., 1979); University of California at Los Angeles (M.A., 1981); Stanford Law School (J.D., 1986). ***COURSES: Moot Court Competitions, Solving Legal Problems.

J. LANI BADER*, (Professor of Law)**, born Honolulu, Hawaii, December 11, 1932; admitted to bar, 1961, New York; 1963, California. *Education:* University of Hawaii (B.B.A., 1956); University of Chicago (J.D., 1960). ***COURSES: Commercial Finance, Alternative Dispute Resolution, Sales, Corporations.

ROGER BERNHARDT*, (Professor of Law)**, born Cleveland, Ohio, 1934; admitted to bar, 1960, California; 1990, New York. *Education:* University of Chicago (A.B., 1955; A.M., 1957; J.D., 1960). ***COURSES: Property, Commercial Finance, Real Estate Clinic, Sales.

***ALLAN BROTSKY*, (Professor of Law Emeritus)**, born Detroit,

(This Listing Continued)

GOLDEN GATE UNIVERSITY SCHOOL OF LAW —Continued

Michigan, July 27, 1920; admitted to bar, 1942, New York; 1946, California. *Education:* University of California at Los Angeles (A.B., 1939); Columbia Law School (LL.B., 1942). ***COURSES:*** Civil Practice Clinic, Trial Advocacy.

LESLIE A. BURTON*, (Lecturer)**, *Education:* University of Portland (B.A., 1976); Santa Clara University (J.D., 1979). ***COURSES: Bankruptcy, Solving Legal Problems, Writing and Research.

ALLAN CADGENE*, (Professor of Law)**, born Paterson, New Jersey, March 27, 1946; admitted to bar, 1972, California. *Education:* Stanford University (B.A., 1969); Yale University (LL.M., 1972). ***COURSES: Tax, Real Estate.

ROBERT K. CALHOUN, JR.*, (Professor of Law)**, born Harrisburg, Pennsylvania, March 20, 1942; admitted to bar, 1971, California. *Education:* University of Rochester (A.B., 1964); Yale Law School (LL.B., 1970). ***COURSES: Criminal Procedure, Evidence, Trial Advocacy.

MORTON P. COHEN*, (Professor of Law)**, born Brooklyn, New York, August 10, 1935; admitted to bar, 1961, New York; 1972, Michigan; 1975, California. *Education:* New York University (B.S., 1957); Brooklyn Law School (LL.B., 1960); Harvard University Law School (LL.M., 1971). ***COURSES: Criminal, Civil Procedure, Health.

MARKITA D. COOPER*, (Professor of Law)**, born Cleveland, Ohio, May 20, 1957; admitted to bar, 1982, California. *Education:* Stanford University (A.B., 1979); University of Virginia (J.D., 1982). ***COURSES: Employment Law, Torts, Corporations.

ANNE LEE ENG*, (Associate Professor and Clinical Staff Attorney)**, born Newark, New Jersey, August 14, 1955; admitted to bar, 1988, California. *Education:* Rutgers University (B.S.W., 1978); Columbia University School of Law (J.D., 1988). ***COURSES: Environmental. ***Email:*** aeng@ggo.edu

THOMAS M. GOETZL*, (Professor of Law)**, born Chicago, Illinois, May 31, 1943; admitted to bar, 1970, California. *Education:* University of California (A.B., 1965; J.D., 1969). ***COURSES: Property, Art and the Law, Remedies.

MARC GREENBERG*, (Visiting Professor and Director, Intellectual Property Program)**, admitted to bar, California. *Education:* University of California, Berkeley (B.A.); Hastings College of the Law (J.D., 1979). ***COURSES: Entertainment Law, Internet and Online Law.

HELEN HARTNELL*, (Associate Professor)**, admitted to bar, 1981, Illinois; 1985, Wisconsin. *Education:* University of Illinois (B.S., 1976; J.D., 1980). ***COURSES: International Business Transactions, International Trade Law, Private International Law.

JOAN HOWARTH*, (Professor of Law)**, born Morristown, New Jersey, November 23, 1950; admitted to bar, 1980, California. *Education:* Smith College (A.B., 1972); University of Southern California (J.D., 1980). ***COURSES: Constitutional Law, Torts, Sexual Orientation and the Law, Women and the Law, Remedies.

LAWRENCE JONES*, (Professor of Law)**, born Spokane, Washington, December 8, 1936; admitted to bar, 1961, California. *Education:* Washington State University (B.A., 1958); Stanford University (J.D., 1961). ***COURSES: Contracts, Conflict of Laws, Torts.

MARCI KELLY*, (Associate Dean and Director, LL.M. (Tax) Program; Professor of Law)**, born Chicago, Illinois, April 29, 1951; admitted to bar, 1978, New York. *Education:* Vassar College (B.A., 1973); University of Virginia (J.D., 1977); New York University School of Law (LL.M., 1983). ***COURSES: Federal Income Tax, Corporate Tax, Estate and Gift Tax, Wills and Trusts.

JANICE E. KOSEL*, (Professor of Law)**, born Oakland, California, June 24, 1948; admitted to bar, 1972, California. *Education:* University of California at Berkeley (A.B., 1968); University of California, Berkeley, Boalt Hall School of Law (J.D., 1971). ***COURSES: Commercial Law, Community Property, Contracts.

SARAH HOOKE LEE*, (Associate Professor and Associate Dean for Library Services)**, born Bangor, Maine, July 15, 1953; admitted to bar, 1982, Maine; 1989, Massachusetts. *Education:* University of Maine (B.A., 1974; M.L.S., 1976); University of Maine School of Law (J.D., 1982). ***COURSES: Legal Research. ***Email:*** shlee@ggu.edu

NEIL LEVY*, (Professor of Law Emeritus)**, admitted to bar, 1969, California. *Education:* Cornell University (A.B.); University of Chicago (J.D.). ***COURSES: Torts.

LESLIE A. MINKUS*, (Professor of Law)**, born San Francisco, California, June 9, 1935; admitted to bar, 1963, California. *Education:* University of California at Berkeley (A.B., 1955); Stanford University (LL.B., 1962). ***COURSES: Professional Responsibility, Corporations, Community Property.

MYRON MOSKOVITZ*, (Professor of Law)**, born San Francisco, California, November 23, 1938; admitted to bar, 1964, California. *Education:* University of California at Berkeley (B.S., 1960); University of California, Boalt Hall School of Law (LL.B., 1964). ***COURSES: Criminal Law, Criminal Procedure, Civil Procedure, Appellate Advocacy, Landlord-Tenant.

CHRISTIAN NWACHUKWU OKEKE*, (Visiting Professor of Law)**, born Obinofia, Ndiuno, August 6, 1941; admitted to bar, 1980, Nigeria. *Education:* St. Joseph's College (Teachers' Diploma, 1961); Kiev State University (LL.M., 1969) Free University (Ph.D., 1973). ***COURSES: International Law, Comparative Law, International Organization, International Investment Law. ***Email:*** cokeke@ggu.edu

MARIA ONTIVEROS*, (Professor of Law)**, born Whittier, California, March 2, 1961; admitted to bar, 1984, California. *Education:* University of California at Berkeley (A.B., 1981); Harvard University Law School (J.D., 1984); Cornell University (M.I.L.R., 1986); Stanford University (J.S.D., 1992). ***COURSES: Employment Discrimination, Labor Law, Evidence.

DAVID OPPENHEIMER*, (Professor of Law and Associate Dean, Academic Affairs)**, born New York, March 18, 1950; admitted to bar, 1978, California. *Education:* Beloit College; Goddard College; University Without Walls, Berkeley (B.A., 1972); Harvard University Law School (J.D., 1978); University of California, Boalt Hall School of Law. ***COURSES: Civil Procedure, Employment Discrimination.

ANTHONY J. PAGANO*, (Professor of Law)**, born West New York, New Jersey, June 29, 1939; admitted to bar, 1963, California. *Education:* Fordham University (B.S., 1960); University of Michigan (J.D., 1963). ***COURSES: Wills & Trusts.

ALAN MARTIN RAMO*, (Professor of Law; Co-Director, Environmental Law and Justice Clinic)**, born Los Angeles, California, October 26, 1949; admitted to bar, 1974, California. *Education:* Stanford University (B.A., 1971); University of California, Berkeley (M.J., 1982); Boalt Hall School of Law, University of California, Berkeley (J.D., 1974). ***COURSES: Environmental Law Practice.

CLIFFORD L. RECHTSCHAFFEN*, (Professor of Law)**, born Brooklyn, New York, December 22, 1957; admitted to bar, 1986, California. *Education:* Princeton University (A.B., 1978); Yale Law School (J.D., 1984). ***COURSES: Environmental Law.

***SUSAN RUTBERG*, (Professor of Law)**, born Washington, D.C.,

(This Listing Continued)

GOLDEN GATE UNIVERSITY SCHOOL OF LAW —Continued

September 13, 1948; admitted to bar, 1975, California. *Education:* Cornell University (B.S., 1971); Golden Gate University School of Law (J.D., 1975). ***COURSES:*** Trial Advocacy, Lawyering Skills: Interviewing, Counseling and Negotiation, Criminal Law Clinic, Criminal Law.

DONNA MIAE RYU*, (Associate Professor; Associate Director, Women's Employment Rights Clinic)**, born Monterey, California, 1960; admitted to bar, 1986, California. *Education:* Yale University (B.A., 1982); University of California at Berkeley (J.D., 1986). ***COURSES: Women's Employment Rights Clinic.

***SUSAN BETH SCHECHTER*, (Interim Assistant Dean for Student Services and Clinical Professor)**, *Education:* Washington University (B.A. 1983); University of Pittsburgh (J.D., 1988).

BERNARD L. SEGAL*, (Professor of Law)**, born Philadelphia, Pennsylvania, July 26, 1930; admitted to bar, 1960, Pennsylvania. *Education:* Temple University (B.S., 1952); University of Pennsylvania (M.A., 1954; J.D., 1959). ***COURSES: Litigation, Evidence, Mock Trial, Trial Advocacy, Criminal Law.

MARCI SEVILLE*, (Associate Professor of Law; Director, Women's Employment Rights Clinic)**, born New York, January 27, 1950; admitted to bar, 1975, California; 1983, New York. *Education:* New York University (B.A., 1971); University Heights College, Colgate University; Rutgers Law School (J.D., 1975). ***COURSES: Women's Employment Rights, Clinic.

MARC STICKGOLD*, (Professor of Law)**, born Washington, D.C., November 24, 1939; admitted to bar, 1963, Illinois; 1964, Wisconsin; 1968, Michigan; 1978, California. *Education:* University of Illinois (B.S., 1960); Northwestern University School of Law (J.D., 1963); University of Wisconsin. ***COURSES: Constitutional Law, Civil Procedure, Lawyering Skills.

SOMPONG SUCHARITKUL*, (Assoc. Dean and Dir., LLM Program in Intl. Law and Distinguished Assoc. Prof. of Intl. and Comparative Law)**, born Bangkok, Thailand, December 4, 1931; admitted to bar, 1954, United Kingdom (Barrister-At-Law). *Education:* Oxford University (B.A., 1953; M.A., 1955; D.Phil., 1955; B.C.L., 1990; D.C.L., 1990); University of Paris (Docteur en Droit, 1954); Harvard University Law School (LL.M., 1956). ***COURSES: International Law, International Economic Law, International Relations, International and Comparative Law, Dispute Settlement and International Conflict Resolution.

JON H. SYLVESTER*, (Professor of Law)**, born Berkeley, California, 1952; admitted to bar, 1981, California; 1982, District of Columbia. *Education:* Stanford University (B.A., 1973); University of California at Berkeley (M.J., 1975); Harvard Law School (J.D., 1981). ***COURSES: Contracts, International Business Transactions.

JOHN P. WILSON*, (Professor of Law)**, born Newark, New Jersey, April 7, 1933; admitted to bar, 1963, New Jersey and Massachusetts. *Education:* Princeton University (A.B., 1955); Harvard University Law School (LL.B., 1962). ***COURSES: Criminal Law, Torts, Health Law.

MARYANN WOLCOTT*, (Lecturer)**, born Toledo, Ohio, May 17, 1939; admitted to bar, 1978, Ohio; 1986, California. *Education:* Marygrove College (B.A., 1961); University of Toledo (J.D., 1977). ***COURSES: Writing and Research.

MICHAEL A. ZAMPERINI*, (Professor of Law/Director of Writing and Research)**, born Providence, Rhode Island, April 22, 1947; admitted to bar, 1973, California; 1974, Virginia. *Education:* George Washington University (B.A., 1967); National Law Center, George Washington University (J.D., 1973). ***COURSES: Writing and Research, Remedies, Sexual Orientation and the Law.

GONZAGA UNIVERSITY SCHOOL OF LAW

P. O. BOX 3528
SPOKANE, WASHINGTON 99220-3528
Telephone: (509) 328-4220
Fax: (509) 323-5744

ABA Approved Since 1951.

Gonzaga University School of Law belongs to a long and distinguished tradition of humanistic, Catholic, and Jesuit education. It is an integral part of Gonzaga University which was founded in 1887 and continues to maintain the tradition of academic excellence in education which is at the heart of the mission of the more than four and a half century old Jesuit order. The School of Law, which is accredited by the American Bar Association and the American Association of Law Schools is located in the new Law Center on the bank of the Spokane River. This riverside setting provides a stunning atmosphere for research and learning.

The Law School's 500 students bring a rich mixture of backgrounds and perspectives to their legal studies. Each fall approximately 170 entering scholars from the majority of the states, as well as trust territories and foreign countries, are met by a talented and dedicated law faculty. The faculty share a commitment to teaching excellence, scholastic endeavors, and active contribution to the legal community. A student faculty ratio of approximately 21/1 makes the faculty readily accessible to the students on a personal and professional level.

For more than two decades, Gonzaga law students have contributed to the development of the law through scholarly criticism and analysis in the highly regarded *Gonzaga Law Review*. Gonzaga's moot court teams have a long standing reputation for excellence with students having earned honors for Best Speaker and Best Brief in the nation. The National Appellate Advocacy Team has placed second in the nation on two occasions and the National Moot Court Team captured second place in the 1993 National Championship. Numerous other activities are available to students offering opportunities to explore social, cultural, and political issues.

A pro-active Career Services Office assists students in their professional job search and in finding internships during law school. Each year law firms, government agencies, and businesses conduct on-campus interviews. Supported by a unique and generous state work study program, intern experiences are financially and educationally profitable for the law students and their employers. Rule 9 of Washington State law enhances the educational value of these internships by providing third year students the opportunity to try cases in Washington courts.

At Gonzaga students have an opportunity to construct a personal framework upon which to build a productive future legal career--a framework based upon a foundation of a solid theoretical curriculum and extensive practical experience gained through the Law School's award winning, multi-faceted clinical program and community internship program. Appropriate to its Inland Northwest setting the

(This Listing Continued)

GONZAGA UNIVERSITY SCHOOL OF LAW—Continued

Law School offers many courses that address natural resource issues. Other outstanding features of the curriculum include an intensive two-year legal writing and research program, private and public sector labor law courses, and a JD/MBA Joint Degree Program.

The Law Library plays an integral role in the educational pursuits of its students by sustaining and supporting the curriculum and student and faculty instructional and research needs. Students have access to an array of software applications and databases, including LEXIS and WESTLAW.

The legal training and experience provided Gonzaga students has facilitated their success in finding employment in a wide variety of legal positions throughout the United States and internationally. Many graduates of the nationally recognized taxation program have received employment opportunities with the U.S. Tax Court and admission to LL.M. programs in taxation. Other graduates have gone on to play key roles in the judiciary, business, politics, and public service.

Dean and Professor of Law: Daniel Morrissey (509) 323-3693
Associate Dean for Academic Affairs: Amy Kelley (509) 323-3720
Associate Dean for Students Affairs: M. Lisa Bradley (509) 323-3762
Registrar: Sharon Day (509) 323-3731
Coordinator of Financial Aid: Joan Henning (509) 323-3859
Director, Law Library: June Stewart (509) 323-3782
Director, Admissions: Tamara Martinez-Anderson (509) 323-5532
Associate Director, Career Services: Robert Scott (509) 323-6122
Director, Development and Alumni Affairs: Karin Olsen (509) 323-3605

FULL TIME FACULTY

DANIEL MORRISSEY*, (Dean and Professor of Law)**, born Chicago, Illinois, September 14, 1948; admitted to bar, 1974, Illinois; 1979, California; 2000, Florida. *Education:* Georgetown University (A.B., 1971; J.D., 1974). ***COURSES: Corporations, Securities Regulation, Jurisprudence. ***Email:*** dmorrissey@lawschool.gonzaga.edu

ROBERT J. ARAUJO, S.J.*, (Professor of Law)**, born Taunton, Massachusetts, October 30, 1948; admitted to bar, 1973, Massachusetts; 1975, District of Columbia. *Education:* Georgetown University (A.B., 1970; J.D., 1973); Columbia University (LL.M., 1980; J.S.D., 1992); Weston School of Theology (M.Div, 1993; S.T.L., 1994); Oxford (B.C.L., 1994). ***COURSES: Public, International Law, Constitutional Law, Contracts, International Organizations. ***Email:*** raraujo@lawschool.gonzaga.edu

CHERYL A. BECKETT*, (Director, Legal Research and Writing Program; Instructor, Legal Research and Writing)**, born Philadelphia, Pennsylvania, June 17, 1952; admitted to bar, 1981, Washington. *Education:* Rutgers University (A.B., 1974); Gonzaga University (J.D., 1981). ***COURSES: Legal Research and Writing, Labor Law, Employment Law. ***Email:*** cbeckett@lawschool.gonzaga.edu

MARY LISA BRADLEY*, (Associate Dean of Students and Instructor)**, born Billing, Montana, May 31, 1957; admitted to bar, 1991, Washington. *Education:* University of Montana (E.D.U.C. 1980); Gonzaga (J.D., 1991, *magna cum laude*). ***COURSES: Legal Research & Writing, Academic Resource Program, Coach Jessup Cup Moot Court Team. ***Email:*** lbradley@lawschool.gonzaga.edu

WILLIAM H. CLARKE*, (Professor of Law)**, born New York, New York, November 29, 1942; admitted to bar, 1969, Washington. *Education:* Washington State University (B.S., 1966); University of Washington (J.D., 1969). ***COURSES: Antitrust, Federal Taxation, Professional Responsibility, Real Property. ***Email:*** wclarke@lawschool.gonzaga.edu

JOHN E. CLUTE*, (Professor of Law)**, born Kooskia, Idaho, October 28, 1934; admitted to bar, 1965, Washington. *Education:* Gonzaga University (B.A., 1960; J.D., 1963). ***COURSES: Contracts. ***Email:*** jclute@lawschool.gonzaga.edu

FRANK CONKLIN*, (Professor of Law)**, born Butte, Montana, June 3, 1925; admitted to bar, 1961, Washington. *Education:* Gonzaga University (B.A., 1946; M.A., 1947); Alma College (M.A., 1956); Georgetown University (J.D., 1961); Yale University (LL.M., 1962; J.S.D., 1963). ***COURSES: Constitutional Law, Evidence, Bankruptcy, Conflicts of Law, Real Estate Transactions. ***Email:*** fconklin@lawschool.gonzaga.edu

GEORGE A. CRITCHLOW*, (Associate Professor of Law, Director of Clinical Law Program)**, born Spokane, Washington, April 4, 1949; admitted to bar, 1977, Washington. *Education:* University of Washington (B.A., 1972); Gonzaga University (J.D., 1977). ***COURSES: Criminal Procedure, Clinical Law. ***Email:*** gcritchlow@lawschool.gonzaga.edu

LYNN M. DAGGETT*, (Associate Professor of Law; Adjunct Professor, School of Education)**, born Detroit, Michigan, April 7, 1961; admitted to bar, 1987, Connecticut. *Education:* The Johns Hopkins University (B.A., 1980); Duke University (Ph.D., 1984); University of Connecticut (J.D., 1987). ***COURSES: Torts, Education Law, Labor Law. ***Email:*** ldaggett@lawschool.gonzaga.edu

VERN G. DAVIDSON*, (Professor of Law)**, born California, August 6, 1929; admitted to bar, 1963, California. *Education:* University of California at Los Angeles (B.A., 1959; J.D., 1962). ***COURSES: Contract, Conflict of Laws, Wills, Trusts. ***Email:*** vdavidson@lawschool.gonzaga.edu

DAVID K. DEWOLF*, (Professor of Law)**, born Oakland, California, August 23, 1949; admitted to bar, 1980, Washington; 1987, California. *Education:* Stanford University (B.A., 1971); Yale University (J.D., 1979). ***COURSES: Torts, Product Liability. ***Email:*** ddewolf@lawschool.gonzaga.edu

MARK EDWARD DEFORREST*, (Visiting Instructor)**, born Anacortes, Washington, November 26, 1969; admitted to bar, 1997, Washington. *Education:* Western Washington University (B.A., 1992); Gonzaga University School of Law (J.D., 1997). ***COURSES: Legal Research and Writing. ***Email:*** mdeforrest@lawschool.gonzaga.edu

HELEN DONIGAN*, (Professor of Law)**, born Nebraska, October 13, 1942; admitted to bar, 1976, Washington. *Education:* University of Nebraska (B.S., 1963); Gonzaga University (J.D., 1976). ***COURSES: Family Law, Uniform Commercial Code. ***Email:*** hdonigan@lawschool.gonzaga.edu

KEVIN PAUL GRAY*, (Assistant Professor & Associate Director of the Chastek Law Library)**, born Queens, New York, May 30, 1961. *Education:* New York Institute of Technology (B.F.A., 1983); State University of New York at Buffalo (M.L.S., 1985); Southern Illinois University School of Law (J.D., 1994). ***Email: kgray@lawschool.gonzaga.edu

(This Listing Continued)

GONZAGA UNIVERSITY SCHOOL OF LAW—Continued

GAIL ANNE HAMMER*, (Visiting Instructor-Clinical Law and Director, Family Law Project)**, born Minot, North Dakota, July 17, 1953; admitted to bar, 1989, Idaho; 1990, Washington; 1993, Montana. *Education:* The University of Montana (B.A., 1978; J.D., 1988). ***COURSES: Clinical Law, Trial Practice, Pretrial Practice, Dispute Resolution, Children and the Law. ***Email:*** ghammer@lawschool.gonzaga.edu

GERALD F. HESS*, (Director, Institute for Law School Teaching; Professor of Law)**, born Two Rivers, Wisconsin, May 6, 1952; admitted to bar, 1982, Wisconsin. *Education:* University of Wisconsin (B.S., 1975; J.D., 1982). ***COURSES: Civil Procedure, Environmental Law, Remedies. ***Email:*** ghess@lawschool.gonzaga.edu

AMY KELLEY*, (Associate Dean for Academic Affairs and Professor of Law)**, born Wausau, Wisconsin, June 4, 1952; admitted to bar, 1977, South Dakota. *Education:* College of St. Catherine (B.A., 1973); University of South Dakota (J.D., 1977). ***COURSES: Property, Water, Mining, Constitutional Law. ***Email:*** akelley@lawschool.gonzaga.edu

MARY KAY LUNDWALL*, (Associate Professor of Law)**, born Indianapolis, Indiana, July 10, 1944; admitted to bar, 1978, Washington. *Education:* University of Florida (B.A., 1964); University of Florida (M.A., 1966); Gonzaga University (M.A., 1984); University of Wyoming (J.D., 1978). ***COURSES: Wills and Trusts, Legal Research and Writing. ***Email:*** mlundwall@lawschool.gonzaga.edu

JOHN MOREY MAURICE*, (Director, Continuing Legal Education and Thomas More Scholarship Program; Professor of Law)**, born Fort Collins, Colorado, April 12, 1939; admitted to bar, 1966, Colorado and Idaho. *Education:* University of Colorado (B.A., 1961); New York University (J.D., 1964). ***COURSES: Corporations, Securities, Regulation, Corporate Taxation. ***Email:*** jmaurice@lawschool.gonzaga.edu

MICHAEL C. MCCLINTOCK*, (Professor of Law)**, born March 28, 1939; admitted to bar, 1969, Oklahoma; 1978, Washington. *Education:* University of Tulsa (B.A., 1965; J.D., 1969); Southern Methodist University (LL.M., 1972; S.J.D., 1975). ***COURSES: International Business Transactions, NAFTA Law and Business Associations 1 (Agency and Partnership). ***Email:*** mmcclintock@lawschool.gonzaga.edu

JAMES R. MCCURDY*, (Professor of Law)**, born Dallas, Texas, January 11, 1947; admitted to bar, 1974, South Dakota. *Education:* University of Houston (B.B.A., 1970); University of Texas (J.D., 1974). ***COURSES: Administrative Law, Environmental Law, Environmental Litigation, Environmental Mediation and Negotiation, Environmental Clinic, Sports Law, Oil and Gas, Indian Law. ***Email:*** jmccurdy@lawschool.gonzaga.edu

ALAN MCNEIL*, (Clinical Law Supervising Attorney and Associate Professor)**, born Dayton, Ohio, July 25, 1947; admitted to bar, 1977, Washington. *Education:* Ohio University (B.A., 1970); Gonzaga University (J.D., 1977). ***COURSES: Clinical Law Supervising Attorney. ***Email:*** amcneil@lawschool.gonzaga.edu

ANN MARIE MURPHY*, (Associate Professor)**, born Chicago, Illinois, January 28, 1958; admitted to bar, 1985, Illinois. *Education:* Western Illinois University (B.A.S., 1979; M.S., 1980); DePaul University (J.D., 1985). ***COURSES: Taxation, Evidence, Wills and Trusts. ***Email:*** amurphy@lawschool.gonzaga.edu

LEWIS H. ORLAND*, (Associate Dean and Professor Emeritus)**, born Moscow, Idaho, September 12, 1915; admitted to bar, 1940, Idaho; 1950, Washington. *Education:* University of Idaho (A.B., 1937); Harvard University (J.D., 1940); Gonzaga University (LL.D., 1967); Post-graduate studies, University of Geneva, Geneva, Switzerland, 1947-49. ***COURSES: Civil Procedure, Contracts, Environmental Law, Evidence, Future Interests, International Transactions, Introduction to Law, Law and Psychiatry, Pleadings and Procedures, Real Property. ***Email:*** lorland@lawschool.gonzada.edu

SPEEDY RICE*, (Dir., Externship Program & Supervising Attorney & Dir. Int'l Human Rights Law Clinic)**, born Richmond, Virginia, April 10, 1954; admitted to bar, 1986, California; 1994, Washington. *Education:* Furman University (B.A., 1976); California Western (J.D., 1986). ***COURSES: Externship, Trial Advocacy, Evidence, Aviation Law, International Human Rights Law. ***Email:*** srice@lawschool.gonzaga.edu

LYNN R. ROBINSON*, (Bibliographic & Collection Mgmt. Librarian & Assistant Professor of Law)**, born Bellingham, Washington, August 7, 1962. *Education:* Central College (B.A., 1984); University of Iowa (M.A., 1988). ***Email: lrobinson@lawschool.gonzaga.edu

STEPHEN L. SEPINUCK*, (Professor of Law)**, born Boston, Massachusetts, September 14, 1959; admitted to bar, 1984, Florida; 1985, Massachusetts. *Education:* Brown University (A.B., 1981); Boston University (J.D., 1984); New York University (LL.M., 1987). ***COURSES: Bankruptcy, Contracts, Creditors Rights (aka Secured Transactions), Moot Court, Sales. ***Email:*** ssepinuck@lawschool.gonzaga.edu

KEVIN GENE SHELLEY*, (Instructor)**, born Dothan, Alabama, June 3, 1961; admitted to bar, 1986, Alabama; 1993, Georgia. *Education:* Auburn University (B.A., 1983); University of Alabama (J.D., 1988). ***COURSES: Legal Research and Writing. ***Email:*** kshelley@lawschool.gonzaga.edu

JUNE STEWART*, (Director, Chastek Library and Associate Professor)**, born Pecos, Texas, June 1, 1945; admitted to bar, 1985, Colorado. *Education:* University of Colorado (B.A., 1967); University of Denver (M.L.L. and J.D., 1985). ***Email: jstewart@lawschool.gonzaga.edu

ELIZABETH THWEATT*, (Collections & Information Access Librarian and Associate Professor of Law)**, born Paris, Texas, May 8, 1939. *Education:* University of Washington (B.A., 1966; M.L.S., 1972). ***Email: ethweatt@lawschool.gonzaga.edu

MARY PATRICIA TREUTHART*, (Professor of Law)**, born Peoria, Illinois, December 9, 1952; admitted to bar, 1978, Pennsylvania and New York. *Education:* Douglass College (A.B., 1975); Rutgers University School of Law, Camden (J.D., 1978); Columbia Law School (LL.M., 1989). ***COURSES: Criminal Procedure, Constitutional Law, Professional Responsibility, Foundations of Law, Clinical, Women in the Law. ***Email:*** mtreuthart@lawschool.gonzaga.edu

JAMES M. VACHE*, (Professor of Law)**, born Richland, Washington, April 17, 1946; admitted to bar, 1972, Washington. *Education:* Washington State University (B.A., 1969, *Phi Beta Kappa*); University of Washington (J.D., 1972, *order of the Coif*). ***COURSES: Civil Rights, Constitutional Law, Criminal Law, Employment Law, Jurisprudence, Professional Responsibility. ***Email:*** jvache@lawschool.gonzaga.edu

LARRY A. WEISER*, (Clinical Law Supervising Attorney and Associate Professor)**, born Fall River, Massachusetts, February 8, 1949; admitted to bar, 1976, Washington. *Education:* Boston University (B.A., 1971); Gonzaga University School of Law (J.D., 1976). ***COURSES: Elder Law, Negotiation and Mediation, Clinical Law. ***Email:*** lweiser@lawschool.gonzaga.edu

MARK E. WILSON*, (Professor of Law)**, born North Platte, Nebraska, August 10, 1938; admitted to bar, 1967, Minnesota; 1970, Wisconsin; 1975, Washington. *Education:* University of South Dakota (A.B., 1960); University of Minnesota (J.D., 1967). ***COURSES: Clinic,

(This Listing Continued)

GONZAGA UNIVERSITY SCHOOL OF LAW—Continued

Advocacy, Legal Writing, Professional Responsibility, Comparative Law. ***Email:*** mwilson@lawschool.gonzaga.edu

KATHRYN CHRISTINE ZIMMERMAN*, (Instructor)**, born Urbana, Illinois, September 27, 1958; admitted to bar, 1990, Illinois. *Education:* University of Illinois (B.S., 1980); Northern Illinois (M.A., 1983); Chicago Kent College of Law (J.D., 1990). ***COURSES: Legal Research and Writing. ***Email:*** kwyatt@lawschool.gonzaga.edu

HAMLINE UNIVERSITY SCHOOL OF LAW

1536 HEWITT AVENUE

ST. PAUL, MINNESOTA 55104-1284

HARVARD LAW SCHOOL

CAMBRIDGE, MASSACHUSETTS 02138

Telephone: (617) 495-3100

http://www.law.harvard.edu

ABA Approved Since 1923

Established in 1817, Harvard is the oldest existing law school in the United States. The School provides comprehensive and enlightened training to prepare its graduates for law practice, for public service at the local, state, federal and international levels, and for law teaching and legal scholarship. Through its faculty, students, and graduates, Harvard Law School seeks to make substantial contributions toward improving our knowledge and understanding of the legal system.

Harvard Law School is a vibrant, dynamic place with a talented and diverse student body of nearly 1900 students, a distinguished full-time faculty of 80 professors and assistant professors, two adjunct professors and 68 lecturers, visiting professors and professors emeriti. The School's curriculum includes such diverse courses as Constitutional Law, Criminal Law, Corporate Finance, Environmental Law, Negotiation, Family Law, and International and Comparative Law. One of the largest Clinical Programs in the U.S. offers students a wide range of fieldwork and simulation courses as well as opportunities to participate in extracurricular practice-related activities in Harvard-operated legal services clinics. Among its 18 research programs are programs relating to such subjects as law and economics, international financial systems, East Asian legal studies, human rights, the legal profession, and negotiation and alternative dispute resolution.

In addition to a challenging curriculum, students can choose among numerous extracurricular activities, including more than seventy student organizations and twelve student-edited journals. Activities range from a battered women's advocacy project to a law and technology society to intramural sports and dramatic productions. There are currently twenty-five special interest and ethnic organizations at the School.

Shaped by its role as a preeminent national law school, the School is working to strengthen its already significant global orientation. The curriculum contains over 50 courses in the international and comparative law field. With approximately 240 lawyers from more than fifty countries in the LL.M. program the S.J.D. program, and the International Tax program, the School is deeply committed to advanced legal study and scholarship.

The Harvard Law Library is the largest academic law library in the world. Its collections, numbering approximately 1.8 million volumes, support the teaching and research activities of the School and serve as a resource for legal scholars throughout the world.

The Office of Career Services provides a wide variety of placement and career counseling services to students, employers and graduates. A separate Office of Public Interest Advising helps students find government and public interest opportunities. The School's more than 30,000 living alumni have distinguished careers in practice, legal education, the judiciary, government, business, and public interest organizations. Five of the current members of the Supreme Court attended Harvard Law School.

Harvard Law School's outstanding faculty and extraordinarily gifted students, its size and prodigious resources and its location at the heart of Harvard University and Cambridge contribute to its leadership role in American and international legal education.

Dean: Robert C. Clark (617) 495-4601
Admissions: Joyce Curll (617) 495-3109
Financial Aid: Elizabeth Rankin (617) 495-4606
Library: Harry Stratton Martin, III (617) 495-3170
Career Services: Mark Weber (617) 495-3119
Alumni Affairs: Scott Nichols (617) 495-3113

FULL TIME FACULTY

ROBERT C. CLARK*, (Dean and Royall Professor of Law)**, born New Orleans, Louisiana, February 26, 1944; admitted to bar, 1972, Massachusetts. *Education:* Maryknoll College (B.A., 1966); Columbia University (Ph.D., 1971); Harvard Law School (J.D., 1972). ***COURSES: Corporate Law, Regulation of Financial Institutions, Health Care Regulation.

WILLIAM P. ALFORD*, (Henry L. Stimson Professor of Law and Director, East Asian Legal Studies)**, born Brookline, Massachusetts, May 29, 1948; admitted to bar, 1977, District of Columbia; 1980, U.S. Supreme Court. *Education:* Amherst College (B.A., 1970); University of Cambridge (LL.B., 1972); Yale University (M.A., 1974; M.A., 1975); Harvard Law School (J.D., 1977). ***COURSES: International Law, International Business Transactions, Comparative Law.

WILLIAM D. ANDREWS*, (Eli Goldston Professor of Law)**, born New York, N.Y., February 25, 1931; admitted to bar, 1956, New York; 1959, Massachusetts. *Education:* Amherst College (A.B., 1952); Harvard Law School (LL.B., 1955). ***COURSES: Federal Income Taxation. ***Email:*** Andrews@law.harvard.edu

(This Listing Continued)

HARVARD LAW SCHOOL—Continued

SAMUEL ROBERT BAGENSTOS*, (Assistant Professor of Law)**, born St. Louis, Missouri, January 5, 1970; admitted to bar, 1994, California. *Education:* University of North Carolina (B.A., 1990); Harvard Law School (J.D., 1993). ***COURSES: Criminal Law, Civil Rights, Litigation, Disability Law. ***Email:*** bagensto@law.harvard.edu

DAVID JEREMIAH BARRON*, (Assistant Professor of Law)**, born Washington, D.C., July 7, 1967; admitted to bar, 1996, New York. *Education:* Harvard (B.A., 1989; J.D., 1994). ***COURSES: Property, Administrative Law, Local Government Law. ***Email:*** dbarron@law.harvard.edu

ELIZABETH BARTHOLET*, (Morris Wassenstein Public Interest Professor of Law)**, born New York, N.Y., September 9, 1940; admitted to bar, 1965, New York; 1967, District of Columbia; 1978, Massachusetts. *Education:* Radcliffe College (B.A., 1962); Harvard Law School (LL.B., 1965). ***COURSES: Family Law, Adoption and Reproduction, Employment Discrimination. ***Email:*** ebarthol@law.harvard.edu

LUCIAN A. BEBCHUK*, (William J. Friedman & Alicia Townsend Friedman Professor of Law, Economics, and Finance)**, born Poland, December 4, 1955. *Education:* University of Haifa (B.A., 1977); University of Tel-Aviv (LL.B., 1979); Harvard Law School (LL.M., 1980; S.J.D., 1984); Harvard Society of Fellows (1982-1985); Harvard University Department of Economics (M.A., 1992; Ph.D., 1993). ***COURSES: Corporations, Corporate Finance, Law and Economics, Law and Finance.

SCOTT BREWER*, (Professor of Law)**, born New York, N.Y. *Education:* State University of New York at Stony Brook (B.A., 1979); Yale University (M.A., 1980); Yale Law School (J.D., 1988); Harvard University (Ph.D., 1997). ***COURSES: Contracts, Jurisprudence.

DAVID CHARNY*, (David Berg Professor of Law)**, born September 16, 1955; admitted to bar, 1983, District of Columbia. *Education:* Yale University (B.A., 1977); Harvard Law School (J.D., 1982). ***COURSES: Contracts, Corporations, Employment Law, Statutory Construction, Health Insurance Regulation and Reform.

JOHN C. COATES*, (Assistant Professor of Law)**, born Lynchburg, Virginia, September 15, 1964; admitted to bar, 1989, New York. *Education:* University of Virginia (B.A., 1986); New York University Law School (J.D., 1989). ***COURSES: Corporations, Securities. ***Email:*** jcoates@law.harvard.com

ALAN M. DERSHOWITZ*, (Felix Frankfurter Professor of Law)**, born Brooklyn, New York, September 1, 1938; admitted to bar, 1963, District of Columbia; 1967, U.S. Supreme Court; 1968, Massachusetts. *Education:* Brooklyn College (B.A., 1959); Yale Law School (LL.B., 1962). ***COURSES: Criminal Law, Tactics and Ethics in Criminal Litigation, Thinking about Thinking, Psychiatry and Law, Civil Liberties, Prediction and Prevention of Crime.

CHRISTINE DESAN*, (Professor of Law)**, born Washington, D.C., March 20, 1959; admitted to bar, 1987, Massachusetts; 1989, District of Columbia. *Education:* Princeton University (A.B., 1981); Tufts University (M.A.L.D., 1987); Yale Law School (J.D., 1987). ***COURSES: Legislation, Legal History, Civil Procedure.

CHARLES DONAHUE, JR.*, (Paul A. Freund Professor of Law)**, born New York, N.Y., October 4, 1941; admitted to bar, 1966, New York; 1970, Michigan. *Education:* Harvard University (A.B., 1962); Yale Law School (LL.B., 1965). ***COURSES: Legal History, Property.

CHRISTOPHER F. EDLEY, JR.*, (Professor of Law, Co-Director, Civil Rights Project)**, born Boston, Massachusetts, January 13, 1953; admitted to bar, 1980, District of Columbia. *Education:* Swarthmore College (B.A., 1973); Kennedy School of Government (J.P.P., 1978); Harvard Law School (J.D., 1978). Special Counsel to President Clinton, 1995; Associate Director, White House OMB, 1993-1995; Domestic Policy Staff, Carter White House, 1978-1980. ***COURSES: Administrative Law, Problems of Governance and Public Policy, Affirmative Action.

EINER RICHARD ELHAUGE*, (Professor of Law)**, born New York, New York, May 28, 1961; admitted to bar, 1986, Pennsylvania. *Education:* Harvard (A.B., 1982; J.D., 1986). ***COURSES: Antitrust, Contracts, Corporations, Health Care Law, Public Choice Theory and Law.

RICHARD H. FALLON, JR.*, (Professor of Law)**, born Augusta, Maine, January 4, 1952; admitted to bar, 1988, Massachusetts. *Education:* Yale University (B.A., 1975); Oxford University (B.A., 1977); Yale Law School (J.D., 1980). ***COURSES: Constitutional Law, Federal Courts, Administrative Law.

ALLEN F. FERRELL*, (Assistant Professor of Law)**, born Lankenan, Pennsylvania, January 23, 1970. *Education:* Brown University (A.B./A.M., 1992); Harvard Law School (J.D., 1995). ***COURSES: Securities, Contracts, Financial Institutions. ***Email:*** fferrell@law.harvard.edu

MARTHA A. FIELD*, (Langdell Professor of Law)**, born Boston, Massachusetts, August 20, 1943; admitted to bar, 1969, District of Columbia. *Education:* Radcliffe College (B.A., 1965); University of Chicago (J.D., 1968). ***COURSES: Constitutional Law, Family Law, Federal Courts, Reproductive Technology.

WILLIAM W. FISHER III*, (Professor of Law)**, born Portland, Maine, October 12, 1953. *Education:* Amherst College (B.A., 1976); Harvard Law School (J.D., 1984); Harvard University (Ph.D., 1991). ***COURSES: Property, Intellectual Property, American Legal History. ***Email:*** tfisher@law.harvard.edu

CHARLES FRIED*, (Beneficial Professor of Law)**, born Prague, Czech Republic, April 15, 1935; admitted to bar, 1961, District of Columbia; 1966, Massachusetts. *Education:* Princeton University (A.B., 1956); Oxford University (M.A., 1960); Columbia Law School (J.D., 1960). ***COURSES: Constitutional Law Supreme Court Litigation, Comparative Constitutional Law. ***Email:*** fried@law.harvard.edu

GERALD FRUG*, (Louis Brandeis Professor of Law)**, born Berkeley, California, July 31, 1939; admitted to bar, 1964, California; 1969, New York. *Education:* University of California (A.B., 1960); Harvard Law School (LL.B., 1963). ***COURSES: Contracts, Legal Theory, Local Government Law.

HEATHER KRISTIN GERKEN*, (Assistant Professor of Law)**, born Boston, Massachusetts, February 19, 1969; admitted to bar, 1997, Maryland; 1998, District of Columbia. *Education:* Princeton University (A.D., 1991); University of Michigan (J.D., 1994). ***COURSES: Civil Procedure, Election Law. ***Email:*** gerken@law.harvard.edu

MARY ANN GLENDON*, (Learned Hand Professor of Law)**, born Pittsfield, Massachusetts, October 7, 1938; admitted to bar, 1964, Illinois; 1980, Massachusetts. *Education:* University of Chicago (B.A., 1959; J.D., 1961; M.C.L., 1963). ***COURSES: Comparative Law, Property, Constitutional Law and Legal Theory.

LANI GUINIER*, (Professor of Law)**, *Education:* Radcliff College (B.A., 1971); Yale Law School (J.D., 1974). ***COURSES: Law and the Political Process, Legal Profession: The Responsibilities of Public Lawyers, Seminar: Critical Perspective on the Law: Issues of Race, Gender, Class and Social Change, Seminar: Lawyering for Social Justice in Theatres of Power.

***DANIEL I. HALPERIN*, (Stanley S. Surrey Professor of Law)**, born

(This Listing Continued)

HARVARD LAW SCHOOL—Continued

Brooklyn, New York, January 2, 1937; admitted to bar, 1962, New York; 1977, Pennsylvania; 1984, District of Columbia. *Education:* City College of New York at Baruch College (B.B.A., 1957); Harvard (J.D., 1961). ***COURSES:*** Taxation. ***Email:*** halperin@law.harvard.edu

JON D. HANSON, **(Professor of Law)**, born Houston, Texas, December 24, 1960. *Education:* Rice University (B.A., 1986); Yale University (J.D., 1990). ***COURSES:*** Torts, Products Liability, Corporations.

BRUCE L. HAY, **(Professor of Law)**, born Northampton, Massachusetts, January 9, 1963; admitted to bar, 1991, Pennsylvania. *Education:* University of Wisconsin (B.A., 1985); Harvard Law School (J.D., 1988). ***COURSES:*** Environmental Law, Civil Procedure.

DAVID R. HERWITZ, **(Austin Wakeman Scott Professor of Law; Director, Program of Instruction for Lawyers)**, born 1925; admitted to bar, 1949, Massachusetts. *Education:* Massachusetts Institute of Technology (B.S., 1946); Harvard Law School (LL.B., 1949). ***COURSES:*** Accounting, Business Planning, Professional Responsibility.

PHILIP BENJAMIN HEYMANN, **(James Barr Ames Professor of Law)**, born Pittsburgh, Pennsylvania, October 30, 1932; admitted to bar, 1960, District of Columbia; 1970, Massachusetts. *Education:* Yale University (A.B., 1954); Harvard Law School (J.D., 1960). ***COURSES:*** Criminal Law and Procedure, Federal Law Enforcement, Comparative Criminal Procedure.

MORTON J. HORWITZ, **(Charles Warren Professor of American Legal History)**, born 1938; admitted to bar, 1970, Massachusetts. *Education:* City College of the City University of New York (A.B., 1959); Harvard University (Ph.D., 1964); Harvard Law School (LL.B., 1967). ***COURSES:*** Torts, Critical Legal Studies, American Legal History.

HOWELL E. JACKSON, **(Household International and Finn M.W. Caspersen Professor of Law)**, born New York, N.Y., January 4, 1954; admitted to bar, 1984, District of Columbia. *Education:* Brown University (B.A., 1976); Harvard Business School (M.B.A., 1982); Harvard Law School (J.D., 1982). ***COURSES:*** Financial Institutions Regulation, Securities Regulation, Federal Budgetary Process, Pension Law.

CHRISTINE MARGARET JOLLS, **(Assistant Professor of Law)**, born White Plains, New York, October 1, 1967. *Education:* Stanford University (B.A., 1989); Harvard Law School (J.D., 1993); Massachusetts Institute of Technology (Ph.D., 1995). ***COURSES:*** Contracts, Employment Law, Corporations.

LOUIS KAPLOW, **(Professor of Law)**, born Chicago, Illinois, June 17, 1956; admitted to bar, 1983, Massachusetts. *Education:* Northwestern University (A.B., 1977); Harvard University (A.M., 1981; Ph.D., 1987); Harvard Law School (J.D., 1981). ***COURSES:*** Antitrust, Law and Economics, Taxation.

ANDREW L. KAUFMAN, **(Charles Stebbins Fairchild Professor of Law)**, born Newark, New Jersey, February 1, 1931; admitted to bar, 1954, District of Columbia; 1979, Massachusetts. *Education:* Harvard University (A.B., 1951); Harvard Law School (LL.B., 1954). ***COURSES:*** Constitutional Law, Professional Responsibility, Commercial Law.

DAVID KENNEDY, **(Henry L. Shattuck Professor of Law; Director, European Law Research Center)**, born Philadelphia, Pennsylvania, April 5, 1954; admitted to bar, 1980, District of Columbia. *Education:* Brown University (B.A., 1976); Fletcher School of Law and Diplomacy (M.A.L.D., 1979; Ph.D., 1984); Harvard Law School (J.D., 1980). ***COURSES:*** European Community Law, Evidence, International Law, Legal Theory.

DUNCAN KENNEDY, **(Carter Professor of General Jurisprudence)**, born Washington, D.C., March 4, 1942. *Education:* Harvard University (B.A., 1964); Yale Law School (LL.B., 1970). ***COURSES:*** Torts, Legal History, Housing.

RANDALL L. KENNEDY, **(Professor of Law)**, born Columbia, South Carolina, 1954; admitted to bar, 1983, District of Columbia. *Education:* Princeton University (B.A., 1977); Balliol College, Oxford University; Yale Law School (J.D., 1982). ***COURSES:*** Civil Rights Law, Contracts.

REINIER KRAAKMAN, **(Ezra Ripley Thayer Professor of Law)**, born Santa Monica, California, June 15, 1949. *Education:* Harvard University (A.B., 1971); University of Frankfurt; Yale Law School (J.D., 1979). ***COURSES:*** Corporations, Corporate Finance, Corporate Theory.

MICHAEL E. LEVINE, **(Adjunct Professor of Law)**, born New York, New York, April 8, 1941. *Education:* Reed College (B.A., 1962); Yale Law School (J.D., 1965). ***COURSES:*** Regulated Industries, International Business. ***Email:*** melevine@law.harvard.edu

KENNETH W. MACK, **(Assistant Professor of Law)**, born Harrisburg, Pennsylvania, December 14, 1964; admitted to bar, 1992, Pennsylvania; 1993, District of Columbia. *Education:* Drexel University (B.S., 1987); Princeton University (M.A., 1996); Harvard Law School (J.D., 1991). ***COURSES:*** American Legal History, Legal Profession, Property. ***Email:*** kmack@law.harvard.edu

JOHN MANSFIELD, **(John H. Watson, Jr. Professor of Law)**, born Morristown, New Jersey, October 12, 1928; admitted to bar, 1956, California; 1962, Massachusetts. *Education:* Harvard University (A.B., 1952; LL.B., 1956). ***COURSES:*** Constitutional Law, Church and State, Evidence, Comparative Law.

HARRY STRATTON MARTIN, III, **(Librarian and Professor of Law)**, born Hartford, Connecticut, January 22, 1943; admitted to bar, 1968, Minnesota. *Education:* Harvard University (A.B., 1965); University of Pittsburgh (M.L.S., 1971); University of Minnesota (J.D., 1968). ***COURSES:*** Computational Analysis of Legal Research, Advanced Legal Research, Information Policy.

DANIEL J. MELTZER, **(Story Professor of Law)**, born Chicago, Illinois, December 17, 1951; admitted to bar, 1975, Illinois; 1978, District of Columbia; 1983, Massachusetts. *Education:* Harvard University (A.B., 1972); Harvard Law School (J.D., 1975). ***COURSES:*** Federal Courts, Criminal Law. ***Email:*** meltzer@law.harvard.edu

FRANK I. MICHELMAN, **(Robert Walmsley University Professor)**, born New Rochelle, New York, May 26, 1936; admitted to bar, 1961, New York; 1967, Massachusetts. *Education:* Yale University (B.A., 1957); Harvard Law School (LL.B., 1960). ***COURSES:*** Property, Constitutional Law and Theory.

ARTHUR R. MILLER, **(Bruce Bromley Professor of Law)**, born Brooklyn, New York, June 22, 1934; admitted to bar, 1959, New York; 1979, Massachusetts. *Education:* University of Rochester (A.B., 1955); Harvard Law School (LL.B., 1958). ***COURSES:*** Civil Procedure, Copyright, Complex Litigation.

MARTHA MINOW, **(Professor of Law)**, born Highland Park, Illinois, December 6, 1954; admitted to bar, 1981, Massachusetts. *Education:* University of Michigan (A.B., 1975); Harvard University (Ed.M., 1976); Yale Law School (J.D., 1979). ***COURSES:*** Civil Procedure, Family Law.

ROBERT H. MNOOKIN, **(Samuel Williston Professor of Law and**

(This Listing Continued)

HARVARD LAW SCHOOL—*Continued*

Chair, Steering Committee, Program on Negotiation), born Kansas City, Missouri, February 4, 1942; admitted to bar, 1970, District of Columbia; 1971, California. *Education:* Harvard University (A.B., 1964); Harvard Law School (LL.B., 1968). ***COURSES:*** Dispute Resolution, Negotiation, Mediation, Family Law.

CHARLES NESSON*, (Weld Professor of Law, Director, Berkman Center for Internet and Society)**, born February 11, 1939. *Education:* Harvard University (A.B., 1960); Harvard Law School (J.D., 1963). ***COURSES: Evidence, Introduction to Lawyering, Law, Information and Technology. ***Email:*** nesson@law.harvard.edu

CHARLES J. OGLETREE, JR.*, (Jessie Climenko Professor of Law, Faculty Director of Clinical Programs)**, born California, December 31, 1952; admitted to bar, 1979, District of Columbia; 1983, U.S. Supreme Court. *Education:* Stanford University (B.A., 1974; M.A., 1975); Harvard Law School (J.D., 1978). ***COURSES: Criminal Law, Juvenile Justice, Trial Advocacy Workshops.

RICHARD DAVIES PARKER*, (Paul W. Williams Professor of Criminal Justice)**, born Boston, Massachusetts, April 3, 1945; admitted to bar, 1973, Massachusetts. *Education:* Swarthmore College (B.A., 1967); Harvard Law School (J.D., 1970). ***COURSES: Law and Literature: Spiritual Hygiene for Lawyers, Claims/Priorities/Argument, Criminal Law, Constitutional Law.

TODD D. RAKOFF*, (Byrne Professor of Administrative Law, Dean of J.D. Students)**, born Philadelphia, Pennsylvania, February 8, 1946; admitted to bar, 1977, Massachusetts. *Education:* Harvard University (B.A., 1967); Oxford University (B.Phil., 1969); University of Pennsylvania (M.S.Ed., 1971); Harvard Law School (J.D., 1975). ***COURSES: Contracts, Administrative Law, Consumer Protection.

J. MARK RAMSEYER*, (Mitsubishi Professor of Japanese Legal Studies)**, born 1954; admitted to bar, 1983, Illinois. *Education:* Goshen College (B.A., 1976); University of Michigan (M.A., 1978); Harvard (J.D., 1982). ***COURSES: Corporate, Japanese Law.

DIANE M. RING*, (Assistant Professor of Law)**, born Baltimore, Maryland, June 21, 1965; admitted to bar, 1991, New York and District of Columbia. *Education:* Harvard University (A.B., 1986); Harvard Law School (J.D., 1990). ***COURSES: Taxation.

***D. ROSENBERG*, (Professor of Law)**

FRANK E.A. SANDER*, (Bussey Professor of Law)**, born Stuttgart, Germany, July 22, 1927; admitted to bar, 1952, Massachusetts. *Education:* Harvard University (B.A., 1949); Harvard Law School (LL.B., 1952). ***COURSES: Negotiation, Mediation, ADR, Lawyering.

LEWIS D. SARGENTICH*, (Professor of Law)**, born February, 1944; admitted to bar, 1972, District of Columbia. *Education:* Occidental College (A.B., 1965); Sussex University (B.A., 1967); Harvard Law School (J.D., 1970). ***COURSES: Torts, Jurisprudence, Theories About Law, Accident Law.

MARGO SCHLANGER*, (Assistant Professor of Law)**, born New York, New York, December 20, 1967; admitted to bar, 1995, New York. *Education:* Yale College (B.A., 1989); Yale Law School (J.D., 1993). ***COURSES: Torts, Constitutional Law, Civil Rights, Institutional Reform Litigation. ***Email:*** mschlang@law.harvard.edu

HAL S. SCOTT*, (Nomura Professor of International Financial Systems, Dir., Ctr for International Financial Systems)**, born Chicago, Illinois, November 25, 1943; admitted to bar, 1982, Massachusetts. *Education:* Princeton University (A.B., 1965); Stanford University (M.A., 1967); University of Chicago (J.D., 1972). ***COURSES: Banking Regulation, International Finance, Payment Systems.

DAVID L. SHAPIRO*, (William Nelson Cromwell Professor of Law)**, born New York, N.Y., October 12, 1932; admitted to bar, 1957, District of Columbia; 1964, Massachusetts. *Education:* Harvard University (B.A., 1954); Harvard Law School (LL.B., 1957). ***COURSES: Federal Jurisdiction, Civil Procedure, Legal Profession, Statutory Interpretation.

STEVEN SHAVELL*, (Professor of Law and Economics; Director, John M. Olin Center for Law, Economics and Business)**, born Washington, D.C., May 29, 1946. *Education:* University of Michigan (A.B., 1968); Massachusetts Institute of Technology (Ph.D., 1973); Harvard Law School (Liberal Arts Fellow, 1977-1978). ***COURSES: Economic Analysis of Law.

JOSEPH WILLIAM SINGER*, (Professor of Law)**, born Long Branch, New Jersey, May 23, 1954; admitted to bar, 1981, Massachusetts; 1982, New Jersey. *Education:* Williams College (B.A., 1976); Harvard University (A.M., 1978); Harvard Law School (J.D., 1981). ***COURSES: Property, Conflict of Laws.

ANNE-MARIE SLAUGHTER*, (J. Sinclair Armstrong Prof. of Intl., Foreign and Comparative Law; Dir, Grad. & Intl. Legal Studies)**, born Charlottesville, Virginia, September 27, 1958; admitted to bar, 1987, Massachusetts. *Education:* Princeton University (A.B., 1980); Oxford University, Oxford, England (M.Phil., 1982; D.Phil., 1992); Harvard University (J.D., 1985). ***COURSES: International Law, Civil Procedure, International Litigation and Arbitration. ***Email:*** slaughtr@law.harvard.edu

CAROL S. STEIKER*, (Professor of Law, Associate Dean)**, born Philadelphia, Pennsylvania, May 31, 1961; admitted to bar, 1987, New York; 1988, District of Columbia. *Education:* Harvard-Radcliffe Colleges (A.B., 1982); Harvard Law School (J.D., 1986). ***COURSES: Criminal Law, Criminal Procedure, Capital Punishment. ***Email:*** steiker@law.harvard.edu

HENRY J. STEINER*, (Jeremiah Smith, Jr. Professor of Law; Director Human Rights Program)**, born Mt. Vernon, New York, June 14, 1930; admitted to bar, 1956, New York; 1963, Massachusetts. *Education:* Harvard University (B.A., 1951; M.A., 1955); Harvard Law School (LL.B., 1955). ***COURSES: Human Rights.

***ALAN A. STONE M.D.*, (Touroff-Glueck Professor of Law and Psychiatry)**

WILLIAM STUNTZ*, (Professor of Law)**, *Education:* College of William and Mary (B.A., 1980); University of Virginia School of Law (J.D., 1984). ***COURSES: Criminal Law, Criminal Procedure: Advanced, Seminar: Policing the Police.

LAURENCE HENRY TRIBE*, (Ralph S. Tyler Professor of Constitutional Law)**, born Shanghai, China, October 10, 1941; admitted to bar, 1966, California; 1978, Massachusetts, U.S. Supreme Court and U.S. Court of Appeals for the District of Columbia Circuit; 1979, U.S. Court of Appeals, Ninth Circuit; 1980, U.S. Court of Appeals, First Circuit; 1982, U.S. Court of Appeals, Second Circuit; 1991, U.S. Court of Appeals, Third Circuit; 1993, U.S. Court of Appeals, Fourth and Federal Circuits. *Education:* Harvard University (A.B., 1962); Harvard Law School (J.D., 1966); Gonzaga University (LL.D., Honorary, 1980); University of the Pacific (LL.D., Honorary, 1987); American University (LL.D., Honorary, 1987); Illinois Institute of Technology (LL.D., Honorary, 1988). ***COURSES: Constitutional Law and Theory, Law and Technology, Privacy.

***ROBERTO MANGABEIRA UNGER*, (Professor of Law)**

DETLEV VAGTS*, (Bemis Professor of Law)**, born Washington, D.C., February 13, 1929; admitted to bar, 1961, Massachusetts. *Education:* Harvard University (A.B., 1948); Harvard Law School (LL.B., 1951). ***COURSES: Corporations, International Law. ***Email:*** vagts@law.harvard.edu

(This Listing Continued)

HARVARD LAW SCHOOL—Continued

W. KIP VISCUSI*, (John F. Cogan Jr. Professor of Law & Economics)**, born Trenton, New Jersey, October 1949. *Education:* Harvard College (A.B., 1971); Harvard University (M.P.P., 1973; A.M., 1974; Ph.D., 1976). ***COURSES: Law and Economics.

FRANK E. VOGEL*, (Custodian of Two Holy Mosques, Adj. Prof. of Islamic Legal Studies, Director, Islamic Legal Studies Program)**, born 1949; admitted to bar, 1975, District of Columbia. *Education:* Harvard University (A.B., 1972; Ph.D., 1993); Washington College of Law, American University (J.D., 1975). ***COURSES: Islamic Law, the Law of Modern Muslim Countries, Comparative Law and Religion, Contracts. ***Email:*** vogel@law.harvard.edu

ALVIN WARREN*, (Ropes & Gray Professor of Law)**, born Daytona Beach, Florida, May 14, 1944; admitted to bar, 1970, Connecticut; 1978, Pennsylvania. *Education:* Yale University (A.B., 1966); University of Chicago Law School (J.D., 1969). ***COURSES: Taxation.

ELIZABETH WARREN*, (Leo Gottlieb Professor of Law)**, born Oklahoma City, Oklahoma, June 22, 1949; admitted to bar, 1977, New Jersey; 1983, Texas. *Education:* University of Houston (B.S., 1970); Rutgers University Law School (J.D., 1976). ***COURSES: Bankruptcy, Commercial Law, Contract Law.

JOSEPH H.H. WEILER*, (Manley Hudson Prof. of Law; Jean Monnet Chair)**, born Johannesburg, South Africa, September 2, 1951. *Education:* Sussex University (B.A., 1976); Cambridge University (LL.B., 1977; LL.M., 1982); Hague Academy (Dip. Int. Law, 1978); European University Institute (Ph.D., Europ.Law, 1982). ***COURSES: European Community Law, Public International Law, NAFTA and International Trade Law.

PAUL C. WEILER*, (Henry J. Friendly Professor of Law)**, born Port Arthur, Ontario, Canada, January 28, 1939; admitted to bar, 1967, Ontario. *Education:* University of Toronto (B.A., 1960; M.A., 1961); Osgoode Hall Law School (LL.B., 1964); Harvard Law School (LL.M., 1965). ***COURSES: Labor and Employment Law, Torts and Personal Injury, Sports and the Law, Entertainment Law.

LLOYD WEINREB*, (Dane Professor of Law)**, born New York, N.Y., October 9, 1936; admitted to bar, 1963, New York; 1968, Massachusetts. *Education:* Dartmouth College (B.A., 1957); University of Oxford (B.A., 1959); Harvard Law School (LL.B., 1962). ***COURSES: Intellectual Property, Criminal Law, Criminal Procedure, Legal Philosophy.

DAVID WESTFALL*, (John L. Gray Professor of Law and Carl F. Schipper, Jr. Professor of Law)**, born Columbia, Missouri, April 16, 1927; admitted to bar, 1950, Illinois; 1956, Massachusetts. *Education:* University of Missouri (A.B., 1947); Harvard Law School (LL.B., 1950). ***COURSES: Employment Law, Family Law, Labor Law.

LUCIE E. WHITE*, (Louis A. Horvitz Professor of Law)**, born North Carolina, June 13, 1949; admitted to bar, 1981, North Carolina and District of Columbia; 1987, California. *Education:* Radcliffe (B.A., 1972); Yale Graduate School (1972-1975); Harvard (J.D., 1981). ***COURSES: Civil Procedure, Social Welfare Law, Community Based Advocacy.

DAVID B. WILKINS*, (Kirkland & Ellis Professor of Law and Director of the Program on the Legal Profession)**, born Chicago, Illinois, January 22, 1956; admitted to bar, 1982, District of Columbia. *Education:* Harvard University (B.A., 1977); Harvard Law School (J.D., 1980). ***COURSES: Legal Profession and Civil Procedure.

BERNARD WOLFMAN*, (Fessenden Professor of Law)**, born Philadelphia, Pennsylvania, July 8, 1924; admitted to bar, 1949, Pennsylvania; 1976, Massachusetts. *Education:* University of Pennsylvania (A.B., 1946; J.D., 1948); Jewish Theological Seminary of America (LL.D. (hon.), 1971); Capital University (LL.D. (hon.), 1990). ***COURSES: Federal Income Taxation (Individual and Corporate), Ethics and Professional Responsibility in Federal Tax Practice. ***Email:*** wolfman@law.harvard.edu

JONATHAN L. ZITRAIN*, (Assistant Professor of Law, Faculty Co-Dir., Berkman Center for Internet & Society)**, born Pittsburgh, Pennsylvania, December 24, 1969; admitted to bar, 1995, Pennsylvania; 1996, District of Columbia. *Education:* Yale University (B.S., 1991); Harvard Law School (J.D., 1995); JFK School of Government (M.P.A., 1995). ***COURSES: Cyberlaw, Torts, Intellectual Property, Internet. ***Email:*** zittrain@law.harvard.edu

---

HOFSTRA UNIVERSITY SCHOOL OF LAW

121 HOFSTRA UNIVERSITY
HEMPSTEAD, LONG ISLAND, NEW YORK 11549-1210
Telephone: (516) 463-5858
Fax: (516) 463-6091
Website: www.hofstra.edu/law

ABA Approved Since 1971.

The Hofstra University School of Law, which is approved by the ABA and is a member of the AALS, is an independent, nonsectarian institution in Hempstead, New York, on suburban Long Island, a short distance from Manhattan.

The first thirty years in the life of the Hofstra University School of Law presents a story of vision, commitment to excellence and extraordinary success. The Law School was founded to create something special--a place which provides a superb legal education, in the broadest sense, to generations of competent and ethical attorneys; a place which makes meaningful contributions to the dialogue on pressing social issues of national and local importance and which brings together a diversity of students, faculty, judges, lawyers, scholars and professionals from a variety of disciplines in an effort to broaden the perspectives of all. The Law School has developed a number of institutes that sponsor research, advanced courses, and lectures and conferences in specialized areas. These institutes include the Institute for the Study of Legal Ethics and the Institute for Trial Advocacy and Dispute Resolution. The Law School has also established a new interdisciplinary Center for Children, Families and the Law, in which professionals from law, medicine and mental health collaborate in a clinical program, conferences and training to improve the welfare of children and their families. The result is a law school community that is constantly engaged in intellectual discussion and debate as faculty and students critically examine the law, the legal profession and legal education itself.

The Law School is located in an air-conditioned, three-level building, designed to be in harmony with the brick neoclassic buildings on the South Campus. A significant building expansion was completed in 1991 to house the school's growing library and faculty and to accommodate new programs. A new state-of-the-art building has been constructed for the Law School's clinical programs and Career Services Offices. In the Law School's newly constructed trial courtroom/classroom, students view and criticize their own trial practice through the use of advanced

(This Listing Continued)

audio-visual equipment, including remote-control, closed-circuit television cameras and recording devices. The new moot courtroom is an attractively designed amphitheater, with a professional judge's and jury box, and sophisticated computer and video equipment. The law library contains approximately 516,000 volumes or equivalents. The library has two computer labs and additional workstations throughout the library. A wireless network has been installed throughout the Law School, which allows laptop access to the network (internet, e-mail, LEXIS and WESTLAW) from any site in the building.

In achieving a national reputation for academic excellence, the Law School has always emphasized teaching as well as research and publication. The faculty are persons of academic distinction, and many of them are recognized as national authorities in their fields. They are also committed to excellence in teaching. The faculty care deeply about legal education in general and about their students in particular. They make it a point to be accessible to students outside of the traditional classroom setting.

The curriculum at Hofstra is designed to provide a broad-based legal education that will equip students to practice law in every state and federal court in the nation. The emphasis is primarily on the teaching of legal analysis, lawyering skills and professional responsibility. The first-year curriculum includes a course on "Lawmaking Institutions in Context" which explores the process of lawmaking through an examination of recent legislation. The Law School takes special care to provide the rigorous first-year legal training in as personal an atmosphere as possible. For example, each first-year student has one class in a section of fewer than 30 students; this experience enables a closer relationship between students and faculty in a seminar-like environment. In the second and third years, the Law School provides the opportunity for interested students to develop expertise in a number of particular areas of the law. For example, extensive offerings in litigation and trial practice consist of a mix of classroom, simulation, skills training and strategy sessions. Other areas of possible concentration include corporate, constitutional, criminal, family, health, labor and tax law as well as alternative dispute resolution.

Learning takes place not only in the classroom and clinical settings, but also at frequent special lectures when prominent judges, scholars and practitioners address students and faculty and during more informal exchanges among faculty and students in faculty offices and students lounges. This intellectually challenging atmosphere makes Hofstra a very special place at which to obtain a high quality and rigorous legal education in a diverse and nurturing atmosphere.

Dean: David Yellen (516) 463-5854
Admissions: Tina Sneed (516) 463-5916
Financial Aid: Rosemary Ferrucci (516) 463-5929
Library: Judith Anspach (516) 463-5900
Career Services: Caroline Levy (516) 463-5871
Alumni Affairs: Lilli Weinger (516) 463-5306

FULL TIME FACULTY

DAVID N. YELLEN*, (Dean & Professor of Law)**, born 1957; admitted to bar, 1985, District of Columbia and New Jersey. *Education:* Princeton University (B.A., 1979); Cornell Law School (J.D., 1984). ***COURSES: Criminal Law, Criminal Procedure, Sentencing Reform, White Collar Crime.

JUDITH FORD ANSPACH*, (Law Library Director and Professor of Law)**, born Akron, Ohio, October 29, 1940. *Education:* Kent State University (B.S.E.D., 1962; M.L.S., 1977); Mississippi College (J.D., 1983). ***COURSES: Legal Research, Legal Writing. ***Email:*** lawjfa@hofstra.edu

ALAFAIR S. BURKE*, (Associate Professor of Law)**, born Fort Lauderdale, Florida, October 16, 1969; admitted to bar, 1995, Oregon; 2000, New York. *Education:* Reed College (B.A., 1991); Stanford University Law School (J.D., 1994). ***COURSES: Criminal Law, Evidence, Criminal Procedure. ***Email:*** lawasb@hofstra.edu

ROBERT A. BARUCH BUSH*, (Professor of Law)**, born 1948; admitted to bar, 1974, California. *Education:* Harvard University (B.A., 1969); Stanford University Law School (J.D., 1974). ***COURSES: Alternative Dispute Resolution, Alternatives to Litigation, Comparative Law, Economic Analysis and Law, Mediation Clinic, Torts.

ROBIN CHARLOW*, (Professor of Law)**, born 1951; admitted to bar, 1982, New York. *Education:* Vassar College (A.B., 1971); Cornell University (J.D., 1981). ***COURSES: Appellate Advocacy, Constitutional Law, Criminal Law, Mass Media and the First Amendment, Sex-Based Discrimination.

NORA V. DEMLEITNER*, (Visiting Professor of Law)**, born Schwabach, Germany, December 11, 1966; admitted to bar, 1993, Massachusetts, New York. *Education:* Bates College (B.A., 1989); Yale Law School (J.D., 1992); Georgetown University Law Center (LL.M., 1994). ***COURSES: Criminal Law, Sentencing, Evidence, Comparative Law. ***Email:*** bell01211@aol.com

J. HERBIE DIFONZO*, (Associate Professor of Law)**, born Buenos Aires, Argentina, March 19, 1953; admitted to bar, 1977, Virginia; 1978, District of Columbia. *Education:* St. Joseph's University (B.S., 1974); University of Virginia (M.A., 1977; J.D., 1977; Ph.D., 1993). ***COURSES: Criminal Justice Clinic, Family Law.

DAVID A. DIAMOND*, (Professor of Law)**, born 1937; admitted to bar, 1963, New York. *Education:* Harvard University (A.B.); Harvard University Law School (LL.B., 1962); New York University School of Law (LL.M., 1963). ***COURSES: Civil Procedure, Conflict of Laws, Domestic Relations, Education, Legal Problems of Federal Jurisdiction, Trial Practice.

JANET L. DOLGIN*, (Maurice A. Deane Distinguished Professor of Constitutional Law)**, born 1947; admitted to bar, 1982, New York. *Education:* Barnard College (B.A., 1968); Princeton University (M.A., 1971; Ph.D., 1974); Yale Law School (J.D., 1981). ***COURSES: Family Law, Health Law, Law and Society, Selected Problems in Reproductive Technology, Wills, Trusts & Estates.

ERIC M. FREEDMAN*, (Professor of Law)**, born 1953; admitted to bar, 1980, New York; 1985, District of Columbia. *Education:* Yale University (B.A., 1975); Victoria University (M.A., 1977); Yale Law School (J.D., 1979). ***COURSES: Civil Procedure, Civil Rights, Constitutional Law, Legal History, Mass Communications Law.

MONROE H. FREEDMAN*, (Howard Lichtenstein Distinguished Professor of Legal Ethics)**, born 1928; admitted to bar, 1954, Massachusetts; 1957, Pennsylvania; 1960, District of Columbia; 1978, New York. *Education:* Harvard University (A.B., 1951); Harvard University Law School (LL.B., 1954; LL.M., 1956). ***COURSES: Appellate Advocacy, Contracts, Legal Ethics, Legal Profession, Trial Advocacy.

(This Listing Continued)

HOFSTRA UNIVERSITY SCHOOL OF LAW—Continued

LEON FRIEDMAN*, (Joseph Kushner Distinguished Professor of Civil Liberties Law)**, admitted to bar, 1961, New York. *Education:* Harvard University (A.B., 1954); Harvard University Law School (LL.B., 1960). ***COURSES: Constitutional Law, Copyright, Criminal Procedure, Federal Courts.

VICTOR FUTTER*, (Special Consultant to the Dean & Special Professor)**, born Brooklyn, New York, January 22, 1919; admitted to bar, 1942, New York; 1948, U.S. Supreme Court. *Education:* Columbia (B.A., 1939); Columbia (J.D., 1942). ***COURSES: Nonprofit Organizations, Corporate Governance, Corporations. ***Email:*** lawvzf@hofstra.edu

LINDA GALLER*, (Professor of Law)**, born 1959; admitted to bar, 1982, Massachusetts; 1983, New York. *Education:* Wellesley College (B.A., 1979); Boston University (J.D., 1982); New York University School of Law (LL.M., 1986). ***COURSES: Business Organizations, Corporate Tax, Federal Taxation, International Taxation, Tax Policy.

MITCHELL GANS*, (Professor of Law)**, born 1949; admitted to bar, 1975, New York. *Education:* Hofstra University (B.B.A., 1971); Hofstra University School of Law (J.D., 1974). ***COURSES: Estate & Gift Tax Partnership Law, Estate Planning, Federal Tax, Wills, Trusts and Estates.

WILLIAM R. GINSBERG*, (Rivkin, Radler, Bayh, Hart & Kremer Distinguished Professor of Environmental Law)**, born 1930; admitted to bar, 1956, New York. *Education:* Antioch College (B.A., 1952); Yale Law School (J.D., 1955). ***COURSES: Environmental Law, Local Government, Preservation Law, Property, Real Estate Transactions.

JOHN DEWITT GREGORY*, (Sidney and Walter Siben Distinguished Professor of Family Law)**, born 1931; admitted to bar, 1960, New York. *Education:* Howard University (B.A., 1952); Harvard University Law School (J.D., 1959). ***COURSES: Criminal Law, Domestic Relations, Education, Legal Problems of Local Government, Family Law.

JOANNA L. GROSSMAN*, (Associate Professor)**, born Madison, Wisconsin, August 5, 1968; admitted to bar, 1995, California; 1996, District of Columbia. *Education:* Amherst College (B.A., 1990); Stanford Law School (J.D., 1994). ***COURSES: Sex Discrimination, Contracts, Trusts & Estates, Family Law. ***Email:*** lawjlg@hofstra.edu

GRANT M. HAYDEN*, (Associate Professor)**, born Los Angeles, California, May 2, 1964; admitted to bar, 1997, Maryland. *Education:* Kansas (B.A., 1989; M.A., 1991); Stanford (J.D., 1995). ***COURSES: Labor Law, Employment Law, Lawmaking Institutions.

JAMES EDWARD HICKEY, JR.*, (Professor of Law)**, born 1944; admitted to bar, 1970, Georgia; 1971, District of Columbia. *Education:* University of Florida (B.S., 1966); University of Georgia (J.D., 1970); University of Cambridge (Ph.D., 1977). ***COURSES: Energy Law, International Human Rights, International Law, Law of the Sea, Personal Property, Real Property.

BERNARD E. JACOB*, (Professor of Law and Alexander M. Bickel Distinguished Professor of Communications Law)**, born 1932; admitted to bar, 1962, California; 1969, New York. *Education:* St. John's College (A.B., 1954); University of California at Berkeley, Boalt Hall School of Law (J.D., 1960); New School for Social Research (M.A., 1991; Ph.D., 1991). ***COURSES: Constitutional Law, Estates, Jurisprudence, Legal History, Real Estate Transactions, Real Property.

LAWRENCE W. KESSLER*, (Richard J. Cardali Distinguished Professor of Trial Advocacy)**, born 1942; admitted to bar, 1967, New York; 1974, Ohio. *Education:* Columbia University (B.A., 1964; J.D., 1967). ***COURSES: Clinical Teaching, Criminal Law, Criminal Procedure, Environmental Law, Evidence, Torts, Trial Practice.

STEFAN H. KRIEGER*, (Professor of Law)**, born 1946; admitted to bar, 1975, Illinois; 1987, Texas. *Education:* University of Chicago (A.B., 1968); University of Illinois (J.D., 1975). ***COURSES: Clinical Teaching, Trial Advocacy.

ERIC LANE*, (Eric J. Schmertz Distinguished Professor of Public Law and Public Service; Professor of Law)**, born 1943; admitted to bar, 1971, New York. *Education:* Brown University (B.A., 1965); State University of New York at Stony Brook (M.A., 1967); Fordham University (J.D., 1970); New York University School of Law (LL.M., 1979). ***COURSES: Administrative Law, Legislative Process, International Law, Legal History.

MALACHY T. MAHON*, (Siggi B. Wilzig Distinguished Professor of Banking Law)**, born 1934; admitted to bar, 1960, New York. *Education:* Manhattan College (B.A., 1954); Fordham University (J.D., 1960). ***COURSES: Antitrust, Banking, Commercial Law, Contracts, Remedies.

LINDA C. MCCLAIN*, (Professor of Law)**, born 1958; admitted to bar, 1986, New York. *Education:* Oberlin College (A.B., 1980); University of Chicago (A.M., 1981); Georgetown University Law Center (J.D., 1985); New York University School of Law (LL.M., 1991). ***COURSES: Jurisprudence, Property, Women and the Law.

MARK MOVSESIAN*, (Professor of Law)**, born Kew Gardens, New York, February 10, 1964; admitted to bar, 1989, New York; 1991, District of Columbia. *Education:* Harvard University (A.B., 1985); Harvard University Law School (J.D., 1988). ***COURSES: Contracts, International Law.

RICHARD K. NEUMANN, JR.*, (Professor of Law)**, born 1947; admitted to bar, 1975, Maryland; 1981, New York. *Education:* Pomona College (B.A., 1969); University of Stockholm (Dipl., 1971); American University Washington College of Law (J.D., 1975); Temple University (LL.M., 1978). ***COURSES: Civil Procedure, Clinical Teaching, Legal Writing, Pre-Trial Litigation, Trial Techniques.

ALAN N. RESNICK*, (Benjamin Weintraub Distinguished Professor of Bankruptcy Law)**, born 1947; admitted to bar, 1973, New York. *Education:* Rider College (B.A., 1969); Georgetown University Law Center (J.D., 1972); Harvard University Law School (LL.M., 1974). ***COURSES: Commercial Law, Commercial Paper, Contracts, Debtor-Creditor Law.

ANDREW SCHEPARD*, (Professor of Law)**, born 1948; admitted to bar, 1974, California; 1980, New York. *Education:* City College of the City University of New York (B.A., 1968); Columbia University (M.A., 1969); Harvard University Law School (J.D., 1972). ***COURSES: Civil Procedure, Education Law, Family Law.

NORMAN I. SILBER*, (Professor of Law)**, born 1951; admitted to bar, 1986, New Jersey; 1987, District of Columbia, Massachusetts and New York. *Education:* Washington University (B.A., 1972); Yale University (M.A., 1978; Ph.D., 1978); Columbia University (J.D., 1986). ***COURSES: Commercial Transactions, Consumer Law, Legal History, Not-for-Profit Corporations.

RONALD H. SILVERMAN*, (Peter S. Kalikow Distinguished Professor of Real Estate Law)**, born 1940; admitted to bar, 1964, Illinois; 1981, New York. *Education:* University of Michigan (B.A., 1961); University of Chicago (J.D., 1964). ***COURSES: Constitutional Law, Housing and Community Development, Land Use Regulation, Local Government, Real Estate Transactions, Real Property.

ROY D. SIMON, JR.*, (Professor of Law)**, born 1949; admitted to bar, 1983, Missouri; 1990, Illinois. *Education:* Williams College (B.A., 1973); New York University School of Law (J.D., 1977). ***COURSES: Agency and Partnership, Clinical Teaching, Complex Litigation, Legal Profession, Pretrial Practice and Procedure.

(This Listing Continued)

HOFSTRA UNIVERSITY SCHOOL OF LAW—Continued

PETER J. SPIRO,* (Professor of Law)**, born Boston, Massachusetts, April 14, 1961; admitted to bar, 1988, New York; 1992, District of Columbia. *Education:* Harvard College (B.A., 1982); University of Virginia (J.D., 1987). ***COURSES: Immigration, Foreign Relations Law, Corporations.

PETER T. SYLVER,* (Associate Dean & Special Professor of Law)**, born New York, October 25, 1968; admitted to bar, 1998, New York. *Education:* John Jay College (B.S., 1994); Hofstra Law School (J.D., 1997). ***COURSES: Critical Race Theory. ***Email:*** lawpts@hofstra.edu

MARSHALL TRACHT,* (Vice Dean & Professor of Law)**, born New York, N.Y., September 18, 1961; admitted to bar, 1990, Pennsylvania; 1991, District of Columbia. *Education:* Yale University (B.A., 1983); University of Pennsylvania (J.D., 1990); University of Pennsylvania, The Wharton School (M.B.A., 1990). ***COURSES: Property, Real Estate, Real Estate Finance, Environmental Issues in Commercial Practice.

CHERYL L. WADE,* (Professor of Law)**, born 1956; admitted to bar, 1989, New York. *Education:* State University of New York at Stony Brook (B.A., 1976); St. John's University (M.A., 1980); Hofstra University School of Law (J.D., 1988). ***COURSES: Business Organizations, Securities Regulation, Torts.

VERN R. WALKER,* (Professor of Law)**, born 1945; admitted to bar, 1980, District of Columbia. *Education:* University of Detroit (B.A., 1967); University of Notre Dame (M.A., 1969; Ph.D., 1975); Yale Law School (J.D., 1980). ***COURSES: Health and Safety Regulation, Products Liability, Scientific Evidence, Torts.

HOWARD UNIVERSITY SCHOOL OF LAW

2900 VAN NESS STREET, N.W.
WASHINGTON, D.C. 20008
Telephone: (202) 806-8000
Fax: (202) 806-8424
http://www.law.howard.edu/

ABA Approved Since 1931.

The Howard University School of Law started as the Howard University Law Department on January 6, 1869 under the leadership of Professor John Mercer Langston. In 1870, Langston was appointed dean. The department opened with six students and increased to twenty-two by the close of the session on June 30, 1869.

Initially, two years were required for the LL.B. degree. Ten of the two-year students graduated on February 3, 1871, eight of whom were admitted to practice in the District of Columbia on the following day. The school officially extended its requirements for graduation from two years to three years during the 1877-1878 academic term. The new three-year program began in 1900.

During this fledgling period, classes were held three nights a week in the homes and offices of the four instructors. Arrangements were later made for the department to use a room in the Second National Bank at 509 Seventh Street, N.W. Classes were later held in the Lincoln Hall building on Ninth and D Streets, N.W., until December 5, 1886, when the building was destroyed by fire. Then classes moved to a room located at Seventh and E Street, N.W. On June 23, 1887, the University purchased a house at 420 Fifth Street, N.W., which served as the law school site until it was moved to the main campus in 1936. In 1974, the school purchased the Dunbarton College at 2900 Van Ness Street, N.W., where it has remained to date.

In 1931, the School of Law was accredited by the American Bar Association (ABA). In the same year, the school was granted membership in the Association of American Law Schools, (AALS).

Today, Howard University School of Law confers an average of 140 Juris Doctor and Master of Comparative Jurisprudence degrees annually to students from the United States and countries in South America, the Caribbean, Africa and Asia. It has a faculty of thirty-five full-time instructors and sixteen adjunct instructors.

From its small beginnings, the school has grown in size and structure under the leadership of its deans. Among the more nationally noted are Charles Hamilton Houston, 1930-1935; William Henry Hastie, 1939-1946; James M. Nabrit, 1958-1960; Spotswood Robinson III, 1960-1963; and Wiley A. Branton, Sr., 1978-1983. In 1872, the law school graduated the first black woman lawyer, Charlotte E. Ray. She is also recognized as the first woman to be admitted to practice law before the Supreme Court of the District of Columbia. James C. Napier, another 1872 graduate, was the Registrar of the United States Treasury, 1911-1913, and a member of Howard's Board of Trustees, 1911-1940. Other graduates who have received merited recognition and distinctions include Thurgood Marshall, the first black United States Supreme Court Justice (LL.B. 1933); Vernon E. Jordan, Jr. former president of the National Urban League, (LL.B. 1960); Damon Keith, Judge, United States Court of Appeals for the Sixth Circuit, (LL.B. 1949); William Bryant, Judge, United States District Court for the District of Columbia, (LL.B. 1936); Spotswood W. Robinson III, Chief Judge, United States Court of Appeals for the District of Columbia, (LL.B. 1939); Douglas Wilder, former Governor of the State of Virginia; Julia Cooper Mack, Judge, District of Columbia Court of Appeals (LL.B., 1952); H. Patrick Swygert, President of Howard University (LL.B., 1968); and Sharon Pratt Kelly, former Mayor of the District of Columbia. The school has produced a large number of distinguished law professors and members of the practicing bar.

The School of Law was created to provide legal education for African Americans and other disadvantaged persons. The School of Law's mission is to produce superior professionals, capable of achieving positions of leadership in law, business, government, education, and public service. More important, Howard University School of Law is dedicated to producing "social engineers." As Charles Hamilton Houston stated, "A lawyer's either a social engineer or...a parasite on society...A social engineer [is] a highly skilled, perceptive, sensitive lawyer who [understands] the Constitution of the United States and [knows] how to explore its uses in the solving of problems of local communities and in bettering conditions of the underprivileged citizens."

In May 2001, the School of Law moved into a new state-of-the-art law library. This four-story, 76,000 square foot building provides for a book collection of up to 215,000 volumes; seating for over 295 students (more than 50% of the student population), including 90 open carrels, with all locations wired for computer use. The first floor features a fifty-six seat classroom equipped with individually designated data ports and a SMART board. The first floor also houses the reserve reading room, audiovisual and microform suites, and rooms for videotaping. The second floor houses the main reading room, the reference area, seven study rooms, and thirty individual carrels. The third floor houses lounges, study rooms and thirty additional individual carrels. The fourth floor of this beautiful edifice houses additional reading rooms, a special Collections room, and additional individual carrels

(This Listing Continued)

HOWARD UNIVERSITY SCHOOL OF LAW—Continued

Among the many things that make the Howard University School of Law a special place to study law are the opportunities it affords its students to enrich their educational experience with all of the resources afforded in the nation's capital and by traveling and studying abroad. The *South Africa Summer Program*, approved by the American Bar Association, allows students to earn up to six semester hours of law school credit. Courses in International Business Transaction, South Africa's Constitution in Comparative Perspective, and Contemporary Developments in Comparative and International Law. The program offers an extraordinary opportunity for students to witness, firsthand, the historic legal and political changes in South Africa. The Howard program is unique because of the opportunity it provides for interaction with South African law students and graduates who also participate in the program.

Dean: Alice Gresham Bullock (202) 806-8000
Associate Dean for Academic Affairs: Patricia M. Worthy (202) 806-8003
Director of the Law Library: Rhea Ballard-Thrower (202) 806-8045
Associate Dean for Administration and Operations: Samuel McClendon (202) 806-8021
Assistant Dean for Admissions and Financial Aid: Ruby Sherrod (202) 806-8009
Assistant Dean for Student Affairs and Records: Denise L. Spriggs (202) 806-8006
Financial Aid: Norman James (202) 806-8005
Placement: LuEllen Conti (202) 806-8135

FULL TIME FACULTY

ALICE GRESHAM BULLOCK*, (Dean)**, admitted to bar, Georgia and District of Columbia. *Education:* Howard University (B.A., 1972; J.D., 1975). ***COURSES: Advanced Tax Problems, Federal Tax, Wills, Trusts and Estates, Professional Ethics. ***Email:*** abullock@law.howard.edu

LORETTA C. ARGRETT*, (Professor)**, born 1937; admitted to bar, 1976, District of Columbia. *Education:* Howard University (B.S., 1958); Harvard University (J.D., 1976). ***COURSES: Advanced Corporate Tax Problems, Federal Income Taxation, Professional Responsibility, State & Local Tax. ***Email:*** largrett@law.howard.edu

RHEA BALLARD-THROWER*, (Associate Professor, Director of the Law Library)**, born Toledo, Ohio, April 5, 1961. *Education:* University of Cincinnati (B.A., 1983); University of Kentucky (J.D., 1986); University of Michigan (M.I.L.S., 1988). ***COURSES: Advanced Legal Research. ***Email:*** rballard@law.howard.edu

GREGORY BERRY*, (Legal Writing Instructor)**, born 1956; admitted to bar, 1980, Pennsylvania; 1981, District of Columbia. *Education:* University of Washington (B.A., 1977); University of Pennsylvania (J.D., 1980);. ***COURSES: Legal Reasoning, Research & Writing, Legal Writing II.

SPENCER H. BOYER*, (Professor)**, born 1938; admitted to bar, 1967, District of Columbia. *Education:* Howard University (B.S. in E.E., 1960); George Washington University (LL.B., 1965); Harvard University (LL.M., 1966). ***COURSES: Federal Income Taxation, Contracts, Entertainment Law. ***Email:*** sboyer@law.howard.edu

PATRICIA BROUSSARD*, (Legal Writing Instructor)**, born 1950; admitted to bar, 1985, District of Columbia. *Education:* Northwestern University (B.S., 1972); Howard University (J.D., 1983). ***COURSES: Legal Reasoning, Research and Writing, Legal Writing II.

LISA ANN CROOMS*, (Associate Professor)**, born 1962; admitted to bar, 1991, California. *Education:* Howard University (B.A., 1984); University of Michigan (J.D., 1991). ***COURSES: Constitutional Law, Contracts, Gender and the Law, Critical Race Theory. ***Email:*** lcrooms@law.howard.edu

ELIZABETH CHRISTI CUNNINGHAM*, (Associate Professor)**, born 1967; admitted to bar, 1993, New York. *Education:* Southern Methodist University (B.S.B.A., 1989); Yale Law School (J.D., 1992). ***COURSES: Equal Employment Law, Labor Law, Collective Bargaining and Arbitration, Poverty Law, National Moot Court, Legal Methods. ***Email:*** ecunningham@law.howard.edu

OKIANER CHRISTIAN DARK*, (Professor of Law)**, born Petersburg, Virginia, December 8, 1954; admitted to bar, 1979, Pennsylvania, New Jersey; 1984, Virginia. *Education:* Upsala College (B.A., 1976); Rutgers University Newark School of Law (J.D., 1979). ***COURSES: Torts, Products Liability.

KIRSTEN ANNE DAUPHINAIS*, (Instructor)**, born Oswego, New York, August 8, 1971; admitted to bar, 1998, New York. *Education:* Colgate University (B.A., 1993); Columbia University School of Law (J.D., 1997). ***COURSES: Legal Reasoning, Research & Writing.

MARSHA A. ECHOLS*, (Professor)**, *Education:* Howard University (B.A., 1965); Phi Beta Kappa; Georgetown University (J.D., 1968); Free University of Brussels (LL.M., 1973). ***COURSES: International Business Transactions, Problems of World Order, International Economic Law, International Sales. ***Email:*** mechols@law.howard.edu

ANDREW I. GAVIL*, (Professor)**, born 1957; admitted to bar, 1981, Illinois; 1986, Colorado; 1993, District of Columbia. *Education:* Queens College, CUNY (B.A., 1978); Northwestern University (J.D., 1981). ***COURSES: Antitrust, Civil Procedure, Consumer Law, Federal Courts, Complex Litigation. ***Email:*** agavil@law.howard.edu

AMINATA N. IPYANA*, (Associate Professor of Law)**, born Groton, Massachusetts, February 14, 1962; admitted to bar, 1991, District of Columbia. *Education:* Howard University (B.A., 1984); Washington University, St. Louis (J.D., 1989). ***COURSES: Criminal Justice Clinic. ***Email:*** aipyana@law.howard.edu

MICHELLE S. JACOBS*, (Visiting Professor)**, born 1954; admitted to bar, 1983, New Jersey and New York. *Education:* Princeton University (A.B., 1977); Rutgers School of Law-Newark (J.D., 1982). ***COURSES: Criminal Justice Clinic, Criminal Law, Women Defendants in the Criminal Justice System, Critical Race Theory. ***Email:*** mjacobs@law.howard.edu

STEVEN D. JAMAR*, (Professor)**, born 1953; admitted to bar, 1979, Minnesota; 1994, District of Columbia. *Education:* Carleton College (B.A., 1975); Hamline University (J.D., 1979); George Washington University (LL.M., 1994). ***COURSES: International Law of Human Rights, International Moot Court, Legal Writing. ***Email:*** sjamar@law.howard.edu

HENRY H. JONES*, (Professor)**, born 1926; admitted to bar, 1957, District of Columbia. *Education:* Howard University (J.D., 1956). ***COURSES: Conflict of Laws, Race Law and Change, Remedies. ***Email:*** hjones@law.howard.edu

***ADAM HARRIS KURLAND*, (Professor)**, born 1957; admitted to bar,

(This Listing Continued)

HOWARD UNIVERSITY SCHOOL OF LAW—Continued

1981, California; 1994, District of Columbia. *Education:* University of California at Los Angeles (B.A., 1978; J.D., 1981). ***COURSES:*** Criminal Law, Criminal Procedure I, Evidence, Federal Criminal Law. ***Email:*** akurland@law.howard.edu

HOMER C. LARUE,* (Professor)**, born 1948; admitted to bar, 1975, New York; 1980, U.S. Supreme Court; 1992, Maryland; 1994, District of Columbia. *Education:* Purdue University (B.A., 1970); Cornell University (J.D., 1974; M.I.L.R., 1975). ***COURSES: Civil Procedure, Alternative Dispute Resolution Clinic, Alternative Dispute Resolution. ***Email:*** hclarue@law.howard.edu

WARNER LAWSON, JR.,* (Professor)**, born 1940; admitted to bar, 1970, New York. *Education:* Howard University (B.A., 1962; J.D., 1969). ***COURSES: Sales and Secured Transactions, Remedies, Contracts. ***Email:*** wlawson@law.howard.edu

ISIAH LEGGETT,* (Professor)**, admitted to bar, 1974, Iowa and Pennsylvania; 1975, District of Columbia and Louisiana. *Education:* Southern University (B.A., 1967); Howard University (M.A., 1972; J.D., 1974); George Washington University (1976). ***COURSES: Torts I and II, Law and Medicine. ***Email:*** ileggett@law.howard.edu

CYNTHIA REGINA MABRY,* (Associate Professor)**, born 1957; admitted to bar, 1983, District of Columbia. *Education:* Howard University (B.A., 1979; J.D., 1983); New York University (LL.M., 1996). ***COURSES: Family Law, Children and the Law, Civil Procedure, Advanced Discovery. ***Email:*** cmabry@law.howard.edu

GWENDOLYN MAJETTE,* (Legal Writing Instructor)**, born 1967; admitted to bar, 1993, Maryland; 1994, District of Columbia. *Education:* Emory (B.A., 1989); George Washington University (J.D.,1993). ***COURSES: Legal Reasoning, Research & Writing, Legal Writing II.

HAROLD MCDOUGALL,* (Professor)**, born 1945; admitted to bar, 1972, New York; 1983, District of Columbia. *Education:* Harvard (B.A., 1967); Yale (J.D., 1971). ***COURSES: Land Finance, Land Development, Property, Civil Rights Planning.

ZIYAD MOTALA,* (Professor, Director of LLM Program, Director of South Africa Program)**, born 1962. *Education:* University of Natal (B.A., 1983; LL.B., 1985); Northwestern University (LL.M., 1987; S.J.D., 1991). ***COURSES: Constitutional Law, Comparative Law, International Law. ***Email:*** zmotala@law.howard.edu

LATEEF MTIMA,* (Associate Professor)**, born 1960; admitted to bar, New York; Pennsylvania. *Education:* Amherst College (B.A., 1982); Harvard Law School (J.D., 1985). ***COURSES: Sales and Secured Transactions, Creditors and Debtors Rights and Remedies, Computer Law, Torts. ***Email:*** lmtima@law.howard.edu

MICHAEL D. NEWSOM,* (Professor)**, born 1943; admitted to bar, 1967, Illinois; 1980, District of Columbia. *Education:* Amherst College (B.A., 1964); Harvard Law School (LL.B., 1967). ***COURSES: Property, Church-State, Wills, Trusts & Estates. ***Email:*** mnewsom@law.howard.edu

LAURENCE NOLAN,* (Professor)**, admitted to bar, 1974, Michigan; 1981, District of Columbia; 1983, Maryland. *Education:* Howard University (B.S., 1981); University of Michigan (J.D., 1974). ***COURSES: Wills, Trusts and Estates, Family Law, Law and Aging. ***Email:*** lnolan@law.howard.edu

REGINALD L. ROBINSON,* (Professor)**, born 1955; admitted to bar, 1983, New York. *Education:* Howard University (B.A., 1981); University of Pennsylvania (J.D., 1989). ***COURSES: Property, Jurisprudence, Critical Race Theory, National Moot Court. ***Email:*** rrobinson@law.howard.edu

W. SHERMAN ROGERS,* (Associate Professor)**, born 1951; admitted to bar, Alabama and New York. *Education:* Oakwood College (B.A., 1973); Howard University (J.D., 1976). ***COURSES: Business Organizations, Corporations, Conflict of Laws. ***Email:*** srogers@law.howard.edu

J. CLAY SMITH, JR.,* (Professor)**, born 1942; admitted to bar, 1967, Nebraska; 1968, District of Columbia. *Education:* Creighton University (B.A., 1964); Howard University (J.D., 1967); George Washington University (LL.M., 1970; S.J.D., 1977). ***COURSES: Constitutional Law, Administrative Law, Federal Elections Law, Advanced Constitutional Law. ***Email:*** csmith@law.howard.edu

ANDREW ERIC TASLITZ,* (Professor)**, born 1956; admitted to bar, 1981, Pennsylvania and District of Columbia. *Education:* Queens College, City University of New York (B.A., 1978); University of Pennsylvania (J.D., 1981). ***COURSES: Criminal Procedure, Evidence, Criminal Law, Pretrial Litigation. ***Email:*** ataslitz@law.howard.edu

BONNY TAVARES,* (Legal Writing Instructor)**, born 1961; admitted to bar, 1994, District of Columbia. *Education:* Howard University (B.B.A., 1990; J.D., 1993). ***COURSES: Legal Reasoning, Research and Writing, Legal Writing II. ***Email:*** btavares@law.howard.edu

RICHARD P. THORNELL,* (Professor)**, born 1936; admitted to bar, 1974, New York; 1979, District of Columbia. *Education:* Fisk University (B.A., 1956); Princeton University (M.P.A., 1958); Yale (J.D., 1971). ***COURSES: Torts II, Professional Responsibility, Advanced Torts, Environmental Law. ***Email:*** rthornell@law.howard.edu

PATRICIA M. WORTHY,* (Associate Professor and Associate Dean for Academic Affairs)**, born 1944; admitted to bar, 1971, District of Columbia. *Education:* Brooklyn College (B.A., 1966); Howard University (J.D., 1969). ***COURSES: Administrative Law, Legal Methods, Professional Responsibility, Telecommunications Law. ***Email:*** pworthy@law.howard.edu

FRANK H. WU,* (Associate Professor and Director of the Clinical Law Center)**, born 1967; admitted to bar, 1992, California; 1995, District of Columbia. *Education:* Johns Hopkins (B.A., 1988); Michigan (J.D., 1991). ***COURSES: Elder Law Clinic, Civil Procedure, Federal Courts, Immigration Law. ***Email:*** fwu@law.howard.edu

---

INDIANA UNIVERSITY SCHOOL OF LAW - BLOOMINGTON

211 SOUTH INDIANA AVENUE
BLOOMINGTON, INDIANA 47405
Telephone: (812) 855-7995
Fax: (812) 855-0555
http://www.law.indiana.edu

(This Listing Continued)

INDIANA UNIVERSITY SCHOOL OF LAW-BLOOMINGTON—Continued

ABA Approved Since 1923.

The Indiana University School of Law - Bloomington

For more than 150 years, the Indiana University School of Law-Bloomington has offered students the highest quality legal education in a college setting. With over 650 students, drawn from over 200 undergraduate schools in the United States and from five continents, the Law School is small enough to retain its distinctive sense of community while large enough to provide a stimulating, cosmopolitan environment.

The Law School stresses innovative, interdisciplinary education which seeks to broaden students' practical understanding of legal issues in an increasingly complex, global society. With 38 full-time faculty members and a number of practitioners and judges who serve as adjunct faculty, the Law School features a student-faculty ratio of 15 to one, which provides significant faculty-student interaction.

The Law School's comprehensive curriculum is taught by internationally recognized faculty and includes leading programs in a variety of important specialties such as bankruptcy, securities, tax, environmental law, communications and information law, and global and international law, just to name a few. Through partnerships with the Kelley School of Business, the School of Public and Environmental Affairs, the Department of Telecommunications, and other departments of Indiana University, the Law School offers a number of joint law degree programs, minors, and opportunities for interdisciplinary study. Visiting faculty from the international legal community teach courses each year at the Law School, bringing their world view and experience to the classroom.

The curriculum extends far beyond the classroom. Each year distinguished jurists, scholars, and practitioners from around the world visit the school to lecture and work with students. In recent years these visitors have included Chief Justice William H. Rehnquist, Justice Ruth Bader Ginsburg, U.S. Attorney General Janet Reno, U.S. Solicitor General Seth Waxman, Filipino Supreme Court Justice Flerida Romero, retired Japanese Supreme Court Justice Shigemitsu Dando, consumer advocate Ralph Nader, civil rights activist and NYU professor Derrick Bell, Chief Judge Richard Posner, former Environmental Protection Agency Administrator William Ruckelshaus, Cambridge University Vice Chancellor Sir David G.T. Williams, Southern Poverty Law Center co-founder Morris Dees, death penalty defense lawyer Stephen Bright, and many more.

Students and faculty have access to one of the finest legal research facilities in the nation. The Law Library, which is among the 20 largest in the country, offers more than half a million volumes and cutting-edge electronic technology. The library hosts the Virtual Law Library, the world's leading Internet legal research tool.

The Law School also offers these distinctive features:

* An innovative legal writing and advocacy program provides students with the skills necessary to meet the demands of a successful law practice.
* An internship program guarantees a summer internship to every interested student following the first year of law school.
* The School's graduate study program attracts postgraduate students from around the world and adds a global perspective to the community.
* International study opportunities include the school's London Study Program and exchange programs with universities in Paris and Barcelona.
* An accelerated program enables students to begin law school in the summer and/or graduate in 27 months.
* A mentoring program links interested students with practicing attorneys throughout the country, providing valuable contacts and advice.
* Three law journals provide writing and editing opportunities for students in their second and third years of law school.
* In-house clinics and externship programs offer students a wide range of opportunities to gain practical experience.
* The Law School's tuition represents one of the best values in legal education, and numerous scholarships and grants are available.

Dean: Alfred C. Aman, Jr. (812) 855-8885
Assistant Dean, Admissions: Kevin R. Robling (812) 855-4765
Assistant Dean, International Programs: Scott J. Palmer (812) 856-5661
Director, Library: Colleen K. Pauwels (812) 855-9666
Assistant Dean, Career Services: Rachael Kearney (812) 855-0258
Assistant Dean, Alumni Affairs: Angela S. Lieurance (812) 855-9953
Assistant Dean, Finance and Administration: Mark S. Hilycord
Associate Dean, Academic Affairs: Lauren K. Robel
Associate Dean, Student Affairs: Leonard D. Fromm

FULL TIME FACULTY

ALFRED C. AMAN, JR.*, (Dean & Rosco C. O'Byrne Professor of Law)**, born Rochester, New York, July 7, 1945; admitted to bar, 1972, District of Columbia, Georgia; 1982, New York; 1993, Indiana. *Education:* University of Rochester (A.B., 1967); University of Chicago (J.D., 1970). ***COURSES: Admin. Law; Globalization, Law & the State; Energy & Natural Resources Law, Comparative Constitutional Law. ***Email:*** aaman@law.indiana.edu

---

AMY G. APPLEGATE*, (Clinical Associate Professor, Director, Child Advocacy Clinic)**, admitted to bar, 1981, District of Columbia; 1985, U.S. Supreme Court; 1988, Ohio; 1998, Indiana. *Education:* Universita di Bologna; Cornell University (B.A., 1978); Harvard Law School (M.A.; J.D., 1981). ***COURSES: Family Law. ***Email:*** aga@indiana.edu

JOHN S. APPLEGATE*, (Professor)**, born Elmira, New York, March 20, 1957; admitted to bar, 1981, District of Columbia. *Education:* Haverford College (B.A., 1978); Harvard Law School (J.D., 1981). ***COURSES: Toxic Substances & Hazardous Wastes; International Environmental Law; Property. ***Email:*** jsapple@law.indiana.edu

PATRICK L. BAUDE*, (Professor)**, born Independence, Kansas, April 7, 1943; admitted to bar, 1966, Wisconsin; 1990, Indiana. *Education:* University of Kansas (A.B., 1964; J.D., 1966); Harvard University (LL.M., 1968). ***COURSES: Constitutional Law; Federal Courts; Legal Profession. ***Email:*** baude@indiana.edu

JEANNINE BELL*, (Associate Professor)**, born Southfield, Michigan, August 20, 1969. *Education:* Harvard University (A.B., 1991; M.A., 1995); University of Michigan (Ph.D., 1999; J.D., 1999). ***COURSES: Seminar in First Amendment; Law, Politics and Society; Seminar in Law and Society; Criminal Procedure. ***Email:*** jeabell@indiana.edu

TERRY A. BETHEL*, (Professor)**, born September 18, 1946; admitted to bar, 1971, Ohio. *Education:* Ohio State University (B.A., 1968; J.D., 1971). ***COURSES: Labor Law; Labor Arbitration; Contracts. ***Email:*** bethel@indiana.edu

(This Listing Continued)

INDIANA UNIVERSITY SCHOOL OF LAW-BLOOMINGTON—Continued

CRAIG M. BRADLEY*, (James Louis Calamaras Professor of Law)** , born Downer's Grove, Illinois, December 5, 1945; admitted to bar, 1970, Virginia; 1972, District of Columbia. *Education:* University of North Carolina (A.B., 1967); University of Virginia (J.D., 1970). ***COURSES: Constitutional Law; Criminal Procedure; Criminal Law; Federal Criminal Law. ***Email:*** bradleyc@indiana.edu

KEVIN D. BROWN*, (Professor)**, born October 13, 1956; admitted to bar, 1982, Indiana. *Education:* Indiana University (B.S., 1978); Yale Law School (J.D., 1982). ***COURSES: Civil Rights; Law & Education; Torts; Race, American Society & Law. ***Email:*** brownkd@indiana.edu

HANNAH L. BUXBAUM*, (Associate Professor)**, born Cologne, Germany, January 9, 1966; admitted to bar, 1993, New York. *Education:* Cornell University (B.A., 1987); Cornell Law School (J.D., 1992); University of Heidelberg (LL.M., 1993). ***COURSES: International Business Transactions; Secured Transactions; Securities Regulation. ***Email:*** hbuxbaum@indiana.edu

FRED H. CATE*, (Professor)**, born McRae, Georgia, May 20, 1963; admitted to bar, 1987, California; 1988, District of Columbia; 1998, Indiana. *Education:* Stanford University (A.B., 1984); Stanford Law School (J.D., 1987). ***COURSES: Communications; Information Law; Internet Law; Privacy Law; Intellectual Property. ***Email:*** fcate@indiana.edu

DANIEL O. CONKLE*, (Robert H. McKinney Professor)** , born Marion, Ohio, November 10, 1953; admitted to bar, 1979, Ohio; 1989, Indiana. *Education:* Ohio State University (B.A., 1976; J.D., 1979). ***COURSES: Civil Procedure; Constitutional Law; Law & Religion. ***Email:*** conkle@indiana.edu

STEVEN A. CONRAD*, (Professor)**, born Winston-Salem, North Carolina, August 16, 1951; admitted to bar, 1982, Massachusetts. *Education:* Haverford College (B.A., 1973); Harvard University (Ph.D., 1980); Yale Law School (J.D., 1982). ***COURSES: Equity; Family Law; Legal History; Legal Profession; Remedies. ***Email:*** conrads@indiana.edu

YVONNE M. CRIPPS*, (Harry T. Ice Chair in Law)** , born United Kingdom, January 26, 1957. *Education:* Victoria University of Wellington (LL.B., 1977; LL.M., 1978); University of Cambridge (Ph.D., 1981). ***COURSES: Biotechnology and the Law; Law, Technology and Science; Comparative Administrative and Constitutional Law. ***Email:*** ycripps@indiana.edu

CATHY E. CROSSON*, (Lecturer)** , born November 21, 1953; admitted to bar, 1983, Indiana; 1987, California. *Education:* Indiana University (B.A., 1975); Indiana University School of Law (J.D., 1982). ***COURSES: Legal Research & Writing. ***Email:*** ccrosson@indiana.edu

LAURA B. DAGHE*, (Lecturer)**, born Urbana, Illinois, August 5, 1967; admitted to bar, 1992, Indiana. *Education:* Illinois State University (B.S., 1989); University of Illinois College of Law (J.D., 1992). ***COURSES: Legal Research & Writing. ***Email:*** ldaghe@indiana.edu

KENNETH G. DAU-SCHMIDT*, (Willard and Margaret Carr Professor of Labor & Employment Law)** , born Des Moines, Iowa, October 12, 1956; admitted to bar, 1982, Wisconsin; 1984, Minnesota; 1988, Ohio; 1996, Indiana. *Education:* University of Michigan (M.A., 1981; Ph.D., 1984). ***COURSES: Law & Economics; Labor law; Antitrust; Employment Law; Poverty Law. ***Email:*** kdauschm@indiana.edu

ROGER BARNETT DWORKIN*, (Robert A. Lucas Professor)** , born Cincinnati, Ohio, January 19, 1943; admitted to bar, 1967, California. *Education:* Princeton University (A.B., 1963); Stanford Law School (J.D., 1966). ***COURSES: Law & Biomedical Advance; Law & Medicine; Torts. ***Email:*** dworkin@indiana.edu

LISA A. FARNSWORTH*, (Lecturer)** , born Indianapolis, Indiana, July 1, 1955; admitted to bar, 1982, Indiana. *Education:* Indiana University (B.A., 1977); Indiana University School of Law (J.D., 1982). ***COURSES: Legal Research & Writing. ***Email:*** farnswor@indiana.edu

DAVID PAUL FIDLER*, (Professor)**, born Amarillo, Texas, March 29, 1964; admitted to bar, 1992, New York; 1994, Missouri. *Education:* University of Kansas (B.A., 1986); University of Oxford (M.Ph.L., 1988; B.C.L., 1991); Harvard Law School (J.D, 1991). ***COURSES: International Law; International Transactions. ***Email:*** dfidler@indiana.edu

ROBERT L. FISCHMAN*, (Professor)**, born New York, New York, April 17, 1962; admitted to bar, 1988, California; 1990, District of Columbia. *Education:* Princeton University (A.B., 1984); University of Michigan School of Natural Resources (M.S., 1987); University of Michigan School of Law (J.D., 1987). ***COURSES: Environmental Law; Administrative Law; Public Land & Natural Resources; Seminar in Advanced Environmental Law; Water Law. ***Email:*** rfischma@indiana.edu

ANN J. GELLIS*, (Professor)**, born Rockville Center, New York, December 22, 1946; admitted to bar, 1972, New York. *Education:* Case Western Reserve University (B.A., 1968); New York University (J.D., 1971). ***COURSES: Corporations; Land Use; Local Government Law; Municipal Finance; Real Estate Finance. ***Email:*** gellis@indiana.edu

CHARLES G. GEYH*, (Professor)**, born Buffalo, New York, March 6, 1958; admitted to bar, 1985, District of Columbia. *Education:* University of Wisconsin (B.A., 1980; J.D., 1983). ***COURSES: Civil Procedure; Federal Jurisdiction; Trademarks and Unfair Competition, Legal Profession. ***Email:*** cgeyh@indiana.edu

DONALD H. GJERDINGEN*, (Professor)**, born Glenwood, Minnesota, May, 22, 1950; admitted to bar, 1976, Minnesota; 1979, District of Columbia. *Education:* Carleton College (B.A., 1971); William Mitchell College of Law (J.D., 1976); Yale Law School (LL.M., 1978). ***COURSES: Constitutional Law; Environmental Law; Estates; Legal Theory; Jurisprudence; Torts. ***Email:*** dongjerd@indiana.edu

SOPHIA C. GOODMAN*, (Lecturer and Director, Legal Research and Writing)** , born Washington, D.C., July 12, 1964; admitted to bar, 1990, Indiana. *Education:* Bryn Mawr College (A.B., 1985); Case Western Reserve University (J.D., 1990). ***COURSES: Legal Research and Writing. ***Email:*** sgoodman@indiana.edu

EDWIN H. GREENEBAUM*, (Professor Emeritus)** , born January 1, 1936; admitted to bar, 1961, Illinois. *Education:* Harvard University (A.B., 1958; LL.B., 1961); University of Michigan (LL.M., 1967). ***COURSES: Alternative Dispute Resolution; Roles & Relations in Legal Practice; Understanding Clinical Experience. ***Email:*** greeneba@indiana.edu

ROBERT H. HEIDT*, (Professor)**, born October 10, 1948; admitted to bar, 1972, Wisconsin; 1976, California. *Education:* University of Wisconsin (B.A., 1972; J.D., 1972). ***COURSES: Antitrust & Trade Regulation; Torts; Products Liability; Legal Drafting; Law & Economics. ***Email:*** heidt@indiana.edu

J. WILLIAM HICKS*, (C. Ben Duton Professor)** , born St. Louis, Missouri, October 26, 1940; admitted to bar, 1966, New York. *Education:* University of Notre Dame (B.A., 1962); University of Michigan (J.D., 1965); New York University (A.M., 1968). ***COURSES: Securities Regulation; Corporations; Contracts; Corporate Finance; International Securities Regulation. ***Email:*** hicks@indiana.edu

(This Listing Continued)

INDIANA UNIVERSITY SCHOOL OF LAW-BLOOMINGTON—Continued

ELIZABETH PERRY HODGES*, (Assistant Professor part-time)**, born July 18, 1943. *Education:* Hollins College (B.A., 1966); Columbia University (M.Phil., 1976; Ph.D, 1980). ***COURSES: Strategies of Legal Writing; Law & Literature. ***Email:*** hodgese@indiana.edu

JOSEPH L. HOFFMANN*, (Professor)**, born Chicago, Illinois, March 1, 1957; admitted to bar, 1985, Pennsylvania. *Education:* Harvard University (B.A., 1978); University of Washington (J.D., 1984). ***COURSES: Criminal Law; Criminal Procedure; Death Penalty; the Law & Society of Japan; Seminar in Law & Psychology of Criminal Law. ***Email:*** hoffma@indiana.edu

SARAH JANE HUGHES*, (University Scholar & Fellow in Commercial Law)**, born June 26, 1949; admitted to bar, 1974, Washington; 1975, District of Columbia. *Education:* Mount Holyoke College (A.B., 1971); University of Washington (J.D., 1974). ***COURSES: Regulated Industries-Banking Law; Negotiable Instruments; Secured Transactions; Sales. ***Email:*** sjhughes@indiana.edu

DAWN E. JOHNSEN*, (Associate Professor)**, born Manhasset, New York, August 14, 1961; admitted to bar, 1987, New York; 1990, District of Columbia. *Education:* Yale University (B.A., 1983); Yale Law School (J.D., 1986). ***COURSES: Constitutional Law, Seminar in the Separation of Powers. ***Email:*** djohnsen@indiana.edu

STEVE R. JOHNSON*, (Professor)**, born Queens, New York, July 27, 1949; admitted to bar, 1982, New York. *Education:* St. Francis College (B.A., 1976); New York University (J.D., 1981). ***COURSES: Federal Income Tax; U.S. Taxation of International Transactions; Tax Procedure; Tax Crimes; Taxation of Business Entities; Advocacy. ***Email:*** srjohnso@indiana.edu

SETH LAHN*, (Lecturer)**, born Hartford, Connecticut, August 17, 1957; admitted to bar, 1984, New York; 1990, Indiana. *Education:* Yale University (B.A. 1979); Yale Law School (J.D., 1982). ***COURSES: Legal Research & Writing; First-year Advocacy. ***Email:*** slahn@indiana.edu

JULIA C. LAMBER*, (Professor)**, born February 27, 1947; admitted to bar, 1972, Indiana. *Education:* De Pauw University (B.A., 1969); Indiana University-Bloomington (J.D., 1972). ***COURSES: Administrative Law; Employment Discrimination; Family Law; Civil Rights; Women & the Law. ***Email:*** lamber@indiana.edu

MARSHALL A. LEAFFER*, (Distinguished Scholar)**, born Ft. Worth, Texas, January 31, 1943; admitted to bar, 1972, Texas; 1977, New York. *Education:* University of Texas (B.A., 1964; J.D., 1971); University of Illinois (M.A., 1969); New York University (LL.M., 1997). ***COURSES: Intellectual Property. ***Email:*** mleaffer@indiana.edu

AVIVA A. ORENSTEIN*, (Professor)**, born Jerusalem, January 27, 1960; admitted to bar, 1996, New Jersey. *Education:* Cornell University (A.B., 1981); Cornell Law School (J.D., 1986). ***COURSES: Evidence; Legal Profession; Children and the Law. Educational Director, Child Advocacy Clinic. ***Email:*** aorenste@indiana.edu

SCOTT JOSEPH PALMER*, (Assistant Dean of International Programs)**, born Chicago, Illinois, May 3, 1968; admitted to bar, 2001, New York. *Education:* Northern Arizona University (B.A., 1992); Indiana University, Bloomington (J.D., 2001). ***Email: sjpalmer@indiana.edu

COLLEEN K. PAUWELS*, (Associate Professor & Director of the Law Library)**, born Chicago, Illinois, January 25, 1946; admitted to bar, 1988, Indiana. *Education:* Barat College (B.A., 1968); Indiana University (M.L.S., 1975); Indiana University School of Law (J.D., 1986). ***COURSES: Legal Research; Legal Bibliography; Law Library Administration. ***Email:*** pauwels@indiana.edu

WILLIAM D. POPKIN*, (Walter W. Foskett Professor Emeritus)**, born October 28, 1937; admitted to bar, 1961, New York. *Education:* Harvard University (A.B., 1958); Harvard Law School (J.D., 1961). ***COURSES: Income Tax; Corporate Tax; Legislation; Tax Policy. ***Email:*** popkin@indiana.edu

LAUREN K. ROBEL*, (Val Nolan Professor & Associate Dean for Academic Affairs)**, born Omaha, Nebraska, December 8, 1953; admitted to bar, 1995, Indiana; 1984, Illinois. *Education:* Auburn University (B.A., 1978); Indiana University (J.D., 1983). ***COURSES: Civil Rights; Civil Procedure; Federal Jurisdiction; Federal Courts Clinic. ***Email:*** lrobel@indiana.edu

JOHN M. ROGERS*, (Lecturer)**, born St. Louis, Missouri, February 6, 1951; admitted to bar, 1979, Indiana. *Education:* Northwestern University (B.A., 1973); Indiana University (M.A., 1976); Indiana University School of Law (J.D., 1979). ***COURSES: Legal Research and Writing. ***Email:*** jorogers@indiana.edu

JOHN A. SCANLAN*, (Professor)**, born Milwaukee, Wisconsin, July 18, 1944; admitted to bar, 1978, Indiana. *Education:* University of Chicago (M.A., 1967); University of Iowa (Ph.D., 1975); Notre Dame Law School (J.D., 1978). ***COURSES: Immigration Law; Law & Sports; Law & Political Theory; Introduction to American Legal Institutions; Constitutional Law. ***Email:*** scanlan@indiana.edu

GENE R. SHREVE*, (Richard S. Melvin Professor of Law)**, born San Diego, California, August 6, 1943; admitted to bar, 1969, Massachusetts; 1981, Vermont. *Education:* University of Oklahoma (A.B., 1965); Harvard Law School (LL.B., 1968; LL.M., 1975). ***COURSES: Civil Procedure; Conflict of Laws; Jurisprudence. ***Email:*** shreve@indiana.edu

EARL R.C. SINGLETON*, (Clinical Associate Professor)**, born New York, New York, October 5, 1948; admitted to bar, 1987, Michigan; 1989, Indiana. *Education:* Oberlin College (B.A., 1972); Indiana University School of Law (J.D., 1986). ***COURSES: Family Law; Seminar in Clinical Experience. ***Email:*** singlet@indiana.edu

JEFFREY E. STAKE*, (Professor)**, born Osmond, Nebraska, August 19, 1953; admitted to bar, 1981, District of Columbia. *Education:* University of Illinois (B.A,, 1975); Georgetown University Law Center (J.D., 1981). ***COURSES: Property; Trusts & Estates; Land-Use Controls; Landlord-Tenant. ***Email:*** stake@indiana.edu

J. ALEXANDER TANFORD*, (Professor)**, born Iowa City, Iowa, January 23, 1950; admitted to bar, 1976, North Carolina; 1977, New York; 1993, Indiana. *Education:* Princeton University (A.B., 1972); Duke University Law School (J.D., 1976; LL.M., 1979). ***COURSES: Civil & Criminal Trial Process; Law & Psychology; Evidence; Insurance Law; Clinical Education. ***Email:*** tanford@indiana.edu

DAVID C. WILLIAMS*, (Professor)**, born Chicago, Illinois, April 25, 1960. *Education:* Haverford College (B.A., 1982); Harvard Law School (J.D., 1985). ***COURSES: Constitutional Law; Native American Law. ***Email:*** dacwilli@indiana.edu

SUSAN HOFFMAN WILLIAMS*, (Professor)**, born Philadelphia, Pennsylvania, July 12, 1960. *Education:* Harvard University (B.A., 1982); Harvard Law School (J.D., 1985). ***COURSES: AIDS & The Law; First Amendment Law; Family Law; Feminist Legal Theory. ***Email:*** shwillia@indiana.edu

INDIANA UNIVERSITY
SCHOOL OF LAW - INDIANAPOLIS

LAWRENCE W. INLOW HALL
530 WEST NEW YORK STREET
INDIANAPOLIS, INDIANA 46202
Telephone: (317) 274-8523
Fax: (317) 274-3955
www.indylaw.indiana.edu

ABA Approved Since 1936

The Indiana University School of Law-Indianapolis prepares its students for a wide range of legal careers. Our success in training our students to uphold the fine traditions of good lawyering is evidenced by the outstanding professional and civic achievements of our alumni, who practice in every state as well as abroad.

One of Indiana University's two independent law schools, the IU School of Law-Indianapolis traces its origins to the late nineteenth century when the first of its private predecessor schools, the Indiana Law School was established in 1894. Fifty years later, the school became an integral part of Indiana University. With more than 800 students, the IU School of Law-Indianapolis is the largest law school in the state of Indiana, and one of the few Big Ten law schools to offer the cultural, recreational and professional advantages of an urban educational environment. Additionally, it is the only law school in Indiana to offer a part-time evening program.

Located on the campus of Indiana University-Purdue University at Indianapolis and the IU Medical Center, the school is just minutes away from the state's courts, legislature, and major law firms, giving students opportunities not only to observe the legal process in action, but also to participate in that process as law clerks, judicial interns and legislative staff assistants.

In the spring of 2001, the school moved into a new, state-of-the-art facility that is now one of the most technologically-advanced schools in the country.

In addition to the JD degree, students may pursue joint degrees through programs offered in cooperation with the IU School of Business, the IU School of Public and Environmental Affairs, and the IU School of Medicine.

Students at the IU School of Law-Indianapolis have a wide range of backgrounds, bringing diverse professional and personal experience to the classroom. The most recent entering class included students from nearly 185 colleges and universities across the country. The median credentials for entering students were a GPA of 3.3 and an LSAT score of 155.

The school's library contains more than 400,000 volumes or volume equivalents and is a depository for U.S. government and United Nations publications. Every student is given instruction in information retrieval systems, including LEXIS and WESTLAW.

The school's clinical programs train students in basic lawyering skills. With faculty supervision, students participate in a General Civil Practice Clinic, a Civil Practice Disability Clinic, and a Criminal Defense Clinic.

Each year the school sponsors a month-long China Summer Program at Renmin University in Beijing. The school also offers a Program in European Law in Lille, France.

Additionally, our Program in International Human Rights Law is designed to promote legal study and scholarship in international human rights. Another special program of interest is the school's Center for Law and Health. Established in 1986, the Center is a resource for the study of critical issues in health care. The school's location, on the same campus as the world-renowned IU Medical Center, allows interaction among noted scholars and practitioners in both disciplines.

Activities available to students include the *Indiana Law Review,* the *Indiana International and Comparative Law Review,* intramural, regional and national moot court and client counseling competitions, the International Law Society, the Environmental and Health Law Societies, the Federalist Society, the Republican Law Coalition, the Democratic Law Society, the Law and Technology Society, the Lambda Law Society, the Criminal Law Association, the Women's Caucus, and the Dean's Tutorial Society. These organizations serve to complement the rigorous academic instruction at the school. The average grade for coursework at the school is in the range of 2.9-3.1 on a 4.0 scale.

Dean: Norman Lefstein (317) 274-2581
Academic Affairs - Associate Dean: Susanah Mead (317) 274-2600
Graduate Studies - Associate Dean: Jeffrey Grove (317) 274-4900
Technology - Associate Dean: Thomas Allington (317) 274-4985
Admissions - Assistant Dean: Angela Espada (317) 274-2459
External Affairs - Assistant Dean: Jonna Kane (317) 274-1908
Student Affairs - Assistant Dean: Elizabeth DeCoux (317) 274-1907
Career Services - Director: Shannon Williams (317) 278-2172
Library - Director: James Bailey (317) 274-1931

FULL TIME FACULTY

NORMAN LEFSTEIN,* (Dean and Professor of Law)**, born Rock Island, Illinois, July 16, 1937; admitted to bar, 1961, Illinois; 1963, District of Columbia. *Education:* Augustana College; Georgetown University (LL.M., 1964); University of Illinois (LL.B., 1961). ***COURSES: Professional Responsibility, Criminal Law, Evidence, Criminal Procedure, Trial Advocacy.

CYNTHIA MATSON ADAMS,* (Lecturer in Law)**, born Minneapolis, Minnesota, July 20, 1955; admitted to bar, 1983, Indiana. *Education:* Kentucky Wesleyan College (B.A., 1977); Indiana University-Indianapolis (J.D., 1983). ***COURSES: Legal Analysis, Research and Communication.

THOMAS B. ALLINGTON,* (Professor of Law and Associate Dean)**, born Lincoln, Nebraska, April 25, 1942; admitted to bar, 1966, Nebraska; 1985, Indiana. *Education:* University of Nebraska (B.S., 1964; J.D., 1966); New York University (LL.M., 1977). ***COURSES: Taxation, Debtor-Creditor Law.

(This Listing Continued)

INDIANA UNIVERSITY SCHOOL OF LAW-INDIANAPOLIS—Continued

JAMES FRANCIS BAILEY*, (Professor of Law and Director of the Law Library)**, born Ann Arbor, Michigan, April 14, 1939; admitted to bar, 1965, Michigan. *Education:* University of Michigan (B.A., 1961; J.D., with distinction, 1964; M.A.L.S., 1970); University of Madrid (1964-1965). ***COURSES: International Law, Comparative Law, Latin American Law, Legal Research.

FRANK O. BOWMAN, III*, (Associate Professor of Law)**, born Midland, Texas, July 13, 1955; admitted to bar, 1979, Colorado. *Education:* Colorado College (B.A., 1976); Harvard Law School (J.D., 1979). ***COURSES: Criminal Law, Criminal Procedure.

ROBERT BROOKINS*, (Professor of Law)**, *Education:* University of South Florida (B.S., 1974); Cornell University (J.D., 1978; Ph.D., 1990). ***COURSES: Sex Discrimination, Employment Law, Torts.

DANIEL H. COLE*, (M. Dale Palmer Professor of Law)**, born Chicago, Illinois, September 7, 1958; admitted to bar, 1987, New Mexico. *Education:* Occidental College (A.B., 1980); University of Chicago (A.M., 1981); Lewis and Clark College (J.D., 1986); Stanford University (J.S.M., 1991; J.S.D., 1996). ***COURSES: Environmental and Natural Resources Law, Property, International Environmental Law.

JEFFREY COOPER*, (Assistant Professor of Law)**, born July 1, 1964; admitted to bar, 1992, Pennsylvania; 1994, District of Columbia. *Education:* Harvard (A.B., 1986); University of Pennsylvania (J.D., 1991). ***COURSES: Civil Procedure, Products Liability.

PAUL N. COX*, (Centennial Professor of Law)**, born Salt Lake City, Utah, March 17, 1949; admitted to bar, 1974, Utah. *Education:* Utah State University (B.S., 1971); University of Utah (J.D., 1974); University of Virginia (LL.M., 1980). ***COURSES: Corporations, Corporate Finance, Securities Regulation, Employment Discrimination.

KENNETH D. CREWS*, (Professor of Law and Library Information Science, and Director, Copyright Management Office)**, born Fairborn, Ohio, February 14, 1955; admitted to bar, 1980, California. *Education:* Northwestern University (B.A., 1977); Washington University (J.D., 1980); University of California, Los Angeles (M.L.S., 1987); University of California, Los Angeles (Ph.D., 1990). ***COURSES: Copyright Law.

JAMES DAVIS DIMITRI*, (Lecturer in Law)**, born Valparaiso, Indiana, September 4, 1967; admitted to bar, 1993, Indiana. *Education:* Indiana University (B.S., 1990); Valparaiso University School of Law (J.D., 1993). ***COURSES: Legal Analysis, Research and Communication.

JENNIFER ANN DROBAC*, (Associate Professor of Law)**, admitted to bar, 1992, California. *Education:* Stanford University (B.A., 1981; M.A., 1987); Stanford Law School (J.D., 1987; J.S.D., 2000). ***COURSES: Family Law, Professional Responsibility.

GEORGE EUGENE EDWARDS*, (Associate Professor of Law and Director, Program in International Human Rights Law)**, born Raleigh, NC, August 26, 1959. *Education:* North Carolina State University (B.A., 1981); Harvard Law School (J.D., 1986). ***COURSES: International Human Rights Law.

PAUL J. GALANTI*, (Professor of Law)**, born Hackensack, New Jersey, August 8, 1938; admitted to bar, 1963, Illinois. *Education:* Bowdoin College (B.A., 1960); University of Chicago (J.D., 1963). ***COURSES: Business Associations, Corporations, Antitrust, Trade Regulation, Intellectual Property.

HAROLD GREENBERG*, (Professor of Law)**, born Philadelphia, Pennsylvania, January 19, 1938; admitted to bar, 1963, Pennsylvania; 1979, Indiana. *Education:* Temple University (A.B., 1959); University of Pennsylvania (J.D., 1962). ***COURSES: Contracts, Sales, Negotiable Instruments, Sports and Entertainment Law.

JEFFREY W. GROVE*, (Professor of Law and Associate Dean)**, born Pennsylvania, October 17, 1943; admitted to bar, 1969, District of Columbia. *Education:* Juniata College (A.B., 1965); George Washington University (J.D., 1969). ***COURSES: Civil Procedure, Complex Litigation, Federal Jurisdiction.

FRANCES WATSON HARDY*, (Clinical Associate Professor)**, born Jeffersonville, Indiana, January 6, 1955; admitted to bar, 1980, Indiana. *Education:* Ball State University (B.S., 1976); Indiana University School of Law-Indianapolis (J.D., 1980). ***COURSES: Criminal Defense Clinic.

LAWRENCE A. JEGEN, III*, (Thomas F. Sheehan Professor of Tax Law and Policy)**, born Chicago, Illinois, November 16, 1934; admitted to bar, 1959, Illinois; 1963, Indiana. *Education:* Beloit College (B.A., 1956); University of Michigan (J.D., 1959; M.B.A., 1960); New York University (LL.M., 1963). ***COURSES: Civil and Criminal, Federal and State Taxation, Business and Estate Planning, Philanthropy.

HENRY CARL KARLSON*, (Professor of Law)**, born Evanston, Illinois, August 17, 1943; admitted to bar, 1968, Illinois; 1972, United States Supreme Court. *Education:* University of Illinois (B.A., 1965; J.D., 1968); Judge Advocate General's School. ***COURSES: Evidence, Criminal Law, Litigation.

ROBERT A. KATZ*, (Associate Professor of Law)**, admitted to bar, 1992, Massachusetts. *Education:* Harvard College (A.B., 1987); University of Chicago (J.D., 1992). ***COURSES: Trusts, Estates, Nonprofit Organizations.

ELEANOR D. KINNEY*, (Samuel R. Rosen Professor of Law and Co-Director of the Center for Law and Health)**, born Boston, Massachusetts, January 17, 1947; admitted to bar, 1973, Ohio; 1977, North Carolina. *Education:* Duke University (A.B., 1969; J.D., 1973); University of Chicago (M.A., 1970). ***COURSES: Health Law, Administrative Law, Insurance Law and Torts.

ANDREW R. KLEIN*, (Professor of Law)**, born March, 9, 1963; admitted to bar, 1988, Illinois. *Education:* University of Wisconsin (B.A., 1985); Emory University School of Law (J.D., 1988). ***COURSES: Torts, Environmental Law.

ROBERT EDWARD LANCASTER*, (Clinical Associate Professor)**, admitted to bar, 1993, Indiana; 1998, Connecticut. *Education:* Millsaps College (B.A., 1989); Tulane Law School (J.D., 1993). ***COURSES: Clinical Teaching, Skills Training, Poverty Law, Criminal Law & Procedure.

GERARD N. MAGLIOCCA*, (Assistant Professor of Law)**, admitted to bar, 1998, New Jersey; 1999, District of Columbia. *Education:* Stanford University (B.A., 1995); Yale Law School (J.D., 1998). ***COURSES: Intellectual Property, Torts, Criminal Law, Legal History, Environmental Law, Constitutional Law.

LYNN MCDOWELL*, (Clinical Associate Professor of Law)**, born Indianapolis, Indiana, April 14, 1949; admitted to bar, 1976, Indiana. *Education:* Indiana University (B.S., 1971); Indiana University School of Law-Indianapolis (J.D., 1976). ***COURSES: Criminal Defense Clinic.

DEBORAH B. MCGREGOR*, (Assistant Director for Legal Analysis, Research and Communication)**, born Indiana, December 9, 1951; admitted to bar, 1983, Virginia; 1984, Colorado. *Education:* University of Evansville (B.A., 1973); Georgetown University (J.D., 1983). ***COURSES: Legal Analysis, Research and Communication.

***SUSANAH M. MEAD*, (Professor of Law and Associate Dean)**, born Indianapolis, Indiana, August 10, 1947; admitted to bar, 1976, Indiana.

(This Listing Continued)

INDIANA UNIVERSITY SCHOOL OF LAW-INDIANAPOLIS—Continued

Education: Smith College (B.A., 1969); Indiana University School of Law-Indianapolis (J.D., 1976). ***COURSES:*** Torts, Products Liability.

MARY HARTER MITCHELL*, (Professor of Law)**, born Ashland, Ohio, March 9, 1953; admitted to bar, 1978, Indiana. *Education:* Butler University (B.A., 1975); Cornell University (J.D., 1978). ***COURSES: Church - State, Contracts, Family Law.

JAMES P. NEHF*, (Cleon H. Foust Fellow and Professor of Law)**, born Oak Park, Illinois, April 5, 1957; admitted to bar, 1984, District of Columbia. *Education:* Knox College (B.A., 1979); University of North Carolina (J.D., 1983). ***COURSES: Contracts, Consumer Protection, Secured Transactions.

DAVID ORENTLICHER*, (Samuel R. Rosen Professor of Law and Co-Director of the Center for Law and Health)**, born Washington, D.C., May 2, 1955; admitted to bar, 1988, District of Columbia; 1993, Illinois. *Education:* Brandeis University (A.B., 1977); Harvard Medical School (M.D., 1981); Harvard Law School (J.D., 1986). ***COURSES: Bioethics and Law, Constitutional Law.

JOANNE ORR*, (Clinical Associate Professor of Law)**, born Manchester, New Hampshire, December 26, 1955; admitted to bar, 1986, Indiana. *Education:* Indiana State University (B.S., 1977); California Western School of Law (J.D., 1986). ***COURSES: Disability Clinic.

DAVID R. PAPKE*, (R. Bruce Townsend Professor of Law and Professor of Liberal Arts)**, born Milwaukee, Wisconsin, January 1, 1947. *Education:* Harvard University (A.B., 1969); Yale University (J.D., 1973); University of Michigan (Ph.D., 1984). ***COURSES: Jurisprudence, Legal History, Law and Literature, Sales, Family Law.

H. KATHLEEN PATCHEL*, (Associate Professor of Law)**, born Montgomery, Alabama, August 24, 1956; admitted to bar, 1981, Georgia. *Education:* Huntingdon College (A.B., 1978); University of North Carolina (J.D., 1981); Yale Law School (LL.M., 1987). ***COURSES: Commercial Law, Constitutional Law.

FLORENCE WAGMAN ROISMAN*, (Professor of Law and Paul Beam Fellow)**, born New York, NY, February 21, 1939; admitted to bar, 1963, New York; District of Columbia. *Education:* University of Connecticut (B.A., 1959); Harvard Law School (LL.B., 1963). ***COURSES: Property, Civil Procedure, Housing Discrimination, Homelessness.

JOAN RUHTENBERG*, (Clinical Professor of Law and Director of Legal Analysis, Research and Communication)**, born Memphis, Tennessee; admitted to bar, 1980, Indiana. *Education:* Mississippi State University for Women (B.A., 1959); Indiana University School of Law--Indianapolis (J.D., 1980). ***COURSES: Legal Analysis, Research and Communication.

JOEL M. SCHUMM*, (Lecturer in Law)**, admitted to bar, 1998, Indiana. *Education:* Ohio Wesleyan University (B.A., 1992); University of Cincinnati (M.A., 1994); Indiana University School of Law - Indianapolis (J.D., 1998). ***COURSES: Legal Analysis, Research and Communication.

E. GARY SPITKO*, (Associate Professor of Law)**, born Norristown, PA, February 7, 1965; admitted to bar, 1992, Pennsylvania; 1992 District of Columbia; 1994, Georgia. *Education:* Cornell (A.B., 1987); Duke University law School (J.D., 1991). ***COURSES: Trusts & Estates. ***Email:*** espitko@iupui.edu

JAMES W. TORKE*, (Carl M. Gray Professor of Law)**, born Milwaukee, Wisconsin, December 23, 1941; admitted to bar, 1968, Wisconsin; 1969, Minnesota. *Education:* University of Wisconsin (B.S., 1963; J.D., 1968). ***COURSES: Civil Procedure, Constitutional Law.

JAMES P. WHITE*, (Professor of Law and Advisor to the ABA Consultant on Legal Education)**, born Iowa City, Iowa, September 29, 1931; admitted to bar, 1956, Iowa; 1969, District of Columbia. *Education:* University of Iowa (B.A., 1953; J.D., 1956); George Washington University (LL.M., 1959); Honorary Degrees: University of Pacific; John Marshall Law School; Widener University; Whittier College. ***COURSES: Legal Profession.

LAWRENCE P. WILKINS*, (Professor of Law and John S. Grimes Fellow)**, born Columbus, Ohio, March 15, 1945; admitted to bar, 1973, Ohio. *Education:* Ohio State University (B.A., 1968); Capital University Law School (J.D., 1973); University of Texas School of Law (LL.M., 1974). ***COURSES: Torts, Law and Medicine, Legislation, Negotiation.

LLOYD T. WILSON, JR.*, (Lecturer in Law)**, born Crawfordsville, Indiana, February 6, 1955; admitted to bar, 1982, Indiana. *Education:* Wabash College (B.A., 1977); Duke University (M.A., 1978); Indiana University School of Law (J.D., 1982). ***COURSES: Legal Analysis, Research and Communication.

MARY THERESE WOLF*, (Clinical Professor of Law and Director of Clinical Programs)**, born Chicago, Illinois, November 8, 1946; admitted to bar, 1974, Illinois and Iowa; 1985, Indiana. *Education:* St. Xavier College (B.A., 1969); University of Iowa (J.D., 1974). ***COURSES: Interviewing and Counseling, Civil Practice Clinic.

R. GEORGE WRIGHT*, (Professor of Law)**, admitted to bar, 1982, Indiana. *Education:* University of Virginia (A.B., 1972); Indiana University (Ph.D., 1976); Indiana University School of Law - Indianapolis (J.D., 1982). ***COURSES: Constitutional Law, Administrative Law, Jurisprudence.

INTER-AMERICAN UNIVERSITY OF PUERTO RICO - SCHOOL OF LAW

P.O. BOX 70351
SAN JUAN, PUERTO RICO 00936-8351
Telephone: (787) 751-1912(2004)
Fax: (787) 751-2975
http://www.derecho.inter.edu

ABA Approved Since 1935.

Established in 1912 in San German, Puerto Rico, as an elementary and secondary school, the Inter American University of Puerto Rico, has grown to become one of the largest private institutions in the United States. Under the direction of its founder, the Rev. J. Will Harris, the University, originally called the Puerto Rico Politechnical Institute, established itself as a non-profit, Christian and Ecumenical, private institution. In 1921 university level courses were offered for the first time and in 1927 the first degrees were awarded. Accredited for the first time in 1944 by the Middle States Association of Colleges and Schools, Inter American University has kept its accreditation in good standing ever since.

Located in San Juan, Puerto Rico, the Inter American University School of Law was established in 1961 as an evening program with 9

(This Listing Continued)

INTER-AMERICAN UNIVERSITY OF PUERTO RICO-SCHOOL OF LAW—Continued

professors and 200 students. From such modest origins, the School of Law has grown--specially qualitatively--to become a major option for the study of law in Puerto Rico. Located in recently-built ultra-modern facilities, the School of Law at present has 600 students and 25 full-time professors. The fact that a small class of 175 students is selected from over 1,000 candidates in recent years, has contributed to the adoption of higher admission standards. The School of Law was fully approved by the ABA in 1978 and has kept its accreditation in good standing thereafter.

In 1986 the School of Law adopted a new curriculum which implemented the clinical approach for the instruction of law. In the first year of studies, education process emphasizes on the importance of acquiring sound research skills, through a two-semester course on research, analysis and writing.

The new library holds over 160,000 volumes and occupies about 35,000 square feet. It is equipped with the most recent technological developments in order to facilitate study and investigation to students, professors and practitioners.

The development of sound litigation skills is one of the distinctive characteristics of the School of Law curriculum. Students enroll in a required three-credit course on the theory of litigation. Subsequently they have the opportunity to practice for one or two semesters with actual cases in the Legal Aid Clinic. The Clinic is integrated to the San Juan Community Law Office, a Legal Services funded program. This joint venture between the University and Legal Services Corp. has contributed to the development of innovative clinical projects which provide services to groups such as the elderly, juveniles, and AIDS victims. Not only do students work on trial litigation skills; they also have the opportunity to get acquainted with some of the problems faced by the underprivileged. In fact for the last several years the Inter American School of Law has been implementing through its curriculum, strategies that have recently been adopted by the ABA.

Several student organizations provide opportunities for engaging in professionally and personally gratifying experiences. The Law Journal hosted the celebration of the National Conference of Law Reviews in April, 1994. The National Association of Law Students, the Student Council, the ABA Law Students Division, the Phi Alpha Delta Law Fraternity and the Hispanic National Bar Association share the enthusiastic participation of a large portion of the student body. Students have effectively participated in litigation skills competitions held locally and in the mainland. Others take advantage of summer studies arrangements with European schools of law.

Dean: Luis M. Negron-Portillo (787) 751-1912(2000)
Admissions: Alida Rivera (787) 751-1912(2013)
Financial Aid: Ricardo Crespo (787) 751-1912(2014)
Library: Ivette Rossello (787) 751-1912(2042)
Placement: Marilucy Gonzalez-Baez (787) 751-1912(2011)
Alumni Affairs: Sheila Gomez (787) 751-1912(2032)

FULL TIME FACULTY

LUIS M. NEGRON-PORTILLO*, (Dean and Professor of Law)**, born Puerto Rico, May 13, 1956; admitted to bar, 1981, Puerto Rico. *Education:* University of Puerto Rico (B.A., 1978; J.D., 1981; M.P.A., 1983); Yale University (LL.M., 1984); Stanford University (J.S.D., 1994). ***COURSES: Corporations, Commercial Law, Jurisprudence, Professional Responsibility, Comparative Law, Sociology of Law. ***Email:*** lmnegron@inter.edu

SYLVIA E. CANCIO*, (Professor of Law)**, born Aquadilla, Puerto Rico, July 20, 1950; admitted to bar, 1975, Puerto Rico. *Education:* Colegio Universitario del Sagrado Corazon (B.A., 1972); Inter-American University of Puerto Rico School of Law (J.D., 1974); Tulane University (M.C.L., 1982). ***COURSES: Family Law, Inheritance Law, Wills and Testaments.

IVETTE COLL DE PESTANA*, (Professor of Law)**, born San Juan, Puerto Rico, July 30, 1942; admitted to bar, 1973, Puerto Rico. *Education:* University of Puerto Rico (B.A., 1964); Inter-American University (J.D., 1972); Tulane University (M.C.L., 1984). ***COURSES: Family Law, Successions, Contracts.

ANDRES CORDOVA*, (Associate Professor)**, born Tulsa, Oklahoma, October 29, 1960; admitted to bar, 1995, Puerto Rico. *Education:* College of the Holy Cross (B.A., 1982); Boston College (M.A., 1985); University of Puerto Rico Law School (J.D., 1994). ***COURSES: Contracts, Sociology of Law.

JUAN FRANCISCO CORREA LUNA*, (Assistant Professor)**, born Brooklyn, New York, August 17, 1957; admitted to bar, 1982, Puerto Rico. *Education:* University of Puerto Rico (B.A., 1978); Inter-American University of Puerto Rico (J.D., 1982); Boston College Law School (1981). ***COURSES: Clinical Program. ***Email:*** jcorrea@inter.edu

MARIA DE LOS ANGELES DIEZ-FULLADOSA*, (Assistant Professor)**, born San Juan, Puerto Rico, January 9, 1948; admitted to bar, 1989, Puerto Rico; 1990, U.S. District Court, District of Puerto Rico; Court of Appeals, First Circuit; 1994, U.S. Supreme Court. *Education:* Manhattanville College (B.A., 1969); Inter-American University (J.D., 1988). ***COURSES: Family Law, Property Law, Obligations and Contracts, Clinic in Negotiation & Mediation. ***Email:*** mdlangel@inter.edu

ANTONIO FERNOS*, (Professor of Law)**, born San Juan, Puerto Rico, December 20, 1944; admitted to bar, 1970, Puerto Rico. *Education:* University of Puerto Rico (B.A., 1966; J.D., 1969); New York University (LL.M., 1970); University Complutense (J.S.D., 1971). ***COURSES: Constitutional Law, International Private Law, History of Puerto Rican Law, Organization and Legal Method.

MARIA D. FERNOS*, (Assistant Professor)**, born San Juan, Puerto Rico, June 6, 1946; admitted to bar, 1971, Puerto Rico. *Education:* University of Puerto Rico (B.A., 1966; J.D., 1970); Columbia University (LL.M., 1971). ***COURSES: Constitutional Law, Administrative Law. ***Email:*** mdfernos@inter.edu

ALBERTO FERRER*, (Emeritus Professor, Former Dean)**, born San Juan, Puerto Rico, December 13, 1919; admitted to bar, 1943, Puerto Rico; 1977, District of Columbia. *Education:* Cornell University (A.B., 1940; J.D., 1943). ***COURSES: Corporations, Basic and Advanced, Real Property, Securities Regulation, Civil Procedure.

JULIO FONTANET-MALDONADO*, (Associate Professor)**, born Mayaguez, Puerto Rico, May 19, 1962; admitted to bar, 1987, Puerto Rico. *Education:* University of Central Florida (B.A., 1983); Inter-American University (J.D., 1986). ***COURSES: Criminal Law, Criminal Procedure, Clinics and Trial Advocacy.

***MIGDALIA FRATICELLI-TORRES*, (Professor of Law)**, born Ponce, Puerto Rico, September 24, 1950; admitted to bar, 1974, Puerto

(This Listing Continued)

INTER-AMERICAN UNIVERSITY OF PUERTO RICO-SCHOOL OF LAW—Continued

Rico. *Education:* Catholic University of Puerto Rico (B.A., 1970); University of Puerto Rico School of Law (J.D., 1973); University de Droit, D'Economie et des Sciences Sociales de Paris (Diplome, 1979); Harvard University Law School. ***COURSES:*** Family Law, Succession Law, Contracts, Comparative Law, Seminars, Civil Law, Legal Research, Writing and Advocacy.

MARGARITA E. GARCIA-CARDENAS, **(Professor of Law)**, born Rio Piedras, San Juan, Puerto Rico, August 26, 1953; admitted to bar, 1978, Puerto Rico. *Education:* University of Puerto Rico (B.A., 1973; J.D., 1977). ***COURSES:*** Real Property, General Theory of Obligations and Contracts, Contracts--Typical and Atypical and Mortgage Law.

BLANCA GARI-PEREZ, **(Assistant Professor)**, born Rio Piedras, Puerto Rico, December 9, 1946; admitted to bar, 1988, Puerto Rico. *Education:* University of Puerto Rico (B.A., 1968; M.A., 1977); Inter-American University School of Law (J.D., 1986). ***COURSES:*** Clinical Education. ***Email:*** bmgari@inter.edu

MARILUCY GONZALEZ-BAEZ, **(Dean of Students)**, born Puerto Rico, December 19, 1960; admitted to bar, 1989, Puerto Rico. *Education:* University of Puerto Rico (B.A.,1984); Inter American University (J.D.,1987). ***COURSES:*** Clinical. ***Email:*** maridonza@inter.edu

CARLOS I. GORRIN-PERALTA, **(Professor of Law)**, born San Juan, Puerto Rico, August 28, 1950; admitted to bar, 1974, Puerto Rico. *Education:* College of the Holy Cross (B.A., 1971); University of Puerto Rico (J.D., 1974); Harvard University (LL.M., 1985). ***COURSES:*** Constitutional Law, Family Law, Legal Research, Analysis and Writing.

CARLOS J. IRIZARRY-YUNQUE, **(Distinguished Professor)**, born Sabana Grande, Puerto Rico, June 24, 1922; admitted to bar, 1949, Puerto Rico; 1967, U.S. Supreme Court. *Education:* University of Puerto Rico (B.A., 1943; LL.B., 1949). ***COURSES:*** Torts, Remedies.

ALBERTO O. JIMENEZ-SANTIAGO, **(Associate Professor of Law)**, born San Juan, Puerto Rico, February 26, 1950; admitted to bar, 1974, Puerto Rico; 1978, Massachusetts. *Education:* University of Puerto Rico (B.A., 1970; J.D., 1973); Harvard Law School (LL.M., 1976). ***COURSES:*** Civil Procedure, Evidence, Remedies.

MANUELITA MUNOZ-RIVERA, **(Professor of Law)**, born Puerto Rico, August 13th; admitted to bar, 1971, Puerto Rico. *Education:* University of Puerto Rico (B.B.A., 1958; J.D., 1970); Georgetown University Law Center (M.L.T., 1982). ***COURSES:*** Tax, Corporate, Banking. ***Email:*** mamunoz@ns.inter.edu

DORA NEVARES, **(Professor of Law)**, born San Juan, Puerto Rico, June 7, 1948; admitted to bar, 1973, Puerto Rico; 1975, U.S. District Court for Puerto Rico. *Education:* University of Puerto Rico (B.A., 1968; J.D., 1972); University of Pennsylvania (M.A., 1976; Ph.D., 1981). ***COURSES:*** Criminal Law and Procedure, Criminology, Juvenile Justice.

HERIBERTO QUINONES, **(Associate Professor)**, born Utuado, Puerto Rico, August 7, 1950; admitted to bar, 1977, Puerto Rico. *Education:* University of Puerto Rico (B.B.A., 1972; J.D., 1977); Pontifical Catholic University of Puerto Rico (LL.M., 1993). ***COURSES:*** Juvenile Law, Introduction to the Law, Trial Advocacy, Trial Practice, Law Research.

DOEL R. QUINONES-NUNEZ, **(Dean of Academic Affairs/Associate Professor)**, born San Juan, Puerto Rico, August 29, 1948; admitted to bar, 1976, Puerto Rico. *Education:* State University of New York at Buffalo (B.A., 1969); Boston University (M.A., 1970); University of Puerto Rico (J.D., 1976). ***COURSES:*** Ethics, Alternative Dispute, Litigation Skills, Consumer Law, Mediation Clinic. ***Email:*** doquinon@ns.inter.edu

CARLOS E. RAMOS-GONZALEZ, **(Professor of Law, Former Dean)**, born Caguas, Puerto Rico, October 20, 1952; admitted to bar, 1978, Puerto Rico. *Education:* University of Puerto Rico (B.A., 1974); Stockholm University (Diploma, 1975); University of Puerto Rico (J.D., 1978); University of California, Berkeley (LL.M., 1987). ***COURSES:*** Constitutional Law, Civil Rights, Prisoners' Rights, Litigation Theory and Practice. ***Email:*** ceramos@inter.edu

LUIS RIVERA, **(Associate Professor)**, born Puerto Rico, November 6, 1953; admitted to bar, 1988, Puerto Rico. *Education:* University of Puerto Rico (B.A., 1974; Master in Planning, 1980; J.D., 1987; Ph.D., 1997); Universidad Complutense. ***COURSES:*** Estate Planning, Property.

JESSICA RODRIGUEZ, **(Associate Professor)**, born San Juan, Puerto Rico, October 2, 1964; admitted to bar, 1989, Puerto Rico. *Education:* University of Puerto Rico (B.A., 1985; J.D., 1988). ***COURSES:*** Environmental Law. ***Email:*** jrodrig@inter.edu

IVETTE M. ROSSELLO-GONZALEZ, **(Director Law Library/Assistant Professor)**, born San Juan, Puerto Rico, January 4, 1951; admitted to bar, 1977, 1983, District of Columbia; 1984, Pennsylvania. *Education:* Pratt Institute (B.F.A., 1974); University of Pittsburgh (M.L.S., 1987); University of Puerto Rico (J.D., 1977). ***COURSES:*** Legal Research. ***Email:*** irosello

LUIS H. SANCHEZ-CASO, **(Associate Professor)**, born San Juan, Puerto Rico, November 23, 1953; admitted to bar, 1978, Puerto Rico. *Education:* University of Puerto Rico (B.A., 1975); Inter-American University (J.D., 1978); Georgetown University Law School (LL.M., 1983). ***COURSES:*** Administrative Law, Labor and Employment Law, Clinical Courses, Legal Research.

RAUL SERRANO GEYLS, **(Emeritus Professor of Law)**, born Arecibo, Puerto Rico, May 6, 1921; admitted to bar, 1944, Puerto Rico. *Education:* University of Puerto Rico (B.A., 1941; LL.B., 1944); Columbia University (LL.M., 1945); Harvard University (M.P.A., 1958). ***COURSES:*** Constitutional Law, Family Law.

CANDIDA ROSA URRUTIA-BASORA, **(Professor of Law)**, born San Juan, Puerto Rico, February 28, 1938; admitted to bar, 1970, Puerto Rico. *Education:* University of Puerto Rico (B.A., 1958; J.D., 1970). ***COURSES:*** Civil Procedure, Notarial Law, Contracts, Family Law.

ALEIDA VARONA, **(Associate Professor)**, born Santurce, Puerto Rico, July 31, 1953; admitted to bar, 1976, Puerto Rico. *Education:* University of Puerto Rico (B.A., 1973; J.D., 1976). ***COURSES:*** Clinical Education.

ENRIQUE VELEZ-RODRIGUEZ, **(Professor of Law)**, born San Juan, Puerto Rico, February 16, 1950; admitted to bar, 1975, Puerto Rico; 1982, U.S. Court of Appeals, First Circuit. *Education:* St. Louis University (B.A., 1971); University of Puerto Rico (J.D., 1974); New York University (M.A., 1978); University of Madrid (Doctoral Program, 1998). ***COURSES:*** Evidence, Criminal Procedure, Trial Advocacy, Law and Literature.

ESTHER RIVERA VICENTE, **(Assistant Professor)**, born Puerto Rico, March 15, 1953; admitted to bar, 1977, Puerto Rico. *Education:* University of Puerto Rico (B.A., 1973; J.D., 1976); University of London (LL.M., 1991). ***COURSES:*** Clinical Legal Education, Legal Theory, Human Rights. ***Email:*** evicent@inter.edu

CHARLES ZENO, **(Professor of Law)**, born January 22, 1957; admitted to bar, 1981, Puerto Rico. *Education:* University of Puerto Rico (B.B.A., 1978); Inter-American University School of Law (J.D., 1981); Harvard Law School (LL.M., 1990). ***COURSES:*** Discrimination Law, Law Clinic, Trial Practice, Compensation Law, Advanced Civil Practice.

JOHN MARSHALL LAW SCHOOL

1422 W. PEACHTREE N.E.
ATLANTA, GEORGIA 30309
Telephone: (404) 872-3593
Fax: (404) 873-3802

John Marshall Law School was founded in 1933 with a primary purpose of providing quality legal education to a large and significantly underserved segment of society. For the past 70 years, John Marshall reached out to the older student, the working professional seeking part-time study, the minority student, and the student motivated by the love of learning and the majesty of the law. Today, the school remains true to its original mission in all of its programs and policies, while at the same time providing opportunities for those seeking full-time course of study in an urban setting.

The Juris Doctor program at John Marshall Law School, Atlanta, is designed to foster intellectual and practical skill development among students with an emphasis on analytical writing skills and problem solving techniques. The goal of the degree program is to produce highly competent and skilled practicing lawyers who are knowledgeable of and committed to adherence to the highest professional and ethical standards in the legal profession. Our graduates are inculcated with those skills and values deemed important by the legal profession and are committed to representing people and solving their everyday legal problems. The program of study is available in a variety of scheduling options thus allowing students to pursue their career goals on a full or part-time basis with courses being offered in both the day and the evening hours.

Since its founding, the Law School has educated thousands of successful practicing attorneys in the State of Georgia. Graduates of the school serve in a variety of roles expected of attorneys from private practitioners in large and small firms to public service lawyers in government offices throughout the State. Numerous graduates have distinguished themselves as members of the judiciary in the state of Georgia while others have devoted themselves to public service through seeking and winning elective public office. The history of John Marshall Law School, Atlanta, is long and illustrious. We are committed to maintaining our role in the legal community of Georgia and to providing a sound program of high quality legal education to the citizens of this State.

Dean: John E. Ryan
Admissions: Shannon Keef (404) 872-4105
Financial Aid: Michael Owen (404) 872-4106
Library: Michael Lynch (404) 872-4108
Placement & Alumni Affairs: Jennifer Post (404) 872-4120

FULL TIME FACULTY

JOHN E. RYAN*, (Dean)**, born Utica, New York, March, 1937; admitted to bar, 1970, California. *Education:* California State University - San Francisco (B.A., 1963); McGeorge School of Law (J.D., 1970); University of Illinois (LL.M., 1976). ***COURSES: Contracts, Constitutional Law. ***Email:*** jryan@johnmarshall.edu

DEREK ALPHRAN*, (Associate Professor)**, born Atlanta, Georgia, September 14, 1953; admitted to bar, 1984, California; 1985, Georgia. *Education:* Morehouse College (B.A., 1975); University of California - Los Angeles School of Law (J.D., 1981). ***COURSES: Constitutional Law, Criminal Law, Criminal Procedure, Civil Rights. ***Email:*** alphrad@johnmarshall.edu

ROBERT J. D'AGOSTINO*, (Professor)**, born New York, New York, October 14, 1942; admitted to bar, 1971, Georgia; 1972, New Jersey. *Education:* Columbia University (B.A., 1964; M.A., 1966); Emory University School of Law (J.D., 1970). ***COURSES: Bankruptcy, Commercial Law, Contracts. ***Email:*** dagostr@johnmarshall.edu

EDNA C. EGUH*, (Law Professor)**, born Nigeria, October 19, 1960. *Education:* University of Lagos - Nigeria (LL.M., 1987); Harvard Law School (LL.M., 1995). ***COURSES: Conflict of Laws, Environmental Law, Immigration Law. ***Email:*** eeguh@johnmarshall.edu

AVARITA LAUREL HANSON*, (Associate Dean for Academic Affairs)**, born New York, New York, July 21, 1953; admitted to bar, 1979, Texas; 1983, Georgia. *Education:* Harvard-Radcliffe College (A.B., 1975); University of Pennsylvania Law School (J.D., 1978). ***COURSES: Client Counseling and Negotiation, Juvenile Law, Trial Advocacy. ***Email:*** avaritah@johnmarshall.edu

EMMANUEL BDIMA JAMES*, (Associate Professor)**, born Monrovia, Liberia, August 24, 1955. *Education:* University of Liberia (B.A., 1978); University of Liberia Law School (LL.B., 1981); Harvard Law School (LL.M., 1989). ***COURSES: Business Organizations, Evidence, International Law, Introduction to Law, Professional Responsibility.

MICHAEL EVAN LEWYN*, (Associate Professor)**, born Atlanta, Georgia, October 14, 1963; admitted to bar, 1987, Georgia; 1988, District of Columbia; 1998, New York. *Education:* Wesleyan University (B.A., 1983); University of Pennsylvania School of Law (J.D., 1986). ***COURSES: Professional Responsibility, Products Liability, Property, Torts. ***Email:*** mlewyn@hotmail.com

MICHAEL J. LYNCH*, (Professor and Director of the Law Library)**, born Detroit, Michigan, September 14, 1940; admitted to bar, 1965, Michigan. *Education:* University of Detroit (Ph.B., 1962); Emory University (M.L.S., 1976); University of Michigan Law School (J.D., 1965). ***COURSES: Contracts, Copyright, Legal Research. ***Email:*** lynchm@johnmarshall.edu

DAVID B. MELTZ*, (Distinguished Professor and Dean Emeritus)**, born Brooklyn, New York, March 12, 1945; admitted to bar, 1977, Georgia. *Education:* Brooklyn College CUNY (B.A., 1965); University of Rochester (Ph.D., 1970); Woodrow Wilson College of Law (J.D., 1977). ***COURSES: Constitutional Law, Law and Economics, Remedies, Torts. ***Email:*** conprof@aol.com

JAMES KERR SATCHER*, (Director of Legal Research and Writing)**, born Houston, Texas, May 24, 1964; admitted to bar, 1989, Georgia. *Education:* Duke University (B.A., 1986); University of Georgia School of Law (J.D., 1989). ***COURSES: Appellate Advocacy, Legal Drafting, Pretrial Motions, Property, Research and Writing. ***Email:*** jamesksat@msn.com

(This Listing Continued)

JON P. THAMES*, (Professor)**, born 1939; admitted to bar, 1968, Mississippi; 1974, South Carolina. *Education:* University of Mississippi Law School (J.D., 1968); Harvard Law School (LL.M., 1971). ***COURSES: Constitutional Law, Criminal Law, Evidence, ADR, Clinical Law, Family Law, Law Office Management, Legal Profession, Criminal Procedure, Trial and Appellate Advocacy.

JEFFREY ALAN VAN DETTA*, (Associate Professor of Law)**, born Schenectady, New York, July 2, 1962; admitted to bar, 1988, New York; 1989, Georgia. *Education:* Union College (B.A., 1985); Albany Law School (J.D., 1987). ***COURSES: Civil Procedure, Commercial Paper, Employment Discrimination, Labor Law, Torts. ***Email:*** jvandetta@msn.com

THE JOHN MARSHALL LAW SCHOOL

315 SOUTH PLYMOUTH COURT
CHICAGO, ILLINOIS 60604
Telephone: (312) 427-2737
Fax: (312) 427-5134
http://www.jmls.edu

ABA Approved Since 1951.

Overview

The John Marshall Law School has been dedicated to the teaching of law since 1899. From its inception it has sought to maintain diversity in its academic programs, student body, and faculty and to provide a harmonious blend of the theory and practice of law. The school is located in the heart of Chicago's legal, financial, and commercial center and offers a vibrant, cosmopolitan setting for legal study. The federal courthouse is across the street, and the nation's largest circuit court, that of Cook County, is just a few blocks away. Students visit these courthouses to observe the theory and procedure they have learned in the classroom applied in a courtroom setting. Accredited by the American Bar Association, the North Central Association of Colleges and Schools and a member of the Association of American Law Schools, the school maintains high standards relating to entrance requirements, faculty, library, and curriculum. Graduates are eligible to take bar examinations in all jurisdictions of the United States.

Admission and Financial Aid

The John Marshall Law School enrolls entering classes in August and January each year in both full and part-time programs. The part-time program offers both day and evening divisions. A variety of financial aid programs, including loans, scholarships, grants, and need-based aid, is available to John Marshall students. Merit scholarships and grants are awarded to entering students on the basis of academic achievement, undergraduate course work, and LSAT scores.

Enrollment/Student Body

With more than 1,400 students, The John Marshall Law School has a diverse student body. Students range in age from 20 to 69 years old; minorities comprised 16% of the Fall 2000 entering class, and women accounted for 49% of those admitted; more than 265 college and universities are represented by the student body; and 35% of John Marshall students are from outside the state of Illinois.

Faculty

The school's 55 full-time faculty are accomplished teachers and serious scholars and include several nationally-known experts in many areas of law. In addition, John Marshall's adjunct faculty represents a committed group of practicing lawyers and judges who share their unique expertise with students. The vibrant legal environment in Chicago enables the law school to draw upon the talents of these professionals who bring an invaluable perspective to legal education at The John Marshall Law School.

Physical Facilities and Library

The law school's facilities occupy three buildings in Chicago's historic "Loop" district and house: classrooms; faculty offices; a courtroom equipped with a state-of-the-art audio/visual installation; an innovative, computerized classroom; a spacious student lounge; conference meeting and reception space; administrative offices; lounges for full-time and adjunct faculty; and five floors of library collections totaling nearly 50,000 square feet. The library of The John Marshall Law School provides support services for the study of law and for legal research. Library materials include more than 364,787 volumes and 1,619 audiovisual tapes. The John Marshall library is a Selective Depository of Federal Documents. As one of the first law schools to teach legal research on computer, John Marshall continues to provide its students with the most up-to-date computer research and reference services. More than 75 IBM compatible computers are available for student use. The school has also installed a school-wide wireless computer network. This allows all student, faculty, and staff computers access to word processing software, LEXIS, WESTLAW, CALI, e-mail, and the INTERNET.

Curriculum and Specific Special Programs

The John Marshall Law School provides one of the most comprehensive and aggressive professional skills training curricula in the country. The initial program for both day and evening divisions consists of a core curriculum, which provides students with a fundamental store of knowledge about substantive legal concepts. Later, students take courses they believe best suit their interests and career objectives.

Lawyering Skills

All students participate for four semesters in the Lawyering Skills Program. Taught in small groups, this program focuses on legal writing, research, and oral advocacy. The legal writing curriculum plays a critical role in developing the professional skills of the lawyer-to-be. The first three courses are designed to provide experience in drafting many different types of legal documents, teach the basics of legal research and problem analysis, introduce persuasive writing techniques, and develop oral argument skills. The fourth semester course requires the students to use their skills in drafting pleadings, wills, and commercial contracts and prepares John Marshall graduates to perform proficiently the many tasks which often confront newly licensed lawyers.

Moot Court and Law Reviews

Each year The John Marshall Law School enters teams and garners top honors in more than 26 interschool competitions involving appellate advocacy, trial advocacy, client counseling, and negotiations. The law school hosts the annual National Moot Court Competition in Information Technology and Privacy Law, and, with the American Bar Association, a national, invitational mock trial competition.

(This Listing Continued)

THE JOHN MARSHALL LAW SCHOOL—Continued

Based on academic achievement, students may write for *The John Marshall Law Review* or *The John Marshall Journal of Computer and Information Law. The John Marshall Law Review* publishes scholarly work on a broad range of current legal topics written by legal scholars, practitioners, and John Marshall law students. *The John Marshall Journal of Computer and Information Law* is an international law journal focusing upon law and policy with regard to software, databases and information networks.

Center for Advocacy and Dispute Resolution

Recognizing that the lawyer is an advocate at every level of his or her practice, John Marshall established the nationally recognized Center for Advocacy and Dispute Resolution. Coordinating the law school's instruction in all phases of advocacy, the center serves John Marshall students by providing a focused approach to attaining advocacy skills. The courses offered include trial and appellate advocacy, alternative dispute resolution, and client counseling; and there are interscholastic competitions, clinical programs and continuing legal education programs for lawyers.

Clinical Programs

The Clinical Education Program is an academic program for which credit may be received. It has two divisions: the Fair Housing Clinic and the General Externship Program. Students participating in the Fair Housing Clinic complete a two-hour seminar about fair housing law and then go to work in the clinic, learning the substance of fair housing law, participating in federal court litigation, as well as in state and local administrative proceedings. The General Externship Program offers students several programs to learn important lawyering skills while working as externs with members of the bench and bar.

Center for Information Technology and Privacy Law

Established in 1983, the Center for Information Technology and Privacy Law engages in legal research and policy analysis regarding newly developing information and communications technology. The Center offers an LL.M. and an M.S. in Information Technology Law and sponsors the John Marshall Journal of Computer and Information Law. Its activities include research and publication, legal and public education, interdisciplinary dialogues, conferences, advocacy, and legislative awareness programs. Through seminars, students consider policies for dealing with the problems of technology and ethics which face us in our everyday lives.

Center for International Business and Trade Law

The Center for International Business and Trade Law directs and coordinates a wide range of programs of interest to students, lawyers, and scholars dealing with today's increasingly international business law climate. The center has developed an extensive international law curriculum on the J.D. level, introduced an LL.M. Program in Comparative Legal Studies and an LL.M. Program in International Business and Trade Law, coordinated sister school relationships with law faculties in the Czech Republic and Lithuania, and established the first permanent academic joint venture between a U.S. law school and a law faculty at a university in the People's Republic of China.

Center for Intellectual Property Law

The John Marshall Law School offers the most comprehensive program in the U.S. dedicated to training law students and attorneys in the law of intellectual property. The intellectual property law area is one of the fastest growing fields of law today. It crosses all aspects of science, technology, business, the arts, and international trade. The center offers J.D. and LL.M. candidates, practicing attorneys, and paralegals specialized training in all aspects of patent, trademark, and copyright law, as well as in trade secrets and unfair competition.

Center for Real Estate Law

The Center for Real Estate Law offers a comprehensive J.D. curriculum and an LL.M. in Real Estate Law. The Center sponsors the annual Robert Kratovil Memorial Seminar in Real Estate, which considers current issues and policies and brings together leading scholars and highly respected practitioners.

Center for Tax Law & Employee Benefits

The Center for Tax Law and Employee Benefits stresses a transactional approach to educating students. Its J.D. concentration prepares students for the complex nature of tax law. Its LL.M. in Tax Law is one of the few programs in the nation, and its LL.M. in Employee Benefits is the first of its kind in the nation.

Fair Housing Legal Support Center

As one of the nation's leaders in housing law, the Fair Housing Legal Support Center presents annually more than 50 conferences and seminars across the country to eliminate discriminatory practices in housing. It publishes educational materials, presents training programs, and maintains an on-line database (fairhousing.jmls.edu) to assist those in need of legal research.

Graduate Degrees

The John Marshall Law School offers programs leading to the conferment of the following degrees: LL.M. in Comparative Legal Studies, Employee Benefits, Information Technology Law, Intellectual Property Law, International Business and Trade Law, Real Estate Law, Tax Law, and M.S. in Information Technology Law.

Joint and Combined Degree Programs

John Marshall and Dominican University cooperate in offering a combined credit program leading to the degrees of Juris Doctor and Master of Business Administration. John Marshall and Roosevelt University cooperate in offering a combined credit program leading to the degrees of Juris Doctor and either the Master of Public Administration or the Master of Arts in Political Science. John Marshall and Roosevelt University offer a joint degree program leading to both the baccalaureate and Juris Doctor degrees. A combined degree program is offered leading to the conferment of a J.D. and LL.M. degree in Employee Benefits, Information Technology Law, Intellectual Property Law, International Business and Trade Law, Real Estate Law, and Tax Law.

(This Listing Continued)

THE JOHN MARSHALL LAW SCHOOL—Continued

Dean: Robert G. Johnston (312) 987-1429
Associate Dean for Academic Affairs: John E. Corkery (312) 987-1426
Associate Dean for Academic Services: Jane D. Oswald (312) 987-1405
Associate Dean For Administration: James J. Kreminski (312) 987-1407
Associate Dean for Admission and Student Affairs: William B. Powers (312) 987-1435
Associate Dean for Institutional Advancement & Planning: Rory Dean Smith (312) 987-1412
Director of Admissions/Financial Aid: Deborah Meyer (312) 987-1403
Assistant Director of Admissions/Financial Aid: Sherri Berendt (312) 987-1451
Assistant Dean & Director of Career Services: Nancy J. Thompson (312) 987-1404
Assistant Dean for Institutional Development: William K. Beach (312) 360-2665
Assistant Dean for Institutional Affairs: John M. McNamara (312) 987-2393
Director of Library Services: Dorothy Li (312) 987-1414
Director, Public Information: Marilyn Thomas (312) 360-2661

FULL TIME FACULTY

R. GILBERT JOHNSTON*, (Dean of Law School)**, born Waipahu, Hawaii, November 28, 1931; admitted to bar, 1960, Illinois; 1970, Hawaii. *Education:* University of Chicago (J.D., 1960). ***COURSES: Civil Procedure, Federal Courts, Legal Ethics. ***Email:*** 6JOHNSTO@JMLS.EDU

YVETTE MARIE BARKSDALE*, (Associate Professor of Law)**, born Detroit, Michigan, February 5, 1958; admitted to bar, 1994, New York. *Education:* Oberlin College (B.A., 1978); Yale Law School (J.D., 1982). ***COURSES: Administrative Law, Conflict of Laws, Constitutional Law, Law and Diversity. ***Email:*** 7BARKSDA@JMLS.EDU

GERALD BERENDT*, (Professor of Law)**, born Charleston, South Carolina, July 16, 1947; admitted to bar, 1972, South Carolina. *Education:* University of Florida (A.A., 1967); University of South Carolina (A.B., 1969; J.D., 1972); New York University School of Law (LL.M., 1973). ***COURSES: Contracts, Labor Law, Public Employee Labor Law. ***Email:*** 7BERENDT@JMLS.EDU

ALBERTO BERNABE*, (Professor of Law)**, born San Juan, Puerto Rico, June 7, 1962; admitted to bar, 1988, Puerto Rico. *Education:* Princeton University (B.A., 1984); University of Puerto Rico (J.D., 1987); Temple University School of Law (LL.M., 1994). ***COURSES: Torts, Mass Media Law, Professional Responsibility. ***Email:*** 7BERNABE@JMLS.EDU

DONALD L. BESCHLE*, (Professor of Law)**, born Danbury, Connecticut, October 15, 1951; admitted to bar, 1977, New York. *Education:* Fordham University (B.A., 1973); New York University School of Law (J.D., 1976); Temple University School of Law (LL.M., 1983). ***COURSES: Constitutional Law, Property, Antitrust, Law and Religion. ***Email:*** 7BESCHLE@JMLS.EDU

SUSAN L. BRODY*, (Professor of Law)**, born Chicago, Illinois, September 28, 1953; admitted to bar, 1979, Illinois. *Education:* Ohio State University (B.S., 1974); Chicago-Kent College of Law, Illinois Institute of Technology (J.D., 1979). ***COURSES: Civil Procedure, Family Law, Lawyering Skills, Conflicts. ***Email:*** 7BRODY@JMLS.EDU

JOSEPH ROBERT BUTLER*, (Clinical Professor)**, born Illinois, February 5, 1963; admitted to bar, 1995, Illinois. *Education:* Eastern Illinois University (B.A., 1985); John Marshall Law School (J.D., 1995). ***COURSES: Fair Housing. ***Email:*** 6BUTLER@JMLS.EDU

WILLIAM KENNETH CARROLL*, (Professor of Law)**, born Oak Park, Illinois, May 8, 1927; admitted to bar, 1972, Illinois. *Education:* Duquesne University (M.A., 1965); University of Strasbourg (Ph.D., 1968); Northwestern University (J.D., 1972). ***COURSES: Criminal Law, Conflict of Laws, Trial Advocacy, Philosophy of Law. ***Email:*** 7CARROLL@JMLS.EDU

F. WILLIS CARUSO*, (Clinical Professor)**, born Chicago, Illinois, April 26, 1933; admitted to bar, 1962, Illinois. *Education:* Northwestern (B.S., 1955; J.D., 1961). ***COURSES: Fair Housing, Affordable Housing. ***Email:*** 6CARUSO@JMLS.EDU

MICHAEL L. CLOSEN*, (Professor of Law)**, born Peoria, Illinois, January 25, 1949; admitted to bar, 1971, Illinois. *Education:* Bradley University (B.S., 1971; M.A., 1971); University of Illinois (J.D., 1974). ***COURSES: Contracts, Agency & Unincorporated Business Entities, Aids and the Law. ***Email:*** 7CLOSEN@JMLS.EDU

SUSAN MARIE CONNOR*, (Professor of Law)**, born Attleboro, Massachusetts, January 18, 1947; admitted to bar, 1977, Hawaii; 1978, Illinois. *Education:* Albertus Magnus (B.A., 1969); University of Hawaii (M.A., 1970; J.D., 1977). ***COURSES: Constitutional Law, Zoning, Employment Discrimination, Ethics. ***Email:*** 7CONNOR@JMLS.EDU

JOHN E. CORKERY*, (Associate Dean for Academic Affairs, Professor of Law)**, born St. Louis, Missouri, January 22, 1943; admitted to bar, 1967, Illinois. *Education:* Northwestern University School of Law (J.D., 1967); St. Louis University (B.S., 1964). ***COURSES: Evidence, Legal Ethics, Family Law. ***Email:*** 7CORKERY@JMLS.EDU

JOEL R. CORNWELL*, (Professor of Law)**, born Des Moines, Iowa, March 2, 1953; admitted to bar, 1984, Missouri; 1985, Illinois. *Education:* Duquesne University (B.A., 1975); Yale University (M.Div., 1978); St. Louis University (J.D., 1983). ***COURSES: Lawyering Skills, Property, Religion and Law, Psychology and Law. ***Email:*** 7CORNWEL@JMLS.EDU

LINDA R. CRANE*, (Professor of Law)**, born Chicago, Illinois, September 4, 1955; admitted to bar, 1983, Illinois. *Education:* University of Illinois (B.A., 1977); Northwestern University (M.M./M.B.A., 1981); Northwestern University School of Law (J.D., 1981). ***COURSES: Property Law, Payment Systems Law, Securities Regulation. ***Email:*** 7CRANE@JMLS.EDU

RONALD Z. DOMSKY*, (Professor of Law)**, born Racine, Wisconsin, June 20, 1934; admitted to bar, 1957, Wisconsin; 1958, Illinois. *Education:* University of Wisconsin (B.B.A., 1955; J.D., 1957). ***COURSES: Taxation, Estates and Trusts. ***Email:*** 7DOMSKY@JMLS.EDU

JOHN D. GORBY*, (Professor of Law)**, born Chicago, Illinois, July 2, 1939; admitted to bar, 1970, Illinois. *Education:* Knox College (A.B., 1961); University of Michigan (J.D., 1968); Heidelberg, Germany. ***COURSES: Evidence, Counseling and Negotiating, Philosophy of Law, Scientific Evidence, Criminal Procedure, Federal Courts. ***Email:*** 7GORBY@JMLS.edu

***KAREN HALVERSON*, (Associate Professor of Law)**, born East

(This Listing Continued)

THE JOHN MARSHALL LAW SCHOOL—Continued

Orange, New Jersey, February 3, 1963; admitted to bar, 1991, New York. *Education:* University of Wisconsin (B.A., 1986); Harvard Law School (J.D., 1990). ***COURSES:*** Contracts, Counseling and Negotiating, International Business Transactions. ***Email:*** 7HALVERS@JMLS.EDU

ARDATH A. HAMANN, **(Associate Professor of Law)**, born Chicago, Illinois, September 10, 1955; admitted to bar, 1977, Illinois. *Education:* Purdue University (B.S., 1974); College of William & Mary (J.D., 1977); The John Marshall Law School (LL.M., 1986). ***COURSES:*** Antitrust, Corporations, Lawyering Skills, Estates and Trusts. ***Email:*** 7HAMANN@JMLS.edu

CELESTE HAMMOND, **(Professor of Law and Director of Center for Real Estate Law)**, born Chicago, Illinois, April 5, 1945; admitted to bar, 1969, Illinois. *Education:* University of Wisconsin; Loyola University (B.S., 1965); University of Chicago (J.D., 1968). ***COURSES:*** Property, Real Estate, Real Estate Finance, Estates and Trusts. ***Email:*** 7HAMMOND@JMLS.EDU

MICHAEL G. HEYMAN, **(Professor of Law)**, born Newark, New Jersey, June 27, 1945; admitted to bar, 1972, New Jersey; 1978, Illinois. *Education:* Temple University (B.A., 1968); University of Wisconsin (M.A., 1968); George Washington University National Law Center (J.D., 1972); New York University School of Law (LL.M., 1976). ***COURSES:*** Immigration Law, Family Law, Legislation and Political Thought, Criminal Law. ***Email:*** 7HEYMAN@JMLS.EDU

KEVIN L. HOPKINS, **(Associate Professor of Law)**, born Milford, Delaware, September 3, 1959; admitted to bar, 1990, Kentucky. *Education:* University of Delaware (B.A., 1981); Duke University (M.A., 1983); College of William & Mary (J.D., 1989). ***COURSES:*** Lawyering Skills, Torts. ***Email:*** 7HOPKINS@JMLS.EDU

JOHN DWIGHT INGRAM, **(Professor of Law)**, born Chicago, Illinois, March 10, 1929; admitted to bar, 1966, Illinois. *Education:* Harvard University (A.B., 1950); American College of Life Underwriters (C.L.U., 1957); The John Marshall Law School (J.D., 1966). ***COURSES:*** Insurance, Agency and Partnership. ***Email:*** 7INGRAM@JMLS.EDU

ALLEN R. KAMP, **(Professor of Law)**, born Oakland, California, September 3, 1942; admitted to bar, 1969, Illinois; 1975, Ohio. *Education:* University of California at Berkeley (A.B., 1964); University of California at Irvine (M.A., 1967); University of Chicago (J.D., 1969). ***COURSES:*** Civil Procedure, Sales, Pretrial Practice in Civil Litigation. ***Email:*** 7KAMP@JMLS.EDU

KENNETH KANDARAS, **(Professor of Law and Director of the Center for Advocacy and Dispute Resolution)**, born Barquisemeto, Venezuela, December 8, 1947; admitted to bar, 1973, Illinois. *Education:* Southern Illinois University (B.S., 1970); DePaul University College of Law (J.D., 1973). ***COURSES:*** Civil Procedure, Torts, Trial Advocacy, Pretrial Practice in Civil Litigation. ***Email:*** 7KANDARA@JMLS.Edu

DIANE S. KAPLAN, **(Associate Professor)**, born Chicago, Illinois, December 13, 1949; admitted to bar, 1976, California; 1980, Illinois and District of Columbia. *Education:* University of California at Berkeley (B.A., 1970); Yale Law School (J.D., 1975). ***COURSES:*** Civil Procedure, Federal Courts, Corporations, Children in the Legal System. ***Email:*** 7KAPLAN@JMLS.EDU

WALTER J. KENDALL, III, **(Professor of Law)**, born Brooklyn, New York, June 8, 1941; admitted to bar, 1966, New York; 1969, Illinois. *Education:* Brooklyn College (B.A., 1962); St. John's University (J.D., 1965). ***COURSES:*** Administrative Law, Constitutional Law, Public International Law. ***Email:*** 7KENDALL@JMLS.EDU

KATHRYN JENNINGS KENNEDY, **(Assistant Professor of Law and Director of Employee Benefits Program)**, born Chicago, Illinois, December 16, 1952; admitted to bar, 1980, Illinois. *Education:* Drake University (B.S., 1974); Northwestern University School of Law (J.D., 1980). ***COURSES:*** Employee Benefits, Taxation. ***Email:*** 7KENNEDY@JMLS.EDU

MAUREEN STRAUB KORDESH, **(Associate Professor of Law and Director Lawyering Skills)**, born Detroit, Michigan, February 7, 1959; admitted to bar, 1986, Pennsylvania. *Education:* Kalamazoo College (B.A., 1981); Indiana University - Bloomington (M.A., 1984; J.D., 1986). ***COURSES:*** Lawyering Skills, Property, Land Use Planning. ***Email:*** 7KORDESH@JMLS.EDU

DORIS ESTELLE LONG, **(Professor of Law)**, born Albany, New York, April 4, 1955; admitted to bar, 1980, District of Columbia. *Education:* Ithaca College (B.A., 1977); Cornell University (J.D., 1980). ***COURSES:*** Intellectual Property, Contracts. ***Email:*** 7long@jmls.edu

ANN LOUSIN, **(Professor of Law)**, born Chicago, Illinois, February 21, 1943; admitted to bar, 1970, Illinois. *Education:* Grinnell College (B.A., 1964); University of Chicago (J.D., 1968). ***COURSES:*** Uniform Commercial Code (Arts. 1,2,5 & 9). ***Email:*** 7LOUSIN@JMLS.EDU

HOWARD THOMAS MARKEY, **(Dean Emeritus)**, born Chicago, Illinois, November 10, 1920; admitted to bar, 1949, Illinois. *Education:* Loyola University Law School (J.D., 1949); The John Marshall Law School (M.P.L., 1950). ***COURSES:*** Appellate Procedure.

PETER JOHN MCGOVERN, **(Professor of Law and Coordinator of Graduate Programs)**, born New York, New York, December 6, 1938; admitted to bar, 1964, New York; 1972, South Dakota; 1983, Indiana; 1990, Illinois. *Education:* Notre Dame University (A.B., 1961); Fordham University School of Law (J.D., 1964); University of South Dakota (E.D.D., 1980). ***COURSES:*** Elder Law, Trusts & Estates, Counseling & Negotiating, International Dispute Resolution. ***Email:*** 7MCGOVER@JMLS.EDU

WILLIAM B.T. MOCK, **(Professor of Law)**, born Ormond Beach, Florida, March 19, 1952; admitted to bar, 1979, District of Columbia; 1986, Illinois. *Education:* Haverford College (B.A., 1973); Shakespeare Institute, University of Birmingham (1974-1975); Georgetown University Law Center (J.D., 1979). ***COURSES:*** International Trade Law, International Business Law, International Law, Corporations, Agency and Unincorporated Business Entities. ***Email:*** 7MOCK@JMLS.EDU

MARIE A. MONAHAN, **(Assistant Professor of Law)**, born Buffalo, New York, February 26, 1951; admitted to bar, 1981, Illinois. *Education:* State University of New York at Buffalo (A.B., 1973; M.A., 1975); DePaul University College of Law (J.D., 1981); Northwestern University (Ph.D., 1986). ***COURSES:*** Contracts, Clinic, Lawyering Skills, Juvenile. ***Email:*** 7MONAHAN@JMLS.EDU

CORINNE SEITHER MORRISSEY, **(Director of Academic Achievement Program)**, admitted to bar, 1985, Illinois. *Education:* Swarthmore College (B.A., 1959); Loyola University of Chicago (J.D., 1985). ***Email:*** 6morriss@jmls.edu

FRANCIS D. MORRISSEY, **(Distinguished Visiting Professor of Law)**, born Chicago, Illinois, June 28, 1930; admitted to bar, 1958, Illinois. *Education:* Saint Mary on The Lake (A.B., 1952; S.T.B., 1954); Loyola of Chicago (J.D., 1958). ***COURSES:*** Professional Responsibility.

JANICE M. MUELLER, **(Associate Professor of Law)**, born 1963; admitted to bar, 1990, Minnesota; 1991, District of Columbia. *Education:* Virginia Polytechnical Institute (B.S.C.E., 1986); William

(This Listing Continued)

THE JOHN MARSHALL LAW SCHOOL—Continued

Mitchell College of Law (J.D., 1990). ***COURSES:*** Patent Law, Trademark Law. ***Email:*** 7mueller@jmls.edu

ROBERT J. NYE*, (Professor of Law)**, born Chicago, Illinois, February 9, 1931; admitted to bar, 1955, Illinois. *Education:* University of Chicago (A.B., 1953); DePaul College of Law (J.D., 1954); New York University School of Law (LL.M., 1956). ***COURSES: Contracts, Equity, Business Franchise Law, Employment Law, Remedies, Criminal Law. ***Email:*** 7NYE@JMLS.EDU

TIMOTHY P. O'NEILL*, (Professor of Law)**, born Cleveland, Ohio, June 17, 1950; admitted to bar, 1975, Ohio; 1976, Illinois. *Education:* Harvard (A.B., 1972); University of Michigan (J.D., 1975). ***COURSES: Criminal Law, Criminal Procedure. ***Email:*** 7ONEILL@JMLS.EDU

SAMUEL R. OLKEN*, (Associate Professor of Law)**, born Boston, Massachusetts, January 1, 1960; admitted to bar, 1987, Massachusetts. *Education:* Harvard University (A.B., 1982); Emory University School of Law (J.D., 1985). ***COURSES: Constitutional Law, Legal History, Lawyering Skills. ***Email:*** 7OLKEN@JMLS.EDU

DAMIAN ORTIZ*, (Professor)**, born Mexico; admitted to bar, 1997, Illinois. *Education:* Loyola University (B.S., 1990); John Marshall (J.D., 1993). ***COURSES: Fair Housing. ***Email:*** 6ORTIZ@JMLS.EDU

CRAIG A. PETERSON*, (Professor of Law)**, born Chicago, Illinois, November 15, 1941; admitted to bar, 1966, Illinois. *Education:* Cornell University (B.A., 1963); Harvard University Law School (J.D., 1966). ***COURSES: Torts, Corporations, Land Use Control, Business Planning. ***Email:*** 7PETERSO@JMLS.EDU

RANDALL THEODORE PETERSON*, (Associate Professor of Law)**, born Sioux City, Iowa, August 27, 1944. *Education:* Brigham Young University (B.S., 1968); University of Utah (J.D., 1972). ***COURSES: Remedies, Torts, Counseling & Negotiating, Dispute Resolution, Agency and Unincorporated Business Entities. ***Email:*** 7RTP@JMLS.EDU

MICHAEL J. POLELLE*, (Professor of Law)**, born Chicago, Illinois, April 28, 1938; admitted to bar, 1965, Illinois. *Education:* Loyola University (A.B., with honors, 1959); Christian-Albrecht University; Harvard University Law School (J.D., 1963); The John Marshall School of Law (LL.M., 1969). ***COURSES: Torts, Civil Rights, Constitutional Law, Evidence. ***Email:*** 7POLELLE@JMLS.EDU

JACQUELINE E. ROSS*, (Assistant Professor)**, born Berlin, Germany, February, 23 1963; admitted to bar, 1989, Illinois. *Education:* University of Chicago (B.A.,1984; J.D.,1989). ***COURSES: Civil Procedure, Criminal Procedure, Criminal Law. ***Email:*** 7ROSS@JMLS

RALPH RUEBNER*, (Professor of Law)**, born Tel Aviv, Israel, January 11, 1944; admitted to bar, 1969, Illinois. *Education:* University of Illinois (B.A., 1966); The American University, Washington College of Law (J.D., 1969). ***COURSES: Evidence, Criminal Procedure, International Human Rights. ***Email:*** 7RUEBNER@JMLS.EDU

ARTHUR J. SABIN*, (Professor of Law)**, born Chicago, Illinois, September 21, 1930; admitted to bar, 1959, Illinois. *Education:* Roosevelt University (A.B., 1952); Northwestern University (A.M., 1953); The John Marshall Law School (J.D., 1959). ***COURSES: Torts, Products Liability, History of American Law. ***Email:*** 7SABIN@JMLS.EDU

JOHN SCHEID*, (Professor of Law)**, born Chicago, Illinois, February 8, 1935; admitted to bar, 1962, Illinois. *Education:* Loyola University (A.B., 1959; J.D., 1962); New York University School of Law (LL.M., 1970). ***COURSES: Torts, Philosophy of Law, Real Estate Transactions. ***Email:*** 7SCHEID@JMLS.EDU

LEONARD JAY SCHRAGER*, (Professor of Law & Former Dean)**, born New York, New York, November 5, 1935; admitted to bar, 1960, Illinois. *Education:* Northwestern University (B.S., 1956; J.D., 1959). ***COURSES: Contracts, Counseling & Negotiating. ***Email:*** 7SCHRAGE@JMLS.EDU

GLENN P. SCHWARTZ*, (Professor of Law)**, born Chicago, Illinois, 1940; admitted to bar, 1964, Illinois. *Education:* Shimer College (B.A., 1960); Northwestern University School of Law (J.D., 1964); The John Marshall Law School (LL.M., 1969). ***COURSES: Individual Income Tax, Business Planning. ***Email:*** 7SCHWART@JMLS.edu

MICHAEL P. SENG*, (Professor of Law and Director of the Fair Housing Legal Support Center)**, born Cedar Rapids, Iowa, July 7, 1942; admitted to bar, 1967, Oregon; 1968, Illinois. *Education:* St. Ambrose College; University of Notre Dame (B.A., 1964); Notre Dame Law School (J.D., 1967). ***COURSES: Constitutional Law, Fair Housing Law, Federal Courts, Comparative Law. ***Email:*** 7SENG@JMLS.EDU

RONALD C. SMITH*, (Professor of Law and Director, John Marshall/ABA National Criminal Justice Trial Advocacy Competition)**, born Chicago, Illinois, December 9, 1933; admitted to bar, 1965, Illinois. *Education:* Loyola University (B.S., 1955; J.D., 1965). ***COURSES: Criminal Law, Criminal Procedure, Federal Criminal Law. ***Email:*** 7SMITH@JMLS.EDU

DAVID E. SORKIN*, (Associate Professor of Law)**, born Ann Arbor, Michigan, December 19, 1964; admitted to bar, 1989, Indiana; 1991, Illinois. *Education:* Indiana University (B.S.Bus., 1985; B.A., 1985; M.L.S., 1991); Harvard University Law School (J.D., 1988). ***COURSES: Lawyering Skills, Consumer Law, Cyberspace Law. ***Email:*** 7SORKIN@JMLS.EDU

JULIE SPANBAUER*, (Associate Professor of Law)**, born Oshkosh, Wisconsin, March 6, 1960; admitted to bar, 1986, Indiana; 1988, Illinois. *Education:* University of Wisconsin - Oshkosh (B.S., 1983); Valparaiso University School of Law (J.D., 1986); Northwestern University School of Law (LL.M., 1992). ***COURSES: Constitutional Theory, Contracts, Employment Discrimination Law, Lawyering Skills. ***Email:*** 7SPANBAU@JMLS.EDU

DEBRA POGRUND STARK*, (Associate Professor of Law)**, born Chicago, Illinois, July 20, 1961; admitted to bar, 1986, Illinois. *Education:* Brandeis University (B.A., 1982); Northwestern University (J.D., 1985). ***COURSES: Property, Real Estate Transactions. ***Email:*** 7STARK@JMLS.edu

PAUL THEODORE WANGERIN*, (Associate Professor of Law)**, born Madison, Wisconsin, March 24, 1947; admitted to bar, 1978, Illinois. *Education:* University of Missouri (A.B., 1969); John Marshall Law School (J.D., 1978). ***COURSES: Remedies, Contracts. ***Email:*** 7WANGERI@JMLS.EDU

MARK E. WOJCIK*, (Associate Professor of Law)**, born Evergreen Park, Illinois, November 7, 1961; admitted to bar, 1987, Nebraska; 1988, District of Columbia; 1990, New York and Massachusetts. *Education:* Bradley University (B.A., 1983); John Marshall Law School (J.D., 1986); New York University School of Law (LL.M., 1991). ***COURSES: International Business Transactions, AIDS and the Law, Lawyering Skills, Torts. ***Email:*** 7WOJCIK@JMLS.EDU

ANTHONY SALVATORE ZITO, JR.*, (Professor of Law)**, born Cleveland, Ohio, April 17, 1942; admitted to bar, 1967, Ohio; 1975, Illinois. *Education:* Case-Western University (B.A., 1964; J.D., 1967; LL.M., 1968). ***COURSES: Professional Responsibility, Family Law, Corporations. ***Email:*** 7ZITO@JMLS.EDU

LOUISIANA STATE UNIVERSITY LAW CENTER

EAST CAMPUS DRIVE
BATON ROUGE, LOUISIANA 70803

LOYOLA LAW SCHOOL

919 SOUTH ALBANY STREET
LOS ANGELES, CALIFORNIA 90015-1211

LOYOLA UNIVERSITY NEW ORLEANS SCHOOL OF LAW

7214 ST. CHARLES AVENUE, BOX 901
NEW ORLEANS, LOUISIANA 70118
Telephone: (504) 861-5550
Fax: (504) 861-5895

ABA Approved Since 1931

Founded in 1914, Loyola University New Orleans School of Law is the only dual division law school in the United States that offers complete curricular programs in both the civil and common law, the world's two leading legal systems. The recent internationalization of markets worldwide has placed renewed emphasis on the civil law legal system in place in two-thirds of the world. Loyola University School of Law's broad curriculum offers its students the opportunity to study either the common law or the civil law, or both. The students may earn a Joint Certificate in Civil and Common Law, as well as a Certificate in International Legal Studies. Approximately 750 students enroll in Loyola's full-time and part-time divisions each year.

Loyola University School of Law, as a Jesuit institution, also prides itself in its focus on social outreach and community service, through curricular emphasis on ethics and poverty law, as well as the special programs of the Gillis Long Poverty Law Center, the Loyola Law Clinic, and the Loyola Public Interest Law Journal.

Joint degree programs are available in conjunction with other departments of Loyola University and the University of New Orleans, including: J.D./M.B.A., J.D./Masters of Religious Studies, J.D./Masters in Mass Communications, J.D./Masters in Public Administration, J.D./Masters in Urban Planning.

Loyola University School of Law is a member of the Association of American Law Schools and has been approved by the American Bar Association since 1931. The faculty of the law school comprises 31 full-time faculty members and numerous adjunct faculty, chosen from leading lawyers and judges. Faculty members actively publish scholarly research and analysis, in addition to serving on boards and committees of the American Bar Association, the Association of American Law Schools, the American Law Institute, the Louisiana Law Institute, the Louisiana Bar Foundation, the Legal Services Corporation, and many others.

Loyola publishes two student-edited journals, offers an extensive Moot Court program that has produced many victories in national competitions in recent years, and enjoys more than fifteen other student organizations which complement the law students' academic and social experiences. Chapters of the International Law Society, the American Trial Lawyer's Association, and the Black Law Students Association are particularly active at Loyola.

In 1985, the law school moved into its new, picturesque facility on historic St. Charles Avenue in the university section of New Orleans. This modern facility houses all classrooms, faculty offices, and the spacious law library. The law library collection numbers more than 300,000 volumes and over 3,400 serial subscriptions. The library collection is supplemented by access to state of the art electronic data bases, including WESTLAW/Dialog and LEXIS/NEXIS. The law library is a selected federal and state depository for government documents.

Loyola's extensive foreign summer school programs offer students the opportunity to study law abroad. We offer programs on four continents: (1) A five week program in Cuernavaca, Mexico, with an additional two week program in either Sao Paolo, Brazil or San Jose, Costa Rica; (2) Five weeks in Moscow, Russia and Budapest, Hungary; (3) Two to four weeks in Vienna, Austria; (4) Five weeks in Kyoto, Japan; These programs are in addition to the popular regular summer school in New Orleans.

Dean: James M. Klebba (504) 861-5762
Associate Dean for Academic Affairs: Rev. Lawrence Moore, S.J. (504) 861-5677
Associate Dean of Student Affairs: Stephanie W. Jumonville (504) 861-5438
Assistant Dean of Admissions & Minority Affairs: K. Michele Allison-Davis (504) 861-5575
Assistant Director, Financial Aid: Nadine Lewis (504) 861-5551
Director of the Law Library: Edmund P. Edmonds (504) 861-5543
Director, Office of Career Services: Pam Occhipinti (504) 861-5645
Director, Law Alumni Relations: Edward D'Antoni (504) 861-5758
Budget Director: Andrew L. Piacun (504) 861-5552
Instructional Resources Coordinator: Paul Hickey (504) 861-5732
Law Records Coordinator: Shirlene Muckleroy (504) 861-5557

(This Listing Continued)

LOYOLA UNIVERSITY - NEW ORLEANS SCHOOL OF LAW—Continued

FULL TIME FACULTY

JAMES M. KLEBBA*, (Dean and Victor H. Schiro Professor of Law)**, born September 8, 1942; admitted to bar, 1970, Minnesota. *Education:* St. John's University (B.A., 1964); Harvard University (J.D., 1967). ***COURSES: Civil Procedure, Evidence, Federal Courts, Comparative Judicial Systems.

MARY GARVEY ALGERO*, (Associate Professor of Law)**, born New Orleans, Louisiana, December 12, 1964; admitted to bar, 1989, Louisiana. *Education:* University of New Orleans (B.A., 1986); Loyola University School of Law (J.D., 1989). ***COURSES: Legal Research and Writing, Federal Civil Procedure, Legal Ethics, Law & Poverty.

GEORGE L. BILBE*, (Professor of Law)**, born Crowley, Louisiana, January 23, 1947; admitted to bar, 1970, Louisiana. *Education:* Louisiana State University (B.A., 1970; J.D., 1970). ***COURSES: Contracts, Commercial Paper, Family Law, Louisiana Sales, Leases, and Obligations.

DANE S. CIOLINO*, (Associate Professor of Law)**, born New Orleans, Louisiana, January 28, 1964; admitted to bar, 1989, New York, Louisiana. *Education:* Rhodes College (B.A., 1985); Tulane Law School (J.D., 1988). ***COURSES: Copyright, Professional Responsibility, Contracts, Family Law, Criminal Law.

MITCHELL F. CRUSTO*, (Associate Professor of Law)**, born New Orleans, Louisiana, April 22, 1953; admitted to bar, 1982, Louisiana; 1984, Missouri; 1985, Illinois. *Education:* Yale University (B.A., 1975); Oxford University, England (B.A., 1980; M.A., 1985); Yale Law School (J.D., 1981). ***COURSES: Common Law Property I and II, Business Organizations I and II, Contracts II.

DARRYL ANTHONY DERBIGNY*, (Assistant Clinical Professor)**, born New Orleans, Louisiana, February 28, 1951; admitted to bar, 1978, Louisiana. *Education:* Columbia University (B.A., 1973); Holy Cross College; Tulane University (J.D., 1977). ***COURSES: Trial Practice, Criminal Law, Clinical Education.

HENRY D. GABRIEL*, (De Van Daggett Professor of Law)**, born 1954; admitted to bar, 1982, New York. *Education:* York University (B.A.); Gonzaga University (J.D.); University of Pennsylvania (LL.M., 1981). ***COURSES: Contracts, Commercial Transactions, Secured Transactions.

MARCEL GARSAUD, JR.*, (Alvin R. Christovich Professor of Law)**, born New Orleans, Louisiana, September 28, 1932; admitted to bar, 1959, Louisiana; 1960, New York. *Education:* Loyola University (B.B.A., 1954; LL.B., 1959); Yale University (LL.M., 1967). ***COURSES: Constitutional Law, Legal Ethics, Torts.

DAVID W. GRUNING*, (Professor of Law)**, born Orange, New Jersey, May 16, 1951; admitted to bar, 1982, Louisiana. *Education:* Wesleyan University (B.A., 1973); Middlebury College (M.A., 1975); Tulane University (J.D., 1982). ***COURSES: Security Rights, Comparative Law, Marital Property, Contracts, Sales.

BOBBY MARZINE HARGES*, (Professor of Law)**, born Grenada, Mississippi, August 11, 1960; admitted to bar, 1986, Louisiana; 1987, Mississippi. *Education:* Mississippi State University (B.S., 1982); University of Mississippi (J.D., 1986); Harvard Law School (LL.M., 1990). ***COURSES: Evidence, Torts, Criminal Law, Criminal Procedure, Mediation and Arbitration.

PATRICK R. HUGG*, (Professor of Law)**, born Paducah, Kentucky, May 9, 1947; admitted to bar, 1979, Kentucky; 1981, Louisiana. *Education:* Spring Hill College (A.B., 1970); University of Louisville (J.D., 1979); Tulane University (LL.M., 1981). ***COURSES: Appellate Advocacy, Comparative Legal Systems: Austria, Germany, and the United States, Law of the European Union.

CATHERINE LA FLEUR*, (Clinical Professor)**, born Eunice, Louisiana, November 28, 1951. *Education:* Louisiana State University (B.S., 1972; J.D., 1976). ***COURSES: Administrative Advocacy, Trial Advocacy, Appellate Advocacy.

JOSEPH H. LAWSON*, (Professor of Law)**, born Athens, Alabama, August 19, 1932; admitted to bar, 1961, Louisiana. *Education:* Rhodes College (B.A., 1954); Tulane University (J.D., 1961). ***COURSES: Contracts, Property, Creditors' Rights.

BLAINE LE CESNE*, (Associate Professor of Law)**, born August 5, 1955; admitted to bar, 1981, New York. *Education:* Columbia University (B.A., 1977; J.D., 1980). ***COURSES: Criminal Law, Civil Procedure, Trial Practice.

CYNTHIA LEPOW*, (Professor of Law)**, born June 11, 1941; admitted to bar, 1967, New York. *Education:* Hunter College (A.B., 1962); Fordham University (J.D., 1967); New York University (LL.M., 1979). ***COURSES: Federal Taxation, Corporate Tax, Gift and Estate Tax, Partnership Tax.

KATHRYN VENTURATOS LORIO*, (Leon Sarpy Professor of Law)**, born Pittsburgh, Pennsylvania, February 15, 1949; admitted to bar, 1973, Louisiana. *Education:* Newcomb College, Tulane University (B.A., 1970); Loyola Law School (J.D., 1973). ***COURSES: Trusts and Estates, Family Law, Civil Law, Comparative Law.

LESLIE LUNNEY*, (Associate Professor of Law)**, born February 24, 1958; admitted to bar, 1988, Texas. *Education:* University of Texas (B.S.N., 1980); Houston Law Center (J.D., 1988); Tulane University (LL.M., 1993). ***COURSES: Civil Procedure, Torts, Criminal Procedure, Environmental Law.

M. ISABEL MEDINA*, (Professor of Law)**, born Havana, Cuba, January 18, 1952; admitted to bar, 1989, District of Columbia (inactive status). *Education:* Monash University (B.A., 1977); University of New Orleans (M.A., 1979; M.F.A., 1980); Tulane Law School (J.D., 1987). ***COURSES: Constitutional Law, Gender Discrimination, Employment Discrimination, Immigration Law.

LUZ M. MOLINA*, (Clinical Professor)**, born Medellin, Colombia, April 14, 1955; admitted to bar, 1979, Louisiana. *Education:* Tulane University (J.D., 1979); University of New Orleans (B.A., 1984). ***COURSES: Clinic, Externs.

LAWRENCE S.J. MOORE*, (Associate Dean for Academic Affairs and Professor of Law)**, born Kansas City, Missouri, July 17, 1946; admitted to bar, 1981, Missouri. *Education:* St. Louis University (A.B., 1970; M.A., 1972); Jesuit School of Theology (M.Div., 1977); University of Missouri, Kansas City (J.D., 1981); New York University (LL.M., 1982). ***COURSES: Civil Procedure, Federal Courts, Civil Rights.

WILLIAM A. NEILSON*, (Associate Professor)**, born New York, N.Y., February 15, 1948; admitted to bar, 1974, New York; 1980, Louisiana. *Education:* University of Pittsburgh (B.A., 1969); Loyola University (J.D., 1973); New York University (LL.M., 1980). ***COURSES: Federal Taxation, Corporations, Partnerships, Decedents' Estates and Trusts.

DAVID R. NORMANN*, (Professor of Law)**, born New Orleans, Louisiana, November 21, 1925; admitted to bar, 1950, Louisiana. *Education:* Washington & Lee University; Tulane University (B.A., 1948; J.D., 1950). ***COURSES: Maritime Law, Professional Responsibility, Trial Advocacy, Civil Procedure.

(This Listing Continued)

LOYOLA UNIVERSITY - NEW ORLEANS SCHOOL OF LAW—Continued

WILLIAM QUIGLEY*, (Professor and Director of Clinic)**, born Chicago, Illinois, August 14, 1949; admitted to bar, 1977, Louisiana. *Education:* Purdue University (B.A., 1971); Loyola University (J.D., 1977). ***COURSES: Law and Poverty, Clinical Seminar.

RAPHAEL J. RABALAIS JR.*, (Elenor Legein Sarpu Professor of Law)**, born New Orleans, Louisiana, September 23, 1947; admitted to bar, 1972, Michigan; 1991, Texas. *Education:* Princeton University (A.B., 1968); Michigan State University (M.A., 1974); Harvard University (J.D., 1971). ***COURSES: International Commercial Law, Legal History, Financial Institutions Law, Business Organizations.

GERARD RAULT*, (Professor of Law)**, born Washington, D.C., October 17, 1943; admitted to bar, 1969, Louisiana. *Education:* Loyola University; Spring Hill College; Louisiana State University (J.D., 1968). ***COURSES: Evidence, Criminal Law and Procedure, Louisiana Obligations, Trial Practice, Clinic, Chinese Law.

JANET RILEY*, (Professor of Law Emeritus)**, admitted to bar, 1953, Louisiana. *Education:* Loyola University (B.A., 1936); Louisiana State University (B.S., 1940); Loyola University School of Law (J.D., 1952); University of Virginia (LL.M., 1960). ***COURSES: Community Property, Family Law, First Amendment Rights, Insurance.

DENNIS ROUSSEAU*, (Fannie Edith Winn Professor of Law)**, born New Orleans, Louisiana, November 19, 1933; admitted to bar, 1957, Louisiana. *Education:* Loyola University (A.B., 1957; J.D., 1957; B.B.A., 1960); Harvard Law School (LL.M., 1958). ***COURSES: Agency, Partnerships, Limited Liability Companies, Corporations, Business Planning, Jurisprudence.

FREDERICK W. SWAIM JR.*, (Professor of Law)**, born 1934; admitted to bar, 1967, Louisiana. *Education:* Tulane University of Louisiana (B.A.); University of California at Berkeley (LL.M.); Tulane University of Louisiana (J.D.). ***COURSES: Admiralty, Successions, Donations & Trusts, Maritime Personal Injury.

DIAN TOOLEY*, (Professor of Law)**, born May 7, 1955; admitted to bar, 1980, Louisiana. *Education:* Southeastern Louisiana University (B.A., 1977); Louisiana State University (J.D., 1980). ***COURSES: Community Property, Mineral Law, Property, Sales.

BERNARD KEITH VETTER*, (Professor of Law)**, born Louisiana, July 5, 1939; admitted to bar, 1965, Maryland. *Education:* Louisiana State University (B.A., 1962; LL.B., 1963); George Washington University (LL.M., 1964). ***COURSES: Civil Law Property, Common Law Property, Civil Law Security Devices, Comparative Law, State and Government Law, Urban Planning Law.

JAMES ETIENNE VIATOR*, (Associate Professor of Law)**, born Eunice, Louisiana, June 28, 1949. *Education:* University of New Orleans (B.A., 1971); Louisiana State University (J.D., 1985). ***COURSES: Contracts, Torts, American Legal and Constitutional History, Obligations, Sales and Lease.

***P. MICHAEL WHIPPLE*, (Director of Law Library and Professor of Law)**, admitted to bar, 1974, Arizona. *Education:* Arizona State University (B.A., 1969); John Hopkins University (M.A., 1971); University of Iowa (J.D., 1974); University of Denver (M.L.L., 1980).

JEANNE WOODS*, (Associate Professor of Law)**, born August 5, 1952. *Education:* Antioch College (B.A., 1974); Temple University (J.D., 1981). ***COURSES: International Law, Constitutional Law, Human Rights, Property Law, Torts.

LOYOLA UNIVERSITY OF CHICAGO SCHOOL OF LAW

ONE EAST PEARSON STREET
CHICAGO, ILLINOIS 60611

MARQUETTE UNIVERSITY LAW SCHOOL

SENSENBRENNER HALL
PO BOX 1881
MILWAUKEE, WISCONSIN 53201-1881
Telephone: (414) 288-7090
Fax: (414) 288-6403
http://www.marquette.edu/law

ABA Approved Since 1925.

For more than a century, Marquette University Law School has been committed to training men and women to serve the public interest by becoming highly skilled, ethical, and moral attorneys. Traditionally, the Law School's curriculum has emphasized the practical aspects of legal practice. In recent years that emphasis has expanded to include particular excellence in the areas of intellectual property, international law, business law, criminal law and procedure, children and the law, and litigation related courses. The National Sports Law Institute, the premiere sports law program in the U.S., is part of the Law School. Our alumni of over 5,500 serve in a broad range of legal, public, and corporate positions throughout the United States.

Dean: Howard B. Eisenberg (414) 288-1768
Administrative Assistant to the Dean: Nancy Rogers (414) 288-5958
Associate Dean for Academic Affairs: Shirley Wiegand (414) 288-5486
Associate Dean for Administration and Registrar: Bonnie Thomson (414) 288-3641
Assistant Dean for Admissions: Edward Kawczynski (414) 288-6767
Assistant Dean for Career Services: Dr. Paul Katzman (414) 288-5236
Director of the Law Library: Peter Schanck (414) 288-5494
Director, National Sports Law Institute: Matt Mitten (414) 288-5815
Director of Development Programs: Jason Kraiss (414) 288-5285

(This Listing Continued)

MARQUETTE UNIVERSITY LAW SCHOOL—Continued

FULL TIME FACULTY

HOWARD B. EISENBERG*, (Dean and Professor of Law)**, born Chicago, Illinois, December 9, 1946; admitted to bar, 1971, Wisconsin; 1980, District of Columbia; 1985, Illinois. *Education:* Northwestern University (B.A., 1968); University of Wisconsin (J.D., 1971). ***COURSES: Criminal Law, Criminal Procedure, Civil Procedure, Appellate Advocacy. ***Email:*** howard.eisenberg@marquette.edu

RALPH C. ANZIVINO*, (Professor)**, born Youngstown, Ohio, October 26, 1947; admitted to bar, 1972, Ohio; 1976, Wisconsin. *Education:* Bowling Green State University (B.S., 1969); Case Western Reserve (J.D., 1971). ***COURSES: Debtor-Creditor, Commercial Law, Contracts, Bankruptcy. ***Email:*** rcanzivino@aol.com

ALISON BARNES*, (Associate Professor)**, born Philadelphia, Pennsylvania, March 1, 1958; admitted to bar, 1985, Florida. *Education:* University of Cambridge (Dipl. in Law, 1992); University of Florida (B.A., 1979; J.D., 1985). ***COURSES: Health Law, Elder Law, Disability Law, Administrative Law. ***Email:*** alison.barnes@marquette.edu

DANIEL DAVID BLINKA*, (Professor)**, born Milwaukee, Wisconsin, January 27, 1953; admitted to bar, 1978, Wisconsin. *Education:* University of Wisconsin - Milwaukee (B.A., 1975); University of Wisconsin - Madison (J.D., 1978; M.A., 1994; Ph.D., 2001). ***COURSES: Evidence, Criminal Law and Procedure, Legal History and Trial Advocacy.

PATRICIA CLARE BRADFORD*, (Associate Professor)**, born Portland, Oregon, October 25, 1954; admitted to bar, 1981, California; 1982, Wisconsin. *Education:* State University of New York (B.A., 1977); Hastings College of the Law (J.D., 1981). ***COURSES: Taxation, Trusts and Estates, Feminist Legal Theory, Gender Economics.

FRANK CHARLES DE GUIRE*, (Professor)**, born Appleton, Wisconsin, April 10, 1931; admitted to bar, 1960, Wisconsin. *Education:* University of Wisconsin (B.A., 1953); Marquette University Law School (J.D., 1960). ***COURSES: Corporations, Business Entities.

CAROLYN EDWARDS*, (Associate Professor)**, born Toledo, Ohio, May 1, 1942; admitted to bar, 1970, Ohio; 1979, Wisconsin. *Education:* Wells College (B.A., 1964); University of Toledo (J.D., 1970). ***COURSES: Commercial Law, Contracts.

EDWARD A. FALLONE*, (Associate Professor)**, born Rockville, Maryland, May 17, 1964; admitted to bar, 1988, Maryland; 1989, District of Columbia; 1995, Wisconsin. *Education:* Boston University (B.A., 1988; J.D., 1988). ***COURSES: Corporations, Securities, White Collar Crime, Immigration.

JANINE P. GESKE*, (Distinguished Professor of Law)**, born Port Washington, Wisconsin, May 12, 1949; admitted to bar, 1975, Wisconsin. *Education:* Beloit College (B.A. and M.A., 1971); Marquette University Law School (J.D., 1975). ***COURSES: Mediation Clinic, Evidence. ***Email:*** jpg@execpc.com

JAY E. GRENIG*, (Professor)**, born Utah, April 18, 1943; admitted to bar, 1972, California; 1980, Wisconsin. *Education:* Willamette University (B.A., 1966); Hastings College of Law (J.D., 1971). ***COURSES: Civil Procedure, Alternative Dispute Resolution.

THOMAS JOHN HAMMER*, (Associate Professor)**, born Milwaukee, Wisconsin, March 14, 1949; admitted to bar, 1975, Wisconsin. *Education:* Marquette University (B.A., 1971; J.D., 1975). ***COURSES: Criminal Law and Procedure, Trial Advocacy.

JILL KOCH HAYFORD*, (Assistant Professor)**, born 1960; admitted to bar, 1985, Wisconsin. *Education:* University of Wisconsin (B.A., 1982); Harvard Law School (J.D., 1985). ***COURSES: Legal Writing.

JOSEPH GORDON HYLTON*, (Associate Professor)**, born Pearisburg, Virginia, May 29, 1952; admitted to bar, 1977, Virginia; 1980, District of Columbia; 1987, Massachusetts. *Education:* Oberlin College (A.B., 1974); University of Virginia (J.D., 1977); Harvard University (Ph.D., 1986). ***COURSES: Property, Legal History, Intellectual Property, Sports Law.

SCOTT CLARK IDLEMAN*, (Associate Professor)**, born Summit, New Jersey, June 3, 1966; admitted to bar, 1994, Illinois. *Education:* Cornell University (B.S., 1989); Indiana University (M.P.A., 1993; J.D., 1993). ***COURSES: Constitutional Law, Federal Courts, Law & Religion, Federal Indian Law. ***Email:*** scott.idleman@marquette.edu

ALISON E. JULIEN*, (Assistant Professor)**, born 1969; admitted to bar, 1994, Pennsylvania; 1995, Wisconsin. *Education:* Saint Olaf College (B.A., 1991); University of Pittsburgh School of Law (J.D., 1991). ***COURSES: Legal Writing.

JOSEPH D. KEARNEY*, (Associate Professor)**, born Chicago, Illinois, December 28, 1964; admitted to bar, 1989, Illinois. *Education:* Yale University (B.A., 1986); Harvard University (J.D., 1989). ***COURSES: Appellate Advocacy, Civil Procedure, Federal Courts, Administrative Law. ***Email:*** joseph.kearney@Marquette.edu

JEFFREY SCOTT KINSLER*, (Associate Professor)**, born Gary, Indiana, June 8, 1962; admitted to bar, 1989, Illinois. *Education:* Ball State University (B.S., 1985); Valparaiso (J.D., 1989); Yale Law School (LL.M., 1996). ***COURSES: Evidence, Tax, Trusts and Estates.

JOHN JOSEPH KIRCHER*, (Professor)**, born Milwaukee, Wisconsin, July 26, 1938; admitted to bar, 1963, Wisconsin. *Education:* Marquette University (B.A., 1960; J.D., 1963). ***COURSES: Torts, Insurance, Product Liability, Advanced Issues in Torts. ***Email:*** john.kircher@marquette.edu

VADA WATERS LINDSEY*, (Assistant Professor)**, born Niagara Falls, New York; admitted to bar, 1988, Illinois; 1991, District of Columbia. *Education:* Michigan State University (B.A., 1983); DePaul University College of Law (J.D., 1988); Georgetown University Law Center (LL.M., 1992). ***COURSES: Taxation, Real Estate, Development & Finance.

ALAN R. MADRY*, (Associate Professor)**, born Detroit, Michigan, May 5, 1952; admitted to bar, 1983, Michigan. *Education:* University of Michigan (B.A., 1976; J.D., 1981); University of Wisconsin (M.A. Phil., 2001). ***COURSES: Constitutional Law, Property, Land Use, Philosophy of Law. ***Email:*** alan.madry@marquette.edu

MICHAEL K. MCCHRYSTAL*, (Professor of Law)**, born St. Paul, Minnesota, September 8, 1950; admitted to bar, 1975, Wisconsin. *Education:* University of Michigan (B.A., 1972); Marquette University (J.D., 1975). ***COURSES: Legal Ethics, Torts, Privacy.

KATHLEEN HORAN MCMANUS*, (Professor of Law)**, born Milwaukee, Wisconsin, March 4, 1940; admitted to bar, 1985, Wisconsin. *Education:* Marquette University (B.A., 1962; J.D., 1985). ***COURSES: Legal Writing and Research. ***Email:*** kathleen.mcmanus@marquette.edu

JUDITH G. MCMULLEN*, (Associate Professor)**, born Milwaukee, Wisconsin, January 25, 1956; admitted to bar, 1980, Illinois; 1989, Wisconsin. *Education:* University of Notre Dame (A.B., 1977); Yale Law School (J.D., 1980). ***COURSES: Family Law, Trusts & Estates.

***MATTHEW J. MITTEN*, (Professor and Director, National Sports**

(This Listing Continued)

MARQUETTE UNIVERSITY LAW SCHOOL—Continued

Law Institute), born Tiffin, Ohio, April 26, 1959; admitted to bar, 1984, Georgia. *Education:* Ohio State University (B.A., 1981); University of Toledo College of Law (J.D., 1984). ***COURSES:*** Sports Law, Torts, Antitrust. ***Email:*** matt.mitten@marquette.edu

CRAIG ALLEN NARD*, (Associate Professor of Law)**, born Monessen, Pennsylvania, August 16, 1965; admitted to bar, 1990, Texas. *Education:* Washington and Jefferson College (B.A., 1987); Capital University Law and Graduate Center (J.D., 1990); Columbia University School of Law (LL.M., 1995; J.S.D., 1999). ***COURSES: Intellectual Property and Torts. ***Email:*** craig.nard@marquette.edu

MICHAEL M. O'HEAR*, (Assistant Professor of Law)**, born District of Columbia, November 7, 1968; admitted to bar, 1998, Illinois. *Education:* Yale (B.A., 1991; J.D., 1996). ***COURSES: Environmental, Sentencing, Civil Procedure, Legislation. ***Email:*** michael.ohear@marquette.edu

KENNETH L. PORT*, (Professor)**, born Cloquet, Minnesota, October 18, 1960; admitted to bar, 1989, Wisconsin and Illinois. *Education:* Macalester College (B.A., 1982); University of Wisconsin - Madison (J.D., 1989). ***COURSES: Intellectual Property, Comparative Law, Property.

PETER K. ROFES*, (Professor and Director of Part-time Legal Education)**, born New York, New York, March 28, 1956; admitted to bar, 1985, District of Columbia; 1989, Wisconsin. *Education:* Brandeis University (B.A., 1978); Harvard University (A.M., 1981); Columbia University School of Law (J.D., 1983). ***COURSES: Constitutional Law, Professional Responsibility, Contracts. ***Email:*** peter.rofes@marquette.edu

PETER C. SCHANCK*, (Director of the Law Library and Professor)**, born Chicago, Illinois, May 9, 1938; admitted to bar, 1963, Connecticut. *Education:* Dartmouth College (B.A., 1960); Yale Law School (J.D., 1963); University of Maryland (M.L.S., 1972). ***COURSES: Advanced Legal Research. ***Email:*** peter.schanck@marquette.edu

ANDREA KUPFER SCHNEIDER*, (Associate Professor)**, born New York, New York, June 3, 1966; admitted to bar, 1992, Pennsylvania; 1994, District of Columbia. *Education:* Princeton University (A.B., 1988); Harvard Law School (J.D., 1992). ***COURSES: International Law, European Union Law, Negotiation, Law and the Visual Arts, Alternative Dispute Resolution. ***Email:*** andrea.schneider@marquette.edu

BONNIE M. THOMSON*, (Associate Dean for Administration and Registrar)**, born Michigan, November 8, 1952. *Education:* University of Michigan (A.B., 1974); University of Wisconsin - Milwaukee (M.S., 1980). ***Email: bonnie.thomson@marquette.edu

MICHAEL PETER WAXMAN*, (Professor)**, born New York, New York, May 20, 1947; admitted to bar, 1973, Maryland; 1982, Wisconsin. *Education:* Cornell University (B.S., 1969); Boston College Law School (J.D., 1973). ***COURSES: International Trade, Antitrust, International Litigation and Arbitration, Administrative Law. ***Email:*** michael.waxman@marquette.edu

SHIRLEY A. WIEGAND*, (Professor and Associate Dean for Academic Affairs)**, born Appleton, Wisconsin, October 10, 1947; admitted to bar, 1983, Kentucky; 1986, Wisconsin. *Education:* Urbana College (B.A., 1976); University of Kentucky (M.A., 1980; J.D., 1983). ***COURSES: Civil Procedure, Conflict of Laws, Feminist Legal Theory, Law and Literature, Remedies. ***Email:*** shirley.wiegand@marquette.edu

PHOEBE WEAVER WILLIAMS*, (Associate Professor)**, born Memphis, Tennessee, June 14, 1946; admitted to bar, 1981, Wisconsin. *Education:* Marquette University (A.B., 1968; J.D., 1981). ***COURSES: Labor, Employment, Discrimination, Business, History of Women Lawyers. ***Email:*** phoebe.williams@marquette.edu

CHRISTINE M. WISEMAN*, (Professor and Associate Vice President for Academic Affairs, Marquette University)**, born Wisconsin, August 17, 1949; admitted to bar, 1973, Wisconsin; 1988, U.S. Supreme Court. *Education:* Marquette University (A.B., 1971; J.D., 1973). ***COURSES: Civil Procedure, Criminal Procedure, Capital Punishment. ***Email:*** christine.wiseman@marquette.edu

---

MCGEORGE SCHOOL OF LAW, UNIVERSITY OF THE PACIFIC

3200 FIFTH AVENUE
SACRAMENTO, CALIFORNIA 95817

MEMPHIS STATE UNIVERSITY
CECIL C. HUMPHREYS SCHOOL OF LAW

3715 CENTRAL AVENUE
MEMPHIS, TENNESSEE 38152

MERCER UNIVERSITY
WALTER F. GEORGE SCHOOL OF LAW

1400 COLEMAN AVE.
MACON, GEORGIA 31207
Telephone: (478) 301-2602
Fax: (478) 301-2101
www.law.mercer.edu

ABA Approved Since 1925.

Founded in 1873, the Mercer University School of Law is one of the older law schools in the nation. It became a member of the Association of American Law Schools in 1923 and has been accredited by the American Bar Association since 1925.

Atlanta philanthropist George W. Woodruff's 1987 bequest of $15

(This Listing Continued)

MERCER UNIVERSITY WALTER F. GEORGE SCHOOL OF LAW—Continued

million spurred a remarkable growth in Mercer's Law School endowment. This endowment, now valued at more than $75 million, is one of the largest law school endowments in the nation. With the support of the Woodruff bequest, the Law School's curriculum was totally redesigned in the late 1980's. The student body was decreased to 400 students at the same time that the faculty was increased to 29 full-time faculty members and 20 adjunct professors.

The Woodruff Curriculum focuses on the professional skills that students will need in practice. This curriculum contains an intensive three-year legal writing program, structured courses requiring students to progress from introductory to advanced work in particular areas of the law, and a final semester of law school in which students choose from various "pre-practice" elective courses taught by both full-time faculty and adjunct practitioners. Legal writing courses are required in four of the six semesters, and popular research and writing electives are offered in the other two semesters. Students start each of their three years at Mercer with an intensive one-week course. The first-year class takes Introduction to Law, which introduces students to the American legal system and law school. The second-year class learns about, and participates in exercises concerning, interviewing and counseling, while the first week of a student's third year is spent in an intensive one-week course involving alternative dispute resolution.

Mercer's Woodruff Curriculum has received attention both within legal education and within the profession. Because of the focus of Mercer's curriculum on professionalism, the American Bar Association awarded Mercer the Gambrell Professionalism Award in 1996.

The *Mercer Law Review* publishes four issues per year. The *Review* sponsors an annual symposium, which brings leading scholars and practitioners to Mercer to address a timely issue of legal significance. Various other student organizations and activities are offered.

Mercer students have enjoyed great success in national interscholastic moot court competitions in recent years. In four of the last ten years, Mercer has represented the Southeast region in the National Moot Court Competition, receiving the award for best brief in the nation in 1998. The outstanding student advocates in the 1996, 1997, and 2000 Georgia Intrastate Moot Court Competition were Mercer students, while Mercer's team won this competition in 1997, 1998, and 2000 (also winning best brief honors in 1997 and 1998).

Mercer's Furman Smith Law Library contains more than 304,000 volumes, including video and audiotapes and 3300 serial titles dealing with domestic and international law. The Law Library's computer laboratory contains 30 workstations, providing access to computer exercises, interactive CD-ROM trial practice materials, legal research databases, word processing, and the Internet and World Wide Web. Research assistance is available throughout the week, and law students have 24-hour access to the Law Library.

Since 1985, the National Criminal Defense College has been located at Mercer. The dean of the college is also a full-time professor and Director of Trial Practice at the Law School. The College brings to Mercer criminal defense attorneys from across the country to participate in intensive trial skills workshops conducted by the College.

Mercer's Office of Career Services assists students in legal placement. The Office of Career Services participates in annual hiring consortia, sponsors workshops for students, and brings lawyers and judges to Mercer to interview current students. Most Mercer graduates accept employment in the Southeast, although one in five graduates practice in other areas of the United States. Upon their graduation from Mercer, graduates accept federal and state judicial clerkships, positions with large, medium-sized, and small private law firms, work for federal, state, and local governments, become prosecutors and criminal defense attorneys, and accept positions in legal aid and public interest organizations.

Mercer graduates value and actively participate in public service. Mercer alumni have served as Attorney General of the United States, federal and state judges, presidents of state and local bar associations, and as president of such organizations as the American College of Trial Lawyers.

Dean: R. Lawrence Dessem (478) 301-2602
Associate Dean: Michael Sabbath (478) 301-2633
Dean for Student Affairs: Mary Donovan (478) 301-2586
Dean of Admissions: Marilyn Sutton (478) 301-2429
Director of Library: Suzanne Cassidy (478) 301-2665
Placement: Rachael Schell (478) 301-2914
Alumni Affairs: Patricia Bass (478) 301-2647
Registrar: Patsy Crammer (478) 301-2621

FULL TIME FACULTY

R. LAWRENCE DESSEM,* (Dean and Professor)**, born Berea, Ohio, May 16, 1951; admitted to bar, 1976, Ohio; 1979, District of Columbia; 1985, Tennessee. *Education:* Macalester College (B.A., 1973); Harvard University (J.D., 1976). ***COURSES: Alternative Dispute Resolution, Legal Writing. ***Email:*** dessem_rl@mercer.edu

ALICE J. BAKER,* (Assistant Professor)**, born California, November 17, 1963; admitted to bar, 1995, Virginia. *Education:* California State University, Northridge (B.A., 1982); University of Virginia (J.D., 1995). ***COURSES: Civil Procedure, Antitrust. ***Email:*** baker-aj@mercer.edu

ANTHONY R. BALDWIN,* (Professor of Law)**, born May 22, 1947. *Education:* Boston University (B.A., 1968); Harvard Law School (J.D., 1973). ***COURSES: Arbitration, Labor Law, Civil Procedure, Constitutional Law, Employment Discrimination. ***Email:*** baldwin_ar@mercer.edu

SUSAN M. BAY,* (Assistant Professor)**, born Cudahy, Wisconsin, July 19, 1969; admitted to bar, 1995, Wisconsin. *Education:* University of Wisconsin (B.A., 1991); Tulane University Law School (J.D., 1995). ***COURSES: Legal Writing. ***Email:*** bay-sm@mercer.edu

THEODORE Y. BLUMOFF,* (Professor of Law)**, born St. Louis, Missouri, January 27, 1947; admitted to bar, 1982, Missouri. *Education:* St. Louis University (B.S., 1969; Ph.D., 1976); Washington University (J.D., 1982). ***COURSES: Criminal Law, Constitutional Law, Federal Courts, Pretrial Practice. ***Email:*** blumoff_ty@mercer.edu

DAVID ALEXANDER BRENNEN,* (Associate Professor)**, born Gainesville, Florida, October 30, 1966; admitted to bar, 1992, Florida. *Education:* Florida Atlantic University (B.B.A., 1988); University of Florida College of Law (J.D., 1991; LL.M., 1994). ***COURSES: Federal Income Tax, Federal Taxation of Tax - Exempt Organizations, Estate & Gift Tax. ***Email:*** brennen_da@mercer.edu

(This Listing Continued)

MERCER UNIVERSITY WALTER F. GEORGE SCHOOL OF LAW—Continued

SUZANNE LOYD CASSIDY*, (Director of the Law Library)**, born London, England, December 18, 1952; admitted to bar, 1981, Georgia. *Education:* University of Georgia (A.B., 1974); Mercer University School of Law (J.D., 1981). ***COURSES: Legal Research. ***Email:*** cassidy_sl@mercer.edu

JOSEPH E. CLAXTON*, (Professor of Law)**, born Griffin, Georgia, April 12, 1946; admitted to bar, 1972, Georgia. *Education:* Emory University (B.A., 1968); Duke University (J.D., 1972). ***COURSES: Business Associations, Wills & Trusts, Legal Ethics, American Legal History. ***Email:*** claxton_je@mercer.edu

JOHN O. COLE*, (Professor of Law)**, born St. Louis, Missouri, July 22, 1936; admitted to bar, 1970, Pennsylvania; 1972, Indiana; 1992, Georgia. *Education:* Duke University (A.B., 1958); Indiana University (M.A., 1962); University of Pennsylvania (J.D., 1970). ***COURSES: Constitutional Law, Criminal Law, Criminal Procedure, Jurisprudence. ***Email:*** cole_jo@mercer.edu

RICHARD W. CRESWELL*, (Professor of Law)**, born Vicksburg, Mississippi, September 5, 1946; admitted to bar, 1972, Tennessee. *Education:* Emory University (B.A., 1969); Vanderbilt University (J.D., 1972). ***COURSES: Torts, Local Government, Environmental Law. ***Email:*** creswell_rw@mercer.edu

DERYL D. DANTZLER*, (Professor of Law/Dean, National Criminal Defense College)**, born Macon, Georgia, January 26, 1944; admitted to bar, 1970, Georgia. *Education:* Mercer University (B.A., 1964; J.D., 1970). ***COURSES: Advanced Trial Practice, Evidence, Trial Practice, Problems in Trial Evidence. ***Email:*** dantzler_d@mercer.edu

LINDA H. EDWARDS*, (Professor of Law & Coordinator of Legal Writing)**, born Miami, Florida, November 26, 1948; admitted to bar, 1977, Colorado; 1978, Idaho; 1988, New York. *Education:* Carson Newman College; Florida State University (B.A., 1970); University of Tennessee (J.D., 1976). ***COURSES: Property, Legal Writing, Legal Reasoning, Litigation Drafting, Professional Ethics. ***Email:*** edwards_lh@mercer.edu

JAMES PETER FLEISSNER*, (Professor of Law)**, born Milwaukee, Wisconsin, July 19, 1957; admitted to bar, 1986, Illinois. *Education:* Marquette University (B.A., 1979); University of Chicago (J.D., 1986). ***COURSES: Criminal Law and Procedure, Evidence, Trial Practice, Appellate Advocacy. ***Email:*** fleissner_jp@mercer.edu

JAMES LOGAN HUNT*, (Associate Professor)**, admitted to bar, 1988, North Carolina. *Education:* University of North Carolina (A.B., 1981; J.D., 1988); University of Wisconsin (Ph.D., 1990); Harvard Law School (LL.M., 1993). ***COURSES: Legal Writing I and II, American Legal History. ***Email:*** hunt_jl@mercer.edu

STEPHEN M. JOHNSON*, (Professor of Law)**, born Middlesex, New Jersey, May 20, 1963; admitted to bar, 1988, Pennsylvania and New Jersey. *Education:* Villanova University (B.S., 1985; J.D., 1988); George Washington University (LL.M., 1992). ***COURSES: Torts, Environmental Law, Administrative Law, Statutory Analysis. ***Email:*** johnson_s@mercer.edu

MARK LAURENCE JONES*, (Professor of Law)**, born Eastleigh, U.K., May 18, 1953; admitted to bar, 1978, England and Wales. *Education:* University College (B.A., 1974; M.A., 1979); University of Michigan (LL.M., 1983). ***COURSES: Comparative Law, European Community Law, International Business and Trade, Immigration Law, Jurisprudence. ***Email:*** jones_ml@mercer.edu

REYNOLD J. KOSEK*, (Professor of Law)**, born Wilkes-Barre, Pennsylvania, February 25, 1947; admitted to bar, 1975, California; 1976, Pennsylvania. *Education:* West Virginia University (A.B., 1968); State University of New York (M.L.S., 1971); University of North Carolina (J.D., 1975). ***COURSES: Contracts, Remedies, Sales, Mass Media, Introduction to Law Study. ***Email:*** kosek_rj@mercer.edu

HAROLD S. LEWIS, JR.*, (Professor of Law)**, born New York, New York, September 26, 1947; admitted to bar, 1973, New York; 1987, Georgia. *Education:* Columbia University (A.B., 1969) Stanford University (J.D., 1972). ***COURSES: Employment Discrimination, Civil Rights, Civil Procedure. ***Email:*** lewis_hs@mercer.edu

PATRICK EMERY LONGAN*, (W. A. Bootle Chair in Professionalism and Ethics)**, born Little Rock, Arkansas, June 13, 1957; admitted to bar, 1983, Texas. *Education:* Washington University (A.B., 1979); University of Sussex (M.A., 1980); University of Chicago (J.D., 1983). ***COURSES: Law of Lawyering, Judicial Field Placement, Litigation Ethics. ***Email:*** longan_p@mercer.edu

JAMES CREEL MARSHALL*, (Professor of Law)**, born Ithaca, New York, March 31, 1948; admitted to bar, 1977, Georgia. *Education:* Princeton University (A.B., 1972); Boston University (J.D., 1977). ***COURSES: Debtor-Creditor Relations, Bankruptcy, Commercial Transactions, Property, Advising Small Business. ***Email:*** marshall_jc@mercer.edu

ADAM A. MILANI*, (Assistant Professor)**, born Peoria, Illinois, December 15, 1965; admitted to bar, 1991, Indiana. *Education:* University of Notre Dame (B.A., 1988); Duke University (J.D., 1991). ***COURSES: Legal Writing. ***Email:*** milani_a@mercer.edu

DAVID G. OEDEL*, (Professor of Law)**, born Salem, Massachusetts, July 30, 1957; admitted to bar, 1987, Massachusetts. *Education:* Haverford College (B.A., 1979); Boston University (J.D., 1987). ***COURSES: Contracts, Intellectual Property, Banking, Business, Civil Procedure. ***Email:*** oedel_dg@mercer.edu

MICHAEL DEAN SABBATH*, (Associate Dean and Professor of Law)**, born St. Louis, Missouri, October 24, 1950; admitted to bar, 1975, Georgia. *Education:* University of Wisconsin (B.A., 1972); Emory University (J.D., 1975); Columbia University (LL.M., 1985). ***COURSES: Contracts, Commercial Law, Remedies. ***Email:*** sabbath_md@mercer.edu

JACK LEE SAMMONS*, (Professor of Law)**, born Fairfield, Ohio, September 9, 1945; admitted to bar, 1974, Georgia; 1977, District of Columbia. *Education:* Duke University (B.A., 1967); University of Georgia (J.D., 1974); Antioch (M.A.T., 1978). ***COURSES: Legal Ethics, Evidence, Criminal Law, Counseling. ***Email:*** JLSJR@AOL.COM

MICHAEL R. SMITH*, (Associate Professor)**, born Gardner, Massachusetts, July 8, 1961; admitted to bar, 1985, California; 1986, Florida. *Education:* Florida State University (B.S., 1982); University of Florida College of Law (J.D., 1985). ***COURSES: Legal Research & Writing, Appellate Advocacy, Advanced Legal Writing. ***Email:*** smith_mr@mercer.edu

JOAN R. TARPLEY*, (Professor of Law)**, born Dallas, Texas, April 11, 1942; admitted to bar, 1968, Texas; 1995, Georgia. *Education:* Dillard University (B.A., 1962); Southern Methodist (J.D., 1968). ***COURSES: Real Estate, Insurance, Alternate Dispute Resolution, Feminine Jurisprudence. ***Email:*** tarpley_jr@mercer.edu

DAVID D. WALTER*, (Assistant Professor of Legal Writing & Analysis)**, born Iowa, March 2, 1958; admitted to bar, 1989, Washington. *Education:* Eastern Kentucky University (B.A., 1983); University of Iowa (M.A., 1986; J.D., 1988). ***COURSES: Legal Writing, Alternative Dispute Resolution, Legal Analysis, Moot Court. ***Email:*** walter_d@mercer.edu

***JAMES SHAND WATSON*, (Professor of Law)**, born Galashiels,

(This Listing Continued)

MERCER UNIVERSITY WALTER F. GEORGE SCHOOL OF LAW—Continued

Scotland, July 5, 1946. *Education:* Edinburgh University (LL.B., 1969); University of Illinois (LL.M., 1972). ***COURSES:*** International Law, Jurisprudence, Criminal Law. ***Email:*** watson_js@mercer.edu

DONAL CHRISTOPHER WELLS*, (Associate Professor of Law)**, born New York, New York, August 24, 1949; admitted to bar, 1979, California. *Education:* Grinnell College (B.A., 1971); Vanderbilt Divinity School (1971); University of Iowa (J.D., 1978). ***COURSES: Business Associations, Contracts, Securities Regulation. ***Email:*** wells_dc@mercer.edu

VIRGINIA FAIRCLOTH WILLIAMS*, (Associate Professor of Law)**, born Bleckley County, Georgia, August 15, 1942; admitted to bar, 1978, District of Columbia; 1980, Massachusetts. *Education:* Emory University (B.A., 1964); University of California Hastings College of the Law (J.D., 1978); Boston University (LL.M., 1982). ***COURSES: Federal Income Tax, Domestic Relations. ***Email:*** williams_vf@mercer.edu

MICHIGAN STATE UNIVERSITY - DETROIT COLLEGE OF LAW

368 LAW COLLEGE BUILDING
EAST LANSING, MICHIGAN 48824-1300
Telephone: (517) 432-6800
Fax: (517) 432-6801

ABA Approved Since 1941

Michigan State University - Detroit College of Law was established in 1891, making it the oldest continuously operated independent law school in the nation. The College is a privately controlled, non-profit, co-educational institution devoted exclusively to professional education in law. MSU/DCL was fully accredited by the American Bar Association in 1941 and has been a member of the American Association of Law Schools since 1946.

For 109 years, the Law College has provided outstanding educational training opportunities for qualified applicants seeking to enter the legal profession. It continues, through its graduates, to make vital contributions to the legal, commercial and industrial communities throughout the nation. More than seven thousand attorneys, judges, public officials and business executives are graduates of this eminent college.

In April 1995, the College, a private law school, affiliated with Michigan State University, a public university, for the benefit of both institutions. As part of this arrangement, the College relocated to the East Lansing Campus of Michigan State University and has a new $25, 000,000 facility. This 180,000-square-foot, multi-story building houses crucial student services such as admissions, financial aid and career services as well as state of the art law library, a moot courtroom, a computer laboratory, and classrooms designed to offer students the highest quality learning atmosphere. All classrooms are fitted with technology sufficient to allow students to use lap top computers during class. Moreover, students have access to the MSU campus network, the Internet, e-mail, critical legal bases, and law libraries around the world.

Dean: Terence L. Blackburn (517) 432-6804
Assistant Dean of Admissions & Financial Aid: Andrea Heatley (517) 432-0222
Executive Director for Business Affairs: Rick Lameti (517) 432-6813
Executive Director for Planning & Administrative Affairs: Christine M. Hammond, Ph.D.
Acting Director of Law Library: Hildur Hanna (517) 432-6862
Director of Career Services: Caryn Mateer (517) 432-6832
Director of Development and Alumni Relations: Julie Duke (517) 432-6842

FULL TIME FACULTY

TERENCE L. BLACKBURN*, (Dean and Professor)**, born Pittsburgh, Pennsylvania, 1947; admitted to bar, 1973, Ohio; 1976, New York; 1996, New Jersey. *Education:* Duquesne University (B.A., 1970); Columbia (J.D., 1973). ***COURSES: Business Association, Corporate Finance, Securities Regulation.

JOHN P. APOL*, (Professor)**, born District of Columbia, March 20, 1941; admitted to bar, 1972, Michigan. *Education:* Grand Valley State University (B.A., 1969); University of Michigan (J.D., 1972). ***COURSES: Criminal Law, Criminal Procedure and Negotiations.

SUSAN H. BITENSKY*, (Professor)**, born New York, N.Y., January 3, 1948; admitted to bar, 1974, Pennsylvania; 1979, New York; 1988, Michigan. *Education:* Case Western Reserve University (B.A., 1971); University of Chicago Law School (J.D., 1974). ***COURSES: Evidence, Constitutional Law, and Jurisprudence.

DONALD F. CAMPBELL*, (Professor)**, born Detroit, Michigan, August 6, 1936; admitted to bar, 1962, Michigan. *Education:* University of Michigan (A.B., 1958); Detroit College of Law (J.D., 1961). ***COURSES: Decedents' Estates and Trust, Property, Estates and Future Interests, and Basic Will Drafting.

AMY C. CHRISTIAN*, (Professor)**, born St. Louis, Missouri, December 25, 1965; admitted to bar, 1991, California; 1992, District of Columbia. *Education:* Georgetown University (B.S.B.A., 1988); Harvard University (J.D., 1991). ***COURSES: Basic Federal Income Taxation, International Taxation and Estate and Gift Taxation.

DAVID S. FAVRE*, (Professor)**, born Anderson, South Carolina, October 10, 1946; admitted to bar, 1973, Virginia; 1985, Michigan. *Education:* University of Virginia (B.A., 1968); College of William and Mary (J.D., 1973). ***COURSES: Environmental Law, Property, Wildlife Law and International Environmental Law.

ROBERT M. FILIATRAULT*, (Professor)**, born Cleveland, Ohio, October 19, 1944; admitted to bar, 1970, Michigan. *Education:* University of Notre Dame; University of Detroit; Detroit College of Law (J.D., 1970). ***COURSES: Clinical Legal Education, Civil Procedure, Evidence and Federal Jurisdiction.

ELIZABETH FOLEY*, (Professor)**, born 1965; admitted to bar, Texas, 1994. *Education:* Emory (B.A., 1987); Tennessee (J.D., 1994); Harvard (LL.M., 1996). ***COURSES: Civil Procedure, Evidence, Food & Drug Law, Health Care Law, and Law and Medicine.

(This Listing Continued)

MICHIGAN STATE UNIVERSITY - DETROIT COLLEGE OF LAW—Continued

JEREMY T. HARRISON*, (Professor)**, born 1935; admitted to bar, 1961, California; 1986, Hawaii. *Education:* San Francisco (B.S., 1957; J.D., 1960); Harvard (LL.M., 1962). ***COURSES: Community Property, Estates, Evidence, Torts, Conflict of Laws, Landlord and Tenant.

CLARK C. JOHNSON*, (Professor)**, born Traverse City, Michigan, November 19, 1940; admitted to bar, 1970, Michigan and U.S. District Court, Southern and Eastern Districts of Michigan; 1974, U.S. Supreme Court. *Education:* University of Michigan (A.B., 1962); Wayne State University (J.D., 1970; M.S., 1985; Ph.D., 1990). ***COURSES: Equity, Agency and Partnership, Commercial Transactions, Secured Transactions, Creditors Rights, Bankruptcy, Psychiatry and the Law, Corporations, Property, Insurance, Mortgages and Suretyship and Medical Legal Problems.

KEVIN C. KENNEDY*, (Professor)**, born Illinois, February, 28, 1951; admitted to bar, 1977, Hawaii; 1990, Michigan. *Education:* University of Michigan (A.B., 1973); Wayne State University (J.D., 1977); Harvard University Law School (LL.M., 1982). ***COURSES: Civil Procedure, International Trade and International Law.

CHRISTINE A. KLEIN*, (Professor)**, born St. Louis, Missouri, January 29, 1956; admitted to bar, 1987, Colorado; 1989, District of Columbia. *Education:* Middlebury College (B.A., 1978); University of Colorado (J.D., 1987); Columbia University (LL.M., 1994). ***COURSES: Environmental Law, Natural Resources Law, Wetlands Law, Water Law and Property.

MARTIN L. KOTCH*, (Professor)**, born 1936; admitted to bar, 1961, New York; 1972, Michigan. *Education:* University of Miami (B.A., 1958); New York University School of Law (J.D., 1961). ***COURSES: Labor Arbitration, Constitutional Law, Employment Relations Law and Jurisprudence.

MAE KUYKENDALL*, (Professor)**, born Cotulla, Texas, June 29, 1947; admitted to bar, 1986, Massachusetts; 1987, New York. *Education:* University of Houston (B.A., 1969); University of North Carolina (M.A., 1972; Ph.D., 1980); Harvard University Law School (J.D., 1985). ***COURSES: Small Business Enterprises, Corporate Law and Policy, Public Corporations, Corporate Finance and Law & Gender.

MICHAEL A. LAWRENCE*, (Professor)**, born Seattle, Washington, January 24, 1959; admitted to bar, 1992, Illinois and Wisconsin; 1993, 1999, District of Columbia. *Education:* Indiana (B.S., 1981); University of Colorado (M.B.S., 1987); University of Wisconsin (M.S., 1992; J.D., 1992). ***COURSES: Property, Constitutional Law, International Law.

ROBERT A. MCCORMICK*, (Professor)**, born Detroit, Michigan, May 9, 1947; admitted to bar, 1973, Colorado; 1987, Michigan. *Education:* Michigan State University (B.A., 1969); University of Michigan (J.D., 1973). ***COURSES: Labor Law, Constitutional Law, Employment Discrimination, Sports Law and Decedents' Estates.

MATTHEW C. MCKINNON*, (Professor)**, born Hamtramck, Michigan, January 29, 1940; admitted to bar, 1972, Michigan. *Education:* University of Detroit (B.S., 1961); Detroit College of Law (J.D., 1972). ***COURSES: Contracts, Remedies, Antitrust Law, Sports Law and Unfair Trade Practices.

PATRICIA MELL*, (Professor)**, born Cleveland, Ohio, December 15, 1953; admitted to bar, 1979, Ohio; 1987, Pennsylvania; 1992, Michigan. *Education:* Wellesley College (A.B., 1975); Case Western Reserve University (J.D., 1978). ***COURSES: Criminal Law, Commercial Law, Agency and Partnership, Consumer Law, Mediation, Corporations, Negotiations and Interviewing and Client Counseling, White Collar Crime.

HAROLD NORRIS*, (Professor Emeritus)**, born Detroit, Michigan, April 7, 1918; admitted to bar, 1948, Michigan. *Education:* University of Michigan (A.B., 1939; M.A., 1941); Columbia University (J.D., 1948); Wayne State University (D.H.L., 1981); Detroit College of Law (LL.D., 1989) . ***COURSES: Criminal Law, Women and the Law, Constitutional Law, Administrative Law, Criminal Procedure and Federal Jurisdiction.

KATHLEEN E. PAYNE*, (Professor)**, born Chicago, Illinois, July 16, 1946; admitted to bar, 1977, Michigan; 1991, Nevada; 1992, Illinois. *Education:* Michigan State University (B.A., 1967); Eastern Michigan University (M.A., 1970); Detroit College of Law (J.D., 1977); University of Michigan (LL.M., 1981). ***COURSES: Secured Transactions, Bankruptcy, Contracts, Torts, Agency and Partnership, Commercial Law, Debtors' and Creditors' Rights, and Legislative Drafting.

BRENDA QUICK*, (Professor)**, born Ravenna, Kentucky, December 26, 1948; admitted to bar, 1985, Kentucky; 1993, Michigan. *Education:* University of Louisville (B.A., 1981; J.D., 1985). ***COURSES: Legal Profession and Property and Native American Law.

JOHN WILLIAM REIFENBERG*, (Professor)**, born Erie, Pennsylvania, May 8, 1944. *Education:* Brown University (B.A., 1967); University of Denver (J.D., 1972). ***COURSES: Torts, International Law, International Business Transactions, European Community Law and Chinese Law.

C. NICHOLAS REVELOS*, (Professor)**, born Middleton, Ohio, March 1, 1938; admitted to bar, 1965, Ohio; 1975, Michigan. *Education:* Bowdoin College (A.B., 1961); Duke University (J.D., 1965); University of California (LL.M., 1971). ***COURSES: Corporations, Agency and Partnership, Bankruptcy, Reorganizations and Securities.

CYNTHIA L. STARNES*, (Professor)**, born Abilene, Texas, March 23, 1952; admitted to bar, 1984, Indiana. *Education:* Michigan State University (B.S., 1973); Indiana University (J.D., 1983); Columbia University (LL.M., 1989). ***COURSES: Commercial Transactions, Contracts and Domestic Relations.

ALVIN L. STORRS*, (Professor)**, born Detroit, Michigan, July 20, 1950; admitted to bar, 1981, Michigan. *Education:* Mercy College (B.A., 1975); University of Detroit (M.B.A., 1981; J.D., 1981); New York University School of Law (LL.M., 1984). ***COURSES: Corporate Taxation, Deferred Compensation, Estate and Gift Taxation, International Tax and Taxation.

MISSISSIPPI COLLEGE SCHOOL OF LAW

151 EAST GRIFFITH STREET
JACKSON, MISSISSIPPI 39201
Telephone: (601) 925-7104
Fax: (601) 925-7115
http://www.mc.edu/

(This Listing Continued)

MISSISSIPPI COLLEGE SCHOOL OF LAW—Continued

ABA Approved Since 1980.

Mississippi College School of Law is conveniently located in downtown Jackson, the state capital, and is within walking distance of the legislature, as well as all federal and state administrative agencies and courts. Jackson is the legal and commercial center of the state. The main campus of Mississippi College, the oldest institution of higher education in Mississippi, is located in Clinton, a suburb of Jackson.

In the fall of 1975, the law school officially opened its doors, with the convening of its first classes in Clinton. A number of outstanding practitioners and leaders of the state bar were recruited to serve as faculty, and the school immediately began the task of obtaining ABA approval.

Within five years, accreditation had been achieved and the school moved into its permanent five-story facility in Jackson. The building houses administrative, faculty and student organization offices, classrooms, trial and appellate courtrooms, and the law library. An integral part of the total law school program, the law library has a collection of more than 303,000 volumes. The law library offers computer labs with access to Westlaw, Lexis and several CD-ROM databases; is a member of the American Association of Law Libraries; and is a selective U.S. Government depository library.

The development of the law school since 1980 has been remarkable. Achievement of accreditation made possible the expansion of both faculty and student recruitment to a national scale, moving the school toward its goal of building a strong, regional law school. The law school's success has been reflected in state and regional recognition it has received through its law review, outstanding performances by its appellate and trial teams, and placement of its graduates.

Fully accredited by the American Bar Association and a member of the Association of American Law Schools, MCSOL is, by design, one of the smallest law schools in the nation. The school limits its entering classes to 150. The overall student body is approximately 400 and the student-to-faculty ratio is 22.6:1. The students represent over one-half of the states and 110 undergraduate institutions.

The school's faculty is diverse in both professional and educational backgrounds. Sixteen full-time faculty members, several of whom have national reputations in their specialties, hold degrees from a number of excellent law schools and have legal experience in either private practice or public service. Students are challenged, encouraged, and supported by educators who have a genuine interest in seeing them succeed in school and beyond.

Recognizing the law school's responsibility to the legal community and the larger society, individuals on the faculty serve or have served in the following positions: United States Supreme Court Fellow; Guest Lecturer in the Harvard Trial Advocacy Program; National Panelist on the American Arbitration Association; Fellow of the American Bar Foundation; Member of the Board of Directors, Christian Legal Society; Member of the Board of Directors, Antitrust Section of the Association of American Law Schools; Member, Mississippi Bankruptcy Conference; Assistant Secretary for Congressional Relations, United States Department of Agriculture; Reporter, Appellate Rules Subcommittee, Mississippi Supreme Court Advisory Committee on Rules; Reporter, Commission on Courts in the Twenty-First Century; Chair, Mississippi Supreme Court Advisory Committee on Rules; Member, Mississippi Judicial Advisory Committee.

MCSOL seeks to provide a superior legal education and create an environment that promotes intellectual and practical learning. Because of the location in a major legal center, the school is able to draw on leading practitioners and judges as adjunct professors and as supervisors of externship programs. The curriculum trains students to become skilled and ethical lawyers capable of adapting their practice to a changing legal world. To accomplish this, the school has looked to a liberal arts model in shaping the curriculum. The courses emphasize individual responsibility for learning, while providing every student instruction in the substantive and analytical skills necessary for successful practice. In addition to courses in legal doctrine, the school offers a wide range of instruction in the skills of modern practice. Since writing is viewed as the most fundamental of these skills, the teaching of writing is stressed at every stage of legal training.

The goals of the law school and the founding institution reflect the belief that human beings are God's creations, equally entitled to dignity and respect. In every setting, MCSOL wants to train lawyers of high intellectual and practical ability, who are committed to ethical practice; to assisting the disadvantaged; and to free and open discussion of issues of law, policy and value.

Interim Dean: J. Larry Lee (601) 925-7104
Assistant Dean for Career Services & External Affairs: J. Michael Maloney (601) 925-7107
Director of Law Library: Mary E. Miller (601) 925-7125
Director of Admissions & Public Relations: Patricia H. Evans (601) 925-7150
Coordinator of Administrative Services: Emily P. Kennedy (601) 925-7103
Assistant Dean for Student Services: Whitney B. Byars (601) 925-7102

FULL TIME FACULTY

JAMES LARRY LEE*, (Professor of Law & Interim Dean)**, born Jackson, Mississippi, March 7, 1943; admitted to bar, 1967, Mississippi. *Education:* Mississippi State University; Mississippi College (B.S., 1965); University of Mississippi (J.D., 1967); New York University (LL.M. in Taxation, 1972). ***COURSES: Taxation. ***Email:*** llee@mc.edu

PATRICIA W. BENNETT*, (Professor of Law)**, born Mississippi, August 31, 1953; admitted to bar, 1979, Mississippi. *Education:* Tougaloo College (B.A., 1975); Mississippi College (J.D., 1979). ***COURSES: Criminal Procedure, Federal Courts, Advocacy. ***Email:*** pbennett@mc.edu

WHITNEY BLAIR BYARS*, (Director of Legal Writing & Assistant Dean for Student Services)**, born Richmond, Virginia, September 22, 1966; admitted to bar, 1992, Mississippi. *Education:* University of Georgia (A.B.J., 1988); Mississippi College (J.D., 1992). ***COURSES: Legal Writing, Appellate Advocacy. ***Email:*** byars@mc.edu

CRAIG RANDALL CALLEN*, (Professor of Law)**, born Des Moines, Iowa, June 12, 1950; admitted to bar, 1974, Wisconsin; 1976, Illinois. *Education:* University of Iowa (B.A., 1971); Harvard Law School (J.D., 1974). ***COURSES: Civil Procedure, Evidence, Federal Courts, Constitutional Law. ***Email:*** callen@mc.edu

CECILE CHAMPION EDWARDS*, (Professor of Law)**, born Pensacola, Florida, December 5, 1955; admitted to bar, 1979, Mississippi. *Education:* University of Mississippi (B.B.A., 1976; J.D., 1979); New York University (LL.M., 1980). ***COURSES: Business Associations, Securities Regulation, Professional Responsibility and Ethics. ***Email:*** edwards@mc.edu

(This Listing Continued)

MISSISSIPPI COLLEGE SCHOOL OF LAW—Continued

N. SHELTON HAND, JR.*, (Professor of Law)**, born Hattiesburg, Mississippi, August 24, 1940; admitted to bar, 1967, Mississippi. *Education:* Mississippi College (B.S., 1965); University of Mississippi (J.D., 1967). ***COURSES: Domestic Relations, Local Court Practice, Education Law, Juvenile Law, Commercial Paper. ***Email:*** hand@mc.edu

H. LEE HETHERINGTON*, (Professor of Law)**, born Kankakee, Illinois, February 13, 1948; admitted to bar, 1973, Mississippi; 1975, New York. *Education:* Millsaps College (B.A., 1970); University of Mississippi (J.D., 1973); New York University (LL.M., 1976). ***COURSES: Torts, Intellectual Property, Negotiation, Remedies. ***Email:*** hetherin@mc.edu

JEFFREY JACKSON*, (Professor of Law)**, born Carmichael, Pennsylvania, May 2, 1956; admitted to bar, 1983, West Virginia; 1986, Pennsylvania. *Education:* Haverford College (B.A., 1978); University of Pittsburgh (J.D., 1983). ***COURSES: Civil Procedure, Conflicts, Insurance, Ethics. ***Email:*** jjackson@mc.edu

JUDITH JONES JOHNSON*, (Professor of Law)**, born Gonzales, Texas, July 30, 1948; admitted to bar, 1974, Mississippi. *Education:* University of Texas at Austin (B.A., 1969); University of Mississippi (J.D., 1974). ***COURSES: Labor, Employment Discrimination, Criminal Law, Criminal Procedure. ***Email:*** jjohnson@mc.edu

SHIRLEY NORWOOD JONES*, (Owen Cooper Professor of Law Emeritus)**, born Gulfport, Mississippi, August 16, 1930; admitted to bar, 1952, Mississippi. *Education:* Millsaps College (B.A., 1950); University of Mississippi (J.D., 1952). ***COURSES: Property, Wills and Estates, Trusts. ***Email:*** jones@mc.edu

GREGG WILLIAM KETTLES*, (Assistant Professor of Law)**, born Heraklion, Greece, April 7, 1966; admitted to bar, 1994, California. *Education:* Washington and Lee University (B.A., 1988); Yale Law School (J.D., 1991). ***COURSES: Contracts, Property, Environmental Land Use. ***Email:*** kettles@mc.edu

LAURA SKEEN KUNS*, (Instructor of Law)**, born Mansfield, Ohio, May 3, 1967; admitted to bar, 1998, Mississippi. *Education:* Memphis State University (B.B.A., 1989); Mississippi College School of Law (J.D., 1995). ***COURSES: Legal Writing, Appellate Advocacy. ***Email:*** kuns@mc.edu

ANGELA MAE KUPENDA*, (Associate Professor of Law on leave)**, born Jackson, Mississippi, September 13, 1956; admitted to bar, 1991, Mississippi; 1993, District of Columbia. *Education:* Jackson State University (B.S., 1979); The Wharton School, University of Pennsylvania (M.A., 1984); Mississippi College (J.D., 1991). ***COURSES: Contracts, Constitutional Law, First Amendment, Civil Rights, Race and the Law. ***Email:*** akupenda@mc.edu

PHILLIP LEE MCINTOSH*, (Professor of Law)**, born Mississippi, October 15, 1954; admitted to bar, 1979, Louisiana. *Education:* Louisiana State University (B.S., 1977; J.D., 1978); New York University (LL.M., 1981). ***COURSES: Torts, Products Liability, Civil Law Obligations, Property, Successions, Commercial Paper. ***Email:*** mcintosh@mc.edu

MARY ELLA MILLER*, (Director of Law Library)**, born South Bend, Indiana, May 14, 1960; admitted to bar, 1985, Mississippi. *Education:* Asbury College (B.A., 1982); University of Southern Mississippi (M.L.S., 1993); Mississippi College School of Law (J.D., 1985). ***COURSES: Legal Research.

MARK C. MODAK-TRURAN*, (Assistant Professor of Law)**, born Grosse Point, Michigan, February 19, 1961; admitted to bar, 1984, Illinois. *Education:* Gustavus Adolphus College (B.A., 1983); University of Chicago (M.A., 1988); Northwestern University School of Law (J.D., 1989). ***COURSES: Business Association, Legal Ethics, Law & Religion, Jurisprudence, Secured Transactions. ***Email:*** mmodak@mc.edu

SID L. MOLLER*, (Professor of Law)**, born Baton Rouge, Louisiana, May 29, 1952; admitted to bar, 1982, Colorado; 1983, Wyoming. *Education:* Louisiana State University (B.A., 1974); Cornell University (M.I.L.R., 1976); University of Wyoming (J.D., 1982). ***COURSES: Contracts, Employment & Labor, Law & Medicine. ***Email:*** moller@mc.edu

MATTHEW SCOTT STEFFEY*, (Professor of Law)**, born Washington, D.C., April 17, 1962; admitted to bar, 1987, Florida. *Education:* University of South Florida (B.A., 1984); Florida State University (J.D., 1987); Columbia University (LL.M., 1990). ***COURSES: Constitutional Law, Evidence, Criminal Law, Admiralty. ***Email:*** steffey@mc.edu

CAROL CATHERINE WEST*, (Professor of Law)**, born Philadelphia, Pennsylvania, May 23, 1944; admitted to bar, 1970, Mississippi. *Education:* Mississippi University for Women (B.A., 1966); University of Southern Mississippi (M.L.S., 1984); University of Mississippi (J.D., 1970). ***COURSES: Criminal Law, Legislation, Domestic Relations, Women & The Law.

NASHVILLE SCHOOL OF LAW

2934 SIDCO DRIVE
NASHVILLE, TENNESSEE 37204
Telephone: (615) 256-3684
Fax: (615) 244-2383

Nashville School of Law began in 1911 when four graduates of Vanderbilt Law School opened night law classes at the Y.M.C.A. The mission, then and now, was to provide an affordable legal education for working men and women who could not attend school during the day. The school was incorporated under the laws of the State of Tennessee on January 19, 1927 and is authorized to confer the degree of Doctor of Jurisprudence.

The school is exclusively a night school offering high quality legal education at an affordable tuition. A large percentage of the law students are employed full-time in fields such as business, trades, education and various professions. Nashville School of Law students are trained to practice law in the state of Tennessee by a faculty of working members of the legal community. Included in this faculty are judges and practicing attorneys who are recognized as masters in their chosen fields. Graduates of Nashville School of Law hold positions of prominence throughout the state.

The law course spans a minimum of four years with classes held each Monday, Tuesday and Thursday nights from 6:45 p.m. to 8:25 p.m. and 8:35 p.m. to 10:15 p.m. A student must attend at least two nights each week in order to complete the course of study in four years. Moot Courts I and II, under direction of an instructor, are held for third and fourth year students on an additional evening from 6:30 p.m. to 10:00 p.m.

(This Listing Continued)

NASHVILLE SCHOOL OF LAW—Continued

Class scheduling only allows students to enter in the fall. There are no quarter or semester divisions. Entrance requirements include a bachelor's degree from an accredited college or university, three letters of recommendation, a recent exam score and other pertinent information from the Law School Data Assembly Service. A proper application with an application fee must be submitted. The application form and all the basic information about the Nashville School of Law is found in the school bulletin, which may be obtained by calling 615-256-3684.

Dean: Joe C. Loser, Jr. (615) 256-3684
Assistant Dean: Virginia M. Townsen (615) 256-3684
Admissions: Joe C. Loser, III (615) 256-3684
Library: Janet Naff (615) 256-3684
Placement: Janet Naff (615) 256-3684
Alumni Affairs: Elizabeth McDonald (615) 256-3684
Registrar: Elizabeth McDonald (615) 256-3684

FULL TIME FACULTY

JOE C. LOSER, JR.*, (Dean and President)**, admitted to bar, 1959, Tennessee. *Education:* Vanderbilt University; Nashville School of Law (J.D., 1959). ***COURSES: Workers' Compensation.

C. DEWEES BERRY, IV, ESQ.*, (Faculty Member/Practicing Attorney)**, admitted to bar, 1976, Tennessee. *Education:* Vanderbilt University (1973); Vanderbilt University School of Law (J.D., 1976). ***COURSES: Real Property.

HON. ADOLPHO A. BIRCH, JR.*, (Faculty/Associate Justice, Supreme Court of Tennessee)**, born Washington, D.C., September 22, 1932; admitted to bar, 1957, Tennessee. *Education:* Howard University (B.A., 1957); Howard University Law School (J.D., 1957). ***COURSES: Lawyering Skills & Values for the Criminal Defense Counsel and Constitutional Criminal Law.

HON. CHERYL A. BLACKBURN*, (Faculty/Judge of Criminal Court, Davidson County, Tennessee)**, admitted to bar, 1979, Tennessee. *Education:* Vanderbilt University (B.A., 1969); Nashville School of Law (J.D., 1979). ***COURSES: Crimes.

CYRUS L. BOOKER, ESQ.*, (Faculty Member/Practicing Attorney)**, born Franklin, Tennessee; admitted to bar, 1981, District of Columbia; 1984, Tennessee. *Education:* Harvard University (A.B., 1978); Georgetown University School of Law (J.D., 1981). ***COURSES: Legal Ethics.

HON. JOE B. BROWN*, (Faculty Member/U.S. Magistrate Judge)**, born Louisville, Kentucky, December 9, 1940; admitted to bar, 1965, Kentucky; 1972, Tennessee. *Education:* Vanderbilt University (B.A., 1962); Vanderbilt University Law School (J.D., 1965). ***COURSES: Federal Crimes. ***Email:*** joe_b._brown@ck6.uscourts.gov

JACK A. BUTLER, ESQ.*, (Faculty Member/Practicing Attorney)**, admitted to bar, 1962, Tennessee. *Education:* Vanderbilt University (B.A.); Nashville School of Law (J.D., 1962). ***COURSES: Moot Court II.

HON. BEN H. CANTRELL*, (Faculty Member/Court of Appeals Judge)**, admitted to bar, 1966, Tennessee. *Education:* Vanderbilt University (B.S., 1957); University of Tennessee (J.D., 1966). ***COURSES: Restitution and Remedies.

THOMAS J. CARLTON, JR.*, (Faculty Member/Private Practice)**, born Nashville, Tennessee, May 3, 1937; admitted to bar, 1965, Tennessee. *Education:* Vanderbilt University (B.A., 1960); Nashville School of Law (J.D., 1965). ***COURSES: Moot Court I.

ROBERT E. CORLEW, III*, (Faculty Member/NS of Law and Chancellor, Tenn. 16th Jud. Dist.)**, born Tuscaloosa, Alabama, December 23, 1952; admitted to bar, 1978, Tennessee. *Education:* Davidson College (B.A., 1975); St. Mary's University of San Antonio (J.D., 1977). ***COURSES: Negotiable Instruments & Secured Trans.. ***Email:*** bob@corlew.com

NANCY K. CORLEY, ESQ.*, (Faculty Member/Private Practicing Attorney)**, admitted to bar, 1970, Tennessee. *Education:* Vanderbilt University (B.A., 1964); Nashville School of Law (J.D., 1970). ***COURSES: Workers' Compensation.

JIM G. CREECY, ESQ.*, (Faculty Member/Special Counsel, State of Tennessee Attorney General)**, admitted to bar, 1974, Tennessee. *Education:* University of Tennessee (B.S., 1970); Vanderbilt University School of Law (J.D., 1974). ***COURSES: State and Local Taxation and Accounting for Lawyers.

JAMES C. DALE, III, ESQ.*, (Faculty Member/Private Practice)**, admitted to bar, 1963, Tennessee. *Education:* Vanderbilt University (B.A., 1957); Vanderbilt University Law School (J.D., 1963). ***COURSES: Business Associations.

HON. J. S. DANIEL*, (Faculty/Circuit Court Judge for Sixteenth Judicial District)**, born Milan, Tennessee, July 13, 1946; admitted to bar, 1971, Tennessee. *Education:* Louisiana State University (B.S., 1969); University of Tennessee College of Law (J.D., 1971). ***COURSES: Conflict of Laws. ***Email:*** tlawdaniel@aol.com

MARSHALL DAVIDSON, III, ESQUIRE*, (Faculty Member/Practicing Attorney/Tennessee Supreme Court Clerk)**, admitted to bar, 1989, Tennessee. *Education:* Middle Tennessee State University (B.S., 1986); University of Tennessee College of Law (J.D., 1989). ***COURSES: Torts and Introduction to Law.

STEVE DAVIS, ESQUIRE*, (Faculty Member/Practicing Attorney)**, admitted to bar, 1980 Tennessee. *Education:* Colgate University (B.A., 1971); Nashville School of Law (J.D., 1980). ***COURSES: T.B.A..

GEORGE A. DEAN, ESQUIRE*, (Faculty Member and Practicing Attorney)**, admitted to bar, 1979 Tennessee. *Education:* Lafayette College (A.B., 1976); Vanderbilt University Law School (J.D., 1979). ***COURSES: Land Use Planning.

K. HARLAN DODSON, III, ESQUIRE*, (Faculty Member and Practicing Attorney)**, born Nashville, Tennessee, August 3, 1944; admitted to bar, 1969, Tennessee. *Education:* Duke University (B.A., 1966); Vanderbilt University Law School (J.D., 1969). ***COURSES: Estate Planning and Administration of Decedents' Estates.

HON. STEVEN R. DOZIER*, (Faculty Member/Criminal Court Judge)**, admitted to bar, 1984. *Education:* Vanderbilt University (B.A.L.); Nashville School of Law (J.D., 1984). ***COURSES: Evidence.

KATHRYN REED EDGE, ESQ.*, (Faculty Member/Practicing Attorney)**, admitted to bar, 1983, Tennessee. *Education:* George Peabody College (1967); Nashville School of Law (J.D., 1983). ***COURSES: Banking Law.

(This Listing Continued)

NASHVILLE SCHOOL OF LAW—Continued

MARK FRALEY, ESQUIRE, **(Faculty Member and Practicing Attorney)**, admitted to bar, 1983, Tennessee. *Education:* University of Cincinnati (B.S., 1974); Nashville School of Law (J.D., 1983). ***COURSES:*** Social Security Disability Law and Practice.

HAL D. HARDIN, ESQUIRE, **(Faculty Member/Practicing Attorney)**, born Nashville, Tennessee, June 29, 1941; admitted to bar, 1969, Tennessee, Texas and District of Columbia. *Education:* Olympic College, George Washington University and Middle Tennessee State University; Vanderbilt University Law School (J.D., 1968). ***COURSES:*** Criminal Procedure. ***Email:*** halhardin@aol.com

KAL HELOU, ESQUIRE, **(Faculty Member/Practicing Attorney)**, admitted to bar, 1990, Tennessee. *Education:* Thiel College (B.A.); Vanderbilt University Law School (J.D., 1990). ***COURSES:*** Alternative Dispute Resolution. ***Email:*** kwhlou@aol.com

HENRY E. HILDEBRAND, III, **(Faculty Member/Private Practice)**, admitted to bar, 1976. *Education:* Vanderbilt University (B.A.); George Washington University (J.D.). ***COURSES:*** Bankruptcy.

TREVOR W. HOWELL, ESQUIRE, **(Faculty Member/Practicing Attorney)**, admitted to bar, 1981, Tennessee. *Education:* Samford University (B.S., 1974); Cumberland School of Law at Samford University (J.D., 1980). ***COURSES:*** Employment and Labor Law.

JOHN D. KITCH, ESQUIRE, **(Faculty Member and Practicing Attorney)**, born Plymouth, Indiana, July 26, 1946; admitted to bar, 1976, Tennessee. *Education:* Purdue University (B.A., 1973); Vanderbilt University (J.D., 1976). ***COURSES:*** Law Office Management. ***Email:*** jdkitch@edge.net

HON. WILLIAM C. KOCH, JR., **(Faculty Member and Judge, Tennessee Court of Appeals)**, born Honolulu, Hawaii, February 12, 1947; admitted to bar, 1972, Tennessee. *Education:* Trinity College (B.A., 1969); University of Virginia School of Law (LL.M., 1996); Vanderbilt University School of Law (J.D., 1972). ***COURSES:*** Constitution Law. ***Email:*** ib011c1@smtpaoc.tsc.state.tn.us

JOHN LEWIS, ESQUIRE, **(Faculty Member and Practicing Attorney)**, admitted to bar, 1972, Tennessee. *Education:* Tulane University (B.A., 1970); Georgetown University School of Law (J.D., 1972). ***COURSES:*** Contracts.

JAMES C. MCBROOM, ESQUIRE, **(Faculty Member and Practicing Attorney)**, born Nashville, Tennessee, November 17, 1942; admitted to bar, 1971, Tennessee. *Education:* Middle Tennessee State University (B.S., 1967); Nashville School of Law (J.D., 1971). ***COURSES:*** Personal Property and Agency. ***Email:*** jmcbroom@edge.net

ROBERT B. NADLER, ESQUIRE, **(Faculty Member & Assistant District Counsel, Internal Revenue Service)**, admitted to bar, 1978, Tennessee; 1972 Illinois (inactive). *Education:* University of Illinois (B.S., 1968); University of Illinois Law School (J.D., 1972). ***COURSES:*** Tax Practice and Procedure.

PHILLIP NORTH, **(Faculty Member)**, born Baton Rouge, Louisiana, March 10, 1950; admitted to bar, 1975, Tennessee. *Education:* David Lipscomb College (B.A., 1972); Pepperdine University School of Law (J.D., 1975). ***COURSES:*** Civil Procedure.

WILLIAM L. PENNY, ESQUIRE, **(Faculty Member and Practicing Attorney)**, born Memphis, Tennessee, September 4, 1953; admitted to bar, 1981, Tennessee. *Education:* University of Tennessee (B.A., 1975); Nashville School of Law (J.D., 1981). ***COURSES:*** Environmental Law. ***Email:*** wpenny@wyattfirm.com

REX H. ROBERTS, ESQUIRE, **(Faculty Member; V-P, General Counsel and Sec. American General Life Ins. Co.)**, admitted to bar, 1968, Tennessee. *Education:* Darmouth College (A.B., 1965); Vanderbilt University School of Law (J.D., 1968). ***COURSES:*** Insurance Law.

HONORABLE MURIEL ROBINSON, **(Faculty Member and Judge Fourth Circuit Court 20th Judicial Circuit)**, admitted to bar, 1969, Tennessee. *Education:* Nashville School of Law (J.D., 1968). ***COURSES:*** Domestic Relations.

ANNE L. RUSSELL, **(Faculty Member / Private Practice)**, admitted to bar, 1984, Tennessee. *Education:* Peabody College of Vanderbilt University (B.S., 1969); University of Tennessee (Ph.D., 1975); Nashville School of Law (J.D., 1984). ***COURSES:*** Wills.

HONORABLE JERRY SCOTT, **(Faculty Member and Practicing Attorney, Retired, Tennessee Court of Appeals)**, born Nashville, Tennessee, November 11, 1941; admitted to bar, 1965, Tennessee. *Education:* Austin Peay State University (B.S., 1962); Vanderbilt University School of Law (J.D., 1965); University of Virginia (L.L.M., 1986). ***COURSES:*** Advanced Legal Writing and Tennessee Constitutional Law. ***Email:*** jerrys1234@aol.com

VIRGINIA TOWNZEN, **(Assistant Dean)**, admitted to bar, 1996, Tennessee. *Education:* University of Arkansas (B.S.E.); Nashville School of Law (J.D., 1996). ***COURSES:*** Criminal Defense Skills and Values.

WESLEY D. TURNER, **(Faculty Member/Private Practice)**, admitted to bar, 1978. *Education:* University of Tennessee (B.A., 1974); Memphis State University, Cecil C. Humphreys School of Law (J.D., 1978). ***COURSES:*** Mortgages.

MARK WESTLAKE, ESQUIRE, **(Faculty Member/Practicing Attorney)**, born Sycamore, IL, March 28, 1951; admitted to bar, 1977, Ohio; 1978, Tennessee. *Education:* Wittenberg University (B.A., 1973); Vanderbilt University (J.D., 1977). ***COURSES:*** Federal Taxation.

NEW ENGLAND SCHOOL OF LAW

154 STUART STREET
BOSTON, MASSACHUSETTS 02116
Telephone: (617) 451-0010
Fax: (617) 422-7333
HTTP://WWW.NESL.EDU

ABA Approved Since 1969.

New England School of Law was founded in 1908 as Portia Law School, the only school in the nation dedicated exclusively to the legal education of women. The institution became coeducational in 1938, but it has remained sensitive to the needs of those underrepresented in the legal profession. New England is fully accredited by the American Bar Association (ABA) and is a member of the Association of American Law Schools (AALS).

The school occupies a completely modern, downtown facility near Boston's government, business, and theater districts. New England

(This Listing Continued)

NEW ENGLAND SCHOOL OF LAW—Continued

capitalizes on its advantageous location by providing an extensive clinical program and by using members of the city's legal community as adjunct faculty and lecturers. The student body is diverse with 44 states and foreign countries as well as 367 undergraduate schools represented. More than 2,300 applicants competed for the 344 seats in the entering class of 2000. Of the 981 students enrolled in 2000-2001, 57% were women and 14% were minority group members.

At the heart of the school is the law library, which plays an essential role in the legal education and research process at New England. The tri-level facility accommodates computerized legal research equipment, 357 seats and study carrels, 7 collaboration rooms, and lounge areas. The library's collection of 310,000 volumes and volume equivalents also includes substantial microforms, a growing video and audiotape collection, and interactive videodiscs that emphasize courtroom and practical lawyering skills. In addition to WESTLAW and LEXIS, the library offers extensive in-house computer research services. These include CALI programs (Center for Computer-Assisted Legal Instruction), in-house World Wide Web access and training, and a network of CD-Roms with more than 60 titles. The library's fully up-to-date, integrated on-line catalog is available from all terminals and home computers via World Wide Web, modem, or telnet. The library also provides student Internet access and maintains a tie-in to OCLC and RLIN (national bibliographic databases providing cataloging and interlibrary loan and document delivery services).

As a national law school, New England's curriculum is designed to prepare graduates to practice in any jurisdiction in the United States. The school has both a day and evening division, each offering the J.D. degree. The day program requires 84 credit hours over three academic years. The work of the first year is prescribed. Second-year day students are required to take criminal procedure, evidence, legal research and writing and ethics. Remaining courses are elective. The curriculum for the evening program which also requires 84 credits is prescribed for the first and second years; the third and fourth years are elective.

In addition to its day and evening programs, New England offers a third program of study for persons whose child-care responsibilities permit only part-time study with more flexibility.

A wide variety of course electives run the gamut from philosophical courses such as Jurisprudence to simulated practice courses and live-client clinics. New England prides itself on the great variety of high quality clinical programs available to its students. The school offers 20 clinics and maintains its own fully equipped Clinical Law Office, in which supervised students handle actual cases. Besides its civil and criminal practice clinics, the school offers clinical programs in such diverse areas as health and hospital law, mental health law, immigration law, tax law, land use, environmental law, administrative law, and prisoner's rights.

Students publish two scholarly journals, The New England Law Review and the New England Journal on Criminal and Civil Confinement, as well as the New England International and Comparative Law Annual, published on the Internet.

The school participates in several moot court programs, including the National Moot Court, the Jessup (international law), the National Environmental Law, and the National Tax Moot Court competitions. The Jessup and Tax Moot Court teams have each won "brief" awards each of the past five years, and in 2000-2001, the Jessup team placed first in the regional competition, advancing to the nation rounds. The team's brief captured two awards in the international competition. Other student organizations include the Black Law Students Association, Environmental Law Society, International Law Society, Law Student Division of the ABA, Les-Bi-Gay-Trans Caucus, Minority Students' Association, Public Interest Law Association and the Women's Law Caucus.

Dean: John F. O'Brien (617) 422-7221
Chief Financial Officer: Frank A. Scloli (617) 422-7205
Admissions Director: Pamela J. Jorgensen (617) 422-7210
Financial Aid Director: Doug Lemon (617) 422-7232
Director of Law Library and Professor of Law: Frank S.H. Bae (617) 422-7284
Career Services Director: Alyssa S. Hammond (617) 422-7499

FULL TIME FACULTY

JOHN F. O'BRIEN*, (Dean, Professor of Law)**, born New York, N.Y., January 3, 1951; admitted to bar, 1977, Massachusetts. *Education:* Manhattan College (B.A., 1973); New England School of Law (J.D., 1977); Boston University (LL.M., 1980). ***COURSES: Constitutional Law and Tax. ***Email:*** jobrien@fac.nesl.edu

FRANK S.H. BAE*, (Professor of Law, Director of Law Library)**, born Chung King, China, December 19, 1941. *Education:* National Chung Shing University, School of Law, Taipei (LL.B., 1965); University of Miami, School of Law (M.C.L., 1968); University of Wisconsin (M.S., 1970). ***COURSES: Legal Research. ***Email:*** fbae@library.nesl.edu

MARK BOBROWSKI*, (Professor of Law)**, born New Britain, Connecticut, February 11, 1951; admitted to bar, 1985, Massachusetts. *Education:* Ithaca College (B.A., 1973); University of Oregon (M.A., 1975); New England School of Law (J.D., 1985). ***COURSES: Property, Land Use, Local Government, Administrative Law. ***Email:*** mbobrowski@fac.nesl.edu

CHARLES RONALD CHESTER*, (Professor of Law)**, born Jacksonville, Illinois, September 20, 1944; admitted to bar, 1972, Massachusetts. *Education:* Harvard University (A.B., 1966); Columbia University (J.D., 1970; Masters of International Affairs, 1970); Cambridge University (Dip. Crim., 1971). ***COURSES: Wills, Estates and Trusts, Contracts, Property. ***Email:*** rchester@fac.nesl.edu

RICHARD B. CHILD*, (Professor of Law)**, born New Haven, Connecticut, December 27, 1943; admitted to bar, 1968, Connecticut; 1970, Massachusetts. *Education:* Harvard University (A.B., 1965); Harvard University Law School (J.D., 1968). ***COURSES: Bankruptcy, Business Organizations, Commercial Law. ***Email:*** rchild@fac.nesl.edu

DAVALENE COOPER*, (Professor of Law, Director of Legal Research and Writing)**, born Columbus, Ohio, April 17, 1954; admitted to bar, 1988, Kentucky; 1991, Massachusetts. *Education:* University of South Florida (B.A., 1974); Northern Illinois University (M.A., 1979); University of Kentucky (J.D., 1988). ***COURSES: Legal Research and Writing, Criminal Law, Drafting, Ethics. ***Email:*** dcooper@fac.nesl.edu

STAN COX*, (Professor of Law)**, born 1952; admitted to bar, 1987, Kentucky. *Education:* Harvard (A.B., 1974); Duke (M.A.T., 1975); University of Dublin (H.Dip., 1978); Kentucky (J.D., 1987). ***COURSES: Administrative Law, Civil Procedure, Conflict of Laws, Environmental Law, International Environmental Law. ***Email:*** scox@fac.nesl.edu

(This Listing Continued)

NEW ENGLAND SCHOOL OF LAW—Continued

CORNELIUS DALY, **(Professor of Law)**, born 1935; admitted to bar, 1960, Massachusetts. *Education:* College of the Holy Cross (A.B., 1956); Boston College (J.D., 1959); New England (S.J.D., 1978). ***COURSES:*** Administrative Law, Clinical Evidence, Evidence, Torts. ***Email:*** cdaly@fac.nesl.edu

GEORGE DARGO, **(Professor of Law)**, born 1935; admitted to bar, 1982, Massachusetts. *Education:* Columbia (B.A., 1957; M.A., 1958; Ph.D., 1970); Northeastern (J.D., 1981). ***COURSES:*** Administrative Law, Constitutional Law, Law & Literature, Legal History, Comparative Constitutionalism: The Canadian Perspective. ***Email:*** gdargo@fac.nesl.edu

ALLISON M. DUSSIAS, **(Professor of Law)**, born Grand Rapids, Michigan, May 18, 1963; admitted to bar, 1988, New York. *Education:* Georgetown University (B.A., 1984); University of Michigan (J.D., 1987). ***COURSES:*** Business Organizations, Secured Transactions, American Indian Law. ***Email:*** adussias@fac.nesl.edu

RUSSELL ENGLER, **(Director, Clinical Programs, Professor of Law)**, born Ridgewood, New Jersey, January 29, 1957; admitted to bar, 1984, Maryland; 1985, Massachusetts and New York. *Education:* Yale University (B.A., 1979); Harvard University Law School (J.D., 1983). ***COURSES:*** Lawyering Process. ***Email:*** rengler@fac.nesl.edu

SUSAN R. FINNERAN, **(Professor of Law)**, born Lynn, Massachusetts, October 12, 1947; admitted to bar, 1978, New York; 1980, Massachusetts. *Education:* University of Massachusetts (B.A., 1969); Notre Dame Law School (J.D., 1977). ***COURSES:*** Secured Transactions, Contracts, Theory of Regulation, Law Practice Management, Small Business Practice. ***Email:*** sfinneran@fac.nesl.edu

THOMAS COVELL FISCHER, **(Professor of Law)**, born Cincinnati, Ohio, May 2, 1938. *Education:* University of Cincinnati (A.B., 1960); University of Washington; Georgetown University Law Center (J.D., 1966); Loyola University. ***COURSES:*** Conflict of Laws, European Union Law. ***Email:*** tfischer@fac.nesl.edu

RICHARD D. GOULD, **(Professor of Law)**, born Hartford, Connecticut, September 19, 1943; admitted to bar, 1968, Connecticut; 1974, Massachusetts. *Education:* Trinity College (B.A., 1965); Boston University School of Law (J.D., 1968); Harvard University Law School (LL.M., 1974). ***COURSES:*** Wills and Trusts, Estate Planning, Estate and Gift Taxation. ***Email:*** rgould@fac.nesl.edu

JUDITH G. GREENBERG, **(Professor of Law)**, born New York, N.Y., September 30, 1948; admitted to bar, 1972, Wisconsin; 1976, New York; 1988, Massachusetts. *Education:* Cornell University (B.A., 1969); University of Wisconsin (J.D., 1972); Harvard University Law School (LL.M., 1979). ***COURSES:*** Corporations, Partnership, Agency, Women and the Law, Torts, Family Law, Domestic Violence. ***Email:*** jgreenbe@fac.nesl.edu

PHILIP K. HAMILTON, **(Professor of Law, Associate Dean)**, born Buffalo, New York, June 5, 1945; admitted to bar, 1973, Massachusetts. *Education:* Harvard University (A.B., 1967); Harvard University Law School (J.D., 1973). ***COURSES:*** Evidence, Trial Skills, Clinical Teaching. ***Email:*** phamilto@fac.nesl.edu

CYNTHIA G. HAWKINS-LEON, **(Associate Professor)**, born Ft. Meade, Maryland; admitted to bar, 1986, Pennsylvania; 1987, District of Columbia. *Education:* Wellesley College (B.A., 1981); Harvard Law School (J.D., 1985). ***COURSES:*** Criminal Law, Family Law, Adoption Law, Race & the Law. ***Email:*** cghleon@fac.nesl.edu

ILENE S. KLEIN, **(Clinical Professor)**, born New York, N.Y., April 4, 1953; admitted to bar, 1978, Ohio; 1979, West Virginia; 1989, Massachusetts. *Education:* Queens College of the City of New York (B.A., 1974); Cleveland Marshall College of Law (J.D., 1977). ***COURSES:*** Interviewing, Counseling, Negotiation, Trial Skills, Case Planning, Law and the Elderly. ***Email:*** iklein@fac.nesl.edu

ERIC A. LUSTIG, **(Professor of Law)**, born West Palm Beach, Florida, September 20, 1958; admitted to bar, 1987, Florida; 1990, District of Columbia. *Education:* University of Florida (B.S., Accounting, 1980; LL.M., Taxation, 1988); University of Baltimore (M.S., 1983); University of Miami (J.D., 1987). ***COURSES:*** Tax, Corporations. ***Email:*** elusting@fac.nesl.edu

PETER MANUS, **(Professor of Law, Co-Director, Center for Law and Social Responsibility)**, born New York, N.Y., January 26, 1958; admitted to bar, 1988, Massachusetts. *Education:* Dartmouth College (B.A., 1980); Cornell University Law School (J.D., 1987). ***COURSES:*** Environmental Law, Property, Administrative Law. ***Email:*** pmanus@fac.nesl.edu

GARY MONSERUD, **(Professor of Law)**, born Waukon, Iowa, February 1, 1946; admitted to bar, 1976, South Dakota; 1989, Massachusetts. *Education:* Wartburg College (B.A., 1968); Bonn University; University of South Dakota School of Law (J.D., 1976); New York University School of Law (LL.M., 1985). ***COURSES:*** Contracts, Sales and Commercial Paper. ***Email:*** gmonseru@fac.nesl.edu

JOELLE ANNE MORENO, **(Assistant Professor of Law)**, born New York, November 21, 1962; admitted to bar, 1989, Connecticut; 1990, New York; 1991, District of Columbia. *Education:* Swartmore College (B.A, 1984); University of Pennsylvania (J.D., 1989). ***COURSES:*** Evidence, Alternative Dispute Resolution, Criminal Law and Criminal Procedure. ***Email:*** jmoreno@fac.nesl.edu

WENDY J. MURPHY, **(Mary Joe Frug Visiting Assistant Professor of Law, Spring 2002)**, born Brighton, Massachusetts, August 13, 1960; admitted to bar, 1987, Massachusetts. *Education:* Boston College (B.A., 1983); New England School of Law (J.D., 1987). ***COURSES:*** Criminal Procedure, Reproductive Technologies and Rights. ***Email:*** wmurphy@fac.nesl.edu

CURTIS W. NYQUIST, **(Professor of Law)**, born 1947; admitted to bar, 1974, Illinois; 1981, Massachusetts. *Education:* No. Park College (B.A., 1969); Harvard (J.D., 1974). ***COURSES:*** Commercial Law, Commercial Paper, Contracts, Jurisprudence. ***Email:*** cnyquist@fac.nesl.edu

ROBERT E. O'TOOLE, **(Professor of Law)**, born Boston, Massachusetts, March 18, 1937; admitted to bar, 1964, Massachusetts; 1966, U.S. District Court, District of Massachusetts; 1976, U.S. Supreme Court. *Education:* Suffolk University (B.S., 1961); Suffolk University School of Law (J.D., 1964); Harvard University School of Law (LL.M., 1977). ***COURSES:*** Constitutional Law, Freedom of the Press, Freedom of Religion and Speech, Conflict of Laws. ***Email:*** rotoole@fac.nesl.edu

BARBARA ORO, **(Clinical Professor)**, born Medford, Massachusetts, November 2, 1958; admitted to bar, 1987, Massachusetts; 1989, New Hampshire. *Education:* Emmanuel College (B.A., 1981); Northeastern University (J.D., 1987). ***COURSES:*** Lawyering Process, Family Law. ***Email:*** boro@fac.nesl.edu

BARBARA PLUMERI, **(Professor of Law)**, admitted to bar, 1982, Massachusetts. *Education:* Rutgers University (B.A., 1969); University of Florida (M.A., 1970); New England School of Law (J.D., 1982). ***COURSES:*** Torts, Products Liability, Remedies, Healthcare Law. ***Email:*** bplumeri@fac.nesl.edu

SARAH SALTER, **(Professor of Law)**, born September 13, 1941; admitted to bar, 1970, New York. *Education:* Radcliffe College (A.B., 1962); Georgetown University (J.D., 1970). ***COURSES:*** Tax,

(This Listing Continued)

NEW ENGLAND SCHOOL OF LAW—Continued

Corporations, Property, International Business Transactions. ***Email:*** ssalter@fac.nesl.edu

MICHAEL SCHARF*, (Professor of Law, Director, Center for International Law and Policy)**, born Pittsburgh, Pennsylvania, April 25, 1963; admitted to bar, 1988, District of Columbia. *Education:* Duke University (A.B., 1988); Duke University School of Law (J.D., 1985). ***COURSES: International Law, Criminal Law, International Criminal Law, Human Rights Law. ***Email:*** mscharf@fac.nesl.edu

DAVID MARC SIEGEL*, (Professor of Law, Co-Director, Center for Law and Social Responsibility)**, born Washington, June 1, 1962; admitted to bar, 1991, Tennessee; 1993, District of Columbia. *Education:* University of Chicago (B.A., 1984; J.D., 1989). ***COURSES: Criminal Law, Criminal Procedure, Evidence, Mental Health Issues in the Criminal Process. ***Email:*** dsiegel@fac.nesl.edu

W.P. COLIN SMITH, JR.*, (Professor of Law)**, born Boston, Massachusetts, April 7, 1944; admitted to bar, 1969, Massachusetts. *Education:* Boston University (B.A., 1966); Boston University School of Law (J.D., 1969). ***COURSES: Civil Procedure, Land Use, Real Estate, Law Practice Management. ***Email:*** csmith@fac.nesl.edu

CHARLES WILLIAM SORENSON, JR.*, (Professor of Law)**, born Denver, Colorado, September 17, 1950; admitted to bar, 1981, Nebraska. *Education:* University of Colorado (B.A., 1972); University of California (M.A., 1977); University of Nebraska (J.D., 1981). ***COURSES: Civil Procedure, Administrative Law, Ethics, Federal Courts. ***Email:*** csorenson@fac.nesl.edu

ELIZABETH K. SPAHN*, (Professor of Law)**, born Chicago, Illinois; admitted to bar, 1976, Connecticut. *Education:* Yale University (A.B., 1972); Temple University School of Law (J.D., 1976). ***COURSES: Constitutional Law, Employment Law, International Women's Issues, Reproductive Freedom. ***Email:*** espahn@fac.nesl.edu

PAUL F. TEICH*, (Professor of Law, Associate Dean)**, born 1949; admitted to bar, 1976, Michigan. *Education:* Michigan (A.B., 1971; J.D., 1975). ***COURSES: Legal Profession, Property, Real Estate Transactions. ***Email:*** pteich@fac.nesl.edu

DANIEL TICCIONI*, (Professor of Law)**, born Milwaukee, Wisconsin, December 1, 1944; admitted to bar, 1969, Wisconsin; 1975, Massachusetts. *Education:* Marquette University (B.A., 1966; J.D., 1969). ***COURSES: Evidence, Civil Procedure, Conflict of Laws, Clinical Evidence, Criminal Procedure, Remedies. ***Email:*** dticcion@fac.nesl.edu

RUSS VERSTEEG*, (Professor of Law)**, born Columbus, Ohio, February 19, 1957; admitted to bar, 1987, Connecticut. *Education:* North Carolina State University; University of North Carolina at Chapel Hill (B.A., 1979); University of Connecticut (J.D., 1987). ***COURSES: Torts, Contracts, Copyright, Computer Law, Law and the Visual Arts, Law in the Ancient World, Trademarks and Unfair Competition. ***Email:*** rversteeg@fac.nesl.edu

NEW YORK LAW SCHOOL

57 WORTH STREET
NEW YORK, NEW YORK 10013
Telephone: (212) 431-2872
Fax: (212) 406-0103
E-Mail: admissions@nyls.edu Website: http://www.nyls.edu

ABA Approved Since 1954

New York Law School has been an integral and innovative member of New York's legal community for over 100 years. Founded in 1891, the School incorporates the practitioner's perspective into doctrinal and theoretical analysis to produce a truly well-rounded and effective legal education. In this pursuit, the School has benefited from proximity to the courts, government agencies, the financial district, and major law firms in which students enjoy a wide variety of clerkship and externship opportunities. The School offers a full-time day program, a part-time day program, and a part-time evening program. Its location in TriBeCa, one of the City's most colorful and dynamic communities, provides ready access to art galleries, some of the City's most interesting and finest restaurants, and a growing number of cultural and entertainment resources. New York Law School is a member of the Association of American Law Schools and is fully approved by the ABA and the New York State Board of Regents.

ENROLLMENT/STUDENT BODY

New York Law School reflects the cosmopolitan nature of its setting. Today's 1,450 students are diverse in their backgrounds, experiences, talents, and viewpoints; they reflect New York Law School's long-standing interest in serving older students, minority students, women, people seeking second careers, end public servants. Students range in age from 21 to 65, with the average age being 26. Over the past several years, students have represented 45 of the 50 states and many foreign countries and over 250 colleges and universities. Historically, approximately 12 percent of the student body has entered with a graduate or professional degree. Minority students account for approximately 29 percent of the student population, and approximately 55 percent of the students are women.

FACULTY

The School's required and core courses are taught by a distinguished faculty of approximately 50 dedicated teachers and was recently ranked among the nations top 50 most productive faculties. The School's extensive elective offerings are taught both by full-time faculty, and over 70 adjunct faculty composed of leading jurists and attorneys who teach courses in their areas of expertise.

PHYSICAL FACILITIES AND LIBRARY

The Law School's newly expanded and renovated urban campus is comprised of four connected buildings on a single block in lower Manhattan. The student center features a sky-lit cafeteria, student organization offices, and a spacious lounge area, providing inviting spaces for student extracurricular activities, social life and art exhibits. The School's fully-automated Mendik Library houses a collection of more than 475,000 volumes, as well as a variety of computer research services and technological enhancements. The five-story facility provides study space for more than 600 users. A member of several consortia linking the resources of various research libraries, the library uses OCLC and RLIN, in addition to LEXIS and WESTLAW, as well as numerous nonlegal databases.

CURRICULUM AND SPECIAL PROGRAMS

The curriculum is distinguished by its systematic effort to integrate the study of theory and practice and to include in the traditional study of legal doctrine and institutions the perspectives of legal practitioners.

(This Listing Continued)

The program of study is designed to prepare students to lead effective, productive, and responsible professional lives, whether in law itself or in businesses or professions in which understanding law and lawyers is a significant advantage. The educational approach that studies legal skills, strategy, and ethics, along with legal doctrine, policy, and theory begins in the first year along with requirements aimed at developing professional skills. The required curriculum comprises the entire first year and part of the second year, providing a foundation in legal reasoning and in areas of law that are considered the indispensable building blocks of a legal education. In the second year and thereafter, students may design their programs by selecting from over 150 elective courses that may be offered during a student's academic career. Innovative "workshops" --a means of teaching professional skills distinctive to New York Law School--link an advanced seminar in a specialized body of law to supervised field placements in offices and agencies practicing that area of law.

The Lawyering Skills Program:

Legal reasoning and legal writing, counseling, interviewing, negotiation, advocacy, planning, and strategizing are the subjects of the School's Lawyering Skills and Legal Writing Programs. These programs integrate skills training into the required first-year sequence as well as offering upper-class electives. The School also offers externships and judicial internships, clinics, and practice workshops tied to subject areas such as alternative dispute resolution, employment, bankruptcy, environmental, immigration, and media law. The School's Civil and Human Rights Clinic offers Pro Bono legal services on cases involving such matters as race, sex, housing and banking discrimination, and applications for political asylum.

Center for New York City Law:

In 1993, the School established a unique Center for New York City Law. The Center's objectives are to gather and disseminate information about New York City's laws, rules, and procedures; to sponsor publications, symposia, and conferences on topics related to governing the City, and to suggest reforms to make City government more effective and efficient. This is the only program in the United States focusing on the administration of a specific municipality. The program also furthers the School's educational goal of integrating concerns arising from practice into the study of legal rules and policies through a variety of courses about municipal government, in general, and New York City, in particular.

Center for International Law:

In mid-1996, New York Law School created its Center for International Law. The Center supports teaching and research in all areas of international law but concentrates on the law of international trade and finance, deriving much of its strength from interaction with New York's business, financial, and legal communities. The Center organizes conferences and symposia, sponsors forums, provides extensive on-line resources, and offers complete on-line transcripts from symposia.

Communications Media Center:

In response to the explosive growth of new communication technologies, the Law School established a Communications Media Center in 1977. The Center promotes education, research, and writing, and discussion about the laws governing mass communication, telecommunications, and computers. It sponsors seminars, conferences, lectures, on current issues in communications law. In addition, the Center produces "The Media Reporter," a television series featuring lively discussion on important issues, trends and technology.

In addition to these Centers, new initiatives will draw on the School's traditions and strengths in the areas of civil liberties and human rights, immigration law, gay and lesbian law, and litigation. The School's outreach programs link members of the School community as volunteers and resources to assist individuals and institutions throughout the metropolitan area.

COCURRICULAR ACTIVITIES

The student-run Moot Court Association participates in intermural competitions and hosts the prestigious Wagner Labor and Employment Law Competition, which annually attracts more than 30 schools as competitors, and draws jurists such as United States Supreme Court Justice Clarence Thomas to judge the competition. Students also edit and staff three scholarly publications that are integral parts of the Law School's program, offering opportunities for academic credit -- New York Law School Law Review, New York Law School Journal of International and Comparative Law, and New York Law School Journal of Human Rights. Students participate in more than 30 national and local organizations.

ADMISSIONS, FINANCIAL AID, AND CAREER SERVICES

The admission process takes into account a range of factors including the applicant's academic record and Law School Admission Test scores. The School seeks to admit students who, in addition to possessing strong academic credentials, also have demonstrated leadership ability, motivation, and a sense of service and responsibility to society. New York Law School has a program of financial aid to assist students in meeting the costs of a legal education, including scholarships awarded on the basis of academic merit and financial needs. The School's Office of Career Services provides a wide range of services to assist students and alumni in identifying career opportunities and conducting successful job searches. Services include an on-line subscription for job listing and career information, individual career counseling, recruitment programs, career panels and workshops, alumni services and network/mentoring programs, mock interviews, and access to job search-related resources.

Dean: Richard A. Matasar (212) 431-2840
Associate Dean for Public Interest & Community Service: Matthew Wilkes (212) 431-2894
Associate Dean for Academic Affairs: Jethro K. Lieberman (212) 431-2842
Associate Dean for Faculty Development: Stephen J. Ellmann (212) 431-2392
Associate Dean for Institutional Advancements: Barbara L. Leshinsky (212) 431-2800
Associate Dean for Finance and Administration: Fred P. DeJohn (212) 431-2881
Associate Dean for Special Projects: Joan R. Fishman (212) 431-2850
Associate Dean for Public Affairs: Altagracia DiLone Levat (212) 431-2872
Director of Library: Joyce Saltalamachia (212) 431-2360
Senior Director of Career and Student Affairs: Lori Freudenberger (212) 431-2345
Senior Director of Academic Affairs: Brenda Holzinger (212) 431-2870
Director of Admissions: Thomas Matos (212) 431-2888
Director of Academic Affairs: Kenneth Norz (212) 431-2854
Director of Academic Affairs for New Projects: Margaret Reuter (212) 431-2158

(This Listing Continued)

NEW YORK LAW SCHOOL—Continued

FULL TIME FACULTY

RICHARD A. MATASAR*, (Dean and President)**, born Chicago, June 4, 1952; admitted to bar, 1977, Pennsylvania; 1978, District of Columbia. *Education:* University of Pennsylvania (B.A., 1974; J.D., 1977). ***COURSES: Civil Procedure, Federal Courts. ***Email:*** rmatasar@nyls.edu

---

RICHARD C.E. BECK*, (Professor of Law)**, born Baltimore, Maryland, October 19, 1943; admitted to bar, 1982, New York. *Education:* University of Chicago (B.A., 1962; Ph.D., 1973); Yale University (J.D., 1980); New York University (LL.M., 1984). ***COURSES: Taxation.

LENNI BETH BENSON*, (Professor of Law)**, born Superior, Arizona, September 27, 1958; admitted to bar, 1983, Arizona; 1990, California. *Education:* Arizona State University (B.S., 1980; J.D., 1983). ***COURSES: Civil Procedure, Immigration Law, Administrative Law.

ROBERT BLECKER*, (Professor of Law)**, born New York, January 31, 1948; admitted to bar, 1974, New York. *Education:* Tufts University (B.A., 1969); Harvard University (J.D., 1974). ***COURSES: Criminal Law, Constitutional History.

MICHAEL BOTEIN*, (Professor of Law and Founding Director, Communications Media Center)**, born New York, New York, January 10, 1945; admitted to bar, 1969, New York. *Education:* Wesleyan University (B.A., 1966); Cornell University (J.D., 1969); Columbia University (LL.M., 1972; J.S.D., 1979). ***COURSES: Administrative Law, Antitrust, Communications Law, Civil Procedure, Constitutional Law.

JAMES BROOK*, (Professor of Law)**, born Buffalo, New York, December 1, 1946; admitted to bar, 1972, Massachusetts. *Education:* Harvard College (B.A., 1968); Harvard Law School (J.D., 1972); Columbia Law School (LL.M., 1983). ***COURSES: Commercial Law, Torts.

CAMILLE BROUSSARD*, (Adjunct Professor/Head of Reference Services)**, born Kaplan, Louisiana, January 1, 1954; admitted to bar, 1981, Oregon. *Education:* University of Nevada (B.S., 1976); Northwestern School of Law of Lewis & Clark College (J.D., 1981). ***COURSES: Advanced Legal Research.

CAROL A. BUCKLER*, (Professor of Law)**, born Pittsburgh, Pennsylvania, August 18, 1956; admitted to bar, 1983, New York. *Education:* Yale University (B.A., cum laude, 1978); Harvard University (J.D., cum laude, 1982). ***COURSES: Civil Law Clinic, Legal Ethics, Lawyering.

EUGENE CERRUTI*, (Professor of Law)**, born Paterson, New Jersey, July 6, 1944; admitted to bar, 1971, New York. *Education:* Harvard University (B.A., 1966); University of Pennsylvania (J.D., 1970). ***COURSES: Criminal Law, Criminal Procedure, Evidence, Trial Advocacy.

PAMELA R. CHAMPINE*, (Associate Professor)**, born Fort Mead, Maryland, June 1, 1964; admitted to bar, 1988, Illinois; 1991, New York. *Education:* University of Illinois (B.S., 1985); Northwestern University (J.D., 1988); New York University (LL.M., 1990). ***COURSES: Wills Trusts & Estates, Property.

DAVID CHANG*, (Professor of Law)**, born Poughkeepsie, New York, May 25, 1957. *Education:* Haverford College (B.A., 1979); Yale University (J.D., 1982). ***COURSES: Constitutional Law, Criminal Law, Conflict of Laws, Torts.

LUNG-CHU CHEN*, (Professor of Law)**, born Taiwan, December 30, 1935; admitted to bar, 1985, New York. *Education:* National Taiwan University (LL.B., 1958); Northwestern University (LL.M., 1961); Yale University (LL.M., 1962; J.S.D., 1964). ***COURSES: International Law, Constitutional Law, Conflict of Laws, Human Rights.

SYDNEY M. CONE, III*, (C.V. Starr Professor of Law/Director, Center for International Law)**, born Greensboro, North Carolina, November 30, 1930; admitted to bar, 1959, North Carolina; 1960, District of Columbia; 1970, New York; 1992, Paris, France. *Education:* Haverford College (A.B., 1952); Yale (LL.B., 1959). ***COURSES: International Trade Law, International Finance Law.

PAUL DUBINSKY*, (Associate Professor)**, born New York, New York, 1963; admitted to bar, 1991, New York, Connecticut; 1993, District of Columbia. *Education:* Yale (B.A., 1985); Harvard (J.D., 1989). ***COURSES: European Community Law, International Arbitration & Litigation, Contracts.

STEPHEN J. ELLMANN*, (Professor of Law and Associate Dean for Faculty Development)**, born Boston, Massachusetts, June 20, 1951; admitted to bar, 1977, Massachusetts; 1978, Alabama; 1987, New York. *Education:* Harvard University (B.A., 1972; J.D., 1976). ***COURSES: Legal Ethics, Constitutional Law, Clinical Skills, South African Law.

ALETA G. ESTREICHER*, (Professor of Law)**, born New York, New York, May 27, 1948; admitted to bar, 1982, New York; 1983, New Jersey. *Education:* Bryn Mawr College (A.B., 1970); Columbia Law School (J.D., 1981). ***COURSES: Corporations, Securities Regulation, Property.

ANTHONY QUENTIN FLETCHER*, (Associate Professor)**, born New York, New York, April 3, 1970; admitted to bar, 1997, New York. *Education:* Columbia College (A.B., 1992); Harvard Law School (J.D., 1995). ***COURSES: Corporations, Securities Regulation. ***Email:*** afletcher@nyls.edu

B. JAMES GEORGE*, (Professor of Law Emeritus)**, born Kansas City, Missouri, October 16, 1925; admitted to bar, 1952, Missouri; 1978, Texas; 1981, New York. *Education:* University of Michigan (B.A., 1949; J.D., 1951). ***COURSES: Criminal Law, Criminal Procedure, Sentencing and Corrections Law, Comparative Law: Japan, Comparative Law: PRC.

I. CATHY GLASER*, (Associate Director of the Writing Program and Adjunct Professor)**, born New York, New York, June 17, 1952; admitted to bar, 1978, New York. *Education:* Cornell University (B.S., 1974); Syracuse University (J.D., 1977). ***COURSES: Writing.

ANNETTE GORDON-REED*, (Professor of Law)**, born Livingston, Texas, November 19, 1958; admitted to bar, 1985, New York. *Education:* Dartmouth College (A.B., 1981); Harvard Law School (J.D., 1984). ***COURSES: Property, Legal Ethics, Criminal Procedure, American Legal History.

LAWRENCE M. GROSBERG*, (Professor of Law; Director, Lawyering Skills Center)**, born Detroit, Michigan, June 4, 1943; admitted to bar, 1969, New York. *Education:* University of Southern California (B.A., 1965); Columbia University (J.D., 1969). ***COURSES: Lawyering, Trial Advocacy, Civil Law Clinic and Negotiating, Counseling and Interviewing, ADR, Mediation Clinic.

KAREN GROSS*, (Professor of Law)**, born Illinois, April 27, 1952; admitted to bar, 1977, Illinois; 1982, New York. *Education:* Smith College (B.A., 1974); Temple Law School (J.D., 1977). ***COURSES: Bankruptcy, Corporate Reorganization, Commercial Law, Contracts, Feminist Theory.

***JEFFREY J. HAAS*, (Professor of Law)**, born Oaklawn, Illinois,

(This Listing Continued)

NEW YORK LAW SCHOOL—Continued

August 18, 1961; admitted to bar, 1989, New York. *Education:* Florida State University (B.S., 1984); University of Melbourne, Australia; University of Pennsylvania (J.D., 1988). ***COURSES:*** Securities Law, Corporate Finance, Mergers and Acquisitions, Contracts.

SETH DAVID HARRIS*, (Associate Professor)**, born Manhasset, New York, October 12, 1962; admitted to bar, 1991, New York; 1992, District of Columbia. *Education:* Cornell University (B.S.I.L.R., 1983); New York University (J.D., 1990). ***COURSES: Labor Law, Employment Law, Torts.

MARIANA J. HOGAN*, (Associate Professor and Director of Externship Programs)**, born Washington, D.C., March 8, 1954; admitted to bar, 1980, New York. *Education:* Brown University (A.B., 1976); Georgetown University Law Center (J.D., 1979); New York University, Visiting Student, 1978-1979. ***COURSES: Lawyering Skills, Trial Advocacy, Legal Ethics.

RANDOLPH N. JONAKAIT*, (Professor of Law)**, born Sheboygan, Wisconsin, May 10, 1945; admitted to bar, 1971, New York. *Education:* Princeton University (A.B., 1967); University of Chicago (J.D., 1970); New York University (LL.M., 1971). ***COURSES: Evidence, Criminal Procedure, Criminal Law.

FAITH STEVELMAN KAHN*, (Professor of Law)**, born Charlottesville, Virginia; admitted to bar, 1990, New York. *Education:* Yale University (B.A., 1982); Yale Graduate School (M.Phil., 1985); New York University School of Law (J.D., 1989). ***COURSES: Corporations.

KENNETH C. KETTERING*, (Associate Professor)**, born Pittsburgh, Pennsylvania, December 3, 1957; admitted to bar, 1981, Pennsylvania. *Education:* Carnegie Mellon University (B.S., 1977); Harvard Law School (J.D., 1980). ***COURSES: Commercial Law, Bankruptcy Debtor-Creditor.

JOSEPH H. KOFFLER*, (Professor of Law Emeritus)**, born Stamford, Connecticut; admitted to bar, 1949, New York and Connecticut. *Education:* City College of New York (B.S.S., 1943); Harvard Law School (LL.B., 1948). ***COURSES: Torts, Products Liability.

WILLIAM P. LAPIANA*, (Rita and Joseph Solomon Professor of Wills, Trusts and Estates)**, born Buffalo, New York, March 7, 1952; admitted to bar, 1980, New York. *Education:* Harvard University (A.B., 1973; A.M., 1975; J.D., 1978; Ph.D., 1987). ***COURSES: Property, Wills and Trusts, Estate Planning, American Legal History, Federal Estate with Gift Tax.

JOEL S. LEE*, (Professor of Law)**, born New York, New York; admitted to bar, 1950, New York. *Education:* New York University (A.B., 1948; LL.B., 1950). ***COURSES: Wills, Trusts and Estates, Contracts, Conflict of Laws, Evidence, Corporations, Property.

ARTHUR S. LEONARD*, (Professor of Law)**, born Brooklyn, New York, January 17, 1952; admitted to bar, 1978, New York. *Education:* Cornell University (B.S., 1974); Harvard University (J.D., 1977). ***COURSES: Contracts, Labor and Employment Law, Sexuality and the Law, Torts.

JETHRO K. LIEBERMAN*, (Professor of Law and Associate Dean for Academic Affairs)**, born Washington, D.C., October 23, 1943; admitted to bar, 1967, New York; 1968, District of Columbia. *Education:* Yale University (B.A., 1964); Harvard Law School (J.D., 1967); Columbia University (M.Phil., 1994; Ph.D., 1995). ***COURSES: Constitutional Law, Writing.

JOSEPH L. MARINO*, (Professor, Associate Director of the Academic Skills Program)**, born Canton, Illinois, July 6, 1950; admitted to bar, 1976, New York, Florida. *Education:* CW Post College (B.A., 1972); St. John's University School of Law (J.D., 1975). ***COURSES: New York Civil Procedure, New York Law in National Perspective. ***Email:*** jmarino@nyls.edu

RICHARD MARSICO*, (Professor of Law)**, born New York, September 29, 1960; admitted to bar, 1986, New York. *Education:* Fordham University (B.A., 1982); Harvard University (J.D., 1985). ***COURSES: Clinical, Lawyering Skills, Legal Ethics.

CARLIN MEYER*, (Professor of Law)**, born Chicago, Illinois, September 7, 1948; admitted to bar, 1975, New York. *Education:* Harvard University (B.A., 1970); Rutgers University (J.D., 1974); Yale University (LL.M., 1988). ***COURSES: Employment Law, Family Law.

ELAINE P. MILLS*, (Associate Professor/Director of the Academic Skills Program)**, born Vincennes, Indiana, January 14, 1943; admitted to bar, 1976, New York. *Education:* Indiana University (A.B., 1965); University of Illinois (M.A., 1969); Rutgers University (J.D., 1975). ***COURSES: Legal Analysis.

WILLIAM R. MILLS*, (Adjunct Professor/Associate Library Director)**, born Brooklyn, New York, June 4, 1950; admitted to bar, 1983, New York. *Education:* State University of New York at Stony Brook (B.S., 1971); Columbia University (M.S.L.S., 1978); Fordham University (J.D., 1982). ***COURSES: Legal Research.

DENISE C. MORGAN*, (Professor of Law)**, born New York, New York, April 4, 1965; admitted to bar, 1990, Connecticut; 1991, New York and District of Columbia. *Education:* Yale College (B.A., 1986); Yale Law School (J.D., 1990). ***COURSES: Civil Procedure, Education Law, Federal Courts.

FRANK W. MUNGER*, (Visiting Professor of Law)**, born California, December 19, 1942; admitted to bar, 1969, Michigan and District of Columbia. *Education:* Kenyon College (A.B., 1964); University of Michigan (J.D., 1968; Ph.D., 1977). ***COURSES: Constitutional law, Land Use; Welfare Law; Legal Profession.

STEPHEN A. NEWMAN*, (Professor of Law)**, born New York, New York, November 13, 1946; admitted to bar, 1971, New York. *Education:* University of Pennsylvania (B.A., 1967); Columbia Law School (J.D., 1970). ***COURSES: Family Law, Children and Law, Civil Procedure, Persuasion.

RUDOLPH J. PERITZ*, (Professor of Law)**, admitted to bar, 1975, Texas. *Education:* Penn State University (B.S., 1969); University of Texas (J.D., 1975); Langdell Fellow, Harvard Law School, 1981-1982. ***COURSES: Antitrust, Regulated Industries, Computers and Law, Contracts, Jurisprudence.

MICHAEL L. PERLIN*, (Professor of Law)**, born Perth Amboy, New Jersey, March 30, 1946; admitted to bar, 1969, New Jersey; 1983, New York. *Education:* Rutgers University (A.B., 1966); Columbia University (J.D., 1969). ***COURSES: Mental Disability Law, Criminal Law, Civil Procedure, Therapeutic Jurisprudence, Criminal Procedure.

EDWARD A. PURCELL, JR.*, (Joseph Solomon Distinguished Professor of Law)**, born Kansas City, Missouri, July 20, 1941; admitted to bar, 1980, New York. *Education:* Rockhurst College (A.B., 1962); University of Wisconsin (Ph.D., 1968); Harvard Law School (J.D., 1979). ***COURSES: Civil Procedure, Federal Courts, Complex Litigation.

SADIQ REZA*, (Associate Professor)**, born New York, New York, November 5, 1964; admitted to bar, 1993, Pennsylvania and District of Columbia. *Education:* Princeton University (A.B., 1986); Harvard Law School (J.D., 1991). ***COURSES: Criminal Procedure, Criminal Law.

(This Listing Continued)

NEW YORK LAW SCHOOL—Continued

ELIZABETH ROSEN*, (Assistant Director Writing Program)**, born New York, New York, January 19, 1955; admitted to bar, 1983, New York. *Education:* Bennington College (B.A., 1978); Benjamin N. Cardozo School of Law Yeshiva University (J.D., 1982); City University of New York Graduate Center (Ph.D., 2000). ***COURSES: Legal Writing, Appellate Advocacy. ***Email:*** erosen@nyls.edu

TANINA ROSTAIN*, (Associate Professor)**, born New York, New York, July 15, 1960; admitted to bar, 1987, Connecticut. *Education:* Swarthmore (B.A., 1981); Yale University (M.A., 1983); Yale Law School (J.D., 1987). ***COURSES: Legal Ethics, Evidence, Lawyer's & Public Life.

JOYCE D. SALTALAMACHIA*, (Library Director and Professor of Law)**, born California, July 7, 1947; admitted to bar, 1976, California. *Education:* University of California at Berkeley (A.B., 1969; M.L.S., 1970); Golden Gate University (J.D., 1976). ***COURSES: Torts.

EDWARD SAMUELS*, (Professor of Law)**, born Memphis, Tennessee, January 29, 1949; admitted to bar, 1975, New York. *Education:* Yale University (B.A., 1971); Columbia University (J.D., 1974). ***COURSES: Copyright, Intellectual Property, Commercial Law, Contracts, Bankruptcy.

ROSS SANDLER*, (Professor of Law/ Director, Center for New York City Law)**, born Milwaukee, Wisconsin, January 31, 1939; admitted to bar, 1965, New York and Florida. *Education:* Dartmouth College (A.B., 1961); New York University School of Law (LL.B., 1965). ***COURSES: State and Local Government, New York City Law.

DAVID SCHOENBROD*, (Professor of Law)**, born Chicago, Illinois, August 18, 1942; admitted to bar, 1971, New York. *Education:* Yale University (B.A., 1963; LL.B., 1968); Oxford University (B.Phil., 1965). ***COURSES: Environmental Law, Remedies.

E. DONALD SHAPIRO*, (Dean Emeritus & Professor of Law Emeritus)**, born York, Pennsylvania, November 1, 1931; admitted to bar, 1957, District of Columbia and Pennsylvania; 1967, Michigan; 1981, New York. *Education:* Dickinson College (A.B., 1953); Harvard Law School (J.D., 1956); New York Law School (LL.D., 1973); Dickinson College (LL.D., 1975); York College of Pennsylvania (H.L.D., 1980); Oxford University (M.A., 1986). ***COURSES: Torts I, Torts II, Legal Medicine, Medical Malpractice, Law and Forensic Science, Law and Bioethics.

RICHARD K. SHERWIN*, (Professor of Law)**, born New York, June 23, 1953; admitted to bar, 1981, New York. *Education:* Brandeis University (B.A., 1975); Boston College (J.D., 1981); Columbia University (LL.M., 1986; J.S.D., 1989). ***COURSES: Criminal Procedure, Torts, Legal Ethics, Jurisprudence, Lawyering.

JAMES F. SIMON*, (Dean Emeritus & Martin Professor of Law)**, born Ft. Worth, Texas, November 26, 1938; admitted to bar, 1965, Texas; 1992, New York. *Education:* Yale University (B.A., 1961; LL.B., 1964). ***COURSES: Constitutional Law, Legal Journalism.

MICHAEL B.W. SINCLAIR*, (Professor of Law)**, born Manurewa, New Zealand, November 8, 1942; admitted to bar, 1978, Michigan. *Education:* Victoria University (B.A., 1968; B.A., with Honors, 1970; Ph.D., 1974); University of Michigan (J.D., 1978). ***COURSES: Contracts, Payment Systems, U.C.C., Banking.

NADINE STROSSEN*, (Professor of Law)**, born Jersey City, New Jersey, August 18, 1950; admitted to bar, 1976, Minnesota; 1979, New York. *Education:* Harvard University (B.A., 1972; J.D., 1975). President, American Civil Liberties Union. ***COURSES: Constitutional Law, International Human Rights, Advanced Constitutional Law and Appellate Advocacy.

LYNN P. BOEPPLE SU*, (Assistant Director, Writing Program and Adjunct Professor, Writing Specialist)**, born Jamaica, New York, July 7, 1960; admitted to bar, 1986, New York; 1989, District of Columbia; 1990, New Jersey. *Education:* New York University (B.A., 1982); Washington & Lee University School of Law (J.D., 1985). ***COURSES: Legal Reasoning, Writing and Advocacy. ***Email:*** lsu@nyls.edu

RUTI G. TEITEL*, (Ernst Stiefel Professor of Comparative Law)**, born Buenos Aires, Argentina; admitted to bar, 1981, New York. *Education:* Georgetown University (B.S., 1977); Cornell Law School (J.D., 1980). ***COURSES: Constitutional Law, Comparative Constitutional Law, Religion and the First Amendment.

ANN F. THOMAS*, (Professor of Law)**, born South Bend, Indiana, August 4, 1951; admitted to bar, 1977, New York; 1980, U.S. Tax Court; 1987, U.S. Supreme Court. *Education:* Radcliffe College (A.B., 1973); Yale Law School (J.D., 1976). ***COURSES: Taxation.

HARRY H. WELLINGTON*, (Dean Emeritus & Professor of Law)**, born New Haven, Connecticut, August 13, 1926; admitted to bar, 1952, District of Columbia. *Education:* University of Pennsylvania (B.A., 1947); Harvard University (LL.B., 1952). ***COURSES: Constitutional Law, Labor Law.

DONALD H. ZEIGLER*, (Professor of Law)**, born New Haven, Connecticut, September 19, 1945; admitted to bar, 1972, New York. *Education:* Amherst College (A.B., 1966); Columbia University (J.D., 1969). ***COURSES: Civil Procedure, Evidence, Federal Courts, Conflicts, Lawyering.

NEW YORK UNIVERSITY SCHOOL OF LAW

40 WASHINGTON SQUARE SOUTH
NEW YORK, NEW YORK 10012
Telephone: (212) 998-6060
Fax: (212) 995-4527
www.law.nyu.edu

ABA Approved Since 1930

At the New York University School of Law, an adventurous intellectual spirit prevails. Our goal, ambitious and maybe a bit impetuous, is to chart the future course for American legal education by developing and refining programs of genuine excellence that encompass the strengths of the traditional curriculum while incorporating interdisciplinary, global, and clinical dimensions.

We are a work in progress, not a final product. But our success to date is remarkable. The breadth of advanced interdisciplinary work occurring at NYU Law is, quite simply, unmatched: thus, for example, there is no law school in the world with our philosophical sophistication; our faculty is on the cutting edge of work in law and economics, game theory, and rational choice theory; we are an important center of research in legal history; and studies in law and society are flourishing as well. NYU Law's groundbreaking Global Law School Program has placed in residence, on a permanent basis, legal scholars and outstanding graduate students from, quite literally, every corner of the world; no other law school has implemented a program of this scope.

(This Listing Continued)

NEW YORK UNIVERSITY SCHOOL OF LAW—Continued

And our clinical program probably needs no introduction; its reputation as the leading program in clinical studies is seldom questioned and well deserved.

At the same time, we have not sacrificed the advantages of the traditional curriculum. On the contrary, the traditional curriculum at NYU Law has been greatly enriched by all of this. The insights of theory surface regularly in class discussions from basic first-year courses to upper-level courses in subjects like Corporations and Constitutional Law to advanced graduate courses in areas like Tax. Moreover, with the advent of the Global Law School Program has come a great range of new offerings in comparative and international law, often co-taught by professors from more than one nation. And, clinical education has made its way into traditional subjects as well, with courses in Evidence, Advanced Procedure, Environmental Law, and Professional Responsibility (to list but a few) being taught in alternative, clinical formats.

NYU Law has a historic commitment to social justice-much of the work in interdisciplinary legal studies is devoted to the ongoing, never-free-from-controversy project of charting the course of a good society. Global studies are an important corrective for the tendency of thinkers and activists in any society to overvalue parochial convention. And clinical education directly engages the enterprises of securing justice for individuals and protecting society from harm. We take pride in being a community of ideas, a community in which orthodoxy is challenged, and invention is celebrated. We ask of our students that they share in and act upon these commitments.

At the heart of any great school is its canonical curriculum, that critical artery of primary knowledge that provides the context for the critical reflection undertaken in all of the educational enterprise. Certain subjects have been, for generations, the canon of American legal education. No school that sought to be an academic leader could compromise the breadth or quality of its offerings in these areas. This canon is, simply, the bedrock upon which excellence in other areas must be built.

NYU Law's most basic commitment is to offer students an opportunity to explore law from all its diverse angles, and to do so in an environment that is cooperative rather than competitive. In part, this simply means providing resources and faculty, and the NYU Law faculty includes men and women who work and teach in an array of fields. But the school offers more than this. A generation ago, interdisciplinary study meant examining law from the perspective of another discipline. Today, it means integrating methodologies and perspectives from more than one discipline in order to gain a multidimensional understanding of legal problems.

NYU Law has pioneered the development of tools to make interdisciplinary work genuinely enriching. Rather than just add faculty members who work in more than one discipline, we have found ways to create a dialogue in which students and faculty with diverse interests and expertise work together; forcing each other to grapple with problems in novel ways.

In these and other ways-independent study, seminars, joint degree programs, courses in other departments, conferences, symposia, and more-students are encouraged to explore the law in the ways that interest them most, aided by faculty with related interests.

The development of interdisciplinary legal studies manifests a recognition that the law does not exist in isolation; that it is formed by, and it affects, other areas of intellectual endeavor. But law does not exist in geographic or cultural isolation, either. As the social, political, and economic systems of different nations become ever more interconnected and interdependent, so too will their legal systems. Already, an increasing proportion of what most lawyers do brings them into contact with this transnational system. The globalization of law is already happening; and judges, lawyers, and legal academics must be prepared to deal with it.

The Global Law School Program is designed to attract faculty and students from many nations into one intellectual community, to make NYU Law a "global" rather than a national law school and, by assimilating these diverse perspectives, to both challenge the most fundamental premises of America's legal system and prepare NYU Law's graduates for the global environment in which they will practice.

At the faculty level, the Global Law School Program supplements the law school's already distinguished American faculty by assembling some of the world's leading law professors from six continents to teach how they think about law and learn how we do. While remaining affiliated with their national universities, these professors have a sustained relationship with NYU Law. This global perspective does not stop with the faculty. NYU Law also recognizes the importance of salting the student body with the finest law students from around the world. Last year, more than 200 full-time students were citizens of countries other than the United States; indeed, the law school's student body is drawn from more than three dozen different countries.

One of the most attractive features of studying law is its applied nature. Legal studies can be as theoretical as the most academic disciplines, but law ultimately must be anchored in the real world. One of the most difficult challenges in studying law is learning how to bridge this gap-how to translate theories into principles that can be understood and used by judges and lawyers in their everyday practice.

Situation-based study at NYU Law begins with the Lawyering course in the first year, and culminates in the upper years in elective fieldwork clinics in which students represent actual clients under close faculty supervision. A distinctive feature of NYU Law's clinics is that the faculty who teach them are tenured or tenure-track professors whose sole professional interest is the research and teaching they do at the law school; the result is not only that the law school attracts the finest clinical faculty but also that our students receive full attention. NYU Law has the nation's premier clinical program, as well as the largest and most diverse.

An important feature of the NYU Law experience flows from our location in New York City, the legal and financial capital of the world. Whether one will practice in Sydney or San Francisco, Zurich or Chicago, studying in New York is an irreplaceable experience. This is especially the case when it can be done, as it can be done at NYU Law, while living in a community as special as Greenwich Village; two-thirds of the NYU Law faculty and over 90% of its law students live within a five minute walk of the law school. The combination of the world's greatest city with one of the world's greatest neighborhoods creates a truly spectacular environment for the study of any subject, but especially for the study of law.

NYU Law has invested heavily in state-of-the-art technology. The result: we are fully wired with the latest equipment-in our faculty offices, student residences, classrooms (podia and seats), library, and in the offices of the law school's administrators. This technology does not sit idle. Faculty has seized the possibilities for new pedagogy it provides: increasingly, classroom activities have a technological component, whether it consists of downloading charts and data prepared in advance by faculty, or researching in real time, or checking current market quotes, or myriad other pedagogical moves. Once class is over, classroom conversation continues not only in the law school's lounges but also on-line.

In each element of the curriculum-the traditional canon, interdisciplinary studies, global studies, and clinical studies-NYU Law is a leader. It is fair to say that no other school offers a better array of opportunities in any of the four individual elements, and clearly no other school offers so much in all of them.

We invite you to look closely at the NYU Law community. Visit our

(This Listing Continued)

NEW YORK UNIVERSITY SCHOOL OF LAW—Continued

campus and speak with our students. To pursue this course of study as part of the special community of faculty and students drawn from around the world to the singular setting of our Greenwich Village campus in New York City is to enjoy a unique academic experience at a level unmatched anywhere.

Dean: John Edward Sexton (212) 998-6000
Assistant Dean - Admissions: Kenneth Kleinrock (212) 998-6060
Associate Director - Financial Aid: John Kelly (212) 998-6050
Director, Law Library: Kathleen Price (212) 998-6300
Assistant Dean - Placement: Irene Dorzback (212) 998-6090
Assistant Dean - Development and Alumni Relations: Joan Petersen (212) 998-6400

FULL TIME FACULTY

JOHN EDWARD SEXTON*, (Dean and Benjamin F. Butler Professor of Constitutional Law & the Courts)**, born 1942; admitted to bar, 1981, New York. *Education:* Fordham University (B.A., 1963; M.A., 1965; Ph.D., 1978); Harvard University Law School (J.D., 1979). ***COURSES: Civil Procedure, Constitutional Law, Lawyering, Religion Clauses of First Amendment. ***Email:*** sextonj@turing.law.nyu.edu

AMY M. ADLER*, (Professor of Law)**, born 1963; admitted to bar, 1993, New York. *Education:* Yale University (B.A., 1985); Yale Law School (J.D., 1990). ***COURSES: Art Law, Contracts, First Amendment Law. ***Email:*** adlera@juris.law.nyu.edu

BARRY E. ADLER*, (Professor of Law)**, born 1960; admitted to bar, 1987, New York. *Education:* Cornell University (B.S., 1982); University of Chicago Law School (J.D., 1985). ***COURSES: Bankruptcy, Business Associations, Corporate Finance. ***Email:*** barry.adler@nyu.edu

WILLIAM T. ALLEN*, (Professor of Law; Clinical Professor of Business, Leonard N. Stern School of Business)**, admitted to bar, 1973, Pennsylvania. *Education:* New York University (B.S., 1969); University of Texas School of Law (J.D., 1972); Pennsylvania State University, Dickenson School of Law (LL.D., 1991). ***COURSES: Corporations. ***Email:*** allenw@turing.law.nyu.edu

ANTHONY G. AMSTERDAM*, (Professor of Law)**, born 1935; admitted to bar, 1960, District of Columbia. *Education:* Haverford College (A.B., 1957); University of Pennsylvania Law School (LL.B., 1960). ***COURSES: Clinical Teaching, Criminal Law, Criminal Procedure, Evidence, Law and Psychiatry. ***Email:*** amsterdam@turing.law.nyu.edu

VICKI L. BEEN*, (Professor of Law)**, born 1956; admitted to bar, 1984, New York. *Education:* Colorado State University (B.S., 1978); New York University School of Law (J.D., 1983). ***COURSES: Empirical Issues in Land Use & Environmental Law, Environmental Justice, Land Use Planning, Local Government, Property, Takings Jurisprudence. ***Email:*** vicki.been@nyu.edu

DERRICK A. BELL, JR.*, (Long Term Visiting Professor of Law)**, born 1930; admitted to bar, 1957, District of Columbia; 1960, Pennsylvania; 1966, New York; 1969, California. *Education:* Duquesne University (A.B., 1952); University of Pittsburgh School of Law (LL.B., 1957). ***COURSES: Constitutional Law & Minority Issues, Constitutional Law, Supreme Court Decision Making. ***Email:*** derrick.bell@nyu.edu

YOCHAI BENKLER*, (Professor of Law)**, born 1964; admitted to bar, 1995, Massachusetts. *Education:* Tel-Aviv University (LL.B., 1991); Harvard Law School (J.D., 1994). ***COURSES: Communications Law, Information Law & Policy, Property. ***Email:*** yochai.benkler@nyu.edu

BROOKES D. BILLMAN*, (Associate Dean and Professor of Law)**, born 1949; admitted to bar, 1974, Ohio; 1976, District of Columbia. *Education:* Princeton University (A.B., 1971); University of Cincinnati College of Law (J.D., 1974); New York University School of Law (LL.M., 1975). ***COURSES: Employee Benefit Plans; Federal Taxation. ***Email:*** brookes.billman@nyu.edu

SARAH E. BURNS*, (Professor of Clinical Law)**, born 1949; admitted to bar, 1979, District of Columbia; 1989, New York. *Education:* University of Oklahoma (B.A., 1971; M.A., 1972); Stanford University (M.A., 1976); Yale University Law School (J.D., 1979). ***COURSES: Civil Litigation, Civil Rights Clinic, Evidence, Litigation Planning, Lawyering, Public Policy Advocacy Clinic, Sex Discrimination Clinic, Women & the Law. ***Email:*** burns@turing.nyu.edu

PAULETTE M. CALDWELL*, (Professor of Law)**, born 1944; admitted to bar, 1972, New York. *Education:* Howard University School of Law (J.D., 1969). ***COURSES: Civil Rights, Lawyering, Non-Profit Corporation, Property, Real Estate Transactions.

OSCAR G. CHASE*, (Professor of Law)**, born 1940; admitted to bar, 1966, New York. *Education:* New York University (B.A., 1960); Yale University Law School (J.D., 1963). ***COURSES: Civil Procedure, Comparative Law, Law & Social Science, Practice. ***Email:*** oscar.chase@nyu.edu

PAUL G. CHEVIGNY*, (Joel S. and Anne B. Ehrenkranz Professor of Law)**, born 1935; admitted to bar, 1961, New York. *Education:* Yale University (B.A., 1957); Harvard University Law School (LL.B., 1960). ***COURSES: Clinic, International Human Rights, Criminal Law, Evidence, Law & Social Science. ***Email:*** chevigny@turing.law.nyu.edu

JEROME A. COHEN*, (Professor of Law)**, born 1930; admitted to bar, 1955, Connecticut; 1957, District of Columbia; 1982, New York. *Education:* Yale University (B.A., 1951); Yale University Law School (J.D., 1955). ***COURSES: Chinese Law, Comparative Law, International Law, International Transactions, Japanese Law.

DANIEL G. COLLINS*, (Professor of Law Emeritus)**, born 1930; admitted to bar, 1955, New York. *Education:* Hofstra University (B.A., 1951); New York University School of Law (LL.B., 1954). ***COURSES: Contracts, Labor Arbitration, Labor Law in the Public Sector, Labor Law, Sports & the Law.

NOEL B. CUNNINGHAM*, (Professor of Law)**, born 1944; admitted to bar, 1974, Connecticut; 1975, New York. *Education:* City College of New York (B.S., 1967); University of Connecticut (M.A., 1971); University of Connecticut School of Law (J.D., 1974); New York University School of Law (LL.M., 1975). ***COURSES: Federal Taxation. ***Email:*** nbc@juris.law.nyu.edu

HARVEY P. DALE*, (Professor of Law)**, born 1937; admitted to bar, 1962, New York; 1966, District of Columbia. *Education:* Cornell University (B.A., 1958); Harvard University Law School (J.D., 1961). ***COURSES: Federal Taxation, International Taxation, Law of Non-Profit Organizations, Philanthropy & the Law, Tax Aspects of Charitable Giving. ***Email:*** hpd1@is2.nyu.edu

(This Listing Continued)

PEGGY COOPER DAVIS*, (John S.R. Shad Professor of Lawyering & Ethics)**, born 1943; admitted to bar, 1969, New York. *Education:* Western College for Women (B.A., 1964); Harvard University Law School (J.D., 1968). ***COURSES: Clinical Teaching, Evidence, Family Law, Law & Social Science, Lawyering Theory. ***Email:*** davisp@turing.law.nyu.edu

NORMAN DORSEN*, (Frederick I. and Grace A. Stokes Professor of Law)**, born 1930; admitted to bar, 1953, District of Columbia; 1954, New York. *Education:* Columbia University (B.A., 1950); Harvard University Law School (LL.B., 1953); Ripon College (LL.D., 1981); John Jay College of Criminal Justice (LL.D., 1992). ***COURSES: Constitutional Law, Legislation. ***Email:*** norman.dorsen@nyu.edu

ROCHELLE C. DREYFUSS*, (Pauline Newman Professor of Law)**, born 1947; admitted to bar, 1982, New York. *Education:* Wellesley College (B.A., 1968); University of California at Berkeley (M.S., 1970); Columbia University Law School (J.D., 1981). ***COURSES: Civil Procedure, Innovation Policy, Intellectual Property, Law & Science.

RONALD M. DWORKIN*, (Frank Henry Sommer Professor of Law)**, born 1931; admitted to bar, 1958, New York. *Education:* Harvard University (A.B., 1953); Oxford University (B.A., 1955); Harvard University Law School (LL.B., 1957). ***COURSES: Jurisprudence.

SAMUEL ESTREICHER*, (Professor of Law)**, born 1948; admitted to bar, 1976, New York; 1978, District of Columbia. *Education:* Columbia University (B.A., 1970); Cornell University (M.S., 1974); Columbia University Law School (J.D., 1975). ***COURSES: Administrative Law, Civil Procedure, Civil Rights (Employment Discrimination), Comparative Labor Law, Constitutional Law, Employment Discrimination Law, Labor Law Theory, Labor Law. ***Email:*** estreicher@turing.law.nyu.edu

JAMES S. EUSTICE*, (Gerald L. Wallace Professor of Taxation)**, born 1932; admitted to bar, 1956, Illinois; 1959, New York. *Education:* University of Illinois (B.S., 1954); University of Illinois College of Law (LL.B., 1956); New York University Law School (LL.M., 1958). ***COURSES: Federal Taxation.

HARRY FIRST*, (Professor of Law)**, born 1945; admitted to bar, 1969, Pennsylvania; 1979, New York. *Education:* University of Pennsylvania (B.A., 1966); University of Pennsylvania Law School (J.D., 1969). ***COURSES: Antitrust, Broadcasting Regulation, Business Crime, Corporations, Criminal Procedure, Regulated Industries. ***Email:*** firsth@turing.law.nyu.edu

ELEANOR M. FOX*, (Walter J. Derenberg Professor of Trade Regulation)**, born 1936; admitted to bar, 1961, New York. *Education:* Vassar College (B.A., 1956); New York University School of Law (LL.B., 1961). ***COURSES: Antitrust, European Union Law, Torts. ***Email:*** eleanor.fox@nyu.edu

THOMAS M. FRANCK*, (Murry & Ida Becker Professor of Law)**, born 1931. *Education:* University of British Columbia (B.A., 1952; LL.B., 1953; LL.D., 1995); Harvard University Law School (LL.M., 1954; S.J.D., 1959). ***COURSES: Comparative German-American Constitutional Protection of Civil Rights, Comparative Law, Congress & the Foreign Relations Power, Constitutional Law of the United Nations, Constitutional Law, International Law, Legitimacy and Justice in the International System, Selected Problems in the Work of International Organizations, The Empowered Self: Law & Society in the Age of Individualism.

BARRY FRIEDMAN*, (Professor of Law)**, born 1958; admitted to bar, 1983, District of Columbia; 1991, Tennessee. *Education:* University of Chicago (A.B., 1978); Georgetown University Law Center (J.D., 1982). ***COURSES: Civil Procedure, Constitutional Law, Criminal Procedure, Federal Courts, Legal Process, Politics of Judicial Review. ***Email:*** barry.friedman@nyu.edu

PAULA GALOWITZ*, (Clinical Professor of Law)**, born 1947; admitted to bar, 1977, New York. *Education:* Rutgers University (B.A., 1968); Yeshiva University (M.S.W., 1971); Brooklyn Law School (J.D., 1976). ***COURSES: Clinical Litigation, Clinical Teaching, Lawyering. ***Email:*** galowitz@turing.law.nyu.edu

MARK GEISTFELD*, (Professor of Law)**, born 1958; admitted to bar, 1990, New York. *Education:* Lewis & Clark University (B.A., 1980); University of Pennsylvania (M.A., 1981); Columbia University Law School (J.D., 1989); Columbia University (Ph.D., Economics, 1990). ***COURSES: Insurance, Law & Economics, Products Liability, Torts. ***Email:*** geistfeld@turing.law.nyu.edu

STEPHEN GILLERS*, (Vice Dean and Professor of Law)**, born 1943; admitted to bar, 1968, New York. *Education:* Brooklyn College (B.A., 1964); New York University School of Law (J.D., 1968). ***COURSES: Evidence, Jurisprudence, Legal Profession. ***Email:*** stephen.gillers@nyu.edu

CLAYTON P. GILLETTE*, (Professor of Law)**, born 1950; admitted to bar, 1977, New York. *Education:* Amherst College (B.A., 1972); University of Michigan Law School (J.D., 1975). ***COURSES: Commercial Law Theory, Commercial Law, Commercial Paper, Contracts, International Sales, Local Government Law, Torts. ***Email:*** gillette@juris.law.nyu.edu

HOWARD L. GREENBERGER*, (Professor of Law Emeritus)**, born 1929; admitted to bar, 1954, District of Columbia; 1955, Pennsylvania; 1969, New York. *Education:* University of Pittsburgh (B.S., 1951); New York University School of Law (LL.B., 1954). ***COURSES: Commercial Law, Contracts, Credit Transactions, Lawyering, Legal Profession.

MARTIN F. GUGGENHEIM*, (Professor of Clinical Law)**, born 1946; admitted to bar, 1972, New York. *Education:* State University of New York at Buffalo (B.A., 1968); New York University School of Law (J.D., 1971). ***COURSES: Child Parent & State, Clinical Teaching, Criminal Procedure, Evidence, Federal Jurisdiction, Juvenile Law. ***Email:*** guggenh@turing.law.nyu.edu

HELEN HERSHKOFF*, (Professor of Law)**, born 1953; admitted to bar, 1979, New York. *Education:* Harvard University (A.B., 1973); Oxford University (B.A., 1975; M.A., 1979); Harvard University Law School (J.D., 1978). ***COURSES: Civil Procedure, Federal Courts. ***Email:*** hershkoff@turing.law.nyu.edu

RANDY A. HERTZ*, (Professor of Clinical Law)**, born 1955; admitted to bar, 1980, District of Columbia; 1986, New York. *Education:* Carleton College (B.A., 1976); Stanford University Law School (J.D., 1979). ***COURSES: Capital Punishment, Evidence, Litigation Planning, Expert Evidence, Juvenile Law, Litigation Skills. ***Email:*** hertzr@turing.law.nyu.edu

STEPHEN HOLMES*, (Professor of Law)**, born 1948. *Education:* Denison University (B.A., 1969); Yale University (Ph.D., 1976). ***COURSES: Comparative Constitutional Law, Origins of the U.S. Constitution, Russian Law. ***Email:*** stephen.holmes@nyu.edu

GRAHAM HUGHES*, (Professor of Law Emeritus)**, born 1928; admitted to bar, 1970, New York. *Education:* Cambridge University (B.A., 1948; M.A., 1949); University of Wales (LL.B., 1951); New York University School of Law (LL.M., 1960). ***COURSES: Criminal Law, Criminal Procedure, Jurisprudence, Torts. ***Email:*** hughesg@turing.law.nyu.edu

***JAMES B. JACOBS*, (Warren E. Burger Professor of Constitutional Law and Courts)**, born 1947; admitted to bar, 1973, Illinois; 1983,

(This Listing Continued)

NEW YORK UNIVERSITY SCHOOL OF LAW—Continued

New York. *Education:* Johns Hopkins University (B.A., 1969); University of Chicago Law School (J.D., 1973); University of Chicago (M.A., 1973; Ph.D., 1975). ***COURSES:*** Corruption, Criminal Law, Criminal Procedure, Drug Law & Policy, Gun Control, Prisons & Legal Culture, Sentencing, State & Local Government. ***Email:*** jacobsj@juris.law.nyu.edu

MARCEL KAHAN*, (Professor of Law)**, born 1962; admitted to bar, 1989, New York. *Education:* Brandeis University (B.A., 1984); Massachusetts Institute of Technology (M.S., 1988); Harvard University Law School (J.D., 1988). ***COURSES: Corporate Finance, Corporations, Securities Litigation. ***Email:*** kahanm@juris.law.nyu.edu

CHARLES L. KNAPP*, (Max E. Greenberg Professor of Contract Law Emeritus)**, born 1935; admitted to bar, 1961, New York. *Education:* Denison University (B.A., 1956); New York University Law School (J.D., 1960). ***COURSES: Commercial Law, Contracts Perspectives, Contracts.

LEWIS A. KORNHAUSER*, (Alfred B. & Gail Engelberg Professor of Law)**, born 1950; admitted to bar, 1976, California. *Education:* Brown University (B.A., and M.A., 1972); University of California - Berkeley School of Law (J.D., 1976); University of California at Berkeley (Ph.D., 1980). ***COURSES: Antitrust, Jurisprudence, Law & Economics, Law & Social Science. ***Email:*** lewis.kornhauser@nyu.edu

LARRY KRAMER*, (Samuel Tilden Professor of Law)**, born 1958. *Education:* Brown University (B.A., 1980); University of Chicago Law School (J.D., 1984). ***COURSES: Civil Procedure, Conflict of Laws, Constitutional Law, Evidence, Federal Courts, Legal History. ***Email:*** larry.kramer@nyu.edu

MATTIAS KUMM*, (Assistant Professor of Law)**, born 1967. *Education:* University of Kiel - Germany (1st and 2nd State Exam, 1994); Harvard University Law School (LL.M., 1996). ***COURSES: Comparative Constitutional Law, European Union Law, Philosophy of International Law.

SYLVIA A. LAW*, (Elizabeth K. Dollard Professor of Law, Medicine & Psychiatry)**, born 1942; admitted to bar, 1968, New York; 1970, Pennsylvania. *Education:* Antioch College (B.A., 1964); New York University School of Law (J.D., 1968). ***COURSES: Constitutional Law, Family Law, Federal Courts, Health Law, Torts, Welfare Law. ***Email:*** sylvialaw@aol.com

GERALD P. LOPEZ*, (Professor of Clinical Law)**, born 1948; admitted to bar, 1974, California. *Education:* University of Southern California (B.A., 1970); Harvard University Law School (J.D., 1974). ***COURSES: Clinical Teaching, Community Outreach Education & Obligation, Contracts, Local Economic Development.

ANDREAS F. LOWENFELD*, (Herbert Rubin & Rose Luttan Rubin Professor of International Law)**, born 1930; admitted to bar, 1955, New York. *Education:* Harvard University (A.B., 1951); Harvard University Law School (LL.M., 1955). ***COURSES: Air Law, Civil Procedure, Conflict of Laws, International Law, International Transactions. ***Email:*** al3@is.nyu.edu

HOLLY MAGUIGAN*, (Professor of Clinical Law)**, born 1945; admitted to bar, 1972, Pennsylvania; 1992, New York. *Education:* Swarthmore College (A.B., 1966); University of California at Berkeley (M.A., 1969); University of Pennsylvania Law School (J.D., 1972). ***COURSES: Clinical Teaching, Comparative Criminal Justice: Focus on Domestic Violence, Criminal Justice, Criminal Procedure. ***Email:*** holly.maguigan@nyu.edu

LAURIE L. MALMAN*, (Professor of Law)**, born 1946; admitted to bar, 1972, New York. *Education:* Vassar College (B.A., 1968); New York University School of Law (J.D., 1971). ***COURSES: Taxation, Federal. ***Email:*** malmanl@turing.law.nyu.edu

LYNN A. MARTELL*, (Professor of Clinical Law)**, born 1946; admitted to bar, 1973, New York. *Education:* City College of New York (B.A., 1969); George Washington University Law School (J.D., 1972). ***COURSES: Clinical Teaching.

GUY B. MAXFIELD*, (Professor of Law Emeritus)**, born 1933; admitted to bar, 1959, New York. *Education:* Augustana College (A.B., 1955); University of Michigan Law School (J.D., 1958). ***COURSES: Estate Planning, Estate & Gift Taxation, Federal Taxation.

PAUL MCDANIEL*, (Professor of Law)**, born 1936; admitted to bar, 1979, Massachusetts. *Education:* University of Oklahoma (B.A., 1958); Harvard University Law School (LL.B., 1961); Uppsala University - Sweden (D. of Law, 1995). ***COURSES: Corporate Taxation, Individual Income Taxation, International Taxation, Tax Policy. ***Email:*** mcdanielp@juris.law.nyu.edu

THEODOR MERON*, (Charles L. Denison Professor of Law)**, born 1930; admitted to bar, 1971, Israel; 1984, New York. *Education:* Hebrew University (M.J., 1954); Harvard University Law School (LL.M., 1955; S.J.D., 1957); Cambridge University (Dip. in Public Intl. Law, 1957). ***COURSES: Human Rights, Humanitarian Law, International Law, Law & Literature, Normative Shakespeare, War Crimes.

GEOFFREY P. MILLER*, (Professor of Law)**, born 1950; admitted to bar, 1979, District of Columbia. *Education:* Princeton University (A.B., 1973); Columbia University School of Law (J.D., 1978). ***COURSES: Banking Law, Constitutional Law, Corporate Finance, Corporations, Legal Profession/Legal Ethics. ***Email:*** gpm1@is4.nyu.edu

CHESTER L. MIRSKY*, (Professor of Clinical Law)**, born 1943; admitted to bar, 1968, New York. *Education:* Emory University (A.B., 1965); New York University School of Law (J.D., 1968). ***COURSES: Criminal Adjudication; Law, Courts & Social Problems, Criminal Procedure & Practice, Criminal Procedure, Federal Defender Clinic, Professional Responsibility in the Practice of Criminal Law. ***Email:*** mirskyc@juris.nyu.edu

NANCY MORAWETZ*, (Professor of Clinical Law)**, born 1954; admitted to bar, 1982, New York. *Education:* Princeton University (A.B., 1976); New York University School of Law (J.D., 1981). ***COURSES: Clinical Teaching, Immigration, Social Legislation. ***Email:*** morawetz@turing.law.nyu.edu

LIAM B. MURPHY*, (Professor of Law)**, born 1960. *Education:* University of Melbourne - Australia (B.A., 1982); University of Melbourne Law School - Australia (LL.B., 1984); Columbia University (M.Phil., 1990; Ph.D., 1991). ***COURSES: Contracts, Jurisprudence, Law's Authority, Topics in Legal Political & Moral Philosophy. ***Email:*** liam.murphy@nyu.edu

THOMAS NAGEL*, (Fiorello La Guardia Professor of Law)**, born 1937. *Education:* Cornell University (B.A., 1958); Oxford University (B.Phil., 1960); Harvard University (Ph.D., 1963). ***COURSES: Ethics, Legal Philosophy, Political Theory. ***Email:*** nagelt@turing.law.nyu.edu

WILLIAM E. NELSON*, (Edward Weinfeld Professor of Law)**, born 1940; admitted to bar, 1966, New York. *Education:* Hamilton College (A.B., 1962); New York University School of Law (LL.B., 1965); Harvard University (Ph.D., 1971). ***COURSES: Contracts, Federal Courts, Legal History, Real Property, Torts.

BURT NEUBORNE*, (John Norton Pomeroy Professor of Law)**, born 1941; admitted to bar, 1965, New York. *Education:* Cornell University (A.B., 1961); Harvard University Law School (LL.B., 1964). ***COURSES: Civil Procedure, Constitutional Law, Evidence, Federal Courts, The Law of Democracy. ***Email:*** neuborne@turing.law.nyu.edu

(This Listing Continued)

NEW YORK UNIVERSITY SCHOOL OF LAW—Continued

RONALD K. NOBLE, **(Professor of Law)**, born 1956; admitted to bar, 1983, New Jersey and Pennsylvania. *Education:* University of New Hampshire (B.A., 1979); Stanford University Law School (J.D., 1982). ***COURSES:*** Criminal Law, Evidence, Gun Control/Gun Rights. ***Email:*** rkn1@nyu.edu

JOHN L. PESCHEL, **(Professor of Law Emeritus)**, born 1935; admitted to bar, 1962, New York. *Education:* University of Minnesota (B.B.A., 1957); University of Michigan Law School (J.D., 1961). ***COURSES:*** Federal Taxation, Real Property, Trusts & Estates.

M. KATHLEEN PRICE, **(Professor of Law and Director of the Library)**, born 1942; admitted to bar, 1973, Illinois. *Education:* University of Florida (B.A., 1963); Florida State University (M.S., 1967); University of Illinois Law School (J.D., 1973). ***COURSES:*** Criminal Law, Law & Medicine, Torts. ***Email:*** pricek@turing.law.nyu.edu

NORMAN REDLICH, **(Dean Emeritus and Edward Weinfeld Professor of Law Emeritus)**, born 1925; admitted to bar, 1951, New York. *Education:* Williams College (B.A., 1947; LL.D., 1976); Yale University Law School (LL.B., 1950); New York University School of Law (LL.M., 1955); John Marshall College (LL.D., 1990). ***COURSES:*** Constitutional Law, Federal Taxation, Law and Medicine, Legal Profession, Local Government.

JOHN PHILLIP REID, **(Russell D. Niles Professor of Law)**, born 1930; admitted to bar, 1955, New Hampshire. *Education:* Georgetown University (B.S.S., 1952); Harvard University Law School (LL.B., 1955); University of New Hampshire (M.A., 1957); New York University School of Law (LL.M., 1960; J.S.D., 1962). ***COURSES:*** American Legal History, English Legal History, Legal History. ***Email:*** john.reid@nyu.edu

RICHARD L. REVESZ, **(Lawrence King Professor of Law)**, born 1958; admitted to bar, 1986, New York and District of Columbia. *Education:* Princeton University (B.S.E., 1979); Massachusetts Institute of Technology (M.S., 1980); Yale University Law School (J.D., 1983). ***COURSES:*** Administrative Law, Advanced Environmental Law, Environmental Law. ***Email:*** revesz@juris.law.nyu.edu

DAVID A.J. RICHARDS, **(Edwin D. Webb Professor of Law; Director, Program for the Study of Law, Philosophy & Social Theory)**, born 1944; admitted to bar, 1972, New York. *Education:* Harvard University (A.B., 1966); Oxford University (Ph.D., 1970); Harvard University Law School (J.D., 1971). ***COURSES:*** Comparative Law, Constitutional Law, Criminal Law, Jurisprudence.

LAURA SAGER, **(Clinical Professor of Law)**, born 1941; admitted to bar, 1969, California; 1973, New York. *Education:* Wellesley College (B.A., 1961); Harvard University (M.A., 1963); University of California at Los Angeles Law School (J.D., 1968). ***COURSES:*** Advocacy of Civil Claims, Civil Rights Clinic, Women's Rights Clinic. ***Email:*** lsager@juris.law.nyu.edu

LAWRENCE G. SAGER, **(Robert B. McKay Professor of Law)**, born 1941; admitted to bar, 1967, California. *Education:* Pomona College (A.B., 1963); Columbia University Law School (LL.B., 1966). ***COURSES:*** Constitutional Law, Constitutional Theory, Legal Philosophy. ***Email:*** sagerl@turing.law.nyu.edu

DEBORAH H. SCHENK, **(Ronald and Marilyn N. Grossman Professor of Taxation)**, born 1947; admitted to bar, 1973, New York. *Education:* Cornell University (B.A., 1969); Columbia University Law School (J.D., 1972); New York University School of Law (LL.M., 1976). ***COURSES:*** Federal Taxation, Legal Profession. ***Email:*** schenk@is3.nyu.edu

MICHAEL H. SCHILL, **(Professor of Law and Urban Planning)**, born 1958; admitted to bar, 1985, New York. *Education:* Princeton University (A.B., 1980); Yale University Law School (J.D., 1984). ***COURSES:*** Land Use Planning, Property, Real Estate Transactions. ***Email:*** schillm@turing.law.nyu.edu

LEO L. SCHMOLKA, **(Professor of Law)**, born 1939; admitted to bar, 1964, New York. *Education:* Harvard University Law School (LL.B., 1963); New York University School of Law (LL.M., 1970). ***COURSES:*** Decedent's Estates, Trusts & Fiduciaries, Taxation.

MICHAEL SCHWIND, **(Professor of Law Emeritus)**, born 1924; admitted to bar, 1949, Ecuador; 1957, New York. *Education:* Central University - Ecuador (Dr. Jur., 1949); New York University School of Law (LL.M., 1953; LL.B., 1957). ***COURSES:*** Comparative Law, Conflict of Laws, International Decedent Estate Law.

HELEN S. SCOTT, **(Professor of Law)**, born 1949; admitted to bar, 1978, District of Columbia and New York. *Education:* Barnard College (B.A., 1970); Columbia University Law School (J.D., 1977). ***COURSES:*** Business Transactions Planning, Contracts, Corporations, Entrepreneurial Finance, Securities Regulation. ***Email:*** scotth@turing.law.nyu.edu

DANIEL N. SHAVIRO, **(Professor of Law)**, born 1957; admitted to bar, 1981, District of Columbia. *Education:* Princeton University (A.B., 1978); Yale University Law School (J.D., 1981). ***COURSES:*** Federal Taxation, Tax Policy Colloquium, Tax Policy. ***Email:*** shavirod@turing.law.nyu.edu

STANLEY SIEGEL, **(Professor of Law)**, born 1941; admitted to bar, 1963, New York; 1964, District of Columbia; 1976, California. *Education:* New York University (B.S., 1960); Harvard University Law School (J.D., 1963). ***COURSES:*** Accounting, Agency & Partnership, Business Planning, Corporate Finance, Corporations, Federal Taxation. ***Email:*** siegals@turing.law.nyu.edu

LINDA J. SILBERMAN, **(Martin Lipton Professor of Law)**, born 1944; admitted to bar, 1969, Illinois. *Education:* University of Michigan (B.A., 1965); University of Michigan Law School (J.D., 1968). ***COURSES:*** Civil Procedure, Conflict of Laws, Family Law, International Litigation.

GEORGE H. SORTER, **(Prof. of Law; Vincent C. Ross Prof. of Accounting, Leonard N. Stern School of Business, University Professor)**, born 1927. *Education:* University of Chicago (Ph.B., 1953; M.B.A., 1955; Ph.D., 1963). ***COURSES:*** Accounting, Analysis of Financial Data for Legal Issues, Corporate Finance. ***Email:*** gsorter@stern.nyu.edu

JOHN P. STEINES, JR., **(Professor of Law)**, born 1948; admitted to bar, 1974, Michigan; 1981, New York. *Education:* General Motors Institute (B.I.E., 1971); Ohio State University Law School (J.D., 1974); New York University School of Law (LL.M., 1978). ***COURSES:*** Federal Taxation. ***Email:*** john.steines@nyu.edu

BRYAN A. STEVENSON, **(Assistant Professor of Clinical Law)**, born 1959; admitted to bar, 1985, Georgia; 1987, Alabama. *Education:* Harvard University (M.P.P., 1985); Harvard University Law School (J.D., 1985); Georgetown University (S.J.D., 1997). ***COURSES:*** Capital Punishment Law & Litigation, Post Conviction Remedies, Race Poverty & Criminal Justice. ***Email:*** ejibryan@aol.com

RICHARD B. STEWART, **(Emily Kempin Professor of Law)**, born 1940; admitted to bar, 1967, District of Columbia. *Education:* Yale University (B.A., 1961); Oxford University (M.A., 1963); Harvard University Law School (LL.B., 1966); Erasmus University - Rotterdam (Dr., 1994). ***COURSES:*** Administrative Law, Environmental Law, International Environmental Law, Torts. ***Email:*** rbs1@1s4.nyu.edu

(This Listing Continued)

NEW YORK UNIVERSITY SCHOOL OF LAW—Continued

HARRY I. SUBIN*, (Professor of Law Emeritus)**, born 1935; admitted to bar, 1961, New York; 1963, District of Columbia. *Education:* Oberlin College (B.A., 1957); Yale University Law School (LL.B., 1960). ***COURSES: Criminal Law Clinic, Criminal Law, Criminal Procedure, Professional Responsibility, Prosecution Clinic, Trial Advocacy. ***Email:*** subin@turing.law.nyu.edu

KIM A. TAYLOR-THOMPSON*, (Professor of Clinical law)**, born 1955; admitted to bar, 1981, District of Columbia. *Education:* Brown University (A.B., 1977); Yale University Law School (J.D., 1980). ***COURSES: Advanced Issues in Criminal Defense & Prosecution, Community Defender Clinic, Criminal Law, Evidence, Litigation & Planning, Juvenile Rights Clinic. ***Email:*** thompsok@juris.law.nyu.edu

ANTHONY C. THOMPSON*, (Professor of Clinical Law)**, born 1960; admitted to bar, 1986, California; 1996, District of Columbia; 1997, New York. *Education:* Northwestern University (B.S., 1982); Harvard University Law School (J.D., 1985). ***COURSES: Civil Litigation, Criminal Defense Clinic, Prosecution Clinic. ***Email:*** thompson@turing.law.nyu.edu

FRANK K. UPHAM*, (Professor of Law)**, born 1945; admitted to bar, 1974, Massachusetts. *Education:* Princeton University (A.B., 1967); Harvard University Law School (J.D., 1974). ***COURSES: Administrative Law, Japanese Law, Land Use Housing & Community Development in New York City, Property. ***Email:*** frank.upham@nyu.edu

HOWARD P. VENABLE JR.*, (Associate Professor of Law)**, born 1959. *Education:* Harvard University (A.B., 1980; A.M., 1980); Yale University Law School (J.D., 1990). ***COURSES: Estates & Trusts, Property.

MICHAEL WISHNIE*, (Associate Professor of Clinical Law)**, born 1966; admitted to bar, 1994, New York. *Education:* Yale University (B.A., 1987); Yale University Law School (J.D., 1993). ***COURSES: Clinical Teaching. ***Email:*** michael.wishnie@nyu.edu

DIANE L. ZIMMERMAN*, (Professor of Law)**, born 1941; admitted to bar, 1977, New York. *Education:* Beaver College (B.A., 1963); Columbia University Law School (J.D., 1976). ***COURSES: Constitutional Law, Patents Copyrights Trademarks, Real Property, Torts. ***Email:*** zimmermd@juris.law.nyu.edu

NORTH CAROLINA CENTRAL UNIVERSITY SCHOOL OF LAW

1512 SOUTH ALSTON AVENUE
DURHAM, NORTH CAROLINA 27707

NORTHEASTERN UNIVERSITY SCHOOL OF LAW

400 HUNTINGTON AVENUE
BOSTON, MASSACHUSETTS 02115
Telephone: (617) 373-5149
Fax: (617) 373-8793
http://www.slaw.neu.edu

ABA Approved Since 1969

Northeastern University School of Law offers students a unique program combining rigorous academic study with practical legal work experience. The law school is accredited by the ABA and is a member of AALS.

Northeastern's unique approach to legal education attracts a diverse and talented student body. Admission to the School of Law is highly competitive. More than 2,000 applicants from across the nation and world compete for 200 seats in the first-year class. Entering students come from all parts of the country, with more than 121 undergraduate schools and 33 states currently represented. Women have comprised at least half of the student body since 1972; currently women comprise 57% of the student population; students of color constitute approximately 26% of the entering class. The most recent entering class had a median age of 24. Forty-four percent had worked for one to three years between undergraduate school and law school and eleven percent entered law school with at least six years of work experience, in a variety of fields. This diverse student body appeals to employers seeking to enhance their own diversity.

Northeastern graduates are consistently successful in obtaining legal employment. Graduates of the School of Law are employed throughout the United States and abroad with private firms, government agencies, legal services and public defender organizations, the judiciary, labor unions and corporate law departments, and are teaching at distinguished law schools.

Northeastern University School of Law and its graduates are particularly committed to public service. Each year, a significant number of graduates from the School of Law begin their legal careers as judicial clerks. Traditionally, Northeastern graduates have entered public interest law positions at a rate five to six times that of the national average for graduates of all law schools. Many of its graduates are awarded fellowships enabling them to pursue careers in public interest law. Graduates of the law school have frequently been recipients of various fellowships, including: Skadden, NAPIL, Soros, Georgetown, Pillsbury, Madison and echoing green.

Participation in the school's unique and extraordinarily successful Cooperative Legal Education ("co-op") Program is an integral part of the academic regimen as well as a requirement for graduation. Students complete a traditional first year of academic study; then, for the remaining two years, they alternate every three months between attending classes and working as full-time legal interns. Co-op employment spans virtually every area of practice in more than 700 settings nationwide, including private firms (small and large), legal service and public defender organizations, judicial clerkships (state and federal), government agencies, corporations, unions and advocacy groups.

Through co-op, students develop practical skills through hands-on experience, gain wide perspectives on the legal profession and the practice of law, and experience firsthand the diversity of opportunities, challenges and satisfactions that are available to them as lawyers. Northeastern believes that the combination of its academic and co-op program produces enthusiastic, realistic and well-trained attorneys who are assets to the profession.

The limited enrollment of approximately 200 students in each entering class encourages individual recognition and participation, as well as

(This Listing Continued)

NORTHEASTERN UNIVERSITY SCHOOL OF LAW —Continued

ensuring access to the 30 full-time faculty members. A distinguished faculty provides students with a thorough grounding in legal doctrine, legal analysis and practical skills, coupled with an exposure to a variety of perspectives. Northeastern's wide range of course offerings introduces students to areas such as environmental law, intellectual property, bioethics, international law, comparative law, legislation, antitrust and domestic violence.

All students must fulfill a public interest requirement as a condition of graduation. Public interest under this rule is defined as employment or service with a government agency; a legal aid, legal services, public defender, victim advocate or similar agency; an organization or attorney advocating law reform or performing pro bono legal representation; or any placement the dominant characteristic of which is service to under-represented groups. Judicial internships and private firms operated for profit are not included in this definition.

The School of Law has no alphabetic or numeric grading system, class ranking or law review competition. Students receive narrative evaluations of their work in each academic course; cooperative employers also submit written appraisals of professional performance which become a part of each student's official transcript. This system, unlike traditional grading systems, helps employers thoroughly evaluate candidates by providing for every student an extensive law school record that indicates clearly the quality of his or her performance.

The Law Library, located on five floors in the Knowles Law Center, includes reserve and reference collections, reading rooms, study carrels and conference rooms for student use. Four computer rooms are available for LEXIS and WESTLAW computerized legal research and support PC-compatible software. The law library collection includes more than 297,000 volumes and more than 3,200 serial titles.

The School of Law has effectively united theory, practice, ethics and social justice, resulting in a challenging, dynamic and innovative method of legal education.

Dean: Roger Abrams (617) 373-3307
Associate Dean: Diane L. Tsoulas (617) 373-3307
Associate Dean of Academic Affairs: Mary E. O'Connell (617) 373-3918
Assistant Dean of Student and Academic Affairs: Bettye C. Freeman (617) 373-5148
Assistant Dean & Director of Admissions: M.J. Knoll (617) 373-2395
Assistant Dean & Cooperative Legal Education Director: Alice D. Alexander (617) 373-3002
Associate Professor & Director of Information Services: Filippa Marullo Anzalone (617) 373-3394
Assistant Dean & Director of Career Services: Randi Friedman (617) 373-3707
Development and Alumni/ae Affairs Director: Cornell L. Stinson (617) 373-3269
Communications Director: Deborah E. Feldman (617) 373-3288
Director of Fiscal Affairs and Administration: Janis Galligan (617) 373-4933
Associate Director of Financial Aid: Lori A. Moore (617) 373-2390

FULL TIME FACULTY

***ROGER I. ABRAMS*, (Dean and Professor of Law)**, *Education:* Cornell (B.A., *cum laude*, 1967); Harvard Law School (J.D., *cum laude*, 1970).

LIBBY S. ADLER*, (Assistant Professor)**, born Rochester, New York, September 11, 1967; admitted to bar, 1994, Massachusetts. *Education:* University of Michigan (A.B., 1989); Northeastern University (J.D., 1994); Harvard Law School (LL.M., 1998). ***COURSES: Constitutional Law, Administrative Law. ***Email:*** l.adler@nunet.neu.edu

FILIPPA MARULLO ANZALONE*, (Associate Professor & Director, Law Library)**, born Massachusetts, September 27, 1953; admitted to bar, 1985, Massachusetts. *Education:* Smith College (A.B., 1975); Simmons College (S.M., 1977); Suffolk University Law School (J.D., 1985). ***COURSES: Advanced Legal Research. ***Email:*** fanzalone@nunet.neu.edu

BROOK K. BAKER*, (Professor of Law)**, born Melrose, Massachusetts, February 23, 1947; admitted to bar, 1977, Massachusetts. *Education:* Harvard University (B.A., 1969); Northeastern University (J.D., 1976). ***COURSES: Legal Practice, Negotiation, Analytical Skills Workshop for first-year students. ***Email:*** bbaker@nunet.neu.edu

NATHANIEL BERMAN*, (Professor of Law)**, born New York, New York, November 2, 1957; admitted to bar, 1987, Massachusetts. *Education:* Yale University (B.A., 1980); Harvard University (J.D., 1985). ***COURSES: International Law, Conflicts of Law, European Community Law, Human Rights Systems. ***Email:*** nberman@nunet.neu.edu

LEE P. BRECKENRIDGE*, (Professor of Law)**, born Rochester, New York, November 10, 1951; admitted to bar, 1976, New Jersey; 1978, Tennessee; 1983, Massachusetts. *Education:* Yale University (B.A., 1973); Harvard University (J.D., 1976). ***COURSES: Environmental Law, Land Use Planning, Water & Wetlands. ***Email:*** lbrecken@nunet.neu.edu

CLARE DALTON*, (Matthews Distinguished Professor of Law & Executive Director, Domestic Violence Institute)**, born Kent, England, November 20, 1950; admitted to bar, 1975, District of Columbia. *Education:* Somerville College, Oxford University (B.A., Hon., 1971); Harvard University (LL.M., 1973). ***COURSES: Torts, Modern Legal, Domestic Violence, Battered Women and the Law. ***Email:*** cdalton@nunet.neu.edu

RICHARD A. DAYNARD*, (Professor of Law)**, born New York, New York, July 19, 1943; admitted to bar, 1967, New York. *Education:* Columbia University (B.A., 1964; M.A., 1970); Harvard University (J.D., 1967); Massachusetts Institute of Technology (Ph.D., 1980). ***COURSES: Products Liability, Toxic Torts, Administrative Law, Law, Policy and Society, Strategic Litigation. ***Email:*** rdaynard@nunet.neu.edu

STACEY L. DOGAN*, (Assistant Professor)**, born Woonsocket, Rhode Island, February 3, 1968; admitted to bar, 1992, California; 1994, District of Columbia. *Education:* Massachusetts Institute of Technology (B.S., 1988); Harvard Law School (J.D., 1992). ***COURSES: Intellectual Property, Computer Law, Antitrust. ***Email:*** sdogan@nunet.neu.edu

MELINDA F. DREW*, (Lecturer and Director, Academic Success Program)**, born Connecticut, August 2, 1946; admitted to bar, 1987, Massachusetts. *Education:* St Joseph's College (B.S., 1974); Boston University (Ed.M., 1978); Northeastern University (J.D., 1987). ***COURSES: Legal Practice, Legal Reasoning. ***Email:*** mdrew@nunet.neu.edu

***PETER D. ENRICH*, (Professor of Law)**, born New York, New York, June 18, 1950; admitted to bar, 1983, Massachusetts. *Education:* Yale

(This Listing Continued)

NORTHEASTERN UNIVERSITY SCHOOL OF LAW —Continued

University (A.B., 1972); Princeton Graduate School (A.B.D., 1977); Harvard University (J.D., 1983). ***COURSES:*** State and Local Tax, State and Local Government, Contracts. ***Email:*** penrich@nunet.neu.edu

JORGE LUIS ESQUIROL*, (Associate Professor of Law)**, born Havana, Cuba, November 19, 1964; admitted to bar, 1992, New York. *Education:* Georgetown University (B.S.B.A., 1986); Harvard Law School (J.D., 1989; S.J.D., Candidate). ***COURSES: Corporations, Comparative Law, International Business Transactions, Law & Politics in Latin America, CL: Payment Systems. ***Email:*** jesquirol@nunet.neu.edu

JOHN G.S. FLYM*, (Professor of Law)**, born Algeria, August 5, 1936; admitted to bar, 1964, Colorado; 1966, Massachusetts. *Education:* Columbia University (B.S., 1961); Harvard University (LL.B., 1964). ***COURSES: Criminal Advocacy, Professional Responsibility, Urban Violence, Post Conviction Remedies. ***Email:*** jflym@nunet.neu.edu

DANIEL GIVELBER*, (Professor of Law)**, born Cleveland, Ohio, February 9, 1940; admitted to bar, 1965, New York; 1967, District of Columbia; 1973, Massachusetts. *Education:* Harvard University (B.A., 1961; J.D., 1964). ***COURSES: Torts, Criminal Law, Certiorari Clinic, Evidence. ***Email:*** dgivelber@nunet.neu.edu

JAMES R. HACKNEY, JR.*, (Professor of Law)**, born West Palm Beach, Florida, September 9, 1964; admitted to bar, 1989, California. *Education:* University of Southern California (A.B., 1986); Yale University (J.D.,1989). ***COURSES: Law and Political Economy, Banking Law, Torts, Corporate Finance. ***Email:*** jhackney@nunet.neu.edu

WALLACE E. HOLOHAN*, (Senior Clinical Specialist and Director, Prisoners' Rights Clinic)**, born Massachusetts, September 30, 1944. *Education:* Fitchburg State College (B.S., 1976); Bentley College (Paralegal, 1977). ***COURSES: Prisoners' Rights Clinic, Poverty Law. ***Email:*** wholohan@nunet.neu.edu

LOIS H. KANTER*, (Senior Clinical Specialist and Director, Domestic Violence Institute)**, born New York, September 18, 1946; admitted to bar, 1977, Massachusetts. *Education:* Radcliffe College (B.A., 1968); Harvard University (J.D., 1976). ***COURSES: Domestic Violence Clinic, Family Law Clinic, Poverty Law. ***Email:*** lkanter@nunet.neu.edu

KARL E. KLARE*, (Matthews Distinguished Professor of Law)**, born New York, New York, January 8, 1947; admitted to bar, 1975, Massachusetts. *Education:* Columbia University (B.A., 1967); Yale University (M.A., 1968); Harvard University (J.D., 1975). ***COURSES: Contracts, Labor Law, Employment Law, Legal Theory. ***Email:*** klare@nunet.neu.edu

HOPE LEWIS*, (Professor of Law)**, born Brooklyn, New York, May 14, 1962; admitted to bar, 1987, New York; 1989, District of Columbia. *Education:* Harvard University (A.B., cum laude, 1983; J.D., 1986). ***COURSES: Securities Regulation, Gender & International Human Rights. ***Email:*** hlewis@nunet.neu.edu

MICHAEL MELTSNER*, (Matthews Distinguished Professor of Law)**, born New York, New York; admitted to bar, 1961, New York; 1983, Massachusetts. *Education:* Oberlin College (B.A., 1957); Yale University (LL.B., 1960). ***COURSES: Criminal Law and Procedure, Constitutional Law, Leadership and the Profession, Constitutional Litigation, Perspectives on Lawyering, Legal Profession: Challenges of the 21st Century. ***Email:*** mmeltsner@nunet.neu.edu

MARY E. O'CONNELL*, (Associate Dean of Academic Affairs & Professor of Law)**, born Clinton, Massachusetts, October 13, 1948; admitted to bar, 1975, Massachusetts. *Education:* Brandeis University (A.B., 1970); Northeastern University (J.D., 1975). ***COURSES: Contracts, Family Law, Children, Parents & the State. ***Email:*** Oconnell@nunet.neu.edu

WENDY E. PARMET*, (Professor of Law)**, born New York, New York, November 12, 1957; admitted to bar, 1982, Massachusetts. *Education:* Cornell University (B.A., 1979); Harvard University (J.D., 1982). ***COURSES: Constitutional Law, Health Law, Bioethics, Federal Courts, Disability Law. ***Email:*** wparmet@nunet.neu.edu

DAVID M. PHILLIPS*, (Professor of Law)**, born Trenton, New Jersey, May 19, 1943; admitted to bar, 1967, Illinois; 1971, New York; 1980, Massachusetts. *Education:* Brandeis University (B.A., 1964); Columbia University (J.D., 1967). ***COURSES: Corporate Law, Commercial Law, Secured Transactions. ***Email:*** dphillips@nunet.neu.edu

DEBORAH A. RAMIREZ*, (Professor of Law)**, born Chicago, Illinois; admitted to bar, 1981, Massachusetts. *Education:* Northwestern University (B.A., 1977); Harvard University (J.D., 1981). ***COURSES: Criminal Justice, Juries, Professional Responsibility, Race, Gender, Juries & Justice, Advanced Criminal Procedure. ***Email:*** dramirez@nunet.neu.edu

JAMES V. ROWAN*, (Professor of Law, Director of Clinical Education)**, born Brooklyn, New York, July 4, 1943; admitted to bar, 1970, North Carolina. *Education:* Georgetown University (A.B., 1967); Duke University (J.D., 1970; LL.M., 1978). ***COURSES: Clinical Education, Welfare Law, Professional Responsibility, Poverty Law. ***Email:*** jrowan@nunet.neu.edu

JANE L. SCARBOROUGH*, (Associate Professor of Law)**, born Houston, Texas, February 26, 1942; admitted to bar, 1986, New York. *Education:* Rice University (B.A., 1964); Purdue University (M.A., 1967); Rice University (Ph.D., 1972); Northeastern University (J.D., 1985). ***COURSES: Constitutional Law, Professional Responsibility, Sexual Orientation and the Law, Leadership and the Profession. ***Email:*** jscarborough@nunet.neu.edu

DANIEL C. SCHAFFER*, (Professor of Law)**, born Brooklyn, New York, June 7, 1938; admitted to bar, 1964, New York. *Education:* Harvard University (A.B., 1959; LL.B., 1962); London School of Economics (1963). ***COURSES: Federal Income Tax, Corporate Tax, Basic Income Taxation, Non-profit Organizations, Advanced Income Taxation. ***Email:*** dschaffer@nunet.neu.edu

STEPHEN N. SUBRIN*, (Professor of Law)**, born Akron, Ohio, September 8, 1936; admitted to bar, 1963, Massachusetts. *Education:* Harvard University (B.A., 1958; LL.B., 1963). ***COURSES: Civil Procedure, Complex Litigation, Federal Courts. ***Email:*** ssubrin@nunet.neu.edu

LUCY A. WILLIAMS*, (Professor of Law)**, born Fort Worth, Texas, January 4, 1948; admitted to bar, 1974, Illinois. *Education:* Baylor University (B.A., 1969); University of Chicago (J.D., 1974). ***COURSES: Federal Courts, Welfare Law. ***Email:*** lwilliams@nunet.neu.edu

MARGARET Y.K. WOO*, (Professor of Law)**, born Hong Kong, March 4, 1957; admitted to bar, 1983, Massachusetts; 1985, District of Columbia. *Education:* Brown University (B.A., 1979); New York University (J.D., 1983); Georgetown University (LL.M., 1989). ***COURSES: Comparative Law, Civil Procedure. ***Email:*** mwoo@nunet.neu.edu

NORTHERN ILLINOIS UNIVERSITY COLLEGE OF LAW

SWEN PARSON HALL
DEKALB, ILLINOIS 60115
Telephone: (815) 753-1067
Fax: (815) 753-8552
www.niu.edu/col

ABA Approved Since 1978.

The Northern Illinois University College of Law marked its twenty fifth year in 1999. It was established at Lewis University in Glen Ellyn, Illinois in 1974, was acquired by Northern Illinois University in 1979 by authorization of the Illinois General Assembly, and was moved to NIU's DeKalb, Illinois campus in 1982. In that year, the College of Law was fully accredited by the American Bar Association and became a member of the Association of American Law Schools in 1985.

The College of Law is the only public law school in the Northern tier of Illinois and is within easy driving distance of the major population centers of Chicago, its rapidly growing western suburbs, and Rockford. It operates a full-time day program with a part-time option and maintains an enrollment of approximately 300 students. In addition to the J.D. degree, a joint J.D.-M.B.A. degree is offered in conjunction with the College of Business. A foreign summer program on Comparative and European Union Law has been established in Agen, France. Summer school courses are also offered at the NIU Naperville, IL facility.

A highly qualified and diverse student body and faculty is a source of great pride to NIU's young law school. The 2001 entering class had an enrollment of 111, selected from an applicant pool of 897. The median undergraduate G.P.A. of this class is 3.09 and the median LSAT is 153. Seventy-Five percent of the class are Illinois residents, 46% are women, and 21% are students of color. For the 2001/02 academic year, the College of Law had a full-time, tenure-track faculty of 18, excluding the dean, associate dean, and the director of the law library. Thirty three percent of the tenure-track faculty are of color, and 39% are women.

The College of Law is committed to providing students with numerous opportunities to develop law practice skills. Courses in Lawyering Skills, Trial Advocacy and Mediation Practice are offered every semester. Courses with drafting components such as Estate Planning, Business Planning and a variety of seminars are regularly offered. Additionally the law school has a live client clinic located in Rockford, IL across the street from the courthouse. Clinic students represent clients under the supervision of an attorney in a range of matters which allows them to apply the legal and professional responsibility principles learned in class to real life settings. Finally, the law school has numerous externship opportunities for students wherein they can gain practice experience working for judges and other public officials.

The College of Law prides itself on its strong co-curricular programs. The Law Review publishes three issues each year and has sponsored symposia on Dispute Resolution, Death Penalty Litigation, Minority Recruitment and Retention, Land Use and Environmental law. The NIU College of Law has sponsored programs on International Trade, Agricultural Law, Legal and Judicial Ethics, Medical Negligence Trials and Collective Bargaining in recent years. The College also participates in several regional and national moot court, trial advocacy, client counseling and negotiation competitions. In 1993 and 1996, the NIU team won the regional ABA Client Counseling Competition and placed second in 1993 at the national level. In 1999 the NIU team won the Regional Negotiation Competition and reached the semi-finals in the National Regional Moot Court Competition. In 2000 the NIU team reached the finals in the Illinois State Bar Association Moot Court Competition. In addition to these external programs, there is a strong intramural moot court program in which approximately half of the second year class participated in 2001.

NIU College of Law's David C. Shapiro Memorial Law Library contains over 216,000 volumes and volume equivalents, including the laws, court reports, and other primary source materials for the federal government and all 50 states; regulations and selected agency government documents, and most major legal treatises, texts and looseleaf services. It also provides access to LEXIS and WESTLAW, computerized full-text on-line services for legal and law-related information, and participates in an inter-library loan system that provides access for its users to materials located in other law libraries in the region. In addition to providing support for law students, faculty, and the larger university community, the law library is an important resource for the legal community in northern Illinois.

The NIU College of Law has developed a national reputation for the commitment of its students and graduates to public service and public interest law. Law students volunteer thousands of hours each year through the Pro Bono Students America network of opportunities. The College of Law received the National School Award from Pro Bono Students America in 1998.

Dean: Leroy Pernell (815) 753-1067
Admissions: Judith Malen (815) 753-8595
Financial Aid: Judith Malen (815) 753-9485
Placement: Greg Anderson (815) 753-0589
Alumni Events: Carol Jambor-Smith (815) 753-9655

FULL TIME FACULTY

LEROY PERNELL*, (Dean)**, born Brooklyn, New York, November 16, 1949; admitted to bar, 1974, Ohio. *Education:* Franklin and Marshall (B.A., 1971); Ohio State University (J.D., 1974). ***COURSES: Criminal Procedure, Juvenile Law, Torts, Product Liability, Juvenile and Criminal Clinic, Trial Practice, Mental Health, Racism and Law Seminar. ***Email:*** lpernell@niu.edu

JAMES J. ALFINI*, (Professor)**, born Yonkers, New York, October 12, 1943; admitted to bar, 1973, New York; 1976, Illinois. *Education:* Columbia College (A.B., 1965); Northwestern University (J.D., 1972). ***COURSES: Mediation Theory and Practice, Constitutional Law, Professional Responsibility, Public Lands and Natural Resources. ***Email:*** jalfini@niu.edu

ELVIA R. ARRIOLA*, (Associate Professor)**, born Los Angeles, California, March 2, 1951; admitted to bar, 1985, New York; 1996, Texas. *Education:* California State University (B.A., 1980); University of California Berkeley (J.D., 1983); New York University (M.A., 1991). ***COURSES: Gender and Law, Domestic Abuse Clinic, Family Law, Latino Studies. ***Email:*** earriola@niu.edu

***JOHN R. AUSTIN*, (Director, Law Library and Associate**

(This Listing Continued)

NORTHERN ILLINOIS UNIVERSITY COLLEGE OF LAW —Continued

Professor), born New York, New York, November 17, 1951; admitted to bar, 1983, Illinois. *Education:* Queens College (B.A., 1973); Indiana University (M.L.S., 1976); DePaul University (J.D., 1983). ***COURSES:*** Legal Research. ***Email:*** jaustin@niu.edu

SUSAN M. BOLAND,* (Research and Instructional Services Librarian and Assistant Professor)**, born Des Moines, Iowa; admitted to bar, 1997, Illinois. *Education:* Monmouth College (B.A., 1992); Northern Illinois University College of Law (J.D., 1997). ***COURSES: Basic Legal Research. ***Email:*** sboland@niv.edu

JEFFREY M. BROWN,* (Assistant Professor)**, admitted to bar, 1991, Georgia. *Education:* Davidson College (B.A., 1986); University of Michigan Law School (J.D., 1991). ***COURSES: International Law Commercial Paper, Law & Emerging Democracies.

THERESE A. CLARKE,* (Instructional Services/Reference Librarian & Assistant Professor)**, born Illinois, 1968; admitted to bar, 1993, Illinois. *Education:* Loyola University (B.B.A., 1989); Dominican University (M.L.S., 1997); The John Marshall Law School (J.D., 1993). ***COURSES: Legal Research.

KATHLEEN LOUISE COLES,* (Assistant Professor)**, born Portland, Oregon, January 10, 1949; admitted to bar, 1978, New York; 1982, Washington, D.C.. *Education:* College of William & Mary (B.A., 1971); Oxford University, Somerville College (M.A., 1988); University of Chicago Law School (J.D., 1977). ***COURSES: Business Organizations, Agency, Commercial Law, Securities Regulation. ***Email:*** kcoles@niu.edu

CHARLES J. CONDON,* (Computer Services/Reference Librarian and Assistant Professor)**, born St. Louis, Missouri, October 17, 1947; admitted to bar, 1980, Florida; 1981, Illinois. *Education:* Florida Atlantic University (B.A., 1975); University of Southern Mississippi (M.L.S., 1994); Nova Southeastern University (J.D., 1980); University of Arkansas (L.L.M., 1993). ***Email: ccondon@niu.edu

MARK W. CORDES,* (Professor)**, born Portland, Oregon, December 20, 1950; admitted to bar, 1980, Oregon. *Education:* Portland State University (B.S., 1975); Willamette University (J.D., 1980); Stanford University (J.S.M., 1983). ***COURSES: Property, Land Use, Environmental Law, Real Estate Transactions. ***Email:*** mcordes@niu.edu

DAVID B. GAEBLER,* (Associate Professor)**, born Lowell, Massachusetts, April 11, 1948; admitted to bar, 1973, Wisconsin. *Education:* Harvard University (A.B., 1970); University of Wisconsin (J.D., 1973). ***COURSES: Contracts, Sales, Secured Transactions. ***Email:*** dgaebler@niu.edu

LEONA S. GREEN,* (Associate Professor)**, born Pine Bluff, Arkansas, November 9, 1951; admitted to bar, 1976, Illinois. *Education:* Northwestern University (B.A., 1973; J.D., 1976). ***COURSES: State and Local Government, Alternative Dispute Resolution, Employment Discrimination. ***Email:*** lgreen@niu.edu

SUSAN S. KUO,* (Assistant Professor)**, born Kingsport, Tennessee, May 3, 1969; admitted to bar, 1995, Tennessee; 1997, District of Columbia, Maryland, Kentucky. *Education:* Duke University (A.B., 1991); Vanderbilt University School of Law (J.D., 1994). ***COURSES: Conflict of Laws, Criminal Law, Federal Courts, Race and Law. ***Email:*** sskuo@niu.edu

GUADALUPE T. LUNA,* (Associate Professor)**, born Dallas, Texas, February 23, 1949; admitted to bar, 1987, Minnesota. *Education:* University of Minnesota (B.A., 1981; J.D., 1985). ***COURSES: Immigration Law, Agricultural Law, Voting Rights, Property. ***Email:*** gluna@niu.edu

LEONARD B. MANDELL,* (Assistant Dean)**, born Willimantic, Connecticut, December 6, 1950; admitted to bar, 1976, Massachusetts; 1983, Illinois; 1989, Florida. *Education:* University of Connecticut (B.A., 1972); Boston College Law School (J.D., 1976). ***COURSES: Appellate Advocacy, Criminal Externship, Appellate Defender Clinic. ***Email:*** lmandell@niu.edu

MALCOLM L. MORRIS,* (Professor)**, born New York, N.Y., December 21, 1948; admitted to bar, 1972, New York; 1973, Illinois. *Education:* Cornell University (B.S., 1969); State University of New York at Buffalo (J.D., 1972); Northwestern University (LL.M., 1977). ***COURSES: Taxation (Federal), Property, Trusts and Estates. ***Email:*** mlmorris@niu.edu

ADELE M. MORRISON,* (Assistant Professor)**, born Detroit, Michigan; admitted to bar, 1999, Wisconsin. *Education:* San Francisco State University (B.A., 1993); Stanford Law School (J.D., 1996); University of Wisconsin Law School (LL.M., 2001). ***COURSES: Family Law, Poverty Law, Domestic Violence. ***Email:*** amorrison@niu.edu

JEFFREY A. PARNESS,* (Professor)**, born Providence, Rhode Island, August 8, 1948; admitted to bar, 1975, Illinois. *Education:* Colby College (B.A., 1970); University of Chicago (J.D., 1974). ***COURSES: Civil Procedure, Evidence, Administrative Law, Advanced Civil Procedure, Illinois Civil Practice, Conflict of Laws, Federal Courts, Privacy. ***Email:*** jparness@niu.edu

DANIEL S. REYNOLDS,* (Associate Dean)**, born Duluth, Minnesota, August 5, 1946; admitted to bar, 1975, Nebraska. *Education:* University of Nebraska (A.B., 1968); Creighton University (J.D., 1975). ***COURSES: Contracts, Corporations, Securities Regulation, Agency/Partnership, Legal Profession. ***Email:*** danreynolds@niu.edu

LAWRENCE SCHLAM,* (Professor)**, born New York, N.Y., October 24, 1942; admitted to bar, 1968, Illinois. *Education:* City College of New York (B.B.A., 1964); New York University (J.D., 1967). ***COURSES: Constitutional Law, Criminal Law, Juvenile Law, State Constitutional Law, Civil Rights Litigation. ***Email:*** lschlam@niu.edu

LORRAINE A. SCHMALL,* (Professor)**, born Chicago, Illinois, February 16, 1950; admitted to bar, 1981, Illinois. *Education:* University of Illinois (B.A., 1971); Teachers College, Columbia University (M.A., 1974); George Washington University (J.D., 1981). ***COURSES: Criminal Law, Labor and Employment Law, Health Law, Law and Feminism. ***Email:*** lschmall@niu.edu

DANIEL M. SCHNEIDER,* (Professor)**, born Cincinnati, Ohio, September 13, 1948; admitted to bar, 1973, Ohio; 1978, New York; 1992, Illinois. *Education:* Washington University (A.B., 1970); University of Cincinnati (J.D., 1973); New York University (LL.M., 1976). ***COURSES: Federal Income Tax, Business Tax, International Tax, Elder Law, Business Planning, Tax Policy Seminar. ***Email:*** dschneider@niu.edu

GORDON B. SHNEIDER,* (Professor)**, born Indiana, November 25, 1933; admitted to bar, 1975, Illinois. *Education:* Northwestern University (B.S., 1954); DePaul University (J.D., 1974); University of Chicago (LL.M., 1975). ***COURSES: Torts, Corporations, Securities Regulation. ***Email:*** gshneider@niu.edu

DAVID H. TAYLOR,* (Professor)**, born Chicago, Illinois, March 9, 1953; admitted to bar, 1981, Illinois. *Education:* Duke University (B.A., 1976); Washington University (J.D., 1980). ***COURSES: Civil Procedure, Lawyering Skills, Debtor/Creditor Remedies, Evidence. ***Email:*** dtaylor@niu.edu

***ELLEN K. VANDYKE,* (Assistant Professor)**, born Chicago, Illinois; admitted to bar, 1989, Connecticut; 1990, New York. *Education:*

(This Listing Continued)

NORTHERN ILLINOIS UNIVERSITY COLLEGE OF LAW —Continued

University of Virginia (B.A., 1986); Catholic University of America (J.D., 1989). ***COURSES:*** Bioethics and the Law, Criminal Procedure, Lawyering Skills, Trial Advocacy. ***Email:*** evandyke@niu.edu

GARY L. VANDERMEER, **(Associate Director of Law Library, and Technical Services Librarian and Assistant Professor)**, born Grand Rapids, Michigan, October 12, 1949. *Education:* University of Illinois (B.A., 1971); Western Michigan University (M.S.L., 1980); Northern Illinois University (M.A.P.A., 1985). ***Email:*** gvandermeer@niu.edu

JOHN A. WALTON, **(Associate Professor)**, born Chicago, Illinois, October 24, 1954; admitted to bar, 1987, Colorado; 1991, District of Columbia. *Education:* Illinois State University (B.S., 1976; M.S., 1978); Northwestern University (J.D., 1986). ***COURSES:*** Agency and Partnership, Business Organization/Corporations, Lawyering Skills, Sports and Entertainment. ***Email:*** jwalton@niu.edu

NORTHERN KENTUCKY UNIVERSITY SALMON P. CHASE COLLEGE OF LAW

NUNN HALL
HIGHLAND HEIGHTS, KENTUCKY 41076

NORTHWESTERN SCHOOL OF LAW OF LEWIS AND CLARK COLLEGE

10015 SW TERWILLIGER BOULEVARD
PORTLAND, OREGON 97219
Telephone: (503) 768-6600
Fax: (503) 768-6671
World Wide Web: http://www.lclark.edu/law

ABA Approved Since 1970.

Northwestern School of Law of Lewis and Clark College was founded in 1884. In 1965, the school merged with Lewis and Clark College, a private liberal arts institution known for its overseas programs and its innovative core curriculum. Northwestern School of Law of Lewis and Clark College is fully accredited by the American Bar Association and is a member of the Association of American Law Schools. The Law School grants J.D. and LL.M. degrees. The master of laws degree is in environmental and natural resources law.

The Law School is very selective in the admissions process, receiving more than eight applications for each seat in the entering class. The 2000 entering class had a median LSAT of 157, approximately the seventy-fourth percentile nationally, and a median GPA of 3.24. The quality of the entering students places the school well within the top quarter of the law schools in the country.

The quality of the students and applicants goes beyond objective numbers. The class reflects a rich diversity of backgrounds. Students are drawn nationally, with more than 72 percent of students coming from outside Oregon, and an increasing number of students coming from outside the United States. The student body represents a wide spectrum of ages with a higher level of maturity and professional experience than is often typical in law school student populations. 49 percent of the students and 35 percent of the tenure track faculty are women. More than 12 percent of the 2000 entering class are members of ethnic minority groups.

The Law School has strong core programs in private and public law. The school emphasizes a solid theoretical foundation and also provides opportunities for practical experience. The curriculum provides a strong foundation for success in the profession of law.

The Law School has a day and an evening division. The day program is three years; the evening program is four years. Tenure track, full-time faculty rotate teaching loads through the evening division so that faculty, graduation requirements and grading are the same in the two divisions.

The Law School presents its students with the opportunity to specialize at the J.D. level. It offers four certificate programs, one to acknowledge a concentration in environmental and natural resources law, one to acknowledge a concentration in federal tax law, one to acknowledge a concentration in business law and one to acknowledge a concentration in criminal law. The school has a strong national reputation in environmental law, with the most extensive environmental and natural resources curriculum in the country. For four years the school was ranked first in the nation among law school environmental programs and was ranked second in 2000. Also the Law School's intellectual property program is recognized as one of the top programs in the nation. The law reviews of Northwestern School of Law of Lewis and Clark College include *Environmental Law,* the nation's oldest law journal dedicated to natural resource and environmental issues, a recognized leader in this field, and *The Journal of Small and Emerging Business Law,* the first scholarly law journal dedicated to issues of peculiar interest to small and emerging businesses. *Animal Law*, an externally funded, student-run law review, is also on campus. The Law School's tax curriculum is also unusually rich, with 10 course offerings devoted solely to federal tax law and several seminars that include tax considerations as part of transactional study.

Beyond environmental law, business law and tax law, the Law School also offers a rich and extensive curriculum in traditional areas of law, including international, criminal and civil litigation. The Law School conducts a clinical program for students to gain "hands-on" practical experience to complement their theoretical understanding. Under the supervision of the Clinical Faculty, students assist in the representation of low-income clients, including interviewing, negotiation and appearing in court and administrative hearings. The Lewis and Clark Legal Clinic is located in downtown Portland and allows students to serve low-income clients and offers excellent experience for academic credit. The Clinic currently focuses in areas of bankruptcy and consumer, family, landlord-tenant, employment, tax law, and investigates alleged unlawful practice of law for the Oregon State Bar.

The Law School offers many other special opportunities to students beyond the classroom and clinical curriculum. Programs include appellate advocacy, mock trial, international law, and client counseling. The school's extensive moot court offerings include a course in trial advocacy taught by a Circuit Court judge which allows students to actually conduct a mock jury trial in front of prominent local judges. Students have recently won a number of competitions, with the most recent national win being first place in the prestigious Environmental Law Moot Court Competition for two consecutive years. Another moot court program focuses specifically on tax cases. Clinical internships, including corporate internships with corporate legal departments, externships, the Higgins Visitor, the Business Roundtables, the

(This Listing Continued)

NORTHWESTERN SCHOOL OF LAW OF LEWIS AND CLARK COLLEGE—Continued

Distinguished Natural Resources Visitor and an active Continuing Legal Education program offer additional learning opportunities.

The Paul Boley Law Library, the largest law library in Oregon, contains more than 455,000 volumes. The library has extensive microform materials and advanced computer retrieval systems, including LEXIS, WESTLAW, DIALOG, OLIS, and OLIC. The library is also a United States Patent and Trademark Depository Library. New computer laboratories in the library offer LEXIS and WESTLAW connectivity along with a variety of other services available on the school network. These services are also available from a number of networked study seats spread throughout the library. Student access to the Internet is also available, with students being able to obtain personal Internet addresses.

The Law School's graduates take jobs throughout the nation. Our alumni practice in every part of the United States and in several foreign countries, using their legal training in a diverse range of specialties. The Law School's graduates make their careers as attorneys in law firms, in offices of public defenders and public prosecutors, and legal aid and public interest organizations. They work in corporations, for state and public agencies, and in areas that combine experience gained before law school with their law degrees. A significant proportion obtain judicial clerkships, and some pursue further academic studies in graduate legal education.

Dean: James L. Huffman (503) 768-6601
Associate Dean for Academic Affairs: Martha W. Spence (503) 768-6634
Associate Dean for Administrative Affairs: David Ellis (503) 768-6827
Assistant Dean for Career Services: Lisa LeSage (503) 768-6608
Director of Admissions: Emily Allen (503) 786-6613
Asst. Dean, Environmental and Natural Resources Law Prog.: Janice Weis (503) 768-6649
Director of Business Law Program: David Ellis (503) 768-6827
Student Financial Services: Diana Meyer (503) 768-7079

FULL TIME FACULTY

JAMES L. HUFFMAN*, (Dean and Professor of Law)**, born Ft. Benton, Montana, March 25, 1945; admitted to bar, 1988, Montana. *Education:* Montana State University (B.S., 1967); Fletcher School of Law and Diplomacy (M.A., 1969); University of Chicago (J.D., 1972). ***COURSES: Constitutional History, Constitutional Law, Government Tort Liability, Jurisprudence, Natural Resources, Torts, Water Law.

PAULA ABRAMS*, (Associate Professor of Law)**, born Philadelphia, Pennsylvania, June 20, 1953; admitted to bar, 1979, California; 1982, Oregon. *Education:* University of Michigan (B.G.S., 1974); University of California at Berkeley (J.D., 1979). ***COURSES: Civil Procedure, Constitutional Law, Population and Reproduction.

TOM N. AMBROSE*, (Visiting Professor of Law)**, born 1950; admitted to bar, 1975, Idaho. *Education:* Harvard University (A.B., 1972); Northwestern School of Law of Lewis & Clark College (J.D., 1975). ***COURSES: Agricultural Law, Commercial Law, Sales, Family Business, Wills & Trusts. ***Email:*** ambrose@lclark.edu

DOUGLAS E. BELOOF*, (Associate Professor and Director, Crime Victims Law Institute)**, born 1955; admitted to bar, 1982, Oregon. *Education:* University of California - Berkeley (B.A., 1978); Northwestern School of Law of Lewis & Clark College (J.D., 1981). ***COURSES: Criminal Law, Criminal Procedure, Evidence, Torts. ***Email:*** beloof@lclark.edu

TONI BERRES-PAUL*, (Instructor, Legal Writing Program)**, born New York, New York, June 22, 1947; admitted to bar, 1986, Oregon. *Education:* University of Wisconsin-Madison (B.A., 1969); University of Michigan (M.A., 1973); Portland State University (M.S., 1980); Northwestern School of Law of Lewis and Clark College (J.D., 1986). ***COURSES: Legal Analysis and Writing, Advanced Legal Writing.

BRIAN ANTHONY BLUM*, (Professor of Law)**, born Johannesburg, South Africa, November 29, 1946; admitted to bar, 1972, Republic of South Africa. *Education:* University of Witwatersrand (B.A., 1969; LL.B., 1971); University of Michigan (LL.M., 1978). ***COURSES: Commercial Law, Commercial Paper, Comparative Law, Contracts, Creditors Rights, Remedies.

MICHAEL C. BLUMM*, (Professor of Law)**, born Detroit, Michigan, March 3, 1950; admitted to bar, 1976, Pennsylvania; 1977, District of Columbia. *Education:* Williams College (B.A., 1972); George Washington University (J.D., 1976; LL.M., 1979). ***COURSES: American Legal History, Native Natural Resources Law, Pacific Salmon Law, Property, Public Lands Law, Water Law.

JOHN A. BOGDANSKI*, (Professor of Law)**, born Newark, New Jersey, January 15, 1954; admitted to bar, 1978, California; 1980, Oregon. *Education:* St. Peter's College (A.B., 1975); Yale University; Stanford University (J.D., 1978). ***COURSES: Federal Income Taxation, Corporate Taxation, Partnership Taxation, Estate and Gift Taxation, Advanced Tax Seminar (Valuation). ***Email:*** bojack@lclark.edu

LAWRENCE R. BROWN*, (Professor of Law)**, born Ann Arbor, Michigan, April 6, 1947; admitted to bar, 1972, California; 1979, Oregon. *Education:* Stanford University (A.B., 1969); University of California at Berkeley (J.D., 1972). ***COURSES: Federal Income Taxation, Corporate Taxation, Partnership Taxation, International Taxation, Estate and Gift Tax.

EDWARD J. BRUNET*, (Henry J. Casey Professor of Law)**, born February 21, 1944; admitted to bar, 1969, Illinois; 1985, Oregon. *Education:* Northwestern University (B.A., 1966); University of Illinois (J.D., 1969); University of Virginia (LL.M., 1972). ***COURSES: Administrative Law, Alternative Dispute Resolution, Antitrust, Civil Procedure, Complex Litigation. ***Email:*** brunet@lclark.edu

AMY C. BUSHAW*, (Associate Professor of Law)**, born Pullman, Washington, November 21, 1958; admitted to bar, 1984, Texas. *Education:* Princeton University (A.B., 1981); Yale University (J.D., 1984). ***COURSES: Contracts, Sales and Leases, Payment Systems, Secured Transactions, Central and Eastern European Law, Commercial Transactions, International Business Transactions. ***Email:*** bushaw@lclark.edu

BILL Y. CHIN*, (Instructor, Legal Writing Program)**, born Hong Kong, August 31, 1963; admitted to bar, 1995, Oregon. *Education:* Portland State University (B.S., 1990; M.S., 1996); Northwestern School of Law of Lewis and Clark College (J.D., 1995). ***COURSES: Legal Analysis and Writing, Advanced Legal Writing. ***Email:*** chin@lclark.edu

***AARON COURTNEY*, (Clinical Professor and Staff Attorney,**

(This Listing Continued)

NORTHWESTERN SCHOOL OF LAW OF LEWIS AND CLARK COLLEGE—Continued

Pacific Environmental Advocacy Center), born Istanbul, Turkey, February 7, 1967. *Education:* University of Virginia (B.A., 1989; M.S., 1993); University of Virginia School of Law (J.D., 1992). ***COURSES:*** Environmental Clinic. ***Email:*** aaron@lclark.edu

MARILYN R. COVER*, (Street Law Program Director)**, born Ravenna, Ohio, October 4, 1953. *Education:* Hiram College (B.A., 1975); Cleveland Marshall College of Law (J.D., 1975). ***COURSES: Client Counseling, Street Law, Law and Education.

HENRY H. DRUMMONDS*, (Professor of Law)**, born South Gate, California, February 24, 1945; admitted to bar, 1972, California; 1973, Oregon. *Education:* University of Oregon (B.A., 1969); Harvard University (J.D., 1972). ***COURSES: Employment Law, Labor Law, Torts, Toxic Torts, Individual Employee Rights.

P. BETH ENOS*, (Instructor, Legal Writing Program)**, born Memphis, Tennessee, January 9, 1952; admitted to bar, 1981, Tennessee; 1991, Oregon. *Education:* Memphis State University (B.A., 1978; J.D., 1981). ***COURSES: Legal Analysis and Writing.

WILLIAM F. FUNK*, (Professor of Law)**, born Boston, Massachusetts, November 29, 1945; admitted to bar, 1974, New York; 1980, District of Columbia. *Education:* Harvard University (B.A., 1967); Columbia University (J.D., 1973). ***COURSES: Administrative Law, Constitutional Law, Environmental Law. ***Email:*** funk@lclark.edu

JOHN P. GRANT*, (Professor of Law)**, born 1944. *Education:* University of Edinburgh - Scotland (LL.B., 1966); University of Pennsylvania Law School (LL.M., 1967). ***COURSES: European Union Law, Human Rights, International Law. ***Email:*** jg@lclark.edu

SANDRA A. HANSBERGER*, (Clinical Professor)**, born Oak Park, Illinois, July 13, 1956; admitted to bar, 1983, Oregon and Washington. *Education:* Pitzer College (B.A., 1978); Northwestern School of Law of Lewis and Clark College (J.D., 1982). ***COURSES: Legal Clinic (administrative and employment law), Legal Ethics.

STEVEN J. JOHANSEN*, (Assistant Professor of Law, Legal Writing Program)**, born Portland, Oregon, February 20, 1956; admitted to bar, 1987, Oregon. *Education:* Portland State University (B.S., 1981); Northwestern School of Law of Lewis and Clark College (J.D., 1987). ***COURSES: Legal Analysis and Writing, Advanced Legal Writing, Regulations and Ethics of Law. ***Email:*** tvj@lclark.edu

JENNIFER J. JOHNSON*, (Professor of Law)**, born Salem, Oregon, November 1, 1951; admitted to bar, 1977, Oregon. *Education:* Mills College (B.A., 1973); Yale University (J.D., 1976). ***COURSES: Business Associations, Corporate Finance, Mergers and Acquisitions, Real Property, Securities Regulation.

CRAIG JOHNSTON*, (Professor of Law)**, born Boston, Massachusetts, July 13, 1956. *Education:* University of Rochester (B.A., 1978); Northwestern School of Law of Lewis and Clark College (J.D., 1985). ***COURSES: Environmental Enforcement, Environmental Law, Hazardous Waste, Environmental Regulation, Torts.

STEPHEN KANTER*, (Professor of Law)**, born Cincinnati, Ohio, June 30, 1946; admitted to bar, 1971, Oregon. *Education:* Massachusetts Institute of Technology (B.S., 1968); Yale University (J.D., 1971). ***COURSES: Constitutional Law, Criminal Law and Procedure, Constitutional Theory, Law and Psychiatry.

JOHN R. KROGER*, (Assistant Professor)**, admitted to bar, 1997, Connecticut. *Education:* Yale College (B.A., 1990); Yale University (M.A., 1990); Harvard University Law School (J.D., 1996). ***COURSES: Criminal Law.

ARTHUR B. LAFRANCE*, (Professor of Law)**, born Manchester, New Hampshire, February 26, 1939; admitted to bar, 1964, Pennsylvania; 1965, Connecticut; 1973, Maine; 1979, Hawaii; 1986, Oregon. *Education:* Dartmouth College (B.A., 1960); Yale University (LL.B., 1963). ***COURSES: Criminal Law, Criminal Procedure, Evidence, Law and Medicine, Bioethics.

RONALD B. LANSING*, (Professor of Law)**, born Chicago, Illinois, January 28, 1932; admitted to bar, 1960, Oregon. *Education:* Valparaiso University (B.A., 1954); Willamette University (J.D., 1960). ***COURSES: Evidence, Torts. ***Email:*** lansing@lclark.edu

DONALD W. LARGE*, (Professor of Law)**, born Kew Gardens, New York, October 27, 1942; admitted to bar, 1967, Delaware; 1968, Ohio. *Education:* Cornell University (B.A., 1964; LL.B., 1967). ***COURSES: Conflicts of Laws, Environmental Law, Land Use, Natural Resources, Property Transactions, Property Mining and Minerals. ***Email:*** large@lclark.edu

LYDIA PALLAS LOREN*, (Associate Professor of Law)**, born Detroit, Michigan, August 3, 1966; admitted to bar, 1992, Michigan. *Education:* University of Michigan (A.B., 1987; J.D., 1992). ***COURSES: Intellectual Property, Civil Procedure, Copyright, Cyberspace Law. ***Email:*** loren@lclark.edu

SUSAN MANDIBERG*, (Professor of Law)**, born Los Angeles, California, August 20, 1947; admitted to bar, 1975, Oregon. *Education:* Oberlin College (B.A., 1968); University of Illinois (M.A., 1970); University of California at Berkeley (J.D., 1975). ***COURSES: Criminal Law, Investigative Criminal Procedure, Environmental Enforcement, Federal Courts. ***Email:*** sfm@lclark.edu

GINA S. MCCLARD*, (Clinical Professor and Associate Director, Crime Victims Law Institute)**, ***COURSES: Crime Victims Law Clinic. ***Email:*** mcclard@lclark.edu

ROBERT J. MILLER*, (Assistant Professor of Law)**, born Portland, Oregon, May 14, 1951; admitted to bar, 1991, Oregon. *Education:* Eastern Oregon University (B.S., 1988); Northwestern School of Law Lewis & Clark College (J.D., 1991). ***COURSES: Indian Law, Cultural Resources, Civil Procedure, Torts. ***Email:*** rmiller@lclark.edu

JANET C. NEUMAN*, (Associate Professor of Law)**, born Minneapolis, Minnesota, August 26, 1954; admitted to bar, 1980, Minnesota; 1981, Oregon. *Education:* Drake University (B.A., 1976); Stanford University (J.D., 1979). ***COURSES: Civil Procedure, Water Law, Administrative Law, Public Lands Law. ***Email:*** neuman@lclark.edu

DOUGLAS K. NEWELL*, (Edmund O. Belsheim Professor of Law)**, born Glendale, California, March 15, 1940; admitted to bar, 1966, California; 1984, Oregon. *Education:* Pomona College (B.A., 1962); Harvard University (J.D., 1965). ***COURSES: Commercial Law, Contracts, Contract Theory, Credit Transactions, Legal Profession, Sports Law.

PETER S. NYCUM*, (Associate Dean)**, born March 30, 1941. *Education:* University of Pittsburgh (B.A., 1962; M.L.S., 1968; LL.B., 1967). ***COURSES: Legal History, Regulations and Ethics of Law.

STEPHANIE MARIE PARENT*, (Environmental Clinic Staff Attorney)**, born Sheboygan, Wisconsin, May 23, 1964; admitted to bar, 1992, Oregon. *Education:* University of Wisconsin (B.S., 1987); Northwestern School of Law of Lewis & Clark College (J.D., 1992). ***COURSES: Environmental Clinic. ***Email:*** parent@lclark.edu

MARK ALLEN PETERSON*, (Clinical Professor)**, born Oregon City, Oregon, September 29, 1949; admitted to bar, 1977, Illinois; 1982, Oregon. *Education:* Portland State University (B.A., 1973); University of Toledo (J.D., 1976). ***COURSES: Legal Clinic (housing law and ethics), Oregon Pleading and Practice. ***Email:*** mpeterson@lclark.edu

(This Listing Continued)

NORTHWESTERN SCHOOL OF LAW OF LEWIS AND CLARK COLLEGE—Continued

JAN RILEY PIERCE*, (Clinical Professor)**, born Fort Riley, Kansas, January 16, 1943; admitted to bar, 1971, Kansas. *Education:* Washburn University (B.S., 1968); Washburn University School of Law (J.D., 1971). ***COURSES: Low-Income Taxpayer Clinic. ***Email:*** pierc@lclark.edu

DANIEL JOHN ROHLF*, (Associate Professor of Law; Director, Pacific Environmental Advocacy Center)**, born Denver, Colorado, September 16, 1961; admitted to bar, 1987, Colorado; 1999, Oregon. *Education:* Colorado College (B.A., 1984); Stanford University (J.D., 1987). ***COURSES: Environmental Clinic, Wildlife Law, Environmental Litigation, Legal Ecology.

RICHARD A. SLOTTEE*, (Professor of Law and Director of Clinical Program)**, born Portland, Oregon, July 1, 1947; admitted to bar, 1972, Oregon. *Education:* University of Oregon (B.S., 1969; J.D., 1972). ***COURSES: Legal Clinic (bankruptcy and consumer), Consumer Law, Contracts, Debtor/Creditor Rights, Lawyering Process. ***Email:*** slottee@lclark.edu

D. GORDON SMITH*, (Associate Professor of Law)**, born Bremerton, Washington, November 16, 1962; admitted to bar, 1991, Delaware. *Education:* Brigham Young University (B.S., 1986); The University of Chicago (J.D., 1990). ***COURSES: Bankruptcy, Business Associations, Corporate Finance, European Union Business Law, Venture Capital. ***Email:*** dgsmith@lclark.edu

MARTHA W. SPENCE*, (Associate Dean)**, born Charleston, West Virginia, June 10, 1949; admitted to bar, 1986, Oregon. *Education:* West Virginia State College (B.A., 1981); Northwestern School of Law of Lewis and Clark College (J.D., 1984). ***COURSES: Jurisprudence and Gender.

JANET STEVERSON*, (Associate Professor of Law)**, born Rochester, New York, May 12, 1961; admitted to bar, 1987, New York and District of Columbia. *Education:* State University of New York at Brockport (B.A., 1982); Harvard University (J.D., 1986). ***COURSES: Contracts, Family Law, Children and the Law Seminar.

ELAINE E. SUTHERLAND*, (Professor of Law)**, born 1957. *Education:* University of Glasgow - Scotland (LL.B., 1978); University of British Columbia (LL.M., 1985). ***COURSES: Family Law, Juvenile Law. ***Email:*** es@lclark.edu

MICHELLE A. TRAVIS*, (Assistant Professor of Law)**, born Alexandria, Virginia, March 22, 1969; admitted to bar, 1995, California. *Education:* Cornell University (B.A., 1991); Stanford Law School (J.D., 1994). ***COURSES: Employment Discrimination, Employment Law, Torts, Remedies. ***Email:*** travis@lclark.edu

BERNARD F. VAIL*, (Professor of Law)**, born Breese, Illinois, March 28, 1942; admitted to bar, 1975, Oregon. *Education:* DePaul University (B.A., 1967; J.D., 1968). ***COURSES: Credit Transactions, Decedents' Estates, Elder Law, Estate and Gift Tax, Family Law, Public International Law, Real Property, Wills and Trusts. ***Email:*** vail@lclark.edu

BILL L. WILLIAMSON*, (Professor of Law)**, born Twin Falls, Idaho, January 7, 1938; admitted to bar, 1965, Oregon. *Education:* University of Oregon (B.A., 1962); Harvard University (J.D., 1965). ***COURSES: Criminal Law, Criminal Procedure Seminars, Jurisprudence. ***Email:*** watashi@lclark.edu

DARYL D. WILSON*, (Instructor, Legal Writing Program)**, born Evanston, Illinois, August 8, 1949; admitted to bar, 1980, Oregon. *Education:* Brown University (A.B., 1971); Wesleyan University (M.A., 1974); Northwestern School of Law of Lewis and Clark College (J.D., 1980). ***COURSES: Legal Analysis and Writing, Advanced Legal Writing.

CHRIS A. WOLD*, (Clinical Professor of Law)**, born Minneapolis, Minnesota, May 25, 1963; admitted to bar, 1992, Oregon. *Education:* St. Olaf College (B.A., 1986); Northwestern School of Law of Lewis & Clark (J.D., 1990). ***COURSES: Comparative Environmental Law, Coastal Law and Ecology, International Environmental Law, International Environmental Practicum, Ocean and Coastal Law, Trade and the Environment. ***Email:*** wold@lclark.edu

THERESA L. WRIGHT*, (Clinical Professor)**, born New Haven, Connecticut, January 20, 1955; admitted to bar, 1981, Oregon; 1985, U.S. District Court, Oregon; 1987, Washington. *Education:* The Evergreen State College (B.A., 1977); Willamette University (J.D., 1981). ***COURSES: Legal Clinic (Family Law, Legal Ethics), Client Interviewing and Counseling, Externship Classroom Component. ***Email:*** twright@lclark.edu

---

NORTHWESTERN UNIVERSITY SCHOOL OF LAW

357 EAST CHICAGO AVENUE
CHICAGO, ILLINOIS 60611
Telephone: (312) 503-8462
Fax: (312) 503-2035

ABA Approved Since 1923.

Northwestern University School of Law is a nationally oriented private institution dedicated to advancing the understanding of law and to producing graduates prepared to excel in a rapidly changing world. Legal education at Northwestern uniquely blends a rigorous intellectual environment within a collegial and supportive community. With one of the lowest student-faculty ratios in the country, Northwestern provides students with unusually close contact with full-time professors who are noted scholars and with an opportunity to participate in the design of their own courses of study.

Founded in 1859, the Law School has a rich and storied history. Among its graduates are U.S. Supreme Court justices, governors, senators, United Nations ambassadors, cabinet members, chairs of regulatory commissions, leading scholars and business executives, the first commissioner of baseball and the first woman to receive a law degree in the United States.

Northwestern is small and highly selective, enrolling 200 JD students each year from around the United States and abroad. A significant number of students enter the law school with full-time work experience and many possess other graduate or professional degrees. Northwestern seeks a student body not only with unparalleled academic ability and achievement, but also with strong interpersonal skills, ambition, work experience and substantial maturity. These characteristics enable students to thrive in the Northwestern community and to excel in their careers. To fulfill this goal, Northwestern is the only major law school that strongly encourages applicants to interview, either on-campus and through its alumni network throughout the nation and the world.

In addition to its JD Program, Northwestern also offers a four-year JD-Master of Management (with Northwestern's Kellogg Graduate School of Management) and a JD-Phd program. Northwestern offers

(This Listing Continued)

NORTHWESTERN UNIVERSITY SCHOOL OF LAW —Continued

two primary programs for graduate students, a nine-month LLM (Master of Laws) program and a one-year Graduate Program in Law and Business, sponsored jointly with Kellogg. The Law School also offers an SJD program to a limited number of students as well as two non-degree programs for international students: the Research Associate Program and the Summer Program in Law and Business.

The Northwestern faculty is composed of a group of the finest scholars, diverse in background and perspective, whose research and writing makes majors contributions to important academic and public policy debates. Today's faculty carries on the tradition of John Henry Wigmore, a professor and Dean of the law school, who is considered by many to have been America's foremost legal scholar. Northwestern professors have a passion for teaching and for engaging students in both theoretical and practical legal applications.

The faculty includes scholars with advanced degrees in anthropology, economics, linguistics, history, philosophy, political science and sociology, as well as law; it includes a former chairman of the United States Securities and Exchange Commission, a former deputy solicitor general of the United States, the first American attorney to argue before the European Court of Human Rights and the senior author of the most widely used casebook on American legal history. The full-time faculty is supplemented by a distinguished group of adjunct professors who teach a wide variety of specialized courses and by a number of visiting professors from the U.S. and abroad.

Northwestern's flexible curriculum allows students to continue a broad range of study after their first year of law school or to focus on a specific area of interest, many within seminars or classes from 10 to 50 students. The Senior Research Program enables third year students to do individual research under the direct supervision of a professor, using library, field and interdisciplinary research methods.

Northwestern's nationally recognized clinical program includes five full-time professors and seven staff attorneys and enables students not only to obtain experience representing clients but also allows them to learn legal practice skills in highly regarded simulation courses or in externships. Clinic attorneys and students handle both civil and criminal cases representing indigents and prisoners on death row and are intensively involved in a major reform of the juvenile justice system.

Northwestern's law students take an intense and energetic interest in their community and their education. Several student-edited scholarly journals are available for research, writing and editing, including the *Northwestern University Law Review, Journal of Criminal Law and Criminology* and *Northwestern Journal of International Law & Business*. Over 30 student-run organizations, ranging from advocacy groups to those focused on careers to social organizations, enrich the community.

Northwestern's law library, the Pritzker Legal Research Center, has an excellent, service-oriented staff and its study carrels and tables are wired so that students can take advantage of a computer network that includes Internet access, word processing software, and legal research databases. The library's collection is one of the finest in the nation. It houses over 600,000 volumes and includes outstanding collections in international, foreign and Anglo-American law and rare books.

The Law School is located along the shores of Lake Michigan in Chicago, a truly spectacular setting in which to study law. Its proximity to courts, commerce and public interest activities enables students to experience the practice of law as well as its theory. The Law School's three interconnected buildings along Chicago's lakefront also house the national headquarters of the American Bar Association and the American Bar Foundation.

Dean: David E. Van Zandt (312) 503-8460
Admissions: Donald L. Rebstock (312) 503-8465
Financial Aid: Donald L. Rebstock (312) 503-8465
Library: Christopher Simoni (312) 503-8451
Placement: Donald Rebstock (312) 503-8438
Alumni Affairs: Timothy Brennan (312) 503-8494
Student Affairs: Theresa Cropper (312) 503-0785
Student Affairs: Amy Sherman (312) 503-0785
Communications: R.A. Pete Wentz (312) 503-1828

FULL TIME FACULTY

DAVID E. VAN ZANDT*, (Dean and Professor of Law)**, born Princeton, New Jersey, February 17, 1953; admitted to bar, 1985, New York. *Education:* Princeton University (A.B., 1975); Yale Law School (J.D., 1981); London School of Economics (Ph.D., 1985). ***COURSES: Corporations, Property, International Finance. ***Email:*** d-vanz@northwestern.edu

KENNETH W. ABBOTT*, (Elizabeth Froehling Horner Professor of Law and Commerce)**, born Albany, New York, July 25, 1944; admitted to bar, 1969, Massachusetts; 1971, New York. *Education:* Cornell University (B.A., 1966); Harvard University (J.D., 1969). ***COURSES: International Law, International Trade and Business Law, Legislation. ***Email:*** k-abbott@northwestern.edu

RONALD J. ALLEN*, (John Henry Wigmore Professor of Law)**, born Chicago, Illinois, July 14, 1948; admitted to bar, 1974, Nebraska; 1979, Iowa; 1986, Illinois. *Education:* Marshall University (B.S., 1970); University of Michigan (J.D., 1973). ***COURSES: Evidence, Criminal Law, Criminal Procedure, Jurisprudence. ***Email:*** rjallan@law.northwestern.edu

ROBERT W. BENNETT*, (Professor of Law)**, born Chicago, Illinois, March 30, 1941; admitted to bar, 1966, Illinois. *Education:* Harvard University (B.A., 1962; LL.B., 1965). ***COURSES: Constitutional Law, Contracts, Legislation. ***Email:*** r-bennett@law.northwestern.edu

LEIGH BUCHANAN BIENEN*, (Senior Lecturer)**, born Berkeley, California, April 24, 1938; admitted to bar, 1975, New Jersey; 1977, Pennsylvania; 1982, New York, District of Columbia and U.S. Supreme Court. *Education:* Cornell University (B.A., honors, 1960); University of Iowa (M.A., 1963); Rutgers School of Law (J.D., 1975). ***COURSES: Homicide; Persuasion; The Not For Profit Institution; Annual Subjects, Human Regulators. ***Email:*** lbbienen@law.northwestern.edu

CYNTHIA GRANT BOWMAN*, (Professor of Law)**, born Binghamton, N.Y., April 14, 1945; admitted to bar, 1982, Illinois. *Education:* Swarthmore College (B.A., 1966); Columbia University (Ph.D., 1972); Northwestern University (J.D., 1982). ***COURSES: Torts, Family Law, Civil Procedure, Feminist Legal Theory. ***Email:*** cgbowman@law.northwestern.edu

BRUCE A. BOYER*, (Senior Lecturer/Staff Attorney)**, born Washington, D.C., September 15, 1960; admitted to bar, 1986, Illinois. *Education:* Dartmouth College (B.A., 1982); Northwestern University (J.D., 1986). ***COURSES: Clinical Practice, Trial Advocacy, Juvenile.

(This Listing Continued)

NORTHWESTERN UNIVERSITY SCHOOL OF LAW —Continued

ROBERT P. BURNS*, (Professor of Law)**, born New York, N.Y., March 23, 1947; admitted to bar, 1974, Illinois; U.S. Supreme Court; U.S. Court of Appeals, Seventh Circuit; U.S. District Court, Northern District of Illinois. *Education:* Fordham University (A.B., 1969); University of Chicago (J.D., 1974; Ph.D., 1982). ***COURSES: Evidence, Legal Ethics, Clinical Teaching, Health Care Law. ***Email:*** r-burns@law.northwestern.edu

STEVEN G. CALABRESI*, (Professor of Law)**, born Madison, Wisconsin, March 1, 1958. *Education:* Yale University (B.A., 1980); Yale Law School (J.D., 1983). ***COURSES: Antitrust, Comparative Law, Constitutional Law, Federal Jurisdiction. ***Email:*** s-calabresi@law.northwestern.edu

LYNN P. COHN*, (Senior Lecturer)**, born Evanston; admitted to bar, 1987, Illinois. *Education:* University of Illinois (B.S., 1982); Northwestern (J.D., 1987). ***COURSES: Negotiation, Mediation, ADR. ***Email:*** l-cohn@law.northwestern.edu

ANGELA M. COIN*, (Director, Community Law Clinic)**, born Louisville, Kentucky, July 29, 1970; admitted to bar, 1995, Illinois. *Education:* University of Carolina-Chapel Hill (B.A., 1992); Northwestern University School of Law (J.D., 1995). ***COURSES: Juvenile Justice, Criminal Law, Public Interest. ***Email:*** a-coin@law.northwestern.edu

LISA ANNETTE COPLAND*, (Senior Lecturer)**, born Ft. Eustis, Virginia, August 16, 1972; admitted to bar, 1997, Illinois and U.S. District Court Northwestern District. *Education:* Princeton University (A.B., 1994); Northwestern University (J.D., 1997). ***COURSES: Criminal, Family. ***Email:*** acy047@lvlv.achs.nwu.edu

CHARLOTTE CRANE*, (Professor of Law)**, born Hanover, New Hampshire, August 30, 1951; admitted to bar, 1977, New Hampshire; 1978, Illinois. *Education:* Radcliffe College (A.B., 1973); University of Michigan (J.D., 1976). ***COURSES: Tax, State and Local Government. ***Email:*** ccrane@law.northwestern.edu

ANTHONY D'AMATO*, (Judd and Mary Morris Leighton Professor of Law)**, born New York, N.Y., January 10, 1937; admitted to bar, 1963, New York. *Education:* Cornell University (A.B., 1958); Harvard University (J.D., 1961); Columbia University (Ph.D., 1968). ***COURSES: Constitutional Law, Justice, International Law, Environmental Law, Torts, Jurisprudence, Legal Ethics, International Human Rights. ***Email:*** d-damato@law.northwestern.edu

SHARI SELDMAN DIAMOND*, (Professor of Law and Psychology)**, born Chicago, Illinois, March, 17, 1947; admitted to bar, 1985, Illinois. *Education:* University of Michigan (B.A., 1968); Northwestern University (M.A, 1970; Ph.D, 1972); University of Chicago (J.D., 1985). ***COURSES: Intellectual Property, Psychology and Law, Scientific Evidence. ***Email:*** s-diamond@nwu.edu

GRACE M. DODIER*, (Senior Lecturer)**, born December 2, 1959; admitted to bar, 1987, Connecticut; 1995, Illinois. *Education:* Barnard College, Columbia University (A.B., 1982); Harvard University (J.D., 1987). ***COURSES: Legal Writing. ***Email:*** g-dodier@law.northwestern.edu

STEVEN A. DRIZIN*, (Lecturer/Staff Attorney)**, born Philadelphia, Pennsylvania, August 6, 1961; admitted to bar, 1986, Illinois. *Education:* Haverford College (B.A., 1983); Northwestern University (J.D., 1986). ***COURSES: Juvenile Law. ***Email:*** s-drizin@law.northwestern.edu

JOHN S. ELSON*, (Professor of Law)**, born St. Louis, Missouri, September 13, 1943; admitted to bar, 1967, Illinois. *Education:* Harvard University (B.A., 1964); University of Chicago (J.D., 1967). ***COURSES: Clinical Practice. ***Email:*** j-elson@law.northwestern.edu

THOMAS L. EOVALDI*, (Professor of Law)**, born Benton, Illinois, May 9, 1940; admitted to bar, 1965, Illinois. *Education:* University of Illinois (B.S., 1962; LL.B., 1965). ***COURSES: Bankruptcy, Consumer Credit Regulation, Negotiating Corporate Financial Restructuring. ***Email:*** t-eovaldi@law.northwestern.edu

CLINTON W. FRANCIS*, (Professor of Law)**, born New Zealand, August 29, 1951; admitted to bar, 1975, New Zealand. *Education:* Victoria University (LL.B., 1973; LL.M., 1978); University of Virginia (S.J.D., 1983). ***COURSES: Commercial Law, Bankruptcy, Legal History. ***Email:*** cwfrancis@law.northwestern.edu

MAYER G. FREED*, (Associate Dean for Academic Affairs and Curriculum Professor of Law)**, born Philadelphia, Pennsylvania, October 26, 1945; admitted to bar, 1970, New York; 1975, Illinois. *Education:* Columbia College (A.B., 1967); Columbia University (J.D., 1970). ***COURSES: Employment Discrimination, Constitutional Law, Labor Law. ***Email:*** mfreed@law.northwestern.edu

THOMAS F. GERAGHTY*, (Associate Dean for Clinical Education; Professor of Law; Director, Legal Clinic)**, born Chicago, March 17, 1944; admitted to bar, 1970, Illinois. *Education:* Harvard University (A.B., 1966); Northwestern University (J.D., 1970). ***COURSES: Clinical Practice, Criminal Process, Formal Proceedings, Legal Ethics. ***Email:*** tgeraghty@law.northwestern.edu

STEPHEN B. GOLDBERG*, (Professor of Law)**, born Cambridge, Massachusetts, October 20, 1932; admitted to bar, 1961, California; 1967, Illinois. *Education:* Harvard University (A.B., 1954; LL.B., 1959). ***COURSES: Negotiation, Dispute Resolution. ***Email:*** stephengoldberg@law.northwestern.edu

CHERYL M. GRAVES*, (Lecturer/Staff Attorney)**, born July 22, 1955; admitted to bar, 1984, Illinois. *Education:* Carleton College (B.A., 1976); University of Illinois (MPH, 1977); Illinois Institute of Technology, Chicago-Kent College of Law (J.D., 1984). ***COURSES: Clinical Practice.

DAVID D. HADDOCK*, (Professor of Law)**, born Erick, Oklahoma, March 28, 1944. *Education:* Oklahoma State University (B.A., 1966); University of Chicago (Ph.D., 1980). ***COURSES: Advanced Law and Economics, American Indian, Federal and Reservation Law Seminar, Broadcast Regulation, Economics for Lawyers. ***Email:*** dhaddock@law.northwestern.edu

JOHN P. HEINZ*, (Owen L. Coon Professor of Law; Professor of Sociology)**, born Carlinville, Illinois, August 6, 1936; admitted to bar, 1962, District of Columbia; 1966, Illinois. *Education:* Washington University (A.B., 1958); Yale University (LL.B., 1962). ***COURSES: Criminal Law, Law and the Social Order. ***Email:*** j-heinz@nwu.edu

CHRISTINA RAFINSKI HEYDE*, (Legal Writing Instructor)**, born Chicago, Illinois, July 27, 1966; admitted to bar, 1992, Illinois. *Education:* Harvard University (A.B., 1988); Northwestern University (J.D., 1992). ***COURSES: Legal Writing. ***Email:*** c-heyde@law.northwestern.edu

RICHARD J. HOSKINS*, (Senior Lecturer)**, born Ft. Smith, Arizona, June 19, 1945; admitted to bar, 1971, New York; 1976, Illinois. *Education:* University of Kansas (B.A., 1967); Northwestern University (J.D., 1970). ***COURSES: Business Regulations, Civil Litigation, Antitrust. ***Email:*** r-hoskins@law.northwestern.edu

LISA HUESTIS*, (Senior Lecturer)**, born Washington, D.C., July 31, 1956; admitted to bar, 1984, New York; 1994, Illinois. *Education:* Kirkland College (B.A., 1978); Brooklyn Law School (J.D., 1983). ***Email: l-huestus@law.northwestern.edu

***JOYCE A. HUGHES*, (Professor of Law)**, born Gadsden, Alabama,

(This Listing Continued)

NORTHWESTERN UNIVERSITY SCHOOL OF LAW —Continued

February 7, 1940; admitted to bar, 1965, Minnesota; 1976, Illinois. *Education:* Carleton College (B.A., 1961); University of Madrid, Spain (Cert. 1962); University of Minnesota (J.D., 1965). ***COURSES:*** Evidence, Immigration, Refugees & Asylum. ***Email:*** jahughes@law.northwestern.edu

ELIZABETH LYNN INGLEHART*, (Legal Writing Instructor)**, born Chicago, Illinois, April 7, 1965; admitted to bar, 1991, New York; 1993, Illinois. *Education:* University of Michigan (B.A., 1987); University of Michigan Law School (J.D., 1990). ***COURSES: Legal Research and Writing. ***Email:*** e-inglehart@law.northwestern.edu

ANDREW MARTIN MAYER KOPPELMAN*, (Associate Professor of Law and Political Science)**, born Nyack, New York, August 29, 1957; admitted to bar, 1990, Connecticut; 1991, New York. *Education:* University of Chicago (A.B., 1979); Yale University (Ph.D., 1991; J.D., 1989). ***COURSES: Constitutional Law, Law and Religion. ***Email:*** akoppelman@law.northwestern.edu

JAMES LINDGREN*, (Professor of Law)**, born Rockford, Illinois, August 8, 1952; admitted to bar, 1977, Illinois. *Education:* Yale University (B.A., 1974); University of Chicago Law School (J.D., 1977). ***COURSES: Criminal Law, Ethics, Wills & Estates, Social Science. ***Email:*** jlindgren@law.northwestern.edu

STEVEN LUBET*, (Professor of Law; Director, Program on Advocacy and Professionalism)**, born Chicago, Illinois, February 4, 1949; admitted to bar, 1973, Illinois. *Education:* Northwestern University (B.A., 1970); University of California, Berkeley (J.D., 1973). ***COURSES: Advanced Trial Practice, Clinical Trial Advocacy, Legal Ethics, Negotiation Workshop, Pretrial Litigation. ***Email:*** slubet@law.northwestern.edu

LAWRENCE C. MARSHALL*, (Professor of Law)**, born Boston, Massachusetts, January 10, 1959; admitted to bar, 1987, Illinois. *Education:* Beth Hatalmud (B.S., 1979); Northwestern University (J.D., 1985). ***COURSES: Civil Procedure, Appellate Practice. ***Email:*** lmarshall@law.northwestern.edu

FRED SANDERSON MCCHESNEY*, (Class of 1967 James B. Haddad Professor of Law)**, born Washington, D.C., November 19, 1948; admitted to bar, 1978, Florida; 1980, District of Columbia. *Education:* Holy Cross College (A.B., 1970); University of Virginia (Ph.D., 1982); University of Miami (J.D., 1978). ***COURSES: Antitrust Corporations, Corporate Finance Statistics. ***Email:*** f-mcchesney@law.northwestern.edu

VANESSA MELENDEZ*, (Senior Lecturer)**, born San Juan, Puerto Rico, October 24, 1970; admitted to bar, 1997, New York; 1999, Illinois. *Education:* Yale University (B.A., 1993); Fordham University School of Law (J.D., 1996). ***COURSES: Domestic Relations, Immigration. ***Email:*** v-melendez@law.northwestern.edu

THOMAS W. MERRILL*, (John Paul Stevens Professor of Law)**, born Bartlesville, Oklahoma, May 3, 1949; admitted to bar, 1980, Illinois. *Education:* Grinnell College (B.A., 1971); Oxford University (B.A., 1973); University of Chicago (J.D., 1977). ***COURSES: Administrative Law, Property, Natural Resources Law. ***Email:*** t-merrill@law.northwestern.edu

JANICE NADLER*, (Assistant Professor)**, born New York, New York, October 3, 1963; admitted to bar, 1990, New York; 1992, Illinois. *Education:* Cornell University (A.B., 1985); Boalt Hall School of Law, University of California - Berkeley (J.D., 1989); University of Illinois (Ph.D., 2000). ***COURSES: Criminal Law, Negotiation, Law and Psychology. ***Email:*** jnadler@law.northwestern.edu

KATHLEEN DILLON NARKO*, (Legal Writing Instructor)**, born Akron, Ohio; admitted to bar, 1989, Illinois. *Education:* Yale University (B.A., 1985); Cornell University (J.D., 1989). ***Email: k-narko@law.northwestern.edu

DAWN CLARK NETSCH*, (Professor of Law Emeritus)**, born Cincinnati, Ohio, September 16, 1926; admitted to bar, 1952, Illinois; 1953, District of Columbia. *Education:* Northwestern University (B.A., 1948; J.D., 1952). ***COURSES: State and Local Government. ***Email:*** d-netsch@law.northwestern.edu

LISA B. GREENFIELD PEARL*, (Senior Lecturer in Legal Writing)**, born Rochester, New York, October 6, 1967; admitted to bar, 1992, Illinois. *Education:* University of Michigan (B.A., 1989); Northwestern University School of Law (J.D., 1992). ***COURSES: Legal Research and Writing. ***Email:*** p-greenfield@law.northwestern.edu

PHILIP F. POSTLEWAITE*, (Professor of Law)**, born Modesto, California, May 30, 1945; admitted to bar, 1970, Wisconsin; 1973, Washington; 1993, Illinois. *Education:* Texas Christian University (B.B.A., 1967); University of California, Berkeley (J.D., 1970); New York University (LL.M., 1971). ***COURSES: Taxation. ***Email:*** p-postlewaite@law.northwestern.edu

STEPHEN B. PRESSER*, (Raoul Berger Professor of Legal History)**, born Chattanooga, Tennessee, August 10, 1946; admitted to bar, 1971, Massachusetts; 1972, District of Columbia. *Education:* Harvard University (A.B., 1968; J.D., 1971). ***COURSES: Corporations, Contracts, American Legal History. ***Email:*** s-presser@law.northwestern.edu

MARTIN H. REDISH*, (Louis and Harriet Ancel Professor of Law and Public Policy)**, born Lynbrook, New York, August 16, 1945; admitted to bar, 1971, New York; 1992, Illinois. *Education:* University of Pennsylvania (A.B., 1967); Harvard University (J.D., 1970). ***COURSES: Civil Procedure, Constitutional Law, Federal Jurisdiction. ***Email:*** m-redish@law.northwestern.edu

ANNELISE RILES*, (Associate Professor)**, born Peoria, November 23, 1966; admitted to bar, 1993, New York. *Education:* Princeton University (A.B., 1988); London School of Economics (MSC, 1990); Harvard Law School (J.D., 1993); Cambridge University (Ph.D., 1997). ***COURSES: Conflict of Laws, Comparative Law, Securities, International Law. ***Email:*** a-riles@law.northwestern.edu

DOROTHY ROBERTS*, (Professor of Law)**, born Chicago, Illinois, Marcg 8, 1956; admitted to bar, 1981, New York. *Education:* Yale (B.A., 1977); Harvard (J.D., 1980). ***COURSES: Criminal Law, Family Law. ***Email:*** d-roberts@northwestern.edu

PAUL H. ROBINSON*, (Edna B. and Ednyfed H. Williams Professor of Law)**, born Waterbury, Connecticut, November 12, 1948; admitted to bar, 1974, Massachusetts; 1989, New Jersey. *Education:* Rensselaer Polytechnic Institute (B.S., 1970); University of California, Los Angeles (J.D., 1973); Harvard University (LL.M., 1974); Cambridge University. ***COURSES: Criminal Law, Criminal Law Theory.

JUDITH A. ROSENBAUM*, (Director of Legal Writing)**, born Chicago, Illinois, June 12, 1951; admitted to bar, 1976, Illinois. *Education:* University of Rochester (B.A., 1973); University of Michigan (J.D., 1976). ***COURSES: Legal Writing.

VICTOR G. ROSENBLUM*, (Nathaniel L. Nathanson Professor of Law)**, born New York, N.Y., June 2, 1925; admitted to bar, 1949, New York; 1960, Illinois. *Education:* Columbia University (A.B., 1945; LL.B., 1948); University of California, Berkeley (Ph.D., 1953). ***COURSES: Administrative Law, Constitutional Law, Law and Education, Torts. ***Email:*** v-rosenblum@law.northwestern.edu

***LEONARD S. RUBINOWITZ*, (Professor of Law)**, born Washington, D.C., April 8, 1943; admitted to bar, 1968, Connecticut. *Education:*

(This Listing Continued)

NORTHWESTERN UNIVERSITY SCHOOL OF LAW —Continued

University of Wisconsin (B.A., 1965); Yale University (LL.B., 1968). ***COURSES:*** Law and Social Change, Civil Rights, Public Interest Law. ***Email:*** l-rubinowitz@law.northwestern.edu

DAVID S. RUDER*, (William W. Gurley Memorial Professor of Law)**, born Wausau, Wisconsin, May 25, 1929; admitted to bar, 1957, Wisconsin; 1962, Illinois. *Education:* Williams College (B.A., 1951); University of Wisconsin (J.D., 1957). ***COURSES: Corporations, Securities Regulation, Corporate Finance.

ORA SCHUB*, (Clinical Faculty)**, born Chicago, Illinois, October 22, 1949; admitted to bar, 1977, Illinois. *Education:* University of Illinois (B.A., 1971); Loyola (J.D., 1976). ***COURSES: Domestic Violence, Human Rights, Disability Right, GLBT. ***Email:*** o-schub@law.northwestern.edu

HELENE S. SHAPO*, (Professor of Law)**, born New York, N.Y., June 5, 1938; admitted to bar, 1976, Virginia; 1993, Illinois. *Education:* Smith College (B.A., 1959); Harvard University (M.A., 1960); University of Virginia (J.D., 1976). ***COURSES: Legal Writing, Estates and Trusts. ***Email:*** h-shapo@law.northwestern.edu

MARSHALL S. SHAPO*, (Frederic P. Vose Professor of Law)**, born Philadelphia, Pennsylvania, October 1, 1936; admitted to bar, 1964, Florida; 1977, Virginia; 1993, Illinois. *Education:* University of Miami (A.B., 1958); Harvard University (A.M., 1961); University of Miami (LL.B., 1964); Harvard University (S.J.D., 1974). ***COURSES: Law of Dangerous Products, Perspectives on Injury Law, Tort Reform and Products Liability Seminar, Torts. ***Email:*** m-shapo@law.northwestern.edu

CAROLE B. SILVER*, (Senior Lecturer)**, born Indiana, May 14, 1956; admitted to bar, 1980, Illinois. *Education:* University of Michigan (B.A., 1977); Indiana University (J.D., 1980). ***COURSES: International and Securities Regulations. ***Email:*** c-silver@law.northwestern.edu

CHRISTOPHER SIMONI*, (Associate Dean for Library & Information Services & Professor of Law)**, born Pittsburgh, Pennsylvania, May 5, 1946; admitted to bar, 1980, Oregon. *Education:* University of Michigan (A.B., 1968); Marquette University (M.A., 1970; Ph.D., 1977); Lewis & Clark University School of Law (J.D., 1980); University of Texas, Austin (M.L.I.S., 1989). ***COURSES: Legal Research. ***Email:*** csimoni@law.northwestern.edu

ROBERT HENRY SITKOFF*, (Assistant Professor of Law)**, born New York, August, 28, 1974. *Education:* The University of Virginia (B.A., 1996); The University of Chicago (J.D., 1999). ***COURSES: Business Associations, Contracts, Estates & Trusts. ***Email:*** r-sitkoff@law.northwestern.edu

HENRY EDWARD SMITH*, (Assistant Professor)**, born Chicago, October 24, 1965; admitted to bar, 1997, Illinois. *Education:* Harvard University (A.B., 1986); Stanford University (Ph.D., 1992); Yale Law School (J.D., 1996). ***COURSES: Contracts, Federal Income Taxation, Contract Theory. ***Email:*** hesmith@law.northwestern.edu

RICHARD E. SPEIDEL*, (Beatrice Kuhn Professor of Law)**, born Cincinnati, Ohio, May 27, 1933; admitted to bar, 1957, Ohio; 1966, Virginia. *Education:* Denison University (B.A., 1954); University of Cincinnati (LL.B., 1957); Northwestern University (LL.M., 1958). ***COURSES: Contracts, Commercial Law, Arbitration. ***Email:*** r-speidel@law.northwestern.edu

CATHRYN ELIZABETH STEWART*, (Senior Lecturer)**, born Dallas, Texas, August 30, 1968; admitted to bar, 1996, Illinois. *Education:* University of Texas 9B.A., 1992); Northwestern University (J.D., 1996). ***COURSES: Clinic, Trial Advocacy. ***Email:*** cestewart@law.northwestern.edu

---

NOTRE DAME LAW SCHOOL

P.O. BOX R
NOTRE DAME, INDIANA 46556-0780
Telephone: (219) 631-6627
Fax: (219) 631-6371
http://www.law.nd.edu

ABA Approved Since 1925.

Founded in 1869, the Notre Dame Law School is the oldest Roman Catholic law school in the United States. Its national program is designed to equip graduates to practice law in any jurisdiction. Among its graduates are members of the bar in every state and numerous foreign nations. The school is approved by the American Bar Association and is a member of the Association of American Law Schools. In addition to offering the Juris Doctor degree, Notre Dame has LL.M. and J.S.D. programs in international human rights law and a second LL.M. program in comparative law offered in London and designed for non-American lawyers.

The Notre Dame program strives to educate men and women to become lawyers of extraordinary professional competence who possess a partisanship for justice, an ability to respond to human need, and compassion for their clients and colleagues.

Notre Dame Law School is a small law school. It is a community of faculty and students of every race and creed from throughout the nation and the world. Each fall approximately 180 full-time J.D. students begin their studies at Notre Dame. The law school has four formalized joint degree programs, a J.D./M.B.A. program, a J.D./Master of Engineering program, a J.D./M.A. in English program, and a J.D./M.A. in Peace Studies program. Where appropriate and with the approval of the department involved, other joint degree programs may be fashioned to suit individual students' interests or needs.

Methods of instruction are both traditional and innovative. The first-year required curriculum is rigorous and traditional. In the second and third years, traditional teaching methods are supplemented by experience-based techniques (actual clinical and simulated), seminars, interdisciplinary study, courses in other graduate departments of the University and directed readings.

Notre Dame offers study in London for credit on both a summer-school and academic-year basis. The London program has been in continuous operation since 1968. Each year approximately 30 J.D. students elect to spend their second year at the Notre Dame London Law Centre. Some 50 hours of credit are generally available including standard American law courses and a variety of international and comparative law courses. Since 1970, Notre Dame also has operated a separate London summer program for credit for its own students and for students from other American law schools.

A wide range of student activities is available. Students participate in the production of four law journals, including the *Notre Dame Law Review*, the *Journal of College and University Law*, the *Notre Dame Journal of Law, Ethics and Public Policy*, and the *Journal of Legislation*. The school also sponsors trial- and appellate-level moot

(This Listing Continued)

NOTRE DAME LAW SCHOOL—Continued

court programs, an international moot court program, and an outstanding trial advocacy program. Cocurricular opportunities that combine classroom learning with practical experience include the Notre Dame Legal Aid Clinic, and it's Immigration Clinic component, and internships with the local prosecutor's, public defender's, and U.S. Attorney's offices. A variety of student organizations provide opportunities to explore social, cultural, religious and political issues. A full-service career services office assists students in finding permanent and summer employment.

The faculty includes 43 full-time teaching-and-research and library faculty. The faculty are actively involved in research and regularly produce books and articles receiving national and international attention. The hallmark of legal education at Notre Dame is the meaningful interaction between faculty and students. The faculty members are accessible and spend more hours in private student conferences than in the classroom.

The Kresge Law Library holds over half a million volumes and microform equivalents and is a leader in developing computer-based legal-research methodologies, especially using emerging technologies. The Library subscribes to all major computer-assisted research services, including LEXIS/NEXIS and WESTLAW. Law students and faculty also have immediate access to the more than two million volumes in the research collections of the University's Theodore M. Hesburgh Library and, via the OCLC and RLIN national data bases, have the capability to identify and procure materials from over 26,000 associated libraries. The professional staff of nine librarians, including five lawyer/librarians assists students and faculty with a wide range of research needs. The library collection is available to students and faculty 24 hours a day, seven days a week.

Dean: Patricia A. O'Hara (219) 631-6789
Associate Dean: Walter F. Pratt, Jr. (219) 631-6984
Associate Dean for Academic Affairs: Vincent D. Rougeau (219) 631-8610
Associate Dean and Library Director: Roger F. Jacobs (219) 631-5916
Administration Director: M. Catherine Roemer (219) 631-6241
Admissions Director: Charles W. Roboski (219) 631-4108
Career Services Director: Gail G. Peshel (219) 631-7625
Alumni Relations Director: Catherine Pieronek (219) 631-6891
Advancement Director: Glenn J. Rosswurm (219) 631-3781

FULL TIME FACULTY

PATRICIA A. O'HARA*, (The Joseph A. Matson Dean and Professor of Law)**, born Berkeley, California, August 26, 1949; admitted to bar, 1974, California. *Education:* University of Santa Clara (B.A., 1971); University of Notre Dame (J.D., 1974). ***COURSES: Business Associations, Securities Regulation. ***Email:*** patricia.a.o'hara.3@nd.edu

MATTHEW J. BARRETT*, (Associate Professor)**, born Youngstown, Ohio, May 31, 1960; admitted to bar, 1985, Ohio. *Education:* University of Notre Dame (B.B.A., 1982; J.D., 1985). ***COURSES: Business Associations (Agency, Partnerships, Corporations), Accounting for Lawyers, Federal Income Tax (Individuals), Business Planning. ***Email:*** matthew.j.barrett.1@nd.edu

JOSEPH P. BAUER*, (Professor)**, born New York, New York, November 3, 1945; admitted to bar, 1970, New York. *Education:* University of Pennsylvania (B.A., 1965); Harvard University (J.D., 1969). ***COURSES: Civil Procedure, Antitrust, Intellectual Property. ***Email:*** joseph.p.bauer.1@nd.edu

ANTHONY J. BELLIA*, (Assistant Professor)**, born Buffalo, New York, June 16, 1969; admitted to bar, 1995, New York; 1999, District of Columbia. *Education:* Canisius College (B.A., 1991); University of Notre Dame (J.D., 1994). ***COURSES: Contracts. ***Email:*** anthony.j.bellia.3@nd.edu

PATRICIA L. BELLIA*, (Assistant Professor)**, born Medford, Massachusetts, August 26, 1969; admitted to bar, 1995, Massachusetts; 1997, District of Columbia. *Education:* Harvard and Radcliffe Colleges (A.B., 1991); Yale Law School (J.D., 1995). ***COURSES: Cyberspace and the Law. ***Email:*** patricia.l.bellia.2@nd.edu

GEOFFREY J. BENNETT*, (Professor and Director of the London Law Centre)**, born Uxbridge, England, June 4, 1952; admitted to bar, 1974, England. *Education:* St. Catherines College at Cambridge University (B.A., 1974); Cambridge University (M.A., 1978). ***COURSES: Evidence, Comparative Law. ***Email:*** geoffrey.j.bennett.24@nd.edu

G. ROBERT BLAKEY*, (William J. and Dorothy O'Neill Professor of Law)**, born Burlington, North Carolina, January 7, 1936; admitted to bar, 1960, North Carolina and District of Columbia; 1986, Colorado. *Education:* University of Notre Dame (A.B., 1957; J.D., 1960). ***COURSES: Criminal Law, Criminal Procedure, Federal Criminal Law, Federal Criminal Procedure, Jurisprudence. ***Email:*** g.r.blakey.1@nd.edu

GERARD V. BRADLEY*, (Professor)**, born Brooklyn, New York, May 31, 1954; admitted to bar, 1981, New York. *Education:* Cornell University (B.A., 1976; J.D., 1980). ***COURSES: Constitutional Law, Criminal Procedure, Trial Advocacy, Law and Religion. ***Email:*** gerard.v.bradley.1@nd.edu

PAOLO G. CAROZZA*, (Associate Professor)**, born Maryland, June 4, 1963. *Education:* Harvard College (A.B., 1985); Harvard Law School (J.D., 1989). ***COURSES: International Law. ***Email:*** paolo.g.carozza.1@nd.edu

LISA L. CASEY*, (Associate Professor of Law)**, born Denver, Colorado, August 8, 1963; admitted to bar, 1987, Colorado. *Education:* Stanford University (A.B., 1984); Stanford Law School (J.D., 1987). ***COURSES: Securities Regulation, Business Associations, Commercial Law. ***Email:*** lcasey@nd.edu

FERNAND N. DUTILE*, (Professor)**, born Lewiston, Maine, February 15, 1940; admitted to bar, 1965, Maine. *Education:* Assumption College (A.B., 1962); University of Notre Dame (J.D., 1965). ***COURSES: Criminal Law and Procedure, Law of Education. ***Email:*** fernand.n.dutile.1@nd.edu

BARBARA J. FICK*, (Associate Professor)**, born St. Louis, Missouri, April 8, 1951; admitted to bar, 1976, Wisconsin. *Education:* Creighton University (B.A., 1972); University of Pennsylvania (J.D., 1976). ***COURSES: Labor and Employment Law, Dispute Resolution. ***Email:*** barbara.j.fick.1@nd.edu

JOHN M. FINNIS*, (Biolchini Family Professor of Law)**, born Adelaide, Australia, July 28, 1940. *Education:* Adelaide University (LL.B., 1961); Oxford University (D.Phil., 1965). ***COURSES: Jurisprudence. ***Email:*** john.m.finnis.1@nd.edu

(This Listing Continued)

NOTRE DAME LAW SCHOOL—Continued

JUDITH L. FOX, **(Associate Professional Specialist)**, born Pittsburgh, Pennsylvania, October 19, 1960; admitted to bar, 1993, Indiana, Michigan. *Education:* Wilkes University (B.S., 1985); University of Notre Dame (J.D., 1993). ***COURSES:*** Clinical Education. ***Email:*** judith.l.fox.30@nd.edu

NICOLE STELLE GARNETT, **(Assistant Professor)**, born Wichita, Kansas, January 7, 1970; admitted to bar, 1996, Arizona; 1998, District of Columbia. *Education:* Stanford University (A.B., 1992); Yale Law School (J.D., 1995). ***COURSES:*** Property. ***Email:*** nicole.garnett.5@nd.edu

RICHARD WINGFIELD GARNETT, **(Assistant Professor)**, born Bryn Mawr, Pennsylvania, November 6, 1968; admitted to bar, 1997, Arizona; 1998, District of Columbia. *Education:* Duke University (A.B., 1990); Yale Law School (J.D., 1995). ***COURSES:*** Criminal Law, Criminal Procedure. ***Email:*** rick.garnett.4@nd.edu

ALAN GUNN, **(John N. Matthews Professor of Law)**, born Syracuse, New York, April 8, 1940; admitted to bar, 1970, District of Columbia. *Education:* Rensselaer Polytechnic Institute (B.S., 1961); Cornell University (J.D., 1970). ***COURSES:*** Taxation, Torts, Contracts, Insurance, Law and Economics. ***Email:*** alan.gunn.1@nd.edu

JIMMY GURULE, **(Professor on leave, 2001-03)**, born Salt Lake City, Utah, June 14, 1951; admitted to bar, 1980, Utah. *Education:* University of Utah (B.A., 1974; J.D., 1980). ***COURSES:*** Criminal Law, Criminal Procedure and Criminal Trial Advocacy. ***Email:*** jimmy.gurule.1@nd.edu

ROGER F. JACOBS, **(Associate Dean, Professor, Kresge Law Library Director)**, born Detroit, Michigan, January 1, 1937; admitted to bar, 1970, Michigan. *Education:* University of Detroit (A.B., 1962; J.D., 1970); University of Michigan (A.M.L.S., 1964). ***COURSES:*** Legal Research. ***Email:*** roger.f.jacobs.1@nd.edu

M. CATHLEEN KAVENY, **(John N. Murphy Foundation Professor of Law and Professor of Theology)**, born Providence, Rhode Island, April 23, 1962; admitted to bar, 1993, Massachusetts. *Education:* Princeton University (A.B., 1984); Yale Law School (J.D., 1990); Yale University (Ph.D., 1991). ***COURSES:*** Contracts, Health Care Law, Jurisprudence. ***Email:*** m.catheleen.kaveny.1@nd.edu

CONRAD L. KELLENBERG, **(Professor)**, born New York, New York, February 12, 1928; admitted to bar, 1952, New York. *Education:* St. John's University (A.B., 1949); Columbia University (J.D., 1952). ***COURSES:*** Natural Resources Law. ***Email:*** conrad.l.kellenberg.1@nd.edu

WILLIAM K. KELLEY, **(Associate Professor)**, born Columbus, Ohio, February 8, 1963; admitted to bar, 1990, Ohio. *Education:* Marquette University (B.A., 1984); Harvard Law School (J.D., 1987). ***COURSES:*** Constitutional Law, Administrative Law. ***Email:*** william.k.kelley.24@nd.edu

DWIGHT B. KING, JR., **(Librarian, Head of Research Services)**, born Kalamazoo, Michigan, May 7, 1955. *Education:* University of Michigan (B.A., 1977; J.D., 1980; M.L.S., 1981). ***COURSES:*** Legal Research. ***Email:*** dwight.b.king.1@nd.edu

CARMELA R. KINSLOW, **(Associate Librarian and Head of Access Services)**, born Philadelphia, Pennsylvania, August 15, 1945. *Education:* Indiana University (B.A., 1987; M.L.S., 1989); University of Notre Dame (M.S.A., 1991). ***Email:*** carmela.r.kinslaw.1@nd.edu

MICHAEL S. KIRSCH, **(Associate Professor of Law)**, born Quincy, Illinois, December 10, 1962; admitted to bar, 1988, California. *Education:* Cornell University (A.B., 1985); Harvard Law School (J.D., 1988); New York University School of Law (LL.M., 1989). ***COURSES:*** Federal Income Taxation, International Taxation. ***Email:*** mkirsch@nd.edu

SANDRA SUE KLEIN, **(Associate Librarian Technical Services)**, born Union City, New Jersey, October 28, 1959. *Education:* University of Illinois (B.A., 1981; M.L.S., 1988; Ed.M., 1983). ***Email:*** sandra.s.klein.26@nd.edu

DONALD PAUL KOMMERS, **(Joseph and Elizabeth Robbie Professor of Government and International Studies and Concurrent Professor of Law)**, born Green Bay, Wisconsin, August 26, 1932. *Education:* Catholic University of America (B.A., 1954); University of Wisconsin (M.A., 1957; Ph.D., 1962). ***COURSES:*** American and Comparative Constitutional Law. ***Email:*** donald.p.kommers.1@nd.edu

GARTH MEINTJES, **(Associate Director, Center for Civil and Human Rights)**, born Durban, South Africa, July 22, 1965; admitted to bar, 1990, South Africa. *Education:* University of Stellenbosch (B.A., 1986); University of Cape Town (LL.B., 1989); University of Notre Dame (LL.M., 1991). ***COURSES:*** International Law, Ethics of Human Rights, Introduction to Human Rights Research Methodology. ***Email:*** garth.meintjes.1@nd.edu

JUAN ERNESTO MENDEZ, **(Professor and Director, Center for Civil & Human Rights)**, born Argentina, December 11, 1944; admitted to bar, 1981; District of Columbia. *Education:* Univ. Catolica Stella Maris (J.D., 1970); Washington College Law American University (Cert., 1980). ***COURSES:*** International Law of Human Rights. ***Email:*** juan.mendez.5@nd.edu

CAROL ANN MOONEY, **(Professor, Vice President and Associate Provost)**, born Kingston, New York, February 11, 1950; admitted to bar, 1977, District of Columbia; 1979, Indiana. *Education:* Saint Mary's College (B.A., 1972); University of Notre Dame (J.D., 1977). ***COURSES:*** Wills and Trusts, Estate Planning. ***Email:*** carol.a.mooney.1@nd.edu

JOHN COPELAND NAGLE, **(Professor)**, born Pittsburgh, Pennsylvania, May 27, 1960; admitted to bar, 1987, Kansas. *Education:* Indiana University (B.A., 1982); University of Michigan Law School (J.D., 1986). ***COURSES:*** Property, Environmental, Legislation. ***Email:*** john.c.nagle.8@nd.edu

PATTI J. OGDEN, **(Research Librarian)**, born Texas, December 8, 1955. *Education:* Northwestern University (B.A., 1977); University of Texas (J.D., 1980; M.L.S., 1985). ***COURSES:*** Legal Research. ***Email:*** patti.j.ogden.1@nd.edu

LUCY SALSBURY PAYNE, **(Research Librarian)**, born Utica, New York, July 5, 1952; admitted to bar, 1988, Indiana and Michigan. *Education:* Andrews University (B.Mus., 1974); Loma Linda University (M.A., 1979); University of Notre Dame (J.D., 1988); University of Michigan (M.I.L.S., 1990). ***COURSES:*** Legal Research. ***Email:*** lucy.s.payne.1@nd.edu

JOHN H. PEARSON, C.S.C., **(Director, Thomas J. White Center on Law and Government)**, born Evergreen Park, Illinois, January 7, 1945; admitted to bar, 1986, California. *Education:* University of Notre Dame (A.B., 1968; M.Th., 1971); University of California, Berkeley (J.D., 1985). ***COURSES:*** Property. ***Email:*** john.h.pearson.1@nd.edu

TERESA GODWIN PHELPS, **(Professor)**, born Bournemouth, England, May 29, 1944. *Education:* University of Notre Dame (B.A., 1973; M.A., 1975; Ph.D., 1980); Yale University (M.S.L., 1989). ***COURSES:*** Legal Writing, Law and Literature, Women and the Law. ***Email:*** teresa.g.phelps.1@nd.edu

NANCY M. POEHLMANN, **(Assistant Librarian)**, born Winston-Salem, North Carolina, April 13, 1955. *Education:* Agnes

(This Listing Continued)

NOTRE DAME LAW SCHOOL—Continued

Scott College (B.A., 1976); Indiana University (M.A., 1982; M.L.S., 1985). ***Email:*** nancy.m.poehlmann.2@nd.edu

WALTER F. PRATT, JR.*, (Associate Dean and Professor)**, born Jackson, Mississippi, September 17, 1946. *Education:* Vanderbilt University (B.A., 1968); Oxford University (D.Phil., 1974); Yale University (J.D., 1977). ***COURSES: American Legal History, Contracts. ***Email:*** walter.f.pratt.1@nd.edu

WARREN DAVID REES*, (Research Librarian)**, born Carlinville, Illinois, August 27, 1956; admitted to bar, 1985, Wisconsin. *Education:* Minnesota Bible College (B.A., 1978); University of Michigan (A.M.L.S., 1986); Southern Illinois University (J.D., 1985). ***COURSES: Legal Research. ***Email:*** warren.d.rees.2@nd.edu

JOHN H. ROBINSON*, (Associate Professor)**, born Providence, Rhode Island, April 4, 1943; admitted to bar, 1980, Rhode Island. *Education:* Boston College (B.A., 1967); University of Notre Dame (M.A., 1972; Ph.D., 1975); University of California at Berkeley (J.D., 1979). ***COURSES: Civil Procedure, Legal Ethics, Estates and Trusts. ***Email:*** john.h.robinson.1@nd.edu

ROBERT E. RODES, JR.*, (Paul J. Schierl/Fort Howard Company Professor of Law)**, born New York, New York, May 29, 1927; admitted to bar, 1952, Massachusetts; 1959, Indiana. *Education:* Brown University (A.B., 1947); Harvard University (LL.B., 1952). ***COURSES: Administrative Law, Civil Procedure, Jurisprudence, Ethics. ***Email:*** robert.e.rodes.1@nd.edu

VINCENT D. ROUGEAU*, (Associate Dean for Academic Affairs and Associate Professor)**, born Miami Beach, Florida June, 17, 1963; admitted to bar, 1989, Maryland; 1990, District of Columbia. *Education:* Brown University (A.B., 1985); Harvard Law School (J.D., 1988). ***COURSES: Contracts, Real Estate, Banking, International. ***Email:*** vinent.d.rougeau.1@nd.edu

JAMES H. SECKINGER*, (Professor)**, born New Rockford, North Dakota, October 16, 1942; admitted to bar, 1968, Colorado; 1976, Indiana. *Education:* St. John's University (B.S., 1964); Vanderbilt University (M.S., 1968); University of Notre Dame (J.D., 1968). ***COURSES: Litigation, Trial Advocacy, Evidence, Pretrial Procedure. ***Email:*** james.h.seckinger.1@nd.edu

DINAH L. SHELTON*, (Professor)**, born New London, Connecticut, September 19, 1944; admitted to bar, 1970, California. *Education:* University of California, Berkeley (B.A., 1967; J.D., 1970). ***COURSES: International Law. ***Email:*** dinah.l.shelton.6@nd.edu

STEVEN D. SMITH*, (Robert and Marion Short Professor of Law)**, born Salt Lake City, Utah, June 6, 1952; admitted to bar, 1981, Utah. *Education:* Brigham Young University (B.A., 1970); Yale (J.D., 1979). ***COURSES: Torts, Constitutional Law, Religious Freedom, Jurisprudence. ***Email:*** steven.d.smith.379@nd.edu

JOHN ERIC SMITHBURN*, (Professor)**, born Noblesville, Indiana, November 21, 1944; admitted to bar, 1974, Indiana; 1989, England and Wales. *Education:* Indiana University (B.S., 1966; M.A., 1970; J.D., 1973). ***COURSES: Family Law, Juvenile Law, Mental Health Law, Evidence. ***Email:*** john.e.smithburn.1@nd.edu

BARBARA M. SZWEDA*, (Associate Professional Specialist in Law)**, born Beaver Dam, Wisconsin, July 25, 1953; admitted to bar, 1980, California; 1987, Oklahoma; 1990, Indiana. *Education:* Lawrence University (B.A., 1975); Pepperdine University (J.D., 1980). ***COURSES: Poverty Law, Family Law, Immigration. ***Email:*** barbara.m.szweda.5@nd.edu

JOSEPH W. THOMAS*, (Associate Librarian and Head of Technical Services)**, born Ramey Air Force Base, Puerto Rico, December 13, 1958. *Education:* University of Kentucky (B.A., 1980); University of Chicago (M.A., 1983). ***Email: joseph.w.thomas.2@nd.edu

JAY TIDMARSH*, (Professor)**, born Milwaukee, Wisconsin, February 20, 1957; admitted to bar, 1982, Wisconsin. *Education:* University of Notre Dame (A.B., 1979); Harvard University (J.D., 1982). ***COURSES: Torts, Civil Procedure, Remedies, Federal Courts, Products Liability, Complex Civil Litigation. ***Email:*** jay.h.tidmarsh.1@nd.edu

JULIAN VELASCO*, (Associate Professor)**, born Perth Amboy, New Jersey, October 5, 1969; admitted to bar, 1995, New York, New Jersey. *Education:* Georgetown University (B.S.B.A., 1991); Columbia University (J.D., 1994). ***COURSES: Corporate and Securities Law. ***Email:*** jvelasco@nd.edu

---

NOVA SOUTHEASTERN UNIVERSITY
SHEPARD BROAD LAW CENTER

LEO GOODWIN, SR., HALL
3305 COLLEGE AVENUE
FORT LAUDERDALE, FLORIDA 33314-7721
Telephone: (954) 262-6100
Fax: (954) 262-3834

ABA Approved Since 1975.

Founded in 1974, the Law Center grants JD, JD/MBA, JD/MS (Dispute Resolution), JD/MURP, JD/MS (Computer Science) and JD/MS (Psychology) degrees. It is accredited by the ABA and is a member of the AALS. Our parent university, founded in 1964, is accredited by the Southern Association of Colleges and Schools.

Shepard Broad Law Center has over 900 students in its full-time day and part-time evening programs. Over 1,300 individuals applied for the 318 seats in the 2000 entering class. Reflecting its appeal to the mature student, for whom law is a second career, students range in age from the early 20's to the 60's. Approximately 32% are members of minority groups. Our students come from all over the United States as well as from several foreign countries.

In 1992 the Law Center moved to the main university campus in Davie, a western suburb of Fort Lauderdale. The spacious atrium in our new facility joins two multi-story wings, a library wing and an office/classroom wing. The Law Center building overlooks a lake and is within walking distance of cafeteria, bookstore, and apartment/dormitory facilities. Its courtrooms and classrooms are equipped to utilize technological innovations as well as traditional teaching methods.

Our classroom/office wing reflects one of our most important traditions, attention to the student as an individual. Small classrooms allow us to offer all first year classes in sections of 60 or fewer students. Upperclass sections rarely exceed 75 students, and numerous workshop and seminar electives are available to groups of 20 or fewer students. Faculty offices are clustered across from the library entrance, facilitating student-faculty interaction. Law Center faculty members

(This Listing Continued)

NOVA SOUTHEASTERN UNIVERSITY SHEPARD BROAD LAW CENTER—Continued

are known for their open door office policy and their commitment to our students.

Our Law Library is one of the few in the United States serving as a depository for state, federal, and United Nations documents. Its resources include over 322,000 volume equivalents, including specialized collections for taxation, international law, criminal law, admiralty, children's rights, jurisprudence, law and popular culture, and trial practice. Its Learning Technology Center includes an extensive collection of media material, computer data bases, and microform and CD-ROM technology. All entering students bring laptop computers and use our wireless technology to access the NSU Law Net.

No one method of instruction predominates; our 49 full-time faculty members engage students in traditional Socratic dialogue, guide them through problem and simulation exercises, and supervise them in live-client clinical placements. Prominent local practitioners and judges serve as adjunct faculty and enrich our curriculum in their areas of expertise.

Our innovative four semester Lawyering Skills and Values curriculum introduces students to legal research and writing, client interviewing, negotiating, and pretrial practice. Students select between litigation and transactional tracks in their second year.

Our skills curriculum includes numerous workshops, pre-trial and trial advocacy courses, and clinical offerings. Seminars consider topics ranging from AIDS to Bias Crimes; workshops include Bankruptcy, Business Planning, and Probate. In addition to offerings traditionally thought of as "bar" courses, students are exposed to courses as diverse as Admiralty, Construction Law, and Immigration Law. Our international offerings include summer programs in San Jose, Costa Rica, and Cambridge, England.

Externships offer students hands-on experience in many facets of lawyering. Every student entering since fall 1997 has been able to enroll in a full semester clinical placement. Placements include Criminal, ADR, Family, Business, Personal Injury Litigation, International, and Environmental. In addition, many of our students are assigned to state and federal judges as part of our highly-acclaimed judicial internship program. Our guardian ad litem program and individuals with disabilities project provide valuable academic experiences, and our street law program introduces middle and high school students to the legal system. A Career Development Academy includes courses such as Spanish for Lawyers and Law Office Management.

The student-run *Nova Law Review* is published three times per year. Its highly-acclaimed symposium issues have covered such important topics as drug testing; reproductive rights; and the Rehnquist Court. Other students participate in the *Journal of International & Comparative Law,* which annually publishes a bilingual issue, or the *International Travel Law Journal*. Active moot court and ATLA groups allow students to participate in intramural and interscholastic moot court, counseling, negotiating, and trial competitions.

Several research and advocacy institutes are affiliated with the Law Center. These include Public Interest Law Center, the Center for the Study of Youth Policy, Environmental & Land Use Law Center, Inter-American Center for Human Rights, Children First, and the Disability Law Institute. These institutes offer opportunities for students and faculty to make important contributions to the administration of justice.

Law Center alumni are represented in major law firms in Florida as well as in other states. Several serve as judges, legislators, and city officials. An active mentoring program pairs attorneys with law students interested in particular areas of practice.

Dean: Joseph D. Harbaugh (954) 262-6105
Admissions Director: Nancy Kelly Sanguigni (954) 262-6120
Library Director: Billie Jo Kaufman (954) 262-6211
Career Development Director: Janet Mosseri (954) 262-6122

FULL TIME FACULTY

JOSEPH D. HARBAUGH**, (Dean and Professor of Law)**, born Harrisburg, Pennsylvania, June 15, 1939; admitted to bar, 1965, Connecticut and District of Columbia; 1978, Pennsylvania. *Education:* St. Joseph's College (B.S., 1961); University of Pittsburgh (LL.B., 1964); Georgetown University (LL.M., 1967). ***COURSES:*** Alternative Dispute Resolution, Clinical Teaching, Criminal Law and Procedure, Evidence, Negotiating.

WILLIAM E. ADAMS, JR.**, (Professor of Law)**, born Bloomington, Indiana, May 20, 1954; admitted to bar, 1978, Indiana; 1980, Florida. *Education:* Indiana University (A.B., 1975; J.D., 1978). ***COURSES:*** Clinic, AIDS Seminar, Pretrial Practice, Criminal Law, Family Law, Torts, Constitutional Law, Criminal Procedure, Negotiable Instruments.

JOHN B. ANDERSON**, (Professor of Law (Distinguished Visiting))**, born Rockford, Illinois, February 15, 1922; admitted to bar, 1946, Illinois; 1973, District of Columbia. *Education:* University of Illinois (A.B., 1942; J.D., 1946); Harvard University (LL.M., 1949). ***COURSES:*** Constitutional Law, Conflicts, Electoral Process.

CATHERINE ARCABASCIO**, (Associate Professor of Law)**, born New York, N.Y., August 6, 1961; admitted to bar, 1988, Massachusetts and New York; 1990, District of Columbia; 1992, Florida. *Education:* New York University (B.A., 1983); Boston College (J.D., 1987). ***COURSES:*** Lawyering Skills and Values, Criminal Procedure, Advanced Criminal Procedure, Clinic, Post Conviction Remedies.

TIMOTHY LEE ARCARO**, (Assistant Professor of Law)**, born Jackson, Michigan, November 3, 1964; admitted to bar, 1989, Pennsylvania and Florida. *Education:* Pennsylvania State University (B.S., 1986); Thomas M. Cooley Law School (J.D., 1989). ***COURSES:*** Clinic, Professional Responsibility, Domestic Violence, Family Law.

STEVEN KEITH BERENSON**, (Assistant Professor of Law)**, born White Plains, New York, February 20, 1963; admitted to bar, 1989, Massachusetts; 1999, Florida. *Education:* Franklin and Marshall College (B.A., 1985); Harvard Law School (J.D., 1989; LL.M., 1998). ***COURSES:*** Clinic, Professional Responsibility, Elder Law.

BRION BLACKWELDER**, (Assistant Professor of Law)**, born Washington, D.C., March 13, 1950; admitted to bar, 1984, Florida. *Education:* Duke University (B.S., 1972); Nova University (J.D., 1984). ***COURSES:*** Clinic, Natural Resources, Property.

RANDOLPH BRACCIALARGHE**, (Professor of Law)**, born New York, New York, October 1, 1948; admitted to bar, 1977, Florida; 1979, District of Columbia Court of Appeals. *Education:* University of Michigan (A.B., 1970); University of Miami (J.D., 1977). ***COURSES:*** Evidence, Professional Responsibility, Trial Advocacy, Criminal Law, Civil Procedure.

RONALD BENTON BROWN**, (Professor of Law)**, born Providence, Rhode Island, March 23, 1948; admitted to bar, 1973, Connecticut;

(This Listing Continued)

NOVA SOUTHEASTERN UNIVERSITY SHEPARD BROAD LAW CENTER—Continued

1983, Florida. *Education:* Northeastern University (B.S.M.E., 1970); University of Connecticut (J.D., 1973); Temple University (LL.M., 1973). ***COURSES:*** Property, Real Estate Finance, Landlord/Tenant, Contracts, Legislation.

JOHNNY C. BURRIS*, (Professor of Law)**, born Paris, Kentucky, May 21, 1953; admitted to bar, 1978, Kentucky; 1979, Ohio. *Education:* University of Kentucky (B.G.S., 1975); Northern Kentucky University (J.D., 1978); Columbia University (LL.M., 1984). ***COURSES: Administrative Law, Constitutional Law, First Amendment, Criminal Procedure, Uniform Commercial Code, Clinic, Property.

MARILYN BLUMBERG CANE*, (Professor of Law)**, born Rockville Centre, New York, February 26, 1949; admitted to bar, 1975, New York; 1977, Connecticut; 1981, Florida. *Education:* Cornell University (B.A., 1971); Boston College (J.D., 1974). ***COURSES: Corporations, Corporate Workshop, Securities Regulation, Corporate Finance, Banking, Torts, Clinic.

KATHY L. CERMINARA*, (Assistant Professor of Law)**, born McKeesport, Pennsylvania, December 6, 1961; admitted to bar, 1987, Pennsylvania. *Education:* Ohio University (B.S., 1983); University of Pittsburgh (J.D., 1987); Columbia University (LL.M., 1996). ***COURSES: Health Law, Property, Lawyering Skills and Values, Complex Litigation, Law of Managed Care.

ANTHONY CHASE*, (Professor of Law)**, born Paris, Illinois, December 9, 1948. *Education:* Antioch College; University of Wisconsin-Madison (B.A., 1972); Wayne State University (J.D., 1978); Harvard University (LL.M., 1979). ***COURSES: Japanese Legal History, American Legal History, Constitutional Law, Criminal Law, Legal Process, International Law, Law and Psychiatry.

PHYLLIS G. COLEMAN*, (Professor of Law)**, born New York, New York, July 24, 1948; admitted to bar, 1978, Florida. *Education:* University of Florida (B.S., 1970; M.Ed., 1975; J.D., 1978). ***COURSES: Bioethics, Contracts, Family Law, Law and Psychiatry, Sports Law, Media Law.

LESLIE LARKIN COONEY*, (Associate Professor of Law)**, born Steubenville, Ohio, May 24, 1949; admitted to bar, 1978, Pennsylvania; 1989, Florida. *Education:* Duquesne University (B.S., 1971; J.D., 1978). ***COURSES: Corporations, Sales and Sales Financing, Agency and Partnership, Lawyering Skills and Values, Clinic.

JANE ELLEN CROSS*, (Assistant Professor of Law)**, born Newark, New Jersey, August 6, 1961; admitted to bar, 1986, New York; 1990, Illinois; 2000, Florida. *Education:* University of California, Davis (B.A., 1982); University of Michigan (J.D., 1985). ***COURSES: Lawyering Skills and Values, Commercial Law.

DEBRA MOSS CURTIS*, (Visiting Assistant Professor of Law)**, born Lake Ronkonkoma, New York, April 11, 1969; admitted to bar, 1993, Florida. *Education:* Tufts University (B.A., 1990); Boston College Law School (J.D., 1993). ***COURSES: Lawyering Skills and Values, Sales Financing.

MICHAEL J. DALE*, (Professor of Law)**, born Passaic, New Jersey, September 4, 1945; admitted to bar, 1972, New York; 1978, Arizona; 1980, New Mexico; 1987, Florida. *Education:* Colgate University (B.A., 1967); Boston College (J.D., 1970). ***COURSES: Civil Procedure, Conflicts, Trial Advocacy, Pretrial Practice, Juvenile Law, Judicial Externship, Family Law, Children's Rights.

MARK DOBSON*, (Professor of Law)**, born Washington, D.C., July 21, 1948; admitted to bar, 1973, Maryland; 1974, Kansas; 1977, Florida. *Education:* Georgetown University (A.B., 1970); Catholic University of America (J.D., 1973); Temple University (LL.M., 1977). ***COURSES: Criminal Law, Criminal Procedure, Evidence, Professional Responsibility, Trial Advocacy, Clinic.

DOUGLAS LEE DONOHO*, (Professor of Law)**, born Benton Harbor, Michigan, April 12, 1955; admitted to bar, 1984, New York; 1989, California. *Education:* Kalamazoo College (B.A., 1977); Rutgers University (J.D., 1981); Harvard University (LL.M., 1989). ***COURSES: International Law, International Business Transactions, Clinic, International Human Rights, Torts, Pretrial Practice, Constitutional Law.

LYNN A. EPSTEIN*, (Associate Professor of Law)**, born Miami, Florida, March 28, 1958; admitted to bar, 1986, Florida. *Education:* C. W. Post College (B.S., Marketing, 1982); Nova University (J.D., 1986). ***COURSES: Lawyering Skills and Values, Professional Responsibility, Interviewing, Counseling and Negotiating, Pretrial Practice, Evidence, Clinic.

CLEVELAND FERGUSON, III*, (Visiting Assistant Professor of Law)**, born Long Branch, New Jersey, August 24, 1971; admitted to bar, 1998, Florida. *Education:* Nova Southeastern University (B.S., 1994); Florida State University (J.D., 1997). ***COURSES: Administrative Law, Lawyering Skills and Values.

MICHAEL FLYNN*, (Professor of Law)**, born Seattle, Washington, August 17, 1951; admitted to bar, 1977, Washington; 1994, Florida. *Education:* Gonzaga University (B.A., 1973; J.D., 1977). ***COURSES: Torts, Uniform Commercial Code, Consumer Protection, Pretrial Practice, Trial Advocacy, Interviewing, Counseling and Negotiating, Clinic, Medical Malpractice, Products Liability, Mass Tort Litigation.

STEVEN FRIEDLAND*, (Professor of Law)**, born New York, New York, August 5, 1956; admitted to bar, 1983, Massachusetts; 1985, District of Columbia; 1989, Florida. *Education:* State University of New York, Binghamton (B.A., 1978); Harvard University (J.D., 1981); Columbia University (LL.M., 1994; J.S.D., 1999). ***COURSES: Evidence, Constitutional Law, Criminal Law, Law and Medicine, Public Interest Law, Law and Psychiatry, Property.

ANGELA GILMORE*, (Professor of Law)**, born Dayton, Ohio, April 18, 1963; admitted to bar, 1988, Maryland. *Education:* Houghton College (B.A., 1985); University of Pittsburgh (J.D., 1988). ***COURSES: Property, Race and Gender Discrimination, Sales, Sales Financing, Professional Responsibility, Contracts, Non-Profit Organizations.

PEARL GOLDMAN*, (Associate Professor of Law)**, born Montreal, Quebec, November 16, 1952; admitted to bar, 1986, Florida. *Education:* McGill University (B.C.L., 1976; LL.B., 1977; LL.M., 1978); Nova University (J.D., 1986); University of Cambridge (M.Phil., 1979). ***COURSES: Lawyering Skills and Values, Interviewing, Counseling and Negotiating.

JOSEPH M. GROHMAN*, (Professor of Law)**, born Atlantic City, New Jersey, September 19, 1944; admitted to bar, 1975, Florida. *Education:* Glassboro State College (B.A., 1966); California State University (M.A., 1971); University of Miami (J.D., 1975). ***COURSES: Property, Real Estate Workshop, Contracts, Corporations, Family Law.

RICHARD JOSEPH GROSSO*, (Assistant Professor of Law)**, born Pittsburgh, Pennsylvania, March 16, 1961; admitted to bar, 1986, Florida. *Education:* Florida State University (B.S., 1983; J.D., 1986); Miami-Dade Community College (A.A., 1981). ***COURSES: Clinic, Environmental Law, Land Use, Natural Resources.

GWEN THAYER HANDELMAN*, (Scholar in Residence)**, born Detroit, Michigan, December 26, 1946; admitted to bar, 1983, District of Columbia. *Education:* The University of Michigan (A.B., 1968; J.D., 1981). ***COURSES: Employee Benefits, Ethics, Taxation.

(This Listing Continued)

NOVA SOUTHEASTERN UNIVERSITY SHEPARD BROAD LAW CENTER—Continued

LINDA FRANCES HARRISON*, (Assistant Professor of Law)**, born New Jersey, June 9, 1950; admitted to bar, 1983, Florida. *Education:* University of North Florida (B.A., 1979); American University (J.D., 1982). ***COURSES: Contracts, Corporations, Disability Law, Sexual Identity Law, Lawyering Skills and Values.

CAROL HENDERSON*, (Professor of Law)**, born Smithtown, New York, April 11, 1956; admitted to bar, 1981, Florida. *Education:* University of Florida (B.A., 1976); George Washington University (J.D., 1980). ***COURSES: Corporations, Criminal Law, Professional Responsibility, Scientific Evidence, Evidence.

ROBERT M. JARVIS*, (Professor of Law)**, born New York, New York, October 17, 1959; admitted to bar, 1984, New York; 1990, Florida. *Education:* Northwestern University (B.A., 1980); University of Pennsylvania (J.D., 1983); New York University (LL.M., 1986). ***COURSES: Admiralty, Florida Constitutional Law, International Litigation, Professional Responsibility, Sports Law, Travel Law, Art Law.

PAUL R JOSEPH*, (Associate Dean-International & External Programs and Professor of Law)**, born Los Angeles, California, April 30, 1951; admitted to bar, 1977, California. *Education:* Goddard College (B.A., 1973); University of California, Davis (J.D., 1977); Temple University (LL.M., 1979). ***COURSES: Criminal Procedure, Torts, Products Liability, Civil Liberties, Constitutional Law, Jurisprudence, Law and Popular Culture.

LAWRENCE KALEVITCH*, (Professor of Law)**, born Fall River, Massachusetts, July 21, 1944; admitted to bar, 1969, Missouri; 1979, Illinois; 1986, Florida. *Education:* University of Massachusetts (B.A., 1966); St. Louis University (J.D., 1969); New York University (LL.M., 1970). ***COURSES: Contracts, Uniform Commercial Code, Bankruptcy, Clinic.

JUDITH R. KARP*, (Assistant Professor of Law)**, born New York, New York, January 26, 1951; admitted to bar, 1986, Florida. *Education:* SUNY at Buffalo (B.A., 1972); Emory University (M.L.S., 1978); University of Miami (J.D., 1986). ***COURSES: Lawyering Skills and Values, Professional Responsibility.

BILLIE JO KAUFMAN*, (Law Library Director and Assistant Professor of Law)**, born New Albany, Indiana, August 20, 1949. *Education:* Indiana University (B.S., 1971; M.S., 1974); Nova University (J.D., 1990). ***COURSES: Moot Court, Appellate Briefwriting, Advanced Legal Research Seminar.

LUNDY RUFFLES LANGSTON*, (Professor of Law)**, born Wilson, North Carolina; admitted to bar, 1989, North Carolina. *Education:* North Carolina Central University (B.S., 1978; J.D., 1989); Columbia University (LL.M., 1991). ***COURSES: Criminal Law, Juvenile Law, Family Law, Jurisprudence, Race and the Law, Torts, Women and the Law, Domestic Violence, International Criminal Law, Cyberlaw.

DONNA LITMAN*, (Professor of Law)**, born New York, New York, February 21, 1951; admitted to bar, 1976, Georgia; 1977, Florida. *Education:* University of Michigan; University of Miami (A.B., 1973); University of Florida (J.D., 1976). ***COURSES: Federal Income Tax, Wills and Trusts, Estate Planning, Business Planning, Jewish Law.

ELENA MARTY-NELSON*, (Professor of Law)**, born Havana, Cuba, February 15, 1960; admitted to bar, 1983, Pennsylvania; 1986, District of Columbia. *Education:* University of Miami (B.A., 1980); Georgetown University Law Center (J.D., 1983; LL.M., Tax, 1986). ***COURSES: Federal Income Tax, International Tax, Property, Securities Regulation, Wills and Trusts.

MICHAEL R. MASINTER*, (Professor of Law)**, born Charleston, West Virginia, August 10, 1946; admitted to bar, 1973, Florida. *Education:* Stanford University (B.A., 1968); Georgetown University (J.D., 1973). ***COURSES: Employment Discrimination, Civil Rights, Federal Jurisdiction, Civil Procedure, Negotiable Instruments.

JANI E. MAURER*, (Associate Professor of Law)**, born New York, New York; admitted to bar, 1979, New York; 1984, Florida. *Education:* Hamilton College (B.A., 1974); New York Law School (J.D., 1978). ***COURSES: Lawyering Skills and Values, Wills and Trusts, Federal Income Tax, Probate Workshop.

HOWARD MESSING*, (Professor of Law)**, born New York, New York, April 2, 1943; admitted to bar, 1973, Florida; 1982, New York. *Education:* Syracuse University (A.B., 1965; J.D., 1973). ***COURSES: Professional Responsibility, Evidence, Torts.

JOEL A. MINTZ*, (Professor of Law)**, born New York, New York, July 24, 1949; admitted to bar, 1975, New York. *Education:* Columbia University (B.A., 1970; LL.M., 1982; J.S.D., 1989); New York University (J.D., 1974). ***COURSES: Environmental Law, Local Government Law, Land Use Planning, Torts, Clinic.

MARK ALLEN PADIN*, (Visiting Assistant Professor of Law)**, born Bronx, New York, June 8, 1953; admitted to bar, 1990, California. *Education:* SUNY Brockport (B.A., 1975); Penn State University (M.S., 1978); University of California Hastings (J.D., 1990). ***COURSES: Lawyering Skills and Values, Property.

GAIL LEVIN RICHMOND*, (Associate Dean-Academic Affairs and Professor of Law)**, born Gary, Indiana, January 9, 1946; admitted to bar, 1971, Ohio. *Education:* University of Michigan (A.B., 1966; M.B.A., 1967); Duke University (J.D., 1971). ***COURSES: Federal Income Tax, Corporate Tax, Tax Research, Wills, Wills Drafting.

MICHAEL L. RICHMOND*, (Professor of Law)**, born Jersey City, New Jersey, May 18, 1945; admitted to bar, 1971, Ohio; 1983, Florida. *Education:* Hamilton College (A.B., 1967); University of North Carolina (M.S.L.S.,1974); Duke University (J.D., 1971). ***COURSES: Torts, Criminal Law, Agency and Partnership, Law and Literature, Defamation and Privacy, Moot Court.

ELOISA C. RODRIGUEZ-DOD*, (Associate Professor of Law)**, born Havana, Cuba, October 14, 1959; admitted to bar, 1990, Florida. *Education:* University of Miami (B.B.A., 1980; J.D., 1990); Florida International University (M.B.A., 1983). ***COURSES: Lawyering Skills and Values, Wills and Trusts.

BRUCE S. ROGOW*, (Professor of Law)**, born Hartford, Connecticut, November 18, 1939; admitted to bar, 1964, Florida. *Education:* University of Miami (B.B.A., 1961); University of Florida (J.D., 1963). ***COURSES: Civil Procedure, Appellate Practice, Constitutional Law, Federal Jurisdiction, Current Constitutional Problems, Criminal Law.

MARC ROHR*, (Professor of Law)**, born New York, New York, February 10, 1947; admitted to bar, 1972, California; 1979, Florida. *Education:* Columbia University (B.A., 1968); Harvard University (J.D., 1971). ***COURSES: Civil Procedure, Constitutional Law, Copyright, Trademark, First Amendment, Law and the Internet.

JOHN SANCHEZ*, (Professor of Law)**, born Los Angeles, California, January 6, 1952; admitted to bar, 1977, California. *Education:* Pomona College (B.A., 1974); University of California at Berkeley; Boalt Hall School of Law (J.D., 1977); Georgetown University (LL.M., 1985). ***COURSES: Elder Law, Labor Law, Constitutional Law, Employment Law, Remedies.

FLORENCE B. SHU-ACQUAYE*, (Assistant Professor of Law)**, *Education:* University of Yaounde (LL.B., 1984; Maitrise, 1985); Harvard Law School (LL.M., 1992); Stanford Law School (J.S.D.; 1996). ***COURSES: Contracts, Sales, Business Associations, Corporate Governance.

(This Listing Continued)

NOVA SOUTHEASTERN UNIVERSITY SHEPARD BROAD LAW CENTER—Continued

JOSEPH F. SMITH, JR.*, (Professor of Law)**, born White Plains, New York, September 18, 1944; admitted to bar, 1970, New York; 1976, Florida; 1979, District of Columbia. *Education:* Alfred University (B.A., 1966); Cornell University (J.D., 1969). ***COURSES: Admiralty, Contracts, Civil Rights of Persons with Disabilities, Special Education Law.

FRAN L. TETUNIC*, (Assistant Professor of Law)**, born New York, New York, April 22, 1951; admitted to bar, 1984, Florida. *Education:* Hunter College (B.A., 1973); Nova Southeastern University (J.D., 1984). ***COURSES: Alternative Dispute Resolution, Clinic, Aids Seminar, Family Law.

JAMES DANIEL WILETS*, (Associate Professor of Law)**, born Seattle, Washington, August 15, 1959; admitted to bar, 1987, California. *Education:* University of Washington (B.A., 1982); Yale University (M.A., 1994); Columbia Law School (J.D., 1987). ***COURSES: International Law, UCC, Contracts, Constitutional Law, Comparative Law, Unincorporated Business Entities, International Human Rights, International Business Transactions, Clinic.

STEVEN WISOTSKY*, (Professor of Law)**, born New York, New York, December 27, 1945; admitted to bar, 1970, Florida. *Education:* University of Pennsylvania (B.A., 1967); University of Miami (J.D., 1970); Yale University (LL.M., 1971). ***COURSES: Criminal Law, Appellate Practice, RICO, Drug Law, Civil Forfeiture, Criminal Procedure.

CHRISTINA ANNE ZAWISZA*, (Legal Director, Children First Project)**, born Amsterdam, New York, June 23, 1947; admitted to bar, 1977, Florida; 1986, New York. *Education:* State University of New York at Albany (B.A., 1969); University of Wisconsin (M.A., 1971); University of Virginia (J.D., 1977). ***COURSES: Clinic.

OHIO NORTHERN UNIVERSITY CLAUDE W. PETTIT COLLEGE OF LAW

525 SOUTH MAIN STREET
ADA, OHIO 45810
Telephone: (419) 772-2205
Fax: (419) 772-1875
www.law.onu.edu

ABA Approved Since 1948

The Claude W. Pettit College of Law, the second-oldest law school in Ohio, was established in 1885 and is fully accredited by the American Bar Association. The College of Law is a member of the Association of American Law Schools and a founding member of the League of Ohio Law Schools. For more than a century, the College of Law has prepared men and women for the practice of law across the country.

Throughout its distinguished history, the College of Law's national reputation has grown stronger as Ohio Northern University graduates have established successful careers in a variety of fields. Over 4,200 graduates are currently practicing law in virtually every state in the United States and several foreign countries. While the majority of our alumni engage in the private practice of law, many serve in different positions in local, state, and federal government. Among the College of Law alumni are over 125 state and federal judges. One of the most distinguished graduates was Frank B. Willis, former governor of Ohio and U.S. Senator until his death in 1928. The Willis Society is the highest academic honor society at the College of Law, and students who have excelled academically are invited to join the Willis Society during their third year of law school.

The College of Law faculty takes a uniquely personalized approach to teaching. With one of the lowest student-faculty ratios among law schools nationwide, the College of Law is committed to providing an environment where students and faculty easily interact both in and outside the classroom. As published scholars and legal practitioners, the faculty brings a variety of experiences and research interests into the classroom. Human values and personal dignity are stressed as paramount aspects of the practice of law. Thus, through its teaching, the College of Law faculty imbues in each student the highest standards of professionalism and ethical and moral responsibility.

The students represent over 100 undergraduate institutions and come from different parts of the United States and several foreign countries. Ohio Northern University is committed to cultural and ethnic diversity, with women and other minority groups well-represented in each entering class.

The Tilton Law Building is a newly-remodeled, handicapped-accessible facility which houses two moot court rooms, two student lounges, faculty and administrative offices, and a research-oriented law library. The Jay P. Taggart Law Library, a government depository library, offers quality research facilities. It contains over 270,000 volumes and has state-of-the-art network access throughout, including a new computer lab providing over 30 computers. All student-use computers provide access to a variety of online legal databases, including both WESTLAW and LEXIS. In addition, the library holds an extensive collection of volumes covering United States federal and state law and commonwealth materials focusing on Canada and the United Kingdom.

Throughout their three years of study, students participate in a variety of co-curricular and extracurricular activities. The Legal Clinic allows third-year students who have obtained internship certificates from the Supreme Court of Ohio to provide legal representation to low-income residents through the Ohio Northern University Legal Clinic with offices in both Ada and Lima, Ohio. These students may also serve as attorneys in criminal misdemeanor cases through local prosecutor and public defender offices. The Moot Court programs provide students with an opportunity for practicing oral advocacy and brief-writing skills by participation in appellate and trial advocacy competitions. In addition, the Moot Court selects and prepares advocates to represent the University in many national competitions. Each Spring semester the Law Review hosts a special symposium and Moot Court hosts a national competition. One unique, extra- curricular program offered to qualifying students at the College of Law is the Icelandic Exchange Program. Each fall a group of Icelandic students visits Ohio Northern University and, in turn, Ohio Northern students travel to Iceland where they are exposed to a full range of experiences relating to the legal education and judicial and social systems.

The College of Law recognizes its responsibility to assist students in obtaining legal employment for summer and for permanent positions. The activities of the Career Services office are coordinated by a full-time director with the assistance of a Placement Committee composed of faculty members and student representatives. The College of Law, as a member of the Ohio Law Placement Consortium, cosponsors a variety of joint recruiting projects throughout the year. On-campus interviews are also conducted in the fall and spring.

(This Listing Continued)

OHIO NORTHERN UNIVERSITY CLAUDE W. PETTIT COLLEGE OF LAW—Continued

Dean: David C. Crago (419) 772-2205
Associate Dean for Academic Affairs: John Paul Christoff (419) 772-2206
Assist. Dean and Dir. of Law Admissions: Linda English (419) 772-2211
Director of Financial Aid: Wendell Schick (419) 772-2272
Law Library Director: Nancy A. Armstrong (419) 772-2692
Director of Law Career Services: Cheryl A. Kitchen (419) 772-2249
Coordinator of External Affairs: J. Hope Raschke (419) 772-1980

FULL TIME FACULTY

DAVID C. CRAGO*, (Dean and Professor of Law)**, born Findlay, Ohio, January 7, 1952; admitted to bar, 1977, Ohio; 1987, United States Supreme Court. *Education:* Duke University (A.B., 1974); University of Michigan (J.D., 1977). ***COURSES: Business Associations, Corporations, Constitutional Law. ***Email:*** d-crago@onu.edu

NANCY A. ARMSTRONG*, (Director of the Law Library and Assistant Professor of Law)**, born Bayshore, New York, July 8, 1960; admitted to bar, 1985, Pennsylvania, New Jersey. *Education:* Vassar College (A.B., 1982); Boston College (J.D., 1985); Drexel University (M.S., 1987). ***COURSES: Advanced Legal Research. ***Email:*** n-armstrong@onu.edu

JOANNE C. BRANT*, (Professor of Law, Ella and Ernest Fisher Chair in Law)**, born Grand Island, New York, August 13, 1961; admitted to bar, 1986, Ohio. *Education:* Cornell University (A.B., 1983); Case Western Reserve University (J.D., 1986). ***COURSES: Federal Courts, Constitutional Law I & II, Church-State Seminar, Corporations. ***Email:*** j-brant@onu.edu

JOHN PAUL CHRISTOFF*, (Associate Dean for Academic Affairs and Professor of Law)**, born Lima, Ohio, November 4, 1943; admitted to bar, 1977, Ohio. *Education:* St. Alphonsus College (B.A., 1966); University of Notre Dame (M.A., 1967); Ohio Northern University (J.D., 1976). ***COURSES: Criminal Law, Criminal Procedure, Evidence. ***Email:*** j-christoff@onu.edu

C. ANTOINETTE CLARKE*, (Associate Professor)**, born Syracuse, New York, November 5, 1954; admitted to bar, 1992, Ohio. *Education:* Saint Lawrence University (1972); Rochester Institute of Technology (B.S., 1976); University of Toledo (J.D., 1992). ***COURSES: Criminal Law, Criminal Procedure, Domestic Relations, Juvenile Law. ***Email:*** c-clarke@onu.edu

CECILY A. CRIDER*, (Director of Legal Research and Writing)**, born Atlanta, Georgia, September 4, 1952; admitted to bar, 1993, Ohio. *Education:* Ohio Northern University (B.A., 1973; J.D., 1993). ***COURSES: Legal Research and Writing. ***Email:*** c-crider@onu.edu

KAREN E. ELLIOTT*, (Legal Writing Instructor)**, born Salem, Ohio, April 18, 1954; admitted to bar, 1983, Ohio. *Education:* Youngstown State (A.B., 1980); Ohio Northern (J.D., 1983). ***COURSES: Research and Writing. ***Email:*** k-elliott@onu.edu

WILLIAM L. EVANS*, (Professor of Law)**, born Kenton, Ohio, June 19, 1935. *Education:* Ohio Northern University (B.A., 1957; J.D., 1971). ***COURSES: Property, Decedents Estates & Trusts, Law & Medicine. ***Email:*** w-evans@onu.edu

HOWARD N. FENTON*, (Professor of Law)**, born Toledo, Ohio, May 6, 1950; admitted to bar, 1975, Texas; 1976, District of Columbia; 1990, Ohio. *Education:* University of Texas at Austin (B.S., 1971); University of Texas School of Law (J.D., 1975). ***COURSES: International Business Transactions, Public International Law, Contracts, Administrative Law. ***Email:*** h-fenton@onu.edu

BRUCE COMLY FRENCH*, (Professor of Law)**, born Philadelphia, Pennsylvania, June 22, 1947; admitted to bar, 1975, Pennsylvania; 1976, District of Columbia, 1985, Ohio. *Education:* American University (B.A., 1969; M.A., 1970); Antioch School of Law (J.D., 1975). ***COURSES: Constitutional Law, Civil Procedure, Remedies, Evidence, Legislative Process and Drafting. ***Email:*** b-french@onu.edu

RICHARD L. HAIGHT*, (Professor of Law)**, born Boston, Massachusetts, April 15, 1941; admitted to bar, 1965, Massachusetts; 1982, District of Columbia. *Education:* Boston University (A.B., 1962; LL.M., 1966); Suffolk University (J.D., 1965). ***COURSES: Federal Income Taxation, Federal Estate and Gift Taxation, Decedents' Estates and Trusts, Estate Planning. ***Email:*** r-haight@onu.edu

KEVIN D. HILL*, (Professor of Law)**, born San Antonio, Texas, July 2, 1950; admitted to bar, 1980, Kentucky. *Education:* University of Kentucky (B.S., 1973); Northern Kentucky University (J.D., 1979); Temple University (LL.M., 1985). ***COURSES: Civil Procedure, Environmental Law, Evidence. ***Email:*** k-hill@onu.edu

LOUIS F. LOBENHOFER*, (Professor of Law)**, born Denver, Colorado, March 24, 1950; admitted to bar, 1975, Colorado. *Education:* College of William and Mary (A.B., 1972); University of Colorado at Boulder (J.D., 1975); University of Denver (LL.M., 1979). ***COURSES: Federal Taxation, Business Planning, Corporate Tax, Partnership Tax. ***Email:*** l-lobenhofer@onu.edu

LIAM S. O'MELINN*, (Assistant Professor of Law)**, *Education:* University of California Santa Cruz (B.A., 1981); Yale University (Ph.D., 1991); Columbia Law School (J.D., 1995). ***COURSES: Contracts, Intellectual Property, Constitutional Law, Business Organizations. ***Email:*** l-omelinn@onu.edu

DAVID W. RAACK*, (Professor of Law)**, born St. Louis, Missouri, April 30, 1954; admitted to bar, 1979, Missouri. *Education:* University of Kansas (B.A., 1976); University of Missouri at Kansas City (J.D., 1979); Temple University (LL.M., 1985); Columbia University (LL.M., 1988). ***COURSES: Environmental Law, Natural Resources Law, Property, Legal Ethics. ***Email:*** d-raack@onu.edu

NANCY PAINE SABOL*, (Assistant Professor and Director of Academic Support Services)**, born Bay Village, Ohio, May 1, 1962; admitted to bar, 1987, Ohio. *Education:* Ohio University Honors Tutorial College (B.A., 1984); Ohio State University College of Law (J.D., 1987). ***COURSES: Employment Discrimination, Academic Support. ***Email:*** n-sabol@onu.edu

VICTOR L. STREIB*, (Professor of Law)**, born Marion, Indiana, October 8, 1941; admitted to bar, 1970, Indiana. *Education:* Auburn University (B.S., 1966); Indiana University (J.D., 1970). ***COURSES: Capital Punishment, Criminal Law, Criminal Procedure, Juvenile Law. ***Email:*** v-streib@onu.edu

VERNON L. TRASTER*, (Professor of Law)**, born Des Moines, Iowa, October 22, 1947; admitted to bar, 1973, Iowa. *Education:* Drake University (B.S. in B.A., 1969; J.D., 1973). ***COURSES: Torts, Insurance, Evidence, Insurance Bad-faith Litigation.

STEPHEN C. VELTRI*, (Professor of Law)**, born Pittsburgh, Pennsylvania, March 29, 1955; admitted to bar, 1981, Pennsylvania. *Education:* University of Pittsburgh (B.A., 1977); Georgetown University (J.D., 1981); Columbia University (LL.M., 1986). ***COURSES: Commercial Law and Property. ***Email:*** s-veltri@onu.edu

(This Listing Continued)

OHIO NORTHERN UNIVERSITY CLAUDE W. PETTIT COLLEGE OF LAW—Continued

BRYAN H. WARD*, (Interim Director of Law Clinics and Instructor of Law)**, born Ashland, Kentucky, August 25, 1961; admitted to bar, 1993, Ohio. *Education:* Ohio Northern University (B.A.,1983); University of North Carolina (J.D., 1986); Ohio State University (Ph.D., 1993). ***COURSES: Legal Clinics. ***Email:*** b-ward1@onu.edu

SHERRY YOUNG*, (Professor of Law)**, born Columbus, Ohio, February 10, 1960; admitted to bar, 1984, Ohio. *Education:* Michigan State University (B.A., 1981); Harvard University (J.D., 1984). ***COURSES: Torts, Products Liability, Domestic Relations, Sports Law. ***Email:*** s-young@onu.edu

THE OHIO STATE UNIVERSITY MICHAEL E. MORITZ COLLEGE OF LAW

55 WEST 12TH AVENUE
COLUMBUS, OHIO 43210
Telephone: (614) 292-2631
Fax: (614) 292-1383
www.osu.edu/units/law

ABA Approved Since 1923.

The College of Law's missions, like those of its parent University, are scholarship, education, and service. The College offers a rigorous academic program, encompassing both a traditional law school curriculum and electives in a wide range of topics. First-year students enroll in at least one "small section" class designed to enhance the learning process, and each first-year student experiences an intensive writing and analysis course taught by a full-time faculty member. Advanced students can elect courses offered through the clinical programs, which are among the oldest and finest in the country. Students also can develop professional skills through service on one of two highly respected academic journals, the *Ohio State Law Journal* and the *Ohio State Journal on Dispute Resolution.* The College also has a large Moot Court and Lawyering Skills Program, in which students can hone their practical legal skills. The College of Law has an active public service program, including a large Street Law program and the Pro Bono Research Group, which provides legal research assistance to public service attorneys in Ohio.

The College has established the Center for Law, Policy, and Social Science, which supports faculty whose teaching and scholarship explore law using tools and concepts developed in the social sciences. This Center has permitted the development of a transatlantic partnership with the Socio-Legal Centre at Oxford University in Oxford, England. The law and pre-law summer programs at Oxford enhance the international and comparative dimensions of the College's program. Extensive involvement in alternative dispute resolution has made the College a leader in this important and developing aspect of the law, and the *Ohio State Journal on Dispute Resolution* has already made its mark in this arena. The College offers joint degree programs with other colleges and departments at the University, including Business Administration and Health Administration, and a number of faculty members hold joint appointments in law and other units.

The educational enterprise of the College of Law is well supported by the physical facilities. A twenty million dollar addition to and renovation of the existing building, funded largely by private donations, has created space for the growing library collection, which is already the fourteenth largest academic law library in the country.

The College of Law is accredited by the American Bar Association and is a charter member of the Association of American Law Schools. Four members of the faculty have been President of this Association. Former faculty members, administrators, and students also have assumed leadership roles in legal education as deans of this and other law schools, in higher education as university presidents, and in the profession as distinguished members of the bar and bench. A significant number have served as elected and appointed public officials at the local, state, and national levels and in executive and management positions in business and industry.

Dean: Nancy Hardin Rogers (614) 292-2631
Academic Affairs: Alan C. Michaels (614) 688-3451
Admissions: Kathy S. Northern (614) 292-8810
Financial Aid: Robert L. Solomon (614) 292-5354
Library Director: Bruce S. Johnson (614) 292-6691
Placement: Amee R. McKim (614) 292-0087
Alumni Affairs: Pam Lombardi (614) 292-2937

FULL TIME FACULTY

NANCY HARDIN ROGERS*, (Dean and Michael E. Moritz Chair in Alternative Dispute Resolution)**, born Lansing, Michigan, September 18, 1948; admitted to bar, 1972, Ohio; 1975, District of Columbia. *Education:* University of Kansas (B.A., 1969); Yale Law School (J.D., 1972). ***COURSES: Mediation, Dispute Resolution, Evidence. ***Email:*** rogers.23@osu.edu

MARY BETH BEAZLEY*, (Associate Professor of Law)**, born Evergreen Park, IL, February 11, 1957; admitted to bar, 1984, Ohio. *Education:* Bowling Green State University (B.A., 1979); University of Notre Dame (J.D., 1983). ***COURSES: Legal Writing and Analysis, Appellate Advocacy, Advanced Legal Writing. ***Email:*** beazley.1@osu.edu

DOUGLAS AARON BERMAN*, (Associate Professor of Law)**, born Washington, D.C., October 21, 1968; admitted to bar, 1997, New York. *Education:* Princeton University (A.B., 1990), Harvard Law School (J.D., 1993). ***COURSES: Criminal Law, Criminal Procedure, Sentencing & Punishment, Legal Writing, Intellectual Property. ***Email:*** berman.43@osu.edu

MICHAEL BRAUNSTEIN*, (Professor of Law)**, born New Orleans, Louisiana, May 21, 1947; admitted to bar, 1974, California. *Education:* Louisiana State University (B.A., 1970); Tulane University School of Law (J.D., 1974). ***COURSES: Estate Planning, Mining Law, Natural Resources, Oil and Gas, Property, Real Estate Finance. ***Email:*** braunstein.1@osu.edu

***JAMES J. BRUDNEY*, (Newton D. Baker- Baker & Hostetler Chair in Law)**, born New York, N.Y., July 6, 1950; admitted to bar, 1981,

(This Listing Continued)

THE OHIO STATE UNIVERSITY MICHAEL E. MORITZ COLLEGE OF LAW—Continued

District of Columbia. *Education:* Amherst College (B.A., 1971); Oxford University (M.A.B.A., 1973); Yale Law School (J.D., 1979). ***COURSES:*** Age Discrimination in the Workplace, Employment Law, Labor Law, Legislation. ***Email:*** brudney.1@osu.edu

SANFORD N. CAUST-ELLENBOGEN*, (Associate Professor of Law)**, born New York, New York, February 21, 1954; admitted to bar, 1986, New York. *Education:* State University of New York at Albany (B.A., 1974); Harvard University (M.C.R.P., 1977); New York University (J.D., 1985). ***COURSES: Civil Procedure, Conflict of Laws, Federal Courts, Administrative Law. ***Email:*** caust-ellenbogen.1@osu.edu

DANIEL C.K. CHOW*, (Professor of Law)**, born Hong Kong, March 12, 1957; admitted to bar, 1984, New York. *Education:* Yale University (B.A., 1979); Yale Law School (J.D., 1982). ***COURSES: Gratuitous Transfers, International Transactions, Jurisprudence, Property, Trusts and Future Interests. ***Email:*** chow.1@osu.edu

DOUGLAS R. COLE*, (Assistant Professor of Law)**, born June 26, 1964; admitted to bar, 1994, Illinois; 1999, Ohio. *Education:* Ripon College (B.A., 1986); University of Wisconsin (B.S., 1988); University of Chicago Law School (J.D., 1993). ***COURSES: Contracts, Business Associations.

SARAH RUDOLPH COLE*, (Associate Professor of Law)**, born Lincoln, Nebraska, September 11, 1966; admitted to bar, 1993, Illinois. *Education:* University of Puget Sound (B.A., 1986); University of Chicago (J.D., 1990). ***COURSES: Alternative Dispute Resolution, Torts, Administrative Law. ***Email:*** cole.228@osu.edu

RUTH COLKER*, (Heck-Faust Memorial Chair in Constitutional Law)**, born Pittsburgh, PA, May 4, 1956; admitted to bar, 1981, Washington. *Education:* Harvard-Radcliffe (A.B., 1978); Harvard University (J.D., 1981). ***COURSES: Constitutional Law, Disability Discrimination, Feminist Theory, Gay Rights. ***Email:*** colker.2@osu.edu

ELIZABETH COOKE*, (Supervising Attorney Clinical Programs)**, born Champaign, Illinois, June 20, 1969; admitted to bar, 1994, Ohio. *Education:* Miami University (B.A., 1991); The Ohio State University College of Law (J.D., 1994). ***COURSES: Civil Law Practicum.

SHARON L. DAVIES*, (Associate Professor of Law)**, born Springfield, Massachusetts, October 22, 1960; admitted to bar, 1988, New York. *Education:* University of Massachusetts (B.A., 1984); Columbia University (J.D., 1987). ***COURSES: Criminal Law, Criminal Procedure, Evidence. ***Email:*** davies.49@osu.edu

ANITA A. DISASQUALE*, (Supervising Attorney, Clinical Programs)**, born Columbus, Ohio, April 1, 1960; admitted to bar, 1988, Ohio; 1990, New York. *Education:* The Ohio State University (B.A., 1982); Case Western Reserve University (J.D., 1987). ***COURSES: Justice for Children Clinic. ***Email:*** disasquale.4@osu.edu

ANNE DOYLE*, (Director, Bar Passage Support Program)**, born Madison, Wisconsin, August 5, 1954; admitted to bar, 1988, Pennsylvania. *Education:* New York University (B.A., 1984); Georgetown University (J.D., 1987). ***COURSES: Bar Passage Support Program. ***Email:*** doyle.64@osu.edu

JOSHUA DRESSLER*, (Professor of Law)**, born New York, March 30, 1947; admitted to bar, 1973, California. *Education:* UCLA (B.A., 1968; J.D., 1973). ***COURSES: Criminal Law, Criminal Procedure, Adjudication. ***Email:*** dressler.11@osu.edu

TERRI L. ENNS*, (Supervising Attorney Clinical Program)**, born Santa Barbara, California, April 3, 1958; admitted to bar, 1996, Ohio. *Education:* Goshen College (B.A., 1980); Associated Mennonite Biblical Seminary (M. Div., 1986); The Ohio State University College of Law (J.D., 1996). ***COURSES: Legislation Practicum. ***Email:*** enns.1@osu.edu

CHRISTOPHER M. FAIRMAN*, (Assistant Professor of Law)**, born July 26, 1960; admitted to bar, 1994, Texas. *Education:* University of Texas at Austin (B.A., 1982); University of Texas School of Law (J.D., 1994). ***COURSES: Civil Procedure, Professional Responsibility, Constitutional Law.

KATHERINE HUNT FEDERLE*, (Associate Professor of Law & Director, Justice for Children)**, born Alton, Illinois, August 5, 1958; admitted to bar, 1984, District of Columbia; 1986, Hawaii. *Education:* Pomona College (B.A., 1980); Seattle University (J.D., 1983); Georgetown University (LL.M., 1986). ***COURSES: Children & the Law, Clinical Teaching. ***Email:*** federle.1@osu.edu

EDWARD B. FOLEY*, (Professor of Law)**, born West Palm Beach, Florida, September 2, 1961; admitted to bar, 1988, District of Columbia. *Education:* Yale University (B.A., 1983); Columbia University (J.D., 1986). ***COURSES: Constitutional Law, Jurisprudence, Children's Rights, Election Law, Religion and the Law.

THOMAS P. GALLANIS, JR.*, (Associate Professor of Law)**, born Chicago, Illinois, November 22, 1965; admitted to bar, 1990, Illinois. *Education:* Yale University (B.A., 1987); University of Chicago (J.D., 1990), Cambridge University (LL.M., 1993; Ph.D., 1997). ***COURSES: Wills, Trusts and Estates, Estate and Gift Taxation, Elder Law. ***Email:*** gallanis.2@osu.edu

DAVID GOLDBERGER*, (Isador and Ida Topper Professor of Law and Director of Clinical Programs)**, born Chicago, Illinois, July 13, 1941; admitted to bar, 1968, Illinois; 1981, Ohio. *Education:* University of Chicago (B.A., 1963; J.D., 1967). ***COURSES: Constitutional Law, First Amendment, Clinic. ***Email:*** goldberger.1@osu.edu

ARTHUR F. GREENBAUM*, (Professor of Law)**, born Toledo, Ohio, November 17, 1951; admitted to bar, 1976, Virginia; 1977, District of Columbia. *Education:* Yale University (B.A., 1973); University of Virginia (J.D., 1976). ***COURSES: Administrative Law, Civil Procedure, Legal Education, Professional Responsibility. ***Email:*** greenbaum.1@osu.edu

SHELDON W. HALPERN*, (C. William O'Neil Professor of Law)**, born New York, New York, December 16, 1935; admitted to bar, 1959, New York; 1973, Minnesota. *Education:* Cornell University (A.B., 1957; LL.B., 1959). ***COURSES: Copyright, Defamation and Privacy, Contracts. ***Email:*** halpern.1@osu.edu

L. CAMILLE HEBERT*, (Carter C. Kissell Professor of Law and Director, Center for Law, Policy, and Social Science)**, born Elk City, Oklahoma, May 15, 1959; admitted to bar, 1982, Kansas; 1983, Missouri; 1989, Ohio. *Education:* Kansas State University (B.A., 1979); University of Kansas (J.D., 1982). ***COURSES: Pretrial Litigation, Employment Discrimination, Sexual Harassment Seminar, Worker Privacy Seminar, Legal Writing and Analysis. ***Email:*** hebert.2@osu.edu

STEVEN F. HUEFNER*, (Assistant Professor of Law)**, born July 2, 1962; admitted to bar, 1991, Utah; 1992 District of Columbia. *Education:* University of Utah (1984); Harvard University (A.B., 1986); Columbia University School of Law (J.D., 1991). ***COURSES: Legislation, Jurisprudence.

LOUIS A. JACOBS*, (Professor of Law)**, born Alliance, Ohio, October 25, 1948; admitted to bar, 1973, Ohio. *Education:* Syracuse University (B.A., 1970); American University, Washington College of Law (J.D., 1973); New York University (LL.M., 1978). ***COURSES: Evidence, Constitutional Law, Employment Discrimination, Clinical Programs (Prosecution Practicum). ***Email:*** jacobs.4@osu.edu

(This Listing Continued)

THE OHIO STATE UNIVERSITY MICHAEL E. MORITZ COLLEGE OF LAW—Continued

BRUCE S. JOHNSON*, (Professor of Law and Associate Dean for Information Services)**, born Glen Ridge, New Jersey, December 6, 1948; admitted to bar, 1973, New Jersey. *Education:* Amherst College (B.A., 1970); New York University School of Law (J.D., 1973); Rutgers University (M.L.S., 1978). ***COURSES: Legal Research, Legal Writing and Analysis. ***Email:*** johnson.726@osu.edu

CREOLA JOHNSON*, (Assistant Professor of Law)**, born Independence, Louisiana, December 8, 1963; admitted to bar, 1994, Pennsylvania. *Education:* Louisiana State University (B.S., 1989); West Virginia University (J.D., 1994). ***COURSES: Contracts, Debtor-Creditor Law, Legal Writing. ***Email:*** johnson.1904@osu.edu

ROBERT KRIVOSHEY*, (Supervising Attorney, Clinical Programs)**, born Brooklyn, New York, November 4, 1942; admitted to bar, 1978, Ohio. *Education:* Yeshiva University (B.A., 1964); University of Chicago (M.A., 1966; Ph.D, 1973); Ohio State University (J.D., 1978). ***COURSES: Prosecution & Defense Clinic, Trial Practice. ***Email:*** krivoshey.1@osu.edu

STANLEY K. LAUGHLIN, JR.*, (Professor of Law)**, born Dayton, Ohio; admitted to bar, 1961, California; 1961, Ohio. *Education:* Miami University (A.B., 1955); Ohio State University (J.D., 1960). ***COURSES: Foreign Relations Law, Constitutional Law, Anthropology and Law, Advanced Constitutional Law, Ethical Issues, Economic Regulation and the Constitution. ***Email:*** laughlin.1@osu.edu

JAMES E. MEEKS*, (Jacob E. Davis Professor of Law)**, born Morgantown, West Virginia, November 8, 1938; admitted to bar, 1963, Ohio. *Education:* Oberlin College (B.A., 1960); Columbia University (J.D., 1963). ***COURSES: Torts, Antitrust, Public Utilities, Law and Economics. ***Email:*** meeks.2@osu.edu

DEBORAH JONES MERRITT*, (Dir., John Glenn Inst. for Public Service & Pub. Policy and John Deaver Drinko/Baker & Hostetler Chair in Law)**, born New York, New York, October 15, 1955; admitted to bar, 1981, Georgia. *Education:* Harvard University (A.B., 1977); Columbia University (J.D., 1980). ***COURSES: Torts, Law and Social Science, Women in Law, Legal Writing. ***Email:*** merritt.52@osu.edu

ALAN C. MICHAELS*, (Associate Dean for Faculty and Associate Professor of Law)**, born New York, New York, May 5, 1961; admitted to bar, 1987, New York. *Education:* Harvard University (A.B., 1983); Columbia University (J.D., 1986). ***COURSES: Criminal Law, Criminal Procedure, White Collar Crime. ***Email:*** michaels.23@osu.edu

KATHY SEWARD NORTHERN*, (Associate Dean for Admissions and Financial Aid and Associate Professor of Law)**, born Columbus, Ohio, March 11, 1958; admitted to bar, 1983, Ohio. *Education:* Williams College (B.A., 1980); Harvard University (J.D., 1983). ***COURSES: Torts, Products Liability, Complex Litigation, Environmental Law, Environmental Torts. ***Email:*** northern.1@osu.edu

MARY ELLEN O'CONNELL*, (Professor of Law)**, born Milwaukee, Wisconsin, May 25, 1958; admitted to bar, 1986, New York, Washington D.C.. *Education:* Northwestern University (B.A., 1980); London School of Economics (M.Sc., 1981); Cambridge University (L.L.B., 1982); Columbia University (J.D., 1985). ***COURSES: International Law, Contracts. ***Email:*** oconnell.44@osu.edu

JOHN QUIGLEY*, (President's Club Professor of Law)**, born St. Louis, Missouri, October 1, 1940; admitted to bar, 1967, Massachusetts; 1973, Ohio. *Education:* Harvard University (A.B., 1962; M.A., 1966; LL.B., 1966). ***COURSES: Criminal Law, International Law, Comparative Law. ***Email:*** quigley.2@osu.edu

ALLAN J. SAMANSKY*, (Professor of Law)**, born St. Paul, Minnesota, June 7, 1945; admitted to bar, 1974, Pennsylvania. *Education:* Harvard University (B.A., 1967); University of California at Berkeley (M.A., 1968); University of Pennsylvania (J.D., 1974). ***COURSES: Accounting, Business Planning, Corporations, Estate and Gift Taxation, Income Taxation. ***Email:*** samansky.1@osu.edu

MORGAN SHIPMAN*, (John W. Bricker Professor of Law)**, born Memphis, Texas, December 4, 1933; admitted to bar, 1958, Texas. *Education:* University of Texas (B.B.A., 1955); University of Texas (LL.B., 1958). ***COURSES: Accounting, Agency and Partnership, Business Organizations, Creditors' and Debtors' Rights, Legal Profession, Securities Regulation, Federal Taxation.

BARBARA ROOK SNYDER*, (University Vice Provost and Joanne Wharton Murphy/Class of 1965 Professor of Law)**, born Columbus, Ohio, July 23, 1955; admitted to bar, 1980, Illinois. *Education:* Ohio State University (B.A., 1976); University of Chicago (J.D., 1980). ***COURSES: Constitutional Law, Evidence. ***Email:*** snyder.7@osu.edu

MARC SPINDELMAN*, (Assistant Professor of Law)**, born New York, March 15, 1968. *Education:* Johns Hopkins University (B.A., 1990); University of Michigan Law School (J.D., 1995). ***COURSES: Health Law, Bioethics, Legal Writing.

JOSEPH B. STULBERG*, (Professor of Law)**, born Lansing, Michigan, April 21, 1945; admitted to bar, 1971, New York. *Education:* Kalamazoo College (B.A., 1967); University of Rochester (M.A., 1974; Ph.D., 1975); New York University (J.D., 1970). ***COURSES: Alternative Dispute Resolution, Employment Law. ***Email:*** stulberg.2@osu.edu

PETER P. SWIRE*, (Professor of Law)**, born New York, May 15, 1958; admitted to bar, 1986, Pennsylvania; 1987, District of Columbia. *Education:* Princeton University (A.B., 1980); Yale, (J.D., 1985). ***COURSES: Cyberspace, Privacy, Business Associations, Banking. ***Email:*** www.osu.edu/units/law/swire.htm

DONALD BRUCE TOBIN*, (Assistant Professor of Law)**, born Maryland, January 8, 1967; admitted to bar, 1996, Maryland. *Education:* Duke University (B.A., 1988); Georgetown University (J.D., 1996). ***COURSES: Federal Income Tax, Tax Policy.

GREGORY M. TRAVALIO*, (Associate Dean for Professional Relations & Lawrence D. Stanley Professor of Law)**, born Harrisburg, Pennsylvania, April 22, 1947; admitted to bar, 1975, Pennsylvania; 1984, Ohio. *Education:* University of Pittsburgh (B.A., 1969; J.D., 1975); Columbia University (LL.M., 1979). ***COURSES: Contracts, Commercial Law, Consumer Law. ***Email:*** travalio.1@osu.edu

VINCENE VERDUN*, (Associate Professor of Law)**, born Flint, Michigan, April 4, 1954; admitted to bar, 1978, Michigan; 1990, Ohio. *Education:* University of Michigan (B.A., 1975; J.D., 1978). ***COURSES: Agency and Partnership, Commercial Paper, Corporations, Remedies. ***Email:*** verdun.1@osu.edu

DOUGLAS JOHN WHALEY*, (James W. Shocknessy Professor of Law)**, born Huntingburg, Indiana, September 25, 1943; admitted to bar, 1968, Illinois; 1970, Indiana; 1985, Ohio. *Education:* University of Maryland (B.A., 1965); University of Texas (J.D., with honors, 1968). ***COURSES: Contracts, Commercial Law, Debtor-Creditor Law, Consumer Law, Sales, Commercial Paper, Secured Transactions. ***Email:*** dglswhaley@aol.com

CHARLES E. WILSON*, (Associate Professor of Law)**, born Denver, Colorado, April 24, 1952; admitted to bar, 1977, New York; 1986, Ohio. *Education:* University of Kansas (B.S., 1973); New York University School of Law (J.D., 1976). ***COURSES: Advanced Labor Law, Civil Procedure, Employment Law, Evidence, Labor Law, Legal Negotiation. ***Email:*** wilson.49@osu.edu

OKLAHOMA CITY UNIVERSITY SCHOOL OF LAW

2501 NORTH BLACKWELDER
OKLAHOMA CITY, OKLAHOMA 73106-1493
Telephone: (405) 521-5337
Fax: (405) 521-5802
http://www.okcu.edu/law/

ABA Approved Since 1960

Oklahoma City University School of Law traces its lineage to 1907, making it the state's oldest law school. Since that time its graduates have held positions of distinction throughout the state and the nation. The School today is especially strong in many fields, including American Indian law, alternative dispute resolution, bankruptcy and commercial law, and legal research and writing.

THE STUDENTS

The School of Law is a national law school. Its 500 students are drawn from more than thirty states and several foreign countries, and were educated at over 215 universities and colleges. While many students enter the Law School immediately after graduation, others enter after a period, often substantial, spent in another career. The student body commonly includes present and former doctors, university professors, engineers, military officers, businesspersons, and professionals from other fields.

THE PROGRAM OF EDUCATION

The program of education is partly traditional, teaching critical and analytical skills in a broad array of subjects. But it is progressive as well, providing essential practical, writing and problem-solving skills, and inculcating the strong sense of professional responsibility that graduates will need as effective lawyers and leaders. The curriculum is well balanced, offering both foundational courses and courses in emerging or currently important fields. In addition, the School offers an array of seminars, practice-oriented courses, and clinical and internship opportunities. The School also stresses writing skills, providing a three-semester introductory program and a host of upper-level writing-related requirements and electives.

The faculty is the greatest resource of any institution; the faculty of the School of Law is a distinguished and energetic group of scholar-teachers. The faculty consists of 31 full-time professors plus adjunct professors who teach a limited number of specialized courses. Full-time faculty members hold law degrees from 20 law schools. Half hold advanced degrees in law or other fields. The faculty includes national leaders in fields such as corporation law, commercial law, health care law, professional responsibility, and Indian law.

THE FACILITIES

Law School activities are conducted in the Sarkeys Law Center and in the Gold Star Building. The Sarkeys Law Center is a spacious, handsome structure housing classrooms, administrative offices, the Law Review, and student organizations. Its classrooms are designed for effective teaching; its upper and lower plazas provide a forum for social interaction. The Gold Star Building is a four-story center housing the library and faculty offices. It has been designed to promote research and study as well as easy interchange with the faculty.

The Law Library's collection includes over 271,000 volumes with 67,749 titles. The Library subscribes to over 3,800 law reviews, journals, and looseleaf services. In addition to holding extensive resource material in state and federal law, it also has a broad collection of foreign and international law texts and sources, and expansive collections in selected non-legal areas. There are also special collections housed in the Library including the Native American Collection.

The Law Library has a fully networked computer lab. Students may use workstations to write briefs and research papers, prepare spreadsheets, and engage in other computing tasks. Students also have access, both in the computer lab and through their own computers, to WESTLAW, LEXIS, and resources on the Internet. The Library also has a substantial holding of databases on CD-ROM in such areas as health law, tax law, and state civil and criminal procedure. OLIB, an on-line database, provides access to the collections of the Law Library and the main University library.

CENTERS FOR RESEARCH AND SERVICE

The School of Law is the home of the Native American Legal Resource Center. The Center makes sources of American Indian law available to the public, and counseling governments and businesses on matters of Indian law and Indian economic development.

The School also has a Center on Alternative Dispute Resolution, which provides mediation services and programs to train mediators in various fields. Faculty, students, lawyers, and interested lay persons have participated in the Center's frequently offered training programs and have been able to serve as mediators in the Early Settlement Program. The Center also develops curricula for integrating ADR methods into the teaching of substantive law school courses and sponsors research in the ADR field.

The Law School's Center for the Study of State Constitutional Law and Government was founded to develop and implement programs dedicated to the improvement of state constitutions and state governance. By sponsoring workshops, scholarly writing, and public lectures, the Center promotes scholarship and discussion on important issues relating to state government.

GRADUATES AND EMPLOYMENT

Graduates of the School of Law have a firm foundation in legal theory, practical legal skills, a strong sense of professional responsibility, a high level of writing ability, technological literacy, and a commitment to the community and public service. The School of Law has a professional Career Services Office that assists students with career planning and locating and securing job opportunities. The Office of Career Services assists employers to find and attract entry-level and experienced graduates of the Law School through job postings, on-campus interviews, market research, resume forwarding, and other services.

(This Listing Continued)

OKLAHOMA CITY UNIVERSITY SCHOOL OF LAW —Continued

Dean: Lawrence K. Hellman (405) 521-5440
Associate Dean: Norwood Beveridge (405) 521-5337
Assistant Dean for Students: Deborah Fathree (405) 521-5334
Assistant Dean, Career Services: Gina Rowsam (405) 521-5332
Director, Admissions: Peter Storandt (405) 521-5354
Director, Native American Legal Resource Center: C. Blue Clark (405) 521-5188
Director, Financial Aid: Molly Roberts (405) 521-5211
Director, Library: Judy Morgan (405) 521-5062
Director, Finance and Administration: Pam Ray (405) 521-5338
Registrar: Sharon Hayes (405) 521-5333

FULL TIME FACULTY

LAWRENCE KENT HELLMAN*, (Dean and Professor of Law)**, born Chandler, Oklahoma, May 30, 1944; admitted to bar, 1970, Oklahoma. *Education:* Washington and Lee (B.S., 1966); Northwestern University (M.B.A., 1967; J.D., 1970). ***COURSES: Anti-Trust, Civil Procedure, Professional Responsibility. ***Email:*** lhellman@okcu.edu

DENNIS W. ARROW*, (Professor of Law, Assoc. Dir., Ctr., Study of St. Con. Law & Gov't, & Assoc. Dir., Nat. Am. Leg. Res. Ctr.)**, born Chicago, Illinois, July 27, 1949; admitted to bar, 1974, California. *Education:* George Washington University (B.A., 1970); California Western School of Law (J.D., 1974); Harvard (LL.M., 1975). ***COURSES: American Indian Law, Civil Rights, Constitutional Law.

PHYLLIS ELAINE BERNARD*, (Professor of Law & Director, Center of ADR)**, born New York, New York, August 24, 1954; admitted to bar, 1982, District of Columbia. *Education:* Bryn Mawr College (A.B., 1976); Columbia University (M.A., 1978); University of Pennsylvania (J.D., 1981). ***COURSES: Administrative Law, ADR, Health Law, Professional Responsibility. ***Email:*** pbernard@okcu.edu

NORWOOD PIERSON BEVERIDGE*, (Associate Dean for Academic Affairs and Professor of Law)**, born Boston, Massachusetts, November 5, 1936; admitted to bar, 1963, New York. *Education:* Harvard (A.B., 1958; LL.B., 1962); New York University (LL.M., 1985). ***COURSES: Corporations, Securities Regulation, Corporate Finance. ***Email:*** paladin@okcu.edu

CHARLES LEONARD CANTRELL*, (Professor of Law)**, born Waco, Texas, August 24, 1948; admitted to bar, 1972, Texas; 1978, Wisconsin. *Education:* Texas A&M; University of Texas, Austin; Baylor University (J.D., 1972); University of Texas, Austin (LL.M., 1976). ***COURSES: Constitutional Law, Criminal Procedure. ***Email:*** ccantrell@okcu.edu

RICHARD EARL COULSON*, (Professor of Law)**, born Panhandle, Texas, September 17, 1942; admitted to bar, 1968, Oklahoma. *Education:* Oklahoma City University (B.A., 1972; J.D., 1968). ***COURSES: Bankruptcy, Evidence, Legal History, Comparative Law. ***Email:*** rcoulson@okcu.edu

VON RUSSELL CREEL*, (Professor of Law)**, born Ardmore, Oklahoma, March 9, 1942; admitted to bar, 1969, Oklahoma. *Education:* University of Oklahoma (B.A., 1964; J.D., 1968). ***COURSES: Civil Procedure, Legal History, Conflict of Laws. ***Email:*** vcreel@okcu.edu

PAULA J. DALLEY*, (Professor of Law)**, born New Brunswick, New Jersey, November 23, 1963; admitted to bar, 1989, New York. *Education:* Princeton University (A.B., 1985); Harvard Law School (J.D., 1988); New York University School of Law (LL.M., 1994). ***COURSES: Agency and Partnership, Corporations, Property. ***Email:*** pdalley@okcu.edu

PETER GARDNER DILLON*, (Associate Professor of Law)**, born September 25, 1945; admitted to bar, 1973, Colorado. *Education:* Syracuse University (B.A., 1967); Fordham University School of Law (J.D., 1970); University of Texas School of Law (LL.M., 1976). ***COURSES: Contracts, Sales, Leases, Secured Transactions.

MARJORIE P. DOWNING*, (Professor Emeritus)**, born Denver, Colorado, June 16, 1933; admitted to bar, 1959, Oklahoma. *Education:* University of Oklahoma (B.A., 1955; LL.B., 1959). ***COURSES: Property, Trusts & Estates, Land Finance. ***Email:*** mdowning@okcu.edu

KAREN EBY*, (Instructor, Legal Research and Writing)**, born Stillwater, Oklahoma, November 20, 1957; admitted to bar, 1984, Oklahoma. *Education:* Oklahoma State University (B.S., 1979); University of Tulsa (J.D., 1984). ***COURSES: Legal Research and Writing, Appellate Advocacy. ***Email:*** keby@okcu.edu

GREGORY NEIL EDDINGTON*, (Instructor, Legal Research and Writing)**, born Norman, Oklahoma, October 1, 1956; admitted to bar, 1987, Oklahoma. *Education:* University of Oklahoma (B.B.A., 1978); University of Oklahoma College of Law (J.D., 1986); New York University (LL.M., 1992). ***COURSES: Legal Research, Legal Writing, Appellate Advocacy. ***Email:*** geddington@okcu.edu

MICHAEL T. GIBSON*, (Professor of Law)**, born Omaha, Nebraska, March 25, 1958; admitted to bar, 1982, Nebraska. *Education:* University of Nebraska - Lincoln (B.A., 1979); Yale (J.D., 1982). ***COURSES: Contracts, Sales, Legal Analysis, Federal Jurisdiction. ***Email:*** mgibson@okcu.edu

JEAN ELIZABETH GILES*, (Instructor)**, born Indiana, August 31, 1974; admitted to bar, 1999, Indiana. *Education:* Indiana University (B.A., 1995; M.L.S., 1996); Yale University Law School (J.D., 1999). ***COURSES: Legal Research and Writing. ***Email:*** jgiles@okcu.edu

ALVIN C. HARRELL*, (Professor of Law)**, born Santa Monica, California, November 4, 1945; admitted to bar, 1972, Oklahoma. *Education:* Oklahoma City University (B.S., 1967; M.B.A., 1978; J.D., 1972); Southern Methodist University (LL.M., 1982). ***COURSES: Bankruptcy, Sales, Commercial Paper, Secured Transactions, Electronic Commerce, Consumer Law.

PATRICIA WICK HATAMYAR*, (Professor of Law)**, born Mankato, Minnesota, October 12, 1957; admitted to bar, 1983, Illinois; 1995, Oklahoma. *Education:* Northwestern University (B.A., 1980); University of Chicago (J.D., 1983). ***COURSES: Civil Procedure, Pretrial Litigation, Complex Litigation, Evidence. ***Email:*** phatamyar@okcu.edu

BARRY L. JOHNSON*, (Professor of Law)**, born Ottumwa, Iowa, January 4, 1963; admitted to bar, 1990, Illinois. *Education:* Northwestern University (B.A., 1985); University of Michigan (J.D., 1988). ***COURSES: Criminal Law and Procedure, Federal Criminal Law, Mass Tort Litigation, Torts. ***Email:*** bjohnson@okcu.edu

LAURIE W. JONES*, (Instructor, Legal Research and Writing)**, born Oklahoma City, Oklahoma, September 6, 1955; admitted to bar, 1984, Oklahoma. *Education:* Oklahoma State University (B.A., 1977); University of Oklahoma (J.D., 1984). ***COURSES: Legal Research and Writing, Appellate Advocacy. ***Email:*** ljones@okcu.edu

(This Listing Continued)

OKLAHOMA CITY UNIVERSITY SCHOOL OF LAW —Continued

NANCY I. KENDERDINE, **(Professor of Law)**, born Rockwood, Tennessee, February 5, 1942; admitted to bar, 1973, Oklahoma. *Education:* Duke University (B.A., 1964); University of Oklahoma (J.D., 1973). ***COURSES:*** Wills & Estates, Oil & Gas, Elder Law. ***Email:*** nkenderdine@okcu.edu

ERIC T. LAITY, **(Professor of Law)**, born Alton, Illinois, January 14, 1953; admitted to bar, 1979, Texas. *Education:* Harvard University (B.A., 1975; J.D., 1979). ***COURSES:*** Corporate Taxation, Partnership Taxation, International Aspects of U.S. Income Tax, International Law, International Business Transactions. ***Email:*** elaity@okcu.edu

MARIBOB L. LEE, **(Instructor, Legal Research and Writing)**, born 1953; admitted to bar, 1986, Oklahoma. *Education:* University of Oklahoma (B.A.; J.D.). ***COURSES:*** Legal Research and Writing, Appellate Advocacy. ***Email:*** mlee@okcu.edu

ARTHUR GARDNER LEFRANCOIS, **(Professor of Law)**, born State College, Pennsylvania, September 25, 1951; admitted to bar, 1978, Pennsylvania. *Education:* Beloit College (B.A., 1973); University of Chicago (J.D., 1978). ***COURSES:*** Criminal Law, Criminal Procedure, Jurisprudence. ***Email:*** alefrancois@okcu.edu

SILAS R. LYMAN, **(Professor Emeritus)**, born Westpoint, Nebraska, September 24, 1932; admitted to bar, 1960, Wyoming; 1976, Oklahoma. *Education:* University of Wyoming (B.S.L., 1958; LL.B., 1960); University of Wisconsin (LL.M., 1969). ***COURSES:*** Evidence, Trial Practice.

VICKI LAWRENCE MACDOUGALL, **(Professor of Law)**, born Oklahoma City, Oklahoma, August 21, 1952; admitted to bar, 1977, Oklahoma and California. *Education:* University of Oklahoma (B.A., 1974); Oklahoma City University School of Law (J.D., 1976). ***COURSES:*** Torts, Products Liability, Health Care Law. ***Email:*** vmacdougall@okcu.edu

MICHAEL MITCHELSON, **(Director, Externship Programs & Instructor of Law)**, born 1952; admitted to bar, 1979, Oklahoma. *Education:* William College (B.A.); Columbia University (J.D.). ***COURSES:*** Externship Programs. ***Email:*** mmitchelson@okcu.edu

DANIEL J. MORGAN, **(Professor of Law, Director, Lawyering Skills Program)**, born Sterling, Colorado, November 19, 1944; admitted to bar, 1970, Wyoming; 1988, Oklahoma. *Education:* University of Wyoming (B.A., 1967; J.D., 1970). ***COURSES:*** Torts, Trial Practice, Consumer Law. ***Email:*** dmorgan@okcu.edu

JUDITH ANN MORGAN, **(Professor of Law & Director of the Law Library)**, born Des Moines, Iowa, June 28, 1939; admitted to bar, 1982, Oklahoma. *Education:* St. Norbert College (B.A., 1962); University of Wisconsin, Madison (M.A.L.S., 1967); George Mason University School of Law (J.D., 1982). ***COURSES:*** Advanced Legal Research. ***Email:*** jmorgan@okcu.edu

THOMAS H. ODOM, **(Assistant Professor of Law)**, born Jersey City, New Jersey, March 8, 1962; admitted to bar, 1988, New Jersey and Pennsylvania; 1990, District of Columbia, U.S. Supreme Court. *Education:* Rutgers College (B.A., magna cum laude, 1984); University of Pennsylvania (J.D., cum laude, 1988). ***COURSES:*** Administrative Law, Civil Procedure, Federalism Seminar, Legal Profession. ***Email:*** todom@okcu.edu

FREDERIC S. SCHWARTZ, **(Professor of Law)**, born Philadelphia, Pennsylvania, March 12, 1951; admitted to bar, 1976, California. *Education:* Stanford University (B.S., 1973); Harvard Law School (J.D., 1976); Washington University School of Law (LL.M., 1986). ***COURSES:*** Property, Wills and Estates. ***Email:*** fschwartz@okcu.edu

ANDREW C. SPIROPOULOS, **(Professor of Law and Director, Center for the Study of State Constitutional Law and Government)**, born Queens, New York, November 5, 1962; admitted to bar, 1988, Illinois. *Education:* Carleton College (B.A., 1984); University of Chicago (M.A., 1988; J.D., 1988). ***COURSES:*** Constitutional Law, Legal Analysis, Legislation, State and Local Government. ***Email:*** aspiropoulos@okcu.edu

JUDSON LOREN TEMPLE, **(Professor of Law)**, born New Brunswick, New Jersey, July 12, 1946; admitted to bar, 1974, Montana; 1978, Michigan. *Education:* Montana State University (B.S., 1968); University of Maryland (M.A., 1971); University of Montana (J.D., 1974); University of Florida (LL.M., 1976). ***COURSES:*** Federal Income Taxation, Estate and Gift Tax, Taxation of Business Entities. ***Email:*** jtemple@okcu.edu

DEBORAH S. TUSSEY, **(Assistant Professor)**, born Wadesboro, North Carolina, February 4, 1951; admitted to bar, 1977, New York. *Education:* The College of William & Mary (B.A., 1973); University of Virginia School of Law (J.D., 1976); Harvard Law School (LL.M., 1998). ***COURSES:*** Computer Law, Intellectual Property, Property. ***Email:*** dtussey@okcu.edu

JOSEPH RIGHTON WEEKS, **(Professor of Law)**, born Savannah, Georgia, September 3, 1948; admitted to bar, 1977, Texas; 1983, Colorado; 1992, Oklahoma. *Education:* University of Georgia (B.B.A., 1974); University of Virginia (J.D., 1977); Georgetown University (LL.M., 1985); Columbia University (J.S.D., 1992). ***COURSES:*** Contracts, Evidence, Litigation and Labor Law. ***Email:*** jweeks1160@aol.com

---

PACE UNIVERSITY SCHOOL OF LAW

78 NORTH BROADWAY
WHITE PLAINS, NEW YORK 10603
Telephone: (914) 422-4128
Fax: (914) 422-4015
http://www.law.pace.edu

ABA Approved Since 1978

Founded in 1976 and located in White Plains, New York, about 30 minutes from New York City, Pace University School of Law offers both a full-time (three year) and part-time day and evening (four year) J.D. program, the LL.M. and S.J.D. in Environmental Law, and the LL.M. in Comparative Legal Studies. Enrollment in the School totals 752.

The curriculum and quality of the full-time and part-time programs do not differ except in scheduling. Of the 90 credits required for graduation, 41 are in required courses, including the entire first-year curriculum. Legal research, analysis and writing skills are taught by integrating them into the basic criminal law course. Constitutional Law II, Federal Income Taxation, and Professional Responsibility are upper-level required courses. Approximately 55 elective courses are offered each semester, allowing students to build their own program of legal study on the foundation of basic legal principles and skills, sampling from a variety of areas, or focusing in an area of particular interest. J.D. candidates may earn certificates demonstrating their

(This Listing Continued)

PACE UNIVERSITY SCHOOL OF LAW—Continued

proficiency in specialized areas of law: Environmental Law, Health Law and Policy, and International Law. In addition, J.D. students may enroll in joint degree programs with the Pace University Lubin School of Business (M.B.A.) or the Department of Public Administration of the University's Graduate Division of the College of Arts and Sciences (M.P.A.).

The LL.M. program in Environmental Law is designed to meet the needs of practicing lawyers seeking a greater depth of knowledge in this expanding field. Enrollment in the LL.M. program averages twenty students per year, on either a full-time or part-time basis.

The LL.M. in Comparative Legal Studies is designed for students who have a law degree from a foreign law institution. This new degree program begins with a summer orientation program to the United States legal system.

The Law School has 35 full-time faculty members and approximately 30 adjunct professors. The majority of the full-time faculty has had significant careers in legal practice prior to becoming legal educators and use their experience to add important perspectives to the theoretical principles of law. They maintain high standards of productivity and quality in legal scholarship and take active roles in service to the bar and bench. The adjunct faculty consists of leading practitioners, judges, and government officials.

The Law School is fully accredited by the American Bar Association and is a member of the Association of American Law Schools.

Dean: David Cohen (914) 422-4407
Associate Dean for Academic Affairs: Michelle Simon (914) 422-4258
Director of Admissions: Cathy Alexander (914) 422-4210
Library Director: Marie Newman (914) 422-4169
Assistant Dean for Career Development: Joy Beane (914) 422-4217
Assistant Dean for External Relations: Alta Levat (914) 422-4128

FULL TIME FACULTY

DAVID COHEN*, (Dean and Professor of Law)**, born Ottawa, Canada, 1950. *Education:* McGill University (B.Sc., 1971); University of Toronto (LL.B., 1975); Yale Law School (LL.M., 1979). ***COURSES: Contracts.

BARBARA ATWELL*, (Associate Professor of Law)**, born Brooklyn, New York, October 4, 1956; admitted to bar, 1984, New York; 1985, District of Columbia. *Education:* Queens College; Smith College (B.A., 1977); Columbia Law School (J.D., 1983). ***COURSES: Health Law, Torts, Contracts, Elder Law.

***ERIC EUGENE BERGSTEN*, (Professor Emeritus)**, born Evanston, Illinois, July 17, 1931; admitted to bar, 1963, Iowa. *Education:* Northwestern University (B.S., 1953); Georgetown University (M.S., 1960); University of Michigan (J.D., 1956); University of Chicago (D.C.L., 1972).

ADELE BERNHARD*, (Associate Professor of Law)**, born New York, New York; admitted to bar, 1977, New York. *Education:* Reed College; New York University, Washington Square College (B.A., 1972); New York University (J.D., 1976). ***COURSES: Criminal, Clinical.

BARBARA BLACK*, (Professor of Law)**, born Cleveland, Ohio, April 8, 1947; admitted to bar, 1974, New York; 1976, District of Columbia. *Education:* Barnard College (B.A., 1970); Columbia University (J.D., 1973). ***COURSES: Contracts, Corporations and Partnerships, Securities Regulation, Securities Arbitration Clinic.

JAY C. CARLISLE*, (Professor of Law)**, born Washington, D.C., April 8, 1942; admitted to bar, 1970, New York; 1972, New Mexico. *Education:* University of California at Los Angeles (A.B., 1965); Columbia University; Exeter, England; University of California at Davis (J.D., 1969). ***COURSES: Civil Procedure, New York Civil Practice, Professional Responsibility, Negotiations, Criminal Procedure.

KARL STEPHEN COPLAN*, (Associate Professor of Law and Co-director of the Environmental Litigation Clinic)**, born New York, New York, April 12, 1958; admitted to bar, 1985, New York. *Education:* Middlebury College (B.A., 1980); Columbia University (J.D., 1984). ***COURSES: Environmental Litigation Clinic.

DON DOERNBERG*, (Professor of Law)**, born Chicago, Illinois, May 21, 1945; admitted to bar, 1969, New York; 1985, California. *Education:* Yale University (B.A., 1966); Columbia University (J.D., 1969). ***COURSES: Federal Courts, Civil Procedure, Conflict of Laws, Criminal Law.

DAVID DORFMAN*, (Assistant Professor of Law)**, *Education:* Queens College, CUNY (B.A., 1977); University of Chicago (M.A., 1980); Chicago/Kent College of Law (J.D., 1987). ***COURSES: Criminal Law, Legal Analysis and Writing.

LINDA C. FENTIMAN*, (Professor of Law and Director of Health Law Program)**, born Washington, D.C., February 15, 1949; admitted to bar, 1976, California; 1985, Massachusetts; 1995, District of Columbia and New York. *Education:* Cornell University (B.S., 1970); State University of New York at Buffalo School of Law (J.D., 1975); Harvard University Law School (LL.M., 1983). ***COURSES: Health Law, Mental Disability and the Law, Bioethics, Criminal Law, White Collar Crime, Public Health Law.

JAMES J. FISHMAN*, (Professor of Law)**, born Philadelphia, Pennsylvania, June 18, 1942; admitted to bar, 1969, New York. *Education:* University of Pennsylvania (A.B., 1964; A.M., 1965); New York University (J.D., 1968; Ph.D., 1979). ***COURSES: Contracts, Corporations, Corporate Finance, Remedies, Nonprofit Organizations.

LESLIE YALOF GARFIELD*, (Associate Professor of Law, Director Academic Support Program)**, born New York, N.Y., June 5, 1960; admitted to bar, 1986, Florida and New York. *Education:* University of Florida (B.A., 1982; J.D., 1985). ***COURSES: Criminal Law, Legal Research and Writing.

BENNETT L. GERSHMAN*, (Professor of Law)**, born New York, N.Y., January 21, 1942; admitted to bar, 1966, New York. *Education:* Princeton University (A.B., 1963); New York University (J.D., 1966). ***COURSES: Criminal Procedure, Evidence, Constitutional Law, Criminal Law.

STEVEN H. GOLDBERG*, (Professor of Law)**, born Winona, Minnesota, March 16, 1941; admitted to bar, 1968, Minnesota; 1991, New York. *Education:* Northwestern University (B.A., 1963); University of Minnesota (J.D., 1968). ***COURSES: Trial Advocacy, Professional Responsibility, Dispute Resolution, Evidence.

***SHELBY D. GREEN*, (Associate Professor of Law)**, born Georgetown, South Carolina, September 18, 1955; admitted to bar, 1981, New York; 1982, District of Columbia. *Education:* Towson State

(This Listing Continued)

PACE UNIVERSITY SCHOOL OF LAW—Continued

College (B.S., 1976); Georgetown University (J.D., 1980). ***COURSES:*** Corporations, Property, Communications and Entertainment Law.

LISSA GRIFFIN, **(Professor of Law)**, born New York, N.Y., May 31, 1952; admitted to bar, 1978, New York. *Education:* University of Michigan (B.A., 1972). ***COURSES:*** Clinical Education, Criminal Procedure, Appellate Advocacy, Lawyering, Criminal Law.

JO ANN HARRIS, **(Scholar in Residence)**, born 1933. *Education:* State University of Iowa (B.A., 1955); New York University School of Law (J.D., 1972). ***COURSES:*** Trial Practice, Evidence, Federal Clerkship.

JOHN A. HUMBACH, **(Professor of Law)**, born Hamilton, Ohio, December 2, 1943; admitted to bar, 1966, Ohio; 1967, New York. *Education:* Miami University (B.A., 1963); Ohio State University (J.D., 1966). ***COURSES:*** Property, Land Use, Criminal Law, Professional Responsibility, Corporations.

RONALD H. JENSEN, **(Professor of Law)**, born Oakland, California, August 2, 1939; admitted to bar, 1964, New York. *Education:* Yale University (B.A., 1961); Harvard Law School (LL.B., 1964). ***COURSES:*** Income Taxation, Federal Corporate Tax, Federal Estate and Gift Taxation, Corporations and Partnerships, Partnership Taxation, Wills, Trusts & Interstate Succession.

IRENE DEAVILLE JOHNSON, **(Professor of Law)**, born Chicago, Illinois, April 5, 1947; admitted to bar, 1978, New York. *Education:* Knox College (B.A., 1969); Teachers College, Columbia University (M.A., 1970); Columbia University (LL.M., 1977). ***COURSES:*** Commercial Law, Creditors' Rights and Bankruptcy, Wills and Trusts, Civil Procedure.

JANET A. JOHNSON, **(Professor of Law)**, born Adair County, Iowa, March 10, 1940; admitted to bar, 1972, Iowa. *Education:* University of Illinois (A.B., 1968); Drake University (J.D., 1972); University of Virginia (LL.M., 1984). ***COURSES:*** Family Law, Remedies, Torts, Women and the Law.

ROBERT F. KENNEDY, JR., **(Professor of Law for Environmental Law & Co-Director of Pace Environmental Litigation Clinic)**, born January 17, 1954; admitted to bar, 1985, New York. *Education:* Harvard University (B.A., 1977); University of Virginia (J.D., 1982); Pace University School of Law (LL.M., 1987). ***COURSES:*** Environmental Law Litigation Clinic.

JOSEPHINE Y. KING, **(Professor of Law Emerita in Residence)**, born Pennsylvania; admitted to bar, 1965, New York. *Education:* University of Pennsylvania (A.B., 1942); Bryn Mawr College (A.M., 1943; Ph.D., 1950); State University of New York at Buffalo (J.D., 1965). ***COURSES:*** Constitutional Law, Torts, Procedure, Conflict of Laws, Health Law, Jurisprudence.

NORMAN B. LICHTENSTEIN, **(Professor of Law)**, born Paterson, New Jersey, October 20, 1934; admitted to bar, 1960, New York. *Education:* Rutgers University (B.A., 1956); Yale Law School (J.D., 1959). ***COURSES:*** Family Law, Administrative Law, Law and Education, Professional Responsibility.

M. STUART MADDEN, **(Distinguished Professor of Law)**, born Washington, D.C., December 1, 1948; admitted to bar, 1976, District of Columbia. *Education:* University of Pennsylvania (B.A., 1971); London School of Economics and Political Science (M.A., 1972); Georgetown University Law Center (J.D., 1976). ***COURSES:*** Torts, Environmental and Toxic Torts, Products Liability, Individual Rights & Liberty.

THOMAS MCDONNELL, **(Associate Professor)**, born Brooklyn, New York, June 9, 1950; admitted to bar, 1976, New York; 1979, California. *Education:* Fordham University (B.A., 1972; J.D., 1975). ***COURSES:*** Criminal Law, Appellate Advocacy, Legal Writing and Legal Research.

RANDOLPH M. MCLAUGHLIN, **(Professor of Law)**, born New York, N.Y., June 9, 1953; admitted to bar, 1979, New York. *Education:* Columbia University (B.A., 1971); Harvard University (J.D., 1978). ***COURSES:*** Civil Procedure, Labor Law, Civil Rights Litigation.

VANESSA MERTON, **(Associate Dean for Clinical Education & Professor of Law)**, admitted to bar, 1973, New York. *Education:* Radcliffe College (B.A., 1970); New York University School of Law (J.D., 1973). ***COURSES:*** Lawyering, Health Law, Litigation, Professional Responsibility, Torts, Evidence, Criminal Law, Poverty Law, Clinical Education, Women's Rights, Family Violence.

JEFFREY MILLER, **(Professor of Law and James D. Hopkins Professor of Law)**, born Muncie, Indiana, August 15, 1941; admitted to bar, 1968, Massachusetts; 1982, District of Columbia. *Education:* Princeton University (A.B., 1963); Harvard Law School (LL.B., 1967). ***COURSES:*** Environmental Law, Torts, Water Law, Hazardous Waste.

GARY A. MUNNEKE, **(Professor of Law)**, born Cedar Rapids, Iowa, December 29, 1947; admitted to bar, 1973, Texas; 1987, Pennsylvania. *Education:* University of Texas (B.S., 1970); University of Texas Law School (J.D., 1973). ***COURSES:*** Torts, Professional Responsibility, Law Office Management, Legal Malpractice.

MICHAEL B. MUSHLIN, **(Associate Professor of Law)**, born New York, N.Y., February 11, 1944; admitted to bar, 1971, New York. *Education:* Vanderbilt University (B.A., 1966); Northwestern University (J.D., 1970). ***COURSES:*** Civil Procedure, Federal Courts, Evidence.

MARIE STEFANINI NEWMAN, **(Library Director and Associate Professor of Law)**, born Boston, Massachusetts, August 30, 1951; admitted to bar, 1984, New York. *Education:* Smith College (A.B., 1973); Columbia University (M.S.. 1974); Rutgers University School of Law (J.D., 1983). ***COURSES:*** Legal Research. ***Email:*** mnewman@law.pace.edu

JOHN R. NOLON, **(Professor of Law and Charles A. Frueauff Research Professor)**, born Colorado Springs, Colorado, November 1, 1941; admitted to bar, 1971, New York. *Education:* University of Nebraska (B.A., 1963); University of Michigan (J.D., 1966). ***COURSES:*** Property, Land Use, Real Estate Transactions and Finance, Local Environmental Law.

PAUL O'NEIL, **(Professor of Law)**, born San Francisco, California, July 11, 1944; admitted to bar, 1975, Washington; 1985, New York. *Education:* University of California (B.A., 1971); University of Oregon (J.D., 1975). ***COURSES:*** Civil Litigation, Clinical Teaching, Health Law, Torts.

RICHARD L. OTTINGER, **(Dean Emeritus)**, born New York, N.Y., January 27, 1929; admitted to bar, 1955, New York; 1960, District of Columbia. *Education:* Cornell University (B.A., 1950); Harvard University (LL.B., 1953).

ANN POWERS, **(Associate Professor of Law)**, born Durant, Oklahoma, January 12, 1946; admitted to bar, 1975, District of Columbia; 1986, Maryland. *Education:* Indiana University (B.A., 1967); Georgetown University Law Center (J.D., 1974). ***COURSES:*** Environmental Law. ***Email:*** apowers@genesis.law.pace.edu

NICHOLAS A. ROBINSON, **(Prof. of Law; Gilbert and Sarah Kerlin Distin. Prof of Law and Co-Dir., Ctr. for Envir. Lgl. Stud.)**, born New York, N.Y., January 20, 1945; admitted to bar, 1971, New York. *Education:* Brown University (A.B., 1967); Columbia University (J.D., 1970). ***COURSES:*** Environmental Law, International and Comparative Environmental Law, Real Property, Historic Preservation, International Law, State and Local Environmental Law.

(This Listing Continued)

PACE UNIVERSITY SCHOOL OF LAW—Continued

AUDREY ROGERS,* (Associate Professor of Law)**, born Bronx, New York, May 18, 1956; admitted to bar, 1981, New York. *Education:* State University of New York at Albany (B.S., 1977); St. John's University (J.D., 1980). ***COURSES: Criminal Law, Legal Analysis and Writing, Advanced Appellate Advocacy, Health Law.

ERIC J. SCHMERTZ,* (Scholar in Residence)**, born New York, New York, December 24, 1925; admitted to bar, 1955, New York. *Education:* Union College (A.B.; LL.D.); New York University School of Law (J.D.). ***COURSES: Collective Bargaining, Dispute Settlement Techniques, Labor Arbitration, Labor Law, Public Sector Labor Law, Remedies.

MICHELLE S. SIMON,* (Associate Dean of Academic Affairs and Professor of Law)**, born New York, N.Y., September 1, 1956; admitted to bar, 1982, New York. *Education:* State University of New York at Albany (B.A., 1977); Syracuse University (J.D., 1981). ***COURSES: Criminal Law, Legal Writing, Local Government, Civil Procedure, Advanced Appellate Practice.

DAVID SIVE,* (Professor of Environmental Law)**, born Brooklyn, New York, September 22, 1922; admitted to bar, 1948, New York. *Education:* Brooklyn College (A.B., 1943); Columbia Law School (LL.B., 1948). ***COURSES: Environmental Law.

MERRIL SOBIE,* (Professor of Law)**, born New York, N.Y., May 22, 1939; admitted to bar, 1965, New York. *Education:* Brooklyn College (B.A., 1961); New York University (J.D., 1964). ***COURSES: Family Law, Juvenile Justice, Criminal Procedure, Judicial Administration, Children and the Law, Jurisprudence.

RALPH MICHAEL STEIN,* (Professor of Law)**, born Far Rockaway, New York, July 14, 1943; admitted to bar, 1980, Pennsylvania. *Education:* New School for Social Research (B.A., 1971); Hofstra University (J.D., 1974). ***COURSES: Constitutional Law, Legal History, Criminal Law, Remedies, Defamation and Privacy, Torts, National Security.

GAYL S. WESTERMAN,* (Professor of Law and Director of International Law Programs)**, born New Mexico, July 17, 1939; admitted to bar, 1986, Connecticut. *Education:* Stanford University (B.A., 1961); University of Pennsylvania (M.S., 1965); Pace University School of Law (J.D., 1981); Yale Law School (LL.M., 1982; J.S.D., 1984). ***COURSES: Admiralty, Antitrust, Contracts, Commercial Law: Domestic and International, International Law, Law of the Sea.

DAVID WOOLEY,* (Professor for Environmental and Energy Law and Executive Director, Center for Environmental Legal Studies)**, born Neptune, New Jersey, September 8, 1951; admitted to bar, 1975, New Jersey and Pennsylvania; 1977, West Virginia; 1981, New York. *Education:* Rutgers University (B.A., 1972); Rutgers University Law School (J.D., 1975). ***COURSES: Energy Law, Environmental Law, Air Quality Law.

PEPPERDINE UNIVERSITY SCHOOL OF LAW

24255 PACIFIC COAST HIGHWAY
MALIBU, CALIFORNIA 90263
Telephone: (310) 506-4611
Fax: (310) 506-4266

ABA Approved Since 1972.

Founded in 1969, Pepperdine University School of Law has distinguished itself for its quality programs and faculty, and excellent facilities and location. Accredited by the ABA and the AALS, the school grants JD and JD/MBA degrees, a Masters in Dispute Resolution (MDR) degree, a Masters in Public Policy (MPP) degree and joint degrees: JD/MPP, JD/MDR, and MDR/MPP.

With more than 600 students, Pepperdine University School of Law is located in the Odell McConnell Law Center on the university's 830-acre Malibu campus in Los Angeles County. The student body is diverse, with almost half of its students coming from states other than California representing 250 colleges and universities.

Pepperdine offers a unique opportunity for the student who wishes to pursue a legal education in an institution that stresses academic excellence while supporting Christian values. Pepperdine is an independent, private university with a long-standing relationship with the Churches of Christ.

The backgrounds of the faculty, almost all of whom have been practicing members of the bench or bar, contribute substantially to the students' understanding of the profession. The opportunity for personal relationships between faculty and students increase the effectiveness of the entire educational experience.

All law school classes, administrative functions, and faculty and student activities are accommodated within the Odell McConnell Law Center, one of the finest physical facilities in the nation. The facility contains a large auditorium classroom, lecture halls, seminar classrooms, an administrative center, faculty and student offices, offices for student services and activities, an appellate courtroom, a trial courtroom, the Salathe' Library Wing, the Odell McConnell Study, a bookstore, and a dining center. The Jerene Appleby Harnish Library is the focal point of the School of Law. Containing in excess of 310,000 volumes, the library boasts three innovative computer labs, offering curricular and practice-oriented software and services. The labs feature full Internet access, high-end computer operating systems and software, roaming network profiles, student notebook connectivity, and high-speed printers.

In 1986, the School established the Straus Institute for Dispute Resolution, recognizing the needs for effective, timely, and affordable resolution of legal disputes. As one of the leading programs in the country, the Institute's activities include academic programs including a certificate and masters degree in dispute resolution. The Institute conducts research, offers training throughout the world, and administers the school's extensive clinical education program in which students engage in a wide variety of practical legal activities under the supervision of experienced attorneys.

The School of Law operates a year-round International Law Program in London, England, with an excellent selection of American and International law courses. Students edit and publish the *Pepperdine Law Review,* which includes writing by outstanding legal scholars and Pepperdine students. In 2001 the Law School launched the Pepperdine Resolution Journal, which features scholastic contributions similar to those found in traditional law reviews. In addition, the Law School publishes the National Association of Administrative Law Judges Journal in collaboration with the National Association of Administrative Law Judges.

The Center for Entrepreneurship and Technology law is a new institution that offers a multidisciplinary certificate program that integrates the study of law, business, and technology. Also, one public

(This Listing Continued)

interest opportunity offered by the Law School is working at Pepperdine Union Reserve Mission Legal Aid Clinic, where students, professors, and alumni assist students with legal concerns.

The School has an outstanding moot court program and has distinguished itself in many national competitions. Several national legal fraternities have chapters on campus, and students are encouraged to join one of the many student organizations that offer social activities centered on the profession of the law.

Admission to the School of Law is based on the applicant's academic record, LSAT score, a written personal statement, a response to the University's admission, and other information that reflects outstanding academic and professional promise. Pepperdine seeks to attract students who bring variety, diversity, character, and excellence to the study of law. The School's active financial aid program provides some type of financial aid to more than 85% of the students.

Dean: Richardson R. Lynn (310) 506-4621
Admissions Director: Shannon Phillips (310) 506-4631
Financial Aid Director: Janet Lockhart (310) 506-4633
Associate Dean, Library and Information: Dan Martin (310) 506-4847
Career Services Director: Carol Allemeier (310) 506-4634
Assistant Dean, Alumni and Boards: Hazel Harrington (310) 506-4492
Director of Overseas Programs: Charles Nelson (310) 506-4666

FULL TIME FACULTY

RICHARDSON R. LYNN*, (Dean and Professor of Law)**, born Harrisburg, Arkansas, July 29, 1950; admitted to bar, 1976, Tennessee; 1989, Nebraska. *Education:* Abilene Christian University (B.A., 1973); Vanderbilt University (J.D., 1976). ***COURSES: Appellate Advocacy, Civil Procedure, Conflicts, Intellectual Property.

ROGER P. ALFORD*, (Associate Professor of Law)**, *Education:* Baylor University (B.A., 1985); Southern Seminary (M.Div., 1998), New York University (J.D., 1991); Edinburch University (LL.M., 1992). ***COURSES: Contracts, Commercial & International Dispute Resolution, International Litigation, International Trade & Finance.

W. HAROLD BIGHAM*, (Professor of Law)**, born Petersburg, Tennessee, November 6, 1932; admitted to bar, 1960, Tennessee. *Education:* The University of the South (B.A., 1954); Vanderbilt University (J.D., 1960). ***COURSES: Admiralty, Civil Procedure, Commercial Law, Evidence, Remedies.

THOMAS G. BOST*, (Professor of Law)**, born Oklahoma City, Oklahoma, July 13, 1942; admitted to bar, 1967, Tennessee; 1968, California. *Education:* Abilene Christian University (B.S., *summa cum laude*, 1964); Vanderbilt School of Law (J.D., 1967). ***COURSES: Business Planning, Corporations, Taxation of Business Entities, Securities Regulation.

KATHRYN LEE BOYD*, (Associate Professor of Law)**, admitted to bar, California, New York. *Education:* University of Virginia (B.A., with highest honors, 1986); Harvard Law School (J.D., *cum laude*, 1989). ***COURSES: Civil Pleading and Procedure, Complex Litigation, Human Rights Litigation, International Litigation, Trial Practice.

***LAURIE BUCHAN*, (Director of Clinical Education and Assistant Professor of Law)**, admitted to bar, California, American State Bar Association. *Education:* University of California, Davis (B.A., 1974); Southwestern University School of Law (J.D., *cum laude*, 1979).

HARRY M. CALDWELL*, (Professor of Law)**, born Bell, California, October 5, 1949; admitted to bar, 1976, California. *Education:* California State University, Long Beach (B.A., *cum laude*, 1972); Pepperdine University School of Law (J.D., 1976). ***COURSES: Criminal Law, Criminal Procedure, Evidence, Honors Trial Practice.

CAROL A. CHASE*, (Associate Professor of Law)**, born Santa Monica, California, December 28, 1953; admitted to bar, 1978, California. *Education:* University of California, Los Angeles (A.B., *summa cum laude* 1975; J.D., 1978). ***COURSES: Criminal Procedure, Evidence, Criminal Law, Trial Practice.

ROBERT F. COCHRAN, JR.*, (Professor of Law)**, born Greenville, South Carolina, May 29, 1951; admitted to bar, 1976, Virginia; West Virginia. *Education:* Carson-Newman College (B.A., *magna cum laude*, 1973); University of Virginia (J.D., 1976). ***COURSES: Alternative Dispute Resolution, Family Law, Professional Responsibility, Religion and Law, Torts.

JACK J. COE, JR.*, (Professor of Law)**, born Glendale, California, 1953; admitted to bar, 1979, California; 1980, Washington. *Education:* University of California, Los Angeles (B.A., with distinction 1975); Loyola Marymount School of Law (J.D., 1979) University Exeter (LL.M., 1982); London School of Economics (Ph.D., Law Dept., 1999). ***COURSES: Commercial Law, Corporations, International Business Transactions, International Dispute Resolution, International Litigation, Private International Law, Public International Law, Remedies.

RICHARD L. CUPP, JR.*, (Professor of Law)**, born Muncie, Indiana, June 4, 1961; admitted to bar, 1987, California. *Education:* Pepperdine University (B.A., *magna cum laude*, 1983); University of California School of Law, Davis (J.D., 1987). ***COURSES: Products Liability, Torts.

R. WAYNE ESTES*, (Professor of Law)**, born Milan, Tennessee, February 5, 1931; admitted to bar, 1956, Tennessee. *Education:* David Lipscomb University (B.A., *cum Laude*, 1953); Vanderbilt University (J.D., 1956). ***COURSES: Contracts, Labor Law, Labor Arbitration.

DARYL FISHER-OGDEN*, (Visiting Assistant Professor of Law)**, admitted to bar, 1976, California. *Education:* University of California at Berkeley (B.A., 1973); Hastings College of Law (J.D., 1976); Fuller Theological Seminary (M.Div., 1987); University of Notre Dame (Ph.D., 1997). ***COURSES: Legal Research and Writing. ***Email:*** daryl.fisher-ogden@pepperdine.edu

JAMES ALLAN GASH*, (Associate Professor of Law)**, admitted to bar, California; District of Columbia. *Education:* Abilene Christian University (B.A., *summa cum laude*); Pepperdine University (J.D., *summa cum laude*). ***COURSES: Evidence, Torts, Trial Preparation and Settlement.

CHRISTINE CHAMBERS GOODMAN*, (Associate Professor of Law)**, born Los Angeles, California, September 8, 1966; admitted to bar, 1992, California. *Education:* Harvard University (B.A., *cum laude*, 1987); Stanford University Law School (J.D., 1991). ***COURSES: Race and the Law, Criminal Law, Pretrial Practice. ***Email:*** christine.goodman@pepperdine.edu

***MICHAEL R. GRADISHER*, (Assistant Professor of Law)**, born

(This Listing Continued)

Columbus, Ohio; admitted to bar, 1986, California. *Education:* California State University (B.A., 1982); Pepperdine University School of Law (J.D., *cum Laude*, 1986). ***COURSES:*** Legal Research and Writing.

COLLEEN P. GRAFFY*, (Director, London Program and Assistant Professor of Law)**, *Education:* Pepperdine University (B.A., 1979); Boston University (M.A., 1982); City of London University and Inns of Court School of Law (Diploma in Law, 1991); King's College, University of London (LL.M., 1996). ***COURSES: International Public Law, International Environmental Law.

WILLIAM D. HENSLEE*, (Assistant Professor of Law)**, born Beeville, Texas, January 14, 1954; admitted to bar, 1984, California; 1986, New Mexico; 1988, Arizona; 1990, Pennsylvania. *Education:* University of Hawaii (B.A., 1977); Pepperdine University School of Law (J.D., 1984); University of California, Los Angeles (M.F.A., 1996). ***COURSES: Legal Research and Writing.

BERNARD JAMES*, (Professor of Law)**, born Magnolia, Arkansas, November 6, 1955. *Education:* University of Michigan (B.G.S., 1977; J.D., 1983). ***COURSES: Constitutional Law, State Constitutional Law, Federalism, Civil Rights, Education Law.

CATHERINE L. KERR*, (Associate Director for Library Services and Assistant Professor of Law)**, born Pasadena, California, April 11, 1959; admitted to bar, 1990, Pennsylvania. *Education:* Seattle Pacific University (B.A., *cum laude*, 1981); University of California, Berkeley (M.L.I.S., 1985); Loyola Law School, Los Angeles (J.D., 1989). ***COURSES: Legal Research.

JANET E. KERR*, (Professor of Law)**, born Los Angeles, California, August 10, 1954; admitted to bar, 1978, California; 1981, New York. *Education:* Pepperdine University (B.A., *summa cum laude*, 1975; J.D., 1978); New York University Law School (LL.M., 1979). ***COURSES: Corporations, Poverty Law, Securities Regulation.

L. RANDOLPH LOWRY*, (Director, Straus Institute for Dispute Resolution Institute & Professor of Law)**, born Long Beach, California, December 2, 1951; admitted to bar, 1986, Idaho. *Education:* Pepperdine University (B.A., 1974; M.P.A., 1977); Hamline University School of Law (J.D., 1981). ***COURSES: Alternative Dispute Resolution, Arbitration, Clinical Education, Mediation, Negotiation.

DANIEL W. MARTIN*, (Associate Dean, Library and Information Services and Professor of Law)**, born Crawfordsville, Indiana, August 22, 1950; admitted to bar, 1989, Texas; 1993, California. *Education:* Cedarville College (B.A., 1972); Indiana University (M.L.S., 1976); University of Texas at Austin (J.D., 1989). ***COURSES: Advanced Legal Research.

JOHN P. MCCRORY*, (Professor of Law)**, born Milwaukee, Wisconsin, January 1, 1933; admitted to bar, 1960, Wisconsin; 1969, Montana. *Education:* University of Wisconsin-Madison (B.S., 1955); University of Wisconsin Law School (J.D., 1960). ***COURSES: Arbitration Practice, Alternative Dispute Resolution, Environmental and Public Policy Dispute Resolution, Selected Issues in Dispute Resolution Advocacy.

ANTHONY X. MCDERMOTT*, (Professor of Law)**, born Teaneck, New Jersey, July 2, 1939; admitted to bar, 1966, California. *Education:* University of California, Los Angeles (A.B., 1961; LL.B., 1965). ***COURSES: Civil Procedure, Tax, Mergers and Acquisitions.

BARRY P. MCDONALD*, (Associate Professor of Law)**, born Chicago Heights, Illinois, October 8, 1959; admitted to bar, 1991, California; 1993, Washington D.C.. *Education:* Loyola University of Chicago (B.B.A., 1981); Northwestern University School of Law (J.D., *cum laude*, 1988). ***COURSES: Contracts, Intellectual Property, Law and Biotechnology.

NANCY L.N. MCGINNIS*, (Assistant Professor of Law)**, born Fullerton, California, February 22, 1947; admitted to bar, 1985, California. *Education:* California State University, Fullerton (B.A., 1968); Pepperdine University School of Law (J.D., *cum laude*, 1985). ***COURSES: Appellate Advocacy, Legal Research and Writing, Moot Court.

JAMES M. MCGOLDRICK, JR.*, (Professor of Law)**, born Cureall, Missouri, March 25, 1944; admitted to bar, 1970, California. *Education:* Pepperdine University (B.A., 1966); University of Chicago (J.D., 1969). ***COURSES: Constitutional Law.

ANTONIO MENDOZA*, (Professor of Law)**, born San Antonio, Texas, August 25, 1945; admitted to bar, 1978, Texas. *Education:* St. Mary's University (B.B.A., 1973; J.D., 1978). ***COURSES: International Business Transactions, International Tax.

ANTHONY MILLER*, (Professor of Law)**, born Los Angeles, California, July 17, 1945; admitted to bar, 1977, California. *Education:* California State University at Long Beach (B.A., 1967; M.A., 1972); Pepperdine University School of Law (J.D., 1977). ***COURSES: Community Property, Family Law, Labor Law, Torts.

CHARLES I. NELSON*, (Director, Overseas Programs and Professor of Law)**, born Houston, Texas, January 23, 1941; admitted to bar, 1965, Texas. *Education:* Abilene Christian University (B.S., 1962); University of Texas, Austin (J.D., 1965). ***COURSES: Community Property, Land Use Planning, Property, Real Estate Finance, Wills and Trusts.

GREGORY L. OGDEN*, (Professor of Law)**, born Fresno, California, January 5, 1948; admitted to bar, 1973, California. *Education:* University of California, Los Angeles (B.A., *cum laude*, 1970); University of California, Davis (J.D., 1973); Temple University (LL.M., 1978); Columbia University (LL.M., 1981). ***COURSES: Administrative Law, Civil Procedure, Professional Responsibility, Remedies.

L. TIMOTHY PERRIN*, (Associate Professor of Law)**, born Lubbock, Texas, December 29, 1961; admitted to bar, 1987, Texas. *Education:* Lubbock Christian University (B.A., 1984); Texas Tech University (J.D., 1987). ***COURSES: Commercial Sales Law, Evidence, Honors Trial Practice, Trial Practice.

PHIL E. PHILLIPS*, (Associate Dean, Administration and Assistant Professor of Law)**, *Education:* Pepperdine University (B.S., 1988); Pepperdine University School of Law (J.D., 1992). ***COURSES: Environmental Law.

RONALD F. PHILLIPS*, (Vice Chancellor, Dean Emeritus and Professor of Law)**, born Houston, Texas, November 25, 1934; admitted to bar, 1965, Texas; 1972, California. *Education:* Abilene Christian University (B.S., 1955); University of Texas (J.D., 1965). ***COURSES: Agency/Partnership, Contracts, Professional Responsibility.

ROBERT G. POPOVICH*, (Associate Professor of Law)**, born Los Angeles, California, June 18, 1953; admitted to bar, 1989, California. *Education:* California State University, Northridge (B.S., 1975); University of Southern California (M.B.T., 1977); Pepperdine University School of Law (J.D., +summa cum laude, 1989). ***COURSES: Accounting, Community Property, Tax.

ROBERT J. PUSHAW*, (Visiting Professor of Law)**, *Education:* La Salle College (B.A., summa cum laude, 1980); Yale University Law School (J.D., 1988). ***COURSES: Constitutional Law, Contracts, Federal Courts.

***PETER ROBINSON*, (Associate Director, Straus Institute for Dispute Resolution and Assistant Professor of Law)**, born Coronado,

(This Listing Continued)

PEPPERDINE UNIVERSITY SCHOOL OF LAW—Continued

California, August 30, 1955; admitted to bar, 1980, California. *Education:* University of California, San Diego (B.A., *magna cum laude*, 1977); Hastings College of Law (J.D., 1980). ***COURSES:*** Alternative Dispute Resolution, Mediation, Negotiation.

SHELLEY ROSS SAXER*, (Associate Dean, Academics and Professor of Law)**, born Washington, D.C., November 12, 1952; admitted to bar, 1990, California. *Education:* Pepperdine University (B.S., *summa cum laude*, 1980); University of California at Los Angeles (J.D., 1989). ***COURSES: Property, Environmental Law, Land Use Planning.

MARK S. SCARBERRY*, (Professor of Law)**, born Bakersfield, California, May 13, 1953; admitted to bar, 1978, California. *Education:* Occidental College (A.B., *magna cum laude*, 1975); University of California at Los Angeles (J.D., 1978). ***COURSES: Business Reorganizations in Bankruptcy, Creditors Rights and Bankruptcy, Contracts, Commercial Law.

PETER T. WENDEL*, (Professor of Law)**, born St. Louis, Missouri, November 30, 1956; admitted to bar, 1983, Missouri; 1984, Illinois. *Education:* University of Chicago (B.S., *cum laude*, 1979; J.D., 1983); St. Louis University (M.A., 1980). ***COURSES: Property, Trusts and Estates, Water Law.

MAUREEN ARELLANO WESTON*, (Associate Professor of Law)**, born Pueblo, Colorado, January 12, 1965; admitted to bar, 1992, Colorado. *Education:* University of Denver (B.A., 1987); University of Colorado School of Law (J.D., 1992). ***COURSES: Alternative Dispute Resolution, Civil Procedure, Mediation, Negotiation, Sports Law, Disability Law, Pretrial Litigation.

PONTIFICAL CATHOLIC UNIVERSITY OF PUERTO RICO SCHOOL OF LAW

2250 LAS AMERICAS AVENUE, SUITE 543
PONCE, PUERTO RICO 00717-0777

QUINNIPIAC COLLEGE SCHOOL OF LAW

275 MOUNT CARMEL AVENUE
HAMDEN, CONNECTICUT 06518

REGENT UNIVERSITY SCHOOL OF LAW

1000 REGENT UNIVERSITY DRIVE
VIRGINIA BEACH, VIRGINIA 23464-9880
Telephone: (757) 226-4040
Fax: (757) 226-4595
http://www.regent.edu/acad/schlaw/

ABA Approved Since 1989.

Regent University is located on a beautiful campus in Virginia Beach, which is famed for its 28 miles of ocean and bay beaches. It is within an hour's drive of historic Yorktown, Jamestown and Colonial Williamsburg and within four hours of Washington, D.C., the Blue Ridge Mountains and North Carolina's Outer Banks.

Regent University School of Law is unique in that its curriculum is taught in the context of the historical and biblical foundations and framework of the Anglo-American legal system. The curriculum includes the typical law courses taught at other law schools, plus a variety of special electives including Non-Profit Organizations and the Law, Charitable Trusts, and Inalienable Rights and Liberties. The foundational course for the initial year of study is The Common Law. This course includes a historical survey of the biblical principles incorporated into the Anglo-American common law and their application to current legal issues.

During each of the three years, students receive training in professional skills designed to equip them for entrance into the legal profession. This preparation includes a law practice requirement, fulfilled by taking either Trial Practice or Negotiations.

A joint-degrees program is also available for those who desire to integrate their legal studies with graduate work in public policy, business administration counseling, or communication. Completion of such a program normally takes four years for full time students and five years for part time students; after which time, a student receives a J.D. and either an M.A. in public policy, or an M.B.A., M.A. in Management or an M.A. in Communication, or an M.A. in Counseling.

The law library has a collection of over 290,000 volumes and volume equivalents. It features not only all the materials necessary for training students for the practice of law, but it also includes significant materials for research in public policy and law. For example, it contains several comprehensive collections of microfiche from the Congressional Information Service (CIS) such as U.S. Supreme Court Records and Briefs and U.S. Congressional Committee Prints and Hearings. Students have access to LEXIS, WESTLAW, NEXIS, LEGALTRAC and other computer assisted legal research systems. Other automated information is also available, including computer catalog access to all items in the legal collection.

The student body at Regent University School of Law is a diverse group of over 500 students from almost every state in the country and from over 100 undergraduate colleges and universities. The students have a wide variety of undergraduate degrees and many of them have substantial experience in other professions. The average LSAT score has been 150 and the average undergraduate grade point average has been 3.0. Graduates of the School of Law are now serving the legal profession in a variety of capacities in over 45 states.

The student-edited *Regent University Law Review* was first published in 1991.

In August, 1998 the School of Law initiated a four-year part-time program leading to the J.D. degree.

In July 1998, the law school also established an international human rights summer program which is held at the University of Strasbourg, France.

(This Listing Continued)

REGENT UNIVERSITY SCHOOL OF LAW—Continued

The law school offers an LL.M. in International Taxation by distance education. Instruction is provided through a state-of-the-art, user-friendly electronic delivery system. The degree was designed for attorneys who practice in the area of international tax or who are looking to expand their practice to include international tax.

Dean and Professor of Law: Jeffrey A. Brauch (757) 226-4040
Admissions and Financial Aid - Director: Bonnie Creef (757) 226-4584
Library - Director & Professor: Charles H. Oates (757) 226-4195
Alumni Relations: Laura J. Hanson (757) 226-4300
Admissions & Financial Aid Counselor: Militza Lyden (757) 226-4559
Student Affairs - Assistant Dean: Rebekah S. Woods (757) 226-4640
Administration - Associate Dean: James E. Murphy (757) 226-2814
Career Services - Director: Laura J. Hanson (757) 226-4300
Academic Affairs - Associate Dean: Douglas H. Cook (757) 226-4331
Academic Support - Assistant Professor: L. O. Natt Gantt (757) 226-4326
International Tax - Associate Dean: Thomas M. Diggs (757) 226-4301

FULL TIME FACULTY

JEFFREY A. BRAUCH*, (Dean and Professor of Law, Director of International Human Rights Summer Program)**, born Redwood City, California, February 18, 1963; admitted to bar, 1988, Wisconsin. *Education:* University of Wisconsin (B.A., 1985); University of Chicago (J.D., 1988). ***COURSES: Common Law, Civil Procedures, Criminal Law.

JAMES MICHAEL BOLAND*, (Assistant Professor)**, born Ontario, Cananda, September 16, 1947; admitted to bar, 1994, Virginia. *Education:* Wheaton College (B.A., 1969); Gordon-Conwell Theological Seminary (M.T.S., 1975); Regent University School of Law (J.D., 1994). ***COURSES: Legal Research and Writing.

DOUGLAS HOWARD COOK*, (Associate Dean for Academic Affairs and Professor of Law)**, born Mansfield, Ohio, February 26, 1957; admitted to bar, 1983, Arizona; 1994, District of Columbia. *Education:* Miami University (B.A., 1978); Ohio State University (J.D., 1983). ***COURSES: Torts, Nonprofit Tax-Exempt Organizations, Health Care, Insurance.

ALICE M. CURTIS*, (Associate Professor of Law)**, born Washington, D.C., January 17, 1946; admitted to bar, 1984, Washington, D.C.. *Education:* Howard University (B.A., 1974); Georgetown University (J.D., 1980); Anitoch School of Law (M.A., 1983). ***COURSES: Family Law and Negotiations, Mediation, Litigation Clinic.

ERIC ALAN DEGROFF*, (Associate Professor)**, born Kansas City, Kansas, March 22, 1949; admitted to bar, 1989, Virginia; 1991, District of Columbia. *Education:* University of Kansas (B.A., 1971); University of Southern California (M.P.A., 1982); Regent University (J.D., 1989). ***COURSES: Property, Environmental Law.

THOMAS M. DIGGS*, (Associate Dean, Director, International Tax Program, and Associate Professor of Law)**, born Bethesda, Maryland, April 2, 1953; admitted to bar, 1993, Virginia. *Education:* Liberty University (B.S., 1974); Lynchburg College (M.Ed., 1979); University of Virginia (Ed.D., 1986); College of William and Mary (J.D., 1993). ***COURSES: Trusts and Other Entities, Thesis.

JAMES JOSEPH DUANE*, (Professor of Law)**, born Buffalo, New York, July 30, 1959; admitted to bar, 1985, New York. *Education:* Harvard University (B.A., 1981; J.D., 1984). ***COURSES: Evidence, Law & Professional Responsibility, Trial Practice, Civil Procedure.

EUGENE CONRAD ELSER*, (Professor of Law)**, born Brooklyn, New York, May 22, 1944; admitted to bar, 1980, Missouri. *Education:* Roberts Wesleyan College (B.A., 1968); Ohio State University (M.A., 1970; Ph.D., 1972); University of Tennessee (J.D., 1979). ***COURSES: Contracts, Negotiations.

STEVEN WERNER FITSCHEN*, (Legal Research and Writing Instructor)**, born Baltimore, Maryland, January 1, 1957; admitted to bar, 1999, Virginia. *Education:* North Carolina State University (B.S.F and B.S., 1979); Regent University (M.Div. and M.A., 1992); Regent University School of Law (J.D., 1999). ***COURSES: Legal Research and Writing.

L.O. NATT GANTT*, (Assistant Professor)**, born Henderson, Kentucky, July 14, 1969; admitted to bar, 1994, North Carolina. *Education:* Duke University (A.B., 1991); Harvard Law School (J.D., 1994); Gordon-Conwell Theological Seminary (M.Div., 2000). ***COURSES: Academic Asstance, Professional Responsibility.

LOUIS W. HENSLER, III*, (Assistant Professor of Law)**, born Biloxi, Mississippi, November 29, 1962; admitted to bar, 1989, Pennsylvania. *Education:* Bob Jones University (B.A., 1985); University of Chicago (J.D., 1988). ***COURSES: Evidence and Torts.

MICHAEL VINCENT HERNANDEZ*, (Associate Professor of Law)**, born Richmond, Virginia, April 29, 1962; admitted to bar, 1987, Virginia. *Education:* University of Virginia (B.A., with high distinction, 1984; J.D., 1987). ***COURSES: Property, Appellate Advocacy.

BRADLEY P. JACOB*, (Associate Professor)**, born Bloomington, Illinois, June 4, 1958; admitted to bar, 1983, Maryland; 1988, Distrtict of Columbia; 1994, Pennsylvania. *Education:* University of Delaware (B.A., 1980); University of Chicago (J.D., 1983). ***COURSES: Constitutional Law, Contract Drafting, Common Law, Business Associations, Legal Writing.

DARLENE ADDIE KENNEDY*, (Assistant Professor of Law)**, born New York, March 19, 1966; admitted to bar, 1995, New Jersey. *Education:* John Jay College (B.A., 1988); Syracuse University (J.D., 1991); Baltimore (LL.M., 1996). ***COURSES: Federal Income Taxation, Corporate Taxation Business Planning and Insurance.

JANIS LYNN KIRKLAND*, (Instructor)**, born Arlington, Virginia, October 8, 1954; admitted to bar, 1987, Virginia. *Education:* College of William and Mary (B.S., 1976); T.C. Williams School of Law (J.D., 1987). ***COURSES: Legal Research and Writing.

LYNNE MARIE KOHM*, (Professor of Law)**, born Albany, New York, August 26, 1959; admitted to bar, 1989, New York and Massachusetts; 1990, Florida and District of Columbia; 1995, Virginia. *Education:* University of Albany (B.A., 1980); Syracuse University (J.D., 1988). ***COURSES: Legal Research, Family Law, Wills, Trusts & Estates, Real Estate Transactions.

***KATHLEEN A. MCKEE*, (Associate Professor of Law)**, born December 6, 1944; admitted to bar, 1977, Virginia, North Carolina,

(This Listing Continued)

REGENT UNIVERSITY SCHOOL OF LAW—Continued

District of Columbia. *Education:* SUNY (B.A., 1966); Catholic University (J.D., 1977); Georgetown University (LL.M., 1984). ***COURSES:*** PI Law, Legal Externship, Administration Law, Litigation Clinic.

STEPHEN L. MCPHERSON,* (Legal Research and Writing Instructor)**, born Norfolk, Virginia, May 26, 1969; admitted to bar, 1996, Virginia. *Education:* Old Diminion University (B.M., 1991); Regent University School of Business (M.B.A., 1996); Regent University School of Law (J.D., 1996). ***COURSES: Legal Research and Writing, Appellate, Advocacy.

SAMUEL PYEATT MENEFEE,* (Professor of Law and Scholar-at-Large)**, born Denver, Colorado, June 8, 1950; admitted to bar, 1981, Georgia; 1983, Virginia and Louisiana; 1985 District of Columbia, Nebraska, Florida and U.S. Supreme Court; 1986, Maine and Pennsylvania. *Education:* Yale University (B.A., summa cum laude, 1972); Oxford University (Dip. Soc. Anth., 1973; B.Litt., 1975); Harvard Law School (J.D., 1981); University of Virginia School of Law (LL.M., 1982; S.J.D., 1988); University of Cambridge (M.Phil., 1995) Scholar-at-Large. ***COURSES: International Law, Law & Literature, Legal History - Directed Research.

JAMES E. MURPHY,* (Associate Dean for Administration)**, born Estherville, Iowa, December 19, 1951; admitted to bar, 1980, Iowa; 1989, Kentucky; 1993, U.S. Supreme Court; 1995, Virginia. *Education:* University of Iowa (B.A., 1974); University of Oklahoma College of Law (J.D., 1977). ***COURSES: Constitutional Criminal Procedure.

CHARLES H. OATES,* (Director of Law Library and Professor of Law)**, born Frankfurt, Kentucky, February 20, 1941; admitted to bar, 1967, Florida. *Education:* University of Florida (B.A., 1963); Stetson University College of Law (J.D., 1967); Catholic University of America (M.L.S., 1997). ***COURSES: Wills, Trusts, Estate Planning, Charitable Tusts, Professional Responsibility, Real Estate Transactions, Insurance and Sports Law.

C. SCOTT PRYOR,* (Associate Professor of Law)**, born Mawr, Pennsylvania, March 28, 1954; admitted to bar, 1980, Wisconsin; 1996, Florida. *Education:* Dordt College (B.A., 1976); University of Wisconsin (J.D., 1980); Reformed Theological Seminary (M.A., 1997). ***COURSES: Contracts, UCC, Bankruptcy.

MICHAEL P. SCHUTT,* (Associate Professor of Law)**, born Chandler, Arizona, July 31, 1962; admitted to bar, 1987, Texas. *Education:* Stephen F. Austin State University (B.A., cum laude, 1984); University of Texas School of Law (J.D., with honors, 1987). ***COURSES: Torts, Law & Professional Responsibility, Appellate Advocacy, Legal Research.

ROBERT M.M. SETO,* (Professor of Law)**, born Canton, China, May 12, 1936; admitted to bar, 1968, Missouri; 1971, Hawaii; 1979, District of Columbia. *Education:* St. Louis University (B.S., 1962; J.D., 1968); George Washington University School of Law (LL.M., 2001). ***COURSES: Government Contracts, Patent Law, Trademark Law, Intellectual Property and Drafting of Contracts, Government Procurement Law, Copyright Law.

JOHN WILLIAM STANFORD,* (Professor of Law)**, born Meadville, Pennsylvania, September 2, 1926; admitted to bar, 1954, Florida. *Education:* University of Florida (B.A., 1949; J.D., 1954). ***COURSES: Criminal Procedure, Trial Practice, Drafting of Contracts, VCCI Drafting of Contracts, Business Associations & Law & Professional Responsibility.

CRAIG ALLEN STERN,* (Professor of Law)**, born Cleveland, Ohio, April 26, 1954; admitted to bar, 1978, Virginia and District of Columbia. *Education:* Yale University (B.A., 1975); University of Virginia (J.D., 1978). ***COURSES: Federal Courts, Criminal Law, Common Law, Conflict of Laws.

MARY C. SZTO,* (Associate Professor of Law)**, born New York, New York, October 12, 1960; admitted to bar, 1987,New York. *Education:* Wellesley College (B.A., 1981); Westminster Theological Seminary (M.A., 1983); Columbia University School of Law (J.D., 1986). ***COURSES: Uniform Commercial Code, Business Associations, Contracts, Law and Theology, Jurisprudence and Chinese Law.

JOE A. TUCKER,* (Professor of Law)**, born Victoria, Texas, October 12, 1955; admitted to bar, 1982, Texas. *Education:* Victoria College (A.A., 1976); University of Houston (B.A., 1977); University of Texas (J.D., 1981). ***COURSES: Contracts, Administrative Law, Immigration Law, Legislation.

JOHN P. TUSKEY,* (Assistant Professor of Law)**, born South Bend, Indiana, November 19, 1957; admitted to bar, 1983, Indiana; 1993, Illinois. *Education:* University of Notre Dame (B.A., 1980); Notre Dame Law School (J.D., 1983). ***COURSES: Civil Procedure, Legal Research and Writing, Employment Discrimination and Appellate Advocacy & Federal Courts, First Amendment Law.

DAVID M. WAGNER,* (Associate Professor of Law)**, born New York City, New York, March 21, 1958; admitted to bar, 1993, Pennsylvania. *Education:* Yale College (B.A., 1980); Yale University (M.A., 1984); George Mason University School of Law (J.D., 1992). ***COURSES: Administrative Law, Legal History Constitutional Law, Criminal Law & Constitutional History.

ROGER WILLIAMS UNIVERSITY
RALPH R. PAPITTO SCHOOL OF LAW

TEN METACOM AVENUE
BRISTOL, RHODE ISLAND 02809-5171
Telephone: (401) 254-4500
Fax: (401) 254-3525
www.law.rwu.edu

Roger Williams University Ralph R. Papitto School of Law offers a challenging legal education at an institution whose hallmark is excellence. There is close interaction between students, faculty and staff; interaction uniquely available in a small institution where all are working toward a common goal. With a faculty/student ratio of approximately 15:1, the faculty is very accessible to students.

The School of Law faculty reflects a wide diversity in experience and interests. With 29 full-time faculty members, there is a broad range of expertise including admiralty, intellectual property, international law, labor, marine affairs and products liability. In addition, 33 adjunct professors augment the curriculum.

Currently, there are approximately 500 students enrolled, 70 percent of whom are attending the three-year, full-time day program and 30 percent in the four-year, part-time evening program. Twenty-seven states and are represented in the student body. The School strives for a diverse student body drawn from throughout the nation. For students

(This Listing Continued)

ROGER WILLIAMS UNIVERSITY RALPH R.PAPITTO SCHOOL OF LAW—Continued

who have demonstrated exceptional ability and achievement before coming to law school, Roger Williams University School of Law offers an honors program which involves a multi-year program of seminars, clinics, international training and externships. The honors program provides every honors student a scholarship of half or full tuition.

The School of Law, with its vision for excellence in legal education, is a major contributor in promoting the administration of justice in Rhode Island. As the only law school in the state, Roger Williams is an integral partner with the bench, bar and community. The *Roger Williams University Law Review* features an annual Survey of Rhode Island Supreme Court decisions and R.I. law. The Law Review also sponsors an annual symposium on a topic of current importance.

A significant aspect of the School of Law curriculum is the comprehensive skills training program which enables law students to master those analytical, communication and other lawyering skills that facilitate effective legal problem solving. Simulation courses provide practical training in trial advocacy, client interviewing, counseling and appellate advocacy. The Lawyering Skills Program brings pragmatic application to a solid foundation of legal doctrine, preparing students for their clinical experience.

Through the Louis Feinstein Legal Clinic, supervised law students provide *pro bono publico* legal service in the areas of criminal and disability law to individuals and organizations in the community which might not have access to legal representation. The law clinics are housed in new facilities at the Roger Williams University Metropolitan Center for Education and Law in Providence.

The Feinstein Institute for Legal Service program at the School of Law requires that all students participate in a meaningful project during their law school career. Law students may accomplish this community service experience by working as student-attorneys in one of the client-service clinics, assisting the elderly with income taxes, helping nonprofit groups meet governmental requirements, counseling senior citizens on health care, teaching secondary school students about the law, or through other outreach efforts.

Three Joint degrees are offered in conjunction with the University of Rhode Island: J.D./Master of Community Planning. J.D./Master of Marine Affairs; and J.D./Master of Science in Labor Relations and Human Resources.

The School of Law offers two study abroad programs in Europe. Two sessions are offered in conjunction with the Inns of Court School of Law in London, England one of which assigns law students to a pupilage with a barrister. The Lisbon, Portugal program offers Comparative Law, Human Rights and European Community Law.

Created in 1996, the Marine Affairs Institute is a focal point for the research and study of legal and policy issues surrounding the use of the oceans and coastal zones. With emphasis on traditional admiralty law and practice, environmental regulation, and the international law of the sea, the Institute provides a forum for discussion through a lecture series, a biennial symposium, faculty exchanges, and scholarly publications.

The four-level law building, designed exclusively for the study of law, contains the latest technology in legal education and is completely self-contained. In addition to the extensive law library, the law building contains class and seminar rooms, a law practice center including trial advocacy and appellate moot court rooms, career services, registrar and bursar, student activities center, bookstore, mail and copy centers, and complete food service. The School of Law is located on the University's waterfront campus in historic Bristol, 25 minutes from Providence, the state's legal center, and one hour from Boston.

The Law Library is an excellent research facility designed to meet the needs of students, faculty, bench and bar. The Library collection contains in excess of 260,000 volumes and more than 3,500 serial subscriptions and plays a vital role in the study of law providing a multitude of legal resources available in electronic format from the on-line catalog INNOPAC to the LegalTrac CD-ROM which indexes legal publications. Both WESTLAW and LEXIS, the two national online legal information systems, are available to students in three labs.

The well-designed Law Library occupies 35,000 square feet on the first floor of the School of Law building. It has 380 seats available, including group study rooms, private rooms for viewing videotapes, individual carrels, and lounges.

Roger Williams University School of Law is fully accredited by the American Bar Association.

Dean: Bruce I. Kogan (401) 254-4502
Associate Dean for Academic Affairs: Diana J. Hassel (401) 254-4618
Director, Library: Gail Winson (401) 254-4530
Dean, Admissions: Christel L. Ertel (401) 254-4515
Director, Alumni, Programs and Events: Chelsie Horne (401) 254-4652
Director, Career Services: Nancy Waggner (401) 254-4651
Financial Aid: Amanda Cicciarella (401) 254-4510
Director, Feinstein Institute for Legal Service: Laurie Barron (401) 254-4600
International Studies: Robert M.C. Webster
President: Dr. Roy J. Nirschel (401) 254-3201

FULL TIME FACULTY

BRUCE I. KOGAN*, (Interim Dean and Professor of Law)**, born New York, New York, November 19, 1944; admitted to bar, 1970, Pennsylvania. *Education:* Syracuse University (B.A., 1967); Dickinson School of Law (J.D., 1970); Georgetown University Law Center (LL.M., 1972). ***COURSES: Alternative Dispute Resolution, Estate Planning, Property, Federal Income Tax. ***Email:*** bkogan@law.rwu.edu

BARBARA L. BERNIER*, (Associate Professor of Law)**, admitted to bar, 1978, West Virginia; 1980, Pennsylvania; 1985, District of Columbia. *Education:* State University of New York (B.A., 1972); Adelphi University (M.S.W., 1974); Howard University (J.D., 1978); Temple University (LL.M., 1980). ***COURSES: Property, Real Estate Transactions, Women & the Law, Torts, Wills & Trusts. ***Email:*** bbernier@law.rwu.edu

CARL T. BOGUS*, (Associate Professor of Law)**, born Fall River, Massachusetts, May 14, 1948; admitted to bar, 1973, Pennsylvania. *Education:* Syracuse University (A.B., 1970; J.D., 1972). ***COURSES: Torts, Products Liability, Civil Procedure, Evidence. ***Email:*** cbogus@law.rwu.edu

***ESTHER F. CLARK*, (Distinguished Visiting Professor of Law)**, born Philadelphia, Pennsylvania, August 29, 1929; admitted to bar, 1956, Pennsylvania. *Education:* Temple University (A.B., 1950); Rutgers

(This Listing Continued)

ROGER WILLIAMS UNIVERSITY RALPH R.PAPITTO SCHOOL OF LAW—Continued

School of Law (J.D., 1955). ***COURSES:*** Advanced Criminal Law, Criminal Law, Evidence. ***Email:*** eclark@law.rwu.edu

DEBRA R. COHEN*, (Visiting Associate Professor of Law)**, admitted to bar, 1988, Rhode Island; 1989, New York. *Education:* Brown University (A.B., 1985); Emory University School of Law (J.D., 1988). ***COURSES: Business Organizations, Commercial Law, Consumer Protection. ***Email:*** dcohen@law.rwu.edu

ELIZABETH COLT*, (Professor of Legal Writing)**, admitted to bar, 1985, Georgia; 1990, Rhode Island; 1992, Massachusetts. *Education:* Columbia University (B.A., 1980); Emory University School of Law (J.D., 1985). ***COURSES: Legal Writing. ***Email:*** ecolt@law.rwu.edu

EDWARD J. EBERLE*, (Professor of Law)**, born 1955; admitted to bar, 1983, Massachusetts; 1984, Minnesota; 1986, Rhode Island. *Education:* Columbia College (B.A., 1978); Northwestern University (J.D., 1982). ***COURSES: Administrative Law, Comparative Law, Constitutional Law, International Business Transactions. ***Email:*** eeberle@law.rwu.edu

JESSICA ELLIOT*, (Director of Legal Writing and Professor of Legal Writing)**, admitted to bar, 1995, Connecticut. *Education:* Cornell University (B.S., 1992); Boston College Law School (J.D., 1995). ***COURSES: Legal Writing. ***Email:*** jelliot@law.rwu.edu

CHRISTEL L. ERTEL*, (Dean of Admissions and Associate Professor of Law)**, born State College, Pennsylvania, October 12, 1960. *Education:* The Pennsylvania State University (B.S., 1982); Widener University School of Law (J.D., 1985). ***COURSES: Client Interviewing and Counseling, Negotiation. ***Email:*** certel@law.rwu.edu

JONATHAN M. GUTOFF*, (Associate Professor of Law)**, born Boston, Massachusetts, January 28, 1960; admitted to bar, 1990, New York. *Education:* Brown University (A.B., 1983); University of Chicago Law School (J.D., 1987). ***COURSES: Legal Methods, Administrative Law, Admiralty, Federal Courts. ***Email:*** jgutoff@law.rwu.edu

MATTHEW P. HARRINGTON*, (Professor of Law & Director, Marine Affairs Institute)**, born Boston, Massachusetts, September 5, 1959; admitted to bar, 1990, Pennsylvania. *Education:* McGill University (B.Th., 1987); Boston University (J.D., 1990); University of Pennsylvania (S.J.D., 2000). ***COURSES: Admiralty, Contracts, Secured Transactions, Bankruptcy, Legal History. ***Email:*** mharrington@law.rwu.edu

DIANA HASSEL*, (Associate Dean for Academic Affairs and Associate Professor of Law)**, born Pittsburgh, Pennsylvania, August 1, 1957; admitted to bar, 1986, New York; 1996, Rhode Island. *Education:* Mt. Holyoke College (B.A., 1979); Rutgers University School of Law (J.D., 1985). ***COURSES: Civil Rights, Constitutional Law. ***Email:*** dhassel@law.rwu.edu

ANDREW HORWITZ*, (Associate Professor of Law, Director of Law Clinic)**, born Boston, Massachusetts, November 7, 1961; admitted to bar, 1987, Massachusetts and New York; 1996, Rhode Island. *Education:* Haverford College (B.A., 1983); New York University School of Law (J.D., 1986). ***COURSES: Criminal Defense Clinic, Criminal Law, Criminal Procedure. ***Email:*** ahorwitz@law.rwu.edu

PETER C. KOSTANT*, (Associate Professor of Law)**, born Brooklyn, New York, May 13, 1947; admitted to bar, 1979, New York. *Education:* Yale (B.A., 1968); Washington University (M.A., 1971); Fordham University School of Law (J.D., 1978). ***COURSES: Professional Responsibility, Secured Transactions, Business Organizations. ***Email:*** pkostant@law.rwu.edu

JOHN C. KUNICH*, (Associate Professor of Law)**, admitted to bar, 1985, Illinois and Court of Military Appeals; 1990, US Supreme Court. *Education:* University of Illinois at Chicago (B.S., 1975; M.S., 1979); Harvard Law School (J.D., 1985); George Washington University School of Law (LL.M., 1993). ***COURSES: Environmental Law, Property. ***Email:*** jkunich@law.rwu.edu

PETER MARGULIES*, (Professor)**, admitted to bar, 1981, New York. *Education:* Colgate University (B.A., 1978); Columbia University School of Law (J.D., 1981). ***COURSES: Disability Law Clinic, Professional Responsibility. ***Email:*** pmargulies@law.rwu.edu

LISA T. MCELROY*, (Professor of Legal Writing)**, born February 22, 1968; admitted to bar, 1996, Massachusetts. *Education:* Dartmouth College (B.A., 1989); Harvard University Law School (J.D., 1995). ***COURSES: Client Interviewing and Counseling, Legal Writing. ***Email:*** lmcelroy@law.rwu.edu

COLLEEN P. MURPHY*, (Professor of Law)**, born 1962; admitted to bar, 1986, Massachusetts. *Education:* University of Virginia (B.A., 1983); Yale Law School (J.D., 1986). ***COURSES: Remedies, Administrative Law, Civil Procedure. ***Email:*** cmurphy@law.rwu.edu

DAVID A. RICE*, (Professor of Law)**, born Oconomowoc, Wisconsin, May 25, 1940; admitted to bar, 1965, New York; 1972, Massachusetts. *Education:* University of Wisconsin (B.B.A., 1962); Columbia University School of Law (LL.B., 1965). ***COURSES: Commercial Code, Intellectual Property, Contracts, Secured Transactions. ***Email:*** drice@law.rwu.edu

HARVEY RISHIKOF*, (Professor of Law)**, born Montreal, Quebec, Canada, March 7, 1954; admitted to bar, 1986, New York; 1989, Massachusetts. *Education:* McGill University (B.A., 1975); Brandeis University (M.A., 1978); New York University (J.D., 1986). ***Email: hrishikof@law.rwu.edu

LARRY J. RITCHIE*, (Professor of Law)**, born Columbia, South Carolina, March 21, 1944; admitted to bar, 1967, South Carolina; 1968, District of Columbia; 1981, Maryland. *Education:* University of South Carolina (A.B., 1965; J.D., 1967); Georgetown University Law Center (LL.M., 1971). ***COURSES: Criminal Law, Advanced Criminal Procedure, Torts, Trial Advocacy. ***Email:*** lritchie@law.rwu.edu

EMILY J. SACK*, (Associate Professor of Law)**, born Massachusetts, November 9, 1959; admitted to bar, 1992, New York. *Education:* Swarthmore College (B.A., 1980); Columbia University (M.A., 1983; M.Phil., 1984); New York University School of Law (J.D., 1991). ***COURSES: Contracts, Domestic Violence, Family Law. ***Email:*** esack@law.rwu.edu

ELLEN M. SAIDEMAN*, (Professor of Legal Writing)**, admitted to bar, 1983, New York. *Education:* Barnard College (B.A., 1979); Columbia Law School (J.D., 1982). ***COURSES: Legal Methods I and II. ***Email:*** esaidman@law.rwu.edu

ANTHONY J. SANTORO*, (Senior Professor of Law)**, born 1942; admitted to bar, 1967, Massachusetts. *Education:* Boston College (A.B., 1964); Georgetown University Law Center (J.D., 1967; LL.M., 1968). ***COURSES: Federal Income Taxation. ***Email:*** asantoro@law.rwu.edu

B. MICHAEL SIMPSON III*, (Professor of Legal Writing)**, born Philadelphia, Pennsylvania, February 16, 1937; admitted to bar, 1980, Rhode Island and US District Court, Rhode Island. *Education:* Colgate University (B.A., 1953); Fletcher School Tufts University (Ph.D., 1968); University of Pennsylvania (LL.B., 1956). ***COURSES: Legal Methods, Legal Drafting. ***Email:*** bsimpson@law.rwu.edu

***LOUISE ELLEN TEITZ*, (Associate Professor of Law)**, born Newport, Rhode Island, July 25, 1952; admitted to bar, 1981, Texas; 1989, Pennsylvania; 1991, District of Columbia. *Education:* Yale College (B.A., 1974); Southern Methodist University (J.D., 1981).

(This Listing Continued)

ROGER WILLIAMS UNIVERSITY RALPH R.PAPITTO SCHOOL OF LAW—Continued

COURSES: Civil Procedure, Antitrust, Complex Litigation, Conflicts of Law, Federal Courts. ***Email:*** lteitz@law.rwu.edu

GAIL I. WINSON*, (Associate Professor of Law, Director of Law Library)**, born East Stroudsburg, Pennsylvania, May 20, 1944; admitted to bar, 1979, Florida; 1980, California. *Education:* Moravian College (B.A., 1966); Drexel University (M.S., 1971); University of Florida (J.D., 1979). ***COURSES: Legal Research. ***Email:*** gwinson@law.rwu.edu

MICHAEL J. YELNOSKY*, (Associate Professor of Law)**, born Philadelphia, Pennsylvania, February 13, 1961; admitted to bar, 1987, Pennsylvania. *Education:* University of Vermont (B.S., 1982); University of Pennsylvania (J.D., 1987). ***COURSES: Employment Law, Civil Procedure, Labor Law. ***Email:*** myelnosky@law.rwu.edu

DAVID M. ZLOTNICK*, (Associate Professor of Law)**, born Queens, New York, May 23, 1960; admitted to bar, 1987, New York; 1988, District of Columbia; 1995, Florida. *Education:* State University of New York at Binghamton (B.A., 1982); Harvard University Law School (J.D., 1986). ***COURSES: Clinical Education, Advanced Criminal Procedure, Trial Advocacy, Criminal Procedure. ***Email:*** dzlotnick@law.rwu.edu

---

RUTGERS, THE STATE UNIVERSITY OF NEW JERSEY SCHOOL OF LAW, CAMDEN

217 N. 5TH STREET
CAMDEN, NEW JERSEY 08102
Telephone: (856) 225-6191
Fax: (856) 225-6487

ABA Approved Since 1951.

Overview:

Founded in 1926, the School of Law was incorporated into Rutgers--The State University of New Jersey in 1950. The school is approved by the ABA and is a member of the AALS. Along with the undergraduate College of Arts and Sciences, School of Business, and Graduate School, the School of Law is an integral part of the Rutgers-Camden campus. The campus is located along the Delaware River in the heart of the Philadelphia-Camden metropolitan area.

The Faculty:

The law school faculty is engaged in a dynamic program of scholarship, teaching and service to the bar and community. The faculty has authored leading casebooks and treatises in health law, international law, commercial law, constitutional law, criminal law, urban law, civil procedure, and admiralty. Faculty scholarship has been cited by numerous courts including the United States Supreme Court and the New Jersey Supreme Court. Faculty members also serve as consultants and reporters for the American Bar Association, the American Law Institute, several federal and state commissions, and counsel in important public interest litigation. The full-time faculty of 38 is assisted by 5 full-time research and writing instructors, 43 adjunct professors, and five clinical staff members.

The Students:

The total enrollment of the law school is between 725 and 750, with about 600 in the full-time program and about 150 enrolled in the part-time evening program. The total student body is represented by more than 300 undergraduate institutions and several international universities. Students are drawn from 44 states and Puerto Rico and several foreign countries. About 20 percent of the total enrollment are students of color and 50 percent are women. Admission to the law school is highly selective with about 9 applications for each seat in the entering class. For the class entering in the fall of 2000, regularly admitted students had a median LSAT of 158 and a median undergraduate GPA of 3.2.

The Educational Program:

The program of Rutgers School of Law - Camden prepares students to enter the practice of law as capable, reflective, ethical professionals and to engage in informed, thoughtful inquiry about law and the legal process. In their first year (or the first and second years of the part-time program) students pursue a basic, required curriculum that examines core subjects and develops the skills that are essential to the study and practice of law. After the first year, students are free to pursue a mainly elective program. The law school offers a wide range of upper level elective courses. The curriculum is especially rich in the areas of commercial law, health law, litigation, public international and comparative law, and public interest law. The school also offers a variety of joint degree programs with other units of Rutgers including programs in business, social work, public policy, and a J.D./M.D. program with the University of Medicine and Dentistry of New Jersey. Throughout the course of study, the curriculum integrates the study of substantive legal doctrine, theory and perspectives on law and the legal process, the operation of law in practice, and the activities and skills of the practicing lawyer. The curriculum uses a wide variety of teaching methods and educational settings, including large courses with challenging teacher-student discussion, small seminars that provide a forum for student research, simulations that require students to function in lawyer roles, and clinical opportunities in which students engage in actual client representation, under attorney supervision. A central and unique feature of the curriculum is the lawyering program. The lawyering program is composed of a series of courses, experiences within courses, and co-curricular activities that engage students in the intellectual, pragmatic, ethical, and personal issues that arise in the practice of law. In particular, each student must take four courses with major writing components. In most of the program's activities, students simulate the role of lawyers and participate in activities such as litigating or counseling clients.

The school offers many client-based courses and experiences in areas such as trial advocacy, bankruptcy, business organizations, labor, family/domestic violence, and environmental law. Many customary courses such as business organizations and family law have significant drafting and lawyering components. Third-year students in the Civil Practice Clinic represent clients, under attorney supervision, in a variety of legal matters such as social security and landlord-tenant cases. The Externship program furnishes third-year students with the opportunity to work in federal and state judicial chambers, public agencies, and public interest organizations and to participate in a clinical seminar to reflect on their experiences. Students in Small Business Counseling advise clients on legal issues involved in starting new businesses. The law school also supports an active pro bono program that provides opportunities to represent clients, under attorney supervision, in such areas as personal bankruptcies and domestic violence cases. Students also may serve as mediators in the alternative dispute resolution program of the Camden Municipal Court.

(This Listing Continued)

RUTGERS, THE STATE UNIVERSITY OF NEW JERSEY SCHOOL OF LAW, CAMDEN—Continued

Facilities:

The law school is located in a six-story structure which was extensively renovated in 1990. A major addition to the building for additional library space was completed in 1994. Student activities are housed in a historic townhouse adjacent to the law school. Two hundred students live on campus in a graduate residence hall.

Dean: Rayman L Solomon (856) 225-6191
Academic Affairs - Associate Dean: John S. Beckerman (856) 225-6546
Administration - Associate Dean: John S. Podolski (856) 225-6252
Admissions - Associate Dean: Camille S. Andrews (856) 225-6102
Director of Development: Scott Schaffer (856) 225-6396
Financial Aid - Manager: Richard L. Woodland (856) 225-6039
Library - Director: Anne Dalesandro (856) 225-6182
Assistant Dean of External Affairs & Career Services: Mary Beth Daisey (856) 225-6178
Student Affairs - Assistant Dean: Sybil James (856) 225-6454

FULL TIME FACULTY

RAYMAN LOUIS SOLOMON*, (Dean, Rutgers-Camden)**, born Helena, Arkansas, June 5, 1947; admitted to bar, 1976, Illinois. *Education:* Wesleyan University (B.A., 1968); University of Chicago (J.D., 1976; Ph.D., 1986). ***COURSES: Legal History Arkansas, Trusts & Estates. ***Email:*** raysol@camlaw.rutgers.edu

RANDALL STEPHEN ABATE*, (Legal Writing Faculty)**, born New Haven, Connecticut, January 24, 1964. *Education:* University of Rochester (B.A., 1986); Vermont Law School (J.D., 1989; M.S.L., 1989). ***COURSES: Legal Research and Writing, Moot Court, Advanced Brief Writing, International Environmental Law. ***Email:*** rabate@camden.rutgers.edu

AARON ARI AFILALO*, (Assistant Professor of Law)**, born Paris, France, April 12, 1966; admitted to bar, 1992, Massachusetts; 1994, New York. *Education:* Harvard (A.B., 1989; LL.M., 1997); Boston University (J.D., 1992). ***COURSES: Contracts, International Trade, International Business Transactions, E.U. Law. ***Email:*** afilalo@camlaw.rutgers.edu

CAMILLE SPINELLO ANDREWS*, (Instructor at Law School and Associate Dean for Enrollment)**, born Meadville, Pennsylvania, November 26, 1959; admitted to bar, 1986, Pennsylvania, New Jersey and U.S. District Court, Eastern District of Pennsylvania; 1988, U.S. Court of Appeals, 3rd Circuit. *Education:* University of Pittsburgh (B.A., 1980); Rutgers Law - Camden (J.D., 1986). ***COURSES: Federal Practice & Procedure, Complex Commercial Litigation. ***Email:*** csa@camden.rutgers.edu

STEPHEN M. BALL*, (Assistant Director-Career Services)**, born New Jersey, July 12, 1957; admitted to bar, 1996, Pennsylvania; 1996, New Jersey. *Education:* Rutgers College (B.A., 1979); Rutgers Graduate School of Management (M.B.A., 1984); Rutgers School of Law-Camden (J.D., 1996). ***Email: smball@camden.rutgers.edu

JOHN STEPHEN BECKERMAN*, (Associate Dean for Academic Affairs)**, born New York, New York, October 26, 1945; admitted to bar, 1983, Connecticut; 1984, New York. *Education:* Union College (A.B., 1966); University of Iowa (M.A., 1968); University of London (England) (Ph.D., 1972); Yale Law School (J.D., 1983). ***COURSES: Civil Procedure, Complex Litigation, Business Organizations, Securities Regulation, Professional Responsibility. ***Email:*** john.beckerman@camden.rutgers.edu

LINDA S. BOSNIAK*, (Professor of Law)**, born Cambridge, England, July 4, 1958; admitted to bar, 1989, New York. *Education:* Wesleyan University (B.A., 1980); University of California at Berkeley (M.A., 1988); Stanford University (J.D., 1988). ***COURSES: Immigration and Nationality, Employment Discrimination, Administrative Law, Refugee Law. ***Email:*** bosniak@camden.rutgers.edu

MICHAEL A. CARRIER*, (Assistant Professor)**, born New York, New York, March 22, 1969; admitted to bar, 1996, Maryland; District of Columbia. *Education:* Yale College (B.A., 1991); University of Michigan at Ann Arbor (J.D., 1995). ***COURSES: Intellectual Property, Evidence. ***Email:*** mcarrier@camlaw.rutgers.edu

EDWARD CHASE*, (Professor of Law)**, born Franklin, Louisiana, October 26, 1942; admitted to bar, 1968, Louisiana; 1973, New Jersey. *Education:* Williams College (B.A., 1965); Tulane Law School (J.D., 1968). ***COURSES: Property, Landlord and Tenant, Remedies, Contracts, Law and Theology. ***Email:*** echase@camden.rutgers.edu

ROGER S. CLARK*, (Board of Governors Professor)**, born Wanganui, New Zealand, April 14, 1940; admitted to bar, 1964, New Zealand. *Education:* Victoria University (B.A., 1964; LL.B., 1964; LL.M., 1967; LL.D., 1997); Columbia Law School (LL.M., 1968; J.S.D., 1972). ***COURSES: International Law, Human Rights, Criminal Law. ***Email:*** rsclark@camden.rutgers.edu

RUSSELL M. COOMBS*, (Associate Professor of Law)**, born April 18, 1938; admitted to bar, 1966, Massachusetts; 1971, Pennsylvania; 1977, Kansas. *Education:* Stanford University (B.A., 1961); Harvard University (J.D., 1966). ***COURSES: Criminal Procedure, Evidence, Juvenile Law, Family Law. ***Email:*** rmcoombs@camden.rutgers.edu

MARY BETH DAISEY*, (Assistant Dean of Alumni Affairs and Career Services)**, born Atlantic City, New Jersey, August 22, 1962. *Education:* University of Pennsylvania (B.A., 1984); Rutgers University Graduate School of Education (M.Ed., 1987). ***Email: daisey@camden.rutgers.edu

ANNE DALESANDRO*, (Director of the Law Library)**, born Brooklyn, New York, September 24, 1949; admitted to bar, 1975, New Jersey. *Education:* Fordham University (A.B., 1971); Rutgers, The State University of New Jersey School of Law, Camden (J.D., 1975); Rutgers University (M.L.S., 1977). ***Email: dalesand@camden.rutgers.edu

PERRY DANE*, (Professor of Law)**, born Tel Aviv, Israel, September 16, 1956. *Education:* Yale University (B.A., 1978; J.D., 1981). ***COURSES: Conflict of Laws, Religion and the Law, American Indian Law, Jurisdiction, Contracts, Jewish Law. ***Email:*** dane@camden.rutgers.edu

JOHN H. DAVIES*, (Professor of Law)**, born January 14, 1940; admitted to bar, 1965, Illinois; 1972, Pennsylvania; 1976, New Jersey. *Education:* University of Illinois (B.S., 1963; LL.B., 1965); Harvard University (LL.M., 1968). ***COURSES: Partnership Taxation, Introduction to F.I.T., Income Tax Planning. ***Email:*** jdavies@camden.rutgers.edu

***ROGER J. DENNIS*, (Provost and Professor of Law)**, born

(This Listing Continued)

RUTGERS, THE STATE UNIVERSITY OF NEW JERSEY SCHOOL OF LAW, CAMDEN—Continued

Cleveland, Ohio, January 17, 1950; admitted to bar, 1974, Illinois. *Education:* Northwestern University (B.S., 1971; J.D., 1974). ***COURSES:*** Antitrust, Business Organizations. ***Email:*** rjdennis@camden.rutgers.edu

MICHAEL B. DORFF*, (Assistant Professor of Law)**, born New York, New York, September 29, 1970; admitted to bar, 1996, Texas; 1999, New York. *Education:* Harvard College (A.B., 1992); Harvard Law School (J.D., 1996). ***COURSES: Contracts, Civil Procedure, Business N.S., Commercial Law, Creditors & Debtors Rights, Remedies, Torts.

ALICE DUEKER*, (Director, Clinical Programs)**, born Connecticut, March 25, 1957; admitted to bar, 1985, District of Columbia; 1991, New Jersey. *Education:* Bryn Mawr College (B.A., 1979); New York University (J.D., 1985); Georgetown University (LL.M., 1991). ***COURSES: Clinic, Elder Law, Disability Law. ***Email:*** dueker@camden.rutgers.edu

JO ANNE DURAKO*, (Director of Legal Research & Writing Program)**, born Philadelphia, Pennsylvania, February 24, 1949; admitted to bar, 1981, District of Columbia; 1987, Pennsylvania. *Education:* University of Florida (B.A., 1970; J.D.,1979). ***Email: durako@camden.rutgers.edu

JAY M. FEINMAN*, (Distinguished Professor of Law)**, born Easton, Pennsylvania, January 22, 1951; admitted to bar, 1975, Pennsylvania; 1986, New Jersey. *Education:* American University (B.A., 1972); University of Chicago (J.D., 1975). ***COURSES: Contracts, Torts, Jurisprudence, Clinical Teaching. ***Email:*** feinman@camden.rutgers.edu

KIMBERLY K. FERZAN*, (Assistant Professor of Law)**, admitted to bar, 1996, Pennsylvania. *Education:* University of North Carolina (B.A., 1991); University of Pennsylvania School of Law (J.D., 1995). ***COURSES: Evidence, Criminal Law. ***Email:*** kferzan@camden.rutgers.edu

SHEILA FOSTER*, (Professor of Law)**, born Detroit, Michigan, December 7, 1963; admitted to bar, 1988, California. *Education:* University of Michigan (B.A., 1985); University of California, Berkeley (J.D., 1988). ***COURSES: Torts, Race and American Law, Sex-Based Discrimination. ***Email:*** srfoster@camden.rutgers.edu

DAVID M. FRANKFORD*, (Professor of Law)**, born Philadelphia, Pennsylvania, July 22, 1954; admitted to bar, 1981, District of Columbia; 1989, Pennsylvania. *Education:* Tufts University (B.A., 1976); University of Chicago (J.D., 1979). ***COURSES: Antitrust, Health Care, Property, Regulation. ***Email:*** frankfor@camden.rutgers.edu

ANN ELIZABETH FREEDMAN*, (Associate Professor of Law)**, born October 18, 1947; admitted to bar, 1971, Connecticut; 1972, District of Columbia; 1974, Pennsylvania. *Education:* Radcliffe College (B.A., 1968); Yale University (J.D., 1971). ***COURSES: Family Law, Constitutional Law, Sex Discrimination Law. ***Email:*** aefreedm@camden.rutgers.edu

STEVEN F. FRIEDELL*, (Professor of Law)**, born Tyler, Minnesota, January 14, 1949; admitted to bar, 1974, Michigan; 1989, New Jersey. *Education:* University of Minnesota; Brandeis University (B.A., 1971); University of Michigan (J.D., 1974). ***COURSES: Admiralty, Torts, Jewish Law, Insurance. ***Email:*** friedell@camden.rutgers.edu

SANDRA FEGAN GAVIN*, (Director of Advocacy Programs)**, born Lebanon, Pennsylvania, May 20, 1951; admitted to bar, 1978, Ohio; 1980, Pennsylvania; 1983, New Jersey. *Education:* Case Western Reserve University (B.A., 1972); Cleveland State University (J.D. 1978). ***COURSES: Trial Advocacy, Pretrial Advocacy, Alternative Dispute Resolution. ***Email:*** redgav@crab.rutgers.edu

SALLY GOLDFARB*, (Associate Professor of Law)**, born New Jersey, 1957; admitted to bar, 1983, Wisconsin; 1985, District of Columbia; 1986, U.S. Supreme Court. *Education:* Yale University (B.A., 1978); Yale Law School (J.D., 1982). ***COURSES: Family Law, Torts, Professional Responsibility, Women and the Law. ***Email:*** sfg@camden.rutgers.edu

PHILIP L. HARVEY*, (Associate Professor of Law)**, born New York, New York, February 18, 1946; admitted to bar, 1989, New York. *Education:* Yale College (B.A., 1968); New York For Social Research (Ph.D., 1976); Yale Law School (J.D., 1988). ***COURSES: Employment Law, Labor Law, Law & Economics, Social Welfare Law, Human Rights. ***Email:*** pharvey@camden.rutgers.edu

ELIZABETH LUTES HILLMAN*, (Assistant Professor of Law)**, *Education:* Duke University (B.S., 1989); University of Pennsylvania (M.A., 1994); Yale Law School (J.D., 2000); Yale Graduate School of Arts & Science (Ph.D., 2001). ***COURSES: Legal History, Military Law, Women & the Law, Criminal Law & Procedure, Law & Sexuality, Evidence. ***Email:*** hillman@camden.rutgers.edu

N.E.H. HULL*, (Distinguished Professor of Law)**, born New York, New York, August 27, 1949; admitted to bar, 1985, Georgia. *Education:* Ohio State University (B.A., 1974); Columbia University (Ph.D., 1981);University of Georgia (J.D., 1985). ***COURSES: Contracts, Law and the Elderly, American Legal History, Jurisprudence. ***Email:*** nehhull@camden.rutgers.edu

RICHARD HYLAND*, (Distinguished Professor of Law)**, born San Diego, California, January 17, 1949; admitted to bar, 1981, California; 1984, District of Columbia; 1989, Florida. *Education:* Harvard University (A.B., 1970); University of California, Boalt Hall School of Law (J.D., 1980); University of Paris 2 (D.E.A., 1982). ***COURSES: Commercial Law, Comparative Law, Contracts, Restitution, Jurisprudence. ***Email:*** hyland@camden.rutgers.edu

SYBIL M. JAMES*, (Dean of Students)**, born Bronx, New York, July 12, 1966; admitted to bar, 1991, Pennsylvania; 1992, U.S. District Court of Eastern Pennsylvania. *Education:* Rutgers College-Rutgers University (B.A., 1988); University of Pennsylvania (J.D., 1991). ***Email: Sybilj@camden.rutgers.edu

HARRIET N. KATZ*, (Director, Legal Externship Program)**, born Dayton, Ohio, May 14, 1947; admitted to bar, 1972, Pennsylvania; 1974, California; 1980, New Jersey. *Education:* University of Michigan (B.A., 1969); Yale University (J.D., 1972). ***COURSES: Interview, Counseling, Negotiation, Pretrial Process, Lawyering Skills. ***Email:*** hnkatz@camden.rutgers.edu

A. KODZO PAAKU KLUDZE*, (Distinguished Professor of Law)**, born Gbi-Kpeme, Ghana, March 12, 1934; admitted to bar, 1965, Ghana; 1984, New York. *Education:* University of Ghana (B.A., 1963; LL.B., 1965); University of London (Ph.D., 1969). ***COURSES: Property, Equity, Decedents' Estates, Trusts, African Law, Comparative Law. ***Email:*** kludze@camden.rutgers.edu

DONALD R. KOROBKIN*, (Professor of Law)**, born Highland Park, Illinois Lake, March 24, 1956. *Education:* University of Michigan (B.A., 1978; J.D., 1983); Harvard University (A.M., 1981). ***COURSES: Commercial Law, Sales, Secured Transactions, Bankruptcy. ***Email:*** korobkin@camden.rutgers.edu

DARREN R. LATHAM*, (Legal Research and Writing Faculty)**, born Clearwater, Florida, January 27, 1966; admitted to bar, 1992, Florida. *Education:* University of California, Berkeley (A.B, 1988); University of Florida (J.D., 1992). ***COURSES: Legal Research & Writing, Judicial Writing. ***Email:*** latham@camden.rutgers.edu

***MICHAEL A. LIVINGSTON*, (Professor of Law)**, born Brooklyn,

(This Listing Continued)

RUTGERS, THE STATE UNIVERSITY OF NEW JERSEY SCHOOL OF LAW, CAMDEN—Continued

New York, July 19, 1956; admitted to bar, 1982, New York. *Education:* Cornell University (A.B., 1977); Yale University (J.D., 1981). ***COURSES:*** Taxation, Tax Policy, Business Planning, Corporations. ***Email:*** maliving@camden.rutgers.edu

EARL MICHAEL MALTZ*, (Distinguished Professor of Law)**, born December 3, 1950; admitted to bar, 1976, Wisconsin. *Education:* Northwestern University (B.A., 1972); Harvard University (J.D., 1975). ***COURSES: Advanced Constitutional Law, Constitutional Law, Conflicts. ***Email:*** emaltz@camden.rutgers.edu

ANNE M. MULLAN*, (Clinical Attorney)**, born Abington, Pennsylvania; admitted to bar, 1988, New Jersey; 1988, Pennsylvania. *Education:* LaSalle University (B.A., 1985); Rutgers University School of Law - Camden (J.D., 1988). ***COURSES: Civil Practice Clinic, Domestic Violence Project. ***Email:*** ammullan@camden.rutgers.edu

CRAIG N. OREN*, (Professor of Law)**, born Floral Park, New York, July 11, 1951; admitted to bar, 1976, California; 1977, Illinois; 1979, District of Columbia. *Education:* University of California, Berkeley (A.B., 1973); University of California, Boalt Hall School of Law (J.D., 1976). ***COURSES: Property, Environmental Law and Administrative Law. ***Email:*** oren@camden.rutgers.edu

TRACI L. OVERTON*, (Clinic Staff Attorney)**, admitted to bar, 1990, Massachusetts; 1998, New Jersey and Pennsylvania. *Education:* Wellesley College (B.A., 1983); University of California-Boalt Hall School of Law (J.D., 1988). ***Email: overton@camden.rutgers.edu

DENNIS M. PATTERSON*, (Distinguished Professor of Law)**, born New York City, New York, September 29, 1955; admitted to bar, 1981, New York; 1981, Maine; 1984, U.S. Supreme Court. *Education:* State University of New York at Buffalo (B.A., 1976; M.A., 1978; Ph.D., 1980; J.D., 1980). ***COURSES: Commercial Law and Jurisprudence. ***Email:*** dpatters@camden.rutgers.edu

JOHN S. PODOLSKI*, (Associate Dean for Administration)**, born Philadelphia, Pennsylvania, October 26, 1949. *Education:* Rutgers University College of Arts and Sciences (A.B., 1971); Rutgers University The Graduate School (M.B.A., 1978). ***Email: podolski@camden.rutgers.edu

STANISLAW POMORSKI*, (Distinguished Professor of Law)**, born Poland, November 23, 1934; admitted to bar, 1961, Poland. *Education:* University of Warsaw (Master, 1956; LL.D., 1968). ***COURSES: Comparative Law, Criminal Law, Criminal Procedure, Law and Economy, Polish Law, Soviet Law, Economic Criminality in Cooperative Trade. ***Email:*** pomorski@camden.rutgers.edu

SARAH ELIZABETH RICKS*, (Legal Writing Instructor)**, born Boston, Massachusetts, September 6, 1962; admitted to bar, 1990, Pennsylvania; New Jersey. *Education:* Barnard College, Columbia University (B.A., 1985); Yale Law School (J.D., 1990). ***COURSES: Research & Writing. ***Email:*** sricks@camden.rutgers.edu

RUTH ANNE ROBBINS*, (Clinical Staff Attorney)**, born Philadelphia, Pennsylvania, November 21, 1966; admitted to bar, 1991, Pennsylvania; 1991, New Jersey; 1992, District of New Jersey; 1992 E.D. of Pennsylvania; 1992, Third Circuit of Appeals. *Education:* University of Pennsylvania (B.A., 1988); Rutgers Law-Camden (J.D., 1991). ***COURSES: Domestic Violence, Practice & Procedure, Advanced Brief Writing. ***Email:*** ruthanne@camden.rutgers.edu

RAND E. ROSENBLATT*, (Professor of Law)**, born June 21, 1945; admitted to bar, 1972, Pennsylvania. *Education:* Harvard University (B.A., 1966); Yale University (J.D., 1971). ***COURSES: Constitutional Law, Health Care Law, Law, Justice and Society. ***Email:*** rrosenbl@camden.rutgers.edu

PATRICK JOHN RYAN*, (Associate Professor of Law)**, born Los Angeles, California, March 18, 1955; admitted to bar, 1980, California; 1981, Colorado. *Education:* Loyola Marymount University (B.A., 1976; M.A., 1977; J.D., 1980); Columbia University (LL.M., 1987; J.S.D., 1991). ***COURSES: Civil Procedure, Corporations. ***Email:*** pryanb@camden.rutgers.edu

DEBORAH A. SHORE*, (Legal Writing Faculty)**, born Philadelphia, Pennsylvania, August 9, 1967; admitted to bar, 1992, Pennsylvania, New Jersey. *Education:* The Wharton School of the University of Pennsylvania (B.S., 1989); University of Pennsylvania School of Law (J.D., 1992). ***COURSES: Legal Research and Writing, Moot Court. ***Email:*** debshore@camden.rutgers.edu

RICHARD G. SINGER*, (Distinguished Professor of Law)**, born August 20, 1943; admitted to bar, 1967, Maryland; 1974, New Jersey. *Education:* Amherst College (B.A., 1963); University of Chicago Law School (J.D., 1966); Columbia University (LL.M., 1970; S.J.D., 1977). ***COURSES: Criminal Law, Torts, Advanced Substantive Criminal Law, Federal Jurisdiction, Criminal Law Administration, Corrections. ***Email:*** rsinger.@camden.rutgers.edu

ALLAN R. STEIN*, (Professor of Law)**, born Newark, New Jersey, June 19, 1953; admitted to bar, 1978, Pennsylvania. *Education:* Haverford College (B.A., 1975); New York University (J.D., 1978). ***COURSES: Civil Procedure, Federal Jurisdiction, Advanced Civil Procedure, Problem in Civil Liberties, Appellate Advocacy, Professional Responsibility. ***Email:*** alstein@camden.rutgers.edu

BETH STEPHENS*, (Associate Professor of Law)**, born New York, New York, July 7, 1954; admitted to bar, 1981, California; 1996, New York; 1997, New Jersey. *Education:* Harvard University (B.A., 1976); University of California-Berkeley (J.D., 1980). ***COURSES: Civil Procedure, Evidence, International law. ***Email:*** bstephen@crab.rutgers.edu

CAROL LYNN WALLINGER*, (Legal Writing faculty)**, born New Jersey, April 13, 1957; admitted to bar, 1989, New Jersey and Pennsylvania. *Education:* Rutgers College (B.S., 1982); Temple University (J.D., 1989). ***COURSES: Legal Writing. ***Email:*** cwalling@camden.rutgers.edu

ROBERT M. WASHBURN*, (Professor of Law)**, born February 19, 1945; admitted to bar, 1968, New Jersey; 1969, Pennsylvania; 1971, Delaware. *Education:* Rutgers University (A.B., 1966); Washington University (J.D., 1968); University of Pennsylvania (LL.M., 1971). ***COURSES: Housing and Urban Development, Land Finance Law, Land Use, Land Transactions, Real Estate Development, Law and Urban Problems.

LINDA J. WHARTON*, (Clinical Staff Attorney)**, born Camden, New Jersey, February 9, 1955; admitted to bar, 1981, New Jersey, Pennsylvania. *Education:* Bryn Mawr College (B.A., 1977); Rutgers School of Law-Camden (J.D., 1981). ***COURSES: Sex Discrimination, Public Interest & Law, Education, Sports Law. ***Email:*** ljwharton@aol.com

ROBERT F. WILLIAMS*, (Distinguished Professor of Law)**, born Miami, Florida, August 20, 1945; admitted to bar, 1970, Florida; 1980, New Jersey. *Education:* Florida State University (B.A., 1967); University of Florida (J.D., 1969); New York University (LL.M., 1971); Columbia University (LL.M., 1980). ***COURSES: Civil Procedure, Legislation, State and Local Tax, State Constitutional Law. ***Email:*** rfw@camden.rutgers.edu

RUTGERS, THE STATE UNIVERSITY OF NEW JERSEY SCHOOL OF LAW, NEWARK

CENTER FOR LAW AND JUSTICE
123 WASHINGTON STREET
NEWARK, NEW JERSEY 07102
Telephone: (973) 353-5561
Fax: (973) 353-1248
http://rutgers-newark.rutgers.edu/law

ABA Approved Since 1941.

The School of Law-Newark is an institution with a talented and diverse faculty and student body. Rutgers living alumni, now numbering over 8,000, hold positions of prominence in legal and political circles. Our graduates serve in the U.S. Senate and House of Representatives, as the Director of the F.B.I., and in many other policy positions in federal, state, and local governments. As leaders of the bench and the bar, Rutgers graduates have established a national reputation for public service and the highest ethical standards. As an institution, the School of Law-Newark is dedicated to improving the quality of justice for all persons in society.

At the law school there is the opportunity to develop the analytical and practical skills needed in law practice and in related fields. Students work on pending law cases in our nine law clinics. Faculty members, who are nationally recognized scholars and experts in their fields, work to help achieve the students greatest potential. Rutgers is a challenging and exciting place to learn the law.

Rutgers School of Law-Newark aspires to be the premier public law school in the Northeast. We attract students who want to make a difference in society. Our progressive tradition reaches back over many decades. With added strengths in business and transactional law, Rutgers graduates are prepared to work on Wall Street or the Main Streets of cities and towns across the country. Our new international studies program allow students to study abroad with some of the finest law faculties in the world.

The School of Law-Newark, the oldest law school in the state, opened in 1908 in an imposing Victorian town house as a proprietary institution, the New Jersey Law School. Over the next decades the school became an institution of national stature. Its library expanded to become the most comprehensive collection in northern New Jersey, and its faculty tripled in size. In the 1960s, the law school pioneered in developing clinical education and in providing the opportunity to study law to women and minority groups. After using and outgrowing several buildings in downtown Newark, it moved in 1978 to the skyscraper that has since become the S.I. Newhouse Center for Law and Justice. In 1999, a new $49 million Center for Law and Justice opened on the University's Newark campus, and Rutgers-Newark now occupies one of the most advanced academic facilities among American Law Schools..

Part of the Newark campus of Rutgers, The State University of New Jersey, the Law School is adjacent to the Newark Public Library, a few steps away from the Newark Museum, and only a short distance form the New Jersey Performing Arts Center. The social, cultural, vocational, and educational opportunities of the area combine to provide a fitting location for the study of law.

Qualities that typify Rutgers School of Law-Newark include its informal atmosphere, its nationally recognized faculty, favorable tuition rates, and a very diverse student body. The professional interests, goals, and outlooks of students are more varied here than at most law schools. Similarly, there is diversity in the background, professional experience, extracurricular work, and scholarship of the faculty. Rutgers School of Law-Newark has the first New Jersey chapter of the Order of the Coif, the national honor society for law students.

The Faculty of Law

Members of Rutgers School of Law-Newark faculty are committed to the law and to excellence in legal education. These shared commitments unite a group of independent individuals otherwise known for their diversity. They are graduates of law schools throughout the country and have brought to Rutgers a variety of backgrounds in private law practice, public interest law practice, and government service. These differences in legal training and experience enable the faculty to expose students to different teaching methods and different approaches to law. The faculty's research and writing is focused on new and developing issues of law, such as feminist and race studies, alternate methods of dispute resolution, law and medicine, and new theories of the corporation. Their work takes them around the globe on matters such as constitutional rights in developing countries, international environmental law, and models of transnational organization in the post-Cold War world. Outside the law school, many faculty members serve on professional committees and participate in community activities.

Dean: Stuart L. Deutsch
Academic Affairs: Ronald K. Chen
Admissions: Anita Walton
Library Director: Carol A. Roehrenbeck
Placement: Dawne Smith
Alumni Affairs: Sheilah McLean Louis
Student Affairs: Andrew Rothman
Publications & Events: Deborah Smith

FULL TIME FACULTY

STUART L. DEUTSCH*, (Dean and Professor of Law)**, *Education:* University of Michigan (B.A.); Yale (J.D.). ***COURSES: Environmental Law, Property, Land Use, Local Government, Hazardous Waste Regulation, Urban Environmental Problems.

***ANN ALEXANDER*, (Staff Attorney, Environmental Law Clinic)**, *Education:* Yale (B.A.); Columbia (J.D.).

FRANK ASKIN*, (Professor of Law and Robert Knowlton Scholar)**, *Education:* City College of New York (B.A.); Rutgers (J.D.). ***COURSES: Constitutional Litigation Clinic, Civil Procedure, Election Law.

(This Listing Continued)

RUTGERS, THE STATE UNIVERSITY OF NEW JERSEY SCHOOL OF LAW, NEWARK—Continued

PAUL AXEL-LUTE*, (Collection Development Librarian)**, born 1945. *Education:* Brandeis University (B.A., 1968). ***Email: axellute@andromeda.rutgers.edu

BERNARD W. BELL*, (Associate Professor of Law)**, *Education:* Harvard (B.A., *cum laude*); Stanford (J.D.). ***COURSES: Torts, Legislation, Administrative Law, Mass Media and the Law.

CYNTHIA BLUM*, (Professor of Law)**, *Education:* Harvard Law School (*magna cum laude*, 1976). ***COURSES: Federal Income Taxation, Federal Income Tax-Corporations and Shareholders, International Tax Seminar, Federal Tax Clinic.

ALFRED W. BLUMROSEN*, (Thomas A. Cowan Professor of Law)**, *Education:* University of Michigan (B.A., J.D.). ***COURSES: Legislation, Administrative Process, Employment Discrimination.

SUSANA IRENE CAMARGO-POHL*, (Reference Librarian)**, born New York, New York, March, 11, 1972; admitted to bar, 1999, New Jersey. *Education:* Ursinus College (B.A., 1994); Rutgers University (M.L.S., 1999); The Dickinson School of Law (J.D., 1997). ***COURSES: Legal Research. ***Email:*** scamargo-pohl@kinoy.rutgers.edu

DANIEL ROBERT CAMPBELL*, (Head of Circulation)**, born New York City, New York, May 20, 1964. *Education:* Jersey City State College (B.A., 1992); Seton Hall Law School (J.D., 1997). ***Email: dcampbell@kinoy.rutgers.edu

NORMAN L. CANTOR*, (Professor of Law and Justice Nathan L. Jacobs Scholar)**, *Education:* Princeton (A.B.); Columbia (J.D., *magna cum laude*). ***COURSES: Constitutional Law, Contracts, Legal Aspects of Death and Dying.

***ESTER CANTY-BARNES*, (Staff Attorney, Special Education Law Clinic)**, *Education:* Bennett College (B.A.); Rutgers University School of Law-Newark (J.D.).

ROBERT A. CARTER*, (Professor of Law and Judge Alexander P. Waugh, Sr. Scholar)**, *Education:* Yale (B.A.; LL.B.). ***COURSES: Civil Procedure, Equity, Federal Jurisdiction, Torts.

RONALD K. CHEN*, (Associate Dean for Academic Affairs)**, *Education:* Darmouth (A.B.); Rutgers (J.D.). ***COURSES: Contracts, Church-State Relations, Federal Courts.

ROBERT CHU*, (Associate Professor of Law)**, *Education:* Massachusetts Institute of Technology (S.B.; S.M.); Harvard Law School (J.D.). ***COURSES: International Business Transactions, International Law and a Just World Order, International Trade Seminar.

SHERRY COLB*, (Professor of Law)**, *Education:* Columbia College (A.B., *summa cum laude*); Harvard Law School (J.D., *magna cum laude*, 1991). ***COURSES: Criminal Procedure, Evidence and Mental Health Law.

DRUCILLA L. CORNELL*, (Professor of Law)**, *Education:* Antioch College (B.A.); University of California (J.D.). ***COURSES: Feminist Jurisprudence.

MARJORIE E. CRAWFORD*, (Head of Technical Services)**, born Memphis, Tennessee, July 30, 1949. *Education:* Rutgers (B.A., 1989). ***Email: mcrawford@kinoy.rutgers.edu

CHARLES DAVENPORT*, (Professor of Law and Arthur L. Dickson Scholar)**, *Education:* Chico State College (A.B., 1954); Harvard (LL.B., 1957). ***COURSES: Federal Income Taxation, Federal Income Tax-Corporations and Shareholders, Estate and Gift Taxation, Estate Planning, Tax Policy.

***CYNTHIA DENNIS*, (Director and Staff Attorney, Women and AIDS Clinic)**, *Education:* Rutgers College (B.A.); Villanova University (J.D.).

JON DUBIN*, (Professor of Law)**, *Education:* Dartmouth (A.B.); New York University (J.D.). ***COURSES: Administrative Law, Urban Legal Clinic.

SHANNON MARK ENGLEMAN*, (Acquisitions/Serials Librarian)**, born Westwood, New Jersey, May 8, 1975. *Education:* Vassar College (B.A., 1997); Rutgers University School of Law (J.D., 2000 (anticipated)). ***Email: smeesq@pegasus.rutgers.edu

***JACK FEINSTEIN*, (Staff Attorney, Urban Legal Clinic)**, *Education:* Rutgers College (B.A.); Rutgers School of Law-Newark (J.D.).

GARY L. FRANCIONE*, (Professor of Law and Nicholas de. B. Katzenbach Scholar, Dir., Animals Rights Law Clinic)**, *Education:* University of Rochester (B.A.); University of Virginia (M.A.; J.D.). ***COURSES: Torts, Law, Science, and Medicine, Jurisprudence, Criminal Law and Procedure, Seminar on Animal Rights Law.

***SANDY FREUND*, (Co-Director and Staff Attorney, Federal Taxation Clinic)**, *Education:* SUNY at Stony Brook (B.A.); Hofstra Law School (J.D.); New York University (LL.M.).

HELEN A. GARTEN*, (Professor of Law)**, *Education:* Princeton (A.B.); Harvard (J.D.). ***COURSES: Business Associations, Securities Regulation.

SUZANNE B. GOLDBERG*, (Assistant Professor of Law)**, *Education:* Brown (A.B., 1986); Harvard (J.D., 1990). ***COURSES: Civil Procedure, Jurisprudence.

CARLOS GONZALEZ*, (Associate Professor of Law)**, *Education:* University of Michigan (B.A.); Yale (J.D.). ***COURSES: Civil Procedure, Torts, Legislation, Statutory Interpretation.

***MARY F. HARNETT*, (Director and Staff Attorney, Special Education Clinic)**, *Education:* Rutgers College (B.A.); Seton Hall University (J.D.).

***ROBERT C. HOLMES*, (Director and Staff Attorney, Community Law Program)**, *Education:* Cornell University (A.B.); Harvard Law School (J.D.).

ALAN HYDE*, (Professor of Law and Sidney Reitman Scholar)**, *Education:* Stanford (A.B.); Yale (J.D.). ***COURSES: Labor Law, Employment Law, Contracts, Federal Jurisdiction.

JONATHAN M. HYMAN*, (Professor of Law)**, *Education:* Harvard (A.B.); Yale (LL.B.). ***COURSES: Clinic in Constitutional Litigation, Contracts, Negotiation, Mediation, and Alternate Dispute Resolution, Criminal Law, Federal Jurisdiction, Lawyering Process.

CHARLES JONES*, (Associate Professor of Law)**, *Education:* University of Illinois (J.D.); Harvard (M.P.A.). ***COURSES: Criminal Law, Criminal Procedure.

***SUSAN KRAHAM*, (Staff Attorney, Environmental Law Clinic)**, *Education:* Columbia (B.A.; J.D.); New York University (M.A.).

***THERESE LANGER*, (Staff Scientist, Environmental Law Clinic)**, *Education:* Harvard (B.A.); University of California (Ph.D.).

HOWARD LATIN*, (Professor of Law and Justice John J. Francis Scholar)**, *Education:* Brandeis (B.A.); University of California Berkeley (J.D.). ***COURSES: Environmental Law, International Environmental Law, Torts, Product Liability, Law and Economics.

(This Listing Continued)

RUTGERS, THE STATE UNIVERSITY OF NEW JERSEY SCHOOL OF LAW, NEWARK—Continued

JOHN LEUBSDORF*, (Professor of Law and Judge Frederick B. Lacey Scholar)**, *Education:* Harvard (B.A., 1963; J.D., 1967); Stanford (M.A., 1964). ***COURSES: Civil Procedure, Legal Profession, Evidence.

***MARCIA LEVY*, (Staff Attorney, Urban Legal Clinic)**, *Education:* SUNY at Albany (B.S.); Lewis and Clark College (J.D.).

GREGORY A. MARK*, (Professor of Law)**, *Education:* Butler University (B.A.); Harvard University (M.A.); University of Chicago (J.D.). ***COURSES: Business Associations, Corporate Finance, American Legal History.

SAUL MENDLOVITZ*, (Dag Hammarskjold Professor of Peace and World Order Studies Emeritus)**, *Education:* Syracuse University (B.A.); University of Chicago (M.A.; J.D.). ***COURSES: International Law, United Nations, World Order.

***ERNEST NARDONE*, (Director of Legal Writing)**, *Education:* Rutgers-Newark (J.D.).

JOHN M. PAYNE*, (Professor of Law and Justice Fred Hall Scholar)**, *Education:* Yale (B.A.); Harvard (J.D.). ***COURSES: Land Use, Municipal Corporations, State and Local Taxation, Constitutional Law.

TWILA L. PERRY*, (Professor of Law)**, *Education:* Mount Holyoke College (B.A.); Columbia University School of Social Work (M.S.W.); New York University (J.D.). ***COURSES: Torts, Family Law Seminar on Children and the Law, Seminar on Race, Gender, and Tort Law.

JAMES POPE*, (Professor of Law)**, *Education:* Harvard (A.B., 1974; J.D., 1983). ***COURSES: Constitutional Law, Labor Law, Property, Constitutional Theory.

LOUIS RAVESON*, (Professor of Law)**, *Education:* School of Law-Newark (1976). ***COURSES: Urban Legal Clinic, Evidence, Constitutional Litigation Clinic, AIDS and the Law, Fact Investigation.

CAROL A. ROEHRENBECK*, (Associate Dean & Law Library Director)**, born Montclair, New Jersey. *Education:* University of Delaware (B.A.); Rutgers University (M.L.S.; J.D.). ***COURSES: Advanced Legal Research. ***Email:*** carolr@andromeda.rutgers.edu

DIANA SCLAR*, (Associate Professor of Law)**, *Education:* Stanford University (A.B.); University of California-Berkeley (J.D.). ***COURSES: Conflict of Laws, Federal Courts, Property.

KEITH SHARFMAN*, (Associate Professor of Law)**, *Education:* Johns Hopkins (B.A., 1993); University of Chicago (J.D., 1997). ***COURSES: Antitrust, Debtor-Creditor Law, Law & Economics.

PHILIP SHUCHMAN*, (Justice Joseph Weintraub Professor of Law Emeritus)**, *Education:* University of Pennsylvania (J.D.). ***COURSES: Civil Procedure, Bankruptcy, Jurisprudence,.

PETER SIMMONS*, (University Professor)**, *Education:* University of California-Berkeley (A.B.; LL.B.). ***COURSES: Property, Land-Use Planning, Housing.

ALFRED SLOCUM*, (Professor of Law)**, *Education:* Newark College of Engineering (B.S.); Rutgers School of Law-Newark (J.D.); Yale (LL.M.). ***COURSES: Property, Real Estate Transactions, Future Interests.

NADINE TAUB*, (Professor of Law and S.I. Newhouse Scholar)**, *Education:* Swarthmore College (B.A.); Yale (LL.B.). ***COURSES: Civil Liberties, Constitutional Law, Social Welfare Legislation, Women and the Law, Women's Rights Litigation Clinic.

GEORGE THOMAS*, (Professor of Law)**, *Education:* University of Tennessee (B.S.); University of Iowa (M.F.A.; J.D.); Washington University-St. Louis (LL.M.; S.J.D.). ***COURSES: Criminal Law, Criminal Procedure, Law and Humanities, Trusts and Estates.

PAUL L. TRACTENBERG*, (Professor of Law and Alfred C. Clapp Public Service Professor)**, *Education:* Wesleyan (B.A.); University of Michigan (J.D.). ***COURSES: Education Law, Contracts, Negotiations, Client Interviewing and Counseling, Alternate Dispute Resolution.

DAVID D. TROUTT*, (Associate Professor of Law)**, *Education:* Stanford University (B.A.); Harvard Law School (J.D., *cum laude*). ***COURSES: Torts, Business Torts, Seminar on Inner City Economic Development.

***PENNY VENETIS*, (Staff Attorney, Constitutional Litigation Clinic)**, *Education:* Barnard College, Columbia University (B.A. 1983); Columbia University (M.A., 1986); Boston College Law School (J.D., *cum laude*, 1989).

ST. JOHN'S UNIVERSITY SCHOOL OF LAW

8000 UTOPIA PARKWAY
JAMAICA, NEW YORK 11439
Telephone: (718) 990-6600
Fax: (718) 591-1855

ABA Approved Since 1937.

Established in 1925, St. John's University School of Law has an enrollment of approximately 1000, representing students with diverse backgrounds who have excelled in undergraduate and graduate institutions.

The School of Law offers an excellent academic program that provides students with a solid foundation in fundamental areas of substantive and procedural law with significant elective offerings in many areas, including tax, labor, environmental, real estate and intellectual property. It holds the honor of being the first (and only) Law School in the nation to offer a Bankruptcy LL.M. program. The faculty has a distinguished background in published scholarship and professional activities. In addition, an adjunct faculty comprised of instructors who have achieved prominence as judges, government officials or private practitioners offer courses in their respective areas of expertise.

St. John's publications -- the *Law Review, Journal of Legal Commentary,* the *New York State Bar Association International Law Review* and the *American Bankruptcy Institute Bankruptcy Law Review* -- and the Moot Court programs have achieved national prominence. Civil and criminal trial institutes also afford students excellent experience in trial practice.

Students may participate in civil and criminal internships with district attorneys' offices, U.S. Attorney's offices and other governmental agencies or serve as judicial interns with federal and state judges. Clinical academic credit and practical experience can be earned through participation in the School's on-site Elder Law Clinic or its newest venture -- a Domestic Violence Clinic -- which is the result of a partnership between St. John's and the New York Legal Assistance Group.

St. John's University School of Law takes pride in its many graduates

(This Listing Continued)

ST. JOHN'S UNIVERSITY SCHOOL OF LAW—Continued

who are partners in the tri-state area's most prestigious law firms, who are counsel or senior executives in Fortune 500 companies or who have dedicated themselves to public service. Recent graduates continue to join major firms, often after having served in clerkships with federal judges. Alumni are also prominent members of various branches of the government and include many state and federal judges, several governors and other political figures.

A major building expansion and renovation project that nearly doubled the size of the Law School's facilities has been completed. This venture will allow for further development of the 500,000 volume Rittenberg Law Library, which has recently been enhanced by the addition of a state-of-the-art computer laboratory. Renovations are under way on two classrooms and a new moot court room, all of which will contain state-of-the-art technology. Several classrooms are already equipped with instructional technology, and a wireless network will soon be implemented to accommodate student computing needs. St. John's is accredited by the American Bar Association and is a member of the Association of American Law Schools.

Dean: Joseph W. Bellacosa (718) 990-6601
Associate Academic Dean: Andrew J. Simons (718) 990-6098
Assistant Dean for Students: Katherine G. Sullivan (718) 990-6045
Registrar: Janet M. Keogan (718) 990-1388
Assistant Dean for CLE and Alumni Relations: Claire C. McKeever (718) 990-6028
Assistant Dean for Admissions: Robert M. Harrison (718) 990-2310
Assistant Dean for Career Services: Albert Lorenzo (718) 990-2337
Law Library; Assist. Dean, Library & Information Resources: Linda M. Ryan (718) 990-1578

FULL TIME FACULTY

JOSEPH W. BELLACOSA*, (Dean and Professor)**, born Brooklyn, New York, 1937; admitted to bar, 1961, New York. *Education:* St. John's University (B.A., 1959; J.D., 1961). ***COURSES: Criminal Justice, Criminal Procedure, Judicial Administration, Legal Ethics, Trial & Appellate Advocacy, Professional Responsibility. ***Email:*** jbella@stjohns.edu

VINCENT C. ALEXANDER*, (Professor)**, born 1949; admitted to bar, 1976, New York. *Education:* Yale University (B.A., 1971); St. John's University School of Law (J.D., 1975); Columbia University (LL.M., 1985; J.S.D., 1990). ***COURSES: Evidence, New York Practice. ***Email:*** alexandv@stjohns.edu

JOHN Q. BARRETT*, (Professor)**, born 1961; admitted to bar, 1986, Pennsylvania; 1989, District of Columbia. *Education:* Georgetown (A.B., 1983); Harvard (J.D., 1986). ***COURSES: Criminal Procedure, Professional Responsibility, Legal History, White Collar Crime. ***Email:*** barrettj@stjohns.edu

JOSEPH JAMES BEARD*, (Professor)**, born 1933; admitted to bar, 1970, Massachusetts; 1989, New York. *Education:* Tufts University (B.S., 1956); Suffolk University (J.D., 1969); Babson College (M.B.A., 1971); Boston University (LL.M., 1974); Harvard Law School (S.J.D., 1981). ***COURSES: Entertainment Law, Trademark/Copyright Law. ***Email:*** beardj@stjohns.edu

CHARLES EDWARD BIBLOWIT*, (Professor)**, born 1947; admitted to bar, 1974, Massachusetts; 1975, District of Columbia. *Education:* Tufts University (B.A., 1968); Northeastern University (J.D., 1974); Columbia University (LL.M., 1981). ***COURSES: Civil Procedure, Conflict of Laws, International Law, International Business Transactions, International Litigation. ***Email:*** biblowic@stjohns.edu

CHARLES S. BOBIS*, (Professor)**, born 1944; admitted to bar, 1968, New York. *Education:* Harpur College, State University of New York at Binghamton (B.A., 1966); St. John's University (J.D., 1968); University of London (LL.M., 1971). ***COURSES: Criminal Law, Criminal Procedure, Legal Method. ***Email:*** bobisc@stjohns.edu

ROBIN A. BOYLE*, (Assistant Legal Writing Professor)**, born Amityville, New York, September 30, 1958; admitted to bar, 1990, New York. *Education:* Vassar College (B.A., 1980); Fordham Law School (J.D., 1989). ***COURSES: Legal Writing. ***Email:*** boyler@stjohns.edu

GINA M. CALABRESE*, (Assistant Professor for Clinical Education)**, born 1965; admitted to bar, 1992, California; 1997, New York; 2000, U.S. District Court, Eastern and Southern Districts of New York. *Education:* Columbia University (B.A., 1987); Fordham University School of Law (J.D., 1991). ***COURSES: Elder Law. ***Email:*** calabreg@stjohns.edu

EDWARD D. CAVANAGH*, (Professor)**, born 1949; admitted to bar, 1975, New York. *Education:* University of Notre Dame (A.B., 1971); Cornell University (J.D., 1974); Columbia University (LL.M., 1986; J.S.D., 1988). ***COURSES: Antitrust, Civil Procedure, Federal Practice, Law and Economics. ***Email:*** cavanage@stjohns.edu

REV. JOHN J. COUGHLIN, O.F.M.*, (Assistant Professor)**, born 1954; admitted to bar, 1988, New York. *Education:* Niagara University (B.A., 1977); Columbia University Teachers College (M.A., 1982); Princeton Theological Seminary (Th.M., 1984); Harvard University Law School (J.D., 1987); Pontifical Gregorian University, Rome (J.C.L., 1990; J.C.D., 1994). ***COURSES: Administrative Law, Canon Law, Family Law, Professional Responsibility. ***Email:*** coughlij@stjohns.edu

NINA J. CRIMM*, (Professor)**, born 1952; admitted to bar, 1979, District of Columbia; 1988, New York. *Education:* Washington University (A.B., 1972); Tulane University (M.B.A., 1979; J.D., 1979); Georgetown University Law Center (LL.M., 1982). ***COURSES: Taxation of Corporations, Basic and Advanced Personal Income Taxation, U.S. Taxation of International Transactions, Nonprofit Organizations. ***Email:*** crimmn@stjohns.edu

JOHN EDWARD DAVIDIAN*, (Professor)**, born 1949; admitted to bar, 1976, New York. *Education:* St. John's University (B.S., 1971); St. John's University School of Law (J.D., 1975); New York University School of Law (LL.M., 1985). ***COURSES: Basic and Advanced Personal Income Taxation, Basic and Advanced Corporate Income Taxation, Partnership Taxation. ***Email:*** davidiaj@stjohns.edu

VINCENT M. DILORENZO*, (Professor)**, born 1953; admitted to bar, 1979, New York; 1985, Pennsylvania. *Education:* Pace University (B.A., 1975); Columbia University (J.D., 1978). ***COURSES: Banking Law, Property, Condominiums, Cooperatives and Homeowner Association, Legislative Advocacy. ***Email:*** dilorenv@stjohns.edu

FRANCIS J. FACCIOLO*, (Assistant Legal Writing Professor)**, born New York City, August 28, 1949; admitted to bar, 1984, New York. *Education:* Columbia College (B.A., 1974); Hunter College (M.A., 1977); City University of New York (M.Phil., 1979); Columbia Law School (J.D., 1983). ***COURSES: Legal Research & Writing. ***Email:*** facciolf@stjohns.edu

(This Listing Continued)

ST. JOHN'S UNIVERSITY SCHOOL OF LAW—Continued

MICHELE G. FALKOW, **(Assistant Legal Writing Professor),** admitted to bar, 1986, New York. *Education:* Harvard University (B.A., 1979); New York University School of Law (J.D., 1985); Columbia University (M.L.S., 1988). ***COURSES:*** Legal Research and Writing. ***Email:*** falkowm@stjohns.edu

BERNARD E. GEGAN, **(Professor),** born 1937; admitted to bar, 1962, New York. *Education:* St. John's University (B.S., 1959); St. John's University School of Law (LL.B., 1961); Harvard Law School (LL.M., 1962). ***COURSES:*** Contracts, Remedies. ***Email:*** geganb@stjohns.edu

ANN L. GOLDWEBER, **(Assistant Professor for Clinical Education and Director, Elder Law Clinic),** born Hewlett, New York, February 21, 1952; admitted to bar, 1977, Wisconsin, U.S. District Court, Western and Eastern Districts of Wisconsin; 1984, New York; 1987, U.S. District Court, Eastern District of New York; 1989, U.S. District Court, Southern District of New York; 1991, U.S. District Court, Western District of New York; 1990, U.S. Court of Appeals, Second Circuit. *Education:* University of Wisconsin-Madison (B.A., 1974); University of Wisconsin Law School (J.D., 1977). ***COURSES:*** Elder Law. ***Email:*** goldweba@stjohns.edu

KERI K. GOULD, **(Assistant Clinical Professor & Assistant Dean for Externships),** born Manhasset, New York, June 22, 1956; admitted to bar, 1983, New York, 1995, Utah. *Education:* Union College (B.S., 1978); Washington College of Law, American University (J.D., 1982). ***COURSES:*** Clinical, Mental Health Law. ***Email:*** gouldk@stjohns.edu

DAVID L. GREGORY, **(Professor),** born 1951; admitted to bar, 1981, Michigan; 1988, New York. *Education:* Catholic University (B.A., 1973); Wayne State University (M.B.A., 1977); University of Detroit (J.D., 1980); Yale Law School (LL.M., 1982; J.S.D., 1987). ***COURSES:*** Constitutional Law, Advanced Labor Law, Employment Law, Employment Discrimination, Constitutional Theory, Jurisprudence. ***Email:*** gregoryd@stjohns.edu

WILLIAM D. HARRINGTON, **(Professor),** born 1945; admitted to bar, 1970, New York. *Education:* Holy Cross University (A.B., 1966); Columbia University (J.D., 1969; M.B.A., 1970). ***COURSES:*** Business Organizations, Business Planning, Corporate Finance, Corporations, Federal Securities Regulation. ***Email:*** harringw@stjohns.edu

JOHN P. HENNIGAN, JR., **(Professor),** born 1947; admitted to bar, 1975, New York; 1982, California. *Education:* Harvard University (A.B., 1969); Harvard Law School (J.D., 1974). ***COURSES:*** Civil Procedure, Commercial Transactions, Secured Transactions, Creditor's Rights. ***Email:*** hennigaj@stjohns.edu

TANYA K. HERNANDEZ, **(Professor),** born 1963; admitted to bar, 1991, Connecticut; 1994, New York. *Education:* Brown (A.B., 1986); Yale (J.D., 1990). ***COURSES:*** Estates and Trusts, Law and Policy of Health Care Delivery Systems. ***Email:*** hernandt@stjohns.edu

LAWRENCE JOSEPH, **(Professor),** born 1948; admitted to bar, 1976, Michigan; 1982, New York. *Education:* University of Michigan (B.A., 1970; J.D., 1975); Cambridge University (B.A., 1972; M.A., 1976). ***COURSES:*** Employment Law, Legal Process, Torts, Jurisprudence. ***Email:*** josephl@stjohns.edu

PAUL F. KIRGIS, **(Assistant Professor),** born Washington, D.C., June 7, 1967; admitted to bar, 1995, Washington, D.C.. *Education:* Colgate University (B.A., 1989); Washington & Lee University (J.D., 1994). ***COURSES:*** Evidence. ***Email:*** kirgisp@stjohns.edu

MARGARET N. KNIFFIN, **(Professor),** born 1940; admitted to bar, 1973, New York. *Education:* Barnard College (A.B., 1961); Harvard Law School (J.D., 1972). ***COURSES:*** Contracts, The Legal Process, Remedies. ***Email:*** mkniff@aol.com

SAMUEL J. LEVINE, **(Research Professor),** born 1967; admitted to bar, 1995, New York, New Jersey; 1996, U.S. Court of Appeals, Second Circuit. *Education:* Yeshiva University (B.A., 1990); Fordham University School of Law (J.D., 1994); Columbia University School of Law (LL.M., 1996). ***COURSES:*** Professional Responsibility and Jewish Law. ***Email:*** levines@stjohns.edu

MARY LORING LYNDON, **(Professor),** born 1947; admitted to bar, 1974, New Jersey; 1975, District of Columbia; 1976, New York. *Education:* Manhattanville College (B.A., 1969); Northeastern University (J.D., 1974); Columbia University (J.S.D., 1995). ***COURSES:*** Environmental Law, International Environmental Law, Torts, Toxic Torts Seminar. ***Email:*** lyndonm@stjohns.edu

ROBERT E. MALCHMAN, **(Assistant Legal Writing Professor),** born New York, New York, April 25, 1963; admitted to bar, 1989, Massachusetts; 1990, New York. *Education:* Massachusetts Institute of Technology (S.B., 1985); University of Michigan (J.D., 1989). ***COURSES:*** Legal Research and Writing. ***Email:*** rmalchman@alum.mit.edu

ROBERT E. PARELLA, **(Keenan Professor),** born 1935; admitted to bar, 1963, New York. *Education:* St. Peter's College (A.B., 1957); New York University School of Law (J.D., 1960). ***COURSES:*** Administrative Law, Property, Real Estate Drafting, Trusts & Estates. ***Email:*** parellar@stjohns.edu

MICHAEL ANTHONY PERINO, **(Associate Professor),** born New York, New York, August 13, 1963; admitted to bar, 1988, New York. *Education:* Rutgers College (B.A., 1985); Columbia Law School (LL.M., 1995); Boston College Law School (J.D., 1988). ***COURSES:*** Securities, Business Associations. ***Email:*** perinom@stjohns.edu

EDWARD D. RE, **(Distinguished Professor),** born 1920; admitted to bar, 1943, New York. *Education:* St. John's University (B.S., 1941); St. John's University School of Law (LL.B., 1943); New York University School of Law (J.S.D., 1950); Pace University (D.H.L., 1985); University of Bologna, Italy (J.D., 1988). ***COURSES:*** Appellate Advocacy, International Law, Remedies, Constitutional Law.

PATRICK J. ROHAN, **(Dean Emeritus and Professor),** born 1933; admitted to bar, 1956, New York. *Education:* St. John's University (B.A., 1954); St. John's University School of Law (LL.B., 1956); Harvard Law School (LL.M., 1957); Columbia University (J.S.D., 1965). ***COURSES:*** Condominiums and Cooperatives, Homeowners Associations, Land Use Planning, Real Property, Trusts and Estates. ***Email:*** rohanp@stjohns.edu

ALBERT J. ROSENTHAL, **(Distinguished Professor),** born 1919; admitted to bar, 1942, New York. *Education:* University of Pennsylvania (A.B., 1938); Harvard Law School (LL.B., 1941). ***COURSES:*** Commercial Transactions, Constitutional Law, Contracts. ***Email:*** brosent75@aol.com

ROBERT A. RUESCHER, **(Assistant Legal Writing Professor),** born 1955; admitted to bar, 1981, New York, U.S. District Court, Eastern and Southern Districts of New York. *Education:* Columbia University (B.A., 1976); Columbia University School of Law (J.D., 1994). ***COURSES:*** Legal Research and Writing. ***Email:*** ruescher@stjohns.edu

ROSEMARY C. SALOMONE, **(Professor),** born 1946; admitted to bar, 1981, New York. *Education:* Brooklyn College of the City University of New York (B.A., 1967); Hunter College of the City University of New York (M.A., 1969); Columbia University (Ph.D., 1976; LL.M., 1984); Brooklyn Law School (J.D., 1980). ***COURSES:*** Administrative Law, Constitutional Law, State Constitutional Law, Local Government Law. ***Email:*** salomonr@stjohns.edu

THOMAS F. SHEA, **(Professor),** born 1935; admitted to bar, 1961,

(This Listing Continued)

ST. JOHN'S UNIVERSITY SCHOOL OF LAW—Continued

New York. *Education:* Cathedral College (B.A., 1957); St. John's University School of Law (LL.B., 1960); New York University School of Law (LL.M., 1968). ***COURSES:*** Antitrust, Constitutional Law, Contracts, Evidence, Advocacy Skills, Legal Research & Writing.

ANDREW J. SIMONS*, (Associate Academic Dean)**, born January 21, 1939; admitted to bar, 1965, New York, U.S. District Court, Eastern and Southern Districts of New York; 1970, U.S. Supreme Court, U.S. Court of Claims, U.S. Court of Appeals for the Federal Circuit and U.S. Court of Military Appeals; 1972, U.S. Court of Appeals, Second Circuit. *Education:* College of the Holy Cross (A.B., 1960); St. John's University (J.D., 1965). ***COURSES: New York Practice, Civil Practice Seminar. ***Email:*** simonsa@stjohns.edu

MICHAEL A. SIMONS*, (Associate Professor)**, born Bronx, New York, November 22, 1964; admitted to bar, 1991, New York. *Education:* College of the Holy Cross (B.A., 1986); Harvard Law School (J.D., 1989). ***COURSES: Criminal Law, Evidence, Sentencing and Post-Conviction Relief. ***Email:*** simonsm@stjohns.edu

JEFF SOVERN*, (Professor)**, born 1956; admitted to bar, 1982, New York. *Education:* Columbia University (A.B., 1977; J.D., 1980). ***COURSES: Civil Procedure, Commercial Transactions, Consumer Protection, Legal Method. ***Email:*** sovernj@stjohns.edu

SUSAN J. STABILE*, (Professor)**, born 1957; admitted to bar, 1983, New York. *Education:* Georgetown University (B.A., 1979); New York University School of Law (J.D., 1982). ***COURSES: Business Organizations, Pension and Employee Benefits Law, Employment Law, Introduction to Law and the Legal Profession. ***Email:*** stabiles@stjohns.edu

BRIAN Z. TAMANAHA*, (Professor)**, admitted to bar, 1984, Massachusetts; 1986, Hawaii. *Education:* Oregon (B.S., 1980); Boston University (J.D., 1983); Harvard (S.J.D., 1992). ***COURSES: Comparative Law, Torts, Law and the Social Sciences, Jurisprudence. ***Email:*** tamanahb@stjohns.edu

JACOB L. TODRES*, (Professor)**, born 1948; admitted to bar, 1973, New York. *Education:* Baruch College, City University of New York (B.B.A., 1969); New York University School of Law (J.D., 1972; LL.M., 1976). ***COURSES: Bankruptcy Taxation, Corporate Income Taxation, Estate and Gift Taxation, Personal Income Taxation, Taxation Seminar. ***Email:*** todresj@stjohns.edu

MARGARET VALENTINE TURANO*, (Professor)**, born 1948; admitted to bar, 1978, New York. *Education:* College of New Rochelle (B.A., 1969); University of Wisconsin (M.A., 1970); St. John's University School of Law (J.D., 1977); Yale Law School (LL.M., 1983). ***COURSES: Trusts and Estates, Law and Literature, Estate Planning, Federal Estate and Gift Taxation. ***Email:*** turanom@stjohns.edu

JANICE D. VILLIERS*, (Associate Professor)**, born 1951; admitted to bar, 1990, New York. *Education:* Pace University (B.A., 1975); New York University (M.A., 1979); Columbia University (J.D., 1989). ***COURSES: Immigration Law, Immigration Law Seminar, Legal Method, Torts I&II. ***Email:*** villierj@stjohns.edu

ETTIE WARD*, (Professor)**, born 1951; admitted to bar, 1975, New York. *Education:* Barnard College (A.B., 1971); Columbia University (J.D., 1974). ***COURSES: Civil Procedure, International Litigation, Legal Method, Torts, Federal Practice, Federal Courts. ***Email:*** warde@stjohns.edu

PHILIP WEINBERG*, (Professor)**, born 1935; admitted to bar, 1958, New York. *Education:* University of Pennsylvania (A.B., 1955); Columbia University (J.D., 1958). ***COURSES: Constitutional Law, Constitutional Rights Seminar, Environmental Law. ***Email:*** weinberp@stjohns.edu

NICHOLAS R. WEISKOPF*, (Professor)**, born 1945; admitted to bar, 1969, New York. *Education:* Columbia University (B.A., 1966; J.D., 1969). ***COURSES: Contracts, Drafting Legal Instruments, Legal Writing Seminar. ***Email:*** weiskopn@stjohns.edu

ROBERT M. ZINMAN*, (Professor and Director, Bankruptcy LL.M. Program)**, born 1931; admitted to bar, 1961, New York. *Education:* Tufts University (A.B., 1953); Harvard Law School (J.D., 1960); New York University School of Law (LL.M., 1965). ***COURSES: Advanced Bankruptcy Research Seminar, Creditor's Rights, Property, Real Estate Transactions, Real Estate Workouts and Bankruptcy, Real Estate Drafting. ***Email:*** zinmanr@stjohns.edu

---

SAINT LOUIS UNIVERSITY SCHOOL OF LAW

3700 LINDELL BOULEVARD
ST. LOUIS, MISSOURI 63108
Telephone: (314) 977-2766
Fax: (314) 977-3333
http://law.slu.edu

ABA Approved Since 1924

Saint Louis University School of Law offers an atmosphere that is the result of a number of factors, including the Jesuit educational traditions, our outstanding faculty and students, and the rich quality of life in a thriving midwestern city. The Jesuit nature of the institution is manifested by our commitment to academic excellence and freedom of inquiry, a genuine concern for the development of each student as a person, and an effort to sensitize students to the moral and ethical dimensions of law and lawyering.

Unique to the School of Law is the special rapport among students, faculty and staff. Over the years, the School has built a reputation for a close-knit community founded on mutual support and friendship. Members of our faculty have authored countless casebooks, treatises, monographs, anthologies, articles, essays and other materials in prominent presses and law journals around the nation and the world. Distinguished Visiting Professors have come form Columbia, Berkeley, Virginia, Oxford, and from the Polish and South African Constitutional Courts.

This remarkable group of people produces a rich and diverse curriculum in which students can receive a broad, general legal education or can specialize. We have leading Centers and Certificates in International and Comparative Law, Health Law and Employment Law. The School also has a great strength in litigation, corporate law, tax, intellectual property, and professional skills.

A student may pursue the J.D. degree as a full-time day student for three years, or as a part-time evening student for four years (including summers) or five years (no summers). The part-time program of legal education is identical to the full-time program in terms of academic quality, rigor and admissions standards. The same faculty members are involved in teaching in both the full and part-time programs.

(This Listing Continued)

SAINT LOUIS UNIVERSITY SCHOOL OF LAW—Continued

Placement for the Class of 2000 was 93.5 percent placed with 93 percent reporting six months after graduation. Tuition is below the national median for private schools and approximately half of the entering class are awarded merit scholarships.

Over the past few years, approximately 50-55 percent of our entering class have come from Missouri, 16-19 percent from Illinois and about 26-30 percent from 24-29 other states and Canada; 46-48 percent are female, 15-18 percent are minority.

The School of Law offers a small, highly selective LL.M. program in health law. The School also offers an LL.M. for Foreign Lawyers which has attracted students from around the world, including Germany, China, France, India, Israel, Russia, and Nepal.

The School of Law is located on the main campus of Saint Louis University, founded as St. Louis College in 1818. It received its University charter in 1832 and became the first university west of the Mississippi. The law faculty offices are located in the law library, which contributes significantly to the collegial atmosphere of the School. The School of Law has undergone a major renovation & expansion program 1998.

The campus is located in the part of the city of St. Louis known as midtown, just a few blocks from the Powell Symphony Hall, part of the Grand Center arts and entertainment district and only ten minutes from the Arch, the riverfront and downtown. St. Louis offers the amenities of urban living without the inconveniences and high costs normally associated with living in a major metropolitan area.

Dean and Professor of Law: Jeffrey E. Lewis (314) 977-8172
Associate Dean/Faculty: Joel K. Goldstein (314) 977-2782
Associate Dean/Academic Programs: Dana Underwood (314) 977-3955
Associate Dean/Evening Program: Stephen D. Smith (314) 977-2763
Law Librarian and Professor of Law: Patricia A. Cervenka (314) 977-3393
Assistant Dean/Administration: Denise M. Woods (317) 977-2766
Assistant Dean and Director/Admissions: Michael J. Kolnik (314) 977-2800
Assistant Dean/Development and Alumni Affairs: Gina M. Sholtis (314) 977-3300
Assistant Dean/Career Services: Mary P. McInnis (314) 977-7100

FULL TIME FACULTY

JEFFREY E. LEWIS*, (Dean & Professor)**, born Oregon, September 23, 1944; admitted to bar, 1969, Ohio. *Education:* Duke University (A.B., 1966; J.D., 1969). ***COURSES: Evidence, Remedies.

JOHN J. AMMANN*, (Associate Professor and Director, Civil Clinic)**, born St. Louis, Missouri, July 2, 1958; admitted to bar, 1984, Missouri; 1985, Illinois. *Education:* Southern Illinois University (B.A., 1979); St. Louis University (J.D., 1984). ***COURSES: Civil Practice, Urban Issues.

PATRICIA ANN CERVENKA*, (Director of the Law Library)**, born Decorah, Iowa, September 28, 1944; admitted to bar, 1984, Idaho. *Education:* Notre Dame College (B.A., 1967); University of Idaho (J.D., 1983); University of Iowa (M.L.S., 1987). ***COURSES: Legal Research. ***Email:*** cervenka@slu.edu

ERIC R. CLAEYS*, (Assistant Professor of Law)**, born Hartford, Connecticut, April 5, 1968; admitted to bar, 1996, California; 1997, District of Columbia. *Education:* Princeton University (A.B., 1989); University of Southern California (J.D., 1994). ***COURSES: Property, Administrative Law, Food and Drug Law.

MELISSA COLE*, (Assistant Professor)**, born Alexandria, Virginia, August 26, 1966; admitted to bar, 1993, California; 1995, District of Columbia. *Education:* Brown University (A.B., 1988); William and Mary (A.B.D., 1998); Columbia University (J.D., 1993). ***COURSES: Civil Procedure, Disability Discrimination, Employment Discrimination.

ISAAK DORE*, (Professor of Law)**, born Lusaka, Zambia, September 21, 1950; admitted to bar, 1973, Zambia. *Education:* University of Zambia (LL.B., 1972; LL.M., 1975); Yale Law School (LL.M., 1976; J.S.D., 1978). ***COURSES: Constitutional Law, International Commercial Arbitration, International Economic Law, International Law and Human Rights, International Law, Jurisprudence.

GERALD T. DUNNE*, (Professor Emeritus)**, born St. Louis, Missouri, September 24, 1919; admitted to bar, 1948, Missouri. *Education:* Georgetown University (B.S.B.A., 1943); St. Louis University School of Law (J.D., 1948). ***COURSES: Commercial Law, Constitutional Law, Jurisprudence, Legal History, Regulated Industries.

JOHN E. DUNSFORD*, (Chester A. Myers Professor of Law)**, admitted to bar, 1956, Missouri. *Education:* St. Louis University (B.S., 1950); St. Louis University School of Law (J.D., 1956); Harvard University Law School (LL.M., 1961). ***COURSES: Arbitration, Jurisprudence, Labor Law, Public Employees Law, Religion, Morality and Law.

SUSAN A. FITZGIBBON*, (Professor of Law and Director, William C. Wefel Center for Employment Law)**, born St. Louis, Missouri, October 22, 1949; admitted to bar, 1984, Missouri. *Education:* Barat College (B.A., 1971); St. Louis University School of Law (J.D., 1984). ***COURSES: Alternative Dispute Resolution, Contracts, Public Employment.

BRADLEY E.S. FOGEL*, (Assistant Professor)**, born New York, New York; admitted to bar, 1994, New York. *Education:* New York University (B.A., 1990; L.L.M., 1988)); Columbia (J.D., 1994). ***COURSES: Tax, Estate & Gift Tax, Trusts & Estates, Estate Planning.

STANISLAW FRANKOWSKI*, (Professor of Law)**, born Warsaw, Poland, November 13, 1939. *Education:* University of Warsaw (LL.M., 1962; Ph.D., 1968; J.S.D., 1976); New York University School of Law (LL.M., 1973). ***COURSES: Criminal Law, Family Law, Juvenile Law.

BARBARA J. GILCHRIST*, (Clinical Professor)**, born Evansville, Indiana, November 6, 1949; admitted to bar, 1976, Missouri. *Education:* Wichita State University (B.A., 1971); Washington University (J.D., 1976); St. Louis University (Ph.D., 1999). ***COURSES: Civil Clinic, Judicial Process Clinic, Client Counseling, Elder Law, Legal Aspects of Health Care Administration.

ROGER L. GOLDMAN*, (Professor of Law)**, born St. Louis, Missouri, June 13, 1941; admitted to bar, 1966, Missouri. *Education:* Harvard College (A.B., 1963); University of Pennsylvania (J.D., 1966). ***COURSES: Constitutional Law, Federal Courts, Criminal Procedure.

***JESSE A. GOLDNER*, (Professor of Law and Co-editor-in-chief, Journal of Health Law)**, born New York, N.Y., August 6, 1948;

(This Listing Continued)

SAINT LOUIS UNIVERSITY SCHOOL OF LAW—Continued

admitted to bar, 1973, Missouri. *Education:* Columbia University (A.B., 1969; M.A., 1971); Harvard Law School (J.D., 1973). ***COURSES:*** Health Law, Evidence, Family, Clinical.

JOEL K. GOLDSTEIN*, (Associate Dean for Faculty and Professor of Law)**, born St. Louis, Missouri, April 18, 1953; admitted to bar, 1981, Missouri; 1982, Illinois. *Education:* Princeton University (A.B., 1975); Rhodes Scholar, Oxford University (B.Phil, 1977; D.Phil. 1978); Harvard University Law School (J.D., 1981). ***COURSES: Contracts, Admiralty, Constitutional Law, Federal Jurisdiction.

THOMAS L. GREANEY*, (Prof. of Law and Co-Dir., Ctr. for Health Law Studies and Co-editor-in-chief, Journal of Health Law Studies)**, born December 2, 1948; admitted to bar, 1974, District of Columbia. *Education:* Wesleyan University (B.A., 1970); Harvard University Law School (J.D., 1973). ***COURSES: Antitrust, Corporations, Health Care Law, Mergers and Joint Ventures, Regulated Industries, Non-Profit Organizations.

JOHN M. GRIESBACH*, (Associate Professor)**, born Toronto, Canada, April 13, 1948. *Education:* Marquette University (B.A., 1970); Harvard University Law School (J.D., 1976; LL.M., 1977). ***COURSES: Torts, Administrative Law, Jurisprudence, Natural Resources Regulation, State and Local Government Law.

CARL R. HELFRICH*, (Instructor-Legal Research and Writing)**, born Chicago, Illinois, December 03, 1949; admitted to bar, 1991, Missouri; 1992, Illinois. *Education:* De Paul University (B.A., 1971); University of Missouri (M.Ed., 1973); Saint Louis University (J.D., 1991). ***COURSES: Legal Research and Writing.

JOYCE SAVIO HERLETH*, (Director/Academic Support)**, born St. Louis, Missouri, March 22, 1953; admitted to bar, 1979, Missouri. *Education:* Saint Louis University School of Law (B.A., 1975; J.D., 1979);. ***COURSES: Academic Support, Legal Methods, Foundations of Law, Legal Research & Writing. ***Email:*** herlethj@slu.edu

ALAN J. HOWARD*, (Professor of Law)**, born Washington, D.C., March 25, 1947; admitted to bar, 1972, Illinois; 1973, District of Columbia. *Education:* Cornell University (B.S., 1969); University of Chicago (J.D., 1972). ***COURSES: Constitutional Law, First Amendment, Legal History.

DANIEL J. HULSEBOSCH*, (Assistant Professor)**, born Scarsdale, New York, November 6, 1965. *Education:* Colgate University (A.B., 1987); Columbia University (J.D., 1991); Harvard University (A.M., 1993; Ph.D., 1999). ***COURSES: Property, Constitutional Law, American Legal History, English Legal History, Native Land Rights.

VINCENT C. IMMEL*, (Professor of Law Emeritus)**, born Gibsonburg, Ohio, March 15, 1920; admitted to bar, 1949, Ohio; 1962, Missouri. *Education:* University of Toledo; Bowling Green State University (B.S.Ed., 1941); University of Michigan (J.D., 1948). ***COURSES: Contracts, Remedies.

DEREK P. JINKS*, (Assistant Professor of Law)**, born Alexandria, Louisiana, September 26, 1967. *Education:* University of Texas at Austin (B.A., 1991); Yale University (M.A., 1998; J.D., 1998). ***COURSES: Criminal Law, Civil Procedure.

SANDRA H. JOHNSON*, (Provost, Saint Louis University and Tenet Chair in Health Care, Law and Ethics)**, born St. Louis, Missouri, January 20, 1952; admitted to bar, 1978, New York. *Education:* St. Louis University (B.A., 1973); New York University School of Law (J.D., 1976); Yale Law School (LL.M., 1977). ***COURSES: Health Law, Bioethics.

NANCY H. KAUFMAN*, (Professor of Law and Director, Center for International and Comparative Law)**, born Baltimore, Maryland, May 19, 1951; admitted to bar, 1984, Wisconsin and Illinois. *Education:* George Washington University (B.A., 1973); University of Wisconsin-Madison (J.D., 1984). ***COURSES: Taxation, International Law.

KATHLEEN A. KELLEY*, (Director and Instructor)**, born Ames, Iowa, December 6, 1947; admitted to bar, 1990, Georgia. *Education:* Loyola University (B.A., 1970); University of Wisconsin-Madison (M.A., 1972; Ph.D., 1975); Emory University School of Law (J.D., 1990). ***COURSES: Legal Research and Writing. ***Email:*** kelleyka@slu.edu

DONALD B. KING*, (Professor Emeritus)**, born Corvallis, Oregon, July 11, 1932; admitted to bar, 1958, Washington; 1970, Missouri. *Education:* Washington State University (B.S., 1954); Harvard University Law School (J.D., 1957); New York University School of Law (LL.M., 1963); St. Louis University (M.S.W., 1979). ***COURSES: Commercial Law, Comparative Law, Consumer Law, Corporations, Creditors' and Debtors' Rights, Law and Society, Products Liability.

MICHAEL JOHN KOLNIK*, (Assistant Dean and Director of Admissions)**, born Metairie, Louisiana, December 28, 1969; admitted to bar, 1994, Missouri; 1995, Illinois. *Education:* University of Notre Dame (B.A., 1991); Saint Louis University School of Law (J.D., 1994). ***Email: kolnikmj@slu.edu

MICHAEL MAFFITT KORYBUT*, (Assistant Professor)**, born New York, New York, December 26, 1962; admitted to bar, 1990, California. *Education:* Claremont McKenna College (B.A., 1985); Stanford Law School (J.D., 1990). ***COURSES: Commercial Law, Secured Transactions; Bankruptcy, Creditors' & Debtors' Rights.

***MARY P. MCINNIS*, (Assistant Dean of Career Services/Placement)**, admitted to bar, 1987, Missouri. *Education:* Saint Louis University (B.A., 1982; B.S., 1982; J.D., 1987).

MICHAEL D. MURRAY*, (Instructor and Director of Moot Court)**, born Troy, New York, July 15, 1965; admitted to bar, 1990, Missouri, 1991, Illinois. *Education:* Fudan University (Certif., 1986); Loyola College (B.A., 1987); Columbia University School of Law (J.D., 1990). ***COURSES: Legal Research and Writing, Moot Court I and II.

CAROL A. NEEDHAM*, (Professor of Law, Executive Editor,** *Northwestern University Law Review*), born Chicago, Illinois, November 1, 1957; admitted to bar, 1985, Illinois; 1987, California; 1989, District of Columbia. *Education:* Northwestern University (B.A., 1979); University of Virginia (M.A., 1982); Northwestern University School of Law (J.D., 1985). ***COURSES: Remedies, Business Law and Ethics, Alternative Dispute Resolution, Civil Procedure, Legal Profession, Negotiation Theory and Strategy.

CAMILLE A. NELSON*, (Assistant Professor)**, born Kingston, Jamaica, August 22, 1968; admitted to bar, 1996, Ontario, Canada. *Education:* University of Toronto (B.A., 1987); University of Ottawa (LL.B., 1994); Columbia University School of Law (LL.M., 2000). ***COURSES: Contracts, Torts, Women & the Law, Critical Race Theory. ***Email:*** nelsonca@slu.edu

FRANCIS M. NEVINS*, (Professor of Law)**, born Bayonne, New Jersey, January 6, 1943; admitted to bar, 1967, New Jersey. *Education:* St. Peter's College (A.B., 1964); New York University School of Law (J.D., 1967). ***COURSES: Estates and Administration, Copyright, Law and Electronic Media, Constitutional Law, Jurisprudence.

JOHN C. O'BRIEN*, (Professor of Law)**, born Troy, New York, November 12, 1942; admitted to bar, 1967, New York; 1970, District of Columbia; 1974, Illinois; 1977, Missouri. *Education:* Yale University (B.A., 1964); Harvard University Law School (J.D., 1967). ***COURSES: Evidence, Trial Advocacy, Legal Profession, Torts, Administrative Law.

(This Listing Continued)

SAINT LOUIS UNIVERSITY SCHOOL OF LAW—Continued

HENRY M. ORDOWER*, (Professor of Law)**, born Chicago, Illinois, January 31, 1947; admitted to bar, 1975, Illinois; 1978, Missouri. *Education:* Washington University (A.B., 1967); University of Chicago (M.A., 1970; J.D., 1975). ***COURSES: Corporate Finance, International Transactions, Law and Literature, Taxation.

JOSEF ROHLIK*, (Professor of Law)**, born Brno, Czechoslovakia, April 21, 1940; admitted to bar, 1962, Czechoslovakia. *Education:* Charles University (LL.B., 1962; Judr., 1965; CSc., 1968); Columbia University School of Law (LL.M., 1969). ***COURSES: Arbitration, Commercial Law, Comparative Law, Conflict of Laws, International Law, International Organizations, International Transactions.

PETER W. SALSICH, JR.*, (McDonnell Professor of Justice)**, born New York, October 23, 1937; admitted to bar, 1966, Missouri. *Education:* Notre Dame University (A.B., 1959); St. Louis University School of Law (J.D., 1965). ***COURSES: Property, Land Use Regulation, Real Estate Transactions, Housing, Local Government, Contracts.

EILEEN H. SEARLS*, (Professor Emeritus)**, born Madison, Wisconsin, April 27, 1925; admitted to bar, 1950, Wisconsin. *Education:* University of Wisconsin (B.A., 1948; J.D., 1950; M.S.L.S., 1951). ***COURSES: Legal Research & Writing.

DAVID L. SLOSS*, (Assistant Professor of Law)**, born Washington, D.C., April 17, 1957; admitted to bar, 1997, California. *Education:* Hampshire College (B.A., 1981); Harvard University (M.P.P., 1983); Stanford Law School (J.D., 1996). ***COURSES: Civil Procedure, Antitrust, International Human Rights.

STEPHEN D. SMITH*, (Associate Dean for the Evening Program)**, born Warrensburg, Missouri, June 7, 1949; admitted to bar, 1976, Missouri. *Education:* Central Missouri State College (B.A., 1971); Saint Louis University (J.D., 1976). ***Email: smithsd@slu.edu

NICOLAS P. TERRY*, (Professor of Law and Co-Director, Center for Health Law Studies)**, born London, England, December 5, 1952. *Education:* Kingston University (B.A., 1975); University of Cambridge (LL.M., 1976). ***COURSES: Torts, Products Liability, Cyberspace Law, Health Law, Professional Malpractice, Computer Law.

STEPHEN C. THAMAN*, (Associate Professor)**, born Berkeley, California, August 23, 1946; admitted to bar, 1975, California. *Education:* University of California, Berkeley (B.A., 1968; M.A., 1969; J.D., 1975); University of Freiburg, Germany (Dr.iur., 1992). ***COURSES: Criminal Law and Procedure.

DENNIS TUCHLER*, (Professor of Law)**, born Berlin, Germany, December 25, 1938; admitted to bar, 1964, District of Columbia and Maryland; 1971, Missouri. *Education:* Reed College (B.A., 1960); University of Chicago (J.D., 1963). ***COURSES: Remedies, Legal Profession, Conflict of Laws, Legislation, Civil Procedure.

DANA UNDERWOOD*, (Associate Dean for Academic Programs)**, born Ann Arbor Michigan, February 20, 1961; admitted to bar, 1987, Minnesota; 1988 Illinois, 1989, Missouri. *Education:* University of Michigan (A.B., 1983); Case Western Reserve School of Law (J.D., 1987). ***COURSES: Legal Research and Writing, Academic Support.

KENT T. VAN DEN BERG*, (Instructor)**, born Minneapolis, Minnesota, March 17, 1942; admitted to bar, 1984, Washington. *Education:* Yale University (B.A., 1964; Ph.D., 1970; J.D., 1984). ***COURSES: Legal Research and Writing. ***Email:*** vandenkt@slu.edu

CONSTANCE Z. WAGNER*, (Assistant Professor)**, born Chicago, Illinois, February 17, 1954; admitted to bar, 1981, New York; 2000, Missouri. *Education:* Northwestern University (B.A., 1976); Columbia University (J.D., 1980); University of Konstanz (Germany) (L.L.M., 1994). ***COURSES: International Business, International Financial Regulations, International Trade Law, Banking, Corporations, Securities Regulation.

SIDNEY D. WATSON*, (Professor of Law)**, born Philadelphia, Mississippi, January 5, 1952; admitted to bar, 1977, Louisiana; 1986, Alaska. *Education:* University of Southwestern Louisiana (B.A., 1974); Harvard University (J.D., 1977). ***COURSES: Health Care Law, Bioethics and Law, Access to Health Care Seminar.

ALAN M. WEINBERGER*, (Professor of Law)**, born Bayonne, New Jersey, September 2, 1950; admitted to bar, 1975, Michigan; 1980, District of Columbia. *Education:* University of Michigan (B.A., 1972; J.D., 1975). ***COURSES: Property, Business Associations, Securities Regulation, Real Estate Transactions.

DOUGLAS R. WILLIAMS*, (Professor)**, born May 25, 1955; admitted to bar, 1987, North Carolina; 1988, District of Columbia. *Education:* Augustana College (B.A., 1984); Duke University (M.A., 1987); Duke University School of Law (J.D., 1987). ***COURSES: Administrative Law, Environmental Law, Environmental Law & Business, International Environmental Law.

ST. THOMAS UNIVERSITY SCHOOL OF LAW

16400 N.W. 32ND AVENUE
MIAMI, FLORIDA 33054
Telephone: (305) 623-2320
Fax: (305) 623-2397

ABA Approved Since 1988

St. Thomas University is located on a 140-acre campus in Northwest Miami-Dade county. In addition to traditional undergraduate programs, the University offers a variety of post-baccalaureate degrees, including programs in business, counseling, management and pastoral ministries. In 1984, the School of law was founded. St. Thomas is the only ABA accredited Catholic law school in the Southeastern United States. In 1995, St. Thomas University School of Law was granted full accreditation by the American Bar Association. The School of Law embraces the duties and obligations of the Judeo-Christian ethic and endeavors to instill the values and ethics of that tradition and of the Catholic Church in its students. Furthermore, the School of Law has a special commitment to training lawyers who are members of South Florida's Hispanic and Black communities traditionally served by the legal profession.

The Law School is located on the main campus of St. Thomas University. The School, containing 62,000 square feet, includes a multi-level library, a moot court amphitheater, a student lounge, faculty and administrative offices and classrooms. The stylish architecture, combining buildings and breezeways, provides a comfortable setting for the study of law.

The law library is the heart of a law school; law students spend much of their academic careers there. The facility houses over 302,000 volumes

(This Listing Continued)

ST. THOMAS UNIVERSITY SCHOOL OF LAW—Continued

and volume equivalencies, and is one of the most technologically advanced libraries of its kind. St. Thomas has ranked first among major law school libraries in student use of computerized research services. In addition to the traditional method of legal research, students receive extensive instruction in computerized research.

To be eligible for the degree of Juris Doctor (J.D.), a student must successfully complete 87 credits with a cumulative grade point average of 2.5 or above. As a requirement for graduation, a student must write a significant analytical paper reflecting substantial legal research, original thought, proper writing style and correct citation form.

In accordance with its mission, the School of Law offers students the opportunity to participate in a variety of clinics which not only bridge the gap between legal studies and the practice of law, but also serve underrepresented segments of the South Florida community. In the Clinical Field Placement Program, students are exposed to actual legal problems in the community in both civil and criminal matters by working with a supervising attorney. The classroom portion of the course gives students the opportunity to learn both substantive and procedural law that relates to their case assignments. The Immigration Clinic, a year-long program, allows third-year students, under the supervision of a law professor/attorney, to represent immigrants or aliens detained at the Krome North Processing Center, a federal facility located in Dade County, in deportation or exclusion hearings before immigration judges. The Bankruptcy Clinic, a year-long program, allows third-year students the opportunity to represent litigant in United States Bankruptcy Court under the close supervision of a bankruptcy expert. The Family Court Clinic is also a year-long clinic in which third-year law students have the opportunity to represent clients in both the Family Court and the Domestic Violence Court. Students learn the inner working of the family court and explore the basis for Family Court matters in Florida. In the Tax Clinic, the mission is two-fold: it provides legal assistance to low income tax payers and informs individuals for whom English is a second language of their tax rights and responsibilities, and provides practical training in a rigorous academic and clinical setting for law students. Students have the opportunity to handle controversies with the Internal Revenue Service, including interviewing clients, preparing offers-in-compromise, filing petitions with the United States Tax Court, negotiating settlements with the Internal Revenue Service and appearing before the Tax Court.

The Law School offers four joint degree programs in cooperation with other graduate divisions of the University. A joint J.D./M.B.A. in Accounting couples skills traditionally in great demand in the corporate, tax and accounting worlds. The joint J.D./M.B.A. in International Business opens the burgeoning field of international transactional law to the new attorney. A joint J.D./M.S. in Sports Management prepares participants for a diverse set of positions in the world of sports. The University's Sports Management program is nationally recognized and the joint degree program has received favorable review in the leading sports management journal. The joint J.D./M.S. in Marriage and Family Counseling, one of the only programs of its kind in the country, fills a serious need in the family lawyer's repertory of skills.

Two Master of Law Degree Programs are also offered at St. Thomas University School of Law: the LL.M./M.I.T. in International Taxation and the LL.M/M.A. in Intercultural Human Rights. The LL.M. or M.I.T. program is the first LL.M. degree delivered via the Internet by a law school accredited by the American Bar Association. The program focuses on the global tax aspects of compliance and planning for both individuals and corporations. The courses are designed to prepare the practitioner to identify issues, perform searches, use problem-solving skills, and provide independent compliance and planning advises. This degree is earned in a minimum of one and a maximum of four years, upon completion of 32 academic credits, four of which comprise the thesis. The program's distinguished faculty members reside in numerous countries and include international revenue department officials, participating and retired professionals from both small firms and the Big Five, and professors. The LL.M/M.A. in Intercultural Human Rights is an innovative program which offers in-depth instruction on the critical issues of our time: the protection of human dignity across political, religious, social, economic and cultural lines. The faculty of global distinction includes top-level United Nations officials and outstanding scholars, judges and practitioners in the field. Students are trained to conduct effective research and advocacy in the field of human rights. Human rights law and complaint procedures are addressed, as well as issues of refugees, women, children, indigenous people, religion, criminal law and international trade. The program offers more than 25 compact courses in intercultural human rights, most of which are one week in duration. This degree is earned in one year upon completion of 24 academic credits.

St. Thomas University School of Law offers a diversity of extra-curricular activities. The Moot Court Board promotes excellence in legal research and written and oral advocacy. Members of the International Moot Court Board compete in international competition, including the Philip Jessup International Moot Court Competition. The Trial Court Board encourages excellence in litigation and trial advocacy. This purpose is carried out by participation in state, regional and national advocacy competitions. The St. Thomas Law Review is a student-operated scholarly journal which publishes articles submitted by students, faculty and members of the Bench and Bar. The Peter T. Fay American Inn of Court at St. Thomas is a chapter of the American Inns of Court founded in 1980 by former Supreme Court Chief Justice Warren E. Burger.

Student organizations reflect the rich diversity of St. Thomas University School of Law. Such organizations include the American Bar Association/Law Student Division, the Student Bar Association (SBA), the American Trial Lawyers Association (ATLA), the Black Law Student Association (BLSA), the Phi Delta Phi Spellman Inn, the Florida Association of Women Lawyers (FAWL), the Hispanic American Law Society, the International Law Society, Opinio Juris (the student newspaper), the Phi Alpha Delta Fraternity (PAD) and the Catholic Lawyers Guild.

Dean: John Makdisi (305) 623-2306
Associate Dean: Jay Silver (305) 623-2318
Director of Law Library: Gordon Russell (305) 623-2303
Assistant Dean for Enrollment and Career Services: Lydia Amy (305) 623-2384
Director of Career Services: Joan Beck (305) 623-2350
Assistant Dean for Student Affairs: Gilda M. Marin (305) 623-2354
Assistant Dean for Academic Support: Barbara Singer (305) 474-2472
Assistant Dean for Development and Alumni Affairs: Cheryl Chapman (305) 474-2432
Associate Director for Development and Alumni Relations: Karen Arch (305) 474-2435
Building and Budget Manager: Olga Leyva (305) 623-2346
Registrar: Iraida Acebo (305) 623-2329

(This Listing Continued)

ST. THOMAS UNIVERSITY SCHOOL OF LAW—Continued

FULL TIME FACULTY

JOHN MAKDISI*, (Dean and Professor of Law)**, born Washington, D.C., March 12, 1949; admitted to bar, 1974, Pennsylvania; 1992, Oklahoma. *Education:* Harvard College (B.A., 1971); University of Pennsylvania (J.D., 1974); Harvard Law School (S.J.D., 1985). ***COURSES: Property, Evidence.

GORDON T. BUTLER*, (Professor of Law)**, born Baltimore, Maryland, November 13, 1943; admitted to bar, 1972, Texas and Georgia; 1977, Ohio; 2000, Florida. *Education:* Georgia Tech (B.S.E.E., 1966); University of Texas (J.D., 1971); New York University (LL.M., 1991); University of Dayton (M.B.A., 1994). ***COURSES: Tax, Corporations, Wills and Trusts. ***Email:*** gbutler@stu.edu

ANDREW J. CAPPEL*, (Associate Professor of Law)**, born Chicago, Illinois, December 21, 1956; admitted to bar, 1992, Connecticut. *Education:* Yale University (B.A., 1979); Yale University (J.D., 1992). ***COURSES: Property, Land Use, Tax. ***Email:*** acappel@stu.edu

ANNA M. CHAN*, (Associate Professor)**, admitted to bar, 1982, Florida. *Education:* University of California at Berkeley (A.B., 1972); University of Pennsylvania (J.D., 1980). ***COURSES: Legal Analysis, Research and Writing, Property.

ALFREDO GARCIA*, (Professor of Law)**, born Santiago, Cuba, January 13, 1952; admitted to bar, 1981, Florida. *Education:* Jacksonville University (B.A., 1973); University of Florida (M.A., 1974; J.D., 1981). ***COURSES: Criminal Law, Criminal Procedure, Torts, Evidence.

DANIEL R. GORDON*, (Professor of Law)**, born Sussex, New Jersey, October 30, 1947; admitted to bar, 1982, Florida; 1983, California. *Education:* Haverford College (B.A., 1970); Boston University (M.S., 1973); Northeastern University (M.P.A., 1974); Boston College (J.D., 1982). ***COURSES: Civil Procedure, Professional Responsibility, State Constitutional Law.

JOHN LAWRENCE HILL*, (Professor of Law)**, born Chicago, Illinois, February 29, 1960; admitted to bar, 1988, Illinois; 1993, California. *Education:* Northern Illinois University (B.A., 1982; M.A., 1985); Georgetown University (J.D., 1988; Ph.D., 1989). ***COURSES: Constitutional Law, Torts, Jurisprudence, Law and Medicine.

BEVERLY HORSBURGH*, (Professor of Law)**, admitted to bar, 1987, Florida. *Education:* Smith College (B.A., 1964); University of Miami (J.D., 1987). ***COURSES: Contracts, Family Law, Women and the Law.

LINDA ANN KELLY*, (Professor of Law)**, born Connecticut, August 31, 1966; admitted to bar, 1992, Florida. *Education:* University of Virginia (B.A., 1988; J.D., 1992). ***COURSES: Immigration Clinic, Wills and Trusts. ***Email:*** lkelly@stu.edu

LENORA P. LEDWON*, (Professor of Law)**, born May 15, 1958; admitted to bar, 1983, Michigan. *Education:* Oakland University (M.A., 1981); University of Michigan (J.D., 1983); University of Notre Dame (Ph.D., 1993). ***COURSES: Evidence, Contracts, Law and Literature.

ALFRED ROBERT LIGHT*, (Professor of Law)**, born Atlanta, Georgia, December 14, 1949; admitted to bar, 1981, District of Columbia; 1982, Virginia. *Education:* Johns Hopkins University (B.A., 1971); University of North Carolina, Chapel Hill (Ph.D., 1976); Harvard University (J.D., 1981). ***COURSES: Civil Procedure, Administrative Law, Constitutional Law, Environmental Law. ***Email:*** ALIGHT@STU.EDU

KATHLEEN MAHONEY*, (Associate Professor)**, born Jersey City, New Jersey; admitted to bar, 1982, Florida. *Education:* Newton College of the Sacred Heart (B.A., 1971); Florida International University (M.S., 1975); University of Miami (J.D., 1982). ***COURSES: Legal Research and Writing, Interviewing, Counseling and Negotiation.

JUNE MARY ZEKAN MAKDISI*, (Assistant Professor of Law)**, born McKeesport, Pennsylvania, November 1, 1953; admitted to bar, 1996, Oklahoma; 1998, Louisiana. *Education:* University of Pennsylvania (B.A., 1973; M.S., 1974); University of Tulsa (J.D., 1995). ***COURSES: Torts, Agency & Partnership, Family Law.

RICHARD H.W. MALOY*, (Associate Professor)**, born New York, New York, August 5, 1926; admitted to bar, 1953, Florida. *Education:* Dartmouth (A.B., 1949); Columbia (J.D., 1953); University of Miami (LL.M., 1974). ***COURSES: Legal Analysis, Research and Writing, Bankruptcy, Debtor-Creditor, Wills-Trusts, Remedies.

ELIZABETH A. PENDO*, (Assistant Professor of Law)**, born San Jose, CA, July 6, 1967; admitted to bar, 1993, California; 1994, New York. *Education:* UCLA (B.A., 1990); UC Berkeley (J.D., 1993). ***COURSES: Civil Procedure, Federal Courts, Employee Benefits Law, Health and Human Rights. ***Email:*** ependo@stu.edu

LEONARD PERTNOY*, (Professor of Law)**, born Pennsylvania, May 19, 1944; admitted to bar, 1969, Florida. *Education:* University of Louisville (B.A., 1966); University of Miami (J.D., 1969). ***COURSES: Florida Constitutional Law, Products Liability, Real Estate Transactions.

STEPHEN PLASS*, (Professor of Law)**, born Guyana. *Education:* Fairleigh Dickinson University (B.A., 1982); Howard University Law School (J.D., 1985); Georgetown University (LL.M., 1988). ***COURSES: Contracts, Employment Discrimination, Labor Law.

EDIBERTO ROMAN*, (Professor of Law)**, born New York. *Education:* Lehman College (B.A., 1985); University of Wisconsin (J.D., 1988). ***COURSES: Corporations, Comparative Corporate Law, Agency and Partnerships, Antitrust, Law and Accounting, Torts, Product Liability, Street Law, Race and the Law.

AMY DEBRA RONNER*, (Professor of Law)**, born New York, September 15, 1953; admitted to bar, 1985, Florida. *Education:* Beloit College (B.A., 1978); University of Michigan (M.A., 1976; Ph.D., 1980); University of Miami (J.D., 1985). ***COURSES: Property, Wills and Trusts.

GORDON ROBERT RUSSELL*, (Associate Professor of Law and Law Librarian)**, born London, Ontario, July 23, 1954. *Education:* Brigham Young University (B.A., 1978; M.L.S., 1982); University of Western Ontario (L.L.B., 1987); University of New Mexico (J.D., 1994). ***COURSES: Computer Assisted Legal Research, Interviewing, Counseling and Negotiation. ***Email:*** grussell@stu.edu

OMAR SALEEM*, (Professor of Law)**, born Lumberton, North Carolina, April 30, 1957; admitted to bar, 1989, North Carolina. *Education:* City University of New York at Queens College (B.A., 1985); North Carolina Central University (J.D., 1988); Columbia University (LL.M., 1990). ***COURSES: Criminal Procedure 1 , Torts, Cyberlaw.

JAY STERLING SILVER*, (Associate Dean and Professor of Law)**, born Chicago, Illinois, September 18, 1952; admitted to bar, 1982, Pennsylvania. *Education:* Washington University (B.A., 1975); Vanderbilt University (J.D., 1981); University of Pennsylvania (LL.M., 1986). ***COURSES: Torts, Criminal Law, Legal Ethics.

***ALYCE JEAN THOMAS*, (Assistant Professor of Law)**, born Washington, D.C., November 20, 1963. *Education:* Swarthmore

(This Listing Continued)

College (B.A., 1987); University of Connecticut (J.D., 1992); Harvard University (LL.M., 1999; S.J.D., 1999). ***COURSES:*** Property, Legal History, Criminal Law, Sexual Identity and the Law.

SIEGFRIED WIESSNER*, (Professor of Law)**, born Neustadt/Aisch, Germany, February 26, 1953; admitted to bar, 1984, Germany. *Education:* University of Tuebingen (J.D., 1977; Dr.iur., 1989); Yale University (LL.M., 1983). ***COURSES: Constitutional Law, International Law.

MARK JOSEPH WOLFF*, (Professor of Law)**, born Syracuse, New York; admitted to bar, 1977, Florida. *Education:* Wadhams Hall Seminary-College (B.A., 1973); Nova Southeastern (J.D., 1977); New York University (LL.M., Taxation, 1978). ***COURSES: Income Tax, Corporations, Estate and Gift Tax. ***Email:*** MWolffe@STU.EDU

SANTA CLARA UNIVERSITY SCHOOL OF LAW

500 EL CAMINO REAL
SANTA CLARA, CALIFORNIA 95053-0435

SEATTLE UNIVERSITY SCHOOL OF LAW

900 BROADWAY
SEATTLE, WASHINGTON 98122-4340
Telephone: (206) 398-4000
Fax: (206) 398-4310
website: http://www.law.seattleu.edu

ABA Approved Since 1994

When the founders of our School of Law set its direction more than two decades ago, they envisioned a school with rigorous academic standards and impeccable ethics, a solid commitment to public service, and a firm resolve to serve as a school of opportunity for persons from diverse backgrounds and economic circumstances.

Working together in those early years, faculty, staff, students, and graduates helped build and nurture a program of legal education based on these principles. In 1994, the School of Law became part of Seattle University, a parent institution committed to remarkably similar values, in a merger that one community member called "an ideal academic marriage." Today, it is an integral part of a great university informed by Jesuit values and traditions that serves the Great Northwest as a superb center for teaching and learning, an ethical training ground, and a place to prepare for a lifetime of service.

Located in a spectacularly beautiful region that serves as a "gateway to Asia," the school is marked by: a student body of 900; a blend of traditional textbook and innovative hands-on legal education; a ranking "among America's 56 best law programs" in the latest edition of *Top Law Schools: The Ultimate Guide.*

As the region's largest, most diverse independent law school enters its third year in Sullivan Hall, a new, state-of-the-art building on the Seattle University campus, it enjoys what many observers have described as the most exciting era in its history.

Students. SU law students range in age from 19 to 60. While the average age at entry is 28, about 30 percent pursue legal studies directly after undergraduate school. The remainder come from an impressive array of professional careers. They represent nearly 300 colleges and universities from across the country and beyond. On average, they rank in the top quarter of their graduating class and rank comfortably in the top third of all LSAT test takers in the nation. Slightly more than half are women and 23 percent represent ethnic minority groups. Some 15 percent already hold at least one post-baccalaureate degree.

Co-curricular activities. A partial listing of student organizations gives an idea of the scope of interests held by law students: Alaska Student Bar Association; Asian/Pacific Islander Law Student Association; Black Law Student Association; Christian Legal Society; Environmental Law Society; Entertainment/Sports Law Association; Hispanic Organization for Legal Advancement; Intellectual Property Legal Society; International Law Society; Jewish Legal Society; Law Review; Lesbian and Gay Legal Society; Moot Court; Public Interest Law Foundation; St. Thomas Moore Society; Seattle Journal of Social Justice; Student Bar Association; and Women's Law Caucus.

Faculty. In selecting, promoting, and tenuring their faculties, American law schools generally have valued publication more highly than teaching. SU Law School stands out in sharp contrast. When the law faculty meet to decide on these issues, they first consider teaching aptitude and performance. Against this backdrop, the faculty's production of significant scholarship is impressive, and has earned them a place among the nation's "top 50" faculties for scholarly productivity. In the past several years, professors have published 15 books, including six national texts, and over 100 law review articles, book chapters, and book reviews, many of which have appeared in the nation's most prestigious legal journals.

More than two-thirds of the faculty hold J.D. degrees from the top national law schools; the remainder are high-ranking graduates of major state law schools. Their credentials accrue from beyond the academy as well. Virtually all have distinguished themselves in law practice. They have come to the law school from Wall Street megafirms and prestigious smaller practices; from offices of the prosecutor and the public defender; from corporate careers and poverty law practices. What these 35 faculty share is a common commitment to carefully conceived, intellectually stimulating teaching.

Program of Study. In the first intensive year, the curriculum concentrates on the highly traditional and prescribed basic courses, and on an intensive, year-long course refining legal analysis, research, and writing skills that the ABA has called "among the finest legal writing programs in the nation." The 110 upper-level courses allow for choice, innovation, and diversity. Students may choose either a broad, balanced program of study, or focus on a particular area. For students who choose to focus their legal studies in a particular area, the upper division curriculum is divided into 13 focus areas: Business Law, Civil Advocacy, Commercial Law, Criminal Practice, Environmental Law, Estate Planning, Health Law, Intellectual Property, International Law, Labor and Employment Law, Inequality and Poverty Law, Real Estate Law, and Taxation Law. The focus areas are designed to provide students with an integrated educational experience containing a body of knowledge and lawyering skills that demonstrate the interrelationships of different legal subjects and how they build upon one another. For example, a student who chooses the Intellectual Property Focus Area will select from among traditional courses such as Trademark,

(This Listing Continued)

SEATTLE UNIVERSITY SCHOOL OF LAW—Continued

Copyright, and Patent Law, cutting-edge courses such as Electronic Commerce and Internet Law, and integrated skills courses such as the Intellectual Property Clinic, the Technology Licensing Lab, and the Intellectual Property Audit Lab.

Law Library. The Seattle University Law Library--among the largest in the Northwest--houses a collection of 340,000 volumes, including extensive microform materials. In addition, the library offers students and faculty the latest in computer technology and related legal information systems. Training in computer-assisted legal research is available for all law students.

Graduates. More than 7,000 alumni are employed throughout the U.S., its territories, and in 15 nations around the world. Recently compiled employment statistics reveal that our graduates are engaged in: *private practice* -- 53 percent; *public service/public interest* -- 20 percent; *business and industry* - 18 percent; *judicial service* -- 7 percent; *academics* -- 1 percent.

Career Services. The Office of Career Services coordinates many activities to assist legal employers in their efforts to hire new associates, summer clerks, school-year interns, contract attorneys and graduates interested in lateral moves. In addition to the traditional *fall on-campus interviews,* the school also sponsors a *spring interview program.* Career Services maintains a comprehensive *"Now Hiring" Guide* in which they regularly update listings of firms and agencies wishing to receive resumes directly from our students and graduates for position vacancies. Office staff also post announcements of job opportunities each day on the school's *Job Board,* and include such notices in the monthly *Job Watch Newsletter* distributed to graduates and subscribers. In addition, job opportunities are publicized via our *telephone hotline and the internet.* Employers wishing more information on the range of services available to them should contact the Office of Career Services directly.

Dean: Rudolph C. Hasl (206) 398-4300
Associate Dean for Academic Affairs: John Weaver (206) 398-4308
Associate Dean for External Affairs: Joan Duffy Watt (206) 398-4306
Associate Dean for Information Services: Stephen L. Burnett (206) 398-4023
Associate Dean for Student Affairs: Donna Claxton Deming (206) 398-4307
Admissions Director: Carol Cochran (206) 398-4200
Financial Aid Director: Kathleen Koch (206) 398-4250
Library Acting Director: Kristin Cheney (206) 398-4091
Career Services Director: Linda Zahrly (206) 398-4104
Alumni Programs Director: Alison Judd (206) 398-4210

FULL TIME FACULTY

RUDOLPH C. HASL*, (Dean and Professor of Law)**, born 1942; admitted to bar, 1967, Illinois; 1980, Missouri. *Education:* Xavier (H.A.B., 1964); St Louis (J.D., 1967); New York University (L.L.M., 1973). ***COURSES: Evidence, Trial Practice. ***Email:*** hasl@seattleu.edu

JANET E. AINSWORTH*, (Professor)**, born Wilmington, Delaware, July 17, 1953; admitted to bar, 1980, Massachusetts; 1981, Washington. *Education:* Brandeis University (B.A., 1974); Yale University (M.A., 1977); Harvard University (J.D., 1980). ***COURSES: Criminal Procedure, Torts, Chinese Law, Child, Family & State.

MARILYN JOAN BERGER*, (Professor)**, born New York, New York, December 7, 1943; admitted to bar, 1971, New York; 1973, California. *Education:* Cornell University (B.S., 1965); University of California at Berkeley (J.D., 1970). ***COURSES: Civil Procedure, Pretrial and Trial Advocacy, Gender and Justice.

DAVID BOERNER*, (Associate Professor)**, born Chicago, Illinois, July 27, 1939; admitted to bar, 1963, Washington. *Education:* University of Illinois (B.S., 1962; LL.B., 1963). ***COURSES: Professional Responsibility, Administrative Law, Criminal Law.

JAMES E. BOND*, (Professor)**, born Omaha, Nebraska, January 4, 1943; admitted to bar, 1967, Illinois. *Education:* Wabash College (A.B., 1964); Harvard University (J.D., 1967); University of Virginia (LL.M., 1971; S.J.D., 1972). ***COURSES: Administrative Law, Criminal Law and Procedure, Constitutional Law, Jurisprudence.

MELINDA J. BRANSCOMB*, (Associate Professor)**, born Nashville, Tennessee, August 28, 1950; admitted to bar, 1980, Tennessee. *Education:* Vanderbilt University (B.A., 1972); University of Tennessee (J.D., 1980). ***COURSES: Employment Discrimination, Labor Law, Employment Law, Alternative Dispute Resolution, Mediation, Torts.

LISA E. BRODOFF*, (Clinical Professor)**, born Brooklyn, New York, June 25, 1955; admitted to bar, 1981, Washington. *Education:* University of Vermont (B.A., 1977); Hofstra University (J.D., 1980). ***COURSES: Law Practice Clinic, Trusts and Estates Clinic, Administrative Law Clinic, Elder Law.

STEPHEN L. BURNETT*, (Associate Dean for Information Services, Professor)**, born Lafayette, Indiana, May 4, 1948; admitted to bar, 1986, Virginia. *Education:* University of California - Los Angeles (B.A., 1969); University of Connecticut (J.D., 1973); Southern Connecticut State College (M.S.L.S., 1975). ***Email: sburnett@seattleu.edu

KRISTIN A. CHENEY*, (Acting Library Director)**, born Seattle, Washington, August 14, 1951; admitted to bar, 1984, Washington. *Education:* Northern Michigan University (B.S., 1973); Seattle University School of Law (J.D., 1984); University of Washington (M.L.S., 1987). ***COURSES: Advanced Legal Research.

ERIC A. CHIAPPINELLI*, (Professor)**, born Santa Monica, California, March 22, 1953; admitted to bar, 1978, California. *Education:* Claremont Mens College (B.A., 1975); Columbia University (J.D., 1978). ***COURSES: Corporate Acquisitions, Business Entities, Securities Regulation, American Legal Historiography, Civil Procedure.

MARK ALLEN TOYOMASA CHINEN*, (Associate Professor)**, born Riverside, California, June 28, 1959; admitted to bar, 1989, District of Columbia. *Education:* Pomona College (B.A., 1981); Yale Divinity School (M.Div., 1984); Harvard Law School (J.D., 1988). ***COURSES: Contracts, International Business Transactions, International Law, Business Transactions Simulation.

MARGARET CHON*, (Associate Professor)**, born Ann Arbor, Michigan, November 26, 1958; admitted to bar, 1986, Pennsylvania. *Education:* Cornell University (A.B., 1979); University of Michigan (J.D., 1986). ***COURSES: Administrative Law, Intellectual Property, Civil Procedure, Internet Law, Race and the Law.

ANNETTE E. CLARK, born Great Falls, Montana, April 3, 1959; admitted to bar, 1989, Washington. *Education:* Washington State

(This Listing Continued)

SEATTLE UNIVERSITY SCHOOL OF LAW—Continued

University (B.S., 1981); University of Washington School of Medicine (M.D., 1985); Seattle University School of Law (J.D., 1989). ***COURSES:*** Medical Liability, Bioethics and the Law, Civil Procedure. ***Email:*** annclark@seattleu.edu

SIDNEY W. DELONG*, (Associate Professor)**, born Franklin, Kentucky, May 12, 1947; admitted to bar, 1974, Colorado. *Education:* Vanderbilt University (B.A., 1969); Yale University (J.D., 1974). ***COURSES: Contracts, Commercial Law, Jurisprudence.

DAVID E. ENGDAHL*, (Professor)**, born Grinnell, Iowa, January 4, 1940; admitted to bar, 1965, Michigan; 1971, Colorado. *Education:* Wheaton College; University of Kansas (A.B., 1961; LL.B., 1964); University of Michigan (S.J.D., 1969). ***COURSES: Constitutional Law, Public Lands, Advanced Constitutional Law.

ANNE MELERING ENQUIST*, (Writing Advisor)**, born Roswell, New Mexico, February 20, 1950. *Education:* University of New Mexico (1968-69); New Mexico State University (B.A., B.S., 1972); University of Washington (M.A.T., 1977). ***COURSES: Legal Writing. ***Email:*** ame@seattleu.edu

SHELDON S. FRANKEL*, (Professor)**, born Bridgeport, Connecticut, December 24, 1938; admitted to bar, 1964, Massachusetts; 1965, Connecticut; 1975, Washington. *Education:* University of Connecticut (B.A., 1961); Boston University (J.D., 1964; LL.M., 1968). ***COURSES: Business Entities, Charitable Organizations, Federal Taxation.

CARMEN G. GONZALEZ*, (Assistant Professor)**, born 1962; admitted to bar, 1988, California. *Education:* Yale (B.A., 1985); Harvard (J.D., 1988). ***COURSES: Torts, Hazardous Waste , Environmental Law, Administrative Law. ***Email:*** gonzalez@seattleu.edu

THOMAS J. HOLDYCH*, (Professor)**, born Rockford, Illinois, December 17, 1944; admitted to bar, 1971, California. *Education:* Rockford College (B.A., 1966); University of Illinois (J.D., 1970). ***COURSES: Contracts, Commercial Law, Law and Economics.

BETSY R. HOLLINGSWORTH*, (Clinical Professor and Director, Law Practice Clinic)**, born Denton, Texas, August 30, 1948; admitted to bar, 1975, Washington. *Education:* Occidental College (B.A., 1970); University of Washington (J.D., 1975). ***COURSES: Law Practice Clinic, Professional Responsibility, Consumer Protection, Evidence.

LILY KAHNG*, (Associate Professor)**, born 1960; admitted to bar, 1986, New York. *Education:* Princeton University (A.B., 1980); Columbia University (J.D., 1984); New York University (LL.M., 1991). ***COURSES: Federal Income Tax, Gift and Estate Tax, Tax Policy Seminar. ***Email:*** kahngl@seattleu.edu

RAVEN CLARKE LIDMAN*, (Clinical Professor)**, born Rochester, New York, November 18, 1945; admitted to bar, 1978, Washington. *Education:* Cornell University (B.A., 1967); Seattle University School of Law (J.D., 1977). ***COURSES: Law Practice Clinic, Family Law.

PAULA LUSTBADER*, (Director, Academic Resource Center)**, born Chicago, Illinois, 1958; admitted to bar, 1988, Washington. *Education:* Southern Oregon State College (B.S., 1982); Seattle University School of Law (J.D., 1988). ***COURSES: Legal Education, Learning Theory. ***Email:*** lusty@seattleu.edu

HENRY W. MCGEE, JR.*, (Professor)**, born Chicago, Illinois, December 31, 1932; admitted to bar, 1957, Illinois; 1975, California. *Education:* Northwestern University (B.S., 1954); De Paul University (J.D., 1957); Columbia University (LL.M., 1970). ***COURSES: Civil Rights, Housing and Community Development, Environmental Law, Land Use, International Environmental Law.

JOHN B. MITCHELL*, (Associate Professor)**, born Germantown, Pennsylvania, October 16, 1944; admitted to bar, 1971, California. *Education:* University of Wisconsin (B.A., 1967); Stanford University (J.D., 1970). ***COURSES: Criminal Procedure, Evidence, Evidence Lab, Forensics.

CATHERINE A. O'NEILL*, (Associate Professor)**, *Education:* University of Notre Dame (B.A., 1987); University of Chicago (J.D., 1990). ***COURSES: Property, Environmental Law, Environmental Justice. ***Email:*** oneillc@seattleu.edu

LAUREL CURRIE OATES*, (Director, Legal Writing Program)**, born Seattle, Washington, April 17, 1951; admitted to bar, 1979, Washington. *Education:* Western Washington University (B.A., 1973); Seattle University School of Law (J.D., 1978). ***COURSES: Legal Writing.

WILLIAM C. OLTMAN*, (Professor)**, born Detroit, Michigan, December 14, 1943; admitted to bar, 1970, Wisconsin; 1972, Washington. *Education:* University of Wisconsin (B.A., 1966); University of Michigan (J.D., 1969). ***COURSES: Trusts and Estates, Community Property, Property.

MARK REUTLINGER*, (Professor)**, born San Francisco, California, May 12, 1944; admitted to bar, 1969, California. *Education:* University of California, Berkeley (A.B., 1965; J.D., 1968). ***COURSES: Trusts and Estates, Evidence, Torts.

J. CHRISTOPHER RIDEOUT*, (Associate Director, Legal Writing Program)**, born Wendell, Idaho, March 29, 1950. *Education:* University of Puget Sound (B.A., 1977); University of Washington (M.A., 1977; Ph.D., 1982). ***COURSES: Advanced Writing Seminar, Law Language & Literature, Legal Drafting.

JULIE SHAPIRO*, (Associate Professor)**, born New York, New York, September 10, 1955; admitted to bar, 1982, Pennsylvania. *Education:* Wesleyan University (B.A., 1977); University College of Wales; University of Pennsylvania (J.D., 1982). ***COURSES: Civil Procedure, Family Law, Constitutional Litigation, Law and Sexuality.

GREGORY M. SILVERMAN*, (Assistant Professor)**, born July 5, 1956; admitted to bar, 1991, Massachusetts. *Education:* Vassar (A.B., 1978); Columbia (M.A., 1984; J.D., 1987; M.Phil., 1991). ***COURSES: Intellectual Property, Property, Electronic Commerce. ***Email:*** gmsilver@seattleu.edu

DAVID M. SKOVER*, (Professor)**, born Racine, Wisconsin, December 4, 1951; admitted to bar, 1981, California. *Education:* Princeton University (A.B., 1974); Yale University (J.D., 1978). ***COURSES: Civil Procedure, Conflict of Laws, Federal Constitutional Law, Federal Courts, Mass Communications Theory, Free Speech Jurisprudence.

RONALD C. SLYE*, (Associate Professor)**, born Cleveland, Ohio, January 25, 1962; admitted to bar, 1990, New York; 1990, Connecticut. *Education:* Columbia (B.A., 1984); Christs College Cambridge (M.Phil., 1985); Yale Law School (J.D., 1989). ***COURSES: Property, International Law of Human Rights, Poverty Law, Public International Law.

JOHN A. STRAIT*, (Associate Professor)**, born San Francisco, California, June 19, 1943; admitted to bar, 1970, Oregon; 1970, California; 1972, Washington. *Education:* University of California at Davis (B.A., 1966); Yale University (J.D., LL.B., 1969). ***COURSES: Criminal Law, Professional Responsibility, Criminal Procedure, Trial Advocacy.

KELLYE Y. TESTY*, (Associate Professor)**, born Brazil, Indiana, October 3, 1960; admitted to bar, 1991, Illinois. *Education:* Indiana University (B.A., 1982; J.D., 1991). ***COURSES: Contracts, Commercial Law, Business Entities, Law and Sexuality, Feminist Theory, Securities Regulation.

(This Listing Continued)

SEATTLE UNIVERSITY SCHOOL OF LAW—Continued

JOHN W. WEAVER, **(Associate Dean and Professor)**, born Columbus, Ohio, February 20, 1945; admitted to bar, 1969, Indiana; 1978, Washington. *Education:* Dartmouth College (A.B., 1966); University of Michigan (J.D., 1969). ***COURSES:*** Real Property, Basic and Advanced Real Estate, Legal Drafting, Remedies.

KENNETH R. WING, **(Professor)**, born Oakland, California, November 25, 1946; admitted to bar, 1971, Massachusetts; 1972, California. *Education:* Foothill Junior College (A.A., 1966); University of California at Santa Cruz (B.A., 1968); Harvard University (J.D., 1971; M.P.H., 1972). ***COURSES:*** Constitutional Law, Health Law, Advanced Health Law.

SETON HALL UNIVERSITY SCHOOL OF LAW

ONE NEWARK CENTER
NEWARK, NEW JERSEY 07102-5210
Telephone: (973) 642-8500
Fax: (973) 642-8031
http://www.shu.edu/law

ABA Approved Since 1951.

Founded in 1951, the law school is an integral part of Seton Hall University, which was chartered in 1856. Accredited by the ABA and the AALS, the law school grants JD, JD/MBA, JD/MD, and JD/MA in Diplomacy & International Relations degrees. It also awards M.S.J. degrees and LL.M. degrees in Health Law.

The Seton Hall Law School has both a full time day program and a part time evening program. The student body is diverse. Nearly 2,500 applicants competed for the 380 seats in the entering class of 2000. The 2001 entering class attended more than 150 universities and colleges in the United States and abroad. Minorities comprise nearly 20% of that entering class.

In pursuit of its mission, the School of Law aspires to maintain and inculcate a nurturing spirit for those involved in its enterprise. Springing from its Catholic origins, identity, and tradition, this spirit requires treating all individuals with dignity, justice and compassion. In this regard, the School of Law is especially committed to teaching and service as an urban law school, an objective which requires an appreciation of the diversity and richness of human experience across racial, ethnic, national, gender and class lines.

The law school demonstrated its commitment to service by deciding to stay in its urban environment. Located in the Gateway district of a revitalized downtown Newark adjacent to Penn Station and near the new New Jersey Performing Arts Center, the law school in 1991 opened a new, $37 million state-of-the-art building. With over 200,000 square feet of space occupying and wrapping around the lower 5 floors of the 22 story One Newark Center office tower, the new law building is a magnificent urban campus. A five story atrium joins the classroom and faculty and administrative office wings to the tower that houses the 65,000 square foot high tech law library, the clinics, two moot court rooms and student space dedicated to the journals and organizations, the lounge, cafeteria and bookstore. There is a spectacular 350 seat auditorium.

In implementing its teaching mission, the Law School seeks to provide rigorous training in legal texts, including full exposition of different modes of analysis of precedents and positive law such as statutes and the constitution. The School of Law, however, views textual analysis as only a starting point. A more comprehensive legal education must enable students to bring to bear on real world problems a variety of jurisprudential perspectives, ranging from Natural Law to Critical Studies. Further, a central goal of the Seton Hall educational experience is to enable our students to identify, articulate, and sharpen their own individual values. In the process the Law School consciously seeks to further the values of adherence to ethical and moral precepts governing lawyers and of the legal profession as one whose primary mission is service to others. These values spring not only from the Law School's origins, identity, and tradition but also from the highest aspirations of the legal profession itself.

Students are taught using a variety of methodologies from traditional socratic classroom instruction to the use of problems, simulations, seminars and clinical experiences. The curriculum includes 120 courses that cover the spectrum of legal learning.

The school's clinics represent more than 2,000 disadvantaged and underrepresented clients each year in a wide range of areas including housing and shelter, consumer protection, family law, public entitlements, juvenile justice, disability law and immigration.

The law school offers a wide range of special academic programs, including four student journals: *The Seton Hall Law Review, Seton Hall Legislative Journal, Seton Hall Constitutional Law Journal* and the *Sports Law Journal.* The law school also offers judicial internships with justices of the New Jersey Supreme Court, judges of the New Jersey Superior Court, the Third Circuit Court of Appeals, the U.S. District Courts and the U.S. Bankruptcy Courts. Each summer the law school co-sponsors with the University of Parma a course of international studies for American law students in Parma, Milan and Genoa. Starting in 1997, the law school has also offered a program in Cairo, Egypt focusing on Islamic Law.

The law school is also very involved in building the idea of law and legal careers among college and high school students. Its MENTOR program has become a national model to inspire high school students to careers in the law. High schools are paired with law firms, public sector attorneys and the law school to show students how law is practiced and to allow them to participate in a moot court competition. The law school also co-sponsors the Summer Institute for Pre-Legal Studies with the Rutgers Law School to enable college students from economically disadvantaged backgrounds to receive evaluation, counseling and guidance in planning their education in the context of a modified law curriculum.

(This Listing Continued)

SETON HALL UNIVERSITY SCHOOL OF LAW—Continued

Dean: Patrick E. Hobbs (973) 642-8750
Associate Dean: Kathleen M. Boozang (973) 642-8501
Admissions: William D. Perez (973) 642-8736
Financial Aid: Sharon Williams (973) 642-8744
Library: Deborah Herrera (973) 642-8766
Career Development: Debra King (973) 642-8746
Student Services: Lori Miller (973) 642-8880
Alumni & Development: Lisa B. Hoyt (973) 642-8512

FULL TIME FACULTY

PATRICK E. HOBBS*, (Dean and Professor of Law)**, born Orange, New Jersey, March 29, 1960; admitted to bar, 1985, New Jersey. *Education:* Seton Hall University (B.S., 1982); University of North Carolina (J.D., 1985); New York University (LL.M., 1988). ***COURSES: Taxation. ***Email:*** HOBBSPAT@SHU.EDU

MICHELLE V. ADAMS*, (Professor of Law)**, born Detroit, Michigan, October 24, 1963; admitted to bar, 1990, New York. *Education:* Brown University (B.A., 1985); City University of New York (J.D., 1989); Harvard Law School (LL.M., 1994). ***COURSES: Civil Procedure, Housing Law, Civil Rights. ***Email:*** ADAMSMCH@SHU.EDU

MARK C. ALEXANDER*, (Associate Professor of Law)**, born Washington, D.C., August 5, 1964; admitted to bar, 1992, California; 1994, Washington, D.C.. *Education:* Yale University (B.A., 1986; J.D., 1992). ***COURSES: Constitutional Law, First Amendment, Criminal Law, Criminal Procedure. ***Email:*** ALEXANMA@SHU.EDU

MICHAEL P. AMBROSIO*, (Professor of Law)**, born Jersey City, New Jersey, November 8, 1941; admitted to bar, 1967, New Jersey. *Education:* Montclair State College (B.A., 1963); Catholic University of America (J.D., 1966). ***COURSES: Jurisprudence, Professional Ethics. ***Email:*** AMBROSMI@SHU.EDU

BAHER A. AZMY*, (Assistant Clinical Professor of Law)**, born Egypt, April 15, 1970; admitted to bar, 1997, New Jersey and New York. *Education:* University of Pennsylvania (B.A., 1992); New York University (J.D., 1996); Columbia University (M.P.A., 1996). ***COURSES: Civil Practice, Procedure. ***Email:*** ASMYBAHE@SHU.EDU

LIVINGSTON BAKER*, (Associate Professor of Law)**, born Newark, New Jersey, March 9, 1936; admitted to bar, 1966, New York. *Education:* Yale University (B.A., 1958); University of Michigan (J.D., 1962); New York University (LL.M., 1975). ***COURSES: International Law, Comparative Law, Advanced Constitutional Law, Torts. ***Email:*** BAKERLIV@SHU.EDU

DAVID W. BARNES*, (Distinguished Research Professor of Law)**, born Connecticut, February 17, 1950; admitted to bar, 1979, Pennsylvania; United States Supreme Court. *Education:* Dartmouth College (A.B., 1972); University of Pennsylvania Law (J.D., 1979); Virginia Polytechnic Inst. and St. U. (Ph.D., 1980). ***COURSES: Torts, Intellectual Property, Antitrust, Law and Science. ***Email:*** BARNESDA@SHU.EDU

LAWRENCE BERSHAD*, (Professor of Law)**, born New Haven, Connecticut, June 25, 1939; admitted to bar, 1964, Virginia; 1978, New Jersey. *Education:* University of Connecticut (B.A., 1961); Georgetown University (J.D., 1964). ***COURSES: Criminal Law, Criminal Procedure, Sports Law. ***Email:*** BERSHALA@SHU.EDU

KATHLEEN M. BOOZANG*, (Professor of Law and Associate Dean)**, born Galveston, Texas, April 21, 1959; admitted to bar, 1984, Missouri. *Education:* Boston College (B.S., 1981); Washington University (J.D., 1984); Yale University (LL.M., 1991). ***COURSES: Contracts, Torts, Health, Feminist Jurisprudence. ***Email:*** BOOZANKA@SHU.EDU

AHMED I. BULBULIA*, (Professor of Law)**, born Johannesburg, South Africa, December 12, 1943; admitted to bar, 1965, United Kingdom; 1966, Republic of South Africa; 1970, Canada. *Education:* London School of Economics (LL.B., 1965); University of Michigan (LL.M., 1966). ***COURSES: Criminal Law, Conflicts, Business Associations, Contracts, Public International Law. ***Email:*** BULBULAH@SHU.EDU

WILFREDO CARABALLO*, (Professor of Law)**, born Puerto Rico, January 1, 1947; admitted to bar, 1975, New York; 1990, New Jersey. *Education:* St. Joseph's Seminary College (B.A., 1969); New York University (J.D.,1974). ***COURSES: Bankruptcy, Commercial Transactions, Contracts. ***Email:*** CARABAWI@SHU.EDU

***GERARD M. CAREY*, (Professor of Law Emeritus)**, born Brooklyn, New York, October 3, 1921; admitted to bar, 1950, New York; New Jersey. *Education:* St. John's College (B.A., magna cum laude, 1942); Columbia University (J.D., 1949); New York University (LL.M., 1959).

ANGELA C. CARMELLA*, (Professor of Law)**, born Rahway, New Jersey, July 29, 1958; admitted to bar, 1983, Massachusetts. *Education:* Princeton University (A.B., 1980); Harvard University (J.D., 1983; M.T.S., 1984). ***COURSES: First Amendment, Religious Liberty, Property. ***Email:*** CARMELAN@SHU.EDU

CHRISTOPHER H. CLANCY*, (Professor of Law)**, born Miami Beach, Florida, April 1, 1935; admitted to bar, 1963, Maine; 1980, New Jersey. *Education:* University of Maine (A.B., 1960; LL.B., 1963). ***COURSES: Labor Law, Employment Discrimination, Torts. ***Email:*** CLANCYCH@SHU.EDU

CARL H. COLEMAN*, (Associate Professor of Law)**, born New York, October 20, 1964; admitted to bar, 1991, New York. *Education:* Georgetown University (B.S.F.S., 1986); Harvard University (A.M., 1990); Harvard Law School (J.D., 1990). ***COURSES: Torts, Health Law. ***Email:*** COLEMCA@SHU.EDU

JOHN KIP CORNWELL*, (Professor of Law)**, born New Haven, Connecticut, October 21, 1961; admitted to bar, 1990, Pennsylvania. *Education:* Harvard University (A.B., 1983); Cambridge University (M.Phil., 1985); Yale Law School (J.D., 1988). ***COURSES: Criminal Law and Procedure, Employment Discrimination and Employment Law. ***Email:*** CORNWEKI@SHU.EDU

JOHN COVERDALE*, (Professor of Law)**, born Chicago, Illinois, June 20, 1940; admitted to bar, 1985, Pennsylvania; 1986, District of Columbia. *Education:* University of Navone (M.A., 1966); University of Wisconsin (Ph.D., 1971); University of Chicago (J.D., 1984). ***COURSES: Federal, State and Local Tax. ***Email:*** COVERDJO@SHU.EDU

ELIZABETH F. DEFEIS*, (Professor of Law)**, admitted to bar, 1958, New York; 1971, New Jersey. *Education:* St. John's University (B.A., 1956; J.D., 1958); New York University (LL.M., 1971). ***COURSES: Constitutional Law, International Law, International Human Rights, Gender and the Law. ***Email:*** DEFEISEL@SHU.EDU

***MARK DENBEAUX*, (Professor of Law)**, born Gainesville, Florida,

(This Listing Continued)

SETON HALL UNIVERSITY SCHOOL OF LAW—Continued

July 30, 1943; admitted to bar, 1969, New York; 1978, New Jersey. *Education:* College of Wooster (B.A., 1965); New York University (J.D., 1968). ***COURSES:*** Constitutional Law, Insurance, Professional Responsibility, Evidence. ***Email:*** DENBEAMA@SHU.EDU

ROBERT A. DIAB*, (Professor of Law Emeritus)**, born Bombay, India, April 30, 1928; admitted to bar, 1958, United Kingdom. *Education:* University of Allahabad (I.Sc., 1947); Fordham University (B.S., 1949;LL.B., 1952); Inns of Court (Barrister at Law, 1958). ***COURSES: Decedents' Estates and Trusts, Wealth Transfer Taxation (Estate and Gift Tax), Estate Administration, Future Interests. ***Email:*** DIABROBE@SHU.EDU

HOWARD M. ERICHSON*, (Professor of Law)**, born New York, New York, November 6, 1962; admitted to bar, 1990, New Jersey; 1991, New York. *Education:* Harvard University (A.B., 1985); New York University (J.D., 1990). ***COURSES: Civil Procedure, Professional Responsibility. ***Email:*** ERICHSHO@SHU.EDU

LINDA E. FISHER*, (Associate Professor of Law & Director, Center for Social Justice)**, born Chicago, Illinois, February 6, 1953; admitted to bar, 1980, Illinois; 1990, Pennsylvania. *Education:* Macalester College (B.A., 1976); University of Chicago (J.D., 1980); Northwestern University (LL.M., 1989). ***COURSES: Clinical Education. ***Email:*** FISHERLN@SHU.EDU

PAULA A. FRANZESE*, (Professor of Law)**, born New York, New York, May 12, 1960; admitted to bar, 1984, New York; 1984, New Jersey. *Education:* Columbia University (B.A., 1980; J.D., 1983). ***COURSES: Property, Commercial Law, Land Use and Zoning. ***Email:*** FRANZEPA@SHU.EDU

BERNARD K. FREAMON*, (Professor of Law)**, born East Meadow, New York, June 18, 1947; admitted to bar, 1974, New Jersey. *Education:* Wesleyan University (B.A., 1970); Rutgers University - Newark (J.D., 1974). ***COURSES: Legal Medicine, Evidence, Law and Psychiatry, Post-Conviction Remedies. ***Email:*** FREAMOBE@SHU.EDU

***GERALD A. GARAFOLA*, (Associate Professor of Law Emeritus)**, born Newark, New Jersey, November 21, 1929. *Education:* University of Alabama (B.Sc., 1951); Seton Hall University School of Law (J.D., 1956).

WILLIAM E. GARLAND*, (Professor of Law)**, born Summit, New Jersey, September 18, 1944; admitted to bar, 1969, New Jersey. *Education:* Fairfield University (A.B., 1966); Seton Hall University (J.D., 1969). ***COURSES: Land Finance, Debtor-Creditor, Property, Drafting. ***Email:*** GARLANWI@SHU.EDU

JOHN J. GIBBONS*, (Richard J. Hughes Professor of Constitutional Law Emeritus)**, born Newark, New Jersey, December 8, 1924; admitted to bar, 1950, New Jersey. *Education:* Holy Cross College (B.S., 1947); Harvard University (LL.B., 1950). ***COURSES: Constitutional Law, Information and Publication Law. ***Email:*** GIBBONJO@SHU.EDU

MARGARET GILHOOLEY*, (Professor of Law)**, born Brooklyn, New York, March 2, 1942; admitted to bar, 1967, New York; 1987, New Jersey; 1980, District of Columbia. *Education:* Fordham University (B.S.Ed., 1963); Columbia University (LL.B., 1966). ***COURSES: Torts, Food and Drug Law, Administrative Law and Environmental (Clean Air). ***Email:*** GILHOOMA@SHU.EDU

TIMOTHY P. GLYNN*, (Associate Professor of Law)**, born Minneapolis, Minnesota, February 5, 1967; admitted to bar, 1994, Minnesota. *Education:* Harvard University (B.A., 1989); University of Minnesota Law School (J.D., 1994). ***COURSES: Business Associations, Civil Procedure, Employment Law. ***Email:*** GLYNNPAT@SHU.EDU

RACHEL D. GODSIL*, (Associate Professor of Law)**, born St. Louis, Missouri, October 27, 1967; admitted to bar, 1994, New York. *Education:* University of Wisconsin Madison (B.A., 1988); University of Michigan (J.D., 1992). ***COURSES: Property, Civil Rights, Environmental. ***Email:*** GODSILRA@SHU.EDU

TRISTIN K. GREEN*, (Assistant Professor of Law)**, born December 12, 1968; admitted to bar, 1998, California. *Education:* UCLA (B.A., 1991); Northwestern University (M.S.J., 1993); UC Berkeley - Boalt Hall (J.D., 1998). ***COURSES: Civil Procedure, Employment Discrimination. ***Email:*** GREENTRI@SHU.EDU

BRENDA SAUNDERS HAMPDEN*, (Associate Professor of Law)**, born High Point, North Carolina, September 18, 1946; admitted to bar, 1980, New Jersey. *Education:* Howard University (B.M.E., 1967; M.M.E., 1974); Seton Hall University School of Law (J.D., 1977). ***COURSES: Property, Copyright Law, Entertainment Law. ***Email:*** SAUNDEBR@SHU.EDU

EDWARD HARTNETT*, (Professor of Law)**, born Jersey City, New Jersey, September 26, 1960; admitted to bar, 1985, Pennsylvania; 1986, New Jersey. *Education:* Harvard University (A.B., 1982); New York University (J.D., 1985). ***COURSES: Civil Procedures, Federal Jurisdiction. ***Email:*** HARTNEED@SHU.EDU

DEBORAH D. HERRERA*, (Director, Law Library and Associate Professor of Law)**, born New Jersey, July 15, 1951. *Education:* Seton Hall University (B.A., 1973; J.D., 1976); Rutgers University (M.L.S., 1985). ***Email: HERRERDE@SHU.EDU

***THOMAS HOLTON*, (Professor of Law Emeritus)**, born Philadelphia, Pennsylvania; admitted to bar, 1952, California; 1953, New York. *Education:* Mount St. Mary's College (A.B., 1943); Stanford University (LL.B., 1951); Yale University (J.S.D., 1965); Angelicom (J.C.D., 1988).

JOHN JACOBI*, (Professor of Law)**, born Buffalo, New York, July 8, 1954; admitted to bar, 1985, New Jersey and Pennsylvania. *Education:* State University College of New York at Buffalo (B.A., 1981); Harvard University Law School (J.D., 1984). ***COURSES: Health Law, Torts. ***Email:*** JACOBIJO@SHU.EDU

E. JUDSON JENNINGS*, (Professor of Law)**, born Orange, New Jersey, January 26, 1943; admitted to bar, 1968, New York; 1968, District of Columbia; 1982, New Jersey. *Education:* Princeton University (A.B., 1964); Georgetown University (J.D., 1967). ***COURSES: Civil Procedure, Evidence, Remedies, Computer Law, Constitutional Law. ***Email:*** JENNINJU@SHU.EDU

TRACY A. KAYE*, (Professor of Law)**, born New Orleans, Louisiana, May 28, 1959. *Education:* University of Illinois (B.S., 1981); De Paul University (M.S.T., 1984); Georgetown University (J.D., 1991). ***COURSES: Tax, Tax Policy. ***Email:*** KAYETRAC@SHU.EDU

***DANIEL C. KNICKERBOCKER, JR.*, (Professor of Law Emeritus)**, born Glen Ridge, New Jersey, April 16, 1919; admitted to bar, 1951, New York; 1964, Massachusetts. *Education:* Syracuse University (A.B., 1940); Cornell University (J.D., 1950).

RAYMOND KU*, (Associate Professor of Law)**, born Rockville Center, New York, June 4, 1970; admitted to bar, 1976, New York; 1997, District of Columbia. *Education:* Brown University (A.B., 1992); New York University (J.D., 1995). ***COURSES: Internet Law, Intellectual Property, Constitutional Law. ***Email:*** KURAYMON@SHU.EDU

***MARINA LAO*, (Professor of Law)**, born Hongkong, August 14, 1952; admitted to bar, 1980, Georgia; 1981, New York; 1984, District of

(This Listing Continued)

SETON HALL UNIVERSITY SCHOOL OF LAW—Continued

Columbia. *Education:* State University of New York at Stony Brook (B.A., 1974); Albany Law School (J.D., 1980); Temple University School of Law (LL.M., 1994). ***COURSES:*** Common Law, Business Association, Antitrust. ***Email:*** LAOMARIN@SHU.EDU

R. ERIC LILLQUIST*, (Assistant Professor of Law)**, born New York, New York, December 9, 1966; admitted to bar, 1997, New York. *Education:* Stanford University (B.A. & B.S., 1989); University of Virginia (1995). ***COURSES: Contracts, Criminal Law and Procedure, Employment Discrimination. ***Email:*** LILLQUER@SHU.EDU

***JOSEPH M. LYNCH*, (Professor of Law Emeritus)**, born Jersey City, New Jersey, August 28, 1924; admitted to bar, 1952, New Jersey. *Education:* St. Peter's College (A.B., 1948); Harvard University (LL.B., 1951).

SOLANGEL MALDONADO*, (Assistant Professor of Law)**, born New York, October 10, 1971; admitted to bar, 1997, New Jersey and New York. *Education:* Columbia College (B.A., 1993); Columbia Law School (J.D., 1996). ***COURSES: Family Law, Torts. ***Email:*** MALDONSO@SHU.EDU

ROBERT MARTIN*, (Visiting Professor of Law)**, born Newark, New Jersey, January 13, 1947; admitted to bar, 1979, New Jersey. *Education:* Dickinson College (B.A., 1969); Lehigh University (M.A., 1973); Seton Hall University (J.D., 1979). ***COURSES: Property, State and Local Government Legislation. ***Email:*** MARTINRO@SHU.EDU

CATHERINE M.A. MCCAULIFF*, (Professor of Law)**, born Massachusetts, June 12, 1944; admitted to bar, 1976, New York. *Education:* Bryn Mawr College (A.B., 1965); University of Toronto (M.A., 1966; Ph.D., 1969); University of Chicago (J.D., 1975). ***COURSES: Corporations, Corporate Finance, Contracts, Legal History. ***Email:*** MCCAULCA@SHU.EDU

DENIS F. MCLAUGHLIN*, (Professor of Law)**, born Brooklyn, New York, January 19, 1949; admitted to bar, 1973, Pennsylvania; 1975, New Jersey. *Education:* Villanova University (A.B., 1970; J.D., 1973). ***COURSES: Civil Procedure, Professional Responsibility. ***Email:*** MCLAUGDE@SHU.EDU

***FRANCIS P. MCQUADE*, (Professor of Law Emeritus)**, born June 11, 1920; admitted to bar, 1956, New York; 1966, New Jersey. *Education:* Catholic University (B.A., M.A., Ph.D.); Fordham University (J.D.); New York University (LL.M.).

GWEN E. ORLOWSKI*, (Bar Fellow)**, born New Jersey, May 3, 1963; admitted to bar, 1990, New Jersey. *Education:* Georgetown University (A.B., 1985); Rutgers-Newark (J.D., 1990). ***COURSES: Housing Clinic. ***Email:*** ORLOWSGW@SHU.EDU

MARC R. POIRIER*, (Professor of Law)**, born Chicago, Illinois, April 1, 1952; admitted to bar, 1978, District of Columbia. *Education:* Yale University (B.A., 1974; LL.M., 1991); Harvard University (J.D., 1978). ***COURSES: Environmental. ***Email:*** POIRIEMA@SHU.EDU

RONALD J. RICCIO*, (Professor of Law)**, born Jersey City, New Jersey, July 18, 1946; admitted to bar, 1971, New Jersey; 1981, New York. *Education:* Seton Hall University (B.A., 1968; J.D., 1971). ***COURSES: Civil Procedure, Constitutional Law. ***Email:*** RICCIORO@SHU.EDU

D. MICHAEL RISINGER*, (Professor of Law)**, born Kansas City, Missouri, March 31, 1945; admitted to bar, 1978, New Jersey; 1983, New York. *Education:* Yale University (B.A., 1966); Harvard University (J.D., 1969). ***COURSES: Evidence, Conflicts, Remedies, Administrative Law. ***Email:*** RISINGMI@SHU.EDU

HOLLY L. ROBINSON*, (Associate Professor of Law)**, born Baltimore, Maryland, December 21, 1949; admitted to bar, 1976, New York. *Education:* Swarthmore College (B.A., 1971); New York University (J.D., 1975). ***COURSES: Trusts and Estates, Family Law, Property. ***Email:*** ROBINSHO@SHU.EDU

PETER W. RODINO, JR.*, (Professor of Constitutional Law and Public Policy)**, born Newark, New Jersey, June 7, 1909; admitted to bar, 1937, New Jersey. *Education:* New Jersey School of Law [Rutgers] (LL.B., 1937). ***COURSES: Constitutional Law and Public Policy. ***Email:*** RODINOPE@SHU.EDU

HARVEY SKLAW*, (Professor of Law Emeritus)**, born Newark, New Jersey, February 8, 1929; admitted to bar, 1963, New Jersey. *Education:* Rutgers University (B.A., 1952); Montclair State College (M.A., 1959); Seton Hall University School of Law (J.D., 1963). ***COURSES: Torts, Commercial Law, Products Liability, Comparative Law. ***Email:*** SKLAWHAR@SHU.EDU

***JOSEPH SLOWINSKI*, (Professor of Law Emeritus)**, born Newark, New Jersey, May 3, 1919; admitted to bar, 1948, New Jersey. *Education:* Seton Hall University (B.A., 1941); Rutgers University (LL.B., 1948); New York University (LL.M., 1950); Yale University (LL.M., 1971).

DANIEL J. SOLOVE*, (Assistant Professor of Law)**, born Lancaster, Pennsylvania, April 4, 1972; admitted to bar, 1998, District of Columbia and Pennsylvania. *Education:* Washington University (A.B., 1994); Yale Law School (J.D., 1997). ***COURSES: Privacy Law, Internet Law & Literature, Criminal Law. ***Email:*** soloveda@shu.edu

CHARLES A. SULLIVAN*, (Professor of Law)**, born New York, New York, March 10, 1943; admitted to bar, 1969, New York; 1983, New Jersey. *Education:* Siena College (B.A., 1965); Harvard University (LL.B., 1968); New York University (LL.M., 1972). ***COURSES: Employment Discrimination, Employment Law, Antitrust, Contracts. ***Email:*** SULLIVCH@SHU.EDU

***MARTHA TRAYLOR*, (Professor of Law Emeritus)**, born Clayton, Indiana, June 24, 1922; admitted to bar, 1946, Indiana; 1971, Pennsylvania; 1980, New Jersey. *Education:* Purdue University (B.S., 1943; M.A., 1966); Indiana University (J.D., 1946; Ph.D., 1980).

SARAH E. WALDECK*, (Assistant Professor of Law)**, born Milwaukee, Wisconsin, June 30, 1969; admitted to bar, 1998, Wisconsin. *Education:* Cornell University (B.A., 1991); University of Wisconsin (J.D., 1997). ***COURSES: Estates and Trusts, Criminal Law. ***Email:*** WALDECSA@SHU.EDU

JOHN B. WEFING*, (Professor of Law)**, born Teaneck, New Jersey, January 29, 1943; admitted to bar, 1967, New Jersey. *Education:* St. Peter's College (A.B., 1964); Catholic University of America (J.D., 1967); New York University (LL.M., 1971). ***COURSES: Criminal Law, Criminal Procedure, Jurisprudence, New Jersey Constitutional Law.

MICHAEL J. ZIMMER*, (Professor of Law)**, born Milwaukee, Wisconsin, October 16, 1942; admitted to bar, 1967, Wisconsin. *Education:* Marquette University (A.B., 1967; J.D., 1967); Columbia University (LL.M., 1976). ***COURSES: Torts, Employment Discrimination, Employment Law, Labor Law, Employee Benefits Law. ***Email:*** ZIMMERMI@SHU.EDU

SOUTH TEXAS COLLEGE OF LAW

1303 SAN JACINTO STREET
HOUSTON, TEXAS 77002-7000
Telephone: (713) 659-8040
Fax: (713) 659-2217
Web Site: www.stcl.edu

ABA Approved Since 1959.

South Texas College of Law is located in the heart of Houston's downtown legal and financial district. In addition to being the only private law school in the city, it is also the oldest. Its student body is one of the largest and the most diverse in Texas. Since the college is situated in the center of the nation's fourth-largest city, it is uniquely suited to serve the needs of its students while cultivating a rich and rewarding learning environment. A dynamic synergism exists among the faculty, student body, and the community's 6,000 practicing attorneys who are within walking distance of the law school.

The college has grown enormously since its founding in 1923. It now boasts a full-time faculty of 55 and an adjunct faculty of approximately 35 practitioners. This deep faculty base allows the school to maintain a 21.4 - 1 student to faculty ratio, while building a strong student body of about 1,200 students. More than 65 percent of the current students attend South Texas on a full-time basis. Many of the part-time students are second-career professionals - the very students for whom the law school was founded. The part-time program remains flexible enough to allow part-time students to attend day and/or evening classes while fulfilling their obligations at home or office.

The college's mission to provide the best combination of practical skills and scholarly training is most evident in the school's winning legacy at national moot court and mock trial competitions. Indisputably, South Texas is the best in the country, with 77 national titles to its credit. This winning record far exceeds what any other law school in the nation has been able to accomplish. The program is further complemented by a strong curricular emphasis on skills training, giving students a firm foundation from which to excel in the courtroom.

Curricular emphasis on skills training takes many forms, beginning in the first year with rigorous mandatory courses in legal analysis, research, writing, and oral communications. It extends into the upper division curriculum with a range of clinical course offerings spanning from direct representation clinics to field placement externships and simulated advocacy and mediation courses. In the law school's various direct client representation clinics, students work with actual clients on pending disputes under the supervision of full-time faculty and staff members. A host of off-site externships are available to allow students to experience the actual practice of law in settings as diverse as pro bono law firms and government agencies, state and federal courts, and prosecutors' offices. Students use the experiences garnered in these placements as the "text" of seminars which explore skills development and system design. Additionally, in simulation courses, students are able to expand their mediation, pre-trial and trial level skills through a combination of lectures, demonstrations, role playing activities and professor critiques. Full time faculty involvement, along with a strong cadre of local jurists and leading practitioners, allows the law school to take full advantage of its urban location for these skill courses.

To complement its strong tradition of excellence in advocacy and skills development, the law school founded the Center for Legal Responsibility. This teaching and research center is dedicated to alternative dispute resolution and professionalism. It supplements and enhances traditional first year course experiences by exposing students to methods of resolving the same disputes they are studying in class by means other than litigation. The Center also aids in designing course offerings for second and third year students that build on these experiences, while additionally helping to foster community involvement by providing opportunities for students to teach peer mediation at local grade and middle schools. Legal education at South Texas is also complemented by the Law Institute for Medical Studies which works closely with local hospitals and health providers on a variety of course offerings, research projects, and volunteer activities.

The law school has a long-standing commitment to practical as well as theoretical education. An increased emphasis has been placed on international and environmental law, and evolving technology. The law school sponsors a variety of summer study abroad programs and hosts professors from Denmark to teach courses in European law. Environmental law offerings have been expanded and emphasis on technology is being incorporated through the expansion of the curriculum and enhanced computer support. A new high tech classroom functions as a prototype for utilizing present and demonstrating future computer capabilities.

South Texas students are engaged in a variety of co-curricular activities, including publishing the *Corporate Counsel Review, Currents* (an international trade law journal), and the *Law Review.* The college is home to the First and Fourteenth Courts of Appeals and is the only American law school to house two appellate courts on a permanent basis. This arrangement allows students to observe live appellate arguments by some of the best attorneys in the country.

The South Texas Law Library is one of the largest in Texas, housing more than 401,000 volumes. Particular strengths of the collection include materials in English law, international business, and trial and appellate advocacy. The South Texas law library's rare book collection features the Shannon Papers. The collection also contains research material, original transcripts, trial exhibits and video-taped depositions from the famous Texaco v. Pennzoil case. These unique materials provide students and legal researchers the opportunity to study in-depth one of the landmark cases in the arena of complex litigation. As a further complement to the campus, the college completed The Fred Parks Law Library, a 70,000 square foot, state-of-the-art library expansion project. The new six-story structure, completed in May 2001, has twice the space of the old library, including 750 seats equipped with computer connections; an abundance of study, seminar and conference rooms; a new computer center; a multi-use penthouse suite; and a rooftop terrace for relaxation and recreational use. Former President George H.W. Bush will preside over the formal dedication of The Fred Parks Law Library on November 14, 2001.

South Texas regularly hosts large or highly publicized trials, such as the Texaco v. Pennzoil case mentioned above. Judges often conduct these trials in the law school's Joe M. Green Jr. Auditorium, the largest courtroom in Texas. It includes more than 700 seats, a judge's chamber, jury room and attorney conference rooms. The 240-seat Garrett-Townes Hall also serves as a courtroom and is equipped with remote control video capability.

All told, the exemplary facilities, access to practicing attorneys and top-notch faculty coalesce to educate well-rounded attorneys.

(This Listing Continued)

SOUTH TEXAS COLLEGE OF LAW—Continued

President and Dean: Frank T. Read (713) 646-1819
Academic Affairs - Associate Dean: Jeffrey L. Rensberger (713) 646-1853
Admissions Director: Alicia Cramer (713) 646-1810
Alumni Services - Director: Ann L. Reinig (713) 646-1801
Career Services - Director: Reginald Green (713) 646-1806
Continuing Legal Education - Director: Jean Fleming Powers (713) 646-1851
Law Library - V.P., Dir. of Library Services and Professor: David G. Cowan (713) 646-1711
Scholarships and Financial Aid - Director: Jennifer N. Pham (713) 646-1823
Student Services - Assistant Dean & Registrar: Lylene Pilkenton (713) 646-1701

FULL TIME FACULTY

FRANK "TOM" READ*, (President, Dean and Professor of Law)**, born Ogden, Utah, July 16, 1938; admitted to bar, 1963, Minnesota; 1966, Missouri; 1968, New York; 1975, Oklahoma. *Education:* Brigham Young University (B.S., 1960); Duke University School of Law (J.D., 1963). ***COURSES: Evidence, Professional Responsibility, Trial Advocacy.

JOHN L. BARNES*, (Assistant Professor of Legal Research and Writing)**, born Orange, Texas, August 12, 1945; admitted to bar, 1990, Texas. *Education:* University of North Texas (B.A., 1968); Oklahoma State University (B.S., 1982); University of Houston Law Center (J.D., 1990). ***COURSES: Legal Research and Writing.

JOHN H. BAUMAN*, (Professor of Law)**, born Albuquerque, New Mexico, May 14, 1953; admitted to bar, 1978, California. *Education:* Pomona College (B.A., 1975); Stanford University (J.D., 1978). ***COURSES: Torts, Insurance, Remedies, Federal Courts.

CANDYCE THOMPSON BENEKE*, (Assistant Professor of Legal Research & Writing)**, born Roxboro, North Carolina, May 4, 1957; admitted to bar, 1995, Texas. *Education:* University of Notre Dame (B.B.A., 1979); University of Houston (M.B.A., 1988); South Texas College of Law (J.D., 1994). ***COURSES: Legal Research & Writing.

CATHERINE GREENE BURNETT*, (Vice President, Associate Dean and Professor of Law)**, born Thunder Bay, Ontario, Canada, April 18, 1951; admitted to bar, 1976, Texas. *Education:* University of Texas (B.A., 1973; J.D., 1976). ***COURSES: Criminal Procedure, International Criminal Law, Clinical Courses.

ELAINE A. CARLSON*, (The Stanley J. Krist Distinguished Professor of Texas Law)**, born St. Louis, Missouri, April 26, 1954; admitted to bar, 1979, Texas. *Education:* Southern Illinois University (B.S., 1974); McMaster University (M.A., 1975); South Texas College of Law (J.D., 1979). ***COURSES: Civil Procedure (Texas and Federal), Professional Responsibility, Commercial Law.

RICHARD R. CARLSON*, (Professor of Law)**, born Columbus, Ohio, May 28, 1954; admitted to bar, 1979, Georgia; 1986, Texas. *Education:* Wake Forest University (B.A., 1976); University of Georgia (J.D., 1979). ***COURSES: Contracts, Labor, Employment Discrimination, Family Law.

SANDRA J. CARNAHAN*, (Assistant Professor of Law)**, born Los Angeles, California; admitted to bar, 1987, Texas. *Education:* University of Arkansas (B.A., 1976); South Texas College of Law (J.D., 1986); University of Houston Law Center (LL.M., 2000). ***COURSES: Criminal Procedure and Health Law.

TERESA S. COLLETT*, (Professor of Law)**, born Oklahoma City, Oklahoma, December 21, 1956; admitted to bar, 1986, Oklahoma. *Education:* University of Oklahoma (B.A., 1978; J.D., 1986). ***COURSES: Professional Responsibility, Property.

DAVID G. COWAN*, (Vice President, Director of Library Services and Professor of Law)**, born Mountain Home, Arkansas, November 12, 1953; admitted to bar, 1979, Arkansas. *Education:* University of Arkansas at Fayetteville (B.A., 1975; J.D., 1978); University of Missouri, Columbia (M.A.L.S., 1984). ***COURSES: Legal Research.

SUSAN W. CRUMP*, (Professor of Law)**, born Fresno, California, February 24, 1947; admitted to bar, 1975, Texas. *Education:* University of Bordeaux; University of California (B.A., 1968); Southern Methodist University; University of Houston (J.D., 1974). ***COURSES: Evidence, Criminal Law, Procedure.

BYRON PRESTON DAVIS*, (Professor of Law)**, born Harlingen, Texas, May 8, 1944; admitted to bar, 1972, Texas. *Education:* University of Houston (B.S., 1967); South Texas College of Law (J.D., 1972). ***COURSES: Civil Procedure.

SANDRA L. DEGRAW*, (Professor of Law)**, born Milwaukee, Wisconsin, June 7, 1940; admitted to bar, 1975, Wisconsin; 1977, Arizona; 1979, Illinois; 1981, California; 1986, Texas. *Education:* University of Wisconsin-Madison (B.B.A., 1966; M.S., 1971); Marquette University (J.D., 1975); Harvard University (LL.M., 1984). ***COURSES: Taxation, Estate Planning, Wills, Trusts and Estates, Professional Responsibility.

ELIZABETH A. DENNIS*, (Assistant Dean; Director of Off-Site Clinics; and Assistant Professor of Clinical Studies)**, born Louisville, Kentucky, June 7, 1955; admitted to bar, 1984, Texas. *Education:* Hollins College (B.A., 1977); South Texas College of Law (J.D., 1984). ***COURSES: Legal Method, Legal Research and Writing.

W. DAVID EAST*, (Professor of Law)**, born Madill, Oklahoma, March 18, 1945; admitted to bar, 1973, Texas; 1974, Nevada; 1979, California. *Education:* Baylor University (B.A., 1971; J.D., 1973); George Washington University (LL.M., 1978). ***COURSES: Contracts, Commercial Law (UCC), Bankruptcy, Property.

PAMELA E. GEORGE*, (Professor of Law)**, born Los Angeles, California, December 14, 1952; admitted to bar, 1977, Texas. *Education:* University of Texas (B.S., 1973; M.L.S., 1974; J.D., 1977). ***COURSES: Marital Property, Texas Trial and Appellate Procedure, Family Law.

RICHARD J. GRAVING*, (Professor of Law)**, born Duluth, Minnesota, August 24, 1929; admitted to bar, 1953, Minnesota; 1956, New York; 1968, Pennsylvania; 1982, Texas. *Education:* University of Minnesota (B.A., 1950); Harvard University (J.D., 1953);. ***COURSES: International Law, Comparative Law, Contracts, Conflict of Laws.

HELEN BISHOP JENKINS*, (Professor of Law)**, born Baltimore, Maryland, November 26, 1947; admitted to bar, 1984, Texas. *Education:* Peabody Conservatory of Johns Hopkins Institute (B.Mus.Ed., 1969); Howard University (M.M.Ed., 1975); University of Houston (J.D., 1983). ***COURSES: Wills, Trusts, Estate Administration, Property.

R. RANDALL KELSO*, (Professor of Law)**, born Indianapolis, Indiana, November 12, 1955. *Education:* University of Chicago (B.A., 1976); University of Wisconsin-Madison (J.D., 1979). ***COURSES: Constitutional Law, Contracts, Jurisprudence.

(This Listing Continued)

SOUTH TEXAS COLLEGE OF LAW—Continued

R. HANSON LAWTON*, (Professor of Law and Executive Director of the Center for Legal Responsibility)**, born Fort Madison, Iowa, November 5, 1941; admitted to bar, 1967, Iowa. *Education:* University of Iowa (B.A., 1963; J.D., 1966). ***COURSES: Corporations, Alternative Dispute Resolution, Corporate Finance, Negotiation and Settlement, Law Practice Management.

PETER W. LEWIS*, (Professor of Law)**, born 1939; admitted to bar, 1982, Texas; 1986, Pennsylvania; 1988, Michigan; 1989, Colorado. *Education:* University of Miami (B.A., 1967); Florida State University (M.A., 1970; Ph.D., 1972); Loyola University (J.D., 1974). ***COURSES: Evidence, Criminal Law, Criminal Procedure, Constitutional Law.

BETTY J. LUKE*, (Director of On-Site Clinics and Assistant Professor of Clinical Studies)**, born Rosenberg, Texas, March 5, 1954; admitted to bar, 1992, Texas. *Education:* Lamar University (B.S., 1977); University of Texas Medical Branch (B.S., 1978); South Texas College of Law (J.D.,1992); University of Houston (LL.M., 1996). ***COURSES: Live Legal Clinics.

NEIL COLMAN MCCABE*, (Professor of Law)**, born Philadelphia, Pennsylvania, January 2, 1948; admitted to bar, 1982, Texas. *Education:* University of Texas (B.A., 1972); South Texas College of Law (J.D., 1982). ***COURSES: Constitutional Law, Criminal Law and Procedure, Appellate Advocacy.

TRACY LEIGH MCGAUGH*, (Visiting Assistant Professor of Legal Research & Writing)**, born Jacksonville, Florida, July 26, 1968; admitted to bar, 1994, Texas. *Education:* University of North Texas (1991); Baylor University School of Law (J.D., 1994). ***COURSES: Legal Research & Writing; Alternative Dispute Resolution.

BRUCE ALAN MCGOVERN*, (Associate Professor of Law)**, born Portland, Maine, 1962; admitted to bar, 1989, Connecticut; 1990, New York; 1991, D.C.; 1994, Maine. *Education:* Columbia University (B.A., 1984); Fordham University School of Law (J.D., 1989); University of Florida College of Law (LL.M., 1996). ***COURSES: Tax, Business Organizations.

PAUL E. MCGREAL*, (Associate Professor of Law)**, born New York, New York, July 21, 1967; admitted to bar, 1992, Texas. *Education:* Williams College (B.A., 1989); Southern Methodist University Law School (J.D., 1992); Yale Law School (LL.M., 1994). ***COURSES: Constitutional Law, Civil Procedure, Legislation.

DOUGLAS S. MILLER*, (Director and Assistant Professor of Legal Research and Writing)**, born Oakland, California, April 28, 1956; admitted to bar, 1984, Alaska; 1988, Pennsylvania. *Education:* University of California at Santa Barbara (B.A., 1978); University of California at Berkeley (J.D., 1983). ***COURSES: Legal Research and Writing.

MATTHEW C. MIROW*, (Assistant Professor of Law)**, born New York, New York, December 19, 1962; admitted to bar, 1986, Florida. *Education:* Boston University (B.A., 1983); Cornell University (J.D., 1986); Cambridge University (Ph.D., 1993). ***COURSES: Property II, Legal Research & Writing, American Legal History, Comparative Law.

MS. SHELBY A.D. MOORE*, (Professor of Law)**, born Baltimore, Maryland, February 16, 1959; admitted to bar, 1985, Maryland. *Education:* Towson State University (B.A., 1981); University of Baltimore (J.D., 1983); Harvard University Law School (LL.M., 1992). ***COURSES: Property, Criminal Law, Criminal Trial Advocacy.

RAY E. MOSES*, (Professor of Law)**, born Sedge, Texas, January 9, 1941; admitted to bar, 1965, Texas. *Education:* University of Texas at Austin (B.A., 1963; J.D., 1965); Northwestern University (LL.M., 1970); Southern Methodist University (S.J.D., 1978). ***COURSES: Criminal Law.

OLGA LYDIA MOYA*, (Professor of Law)**, born Weslaco, Texas, December 27, 1959; admitted to bar, 1984, Texas. *Education:* University of Texas at Austin (B.A., 1981; J.D., 1984). ***COURSES: Environmental Law, Administrative Law, Legislation.

PETER W. MURPHY*, (Professor of Law)**, born Boston, England, February 10, 1946; admitted to bar, 1968, England; 1981, California; 1985, Texas. *Education:* University of Cambridge (B.A., 1966; LL.B., 1967; M.A., 1970). ***COURSES: Evidence, Trial Advocacy.

JAMES L. MUSSELMAN*, (Professor of Law)**, born Peoria, Illinois, August 4, 1951; admitted to bar, 1980, Colorado; 1985, Arizona; 1990, Texas. *Education:* Illinois Central College (A.A., 1972); Illinois State University (B.S., 1973); J. Rueben Clark Law School, Brigham Young University (J.D., 1979). ***COURSES: Taxation and Commercial Law.

FRANCESCA ORTIZ*, (Associate Professor of Law)**, born San Antonio, Texas, October 11, 1964; admitted to bar, 1989, Texas. *Education:* University of Texas at Austin (B.A., 1986); Harvard Law School (J.D., 1989). ***COURSES: Property.

PHILLIP EDWARD PAGE*, (Professor of Law)**, born Memphis, Tennessee, August 3, 1949; admitted to bar, 1980, Tennessee. *Education:* University of Tennessee (B.S., 1971); Memphis State University (J.D., 1980); New York University (LL.M., 1983). ***COURSES: Copyright, Trademark, Communications, Art Law, Contracts.

JAMES W. PAULSEN*, (Professor of Law)**, born Eau Claire, Wisconsin, February 17, 1954; admitted to bar, 1984, Texas. *Education:* Texas Christian University (B.F.A., 1976); Baylor University (J.D., 1984); Harvard University Law School (LL.M., 1992). ***COURSES: Civil Procedure, Community Property, Legal History.

JEAN FLEMING POWERS*, (Professor of Law and Director of Continuing Legal Education)**, born Newark, Ohio, October 6, 1948; admitted to bar, 1978, Texas. *Education:* University of Texas (B.A., 1970); University of Houston (J.D., 1978). ***COURSES: Contracts, Professional Responsibility.

HARRY L. REED*, (Professor of Law)**, born Houston, Texas, December 16, 1923; admitted to bar, 1948, Texas. *Education:* University of Texas (B.A., 1943; J.D., 1948). ***COURSES: Oil and Gas, Federal Courts.

JEFFREY L. RENSBERGER*, (Vice President, Associate Dean and Professor of Law)**, born Goshen, Indiana, June 20, 1958; admitted to bar, 1984, Indiana. *Education:* Wabash College (B.A., 1980); Indiana University at Bloomington (J.D., 1983). ***COURSES: Civil Procedure, Conflict of Laws, Torts.

CHARLES W. "ROCKY" RHODES, IV*, (Assistant Professor)**, born Arlington, Texas, December 8, 1967; admitted to bar, 1992, Texas. *Education:* Baylor University (B.B.A., 1990; J.D., 1992). ***COURSES: Civil Procedure, Constitutional Law, Federal Courts, Torts.

VAL D. RICKS*, (Associate Professor of Law)**, born Rexburg, Idaho, December 20, 1965; admitted to bar, 1992, Utah. *Education:* Ricks College (A.A., 1987); Brigham Young University (B.A., 1989; J.D., 1992). ***COURSES: Contracts.

GARY S. ROSIN*, (Professor of Law)**, born San Antonio, Texas, September 25, 1950; admitted to bar, 1975, Texas. *Education:* Texas A & M University (B.S., 1972); University of Texas (J.D., 1975). ***COURSES: Agency and Partnership, Banking Law, Corporations, Payment Systems and Securities Regulation.

***MARK R. SIEGEL*, (Professor of Law)**, born New Rochelle, New York, April 21, 1958; admitted to bar, 1983, Georgia; 1985, Florida.

(This Listing Continued)

SOUTH TEXAS COLLEGE OF LAW—Continued

Education: University of Florida (B.S. in B.A., 1979); Florida State University (J.D., 1983); Emory University (LL.M., 1988). ***COURSES:*** Federal Income Taxation, Estate and Gift Taxation, Estate Planning.

ANDREW T. SOLOMON*, (Assistant Professor of Legal Research and Writing)**, born New York, June 2, 1965; admitted to bar, 1991, New York. *Education:* University of Michigan (B.A., 1987); Boston University School of Law (J.D., 1990). ***COURSES: Legal Research and Writing. ***Email:*** asolomon@stcl.edu

TOBIN ANDREWS SPARLING*, (Assistant Professor of Legal Research and Writing)**, born Glens Falls, New York, September 28, 1953; admitted to bar, 1989, New York; 1994, Texas. *Education:* Dartmouth College (B.A., 1975); Columbia University (J.D., 1988). ***COURSES: Legal Research & Writing, Privacy Law. ***Email:*** sparling@stcl. edu

MARK E. STEINER*, (Assistant Professor of Law)**, born New Orleans, Louisiana, April 30, 1955; admitted to bar, 1983, Texas. *Education:* University of Texas (B.A., 1978); University of Houston (J.D., 1982; Ph.D., 1993). ***COURSES: Torts, Civil Procedure, and Internet Legal Research.

CHERIE O'NEAL TAYLOR*, (Professor of Law)**, born Columbia, South Carolina, March 7, 1958; admitted to bar, 1983, Georgia. *Education:* Harvard University, Radcliffe (A.B., 1980); University of Georgia (J.D., 1983); Georgetown University (LL.M., 1990). ***COURSES: International Business Transactions, International Civil Litigation, Civil Procedure.

BUFORD C. TERRELL*, (Professor of Law)**, born Lubbock, Texas, May 27, 1940; admitted to bar, 1970, Texas; 1983, Louisiana. *Education:* Massachusetts Institute of Technology; Texas Tech University (B.A., 1965; J.D., 1969); Harvard University (LL.M., 1983). ***COURSES: Law and Technology, Computer Law, Professional Responsibility, Property.

T. GERALD TREECE*, (Vice President, Associate Dean, and The W. James Kronzer, Jr. Distinguished Professor of Advocacy)**, born Midland, Texas, April 9, 1945; admitted to bar, 1971, Texas. *Education:* University of Houston (B.A., 1967; J.D., 1969). ***COURSES: Torts, Constitutional Law, Advocacy.

CHARLES J. WEIGEL, II*, (Exec. Dir. of the Law Institute for Medical Studies, & The Spurgeon E. Bell Dist. Prof. of Law)**, born Chicago, Illinois, May 24, 1932; admitted to bar, 1960, Texas. *Education:* Knox College (B.A., 1953); University of Texas (J.D., 1960); John Marshall Law School (1962-1963); University of Texas (LL.M., 1975). ***COURSES: Torts, Legal Medicine, Hospital Law, Admiralty, Family Law.

MICHAEL E. WHEELER*, (Vice President, Associate Dean and Professor of Law)**, born Fort Smith, Arkansas, August 24, 1949; admitted to bar, 1979, Arkansas. *Education:* Arkansas Tech University (B.A., 1972); University of Arkansas at Little Rock (J.D., 1979). ***COURSES: Criminal Law, Criminal Procedure, Juvenile Law.

WILLIAM L. WILKS*, (Dean Emeritus and Professor of Law)**, born Fort Wayne, Indiana, November 12, 1931; admitted to bar, 1955, Indiana and Michigan. *Education:* Yale University (B.A., 1952); University of Michigan (J.D., 1955); George Washington University (LL.M., 1973). ***COURSES: Evidence, Insurance, Civil Procedure.

JOHN J. WORLEY*, (Professor of Law)**, born Elberton, Georgia, July 14, 1954; admitted to bar, 1981, Georgia. *Education:* University of Georgia (A.B., 1975; J.D., 1980). ***COURSES: Bankruptcy, Commercial Law, Contracts.

KEVIN M. YAMAMOTO*, (Associate Professor of Law)**, born Los Angeles, California, August 4, 1963; admitted to bar, 1993, California. *Education:* University of California at Davis (B.S., 1987); University of San Diego (J.D., 1992); University of Florida (LL.M., 1995). ***COURSES: Tax.

TIMOTHY ROBERT ZINNECKER*, (Professor of Law)**, born Owosso, Michigan, July 20, 1959; admitted to bar, 1989, Texas. *Education:* Central Missouri State University (B.S.B.A., 1981); Brigham Young University (J.D., 1986). ***COURSES: UCC, Banking.

SOUTHERN ILLINOIS UNIVERSITY SCHOOL OF LAW

LESAR LAW BUILDING, DOUGLAS DRIVE
CARBONDALE, ILLINOIS 62901
Telephone: (618) 536-7711
Fax: (618) 453-8769

ABA Approved Since 1974.

HISTORY

The Southern Illinois University School of Law began instruction in the fall of 1973, and graduated its first class in the spring of 1976. Hiram H. Lesar, for whom the law building is named, was the founding dean. Since 1976, the School of Law has graduated some 2500 students. The School of Law is fully accredited by the American Bar Association and is a member of the Association of American Law Schools.

Twenty-nine full-time teaching faculty are involved in research and publication in addition to their teaching duties. A dynamic, personalized educational environment is the result of a student body of 360 and a faculty-student ratio 1:12. The group is small enough so that faculty and students can know each other but large enough to justify the variety of courses that should be available in a modern law school. Clinical, library and visiting professors add additional depth to the faculty and curriculum.

The School has particular strengths in the areas of health law and environmental law. It also has an outstanding clinical/skills program and a remarkable law library.

PURPOSES

As the School of Law has grown and matured, its mission has followed. The primary initial focus of the School was providing lawyers and legal services to Southern Illinois, a mission that the School of Law has accomplished to a remarkable extent. The SIU School of Law now seeks no less than to become the best small (enrollments of 450 or less) public law school in the nation. As a corollary to this basic mission, the SIU School of Law seeks to be viewed as the best school to attend for those who wish to practice in the state of Illinois. The achievement of this mission has three components. They are: fully preparing its students to enter the legal profession or other intellectually demanding work; contributing to legal scholarship; and serving the legal profession and the general public.

The school believes that all of its graduates must have the basic substantive knowledge and legal skills to become competent to practice law or to perform other work involving legal doctrine and skills, both

(This Listing Continued)

SOUTHERN ILLINOIS UNIVERSITY SCHOOL OF LAW —Continued

at the time of graduation and throughout their working lifetime. Thus, SIU graduates should possess a broad knowledge or legal doctrine which serves as the foundation for the abilities to recognize legal issues, manipulate legal concepts and build a strong body of substantive knowledge in their chosen specialty. Each student should have a knowledge of the American legal institutions and traditions in role of lawyers in our society. Each student should possess a basic grounding in the fundamental lawyering skills and a strong sense of professional responsibility and professionalism. Finally, SIU graduates are expected to have the ability to integrate non-legal disciplines into their legal analysis. The primary aspect of the law school's mission is to provide a program sufficiently broad in scope that its students are introduced to these skills and qualities by the time they graduate.

Dean: Thomas F. Guernsey (618) 453-8761
Assistant Dean for Administration: Alicia Ruiz (618) 453-8700
Associate Dean for Administration: Mary Rudasill (618) 453-8717
Assistant Dean-Admissions: Michael Ruiz (618) 453-8768
Assistant Dean for Career Services: Carmen Suarez (618) 453-8749
Director of Alumni Affairs: Elizabeth Murphy (618) 453-4811
Director of Development: Scott Kruger (618) 453-8723
Financial Aid: (618) 453-4334
Library Director: Frank Houdek (618) 453-8796

FULL TIME FACULTY

THOMAS F. GUERNSEY*, (Dean and Professor of Law)**, born Battle Creek, Michigan, November 3, 1951; admitted to bar, 1976, New Hampshire; 1983, Virginia. *Education:* University of Michigan (B.A., 1973); Wayne State University (J.D., 1976); Temple University (LL.M., 1980). ***COURSES: Evidence, Negotiation, Trial Practice. ***Email:*** guernsey@siu.edu

---

JILL ADAMS*, (Associate Professor of Law)**, born Durham, North Carolina, July 9, 1952; admitted to bar, 1982, New Mexico; 1986, Illinois. *Education:* University of North Carolina (B.A., with highest honors, 1974); University of Massachusetts (M.A.T., 1978); University of New Mexico (J.D., summa cum laude, 1982). ***COURSES: Civil Procedure, Civil Rights, Legal Profession, Alternative Dispute Resolution, Legal Writing and Argumentation. ***Email:*** jeadams@siu.edu

CHERYL L. ANDERSON*, (Assistant Professor of Law)**, born January 23, 1964; admitted to bar, 1988, State-Minnesota, North Dakota; 1989, Federal-Minnesota, North Dakota; 1992, Washington. *Education:* University of North Dakota (B.A., 1985; J.D., 1988); Temple University School of Law (LL.M., 1995). ***COURSES: Labor Law, Employment Law, Products Liability. ***Email:*** cheryla@siu.edu

W. EUGENE BASANTA*, (Professor of Law)**, born Norwalk, Connecticut, January 21, 1950; admitted to bar, 1975, Kentucky. *Education:* Williams College (B.A., 1972); University of Kentucky (J.D., 1975); Temple University School of Law (LL.M., 1980). ***COURSES: Health Law, Contracts. ***Email:*** basanta@siu.edu

ROBERT E. BECK*, (Professor)**, born Aitkin, Minnesota, April 24, 1937; admitted to bar, 1960, Minnesota. *Education:* University of Minnesota (B.S.L., 1958; LL.B., 1960); New York University School of Law (LL.M., 1966). ***COURSES: Natural Resources and Environmental Law. ***Email:*** bobbeck@siu.edu

KEITH H. BEYLER*, (Professor of Law)**, born Indianapolis, Indiana, August 11, 1947; admitted to bar, 1974, California. *Education:* Princeton University (A.B., 1969); University of Chicago (J.D., 1974). ***COURSES: Civil Procedure, Conflict of Laws, Federal Courts, Legal Argumentation, Pretrial Advocacy. ***Email:*** kbeyler@siu.edu

THOMAS C. BRITTON*, (Associate Professor)**, born Evansville, Indiana, November 12, 1948; admitted to bar, 1976, Illinois. *Education:* Southern Illinois University (B.A., 1970; M.S.Ed., 1973; J.D., 1976). ***COURSES: Administrative Law, Education Law. ***Email:*** tbritton@siu.edu

CINDY GALWAY BUYS*, (Assistant Professor of Law)**, admitted to bar, 1992, New York. *Education:* Syracuse University (M.A., 1991; J.D., 1991); State University of NY at Albany (B.A., 1987); Georgetown Law Center (LL.M., 1999). ***COURSES: International Law.

BRANNON PADGETT DENNING*, (Assistant Professor of Law)**, born Ownesboro, Kentucky , October 13, 1970; admitted to bar, 1995, Tennessee. *Education:* University of the South (B.A., 1992); University of Tennessee (J.D., 1995); Yale Law School (LL.M., 1999). ***COURSES: Constitutional Law, Legal Ethics, Legislation. ***Email:*** bdenning@siu.edu

JAMES EDGAR DUGGAN*, (Professor and Computer Services Librarian)**, born Roanoke, Virginia, March 24, 1961; admitted to bar, 1987, Mississippi. *Education:* Virginia Polytechnic Institute and State University (B.A., 1983); University of Mississippi (J.D., 1986); Louisiana State University (M.L.I.S., 1987). ***COURSES: Legal Research I, Legal Research II, Advanced Electronic Legal Research. ***Email:*** duggan@siu.edu

DARRELL W. DUNHAM*, (Professor of Law)**, born Anchorage, Alaska, August 29, 1946; admitted to bar, 1971, Washington; 1978, Illinois. *Education:* Williamette University (B.A., 1968; J.D., 1971); Harvard University Law School (LL.M., 1972). ***COURSES: Bankruptcy, Commercial Law, Intellectual Property. ***Email:*** dwd1@siu.edu

JOHN F. ERBES*, (Assistant Clinical Professor)**, born Rockford, Illinois, January 27, 1954; admitted to bar, 1979, Illinois. *Education:* Western Illinois University (B.A., 1976); Southern Illinois University (J.D., 1979). ***COURSES: Elder Law. ***Email:*** erbes@siu.edu

DONALD GARNER*, (Professor of Law)**, born Little Rock, Arkansas, February 6, 1943; admitted to bar, 1971, Texas. *Education:* University of Texas (B.A., 1967); Williamette University; University of Texas (J.D., 1971). ***COURSES: Torts, Product Liability, Education Law. ***Email:*** dgarner@siu.edu

LEONARD GROSS*, (Professor of Law)**, born Brooklyn, New York, December 15, 1951; admitted to bar, 1977, Massachusetts; 1977, New York; 1984, Illinois. *Education:* State University of New York at Binghamton (B.A., 1973); Boston University (J.D., 1976); New York University. ***COURSES: Legal Profession, Corporations, Agency and Partnership, Remedies. ***Email:*** lgross@siu.edu

FRANK G. HOUDEK*, (Law Library Director and Professor of Law)**, born Long Beach, California, December 22, 1948; admitted to bar, 1974, California. *Education:* University of California at Los Angeles (B.A., 1971; J.D., 1974; M.L.S., 1976). ***COURSES: Legal Research, Law Librarianship. ***Email:*** houdek@siu.edu

(This Listing Continued)

SOUTHERN ILLINOIS UNIVERSITY SCHOOL OF LAW —Continued

DAVID C. JOHNSON*, (Professor of Law)**, born North Dakota, December 11, 1937; admitted to bar, 1961, North Dakota; 1967, Georgia. *Education:* University of North Dakota (B.S.B.A., 1959; J.D., 1961); University of Pennsylvania (LL.M., 1964). ***COURSES: Taxation, Estate Planning, Property. ***Email:*** djohnson@siu.edu

PATRICK J. KELLEY*, (Professor of Law)**, born Ames, Iowa, July 24, 1943; admitted to bar, 1969, Iowa and Illinois; 1978, Missouri. *Education:* University of Notre Dame (B.A., 1965); University of Iowa College of Law (J.D., 1969). ***COURSES: Torts, Legislation, State and Local Government, Jurisprudence. ***Email:*** pkelley@siu.edu

EDWARD J. KIONKA*, (Professor of Law)**, born Oak Park, Illinois, February 18, 1939; admitted to bar, 1962, Illinois; 1977, Missouri. *Education:* University of Illinois (B.S., 1960); University of Illinois College of Law (J.D., 1962); Columbia University Law School (LL.M., 1974). ***COURSES: Torts, Evidence, Appellate Courts. ***Email:*** ejkionka@siu.edu

MARK R. LEE*, (Professor of Law)**, born St. Louis, Missouri, January 23, 1949; admitted to bar, 1974, Texas. *Education:* Yale University (B.A., 1971); University of Texas (J.D., 1974). ***COURSES: Antitrust, Corporations, Agency and Partnership, Securities Regulation, Regulated Industries, Law and Economics, Criminal Law. ***Email:*** markrlee@siu.edu

BRYAN ALBERT LIANG*, (Professor)**, born Wilmington, Delaware, September 8, 1962; admitted to bar, 1995, Connecticut. *Education:* M.I.T. (B.S., 1983); University of Chicago (Ph.D., 1989); Columbia University (M.D., 1991); Harvard University (J.D., 1995). ***COURSES: Health Law, Contracts, Public Policy. ***Email:*** baliang@alum.mit.edu

SUSAN P. LIEMER*, (Director of Lawyering Skills and Assistant Professor)**, born Chicago, Illinois, May 14, 1958; admitted to bar, 1986, Connecticut; 1987, New York. *Education:* Princeton University (B.A., 1979); University of Virginia (J.D., 1986). ***COURSES: Lawyering Skills (Legal Writing). ***Email:*** sliemer@siu.edu

PATRICIA ROSS MCCUBBIN*, (Assistant Professor)**, admitted to bar, 1990, Georgia; 1991, District of Columbia. *Education:* University of Virginia (B.A., 1985; J.D., 1990). ***COURSES: Environmental Law. ***Email:*** mccubbin@siu.edu

ALICE M. NOBLE-ALLGIRE*, (Associate Professor of Law)**, born Woodstock, Illinois, January 11, 1957; admitted to bar, 1990, Illinois. *Education:* Southern Illinois University (B.S., 1980; J.D., 1990). ***COURSES: Property, Professional Responsibility. ***Email:*** nobleall@siu.edu

REBECCA O'NEILL*, (Associate Clinical Professor)**, born Benton, Illinois, April 2, 1963; admitted to bar, 1988, Illinois; 1990, U.S. District Court, Southern District of Illinois; 1993, U.S. Court of Appeals, Seventh Circuit; 1994, U.S. Supreme Court and U.S. Court of Veterans Appeals. *Education:* Southern Illinois University (B.S., 1985; J.D., 1988). ***COURSES: Clinical Courses, Family Law. ***Email:*** rjoneill@siu.edu

RALPH J. ROBERTSON, JR.*, (Professor of Law)**, born Humansville, Missouri, July 9, 1951; admitted to bar, 1976, Missouri. *Education:* University of Missouri (A.B., 1973; J.D., 1976). ***COURSES: Contracts, Insurance, Remedies, Sales, Negotiable Instruments. ***Email:*** rjrobert@siu.edu

MARY C. RUDASILL*, (Clinic Director, Associate Professor of Law and Associate Dean for Administration)**, born Champaign, Illinois, May 13, 1949; admitted to bar, 1980, Illinois. *Education:* Illinois State University (B.S., 1971); University of Illinois (M.S., 1975); Southern Illinois University School of Law (J.D., 1980). ***COURSES: Clinical Courses, Aging and the Law, Pre-Trial Advocacy. ***Email:*** rudasill@siu.edu

HEIJA B. RYOO*, (Professor/Head of Technical Services)**, born Seoul, Korea, November 22, 1943. *Education:* Sook Myung Women's University (B.B.A., 1966); Indiana University (M.L.S., 1980). ***Email: hryoo@siu.edu

SUZANNE J. SCHMITZ*, (Alternative Dispute Resolution Project Coordinator and Clinical Associate Professor)**, born Breese, Illinois, December 3, 1947; admitted to bar, 1981, Illinois and U.S. District Court, Central District of Illinois; 1988, U.S. District Court, Southern District of Illinois; 1990, Missouri. *Education:* St. Xavier College (B.A., 1969); Southern Illinois University (M.S.Ed., 1976); St. Louis University School of Law (J.D., 1981). ***COURSES: Advanced ADR; ADR Clinic. ***Email:*** sschmitz@siu.edu

WILLIAM A. SCHROEDER*, (Professor of Law)**, born Chicago, Illinois, March 19, 1943; admitted to bar, 1972, Massachusetts; 1990, Missouri. *Education:* University of Illinois (A.B., 1966); University of Illinois College of Law (J.D., 1969); Harvard University Law School (LL.M., 1977). ***COURSES: Criminal Procedure, Criminal Law, Evidence. ***Email:*** wschroe@siu.edu

MELISSA SHAFER*, (Assistant Professor)**, born April 5, 1970; admitted to bar, 1996, Illinois. *Education:* Southern Illinois University at Carbondale (B.S., 1991); Southern Illinois University School of Law (J.D., 1996). ***COURSES: Lawyering Skills. ***Email:*** shafer@siu.edu

SHEILA SIMON*, (Clinical Assistant Professor)**, born Troy, Illinois, March 13, 1961; admitted to bar, 1987, Illinois. *Education:* Wittenberg University (B.A., 1983); Georgetown University Law Center (J.D., 1987). ***COURSES: Lawyering Skills. ***Email:*** ssimon@siu.edu

NORMAN VIEIRA*, (Professor of Law)**, born New Bedford, Massachusetts, March 18, 1937; admitted to bar, 1963, Illinois. *Education:* Columbia University (A.B., 1959); University of Chicago (J.D., 1962). ***COURSES: Constitutional Law, Criminal Law. ***Email:*** vieira@siu.edu

LAUREL WENDT*, (Associate Director of the Law Library and Associate Professor)**, admitted to bar, 1978, Indiana. *Education:* Indiana University (B.A., 1967; M.L.S., 1968); Indiana University - Indianapolis School of Law (J.D., 1978). ***COURSES: Legal Research. ***Email:*** lwendt@siu.edu

WENONA Y. WHITFIELD*, (Associate Professor of Law)**, born Chicago, Illinois, January 23, 1949; admitted to bar, 1977, Illinois. *Education:* Illinois Wesleyan University (B.A., 1970); Southern Illinois University School of Law (J.D., 1977). ***COURSES: Property, Alternative Dispute Resolution, Family Law, Mental Health Law, Oral Advocacy, Real Estate Finance, Legal Writing. ***Email:*** wenona@siu.edu

SOUTHERN METHODIST UNIVERSITY SCHOOL OF LAW

STOREY HALL, 3315 DANIEL STREET
DALLAS, TEXAS 75275
Telephone: (214) 768-8999
Fax: (214) 768-2182

ABA Approved Since 1927

The School of Law of Southern Methodist University has a tradition of excellence in legal education and legal scholarship. The school has a nationally regarded and diverse group of 40 full-time faculty who represent a broad spectrum of social and scholarly views. The faculty work together in a spirit of collegiality and share a devotion to excellence in classroom teaching and legal scholarship. The highly accomplished and diverse student body consists of approximately 765 J.D. candidates from over 200 undergraduate institutions throughout the United States, as well as 80 candidates for graduate degrees from approximately 20 countries. The School's exemplary physical complex is a quadrangle of four buildings that occupies six acres on the SMU campus. The largest of the buildings is Underwood Law Library, which features a over a half a million volume open-stack collection, the largest private legal collection in the Southwest.

The school offers a broad and rich Juris Doctor curriculum and awards combined degrees in business (J.D./M.B.A.) and economics (J.D./M.A.). The school offers strong civil and criminal clinical education programs and a clinical program in taxation. The school also has a tradition of strength in its International Law program. The latter is enhanced by the school's summer program at Oxford University, and by the Center for Pacific Rim Legal Studies and the Center for NAFTA and Latin American Studies.

For more information about SMU School of Law, please visit our webpage at http://www.smu.edu/~law/.

Dean & William Hawley Atwell Professor of Constitutional Law: John B. Attanasio (214) 768-8999
Administration-Assistant Dean: Christine Szaj
Admissions & Assistant Dean: Lynn Switzwer Bozalis (214) 768-2540
Financial Aid-Associate Dean: William DeLoach (214) 768-4178
Library-Associate Dean: Gail Daly (214) 768-1873
Director of Alumni Development: Douglas Yeager (214) 768-8617
Student Affairs-Associate Dean: William DeLoach (214) 768-4178
Career Services-Assistant Dean: Kelly Noblin (214) 768-3893
Public Services-Director: Rebecca Greenan (214) 768-2567
Registrar: Laura Amberson (214) 768-2551
Director of Legal Research and Writing and Lawyering: Ruth Cross (214) 768-2569

FULL TIME FACULTY

***JOHN B. ATTANASIO*, (Dean and William Hawley Atwell Professor of Constitutional Law)**, born Jersey City, New Jersey, October 19, 1954; admitted to bar, 1979, Maryland. *Education:* University of Virginia (B.A., 1976); New York University (J.D., 1979); University of Oxford, Oriel College (Diploma of Law, 1982); Yale University (LL.M., 1985).

ROY RYDEN ANDERSON*, (Professor)**, born Lecompte, Louisiana, July 28, 1944; admitted to bar, 1969, Texas. *Education:* Texas Christian University (B.A., 1966); Southern Methodist University (J.D., 1969); Yale University (LL.M., 1975). ***COURSES: Contracts, Commercial and Consumer, Law Remedies. ***Email:*** rranders@mail.smu.edu

MAUREEN N. ARMOUR*, (Associate Dean for Clinical Education-Associate Professor)**, born October 9, 1948. *Education:* University of California, Santa Cruz (B.A., 1970); University of California at Berkeley (M.S.W., 1974); Southern Methodist University (J.D., 1981). ***Email: marmour@mail.smu.edu

LACKLAID H. BLOOM*, (Professor)**, born September 17, 1948. *Education:* Southern Methodist University (B.A., 1970); University of Michigan (J.D., 1973). ***Email: lbloom@mail.smu.edu

WILLIAM J. BRIDGE*, (Associate Professor)**, born Lewistown, Pennsylvania, August 3, 1948; admitted to bar, 1975, District of Columbia; 1984, Pennsylvania. *Education:* Georgetown University (B.S.F.S., 1970; J.D., 1974). ***COURSES: Criminal Law, Evidence, Professional Responsibility, Comparative Law. ***Email:*** wbridge@mail.smu.edu

ALAN R. BROMBERG*, (Professor-University Distinguished Professor of Law)**, born Dallas, Texas, November 24, 1928; admitted to bar, 1952, Texas. *Education:* Harvard University (A.B., 1949); Yale University (J.D., 1952). ***COURSES: Business Enterprise, Securities Regulation, Corporate Planning. ***Email:*** abromber@mail.smu.edu

REGIS W. CAMPFIELD*, (Professor of Law and Marilyn Jeanne Johnson Distinguished Law Faculty Fellow)**, born Pittsburgh, Pennsylvania, January 8, 1942; admitted to bar, 1966, Ohio; 1966, Virginia; 1974, Indiana. *Education:* University of Notre Dame (B.B.A., 1963); University of Virginia (LL.B., 1966). ***COURSES: Wills & Trusts, Taxation, Estate Planning. ***Email:*** rcampfie@mail.smu.edu

MICHAEL THOMAS COLATRELLA, JR.*, (Lecturer-in-Law)**, born Newark, New Jersey, June 29, 1963; admitted to bar, 1991, New Jersey. *Education:* Rutgers University (B.A., 1987); Seton Hall University (J.D., 1991); New York University (LL.M., 1999). ***COURSES: Legal Research & Writing; ADR. ***Email:*** mcolatre@mail.smu.com

MICHAELA EILEEN CONWAY*, (Lecturer-in-Law)**, born Rock Island, Illinois, August 9, 1958; admitted to bar, 1984, Texas. *Education:* Augustana College (B.A., 1981); University of Illinois (J.D., 1984). ***COURSES: Legal Research, Writing and Advocacy. ***Email:*** mconway@mail.smu.com

GREGORY S. CRESPI*, (Associate Professor)**, born Princeton, New Jersey, February 8, 1948; admitted to bar, 1985, Iowa; 1987, Pennsylvania; 1987, Washington D.C.. *Education:* Michigan State University (B.S., 1969); George Washington University (M.S., 1974); University of Iowa (Ph.D., 1978); Yale Law School (J.D., 1985). ***COURSES: Contracts, Law-and-Economics. ***Email:*** gcrespi@mail.smu.edu

***RUTH A. CROSS*, (Director Legal Research Writing and Advocacy)**, born Cairo, Egypt, March 28, 1954; admitted to bar, 1978, Texas. *Education:* University of Texas at Austin (B.A., 1975); University of

(This Listing Continued)

SOUTHERN METHODIST UNIVERSITY SCHOOL OF LAW —Continued

Texas School of Law (J.D., 1978). ***COURSES:*** Research, Procedure. ***Email:*** rccross@mail.smu.com

GAIL M. DALY*, (Associate Dean for Library and Technology and Associate Professor)**, born Detroit, Michigan; admitted to bar, 1989, Minnesota. *Education:* University of Michigan (B.A., 1968; M.A., 1969); University of Minnesota (J.D., 1989). ***COURSES: Advanced Legal Research, Copyright. ***Email:*** gdaly@mail.smu.edu

JANE L. DOLKART*, (Associate Professor)**, born April 19, 1948. *Education:* Mount Holyoke College (B.A., 1969); Columbia University (J.D., 1972); Georgetown University (LL.M., 1973). ***Email: jdolkart@mail.smu.edu

WILLIAM V. DORSANEO III*, (Professor, Chief Justice John and Lena Hickman Distinguished Faculty Fellow)**, born Norristown, Pennsylvania, December 17, 1945; admitted to bar, 1970, Texas. *Education:* University of Pennsylvania (B.A., 1967); University of Texas (J.D., 1970). ***COURSES: Civil Procedure Appellate Advocacy, Torts, Product Liability. ***Email:*** wdorsaneo@mail.smu.edu

BEVERLY CARO DUREUS*, (Lecturer-in-Law)**, born Kansas City, Kansas, June 3, 1961; admitted to bar, 1987, Texas. *Education:* Drake University (B.A., 1983; J.D., 1986); Dallas Theological Seminary (Th.M., 1999);. ***COURSES: Legal Research & Writing. ***Email:*** bcaro@mail.smu.com

LINDA S. EADS*, (Associate Professor)**, born Pittsburgh, Pennsylvania, November 24, 1949; admitted to bar, 1975, Texas; 1976, District of Columbia. *Education:* American University (B.A., 1971); University of Texas J.D.,1975). ***COURSES: Evidence, Ethics, Women & Law, Constitutional Law, Trial Advocacy. ***Email:*** leads@mail.smu.edu

JULIA P. FORRESTER*, (Associate Professor)**, born Dallas, Texas, August 22, 1959; admitted to bar, 1986, Texas. *Education:* University of Texas (B.S.E.E., 1981; J.D., 1985). ***COURSES: Property, Real Estate Transactions, Land Use. ***Email:*** jforrest@mail.smu.edu

***JEFFREY M. GABA*, (Professor)**, born September 20, 1950. *Education:* University of California at Santa Barbara (B.A., 1972); Columbia University (J.D., 1976); Harvard University (M.P.H., 1989).

CHRISTOPHER H. HANNA*, (Professor of Law)**, born Tampa, Florida, August 19, 1962; admitted to bar, 1988, Florida; 1991 District of Columbia (inactive). *Education:* University of Florida (B.S., 1984; J.D., 1988); New York University (LL.M., 1989). ***COURSES: Taxation, International. ***Email:*** channa@mail.smu.edu

JOANN A. HUBBARD*, (Lecturer-in-Law)**, born Ardmore, Oklahoma; admitted to bar, 1987, Texas. *Education:* University of Oklahoma (B.S.); (J.D., 1987)). ***COURSES: Legal Research & Writing, Advocacy. ***Email:*** joannh@mail.smu.com

DARREN HUTCHINSON*, (Assistant Professor)**, born Gainesville, Florida, October 4, 1968; admitted to bar, 1994, New York. *Education:* University of Pennsylvania (B.A., 1990); Yale University Law School (J.D., 1993). ***COURSES: Constitutional Law, Jurisprudence, Critical Race Theory, Civil Rights. ***Email:*** dhutchin@mail.smu.edu

NDIVA KOFELE-KALE*, (Associate Professor)**, born Lagos, Nigeria, December 18, 1946; admitted to bar, 1984, Illinois. *Education:* Beloit College (B.A., 1970); Northwestern University (M.A., 1972; Ph.D., 1974; J.D., 1984). ***COURSES: Public International Law, International Trade & Investment, Human Rights. ***Email:*** nkofele@mail.smu.edu

HENRY J. LISCHER JR.*, (Professor of Law)**, born Washington, D.C., September 29, 1945; admitted to bar, 1970, Iowa; 1974, California; 1982, Texas. *Education:* University of Iowa (B.B.A.,1967; J.D., 1970); New York University (LL.M., 1974). ***COURSES: Taxation. ***Email:*** hlischer@mail.smu.edu

JOHN S. LOWE*, (Professor and George W. Hutchison Professor of Energy Law)**, born May 11, 1941. *Education:* Denison University (B.A., 1963); Harvard University (LL.B., 1966). ***Email: jlowe@mail.smu.edu

GEORGE A. MARTINEZ*, (Professor)**, born September 10, 1954. *Education:* Arizona State University (B.A., 1976); University of Michigan (M.A., 1979); Harvard University (J.D., 1985). ***Email: gmartine@mail.smu.edu

THOMAS WILLIAM MAYO*, (Associate Professor)**, born Bangor, Maine, September 7, 1949; admitted to bar, 1978, New York; 1980, District of Columbia. *Education:* Amherst College (B.A., 1971); Syracuse University (J.D., 1977). ***COURSES: Health Law, Bioethics, Legislation, Constitutional Law, Civil Procedure. ***Email:*** tmayo@mail.smu.edu

JOSEPH W. MCKNIGHT*, (Professor)**, born San Angelo, Texas, February 17, 1925; admitted to bar, 1951, Texas. *Education:* University of Texas (B.A., 1947); Oxford University (B.A., 1949; B.C.L., 1950; M.A., 1943); Columbia University (LL.M., 1959). ***COURSES: Legal History, Family and Martial Property Law.

FREDERICK C. MOSS*, (Associate Professor)**, born Washington, D.C., April 1, 1943; admitted to bar, 1969, District of Columbia; 1980, Texas. *Education:* Georgetown University (A.B., 1965); Villanova University (J.D., 1968); Harvard University (LL.M., 1977). ***COURSES: Professional Ethics, Evidence, Criminal Law, Trial Practice. ***Email:*** fmoss@mail.smu.edu

JOHN J. MYLAN*, (Professor)**, born New York, New York, August 20, 1939; admitted to bar, 1965, California. *Education:* Fordham University (B.S., 1961); Stanford Law School (J.D., 1964); New York University (LL.M., 1965). ***COURSES: Federal Taxation. ***Email:*** jmylan@mail.smu.edu

JOSEPH J. NORTON*, (Professor and James L. Walsh Distinguished Faculty Fellow in Financial Institutions)**, born Rhode Island, September 15, 1945; admitted to bar, 1970, Texas. *Education:* Providence College (A.B., 1966); University of Edinburgh (LL.B., 1969); University of Texas (LL.M., 1970); University of Michigan (S.J.D., 1973); Oxford University (D.Phil., 1994). ***COURSES: Domestic & International Business & Banking. ***Email:*** jnorton@mail.smu.edu

VICTORIA PALACIOS*, (Associate Professor)**, born September 5, 1947. *Education:* University of Nebraska (J.D., 1975). ***Email: vpalacio@mail.smu.edu

ELLEN SMITH PRYOR*, (Associate Professor)**, born June 24, 1956. *Education:* Rice University (B.A., 1978); University of Texas (J.D., 1982). ***Email: epryor@mail.smu.edu

ROARK M. REED*, (Professor)**, born Elizabeth, New Jersey, February 20, 1940; admitted to bar, 1969, District of Columbia. *Education:* Georgetown University (B.S. B.A., 1965, J.D., 1969). ***COURSES: Criminal Procedure, Litigation, Evidence, Expert Testimony, Japanese Legal System. ***Email:*** rreed@mail.smu.edu

C. PAUL ROGERS III*, (Professor)**, born NYC, New York, April 19, 1948; admitted to bar, 1973, Pennsylvania; 1984, Texas. *Education:* University of Texas (B.A., 1970; J.D., 1973); Columbia University (LL.M., 1977). ***COURSES: Antitrust, Contracts, Business Torts. ***Email:*** crogers@mail.smu.edu

***SUSAN SCAFIDI*, (Assistant Professor)**, born Washington, D.C.,

(This Listing Continued)

SOUTHERN METHODIST UNIVERSITY SCHOOL OF LAW —Continued

December 16, 1968; admitted to bar, 1993, Maryland. *Education:* Duke University (B.A., 1990); Yale Law School (J.D., 1993). ***COURSES:*** Intellectual Property, Property, Legal History, Native American Law. ***Email:*** sscafidi@mail.smu.com

DANIEL W. SHUMAN, **(Professor)**, born May 4, 1948. *Education:* University of Arizona (B.S., 1969; J.D., 1972). ***Email:*** dshuman@mail.smu.edu

MARY BRYNA SPECTOR, **(Associate Professor)**, born Texas, October 3, 1957; admitted to bar, 1987, New York; 1987, Texas. *Education:* Simmons College (B.A., 1979); Benjamin N. Cardozo School of Law (J.D., 1986). ***COURSES:*** Clinical Education. ***Email:*** mspector@mail.smu.edu

MARC I. STEINBERG, **(Senior Associate Dean for Academics and Rupert & Lillian Radford Professor of Law-Professor)**, born Detroit, Michigan, June 15, 1950; admitted to bar, 1975, California; 1979, District of Columbia; 1987, Maryland; 1991, Texas. *Education:* University of Michigan (A.B., 1972); UCLA (J.D., 1975); Yale University (LL.M., 1977). ***COURSES:*** Business, Enterprise, Corporations, Securities. ***Email:*** msteinbe@mail.smu.edu

ELIZABETH G. THORNBURG, **(Professor)**, born Norwalk, Connecticut, May 3, 1954; admitted to bar, 1979, Texas. *Education:* College of William and Mary (B.A., 1976); Southern Methodist University (J.D., 1979). ***COURSES:*** Civil Procedure, Remedies, Conflict of Laws. ***Email:*** ethornbu@mail.smu.eud

ERNEST B. WHITE, **(Director of Criminal Clinic)**, born New York, New York, October 9, 1955; admitted to bar, 1985, Texas. *Education:* San Diego State University (B.A., 1981); (J.D., 1985). ***COURSES:*** Criminal Clinic. ***Email:*** ebwhite@mail.smu.com

HARVEY WINGO, **(Professor)**, born Birmingham, Alabama, June 15, 1936; admitted to bar, 1962, Tennessee. *Education:* Birmingham-Southern College (B.A., 1958); Vanderbilt University (M.A., 1960; J.D., 1962). ***COURSES:*** Sabbatical.

JANE KAUFMAN WINN, **(Professor)**, born April 30, 1957; admitted to bar, 1988, New York. *Education:* Queen Mary College, University of London (B.S., 1980); Harvard Law School (J.D., 1987). ***Email:*** jwinn@mail.smu.edu

PETER WINSHIP, **(James Cleo Thompson Sr. Trustee Professor of Law)**, born January 5, 1944. *Education:* Harvard University (B.A., 1965; LL.B., 1968); University of London (LL.M., 1973). ***Email:*** pwinship@mail.smu.edu

---

SOUTHERN UNIVERSITY LAW CENTER

P. O. BOX 9294
BATON ROUGE, LOUISIANA 70813
Telephone: (225) 771-2552
Fax: (225) 771-2474

ABA Approved Since 1953.

On October 22, 1946, the State of Louisiana Board of Education approved the report and recommendation of a committee of the State Board of Education for the establishment of a law school at Southern University, Baton Rouge. In September 1947, the Southern University School of Law was officially opened.

Accredited by the American Bar Association, the Supreme Court of Louisiana, and the Southern Association of Colleges and Secondary Schools, the Law Center maintains a high standard of professional education. It is fully approved by the Veterans Administration for the training of eligible veterans. The Southern University Law Center adheres to the principle of equal opportunity without regard to race, sex, color, creed, national origin, age, handicap, or marital status.

Library and Physical Facilities: The Law Center is housed in the A.A. Lenior Hall, named after the first dean of the originally established School of Law.

A $4 million expansion and improvement of the Law Center was completed in September 1993. The new facility gives the Law Center a total area of approximately 80,000 square feet.

In December 1992, administrative and faculty offices were relocated on the second floor of the newly renovated Law Center facility and the library staff was re-located on the first floor of that facility. Other renovations to the original Law Center building includes classrooms, study areas, offices for student organizations, faculty, staff and student lounges, seminar rooms and a Moot Court/Auditorium.

The Law Center has established the Institute for Civil Rights with plans for establishing other Centers for Legal Studies and Law and Artificial Intelligence. The Law Center has an outstanding Clinical Education program. A fully equipped law office within the Law Center enables students to develop lawyering skills by representing indigent clients in court and before administrative agencies.

The law library is housed in the Law Center building and contains more than 400,000 volumes of legal materials. These materials have been carefully selected to offer a basic working collection for both students and faculty. Systematic additions to the collection are being made in accordance with a definite program of growth. The Law Library consists of two large reading rooms, two large computer aided research rooms, computer lab, microform area, five group study rooms and a special Civil Rights reading room.

Special arrangements have been made with the Louisiana State University Library, which has one of the largest collections of Anglo-American and civil law materials in the South, to make its resources available for research purposes through the Southern University Law Library.

The Law Center subscribes to WESTLAW and LEXIS computerized legal research system. Training sessions are conducted each semester by library staff to assist students in the proper utilization of the system.

Basic Program of Study/Degree Requirements: The program of study is designed to give students a comprehensive knowledge of both the civil law and common law. While emphasis is given to the substantive and procedural law of Louisiana with its French and Spanish origins, Anglo-American law is strongly integrated into the curriculum. Fundamental differences in method and approach and the results reached in the two systems are analyzed.

The civil law system of Louisiana offers the law student a unique educational opportunity. The program of instruction examines the historical background of the civil law system and its development in the Anglo-American setting.

Students are trained in the art of advocacy, legal research, and the sources and social purposes of legal principles. Techniques to discipline

(This Listing Continued)

SOUTHERN UNIVERSITY LAW CENTER—Continued

the students' minds in legal reasoning are an integral part of the educational objectives of the Law Center. Students are instructed in the ethics of the legal profession and the professional responsibility of the lawyer to society.

The three-year curriculum is based upon the standard professional courses usually given in member schools of the ABA. It requires the satisfactory completion of at least 96 semester hours including required courses. The curriculum further requires a full six semesters of residence. Any study undertaken in a summer session shall not count toward residence requirements. Electives have been integrated as part of the curriculum, and students are required to take courses specified for the respective years.

Activities: The Student Bar Association, an affiliate of the American Law Student Association, is a self-governing organization that receives the full cooperation of the Law Center faculty and to which a member of the faculty is appointed as adviser. Any student in good standing enrolled in the Law Center is eligible for membership in the association. The purposes of the association are to promote the general welfare of the Law Center, encourage among its members high scholarship, and cultivate rapport and cooperation among the students, faculty, and members of the legal profession.

The Law Center publishes a law review. A board of editors composed of students with high academic standing edits the publication. At the present time, two issues a year are published.

Students with advanced standing are eligible to enroll in the Clinical Education Program, which allows students to handle cases under the direct supervision of a full-time faculty member of the Law Center.

Admission: The Law Center does not prescribe any prelegal courses but strongly recommends a foundation in such courses as English, Speech, Political Science, History, Economics, Psychology, Logic, Mathematics and Analytical Courses, and Science. It will be necessary for such students to show satisfactory improvement in order to remain in the Law Center.

Students beginning the study of law are admitted only in the fall semester. The Law Center operates a full-time day program. To be considered for admission, an applicant must have received a bachelor's degree from an approved college or university and must have received an acceptable score on the LSAT. Applicants are advised to take the LSAT prior to the March test date of the expected year of enrollment. Under no circumstances will a score received on the test administered more than three years prior to the anticipated date of acceptance be considered. A $25 application fee will be required for all applicants applying for admission. All applications for admissions are reviewed by a special committee. Though many variables are taken into consideration for admission, primary emphasis is given to the undergraduate grade-point average and scores from the Law School Admission Test (LSAT). Work experience and past pursuits are also reviewed. Transcript evaluation by LSDAS is required.

Completed application forms, in addition to two letters of recommendation and one copy of an official transcript, should be filed with the Admissions Office during the fall semester prior to the year in which admission is sought. The application deadline is March 31.

Expenses and Financial Aid: Tuition for residents of Louisiana is $1,664 per semester. The tuition for nonresident students is $3,944 per semester.

Applicants seeking loans under the State Financial Assistance Act should apply to the Financial Aid Office, Southern University Law Center. Short-term loans to meet emergency needs are available from the Law Center loan fund. All students are expected to pay the required fees on the day of registration.

Housing: Limited dormitory accommodations are available for law students. All students desiring to live in campus housing are required to submit an application to the Housing Office, in addition to a security deposit of $50. Applications should be made to the Director of Housing, Southern University, as early as possible.

Placement: A placement office assists students and alumni in obtaining meaningful employment opportunities. Information on part-time employment before graduation is available through this office. Assistance is also given in job-seeking skills and interviewing techniques.

Correspondence: Inquiries should be addressed to Office of Admissions, Southern University Law Center, Baton Rouge, LA 70813. Phone (225) 771-5340 or 1-800-537-1135.

Chancellor: B. K. Agnihotri (225) 771-2552
Registrar: Elaine Simmons (225) 771-5340
Financial Aid Director: Jerome Harris (225) 771-2141
Law Librarian: Alvin Roche, Jr. (225) 771-2139
Vice Chancellor: Arthur E. Stallworth (225) 771-2552
Coordinator of Admissions: Velma Wilkerson (225) 771-5340
Coordinator of Recruitment: Andrea Love (225) 771-5340
Coordinator of Academic Counseling and Academic Assistance: Olliviette E. Mencer (225) 771-4913

FULL TIME FACULTY

BHISHMA K. AGNIHOTRI*, (Chancellor and Professor of Law)**, born Punjab, India, January 5, 1933; admitted to bar, 1956, New Delhi; 1985, New York. *Education:* Punjab University (B.A., 1951; M.A., 1955; LL.B., 1954); University of California, Berkeley (LL.M., 1967); New York University (LL.M., 1973). ***COURSES: Torts, Law and Medicine, International Trade Law.

STEVE V. BARBRE*, (Associate Professor of Law)**, born New Orleans, Louisiana, March 19, 1947; admitted to bar, 1976, Louisiana. *Education:* University of Wisconsin (B.A., 1972); University of Chicago (J.D., 1975). ***COURSES: Corporations, Commercial Paper, Securities Regulation, Legal History, Special Problems in Business Law.

CLEVELAND COON*, (Assistant Professor of Law)**, born Monroe, Louisiana, October 8, 1954; admitted to bar, 1981, Louisiana. *Education:* Southern University (B.S., 1976); Southern University Law Center (J.D., 1981). ***COURSES: Advanced Legal Writing and Civil Procedure I, Trust.

CARY DEBESSONET*, (Professor of Law)**, born Donaldsonville, Louisiana, December 11, 1941; admitted to bar, 1968, Louisiana. *Education:* Louisiana State University (J.D., 1968); University of Illinois (LL.M., 1977). ***COURSES: Contracts, Obligations, Law and Artificial Intelligence.

***ERNEST S. EASTERLY, III*, (Professor of Law)**, born Denham

(This Listing Continued)

SOUTHERN UNIVERSITY LAW CENTER—Continued

Springs, Louisiana, December 3, 1952; admitted to bar, 1978, Louisiana. *Education:* Louisiana State University (B.A., 1973; Ph.D., 1980; J.D., 1977); Salzburg University (D.E.S., 1981). ***COURSES:*** International Law, Comparative Law, Mineral Rights, Federal Jurisdiction and Procedure, Louisiana Sales and Leases.

MAURICE FRANKS, **(Associate Professor of Law)**, born Chicago, Illinois, April 11, 1942; admitted to bar, 1968, Louisiana; 1968, Tennessee. *Education:* University of Memphis (B.S., 1966; J.D., 1968). ***COURSES:*** Family Law, Conflict of Laws, Antitrust Law, Constitutional Law, Agency and Partnership.

MICHELLE WARD GHETTI, **(Associate Professor of Law)**, born Baton Rouge, Louisiana, August 8, 1953; admitted to bar, 1983, Texas; 1988, Louisiana. *Education:* Louisiana State University (B.S., 1978; J.D., 1983); Southern Methodist University. ***COURSES:*** Evidence, Law Office Practice, Criminal Procedure.

STANLEY A. HALPIN, JR., **(Professor of Law)**, *Education:* University of Southwestern Louisiana (B.A.); George Washington University (Ph.D., 1978); Tulane University (J.D., 1965). ***COURSES:*** Constitutional Law, Federal Jurisdiction and Procedure, Criminal Procedure, Civil Procedure.

DOROTHY F. JACKSON, **(Managing Attorney, Elder Law Clinic)**, born Shreveport, Louisiana, April 29, 1963; admitted to bar, 1991, Louisiana. *Education:* Louisiana Tech University (B.A., 1986); Southern University Law Center (J.D., 1990). ***COURSES:*** Clinical Education.

EILEEN JONES, **(Assistant Professor of Law)**, born Woodbury, New Jersey, February 2, 1962; admitted to bar, 1988, New Jersey and Pennsylvania. *Education:* Temple University (B.A., 1985; J.D., 1988). ***COURSES:*** Professional Responsibility, Legal Research, Basic Civil Procedure, Family Law, Trial Advocacy.

RUSSELL L. JONES, **(Professor of Law)**, born Wisner, Louisiana, June 18, 1953; admitted to bar, 1982, Louisiana. *Education:* Northeast Louisiana University (B.A., 1974); Southern University (J.D., 1982; LL.M., 1992). ***COURSES:*** Clinical Education, Professional Responsibility, Appellate Advocacy.

VIRGINIA LISTACH, **(Managing Attorney (Administrative Civil))**, born Shreveport, Louisiana, May 29, 1960; admitted to bar, 1988, Louisiana. *Education:* Shippenburg University (B.A., 1982); Southern University Law Center (J.D., 1988). ***COURSES:*** Clinical Education.

WASHINGTON MARSHALL, **(Professor of Law)**, born Brunswick, Georgia, February 10, 1942; admitted to bar, 1972, Louisiana. *Education:* Southern University (B.A., 1967; J.D., 1971). ***COURSES:*** Louisiana Family Law, Louisiana Sales and Leases, Civil Law Property.

WILLIAM MAYFIELD, **(Professor of Law)**, born Gary, Indiana, March 2, 1919; admitted to bar, 1949, Michigan. *Education:* Detroit Institute of Technology (A.B., 1946); Detroit College (J.D., 1949). ***COURSES:*** Civil Rights, Social Legislation, Constitutional Law, Consumer Law.

OLLIVETTE MENCER, **(Director of Academic Counseling and Academic Assistance, Assistant Professor)**, born Baton Rouge, Louisiana, April 24, 1953; admitted to bar, 1983, Louisiana. *Education:* Southern University (B.S., 1974); Louisiana State University (M.Ed., 1979); Southern University Law Center (J.D., 1983). ***COURSES:*** Legal Writing.

JACQUELINE NASH, **(Managing Attorney)**, born Shreveport, Louisiana, February 13, 1959; admitted to bar, 1983, Louisiana. *Education:* Southern University (B.A., 1980, J.D., 1983). ***COURSES:*** Clinical Education.

DONALD NORTH, **(Associate Professor)**, born Mobile, Alabama, March 9, 1958; admitted to bar, 1984, Louisiana. *Education:* Grambling State University (A.S., 1980; B.S., 1980; Southern University Law Center (J.D., 1983). ***COURSES:*** Clinical Education, Social Legislation.

OKECHUKWU OKO, **(Associate Professor of Law)**, born Awka, Nigeria, November 12, 1958; admitted to bar, 1994, Louisiana; 1982, Supreme Court of Nigeria. *Education:* University of Nigeria (LL.B., 1981; LL.M., 1985); Yale Law School (LL.M., 1989; J.S.D., 1992). ***COURSES:*** Commercial Paper, Comparative Law, Advanced Legal Writing I, Corporations.

JUDITH PERHAY, **(Assistant Professor of Law)**, born Cleveland, Ohio, April 25, 1949; admitted to bar, 1985, Louisiana. *Education:* John Carroll University (B.A., 1970); Loyola Law School, Louisiana (J.D., 1985). ***COURSES:*** Torts, Professional Responsibility, Basic Civil Procedure, Toxic Torts.

CYNTHIA PICOU, **(Professor of Law)**, born West Feliciana, Louisiana, December 20, 1943; admitted to bar, 1970, Louisiana. *Education:* Louisiana State University (B.A., 1965; J.D., 1970). ***COURSES:*** Successions and Donations, Torts, Bankruptcy, Civil Procedure.

JOHN K. PIERRE, **(Associate Professor of Law)**, born Loreauville, Louisiana, March 10, 1959; admitted to bar, 1986, Texas; 1990, Louisiana. *Education:* Southern University (B.S., 1980); Texas Tech University (M.S., 1982); Southern Methodist University (J.D., 1985). ***COURSES:*** Federal Taxation, Secured Transactions, Commercial Paper, Agency Partnership.

THOMAS RICHARD, **(Associate Professor of Law)**, born Springhill, Louisiana, August 28, 1950; admitted to bar, 1976, Louisiana. *Education:* Louisiana State University (B.A., 1972); Louisiana State University Law Center (J.D., 1975). ***COURSES:*** Sports Law, Security Devices, Torts II, Obligations.

WINSTON RIDDICK, **(Professor of Law)**, born Crowley, Louisiana, February 11, 1941; admitted to bar, 1974, Louisiana. *Education:* University of Southwestern Louisiana (B.A., 1962); University of North Carolina (M.A., 1964); Columbia University (Ph.D., 1973); Louisiana State University (J.D., 1973). ***COURSES:*** Advanced Constitutional Law, Administrative Law, Insurance Law, Mineral Law, Alternative Dispute Resolution.

ALFREDA A. SELLERS-DIAMOND, **(Professor of Law)**, born Baton Rouge, Louisiana, September 3, 1954; admitted to bar, 1986, Louisiana. *Education:* Louisiana State University (B.M., 1976; M.Ed., 1978; J.D., 1986). ***COURSES:*** Introduction to Law, Constitutional Law, Agency and Partnership, Products Liability, Federal Rules & Jurisdiction.

ARTHUR E. STALLWORTH, **(Vice Chancellor Professor of Law)**, born Mobile, Alabama, December 9, 1950; admitted to bar, 1976, Louisiana. *Education:* Vanderbilt University (B.S., 1972); Southern University (J.D., 1975). ***COURSES:*** Civil Procedure.

CLYDE C. TIDWELL, **(Professor of Law)**, born West Monroe, Louisiana; admitted to bar, 1967, Louisiana. *Education:* Southern University (B.A., 1961; J.D., 1966). ***COURSES:*** Legal Research, Advanced Research, Civil Law Property, Criminal Law, Conflict of Laws.

SHAWN D. VANCE, **(Instructor of Legal Writing)**, born Baton Rouge, Louisiana, January 29, 1971; admitted to bar, 1996, Louisiana. *Education:* Southern University A&M College (B.S., 1993); Southern University Law Center (J.D., 1996); Georgetown University Law Center (L.L.M., 1999). ***COURSES:*** Legal Writing. ***Email:*** svance@sulc.sus.edu

(This Listing Continued)

SOUTHERN UNIVERSITY LAW CENTER—Continued

PRENTICE LANG WHITE,* (Legal Writing Instructor)**, born New Orleans, Louisiana, October 6, 1969; admitted to bar, 1996, Louisiana. *Education:* Xavier University of Louisiana (B.A., 1991); Southern University (J.D., 1995). ***COURSES: Legal Writing and Oral Advocacy.

ROEDERICK CAMERON WHITE,* (Associate Professor of Law)**, born Baton Rouge, Louisiana, August 13, 1961; admitted to bar, 1992, Michigan. *Education:* Southern University (B.S., 1985); Wayne State University (M.B.A., 1987; J.D., 1992). ***COURSES: Constitutional Law, Ethics, Contracts, Conflict of Laws.

EVELYN L. WILSON,* (Professor of Law)**, born Parkersburg, West Virginia, July 7, 1949; admitted to bar, 1983, Louisiana. *Education:* Oberlin College (A.B., 1971); University of Utah (M.S., 1975); Louisiana State University (J.D., 1983). ***COURSES: Criminal Law, Federal Rules and Jurisdiction and Civil Law Property.

SOUTHWESTERN UNIVERSITY SCHOOL OF LAW

675 S. WESTMORELAND AVENUE
LOS ANGELES, CALIFORNIA 90005-3992

STANFORD UNIVERSITY LAW SCHOOL

STANFORD, CALIFORNIA 94305-8610

STETSON UNIVERSITY COLLEGE OF LAW

1401 61ST STREET SOUTH
ST. PETERSBURG, FLORIDA 33707
Telephone: (727) 562-7800
Fax: (727) 345-6428

ABA Approved Since 1930

Founded in 1900, the Stetson University College of Law is Florida's first law school. Stetson boasts a long history of educating and training lawyers, judges, scholars, and business and civic leaders. This strong tradition is enhanced by the College of Law's devotion to developing the lawyering skills necessary to become an effective member of the legal profession. The College of Law operates an LL.M. program in International Law and Business, and summer study programs in Tallinn, Estonia and Granada, Spain. A part-time J.D. program will begin in August 2002.

Located on its own twenty-one acre campus, Stetson is patterned after a medieval Spanish Village. Its principal buildings are of Spanish architecture, clustered around a plaza of fountains and palm trees. The campus is centrally located in the city of Gulfport, a residential beachfront community adjacent to St. Petersburg, in the dynamic Tampa Bay Area, one of the nation's largest metropolitan areas.

The faculty at Stetson continues to grow in strength and number. Because of its strong academic reputation, Stetson is able to attract distinguished scholars to its faculty. Many members of the faculty hold advanced law degrees or Master's or Ph.D. degrees in other disciplines. The majority of the faculty have engaged in the full-time practice of law. Adding to the strength of the full-time faculty is an outstanding adjunct faculty, comprised of prominent practicing attorneys and judges, who teach highly specialized elective courses, conduct seminars, and deliver lectures.

A new Legal Information Center was dedicated in 1998, housing a cutting-edge law library containing over 366,000 volumes. The Law Library's resources are enriched by subscriptions to LEXIS/NEXIS, WESTLAW and other electronic information systems. Study carrels are wired for access to the Internet and the advanced legal research systems, as are most classroom seats.

The College of Law serves the legal profession and the community as a center for continuing legal education (CLE). Stetson offers a variety of programs ranging from half-day seminars to multi-day conferences. The CLE Office attracts nationally-recognized practitioners and jurists to attend and participate in these programs. Through the CLE programs, the College of Law extends its educational mission beyond students pursuing legal degrees.

The Center for Dispute Resolution was established in 1983, an Elder Law Center was established in 1995, an Advocacy Center was established in 2000, and a Consortium on Health Law and Policy was established with the University of South Florida in 2000. They provide forums for the examination of law and public policy issues, and promote harmonious relationships among diverse constituencies through training programs, publications, and information exchange.

Stetson attracts a national student body. More than 150 different undergraduate colleges and universities and 36 states are represented in the current enrollment of approximately 630 students. Last year almost 1900 applicants vied for about 260 seats in the entering class. Approximately 55% of the students are women and about 19% are members of minority groups.

One of Stetson College of Law's greatest assets is the practical experience offered to students through trial team competitions and clinical programs. Over the years Stetson has built an impressive tradition of winning. During 1993-1994 Stetson won all five national level trial competitions, making it the only law school in the nation ever to win all five in one academic year. Stetson is consistently ranked as one of the top law schools in the nation in advocacy training.

The Stetson Lawyers Association ensures that our 6000 alumni are kept informed about the College of Law through publications, regional gatherings, Alumni Weekends, and class reunions. Alumni are encouraged to participate in a wide variety of activities. Stetson fosters close relationships among students and faculty, as well as among the students themselves.

(This Listing Continued)

STETSON UNIVERSITY COLLEGE OF LAW—Continued

Dean: W. Gary Vause (727) 562-7809
Admissions: Pamela B. Coleman (727) 562-7802
Financial Aid: Emily Schmidt (727) 562-7813
Library: Madison Mosley, Jr. (727) 562-7833
Placement: Catherine K. Fitch (727) 562-7815
Alumni Affairs: Dorothy E. Bressi (727) 562-7818
Student Services: Lynn A. Howell (727) 562-7808

FULL TIME FACULTY

W. GARY VAUSE*, (Vice President, Dean and Professor of Law)**, born Tallahassee, Florida, October 26, 1942; admitted to bar, 1970, Connecticut; 1975, Florida. *Education:* Yale University (Certificate in Mandarin Chinese, 1963); University of Connecticut (B.A., 1967; J.D., 1970); University of Virginia (LL.M., 1980; S.J.D., 1985). ***COURSES: Labor Law, Arbitration, International Business Transactions. ***Email:*** vause@law.stetson.edu

---

MICHAEL P. ALLEN*, (Assistant Professor of Law)**, born March 14, 1967; admitted to bar, 1992, Massachusetts. *Education:* University of Rochester (B.A., 1989); Columbia University (J.D., 1992). ***COURSES: Civil Procedure, Remedies. ***Email:*** allen@law.stetson.edu

THOMAS E. ALLISON*, (Vice Dean and Professor of Law)**, born St. Petersburg, Florida; admitted to bar, 1977, Florida. *Education:* Tulane University (B.S., 1973); Florida State University (M.B.A., 1974); Stetson University (J.D., 1977); University of Florida (LL.M., 1978). ***COURSES: Trusts and Estates, Federal Taxation of Estates, Trusts and Gifts, Property. ***Email:*** allison@law.stetson.edu

ROBERT BATEY*, (Professor of Law)**, born Corpus Christi, Texas, June 14, 1948. *Education:* Yale University (B.A., 1970); University of Virginia (J.D., 1974); University of Illinois (LL.M., 1976). ***COURSES: Criminal Law, Law and Literature. ***Email:*** batey@law.stetson.edu

DOROTHEA A. BEANE*, (Professor of Law)**, born Plainfield, New Jersey, March 30, 1952; admitted to bar, 1980, New Jersey. *Education:* Drew University (B.A., 1974); Rutgers University (J.D., 1977). ***COURSES: Civil Procedure, Pretrial Practice, Legal Medicine. ***Email:*** beane@law.stetson.edu

ROBERT DALE BICKEL*, (Professor of Law)**, born Easton, Pennsylvania, December 24, 1942; admitted to bar, 1969, Florida. *Education:* University of South Florida (B.A., 1964); Florida State University (J.D., 1968). ***COURSES: Torts, Employment Discrimination, Civil Procedure, Law and Education, Trial Practice. ***Email:*** bickel@law.stetson.edu

JAMES JAY BROWN*, (Professor of Law)**, born Cleveland, Ohio, December 22, 1937; admitted to bar, 1964, Ohio; 1978, Florida. *Education:* University of Pennsylvania (B.Sc., 1960); Cleveland State University (J.D., 1964); Washington University at St. Louis (LL.M., 1970). ***COURSES: Real Property, Environmental Law, Land Use Planning and Zoning. ***Email:*** brownj@law.stetson.edu

MARK R. BROWN*, (Professor of Law)**, born Louisville, Kentucky, August 13, 1959; admitted to bar, 1984, Kentucky. *Education:* University of Dayton (B.S., 1981); University of Louisville (J.D., 1984); University of Illinois (LL.M., 1988). ***COURSES: Civil Rights, Criminal Procedure, Constitutional Law, Administrative Law. ***Email:*** brownm@law.stetson.edu

KRISTEN D.A. CARPENTER*, (Assistant Professor of Law)**, born Des Moines, Iowa, July, 1971; admitted to bar, 1995, Georgia. *Education:* Rice University (B.A., 1992); Emory University School of Law (J.D., 1995); Yale Law School (LL.M., 2000). ***COURSES: Contracts I. ***Email:*** carpenter@law.stetson.edu

JOHN F. COOPER*, (Professor of Law)**, born Yokohama, Japan, October 3, 1950; admitted to bar, 1979, Oklahoma. *Education:* College of William & Mary (B.A., 1972); University of Oklahoma (J.D., 1979); University of Florida (LL.M., 1988). ***COURSES: Federal Income Taxation, State Constitutional Law. ***Email:*** cooper@law.stetson.edu

ROBERT N. DAVIS*, (Visiting Professor of Law)**, born Kewanee, Illinois, September 20, 1953; admitted to bar, 1980, Iowa; 1993, Virginia. *Education:* University of Hartford (B.A., 1975); Georgetown University (J.D., 1978). ***COURSES: Constitutional Law, Administrative. ***Email:*** davisr@law.stetson.edu

A. DARBY DICKERSON*, (Associate Dean, Professor of Law and Director of Research & Writing)**, born Columbia, South Carolina, December 31, 1963; admitted to bar, 1988, Texas. *Education:* College of William & Mary (B.A., 1984; M.A., 1985); Vanderbilt Law School (J.D., 1988). ***COURSES: Legal Research and Writing. ***Email:*** darby@law.stetson.edu

WILLIAM R. ELEAZER*, (Distinguished Professor Emeritus)**, born Springfield, Georgia, June 18, 1932; admitted to bar, 1968, District of Columbia; 1974, Florida and Georgia. *Education:* Vanderbilt University (B.A., 1953); George Washington University (J.D., 1967); Emory University (LL.M., 1987). ***COURSES: Trial Practice, Evidence, Criminal Law. ***Email:*** eleazer@law.stetson.edu

STEPHEN MICHAEL EVERHART*, (Professor of Law)**, born Elyria, Ohio, March 13, 1946; admitted to bar, 1972, Florida. *Education:* Florida State University (B.A., 1968); University of Florida (J.D., 1971). ***COURSES: Trial Advocacy, Criminal Procedure, Public Defender Clinic. ***Email:*** everhart@law.stetson.edu

KELLY M. FEELEY*, (Visiting Instructor of Legal Research and Writing)**, born Stoughton. Massachusetts, August 24, 1970; admitted to bar, 1995, Florida. *Education:* Florida State University (B.S., 1992); Stetson University College of Law (J.D., 1995). ***COURSES: Research and Writing I, Pre-Trial Practice. ***Email:*** feeley@law.stetson.edu

MICHAEL FINCH*, (Professor of Law)**, born 1952; admitted to bar, 1978, Connecticut. *Education:* Oberlin College (B.A., 1975); Boston University (J.D., 1978); Harvard University (S.J.D., 1982). ***COURSES: Civil Procedure, Federal Courts, Civil Rights, Conflict of Laws. ***Email:*** finch@law.stetson.edu

PETER FITZGERALD*, (Associate Professor of Law)**, born Washington, D.C., June 9, 1951; admitted to bar, 1977, Texas; 1982, New York. *Education:* College of William & Mary (B.A., 1973); Hastings College of Law (J.D., 1976); University of Exeter (LL.M., 1981). ***COURSES: International Business Transactions, Computer Law. ***Email:*** fitz@law.stetson.edu

ROBERTA KEMP FLOWERS*, (Professor of Law)**, born Denver, Colorado, October 26, 1957; admitted to bar, 1984, Colorado; 1992, Florida. *Education:* Baylor University (B.A., 1979); University of Colorado (J.D., 1984). ***COURSES: Trial Advocacy and Evidence. ***Email:*** flowers@law.stetson.edu

***JAMES W. FOX, JR.*, (Assistant Professor of Law)**, born Akron, Ohio, July 19, 1964; admitted to bar, 1991, Pennsylvania; 1993, District of Columbia. *Education:* University of North Carolina-Chapel Hill

(This Listing Continued)

STETSON UNIVERSITY COLLEGE OF LAW—Continued

(B.A., 1986); University of Michigan Law School (J.D., 1990). ***COURSES:*** Contracts I. ***Email:*** fox@law.stetson.edu

ROYAL C. GARDNER*, (Professor of Law and Director of Graduate and International Programs)**, born Buffalo, New York, March 10, 1963; admitted to bar, 1988, Massachusetts. *Education:* Georgetown University (B.A., 1985); Boston College (J.D., 1988). ***COURSES: Environmental Law. ***Email:*** gardner@law.stetson.edu

RICHARD B. GRAVES III*, (Instructor)**, admitted to bar, 1991, Texas. *Education:* Washington & Lee University (B.A., 1987); Tulane University (J.D., 1991); University of Houston (LL.M., 1998). ***COURSES: Research & Writing. ***Email:*** graves@law.stetson.edu

BRUCE ROBERT JACOB*, (Dean Emeritus and Professor of Law)**, born Chicago, Illinois, March 26, 1935; admitted to bar, 1959, Florida; 1965, Illinois; 1970, Massachusetts; 1972, Ohio. *Education:* Florida State University (B.A., 1957); Stetson University (J.D., 1959); Northwestern University (LL.M., 1965); Harvard University (S.J.D., 1980); University of Florida (LL.M., 1995). ***COURSES: Taxation, Administrative Law. ***Email:*** jacob@aw.stetson.edu

JULIAN R. KOSSOW*, (Visiting Associate Professor of Law)**, born 1932; admitted to bar, 1968, District of Columbia; 1976, Pennsylvania. *Education:* University of Pennsylvania (B.A., 1955); Georgetown Law School (J.D., 1967). ***COURSES: Estates & Trusts, Property. ***Email:*** kossow@law.stetson.edu

PETER F. LAKE*, (Professor of Law)**, born Marlboro, Massachusetts, November 27, 1958; admitted to bar, 1987, New York. *Education:* Harvard University (A.B., 1981; J.D., 1984). ***COURSES: Torts, Insurance, Jurisprudence. ***Email:*** lake@law.stetson.edu

JEROME C. LATIMER*, (Professor of Law)**, born Tampa, Florida, October 11, 1946; admitted to bar, 1970, Florida. *Education:* Florida State University (B.A., 1967); University of Florida (J.D., 1970). ***COURSES: Evidence, Criminal Law, Clinics. ***Email:*** latimer@law.stetson.edu

JANICE KAY LAWRENCE*, (Assistant Professor of Law)**, born Harlington, Texas; admitted to bar, 1997, New Jersey; 1999, District of Columbia. *Education:* University of Texas (B.A.,, 1987); University of Utah (J.D., 1996); New York University (LL.M., 1997). ***COURSES: Federal Income Taxation. ***Email:*** lawrence@law.stetson.edu

THOMAS CLARK MARKS, JR.*, (Professor of Law)**, born Tampa, Florida, December 14, 1938; admitted to bar, 1963, Florida. *Education:* Florida State University (B.S., 1960); University of Florida (Ph.D., 1971); Stetson University (LL.B., 1963). ***COURSES: United States Constitutional Law, State Constitutional Law. ***Email:*** marks@law.stetson.edu

LIZABETH A. MOODY*, (Distinguished University Professor and Dean Emeritus)**, born Johnson City, Tennessee, July 11, 1934; admitted to bar, 1959, Connecticut; 1960, Ohio. *Education:* Columbia University (A.B., 1956); Yale University (J.D., 1959). ***COURSES: Corporation and Securities Law, Nonprofit Organizations, Legal Profession. ***Email:*** moody@law.stetson.edu

REBECCA C. MORGAN*, (Professor of Law)**, born Missouri, June 4, 1953; admitted to bar, 1981, Florida. *Education:* Central Missouri State University (B.S.B.A., 1975); Stetson College of Law (J.D., 1980). ***COURSES: Elder Law, Interviewing, Counseling, Negotiations, Clinics. ***Email:*** morgan@law.stetson.edu

MADISON MOSLEY, JR.*, (Associate Professor of Law, Law Librarian and Director of Information Services)**, born Leesburg, Florida, January 17, 1950; admitted to bar, 1993, Florida. *Education:* Florida State University (B.A., 1971; Ph.D., 1980); University of North Carolina - Greensboro (M.L.S., 1974); Stetson University (J.D., 1992). ***Email: mosley@law.stetson.edu

LUZ E. ORTIZ NAGLE*, (Associate Professor of Law)**, born Columbia, South America; admitted to bar, Columbia. *Education:* Universidad Pontificia Bolivariana (LL.D., 1981); University of California, Los Angeles (LL.M., 1991; M.A., 1992); College of William and Mary (J.D., 1995). ***COURSES: Latin American Business Law, International Criminal Law, Criminal Law. ***Email:*** nagle@law.stetson.edu

CAROLYN J. NYGREN*, (Visiting Assistant Professor of Law)**, admitted to bar, 1985, Massachusetts. *Education:* Tufts University (B.A., 1963); Northeastern Illinois State University (M.Ed, 1969); University of Chicago (Ph.D., 1972); Harvard (J.D., 1985). ***COURSES: Real Property. ***Email:*** nygren@law.stetson.edu

MARLEEN O'CONNOR*, (Professor of Law)**, born Chicago, Illinois, November 15, 1962; admitted to bar, 1987, Georgia. *Education:* DePaul University (B.S., 1984); Duke University (J.D., 1987). ***COURSES: Business Associations, Law and Economics, Securities Regulation. ***Email:*** oconnor@law.stetson.edu

ANN M. PICCARD*, (Research & Writing Instructor)**, born Tallahassee, Florida, April 11, 1956; admitted to bar, 1986, Florida. *Education:* Florida State University (B.A., 1977); Stetson University College of Law (J.D., 1985). ***COURSES: Legal Research and Writing. ***Email:*** piccard@law.stetson.edu

THERESA PULLEY-RADWAN*, (Assistant Professor of Law)**, admitted to bar, 1995, Ohio. *Education:* University of Dayton (B.A., 1992); College of William and Mary (J.D., 1995). ***COURSES: Commercial Law. ***Email:*** radwan@law.stetson.edu

J. TIM REILLY*, (Distinguished Professorial Lecturer)**, born Milwaukee, Wisconsin, August 6, 1928; admitted to bar, 1959, Florida; 1961, Wisconsin. *Education:* Marquette University (B.A., 1950; M.A., 1952); Stetson College of Law (J.D., 1958). ***COURSES: Remedies, Criminal Procedure, Comparative Legal Systems. ***Email:*** reilly@law.stetson.edu

LAWRENCE D. ROSENTHAL*, (Instructor)**, admitted to bar, 1993, Florida; 1997, District of Columbia. *Education:* Union College (B.A., 1990); Vanderbilt University (J.D., 1993); Georgetown University (LL.M., 1998). ***COURSES: Research & Writing. ***Email:*** rosenthal@law.stetson.edu

JOHN M. SCHEB*, (Distinguished Professorial Lecturer)**, born Orlando, Florida, April 25, 1926; admitted to bar, 1950, Florida. *Education:* University of Florida (J.D., 1950); Florida Southern College (B.A., 1980); University of Virginia (LL.M., 1984); Florida Southern College (D.H.L., Hon.); Stetson University (LL.D., Hon.). ***COURSES: Appellate Practice.

CARY R. SINGLETARY*, (Distinguished Professorial Lecturer)**, born October 14, 1944; admitted to bar, 1973, Florida. *Education:* University of Tampa (B.S., 1968); Rollins College (M.C.S., 1970); Stetson University (J.D., 1973). ***COURSES: Alternative Dispute Resolution. ***Email:*** singletary@law.stetson.edu

W. MCKINLEY SMILEY, JR.*, (Professor of Law)**, born Arcadia, Florida, September 28, 1935; admitted to bar, 1963, Florida. *Education:* Duke University (A.B., 1957); Emory University (J.D., 1962); University of Miami (LL.M., 1967); Yale Visiting Scholar, 1974. ***COURSES: Medical Jurisprudence, Civil Trial Skills. ***Email:*** smiley@law.stetson.edu

***WILLIAM REECE SMITH, JR.*, (Distinguished Professorial Lecturer)**, born Athens, Tennessee, September 19, 1925; admitted to

(This Listing Continued)

STETSON UNIVERSITY COLLEGE OF LAW—Continued

bar, 1949, Florida. *Education:* University of South Carolina (B.S., 1946); University of Florida (J.D., 1949); Oxford University, Oxford, England (Rhodes Scholar, 1952). ***COURSES:*** Professional Responsibility, Contracts.

BRADFORD STONE*, (Charles A. Dana Professor of Law)**, born Detroit, Michigan, April 26, 1929; admitted to bar, 1955, Michigan. *Education:* University of Michigan (A.B., 1951; J.D., 1954); London School of Economics. ***COURSES: Commercial Transactions, Uniform Commercial Code. ***Email:*** stone@law.stetson.edu

MICHAEL I. SWYGERT*, (Professor of Law)**, born Hammond, Indiana, November 20, 1939; admitted to bar, 1968, Illinois. *Education:* Valparaiso University (A.B., 1965; J.D., 1967); Yale University (LL.M., 1968). ***COURSES: Contracts, Commercial Law, Jurisprudence. ***Email:*** swygert@law.stetson.edu

RUTH FLEET THURMAN*, (Professor of Law)**, born St. Petersburg, Florida; admitted to bar, 1963, Florida. *Education:* Smith College (B.A., 1951); Stetson University (J.D., 1963); Columbia University (LL.M., 1984); Cambridge University (Visiting Scholar). ***COURSES: Professional Responsibility, Domestic Relations, Family Law. ***Email:*** thurman@law.stetson.edu

STEPHANIE VAUGHAN*, (Associate Director of Research & Writing & Moot Court Advisor)**, born San Diego, California, February 16, 1966; admitted to bar, 1991, Florida. *Education:* University of Alabama (B.A., 1988); Stetson University (J.D., 1991). ***COURSES: Research & Writing. ***Email:*** vaughan@law.stetson.edu

KAREN A. WILLIAMS*, (Trial Advocacy Fellow)**, born 1955; admitted to bar, 1994, Florida. *Education:* Florida State University (B.S., 1976); University of Central Florida (M.S., 1983); Stetson University (J.D., 1994). ***COURSES: Trial Advocacy, Mock Trial Board. ***Email:*** williams@law.stetson.edu

DARRYL C. WILSON*, (Professor of Law)**, born Chicago, Illinois, November 5, 1961. *Education:* Southern Methodist University (B.F.A. and B.B.A., 1982); University of Florida (J.D., 1984); John Marshall Law School (LL.M., 1989). ***COURSES: Intellectual Property, Real Property, Sports Law. ***Email:*** wilson@law.stetson.edu

JOSEPH LAMAR WOODARD*, (Professor of Law Emeritus and Law Librarian Emeritus)**, born Auburndale, Florida, December 28, 1937; admitted to bar, 1962, Florida. *Education:* University of Florida (B.A., 1959; J.D., 1962); Columbia University (M.L.S., 1964). ***COURSES: Legal Research. ***Email:*** woodard@law.stetson.edu

SUFFOLK UNIVERSITY LAW SCHOOL

120 TREMONT STREET
BOSTON, MASSACHUSETTS 02108-4977
Telephone: (617) 573-8000
Fax: (617) 723-5109

ABA Approved Since 1953.

For over 90 years Suffolk University Law School has been devoted to the education of lawyers. It is now a major legal center with a growing national reputation. The goal of Suffolk University Law School is to educate informed, ethical and effective legal practitioners capable of positively influencing the profession. The curriculum builds upon a strong core of substantive courses that provide extensive exposure to all fundamental areas of the law. This solid base of knowledge is amplified by more than one hundred elective courses covering every area of legal practice.

Innovative concentrations have been developed in High Technology Law, Civil Litigation, Financial Services and Health and Biomedical Law where students interested in these fields have an opportunity to develop substantial depth and breadth of knowledge. Students who complete these concentrations while satisfying certain minimum grade requirements are recognized on graduation as distinguished students in the respective field.

Suffolk Law School faculty combines scholarly attainment and professional achievement with a strong commitment to classroom teaching. Faculty members write widely-used legal texts and articles for major law reviews. They also teach all the required courses. The school's downtown Boston location also allows it to call upon outstanding leaders of the judiciary and practicing bar community as distinguished lecturers and faculty.

The scholarly and theoretical focus of the classroom is complemented by significant opportunities to develop practical skills. Two law reviews and a Trial Law Journal offer intensive writing experience on topics of national and international importance. Trial advocacy competitions provide opportunities to develop advocacy skills while exploring emerging legal policy issues. Nine clinical and internship programs offer Suffolk students hands-on experience in preparing cases and representing clients. The Public Internship Program offers over 250 placement opportunities in Courts, Federal and State Agencies, and with non-profit legal aid providers throughout New England. The private internship program provides corporate and law firm experience for 75 students throughout the region.

In 1999, the law school moved into a new $65 million 300,000 sq. ft. technologically precedent setting state of the art law school building located on Beacon Hill at the Tremont and Park streets corner of historic Boston Common, establishing a new standard for American legal education.

The Law School program is fully accredited by both the American Bar Association and the Association of American Law Schools. Faculty, courses, academic standards and competitive opportunities are identical for both Day and Evening Divisions.

The Law School is surrounded by Boston's financial and business districts, the Massachusetts State House, Government Center, and federal, state and municipal courts. This location makes the school an integral part of Boston's legal community. A wealth of nearby business, government and judicial institutions offer outstanding opportunities for professional experience.

Suffolk University Law School's student body includes graduates of more than 340 colleges and universities, including many of the most prestigious in the nation. Women make up more than half the student body, and 15% of entering students are members of minority groups.

One of the best law libraries in New England, Suffolk's Law Library provides students with outstanding opportunities to develop their research skills. Two computer laboratories and a computerized library facility offer the instruction and equipment necessary to develop skills in the growing field of computerized research and computer applications.

The Day Division enrolls students who are able to devote substantially

(This Listing Continued)

SUFFOLK UNIVERSITY LAW SCHOOL—Continued

all their time to the study of law. This program requires the traditional three years (six semesters) to complete. The Evening Division is designed for students who pursue a legal education on a part-time basis. It can be completed in four years (eight semesters) of part-time study. Graduates of both Divisions receive the Juris Doctor (J.D.) Degree.

The J.D./M.B.A., J.D./M.P.A. and J.D./M.S.F. four-year programs, sponsored by the Suffolk University Law School and the Suffolk University Sawyer School of Management, offer an integrated professional education in law management; and law and public administration law and finance. Students pursue coursework in both the Law School and the School of Management, with curriculum requirements determined jointly by both schools. The J.D./M.S.C.J. and J.D./M.S.I.E. four-year program offers an integrated education in law and criminal justice and law and international economics.

Dean: Robert H. Smith (617) 573-8155
Associate Dean: John C. Deliso (617) 573-8155
Associate Dean: Bernard V. Keenan (617) 573-8157
Associate Dean: Marc G. Perlin (617) 573-8157
Dean of Students: Bernadette T. Feeley (617) 573-8157
Dean of Admissions: Gail N. Ellis (617) 573-8144

FULL TIME FACULTY

ROBERT H. SMITH,* (Dean and Professor)**, born Maplewood, New Jersey, 1946; admitted to bar, 1972, Illinois; 1978, Massachusetts. *Education:* Wesleyan University (B.A., 1968); University of Chicago (J.D., 1972). ***COURSES: Mediation, Civil Procedure.

MARIE ASHE,* (Professor)**, born Worcester, Massachusetts, May 23, 1943; admitted to bar, 1980, Nebraska; 1986, West Virginia; 1992, Massachusetts. *Education:* Clark University (B.A., 1965); Tufts University (M.A., 1980); University of Nebraska (J.D., 1979). ***COURSES: Constitutional Law, Criminal Law, Jurisprudence, Clinical.

JEFFERY CYRIL ATIK,* (Professor)**, born Cleveland, Ohio, June 5, 1956; admitted to bar, 1983, New York and Connecticut; 1984, Massachusetts; 1989, Missouri. *Education:* University of California at Berkeley (A.B., 1976); Yale University (J.D., 1982). ***COURSES: International Business Transactions, European Community Law, Regulated Industries.

MICHAEL A. AVERY,* (Associate Professor)**, born Chicago, Illinois, December 5, 1944; admitted to bar, 1970, Connecticut; 1977, Massachusetts. *Education:* Yale (B.A, 1966, LL.B., 1970). ***COURSES: Evidence, Civil Procedure I, Pre-Trial Litigation.

R. LISLE BAKER,* (Professor)**, born Louisville, Kentucky, August 2, 1942; admitted to bar, 1968, Massachusetts. *Education:* Williams College (A.B., 1964); Harvard University Law School (LL.B., 1966). ***COURSES: Property, Land Use, Law Practice Management, Mediation.

CARTER G. BISHOP,* (Professor)**, born 1948; admitted to bar, 1976, Iowa; 1979, District of Columbia: 1979, Minnesota. *Education:* Ball State University (B.S., 1971); Drake (M.B.A., 1973; J.D., 1975); New York University (LL.M., 1977). ***COURSES: Contracts, Basic Federal Income Taxation.

KAREN MICHELE BLUM,* (Professor)**, born New Haven, Connecticut, September 24, 1946; admitted to bar, 1974, Massachusetts. *Education:* Wells College (B.A., 1968); Suffolk University Law School (J.D., 1974); Harvard University Law School (LL.M., 1976). ***COURSES: Civil Procedure, Civil Rights. ***Email:*** kblum@acad.suffolk.edu

ERIC BLUMENSON,* (Professor)**, born New York, New York, February 23, 1948; admitted to bar, 1972, Washington and California; 1974, Massachusetts. *Education:* Wesleyan University (B.A., 1968); Harvard University Law School (J.D., 1972). ***COURSES: Criminal Law, Trial Advocacy, Clinical.

BARRY BROWN,* (Professor)**, born 1946; admitted to bar, 1973, Massachusetts. *Education:* Harvard (A.B., 1968; Ed.M., 1969; J.D., 1972). ***COURSES: Property, Biomedical Ethics and Public Policy.

STEPHEN J. CALLAHAN,* (Professor)**, born Norwood, Massachusetts, December 10, 1945; admitted to bar, 1976, Massachusetts and Texas. *Education:* Middlebury College (A.B., 1968); Suffolk University (J.D., 1975). ***COURSES: Criminal Law, Constitutional Law, Clinical Programs.

ROSANNA CAVALLARO,* (Professor)**, born Brooklyn, New York, November 1, 1961; admitted to bar, 1986, Massachusetts. *Education:* Harvard University (A.B., 1983); Harvard University Law School (J.D., 1986). ***COURSES: Criminal Law, Criminal Procedure.

GERARD J. CLARK,* (Professor)**, born New Jersey, June 16, 1944; admitted to bar, 1970, New York and New Jersey; 1976, Massachusetts. *Education:* Seton Hall University (B.A., 1966); Columbia University (J.D., 1969). ***COURSES: Constitutional Law, Federal Courts, Professional Responsibility.

WILLIAM T. CORBETT,* (Professor)**, born Boston, Massachusetts, May 16, 1946; admitted to bar, 1975, Massachusetts; 1976, Maine. *Education:* Providence College (A.B., 1969); Boston College (M.B.A., 1972); Suffolk University (J.D., 1975); Boston University (LL.M., 1981). ***COURSES: Taxation.

JOSEPH D. CRONIN,* (Professor)**, born Newton, Massachusetts, August 10, 1937; admitted to bar, 1967, Massachusetts. *Education:* Boston College (A.B., 1961; M.A., 1962); Boston University (J.D., 1967). ***COURSES: Constitutional Law.

KATE NACE DAY,* (Professor)**, born 1948; admitted to bar, 1981, District of Columbia; 1983, California. *Education:* Cal. Berkeley (J.D., 1980). ***COURSES: Constitutional Law, Constitutional Law and the Constructions of Childhood, Constitutional Theory..

VICTORIA JEANNETTE DODD,* (Professor)**, born Los Angeles, California, July 8, 1948; admitted to bar, 1978, California; 1986, Massachusetts. *Education:* Radcliffe College (B.A., 1970); University of Southern California (J.D., 1978). ***COURSES: Civil Procedure, Constitutional Law, Law and Education.

MALCOLM M. DONAHUE,* (Professor)**, born Boston, Massachusetts, April 4, 1921; admitted to bar, 1951, Massachusetts. *Education:* Harvard University (A.B., 1944); Boston University (J.D., 1950). ***COURSES: Conflict of Laws and Administrative Law.

STEVEN EISENSTAT,* (Professor)**, born New York, September 27, 1951; admitted to bar, 1980, Massachusetts. *Education:* State University of New York at Buffalo (B.A., 1972; M.Ed., 1974); Northeastern University (J.D., 1980). ***COURSES: Torts, Civil Procedures.

(This Listing Continued)

SUFFOLK UNIVERSITY LAW SCHOOL—Continued

CLIFFORD E. ELIAS*, (Professor)**, born Lawrence, Massachusetts; admitted to bar, 1958, Massachusetts. *Education:* Yale University (B.A., 1952); Boston University (J.D., 1958). ***COURSES: Evidence, Health Care Law.

VALERIE EPPS*, (Professor)**, born United Kingdom, March 6, 1943; admitted to bar, 1972, Massachusetts; U.S. District Court, District of Massachusetts; U.S. Court of Appeals, 1st Circuit; U.S. Supreme Court. *Education:* Birmingham University (B.A., with honors, 1965); Boston University (J.D., 1972); Harvard University Law School (LL.M., 1978). ***COURSES: International Law, Immigration Law, Constitutional Law.

JOHN E. FENTON, JR.*, (Professor)**, born Lawrence, Massachusetts, October 28, 1930; admitted to bar, 1954, Massachusetts. *Education:* College of the Holy Cross (A.B., 1951); Boston College (J.D., 1954); Harvard University (LL.M., 1955). ***COURSES: Evidence, Advanced Evidence.

STEVEN FERREY*, (Professor)**, born Bloomington, Indiana, May 17, 1950; admitted to bar, 1976, California; 1978, Massachusetts. *Education:* Pomona College (B.A., 1972); University of California at Berkeley (M.A., 1977); University of California at Boalt Hall (J.D., 1975); University of London (Fulbright Fellow, 1976). ***COURSES: Environmental and Energy Law, Contracts.

THOMAS FINN*, (Professor)**, born Chicago, Illinois, July 26, 1950; admitted to bar, 1976, Rhode Island; 1985, Massachusetts. *Education:* Brown University (B.A., 1972); Georgetown (J.D., 1975). ***COURSES: Criminal, Civil Procedure, Children's Law. ***Email:*** tfinn@acad.suffolk.edu

KEITH R. FISHER*, (Associate Professor)**, admitted to bar, 1980, District of Columbia. *Education:* Princeton University (A.B., 1975); Georgetown University (J.D., 1980). ***COURSES: Contracts, Banking Law.

JOSEPH A. FRANCO*, (Associate Professor)**, born Salt Lake City, Utah, October 16, 1957; admitted to bar, 1986, New York. *Education:* University of Notre Dame (B.A., 1979); Yale University (M.A., 1984; J.D., 1984). ***COURSES: Securities Regulation, Corporate Finance. ***Email:*** jfranco@acad.suffolk.edu

JOSEPH WILLIAM GLANNON*, (Professor)**, born New York, New York, March 22, 1946; admitted to bar, 1977, Massachusetts. *Education:* Harvard University (B.A., 1968; M.A.T., 1971; J.D., 1977). ***COURSES: Torts, Civil Procedure.

DWIGHT GOLANN*, (Professor)**, born Rochester, New York, September 1, 1947; admitted to bar, 1973, Massachusetts. *Education:* Amherst College (B.A., 1969); Harvard University (J.D., 1973). ***COURSES: Financial Services, Alternative Dispute Resolution, Remedies.

LORIE M. GRAHAM*, (Assistant Professor)**, admitted to bar, Massachusetts and New York. *Education:* Syracuse University (B.S., 1985); Syracuse University College of Law (J.D., 1990); Howard Law School (LL.M., 1995). ***COURSES: Property, International Union Rights, Native American Law.

MARC D. GREENBAUM*, (Professor)**, born Jersey City, New Jersey, October 1, 1951; admitted to bar, 1977, Massachusetts. *Education:* Rutgers University (B.A., 1973); Boston College (J.D., 1976). ***COURSES: Labor Law, Employment Law, Employment Discrimination, Public Sector Labor Law.

STEPHEN C. HICKS*, (Professor)**, born Halifax, Yorkshire, United Kingdom, March 6, 1949; admitted to bar, 1979, Ohio. *Education:* Downing College (M.A., 1971; LL.B., 1972); University of Virginia (LL.M., 1977). ***COURSES: Torts, Comparative Law, Legal Theory.

CECIL J. HUNT, II*, (Associate Professor)**, born 1952; admitted to bar, 1980, Massachusetts. *Education:* Harvard (A.B., 1975); Boston College (J.D., 1980). ***COURSES: Property, Banking Law.

CATHERINE T. JUDGE*, (Professor)**, born Lowell, Massachusetts, March 7, 1928; admitted to bar, 1958, Massachusetts. *Education:* Boston University (B.B.A., 1950); Suffolk University Law School (J.D., 1957; LL.M., 1960). ***COURSES: Contracts, Equitable Remedies.

BERNARD V. KEENAN*, (Associate Dean and Professor)**, born Worcester, Massachusetts, September 17, 1947; admitted to bar, 1973, Massachusetts. *Education:* College of the Holy Cross (B.A., 1970); Georgetown University (J.D., 1973); Columbia University (LL.M., 1981). ***COURSES: Property, Land Use.

CHARLES P. KINDREGAN, JR.*, (Professor)**, born Philadelphia, Pennsylvania, June 18, 1935; admitted to bar, 1966, Illinois; 1968, Massachusetts. *Education:* LaSalle University (B.A., 1957; M.A., 1957); Chicago-Kent University (J.D., 1966); Northwestern University (LL.M., 1967). ***COURSES: Family Law, Torts, Professional Responsibility.

HERBERT LEMELMAN*, (Professor)**, born Boston, Massachusetts, June 13, 1933; admitted to bar, 1957, Massachusetts; 1959, New York. *Education:* Northeastern University (B.A., 1954); Boston University (J.D., 1957); New York University (LL.M., 1958). ***COURSES: Commercial Law, Property, Bankruptcy. ***Email:*** hlemelma@acad.suffolk.edu

JOSEPH P. MCETTRICK*, (Professor)**, born Boston, Massachusetts, March 10, 1946; admitted to bar, 1971, Massachusetts. *Education:* Boston College (A.B., 1967; J.D., 1971); Harvard University (M.P.A., 1987). ***COURSES: Contracts, Consumer Law, Equitable Remedies.

STEPHEN MCJOHN*, (Professor)**, born Chicago, Illinois, March 29, 1959; admitted to bar, 1985, Illinois. *Education:* Northwestern University (B.A., 1981; J.D., 1985). ***COURSES: Commercial Law, Law and Economics.

ELIZABETH M. MCKENZIE*, (Law Library Director and Associate Professor)**, born Lexington, Kentucky, June 27, 1954; admitted to bar, 1981, Kentucky and Federal Court. *Education:* Transylvania University (B.A., 1975); University of Kentucky (J.D., 1981; M.S.L.S., 1984). ***COURSES: Advanced Legal Research. ***Email:*** emckenzi@acad.suffolk.edu

RUSSELL G. MURPHY*, (Professor)**, born South Weymouth, Massachusetts, March 16, 1944; admitted to bar, 1973, Massachusetts. *Education:* University of Massachusetts (B.A., 1966); Suffolk University Law School (J.D., 1973). ***COURSES: Constitutional Law, Civil Procedure, Federal Jurisdiction, Criminal Law.

JOHN J. NOLAN*, (Professor)**, born Derby, Connecticut, November 1, 1928; admitted to bar, 1955, Connecticut and Massachusetts. *Education:* College of the Holy Cross (B.S., 1950); Cornell University Medical College (1950-1951); Suffolk University Law School (J.D., 1955); Harvard University (LL.M., 1962). ***COURSES: Administrative Law, Workers Compensation.

JOSEPH NOLAN*, (Judge/University Professor)**, born Boston, Massachusetts, June 14, 1925. *Education:* Boston College (B.S., 1950; LL.B., 1954). ***COURSES: Jurisprudence, Trial Practice, Constitutional Law, Real Estate Mortgages. ***Email:*** jnolan@acad.suffolk.edu

BERNARD M. ORTWEIN*, (Professor)**, born Bethlehem, Pennsylvania, July 2, 1944; admitted to bar, 1972, Massachusetts. *Education:* University of Richmond (B.A., 1966); Suffolk University Law School (J.D., 1972); Harvard University (LL.M., 1974). ***COURSES: Criminal Law, Evidence, Professional Responsibility.

(This Listing Continued)

SUFFOLK UNIVERSITY LAW SCHOOL—Continued

MARC G. PERLIN*, (Associate Dean and Professor)**, born Brookline, Massachusetts, July 15, 1948; admitted to bar, 1973, Massachusetts. *Education:* McGill University (1966-1967); Boston University (B.A., 1970); Northeastern University (J.D., 1973). ***COURSES: Family Law, State Civil Practice.

RICHARD M. PERLMUTTER*, (Professor)**, born Cambridge, Massachusetts, December 3, 1942; admitted to bar, 1967, Massachusetts. *Education:* Tufts University (A.B., 1964); Harvard University (LL.B., 1967). ***COURSES: Contracts, Equity, Remedies, Sports Law, Negotiation.

RICHARD G. PIZZANO*, (Professor)**, born Boston, Massachusetts; admitted to bar, 1966, Massachusetts. *Education:* Suffolk University (B.A., 1963; J.D., 1966); Harvard University (Visiting Scholar 1979-1980). ***COURSES: Business Associations (Corporations), Legal Interviewing and Counseling, Agency.

ANTHONY P. POLITO*, (Associate Professor)**, born 1964; admitted to bar, 1990, New York. *Education:* Harvard (S.B., 1986; M.I.T., J.D., 1989); New York University (LL.M., 1995). ***COURSES: Basic Federal Income Taxation, Corporate Taxation, Taxation of International Transactions.

ELBERT L. ROBERTSON*, (Associate Professor)**, admitted to bar, Illinois. *Education:* Brown University (B.A., 1980); Columbia (J.D., 1989); Pennsylvania (M.A., 1992). ***COURSES: Antitrust Law.

CHARLES E. ROUNDS, JR.*, (Professor)**, born Middletown, Connecticut, December 16, 1946; admitted to bar, 1976, Massachusetts. *Education:* Columbia University (B.A., 1969); Suffolk University Law School (J.D., 1976). ***COURSES: Trusts.

MICHAEL RUSTAD*, (Professor)**, born Humboldt, Minnesota, July 9, 1949; admitted to bar, 1986, Massachusetts. *Education:* University of North Dakota (B.A., 1971); University of Maryland (M.A., 1973); Boston College (Ph.D., 1981); Suffolk University (J.D., 1984); Harvard University (LL.M., 1986). ***COURSES: Commercial Law, Torts.

ANTHONY BENSON SANDOE*, (Professor)**, born Bristol, Virginia, June 18, 1944; admitted to bar, 1971, New York; 1972, Massachusetts. *Education:* Williams College (A.B., 1966); Boston College (J.D., 1970); Boston University. ***COURSES: Estates and Trusts, Estate Administration.

LINDA SANDSTROM SIMARD*, (Professor)**, born Dover, New Jersey, August 18, 1964; admitted to bar, 1989, Massachusetts. *Education:* University of Delaware (B.S., 1986); Boston College (J.D., 1989). ***COURSES: Civil Procedure, Federal Courts.

TOMMY F. THOMPSON*, (Professor)**, born Medina, New York, May 21, 1947; admitted to bar, 1975, Indiana. *Education:* University of Notre Dame (B.S., 1968); Indiana University at Bloomington (J.D., 1975). ***COURSES: Federal Taxation.

RICHARD VACCO*, (Professor)**, born Bridgeport, Connecticut, August 27, 1940; admitted to bar, 1967, Massachusetts; 1968, New Hampshire. *Education:* Colby College (B.A. 1962); Suffolk Law (J.D., 1967). ***COURSES: Business Associations, Business Planning. ***Email:*** rvacco@acad.suffolk.edu

***ROBERT P. WASSON JR.*, (Professor)**, born 1954; admitted to bar, Illinois, 1979; Massachusetts, 1981. *Education:* Harvard (B.A., 1976; J.D., 1979).

TIMOTHY WILTON*, (Professor)**, born New York, New York, October 3, 1946; admitted to bar, 1971, Massachusetts; 1983, Michigan. *Education:* Harvard University (A.B., 1968; J.D., 1971; LL.M., 1977). ***COURSES: Trial Advocacy, Evidence, Constitutional Law.

JEFFREY D. WITTENBERG*, (Professor)**, born 1945; admitted to bar, Illinois, 1973; Minnesota, 1973. *Education:* San Francisco State College (B.A., 1968); Cal (J.D., 1972). ***COURSES: Contracts, Products Liability Seminar.

DAVID YAMADA*, (Associate Professor)**, born East Chicago, Indiana, July 22, 1959; admitted to bar, 1986, New York. *Education:* Valparaiso University (B.A., 1981); New York University (J.D., 1985). ***COURSES: Employment and Labor Law, Torts, Lawyering Skills.

SYRACUSE UNIVERSITY COLLEGE OF LAW

E.I. WHITE HALL
SYRACUSE, NEW YORK 13244-1030
Telephone: (315) 443-2524
Fax: (315) 443-4213

ABA Approved Since 1923

The Syracuse University College of Law was founded in 1895 as the second college at Syracuse University. As one of the older law schools in the United States it was a charter member of the Association of American Law Schools (AALS) and one of only three law schools in New York state on the original approved list of the American Bar Association (1923). Today the College enrolls 777 students in a day-only program. The J.D. may be pursued over three or four years.

Syracuse Law is committed to providing innovative approaches to the study of law, building on the framework of a traditional legal education. Our curriculum seeks to bridge the gap between theory and practice by providing law students with opportunities for applied learning - learning that focuses on real world problems and issues. The Applied Learning Program at Syracuse Law offers students hands-on experience throughout their law school education. The curriculum includes advocacy training; clinical experiences; specialization within selected areas of the law, including Family Law, Global Law, Business Law and Law, Technology and Management. In addition, Syracuse offers a wide range of interdisciplinary opportunities which integrate traditional lawyering skills with insights from other professions and disciplines.

The College of Law has 40 full-time tenure track faculty and 43 adjunct faculty. The full-time faculty is a diverse group of men and women who bring wide-ranging experiences in practice, scholarship, and community service to the classroom. Valuing teaching and scholarship equally, the faculty is concerned with preparing students for the diverse opportunities available to them. The adjunct ranks are drawn from distinguished jurists and practitioners.

From its very beginning, the College has believed in an admission decision process that is more complex than merely rank-ordering applicants based on a numerical formula. This has resulted in a student body that is motivated, well-qualified for the study of law, and includes geographic and ethnic diversity. While the LSAT scores and undergraduate grade point average of the 2,100 applicants who apply to Syracuse Law are important, the College also takes into account other factors of importance, such as significant progression in grades earned or unusually difficult coursework in undergraduate or graduate

(This Listing Continued)

SYRACUSE UNIVERSITY COLLEGE OF LAW—Continued

programs or a special experience that the faculty considers important. Past successes in overcoming personal hardship, including such burdens as poverty or disability are also considered. Today, about 50% of the student body is women, less than 50% of the student body comes from New York state (with California the second largest feeder state), and 20% of the student body is made up of students of color.

The College of Law is located on the Syracuse University 200 acre main campus, overlooking downtown Syracuse. Often cited as one of the best twenty-five places in the nation to live, Syracuse's 500,000 residents enjoy a full range of cultural and sporting activities--from symphony and opera to NCAA Division I football and basketball.

Dean: Daan Braveman (315) 443-2524
Director, Admissions: Patricia K. Golla (315) 443-1962
Associate Director, Financial Aid: Gina M. Soliz (315) 443-1963
Director, Library: Thomas R. French (315) 443-9571
Placement: Alexandra Epsilanty (315) 443-1941
Alumni Affairs: Richard Ingles (315) 443-1965

FULL TIME FACULTY

DAAN BRAVEMAN*, (Dean and Professor of Law)**, born 1947; admitted to bar, 1972, Pennsylvania; 1982, New York. *Education:* University of Rochester (A.B., 1969); University of Pennsylvania (J.D., 1972). ***COURSES: Civil Procedure, Civil Rights, Constitutional Law, Federal Courts, Federal Litigation.

DONNA E. ARZT*, (Professor)**, born 1954; admitted to bar, 1979, Massachusetts; 1988, New York. *Education:* Brandeis University (B.A., 1976); Harvard University (J.D., 1979); Columbia University (LL.M., 1988). ***COURSES: Comparative Law, Consumer Law, International Human Rights, Legal Method, Refugee Law, Religion and State Soviet Law.

ROBERT H.A. ASHFORD*, (Professor)**, born 1943; admitted to bar, 1970, California; 1979, District of Columbia; 1980, New York. *Education:* University of South Florida (B.A., 1965); Harvard University (J.D., 1969). ***COURSES: Administrative Law, Binary Economics, Corporations, Business Planning, Professional Responsibility, Securities Regulation.

LAUREN A. AUSTIN*, (Legal Writing Professor)**, admitted to bar, New York. *Education:* Dartmouth College (B.A., 1981); Syracuse University (J.D., 1993). ***COURSES: Legal Writing & Research. ***Email:*** laaustin@law.syr.edu

WILLIAM C. BANKS*, (Professor)**, born 1948; admitted to bar, 1974, Colorado; 1980, New York. *Education:* University of Nebraska (B.A., 1971; J.D., 1974); University of Denver (M.S.L.S., 1982). ***COURSES: Administrative Law, Clinical Teaching, Constitutional Law, Energy Law, Environmental Law, National Security Law, Public Law Process.

JOSEPH BARRETTE*, (Professor)**, born 1948; admitted to bar, 1973, New York. *Education:* Providence College (B.S., 1969); Catholic University (J.D., 1972). ***COURSES: Advanced Criminal Procedure, Art and Entertainment Clinic, Civil Practice Law and Rules, Civil and Criminal Clinics Law and Lawyering, Law Firm.

PETER A. BELL*, (Professor)**, born 1945; admitted to bar, 1971, California; 1972, District of Columbia. *Education:* Wesleyan University (B.A., 1967); Stanford University (J.D., 1970). ***COURSES: Criminal Law, Evidence, Family Law, Federal Jurisdictions, Law Firm, Torts.

LESLIE BENDER*, (Professor)**, born 1952; admitted to bar, 1979, West Virginia; 1985, Massachusetts; 1992, New York. *Education:* Chatham College (B.A., 1973); University of Pittsburgh (J.D., 1979); Harvard University (LL.M., 1985). ***COURSES: Civil Rights, Contemporary Legal Theories, Federal Jurisdiction, Law and Medicine--Bioethics, Real Estate Transactions, Torts.

BARBARA BURNETT*, (Professor)**, born 1947; admitted to bar, 1972, New York. *Education:* University of Kansas (B.A., 1969); New York University (J.D., 1972). ***COURSES: Entertainment Law, Estates, Intellectual Property, Unfair Competition.

ANGELA OLIVIA BURTON*, (Assistant Professor)**, admitted to bar, 1992, New York. *Education:* Cornell University (B.S., 1981); New York University (J.D., 1991). ***COURSES: Family Law, Clinic, Legal Writing & Research. ***Email:*** aoburton@law.syr.edu

CHRISTIAN C DAY*, (Professor of Law)**, born 1946; admitted to bar, 1970, Pennsylvania.. *Education:* Cornell (A.B., 1967); New York University (J.D.,1970).. ***COURSES: Corporations; Land Use Planning, Decedents Estates & Trusts, Real Estate Transactions, Business Finance and Economy..

LISA A. DOLAK*, (Associate Professor)**, born 1961; admitted to bar, 1989, New York. *Education:* Duquesne University (B.S., 1983); Syracuse University College of Law (J.D., 1988). ***COURSES: Patents and Trade Secrets, Federal Courts.

KATHLEEN D. DOLE*, (Legal Writing Professor)**, *Education:* St. Lawrence University (M.A., 1987); Albany Law School (J.D., 1990). ***COURSES: Legal Writing & Research. ***Email:*** kddole@law.syr.edu

SAMUEL J.M. DONNELLY*, (Professor)**, born 1934; admitted to bar, 1961, New Jersey; 1963, New York. *Education:* Fordham University (A.B., 1956); Harvard University (LL.B., 1960); New York University (LL.M., 1966). ***COURSES: Capital Punishment, Commercial Law, Consumer Protection.

DAVID M. DRIESEN*, (Associate Professor of Law)**, born 1958; admitted to bar, 1990, Washington; 1992, Pennsylvania; 1993, District of Columbia. *Education:* Oberlin Conservatory of Music (B.M., 1980); Yale School of Music (M.M., 1983); Yale Law School (J.D., 1989). ***COURSES: Environmental Law, Law Firm, International Environmental Law.

RICHARD A. ELLISON*, (Professor)**, born 1940; admitted to bar, 1966, New York. *Education:* Community College of New York (B.B.A., 1962); St. John's University (LL.B., 1965). ***COURSES: Conflict Resolution through Negotiation, Constitutional Law, Family Law, Health Law, Juvenile Law, Law and Education, Developmental Disabilities Law.

THOMAS R. FRENCH*, (Associate Professor & Director, Law Library)**, born Bath, New York, August 5, 1948; admitted to bar, 1987, Kentucky. *Education:* SUNY Oswego (B.A., 1971); SUNY Geneseo (M.L.S., 1975); University of Cincinnati (M.A., 1978); Northern Kentucky University Chase College of Law (J.D., 1987). ***COURSES: Intro to American Law, Advanced Legal Research. ***Email:*** trfrench@law.syr.edu

(This Listing Continued)

SYRACUSE UNIVERSITY COLLEGE OF LAW—Continued

THOMAS R. FRENCH*, (Associate Professor and Director, Law Library)**, born Bath, NewYork, 1948; admitted to bar, 1987, Kentucky. *Education:* SUNY at Oswego (B.A., 1971); SUNY at Geneseo (M.L.S., 1975); University of Cincinnati (M.A., 1978); Northern Kentucky, Chase College of Law (J.D., 1987). ***COURSES: Legal Research.

MARTIN L. FRIED*, (Crandall Melvin Professor of Wills and Trusts)**, born New York, N.Y., February 11, 1934; admitted to bar, 1959, New York. *Education:* Antioch College (B.A., 1955); Columbia Law School (LL.B., 1958); New York University School of Law (LL.M., 1968). ***COURSES: Estates and Trusts, Federal Income Taxation, Property.

RICHARD I. GOLDSMITH*, (Professor)**, born 1942; admitted to bar, 1966, New York. *Education:* University of Rochester (A.B., 1962); New York University (LL.B., 1965). ***COURSES: Administrative Law, Civil Procedure, Environmental Law, Public Law Process.

THEODORE HAGELIN*, (Professor)**, born 1943; admitted to bar, 1970, Pennsylvania. *Education:* University of Pennsylvania, Wharton School (B.S., 1965); Temple University (J.D., 1970); Harvard University (LL.M., 1972). ***COURSES: Computers and the Law, Regulated Industries, Telecommunications Law.

MARGARET M. HARDING*, (Associate Professor)**, born 1960; admitted to bar, 1987, New York. *Education:* Boston University (B.A., 1982); Georgetown University Law Center (J.D., 1986). ***COURSES: Torts, Alternative Dispute Resolution; & Courses in the Business Law Area; Con Law. ***Email:*** mharding@law.syr.edu

PATRICIA HASSETT*, (Professor)**, born 1940; admitted to bar, 1966, New York; 1992, United Kingdom. *Education:* Elmira College (A.B., 1962); Syracuse University (LL.B., 1966); Harvard University (LL.M., 1973). ***COURSES: Criminal Law, Criminal Procedure.

PETER E. HERZOG*, (Crandall Melvin Professor of Law Emeritus)**, born Vienna, Austria, December 25, 1925; admitted to bar, 1957, New York. *Education:* Hobart College (B.A., cum laude, 1952); Syracuse University College of Law (J.D., summa cum laude, 1955); Columbia University School of Law (LL.M., 1956). ***COURSES: Torts, Conflict of Laws, Comparative Law, European Union Law.

PAULA C. JOHNSON*, (Associate Professor)**, born 1959; admitted to bar, 1985, Massachusetts; 1988, District of Columbia. *Education:* University of Maryland (B.A., 1981); Temple University (J.D., 1985); Georgetown University (LL.M., 1990). ***COURSES: Clinical Teaching, Criminal Procedure, Property.

HILARY KROMELOW JOSEPHS*, (Professor of Law)**, born February 23, 1945; admitted to bar, 1978, Hawaii; 1980, New York. *Education:* Radcliffe College (A.B., 1966); University of Hawaii (J.D., 1978). ***COURSES: Contracts, Comparative Law, International Law, International Transactions.

ARLENE KANTER*, (Professor, Director, Clinical Legal Education)**, born 1954; admitted to bar, 1982, New York; 1984, Pennsylvania; 1985, District of Columbia. *Education:* Trinity College (B.A., 1976); New York University (J.D., 1981); Georgetown University (LL.M., 1983). ***COURSES: Civil Rights, Employment Discrimination, Federal Rights, Health Care Law.

GARY KELDER*, (Professor)**, born 1948; admitted to bar, 1971, Massachusetts. *Education:* Boston University (J.D., 1971); New York University (LL.M., 1972). ***COURSES: Administration of Criminal Justice, American Indian Law, Conflict of Laws, Criminal Law.

DEBORAH KENN*, (Associate Professor and Director, Housing Finance Clinic)**, born New York, N.Y., December 1, 1955; admitted to bar, 1981, New York. *Education:* Eisenhower College (B.A., 1977); State University of New York at Buffalo (J.D., 1980). ***COURSES: Affordable Housing Development, Community Development Law.

M. LOUISE LANTZY*, (Professor)**, born Philadelphia, Pennsylvania, March 8, 1943. *Education:* Pennsylvania State University (B.S., 1965); Drexel University (M.L.S., 1976); Syracuse University (J.D., 1991). ***COURSES: Legal Writing, Law Firm.

LAURA G. LAPE*, (Associate Professor)**, born 1952; admitted to bar, 1986, Massachusetts. *Education:* University of North Carolina (M.A., 1985; J.D., 1986). ***COURSES: Estates, Intellectual Property, Property.

TRAVIS H.D. LEWIN*, (Professor)**, born Long Beach, California, August 24, 1933; admitted to bar, 1958, South Dakota; 1968, New York. *Education:* Southern State Teachers College (B.A., 1958); South Dakota University (LL.B., 1958); University of Michigan (S.J.D., 1968). ***COURSES: Trial, Evidence, Criminal Law and Procedure, Law and Psychiatry.

ROBIN PAUL MALLOY*, (Professor of Law and Economics)**, born 1956; admitted to bar, 1980, Florida. *Education:* Purdue University (B.S., 1977); University of Florida (J.D., 1980); University of Illinois (LL.M., 1983). ***COURSES: Contracts, Law and Economics, Property, Real Estate Transactions, Sales, Secured Transactions.

STEVEN MARCHESE*, (Legal Writing Professor)**, admitted to bar, 1993, Michigan; 1994, New York. *Education:* Yale University (B.A., 1998); New York University School of Law (J.D., 1993). ***COURSES: Legal Writing & Research. ***Email:*** smmarch1@law.syr.edu

THOMAS J. MARONEY*, (Professor)**, born 1938; admitted to bar, 1963, New York. *Education:* Syracuse University (B.A., 1961; LL.B., 1963). ***COURSES: Alternative Dispute Resolution, Antitrust, Civil Rights, Constitutional Law.

JANIS MCDONALD*, (Associate Professor)**, born 1948; admitted to bar, 1977, District of Columbia. *Education:* George Washington University (B.A., 1972); Hofstra University (J.D., 1977); Yale University (LL.M., 1988). ***COURSES: Constitutional Law, Criminal Law, Employee Discrimination, Legal Ethics, Legal History, Trial Advocacy.

JILL M. PAQUETTE*, (Legal Writing Professor)**, *Education:* Fordham University - Fordham College (B.A., 1998); Harvard Law School (J.D., 1991). ***COURSES: Legal Writing & Research. ***Email:*** jmpaquet@law.syr.edu

ROBERT J. RABIN*, (Professor)**, born 1939; admitted to bar, 1965, New York. *Education:* Cornell University (A.B., 1961); Harvard University (LL.B., 1964); New York University (LL.M., 1965). ***COURSES: Administrative Law, Commercial Transactions, Conflict Resolution, Contracts, Labor Law, Law Firm.

SARAH H. RAMSEY*, (Professor of Law)**, born 1943; admitted to bar, 1974, North Carolina, 1988, New York. *Education:* Duke University (B.A., 1965); University of North Carolina at Chapel Hill (M.A., 1966; J.D., 1973); University of Michigan (LL.M., 1982). ***COURSES: Family Law, Children and the Law, Family Issues.

WILHELMINA REUBEN-COOKE*, (Professor)**, born 1946; admitted to bar, 1973, Michigan; 1975, District of Columbia. *Education:* Duke University (B.A., 1967); University of Michigan (J.D., 1973). ***COURSES: Administrative Law, Estates, Property, Regulated Industries, Women and the Law.

RICHARD S. RISMAN*, (Assistant Professor of Law & Director, Law Firm)**, born Buffalo, New York, January 26, 1960; admitted to bar, 198, New York. *Education:* Suny Buffalo (B.A., 1981). ***COURSES: Skills. ***Email:*** rsrisman@law.syr.edu

(This Listing Continued)

SYRACUSE UNIVERSITY COLLEGE OF LAW—Continued

RICHARD D. SCHWARTZ*, (E.I. White Professor of Law and Social Science)**, born 1925. *Education:* Yale University (A.B., 1947; Ph.D., 1952). ***COURSES: Criminal Law, Environmental Law, Interdisciplinary Legal Methods, Society and the Legal Order.

RODERICK SURRATT*, (Professor)**, born 1943; admitted to bar, 1969, Texas. *Education:* Baylor University (B.A., 1966); University of Texas (J.D., 1969). ***COURSES: Contracts, Evidence, Products Liability, Torts.

STEVEN WECHSLER*, (Professor of Law)**, born Washington, D.C., June 24, 1945; admitted to bar, 1976, Colorado; 1984, New York. *Education:* Cornell University (B.S., 1967); University of Michigan (M.B.A., 1973; J.D., 1975). ***COURSES: Contracts, Professional Responsibility, Negotiation.

JAMES K. WEEKS*, (Professor)**, born 1934; admitted to bar, 1958, South Dakota; 1960, Colorado; 1970, New York. *Education:* University of South Dakota (A.B., 1956; LL.B., 1958); New York University (LL.M., 1962). ***COURSES: Advanced Trial Practice, Criminal Law, Family Court Procedure, Immigration Law, Insurance, Trial Practice.

WILLIAM M WIECEK*, (Congdon Professor of Public Law and Legislation)**, born Cleveland, Ohio, January 31, 1938; admitted to bar, 1962, New Hampshire. *Education:* The Catholic University of America (A.B., 1959); Harvard University (LL.B., 1962); University of Wisconsin, Madison (Ph.D., 1968). ***COURSES: Legal History (American and Roman), Constitutional Law, Civil Procedure, Corporations.

TEMPLE UNIVERSITY BEASLEY SCHOOL OF LAW

1719 NORTH BROAD STREET
PHILADELPHIA, PENNSYLVANIA 19122
Telephone: (215) 204-7861
Fax: (215) 204-1185
E-mail: law@astro.ocis.temple.edu *http://www.temple.edu/lawschool*

ABA Approved Since 1933

Temple Law School began in 1895 as a small evening program. Today it is one of the finest law schools in the nation, with 1200 students from around the world and programs of study in Philadelphia, Tokyo, Rome, Athens, Tel Aviv and Beijing. The law school is located on the main campus of Temple University, a Pennsylvania state-related school that is one of the nation's largest centers for graduate and professional education.

Temple stands apart from other law schools. We have a unique student-centered curriculum that integrates both critical thinking and practical legal skills. Rigorous study is complemented by actual practice experience. Students at Temple build lawyering skills both in the classroom and in the readily accessible law firms, courts, civic organizations and financial institutions of center city Philadelphia and the surrounding region. As a result, Temple students graduate ready to perform skillfully in the legal marketplace.

CURRICULUM

At Temple Law School, we believe that a legal education must provide both practical and theoretical knowledge. Temple is a national leader in training lawyers through innovative teaching and award-winning skills courses like the Integrated Business Law Program and the Integrated Trial Advocacy Program. These programs combine the teaching of traditional law school course-work with practical skills training in interviewing, negotiating, drafting legal documents, arguing before a jury and cross-examining a witness. These skills are developed early by the work students perform in the first-year legal research and writing program. This required year-long program is staffed by five full-time professors and is acknowledged to be among the best in the nation. Participation in these courses prepares students for the challenges of the clinical program, in which students represent real clients with real legal problems while earning academic credit.

TRIAL ADVOCACY

Temple Law School has a national reputation for its prize-winning trial advocacy programs. Temple provides programs in basic, integrated and advanced trial advocacy and is the only school in the country to offer an LL.M. in Trial Advocacy to full-time practitioners.

Temple's National Trial Team won the National Institute of Trial Advocacy Tournament of Champions in 1997, 1998 and 1999, the National Trial Championship Competition in 1995, 1998 and 1999 and the Association of Trial Lawyers Competition in 1998 and 2001. Since 1989, our Trial Team has won 13 consecutive National Trial Competition regional championships in a row. Professor Edward D. Ohlbaum, Director of Trial Advocacy and Clinical Legal Education, was named the top teacher of trial advocacy in the country in 1997. He was the recipient of the prestigious Richard S. Jacobson Award given by the Roscoe Pound Foundation to a full-time professor of trial advocacy, for teaching ability, and for the overall success of the program. In 2001, Professor David Sonenshein won the American Bar Association's Francis Rawlc Award for outstanding contributions to continuing legal education in skills training.

The cornerstone of Temple's litigation curriculum is the Integrated Trial Advocacy Program. This innovative program, combines the teaching of evidence, trial advocacy, and professional responsibility in an integrated year-long course. In 1989, Temple received the Emil Gumpert Award from the American College of Trial Lawyers for excellence in teaching trial advocacy. In 1993, the Law School won the American Bar Association's E. Smythe Gambrell Award for excellence in the teaching of trial advocacy and professionalism.

BUSINESS AND TAX LAW

Temple's reputation for superior training in business and tax law is bolstered by an innovative program which combines the teaching of professional responsibility, substantive law courses, and business skills, such as interviewing, negotiating, and drafting. Students use these skills in several clinicals, including the Representing Charitable Organizations Clinical, the Federal Estate and Gift Tax Clinical and the Business Law Clinical. Prospective business lawyers can also pursue the J.D./M.B.A. dual degree program, offered in conjunction with the School of Business and Management, or the J.D./LL.M. in Taxation.

INTERNATIONAL LAW

For students interested in international law, Temple offers a unique semester abroad program in Tokyo, Japan (see Study Abroad below). The Japan program capitalizes on Temple's strengths in international law - a distinguished international law faculty; a diverse curriculum in international and comparative law; the opportunity for summer study in

(This Listing Continued)

TEMPLE UNIVERSITY BEASLEY SCHOOL OF LAW —Continued

Rome, Athens, and Tel Aviv; a Master of Laws (LL.M.) Program for international students holding foreign law degrees; an LL.M. in Transnational Law for lawyers who want to practice in the global market; and active student organizations, such as the International Law Journal, the International Law Society and the Japan America Law Student Alliance. Knowing of Temple's success in Japan, the Chinese Ministry of Justice collaborated with the Law School in creating innovative program for Chinese lawyers, judges and government officials, leading to an LL.M. in American and international law. The program was launched in the fall of 1999 in Beijing, and included one summer of study in Philadelphia. The First group of Chinese students graduated from the program in May, 2001.

TECHNOLOGY AND INTELLECTUAL PROPERTY LAW

Temple Law School offers a first-rate course of study in intellectual property and technology law. Through course work, hands-on activities outside the classroom, and faculty members who are experts in the field, Temple prepares students to help fill the gap between technology and the law. Course offerings include Computer Law; Copyrights; Cyberspace; Intellectual Property Licensing Law; International Intellectual Property; Law, Science and Technology; Patents; and Trademarks. In addition, the Cyberspace Law Institute, housed at Temple Law School, provides both students and practitioners with a forum to define intellectual property on the Internet, protect individual and corporate privacy in cyberspace, and apply laws in a world without borders.

PUBLIC SERVICE

Public service is a Temple tradition. Students provide much-needed legal services in the Philadelphia area through the clinical program, the Temple Legal Aid Office, located in the law school building, and the Temple Law, Education and Participation Program (LEAP), which offers programs designed to teach children about the law. Public interest careers are supported by the Student Public Interest Network, which provides grants for summer internships, and the Barrack Public Interest Fellowships, a loan repayment assistance program for Temple graduates in public interest jobs. Additionally, Temple now offers substantial scholarships to entering students committed to public interest through the Public Interest Scholars Program. The Office of Public Interest Programs administers the scholarship program and provides an administrative home base for a variety of public service opportunities, including the Public Interest Experience (PIE), a student directed program for public interest volunteers.

FACULTY

Our faculty members are an outstanding group of teacher-scholars. They bring real world practice experience to the law school classroom. Educated at the nation's top law schools, they have worked in law firms, judicial clerkships, government service and public interest agencies. They are committed to scholarship and public service, but their first commitment is to teaching.

STUDENT BODY

Temple Law students are not easy to describe. They arrive at the law school each fall from across the country and around the world. They bring with them a rich array of academic and professional experience. Temple Law students contribute an energy and diversity of opinion to the classroom experience that animates the learning atmosphere and defines the Temple community.

Temple received over 3000 applications for the 346 seats in the 2000 entering class. The 2000-2001 entering class came to Temple from 143 different undergraduate schools and 34 states and foreign countries. Women comprise 54 percent of the entering class, and 20 percent are minority students.

STUDENT ACTIVITIES

Students are an integral part of policy-making and governance at the Law School. The Student Bar Association is the umbrella organization that oversees over 30 student groups. Student publications include the *Temple Law Review, the Temple Environmental Law and Technology Journal, the Temple International and Comparative Law Journal, and the Temple Political and Civil Rights Law Review.* Students who excel in trial advocacy may participate in the National Trial Team, the Moot Court Honor Society, and the Barrister's Society. Other student organizations include the Women's Law Caucus, the Black Law Students Association, the Asian/Pacific Islander American Law Student Association, the Latino Law Students Association, Law Students for Lesbian, Gay, Bisexual and Transgender Rights, the Student Public Interest Network, the International Law Society, the Japan America Law Student Alliance, and the Technology Law Society.

PLACEMENT

The exceptional quality of the Law School is reflected in the achievement of its graduates. The 2000 graduating class had a placement rate of 93 percent. Of those employed, 45 percent entered private law firm practice, 13 percent began their legal careers as judicial clerks, 16 percent launched careers in government, 5 percent accepted positions with public interest organizations, 18 percent went into business and industry, and the remainder pursued other careers or advanced degrees. As a result of their diverse geographic origins, talents and interests, Temple students seek positions throughout the country. The ability of Temple alumni/ae to make a difference is evidenced by their achievements in every branch of local and federal government, the judiciary and private and public practice.

STUDY ABROAD

Recognizing that an international experience is best gained by actually living, learning and working abroad, the Law School has established a semester-abroad program in Tokyo, Japan. This is the first and only ABA-accredited semester abroad program offered by an American law school in Asia. The curriculum, taught by U.S. and Japanese law professors to U.S. and Japanese students, includes a mix of standard law courses and specialty courses focusing on comparative, Japanese, and Asian legal studies. Internships in Japanese law firms and corporations are also available.

Every summer for over 24 years, students from law schools all over the United States have gathered at Temple Law School's summer program in Rome, Italy. Encouraged by the popularity of the Rome summer session, Temple started summer sessions in Athens, Greece, and Tel Aviv, Israel. At each of these programs, students study comparative and international law in classes co-taught by Temple faculty and by professors, judges, and prominent lawyers from the host country. Visits to the courts and other legal institutions of the host country enrich classroom studies.

LL.M. PROGRAMS

Temple Law School currently offers a Master of Laws (LL.M.) through five specialized programs: Taxation, Trial Advocacy, Teaching Fellowships, Transnational Law, and the Program for graduates of International Law Schools.

Founded in 1973, Temple's Graduate Tax program has a well-deserved reputation for excellence. Courses are taught by Temple's distinguished full-time faculty and prominent tax practitioners. Students can attend on a full or part-time basis. J.D./LL.M. students can obtain up to half the credits toward the LL.M. while they are J.D. students.

The LL.M. in Trial Advocacy embodies Temple's award-winning concept of advocacy training in a unique, one-year program designed for the practicing lawyer. Nationally prominent trial lawyers, law

(This Listing Continued)

TEMPLE UNIVERSITY BEASLEY SCHOOL OF LAW —Continued

professors and communications experts guide students through the intricacies of complex litigation using lectures and critiques of student performances.

Each year Temple admits up to four lawyers with an interest in teaching law into its prestigious Graduate Teaching Fellowship program where fellows spend two years developing their teaching and scholarship in preparation for a career in teaching law.

Twenty-five years ago, Temple was among the first law schools to recognize the need for globally-trained lawyers when it created its LL.M. degree program for lawyers holding a first degree in law from a recognized law faculty outside the U.S. Today, Temple's program provides an excellent traditional legal education as well as opportunities not available at other law schools, such as the option to study at the Philadelphia or Tokyo campus and to participate in Temple's award-winning trial advocacy program.

In 1997 the faculty instituted an LL.M. in Transnational Law for lawyers who want to practice in the global market. This innovative program, which can be completed in Philadelphia and/or Tokyo, gives students the cultural understanding and legal skills necessary to practice internationally.

Dean: Robert J. Reinstein (215) 204-7863
Asst. Dean for Admissions, Financial Aid & Student Affairs: Marylouise Esten (215) 204-8574
Assistant Dean for Graduate and International Programs: Adelaide Ferguson (215) 204-1448
Assistant Dean for Career Planning: Karen Jackson Vaughn (215) 204-1285
Assistant Dean for Computer and Information Services: Shyam Nair (215) 204-1273
Assistant Dean for External Services: Deborah A. Feldman (215) 204-8979
Law Librarian: John Necci (215) 204-4538

FULL TIME FACULTY

ROBERT J. REINSTEIN*, (Dean & Professor of Law)**, born Baltimore, Maryland, March 17, 1945; admitted to bar, 1968, Maryland; 1983, Pennsylvania. *Education:* Cornell (B.S., 1965); Harvard (J.D., 1968). ***COURSES: Constitutional Law. ***Email:*** rreinst@vm.temple.edu

ALICE G. ABREU*, (Professor of Law)**, born Havana, Cuba, November 11, 1951; admitted to bar, 1978, Pennsylvania. *Education:* Cornell University (B.A., 1973; J.D., 1978). ***COURSES: Taxation, Contracts. ***Email:*** ABREU@VM.TEMPLE.EDU

DAVID ADAMANY*, (University President and Laura H. Carnell Professor of Law & Political Science)**, born Janesville, Wisconsin, September 23, 1936; admitted to bar, 1961, Wisconsin. *Education:* Harvard College (A.B., 1958); Harvard Law School (J.D., 1961); University of Wisconsin (M.S., 1963; Ph.D., 1967). ***COURSES: Constitutional Law.

MARK F. ANDERSON*, (Associate Professor of Law)**, born Brainerd, Minnesota, November 5, 1954; admitted to bar, 1984, Massachusetts; 1993, Pennsylvania. *Education:* Colorado College (B.A., 1976); University of Michigan (J.D., 1983). ***COURSES: Contracts, Environmental Law, Bioethics, Health Care Law, Secured Transactions. ***Email:*** ANDERSON@VM.TEMPLE.EDU

MARINA ANGEL*, (Professor of Law)**, born New York, New York, July 21, 1944; admitted to bar, 1969, New York; 1971, Pennsylvania. *Education:* Barnard College (B.A., 1965); Columbia University (J.D., 1969); University of Pennsylvania (LL.M., 1977). ***COURSES: Labor and Employment, Criminal Law, Juvenile Law, Legal Education, Legal Process.

JANE B. BARON*, (Professor of Law)**, born New York, N.Y., November 9, 1953; admitted to bar, 1979, New York; 1981, Tennessee. *Education:* Radcliffe College (A.B., 1975); Harvard University Law School (J.D., 1978). ***COURSES: Property, Trusts and Estates Contracts, Jurisprudence. ***Email:*** BARON@VM.TEMPLE.EDU

ROBERT J. BARTOW*, (Laura H. Carnell Professor of Law)**, born Mobile, Alabama, October 10, 1945; admitted to bar, 1971, Pennsylvania. *Education:* Oberlin College (A.B., 1967); Temple University School of Law (J.D., 1971); Yale Law School (LL.M., 1973). ***COURSES: Federal Income Taxation, Property, Trusts and Estates; Secured Transactions. ***Email:*** RBARTOW@VM.TEMPLE.EDU

ANTHONY J. BOCCHINO*, (Professor of Law)**, born Meriden, Connecticut, July 31, 1947; admitted to bar, 1972, Connecticut; 1973, North Carolina. *Education:* Bucknell University (A.B., 1969); University of Connecticut (J.D., 1972). ***COURSES: Evidence, Trial Advocacy, Criminal Law, Civil Procedure, Professional Responsibility. ***Email:*** ABOCCHIN@VM.TEMPLE.EDU

AMELIA H. BOSS*, (Charles Klein Professor of Law and Government)**, born Baltimore, Maryland, April 3, 1949; admitted to bar, 1975, New Jersey; 1976, Pennsylvania. *Education:* Bryn Mawr College (B.A., 1970); Rutgers University (J.D., 1975). ***COURSES: Commercial Law, Bankruptcy, International Business, Electronic Communications. ***Email:*** ABOSS@VM.TEMPLE.EDU

SCOTT BURRIS*, (Professor of Law)**, born Chicago, Illinois, December 30, 1956; admitted to bar, 1988, Pennsylvania. *Education:* Washington University (B.A., 1980); Yale Law School (J.D., 1987). ***COURSES: Torts, Civil Procedure, Public Health Law. ***Email:*** Burris@VM.TEMPLE.EDU

BURTON CAINE*, (Professor of Law)**, born Darby, Pennsylvania, April 4, 1928; admitted to bar, 1952, Pennsylvania and District of Columbia. *Education:* University of Pennsylvania (B.A., 1949); Harvard University Law School (J.D., 1972). ***COURSES: Antitrust and Trade, Comparative American-Israeli Constitutional Law, Constitutional Law, Political and Civil Rights. ***Email:*** B-CAINE@VM.TEMPLE.EDU

RICHARD B. CAPPALLI*, (Professor of Law)**, born December 3, 1940; admitted to bar, 1966, District of Columbia; 1968, Puerto Rico; 1978, Pennsylvania. *Education:* Williams College (B.A., 1962); Columbia University (J.D., 1965); Yale Law School (LL.M., 1972). ***COURSES: Administrative Law, Alternative Dispute Resolution, Civil Procedure, Legal Process. ***Email:*** rcappali@vm.temple.edu

SUSAN L. DEJARNATT*, (Associate Professor of Law)**, born Sterling, Colorado, February 10, 1953; admitted to bar, 1980, Pennsylvania. *Education:* Oberlin College (B.A., 1974); Temple University School of Law (J.D., 1980). ***COURSES: Research & Writing. ***Email:*** SDEJARN@VM.TEMPLE.EDU

JOHN THEODORE DROST*, (Director LL.M. in Trial Advocacy)**, born McKeesport, Pennsylvania, January, 28, 1951; admitted to bar, 1975, Pennsylvania. *Education:* University of Notre Dame (B.A., 1972); Catholic University of America (J.D., 1975). ***COURSES: Trial Advocacy.

(This Listing Continued)

TEMPLE UNIVERSITY BEASLEY SCHOOL OF LAW —Continued

JEFFREY L. DUNOFF*, (Director of LL.M. in Transactional Law Program and Professor of Law)**, born New York, January 15, 1960; admitted to bar, 1986, Pennsylvania. *Education:* Haverford (B.A., 1982); New York University (J.D., 1986); Georgetown (LL.M., 1992). ***COURSES: International, Civil Procedure. ***Email:*** dunoff@vm.temple.edu

JOANNE A. EPPS*, (Associate Dean for Academic Affairs and I. Herman Stern Professor of Law)**, born Abington, Pennsylvania, May 28, 1951; admitted to bar, 1976, California; 1982, District of Columbia; 1991, Pennsylvania. *Education:* Trinity College (B.A., 1973); Yale Law School (J.D., 1976). ***COURSES: Criminal Procedure, Criminal Law, Evidence. ***Email:*** JEPPS@VM.TEMPLE.EDU

KRISTIN BETH GERDY*, (Visiting Assistant Professor of Law)**, born Boulder, Colorado, November 18, 1969; admitted to bar, 1995, Utah. *Education:* Brigham Young University (J.D., 1995). ***COURSES: Legal Research & Writing. ***Email:*** kgerdy@vm.temple.edu

THERESA GLENNON*, (Associate Professor of Law)**, born Jersey City, New Jersey, June 12, 1958; admitted to bar, 1985, Pennsylvania; 1989, Maryland. *Education:* Yale University (B.A., 1980; J.D., 1984). ***COURSES: Professional Responsibility, Education Law, Children, Parents, State. ***Email:*** GLENNON@VM.TEMPLE.EDU

RICHARD K. GREENSTEIN*, (Professor of Law)**, born Lancaster, Pennsylvania, May 2, 1948; admitted to bar, 1973, Georgia. *Education:* Wesleyan University (B.A., 1970); Vanderbilt University (J.D., 1973); Temple University School of Law (LL.M., 1982). ***COURSES: Jurisprudence, Criminal Law, Conflict of Laws. ***Email:*** RKG@VM.TEMPLE.EDU

SAMUEL J. GYANDOH, JR.*, (Professor of Law)**, born Ghana, June 2, 1933; admitted to bar, 1960, England; 1961, Ghana. *Education:* University of Southampton (B.A., 1960); Yale Law School (LL.B., 1964). ***COURSES: Administrative Law, Comparative Law, Constitutional Law. ***Email:*** SGYANDOH@VM.TEMPLE.EDU

PHOEBE A. HADDON*, (Professor of Law)**, born August 29, 1950; admitted to bar, 1977, Pennsylvania. *Education:* Smith College (B.A., 1972); Duquesne University (J.D., 1977); Yale Law School (LL.M., 1985). ***COURSES: Constitutional Law, Constitutional Remedies, Domestic Relations, Product Liability, Torts. ***Email:*** PHADDON@VM.TEMPLE.EDU

SHARON S. HARZENSKI*, (Professor of Law)**, born February 22, 1943; admitted to bar, 1976, Pennsylvania. *Education:* Kean College of New Jersey (B.A., 1965); Temple University School of Law (J.D., 1974); Yale Law School (LL.M., 1975). ***COURSES: Civil Rights, Constitutional Law, Contracts, Jurisprudence, Women and the Law, Federalism. ***Email:*** SHARZENS@VM.TEMPLE,EDU

CASSANDRA JONES HAVARD*, (Associate Professor of Law)**, born North Carolina, June, 16, 1956; admitted to bar, 1981, Pennsylvania. *Education:* Bennett College (B.A., 1978); University of Pennsylvania (J.D., 1981). ***COURSES: Banking, Corporate, Contracts. ***Email:*** cjonesha@nimbus.ocis.temple.edu

MELISSA B. JACOBY*, (Assistant Professor of Law)**, born Abington, Pennsylvania, April 8, 1969; admitted to bar, 1995, Pennsylvania. *Education:* University of Pennsylvania (B.A., 1991; J.D., 1994). ***COURSES: Contracts, Secured Transactions, Bankruptcy. ***Email:*** mjacoby@vm.temple.edu

DAVID KAIRYS*, (James E. Beasley Professor of Law)**, born Baltimore, Maryland, April 16, 1943; admitted to bar, 1969, District of Columbia and Pennsylvania. *Education:* Cornell University (B.S., 1965); Cornell Law School (LL.B., 1968); Columbia University (LL.M., 1971). ***COURSES: Civil Rights, Constitutional Law, Law and Technology, Privacy. ***Email:*** DKAIRYS@VM.TEMPLE.EDU

NANCY KNAUER*, (Professor of Law)**, born Philadelphia, Pennsylvania, July 27, 1961; admitted to bar, 1984, Pennsylvania. *Education:* University of Pennsylvania (B.A., 1981; J.D., 1984). ***COURSES: Estate and Gift Taxation, Income Taxation. ***Email:*** NKNAUER@VM.TEMPLE.EDU

JAN M. LEVINE*, (Director of Legal Research and Writing Program Associate and Professor of Law)**, born Brooklyn, New York, May 23, 1954; admitted to bar, 1978, Massachusetts. *Education:* State University of New York at Albany (B.A., 1975); Boston University School of Law (J.D., 1978). ***COURSES: Research & Writing. ***Email:*** LEVINE@Thunder.OCIS.TEMPLE.EDU

PETER J. LIACOURAS*, (University Chancellor and Professor of Law)**, born 1931; admitted to bar, 1957, Pennsylvania. *Education:* Drexel Institute (B.S., 1953); Fletcher School of Law and Diplomacy (M.A., 1958); University of Pennsylvania (J.D., 1956); Harvard University Law School (LL.M., 1959). ***COURSES: Conflict of Law, International Law, International Protection of Human Rights, International Transactions, Jurisprudence.

MICHAEL E. LIBONATI*, (Laura H. Carnell Professor of Law)**, born May 25, 1944; admitted to bar, 1968, District of Columbia; 1975, Illinois. *Education:* Yale Law School (LL.B., 1967; LL.M., 1969). ***COURSES: Administrative Law, Comparative Law, Constitutional Law, Government Contracts, Legislation.

LAURA E. LITTLE*, (Professor of Law)**, born Wilmington, Delaware, November 12, 1957; admitted to bar, 1985, Pennsylvania. *Education:* University of Pennsylvania (B.A., 1979); Smith College; Temple University School of Law (J.D., 1985). ***COURSES: Federal Courts, Remedies, Civil Procedure, Conflict of Laws. ***Email:*** Llittle@vm.temple.edu

OLAN B. LOWREY*, (Professor of Law Emeritus)**, born May 11, 1930; admitted to bar, 1958, Texas; 1969, Pennsylvania. *Education:* Southwest Texas State College (B.A., 1950); University of Iowa (M.A., 1951); Baylor University (LL.B., 1956). ***COURSES: Environmental Law, Land Use.

DIANE C. MALESON*, (Professor of Law and University Vice Provost)**, born Hartford, Connecticut, July 7, 1942; admitted to bar, 1971, Massachusetts; 1972, Pennsylvania. *Education:* Bryn Mawr College (A.B., 1964); Temple University School of Law (J.D., 1969). ***COURSES: American Legal History, Constitutional Law, Environmental Law, Torts.

KATHY C. MANDLEBAUM*, (Director of Graduate Tax Program, Associate Professor of Law)**, born Boston, Massachusetts, December 31, 1958; admitted to bar, 1983, Pennsylvania. *Education:* Radcliffe College (A.B., 1980); Harvard Law School (J.D., 1983). ***COURSES: Estate and Gift Tax, Nonprofit and Charitable Organizations, Foundations. ***Email:*** kmandleb@vn.temple.edu

ELLIE MARGOLIS*, (Associate Professor)**, born Minneapolis, Minnesota, July 11, 1965; admitted to bar, 1990, Massachusetts. *Education:* Wesleyan (B.A., 1987); Northeastern University School of Law (J.D., 1990). ***COURSES: Legal Research & Writing. ***Email:*** EMARGOLI@VM.Temple.EDU

JOSEPH W. MARSHALL*, (Professor of Law Emeritus)**, born February 19, 1926; admitted to bar, 1955, Pennsylvania. *Education:* University of Pennsylvania (B.S., 1949); Temple University School of Law (J.D., 1954). ***COURSES: Business Planning, Estate Planning, Sports Law, Taxation, Federal.

***FINBARR MCCARTHY*, (Associate Professor of Law)**, born Dublin,

(This Listing Continued)

TEMPLE UNIVERSITY BEASLEY SCHOOL OF LAW —Continued

Ireland, September 23, 1952. *Education:* Trinity College (B.A., 1976); Tulane University (Ph.D., 1988; J.D., 1989). ***COURSES:*** Property, Trusts and Estates, Theories of Property, Employment Discrimination. ***Email:*** MCCARTHY@VM.TEMPLE.EDU

FRANK M. MCCLELLAN,* (I. Herman Stern Professor of Law)**, born Marion, South Carolina, February 5, 1945; admitted to bar, 1971, Pennsylvania and District of Columbia. *Education:* Rutgers University (A.B., 1967); Duquesne University (J.D., 1970); Yale Law School (LL.M., 1974). ***COURSES: Torts, Medical Malpractice, Bioethics. ***Email:*** FRANK@VM.TEMPLE.EDU

SALIL KUMAR MEHRA,* (Assistant Professor of Law)**, born Brooklyn, New York, September 8, 1969; admitted to bar, 1997, New York. *Education:* Harvard College (A.B., 1991); University of California (M.A., 1992); University of Chicago (J.D., 1995). ***COURSES: Antitrust, Contracts, Corporations, Japanese Law. ***Email:*** smehra@vm.temple.edu

STEPHEN L. MIKOCHIK,* (Professor of Law)**, born April 26, 1948; admitted to bar, 1976, New York; 1982, Pennsylvania. *Education:* New York University (B.A., 1972); Fordham University (J.D., 1975); Harvard University Law School (LL.M., 1976). ***COURSES: Constitutional Law, Civil Procedure, Religious Rights Under the U.S. Constitution, Civil Rights of Handicapped Persons. ***Email:*** Mikochik@VM.TEMPLE.EDU

MURIEL MORISEY,* (Associate Professor of Law)**, born Greensboro, North Carolina, September 7, 1947; admitted to bar, 1978, District of Columbia. *Education:* Radcliffe College (B.A., 1969); Georgetown University Law Center (J.D., 1977). ***COURSES: Administrative Law, Contracts, Legislation, Professional Responsibility. ***Email:*** MMORISEY@VM.TEMPLE.EDU

ELEANOR W. MYERS,* (Associate Professor of Law)**, born November 15, 1947; admitted to bar, 1976, Pennsylvania. *Education:* University of Pennsylvania (B.A., 1969; J.D., 1976). ***COURSES: Corporations, Professional Responsibility, Securities Regulation. ***Email:*** EMYERS@VM.TEMPLE.EDU

LOUIS M. NATALI, JR.,* (Jack E. Feinberg Professor of Litigation)**, born 1942; admitted to bar, 1967, Pennsylvania; 1984, California. *Education:* Georgetown University Law Center (LL.B., 1966). ***COURSES: Criminal Law, Criminal Practice, Ethics, Interviewing, Negotiation and Counseling, Evidence, Evidence for Trial Lawyers, Trial Advocacy. ***Email:*** LNATALI@VM.TEMPLE.EDU

ANTHONY S. NIEDWIECKI,* (Assistant Professor)**, born Detroit, Michigan, March 18, 1967; admitted to bar, 1995, Texas. *Education:* Wayne State University (B.A., 1989); Tulane Law School (J.D., 1995); Temple University Beasley School of Law (LL.M., 2000). ***COURSES: Legal Research and Writing, Appellate Advocacy, Law and Genetics. ***Email:*** aniedwie@vm.temple.edu

EDWARD D. OHLBAUM,* (Professor of Law and Director Clinical Legal Education)**, born New York, N.Y., January 22, 1950; admitted to bar, 1976, Pennsylvania; 1983, New York. *Education:* Wesleyan University (B.A., 1972); Temple University School of Law (J.D., 1976). ***COURSES: Evidence, Criminal Law, Professional Responsibility, Trial Advocacy. ***Email:*** ohlbaum@vm.temple.edu

JOSEPH I. PASSON,* (Professor of Law)**, born October 27, 1940; admitted to bar, 1970, Pennsylvania. *Education:* Temple University (B.S., 1962); Temple University School of Law (LL.B., 1965). ***COURSES: Damages, Estates and Trusts, Family Law, Legal Writing and Research, Property, Real Estate Transactions, Torts, Workers Compensation. ***Email:*** JPASSON@VM.TEMPLE.EDU

K. G. JAN PILLAI,* (Professor of Law)**, born India, January 23, 1936; admitted to bar, 1975, District of Columbia. *Education:* University of Kerala (B.A., 1965; LL.B., 1965; LL.M., 1965); Yale Law School (LL.M., 1967; J.S.D., 1969). ***COURSES: Administrative Law, Corporations, Civil Rights, Small Businesses. ***Email:*** JPillai@VM.TEMPLE.EDU

RAFAEL PORRATA-DORIA, JR.,* (Professor of Law)**, born Santurce, Puerto Rico, November 23, 1952; admitted to bar, 1977, Pennsylvania and Puerto Rico; 1982, Florida; 1984, New York. *Education:* University of Pennsylvania (B.A., 1974; M.A., 1974); Yale Law School (J.D., 1977). ***COURSES: Comparative Law, Contracts, Corporations, International Business Transactions, Remedies, Securities Regulation. ***Email:*** PORRATA1@VM.TEMPLE.EDU

DAVID GORDON POST,* (Associate Professor of Law)**, born New York City, September 26, 1951; admitted to bar, 1987, Pennsylvania; 1988, District of Columbia. *Education:* Yale University (B.A., 1972; Ph.D., 1978); Georgetown University Law Center (J.D., 1986). ***COURSES: Intellectual Property; Computers & Law, Law of Cyberspace. ***Email:*** DPost@VM.TEMPLE.EDU

CHARLES R.P. POUNCY,* (Associate Professor of Law)**, born Blenhiem, South Carolina, June 4, 1954; admitted to bar, 1980, District of Columbia. *Education:* Fordham University (B.A., 1976); Cornell Law School (J.D., 1979); Temple Law School (LL.M., 1995). ***COURSES: Corporations, Banking, Corporate Finance. ***Email:*** cpouncy@vm.temple.edu

DONALD R. PRICE,* (Professor of Law Emeritus)**, born Sellersville, Pennsylvania, December 7, 1936; admitted to bar, 1967, Pennsylvania. *Education:* Elizabethtown College (B.A., 1958); Temple University School of Law (J.D., 1966). ***COURSES: Contracts, Creditors' Rights, Legal Writing and Research, Sales and Secured Transactions. ***Email:*** DPRICE@VM.TEMPLE.EDU

MARK C. RAHDERT,* (Associate Dean for Academic Affairs and Professor of Law)**, born February 7, 1936; admitted to bar, 1980, Pennsylvania. *Education:* Harvard University (B.A., 1974); Yale Law School (J.D., 1978). ***COURSES: Appellate Advocacy, Constitutional Law, Federal Jurisdiction, Insurance, Torts. ***Email:*** MRAHDERT@VM.TEMPLE.EDU

HENRY J. RICHARDSON, III,* (Peter J. Liacouras Professor of Law)**, born March 24, 1941; admitted to bar, 1966, Indiana. *Education:* University de Besancon (Certificat en Histoire, 1962); Antioch College (A.B., 1963); Yale Law School (LL.B., 1966; LL.M., 1971). ***COURSES: Constitutional Law and Foreign Policy, International Business Transactions, International Law, International Organization, International Protection of Human Rights, Law and Social Change, Torts.

CHARLES H. ROGOVIN,* (Professor of Law)**, born January 24, 1931; admitted to bar, 1956, New York; 1957, Pennsylvania. *Education:* Wesleyan University (B.A., 1952); Columbia University (LL.B., 1956). ***COURSES: Clinical Prosecution, Criminal Law, Criminal Procedure, Organized White Collar Crime, Professional Responsibility. ***Email:*** CROGOVIN@VM.TEMPLE.EDU

PETER SEVAREID,* (Professor of Law)**, born April 25, 1940; admitted to bar, 1966, District of Columbia. *Education:* Harvard University (A.B., 1962); Georgetown University Law Center (J.D., 1966); Yale Law School (LL.M., 1972). ***COURSES: Administrative Law, Civil Procedure, Comparative Law, Family Law, Federal Jurisdiction, Jurisprudence, Legal Process. ***Email:*** SEVAREID@VM.TEMPLE.EDU

***JAMES A. SHELLENBERGER,* (Professor of Law)**, born Doylestown, Pennsylvania, July 13, 1947; admitted to bar, 1972, Pennsylvania. *Education:* Lafayette College (A.B., 1969); Villanova

(This Listing Continued)

TEMPLE UNIVERSITY BEASLEY SCHOOL OF LAW —Continued

University (J.D., 1972). ***COURSES:*** Criminal Law and Procedure, Legal Methods. ***Email:*** JSHELL@VM.TEMPLE.EDU

AMY SINDEN*, (Assistant Professor)**, born Morristown, New Jersey, June 17, 1961; admitted to bar, 1991, Pennsylvania; 1992, New Jersey; 1997, Washington. *Education:* Swarthmore College (B.A., 1984); University of Pennsylvania Law School (J.D., 1991). ***COURSES: Environmental Law, Property, Civil Procedure.

CARL E. SINGLEY*, (Professor of Law)**, born March 26, 1946; admitted to bar, 1972, Pennsylvania. *Education:* Talladega College (B.A., 1968); Temple University School of Law (J.D., 1972); Yale Law School (LL.M., 1974). ***COURSES: Civil Procedure, Criminal Law, Criminal Procedure, Local Government. ***Email:*** CSINGLEY@VM.TEMPLE.EDU

DAVID A. SONENSHEIN*, (Professor of Law)**, born Washington, D.C., August 7, 1947; admitted to bar, 1972, Massachusetts; 1981, Illinois; 1986, Pennsylvania. *Education:* Cornell University (B.A., 1967); New York University School of Law (J.D., 1972). ***COURSES: Evidence, Civil Procedure, Criminal Procedure, Trial Advocacy. ***Email:*** DSonensh@VM.Temple.edu

KATHRYN M. STANCHI*, (Associate Professor of Law)**, born Englewood, New Jersey, February 11, 1966; admitted to bar, 1990, New Jersey; 1991, New York. *Education:* University of Pennsylvania (B.A., 1987); Boston University School of Law (J.D., 1990). ***COURSES: Research & Writing. ***Email:*** KSTANCHI@VM.TEMPLE.EDU

JAMES A. STRAZZELLA*, (James G. Schmidt Professor of Law)**, born Hanover, Pennsylvania, May 18, 1939; admitted to bar, 1964, Pennsylvania; 1966, District of Columbia. *Education:* Villanova University (A.B., 1961); University of Pennsylvania (J.D., 1964). ***COURSES: Criminal Law and Procedure, Appellate, Litigation. ***Email:*** STRAZ@VM.TEMPLE.EDU

GERALD F. TIETZ*, (Professor of Law Emeritus)**, born December 13, 1937; admitted to bar, 1970, Pennsylvania. *Education:* University of Illinois (B.S., 1960; M.A., 1964); Temple University School of Law (J.D., 1970). ***COURSES: Civil Procedure, Civil Procedure II, Product Liability. ***Email:*** GFTIETZ@VM.TEMPLE.EDU

JAN C. TING*, (Professor of Law, Director of Graduate Tax Program)**, born Ann Arbor, Michigan, December 17, 1948; admitted to bar, 1975, Pennsylvania. *Education:* Oberlin College (B.A., 1970); University of Hawaii (M.A., 1972); Harvard University Law School (J.D., 1975). ***COURSES: Taxation, Immigration Law. ***Email:*** JANTING@VM.TEMPLE.EDU

DAVID WEINSTEIN*, (Professor of Law Emeritus)**, born April 7, 1938; admitted to bar, 1962, Connecticut. *Education:* Yale University (B.A., 1959); University of Hartford (M.P.A., 1972); Harvard University Law School (J.D., 1962). ***COURSES: Administrative Law, Collective Bargaining, Contract Remedies, Contracts, Employment Law, Labor Law, Public Employee Labor Relations.

WILLIAM J. WOODWARD, JR.*, (I. Herman Stern Professor of Law)**, born New York, N.Y., April 9, 1947; admitted to bar, 1975, Pennsylvania. *Education:* University of Pennsylvania (B.A., 1968); Rutgers University (J.D., 1975). ***COURSES: Contracts, Torts, Bankruptcy, Remedies, Commercial Law. ***Email:*** woodward@vm.temple.edu

MO ZHANG*, (Director of Temple Law China and Associate Professor of Law)**, *Education:* China University of Political Science & Law (LL.B., 1983; LL.M., 1986, Ph.D., 1989); University of Michigan (LL.M., 1991). ***COURSES: Corporate Law, International Commercial Transactions, Contracts. ***Email:*** mztemple@ihw.com.cn

---

TEXAS SOUTHERN UNIVERSITY
THURGOOD MARSHALL SCHOOL OF LAW

3100 CLEBURNE AVENUE
HOUSTON, TEXAS 77004
Telephone: (713) 313-1076
Fax: (713) 313-1049

ABA Approved Since 1949.

Introduction

Texas Southern University Thurgood Marshall School of Law is located in Houston, Texas, the fourth largest city with a population of approximately 1.7 million. The metropolitan area with a population of 3.3 million offers all of the arts and leisure amenities associated with an urban environment as well as the opportunity to live in a number of surrounding suburban communities. The University and the Law School are located within the city limits, just outside the downtown business district. It is a convenient distance from all major thoroughfares into the City of Houston. In addition, law students receive priority consideration for on-campus private apartments.

The School of Law is housed in an attractive, modern building located at the east end of the Texas Southern University campus. The building is a tri-level structure with classrooms and administrative offices on the first and second floors, and the law library on the first floor and basement level. Numerous study carrels are located on the lower level of the library which, along with the entire law school, has been recently renovated and is a state-of-the-art facility.

Many attributes contribute to the making of an institution. At Texas Southern University, two of the most important attributes are the faculty and the law library. The faculty consists of 33 full-time instructors, including the dean and two associate deans. The faculty members hold degrees from leading law schools across the nation. Nearly half hold LL.M. degrees from schools such as Stanford, University of Pennsylvania, Georgetown, Harvard, University of California at Berkeley, University of Texas and Yale. In addition, the School of Law benefits from the association of several adjunct faculty members prominent in the Houston bar and judiciary, as well as writing skills specialists and a distinguished visiting professor.

The School of Law affords its students an opportunity to pursue a complete and systematic course of legal study in preparation for the practice of law.

History

Texas Southern University was established in 1947 under Texas State Senate Bill 140, granting it authority to offer courses of higher learning in pharmacy, dentistry, journalism, education, arts and sciences, literature, law, medicine, and other professional courses. The University, as established by the Fiftieth Texas Legislature, was originally known as "Texas State University for Negroes." However, the name was changed by the legislature in 1951 to Texas Southern University. The School of Law, as well as the University at large, was undoubtedly created as a consequence of a 1946 lawsuit brought by

(This Listing Continued)

TEXAS SOUTHERN UNIVERSITY
THURGOOD MARSHALL SCHOOL OF LAW—Continued

Heman M. Sweatt. Under the Texas Constitution, which required separate but equal treatment, Mr. Sweatt was refused admission to the University of Texas School of Law because he was black. As a result, the legislature provided for an interim and separate law school for Negroes. During its first academic year, the law school was housed in Austin, Texas, and was subsequently transferred to the new university campus in Houston. In the famous case of Sweatt v. Painter, the United States Supreme Court ruled in 1950 that the creation of a separate law school for a black student violated the Equal Protection Clause of the US constitution.

Since that time, the School of Law has become an integral part of the university campus. Prior to 1976, the law school was housed in Hannah Hall - the University's administrative complex. On February 14, 1976, the school was formally designated as the Thurgood Marshall School of Law in honor of the distinguished former U.S. Supreme Court Justice and was moved to its present location. It is appropriate to note that Justice Marshall, at the time chief counsel for the NAACP Legal Defense Fund, successfully argued Heman M. Sweatt's case before the United States Supreme Court.

The history of the law school has been greatly enriched by the contribution of students and faculty of diverse cultural heritage. Texas Southern University Thurgood Marshall School of Law is proud that it has produced a substantial number of attorneys whose ethnicity covers all minority categories and significantly impacts upon the national pool of such attorneys.

Purpose

In 1973, the University was designated by the State Legislature as a special purpose institution for urban programming. The Law School established a curriculum designed to meet not only the needs of students in general but also those special needs of minority and disadvantaged students. Graduates receive thorough training in the fundamental principles of law, enabling them to practice not only in the State of Texas, but throughout the United States.

In addition to traditional legal careers, the School of Law provides training for those who plan careers in business, government, politics, the foreign service, journalism, and many other fields in which a knowledge of the law is increasingly necessary.

Special attention is placed on the legal problems of the poor and disadvantaged. This is accomplished through enrichment courses and the clinical program.

Dean: John C. Brittain (713) 313-1076
Admissions: Edward W. Rene (713) 313-1004
Financial Aid: DeCarlous Spearman (713) 313-7328
Library: Marguerite Butler (713) 313-1010
Placement: Faith Joseph (713) 313-4313
Alumni Affairs: Mia Settle-Vinson (713) 313-1014
Associate Dean: Donald K. Hill (713) 313-7126
Associate Dean: Dannye Holley (713) 313-7126

FULL TIME FACULTY

JOHN C. BRITTAIN*, (Dean & Professor)**, admitted to bar, 1969, Connecticut; 1971, Mississippi, 1974, California. *Education:* Texas Southern (B.A., 1966); Howard (J.D., 1969). ***COURSES: Administrative Law, Civil Procedure, Civil Rights, Torts.

JAMES WILLIAM BEARD, JR.*, (Associate Professor of Law)**, born Chillicothe, Ohio, September 16, 1941; admitted to bar, Texas. *Education:* Hardin-Simmons University (B.S., 1967); Texas Southern University (J.D., 1973); University of Texas (LL.M., 1976). ***COURSES: Tax, Income, Estate & Gift.

JAMES BULLOCK*, (Associate Professor)**, born Charleston, Mississippi, August 22, 1926; admitted to bar, 1970, Texas. *Education:* Texas Southern University (B.A., 1970; J.D., 1970). ***COURSES: Contracts, Wills and Trust, Oil and Gas.

MARGUERITE LOUISE BUTLER*, (Law Library Director)**, born Kansas City, Kansas, October 19, 1952; admitted to bar, 1981, New York; 1982, Missouri. *Education:* Wilberforce University (B.A., 1974); Syracuse University (J.D., 1979); University of Texas (M.LIS., 1992). ***COURSES: Legal Research, Appellate Litigation, Torts.

MCKEN V. CARRINGTON*, (Professor)**, born St. Vincent, West Indies, December 22, 1949; admitted to bar, 1983, New York. *Education:* Brooklyn College (B.S., 1979); City College of New York; Albany Law School (J.D., 1982). ***COURSES: Wills, Estates, Trusts, Estate Planning. ***Email:*** mcarring@tsulaw.edu

WALTER CHAMPION*, (Professor)**, born Philadelphia, Pennsylvania, November 22, 1950; admitted to bar, 1982, Pennsylvania; 1993, Texas. *Education:* St. Joseph's University (B.A., 1973); Western Illinois University (M.A., 1975); Drexel University (M.S., 1977); Temple University (J.D., 1982). ***COURSES: Sports Law, Torts, Recreational Injuries.

FERNANDO COLON-NAVARRO*, (Associate Professor)**, born Arroyo, Puerto Rico, October 8, 1952; admitted to bar, 1982, Minnesota; 1983, Illinois; 1988, Massachusetts. *Education:* St. John's University (B.A., 1974); University of Minnesota (J.D., 1981); Harvard (M.Ed., 1990; LL.M., 1991). ***COURSES: Property, Contracts, Immigration, Clinical.

JULIAN COOK, III*, (Assistant Professor)**, born Highland Park, Michigan, May 14, 1961; admitted to bar, 1991. *Education:* Duke University (B.A., 1983); Columbia University (M.P.A., 1985); University of Virginia (J.D. 1988). ***COURSES: Evidence, Criminal Procedure, Criminal Law.

JAMES ALEXANDRE COTTON*, (Associate Professor)**, born Pt. Riley, Kansas, November 22, 1939; admitted to bar, 1973, New York. *Education:* The Colorado College (A.B., 1963); University of Colorado (J.D., 1970). ***COURSES: Business Association, Securities Regulation.

MARTHA S. DAVIS*, (Professor)**, born Austin, Texas, January 7, 1939; admitted to bar, 1981, Texas; 1986, South Dakota. *Education:* University of Texas (B.A., 1964); Baylor (J.D., 1981); Harvard (LL.M., 1982). ***COURSES: Property, Labor & Employment, Civil Rights. ***Email:*** MDAVIS@TSULAW.EDU

JAMES MATTHEW DOUGLAS*, (Distinguished Professor)**, born Onalaska, Texas, February 11, 1944; admitted to bar, 1970, Texas. *Education:* Texas Southern University (B.A., 1966; J.D., 1970); Stanford University (J.S.M., 1971). ***COURSES: Contracts, Computer Law, Legislation.

***CONSTANCE FRISBY FAIN*, (Professor)**, born Philadelphia,

(This Listing Continued)

TEXAS SOUTHERN UNIVERSITY
THURGOOD MARSHALL SCHOOL OF LAW—Continued

Pennsylvania, February 11, 1949; admitted to bar, 1975, Texas; 1981, Pennsylvania. *Education:* Cheyney University (B.S., 1966); Texas Southern University Law School (J.D., 1974); University of Pennsylvania (LL.M., 1981). ***COURSES:*** Torts, Constitutional Law, Medical Liability.

LONNIE JOHN GOODEN*, (Associate Professor)**, born Galveston, Texas, June 12, 1939; admitted to bar, 1965, Texas. *Education:* Texas Southern University (B.A., 1962); Thurgood Marshall (LL.B., 1965). ***COURSES: Clinical.

GROVER G. HANKINS*, (Professor of Law)**, born Waukegan, Illinois, November 18, 1940; admitted to bar, 1973, Nebraska; 1981, Missouri; 1983, Kansas; 1990, Maryland; 1996, Texas. *Education:* Augustana College (A.B., 1962); University of Illinois College of Law (J.D., 1972). ***COURSES: Constitutional Law, Criminal Law, Environmental Law, International Environmental Law, Environmental Justice Clinic, Trial Advocacy.

EUGENE M. HARRINGTON*, (Professor)**, born New York, New York, April 6, 1939; admitted to bar, 1963, New York. *Education:* St. John's College (B.A., 1960); St. John's Law School (LL.B., 1963); University of California, Berkeley (LL.M., 1970). ***COURSES: Commercial Law, Consumer Protection, Aids, Sexual Orientation.

DONALD KENNETH HILL*, (Professor of Law)**, born Houston, Texas, September 30, 1937; admitted to bar, 1967, Texas. *Education:* University of Texas; Texas Southern University (J.D., 1967); Yale University (LL.M., 1970). ***COURSES: Contracts, Administrative Law, Law and National Security, Regulatory Process.

DANNYE HOLLEY*, (Professor)**, born Buffalo, New York, July 23, 1945; admitted to bar, 1971, New York. *Education:* State University of New York at Buffalo (B.A., 1967; J.D., 1970); University of California at Berkeley (LL.M., 1971). ***COURSES: Evidence, Criminal Law, Criminal Procedure.

CRAIG LEONARD JACKSON*, (Associate Professor)**, born Beaumont, Texas, September 21, 1955; admitted to bar, 1980, Texas. *Education:* Rice University (B.A., 1977); University of Texas (J.D., 1980). ***COURSES: International Law, International Trade, Contracts. ***Email:*** cjackson@tsulaw

ANNA TAYLOR JAMES*, (Associate Professor)**, born Texas. *Education:* Texas Southern University (B.A., 1969); Thurgood Marshall School of Law (J.D., 1969); University of Washington (M.L.L., 1973). ***COURSES: Professional Responsibility, Domestic Relations, Texas Marital Property.

OTIS H. KING*, (Professor)**, born Texarcana, Texas, February 3, 1935; admitted to bar, 1961, Texas. *Education:* Texas Southern University (B.S., 1956; LL.B., 1961); Harvard University (LL.M., 1970). ***COURSES: Property, Oil and Gas, Labor Law.

DIANE JULIA KLEIN*, (Assistant Professor)**, born Los Angeles, California, March 30, 1966; admitted to bar, 1999, California. *Education:* Harvard (A.B., 1987); UCLA (J.D., 1997); University of California Berkeley (Ph.D., ABD.). ***COURSES: Civil Procedure, Wills & Trusts, Professional Responsibility. ***Email:*** diklein@tsulaw.edu

THOMAS KLEVEN*, (Professor of Law)**, born Cambridge, Massachusetts, August 30, 1942; admitted to bar, 1968, Massachusetts. *Education:* Yale (B.A., 1964; LL.B., 1967). ***COURSES: Property, Local Government, Public Education, Environmental Law.

MARTIN L. LEVY*, (Professor)**, born South Bend, Indiana, July 19, 1945; admitted to bar, 1974, Texas. *Education:* Indiana University (A.B., 1967); Indiana University (J.D., 1970). ***COURSES: Constitutional Law, Jurisprudence, Criminal Procedure, Federal Courts. ***Email:*** MLEVY@IBM.NET

RUBEN LUGO-RIGAU*, (Associate Professor)**, born July 22, 1928; admitted to bar, 1968, Texas. *Education:* Davis and Elkins College (B.S., 1956); Texas Southern University (J.D., 1965). ***COURSES: Criminal Law, Insurance, Juvenile Torts.

DEANNA POLLARD*, (Assistant Professor of Law)**, born Tacoma, Washington, March 5, 1964; admitted to bar, 1989, California; 1994, Washington. *Education:* University of Washington (B.A., 1986); University of Southern California (J.D., 1989); University of California Berkeley (LL.M., 1999). ***COURSES: Torts, Civil Rights. ***Email:*** pollardda@aol.com

ELSA YVETTE RANSOM*, (Associate Professor)**, born Houston, Texas, August 12, 1947; admitted to bar, 1990, Texas. *Education:* Indiana University (B.S., 1969); Syracuse University (M.S., 1970); University of Texas (J.D., 1987). ***COURSES: Torts, Mass Media Law, Intellectual Property Law. ***Email:*** eransom@tsulaw.edu

CATHERINE E. SMITH*, (Assistant Professor)**, born Ft. Monmouth, New Jersey, February 24, 1969; admitted to bar, 1996, South Carolina. *Education:* Wofford College (B.A., 1991); University of South Carolina (M.P.A., 1993; J.D., 1996). ***COURSES: Criminal Law, Torts. ***Email:*** casmith@tsulaw.edu

LARRY DARNELL WEEDEN*, (Professor)**, born Tunica, Mississippi, April 20, 1972; admitted to bar, 1975, Mississippi. *Education:* University of Mississippi (B.A., 1972; J.D., 1975). ***COURSES: Criminal Procedure, Employment Discrimination, Constitutional Law. ***Email:*** lweeden@tsu.edu

KENNETH ANTHONY WILLIAMS*, (Associate Professor)**, born New Orleans, February 12, 1961; admitted to bar, 1986, Pennsylvania; 1989, Louisiana. *Education:* University of San Francisco (B.A., 1983); University of Virginia (J.D., 1986). ***COURSES: Criminal Law, Civil Procedure, Evidence, International Law, International Human Rights, Death Penalty. ***Email:*** kwill@tsulaw.edu

---

TEXAS TECH UNIVERSITY SCHOOL OF LAW

18TH AND HARTFORD
LUBBOCK, TEXAS 79409
Telephone: (806) 742-3793
Fax: (806) 742-4014
www.law.ttu.edu

ABA Approved Since 1969.

The Texas Tech University School of Law was established in 1966 as a result of the efforts of attorney Alvin R. Allison, who saw a need for a state-supported law school in West Texas. The first class of 72 entering students was enrolled in 1967. Accredited by the Supreme Court of Texas in 1968 and approved by the American Bar Association in 1970, the Law School was granted an Order of the Coif Chapter in 1974.

(This Listing Continued)

TEXAS TECH UNIVERSITY SCHOOL OF LAW —Continued

The objective of the Law School faculty is to train men and women for the practice of law anywhere in the United States as advocates, counselors, judges, or law teachers, in accordance with the highest traditions of professional responsibility. The curriculum and the instructional methods of the law school faculty are designed to develop the students' highest potential, whatever their reasons for studying the law.

The smaller size of the Law School, which has a 19:1 student-faculty ratio, provides an atmosphere of informality and accessibility. The faculty's "open door" policy allows students to visit faculty as needed beyond classroom hours.

The Law School's physical facilities enhance the learning experience. The Law School has an outstanding law library, a new criminal and civil law clinic, a recently renovated courtroom, computer laboratory, a recently renovated office of career services, classrooms, seminar rooms, lounge and snack areas, student organization offices, and faculty and administrative offices. The Law School is accessible for students with disabilities.

Law libraries figure prominently in legal education, and facilities of the Texas Tech Law Library are among the best in the nation. Students have wide-ranging access to legal information resources, both print and on-line. An addition to the Law Library gives Texas Tech students unparalleled access to computer equipment and facilities. Traditional study carrels were transformed into computer-based workstations, enabling students to perform computer-assisted legal research, word processing, and a number of other functions in an office-like setting. These resources prepare students for the practice of law in technologically sophisticated environments. Our continuing goal is to update the computer network to provide our students with knowledge of technologies shaping the future of the legal community.

The student computer network consists of 220 computers in student study carrels, a 13-station computer lab, and multiple high-speed, high capacity laser printers. Each computer has access to electronic mail, word processing, legal research databases and utilities, Internet browsers, on-line library catalogs, and the CALI library of over 90 legal instruction tutorials and exercises.

These superior on-line facilities complement the substantial collection of print materials available in the Law Library. The collection contains over 200,000 bibliographic items, including bound volumes, microforms, government documents and CD-ROMs. The collection includes the reported cases of the federal and state courts, the statutes of Congress and all state legislatures, and the rules and decisions of federal and Texas state administrative agencies. As a selective U.S. Government Documents Depository, the Law Library collects a wide array of government documents relating to the law.

The Law Library staff is comprised of knowledgeable and experienced librarians and paraprofessionals who provide superior assistance and service to students and faculty. The staff includes four members with professional library education and two of whom are also lawyer-librarians.

Students at the Texas Tech University School of Law have significant opportunities to develop lawyering skills which contribute to the making of competent practitioners. The Law School curriculum includes courses that emphasize skills such as client interviewing and counseling, trial and appellate advocacy, negotiation, mediation, and arbitration. These courses bridge the gap between the law students' theoretical education and the practice of law. Students also have opportunities to enhance their skills training through participation in intraschool competitions in moot court, mock trial, client counseling, and negotiation. These competitions are administered by the student-run Board of Barristers. Every student, including first-year students, can participate each year in a competition in one or more of these four areas.

The Texas Tech Law School actively participates in interscholastic skills competitions and boasts one of the best records in the nation for outstanding performance in regional and national competitions. National championships have been achieved in moot court, mock trial, client counseling, and negotiation.

The Law School has a variety of other programs of interest. International study is afforded to our students through its program with the Universidad de Guanajuato. Several joint degree programs are offered leading to a Juris Doctorate and a Masters of Business Administration (School of Business Administration); Masters of Science in Accounting (School of Business Administration-Taxation); Master of Public Administration (Center for Public Service); or Masters of Science in Agricultural and Applied Economics (Department of Agricultural and Applied Economics); Masters in Financial Planning (College of Human Science).

Two Journals are published at the law school: *Texas Tech Law Review* and the newly established *Administrative Law Journal.* Several law professors along with a corps of student assistants compile and update bench books for Texas district judges and county judges under the auspices of each of their respective statewide organizations.

FULL TIME FACULTY

W. FRANK NEWTON*, (Dean and Professor of Law)**, admitted to bar, 1967,Texas. *Education:* Baylor University (B.A., 1965; J.D., 1967); New York University (LL.M., 1969); Columbia University (LL.M., 1978). ***COURSES: Public International Law, Conflict of Laws, Commercial Law, Legal Practice.

DANIEL H. BENSON*, (Horn Professor of Law, Adjunct Professor of Sociology)**, admitted to bar, 1961, Texas; 1965 District of Columbia. *Education:* University of Texas (B.A., 1958; J.D., 1961); Texas Tech University (M.A., 1974). ***COURSES: Evidence, Family Law, Texas Pre-trial Procedure, Texas Trial and Appellate Procedure.

CHARLES P. BUBANY*, (George Herman Mahon Professor of Law)**, admitted to bar, 1965, Missouri. *Education:* Saint Ambrose University (B.A., 1962); Washington University (J.D., 1965). ***COURSES: Family Law, Criminal Law, Criminal Procedure.

BRYAN THOMAS CAMP*, (Associate Professor)**, born Texas, 1960; admitted to bar, 1987, Virginia. *Education:* Haverford (B.A., 1982); University of Virginia (J.D., 1987; M.A., 1988); Columbia (L.L.M., 1993). ***COURSES: Tax Admin Bankruptcy.

WILLIAM R. CASTO*, (Alvin R. Allison Professor of Law)**, admitted to bar, 1973, Tennessee. *Education:* University of Tennessee at Knoxville (B.A., 1970; J.D., 1973); Columbia University (J.S.D., 1983). ***COURSES: Federal Jurisdiction, Contracts, Business Torts, National Security Law.

J. WESLEY COCHRAN*, (Professor of Law)**, admitted to bar, 1979, Texas. *Education:* Austin College (B.A., 1976); University of Houston (J.D., 1978); University of Washington (M.L.L., 1980). ***COURSES: Copyright Law, Native American Law, Gaming and Racing Law, Torts, Legislation, Business Torts.

***JOSEPH B. CONBOY*, (Associate Dean)**, admitted to bar, 1958, New York, Texas. *Education:* Canisius College (B.S., 1954); Georgetown

(This Listing Continued)

TEXAS TECH UNIVERSITY SCHOOL OF LAW —Continued

University Law Center (J.D., 1958); George Washington National Law Center (LL.M., 1972). ***COURSES:*** Trial Advocacy, Sports Law.

JAMES R. EISSINGER, **(Professor of Law)**, admitted to bar, 1964, North Dakota, Texas. *Education:* Wartburg College (B.A., 1960); University of North Dakota (J.D., 1964). ***COURSES:*** Labor Law, Constitutional Law, Discrimination in Employment, Constitutional Torts.

KAY PATTON FLETCHER, **(Assistant Dean)**, admitted to bar, 1980, Texas. *Education:* Bayor (B.S., 1971); Texas Tech University School of Law (J.D., 1980). ***COURSES:*** Law Office Management.

DAISY HURST FLOYD, **(Associate Dean and Professor of Law)**, admitted to bar, 1980, Georgia, Texas. *Education:* Emory University (B.A., 1977;M.A., 1977); University of Georgia (J.D., 1980). ***COURSES:*** Civil Procedure, Evidence, Dispute Resolution, Juvenile Justice, Pretrial Litigation.

TIMOTHY W. FLOYD, **(J. Nadley Edgar Professor of Law)**, admitted to bar, 1980, Georgia, Texas. *Education:* Emory University (B.A., 1977; M.A., 1977); University of Georgia (J.D., 1980). ***COURSES:*** Criminal Law, Legal Ethics, various lawyering skills courses.

SUSAN SAAB FORTNEY, **(Professor of Law)**, admitted to bar, 1977, Texas. *Education:* Trinity University (B.A., 1974); Antioch School of Law (J.D., 1977); Columbia University School of Law (LL.M., 1992; J.S.D., 1997). ***COURSES:*** Texas Civil Pre-Trial Procedure, Texas Trial and Appellate Procedure, Professional Responsibility, Pre-Trial Litigation.

JUDITH FULLINGIM, **(Legal Practice Professor)**, born Garden City, Michigan, March 03, 1946; admitted to bar, 1994, Texas. *Education:* Oakland University (B.A., 1974); University of Detroit (M.A., 1976); University of Michigan (Ph.D, 1978; J.D., 1983). ***COURSES:*** Legal Practice.

D. MURRAY HENSLEY, **(Adjunct Professor of Law)**, admitted to bar, 1982, Texas. *Education:* Texas Tech University (B.B.A., 1979); Texas Tech University School of Law (J.D., 1982). ***COURSES:*** Advises--Trial and Appellate Advocacy Teams.

DONALD M. HUNT, **(Adjunct Professor of Law)**, admitted to bar, 1961, Texas. *Education:* McMurry University (B.A., 1956); University of Texas (LL.B., 1961). ***COURSES:*** Appellate Advocacy; Advises--Trial and Appellate Advocacy Teams.

VAUGHN E. JAMES, **(Associate Professor)**, born Dominica; admitted to bar, 1999, New York. *Education:* University of the Virgin Islands (B.A., 1986); Andrews University (M.Div.,1991); University at Albany-SUNY (M.B.A., 1993); Syracuse University (J.D., 1998). ***COURSES:*** Wills and Trusts, Estate and Gift Tax, Law and Religion, Estate Planning.

JOHN E. KRAHMER, **(Foundation Professor of Commercial Law)**, admitted to bar, 1966, Iowa. *Education:* University of Iowa (B.A., 1965; J.D., 1966); Harvard University (LL.M., 1967). ***COURSES:*** Contracts, Commercial Law, Consumer Law.

BRUCE M. KRAMER, **(Maddox Professor of Law)**, admitted to bar, 1972, California; 1985, Texas. *Education:* University of California at Los Angeles (A.B., 1968; J.D., 1972); University of Illinois (LL.M., 1975). ***COURSES:*** Property, Oil and Gas Law, International Petroleum Transactions, Land-Use Planning, State and Local Government Law, Public Lands Law, Entertainment Law.

DELLAS W. LEE, **(Professor of Law)**, admitted to bar, 1960, British Columbia. *Education:* University of British Columbia (LL.B., 1959); University of Illinois (LL.M, 1962); University of Michigan (S.J.D., 1969). ***COURSES:*** Torts, Commercial Law, Creditors' Rights, Jewish Law.

FRANK RENE LOPEZ, **(Associate Professor)**, born El Paso, Texas, May 28, 1961; admitted to bar, 1990, California; 1995, Texas. *Education:* University of Texas at Austin (B.B.A., 1984); University of California, Berkeley, Boalt Hall School of Law (J.D., 1990). ***COURSES:*** Business Entities, Race and Law, Securities Regulation, Legal Problems- Small Business.

ALFREDO MIRANDE, **(Associate Professor)**, born Mexico City; admitted to bar, 1996, California. *Education:* Illinois State (B.S., 1963); University of Nebraska (Ph.D., 1967); Stanford (J.D., 1994). ***COURSES:*** Con Law, Immigration, Civil Rights, Race and Racism.

ALISON G. MYHRA, **(Professor of Law)**, admitted to bar, 1985, Minnesota, North Dakota. *Education:* University of North Dakota (B.A., B.S.Ed., 1982; J.D., 1985); Harvard University (LL.M., 1991). ***COURSES:*** Civil Procedure, Constitutional Law, Criminal Law, Criminal Procedure, Jurisprudence, Internships, Privacy Law.

DEAN G. PAWLOWIC, **(Professor of Law)**, admitted to bar, 1979, Nebraska. *Education:* Creighton University (B.A., 1970; M.A., 1972; J.D., 1979). ***COURSES:*** Advanced Bankruptcy Law, Banking Law, Business Entities, Contracts, Creditors' Rights, Bankruptcy, Remedies.

MARILYN PHELAN, **(Bean Professor of Law)**, admitted to bar, 1962, Texas. *Education:* Texas Tech University (B.A., 1959; M.B.A., 1967; Ph.D., 1971); University of Texas (J.D., 1972). ***COURSES:*** Accounting for Lawyers, Business Entities, Museums & the Law, Non-profit Organizations, Federal Income Taxation, Advanced Income Taxation.

JORGE ALBERTO RAMIREZ, **(Associate Professor)**, born McAllen, Texas, November 2, 1961; admitted to bar, 1990, Texas. *Education:* Harvard College (B.A., 1984); Harvard Law School (J.D., 1990). ***COURSES:*** Public International Law, International Business Transactions, Professional Responsibility. ***Email:*** jorge.ramirez@ttu.edu

BRIAN D. SHANNON, **(Associate Dean and Charles "Tex" Thornton Professor of Law)**, admitted to bar, 1982, Texas. *Education:* Angelo State University (B.S., 1979); University of Texas (J.D., 1982). ***COURSES:*** Administrative Law, Contracts, Dispute Resolution, Law and Psychiatry, Products Liability, Law and Disabilities; Coaches--ABA National Negotiation Team.

FRANK F. SKILLERN, **(George W. McCleskey Professor of Water Law)**, admitted to bar, 1966, Colorado, Texas. *Education:* University of Chicago (A.B., 1964); University of Denver (J.D., 1966); University of Michigan (LL.M., 1969). ***COURSES:*** Property, Wills and Trusts, Natural Resources Law, Water Law, Environmental Law.

NANCY JOANN SOONPAA, **(Associate Professor & Director, Legal Practice)**, born Minneapolis, Minnesota, July 28, 1961; admitted to bar, 1988, North Dakota. *Education:* University of North Dakota (B.A., 1983; J.D., 1987; M.A., 1990). ***COURSES:*** Legal Writing, Research, Appellate Ad., Negotiation, Health Law.

LARRY R. SPAIN, **(Associate Professor)**, born Newton, Iowa, April 20, 1951; admitted to bar, 1976, Nebraska; 1983, North Dakota; 2001, Texas. *Education:* University of Iowa (B.A., 1973); Creighton University (J.D., 1976). ***COURSES:*** Clinical, Interviewing and Counseling, Poverty Law.

VICTORIA V. SUTTON, **(Associate Professor)**, born North Carolina, April 9, 1956; admitted to bar, 1999, District of Columbia. *Education:* North Carolina University (B.S., 2 year, 1977); Old Dominion University (M.P.A., 1986); University of Texas at Dallas (Ph.D., 1989);

(This Listing Continued)

TEXAS TECH UNIVERSITY SCHOOL OF LAW —Continued

American University Washington School of Law (J.D., 1998). ***COURSES:*** Environmental Law, Administrative Law, American Indian Law, Law & Science. ***Email:*** xwsbb@ttu.edu

ARTURO LOPEZ TORRES*, (Associate Dean, Professor & Director, Law Library)**, born Mercedes, Texas; admitted to bar, 1981, Oregon. *Education:* University Nevada Las Vegas (B.S., 1971; M.E.D., 1973); Willamette University (J.D., 1979); University of Arizona (Ph.D., 1980); University Washington (M.L.S., 1984). ***Email: arturo.torres@ttu.edu

RACHEL A. VAN CLEAVE*, (Professor of Law)**, admitted to bar, 1989, California. *Education:* Stanford University (B.A., 1986); University of California, Hastings College of Law (J.D., 1989); Stanford Law School (J.S.M., 1994). ***COURSES: Property, Wills and Trusts, Criminal Law, Comparative Criminal Procedure.

ROBERT A. WENINGER*, (Professor of Law)**, admitted to bar, 1960, Wisconsin; 1970, California. *Education:* University of Wisconsin (B.B.A., 1955; LL.B., 1960); University of Chicago (LL.M., 1964). ***COURSES: Evidence, Civil Procedure, Trial Advocacy.

DONALD R. WILLIAMS*, (Director of Clinical Tax Studies)**, born Seminole, Texas, November 13, 1943; admitted to bar, 1987, Texas. *Education:* Texas Tech University (B.B.A., 1976); Texas Tech School of Law (J.D., 1987). ***COURSES: Tax Clinic.

TEXAS WESLEYAN UNIVERSITY SCHOOL OF LAW

1515 COMMERCE STREET
FORT WORTH, TEXAS 76102

THOMAS JEFFERSON SCHOOL OF LAW

2121 SAN DIEGO AVENUE
SAN DIEGO, CALIFORNIA 92110
Telephone: (619) 297-9700
Fax: (619) 294-4713
http://www.tjsl.edu E-mail: info@tjsl.edu

ABA Approved Since 1996.

Thomas Jefferson School of Law is a private, nonprofit, independent law school located in San Diego. Its mission is to provide an outstanding legal education for a nationally-based student body in a collegial and supportive environment. with attention to emerging new areas of law, particularly those relating to technological development, globalization and the quest for social justice.

The distinguished and dedicated members of the faculty have many years of experience as attorneys in the private and public sectors. They have participated in litigation at every level of the judicial system, from mediation sessions and local trial courts to the United States Supreme Court and the International Court of Justice The faculty includes scholars of national and international reputation whose numerous books and articles are used in classrooms and law offices throughout the United States and abroad. Faculty members have testified before Congress and the California legislature, have appeared as experts on national and local television and radio news broadcasts, and have served as legal consultants to the United States government, the United Nations, and several foreign governments.

The law school offers a balanced and comprehensive curriculum to prepare students to practice in any of the traditional areas of law, such as business law, family law, intellectual property, environmental law, civil rights law, civil litigation, criminal prosecution and criminal defense. Three academic centers ensure that students are prepared to practice in new fields of law as well as to address new trends that are transforming long established areas of law

The Center for Global Legal Studies prepares students to address the increasingly international dimension of law practice, as well as to specialize in international law. Courses include a wide range of international courses, including international business transactions, international environmental law, international criminal law, international dispute resolution, international human rights, European Union law, and international intellectual property law.

The center for Law, Technology and Communications considers the legal implications of the revolutions in information, communications and biological technology. Courses include traditional intellectual property law, cyberspace law, biotechnology law, bioethics, tele-communications law, e-commerce, media law, and sports and entertainment law.

The Center for Law and Social Justice addresses the continuing struggle to define and preserve the values of liberty and equality in a constantly changing world. Courses include traditional courses in civil rights, civil liberties, and international human rights, and courses that address the circumstances of those whom the law has sometimes treated differently, such as racial and ethnic minorities, and gays and lesbians.

The curriculum educates students in both the theory and practice of law. Each year the law school offers practical skills courses in trial practice, appellate advocacy, negotiation, mediation, arbitration, legal drafting, and client counseling. To supplement this classroom instruction, judicial internships and clinical field placement programs enable students to work directly for federal and state judges and attorneys in public agencies and with selected private law firms and companies for academic credit. These include agencies such as the California Attorney General, San Diego's City Attorney and District Attorney, the Federal Defender, the Public Defender, and the United States Attorney. A new public interest law program has been developed, as well as a new Honors Pro Bono program.

The curriculum is enriched by programs such as the Jefferson Lecture. U.S. Supreme Court Justice Antonin Scalia inaugurated the lecture series in January 2001. During his visit, Justice Scalia taught a constitutional law class, held a round table discussion with the faulty and delivered an address to students, alumni and members of the San Diego legal and business communities.

Thomas Jefferson's collegial and supportive environment is one of the truly distinguishing features of the law school. The *Princeton Review 2000 edition of The Best Law Schools* ranked Thomas Jefferson fifth in the nation for the quality of life on campus, as measured by the degree of student-faculty interaction, the sense of community on campus, and the lack of competitiveness among students.

Classes are kept small with the average class section in 2000-2001

(This Listing Continued)

THOMAS JEFFERSON SCHOOL OF LAW—Continued

having fewer than 30 students. Support services for students include faculty advisors; survival skills lectures and workshops presented by faculty and upper class students for all first year students; career planning and development services; and assistance in locating professional law-related employment. Student accessibility to the faculty is a top priority.

A flexible curriculum helps students tailor their schedules to their particular needs. Students may begin classes in January or August, attend the three year full-time program or the four year part-time program, and accelerate graduation one semester by taking additional classes during the summer.

Many students enhance their legal education by participation in extracurricular activities, such as the *Thomas Jefferson Law Review* and the moot court or mock trial teams. The Thomas Jefferson team took first place in the 1997 Roger J. Traynor Moot Court Competition against 20 other California law schools. The large number of student organizations on campus annually reflects not only a wide range of student interests, but also valuable networking opportunities with professional law organizations.

A significant number of the almost 600 students enrolled at Thomas Jefferson are second career students, including physicians, nurses, law enforcement officers, real estate and stock brokers, engineers, accountants and administrators, among others, who bring a wealth of professional and personal experience to the classroom. Due to Thomas Jefferson's growing national and international reputation, about sixty percent of the fall 2000 class came from outside California, representing about 40 states and several foreign countries The student body also is racially and ethnically diverse, with more than 20 percent of the fall class representing members of racial or ethnic minority groups.

The law school is extremely proud of its nearly 4,200 alumni, who include partners in major law firms, numerous judges, a member of the United States Congress, and the 1997-98 president of the 155,000-member State Bar of California. The school's Alumni Relations Office encourages networking between the students and the alumni through various activities, including an alumni association mentor program.

The law school is housed in two modern buildings in the historic Old Town section of San Diego: the Law Library Building and the Courtyard Building. The campus is near the courthouses, law offices, and corporate headquarters which adorn the downtown San Diego horizon.

One of the benefits of attending Thomas Jefferson School of Law is the opportunity to study law in beautiful San Diego, one of America's largest and finest cities. Bordered on the west by 70 miles of glistening Pacific Ocean beaches, San Diego can boast of a near perfect climate and an array of spectacular scenery to be enjoyed year around. Fabulous white sand beaches and bays offering water sports, picnic areas, running and biking paths, and playgrounds are within minutes of campus. A short distance to the east are majestic mountains and deserts, admired by residents and visitors alike. Other popular attractions include the world-famous San Diego Zoo and Wild Animal Park, Sea World, historic Balboa Park with its acclaimed museums and landscaping, early Spanish settlements and missions, and professional sporting events. The Student Services Office is available to assist students with housing options near campus and throughout the San Diego area.

In addition to its seemingly endless selection of physical, cultural, and recreational attractions, San Diego also provides an abundance of professional opportunities for Thomas Jefferson students and alumni due to its continued growth and economic vitality. Legal services are one of San Diego's most prosperous industries.

Dean: Kenneth J. Vandevelde (619) 297-9700(1430)
Admissions: Jennifer Keller (619) 297-9700(1472)
Financial Assistance: Nancy Vu (619) 297-9700(1302)
Library: Karla Castetter (619) 297-9700(1110)
Placement: Andrea Lamb (619) 297-9700(1492)
Alumni Relations: Lisa Kellogg (619) 297-9700(1491)
Student Services: Lisa Ferreira (619) 297-9700(1481)
Academics: Kay Henley (619) 297-9700(1400)
Communications: Lori Wulfemeyer (619) 297-9700(1840)

FULL TIME FACULTY

KENNETH JOSEPH VANDEVELDE*, (Dean and Professor of Law)**, born Louisville, Kentucky, August 19, 1953; admitted to bar, 1979, District of Columbia; 1988, California. *Education:* University of Louisville (B.A., 1975); Harvard Law School (J.D., 1979). ***COURSES: International Law, Constitutional Law, American Legal History. ***Email:*** kennethv@tjsl.edu

LAURA S. ADAMS*, (Assistant Professor of Law)**, born London, England, December 24, 1966; admitted to bar, 1993, New York; 1998, California. *Education:* Princeton University (A.B., 1988); Harvard University (J.D., 1992). ***COURSES: Contracts, Family Law.

H. HADLEY BATCHELDER*, (Professor of Law)**, born San Diego, California, May 18, 1939; admitted to bar, 1965, California. *Education:* Pomona College (B.A., 1961); University of California, Berkeley (Boalt Hall) (J.D.,1964). ***COURSES: Alternative Dispute Resolution, Arbitration, Community Property, Remedies. ***Email:*** hadleyb@tjsl.edu

LINDA L. BERGER*, (Associate Professor of Law)**, born Akron, Colorado; admitted to bar, 1985, California. *Education:* University of Colorado-Boulder (B.S., 1970); Case Western Reserve University (J.D., 1985). ***COURSES: Legal Writing, Legal Drafting, Legal Rhetoric. ***Email:*** lindab@tjsl.edu

SUSAN BISOM-RAPP*, (Associate Professor of Law)**, born Plainview, New York, October 29, 1961; admitted to bar, 1987, New York. *Education:* Cornell University (B.S., 1983); University of California, Berkeley (Boalt Hall) (J.D., 1987); Columbia University School of Law (LL.M., 1994; J.S.D., 1997). ***COURSES: Employment Discrimination Law, Employment Law, Labor Law, Torts. ***Email:*** susanb@tjsl.edu

KARLA MARLENE CASTETTER*, (Professor of Law & Library Director)**, born Kingsport, Tennessee, February 7, 1950. *Education:* University of Cincinnati (B.A., 1972); Kent State University (M.L.S., 1973); California Western School of Law (J.D., 1980). ***Email: karlac@tjsl.edu

***MARJORIE COHN*, (Associate Professor of Law)**, born Pomona, California, November 1, 1948; admitted to bar, 1975, California.

(This Listing Continued)

THOMAS JEFFERSON SCHOOL OF LAW—Continued

Education: Stanford University (B.A., 1970); Santa Clara University School of Law (J.D., 1975). ***COURSES:*** Criminal Law, Criminal Procedure, Evidence, International Human Rights Law. ***Email:*** marjorie@tjsl.edu

COLIN CRAWFORD, **(Associate Professor of Law),** born Denver, Colorado, November 17, 1958; admitted to bar, 1989, New York. *Education:* Columbia University (B.A., 1980); Corpus Christi College, Cambridge (M.A., 1982); Harvard (J.D., 1988). ***COURSES:*** Environmental Law, International Environmental Law, Land Use Planning, Local Government Law, Property. ***Email:*** colinc@tjsl.edu

JOY L. DELMAN, **(Professor of Law),** born Philadelphia, Pennsylvania, February 5, 1954; admitted to bar, 1979, Pennsylvania; 1982, California. *Education:* University of Pennsylvania (B.A., 1974); Georgetown University Law Center (J.D., 1979). ***COURSES:*** Torts, Law & Medicine, Wills. ***Email:*** joyd@tjsl.edu

ILENE BETH DURST, **(Associate Professor of Law),** born New York, NY, March 9, 1956; admitted to bar, 1984, New York. *Education:* S.U.N.Y. at Albany (B.A., 1977); University of California, Irvine (M.F.A., 1994); New York Law School (J.D., 1983). ***COURSES:*** Legal Writing, Law & Literature, Immigration Law. ***Email:*** ilened@tjsl.edu

ALFRED THOMAS GOLDEN, **(Professor of Law),** born East Liverpool, Ohio, February 20, 1950; admitted to bar, 1975, California. *Education:* Kent State University (B.A., 1972); UCLA (J.D., 1975). ***COURSES:*** Remedies, Contracts, Antitrust. ***Email:*** thomasg@tjsl.edu

JULIE A. GREENBERG, **(Professor of Law),** born Detroit, Michigan, December 14, 1951; admitted to bar, 1980, California. *Education:* University of Michigan (B.A., 1972; J.D., 1979). ***COURSES:*** Corporations, Business Drafting, Women and the Law. ***Email:*** julieg@tjsl.edu

KEVIN JEROME GREENE, **(Assistant Professor of Law),** born New York, NY; admitted to bar, 1991, New York. *Education:* S.U.N.Y., Old Westbury (B.A., 1986); Yale Law School (J.D., 1989). ***COURSES:*** Contracts, Intellectual Property, Entertainment Law.

MARYBETH HERALD, **(Associate Dean and Professor of Law),** born Buffalo, New York, March 16, 1956; admitted to bar, 1982, California. *Education:* Michigan State University (B.A., 1977); Harvard (J.D., 1980). ***COURSES:*** Constitutional Law, Contracts. ***Email:*** marybeth@tjsl.edu

MAUREEN E. MARKEY, **(Professor of Law),** born Glendale, West Virginia, November 25, 1947; admitted to bar, 1981, California. *Education:* Bowling Green State University (B.A., 1970); Duquesne University (1970-1972); University of San Diego (J.D., 1981). ***COURSES:*** Jurisprudence, Law and Literature, Property, Wills and Trusts. ***Email:*** maureenm@tjsl.edu

ERIC J. MITNICK, **(Assistant Professor of Law),** born New Jersey, 1966; admitted to bar, 1991, New Jersey; 1992, New York. *Education:* Cornell University (A.B., 1988); Princeton University (M.A., 1998); University of Michigan Law School (J.D., 1991). ***COURSES:*** Administrative Law, Torts, Professional Responsibility.

RUTH B. PHILIPS, **(Visiting Assistant Professor of Law),** born Bethpage, New York, 1956; admitted to bar, 1989, Massachusetts; 1990, New York. *Education:* State University of New York (B.F.A., 1980); Harvard Law School (J.D., 1989). ***COURSES:*** Evidence, International Criminal Law. ***Email:*** ruthp@tjsl.edu

ARNOLD S. ROSENBERG, **(Assistant Professor),** born Rochester, New York, June 22, 1951; admitted to bar, 1976, Illinois; 1979, California; 1982, New York. *Education:* Cornell University (B.A., 1972); Harvard Law School (J.D., 1976). ***COURSES:*** Bankruptcy, Commercial Law, E-Commerce, Real Estate Transactions. ***Email:*** arosenberg@tjsl.edu

AARON SCHWABACH, **(Associate Professor of Law),** born Chicago, Illinois, March 3, 1963; admitted to bar, 1989, California; 1993, Florida. *Education:* Antioch College (B.A., 1985); University of California, Berkeley (Boalt Hall) (J.D., 1989). ***COURSES:*** International Business Transactions, International Dispute Resolution, International Environmental Law, International Law, Legal Writing. ***Email:*** aarons@tjsl.edu

RICHARD F. SCOTT, **(Distinguished Professor of International Law),** born Altadena, California, February 28, 1928; admitted to bar, 1954, California. *Education:* University of Chicago Law School (J.D., 1952); University of Paris (Docteur en Droit de L' Universite in International Law, 1964). ***COURSES:*** International Economic Law, International Law, European Union Law. ***Email:*** richards@tjsl.edu

STEVEN SEMERARO, **(Assistant Professor of Law),** born New Jersey, April 5, 1962; admitted to bar, 1989, New York and District of Columbia; 1990 U.S., Court of Appeals for the Fifth Circuit; 1991, U.S. District Court for the District of Columbia. *Education:* Rutgers College (B.A., 1984); Stanford University Law School (J.D., 1987). ***COURSES:*** Civil Procedure, Criminal Law, Death Penalty Seminar, Intellectual Property & Competition Law, Property, Telecommunications Law. ***Email:*** ssemeraro@tjsl.edu

WILLIAM REED SLOMANSON, **(Professor of Law),** born Johnstown, Pennsylvania, May 1, 1945; admitted to bar, 1975, California. *Education:* University of Pittsburgh (B.A., 1967); California Western School of Law (J.D., 1974); Columbia University School of Law (LL.M., 1975). ***COURSES:*** Civil Procedure, California Civil Procedure, International Law. ***Email:*** bills@tjsl.edu

DAVID E. STEINBERG, **(Associate Professor of Law),** born San Francisco, California, September, 24, 1960; admitted to bar, 1988, Illinois; 1996, Pennsylvania. *Education:* Northwestern University (B.A., 1982); Stanford University Law School (J.D., 1986). ***COURSES:*** Civil Rights Law, Constitutional Law, Criminal Law, Criminal Procedure, Cybercrimes. ***Email:*** davids@tjs;.edu

SUSAN W. TIEFENBRUN, **(Associate Professor of Law),** born New York, 1943; admitted to bar, 1987, New York; 1987, Connecticut. *Education:* University of Wisconsin (B.S., 1965; M.A., 1966); Columbia University (Ph.D., 1971); New York University School of Law (J.D., 1986). ***COURSES:*** Business Planning, Corporations, International Business Transactions, International Intellectual Property Law, Securities Regulation. ***Email:*** susant@tjsl.edu

ELLEN A. WALDMAN, **(Professor of Law),** born New York, December 20, 1961; admitted to bar, 1988, Maryland; 1990, Washington D.C.. *Education:* Brown University (B.A., 1983); New York University School of Law (J.D., 1987); University of Virginia (LL.M., 1991). ***COURSES:*** Torts, Bioethics, Mediation, Director of Clinical Education and Judicial Internships. ***Email:*** ellenw@tjls.edu

BRYAN H. WILDENTHAL, **(Associate Professor of Law),** born Houston, Texas, 1964; admitted to bar, 1990, Michigan; 1993, Washington D.C.. *Education:* Stanford University (A.B., 1986); Stanford University Law School (J.D., 1989). ***COURSES:*** Civil Procedure, Constitutional Law, Federal Indian Law, Sexual Orientation and the Law. ***Email:*** bryanbhw@ix.netcom.com

THOMAS M. COOLEY LAW SCHOOL

300 S. CAPITOL AVENUE
LANSING, MICHIGAN 48933
Telephone: (517) 371-5140
Fax: (517) 334-5718
http://www.cooley.edu

ABA Approved Since 1975

America's leader in part-time, year-round legal education, Thomas M. Cooley Law School was established by former Michigan Supreme Court Chief Justice Thomas E. Brennan and a group of dedicated lawyers and judges.

Named for Michigan's renowned Judge Cooley, the school is committed to liberal admissions, practical scholarship, and uncompromising professionalism. The American Bar Association approved Thomas Cooley Law School in 1978. As an independent, non-profit, graduate institution, Thomas Cooley enjoys the reputation of a tough law school, run by experienced lawyers and judges. Its faculty, students and alumni take pride in the school's close contacts with the bench and bar.

In 1993, Thomas M. Cooley Law School received the Outstanding School Award from the American Bar Association Law Student Division. This recognition was attributed to Thomas Cooley's participation in many ABA-sponsored functions, including hosting the 6th Circuit Summer Caucus, and student competitions in client counseling and negotiation. Nearly 50 percent of all Thomas Cooley students belong to the ABA Law Student Division, a fact which gained further recognition from the association. In the same ceremony, a Thomas Cooley student was awarded the Silver Key Award by the 6th Circuit, its highest award; an alumnus was awarded the 1992-93 National Award for VITA, a volunteer income tax assistance program; and the Pillar, the student newspaper, received a second place award for its humor column. Thomas Cooley's law review has received national recognition for promoting the use of plain English in lawsuit papers. The school's courtroom advocacy course, trial workshops and moot court classes emphasize professional skills.

Thomas Cooley's massive, seven-story air-conditioned main building contains modern lecture halls, classrooms, seminar and conference rooms, faculty offices and a student lounge area. The Administration Building and bookstore are in separate, nearby buildings.

The law school's 65,000-square-foot library building has four floors and a basement. Comfortable seating for 559 is provided at tables and spacious carrels in group study-audio-visual viewing rooms, stack and casual seating areas, and the Strosacker Commons, the magnificent main reading room.

Most of the library's functions and services have been automated to increase efficiency and improve the quality of information services delivered to patrons. For example, the library employs INNOPAC, an automated library system which provides access to the on-line catalog by personal computer from homes and law offices, as well as the library.

The law school is organized on a 12 month academic year, consisting of three full 15-week terms of school. Each term meets the definition of a full semester. Like the terms of the English Courts of Common Law, Thomas Cooley's three academic terms are designated Hilary Term (January to April), Trinity Term (May to August), and Michaelmas Term (September to December).

Thomas Cooley students typically attend classes only 10 hours per week which permits full-time employment. Still, they graduate in three years or less.

The Sixty Plus, Inc., Elderlaw Clinic, Thomas Cooley's award-winning clinic for elderly citizens, permits students to earn academic credit representing real clients. Directed studies, trial workshops, law review, and moot court programs enrich the curriculum. Because Thomas Cooley has a national student body, civil and criminal practice courses for New York, New Jersey, Pennsylvania, Florida, Indiana and Illinois are offered.

Thomas Cooley's diverse student body nears 1,600; more than 30 percent are women; 72 percent hail from out-of-state; about 15 percent are racial minorities; and 12 percent hold advanced degrees. Thomas Cooley's externship program places final-year students in real-life work settings to gain practical experience in the legal settings of their choice. This dynamic program provides students with experience, confidence and contacts to provide a seamless transition from school to career.

Dean: Don LeDuc
Associate Dean of Faculty: John Nussbaumer
Associate Dean of Students: Amy Timmer
Associate Dean of Planning & Programs: M. Ann Miller
Associate Dean, Professor and Director of Library Services: Roberta Studwell
Admissions Director: Stephanie Gregg
Financial Aid Director: Richard Boruszewski
Director of Career Services: Bernice Davenport
Alumni Director: Darryl J. Parsell
Registrar: Sherida Wysocki

FULL TIME FACULTY

DON LEDUC*, (Dean)**, born Flint, Michigan, April 7, 1942; admitted to bar, 1968, Michigan. *Education:* Kalamazoo College (B.A., 1964); Wayne State University (J.D., 1967). ***COURSES: Administrative Law, Torts, Correctional Law.

GARY BAUER*, (Assistant Professor)**, born Ft. Wayne, Indiana, November 1, 1948; admitted to bar, 1988, Michigan. *Education:* Purdue University (B.S., 1971); Central Michigan University (M.A., 1976); Thomas Cooley (J.D., 1988). ***COURSES: Elderlaw, Environmental Law. ***Email:*** bauerg@cooley.edu

***HONORABLE THOMAS E. BRENNAN*, (President and Chairman of the Board)**, born Detroit, Michigan, May 27, 1929; admitted to bar, 1953, Michigan. *Education:* University of Detroit (LL.B., 1952).

***JOHN S. BRENNAN*, (Associate Professor and Vice President of**

(This Listing Continued)

THOMAS M. COOLEY LAW SCHOOL—Continued

Information Services), born Detroit, Michigan, March 21, 1956; admitted to bar, 1984, Illinois; 1991, Minnesota; 1996, Michigan. *Education:* University of Detroit (A.B., 1977); Boston College Law School (J.D., 1984). ***COURSES:*** Civil Procedure, Remedies, Professional Responsibility.

RONALD J. BRETZ, **(Associate Professor)**, born Detroit, November 11, 1951; admitted to bar, 1976, Michigan. *Education:* Michigan State University (B.A., 1973); Wayne State University Law School (J.D., 1976). ***COURSES:*** Criminal Procedure, Criminal Law, Evidence.

DENA M. BROWN, **(Assistant Professor)**, admitted to bar, 1995, Michigan; 1996 Illinois. *Education:* Davenport College; Thomas M. Cooley Law School. ***COURSES:*** Research & Writing.

KATHLEEN CONNOLLY BUTLER, **(Associate Professor)**, born Champaign, Illinois, November 15, 1954; admitted to bar, 1989, Indiana; 1992, Illinois. *Education:* Northwestern University (B.S.S., 1976; M.A.T., 1979); University of Illinois College of Law (J.D., 1989). ***COURSES:*** Torts I, Torts II.

JEANETTE BUTTREY, **(Associate Professor)**, ***COURSES:*** Research & Writing.

TERRENCE F. CAVANAUGH, **(Associate Professor)**, born Detroit, February 14, 1948; admitted to bar, 1978, Michigan. *Education:* University of Michigan (B.S.E., 1971); The University of Toledo College of Law (J.D., 1978). ***COURSES:*** Criminal Law Clinic, Elder Law Clinic. ***Email:*** cavanaut@cooley.edu

CHARLES P. CERCONE, **(Associate Professor)**, *Education:* Williams College (B.A., 1980); State University of New York School of Law (J.D., 1984). ***COURSES:*** Civil Procedure, Taxation.

DENNIS E. CICHON, **(Professor)**, *Education:* Grand Rapids Junior College (A.A., 1974); Grand Valley State College (B.S., 1976); Ohio State University College of Law (J.D., 1981); Temple University School of Law (LL.M., 1987). ***COURSES:*** Secured Transactions, Disabilities Law, Contracts.

PATRICK EDWARD CORBETT, **(Associate Professor)**, born Michigan, November 23, 1960; admitted to bar, 1987, Michigan. *Education:* Michigan State University (B.A., 1983); Notre Dame Law School (J.D., 1987). ***COURSES:*** Criminal Law, Procedure. ***Email:*** corbettp@cooley.edu

DAVID G. COTTER, **(Professor)**, born Lansing, Michigan, November 8, 1948; admitted to bar, 1976, Michigan. *Education:* University of Michigan (B.S.E., 1971); Thomas M. Cooley Law School (J.D., 1976). ***COURSES:*** Civil Procedure, Jurisdiction, Agency & Partnership, Corporations.

MICHAEL P. COX, **(Professor & Dean Emeritus)**, born Lexington, Kentucky, May 18, 1943; admitted to bar, 1968, Kentucky; 1980, Oklahoma; 1989, Michigan. *Education:* University of Kentucky (B.S., 1965; J.D., 1968); Columbia University (LL.M., 1974; J.S.D., 1981). ***COURSES:*** Contracts, Administrative Law, Conflict of Laws, Regulated Industries.

MARY ELIZABETH D'ISA, **(Professor)**, born Iowa City, Iowa, September 18, 1958; admitted to bar, 1984, Iowa; 1984, Nebraska; 1990, Michigan. *Education:* St. Mary's College (B.A., 1981); Creighton University (J.D., 1984); Northwestern University (M.S.J., 1988). ***COURSES:*** Legal Research and Writing, Criminal Law, Faculty Advisor Law Review.

MARK DOTSON, **(Associate Professor)**, born Flint, Michigan, April 23, 1957; admitted to bar, 1990, Wisconsin. *Education:* University of Michigan (B.S., 1980); Thomas M. Cooley (J.D., 1990). ***COURSES:*** Torts, Criminal Procedure. ***Email:*** dotsonm@cooley.edu

BARRY HART DUBNER, **(Professor)**, born Brooklyn, New York, November 22, 1940; admitted to bar, 1969, New York; 1974, Florida; 1991, Michigan. *Education:* B.A. Hunter College (B.A., 1965); University of Miami (LL.M., 1974); New York University (J.S.D., 1975; LL.M., 1975). ***COURSES:*** Contracts, Admiralty, International Law of the Sea, Commercial Law, Secured Transactions.

NORMAN FELL, **(Professor)**, born Detroit, Michigan, September 8, 1942; admitted to bar, 1969, California; 1972, Michigan. *Education:* Wayne State University (B.S., 1965; J.D., 1968). ***COURSES:*** Clinical Education, Criminal Law, Professional Responsibility, Skills Program.

HONORABLE JOHN W. FITZGERALD, **(Professor)**, born Grand Ledge, Michigan, November 14, 1924; admitted to bar, 1954, Michigan; 1971, U.S. Supreme Court. *Education:* Michigan State University (B.S., 1947); University of Michigan (J.D., 1954). ***COURSES:*** Property, Land Titles.

JUDITH A. FRANK, **(Professor)**, born Detroit, Michigan, March 1, 1945; admitted to bar, 1986, Michigan. *Education:* University of Michigan (B.A., 1966); Michigan State University (M.A., 1970); Thomas M. Cooley Law School (J.D., 1986). ***COURSES:*** Clinic, Lawyering Skills.

ELLIOT B. GLICKSMAN, **(Professor)**, born Detroit, Michigan, January 25, 1942; admitted to bar, 1969, Michigan. *Education:* Eastern Michigan University (B.A., 1964); Wayne State University (M.A., 1966); University of Detroit (J.D., 1969). ***COURSES:*** Evidence, Constitutional Law, Evidence Seminars.

RICHARD C. HENKE, **(Associate Professor)**, born Red Bank, New Jersey, October 3, 1961; admitted to bar, 1986, New Jersey; 1987, New York. *Education:* University of Notre Dame (B.A., 1983); Syracuse University College of Law (J.D., 1986). ***COURSES:*** Torts II.

KEITH J. HEY, **(Professor)**, born Marcus, Iowa, August 4, 1934; admitted to bar, 1963, Iowa; 1963, Nebraska; 1980, Michigan. *Education:* Creighton University (B.S.C., 1955; J.D., 1963); Georgetown University (LL.M., 1969). ***COURSES:*** Contracts, Commercial Law, Health Law, Torts, Remedies, Sales and Negotiable Instruments.

JAMES HICKS, **(General Counsel and Visiting Professor)**, born Bay Shore, New York, January 1, 1958; admitted to bar, 1984, Illinois; 1988, Connecticut; 1992 Michigan. *Education:* Williams College (B.A., 1980); Washington and Lee University (J.D., 1984). ***COURSES:*** Civil Procedure, Lawyering Before Trial. ***Email:*** hicksj@cooley.edu

MARION M. HILLIGAN, **(Assistant Professor)**, born Germany; admitted to bar, 1990, Michigan. *Education:* Michigan State University (B.A., 1986); Thomas M. Cooley Law School (J.D., 1989). ***COURSES:*** Research/Writing.

PETER D. JASON, **(Professor)**, born Detroit, Michigan, July 9, 1941; admitted to bar, 1968, Michigan. *Education:* University of Notre Dame (B.B.A., 1963); St. John's Seminary (M.T.S., 1986); University of Detroit (J.D., 1967). ***COURSES:*** Contracts, Torts, Remedies, Sales and Negotiable Instruments, Legal History.

EILEEN KAVANAGH, **(Associate Professor)**, born Detroit, Michigan, June 6, 1950; admitted to bar, 1977, Illinois; 1989, Michigan. *Education:* University of Michigan (B.A., 1973); DePaul University College of Law (J.D., 1977). ***COURSES:*** Research & Writing, Property II. ***Email:*** kavanage@cooley.edu

PETER M. KEMPEL, **(Professor)**, born Detroit, Michigan, March 5, 1943; admitted to bar, 1971, Michigan. *Education:* University of

(This Listing Continued)

THOMAS M. COOLEY LAW SCHOOL—Continued

Detroit (A.B., 1965; J.D., 1971); University of Michigan (A.M.L.S., 1967). ***COURSES:*** Professional Responsibility, Contracts, Commercial Law, Legislation, Jurisprudence, Evidence.

MARA ELENA KENT*, (Visiting Assistant Professor)**, born Ann Arbor, Michigan, November 23, 1970; admitted to bar, 1996, Michigan. *Education:* University of Michigan (B.F.A., 1993); University of Detroit Mercy (J.D., 1996). ***COURSES: Research & Writing. ***Email:*** kentm@cooley.edu

JOSEPH KIMBLE*, (Professor)**, born Howell, Michigan, July 1, 1945; admitted to bar, 1982, Michigan. *Education:* Amherst College (B.A., 1967); University of Michigan (J.D., 1972). ***COURSES: Research and Writing, Drafting, Legal Methods Program.

DOREAN M. KOENIG*, (Professor)**, born Bay City, Michigan, August 1, 1934; admitted to bar, 1968, Michigan. *Education:* University of Detroit (Ph.B., 1956; J.D., 1967). ***COURSES: Constitutional Law, Civil Procedure, Criminal Law.

***PAULA R. LATOVICK*, (Professor)**, born Detroit, Michigan, February 17, 1954; admitted to bar, 1980, Michigan. *Education:* Michigan State University (B.A., 1976); University of Michigan (J.D., 1980; LL.M., 1999).

GERALD G. MACDONALD*, (Professor)**, born Beverly, Massachusetts, June 11, 1959; admitted to bar, 1984, District of Columbia; 1985, Massachusetts. *Education:* University of Michigan (B.A., 1981); Case Western Reserve University (J.D., 1984). ***COURSES: Civil Procedure, Jurisdiction.

JOHN H. MARKS*, (Associate Professor)**, born Detroit, Michigan, July 19, 1959; admitted to bar, 1989, California. *Education:* Michigan State University (B.S., 1981); University of California (J.D., 1989). ***COURSES: Legal Writing, Reasoning and Research.

DAN L. MCNEAL*, (Professor)**, born Kenosha, Wisconsin, November 14, 1940; admitted to bar, 1968, Michigan. *Education:* Michigan State University (B.A., 1962); Detroit College of Law (J.D., 1967); Wayne State University (LL.M., 1986). ***COURSES: Taxation.

HELEN PRATT MICKENS*, (Professor)**, born Kalamazoo, Michigan, June 1, 1952; admitted to bar, 1980, Michigan; 1985, Louisiana. *Education:* Kalamazoo College (B.A., 1976); Thomas M. Cooley Law School (J.D., 1980); Michigan State University (M.A., 1999). ***COURSES: Professional Responsibility, Admiralty, Maritime Law.

M. ANN MILLER*, (Associate Dean of Planning & Programs and Professor)**, born Indianapolis, Indiana, February 5, 1952; admitted to bar, 1979, Michigan; 1989, California. *Education:* State University of New York at Binghamton (B.A., 1974); University of Michigan (J.D., 1979). ***COURSES: Clinical Law, Professional Responsibility.

MARLA MITCHELL*, (Associate Professor)**, born San Bernardino, California, November 2, 1958; admitted to bar, 1984, Ohio; 1996, Michigan. *Education:* San Barnardino Community College (1978); Youngstown State University (B.S., 1981); The University of Akron (J.D., 1984). ***COURSES: Clinic, Appellate Advocacy. ***Email:*** mitchelm@cooley.edu

LAWRENCE W. MORGAN*, (Professor)**, born Detroit, Michigan, July 17, 1941; admitted to bar, 1968, Michigan. *Education:* University of Notre Dame (B.B.A., 1963); University of Michigan (M.B.A., 1964); University of Detroit (J.D., 1968). ***COURSES: Sales, Secured Transactions, Bankruptcy, Contracts, State and Local Government, State and Local Tax.

MAURICE E. R. MUNROE*, (Professor)**, born London, England; admitted to bar, 1977, United Kingdom. *Education:* University of Birmingham (LL.B., 1976); University of London (LL.M., 1980); University of Michigan (LL.M., 1992). ***COURSES: Contracts, Employment Discrimination, Torts.

JOHN R. NUSSBAUMER*, (Associate Dean of Faculty & Professor)**, born Oak Park, Illinois, December 23, 1950; admitted to bar, 1977, Michigan. *Education:* Denison University (B.A., 1973); University of Michigan (J.D., 1976). ***COURSES: Criminal Procedure, Criminal Law and Appellate Practice.

KIMBERLY E. O'LEARY*, (Associate Professor of Law)**, born Kentucky, January 30, 1958; admitted to bar, 1982, Indiana; 1994, Ohio. *Education:* Oberlin College (B.A., 1979); Northeastern University (J.D., 1982). ***COURSES: Clinical, Interviewing & Counseling. ***Email:*** olearyk@cooley.edu

CHARLES A. PALMER*, (Professor)**, born Jackson, Michigan, January 25, 1945; admitted to bar, 1970, Michigan. *Education:* University of Michigan (B.B.A., 1967; J.D., 1970). ***COURSES: Contracts, Property, Products Liability, Torts, Lawyering Before Trial (Pretrial Skills Course), Unfair Trade Practices.

NORA J. PASMAN-GREEN*, (Professor)**, born Detroit, Michigan, November 30, 1951; admitted to bar, 1977, Michigan. *Education:* University of Michigan (B.S., 1973); Wayne State University (J.D., 1977). ***COURSES: Administrative Law, Clinic, Trial Advocacy, Torts.

JAMES M. PEDEN*, (Professor)**, born Angola, Indiana, October 26, 1950; admitted to bar, 1976, Ohio; 1987, Texas; 1989, Michigan. *Education:* University of Michigan (B.A., 1972); University of Toledo (J.D., 1976). ***COURSES: Clinic, Lawyering Before Trial, Criminal Law.

ERNEST A. PHILLIPS*, (Professor)**, born New Kensington, Pennsylvania, January 17, 1941; admitted to bar, 1972, Pennsylvania; 1973, Michigan. *Education:* College of William & Mary (B.A., 1962); Duquesne University (J.D., 1972). ***COURSES: Torts, Alternative Dispute Resolution, Sports Law.

PHILIP J. PRYGOSKI*, (Professor)**, born Michigan, December 7, 1947; admitted to bar, 1973, Michigan. *Education:* University of Michigan (B.A., 1969; M.A., 1978; J.D., 1973; LL.M., 1983). ***COURSES: Constitutional Law, Federal Courts, American Indian Law.

JOHN P. ROONEY*, (Professor Emeritus)**, born Evanston, Illinois, May 1, 1932; admitted to bar, 1958, Illinois; 1961, California; 1975, Michigan. *Education:* University of Illinois (B.A., 1953); Harvard University (J.D., 1958). ***COURSES: Property, Remedies, Jurisprudence.

MARJORIE P. RUSSELL*, (Associate Professor)**, born New York, New York, October 7, 1954; admitted to bar, 1983, Michigan. *Education:* Michigan State University (B.A., 1976); Thomas M. Cooley School of Law (J.D., 1983). ***COURSES: Evidence, Trial Advocacy, Legal Clinics.

JOHN N. SCOTT*, (Professor)**, born Detroit, Michigan, March 7, 1945; admitted to bar, 1974, Michigan. *Education:* University of Michigan (B.A., 1967; M.A., 1969; J.D., 1974). ***COURSES: Evidence, Trial Advocacy, Property, Land Use.

CHARLES J. SENGER*, (Professor)**, born Rock Island, Illinois, July 15, 1945; admitted to bar, 1974, Michigan. *Education:* Immaculate Conception (B.A., 1968); Michigan State University (M.A., 1982; Ph.D., 1989); University of Detroit (J.D., 1973). ***COURSES: Debtors and Creditors Rights, Property, Secured Transactions.

***CHRIS A. SHAFER*, (Associate Professor)**, born Sikeston, Montana, November 1, 1950; admitted to bar, 1993, Michigan. *Education:*

(This Listing Continued)

THOMAS M. COOLEY LAW SCHOOL—Continued

Michigan State University (B.S., 1973; M.S., 1975); Thomas M. Cooley Law School (J.D., 1993). ***COURSES:*** State & Federal Administrative Law, Property Law, Environmental Law. ***Email:*** shaferc@cooley.edu

BRENT E. SIMMONS,* (Professor)**, born Albion, Michigan, March 17, 1949; admitted to bar, 1977, Michigan. *Education:* Albion College (B.A., 1971); University of Michigan Law School (J.D., 1977); George Washington University (M.A., 1981). ***COURSES: Constitutional Law.

NORMAN OTTO STOCKMEYER, JR.*, (Professor)**, born Detroit, Michigan, May 24, 1938; admitted to bar, 1963, Michigan; 1974, U.S. Supreme Court. *Education:* Oberlin College (A.B., 1960); University of Michigan (J.D., 1963). ***COURSES: Contracts, Remedies, Legal Writing. ***Email:*** stockmen@cooley.edu

ROBERTA STUDWELL*, (Associate Dean, Professor and Director, Library Services)**, born Phoenix, Arizona, October 31, 1951. *Education:* Arizona State University (B.A., 1973); University of Washington (M.L.S., 1980); University of Miami (J.D., 1989). ***COURSES: Legal Research.

AMY TIMMER*, (Associate Dean of Students & Professor)**, born Grand Rapids, Michigan, August 7, 1956; admitted to bar, 1989, Michigan. *Education:* Michigan State University (B.A., 1978); Thomas M. Cooley Law School (J.D., 1988). ***COURSES: Torts.

EVELYN C. TOMBERS*, (Assistant Professor)**, born Philadelphia, Pennsylvania, November 7, 1956; admitted to bar, 1991, Michigan; 1994, ED Michigan and 6th Circuit Court of Appeals. *Education:* Temple University (B.A, 1977); Thomas M. Cooley Law School (J.D., 1991). ***COURSES: Research & Writing.

RONALD J. TROSTY*, (Professor)**, born Brooklyn, New York, February 26, 1935; admitted to bar, 1959, Alabama; 1960, New York; 1975, Michigan. *Education:* University of Alabama (B.A., 1957; J.D., 1959); Grand Valley State College (M.S.T., 1986). ***COURSES: Corporations, Agency and Partnership, Securities Regulation.

WILLIAM P. WEINER*, (Professor)**, born Three Rivers, Michigan, May 14, 1947; admitted to bar, 1972, Michigan. *Education:* Kalamazoo College (B.A., 1969); University of Michigan (M.A., 1972; J.D., 1972); Cambridge University (LL.M., 1985). ***COURSES: Criminal Law, Criminal Procedure, Constitutional Law, International Law.

F. GEORGANN WING*, (Professor)**, born Clare, Michigan; admitted to bar, 1977, Michigan. *Education:* Michigan State University (B.A., 1970; M.A., 1972); Thomas M. Cooley School of Law (J.D., 1977). ***COURSES: Legal Research and Writing, Advocacy, Criminal Law.

TOURO COLLEGE JACOB D. FUCHSBERG LAW CENTER

300 NASSAU ROAD
HUNTINGTON, NEW YORK 11743
Telephone: (631) 421-2244
Fax: (631) 421-2675
Web: www.tourolaw.edu

ABA Approved Since 1983.

The School: Touro Law Center was established in 1980 as part of Touro College, an independent institution of higher and professional education, chartered by the Board of Regents of the State of New York in 1970. Expanding rapidly since its inception, the College now has 8,500 students enrolled in ten divisions in the New York City metropolitan area, in California, in Israel, and in Russia. The Law Center is fully accredited by the American Bar Association and is a member of the Association of American Law Schools. Touro offers the degrees of Juris Doctor (J.D.), Master of Laws (LL.M.), and Master of Laws (LL.M.) in U.S. Legal Studies (for foreign law graduates). In addition, students may combine the J.D. degree with a Master of Business Administration (M.B.A.), a Master of Public Administration (M.P.A.) in Health Care, and a Master of Social Work (M.S.W.).

Location: The Law Center's campus is located in Huntington, on the north shore of Long Island, New York, in the heart of a vibrant suburban community approximately a one-hour drive or commuter train ride from Manhattan.

Students: Approximately 65% of the Law Center's 650 students are enrolled in the full-time day program; the remainder are enrolled in part-time day or part-time evening programs. The increasingly diverse student body represents over 100 undergraduate institutions; students come from all over the U.S. and from several foreign countries. Women represent over 50% of the total enrollment; African-American, Hispanic, and Asian students comprise 25% of the student body. Admission to the Law Center is competitive, with approximately 1700 applications for the 215 seats in the entering class.

Faculty: The Law Center's thirty-five full-time faculty members are committed to teaching both the theory of law and its practical application. The faculty's rich background in private practice, public service, and scholarship enhances the learning experience. Touro's 16:1 student/faculty ratio enables professors to take an active role in the broader learning experience, through clinics, externships, support of student organizations, and so on.

Library: The Law Library continues to be one of the fastest growing legal research collections in the country. Holdings now include over 405,000 volumes and microform equivalents. WESTLAW and LEXIS/NEXIS and the internet are available for student use, and all students receive extensive instruction in traditional and computer research techniques.

Curriculum Emphasizes Writing, Practice Training: The Law Center's curriculum features a strong emphasis on practice training and writing skills. Intensive writing work begins in first year, with all students assigned to small sections devoted exclusively to written communication skills. That commitment continues through the Second Year Writing Tutorial, where students work in groups of five, under faculty supervision, to produce assignments modeled on the Multistate Performance Test (MPT). Practice training is an integral part of first-year substantive courses and students hone these skills in an extensive array of upper-level courses, clinics, rotations, and practice modules (offering a unique synergy of classroom instruction and supervised practical experience).

Academic Support Programs: The Law Center provides a unique program of outside-the-classroom assistance. Teaching Assistants (TAs), assigned to most required courses, present weekly review sessions on material covered in class. TAs also offer sessions on basic study and examination skills, as well as writing skills. For graduating students, there is a series of workshops to review the multistate bar examination topics. In addition, the Legal Education Access Program (LEAP) is designed to offset barriers to success that often are experienced by students of color. LEAP comprises a four-week summer program prior to the start of classes, TA sessions, a mentor program, and individualized assistance for all participants.

(This Listing Continued)

TOURO COLLEGE JACOB D. FUCHSBERG LAW CENTER —Continued

Commitment to the Public Interest: The Law Center is one of a handful of law schools in the country that expect students to develop an appreciation of the legal needs of traditionally underserved populations. Students must satisfy the Public Interest Requirement as a condition of graduation. They may do so in one of three ways: by doing *pro bono* legal work, by taking a course on public interest law combined with *pro bono* legal work, or by participating in one of the Law Center's clinics. Law Center clinics offer students valuable hands-on, real world experience in handling cases under the close supervision of members of the clinical faculty expert in the relevant field. The Law Center offers clinics in Civil Practice, Elder Law, Civil Rights Litigation, Family Law, Judicial Clerkships, Criminal Law, Not-For-Profit Corporation Law, and International Human Rights Immigration Litigation, the last two of which are among relatively few nationwide designed for part-time evening students. An innovation in clinical education, the Civil Practice Clinic affords students the opportunity to earn academic credit while working for private law firms, corporate law departments, government agencies, or public interest legal groups.

International Programs: The centerpiece of the Law Center's international focus is its summer programs in Russia, India, and China. The Russia program is based at, and conducted in cooperation with, Moscow State University, the oldest, largest, and most prestigious university in the former Soviet Union. The program offers international law courses taught by distinguished American and Russian professors, concentrating primarily on the Russian legal system in transition. In summer 1995, the Law Center became the first American law school to conduct a summer program on the Indian subcontinent, with its "New India" program in Shimla, in the foothills of the Himalayas. This program examines India's religious and cultural pluralism, as well as the challenges posed by economic liberalization and expanding participation in the world economy. The Law Center's newest program provides a variety of cultural and educational experiences as it explores the historical, philosophical, and sociological underpinnings of Chinese society. While based in Xiamen, a port city in Fujian province, the program takes students, also, to Beijing and Hong Kong. All of the international summer programs include the option to work in local law offices at the end of the school session.

The Law Center also offers an international summer law internship program. Law firms and government law offices in Lisbon, London, Paris, Brussels, Tel Aviv, and Jerusalem have summer positions exclusively for Law Center students. Students selected for the program have the opportunity to work on both international and local matters under the supervision of experienced host-country lawyers.

Extracurricular Opportunities: At the Law Center, the student experience is not limited to the classroom. Students play an active role in governing the entire institution, through the Student Bar Association and through service on many faculty-student committees. Students also participate in many professional and social organizations, most notably the *Touro Law Review*, which publishes a highly regarded, student-edited scholarly journal, and the Moot Court Board, which takes part in interschool competitions in appellate advocacy. The Law Center also sponsors the *Journal of the Suffolk Academy of Law,* which is dedicated to issues of interest to local practitioners and is published in conjunction with the local bar association. Other student groups produce newsletters and present symposiums and lectures related to health law, entertainment law, and women's issues, among other subjects.

Specialized Institutes: The Law Center hosts the Institute of Local and Suburban Law, the Institute of Jewish Law, and the Institute on the Holocaust and the Law. The first is dedicated to research and education in municipal, environmental, planning, and local government law. The second, in keeping with Touro's establishment under Jewish auspices, is concerned with research, scholarship, and publications in Jewish law. The third is devoted to investigating and preserving the experience of the Holocaust.

Dean: Howard A. Glickstein
Vice-Dean: Gary Shaw
Associate Dean for Special Projects: Nicola Lee
Director of Enrollment: Susan Thompson
Financial Aid Director: Lydia Marcantonio
Head Law Librarian: Daniel P. Jordan
Career Planning & Placement Director: Barbara J. Mehrman
Development & Alumni Affairs Director: Linda Howard Weissman

FULL TIME FACULTY

HOWARD A. GLICKSTEIN*, (Dean; Professor of Law)**, born New York, New York, September 14, 1929; admitted to bar, 1954, New York; 1980, District of Columbia. *Education:* Dartmouth College (B.A., 1951); Yale University (LL.B., 1954); Georgetown University (LL.M., 1962). ***COURSES: Constitutional Law, Employment Discrimination, Civil Rights, Administrative Law.

HAROLD I. ABRAMSON*, (Professor of Law)**, born Binghamton, New York, November 22, 1949; admitted to bar, 1975, New York; 1980, District of Columbia. *Education:* University of Wisconsin (1967-1969); University of Michigan (B.B.A., 1971); Syracuse University (J.D., 1974); Harvard University (LL.M., 1983; M.P.A., 1982). ***COURSES: Alternative Dispute Resolution, Administrative Law.

MARIANNE ARTUSIO*, (Associate Professor of Law; Director of Clinical Programs)**, born Jersey City, New Jersey, September 3, 1946; admitted to bar, 1972, New York. *Education:* Vassar College (A.B., 1968); Cornell University (J.D., 1971). ***COURSES: Disability and Health Law, Elder Law, Clinical Teaching, Interview and Counseling.

ILENE HALLY BARSHAY*, (Professor of Legal Methods)**, born New York, New York; admitted to bar, 1988, New York; 1988, District of Columbia. *Education:* Long Island University (B.S., 1963); Hofstra University (M.S., 1965); Touro College, Jacob D. Fuchsberg Law Center (J.D., 1987); New York University (LL.M., 1995). ***COURSES: Legal Methods and Legal Writing.

WILLIAM M. BROOKS*, (Associate Professor of Law; Director of Civil Rights Litigation Clinic)**, born New York, New York, June 12, 1954; admitted to bar, 1980, New York. *Education:* Ohio Wesleyan University (B.A., 1976); State University of New York at Buffalo (J.D., 1979). ***COURSES: Mental Disability Law, Clinical Teaching.

PETER L. DAVIS*, (Associate Professor of Law)**, born New York, New York, June 23, 1948; admitted to bar, 1973, New York. *Education:* Harvard University (B.A., 1969); New York University (J.D., 1972). ***COURSES: Criminal Procedure, Professional Responsibility, Clinical Teaching.

***DANIEL H. DERBY*, (Professor of Law; Director of International Programs)**, born Chicago, Illinois, August 28, 1947; admitted to bar,

(This Listing Continued)

TOURO COLLEGE JACOB D. FUCHSBERG LAW CENTER —Continued

1978, Illinois. *Education:* United States Military Academy (1965-1968); University of Illinois (B.A., 1974); De Paul University (J.D., 1978); Columbia University (LL.M., 1980). ***COURSES:*** Conflict of Laws, International Law, Comparative Law, Civil Procedure, Criminal Law.

J. KIRKLAND GRANT, **(Professor of Law)**, born Monroe, Michigan, February 14, 1943; admitted to bar, 1968, Michigan; 1971, New York; 1975, South Carolina. *Education:* University of Michigan (B.B.A., 1965; J.D., cum laude, 1967). ***COURSES:*** Corporations, Securities Regulation, Contracts, Partnership, Real Estate, Arbitration.

LOUISE HARMON, **(Professor of Law)**, born Columbus, Ohio, October 27, 1949; admitted to bar, 1979, Illinois. *Education:* Indiana University (B.A., 1971); University of Texas (J.D., 1979); Harvard University (LL.M., 1983); Columbia University (Ph.D., 1998). ***COURSES:*** Property, Legal History, Jurisprudence.

BRANNON HEATH, **(Associate Professor of Legal Methods)**, born Cleveland, Ohio, December 21, 1941; admitted to bar, 1977, Illinois. *Education:* Bennington College (B.A., 1964); University of Arizona (M.A., 1967); Loyola University of Chicago (J.D., 1977). ***COURSES:*** Legal Methods.

DANIEL P. JORDAN, JR., **(Assistant Professor of Law; Head Law Librarian)**, born Brooklyn, New York, July 15, 1951; admitted to bar, 1982, California. *Education:* Brooklyn College (B.A., 1975); Pratt Institute (M.L.S., 1982); University of the Pacific, McGeorge School of Law (J.D., 1980). ***COURSES:*** Legal Research.

EILEEN KAUFMAN, **(Professor of Law)**, born New York, New York, January 6, 1949; admitted to bar, 1976, New York. *Education:* Skidmore College (B.A., 1970); New York University (J.D., 1975; LL.M., 1991). ***COURSES:*** Torts, Family Law, Sex Discrimination, Constitutional Law.

RICHARD KLEIN, **(Professor of Law)**, born New York, New York, June 21, 1943; admitted to bar, 1973, New York. *Education:* University of Wisconsin-Madison (B.S., 1964); Columbia University (M.I.A., 1968); Harvard University (J.D., 1972). ***COURSES:*** Criminal Law, Trial Practice, Labor Law.

SIDNEY KWESTEL, **(Professor of Law)**, born April 7, 1938; admitted to bar, 1962, New York. *Education:* Yeshiva University (B.A., 1958); New York University (J.D., 1961). ***COURSES:*** Contracts, Remedies, Pretrial Litigation.

LEON D. LAZER, **(Visiting Prof. of Law; Dir. of Institute of Local and Suburban Law; Assoc. Dean for Continuing Legal Education)**, born New York, New York, July 4, 1921; admitted to bar, 1948, New York. *Education:* City College of the City University of New York (B.S.S., 1942); New York University (LL.B., 1948). ***COURSES:*** Land Use, State and Local Government, Judicial Clerkship, Torts.

NICOLA LEE, **(Associate Dean for Special Projects; Professor of Legal Methods)**, born Stockton Heath, England, March 14, 1958; admitted to bar, 1982, England, Wales, N. Ireland and the Commonwealth; 1989, New York. *Education:* Brunel University (LL.B., *honors,* 1981); Cambridge University (M.Phil., 1983);Inns of Court School of Law (Barrister at Law, 1982). ***COURSES:*** International Law, Legal Methods.

HEATHER MELNIKER, **(Coordinator of Legal Methods; Associate Professor of Legal Methods)**, born New York, New York, August 25, 1949; admitted to bar, 1982, New York. *Education:* Tufts University (B.A., 1971); Northeastern University (M.Ed., 1972); Hofstra University (J.D., 1982). ***COURSES:*** Legal Methods.

JEFFREY B. MORRIS, **(Professor of Law)**, born New York, New York, January 8, 1941; admitted to bar, 1967, New York; 1978, District of Columbia. *Education:* Princeton University (B.A., 1962); Columbia University (J.D., 1965; Ph.D., 1972). ***COURSES:*** Constitutional Law, Criminal Law, Criminal Procedure, Legal History.

DEBORAH WAIRE POST, **(Professor of Law)**, born Auburn, New York, July 27, 1949; admitted to bar, 1979, Texas. *Education:* Hofstra University (B.A., 1971); Harvard University (J.D., 1978). ***COURSES:*** Contracts, Partnership, Corporations, Sociology of Law.

CHAIM POVARSKY, **(Professor of Law; Director of Institute of Jewish Law)**, born Poland, July 19, 1933; admitted to bar, 1967, Israel. *Education:* Hebrew University (LL.B., 1966); Tel Aviv University (LL.M., 1978; J.S.D., 1986). ***COURSES:*** Jewish Law, Comparative Law.

GEORGE C. PRATT, **(Professor of Law)**, born Corning, New York, May 22, 1928; admitted to bar, 1953, New York. *Education:* Yale University (B.A., 1950; J.D., 1953). ***COURSES:*** Civil Procedure, Civil Rights, Appellate Advocacy, Federal Courts.

JEFFREY I. ROTH, **(Professor of Law)**, born Chicago, Illinois, September 12, 1947; admitted to bar, 1975, New York. *Education:* Yeshiva University (B.A., 1968); Columbia University (M.A., 1969); Yale University (J.D., 1974). ***COURSES:*** Wills, Trusts, Property, Jewish Law.

DOUGLAS D. SCHERER, **(Professor of Law; Director of Academic Support Programs)**, born Lima, Ohio, June 29, 1940; admitted to bar, 1969, Massachusetts. *Education:* Case Western Reserve University (B.A., 1962); Suffolk University (J.D., 1969); Harvard University (LL.M., 1978). ***COURSES:*** Constitutional Law, Employment Discrimination Law, Administrative Law, Torts.

MARTIN A. SCHWARTZ, **(Professor of Law)**, born Bronx, New York, August 28, 1943; admitted to bar, 1968, New York. *Education:* City College of the City University of New York (B.B.A., 1966); Brooklyn Law School (J.D., 1968); New York University (LL.M., 1973). ***COURSES:*** Constitutional Law, Evidence, Federal Courts, Appellate Advocacy, Poverty Law.

THOMAS A. SCHWEITZER, **(Professor of Law)**, born New York, New York, June 19, 1944; admitted to bar, 1978, New York. *Education:* College of the Holy Cross (A.B., 1966); Yale University (J.D., 1977); University of Wisconsin-Madison (M.A., 1968; Ph.D., 1971). ***COURSES:*** Civil Procedure, Education Law, First Amendment, Conflict of Laws, International Law.

RENA C. SEPLOWITZ, **(Professor of Law)**, born New York, New York, April 3, 1952; admitted to bar, 1976, New York. *Education:* Barnard College (A.B., 1973); Columbia University (J.D., 1975). ***COURSES:*** Trusts and Estates, Property and Intellectual Property.

CAROLE SHAPIRO, **(Professor of Legal Methods)**, born New York, New York, October 6, 1949; admitted to bar, 1973, New York. *Education:* Brown University (B.A., 1969); New York University (J.D., 1972). ***COURSES:*** Legal Methods, Law and Literature.

GARY SHAW, **(Vice Dean; Professor of Law)**, born Chicago, Illinois, March 24, 1952; admitted to bar, 1979, Illinois. *Education:* University of Illinois (A.B., 1975); John Marshall Law School (J.D., 1979); Temple University (LL.M., 1983). ***COURSES:*** Constitutional Law, Evidence, Bankruptcy, Computer Law.

MARJORIE A. SILVER, **(Professor of Law)**, born New York, New York, April 11, 1948; admitted to bar, 1973, Pennsylvania; 1981, New York. *Education:* Brandeis University (B.A., 1970); University of Pennsylvania (J.D., 1973). ***COURSES:*** Civil Procedure, Administrative Law, Education Law, Professional Responsibility.

(This Listing Continued)

TOURO COLLEGE JACOB D. FUCHSBERG LAW CENTER —Continued

THEODORE SILVER*, (Associate Professor of Law)**, born New York, New York, February 24, 1953; admitted to bar, 1978, Connecticut. *Education:* Yale University (B.A., 1975; M.D., 1984); University of Connecticut (J.D., 1978). ***COURSES: Contracts, Taxation, Medical Jurisprudence.

LEWIS A. SILVERMAN*, (Assistant Professor of Clinical Law; Director of Family Law Clinic)**, born Brooklyn, New York, January 26, 1951; admitted to bar, 1977, New York. *Education:* New York University (B.A., 1973); Boston University School of Law (J.D., 1976). ***COURSES: Family Law, Family Law Clinic.

BEVERLY MCQUEARY SMITH*, (Professor of Law)**, born Jersey City, New Jersey, August 10, 1947; admitted to bar, 1978, District of Columbia; 1982, West Virginia; 1986, Texas; 1989, New Jersey. *Education:* Jersey City State College (B.A., 1970); Rutgers University (M.A., 1974); New York University (J.D., 1977); Harvard University (LL.M., 1988). ***COURSES: Torts, Contracts, Environmental Law, Consumer Law and Legislation.

DAN SUBOTNIK*, (Professor of Law)**, born New Jersey, January 5, 1942; admitted to bar, 1967, New York. *Education:* Columbia University (B.A., 1963; J.D., 1966; M.B.A., 1966). ***COURSES: Tax, Estate Planning, Accounting.

BARBARA SWARTZ*, (Bruce K. Gould Professor of Law)**, born Bridgeport, Connecticut, July 23, 1945; admitted to bar, 1972, New York. *Education:* Temple University (B.A., 1966); London School of Economics; University of Michigan (M.A., 1967); New York University School of Law (J.D., 1971); Columbia University (M.P.H., 1991). ***COURSES: Law and Medicine, Family Law, Criminal Law, Rights of Children.

PETER ZABLOTSKY*, (Professor of Law)**, born Binghamton, New York, April 18, 1955; admitted to bar, 1981, New York; 1986, Pennsylvania. *Education:* Penn State University (B.A., 1977); Columbia University (J.D., 1980). ***COURSES: Torts, Entertainment Law, Products Liability.

TULANE UNIVERSITY LAW SCHOOL

JOHN GIFFEN WEINMANN HALL
6329 FRERET STREET
NEW ORLEANS, LOUISIANA 70118

THE UNIVERSITY OF AKRON SCHOOL OF LAW

150 UNIVERSITY AVENUE
AKRON, OHIO 44325-2901
Telephone: (330) 972-7331
Fax: (330) 258-2343
www.uakron.edu/law

ABA Approved Since 1961.

The University of Akron School of Law was founded in 1921 as a private evening law school, the Akron Law School. In 1959 it merged with The University of Akron, a public university which enjoys an international reputation, especially in Polymer Science and Engineering. In 1966, the School added a full-time day program. From its inception, the School of Law has been dedicated to providing access into the legal profession for working people, women and people of color. This mission has led the school to retain a four-year, part-time course of study with equal status to the three-year, full-time course of study it offers, and to deliver high-quality legal education at reasonable cost.

As indicated in its Mission Statement, the University of Akron believes there is no higher calling than that of promoting justice and the protection of individual liberty through adherence to the rule of law. Through its high quality legal education that focuses upon teaching both the purposes of the law and client-service skills, the school lives up to its tradition of excellence. The school is nationally acclaimed for its Trial Advocacy program, fielding perennial winners of regional competitions and participants in national competitions. Its Trial Advocacy teams have been selected by the National Invitational Trial Tournament as one of the country's top sixteen teams for twelve straight years. The school is fully accredited by the American Bar Association and is a member in good standing of the Association of American Law Schools.

The School of Law is home to the Seiberling Center for Constitutional Law, one of only four centers nationally funded by a grant from Congress, and the Miller Institute of Professional Responsibility. It is continuing to expand its Center for Intellectual Property and Technology, which houses the Brennan Professorship, the Giles Sutherland Rich Professorship, and an endowed chair from Goodyear. The school's Intellectual Property curriculum is one of the richest in the country. The school's location in the Polymer Valley, next door to the internationally acclaimed College of Polymer Science and Engineering and across the street from Inventure Place, the National Inventors' Hall of Fame, enhances its intellectual property program. The Akron Public Library is a Patent Depository, and the Law Library is a Government Documents Repository, as well as having an enriched collection of intellectual property materials.

The school achieves its mission by devoting resources and talent to four central elements: teaching, scholarship, service to the bench, bar and broader community, and providing access to legal education. The school is fortunate to have full-time and part-time faculty who are dedicated to excellence in classroom teaching. The vast majority of faculty have varied practice backgrounds, and use this experience to integrate lawyerly skills training, ethics, client service and theory into both traditional classes and practical skills classes.

Believing that active and interactive learning is superior for students, the school devotes significant faculty resources to the all-important foundational courses required during the first and second year of study. All required courses are offered in sections of approximately 50 students each, and the writing classes are sectioned into groups of approximately 15 students each. Upper class courses include a wide variety of electives taught in groups that rarely exceed 60 students each, and often comprise 20 or fewer students. No class exceeds 100 students. The school strives to promote learning and professionalism by maintaining an atmosphere of friendliness, collegiality and collaboration, possible because of its smallness and its emphasis upon small and interactive classes.

The faculty produce legal scholarship in a wide variety of areas. The Law Library is a state-of-the-art facility whose own collection of legal

(This Listing Continued)

THE UNIVERSITY OF AKRON SCHOOL OF LAW —Continued

materials is enhanced by on-line access to the entire University collection (through ZipLink) and the collections of at least 52 of the universities and colleges in Ohio (through OhioLink), from which students and faculty can obtain books and journals on request. The school publishes the *Akron Law Review,* which has special editions devoted to taxation and capital punishment law.

The school enjoys an outstanding relationship with the local bench and bar. It co-sponsors continuing legal education with the Akron Bar Association. First-year students are paired with practicing attorneys in their areas of interest through the Mentoring Program sponsored by the bar association. In addition to having some of the finest and most well-respected practitioners teach skills or specialty courses, the school is able to invite practitioners to participate in other classes and in the life of the law school on a regular basis, adding immeasurably to the professional education of its students.

The school takes pride in its importance to the region in which it is located. From local School Board members, local trial and appellate judges, mayors and state legislators to federal judges, Ohio Supreme Court Justices and law faculty members, the school's graduates serve the public interest. In addition, graduates serve in Fortune 500 companies, prestigious large law firms, government positions, and small firms.

The University of Akron currently offers the J.D. degree, certificate programs in Intellectual Property and in Litigation, as well as joint degrees of J.D./M.Tax (Master of Taxation), J.D./M.B.A. (Master of Business Administration), J.D./M.B.A.-H.R. (Master of Business Administration, Human Resources), and J.D./M.P.A. (Master of Public Administration). Its student body comprises 600 students, approximately 200 of whom are enrolled in the part-time program. Curricular opportunities to specialize exist in business, taxation and litigation, with additional opportunities to concentrate in other areas.

Dean: Richard L. Aynes (330) 972-6359
Admissions / Financial Aid: Lauri S. File (800) 425-7668
Library: Paul Richert (330) 972-7330
Placement: Jay Levine (330) 972-5321
Alumni Affairs: William Rickett (330) 972-7246
Academic Affairs: Elizabeth Reilly (330) 972-6197
Student Affairs: Malina Coleman (330) 972-6797
Internal Affairs: Rosemary Cannon (330) 972-6366
Center for Intellectual Property: Jeffrey Samuels (330) 972-7972

FULL TIME FACULTY

RICHARD L. AYNES,* (Professor, Dean)**, born Dayton, Ohio, June 12, 1949; admitted to bar, 1975, Ohio. *Education:* Miami of Ohio, University (B.S., 1971); Cleveland-Marshall College of Law, Cleve. St. U. (J.D., 1974). ***COURSES: Constitutional Law I & II, Constitutional Litigation Seminar, Legal History. ***Email:*** raynes@uakron.edu

---

LLOYD C. ANDERSON,* (McDowell Professor)**, born Saginaw, Michigan, November 6, 1947; admitted to bar, 1973, Kentucky. *Education:* University of Michigan (B.A., 1969); Harvard Law School (J.D., 1973). ***COURSES: Civil Procedure I & II, Federal Jurisdictions, Procedure. ***Email:*** lca@uakron.edu

WILLIAM C. BECKER,* (Professor Emeritus, Director, Miller Institute of Professional Responsibility)**, born Erie, Pennsylvania, September 1, 1929; admitted to bar, 1957, Ohio. *Education:* Harvard University (A.B., 1951); University of Michigan (J.D., 1956). ***COURSES: Professional Responsibility, Alternative Dispute Resolution, Lawyer as Negotiator. ***Email:*** wbecker@uakron.edu

J. DEAN CARRO,* (Professor, Director of the Legal Clinic Offices)**, born Brooklyn, New York, July 31, 1952; admitted to bar, 1978, Ohio. *Education:* SUNY New Paltz (B.A., 1974); University of Akron School of Law (J.D., 1978). ***COURSES: Clinical Seminar I & II, Appellate Advocacy, Criminal Law, Moot Court. ***Email:*** carro1@uakron.edu

RICHARD C. COHEN,* (Associate Professor)**, born Bridgeport, Connecticut, October 22, 1950; admitted to bar, 1975, Connecticut. *Education:* Emory University (B.A., 1972); University of Connecticut (J.D., 1975). ***COURSES: Basics, Intermediate Legal Communications, Legal Analysis, Research and Writing I & II, Legal Drafting, Contracts I & II. ***Email:*** rcohen@uakron.edu

DANA K. COLE,* (Associate Professor)**, born Dayton, Ohio, May 16, 1956; admitted to bar, 1986, Ohio. *Education:* University of Cincinnati (B.S., 1980); University of Dayton School of Law (J.D., 1986). ***COURSES: Evidence, Criminal Law, Trial Advocacy I & II. ***Email:*** dkc@uakron.edu

MALINA COLEMAN,* (Associate Professor, Associate Dean)**, born Akron, Ohio, September 23, 1954; admitted to bar, 1987, Pennsylvania. *Education:* Central State University (B.S., 1980); Yale Law School (J.D., 1985). ***COURSES: Contracts I & II, Family Law, Basic Business Associations. ***Email:*** mcoleman@uakron.edu

CAROLYN L. DESSIN,* (Associate Professor)**, born Philadelphia, Pennsylvania, March 10, 1957; admitted to bar, 1987, Pennsylvania. *Education:* Temple University (B.M.Ed.; 1978); Westminster Choir College (M.M., 1980); Villanova University (J.D., 1987). ***COURSES: Federal Individual Taxation, Estate & Gift Tax, Business Planning, Estate Planning, Contracts I & II. ***Email:*** cld3@uakron.edu

JAY DRATLER, JR.,* (Goodyear Professor of Intellectual Property)**, born Los Angeles, California, June 11, 1945; admitted to bar, 1978, California; 1987, Hawaii. *Education:* University of California, Berkeley (A.B., 1966); University of California, San Diego (M.S., 1968; Ph.D., 1971); Harvard Law School (J.D., 1978). ***COURSES: Copyright Law, Patent Law & Policy, Cyberspace Law, Intellectual Property Law, Trade Secrets, Remedies, Antitrust. ***Email:*** dratler@uakron.edu

STEVEN R. DUVALL,* (Technical Services Librarian)**, born Canton, Ohio, March 7, 1967. *Education:* University of Florida (B.A., 1989); University of South Florida (M.L.S., 1992). ***Email: duvalls@uakron.edu

BERNADETTE BOLLAS GENETIN,* (Assistant Professor)**, born Canton, Ohio, December 14, 1959; admitted to bar, 1988, Ohio. *Education:* University of Notre Dame (B.A., 1982); The Ohio State University College of Law (J.D., 1988). ***COURSES: Civil Procedure I & II, Legal Drafting, Business Regulation. ***Email:*** genetin@uakron.edu

WILLA E. GIBSON,* (Associate Professor)**, born Presque Isle, Maine, August 16, 1960; admitted to bar, 1991, Iowa. *Education:* Tulane University (B.A., 1982); Drake University Law School (J.D., 1991). ***COURSES: Commercial Law I & II, Consumer Law, Securities Regulation. ***Email:*** willa1@uakron.edu

(This Listing Continued)

THE UNIVERSITY OF AKRON SCHOOL OF LAW —Continued

WILSON R. HUHN*, (Professor)**, born Jamestown, New York, January 1, 1950; admitted to bar, 1977, Ohio. *Education:* Yale University (B.A., 1972); Cornell Law School (J.D., 1977). ***COURSES: Constitutional Law I & II, Administrative Law, Commercial Law I & II, Evidence, Health Law. ***Email:*** whuhn@uakron.edu

WILLIAM S. JORDAN, III*, (McDowell Professor)**, born Ohio, September 16, 1949; admitted to bar, 1974, Michigan; 1979, District of Columbia. *Education:* Stanford (B.A., 1971); University of Michigan (J.D., 1974). ***COURSES: Property I & II, Administrative Law, Environmental Law. ***Email:*** jordan@uakron.edu

MARGERY B. KOOSED*, (Professor)**, born Cleveland, Ohio, 1948; admitted to bar, 1974, Ohio. *Education:* Miami of Ohio, University (B.S.Ed., 1971); Case Western Reserve University, Franklin Thomas Backus School of Law (J.D., 1974). ***COURSES: Criminal Law, Administration of Criminal Justice, Criminal Process, Capital Litigation. ***Email:*** mkoosed@uakron.edu

RICHARD J. KOVACH*, (McDowell Professor)**, born Berea, Ohio, January 18, 1947. *Education:* Oberlin College (A.B., 1970); Harvard Law School (J.D., 1974). ***COURSES: Qualified Pension & Profit Sharing, Corporate Taxation I, Wills, Trusts and Estates, Basic Business Associations, Taxation of Nonprofit Entities, Intellectual Property Taxation. ***Email:*** kovach2@uakron.edu

BRANT T. LEE*, (Assistant Professor)**, born San Francisco, February 17, 1962; admitted to bar, 1992, California. *Education:* University of California, Berkeley (B.A., 1985); John F. Kennedy School of Government, Harvard University (M.P.P., 1994); Harvard Law School (J.D., 1990). ***COURSES: Property I & II, Feminist & Race Theory, Cyberlaw. ***Email:*** btlee@uakron.edu

LYNN M. LENART*, (Assistant Librarian, Reference Services)**, born Cuyahoga County, Ohio. *Education:* University of Akron (B.A., 1982); Kent State University (M.L.S., 1990); University of Akron (J.D., 1999). ***COURSES: Specialized Areas of Legal Research. ***Email:*** lynnlenart@uakron.edu

JAY LEVINE*, (Director, Career Planning & Placement)**, born Akron, Ohio, September 8, 1954. *Education:* Kent State University (B.A., 1975; M.P.A., 1976); University of Akron (M.A., 1990; Ph.D., 1991). ***Email: jay10@uakron.edu

JANE C. MORIARTY*, (Associate Professor)**, born Waterbury, Connecticut, January 7, 1959; admitted to bar, 1983, Massachusetts; 1987, Pennsylvania. *Education:* Boston College (B.A., 1980); Boston College Law School (J.D., 1983). ***COURSES: Employment Discrimination, Disability Discrimination, Expert Evidence, Professional Responsibility, Evidence. ***Email:*** moriart@uakron.edu

E. STEWART MORITZ*, (Assistant Professor of Law)**, born 1968; admitted to bar, 1996, California. *Education:* Yale University (B.A., 1990); Vanderbilt University School of Law (J.D., 1995). ***COURSES: Legislative Process, Pretrial Advocacy, Corporations. ***Email:*** moritzes@uakron.edu

C. ALAN NEWMAN*, (Associate Professor)**, born Dallas, Texas, January 26, 1951; admitted to bar, 1980, Oklahoma. *Education:* University of Oklahoma (B.A., 1977): University of Oklahoma (J.D., 1980). ***COURSES: Wills, Trusts, and Estates I & II, Estate Planning, Property. ***Email:*** newman2@uakron.edu

MOLLY TOWNES O'BRIEN*, (Associate Professor of Law)**, born Nashville, Tennessee, February 2, 1959; admitted to bar, 1987, Georgia; 1992, Pennsylvania. *Education:* Brown University (A.B., 1982); Northeastern University (J.D., 1986); Temple University (LL.M., 1997). ***COURSES: Education Law, Criminal Law, Evidence, Trial Advocacy, Alternative Dispute Resolution. ***Email:*** mobrien@uakron.edu

T. MODIBO OCRAN*, (Professor)**, born Tarkwa-Nsuaem, Ghana, September 12, 1942; admitted to bar, 1970, Ghana. *Education:* University of Ghana (LL.B., 1966; B.L., 1967); University of Wisconsin (M.L.I., 1968; Ph.D., 1971). ***COURSES: Corporations, Commercial Law, International Law, International Trade: GATT, NAFTA, European Union, International Investments and Commercial Transactions. ***Email:*** ocran@uakron.edu

A. SAMUEL ODDI*, (Giles Sutherland Rich Professor)**, born 1936; admitted to bar, 1964, Pennsylvania; 1990, Illinois. *Education:* Carnegie Mellon University (B.S., 1958); University of Pittsburgh (J.D., 1963); George Washington University (LL.M., 1971). ***COURSES: Patent Law & Policy, Intro to Intellectual Property, Torts I & II, Jurisprudence, Law & Medicine, International Law. ***Email:*** oddi@uakron.edu

CAROL A. OLSON*, (Associate Professor)**, born Detroit, Michigan, October 11, 1949; admitted to bar, 1983, California. *Education:* Washington College (B.A., 1971); University of Delaware (M.A., 1973; M.Ed., 1975); McGeorge School of Law (LL.B., 1983). ***COURSES: Torts I & II, Legal Method, Advanced Torts, Products Liability, Administrative Law. ***Email:*** colson@uakron.edu

KYLE S. PASSMORE*, (Associate Law Librarian)**, born Columbus, Ohio, November 5, 1952; admitted to bar, 1993, Ohio. *Education:* Capital University (B.A., 1975); Kent State University (M.L.S., 1977); University of Akron (J.D., 1993). ***COURSES: Legal Research. ***Email:*** passmore@uakron.edu

ELIZABETH A. REILLY*, (McDowell Professor, Associate Dean)**, born South Bend, Indiana, September 9, 1951; admitted to bar, 1978, Ohio. *Education:* Princeton University (A.B., 1973); University of Akron (J.D., 1978). ***COURSES: Torts I & II, Introduction to Law, Pretrial Advocacy, Seminar in Feminist & Race Theory, Constitutional Law. ***Email:*** reilly@uakron.edu

WILLIAM D. RICH*, (Associate Professor)**, born New York, New York, January 14, 1953; admitted to bar, 1977, Colorado. *Education:* University of Rochester (B.A., 1974); University of Denver (J.D., 1977); Harvard University (LL.M., 1986). ***COURSES: Constitutional Law I & II, First Amendment Seminar, AIDS and the Law. ***Email:*** rich@uakron.edu

PAUL RICHERT*, (Professor, Law Librarian)**, born Elwood, Indiana, August 31, 1948; admitted to bar, 1977, Ohio. *Education:* University of Illinois (A.B., 1970; M.S., 1971); Tulane University School of Law (J.D., 1977). ***COURSES: Legal Research. ***Email:*** richert@uakron.edu

JOHN P. SAHL*, (Associate Professor, Deputy Director of the Miller Institute of Professional Responsibility)**, born New York City, New York, July 26, 1951; admitted to bar, 1982, Connecticut. *Education:* Boston College (B.A., 1974); Monmouth College; Vermont Law School (J.D., 1979); Yale Law School (LL.M., 1989). ***COURSES: Evidence, Entertainment Law, Sports Law, Professional Responsibility, Antitrust. ***Email:*** jps@uakron.edu

JEFFREY M. SAMUELS*, (Brennan Professor, Director, Center for Intellectual Property Law)**, born Brooklyn, New York, May 8, 1950; admitted to bar, 1976, New York; 1977, Virginia; 1978, District of Columbia; 1996, U.S. Court of Appeals for the Federal Circuit. *Education:* Colgate University (B.A., 1972); Albany Law School of Union College (J.D., 1975). ***COURSES: Patent Law, Trademark Law, International Intellectual Property Law, Introduction to Intellectual Property Law. ***Email:*** samuels@uakron.edu

ANNETTE A. SOUARE*, (Public Services Librarian)**, born Cleveland, Ohio, May 19, 1959. *Education:* Cleveland State University (B.A., 1983); University of Pittsburgh (M.L.S., 1994); University of Akron (M.Ed., 1998). ***COURSES: Specialized Areas of Legal Research. ***Email:*** amckissick@uakron.edu

(This Listing Continued)

THE UNIVERSITY OF AKRON SCHOOL OF LAW —Continued

TRACY A. THOMAS*, (Assistant Professor)**, born Columbus, Ohio, September 6, 1965; admitted to bar, 1991, California; 1992, District of Columbia. *Education:* Miami University (Ohio) (B.A., 1987); California State University (M.P.A., 1991); Loyola Law School, Los Angeles (J.D., 1991). ***COURSES: Remedies, Family Law, Antitrust Law. ***Email:*** thomast@uakron.edu

C. MICHAEL WALSH*, (Director, Trial Litigation Clinic, Staff Attorney)**, born East Liverpool, Ohio, February 23, 1966; admitted to bar, 1991, Ohio. *Education:* University of Akron (B.S., 1988); University of Akron (J.D., 1991). ***COURSES: Clinical Seminar I, Trial Advocacy I. ***Email:*** walsh@uakron.edu

---

UNIVERSITY OF ALABAMA SCHOOL OF LAW

BOX 870382
TUSCALOOSA, ALABAMA 35487
Telephone: (205) 348-5117
Fax: (205) 348-3917
http://www.law.ua.edu

ABA Approved Since 1926.

The University of Alabama School of Law combines great traditions with great promise. As the only public law school in the State, The University of Alabama has educated premier lawyers, business and civic leaders, and state and national leaders for over 125 years. The school was established in 1872, and in 1913 moved into its first permanent home, Farrah Hall. In 1978 the School moved into the Law Center -- a modern spacious building. The facilities are among the nation's finest -- graphic evidence of the School's dynamic growth and progressive spirit.

Never content with its past success, our Law School today offers state-of-the-art facilities and technology, an updated curriculum, increased opportunity for skills training, and expanded career services for students. Alabama is considered one of the best law schools in the Southeast, and is ranked in the top fifty law schools in the country by national surveys.

Our student body of about 524 students is talented, diverse, academically strong, and friendly. The average UGPA of our first-year class of about 180 is 3.3, and their average LSAT is 159. While the Admissions Committee, of course, considers the LSAT and UGPA, they also consider other factors which indicate a student will perform well academically in law school. The Admissions Committee looks for determination, diligence, the ability to solve problems and deal with difficult situations, and perseverance.

The Admissions Committee is also sensitive to the idea that a diverse student body -- a group with different life experiences and from different academic and economic backgrounds -- creates a stronger law school. Each class usually includes about 40% women, 11% minority persons, and 15% non-residents and graduates from more than 50 colleges and universities.

On the average, more than 95% of those students who enter the Law School graduate in three years. Generally the law school employment rate is 98-99% within nine months of graduation. Our students are prepared to practice law in various types of work or to enter other professions.

The University of Alabama is accredited by the Commission on Colleges of the Southern Association of Colleges and Schools to award baccalaureate, master's, and doctoral degrees. The University of Alabama School of Law is accredited by the American Bar Association and is a member of the Association of American Law Schools. The School of Law is a member of the Order of the Coif. This prestigious organization has extended membership to only about 75 of America's ABA accredited law schools, based on demonstrated academic excellence.

The tuition at The University of Alabama remains reasonable, yet the Law School provides approximately $700,000 a year in student scholarships, financial aid, and upper-class student employment.

Alabama's trial and appellate advocacy teams are among the nation's best and have won numerous awards. Since winning the Association of Trial Lawyers of America National Championship in 1990, Alabama trial advocacy teams have set a standard few schools can match: advancing 15 teams from regional to national competition in the last ten years and consistently placing teams in national competition.

Alabama's Jessup International Moot Court Team also has established itself as one of the most competitive in the nation, boasting five regional championships, several Best Brief Awards, and numerous individual honors. In 1994 and 1995, the law school received the prestigious Dillard and Baxter Awards for having written the best appellate briefs in the World Competition.

The Law School also sponsors at Douglass Moot Court, a Duberstein Banckruptcy Moot Court Team, and moot court teams in intellectual property, criminal law, tax, and environment law.

Student teams from Alabama also have won team and individual awards in many of these competitions.

Students have several opportunities to write for a scholarly journal while in law school at The University of Alabama. The *Alabama Law Review* is published three times a year and is ranked in the top 25 law journals in the country. In addition to the *Law Review* there are two other journals published at the Law School: *The Journal of the Legal Profession and the Law and Psychology Review.*

The guiding philosophy of The University of Alabama School of Law is that the institution must not only prepare future lawyers, it must become a dynamic part of the community. That philosophy is embodied in the concept of the "Law Center" which envisions a broader role of service to the state, the region, and the nation by the application of the School's resources and expertise to problems that affect the way people live.

The Law Center includes the best law library in the state and one of the best in the region. The Alabama Law Institute, which works on progressive state law reform and employs law students, and the state's largest provider of continuing legal education are housed in the Law Center. The Law School hosts numerous conferences, lectures, and visits. In a word, it is the center of legal developments and progress in the State of Alabama.

Future building plans include new facilities to house the school's extensive clinical program and to provide more classrooms and faculty offices. An expansion of the Law Library also is planned.

The curriculum of The University of Alabama School of Law is traditional, but certainly includes offerings in emerging areas of the law, including electives in environmental law, international law, intellectual

(This Listing Continued)

UNIVERSITY OF ALABAMA SCHOOL OF LAW —Continued

property, business crime, and business. The curriculum also is rich in clinical, advocacy, and skills offerings. Perspective offerings, such as legal history, legal philosophy, and law in literature also are taught.

The law curriculum has been expanded -- particularly in the third year -- to include more seminars and elective courses that cut across traditional course lines and expose students to the complex problems with which lawyers and lawmakers must deal in modern life and that aim to increase students' understanding of the development of the legal order.

All first-year students are required to take Civil Procedure, Contracts I, Legal Writing and Research, Torts and Criminal Law in the fall semester. In the spring of the first year students take Moot Court, Constitutional Law, Federal Income Tax, Property, and Contracts II. During the second year students are required to take Evidence and Legal Profession. All other courses taken during the second and third years are electives.

Students may follow a tract of particular courses in the business, estate planning, or criminal law areas among other areas or may design their own programs of study after the first year. Most students participate in trial and appellate advocacy, an important part of the curriculum. The curriculum also includes extensive clinical offerings.

The Clinical Program offers second- and third-year students an opportunity to acquire first-hand practical experience by direct involvement in actual client cases handled through the Clinical Program. Through its various legal assistance programs, the Clinical Program also helps the Law School meet its commitment of service to the community and state while providing tomorrow's lawyers with a taste of the real practice of law. Students may enroll in the Elder Law Clinic, the Criminal Law Clinic, the Disability Litigation Clinic, the Pension Clinic, the Children's Rights Clinic, and the Student Law Clinic.

Located in Beautiful Tuscaloosa, Alabama

A wonderful and relatively inexpensive place to live, Tuscaloosa is rich in tradition and committed to academic and community excellence. Tuscaloosa is rich in Native American history; some of the largest and best-preserved Indian mounds in the Southeast are located in Moundville, Alabama, about 15 miles south of the University. Mound State Monument is administered by The University of Alabama. Tuscaloosa is an exciting city of about 100,000, and The University of Alabama has a student population of approximately 19,000. The city is in a part of the state full of lakes and rivers. It was built on the banks of the Black Warrior River, now a link in the Tennessee-Tombigbee Waterway. Lake Tuscaloosa and nearby Lake Lurleen State Park provide ample opportunity for water sports, camping, and other outdoor recreation. Tuscaloosa's cooperation with the University has allowed for a rich cultural life as well. Tuscaloosa combines a small-town atmosphere with big-town activities, sports, and culture.

International Summer Programs

The Law School offers five-week summer programs at the University of Fribourg in Fribourg, Switzerland and at Australian National University in Canberry, Australia. During the program, students participate in two credited classes: a course surveying Swiss or Australian law and a comparative doctrinal course. In the comparative law course students learn about the Swiss or Australian legal system through presentations by Swiss and Australian professors. The doctrinal course, team-taught in English by a professor from the home law school and a law school professor, allows students to compare the two legal systems in a specific area of law. Students from the home law schools are also involved in the doctrinal courses.

Joint J.D./M.B.A. Program

The School of Law and the Manderson Graduate School of Business at The University of Alabama offer select students an opportunity to earn joint Masters of Business Administration (M.B.A.) and J.D. degrees in a four-year program of study. The first year is the first year of law school. The second year is the first year of the M.B.A. Program. The third and fourth years consists of courses in both law and business.

International Graduate Program

The School of Law offers a one-year program leading to the LL.M. degree. The program is for persons who have completed a basic legal education and received a university degree in law in another country. The program's purpose is to afford students whose legal background is not the common law tradition an opportunity to acquire a basic understanding of Anglo-American legal institutions and concepts, prior to returning to their respective legal communities. Enrollment in the LL.M. program is quite limited; a few highly qualified applicants are accepted.

Dean: Ken Randall (205) 348-5117
Admissions: Betty McGinley (205) 348-5440
Career Services: Susie Carver (205) 348-6479
Continuing Legal Education: Steven C. Emens (205) 348-4960
Development & Alumni Affairs: Elizabeth U. Sadler (205) 348-5756
Financial Aid: J. Noah Funderburg (205) 348-4508
Library: James B. Leonard (205) 348-5927
Recruiting and Scholarships: Claude Beers (205) 348-2728
Students/Academic Affairs: Jenelle Mims Marsh (205) 348-5751
Clinical Programs: Robert R. Kuehn (205) 348-4960

FULL TIME FACULTY

KEN RANDALL*, (Dean & Thomas E. McMillan Professor of Law)**, born 1956; admitted to bar, 1983, New York; 1991, Alabama. *Education:* Hofstra (J.D., 1981); Yale (LL.M., 1982); Columbia (LL.M., 1985; J.S.D., 1988). ***COURSES: Constitutional Law, International Law, International Transactions. ***Email:*** kcrandal@law.ua.edu

WILLIAM L. ANDREEN*, (Edgar L. Clarkson Professor)**, born 1953; admitted to bar, 1977, Georgia. *Education:* College of Wooster (B.A., 1975); Columbia (J.D., 1977). ***COURSES: Administrative Law, Environmental Law, International Law, Torts. ***Email:*** wandreen@law.ua.edu

CAROL RICE ANDREWS*, (Professor)**, born 1958; admitted to bar, 1983, Illinois. *Education:* Illinois (B.S., 1980; J.D., 1983). ***COURSES: Civil Procedure, Advanced Civil Procedure, Legal Profession. ***Email:*** candrews@law.ua.edu

(This Listing Continued)

UNIVERSITY OF ALABAMA SCHOOL OF LAW —Continued

DONALD W. BAKER,* (Ira Drayton Pruitt Sr. Professor)**, born 1943; admitted to bar, 1973, Virginia. *Education:* Southern Methodist University (B.A., 1967); University of Texas (J.D., 1970). ***COURSES: Secured Credit Transactions, Contracts, Creditors' & Debtors' Rights. ***Email:*** dbaker@law.ua.edu

JONATHAN S. BERCK,* (Assistant Professor)**, born 1959; admitted to bar, 1986, New Jersey; 1987, New York; 1988, District of Columbia; 1997, United Kingdom. *Education:* Swarthmore College (B.A., 1981); Columbia University (M.A., 1983); Harvard University (J.D., 1986). ***COURSES: Public International Law, International Business Transactions, Immigration Law, International Trade. ***Email:*** jberck@law.ua.edu

KIMBERLY KEEFER BOONE,* (Legal Writing Lecturer)**, born Ocala, Florida, July 30, 1970; admitted to bar, 1995, Alabama. *Education:* Huntingdon College (B.A., 1992); The University of Alabama (J.D., 1995). ***COURSES: Legal Writing. ***Email:*** kboone@law.ua.edu

WILLIAM S. BREWBAKER, III,* (Professor)**, born 1959; admitted to bar, 1986, Alabama. *Education:* Vanderbilt (B.A., 1981); University of Virginia (J.D., 1986); Duke (LL.M., 1993). ***COURSES: Antitrust Law, Health Care Law, Property Law. ***Email:*** wbrewbak@law.ua.edu

ALFRED L. BROPHY,* (Professor)**, born Champaign, Illinois, September 6, 1966; admitted to bar, 1992, New York. *Education:* University of Pennsylvania (A.B., 1987); Columbia University (J.D., 1990); Harvard University (A.M., 1993). ***COURSES: Constitutional Law, Estates, Damages. ***Email:*** abrophy@law.ua.edu

CAROL NECOLE BROWN,* (Assistant Professor of Law)**, born Greensboro, North Carolina, December 30, 1969; admitted to bar, 1995, Virginia; 1998, Alabama. *Education:* Duke University (A.B., 1992); Duke Law (J.D.; L.L.M., 1995). ***COURSES: Real Property, Land Use, Real Property Security. ***Email:*** cbrown@law.ua.edu

JAMES D. BRYCE,* (Joseph D. Peeler Professor)**, born 1939; admitted to bar, 1974, New York; 1982, Alabama. *Education:* Columbia College (B.A., 1961; J.D., 1970); New York University (LL.M., 1974). ***COURSES: Federal Income Taxation, Partnership Tax, State & Local Taxation, Tax Shelters. ***Email:*** jbryce@law.ua.edu

PAMELA HARNEST BUCY,* (Frank M. Bainbridge Professor and Director of Legal Writing)**, born 1953; admitted to bar, 1978, Missouri; 1991, Alabama. *Education:* Austin College (B.A., 1975); Washington, St. Louis (J.D., 1978). ***COURSES: Criminal Law, Criminal Procedure, Business Crime. ***Email:*** pbucy@law.ua.edu

SUSIE TAYLOR CARVER,* (Assistant Dean for Career Services)**, born Fayette, Alabama, August 18, 1949; admitted to bar, 1986, Alabama. *Education:* The University of Alabama (B.A., 1971); The University of Alabama School of Law (J.D., 1986). ***Email: scarver@law.ua.edu

JOSEPH A. COLQUITT,* (Jere L. Beasley Professor & Director, Trial Advocacy Program)**, born 1940; admitted to bar, 1970, Alabama. *Education:* Alabama (B.S., 1967; J.D., 1970); Nevada-Reno (M.J.S., 1987). ***COURSES: Criminal Justice, Criminal Procedure, Evidence, Trial Advocacy. ***Email:*** jcolquit@law.ua.edu

ALAN DURHAM,* (Associate Professor)**, born 1963; admitted to bar, 1988, California. *Education:* Berkeley (J.D., 1988); Pomona College (B.A., 1985). ***COURSES: Patents and Copyrights, Antitrust, Trademarks and Unfair Trade Practices. ***Email:*** adurham@law.ua.edu

STEVEN COUNTISS EMENS,* (Assoc. Dean; Director, CLE Programs & Prof. of Clin. Legal Instruction)**, born 1950; admitted to bar, 1976, Alabama. *Education:* University of North Alabama (B.S., 1973); Alabama (M.B.A., 1976; J.D., 1976). ***COURSES: Clinical Teaching, Evidence, Trial & Appellate Advocacy. ***Email:*** semens@law.ua.edu

DAVID EPSTEIN,* (Charles E. Tweddy, Jr. Chair of Law)**, born Alexandria, Louisiana, December 7, 1943; admitted to bar, 1966, Texas; 1967, Arizona; 1979, Arkansas; 1989, Georgia. *Education:* University of Texas (B.A., 1964; J.D., 1966); Harvard University (LL.M., 1969). ***COURSES: Bankruptcy, Business Organizations, Contracts, Agency and Partnership. ***Email:*** depstein@law.ua.edu

BRYAN KEITH FAIR,* (Thomas E. Skinner Professor)**, born 1960; admitted to bar, 1986, California. *Education:* Duke (A.B., 1982); U.C.L.A. (J.D., 1985). ***COURSES: Civil Rights, Constitutional Law, Gender & the Law, First Amendment. ***Email:*** bfair@law.ua.edu

DAN FILLER,* (Associate Professor)**, born 1962; admitted to bar, 1990, Pennsylvania; 1994 New York. *Education:* Brown University (A.B., 1984); New York University (J.D., 1990). ***COURSES: Juvenile Law, Clinical Program. ***Email:*** dfiller@law.ua.edu

TONY A. FREYER,* (Resident Professor, History & Law)**, born 1947. *Education:* San Diego State University (A.B., 1970); Indiana University (M.A., 1972; Ph.D., 1975). ***COURSES: American Legal History, English Legal History. ***Email:*** tfreyer@law.ua.edu

J. NOAH FUNDERBURG,* (Professor, Clinical Legal Instruction; Senior Assistant Dean of Administration)**, born 1951; admitted to bar, 1977, Alabama. *Education:* Auburn University (B.A., 1974); Alabama (J.D., 1977). ***COURSES: Clinical Teaching, Trial Advocacy. ***Email:*** nfunderb@law.ua.edu

CHARLES W. GAMBLE,* (Upson Sims Professor)**, born 1942; admitted to bar, 1968, Alabama. *Education:* Jacksonville State University (B.S., 1965); Alabama (J.D., 1968); Harvard (LL.M., 1971). ***COURSES: Advanced Evidence, Bankruptcy, Contracts, Evidence, Restitution, Torts. ***Email:*** cgamble@law.ua.edu

SUSAN PACE HAMILL,* (Professor)**, born 1960; admitted to bar, 1987, New York. *Education:* Oxford College of Emory (A.A., 1980); Emory (B.A., 1982); Tulane (J.D., 1985); New York University (LL.M., 1986). ***COURSES: Business Organizations, Business Planning, Corporate Finance, Limited Liability Companies & Other Closely Held Businesses, Partnership Taxation, Securities Regulation. ***Email:*** shamill@law.ua.edu

STEVEN H. HOBBS,* (Tom Bevill Chair of Law)**, born Summerville, New Jersey, October 7, 1952; admitted to bar, 1980, New Jersey, Pennsylvania. *Education:* Harvard University (B.A., 1975); University of Pennsylvania (J.D., 1979). ***COURSES: Legal Profession, Family Law, Small Business Development. ***Email:*** shobbs@law.ua.edu

TIMOTHY HOFF,* (Gordon Rosen Professor)**, born 1941; admitted to bar, 1967, Florida; 1973, Alabama. *Education:* Tulane (A.B., 1963; J.D., 1966); Harvard (LL.M., 1970). ***COURSES: Admiralty, Civil Procedure, Conflict of Laws, Contracts, Federal Jurisdiction, The Law in Literature. ***Email:*** thoff@law.ua.edu

JEROME ALLAN HOFFMAN,* (Elton B. Stephens Professor of Law)**, born 1935; admitted to bar, 1965, California; 1974, Alabama. *Education:* Nebraska (A.B., 1962; J.D., 1965). ***COURSES: Civil Procedure. ***Email:*** jhoffman@law.ua.edu

WYTHE HOLT,* (University Research Professor)**, born 1942; admitted to bar, 1966, Virginia; 1970, Alabama. *Education:* Amherst College (B.A., 1963); University of Virginia (J.D., 1966; Ph.D., 1979). ***COURSES: Conflict of Laws, Estates & Trusts, Federal Courts, Legal History. ***Email:*** wholt@law.ua.edu

(This Listing Continued)

UNIVERSITY OF ALABAMA SCHOOL OF LAW —Continued

THOMAS L. JONES*, (Alumni Class of 1936 Professor of Law)**, born 1931; admitted to bar, 1961, Kentucky; 1968, Alabama. *Education:* Kentucky (B.S., 1959; J.D., 1961); Michigan (LL.M., 1965). ***COURSES: Contracts, Corporations, Decedents' Estates, Equity, Estate & Gift Taxation, Estate Planning, Trusts & Estates. ***Email:*** tjones@law.ua.edu

ROBERT R. KUEHN*, (Director of Clinical Programs, Professor)**, born South Bend, Indiana, April 30, 1952; admitted to bar, 1981, Florida; 1989, Louisiana; 1991, District of Columbia. *Education:* Duke University (B.A., 1974); George Washington University National Law Center (J.D., 1981); Columbia University (LL.M., 1983). ***COURSES: Legal Profession. ***Email:*** rkuehn@law.ua.edu

JAMES B. LEONARD*, (Professor of Law and Director, Law Library)**, born Hot Point, North Carolina, June 27, 1954; admitted to bar, 1987, Ohio; 1988, District of Columbia. *Education:* University of North Carolina (B.A., 1975; M.L.S., 1980; J.D., 1986). ***COURSES: Disability Law, Legal Research. ***Email:*** jleonard@law.ua.edu

GENE A. MARSH*, (James M. Kidd, Sr. Professor)**, born 1951; admitted to bar, 1981, Alabama. *Education:* Ohio State (B.S./M.S., 1978); Washington & Lee University (J.D., 1981). ***COURSES: Commercial Law, Commercial Paper, Consumer Law, Contracts, Corporate Finance, Corporations. ***Email:*** gmarsh@law.ua.edu

JENELLE MIMS MARSH*, (Senior Assistant Dean for Students/Academic Services)**, born 1956; admitted to bar, 1981, Alabama. *Education:* Auburn (B.S., 1978); Washington & Lee University (J.D., 1981). ***Email: jmarsh@law.ua.edu

ROBERT L. MARSHALL*, (Associate Director, Library & Lecturer)**, born Mobile, Alabama, June 26, 1956. *Education:* Rhodes College (B.A., 1978); University of Memphis (J.D., 1986); Emory University (M.L.N., 1987). ***COURSES: Legal Research. ***Email:*** rmarshal@law.ua.edu

ALLISON D. MARTIN*, (Director and Lecturer of Legal Writing)**, born 1964; admitted to bar, 1992, Illinois. *Education:* University of Illinois (B.S., 1986; J.D., 1992). ***COURSES: Legal Writing. ***Email:*** amartin@law.ua.edu

LAURA E. MCNALLY*, (Lecturer in Clinical Legal Education)**, born Loma Linda, California, June 8, 1974; admitted to bar, 2000, Alabama. *Education:* Hobart and William Smith Colleges (B.A., 1996); Syracuse University (J.D., 1999). ***COURSES: Clinic, Children's Rights. ***Email:*** mcnally@law.ua.edu

MARTHA I. MORGAN*, (Robert S. Vance Professor)**, born 1950; admitted to bar, 1977, District of Columbia; 1995, Alabama. *Education:* Alabama (B.S., 1972); George Washington University (J.D., 1977). ***COURSES: Civil Rights, Comparative Constitutional Law, Constitutional Law, Legal Education. ***Email:*** mmorgan@law.ua.edu

JOE C. MORRISON*, (Professor, Clinical Legal Instruction & Dir., Public Defender Program)**, born 1947; admitted to bar, 1975, Alabama. *Education:* Alabama (B.A., 1969; J.D., 1975). ***COURSES: Clinical Programs, Legal Counseling, Trial Advocacy. ***Email:*** jmorriso@law.ua.edu

DANIEL C. POWELL*, (Legal Writing Lecturer)**, born Tuscaloosa, Alabama, January 10, 1969; admitted to bar, 1998, Alabama. *Education:* Vanderbilt University (B.A., 1991); University of Virginia (M.A., 1994); The University of Alabama (J.D., 1998). ***COURSES: Legal Writing. ***Email:*** dpowell@law.ua.edu

SUSAN LYONS RANDALL*, (Professor)**, born 1956; admitted to bar, 1983, New York. *Education:* University of North Carolina (B.A., 1978); Columbia (J.D., 1982). ***COURSES: Insurance, Jurisprudence, Torts. ***Email:*** srandall@law.ua.edu

ELIZABETH UTSEY SADLER*, (Assistant Dean for Advancement)**, admitted to bar, 1997, Alabama. *Education:* University of Alabama (B.A., 1992); University of Alabama School of Law (J.D., 1996). ***Email: lsadler@law.ua.edu

NORMAN J. SINGER*, (Charles O. Stokes Professor of Law & Anthropology)**, born 1938; admitted to bar, 1964, Massachusetts; 1974, Alabama. *Education:* Pennsylvania, (B.S., 1960); Boston University (J.D., 1964); Harvard (S.J.D., 1975). ***COURSES: Comparative Law, Conflict of Laws, Family Law, Law & Society, Legislation, Sports Law, Workers' Compensation, Legal Anthropology. ***Email:*** nsinger@law.ua.edu

NORMAN P. STEIN*, (Douglas Arant Professor)**, born 1951; admitted to bar, 1978, District of Columbia; 1981, Georgia. *Education:* New College (B.A., 1973); Duke (J.D., 1978). ***COURSES: Corporate Tax, Federal Income Taxation I, Labor Law, Law & Literature. ***Email:*** nstein@law.ua.edu

PAUL E. TOPPINS*, (Legal Writing Lecturer)**, born Gando, Texas, October 24, 1956; admitted to bar, 1982, Alabama; 1990, District of Columbia, US District Court, Northern District of Alabama, US Court of Appeals, Eleventh Circuit, U.S. Supreme Court. *Education:* University of Alabama (B.A., 1979); University of Alabama School of Law (J.D., 1982); Columbia University School of Law (LL.M., 1998). ***COURSES: Legal Writing. ***Email:*** ptoppins@law.ua.edu

THE UNIVERSITY OF ARIZONA, JAMES E. ROGERS COLLEGE OF LAW

1201 E. SPEEDWAY
P.O. BOX 210176
TUCSON, ARIZONA 85721-0176
Telephone: (520) 621-1373
Fax: (520) 621-9140

ABA Approved Since 1930.

The University

The University of Arizona was founded in 1885 and is one of the nation's leading research universities, ranking 13th among public universities in 1999 by the National Science Foundation. The Faculty of the University of Arizona includes scores of nationally recognized scholars and teachers, including a Nobel laureate, many Sloan, Guggenheim and MacArthur Fellows, Fulbright scholars and members of the National Academy of Sciences and Institute of Medicine. The College of Law, founded in 1915, is the oldest law school in Arizona and has a rich and distinguished history. We have a full-time JD and LLM program, with a total of approximately 470 enrolled students each year. The College of Law Library is one of the best legal research facilities in the Southwest, with a collection of over 383,000 volumes and the latest in computer-based legal research through Lexis, Westlaw and Internet access.

(This Listing Continued)

THE UNIVERSITY OF ARIZONA, JAMES E. ROGERS COLLEGE OF LAW—Continued

The Students

The students of the College of Law are a talented and diverse group culturally, educationally and geographically with rich work and volunteer experience. Each year about 150 JD candidates enroll in an entering class, and 30 students with law degrees enroll in our two LL.M. programs in International Trade Law and in Indigenous Peoples Law and Policy. Admission is very competitive; the 150 members of the 2000 Fall entering class were selected from 1,660 applicants and represent 81 different undergraduate schools and 18 graduate schools. The law school LSAT median is 160 (the 85th percentile rank), and the median undergraduate GPA is 3.49. Fifty-four percent of the Fall 2000 entering class are women, 27 percent come from minority backgrounds, 16 percent have graduate degrees. Nineteen percent of our graduates enter judicial clerkships after graduation, one of the highest percentages of all public law schools.

The Faculty

The College of Law has 30 full-time faculty, complemented by a diverse adjunct faculty. With a ratio of 14 to 1, the College has one of the most favorable student-faculty ratios of any American law school. Many members of the Faculty are nationally recognized legal scholars, and 18 members of the faculty hold named professorships.

An extraordinary number of major texts are authored and edited by our faculty (e.g., Mauet on *Trial Techniques*; Dobbs on *Torts* and the *Law of Remedies*), with more than twelve nationally used casebooks and another half-dozen hornbooks written by our 30 full-time faculty members. Practicing attorneys readily recognize such classics as Dobbs on *Torts* and McCormick's *Evidence*, both written and updated by Arizona faculty.

Costs

The tuition structure of the University of Arizona College of Law affords students the opportunity to pursue a legal education of outstanding quality without extraordinary debt burden. Tuition and fees for the 2001-2002 academic year are $5,240 for Arizona residents and $13, 106 for non-residents.

Clinical Programs

The College of Law offers varied clinical programs which provide students the opportunity to work under the supervision of attorneys and judges in private law firms, government agencies, public interest organizations and the federal and state courts. Four in-house clinics (Immigration Law, Domestic Violence, Child Advocacy and Tribal Law) are directed and staffed by full-time directors and attorneys. Additionally, the College sponsors two United States Senate internships, various congressional and legislative internships, prosecution and defense clinics, a Ninth Circuit pro bono appellate project, and internships with the Navajo, Tohono O'odham, White Mountain Apache and Pascua Yaqui tribal governments.

Career Services

The professionally staffed Career Services Office provides employers, students and alumni with a variety of support and information services. In 2000-01, 125+ firms, agencies and corporations visited the College of Law to interview our students. The Career Services Office staff are pleased to assist employers with their hiring needs, whether summer associate, permanent attorney, or short-term research projects. Facilities and assistance are provided for employers who wish to interview *on-campus, off-campus* or via *teleconferencing*. College of Law alumni and other subscribers can be reached by employers through our bi-weekly job publication, *The Career AdvoCAT*. The Class of 2000 found 95% employment six months after graduation, with the largest percentage (87%) choosing traditional law firm, judicial clerkship and government practice. Geographically, 65% of the Class of 1999 found employment in Arizona, while the remaining 35% found employment in 18 other states.

Dean & Milton O. Riepe Chair in Constitutional Law: Toni M. Massaro (520) 621-1498
Associate Dean, Academic Affairs: Kay Kavanagh (520) 621-1720
Director, Law Library & Professor of Law: Michael G. Chiorazzi (520) 621-5477
Assistant Dean, Student Affairs: Dr. Willie M. Jordan-Curtis (520) 621-8602
Assistant Dean, Admissions: Terry S. Holpert (520) 621-7666
Assistant Dean, Finance & Administration: Henrietta A. Stover (520) 621-3783
Assistant Dean, Career Services: Mary N. Birmingham (520) 621-5060
Associate Director, Professional Development: Paula Nailon (520) 626-6107
Registrar: Janice Marotta (520) 621-7667
Assistant Dean for External Relations: Vicki Fleischer (520) 621-8430
Assistant Director, Development & External Affairs: Christine M. Thompson (520) 626-9223
Director of Information Technology: Mohyeddin K. Abdulaziz (520) 621-3053
Internet Developer: Paul Kealey (520) 626-7258
Coordinator, Special Projects: Martha Fenn (520) 621-1166

FULL TIME FACULTY

TONI M. MASSARO*, (Dean and Milton O. Riepe Chair in Constitutional Law)**, born 1955; admitted to bar, 1980, Illinois; 1990, Arizona. *Education:* Northwestern (B.S., 1977); College of William and Mary (J.D., 1980). ***COURSES: Civil Procedure, Constitutional Law. ***Email:*** massaro@law.arizona.edu

DAVID E. ADELMAN*, (Associate Professor of Law)**, born Saskatoon, Canada, November 10, 1965; admitted to bar, 1996, California; 1998, District of Columbia. *Education:* Reed College (B.A., 1988); Stanford University (PhD, 1993; J.D., 1996). ***COURSES: Environmental Law, Law & Science, Intellectual Property. ***Email:*** adelman@law.arizona.edu

JAMES S. ANAYA*, (Samuel M. Fegtly Professor of Law)**, admitted to bar, 1983, New Mexico. *Education:* University of New Mexico (B.A., 1980); Harvard Law School (J.D., 1983). ***COURSES: Constitutional Law, Indigenous Human Rights, International Human Rights, Property. ***Email:*** anaya@law.arizona.edu

ARTHUR W. ANDREWS*, (Rosenstiel Distinguished Professor of Law)**, born 1937; admitted to bar, 1963, New York; 1964 Iowa; 1973, Arizona. *Education:* University of Iowa (B.A., 1959); New York University (LL.B., 1963; LL.M., 1964). ***COURSES: Administrative Law, Business Planning, Criminal Procedure, Federal Tax Procedure, Taxation (Federal). ***Email:*** andrews@law.arizona.edu

***CHARLES E. ARES*, (J. Byron McCormick Professor of Law Emeritus)**, born 1926; admitted to bar, 1953, Arizona. *Education:*

(This Listing Continued)

THE UNIVERSITY OF ARIZONA, JAMES E. ROGERS COLLEGE OF LAW—Continued

University of Arizona (J.D., 1952). ***COURSES:*** Civil Procedure, Research & Writing. ***Email:*** ares@law.arizona.edu

BARBARA A. ATWOOD*, (Mary Anne Richey Professor of Law)**, born 1947; admitted to bar, 1976, Arizona. *Education:* Mary Baldwin College (B.A., 1969); University of Arizona (J.D., 1976). ***COURSES: Civil Procedure, Community Property, Conflict of Laws, Family Law, Federal Jurisdiction. ***Email:*** atwood@law.arizona.edu

GRAEME W. AUSTIN*, (Professor of Law)**, born Wellington, New Zealand, March 11, 1963; admitted to bar, 1991, New Zealand. *Education:* Victoria University of Wellington (B.A. Hons., 1985; LL.B., 1989; LL.M. Hons., 1991); Columbia University (LL.M., 1998; J.S.D., 2001). ***COURSES: Intellectual Property, Torts. ***Email:*** austin@law.arizona.edu

PAUL D. BENNETT*, (Director, Child Advocacy Clinic, Associate Clinical Professor)**, born Quincy, Massachusetts, January 12, 1951; admitted to bar, 1977, New York. *Education:* Bates College (B.A., 1973); Cornell (J.D., 1976). ***COURSES: Clinical Education, Family Law, Legal Reasoning & Analysis, Legal Research & Writing, Professional Responsibility, Trial Advocacy. ***Email:*** bennett@law.arizona.edu

WILLIAM E. BOYD*, (Chester H. Smith Professor of Law)**, born 1941; admitted to bar, 1967, Michigan; 1970, Arizona, U.S. District Court Arizona, U.S. Court of Appeals 9th Cir.. *Education:* Michigan (A.B., 1963); Wayne State (J.D., 1966); Harvard (LL.M., 1967). ***COURSES: Commercial Law, Commercial Paper, Consumer Law, Contracts, Creditor's Rights, Law and Technology. ***Email:*** boyd@law.arizona.edu

JEAN BRAUCHER*, (Roger Henderson Professor of Law)**, born 1950; admitted to bar, 1978, Wisconsin; 1979, Maine. *Education:* Brown University (A.B., 1972); Boston University (J.D., 1978). ***COURSES: Contracts, Commercial Law, Creditor & Debtor Rights, Commercial Paper, Introduction to Law. ***Email:*** braucher@law.arizona.edu

ELLEN MICHELLE BUBLICK*, (Associate Professor of Law)**, born Chicago, Illinois, April 10, 1966; admitted to bar, 1991, Illinois. *Education:* Duke (A.B., 1987); Harvard (J.D., 1991). ***COURSES: Employment Law, Genetics and the Law, Torts, Civil Rights Law, Economic & Dignitary Torts. ***Email:*** bublick@law.arizona.edu

MICHAEL G. CHIORAZZI*, (Professor of Law and Director of the Law Library)**, born Jersey City, N.J., December 3, 1954. *Education:* Miami (B.A., 1976); Gonzaga (J.D., 1980); Washington (M.L.L., 1981). ***COURSES: Legal Research and Writing, Advanced Legal Research. ***Email:*** chiorazzi@law.arizona.edu

DAN B. DOBBS*, (Regents and Rosenstiel Distinguished Professor of Law)**, born 1932; admitted to bar, 1956, Arkansas. *Education:* Arkansas, Fayetteville (B.A., 1956; J.D., 1956); Illinois (LL.M., 1961; J.S.D., 1966). ***COURSES: Remedies, Torts. ***Email:*** dobbs@law.arizona.edu

JULIE FERDON*, (Adjunct Assistant Professor of Law & Moot Court Advisor)**, born Santa Fe, New Mexico, December 25, 1950; admitted to bar, 1986, Arizona. *Education:* The University of Arizona (B.A., 1972; L.B., 1985). ***COURSES: Moot Court, Appellate Advocacy. ***Email:*** ferdon@law.arizona.edu

DAVID A. GANTZ*, (Dir. of Intl. Trade Law Program., Prof. of Law and Assoc. Dir., Nat. Law Ctr. for Intl. American Free Trade)**, born 1942; admitted to bar, 1967, Ohio; 1971, District of Columbia; 1995, Arizona. *Education:* Harvard (A.B., 1964); Stanford (J.D., 1967; J.S.M., 1970). ***COURSES: International Environmental Law, Intl. Investment Law, Intl. Public Law, Intl. Trade Law, Intro to US Legal System, Law of Regional Economic Integration. ***Email:*** gantz@law.arizona.edu

ROBERT J. GLENNON*, (Morris K. Udall Professor of Law & Public Policy)**, born 1944; admitted to bar, 1969, Massachusetts; 1982, Michigan. *Education:* Boston College (A.B., 1966); Brandeis (M.A., 1972; Ph.D., 1981); Boston College (J.D., 1969). ***COURSES: American Legal History, Constitutional Law, Criminal Procedure, Federal Jurisdiction, Water Rights, Legal History. ***Email:*** glennon@law.arizona.edu

BERNARD E. HARCOURT*, (Associate Professor of Law)**, born 1963; admitted to bar, 1990, New York; 1991, Alabama, District of Columbia; 1996, Massachusetts. *Education:* Princeton (A.B., 1984); Harvard (J.D., 1989; Ph.D., 2000; S.J.D.). ***COURSES: Capital Punishment, Criminal Law Theory, Gun Control Seminar, Criminal Justice, Criminal Procedure, Legal and Political Theory. ***Email:*** harcourt@law.arizona.edu

ZELDA B. HARRIS*, (Director, Domestic Violence Clinic, Associate Clinical Professor)**, born Princeton, New Jersey, 1966; admitted to bar, 1991, Illinois. *Education:* Syracuse University (B.S., 1988); Washington University (St. Louis) (J.D., 1991). ***COURSES: Clinical Training, Family Law, Domestic Violence Law, Poverty Law. ***Email:*** harris @law.arizona.edu

KENNEY F. HEGLAND*, (James E. Rogers Professor of Law)**, born 1940; admitted to bar, 1967, California; 1976, Arizona. *Education:* Stanford (A.B., 1963); Cal. Berkeley (LL.B., 1966); Harvard (LL.M., 1974). ***COURSES: Clinical Teaching, Contracts, Health Care Law, Legal Research and Writing, Sports Law, Elder Law, Law & Humanities. ***Email:*** hegland@law.arizona.edu

ROGER C. HENDERSON*, (Ralph W. Bilby Professor of Law)**, born 1938; admitted to bar, 1965, Texas; 1977, Arizona, Nebraska. *Education:* University of Texas (B.B.A., 1960; LL.B., 1965); Harvard (LL.M., 1969). ***COURSES: Evidence, Insurance, Products Liability, Torts. ***Email:*** henderson@law.arizona.edu

ROBERT ALAN HERSHEY*, (Adjunct Assistant Professor, Specialist in Indian Programs, Director of Tribal Law Clinic)**, born Los Angeles, California, December 23, 1947; admitted to bar, 1972, Arizona; 1990, Montana. *Education:* University of California Irvine (B.S., 1969); University of Arizona (J.D., 1972). ***COURSES: Indian Law, Globalization and Preservation (Transformation) of Culture. ***Email:*** hershey@law.arizona.edu

JUNIUS HOFFMAN*, (Professor of Law Emeritus)**, born Augusta Maine, April 14, 1924; admitted to bar, 1951, Ohio; 1970, Arizona. *Education:* Dartmouth College (B.A., 1943); Harvard University (M.A., 1946); Yale Law School (LL.B., 1951). ***COURSES: Corporate Finance, Securities Regulation, Corporations.

JAMES C. HOPKINS*, (Associate Clin. Professor, Director, Indigenous Peoples Law & Policy Program)**, born Ottawa, Canada, December 3, 1971. *Education:* University of Toronto (B.A., 1993; J.D., 1996); Harvard University (LL.M., 2000). ***COURSES: Indigenous Law. ***Email:*** hopkins@lawarizona.edu

MONA L. HYMEL*, (Associate Professor of Law)**, born Baton Rouge, Louisiana, January 22, 1960; admitted to bar, 1992, Texas; 1994, District of Columbia. *Education:* University of Texas (B.B.A., 1981; J.D., 1992). ***COURSES: Estates and Trusts, Federal Income Tax, Partnership Taxation, Tax Policy. ***Email:*** hymel@law.arizona.edu

KAY KAVANAGH*, (Associate Dean for Academic Affairs)**, born Baton Rouge, Louisiana, March 2, 1950; admitted to bar, 1981, Arizona. *Education:* Emory University (B.A., 1972); University of Arizona College of Law (J.D., 1981). ***COURSES: Legal Research & Writing, Legal Profession. ***Email:*** kavanagh@law.arizona.edu

(This Listing Continued)

THE UNIVERSITY OF ARIZONA, JAMES E. ROGERS COLLEGE OF LAW—Continued

JANE B. KORN*, (Professor of Law)**, born 1950; admitted to bar, 1983, Colorado; 1985, New York. *Education:* Rutgers University (B.A., 1972); University of Colorado (J.D., 1983). ***COURSES: Civil Procedure, Contracts, Corporations, Employment Law. ***Email:*** korn@law.arizona.edu

BORIS KOZOLCHYK*, (Director of National Law Center for Inter-American Free Trade, Evo A. DeConcini Professor of Law)**, born 1934; admitted to bar, 1972, Arizona. *Education:* University of Havana (D.C.L., 1956); University of Miami (LL.B., 1959); University of Michigan (LL.M., 1960; S.J.D., 1966). ***COURSES: Commercial Law, Comparative law, Intl. Transactions, Jurisprudence, Law and Socio-Economic Development. ***Email:*** b:kozolchyk@worldnet.att.net

JOSEPH M. LIVERMORE*, (Visiting Professor)**, born February 5, 1937; admitted to bar, 1962, California; 1974, Arizona. *Education:* Dartmouth (A.B., 1958); Stanford University (LL.B., 1961). ***COURSES: Copyright (Unfair Competition), Criminal Procedure, Evidence. ***Email:*** livermore@lawarizona.edu

LYNN MARCUS*, (Director, Immigration Law Clinic, Adjunct Assistant Professor)**, born Washington, D.C., April 10, 1964; admitted to bar, 1990, Supreme Court of Arizona; 1992, Fed. District Court; 1993, 9th Circuit. *Education:* Stanford University (B.S., 1986); New York University (J.D., 1989). ***COURSES: Director- Immigration Law Clinic. ***Email:*** marcus@law.arizona.edu

THOMAS A. MAUET*, (Milton O. Riepe Professor of Law; Director, Trial Advocacy)**, born Rendsburg, Germany, January 8, 1945; admitted to bar, 1970, Illinois; 1980, Arizona; 1982, New York. *Education:* Dartmouth (A.B., 1967); Northwestern (J.D., 1970). ***COURSES: Trial and Appellate Advocacy, Evidence, Civil Procedure, Criminal Procedure. ***Email:*** mauet@law.arizona.edu

ANA MARIA MERICO-STEPHENS*, (Associate Professor of Law)**, born 1961; admitted to bar, 1996, Ohio. *Education:* University of Cincinnati (B.A., 1992); University of Michigan (J.D. 1995). ***COURSES: Civil Procedure, Federal Courts, Legal Research & Writing. ***Email:*** stephens@law.arizona.edu

LESLYE A. OBIORA*, (Professor of Law)**, born Nigeria, 1963; admitted to bar, 1988, Connecticut. *Education:* University of Nigeria (LL.B., 1984); Yale (LL.M., 1988). ***COURSES: Business Associations, Feminist Legal Theory, International Law, Property, Corporations, Gender & Law, Jurisprudence. ***Email:*** obiora@law.arizona.edu

SUZANNE M. RABE*, (Director of Legal Writing and Associate Clinical Professor)**, born Portland, Oregon, May 26, 1953; admitted to bar, 1979, Arizona; 1981, California. *Education:* Arizona State University (B.A., 1976); University of Arizona (J.D., 1979). ***COURSES: Criminal Procedure, Family Law, Legal Research & Writing. ***Email:*** rabe@law.arizona.edu

JAMES R. RATNER*, (Professor of Law)**, born Los Angeles, California, February 2, 1953; admitted to bar, 1980, California. *Education:* Cal Berkeley (A.B., 1974; M.A., 1980); Cal Berkeley Boalt Hall (J.D., 1980). ***COURSES: Administrative Law, Antitrust, Community Property, Contracts, Law and Economics, Regulated Industries. ***Email:*** ratner@law.arizona.edu

THEODORE J. SCHNEYER*, (Milton O. Riepe Professor of Law)**, born 1943; admitted to bar, 1971, California. *Education:* John Hopkins University (A.B., 1965); Harvard University (LL.B., 1968); Stanford (J.S.M., 1971); University of Stockholm (Dip. C.L., 1969). ***COURSES: Law and Behavioral Sciences, Legal Process, Legal Profession, Torts. ***Email:*** schneyer@law.arizona.edu

ANDREW SILVERMAN*, (Director of Clinical Programs, Professor of Law)**, born 1943; admitted to bar, 1969, Arizona. *Education:* University of Arizona (J.D., 1969). ***COURSES: Clinical Practice, Immigration Law, Interviewing, Counseling and Negotiating, Trial Practice. ***Email:*** silverman@law.arizona.edu

ROY G. SPECE, JR.*, (Professor of Law)**, born 1948; admitted to bar, 1972, California; 1978, Arizona. *Education:* California State University, Long Beach (B.A., 1972); University of Southern California (J.D., 1972). ***COURSES: Biomedical Technology and Law (Bioethics and Law), Law and Medicine, Civil Procedure, Constitutional Law, Employment Discrimination, Jurisprudence. ***Email:*** spece@law.arizona.edu

JOHN W. STRONG*, (Rosentiel Distinguished Professor of Law Emeritus)**, born Iowa, August 18, 1935; admitted to bar, 1963, Illinois; 1976, Oregon. *Education:* Yale (B.A., 1957); University of Illinois (J.D., 1962). ***COURSES: Copyright, Evidence, Insurance, Practice & Procedure, Practice Court, Property. ***Email:*** strong@law.arizona.edu

JOHN A. SWAIN*, (Associate Professor of Law)**, born Lynchburg, Virginia, September 12, 1956; admitted to bar, 1987, Arizona. *Education:* Dartmouth College (A.B., 1978); Yale (J.D., 1984). ***COURSES: Estates & Trusts, Taxation, State & Local Property, Federal Taxation, Legal Profession (Professional Responsibility). ***Email:*** swin@law.arizona.edu

DALIA TSUK*, (Associate Professor of Law)**, admitted to bar, 1993, Israel. *Education:* Tel Aviv University School of Law (LL.B., 1992); Harvard Law School (S.J.D., 1998). ***COURSES: Corporations, American Legal History, Constitutional Law. ***Email:*** tsuk@law.arizona.edu

ELLIOTT J. WEISS*, (Charles E. Ares Professor of Law)**, born 1939; admitted to bar, 1965, California; 1966, New York. *Education:* Dartmouth College (B.A., 1961); Yale (LL.B., 1964). ***COURSES: Accounting for Lawyers, Corporate Governance, Corporations, Securities Regulation, Health Care Law, Torts. ***Email:*** weiss@law.arizona.edu

DAVID B. WEXLER*, (John D. Lyons Professor of Law and Psychology)**, born 1941; admitted to bar, 1964, New York; 1970, Arizona. *Education:* SUNY at Binghamton (B.A., 1961); New York University (J.D., 1964). ***COURSES: Criminal Law, Criminal Procedure, Law and Psychiatry, Law and Social Sciences, Therapeutic Jurisprudence. ***Email:*** dwexler@compuserve.com

ROBERT A. WILLIAMS, JR.*, (E. Thomas Sullivan Professor of Law)**, born 1955; admitted to bar, 1980, Massachusetts. *Education:* Loyola (A.B., 1977); Harvard (J.D., 1980). ***COURSES: Energy and Natural Resources Law, Federal Indian Law, Indigenous Human Rights, Land Planning, Real Property, Indigenous Peoples Law & Policy Clinic. ***Email:*** williams@law.arizona.edu

WINTON D. WOODS*, (Professor of Law)**, born 1938; admitted to bar, 1965, Indiana; 1971, Arizona. *Education:* Indiana University (A.D.; J.D., 1965). ***COURSES: Arbitration Dispute Resolution, Law Office Management and Technology. ***Email:*** courtroom@mail.com

UNIVERSITY OF ARKANSAS AT FAYETTEVILLE SCHOOL OF LAW

LEFLAR LAW CENTER
FAYETTEVILLE, ARKANSAS 72701
Telephone: (501) 575-5601
Fax: (501) 575-3320
http://law.uark.edu

The School of Law was established in 1924. Our rich history is exemplified by the outstanding contributions of faculty and alumni to the world, the nation and the state. President Bill Clinton and First Lady Hillary Rodham Clinton were both members of the faculty. The late Senators J. William Fulbright and Claude Pepper served on the faculty. Alumni have held and continue to occupy important federal and state judicial posts, including George Haley ('52), currently serving as U.S. Ambassador to Nambia; Rodney Slater ('80), the U.S. Secretary of Transportation; and U.S. Congressmen Jay Dickey ('63) and W. Asa Hutchinson ('75). In addition to the regular law program, the school offers the only LL.M. degree in Agricultural Law in the nation. In this connection, the law school houses the National Center for Agricultural Law Research and Information.

The law school admits a class of approximately 135 students every year in the fall. Additionally, approximately 10 graduate students are admitted into the Agricultural Law LL.M. program. A full-time faculty of 36 assures a low student-teacher ratio and enables faculty and students to form close and beneficial professional relationships.

In addition to the Arkansas Law Review, published quarterly, the law school publishes the Arkansas Law Notes annually. The National Center for Agricultural Law Research and Information publishes specialized monographs from time to time.

The Board of Student Advocates is an integrated advocacy organization that supports moot court, trial, negotiation, and counseling competitions, both intra- and extra-mural. Our Moot Court teams have advanced to the finals of the National Moot Court competition in New York City three times since 1994. In addition, since 1994, Arkansas has won six best oralist awards; three best brief awards; and won, placed or advanced in 11 national invitational competitions including multiple distinctions at both Vanderbilt First Amendment Moot Court Competition and the National Juvenile Law Moot Court Competition. In 1996, our client Counseling Team advanced from regional competition to the National Championship Rounds in Pennsylvania. In 1998, our Negotiation Team won the regional competition and advanced to the National Championship Rounds in Los Angeles.

The law school is located in Fayetteville--a town of 52,000 in the Ozarks. The University has a total enrollment of about 16,000.

Dean: Robert Moberly (501) 575-4504
Admissions: James K. Miller (501) 575-3102
Financial Aid: James K. Miller (501) 575-3102
Library: Glen-Peter Ahlers (501) 575-5604
Placement: Claudia Driver (501) 575-7644
Alumni Affairs: Malcolm McNair (501) 575-7735

FULL TIME FACULTY

ROBERT B. MOBERLY*, (Dean of the Law School and Professor of Law)**, born Madison, Wisconsin, September 17, 1941; admitted to bar, 1966, Wisconsin; 1977, Tennessee; 1984, Florida. *Education:* University of Wisconsin (B.S., 1963); University of Wisconsin Law School (J.D., 1966). ***COURSES: Labor Law and Alternative Dispute Resolution. ***Email:*** moberly@comp.uark.edu

GLEN-PETER AHLERS*, (Law Library Director and Associate Professor)**, born New York, New York, March 15, 1955; admitted to bar, 1987, Kansas; 1988, U.S. Court of Military Appeals; 1990, District of Columbia. *Education:* University of New Mexico (B.U.S., 1977); University of South Florida (M.L.S., 1983); Washburn University (J.D., 1987). ***COURSES: Advanced Legal Research. ***Email:*** gahlers@comp.uark.edu

RICHARD B. ATKINSON*, (Associate Professor of Law)**, born Pittsburgh, Pennsylvania, September 3, 1946; admitted to bar, 1974, Georgia. *Education:* Duke University (A.B., 1968); Yale Divinity School (M.Div., 1971); Yale Law School (J.D., 1974). ***COURSES: Property, Real Estate Transactions, Decedents' Estates, AIDS and the Law. ***Email:*** ratkins@comp.uark.edu

CARLTON BAILEY*, (Associate Professor of Law)**, born Birmingham, Alabama, February 28, 1948; admitted to bar, 1973, Minnesota; 1979, Arkansas. *Education:* Talladega College (B.S., 1969); University of Chicago (J.D., 1972). ***COURSES: Evidence, Criminal Procedure, Trial Advocacy, Lawyering Practice Skills. ***Email:*** cbailey@comp.uark.edu

LONNIE R. BEARD*, (Professor of Law and Associate Dean for Academic Affairs)**, born Keiser, Arkansas, June 23, 1948; admitted to bar, 1975, Iowa and Arkansas; 1979, California. *Education:* Arkansas State University (B.A., 1970); University of Arkansas, Fayetteville (J.D., 1975); New York University (LL.M., 1978). ***COURSES: Federal Taxation, Taxation of Business Enterprises, Business Planning, Agricultural Taxation. ***Email:*** lrbeard@comp.uark.edu

HOWARD W. BRILL*, (Vincent Foster Professor of Legal Ethics and Professional Responsibility)**, born Englewood, New Jersey, October 18, 1943; admitted to bar, 1970, Florida; 1973, Illinois; 1977, Arkansas. *Education:* Duke University (A.B., 1965); University of Florida (J.D., 1970); University of Illinois (LL.M., 1978). ***COURSES: Professional Responsibility, Remedies, Civil Procedure, Law and Baseball. ***Email:*** hbrill@comp.uark.edu

CHAUNCEY E. BRUMMER*, (Associate Professor)**, born Louisville, Kentucky, November 22, 1948; admitted to bar, 1973, Kentucky. *Education:* Howard University (B.A., 1970); University of Kentucky (J.D., 1973). ***COURSES: Torts, Family Law, Juvenile Law, Professional Responsibility. ***Email:*** cbrummer@comp.uark.edu

KIM COATS*, (Research Assistant Professor of Legal Writing)**, born Oklahoma City, Oklahoma, July 5, 1960; admitted to bar, 1992, Oklahoma; 1966, Arkansas. *Education:* Arizona State University (B.S., 1981); Oklahoma City University School of Law (J.D., 1991). ***COURSES: Legal Research and Writing. ***Email:*** kcoats@comp.uark.edu

***JANET A. FLACCUS*, (Professor of Law)**, born Pittsburgh, Pennsylvania, December 31, 1949; admitted to bar, 1978, Illinois. *Education:* Wheaton College (B.A., 1971); University of California,

(This Listing Continued)

UNIVERSITY OF ARKANSAS AT FAYETTEVILLE SCHOOL OF LAW—Continued

Davis (M.S., 1973; J.D., 1978); University of Illinois (LL.M., 1985). ***COURSES:*** Contracts, Bankruptcy, Secured Transactions, Sales and Leasing. ***Email:*** jflaccus@comp.uark.edu

SHARON E. FOSTER, **(Research Professor of Legal Writing),** *Education:* University of California at Los Angeles (B.A., 1983); Loyola Law School (J.D., 1987); University of Edinburgh (LL.M., 1997). ***COURSES:*** Legal Writing, Appellate Advocacy, International Business Transactions.

MORTON GITELMAN, **(Distinguished Professor of Law),** born Chicago, Illinois, February 7, 1933; admitted to bar, 1959, Illinois; 1972, Arkansas. *Education:* Roosevelt University (Certificate, 1954); De Paul University (J.D., 1959); University of Illinois (LL.M., 1965). ***COURSES:*** Land Use, Evidence, Legal History. ***Email:*** gitelman@comp.uark.edu

CAROL R. GOFORTH, **(Clayton N. Little Professor of Law),** born Fayetteville, Arkansas, October 12, 1960; admitted to bar, 1984, Oklahoma. *Education:* University of Arkansas (B.A., 1981; J.D., 1984). ***COURSES:*** Corporations, Corporate Finance, Securities Regulation, Business Planning. ***Email:*** cgoforth@comp.uark.edu

RAFAEL GUZMAN, **(Professor of Law),** born Pennsylvania, June 27, 1935; admitted to bar, 1964, District of Columbia. *Education:* University of Dayton (B.A., 1961); George Washington University (LL.B., 1964). ***COURSES:*** Criminal Law, Criminal Procedure, Evidence.

JOHN STEPHEN HARBISON, **(Research Associate Professor),** born Kentucky, December 15, 1951; admitted to bar, 1983, Massachusetts. *Education:* University of Kentucky (J.D., 1981); University of Arkansas (LL.M., 1991); Stanford Law School. ***COURSES:*** Environmental Law, Public Lands, Natural Resources. ***Email:*** jharbiso@comp.uark.edu

JOSEPH H. HOBSON, JR., **(Director of the Graduate Agriculture Law Program),** born Nampa, Idaho, December 8, 1949. *Education:* Northwest Nazarene College (B.A., 1972); Willamette University (J.D., 1975). ***COURSES:*** Agriculture Law. ***Email:*** josephh@comp.uark.edu

DONALD JUDGES, **(Professor),** born Baltimore, Maryland, April 13, 1955; admitted to bar, 1985, District of Columbia; 1986, Colorado. *Education:* Johns Hopkins University (B.A., 1978); University of Maryland (J.D., 1983). ***COURSES:*** Constitutional Law, Torts, Civil Rights, Jurisprudence. ***Email:*** djudges@comp.uark.edu

CHRISTOPHER R. KELLEY, **(Assistant Professor of Law),** born Atlanta, Georgia, July 21, 1947; admitted to bar, 1975, Minnesota; 1982, Arkansas; 1992, North Dakota; 1993, District of Columbia. *Education:* Louisiana State University (B.A., 1969); University of Arkansas School of Law (LL.M., 1986); Howard University (J.D., 1975). ***COURSES:*** Agricultural Law. ***Email:*** ckelley@comp.uark.edu

MARK R. KILLENBECK, **(Wylie H. Davis Professor of Law),** born Rochester, New York, September 29, 1948. *Education:* Boston College (A.B., 1970); University of Nebraska (Ph.D., 1987; J.D., 1987). ***COURSES:*** Constitutional Law, First Amendment, Supreme Court. ***Email:*** mkillenb@comp.uark.edu

JUDITH KILPATRICK, **(Associate Professor),** born Milwaukee, Wisconsin, December 15, 1946; admitted to bar, 1975, California. *Education:* University of California-Berkeley (B.A., 1971); Boalt Hall School of Law, University of California-Berkeley (J.D., 1975); Columbia University (LL.M., 1992). ***COURSES:*** Professional Responsibility, Skills (Interviewing/Counseling, Negotiation, Alternative Dispute Resolution, Trial Practice, etc.). ***Email:*** jkilpat@comp.uark.edu

ROBERT TODD LAURENCE, **(Robert A. Leflar Professor of Law),** born Newport News, Virginia, September 19, 1945; admitted to bar, 1978, New Mexico. *Education:* Ohio State University (B.Sc., 1967); University of Alberta (M.Ed., 1973); University of New Mexico (J.D., 1977); University of Illinois (LL.M., 1981). ***COURSES:*** Property, Commercial Law, American Indian Law. ***Email:*** rlaurenc@comp.uark.edu

ROBERT B. LEFLAR, **(Professor),** born Little Rock, Arkansas, January 23, 1951; admitted to bar, 1978, Arkansas; 1980, District of Columbia. *Education:* Harvard College (A.B., 1972); Tokyo University; Harvard Law School (J.D., 1977); Harvard School of Public Health (M.P.H., 1982). ***COURSES:*** Torts, Contracts, Health Law, Products Liability, Food and Drug Law, Workers' Compensation. ***Email:*** rbleflar@comp.uark.edu

MARY E. MATTHEWS, **(Professor),** born Rogers, Arkansas, January 20, 1954; admitted to bar, 1978, Arkansas. *Education:* University of Arkansas (B.S.E., 1975; J.D., 1978). ***COURSES:*** Corporations, Agency and Partnership, Negotiable Instruments, Agricultural Cooperatives. ***Email:*** mmatthew@comp.uark.edu

MICHAEL W. MULLANE, **(Director of the Legal Clinic and Professor of Law),** born 1943; admitted to bar, 1972, Arizona; 1987, Maine. *Education:* Notre Dame (B.A., 1964; J.D., 1964). ***COURSES:*** Advanced Trial Advocacy, Clinical Legal Education, Criminal Law, Evidence, Trial Practice. ***Email:*** mullane@comp.uark.edu

CYNTHIA E. NANCE, **(Associate Professor),** born Chicago, Illinois, September 3, 1958; admitted to bar, 1990, Iowa. *Education:* University of Iowa (M.A., 1990); Chicago State University (B.S., 1986); University of Iowa (J.D., 1990). ***COURSES:*** Torts, Labor Law, Employment Law, Social Science and Law. ***Email:*** cnance@comp.uark.edu

LINDLEE BAKER NORVELL, **(Research Assistant Professor),** born Arkansas, July 19, 1959. *Education:* Georgetown University (A.B., 1981); The London School of Economics (MSc., 1985); University of Arkansas School of Law (J.D., 1988). ***COURSES:*** Criminal Defense, Domestic Relations, Appellate Practice. ***Email:*** lbaker@comp.uark.edu

PHILLIP E. NORVELL, **(Professor of Law),** born Oklahoma City, Oklahoma, November 28, 1944; admitted to bar, 1973, Oklahoma; 1983, Arkansas. *Education:* University of Oklahoma (B.A., 1968; J.D., 1973). ***COURSES:*** Real Property, Oil and Gas, Water Law, Future Interests, Antitrust. ***Email:*** pnorvel@comp.uark.edu

RICHARD F. RICHARDS, **(Professor of Law),** born Champaign, Illinois, August 10, 1938. *Education:* University of Minnesota (B.A., 1964; J.D., 1967). ***COURSES:*** Employment Discrimination, Civil Procedure, Administrative Law.

SUSAN A. SCHNEIDER, **(Assistant Professor and Director of the Graduate Agricultural Law Program),** admitted to bar, 1985, Minnesota. *Education:* University of Minnesota School of Law (J.D., 1985); University of Arkansas School of Law (LL.M., 1990). ***COURSES:*** Agricultural Bankruptcy and Agricultural Labor Law, Agricultural Finance and Credit. ***Email:*** sschneider@comp.uark.edu

TERRY JEAN SELIGMANN, **(Associate Professor & Director of Legal Research and Writing Program),** born New York, New York, January 21, 1949; admitted to bar, 1974; Massachusetts; 1998, Arkansas. *Education:* Mount Holyoke College (B.A., 1970); New York University Law School (J.D., 1974). ***COURSES:*** Legal Research and Writing Curriculum, Special Education Law. ***Email:*** tselig@comp.uark.edu

JOHN G. STEINKAMP, **(Professor of Law),** born Quincy, Illinois, October 6, 1952; admitted to bar, 1977, Colorado. *Education:* University of Illinois (B.A., 1974); University of Colorado (J.D., 1977);

(This Listing Continued)

UNIVERSITY OF ARKANSAS AT FAYETTEVILLE SCHOOL OF LAW—Continued

University of Denver (LL.M., 1984). ***COURSES:*** Decedents' Estate, Estate Planning, Federal Estate and Gift Tax, Federal Income Tax. ***Email:*** jsteinka@comp.uark.edu

KATHRYN A. SAMPSON STINSON,* (Research Associate Professor of Legal Writing)**, born Belmond, Iowa, July 29, 1959; admitted to bar, 1990, Iowa. *Education:* University of Northern Iowa (B.A., 1982); University of Iowa (J.D., 1989). ***COURSES: Legal Research, Reasoning and Writing, Appellate Practice, Advanced Litigation Drafting, Moot Court, Insurance Law. ***Email:*** ksampson@comp.uark.edu

LEONARD P. STRICKMAN,* (Professor of Law)**, born Brooklyn, New York, April 14, 1942; admitted to bar, 1967, New York; 1972, U.S. Supreme Court. *Education:* University of Rochester (A.B., 1963); Yale University (J.D., 1966). ***COURSES: Constitutional Law, Administrative Law, Education Law. ***Email:*** lstrickm@comp.uark.edu

TIMOTHY R. TARVIN,* (Research Assistant Professor)**, born Kansas City, Missouri, December 28, 1950; admitted to bar, 1976, Arkansas. *Education:* Hendrix College (B.A., 1972); Southern Methodist University; University of Arkansas, Fayetteville (J.D., 1976). ***COURSES: Clinical Law. ***Email:*** ttarvin@comp.uark.edu

JOHN J. WATKINS,* (William H. Enfield Professor of Law)**, born Fort Worth, Texas, April 26, 1949; admitted to bar, 1977, Texas. *Education:* University of Texas (B.J., 1970; M.A., 1971; J.D., 1976). ***COURSES: Civil Procedure, Communications Law, Conflict of Laws, Federal Courts. ***Email:*** jwatkins@comp.uark.edu

ALBERT M. WITTE,* (Professor Emeritus)**, born 1923; admitted to bar, 1955, Wisconsin; 1979, Arkansas. *Education:* Chicago (Ph.B., 1947; M.A., 1950); University of Chicago (J.D., 1955). ***COURSES: Contracts abd Constitutional Law, Sports Law, Law and Literature.

MARGARET MACFARLANE WRIGHT,* (Research Assistant Professor of Legal Research & Writing)**, admitted to bar, 1978, California. *Education:* California State University (B.A., 1975); Pepperdine University School of Law (J,D., 1978); New York University School of Law (LL.M., 1979). ***COURSES: Employment and Corporate Law, Legal Writing.

UNIVERSITY OF ARKANSAS AT LITTLE ROCK SCHOOL OF LAW

1201 MCALMONT
LITTLE ROCK, ARKANSAS 72202-5142

UNIVERSITY OF BALTIMORE SCHOOL OF LAW

1420 NORTH CHARLES STREET
BALTIMORE, MARYLAND 21201-5779
Telephone: (410) 837-4200
Fax: (410) 837-4450

ABA Approved Since 1972.

The University of Baltimore School of Law has a past rooted in a commitment to provide broad access to an excellent legal education. Founded in 1925 as a private college, it became a public institution in 1975 and a member of the University System of Maryland in 1988. Its location in the heart of the city's cultural center is convenient not only to state and federal courts and the business district but also to the attractions of Harborplace and Oriole Park at Camden Yards. The School of Law is accredited by the American Bar Association and is a member of the Association of American Law Schools.

The day division enrolls approximately two-thirds of the 904 students in the J.D. program. Over one-half of the student body is comprised of women, and about 20% are members of minority groups. Joint degree programs offered include the J.D./M.B.A., J.D./M.P.A., J.D./M.S. in Criminal Justice, J.D./M.S. in Negotiations and Conflict Management, and J.D./Ph.D. in Policy Science. The faculty conducts a summer program on international and comparative law in Aberdeen, Scotland. This program is taught in conjunction with faculty of the University of Aberdeen and the University of Maryland Law School. In conjunction with the University of Haifa and the University of Arkansas at Little Rock, the School of Law also offers a summer program on comparative law in Haifa, Israel. Baltimore also offers a widely-recognized Graduate Tax Program leading to the LL.M. in Taxation.

The University of Baltimore School of Law has an innovative curriculum designed to follow the ABA MacCrate Report's recommendation to better prepare students for the transition from law school to the practice of law and for law related careers.

The curriculum contains a strong mix of the traditional and the innovative, including numerous course offerings in such expanding fields as environmental law, international law and intellectual property. In addition, an extensive range of courses enables students to develop the essential lawyering skills they will employ daily in the practice of law. The Legal Clinics offer upper-level students an opportunity to develop their litigation, negotiating and counseling skills by representing indigent clients under the supervision of members of the faculty. An internship program, also directed by members of the faculty, enables students to work in a variety of legal settings under the direct supervision of members of the bar and judiciary. A broad array of simulation skills courses, including planning and drafting courses and litigation skills courses such as Trial Advocacy and Litigation Process, also are available. Students produce a respected law review, specialized journals of environmental and intellectual property law, and a periodical devoted to analyzing developing trends in the law.

In the second and third years (third and fourth years for evening students) a student may combine traditional substantive courses with courses required for recognition of a concentration in a particular area of the law. The option to earn recognition as having concentrated in a particular area of the law will involve the student in a sequence of courses of increasing depth and assist the student in developing more complex professional skills. It is not intended to make the student a "specialist" in specific areas. The University of Baltimore School of Law will recognize students as having concentrated in one or two of the following areas: Business Law, Criminal Practice, Electronic Commerce, Environmental Law, Estate Planning, Family Law, General Practice, Intellectual Property, International and Comparative Law, Litigation and Advocacy, Public and Government Service, Real Estate Practice and Theories of the Law.

Students are required to choose at least one perspective course from among those offered so that they get a broader view of the law and how it interacts with other disciplines. There is an upper-level requirement that each student produce two written works.

(This Listing Continued)

UNIVERSITY OF BALTIMORE SCHOOL OF LAW —Continued

University of Baltimore has forty-five full-time faculty members, and they teach the majority of courses in both the day and evening divisions. Each year, the full-time faculty are joined by one or more outstanding visiting professors as well as a fine adjunct faculty that includes some of the foremost practicing attorneys, judges and government officials in Maryland.

Students are assisted by a dedicated and supportive law school staff, including an expanded Career Services Center and Office of Student Affairs. The Office of Student Affairs advises students and works with the school's large and active group of student organizations.

For the 2000 graduating class, the total employment rate six months after graduation was 88.3%. Forty-nine of the 252 2000 graduates were employed in prestigious judicial clerkships.

The Law Library offers an extensive collection of primary and secondary materials on Anglo-American law, with a strong complement of international materials. There are two large microcomputer laboratories that provide access to the two computer-assisted legal research systems (LEXIS and WESTLAW), computer-assisted legal instruction, word processing systems and other software.

Alumni of the University of Baltimore School of Law are prominent in the legal, governmental and business communities of Maryland and the Middle-Atlantic area, and an increasing number are taking positions around the country. In Maryland, UofB law graduates have recently served or are serving as governor, lieutenant governor, and attorney general. Alumni also include many members of the legislature and judges at every level of the Maryland judiciary.

The School of Law is housed in the John and Frances Angelos Law Center. The four-story building encompasses the Law Library; classrooms; faculty, administrative and student offices and lounges; moot courtrooms; and a dining and conference complex. The Law Clinics occupy an attractive, newly-renovated facility nearby containing offices for interviewing clients, a library, student work areas and computers, faculty offices and a classroom.

Dean: Gilbert A. Holmes (410) 837-4458
Vice Dean: Arnold Rochvarg (410) 837-4620
Associate Dean, Career Services and Publications: Karen Rae Hammer (410) 837-4404
Associate Dean, Student Affairs: Tony W. Torain (410) 837-4529
Assistant Dean, Admissions and Financial Aid: Gary L. Wimbish (410) 837-4469
Director, Law Library: Emily R. Greenberg (410) 837-4566
Director, Clinical Programs: Jane C. Murphy (410) 837-5657

FULL TIME FACULTY

***GILBERT A. HOLMES*, (Dean & Professor of Law)**, born 1947; admitted to bar, 1973, New York. *Education:* Bucknell University (B.A., 1969); New York University (J.D., 1972).

JULIE KATHLEEN ABBATE*, (Clinical Fellow)**, born 1966; admitted to bar, 1993, Maryland; 1994, District of Columbia. *Education:* University of Michigan (B.A., 1989); Howard University (J.D., 1993). ***COURSES: Civil Clinic.

JOSE F. ANDERSON*, (Professor of Law and Director, Litigation Skills Program)**, born 1960; admitted to bar, 1984, Maryland. *Education:* University of Maryland (B.A., 1981; J.D., 1984). ***COURSES: Criminal Law, Constitutional Criminal Procedure I, Litigation Process.

BARBARA A. BABB*, (Associate Professor of Law & Director, Center for Families, Children & the Courts)**, born 1951; admitted to bar, 1982, New York; 1988, Maryland. *Education:* Pennsylvania State University (B.S., 1973); Cornell University (M.S., 1978; J.D., 1981). ***COURSES: Family Law Clinic, Child and the Family, Domestic Relations.

CHARLES BOREK*, (Visiting Assistant Professor of Law, 2002 Spring Semester)**, admitted to bar, 1993, Maryland. *Education:* Mary Washington College (B.A., 1985); University of Baltimore (J.D., M.B.A., 1993). ***COURSES: Business Organizations, Tax Clinic.

RICHARD W. BOURNE*, (Professor of Law)**, born 1942; admitted to bar, 1968, Virginia. *Education:* Harvard University (B.A., 1964); University of Virginia (LL.B., 1968); Harvard University (LL.M., 1975). ***COURSES: Civil Procedure, Conflicts of Law, Remedies, Professional Responsibility.

FRED B. BROWN*, (Associate Professor of Law and Director, Graduate Tax Program)**, born 1959; admitted to bar, 1987, New Jersey. *Education:* Rutgers University (B.S., 1982); Georgetown University (J.D., 1985); New York University (LL.M., 1986). ***COURSES: Foreign Taxation, Fundamentals of Federal Income Tax, Tax Clinic.

STEVEN A.G. DAVISON*, (Professor of Law)**, born 1946; admitted to bar, 1971, Colorado. *Education:* Cornell University (B.S.,1968); Yale University (J.D., 1971). ***COURSES: Environmental Law, International Environmental Law, Environmental and Toxic Torts.

ERIC EASTON*, (Associate Professor of Law and Co-Director, Legal Skills Program)**, born 1946; admitted to bar, 1989, Maryland. *Education:* Northwestern University (B.S., 1968); University of Maryland (J.D., 1989). ***COURSES: Communications Law, Cyberspace Law, Legal Analysis, Research and Writing.

MORAD EGHBAL*, (Visiting Assistant Professor of Law)**, born 1952. *Education:* George Washington University (B.A., 1975; M.A., 1977); Howard University School of Law (J.D., 1989); McGeorge School of Law (L.L.M., 1991). ***COURSES: Comparative Law, International Business Transactions, International Finance.

WILLIAM T. FRYER, III*, (Professor of Law)**, born 1933; admitted to bar, 1960, Maryland; 1961, District of Columbia; 1963, Texas; 1967, Ohio; 1978, South Dakota. *Education:* Lafayette College (B.S.E.E., 1955); George Washington University (J.D., 1960). ***COURSES: Business Planning, Patent, Trademark and Technology Law, and a Seminar in Patent, Copyright and Trademark Law.

WENDY GERZOG*, (Professor of Law)**, born 1947; admitted to bar, 1977, District of Columbia and Ohio. *Education:* Clark University (B.A., 1968); Assumption College (M.A., 1971); University of Akron (J.D., 1976); George Washington University (LL.M., 1979). ***COURSES: Federal Estate and Gift Tax, Federal Income Tax, Seminar in Tax Policy.

MICHELE GILLIGAN*, (Associate Professor of Law)**, born 1947; admitted to bar, 1975, District of Columbia; 1976, Maryland. *Education:* Smith College (B.A., 1969); George Washington University (J.D., 1974; LL.M., 1977). ***COURSES: Professional Responsibility, Property, Real Estate Finance.

(This Listing Continued)

UNIVERSITY OF BALTIMORE SCHOOL OF LAW —Continued

MICHELE ESTRIN GILMAN*, (Assistant Professor of Law),** *Education:* Duke University (B.A., 1990); University of Michigan (J.D., 1993). ***COURSES: Civil Clinic.

***ROBERT GONZALES*, (Visiting Assistant Professor, 2002 Spring Semester)**, born 1948; admitted to bar, 1983, Maryland. *Education:* University of Maryland (B.A., 1976); University of Baltimore (J.D., 1976).

***EMILY R. GREENBERG*, (Law Librarian)**, born 1948; admitted to bar, 1983, Maryland. *Education:* Brandeis University (B.A., 1970); University of Pennsylvania (M.A., 1973); Rutgers University (M.L.S., 1974); University of Baltimore (J.D., 1982).

STEVEN P. GROSSMAN*, (Dean Julius Isaacson Professor of Law)**, born 1949; admitted to bar, 1974, New York. *Education:* City College of New York (B.A., 1969); Brooklyn Law School (J.D., 1973); New York University (LL.M., 1977). ***COURSES: Constitutional Criminal Procedure I, Sentencing and Plea Bargaining, Trial Advocacy.

MICHAEL HAYES*, (Assistant Professor of Law)**, born 1963; admitted to bar, 1989, New York; 1990, District of Columbia. *Education:* Cornell University (B.S., 1985); University of Virginia (J.D., 1988). ***COURSES: Collective Bargaining, Employment Discrimination, Employment Law, Labor Law.

F. MICHAEL HIGGINBOTHAM*, (Professor of Law)**, born 1957; admitted to bar, 1983, Illinois; 1984, District of Columbia. *Education:* Brown University (A.B., 1979); Yale University (J.D., 1982); Cambridge University (LL.M., 1985). ***COURSES: Constitutional Law, Race and the Law,.

SUZANNE H. JACKSON*, (Clinical Fellow)**, born 1963; admitted to bar, 1990, District of Columbia; 1990, California; 2000, Maryland. *Education:* Wellesley College (B.A., 1985); Harvard Law School (1988). ***COURSES: Family Law Clinic.

LAURENCE M. KATZ*, (Professor of Law and Dean Emeritus)**, born 1940; admitted to bar, 1963, Florida and Maryland. *Education:* University of Maryland (J.D., 1963). ***COURSES: Contracts, Payment Systems, Secured Transactions.

REBECCA KORZEC*, (Professor of Law)**, born 1948; admitted to bar, 1972, Maryland. *Education:* Goucher College (B.A., 1969); Temple University (J.D., 1972). ***COURSES: Sales and Leases, Gender and the Law Seminar.

***JEFFREY A. KUHN*, (Senior Fellow, UB Center on Children, Families & the Courts)**, *Education:* University of Nevada (B.A., 1975); McGeorge School of Law (J.D., 1981).

ROBERT H. LANDE*, (Venable Professor of Law)**, born 1952; admitted to bar, 1978, District of Columbia. *Education:* Northwestern University (B.A., 1974); Harvard University (M.P.P., J.D., 1978). ***COURSES: Antitrust, Torts.

KENNETH LASSON*, (Professor of Law, and Director, Haifa Summer Program)**, born 1943; admitted to bar, 1967, Maryland. *Education:* Johns Hopkins University (A.B., 1963; M.A., 1967); University of Maryland (J.D., 1966). ***COURSES: Advanced Legal Research, Alternative Dispute Resolution Workshop, Seminar in Civil Liberties.

JONATHAN CHARLES LIPSON*, (Assistant Professor of Law)**, born 1964; admitted to bar, 1991, New York and Wisconsin. *Education:* University of Wisconsin (B.A., 1986; J.D., 1990);. ***COURSES: Commercial Transactions Workshop, Payment Systems, Secured Transactions Law.

JOHN A. LYNCH, JR.*, (Professor of Law)**, born 1949; admitted to bar, 1975, District of Columbia. *Education:* St. Anselm's College (A.B., 1971); George Washington University (J.D., 1974; LL.M., 1978). ***COURSES: Civil Procedure, Conflict of Laws, Federal Income Tax, and Federal Jurisdiction.

AUDREY MCFARLANE*, (Assistant Professor of Law)**, born 1964; admitted to bar, 1992, Pennsylvania; 1993, District of Columbia. *Education:* Harvard-Radcliffe Colleges (A.B., 1986); Stanford University (J.D., 1990). ***COURSES: Local Economic Development, Seminar, Local Government Law, Property.

LYNN MCLAIN*, (Professor of Law and Dean Joseph Curtis Faculty Fellow)**, born 1949; admitted to bar, 1974, Maryland. *Education:* University of Pennsylvania (B.A., 1971); Duke University (J.D., 1974). ***COURSES: Copyright and the Arts, Evidence, Problems in Evidence Seminar.

MICHAEL I. MEYERSON*, (Professor of Law and Piper & Marbury Faculty Fellow)**, born 1955; admitted to bar, 1980, New York. *Education:* Hampshire College (B.A. 1976); University of Pennsylvania (J.D., 1979). ***COURSES: American Legal History, Constitutional Law, Contracts.

JOHN H. MORRIS JR.*, (Visiting Assistant Professor of Law)**, admitted to bar, 1978, Maryland. *Education:* Yale College (B.A., 1975); Yale Law School (J.D., 1978). ***COURSES: Civil Procedure, Interviewing Negotiating & Counseling.

JANE C. MURPHY*, (Professor of Law, and Director, Clinical Education)**, born 1953; admitted to bar, 1979, New York; 1981, District of Columbia; 1984, Maryland. *Education:* Boston College (B.A., 1975); New York University (J.D., 1978). ***COURSES: Domestic Relations, Family Law Clinic.

ODEANA R. NEAL*, (Associate Professor of Law and Director, Attorney Practice Internship Program)**, born 1961; admitted to bar, 1987, District of Columbia and Massachusetts. *Education:* Harvard-Radcliffe College (A.B., 1983); Harvard University (J.D., 1986). ***COURSES: Attorney Practice Internship Program, Juvenile Justice, Property, Sexual Orientation and the Law.

ANNE K. PECORA*, (Associate Professor of Law)**, born 1946; admitted to bar, 1974, Maryland. *Education:* University of Maryland (B.A., 1968); Johns Hopkins University (M.L.A., 1982); University of Baltimore (J.D., 1973). ***COURSES: Litigation Process, Maryland Civil Procedure, Trial Advocacy.

CHARLES A. REES*, (Professor of Law)**, born 1938; admitted to bar, 1970, Maryland. *Education:* Portland State University (B.S., 1961); Johns Hopkins University (M.L.A., 1964); Harvard University (J.D., 1970). ***COURSES: Civil Procedure, Constitutional Law, Federal Jurisdiction.

ARNOLD ROCHVARG*, (Vice Dean and Professor of Law)**, born 1952; admitted to bar, 1976, District of Columbia; 1980, Florida; 1992, Maryland. *Education:* University of Pennsylvania (B.A., 1973); George Washington University (J.D., 1976). ***COURSES: Administrative Law, Maryland Administrative Law.

MATTHEW JOSEPH ROSSMAN*, (Clinical Fellow)**, born 1970; admitted to bar, 1997, New York; 2000, Maryland. *Education:* Miami University (B.A., 1992); New York University School of Law (J.D., 1996). ***COURSES: Community Development Clinic.

ROBERT JEFFREY RUBINSON*, (Associate Professor of Law)**, born 1962; admitted to bar, 1989, New York. *Education:* Columbia University (B.A., 1984); New York University (J.D., 1988). ***COURSES: Civil Clinic, Professional Responsibility.

(This Listing Continued)

UNIVERSITY OF BALTIMORE SCHOOL OF LAW —Continued

ELIZABETH J. SAMUELS*, (Associate Professor of Law)**, admitted to bar, 1981, Alabama. *Education:* Harvard College (A.B., 1975); University of Chicago (J.D., 1980). ***COURSES: Constitutional Law, Property, Legal Writing Lab, Supreme Court Seminar.

ERIC C. SCHNEIDER*, (Professor of Law & Assoc. Dir., Center for International & Comparative Law)**, born 1937; admitted to bar, 1963, California. *Education:* University of Connecticut (B.A., 1959); University of California, Hastings (LL.B., 1962); New York University (LL.M., 1968). ***COURSES: Contracts, European Community Law.

***JANE E. SCHUKOSKE*, (Associate Professor of Law)**, born 1951; admitted to bar, 1978, Virginia; 1987, District of Columbia; 1989, Maryland. *Education:* Boston University (B.A, 1973); Vanderbilt University (J.D., 1977); Georgetown University (LL.M., 1988).

WALTER D. SCHWIDETZKY*, (Professor of Law)**, born 1952; admitted to bar, 1979, Colorado. *Education:* University of Denver (B.A., 1974; M.B.A., 1978; J.D., 1978; LL.M., 1984). ***COURSES: Estate Planning, Corporate Taxation, Fundamentals of Federal Income Tax, Partnership Taxation.

MORTIMER SELLERS*, (Professor of Law and Director, Center for International & Comparative Law)**, born 1959; admitted to bar, 1989, New Jersey and Pennsylvania; 1990, District of Columbia and Maryland. *Education:* Harvard University (A.B., 1980; J.D., 1988); Oxford University (B.C.L., D.Phil., 1986). ***COURSES: International Law, Jurisprudence.

CHARLES B. SHAFER*, (Professor of Law)**, born 1945; admitted to bar, 1979, New York; 1992, Maryland. *Education:* Marietta College (B.A., 1967); Rutgers University, Newark (J.D., 1978); University of Illinois (LL.M., 1984). ***COURSES: Business Bankruptcy, Consumer Law, Debtor-Creditor Relations, Seminar on Law and Social Reform, Torts.

STEPHEN J. SHAPIRO*, (Professor of Law)**, born 1949; admitted to bar, 1976, Pennsylvania; 1977, Ohio; 1985, Maryland. *Education:* Haverford College (B.A., 1971); University of Pennsylvania (J.D., 1976). ***COURSES: Civil Procedure, Civil Rights Litigation, Evidence.

AMY E. SLOAN*, (Associate Professor of Law & Co-Director, Legal Skills Program)**, born 1964; admitted to bar, 1993, Pennsylvania; 1994, District of Columbia. *Education:* University of Texas (B.A., 1985); George Washington University (J.D., 1992). ***COURSES: Legal Analysis, Research & Writing.

DONALD H. STONE*, (Professor of Law and Director, Aberdeen Summer Abroad Program in Comparative Law)**, born 1952; admitted to bar, 1977, Virginia; 1990, Maryland. *Education:* Rutgers College (B.A., 1974); Temple University (J.D., 1977). ***COURSES: Criminal Law, Criminal Practice Clinic, Disability Law Clinic, Law and Disabilities Seminar.

CHARLES TIEFER*, (Professor of Law)**, born 1954; admitted to bar, 1981, District of Columbia. *Education:* Columbia College (B.A., 1974); Harvard University (J.D., 1977). ***COURSES: Contracts, Government Contracts Seminar.

ANGELA M. VALLARIO*, (Assistant Professor of Law)**, born 1961; admitted to bar, 1991, Maryland. *Education:* University of Florida (B.S.A., 1985); University of Baltimore School of Law (J.D., 1991); Georgetown University Law Center (L.L.M., 1995). ***COURSES: Trusts & Estates, Planning for Families & Seniors.

HOWARD E. WALLIN*, (Professor of Law)**, born 1938; admitted to bar, 1965, Maryland. *Education:* Ner Israel Rabbinical College (Rabbinics, 1958); Beth Medorash Elyon (Advanced Rabbinics, 1963); University of Maryland (LL.B., 1965). ***COURSES: Constitutional Criminal Procedure I, Products Liability, Torts.

BYRON L. WARNKEN*, (Associate Professor of Law and Director, Judicial Internship Program)**, born 1946; admitted to bar, 1977, Maryland. *Education:* Johns Hopkins University (B.A., 1968); University of Baltimore (J.D., 1977). ***COURSES: Attorney Practice Internship Program, Criminal Law, Constitutional Criminal Procedure I & II, Issues in Law Enforcement, Judicial Internship Program.

BARBARA ANN WHITE*, (Associate Professor of Law)**, *Education:* Hunter College (B.A.); Cornell University (Ph.D., 1980); State University of New York (J.D., 1985). ***COURSES: Advanced Business Organizations, Business Organizations.

UNIVERSITY OF CALIFORNIA AT DAVIS SCHOOL OF LAW

KING HALL
DAVIS, CALIFORNIA 95616-5201

UNIVERSITY OF CALIFORNIA AT LOS ANGELES SCHOOL OF LAW

405 HILGARD AVENUE
LOS ANGELES, CALIFORNIA 90024-1476

UNIVERSITY OF CALIFORNIA HASTINGS COLLEGE OF THE LAW

200 MCALLISTER STREET
SAN FRANCISCO, CALIFORNIA 94102

UNIVERSITY OF CALIFORNIA, BERKELEY SCHOOL OF LAW (BOALT HALL)

BERKELEY, CALIFORNIA 94720-7200

UNIVERSITY OF CHICAGO LAW SCHOOL

1111 EAST 60TH STREET
CHICAGO, ILLINOIS 60637
Telephone: (773) 702-9494
http://www.law.uchicago.edu

The University of Chicago Law School occupies a unique niche among this country's premier law schools. Located on a residential campus in one of America's great cities, Chicago offers a rigorous professional education that blends the study of law with the humanities, the social sciences, and the natural sciences. Students, faculty and staff form a small, tightly-knit community devoted to the life of the mind. Learning is participatory. Chicago does not seek to impose a single viewpoint or style of thought on its students. Instead, faculty expose students to contrasting views, confident in their abilities to choose their own paths.

History of The Law School

The University of Chicago, one of the youngest of the major American universities, was granted its charter in 1890 and opened its doors for classes in October 1892. The generosity of its founding donors, led by John D. Rockefeller, enabled the first president of the University, William Rainey Harper, to realize his bold ideas and extraordinary standards in the creation of a new university. Harper insisted that the new institution must be a true university, with a strong emphasis on both education and scholarship.

The Law School, part of Harper's original plan but delayed in fulfillment until 1902, was a product of an innovative spirit and a devotion to intellectual inquiry. The objective, in the view of Harper and faculty members associated with him in the project, was to create a new kind of law school, professional in its purpose, but with a broader outlook than was then prevalent in the leading American law schools. The aspirations of the new school were set by Harper's conception of legal education in a university setting: education in law "implies a scientific knowledge of law and of legal and juristic methods. These are the crystallization of ages of human progress. They cannot be understood in their entirety without a clear comprehension of the historic forces of which they are the product, and of the social environment with which they are in living contact. A scientific study of law involves the related sciences of history, economics, philosophy - the whole field of man as social being."

This animating philosophy has resulted in the Law School playing a leading role in both legal education and legal scholarship since its founding. Chicago was pivotal in almost all of the innovations made in legal education during the last century: the recognition of administrative law, legislation and comparative law as legitimate fields of legal study; the introduction of other disciplines into the law school curriculum and the appointment of faculty outside the law; the extension of the field of legal research from concern with the rules of the law to empirically oriented investigations of the legal system; and the broadening of the curriculum to include clinical as well as academic offerings.

Education at The Law School

Chicago aims to train well-rounded, critical and socially conscious thinkers and doers. The cornerstones that provide the foundation for Chicago's educational mission are: the life of the mind, participatory learning, interdisciplinary inquiry and an education for generalists.

What sets Chicago apart from other law schools is its unabashed enthusiasm for the life of the mind - the conviction that ideas matter, that they are worth discussing and that legal education should devote itself to learning for learning's sake.

Learning the law at Chicago therefore is a passionate - even intense - venture between and among faculty and students. It begins in the classroom where students share the stage with the professor. The professor does not lecture, but instead engages the group in a dialogue. Known as the Socratic Method, this dialogue presents students with questions about thorny legal concepts and principles. Energized by this dialogue within the classroom, students seek opportunities outside the classroom for further conversation and learning in one of Chicago's clinical programs, with one of Chicago's four student-edited journals, or in one of Chicago's many extracurricular offerings.

Honoring Chicago's history and commitment to interdisciplinary inquiry, faculty draw students' attention to insights from the social sciences, the humanities, and the natural sciences beginning on the first day of class. Chicago's unique first year required course, "Elements of the Law", introduces student to the law as an interdisciplinary field and gives students the tools to continue the interdisciplinary inquiry throughout their legal education.

Although it is currently in vogue for law schools to promote "specialties" and Chicago could credibly claim more than 15 areas with a depth of curriculum warranting a "specialty" label, Chicago remains committed to legal education as an education for generalists. Emphasizing the acquisition of broad and basic knowledge of law, an understanding of the functioning of the legal system, and the development of analytic abilities of the highest order, a Chicago legal education prepares students for any professional role they might choose --legal practice or legal education, entrepreneurial ventures, corporations, government, or non-profit organizations.

Scholarship at The Law School

Every professor at Chicago is a distinguished scholar in addition to being a dedicated teacher. Recognized as the most productive and influential faculty of any law school, Chicago's academic faculty is a group of about 40 professors engaged in research and writing on the most important topics of the day. The clinical faculty of about 8-10 pursue a specialized niche of legal scholarship by engaging in ground-breaking advocacy efforts. The brief biographies of the faculty below provide an introduction to their individual areas of expertise.

Dean and William B. Graham Professor of Law: Saul Levmore
Assistant Dean for Admissions: Genita Robinson
Associate Dean & Dean of Students: Ellen Cosgrove
Associate Dean for Library & Information Services: Judith Wright
Assistant Dean for Career Services: Diane Downs
Assistant Dean for LL.M. Program & Alumni Development: Richard Badger
Assistant Dean for Financial Aid: Heike Spahn
Associate Dean for External Affairs: Jonathan S. Stern

(This Listing Continued)

UNIVERSITY OF CHICAGO LAW SCHOOL—Continued

FULL TIME FACULTY

SAUL LEVMORE*, (Dean and William B. Graham Professor of Law)**, born 1953; admitted to bar, 1983, Virginia. *Education:* Columbia College (B.A., 1973); Yale (Ph.D., 1978; J.D., 1980); Chicago-Kent (LL.D., 1995). ***COURSES: Commercial Law, Comparative Law, Corporate Tax, Corporations, Public Choice & the Law, Torts.

ALBERT W. ALSCHULER*, (Wilson-Dickinson Professor)**, born 1940; admitted to bar, 1965, Illinois. *Education:* Harvard (A.B., 1962; LL.B., 1965). ***COURSES: Criminal Law, Criminal Procedure, Jurisprudence.

DOUGLAS G. BAIRD*, (Harry A. Bigelow Distinguished Serv. Professor)**, born 1953. *Education:* Yale (B.A., 1975); Stanford (Ll.D., 1994). ***COURSES: Civil Procedure, Commercial Law, Contracts, Creditor's Rights.

LISA E. BERNSTEIN*, (Professor)**, born 1964; admitted to bar, 1994, New York. *Education:* University of Chicago (B.A., 1986); Harvard (J.D., 1990). ***COURSES: Contracts, Corporate Governance, Corporations, Law & Economics.

ANDREA KAY BJORKLUND*, (Bigelow Teaching Fellow)**, born Lincoln, Nebraska, January 22, 1965. *Education:* University of Nebraska (B.A., 1986); New York University (M.A., 1988); Yale Law School (J.D., 1994). ***COURSES: Legal Writing. ***Email:*** abjorklu@law.uchicago.edu

EMILY BUSS*, (Professor)**, born 1960; admitted to bar, 1988, Pennsylvania; 1989, Maryland, 1997, Illinois. *Education:* Yale (B.A., 1982; J.D., 1986). ***COURSES: Children's Law, Civil Procedure, Evidence, Parent, Child, State.

MARY ANNE C. CASE*, (Professor)**, born 1957; admitted to bar, 1986, New York. *Education:* Yale (B.A., 1979); Harvard (J.D., 1985). ***COURSES: Comparative Law, Constitutional Law, Employment Law, Family Law (Regulating Family, Sex & Gender), International Transactions, Jurisprudence, Women & the Law.

R.H. COASE*, (Clifton R. Musser Professor of Economics Emeritus & Senior Fellow in Law & Economics)**, born 1910. *Education:* University of London (B. Com., 1932; D. Sc., 1951); University of Cologne (Dr. Rep. Pol. h.c., 1988); Yale (D. So.Sc., 1989); Washington (LL.D., 1990). ***COURSES: Economic Analysis & Public Policy I, Economic Analysis & Public Policy II, Regulated Industries.

THOMAS B. COLBY*, (Bigelow Teaching Fellow)**, *Education:* Duke University (A.B., 1992); Harvard Law School (J.D., 1996). ***COURSES: Legal Writing.

DAVID P. CURRIE*, (Edward H. Levi Distinguished Serv. Professor)**, born 1936; admitted to bar, 1963, Illinois. *Education:* University of Chicago (A.B., 1957); Harvard (LL.B., 1960). ***COURSES: Civil Procedure, Constitutional Law, Federal Courts, Property.

KENNETH W. DAM*, (Max Pam Professor of American & Foreign Law)**, born 1932; admitted to bar, 1959, New York. *Education:* Kansas (S.B., 1954); University of Chicago (J.D., 1957). ***COURSES: Antitrust, Civil Procedure, Constitutional Law, Financial Institutions, Intellectual Property, International Commercial Arbitration, International Transactions.

RICHARD A. EPSTEIN*, (James Parker Hall Distinguished Serv. Professor & Ed. Jour. of Law & Economics)**, born 1943; admitted to bar, 1969, California. *Education:* Columbia (A.B., 1964); Oxford University (B.A., 1966); Yale (LL.B., 1968). ***COURSES: Communications, Contracts, Land Use Planning, Property, Real Estate Transactions, Torts.

ADAM K. FEIBELMAN*, (Bigelow Teaching Fellow)**, *Education:* Wesleyan University (B.A., 1992); University of Memphis School of Law; Yale Law School (J.D., 2000). ***COURSES: Legal Writing.

DANIEL R. FISCHEL*, (Lee & Brena Freeman Professor of Law & Business)**, born 1950; admitted to bar, 1977, Illinois. *Education:* Cornell (B.A., 1972); Brown (M.A., 1974); University of Chicago (J.D., 1977). ***COURSES: Agency & Partnerships, Corporate Finance, Corporations, Current Problems in Corporation Law, Non Profits.

CRAIG B. FUTTERMAN*, (Assistant Clinical Professor of Law)**, born Chicago, Illinois, March 2, 1966; admitted to bar, 1991, Illinois. *Education:* Northwestern University (B.A., 1988); Stanford Law School (J.D., 1991). ***COURSES: Civil Rights. ***Email:*** futterman@uchicago.edu

ELIZABETH GARRETT*, (Professor)**, born 1963; admitted to bar, 1988, Texas; 1989, District of Columbia. *Education:* University of Oklahoma (B.A., 1985); University of Virginia (J.D., 1988). ***COURSES: Administrative Law, Civil Procedure, Federal Budget Process, Federal Income Taxation, Legislation.

JACK LANDMAN GOLDSMITH, III*, (Professor)**, born 1962; admitted to bar, 1993, District of Columbia. *Education:* Washington & Lee (B.A., 1984); Oxford (B.A., 1986); Yale (J.D., 1989). ***COURSES: Civil Procedure, Conflicts of Law, Foreign Affairs & the Constitution, International Arbitration, International Litigation.

RYAN GOODMAN*, (Bigelow Teaching Fellow)**, born South Africa, May 26, 1970. *Education:* University of Texas at Austin (B.A., 1992); Yale University Graduate School of Arts and Science (M.A., 1998; M.Phil, 1999); Yale Law School (J.D., 1999). ***COURSES: Legal Writing.

GIDON A.G. GOTTLIEB*, (Leo Spitz Professor of International & Dip.)**, born 1932; admitted to bar, 1958, England. *Education:* London School of Economics (LL.B., 1954); Trinity College of Cambridge (LL.B., 1956); Harvard (LL.M., 1957). ***COURSES: International Law, International Organizations, Jurisprudence, Negotiation.

PHILIP A. HAMBURGER*, (John P. Wilson Professor of Law)**, born 1957; admitted to bar, 1982, Pennsylvania. *Education:* Princeton University (B.A., 1979); Yale University (J.D., 1982). ***COURSES: Contracts, Legal History, Corporations, Trusts Estates.

JILL ELAINE HASDAY*, (Assistant Professor)**, born New Haven, Connecticut, November 30, 1972; admitted to bar, 1998, New York. *Education:* Yale (B.A., 1994; J.D., 1997);. ***COURSES: Family Law, Employment Discrimination, National Security Law, Women's Legal History. ***Email:*** j-hasday@uchicago.edu

R.H. HELMHOLZ*, (Ruth Wyatt Rosenson Professor and Arnold & Frieda Shure Scholar)**, born 1940; admitted to bar, 1965, Missouri. *Education:* Princeton University (A.B., 1962); Harvard (LL.B., 1965); California, Berkeley (Ph.D., 1966); Trinity College (LL.D., 1992). ***COURSES: Estates, Legal History, Natural Resources, Oil & Gas, Real Property.

MARK J. HEYRMAN*, (Clinical Professor and Interim Director of Clinical Programs)**, born 1949; admitted to bar, 1977, Illinois. *Education:* Illinois (B.A., 1974); University of Chicago (J.D., 1977). ***COURSES: Clinical Teaching, Law & Psychiatry, Trial & Appellate Advocacy.

***JOSEPH ISENBERGH*, (Harold J. and Marion F. Green Professor of Law)**, born 1945; admitted to bar, 1976, District of Columbia.

(This Listing Continued)

UNIVERSITY OF CHICAGO LAW SCHOOL—Continued

Education: Columbia (B.A., 1966); University of Rochester (A.M., 1967); Yale (J.D., 1976). ***COURSES:*** International Transactions, Taxation, Federal.

WILLIAM M. LANDES*, (Clifton R. Musser Professor of Law & Economics)**, born 1939. *Education:* Columbia (A.B., 1960; Ph.D., 1966). ***COURSES: Antitrust, Art Law, Economic Analysis of Law, Intellectual Property.

DOUGLAS G. LICHTMAN*, (Assistant Professor)**, born Connecticut, January 13, 1972; admitted to bar, 1998, Illinois. *Education:* Duke University (B.S.E., 1994); Yale Law (J.D., 1997). ***COURSES: Telecommunications, Intellectual Property, First Amendment. ***Email:*** dgl@uchicago.edu

JO DESHA LUCAS*, (Professor Emeritus)**, born 1921; admitted to bar, 1952, Virginia. *Education:* Syracuse University (A.B., 1947; M.P.A., 1951); University of Virginia (LL.B., 1951); Columbia (LL.M., 1952). ***COURSES: Admiralty, Civil Procedure, Local Government, State & Local Taxation, Torts.

CATHARINE A. MACKINNON*, (Visiting Professor)**, born 1946; admitted to bar, 1978, Connecticut. *Education:* Smith (B.A., 1969); Yale (J.D., 1977, Ph.D., 1987); Reed (LL.D., 1989); Haverford (LL.D., 1991). ***COURSES: Constitution Law, Feminist Legal Theory, Sex Equality, Sexual Harassment, Speech, Sexual Harassment of Working Women.

JAMES P. MADIGAN*, (Bigelow Teaching Fellow and Lecturer in Law)**, born Warren, Ohio, May 3, 1974. *Education:* Case Western Reserve (B.A., 1996); University of Chicago (J.D., 2000). ***COURSES: Legal Writing.

TRACEY LOUISE MEARES*, (Professor)**, born 1967; admitted to bar, 1991, Illinois. *Education:* University of Illinois (B.A., 1998); University of Chicago (J.D., 1991). ***COURSES: Criminal Justice System, Issues in Poverty & Law, Law & Lawyering, Remedies.

BERNARD DAVID MELTZER*, (Edward H. Levi Distinguished Serv. Professor Emeritus)**, born 1914; admitted to bar, 1938, Illinois. *Education:* University of Chicago (A.B., 1935; J.D., 1937); Harvard (LL.M., 1938). ***COURSES: Evidence, Labor Law.

NORVAL MORRIS*, (Julius Kreeger Professor Emeritus of Law & Criminology)**, born 1923; admitted to bar, 1954, Victoria; 1958, South Australia. *Education:* University of Melbourne (LL.B., 1946; LL.M., 1947); London University (Ph.D., 1949); Villanova (LL.D., 1982). ***COURSES: Criminal law, Criminal Procedure, law & Literature, Law & Psychiatry.

JONATHAN R. NASH*, (Bigelow Teaching Fellow and Lecturer in Law)**, born New York, New York, December 5, 1966; admitted to bar, 1993, New York. *Education:* Columbia College (B.A., 1988); New York University (J.D., 1992); Harvard Law School (LL.M. 1999). ***COURSES: Legal Writing.

PHIL CALDWELL NEAL*, (Harry A. Bigelow Professor Emeritus)**, born 1919; admitted to bar, 1943, Illinois. *Education:* Harvard (A.B., 1940; LL.B., 1943). ***COURSES: Antitrust, Civil Procedure, Conflict of Laws, Constitutional Law.

MARTHA NUSSBAUM*, (Ernst Freund Professor of Law & Ethics)**, born 1947. *Education:* New York University (B.A., 1969); Harvard (M.A., 1971; Ph.D., 1975). ***COURSES: Aesthetics, Ancient Greek Philosophy, Feminism, Law & Literature, Moral Philosophy, Political Philosophy.

RANDAL C. PICKER*, (Paul & Theo Leffmann Professor)**, born 1959; admitted to bar, 1986, Illinois. *Education:* University of Chicago (B.A, 1980; M.A., 1982; J.D., 1985). ***COURSES: Bankruptcy, Commercial Transactions, Corporation Reorganizations, Game Theory & the Law, Regulated Industries, Secured Transactions.

ERIC A. POSNER*, (Professor)**, born 1965; admitted to bar, 1991, Maryland. *Education:* Yale (B.A., 1988); Harvard (J.D., 1991). ***COURSES: Bankruptcy, Commercial Law, Copyright Law.

JULIE ROIN*, (Professor)**, born 1955; admitted to bar, 1981, District of Columbia. *Education:* Radcliffe College (B.A., 1977); Yale (J.D., 1980). ***COURSES: Contracts, Federal Taxation, International Taxation, Property.

RANDALL D. SCHMIDT*, (Clinical Professor)**, born 1954; admitted to bar, 1979, Illinois. *Education:* Illinois (B.A., 1976); University of Chicago (J.D., 1979). ***COURSES: Clinical Teaching, Employment Discrimination, Evidence, Trial Practice.

GEOFFREY R. STONE*, (Harry Kalven, Jr. Distinguished Serv. Professor & Provost)**, born 1946; admitted to bar, 1972, New York. *Education:* Pennsylvania (B.S., 1968); University of Chicago (J.D., 1971). ***COURSES: Civil Procedure, Constitutional Law, Criminal Procedure.

RANDOLPH N. STONE*, (Clinical Professor)**, born 1946; admitted to bar, 1975, District of Columbia; 1975, Wisconsin; 1977, Illinois. *Education:* Wisconsin-Milwaukee (B.A., 1972); Wisconsin (J.D., 1975). ***COURSES: Clinical Teaching, Evidence, Legal Profession, Trial Advocacy,.

DAVID A. STRAUSS*, (Harry N. Wyatt Professor)**, born 1952; admitted to bar, 1980, District of Columbia. *Education:* Harvard (A.B., 1973; J.D., 1978); Oxford (B.Phil., 1975);. ***COURSES: Administrative Law, Civil Procedure, Constitutional Law, Federal Jurisdiction, Torts.

CASS R. SUNSTEIN*, (Karl N. Llewellyn Distinguished Service Professor of Jurisprudence)**, born 1954; admitted to bar, 1980, District of Columbia. *Education:* Harvard (A.B., 1975; J.D., 1978);. ***COURSES: Administrative Law, Civil Procedure, Constitutional Law, Elements of the Law, Environmental Law, Law & Human Behavior.

ALAN O'NEIL SYKES, JR.*, (Frank and Bernice Greenburg Professor)**, born 1954; admitted to bar, 1984, Massachusetts. *Education:* William & Mary (B.A., 1976); Yale (M.A., 1977; M.Phil., 1978; J.D., 1982; Ph.D., 1987). ***COURSES: Contracts, Insurance Law, International Trade, Law & Economics, Torts.

ADRIAN VERMEULE*, (Professor)**, born 1968; admitted to bar, 1998, District of Columbia. *Education:* Harvard (B.A., 1990, J.D., 1993). ***COURSES: Legislation.

DAVID A. WEISBACH*, (Professor and Director, Law & Economics Program)**, born 1963; admitted to bar, 1989, Illinois; 1990, District of Columbia. *Education:* Michigan (B.S., 1985); Harvard (J.D., 1989). ***COURSES: Tax.

***JUDITH MARGARET WRIGHT*, (Associate Dean for Library & Information Services and Lecturer in Law)**, born 1944; admitted to bar, 1980, Illinois. *Education:* Memphis State (B.S., 1966); University of Chicago (M.A., 1971, Grad. Lib. Sch.); De Paul (J.D., 1980).

UNIVERSITY OF CINCINNATI COLLEGE OF LAW

CLIFTON AND CALHOUN STREETS
CINCINNATI, OHIO 45221

UNIVERSITY OF COLORADO SCHOOL OF LAW

KITTREDGE LOOP DRIVE, 401 UCB
BOULDER, COLORADO 80309-0401
Telephone: (303) 492-8047
Fax: (303) 492-1757

ABA Approved Since 1923.

The University of Colorado School of Law is a state institution located at the foot of the Rocky Mountains. It has high admission standards, a relatively small **student body**, and a favorable student-to-faculty ratio of 12 to 1, assuring a stimulating and challenging academic environment that encourages in-class participation and informal consultations with faculty. Admission to the CU School of Law is competitive, with about 2000 applicants for 165 positions in the entering class. Typically the class is drawn from over 100 undergraduate schools, about 40 states, and includes about 50% women and 15-20% minority students. The CU **Law Library** collection includes over 400,000 volumes and contains statutes and cases from all 50 states, the federal government, and many foreign jurisdictions. Professional librarians and a computer lab are available to students, who may also access computer services from their homes. The **faculty** has a demonstrated record of excellence in teaching, research, and public service. Particular areas of strength include natural resources and constitutional law, but the faculty also includes some of the nation's leading scholars on such subjects as alternative dispute resolution, evidence, international law, race relations, securities law and telecommunications. These great scholars are also highly-regarded teachers as well.

The CU School of Law offers over 100 courses leading to the Juris Doctor degree, with joint JD/MBA, JD/Master of International Affairs, and JD/Master of Public Affairs degrees available, as well as certificates in tax and in environmental policy. Students may select courses to emphasize areas such as litigation, natural resources, environmental law, American Indian law, criminal law, commercial law, constitutional law, taxation, jurisprudence, and public law.

Special programs at the CU School of Law include the Natural Resources Law Center, offering research and publication, legal education, and the distinguished visitors and fellows program; the National Wildlife Federation's Natural Resources Litigation Clinic involves students in complex administrative and judicial environmental litigation; the Legal Aid and Defender Program allows students to represent low-income clients in civil and criminal cases under faculty supervision; the Indian Law Clinic provides students the opportunity to work with Native Americans on their unique legal problems. The Byron R. White Center for American Constitutional Study was established to further the study, teaching and publication of Constitutional law. The White Center hosts the Ira C. Rothgerber Constitutional Law Conference annually which exposes students to analysis and debate of contemporary constitutional issues. The Entrepreneurial Law Center operates a clinic for startup businesses and supports teaching, research, and conferences on legal issues relating to new and expanding businesses. The Silicon Flatirons Telecommunication Program supports interdisciplinary teaching, research, and conferences on the increasingly important area of telecommunications law. In addition, the Law School sponsors the Rothgerber Moot Court competition, and law students participate in appellate moot court competitions such as Jessup International Law, Hispanic National Bar, Pace Environmental Law, and Indian Law, as well as several trial practice competitions. These competitions provide students with valuable experience in written and oral advocacy. Further writing experience is provided by the *University of Colorado Law Review* and the newly created *Colorado Telecom Law Journal*, professional journals edited entirely by students, and the *Colorado Journal of International Environmental Law and Policy*, one of only two such journals in the nation. Over twenty student organizations provide opportunities for outreach and leadership in projects, programs, and social activities.

Offers of **admission** are heavily based on GPA and LSAT (typical classes have a 3.5 median GPA and an LSAT median around the 90th percentile), but these scores are considered in the context of the entire application. We give substantial weight to special qualities such as motivation, undergraduate program, diversity in economic, social, or cultural background, unusual employment or other experience, leadership, and perseverance in overcoming personal handicaps or disadvantages. The CU School of Law seeks ethnic, cultural, and other diversity of its student body. Several positions are offered each year to transfer and visiting students, based on space available in the second and third-year classes.

Non resident students may establish Colorado residence by maintaining their legal residence in Colorado for 12 consecutive months. A limited number of scholarships are available from state and private funds, and students may qualify for federal and private loan programs. Financial aid is available to both resident and non resident students.

The CU School of Law has an active Office of **Career Services** that provides a broad range of employment and career counseling services. Liaison is maintained with law firms, government agencies, public interest organizations, courts, businesses, and other employers that seek the services of students and graduates. Graduates of the CU School of Law live throughout the United States and Canada. Typically a higher percentage of our students pass the bar exam than do applicants for the bar generally.

Dean: Harold H. Bruff (303) 492-3087
Admissions, Assistant Dean: Carol Nelson-Douglas (303) 492-7203
Admissions: Cindy Gibbons (303) 492-3092
Alumni Relations, Assistant Dean: David Gosser (303) 492-3124
Career Services, Assistant Dean: Anthony Bastone (303) 492-8651
Career Services, Director: Connie Zubler (303) 492-4332
Development, Director: Carolyn M. Whitehead (303) 492-5366
Financial Aid: Jamy Coulson (303) 492-0647
Law Library Director: Barbara Bintliff (303) 492-7534

(This Listing Continued)

UNIVERSITY OF COLORADO SCHOOL OF LAW
—Continued

FULL TIME FACULTY

HAROLD H. BRUFF*, (Dean)**, admitted to bar, 1969, California. *Education:* Williams College (B.A., 1965); Harvard (J.D., 1968). ***COURSES: Administrative Law. ***Email:*** bruffh@stripe.colorado.edu

***NORMAN F. AARONSON*, (Clinical Professor, Legal Aid and Defender Program)**, admitted to bar, 1974, Colorado. *Education:* Brandeis University (B.A., 1967); Boston University (J.D., 1973).

COURSES: Civil Practice, Evidence, Trial Advocacy. ***Email:*** norman.aaronson@colorado.edu

BEVERLY CUMMINGS AGNEW*, (Reference Librarian)**, admitted to bar, 1983, Indiana; 1994, Colorado. *Education:* Indiana University (A.B., 1969; M.L.S., 1971; J.D., 1983). ***Email: beverly.agnew@colorado.edu

BARBARA ANN BINTLIFF*, (Professor, Director of the Law Library)**, born Houston, Texas; admitted to bar, 1979, Washington; 1983, Colorado. *Education:* Central Washington University (B.A., 1975); University of Washington (J.D., 1978; M.L.L., 1979). ***COURSES: Advanced Legal Research., Legal History. ***Email:*** barbara.bintliff@colorado.edu

KARI L. BOURG*, (Instructor, Legal Writing & Appellate Advocacy)**, admitted to bar, 1994, Florida; 1995 District of Columbia; 1997, Colorado. *Education:* University of North Carolina (B.S., 1990); University of Virginia (J.D., 1994). ***COURSES: Legal Writing, Research, and Appellate Advocacy. ***Email:*** bourgk@stripe.colorado.edu

GEORGIA K. BRISCOE*, (Associate Director of the Law Library)**, *Education:* Washington State University (B.S., 1968); University of Michigan (A.M.L.S., 1974); University of San Diego (M.A., 1985 and 1989);. ***COURSES: Bibliography Control. ***Email:*** briscoe@colorado.edu

EMILY M. CALHOUN*, (Professor of Law)**, *Education:* Texas Tech. University (B.A., 1945; M.A., 1968); University of Texas (J.D., 1971). ***COURSES: Advanced Torts, Alternative Dispute Resolution, Civil Rights, Federal Courts, Torts. ***Email:*** emily.calhoun@colorado.edu

PAUL F. CAMPOS*, (Professor of Law)**, *Education:* University of Michigan (A.B., 1982; M.A., 1983; J.D., 1989). ***COURSES: Criminal Justice, Legislation, Property. ***Email:*** paul.campos@colorado.edu

RICHARD B. COLLINS*, (Professor of Law)**, admitted to bar, 1966, California; 1972, Arizona,; 1973, New Mexico. *Education:* Yale (B.A., 1960); Harvard (LL.B., 1966). ***COURSES: Property, Constitutional Law, American Indian Law. ***Email:*** richard.collins@colorado.edu

JAMES N. CORBRIDGE*, (Professor Emeritus)**, admitted to bar, 1964, New York; 1975, Colorado. *Education:* Brown University (LL.B., 1963). ***COURSES: Property, Water Law, Natural Resources. ***Email:*** james.corbridge@colorado.edu

RICHARD DELGADO*, (Jean N. Lindsley Professor of Law)**, *Education:* University of Washington (A.B.); University of California, Berkeley (J.D., 1974). ***COURSES: Civil Procedure, Civil Rights, Biotechnology & Law, Civil Rights Seminar, Civil Procedure Seminar, Law & the Life Sciences Seminar. ***Email:*** richard.delgado@colorado.edu

ROBERT JOHANN DIETER*, (Clinical Professor, Legal Aid & Defender Program)**, admitted to bar, 1972, Colorado. *Education:* Yale University (B.A., 1968); University of Denver (J.D., 1972). ***COURSES: Criminal Practice, Trial Advocacy, Evidence. ***Email:*** dieter@spot.colorado.edu

ALLISON HARTWELL EID*, (Associate Professor of Law)**, admitted to bar, Stanford University (A.B., 1987); University of Chicago Law School (J.D., 1991). *Education:* Stanford University (A.B., 1987); University of Chicago Law School (J.D., 1991). ***COURSES: Torts, Bioethics, Legislation. ***Email:*** allison.eid@colorado.edu

TED J. FIFLIS*, (Professor of Law)**, *Education:* Northwestern University (B.S., 1954); Harvard University (LL.B., 1957). ***COURSES: Corporations, Securities Regulation, Accounting Issues of Lawyers, Mergers & Acquisitions, Responsibility of Advisors of Management, Mentors in Public Policy.

MITCHELL JOHN FONTENOT*, (Head of Public Services, Law Library)**, *Education:* Louisiana University (B.A., 1983); University of Texas (M.L.I.S., 1986). ***Email: mitch.fontenot@colorado.edu

REBECCA R. FRENCH*, (Associate Professor of Law)**, admitted to bar, 1974, Washington. *Education:* University of Michigan (B.A., 1971); University of Washington (J.D., 1974); Yale University (L.L.M., 1988; Ph.D., 1990. ***COURSES: Property, Anthropology, Comparative Law, Modern Legal Theory.

PATRICK FURMAN*, (Clinical Professor, Director of Clinical Programs)**, admitted to bar, 1980, Oklahoma. *Education:* University of Colorado (B.A., 1976); University of Colorado (J.D., 1980). ***COURSES: Criminal Law, Criminal Procedure, Trial Advocacy, Evidence. ***Email:*** furman@colorado.edu

WAYNE M. GAZUR*, (Associate Professor)**, admitted to bar, 1981, Colorado. *Education:* University of Wyoming (B.S., 1976); University of Colorado School of Law (J.D., 1981); University of Denver College of Law (LL.M., 1984). ***COURSES: Taxation. ***Email:*** wayne.gazur@colorado.edu

DAVID HARDING GETCHES*, (Raphael J. Moses Professor of Natural Resources Law)**, admitted to bar, 1968, California; 1973, District of Columbia; 1973, Colorado. *Education:* Occidental College (A.B., 1964); University of Southern California (J.D., 1967). ***COURSES: Environmental, Water, Indian Law. ***Email:*** getches@colorado.edu

JULIET C. GILBERT*, (Clinical Professor, Legal Aid and Defender Program)**, *Education:* Valparaiso University (B.S.W., 1974); University of Denver (J.D., 1978). ***COURSES: Clinical Teaching. ***Email:*** juliet.gilbert@colorado.edu

LAKSHMAN D. GURUSWAMY*, (Professor of Law)**, *Education:* University of Ceylon (LL.B., 1962); University of Durham (Ph.D., 1977). ***COURSES: International Environmental, US Environmental, International. ***Email:*** guruswam@colorado.edu

MELISSA HART*, (Associate Professor of Law)**, *Education:* Harvard College (B.A., 1991); Harvard Law School (J.D., 1995). ***COURSES: Employment Law, Civil Procedure, Evidence. ***Email:*** melissa.hart@colorado.edu

DAVID S. HILL*, (Professor of Law)**, admitted to bar, 1970, Nebraska and Minnesota. *Education:* University of Nebraska (B.S., 1967; J.D., 1970). ***COURSES: Property, Corporations. ***Email:*** dhill@spot.colorado.edu

J. DENNIS HYNES*, (Nicholas Rosenbaum Professor of Law, Emeritus)**, admitted to bar, 1961, Colorado; 1961, New York. *Education:* University of Colorado (B.A., 1958); University of Colorado School of Law (LL.B., 1960). ***COURSES: Contracts, Agency, Partnership, LLC. ***Email:*** dennis.hynes@colorado.edu

(This Listing Continued)

UNIVERSITY OF COLORADO SCHOOL OF LAW —Continued

SARAH A. KRAKOFF*, (Associate Professor)**, *Education:* Yale University (B.A., 1986); University of California at Berkeley (LL.B., 1991). ***COURSES: Indian Law, Civil Procedure, Environmental Philosophy. ***Email:*** sarah.hrakoff@colorado.edu

JAMES B. LEVY*, (Instructor, Legal Writing & Appellate Advocacy)**, admitted to bar, 1986, Massachusetts; 1995, Colorado. *Education:* Colby College (B.A, 1982); Suffolk University School of Law (J.D., 1986). ***COURSES: Legal Writing. ***Email:*** james.levy@colorado.edu

MARK J. LOEWENSTEIN*, (Associate Dean for Research and Professor of Law)**, born Chicago, Illinois, March 30, 1948; admitted to bar, 1979, Illinois and California; 1980, Colorado. *Education:* University of Illinois (A.B., 1969; J.D., 1974). ***COURSES: Corporations, Securities, Contracts. ***Email:*** mark.loewenstein@colorado.edu

HIROSHI MOTOMURA*, (Nicholas Doman Professor of International Law)**, admitted to bar, 1979, District of Columbia; 1986, Colorado. *Education:* Yale College (B.A., 1974); University of California (J.D., 1978). ***COURSES: Civil Procedure, Immigration & Citizenship. ***Email:*** hiroshi.motomura@colorado.edu

CHRISTOPHER B. MUELLER*, (Henry S. Lindsley Professor of Procedure and Advocacy)**, admitted to bar, 1970, California; 1986, Colorado. *Education:* Haverford College (B.A., 1966); University of California (Boalt) (J.D., 1969). ***COURSES: Civil Procedure, Evidence, Complex Civil Litigation. ***Email:*** mueller@spot.colorado.edu

ROBERT F. NAGEL*, (Ira C. Rothgerber, Jr. Prof. of Constitutional Law & Dir., Byron R. White Ctr. for Amer. Constitutional Study)**, admitted to bar, 1972, Pennsylvania; 1982, Colorado. *Education:* Swarthmore College (B.A., 1968); Yale University (J.D., 1972). ***COURSES: Constitutional Law. ***Email:*** robert.nagel@colorado.edu

DALE A. OESTERLE*, (Monfort Professor of Law)**, admitted to bar, 1977, Virginia; 1990, New York. *Education:* University of Michigan (J.D., 1975; M.P.P, 1973; B.A., 1972). ***COURSES: Corporations, Mergers & Acquisitions, International Transactions. ***Email:*** oesterle@colorado.edu

SCOTT RUSSELL PEPPET*, (Associate Professor of Law)**, admitted to bar, 1996, Massachusetts. *Education:* Cornell University (B.A., 1991); Harvard Law School (J.D. 1996). ***COURSES: Negotiation, Alternative Dispute, Resolution, Contracts, Criminal Law. ***Email:*** peppet@stripe.colorado.edu

WILLIAM T. PIZZI*, (Professor of Law)**, admitted to bar, 1971, New Jersey. *Education:* Holy Cross College (B.A., 1965); University of Massachusetts (M.A. 1971); Harvard Law School (J.D., 1971). ***COURSES: Criminal Law. ***Email:*** pizzi@colorado.edu

CAROLYN RAMSEY*, (Associate Professor of Law)**, *Education:* University of California-Irvine (B.A., 1990); Stanford Law School (J.D., 1998). ***COURSES: Criminal Law, Employment Discrimination, Legal History, Women and the Law. ***Email:*** ramsey@colorado.edu

KEVIN R. REITZ*, (Professor of Law)**, admitted to bar, 1983, Pennsylvania. *Education:* Darmouth College (B.A., 1979); University of Pennsylvania (J.D., 1982). ***COURSES: Criminal law, Criminal Justice. ***Email:*** Reitz@spot.colorado.edu

ROBERT C. RICHARDS*, (Technical Services Librarian)**, *Education:* Yale (B.A., 1992); University of Iowa (M.D., 1994); University of Illinois at Urbana-Champaign (M.S. Library & Information Sciences, 1996). ***Email: robert.c.richards@colorado.edu

PIERRE SCHLAG*, (Byron White Professor of Constitutional Law)**, admitted to bar, 1983, District of Columbia. *Education:* Yale (B.A., 1975); UCLA School of Law (J.D., 1978). ***COURSES: Jurisprudence, Constitutional Law Torts. ***Email:*** schlag@stripe.colorado.edu

AMY J. SCHMITZ*, (Associate Professor of Law)**, born Racine, Wisconsin, April 28, 1970; admitted to bar, 1995, Minnesota; 1999, Washington. *Education:* Drake University (B.A., 1992); University of Minnesota Law School (J.D., 1995). ***COURSES: Commercial Law, Contracts, Commercial Arbitration. ***Email:*** achristo@stripe.colorado.edu

KAREN E. SELDEN*, (Catalog Librarian)**, *Education:* Pennsylvania State University (B.S., 1984); Simmons College (M.L.S., 1995). ***Email: karen.selden@colorado.edu

PETER N. SIMON*, (Associate Professor of Law, Emeritus)**, *Education:* University of Wisconsin (B.S., 1962); M.D., 1969); University of California, Berkeley (J.D., 1970). ***COURSES: Administrative Law, Civil Procedure, Conflict of Laws, Constitutional law, Creditors' Rights, Evidence.

GABRIELLE MARKS STAFFORD*, (Instructor, Legal Writing & Appellate Advocacy)**, admitted to bar, 1991, New Mexico; 1992, U.S. District Court for New Mexico; 1995 U.S. Court of Appeals for 10th Circuit. *Education:* Boston University School of Law (J.D., 1991). ***COURSES: Legal Writing. ***Email:*** staffog@stripe.colorado.edu

TODD MICHAEL STAFFORD*, (Instructor of Legal Writing and Appellate Advocacy)**, admitted to bar, 1992, New Mexico; 1999, Illinois & Colorado. *Education:* Southern Methodist University (B.A., 1989); Duke University (J.D., 1992). ***COURSES: Legal Writing, Appellate Advocacy.

NORTON L. STEUBEN*, (Nicholas Rosenbaum Professor)**, admitted to bar, 1962, New York; 1975, Colorado. *Education:* University of Michigan (A.B., 1958; J.D., 1961);. ***COURSES: Taxation, Real Estate. ***Email:*** norton.steuben@colorado.edu

JANE E. THOMPSON*, (Head of Faculty Services Law Library)**, *Education:* University of Missouri (B.A., 1977); University of Denver (M.A., 1977, J.D., 1984). ***COURSES: Legal Research. ***Email:*** jane.thompson@colorado.edu

ARTHUR H. TRAVERS*, (Professor of Law, Emeritus)**, admitted to bar, 1962, Illinois; 1976, Colorado. *Education:* Grinnell College (B.A., 1957); Harvard Law School (LL.B (JD), 1962). ***COURSES: Copyright, Commercial Law, Antitrust. ***Email:*** arthur.travers@spot.colorado.edu

DANIEL A. VIGIL*, (Associate Dean and Adjunct Professor)**, admitted to bar, 1982, Colorado. *Education:* University of Colorado (B.A., 1978; J.D., 1982). ***COURSES: Criminal Law, Professional Responsibility, Legal Method. ***Email:*** daniel.vigil@colorado.edu

MICHAEL J. WAGGONER*, (Associate Dean and Associate Professor)**, admitted to bar, 1968, District of Columbia. *Education:* Stanford University (A.B., 1964); Harvard (LL.B., 1967). ***COURSES: Tax, Civil Procedure. ***Email:*** michael.waggoner@colorado.edu

PHILIP J. WEISER*, (Associate Professor of Law)**, admitted to bar, 1995, New York. *Education:* Swarthmore College (B.A., 1990); New York University (J.D., 1994). ***COURSES: Telecommunications, Antitrust. ***Email:*** phil.weiser@colorado.edu

MARIANNE WESSON*, (Professor of Law and Wolf-Nichol Fellow)**, admitted to bar, 1974, Texas; 1977, Colorado; 1999 U.S. Supreme Court. *Education:* Vassar College (A.B., 1970); University of Texas (J.D., 1973). ***COURSES: Criminal Law, Evidence, Trial Advocacy, Law and Literature. ***Email:*** marianne-wesson@colorado.edu

***AHMED A. WHITE*, (Associate Professor)**, admitted to bar, 1999,

(This Listing Continued)

UNIVERSITY OF COLORADO SCHOOL OF LAW —Continued

Louisiana. *Education:* Southern University (B.A., 1991); Yale (J.D., 1994). ***COURSES:*** Labor and Employment, Criminal. ***Email:*** ahmed.white@colorado.edu

CHARLES F. WILKINSON*, (University's Distinguished Professor and Moses Lasky Professor of Law),** *Education:* Denison University (B.A., 1963); Stanford University (LL.B., 1966). ***COURSES: Public Land Law, Indian Law, Water Law, Administrative Law, Environmental law, Constitutional Law. ***Email:*** charles.wilkinson@colorado.edu

SIENHO YEE*, (Associate Professor of Law),** *Education:* Brandeis University (B.A., 1989); Columbia University (J.D., 1993); Oxford University (D.Phil., 1997). ***COURSES: Public International Law, International Dispute Settlement, Human Rights, Crime and Punishment in International Law. ***Email:*** sienho@yahoo.com

UNIVERSITY OF CONNECTICUT SCHOOL OF LAW

55 ELIZABETH STREET
HARTFORD, CONNECTICUT 06105-2296
Telephone: (860) 570-5127
Fax: (860) 570-5128
http://www.uconn.law.edu

ABA Approved Since 1933

The University of Connecticut School of Law was founded in 1921. Its 20-acre campus in the West End of Hartford, listed in the National Register of Historic Sites, is probably the most handsome of any law school in the United States. Its graduates constitute about half of the state judiciary, and include principal officers of the state government, legislators, presidents and general counsels of major insurance companies, partners in all of the state's leading law firms, and federal judges. Historically Connecticut's 6,000 graduates have been concentrated between Boston and New York. In the past ten years, however, as the ambition of its graduates has kept pace with the growth of the School's reputation, they have begun to spread across the country and abroad.

Connecticut is highly selective. The 190 first-year students (135 in the Day Division, 55 in the Evening Division) have a median LSAT score that places them in the top 15% nationally. With a full-time faculty of 41 for a student body of 660, the student-faculty ratio is 16:1. The faculty, diverse in its scholarly interests, consists of graduates of the country's leading schools. Most have experience in practice and judicial clerkships; collectively they hold 17 master's degrees, and 8 doctorates in addition to the basic law degree. Faculty exchanges with Exeter (U.K.), Tilburg (Netherlands), Leiden (Netherlands), Budapest, the University of International Business and Economics in Beijing and Aix-Marseilles reinforce the faculty's strength in international and comparative law. Connecticut also offers a program in United States Legal Studies for Foreign Lawyers, leading to the LL.M. degree, and a graduate program in Insurance Law, also leading to the LL.M. degree, under the auspices of the Insurance Law Center. Together with an adjunct faculty of 35 lawyers and judges, the faculty offers 175 courses and seminars each year. No course enrollment may exceed 70, and the average for all courses is 30. Each student takes one first-year course and the intensive legal writing program in a small section of 20. In addition to the standard required courses (including Moot Court and Professional Responsibility) and a broad range of electives, the students have available six dual degree programs with other schools of the University and nearby private colleges (J.D./M.A., J.D./M.S.W., J.D./M.B.A., J.D./M.P.H., J.D./M.L.S., J.D./M.P.A.), five in-house clinical programs involving supervised client representation in judicial and administrative proceedings (Criminal-Trial and Appellate, Civil-Civil Rights and Advanced Civil Rights, Disability Law), and five externship clinics (Judicial Clerkship, Administrative Clerkship, Labor Relations, Legislative Clinic, Women's Law Clinic). The Moot Court Board administers an extensive program of intra-mural and inter-scholastic moot court competitions, and all students may compete for election to the three student-edited journals, the *Connecticut Law Review,* the *Connecticut Journal of International Law,* and the *Connecticut Insurance Law Journal.* Students also have the opportunity to participate in exchange programs with Exeter, Leiden, The University of London, Trinity College Dublin, and the University of Puerto Rico. Before graduation, each student must complete a substantial original research project, supervised through as many drafts as needed to reach near-publishable quality.

The $20 million Law Library Building, dedicated in 1996, houses a collection of over 400,000 volumes, including microforms, state-of-the-art electronic databases and an on-line catalogue.

In addition to its traditional strengths in fields such as tax, commercial law, and jurisprudence, Connecticut provides unusual curricular opportunities in clinical education, where the School has been an innovator for 30 years, in its international and comparative offerings supplemented by increased opportunities both for study abroad and for instruction by foreign experts in residence, and in its growing emphasis on environmental law and interdisciplinary work. Connecticut's success in these areas and more generally owes much to the intimate scale of the School, with small classes and a culture of support among students and faculty alike.

Dean: Nell Jessup Newton (860) 570-5127
Associate Dean for Finance and Administration: Laurie Werling (860) 570-5130
Associate Dean for Admissions and Career Services: Ellen Keane Rutt (860) 570-5159
Director of Development: C. Ann Merriam (860) 570-5340
Director of Admissions: Karen DeMcola (860) 570-5159
Director of Financial Aids: Roberta Frick (860) 570-5147
Law Librarian: Darcy Kirk (860) 570-5109
Director of Career Services: Robin Cecere (860) 570-5320
Director of Alumni Relations: Julia Dunlop (860) 570-5149

(This Listing Continued)

UNIVERSITY OF CONNECTICUT SCHOOL OF LAW —Continued

FULL TIME FACULTY

NELL JESSUP NEWTON*, (Dean and Professor of Law)**, born St. Louis, Missouri, April 30, 1944; admitted to bar, 1977, California; 1980, District of Columbia. *Education:* University of California-Berkeley (B.A., 1973); University of California, Hastings College of Law (J.D., 1976). ***COURSES: American Indian Law, Constitutional Law, Contracts, International Law, Property. ***Email:*** nnewton@law.uconn.edu

---

TOM BAKER*, (Connecticut Mutual Professor of Law, and Director, Insurance Law Center)**, born 1959; admitted to bar, 1987, Massachusetts; 1988, District of Columbia. *Education:* Harvard University (B.A. 1982; J.D., 1986). ***COURSES: Insurance Regulation, Torts/Insurance Law in Action.

ROBIN D. BARNES*, (Professor of Law)**, admitted to bar, 1990, New York. *Education:* Spelman College (1978-1980); University of Buffalo (B.A., 1986; J.D., 1989); University of Wisconsin (LL.M., 1991). ***COURSES: Constitutional Law II, Professional Responsibility, Theories of Free Speech, Trusts and Estates.

JON BAUER*, (Clinical Professor of Law and Director, Civil Clinical Programs)**, born Hempstead, New York, January 19, 1960; admitted to bar, 1985, New York; 1989, Connecticut. *Education:* Cornell University (A.B., 1980); Yale University (J.D., 1984). ***COURSES: Civil Rights Clinic, Employment Discrimination, Evidence, Labor Law Clinic.

LOFTUS E. BECKER, JR.*, (Professor of Law)**, born Pittsburgh, Pennsylvania, December 28, 1944; admitted to bar, 1970, District of Columbia; 1982, United States Supreme Court. *Education:* Harvard University (A.B., 1965); University of Pennsylvania (LL.B., 1969). ***COURSES: Computers and the Law, Constitutional Law, Criminal Law, Federal Courts.

BETHANY RUTH BERGER*, (Research Professor Indian Law)**, born April 18, 1968; admitted to bar, 1997, Arizona; 2000, New York. *Education:* Wesleyan University (B.A., 1990); Yale Law School (J.D., 1996). ***COURSES: Indian Law.

PAUL SCHIFF BERMAN*, (Associate Professor of Law)**, born New York City, New York, December 12, 1966. *Education:* Princeton University (A.B., 1988); New York University School of Law (J.D., 1995). ***COURSES: Cyberlaw, Conflicts, Copyright, Cyberlaw and Culture.

ROBERT L. BIRMINGHAM*, (Professor of Law)**, born 1938; admitted to bar, 1966, Pennsylvania; 1985, New York. *Education:* University of Pittsburgh (A.B., 1960; J.D., 1963; Ph.D., 1967; Ph.D., 1976); Harvard University (LL.M., 1965). ***COURSES: Contracts, Jurisprudence, Law and Economics, Procedure.

PHILLIP I. BLUMBERG*, (Professor of Law and Business, Emeritus)**, born Baltimore, Maryland, September 6, 1919; admitted to bar, 1942, New York; 1970, Massachusetts. *Education:* Harvard University (A.B., 1939); Harvard University Law School (LL.B., 1942); University of Connecticut (LL.D., 1994). ***COURSES: Corporate Finance, Corporations.

DEBORAH ANN CALLOWAY*, (Professor of Law)**, born Berwyn, Illinois, April 15, 1949; admitted to bar, 1980, District of Columbia. *Education:* Middlebury College (B.A., 1970); Georgetown University (J.D., 1978). ***COURSES: Constitutional Law, Criminal Law, Employment Discrimination, Employment Law.

PAUL CHILL*, (Clinical Professor of Law)**, born New York, New York, April 9, 1956; admitted to bar, 1985, Connecticut. *Education:* Wesleyan University (B.A., 1979); University of Connecticut (J.D., 1985). ***COURSES: Disability Law Clinic, Torts, Civil Rights Clinic.

ALAN D. CULLISON*, (Oliver Ellsworth Research Professor of Law)**, born 1936; admitted to bar, 1962, Iowa. *Education:* University of Chicago (B.S., 1959); University of Iowa (J.D., 1962); Yale University (LL.M., 1966). ***COURSES: Civil Procedure, Commercial Law, Contracts, Evidence.

ANNE COMER DAILEY*, (Professor of Law)**, born 1960; admitted to bar, 1988, Connecticut. *Education:* Yale University (B.A., 1983); Harvard University (J.D., 1987). ***COURSES: Constitutional Law, Family Law, Federal Courts, Women and the Law.

JOHN G. DAY*, (Professor in Residence)**, born Cleveland, Ohio, October 11, 1936; admitted to bar, 1961, Ohio; 1965, District of Columbia; 1990, Connecticut. *Education:* Oberlin College (1957); Case Western Reserve (J.D., 1961). ***COURSES: Regulation of Health Care, Financial Institution. ***Email:*** jday@law.uconn.edu

LAURA DICKINSON*, (Associate Professor of Law)**, born October 31, 1970; admitted to bar, 1999, Connecticut. *Education:* Harvard College (A.B., 1992); Yale Law School (J.D., 1996). ***COURSES: Constitutional Law, International Human Rights, Immigration Law, First Amendment Law. ***Email:*** ldickins@law.uconn.edu

MARK A. DUBOIS*, (Assistant Clinical Professor of Law)**, born October 10, 1950. *Education:* Holy Cross (B.A., 1972); University of Connecticut (J.D., 1977). ***COURSES: Lawyering Process.

TIMOTHY H. EVERETT*, (Clinical Professor of Law)**, born Flushing, New York, October 28, 1951; admitted to bar, 1984, Connecticut. *Education:* Clark University (B.A., 1975; M.A., 1977); University of Connecticut (J.D., 1984). ***COURSES: Clinical Teaching - Criminal, Trial and Appellate, Criminal Procedure.

TODD D. FERNOW*, (Director Criminal Clinics; Professor of Law)**, born Bronxville, New York, December 26, 1954; admitted to bar, 1983, Connecticut. *Education:* Cornell University (B.A., 1977); University of Connecticut (J.D., 1983). ***COURSES: Clinical Teaching, Criminal Justice, Criminal Procedure, Trial and Appellate Advocacy.

NICHOLAS L. GEORGAKOPOULOS*, (Professor of Law)**, born Athens, Greece, October 1, 1964; admitted to bar, 1989, New York; 1992, Greece (Inc. Reciprocal EEC). *Education:* Athens University (J.D., 1987); Harvard University Law School (LL.M., 1988; S.J.D., 1992). ***COURSES: Bankruptcy, Corporations, Law and Economics.

CAROLYN GROSE*, (Assistant Clinical Professor of Law)**, born November 26, 1966; admitted to bar, 1996, Massachusettes. *Education:* Middlebury College (B.A., 1988); Brooklyn Law School (J.D., 1994). ***COURSES: Lawyering Process.

***OLIMPIAD S. IOFFE*, (William F. Starr Professor of Law Emeritus)**, born 1920. *Education:* Leningrad University (D.J.S., 1954); Lodz University (D.J., 1965).

MARK WESTON JANIS*, (William F. Starr Professor of Law)**, born Chicago, Illinois, September 25, 1947; admitted to bar, 1978, New York. *Education:* Princeton University (A.B., 1969); Oxford University (M.A., 1975); Harvard University (J.D., 1977). ***COURSES: Conflict of Laws, Constitutional Law, International Law, International Transactions.

CAROLYN C. JONES*, (Professor of Law)**, born Lincoln, Nebraska, June 12, 1955; admitted to bar, 1979, Iowa. *Education:* University of Iowa (B.A., 1976; J.D., 1979); Yale University (LL.M., 1982). ***COURSES: Estate and Gift Taxation, Federal Taxation, Legal History of American Women, Non-Profit Institutions, State and Local Taxation.

(This Listing Continued)

UNIVERSITY OF CONNECTICUT SCHOOL OF LAW —Continued

RICHARD STEVEN KAY*, (George and Helen England Professor of Law)**, born Jersey City, New Jersey, September 5, 1946; admitted to bar, 1973, Massachusetts. *Education:* Brandeis University (A.B., 1968); Harvard University (J.D., 1973); Yale University (M.A., 1974). ***COURSES: Commercial Law, Comparative Constitutional Law, Contracts, Evidence, Human Rights.

DARCY KIRK*, (Director of The Law Library and Professor of Law)**, born London, England, November 14, 1948. *Education:* Vassar College (A.B., 1970); Simmons College (M.L.S., 1973; M.B.A., 1979); Boston College (J.D., 1989). ***COURSES: Advanced Legal Research. ***Email:*** DKIRK@LAW.UCONN.EDU

LEWIS S. KURLANTZICK*, (Professor of Law)**, born Paterson, New Jersey, October 28, 1944; admitted to bar, 1969, New York. *Education:* Wesleyan University (B.A., 1965); Harvard University (LL.B., 1968). ***COURSES: Arbitration, Contracts, Copyright, Law and Literature, Legal Process, Sports and the Law.

LESLIE C. LEVIN*, (Professor of Law and Director, Lawyering Skills Program)**, born Kansas City, Missouri, 1955; admitted to bar, 1981, New York. *Education:* Northwestern University (B.S., 1976); Columbia University (J.D., 1979). ***COURSES: Legal Profession, Lawyering Process.

PETER LINCOLN LINDSETH*, (Associate Professor of Law)**, born Waynesboro, Virginia, February 25, 1962; admitted to bar, 1988, New York. *Education:* Cornell University (B.A., 1984; J.D., 1987); Columbia University (Ph.D., 1994). ***COURSES: Administrative Law, International Business, Transactions, European Community Law.

H. C. MACGILL*, (Professor of Law)**, born Baltimore, Maryland, May 1, 1940; admitted to bar, 1990, Connecticut. *Education:* Yale University (B.A., 1965); University of Virginia (LL.B., 1968). ***COURSES: Constitutional Law, Federal Jurisdiction, Legal History (U.S.), Political and Civil Rights, Torts.

JENNIFER BROWN MAILLY*, (Assistant Clinical Professor of Law)**, born September 4, 1960; admitted to bar, 1986, New York. *Education:* Ohio State (J.D., 1986). ***COURSES: Lawyering Process.

WILLAJEANNE F. MCLEAN*, (Professor of Law)**, born Rocky Mountain, North Carolina, August 28, 1956; admitted to bar, 1987, Massachusetts and New York. *Education:* Wellesley College (B.A., 1977); University of Massachusetts (B.S., 1979); Fordham University (J.D., 1986); Free University of Brussels (LL.C., 1989). ***COURSES: European Commodity Law, Intellectual Property, Torts, Trademark.

***C. ANN MERRIAM*, (Director of Development)**, born December 8, 1946. *Education:* University of Massachusettes (B.A., 1968); University of Hawai (M.Ed., 1970); University of Connecticut School of Law (J.D., 1989).

THOMAS H. MORAWETZ*, (Tapping Reeve Professor of Law and Ethics)**, born 1942. *Education:* Harvard University (A.B., 1963); Yale University (J.D., 1968, M. Phil., 1968, Ph.D., 1969). ***COURSES: Criminal Law, Criminal Procedure, Jurisprudence, Legal Profession, Legal Theory, Law and Literature.

R. KENT NEWMYER*, (Law Lecturer)**, born Alliance, Nebraska, May 18, 1930. *Education:* Doane College (B.A., 1952); University of Nebraska (Ph.D., 1959). ***COURSES: Constitution and Legal History.

ANGEL R. OQUENDO*, (Professor of Law)**, born Guaynabo, Puerto Rico, 1961; admitted to bar, 1986, Puerto Rico. *Education:* Harvard University (A.B., 1983; Ph.D., 1993); Yale University (J.D., 1986). ***COURSES: Civil Procedure, Corporations, Comparative Law.

LEONARD ORLAND*, (Professor of Law)**, born Trenton, New Jersey, 1936; admitted to bar, 1963, New York. *Education:* Rutgers University (B.A., 1957); University of Pennsylvania (LL.B., 1960). ***COURSES: Antitrust, Corporate Crime, Criminal Corrections, Criminal Law, Criminal Procedure, Federal Criminal Law, Trade Regulation.

RICHARD W. PARKER*, (Professor of Law)**, born Dallas, Texas, May 21, 1956; admitted to bar, 1985, Pennsylvania; 1990, District of Columbia. *Education:* Princeton University (B.A., 1978); Oxford University (D. Phil., 1982); Yale Law School (J.D., 1985). ***COURSES: Administrative Law, Environmental Law, International Environmental Law.

JEREMY R. PAUL*, (Professor of Law and Associate Dean of Academic Affairs)**, born New York, New York, July 22, 1956; admitted to bar, 1982, New York. *Education:* Princeton University (A.B., 1978); Harvard University (J.D., 1981). ***COURSES: Administrative Law, Constitutional Law, Eminent Domain, Corporate Finance, Jurisprudence, Property.

ELLEN ASH PETERS*, (Visiting Professor of Law)**, born Berlin, Germany, March 21, 1930; admitted to bar, 1957, Connecticut; 1984, State Court Chief Justice Connecticut Supreme Court; 1996, Senior Justice. *Education:* Swarthmore College (B.A., 1951); Yale (LL.B., 1954). ***COURSES: Comparative Federalism, Contracts.

RICHARD DAVID POMP*, (Alva P. Loiselle Professor of Law)**, born January 11, 1946; admitted to bar, 1972, Massachusetts. *Education:* University of Michigan (S.B., 1967); Harvard University (J.D., 1972). ***COURSES: Corporate Tax, International Tax, State and Local Tax, Tax Administration, Tax Policy, Federal Taxation.

ALAN RITTER*, (Visiting Professor of Political Philosophy)**, born 1937. *Education:* Yale University (A.B., 1958); Harvard University (Ph.D., 1966). ***COURSES: Obedience and Disobedience, Social Justice.

JESSICA RUBIN*, (Assistant Clinical Professor)**, born December 23, 1968; admitted to bar, 1993, Connecticut; 1994, New York. *Education:* Cornell University (B.S., 1990); Cornell Law School (J.D., 1993). ***COURSES: Lawyering Process.

***ELLEN KEANE RUTT*, (Associate Dean Admissions and Career Services)**, born February 08, 1955. *Education:* University of Notre Dame (B.A., 1977); Fairfield University (M.A., 1985); University of Connecticut (J.D., 1990).

EILEEN SILVERSTEIN*, (Zephaniah Swift Professor of Law)**, born 1945; admitted to bar, 1972, California. *Education:* University of Nebraska (A.B., 1968); University of Chicago (J.D., 1972). ***COURSES: Civil Rights, Labor Law, Property, Torts.

JAMES H. STARK*, (Professor of Law)**, born New York, New York, April 6, 1947; admitted to bar, 1974, District of Columbia; 1980, Connecticut. *Education:* Cornell University (B.A., 1968); Columbia University (J.D., 1971). ***COURSES: Clinical Teaching, Evidence, Torts, Juvenile Law, Interviewing, Counseling and Negotiation, Law and Social Science, Legal Profession.

KURT A. STRASSER*, (Phillip I. Blumberg Professor of Law)**, born 1947; admitted to bar, 1972, Tennessee; 1976, Georgia; 1987, Connecticut. *Education:* Vanderbilt University (B.A., 1969; J.D., 1972; LL.M., 1979); Columbia University (J.S.D., 1986). ***COURSES: Administrative Law, Antitrust, Contracts, Environmental Law, Law and Economics, Regulated Industries.

COLIN C. TAIT*, (Oliver Ellsworth Research Professor of Law)**, born 1932; admitted to bar, 1959, Connecticut. *Education:* Cornell University (B.A., 1954); Yale University (LL.B., 1959). ***COURSES: Civil Procedure, Conflict of Laws, Environmental Law, Evidence, Insurance, Torts.

(This Listing Continued)

UNIVERSITY OF CONNECTICUT SCHOOL OF LAW —Continued

TERRY J. TONDRO*, (Thomas F. Gallivan Professor of Law)**, born Santa Monica, California, May 7, 1938; admitted to bar, 1968, New York; 1981, Connecticut. *Education:* Cornell University (A.B., 1961); New York University (LL.B., 1967); Yale University (M.Phil., 1972). ***COURSES: Housing Law and Economics, Land Use Planning, Law and the Visual Arts, Local Government, Real Estate Planning, Real Estate Transactions, Real Property, Environmental Law.

STEPHEN G. UTZ*, (Professor of Law)**, born Baton Rouge, Louisiana, June 8, 1947; admitted to bar, 1979, Texas; 1980, District of Columbia; 1988, Connecticut. *Education:* Louisiana State University (B.A., 1967); Cambridge University (Ph.D., 1977); University of Texas (J.D., 1979). ***COURSES: Corporate Finance, Partnership Tax, Real Property, Federal Taxation.

CAROL ANN WEISBROD*, (Ellen Ash Peters Professor of Law)**, born New York, New York, April 12, 1939; admitted to bar, 1962, New York. *Education:* Vassar College; Columbia University (J.D., 1961). ***COURSES: Commercial Law, Church and State, Contracts, Domestic Relations, U.S. Law and Legal Studies, Property.

***LAURIE WERLING*, (Associate Dean Finance and Administration)**, born 1953. *Education:* University of Connecticut (B.A., 1975; M.B.A., 1983).

ROBERT WHITMAN*, (Professor of Law)**, born 1936; admitted to bar, 1959, New York; 1967, Connecticut. *Education:* Bernard M. Baruch College of the City University of New York (B.B.A., 1956); Columbia University (J.D., 1959); New York University (LL.M., 1970). ***COURSES: Commercial Law, Contracts, Credit Transactions, Decedents Estates, Estate Planning, Family Law, Trusts and Estates.

STEVEN R. WILF*, (Associate Professor of Law)**, born Philadelphia, Pennsylvania, November 21, 1956. *Education:* Arizona State University (B.S., 1977); Yale University (Ph.D., 1995); Yale Law School (J.D., 1995). ***COURSES: Criminal Law, Legal History, Introduction to Intellectual Property, Defamation, Privacy and Publicity, Legal Regulation of Art and Culture. ***Email:*** swilf@law.uconn.edu

***NICHOLAS WOLFSON*, (Professor of Law Emeritus)**, born New York, New York, February 29, 1932; admitted to bar, 1956, New York; 1966, Massachusetts. *Education:* Columbia University (A.B., 1953); Harvard University (J.D., 1956).

UNIVERSITY OF DAYTON SCHOOL OF LAW

300 COLLEGE PARK DRIVE
DAYTON, OHIO 45469-2772

UNIVERSITY OF DENVER COLLEGE OF LAW

7039 EAST 18TH AVENUE
DENVER, COLORADO 80220
Telephone: (303) 871-6000
Fax: (303) 871-6378
www.law.du.edu

ABA Approved Since 1928.

The University of Denver College of Law is located under the wide-open blue skies of Colorado, in the thriving and progressive capital of the Rocky Mountains, on a campus just a short drive from the foothills of the Rockies. The law school emphasizes practical legal skills through its highly developed clinical programs, its extensive internship program, the judicious use of adjunct faculty who bring real-world experience to the classroom, and its well-regarded moot court program.

The University of Denver began offering clinical legal education in 1904, one of the first law schools in the nation to do so. That tradition continues today through seven clinical opportunities offered at the law school.

In the Civil Representation Clinic, students work on cases involving restraining orders, housing, public benefits, wills, paternity, consumer affairs, and the rights of the elderly and disabled.

In the Criminal Representation Clinic, cases involve misdemeanor criminal charges. In the Mediation/Arbitration Clinic, students learn mediation skills and mediate cases in county court and in the Clinic itself.

In the Domestic Violence Civil Justice Project (one of only four such clinics funded by the U.S. Department of Justice Violence Against Women Office), students provide legal assistance to victims of domestic violence.

Students in the Low-Income Taxpayer Representation Clinic represent clients in disputes with tax authorities and provide education on taxpayer rights and responsibilities in immigrant communities.

In the Family Law Clinic, students represent underserved populations in family law matters.

In the Rocky Mountain Children's Law Center, students tackle issues such as child abuse, domestic violence, guardianship, custody, and adoption proceedings.

Earthjustice (formerly the Sierra Club Legal Defense Fund) operates a clinic at the University of Denver, which allows students to work on the front lines of environmental law, whether by stopping tree cutting in national forests, protecting animal species or native prairies, or working on other environmental issues.

Students who want to work in the community can do so through the countless part-time jobs available in Denver or through DU's extensive internship program. The College of Law makes more than 250 internship placements each year throughout the Denver area, elsewhere in the U.S., and even abroad. Students serve as clerks with federal judges or work in private law firms, government or non-profit agencies, or corporate counsel offices. The U.S. Court of Appeals for the Tenth Circuit is located in Denver, as is the U.S. District Court and the Colorado Supreme Court. Most U.S. government agencies have regional offices in Denver, and many national law firms locate offices here as well.

The University of Denver College of Law produces the following scholarly journals, all of which are student-run and edited. *Denver University Law Review, Denver Journal of International Law, Preventive Law Reporter, Transportation Law Journal* and *Water Law*

(This Listing Continued)

UNIVERSITY OF DENVER COLLEGE OF LAW
—Continued

Review. Each addresses unique issues, and students have many topics on which they can write.

In addition to the J.D. degree, the College of Law offers a Master of Laws (LL.M.) in Natural Resources Law and Policy. It is designed for attorneys who need cutting-edge information and skills and responds to the recent proliferation of resource and environmental laws throughout the world.

The Master of Laws (LL.M.) in American and Comparative Law allows foreign lawyers, judges, and law students to study the U.S. common law system. Students in the program take classes with the J.D. students and visit U.S. courts, law firms, and other legal institutions.

The Master of Science in Legal Administration (MSLA) is a joint offering of the College of Law and the Daniels College of Business. MSLA course work presents business management principles and fosters an understanding of the legal culture and the court and practice environments.

The University of Denver is an ideal setting in which to pursue a J.D. along with an advanced degree in another field. Dual degrees are offered in Business Administration, Economics, Geography, History, Intermodal Transportation, International Management, International Studies, Legal Administration, Mass Communications, Mineral Economics (with the Colorado School of Mines), Professional Psychology, Psychology, Real Estate and Construction Management, Social Work, Sociology, and Urban and Regional Planning.

Dean: Mary Ricketson (303) 871-6103
Associate Dean: J. Robert Brown Jr. (303) 871-6105
Assistant Dean of Administration: Stephen F. Favreau (303) 871-6101
Admissions: Forrest Stanford (303) 871-6135
Financial Aid: Iain Davis (303) 871-6136
Library & Assistant Dean of Information Services: Gary Alexander (303) 871-6188
Career Services: (303) 871-6124
Alumni Relations: Laura Dean (303) 871-6122
Assistant Dean of Student Affairs: Patricia H. Powell (303) 871-6120
Assistant Dean of Development: Johanna E. Kelly (303) 871-6117
Registrar: David Ricciardi (303) 871-6132
Clinics: Julie Field (303) 871-6923

FULL TIME FACULTY

MARY E. RICKETSON*, (Dean)**, born October 8, 1947. *Education:* University of Denver College of Law (J.D., 1978). ***Email: mrickets@law.du.edu

GARY ALEXANDER*, (Assistant Dean of Information Services; Director of the Law Library)**, born 1950; admitted to bar, 1982, Colorado. *Education:* University of Denver (M.L.L., 1982; J.D., 1981). ***Email: galexand@law.du.edu

THOMAS A. BARNES*, (Legal Writing Professor)**, *Education:* University of Colorado (B.A., 1971); Ohio Northern University (J.D., 1974). ***COURSES: Legal Writing. ***Email:*** tbarnes@law.du.edu

ARTHUR BEST*, (Professor of Law)**, born 1945; admitted to bar, 1969, District of Columbia; 1974, New York; 1989, Colorado. *Education:* Columbia College (A.B., 1966); University of Pennsylvania (J.D., 1969). ***COURSES: Torts, Evidence. ***Email:*** abest@law.du.edu

ANDREA BLOOM*, (Lawyer Process Professor)**, born Clarksdale, Missouri, December 04, 1951; admitted to bar, 1979, Colorado. *Education:* University of Michigan (B.A., 1972); University of Colorado (J.D., 1978). ***COURSES: Legal Writing and Research. ***Email:*** abloom@law.du.edu

JEROME BORISON*, (Associate Professor)**, born 1946; admitted to bar, 1977, Pennsylvania; 1981, California; 1985, Colorado. *Education:* Temple University (B.S., 1967); Gonzaga University (J.D., 1977); New York University (LL.M., 1982). ***COURSES: Public Interest Law, Basic Tax, Estate and Gift Tax. ***Email:*** jborison@law.du.edu

BURTON F. BRODY*, (Professor of Law)**, born 1937; admitted to bar, 1962, Illinois. *Education:* DePaul University (B.Sc., 1959; J.D., 1961); Northwestern University (LL.M., 1978). ***COURSES: Contracts, Remedies. ***Email:*** bbrody@law.du.edu

J. ROBERT BROWN, JR.*, (Associate Dean and Professor of Law)**, born 1957; admitted to bar, 1981, District of Columbia. *Education:* College of William and Mary (B.A., 1978); Georgetown University (M.A., 1984; Ph.D., 1993); University of Maryland (J.D., 1980). ***COURSES: Corporations, Administrative Law, Russian Commercial Environment. ***Email:*** jbrown@law.du.edu

PENELOPE BRYAN*, (Associate Professor)**, born 1944; admitted to bar, 1983, Florida. *Education:* Rollins College (B.S., 1978); University of Florida (J.D., 1981; M.A., 1989). ***COURSES: Civil Procedure, Federal Courts, Family Law, Alternative Dispute Resolution. ***Email:*** pbryan@law.du.edu

FREDERICO CHEEVER*, (Associate Professor)**, born 1957; admitted to bar, 1986, California; 1988, Colorado. *Education:* Stanford University (B.A/M.A., 1981); UCLA (J.D., 1986). ***COURSES: Property, Environmental Law, Public Land Use. ***Email:*** fcheever@law.du.edu

ALAN CHEN*, (Associate Professor)**, born 1960; admitted to bar, 1985, California; 1988, Illinois. *Education:* Case Western Reserve University (B.A., 1982); Stanford (J.D., 1985). ***COURSES: Constitutional Law, Constitutional Litigation, Criminal Procedure, Federal Jurisdiction. ***Email:*** achen@law.du.edu

CHRISTINE CIMINI*, (Assistant Professor)**, born 1967; admitted to bar, 1992, Connecticut; 1996, Oregon; 1998, Colorado. *Education:* Clark University (B.A., 1989); University of Connecticut (J.D., 1992). ***COURSES: Basic and Advanced Civil Representation. ***Email:*** ccimini@law.du.edu

ROBERTO L. CORRADA*, (Associate Professor)**, born 1960; admitted to bar, 1985, District of Columbia; 1990, Michigan. *Education:* George Washington University (B.A., 1982); Catholic University School of Law (J.D., 1985). ***COURSES: Employment Law, Labor Law, Contracts, Administrative Law, Critical Race Theory. ***Email:*** rcorrada@law.du.edu

TAMI D. COWDEN*, (Legal Writing Professor)**, *Education:* Arizona University (B.A., 1982); University of Colorado School of Law (J.D., 1987). ***COURSES: Legal Writing. ***Email:*** tcowden@law.du.edu

(This Listing Continued)

UNIVERSITY OF DENVER COLLEGE OF LAW —Continued

EDWARD A. DAUER*, (Dean Emeritus; Professor of Law)**, born 1944; admitted to bar, 1978, Connecticut; 1986 Colorado. *Education:* Brown University (A.B., 1966); Yale Law School (LL.B., 1969). ***COURSES: Alternative Dispute Resolution, Preventive Law, Medicine and Health Law. ***Email:*** edauer@law.du.edu

PAUL STEPHEN DEMPSEY*, (Professor of Law; Director, Transportation Law Program)**, born Atlanta, Georgia, August 27, 1950; admitted to bar, 1975, Georgia; 1977, District of Columbia; 1978, Colorado. *Education:* University of Georgia (A.B.J., 1972; J.D., 1975); George Washington University (LL.M., 1978); McGill University (D.C.L. 1986). ***COURSES: Transportation Law, Torts, Aviation Law. ***Email:*** pdempsey@law.du.edu

KATHERINE K. DUVIVIER*, (Assistant Professor; Director Lawyering Process Program)**, born Alton, Illinois, January 1, 1953; admitted to bar, 1982, Colorado. *Education:* Williams College (B.A., 1975); University of Denver College of Law (J.D., 1982). ***COURSES: Lawyering Process, Local Government, Trust and Estates. ***Email:*** kkduvivie@mail.law.du.edu

M. CATHERINE DUBA*, (Legal Writing Professor)**, admitted to bar, 1990, Colorado; 1995, District of Columbia. *Education:* University of Colorado (B.A., 1977); University of Denver College of Law (J.D., 1990). ***COURSES: Legal Writing, Advanced Legal Analysis. ***Email:*** cduba@mail.law.du.edu

NANCY S. EHRENREICH*, (Associate Professor)**, born 1952; admitted to bar, 1979, Virginia; 1996, Colorado. *Education:* Yale University (B.A., 1974); University of Virginia (J.D., 1979; LL.M., 1982). ***COURSES: Criminal Law, Jurisprudence, Reproductive Rights, Torts, Feminist Legal Theory. ***Email:*** nehrenre@mail.law.du.edu

MARTHA M. ERTMAN*, (Associate Professor)**, born 1963; admitted to bar, 1990, Washington; 1991, Colorado. *Education:* Wellesley College (B.A., 1985); Northwestern University College of Law (J.D., 1990). ***COURSES: Commercial Law, Contracts, Sales, Payments, Secured Transactions. ***Email:*** mertman@mail.law.du.edu

STEPHEN F. FAVREAU*, (Assistant Dean of Administration)**, *Education:* Central Connecticut State University (B.A., 1979); University of New Haven (M.S., 1989). ***Email: sfaureau@mail.law.du.edu

CHRISTOPHER A. GEHRING*, (Lawyering Process Professor)**, born Baltimore, May 25, 1970; admitted to bar, 1996, Colorado. *Education:* Albright College (B.A., 1992); Cornell University (J.D., 1996). ***COURSES: Legal Research Writing. ***Email:*** cgehring@mail.law.du.edu

J. WADINE GEHRKE*, (Assistant Professor)**, born Williamson, West Virginia, August 8, 1942; admitted to bar, 1984, Colorado. *Education:* Colorado State University (B.A., 1965); University of Denver College of Law (J.D., 1984). ***COURSES: Clinical Education, Basic and Advanced Civil and Criminal Representation. ***Email:*** wgehrke@law.du.edu

ROBERT M. HARDAWAY*, (Professor of Law)**, born 1946; admitted to bar, 1971, Colorado. *Education:* New York University (J.D., 1971). ***COURSES: Evidence, Civil Procedure, Preventive Law. ***Email:*** rhardawa@law.du.edu

JEFFREY H. HARTJE*, (Associate Professor)**, born 1942; admitted to bar, 1967, Minnesota; 1976, Washington. *Education:* University of Minnesota (B.A., 1964; J.D., 1967). ***COURSES: Clinical Teaching, Evidence. ***Email:*** jhartje@law.du.edu

TIMOTHY M. HURLEY*, (Legal Writing Professor)**, born 1955; admitted to bar, 1987, Ohio. *Education:* University of Wisconsin (B.A., 1981); Southern Illinois University Lesar College of Law (J.D., 1985). ***COURSES: Legal Writing, Advanced Legal Research. ***Email:*** thurley@law.du.edu

SHEILA K. HYATT*, (Professor of Law)**, born 1950; admitted to bar, 1974, Missouri; 1980, Colorado. *Education:* Miami University (B.A., 1971); Washington University (J.D., 1974). ***COURSES: Evidence, Civil Procedure, Trial Practice, Gender and the Law. ***Email:*** shyatt@law.du.edu

SAM KAMIN*, (Assistant Professor)**, born 1969; admitted to bar, 1996, California. *Education:* Amherst College (B.A., 1992); University of California (J.D., 1996; Ph.D., 2000). ***COURSES: Criminal Law, Basic Criminal Procedure, Administration of Criminal Justice Seminar. ***Email:*** skamin@law.du.edu

MARTIN J. KATZ*, (Assistant Professor)**, born New York City, New York, February 6, 1965; admitted to bar, 1993, Colorado. *Education:* Harvard College (B.A., 1987); Yale Law School (J.D., 1991). ***COURSES: Constitutional Law, Employment Law, Intellectual Property. ***Email:*** mkatz@law.du.edu

JOHANNA E. KELLY*, (Assistant Dean of Development and External Affairs)**, *Education:* Vassar College (A.B., 1981); University of Denver (M.B.A., 2000). ***Email: jkelly@mail.law.du.edu

JAN G. LAITOS*, (John A. Carver Professor of Law; Director, Natural Resources & Environmental Law Program)**, born 1946; admitted to bar, 1971, Colorado; 1974, District of Columbia. *Education:* Yale University (B.A., 1968); University of Colorado (J.D., 1971); University of Wisconsin (S.J.D., 1975). ***COURSES: Environmental and Natural Resources Law, Constitutional Law. ***Email:*** jlaitos@law.du.edu

LUCY A. MARSH*, (Professor of Law)**, born 1941; admitted to bar, 1967, Connecticut; 1971, Colorado. *Education:* Smith College (B.A., 1963); University of Michigan (J.D., 1966). ***COURSES: Civil Procedure, Future Interests, Property, Trusts, and Estates. ***Email:*** lmarsh@law.du.edu

VED P. NANDA*, (Vice President for Internationalization; Evans University Professor; Thompson G. Marsh Professor of Law)**, born Gujranwala, India, November 20, 1934. *Education:* Punjab University (B.A./M.A., 1952); Delhi University (LL.B., 1955; LL.M., 1958); Northwestern University (LL.M., 1962). ***COURSES: International Law, Conflicts of Law, Human Rights Law, International Conflict Resolution, International Business Trade Law. ***Email:*** vnanda@mail.law.du.edu

JULIE A. NICE*, (Associate Professor)**, born 1960; admitted to bar, 1986, Illinois. *Education:* Northwestern University (B.S., 1982; J.D., 1986). ***COURSES: Constitutional Law, Civil Procedure, Poverty Law, Sexual Orientation Law, Administrative Law, American Legal History. ***Email:*** jnice@law.du.edu

JAMES OTTO*, (Director, Graduate Program in International Natural Resources and Environmental Law)**, born Ohio, February 10, 1954; admitted to bar, 1983, Colorado. *Education:* University of Colorado (B.S., 1976); Colorado School of Mines (M.S., 1982); University of Denver. ***COURSES: Natural Resources. ***Email:*** jotto@law.du.edu

STEPHEN L. PEPPER*, (Professor of Law)**, born 1947; admitted to bar, 1973, Colorado. *Education:* Stanford University (A.B., 1969); Yale University (J.D., 1973). ***COURSES: Torts, Legal Profession, Professional Ethics. ***Email:*** spepper@law.du.edu

***GEORGE (ROCK) PRING*, (Professor of Law)**, born Manhattan, Kansas, September 1, 1942; admitted to bar, 1968, Ohio; 1974, Colorado. *Education:* Harvard College (B.A., 1963); University of

(This Listing Continued)

UNIVERSITY OF DENVER COLLEGE OF LAW —Continued

Michigan (J.D., 1968). ***COURSES:*** Environmental Law, International Environmental Law, Administrative Law, Constitutional Law. ***Email:*** rpring@law.du.edu

JOHN H. REESE, **(Professor of Law)**, born 1931; admitted to bar, 1954, Texas. *Education:* Southern Methodist University (B.B.A./LL.B., 1954); George Washington University (LL.M., 1965; S.J.D.,1969). ***COURSES:*** Constitutional Law, Administrative Law. ***Email:*** jreese@law.du.edu

PAULA RHODES, **(Associate Professor; Director, LL.M. in American and Comparative Law Program)**, born 1949; admitted to bar, 1975, Louisiana; 1979, District of Columbia. *Education:* American University (B.A., 1971); Harvard University (J.D., 1974). ***COURSES:*** International Law, Human Rights, International Organizations, Comparative Law. ***Email:*** prhodes@law.du.edu

EDWARD J. ROCHE, **(Professor of Law)**, born 1951; admitted to bar, 1976, Illinois; 1982, Colorado. *Education:* University of Notre Dame (B.B.A., 1973); University of Chicago (J.D., 1976). ***COURSES:*** Tax Law. ***Email:*** eroche@law.du.edu

HOWARD ROSENBERG, **(Professor of Law)**, born Chicago, Illinois, April 10, 1927; admitted to bar, 1952, Illinois; 1954, Colorado. *Education:* Roosevelt College (B.A., 1949); DePaul University (LL.B., 1952). ***COURSES:*** Legal Profession, Bankruptcy and Creditor-Debtor Law, Student Law Office (clinical). ***Email:*** hrosenbe@law.du.edu

THOMAS DAVID RUSSELL, **(Professor of Law)**, born Pittsburgh, Pennsylvania, April 4, 1962; admitted to bar, 1989, California. *Education:* Northwestern University (B.A., 1983); Stanford University (M.A., 1986; J.D., 1989; Ph.D., 1993). ***COURSES:*** Legal History, Torts, Criminal Justice, Contracts. ***Email:*** trussell@law.du.edu

JOHN T. SOMA, **(Professor of Law)**, born 1948; admitted to bar, 1973, Illinois; 1976, District of Columbia; 1984, Colorado. *Education:* Augustana College (B.A., 1970); University of Illinois (M.A., 1973; J.D., 1973; Ph.D., 1975). ***COURSES:*** Corporations, Antitrust, Internet and Computer Law, Cybercommunications, Copyright, Trademarks, and Unfair Competition. ***Email:*** jsoma@law.du.edu

JACQUELINE ST. JOAN, **(Assistant Professor; Director of Clinical Education)**, born 1945; admitted to bar, 1977, District of Columbia; 1997, Colorado. *Education:* Brooklyn College, City University of New York (B.A., 1969); University of Colorado (M.A., 1997); University of Denver (J.D., 1977). ***COURSES:*** Domestic Violence Clinic, Battered Women's Clemency Reform Project, Civil Representation Clinic, Internship Classes. ***Email:*** jstjoan@law.du.edu

MARY A. STEEFEL, **(Legal Writing Professor)**, admitted to bar, 1979, Colorado. *Education:* University of Illinois (B.A., 1973); University of Colorado (J.D., 1979); University of Denver Graduate Tax Program (LL.M., 1984). ***COURSES:*** Legal Writing. ***Email:*** msteefel@law.du.edu

JOYCE S. STERLING, **(Professor of Law)**, born 1945. *Education:* University of California (B.A., 1967); University of Hawaii (M.A., 1970); University of Denver (Ph.D., 1977). ***COURSES:*** American Legal History, Law and Society, Scientific Evidence. ***Email:*** jsterlin@law.du.edu

CELIA TAYLOR, **(Associate Professor)**, born 1964; admitted to bar, 1989, California. *Education:* George Washington University (B.A., 1986); New York University (J.D., 1989); Columbia University (LL.M., 1994). ***COURSES:*** Contracts, Corporations, International Human Rights and Economic Development, Securities Regulation. ***Email:*** ctaylor@law.du.edu

MARK A. VOGEL, **(Associate Professor; Director, Graduate Program in Taxation)**, born 1948; admitted to bar, 1975, Colorado. *Education:* University of Notre Dame (B.B.A., 1969); University of Denver (J.D., 1975; LL.M., 1976). ***COURSES:*** Taxation. ***Email:*** mvogel@law.du.edu

JAMES L. WINOKUR, **(Professor of Law)**, born 1945; admitted to bar, 1970, Pennsylvania; 1983, Colorado. *Education:* University of Pennsylvania (B.A., 1966; LL.B., 1969). ***COURSES:*** Property, Community Associations Law, Real Estate Transactions. ***Email:*** jwinokur@law.du.edu

ROBERT B. YEGGE, **(Dean Emeritus; Professor of Law; Director, Legal Administration Program)**, born Denver, Colorado, June 17, 1934; admitted to bar, 1959, Colorado; 1978, District of Columbia. *Education:* Princeton University (A.B., 1956); University of Denver (M.A., 1958; J.D., 1959). ***COURSES:*** Law and Society, Law Firm Administration, Clinical Education. ***Email:*** ryegge@law.du.edu

EDWARD H. ZIEGLER, **(Professor of Law)**, born 1948; admitted to bar, 1975, Kentucky. *Education:* University of Notre Dame (B.A., 1970); University of Kentucky (J.D., 1973); George Washington University (LL.M., 1975). ***COURSES:*** Property, Land-Use Planning, Real Estate, Legal Profession. ***Email:*** eziegler@law.du.edu

UNIVERSITY OF DETROIT MERCY SCHOOL OF LAW

651 EAST JEFFERSON AVENUE
DETROIT, MICHIGAN 48226
Telephone: (313) 596-0200
Fax: (313) 596-0280
www.law.udmercy.edu

ABA Approved Since 1933.

Founded in 1912, the University of Detroit Mercy School of Law is the only Michigan law school affiliated with a private university, and it shares the Jesuit and Mercy tradition of value-oriented education. The School of Law emphasizes a rigorous legal education coupled with a curriculum that stresses the public responsibility of lawyers to the larger community. Degrees offered include a three-year, full-time program and a four-year, part-time evening program. Also offered is a joint J.D. - M.B.A. program, that requires four years to complete.

The school's Law Library, a U.S. government depository, has been housed in its present quarters for more than 15 years. The extensive collection includes federal, state and British Commonwealth materials, as well as records and briefs of cases argued before the Supreme Courts of the U.S. and Michigan.

The array of student activities at the School of Law includes Law Review, the *Michigan Business Law Journal*, Moot Court, The American Inn of Court, the Justice Frank Murphy Honor Society, the Black Law Student Association, the St. Thomas More Society, the Student Bar Association, and several other organizations.

The School of Law sponsors several types of special programs for academic and professional development, such as the Intellectual Property Institute, the Urban Law Clinic, and various continuing legal education seminars.

(This Listing Continued)

UNIVERSITY OF DETROIT MERCY SCHOOL OF LAW —Continued

The School of Law also participates in an exchange program with the University of Clermont-Ferrand in France, by which a recent graduate of each school visits the other institution for a year of teaching French or American law. Canadian contacts are maintained through the availability of cross-registration for elective courses between the School of Law and the University of Windsor (Ontario) Law School and a joint JD/LLB program with the Faculty of Law at the University of Windsor.

Graduates of the School of Law sit on the Michigan Supreme Court, the Michigan Court of Appeals, the U.S. Court of Appeals for the Sixth Circuit, and other benches throughout Michigan and beyond. Alumni have held major elective offices, including mayor of the City of Detroit, County Commissioner, County Sheriff, and a host of other executive positions. UDM graduates will continue to distinguish themselves in the practice of law, bringing respect and recognition not only to themselves, but also to the University of Detroit Mercy School of Law.

Dean: Stephen A. Mazurak (313) 596-0210
Assistant Dean of Admissions and Student Affairs: Kathleen H. Caprio (313) 596-0287
Financial Aid: Denise Daniel (313) 596-0214
Library: Byron Cooper (313) 596-0240
Career Services: Ann Griffin (313) 596-0260
Registrar: Loretta Lewis-Peck (313) 596-0212

FULL TIME FACULTY

STEPHEN ANDREW MAZURAK*, (Dean and Professor of Law)**, born Berkeley, California, October 11, 1944; admitted to bar, 1970, Nebraska; 1971, California; 1996, Michigan. *Education:* University of Nebraska (B.A., 1967; J.D., 1970). ***COURSES: Private and Public Sector Labor Law, Employment Discrimination Law, Contracts, Alternative Dispute Resolution.

HOWARD B. ABRAMS*, (Professor of Law)**, born Chicago, Illinois, April 26, 1940; admitted to bar, 1966, Illinois; 1980, Michigan. *Education:* University of Michigan (B.A., 1963); University of Chicago (J.D., 1966). ***COURSES: Copyright, Entertainment Law, Intellectual Property, Secured Transactions.

ROBERT NEIL BROWN*, (Professor of Law)**, born St. Joseph, Michigan, May 23, 1944; admitted to bar, 1969, Michigan; 1970, District of Columbia. *Education:* University of Michigan (A.B., 1966; J.D., 1969); George Washington University (LL.M., 1973). ***COURSES: Constitutional Law, Administrative Law, Aging and the Law.

***MICHAEL C. BRYCE*, (Director, Urban Law Clinic)**, *Education:* Fordham University (B.A., 1972); University of Detroit (J.D., 1977).

BYRON D. COOPER*, (Law Library Director; Associate Dean and Associate Professor of Law)**, born Wabash, Indiana, July 13, 1945; admitted to bar, 1977, Indiana. *Education:* Indiana University (A.B., 1968; M.S., 1973; J.D., 1977; M.L.S., 1978). ***COURSES: Legal Research, English Legal History.

LAWRENCE DUBIN*, (Professor of Law)**, born Detroit, Michigan, March 9, 1943; admitted to bar, 1966, Michigan. *Education:* University of Michigan (B.A., 1963; J.D., 1966). ***COURSES: Professional Responsibility, Evidence, Trial Practice, Civil Procedure.

LOIS E. FIELDING*, (Associate Professor)**, born Waco, Texas, May 19, 1954; admitted to bar, 1980, Texas. *Education:* Rice University (B.A., 1977); University of Texas (J.D., 1980); University of Virginia (LL.M., 1989). ***COURSES: International Law, Property, Sales, Consumer Transactions, Commercial Law.

LEE GOLDMAN*, (Professor of Law)**, born Queens, New York, November 23, 1953; admitted to bar, 1979, California; 1982, Michigan. *Education:* Queens College (B.A., 1976); Stanford University (J.D., 1979). ***COURSES: Antitrust, Civil Procedure, Sports Law, Unfair Competition.

JACQUELINE P. HAND*, (Professor of Law)**, born Reno, Nevada, August 7, 1946; admitted to bar, 1978, Michigan. *Education:* St. Mary's College (B.A., 1968); Northwestern (M.S.J., 1969); Wayne State (J.D., 1978). ***COURSES: Environmental Law, Estates & Trusts, Land Use Planning, Real Property.

HARRY GREENE HUTCHISON*, (Professor of Law)**, born Detroit, Michigan, April 12, 1948; admitted to bar, 1986, Michigan. *Education:* Wayne State University (M.A., 1975; J.D., 1986); University of Michigan (M.B.A., 1977). ***COURSES: Business Organizations, Securities, Labor Law, Torts, Law and Economics (On leave in 2001-02).

PATRICK A. KEENAN*, (Professor of Law)**, born Detroit, Michigan, July 22, 1945; admitted to bar, 1969, Illinois; 1970, Michigan. *Education:* University of Detroit (A.B., 1966); University of Chicago (J.D., 1969); University D'Aix-Marseille (Comp. Law Fellowship, 1970). ***COURSES: Constitutional Law, Criminal Law, Trial Practice, Professional Responsibility, Evidence.

NICKOLAS J. KYSER*, (Associate Professor of Law)**, born Mt. Pleasant, Michigan, August 17, 1946; admitted to bar, 1975, Colorado. *Education:* Michigan State University (B.A., 1972); University of Michigan (J.D., 1975). ***COURSES: Federal Taxation.

LEON J. LYSAGHT, JR.*, (Associate Professor of Law)**, born Butte, Montana, August 25, 1940; admitted to bar, 1966, Montana. *Education:* Whitman College (B.A., 1962); University of Chicago (J.D., 1965). ***COURSES: Contracts, Sale of Goods, Negotiable Instruments, Secured Transactions, Oil and Gas.

GARY M. MAVEAL*, (Associate Professor)**, born Monroe, Michigan, January 13, 1954; admitted to bar, 1982, Michigan. *Education:* Wayne State University (B.A., 1977); University of Detroit (J.D., 1981). ***COURSES: Civil Procedure, Evidence and Trial Practice.

ANDREW FOSTER MOORE*, (Visiting Professor)**, born January 7, 1967; admitted to bar, 1992, Ohio; 1999, Michigan. *Education:* John Carroll University (B.A., 1989); Case Western Reserve University (J.D. 1992); Columbia University (LL.M., 1998). ***COURSES: International Law, Human Rights, Immigration Law. ***Email:*** mooreaf@udmercy.edu

ALAN SALTZMAN*, (Professor of Law)**, born Detroit, Michigan, March 26, 1941; admitted to bar, 1966, California and Michigan. *Education:* Wayne State University (A.B., 1962); University of Chicago School of Law (J.D., 1965). ***COURSES: Criminal Law, Criminal Procedure.

RICHARD A. SEID*, (Professor of Law)**, born New York, December 7, 1933; admitted to bar, 1959, New York; 1969, Massachusetts; 1973, Michigan. *Education:* University of Michigan (M.A., 1955; M.S.W., 1985); New York University (J.D., 1959). ***COURSES: First and Fourteenth Amendment, Federal Jurisdiction, Family Law.

THE UNIVERSITY OF THE DISTRICT OF COLUMBIA SCHOOL OF LAW

4200 CONNECTICUT AVENUE, N.W.
WASHINGTON, D.C. 20008

UNIVERSITY OF FLORIDA FREDRIC G. LEVIN COLLEGE OF LAW

S.W. SECOND AVENUE AND S.W. 25TH STREET
P.O. BOX 117620
GAINESVILLE, FLORIDA 32611-7620
Telephone: (352) 392-9238
Fax: (352) 392-8727
www.law.ufl.edu

ABA Approved Since 1925.

The size, quality and diversity of University of Florida law faculty, combined with quality students and a location that is a major academic and international crossroads, support one of the nation's most comprehensive curriculums leading to the degree of Juris Doctor. Established in 1909 with an emphasis on outstanding teaching, the College of Law has educated numerous state and national leaders in law, business, education and government. Nationally, no other state or law school has produced as many presidents of the American Bar Association, Including current ABA President-elect Martha Barnett (Class of 1973). In Florida, approximately one-fourth of all practicing lawyers are UF Law alumni. The college also has graduated 29 of 47 Florida Bar presidents and numerous state and federal judges.

The college is accredited by the American Bar Association and is a member of the Association of American Law Schools. The University of Florida is a member of the Association of American Universities, comprised of the nation's top 58 public and private comprehensive research institutions.

The state of Florida is home to many of the most prominent, active and skilled lawyers and judges in America. many of whom are actively involved in the teaching and practical skills training of UF Law students. Because writing skills are of critical importance to success in the legal profession, Florida develops those skills through required courses in each year of law study, including a nationally acclaimed Legal Drafting program.

Through programs offered on campus and abroad students gain international experience and a distinguishing edge in today's employment market. Students benefit from an innovative program of Foreign Enrichment Courses offered on campus, and decades of international experience and involvement by faculty in Latin America, Asia and Europe, with specific emphasis on Poland, Brazil, Mexico, China and South Africa Students and faculty also benefit from exchange programs with renowned international institutions of law study around the globe. The college also sponsors summer abroad programs at the renowned Montpellier University in France and the University of Cape Town, South Africa

UF law students help impact state, national and international environmental and social policy by assisting in grant-funded research conducted by the Center for Governmental Responsibility, housed at the law school. The center has influenced more public policy during the past 20 years than any other organization of its nature and scope in the nation.

UF's Legal Information Center, one of the three largest law libraries in the Southeastern United States, houses more than 595,000 volumes and was a pioneer in the development of computer-assisted legal research.

The 60-member law faculty includes nationally and internationally respected legal scholars in areas including dispute resolution, family law, environmental law, criminal law and procedure, constitutional law, socioeconomics, and taxation. A number of faculty are authors of casebooks used extensively at law schools throughout the Radon.

Florida's three-year J.D. curriculum develops students' analytical ability, knowledge of the theory and practice of law, communication skills, and an understanding of the codes of professional responsibility and ethics that are central to the practice of law. Students experience a variety of teaching methods, including the traditional "case" and "Socratic" methods, as well as problems, simulations, role-playing videotaping, computer-assisted instruction and interaction with actual clients. After completing first-year requirements, students can tailor their course load to fit their interests and career plans.

The college's more than 100 courses and 30 seminars offered each year support traditional and contemporary law practice areas, including Administrative Law, Business Law, Criminal Law, Entertainment, Art and Sports Law, Environmental and Land Use Law, Family Law, Government Law, Health Law, Intellectual Property Law, International Law, Labor and Employment Law, Media Law, Mediation, Public Interest Law, Real Property Law, Probate and Trust Law, Securities Law, and Tax Law.

Special Program Offerings
Certificate Programs -- Florida offers J.D. students a "Certificate in Environmental and Land Use Law,- which is the first in the nation to offer a concentration in these two closely linked fields. Also offered is a "Certificate in Estates and Trusts Practice," another popular practice area. The certificate programs enable interested students to graduate with additional knowledge and credentials, including eight more credits than the 88 currently required for the J.D. degree. Details of both programs are available on the "Academic Programs" page of the College of Law
Web site.

Law Clinics -- Florida's "Virgil Hawkins Civil Clinics" include four areas of opportunity for students to work with actual clients: the Full-Representation Clinic, the "Gator Teamchild" Juvenile Law Clinic, the Mediation Clinic, and the *Pro Se* Clinic. The Criminal Clinics allow students to work at various State Attorney and Public Defender Offices.

Externships -- Florida's popular externship program allows selected students to gain practical experience while earning course credits. Placements include:
Environmental Protection Agency, Washington, D.C.
EEOC, U.S. Department of Justice, Washington, D.C.
U.S. Congress
Florida Supreme Court
Legal Services
State Attorney Offices
Various Environmental & Probate Externships

(This Listing Continued)

UNIVERSITY OF FLORIDA FREDRIC G. LEVIN COLLEGE OF LAW—Continued

Joint Degrees -- Because the college is affiliated with one of the nation's most comprehensive universities, J.D. students can earn joint graduate degrees in many subjects, including accounting, business administration, mass communication, exercise and sports sciences, educational leadership, environmental engineering, forest resources and conservation, gender studies, health administration, medicine, medical sciences, history, Latin American studies, political science, psychology, real estate, sociology, and urban and regional planning.

LL.M./J.S.D. in Taxation -- The UF Graduate Tax Program, offering a Master of Laws degree in taxation, is widely recognized as one of the top two such programs in the nation. Each year the program attracts 60 to 75 students from across the country. It is the only program in the nation to offer the S.J.D. in Taxation (Doctor of Juridical Science), aimed at students who plan to teach tax law.

LL.M. in Comparative Law -- Florida also offers a course of study leading to the LL.M. in Comparative Law, designed exclusively for graduates of foreign schools law schools who want to increase their understanding of the American legal system. The program offers certificates in international tax studies, international business and trade law, environmental and land use law, and intellectual properly law.

Centers & Institutes
A number of programs established at the law school complement Florida's rich curriculum, and bring together interdisciplinary students, faculty, and practitioners with shared interests. These include:
Center for Governmental Responsibility
Institute for Dispute Resolution
Center for the Study of Race and Race Relations
OF Center for International Financial Crimes Studies
International Center for Automated Information Research
Legal Technology Institute
Holland & Knight Institute

Student Body
Florida's enrollment of approximately 1,200 students results in a student-teacher ratio of 18:1, which is one of the most favorable among major U.S. law schools. Approximately half of the students are female, and approximately 25 percent are minorities. Students come from colleges and universities throughout the United States, and represent virtually all ethnic ant age groups. The median LSAT score and undergraduate grade point average of a traditional fall class are approximately 159 and 3.5 (4.0 scale). The median LSAT score and UGPA of a typical spring entering class are approximately 155 and 3.4. Dozens of co -curricular and extra-curricular organizations including student-edited journals and successful moot court and trial teams, support a rich and diverse student life.

Journals and Co-Curricular Organizations
Students earn credit and gain experience with a variety of legal skills through the following organizations. Participation is based on academic achievement, writing skills and/or open competitions.
Florida Law Review. The Florida Law Review is student-edited and contains articles by legal scholars expert in various areas of the law and works by students.
Florida Journal of International Law. The student-edited Florida Journal of International Law publishes scholarly works by students, professors and practitioners on public and private international law topics.
Journal of Technology Law & Policy. This student-edited online journal publishes scholarly works by students, professors and practitioners on technology issues.
University of Florida Journal of Law & Public Policy. This interdisciplinary publication introduces the legal and social science professions to each other through the publication of two issues a year and a spring symposium. Its members include law, joint-degree and other UF graduate students.
Justice Campbell Thornal Moot Court Team The Moot Court Team, named in honor of the late Florida Supreme Court justice and devoted alumnus, participates in Intramural, state ant national appellate competitions sponsored by organizations and law firms.
Trial Competition Team -- The UF Trial Team competes in intramural, state, regional and national competitions sponsored by individuals, groups and law firms.

Career Services
A full-service career planning office assists students in finding permanent and summer employment. Each year hundreds of employers, including law firms, government agencies and businesses, conduct interviews on campus. Florida graduates are employed in all 50 states and many foreign countries.

Admissions Policy
The college uses two selection methods to allocate the limited number (about 200) of openings each August and January Approximately 50 percent of each entering class is admitted based on LSAT score and undergraduate grade point average. An applicant's multiple LSAT scores are averaged and the UGPA of only the first bachelor's degree earned is considered. The remaining 50 percent of each class is selected by the college's Admissions Committee. which evaluates academic credentials and considers discretionary criteria, including effort in undergraduate or other academic performance, whore and in what disciplines degree were earned; academic accomplishment following the first bachelor's degree; leadership and other relevant activities; evaluations by persons who can objectively judge the applicant's potential for law study and practice; maturing experience (employment, military service, etc.); racial, ethnic and economic background; and geographic origin.

Transfer students must submit a written statement concerning their attendance, a complete transcript, and a statement from their dean indicating class rank and certifying that they are in good standing and eligible to return to the institution For complete details on Florida's admissions policy and procedures, please visit the "Admissions" section of our Web site.

Fees and Financial Aid
The quality and value of a UF law degree are major considerations among students. The 1999-2000 semester credit hour fee is approximately $161 for Florida residents and $537 for non-Florida residents. Financial aid is available through federal ant institutional sources, including more than 70 need. and merit-based scholarships administered by the College of Law.

Dean: Jon L. Mills (352) 392-9238
Admissions: J. Michael Patrick (352) 392-2087
Financial Aid: Patricia Varnes (352) 392-0421
Library Director: Grace W. Taylor (352) 392-0417
Placement: Kathy Urbach (352) 392-0499
Alumni Affairs: Donald Hale (352) 392-9296

(This Listing Continued)

UNIVERSITY OF FLORIDA FREDRIC G. LEVIN COLLEGE OF LAW—Continued

FULL TIME FACULTY

JON MILLS*, (Dean, Prof. & Dir., Center for Governmental Responsibility. Affiliate Faculty, Latin American Studies)**, born Coral Gables, Florida, July 24, 1947; admitted to bar, 1972, Florida. *Education:* Stetson University (B.A., 1969); University of Florida (J.D., 1972). ***COURSES: Florida Constitutional Law, Legislative Drafting Seminar, International Trade, Environmental Law. ***Email:*** Mills@law.ufl.edu

FLETCHER N. BALDWIN, JR.*, (Chesterfield Smith Professor of Law and Director, Center for International and Financial Crimes Studies)**, born Portsmouth, Virginia, January 5, 1933; admitted to bar, 1960, Georgia; 1970, United States Supreme Court. *Education:* University of Georgia (A.B., 1958; J.D., 1961); University of Illinois (LL.M., 1962); Yale University (LL.M., 1968). ***COURSES: Constitutional Law, International Financial Crimes, Media Law, Political and Civil Rights, Criminal Procedure. ***Email:*** BaldwinFn@law.ufl.edu

IRIS A. BURKE*, (Clinical Lecturer)**, born New York, New York, November 22, 1946; admitted to bar, 1977, Florida. *Education:* Brooklyn College (B.A., 1967); Brooklyn Law School (J.D., 1977). ***COURSES: Civil Clinic. ***Email:*** Burke@law.ufl.edu

DENNIS A. CALFEE*, (Professor and Alumni Research Scholar)**, born Pasco, Washington, April 10, 1945; admitted to bar, 1972, Washington. *Education:* Gonzaga University (J.D., 1972); University of Florida (LL.M., 1975). ***COURSES: Taxation - Federal. ***Email:*** Calfee@law.ufl.edu

JONATHAN R. COHEN*, (Assistant Professor)**, born December 28, 1966; admitted to bar, 1993, Massachusetts; 1993, New York. *Education:* Harvard (A.B., 1987; Ph.D., 1989 and 1993; J.D., 1992). ***COURSES: Negotiation, Alternative Dispute Resolution, Ethics, Public Policy, Evidence. ***Email:*** Cohenjr@law.ufl.edu

STUART R. COHN*, (Professor and Gerald A. Sohn Research Scholar)**, born Springfield, Illinois, August 14, 1941; admitted to bar, 1966, Illinois. *Education:* University of Illinois (B.A., 1962); Oxford University (B.A., 1964); Yale University (LL.B., 1966). ***COURSES: Corporations, Securities Regulation, Jurisprudence. ***Email:*** Cohn@law.ufl.edu

CHARLES W. COLLIER*, (Professor)**, born 1950. *Education:* Reed College (B.A., 1972); Yale University (Ph.D., 1978); Stanford University (J.D., 1985). ***COURSES: Constitutional Law, Jurisprudence, Legal Theory. ***Email:*** Collier@law.ufl.edu

THOMAS F. COTTER*, (UF Research Foundation Professor)**, *Education:* University of Wisconsin (B.S., 1982; M.S., 1984; J.D., 1987). ***COURSES: Evidence, Intellectual Property, Law and Economics. ***Email:*** Cotter@law.ufl.edu

JEFFREY DAVIS*, (Professor and Gerald A. Sohn Research Scholar)**, born Indianapolis, Indiana, August 1, 1943; admitted to bar, 1977, California. *Education:* University of California at Los Angeles (B.S., 1965); Loyola University (J.D., 1972); University of Michigan (LL.M., 1973). ***COURSES: Contracts, Bankruptcy. ***Email:*** Davis@law.ufl.edu

GEORGE L. DAWSON*, (Professor)**, born Manchester, Connecticut, July 16, 1944; admitted to bar, 1970, Colorado (Inactive). *Education:* Princeton University (A.B., 1966); University of Chicago (J.D., 1969). ***COURSES: Commercial Law, Contracts, Estates and Trusts. ***Email:*** Dawson@law.ufl.edu

PATRICIA E. DILLEY*, (Professor)**, born Ypsilanti, Michigan, December 4, 1950. *Education:* Swathmore College (B.A., 1973); University of Pennsylvania (M.A., 1976); Georgetown University Law Center (J.D., 1986); Boston University (LL.M., 1993). ***COURSES: Tax, Differed Compensation, Individual & Corporate Taxation, Advanced Employee Benefits, Retirement Income Policy. ***Email:*** Dilley@law.ufl.edu

NANCY E. DOWD*, (Chesterfield Smith Professor)**, born New Jersey, March 11, 1949; admitted to bar, 1982, Massachusetts. *Education:* University of Connecticut (B.A., 1971); University of Illinois (M.A., 1973); Loyola University (J.D., 1981). ***COURSES: Torts, Contracts, Employment Discrimination, Employment Law, Family Law, Women & the Law. ***Email:*** Dowd@law.ufl.edu

MARK A. FENSTER*, (Assistant Professor)**, born New York, New York, April 11, 1963; admitted to bar, 1999, California; 2000, New York. *Education:* University of Virginia (B.A., 1985); University of Illinois (Ph.D., 1992); Yale Law School (J.D., 1998). ***COURSES: Property, Land Use. ***Email:*** fester@law.ufl.edu

ALYSON FLOURNOY*, (Professor)**, born Plainfield, New Jersey, August 11, 1958; admitted to bar, 1983, District of Columbia. *Education:* Princeton University (A.B., 1979); Harvard University (J.D., 1983). ***COURSES: Environmental Law, Property, Administrative Law. ***Email:*** Flournoy@law.ufl.edu

MICHAEL K. FRIEL*, (Associate Dean & Professor)**, born Aruba, Netherlands Antilles, January 20, 1945; admitted to bar, 1969, Massachusetts; 1971, Oregon. *Education:* Harvard University (B.A., 1966; J.D., 1969); New York University (LL.M., 1982). ***COURSES: Taxation. ***Email:*** Friel@law.ufl.edu

F. ALISON GERENCSER*, (Assistant Director/Lecturer)**, born Athens, Ohio, August 28, 1942; admitted to bar, 1985, Florida. *Education:* Purdue University (B.A., 1963); University of Florida (M.A., 1981; J.D., 1984). ***COURSES: Legal Research and Writing, Appellate Advocacy, Mediation Clinic. ***Email:*** Gerencse@law.ufl.edu

MICHAEL GORDON*, (Chesterfield Smith Professor)**, born 1935. *Education:* University of Connecticut (B.S., 1957; LL.B., 1963); Trinity College (M.A., 1968). ***COURSES: Corporate Law, International Business Transactions, Comparative Law, International Litigation.

JEFFREY T. GRATER*, (Clinical Lecturer)**, born Lansing, Michigan, November 4, 1956; admitted to bar, 1985, Florida. *Education:* University of Florida (B.A., with high honors, 1979; J.D., with honors, 1985). ***COURSES: Civil Clinic. ***Email:*** Grater@law.ufl.edu

JEFFREY L. HARRISON*, (Stephen C. O'Connell Professor)**, born Bluefield, West Virginia, April 2, 1946; admitted to bar, 1979, Texas. *Education:* University of Florida (B.S., 1967; M.B.A., 1968; Ph.D., 1970); University of North Carolina (J.D., 1977). ***COURSES: Antitrust, Contracts. ***Email:*** Harrison-Jeff@law.ufl.edu

BERTHA ESPERANZA HERNANDEZ-TRUYOL*, (Professor of Law, Levin, Mabie & Levin Professor)**, born Cuba; admitted to bar, 1979, New York. *Education:* Cornell University (A.B., 1974); Albany Law School (J.D., 1978); New York University (LL.M., 1982). ***COURSES: International Law, Human Rights, Race & Gender, Property. ***Email:*** Hernandez@law.ufl.edu

DAVID M. HUDSON*, (Professor)**, born Washington, District of Columbia, July 12, 1946; admitted to bar, 1974, Florida; 1976, District of Columbia. *Education:* Florida State University (J.D., 1974); University of Florida (LL.M., 1975); University of London (LL.M., 1980). ***COURSES: Tax, Immigration. ***Email:*** Hudson@law.ufl.edu

***THOMAS R. HURST*, (Professor and Sam T. Dell Research**

(This Listing Continued)

UNIVERSITY OF FLORIDA FREDRIC G. LEVIN COLLEGE OF LAW—Continued

Scholar), born Washington, District of Columbia, May 22, 1944; admitted to bar, 1969, Wisconsin. *Education:* University of Wisconsin (B.A., 1966); Harvard University (J.D., 1969). ***COURSES:*** Contracts, Corporations, Corporate Finance. ***Email:*** Hurst@law.ufl.edu

JEROLD H. ISRAEL*, (Ed Rood Eminent Scholar and Professor)**, born Cleveland, Ohio, June 14, 1934; admitted to bar, 1959, Ohio; 1965, Michigan. *Education:* Western Reserve University (B.B.A., 1956); Yale University (L.L.B., 1959). ***COURSES: Criminal Procedure, White Collar Crime. ***Email:*** Israel@law.ufl.edu

JOSEPH S. JACKSON*, (Lecturer, Legal Research & Writing Program)**, born Hartford, Connecticut, December 8, 1957; admitted to bar, Arizona and Florida. *Education:* Princeton University (A.B., 1979); University of Florida (J.D., 1982). ***COURSES: Legal Research & Writing, Appellate Advocacy.

MICHELLE S. JACOBS*, (Professor)**, born Brooklyn, New York, April 2, 1954. *Education:* Princeton University (A.B., 1977); Rutgers University (J.D., 1982). ***COURSES: Criminal Clinics, Criminal Law.

ELIZABETH T. LEAR*, (Professor)**, born Gainesville, Florida, January 10, 1959; admitted to bar, 1989, Pennsylvania. *Education:* University of North Carolina (B.A., 1981); University of Michigan (J.D., 1987). ***COURSES: Civil Procedure, Criminal law, Federal Practice. ***Email:*** Lear@law.ufl.edu

LYRISSA C. LIDSKY*, (Professor)**, *Education:* Texas A & M University (B.A., 1989); University of Texas (J.D., 1993). ***COURSES: Torts, Jurisprudence, Professional Responsibility, Media Law. ***Email:*** Lidsky@law.ufl.edu

JOSEPH W. LITTLE*, (Professor and Alumni Research Scholar)**, born Asheville, North Carolina, March 15, 1935; admitted to bar, 1964, South Carolina; 1965, Georgia; 1974, Michigan and Florida. *Education:* Duke University (B.S., 1957); Worcester Polytechnic Institute (M.S., 1961); University of Michigan (J.D., 1963). ***COURSES: Torts, Local Government, State and Federal Constitutional Law, Workers' Compensation. ***Email:*** Little@law.ufl.edu

LAWRENCE LOKKEN*, (Culverhouse Eminent Scholar in Taxation)**, born November 10, 1939. *Education:* Augsburg College (B.A., 1960); University of Minnesota (J.D., 1967). ***COURSES: Taxation. ***Email:*** Lokken@law.ufl.edu

PEDRO MALAVET*, (Associate Professor)**, born Ponce, Puerto Rico, November 22, 1962; admitted to bar, 1988, Puerto Rico. *Education:* Emory University (B.B.A., 1984); Georgetown University (J.D., 1987; LL.M., 1995). ***COURSES: Comparative Law, Civil Procedure, European Union. ***Email:*** Malavet@law.ufl.edu

AMY R. MASHBURN*, (Professor)**, born Panama City, Florida, October 10, 1955; admitted to bar, 1987, Florida. *Education:* Eckerd College (B.A., 1977); University of Florida (J.D., 1987). ***COURSES: Civil Procedure, Professional Responsibility, Administrative Law. ***Email:*** Mashburn@law.ufl.edu

DIANE H. MAZUR*, (Professor)**, admitted to bar, 1988, New Mexico; U.S. District Court, District of New Mexico. *Education:* State University of New York at Binghamton (B.A., 1977); Pennsylvania State University (M.S., 1979); University of Texas (J.D., 1988). ***COURSES: Evidence, Corporations, Women in Military Service. ***Email:*** Mazur@law.ufl.edu

FRANCIS T. MCCOY*, (Professor Emeritus)**, born 1922. *Education:* University of Florida (B.A., 1944; M.A., 1947; LL.B., 1955). ***COURSES: Admiralty, Legal History, Family Law.

LYNN D. MCGILVRAY-SALTZMAN*, (Lecturer)**, born Manchester, Connecticut, June 20, 1949; admitted to bar, 1985, Florida. *Education:* George Mason University (B.A., 1979); University of Florida (J.D., 1984). ***COURSES: Drafting Legal Documents. ***Email:*** Saltzman@law.ufl.edu

MARTIN J. MCMAHON, JR.*, (Clarence J. TeSelle Professor)**, born Philadelphia, Pennsylvania, May 3, 1949; admitted to bar, 1974, New Hampshire; 1981, Kentucky. *Education:* Rutgers University (B.A., 1971); Boston College (J.D., 1974); Boston University (L.L.M., 1979). ***COURSES: Federal Taxation. ***Email:*** Mcmahon@law.ufl.edu

C. DOUGLAS MILLER*, (Professor and Director, Estates Trusts Practice Program)**, born Salina, Kansas, October 22, 1940; admitted to bar, 1965, Kansas; 1975, Florida. *Education:* University of Kansas (B.S., 1962; J.D., 1965); New York University (LL.M., 1966). ***COURSES: Estate Planning, Estates and Trusts, Federal Taxation, Professional Responsibility. ***Email:*** Miller@law.ufl.edu

ROBERT C. L. MOFFAT*, (Professor and Affiliate Professor of Philosophy)**, born Illinois, March 22, 1937; admitted to bar, 1962, Texas. *Education:* Southern Methodist University (B.A., 1958; M.A., 1962; LL.B., 1962); University of Sydney (LL.M., 1966). ***COURSES: Criminal Law, Jurisprudence, Law & Morality, Law & Public Policy. ***Email:*** Moffat@law.ufl.edu

WINSTON P. NAGAN*, (Professor and Sam T. Dell Research Scholar)**, born Port Elizabeth, South Africa, June 23, 1941. *Education:* University of South Africa (B.A., 1964); Oxford University (M.A., 1970); Duke University (LL.M., 1970; M.C.L., 1970); Yale University (J.S.D., 1977). ***COURSES: International Law, Conflicts, Human Rights, Jurisprudence. ***Email:*** Nagan@law.ufl.edu

JAMES C. NICHOLAS*, (Professor of Urban and Regional Planning and Affiliate Professor of Law)**, born Los Angeles, California, July 24, 1941. *Education:* University of Miami (B.B.A., 1965; M.A., 1967); University of Illinois (Ph.D., 1970). ***COURSES: Growth Management. ***Email:*** Nicholas@law.ufl.edu

LARS NOAH*, (Professor)**, born Miami, Florida, September 2, 1965; admitted to bar, 1990, Pennsylvania; 1991, District of Columbia. *Education:* Harvard University (B.A., 1986); Harvard Law School (J.D., 1990). ***COURSES: Administrative Law, Conflicts, Torts, Products Liability. ***Email:*** Noah@law.ufl.edu

KENNETH B. NUNN*, (Professor)**, born Clark A.F.B., Philippines, January 6, 1958; admitted to bar, 1984, California; 1988, District of Columbia. *Education:* Stanford University (A.B., 1980); University of California, Berkeley (J.D., 1984). ***COURSES: Criminal Law, Criminal Procedure, Civil Rights, Race Relations. ***Email:*** Nunn@law.ufl.edu

MICHAEL A. OBERST*, (Professor)**, born New York, New York, January 1, 1942; admitted to bar, 1969, District of Columbia; 1971, California. *Education:* University of Florida (B.S.B.A., 1964; J.D., 1968). ***COURSES: Taxation. ***Email:*** Oberst@law.ufl.edu

WILLIAM H. PAGE*, (Marshall M. Criser Eminent Scholar)**, born New Orleans, Louisiana, March 21, 1951; admitted to bar, 1975, New Mexico. *Education:* Tulane University (B.A., 1973); University of New Mexico (J.D., 1975); University of Chicago (LL.M., 1979). ***COURSES: Antitrust, Administrative Law, Civil Procedure. ***Email:*** Page@law.ufl.edu

RICHARD N. PEARSON*, (Cone, Wagner, Nugent, Hazouri & Roth Professor Emeritus.)**, born Michigan, September 3, 1928; admitted to bar, 1956, New Hampshire; 1971, Massachusetts. *Education:* University of Michigan (B.B.A., 1950); Boston University (LL.B., 1956); Yale University (LL.M., 1964). ***COURSES: Torts, Remedies, Insurance, Product Liability. ***Email:*** Pearson@law.ufl.edu

(This Listing Continued)

UNIVERSITY OF FLORIDA FREDRIC G. LEVIN COLLEGE OF LAW—Continued

JUAN F. PEREA*, (Cone, Wagner, Nugent et al Professor)**, born Washington, D.C., November 10, 1955; admitted to bar, 1986, Massachusetts. *Education:* University of Maryland (B.A., 1977); Smith College School for Social Work (1979-1980); Boston College (J.D., 1986). ***COURSES: Constitutional Law, Employment Law, Immigration, Race & Race Relations. ***Email:*** Peara@law.ufl.edu

DON C. PETERS*, (Professor, Trustee Research Fellow, and Director, Institute for Dispute Resolution)**, born Iowa, December 9, 1944; admitted to bar, 1968, Iowa; 1968, Colorado; 1969, Florida. *Education:* University of Northern Iowa (B.A., 1965); University of Iowa (J.D., 1968). ***COURSES: Civil Clinics, Civil Procedure, Negotiation, Interviewing, Counseling, Trial Advocacy and Evidence. ***Email:*** Petersdon@law.ufl.edu

LEANNE J. PFLAUM*, (Assistant Director Legal Research and Writing/Lecturer)**, born Miami, Florida, February 25, 1952; admitted to bar, 1980, Florida. *Education:* University of Florida (B.D., 1974); Florida State University (J.D., 1980). ***COURSES: Legal Research and Writing, Appellate Advocacy. ***Email:*** Pflaum@law.ufl.edu

JAMES R. PIERCE*, (Professor Emeritus.)**, born San Antonio, Texas, July 28, 1938; admitted to bar, 1965, Florida. *Education:* University of Florida (B.A., 1961; J.D., 1965). ***COURSES: Evidence, Trial Advocacy, Criminal Trial Practice, Clinic. ***Email:*** Pierce@law.ufl.edu

JAMES C. QUARLES*, (Professor Emeritus.)**, born Charlottesville, Virginia, March 18, 1921; admitted to bar, 1944, Virginia; 1955, Georgia. *Education:* University of Virginia (B.A., 1942; J.D., 1945). ***COURSES: Criminal Law and Constitutional Law. ***Email:*** Quarles@law.ufl.edu

TERESA REID J. RAMBO*, (Assistant Director Legal Research and Writing/Lecturer)**, born Miami Beach, Florida, January 27, 1957; admitted to bar, 1982, California; 1987, Florida. *Education:* University of Florida (B.A., 1978); Santa Clara University (J.D., 1982). ***COURSES: Legal Research & Writing and Appellate Advocacy. ***Email:*** Rambo@law.ufl.edu

DAVID M. RICHARDSON*, (Professor)**, born Panama City, Florida, November 6, 1939; admitted to bar, 1966, Florida. *Education:* Rensselaer Polytechnic Institute (B.S., 1961); Columbia University (LL.B., 1966); New York University (LL.M., 1974). ***COURSES: Taxation. ***Email:*** Richards@law.ufl.edu

BETSY L. RUFF*, (Assistant Director and Lecturer of Legal Research and Writing)**, born Orlando, Florida, March 26, 1956; admitted to bar, 1980, Florida. *Education:* University of Florida (B.A., 1976; J.D., 1979). ***COURSES: Legal Research and Writing, Appellate Advocacy. ***Email:*** Ruff@law.ufl.edu

SHARON E. RUSH*, (Irving Cypen Professor)**, born Indiana, December, 22, 1951; admitted to bar, 1980, District of Columbia. *Education:* Cornell University (B.A., 1974; J.D., 1980). ***COURSES: Constitutional Law, Civil Procedure, Federal Courts, 14th Amendment, Race Relations. ***Email:*** Rush@law.ufl.edu

SHERRIE RUSSELL-BROWN*, (Assistant Professor)**, born Middlesex, New Jersey, November 22, 1967. *Education:* Pomona College (B.A., 1989); Columbia Law School (J.D., 1992; L.L.M., 1999);. ***COURSES: Environmental Law, Evidence Torts, International Law. ***Email:*** RussellB@law.ufl.edu

ANNE RUTLEDGE*, (Director, Legal Drafting Program)**, born Pittston, Pennsylvania, March 6, 1940; admitted to bar, 1979, New Jersey. *Education:* Bucknell University (B.S., 1961); Rutgers University (J.D., 1979). ***COURSES: Legal Drafting. ***Email:*** Rutledge@law.ufl.edu

VALERIE SANCHEZ*, (Assistant Professor)**, born Hollywood, Florida, July 08, 1960. *Education:* Harvard University (J.D., 1986). ***COURSES: Alternative Dispute Resolution, Labor and Property Law. ***Email:*** Sanchez@law.ufl.edu

PEGGY F. SCHRIEBER*, (Clinical Lecturer)**, born Orange, New Jersey, November 18, 1949; admitted to bar, 1980, Florida. *Education:* University of Florida (B.A., 1972; J.D., 1979). ***COURSES: Clinic/skills. ***Email:*** Schriebe@law.ufl.edu

MICHAEL L. SEIGEL*, (Associate Dean & Professor)**, born Philadelphia, Pennsylvania, October 10, 1959; admitted to bar, 1985, Pennsylvania. *Education:* Princeton University (A.B., 1981); Harvard University (J.D., 1984). ***COURSES: Evidence, Criminal Law, Professional Responsibility, Federal Criminal Law.

CHRISTOPHER SLOBOGIN*, (Associate Dean of Faculty Dev., Prof., Stephen C. O'Connell Chair, & Affiliate Prof. of Psychiatry)**, born San Antonio, Texas, April 27, 1951. *Education:* Princeton University (B.A., 1973); University of Virginia (J.D., 1977; LL.M., 1979). ***COURSES: Criminal Law and Procedure, Law and Psychiatry, Evidence, Professional Responsibility, Social Science Law. ***Email:*** Slobogin@law.ufl.edu

DAVID T. SMITH*, (Professor)**, born Pawtucket, Rhode Island, December 11, 1935; admitted to bar, 1961, Massachusetts. *Education:* Yale University (B.A., 1957); Boston University (J.D., 1960). ***COURSES: Estates, Trusts and Property, Fiduciary Administration, Future Interests. ***Email:*** Smithdt@law.ufl.edu

GAYLIN G. SOPONIS*, (Lecturer)**, born Brooklyn, New York, August 22, 1944. *Education:* Mount Holyoke College (B.A., 1962); George Washington University (J.D., 1969). ***COURSES: Legal Drafting. ***Email:*** Soponis@law.ufl.edu

G. W. BETTY TAYLOR*, (Director, Law Library, Clarence J. TeSelle Professor)**, born Butler, New Jersey, June 14, 1926. *Education:* Florida State University (A.B., 1949; M.A., 1950); University of Florida (J.D., 1962). ***COURSES: Computers and the Law. ***Email:*** Taylor@law.ufl.edu

MARGARET TEMPLE-SMITH*, (Lecturer)**, born September 30, 1957; admitted to bar, 1983, North Carolina. *Education:* Wake Forest University (B.A., 1978; J.D., 1983). ***COURSES: Legal (Document) Drafting. ***Email:*** Temples@law.ufl.edu

PATRICIA A. THOMSON*, (Assistant Director/Lecturer)**, born Providence, Rhode Island, July 30, 1957; admitted to bar, 1983, Florida. *Education:* Hollins College (B.A., 1979); University of Florida (J.D., 1983). ***COURSES: Legal Research and Writing. ***Email:*** Thomson@law.ufl.edu

DIANE A. TOMLINSON*, (Lecturer)**, born Philadelphia, Pennsylvania, April 18, 1951. *Education:* University of Florida College of Business (B.S.B.A., 1988); University of Florida College of Law (J.D., 1992). ***COURSES: Legal Research and Writing, Appellate Advocacy. ***Email:*** Tomlinso@law.ufl.edu

MARY P. TWITCHELL*, (Professor)**, born Elmira, New York, February 25, 1944; admitted to bar, 1978, Florida. *Education:* Hollins College (B.A., 1966); University of North Carolina (M.A., 1966); University of Florida (J.D., 1977); Yale University (LL.M., 1982). ***COURSES: Civil Procedure, Federal Practice. ***Email:*** Twitchel@law.ufl.edu

***WALTER O. WEYRAUCH*, (Stephen C. O'Connell Chair and Distinguished Professor)**, born Lindau, Germany, August 27, 1919; admitted to bar, 1949, Germany (Hessen). *Education:* Referendar (1943); Assessor, (1948); Johann Wolfgang Goethe Universitat (Dr.Iur., 1951); Georgetown University (LL.B., 1955); Harvard

(This Listing Continued)

UNIVERSITY OF FLORIDA FREDRIC G. LEVIN COLLEGE OF LAW—Continued

University (LL.M., 1956); Yale University (J.S.D., 1962). ***COURSES:*** Business Organizations, Comparative Law, Family Law, Legal Counseling. ***Email:*** Weyrauch@law.ufl.edu

HENRY T. WIHNYK*, (Director/Lecturer, Legal Research & Writing and Appellate Advocacy Program)**, born Garden City, New York, June 7, 1954; admitted to bar, 1985, Florida. *Education:* Florida Atlantic University (B.A., 1976); Nova University (J.D., 1985); Columbia University (LL.M., 1990). ***COURSES: Legal Research & Writing and Appellate Advocacy. ***Email:*** Wihnyk@law.ufl.edu

WINTON E. WILLIAMS*, (Professor)**, born 1935; admitted to bar, 1962, Mississippi. *Education:* Tulane University (B.B.A., 1957); University of Mississippi (LL.B., 1962); Yale University (LL.M., 1973). ***COURSES: Bankruptcy, Secured Transactions, Sales. ***Email:*** Williams-winton@law.ufl.edu

STEVEN J. WILLIS*, (Professor)**, born Lafayette, Louisiana, October 22, 1952; admitted to bar, 1977, Louisiana; 1987, Florida. *Education:* Louisiana State University (B.S., 1974; J.D., 1977); New York University (LL.M., 1980). ***COURSES: Taxation. ***Email:*** Willis@law.ufl.edu

BARBARA BENNETT WOODHOUSE*, (David H. Levin Chair in Family Law)**, born New York, New York, September 19, 1945; admitted to bar, 1986, New York. *Education:* University of State of New York, Regents College (B.S., 1980); Columbia (J.D., 1983). ***COURSES: Family Law, Children and the Law, Constitutional Law, Children's Rights in International Law. ***Email:*** woodhouse@law.ufl.edu

CLAUDIA WRIGHT*, (Clinical Lecturer)**, born Jacksonville, Florida, June 3, 1946; admitted to bar, 1978, Florida. *Education:* University of Florida (B.A., 1975; J.D., 1977). ***COURSES: Civil Clinic. ***Email:*** Wright@law.ufl.edu

DANAYA C. WRIGHT*, (Associate Professor)**, born Lafayette, Indiana, September 18, 1961. *Education:* Cornell University (A.B., 1983; J.D., 1991); University of Arizona (M.A., 1986); John Hopkins University (Ph.D.). ***COURSES: Property, Trust & Estates, Legal History, Jurisprudence. ***Email:*** Wrightdc@law.ufl.edu

---

UNIVERSITY OF GEORGIA SCHOOL OF LAW

HERTY DRIVE
ATHENS, GEORGIA 30602

UNIVERSITY OF HAWAII
WILLIAM S. RICHARDSON SCHOOL OF LAW

2515 DOLE STREET
HONOLULU, HAWAII 96822

UNIVERSITY OF HOUSTON LAW CENTER

4800 CALHOUN ROAD
HOUSTON, TEXAS 77204-6391
Telephone: (713) 743-2100
Fax: (713) 743-2122

ABA Approved Since 1950.

The University of Houston Law Center is located at the University of Houston--the flagship campus of the University of Houston System. Three miles south of downtown, the campus extends over 550 acres of wooded terrain. The state assisted Law Center, located in the center of the nation's sixth largest legal market, is noted throughout the South and Southwest not only for its excellence, but for its progressive and innovative approach to the teaching of law. The College of Law, the academic branch of the Law Center, is fully accredited by the ABA and AALS and has a chapter of the Order of the Coif. The law school confers a J.D. degree as the first degree in law and a Masters of Law (LL.M) degree to students pursuing work beyond the J.D. degree.

The Law Center is currently undergoing a period of substantial qualitative growth and diversification. Emphasis is placed on current legal and administrative problems confronting this region and the nation. These problems are addressed through nationally recognized programs in energy, environment and natural resources law; intellectual property and information law; international law with a special emphasis on Latin America; and health law.

The Health Law and Policy Institute was established in 1978, and is considered one of the top health law programs in the country. Although the Institute is part of the University of Houston, it works closely with all of the other academic and health institutions in the area. Taught by both full-time faculty and distinguished adjuncts, the UH Law Center has one of the largest number of health law course offerings of any law school in the U.S. In addition, the Institute is guided by an advisory board consisting of leading academicians, practitioners, and representatives of area institutions and the public.

The Institute for Intellectual Property and Information Law Program affords students the opportunity for study, research and writing in patent, trademark, copyright, and trade secret and information law subjects, as well as inter-disciplinary legal protection for computer hardware and software. The UH Law Center's offerings in intellectual property law are the most extensive of any law school in the western half of the United States, and are designed to provide students with a broad exposure to the central concepts of domestic and international protection of proprietary technology in the modern industrial world.

The UH Law Center hosts an annual summer school in Mexico, with a faculty composed of Mexican Law professors and lawyers, special lecturers from the United States and members of the UH Law Center faculty. The UH Law Center also offers a concurrent joint J.D./M.B.A. degree program, a J.D./M.A. program in History with Rice University, a J.D./M.P.H. program with the University of Texas School of Public Health and a J.D./Ph.D. program in Medical Humanities with The University of Texas Medical Branch in Galveston.

The UH Law Center offers a wide variety of experiences in its clinical course offerings. Students can choose among different areas of concentrations, including health law practice, immigration law, judicial

(This Listing Continued)

UNIVERSITY OF HOUSTON LAW CENTER—Continued

internships, environmental law or criminal prosecution or defense. Within each area of concentration, students may find placements that are focused on more specific areas. All told, some 20 or more clinics of various types are available. The UH Law Center also offers skills training in both civil and criminal trial advocacy. Each year more than fifty experienced trial attorneys and judges from the Houston area participate as adjunct faculty for these courses. The Trial Advocacy Institute oversees the design and implementation of these trial advocacy courses and the training of adjunct Faculty for these courses at the UH Law Center. The Institute provides or co-sponsors yearly instruction for approximately 450 law students and 100 attorneys. The moot court and mock trial programs are extensive and available to all that are interested.

The student body consists of approximately 1000 individuals from across the United States and several foreign countries, although most students come from Texas and the Southwest. Of that number, approximately 930 are full-time and the remainder attend part-time. Approximately 41% of the student body are women and 19% are minority students. There are approximately thirty active student organizations including three national legal fraternities. Students also have the opportunity to serve on the editors board for the *Houston Journal of International Law* or the *Houston Law Review.*

The Law Center offers a graduate program leading to the Master of Laws (LL.M.) degree, with concentrations in health law, taxation, energy and natural resources, intellectual property and international economic law. In addition, a Master of Laws program is available to attorneys from foreign countries interested in obtaining exposure to the United States legal system.

The 47 (forty seven) full-time faculty members at the University of Houston Law Center bring to the school wide diversity in background and training. They received their law degrees from 27 different law schools representing every important center of legal education in the country. Fifteen of the faculty have advanced degrees in law; fourteen have additional advanced degrees in disciplines other than law; eight have Ph.D. degrees in addition to their law degrees.

Dean: Stephen Zamora (713) 743-2100
Senior Associate Dean for Academic Affairs: Mary Anne Bobinski (713) 743-2227
Senior Associate Dean for Information Services: Jon S. Schultz (713) 743-2300
Associate Dean for Graduate Studies and Special Programs: Laura F. Rothstein (713) 743-2183
Associate Dean for Information Technology: Gary Hartman (713) 743-2320
Associate Dean for Administration: Michael Karchmer (713) 743-2150
Assistant Dean for Student Affairs: Julia P. McKay (713) 743-2182
Assistant Dean for Student Services and Records: Marion S. Plain (713) 743-2182
Assistant Dean for Admissions: Sondra Richardson (713) 743-2079
Director of Career Services: Jacquelyn Plesnicher (713) 743-2090

FULL TIME FACULTY

STEPHEN ZAMORA*, (Dean and Professor of Law)**, born Los Angeles, California, June 26, 1944; admitted to bar, 1972, California; 1975, District of Columbia. *Education:* Stanford University (B.A., 1966); University of California, Boalt Hall School of Law (J.D., 1972). ***COURSES: International Law, International Business, International Banking, Contracts, Mexican Law, International Transactions.

RICHARD M. ALDERMAN*, (Law Foundation Professor)**, born Passaic, New Jersey, February 18, 1947; admitted to bar, 1972, New York; 1982, Texas. *Education:* Tulane University (B.A., 1968); University of Virginia (LL.M., 1973); Syracuse University (J.D., cum laude, 1971); Survey Editor, Syracuse Law Review; Justinian Honor Society. ***COURSES: Commercial Law, Consumer Law, Sports Law, Contracts, Deceptive Trade Practices.

MARY ANNE BOBINSKI*, (Senior Associate Dean for Academic Affairs and Professor of Law)**, born Cortland, New York, July 29, 1962; admitted to bar, 1988, New York. *Education:* State University of New York at Buffalo (B.A., 1982; J.D., 1987); Harvard University (LL.M., 1989). ***COURSES: Health Law, Torts, AIDS & the Law, Reproductive Health Law, Health Law Reform, Legislation, Special Topics in Discrimination Law.

RAYMOND L. BRITTON*, (Professor of Law)**, born Charleroi, Pennsylvania, August 20, 1924; admitted to bar, 1951, Texas. *Education:* Penn State University (A.B., 1948); Southern Methodist University (LL.B., 1951); Harvard University (LL.M., 1961). ***COURSES: Arbitration, Alternative Dispute Resolution, Securities, Admiralty.

G. SIDNEY BUCHANAN*, (Baker & Botts Professor of Law)**, born Houston, Texas, November 27, 1933; admitted to bar, 1959, Texas. *Education:* Princeton University (A.B., magna cum laude, 1956); University of Michigan Law School (J.D., 1959). ***COURSES: Constitutional Law, Trusts and Wills, First Amendment Rights.

SETH J. CHANDLER*, (Associate Professor of Law)**, born New York, New York, October 22, 1957; admitted to bar, 1984, Pennsylvania; 1986, California. *Education:* Princeton University (A.B., 1979); Harvard University (J.D., 1983). ***COURSES: Insurance Law, Insurance Regulation, Civil Procedure, Corporation, Law & Economics, Contracts, Antitrust.

ANTHONY R. CHASE*, (Associate Professor of Law)**, born Houston, Texas, March 17, 1955; admitted to bar, 1982, Texas. *Education:* Harvard University (A.B., 1977; J.D.-M.B.A. 1981); Harvard Business School (M.B.A., 1981). ***COURSES: Contracts, Environmental Law, Broadcast Regulation, Professional Responsibility.

GARY B. CONINE*, (Associate Professor of Law)**, born Jackson, Mississippi, November 26, 1947; admitted to bar, 1977, Texas. *Education:* Southern Methodist University (B.A., 1970); University of Oklahoma (J.D., 1977); Harvard University (LL.M., 1988). ***COURSES: Federal Energy Law & Policy, International Energy Transactions, Oil & Gas Law, Oil & Gas Contracts, Regulated Industries, Commercial Transactions.

JAMES S. COVINGTON*, (Professor of Law)**, born 1929. *Education:* University of Texas (B.B.A.; J.D.); Yale University (LL.M.). ***COURSES: Accounting in Law, Business Organization, Property, Evidence.

DAVID CRUMP*, (Newell H. Blakely Chair in Law)**, born Macon, Georgia, November 30, 1943; admitted to bar, 1969, Texas. *Education:* Harvard University (A.B., 1966); University of Texas (J.D., 1969). ***COURSES: Civil Procedure, Constitutional Law, Criminal Law, Evidence, Torts.

***RICHARD F. DOLE, JR.*, (B.W. Young Professor of Law)**, born Lowell, Massachusetts, July 12, 1936; admitted to bar, 1961, Maine; 1962, New York; 1966, Iowa; 1979, Texas. *Education:* Bates College

(This Listing Continued)

UNIVERSITY OF HOUSTON LAW CENTER—Continued

(A.B., 1958); Cornell University (LL.B., 1961; LL.M., 1963); University of Michigan (S.J.D., 1966). ***COURSES:*** Commercial Law, Bankruptcy, Business Torts, Creditors Rights, Lender Liability.

JOHN JAY DOUGLASS, **(Professor of Law)**, born Lincoln, Nebraska, March 9, 1922; admitted to bar, 1952, Nebraska; 1952, Michigan; 1975, Texas. *Education:* University of Nebraska (A.B., 1943); Washington University (M.A., 1963); University of Michigan (J.D., 1952); University of Virginia (LL.M., 1973). ***COURSES:*** Criminal Justice, Election Law.

DAVID R. DOW, **(George Butler Professor of Law)**, born Houston, Texas, July 18, 1959; admitted to bar, 1986, Texas. *Education:* Rice University (B.A., 1981; M.A., 1982); Yale University (J.D., 1985). ***COURSES:*** Constitutional Law, Jurisprudence, Contracts, Death Penalty Law, Federal Jurisdiction, law & Literature.

MEREDITH J. DUNCAN, **(Assistant Professor of Law)**, born 1966. *Education:* Northwestern University (B.A., 1988); University of Houston (J.D., 1993). ***COURSES:*** Torts, Professional Responsibility, Criminal Law.

SANFORD E. GAINES, **(Professor of Law and Director, Environmental Program)**, born New York, New York, September 23, 1945; admitted to bar, 1975, Massachusetts. *Education:* Harvard University (A.B., 1967; M.A., 1974; J.D., 1974). ***COURSES:*** Environmental Law, International Law, Torts, Coastal Zone Management, International Environmental Law, International Trade.

SANDRA GUERRA, **(George Butler Research Professor of Law)**, born Laredo, Texas, May 17, 1963; admitted to bar, 1988, New York. *Education:* Yale University (B.A., 1985; J.D., 1988). ***COURSES:*** Evidence, Criminal Law, Criminal Procedure, Sentencing, Prisoners Rights.

STEPHEN K. HUBER, **(University of Houston Law Foundation Professor of Law)**, admitted to bar, 1969, Illinois; 1971, District of Columbia; 1976, Texas. *Education:* Earlham College (B.A., 1963); University of Chicago (J.D., 1966); Yale University (LL.M., 1974). ***COURSES:*** Administrative Law, Contracts, Regulation of Banking, Commercial Law, Regulated Industries.

PAUL M. JANICKE, **(Associate Professor of Law and Co-Director, Institute for Intellectual Property and Information Law)**, born New York, New York, December 20, 1940; admitted to bar, 1964, New York; 1972, Texas. *Education:* Manhattan College (B.E.E., 1961); New York University (J.D., 1964); George Washington University (LL.M., 1971). ***COURSES:*** Patent Law, Intellectual Property, Law Survey, Evidence, Patent Litigation.

MICHAEL T. JOHNSON, **(Professor of Law)**, born Houston, Texas, October 24, 1938; admitted to bar, 1963, Texas. *Education:* Southwestern University (B.A., 1960); University of Texas (J.D., 1963). ***COURSES:*** Torts, Products Liability, Civil Procedure, Legislation, Admiralty, Family Law.

CRAIG JOYCE, **(Univ. of Houston Law Foundation Prof. of Law and Co-Dir., Institute for Intellectual Property and Info. Law)**, born Tempe, Arizona, August 19, 1948; admitted to bar, 1976, Arizona and Tennessee. *Education:* Dartmouth College (B.A., 1970); Oxford University (M.A., 1972); Stanford Law School (J.D., 1975). ***COURSES:*** Copyright, American Legal History, Torts. ***Email:*** CJOYCE@UH.EDU

ELWYN C. LEE, **(Vice Chancellor/President of Student Affairs and Professor of Law)**, born Portsmouth, Virginia, March 4, 1949; admitted to bar, 1975, Connecticut; 1976, District of Columbia; 1978, Texas. *Education:* Yale University (B.A., 1972; J.D., 1975). ***COURSES:*** Administrative Law, Employment Discrimination, Professional Responsibility, Torts.

PETER LINZER, **(University of Houston Law Foundation Professor of Law)**, born New York, New York, September 8, 1939; admitted to bar, 1963, New York; 1974, Ohio; 1982, Michigan; 1986, Texas. *Education:* Cornell University (A.B., 1960); Columbia University (J.D., 1963). ***COURSES:*** Contracts, Constitutional Law, Fourteenth Amendment Law, International Contracting.

ELLEN MARRUS, **(Associate Professor and Director of Clinical Programs)**, born New York, New York, August 7, 1951; admitted to bar, 1991, California. *Education:* Kean College (B.A., 1973); University of San Francisco (J.D., 1990); Georgetown University (LL.M., 1992). ***COURSES:*** Clinical Education.

IRENE MERKER ROSENBERG, **(Professor of Law)**, born New York, New York, June 1, 1939; admitted to bar, 1964, New York; 1974, Texas. *Education:* City College of the City University of New York (B.A., 1961); New York University (LL.B., 1964). ***COURSES:*** Criminal Law, Criminal Procedure, Constitutional Law, Juvenile Justice.

JOHN MIXON, **(Law Alumni Professor of Law)**, born Texas, August 4, 1933; admitted to bar, 1955, Texas. *Education:* Stephen F. Austin State University (B.B.A., 1952); University of Houston (J.D., 1955); Yale University (LL.M., 1962). ***COURSES:*** Property, Contracts, Real Estate, Finance, Land Finance, Oil & Gas Law.

DOUGLAS K. MOLL, **(Associate Professor of Law)**, born 1969. *Education:* University of Virginia (B.A., 1991); Harvard University (J.D., 1994). ***COURSES:*** Commercial Law, Business Organization.

GERALDINE SZOTT MOOHR, **(Associate Professor of Law)**, born Saginaw, Michigan, August 30, 1942; admitted to bar, 1992, Pennsylvania; 1993, District of Columbia. *Education:* University of Illinois (B.S., 1964); Bucknell University (M.S., 1987); American University (J.D., 1991). ***COURSES:*** Criminal Law, While Collar Crime, Employment Discrimination, Employment Law.

JOHN BREWSTER NEIBEL, **(John B. Neibel Professor of Law)**, born Houston, Texas, April 21, 1930; admitted to bar, 1956, Texas. *Education:* University of Houston (B.A., 1952; J.D., 1956); University of Michigan (LL.M., 1959). ***COURSES:*** Remedies, Real Property, Texas Civil Procedure, Law & Medicine.

THOMAS C. NEWHOUSE, **(Professor of Law)**, born Cincinnati, Ohio, May 21, 1935; admitted to bar, 1962, Oklahoma; 1978, Texas. *Education:* University of Notre Dame (B.A., 1957); University of Tulsa (J.D., 1962); New York University (LL.M., 1966). ***COURSES:*** Labor Law, Federal Procedure, Alternate Dispute Resolution, Mediation, Legal Aid Clinic, Civil Procedure, Torts, Workers Compensation.

RAYMOND T. NIMMER, **(Leonard Childs Professor of Law and Co-Director, Institute for Intellectual Property & Information Law)**, *Education:* Valparaiso University (B.A. 1996, J.D., 1968). ***COURSES:*** Commercial Law, Bankruptcy, Intellectual Property, Law and Science, Information Law.

J. THOMAS OLDHAM, **(John H. Freeman Professor of Law)**, born Ohio, December, 1948; admitted to bar, 1974, California; 1977, District of Columbia; 1983, Texas. *Education:* Dennison University (B.A., 1970); University of California at Los Angeles (J.D., 1974). ***COURSES:*** Corporations, Agency/Partnership, Family Law, Community Property, Business Associations, Mediation, Martial Property.

MICHAEL A. OLIVAS, **(William B. Bates Professor of Law and Director, Institute for Higher Education Law and Governance)**, born U.S. Army Hospital, Tokyo, February 24, 1951; admitted to bar, 1981,

(This Listing Continued)

UNIVERSITY OF HOUSTON LAW CENTER—Continued

Pennsylvania. *Education:* Pontifical College Josephinium (B.A., 1972); College of Santa Fe (1968-1969); Georgetown University (J.D., 1981); Ohio State University (M.A., 1974; Ph.D., 1977). ***COURSES:*** Immigration, Education, Legislation, Administrative Law, Professional Responsibility, Immigration & Business Law.

LAURA E. OREN**, (Professor of Law)**, born Brooklyn, New York, December 9, 1945; admitted to bar, 1981, Texas. *Education:* Queens College (B.A., 1966); Yale University (Ph.D., 1974); University of Houston Law Center (J.D., 1980). ***COURSES:*** Civil Rights, Family Law, Constitutional. ***Email:*** LOREN@UH.EDU

ROBERT G. PALMER**, (NEH Cullen Chair in History and Law)**, *Education:* University of Oregon (B.A., 1970); University of Iowa (M.A. 1971; Ph.D., 1977). ***COURSES:*** American Legal History, English Legal History, History of the Bill of Rights, Property.

JORDAN J. PAUST**, (University of Houston Law Foundation Professor of Law)**, born Washington, D.C., October 4, 1943; admitted to bar, 1969, California. *Education:* University of California at Los Angeles (A.B., 1965; J.D., 1968); University of Virginia (LL.M., 1972); Yale University (J.S.D. Cand., 1973-1975). ***COURSES:*** International Law, Human Rights, Constitutional and Foreign Affairs, International, Criminal.

ROBERT A. RAGAZZO**, (George Butler Research Professor of Law)**, born Brooklyn, New York, June 23, 1960; admitted to bar, 1987, New York. *Education:* Fordham University (B.A., 1982); Harvard University (J.D., 1985). ***COURSES:*** Business Organizations, Securities Regulation, Mergers and Acquisitions, Civil Procedure.

IRENE MERKER ROSENBERG**, (Royce R. Till Professor of Law)**, born New York, New York, June 1, 1939; admitted to bar, 1964, New York; 1974, Texas. *Education:* City College of the University of New York (B.A., 1961); New York University (LL.B., 1964). ***COURSES:*** Criminal Law, Criminal Procedure, Constitutional Law, Juvenile Justice.

YALE LEONARD ROSENBERG**, (A.A. White Professor of Law)**, born Houston, Texas, April 19, 1939; admitted to bar, 1964, Texas; 1965, District of Columbia; 1967, New York. *Education:* Rice University (B.A., 1959); New York University (LL.B., 1964). ***COURSES:*** Civil Procedure, Federal Jurisdiction, Administrative Law, Jewish Law.

MARK A. ROTHSTEIN**, (Hugh Roy and Lillie Cranz Cullen Distinguished Law and Policy Institute)**, born Philadelphia, Pennsylvania, May 23, 1949; admitted to bar, 1973, Pennsylvania; 1974, District of Columbia. *Education:* University of Pittsburgh (B.A., 1970); Georgetown University (J.D., 1973). ***COURSES:*** Employment Law, Health Law, Torts, Law & Genetics, Occupational Health Law.

JOSEPH SANDERS**, (A.A. White Professor of Law)**, born 1944. *Education:* Northwestern University (B.A. 1966; J.D., 1969; Ph.D., 1974). ***COURSES:*** Law and Society, Products Liability, Torts.

JON S. SCHULTZ**, (Senior Associate Dean for Information Systems and Professor of Law)**, born Hastings, Nebraska, May 3, 1941. *Education:* Nebraska State Teachers College (B.A., 1963); University of Washington (M.L.L., 1970); University of Denver (J.D., 1966). ***COURSES:*** Legal Bibliography, Legal Research and Writing.

ROBERT PAUL SCHUWERK**, (Professor of Law)**, born Evanston, Illinois, September 12, 1942; admitted to bar, 1972, Illinois; 1985, Texas. *Education:* University of Chicago (B.S., 1964; MATA, 1966; J.D., 1972). ***COURSES:*** Professional Responsibility, Civil Procedure, Remedies, Class Actions, Criminal Law.

IRA SHEPARD**, (Professor of Law)**, born New York, New York, December 14, 1937; admitted to bar, 1964, New York. *Education:* Harvard University (A.B., 1958; LL.B., 1964). ***COURSES:*** Taxation, Professional Responsibility.

WILLIAM P. STRENG**, (Vinson & Elkins Professor of Law)**, born Illinois, October 17, 1937; admitted to bar, 1962, Illinois/Iowa; 1964, Ohio; 1973, Texas. *Education:* Wartburg College (B.A., 1959); Northwestern University (J.D., 1962). ***COURSES:*** Estate Planning, Corporate Taxation, Federal Income Taxation, International Taxation.

RONALD TURNER**, (Associate Professor of Law)**, born 1955. *Education:* Wilberforce University (B.A., 1980); University of Pennsylvania (J.D., 1984). ***COURSES:*** Employment Law, Labor Law, Torts.

JACQUELINE LANG WEAVER**, (A.A. White Professor of Law)**, born Westchester, Pennsylvania, January 18, 1947; admitted to bar, 1975, Texas. *Education:* Harvard University (B.A., 1968); University of California at Los Angeles (C.Phil., in Economics, 1971); University of Houston (J.D., 1975). ***COURSES:*** Oil and Gas, Energy, Water, Environment, Public Land Use.

WILLIAM WINSLADE**, (Distinguished Visiting Professor of Law)**, born Denver, Colorado, November 18, 1941. *Education:* Monmouth College (B.A., 1963; D.H.L./Honorary Doctor of Humane Letters, 1990); Northwestern University (Ph.D., 1967); University of California at Los Angeles (J.D., 1972); Southern California Pschyoanalytic Institute (Ph.D., 1984). ***COURSES:*** Law & Bioethics, Law & Psychiatry.

UNIVERSITY OF IDAHO COLLEGE OF LAW

P.O. BOX 442321
MOSCOW, IDAHO 83844-2321
Telephone: (208) 885-6422
Fax: (208) 885-7609
http://www.uidaho.edu/law

ABA Approved Since 1925

Founded in 1909, the University of Idaho College of Law has established a reputation for excellence throughout the Northwest. It has been a member of the AALS since 1914 and on the ABA's list of "approved schools" since 1925. The school's small size and informal atmosphere provide a supportive, collegial environment for the study of law.

The College of Law enrolls nearly 300 students representing 30 states and more than 100 colleges and universities. The school is committed to increasing representation of women and members of minority groups.

A student-managed *Idaho Law Review* is published three times a year and is open to students who have demonstrated academic distinction or who submit a publishable article. From a voluntary intramural moot court competition a student Board of Advocates selects winning teams to participate in a number of national forensic competitions. Idaho

(This Listing Continued)

UNIVERSITY OF IDAHO COLLEGE OF LAW—Continued

students are extremely active and sponsor many organizations and activities.

Faculty members at the University's law school are committed to high quality teaching in the classroom and to accessibility outside the classroom. They are exceptionally well-qualified, holding degrees from many of the country's finest law schools. Members of our faculty have advised the Legislature, participated on the Idaho Humanities Council, helped revise court rules, and assisted executive and legislative agencies in many reform projects. Among the school's regular faculty are nationally recognized experts who write for publication in a variety of legal fields.

Our curriculum is designed to provide three years of instruction in basic principles generally applicable in the legal system of the United States. Although most of our students intend to practice law, a law degree also serves as a valuable asset to those who desire to pursue a position of leadership in government or business.

The basic method of instruction is the case system, a study of the decisions of appellate courts supplemented by selected readings which provide insight into the nature of judicial and legislative processes. Problem and simulation methods are frequently used in advanced courses. In addition, the University of Idaho offers third year students the opportunity to study law and lawyering skills through the representation of clients in a wide variety of cases under the supervision of clinical faculty.

The College of Law is housed in an outstanding building completed in 1973 and assigned for its exclusive use. The building contains a courtroom, classrooms, a cafe and student recreation center, offices, library, discussion areas, an interactive video classroom, and seminar rooms. TV videotaping equipment, networked computer terminals, and other modern technological advances now having an impact on the practice of law are available for student instruction and use.

The library of the College of Law contains over 125,000 volumes and is maintained as an integral part of the College of Law. The library is designed, through reading areas and open stacks, to insure maximum utilization by students and faculty for studying and research, and its subscriptions to LEXIS and Westlaw allow students to learn the most up-to-date methods for legal research. Membership in the Western Library Network (WLN) allows library staff to ascertain holdings of approximately 300 libraries in the Pacific Northwest and expedites the borrowing of materials from those libraries.

The University of Idaho is the centerpiece of the Palouse, an area of rolling, wheat-covered hills and forested mountains. Moscow, the university's hometown, is a thriving retail and hospitality center, as well as a gateway to a wonderland of recreational opportunities. Washington State University, with an enrollment of 18,000, is located eight miles west. Between these two major universities, an exceptionally wide range of cultural and educational programs are provided. Numerous ski areas are within driving distance of the school, while the Idaho countryside, rivers and lakes provide a rich variety of outdoor activities.

Dean: John A. Miller (208) 885-6208
Business Manager: Linda Kiss (208) 885-6208
Financial Aid - Admissions Officer: Erick Larson (208) 885-6423
Director of Library Services: John Hasko (208) 885-6521
Director of Development: Chandra Zenner Ford (208) 364-4044
Alumni Affairs & Career Services Officer: Leann Phillips (208) 885-5817

FULL TIME FACULTY

JOHN A. MILLER*, (Dean and Professor)**, born Milwaukee, Wisconsin, July 2, 1950; admitted to bar, 1976, Kentucky. *Education:* University of Kentucky (B.A., 1972; J.D., 1976); University of Florida (LL.M., 1987). ***COURSES: Legal Accounting, Business Planning, Estate Planning, Evidence, Legal Research, Taxation, Federal.

MARK DAVID ANDERSON*, (Professor)**, born Minot, North Dakota, August 29, 1951; admitted to bar, 1977, Minnesota. *Education:* Macalester College (B.A., 1973); University of Chicago (J.D., 1977). ***COURSES: Antitrust, Business Associations, Criminal Law, Trademarks and Unfair Competition.

D. BENJAMIN BEARD*, (Professor of Law and Associate Dean)**, born Cleveland, Ohio, November 4, 1954; admitted to bar, 1982, Ohio. *Education:* University of Cincinnati (B.A., 1977); Case Western Reserve University (J.D., 1982). ***COURSES: Commercial Law, Commercial Paper, International Business Transactions, Property, Sales, Surety.

ELIZABETH BARKER BRANDT*, (Professor)**, born Pittsburgh, Pennsylvania, August 26, 1957; admitted to bar, 1982, Ohio. *Education:* College of Wooster (B.A., 1979); Case Western Reserve University (J.D., 1982). ***COURSES: Legal Research and Writing, Trusts, Wills, Community Property, Estates, Family Law.

REBECCA BRATSPIES*, (Associate Professor)**, admitted to bar, 1992, Pennsylvania. *Education:* Wesleyan University (B.A., 1987); University of Pennsylvania (J.D., 1992). ***COURSES: Property, Administrative Law, Environmental Law. ***Email:*** rbratspi@uidaho.edu

DENNIS C. COLSON*, (Professor)**, born Grant, Nebraska, March 9, 1945; admitted to bar, 1971, California; 1971, Colorado. *Education:* University of Northern Colorado (B.A., 1968); University of Denver (J.D., 1971). ***COURSES: Contracts, Native American Law.

NEIL EDWARD FRANKLIN*, (Professor)**, born Orange, California, November 3, 1944; admitted to bar, 1975, California; 1976, Idaho. *Education:* University of Oregon (B.S., 1966); Golden Gate University (J.D., 1974). ***COURSES: Civil Procedure, Clinical Teaching, Community Property, Constitutional Law, Family Law, Law and Politics of South Africa.

DALE D. GOBLE*, (Professor)**, born Boise, Idaho, November 28, 1947; admitted to bar, 1978, Oregon. *Education:* Columbia University (A.B., 1975); University of Oregon (J.D., 1978). ***COURSES: Administrative Law, Energy Law, Environmental Law, Natural Resources, Torts.

JOHN J. HASKO*, (Director of the Law Library and Associate Professor of Law)**, born New York City, New York, January 3, 1945; admitted to bar, 1980, Texas. *Education:* Siena College (B.A., 1965); Fordham University (M.A., 1967, 1970); St. Mary's University (J.D., 1980); University of Illinois, Urbana-Champaign (M.S., 1981). ***COURSES: Legal Research and Writing.

JOANN H. HENDERSON*, (Professor)**, born Bonners Ferry, Idaho, July 30, 1942; admitted to bar, 1973, Washington. *Education:* University of Idaho (B.A., 1971; J.D., 1973). ***COURSES: Contracts, Creditors Rights, Secured Transactions, Bankruptcy.

(This Listing Continued)

UNIVERSITY OF IDAHO COLLEGE OF LAW—Continued

MAUREEN E. LAFLIN**, (Associate Professor and Director of Clinical Programs)**, born St. Louis, Missouri, March 21, 1955; admitted to bar, 1982, Missouri; 1984, Pennsylvania; 1992, Idaho and U.S. Supreme Court. *Education:* University of Dayton (B.S., 1977); St. Louis University (J.D., 1982). ***COURSES:*** Clinical, Skills Training.

D. CRAIG LEWIS**, (Professor)**, born Champaign, Illinois, September 9, 1944; admitted to bar, 1969, Colorado; 1977, Idaho. *Education:* Northwestern University (B.S./B.A., 1966); Yale University (J.D., 1969). ***COURSES:*** Civil Procedure, Clinical Teaching, Evidence, Trial and Appellate Practice.

MONIQUE C. LILLARD**, (Professor)**, born Los Angeles, California, September 22, 1957; admitted to bar, 1983, California. *Education:* Stanford University (B.A., 1979); University of California at Los Angeles (J.D., 1983). ***COURSES:*** Labor and Employment Law, Remedies, Torts.

JAMES S. MACDONALD**, (Professor)**, born Lynwood, California, June 27, 1944; admitted to bar, 1969, Texas. *Education:* Pomona College (B.A., 1966); University of California, Berkeley (J.D., 1969). ***COURSES:*** Legal Accounting, Constitutional Law, Federal Courts, Securities Regulation, Sports Law.

MONICA SCHURTMAN**, (Associate Professor)**, *Education:* State University of New York (B.A., 1982); New York University School of Law (J.D., 1990). ***COURSES:*** Legal Aid Clinic.

ARTHUR D. SMITH, JR.**, (Professor)**, born Logan, Utah, November 6, 1942; admitted to bar, 1968, District of Columbia. *Education:* Utah State University (B.S., 1965); George Washington University (J.D., 1968). ***COURSES:*** Environmental Law, Natural Resource Law.

SHELDON A. VINCENTI**, (Professor & Dean Emeritus)**, born Ogden, Utah, September 4, 1938; admitted to bar, 1963, Utah. *Education:* Harvard University (A.B., 1960; J.D., 1963). ***COURSES:*** Criminal Law, Criminal Procedure, Family Law, Jurisprudence, Conflicts.

UNIVERSITY OF ILLINOIS COLLEGE OF LAW

504 EAST PENNSYLVANIA AVENUE
CHAMPAIGN, ILLINOIS 61820
Telephone: (217) 333-0931
Fax: (217) 244-1478

ABA Approved Since 1923

The University of Illinois College of Law was founded in 1897 and has a long, proud history. Today the College stands at the forefront of legal education, with a reputation for excellence in both teaching and scholarship.

Each entering class of just under 200 students is divided into three sections. Students take classes and study together in these smaller sections -- an arrangement that is conducive to building cooperation and learning from one another. The first-year curriculum concentrates on basic legal areas, with classes in contracts, torts, property, criminal law and procedure, constitutional law, civil procedure, legal research and writing, and introduction to advocacy. A unique feature of the first-year curriculum is the second-semester course Statutory Interpretation. Students are permitted to elect one of several sections of this course, each focusing on a different statutory scheme. Statutes covered have included the federal Bankruptcy Code, the Copyright Act, federal welfare law statutes, and the Americans with Disabilities Act. In each section, students are given an in-depth introduction to the role of statutes in our legal system and the various techniques for statutory interpretation.

Classes in the second and third years are almost entirely elective; only the course in professional responsibility is required. There is also an advanced writing requirement. Most classes after the first year have fewer than thirty students, allowing for more discussion and interaction. The curriculum is broad, offering courses ranging from Law & Regulation of Cyberspace to Modern Environmental Theory to Alternative Dispute Resolution. There are a number of practical skills courses, including Lawyer as a Negotiator, Problems in Estate Planning, and an extensive Trial Advocacy program. The College also has an in-house clinic, serving the needs of low-income clients. Students can also receive credit for clinical experience by working in one of the many legal services offices in the area. Illinois also offers a number of joint degree programs, allowing students to specialize and integrate their law school courses with other disciplines.

Illinois students are especially active. The student body size of approximately 600 fosters camaraderie and support among the students. Although law school is a competitive enterprise, Illinois students seek opportunities to work together and learn from one another. The small size of the College also allows students to become actively involved in the College's more than thirty extracurricular organizations, combining professional training, recreation, and opportunities for making friends. Students bring many speakers to the law school, and co-sponsor many events and activities throughout the year. Illinois students also have a strong commitment to public service; many of the student organizations participate in weekly and annual community service activities, and the Public Interest Law Foundation started a national work-a-day program where law students across the country volunteer for public-service projects on the same day. More than 10,000 students from 100 law schools have participated.

Students also write for the *University of Illinois Law Review,* the *Elder Law Journal,* the *Journal of Law, Technology & Policy*, and the Recent Developments Section of the *Illinois Bar Journal.* They conduct and participate in competitions such as Frederick Green Moot Court, Jessup (International) Moot Court, Frederick Douglass Moot Court, the ABA Client Counseling Competition, and the ABA Negotiations Competition. They participate in law school governance through the Student Bar Association and by serving as student members of faculty committees, including the curriculum committee, the admissions and scholarship committee, the placement and clerkship committee, and the international studies committee.

The faculty at Illinois have an exceptional record of achievement in both teaching and scholarship. *The Ultimate Guide to Top Law Schools* recently awarded Illinois faculty an "A" for both quality of teaching and faculty accessibility. Illinois was one of only a few schools to achieve distinction in both categories. In addition to the faculty providing outstanding classroom instruction, faculty and students at Illinois have an unusually high degree of interaction; students talk with professors in their offices, in the law school's Pavilion, at coffee houses, and at a variety of social events. This interaction contributes to the overall sense of community and camaraderie at the College. While accessible, Illinois faculty also have a strong record of scholarship. An independent survey of faculty scholarship ranked Illinois first in the number of pages published in top-twenty journals, excluding in-house articles. Many of the leading case books and treatises have been authored by Illinois faculty, and often students in Illinois classes use a book written by their professor.

(This Listing Continued)

UNIVERSITY OF ILLINOIS COLLEGE OF LAW —Continued

The building is also conducive to learning. Our law library ranks sixth nationally in number of titles, and is designated as a federal depository. A recent building renovation has resulted in a spacious, comfortable environment, including a new student lounge and dining area, new offices for student organizations, additional smaller classrooms, spaces where students can study together in small groups, and the central pavilion, which is a natural meeting place for students, faculty, and distinguished visitors.

The University of Illinois College of Law continues, 100 years after it was founded, to offer a solid legal education in all aspects.

Dean: Thomas Mengler (217) 333-9857
Admissions: Ann K. Perry (217) 333-1097
Financial Aid: Ann K. Perry (217) 333-1097
Library: Janis Johnston (217) 333-2914
Placement: Virginia Vermillion (217) 244-0736
Alumni Affairs: Jeffrey Fehrenbacher (217) 244-0001

FULL TIME FACULTY

THOMAS M. MENGLER*, (Dean and Professor of Law)**, born Chicago, Illinois, May 18, 1953; admitted to bar, 1981, Illinois; 1982, District of Columbia. *Education:* Carleton College (B.A., 1975); University of Texas, Austin (M.A., 1978; J.D., 1981). ***COURSES: Civil Procedure, Complex Litigation, Class Actions. ***Email:*** tmengler@law.uiuc.edu

CARLOS A. BALL*, (Professor of Law)**, born Caracas, Venezuela, October 3, 1964; admitted to bar, 1990, Massachusetts; 1991, New York. *Education:* Tufts University (B.A., 1986); Columbia University (J.D., 1990); Cambridge University (LL.M., 1995). ***COURSES: Property, Disability, Jurisprudence, Sexual Orientation and the Law. ***Email:*** cball@law.uiuc.edu

FRANCIS A. BOYLE*, (Professor of Law)**, born Chicago, Illinois, March 25, 1950; admitted to bar, 1977, Massachusetts. *Education:* University of Chicago (A.B., 1971); Harvard (A.M., 1978; J.D. (*magna cum laude*), 1976; Ph.D., 1983). ***COURSES: International, Jurisprudence, Criminal, Constitutional, Human Rights, Latinos. ***Email:*** FBOYLE@LAW.UIUC.EDU

LONNIE T. BROWN*, (Assistant Professor)**, born Orlando, Florida, August 29, 1964; admitted to bar, 1989, Georgia. *Education:* Emory University (B.A., 1986); Vanderbilt Law School (J.D., 1989). ***COURSES: Professional Responsibility, Civil Procedure. ***Email:*** brown14@law.uiuc.edu

JOHN DAVID COLOMBO*, (Professor of Law)**, born Herrin, Illinois, April 30, 1956; admitted to bar, 1982, Georgia. *Education:* University of Illinois (B.A., 1978; J.D., 1981). ***COURSES: Tax, Tax-Exempt Organizations.

WILLIAM JAMES DAVEY*, (Edwin M. Adams Professor of Law)**, born Albion, Michigan, April 25, 1949; admitted to bar, 1974, Michigan; 1979, New York. *Education:* University of Michigan (B.A., 1971; J.D., 1974). ***COURSES: International Trade Law. ***Email:*** wdavey@law.uiuc.edu

ELLEN E. DEASON*, (Associate Professor of Law)**, admitted to bar, 1989, District of Columbia. *Education:* Carleton College (B.A., 1972); Oregon State University (M.S., 1975); University of Michigan Law School (J.D., 1985). ***COURSES: Civil Procedure, Alternative Dispute Resolution, Law & Science, Choice of Courts & Law. ***Email:*** edeason@law.uiuc.edu

MATTHEW WILLIAM FINKIN*, (Albert J. Harno Professor of Law)**, born New York, New York, April 7, 1943; admitted to bar, 1968, New York. *Education:* Ohio Wesleyan (B.A., 1963); New York University (LL.B., 1967); Yale (LL.M., 1973). ***COURSES: Labor Law.

ERIC T. FREYFOGLE*, (Max L. Rowe Professor of Law)**, born Decatur, Illinois, January 21, 1952; admitted to bar, 1976, District of Columbia; 1980, Indiana. *Education:* Lehigh University (B.A., 1973); University of Michigan Law School (J.D., 1976). ***COURSES: Property, Environmental Law, Natural Resources.

THOMAS B. GINSBURG*, (Assistant Professor)**, born Berkeley, California, February 22, 1967; admitted to bar, 1997, California. *Education:* Berkeley (B.A., 1989; Ph.D., 1999); Boalt Hall (J.D., 1997). ***COURSES: Torts, Comparative Law, International Law. ***Email:*** tginsbur@law.uiuc.edu

ORA FRED HARRIS, JR.*, (Professor of Law)**, born Camden, Arkansas, May 9, 1948; admitted to bar, 1973, Arkansas. *Education:* University of Arkansas (B.A., 1970; J.D., 1973). ***COURSES: Products Liability, Environmental Law, Insurance, Toxic Torts. ***Email:*** fharris@Law.uiuc.edu

RICHARD LEE KAPLAN*, (Professor of Law)**, born Indianapolis, Indiana, October 28, 1948; admitted to bar, 1976, Texas. *Education:* Indiana University (B.S., 1970); Yale University (J.D., 1976). ***COURSES: Federal Income Taxation, Tax Policy, Elder Law. ***Email:*** rkaplan@law.uiuc.edu

JAY P. KESAN*, (Assistant Professor)**, admitted to bar, 1997, Virginia; 1998, District of Columbia. *Education:* University of Texas (M.S., 1986; Ph.D., 1989); Georgetown University (J.D., 1996). ***COURSES: Patent Law, Internet Law, Intellectual Property. ***Email:*** kesan@uiuc.edu

KIT KINPORTS*, (Professor of Law)**, born Chicago, Illinois, November 28, 1954; admitted to bar, 1982, District of Columbia; 1996, Illinois. *Education:* Brown University (A.B., 1976); University of Pennsylvania (J.D., 1980). ***COURSES: Criminal Law & Procedure, Civil Rights, Feminist Jurisprudence. ***Email:*** KKINPORT@LAW.UIUC.EDU

ANDREW D. LEIPOLD*, (Associate Dean and Professor of Law)**, born Plattsburgh, New York, February, 15, 1960; admitted to bar, 1987, Pennsylvania; 1994, Illinois. *Education:* Boston University (B.S., 1982); University of Virginia (J.D., 1985). ***COURSES: Criminal Law, Criminal Procedure, Supreme Court. ***Email:*** aleipold@law.uiuc.edu

PETER B. MAGGS*, (Peer & Sarah Pedersen Professor of Law)**, born Durham, North Carolina, July 24, 1938; admitted to bar, 1962, District of Columbia. *Education:* Harvard College (A.B., 1957); Harvard Law School (J.D., 1961). ***COURSES: Contracts, Intellectual Property, Statutory Interpretation, Russian Law. ***Email:*** P-maggs@uiuc.edu

PHILIP J. MCCONNAUGHAY*, (Professor of Law)**, born January 5, 1953; admitted to bar, 1978, Illinois; 1979, California; 1983, District of Columbia. ***COURSES: International Litigation and Arbitration, Copyright, International Business Transactions, Law and Economic Development. ***Email:*** pmcconna@law.uiuc.edu

(This Listing Continued)

UNIVERSITY OF ILLINOIS COLLEGE OF LAW —Continued

JOHN HARRISON MCCORD*, (Professor of Law Emeritus)**, born Oceanside, New York, December 22, 1934; admitted to bar, 1960, New York; 1964, Illinois. *Education:* Fordham College (A.B., 1957); St. John's University School of Law (J.D., 1960); University of Illinois (LL.M., 1965). ***COURSES: Federal Taxation, Estate Planning, Wills and Trusts, Business Planning.

DAVID D. MEYER*, (Associate Professor)**, born Grinnell, Iowa, November 4, 1961; admitted to bar, 1992, Michigan; 1995, Illinois. *Education:* University of Michigan (B.A., 1984; J.D., 1990). ***COURSES: Family Law, Constitutional Law.

JOHN E. NOWAK*, (David C. Baum Professor of Law)**, born Chicago, Illinois, January 2, 1947; admitted to bar, 1972, Illinois. *Education:* Marquette University (A.B., 1968); University of Illinois (J.D., 1971). ***COURSES: Constitutional Law, Criminal Procedure, State Taxation. ***Email:*** JNowak@Law.uiuc.edu

RICHARD W. PAINTER*, (Professor)**, born October 3, 1961; admitted to bar, 1988, New York; 1991, Connecticut. *Education:* Harvard College (B.A., 1984); Yale Law School (J.D., 1987). ***COURSES: Professional Responsibility, Partnership & Corporations, Securities Mkt. Reg. & Corporate Finance. ***Email:*** rpainter@law.uiuc.edu

JAMES E. PFANDER*, (Professor of Law)**, born Columbia, Missouri, September 21, 1956; admitted to bar, 1983, District of Columbia; 1989, Illinois. *Education:* University of Missouri (B.A., 1978); University of Virginia (J.D., 1982). ***COURSES: Civil Procedure, Conflicts of Law, Federal Courts.

LAURIE REYNOLDS*, (Professor of Law)**, born Mt. Kisco, New York, September 3, 1950; admitted to bar, 1980, Illinois. *Education:* Georgetown University (B.S., 1972); University of Illinois (M.A., 1974; J.D., 1980). ***COURSES: Property, Land Use, State and Local Government, Federal Indian Law. ***Email:*** lreynold@law.uiuc.edu

DARIA ROITHMAYR*, (Associate Professor of Law)**, admitted to bar, 1990, California; 1992, Arizona. *Education:* UCLA (B.S., 1984); Georgetown University Law Center (J.D., 1990). ***COURSES: Civil Procedure, Evidence, Critical Race Theory. ***Email:*** droithma@law.uiuc.edu

STEPHEN F. ROSS*, (Professor of Law)**, born Hollywood, California, May 20, 1955; admitted to bar, 1979, California; 1981, District of Columbia. *Education:* University of California (B.A., 1976; J.D., 1979). ***COURSES: Sports, Antitrust, Statutory Interpretation, Canadian Law. ***Email:*** sross@law.uiuc.edu

RONALD DANIEL ROTUNDA*, (Albert E. Jenner, Jr. Professor of Law)**, born Blue Island, Illinois, February 14, 1945; admitted to bar, 1971, New York and District of Columbia; 1975, Illinois. *Education:* Harvard University (A.B., 1967; J.D., 1970). ***COURSES: Constitutional Law, Professional Responsibility. ***Email:*** rrotunda@law.uiuc.edu

ELAINE W. SHOBEN*, (Edward W. Cleary Professor of Law)**, born Glen Ridge, New Jersey, January 18, 1948; admitted to bar, 1974, California. *Education:* Barnard College (A.B., 1970); Hastings College of Law (J.D., 1974). ***COURSES: Employment Discrimination, Remedies, Torts.

CHARLES JORDAN TABB*, (Professor)**, born Dallas, Texas, November 1, 1955; admitted to bar, 1980, Texas. *Education:* Vanderbilt University (B.A., 1977); University of Virginia (J.D., 1980). ***COURSES: Bankruptcy, Commercial Law, Contracts. ***Email:*** ctabb@law.uiuc.edu

NINA W. TARR*, (Professor of Law)**, born Boston, Massachusetts, December 15, 1952; admitted to bar, 1979, Minnesota; 1987, Illinois. *Education:* Southern Illinois University (B.S., 1973); Washington University (M.A., 1975); Iowa (J.D., 1979). ***COURSES: Clinic Director. ***Email:*** NTARR@LAW.UIUC.EDU

CHARLES T. TERRY*, (Professor)**, born Washington, D.C.; admitted to bar, 1981, California. *Education:* Stanford University (B.A., 1967); Southwestern (J.D., 1981); New York University (LL.M. 1982). ***COURSES: Federal Income Tax. ***Email:*** cterry@law.uiuc.edu

THOMAS SHAHAN ULEN*, (Alumni Distinguished Professor of Law)**, born Lebanon, Indiana, November 4, 1946. *Education:* Dartmouth College (B.A., 1968); University of Oxford (B.Phil., 1972); Stanford University (Ph.D., 1979). ***COURSES: Law and Economics, Regulation, Quantitative Methods. ***Email:*** tulen@law.uiuc.edu

CYNTHIA ANN WILLIAMS*, (Associate Professor of Law)**, born Rochester, New York, October 25, 1955; admitted to bar, 1990, New York. *Education:* University of Virginia; University of California at Berkeley (B.A., 1981); New York University (J.D., 1989). ***COURSES: Securities Regulation, Business Organizations, Corporate Responsibility, Torts.

UNIVERSITY OF IOWA COLLEGE OF LAW

BOYD LAW BUILDING
IOWA CITY, IOWA 52242
Telephone: (319) 335-9034
Fax: (319) 335-9019

ABA Approved Since 1923.

The University of Iowa College of Law, founded in 1865, is the oldest law school west of the Mississippi River. Over 700 students of the College and a full-time faculty of 50 are engaged in a cooperative study of law, legal institutions, professional ethics, the role of law in public policy matters, and the intersection of law and other disciplines. Six members of the faculty hold Ph.D. degrees in law-related disciplines. The College's 12-1 student-faculty ratio is one of the ten best in American legal education. Through traditional Socratic classes, research seminars, closely-supervised writing exercises, ambitious professional skills training programs and clinical experiences, the College seeks to produce public-spirited leaders who will be thoughtful advisors, forceful advocates, creative policymakers and innovative scholars.

The College conducts business in the magnificent Boyd Law Building, a 200,000 sq. ft. facility opened in 1986. Its spacious library, three courtrooms, clinic suite, building-wide audio-visual system and extensive use of computer technologies are still recognized as state-of-the-art features in an educational facility specially designed for modern legal training.

The College is home to one of the nation's premier law libraries. The Library has the second largest collection of legal titles among public law schools. It has comfortable seating for 700 patrons, including 440 private study carrels. The library staff numbers 25 professionals. The Library boasts a fully computerized information retrieval system. Westlaw and Lexis are available at numerous terminals for training and research activities, while an online access system for information sources provides instant information about all catalogued materials.

(This Listing Continued)

UNIVERSITY OF IOWA COLLEGE OF LAW—Continued

The College celebrates diversity in its students and faculty. It enjoys the full range of racial and ethnic diversity among its students and faculty, with good representation of African-Americans, Asian-Americans, Hispanic-Americans, and Native-Americans. Starting in 1967, the College undertook one of the nation's first and most aggressive affirmative-action programs aimed at attracting a more racially and ethnically diverse student body. Its success in this area is evident given a nearly 16% minority population in the current student body (compared with a 4% minority population in the state of Iowa generally).

The College offers a challenging curriculum that is carefully balanced between substantive courses and skills training programs, including a highly active in-house Legal Clinic. Iowa's writing program--one of the strongest among law schools nationwide--is an integral part of all students' academic experience. Students take one "small section" class both semesters of their first year. In these classes full-time professors focus individually on the development of each student's analytical, research, writing, and advocacy skills. The College also requires five additional writing units at the upper level. This requirement can be fulfilled through a range of options, including writing for one of the school's four law journals, participating in the clinical program, completing exercises in appellate advocacy, or enrolling in specific seminars or independent study projects. A unique Writing Resource Center serves as an extension of classroom writing instruction at the College and offers students assistance with a broad range of writing tasks, from class assignments, seminar papers, articles for law journals and symposium presentations, to letters of application and resumes. The Center and the Writing Program as a whole exemplify the personalized attention and dedication to individual learning for which the College is renowned in legal education circles, as does the recent creation of a full-time position for an Academic Achievement Director, currently filled by a Ph.D. in educational psychology.

The College is proud of its four student-run scholarly journals. The *Iowa Law Review* has served as a scholarly legal journal since 1915, analyzing developments in the law and recommending new paths for the law to follow. It is ranked among the top twenty legal periodicals in the country on the basis of the frequency with which it is cited. The *Journal of Corporate Law* is the nation's oldest student-run legal periodical specializing in corporate law. It provides the legal and academic communities with high-quality articles on corporate issues and business law. *Transnational Law and Contemporary Problems,* which began publishing in 1991, addresses legal issues confronting the global community. It has already earned an excellent reputation for its symposia on such issues as world food policy and global environmental regulation. A fourth journal, The Journal of Gender, Race and Justice, published its first volume in 1996-97.

The College admits a limited number of students each year to pursue studies in international and comparative law leading to the degree of Master of Laws (LL.M.). The College also offers programs abroad. It is one of a consortium of seven American law schools that jointly operates a one-semester program in London each spring. The College also offers a month of intensive coursework in a summer program at Arcachon, France.

Over the years, the College has enjoyed great success in preparing men and women to be professional and civic leaders. Currently three of the seven justices on the Iowa Supreme Court are Iowa graduates. In this century Iowa graduates have served as U.S. senators and representatives, federal circuit and district judges, state governors, and presidents of the ABA, of major universities and of the country's largest corporations. Iowa has also been a leading producer of American law teachers. The College is firmly resolved that its traditional role of training young men and women for positions of leadership will continue at full strength in the 21st Century.

Dean: N. William Hines (319) 335-9034
Associate Dean for Academic Affairs: Eric G. Andersen
Associate Dean for Law Library: Arthur E. Bonfield (319) 335-9016
Associate Dean for International Programs: John C. Reitz
Associate Dean for Student Affairs: Linda McGuire
Acting Admissions and Financial Aid Director: Susan Palmer (319) 335-9142
Career Services Director: Karen Klonda (319) 335-9011
Development Director: Mark Wunder (319) 335-3305
Writing Center Director: Nancy Jones (319) 335-9083
Academic Achievement Director: Martha Peters

FULL TIME FACULTY

N. WILLIAM HINES*, (Dean and Joseph F. Rosenfield Professor)**, born Chicago, Illinois, 1936; admitted to bar, 1961, Kansas; 1965, Iowa. *Education:* Baker University (A.B., 1958; L.L.D., 1999); University of Kansas (LL.B., 1961). ***COURSES: Environmental Law, Land Use, Real Property.

PATRICIA ACTON*, (Clinical Professor)**, born Cedar Rapids, Iowa, 1949; admitted to bar, 1974, Iowa. *Education:* University of Iowa (B.A., 1971; J.D., 1974). ***COURSES: Commercial Law, Entertainment Law, Legal Clinic, Trusts and Estates.

JOHN ALLEN*, (Clinical Associate Professor)**, born Detroit, Michigan, 1955; admitted to bar, 1981, Iowa. *Education:* St. Olaf College (B.A., 1977); University of Illinois (J.D., 1980). ***COURSES: Poverty Law, Trial Advocacy.

ERIC G. ANDERSEN*, (Professor and Associate Dean)**, born Los Angeles, California, March 9, 1950; admitted to bar, 1977, California; 1978, District of Columbia. *Education:* Brigham Young University (B.A., 1974; J.D., 1977). ***COURSES: Contracts, Family Law, Roman Law.

DAVID C. BALDUS*, (Joe B. Tye Professor)**, born Wheeling, West Virginia, June 23, 1935; admitted to bar, 1965, Pennsylvania. *Education:* Dartmouth College (A.B., 1957); University of Pittsburgh (M.A., 1962); Yale University (LL.B., 1964; LL.M., 1969). ***COURSES: Civil Rights, Criminal Law, Evidence, Law and Science.

PATRICK B. BAUER*, (Professor)**, born Minneapolis, Minnesota, December, 1950; admitted to bar, 1975, Minnesota; 1979, Iowa. *Education:* Wesleyan University (B.A., 1972); University of Chicago (J.D., 1975). ***COURSES: Creditors Rights, Real Estate Transactions.

RANDALL PETER BEZANSON*, (Charles E. Floete Professor)**, born 1946; admitted to bar, 1971, Iowa; 1988, Virginia. *Education:* Northwestern University (B.S.B.A., 1968); University of Iowa College of Law (J.D., 1971). ***COURSES: Administrative Law, Constitutional Law, Law & Medicine (Bioethics), Law & Technology, Mass Communication Law.

***STEPHANOS BIBAS*, (Associate Professor)**, born Queens, New York, July 2, 1969; admitted to bar, 1995, Virginia; District of Columbia, 1996. *Education:* Columbia University (B.A., 1989); Oxford University

(This Listing Continued)

UNIVERSITY OF IOWA COLLEGE OF LAW—Continued

(B.A., 1991); Yale Law School (J.D., 1994). ***COURSES:*** Criminal Law, Criminal Procedure. ***Email:*** bibas@philo.org

PETER D. BLANCK,* (Professor)**, born Roslyn, New York, August 27, 1957; admitted to bar, 1986, Massachusetts; 1987, District of Columbia. *Education:* University of Rochester (B.A., 1979); Harvard University (Ph.D., 1982); Stamford University (J.D., 1986). ***COURSES: Contracts, Law and Social Science.

ARTHUR E. BONFIELD,* (John Murray Professor and Associate Dean)**, born New York, New York, May 12, 1936; admitted to bar, 1961, Connecticut; 1966, Iowa. *Education:* Brooklyn College (B.A., 1956); Yale University (J.D., 1960; LL.M., 1961). ***COURSES: Administrative Law, Constitutional Law.

WILLARD LEE BOYD,* (Professor)**, born St. Paul, Minnesota, March 29, 1927; admitted to bar, 1951, Minnesota; 1958, Iowa. *Education:* University of Minnesota (B.S.L., 1949; LL.B., 1951); University of Michigan (LL.M., 1952; S.J.D., 1962). ***COURSES: Philanthropy & Non-Profit Institutions.

MARGARET F. BRINIG,* (Edward Howry Professor)**, born Milwaukee, Wisconsin, April 15, 1949; admitted to bar, 1973, New Jersey; 1976; District of Columbia; 1979, Virginia. *Education:* Duke University (B.A., 1970); Seton Hall University (J.D., 1973); George Mason University (M.A., 1993; Ph.D., 1994). ***COURSES: Alternative Dispute Resolution, Contracts, Family Law.

STEVE J. BURTON,* (William G. Hammond Professor)**, born Los Angeles, California, January 26, 1949; admitted to bar, 1973, California. *Education:* University of California at Los Angeles (B.A., 1970); University of Southern California (J.D., 1973). ***COURSES: Contracts and Sales Transactions, Contracts, Introduction to Legal Reasoning, Jurisprudence.

WILLIAM G. BUSS,* (O.K. Patton Professor)**, born Akron, Ohio, 1933; admitted to bar, 1961, Massachusetts. *Education:* Yale University (B.A., 1955); Harvard University (LL.B., 1960). ***COURSES: Constitutional Law, Education Law.

PATRICIA A. CAIN,* (Aliber Family Professor)**, born Columbus, Georgia, June 10, 1945; admitted to bar, 1974, Alabama; 1982, Texas. *Education:* Vassar College (B.A., 1968); University of Georgia (J.D., 1973). ***COURSES: Estates; Property; Taxation, Federal; Women and the Law.

JONATHAN C. CARLSON,* (Professor)**, born Minot, North Dakota, April 12, 1954; admitted to bar, 1981, District of Columbia. *Education:* McGill College (B.A., 1976); University of Chicago (J.D., 1979). ***COURSES: Commercial Law, Criminal Law, International Transactions.

ENRIQUE R. CARRASCO,* (Professor)**, born Chicago, Illinois, June, 1956; admitted to bar, 1986, District of Columbia. *Education:* Indiana University (B.A., 1980); Georgetown University (J.D., 1986). ***COURSES: Contracts, International Law, Latin American Legal Affairs.

ROBERT N. CLINTON,* (Wiley B. Rutledge Professor)**, born Detroit, Michigan, August 1, 1946; admitted to bar, 1971, Illinois; 1973, Iowa. *Education:* University of Michigan (B.A., 1968); University of Chicago (J.D., 1971). ***COURSES: Copyrights, Federal Jurisdiction, American Indian Law, Constitutional Law.

LOIS K. COX,* (Clinical Professor)**, born Kansas City, Missouri, June, 1949; admitted to bar, 1978, Iowa. *Education:* Rice University (B.A., 1971); Tufts University (M.A., 1973); Boston University (J.D., 1978). ***COURSES: Clinical Teaching, Poverty Law.

MARCELLA DAVID,* (Professor)**, born New York, New York, September 13, 1964; admitted to bar, 1993, New York. *Education:* Rensselaer Polytechnic Institute (B.S., 1986); University of Michigan (J.D., 1989). ***COURSES: Public International Law, Civil Procedure, Trial Skills, Equal Protection.

ANN LAQUER ESTIN,* (Professor)**, born Philadelphia, Pennsylvania, February 3, 1956; admitted to bar, 1983, Colorado. *Education:* University of Pennsylvania (J.D., 1983). ***COURSES: Contracts, Family Law, Professional Responsibility.

JOSEPHINE GITTLER,* (Professor)**, born Richmond, Virginia, May, 1943; admitted to bar, 1969, Connecticut. *Education:* Northwestern University (J.D., 1968). ***COURSES: Criminal Law, Criminal Procedure, Juvenile Law, Mediation, Mediation Clinic.

HERBERT J. HOVENKAMP,* (Ben and Dorothy Willie Professor)**, born Dowagiac, Michigan, August, 1948. *Education:* Calvin College (B.A., 1969); University of Utah (M.A., 1971; Ph.D., 1976); University of Texas (J.D., 1978). ***COURSES: Advanced Antitrust, American Legal History, Property.

MARK DAVID JANIS,* (Professor)**, born Blue Island, Illinois, August 15, 1964; admitted to bar, 1989, Indiana. *Education:* Purdue University (B.S., 1986); Indiana University (J.D., 1989). ***COURSES: Intellectual Property, Natural Resources, Patents, Copyrights.

KENNETH J. KRESS,* (Professor)**, born Hollywood, California, August 27, 1951. *Education:* University of California at Los Angeles (B.A., 1978); University of California at Berkeley (M.A., 1983; J.D., 1985; Ph.D., 1989). ***COURSES: Jurisprudence, Products Liability, Torts, Law & Psychiatry.

SHELDON F. KURTZ,* (Percy Bordwell Professor)**, born Syracuse, New York, May, 1943; admitted to bar, 1967, New York. *Education:* Syracuse University (A.B., 1964; J.D., 1967). ***COURSES: Estates, Health Law, Property, Trusts.

MARC LINDER,* (Professor)**, born New York, New York, March 15, 1946. *Education:* University of Chicago (B.A., 1966); Princeton University (M.A., 1971; Ph.D., 1973); Harvard University (J.D., 1983). ***COURSES: Labor Law, Law of Low-Paid Workers, Contracts.

JEAN C. LOVE,* (Martha Ellen Tye Professor)**, born Bremerton, Washington, September, 1943; admitted to bar, 1968, Wisconsin. *Education:* University of Wisconsin (B.A., 1965; J.D., 1968). ***COURSES: Civil Rights, Federal Courts, Remedies, Sex-Based Discrimination, Torts.

BARRY D. MATSUMOTO,* (Associate Professor)**, born Heart Mountain, Wyoming, March, 1945; admitted to bar, 1970, Washington. *Education:* University of Washington (B.A, 1967; J.D., 1970). ***COURSES: Constitutional Law, Environmental Law, Legal Profession, Local Government.

LINDA MCGUIRE,* (Associate Dean for Student Affairs)**, admitted to bar, 1982, Iowa. *Education:* State University of New York at Oneonta (B.S., 1970); Bowling Green State University (M.A., 1971); University of Iowa (J.D., 1982). ***COURSES: Constitutional Law, Criminal Law, Family Law, Trial Advocacy, Professional Responsibility, Domestic Abuse Law.

RETA NOBLETT-FELD,* (Clinical Professor)**, born Mt. Pleasant, Iowa, April, 1943; admitted to bar, 1983, Iowa. *Education:* University of Iowa (B.A., 1980; J.D., 1983). ***COURSES: Clinical Teaching.

***MARK J. OSIEL,* (Professor)**, born Los Angeles, California, June 5, 1955; admitted to bar, 1988, Massachusetts. *Education:* University of California at Berkeley (B.A., 1977); Harvard University (Ph.D.; J.D.,

(This Listing Continued)

UNIVERSITY OF IOWA COLLEGE OF LAW—Continued

1987). ***COURSES:*** International Transactions, Legal Profession, Remedies.

GEOFFREY W. R. PALMER*, (Visiting Professor)**, born Nelson, New Zealand, April, 1942. *Education:* Victoria University (B.A., 1964; LL.B., 1965); University of Chicago (J.D., 1967). ***COURSES: Torts, Global Environmental, Comparative Constitutional Law.

TODD E. PETTYS*, (Associate Professor)**, born Longview, Washington; admitted to bar, 1997, Washington. *Education:* Seattle Pacific University (B.A., 1988); University of North Carolina (J.D., 1995). ***COURSES: Constitutional Law, Evidence, Federal Courts.

MARGARET RAYMOND*, (Professor)**, born New York, New York, March 7, 1960; admitted to bar, 1986, New York; 1990, Oregon. *Education:* Carleton College (B.A., 1980); Columbia University School of Law (J.D., 1985). ***COURSES: Criminal Law, Criminal Procedure, Professional Responsibility.

JOHN C. REITZ*, (Professor)**, born Chicago, Illinois, December 4, 1948; admitted to bar, 1975, District of Columbia. *Education:* Harvard University (B.A., 1970); University of Michigan (J.D., 1975). ***COURSES: Comparative Law, Contracts.

HILLARY A. SALE*, (Associate Professor)**, born Denver, Colorado, May 14, 1961; admitted to bar, 1994, Massachusetts; 1994, Eighth Circuit; 1995 First Circuit. *Education:* Boston University (B.A., 1983; M.A. 1983); Harvard (J.D., 1993). ***COURSES: Contracts Corporations Securities, Corporate Governance. ***Email:*** hsale@lawnet-po.law.uiowa.edu

LEONARD SANDLER*, (Clinical Professor)**, born New York, New York, February, 1950; admitted to bar, 1981, Maryland. *Education:* Northeastern University (B.S., 1978); University of Maryland (J.D., 1981). ***COURSES: Clinical Teaching, Legal Aspects of AIDS.

BARBARA A. SCHWARTZ*, (Clinical Professor)**, born Detroit, Michigan, June, 1945; admitted to bar, 1975, Michigan. *Education:* University of Michigan (B.A., 1967; M.A., 1968); Wayne State University (J.D., 1975). ***COURSES: Advanced Criminal Procedure, Clinical Teaching, Professional Responsibility, Trial Advocacy.

MARK SIDEL*, (Associate Professor of Law)**, born Boston, Massachusetts, December 12, 1957; admitted to bar, 1987, New York. *Education:* Princeton (A.B., 1979); Yale (M.A., 1982); Columbia (J.D., 1985). ***COURSES: Contracts, Philanthropy/Nonprofits, Comparative Law.

JOHN MARK STENSVAAG*, (Professor)**, born Minneapolis, Minnesota, July, 1947; admitted to bar, 1974, Minnesota. *Education:* Augsburg College (B.A., 1969); Harvard University (J.D., 1974). ***COURSES: Civil Procedure, Environmental Law, Evidence.

JAMES J. TOMKOVICZ*, (Professor)**, born Los Angeles, California, October 10, 1951; admitted to bar, 1976, California. *Education:* University of Southern California (B.A., 1973); University of California at Los Angeles (J.D., 1976). ***COURSES: Criminal Law, Criminal Procedure.

LEA S. VANDER VELDE*, (Josephine Witte Professor)**, born Milwaukee, Wisconsin, November 16, 1950; admitted to bar, 1978, Wisconsin. *Education:* University of Wisconsin (B.A., 1972; B.S., 1974; J.D., 1978). ***COURSES: Land Use Planning, Natural Resources, Real Property, Water Rights.

DAVID H. VERNON*, (Allan D. Vestal Professor)**, born Boston, Massachusetts, August 8, 1925; admitted to bar, 1952, Massachusetts. *Education:* Harvard University (A.B., 1949; LL.B., 1952); New York University (LL.M., 1953; J.S.D., 1960); University of Durham (D.C.L.). ***COURSES: Conflicts, Contracts.

LARRY D. WARD*, (Orville & Ermina Dykstra Professor)**, born Kirksville, Missouri, August, 1944; admitted to bar, 1970, Missouri. *Education:* University of Kansas (B.S., 1966; J.D., 1969). ***COURSES: Accounting, Corporate Taxation, Estate and Gift Taxation, Federal Taxation, Corporation and Finance.

BURNS H. WESTON*, (Bessie Dutton Murray Professor Emeritus)**, born Cleveland, Ohio, November, 1933; admitted to bar, 1963, New York. *Education:* Oberlin College (B.A., 1956); Yale University (LL.B., 1961; J.S.D., 1970). ***COURSES: Constitution and Foreign Relations, Human Rights in the World Community.

GERALD B. WETLAUFER*, (Professor)**, born Springfield, Missouri, March, 1945; admitted to bar, 1973, District of Columbia. *Education:* Princeton University (A.B., 1967); Yale University (J.D., 1972). ***COURSES: Antitrust, Civil Procedure, Jurisprudence, Negotiations.

JOHN BOOKER WHISTON*, (Clinical Associate Professor)**, born Laramie, Wyoming, December 17, 1947; admitted to bar, 1984, Montana; 1994, Iowa. *Education:* Yale University (B.A., 1970); University of Montana (J.D., 1984). ***COURSES: Clinical, Trial Advocacy.

ADRIEN WING*, (Bessie Dutton Murray Professor)**, born California, August, 1956; admitted to bar, 1983, New York. *Education:* Princeton University (A.B., 1978); University of California at Los Angeles (M.A., 1979); Stanford University (J.D., 1982). ***COURSES: Civil Rights, Comparative Law, Constitutional Law.

UNIVERSITY OF KANSAS SCHOOL OF LAW

15th AND BURDICK DRIVE
LAWRENCE, KANSAS 66045

UNIVERSITY OF KENTUCKY COLLEGE OF LAW

209 LAW BUILDING, SOUTH LIMESTONE STREET
LEXINGTON, KENTUCKY 40506
Telephone: (859) 257-1678
Fax: (859) 323-1061
http://www.uky.edu/law/

ABA Approved Since 1925.

The College of Law, which was established in 1908, provides a broad-based professional education designed to prepare students for the private practice of law, for public law practice in state or federal government, and for employment in businesses which utilize legal

(This Listing Continued)

UNIVERSITY OF KENTUCKY COLLEGE OF LAW
—Continued

training. As an integral part of its program, the College, through its faculty, engages in research and writing which supports the teaching function, assists and instructs practicing lawyers, and provides a resource of knowledge and analysis which may be drawn upon by federal and state judicial and legislative bodies in developing and changing the law in response to societal change and current problems. The College of Law's Legal Clinic serves indigent persons in need of legal services. Through its Law Library, Mineral Law Center, the Eastern Mineral Law Foundation and the direct consultation of its faculty, the College provides service and expert assistance to federal and state agencies and legislatures, judges, and practicing lawyers. The school also conducts an extensive program of continuing legal education for the bar and the judiciary. Graduates of the College of Law include state and federal elected officials, members of the state and federal judiciary, law professors, leaders of the organized bar, business and community leaders, and many outstanding practitioners.

Dean: Allan W. Vestal (859) 257-8319
Admissions Financial Aid: Drusilla V. Bakert (859) 257-8321
Library: Susan G. Burch (859) 257-8351
Placement: Susan Bybee Steele (859) 257-8320
Alumni Affairs: Linda B. Talbott (859) 257-3208
Continued Education: Kevin P. Bucknam (859) 257-1083

FULL TIME FACULTY

ALLAN W. VESTAL*, (Dean and Professor)**, born Iowa City, Iowa, December 3, 1953; admitted to bar, 1982, Iowa. *Education:* Yale University (B.A., 1976; J.D., 1979). ***COURSES: Antitrust, Close Business Transactions, Commercial Transactions, Dev. in Business Organization Law, Introduction to Lawyer's Role. ***Email:*** vestal@pop.uky.edu

RICHARD CHRISTIAN AUSNESS*, (Ashland Professor of Law)**, born Oakland, California, January 15, 1945; admitted to bar, 1968, Florida. *Education:* University of Florida (B.A., 1966; J.D., 1968); Yale Law School (LL.M., 1973). ***COURSES: Property, Torts, Trusts & Estates, Products Liability. ***Email:*** rausness@pop.uky.edu

DRUSILLA VANSANT BAKERT*, (Associate Dean for Admissions, Scholarships and Student Affairs)**, born Frankfort, Kentucky, December 8, 1952; admitted to bar, 1977, Georgia; 1983, Kentucky. *Education:* University of North Carolina at Chapel Hill (A.B., 1974); Harvard Law School (J.D., 1977). ***Email: dbakert@pop.uky.edu

JOHN R. BATT*, (Professor)**, born Cumberland, Maryland, May 29, 1934. *Education:* Johns Hopkins (B.A., 1956); William & Mary (J.D., 1959); Yale (LL.M., 1960). ***COURSES: Criminal Law, Criminal Procedure, Law & Psychiatry, Law & Psychological Sciences, Domestic Relations, Family Law, Jurisprudence, Sports Law.

CAROLYN S. BRATT*, (W.L. Matthews Professor of Law)**, born Suffern, New York, May 18, 1943; admitted to bar, 1975, New York; 1976, Kentucky. *Education:* SUNY at Albany (B.A., 1965); Syracuse University College of Law (J.D., 1974). ***COURSES: Property, Trusts and Estates, Future Interests, Constitutional Law, Gender Discrimination, Education Law. ***Email:*** cbratt@pop.uky.edu

RUTHEFORD B. CAMPBELL, JR.*, (Law Alumni Professor of Law)**, born Hyden, Kentucky, April 20, 1944; admitted to bar, 1970, New York; 1975, Kentucky. *Education:* Centre College (B.A., 1966); University of Kentucky (J.D., 1969); Harvard University (LL.M., 1971). ***COURSES: Business Associations, Corporate, Finance, Securities Regulation, Law and Economics. ***Email:*** rcampbel@pop.uky.edu

ALLISON CONNELLY*, (Assistant Professor and Director College of Law Legal Clinic)**, born Ashland, Kentucky, December 22, 1951; admitted to bar, 1983, Kentucky. *Education:* University of Kentucky (B.A., 1980); University of Kentucky College of Law (J.D., 1983). ***COURSES: Legal Clinic, Criminal Procedure, Criminal Trial Process, Litigation Skills, Legal Writing. ***Email:*** connelly@pop.uky.edu

MARY J. DAVIS*, (Stites & Harbison Professor of Law)**, born Martinsville, Virginia, January 29, 1957; admitted to bar, 1985, Virginia; 1988, North Carolina. *Education:* University of Virginia (B.A., 1979); Wake Forest University (J.D., 1985). ***COURSES: Torts, Products Liability, Conflict of Laws. ***Email:*** mjdavis@pop.uky.edu

WILLIAM HILNER FORTUNE*, (Robert G. Lawson Professor of Law)**, born Lexington, Kentucky, May 9, 1940; admitted to bar, 1964, Kentucky; 1975, California. *Education:* University of Kentucky (A.B., 1961; LL.B., 1964). ***COURSES: Evidence, Professional Responsibility, Criminal Procedure, Criminal Law. ***Email:*** fortunew@pop.uky.edu

CHRISTOPHER W. FROST*, (Associate Dean and Frost, Brown, Todd Professor)**, born 1960; admitted to bar, 1986, Illinois; 1999, Kentucky. *Education:* University of Kentucky (B.B.A., 1983; J.D., 1986). ***COURSES: Commercial Law, Contracts, Corporate Finance, Corporate Reorganization, Creditors' & Debtors' Rights, Law and Economics. ***Email:*** cfros1@pop.uky.edu

EUGENE ROGER GAETKE*, (H. Wendell Cherry Professor of Law)**, born St. Paul, Minnesota, September 12, 1948; admitted to bar, 1974, Minnesota. *Education:* University of Minnesota (B.A., 1971; J.D., 1974). ***COURSES: Contracts, Legal Ethics. ***Email:*** ggaetke@pop.uky.edu

ALVIN L. GOLDMAN*, (William T, Lafferty Professor of Law)**, born New York, New York, February 27, 1938; admitted to bar, 1963, New York; 1969, Kentucky. *Education:* Columbia (A.B., 1959); New York University (LL.B., 1962). ***COURSES: Labor Law, Employment Law, Negotiations, Constitutional Law. ***Email:*** agoldman@pop.uky.edu

DARLENE CECILE GORING*, (Assistant Professor of Law)**, born Miami, Florida, November 3, 1961; admitted to bar, 1986, Illinois. *Education:* Howard University (B.B.A., 1983); Northwestern University School of Law (J.D., 1986; LL.M., 1994). ***COURSES: Property, Real Estate Transactions, Anti-Discrimination, Land Use. ***Email:*** dgoring@pop.uky.edu

MARY LOUISE GRAHAM*, (Wendell H. Ford Professor of Law)**, born Beeville, Texas, May 20, 1943; admitted to bar, 1977, Texas; 1984 Kentucky. *Education:* University of Texas (B.A., 1965; J.D., 1977). ***COURSES: Family Law, Contracts, Children and the Law, Law & Literature. ***Email:*** lgraham@pop.uky.edu

WILLBURT D. HAM*, (Emeritus Professor)**, born March 2, 1916; admitted to bar, 1940, Illinois; 1951, Kentucky. *Education:* University of Illinois (B.S., 1937; J.D., 1940); Harvard Law School (LL.M., 1941). ***COURSES: Agency & Partnership, Business Associations, Contracts, Corporation Finance, Federal Corporation Law.

ROBERTA MARIA HARDING*, (Wilburt D. Ham Professor of Law)**, born New York, New York, March 3, 1960; admitted to bar, 1986, California. *Education:* University of San Francisco (B.S., B.A., 1981); Harvard (J.D., 1986). ***COURSES: Civil Procedure, Remedies, Capital

(This Listing Continued)

UNIVERSITY OF KENTUCKY COLLEGE OF LAW —Continued

Punishment, Prisoner's Rights, Human Rights. ***Email:*** rharding@pop.uky.edu

MICHAEL P. HEALY*, (Dorothy Salmon Professor of Law)**, born New York, New York, August 17, 1956; admitted to bar, 1985, Pennsylvania; 1985, District of Columbia. *Education:* Williams College (B.A., 1978); University of Pennsylvania (J.D., 1984). ***COURSES: Environmental Law, Torts, Legislation, Administrative Law, Land Use Planning. ***Email:*** healym@pop.uky.edu

ROBERT G. LAWSON*, (Charles S. Cassis Professor of Law)**, born Logan, West Virginia, July 15, 1938; admitted to bar, 1963, Kentucky. *Education:* Berea College (B.S., 1960); University of Kentucky (J.D., 1963). ***COURSES: Criminal Law, Evidence, Civil Procedure. ***Email:*** lawsonr@pop.uky.edu

THOMAS P. LEWIS*, (Emeritus Professor)**, born Ashland, Kentucky, March 26, 1930; admitted to bar, 1954, Kentucky; 1974, Massachusetts. *Education:* University of Kentucky (B.A., 1957; J.D., 1954); Harvard Law School (S.J.D., 1964). ***COURSES: Constitutional Law, Federal Courts, Civil Procedure. ***Email:*** tlewis@pop.uky.edu

DAYNA BOWEN MATTHEW*, (Associate Professor)**, born New York, New York, October 6, 1959; admitted to bar, 1987, Virginia; 1996, Kentucky. *Education:* Harvard (A.B., 1981); University of Virginia (J.D., 1987). ***COURSES: Health Law, Bioethics, Health Quality Regulation and Litigation, Civil Procedure. ***Email:*** dmatt2@pop.uky.edu

DOUGLAS C. MICHAEL*, (Edward T. Breathitt Professor)**, born Omaha, Nebraska, December 8, 1957; admitted to bar, 1984, California; 1988, District of Columbia. *Education:* Stanford University (A.B., 1979); University of California (M.B.A., 1982; J.D., 1983). ***COURSES: Accounting, Banking, Business Associations. ***Email:*** michaeld@pop.uky.edu

KATHRYN LYNN MOORE*, (Associate Professor)**, born Florida, December 5, 1961; admitted to bar, 1989, Pennsylvania; 1989, Washington D.C.; 1999, Kentucky. *Education:* University of Michigan (A.B., 1983); Cornell Law School (J.D., 1988). ***COURSES: Property, Land Use Planning, Employee Benefits, State & Local Tax. ***Email:*** kmoore@pop.uky.edu

JOHN MARSHALL ROGERS*, (Thomas P. Lewis Professor of Law)**, born Rochester, New York, June 26, 1948; admitted to bar, 1975, District of Columbia; 1980, Kentucky. *Education:* Stanford University (B.A., 1970); University of Michigan Law School (J.D., 1974). ***COURSES: Constitutional Law, International Law, Administrative Law, Torts. ***Email:*** jrogers@pop.uky.edu

PAUL E. SALAMANCA*, (Associate Professor of Law)**, born Boston, Massachusetts, December 3, 1961; admitted to bar, 1989, Massachusetts; 1993, New York. *Education:* Dartmouth College (A.B., 1983); Boston College Law School (J.D., 1989). ***COURSES: Constitutional Law, Federal Courts, Criminal Procedure. ***Email:*** psalaman@pop.uky.edu

ROBERT G. SCHWEMM*, (Ashland Professor of Law)**, born July 9, 1945; admitted to bar, 1971, Illinois, 1977, Kentucky. *Education:* Amherst College (B.A., 1967); Harvard Law School (J.D., 1970). ***COURSES: Constitutional Law, Civil Procedure. ***Email:*** schwemmr@pop.uky.edu

THOMAS J. STIPANOWICH*, (W.L. Mathews Professor of Law)**, born Evanston, Illinois, October 5, 1952; admitted to bar, 1980, Georgia; 1981, Illinois; 1992, Kentucky. *Education:* University of Illinois (B.S., 1974; M.Arch., 1976; J.D., 1980). ***COURSES: Commercial Arbitration, Alternative Dispute Resolution, Advanced Mediation, Contracts. ***Email:*** tstipano@pop.uky.edu

RICHARD HARVEY UNDERWOOD*, (Spears-Gilbert Professor of Law)**, born Columbus, Ohio, December 18, 1948; admitted to bar, 1976, Ohio; 1984, Kentucky. *Education:* Ohio State (B.S., 1969; J.D., 1976). ***COURSES: Ethics, Evidence, Insurance, Trial Advocacy, Health Law.

STEPHEN J. VASEK JR.*, (Associate Professor)**, born Chicago, Illinois, May 29, 1940; admitted to bar, 1966, Illinois; 1974, Kentucky. *Education:* Northwestern University (B.S., 1961; J.D., 1966); Harvard (LL.M., 1969). ***COURSES: Tax, Estates & Trusts, Estate Planning, International Business Law. ***Email:*** vaseks@pop.uky.edu

HAROLD ROY WEINBERG*, (Wyatt, Tarrant & Combs Professor)**, born Louisville, Kentucky, November 15, 1943; admitted to bar, 1969, Ohio (Inactive status); 1985, Kentucky. *Education:* Case Western Reserve University (A.B., 1966; J.D., 1969); University of Illinois (LL.M., 1975). ***COURSES: Antitrust, Intellectual Property, Uniform Commercial Code. ***Email:*** hweinber@pop.uky.edu

SARAH N. WELLING*, (Wendell H. Ford Professor of Law)**, born Chicago, Illinois, September 9, 1952; admitted to bar, 1979, Illinois; 1984, Kentucky. *Education:* University of Wisconsin (B.A., 1974); University of Kentucky (J.D., 1978). ***COURSES: Criminal Law, Criminal Procedure, Federal Criminal Law. ***Email:*** swelling@pop.uky.edu

RICHARD AXEL WESTIN*, (Laramie L. Leatherman Distinguished Professor of Tax Law)**, born 1945; admitted to bar, 1972, California; 1992, Texas. *Education:* Columbia College (B.A., 1967; M.B.A., 1968); University of Pennsylvania (J.D., 1972). ***COURSES: Business Planning, Corporations, Environmental Taxes, Federal Taxation, International Taxation, Income Tax Planning, Tax Policy.

UNIVERSITY OF LOUISVILLE - LOUIS D. BRANDEIS SCHOOL OF LAW

2301 SOUTH THIRD STREET
LOUISVILLE, KENTUCKY 40292
Telephone: (502) 852-6358
Fax: (502) 852-0862
Web Site: http://www.louisville.edu/brandeislaw/

ABA Approved Since 1931.

Institutions, like individuals, have distinct characteristics. The Louis D. Brandeis School of Law at the University of Louisville is Kentucky's national law school--an institution distinguished by a rich history, global perspective, and profound dedication to public service. As America's fifth oldest law school in continuous operation, the School of Law has been preparing lawyers for careers in practice, the judiciary, public administration, and allied professions since 1846. One of America's greatest jurists, Supreme Court Justice Louis D. Brandeis, gave the School his personal library (over 250,000 items) and chose the School's classical portico as his final resting place. With assistance from Justice Brandeis, the School also became custodian of papers of another historic figure: Justice John Marshall Harlan.

(This Listing Continued)

UNIVERSITY OF LOUISVILLE - LOUIS D. BRANDEIS SCHOOL OF LAW—Continued

Justice Brandeis envisioned a "law school of distinction" in his native city of Louisville. His vision focused on collegial teaching and learning, interdisciplinary scholarship, development of innovative ideas in public policy, and cultivating an ethos of public service. Today, the Brandeis School is one of the first five institutions in the country to adopt pro bono service as part of the prescribed course of study. *All* students participate in the public service program, deriving invaluable experience from working with real people and real problems under professional supervision. They also learn the values that make the practice of law a noble profession, not merely a commercial occupation.

Today's students also will find a diverse faculty with outstanding academic credentials as well as remarkable achievements in the "real world" of law and public affairs. Among the law schools represented on the faculty are Harvard, Yale, Chicago, Stanford, Michigan, Virginia, New York University, Georgetown, Duke, Vanderbilt, Iowa and Wisconsin.

The law building, Wilson W. Wyatt Hall, is a gracious blend of colonial and modern architecture located on a park-like campus, where it provides an excellent environment for learning. The surrounding city is ranked by Rand McNally's "Places Rated Almanac" as one of America's ten most livable metropolitan communities; an American Bar Association Journal article has named it as one of the nation's top ten places to practice law.

The School offers four degree programs. One program leads to the Juris Doctor (J.D.) degree; the others lead to combined degrees. Students may pursue a combination of J.D. and Master of Business Administration (M.B.A.) degrees or may choose an innovative combination of the J.D. and Master of Divinity (M.Div.) degrees or J.D. and Master of Science in Social Work (MSSW). The Juris Doctor program is available for both day and evening students.

With an attractive student-faculty ratio of 12:1 and an expansive curriculum of more than 100 courses, the School provides a generous array of educational choices. Students receive a thorough education in core legal subjects, coupled with an opportunity to pursue specialized interests. Graduating students enjoy a higher average bar examination pass rate than the Kentucky statewide average. They also benefit from an academic support program and personalized career advising, resulting in a higher job placement rate than the national average.

Students receive skills training through rigorous writing courses; curricular offerings in trial practice, appellate advocacy, dispute resolution, negotiation and counseling; and thirteen national moot court programs. Brandeis students recently have received national "best brief" awards in the Irving Kaufman Securities Law Competition and the Tax Law Competition, as well as the regional "best brief" award in the National Moot Court Competition. Students produce the Brandeis Law Journal of Family Law the Journal of Law and Education and The Brandeis Brief. Students may participate in several internship programs with federal and state trial judges, federal and state prosecutors, public defender offices, and the Legal Aid Society.

Recognizing the global dimensions of modern legal scholarship and law practice, the Brandeis School has developed an ambitious program of international law courses, special speakers and foreign exchanges. The school exchanges faculty with other law schools in England, France, Germany, Finland, Japan, China, Australia, South Africa, and Morocco. In response to the growing importance of environmental law, the University of Louisville has established an interdisciplinary Kentucky Institute for the Environment and Sustainable Development, with a Center for Environmental Policy located at the School of Law. The School also hosts the annual Carl A. Warns Labor and Employment Law Institute, as well as the annual Brandeis and Harlan lectures.

The Law Library contains approximately 320,000 volumes of books and microforms as well as more than 5,000 legal subscriptions. The library has a computerized catalog system and two computer laboratories for student research or word-processing. LEXIS and WESTLAW services, CD-ROM materials, computer-assisted legal instruction (CALI) programs, and access to the Internet are available. A state-of-the-art courtroom and special seminar room have voice activated video and computer imaging technology.

Admissions are competitive; the 2001 entering class of 129 students was selected from 800 fully completed applications. The priority deadline for admission applications is March 1 of each year. Because the University of Louisville is a public institution, tuition rates are reasonable; in addition, the Brandeis School commits over $650,000 annually to scholarship aid.

The School of Law is fully accredited by the American Bar Association and the Association of American Law Schools. Louisville law alumni/ae serve the legal profession, the business community, and allied professions in 50 states or territories and in numerous foreign countries. More than one-third of all Kentucky lawyers and more than half of all Louisville lawyers are U of L law graduates. The alumni/ae include past or present members of the United States Senate and House of Representatives, past governors of Kentucky, a past president of the American Bar Association, a past commander of the U.S. Strategic Air Command, the deans and faculty of several other law schools, the director of the National Center for Missing and Exploited Children and the chief executive officer of Churchill Downs.

Dean: Laura Rothstein (502) 852-6879
Associate Dean for Academic Affairs: Cedric M. Powell
Associate Dean for External Affairs: Linda S. Ewald (502) 852-7362
Library Director: David Ensign (502) 852-6392
Assistant Dean for Administration: Donald F. Olson (502) 852-6092
Assistant Dean for Admissions: Connie C. Shumake (502) 852-6391
Assistant Dean for Career Services: Jerie L. Torbeck (502) 852-6096
Director of Development: Steven Milburn (502) 852-1138
Public Service Program Director: Dana C. Williams

FULL TIME FACULTY

LAURA F. ROTHSTEIN*, (Dean and Professor of Law)**, born Salina, Kansas, July 8, 1949; admitted to bar, 1974, Pennsylvania; 1976, Ohio. *Education:* University of Kansas (B.A., 1971); Georgetown University Law Center (J.D., 1974). ***COURSES: Disability Law, Property, Torts.

LESLIE W. ABRAMSON*, (Professor of Law)**, born Louisville, Kentucky, January 22, 1946; admitted to bar, 1971, Kentucky. *Education:* Cornell University (A.B., 1968); University of Michigan (J.D., 1971); University of Wisconsin (LL.M., 1978; S.J.D., 1979). ***COURSES: Civil Procedure, Criminal Procedure, Professional Responsibility, Antitrust. ***Email:*** les.abramson@louisville.edu

***KATHLEEN S. BEAN*, (Professor of Law)**, born Peru, Indiana, July 7, 1953; admitted to bar, 1978, Iowa. *Education:* Ball State University

(This Listing Continued)

UNIVERSITY OF LOUISVILLE - LOUIS D. BRANDEIS SCHOOL OF LAW—Continued

(B.S., 1973); Drake University (J.D., 1978). ***COURSES:*** Property, Domestic Relations, Legal Skills. ***Email:*** kathybean@louisville.edu

R. THOMAS BLACKBURN, JR.*, (Professor of Law)**, born Boston, Massachusetts, April 30, 1945; admitted to bar, 1971, Kentucky. *Education:* University of Kentucky (B.S., 1967); Vanderbilt University (J.D., 1971); Harvard University (LL.M., 1988). ***COURSES: Taxation, Corporations, Business and Estate Planning. ***Email:*** tblackburn@louisville.edu

DONALD L. BURNETT, JR.*, (Professor of Law)**, born Pocatello, Idaho, October 1, 1946; admitted to bar, 1972, Idaho. *Education:* Harvard University (A.B., 1968); University of Chicago (J.D., 1971); University of Virginia (LL.M., 1990). ***COURSES: Law and Economics, Judicial Decision-Making, Legal Skills. ***Email:*** don.burnett@louisville.edu

JOHN T. CROSS*, (Professor of Law)**, born Lincoln, Illinois, August 9, 1959; admitted to bar, 1984, Minnesota. *Education:* Bradley University (B.S., 1981); University of Illinois (J.D., 1984). ***COURSES: Civil Procedure, Federal Courts, Bankruptcy, Debtor-Creditor Law, Business Torts, Intellectual Property, Secured Transactions, Law and Computers. ***Email:*** john.cross@louisville.edu

RONALD W. EADES*, (Professor of Law)**, born Lexington, Kentucky, September 6, 1948; admitted to bar, 1974, Tennessee; 1984, Kentucky. *Education:* Rhodes College (B.A., 1970); Memphis State University (J.D., 1973); Harvard University (LL.M., 1977). ***COURSES: Torts, Workers Compensation, Products Liability, First Amendment. ***Email:*** ron.eades@louisville.edu

DAVID JAMES ENSIGN*, (Law Librarian and Professor of Law)**, born Wichita, Kansas, August 10, 1950; admitted to bar, 1983, Kansas. *Education:* University of Kansas (B.A., 1972); Emporia State University (M.L.S., 1976); Washburn University (J.D., 1982). ***COURSES: Legal Research, Domestic Relations. ***Email:*** david.ensign@louisville.edu

LINDA SORENSON EWALD*, (Associate Dean, Professor of Law)**, born Mankato, Minnesota, August 27, 1945; admitted to bar, 1973, Kentucky. *Education:* University of Louisville (B.A., 1967; J.D., 1972); New York University (LL.M., 1979). ***COURSES: Civil Procedure, Professional Responsibility. ***Email:*** lsewald@louisville.edu

JUDITH D. FISCHER*, (Assistant Professor of Law)**, born Cincinnati, Ohio, November 8, 1942; admitted to bar, 1981, California; 1992, Ohio. *Education:* Bradley University (B.A., 1964; M.A., 1971); Loyola Law School (J.D., 1981). ***COURSES: Legal Writing. ***Email:*** j.fischer@louisville.edu

MICHAEL R. FOWLER*, (Associate Professor of Law)**, born Washington, D.C., April 14, 1960; admitted to bar, 1986, Massachusetts. *Education:* Dartmouth College (B.A., 1982); University of Virginia (M.A., 1985); Harvard University (J.D., 1986). ***COURSES: International Law, Negotiations. ***Email:*** m.fowler@louisville.edu

GRACE M. GIESEL*, (Professor of Law)**, born South Carolina, June 13, 1960; admitted to bar, 1985, Kentucky. *Education:* Yale University (B.A., 1982); Emory University (J.D., 1985). ***COURSES: Insurance, Professional Responsibility, Corporations, Criminal Law. ***Email:*** g.giesel@louisville.edu

JAMES T.R. JONES*, (Professor of Law)**, born Richmond, Virginia, December 28, 1953; admitted to bar, 1979, Florida. *Education:* University of Virginia (B.A., 1975); Duke University (J.D., 1978). ***COURSES: Torts, Legal Writing, Legal Methods. ***Email:*** jtrjones@louisville.edu

KAREN JORDAN*, (Professor of Law)**, born Indianapolis, Indiana, March 10, 1958; admitted to bar, 1990, Indiana. *Education:* Indiana University (B.S., 1987; J.D., 1990). ***COURSES: Civil Procedure, Criminal Procedure, Health Law. ***Email:*** karen.jordan@louisville.edu

SUSAN H. KOSSE*, (Assistant Professor of Law)**, born Louisville, Kentucky, March 4, 1966; admitted to bar, 1991, Kentucky; 1993, Tennessee. *Education:* Miami University (B.A., 1987); University of Louisville (J.D., 1991). ***COURSES: Legal Writing. ***Email:*** susan.kosse@louisville.edu

NORVIE L. LAY*, (Professor of Law)**, born Cardwell, Kentucky, April 17, 1940; admitted to bar, 1963, Kentucky. *Education:* University of Kentucky (B.S., 1960); University of Louisville (J.D., 1963); University of Michigan (LL.M., 1964; S.J.D., 1967). ***COURSES: Federal Income Tax, Estate and Gift Tax, Fiduciary Income Tax, Estate Planning, Conflicts. ***Email:*** norvie.lay@louisville.edu

DAVID J. LEIBSON*, (Bernard Flexner Professor of Law)**, born Louisville, Kentucky, March 18, 1944; admitted to bar, 1969, Kentucky. *Education:* Vanderbilt University (B.A., 1966); University of Louisville (J.D., 1969); Harvard University (LL.M., 1970). ***COURSES: Torts, Uniform Commercial Code. ***Email:*** davidjay@louisville.edu

BARBARA B. LEWIS*, (Professor of Law)**, born Campbellsville, Kentucky, May 1, 1938; admitted to bar, 1962, Kentucky. *Education:* University of Louisville (B.A., 1958; J.D., 1962); Tennessee Technological University (M.A., 1972); College of William & Mary (M.L.&T., 1974). ***COURSES: Taxation and Estate Planning. ***Email:*** b.lewis@louisville.edu

SAMUEL ALAN MARCOSSON*, (Associate Professor of Law)**, born New York, September 23, 1961; admitted to bar, 1988, District of Columbia. *Education:* Bradley University (B.S., 1983); Yale (J.D., 1986). ***COURSES: Employment Discrimination, Constitutional Law, Family Law. ***Email:*** smarcosson@louisville.edu

LISA HOPE NICHOLSON*, (Assistant Professor of Law)**, born New York, New York, August 30, 1965; admitted to bar, 1993, New York. *Education:* Virginia Tech (B.S., 1986); William & Mary (J.D., 1993). ***COURSES: Contracts. ***Email:*** l.nicholson@louisville.edu

RICHARD H. NOWKA*, (Professor of Law)**, born Nebraska, August 5, 1951; admitted to bar, 1976, Nebraska. *Education:* Wayne State College (B.S., 1973); Creighton University (J.D., 1976). ***COURSES: Uniform Commercial Code, Contracts, Bankruptcy. ***Email:*** rick.nowka@louisville.edu

CEDRIC M. POWELL*, (Associate Dean, Professor of Law)**, born Cleveland, Ohio, November 8, 1961; admitted to bar, 1988, Ohio; 1990, New York. *Education:* Oberlin College (B.A., 1984); New York University School of Law (J.D., 1987). ***COURSES: Criminal Procedure, Criminal Law, Evidence and Trial Practice. ***Email:*** cedric.powell@louisville.edu

LAVONDA N. REED-HUFF*, (Assistant Professor of Law)**, born Quantico, Virginia, January 20, 1969; admitted to bar, 1997, Maryland; 1999, District of Columbia. *Education:* University of Virginia (B.A., 1990); University of Southern California (J.D., 1997). ***COURSES: Property, Mass Media. ***Email:*** lavonda.reedhuff@louisville.edu

EDWIN R. RENDER*, (Professor of Law)**, born Detroit, Michigan, November 13, 1935; admitted to bar, 1962, Tennessee; 1965, Kentucky. *Education:* Western Kentucky University (B.A., 1958); Vanderbilt University (LL.B., 1962); Harvard University (LL.M., 1970). ***COURSES: Evidence, Labor Clinics. ***Email:*** ed.render@louisville.edu

***MARK A. ROTHSTEIN*, (Boehl Professor of Law and Medicine)**, born Philadelphia, Pennsylvania, May 23, 1949; admitted to bar, 1973,

(This Listing Continued)

UNIVERSITY OF LOUISVILLE - LOUIS D. BRANDEIS SCHOOL OF LAW—Continued

Pennsylvania and District of Columbia. *Education:* University of Pittsburgh (B.A., 1970); Georgetown (J.D., 1973). ***COURSES:*** Employment Law, Genetics and the Law. ***Email:*** mark.rothstein@louisville.edu

LARS S. SMITH*, (Assistant Professor of Law)**, born Hellerup, Denmark, January 4, 1965; admitted to bar, 1992, New Hampshire; 1995, Massachusetts. *Education:* Colby College (B.A., 1986); New England School of Law (J.D., 1992); Franklin Pierce Law Center (LL.M., 1998). ***COURSES: Business Law, Property. ***Email:*** l.smith@louisville.edu

ROBERT L. STENGER*, (Professor of Law)**, born Saint Paul, Minnesota, September 19, 1934; admitted to bar, 1974, Iowa. *Education:* St. Thomas College (B.A., 1956; M.A., 1957); Catholic University of America (S.T.D., 1963); University of Iowa (J.D., 1974). ***COURSES: Constitutional Law, Domestic Relations, Decedents' Estates, Jurisprudence, Legal Method, Introduction to Law, Conflict of Laws, Property, Torts. ***Email:*** bob.stenger@louisville.edu

ENID TRUCIOS-HAYNES*, (Professor of Law)**, born Brooklyn, New York, May 15, 1960; admitted to bar, 1988, New York. *Education:* City University of New York at Queens College (B.A., 1983); Stanford Law School (J.D., 1986). ***COURSES: Constitutional Law, Administrative Law, International Law, Immigration Law. ***Email:*** ethaynes@louisville.edu

MANNING G. WARREN III*, (Harter Professor of Law)**, born Dothan, Alabama, August 20, 1948; admitted to bar, 1973, District of Columbia; 1974, Alabama; 1990, Kentucky. *Education:* University of Georgia (1966-1967); University of Alabama (B.A., 1970);George Washington University (J.D., 1973). ***COURSES: Securities Regulation, Corporations, European Communities Law. ***Email:*** mgw111@louisville.edu

RUSSELL L. WEAVER*, (Professor of Law)**, born Kansas City, Missouri, October 24, 1952; admitted to bar, 1978, Missouri. *Education:* University of Missouri (B.A., 1974; J.D., 1978). ***COURSES: Constitutional Law, Criminal Procedure, Remedies, Administrative Law, International Law. ***Email:*** russ.weaver@louisville.edu

SERENA M. WILLIAMS*, (Associate Professor of Law)**, born Augusta, Georgia, December 13, 1959; admitted to bar, 1985, Maryland; 1989, District of Columbia. *Education:* Smith College (B.A., 1981); Georgetown University Law Center (J.D., 1984); Georgetown University (LL.M., 1992). ***COURSES: Property Law, Environmental Law. ***Email:*** smwilliams@louisville.edu

UNIVERSITY OF MAINE SCHOOL OF LAW

246 DEERING AVENUE
PORTLAND, MAINE 04102
Telephone: (207) 780-4341
www.law.usm.maine.edu

ABA Approved Since 1962.

Our Mission

The School, which fosters close student/faculty interaction, seeks to educate students from a variety of backgrounds through a Juris Doctorate degree program providing the public and private sectors with distinctive members of the legal profession. The University of Maine School of Law is the only law school in Maine. With responsibilities to the statewide University System, it is committed to educational excellence, professionalism, maintaining a strong core curriculum for students, and acting as a resource for the entire state. In addition, the School contributes to the advancement and improvement of the law in a number of ways including providing leadership in scholarly and professional research and writing. The School also engages in extensive public service aimed at improving the law and the legal system.

Our Size

With a total student body of 260, we are among the smallest fully accredited law schools in the United States. Our size, which intentionally remains small, allows for a personal, one-on-one study of the law. The entire first year class meets in one section, and the students value attending class and graduating with their friends. Professors serve as teachers, writing advisors, activity leaders, moot court judges and colleagues.

Program of Study

The three year curriculum is intensive and challenging. It is both broad and general in nature, offering courses in subjects as diverse as international business transactions and environmental law, as well as traditional core courses. The underlying purpose of the curriculum is to give students a solid foundation in legal analysis and practical lawyering skills that will serve them well in any field they choose to pursue. Though teaching methods vary from course to course depending on the instructor and the subject matter, the overall emphasis is on personal contact between student and teacher, as well as among the students themselves. Some upper-level courses have enrollments of between 10-20 students; class sizes of 20-40 are common.

Our Commitment

We take our responsibility as a public institution very seriously. Here faculty and students help create and comment on Maine law. Our students benefit the public through service to low income clients in the Law School's Cumberland Legal Aid Clinic, through summer public interest fellowships with legal services agencies and government offices, and through individual volunteer projects. Our graduates in turn bring a sense of public service into their careers, whether they pursue them in the private or public sectors. Not surprisingly, our alumni include many of Maine's former Governors, Attorneys General, and current United States Attorney and the Chief Justice of the Maine Supreme Judicial Court.

Faculty

Our faculty bring a wide range of experience to the classroom, and are noted for their exceptional ability as teachers. They are graduates of Boston University, Chicago, Columbia, Georgetown, George Washington, Harvard, IIT, Maine, Michigan, Notre Dame, Pennsylvania, Puget Sound, Virginia, Wisconsin and Yale Law Schools. Before our faculty began teaching, they were judicial clerks, private practitioners' government attorneys, and research scholars. Many continue to serve as advisors to legislative, judicial and professional bodies and as members of government commissions. Their research spans matters of state, national and international interest and examines topics as varied as international treaty practice, Maine tort law, coastal zone management, federal tax elections, constitutional controls over the military, rules of evidence, intellectual property and commercial practices.

(This Listing Continued)

UNIVERSITY OF MAINE SCHOOL OF LAW—Continued

Dean: (207) 780-4344
Admissions: (207) 780-4341
Financial Aid: (207) 780-5250
Alumni Affairs: (207) 780-4342

FULL TIME FACULTY

COLLEEN A. KHOURY*, (Dean and Professor)**, *Education:* Colby College (B.A.); Illinois Institute of Technology/Chicago Kent College of Law (J.D.). ***COURSES: Income Tax, Contracts, Business Associations, Land Transactions.

DAVID P. CLUCHEY*, (Associate Dean and Professor)**, *Education:* Yale University (A.B.); State University of New York at Albany (M.A.); Harvard University (J.D.). ***COURSES: Antitrust, Business Associations, Economic Regulation of Business, International Trade Law.

ORLANDO E. DELOGU*, (Professor)**, *Education:* University of Utah (B.S.); University of Wisconsin (M.S.; J.D.). ***COURSES: Land Use, Environmental Law, State and Local Government, Property, Administrative law, Medical Legal Process.

JOHN A. DUFF*, (Associate Research Professor and Co-Director, Marine Law Institute)**, *Education:* University of Lowell (B.S.); Suffolk University (J.D.); University of Washington (LL.M.); University of Mississippi (M.A.). ***COURSES: Coastal Zone Law, International Law of the Sea.

JAMES FRIEDMAN*, (Professor)**, *Education:* Brown University (B.A.); University of Chicago (J.D.). ***COURSES: Constitutional Law, Labor Law, Jurisprudence, Law & Terrorism.

CHRISTINE DAVIK GALBRAITH*, (Associate Professor)**, born Oak Park, Illinois, June 24, 1970; admitted to bar, 1995, Illinois. *Education:* University of Illinois (B.S., 1992; J.D., 1995). ***COURSES: Contracts, Intellectual Property. ***Email:*** galbraith@usm.maine.edu

***BARBARA GAUDITZ*, (Assistant Dean)**, *Education:* Hunter College (B.A.); University of Maine (J.D.).

***EDWARD S. GODFREY*, (Emeritus Dean and Professor)**, *Education:* Harvard College (A.B.); Columbia University (J.D.); Union University, Albany Law School (LL.D.); University of Southern Maine (LH.D.).

L. SCOTT GOULD*, (Associate Professor)**, *Education:* Stanford University (A.B.); University of Northern Colorado (M.A.); University of Idaho (J.D.). ***COURSES: Negotiable Instruments, Trusts & Estates, American Indian Law, Remedies.

H. CABANNE HOWARD*, (Assistant Professor)**, *Education:* Cornell University (B.A.); Georgetown University (J.D.). ***COURSES: Canadian Legal System, Constitutional Law, Professional Responsibility.

MICHAEL B. LANG*, (Professor)**, *Education:* Harvard College (A.B.); University of Pennsylvania (J.D.). ***COURSES: Estate and Gift Taxation, Corporate Tax, Personal Income Tax.

LOIS R. LUPICA*, (Professor)**, *Education:* Cornell University (B.S.); Boston University (J.D.). ***COURSES: Bankruptcy, Secured Transactions, Negotiation, Professional Responsibility, Consumer Law Property.

JUDY R. POTTER*, (Professor)**, *Education:* Cornell University (B.A.); University of Michigan (J.D.). ***COURSES: Negotiation, Trial Practice, Criminal Law Practicum, Clinic, Advanced Trial Advocacy.

ALISON RIESER*, (Professor and Director, Marine Law Institute)**, *Education:* Cornell University (B.A.); George Washington University (J.D.); Yale University (LL.M.). ***COURSES: Coastal Zone Law, Marine Resources Law, Environmental Law, Law of the Sea.

MARTIN A. ROGOFF*, (Professor)**, *Education:* Cornell University (B.A.); University of California at Berkeley (M.A.); Yale University (LL.B.). ***COURSES: Comparative Law, Conflict of Laws, European Community Law, International Business Transactions, International Law, Legal History.

NANCY WANDERER*, (Director of Legal Research and Writing)**, *Education:* Wellesley College (B.A.); George Washington University (M.A.); University of Maine (J.D.). ***COURSES: Legal Research, Writing and Oral Advocacy.

THOMAS M. WARD*, (Professor)**, *Education:* University of Pennsylvania (B.A.); University of Notre Dame (LL.B.); University of Illinois (LL.M.). ***COURSES: Contracts, Commercial Law, Intellectual Property.

***WM. W. WELLS*, (Associate Provost for Technology, Information Systems & Libraries; Law Library Director, and Professor)**, *Education:* Eastern Oregon College (B.S.); University of Puget Sound (J.D.); University of Washington (M.L.L.).

JENNIFER WRIGGINS*, (Associate Professor)**, *Education:* Yale University (A.B.); Harvard University (J.D.). ***COURSES: Torts, Family Law, Clinic, Gender and the Law.

MELVYN ZARR*, (Professor)**, *Education:* Clark University (A.B.); Harvard University (LL.B.). ***COURSES: Civil Procedure, Criminal Law, Criminal Procedure, Federal Courts.

DONALD N. ZILLMAN*, (Godfrey Professor)**, *Education:* University of Wisconsin (B.S., J.D.); University of Virginia (LL.M.). ***COURSES: Constitutional Law, Natural Resources, Torts, Property.

UNIVERSITY OF MARYLAND SCHOOL OF LAW

515 WEST LOMBARD STREET
BALTIMORE, MARYLAND 21201-1786
Telephone: (410) 706-7214
Fax: (410) 706-4045

ABA Approved Since 1930

The University of Maryland School of Law was established in 1816 and began regular instruction in 1824. It is one of the oldest law schools in the nation, but its innovative programs make it one of the freshest and liveliest today. Just a few blocks from Baltimore's famous Inner Harbor and Oriole Park at Camden Yards, the law school is one of six professional schools which comprise the University of Maryland, Baltimore campus. It has taken advantage of this location to become an integral part of the Baltimore-Washington legal and business community.

The law school community is both diverse and congenial. Students come from thirty-one states and two hundred forty-nine different undergraduate institutions. More than one-quarter of the students are students of color. Numerous opportunities for participating in the social, cultural and political life of the school and the city are available through the various student organizations. Students interested in writing can compete for positions on four legal publications--three student-run journals and *The Business Lawyer* published in cooperation between the School of Law and the American Bar Association. The school also has an extensive moot court program and opportunities to participate in trial advocacy, counseling and negotiation competitions. The school's Thurgood Marshall Library is the largest law library in the state.

The curriculum combines traditional offerings with cutting edge programs and a full time menu of elective courses enriched by the use of adjunct faculty from among the state's leading lawyers, judges and academics. Fifty-four full-time faculty members teach the 717-day and 238-evening students. The 15-1 student-faculty ratio promotes close contact between professors and students. The learning environment is enriched by specialized programs and experiential learning opportunities.

Maryland's specialty programs include the Environmental Law Program, and the Law and Health Care Program. There are burgeoning programs in Business Law and Intellectual Property. The emphasis in these programs is interdisciplinary, offering students the opportunity to work with lawyers and professionals in related disciplines toward the resolutions of problems that transcend traditional disciplinary boundaries. For example, a student in the Law and Health Care Program would have the opportunity to supplement a broad and diverse curriculum of classroom courses with clinical opportunities in the Health Care Law or AIDS Clinic, internships with organizations such as the National Institute of Health and editorial positions with the School's *Journal of Health Care Law and Policy*.

The School of Law's experiential programs are among the most extensive in the country. Students have the opportunity to enroll in a wide range of clinical offerings including those specializing in representing emerging business owners, AIDS patients, environmental clinics, and scientists with intellectual property issues. All Day students take a course involving a clinical law experience representing the disadvantaged. Students meet regularly with their professors to review the substantive professional, ethical and craft issues raised by their work and to explore the connections between what is taught in the classroom and the practice of law as they are experiencing it.

Simulation and clinical courses make extensive use of the audio-visual facilities of the school, and students take advantage of the school's large number of computers for research, writing, clinical work and computer-assisted learning exercises. A helpful professional staff, from the Admissions Office to the Director of Academic Support to the Office of Career Development, is committed to students. That devotion is reciprocated by our loyal alumni whose leadership in supporting the school and in service to the community has been outstanding.

Dean: Karen H. Rothenberg (410) 706-2041
Assistant Dean, Registration: James F. Forsyth (410) 706-3492
Assistant Dean for Library Services: Barbara S. Gontrum (410) 706-7270
Associate Dean: Alan D. Hornstein
Associate Dean: Diane E. Hoffmann
Associate Dean, Administrative Affairs: Jose Bahamonde-Gonzalez
Assistant Dean, Development: Shelley Gitomer
Assistant Dean, Career Development: Dana Morris
Assistant Dean, Student Affairs: Tricia O'Neill
Assistant Dean for Academic Technology: Mary Cornaby
Clinic Director: Thomas E. Perez

FULL TIME FACULTY

KAREN H. ROTHENBERG*, (Dean, Marjorie Cook Professor of Law)**, born New York, October 30, 1952; admitted to bar, 1979, District of Columbia. *Education:* Princeton University (A.B., 1973; M.P.A., 1974); University of Virginia (J.D., 1979). ***COURSES: Alternative Dispute Resolution & Health Care, Biotechnology & the Law, Health Care Law, Health Law Practice Workshop, Law & Biomedical Sciences, Law & Medicine, Torts. ***Email:*** krothenberg@law.umaryland.edu

---

TAUNYA LOVELL BANKS*, (Jacob A. France Professor of Equality Jurisprudence)**, born Washington, District of Columbia, February 5, 1945; admitted to bar, 1969, Mississippi. *Education:* Syracuse University (B.A., 1965); Howard University (J.D., 1968). ***COURSES: Civil Rights, Constitutional Law, Criminal Law, Health Care Law, Torts. ***Email:*** tbanks@law.umaryland.edu

BARBARA BEZDEK*, (Associate Professor of Law)**, born New York, New York, January 2, 1954; admitted to bar, 1978, District of Columbia; 1986, New York; 1991, Maryland. *Education:* University of South Carolina (B.A., 1975); Columbia University (J.D., 1978); Georgetown University (LL.M., 1986). ***COURSES: Civil Procedure, Clinical Teaching, Community Teaching, Legal Method, Legal Profession, Property. ***Email:*** bbezdek@law.umaryland.edu

***BRENDA BRATTON BLOM*, (Law School Assistant Professor)**, born Texas, March 16, 1953; admitted to bar, 1993, Maryland. *Education:*

(This Listing Continued)

UNIVERSITY OF MARYLAND SCHOOL OF LAW —Continued

University of Baltimore (B.A., 1989; J.D., 1993); University of Maryland, Baltimore (M.P.S., 1993). ***COURSES:*** Clinical law, Community & Economic Development. ***Email:*** bblom@law.umaryland.edu

DAVID S. BOGEN, **(Professor of Law and T. Carroll Brown Scholar),** born Los Angeles, California, August 24, 1941; admitted to bar, 1965, Massachusetts; 1967, New York. *Education:* Harvard University (B.A., 1962; LL.B., 1965); New York University (LL.M., 1967). ***COURSES:*** Constitutional Law, Contracts, Legal History, Legal Methods, Mass Communication Law. ***Email:*** dbogen@law.umaryland.edu

RICHARD C. BOLDT, **(Professor of Law),** born Louisville, Kentucky, March 24, 1958; admitted to bar, 1983, New York; 1991, Maryland. *Education:* Columbia College (A.B., 1979); Yale University (J.D., 1982). ***COURSES:*** Constitutional Law, Criminal Law, Criminal Procedure, Torts. ***Email:*** rboldt@law.umaryland.edu

RICHARD A. BOOTH, **(Professor of Law),** born Marion, Indiana, November 24, 1950; admitted to bar, 1977, New York; 1985, Texas. *Education:* University of Michigan (A.B., 1973); Yale University (J.D., 1976). ***COURSES:*** Agency & Partnership, Business Planning, Corporate Finance, Corporations, Securities Regulation. ***Email:*** rbooth@law.umaryland.edu

IRVING A. BREITOWITZ, **(Associate Professor of Law),** born New York, New York, April 15, 1954; admitted to bar, 1979, Connecticut; 1980, Illinois. *Education:* Harvard University (J.D., 1979); Ner Israel Rabbinical College (Ph.D., 1991). ***COURSES:*** Contracts, Legal Method and Writing, Creditors' Rights, Sales-Secured Transactions, Commercial Paper, Government Contracts. ***Email:*** ibreitowitz@law.umaryland.edu

C. CHRISTOPHER BROWN, **(Associate Professor of Law),** born Dover, Delaware, December 15, 1941; admitted to bar, 1968, District of Columbia; 1974, Maryland. *Education:* Swarthmore College (B.A., 1963); University of Delaware (M.A., 1965); Georgetown University (J.D., 1968). ***COURSES:*** Appellate Practice, Civil Procedure, Clinical Teaching, Torts. ***Email:*** ccb@browngold.com

ALICE A. BRUMBAUGH, **(Robert Stanton Distinguished Service Professor of Law),** born New York, New York, March 19, 1933; admitted to bar, 1955, New York; 1957, Michigan. *Education:* University of Michigan (A.B., 1953; J.D., with honors, 1955). ***COURSES:*** Criminal Law, Estates & Trusts, Fiduciary Administration, Future Interests, Personal Property, Real Estate Transactions, Real Property, Trusts. ***Email:*** abrumbaugh@law.umaryland.edu

MAXWELL O. CHIBUNDU, **(Professor of Law),** born Nigeria, May 14, 1957; admitted to bar, 1984, District of Columbia. *Education:* Yale University (B.A., 1980); Harvard University (J.D., 1984). ***COURSES:*** Civil Procedure, Federal Jurisdiction, International Civil Litigation, International Transactions, Legal Method. ***Email:*** mchibundu@law.umaryland.edu

HUNGDAH CHIU, **(Professor of Law),** born Shanghai, China, March 23, 1936. *Education:* National Taiwan University (B.L., 1958); Long Island University (M.A., 1962); Harvard University (LL.M., 1962; S.J.D., 1965). ***COURSES:*** Chinese Law, International Law. ***Email:*** hchiu@law.umaryland.edu

DOUGLAS LAWRENCE COLBERT, **(Professor of Law),** born Far Rockaway, December 23, 1946; admitted to bar, 1973, New York; 1995, Maryland. *Education:* State University of New York at Buffalo (B.S., 1968); Rutgers (J.D., 1972). ***COURSES:*** Civil Rights, Clinical Teaching, Constitutional Law, Criminal Justice, Evidence. ***Email:*** dcolbert@law.umaryland.edu

ROBERT J. CONDLIN, **(Professor of Law),** born United States; admitted to bar, 1969, Massachusetts. *Education:* Siena College (B.A., 1966); Boston College (J.D., 1969); Harvard University (LL.M., 1976). ***COURSES:*** Alternative Dispute Resolution, Civil Procedure, Legal Method, Legal Profession, Legislation. ***Email:*** rcondlin@law.umaryland.edu

KAREN CZAPANSKIY, **(Professor of Law),** born Washington, District of Columbia, January 18, 1947; admitted to bar, 1974, Maryland; 1983, District of Columbia. *Education:* University of California at Berkeley (B.A., 1969); Georgetown University (J.D., 1973). ***COURSES:*** Civil Procedure, Clinical Teaching, Family Law, Legal Theory & Practice, Women and The Law. ***Email:*** kczapanskiy@law.umaryland.edu

ABRAHAM A. DASH, **(Professor of Law),** born Camden, New Jersey, December 2, 1927; admitted to bar, 1960, District of Columbia. *Education:* United States Naval Academy; University of Nebraska (B.S., 1957); Georgetown University (J.D., 1960). ***COURSES:*** Administrative Law, Legal Ethics, Criminal Procedure, Trial Practice. ***Email:*** adash@law.umaryland.edu

JEROME E. DEISE, **(Law School Associate Professor),** born Baltimore, Maryland, December 6, 1947; admitted to bar, 1976, Maryland. *Education:* University of Maryland (B.A., 1970); University of Baltimore (J.D., 1975). ***COURSES:*** Criminal Law Clinic, Trial Advocacy. ***Email:*** jdeise@law.umaryland.edu

JOHN W. ESTER, **(Professor of Law Emeritus),** born Oklahoma City, Oklahoma, November 27, 1935; admitted to bar, 1960, California. *Education:* Pasadena College (B.A., 1956); Willamette University (J.D., 1959); University of Illinois (LL.M., 1962). ***COURSES:*** Torts. ***Email:*** jester@law.umaryland.edu

LISA M. FAIRFAX, **(Assistant Professor of Law),** born Bellflower, California, November 13, 1970; admitted to bar, 1995, Massachusetts; 1998, District of Columbia. *Education:* Harvard College (A.B., 1992); Harvard Law School (J.D., 1995). ***COURSES:*** Business Associations. ***Email:*** lfairfax@law.umaryland.edu

LARRY S. GIBSON, **(Professor of Law),** born Washington, District of Columbia, March 22, 1942; admitted to bar, 1967, Maryland. *Education:* Howard University (B.A., 1964); Columbia University (LL.B., 1967). ***COURSES:*** Civil Procedure, Evidence, Trial Practice. ***Email:*** lgibson@law.umaryland.edu

DONALD G. GIFFORD, **(Professor of Law),** born Medina, Ohio, July 26, 1952; admitted to bar, 1976, Ohio; 1984, Florida. *Education:* College of Wooster (B.A., 1973); Harvard University (J.D., 1976). ***COURSES:*** Negotiation, Torts. ***Email:*** dgifford@law.umaryland.edu

DANIEL S. GOLDBERG, **(Professor of Law),** born New York, New York, February 26, 1947; admitted to bar, 1972, New York; 1973, District of Columbia; 1984, Maryland. *Education:* University of Rochester (A.B., magna cum laude, 1968); Harvard University (J.D., cum laude, 1971). ***COURSES:*** Corporate Tax, Estate & Gift Taxation, Federal Income Taxation, International Taxation, Law & Economics, Partnership Taxation, Tax Policy. ***Email:*** dgoldberg@law.umaryland.edu

BARBARA S. GONTRUM, **(Instructor and Assistant Dean for Library Services),** born Indiana, May 18, 1950; admitted to bar, 1978, North Carolina. *Education:* Purdue University (B.A., 1972); University of Illinois (M.L.S., 1973); Duke University (J.D., 1978). ***COURSES:*** Legal Research & Writing, Advanced Legal Research. ***Email:*** bgontrum@law.umaryland.edu

OSCAR S. GRAY, **(Jacob A. France Professor of Torts Emeritus),** born New York, New York, October 18, 1926; admitted to bar, 1951,

(This Listing Continued)

UNIVERSITY OF MARYLAND SCHOOL OF LAW —Continued

Maryland; 1952, District of Columbia. *Education:* Yale University (B.A., 1948; J.D., 1951). ***COURSES:*** Admiralty, Business Associations, Commercial Transactions, Environmental Law, Insurance, Torts. ***Email:*** ogray@law.umaryland.edu

SUSAN HANKIN*, (Law School Associate Professor & Director of Legal Writing)**, born Baltimore, Maryland, February 8, 1959; admitted to bar, 1988, Pennsylvania and Maryland. *Education:* University of Pennsylvania (B.A., 1980); University of Virginia (J.D., 1986). ***COURSES: Legal Method, TA Training, Writing Fellow, Writing in Law Practice. ***Email:*** shankin@law.umaryland.edu

DEBORAH S. HELLMAN*, (Associate Professor of Law)**, born New Haven, Connecticut, July 18, 1963; admitted to bar, 1991, New York and Massachusetts. *Education:* Dartmouth College (B.A., 1985); Columbia University (M.A., in Philosophy, 1987); Harvard Law School (J.D., 1991). ***COURSES: Constitutional Law, Contracts, Jurisprudence, Law & Medicine: Bioethics, Legal Profession. ***Email:*** dhellman@law.umaryland.edu

DIANE E. HOFFMANN*, (Associate Dean, Professor of Law, and Director, Law and Health Care Program)**, born New York, New York, August 10, 1955; admitted to bar, 1986, District of Columbia. *Education:* Duke University (A.B., 1976); Harvard University (M.S., 1980; J.D., 1986). ***COURSES: Critical Issues in Health Care, Health Care Law, Health Care for the Poor, Law & Biomedical Science: Medical Research, Law & Medicine, Legal Problems of the Elderly. ***Email:*** dhoffman@law.umaryland.edu

ALAN D. HORNSTEIN*, (Associate Dean and Professor of Law)**, born Brooklyn, New York, February 16, 1945; admitted to bar, 1971, New York; 1983, Maryland. *Education:* Long Island University (A.B., 1965; M.A., 1967); St. John's College (M.A., 1986); Rutgers University (J.D., 1970). ***COURSES: Contracts, Evidence, Jurisprudence. Legal Method. ***Email:*** ahornstein@law.umaryland.edu

MARINA CING HSIEH*, (Assistant Professor of Law)**, born Waco, Texas, August 30, 1960; admitted to bar, 1991, Pennsylvania. *Education:* Harvard University (A.B., 1982); Boalt Hall (University of California) (J.D., 1988). ***COURSES: Civil Procedure, Criminal Procedure, Civil Rights/Race Discrimination. ***Email:*** mhsieh@law.umaryland.edu

DAVID A. HYMAN*, (Professor of Law)**, born Cambridge, Massachusetts, August 16, 1961; admitted to bar, 1989, Illinois; 1996, District of Columbia. *Education:* University of Chicago (B.A., 1983; J.D., 1989). ***COURSES: Civil Procedure, Health Care Finance, Health Care Law, Insurance Law, Tax Policy. ***Email:*** dhyman@law.umaryland.edu

SHERRILYN A. IFILL*, (Associate Professor of Law)**, born New York, December 17, 1962; admitted to bar, 1988, New York. *Education:* Instituto Internacional; Vassar College (B.A., 1984); New York University School of Law (J.D., 1987). ***COURSES: Civil Procedure, Complex Litigation, Constitutional Law, Environmental Justice. ***Email:*** sifill@law.umaryland.edu

ROBERT I. KELLER*, (Professor of Law)**, born Brooklyn, New York, June 2, 1942; admitted to bar, 1967, Pennsylvania. *Education:* University of Pennsylvania (B.S., 1963); Harvard University (J.D., 1966). ***COURSES: Accounting, Estate Planning, Estates & Gift Taxation, Taxation, Federal, Taxation, State & Local. ***Email:*** rkeller@law.umaryland.edu

ANDREW J. KING*, (Professor of Law)**, born United States, April 23, 1941; admitted to bar, 1966, Illinois. *Education:* Harvard University (LL.B., 1963); Antioch College (B.A., 1966); University of Wisconsin (Ph.D., 1975). ***COURSES: Estates & Trusts, Legal History (Colonial to Civil War and Civil War to Present), Legal Method, Legal Research & Writing, Personal Property, Real Property, Religion & Law. ***Email:*** aking@law.umaryland.edu

SUSAN LEVITON*, (Law School Professor)**, born Baltimore, Maryland, September 21, 1947; admitted to bar, 1972, Maryland. *Education:* University of Maryland (B.S., 1969); University of Maryland School of Law (J.D., 1972). ***COURSES: Clinical Law, Education Law, Family Law. ***Email:*** sleviton@law.umaryland.edu

MICHAEL A. MILLEMANN*, (Jacob A. France Professor of Public Interest Law)**, born Freeport, New Jersey, July 16, 1944; admitted to bar, 1969, Maryland. *Education:* Dartmouth College (B.A., 1966); University of Oregon; Georgetown University (J.D., 1969). ***COURSES: Contracts, Constitutional Law, Clinical Education, Death Penalty, Legal Profession. ***Email:*** mmillemann@law.umaryland.edu

TRICIA DIANE O'NEILL*, (Assistant Dean for Student Affairs)**, born Lansing, Michigan; admitted to bar, 1987, Maryland. *Education:* University of Maryland (B.A., 1984); University of Maryland School of Law (J.D., 1987). ***COURSES: Women & The Law. ***Email:*** toneill@law.umaryland.edu

JOAN L. O'SULLIVAN*, (Law School Associate Professor)**, born New London, Connecticut, April 3, 1946; admitted to bar, 1975, Maryland. *Education:* Butler University (B.A., 1968); University of Maryland School of Law (J.D., 1975). ***COURSES: Guardianship Clinic, Health & Elder Law Clinic, Helath Care for the Elderly Poor, Health Care for the Poor. ***Email:*** josullivan@law.umaryland.edu

ROBERT V. PERCIVAL*, (Professor of Law and Director, Environmental Law Program and Robert Stanton Scholar)**, born Des Moines, Iowa, May 19, 1952; admitted to bar, 1978, California; 1981, District of Columbia; 1988, Maryland. *Education:* Macalester College (B.A., 1972); Stanford University (M.A., 1978; J.D., 1978). ***COURSES: Comparative Law, Environmental & Administrative Law, Environmental Law Clinic, Environmental Law, Environmental Seminar, Lead Poisoning, Torts, Toxic Torts. ***Email:*** rpercival@law.umaryland.edu

THOMAS E. PEREZ*, (Assistant Professor and Director, Clinical Law Program)**, born Buffalo, New York, October 7, 1961; admitted to bar, 1988, New York; 1997, District of Columbia. *Education:* Brown University (A.B., 1983); Harvard University (M.A., 1987); Harvard Law School (J.D., 1987). ***COURSES: Civil Rights, Clinical Programs, Criminal Law. ***Email:*** tperez@law.umaryland.edu

GARRETT POWER*, (Professor of Law)**, born Baltimore, Maryland, October 16, 1938. *Education:* Duke University (B.A., 1960; LL.B., 1962); University of Illinois College of Law (LL.M., 1965). ***COURSES: Land Use Planning, Law & Economics, Legal History, Real Property. ***Email:*** gpower@law.umaryland.edu

PETER E. QUINT*, (Jacob A. France Professor of Constitutional Law)**, born Detroit, Michigan, March 8, 1940; admitted to bar, 1965, Michigan; 1968, New York. *Education:* Harvard University (A.B., 1961; LL.B., 1964); Oxford University (Diploma in Law, 1965). ***COURSES: Comparative Constitutional Law, Constitutional Law, Evidence, First Amendment, International Human Rights, Torts. ***Email:*** pquint@law.umaryland.edu

WILLIAM L. REYNOLDS*, (Jacob A. France Professor of Judicial Process)**, born Baltimore, Maryland, July 26, 1945; admitted to bar, 1972, Maryland. *Education:* Dartmouth College (A.B., 1967); Harvard Law School (J.D., 1970). ***COURSES: Conflicts of Laws, Constitutional Law, International Transactions, Legal Methods, Legal Profession. ***Email:*** wreynolds@law.umaryland.edu

***STEVEN D. SCHWINN*, (Law School Assistant Professor)**, born Dayton, Ohio, August 15, 1969; admitted to bar, 1995, Michigan.

(This Listing Continued)

UNIVERSITY OF MARYLAND SCHOOL OF LAW —Continued

Education: Michigan State University (B.A., 1992); American University, Washington College of Law (J.D., 1995). ***COURSES:*** Legal Analysis and Writing. ***Email:*** sschwinn@law.umaryland.edu

JANA SINGER, **(Professor of Law)**, born Boston, Massachusetts, May 22, 1955; admitted to bar, 1981, District of Columbia. *Education:* Dartmouth College (A.B., 1977); Yale University Law School (J.D., 1982). ***COURSES:*** Children and Law, Civil Procedure, Family Law. ***Email:*** jsinger@law.umaryland.edu

RENA I. STEINZOR, **(Professor of Law & Director, Environmental Law Clinic)**, born Topeka, Kansas, August 9, 1949; admitted to bar, 1977, New York; 1979, District of Columbia; 1995, Maryland. *Education:* University of Wisconsin (B.A., 1971); Columbia University Law School (J.D., 1976). ***COURSES:*** Environmental Law & Science, Environmental Law Clinic, Torts. ***Email:*** rsteinzor@law.umaryland.edu

ROBERT E. SUGGS, **(Professor of Law)**, born Detroit, Michigan, September 6, 1947; admitted to bar, 1974, New York. *Education:* University of Michigan (B.A., 1968); Harvard Law School (J.D., 1973). ***COURSES:*** Contracts, Copyright, Corporations, Local Government, Not for profit Corporations, Race & Markets. ***Email:*** rsuggs@law.umaryland.edu

LAWRENCE M. SUNG, **(Assistant Professor)**, born Montreal, Canada, October 18, 1965; admitted to bar, 1993, Pennsylvania; 1994, District of Columbia; 2001, Oregon. *Education:* University of Pennsylvania (B.A., 1985); United States Department of Defense Uniformed Services (Ph.D., 1990); American University, Washington College of Law (J.D., 1993). ***COURSES:*** Intellectual Property Survey, Licensing and Technology Transfer Policy, Patent Law and Policy. ***Email:*** lsung@law.umaryland.edu

EDWARD A. TOMLINSON, **(Professor of Law)**, born New York, New York, June 4, 1939; admitted to bar, 1965, Maryland. *Education:* Princeton University (A.B., 1961); Harvard Law School (J.D., 1965). ***COURSES:*** Administrative Law, Comparative Law, Contracts, Criminal Justice, Legal Method. ***Email:*** etomlinson@law.umaryland.edu

KATHERINE L. VAUGHNS, **(Professor of Law)**, born Oakland, California, March 27, 1945; admitted to bar, 1971, California. *Education:* University of California at Berkeley (B.A., 1967); University of California, Berkeley School of Law, Boalt Hall (J.D., 1970). ***COURSES:*** Advanced Immigration, Civil Procedure, Conflict of Laws, Immigration Law. ***Email:*** kvaughns@law.umaryland.edu

ANTHONY JON WATERS, **(Professor of Law)**, born London, England, January 24, 1946. *Education:* University of Keele (B.A., 1972); Yale University (LL.M., 1974). ***COURSES:*** Consumer Law, Contracts, Criminal Law, Federal Criminal Law, Judicial Function, Taxation, Federal. ***Email:*** awaters@law.umaryland.edu

DEBORAH WEIMER, **(Law School Professor)**, born Rockville Center, New York, August 7, 1951; admitted to bar, 1979, New York; 1981, South Carolina; 1987, Maryland. *Education:* State University of New York, Old Westbury (B.A., 1975); New York University School of Law (J.D., 1978); Temple University (LL.M., 1987). ***COURSES:*** AIDS and the Law, Clinic, Trial Practice. ***Email:*** dweimer@law.umaryland.edu

MARLEY S. WEISS, **(Professor of Law)**, born Detroit, Michigan, August 25, 1949; admitted to bar, 1974, Michigan; 1985, Maryland. *Education:* Barnard College (B.A., 1971); Harvard Law School (J.D., 1974). ***COURSES:*** Employment Discrimination Law, Labor and Employment Law, Torts. ***Email:*** mweiss@law.umaryland.edu

ROGER C. WOLF, **(Law School Professor)**, born Cincinnati, Ohio, January 10, 1941; admitted to bar, 1968, District of Columbia; 1978, Maryland. *Education:* Harvard University (B.A., 1962); The George Washington University Law School (J.D., 1967). ***COURSES:*** Alternative Dispute Resolution, Clinical Teaching. ***Email:*** rwolf@law.umaryland.edu

GORDON G. YOUNG, **(Professor of Law)**, born June 29, 1946; admitted to bar, 1973, New York. *Education:* Rollins College (A.B., 1967); New York University School of Law (J.D., 1970); Harvard Law School (LL.M., 1972). ***COURSES:*** Administrative Law, Constitutional Law, Contracts, Federal Courts, First Amendment. ***Email:*** gyoung@law.umaryland.edu

UNIVERSITY OF MIAMI SCHOOL OF LAW

1311 MILLER DRIVE
CORAL GABLES, FLORIDA 33146
Telephone: (305) 284-2394
Fax: (305) 284-3210
Web: www.law.miami.edu

ABA Approved Since 1941

A Dynamic Institution

The University of Miami School of Law is located in a beautiful suburban area of a great metropolitan center. Along with a distinguished faculty, a carefully selected and exceptionally diverse student body, and excellent research library, the 72-year-old Law School offers an innovative curriculum that is rich, rigorous, and fully responsive to the needs of tomorrow's lawyers. The school offers the J.D. degree; joint JD programs in business, public health, and marine science; and seven LL.M. programs. The School is accredited by the American Bar Association and is a member of the Association of American Law Schools.

Rich Curriculum with Outstanding Faculty

The School provides some of the most extensive trial advocacy, and clinical programs in the country. Its unique first-year curriculum trains students to master both the theory and the craft of the law.

The faculty's varied legal backgrounds and diverse interests provide students with an intellectually challenging and multifaceted legal education, adding new national, international, and interdisciplinary dimensions to the School's established tradition of sound teaching and scholarship. Over half of the faculty has extensive international legal experience, which is reflected in the School's curriculum as well as in the scholarship of the faculty. The School is the only one in the continental U.S. to offer significant course work on international and comparative law subjects in Spanish.

The teaching and research strengths of the School's faculty, the innovative nature of its educational program, and the quality of its graduates have earned the School a reputation as one of the most exciting law schools in the country.

(This Listing Continued)

UNIVERSITY OF MIAMI SCHOOL OF LAW—*Continued*

Excellent Research Library

The Law School encompasses a complex of buildings which form a quadrangle around an open courtyard. In addition to several large classrooms, these buildings contain a number of smaller classrooms, where seminars and workshops are held; moot court rooms, where trial and appellate advocacy and other competitions take place; and administrative offices. Faculty offices are located in the Law Library. The newly renovated student lounge, snack bar, and courtyard are popular, informal gathering places for students and faculty.

The centerpiece of the Law School complex is the Law Library, one of the largest research law libraries in the Southeast. Law Library collections comprise over 530,000 volumes in print and microform. Taxation and estate planning, labor law, ocean law, environmental law, and international and foreign law are among the special subject strengths represented in the collection. The collection is highly regarded for its holdings on the law of Caribbean and Latin American states. All Law Library collections are available for student use.

An expansion and renovation project increased the Law Library's size to 78,000 square feet, adding substantially to student-oriented facilities such as electronic classrooms, group study rooms and spacious reading areas. Carrels throughout the Law Library contain computers or connections for laptops to communicate with the School of Law's network. The network provides access to a wide variety of on-line information resources, including LEXIS, Westlaw, computer-assisted legal instruction (CALI) materials, plus access to the Internet and e-mail, as well as popular word processing and spreadsheet applications.

The Law Library's staff consists of 13 professional librarians and 15 other staff members. All are committed to providing a high level of service to students and faculty.

In addition to Law Library collections and facilities, students and faculty have access to the University's network of general and specialized libraries. Adjacent to the Law School complex, the University's Otto G. Richter Library contains over 1.6 million volumes, offering important support for interdisciplinary research. Resources of the School of Medicine and School of Marine and Atmospheric Science libraries also are available for research in health and environmental-related areas.

Diverse and Talented Student Body

The Law School admits first-year students only in the fall semester. Its gives careful consideration not only to each applicant's undergraduate record and LSAT, but also to personal information such as obstacles overcome, graduate studies, job history, and significant extracurricular and community activities. Special care is taken to ensure that the entering class is a highly talented and select group, representing a wide variety of cultural, racial, ethnic, religious, and geographic backgrounds. The Law School takes great pride in the diversity of its students and faculty, as attorneys they develop the flexibility and understanding that comes with exposure to viewpoints of persons whose life experiences have been different from their own.

The Law School also accepts students who have undergraduate or law degrees from accredited foreign schools; in 1997, the last year for which statistics are available, the Law School graduated more foreign students from its J.D. program than any other ABA-accredited school. In addition, the LLM program in comparative law typically enrolls over 35 foreign lawyers from 20 or more nations.

Generous Financial Aid

An abundance of financial assistance in the form of scholarships, low interest student loans, and employment opportunities is available for qualified students. In recent years, approximately one-third of admitted students have been awarded scholarships. Over $3.5 million is awarded in financial aid to the Law School's students each year, with over $3 million devoted to scholarships alone.

A Cosmopolitan Community

The Law School is located on the 260-acre main Coral Gables campus of the University of Miami, one of the largest private research universities in the United States. Long regarded as one of Florida's most desirable residential areas and increasingly recognized as an international business center, Coral Gables offers all the benefits of large-city living in a relaxed subtropical setting.

Next door to Coral Gables is the City of Miami, a burgeoning international center for trade and finance. Miami and the greater South Florida region have one of the most dynamic and rapidly expanding legal communities in the country. Thus, the community provides numerous opportunities for internships, clinical programs, and the law clerking experiences. Students can commute quickly and easily between campus and the downtown Miami legal community via Metrorail, an elevated rail system.

The cultural diversity of Miami makes for an extraordinary setting in which to live while attending law school. Greater Miami is comprised of many distinctive neighborhoods, among them: Art Deco-inspired South Beach; "Little Havana;" fashionable Coconut Grove; and South Miami, with its small-town ambiance. In addition, South Florida offers a wealth of cultural attractions, sporting events, and natural treasures to enjoy year-round.

Most students reside in the vicinity of the Law School, where apartments are plentiful and affordable; on-campus housing is limited.

Dean: Dennis O. Lynch (305) 284-2394
Associate Dean: Stephen J. Schnably (305) 284-3976
Admissions: Michael L. Goodnight (305) 284-4859
Student Recruiting: Therese Lambert (305) 284-6746
Financial Aid: Felicita Colon (305) 284-3168
Library: Sally Wise (305) 284-2755
Career Planning: Marcelyn Cox (305) 284-5301
Registrar: Cindy Busch (305) 284-4825
Alumni Relations: Carol Cope (305) 284-4849

FULL TIME FACULTY

DENNIS O. LYNCH,* (Dean and Professor of Law)**, born Caldwell, Idaho, October 4, 1942; admitted to bar, 1969, District of Columbia. *Education:* University of Oregon (B.A., 1965); Harvard Law School (J.D., 1969, *Cum Laude*); Yale Law School (LL.M., 1973; J.S.D., 1979). ***COURSES: Civil Procedure, Labor Law, Labor Arbitration.

***DAVID ABRAHAM,* (Professor of Law)**, born Antwerp, Belgium, November 9, 1946; admitted to bar, 1990, New York and New Jersey.

(This Listing Continued)

UNIVERSITY OF MIAMI SCHOOL OF LAW—Continued

Education: University of Chicago (B.A., 1968; Ph.D., 1977); University of Pennsylvania (J.D., 1989). ***COURSES:*** Property, Immigration, Legal Theory, Democratization Seminar. ***Email:*** dabraham@law.miami.edu

ANTHONY V. ALFIERI,* (Professor of Law and Director, Center for Ethics & Public Service)**, born New York, New York, June 6, 1959; admitted to bar, 1985, New York. *Education:* Brown University (A.B., 1981); Columbia University School of Law (J.D., 1984). ***COURSES: Civil Procedure, Legal Profession, Legal Ethics. ***Email:*** aalfieri@law.miami.edu

TERENCE J. ANDERSON,* (Professor of Law)**, born Chicago, Illinois; admitted to bar, 1967, Illinois; 1973, District of Columbia; 1977, Florida. *Education:* Wabash College (B.A., 1961); University of Chicago Law School (J.D., 1964). ***COURSES: Evidence, Legal Reasoning. ***Email:*** tanderson@law.miami.edu

WILLIAM S. BLATT,* (Professor of Law)**, born Chicago, Illinois, February 20, 1956; admitted to bar, 1984, New York and District of Columbia; 1985, Tax Court. *Education:* Dartmouth College (A.B., 1978); Harvard Law School (J.D., 1982); Georgetown University Law Center (LL.M., 1988). ***COURSES: Federal Income Tax I, Federal Income Tax of Business Entities, Legislation, Tax Policy. ***Email:*** wblatt@law.miami.edu

CAROLINE M. BRADLEY,* (Professor of Law)**, *Education:* Jesus College, Cambridge University (LL.M., 1984). ***COURSES: European Community Law, United States Securities Regulation, Business Associations, Globalization of Law, International Securities. ***Email:*** cbradley@law.miami.edu

KENNETH M. CASEBEER,* (Professor of Law)**, born Barrett, Indiana, August 21, 1949. *Education:* Georgetown University (A.B., 1971); Harvard Law School (J.D., 1974). ***COURSES: Labor Law and History, Constitutional Law, Jurisprudence. ***Email:*** casebeer@law.miami.edu

DONNA K. COKER,* (Associate Professor of Law)**, born Russleville, Arizona, January 8, 1957; admitted to bar, 1991, California. *Education:* Harding University (B.S.W., 1978); University of Arkansas at Little Rock (M.S.W., 1982); Stanford Law School (J.D., 1991). ***COURSES: Family Law, Domestic Violence Seminar, Substantive Criminal Law. ***Email:*** dcoker@law.miami.edu

MARY I. COOMBS,* (Professor of Law)**, *Education:* University of Michigan (B.A., 1965; M.A., 1967; J.D., 1978). ***COURSES: Criminal Law, Women and the Law, Family Law, International Criminal Law. ***Email:*** mcoombs@law.miami.edu

STEPHEN M. DIAMOND,* (Professor of Law)**, born Detroit, Michigan, April 25, 1946; admitted to bar, 1977, New York. *Education:* Swarthmore (B.A., 1967); Harvard (Ph.D., in History, 1976; J.D., 1976); Cambridge University (Certificate in Anthropology, 1970). ***COURSES: American Legal History, Local Government, Alcoholic Beverage Law, Food Law, Torts. ***Email:*** sdiamond@law.miami.edu

MARY DOYLE,* (Dean Emeritus and Professor of Law)**, *Education:* Radcliffe College (B.A., 1965); Columbia Law School (LL.B., 1968). ***COURSES: Property Law, Land Use, Water Law. ***Email:*** mdoyle@law.miami.edu

JOHN HART ELY,* (Richard A. Hausler Professor of Law)**, born New York, New York, December 3, 1938; admitted to bar, 1965, District of Columbia; 1967, California. *Education:* Princeton (A.B., 1960); Yale Law School (LL.B., 1963). ***COURSES: Constitutional Law. ***Email:*** jely@law.miami.edu

MARC A. FAJER,* (Professor of Law)**, *Education:* Stanford University (A.B., 1982); Stanford Law School (J.D., 1985). ***COURSES: Property Law, Antitrust Law, American Legal History, Constitutional Law, Legal Process. ***Email:*** mfajer@law.miami.edu

R. MICHAEL FISCHL,* (Professor of Law)**, born Evanston, Illinois, July 30, 1952; admitted to bar, 1978, District of Columbia. *Education:* Indiana University; University of Illinois (B.A., 1975); Harvard Law School (J.D., 1978). ***COURSES: Labor Law, Employment Law, Contracts, Evidence. ***Email:*** mfischl@law.miami.edu

CLARK J. FRESHMAN,* (Professor of Law)**, born New York, New York, March 2, 1965; admitted to bar, 1992, California. *Education:* Harvard College (B.A., 1986); University College, Oxford (B.A., 1988); Stanford Law School (J.D., 1991). ***COURSES: Civil Procedure, Alternative Dispute Resolution, Civil Rights, Arbitration. ***Email:*** cfreshma@law.miami.edu

A. MICHAEL FROOMKIN,* (Professor of Law)**, born New York, New York, July 14, 1960; admitted to bar, 1988, New York; 1989, District of Columbia. *Education:* Yale College (B.A., 1982); Cambridge University (M.P.H.I., 1984); Yale Law School (J.D., 1987). ***COURSES: Administrative Law, Constitutional Law I, Internet Law, Jurisprudence. ***Email:*** froomkin@law.miami.edu

JOHN T. GAUBATZ,* (Professor of Law)**, born Denver, Colorado, April 21, 1942; admitted to bar, 1967, Colorado. *Education:* Colorado State University (B.S., 1964); University of Chicago (J.D., 1967). ***COURSES: Wills, Trusts, Estate Planning, Employee Benefits, Patents, Legal Process. ***Email:*** jgaubatz@law.miami.edu

MICHAEL H. GRAHAM,* (Professor of Law)**, born Brooklyn, New York, January 31, 1943; admitted to bar, 1967, New York; 1975, Illinois. *Education:* University of Pennsylvania (B.S.E., 1964); Columbia Law School (J.D., 1967). ***COURSES: Evidence, Torts. ***Email:*** mgraham@law.miami.edu

PATRICK O. GUDRIDGE,* (Professor of Law)**, born Mankato, Minnesota, December 23, 1949. *Education:* Harvard College (A.B., 1972); Harvard Law School (J.D., 1976). ***COURSES: Business Associations, Constitutional Law, Agency, Jurisprudence, Reconstruction Legal Theory Seminar. ***Email:*** pgudridge@law.miami.edu

STEPHEN K. HALPERT,* (Professor of Law)**, born Detroit, Michigan, May 3, 1951; admitted to bar, 1978, Massachusetts; 1982, Florida. *Education:* Harvard College (A.B., 1973; J.D., 1978); Emmanual College/Cambridge University (1974). ***COURSES: Securities Regulation, Bankruptcy, Insurance, Torts. ***Email:*** shalpert@law.miami.edu

FRANCES R. HILL,* (Professor of Law)**, born Tomah, Wisconsin, July 26, 1944; admitted to bar, 1985, District of Columbia. *Education:* University of Denver (B.A., 1966); University of Birmingham (M.A., 1967); Harvard (Ph.D., 1973); Yale Law School (J.D., 1984). ***COURSES: Taxation, Bankruptcy, Commercial Law. ***Email:*** fhill@law.miami.edu

ELIZABETH M. IGLESIAS,* (Professor of Law)**, *Education:* University of Michigan (B.A., 1984); Yale (J.D., 1988). ***COURSES: Employment Relations, Criminal Procedure, International Trade, Trade & Investments, Antitrust Law. ***Email:*** iglesias@law.miami.edu

D. MARVIN JONES,* (Professor of Law)**, *Education:* Union College (B.S., 1973); New York University (J.D., 1976). ***COURSES: Constitutional Law, Criminal Procedure, Employment Discrimination. ***Email:*** mjones@law.miami.edu

***SHARON E. KELLER,* (Assistant Dean of Academic Affairs and Research Associate Professor of Law)**, *Education:* Antioch College (B.A., 1972); University of Pennsylvania Law School (J.D., 1987).

(This Listing Continued)

UNIVERSITY OF MIAMI SCHOOL OF LAW—Continued

COURSES: Contract Law, Administrative Law, Agency. ***Email:*** skeller@law.miami.edu

STANLEY I. LANGBEIN*, (Professor of Law)**, *Education:* Yale College (A.B., 1970); Harvard Law School (J.D., 1973). ***COURSES: Administrative Law, Federal Income Taxation, International Tax, Banking Law, Commercial Law. ***Email:*** slangbei@law.miami.edu

LILI LEVI*, (Professor of Law)**, born Istanbul, Turkey, July 24, 1956; admitted to bar, 1981, New York. *Education:* Bryn Mawr College (A.B., 1977); Harvard Law School (J.D., 1981). ***COURSES: Broadcast Regulation, Business Associations, Copyright, Defamation. ***Email:*** llevi@law.miami.edu

MARTHA R. MAHONEY*, (Professor of Law)**, *Education:* Regents College (B.A., 1981); Tulane (M.A., 1985); Stanford Law School (J.D., 1989). ***COURSES: Property, Land Use, Public Interest Law, Criminal Law, Desegregation & Urban Development. ***Email:*** mmahoney@law.miami.edu

ELLIOTT MANNING*, (Professor of Law)**, born Atlanta, Georgia, June 7, 1935; admitted to bar, 1957, Georgia; 1959, New York; 1985, Florida. *Education:* Columbia College (A.B., 1955); Harvard (J.D., 1958). ***COURSES: Federal Tax, Corporate, Business Planning. ***Email:*** emanning@law.miami.edu

M. MINNETTE MASSEY*, (Professor of Law)**, born Oakland, California, May 5, 1929; admitted to bar, 1951, Florida. *Education:* University of Miami (B.B.A., 1948; LL.B., 1951; M.A., 1952); New York University (LL.M., 1958). ***COURSES: Civil Procedure, Federal Jurisdiction. ***Email:*** mmassey@law.miami.edu

BERNARD H. OXMAN*, (Professor of Law)**, *Education:* Columbia College (A.B., 1962); Columbia Law School (J.D., 1965). ***COURSES: International Law, Civil Procedure, Conflict of Laws, Torts, Law of the Sea. ***Email:*** bhoxman@law.miami.edu

THOMAS A. ROBINSON*, (Professor of Law)**, born Coronado, California, July 24, 1943; admitted to bar, 1973, California; 1982, Florida. *Education:* University of Idaho (B.S.E.E., 1966); University of California at Los Angeles (J.D., 1969); Oxford University (B.Litt., 1975). ***COURSES: Federal Income Taxation, Trust & Estates, Professional Management. ***Email:*** trobinso@law.miami.edu

LAURENCE M. ROSE*, (Professor of Law)**, born Brooklyn, New York, July 22, 1947; admitted to bar, 1972, Vermont; 1976, Kansas. *Education:* State University of New York at Stony Brook (B.A., 1969); New York University (J.D., 1972). ***COURSES: Litigation Skills, Clinical Programs. ***Email:*** lrose@law.miami.edu

ROBERT E. ROSEN*, (Professor of Law)**, born New York, New York, June 14, 1952; admitted to bar, 1981, California. *Education:* Harvard College (A.B., 1974); Harvard Law School (J.D., 1979). ***COURSES: Legal Ethics, Contracts. ***Email:*** rrosen@law.miami.edu

KEITH S. ROSENN*, (Professor of Law)**, born Wilkesbarre, Pennsylvania, December 9, 1938; admitted to bar, 1964, Pennsylvania; 1981, Florida. *Education:* Amherst College (B.A., 1960); Yale Law School (LL.B., 1963). ***COURSES: Constitutional Law, Comparative Law, Latin American Law. ***Email:*** krosenn@law.miami.edu

STEPHEN J. SCHNABLY*, (Associate Dean and Professor of Law)**, born Oak Park, Illinois, February 17, 1955; admitted to bar, 1981, District of Columbia. *Education:* Harvard College (A.B., 1976); Harvard Law School (J.D., 1981). ***COURSES: Property, Constitutional Law, International Human Rights Law. ***Email:*** schnably@law.miami.edu

JONATHAN SIMON*, (Professor of Law)**, *Education:* University of California at Berkeley (A.B., 1981; J.D., 1987; Ph.D., 1991). ***COURSES: Criminal Law and Procedure, Constitutional Law, Insurance Law. ***Email:*** jsimon@law.miami.edu

IRWIN P. STOTZKY*, (Professor of Law)**, *Education:* Wayne State University (A.B., 1969); University of Chicago Law School (J.D., 1974). ***COURSES: Constitutional Law, Criminal Law & Procedure, Elements, Jurisprudence & Legal Theory. ***Email:*** istotzky@law.miami.edu

ALAN C. SWAN*, (Professor of Law)**, born Kalimpong, India, December 29, 1933; admitted to bar, 1958, New York. *Education:* Albion College (B.A., 1954); University of Chicago (J.D., 1957). ***COURSES: International Economic Law, International Business Transactions, Contracts, Antitrust. ***Email:*** aswan@law.miami.edu

SAMUEL C. THOMPSON, JR.*, (Dean Emeritus and Professor of Law)**, born Harrisburg, Pennsylvania, October 25, 1943; admitted to bar, 1972, New York; 1981, Virginia; 1983, Illinois. *Education:* Westchester University (B.S., 1965); University of Pennsylvania (M.A., 1969; J.D., 1971); New York University (LL.M., 1973). ***COURSES: Tax, Mergers & Acquisitions. ***Email:*** thompson@law.miami.edu

FRANCISCO VALDES*, (Professor of Law)**, *Education:* University of Florida (J.D., 1984); Stanford Law School (J.S.M., 1991; J.S.D., 1994). ***COURSES: Civil Procedure I, Constitutional Law, Critical Race Theory Seminar. ***Email:*** fvaldes@law.miami.edu

ROBERT H. WATERS*, (Professor of Law)**, born Kansas City, Kansas, October 25, 1926; admitted to bar, 1964, Kansas. *Education:* Northwestern University (Ph.B., 1953); University of Missouri (J.D., 1964). ***COURSES: Economic Regulation of Sports, Florida Constitutional Law. ***Email:*** rwaters@law.miami.edu

RICHARD L. WILLIAMSON, JR.*, (Professor of Law)**, born Buffalo, New York, September 19, 1943; admitted to bar, 1984, District of Columbia. *Education:* University of Southern California (A.B., 1967); American University (M.A., 1977); Harvard Law School (J.D., 1984). ***COURSES: Environmental Law, Administrative Law, Alternative Dispute Resolution, Public International Law, International Environmental Law. ***Email:*** rwilliam@law.miami.edu

BRUCE J. WINICK*, (Professor of Law)**, born New York, New York; admitted to bar, 1968, New York. *Education:* Brooklyn College, City University of New York (A.B., 1965); New York University (J.D., 1968). ***COURSES: Criminal Procedure, Constitutional Law, Administrative Law, Mental Health Law. ***Email:*** bwinick@law.miami.edu

SALLY H. WISE*, (Director of the Library and Professor of Law)**, born Oak Park, Illinois; admitted to bar, 1976, Washington. *Education:* Lake Forest College (B.S., 1972); Seattle University (J.D., 1976); University of Washington (M.L.L., 1977). ***COURSES: Legal Research Techniques. ***Email:*** swise@law.miami.edu

UNIVERSITY OF MICHIGAN LAW SCHOOL

625 SOUTH STATE STREET
ANN ARBOR, MICHIGAN 48109

UNIVERSITY OF MINNESOTA LAW SCHOOL

229 19th AVENUE SOUTH
MINNEAPOLIS, MINNESOTA 55455

UNIVERSITY OF MISSISSIPPI SCHOOL OF LAW

LAMAR LAW CENTER
UNIVERSITY, MISSISSIPPI 38677
Telephone: (662) 915-7361
Fax: (662) 915-5313
http://www.olemiss.edu/depts/law_school/law-hom.html

ABA Approved Since 1930.

Recognizing the need for formal law instruction in the state of Mississippi, the legislature in 1854 established the Department of Law at The University of Mississippi. Over the years, the law department has evolved into today's modern Law Center. Located in Oxford, Mississippi, on the main campus of The University of Mississippi, the Law Center is housed in Lamar Hall, named in honor of the late Mississippian, L.Q.C. Lamar, former Associate Justice of the United States Supreme Court and first law professor at the university. Oxford, a small town of approximately 10,000 people, lies nestled in the quiet hills of North Mississippi, just 75 miles southeast of bustling Memphis, Tennessee, and 180 miles north of the state capital of Jackson.

The University of Mississippi is the fourth oldest state-supported law school in the nation. The School of Law is fully approved by the American Bar Association and is a long-standing member of the Association of American Law Schools.

The law school library collection consists of 300,000 volumes and equivalents. The Library's website (http://library.law.olemiss.edu) provides access to the online catalog and other legal resources, including decisions of the U.S. District Court for the Northern District of Mississippi.

The law school student body numbers approximately 500, with a recent entering class of 179 for the fall 2000 term. The faculty numbers thirty-one, nine of whom are women.

Admission to law school is gained by committee approval, based upon an applicant's credentials. Although the LSAT and GPA are the most important factors in the admissions process, other considerations are: grade progression, quality of undergraduate institution, difficulty of major field of study, socio-economic circumstances, letters of recommendation and residency.

Since the first seven students entered The University of Mississippi's fledgling Department of Law in 1854, thousands of eager students have streamed into the law school, some already solid in their ambitions, others still searching. For these new students, the school has served both as a source of inspiration and as a pragmatic preparation for the task at hand.

Dean: Samuel M. Davis (662) 915-6901
Director of Admissions: Barbara Vinson (662) 915-6910
Financial Aid Director: Larry Ridgeway (662) 915-5788
Director of the Law Library: Kris Gilliland (662) 915-6817
Director of Career Services: Joyce Whittington (662) 915-6830
Associate Director, Alumni Affairs: Timothy L. Walsh (662) 915-7375

FULL TIME FACULTY

SAMUEL MARION DAVIS*, (Dean - School of Law; Director of Law Center, Jamie L. Whitten Chair of Law & Gov. and Professor of Law)**, born Pascagoula, Mississippi, November 24, 1944; admitted to bar, 1969, Mississippi. *Education:* University of Southern Mississippi (B.A., 1966); University of Mississippi (J.D., 1969); University of Virginia (LL.M., 1970). ***COURSES: Criminal Law, Children in the Legal System, Family Law, Juvenile Courts Seminar. ***Email:*** smdavis@olemiss.edu

---

GUTHRIE TURNER ABBOTT*, (Professor Emeritus & Butler, Snow, O'Mara, Stevens & Cannada Lecturer Emeritus)**, born Washington, D.C., December 13, 1942; admitted to bar, 1967, Mississippi. *Education:* University of Mississippi (B.A., 1964; J.D., 1967). ***COURSES: Real Property, Federal Procedure, Mississippi Practice and Procedure. ***Email:*** gtabbott@olemiss.edu

DONNA D. ADLER*, (Associate Professor of Law)**, born Hornell, New York, August 25, 1961; admitted to bar, 1986, Massachusetts. *Education:* Harvard University (B.A., 1983); Boston College Law School (J.D., 1986); University of Florida College of Law (LL.M., 1988). ***COURSES: Accounting and Taxation. ***Email:*** dadler@olemiss.edu

RICHARD LEE BARNES*, (Professor of Law & Leonard B. Melvin Distinguished Lecturer)**, born Willcox, Arizona, December 14, 1954; admitted to bar, 1979, Arizona. *Education:* University of Arizona (B.A., 1976; J.D., 1979); Northwestern University (LL.M., 1983). ***COURSES: Contracts, Commercial Law, Indian Law, Agricultural Law. ***Email:*** rbarnes@olemss.edu

DEBORAH HODGES BELL*, (Professor of Law & MS Defense Lawyers Assoc. Distinguished Lecturer)**, born Mississippi, November 8, 1953; admitted to bar, 1979, Mississippi; 1981, Georgia. *Education:* Mississippi College (B.A., 1975); University of Mississippi (J.D., 1979). ***COURSES: Property, Family Law, Housing Law. ***Email:*** dbell@olemiss.edu

***JOHN R. BRADLEY, JR.*, (Professor of Law)**, born Mississippi, January 10, 1938; admitted to bar, 1962, Mississippi. *Education:* Mississippi College (B.A., 1959); University of Vienna; Tulane

(This Listing Continued)

UNIVERSITY OF MISSISSIPPI SCHOOL OF LAW —Continued

University; University of Mississippi (J.D., 1962). ***COURSES:*** Workers' Compensation, Contracts, Corporations. ***Email:*** jbradley@olemiss.edu

CHARLES HENDRICKSON BROWER II*, (Croft Assistant Professor of International Law and Jessie D. Puckett, Jr., Lecturer)**, born New York, New York, March 13, 1967; admitted to bar, 1996, Minnesota; 1998, District of Columbia. *Education:* University of Vermont (B.A., 1989); University of Virginia (J.D., 1995). ***COURSES: International Litigation and Arbitration, International Trade, Public International Law. ***Email:*** cbrower@olemiss.edu

LARRY STEVEN BUSH*, (Professor of Law)**, born Ozark, Alabama, May 3, 1946; admitted to bar, 1974, Florida. *Education:* University of Florida (B.A., 1968; J.D., 1974); University of Cambridge (LL.M., 1979). ***COURSES: Labor, Employment, International Comparative. ***Email:*** lwbush@olemiss.edu

WILLIAM MONTGOMERY CHAMPION*, (Professor Emeritus and MS Defense Lawyers Assoc. Distinguished Lecturer Emeritus)**, born Edwards, Mississippi, January 31, 1932; admitted to bar, 1961, Mississippi. *Education:* Hinds Jr. College (A.A., 1951); Mississippi State College (B.S., 1953); University of Mississippi (LL.B., 1961); George Washington University (LL.M., 1962). ***COURSES: Property, Trusts, Future Interests, Legal Profession.

THOMAS K. CLANCY*, (Director, National Center for Justice and Visiting Professor of Law)**, admitted to bar, 1983, Maryland and District of Columbia. *Education:* University of Notre Dame (B.A., 1974); Vermont Law School (J.D., cum laude,1980). ***COURSES: Criminal Justice, Criminal Law, Constitutional Law. ***Email:*** ncjrl@olemiss.edu

GEORGE C. COCHRAN*, (Professor of Law)**, born Maysville, Kentucky, December 1, 1936; admitted to bar, 1965, District of Columbia. *Education:* North Carolina State University (B.S., 1958); University of North Carolina (J.D., 1964). ***COURSES: Constitutional Law, Federal Jurisdiction, Admiralty, Conflict of Laws, Administrative Law. ***Email:*** 1wgcc@olemiss.edu

AARON STORER CONDON*, (Professor Emeritus of Law)**, born Kosciusko, Mississippi, April 23, 1927; admitted to bar, 1952, Mississippi. *Education:* University of Alabama (A.B., 1950); University of Mississippi (J.D., 1968). ***COURSES: Legal Profession, General Practice, Criminal Law, Civil Procedure.

JOHN MICHAEL CZARNETZKY*, (Associate Professor of Law and Mitchell, McNutt, Threadgill, Smith & Sams Lecturer)**, born Beacon, New York, September 15, 1960; admitted to bar, 1989, Illinois; 1991, Virginia; 1992, District of Columbia. *Education:* Massachusetts Institute of Technology (B.S., 1982); University of Virginia (J.D., 1989). ***COURSES: Bankruptcy, Commercial Law, Civil Procedure, International Trade. ***Email:*** johnmc@olemiss.edu

ROBERT N. DAVIS*, (Professor of Law)**, born Kewanee, Illinois, September 20, 1953; admitted to bar, 1980, Iowa; 1993, Virginia. *Education:* University of Hartford (B.A., 1975); Georgetown University Law Center (J.D., 1978). ***COURSES: Constitutional Law & Administrative Law, Sports Law & International Security Law. ***Email:*** rdavis@olemiss.edu

JASON DERRICK*, (Acting Assistant Professor in Legal Writing)**, born McComb, Mississippi, October 26, 1973. *Education:* Mississippi College (B.A., 1996); University of Mississippi (J.D., 2000). ***COURSES: Legal Writing. ***Email:*** wjderric@olemiss.edu

MICHAEL FEATHERSTONE*, (Professor Emeritus)**, born Mt. Holly, North Carolina, January 14, 1941; admitted to bar, 1970, South Carolina. *Education:* Davidson College (A.B., 1963); University of South Carolina (J.D., 1970); University of Georgia (LL.M., 1971). ***COURSES: Family Law, Eminent Domain, Property.

MOLLY ELEANOR FERGUSSON*, (Assistant Professor of Law)**, born Columbia, South Carolina, August 20, 1973; admitted to bar, 2001, Mississippi. *Education:* Randolph-Macon Woman's College (B.A., 1995); University of Mississippi (J.D., 2001). ***COURSES: Legal Writing and Research. ***Email:*** mefergu1@olemiss.edu

GAIL M. FLATOW*, (Law Faculty)**, born Montpelier, Vermont, September 25, 1952; admitted to bar, 1996, Indiana; 1997, Florida. *Education:* Indiana University (A.B., 1988; M.A., 1993; J.D., 1996). ***COURSES: Writing. ***Email:*** gflatow@olemiss.edu

DON L. FRUGE*, (Professor Emeritus and President & CEO of the University of MS Foundation)**, born Meridian, MS August 19, 1945; admitted to bar, 1970, Mississippi. *Education:* University of Mississippi (B.B.A., Accounting, 1967; J.D., 1970); New York University (LL.M., in Taxation, 1971). ***COURSES: Estate Planning, Taxation. ***Email:*** dfruge@olemiss.edu

JOANNE IRENE GABRYNOWICZ*, (Research Professor and Director of the Remote Sensing & Space Law Center of Excellence)**, born Brooklyn, New York, July 27, 1949; admitted to bar, 1980, New York. *Education:* Hunter College (B.A., 1977); Yeshiva University Cardoza School of Law (J.D., 1980). ***COURSES: Space Law, Remote Sensing Law, Earth Observations. ***Email:*** jgabryno@olemiss.edu

KRIS GILLILAND*, (Director, Law Library; Assistant Professor)**, born Fayetteville, Arkansas, December 30, 1963; admitted to bar, 1991, Alabama. *Education:* Vanderbilt University (B.A., 1986); University of Alabama (J.D., 1991); University of Washington (M.L.S., 1992). ***COURSES: Legal Research. ***Email:*** gillilan@olemiss.edu

KAREN O. GREEN*, (Professor and MS Defense Lawyers Assoc. Distinguished Lecturer)**, born Grenada, Mississippi, May 31, 1949; admitted to bar, 1974, Mississippi. *Education:* University of Mississippi (B.S., 1971; J.D., 1974); New York University (LL.M., 1976). ***COURSES: Estate and Gift Taxation, Federal Income Taxation. ***Email:*** kgreen@olemiss.edu

***MATTHEW R. HALL*, (Assistant Professor)**, born July 7, 1964; admitted to bar, 1997, Kentucky. *Education:* Harvard University (A.B., 1987); University of Kentucky College of Law (J.D., 1997).

TIMOTHY LEE HALL*, (Professor of Law)**, born Tyler, Texas, October 28, 1955; admitted to bar, 1983, Texas. *Education:* University of Houston (B.A., 1978); Rice University; University of Texas (J.D., 1983). ***COURSES: Constitutional Law, Legal Ethics. ***Email:*** lwhall@olemiss.edu

MICHAEL H. HOFFHEIMER*, (Professor of Law & MS Defense Lawyers Assoc. Distinguished Lecturer)**, born Cincinnati, Ohio, December 21, 1954; admitted to bar, 1984, Ohio; 1985, District of Columbia (inactive). *Education:* The Johns Hopkins University (B.A., with honors in Philosophy, 1977); University of Chicago (Ph.D., 1981); University of Michigan (J.D., cum laude, 1984). ***COURSES: Civil Procedure, Criminal Law, Conflicts, Legal History.

WENDY KEITH*, (Visiting Professor of Law)**, born Cherry Point, North Carolina, November 14, 1967; admitted to bar, 1993, Mississippi; 1995, Wisconsin; 1996, Illinois. *Education:* University of Mississippi (B.S., 1990; J.D., 1993); New York School of Law (LL.M., 1994). ***COURSES: Tax, Corporations. ***Email:*** wabbott@olemiss.edu

ROBERT C. KHAYAT*, (Chancellor and Professor of Law)**, born Moss Point, MS, April 18, 1938; admitted to bar, 1966, Mississippi. *Education:* University of Mississippi (B.A.E., 1961; J.D., 1966); Yale University (LL.M., 1981). ***COURSES: Torts.

(This Listing Continued)

UNIVERSITY OF MISSISSIPPI SCHOOL OF LAW —Continued

PATRICIA KRUEGER*, (Acting Assistant Professor, Acting Legal Writing Specialist)**, born Durham, North Carolina, December 31, 1962; admitted to bar, 1991, Oregon; 1993, Mississippi. *Education:* Western Washington University (B.A., 1986); Willamette University College of Law (J.D., 1991). ***COURSES: Legal Writing, Legal Research. ***Email:*** pkrueger@olemiss.edu

TOM R. MASON*, (Professor of Law)**, born Duncan, Oklahoma, August 1, 1934; admitted to bar, 1962, Oklahoma; 1972, Colorado; 1975, Mississippi. *Education:* University of Oklahoma (B.S., 1957; J.D., 1962). ***COURSES: Torts, Oil and Gas, Evidence, Trial Practice, Pretrial Practice. ***Email:*** tmason@olemiss.edu

RICHARD JOSEPH MCLAUGHLIN*, (Associate Professor and Mitchell, McNutt, Threadgill, Smith & Sams Lecturer)**, born Urbana, Illinois, September 29, 1955; admitted to bar, 1986, Washington; 1988, Mississippi. *Education:* Humboldt State University (A.B., 1978); Tulane University (J.D., 1985); University of Washington (LL.M., 1987). ***COURSES: International, Environmental, Coastal, Land Use Planning, Admiralty. ***Email:*** lwrjm@olemiss.edu

GARY MYERS*, (Professor of Law)**, born Bellflower, California, September 10, 1962; admitted to bar, 1987, Georgia. *Education:* New York University (B.A., 1984); Duke University (J.D., 1986). ***COURSES: Antitrust, Intellectual Property, Media Law, Torts. ***Email:*** gmyers@olemiss.edu

JACK WADE NOWLIN*, (Assistant Professor and Jessie D. Puckett, Jr., Lecturer)**, born San Angelo, Texas, December 24, 1966; admitted to bar, 1994, Texas. *Education:* Angelo State University (B.A., 1991); University of Texas School of Law (J.D., 1994); Princeton University (Ph.D., 1999). ***COURSES: Constitutional Law, Jurisprudence, Criminal Procedure, Criminal Law. ***Email:*** jnowlin@olemiss.edu

E. FARISH PERCY*, (Assistant Professor of Law)**, born Greenville, Mississippi, August 26, 1966; admitted to bar, Mississippi; District of Columbia. *Education:* University of North Carolina, Chapel Hill (B.A., 1988); University of Virginia (J.D., 1991). ***COURSES: Torts, Civil Procedure. ***Email:*** farish@tollisonlaw.com

LARRY J. PITTMAN*, (Associate Professor and Jessie D. Puckett, Jr., Lecturer)**, born Charleston, Mississippi, October 25, 1960; admitted to bar, 1986, Michigan. *Education:* University of Mississippi (B.B.A., 1983; J.D., 1986); Harvard Law School (LL.M., 1992). ***COURSES: Law and Medicine, Health Law, Torts, Civil Procedure, Pretrial Practice, Alternative Dispute Resolution Process. ***Email:*** lpittman@olemiss.edu

LISA SHAW ROY*, (Assistant Professor)**, born Long Beach, California, November 10, 1970; admitted to bar, 1996, California. *Education:* University of California, Riverside (B.A., 1992); University of Southern California (J.D., 1996). ***COURSES: Contracts. ***Email:*** lisaroy@olemiss.edu

RONALD JOSEPH RYCHLAK*, (Professor of Law & Associate Dean, MS Defense Lawyers Assoc. Lecturer)**, born Columbus, Ohio, September 23, 1957; admitted to bar, 1983, Illinois. *Education:* Wabash College (B.A., 1980); Vanderbilt University School of Law (J.D., 1983). ***COURSES: Criminal Law, Criminal Procedure, Environmental Law, Trial Practice, Gaming Law. ***Email:*** rrychlak@olemiss.edu

CAROLYN ELLIS STATON*, (Provost and Professor of Law)**, born Vicksburg, Mississippi, January 25, 1946; admitted to bar, 1972, New Jersey; 1974, New York; 1978, Mississippi. *Education:* Tulane (B.A., 1967); Teachers College, Columbia University (M.A., 1969); Yale (J.D., 1972). ***COURSES: Evidence, Criminal Procedure, Sex Discrimination. ***Email:*** ces@olemiss.edu

ROBERT A. WEEMS*, (Professor of Law & Butler, Snow, O'Mara, Stevens & Cannada Lecturer)**, born Morton, Mississippi, January 8, 1937; admitted to bar, 1966, Mississippi. *Education:* Millsaps (B.S., 1959); University of Mississippi (J.D., 1966). ***COURSES: Torts, Evidence, Wills. ***Email:*** rweems@olemiss.edu

UNIVERSITY OF MISSOURI - COLUMBIA SCHOOL OF LAW

MISSOURI AND CONLEY AVENUES
COLUMBIA, MISSOURI 65211

UNIVERSITY OF MISSOURI - KANSAS CITY SCHOOL OF LAW

5100 ROCKHILL ROAD
KANSAS CITY, MISSOURI 64110
Telephone: (816) 235-1644
Fax: (816) 235-5276
http://www.law.umkc.edu

ABA Approved Since 1936.

The University of Missouri-Kansas City (UMKC) School of Law is part of an urban university located on a landscaped campus in a dynamic and diverse metropolitan area. The School was founded in 1895 by three young lawyers with the assistance of leading members of the Bench and Bar. It merged with the University of Kansas City in 1938 and became part of the University of Missouri in 1963. UMKC is the only law school located in Kansas City, the key city of the metroplex and takes advantage of its urban setting through active involvement with the legal, civic and social community surrounding it.

The School of Law offers both a full-time and a flexible part-time day program (Flex Program). The full-time program is the traditional three year program. Most students at the school are enrolled full-time.

The Law School is committed to providing sound legal training in a supportive, professional environment. Teaching, research and service are its hallmarks. Classes are small and student-faculty interaction is encouraged. Such interaction is facilitated in our modern law building by a physical structure that is unique to legal education. Student offices and carrels, located in suites adjoining the faculty offices are available to second and third year students. The law library contains a state-of-the-art Electronic Resource Center. Among other electronic equipment, the Center contains: The Virtual Classroom comprised of Pentium computers, which provides a teaching resource for instruction in the use of digital/optical databases; the Internet and World Wide Web; and multiple software applications of use to law students and lawyers. The Center also provides additional Pentium computers exclusively reserved for use by law students. All of the resources available in the Virtual Classroom, plus additional law student-related software, are also available on these machines. Having electronically

(This Listing Continued)

UNIVERSITY OF MISSOURI - KANSAS CITY SCHOOL OF LAW—Continued

established a Virtual Classroom in the law library, the school's plans call for expanding this access point to the World Wide Web and legal data bases to include faculty offices, classrooms, and student offices. The concept of the Virtual Classroom has been extended to the suites via the Virtual Law Office Project, which provides computers for use by students and faculty in the suites in conjunction with specialized instructional programs offered by the School of Law. It also has been extended to the faculty offices and plans call for expanding this access point to the World Wide Web and legal data bases to the classrooms and student offices. The School has programs leading to both the J.D. and LL.M. degrees.

Through a cooperative arrangement with the Bloch School of Business Administration, students may simultaneously pursue the J.D. and M.B.A. degrees. Students interested in taxation may earn both the J.D. and the LL.M. in Taxation on an accelerated basis, generally requiring only one additional semester (or two summer sessions) beyond that required for the J.D. degree. Similarly, students interested in Estate Planning have an accelerated J.D./LL.M. program with an estate planning emphasis. The School's Interdisciplinary urban legal affairs program leading to a Master of Laws in Urban Affairs prepares lawyers for specializing in practice, public service and corporate and financial institutions dealing with metropolitan area problems.

The curriculum is rich and diverse, with opportunities to obtain both depth and breadth. Teaching methods are varied and many faculty use real problems and "hands on" activities in required as well as elective classes. Our research and writing program is particularly strong, with an intensive full-year program for first year students, a research and writing requirement necessary for graduation, and upper-level writing and drafting electives. Students desiring an interdisciplinary focus are able to take courses toward the law degree in other graduate divisions of the university. The School is responsive to our rapidly changing legal world, adding new courses and adapting existing programs as the need arises.

Scholarship is an important part of the School. Faculty are actively involved in scholarly activity, producing law review articles and books for the academic community as well as materials of interest to practicing lawyers. The three journals published at the school, *The UMKC Law Review, The Urban Lawyer* (the official publication of the American Bar Association Section of Urban, State and Local Government), and the *Journal of the American Academy of Matrimonial Lawyers,* provide students with opportunities for active roles in shaping the course and pace of legal change.

Such service is an expected part of the esperit de corp of an urban-oriented law school. Accordingly, faculty, students and staff are active in the Kansas City community. Our externship program allows students to provide service to the Public Defender's Office, Legal Aid, and various state and federal courts while developing and honing their lawyering skills. Law school graduates are well represented in the Kansas City community as well. More than half the active judges of the state and federal courts in the Western District of Missouri are UMKC alums, as are two of the states Supreme Court Justices. Although most of our graduates practice in Missouri, we have alumni around the country. Graduates enter all varieties of public and private practice and increasingly use their legal training to make contributions to the business world, government and politics.

The Law School has a highly motivated, academically talented student body of approximately 500 J.D. and LL.M. students. While most of the students come from western Missouri and eastern Kansas, the School also draws excellent students from throughout the United States. The students consistently distinguish themselves in competition with other schools, often placing first or second in the region and achieving substantial success at the national level.

The Law School is housed in a modern, comfortable building well suited to professional training. The law library contains a complete collection of basic research materials and a growing collection of material in alternative formats. As has already been noted with respect to establishment of the Virtual Classroom, the library makes extensive use of technology to enhance users' access to research sources. It houses a Computer Media Center that contains LEXIS and WESTLAW training centers and a computer lab making word processing, computer-assisted learning exercises, interactive video, CD-ROM and other on-line research products and Internet access available for student use. The library staff is accessible and helpful.

As we enter our second century, the Law School remains committed, as a public, urban institution, to providing a high quality legal education for our students, a supportive environment for faculty teaching and research, and a valuable resource for the community.

Dean: Burnele V. Powell (816) 235-1007
Associate Dean: Jeffrey Berman (816) 235-1640
Assistant Dean: Matthew Davis (816) 235-5739
Director of Admissions: Jean Klosterman (816) 235-1672
Director of Student Support Services: Nicole Francis (816) 235-1654
Library Director: Patricia O'Connor (816) 235-2440
Director of Career Services: Linda Trout (816) 235-1669
Development Communications Officer: Debra Simon (816) 235-5361
Business Manager: Tom Green (816) 235-1646
Director, Continuing Legal Education: Fred Green (816) 235-1647

FULL TIME FACULTY

BURNELE VENABLE POWELL,* (Dean)**, born Kansas City, Missouri, March 5, 1947; admitted to bar, 1973, Wisconsin; 1979, Massachusetts. *Education:* University of Missouri, Kansas City (B.A., 1970); University of Wisconsin (J.D., 1973); Harvard University (LL.M., 1979). ***COURSES: Administrative Law, Real Property, Professional Responsibility. ***Email:*** powellb@umkc.edu

DAVID JACKS ACHTENBERG,* (Associate Professor)**, born Kansas City, Missouri, October 10, 1948; admitted to bar, 1973, Missouri. *Education:* Harvard University (B.A., 1970); University of Chicago (J.D., 1973). ***COURSES: Civil Procedure, Evidence, Civil Rights, Supreme Court. ***Email:*** achtenbd@umkc.edu

MARK BERGER,* (Professor)**, born New York, New York, January 23, 1946; admitted to bar, 1969, Connecticut; 1974, Missouri. *Education:* Columbia University (A.B., 1966); Yale University (J.D., 1969). ***COURSES: Labor, Employment, Criminal Law and Procedure, Arbitration. ***Email:*** bergerm@umkc.edu

JEFFREY B. BERMAN,* (Associate Dean)**, born New York, New York, March 20, 1942; admitted to bar, 1966, New York; 1972, Colorado; 1973, Missouri. *Education:* City University of New York (B.S., 1963); Brooklyn Law School (J.D., 1966); University of Denver (M.S.L.S., 1973). ***COURSES: Civil Procedure, Evidence, Trial Advocacy. ***Email:*** bermanj@umkc.edu

(This Listing Continued)

UNIVERSITY OF MISSOURI - KANSAS CITY SCHOOL OF LAW—Continued

JULIE M. CHESLIK*, (Associate Professor)**, born St. Paul, Minnesota, May 10, 1960; admitted to bar, 1985, Missouri. *Education:* University of Iowa (B.A., 1982; J.D., 1985). ***COURSES: Property, Estates & Trusts, Land Use Planning. ***Email:*** cheslikj@umkc.edu

MARCIA S. COOK*, (Assistant Clinical Professor of Law)**, born Monticello, Iowa, October 20, 1967; admitted to bar, 1993, Missouri; 1994, Kansas. *Education:* University of Northern Iowa (B.A., 1990); University of Arkansas-Fayetteville (J.D., 1993). ***COURSES: Introduction to Law, Lawyering Process. ***Email:*** cookm@umkc.edu

CORINNE COOPER*, (Professor)**, born Albuquerque, New Mexico, July 12, 1952; admitted to bar, 1978, Arizona; 1985, Missouri. *Education:* University of Arizona (B.A., 1975; J.D., 1978). ***COURSES: Contracts, Commercial Transactions, Sales & Leasing. ***Email:*** cooperc@umkc.edu

ROBERT C. DOWNS*, (Professor)**, born Aurora, Missouri, May 27, 1941; admitted to bar, 1966, Nebraska; 1986, Missouri. *Education:* Kansas State University (B.A.); University of Nebraska (J.D.); University of Missouri, Kansas City (LL.M.). ***COURSES: Business Organizations, Contracts, Negotiating, Securities Regulation, Jurisprudence. ***Email:*** downsr@umkc.edu

WILLIAM GEORGE ECKHARDT*, (Clinical Professor of Law, Director of Urban Affairs Outreach)**, born Ames, Iowa, January 7, 1941; admitted to bar, 1966, Virginia. *Education:* University of Mississippi (B.A., 1963); University of Virginia (LL.B., 1966); The Judge Advocate General's School (LL.M., Equivalent, 1970). ***COURSES: Clinical Law, Administrative Law, Evidence, National Security Law, Introduction to Law. ***Email:*** eckhardw@umkc.edu

KENNETH D. FERGUSON*, (Associate Professor)**, born Georgetown, Guyana, April 9, 1953; admitted to bar, 1986, Missouri. *Education:* Drake University (B.A., 1975); Oral Roberts University (J.D., 1986). ***COURSES: Contracts, Secured Transactions, Commercial Transactions, Debtor/Creditor Rights, Sports & Entertainment Law. ***Email:*** fergusok@umkc.edu

BARBARA GLESNER-FINES*, (Associate Professor)**, born Texas, March 20, 1957; admitted to bar, 1983, Wisconsin. *Education:* Thomas Jefferson College (B.Ph., 1980); University of Wisconsin-Madison (J.D., 1983); Yale University Law School (LL.M., 1986). ***COURSES: Professional Ethics, Remedies, Civil Procedure, Family Law, Seminar Legal Education. ***Email:*** glesnerb@umkc.edu

FRANCIS M. HANNA*, (Professor)**, born Tulsa, Oklahoma, August 10, 1935; admitted to bar, 1962, Missouri. *Education:* Chicago State University (B.Ed., 1959); Northwestern University (J.D., 1962). ***COURSES: Estates and Trusts, Administration of Estates and Trusts, Estate Planning, Professional Malpractice Litigation. ***Email:*** hannaf@umkc.edu

EDWIN T. HOOD*, (Professor and Director of LL.M. Tax Program)**, born Ft. Dodge, Iowa, August 2, 1940; admitted to bar, 1966, Iowa; 1969, California; 1978, Missouri. *Education:* University of Iowa (B.B.A., 1962; J.D., 1966); New York University School of Law (LL.M. in Taxation, 1967). ***COURSES: Federal Taxation, Taxation of Estates, Gift & Trusts, Estates and Trusts, Corporate Taxation, International Taxation. ***Email:*** hoode@umkc.edu

CHRISTOPHER R. HOYT*, (Professor)**, born Milwaukee, Wisconsin, November 7, 1953; admitted to bar, 1979, Missouri. *Education:* Northwestern University (B.A.); University of Wisconsin (M.S.; J.D.). ***COURSES: Tax, Deferred Compensation, Business Organizations, Charitable Organizations. ***Email:*** hoytc@umkc.edu

MARY KAY KISTHARDT*, (Associate Professor)**, born Pennsylvania, May 24, 1953; admitted to bar, 1978, Pennsylvania. *Education:* Kings College (B.A., 1975); Dickinson School of Law (J.D., 1978); Yale Law School (LL.M., 1985). ***COURSES: Family Law, Children in the Law, Alternative Dispute Resolution, Mediation. ***Email:*** kistharm@umkc.edu

KRIS W. KOBACH*, (Professor)**, born Madison, Wisconsin, March 26, 1966; admitted to bar, 1995, Kansas. *Education:* Harvard (A.B., 1988); Oxford University (D.Phil. and M.Phil., 1992); Yale (J.D., 1995). ***COURSES: Constitutional Law, Legal History, Legislation. ***Email:*** kobachk@umkc.edu

JOHN Q. LAFOND*, (Edwards A. Smith/Missouri Chair in Law, the Constitution and Society)**, born Chicago, Illinois, 1943; admitted to bar, 1969, New York. *Education:* Yale (B.A., 1965; J.D., 1968). ***COURSES: Criminal Law, Criminal Procedure, Constitutional Law, Law & Mental Health, Professional Responsibility, Seminar in Sex Offenders. ***Email:*** lafondj@umkc.edu

NANCY LEVIT*, (Professor)**, born Kansas City, Missouri, September 28, 1958; admitted to bar, 1984, Kansas. *Education:* Bates College (B.A., 1980); University of Kansas (J.D., 1984). ***COURSES: Torts, Jurisprudence, Criminal Law, Constitutional Law. ***Email:*** levitn@umkc.edu

DOUGLAS OWEN LINDER*, (Professor)**, born Mankato, Minnesota, March 5, 1952; admitted to bar, 1976, Minnesota. *Education:* Gustavus Adolphus College (B.A., 1973); Stanford Law School (J.D., 1976). ***COURSES: Constitutional Law, Environmental Law, Famous Trials, Communications Law. ***Email:*** linderd@umkc.edu

ANDRE A. MOENSSENS*, (Douglas Stripp Missouri Professor of Law)**, born Belgium, January 13, 1930; admitted to bar, 1966, Illinois; 1974, Virginia. *Education:* St. Jan Berchmans College, Belgium (1950); Chicago-Kent College of Law (J.D., 1966); Northwestern University (LL.M., 1967). ***COURSES: Trial Practice, Scientific Evidence, Criminal Law, Forensic Dispute Resolution. ***Email:*** moenssensa@umkc.edu

PATRICIA JEAN O'CONNOR*, (Director of the Law Library and Associate Professor)**, born March 7, 1952. *Education:* University of Oklahoma (B.A., 1973; M.L.S., 1974); University of Texas (J.D., 1982). ***COURSES: Legal Research, Computers and the Law. ***Email:*** oconnorp@umkc.edu

JENNIFER O'HARE*, (Associate Professor)**, born Flushing, New York, May 12, 1964; admitted to bar, 1991, New York. *Education:* The Wharton School of the University of Pennsylvania (B.S., 1986); George Washington University Law School (J.D., 1990). ***COURSES: Securities Regulation, Business Planning, Federal Income Taxation. ***Email:*** oharej@umkc.edu

COLIN BENJAMIN PICKER*, (Associate Professor)**, born Santa Barbara, California, October 12, 1965; admitted to bar, 1997, Maryland and District of Columbia. *Education:* Bowdoin College (A.B., 1992); Yale Law School (J.D., 1996). ***COURSES: International Business Transactions, International Trade & Finance, Conflict of Laws, Comparative Law. ***Email:*** pickerc@umkc.edu

JOHN W. RAGSDALE, JR.*, (Professor)**, born Neosha, Missouri, October 14, 1944; admitted to bar, 1969, Colorado. *Education:* Middlebury College; University of Colorado (J.D., 1969); University of Missouri-Kansas City (LL.M., 1972); Northwestern University (S.J.D., 1985). ***COURSES: Law and the American Indian, Natural Resources, Preservation Law, Water Law. ***Email:*** ragsdalj@umkc.edu

PATRICK A. RANDOLPH, JR.*, (Professor)**, born Pasadena, California, September 2, 1944; admitted to bar, 1970, California; 1981, Oregon and Missouri. *Education:* Yale University (B.A., 1966); University of California, Berkeley (J.D., 1969). ***COURSES: Property Law, Real Estate Law: Transactions, Finance, Leasing. ***Email:*** randolpp@umkc.edu

(This Listing Continued)

UNIVERSITY OF MISSOURI - KANSAS CITY SCHOOL OF LAW—Continued

EDWARD P. RICHARDS, III,* (Professor)**, born Baton Rouge, Louisiana, January 5, 1950; admitted to bar, 1979, Texas. *Education:* Rice University (B.A., 1972); University of Houston Law Center (J.D., 1978); University of Texas School of Public Health (M.Ph., 1983). ***COURSES: Torts, Products Liability, FDA Law, Health Law. ***Email:*** richarde@umkc.edu

ELLEN YANKIVER SUNI,* (Professor)**, born New York, New York, April 27, 1950; admitted to bar, 1974, Massachusetts; 1987, Missouri. *Education:* City College of New York (B.A., 1970); Boston University School of Law (J.D., 1974). ***COURSES: Criminal Law and Procedure, Professional Responsibility, Appellate Advocacy, Law Practice Management, Death Penalty Clinic. ***Email:*** sunie@umkc.edu

WANDA M. TEMM,* (Associate Clinical Professor and Director, Legal Writing)**, born Chicago, Illinois, September 12, 1955; admitted to bar, 1988, Kansas; 1989, Missouri. *Education:* Ottawa University (B.A., 1977); Purdue University (M.S., 1979); University of Kansas (J.D., 1988). ***COURSES: Legal Research and Writing, Family Law, Introduction to Law, Advanced Drafting. ***Email:*** temmw@umkc.edu

JEFFREY ELLIS THOMAS,* (Associate Professor)**, born Inglewood, California, July 3, 1959; admitted to bar, 1988, California. *Education:* Loyola Marymount University (B.A., 1983); University of California, Berkeley (J.D., 1986). ***COURSES: Torts, Civil Procedure, Law & Economics, Insurance, Appellate Advocacy. ***Email:*** thomasj@umkc.edu

ROBERT REED VERCHICK,* (Associate Professor)**, born Las Vegas, Nevada, October 5, 1964; admitted to bar, 1990, Washington. *Education:* Stanford University (A.B., 1986); Harvard Law School (J.D., 1989). ***COURSES: Property, Land Use, Gender & Justice, Environmental Law. ***Email:*** verchicr@umkc.edu

GEORGE RAY WARNER,* (Professor)**, born Columbia, South Carolina, December 16, 1955; admitted to bar, 1980, Georgia; 1982, Illinois. *Education:* Emory University (B.A., 1977); Northwestern University (J.D., 1980); New York University (LL.M., 1985). ***COURSES: Bankruptcy, Consumer Law, Commercial Law, Debtor-Creditor Rights. ***Email:*** warnerr@umkc.edu

DAN WEDDLE,* (Assistant Clinical Professor)**, born Kansas City, Missouri, June 29, 1955; admitted to bar, 1995, Kansas; Missouri 1996. *Education:* University of Kansas (B.S., 1978); University of Kansas School of Law (J.D., 1995). ***COURSES: Introduction to Law & Lawyering Processes, Advanced Legal Writing--Litigation Drafting, Advanced Lawyering Processes, Education Law. ***Email:*** weddle@umkc.edu

BARBARA ELIZA WILSON,* (Assistant Clinical Professor)**, born Minneapolis, Minnesota, February 4, 1959; admitted to bar, 1997, Missouri; 1998, Kansas. *Education:* University of Missouri-Columbia (B.A., 1982); University of Missouri-Columbia (J.D., 1997). ***COURSES: Advanced Legal Writing, Introduction to Law and Lawyering Processes.

JUDITH F. WISEMAN,* (Associate Clinical Professor and Associate Director of LL.M. Tax Program)**, born St. Louis, Missouri, October 31, 1957; admitted to bar, 1990, Oklahoma; 1991, Kansas. *Education:* The University of Wisconsin (B.B.A. (in accounting, 1979); The University of Tulsa College of Law (J.D., 1990); New York University College of Law (LL.M., (in taxation, 1991). ***COURSES: Tax Practicum, Federal Taxation, Taxation of Estates, Gifts & Trusts, Taxation of Property Transactions, Corporate Tax, Estate Planning & Practice. ***Email:*** wisemanj@umkc.edu

UNIVERSITY OF MONTANA SCHOOL OF LAW

MISSOULA, MONTANA 59812

UNIVERSITY OF NEBRASKA COLLEGE OF LAW

P.O. BOX 830902
103 ROSS MCCOLLUM HALL
LINCOLN, NEBRASKA 68583-0902
Telephone: (402) 472-2161
Fax: (402) 472-5185
http://www.unl.edu/lawcoll/

ABA Approved Since 1923

Large enough to offer students a diverse curriculum yet small enough to ensure that students are not lost in a faceless crowd, the College of Law of the University of Nebraska-Lincoln offers an educational program designed to provide its students with the intellectual and practical skills necessary to meet the diverse challenges of a legal career.

The College of Law was founded in 1888 and became part of the University of Nebraska in 1891. The College was among the first law schools to be fully accredited by the American Bar Association and was a charter member of the Association of American Law Schools. One of the College's early deans, native Nebraskan Roscoe Pound, earned a reputation as one of the foremost scholars and educators in the history of legal education.

From the days of Dean Pound to the present, the College of Law has been the professional home of an energetic and nationally recognized faculty, drawn from a variety of backgrounds and educational experiences. The current faculty is strongly committed to both teaching and scholarship. Students therefore have the opportunity to take classes from dedicated teachers who are exploring the frontiers of the law and who are also freely available to students outside the classroom.

The Law College is housed in a modern, comfortable building that includes the Marvin and Virginia Schmid Law Library and the Sherman Welpton Courtroom complex. The Schmid Law Library is the largest collection of legal materials in the state of Nebraska. In addition to its own extensive collection, it permits student access to Westlaw and Lexis electronic databases and houses a computer laboratory for student use of word processing, data base, and spread sheet programs in addition to computer-assisted instruction. A staff of skilled professional librarians and an online catalogue provide access to materials throughout the University system and the world. The Sherman Welpton Courtroom Building houses the College's clinical law program and provides a real-life setting for courses in trial advocacy as well as a site for local courts to hear cases.

The approximately 400 students at the College of Law come from

(This Listing Continued)

UNIVERSITY OF NEBRASKA COLLEGE OF LAW —Continued

diverse backgrounds. Although a substantial number are residents of Nebraska, the College draws roughly one quarter of its students from across the country, and the student body collectively holds graduate and undergraduate degrees in a variety of fields from over 60 colleges and universities. Women constitute about 50 percent of the student body and members of minority groups constitute over 8 percent of the student body.

The College offers numerous joint degree programs with other units of the University of Nebraska, including a long-established and nationally recognized Law and Psychology program.

Dean: Steven L. Willborn (402) 472-2161
Student Services: Glenda J. Pierce (402) 472-2161
Admissions: Denice Archer (402) 472-2161
Financial Aid: Rebecca Colberg (402) 472-8263
Library: Richard Leiter (402) 472-5737
Career Services and Alumni Relations: Sue Kirkland (402) 472-5525
Development: Tony Dworak (402) 472-8265

FULL TIME FACULTY

STEVEN L. WILLBORN*, (Dean and Richard C. and Catherine Stuart Schmoker Professor)**, born Dodgeville, Wisconsin, January 18, 1952; admitted to bar, 1976, Ohio and Wisconsin; 1979, Nebraska. *Education:* Northland College (B.A., 1974); University of Wisconsin at Madison (M.S.; J.D., 1976). ***COURSES: Employment Law, Employment Discrimination Law, Labor Law, Pensions and Employee Benefits. ***Email:*** willborn@unl.edu

LAWRENCE BERGER*, (Robert J. Kutak Professor of Law)**, born Newark, New Jersey, May 21, 1928; admitted to bar, 1953, District of Columbia and New Jersey; 1973, Nebraska. *Education:* University of Pennsylvania (B.S., 1949); Rutgers University (J.D., 1952). ***COURSES: Property, Real Estate. ***Email:*** lberger1@unl.edu

C. STEVEN BRADFORD*, (Cline Williams - Flavel A. Wright and Warren C. (Bud) Johnson Professor of Law)**, born Waxahachie, Texas, March 14, 1956; admitted to bar, 1982, Texas; 1989, Nebraska. *Education:* Utah State University (B.S., 1978); Harvard University (M.P.P., 1982; J.D., 1982). ***COURSES: Corporations, Securities Regulation, Investment Companies and Investment Advisers, Conflict of Laws, Law and Economics. ***Email:*** sbradford1@unl.edu

***TERESA LOUISE CONAWAY*, (Assistant Professor & Electronic Services Librarian)**, born Norfolk, Virginia, October 19, 1955; admitted to bar, 1985, Maryland; 1993, Tennessee. *Education:* Pikeville College (B.A., 1977); Virginia Tech (M.A.Ed., 1981); Dickinson School of Law of Penn State University (J.D., 1980); University of Tennessee (M.S., 1996).

ROBERT C. DENICOLA*, (Margaret Larson Professor of Law)**, born Union City, New Jersey, October 15, 1949; admitted to bar, 1974, Massachusetts; 1976, Nebraska. *Education:* Princeton University (B.S.E., 1971); Harvard University (J.D., 1974; LL.M., 1976). ***COURSES: Copyright, Unfair Competition, Contracts. ***Email:*** rdenicola1@unl.edu

RICHARD F. DUNCAN*, (Sherman S. Welpton, Jr. Professor of Law)**, born Fall River, Massachusetts, June 6, 1951; admitted to bar, 1976, New York. *Education:* University of Massachusetts (B.A., 1973); Cornell University (J.D., 1976). ***COURSES: Constitutional Law, Property. ***Email:*** conlawprof@yahoo.com

ALAN H. FRANK*, (Professor of Law)**, born Milwaukee, Wisconsin, September 14, 1944; admitted to bar, 1972, Wisconsin. *Education:* Duke University (A.B., 1966); University of Wisconsin (J.D., 1972). ***COURSES: Family Law, Client Counseling, Mediation, Family Law Practice. ***Email:*** afrank2@unl.edu

MARTIN R. GARDNER*, (Steinhart Foundation Professor of Law)**, born Salt Lake City, Utah, November 3, 1944; admitted to bar, 1972, Utah; 1979, Nebraska. *Education:* University of Utah (B.S., 1969; J.D., 1972). ***COURSES: Criminal Law and Procedure, Juvenile Law, Family Law. ***Email:*** mgardner1@unl.edu

JOHN M. GRADWOHL*, (Ross McCollum Professor of Law)**, born Lincoln, Nebraska, May 2, 1930; admitted to bar, 1953, Nebraska. *Education:* University of Nebraska - Lincoln (B.S., 1951; LL.B., 1953); Harvard University (LL.M., 1957). ***COURSES: Arbitration, Legislation, Judicial Seminar. ***Email:*** jgradwohl1@unl.edu

ALICIA BLUMER HENDERSON*, (Assistant Clinical Professor of Law)**, born Mountainside, New Jersey, January 5, 1959; admitted to bar, 1986, Nebraska. *Education:* University of Nebraska - Lincoln (B.M.E., 1981; J.D., 1986). ***COURSES: Criminal Clinic. ***Email:*** ahenderson1@unl.edu

PETER TOLL HOFFMAN*, (Earl Dunlap Distinguished Professor of Law and Coordinator of Clinical Legal Education)**, born Schenectady, New York, May 5, 1946; admitted to bar, 1971, Illinois; 1972, Michigan; 1974, Nebraska. *Education:* Michigan State University (B.A., 1968); University of Michigan (J.D., 1971). ***COURSES: Evidence, Trial Advocacy, Clinical Legal Education, Pretrial Litigation. ***Email:*** phoffman1@unl.edu

STEPHEN E. KALISH*, (Margaret R. Larson Professor of Legal Ethics; Director, Center for the Teaching and Study of Applied Ethics)**, born St. Louis, Missouri, January 14, 1942; admitted to bar, 1969, California; 1971, Nebraska. *Education:* Harvard University (B.A., 1964; J.D., 1967; LL.M., 1974). ***COURSES: Legal Profession, Business Organizations, Ethics, History. ***Email:*** skalish1@unl.edu

ROGER W. KIRST*, (Henry Grether Professor of Law)**, born 1945; admitted to bar, 1971, New York; 1974, Nebraska. *Education:* Massachusetts Institute of Technology (B.S., 1967); Stanford University (J.D., 1970). ***COURSES: Civil Procedure, Evidence, Civil Rights. ***Email:*** rkirst@unlserve.unl.edu

CRAIG M. LAWSON*, (Professor of Law)**, born Salem, Massachusetts, November 28, 1948; admitted to bar, 1974, California. *Education:* Yale University (A.B., 1970); Hastings College of the Law (J.D., 1974). ***COURSES: Torts, Law and Medicine, Law and Literature, Law of Patient and Provider, Professional Responsibility, Legal Writing. ***Email:*** clawson1@unl.edu

RICHARD A. LEITER*, (Director of Law Library & Professor)**, born Sacramento, California, March 21, 1952. *Education:* University of California at Santa Cruz (B.A., 1976); University of Texas at Austin (M.L.I.S., 1986); Southwestern University School of Law (J.D., 1981). ***COURSES: Legal Research. ***Email:*** rleiter2@unl.edu

***JOHN P. LENICH*, (Associate Professor of Law)**, born Chicago, Illinois, May 30, 1955; admitted to bar, 1981, California; 1985,

(This Listing Continued)

UNIVERSITY OF NEBRASKA COLLEGE OF LAW —Continued

Nebraska. *Education:* University of Illinois (B.A., 1977); Northwestern University (J.D., 1980). ***COURSES:*** Antitrust, Appellate Advocacy, Civil Procedure, Remedies. ***Email:*** jlenich2@unl.edu

BRIAN D. LEPARD,* (Associate Professor of Law)**, born Hollywood, California, June 16, 1962; admitted to bar, 1989, Pennsylvania and New Jersey; 1995, Nebraska. *Education:* Princeton University (A.B., 1983); Yale Law School (J.D., 1989). ***COURSES: Federal Income Tax, International Tax, Corporate Tax, Business Planning, International Human Rights Law. ***Email:*** blepard1@unl.edu

WILLIAM H. LYONS,* (Richard H. Larson Professor of Tax Law)**, born Fitchburg, Massachusetts, March 5, 1947; admitted to bar, 1973, Maine and Massachusetts; 1985, Nebraska. *Education:* Colby College (B.A., 1969); Boston College (J.D., 1973). ***COURSES: Estate Planning, Federal Income Taxation, Business Planning, Wills and Trusts. ***Email:*** wlyons2@unl.edu

HARVEY S. PERLMAN,* (Chancellor, University of Nebraska and Harvey & Susan Perlman Alumni Professor of Law)**, born Lincoln, Nebraska, January 17, 1942; admitted to bar, 1966, Nebraska. *Education:* University of Nebraska - Lincoln (B.A., 1963; J.D., 1966). ***COURSES: Torts, Unfair Competition, Cyberlaw, Patent Law, International Intellectual Property Law and Construction Law. ***Email:*** hsperlman@unl.edu

SANDRA B. PLACZEK,* (Assistant Professor, Head of Public Services)**, born Omaha, Nebraska, October 21, 1961; admitted to bar, 1996, Nebraska. *Education:* University of Nebraska-Lincoln (B.A., 1986); Creighton University Law School (J.D., 1993); University of Texas-Austin (M.L.I.S., 1995). ***Email: splaczek2@unl.edu

SUSAN POSER,* (Assistant Professor of Law)**, born Washington, D.C., September 7, 1963; admitted to bar, 1993, Pennsylvania; 1994, Nebraska. *Education:* Swarthmore College (B.A, 1985); University of CA Berkeley (J.D., 1991; Ph.D., 2000). ***COURSES: Torts, Wills & Trusts, Professional Responsibility. ***Email:*** sposer1@unl.edu

JOSEPHINE R. POTUTO,* (Richard H. Larson Professor of Constitutional Law)**, born Newark, New Jersey, March 5, 1947; admitted to bar, 1974, New Jersey; 1977, Nebraska. *Education:* Douglass College (B.A., 1967); Seton Hall University (M.A., 1971); Rutgers University (J.D., 1974). ***COURSES: Constitutional Law, Federal Jurisdiction, Criminal Procedure, Conflict of Laws, Sports Law. ***Email:*** jpotuto1@unl.edu

KEVIN RUSER,* (Clinical Professor of Law)**, born Ogallala, Nebraska, June 3, 1953; admitted to bar, 1979, Nebraska. *Education:* University of Nebraska - Lincoln (B.A., 1975; J.D., 1979). ***COURSES: Pretrial Litigation, Clinical Law. ***Email:*** keruser@unl.edu

MATTHEW P. SCHAEFER,* (Associate Professor of Law)**, born Ann Arbor, Michigan, July 26, 1965; admitted to bar, 1994, Michigan. *Education:* University of Chicago (B.A., Economics, 1987); University of Michigan Law School (J.D., 1991 and LL.M., International Law, 1993). ***COURSES: International Trade Law, Public International Law, International Business Transactions. ***Email:*** mschaefer1@unl.edu

ROBERT F. SCHOPP,* (Professor of Law and Psychology)**, born Teaneck, New Jersey, January 9, 1948; admitted to bar, 1990, Nebraska. *Education:* North Carolina State University (Ph.D. in Psychology, 1977); University of Arizona (J.D., 1988; Ph.D. in Philosophy, 1989). ***COURSES: Criminal Law, Criminal Procedure, Law and Psychology, Jurisprudence. ***Email:*** rschopp1@unl.edu

ANNA WILLIAMS SHAVERS,* (Associate Professor of Law)**, born Little Rock, Arkansas, February 12, 1946; admitted to bar, 1979, Minnesota; 1989, Nebraska. *Education:* Central State University (B.S., 1967); University of Wisconsin (M.S., 1973); University of Minnesota (J.D., 1979). ***COURSES: Civil Procedure, Administrative Law, Gender Issues, Refugee Law, Immigration. ***Email:*** ashavers@unl.edu

JOHN ROCKWELL SNOWDEN,* (Professor of Law)**, born Everett, Washington, August 24, 1943; admitted to bar, 1971, Nebraska. *Education:* University of Nebraska - Lincoln (B.A., 1966; J.D., 1971). ***COURSES: Native American Law, Legal Process, Mass Communications Law, Criminal Law.

BRIAN D. STRIMAN,* (Associate Professor of Law Library, Head of Technical Services)**, born Columbus, Ohio, February 29, 1952. *Education:* University of Nebraska - Lincoln (B.S., 1974); University of Missouri at Columbia (M.A., 1978). ***Email: bstriman1@unl.edu

NORMAN W. THORSON,* (Judge Harry A. Spencer Professor of Law)**, born Omaha, Nebraska, September 16, 1949; admitted to bar, 1977, Nebraska. *Education:* University of Nebraska - Lincoln (B.S., 1971; M.S., 1974; J.D., 1977; Ph.D., 1979). ***COURSES: Environmental and Natural Resources Law, Water Law, Agricultural Law, Public Lands, Law and Economics, Oil and Gas, International Environmental Law. ***Email:*** nthorson1@unl.edu

CATHERINE LEE WILSON,* (Assistant Professor of Law)**, born Hastings, Nebraska, November 6, 1961; admitted to bar, 1988, Georgia. *Education:* Hastings College; Creighton University (B.A., 1984); Creighton University School of Law; University of Alabama School of Law (J.D., 1987). ***COURSES: Sales, Payment Systems, Creditor's Rights, Secured Transactions, Banking Law. ***Email:*** cwilson2@unl.edu

ROBERT G. WORKS,* (Margaret R. Larson Professor of Insurance Law)**, born San Francisco, California, July 30, 1943; admitted to bar, 1967, Missouri; 1975, Nebraska. *Education:* Kansas State University (A.B., 1966); St. Louis University (J.D., 1967). ***COURSES: Contracts, Insurance, Health Care Finance. ***Email:*** rworks1@unl.edu

UNIVERSITY OF NEW MEXICO SCHOOL OF LAW

1117 STANFORD DRIVE, N.E.
ALBUQUERQUE, NEW MEXICO 87106

UNIVERSITY OF NORTH CAROLINA SCHOOL OF LAW

VAN HECKE-WETTACH HALL CB#3380
CHAPEL HILL, NORTH CAROLINA 27599

UNIVERSITY OF NORTH DAKOTA SCHOOL OF LAW

GRAND FORKS, NORTH DAKOTA 58202

UNIVERSITY OF OKLAHOMA COLLEGE OF LAW
300 TIMBERDELL ROAD
NORMAN, OKLAHOMA 73019-0701

UNIVERSITY OF OREGON SCHOOL OF LAW
1101 KINCAID STREET
EUGENE, OREGON 97403

UNIVERSITY OF PENNSYLVANIA LAW SCHOOL
3400 CHESTNUT STREET
PHILADELPHIA, PENNSYLVANIA 19104-6204
Telephone: (215) 898-7481
Fax: (215) 573-2025
http://www.law.upenn.edu

ABA Approved Since 1923.

The University of Pennsylvania is comprised of 12 undergraduate, graduate and professional schools and offers many amenities to the law student: 12 libraries are open for research and study, faculty collaboration across disciplines is encouraged and enhanced, students join with other professional and graduate students on public service projects, research offers, and social events. Joint degree programs are strong and diverse.

The Law School provides a hospitable and rigorous environment for learning. Each year it selects an able and diverse class of approximately two-hundred and thirty students. Our community combines an excellent student body with an outstanding faculty who have varied educational backgrounds and a wide spectrum of experience. The relatively small scale permits easy and frequent contact between students and faculty, with a ratio of 18:1.

The Law School's intellectual vigor is derived from its students and its faculty. Most of the instruction is provided by full-time faculty members who are accomplished in many fields complementary to the law, including economics, political science, legal history, philosophy, psychiatry, psychology, and sociology. Many of them participate in public interest activities, a number are active in legal education organizations, including the Director of the American Law Institute, a recent president of the Association of American Law Schools, and in American Bar Association activities. In addition, judges and practicing attorneys offer courses in specialized areas. The law faculty maintains a lively and diverse research interest and engages in a wide range of activities in public service and law reform.

Among the formally organized extracurricular activities at the Law School are four student-edited journals, *The University of Pennsylvania Law Review,* the *Journal of Labor and Employment Law,* the *Journal of Constitutional Law,* and the *Journal of International Economic Law.* In addition, national and international moot court programs are available. The Career Planning and Placement Office provides a range of services to assist law students in making career decisions. Each year the recruiting program brings to campus approximately 300 employers, representing law firms, corporations, government, and public interest organizations.

Faculty and students engage in a curriculum of unusual breadth. Courses are presented across a broad spectrum of distinct disciplines. Clinical education is an important part of our program.

Our library collection is 730,809 volumes, among the largest law libraries in the country. We have a sophisticated computer system in the law and provide Westlaw, Lexis, and internet to students and faculty.

The Law School is proud of its graduates and their accomplishments. Several have served as President of the American Bar Association. The Law School numbers among its graduates many judges, law professors, law school deans, CEOs of major corporations, best-selling authors, and leaders of major educational and cultural institutions.

Dean: Michael A. Fitts (215) 898-7061
Assistant Dean for Admissions & Financial Aid: Janice L. Austin (215) 898-7743
Interim Co-Director, Biddle Law Library: Patricia Callahan (215) 898-0230
Interim Co-Director, Biddle Law Library: Edwin Greenlee (215) 898-4169
Assistant Dean for Placement: Jo-Ann M. Verrier (215) 898-6746
Assistant Dean for Development and Alumni Relations: Elizabeth Brown (215) 898-4396

FULL TIME FACULTY

MICHAEL ANDREW FITTS*, (Dean and Bernard G. Segal Professor of Law)**, born Philadelphia, Pennsylvania, March 1, 1953; admitted to bar, 1981, Pennsylvania. *Education:* Harvard University (A.B., 1975); Yale University (J.D., 1979). ***COURSES: Administrative Law, Regulated Industries, Legislation.

MATTHEW ADLER*, (Professor of Law)**, born Philadelphia, Pennsylvania, October 22, 1962; admitted to bar, 1994, Pennsylvania. *Education:* Yale College (B.A., 1984; J.D., 1991); Oxford University (M.Litt., 1986). ***COURSES: Administrative Law, Constitutional Law.

***ANITA L. ALLEN-CASTELLITTO*, (Professor of Law and Philosophy)**, born Fort Worden, Washington, March 24, 1953; admitted to bar, 1985, New York; Pennsylvania. *Education:* New College (B.A., 1974); University of Michigan (M.A., 1978); Harvard University (J.D.,

(This Listing Continued)

UNIVERSITY OF PENNSYLVANIA LAW SCHOOL —Continued

1984). ***COURSES:*** Constitutional Law, Jurisprudence, Privacy in American Law, Torts.

REGINA AUSTIN*, (William A. Schnader Professor of Law)**, born Washington, D.C., September 29, 1948; admitted to bar, 1973, Pennsylvania. *Education:* University of Rochester (B.A., 1970); University of Pennsylvania (J.D., 1973). ***COURSES: Torts, Insurance, International Torts.

C. EDWIN BAKER*, (Nicholas F. Gallicchio Professor of Law)**, born Nashville, Tennessee, May 28, 1947; admitted to bar, 1979, Oregon. *Education:* Stanford University (B.A., 1969); Yale Law School (J.D., 1972). ***COURSES: Constitutional Law, Mass Media Law, First Amendment.

STEPHEN B. BURBANK*, (David Berger Professor for the Administration of Justice)**, born New York, New York, January 8, 1947; admitted to bar, 1973, Massachusetts; 1976, Pennsylvania. *Education:* Harvard University (A.B., 1968; J.D., 1973). ***COURSES: Civil Procedure, Complex Litigation, International Civil Litigation, Judicial Administration.

HOWARD F. CHANG*, (Professor of Law)**, born Lafayette, Indiana, June 30, 1960; admitted to bar, 1989, New York and District of Columbia. *Education:* Harvard College (A.B., 1982); Princeton University (M.A., 1985); Harvard University (J.D., 1987); MIT (Ph.D., 1992). ***COURSES: Environmental Law, Immigration, Intellectual Property, and International Trade.

JACQUES DELISLE*, (Professor of Law)**, born Phoenix, Arizona, June 21, 1961; admitted to bar, 1991, Massachusetts. *Education:* Princeton University (A.B., 1982); Harvard University Law School (J.D., 1990). ***COURSES: Comparative Law (East Asia/China), International Law, Separation of Powers.

COLIN S. DIVER*, (Charles A. Heimbold, Jr. Professor of Law and Economics)**, born Boston, Massachusetts, December 29, 1943; admitted to bar, 1968, Massachusetts. *Education:* Amherst College (B.A., 1965); Harvard University (LL.B., 1968). ***COURSES: Administrative Law, Torts.

WILLIAM B. EWALD*, (Professor of Law and Philosophy)**, born Washington, D.C., September 30, 1954; admitted to bar, 1982, New York. *Education:* Harvard University (B.A., and A.M., 1976; J.D., 1981); Oxford University (D.Phil., 1978). ***COURSES: Introduction to American Legal System, Comparative Law, Public International Law.

ERIC FELDMAN*, (Assistant Professor)**, born New York, New York, October 18, 1959; admitted to bar, 1989, California. *Education:* Vassar College (B.A., 1982); University of California, Berkeley School of Law (Boalt Hall) (J.D., 1989; Ph.D., 1994). ***COURSES: Comparative Law, Health Law, Japanese Law.

CLAIRE O. FINKELSTEIN*, (Professor of Law)**, born Washington, DC, November 04, 1964. *Education:* Harvard College (B.A., 1986); Yale University Law School (J.D., 1993); University of Pittsburgh (Ph.D., 1996). ***COURSES: Contracts, Criminal Law, Jurisprudence, Philosophy of Law.

DOUGLAS N. FRENKEL*, (Practice Professor)**, born New York, New York, July 14, 1947; admitted to bar, 1972, Pennsylvania. *Education:* University of Pennsylvania (B.S., Economics, 1968; J.D., 1972). ***COURSES: Professional Responsibility, Mediation, Interviewing, Counseling and Negotiation.

FRANK GOODMAN*, (Professor of Law)**, born Omaha, Nebraska, November 20, 1932; admitted to bar, 1961, California. *Education:* Harvard University (A.B., 1954); Oxford University (M.A., 1956); Harvard Law School (J.D., 1959). ***COURSES: Constitutional Law, Federal Courts, Constitutional Theory.

SARAH BARRINGER GORDON*, (Associate Dean and Professor of Law)**, born Princeton, New Jersey, March 5, 1955; admitted to bar, 1986, Pennsylvania. *Education:* Vassar College (B.A., 1982); Yale University Law School (J.D., 1986); Yale Divinity School (M.A.R., 1987); Princeton University (J.D., 1991). ***COURSES: Legal History, Property.

GEOFFREY CORNELL HAZARD, JR.*, (Trustee Professor of Law)**, born Cleveland, Ohio, September 18, 1929; admitted to bar, 1954, Oregon; 1960, California; 1982, Connecticut. *Education:* Swarthmore College (B.A., 1953); Columbia University (LL.B., 1954). ***COURSES: Civil Procedure, Professional Responsibility.

PETER H. HUANG*, (Assistant Professor of Law)**, born December 6, 1958; admitted to bar, 1997, California. *Education:* Princeton University (A.B., 1976); Harvard University (S.M., 1978); Harvard University (Ph.D., 1984); Stanford University Law School (J.D., 1997). ***COURSES: Corporate Law, Law & Economics, Securities Regulation.

JASON S. JOHNSTON*, (Robert G. Fuller, Jr. Professor of Law)**, born Dearborn, Michigan, May 5, 1956. *Education:* Dartmouth College (A.B., 1978); University of Michigan (J.D., 1981; Ph.D., 1984). ***COURSES: Contracts, Environmental Law, Law and Economics.

LEO KATZ*, (Professor of Law)**, born Vienna, Austria, July 21, 1957; admitted to bar, 1982, Illinois. *Education:* University of Chicago (B.A., 1979; M.A., 1982; J.D., 1982). ***COURSES: Criminal Law, Corporations.

MICHAEL STEVEN KNOLL*, (Professor of Law and Real Estate)**, born New York, April 23, 1957; admitted to bar, 1984, Illinois; 1988, New York and District of Columbia. *Education:* University of Chicago (A.B., 1977; Ph.D., 1983; J.D., 1984). ***COURSES: Tax, Corporate Finance.

NANCY C. KRAYBILL*, (Lecturer and Clinical Supervisor)**, born Dallas, Texas, January 31, 1954; admitted to bar, 1986, California; 1999, Pennsylvania. *Education:* Princeton University (A.B., 1976); University of Delaware (M.A., 1983); University of California, Los Angeles (J.D., 1986). ***COURSES: Civil Practice Clinic. ***Email:*** mkraybil@law.upenn.edu

SETH F. KREIMER*, (Professor of Law)**, born Pittsburgh, Pennsylvania, September 30, 1952; admitted to bar, 1977, Pennsylvania. *Education:* Yale University (B.A., 1974; J.D., 1977). ***COURSES: Constitutional Law, Constitutional Litigation, Health Law.

ANNE E. KRINGEL*, (Legal Writing Director and Senior Lecturer)**, born New Haven, Connecticut, February 24, 1964; admitted to bar, 1991, Minnesota; 1992, Wisconsin. *Education:* Yale University (B.A., 1986); Yale Law School (J.D., 1991). ***COURSES: Legal Writing and Research, Law and Literature.

FRIEDRICH KUBLER*, (Professor of Law)**, born Reutlingen, Germany, October 19, 1932; admitted to bar, 1961, Germany. *Education:* Tubingen, Germany (Ref., 1956; Dr.iur., 1966). ***COURSES: European Community Law, Corporations, International Banking, Comparative Mass Communication Law.

ALAN M. LERNER*, (Practice Professor)**, born Philadelphia, Pennsylvania, January 24, 1942; admitted to bar, 1966, New York; 1968, Pennsylvania. *Education:* University of Pennsylvania (B.S., 1962; LL.B., 1965). ***COURSES: Civil Practice Clinic, Advanced Civil Practice Clinic, Law and the Workplace.

***HOWARD LESNICK*, (Jefferson B. Fordham Professor of Law)**, born New York, New York, April 22, 1931; admitted to bar, 1958, New

(This Listing Continued)

UNIVERSITY OF PENNSYLVANIA LAW SCHOOL —Continued

York; 1968, Pennsylvania. *Education:* New York University (A.B., 1952); Columbia University (A.M., 1953; LL.B., 1958). ***COURSES:*** Professional Responsibility, Law and Inequality, Religion and Law, Civil Liberties in the Workplace.

KRISTIN M. MADISON, **(Assistant Professor)**, born Minnesota, August 30, 1970; admitted to bar, 2001, Massachusetts. *Education:* University of California at Berkeley (B.A., 1992); Yale University Law School (J.D., 2000). ***COURSES:*** Contracts, Health Law.

BRUCE H. MANN, **(Professor of Law and History)**, born Cambridge, Massachusetts, April 27, 1950; admitted to bar, 1975, Connecticut; 1984, Texas. *Education:* Brown University (A.B., and A.M., 1972); Yale University (M.Phil., and J.D., 1975; Ph.D., 1977). ***COURSES:*** Legal History, Trusts and Estates, Property.

CHARLES W. MOONEY, JR., **(Professor of Law)**, born Shawnee, Oklahoma, August 13, 1947; admitted to bar, 1972, Oklahoma; 1982, New York; 1988, Pennsylvania. *Education:* University of Oklahoma (B.A., 1969); Harvard University (J.D., 1972). ***COURSES:*** Commercial Law, Bankruptcy.

STEPHEN J. MORSE, **(Ferdinand Wakeman Hubbell Professor of Law and Professor of Psychology and Law in Psychiatry)**, born New York, New York, February 28, 1945; admitted to bar, 1972, Massachusetts. *Education:* Tufts University (A.B., 1966); Harvard University (J.D., 1970; Ph.D., 1973). ***COURSES:*** Criminal Law, Mental Health Law.

STEPHEN R. PERRY, **(John J. O'Brien Professor of Law and Professor of Philosophy)**, born Winnipeg, Canada, January 16, 1952. *Education:* University of Toronto, Trinity College (B.A., 1975); University of Toronto, Faculty of Law (LL.B., 1981); Oxford University (D.Phil., 1983). ***COURSES:*** Torts, Legal Theory, Jurisprudence.

NATHANIEL PERSILY, **(Assistant Professor)**, born New York, New York, July 03, 1970. *Education:* Yale University (B.A., M.A., 1992); University of California at Berkeley (M.A., 1994); Stanford University Law School (J.D., 1998). ***COURSES:*** Administrative Law, Constitution Law, Law of the Political Process.

ARTI RAI, **(Assistant Professor)**, born India, November 17, 1966; admitted to bar, 1993, Pennsylvania; 1995, District of Columbia. *Education:* Harvard College (A.B., 1987); Harvard Law School (J.D., 1991). ***COURSES:*** Biotechnology and the Law, Health Law, Intellectual Property, Patents.

CURTIS R. REITZ, **(Algernon Sydney Biddle Professor of Law)**, born Reading, Pennsylvania, November 20, 1929; admitted to bar, 1957, Pennsylvania; 1959, U.S. Supreme Court. *Education:* University of Pennsylvania (B.A., 1951; LL.B., 1956). ***COURSES:*** Commercial Transactions, Domestic and International Sales, Commercial Credit, International Trade Regulation.

EDWARD B. ROCK, **(Saul A. Fox Distinguished Professor of Business Law)**, born Philadelphia, Pennsylvania, June 16, 1956; admitted to bar, 1983, Pennsylvania. *Education:* Yale University (B.S., 1977); Oxford University (B.A., 1980); University of Pennsylvania (J.D., 1983). ***COURSES:*** Antitrust, Corporations.

MATTHEW ROSSMAN, **(Lecturer - Clinical Supervisor)**, born Cleveland, Ohio, February 23, 1970. *Education:* Miami University (B.A., 1992); New York University School of Law (J.D., 1996). ***COURSES:*** Civil Practice Clinic.

EDWARD RUBIN, **(Professor of Law)**, born New York, New York, June 2, 1948; admitted to bar, 1981, New York. *Education:* Princeton University (B.A., 1969); Yale Law School (J.D., 1979). ***COURSES:*** Administrative Law, Constitutional Law, Payments Law, Financial Securities Law.

DAVID RUDOVSKY, **(Senior Fellow)**, born New York, New York, February 10, 1943; admitted to bar, 1967, New York; 1971, Pennsylvania. *Education:* Queens College (B.A., 1964); New York University (LL.B., 1967). ***COURSES:*** Evidence, Criminal Procedure, Criminal Law.

LOUIS S. RULLI, **(Practice Professor)**, born New York, New York, September 19, 1950; admitted to bar, 1974, Pennsylvania; 1975, New Jersey. *Education:* Rutgers University (B.A., 1971); Rutgers University Law School (J.D., 1974). ***COURSES:*** Civil Practice Clinic, Legislative Clinic.

LAWRENCE J. SCHEMPP, **(Lecturer - Clinical Supervisor)**, born Pittsburgh, Pennsylvania, September 17, 1959. *Education:* Temple University (B.A., 1981); Georgetown University Law Center (J.D., 1990). ***COURSES:*** Civil Practice Clinic, Litigation Clinic.

KIM LANE SCHEPPELE, **(Professor of Law and Sociology)**, born Glen Ridge, New Jersey, September 10, 1953. *Education:* Columbia University (A.B., 1975); University of Chicago (M.A., 1977; Ph.D., 1985). ***COURSES:*** Comparative Constitutional Law, Evidence, Privacy, Sociology of Law.

DINA LYNN SCHLOSSBERG, **(Clinical Faculty Supervisor)**, born Cleveland, Ohio, January 14, 1960; admitted to bar, 1985, Pennsylvania. *Education:* Miami University (B.A.P.H., 1982); Temple University (J.D., 1985). ***COURSES:*** Business Law, Clinical Education.

REED SHULDINER, **(Associate Dean and Professor of Law)**, born Berkeley, California, August 20, 1956; admitted to bar, 1983, Massachusetts; 1984, District of Columbia. *Education:* Princeton University (B.S.E., 1977); Harvard Law School (J.D., 1983); Massachusetts Institute of Technology (Ph.D., Economics, 1985). ***COURSES:*** Federal Income Tax, International Taxation, Tax Policy.

DAVID AUTHOR SKEEL, JR., **(Professor of Law)**, born Washington, D.C, September 10, 1961; admitted to bar, 1988, Pennsylvania. *Education:* University of North Carolina (B.A., 1983); University of Virginia School of Law (J.D., 1987). ***COURSES:*** Bankruptcy, Commercial Law, Corporations.

CATHERINE T. STRUVE, **(Assistant Professor)**, admitted to bar, 1996, New York. *Education:* Harvard College (A.B., 1992); Harvard Law School (J.D., 1995). ***COURSES:*** Civil Procedure.

CLYDE WILSON SUMMERS, **(Jefferson B. Fordham Professor of Law Emeritus)**, born Grass Range, Montana, November 21, 1918; admitted to bar, 1951, New York. *Education:* University of Illinois (B.S., 1939; J.D., 1942); Columbia University (J.S.D., 1952). ***COURSES:*** Comparative Labor Law, Contracts, Employment Law, Labor Law.

MICHAEL L. WACHTER, **(William B. Johnson Professor of Law and Economics)**, born New York, N.Y., March 12, 1943. *Education:* Cornell University (B.S., 1964); Harvard University (Ph.D., 1970). ***COURSES:*** Corporate Finance, Law and Economics, Topics in Antitrust and Corporate Law.

R. POLK WAGNER, **(Assistant Professor)**, born 1969; admitted to bar, 1998, California. *Education:* University of Michigan (B.S.E., 1993); College of Charleston (B.S., 1993); Stanford University Law School (J.D., 1998). ***COURSES:*** E-commerce, Intellectual Property.

AMY L. WAX, **(Professor of Law)**, born 1953; admitted to bar, 1988, New York. *Education:* Yale College (B.S., 1975); Harvard Medical School (M.D., 1981); Columbia University School of Law (J.D., 1987). ***COURSES:*** Civil Procedure, Labor and Employment Law, Social Welfare Law & Policy.

UNIVERSITY OF PITTSBURGH SCHOOL OF LAW

3900 FORBES AVENUE
PITTSBURGH, PENNSYLVANIA 15260
Telephone: (412) 648-1400
Fax: (412) 648-2647
Internet: http:\www.law.pitt.edu

ABA Approved Since 1923

The University of Pittsburgh School of Law, founded in 1895, is a leader in legal education. From 1900, when Pitt joined with 31 other schools to form the Association of American Law Schools, until today, when Pitt stands as a founding member of the ABA African Law Initiative, Pitt has upheld the highest traditions of American legal education while continuously innovating educational programs of national and international stature. Its emphases in law and business, environmental law, health law, intellectual property and technology law, international and comparative law, and clinical legal education make a special contribution to the greater Pittsburgh region, while equipping our graduates to have an impact around the world.

The scholarship of the faculty at the University of Pittsburgh School of Law is consistently among the finest in the nation. Over three quarters of the faculty has authored leading casebooks, treatises, or trade books with major university presses, such as Michigan, NYU, and Oxford. Nearly all top law reviews have carried at least some scholarship by Pitt law faculty in the last decade.

Law School faculty currently number 43 full-time and over 50 adjunct professors. The student body consists of approximately 700 students from more than 185 colleges and universities across the nation. The diversity of the student body is a key element to the quality of the educational experience at Pitt. The School is proud of the supportive environment it provides to women students, minority students, older students, and students from nontraditional backgrounds.

The School of Law Building contains tiered classrooms, seminar rooms, a formal courtroom that seats up to 256 observers, a student lounge and student organization offices, administrative and faculty offices, and the Barco Law Library.

The current holdings of the Barco Law Library include more than 375,000 volumes and microform volume equivalents. A rapidly expanding treatise and microform collection is augmented by more than 5,000 legal periodical titles. Library holdings offer depth in all significant areas of law with particularly notable collections in international law, human rights and tax law. Law librarians are available to provide students with research assistance.

The library's Harold Obernauer Computerized Legal Research Center is state-of-the-art. Established in 1983 and significantly expanded in 1993, 1997 and 2000, the center provides students with over sixty personal computers that operate in a Windows environment along with supporting printers. The center offers access to both WESTLAW and LEXIS, and students receive professional training on both systems, as well as CD-Rom and the World Wide Web. The facility also offers students access to a wide variety of national sources and databases through the University's mainframe. An attendant is always on hand to provide students with computer assistance.

Our faculty help to make policy as well as write about it. Pitt law faculty are active in leadership in national organizations engaged in the study and application of law, such as the American Bar Association, the American Judicature Society, the Association of American Law Schools, and the American Society of International Law. Pitt is especially strong in the international area, as evidenced by the creation in 1995 of the University of Pittsburgh Center for International Legal Education. The Center provides students and faculty opportunities to work and study abroad and hosts visiting professors and lecturers from all over the world.

The rich international law curriculum features innovative courses in French, Spanish, German, Japanese and Chinese especially designed for lawyers. Also in 1995, the School of Law created the Master of Laws (LL.M.) Program for Foreign-Trained Lawyers. This program allows lawyers from overseas to learn American law in a U.S. context.

Among Pitt's other special programs are the Health Law Certificate Program, the Civil Litigation Certificate Program, the Environmental Law Certificate Program, and the International and Comparative Law Certificate Program that permit J.D. candidates to establish their particular expertise in a specific field of law. Additionally, Pitt has a so-called "3/3 Program" with Pitt's College of Arts and Sciences, which permits selected undergraduates to earn both a bachelor's degree and a J.D. in six, rather than seven, years.

We are proud to say that the scholar who wants to teach is a hallmark of our School of Law. Our faculty is recruited and evaluated for teaching ability as well as scholarship. We have a sophisticated faculty development process that includes both peer and student evaluations. New faculty members are given reduced teaching assignments and are encouraged to concentrate on developing teaching skills. This emphasis on faculty development helps to explain why thirteen law faculty members have received the Chancellor's Distinguished Teaching Award, first established by the University of Pittsburgh in 1984. This is an amazing achievement for a law faculty of just over 40 in a university with well over 2,000 teachers.

Four specialized legal clinics enable Pitt law students to work with real clients and apply what they have learned in their legal studies and from other disciplines. Students work in teams of two on real cases under the supervision of full-time or adjunct law professors, chiefly on issues of elder law, environmental law, health law and tax law. Pitt also offers a unique corporate counsel clinic. Most of these clinics are multidisciplinary and involve faculty from a number of schools of the University.

The University of Pittsburgh Law Review has received national recognition for the quality of its scholarly articles for more than half a century. It has been ranked among the top 40 most cited law reviews in the nation in a study by the editors of Chicago-Kent Law Review. Published quarterly, it contains articles by law faculty, lawyers, and public officials throughout the country. Each issue also contains student comments and notes on recent developments, legislative initiatives, and other topics of scholarly and practical interest.

In 1981, the Law School initiated a second review, the semi-annual Journal of Law and Commerce. The decision to publish a journal in this area of the law reflects the Law School's strength in the commercial, business, tax, and corporate law areas. Within two years of its inception, the Journal was accepted for inclusion in the prestigious Index to Legal Periodicals. It is now recognized both in the United States and Europe as among the very best sources of scholarship on the United Nations Convention on Contracts for the International Sale of Goods.

The daily interaction of law with economics, public policy and management, health policy, and international affairs places very real

(This Listing Continued)

UNIVERSITY OF PITTSBURGH SCHOOL OF LAW —Continued

demands on attorneys to approach the practice of law with an interdisciplinary perspective. Motivated by the growing management/social science needs of attorneys and the increasingly intricate legal needs of society, the University of Pittsburgh School of Law offers several joint-degree programs that provide rigorous, integrated training effectively merging law and a number of allied fields.

Of the Pitt Law School's almost 7,000 living alumni, approximately 80 are current or former judges. Our alumni have served on all court levels except the United States Supreme Court. Pitt graduates have served as U.S. senators, attorney general, law school deans, corporate CEOs, and general counsel of major corporations -- including Alcoa Inc., HarperCollins, and Saks Fifth Avenue. The National Law Journal's 2000 roster of the 100 most influential private attorneys in the United States included two of our alumni. That's why "Pittsburgh roots, global reach" is a phrase that well captures the combination of local commitment and national stature that Pitt Law School embodies.

Dean: David J. Herring (412) 648-1401
Admissions and Financial Aid: Fredi G. Miller (412) 648-1415
Library: George Pike (412) 648-1322
Placement: Christine Miller (412) 648-1408
Development/ Alumni Affairs: Leslie Heilman (412) 648-1909
Continuing Legal Education: Jui Joshi (412) 624-0083
Student Affairs: Namosha Smith (412) 648-5642
Director, Center for Bioethics and Health Law: Alan Meisel (412) 648-1384
Director, Center for International Legal Education: Ronald A. Brand (412) 648-1307

FULL TIME FACULTY

DAVID JOHN HERRING*, (Dean and Professor)**, born Detroit, Michigan, July 9, 1958; admitted to bar, 1985, Michigan; 1987, Illinois; 1990, Pennsylvania. *Education:* University of Michigan (B.B.A., 1980; J.D., 1985). ***COURSES: Civil Procedure, Child Welfare Law, Law and Biology, Legal Process.

KEVIN D. ASHLEY*, (Professor)**, born New York, New York, February 4, 1951; admitted to bar, 1976, New York; 1982, Massachusetts; 1990, Pennsylvania. *Education:* Princeton University (A.B., 1976); University of Massachusetts (Ph.D., 1989); Harvard University (J.D., 1976). ***COURSES: Computers and Law, Commercial Paper, Intellectual Property.

DEBORAH L. BRAKE*, (Assistant Professor)**, born Detroit, Michigan, May 25, 1967; admitted to bar, 1990, Kentucky; 1992, District of Columbia. *Education:* Stanford University (B.A., 1987); Harvard Law School (J.D., 1990). ***COURSES: Civil Procedure, Constitutional Law, Employment Discrimination.

RONALD A. BRAND*, (Professor and Director of the Center for International Legal Education)**, born McCook, Nebraska, September 19, 1952; admitted to bar, 1997, Pennsylvania. *Education:* University of Nebraska (B.A., 1974); Cornell Law School (J.D., 1977). ***COURSES: International Transactions, International Trade, Probate and Estate, Introduction to American Law.

DOUGLAS M. BRANSON*, (W. Edward Sell Chair in Law)**, born June 10, 1945. *Education:* University of Notre Dame (B.A., 1965); Northwestern University School of Law (J.D., 1970); University of Virginia School of Law (LL.M., 1974). ***COURSES: Corporate Governance, Progressive Corporate Law Seminar, Corporations, Securities Regulation.

TERESA KISSANE BROSTOFF*, (Associate Professor of Legal Writing)**, born New York, New York, May 11, 1958; admitted to bar, 1992, Pennsylvania. *Education:* University of Pittsburgh (B.S., 1984; J.D., 1991). ***COURSES: Legal Analysis and Writing, Advanced Legal Writing, English for Lawyers for LL.M. Students.

THOMAS C. BUCHELE*, (Clinical Assistant Professor)**, born Peoria, Illinois, May 6, 1960; admitted to bar, 1986, Indiana; 1987, California; 1990, Illinois. *Education:* Illinois Weslyan University (B.A., 1982); University of Illinois College of Law (J.D., 1986). ***COURSES: Environmental Clinic.

JOHN MICHAEL BURKOFF*, (Associate Dean and Professor)**, born Louisville, Kentucky, November 16, 1948; admitted to bar, 1974, Michigan; 1979, Pennsylvania. *Education:* University of Michigan (A.B., 1970; J.D., 1973); Harvard University (LL.M., 1976). ***COURSES: Criminal Law, Criminal Procedure, Legal Ethics, Criminal Defense and Prosecutorial Ethics.

MARTHA E. CHAMALLAS*, (Professor)**, born Waltham, Massachusetts, October 2, 1949; admitted to bar, 1975, Louisiana; 1978, District of Columbia. *Education:* Tufts University (B.A., 1971); Louisiana State University Law Center (J.D., 1975). ***COURSES: Torts, Constitutional Law, Employment Discrimination, Feminist Legal Theory, Employment Law.

PAT K. CHEW*, (Professor)**, born El Paso, Texas, September 30, 1950; admitted to bar, 1982, Illinois; 1985, California. *Education:* Stanford University (A.B., 1972); University of Texas (M.Ed., 1975; J.D., 1982). ***COURSES: Corporations, Dispute Resolution.

VIVIAN CURRAN*, (Associate Professor)**, born Philadelphia, Pennsylvania, October 30, 1955; admitted to bar, 1984, Pennsylvania, U.S. District Court, Western District of Pennsylvania and U.S. Court of Appeals, Third Circuit. *Education:* University of Pennsylvania (B.A., 1975); Columbia University (M.A., 1977; M.Phil., 1979; Ph.D., 1980; J.D., 1983). ***COURSES: Comparative Legal Cultures, Torts, Estates and Trusts, Property, U.S. Legal Analysis & Writing for LL.M. Students, Cultures of Law & Justice.

KEVIN MICHAEL DEASY*, (Director, Legal Writing Programs)**, born Pittsburgh, Pennsylvania, September 7, 1953; admitted to bar, 1984, Pennsylvania. *Education:* Pennsylvania State University (B.A.S.W., 1976); University of Pittsburgh School of Social Work (M.S.W., 1978); University of Pittsburgh (J.D., 1984). ***COURSES: Legal Writing, Academic Support, Client Counseling, Legal Methods.

KAREN ENGRO*, (Associate Clinical Professor)**, born Erie, Pennsylvania, December 16, 1958; admitted to bar, 1991, Pennsylvania and Massachusetts; 1992, District of Columbia. *Education:* Gannon University (B.A., 1982); Tulane Law School (J.D., 1990). ***COURSES: Civil Practice Clinic (Disability Discrimination), Health Law Practicum: ADR.

***MARVIN A. FEIN*, (Associate Professor of Legal Writing and Director, Civil Litigation Certificate Program)**, born Pittsburgh, Pennsylvania, October 17, 1938; admitted to bar, 1964, District of Columbia and Pennsylvania. *Education:* University of Pennsylvania (B.S., 1960); University of Pittsburgh (J.D., 1963); New York

(This Listing Continued)

UNIVERSITY OF PITTSBURGH SCHOOL OF LAW —Continued

University (LL.M., 1969). ***COURSES:*** Legal Writing and Analysis, Narrative and Trial Advocacy.

JAMES L. FLANNERY, **(Visiting Assistant Professor of Legal Writing)**, born New York, New York, January 29, 1949; admitted to bar, 1986, Pennsylvania, Indiana. *Education:* Miami University (B.A., 1971); University of Pittsburgh School of Law (J.D., 1982). ***COURSES:*** Legal Analysis and Writing.

HARRY M. FLECHTNER, **(Professor)**, born Fostoria, Ohio, April 8, 1952; admitted to bar, 1981, District of Columbia. *Education:* Harvard University (B.A., 1973; M.A., 1975; J.D., 1981). ***COURSES:*** Contracts, Sales, International Sales, Advanced Bankruptcy, Seminar on International Sales.

CYRIL A. FOX, JR., **(Professor)**, born Pittsburgh, Pennsylvania, February 18, 1937; admitted to bar, 1965, Pennsylvania; 1970, U.S. Supreme Court. *Education:* College of Wooster (A.B., 1958); University of Pittsburgh School of Law (J.D., 1965). ***COURSES:*** Property, Real Estate Finance, Real Estate, Regulation & the Environment, Natural Resources Law.

LAWRENCE A. FROLIK, **(Professor)**, born Lincoln, Nebraska, January 10, 1944; admitted to bar, 1970, New York; 1973, Massachusetts; 1976, Pennsylvania. *Education:* University of Nebraska (B.A., 1966); Harvard Law School (J.D., 1969; LL.M., 1972). ***COURSES:*** Elderly and the Law, Torts, Employee Benefits.

ROBERT BERKLEY HARPER, **(Professor)**, born Pittsburgh, Pennsylvania, March 26, 1939; admitted to bar, 1972, Pennsylvania. *Education:* University of Pittsburgh (B.S., 1962; J.D., 1971). ***COURSES:*** Evidence, Criminal Law, Law and Education, Scientific Evidence.

KATHRYN RITA HEIDT, **(Professor)**, born Philadelphia, Pennsylvania, June 14, 1953; admitted to bar, 1978, Ohio; 1980, Pennsylvania. *Education:* Pennsylvania State University (B.A., 1974); Cleveland State University (J.D., 1978); Yale Law School (LL.M., 1985). ***COURSES:*** Commercial Law (U.C.C.), Bankruptcy, Bankruptcy Seminar, Negotiation, Contracts.

ARTHUR D. HELLMAN, **(Professor)**, born New York, New York, December 9, 1942; admitted to bar, 1967, Minnesota; 1985, Pennsylvania. *Education:* Harvard University (LL.B., 1963); Yale Law School (J.D., 1966). ***COURSES:*** Federal Courts, Civil Procedure, Constitutional Law.

BERNARD JOHN HIBBITTS, **(Professor)**, born Halifax, Nova Scotia, Canada, June 29, 1959; admitted to bar, 1987, Nova Scotia. *Education:* Dalhousie University, Halifax, Nova Scotia (B.A., 1980); Carleton University, Ottawa, Ontario (M.A., 1981); Oxford University, Oxford, England (B.A., 1983); Harvard University (LL.M., 1988). ***COURSES:*** American Legal History, English Legal History, Property, Estates and Trusts.

ANTHONY INFANTI, **(Assistant Professor)**, born Point Pleasant, New Jersey, August 29, 1968; admitted to bar, 1993, California; 1995, New York, New Jersey; 2000, Pennsylvania. *Education:* Drew University (B.A., 1990); University of California - Berkeley (J.D., 1993); New York University (LL.M., 1996). ***COURSES:*** Legal Process, Estate and Gift Tax, Federal Income Tax, International Tax.

DARRYLL JONES, **(Assistant Professor)**, born Los Angeles, California, June 15, 1961; admitted to bar, 1986, Florida; 1995, Illinois. *Education:* University of Florida (B.S., 1983; J.D., 1986; LL.M., 1994). ***COURSES:*** Corporate Taxation, Partnership Taxation, Federal Income Tax.

SANDRA DICKERSON JORDAN, **(Associate Professor)**, born Philadelphia, Pennsylvania, December 3, 1951; admitted to bar, 1979, Pennsylvania. *Education:* Wilberforce University (B.S.Ed., 1973); University of Pittsburgh School of Law (J.D., 1979). ***COURSES:*** White Collar and Corporate Crime, Criminal Law, Pretrial Advocacy, Evidence.

JULES L. LOBEL, **(Professor)**, born New York, New York, September 8, 1951; admitted to bar, 1979, New York. *Education:* New York University (B.A., 1972); Rutgers Law School (J.D., 1978). ***COURSES:*** Constitutional Law, International Law, Human Rights, Comparative Constitutional Law.

WILLIAM V. LUNEBURG, **(Professor)**, born New York, New York, June 9, 1946; admitted to bar, 1971, Massachusetts; 1974, Illinois; 1995, Pennsylvania. *Education:* Carleton College (B.A., 1968); Harvard Law School (J.D., 1971). ***COURSES:*** Administrative Law, Civil Procedure, Legal Process, Environmental Law, Complex Civil Litigation, Litigation with the Federal Government.

MICHAEL J. MADISON, **(Assistant Professor)**, born Redwood City, California, December 13, 1961; admitted to bar, 1987, California. *Education:* Yale University (B.A., 1983); Stanford Law School (J.D., 1987). ***COURSES:*** Intellectual Property, Contracts.

MARGARET M. MAHONEY, **(Professor)**, born Buffalo, New York, October 21, 1948; admitted to bar, 1974, Michigan; 1975, New York. *Education:* LeMoyne College (B.A., 1970); University of Michigan (J.D., 1974). ***COURSES:*** Family Law, Property, Divorce Settlements.

MARTHA MANNIX, **(Clinical Assistant Professor)**, born New Rochelle, New York, September 29, 1959; admitted to bar, 1986, California; 1991, Pennsylvania. *Education:* University of Vermont (B.A., 1981); University of California, Hastings College of Law (J.D., 1986). ***COURSES:*** Civil Practice Clinic (Elder Law), Corporate Counseling Clinic.

FRANCIS BARRY MCCARTHY, **(Professor)**, born Brockton, Massachusetts, April 12, 1946; admitted to bar, 1971, Massachusetts; 1979, Pennsylvania. *Education:* Stonehill College (A.B., 1967); Boston College (J.D., 1971); Columbia University (LL.M., 1975). ***COURSES:*** Criminal Law, Criminal Procedure, Juvenile Law.

ALAN MEISEL, **(Professor of Law and Dickie, McCamey and Chilcote Professor of Bioethics)**, born Newark, New Jersey, December 24, 1946; admitted to bar, 1972, Connecticut; 1973, Pennsylvania. *Education:* Yale University (B.A., 1968; J.D., 1972). ***COURSES:*** Bioethics, Health Law, Torts.

MARK ALAN NORDENBERG, **(Chancellor, Distinguished Service Professor of Law and former Dean)**, born Duluth, Minnesota, July 12, 1948; admitted to bar, 1973, Wisconsin; 1974, Minnesota; 1985, Pennsylvania. *Education:* Thiel College (B.A., 1970); University of Wisconsin (J.D., 1973). ***COURSES:*** Civil Procedure, International Litigation.

SEAN O'CONNOR, **(Assistant Professor)**, born Cleveland, Ohio, May 29, 1965; admitted to bar, 1999, New York; 2001, Massachusetts. *Education:* University of Massachusetts (B.A., 1988); Arizona State University (M.A., 1995); Stanford Law School (J.D., 1998). ***COURSES:*** Biotech Law, Intellectual Property.

JOHN T. PARRY, **(Assistant Professor)**, born Akron, Ohio, June 19, 1964; admitted to bar, 1991, Virginia; 1992, District of Columbia. *Education:* Princeton University (A.B., 1986); Harvard University (J.D., 1991). ***COURSES:*** Constitutional Law, Criminal Law, Legal Process, Civil Rights Litigation.

GEORGE H. PIKE, **(Assistant Professor and Director of the Barco Law Library)**, born Dubuque, Iowa, August 5, 1959; admitted to bar,

(This Listing Continued)

UNIVERSITY OF PITTSBURGH SCHOOL OF LAW —Continued

1985, Idaho. *Education:* Albertson College of Idaho (B.A., 1982); University of Idaho (J.D., 1985); University of Washington (M.L.S., 1988). ***COURSES:*** Legal Research.

THOMAS ROSS,* (Professor)**, born Bridgeton, New Jersey, April 26, 1949; admitted to bar, 1975, Virginia; 1976, District of Columbia. *Education:* University of Virginia (B.A., 1971; J.D., 1974). ***COURSES: Legal Ethics, Lawyering Skills, Constitutional Law, Torts.

WILLIAM EDWARD SELL,* (Distinguished Service Professor of Law and Dean Emeritus)**, born Hanover, Pennsylvania, January 1, 1923; admitted to bar, 1950, District of Columbia; 1952, Pennsylvania; 1958, U.S. Supreme Court. *Education:* Washington and Jefferson College (B.A., 1944); Yale Law School (J.D., 1947). ***COURSES: Corporations, Agency and Partnership, Corporate Finance.

PETER MILO SHANE,* (Professor)**, born Oceanside, New York, July 12, 1952; admitted to bar, 1978, New York; 1979, District of Columbia; 1995, Pennsylvania. *Education:* Harvard University (A.B., 1974); Yale Law School (J.D., 1977). ***COURSES: Constitutional and Administrative Law, Legislation, Law and the Presidency, Telecommunications Law.

ANN M. SINSHEIMER,* (Associate Professor of Legal Writing)**, born Michigan, April 22, 1963; admitted to bar, 1995, Pennsylvania. *Education:* Northwestern University; University of Michigan (A.B., 1985); Howard University (1989); University of Pittsburgh (J.D., 1994). ***COURSES: Legal Writing, English for Lawyers.

STELLA L. SMETANKA,* (Associate Clinical Professor)**, born Latrobe, Pennsylvania, September 22, 1947; admitted to bar, 1980, Pennsylvania. *Education:* Carlow College (B.A., 1970); University of Pittsburgh School of Law (J.D., 1980). ***COURSES: Health Law, Civil Practice Clinic (Health Law).

GEORGE H. TAYLOR,* (Associate Professor)**, born Cambridge, Massachusetts, June 15, 1951. *Education:* Brown University (A.B., 1973); University of Chicago (M.A., 1976); Harvard University (J.D., 1988). ***COURSES: Legislation, Jurisprudence, Property, Jurisprudence Seminar.

LU-IN WANG,* (Associate Professor)**, born Pittsburgh, Pennsylvania, July 6, 1962; admitted to bar, 1986, Illinois; 1988, Michigan. *Education:* Pennsylvania State University (B.S., 1983); University of Pittsburgh (B.A., 1983); University of Michigan (J.D., 1986). ***COURSES: Contracts, Civil Procedure, Antitrust, Violence and the Law Seminar.

RHONDA WASSERMAN,* (Professor)**, born Newark, New Jersey, July 8, 1958; admitted to bar, 1984, New York and New Jersey; 1995, Pennsylvania. *Education:* Cornell University (A.B., 1980); Yale Law School (J.D., 1983). ***COURSES: Civil Procedure, Conflict of Laws, Complex Civil Litigation, Family Law Seminar, Family Law.

WELSH S. WHITE,* (Professor)**, born Philadelphia, Pennsylvania, April 17, 1940; admitted to bar, 1965, Pennsylvania. *Education:* Harvard University (B.A., 1962); University of Pennsylvania (LL.B., 1965). ***COURSES: Criminal Law, Criminal Procedure, Advanced Criminal Procedure, Evidence.

UNIVERSITY OF PUERTO RICO SCHOOL OF LAW

SAN JUAN, PUERTO RICO 00931

UNIVERSITY OF RICHMOND SCHOOL OF LAW

19 RICHMOND WAY
RICHMOND, VIRGINIA 23173
Telephone: (804) 289-8740
Fax: (804) 289-8992
http://law.richmond.edu

ABA Approved Since 1928

The University of Richmond School of Law, formally The T.C. Williams School of Law of the University of Richmond, was founded in 1870 as a constituent school of the University of Richmond. The Law School is located on the university campus, which is about six miles from the center of the city of Richmond and is often said to be one of the loveliest campuses in the country. The Law School building was renovated and expanded in the early 1990's resulting in a facility which is both state of the art and gracious.

The Law School is fairly small; it has a student body from across the nation and abroad of approximately 470 and a full-time teaching faculty of 28. It is also innovative in many respects. The School is in the forefront in the use of computer technology in legal education. The School was the first in the country to require that its entering students have lap-top computers. Each student is assigned a commodious carrel in the library. All of these carrels, and all of the faculty and other offices, are connected to the building computer network. In addition, the classrooms have electric and data ports at each seat. Faculty and students are also able to access the computer network from their homes. There is thus ready access to the Law School and university networks, and via them to the myriad databases and the internet. Some faculty are developing electronic teaching materials and are intensely using computer technology in their courses.

The Law School's curriculum balances traditional courses with a lawyering skills program and several in-house clinical programs. This combination provides both an intellectual and a practical approach to the study of law. Richmond is the state capital, as well as the base of the U.S. Court of Appeals for the Fourth Circuit and of a Federal Reserve District. Due to its location in this city, the Law School is able to offer an extensive range of clinical externship placements with a wide range of judicial and governmental entities. In addition, there is an International Business Practice Course in which law students and MBA students work together in small groups to prepare legal and business solutions to international business or trade issues brought to the clinic by publicly and privately held corporations located in Virginia. The Law School recently enhanced its international law program by establishing a prestigious Chair in Global Law and Business. A four semester (the two semesters of the first and second year) Lawyering Skills Program is required. This program provides in depth training in the various skills of legal research and writing, oral and written advocacy (pre-trial, trial and appellate) and interviewing, counseling and negotiation. The aim is to teach these skills in an integrative way. Another noteworthy aspect of the first year curriculum is that Environmental Law is a required course. This course is intended both to teach some fundamental principles of environmental law and to

(This Listing Continued)

UNIVERSITY OF RICHMOND SCHOOL OF LAW —Continued

introduce students in the first year to basic notions of administrative law and regulation.

The Law School has numerous joint degree programs, including the JD/MBA program offered in conjunction with the university's Business School and the JD/MSW (Master of Social Work), JD/MURP (Master of Urban Planning), JD/MPA (Master of Public Administration) and JD/MHA (Master of Health Administration) programs offered in conjunction with Virginia Commonwealth University, a publicly supported university located in Richmond. In addition, students are allowed to devise, in conjunction with the relevant department in the university, a joint program in areas of their interest, such as a joint JD/Masters in Biology.

Four journals are currently published at the Law School, the Law Review, the Journal of Global Law and Business, Journal of Law and Technology, and Journal of Law and the Public Interest. The latter two of these are published only in electronic form. The Journal of Law and Technology was the first solely "on-line" legal journal in the country.

Dean: John R. Pagan (804) 289-8188
Associate Dean for Academic Affairs: W. Clark Williams (804) 289-8740
Associate Dean for Student Services and Administration: Kristine T. Marzolf (804) 289-8740
Director of the Law Library: Timothy L. Coggins (804) 289-8218
Director of Admissions: Michelle L. Rahman (804) 289-8191
Director of Career Services / Placement: Beverly D. Boone (804) 289-8185
Financial Aid: Michelle Rahman (804) 289-8191

FULL TIME FACULTY

JOHN RUSTON PAGAN, **(Dean and Professor of Law)**, born Little Rock, Arkansas, August 4, 1951; admitted to bar, 1979, Arkansas; 1982, Virginia; 1984, District of Columbia; 1996, New York. *Education:* College of William and Mary (A.B., 1973); University of Oxford (M.Litt., 1975); Harvard University (J.D., 1978); University of Oxford (D.Phil., 1997). ***COURSES:*** Constitutional Law, Federal Courts, Legal History. ***Email:*** pagan@uofrlaw.richmond.edu

MARGARET IVEY BACIGAL, **(Associate Clinical Professor & Administrative Director, Clinical Placement Program)**, born Greensboro, North Carolina, June 29, 1951; admitted to bar, 1979, Virginia. *Education:* Mary Baldwin College (B.A., 1973); University of Richmond (J.D., 1979). ***COURSES:*** Clinical Program and Family Law. ***Email:*** bacigalm@uofrlaw.richmond.edu

RONALD J. BACIGAL, **(Professor of Law)**, born Pittsburgh, Pennsylvania, January 13, 1943; admitted to bar, 1967, District of Columbia; 1985, Virginia. *Education:* Concord College (B.A., 1964); Washington & Lee University (J.D., 1967). ***COURSES:*** Criminal Law and Criminal Procedure. ***Email:*** bacigalr@uofrlaw.richmond.edu

KELLEY H. BARTGES, **(Clinical Professor & Director, Youth Advocacy Clinic)**, born Fitchburg, Massachusetts, November 28, 1958; admitted to bar, 1985, Virginia. *Education:* Converse College (B.A., 1980); Clemson University (M.Ed., 1982); University of Richmond (J.D., 1985). ***COURSES:*** Clinical Program (Juvenile Law). ***Email:*** bartges@uofrlaw.richmond.edu

W. WADE BERRYHILL, **(Professor of Law)**, born Arkansas, September 2, 1946; admitted to bar, 1972, Arkansas; 1979, Virginia. *Education:* Arkansas State University (B.S., 1964); University of Arkansas (J.D., 1972); Columbia University (LL.M., 1976). ***COURSES:*** Real Property, Environmental Law. ***Email:*** berryhill@uofrlaw.richmond.edu

PAUL MATTHEWS BIRCH, **(Computer Services Librarian)**, born Milwaukee, Wisconsin, October 13, 1953; admitted to bar, 1982, Wisconsin. *Education:* University of Wisconsin (B.A., 1976; M.A., 1982; J.D., 1982). ***COURSES:*** Legal Research. ***Email:*** birch@uofrlaw.richmond.edu

KATHLEEN ANN BRADY, **(Assistant Professor of Law)**, born District of Columbia, December 31, 1967; admitted to bar, 1995, Connecticut; 1997, District of Columbia. *Education:* Yale College (B.A., 1989); Yale Divinity School (M.A.R., 1991); Yale Law School (J.D., 1994). ***COURSES:*** Wills & Trusts I, Law and Religion. ***Email:*** kbrady@richmond.edu

WILLIAM HAMILTON BRYSON, **(Professor of Law)**, born Richmond, Virginia, July 29, 1941; admitted to bar, 1967, Virginia. *Education:* Hampden-Sydney College (B.A., 1963); Harvard University (LL.B., 1967); University of Virginia (LL.M., 1968); Cambridge University (Ph.D., 1972). ***COURSES:*** Equity, Legal History, Virginia Civil Procedure. ***Email:*** hbryson@richmond.edu

TIMOTHY COGGINS, **(Director of the Law Library and Associate Professor of Law)**, born Conway, North Carolina, December 7, 1948. *Education:* North Carolina Wesleyan College (B.A., 1972); Simmons College (M.S., 1974); North Carolina Central University School of Law (J.D., 1984). ***COURSES:*** Lawyering Skills, Legal Research, Advanced Legal Research. ***Email:*** coggins@uofrlaw.richmond.edu

JOHN G. DOUGLASS, **(Associate Professor of Law)**, born Lynchburg, Virginia, April 12, 1955; admitted to bar, 1981, Virginia and District of Columbia. *Education:* Dartmouth College (B.A., 1977); Harvard Law School (J.D., 1980). ***COURSES:*** Criminal Law, Criminal Procedure. ***Email:*** douglass@uofrlaw.richmond.edu

JOEL B. EISEN, **(Professor of Law & Director, Robert R. Merhige, Jr. Center of Environmental Law)**, born Reading, Pennsylvania, February 26, 1960; admitted to bar, 1985, California; 1987, District of Columbia. *Education:* Massachusetts Institute of Technology (B.S.C.E., 1981); Stanford Law School (J.D., 1985). ***COURSES:*** Property, Environmental Law, Urban Environmental Law, International Environmental Disputes, Environmental Dispute Resolution. ***Email:*** eisen@uofrlaw.richmond.edu

DAVID FRISCH, **(Professor)**, born New York, New York, April 5, 1949; admitted to bar, 1975, Florida; 1976, Rhode Island. *Education:* University of Pennsylvania (B.S., 1971); University of Miami School of Law (J.D., 1975); Yale University School of Law (LL.M., 1980). ***COURSES:*** Secured Transactions, Commercial Paper, Sales and Leases. ***Email:*** frisch@uofrlaw.richmond.edu

MARY L. HEEN, **(Professor of Law)**, born September 2, 1949; admitted to bar, 1979, California; 1981, Alaska; 1982, New York; 1986, Massachusetts; 1997, Virginia (Associate). *Education:* Yale University (A.B., 1971); Harvard University (M.A.T., 1972); University of California at Boalt Hall (J.D., 1978); New York University (LL.M., 1987). ***COURSES:*** Federal Income Taxation, Corporate Taxation, Tax Policy, Legislation. ***Email:*** mheen@richmond.edu

AZIZAH Y. AL HIBRI, **(Professor of Law)**, born Beirut, Lebanon, January 14, 1943. *Education:* American University of Beirut (B.A., 1966); Wayne State University (M.A., 1968); University of

(This Listing Continued)

UNIVERSITY OF RICHMOND SCHOOL OF LAW —Continued

Pennsylvania (Ph.D., 1975; J.D., 1985). ***COURSES:*** Securities Regulation, Corporations, Corporate Finance, Islamic Jurisprudence. ***Email:*** hibri@richmond.edu

ANN CRANSTON HODGES*, (Professor of Law)**, born Winston-Salem, North Carolina, July 11, 1951; admitted to bar, 1981, Illinois. *Education:* University of North Carolina (B.S.I.R., 1973); University of Illinois (M.A., 1974); Northwestern University (J.D., 1981). ***COURSES: Labor Law, Employment Law, Employment Discrimination, Arbitration, Public Sector Law. ***Email:*** hodges@uofrlaw.richmond.edu

JOYCE MANNA JANTO*, (Associate Director, Law Library)**, born Pittsburgh, Pennsylvania, January 14, 1956; admitted to bar, 1991, Pennsylvania. *Education:* Clarion State University (B.S., 1978); University of Pittsburgh (M.L.S., 1982); University of Richmond (J.D., 1989). ***COURSES: Legal Research, Professional Responsibility. ***Email:*** janto@uofrlaw.richmond.edu

J. RODNEY JOHNSON*, (Professor of Law Emeritus)**, born Richmond, Virginia, July 9, 1939; admitted to bar, 1967, Virginia. *Education:* William & Mary (B.A., 1965; J.D., 1967); New York University (LL.M., 1970). ***Email: johnson@uofrlaw.richmond.edu

JOHN PAUL JONES*, (Professor of Law)**, born Nyack, New York, March 26, 1947; admitted to bar, 1980, California; 1986, Virginia. *Education:* Marquette University (B.A., 1969); University of San Diego (J.D., 1980); Yale Law School (LL.M., 1982). ***COURSES: Constitutional Law, Administrative Law, Admiralty Law. ***Email:*** jjones@richmond.edu

LESLIE M. KELLEHER*, (Associate Professor of Law)**, born Brandon, Manitoba; admitted to bar, 1989, New York. *Education:* Brandon University; University of Manitoba (LL.B., 1985); Columbia University (LL.M., 1988). ***COURSES: Civil Procedure, Federal Courts, Corporations, Mergers & Acquisitions. ***Email:*** kelleher@uofrlaw.richmond.edu

GARY CHARLES LEEDES*, (Professor of Law Emeritus)**, born Philadelphia, Pennsylvania, May 20, 1934; admitted to bar, 1962, Pennsylvania. *Education:* University of Pennsylvania (B.S., Economics, 1960); Temple (LL.B., 1962); Harvard (S.J.D., 1972). ***Email: leedes@uofrlaw.richmond.edu

DANIEL T. MURPHY*, (Professor of Law)**, born Birmingham, Alabama, October 23, 1942; admitted to bar, 1970, New York; 1972, New Jersey; 1979, Virginia. *Education:* Villanova University (B.A., 1965; J.D., 1968); Columbia Law School (LL.M., 1969). ***COURSES: International Law, International Trade, European Union Law, Comparative Law. ***Email:*** dmurphy@richmond.edu

EMMELINE M. PAULETTE*, (Assistant Professor for Academic Success)**, born Fort Hood, Texas, November 10, 1970; admitted to bar, 1996, Virginia. *Education:* University of Virginia (B.A., 1992), University of Virginia School of Law (J.D., 1996). ***Email: epaulette@richmond.edu

ROBERT EDWARD SHEPHERD, JR.*, (Professor of Law Emeritus)**, born Richmond, Virginia, September 22, 1937; admitted to bar, 1961, Virginia; 1976, Maryland. *Education:* Washington and Lee University (B.A., 1959; LL.B., 1961); Georgetown University Law Center (1962 & 1963). ***Email: shepherd@uofrlaw.richmond.edu

RODNEY ALAN SMOLLA*, (Allen Professor of Law)**, born Pueblo, Colorado, March 13, 1953; admitted to bar, 1979, Illinois, 1996, Virginia. *Education:* Yale University (B.A., 1975); Duke University (J.D., 1978). ***COURSES: Constitutional Law. ***Email:*** smolla@uofrlaw.richmond.edu

JONATHAN K. STUBBS*, (Professor of Law)**, born Gloucester, Virginia, August 12, 1952; admitted to bar, 1987, Virginia. *Education:* Haverford College (B.A., 1974); University of Oxford (B.A., 1976); Yale Law School (J.D., 1978); Harvard University (LL..M., 1979); Harvard Divinity School (M.T.S., 1990). ***COURSES: Contracts, Professional Responsibility, Human Rights, Jurisprudence. ***Email:*** stubbs@uofrlaw.richmond.edu

PETER NASH SWISHER*, (Professor of Law)**, born Oxford, England, January 7, 1944; admitted to bar, 1973, California; 1978, Virginia. *Education:* Amherst College (B.A., 1966); Stanford University (M.A., 1967); Hastings College of Law, University of California (J.D., 1973). ***COURSES: Family Law, Insurance Law, Products Liability Law. ***Email:*** swisher@uofrlaw.richmond.edu

ADRIENNE ELAINE VOLENIK*, (Associate Clinical Professor and Director, Mental Disabilities Clinic)**, born Berea, Ohio, December 8, 1946; admitted to bar, 1974, Maryland; 1975, Missouri; 1987, Maine; 1996, Virginia. *Education:* Marietta College (B.A., 1968); University of Maryland (J.D., 1974). ***COURSES: Clinic. ***Email:*** volenik@uofrlaw.richmond.edu

SALLY HILL WAMBOLD*, (Technical Services Librarian)**, born Norfolk, Virginia, February 11, 1947. *Education:* Old Dominion University (B.A., 1969); University of North Carolina at Chapel Hill (M.S.L.S., 1979). ***Email: wambold@uofrlaw.richmond.edu

WILLIAM CLARK WILLIAMS*, (Associate Dean and Professor of Law)**, born Memphis, Tennessee, November 10, 1949; admitted to bar, 1974, Texas; 1979, Virginia. *Education:* Brown University (B.A., 1971); Vanderbilt University (J.D., 1974). ***COURSES: Civil Procedure, Federal Courts, Conflict of Laws, Evidence. ***Email:*** williams@uofrlaw.richmond.edu

MICHAEL ALLAN WOLF*, (Professor of Law and History)**, born Lakeland, Florida, December 12, 1952; admitted to bar, 1978, Florida. *Education:* Emory University (B.A., 1974); Georgetown University (J.D., 1977); Harvard University (A.M., 1979; Ph.D., 1991). ***COURSES: Land-Use Planning, Environmental Law, Property, History. ***Email:*** mwolf@richmond.edu

---

UNIVERSITY OF SAN DIEGO SCHOOL OF LAW

ALCALA PARK

SAN DIEGO, CALIFORNIA 92110

UNIVERSITY OF SAN FRANCISCO SCHOOL OF LAW

2130 FULTON STREET
SAN FRANCISCO, CALIFORNIA 94117-1080
Telephone: (415) 422-6304
Fax: (415) 422-6433

ABA Approved Since 1935

The University of San Francisco School of Law is situated on a 55-acre residential campus adjacent to Golden Gate Park and a short distance from downtown San Francisco. Its graduates, who play leading roles in the bench and bar of the San Francisco Bay Area, practice in over 40 states and 20 foreign countries. The University was founded by the Jesuit fathers in 1855 as San Francisco's first institution of higher learning. The Law School dates from 1912 and is located in its own modern building Kendrick Hall, and newly constructed Dorraine Zief Law Library, both located on the main campus. Approximately 650 students are enrolled in the full-time and part-time divisions each year. The Law School offers a joint J.D./M.B.A. degree with the USF School of Business and Management.

Consistent with its commitment to lawyering skills training, USF offers a number of opportunities for students to experience the dynamics of actual law practice under careful faculty supervision. These highly regarded programs train students in all aspects of litigation and dispute resolution including interviewing, investigating, discovery, mediation, trial techniques and appellate review.

The principal component of the clinical program is the USF Law Clinic, a unique teaching law firm operated under the direction of full-time faculty members. Students enrolled in the civil clinic represent individual plaintiffs in a variety of civil actions, they also work on human rights projects. Students enrolled in the criminal defense clinic represent indigent defendants in all phases of criminal proceedings, from arraignment through trial and appeal as well as juvenile in delinquentcy proceedings.

The Mediation Clinic enables students to apply resolution skills to real world legal disputes. It provides the unusual opportunity for law students to mediate small claims cases and other civil disputes through innovative programs in the local courts as well as to mediate employment discrimination disputes brought before the EEOC.

The Intensive Advocacy Program is a unique two-week summer program which allows students to study pre-trial and advocacy skills under the guidance of nearly 100 outstanding trial attorneys. The program features 80 hours of lecture, demonstration and practice workshops. Students perform individual exercises relating to all phases of advocacy and receive extensive feedback about their performances. At the conclusion of the program, each student conducts a jury trial.

Students may also obtain practical experience outside the law school by interning in one of the numerous courts located in the San Francisco Bay Area. Academic credit can also be earned by participating in a clinical placement at a governmental agency, public interest organization, corporate legal department or private law firm.

Students interested in public interest law may receive a specialization certificate through the Public Interest Law Program. Achievement of the certificate requires completion of core courses and electives as well as significant practical experience in the public interest arena.

An Intellectual Property/Cyberlaw certificate is available to students interested in graduating with a concentration in Intellectual Property Law and Cyberlaw. Certificate students must complete core and elective courses which qualify as advanced study in these fields and meet the minimum scholastic and unit requirements of the program.

Since persuasive writing is of critical importance, all students undergo a rigorous Legal Research & Writing program during the first year. In addition, each student must complete an upper division writing requirement. The Law School publishes two student-edited journals, the *University of San Francisco Law Review* and the *Maritime Law Journal,* one of only two maritime legal journals in the United States. There is an extensive Moot Court program for first year students as well as an advanced Moot Court program for upper division students.

The recently established Center for Applied Legal Ethics is dedicated to fostering ethical behavior in the practice of law. The Center creates a forum for dialogue about teaching and applying legal ethics. Its focus is on the everyday practice of law, with the goal of enriching the legal community's understanding of ethics and morality.

Each year USF co-sponsors foreign summer programs with Trinity College in Dublin, Charles University in Prague, and Udayana University in Bali. In addition to these summer programs, there is a regular faculty exchange with these schools, as well as the East China University of Politics and Law in Shanghai.

The basic curriculum is taught by a faculty of 32 full-time teachers with a strong commitment to effective legal education. In addition, approximately 60 adjunct professors, drawn from judges and leading practitioners in the San Francisco Bay Area, teach specialized courses in their particular areas of expertise. Visiting faculty from Ireland, the Czech Republic and China regularly teach comparative law courses.

Over 2,000 students apply each year for a fall entering class of approximately 230 in the day and evening programs. Applicants represent over 150 undergraduate institutions from all over the United States.

Dean: Jeffrey S. Brand (415) 422-6304
Director, Admissions: Alan Guerrero (415) 422-6586
Financial Aid: Gaby De la Vega (415) 422-6210
Director, Library: Virginia Kelsh (415) 422-6679
Director, Career Services: Lisa Dickinson (415) 422-6757

FULL TIME FACULTY

JEFFREY S. BRAND*, (Dean and Professor of Law)**, born Brooklyn, New York, April 20, 1945; admitted to bar, 1970, California and New York. *Education:* University of California at Berkeley (A.B., 1966); University of California at Berkeley, Boalt Hall School of Law (J.D., 1969). ***COURSES: Civil Procedure, Evidence, Remedies, Constitutional Law, Labor Law.

JOHN M. ADLER*, (Professor of Law)**, born Boston, Massachusetts, January 5, 1947; admitted to bar, 1976, California. *Education:* Colorado College; Harvard University (A.B., 1968); University of New Mexico (J.D., 1976); University of California at Berkeley, Boalt Hall School of Law. ***COURSES: Torts, Bioethics, Legal Ethics.

(This Listing Continued)

UNIVERSITY OF SAN FRANCISCO SCHOOL OF LAW —Continued

RHONDA MAGEE ANDREWS*, (Associate Professor of Law)**, born Kinston, North Carolina, August 25, 1967; admitted to bar, 1993, California. *Education:* University of Virginia College of Arts & Sciences (B.A., 1989; M.A., 1993); University of Virginia School of Law (J.D., 1993). ***COURSES: Torts, Insurance Law.

WILLIAM W. BASSETT*, (Professor of Law)**, born Peoria, Illinois, December 18, 1932; admitted to bar, 1973, District of Columbia; 1978, California; 1984, U.S. Supreme Court. *Education:* St. Mary of the Lake (S.T.L., 1959; B.A., 1956); University of Illinois (M.A., 1959); Gregonian University (J.C.D., 1965); Catholic University of America School of Law (J.D., 1973); Ludwig-Maximilious Universitat. ***COURSES: Property, Wills, Trusts and Estates, Community Property, Churches and Religious Organizations.

JOSHUA PAUL DAVIS*, (Associate Professor of Law)**, *Education:* Brown University (A.B., 1989); New York University (J.D., 1993); Georgetown (LL.M., 1996). ***COURSES: Civil Procedure, Remedies, Legal Ethics. ***Email:*** davisj@usfca.edu

CONSTANCE DE LA VEGA*, (Professor of Law)**, born Mexico, D.F. Mexico, February 5, 1953; admitted to bar, 1979, California. *Education:* Chapman College; Scripps College (B.A., 1975); University of California at Berkeley, Boalt Hall School of Law (J.D., 1978). ***COURSES: Civil Law Clinic, International Human Rights.

JOHN F. DENVIR*, (Professor of Law)**, born Chicago, Illinois, December 17, 1942; admitted to bar, 1967, California. *Education:* College of the Holy Cross (B.S., with honors, 1964); New York University School of Law (J.D., 1967); Harvard University Law School (LL.M., 1972). ***COURSES: Constitutional Law, Legal Theory, Freespeech.

DOLORES A. DONOVAN*, (Professor of Law)**, born Detroit, Michigan, July 26, 1945; admitted to bar, 1971, California; 1972, District of Columbia. *Education:* Stanford University (A.B., 1967); Stanford University Law School (J.D., 1970). ***COURSES: Criminal Procedure, Comparative Law.

H. JAY FOLBERG*, (Professor of Law)**, born East St. Louis, Illinois, July 7, 1941; admitted to bar, 1968, Oregon. *Education:* University of Illinois; San Francisco State University (B.A., 1963); University of California at Berkeley, Boalt Hall School of Law (J.D., 1968). ***COURSES: Dispute Resolution, Family Law.

DAVID I. FRANKLYN*, (Associate Professor of Law)**, *Education:* Evangel College (B.A., 1983); University of Michigan (J.D., 1990). ***COURSES: Intellectual Property, Constitutional Law, International Intellectual Property. ***Email:*** franklyn@usfca.edu

SUSAN A. FREIWALD*, (Associate Professor of Law)**, born Cincinnati, Ohio, December 30, 1964; admitted to bar, 1993, New York. *Education:* Harvard-Radcliffe College (B.A., 1987); Harvard University Law School (J.D., 1991). ***COURSES: Contracts, Cyberspace Law, Information Technology Law.

JACK GARVEY*, (Professor of Law)**, born Chicago, Illinois, November 28, 1942; admitted to bar, 1971, Illinois; 1973, California. *Education:* Harvard University (A.B., 1964); Harvard University Law School (J.D., 1968). ***COURSES: Contracts, Public International Law and Organizations, International Dispute Resolution.

JOSEPH HENKE*, (Professor of Law)**, born Seattle, Washington, July 24, 1938; admitted to bar, 1964, Washington; 1968, Oregon. *Education:* Amherst College (B.A., 1960); University of Washington (J.D., 1964); New York University School of Law (LL.M., 1971). ***COURSES: Property, Wills, Trusts, Community Property.

MICHAEL C. HONE*, (Professor of Law)**, born San Francisco, California, June 21, 1937; admitted to bar, 1964, California. *Education:* University of California at Berkeley (B.S., 1960); University of California at Berkeley, Boalt Hall School of Law (J.D., 1963). ***COURSES: Corporations, Venture Capital, Non-Profit and Public Interest Organizations.

PETER JAN HONIGSBERG*, (Professor of Law)**, born New York, N.Y., June 29, 1943; admitted to bar, 1968, New York; 1982, California. *Education:* City College of New York (B.A., 1965); New York University School of Law (J.D., 1968). ***COURSES: Legal Research and Writing, Legal Drafting, Professional/Practice Skills.

ALICE KASWAN*, (Associate Professor)**, *Education:* UC Berkeley (B.S., 1984); Harvard Law School (J.D., 1991). ***COURSES: Administrative Law Property, Environmental Law, International Environmental Law. ***Email:*** kaswan@usfca.edu

VIRGINIA KELSH*, (Law Librarian and Professor of Law)**, born Portland, Oregon, April 1, 1945. *Education:* Marylhurst College (B.A., 1967); Catholic University of America (M.S.L.S., 1968); Northwestern School of Law of Lewis and Clark College (J.D., 1977). ***COURSES: Art Law (not currently teaching), Law Librarianship.

J. THOMAS MCCARTHY*, (Professor of Law)**, born Detroit, Michigan, July 2, 1937; admitted to bar, 1964, California. *Education:* University of Detroit (B.A., 1960); University of Michigan (J.D., 1963). ***COURSES: Intellectual Property, Copyright Law.

PAUL MCKASKLE*, (Professor of Law)**, born Little Rock, Arkansas, September 29, 1934; admitted to bar, 1964, California. *Education:* University of California at Berkeley (B.S., 1956); University of California at Berkeley, Boalt Hall School of Law (J.D., 1963). ***COURSES: Civil Procedure, Evidence, Conflict of Laws, Administrative Law.

SHARON MEADOWS*, (Professor of Law)**, born Indiana, September 11, 1950; admitted to bar, 1975, California. *Education:* Cornell University (B.A., 1972; M.A., 1972); University of Michigan (J.D., 1975). ***COURSES: Criminal Law Clinic, Criminal Procedure.

RONALD H. MICON*, (Associate Dean for Academic Affairs and Professor of Law)**, born Chicago, Illinois, January 23, 1943; admitted to bar, 1969, California. *Education:* University of California at Los Angeles (A.B., 1966; J.D., 1969). ***COURSES: Contracts, Commercial Law.

SUZANNE MOUNTS*, (Professor of Law)**, born Chicago, Illinois, August 21, 1945; admitted to bar, 1972, California; 1973, Washington. *Education:* University of California at Berkeley (B.A., 1967); University of California at Berkeley, Boalt Hall School of Law (J.D., 1972). ***COURSES: Criminal Law, Criminal Procedure, Evidence.

THOMAS NAZARIO*, (Assistant Professor of Law)**, born New York, N.Y., May 15, 1951; admitted to bar, 1978, California. *Education:* City University of New York (B.A., 1971); New York University (M.A., 1972); University of San Francisco School of Law (J.D., 1975). ***COURSES: Family Law, Children Rights, Civil Rights Litigation and Practical Aspects of California Law.

MARIA LINDA ONTIVEROS*, (Visiting Professor of Law)**, *Education:* UC Berkeley (A.B., 1981); Harvard (J.D., 1984). ***COURSES: Labor Law, Employment Discrimination, Torts.

DELOS PUTZ*, (Professor of Law)**, born Miles City, Montana, October 4, 1937; admitted to bar, 1963, New York; 1964, District of Columbia; 1974, California. *Education:* Gonzaga University (B.A., 1959); New York University School of Law (J.D., 1962). ***COURSES: Civil Procedure, Remedies, Complex Civil Litigation.

(This Listing Continued)

UNIVERSITY OF SAN FRANCISCO SCHOOL OF LAW —Continued

ELDON H. REILEY*, (Professor of Law)**, born Seattle, Washington, May 30, 1933; admitted to bar, 1958, Washington; 1973, California. *Education:* Massachusetts Institute of Technology (B.A., 1955); Harvard University Law School (J.D., 1958). ***COURSES: Contracts, Commercial Law.

JOSHUA ROSENBERG*, (Professor of Law)**, born Montclair, New Jersey, March 3, 1950; admitted to bar, 1974, New York; 1976, Virginia. *Education:* Case Western Reserve University (B.A., 1971); New York University School of Law (J.D., 1974; LL.M., 1982). ***COURSES: Mediation, Negotiation, Taxation.

STEVEN F. SHATZ*, (Philip and Muriel Barnett Professor of Trial Advocacy)**, born Chicago, Illinois, July 18, 1945; admitted to bar, 1970, California; 1979, Washington. *Education:* University of California at Berkeley (A.B., 1966); Harvard University Law School (J.D., 1969). ***COURSES: Criminal Law, Criminal Procedure, Federal Courts, Labor Law.

ROBERT E. TALBOT*, (Professor of Law)**, born New York, N.Y., September 29, 1940; admitted to bar, 1966, California. *Education:* Columbia University (B.A., 1961; J.D., 1964). ***COURSES: Evidence, Trial Practice, Criminal Law, Clinical Mediation, Internet Justice Project.

FREDERICK TUNG*, (Associate Professor of Law)**, born Chicago, Illinois, October 21, 1961; admitted to bar, 1987, California. *Education:* Cornell University (A.B., 1983); Harvard University Law School (J.D., 1987). ***COURSES: Corporations, Bankruptcy, International Business Transactions.

CAROL WILSON*, (Director, Academic Support Program)**, born Roseburg, Oregon, May 15, 1957; admitted to bar, 1988, California. *Education:* University of Oregon (B.A., 1979); School for International Training (M.A., 1981); University of San Francisco School of Law (J.D., 1988). ***COURSES: Legal Research and Writing.

UNIVERSITY OF SOUTH CAROLINA SCHOOL OF LAW

701 S. MAIN STREET
COLUMBIA, SOUTH CAROLINA 29208

UNIVERSITY OF SOUTH DAKOTA SCHOOL OF LAW

414 EAST CLARK STREET
VERMILLION, SOUTH DAKOTA 57069

UNIVERSITY OF SOUTHERN CALIFORNIA LAW SCHOOL

LOS ANGELES, CALIFORNIA 90089-0071

UNIVERSITY OF TENNESSEE COLLEGE OF LAW

1505 WEST CUMBERLAND AVENUE
KNOXVILLE, TENNESSEE 37996-1800

UNIVERSITY OF TEXAS SCHOOL OF LAW

727 EAST DEAN KEETON STREET
AUSTIN, TEXAS 78705
Telephone: (512) 471-5151
Fax: (512) 471-6988
http://www.utexas.edu/law/

ABA Approved Since 1923

Overview of the Law School
Founded in 1883, The University of Texas School of Law is one of the oldest law schools in the nation. With an enrollment of fourteen hundred Doctor of Jurisprudence (JD) degree candidates, the University of Texas School of Law is also one of the nation's largest law schools. In addition, the Law School offers a Master of Laws (LLM) program for graduates of foreign law schools, and another for American lawyers on doing business in Latin-America. Long recognized as one of the nation's leading law schools, it continues a rich tradition of educational excellence.

The University of Texas is a national school. The training received, and the courses offered, provide the necessary legal education for practice in any part of the United States. Legal positions with government, public service organizations, leading corporations, and law firms, throughout Texas, the nation, and the world, are available to its graduates. Graduates, including former U.S. Secretary of State James A. Baker III, former U.S. Ambassador Robert S. Strauss, former Secretary of Treasury Lloyd M. Bentsen, Jr., Fifth Circuit Court of Appeals Judge Reynaldo Garza, U.S. Senator Kay Bailey Hutchison, Secretary of Energy Federico Pena, Mayor Ron Kirk of Dallas, Presidential Advisor Paul Begala, and cartoonist Sam Hurt, have realized distinguished careers outside the traditional practice of law. Over 500 employers, 50 percent of whom were from out-of-state, participated in the Law School's on-campus interviewing and other career service programs in the 1998-99 academic year. Approximately one quarter of the school's 19,000 living alumni practice law outside Texas.

Although a majority of our students are Texas residents, over one-third graduated from a college or university outside of Texas. In fact, more

(This Listing Continued)

UNIVERSITY OF TEXAS SCHOOL OF LAW—Continued

than 250 undergraduate institutions and 45 states plus Washington D.C. are represented in the student body. Aggressive recruiting efforts coupled with the dramatic increase in the number of highly competitive applicants have resulted in diverse and academically distinguished student body.

Mission of the Law School

The University of Texas School of Law is dedicated to the professional training of future lawyers. To accomplish this goal, the Law School strives to provide effective and inspiring faculty who can train students in the process of legal analysis and in the development of clear and persuasive oral and written advocacy skills. In addition to expanding the substantive knowledge of our students, the Law School also seeks to nurture a sense of justice, and convey a vision of our students' responsibilities as citizens and lawyers.

The University of Texas School of Law is also committed to the study of law as an intellectual discipline. Through its world renowned faculty, the Law School seeks to advance knowledge about the law as a social institution and about the way the law effects the social, political, and economic life of our nation. Faculty research involves reexamination of classic jurisprudential problems, analysis of legal doctrines, the integration of social science and law, the evaluation of law as an instrument of social change and for the protection of rights, empirical analysis of the effects of law, a focus on law and legal institutions as a means of resolving disputes, and cross-cultural comparisons of law and legal systems. Twenty faculty are members of the American Law Institute, the nation's leading forum for law reform.

Finally, the School of Law seeks to promote public service. This involves making our legal resources available to assist government agencies, courts, legislatures, and other public interest entities, as well as demonstrating to our students the relationship between law and public policy.

Dean: William C. Powers, Jr. (512) 232-1120
Associate Dean for Student Services: Alexandra Wilson Albright (512) 232-1316
Associate Dean for Academic Affairs: Steven Goode (512) 232-1331
Associate Dean for Research: Douglass Laycock (512) 232-1341
Assistant Dean for Student Affairs: Susana I. Aleman (512) 232-1313
Assistant Dean for Alumni Relations: Nancy A. Brazzil (512) 232-1129
Assistant Dean for Career Services: Kathryn Holt Richardson (512) 232-1155
Assistant Dean for Admissions: Shelli D. Soto (512) 232-1207
Assistant Dean for Continuing Legal Education: William Watson (512) 232-1170
Exec. Dir., Law Sch. Found. and Asst. Dean, Admin.: Juan J. Zabala (512) 232-1117

FULL TIME FACULTY

WILLIAM POWERS, JR.*, (Dean & John Jeffers Res. Chair in Law & Hines H. Baker & Thelma Kelley Baker Chair in Law Dist. Teaching Prof.)**, born 1946; admitted to bar, 1974, Washington; 1980, Texas. *Education:* University of California at Berkeley (B.A., 1967); Harvard (J.D., 1973). ***COURSES: Conflict of Laws, Contracts, Jurisprudence, Legal Process, Products Liability, Torts. ***Email:*** wpowers@mail.law.utexas.edu

ALEXANDRA WILSON ALBRIGHT*, (Senior Lecturer and Associate Dean for Student Services)**, born Austin, Texas, November 9, 1955; admitted to bar, 1980, Texas. *Education:* University of the South (B.A., 1977); University of Texas (J.D., 1980). ***COURSES: Civil Procedure. ***Email:*** aalbright@mail.law.utexas.edu

DAVID A. ANDERSON*, (Thompson & Knight Centennial Professor in Law)**, born Gothenburg, Nebraska, May 27, 1939; admitted to bar, 1972, Texas. *Education:* Harvard College (A.B., 1962); University of Texas (J.D., 1971). ***COURSES: Communications Torts, Mass Communications, Torts. ***Email:*** danderson@mail.law.utexas.edu

MARK L. ASCHER*, (Sylvan Lang Professor in Law of Trust)**, born Junction City, Kansas, September 23, 1953; admitted to bar, 1979, New York; 1980, Florida; 1982, Arizona. *Education:* Marquette University (B.A., 1975); Kansas State University (M.A., 1977); Harvard (J.D., 1978); New York University (LL.M., 1981). ***COURSES: Federal Income Taxation, Trusts & Estates, Wills & Estates. ***Email:*** mascher@mail.utexas.law.edu

HANS W. BAADE*, (Hugh Lamar Stone Chair in Civil Law)**, *Education:* Syracuse University (B.A., 1949); Kiel(Germany) (Dr.Jur., 1951); Duke University (LL.B. and LL.M., 1955). ***COURSES: Commonwealth & Canadian Law, Comparative Law, Conflict of Laws, Domestic Relations, International Law, International Transactions, Texas Legal History. ***Email:*** hbaade@mail.law.utexas.edu

LYNN A. BAKER*, (Thomas Watt Gregory Professor in Law)**, born Pittsburgh, Pennsylvania, June 10, 1957; admitted to bar, 1992, Arizona. *Education:* Yale University (B.A., 1978; J.D., 1985); Oxford University (B.A., 1982). ***COURSES: Family Law & Policy, State & Local Government Law. ***Email:*** lbaker@mail.law.utexas.edu

CARL BAUDENBACHER*, (Visiting Professor of Law)**, *Education:* University of Berne (J.D., 1971; Dr.iur., 1978); University of Zurich (Habilitation, 1982). ***COURSES: Law of European Integration.

ANTONIO H. BENJAMIN*, (Visiting Professor of Law)**, *Education:* Fed. Univ. of Rio de Janeiro (L.L.B., 1980); University of Illinois (L.L.M., 1987). ***COURSES: Comparative Environmental Law, Biodiversity, Agenda 21 and Protection of the Rainforests.

STUART MINOR BENJAMIN*, (Professor)**, born New Orleans, Louisiana, June 18, 1965; admitted to bar, 1992, Pennsylvania; 1993, District of Columbia. *Education:* Yale (B.A., 1987; J.D., 1991). ***COURSES: Telecommunications, Administrative Law. ***Email:*** sbenjamin@mail.law.utexas.edu

MITCHELL N. BERMAN*, (Assistant Professor of Law)**, *Education:* Harvard (A.B., 1988); University of Michigan (Ann Arbor) (J.D., 1993; M.A., Political Science, 1994)). ***COURSES: Constitutional Law, Criminal Law.

LYNN E. BLAIS*, (Professor in Law)**, born Vermont, July 5, 1961; admitted to bar, 1988, Texas. *Education:* Wellesley College (A.B., 1983); Harvard (J.D., 1988). ***COURSES: Environmental Law, Property, Administrative Law. ***Email:*** lblais@mail.law.utexas.edu

PHILIP CHASE BOBBITT*, (A.W. Walker Centennial Chair in Law)**, born 1948; admitted to bar, 1978, Texas. *Education:* Princeton University (A.B., 1971); Yale (J.D., 1975); Oxford University (Ph.D., 1983). ***COURSES: Civil Procedure, Constitutional Law, International Law, Strategic Arms & Arms Control. ***Email:*** pbobbitt@mail.law.utexas.edu

(This Listing Continued)

UNIVERSITY OF TEXAS SCHOOL OF LAW—Continued

KAMELA S. BRIDGES,* (Lecturer)**, born 1966; admitted to bar, 1991, Texas. *Education:* University of Texas (B.A., 1988; J.D., 1991). ***COURSES: Legal Writing. ***Email:*** kbridges@mail.utexas.law.edu

LOFTUS C. CARSON, II,* (Ronald D. Krist Professor in Law)**, born Marion, North Carolina, July 16, 1946; admitted to bar, 1973, Pennsylvania. *Education:* Cornell University (B.S., 1968); Woodrow Wilson School, Princeton (M.Pub.Affrs., 1970); Harvard (J.D., 1973); Wharton School, Pennsylvania (M.B.A., 1980). ***COURSES: Banking Law, Corporate Law, Commercial Law, Securities Regulation, Professional Responsibility. ***Email:*** lcarson@mail.law.utexas.edu

MICHAEL J. CHURGIN,* (Raybourne Thompson Centennial Professor in Law)**, born New York, New York, February 25, 1948; admitted to bar, 1974, Connecticut; 1975, Texas. *Education:* Brown University (A.B., 1970); Yale Law School (J.D., 1973). ***COURSES: Criminal Procedure, Immigration, Legal History, Mental Health Clinic. ***Email:*** mchurgin@mail.law.utexas.edu

SARAH H. CLEVELAND,* (Assistant Professor of Law)**, born Washington, D.C., September 4, 1965; admitted to bar, 1994, Florida. *Education:* Brown University (A.B., 1987); Oxford University (M.St., 1989); Yale (J.D., 1992). ***COURSES: International Law. ***Email:*** sclevela@mail.law.utexas.edu

FRANK B. CROSS,* (Herbert D. Kelleher Centennial Professor of Law and Professor of Law)**, born 1955. *Education:* University of Kansas (B.A., 1977); Harvard University (J.D., 1980). ***COURSES: Administrative Law, Economics of Law & Litigation, Environmental Law. ***Email:*** crossf@mail.law.utexas.edu

ROBERT O. DAWSON,* (Bryant Smith Chair in Law)**, born 1939; admitted to bar, 1963, Missouri; 1972, District of Columbia; 1973, Texas. *Education:* University of Missouri (B.A., 1960); Washington University (J.D., 1963); Wisconsin (S.J.D., 1969). ***COURSES: Clinical Teaching, Criminal Law, Criminal Procedure, Juvenile Law. ***Email:*** rdawson@mail.law.utexas.edu

GEORGE E. DIX,* (A.W. Walker Centennial Chair in Law)**, born Neenah, Wisconsin, December 9, 1941; admitted to bar, 1966, Wisconsin; 1970, Arizona; 1975, Texas. *Education:* Wisconsin (B.S., 1964; J.D., 1966). ***COURSES: Criminal Law, Criminal Procedure, Psychiatry & The Law. ***Email:*** gdix@mail.law.utexas.edu

JOHN S. DZIENKOWSKI,* (John S. Redditt Professor in State & Local Government Law)**, born Ontario, Canada, November 14, 1959. *Education:* University of Miami (B.B.A., 1980); University of Texas (J.D., 1983). ***COURSES: Federal Taxation, International Energy Transactions, Natural Resources Taxation, Oil & Gas, Legal Ethics & Professional Responsibility. ***Email:*** jdzienkowski@mail.law.utexas.edu

LEE ANNE FENNELL,* (Assistant Professor)**, born Oklahoma City, October 4, 1966; admitted to bar, 1990, California; 1991, District of Columbia; 1998, Virginia. *Education:* Baylor University (B.B.A., 1987); Georgetown University Law Center (J.D., 1990). ***COURSES: Property, State and Local Government, Social Welfare Law. ***Email:*** lfennell@mail.law.utexas.edu

JAMES S. FISHKIN,* (Darrell K. Royal Regents Chair in Government, Law, and Philosophy)**, born May 9, 1948. *Education:* Yale University (B.A., 1970; Ph.D., 1975); University of Cambridge (Ph.D., 1976). ***COURSES: Contemporary Issues in Law & Philosophy. ***Email:*** fishkin@mail.utexas.edu

WILLIAM E. FORBATH,* (Angus G. Wynne, Sr. Professor in Civil Jurisprudence and Professor of History)**, *Education:* Harvard (A.B., 1974); Cambridge (B.A., 1976); Yale (J.D., 1983, Ph.D., 1992). ***COURSES: Constitutional Law, Legal History. ***Email:*** wforbath@mail.law.utexas.edu

FRANCES FRANCIONI,* (Visiting Professor of Law)**, *Education:* Florence (Dr. Jur., 1966); Harvard (LL.M., 1968). ***COURSES: Public International Law, International Environmental Law.

MARK P. GERGEN,* (Joseph C. Hutcheson Professor in Law)**, born 1956; admitted to bar, 1983, District of Columbia. *Education:* Yale College (B.A., 1979); University of Chicago (J.D., 1982). ***COURSES: Contracts, Federal Income Tax, Oil & Gas, Partnership Tax, Tax Policy, Commercial Torts, Taxation of Financial Products. ***Email:*** mgergen@mail.law.utexas.edu

JULIUS G. GETMAN,* (Earl E. Sheffield Regents Chair in Law)**, born 1931; admitted to bar, 1959, District of Columbia; 1970, Indiana. *Education:* City College of New York (B.A., 1953); Harvard University (J.D., 1958; LL.M., 1963). ***COURSES: Contracts, Criminal Law, Employment Discrimination, Labor Law. ***Email:*** jgetman@mail.law.utexas.edu

STEVEN J. GOODE,* (Assoc. Dean, Acad. Affrs., Fulbright & Jaworski Prof. in Law, & Univ. Distinguished Teaching Prof.)**, born New York, New York, January 5, 1951; admitted to bar, 1975, District of Columbia; 1977, Texas. *Education:* Williams College (B.A., 1972); Yale Law School (J.D., 1976). ***COURSES: Criminal Justice, Estates & Trusts, Evidence, Legal Profession. ***Email:*** sgoode@mail.law.utexas.edu

LINO A. GRAGLIA,* (A. Dalton Cross Professor in Law)**, born Brooklyn, New York, January 22, 1930; admitted to bar, 1954, New York; 1957, District of Columbia; 1980, Texas. *Education:* City College of New York (B.A., 1952); Columbia University (LL.B., 1954). ***COURSES: Antitrust, Constitutional Law. ***Email:*** lgraglia@mail.law.utexas.edu

DAGMAR S. HAMILTON,* (Professor of Public Affairs (LBJ School) and Law)**, born Philadelphia, Pennsylvania, January 10, 1932; admitted to bar, 1972, Texas. *Education:* Swarthmore College (A.B., 1953); American University (J.D., 1961). ***COURSES: Supreme Court in American History, Race in American Public Education. ***Email:*** dhamilton@mail.law.utexas.edu

ROBERT W. HAMILTON,* (Minerva House Drysdale Regents Chair in Law)**, born Syracuse, New York, March 4, 1931; admitted to bar, 1956, District of Columbia. *Education:* Swarthmore College (B.A., 1952); University of Chicago (J.D., 1955). ***COURSES: Contracts, Corporate, Finance, Corporations, Modern Securities & Transactions. ***Email:*** rhamilton@mail.law.utexas.edu

PATRICIA ISELA HANSEN,* (Assistant Professor of Law)**, born St. Louis, Missouri, May 24, 1960; admitted to bar, 1989, Pennsylvania; 1990, District of Columbia; 1996, Texas. *Education:* Harvard (A.B., 1982); Princeton (M.P.A., 1987); Yale (J.D., 1987). ***COURSES: Civil Procedure, International Trade, NAFTA. ***Email:*** phansen@mail.law.utexas.edu

J. PATRICK HAZEL,* (Tiny Gooch Centennial Professor in Trial Practice)**, born Kilgore, Texas, August 18, 1933; admitted to bar, 1971, Texas. *Education:* Gregorian University (S.T.L., 1960); Loyola University (Chicago) (M.Ed., 1968); University of Texas (J.D., 1971). ***COURSES: Civil Procedure, Trial Advocacy. ***Email:*** phazel@mail.law.utexas.edu

BARBARA C. HINES,* (Lecturer)**, born Chicago, Illinois, October 29, 1947; admitted to bar, 1975, Texas. *Education:* University of Texas (B.A., 1969); Northeastern University Law School (J.D., 1975). ***COURSES: Immigration Clinic.

HENRY T.C. HU,* (Allan Shivers Chair in the Law of Banking and Finance)**, born 1953; admitted to bar, 1979, California. *Education:* Yale (B.S., 1975; M.A., 1976; J.D., 1979). ***COURSES: Commercial

(This Listing Continued)

UNIVERSITY OF TEXAS SCHOOL OF LAW—Continued

Law, Corporations, Law & Science, Securities Regulation. ***Email:*** hhu@mail.law.utexas.edu

STANLEY M. JOHANSON,* (Fannie Coplin Regents Chair in Law and University Distinguished Teaching Professor)**, born 1933; admitted to bar, 1958, Washington; 1973, Texas. *Education:* Yale (B.A., 1955); Washington (Seattle) (LL.B., 1958); Harvard (LL.M., 1963). ***COURSES: Decedents' Estates, Estate Planning, Low-Income Housing, Real Property, Trusts & Estates. ***Email:*** sjohanson@mail.law.utexas.edu

CALVIN H. JOHNSON,* (Andrews & Kurth Centennial Professor in Law)**, born 1944; admitted to bar, 1971, California and New York. *Education:* Columbia University (B.A., 1966); Stanford University (J.D., 1971). ***COURSES: Accounting, Federal Taxation. ***Email:*** chjohnson@mail.law.utexas.edu

CORWIN W. JOHNSON,* (Edward Clark Centennial Professor Emeritus)**, born Hamlet, Indiana, October 5, 1917; admitted to bar, 1941, Iowa; 1946, California; 1957, Texas. *Education:* University of Iowa (A.B., 1939; J.D., 1941). ***COURSES: Land Use, Real Property, Water Rights. ***Email:*** cwjohnson@mail.law.utexas.edu

SUSAN R. KLEIN,* (Baker and Botts Professor in Law)**, born Miami, Florida, February 5, 1962; admitted to bar, 1989, California; 1995, Florida. *Education:* Wellesley College (B.A., 1984); University of California at Berkeley (J.D., 1989). ***COURSES: Criminal Law, Criminal Procedure, Federal Criminal Law. ***Email:*** sklein@mail.law.utexas.edu

JONATHAN JAY KOEHLER,* (Assoc. Prof. of Behavioral Decision Making & Law and Univ. Distinguished Teaching Professor)**, born Chicago, Illinois, November 4, 1960. *Education:* Pomona College (B.A., 1982); University of Chicago (Ph.D., 1989). ***COURSES: Probability & Science in the Courtroom. ***Email:*** koehler@mail.utexas.edu

***KIMBERLEE K. KOVACH,* (Lecturer)**, *Education:* Ohio State (B.S., 1976); Capital University (J.D., 1979).

H. DOUGLAS LAYCOCK,* (Associate Dean for Research and Alice McKean Young Regents Chair in Law)**, born Alton, Illinois, April 15, 1948; admitted to bar, 1973, Illinois; 1974, Texas. *Education:* Michigan State University (B.A., 1970); University of Chicago (J.D., 1973). ***COURSES: Constitutional Law, Religious Liberty, Remedies. ***Email:*** dlaycock@mail.law.utexas.edu

TERRI LECLERCQ,* (Senior Lecturer)**, born Indiana, September 16, 1946. *Education:* Southwest Texas State University (B.S., 1968; M.A., 1970); University of Texas (Ph.D., 1977). ***COURSES: Legal Writing, Editing, Drafting. ***Email:*** tleclercq@mail.law.utexas.edu

BRIAN LEITER,* (Joe A. Worsham Centennial Prof. in Law, Prof. of Philosophy & Dir., Law & Philosophy Prog.)**, born New York, New York, January 14, 1963; admitted to bar, 1988, New York. *Education:* Princeton (A.B., 1984); University of Michigan (J.D., 1987; Ph.D., 1995). ***COURSES: Constitutional Law, Evidence, Jurisprudence, Social Philosophy. ***Email:*** bleiter@mail.law.utexas.edu

SANFORD LEVINSON,* (W. St. John Garwood & W. St. John Garwood, Jr. Centennial Chair in Law and Prof. of Government)**, born 1941; admitted to bar, 1973, California. *Education:* Duke University (A.B., 1962); Harvard University (Ph.D., 1969); Stanford University (J.D., 1973). ***COURSES: Constitutional Law, Legal Profession. ***Email:*** slevinson@mail.law.utexas.edu

BASIL MARKESINIS,* (Jamail Regents Chair in Law)**, *Education:* Arhens (LL.B., 1965; Doctor Iuris, 1968); Cambridge (M.A., Ph.D., 1970, LL.D., 1988); Oxford (DCL, 1995). ***COURSES: Foreign Law and Comparative Methodology, Emergence of Modern European Law, American Torts from a European Perspective.

INGA MARKOVITS,* ("The Friends of Joe Jamail" Regents Chair in Law)**, born 1937. *Education:* Free University, Berlin (Dr.Jur., 1966); Yale University (LL.M., 1969). ***COURSES: Children & The Law, Comparative Family Law, Comparative Legal Systems, Domestic Relations. ***Email:*** imarkovits@mail.law.utexas.edu

RICHARD S. MARKOVITS,* (John B. Connally Chair in Law)**, born 1942; admitted to bar, 1978, Texas. *Education:* Cornell University (B.A., 1963); London School of Economics, (Ph.D., 1966); Yale University (LL.B., 1968). ***COURSES: Antitrust Law, Constitutional Law, Environmental Law, Jurisprudence & Constitutional Law, Law of Economics, Legal Profession, Legal Scholarship. ***Email:*** rmarkovits@mail.law.utexas.edu

THOMAS OWEN MCGARITY,* (W. James Kronzer Chair in Trial & Appellate Advocacy)**, born Charleston, Illinois, April 15, 1949; admitted to bar, 1974, Colorado; 1984, Texas. *Education:* Rice University (B.A., 1971); University of Texas (J.D., 1974). ***COURSES: Administrative Law, Environmental Law, Law & Science, Torts. ***Email:*** tmcgarity@mail.law.utexas.edu

ROY M. MERSKY,* (Wm. Stamps Farish Prof. in Law; Elton & Martha Hyder Jr. Centennial Faculty Fellow in Law; Dir. of Research)**, born New York, New York, 1925; admitted to bar, 1952, Wisconsin; 1972, Texas; 1983, New York. *Education:* University of Wisconsin (B.S., 1948; J.D., 1952; M.A.L.S., 1953). ***COURSES: Computers & The Law, Legal Bibliography, Legal Research & Writing. ***Email:*** rmersky@mail.law.utexas.edu

ROBIN B. MEYER,* (Lecturer)**, born Austin, Texas, November 7, 1954; admitted to bar, 1988, Texas. *Education:* University of Texas (B.A., 1975; M.S., 1981; J.D., 1988). ***COURSES: Legal Writing. ***Email:*** rmeyer@mail.law.utexas.edu

LINDA S. MULLENIX,* (Morris and Rita Altas Chair in Advocacy)**, born 1950; admitted to bar, 1981, District of Columbia; 1991, Texas. *Education:* City College of New York (B.A., 1971); Columbia (M.Phil., 1974; Ph.D., 1977); Georgetown University (J.D., 1980). ***COURSES: Civil Procedure, Complex Litigation, Conflict of Laws, Federal Courts, Mass Tort Litigation, Civil Justice Reform. ***Email:*** lmullenix@mail.law.utexas.edu

NEIL WEINSTOCK NETANEL,* (Arnold, White & Durkee Centennial Professor in Law)**, born Washington, D.C., May 4, 1954; admitted to bar, 1982, California; 1986, Israel. *Education:* Yale (B.A., 1976); University of California at Berkeley (J.D., 1980); Stanford University (J.S.D., 1998). ***COURSES: Intellectual Property, Commercial Paper. ***Email:*** nnetanel@mail.law.utexas.edu

CHRISTY BLAND NISBETT,* (Senior Lecturer)**, born St. Louis, Missouri, September 30, 1947; admitted to bar, 1979, Arkansas. *Education:* University of Missouri (Columbia) (B.A., 1969; M.A., 1971); University of Texas (J.D., 1979). ***COURSES: Legal Writing. ***Email:*** cnisbett@mail.law.utexas.edu

H.W. PERRY, JR.,* (Associate Professor of Government and Law)**, *Education:* Southern Methodist University (B.A., 1974); University of Michigan (Ph.D.,). ***COURSES: Constitutional Law.

L.A. (SCOT) POWE, JR.,* (Anne Green Regents Chair in Law and Professor of Government)**, born 1943; admitted to bar, 1968, Washington; 1980, Texas. *Education:* Yale (B.A., 1965); University of Washington (Seattle) (J.D., 1968). ***COURSES: Broadcasting, Constitutional Law, Federal Jurisdiction, First Amendment, Sports Law. ***Email:*** spowe@mail.law.utexas.edu

(This Listing Continued)

UNIVERSITY OF TEXAS SCHOOL OF LAW—Continued

DAVID M. RABBAN*, (Dahr Jamail, Randall Hage Jamail, and Robert Lee Jamail Centennial Chair in Law and Univ. Dist. Prof.)**, born Brooklyn, New York, December 29, 1949; admitted to bar, 1975, New York; 1980, District of Columbia. *Education:* Wesleyan University (B.A., 1971); Stanford (J.D., 1974). ***COURSES: Labor Law, Law & Higher Education, Legal History, Constitutional Law. ***Email:*** drabban@mail.law.utexas.edu

JACK T. RATLIFF*, (Ben Gardner Sewell Professor in Civil Trial Advocacy)**, born 1934; admitted to bar, 1962, Texas. *Education:* University of Texas (B.A., 1956; LL.B., 1962). ***COURSES: Advanced Civil Litigation, Civil Procedure, Torts. ***Email:*** jratliff@mail.law.utexas.edu

STEVEN R. RATNER*, (Albert Sidney Burleson Professor in Law)**, born New York, New York, December 9, 1959; admitted to bar, 1987, New York. *Education:* Princeton (A.B., 1982); Yale (J.D., 1986); Institute Univ. De Havtes Etudes International, Geneva, Switzerland (M.A., 1993). ***COURSES: International Law, International Organizations, International Transactions. ***Email:*** sratner@mail.law.utexas.edu

ALAN SCOTT RAU*, (Robert F. Windfohr & Anne Burnett Windfohr Professor in Oil, Gas & Mineral Law)**, born New York, New York, December 23, 1942; admitted to bar, 1968, New York. *Education:* Harvard (B.A., 1963; LL.B., 1967). ***COURSES: Alternate Dispute Resolution, Arbitration, Contracts, Copyright, Negotiation. ***Email:*** arau@mail.law.utexas.edu

R. ANTHONY REESE*, (Assistant Professor of Law)**, born November 13, 1964; admitted to bar, 1997, California. *Education:* Yale (B.A., 1986); Stanford (J.D., 1995). ***COURSES: Intellectual Property. ***Email:*** treese@mail.law.utexas.edu

DAVID W. ROBERTSON*, (W. Page Keeton Chair in Tort Law)**, born 1937; admitted to bar, 1961, Louisiana; 1962, District of Columbia; 1977, Texas. *Education:* Louisiana State University (B.A., 1960; LL.B., 1961); Yale (LL.M., 1965; J.S.D., 1968). ***COURSES: Admiralty, Civil Procedure, Federal Jurisdiction, Torts. ***Email:*** drobertson@mail.law.utexas.edu

JOHN A. ROBERTSON*, (Vinson & Elkins Chair in Law)**, born 1943; admitted to bar, 1969, Massachusetts; 1975, Wisconsin; 1993, Texas. *Education:* Dartmouth (B.A., 1964); Harvard (J.D., 1968). ***COURSES: Constitutional Law, Criminal Law, Law & Bioethics, Law & Medicine. ***Email:*** jrobertson@mail.law.utexas.edu

TIFFANY L. ROPER*, (Lecturer)**, born 1966; admitted to bar, 1991, Texas. *Education:* University of Texas (B.A., 1988; J.D., 1991). ***COURSES: Children's Rights Clinic. ***Email:*** troper@mail.law.utexas.edu

JOHN J. SAMPSON*, (William Benjamin Professor in Law)**, born 1935; admitted to bar, 1967, California; 1980, Texas. *Education:* University of Minnesota (B.B.A., 1957; LL.B., 1966). ***COURSES: Children's Right, Family Law, Legal Aid, Legislative Process. ***Email:*** jsampson@mail.law.utexas.edu

WAYNE SCHIESS*, (Lecturer)**, born April 3, 1963; admitted to bar, 1990, Texas. *Education:* Brigham Young University (B.A., 1986); Cornell Law School (J.D., 1989). ***COURSES: Legal Writing. ***Email:*** wschiess@mail.law.utexas.edu

JOSE MARIA SERNA DE LA GARZA*, (Visiting Professor of Law)**, *Education:* National Autonomous University of Mexico (B.Law, 1988); University of Essex (Ph.D., 1995). ***COURSES: Mexican Law, Latin American Legal Systems.

T.K. SEUNG*, (Jesse H. Jones Regents Professor of Liberal Arts, Philosophy, Government & Law)**, born Jungju, Korea, September 20, 1930. *Education:* Yale College (B.A., 1958; Ph.D., 1965). ***COURSES: Jurisprudence. ***Email:*** t.k.seung@mail.utexas.edu

M. MICHAEL SHARLOT*, (Wright C. Morrow Professor in Law)**, born Brooklyn, New York, October 7, 1935; admitted to bar, 1962, District of Columbia; 1974, Texas. *Education:* Antioch College (B.A., 1958); University of Pennsylvania (LL.B., 1962). ***COURSES: Criminal Law, Criminal Procedure, Evidence, Population Policy, Prosecutorial Clinic. ***Email:*** msharlot@mail.law.utexas.edu

CHARLES SILVER*, (Cecil D. Redford Professor in Law)**, born 1957; admitted to bar, 1988, Texas. *Education:* University of Florida (B.A., 1979); University of Chicago (M.A., 1981); Yale (J.D., 1987). ***COURSES: Attorney's Fees Litigation, Civil Procedure, Insurance, Law Ethics & Public Choice, Legal Profession, Litigation. ***Email:*** csilver@mail.law.utexas.edu

ERNEST E. SMITH*, (Rex G. Baker Centennial Chair in Natural Resources Law)**, born 1936; admitted to bar, 1962, Texas. *Education:* Southern Methodist University (B.A., 1958); Harvard University (LL.B., 1962). ***COURSES: Environmental Law, International Transactions, Oil & Gas, Real Property. ***Email:*** esmith@mail.law.utexas.edu

DAVID SIMON SOKOLOW*, (Senior Lecturer)**, born New Jersey, February 8, 1949; admitted to bar, 1980, New York; 1992, Texas. *Education:* Columbia University (B.A., 1970; M.A., 1971; J.D., 1979); University of Texas (M.B.A., 1993). ***COURSES: Contracts, Corporations, Intellectual Property. ***Email:*** dsokolow@mail.law.utexas.edu

JORDAN STEIKER*, (Cooper K. Ragan Regents Professor in Law)**, born 1962; admitted to bar, 1991, Texas. *Education:* Wesleyan University (B.A., 1984); Harvard University (J.D., 1988). ***COURSES: Capital Punishment Clinic, Capital Punishment, Constitutional Law, Property. ***Email:*** jsteiker@mail.law.utexas.edu

MICHAEL F. STURLEY*, (Stanley D. & Sandra J. Rosenberg Centennial Professor in Property Law)**, born Syracuse, New York, February 14, 1955; admitted to bar, 1984, New York. *Education:* Yale University (B.A., 1977; J.D., 1981); Yale University (B.A., 1980); Oxford University, England (M.A., 1985). ***COURSES: Admiralty, Commercial Law, Real Property. ***Email:*** msturley@mail.law.utexas.edu

TERESA A. SULLIVAN*, (Vice-President & Dean of Graduate Studies, and Professor of Sociology & Law)**, born Kewanee, Illinois, July 9, 1949. *Education:* Michigan State University (B.A., 1970); University of Chicago (A.M., 1972; Ph.D., 1975). ***COURSES: Law & Demography. ***Email:*** tsullivan@mail.utexas.edu

JOHN F. SUTTON, JR.*, (A.W. Walker Centennial Chair Emeritus in Law)**, born Alpine, Texas, January 26, 1918; admitted to bar, 1941, Texas. *Education:* University of Texas (J.D., 1941). ***COURSES: Evidence, Legal Profession, Torts. ***Email:*** jsutton@mail.law.utexas.edu

GERALD TORRES*, (H.O. Head Centennial Professor in Real Property Law)**, born Victorville, California, September 29, 1952; admitted to bar, 1978, District of Columbia. *Education:* Stanford University (A.B., 1974); Yale University (J.D., 1977); University of Michigan (Ann Arbor) (LL.M., 1980). ***COURSES: Agricultural Law, Environmental Law, Federal Indian Law, International Environmental Law, Jurisprudence, Property. ***Email:*** gtorres@mail.law.utexas.edu

WENDY ELIZABETH WAGNER*, (Professor)**, born Hindsdale, Illinois, August 26, 1960; admitted to bar, 1988, Michigan; 1989, District of Columbia. *Education:* Hanover College (B.A., 1982); Yale School of Forestry (M.E.S., 1984); Yale Law School (J.D., 1987). ***COURSES: Torts, Environmental Law, Regulation, Law and Science. ***Email:*** wagner@attglobalnet.net

(This Listing Continued)

UNIVERSITY OF TEXAS SCHOOL OF LAW—Continued

LOUISE WEINBERG*, (William B. Bates Chair for the Administration of Justice)**, admitted to bar, 1969, Massachusetts. *Education:* Cornell University (A.B., 1964); Harvard University (J.D., 1969; LL.M., 1974). ***COURSES: Constitutional Law, Federal Courts. ***Email:*** lweinberg@mail.law.utexas.edu

RUSSELL J. WEINTRAUB*, (Ben H. and Kitty King Powell Chair in Business and Commercial Law)**, born New York, New York, December 20, 1929; admitted to bar, 1955, New York; 1961, Iowa; 1980, Texas. *Education:* New York University (B.A., 1950); Harvard University (J.D., 1953). ***COURSES: Conflict of Laws, Contracts, International Litigation. ***Email:*** rweintraub@mail.law.utexas.edu

OLIN GUY WELLBORN, III*, (William C. Liedtke, Sr. Professor in Law)**, born 1947. *Education:* Harvard University (A.B., 1970; J.D., 1973). ***COURSES: Evidence, Torts. ***Email:*** gwellborn@mail.law.utexas.edu

JAY L. WESTBROOK*, (Benno C. Schmidt in Business Law)**, born 1943; admitted to bar, 1968, Texas; 1969, District of Columbia. *Education:* University of Texas (B.A., 1965; J.D., 1968). ***COURSES: Commercial Law, Creditors' Rights, Damages, International Business Litigation, International Transactions, Transnational Bankruptcy. ***Email:*** jwestbrook@mail.law.utexas.edu

ZIPPORAH BATSHAW WISEMAN*, (Thos. H. Law Centennial Professor in Law)**, born 1930; admitted to bar, 1959, Massachusetts. *Education:* McGill University (B.A., 1950); Yale University (LL.B., 1954). ***COURSES: Commercial Law, Commercial Paper, Contracts, Creditors' & Debtors' Rights, Gender, Law & Biography, Women & The Law. ***Email:*** zwiseman@mail.law.utexas.edu

PATRICK WOOLLEY*, (Professor of Law)**, born November 27, 1962; admitted to bar, 1987, California. *Education:* Stanford University (A.B., 1984); Yale (J.D., 1987). ***COURSES: Civil Procedure. ***Email:*** pwoolley@mail.law.utexas.edu

ERNEST A. YOUNG*, (Assistant Professor of Law)**, *Education:* Dartmouth (B.A., 1990); Harvard (J.D., 1993). ***COURSES: Federal Courts, Constitutional Law. ***Email:*** eyoung@mail.law.utexas.edu

---

THE UNIVERSITY OF TOLEDO COLLEGE OF LAW

2801 WEST BANCROFT STREET
TOLEDO, OHIO 43606
Telephone: (419) 530-2882
Fax: (419) 530-2821

ABA Approved Since 1939

The College of Law was founded in 1906 and in 1909 became a degree-granting college of The University of Toledo, a state university. It is accredited by the American Bar Association and is a member of the Association of American Law Schools and the League of Ohio Law Schools. In 1984 it was awarded a chapter of the Order of the Coif.

As an urban law school the college offers both a full-time (day) and part-time (day or evening) program and an integrated summer session. The course of study leads to a Juris Doctor (J.D.) degree. Full-time students normally graduate at the end of the second semester of their third year, but through summer study may graduate as early as the end of the first semester of their third year. Part-time students normally graduate in four years, including summer study. Typically, part-time students attend classes in the evening; however, persons whose work or childcare responsibilities preclude such attendance may attend classes during the day. Total enrollment is approximately 430, with about 302 full-time and 128 part-time students.

The college's modern facility compares favorably with any of its size in the country. Classrooms are designed to facilitate effective teaching and learning. A spacious auditorium is used for special events. A state-of-the-art moot courtroom is available both for trial practice and for appellate advocacy programs. A complex audiovisual system brings many new dimensions to the legal education experience. The student body is drawn from more than 200 colleges and universities from all regions of the country. Persons with diverse cultural backgrounds--ethnic, racial, educational, disadvantaged--are encouraged to apply for admission. Candidates for admission should expect stiff but not impossible competition. Grades and LSAT scores are the most important determinants of admission. Evidence showing that the GPA and LSAT score understate an applicant's ability is carefully considered.

The LaValley Law Library combines modern, well-designed facilities and a carefully chosen and ever expanding collection, with librarians and a support staff committed to meeting the curricular and research needs of students and faculty. The LaVally Law Library contains over 320,000 volumes and volume equivalents, in paper, microform and video and electronic formats. The library holdings also include subscriptions to nearly 3,250 serials. The collection contains the reported decisions of all federal and state courts, federal and state statutes and administrative materials, briefs and records of the U.S. Supreme Court, as well as a wealth of encyclopedias, treatises, looseleaf services, periodicals and access tools. The Library is a Federal Depository Library and receives a wide range of law-related government documents. In addition, the Library contains significant holdings of primary materials for the United Kingdom, Canada, Australia and New Zealand and primary and secondary materials necessary to the study of international law.

Occupying four levels within the Law Center, the Library provides seating for 440 at large tables and individual carrels, as well as in six group study rooms. Exciting capital improvements are under way that will enable the Law Library to collect, manage and deliver digital information more effectively to the University of Toledo research community.

Computerized services available to students and faculty include LEXIS/NEXIS, WESTLAW select collection of CD-ROM materials and many Internet-based data resources. Students receive instruction in the use of computer assisted legal research systems in their first year of legal studies. Desktop computers and printers are available to law students for word processing, computer assisted legal instruction and research applications. The University online public catalog, UTMOST, allows researchers to locate materials held in the University libraries. UTMOST also serves as a gateway to the OHIOLINK Network which enables researchers to access the catalogs and selected research databases maintained at other Ohio state college libraries.

A staff of fourteen, including seven professional law librarians, provide reference services during the day, evenings and on weekends. Library hours are from 7:30 a.m. to midnight, Monday through Friday and 9:00 a.m. to midnight, Saturday and Sunday.

The objective of legal education at The University of Toledo College of Law is to familiarize prospective lawyers with the major areas of the law while at the same time introducing them to the basic skills necessary for effective and competent lawyering. Successful integration of theory and practice is difficult but not impossible to achieve. In the early stages of

(This Listing Continued)

THE UNIVERSITY OF TOLEDO COLLEGE OF LAW —Continued

their law school experience, students are exposed to a variety of fundamental legal concepts as well as being introduced to the "lawyering skills" and instructed in legal analysis, research, writing and oral advocacy. An expansive set of advanced course offerings permits students to build upon the basic required courses and allows for exposure to various specialized areas of the law.

Dean: Phillip J. Closius (419) 530-2379
Associate Dean for Academic Affairs: Beth A. Eisler (419) 530-2937
Assistant Dean for Law Admissions: Carol E. Frendt (419) 530-4131
Financial Aid: Beth Solo (419) 530-7929
Director of Law Library: Bruce M. Kennedy (419) 530-2736
Assistant Dean for Law Career Services: Ricardo A. King (419) 530-2851
Director of Alumni Affairs & Communications: Linda Packo (419) 530-2628

FULL TIME FACULTY

PHILLIP J. CLOSIUS*, (Dean)**, born New York, N.Y., November 10, 1950; admitted to bar, 1975, New York. *Education:* University of Notre Dame (B.A., 1972); Columbia University (J.D., 1975). ***COURSES: Constitutional Law, Sports Law, Law and Literature, First Amendment.

TERRELL ALLEN*, (Instructor)**, born October 18, 1955. *Education:* University of Mississippi (B.A., B.S.W., 1977); Washington University (M.S.W., 1979); University of Michigan (J.D., 1985). ***COURSES: Legal Research & Writing, Appellate Advocacy. ***Email:*** tallen6@utnet.utoledo.edu

ROGER W. ANDERSEN*, (Professor of Law)**, born Chicago, Illinois, October 20, 1948; admitted to bar, 1974, Michigan and Washington. *Education:* Knox College (B.A., 1970); University of Iowa (J.D., 1973); University of Illinois College of Law (LL.M., 1978). ***COURSES: Property, Trusts and Estates, Environmental Law, Elder Law.

JOHN ADAMS BARRETT, JR.*, (Associate Professor)**, born Austin, Texas, December 13, 1962; admitted to bar, 1988, Texas; 1989, Colorado. *Education:* Amherst College (B.A., 1985); Harvard Law School (J.D., 1988). ***COURSES: International (Public & Commercial), Environmental.

RHODA L. BERKOWITZ*, (Professor of Law)**, born New York, New York, November 6, 1939; admitted to bar, 1964, District of Columbia. *Education:* Mount Holyoke College (A.B., 1960); Yale Law School (L.L.B., 1963). ***COURSES: Family Law, Criminal Law, Torts, Juvenile Law. ***Email:*** rberkow@pop3.utoledo.edu

JOAN R. BULLOCK*, (Professor)**, born London, England, Great Britain, January 30, 1959; admitted to bar, 1983, Michigan. *Education:* Michigan State University (B.A., 1980); University of Michigan (M.B.A., 1988); University of Toledo (J.D., 1983). ***COURSES: Contracts, Agency, Partnerships, Corporations, Secured Transactions, Accounting for Lawyers.

BRUCE CAMPBELL*, (Professor of Law)**, born Columbus, Ohio, May 29, 1941; admitted to bar, 1974, Michigan. *Education:* DePauw University (B.A., 1964); Michigan State University (Ph.D., 1973); University of Michigan (J.D., 1973). ***COURSES: Secured Transactions, Commercial Paper, Contracts, Constitutional Law.

DOUGLAS K. CHAPMAN*, (Professor of Law)**, born Cleveland, Ohio, July 11, 1945; admitted to bar, 1974, Ohio. *Education:* Ohio State University (B.S., 1971); Ohio Northern University (J.D., 1974). ***COURSES: Taxation, Estate Planning, Wills and Trusts.

GABRIELLE DAVIS*, (Instructor)**, *Education:* Siena Heights College (B.A., 1985); University of Toledo College of Law (J.D., 1991). ***COURSES: Clinical Education. ***Email:*** gdavis3@pop3.utoledo.edu

RICHARD W. EDWARDS, JR.*, (Professor of Law, Emeritus)**, born Columbus, Ohio, June 2, 1935; admitted to bar, 1959, District of Columbia; 1960, New York. *Education:* Cornell University (A.B., 1957); Cornell Law School (J.D., 1959). ***COURSES: International Law, International Financial Law.

BETH A. EISLER*, (Associate Dean and Professor of Law)**, born New York, N.Y., October 24, 1946; admitted to bar, 1973, District of Columbia; 1978, Michigan. *Education:* George Washington University (A.B., 1968); George Washington University National Law Center (J.D., 1972). ***COURSES: Advanced Sales, Commercial Law, Contracts, Criminal Law, Trusts and Estates, Evidence, Legislation, Secured Transactions.

MAARA FINK*, (Instructor)**, born Columbus, Ohio, April 4, 1970; admitted to bar, 1996, Ohio. *Education:* Clark University (B.A., 1992); University of Toledo (J.D., 1996). ***COURSES: Clinical Education, Dispute Resolution. ***Email:*** maara.fink@toledo.edu

HOWARD M. FRIEDMAN*, (Distinguished Professor of Law)**, born Springfield, Ohio, September 26, 1941; admitted to bar, 1965, Ohio. *Education:* Ohio State University (B.A., 1962); Harvard University Law School (J.D., 1965); Georgetown University Law Center (LL.M., 1967). ***COURSES: Agency and Partnership, Constitutional Law, Corporations, Securities Regulation, White Collar Crime.

LLEWELLYN J. GIBBONS*, (Assistant Professor of Law)**, born 1960; admitted to bar, 1992, Massachusetts; 1993, New York. *Education:* Suny-New Platz (B.A.,1998); Northeastern (J.D., 1991); Temple (LL.M. [LE], 1996); Franklin Pierce (LL.M. [I.P.], 1998). ***COURSES: Cyberlaw, I.P., Torts, Comm. Law, Law & Science, Contracts.

SUSAN E. GILMORE*, (Instructor)**, born 1960; admitted to bar, 1993, Ohio. *Education:* University of Toledo (B.S., 1983; M.B.A., 1989); University of Toledo College of Law (J.D., 1993). ***COURSES: Legal Research & Writing, Appellate Advocacy. ***Email:*** sgilmor@utnet.utoledo.edu

DAVID HARRIS*, (Professor of Law)**, born Chicago, Illinois, December 3, 1957; admitted to bar, 1984, Pennsylvania and District of Columbia; 1986, Maryland; 1988, Illinois; 1992, Ohio. *Education:* Northwestern University (B.A., 1980); Yale Law School (J.D., 1983); Georgetown University Law Center (LL.M., 1988). ***COURSES: Criminal Procedure, Criminal Law, Constitutional Law, Clinic.

ROBERT J. HOPPERTON*, (Professor of Law)**, born Cleveland, Ohio, June 19, 1941; admitted to bar, 1972, Ohio. *Education:* Baldwin-Wallace College (B.A., 1963); University of Toledo (M.A., 1969); Ohio State University College of Law (J.D., 1972). ***COURSES: Property, Land Transactions, Land Use, Environmental, Alternative Dispute Resolution.

MICHAEL G. KADENS*, (Professor of Law Emeritus)**, born Chicago, Illinois, July 20, 1935; admitted to bar, 1960, California and Illinois. *Education:* University of Michigan (B.A., 1956); Stanford University Law School (J.D., 1959). ***COURSES: Insurance Law, Law and the Great Lakes, Accounting for Lawyers, Business Planning.

(This Listing Continued)

THE UNIVERSITY OF TOLEDO COLLEGE OF LAW —Continued

BRUCE KENNEDY,* (Director of Law Library and Associate Professor)**, born Windsor, Ontario, Canada, February 24, 1954; admitted to bar, 1980, Minnesota; 1982, Michigan. *Education:* University of Michigan (A.B., 1976; A.M.L.S., 1984); University of Minnesota (J.D., 1980). ***COURSES: Property.

ROBIN M. KENNEDY,* (Associate Professor of Law)**, born Cleveland, Ohio, June 6, 1945; admitted to bar, 1970, Ohio; 1971, Florida, U.S. District Court, Northern District of Ohio, U.S. Court of Appeals, Sixth Circuit and U.S. Supreme Court. *Education:* University of Notre Dame (A.B., 1967); Case Western Reserve University School of Law (J.D., 1970). ***COURSES: Clinical Training (Prosecution), Civil Procedure, Remedies, Administrative Law, Interviewing, Counseling and Negotiating.

JAMES M. KLEIN,* (Professor of Law)**, born Toledo, Ohio, June 14, 1944; admitted to bar, 1969, Ohio; 1970, California. *Education:* University of Michigan (A.B., 1966); Case Western Reserve University School of Law (J.D., 1969). ***COURSES: Civil Procedure and Legal Clinic.

SUSAN R. MARTYN,* (Professor of Law)**, born Fairbanks, Alaska, November 24, 1947; admitted to bar, 1974, Wisconsin; 1975, Michigan. *Education:* St. Olaf College (B.A., 1969); Marquette University Law School (J.D., 1974). ***COURSES: Torts, Law, Science and Medicine, Legal Ethics.

FRANK MERRITT,* (Professor of Law)**, born Cleveland, Ohio, October 25, 1943; admitted to bar, 1968, Ohio; 1973, Illinois. *Education:* Hiram College (B.A., 1966); Case Western University School of Law (J.D., 1968). ***COURSES: Criminal Law, Criminal Procedure, Criminal Corrections, Local Government Law, Torts.

DEBORAH M. MOSTAGHEL,* (Senior Legal Research and Writing Instructor)**, born Berkeley, California, August 24, 1948; admitted to bar, 1988, Utah; 1991, Ohio. *Education:* University of California (B.A., 1969); Shiraz University, Shiraz, Iran (M.A., 1972); University of Utah College of Law (J.D., 1988). ***COURSES: Legal Writing, Legal Research and Appellate Advocacy.

LEE ANNE PIZZIMENTI,* (Professor)**, born Detroit, Michigan, October 9, 1955; admitted to bar, 1981, Michigan. *Education:* University of Michigan (B.G.S., 1977); Wayne State University (J.D., 1981). ***COURSES: Legal Ethics, Contracts, Agency and Partnership, Sales.

MARILYN FRIEDMAN PRESTON,* (Legal Writing and Research Instructor)**, born Detroit, Michigan, August 3, 1955; admitted to bar, 1981, California; 1982, Michigan. *Education:* Emory University (B.A., 1977); Hastings College of the Law (J.D., 1981). ***COURSES: Legal Writing and Research.

RONALD RAITT,* (Professor of Law)**, born Burton, Nebraska, September 28, 1931; admitted to bar, 1959, Nebraska. *Education:* University of Nebraska (B.S., 1953; LL.B., 1959). ***COURSES: Civil Procedure, Evidence, Trial Practice, Products Liability.

WILLIAM M. RICHMAN,* (Distinguished University Professor)**, born Baltimore, Maryland, November 13, 1949; admitted to bar, 1975, Maryland. *Education:* University of Pennsylvania (B.A., 1970); University of Maryland (J.D., 1975). ***COURSES: Procedure, Conflict of Laws, Evidence.

ROBERT S. SALEM,* (Instructor)**, born Beirut, Lebanon, March 21, 1964; admitted to bar, 1990, Ohio. *Education:* University of Toledo (B.A., 1987); University of Toledo College of Law (J.D., 1990). ***COURSES: Clinical Education. ***Email:*** rsalem@pop3.utoledo.edu

JOSEPH SLATER,* (Assistant Professor)**, born Ann Arbor, Michigan, April 12, 1960; admitted to bar, 1986, Maine; 1988, District of Columbia. *Education:* Oberlin College (B.A., 1983); University of Michigan Law School (J.D., 1986); Georgetown University (Ph.D., 1998). ***COURSES: Torts, Labor Law, Employment Law, Public Sector Labor Law, Employment Discrimination. ***Email:*** jslater@utnet.utoledo.edu

DANIEL J. STEINBOCK,* (Professor of Law)**, born New York, December, 12, 1946; admitted to bar, 1972, New York. *Education:* Yale University (B.A., 1968); Yale Law School (J.D., 1971). ***COURSES: Criminal Procedure, Evidence, Immigration Law, Administrative Law and Trial Practice.

JAMES E. TIERNEY,* (Professor of Law)**, born Perth Amboy, New Jersey, January 15, 1957; admitted to bar, 1982, New York; 1986, District of Columbia. *Education:* Rutgers University (B.A., 1978); New York University School of Law (J.D., 1981; LL.M., 1984). ***COURSES: Federal Income Taxation, Business Associations.

SANDRA K. ZELLMER,* (Associate Professor of Law)**, born 1964; admitted to bar, 1990, Minnesota. *Education:* Morningside College (B.S., 1985); University of South Dakota (J.D., 1990); George Washington University (LL.M., 1996). ***COURSES: natural Resources, Environmental Law, Property, Indian Law.

REBECCA ERNST ZIETLOW,* (Associate Professor of Law)**, born Ann Arbor, Michigan, December 18, 1962; admitted to bar, 1991, Illinois. *Education:* Barnard College of Columbia University (B.A.,1985); Yale Law School (J.D., 1990). ***COURSES: Clinical Instruction, Civil Procedure.

THE UNIVERSITY OF TULSA COLLEGE OF LAW

3120 EAST FOURTH PLACE
TULSA, OKLAHOMA 74104
Telephone: (918) 631-2401
Fax: (918) 631-3556
http://www.utulsa.edu/law

ABA Approved Since 1950.

The University of Tulsa College of Law began as the Tulsa Law School, a city-based program founded in 1923 by a group of Tulsa attorneys. In its early years, the Tulsa Law School was not affiliated with a university, and the faculty consisted of lawyers who practiced during the day and taught at night.

The Tulsa Law School became affiliated with The University of Tulsa in 1943. It was accredited by the American Bar Association in 1953 and admitted to membership in the Association of American Law Schools (AALS) in 1966. The law school continued to be located downtown until 1973, when it moved to the TU campus and its permanent home, John Rogers Hall. In 2000 the College added a new Legal Information Center and is planning a new Clinic Building for 2001.

The University of Tulsa College of Law offers eight areas of excellence: the National Energy Environment Law and Policy Institute (NELPI), the

(This Listing Continued)

THE UNIVERSITY OF TULSA COLLEGE OF LAW
—Continued

Native American Law Certificate Program, the Center for Comparative and International Law, the Center on Dispute Resolution, the Public Policy and Regulation Certificate Program, the Health Law Certificate Program, the Lawyering Skills Certificate Program, and the Entrepreneurial Law Certificate Program.

The National Energy-Environment Law and Policy Institute draws on TU's internationally known reputation in oil and gas, while also examining natural resource and environmental issues. NELPI's flagship publication, the Energy Law Journal, has been co-published since 1985 by the TU College of Law and the Federal Energy Bar based in Washington, D.C.

More than 35 federally recognized Native American tribes are headquartered in Oklahoma. About half of these, including the governments of the Five Civilized Tribes, are within an easy drive of Tulsa. This proximity to tribal headquarters makes it possible for the Native American Law Certificate Program to offer student internships at the heart of modern, evolving tribal governments. Beginning with the Fall 2001 Semester, the Law School is offering an LL.M. program for American Indian & Indigenous Law. The University of Tulsa's McFarlin Library also houses the John W. Shleppey Collection, one of the nation's most complete sets of tribal laws, constitutions and regulations.

The law school's Comparative and International Law Center offers students the opportunity to study with their Argentina counterparts through the Argentina Summer Institute in Law, a program established by the TU College of Law and by Universidad de Palermo of Buenos Aires. In addition to the Argentina Summer Institute in Law, the law school now also offers a summer program in Dublin Ireland and a semester abroad in London, England. An LL.M. degree program in Comparative and International Law for foreign lawyers began in the Spring 2000 semester. The TU center also coordinates visiting faculty members and guest speakers from other countries. TU college of Law is a participant in the multiple spring program in London.

The University of Tulsa College of Law Center on Dispute Resolution was established to educate and offer a resource for students, attorneys, judges and the general public in the field of dispute resolution. The Center offers classes for students on ADR theory and skills, opportunities for students to observe and conduct ADR procedures, and collaboration among students, teachers, practitioners, and judges interested in ADR.

Human resources are the TU law school's most valuable asset. Inquisitive students and a dedicated faculty produce a dynamic atmosphere. As teachers, TU law faculty members are dedicated to training students. As scholars, these professors add to the storehouse of legal knowledge in many fields -- environmental and natural resources law, bioethics, sports law, alternative methods of dispute resolution, Native American law, energy law and international and comparative law.

In addition to taking required courses, students at TU College of Law may choose from a wide variety of electives. Students may also concentrate and obtain certificates in one of several areas including Energy and Environment, Native American Law, International and Comparative Law, Alternate Dispute Resolution, Health Law, Public Policy and Regulation Law, Lawyering Skills and Entrepreneurial Law.

The law school's nine joint degree programs also provide cross-disciplinary education in history, business administration, accounting, modern disciplinary education in history, modern letters, psychology, taxation, anthropology, biological sciences and geosciences.

The law school also offers lawyering skills courses such as pretrial and trial practice, estate planning and evidence workshops. In addition, the law school offers legal and judicial internship programs; client counseling, negotiation and trial advocacy competitions; and the opportunity to serve on the staff of three publications, the Tulsa Law Review, the Energy Law Journal, and the Tulsa Journal of Comparative and International Law.

The Board of Advocates is open to any law student interested in advocacy. It's mission is to develop the communication skills of the lawyer in a broad range of settings. The Board of Advocates provides opportunities for professional development of the oral and written skills required for the legal profession. The Board sponsors two intraschool competitions; a negotiation competition for first-year students, and the Professor John W. Hager Memorial Competition for all students. The Board has hosted regional competitions at the Law School.

The University of Tulsa Legal Clinic offers students academic credit and clinical experience in cases involving landlord-tenant law, Social Security disability, unemployment compensation, welfare benefits, Health Law and other issues. The TU Health Law Project is part of the Legal Clinic. Its mission is to provide free health-care related legal services to Tulsa-area individuals and organizations that otherwise would not be able to afford legal assistance. The Legal Clinic will move into a new building at the end of this year.

The Law School's Taliaferro Savage Law Library contains approximately 260,000 volumes and has a computerized information system to connect TU students with libraries throughout the United States and abroad. The newly completed Mabee Legal Information Center includes another electronic classroom, rooms for special study projects, group study rooms, and sophisticated use of new information technologies including CD Roms, the Internet, multi-media, new student organization offices and a new classroom with the completion of the Mabee Legal Information Center, Tulsa is now in the top third among all ABA approved Law Schools in total net square footage area. In addition, several classrooms in the law school building are fully electronic classrooms.

The TU College of Law, with 36 full-time regular faculty and several distinguished visiting and adjunct faculty members, enrolls more than 575 students in its full-time and part-time divisions. By graduating lawyers who have become noted judges, educators, practitioners and public office holders, the law school has made its mark nationwide. Alumni in every state and several foreign countries attest to the law school's continuing efforts to seek a diverse, multi-talented student body.

Dean: Martin H. Belsky (918) 631-2400
Admissions & Financial Aid: George Justice (918) 631-2709
Library: Richard Ducey (918) 631-2458
Career Services: Vicki Jordan (918) 631-2429
Alumni Affairs: Jane Kolesnik (918) 631-3320

(This Listing Continued)

THE UNIVERSITY OF TULSA COLLEGE OF LAW —Continued

FULL TIME FACULTY

MARTIN HENRY BELSKY*, (Dean and Professor of Law)**, born Philadelphia, Pennsylvania, May 29, 1944; admitted to bar, 1969, Pennsylvania; 1983, Florida; 1987, New York. *Education:* Temple University (B.A., 1965); Columbia University (J.D., 1968); Cambridge University (D.P., 1969). ***COURSES: Legal Ethics, Constitutional Law, International Law, Land Use Law, Law & Theological Ethics. ***Email:*** martin-belsky@utulsa.edu

---

CHARLES W. ADAMS*, (Professor of Law)**, born Elgin, Illinois, June 3, 1948; admitted to bar, 1976, California; 1977, Oklahoma. *Education:* University of California at Santa Barbara (B.A., 1968; M.A., 1970); University of California at Berkeley (M.B.A., 1972); University of California at Berkeley, Boalt Hall School of Law (J.D., 1976). ***COURSES: Civil Procedure, Evidence, Law and Economics, Creditors' Rights and Bankruptcy. ***Email:*** charles-adams@utulsa.edu

GARY DEAN ALLISON*, (Professor of Law)**, born Wichita, Kansas, December 14, 1946; admitted to bar, 1973, Oklahoma. *Education:* University of Tulsa (B.S., 1968); University of Tulsa College of Law (J.D., 1972); Columbia University (LL.M., 1976). ***COURSES: Constitutional Law, Water Law, Regulated Industries, Hazardous Substances. ***Email:*** gary-allison@utulsa.edu

M. THOMAS ARNOLD*, (Professor of Law & Associate Dean of Academic Affairs)**, born Auburn, New York, November 23, 1952; admitted to bar, 1976, Michigan. *Education:* Ohio University (A.B., 1973; M.A., 1973); University of Michigan (J.D., 1976). ***COURSES: Contracts, Civil Procedure, Agency and Partnership, Basic Corporate Law, Unfair Trade Practices. ***Email:*** mark-arnold@utulsa.edu

MORRIS BERNSTEIN*, (Associate Clinical Professor)**, born Bronx, New York, June 27, 1951; admitted to bar, 1983, Pennsylvania; 1994, Oklahoma. *Education:* State University of New York at Binghamton (B.A., 1972); Temple University (M.S.W., 1976); Rutgers University at Camden (J.D., 1983). ***COURSES: Clinical Teaching, Interviewing, Counseling and Negotiation. ***Email:*** morris-bernstein@utulsa.edu

DENNIS BIRES*, (Associate Professor of Law)**, born Rochester, Pennsylvania, May 18, 1954; admitted to bar, 1979, Pennsylvania. *Education:* Allegheny College (B.A., 1976); New York University School of Law (J.D., 1979; LL.M., 1984). ***COURSES: Tax. ***Email:*** dennis-bires@utulsa.edu

CHRIS BLAIR*, (Associate Professor of Law)**, born Martins Ferry, Ohio, March 15, 1949; admitted to bar, 1976, Ohio. *Education:* Muskingum College (B.A., 1971); Ohio State University (J.D., 1976); Columbia University (LL.M., 1981). ***COURSES: Evidence, Criminal Procedure, Criminal Law. ***Email:*** christen-blair@utulsa.edu

D. MARIANNE BLAIR*, (Professor of Law)**, born Chicago, Illinois; admitted to bar, 1982, Oklahoma. *Education:* DePauw University (B.A., 1974); Ohio State University (J.D., 1980). ***COURSES: Civil Procedure, Family Law. ***Email:*** marianne-blair@utulsa.edu

BARBARA BUCHOLTZ*, (Associate Professor of Law)**, born Tulsa, Oklahoma; admitted to bar, 1980, Indiana; 1983, Oklahoma. *Education:* Mount Holyoke (B.A., 1961); Valparaiso University School of Law (J.D., 1980); George Washington University Law Center (LL.M., 1990). ***COURSES: Corporations, Comparative Corporate Law, Agency and Partnership, Reasoning and Writing, Jurisprudence, Legal History, Non-Profit Associations. ***Email:*** barbara-bucholtz@utulsa.edu

NICHOLAS CAPALDI*, (Research Professor of Law)**, *Education:* University of Pennsylvania (B.A., 1960); Columbia University (Ph.D., 1965). ***COURSES: Public Policy, Political Science, Philosophy, Law and Economics. ***Email:*** nicholas-capaldi@utulsa.edu

MARGUERITE ANN CHAPMAN*, (Associate Professor of Law)**, born Heber Springs, Arkansas, April 10, 1951; admitted to bar, 1976, Arkansas. *Education:* University of Arkansas (B.A., 1973; J.D., 1976); George Washington University National Law Center (LL.M., 1985). ***COURSES: Torts, Bioethics and the Law, Health Law, Law and Medicine, Decedents' Estates and Trusts. ***Email:*** marguerite-chapman@utulsa.edu

DAVID S. CLARK*, (Professor of Law)**, born San Diego, California, November 24, 1944; admitted to bar, 1972, California. *Education:* Stanford University (A.B., 1966); Stanford University Law School (J.D., 1969; J.S.M., 1972). ***COURSES: Comparative Law, International Law, Conflict of Laws, Federal Courts, Transnational Litigation. ***Email:*** david-clark@utulsa.edu

CATHERINE CULLEM*, (Associate Professor of Law)**, born New York, May 25, 1954; admitted to bar, 1980, Oklahoma. *Education:* C.W. Post College, Long Island University (B.A., 1977); University of Tulsa College of Law (J.D., 1980). ***COURSES: Legal Reasoning, Authorities and Writing, Professional Responsibility. ***Email:*** catherine-cullen@utulsa.edu

RICHARD DUCEY*, (Associate Professor of Law/Mabee Legal Information Center Director)**, born New Milford, Connecticut, August 21, 1952; admitted to bar, 1977, Connecticut; 1978, District of Columbia; 1979, Massachusetts. *Education:* Western Connecticut State University (B.A., 1974); New England University School of Law (J.D., 1977); Simmons College (M.S., 1983). ***COURSES: Legal Research. ***Email:*** richard-ducey@utulsa.edu

STEPHEN M. FELDMAN*, (Professor of Law)**, born New York, N.Y., December 21, 1955; admitted to bar, 1982, California. *Education:* Hamilton College (B.A., 1977); University of Oregon (J.D., 1982); Stanford University Law School (J.S.M., 1986). ***COURSES: Constitutional Law, Jurisprudence, Federal Courts. ***Email:*** stephen-feldman@utulsa.edu

JOHN HICKS*, (Professor of Law)**, born Houston, Texas, August 9, 1942; admitted to bar, 1967, Texas; 1982, Oklahoma. *Education:* Baylor University (B.A., 1964; J.D., 1967); University of Illinois (LL.M., 1972). ***COURSES: Property, Decedents' Estates and Trusts, Land Use Controls, Real Estate Transactions. ***Email:*** john-hicks@utulsa.edu

RUSSELL HITTINGER*, (Research Professor of Law)**, born Quantico, Virginia, July 27, 1949. *Education:* University of Notre Dame (B.A., 1975); St. Louis University (M.A., 1981); St. Louis University (Ph.D., 1986). ***COURSES: Religion and Law, Jurisprudence, and similar topics. ***Email:*** francis-hittinger@utulsa.edu

TOM HOLLAND*, (Professor of Law)**, born Delaware, Arkansas, September 11, 1938; admitted to bar, 1971, Oklahoma. *Education:* Southwestern College; Friends University (B.A., 1961); University of Tulsa College of Law (J.D., 1970); University of Illinois (LL.M., 1976). ***COURSES: Commercial Law, Consumer Transactions. ***Email:*** tommy-holland@utulsa.edu

WILLIAM HOLLINGSWORTH*, (Professor of Law)**, born Miami, Florida, December 28, 1937; admitted to bar, 1969, Florida. *Education:* University of Florida (B.S.B.A., 1960); Southern Methodist University (B.D., 1967); University of Florida (J.D., 1969); Yale Law School (LL.M., 1972). ***COURSES: Criminal Law, Criminal Procedure, Jurisprudence. ***Email:*** william-hollingsworth@utulsa.edu

LINDA J. LACEY*, (Professor of Law & Director of the Comparative & International Law Center)**, *Education:* University of California at Los Angeles School of Law (J.D., 1978). ***COURSES: Criminal Law,

(This Listing Continued)

THE UNIVERSITY OF TULSA COLLEGE OF LAW —Continued

Family Law, Woman and the Law, Law and Religion, Mass Media Law. ***Email:*** linda-lacey@utulsa.edu

R. DOBIE LANGENKAMP*, (Professor of Law and Interim Director of NELPI)**, born Tulsa, Oklahoma, August 14, 1936; admitted to bar, 1962, District of Columbia; 1964, Oklahoma; 1968, The Supreme Court. *Education:* Stanford University (B.A., 1958); Harvard Law School (J.D., 1961). ***COURSES: Federal Energy, Oil & Gas Law, Regulated Industries, Financing Energy Development, Advanced Oil & Gas.

VICKI J. LIMAS*, (Professor of Law and Associate Dean of Students)**, born Perry, Oklahoma, August 4, 1952; admitted to bar, 1984, Oklahoma. *Education:* University of Illinois (B.A., 1978; M.A., 1980); Northwestern University (J.D., 1984). ***COURSES: Employment Discrimination, Civil Procedure, Mediation. ***Email:*** vicki-limas@utulsa.edu

LESLIE MANSFIELD*, (Assistant Clinical Professor of Law and Director of the Legal Clinic)**, born Cordell, Oklahoma, May 14, 1962; admitted to bar, 1996, New Mexico. *Education:* University of New Mexico (B.A., 1998); University of New Mexico School of Law (J.D., 1996). ***COURSES: Clinical Law Program. ***Email:*** leslie-mansfield@utulsa.edu

MARLA E. MANSFIELD*, (Professor of Law, Professorial Fellow, National Energy-Environment Law and Policy Institute)**, born Connecticut, April 3, 1952; admitted to bar, 1978, Colorado. *Education:* Yale University (B.A., 1974); Bard College; University of Wyoming (J.D., 1978). ***COURSES: Public Lands, Natural Resources, Oil and Gas, Energy, Environmental, Property, Energy. ***Email:*** marla-mansfield@utulsa.edu

JOHNNY PARKER*, (Professor of Law)**, born Mississippi, January 20, 1961; admitted to bar, 1985, Mississippi. *Education:* University of Mississippi (B.A., 1982; J.D., 1984); Columbia University (LL.M., 1987). ***COURSES: Torts, Insurance Law, Agency/Partnership, Civil Rights. ***Email:*** johnny-parker@utulsa.edu

RICHARD A. PASCHAL*, (Assistant Professor of Legal Writing)**, born Paterson, New Jersey, May 9, 1950; admitted to bar, 1977, Oklahoma. *Education:* University of Oklahoma (B.A., 1972); University of Tulsa (J.D., 1976). ***COURSES: Legal Writing, Pretrial Practice, Mediation. ***Email:*** richard-paschal@utulsa.edu

MADELEINE MERCEDES PLASENCIA*, (Associate Professor of Law)**, born March 14, 1962; admitted to bar, 1989, Pennsylvania; 1992, New York and District of Columbia. *Education:* Cornell University (A.B., 1984); University of Pennsylvania (J.D., 1988). ***COURSES: Corporate Finance, Federal Securities, Regulations, Torts. ***Email:*** madeline-plasencia@utulsa.edu

G. WILLIAM RICE*, (Associate Professor of Law & Director of the LL.M. in American Indian & Indigenous Law)**, admitted to bar, 1979, Oklahoma. *Education:* Phillips University (B.A., 1973); University of Oklahoma College of Law (J.D., 1978). ***COURSES: Tribal Government Law, American Indian Law Seminar, Jurisprudence, Constitutional Law. ***Email:*** gwrice@utulsa.edu

JUDITH ROYSTER*, (Professor of Law)**, born Illinois; admitted to bar, 1986, Wisconsin. *Education:* University of Wisconsin (B.A., 1973; M.A., 1978; J.D., 1986). ***COURSES: Environmental Law, Native American Rights, Property, Native American Natural Resources. ***Email:*** judith-royster@utulsa.edu

LANCE STOCKWELL*, (Assistant Professor of Legal Writing)**, born New York, New York, February 21, 1942; admitted to bar, 1968, Oklahoma. *Education:* University of Oklahoma (B.B.A., 1965); University of Tulsa (J.D., 1968); Oklahoma State University (M.A., 1996). ***COURSES: Trial Practice, Oral Communication & Persuasion, Legal Reasoning, Authorities & Writing. ***Email:*** lance-stockwell@utulsa.edu

WINONA M. TANAKA*, (Associate Professor of Law)**, born Honolulu, Hawaii, October 25, 1945; admitted to bar, 1971, New York; 1985, Hawaii; 1993, Oklahoma. *Education:* Wellesley College (B.A., 1967); Columbia University (J.D., 1970). ***COURSES: Contracts, Pretrial Practice, As Director of Academic Support Program & the Legal Intern Program. ***Email:*** winona-tanaka@utulsa.edu

MELISSA TATUM*, (Associate Professor of Law)**, born Florida, July 7, 1968; admitted to bar, 1992, Michigan; U.S. District Court for the Eastern District of MI; U.S. Court of Appeals for 6th Circuit; Federal Bar Association. *Education:* Trinity University (B.A., 1989); University of Michigan (J.D., 1992). ***COURSES: Constitutional Litigation, Criminal Procedure, Indian Law, Juvenile Law. ***Email:*** melissa-tatum@utulsa.edu

JAMES C. THOMAS*, (Professor of Law)**, admitted to bar, 1957, Alabama, Oklahoma. *Education:* University of Alabama (J.D., 1957); New York University (LL.M., 1963). ***COURSES: Antitrust Law, Labor Law, Administrative Law, Legislation, Legal Rights of Children. ***Email:*** james-thomas@utulsa.edu

KATHLEEN WAITS*, (Associate Professor of Law)**, born Washington, D.C., November 4, 1950; admitted to bar, 1975, District of Columbia; 1978, Illinois; 1980, Florida; 1991, New York. *Education:* Cornell University (A.B., 1972); Harvard (J.D., 1975). ***COURSES: Contracts, Professional Responsibility, Civil Procedure, Women & The Law, Domestic Violence. ***Email:*** waitsk@utulsa.edu

RAY YASSER*, (Professor of Law)**, born New York, N.Y., January 16, 1950; admitted to bar, 1974, North Carolina; 1975, Oklahoma. *Education:* University of Delaware (B.A., 1971); Duke University (J.D., 1974). ***COURSES: Torts, Sports Law, Trial Practice. ***Email:*** raymond-yasser@utulsa.edu

REX J. ZEDALIS*, (Professor of Law)**, born Orlando, Florida, July 22, 1949; admitted to bar, 1976, California. *Education:* California State University (B.A., 1973); Pepperdine University School of Law (J.D., 1976); George Washington University National Law Center (LL.M., 1978); Columbia University (J.S.D., 1987). ***COURSES: International Energy and Natural Resources, International Business Transactions, Property, Administrative Law. ***Email:*** rex-zedalis@utulsa.edu

---

UNIVERSITY OF UTAH COLLEGE OF LAW

SALT LAKE CITY, UTAH 84112

UNIVERSITY OF VIRGINIA SCHOOL OF LAW

580 MASSIE ROAD
CHARLOTTESVILLE, VIRGINIA 22903
Telephone: (434) 924-7354
Fax: (434) 924-7536

ABA Approved Since 1923.

The University of Virginia School of Law, founded by Thomas Jefferson in 1826, is a world-renowned training ground for distinguished lawyers and public servants and an integral part of a great university. One of Jefferson's eight original faculties, the Law School advances Jefferson's belief that lawyers should be educated to promote the ideals of leadership, integrity, and community service in their practice.

The Law School is located in Charlottesville, Virginia, a picturesque and thriving metropolitan community located about two hours southwest of Washington, D.C. The Law School facilities recently underwent a transformative, $30 million construction and renovation project that nearly doubled the size of the complex. The Law School's 1,120 students gain an appreciation of the power of law to shape human behavior and to influence our political, social, and cultural experience. Virginia is widely recognized for the collegial environment it affords both students and faculty, and student satisfaction is consistently cited as among the highest in American law schools. Students subscribe to the University of Virginia's student-run honor system, in place for more than 155 years, which enables law students to enjoy the kind of personal freedom that is possible only in an environment where mutual respect and trust exist.

The Law School's faculty includes 64 full-time professors and more than 50 adjunct faculty members. A combination of seasoned experts and promising young teachers and scholars, faculty members have written dozens of casebooks and scholarly works now used in law schools across the country. Faculty members are committed to teaching, offering approximately 145 courses and 100 seminars each academic year. One of the newest curricular innovations is the Mary Morton Parsons Seminars in Ethical Values. Using readings from literature old and new, these seminars offer Virginia students an opportunity to enhance their understanding of ethical issues by bridging the gap between the rules of professional conduct enforced by the organized bar and the broader ethical and moral concerns that confront lawyers as citizens.

The Law School has one of the most successful career planning and placement programs in the country. Approximately 90 percent of the school's graduates generally accept employment offers before graduation. Members of the class of 2000 accepted 63 judicial clerkships; in virtually every year in recent history at least one member of the graduating class has secured a clerkship with a Justice of the Supreme Court of the United States.

The Law School's Mortimer M. Caplin Public Service Center offers career support to students seeking public interest jobs, coordinates student pro bono activities, and serves as an information hub for all Law School public service programs and activities. The center also administers the Law School's public service loan assistance program, which provides grants to graduates who choose to work in public interest law.

The Arthur J. Morris Library, the tenth largest law library in the country, owns more than 800,000 volumes as well as substantial collections of federal, state, and international documents, manuscripts, and archives.

The Law School has 45 student organizations, including eight student-edited scholarly journals, Moot Court, a weekly newspaper, various groups organized around major areas of law, service organizations, student government, and social fraternities.

The Law School is home to five internationally known special programs. The Graduate Program for Judges affords sitting judges the opportunity to take part in a three-summer course of study culminating in the LL.M. degree. The Institute of Law, Psychiatry, and Public Policy offers a multi-disciplinary training, educational, research, and service program in the areas of forensic psychiatry, forensic psychology, and mental health law. The John M. Olin Program in Law and Economics supports research and provides a forum for discussion and debate relating to the economic analysis of legal issues. The Center for Oceans Law and Policy seeks to promote rational choices for managing the future of the oceans, coastal, and polar areas through teaching, research, and the dissemination of information. The Center for National Security Law promotes advanced interdisciplinary research, non-partisan scholarship, and education about the legal aspects of national security issues.

Dean: John C. Jeffries, Jr. (434) 924-7343
Academic Associate Dean: Paul G. Mahoney (434) 924-3996
Associate Dean, Management and Finance: Elaine M. Hadden (434) 924-7343
Associate Dean for Admissions: Albert R. Turnbull (434) 924-4676
Senior Assistant Dean for Financial Aid: Jerome W.D. Stokes (434) 924-7805
Senior Assistant Dean for Career Services: William S. Hopson IV (434) 924-7349
Assistant Dean for Academic Services and Registrar: Cary Bennett (434) 924-4072
Assistant Dean for Student Affairs: Beverly P. Harmon (434) 924-3737
Assistant Dean for Public Service: Kimberly C. Emery (434) 924-1419
Law Librarian: Larry B. Wenger (434) 924-3384
Director of Alumni Affairs: Linda A. Skove (434) 924-3588

FULL TIME FACULTY

JOHN C. JEFFRIES, JR.*, (Dean, Emerson G. Spies Professor of Law and Arnold H. Leon Professor of Law)**, born Raleigh, North Carolina; admitted to bar, 1973, Virginia; 1974, District of Columbia. *Education:* Yale University (B.A., 1970); University of Virginia (J.D., 1973). ***COURSES: Criminal Law, Constitutional Law, Civil Rights, Civil Procedure & Litigation. ***Email:*** jcj3w@virginia.edu

---

KENNETH S. ABRAHAM*, (Class of 1962 Professor of Law)**, born Kearny, New Jersey; admitted to bar, 1977, Maryland; 1988, Virginia. *Education:* Indiana University (A.B., 1967); Yale Law School (J.D., 1971). ***COURSES: Insurance, Torts. ***Email:*** ksa@virginia.edu

***BARBARA ELLEN ARMACOST*, (Professor of Law)**, born Baltimore, Maryland; admitted to bar, 1989, Virginia. *Education:*

(This Listing Continued)

UNIVERSITY OF VIRGINIA SCHOOL OF LAW —Continued

University of Virginia (B.S., 1976; J.D., 1989). ***COURSES:*** Torts, Legislation, Civil Rights. ***Email:*** bea4k@virginia.edu

RICHARD BALNAVE*, (Professor, General Faculty)**, born New Jersey; admitted to bar, 1977, Ohio; 1978, Pennsylvania and U.S. District Court, District of Pennsylvania; 1986, Virginia; 1987, U.S. Military Court of Appeals. *Education:* William and Mary (B.A., 1971); State University of New York at Albany (M.A., 1973); Case Western Reserve University (J.D., 1977). ***COURSES: Child Advocacy Clinic, Professional Responsibility. ***Email:*** rdb@virginia.edu

LILLIAN RIEMER BEVIER*, (Henry L. and Grace Doherty Charitable Foundation Professor of Law)**, born Washington, D.C.; admitted to bar, 1966, California; 1979, Virginia. *Education:* Smith College (B.A., 1961); Stanford Law School (J.D., 1965). ***COURSES: Property, Torts, Constitutional Law, Intellectual Property, Trusts and Estates. ***Email:*** lrb5s@virginia.edu

VINCENT ANTHONY BLASI*, (D. Lurton Massee, Jr. Professor of Law)**, born Chicago, Illinois; admitted to bar, 1968, Texas. *Education:* Northwestern University (B.A., 1964); University of Chicago (J.D., 1967). ***COURSES: First Amendment, Torts. ***Email:*** vab7b@virginia.edu

RICHARD JEFFREY BONNIE*, (John S. Battle Professor of Law and Director, Institute of Law, Psychiatry and Public Policy)**, born Richmond, Virginia; admitted to bar, 1969, Virginia. *Education:* Johns Hopkins University (B.A., 1966); University of Virginia (LL.B., 1969). ***COURSES: Criminal Law, Health Law, Disability Law. ***Email:*** rjb6f@virginia.edu

CURTIS A. BRADLEY*, (Professor of Law)**, born San Francisco, California; admitted to bar, 1989, Colorado; 1992, District of Columbia. *Education:* University of Colorado (B.A., 1985); Harvard Law School (J.D., 1988). ***COURSES: Federal Courts, International Business Transactions, International Law, International Litigation, Trademark & Unfair Competition Law. ***Email:*** cab8u@virginia.edu

KATHRYN WEBB BRADLEY*, (Associate Professor, General Faculty and Co-Director of Legal Research and Writing Program)**, born Oklahoma City, Oklahoma; admitted to bar, 1988, Maryland; 1991, District of Columbia; 1995, Colorado; 2000, Virginia. *Education:* Wake Forest (B.S., 1979); University of Maryland (J.D., 1988). ***COURSES: Legal Research and Writing. ***Email:*** kwb3z@virginia.edu

ROSA EHRENREICH BROOKS*, (Associate Professor of Law)**, *Education:* Harvard University (A.B., 1991); Oxford University (M.ST., 1993); Yale Law School (J.D., 1996). ***COURSES: Human Rights, International Law, Law and Social Science. ***Email:*** reb2d@virginia.edu

D. RUTH BUCK*, (Professor, Gen. Faculty; Co-Director, Legal Research & Writing)**, born Gadsden, Alabama; admitted to bar, 1986, Georgia and Virginia. *Education:* University of Virginia (B.A., 1974; M.Ed., 1976; J.D., 1985). ***COURSES: Legal Research and Writing, Pretrial Litigation. ***Email:*** drb7c@virginia.edu

JONATHAN CANNON*, (Professor, General Faculty & Director, Environmental Law Center)**, born Chestertown, Maryland; admitted to bar, 1975, District of Columbia. *Education:* Williams College (B.A., 1967); University of Pennsylvania Law School (J.D., 1974). ***COURSES: Environmental. ***Email:*** jzc8j@virginia.edu

GEORGE MEREDITH COHEN*, (Professor of Law)**, born Brooklyn, New York. *Education:* Yale University (B.A., 1982); University of Pennsylvania (J.D., 1986; Ph.D., 1992). ***COURSES: Contracts, Antitrust, Professional Responsibility, Agency & Partnership. ***Email:*** gmc3y@virginia.edu

ANNE M. COUGHLIN*, (Professor of Law)**, born New Jersey; admitted to bar, 1987, New York. *Education:* Tufts (B.A., 1978); Columbia University (M.A., 1979); New York University (J.D., 1984). ***COURSES: Criminal Law, Criminal Procedure, Feminist Jurisprudence. ***Email:*** amc6z@virginia.edu

BARRY CUSHMAN*, (Professor of Law)**, born Columbus, Ohio; admitted to bar, 1986, West Virginia; 1987, California. *Education:* Amherst College (B.A., 1982); University of Virginia (M.A., 1986; Ph.D., 1995; J.D., 1996). ***COURSES: American Legal History; Trusts and Estates, Constitutional Law. ***Email:*** bjc2r@virginia.edu

MICHAEL P. DOOLEY*, (William S. Potter Professor of Law & Director of Graduate Studies)**, born Iowa City, Iowa; admitted to bar, 1963, Iowa; 1964, New York; 1971, Illinois; 1979, Virginia. *Education:* University of Iowa (B.A., 1960; J.D., 1963). ***COURSES: Corporate Governance, Mergers and Acquisitions, Securities Regulations. ***Email:*** mpd@virginia.edu

EARL C. DUDLEY*, (Professor, General Faculty)**, born Manila, PI; admitted to bar, 1967, Virginia; 1969, District of Columbia. *Education:* Amherst College (B.A., 1961); University of Virginia (LL.B., 1967). ***COURSES: Civil Procedure, Evidence, Criminal Procedure, Constitutional Law. ***Email:*** ecd3u@virginia.edu

KIM FORDE-MAZRUI*, (Professor of Law)**, born Kampala, Uganda; admitted to bar, 1993, Michigan; 1996, District of Columbia. *Education:* University of Michigan (A.B., 1990; J.D., 1993). ***COURSES: Affirmative Action, Constitutional Law, Criminal Law. ***Email:*** kf9j@virginia.edu

CHARLES J. GOETZ*, (Joseph M. Hartfield Professor of Law)**, born New York, New York. *Education:* Providence College (A.B., 1961); University of Virginia (Ph.D., 1965). ***COURSES: Antitrust Law, Applications of Computers to the Law, Contracts, Law & Economics. ***Email:*** cjg4t@virginia.edu

JOHN C. HARRISON*, (Professor of Law)**, born Columbus, Ohio; admitted to bar, 1980, District of Columbia. *Education:* University of Virginia (B.A., 1977); Yale University (J.D., 1980). ***COURSES: Administrative Law, Federal Jurisdiction, Constitutional Law. ***Email:*** jh8m@virginia.edu

STANLEY D. HENDERSON*, (F.D.G. Ribble Professor of Law)**, born Monona, Iowa; admitted to bar, 1961, Colorado; 1973, Virginia. *Education:* Coe College (A.B., 1957); University of Colorado (J.D., 1961). ***COURSES: Contracts, Labor Law, Labor Arbitration. ***Email:*** sdh6k@virginia.edu

A.E. DICK HOWARD*, (White Burkett Miller Professor of Law and Public Policy)**, born Richmond, Virginia; admitted to bar, 1961, Virginia and District of Columbia. *Education:* University of Richmond (B.A., 1954); University of Virginia (LL.B., 1961); Oxford University (M.A., 1965). ***COURSES: Constitutional Law. ***Email:*** adh3m@virginia.edu

ALEX M. JOHNSON, JR.*, (Vice Provost for Faculty Recruitment and Retention, Mary & Daniel Loughran Professor of Law)**, born Portland, Oregon; admitted to bar, 1978, California. *Education:* Princeton University; Claremont Men's College (B.A., 1975); University of California at Los Angeles School of Law (J.D., 1978). ***COURSES: Property, Trusts & Estates, Modern Real Estate, Critical Race Theory. ***Email:*** amj9y@virginia.edu

EDMUND W. KITCH*, (Joseph M. Hartfield Professor of Law)**, born Wichita, Kansas; admitted to bar, 1964, Kansas; 1965, Illinois; 1984, Virginia. *Education:* Yale College (B.A., 1961); University of Chicago (J.D., 1964). ***COURSES: Agency, Corporations, Intellectual Property, Securities Regulation. ***Email:*** ewk@virginia.edu

(This Listing Continued)

UNIVERSITY OF VIRGINIA SCHOOL OF LAW —Continued

MICHAEL JOSEPH KLARMAN*, (James Monroe Professor of Law)**, born New York, New York. *Education:* University of Pennsylvania (B.A./M.A., 1980); Stanford Law School (J.D., 1983); Oxford University (D.Phil., 1988). ***COURSES: Constitutional Law, Constitutional History, Constitutional Theory. ***Email:*** mjk6s@virginia.edu

KEVIN A. KORDANA*, (Professor of Law)**, *Education:* Yale College (B.A., 1991; J.D., 1995). ***COURSES: Contracts, Corporations, Non-Profits. ***Email:*** kk3t@virginia.edu

JODY S. KRAUS*, (Professor of Law)**, born Indianapolis, Indiana; admitted to bar, 1990, Virginia; 1992, District of Columbia. *Education:* Ohio State University (B.A., 1982); University of Arizona (M.A., 1984; Ph.D., 1987); Yale University (J.D., 1990). ***COURSES: Commercial Law, Contracts, Jurisprudence/Philosophy of Law, Political Theory. ***Email:*** jsk5g@virginia.edu

DOUGLAS L. LESLIE*, (Charles O. Gregory Professor of Law)**, born Des Moines, Iowa; admitted to bar, 1968, Ohio, Maryland and District of Columbia. *Education:* University of Iowa (B.A., 1964); University of Michigan (J.D., 1968). ***COURSES: Contracts, Health Law, Labor Law, Sales, Sports Law. ***Email:*** dll2k@virginia.edu

DARYL J. LEVINSON*, (Professor of Law)**, born Madison, Wisconsin. *Education:* Harvard (A.B., 1990); University of Virginia (M.A., 1995; J.D., 1995). ***COURSES: Constitutional Law, Criminal Law, Remedies, Jurisprudence/Legal Theory. ***Email:*** djl2n@virginia.edu

GRAHAM LILLY*, (Armistead M. Dobie Professor of Law)**, born Welch, West Virginia; admitted to bar, 1963, District of Columbia. *Education:* Virginia Polytechnic Institute (B.S., 1960); University of Virginia (LL.B., 1963). ***COURSES: Evidence, Civil Procedure, Federal Courts, Constitutional Law, Conflict of Laws. ***Email:*** gl@virginia.edu

CLARISA LONG*, (Associate Professor of Law)**, admitted to bar, 1995, Maryland. *Education:* University of Illinois (B.S. and B.A., 1989; Stanford Law School (J.D., 1994). ***COURSES: Intellectual Property, Property. ***Email:*** cl2s@virginia.edu

PETER W. LOW*, (Hardy Cross Dillard Professor of Law)**, born Springfield, Massachusetts; admitted to bar, 1963, Virginia. *Education:* Princeton University (A.B., 1959); University of Virginia (LL.B., 1963). ***COURSES: Criminal Law, Federal Courts, Civil Rights. ***Email:*** pwl@virginia.edu

M. ELIZABETH MAGILL*, (Associate Professor of Law)**, born Fargo, North Dakota. *Education:* Yale (B.A., 1988); University of Virginia (J.D., 1995). ***COURSES: Administrative Law, Criminal Law, Employment Discrimination. ***Email:*** mem2a@virginia.edu

JULIA DELONG MAHONEY*, (Associate Professor of Law)**, born Boston, Massachusetts; admitted to bar, 1988, New York. *Education:* Barnard College (B.A., 1984); Yale Law School (J.D., 1987). ***COURSES: Corporations, Property, Feminist Jurisprudence. ***Email:*** jdm8t@virginia.edu

PAUL G. MAHONEY*, (Brokaw Professor of Corporate Law and Academic Associate Dean)**, born St. Louis, Missouri; admitted to bar, 1987, New York. *Education:* Massachusetts Institute of Technology (B.S., 1981); Yale University (J.D., 1984). ***COURSES: Commercial Law, Contracts, Corporate Finance, Corporations, Law & Economic Developments. ***Email:*** pgm9h@virginia.edu

DAVID A. MARTIN*, (Henry L. and Grace Doherty Charitable Foundation Professor of Law)**, born Indianapolis, Indiana; admitted to bar, 1977, District of Columbia. *Education:* DePauw University (B.A., 1970); Yale Law School (J.D., 1975). ***COURSES: Immigration & Refugee Law, International Law, Constitutional Law. ***Email:*** dam3r@virginia.edu

RICHARD AUSTIN MERRILL*, (Daniel Caplin Professor of Law)**, born Logan, Utah; admitted to bar, 1964, New York; 1966, District of Columbia; 1980, Virginia. *Education:* Columbia College (A.B., 1959); Columbia Law School (LL.B., 1964). ***COURSES: Administrative Law, Food and Drug Law, Environmental Law. ***Email:*** ram@virginia.edu

JENNIFER MNOOKIN*, (Associate Professor of Law)**, born Cambridge, Massachusetts; admitted to bar, 1998, New York. *Education:* Harvard University (A.B., 1988); Yale University (J.D., 1995); Massachusetts Institute of Technology (Ph.D., 1999). ***COURSES: Evidence, Scientific Evidence. ***Email:*** jlm2bc@virginia.edu

JOHN MONAHAN*, (Henry L. & Grace Doherty Charitable Foundation Professor of Law; Professor of Psychology and Legal Medicine)**, born New York, New York. *Education:* SUNY (Stony Brook) (B.A., 1968); Indiana University (Ph.D., 1972). ***COURSES: Social Science in Law. ***Email:*** jtm9p@virginia.edu

JOHN NORTON MOORE*, (Walter L. Brown Professor of Law; Dir., Center for Oceans Law and Dir., Center for National Security Law)**, born New York, New York; admitted to bar, 1962, Florida. *Education:* Drew University (B.A., 1959); Duke Law School (LL.B., 1962); University of Illinois (LL.M., 1965). ***COURSES: International Law, National Security Law, Oceans Law, Rule of Law. ***Email:*** jnm9s@virginia.edu

THOMAS NACHBAR*, (Associate Professor of Law)**, admitted to bar, 1997, Illinois. *Education:* University of Illinois, Urbana-Champaign (A.B., 1989); University of Chicago (J.D., 1997). ***COURSES: Intellectual Property, Constitutional Law, Communications Law. ***Email:*** tbn4n@virginia.edu

CALEB EDWARD NELSON*, (Associate Professor of Law)**, born Cleveland, Ohio; admitted to bar, 1993, Ohio. *Education:* Harvard University (A.B., 1988); Yale Law School (J.D., 1993). ***COURSES: Constitutional Law, Civil Procedure, Legislation. ***Email:*** cen2d@virginia.edu

JEFFREY O'CONNELL*, (Samuel H. McCoy II Professor of Law)**, born Worcester, Massachusetts; admitted to bar, 1954, Massachusetts and Connecticut; 1982, Virginia. *Education:* Dartmouth (A.B., 1951); Harvard (J.D., 1954). ***COURSES: Torts, Insurance. ***Email:*** jo@virginia.edu

ROBERT M. O'NEIL*, (University Professor; Prof. of Law; Director, Thomas Jefferson Center for the Protection of Free Expression)**, born Boston, Massachusetts; admitted to bar, 1962, Massachusetts; 1971, U.S. Court of Appeals, 9th Circuit; 1996, U.S. Court of Appeals, 4th Circuit. *Education:* Harvard University (A.B., 1956; A.M., 1957; LL.M., 1961). ***COURSES: Church & State/Religious Freedom, Copyright, Freedom of Speech & Press, Intellectual Property. ***Email:*** rmo@virginia.edu

DANIEL R. ORTIZ*, (John Allan Love Professor of Law)**, born Pittsburgh, Pennsylvania; admitted to bar, 1988, Virginia. *Education:* Yale University (B.A., 1978; J.D., 1983); Oxford University (M.Phil., 1980). ***COURSES: Constitutional Law, Administrative Law, Civil Procedure, Jurisprudence, ERISA, Electoral Law. ***Email:*** dro@virginia.edu

MARGARET V.W. FOSTER RILEY*, (Associate Professor, General Faculty; Co-Director, Legal Research & Writing)**, born New York, New York; admitted to bar, 1986, New York; 1988, Pennsylvania. *Education:* Duke University (A.B., 1981); Columbia University (J.D., 1985). ***COURSES: Legal Writing, Litigation. ***Email:*** mf9c@virginia.edu

(This Listing Continued)

UNIVERSITY OF VIRGINIA SCHOOL OF LAW
—Continued

GLEN O. ROBINSON*, (David A. Harrison Professor of Law and Associate Dean for Research and Information Services)**, born Salt Lake City, Utah; admitted to bar, 1961, District of Columbia. *Education:* Harvard (A.B., 1958); Stanford (J.D., 1961). ***COURSES: Communications, Property, Administrative Law. ***Email:*** gor@virginia.edu

MILDRED WIGFALL ROBINSON*, (Professor of Law)**, born Charleston, South Carolina; admitted to bar, 1971, Massachusetts. *Education:* Fisk University (B.A., 1965); Howard University School of Law (J.D., 1968); Harvard University School of Law (LL.M., 1971). ***COURSES: Federal Income Tax, State and Local Taxes and Finance, Trusts and Estates. ***Email:*** mwr@virginia.edu

GEORGE RUTHERGLEN*, (O.M. Vicars Professor of Law)**, born Portland, Oregon; admitted to bar, 1979, Virginia. *Education:* University of California at Berkeley (A.B., 1971; J.D., 1974). ***COURSES: Civil Rights, Civil Procedure, Federal Courts, Admiralty, Professional Responsibility. ***Email:*** gar3h@virginia.edu

EDWARD JAMES RYAN*, (Associate Professor of Law)**, born Elizabeth, New Jersey; admitted to bar, 1995, New Jersey. *Education:* Yale (A.B., 1988); University of Virginia (J.D., 1992). ***COURSES: Law & Education, Constitutional Law. ***Email:*** jer6p@virginia.edu

CHRIS SANCHIRICO*, (Associate Professor of Law)**, born Bronx, New York. *Education:* Princeton (A.B., 1984); Yale Law School (J.D., 1990); Yale University (Ph.D., 1994). ***COURSES: Evidence, Income Tax, Civil Procedure, Law & Economics. ***Email:*** cs2aw@virginia.edu

ELIZABETH S. SCOTT*, (University Professor, Class of 1962 Professor of Law)**, born Washington, D.C.; admitted to bar, 1977, Virginia. *Education:* College of William & Mary (B.A., 1967); University of Virginia (J.D., 1977). ***COURSES: Family Law, Property, Criminal Law. ***Email:*** es@virginia.edu

ROBERT EDWIN SCOTT*, (Lewis F. Powell, Jr. Professor of Law)**, born Nagpur, India; admitted to bar, 1968, Virginia. *Education:* Oberlin College (B.A., 1965); William and Mary School of Law (J.D., 1968); University of Michigan School of Law (S.J.D., 1973). ***COURSES: Contracts, Commercial Law, Bankruptcy. ***Email:*** res8f@virginia.edu

JOHN KENNEDY SETEAR*, (Professor of Law)**, born Evanston, Illinois. *Education:* Williams College (B.A., 1981); Yale University (J.D., 1984). ***COURSES: International Law, Contracts. ***Email:*** jks9d@virginia.edu

KENT SINCLAIR*, (Professor of Law and Director of Advocacy and Lawyer Training)**, born San Diego, California; admitted to bar, 1971, California; 1985, Virginia; 1993, New York. *Education:* University of California at Santa Barbara (B.A., 1968); University of California at Berkeley (J.D., 1971). ***COURSES: Civil Procedure, Evidence, Motions Practice, Virginia Procedure. ***Email:*** ks3r@virginia.edu

STEPHEN F. SMITH*, (Associate Professor of Law)**, admitted to bar, 1995, Virginia. *Education:* Dartmouth College (B.A., 1988); University of Virginia (J.D., 1992). ***COURSES: Criminal Law, Criminal Adjudication. ***Email:*** sfs3h@virginia.edu

PAUL BROOKE STEPHAN III*, (Percy Brown, Jr. Professor of Law)**, born Somerville, New Jersey; admitted to bar, 1979, District of Columbia; 1982, Virginia. *Education:* Yale (B.A., 1973; M.A., 1974); University of Virginia (J.D., 1977). ***COURSES: International Business, Taxation, Comparative Law. ***Email:*** pbs@virginia.edu

APRIL W. TRIANTIS*, (Associate Professor, General Faculty; Director, Business Law Program)**, admitted to bar, 1997, California; 1999, New York; 2000, Illinois. *Education:* Eckerd College (B.A., 1991); Pepperdine University (J.D., 1996); New York University (LL.M., 1997). ***COURSES: Public Securities Offerings, Venture Capital, Business Law. ***Email:*** awt2c@virginia.edu

GEORGE G. TRIANTIS*, (Perre Bowen Professor of Law)**, born Toronto, Ontario, Canada. *Education:* University of Toronto (B.A., 1980; LL.B., 1983); University of Virginia (LL.M., 1986); Stanford University (J.S.D., 1989). ***COURSES: Commercial Law, Bankruptcy. ***Email:*** ggt2y@virginia.edu

ALBERT ROBERT TURNBULL*, (Associate Dean for Admissions and Career Services and Professor of Law)**, born Norfolk, Virginia; admitted to bar, 1963, Virginia. *Education:* Princeton (B.A., 1959); University of Virginia (LL.B., 1962). ***COURSES: Professional Responsibility. ***Email:*** art@virginia.edu

J. HOULT VERKERKE*, (Professor of Law and Director, Program for Employment and Labor Law Studies)**, born Charlottesville, Virginia. *Education:* Loyola College (B.A., 1983); Yale University (M.Phil., 1988; J.D., 1990). ***COURSES: Employment Law, Employment Discrimination, Contracts. ***Email:*** ripv@virginia.edu

WALTER J. WADLINGTON*, (James Madison Professor of Law and Professor of Legal Medicine)**, born Biloxi, Mississippi; admitted to bar, 1954, Louisiana; 1965, Virginia. *Education:* Duke (A.B., 1951); Tulane (LL.B., 1954). ***COURSES: Family Law, Law and Medicine, Historic Preservation, Children in the Legal System. ***Email:*** wjw@virginia.edu

W. LAURENS WALKER*, (T. Munford Boyd Professor of Law)**, born Spartanburg, South Carolina; admitted to bar, 1964, Georgia. *Education:* Davidson College (A.B., 1959); Duke Law School (J.D., 1963); Harvard Law School (S.J.D., 1970). ***COURSES: Civil Procedure, Federal Courts, Complex Litigation. ***Email:*** wlw4q@virginia.edu

STEVEN DAVID WALT*, (Professor of Law)**, born Rochester, Minnesota; admitted to bar, 1988, New York. *Education:* Kalamazoo College (B.A., 1976); University of Chicago (M.A. and Ph.D., 1984); Yale Law School (J.D., 1988). ***COURSES: Commercial Law, Contracts. ***Email:*** sdw6a@virginia.edu

LARRY B. WENGER*, (Law Librarian and Professor of Law)**, born Everett, Washington; admitted to bar, 1967, Washington. *Education:* University of Washington (B.A., 1964); Simmons College (M.L.S., 1969); University of Washington (J.D., 1967). ***COURSES: Historic Preservation Law. ***Email:*** lbw@virginia.edu

G. EDWARD WHITE*, (University Professor and John B. Minor Professor of Law and History)**, born Northampton, Massachusetts; admitted to bar, 1970, District of Columbia; 1975, Virginia. *Education:* Amherst College (B.A., 1963); Yale University (M.A., 1964 and Ph.D., 1967); Harvard (J.D., 1970). ***COURSES: Torts, Constitutional Law, Legal History, Mass Media Law. ***Email:*** gew@virginia.edu

THOMAS RAEBURN WHITE III*, (John C. Stennis Professor of Law)**, born Philadelphia, Pennsylvania; admitted to bar, 1964, Pennsylvania; 1971, Virginia. *Education:* Williams College (B.A., 1960); University of Pennsylvania (J.D., 1963). ***COURSES: Employee Benefits, Taxation, Real Estate Finance, Elder Law. ***Email:*** trw@virginia.edu

GEORGE K. YIN*, (Howard W. Smith Professor of Law)**, born New York, New York; admitted to bar, 1977, Virginia; 1978, District of Columbia. *Education:* University of Michigan (B.A., 1970); University of Florida (M.Ed., 1972); George Washington University (J.D., 1977). ***COURSES: Federal Income Tax. ***Email:*** gy8a@virginia.edu

UNIVERSITY OF WASHINGTON SCHOOL OF LAW

CONDON HALL, 1100 N. E. CAMPUS PARKWAY
SEATTLE, WASHINGTON 98105
Telephone: (206) 543-4551
Fax: (206) 543-5671

ABA Approved Since 1924

The University of Washington School of Law offers programs of study leading to the Juris Doctor (J.D.), Master of Law (LL.M.) in Asian and Comparative Law, Law of Sustainable International Development, Taxation, and the Doctor of Philosophy (Ph.D.) in Asian and Comparative Law.

Seattle, home of the University of Washington, is the gateway to the Pacific Rim. Its economic strength, rich cultural resources, physical beauty and moderate climate attract visitors and commerce from around the world. The city of Seattle is located on the eastern shore of Puget Sound, an inland body of water connected to the Pacific Ocean, and is bordered by the Olympic and Cascade mountain ranges.

The active international community in Seattle includes high technology firms, international banks and major corporations such as Boeing and Microsoft. The Port of Seattle is one of the largest container ports in the United States and is the top port for container exports to Asia. In addition to city, state and federal institutions dealing with international commerce and trade, international organizations located in Seattle include the Japan-American Society, the Washington State China Relations Council, the World Affairs Council and the Washington Council on International Trade.

The University of Washington is widely considered one of the leading research universities in the United States. The University is located in a residential area about four miles from the center of Seattle and is bordered by Lake Washington and Portage Bay. Enrollment at the University is approximately 34,000 students with a full-time teaching faculty of 2,800. The University is well known for its strength in areas such as international studies, marine affairs, environmental studies and medicine.

The School of Law was first organized in 1899 and is fully accredited. Condon Hall, three blocks west of the main University campus, houses most of the Law School and the Marian Gould Gallagher Law Library. The University of Washington Law School is recognized as one of the leading law schools in the United States.

The School of Law offers a diverse curriculum. J.D. law students number about 500 and graduate students number about 150. there is an excellent ratio of students to faculty (approximately 13:1) with many small classes and the opportunity for close student-faculty contact. Faculty members generally have an open-door policy to encourage contact and informal discussions with students.

The Marian Gould Gallagher Law Library is one of the finest law libraries in the country. Its collection is among the largest university law collections on the West Coast and currently numbers more than 450,000 volumes. Access to legal and non-legal online databases, CD-Rom products and electronic information is enhanced through use of WESTLAW, LEXIS, DIALOG, NEXIS and other online databases, CD-Rom products and electronic information sources. A superb staff of librarians, technicians and students support the research, writing and curricular needs of law students and faculty.

Dean: W.H. (Joe) Knight, Jr. (206) 685-3846
Admissions: Kathy Swinehart (206) 685-3181
Library: Penny Hazelton (206) 543-4089
Placement: Millicent Newhouse (206) 543-9097
Development and Community Relations: Dexter Bailey (206) 616-5356
Public Relations: Paula Littlewood (206) 685-1998
Student Affairs: Sandra Madrid (206) 543-0199
Academic Affairs: Richard Kummert (206) 543-4937
Financial Aid: To be determined (206) 543-4552

FULL TIME FACULTY

W.H. (JOE) KNIGHT, JR.*, (Dean and Professor)**, born Beckley, West Virginia; admitted to bar, 1980, New York. *Education:* University of North Carolina (B.A., 1976); Columbia University (J.D., 1979). ***COURSES: Banking, Commercial Law, Contracts. ***Email:*** whknight@u.washington.edu

CRAIG H. ALLEN*, (Professor)**, *Education:* Portland State University (B.S., 1979); University of Washington (J.D., 1989). ***COURSES: Torts, Admiralty, Marine Law. ***Email:*** challen@u.washington.edu

WILLIAM R. ANDERSEN*, (Professor)**, born September 29, 1932; admitted to bar, 1961, Colorado. *Education:* University of Denver (B.S., 1954; LL.B., 1956); Yale University (LL.M., 1958). ***COURSES: Antitrust, Administrative Law, Constitutional Law, Legislation. ***Email:*** ander@u.washington.edu

HELEN A. ANDERSON*, (Senior Lecturer)**, born Washington, D.C., January 20, 1958; admitted to bar, 1985, Washington. *Education:* Carleton College (B.A., 1980); University of Washington (J.D., 1984). ***COURSES: Legal Research Writing. ***Email:*** hander@u.washington.edu

ROBERT ANDERSON*, (Assistant Professor)**, born June 21, 1957; admitted to bar, 1983, Minnesota; 1984, Colorado; 1985, Alaska; 1996, District of Columbia; 2000, Washington. *Education:* Bemidji State University (B.A., 1980); University of Minnesota (J.D., 1983). ***COURSES: Indian Law. ***Email:*** boba@u.washington.edu

THOMAS R. ANDREWS*, (Professor)**, born Portland, Oregon, July 11, 1947; admitted to bar, 1980, District of Columbia; 1986, Washington. *Education:* University of Pittsburgh (B.A., 1969); Northwestern University (M.A., 1976); University of Pennsylvania (J.D., 1979). ***COURSES: Professional Responsibility, Torts, Estates and Trusts, Community Property. ***Email:*** tra@u.washington.edu

ROBERT H. ARONSON*, (Professor)**, born Philadelphia, Pennsylvania, 1947; admitted to bar, 1973, California. *Education:* University of Virginia (B.A., 1969); University of Pennsylvania (J.D., 1973). ***COURSES: Evidence, Professional Responsibility Law and Literature. ***Email:*** raron@u.washington.edu

(This Listing Continued)

UNIVERSITY OF WASHINGTON SCHOOL OF LAW —Continued

MELISSA M. BERRY, **(Lecturer)**, admitted to bar, 1993, Illinois; 1997, Washington. *Education:* Tulane University (B.A., 1990); Northwestern University of Law (J.D., 1993). ***COURSES:*** Basic Legal Skills. ***Email:*** mmberry@u.washington.edu

DANIEL M. BODANSKY, **(Professor)**, born Seattle, Washington, July 7, 1956; admitted to bar, 1986, Pennsylvania. *Education:* Harvard University (A.B., 1979); Cambridge University (M.Phil., 1981); Yale University (J.D., 1984). ***COURSES:*** International Environmental Law. ***Email:*** bodansky@u.washington.edu

KAREN BOXX, **(Assistant Professor)**, born Lafayette, LA., February 27, 1954; admitted to bar, 1983, Washington. *Education:* University of New Mexico (B.A., 1976); University of Washington (J.D., 1983). ***COURSES:*** Estate Planning, Trusts, Probate, Family Business Planning, Community Property. ***Email:*** kboxx@u.washington.edu

STEVE P. CALANDRILLO, **(Assistant Professor)**, admitted to bar, 1998, Washington. *Education:* University of California Berkley (B.A., 1994); Harvard Law School (J.D., 1998). ***COURSES:*** Contracts, Secured Transactions. ***Email:*** stevecal@u.washington.edu

DONALD C. CLARKE, **(Professor)**, born Toronto, Ontario, Canada, August 10, 1956; admitted to bar, 1988, New York. *Education:* Princeton University (A.B., 1977); London School of Oriental Studies (M.Sc., 1983); Harvard University (J.D., 1987). ***COURSES:*** Comparative Law - China, Property, International Law, International Transactions. ***Email:*** dclarke@u.washington.edu

SAM A. DONALDSON, **(Assistant Professor)**, admitted to bar, 1994, Arizona. *Education:* Oregon State, (B.A., 1990); University of Arizona College of Law (J.D., 1993); University of Florida College of Law (1994). ***COURSES:*** Tax-Basic, CNS Corporations, State & Gift. ***Email:*** sdonalds@u.washington.edu

G. MEADE EMORY, **(Professor)**, born Seattle, Washington, 1931; admitted to bar, 1958, District of Columbia; 1959, Washington. *Education:* George Washington University (B.A., 1954; J.D., 1958); Boston University (LL.M., 1963). ***COURSES:*** Taxation. ***Email:*** memory@u.washington.edu

JOAN M. FITZPATRICK, **(Professor)**, born El Paso, Texas, September 14, 1950; admitted to bar, 1975, Massachusetts. *Education:* Rice University (B.A., 1972); Harvard University (J.D., 1975); Oxford University (Dipl., 1980). ***COURSES:*** Constitutional Law, Federal Jurisdiction, Immigration Law, International Law. ***Email:*** fitzp@u.washington.edu

JULIA ANN GOLD, **(Senior Lecturer)**, *Education:* University of North Carolina (B.A., 1971); University of South Carolina (J.D., 1983). ***COURSES:*** Mediation, Street Law. ***Email:*** julgold@u.washington.edu

JAMES H. HARDISTY, **(Professor)**, born Minneapolis, Minnesota, February 23, 1941; admitted to bar, 1966, Ohio. *Education:* Harvard University (A.B., 1963; LL.B., 1966). ***COURSES:*** Criminal Justice, Criminal Procedure, Family Law. ***Email:*** hardisty@u.washington.edu

PENELOPE A. HAZELTON, **(Professor and Law Librarian)**, born Yakima, Washington, 1947; admitted to bar, 1975, Washington. *Education:* Linfield College (B.A., 1969); Lewis and Clark College (J.D., 1975); University of Washington (M.L.L., 1976). ***COURSES:*** Legal Research. ***Email:*** pennyh@u.washington.edu

GREGORY ALAN HICKS, **(Professor)**, born Austin, Texas, September 11, 1950; admitted to bar, 1979, Washington. *Education:* Yale University (B.A., 1972); University of Texas (J.D., 1978). ***COURSES:*** Public Land Law, Securities Regulation. ***Email:*** gahicks@u.washington.edu

ROLAND L. HJORTH, **(Professor)**, born Wisner, Nebraska, December 9, 1935; admitted to bar, 1961, New York; 1971, Washington. *Education:* University of Nebraska (A.B., 1957); New York University (LL.B., 1961). ***COURSES:*** Taxation. ***Email:*** hjorth@u.washington.edu

MARY A. HOTCHKISS, **(Senior Lecturer)**, admitted to bar, 1983, Maryland. *Education:* Duke University (B.A., 1975); Catholic University of Maryland (M.S.L.S., 1978); George Washington University (J.D., 1983; L.L.M., 1985). ***COURSES:*** Federal Tax Research, International Legal Research. ***Email:*** hotchma@u.washington.edu

LINDA S. HUME, **(Professor)**, born Philadelphia, Pennsylvania, November 2, 1942; admitted to bar, 1971, California; 1981, Washington. *Education:* California State University (B.A., 1967); University of California (J.D., 1970). ***COURSES:*** Commercial Law, International Contracts, Legal Research and Writing. ***Email:*** humels@u.washington.edu

STEWART M. JAY, **(Professor)**, born Havre, Montana, June 27, 1950; admitted to bar, 1976, District of Columbia. *Education:* Georgetown University (A.B., 1973); Harvard University (J.D., 1976). ***COURSES:*** Constitutional Law, Jurisprudence, Legal History. ***Email:*** smj@u.washington.edu

JOHN M. JUNKER, **(Professor)**, born Vancouver, Washington, 1934; admitted to bar, 1964, California. *Education:* Washington State University (B.A., 1959); University of Chicago (J.D., 1962). ***COURSES:*** Criminal Law, Criminal Procedure, Evidence. ***Email:*** junkerjm@u.washington.edu

ALAN KIRTLEY, **(Associate Professor)**, born 1946; admitted to bar, 1972, Michigan; 1980, Washington. *Education:* Indiana University (B.A., 1969; J.D., 1972). ***COURSES:*** Clinical Legal Education, Alternative Dispute Resolution. ***Email:*** kirtley@u.washington.edu

RICHARD O. KUMMERT, **(Associate Dean and Professor)**, born Chicago, Illinois, November 23, 1932; admitted to bar, 1962, California. *Education:* Illinois Institute of Technology (B.S., 1953); Northwestern University (M.B.A., 1955); Stanford University (LL.B., 1961). ***COURSES:*** Business Planning, Corporations, Federal Taxation. ***Email:*** kummert@u.washington.edu

PATRICIA C. KUSZLER, **(Professor)**, born 1952; admitted to bar, 1991, Connecticut; 1993, District of Columbia. *Education:* Mills College (B.A., 1974); Mayo Medical School (M.D., 1978); Yale University (J.D., 1991). ***COURSES:*** Health Care Law, Law and Biotechnology, Law and Medicine, Torts, Medical Malpractice. ***Email:*** kuszler@u.washington.edu

DEBORAH MARANVILLE, **(Associate Professor)**, born 1949; admitted to bar, 1975, Washington. *Education:* Stanford University (B.A., 1972); Harvard University (J.D., 1975). ***COURSES:*** Clinical Legal Education, Women and The Law. ***Email:*** maran@u.washington.edu

ANNA C. MASTROIANNI, **(Assistant Professor)**, born New Haven, Connecticut; admitted to bar, 1987, Pennsylvania; 1988 District of Columbia. *Education:* University of Pennsylvania (B.A./B.S., 1982; J.D., 1986); University of Washington (MPH, 1997). ***COURSES:*** Health Law, Bioethics, Public Health. ***Email:*** amastroi@u.washington.edu

KATHLEEN M. MCGINNIS, **(Senior Lecturer)**, admitted to bar, 1984, Washington. *Education:* Whitworth College (B.A., 1979); University of California/Berkeley (J.D., 1984). ***COURSES:*** Basic Legal Skills. ***Email:*** mcginnis@u.washington.edu

JACQUELINE MCMURTRIE, **(Senior Lecturer)**, born 1956;

(This Listing Continued)

UNIVERSITY OF WASHINGTON SCHOOL OF LAW —Continued

admitted to bar, 1983, Washington. *Education:* University of Michigan (B.S., 1978; J.D., 1983). ***COURSES:*** Criminal Law, Immigration Law. ***Email:*** jackiem@u.washington.edu

PETER NICOLAS, **(Assistant Professor)**, born 1970; admitted to bar, 2000, New York. *Education:* University of Michigan (B.A., 1991); University of Michigan School of Public Policy (M.P.P., 1992); Harvard Law School (J.D., 1999). ***COURSES:*** International Civil Litigation, Evidence, Federal Courts. ***Email:*** pnicolas@u.washington.edu

KATHLEEN O'NEILL, **(Associate Professor)**, born 1953; admitted to bar, 1981, New York. *Education:* Stanford University (B.A., 1975); Columbia University (J.D., 1980). ***COURSES:*** Basic Legal Skills, Law and Literature. ***Email:*** kateon@u.washington.edu

ANITA RAMASASTRY, **(Assistant Professor)**, *Education:* Harvard University (B.A., 1988; J.D., 1992); University of Sydney (M.A., 1990). ***COURSES:*** Contracts, Commercial Law, Banking. ***Email:*** arama@u.washington.edu

WILLIAM HAMILTON RODGERS, **(Professor)**, born Brockton, Massachusetts, September 16, 1939; admitted to bar, 1965, New York; 1967, Washington, 1973, District of Columbia. *Education:* Harvard University (B.A., 1961); Columbia University (LL.B., 1965). ***COURSES:*** Environmental Law, Torts. ***Email:*** whr@u.washington.edu

ERIC SCHNAPPER, **(Professor)**, born 1942; admitted to bar, 1969, California; 1971, New York. *Education:* Johns Hopkins University (B.A., 1962; M.A., 1963); Yale University (LL.B., 1968). ***COURSES:*** Civil Rights, Constitutional Law, Employment Law, Legal History. ***Email:*** schnapp@u.washington.edu

SCOTT A. SCHUMACHER, **(Lecturer)**, born Seattle, Washington, December 3, 1962; admitted to bar, Washington. *Education:* Loyola Marymount University (B.A., 1986); Seattle University (J.D., 1990); New York University (LL.M., 1991). ***Email:*** sschum@u.washington.edu

WILLIAM B. STOEBUCK, **(Professor)**, born Wichita, Kansas, March 18, 1929; admitted to bar, 1959, Washington. *Education:* Wichita State University (B.A., 1951); Indiana University (M.A., 1953); University of Washington (J.D., 1959); Harvard University (S.J.D., 1973). ***COURSES:*** Land Use, Real Property. ***Email:*** stoebuck@u.washington.edu

TOSHIKO TAKENAKA, **(Associate Professor)**, born Tokyo, July 10, 1958; admitted to bar, 1993, New York. *Education:* Seikei University (B.A., 1981); University of Washington School of Law (LL.M., 1990); University of Washington School of Law (Ph.D., 1992). ***COURSES:*** Intellectual Property, Patents Law, Japanese Law, Comparative Law. ***Email:*** toshiko@u.washington.edu

VERONICA TAYLOR, **(Professor)**, *Education:* Monash University (B.A., 1986; L.L.B., 1988); University of Washington (L.L.M., 1992). ***COURSES:*** Asian Contract Law, Comparative Law, Japanese Law, US/Japanese Corporate Relations. ***Email:*** vtaylor@u.washington.edu

MICHAEL E. TOWNSEND, **(Associate Professor)**, born 1952. *Education:* University of Michigan (B.A., 1973; Ph.D., 1982); Yale University (J.D., 1989). ***COURSES:*** Contracts, Intellectual Property, Law and Science. ***Email:*** met@u.washington.edu

PHILIP A. TRAUTMAN, **(Professor)**, born Butte, Montana, September 10, 1930. *Education:* University of Washington (B.A., 1952; J.D., 1954). ***COURSES:*** Civil Procedure, Conflict of Laws. ***Email:*** trautman@u.washington.edu

LEA B. VAUGHN, **(Professor)**, born Seattle, Washington, July 18, 1953. *Education:* Princeton University (A.B., 1975); University of Michigan (J.D., 1978). ***COURSES:*** Civil Procedure, Labor Law, Alternative Dispute Resolution. ***Email:*** lvaughn@u.washington.edu

MARIA DE LOURDES VICTORIA, **(Lecturer)**, admitted to bar, 1992, Washington. *Education:* University of Washington (B.A., 1988; J.D., 1992). ***COURSES:*** Child Advocacy. ***Email:*** mariavic@u.washington.edu

WALTER J. WALSH, **(Assistant Professor)**, born Dublin, Ireland, June12, 1958; admitted to bar, 1983, Ireland; 1984, California; 1986, New York; 1993, U.S. Supreme Court. *Education:* National University of Ireland (University College Dublin) (B.C.L., 1979); Yale Law School (LL.M., 1989); Harvard Law School (S.J.D., 1997). ***COURSES:*** Torts, Legal History, EU Law, Comparative Constitutional Law, Law & Religion. ***Email:*** wawa@u.washington.edu

LIS W. WIEHL, **(Associate Professor)**, *Education:* Barnard College (A.B., 1983); University of Queensland (M.A., 1985); Harvard University (J.D., 1987). ***COURSES:*** Trial Practice, Criminal Procedure, Evidence, Professional Responsibility. ***Email:*** wiehl@u.washington.edu

LOUIS E. WOLCHER, **(Professor)**, born San Francisco, California, August 27, 1947. *Education:* Stanford University (B.A., 1969); Harvard University (J.D., 1973). ***COURSES:*** Admiralty, Contracts, Torts, Federal Courts, Restitution, Critical Legal Studies. ***Email:*** wolcher@u.washington.edu

---

UNIVERSITY OF WISCONSIN LAW SCHOOL

975 BASCOM MALL
MADISON, WISCONSIN 53706-1399
Telephone: (608) 262-2240
Fax: (608) 262-5485

ABA Approved Since 1923.

Wisconsin Law School, established in 1868, is a leader in legal education. A charter member of the Association of American Law Schools, and among the first approved by the ABA in 1923, the school has a heritage of commitment to interdisciplinary research with other departments in the University. The Wisconsin approach to legal problems, described as "Law-in-Action," emphasizes how the law relates to society as a whole and to social change. The fifty law faculty members encourage innovative teaching methods, supplementing traditional casebooks with role playing, problem solving, drafting exercises, videotapes and computer technology. Clinical programs, which combine research, field work and the hands-on application of legal skills include Legal Assistance to Institutionalized Persons, Legal Defense Program, Center for Public Representation, Consumer Law Clinic, Family Law Clinic, Labor Law Clinical Program, Judicial Internship Program, Prosecution Project, Public Defender Project, Center for Patient Partnerships, Wisconsin Innocence Project, and the NAACP Legal Counsel Summer Placement Program. The General Practice Course uses teaching teams of practicing lawyers under supervision of the General Practice Director, to provide skills training. The success of this program has led to the adoption of similar programs,

(This Listing Continued)

UNIVERSITY OF WISCONSIN LAW SCHOOL
—Continued

following consultation with the Wisconsin faculty responsible for it, in Canada, Ireland and Australia.

Out of a student body of approximately 850 students, about 40% come from outside Wisconsin. Forty-seven percent of the enrolled students are women; 25% are students of color. The Legal Education Opportunities (LEO) Program is a national model for the recruitment and retention of students of color. The average age of incoming students is about 27 years. In the first year program, all students have a small section of no more than 23 students for one of their four required classes. The Student Bar Association is active in governance of the Law School through appointment of students as members of most faculty committees. Specialized student interest organizations, in addition to student divisions of the American Bar Association and the Lawyer's Guild, include chapters of virtually every ethnic, religious and substantive law organization found in American law schools.

In addition to the Juris Doctor degree, the school awards the LL.M., S.J.D. and M.L.I. (Master of Legal Institutions) degrees to those admitted to these specific programs by the committee on graduate studies. In addition to the *Wisconsin Law Review,* one of the leading traditional Law Reviews, Wisconsin Law students also publish the *Wisconsin Women's Law Journal,* the *Wisconsin International Law Journal,* and the *Wisconsin Environmental Law Journal.* There is a student Moot Court Board which oversees the participation of students in most of the national Moot Court competitions.

The school's Institute for Legal Studies supports and facilitates inter-disciplinary research, colloquia and seminars for both the Law School and the larger University community throughout the year. The East Asian Legal Studies Center, established in 1990, undertakes not only research in legal matters of particular pertinence to that part of the world but also provides special courses in training for qualified law students from there.

In addition to the traditional academic year, the school offers a substantial summer program in 3 segments over 13 weeks. Its outreach program offers a five-week intensive summer course for foreign lawyers summarizing the basics of American Legal Institutions that enrolls approximately 60 students from South America, Asia, Europe and Africa each year. The summer is also used for programs designed to assist pre-law minority students in understanding the nature and opportunities of the practice of law and the nature of legal education.

Although the majority of the school's alumni are located in Wisconsin and adjacent states, there are significant numbers of alumni in every major population center in the United States, as well as significant numbers abroad. The commitment of the school to a diverse faculty and student body was recognized when it received an award from the Society of American Law Teachers in 1989 for the steps it had taken to achieve those goals. The Hastie Fellows Program, through which lawyers of color earn LL.M. degrees preparing them for careers in law teaching, is 27 years old.

Dean: Kenneth B. Davis, Jr. (608) 262-0618
Chair, Admissions Committee: John A. Kidwell (608) 262-5914
Financial Aid: Beth Kransberger (608) 262-1815
Library Director: Steven M. Barkan (608) 262-1151
Placement - Director: Jane G. Heymann (608) 262-7856
Alumni Affairs - Development Director: Tricia Wheeler (608) 263-2202

FULL TIME FACULTY

KENNETH B. DAVIS, JR.*, (Dean and James E. and Ruth B. Doyle-Bascom Professor of Law)**, born Louisville, Kentucky, September 1, 1947; admitted to bar, 1974, Ohio; 1975, District of Columbia; 1990, Wisconsin. *Education:* University of Michigan (A.B., 1969); Case Western Reserve University (J.D., 1974). ***COURSES: Agency and Partnership, Corporations, Securities Regulation.

CATHERINE R. ALBISTON*, (Assistant Professor)**, born Seattle, Washington, October 8, 1965; admitted to bar, 1993, California. *Education:* Stanford University (B.A., 1987; M.A., 1989); University of California, Boalt Hall School of Law (J.D., 1993; Ph.D., 2001). ***COURSES: Civil Procedure, Employment Law, Sociology of Law, Women and the Law.

ANN ALTHOUSE*, (Robert W. and Irma M. Arthur-Bascom Professor)**, born Wilmington, Delaware; admitted to bar, 1981, New York. *Education:* University of Michigan (B.F.A., 1973); New York University (J.D., 1981). ***COURSES: Federal Courts, Constitutional Law, Civil Procedure.

GORDON BREWSTER BALDWIN*, (Professor of Law, Emeritus)**, born Binghamton, New York, September 3, 1929; admitted to bar, 1953, New York; 1965, Wisconsin. *Education:* Haverford College (B.A., 1950); Cornell University (LL.B., 1953). ***COURSES: Constitutional Law, International Law, Admiralty, First Amendment.

STEVEN MILES BARKAN*, (Law Library Director & Professor of Law)**, born Cleveland, Ohio, February 10, 1950; admitted to bar, 1975, Ohio. *Education:* University of Wisconsin-Madison (B.A., 1972); Cleveland State University (J.D., 1975); University of Michigan (A.M.L.S., 1980). ***COURSES: Torts, Professional Responsibility. ***Email:*** smbarkan@facstaff.wisc.edu

RICHARD B. BILDER*, (Professor of Law, Emeritus)**, born Newark, New Jersey; admitted to bar, 1956, District of Columbia, New Jersey; 1965, Wisconsin. *Education:* Williams College (B.A., 1949); Harvard University (J.D., 1956). ***COURSES: International Law, Foreign Relations Law, International Business Transactions, Torts, Contracts, Admiralty.

TONYA L BRITO*, (Associate Professor)**, admitted to bar, 1990, Pennsylvania; 1992, Washington, D.C.. *Education:* Barnard College (A.B., 1986); Harvard Law School (J.D., 1989). ***COURSES: Children, Law & Society, Civil Procedure, Family Law, Adoption Law & Policy.

PETER C. CARSTENSEN*, (Associate Dean and George H. Young-Bascom Professor of Law)**, born Ellensberg, Washington, June 6, 1942; admitted to bar, 1968, District of Columbia; 1995, Wisconsin. *Education:* University of Wisconsin-Madison (B.A., 1964); Yale University (M.A., 1968; LL.B., 1968). ***COURSES: Antitrust, Corporations, Torts, Economic Regulation. ***Email:*** pccarste@fastaff.wisc.edu

R. ALTA CHARO*, (Professor of Law and Medical Ethics)**, born Brooklyn, New York, June 6, 1958; admitted to bar, 1983, New York. *Education:* Harvard University (B.A., 1979); Columbia University (J.D., 1982). ***COURSES: Torts, Legislation, Bioethics.

W. LAWRENCE CHURCH*, (Volkman-Bascom Professor of Law)**, born Milwaukee, Wisconsin, June 20, 1938; admitted to bar, 1963, Wisconsin. *Education:* Amherst College (B.A., 1960); University of Wisconsin-Madison (LL.B., 1963). ***COURSES: Property, Constitutional Law.

(This Listing Continued)

UNIVERSITY OF WISCONSIN LAW SCHOOL —Continued

CARIN ANN CLAUSS*, (Nathan P. Feinsinger Labor Law Professor)**, born Knoxville, Tennessee, January 24, 1939; admitted to bar, 1964, New York. *Education:* Vassar College (B.A., 1960); Columbia University (LL.B., 1963). ***COURSES: Labor Relations Law, Sex-Based Discrimination, Protective Labor Legislation, Legal Process, Administrative Law, Civil Procedure.

WILLIAM H. CLUNE*, (Professor, Emeritus)**, born Plainfield, New Jersey, May 17, 1942; admitted to bar, 1967, Illinois. *Education:* Loyola University (B.S., with honors, 1964); Northwestern University (J.D., 1967). ***COURSES: Constitutional Law, Law and Education, Law and Policy.

ANUJ CHANG DESAI*, (Assistant Professor)**, born Ithaca, New York, December 26, 1963; admitted to bar, 1999, Washington. *Education:* Harvard University (A.B., 1987); Columbia University (M.I.A., 1990); University of California, Boalt Hall School of Law (J.D., 1994). ***COURSES: Copyright, Cyberlaw.

WALTER J. DICKEY*, (Evjue-Bascom Professor)**, born Bronx, New York, November 11, 1946; admitted to bar, 1971, Wisconsin; 1974, Minnesota. *Education:* University of Wisconsin (B.A., 1968; J.D., 1971). ***COURSES: Criminal Law, Criminal Procedure, Criminal Justice, Administration, Law and Correctional Institutions, Professional Responsibilities.

HOWARD S. ERLANGER*, (Voss-Bascom Professor of Law, Director, Institute for Legal Studies)**, born San Francisco, California, March 5, 1945; admitted to bar, 1981, Wisconsin. *Education:* University of California, Berkeley (B.A., 1967; Ph.D., 1971); University of Wisconsin (J.D., 1981). ***COURSES: Wills and Trusts, Community Property, Estate Planning, Law and Society, Seminar on Probate Reform. ***Email:*** erlanger@ssc.wisc.edu

MARC GALANTER*, (John and Rylla Bosshard Professor of Law and South Asian Studies Emeritus)**, born Philadelphia, Pennsylvania, February 18, 1931; admitted to bar, 1956, Illinois. *Education:* University of Chicago (B.A., 1950; M.A., 1954; J.D., 1956). ***COURSES: Legal Profession, Sociology of Law, Church and State.

LINDA S. GREENE*, (Evjue - Bascom Professor)**, born May 20, 1948; admitted to bar, 1975, California. *Education:* California State University, Long Beach (A.B., 1970); University of California, Berkeley (J.D., 1974). ***COURSES: Constitutional Law, Civil Procedure, Employment Discrimination, Legislation, Related Seminars. ***Email:*** LSGREENE@FACSTAFF.WISC.EDU

KATHRYN HENDLEY*, (Professor)**, born Pittsburgh, Pennsylvania, November 6, 1958; admitted to bar, 1982, Texas. *Education:* Indiana University (A.B., 1979); Georgetown University (M.A., 1987); University of California at Los Angeles (J.D., 1982); University of California at Berkeley (Ph.D., 1993). ***COURSES: Business Associations, International Business Transactions, Comparative Law.

CHARLES R. IRISH*, (Volkman-Bascom Professor of Law, Director, East Asian Legal Studies Center)**, born May 22, 1944; admitted to bar, 1970, California; 1977, Wisconsin. *Education:* Columbia University (B.A., 1966); Vanderbilt University (J.D., 1969). ***COURSES: Taxation I, Taxation II, International Trade and Investment, International Taxation. ***Email:*** crirish@facstaff.wisc.edu

LEONARD V. KAPLAN*, (Mortimer M. Jackson Professor)**, born September 7, 1941; admitted to bar, 1966, California. *Education:* Temple University (A.B., 1962; J.D., 1965); Yale University (LL.M., 1966); University of Chicago (M.A., 1971; Ph.D., 1977). ***COURSES: Criminal Law, Criminal Procedure, Family Law, Family and State, Human Experimentation, Law, Society and State, Law and Psychiatry, Law and Literature, Legal Process, Jurisprudence.

JOHN A. KIDWELL*, (Haight Professor of Law)**, born Denver, Colorado, April 1, 1945; admitted to bar, 1970, Colorado; 1975, Wisconsin. *Education:* University of Iowa (B.A., 1967); Harvard University (J.D., 1970). ***COURSES: Contracts, Remedies, Copyright, Trademarks. ***Email:*** jkidwell@facstaff.wisc.edu

HEINZ J. KLUG*, (Associate Professor)**, born Durban, South Africa, April 7, 1957; admitted to bar, 1989, California; 1995, Advocate of the High Court of South Africa. *Education:* University of Natal (B.A., 1977; B.A., with honors, 1978); University of California, Hastings (J.D., 1989); University of Wisconsin, Madison (S.J.D.1997). ***COURSES: Constitutional Law, Property, Torts, Renewable Natural Resources. ***Email:*** klug@facstaff.wisc.edu

NEIL K. KOMESAR*, (Burrus-Bascom Professor)**, born July 22, 1941; admitted to bar, 1967, Illinois. *Education:* University of Chicago (A.B., 1963; A.M., 1964; J.D., 1967; Ph.D., 1973). ***COURSES: Property, Torts, Constitutional Law, Law & Economics.

JANE ELIZABETH LARSON*, (Professor)**, born Omaha, Nebraska, September 9, 1958; admitted to bar, 1985, Minnesota; 1988, District of Columbia. *Education:* Macalester College (B.A., 1980); University of Minnesota (J.D., 1985). ***COURSES: Property, Legal History, Conflict of Law, Feminist Legal Theory. ***Email:*** janelarson@facstaff.wisc.edu

STEWART MACAULAY*, (Malcolm Pitman Sharp Professor and Theodore W. Brazeau Professor)**, born Atlanta, Georgia, April 7, 1931; admitted to bar, 1955, California. *Education:* Stanford University (A.B., 1952; LL.B., 1955). ***COURSES: Contracts; Sociology of Law.

ARTHUR F. MCEVOY, III*, (J. Willard Hurst Professor)**, *Education:* Stanford University (A.B., 1973); University of California at San Diego (Ph.d., 1979); Stanford Law School (J.D., 1989). ***COURSES: Jurisprudence, Environmental Law, History of American Law, Torts.

ELIZABETH ELLEN MERTZ*, (Associate Professor)**, born Washington, D.C., February 03, 1955. *Education:* Bryn Mawr College (B.A., 1976); Duke University (PhD, 1982); Northwestern University Law School (J.D., 1988). ***COURSES: Family Law, Legal Process, Law and Language, Law and Anthropology. ***Email:*** eemertz@facstaff.wisc.edu

THOMAS WILSON MITCHELL*, (Assistant Professor)**, born San Francisco, California, June 11, 1965; admitted to bar, 1993, California; 1994, District of Columbia. *Education:* Amherst College (B.A., 1987); Howard University (J.D., 1993); University of Wisconsin (LL.M., 1999). ***COURSES: Real Estate, Remedies, Property. ***Email:*** tmitchell@facstaff.wisc.edu

RICHARD ALAN MONETTE*, (Associate Professor of Law)**, born Seattle, Washington, September 30, 1959. *Education:* Mayville State College (B.S., 1982); University of North Dakota (M.A., 1984); University of Oregon (J.D., 1988); University of Wisconsin-Madison (LL.M., 1997). ***COURSES: Constitutional Law, Federal Laws Affecting Indian Tribes, Property, Torts, Water Rights.

BEVERLY I. MORAN*, (Voss - Bascom Professor)**, admitted to bar, 1982, New York; 1982, New Jersey. *Education:* Vassar College (A.B., 1977); University of Pennsylvania (J.D., 1981); New York University (LL.M., 1986). ***COURSES: Federal Income Taxation of Individuals, Federal Income Taxation of Trusts and Estates, Federal Income Taxation of Partnerships and Agency/Partnership.

VICTORIA F. NOURSE*, (Associate Professor)**, admitted to bar, 1986, New York. *Education:* Stanford University (B.A., 1980); University of California at Berkeley Boalt Hall School of Law (J.D., 1984). ***COURSES: Criminal Law, Criminal Procedure, Legislative Process, Constitutional Law.

(This Listing Continued)

UNIVERSITY OF WISCONSIN LAW SCHOOL —Continued

JOHN K.M. OHNESORGE,* (Assistant Professor)**, born Minneapolis, Minnesota, April 24, 1963; admitted to bar, 1990, Minnesota. *Education:* St. Olaf College (B.A., 1985); University of Minnesota (J.D., 1989); Harvard Law School (LL.M., 1995). ***COURSES: Administrative Law, Business Association, Comparative Law. ***Email:*** ohnesorg@law.harvard.edu

PILAR NICOLE OSSORIO,* (Assistant Professor)**, born November 16, 1959. *Education:* Stanford University (B.S., 1983; Ph.D., 1990); University of California (J.D., 1997). ***COURSES: Intellectual Property, Bioethics, Law and Medicine. ***Email:*** pnossorio@facstaff.wisc.edu

THOMAS M. PALAY,* (Associate Dean and Foley & Lardner - Bascom Professor of Law)**, born Milwaukee, Wisconsin, April 21, 1953. *Education:* Tufts University (B.A., 1975); University of Pennsylvania (J.D., 1981; Ph.D., 1981). ***COURSES: Law and Economics, Property, Torts, Business Organization.

JOEL E. ROGERS,* (Professor)**, born March 19, 1952; admitted to bar, 1982, New York. *Education:* Yale University (B.A., 1972; J.D., 1976); Princeton University (M.A., 1978; Ph.D., 1984). ***COURSES: Administrative Law, Problems of Law and the Welfare State.

RICHARD J. ROSS,* (Assistant Professor)**, born New York, January 28, 1963; admitted to bar, 1989, Connecticut. *Education:* Yale University (B.A., 1980; J.D., 1989). ***COURSES: Trusts and Estates, Legal History.

JANE S. SCHACTER,* (Professor)**, born New Rochelle, New York, June 27, 1958; admitted to bar, 1985, Massachusetts. *Education:* University of Michigan (A.B., 1980); Harvard University (J.D., 1984). ***COURSES: Civil Procedure, Constitutional Law, Legislation, Sexual Orientation and the Law.

DAVID EDWARD SCHULTZ,* (Associate Dean, Professor of Law)**, born Watertown, Wisconsin, March 9, 1946; admitted to bar, 1972, Wisconsin. *Education:* University of Wisconsin (B.S., 1967; J.D., 1972). ***COURSES: Criminal Law, Criminal Procedure.

GREGORY CHARLES SHAFFER,* (Assistant Professor)**, born Cincinnati, Ohio, July 8, 1958; admitted to bar, 1991, California. *Education:* Dartmouth College (B.A., 1980); Stanford Law School (J.D., 1988). ***COURSES: International Trade, European Union, International Business Transactions, Business Organizations. ***Email:*** gshaffer@facstaff.wisc.edu

MICHAEL EDWARD SMITH,* (Associate Professor)**, born New York, N.Y., June 30, 1942; admitted to bar, 1971, New York. *Education:* Princeton University (B.A., 1965); Oxford University, Worcester College (B.A., 1967); Harvard Law School (J.D., 1970). ***COURSES: Criminal Law, Criminal Procedure, Sentencing.

GERALD J. THAIN,* (Consumer Law Professor)**, born Galena, Illinois, October 14, 1935; admitted to bar, 1960, Iowa; 1979, Wisconsin. *Education:* University of Iowa (B.A., 1957; J.D., 1960). ***COURSES: Unfair Trade Practices, Negotiable Instruments, Secured Transactions, Consumer Law, Tobacco and the Law, First Amendment, E-commerce Law. ***Email:*** gjthain@facstaff.wisc.edu

JOSEPH R. THOME,* (Professor of Law Emeritus)**, born San Jose, Costa Rica, January 30, 1935; admitted to bar, 1962, California. *Education:* University of California at Los Angeles (B.A., 1958); Harvard University (LL.B., 1961). ***COURSES: Comparative Law, Contracts, Latin American Legal Institutions, Legal Problems of Economic and Social Change in Latin America, Law and Modernization in the Third World.

CLIFF F. THOMPSON,* (Professor)**, born August 15, 1934; admitted to bar, 1960, Kansas. *Education:* Harvard University (A.B., 1956; J.D., 1960); Magdalen College, Oxford (B.A., 1958; M.A., 1962). ***COURSES: Property, Jurisprudence, Law and Society, Negotiable Instruments, Contracts, Legal Profession, Comparative Law.

DAVID M. TRUBEK,* (Director of WAGE & Voss-Bascom Professor)**, born Hackensack, New Jersey, December 17, 1935; admitted to bar, 1961, Connecticut. *Education:* University of Wisconsin (B.A., 1957); Yale University (LL.B., 1961). ***COURSES: Civil Procedure, Social Theory and Law, Legal Profession, International Political Economy, International Law.

BERNARD R. TRUJILLO,* (Assistant Professor)**, born Pueblo, Colorado, November 9, 1966; admitted to bar, 1994, Pennsylvania; 1996, District of Columbia. *Education:* Princeton University (A.B., 1988); Yale Law School (J.D., 1992). ***COURSES: Bankruptcy, Corporations, Commercial Law, Immigration. ***Email:*** brtrujil@facstaff.wisc.edu

FRANK M. TUERKHEIMER,* (Robert L. Habush-Bascom Professor)**, born July 27, 1939; admitted to bar, 1963, New York; 1971, Wisconsin. *Education:* Columbia College (B.A., 1960); New York University (LL.B., 1963). ***COURSES: Evidence, Trial Advocacy, Appellate Advocacy, Criminal Litigation, Trials of the Holocaust. ***Email:*** fmtuerkh@facstaff.wisc.edu

ALAN J. WEISBARD,* (Associate Professor of Law, of Medical Ethics, and of Jewish and Religious Studies)**, born Miami Beach, Florida, September 21, 1950; admitted to bar, 1978, District of Columbia. *Education:* Harvard College (A.B., 1972); Yale Law School (J.D., 1977). ***COURSES: Torts, Bioethics and the Law, Law Science and Biotechnology, Privacy Law in the Cyber Era, Children, Parents and the State, Caring for the Dying Patient (Medical School), Patients Doctors and Society (Medical School) ,Jewish Law and Ethics in Comparative Perspective. ***Email:*** weisbard@facstaff.wisc.edu

WILLIAM C. WHITFORD,* (Professor of Law Emeritus)**, born Madison, Wisconsin, January 16, 1940. *Education:* University of Wisconsin (B.A., 1961); Yale University (LL.B., 1964). ***COURSES: Contracts, Creditors Rights, Consumer Protection. ***Email:*** whitford@lawmail.law.wisc.edu

UNIVERSITY OF WYOMING COLLEGE OF LAW

P. O. BOX 3035
LARAMIE, WYOMING 82071-3035

VALPARAISO UNIVERSITY SCHOOL OF LAW

WESEMANN HALL
VALPARAISO, INDIANA 46383
Telephone: (219) 465-7829
Fax: (219) 465-7872
Email: valpolaw@valpo.edu http://www.valpo.edu/law

Overview

The Valparaiso University School of Law is a small private law school near Chicago, in Northwest Indiana. The School offers full-time, part-time, and accelerated programs leading to the J.D. It also offers a joint J.D./M.B.A., a joint J.D./M.A. (Master of Arts in Psychology), and an LL.M. for foreign lawyers.

The School of Law has approximately 435 students, drawn from over 100 colleges and universities in the United States and abroad. There are over 3800 alumni throughout the world. Alumni include lawyers in large and small firms, general counsel, federal and state judges, academics, businesspersons, and leaders of nonprofit organizations.

The School of Law is part of a Lutheran-affiliated university. It provides a personalized education, the opportunity for inquiry into fundamental values, preparation for practice, and service to the community.

Special Programs

Valparaiso University School of Law has a number of programs that meet special needs of certain students. A three-year Honors Program, which admits up to 25 new students each year, provides enriched training in legal writing for students who show exceptional promise.

Concentrations are available in the areas of environmental law, labor and employment law, international trade & development law, alternative dispute resolution, criminal practice, civil practice, entertainment litigation and intellectual property/technology, child/family law, elder/healthcare law, and state and local government/civil rights. A student who pursues a concentration takes advanced electives, writes a scholarly paper, and engages in clinic, externship, or other practice opportunities in the chosen field. The first four concentrations listed work closely with the School of Law's Center on Dispute Resolution, which sponsors an annual conference for attorneys and scholars on dispute resolution in specific fields of law.

A summer program of international and comparative law studies is offered annually in Cambridge, England. Courses have included International Finance Law, International Environmental Law, NAFTA, and Comparative Family Law; courses are taught by faculty of the School and distinguished visitors. Visiting faculty have included several United States Supreme Court Justices.

Skills Education

Skills education is an important part of the School of Law's curriculum and programs. The Law Clinic, which was established in 1969, offers a civil clinic, a criminal clinic, a tax clinic, a juvenile clinic, a domestic violence clinic, and a mediation clinic. Approximately 40% of Valparaiso University School of Law students participate in one of these clinics, which provide free legal services to over 650 members of the community each year.

A wealth of externships are available in federal and state agencies, prosecutor and public defender offices, public service organizations, and other institutions. In special cases, a student may be permitted to spend a semester enrolled in an externship at a distant location. Also available is an externship program with federal judges.

The School offers an array of practice courses, such as a trial practice, pretrial skills, drafting, and alternative dispute resolution. In addition, professors may include a one-credit practicum as part of a substantive law course.

Students participate in many practice competitions. The prestigious Luther M. Swygert Moot Court competition is held each year; judges include members of the Seventh Circuit Court of Appeals, Indiana Supreme Court, federal district courts, and in some years the United States Supreme Court. The student Moot Court Society enters student teams in ten national competitions annually. Teams also compete in ATLA competitions, client counseling and negotiating competitions, and other moot court competitions.

International and Comparative law

The Valparaiso University School of Law provides education and programs in international law and trade, including the concentration in international trade & development law, the Cambridge summer abroad program, international law-related externships, conferences, and international moot court competitions. Faculty members publish the journal *Third World Legal Studies* in conjunction with the International Third World Studies Association, and serve on editorial boards of other international law journals. Faculty members have taught at universities in Europe, Africa and Asia, have received Fulbright Fellowships for work in Vietnam, India, Australia, and other countries, and have served as economic and legal advisors to emerging nations.

Speakers

Several endowed annual lectureships enrich the life of the School. The Monsanto Fund Lecture brings a leading scholar in law or economics to speak on issues in tort law or reform. The Seegers Lecture brings a leading legal scholar or philosopher to speak on a topic in jurisprudence or legal theory. The Tabor Institute brings to campus a leading scholar in legal ethics to deliver two lectures, one for practicing lawyers in the community and one for those interested in scholarly issues in the field.

Speakers are also brought to campus as part of the activities of concentrations, for Martin Luther King Day observations, for the newly instituted Indiana Supreme Court lectureship, in connection with student organization activities, and on other occasions.

Pro Bono and Public Service

A graduation requirement is that law students provide 20 hours of pro bono activity in the form of legal service, government, or nonprofit work. Students who perform more than 40 hours receive Public Service Honors.

Students who work in public service during the summer are eligible for financial assistance through the Summer Public Interest Scholarship program. Graduates who commit to working in public interest positions following graduation may apply for loan repayment assistance through the School of Law's Loan Repayment Assistance Program.

A recently instituted program provides law students with opportunities to provide legal and other assistance to Indian tribes and reservations during the summer.

Student Activities

The *Valparaiso University Law Review* is a scholarly journal published by students three times each year. One issue consists of a symposium on

(This Listing Continued)

a major topic of current importance. The *Review* also publishes the annual Monsanto Fund Lecture.

The Moot Court Society coordinates the student competitions described above. The *Forum* is a student newspaper published several times each semester; it provides news about law student activities and concerns, and is a vehicle for the dean and other administrators to communicate with students. The Student Bar Association funds and coordinates the activities of student organizations. Those organizations include the Black Law Student Association, Hispanic Law Student Association, Women Law Students Association, Jewish Law Student Association, Midwest Environmental Law Caucus, Intellectual Property Law Association, Christian Legal Society, law student divisions of national, state and local bar associations, and several law fraternities.

Dean: Jay Conison (219) 465-7834
Associate Dean for Academic Affairs: Rosalie Levinson (219) 465-7854
Associate Dean for Administration: Curtis Cichowski (219) 465-7841
Assistant Dean for Admissions and Student Services: Marilyn Olson (219) 465-7891
Assistant Dean for Career Services: Art Bousel (219) 465-7814
Library Director: Mary G. Persyn (219) 465-7830
Director of Development: Joan White (219) 465-7851
Director of Alumni Relations and Annual Fund: Marilyn Otis (219) 465-7916
Financial Aid: Ann F. Weitgenant (219) 465-7818

FULL TIME FACULTY

JAY CONISON*, (Dean and Professor of Law)**, born October 21, 1953; admitted to bar, 1981, Illinois. *Education:* Yale College (B.A., 1975); University of Minnesota (M.A., 1978; J.D., 1981). ***COURSES: Copyright, Intellectual Property, Employee Benefit Plans, Legal Reasoning. ***Email:*** jay.conison@valpo.edu

MARK L. ADAMS*, (Professor of Law)**, born Chicago, Illinois, December 30, 1960; admitted to bar, 1989, Washington. *Education:* Williams College (B.A., 1983); University of Chicago (J.D., 1988). ***COURSES: Contracts, Employment Law, Labor Law, Labor Arbitration, Legal Writing and Research. ***Email:*** mark.adams@valpo.edu

BRUCE G. BERNER*, (Louis and Anna Seegers Professor of Law)**, born Brooklyn, New York, November 13, 1943; admitted to bar, 1967, New Jersey; 1974, Indiana. *Education:* Valparaiso University (B.A., 1965; LL.B., 1967); Yale University (LL.M., 1978). ***COURSES: Criminal Law and Procedure, Evidence, Torts. ***Email:*** bruce.berner@valpo.edu

ROBERT BLOMQUIST*, (Professor of Law)**, born Elizabeth, New Jersey, October 9, 1951; admitted to bar, 1977, New Jersey; 1986, Indiana. *Education:* University of Pennsylvania (B.S., 1973); Cornell University (J.D., 1977). ***COURSES: Environmental, Legislation, Torts. ***Email:*** robert.blomquist@valpo.edu

IVAN E. BODENSTEINER*, (Professor of Law)**, born February 14, 1943; admitted to bar, 1968, Indiana; 1970, Colorado. *Education:* Loras College (B.A., 1965); University of Notre Dame (J.D., 1968). ***COURSES: Civil Procedure, Civil Rights, Constitutional Law and Evidence. ***Email:*** ivan.bodensteiner@valpo.edu

PAUL H. BRIETZKE*, (Professor of Law)**, born Chicago, Illinois, July 30, 1944; admitted to bar, 1969, Wisconsin. *Education:* Lake Forest College (B.A., 1966); University of Wisconsin (J.D., 1969); University of London (Ph.D., 1981). ***COURSES: Law and Economics, Antitrust, Contracts, International Human Rights. ***Email:*** paul.brietzke@valpo.edu

DERRICK A. CARTER*, (Associate Professor of Law)**, born Detroit, Michigan, January 17, 1950; admitted to bar, 1975, Michigan. *Education:* Eastern Michigan University (B.S., 1972); Valparaiso University (J.D., 1975). ***COURSES: Criminal Law, Criminal Procedure, Legal Process, Trial and Appellate Advocacy, Pretrial Skills. ***Email:*** derrick.carter@valpo.edu

CURTIS W. CICHOWSKI*, (Associate Dean for Administration and Adjunct Professor of Law)**, born Oak Park, Illinois, July 27, 1956; admitted to bar, 1981, Indiana. *Education:* Carroll College (B.A., 1978); Valparaiso University (J.D., 1981). ***COURSES: Intellectual Property. ***Email:*** curt.cichowski@valpo.edu

LAURA GASTON DOOLEY*, (Professor of Law)**, born Little Rock, Arkansas, September 1, 1960; admitted to bar, 1986, Missouri. *Education:* University of Arkansas (B.A., 1982); Washington University (J.D., 1986). ***COURSES: Civil Procedure, Complex Litigation, Legal Ethics, Feminist Legal Theory. ***Email:*** laura.dooley@valpo.edu

EDWARD MCGLYNN GAFFNEY, JR.*, (Professor of Law)**, born San Francisco, California, August 18, 1941; admitted to bar, 1975, District of Columbia; 1991, California. *Education:* St. Patrick's College (B.A., 1963); Gregorian University (S.T.L., 1967); Catholic University of America (J.D., 1974; M.A., 1975); Harvard University (LL.M., 1976). ***COURSES: Appellate Advocacy, Comparative Law, Constitutional Law, International Law, Jurisprudence, and Professional Responsibility.

ALEX GEISINGER*, (Professor of Law)**, born New York, New York, November 6, 1964; admitted to bar, 1992, Connecticut. *Education:* Franklin and Marshall College (B.A., 1987); University of Connecticut (J.D., 1992); Harvard University (LL.M., 1996). ***COURSES: Environmental Law, International Environmental Law, Commercial Law, Regulated Industries. ***Email:*** alex.geisinger@valpo.edu

MARCIA L. GIENAPP*, (Professor of Law)**, born Trenton, Michigan, January 25, 1951; admitted to bar, 1977, Michigan; 1978, Indiana. *Education:* Valparaiso University (B.A., 1973; J.D., 1977). ***COURSES: Clinic. ***Email:*** marcia.gienapp@valpo.edu

RICHARD GORDON HATCHER*, (Senior Research Professor)**, born Michigan City, Indiana, July 10, 1933; admitted to bar, 1959, Indiana. *Education:* Indiana University (B.S., 1956); Valparaiso University (J.D., 1959). ***COURSES: Constitutional Law, Local Government, and Employment Discrimination. ***Email:*** richard.hatcher@valpo.edu

REBECCA JEAN HUSS*, (Assistant Professor of Law)**, born Cedar Rapids, Iowa, July 24, 1967; admitted to bar, 1992, Washington; 1995, Iowa; 1996 Missouri and Kansas. *Education:* University of Northern Iowa (B.A., 1989); University of Richmond (J.D., 1992); University of Iowa (LL.M., 1995). ***COURSES: Business Planning, Business Associations, International Arbitration, Mediation & Litigation, U.C.C., Mergers and Acquisitions. ***Email:*** rebecca.huss@valpo.edu

***ROSALIE BERGER LEVINSON*, (Professor of Law)**, born Gary, Indiana, December 22, 1948; admitted to bar, 1973, Indiana. *Education:* Indiana University (B.A., 1969; M.A., 1970); Valparaiso University

(This Listing Continued)

VALPARAISO UNIVERSITY SCHOOL OF LAW—Continued

(J.D., 1973). ***COURSES:*** Constitutional Law, Federal Practice, Civil Rights. ***Email:*** rosalie.levinson@valpo.edu

JOELLEN LIND, **(Professor of Law)**, born October 30, 1950; admitted to bar, 1975, California; 1986, Utah; 1988, Indiana. *Education:* Stanford University (A.B., 1972); University of California at Los Angeles (J.D., 1975). ***COURSES:*** Civil Procedure, Jurisprudence, Constitutional Theory. ***Email:*** joellen.lind@valpo.edu

SEYMOUR MOSKOWITZ, **(Professor of Law)**, admitted to bar, 1968, New York; 1969, Indiana; 1975, Massachusetts; 1982, Connecticut. *Education:* Columbia University (B.A., 1962); Harvard University (J.D., 1966). ***COURSES:*** Administrative Law, Labor Law, Health Care Law, Pretrial Skills, Family Law. ***Email:*** seymour.moskowitz@valpo.edu

DAVID A. MYERS, **(Professor of Law)**, *Education:* Drake University (B.A., 1973); University of Illinois (J.D., 1976). ***COURSES:*** Property, Entertainment Law. ***Email:*** david.myers@valpo.edu

ADAM JEROME MYERS, III, **(Associate Professor of Law)**, born Gettysburg, Pennsylvania, December 31, 1951; admitted to bar, 1986, California. *Education:* Pennsylvania State University (B.S., 1973); Harvard Law School (J.D., 1985). ***COURSES:*** Business Associations, Corporate Finance, Law and Accounting, Trusts & Estates, Commercial Law. ***Email:*** adam.myers@valpo.edu

MARY G. PERSYN, **(Law Librarian and Associate Professor of Law)**, born Elizabeth, New Jersey, February 25, 1945; admitted to bar, 1982, Indiana. *Education:* Creighton University (A.B., 1967); University of Oregon (M.L.S., 1969); University of Notre Dame (J.D., 1982). ***COURSES:*** Legal Research. ***Email:*** mary.persyn@valpo.edu

JOHN J. POTTS, **(Professor of Law)**, *Education:* University of New Mexico (B.A., 1969); Northeastern University (M.S., 1975); Boston College School of Law (J.D., 1974). ***COURSES:*** Individual Taxation, Corporate & Partnership Taxation, Corporate Reorganization Taxation, Family Taxation. ***Email:*** john.potts@valpo.edu

BARBARA JEAN SCHMIDT, **(Professor of Law)**, born Plymouth, Wisconsin, May 22, 1948; admitted to bar, 1973, Wisconsin and Indiana. *Education:* Valparaiso University (B.A., 1970; J.D., 1973). ***COURSES:*** Clinical Program. ***Email:*** barbara.schmidt@valpo.edu

RICHARD STITH, **(Professor of Law)**, born Corvallis, Oregon, November 17, 1944; admitted to bar, 1974, Indiana. *Education:* Harvard University (A.B., 1965); University of California, Berkeley (M.A., 1967); Yale University (M.Phil., 1971; J.D., 1973; Ph.D., 1973). ***COURSES:*** Jurisprudence, Comparative Law, Legal History, European Union, Criminal Law. ***Email:*** richard.stith@valpo.edu

MICHAEL S. STRAUBEL, **(Associate Professor of Law)**, born Spokane, Washington, November 4, 1957; admitted to bar, 1982, Wisconsin; 1982, Michigan. *Education:* Western Michigan University (B.S., 1979); Marquette University (J.D., 1982); McGill University (LL.M., 1989). ***COURSES:*** International Law, International Business, Air and Space Law, Insurance Law, Legal Writing, and Appellate Advocacy. ***Email:*** michael.straubel@valpo.edu

SUSAN STUART, **(Assistant Professor of Law)**, born Lafayette, Indiana, May 6, 1951; admitted to bar, 1982, Indiana. *Education:* DePauw University (B.A., 1973); Valparaiso University (M.Ed., 1976); Indiana University (J.D., 1982). ***COURSES:*** Legal Research & Writing, Remedies, Education Law. ***Email:*** susan.stuart@valpo.edu

RUTH C. VANCE, **(Professor of Law)**, born Detroit, Michigan, October 4, 1957; admitted to bar, 1982, Indiana. *Education:* Olivet College (B.A., 1979); Valparaiso University (J.D., 1982). ***COURSES:*** Legal Writing Reasoning and Research, Workers Compensation, Employment Rights, Pretrial Skills, Negotiation Alternative Dispute Resolution. ***Email:*** ruth.vance@valpo.edu

DAVID E. VANDERCOY, **(Professor of Law & Director of Clinical Programs)**, born Corry, Pennsylvania, December 12, 1949; admitted to bar, 1974, Pennsylvania; 1980, Indiana. *Education:* Pennsylvania State University (B.A., 1971); Dickinson School of Law (J.D., 1974); New York University (LL.M., 1980). ***COURSES:*** Litigation, Criminal, Ethics, Torts. ***Email:*** david.vandercoy@law.valpo.edu

DAVID MILTON WELTER, **(Professor of Law)**, born Blue Island, Illinois, December 24, 1959; admitted to bar, 1990, Indiana. *Education:* Valparaiso University (B.A., 1983; J.D., 1990). ***COURSES:*** Criminal Law Clinic. ***Email:*** david.welter@valpo.edu

LINDA S. WHITTON, **(Professor of Law)**, born Fort Wayne, Indiana, May 1, 1958; admitted to bar, 1986, Indiana. *Education:* Valparaiso University (B.A., 1979; J.D., 1986). ***COURSES:*** Elder Law, Business Planning, Property. ***Email:*** linda.whitton@valpo.edu

GERI YONOVER, **(Professor of Law)**, born New York, New York, June 5, 1941; admitted to bar, 1983, Illinois. *Education:* University of Chicago (B.A., 1964); Chicago-Kent College of Law (J.D., 1983). ***COURSES:*** Torts, Conflict of Laws, Intellectual Property, Art Law Seminar. ***Email:*** geri.yonover@valpo.edu

---

VANDERBILT UNIVERSITY SCHOOL OF LAW
21st AVENUE SOUTH
NASHVILLE, TENNESSEE 37240

VERMONT LAW SCHOOL
P. O. BOX 96, CHELSEA STREET
SOUTH ROYALTON, VERMONT 05068-0096

VILLANOVA UNIVERSITY SCHOOL OF LAW
299 N. SPRING MILL ROAD
VILLANOVA, PENNSYLVANIA 19085-1682
Telephone: (610) 519-7000
Fax: (610) 519-6472

(This Listing Continued)

VILLANOVA UNIVERSITY SCHOOL OF LAW—Continued

ABA Approved Since 1954.

Founded in 1953, the School of Law is fully accredited by the American Bar Association and the Association of American Law Schools. Villanova University is conducted under the auspices of the Roman Catholic Order of St. Augustine and was founded in 1892. The School of Law was the first within a church-related university to be awarded a chapter of the Order of the Coif, the premier law honor society.

Less than 15 miles from Philadelphia, Villanova's campus is located in the beautiful suburban area known as the Main Line. The Villanova train station is less than 200 yards from the School of Law, providing easy access to the center of Philadelphia.

Students come from approximately 200 universities and colleges. Many have significant work experience outside of law. 47% are women and more than 11% identify themselves as members of minority groups.

The faculty is recognized nationally for its legal scholarship, teaching and significant contributions to the study and practice of law. Faculty members are available to students outside the classroom, and every student has a faculty adviser.

The School of Law draws on its Catholic and Augustinian identity to support a tradition of academic excellence, a tradition of academic freedom, a tradition of inclusion and a tradition of respect for human dignity.

A wide range of special academic programs and activities supplement the educational opportunities at Villanova, including externships and an enhanced clinical program. Clinics include: juvenile justice, immigration and asylum poverty law farmworkers and tax. An international law focus reflects the emerging international dimension of activity and enterprise. The school is a leader in the melding of information technology and the law. The School also is at the forefront of practical applications of technology to daily practice, and the jurisprudence of substantive law application.

Every student at the School of Law attains a minimum level of computer literacy in the first-year legal research and writing program. Approximately total of 180 computers are available for students use and are connected to the University back bone and to the Internet CALI Instruction. Advanced courses on the application of new technologies to law are offered in the elective curriculum.

International law is a particular strength at Villanova. Seven full-time faculty teach numerous courses on a broad variety of international subjects.

The *Villanova Law Review, Environmental Law Journal* and *Re Sports and Entertainment Law Journal* provide training in independent legal research, increase knowledge in legal topics and develop legal writing skills of students who participated. Members are selected on the basis of academic rank at the end of the first and second year of law studies and through writing competitions. The editors of the Journals sponsor symposia each year dealing with cutting edge subjects.

The Reimel Moot Court Competition, The Trial Practice Competition and Client Interviewing and Counseling Competition give law students the opportunity to practice important lawyering skills in hands-on situations. Students also enter national moot court competitions, various specialized intermural moot court competitions.

A joint JD/PhD program in law and psychology is sponsored by Villanova School of Law and the Medical College of Philadelphia. This program is one of three in the U.S. and is the only one with a fully-accredited PhD in clinical psychology along with a law degree. This intersection of the legal and mental health systems is the core of the program that approaches human problems as holistic challenges.

The School of Law and the Villanova University College of Commerce and Finance offer a joint JD/MBA program and conduct the Graduate Tax Program. The College of Commerce and Finance's department of accountancy and MBA program have been approved by the American Assembly of Collegiate Schools of Business. The Graduate Tax Program awards Master's of Laws (LLM) and Master's of Taxation (MT) degrees.

Reflecting the Augustinian heritage of service to the poor, the School of Law sponsors in addition to its extensive clinical programs, and a pro bono service program.

In every aspect of the programs at Villanova School of Law, the effect of legal and political systems on the individual person is of primary concern. The school's commitment to humanistic values is also reflected in its commitment to training lawyers with strong ethical sensibilities.

Dean: Mark A. Sargent (610) 519-7007
Associate Dean for Academic Affairs: Doris Del Tosto Brogan (610) 519-7005
Associate Dean for Information Services: William James (610) 519-7020
Assistant Dean for Admissions: David P. Pallozzi (610) 519-7010
Assistant Dean for Financial Aid: Wendy Barron (610) 519-7015
Assistant Dean for Career Services: Elaine T. Petrossian (610) 519-7031

FULL TIME FACULTY

MARK A. SARGENT, **(Dean and Professor of Law),** *Education:* Wesleyan University (B.A., 1973); Cornell University (M.A., 1975; J.D., 1978). ***COURSES:*** Law and Entrepreneurship, Securities Regulation, Law of Investment Management.

GERALD ABRAHAM, **(Professor of Law Emeritus),** born Germany, October 18, 1930; admitted to bar, 1956, New York. *Education:* New York University (B.A., 1951; LL.B., 1953). ***COURSES:*** Criminal Law, Family Law, Children and the Law.

MICHELLE J. ANDERSON, **(Associate Professor of Law),** *Education:* University of California at Santa Cruz (B.A., 1989); Yale University (J.D., 1994); Georgetown University Law Center (LL.M., 1997). ***COURSES:*** Feminist Jurisprudence, Criminal Law.

LEWIS BECKER, **(Professor of Law),** born Philadelphia, Pennsylvania, November 17, 1937; admitted to bar, 1961, District of Columbia; 1965, Pennsylvania; 1969, New York. *Education:* Temple University (B.S., 1958); University of Pennsylvania (LL.B., 1961). ***COURSES:*** Family Law, Sales, Consumer Transactions, Federal Securities Regulation.

DONALD N. BERSOFF, **(Professor of Law Emeritus),** born New York, New York, March 1, 1939; admitted to bar, 1976, Maryland; 1984, District of Columbia; 1990, Pennsylvania. *Education:* New York University (B.S., 1958; M.A., 1960; Ph.D., 1965); Yale University (J.D., 1976). ***COURSES:*** Mental Health Law, Social Science and Law, Criminal Law.

(This Listing Continued)

VILLANOVA UNIVERSITY SCHOOL OF LAW—Continued

LESLIE M. BOOK*, (Assistant Professor of Law and Director of the Tax Clinic)**, *Education:* Franklin & Marshall College (B.A., 1987); Stanford Law School (J.D., 1990); New York University (LL.M., 1994). ***COURSES: Tax Clinic.

DORIS DEL TOSTO BROGAN*, (Associate Dean for Academic Affairs and Professor of Law)**, born North Arlington, New Jersey, June 17, 1952; admitted to bar, 1981, Pennsylvania. *Education:* Glassboro State College (B.A., 1974); Villanova University (J.D., 1981). ***COURSES: Family Law, Conflict of Laws, Domestic Abuse, Legal Ethics, Torts, First Amendment and the Media.

JOHN J. CANNON*, (Professor of Law)**, born Philadelphia, Pennsylvania, January 10, 1938; admitted to bar, 1962, District of Columbia; 1966, Pennsylvania. *Education:* Villanova University (A.B., 1959; J.D., 1962); Georgetown University. ***COURSES: Civil Procedure, Civil Pretrial Practice, Labor Law, Evidence.

MICHAEL W. CARROLL*, (Assistant Professor of Law)**, born Rhode Island, July 25, 1963; admitted to bar, 1996, Maryland; 1997, District of Columbia. *Education:* University of Chicago (A.B., 1986); Georgetown University Law Center (J.D., 1996). ***COURSES: Contracts, Selected Topics in Cyberspace, Intellectual Property in Cyberspace. ***Email:*** carroll@law.villanova.edu

STEVE CHANENSON*, (Assistant Michael W. Carroll Professor of Law - Spring 2001)**, *Education:* University of Pennsylvania (B.A., M.A.); University of Chicago Law School (J.D., 1992). ***COURSES: Corporate and White Collar Crime, Sentencing.

ARNOLD B. COHEN*, (Professor of Law)**, born Philadelphia, Pennsylvania, April 1, 1939; admitted to bar, 1964, Pennsylvania. *Education:* Brown University (A.B., 1960); University of Pennsylvania (LL.B., 1963). ***COURSES: Bankruptcy, Secured Transactions, Creditors Rights.

FRANK RUDY COOPER*, (Assistant Professor of Law)**, *Education:* Amherst College (B.A., 1991); Duke University School of Law (J.D., 1995). ***COURSES: Criminal Law, Criminal Procedure, Intersection of Race and Law.

JOSEPH W. DELLAPENNA*, (Professor of Law)**, born Detroit, Michigan, December 28, 1942; admitted to bar, 1968, Michigan. *Education:* University of Michigan (B.B.A., 1965); Detroit College of Law (J.D., 1968); George Washington University (LL.M., 1969); Columbia University (LL.M., 1975). ***COURSES: Contracts, Conflicts of Law, Torts, International Law, Admiralty, Chinese Law, Transnational Litigation, Water Law.

JOHN F. DOBBYN*, (Professor of Law)**, born Boston, Massachusetts, August 31, 1937; admitted to bar, 1965, Massachusetts. *Education:* Harvard University (A.B., 1959; LL.M., 1969); Boston College (J.D., 1965). ***COURSES: Corporations, Insurance Law, Criminal Law, Equity.

DONALD W. DOWD*, (Professor of Law Emeritus)**, born 1929. *Education:* Harvard University (A.B., 1951; J.D., 1954). ***COURSES: Criminal Law, Constitutional Law.

STEVEN P. FRANKINO*, (Professor of Law)**, born Butte, Montana, May 12, 1936; admitted to bar, District of Columbia; Nebraska. *Education:* Catholic University of America (A.B., 1959; J.D., 1962). ***COURSES: Higher Education Law, Conflict of Laws.

ABRAHAM J. GAFNI*, (Professor of Law)**, born Brooklyn, New York, June 29, 1939; admitted to bar, 1963, New York; 1965, Pennsylvania. *Education:* Yeshiva University (B.A., B.H.L., 1960); Hebrew University, Jerusalem, Israel; Harvard Law School (J.D., 1963). ***COURSES: Dispute Resolution, Trial Advocacy and Practice, Professional Responsibility.

RUTH E. GORDON*, (Professor of Law)**, born Philadelphia, Pennsylvania, July 7, 1956; admitted to bar, 1980, New York; 1982, District of Columbia. *Education:* New York University (B.A., 1977; J.D., 1980); London School of Economics and Political Science (LL.M., 1987). ***COURSES: International Law, Contracts.

***JOHN Y. GOTANDA*, (Professor of Law)**, born Honolulu, Hawaii, December 30, 1961; admitted to bar, 1987, Hawaii; 1988, District of Columbia; 1994, Massachusetts. *Education:* University of Hawaii (B.A., 1984); William S. Richardson School of Law, University of Hawaii (J.D., 1987).

JOHN M. HYSON*, (Professor of Law)**, born Rockland, Massachusetts, April 6, 1942; admitted to bar, 1967, Massachusetts. *Education:* Boston College (A.B., 1963); University of North Carolina (M.A., 1964); Harvard University (LL.B., 1967). ***COURSES: Environmental Law, Land Use Planning, Civil Procedure.

WILLIAM JAMES*, (Associate Dean for Information Services; Director of Law Library; and Professor of Law)**, born 1945. *Education:* Morehouse College (B.A., 1967); Howard University (J.D., 1972); Atlanta University School of Library Science (M.S.L.S., 1973). ***COURSES: Introduction to Legal Research.

ANN CAREY JULIANO*, (Associate Professor of Law)**, *Education:* University of Pennsylvania (B.A., 1989); Cornell Law School (J.D., 1992). ***COURSES: Civil Procedure, Employment Discrimination.

CATHERINE J. LANCTOT*, (Professor of Law)**, born Woonsocket, Rhode Island, September 17, 1957; admitted to bar, 1981, District of Columbia. *Education:* Brown University (A.B., 1978); Georgetown University (J.D., 1981). ***COURSES: Torts, Legal Ethics, Employment Discrimination, Legal History.

DON W. LLEWELLYN*, (Professor of Law)**, born 1935. *Education:* Dickinson College (B.A., 1957; J.D., 1961); New York University (LL.M., 1967). ***COURSES: Federal Income Taxation, Family Wealth Planning, Post-Mortem Estate Planning, Taxation, Compensation Planning.

HOWARD R. LURIE*, (Professor of Law)**, born Steubenville, Ohio, November 18, 1938; admitted to bar, 1963, West Virginia; 1964, District of Columbia; 1979, Pennsylvania. *Education:* West Virginia University (A.B., 1960); University of Michigan (J.D., 1963). ***COURSES: Antitrust, Administrative Law, Trademarks, Copyrights, Economic Regulation.

M. BETH LYON*, (Assistant Professor of Law; Director, Farmworkers Legal Aid Clinic)**, born Vero Beach, Florida, July 12, 1966; admitted to bar, 1995, New York; 1997, District of Columbia; 2001, Pennsylvania. *Education:* University of North Carolina (B.A., 1988); Georgetown University, School of Foreign Services (M.S., 1994); Georgetown University Law Center (J.D., 1994). ***COURSES: Poverty, Immigration, International; Clinical. ***Email:*** lyon@law.villanova.edu

GREGORY P. MAGARIAN*, (Assistant Professor of Law)**, *Education:* Yale University (B.A., 1989); University of Michigan Public Policy Studies (M.P.P., 1993); University of Michigan Law School (J.D., 1993). ***COURSES: Constitutional Law I & II, Political Speech.

JAMES EDWARD MAULE*, (Professor of Law)**, born Philadelphia, Pennsylvania, November 26, 1951; admitted to bar, 1976, Pennsylvania; 1986, U.S. Tax Court. *Education:* University of Pennsylvania (B.S., 1973); Villanova University School of Law (J.D., 1976); George Washington University (LL.M., 1979). ***COURSES: Federal Income Taxation, Federal Estate and Gift Taxation, Computers and the Law.

(This Listing Continued)

VILLANOVA UNIVERSITY SCHOOL OF LAW—Continued

MICHAEL MULRONEY*, (Professor of Law; Director, Graduate Tax Program)**, born Chicago, Illinois, February 26, 1932; admitted to bar, 1959, Iowa; 1960, District of Columbia. *Education:* State University of Iowa (B.S.C., 1954); Harvard University (J.D., 1959). ***COURSES: Federal Taxation, Professional Responsibility.

JOHN F. MURPHY*, (Professor of Law)**, born Port Chester, New York, April 25, 1937; admitted to bar, 1963, District of Columbia; 1969, Kansas; 1987, Pennsylvania. *Education:* Cornell University (B.A., 1959; LL.B., 1962). ***COURSES: Public International Law, International Business Transactions, Comparative Law, International Human Rights.

***J. WILLARD O'BRIEN*, (Professor & Dean Emeritus)**, born New York, New York, October 19, 1930; admitted to bar, 1957, New York; 1983, Pennsylvania. *Education:* Fordham University (B.S., 1952; J.D., 1957).

JENNIFER O'HARE*, (Professor of Law)**, *Education:* Wharton School of Business, University of Pennsylvania (B.S., 1986); The George Washington University Law School (J.D., 1990). ***COURSES: Corporations I and II, Securities Act of 1933, Securities Act of 1934.

LEONARD PACKEL*, (Professor of Law)**, born Philadelphia, Pennsylvania, April 7, 1935; admitted to bar, 1961, Pennsylvania. *Education:* University of Pennsylvania (B.S., 1957); Harvard University (J.D., 1960). ***COURSES: Trial Advocacy, Evidence, Professional Responsibility, Criminal Law.

MICHELE PISTONE*, (Assistant Professor of Law and Director of Clinical Programs)**, *Education:* New York University (B.S., 1986); St. John's University School of Law (J.D., 1989); Georgetown University Law Center (LL.M., 1999). ***COURSES: Immigration and Asylum Law Clinic.

ANNE BOWEN POULIN*, (Professor of Law)**, born Port Jefferson, New York, October 10, 1948; admitted to bar, 1973, Maine; 1975, Illinois; 1983, Pennsylvania. *Education:* Radcliffe College (B.A., 1969); University of Maine (J.D., 1973); University of Michigan (LL.M., 1975). ***COURSES: Criminal Procedure, Evidence.

RICHARD REDDING*, (Associate Professor of Law; Director, Law and Psychology Program)**, born Miami, Florida, September 17, 1964; admitted to bar, 1992, Virginia. *Education:* Hampden-Sydney College (B.A., 1984); Vanderbilt University (M.S., 1986); Washington and Lee University (J.D., 1992); University of Virginia (PhD, 1997). ***COURSES: Criminal Law, Social Science Applied in Law, Mental Health Law. ***Email:*** redding@law.villanova.edu

FREDERICK P. ROTHMAN*, (Professor of Law Emeritus)**, born Baltimore, Maryland, November 14, 1940; admitted to bar, 1964, Maryland; 1965, District of Columbia. *Education:* Cornell University (A.B., 1962; J.D., 1965). ***COURSES: Corporate Finance, Decedents' Estates and Trusts, Estate Planning, Federal Taxation, Will Drafting, Corporations.

DVEERA SEGAL*, (Assistant Professor of Law; Director, Civil Justice Clinic)**, *Education:* SUNY, Albany (B.A., 1975); Harvard Law School (J.D., 1979). ***COURSES: Villanova Community Legal Service Clinic.

LOUIS J. SIRICO, JR.*, (Professor of Law)**, born New Haven, Connecticut, September 22, 1945; admitted to bar, 1973, Connecticut; 1975, District of Columbia. *Education:* Yale University (B.A., 1967); University of Texas (J.D., 1972). ***COURSES: Property, Constitutional Convention, Legal Writing, Public Interest.

WALTER J. TAGGART*, (Professor of Law)**, born New York, New York, August 4, 1943; admitted to bar, 1968, Pennsylvania. *Education:* Belmont Abbey College (A.B., 1965); Villanova University School of Law (J.D., 1968). ***COURSES: Commercial Law, Bankruptcy, Real Estate, Federal Courts.

RICHARD C. TURKINGTON*, (Professor of Law)**, born Cortland, New York, October 5, 1940; admitted to bar, 1969, Michigan. *Education:* Wayne State University (B.A., 1963; J.D., 1966); New York University (LL.M., 1967). ***COURSES: Constitutional Law, Torts, Privacy.

WILLIAM D. VALENTE*, (Professor of Law Emeritus)**, born Philadelphia, Pennsylvania, October 10, 1924; admitted to bar, 1949, Pennsylvania. *Education:* University of Pennsylvania (A.B., 1947; J.D., 1949). ***COURSES: Constitutional Law, Education Law, Local Government Law.

ELLEN WERTHEIMER*, (Professor of Law)**, born New York, New York, November 29, 1953; admitted to bar, 1980, Pennsylvania. *Education:* Yale University (B.A., 1975; J.D., 1979). ***COURSES: Contracts, Products Liability, Medical Malpractice, Supreme Court.

WAKE FOREST UNIVERSITY SCHOOL OF LAW

P. O. BOX 7206
WINSTON-SALEM, NORTH CAROLINA 27109-7206

WASHBURN UNIVERSITY SCHOOL OF LAW

1700 COLLEGE
TOPEKA, KANSAS 66621

WASHINGTON AND LEE UNIVERSITY SCHOOL OF LAW

SYDNEY LEWIS HALL
LEXINGTON, VIRGINIA 24450
Telephone: (540) 463-8504
Fax: (540) 463-8488

(This Listing Continued)

WASHINGTON AND LEE UNIVERSITY SCHOOL OF LAW —Continued

ABA Approved Since 1923.

The school that is now Washington and Lee University was established in 1749. Its name was changed several times in its early years, but the school has been called Washington Academy or College since 1798, when the Trustees took that name in gratitude for an endowment provided by President George Washington. Washington's gift was then the largest gift made to a private educational institution in America. The University became known as Washington and Lee University in 1871, following the death of General Robert E. Lee, who served as president from 1865 to 1870. It was during General Lee's presidency, and as a result of his strong commitment to professional education, that the Lexington Law School, founded by Judge John White Brockenbrough in 1849, became affiliated with Washington College. The Law School became an integral part of the University in 1870 and soon flourished under the leadership of John Randolph Tucker, a distinguished constitutional scholar who also served as Member of Congress, Attorney General of Virginia, and President of the American Bar Association. The Washington and Lee University School of Law is approved by the American Bar Association and has been a member of the Association of American Law Schools since 1920. A distinctive feature of the University and the Law School is an honor system which dates from the administration of General Lee and is entirely the responsibility of students.

The School of Law, like the University, has always chosen to be small. The School of Law increased the size of its student body in 1976, when it moved into Sydney Lewis Hall, its present building, but it remains the smallest of the national law schools, in terms of student enrollment, with an entering class each year of approximately 120 students. The full-time faculty numbers 34; one faculty member from another division of the University and 12 adjunct faculty also offer courses in the School of Law. Sydney Lewis Hall, funded by a generous gift from Frances and Sydney Lewis of Richmond, Virginia, is a modern facility containing classrooms, a moot courtroom, faculty and administrative offices, clinical facilities, and space for student activities. The building contains no classroom capable of seating more than 75 students, thus ensuring small classes. In recent years, approximately 60% of W&L classes have had 20 students or fewer. A carrel or office space is provided for each student, and a computer cluster is available for word processing and legal research. An addition completed in 1992 includes the Lewis F. Powell, Jr. Archives, which contain the papers of Justice Powell and those of several other alumni, faculty, and friends of the Law School, including the late Walter E. Hoffman, Judge of the United States District Court for the Eastern District of Virginia. The Archives also contain the Bankruptcy Reform Act papers of former Congressman M. Caldwell Butler.

The law library contains more than 382,900 volumes, including microform materials, appellate records and briefs, and government documents. It maintains subscriptions to more than 1,250 journals, over 250 looseleaf reporting services, and more than 500 series of documents issued by international organizations and the U.S. government. Lexis and Westlaw terminals are provided. The stacks, carrels and reading areas are available to students and faculty 24 hours a day, seven days a week.

The Frances Lewis Law Center is the research arm of the School of Law. Each year the Law Center appoints a Frances Lewis Scholar in Residence who spends a semester in residence, working on his or her own research and teaching a seminar. These scholars have included Harold J. Berman of Emory; Hilary Charlesworth of the Australian National University; Richard Delgado of the University of Colorado; Deborah DeMott of Duke University; Herbert Fingarette of the University of California (Santa Barbara); Linda R. Hirshman of Chicago-Kent; Brian P. Levack of the University of Texas; Curtis R. Reitz of the University of Pennsylvania; Victor G. Rosenblum of Northwestern; Yvonne Scannell of Trinity College, Dublin; Thomas L. Shaffer of Notre Dame; and Calvin Woodard of the University of Virginia.

In addition, the Frances Lewis Law Center brings visiting judges and lawyers to the campus for varying periods, sometimes as long as a semester. It supports research by Washington and Lee faculty and students, and it convenes scholarly colloquia on topics of current legal interest.

The instructional program is designed to provide students with a legal education in the fullest sense; not only the technical tools needed for the practice of law, but an understanding of how law operates in our society and a sensitivity to the ethical imperatives of the profession. Intense faculty-student interaction is encouraged. First-year research and writing is taught in small sections of substantive courses by full-time tenured and tenure-track faculty. The regular faculty also teach the upper-level clinical courses as part of their course loads. All first-year courses are required, with the first semester focusing on common law subjects and the second semester on many of the procedural aspects of our legal system. Most second- and third-year courses are elective. There are no "majors," and students are encouraged to obtain a broad-based legal education. Nevertheless, a student who wishes to do so may progress through courses of increasing complexity and intensiveness in areas of particular interest to him or her. Each student is required to complete a major writing project as a condition of graduation.

Dean: David F. Partlett (540) 463-8502
Admissions and Student Affairs: Susan Palmer (540) 463-8503
Financial Aid: Cynthia Hintze (540) 463-8032
Library: Sarah K. Wiant (540) 463-8540
Placement: Elizabeth K. Peck (540) 463-8536
Alumni Affairs: Elizabeth Turley (540) 463-8584

FULL TIME FACULTY

DAVID F. PARTLETT*, (Vice President, Dean and Professor of Law)**, born Sydney, Australia, August 10, 1947; admitted to bar, 1971, New South Wales; 1978 Australian Capital Territory. *Education:* University of Sydney, School of Law (LL.B., 1970); University of Michigan Law School (LL.M., 1974); University of Virginia (S.J.D., 1980). ***COURSES: Torts, Advanced Torts, Child Mental Health and the Law, Judicial Remedies. ***Email:*** partlettd@wlu.edu

DENIS JOLY BRION*, (Professor of Law)**, born 1939; admitted to bar, 1971, Virginia: 1971, District of Columbia. *Education:* Northwestern University (B.S., 1961); University of Virginia (J.D., 1970). ***COURSES: Property, Land Use Regulation, Commercial Law, Law & Economics, Legal Profession. ***Email:*** briond@wlu.edu

DARRYL K. BROWN*, (Associate Professor of Law and Alumni Faculty Fellow)**, born Maryland, January 17, 1962; admitted to bar, 1991, Georgia; 1997, Ohio. *Education:* East Carolina University (B.A., 1984); College of William and Mary (M.A., 1991); University of Virginia (J.D., 1990). ***COURSES: Criminal Law and Procedure, Torts, White-Collar Crime. ***Email:*** browndk@wlu.edu

***SAMUEL WOLFE CALHOUN*, (Professor of Law)**, born 1949;

(This Listing Continued)

WASHINGTON AND LEE UNIVERSITY SCHOOL OF LAW —Continued

admitted to bar, 1974, Georgia. *Education:* Harvard (B.A., 1971); University of Georgia (J.D., 1974). ***COURSES:*** Contracts, Commercial Transactions, Abortion Controversy Seminar, Consumer Bankruptcy. ***Email:*** calhouns@wlu.edu

DAVID S. CAUDILL*, (Professor of Law)**, born 1951; admitted to bar, 1981, Texas; 1982, California. *Education:* Michigan St. University (B.A., 1973); Vrije Universiteit te Amsterdam (Ph.D., 1989); University of Houston Law Center (J.D., 1981). ***COURSES: Contracts, Professional Responsibility, Sports Law, Jurisprudence, Law & Psychology. ***Email:*** caudilld@wlu.edu

MAUREEN B. CAVANAUGH*, (Assistant Professor of Law and Alumni Faculty Fellow)**, born 1955; admitted to bar, 1995, Minnesota. *Education:* Swarthmore College (B.A., 1975); Cornell University (M.A., 1977; Ph.D., 1980); University of Minnesota (J.D., 1995). ***COURSES: Tax, Pensions. ***Email:*** cavanaughm@wlu.edu

ROBERT T. DANFORTH*, (Assistant Professor of Law)**, born 1957; admitted to bar, 1987, North Carolina; 1988, District of Columbia; 1993, Virginia. *Education:* Washington University (B.A., 1980); Duke University School of Law (J.D., 1986). ***COURSES: Trusts & Estates, Estate Planning, Taxation of Trusts & Estates. ***Email:*** danforthr@wlu.edu

LAURA S. FITZGERALD*, (Associate Professor of Law)**, born 1962; admitted to bar, 1989, Pennsylvania; 1990, District of Columbia; 1991, New York. *Education:* Hollins College (B.A., 1984); Yale (J.D., 1987). ***COURSES: Civil Procedure, Juris & Procedure, Constitutional Law. ***Email:*** fitzgeraldl@wlu.edu

WILLIAM S. GEIMER*, (Professor of Law, Emeritus)**, born 1940; admitted to bar, 1969, North Carolina; 1984, Virginia. *Education:* East Tennessee St. University (B.A., 1962); University of North Carolina (J.D., 1969). ***COURSES: Criminal Law, Criminal Procedure, Juvenile Law. ***Email:*** geimerw@wlu.edu

ROGER DOUGLAS GROOT*, (Class of 1975 Alumni Professor)**, born 1942; admitted to bar, 1971, North Carolina; 1986, Virginia. *Education:* Vanderbilt University (B.A., 1962); University of North Carolina (J.D., 1971). ***COURSES: Criminal Law, Criminal Procedure. ***Email:*** grootr@wlu.edu

MARK HOWARD GRUNEWALD*, (Professor of Law)**, born 1947; admitted to bar, 1973, District of Columbia; 1979, Virginia. *Education:* Emory University (B.A., 1969); George Washington University (J.D., 1972). ***COURSES: Employment, Labor Law, Administrative Law, Constitutional Law, Cyberlaw, Information & Privacy Law. ***Email:*** grunewaldm@wlu.edu

LOUISE A. HALPER*, (Professor of Law)**, admitted to bar, 1973, New Jersey; 1981, New York. *Education:* Brandeis University (B.A., 1967); Rutgers University (J.D., 1973); New York University (LL.M., 1991). ***COURSES: Environmental Law, Legal History, Property. ***Email:*** halperl@wlu.edu

EDWARD O. HENNEMAN*, (Associate Professor of Law)**, born 1937; admitted to bar, 1963, New York. *Education:* Yale University (B.A., 1959); Harvard (J.D., 1962). ***COURSES: Estates & Trusts, Estate Planning, Elderlaw, Family, Property, Est. & Gift Taxation. ***Email:*** hennemane@wlu.edu

C. QUINCE HOPKINS*, (Assistant Professor of Law)**, admitted to bar, 1989, Maryland; 1993, District of Columbia, 1995, Arizona; 1994, Pascua Yaqui Tribal Court. *Education:* St. John's College (B.A., 1983); University of Maryland School of Law (J.D., 1989); Stanford Law School (J.S.M., 1998). ***COURSES: Family Law, Law & Society, Legal Ethics, Civil Procedure, Criminal Law. ***Email:*** hopkinsq@wlu.edu

MARGARET HOWARD*, (Professor of Law)**, born Rocky Mount, North Carolina; admitted to bar, 1975, Missouri. *Education:* Duke University (A.B., 1969); Washington University School of Law (M.S.W., 1975; J.D., 1975); Yale Law School (LL.M., 1981). ***COURSES: Bankruptcy, Commercial Law, Contracts, Creditors' Rights. ***Email:*** howardm@wlu.edu

LYMAN PAUL QUENTIN JOHNSON*, (Robert O. Bentley Professor of Law)**, born 1951; admitted to bar, 1978, Minnesota. *Education:* Carleton College (B.A., 1973); University of Minnesota (J.D., 1978). ***COURSES: Corporate Law, Business Law, Corporate Finance, Securities Regulation. ***Email:*** johnsonlp@wlu.edu

TIMOTHY S. JOST*, (Robert L. Willett Family Professor of Law)**, born Reedley, California, November 25, 1948; admitted to bar, 1975, Illinois; 1982, Ohio. *Education:* University of California at Santa Cruz (B.A., 1970); University of Chicago (J.D., 1975). ***COURSES: Health Care Law, Insurance, Law & Medicine, Personal Property, Real Property. ***Email:*** jostt@wlu.edu

FREDERIC LEE KIRGIS*, (Law Alumni Association Professor)**, born 1934; admitted to bar, 1961, Colorado; 1964, District of Columbia; 1983, Virginia. *Education:* Yale (B.A., 1957); University of California-Berkeley (J.D., 1960). ***COURSES: Contracts, International Law, Conflict of Law, International Organizations. ***Email:*** kirgisr@wlu.edu

RONALD J. KROTOSZYNSKI*, (Associate Professor of Law and Ethan Allen Faculty Fellow)**, born Indianapolis, Indiana, November 3, 1967; admitted to bar, 1991, Georgia; 1992, District of Columbia. *Education:* Emory University (B.A., 1987); Emory University (M.A., 1987); Duke Law School (J.D., 1991); Duke Law School (LL.M., 1991). ***COURSES: Administrative Law, Professional Responsibility, Communications Law. ***Email:*** krotoszynskir@wlu.edu

CLIFFORD LARSEN*, (Associate Professor of Law)**, born 1958; admitted to bar, 1987, New York; 1988, Louisiana; 1993, Paris, France. *Education:* Tulane University (B.A., 1980); Oxford University (B.A., 1984; M.A., 1990); University of Virginia (J.D., 1986). ***COURSES: Comparative Law, Contracts, International Transactions. ***Email:*** larsenc@wlu.edu

LEWIS HENRY LARUE*, (Class of 1958 Alumni Professor)**, born 1938; admitted to bar, 1962, Virginia. *Education:* Washington & Lee University (A.B., 1959); Harvard University (LL.B., 1962). ***COURSES: Constitutional Law, Evidence, Jurisprudence, Federal Jurisdiction. ***Email:*** laruel@wlu.edu

ANN MACLEAN MASSIE*, (Professor of Law)**, born 1943; admitted to bar, 1971, Georgia. *Education:* Duke University (B.A., 1966); University of Michigan (M.A., 1967); University of Virginia (J.D., 1971). ***COURSES: Constitutional Law, Criminal Procedure, Health Law, Law & Medicine. ***Email:*** massiea@wlu.edu

ANDREW WOLFE MCTHENIA, JR.*, (James P. Morefield Professor of Law, Emeritus)**, born 1935; admitted to bar, 1963, District of Columbia; 1963, Virginia. *Education:* Washington & Lee University (A.B., 1958; LL.B., 1963); Columbia University (M.A., 1960). ***COURSES: Clinical, Contracts, Remedies, Social Legislation, Law & Psychiatry, Office Practice. ***Email:*** mctheniaa@wlu.edu

DAVID K. MILLON*, (Associate Dean for Academic Affairs and J.B. Stombock Professor of Law)**, born 1953; admitted to bar, 1983, Massachusetts. *Education:* Ohio State University (B.A., 1975; M.A., 1976); Cornell University (M.A., 1978; Ph.D., 1982); Harvard University (J.D., 1983). ***COURSES: Business Organizations, Corporations, English Legal History. ***Email:*** milliond@wlu.edu

***BLAKE DOMINIC MORANT*, (Professor of Law and Director,**

(This Listing Continued)

WASHINGTON AND LEE UNIVERSITY SCHOOL OF LAW —Continued

Frances Lewis Law Center), born 1952; admitted to bar, 1978, Virginia; 1986, District of Columbia. *Education:* University of Virginia (B.A., 1975; J.D., 1978). ***COURSES:*** Contracts, Entertainment Law, Administrative Law, Communications Law. ***Email:*** morantb@wlu.edu

BRIAN CAMERON MURCHISON*, (Professor of Law)**, born 1952; admitted to bar, 1980, District of Columbia. *Education:* Yale (B.A., 1974; J.D., 1979). ***COURSES: Administrative Law, Communications Law, Communicative Torts, Torts. ***Email:*** murchisonb@wlu.edu

MARY ZANOLLI NATKIN*, (Associate Clinical Professor)**, born Pittsburgh, Pennsylvania, October 4, 1957; admitted to bar, 1985, Virginia. *Education:* University of California (B.A., 1979); Washington & Lee (J.D., 1985). ***COURSES: Clinical, Academic Support, Writing. ***Email:*** natkinm@wlu.edu

JAMES MICHAEL PHEMISTER*, (Professor of Law)**, born 1944; admitted to bar, 1969, Ohio; 1977, Virginia. *Education:* Purdue University (B.S., 1966); Northwestern University (J.D., 1969). ***COURSES: Evidence, Pretrial Advocacy, Trial Advocacy. ***Email:*** phemisterj@wlu.edu

DOUG RENDLEMAN*, (Robert E. R. Huntley Professor of Law)**, admitted to bar, 1968, Iowa; 1977, Virginia. *Education:* University of Iowa (B.A., 1963; M.A., 1965; J.D., 1968); University of Michigan (LL.M., 1970). ***COURSES: Civil Procedure, Conflict of Laws, Creditors Rights, Property, Remedies. ***Email:*** rendlemand@wlu.edu

ADAM F. SCALES*, (Assistant Professor of Law)**, born 1969; admitted to bar, 1994, Minnesota. *Education:* University of Massachusetts (B.A., 1991); University of Michigan (J.D., 1993). ***COURSES: Torts, Civil Procedure & Jurisdiction, Insurance, Legal Philosophy. ***Email:*** scalesa@wlu.edu

JOAN M. SHAUGHNESSY*, (Professor of Law)**, born 1953; admitted to bar, 1980, New York. *Education:* State University of New York at Binghamton (B.A., 1975); University of Chicago (J.D., 1978). ***COURSES: Civil Procedure, Complex Litigation, Evidence, Federal Courts, Jurisprudence. ***Email:*** shaughnessyj@wlu.edu

ROY L. STEINHEIMER, JR.*, (Robert E. R. Huntley Professor of Law, Emeritus)**, born 1916; admitted to bar, 1941, New York; 1951, Michigan; 1974, Virginia. *Education:* University of Kansas (A.B., 1937); University of Michigan (J.D., 1940). ***COURSES: Commercial Law, Consumer Protection.

SCOTT E. SUNDBY*, (Professor of Law & Acting Director, Frances Lewis Law Center)**, born 1958; admitted to bar, 1985, California. *Education:* Vanderbilt (B.A., 1980); Cornell (J.D., 1983). ***COURSES: Capital Punishment, Constitutional Law, Criminal Law, Criminal Procedure. ***Email:*** sundbys@wlu.edu

JOSEPH EDWARD ULRICH*, (Professor of Law, Emeritus)**, born 1938; admitted to bar, 1961, Kentucky, Virginia. *Education:* Washington & Lee University (A.B., 1959; L.L.B., 1961). ***COURSES: Business Bankruptcy, Commercial Law, Creditors Rights, Future Interests, Torts.

W. BRADLEY WENDEL*, (Assistant Professor of Law)**, born Reading, Pennsylvania, May 10, 1969; admitted to bar, 1994, Washington. *Education:* Rice University (B.A., 1991); Duke University School of Law (J.D., 1994); Columbia University Law School (LL.M., 1998). ***COURSES: Legal Ethics, Torts. ***Email:*** wendelb@wlu.edu

SARAH KIRSTEN WIANT*, (Law Librarian & Professor)**, born 1946. *Education:* Western State College (B.A., 1968); University North Texas (M.L.S., 1970); Washington & Lee University (J.D., 1978). ***COURSES: Admiralty, Intellectual Property, Torts. ***Email:*** wiants@wlu.edu

WASHINGTON UNIVERSITY SCHOOL OF LAW

ONE BROOKINGS DRIVE, CAMPUS BOX 1120
ST. LOUIS, MISSOURI 63130-4899
Telephone: (314) 935-6400
Fax: (314) 935-6493
http://www.wulaw.wustl.edu

ABA Approved Since 1923.

Founded in 1867, Washington University School of Law is the oldest private law school in continuous operation west of the Mississippi River. A charter member of the AALS and accredited by the ABA, the school was one of the first law schools to graduate women. The law school is located on the beautiful and serene 169-acre Hilltop Campus bordered by Forest Park (the site of the 1904 World's Fair) and the residential communities of Clayton and University City.

The Washington University faculty is dedicated to the professional education and evelopment of its students. The student/faculty ratio of 15:1 and the participation of experienced practicing lawyers in selected skills courses permit many small classes and seminars during the second and third years. Yearly programs presented by the School's Center for Interdisciplinary Studies, Institute for Global Legal Studies and Public Interest Law Speakers Series complement the academic program. Distinctive features include a faculty nationally recognized for its accessibility to students and a respected clinical program in which every student is guaranteed enrollment in at least one clinic.

The School of Law offers a Masters degree (LL.M.) in Taxation and a LL.M. in U.S. Law for International Students, with a new LL.M. program in Intellectual Property beginning in 2001. Combined study programs exist with eight other Washington University graduate departments: Social Work (J.D./M.S.W.); the Health Administration Department of the School of Medicine (J.D./M.H.A.); Business (J.D./M.B.A); Economics (J.D./M.S.Ec.); Political Science (J.D./M.A.); East Asian Studies (J.D./M.A.); European Studies (J.D./M.A.); Engineering and Applied Science (J.D./M.S. or M.A.). Additional combined-degree programs are available by arrangement with other departments.

The School of Law publishes three student-edited law review periodicals, the **Washington University Law Quarterly, Washington University Journal of Law and Policy**, and the new **Washington University Global Studies Law Review**. A very active moot court program, mock trial competitions and competitions on negotiation and client counseling are available. Law students participate in a variety of other programs, including the Women's Law Caucus, the National Association for Public Interest Law, the Black Law Students Association, the Federalist Society, and the Student Bar Association. The student body is self-regulated through the Law School Honor Council. Students are eligible for election to the Order of the Coif. Students also serve on many joint committees with faculty members.

The School of Law moved into its new building, Anheuser-Busch Hall, in December, 1996. The new building combines traditional architecture with a modern, state-of-the-art learning environment.

(This Listing Continued)

WASHINGTON UNIVERSITY SCHOOL OF LAW
—Continued

Dean: Joel Seligman (314) 935-6420
Associate Dean of Faculty: Susan F. Appleton (314) 935-6449
Associate Dean for Academic Affairs: Daniel L. Keating (314) 935-6481
Associate Dean for Student Affairs: Katherine Goldwasser (314) 935-7573
Associate Dean, Information Resources: Philip Berwick (314) 935-4042
Associate Dean for Student Services: Mark Smith (314) 935-6489
Assistant Dean for Admissions & Financial Aid: Janet Bolin (314) 935-4525
Associate Dean for External Relations: David M. Becker (314) 935-6492
Assistant Dean for Graduate & Joint Degree Programs: Michele Shoresman (314) 935-7244
Director of Development: Ronald S. Gray (314) 935-7056
Director of External Affairs: Serena Yee (314) 935-6430
Assistant Dean for Operations: Pete Milne (314) 935-4438

FULL TIME FACULTY

JOEL SELIGMAN*, (Dean and Ethan A.H. Shepley University Professor)**, born New York, New York, January 11, 1950; admitted to bar, 1976, California. *Education:* University of California at Los Angeles (A.B., 1971); Harvard University Law School (J.D., 1974). ***COURSES: Corporate Finance, Corporations, Securities Regulation. ***Email:*** seligman@wulaw.wustl.edu

JANE H. AIKEN*, (Professor of Law)**, born Greenville, South Carolina, April 13, 1955; admitted to bar, 1983, District of Columbia; 1998, Missouri. *Education:* Hollins College (B.A., 1977); New York University School of Law (J.D., 1981); Georgetown University Law Center (LL.M., 1985). ***COURSES: Evidence, Torts, Clinic, Family Law, Alternative Dispute. ***Email:*** aiken@wulaw.wustl.edu

SUSAN FRELICH APPLETON*, (Associate Dean of Faculty and Lemma Barkeloo and Phoebe Couzins Professor of Law)**, born St. Louis, Missouri, January 29, 1948; admitted to bar, 1973, Missouri. *Education:* Vassar College (A.B., 1970); University of California at Berkeley, Boalt Hall School of Law (J.D., 1973). ***COURSES: Reproductive Health and Privacy Law, Family Law, Criminal Law, Conflict of Laws, Reproductive Control. ***Email:*** appleton@wulaw.wustl.edu

STUART BANNER*, (Professor of Law)**, born New York, N.Y., November 20, 1963; admitted to bar, 1990, New York. *Education:* Yale University (B.A., 1985); Stanford University Law School (J.D., 1988). ***COURSES: Supreme Court, American Legal History, Property, Capital Punishment Clinic. ***Email:*** banner@wulaw.wustl.edu

DAVID M. BECKER*, (Associate Dean for External Relations and Joseph H. Zumbalen Professor of the Law of Property)**, born Chicago, Illinois, December 31, 1935; admitted to bar, 1960, Illinois. *Education:* Harvard University (A.B., 1957); University of Chicago (J.D., 1960). ***COURSES: Property Law, Landlord-Tenant Law, Estate Planning Law, Future Interests. ***Email:*** becker@wulaw.wustl.edu

NEIL N. BERNSTEIN*, (Professor of Law)**, born Cheyenne, Wyoming, May 18, 1932; admitted to bar, 1957, Wyoming and District of Columbia; 1962, New York; 1973, Missouri. *Education:* University of Michigan (B.A., 1954); Yale Law School (LL.B., 1957). ***COURSES: Employment Law, Insurance Law, Labor Law. ***Email:*** bernsten@wulaw.wustl.edu

CHRISTOPHER ALAN BRACEY*, (Associate Professor of Law)**, born Washington, D.C., December 17, 1970; admitted to bar, 1995, Maryland; 1997, District of Columbia. *Education:* University of North Carolina (B.S., 1992); Harvard Law School (J.D., 1995). ***COURSES: Civil Procedure, Civil Rights, Criminal Procedure, Race Relations Law. ***Email:*** bracey@wulaw.wustl.edu

KATHLEEN F. BRICKEY*, (James Carr Professor of Criminal Jurisprudence)**, born Austin, Texas, September 16, 1944. *Education:* University of Kentucky (A.B., 1965; J.D., 1968). ***COURSES: White Collar Crime, Criminal Law, Federal Criminal Law. ***Email:*** brickey@wulaw.wustl.edu

KATHLEEN CLARK*, (Professor of Law)**, born Columbus, Ohio, December 20, 1961; admitted to bar, 1990, Pennsylvania; 1993, District of Columbia. *Education:* Yale University (B.A., 1984); Yale Law School (J.D., 1990). ***COURSES: Legal Ethics, Secrecy and Whistle Blowing, Government Ethics. ***Email:*** kathleen@wulaw.wustl.edu

CLARK D. CUNNINGHAM*, (Professor of Law)**, born Detroit, Michigan, September 1, 1953; admitted to bar, 1981, Michigan; 1989, Missouri. *Education:* Dartmouth College (A.B., 1975); Wayne State University (J.D., 1981). ***COURSES: Legal Ethics, Pretrial, Law and Linguistics, Clinic, Law and Social Science, Comparative Constitutional Law, Law, Language & Culture. ***Email:*** cunningc@wulaw.wustl.edu

BILL BURCH DOROTHY, III*, (Lecturer in Law)**, born Keosauqua, Iowa, September 1, 1959; admitted to bar, 1987, Missouri; 1988, Illinois. *Education:* University of Iowa (B.A., 1984); Southern Illinois University (J.D., 1987). ***COURSES: Legal Research and Writing. ***Email:*** bbdorth@wulaw.wustl.edu

REBECCA S. DRESSER*, (Professor of Law and Professor, Humanities in Medicine Program)**, born Annapolis, Maryland, April 5, 1952; admitted to bar, 1979, Wisconsin. *Education:* Indiana University (A.B., 1973; M.S., 1975); Harvard (J.D., 1979). ***COURSES: Biomedical Research Law, Law & Bioethics, Criminal Law. ***Email:*** dresser@wulaw.wustl.edu

JOHN N. DROBAK*, (Professor of Law and Professor of Economics)**, born Binghamton, New York, February, 1947; admitted to bar, 1975, Connecticut; 1976, California. *Education:* Massachusetts Institute of Technology (B.S., 1970); Stanford University Law School (J.D., 1973). ***COURSES: Antitrust Law, Utility Regulation, Civil Procedure, Theory of Property Rights. ***Email:*** drobak@wulaw.wustl.edu

DORSEY D. ELLIS, JR.*, (William R. Orthwein Distinguished Professor of Law)**, born Cape Girardeau, Missouri, May 18, 1938; admitted to bar, 1967, New York; 1976, Iowa. *Education:* Maryville College (B.A., 1960); University of Chicago (J.D., 1963). ***COURSES: Antitrust Law, Torts, Products Liability Law, Law and Economics, Agency and Partnership. ***Email:*** ellis@wulaw.wustl.edu

LEE EPSTEIN*, (Professor of Law and Edward Mallinckrodt Distinguished University Professor of Political Science)**, born New York, March 17, 1958. *Education:* Emory University (B.A., 1980; M.A., 1982; PhD., 1983). ***COURSES: Social Science & Law, Supreme Court, Law & Social Change. ***Email:*** epstein@artsci.wustl.edu

DENISE Z. FIELD*, (Lecturer in Law)**, born Philadelphia, Pennsylvania, April 07, 1954; admitted to bar, 1978, District of Columbia. *Education:* Princeton University; Harvard University (A.B.,1975); Yale Law School (J.D., 1978). ***COURSES: Legal Research and Writing. ***Email:*** dzfields@wulaw.wustl.edu

(This Listing Continued)

WASHINGTON UNIVERSITY SCHOOL OF LAW —Continued

BARBARA FLAGG*, (Professor of Law)**, born San Diego, California, January 30, 1947. *Education:* University of California at Riverside (A.B., 1967; M.A., 1971); University of California at Berkeley, Boalt Hall School of Law (J.D., 1987). ***COURSES: Constitutional Law, Nontraditional Perspectives, Critical Race Theory, Advanced Legal Reasoning. ***Email:*** flagg@wulaw.wustl.edu

FRANCES H. FOSTER*, (Professor of Law)**, born Ann Arbor, Michigan, December 8, 1955. *Education:* Princeton University (A.B., 1977); Yale Law School (J.D., 1981; M.A., 1981); Stanford University (J.S.D., 1987). ***COURSES: Research Topics in Socialist Law, Socialist Law in Transition: China, Cuba and Russia, Trusts and Estates. ***Email:*** foster@wulaw.wustl.edu

KATHERINE GOLDWASSER*, (Associate Dean for Student Affairs and Professor of Law)**, born Oakland, California, June 4, 1949; admitted to bar, 1978, Illinois. *Education:* University of Wisconsin; University of Illinois (B.A., 1971); Temple University School of Law (J.D., 1978). ***COURSES: Criminal Procedure, Trial, Evidence. ***Email:*** goldwask@wulaw.wustl.edu

MICHAEL M. GREENFIELD*, (Walter D. Coles Professor of Law)**, born Chicago, Illinois, August 21, 1944. *Education:* Grinnell College (A.B., 1966); University of Texas (J.D., 1969). ***COURSES: Consumer Protection Law, Commercial Law, Contracts. ***Email:*** greenfim@wulaw.wustl.edu

LEIGH HUNT GREENHAW*, (Lecturer in Law)**, ***COURSES: Business and Legal Research Seminar for International LL.M. students. ***Email:*** greenhaw@wulaw.wustl.edu

JOHN OWEN HALEY*, (Wiley B. Rutledge Professor of Law)**, born Ft. Bragg, North Carolina, March 24, 1942; admitted to bar, 1969, Alabama. *Education:* Princeton (A.B., 1964); Yale (LL.B., 1969); University of Washington (LL.M., 1971). ***COURSES: Japanese Law, Comparative Law, Contracts, Transnational Litigation. ***Email:*** johaley@wulaw.wustl.edu

PETER A. JOY*, (Professor of Law)**, born Youngstown, Ohio, December, 2, 1951; admitted to bar, 1979, District of Columbia. *Education:* Youngstown State University (A.B., 1974); Case Western Reserve (J.D., 1977). ***COURSES: Criminal Justice Clinic, Trial, Professional Responsibility. ***Email:*** joy@wulaw.wustl.edu

DANIEL L. KEATING*, (Associate Dean for Academic Affairs and Tyrrell Williams Professor of Law)**, born Chicago, Illinois, October 14, 1961; admitted to bar, 1986, Illinois. *Education:* Monmouth College (B.A., 1983); University of Chicago (J.D., 1986). ***COURSES: Commercial Paper, Bankruptcy Law, UCC : Article 2, Reorganization Seminar. ***Email:*** keating@wulaw.wustl.edu

F. SCOTT KIEFF*, (Associate Professor)**, born Chicago, Illinois, August 6, 1969; admitted to bar, 1995, New York; 1997, District of Columbia; 1999, Illinois. *Education:* Massachusetts Institute of Technology (S.B., 1991); University of Pennsylvania (J.D., 1994). ***COURSES: Intellectual Property, Contracts, Civil Procedure, Science and Law, Ethics, Business. ***Email:*** kieff@wulaw.wustl.edu

PAULINE KIM*, (Professor of Law)**, born St. Louis, Missouri, September 25, 1962; admitted to bar, 1988, California; 1994, Missouri. *Education:* Harvard University (A.B., 1984; J.D., 1988). ***COURSES: Employment Law, Pretrial Litigation, Civil Justice Clinic, Race, Ethnicity and the Law. ***Email:*** kim@wulaw.wustl.edu

MICHAEL H. KOBY*, (Associate Director of Legal Research & Writing and Senior Lecturer in Law)**, born Santa Clarita, California, November 17, 1966; admitted to bar, 1992, Illinois; 1994, District of Columbia. *Education:* Biola University (B.A., 1988); The American University (J.D., 1992). ***COURSES: Legal Research and Writing. ***Email:*** koby@wulaw.wustl.edu

RICHARD B. KUHNS*, (Professor of Law)**, born Omaha, Nebraska, June 27, 1942; admitted to bar, 1968, California. *Education:* Stanford University (A.B., 1964); Stanford University Law School (LL.B., 1967); University of Michigan (LL.M., 1974; S.J.D., 1978). ***COURSES: Criminal Justice Administration, Evidence, Advanced Evidence, Children and the Law. ***Email:*** kuhns@wulaw.wustl.edu

D. BRUCE LA PIERRE*, (Professor of Law)**, born Bethesda, Maryland, June 1, 1947; admitted to bar, 1973, New Jersey. *Education:* Princeton University (A.B., 1969); Columbia University (J.D., 1973). ***COURSES: Federal Jurisdiction, Constitutional Law, Civil Rights. ***Email:*** lapierre@wulaw.wustl.edu

STEPHEN H. LEGOMSKY*, (Charles F. Nagel Professor of International & Comparative Law)**, born Hartford, Connecticut, June 6, 1947; admitted to bar, 1978, California. *Education:* Worcester Polytechnic Institute (B.S., 1969); University of San Diego (J.D., 1977); Oxford University (D.Phil., 1984). ***COURSES: Immigration Law, Criminal Law, International Human Rights, Torts. ***Email:*** legomsky@wulaw.wustl.edu

RONALD M. LEVIN*, (Henry Hitchcock Professor of Law)**, born St. Louis, Missouri, May 11, 1950; admitted to bar, 1975, Missouri; 1977, District of Columbia. *Education:* Yale University (B.A., 1972); University of Chicago (J.D., 1975). ***COURSES: Administrative Law, Legislation, Civil Procedure. ***Email:*** levin@wulaw.wustl.edu

JO ELLEN D. LEWIS*, (Director of Legal Research & Writing and Senior Lecturer in Law)**, born St. Louis, Missouri, August 20, 1956; admitted to bar, 1986, Maryland; 1987, District of Columbia; 1995, Missouri. *Education:* University of Missouri-Columbia (B.S., 1978; M.Ed., 1979); Georgetown University (J.D., 1986). ***COURSES: Legal Research & Writing. ***Email:*** lewisj@wulaw.wustl.edu

MAXINE I. LIPELES*, (Professor of Law, part-time)**, admitted to bar, 1980, Massachusetts; 1982, Missouri. *Education:* Princeton University (A.B., 1975); Harvard Law School (J.D., 1979). ***COURSES: Environmental Law, Regulation of Toxic and Hazardous Substances, Interdisciplinary Environmental Clinic. ***Email:*** milipeles@seas.wustl.edu

DANIEL R. MANDELKER*, (Howard A. Stamper Professor of Law)**, born Milwaukee, Wisconsin, July 18, 1926; admitted to bar, 1949, Wisconsin. *Education:* University of Wisconsin (B.A., 1947; LL.B., 1949); Yale Law School (J.S.D., 1956). ***COURSES: Land Use Law, Environmental Law, State and Local Government. ***Email:*** mandelker@wulaw.wustl.edu

CHARLES R. MCMANIS*, (Professor of Law)**, born Murphy, North Carolina, September 8, 1941; admitted to bar, 1975, Georgia. *Education:* Birmingham Southern College (B.A., 1964); Duke University (M.A., 1972; J.D., 1972). ***COURSES: Administrative Law, Intellectual Property, Unfair Trade Practices, Torts, Advanced Torts. ***Email:*** mcmanis@wulaw.wustl.edu

JANE MARIE MOUL*, (Lecturer in Law)**, born Hastings, Nebraska, November 24, 1961; admitted to bar, 1989, Missouri; 1990, Illinois. *Education:* University of Nebraska (B.S., 1984); Washington University School of Law (J.D., 1989). ***COURSES: Legal Research & Writing. ***Email:*** jmoul@wulaw.wash.edu

A. PETER MUTHARIKA*, (Professor of Law)**, born Cholo, Malawi, July 18, 1940; admitted to bar, 1970, Tanzania. *Education:* London University (LL.B., 1965); Yale Law School (LL.M., 1966; J.S.D., 1969). ***COURSES: Contracts, International Law, International Trade, International Investment. ***Email:*** mutharip@wulaw.wustl.edu

(This Listing Continued)

WASHINGTON UNIVERSITY SCHOOL OF LAW
—Continued

KIMBERLY JADE NORWOOD*, (Professor of Law)**, born New York, N.Y., August 18, 1960; admitted to bar, 1985, Missouri; 1986, Pennsylvania; 1987, Illinois. *Education:* Fordham University (B.A., 1982); University of Missouri-Columbia (J.D., 1985). ***COURSES: Torts, Pretrial, Products Liability, Advanced Civil Procedure Seminar, Civil Justice Clinic. ***Email:*** norwood@wulaw.wustl.edu

TROY ALLAN PAREDES*, (Associate Professor)**, born San Bernardino, California, February 21, 1971; admitted to bar, 1996, California. *Education:* University of California Berkeley (A.B., 1992); Yale Law School (J.D., 1996). ***COURSES: Corporations, Securities Regulation, Corporate Finance, Property. ***Email:*** paredes@wulaw.wustl.edu

STANLEY L. PAULSON*, (William G. Hammond Professor of Law and Professor of Philosophy)**, born Fergus Falls, Minnesota, May 16, 1941. *Education:* University of Minnesota (B.A., 1964); University of Wisconsin (M.A., 1966; Ph.D., 1968); Harvard Law School (J.D., 1972). ***COURSES: Jurisprudence, Constitutional Law. ***Email:*** paulson@wulaw.wustl.edu

THEODORE W. RUGER*, (Associate Professor of Law)**, born St. Louis, Missouri, November 15, 1968; admitted to bar, 1995, Massachusetts; 1998, District of Columbia. *Education:* Williams College (B.A., 1990); Harvard Law School (J.D., 1995). ***COURSES: Constitutional Law, Health Law, Clinical. ***Email:*** ruger@wulaw.wustl.edu

LEILA NADYA SADAT*, (Professor of Law)**, born Newark, New Jersey, January 24, 1960; admitted to bar, 1986, Louisiana; 1992, Paris, France. *Education:* Rutgers University (B.A., 1980); Tulane University (J.D, 1985); Columbia University (LL.M., 1987); University of Paris (D.E.A., 1988). ***COURSES: European Community Law, Civil Procedure, International Business Planning and Drafting, International Criminal Law. ***Email:*** sadat@wulaw.wustl.edu

ANN D. SHIELDS*, (Associate Director of Legal Research & Writing and Senior Lecturer in Law)**, born Athens, Georgia, May 24, 1963; admitted to bar, 1993, Missouri; 1994, Illinois. *Education:* Washington University (A.B., 1985; J.D., 1993). ***COURSES: Legal Research and Writing. ***Email:*** davis@wulaw.wustl.edu

NANCY C. STAUDT*, (Professor of Law)**, born Akron, Ohio, August 4, 1963; admitted to bar, 1990, California. *Education:* Ohio State University (B.A., 1985); University of Minnesota (J.D., 1989). ***COURSES: Tax, Social Security, Tax Policy. ***Email:*** nstaudt@wulaw.wustl.edu

KAREN L. TOKARZ*, (Professor of Law and Director of Clinical Education)**, born Fall River, Massachusetts, October 28, 1948; admitted to bar, 1976, Missouri. *Education:* Webster University (B.A., 1970); St. Louis University (J.D., 1976); University of California at Berkeley, Boalt Hall School of Law (LL.M., 1985). ***COURSES: Clinic, Employment and Sex Discrimination, Civil Rights Law, Litigation, Alternative Dispute Resolution. ***Email:*** tokarz@wulaw.wustl.edu

PETER WIEDENBECK*, (Professor of Law)**, born Ann Arbor, Michigan, December 31, 1953; admitted to bar, 1979, District of Columbia; 1985, Missouri. *Education:* University of Toronto (B.Sc., 1976); University of Michigan (J.D., 1979). ***COURSES: Pensions and Employee Benefits, Federal Income Tax, Constitutional History, Corporate Tax, Partnership Tax. ***Email:*** wiedenbp@wulaw.wustl.edu

---

WAYNE STATE UNIVERSITY LAW SCHOOL

468 WEST FERRY MALL
DETROIT, MICHIGAN 48202

WEST VIRGINIA UNIVERSITY COLLEGE OF LAW

P.O. BOX 6130
MORGANTOWN, WEST VIRGINIA 26506

WESTERN NEW ENGLAND COLLEGE SCHOOL OF LAW

1215 WILBRAHAM ROAD
SPRINGFIELD, MASSACHUSETTS 01119-2689
Telephone: (413) 782-1412
Fax: (413) 796-2067
http://www.law.wnec.edu

ABA Approved Since 1974

THE SCHOOL

The School of Law at Western New England College is a dynamic institution with an emphasis on exceptional education in a supportive and friendly atmosphere. It is the only Massachusetts law school outside the greater Boston area that is accredited by the American Bar Association. It is also a member of the Association of American Law Schools. The Law School was founded in 1919 and has a long history of graduating students who have excelled in virtually every area of the law. In addition to the full-time day program, the Law School offers part-time programs during the day and evening, with a total enrollment of about 500 students.

THE STUDENTS

During the past two years, Western New England College School of Law has attracted first-year students from approximately 200 undergraduate institutions and 25 states across the nation. A typical entering class is approximately 50% female and 10% people of color. Many students bring to the School a diversity of backgrounds and real-world experiences.

THE FACULTY

The Law School takes pride in the excellence of its faculty members and their dedication to teaching and to the needs of our students. Faculty members are recruited nationally and come from varied backgrounds that include government service, judicial clerkships, and a broad range of private practice. The faculty at the Law School is strongly committed

(This Listing Continued)

WESTERN NEW ENGLAND COLLEGE SCHOOL OF LAW —Continued

to being accessible to their students. Our students consistently indicate great satisfaction with the quality of instruction they receive and the environment in which they study.

THE LIBRARY

The collection at the law library is among the finest in the country, exceeding 380,000 volumes. The collection is a combination of the best of the newest research and reference volumes, along with reprints of historical texts. Westlaw, Lexis, and Loislaw, internet e-mail, and World Wide Web access are available for all students. It is the only research law library in western Massachusetts and is a valued resource for the area's legal community.

A PRACTICAL EDUCATION

The Law School supplements its extensive traditional curriculum with practical experience so students are well prepared to practice law upon graduation. In addition to the required first year legal research and writing program, every student takes an upper level qualified writing course. Students are encouraged to participate in regional and national moot court competitions, including the National Moot Court Competition, the ABA National Trial Competition, the National First Amendment Moot Court Competition, the Tax Moot Court Competition, the Negotiation Moot Court Competition, and the Jessup International Moot Court Competition. Our teams compete quite well against regional and national teams and have received national recognition for their outstanding efforts.

The Law School also offers several clinical and simulation courses that provide practical experience in both live-client and simulated settings. Clinics allow students to work with actual clients under the supervision of faculty and members of the legal community; students can choose from a number of clinical courses including the Criminal Law Clinic, the Civil Law Clinic, the Consumer Protection Clinic, and the Legal Services Clinic where students work with Western Massachusetts Legal Services. Clinic students also meet regularly with faculty to discuss their cases and increase their understanding of professional and ethical obligations. In simulation courses, students work with hypothetical cases and argue on their client's behalf before a panel of faculty, peers, or members of the legal community.

THE ALUMNI

Graduates of the Law School are employed in top law firms and companies, government and public interest agencies, judgeships and clerkships, and small firms. Nearly 5,800 alumni are employed in 48 states, U.S. Territories, Canada, Europe and Asia. The Law School believes that both its curricular approaches and its supportive learning environment work together to develop lawyers who are effective and skilled practitioners of the law.

Please visit us in person or on the Web at http://www.law.wnec.edu.

Dean and Professor of Law: Arthur R. Gaudio (413) 782-1412
Associate Dean and Professor: Arthur Leavens (413) 782-1412
Associate Dean for Admissions and Professor: William Metzger (413) 782-1421
Assistant Dean and Director of Career Services: Charlene M. Allen (413) 782-1416
Director of Financial Aid: Kathleen Chambers (413) 782-1258
Director, Law Library and Professor: Donald J. Dunn (413) 782-1454
Director of Law Alumni Relations: Linda Polhemus (413) 782-1311
Assistant Dean for Law School Affairs: Nancy Sykes (413) 782-1413
Director of Student Records: Mary M. Van Houten (413) 782-1402

FULL TIME FACULTY

ARTHUR RALPH GAUDIO*, (Dean and Professor of Law)**, born Rochester, New York, November 21, 1942; admitted to bar, 1967, New York. *Education:* University of Rochester (B.S., 1964); Syracuse University (J.D., 1967). ***COURSES: Property, Real Estate Finance, Real Estate Development, Oil & Gas. ***Email:*** agaudio@law.wnec.edu

PETER L. ADOMEIT*, (Professor)**, born Oak Park, Illinois, December 17, 1940; admitted to bar, 1967, California; 1978, Connecticut. *Education:* Carleton College (B.A., 1962); University of Minnesota (J.D., 1965). ***COURSES: Arbitration, Civil Procedure, Labor Law, Legal Method, Negotiation, Public Sector Labor Law, Alternative Dispute Resolution.

WILLIAM G. BAKER*, (Professor)**, born New York, New York, January 11, 1950; admitted to bar, 1975, New York. *Education:* Clarkson College (B.S., 1971); Union University, Albany Law School (J.D., 1974). ***COURSES: Estate and Gift Taxation, Estate Planning, Estates, Real Estate Transactions, Real Property, Trusts.

LEONARD M. BAYNES*, (Professor (on leave 2001-2002))**, born East Elmhurst, New York, June 30, 1957; admitted to bar, 1984, New York; 1987, Massachusetts. *Education:* New York University (B.S., 1979); Columbia University (J.D., 1982; M.B.A., 1983). ***COURSES: Agency and Partnership, Corporations, Land Use Planning, Legal Research and Writing, Property, Regulated Industries.

PHILIP W. BOUCHARD*, (Professor)**, born Boston, Massachusetts, December 20, 1930; admitted to bar, 1957, Massachusetts; 1970, Wisconsin. *Education:* Boston University (A.B., 1952; J.D., 1957). ***COURSES: Law and Education, Products Liability, Torts.

TINA WESCOTT CAFARO*, (Assistant Clinical Professor of Law)**, born Springfield, Massachusetts, April 12, 1970; admitted to bar, 1995, Massachusetts. *Education:* University of Massachusetts (B.A., 1992); Western New England College School of Law (J.D., 1995). ***COURSES: Criminal Law, Trial Practice & Techniques.

LAUREN J. CARASIK*, (Director, Anti-Discrimination Clinic and Assistant Professor)**, born Rochester, New York, December 16, 1963; admitted to bar, 1991, Massachusetts. *Education:* Earlham College (B.A., 1986); Northeastern University (J.D., 1991). ***COURSES: Discrimination, Clinical Education, Disability Rights. ***Email:*** lcarasil@law.wnec.edu

AMY B. COHEN*, (Professor)**, born Bronx, New York, August 5, 1952; admitted to bar, 1978, Massachusetts; 1981, Connecticut. *Education:* Connecticut College (B.A., 1974); Harvard University (J.D., 1978). ***COURSES: Contract Law, Corporations, Intellectual Property, Unfair Trade and Trademark.

BETH DIANE COHEN*, (Assistant Professor and Director of Legal Research and Writing Program)**, born New York City, New York, June 22, 1959; admitted to bar, 1995, Massachusetts. *Education:* SUNY at Stony Brook (B.A., 1981); Suffolk University Law School (J.D., 1984). ***COURSES: Legal Research & Writing, Academic Support, Professional Responsibility. ***Email:*** bcohen@11ama.1net.wnec.edu

(This Listing Continued)

WESTERN NEW ENGLAND COLLEGE SCHOOL OF LAW —Continued

RICHARD P. COLE*, (Professor)**, born Punxsutawney, Pennsylvania, November 27, 1944; admitted to bar, 1969, Pennsylvania. *Education:* University of Pennsylvania (B.A., 1966); University of Michigan (J.D., 1969; M.A., 1972). ***COURSES: Torts, Toxic Torts, Legal History, Legislation.

ROBIN K. CRAIG*, (Associate Professor)**, born Long Beach, California, June 18, 1964; admitted to bar, 1996, Oregon. *Education:* Pomona College (B.A., 1985); The John Hopkins University (M.A., 1986); University of California (Ph.D., 1993); Lewis & Clark School of Law (J.D., 1996). ***COURSES: Environmental Law, Administrative Law, Property.

DONALD J. DUNN*, (Director, Law Library and Professor)**, born Tyler, Texas, November 9, 1945. *Education:* University of Texas (B.A., 1969; M.L.S., 1972); Western New England College School of Law (J.D., 1983). ***COURSES: Legal Bibliography.

JOHN DAVID EGNAL*, (Professor)**, born Philadelphia, Pennsylvania, December 16, 1943; admitted to bar, 1968, Pennsylvania. *Education:* Lehigh University (B.A., 1965); Temple University (J.D., 1968; LL.M., 1976). ***COURSES: Civil Procedure, Civil Rights, Clinical Teaching, Conflict of Laws, Constitutional Law, Evidence, Federal Jurisdictions, Land Use Planning.

TAYLOR FLYNN*, (Assistant Professor)**, born Illinois, December 16, 1964; admitted to bar, 1991, California. *Education:* Dartmouth College (B.A., 1986); Columbia Law School (J.D., 1991); Stanford Law School (J.S.M., 1995). ***COURSES: Family Law, Constitutional Law, Sexual Orientation & the Law.

JAMES A. GARDNER*, (Professor (on leave 2001-2002))**, born New York, New York, April 25, 1959; admitted to bar, 1985, District of Columbia and New York. *Education:* Yale University (B.A., 1980); University of Chicago (J.D., 1984). ***COURSES: Administrative Law, Constitutional Law, Election Law, Federal Litigation, First Amendment.

ANNE B. GOLDSTEIN*, (Professor)**, born New York, New York, March 4, 1949; admitted to bar, 1977, Massachusetts. *Education:* Simon Fraser University (B.A., 1972); Reed College; Northeastern University (J.D., 1976). ***COURSES: Conflict of Laws, Criminal Law, Estates, Family Law, Divorce.

JAMES WICE GORDON*, (Professor)**, born Louisville, Kentucky, October 3, 1949; admitted to bar, 1974, Kentucky. *Education:* University of Louisville (A.B., 1971); University of Kentucky (J.D., 1974; Ph.D., 1981). ***COURSES: Constitutional History, Legal History, Legal Profession, Property, Trusts and Estates.

ERIC JOSEPH GOUVIN*, (Professor)**, born Westerly, Rhode Island, February 15, 1961; admitted to bar, 1986, Maine; 1993, Massachusetts. *Education:* Cornell University (A.B., 1983); Boston University (J.D., 1986; LL.M., 1990). ***COURSES: Business Planning, Corporate Finance, Corporations, Secured Transactions, Banking Law.

LENESE CORINE HERBERT*, (Assistant Professor)**, born Washington, D.C., August 25, 1963; admitted to bar, 1990, Pennsylvania. *Education:* Howard University (B.S., 1985); UCLA School of Law (J.D., 1989). ***COURSES: Criminal Law, Torts, Administrative Law.

ARTHUR BOWEN LEAVENS, III*, (Associate Dean and Professor)**, born Kansas City, Missouri, May 18, 1947; admitted to bar, 1977, Massachusetts; 1978, New York. *Education:* Duke University (B.A., 1969); Harvard University (J.D., 1976). ***COURSES: Advanced Criminal Procedure, Clinical Teaching, Criminal Law, Criminal Procedure, Evidence.

ROBERT A. LUSARDI*, (Professor)**, born Newark, New Jersey, May 4, 1946; admitted to bar, 1971, Massachusetts. *Education:* Colgate University (A.B., 1968); Boston College (J.D., 1971). ***COURSES: Advanced Problems in Civil Procedure, Agency and Partnership, Civil Procedure, Corporations, Federal Jurisdiction, Securities Regulation.

JENNIFER S. MARTIN*, (Assistant Professor of Law)**, born Ashland, Ohio, January 22, 1967; admitted to bar, 1993, Texas. *Education:* University of Nevada Las Vegas (B.S., 1988); Vanderbilt University School of Law (J.D., 1993). ***COURSES: Corporate Law, Commercial Law.

WILLIAM D. METZGER*, (Associate Dean and Professor)**, born Leominster, Massachusetts, March 2, 1943; admitted to bar, 1972, Massachusetts. *Education:* Holy Cross College (B.S., 1964); Boston College (J.D., 1972); Georgetown University (LL.M., 1976). ***COURSES: Taxation, Federal.

BRUCE K. MILLER*, (Professor)**, born Evanston, Illinois, March 7, 1945; admitted to bar, 1970, California. *Education:* Stanford University (A.B., 1966); Harvard University (J.D., 1969). ***COURSES: Civil Rights Litigation, Constitutional Law, Federal Courts and Jurisdiction, Federal Litigation, Jurisprudence, First Amendment Rights.

FREDERICK D. ROYAL*, (Professor)**, born Pittsfield, Massachusetts, February 28, 1947; admitted to bar, 1972, Massachusetts. *Education:* University of Massachusetts (B.A., 1968); Cornell University (J.D., 1972); Boston University (LL.M., 1973). ***COURSES: Taxation, Federal.

SAMUEL STONEFIELD*, (Professor)**, born Rockford, Illinois, September 4, 1945; admitted to bar, 1971, Massachusetts. *Education:* Dartmouth College (B.A., 1967); Harvard University (J.D., 1971). ***COURSES: Administrative Law, Civil Rights, Constitutional Law, Evidence, Federal Jurisdiction, Real Estate Transactions.

KATHARINE A. VAN TASSEL*, (Assistant Professor of Law)**, born Austen, Texas, June 24, 1957; admitted to bar, 1986, Ohio. *Education:* Case Western Reserve University (B.S.W., 1990; J.D., 1986). ***COURSES: Torts, Health Law, Law & Biotechnology. ***Email:*** kvantassel@law.wnec.edu

VALORIE K. VOJDIK*, (Assistant Professor)**, born Flint, Michigan, December 24, 1959; admitted to bar, 1987, New York. *Education:* Brown University (A.B., 1982); New York University School of Law (J.D. 1986). ***COURSES: Civil Rights, Creditors Rights. ***Email:*** vvojdik@wnec.edu

ARTHUR D. WOLF*, (Professor)**, born Rochelle Park, New Jersey, April 15, 1940; admitted to bar, 1965, New Jersey; 1966, District of Columbia. *Education:* Tufts University (A.B., 1962); Columbia University (J.D., 1965). ***COURSES: Administrative Law, Civil Procedure, Civil Rights, Evidence, Federal Courts, Federal Litigation, International Human Rights, International Law, Remedies, Injunctions.

WESTERN STATE UNIVERSITY COLLEGE OF LAW

1111 NORTH STATE COLLEGE BOULEVARD
FULLERTON, CALIFORNIA 92831-3000
Telephone: (714) 738-1000
Fax: (714) 525-2786
www.wsulaw.edu

ABA Approved Since 1998.

The mission of *Western State University College of Law* is to provide the highest quality legal education, based on an innovative program of studies designed to develop the tools of careful legal analysis and to foster a broad understanding of law, law practice, and legal theory. Recognizing the importance of technology in the practice of law, the College is developing and expanding technology based learning aids designed to enhance traditional law school instruction methods.

The College of Law emphasizes the study and practice of lawyering skills required for the ethical, skillful, and professional practice of law and is particularly committed to meeting the educational needs of those who seek to practice in small to medium law offices, corporate law departments and governmental and other public service settings.

Approximately 21% of all sitting Orange County judges and commissioners and 25% of all sitting judges and commissioners in nearby Riverside County are WSU grads. Currently, 118 WSU graduates are reported as holding judicial posts, mostly in Southern California. This is a lawyers' law school. Many of its faculty have substantial experience in practice, as well as advanced degrees in law (see the individuals listings below). They are experienced and tested law school instructors.

To further its mission, the College of Law pursues student and faculty diversity, both to enhance the educational program of the school and to address important needs of the legal profession and of society as a whole.

Western State is in Orange County, California - midway between Los Angeles and San Diego. The campus is situated in Fullerton within the city's university district, home to six institutions of higher education. The student body is distinctly cosmopolitan. More than 36% of these students are minorities. About 45% are women. Both full-time and part-time students have the opportunity to participate in the life of the law school community.

Western State is associated with the Argosy Education Group, Inc., the nation's largest for-profit provider of doctoral level programs.

Dean and Chief Executive Officer: Dr. James F. Hogg
Assistant Dean for Administration: June E. Flaim
Director of Admission: Joel H. Goodman
Business Manager: John W. Meyers
Director of Career Services and Public Service Program: Tim Mallory
Director of Student Finance: Donna J. Espinoza
Director of Human Resources: Peg Savala
Director of Alumni Relations & Western State Law Foundation: Amy Kluth
Director of Outreach Services: Phyllis L. Wignall
Director, Criminal Law Practice Center & Associate Professor: Brent Romney
Dir., Academic Success & Enrichment Prog., & Assoc. Prof.: Stuart M. Miller
Director of Externships and Associate Professor: Laura L. Rovner
Acting Assistant Director of Student Services/Registrar: Lourdes Barriga
Director of Library and Assistant Professor: Carol Ebbinghouse

FULL TIME FACULTY

JAMES F. HOGG*, (Dean and Professor)**, *Education:* University of New Zealand (B.A.; LL.B. ; LL.M. first class honors); Harvard University Law School (LL.M.; S.J.D.). ***COURSES: Contracts, Insurance Law, Corporations, Agency & Partnership. ***Email:*** jhogg@wsulaw.edu

TODD BROWER*, (Professor)**, *Education:* Princeton University (A.B., cum laude); Stanford University (J.D.); Yale University (LL.M.). ***COURSES: Advocacy, American Law Seminar, Constitutional Law, Employment Discrimination, First Amendment/Equal Protection, Labor Law, Legal Perspective Seminar, Property. ***Email:*** todd@wsulaw.edu

LESLIE V. DERY*, (Associate Professor)**, *Education:* University of California, San Diego (B.A.); Georgetown University (M.S.); University of California, Hastings College of Law (J.D.). ***COURSES: Constitutional Law, Criminal Procedure, Federal and California Civil Procedure, First Amendment, Immigration Law, Juvenile Justice, Professional Responsibility. ***Email:*** leslied@wsulaw.edu

CAROL EBBINGHOUSE*, (Director of Library and Assistant Professor)**, *Education:* California State University, Los Angeles (B.A.); University of Kentucky (M.S.L.S.); Southwestern University School of Law (J.D.). ***COURSES: Copyright Law, California Legal Research. ***Email:*** carole@wsulaw.edu

NEIL T. GOTANDA*, (Professor)**, *Education:* Stanford University (B.S.); University of California, Berkeley Boalt Hall School of Law (J.D.); Harvard University Law School (LL.M.). ***COURSES: Advocacy, Constitutional Law, Equal Protection and Due Process, Race and the Law, Torts. ***Email:*** neilg@wsulaw.edu

CONSTANCE K. HOOD*, (Associate Professor)**, *Education:* Lewis and Clark College (B.A.); Pepperdine University College of Law (J.D., cum laude); Georgetown University Law Center (LL.M. with distinction). ***COURSES: Advocacy, Professional Skills, Sales, Solving Legal Problems. ***Email:*** connieh@wsulaw.edu

CHEYANNA L. JAFFKE*, (Associate Professor)**, *Education:* University of Idaho (B.S., summa cum laude); University of Idaho College of Law (J.D.); University of Washington School of Law (LL.M.). ***COURSES: American Indian Law, Corporations, Estate and Gift Taxation, Estates, Federal Income Tax, Taxation of Business Entities. ***Email:*** cjaffke@wsulaw.edu

(This Listing Continued)

WESTERN STATE UNIVERSITY COLLEGE OF LAW —Continued

RICHARD E. JENKINS*, (Professor)**, *Education:* Western State University College of Law (B.S.L.; J.D.). ***COURSES: Criminal Law, Criminal Procedure, Education Law, Evidence, Juvenile Law. ***Email:*** richardj@wsulaw.edu

MARYANN JONES*, (Professor)**, *Education:* Trinity College (B.A.); Chicago-Kent College of Law (J.D.). ***COURSES: Administrative Law, Civil Practice Externship, Civil Procedure, Judicial Externship, Professional Skills. ***Email:*** maryannj@wsulaw.edu

WENDY KENNEDY*, (Visiting Associate Professor)**, *Education:* United States International University (B.A.); University of Baltimore School of Law (J.D. cum laude); University of Cambridge (LL.M.). ***COURSES: Agency and Partnership, Contracts. ***Email:*** wendyk@wsulaw.edu

GLENN S. KOPPEL*, (Professor)**, *Education:* City College of New York (B.A.); Harvard University Law School (J.D.). ***COURSES: Advocacy, Civil Procedure, Evidence, Evidence Practice, Professional Skills. ***Email:*** glennk@wsulaw.edu

PHILIP L. MERKEL*, (Professor)**, *Education:* University of Illinois (A.B.); University of Illinois College of Law (J.D.); University of Virginia (M.A.). ***COURSES: Legal History, Professional Skills, Remedies, Torts. ***Email:*** philipm@wsulaw.edu

G. KRISTIAN MICCIO*, (Associate Professor and Director, Domestic Violence Project)**, *Education:* Marymount College (B.A.); The Rockefeller School of Public Policy, University of New York at Albany (M.A.); Antioch University School of Law (J.D.); Columbia University School of Law (LLM). ***COURSES: Criminal Law, Criminal Procedure, Domestic Violence Seminar, Professional Skills, Women and the Law. ***Email:*** kristianm@wsulaw.edu

STUART M. MILLER*, (Visiting Associate Professor and Director, Academic Success & Enrichment Program)**, *Education:* Oberlin College (B.A.); New York University School of Law. ***COURSES: Administrative Law, Environmental Law, Professional Skills, Property. ***Email:*** stuartm@wsulaw.edu

KEVIN EDWARD MOHR*, (Associate Professor)**, *Education:* Harpur College (B.A., magna cum laude); University of Wisconsin (M.S.); Yale University Law School (J.D.). ***COURSES: Contract, Intellectual Property, Professional Skills, Professional Responsibility. ***Email:*** kevinm@wsulaw.edu

BRENT F. ROMNEY*, (Associate Professor and Director, Criminal Law Practice Center)**, *Education:* California State University, Fullerton (B.A.); Brigham Young University, J. Reuben Clark Law School (J.D.). ***COURSES: Advanced Criminal Evidence, Criminal Justice Ethics, Criminal Law, Criminal Procedure, Evidence, Juvenile Law. ***Email:*** brentr@wsulaw.edu

LAURA L. ROVNER*, (Associate Professor and Director, Externship Programs)**, *Education:* University of Pennsylvania (B.A., magna cum laude); Cornell University Law School (J.D.); Georgetown University Law Center (LL.M.). ***COURSES: Advocacy, Civil Procedure, Civil Rights, Externships Seminar, Torts. ***Email:*** laurar@wsulaw.edu

JENNIFER M. RUSSELL*, (Visiting Associate Professor)**, *Education:* City University of New York, Queens College (B.A.); New York University School of Law (J.D.). ***COURSES: Civil Procedure, Corporations, Race and the Law. ***Email:*** jenniferr@wsulaw.edu

MICHAEL HUNTER SCHWARTZ*, (Associate Professor)**, *Education:* University of California, Berkeley (A.B.); University of California, Hastings College of Law (J.D., cum laude). ***COURSES: Academic Success Program, Agency, Contracts, Insurance Law, Legal Methods, Professional Skills, Remedies. ***Email:*** michaels@wsulaw.edu

GREGORY STEVEN SERGIENKO*, (Associate Professor)**, *Education:* Harvard College (B.A., magna cum laude); Harvard University Law School (J.D., magna cum laude). ***COURSES: Administrative Law, Agency and Partnership, Civil Procedure, Contracts, Environmental Law, Property, Remedies, Torts. ***Email:*** gregs@wsulaw.edu

CHARLES B. SHEPPARD*, (Associate Professor)**, *Education:* California State University, Dominguez Hills (B.A.); Loyola University School of Law (J.D.). ***COURSES: Contracts, Estates, Insurance Law, Property, Real Estate Transactions, Secured Land Transactions. ***Email:*** charless@wsulaw.edu

MARCIA B. WILBUR*, (Dean Emeritus and Professor Emeritus)**, *Education:* California State University, Fullerton (B.A.); Pepperdine University School of Law (J.D.). ***COURSES: Conflict of Laws, Contracts, Criminal Law, Criminal Procedure, Externship Programs Supervisor, Juvenile Law, Sales. ***Email:*** marciaw@wsulaw.edu

WHITTIER LAW SCHOOL

3333 HARBOR BLVD.
COSTA MESA, CALIFORNIA 92626

WIDENER UNIVERSITY SCHOOL OF LAW

3800 VARTAN WAY
P.O. BOX 69381
HARRISBURG, PENNSYLVANIA 17106-9381

WIDENER UNIVERSITY SCHOOL OF LAW

4601 CONCORD PIKE
P.O. BOX 7474
WILMINGTON, DELAWARE 19803-0474

WILLAMETTE UNIVERSITY COLLEGE OF LAW

TRUMAN WESLEY COLLINS LEGAL CENTER
245 WINTER STREET SE
SALEM, OREGON 97301-3922
Telephone: (503) 370-6402
Fax: (503) 370-6828
http://www.willamette.edu/wucl

ABA Approved Since 1938

Willamette University is the West's oldest university, celebrating its 158th year in 2000. An independently-supported institution founded by missionaries, it bears the name of one of Oregon's great rivers and is historically related to the United Methodist Church. Willamette is located in Salem, the state capital. The 61-acre campus is home to the College of Liberal Arts, the George H. Atkinson Graduate School of Management, the Master of Arts in Teaching program, and the College of Law. Total enrollment is 2500 students.

Established in 1883, the College of Law holds an honored place in Oregon history. It is the oldest law school in the region and the second oldest in the western United States. Its total enrollment of 420 makes it one of the smaller schools in the West. It gained American Bar Association accreditation in 1938 and membership in the Association of American Law Schools in 1946. Willamette boasts over 4,000 alumni, including 34% of Oregon's judiciary. Historically, about 55% of the graduating class choose private practice. Each year, about 6% of the class accept judicial clerkships.

Willamette offers only a full-time day program. In 2000-01, 645 students competed for 170 first-year seats. In the class, 88 colleges and 22 states are represented. Forty-five percent of the students are women; 12% are minority students. Average age of the entering class is 26. Eighteen per cent of the class is at least 30 years old. There are a variety of student groups including the Multi-Cultural Law Students Association, Environmental Law Society, Federalist Society, Women's Law Caucus, Prime Time Christian Fellowship, Public Interest Law Project, Lambda Legal Organization, and Black Law Students Association.

Access to clerking opportunities and legal research is outstanding. Salem is one of two cities on the West Coast that is home to both a law school and to state government. Adjacent to the campus: State Supreme Court and Library, Court of Appeals, the Governor, and the Legislature. Nearby: Circuit Court, District Court, Municipal Court, and State Tax Court. Federal courts are in Portland, 45 minutes north, and in Eugene, one hour and 15 minutes south. Virtually all state agencies are headquartered in Salem, including the Oregon Department of Justice.

More than 100 courses are taught by 21 full-time faculty, three Legal Research and Writing professors, two clinical professors, and several adjunct professors. Faculty research interests include international and comparative law, conflicts of law, dispute resolution, and commercial law and business law, among others. Recently, the law school was selected to house the Oregon Law Commission, which is the official law-reform agency of the State of Oregon.

A traditional approach to legal education is favored, but aspects of the program are distinctive. Each first-year student is assigned to three classes of less than 30. Two are substantive courses. The other is Legal Research and Writing, which concludes with required Moot Court Competition participation. The curriculum after the first year is elective with exception of Constitutional Law II, Evidence and Professional Responsibility.

Through the Center for Dispute Resolution, students learn dispute resolution methods: client counseling, negotiation, mediation, and arbitration. The College of Law is one of the few law schools in the country that requires a first-year course in dispute resolution. A certificate in dispute resolution is an option within the academic program.

Students admitted to the College of Law and the Atkinson School may pursue a joint degree, enabling the simultaneous receipt of the Doctor of Jurisprudence and Master of Business Administration in four years. The Atkinson School is the only graduate program in the nation accredited by the leading accrediting bodies in both business administration and public administration. The joint degree is a basis for careers in law, business, government and not-for-profit agencies.

Willamette offers summer study at the East China University of Politics and Law in Shanghai. Students study Chinese legal theory and history, observe a trial and a mediation, visit a prison, and meet with officials involved in trade and investment in addition to more traditional course work.

Many third-year students select courses in skills training such as trial practice, negotiation, arbitration and mediation. Other students choose to participate in the Willamette Clinical Law program. Second- and third-year students may participate in a wide variety of Moot Court competitions or write for the school's *Willamette Law Review* or *Willamette Journal of International and Dispute Resolution.*

Dean: Symeon Symeonides (503) 370-6402
Admissions Director: Lawrence Seno, Jr. (503) 370-6282
Financial Aid: (503) 370-6273
Law Librarian: Richard Breen (503) 370-6386
Center for Dispute Resolution Director: Richard Birke (503) 370-6046
Career Services Director: Diane Reynolds (503) 370-6057
Alumni Director: Sharon Blus (503) 370-6492

FULL TIME FACULTY

SYMEON C. SYMEONIDES, **(Dean and Professor of Law),** born Cyprus, April 28, 1949. *Education:* University of Thessaloniki Law School (LL.B., 1972; LL.B., 1973); Harvard Law School (LL.M., 1974; SJD, 1980). ***COURSES:*** Conflict of Laws, Comparative Law, International Litigation, Civil Law, Property. ***Email:*** symeon@willlamette.edu

ROBERT C. ART, **(Professor of Law),** born Chicago, Illinois, March 23, 1948; admitted to bar, 1978, Illinois; 1980, Arizona; 1985, Oregon. *Education:* Beloit College (B.A., 1969); University of Wisconsin (M.A., 1970); De Paul University (J.D., 1978); Columbia University (LL.M., 1981). ***COURSES:*** Securities Regulation, Property, Corporate Finance, Mergers and Acquisitions. ***Email:*** rart@willamette.edu

(This Listing Continued)

WILLAMETTE UNIVERSITY COLLEGE OF LAW —Continued

RICHARD BIRKE*, (Associate Professor; Director, Center for Dispute Resolution)**, born Lowell, Massachusetts, November 30, 1960; admitted to bar, 1986, Massachusetts. *Education:* Tulane University (B.A., 1982); New England School of Law (J.D., 1986); Harvard Law School (LL.M., 1991). ***COURSES: Negotiation, Alternative Dispute Resolution, Mediation, Advanced Topics in Conflict Theory. ***Email:*** rbirke@willamette.edu

***DOUGLAS M. BRANSON*, (Isaac Van Winkle Meltow Endowed Professorship)**, *Education:* Notre Dame (B.A., 1965); Northwestern University (J.D., 1970); University of Virginia School of Law (LL.M., 1974).

RICHARD F. BREEN, JR.*, (Professor of Law and Director, Law Library)**, born Providence, Rhode Island, August 1, 1940; admitted to bar, 1968, Maine; 1969, New Hampshire. *Education:* Dartmouth College (A.B., 1962); University of Maine School of Law (LL.B., 1967); University of Oregon (M.L.S., 1973). ***Email: dbreen@willamette.edu

DAVID L. CAMERON*, (Professor of Law)**, born Edmundston, New Brunswick, Canada, October 27, 1957; admitted to bar, 1986, Massachusetts. *Education:* Massachusetts Institute of Technology (B.S., 1980); Northwestern University (J.D., 1986). ***COURSES: Federal Income Taxation, Property, Real Estate Finance, International Taxation, State and Local Taxation. ***Email:*** dcameron@willamette.edu

GILBERT PAUL CARRASCO*, (Professor of Law)**, born California, June 16, 1953; admitted to bar, 1979, California; 1980, District of Columbia. *Education:* Chami Nade University; University of San Diego (B.A., 1975); University of Santa Clara (J.D., 1978); Georgetown University Law School (LL.M., 1979). ***COURSES: Constitutional Law, Civil Rights Litigation, Public Law and Policy. ***Email:*** carrasco@willamette.edu

VINCE CHIAPPETTA*, (Associate Professor of Law)**, born Detroit, Michigan, June 23, 1951; admitted to bar, 1977, Arizona; 1994, California; 1994, Oregon. *Education:* Massachusetts Institute of Technology (B.S.E.E., 1973); University of Michigan Law School (J.D., 1977). ***COURSES: Business Organization, Intellectual Property, Patent Law, Science, Technology and the Law, Business Planning. ***Email:*** vchiappe@willamette.edu

DAVID S. CLARK*, (Maynard and Bertha Wilson Professor of Law)**, born San Diego, California, November 24, 1944; admitted to bar, 1972, California. *Education:* Stanford University (A.B., 1966); Stanford Law School (J.D., 1969; J.S.M., 1972). ***COURSES: Comparative Law, Procedure, Dispute Resolution. ***Email:*** dsclark@willamette.edu

M. DAVID DANIEL*, (Supervising Attorney, Clinical Law Program)**, born Portsmouth, Virginia, November 7, 1953; admitted to bar, 1986, Oregon. *Education:* Western Oregon State College (B.S., 1983); Willamette University College of Law (J.D., 1986). ***COURSES: Civil Practice Clinic. ***Email:*** ddaniel@willamette.edu

KATHY TODRANK GRAHAM*, (Associate Dean and Professor of Law)**, born Yuba City, California, November 14, 1947; admitted to bar, 1972, California; 1982, Oregon. *Education:* University of California, Berkeley (A.B., 1969); University of California School of Law, Davis (J.D., 1972). ***COURSES: Torts, Domestic Relations. ***Email:*** kgraham@willamette.edu

STEVEN K. GREEN*, (Associate Professor)**, born Texas, September 14, 1955; admitted to bar, 1981, Texas; 1987, Alaska; 1990, Minnesota; 1992 Maryland. *Education:* Texas Christian University (B.A., 1978); University of Texas (J.D., 1981); University of North Carolina (Ph.D., 1997). ***COURSES: Constitutional Law, First Amendment, Criminal Law, Legal History. ***Email:*** sgreen@willamette.edu

RICHARD B. HAGEDORN*, (Professor of Law)**, born Portland, Oregon, July 23, 1948; admitted to bar, 1973, Oregon. *Education:* Oregon State University (B.S., 1970); Willamette University College of Law (J.D., 1973). ***COURSES: Commercial Paper, Contracts, Commercial Transactions. ***Email:*** rhagedor@willamette.edu

EDWARD J. HARRI*, (Assistant Dean and Instructor)**, born Duluth, Minnesota, July 8, 1946; admitted to bar, 1973, Oregon. *Education:* Walla Walla College (B.A., 1968); Montana State University (M.S.A.S., 1970); Willamette University College of Law (J.D., 1973). ***COURSES: Legal Research and Writing, Advanced Legal Research. ***Email:*** eharri@willamette.edu

MARCIA H. (SAM) JACOBSON*, (Instructor)**, born Watertown, South Dakota, September 24, 1950; admitted to bar, 1976, Iowa; 1982, Oregon. *Education:* University of Oregon (B.S., 1972); University of Iowa (J.D., 1976). ***COURSES: Legal Research and Writing. ***Email:*** sjacobso@willamette.edu

TIMOTHY P. KELLY*, (Law Reference Librarian)**, born Leavenworth, Kansas, November 1, 1949; admitted to bar, 1987, Kansas. *Education:* University of Kansas (B.A., 1973); Emporia Kansas State University (M.L.S., 1975); Washburn University (J.D., 1987). ***COURSES: Advanced Legal Research. ***Email:*** tkelly@willamette.edu

DAVID KENAGY*, (Associate Dean)**, born Redmond, Oregon, September 3, 1952; admitted to bar, 1977, California; 1991, Oregon. *Education:* Pomona College (B.A., 1974); University of California at Los Angeles (J.D., 1977). ***COURSES: Pre-Trial Civil Litigation. ***Email:*** dkenagy@willamette.edu

HANS A. LINDE*, (Distinguished Scholar in Residence)**, born Berlin, Germany, April 15, 1924; admitted to bar, 1951, Oregon; retired Justice, Oregon Supreme Court. *Education:* Reed College (B.A., 1947); University of California, Berkeley (J.D., 1950). ***COURSES: State Constitutional Law. ***Email:*** hlinde@willamette.edu

HELEN L. MAZUR-HART*, (Instructor)**, born Helena, Montana, August 2, 1947; admitted to bar, 1983, Oregon. *Education:* Mills College (B.A., 1969); Willamette University College of Law (J.D., 1983). ***COURSES: Legal Research and Writing. ***Email:*** hmazur@willamette.edu

MICHELLE MARIE MHOON*, (Instructor)**, born Portland, Oregon, September 9, 1971; admitted to bar, 1997, Arkansas. *Education:* Linfield College (B.A., 1993); Atkinson Graduate School of Management (M.B.A., 1997); Willamette University College of Law (J.D., 1997). ***COURSES: Legal Research and Writing. ***Email:*** mmhoon@willamette.edu

JAMES A. R. NAFZIGER*, (Thomas B. Stoel Professor of Law, Director, International Programs)**, born Minneapolis, Minnesota, September 24, 1940; admitted to bar, 1967, Wisconsin. *Education:* University of Wisconsin (B.A., 1962; M.A., 1969); Harvard University (J.D., 1967). ***COURSES: International Business Transactions, Comparative Law, Conflict of Laws, International Law and Dispute Resolution, Immigration Law. ***Email:*** jnafzige@willamette.edu

EDWIN J. PETERSON*, (Distinguished Jurist in Residence)**, born Gilmanton, Wisconsin, March 30, 1930; admitted to bar, 1957, Oregon; retired Chief Justice, Oregon Supreme Court. *Education:* University of Oregon (B.S., 1951); University of Oregon School of Law (LL.B., 1957). ***COURSES: Pre-Trial Civil Litigation. ***Email:*** epeterso@willamette.edu

SUSAN L. SMITH*, (Professor of Law)**, born Whittier, California, October 31, 1953; admitted to bar, 1980, Colorado; 1981, District of Columbia; 1991, Oregon. *Education:* Reed College (B.A., 1976); Harvard University (J.D., 1980; M.Public Policy, 1980). ***COURSES:

(This Listing Continued)

WILLAMETTE UNIVERSITY COLLEGE OF LAW —Continued

Environmental Law, Natural Resources Law, Criminal Law, Environmental Criminal Enforcement, Toxic and Hazardous Substances. ***Email:*** smiths@willamette.edu

CARLTON J. SNOW, **(Professor of Law)**, born Lynchburg, Virginia, December 26, 1939; admitted to bar, 1969, Wisconsin. *Education:* Taylor University (B.A., 1962); Fuller Theological Seminary (M.Div., 1965); University of Wisconsin-Madison (M.A., 1966; J.D., 1969). ***COURSES:*** Contracts, Arbitration, Negotiation.

JEFFREY STANDEN, **(Professor of Law)**, born Boston, Massachusetts, February 27, 1960; admitted to bar, 1986, Virginia. *Education:* Georgetown University (A.B., 1982); University of Virginia (J.D., 1986). ***COURSES:*** Criminal Procedure, Remedies, Advanced Criminal Law, Professional Responsibility, Evidence, Jurisprudence. ***Email:*** jstanden@willamette.edu

YVONNE A. TAMAYO, **(Assistant Professor of Law)**, born Havana, Cuba, March 27, 1955; admitted to bar, 1994, District of Columbia; 1998, Florida. *Education:* Louisiana State University (B.S., 1977); Universite' De La Sorbonne (L.C., 1978); Loyola Law School (J.D., 1987). ***COURSES:*** Civil Procedure, Federal Courts, Church and State, Professional Responsibility. ***Email:*** ytamayo@willlamette.edu

LEROY J. TORNQUIST, **(Professor of Law)**, born Chicago, Illinois, April 2, 1940; admitted to bar, 1965, Illinois; 1981, Oregon. *Education:* Northwestern University (B.S., 1962; J.D., 1965). ***COURSES:*** Civil Procedure, Evidence, Trial Practice. ***Email:*** ltornqui@willamette.edu

DONALD L. TURNER, **(Professor of Law)**, born Portland, Oregon, December 30, 1931; admitted to bar, 1959, Oregon. *Education:* Lewis and Clark College (B.S., 1956); Willamette University College of Law (LL.B., 1959). ***COURSES:*** Criminal Law, Evidence, Scientific Proof, Criminal Procedure. ***Email:*** dturner@willamette.edu

VALERIE J. VOLLMAR, **(Professor of Law)**, born Corvallis, Oregon, October 21, 1946; admitted to bar, 1975, Oregon. *Education:* University of Oregon (B.A., 1968); Willamette University College of Law (J.D., 1975). ***COURSES:*** Trusts and Estates, Federal Estate and Gift Taxation, Will and Trust Drafting. ***Email:*** vvollmar@willamette.edu

NORMAN R. WILLIAMS, **(Assistant Professor of Law)**, born Phoenix, Arizona, November 19, 1969; admitted to bar, 1996, New York; 1998, District of Columbia. *Education:* Harvard University (A.B., 1991); New York University (J.D., 1995). ***COURSES:*** Constitutional Law, Administrative Law. ***Email:*** normanw@willamette.edu

MICHAEL B. WISE, **(Professor of Law)**, born Wilmington, Delaware, January 8, 1946; admitted to bar, 1972, California. *Education:* Yale University (B.A., 1968); Stanford University (J.D., 1971). ***COURSES:*** Civil Procedure, Constitutional Law, Law and Education, Comparative Constitutional Law. ***Email:*** mwise@willamette.edu

JENNIFER L. WRIGHT, **(Assistant Professor/Director, Clinical Law Program)**, born Redwood City, California, July 30, 1960; admitted to bar, 1989, Oregon. *Education:* Swarthmore College (A.B., 1982); Stanford Law School (J.D., 1986). ***COURSES:*** Clinical Legal Education. ***Email:*** jlwright@willamette.edu

WILLIAM MITCHELL COLLEGE OF LAW

875 SUMMIT AVENUE
ST. PAUL, MINNESOTA 55105

YALE UNIVERSITY LAW SCHOOL

127 WALL STREET, 401A YALE STATION
NEW HAVEN, CONNECTICUT 06520

SERVICES, SUPPLIERS, CONSULTANTS SECTION

CONNECTICUT, DELAWARE
DISTRICT OF COLUMBIA

The Services, Suppliers, Consultants Section provides information on businesses and professionals serving the legal community. Each volume index is listed alphabetically by category then within each category alphabetically by state, city and service name. Whether you are looking for a court reporter in your own jurisdiction or an expert witness in another state, the Services, Suppliers, Consultants Section is your direct link to legal support services.

SERVICES, SUPPLIERS, CONSULTANTS

List of Categories

Abogado - World Nations League Corporate Code
Abstractors
Accident Investigation & Reconstruction Services
Accident Investigation, Safety-Training-Environmental
Accountants
Accounting
Acoustics Consultants
Actuaries
Actuarial Analysis
Admiralty & Maritime Expert & Consultant
Advertising & Public Relations Firms
Aerial Photography
Affirmative Action Plan Development
Alternative Dispute Resolution
(See Arbitration & Mediation)
Americans With Disabilities Act (ADA)
Ancillary Financial/Trust Services
Appearance by Phone/Court Conferencing
Appellate Consultant
Appraisal & Valuation Services
Appraisal Services
Appraisal Services - Books
Appraisal Services - Estate & Gift Taxes
Appraisal Services - Health Care Property
Appraisal Services - Jewelry & Gems
Appraisal Services - Mines & Quarries
Appraisal Services - Personal Property
Appraisal Services - Real Estate
Arbitration & Mediation Services
Arbitration & Mediation Services - Aviation
Arbitrators - World Nations League Corporate Code
Asset Locators
Asset Management
Association Management
Attorney - Lobbyist
Attorney - World Nations League Corporate Code
Attorney Referral Services
Attorney Services
Auctioneers & Appraisers
Auctioneers & Appraisers - Arts & Letters
Auctioneers & Appraisers Of Autographs, Rare Books
Audio Tape Analysis/Authentication/Voice Identification
Audio/Video Services
Audiology/Hearing & Sound
Autographs, Rare Books
(See Process Servers)
Automated Records Management Software
Automobile & Office Equipment Leasing
Autopsy Service
Aviation Consultants
Aviation Medicine
Aviation-Investigation

Bail Bonds
Bank Associations & Societies
Banking - On Line Internet Access
Bankruptcy Creditor Report Services
Bankruptcy Software
Bankruptcy/Turnaround/Insolvency
Banks & Trust Companies
Bar Associations
Barter & Reciprocal Trade
Bilingual Staffing
Bodyguards
Bonds - Surety & Fidelity
Bowling Centers - Valuation & Financial Analysis
Brain Injury - Rehabilitation Services
Briefs
(See Legal Brief Printers)
Building Evaluation - Due Diligence
Building/Home Inspection
Business & Financial Information Providers
Business & Trade Organizations
Business Finance & Purchase of Receivables
Business Intelligence
Business Valuations
Business Valuations - Marine

CD-ROM Products
Captioning
Career Services
Case Consultants
Case Management Services
Case Management Systems
Civil Rights Under Color of Law
Class Action Locators
Class Action Notice
Class Action Settlement Administration
Closed Captioning
Coins and Currency
Collection Agencies
Commercial Real Estate Services/Brokerage
Computer - Programming & Consulting
Computer Animation, Graphics & Simulation
Computer Consultants
Computer Evidence Investigation
Computer Hardware & Software
Computer Rental & Audio/Visual Equipment
Computer Security Data & Hardware
Computer Software - Text Search
Computer Supplies
Computer Systems Integration
Computer Training
Conference/Seminar Center
Conferencing
Construction & Engineering Litigation
Construction Accidents, Safety
Construction Consultants
Construction Consultants-Construction Defects
Construction Consultants-Structural Damage
Consultant Referral Services
Contact Management
Continuing Legal Education
Copier Services
Corporate Services Companies
Corporate Supplies
Corporation Companies
Cost Recovery
Courier Services
Court House Research
Court Recording Systems
Court Reporters
Courtroom Sketching
Credit Bureaus
Crime Scene Analysis
Crime Scene Reconstruction
Criminal Background Checks
Criminal Investigations
Criminal Records Research

DNA Consulting
DNA Forensic Testing
Dataroom Solutions
Debt Collection Software
Debugging
Delivery Services
Demonstrative Evidence
Demonstrative Exhibits
Deposition Summaries
Depositions - Video & Audio
Depositions on Written Questions
Dictating Equipment & Supplies
Directory/On-Line
Disability Assessment - Learning and/or Behavioral
Discovery and Document Reproduction Services
Dispute Analysis & Investigation
Diversity/Teambuilding
Divorce Financial Software
Document Assembly
Document Delivery Systems
(See Process Servers)
Document Imaging
Document Management Services
Document Research, Retrieval & Filing
Document Scanning
Document/Data Conversion
Drug Detection

E-Business
E-Commerce/Web Hosting
Economic and Statistical Consulting Services
Economic and Statistical Consulting Services - Automobiles
Educational Consultant
Elder Care

Electronic Billing
Electronic Countermeasures
Electronic Discovery Services
Electronic Filing
Electronic Funds
Electronic Librarian
Electronic Packaging & Production
Employment Agencies - Permanent/Temporary
Employment Discrimination & Disparate Impact
Employment Screening
Engineering & Scientific Consulting Services
Engineering - Mechanical Design & Safety
Engineering - Metallurgy/Reconstruction/Forensic Consulting
Engineers/Engineering
Engineers/Engineering - Architectural
Environmental & Ecological Services
Environmental Consultants
Environmental Engineering & Remediation Services
Environmental Health & Safety
Environmental Investigations
Environmental Risk Assessment and Consulting
Environmental Risk Management & Compliance Information
Equine - Appraisers & Consultants
Escrow Services
Estate Planning & Personal Benefits
Estate Valuations
Examiners Of Questioned Documents (Handwriting Experts)
Executive Protective Services
Expert Witness
- Accident Analysis
- Accident Investigation & Reconstruction
- Accident Prevention-Exercise Equipment
- Accident Reconstruction
- Accidents/Fires/Product Liability
- Accounting
  - Business Damages
  - Malpractice
- Acoustics
  - Sound, Noise & Vibration
- Admiralty
- Agri-Horticultural
- Agricultural, Chemical & Equipment Safety
- Agronomy
- Air Bags
- Air Pollution
- Air Safety
- Air Traffic Control
- Americans with Disabilities Act (ADA)
- Animal Behavior
- Antiquity & Art Conservation
- Appraisal Services
  - Gems & Jewelry
- Aquatics
- Arboriculture & Forestry
- Architects
- Audio-Tape Analysis/Authentication/Voice ID
- Audiology
- Automobile
  - Appraiser & Consultant
  - Forensic
  - Occupant Biomechanics
  - Repairs
  - Sales
- Automotive/Dealer
- Banking
  - Finance
  - Trusts & Investments
- Biomechanical Engineering
- Biomedical Engineering
- Blasting Damage
- Bunk Bed Safety
- Burglar & Fire Alarm
- Bus Operations
  - School/Transit/Highway
- Business Valuations
- Carpal Tunnel Syndrome
- Chemical Process
  - Safety
- Chemistry
- Child, Infant, Household Products
- Child Pornography
- Class Action Notice
- Coatings/Paint
- Commercial Law
- Commodity Futures
- Communications
- Compensation
- Computer & Business Information Systems
- Computer Forensics/Data Recovery
- Computer/Litigation
- Computer Programming & Consulting
  - Computer Forensics
- Computer Science/Intellectual Property
- Computer/Systems Support
- Computer Technology Industry
- Computer Valuation
- Construction
  - Building Codes
  - Chimney & Fireplace
  - Defects
  - Scaffolding
- Conveyor Safety
- Cooling Towers
- Corporate Whistle Blowers/Former Employees
- Corrections
  - Jail/Prison/Lockup
  - Corrections (Adult & Juvenile)/Use of Force/Wrongful Death
  - Cranes
  - Criminalistics & Firearms
  - Currency Trading
  - Customs & International Trade
  - DUI
  - Damage Valuation
  - Demolition
  - Document Examination/Comprehension
- Cults & Sects
- Divorce/Marital Dissolution
- Drugs/Alcohol/Toxicology
- Economics/Economists
  - Agricultural/Environmental
  - Financial Valuation
  - Statistics
- Economics/Statistics
- Education/Schools
- Electrical
  - Electrical Utility Problems
  - Electrocution, Explosion & Fire
  - Electronics
- Electronic Countermeasures
- Electronic Devices & Systems
- Electronic Equipment & Circuitry
- Electronics
  - Product & Parts Valuations
- Electrostatic & Radiation
- Elevators
- Eminent Domain/Planning & Engineering
- Employee/Employment
  - Benefits
  - Compensation/Wages
  - Discrimination
  - Negligence Hiring/Retention
  - OSHA Regulations/Procedures
  - Practices
  - Wrongful Termination/Harassment
- Employment Practices
- Energy & Utilities
- Engineering Cryogenics
- Engineers/Engineering
  - Acoustics
  - Agricultural/Mechanical
  - Architecture
  - Automotive
  - Biomechanical
  - Biomedical
  - Chemical
  - Civil/Mechanical/Structural
  - Combustion/Incineration
  - Consultants
  - Control Systems
  - Conveyor Systems
  - Corrosion
  - Electrical
  - Electrical Project Management
  - Electrical/Accidents/Utilities
  - Explosion/Fire
  - Fire Protection
  - Forensic Engineering
  - GeoScience
  - Geotechnical
  - Industrial Refrigeration
  - Lifting Equipment
  - Materials
  - Mechanical/Machine Design
  - Petroleum

Expert Witness - Transportation (continued)
Aviation
Aviation - Air Traffic Control
Aviation - Airline Maintenance
Aviation/Aircraft/Airports
Buses
Public
Railroads
Tire & Wheel
Traffic Engineering & Safety
Trucking
Trees
Unclaimed Property
Underground Tanks
Underground Utilities
Utilities
Vehicle Mechanical Failure
Video Audio Track
Visibility Issues
Vocational
Economic Analysis
Vocational Evaluation
Life Care Plans
Warnings & Instructions
Warnings, Labeling & Product Instructions
Water Accidents
Weather & Climate
Wheelchairs
Windows & Doors
Witness Preparation Consultants
Wood Products (Adhesive-Bonded)
Wood Science & Technology
Wood Utility Poles
Expert Witness Referral Service - Environmental
Expert Witness Referral Services
Expert Witness Testimony Retrieval

Facilities Management
Failure Analysis/Testing Services
Fairness Opinions
Family Business Consultants
Filing Court Documents By Fax
Financial Case Prosecution
Financial Document Services
Financial Investigation/Forensic Accounting
Financial Services
Fingerprint Analysis
Fire Investigators
Fire Loss Experts
Foreign Embassy Services
Forensic Documentation - Demonstrative Evidence
Forensic Engineering - Non-Metallics/Failure Analysis
Forensic Engineering Metallurgy/Failure Analysis
Forensic Engineers
Forensic Financial Analysis
Forensic Geochemistry
Forensic Medicine
Forensic Photography
Forensic Psychiatry
Forensic Psychology
Forensic Services

Gemology
Genealogical Services
Geology
Geriatric and Disability Medicine
Government - Foreign Government Incorporating Offices
Government - Foreign Government Philatelic Bureaus
Government Contract Claims Consultant
Government Regulatory Research Specialists
Graphics Design & Production
Groupware

Handwriting Experts
Hedonic Damages/Loss of Enjoyment of Life
Heir Tracers
Heir/Probate Research
Home Detection Monitoring
Homicide Events
Hotel/Apartment Consultants & Experts
Human Factors & Ergonomics Consulting

Imaging Services
Immigration & Customs Consulting
Immigration Investment
Importer Associations
Incorporating Companies - Overseas Corporations
Incorporation Services
Independent Medical Examiner Referral Services
Independent Medical Examiners
Independent Medical Examiners - Chiropractic
Independent Medical Examiners - National Referral Service
Independent Medical Examiners - Neurology
Independent Medical Examiners - Neurosurgery
Independent Medical Examiners - Orthopaedics
Independent Medical Examiners - Physiatry
Independent Medical Examiners - Psychiatry
Information Brokers
Information Brokers - Medical
Information Clearing House
Information Security Specialists
Information Technology Governance
Insurance
Insurance - Corporate Owned Life Insurance
Insurance - Employment Practices
Insurance - Expert Witness Referral Service
Insurance - Health
Insurance - Intellectual Property
Insurance - Professional Liability
Insurance - Property/Casualty
Insurance - Risk Management Consulting
Insurance/Reinsurance Auditing Services
Intellectual Property Document Services
Intellectual Property Infringement
Intellectual Property Investigations
International Finance/Venture Capital
International Personal Tax Consultant
International Trade Consultants
Internet Advertising
Internet Marketing
Internet On Line Stock Exchange
Internet Services
Internet/Intranet Services
Interpreters
(See also Interpreters & Translators; Translation Services)
Interpreters & Translators
(See also Translation Services)
Interpreting - Deaf/Sign Language
Investigative Consultants
Investigators
Investment Advisory Compliance
Investment Clubs

Jail Mail
Judgement Enforcement
Jury Consultants
Jury Verdict Reporting Services

Labor Relations, Products & Services
Laboratories - Geochemical/Petroleum/Source ID
Laboratories - Parentage Testing
Law Books - New/Used
Law Office Automation Consulting
Law Office Automation Services
Lawyer Coaches
Lawyer Referral Service
Lawyer Search & Placement Consultants
Lease Auditors
Leasing & Financing
Legal Advertising
Legal Associations
Legal Auditors
Legal Brief Printers
Legal Copying
Legal Document Production Services
Legal Editor
Legal Forms - Computerized
Legal Office Support Services
Legal Publications
Legal Research
Legal Research/Appellate Practice
Legal Software
Legal Support Personnel - Temporary & Permanent
Legislative Intent Research
Letters of Credit
Libraries/Books Purchased
Library Management Services
Library Management Software
Life Care Planning
Lighting/Illumination Consultants
Linguistics
Liquidators
Litigation Consulting
Litigation Support - Detecting Deception

Services, Suppliers, Consultants
In This Volume

ACCOUNTANTS
DISTRICT OF COLUMBIA
WASHINGTON .... THE KARDON CORP.
LINDQUIST FORENSIC PARTNERS

ACCOUNTING
DISTRICT OF COLUMBIA
WASHINGTON .... LINDQUIST FORENSIC PARTNERS

APPRAISAL & VALUATION SERVICES
CONNECTICUT
STAMFORD .... THE AXIS GROUP INTERNATIONAL, LLC

APPRAISAL SERVICES - ESTATE & GIFT TAXES
CONNECTICUT
STAMFORD .... THE AXIS GROUP INTERNATIONAL, LLC

ARBITRATION & MEDIATION SERVICES
DISTRICT OF COLUMBIA
WASHINGTON .... JAMS
TASA

ASSET LOCATORS
DISTRICT OF COLUMBIA
WASHINGTON .... THE KARDON CORP.

ATTORNEY SERVICES
DELAWARE
WILMINGTON .... A & E, INC.
DISTRICT OF COLUMBIA
WASHINGTON .... A & E, INC.
AMERICAN LEGAL DOCUMENT COURIERS

BANKRUPTCY/TURNAROUND/INSOLVENCY
DISTRICT OF COLUMBIA
WASHINGTON .... CHARLES RIVER ASSOCIATES INCORPORATED

BANKS & TRUST COMPANIES
DELAWARE
WILMINGTON .... WILMINGTON TRUST COMPANY

BUSINESS VALUATIONS
CONNECTICUT
STAMFORD .... THE AXIS GROUP INTERNATIONAL, LLC
TRUGMAN VALUATION ASSOCIATES INC.
DISTRICT OF COLUMBIA
WASHINGTON .... ADVANCED VALUATION ANALYTICS, LTD. BUSINESS VALUATION CONSULTANTS
THE KARDON CORP.

CASE MANAGEMENT SYSTEMS
DISTRICT OF COLUMBIA
WASHINGTON .... COMPUTER PACKAGES INC.

CLASS ACTION NOTICE

DISTRICT OF COLUMBIA

WASHINGTON .... GCG COMMUNICATIONS
KINSELLA COMMUNICATIONS, LTD.

COMPUTER CONSULTANTS

DISTRICT OF COLUMBIA

WASHINGTON .... THE KARDON CORP.

CONSTRUCTION CONSULTANTS

DISTRICT OF COLUMBIA

WASHINGTON .... RBS CONSULTING GROUP
WARNER CONSTRUCTION CONSULTANTS, INC.

CORPORATION COMPANIES

DELAWARE

DOVER .... HYLIND SEARCH COMPANY, INC.

COURT HOUSE RESEARCH

DISTRICT OF COLUMBIA

WASHINGTON .... MOHR INFORMATION SERVICES

COURT REPORTERS

CONNECTICUT

BRIDGEPORT .... NIZIANKIEWICZ & MILLER REPORTING SERVICES

HARTFORD .... BRANDON SMITH REPORTING SERVICE, LLP
THE CUNNINGHAM GROUP, INC.
DEL VECCHIO REPORTING SERVICES
DOYLE REPORTING, INC.
NIZIANKIEWICZ & MILLER REPORTING SERVICES

NEW HAVEN .... BRANDON SMITH REPORTING SERVICE, LLP
DEL VECCHIO REPORTING SERVICES
NIZIANKIEWICZ & MILLER REPORTING SERVICES

STAMFORD .... THE CUNNINGHAM GROUP, INC.

WATERBURY .... NIZIANKIEWICZ & MILLER REPORTING SERVICES

DELAWARE

WILMINGTON .... CORBETT & ASSOCIATES
ESQUIRE™ DEPOSITION SERVICES
JANE ROSE REPORTING

DISTRICT OF COLUMBIA

WASHINGTON .... 1-800-FOR-DEPO-ALDERSON REPORTING
AA BETA REPORTING
ACE-FEDERAL REPORTERS, INC.
ALEXANDER GALLO & ASSOCIATES, INC.
AMICUS REPORTING
ART MILLER & ASSOCIATES, LLC
BRADFORD ASSOCIATES
CAPITOL REPORTING, INC.
CAROL J. THOMAS STENOTYPE REPORTING SERVICES, INC.
CATHERINE TEACH REPORTING, INC.
CERTIFIED VIDEO SERVICES, INC.
COURT REPORTERS, ETCETERA, INC.
THE CUNNINGHAM GROUP, INC.
DEPOSITION SERVICES, INC.
DIVERSIFIED REPORTING SERVICES, INC.
DOERNER & GOLDBERG INC.
EVANS REPORTING SERVICE, INC.
FOR THE RECORD, INC.

HUDSON REPORTING & VIDEO, INC.
HUTCHINGS COURT REPORTERS, LLC
JANE ROSE REPORTING
LYON REPORTING, INC.
MC CORKLE COURT REPORTERS, INC.
NEAL R. GROSS AND CO., INC.
RIGLER & O'NEILL COURT REPORTERS, INC.

CRIMINAL RECORDS RESEARCH

DISTRICT OF COLUMBIA

WASHINGTON .... MOHR INFORMATION SERVICES

DOCUMENT IMAGING

DISTRICT OF COLUMBIA

WASHINGTON .... ADVANCED IMAGING SOLUTIONS, INC.

DOCUMENT RESEARCH, RETRIEVAL & FILING

DELAWARE

DOVER .... A & E, INC.
HYLIND SEARCH COMPANY, INC.

WILMINGTON .... A & E, INC.

DISTRICT OF COLUMBIA

WASHINGTON .... A & E, INC.
ACCU-FAX SERVICES, A DIVISION OF CEO CORPORATE SECURITY GROUP, INC.
AMERICAN LEGAL DOCUMENT COURIERS
CAPITOL PROCESS SERVICES, INC., CAPITOL INVESTIGATOR SERVICES
MOHR INFORMATION SERVICES

E-BUSINESS

DISTRICT OF COLUMBIA

WASHINGTON .... COMPUTER AND COMMUNICATIONS LAW CONSULTANTS

ECONOMIC AND STATISTICAL CONSULTING SERVICES

DISTRICT OF COLUMBIA

WASHINGTON .... ANALYSIS AND INFERENCE, INC.
ANALYSIS GROUP/ECONOMICS
THE BRATTLE GROUP
CHARLES RIVER ASSOCIATES INCORPORATED
THE KARDON CORP.
LECG, LLC
NERA ECONOMIC CONSULTING
PA CONSULTING GROUP

ELECTRONIC FILING

DISTRICT OF COLUMBIA

WASHINGTON .... COURTLINK®

EMPLOYMENT SCREENING

DISTRICT OF COLUMBIA

WASHINGTON .... ACCU-FAX SERVICES, A DIVISION OF CEO CORPORATE SECURITY GROUP, INC.

ENVIRONMENTAL & ECOLOGICAL SERVICES

DISTRICT OF COLUMBIA

WASHINGTON .... ZYMAX FORENSICS

ENVIRONMENTAL CONSULTANTS

DISTRICT OF COLUMBIA

WASHINGTON .... ZYMAX FORENSICS

ENVIRONMENTAL INVESTIGATIONS
DISTRICT OF COLUMBIA
WASHINGTON .... ZYMAX FORENSICS

ESTATE PLANNING & PERSONAL BENEFITS
DELAWARE
WILMINGTON .... COMMONWEALTH TRUST COMPANY

EXAMINERS OF QUESTIONED DOCUMENTS (HANDWRITING EXPERTS)
CONNECTICUT
HARTFORD .... SEIFER HANDWRITING CONSULTANTS
DISTRICT OF COLUMBIA
WASHINGTON .... GIDEON EPSTEIN, MFS

EXPERT WITNESS
DISTRICT OF COLUMBIA
WASHINGTON .... LINDQUIST FORENSIC PARTNERS

ACCOUNTING
DISTRICT OF COLUMBIA
WASHINGTON .... THE KARDON CORP.
LINDQUIST FORENSIC PARTNERS

BANKING
FINANCE
DISTRICT OF COLUMBIA
WASHINGTON .... ANALYSIS GROUP/ECONOMICS

CHEMICAL PROCESS
SAFETY
CONNECTICUT
HARTFORD .... SAFETY ENGINEERING CONSULTANTS
DISTRICT OF COLUMBIA
WASHINGTON .... GRANBERRY & ASSOCIATES, INC.

COMMUNICATIONS
DISTRICT OF COLUMBIA
WASHINGTON .... COMPUTER AND COMMUNICATIONS LAW CONSULTANTS
TELECOMMUNICATIONS CONSULTING GROUP, INC.

COMPUTER & BUSINESS INFORMATION SYSTEMS
DISTRICT OF COLUMBIA
WASHINGTON .... COMPUTER AND COMMUNICATIONS LAW CONSULTANTS
THE KARDON CORP.

COMPUTER FORENSICS/DATA RECOVERY
DISTRICT OF COLUMBIA
WASHINGTON .... FOUNDSTONE, INC.

COMPUTER SCIENCE/INTELLECTUAL PROPERTY
DISTRICT OF COLUMBIA
WASHINGTON .... COMPUTER AND COMMUNICATIONS LAW CONSULTANTS

CONSTRUCTION
DISTRICT OF COLUMBIA
WASHINGTON .... RBS CONSULTING GROUP
URS/O'BRIEN KREITZBERG

DAMAGE VALUATION
DISTRICT OF COLUMBIA
WASHINGTON .... ANALYSIS GROUP/ECONOMICS
THE KARDON CORP.

ECONOMICS/ECONOMISTS
DISTRICT OF COLUMBIA
WASHINGTON .... ANALYSIS GROUP/ECONOMICS
CHARLES RIVER ASSOCIATES INCORPORATED
LECG, LLC

FINANCIAL VALUATION

DISTRICT OF COLUMBIA

WASHINGTON .... THE BRATTLE GROUP
RICHARD B. EDELMAN, PH.D.
LECG, LLC

STATISTICS

DISTRICT OF COLUMBIA

WASHINGTON .... ANALYSIS AND INFERENCE, INC.

ECONOMICS/STATISTICS

DISTRICT OF COLUMBIA

WASHINGTON .... THE KARDON CORP.

EMPLOYEE/EMPLOYMENT PRACTICES

DISTRICT OF COLUMBIA

WASHINGTON .... ANALYSIS GROUP/ECONOMICS

ENERGY & UTILITIES

DISTRICT OF COLUMBIA

WASHINGTON .... ANALYSIS GROUP/ECONOMICS
PA CONSULTING GROUP

ENGINEERS/ENGINEERING

CONNECTICUT

HARTFORD .... TETRA ENGINEERING GROUP, INC.

ENVIRONMENTAL

DISTRICT OF COLUMBIA

WASHINGTON .... THE BRATTLE GROUP

ENVIRONMENTAL CONSULTANT

CONNECTICUT

WINDSOR .... TRC ENVIRONMENTAL CORPORATION

DISTRICT OF COLUMBIA

WASHINGTON .... ZYMAX FORENSICS

ENVIRONMENTAL CONTAMINATION/SPILLS

DISTRICT OF COLUMBIA

WASHINGTON .... ZYMAX FORENSICS

ENVIRONMENTAL HEALTH & SAFETY

CONNECTICUT

HARTFORD .... SAFETY ENGINEERING CONSULTANTS

DISTRICT OF COLUMBIA

WASHINGTON .... GRANBERRY & ASSOCIATES, INC.

FALL PROTECTION

DELAWARE

WILMINGTON .... DYNAMIC SCIENTIFIC CONTROLS, INC.

FORENSIC ACCOUNTING

DISTRICT OF COLUMBIA

WASHINGTON .... THE KARDON CORP.

FRAUD

DISTRICT OF COLUMBIA

WASHINGTON .... THE KARDON CORP.
LINDQUIST FORENSIC PARTNERS

GOVERNMENT CONTRACT CLAIMS

DISTRICT OF COLUMBIA

WASHINGTON .... SHAW CONSULTING GROUP

HANDWRITING

CONNECTICUT

HARTFORD .... SEIFER HANDWRITING CONSULTANTS

HEALTH CARE PLANS

DISTRICT OF COLUMBIA

WASHINGTON .... MANAGED LIABILITY ASSOCIATES

EXPERT WITNESS - Continued

HUMAN FACTORS & SAFETY

CONNECTICUT

HARTFORD .... SAFETY ENGINEERING CONSULTANTS

INTELLECTUAL PROPERTY/INFRINGEMENT DAMAGES

DISTRICT OF COLUMBIA

WASHINGTON .... ANALYSIS GROUP/ECONOMICS
THE BRATTLE GROUP
CHARLES RIVER ASSOCIATES INCORPORATED
COMPUTER AND COMMUNICATIONS LAW CONSULTANTS
LECG, LLC

OSHA/SAFETY/TOXIC TORT

CONNECTICUT

HARTFORD .... SAFETY ENGINEERING CONSULTANTS

OIL & GAS

DISTRICT OF COLUMBIA

WASHINGTON .... ZYMAX FORENSICS

PETROLEUM SOURCE ID

DISTRICT OF COLUMBIA

WASHINGTON .... ZYMAX FORENSICS

PREMISES SECURITY & LIABILITY

DISTRICT OF COLUMBIA

WASHINGTON .... SECURE SOURCE INC.

PRODUCT LIABILITY

DISTRICT OF COLUMBIA

WASHINGTON .... DAVID F. GOLDSMITH PHD
THE KARDON CORP.

RAPE/SEXUAL ASSAULT

DISTRICT OF COLUMBIA

WASHINGTON .... PAGE VERLANDER R.N., MS, PH.D.

SAFETY

CONNECTICUT

HARTFORD .... SAFETY ENGINEERING CONSULTANTS

SECURITIES LAW

DISTRICT OF COLUMBIA

WASHINGTON .... WILLIAM A. COLLISON, JR., P.A.

SECURITIES/LITIGATION SUPPORT

DISTRICT OF COLUMBIA

WASHINGTON .... ANALYSIS GROUP/ECONOMICS
CHARLES RIVER ASSOCIATES INCORPORATED

SECURITY CONSULTANTS

DISTRICT OF COLUMBIA

WASHINGTON .... SECURE SOURCE INC.

TELECOMMUNICATIONS

DISTRICT OF COLUMBIA

WASHINGTON .... THE BRATTLE GROUP
CPT ASSOCIATES, INC.
TELECOMMUNICATIONS CONSULTING GROUP, INC.

TOXICOLOGY

DISTRICT OF COLUMBIA

WASHINGTON .... PAGE VERLANDER R.N., MS, PH.D.

TRANSPORTATION

DISTRICT OF COLUMBIA

WASHINGTON .... NATIONAL TRUCKING SAFETY CONSULTANTS

AVIATION

DISTRICT OF COLUMBIA

WASHINGTON .... JACOBY AND ASSOCIATES

EXPERT WITNESS REFERRAL SERVICES

DELAWARE

WILMINGTON .... THE CECON GROUP INC.

DISTRICT OF COLUMBIA

WASHINGTON .... EXPERT RESOURCES, INC.®
SILICON VALLEY EXPERT WITNESS GROUP INC.
TASA

FINANCIAL INVESTIGATION/FORENSIC ACCOUNTING

DISTRICT OF COLUMBIA

WASHINGTON .... THE KARDON CORP.
LINDQUIST FORENSIC PARTNERS

FORENSIC FINANCIAL ANALYSIS

DISTRICT OF COLUMBIA

WASHINGTON .... LINDQUIST FORENSIC PARTNERS

FORENSIC GEOCHEMISTRY

DISTRICT OF COLUMBIA

WASHINGTON .... ZYMAX FORENSICS

GENEALOGICAL SERVICES

DISTRICT OF COLUMBIA

WASHINGTON .... HOERNER BANK

HANDWRITING EXPERTS

CONNECTICUT

HARTFORD .... SEIFER HANDWRITING CONSULTANTS

HEIR TRACERS

DISTRICT OF COLUMBIA

WASHINGTON .... HOERNER BANK

INTERPRETERS

DISTRICT OF COLUMBIA

WASHINGTON .... LANGUAGEWORKS
THE LEGAL TRANSLATORS.COM

INTERPRETERS & TRANSLATORS

DISTRICT OF COLUMBIA

WASHINGTON .... JAPAN COMMUNICATION CONSULTANTS, LLC
LANGUAGEWORKS
THE LEGAL TRANSLATORS.COM

INVESTIGATIVE CONSULTANTS

DISTRICT OF COLUMBIA

WASHINGTON .... CAPITOL PROCESS SERVICES, INC., CAPITOL INVESTIGATOR SERVICES

INVESTIGATORS

CONNECTICUT

HARTFORD .... PINKERTON® CONSULTING & INVESTIGATIONS

DISTRICT OF COLUMBIA

WASHINGTON .... HICKEY, MILLER & BAILEY, INC.
INTERFOR, INC.
THE KARDON CORP.
PINKERTON® CONSULTING & INVESTIGATIONS
SECURE SOURCE INC.

JURY CONSULTANTS
DISTRICT OF COLUMBIA
WASHINGTON .... ON TRIAL ASSOCIATES, INC.

LABORATORIES - GEOCHEMICAL/PETROLEUM/SOURCE ID
DISTRICT OF COLUMBIA
WASHINGTON .... ZYMAX FORENSICS

LAW OFFICE AUTOMATION SERVICES
DISTRICT OF COLUMBIA
WASHINGTON .... SAGE

LAWYER SEARCH & PLACEMENT CONSULTANTS
DELAWARE
WILMINGTON .... THE AFFILIATES℠
DISTRICT OF COLUMBIA
WASHINGTON .... THE AFFILIATES℠
HARBOR CONSULTANTS INTERNATIONAL, INC.
LEGALLEADERS, INC.
STAFFWISE LEGAL, INC.

LEGAL PUBLICATIONS
DISTRICT OF COLUMBIA
WASHINGTON .... THE BUREAU OF NATIONAL AFFAIRS
CCH INCORPORATED
U.S. GOVERNMENT PRINTING OFFICE

LEGAL RESEARCH
DISTRICT OF COLUMBIA
WASHINGTON .... COURTLINK®

LEGAL SOFTWARE
DISTRICT OF COLUMBIA
WASHINGTON .... COMPUTER PACKAGES INC.

LEGAL SUPPORT PERSONNEL - TEMPORARY & PERMANENT
DISTRICT OF COLUMBIA
WASHINGTON .... NRI LEGAL RESOURCES
STAFFWISE LEGAL, INC.

LITIGATION SUPPORT SERVICES
DISTRICT OF COLUMBIA
WASHINGTON .... COURTLINK®

MANAGEMENT CONSULTANTS
DISTRICT OF COLUMBIA
WASHINGTON .... THE KARDON CORP.
PA CONSULTING GROUP

MEDICAL EXPERT WITNESS
MANAGED CARE/HMO LITIGATION
DISTRICT OF COLUMBIA
WASHINGTON .... MANAGED LIABILITY ASSOCIATES
PSYCHIATRY
CONNECTICUT
HARTFORD .... ACCREDITED PSYCHIATRY AND MEDICINE

NEWS/MEDIA SERVICES
DISTRICT OF COLUMBIA
WASHINGTON .... U.S. NEWSWIRE

NURSING CONSULTANTS
CONNECTICUT
OXFORD .... J.C. LEVIS AND ASSOCIATES LLC

ONLINE PUBLIC RECORDS SERVICE
DISTRICT OF COLUMBIA
WASHINGTON .... COURTLINK®

PARALEGAL SERVICES
DISTRICT OF COLUMBIA
WASHINGTON .... DAWNA PARKER, PARALEGAL SERVICES
NRI LEGAL RESOURCES
STAFFWISE LEGAL, INC.

PATENT, TRADEMARK & COPYRIGHT SEARCH SERVICES
DISTRICT OF COLUMBIA
WASHINGTON .... COMPUTER PACKAGES INC.
THOMSON & THOMSON

PETROLEUM SOURCE IDENTIFICATION
DISTRICT OF COLUMBIA
WASHINGTON .... ZYMAX FORENSICS

PROCESS SERVERS & DOCUMENT DELIVERY SERVICES
CONNECTICUT
BRIDGEPORT .... A-BEST BAIL BONDS, L.L.C.
CONNECTICUT PROCESS SERVICE
NEW WORLD SERVICES INTERNATIONAL LTD.

HARTFORD .... A & E, INC.
A-BEST BAIL BONDS, L.L.C.
CONNECTICUT PROCESS SERVICE

NEW HAVEN .... CONNECTICUT PROCESS SERVICE

STAMFORD .... A & E, INC.

WATERBURY .... CONNECTICUT PROCESS SERVICE
DELAWARE
DOVER .... A & E, INC.

WILMINGTON .... A & E, INC.
DM PROFESSIONAL SERVICES, INC.
DISTRICT OF COLUMBIA
WASHINGTON .... A & E, INC.
ACCURATE LEGAL SERVICES
AMERICAN LEGAL DOCUMENT COURIERS
CAPITOL PROCESS SERVICES, INC., CAPITOL INVESTIGATOR SERVICES
GUARANTEED SUBPOENA SERVICE, INC.
LEGAL LANGUAGE SERVICES
WASHINGTON DC PROCESS SVC
WASHINGTON PRE-TRIAL SERVICES, INC.

SECRETARIAL SUPPORT
DISTRICT OF COLUMBIA
WASHINGTON .... NRI LEGAL RESOURCES

STATISTICS
DISTRICT OF COLUMBIA
WASHINGTON .... ANALYSIS AND INFERENCE, INC.

STRUCTURED SETTLEMENTS
CONNECTICUT
STAMFORD .... SUMMIT SETTLEMENT SERVICES

SURVEYS & OPINION RESEARCH
DISTRICT OF COLUMBIA
WASHINGTON .... THE KARDON CORP.

TRANSCRIPTION SERVICES
DISTRICT OF COLUMBIA
WASHINGTON .... ACE-FEDERAL REPORTERS, INC.

TRANSLATION SERVICES
DISTRICT OF COLUMBIA
WASHINGTON .... JAPAN COMMUNICATION CONSULTANTS, LLC
LANGUAGEWORKS
THE LEGAL TRANSLATORS.COM
SYNTES LANGUAGE GROUP, INC.

TRIAL CONSULTANTS
DISTRICT OF COLUMBIA
WASHINGTON .... ON TRIAL ASSOCIATES, INC.

TRUST & FIDUCIARY SERVICES
DELAWARE
WILMINGTON .... COMMONWEALTH TRUST COMPANY

TRUST COMPANIES
DELAWARE
WILMINGTON .... COMMONWEALTH TRUST COMPANY

VALUATION SERVICES
CONNECTICUT
STAMFORD .... THE AXIS GROUP INTERNATIONAL, LLC

VIDEO TAPE SERVICES
DISTRICT OF COLUMBIA
WASHINGTON .... ACE-FEDERAL REPORTERS, INC.
CERTIFIED VIDEO SERVICES, INC.

BRIDGEPORT,* 141,686, *Fairfield Co.*

COURT REPORTERS

Niziankiewicz & Miller Reporting Services

Phone (860) 291-9191
Fax (860) 528-1972
Toll-Free: (888) 565-9091
972 Tolland Street
East Hartford, CT 06108-1533

Niziankiewicz & Miller court reporters provide reporting services throughout the state of Connecticut.

Our reporters hold Certificates of Merit and are Registered Professional Reporters. We provide the best reporting specialists in all fields including:

Medical
Technical
Environmental
Construction

We are a full-service reporting firm providing stenography, video and litigation support to the legal community.

Arbitrations	DiscoveryZX
ASCII Disks	Hearings
CAT-Links	Statewide Coverage
Computer-Aided Transcription	Real-Time depositions
Conference Room	Subpoena Service
Courier Service	Translators
Daily Copy	Video Service
	XMAX Condensed Transcripts

Our professional associations include:

National Court Reporters Association
California Court Reporters Association
Connecticut Court Reporters Association
Massachusetts Court Reporters Association

Serving Bridgeport, Hartford, New Haven, Waterbury & Stamford.

PROCESS SERVERS & DOCUMENT DELIVERY SERVICES

A-BEST BAIL BONDS, L.L.C.

Since 1991

P.O. Box 653
Manchester, Connecticut 06045
Phone: 860-646-4333
Fax: 860-646-8877
Toll Free: (800) 646-0384

Services provided:

- SUMMONS, COMPLAINTS, SUBPOENAS
- PERSONAL SERVICE
- REGULAR STATUS UPDATES
- COURIER SERVICE
- COUNTIES SERVED:
  Hartford, Tolland Counties, and the Metro Hartford Area
- SUBPOENA PREPARATION
- SPECIALIZING IN RUSH SERVICE TO MAJOR INSURANCE CARRIERS
- FLAT RATE
- NO MILEAGE CHARGES

MEMBERSHIPS
NAPPS
USPSA

BRIDGEPORT (Continued)

Process Servers & Document Delivery Services (Continued)

HARTFORD,* 139,739, *Hartford Co.*

COURT REPORTERS

HARTFORD (Continued)

Court Reporters (Continued)

SEE OUR AD ON PAGE CT3S

EXAMINERS OF QUESTIONED DOCUMENTS (HANDWRITING EXPERTS)

HARTFORD (Continued)

EXPERT WITNESS

CHEMICAL PROCESS

Specializing in: Safety

Safety Engineering Consultants
19 Settlement Hill
Windsor, CT 06095
Phone: (860) 833-8035
Fax: (860) 298-8472

See Expert Witness-Environmental Health & Safety

ENGINEERS/ENGINEERING

Tetra Engineering Group, Inc.
110 Hopmeadow Street Suite 800
Weatogue, Connecticut USA 06089

1-860-651-4622 dmoelling@tetra-eng.com

Tetra Engineering provides consulting and expert services in:

- Pressure Vessel & Piping Integrity
- Energy System Warranties and Guarantees
- Reliability and Fitness for Service Evaluations
- Economic Assessments for Energy Projects
- Prudence and Due Diligence Assessments

Tetra Engineering can provide specialized services for cases involving pipe failure due to erosion-corrosion or flow accelerated corrosion. Statistical and probabilistic assessments for piping and pressure vessel integrity are a specialty.

Profiles:

Frank J. Berté, PhD

Dr. Berté has over 30 years experience in the electric power industry, including the design, construction, and troubleshooting of power plants.

Peter S. Jackson, PhD, PE

Dr. Jackson has 20 years experience in power plant design and operation and has specialized in the review and management of pressure piping and vessel integrity.

Frederick C. Anderson, PE

Mr. Anderson has over 20 years of experience in power and process industries including service under Admiral Hyman Rickover in the US Navy. He is an experienced metallurgical engineer and is a leading expert on flow accelerated corrosion.

David S. Moelling, PE

Mr. Moelling has 20 years experience in the assessment of capital equipment for warranties, guarantees, technical suitability and financial due diligence.

James W. Malloy

Mr. Malloy has 20 years experience in the assessment of electrical and electronic systems under harsh conditions. He provides support for issues involving failures and performance of these systems for power, process, and aerospace applications.

ENVIRONMENTAL HEALTH & SAFETY

Safety Engineering Consultants
Wes Jordan Associates, Inc.
C.W. Jordan, Ph.D., PE
Certified Safety Professional
Principal Consultant
cwjordan2@home.com
Tel: 860 833-8035
Fax: 860 298-8472

Dr. Wes Jordan is a senior level, registered professional engineer, expert in the **technical** and **regulatory** aspects of **environmental protection, process safety, construction safety, industrial hygiene, loss prevention, and human factors** for chemical, petroleum, pharmaceutical, aerospace, defense and construction industries.

Dr. Jordan has 35 years of industrial experience in the design, construction, maintenance, and auditing of petrochemical process and environmental safety systems to improve operational safety and regulatory compliance. He performs accident investigations and serves as an expert witness on causal factors relating to chemical process, construction and environmental safety. In addition, he has investigated and testified relative to soil contamination claims, toxic exposures or chemical injuries as well as fire and explosion accidents from consumer products.

Dr. Jordan has been consulting for industry and the legal profession for the last ten years. In addition to his consultation practice, Dr. Jordan is Assistant Professor, Safety & Environmental Management & Engineering, at Rensselaer Polytechnic Institute, Hartford, CT. He has been Adjunct Professor, Safety and Health at University of Connecticut.

His firm has the ability to conduct and manage investigations and coordinate the activities of multiple experts or investigators working on a complex case.

Please call or write for information about services or contract information and fees.

HANDWRITING

Seifer Handwriting Consultants
Box 32
Kingston, RI 02881
Phone: (401) 294-2414
Fax: (401) 294-2414

See Examiners Of Questioned Documents (Handwriting Experts)

HUMAN FACTORS & SAFETY

Safety Engineering Consultants
19 Settlement Hill
Windsor, CT 06095
Phone: (860) 833-8035
Fax: (860) 298-8472

See Expert Witness-Environmental Health & Safety

OSHA/SAFETY/TOXIC TORT

Safety Engineering Consultants
19 Settlement Hill
Windsor, CT 06095
Phone: (860) 833-8035
Fax: (860) 298-8472

See Expert Witness-Environmental Health & Safety

SAFETY

Safety Engineering Consultants
19 Settlement Hill
Windsor, CT 06095
Phone: (860) 833-8035
Fax: (860) 298-8472

See Expert Witness-Environmental Health & Safety

HANDWRITING EXPERTS

Seifer Handwriting Consultants
Box 32
Kingston, RI 02881
Phone: (401) 294-2414
Fax: (401) 294-2414

See Examiners Of Questioned Documents (Handwriting Experts)

INVESTIGATORS

PINKERTON®
CONSULTING & INVESTIGATIONS

20 North Plains Industrial Rd., Suite 3
Wallingford, CT 06492
Phone (203) 284-1233
Fax (203) 294-4174
Kevin Cox, Director of Operations
E-mail kevin.cox@ci-pinkerton.com
Website www.pinkertonagency.com

World Headquarters
13950 Ballantyne Corporate Place, Suite 300
Charlotte, NC 28277-2712
Phone (888) 774-9600
International (704) 552-1119

Where More and More Attorneys Are Turning For Credible, Confidential Investigative Support.
Serving the Legal Community Since 1850.

Pinkerton Consulting and Investigations enjoys an established reputation and expertise in protecting and safeguarding the interests of businesses worldwide. We offer comprehensive solutions through proven professionals with global capabilities with offices in 60 locations throughout North and South America, Europe, Asia, Australia, and Africa.

Business Integrity Solutions
- Fraud Investigations
- Financial Investigations
- Data Mining and Fraud Detection
- Legal Support
- Due Diligence Inquires
- Background Investigations
- Employee Vetting

Brand Protection Solutions
- Education and Awareness
- Product Authentication
- Trademark and Patent Infringement
- Internet and Field Monitoring
- Investigations and Enforcement
- Litigation Support

Workplace Compliance Solutions
- AlertLine® Ethics and Compliance Hotlines
- Incident Reporting
- Employee Awareness and Training
- Workplace Violence
- Fair Employment Practices
- Field Research
- Compliance Audits and Monitoring

Crisis Management Solutions
- Risk Evaluation and Analysis
- Crisis Planning, Evacuation Continuity
- Crisis Prevention Programs
- Incident Response
- Personnel Protection
- Executive Protection Services and Programs

Global Intelligence
- Risk Reporting and Analysis
- City and Country Reports
- Travel Advisory and Briefings

Technology Risk Solutions
- Information Technology Security
- Logistics Security
- Computer Forensics

HARTFORD (Continued)

MEDICAL EXPERT WITNESS

PSYCHIATRY

Telephone: (617) 492-8366
FAX: (617) 441-3195
Email: harold_bursztajn@hms.harvard.edu
Website: http://www.forensic-psych.com

Harold J. Bursztajn, M.D.
96 Larchwood Drive
Cambridge, MA 02138

Associate Clinical Professor
Harvard Medical School

ACCREDITED PSYCHIATRY AND MEDICINE

Harold J. Bursztajn, M.D., Co-Director of the Program in Psychiatry and the Law and senior clinical faculty member at Harvard Medical School, is active in direct patient care, teaching, and research. He consults to plaintiff and defense counsel, to insurance companies, and to state and federal agencies as an expert in general and forensic psychiatry, medical malpractice decision analysis, and professional organizational ethics. He also has nationwide experience as a distinguished expert qualified to testify in state and federal courts. Relevant areas of expertise include:

- **Employment: disability, workers' compensation, & sexual harassment, workplace violence**
- **Malpractice, managed care & informed consent: medical & mental health**
- **Emotional & physical damages: pain & suffering, PTSD, neuropsychiatry & brain imaging, psychiatric examinations**
- **Product liability & toxic tort**
- **Criminal justice & diminished capacity**
- **Family issues: divorce & custody, testamentary capacity**
- **Professional ethics in clinical practice and telemedicine**

Dr. Bursztajn is an honors graduate of Princeton University and Harvard Medical School. In addition to his clinical practice involving patient care, he has published numerous articles, and chapters in standard texts in medicine, medical decision making, clinical ethics, psychiatry, neuropsychiatry, and forensic psychiatry. He has authored a number of books including *(1) Divided Staffs, Divided Selves: A Case Approach to Mental Health Ethics; (2) Medical Choices, Medical Chances: How Patients, Families, and Physicians Can Cope With Uncertainty;* and *(3) Decision Making in Psychiatry and the Law.*

A complete curriculum vitae and references are available upon request. All inquiries are confidential.

PROCESS SERVERS & DOCUMENT DELIVERY SERVICES

An **A&E, Inc.** Company
Torri's Legal Services
— **Quality Legal Service** —
BASED ON CONFIDENCE, TRUST AND RESULTS

(800) 990-SERV
(800) 990-7378
Fax: (800) 845-2131
Internet: www.torrilegalservices.com
email: tlsnc@erols.com

We Service:
Hartford • Stamford • Bridgeport •
New Haven and all of Connecticut

*24 Hour Service * 7 Days A Week * Weekends * Holidays*

WE SPECIALIZE IN:

- Nationwide Service of Process
- Summons, Complaints, Subpoenas
- Personal Services
- Document Retrieval
- Court Filings
- Emergency Service
- Defendants And Witness
- Computerized Searches
- International Service

Member:
National Association of Professional Process Servers

A-BEST BAIL BONDS, L.L.C.

Since 1991

P.O. Box 653
Manchester, Connecticut 06045
Phone: 860-646-4333
Fax: 860-646-8877
Toll Free: (800) 646-0384

Services provided:

- SUMMONS, COMPLAINTS, SUBPOENAS
- PERSONAL SERVICE
- REGULAR STATUS UPDATES
- COURIER SERVICE
- COUNTIES SERVED:
  Hartford, Tolland Counties, and the Metro Hartford Area
- SUBPOENA PREPARATION
- SPECIALIZING IN RUSH SERVICE TO MAJOR INSURANCE CARRIERS
- FLAT RATE
- NO MILEAGE CHARGES

MEMBERSHIPS
NAPPS
USPSA

NAPPS

SEE OUR AD ON PAGE CT9S

Connecticut Process Service

Phone (860) 528-2920
Fax (860) 528-2720

9 Beaumont Street
East Hartford, CT 06108-1533

Connecticut Process Service provides process serving throughout the state of Connecticut.

We provide the best Process Serving specialists in Connecticut.

Medical
Technical
Environmental
Construction

We are a full-service agency providing service of process, court reporting, video and litigation support to the legal community.

Courier Service
Statewide Coverage
Subpoena Service
Translators
Video Service

Our professional associations include:
National Association of Professional Process Servers

Serving Bridgeport, Hartford, New Haven, Waterbury & Stamford.

NEW HAVEN,* 130,474, *New Haven Co.*

COURT REPORTERS

SEE OUR AD ON PAGE CT11S

PROCESS SERVERS & DOCUMENT DELIVERY SERVICES

Connecticut Process Service

Phone (860) 528-2920
Fax (860) 528-2720

9 Beaumont Street
East Hartford, CT 06108-1533

Connecticut Process Service provides process serving throughout the state of Connecticut.

We provide the best Process Serving specialists in Connecticut.

Medical
Technical
Environmental
Construction

We are a full-service agency providing service of process, court reporting, video and litigation support to the legal community.

Courier Service
Statewide Coverage
Subpoena Service
Translators
Video Service

Our professional associations include:

National Association of Professional Process Servers

Serving Bridgeport, Hartford, New Haven, Waterbury & Stamford.

OXFORD, 6,634, ***New Haven Co.***

NURSING CONSULTANTS

J.C. Levis and Associates LLC

Legal Nurse Consultants
Health Care Consulting & Educational Services

PO Box 608
Oxford, CT 06478
Telephone/Fax 203-888-0535

Web site: www.jclevis.com
E-mail: jclevis@aol.com

We are Professional Service Organization providing Legal Nurse Consultant services for attorneys and Consulting and Educational Services for Health Care Providers.

We are based in New Haven County, Connecticut and service clients' nationwide and welcome international inquires.

You are invited to view our website www.jclevis.com for a comprehensive description of our exceptional qualifications and services that we offer. If you prefer, call or write to us and request our information packet describing the firm and our services.

If you have an immediate case to discuss with us, please contact us and we will be available to set up a mutually convenient time to discuss it with you.

STAMFORD, 108,056, *Fairfield Co.*

APPRAISAL & VALUATION SERVICES

THE AXIS GROUP INTERNATIONAL, LLC

111 Godfrey Road West
Weston, Connecticut 06883

c.armbrust@axis-group.net
www.axis-group.net

Telephone: (203) 451-3050
Facsimile: (914) 206-7652

The AXIS Group International, LLC specializes in business valuations and merger & acquisition advisory and support services. Our staff's professional experience in valuations, M&A's, and related strategic business analysis spans over 17 years, and includes fair market and investment valuations for businesses ranging from $1 million to $250 million in value.

SERVICES PROVIDED

The AXIS Group's (TAG) business valuation and appraisal services include professional opinions of fair market value, fair value, and investment value for businesses, controlling an minority interests. We provide our clients, consisting of both closely held and publicly held businesses, with accurate, timely, and confidential valuations in the form of Formal Appraisals and Preliminary Reports to meet their needs:

- Employee Stock Ownership Plans (ESOPs)
- Family Limited Partnerships (FLPs)
- Gifting/Estate Planning and Settlement
- Lost Profit Calculations
- Marital Dissolutions
- Mergers & Acquisitions
- Shareholder Agreements

TAG's advisory and support services for mergers, acquisitions, and divestitures are comprehensive and thorough - from targeting buyers and sellers through closing of the transaction. Our experience in M&A's has an aggregate value of $1 billion, including both North America and international businesses:

- Origination/Prospecting
- Offering Memorandums
- Corporate Proposals
- Valuation Benchmarking
- Negotiations
- Due Diligence

INDUSTRY EXPERIENCE

The professionals at The AXIS Group have assimilated considerable expertise and competence in serving a broad array of industries - from distributors to retailers, from high technology to industrial manufacturing, and from professional practices to professional trades.

CREDENTIALS & AFFILIATIONS

The TAG team possesses strong professional credentials, including degrees, designations, and continuing professional education from the following organizations:

MBA - University of New Haven
BA - North Central College
Institute of Business Appraisers (IBA)
American Society of Appraisers (ASA)
Connecticut Bar Association (CBA)
Regional Bar Association of Stamford, Norwalk, Darien, and Wilton

The AXIS Group is committed to providing accurate, timely and professional services to our clients and business partners. Contact us for a confidential consultation, engagement proposal or further information at (203) 451- 3050 or c.armbrust@axis-group.net.

APPRAISAL SERVICES - ESTATE & GIFT TAXES

The AXIS Group International, LLC
111 Godfrey Rd. W.
Weston, CT 06883
Phone: (203) 451-3050
Fax: (914) 206-7652

See Appraisal & Valuation Services

BUSINESS VALUATIONS

The AXIS Group International, LLC
111 Godfrey Rd. W.
Weston, CT 06883
Phone: (203) 451-3050
Fax: (914) 206-7652

See Appraisal & Valuation Services

Trugman Valuation
ASSOCIATES INC.

The certified leader in business valuation expertise™

270A Route 46 East, Rockaway, NJ 07866
6 Landmark Square, 4th Floor, Stamford, CT 06901
3001 N. Rocky Point Drive East, Suite 200, Tampa, FL 33607
8201 Peters Road, Suite 1000, Plantation, FL 33324

Toll Free 800 330-VALU
www.trugmanvaluation.com

Trugman Valuation Associates is regularly called upon by law firms and CPAs to assist in the complex legal and financial matters of their clients. We are often retained by opposing parties with differing valuations of businesses or business interests, and frequently appointed by judges to mediate widely disparate appraisals, or to offer expert testimony. Our firm also performs a wide variety of economic damages analyses ranging from lost profits to personal injury.

Areas of Expertise

- Mergers & Acquisitions
- Stockholder Litigation
- Estate & Gift Tax
- Buy/Sell Agreements
- Intangible Assets
- Sales & Spin-Offs
- Economic Damages
- Marital Dissolution
- ESOPs
- Fairness Opinions

The professionals at Trugman Valuation Associates offer substantial experience and competence in business valuations and economic damages. This experience extends across a wide variety of industries and different size companies. We also have extensive experience in providing court testimony.

All professional staff members are required to pursue accreditations in the firm's areas of specialization. We invite you to review individual credentials of our senior staff members on our Web site.

Staff Credentials

- Certified Public Accountants accredited in Business Valuation by the American Institute of CPAs
- Certified Business Appraisers accredited by The Institute of Business Appraisers, Inc.
- Accredited Senior Appraiser designations in Business Valuation from the American Society of Appraisers

COURT REPORTERS

THE CUNNINGHAM GROUP, INC.

Specialists in Court Reporting and Litigation Management
700 Canal Street
Stamford, CT 06902
Telephones: 203-356-1229
1-800-842-4486 - Nationwide
Fax: 860-524-5021
www.cunninghamreporting.com
cgroup@compuserve.com

Serving the legal and corporate communities since 1965.

Customized document databases, customized software for search and retrieval, document repository and distribution center, imaging, computer-generated document numbers, deposition exhibit databases, deposition digesting.

Complete court reporting and litigation service including: Computer-aided transcription, instant-real-time, daily and expedited delivery, videography, and telecommunications. Diskettes in all standard formats: ASCII, Summation, Discovery, WordPerfect, Word Star, Zyindex, etc. Customized formats on request.

Registered Professional Reporters and Notaries; experienced in federal and state court depositions; patent, medical and public utilities; Environmental litigation a specialty.

Deposition rooms. Subpoena preparation and service.

Member National Court Reporters Association, Connecticut, Massachusetts, New Hampshire, New York, Texas, Ohio and California Court Reporters Associations, Reporters Cooperative, Inc., and American Arbitration Association.

Please have notice read: "Before Margherita R. Cunningham or other competent authority within and for the State of... "

References furnished on request.

STAMFORD (Continued)

Court Reporters (Continued)

Niziankiewicz & Miller Reporting Services

Fax: 860-528-1972
972 Tolland Street
East Hartford, CT 06108-1533

We are a full-service firm providing video and litigation support to the legal community.

- arbitrations
- ASCII disks
- CAT-links
- computer-aided transcription
- conference room
- courier service
- daily copy
- discovery ZX
- hearings
- statewide coverage
- real-time depositions
- subpoena service
- translators
- video service

XMAX condensed transcripts

(888) 565-9191

PROCESS SERVERS & DOCUMENT DELIVERY SERVICES

An **A&E, Inc.** Company

Torri's Legal Services

Quality Legal Service
BASED ON CONFIDENCE, TRUST AND RESULTS

(800) 990-SERV
(800) 990-7378
Fax: (800) 845-2131
Internet: www.torrilegalservices.com
email: tlsnc@erols.com

We Service:
Hartford • Stamford • Bridgeport •
New Haven and all of Connecticut

*24 Hour Service * 7 Days A Week * Weekends * Holidays*

WE SPECIALIZE IN:

- Nationwide Service of Process
- Summons, Complaints, Subpoenas
- Personal Services
- Document Retrieval
- Court Filings
- Emergency Service
- Defendants And Witness
- Computerized Searches
- International Service

Member:
National Association of Professional Process Servers

STAMFORD (Continued)

STRUCTURED SETTLEMENTS

John D. Darer, CLU, ChFC, CSSC
Summit Settlement Services
43 Harbor Drive, Unit 309
Stamford, CT 06902
(888) 325-8640 Toll-free USA
(203) 325-8640 Local and from outside USA
(917) 226-2882 cellular
(203) 969-2303 fax
structures@aol.com or john.darer@4structures.com
Website: www.4structures.com

ABOUT SUMMIT SETTLEMENT SERVICES

Summit Settlement Services provides financial consulting services in conjunction with personal injury litigation. Summit Settlement Services experienced financial consultants work with lawyers, claims personnel and risk managers to effectively design, negotiate and implement solutions that benefit all parties. Summit Settlement Services provides in-depth analysis and comprehensive planning advice that gets results. Summit serves accounts throughout the United States and international insurers on their risks in the United States. With a national presence, we have the flexibility to create service groups to handle virtually any type of loss. Economies of scale enable our clients to have access to a large portfolio of major structured annuity markets and T-Bond structure providers and competitive pricing.

We aim to provide you and your staff with value added service. We would appreciate any feedback that would help us further understand your needs and to help us to serve you better.

Let us be your source **4structures**.com!

SERVICES PROVIDED BY SUMMIT

Pre-Settlement Services

- Develop financial and capital needs analyses
- Calculate actual present value cost
- Coordinate the settlement with public assistance (SSI, Medicaid) and/or private benefit programs
- Apply for medical age ratings based on impaired life expectancy
- Consider estate planning issues such as taxes and/or replacing caregiver(s)
- Design creative settlement proposals to match the claimant's need and integrate with overall financial plan
- "Shop the market" for the best annuity benefits

Settlement Services

- Evaluate structured settlement offers from opposing counsel
- Attendance and availability for consultation at mediations. Will travel.
- Avoid constructive receipt
- Offer full structured settlement annuity and government bond program placement
- Offer resources for all types of trusts
- Provide expert financial testimony
- Provide instructions and guidance for completion of settlement documents

(This Listing Continued)

Summit Settlement Services (Continued)

Post-Settlement Services

- Attorney/claimant communication
- Coordinate receipt of future periodic payments

Our Services are usually provided at no cost to you or your client. As licensed brokers, we are entitled to receive commissions directly from placing or co-brokering the annuities from the life insurance companies issuing the structured annuities.

Mr. Darer is an experienced financial professional who brings a wide range of experience in negotiating personal injury claims settlements as well as the development of innovative applications and solutions for complex claims in jurisdictions throughout the United States. Mr. Darer is a graduate of the Crouse-Hinds School of Management at Syracuse University with a degree in marketing. In addition to holding the NASD Series 7, he has earned the designations of Chartered Life Underwriter and Chartered Financial Consultant from the American College as well as the designation of Certified Structured Settlement Consultant through the executive program at the University of Notre Dame. John is currently in pursuit of the designation of Chartered Life Assistance Planner, the curriculum for which focuses on the practice of financial planning for children with disabilities. His broad background in structured settlements, litigation support, diversified financial planning and securities brings a valuable asset to the table for his clients.

Mr. Darer has published articles in the *AIA Binder (01/00)*, "Structured Settlements: You save, They Prosper" in *International Risk Management* magazine (2/95) and the *Vermont Captive Chronicle* (10/93). He has advised numerous attorneys, corporations, insurance companies, and government entities on issues concerning economic damages and transfer of risk in domestic, London, and French insurance markets. He is a member of the National Structured Settlement Trade Association, the Aviation Insurers Association, the New York Self-Insurer's Association, National Association of Forensic Economists and the New York Claims Association.

You will find John to be highly responsive to your needs. Feel free to contact John at anytime 24 hours/7 days a week via phone, fax or email.

Florida Insurance License: A061450
California Insurance License: 0761076
other state licenses available upon request.

VALUATION SERVICES

The AXIS Group International, LLC
111 Godfrey Rd. W.
Weston, CT 06883
Phone: (203) 451-3050
Fax: (914) 206-7652

See Appraisal & Valuation Services

WATERBURY, 108,961, *New Haven Co.*

COURT REPORTERS

PROCESS SERVERS & DOCUMENT DELIVERY SERVICES

WINDSOR, 25,204, *Hartford Co.*

EXPERT WITNESS

ENVIRONMENTAL CONSULTANT

TRC ENVIRONMENTAL CORPORATION
CUSTOMER-FOCUSED SOLUTIONS

Headquarters:
5 Waterside Crossing
Windsor, CT 06095

Offices in CA, CO, CT, GA, IL, MA, NJ, NM, NY, NC, OH, TN, TX, & WY

Phone: 860-289-8631
Fax: 860-298-6399

Web site: www.trcsolutions.com
Email: info@trcsolutions.com

Litigation Support Sector Leader: Gale F. Hoffnagle, CCM, QEP

Because of our *Customer-Focused Solutions* approach, TRC is different than most environmental engineering firms. Depending on specific case requirements, our involvement ranges from:

- Full service, strategic planning to aid an attorney in developing the most cost-effective case; to
- Value-added services to aid an attorney in fulfilling a clearly defined task, on schedule and at the lowest appropriate cost.

EXPERT CONSULTATION AND TESTIMONY SERVICES:

Air Quality
- Emissions identification & quantification
- Odors
- Material damage
- Clean air act regulations/permitting/enforcement
- Exposure assessment
- Field studies
- Meteorology
- Air quality modeling

Groundwater
- Hydrology/geohydrology
- Remediation/compliance
- Geochemistry
- Civil engineering

Surface Water
- Hydrology
- Chemistry/stream loading
- Supply

Impact Assessment
- Environmental risk assessment
- Human health risk assessment
- Environmental due diligence
- Occupational health & safety
- Cultural resources
- Flora/fauna
- Toxicology

Case Technical Strategy
- Analysis of technical issues
- Assistance in finding the right experts
- Planning/executing field or laboratory tests
- Development of technical approach to jury/judge
- Exhibit management
- Literature surveys
- Analysis of opposing expert fact basis

Expert Report Preparation
- Rule 26 and format compliance
- Clarity of purpose and writing
- Peer review & expert substantiation
- Document control & presentation
- Response to opposing expert's claims
- Deposition preparation

Litigation Services
- Mediation
- Class certification hearings
- EPA/state environmental enforcement actions
- Jury trials
- Fairness hearings
- Hearings before a judge
- Daubert/Frye challenges

Our clients benefit by being assured that each task is completed with full appreciation for regulatory and legal operating requirements.

A list of our litigation support clients is available upon request. For more information on TRC, visit www.trcsolutions.com.

DOVER,* 27,630, *Kent Co.*

CORPORATION COMPANIES

Hylind Search Company, Inc.
304 South State St.
Dover, DE 19901
Phone: (888) 449-5463
Fax: (410) 468-0808

See Document Research, Retrieval & Filing

DOCUMENT RESEARCH, RETRIEVAL & FILING

An **A&E, Inc.** Company

Torri's Legal Services

Quality Legal Service

BASED ON CONFIDENCE, TRUST AND RESULTS

(800) 990-SERV
(800) 990-7378
Fax: (800) 845-2131
Internet: www.torrilegalservices.com
email: tlsnc@erols.com

We Service:
Wilmington • Dover •
and all of Delaware

*24 Hour Service * 7 Days A Week * Weekends * Holidays*

WE SPECIALIZE IN:

- Document Retrieval
- Court Filings
- Computerized Searches
- Nationwide Service of Process
- Summons, Complaints, Subpoenas
- Personal Services
- Emergency Service
- Defendants And Witness
- International Service

Member:
National Association of Professional Process Servers

Hylind Search Company, Inc.

245 West Chase Street
Baltimore MD 21201
Phone: 1-888-4HYLIND
Fax: 410-468-0808
E-mail: info@hylindsearch.com

304 South State Street
Dover, DE 19901
Phone: 1-888-AGENT 57
Fax: (302) 744-9025
E-mail: rcbowser@concentric.net

"We Meet Your Deadlines!"

A *nationwide* public records research company specializing in searches including but not limited to UCC, corporate mortgages preparation, searching and retrieval. Our highest priority is the quick turnaround and accurate results at a reasonable price.

RESIDENT AGENT SERVICES
In
MARYLAND & DELAWARE

ONLINE ACCESS!!!
Volume Discounts Available
Will meet or beat any competitor's price by 10%

EASY ONLINE ORDERING:
WWW.HYLINDSEARCH.COM

Uniform Commercial Code
- State & Local Searches and Filings
- UCC Forms and Preparation
- Litigation & Bankruptcy Case Searches
- Fixture Filings
- Suits and Judgments

Mortgages
- Mortgage Verification
- Mortgage and Assignment Filings
- Assignment Monitoring Services

Motor Vehicle Records
- Nationwide Driving Records
- Vehicle Asset Searches
- Insurance Carrier Services
- Duplicate Titles
- Accident Reports
- Tag & Title Transfers
- License Plate & Vehicle I.D. Searches

Miscellaneous Services
- Patent & Trademark Services
- Workman's Compensation
- Copyright Searches
- FAA Aircraft Searches
- Franchise Offering Circulars

Corporate/Partnership
- Name Availability
- Name Reservation
- Corporate Forms & Guidelines
- Incorporation Filings
- Certificates of Good Standing
- Resident Agent Services

Real Property
- Owner Verification
- Tax Payment & Assessments
- Asset/Ownership Searches
- Appraisals

Investigative Searches
- TRW Business Credit Reports
- Industry SIC Code Searches
- National Corporation Locator
- Corporate Affiliations
- Credit Reports
- Social Security # Trace
- Change of Address Search
- Demographic Search

DOVER (Continued)

PROCESS SERVERS & DOCUMENT DELIVERY SERVICES

An **A&E, Inc.** Company

Torri's Legal Services

Quality Legal Service

BASED ON CONFIDENCE, TRUST AND RESULTS

(800) 990-SERV

(800) 990-7378

Fax: (800) 845-2131

Internet: www.torrilegalservices.com

email: tlsnc@erols.com

We Service:

Wilmington • Dover •
and all of Delaware

*24 Hour Service * 7 Days A Week * Weekends * Holidays*

WE SPECIALIZE IN:

- Nationwide Service of Process
- Summons, Complaints, Subpoenas
- Personal Services
- Document Retrieval
- Court Filings
- Emergency Service
- Defendants And Witness
- Computerized Searches
- International Service

Member:
National Association of Professional Process Servers

WILMINGTON,* 71,529, *New Castle Co.*

ATTORNEY SERVICES

An **A&E, Inc.** Company

Torri's Legal Services

Quality Legal Service

BASED ON CONFIDENCE, TRUST AND RESULTS

(800) 990-SERV

(800) 990-7378

Fax: (800) 845-2131

Internet: www.torrilegalservices.com

email: tlsnc@erols.com

We Service:

Wilmington • Dover •
and all of Delaware

*24 Hour Service * 7 Days A Week * Weekends * Holidays*

WE SPECIALIZE IN:

- Nationwide Service of Process
- Summons, Complaints, Subpoenas
- Personal Services
- Document Retrieval
- Court Filings
- Emergency Service
- Defendants And Witness
- Computerized Searches
- International Service

Member:
National Association of Professional Process Servers

BANKS & TRUST COMPANIES

Wilmington Trust Company

Telephone: 302-651-1000

Ted T. Cecala, Jr. - Chairman and CEO
Robert V.A. Harra, Jr. - President and COO

Private Client Advisory Services Department
Rodney P. Wood - Senior Vice President
Joseph Covas, Jr. - Vice President, Personal Trust Administration
David L. Kloth - Vice President, National Markets & Alliances
Curtis L. Lyman - Co-President, Wilmington Trust FSB - Florida
Michael K. Bloxham - Co-President, Wilmington Trust FSB - Maryland
Peter E. Guernsey, Jr. - Co-President, Wilmington Trust FSB - New York
Alan K. Bonde - Co-President, Wilmington Trust FSB - California
Mark A. Graham - President, WT - Pennsylvania
Matthew J. Lynch, Jr., - Vice President, Planning and Compliance
S. Alan Snook - Vice President, Private Client Advisory Services

Asset Management Department
Robert J. Christian - Senior Vice President
Eric K. Cheung - Vice President, Fixed Income Management
E. Matthew Brown - Vice President, Equity Management Administration

Corporate Financial Services Department
Howard K. Cohen - Senior Vice President
Norma P. Closs - Vice President, Corporate Financial Services Business Development
David W. Dupert - President, Delaware Corporate Management, Inc.
John M. Beesen -Vice President, Corporate Trust
Virginia Karablacas - Vice President, Employee Benefit

Commercial Banking Department
Robert A. Matarese - Senior Vice President
Francis J. Ackerman - Vice President, Delaware Region
Bradley A. Hublein - Vice President, Northern Delaware Region
Michael J. Monaco - Vice President, Southern Delaware Division
Mary V. Murphy - Vice President, Small Business Banking
Karen Thuresson - Vice President, Credit Policy & Administration
Mark A. Graham - President, WT - Pennsylvania

Personal Banking Department
Hugh D. Leahy, Jr. - Senior Vice President
John C. Castle - Vice President, Personal Finance
Edward W. Garrison, Jr. - Vice President, Data Preparation
Jerry A. Mullins - Vice President, Branch Sales
Douglas Harder - Vice President, Deposit Services
Richard K. Wilhide - Vice President, Delivery Systems

COURT REPORTERS

CORBETT & ASSOCIATES

1400 N. French Street
Wilmington, DE 19801
(302) 571-0510 (800) 462-2233
Dover: (302) 734-3534 Fax: (302) 571-1321
Email: ecorbett@erols.com

www.corbettreporting.com

EXCEPTIONAL COURT REPORTING
SINCE 1975

- Registered Professional Reporters
- Real Time Reporting
- Live-Note
- In-House Videographers
- Conference Facilities
- PubNETics Software
- E-mail capabilities

STATE-OF-THE-ART RESOURCES

- **Top Quality Reporting**
- **Daily & Expedited Service**
- **Advanced Litigation Support**

CORBETT & ASSOCIATES—Your Reporting Experts!!!

WILMINGTON (Continued)

Court Reporters (Continued)

ESQUIRE™
DEPOSITION SERVICES

1 Commerce Center
Suite 760
Wilmington, DE 19801
302.426.9857 / 800.345.4940
Fax 800.600.3768
Web Site Address: www.esquirecom.com
Email Address: info@esquirecom.com

A Record of Excellence™

Our *Complimentary* Court Reporting Services and Products Include:

- Worldwide Scheduling
- Spacious Esquire Deposition Suites
- Calendar Management
- Scheduling of Interpreters
- Word Indexes
- ASCII, Discovery$_{TM}$ ^{ZX} and CAT-Links™ Disks
- Transcript Archiving
- Litigation Support Software and Training

We Also Provide:

- E-transcript™ Delivery and Software
- Over 5,000 Court Reporters Nationwide
- In-house Process Serving - Subpoena, Summons and Complaint Services - Worldwide
- In-house Legal Video Services
- Video Teleconferencing
- Video/Text Synchronization
- Compressed Format Transcripts
- LiveNote™ Interactive Realtime Reporting, Software and Training
- Realtime Reporting
- Document Depositories
- X-ray Duplication
- Imaging and Coding Service
- Deposition Summarizing
- Video Synchronizing

DEPONET
Across Town Or Across The Nation™

Fast ... Easy ... Flexible...
The Martindale-Hubbell Law Directory on CD-ROM gives you instant access through multiple search criteria to information on over 900,000 lawyers and law firms. For more details call **1-800-323-3288.**

Jane Rose
President and Managing Reporter
Jane Rose Reporting
Website: www.janerose.net
37 West 16th Street
New York, New York 10011
Telephone: 800-825-3341
Fax: 800-825-9055

Business Focus: Court reporting management of high-profile and complex litigation throughout the United States.

Services: Daily Copy; Realtime Reporting; Exhibit Scanning; Online Transcript Management; Litigation Support Services.

Reporting Experience: Commercial Business Litigation; Antitrust and Trade Regulation; Bankruptcy/Creditors' Rights; Class Actions; Environmental Insurance Coverage Litigation; Patent/Intellectual Property; Products Liability; Mass Tort; Securities and Corporate Governance; Tax Litigation.

Certifications: Certified Realtime Reporter, National Court Reporters Association (1994); Certified Shorthand Reporter, State of California (1992); Certified Shorthand Reporter, State of New Jersey (1994); Registered Professional Reporter, National Court Reporters Association (1990).

Website: www.janerose.net

DOCUMENT RESEARCH, RETRIEVAL & FILING

An **A&E, Inc.** Company
Torri's Legal Services
Quality Legal Service
BASED ON CONFIDENCE, TRUST AND RESULTS

(800) 990-SERV
(800) 990-7378
Fax: (800) 845-2131
Internet: www.torrilegalservices.com
email: tlsnc@erols.com

We Service:
Wilmington • Dover •
and all of Delaware

*24 Hour Service * 7 Days A Week * Weekends * Holidays*

WE SPECIALIZE IN:

- Document Retrieval
- Court Filings
- Computerized Searches
- Nationwide Service of Process
- Summons, Complaints, Subpoenas
- Personal Services
- Emergency Service
- Defendants And Witness
- International Service

Member:
National Association of Professional Process Servers

ESTATE PLANNING & PERSONAL BENEFITS

Commonwealth Trust Company
Bancroft Mills
29 Hill Rd.
Wilmington, DE 19806
Phone: (302) 658-7214
Fax: (302) 658-7219

See Trust & Fiduciary Services

EXPERT WITNESS

FALL PROTECTION

Dynamic Scientific Controls, Inc.
Accident Prevention & Safety: Fall Protection

Dynamic Scientific Controls was founded by J. Nigel Ellis, PhD, CSP, P.E., CPE. It is an organization of experienced safety, engineering and training professionals, dedicated to the study of fall hazards and training those at risk how to avoid danger. DSC has trained over 20,000 managers and workers in fall protection techniques and procedures since 1970.

DSC provides Consulting, Training and Engineering that can be customized to client specific needs.

Legal Support

Dynamic Scientific Controls, Inc. offers the protective services of highly experienced expert witness and court testimony for organizations which have followed good fall protection practice but had an incident that requires skilled legal support.

Headed by Dr. J. Nigel Ellis who has hundreds of cases experience of serious injury and death as consultant through trial for both plaintiff and defense, the nature of injury and site of injury often requires more than one expert; DSC is skilled at putting together a variety of experts in different specialties who can complement each other to resolve a complex situation quickly.

For more information, refer to our website www.FallSafety.com or call 302 571 8470 x21for more information.

EXPERT WITNESS REFERRAL SERVICES

The CECON GROUP inc.

242 N. James Street
Wilmington, DE 19804
Phone: 302-994-8000
Toll-Free: 888-263-8000
FAX: 302-994-8837
e-mail: cecon@cecon.com

The CECON GROUP, a Science, Engineering and Technology Consulting Network with over 600 experts in myriads of specialties offers scientific assistance

to the **defense or plaintiff's attorney** in:

* chemical hazards
* product liability
* assessing the technical merits of a case
* evolving strategies provable in court
* proposing analyzable evidence
* critiquing opposing evidence
* determining causation of product failures
* accident investigations
* examining discovery, interrogatory and deposition documents
* writing affidavits
* providing the best affordable expert witnesses

to the **patent attorney** in questions regarding:

* prior art
* freedom to operate
* alleged infringement

CALL CECON WHEN YOU NEED EXPERTISE IN:

Adhesives, Agricultural Chemicals (Fungicides, Herbicides, Insecticides, Nematicides, Fertilizers), **Air Pollution, Biotechnology, Catalysis, Ceramics, Chemical Toxicology, Chemistry** (Analytical, Biochemistry, Inorganic, Organic, Photochemistry, Physical, Polymer), **Chromatography, Cleaners, Composites, Cost Estimating, Elastomers, Encapsulation, Engineering** (Chemical, Civil, Design, Electrical, Electronics, Materials, Project), **Failure Analysis, Flammability & Flame Resistance, Food, Forensics, Hazardous Materials, High Performance Materials, Imaging Processes, Industrial Hygiene, Industrial Management, Instrumentation, Manufacturing Plant Problems, Materials Identification, Medical Devices, Metallurgy, Petrochemicals, Pharmaceuticals, Pigments, Plastics, Polymers** (All Classes), **Radiation, Regulatory Compliance, Safety, Spectroscopy, Technology** (Coatings, Composites, Concrete, Dyes, Elastomers, Environmental, Film, Foam, Food, Inks, Paints, Paper & Paperboard, Pigments, Plastics, Printing, Rubber, Textiles), **Timed Release Systems, Toxicology, Water Pollution....**

and hundreds more!

Visit us at: www.cecon.com

WILMINGTON (Continued)

LAWYER SEARCH & PLACEMENT CONSULTANTS

The Affiliates[SM]

200 Bellevue Parkway
Suite 140
Wilmington, DE 19809
(302) 791-0571

Located in more than 30 major markets throughout the United States and Canada, including Wilmington, *The Affiliates* is a premier provider of experienced project and full-time professionals for law officers and corporate legal departments. The firm places highly qualified candidates in a wide range of positions for the legal field, including attorney, paralegal, administrator, executive director, litigation support specialist, legal secretary, legal word processor and other legal support professionals.

Through its expertise, diligence and attention to meeting the needs of its clients, *The Affiliates* has earned a reputation for outstanding service and professionalism. Many of *The Affiliates'* account executives are attorneys and administrators who have experience working in law firms and legal departments. They possess an "insider knowledge" of our clients' needs, enabling them to serve as advisors on hiring and personnel management issues. On the candidate side, *The Affiliates* maintains an active referral network, an advanced e-cruiting program and an extensive database of highly qualified legal professionals currently available, all of which offer us access to a large talent pool for fulfilling the staffing needs of law practices and departments.

The Affiliates routinely assists law offices in identifying the appropriate personnel resources required for each particular case or project, and provides specialists whose specific training and experience make them ideal for the assignment, whether it is temporary or full-time.

The Affiliates also serves as a reliable information source on workplace trends and management issues within the legal community. We regularly conduct national surveys of attorneys and other legal professionals about topics ranging from new technologies and flexible work options to the fastest growing areas. In addition, *The Affiliates* has produced a number of informative pamphlets for management within law firms and corporate legal departments, complimentary copies of which may be requested by contacting *The Affiliates.*

For additional information, please visit *The Affiliates'* web site at www.affiliates.com.

PROCESS SERVERS & DOCUMENT DELIVERY SERVICES

An **A&E, Inc.** Company
Torri's Legal Services
Quality Legal Service
BASED ON CONFIDENCE, TRUST AND RESULTS

(800) 990-SERV
(800) 990-7378
Fax: (800) 845-2131
Internet: www.torrilegalservices.com
email: tlsnc@erols.com

We Service:
Wilmington • Dover •
and all of Delaware

*24 Hour Service * 7 Days A Week * Weekends * Holidays*

WE SPECIALIZE IN:

- Nationwide Service of Process
- Summons, Complaints, Subpoenas
- Personal Services
- Document Retrieval
- Court Filings
- Emergency Service
- Defendants And Witness
- Computerized Searches
- International Service

Member:
National Association of Professional Process Servers

SEE OUR AD ON PAGE DE7S

DM PROFESSIONAL SERVICES, INC.

Silverside Carr Executive Center
501 Silverside Road, Suite 133
Wilmington, Delaware 19809

Telephone (302) 792-9695
Toll Free (800) 966-3624
Fax (302) 798-8566

When Calling, Ask To Speak With Either Kathy DeLacy or Robert DeLacy

When you use a professional process service, you need answers - and you need them now. That's why we are linked to one of the most sophisticated national information networks. Coupled with this advanced technology is a professional staff with the intelligence and ingenuity to provide you with a level of service that aims to go beyond everyday, average satisfaction. We make the impossible, possible.

DM Professional Services Offers Services Including:

- **Process Services**
- **Extensive Nationwide Skip Tracing**
- **Hand Deliveries/Courier Services**
- **Surveillance**
- **Foreclosures/Postings**
- **Same Day or Next Day Service**
- **Service 24-Hours A Day, Seven Days A Week**

DM Professional Services serves all three of Delaware's Counties: New Castle, Kent and Sussex, plus the surrounding tri-state areas of Pennsylvania, New Jersey and Maryland.

Member of National Association For Professional Process Servers
Member of New Castle County Chamber of Commerce
Member of American Collectors Association
Member of Seaboard Collectors Association

Call DM PROFESSIONAL SERVICES today and start your relationship with the people you can always count on!

An **A&E, Inc.** Company

Torri's Legal Services

OFFICES NATIONWIDE
24 Hour Service
Weekends & Holidays
7 Days a Week

- **Nationwide Service of Process**
- **Summons, Complaints, Subpoenas**
- **Document Retrieval**
- **Rush Service**
- **Court Filings**
- **Hard to Locate and Serve Defendants and Witnesses**

Quality Legal Service
BASED ON CONFIDENCE, TRUST AND RESULTS

1-800-990-SERV

(or 1-800-990-7378) • Toll Free Fax: 1-800-845-2131
www.torrilegalservices.com • E-mail: tlsnc@erols.com

WILMINGTON (Continued)

TRUST & FIDUCIARY SERVICES

TRUST COMPANIES

Commonwealth Trust Company

Bancroft Mills
29 Hill Rd.
Wilmington, DE 19806
Phone: (302) 658-7214
Fax: (302) 658-7219

See Trust & Fiduciary Services

WASHINGTON, 606,900, *D.C. Co.*

ACCOUNTANTS

The Kardon Corp.
P.O. Box 653
Clemmons, NC 27012
Phone: (336) 766-5608
Fax: (336) 766-5608

See Economic and Statistical Consulting Services

Lindquist Forensic Partners
Suite 800
2121 K St. NW
Washington, DC 20037
Phone: (202) 261-3548
Fax: (202) 261-3508

See Financial Investigation/Forensic Accounting

ACCOUNTING

Lindquist Forensic Partners
Suite 800
2121 K St. NW
Washington, DC 20037
Phone: (202) 261-3548
Fax: (202) 261-3508

See Financial Investigation/Forensic Accounting

ARBITRATION & MEDIATION SERVICES

JAMS

THE RESOLUTION EXPERTS

JAMS, The Resolution Experts, offers its domestic and international clients an exclusive panel of justices, judges and attorneys with proven track records for resolving the most complex and high stakes cases. With over 20 offices nationwide, JAMS and its 200 full-time neutrals are responsible for resolving thousands of cases in the United States and abroad.

The JAMS difference lies in its expert neutrals and highly trained case managers. JAMS selects the world's top judges and attorneys based on their experience, reputation and proven ability to adjudicate cases and settle large and complex disputes. JAMS has neutrals with experience in all case types, and with specialized knowledge in individual practice areas such as employment, construction, real estate, environmental, intellectual property, bankruptcy and insurance coverage. In addition, JAMS case managers excel at getting parties to agree on a neutral, procedure, location, and date — all with a unified agenda of gaining resolution to disputes.

While JAMS neutrals are especially adept at resolving complex, multi-party, and difficult disputes, JAMS offers a full scope of ADR services and can resolve disputes in any price category. Some of the ADR services JAMS provides include: mediation, arbitration, special mastering, neutral fact finding, private jury trials, settlements conferences, ADR training and class action settlement adjudication.

JAMS is united in providing world-class resolution services. The various ADR processes employed by JAMS have proven their merit in case after case.

JAMS can be reached at its corporate headquarters at (949) 224-1810, by dialing (800) 352-5267, or at www.jamsadr.com.

WASHINGTON (Continued)

Arbitration & Mediation Services (Continued)

TASA

SINCE 1961

TECHNICAL ADVISORY SERVICE FOR ATTORNEYS
Headquarters: 1166 DeKalb Pike, Blue Bell, PA 19422-1853
U.S. and Canada: 800-523-2319 Fax: 800-329-8272
United Kingdom: 0800-89-1292
E-mail: experts@tasanet.com
www.tasanet.com

WASHINGTON ATTORNEYS CALL TASA WHEN ONLY AN EXPERT WILL DO®.

Now that you've chosen the efficiency and savings of Alternative Dispute Resolution, choose the efficiency and savings of making TASA your source for ADR panelists and experts.

Throughout our 40-year history, TASA has provided clients with seasoned dispute resolvers, experts with specialized subject knowledge, and individuals who possess both ADR process *and* subject skills.

Our comprehensive roster includes highly qualified arbitrators, mediators, negotiators, private judges, and other neutrals. And we can provide them in virtually any location you choose. Our approach is flexible: You determine the process and parameters; we will refer candidates for your consideration, with no obligation.

When you're looking for the most direct route to experienced ADR professionals, discover what over 200,000 attorneys, insurance firms, corporations, and government agencies already know: **TASA is the best source for experts, worldwide.®**

Call for a FREE CONSULTATION.
And ask for a complimentary copy of
TASA's Directory of Expertise.

800-523-2319

ASSET LOCATORS

The Kardon Corp.
P.O. Box 653
Clemmons, NC 27012
Phone: (336) 766-5608
Fax: (336) 766-5608

See Economic and Statistical Consulting Services

ATTORNEY SERVICES

A & E, Inc.
P.O. Box 18647
Washington, DC 20036-9998
Phone: (800) 990-7378
Fax: (800) 845-2131

See Process Servers & Document Delivery Services

Attention small law firms:
Lawyer HomePages @ lawyers.com
The fast, easy and affordable way to promote your practice on the Web. For details call
1-800-526-4902 x-5095.

AMERICAN LEGAL DOCUMENT COURIERS

10570 Main Street, Suite 123
Fairfax, Virginia 22030

Serving Northern Virginia, Maryland and Washington D.C.

(703) 934-6777
Call 800-747-0820

We believe that technology, paired with the right people, practices and vision, can provide an important competitive edge in today's ever-changing business world. Because we focus on understanding business goals in conjunction with a technological direction , we can manage projects from the planning phase to the production support phase.

We offer our clients a very different approach. We provide services to transform your entire enterprise-your strategy, processes, information technology, and people. In addition, we focus on the realization that changing business processes is necessary to achieve the promised returns from strategy and technology. This approach enables the delivery of very different-results clients can build on because we help make organizations more robust and adaptable to future shifts in the environment.

Our aim is to develop effective and mutually beneficial working partnerships by introducing an innovative yet practical approach towards solving your problems. Our staff succeeds by listening carefully to your needs and then providing world-class products, solutions, and expertise. **We will get the results you need.**

SERVICES PROVIDED

PUBLIC RECORDS RETRIEVAL
POST OFFICE CHECKS
DOCUMENT RETRIEVAL FILING & RESEARCH
DATABASE & REAL PROPERTY SEARCHES
DMV/UCC/CREDIT HEADER SEARCHES
SAME DAY & RUSH SERVICE AVAILABLE
UNDERCOVER/SURVEILLANCE, VIDEO
ATTORNEY SERVICES
LITIGATION SUPPORT
COUNTY, STATE & FEDERAL COURTS
SUBPOENAS BY FAX
CONTACTS/TRAVEL WORLDWIDE
WITNESS STATEMENTS TAKEN
SKIP TRACING, MISSING PERSONS
CHILD CUSTODY, FAMILY, SPOUSAL, MARITAL
PRE-EMPLOYMENT, BACKGROUND CHECKS
POLYGRAPH SERVICES AVAILABLE

MEMBERSHIPS

NAPPS
PISA

BANKRUPTCY/TURNAROUND/INSOLVENCY

Charles River Associates Incorporated

Suite 700
1201 F St., NW
Washington, DC 20004-1204
Phone: (202) 662-3800
Fax: (202) 662-3910

See Economic and Statistical Consulting Services

BUSINESS VALUATIONS

Advanced Valuation Analytics, Ltd.
Business Valuation Consultants

1901 Pennsylvania Avenue, N.W., Suite 400, 20006
Telephone: 202-296-2777
Fax: 202-331-1563
www.advancedval.com

Business Valuation
and
Valuation of Business Damages
The Highest Qualifications:

Chartered Financial Analyst
Certified Business Appraiser
Certified Public Accountant
Accredited In Business Valuation
Accredited Senior Appraiser-American Society of Appraisers
Fellow-Financial Analysts Federation
Certified Financial Planner

We have valued over $3 Billion worth of closely-held securities. Among our engagements, we have valued such securities for the following reasons:

Employee Stock Ownership Plans
Minority Shareholder Disputes
Bankruptcy Cases
Divorces
Damages for Lost Profits
Estate, Gift and Income Tax Returns
Stock Options
Stock Given as an Employee Benefit
Recapitalizations, Mergers & Acquisitions-Fairness Opinions
Investment Limited Partnership Interests
Stock Offerings
Warrant and Option Valuations
Family Partnerships and Corporations
"Estate Freeze" Valuations

We have full computer support for the best litigation presentation, including excellent graphics and other desk-top publishing capabilities.

In addition to the valuation of closely-held securities, we provide expert witness testimony and related support in cases having to do with investment advisory violations. This includes prudent man rule, suitability, due diligence and other related topics for ERISA and non-ERISA cases.

References: Most major Washington, D.C. area law firms as well as many accounting firms. Specifics are available upon request.

The Kardon Corp.

P.O. Box 653
Clemmons, NC 27012
Phone: (336) 766-5608
Fax: (336) 766-5608

See Economic and Statistical Consulting Services

WASHINGTON (Continued)

CASE MANAGEMENT SYSTEMS

CLASS ACTION NOTICE

COMPUTER CONSULTANTS

The Kardon Corp.
P.O. Box 653
Clemmons, NC 27012
Phone: (336) 766-5608
Fax: (336) 766-5608

See Economic and Statistical Consulting Services

CONSTRUCTION CONSULTANTS

RBS Consulting Group
8402 Boxwood Dr.
Tampa, FL 33615-4939
Phone: (800) 909-7692
Fax: (813) 886-6892

See Expert Witness-Construction

WASHINGTON (Continued)

Construction Consultants (Continued)

WARNER

CONSTRUCTION CONSULTANTS, INC.

2275 Research Boulevard, Suite 100
Rockville, MD 20850-3268
Tel. (301) 670-9020 Fax (301) 670-7977
E-mail rraeon@warnercon.com
www.warnercon.com

Warner provides timely, affordable, and effective consulting services to all segments of the construction industry. Warner performs construction and procurement planning, performance management and dispute resolution assistance on a day-to-day basis. As a result, Warner brings a whole industry perspective to its performance. Warner's staff of architectural, engineering, construction management, scheduling, financial and legal professionals all have construction trade or field management experience and possess specialty expertise in construction disputes. For over two decades Warner has been providing high quality consulting and testifying expert services on an international basis. This combination of perspective, expertise and experience enables Warner to select and execute considered, balanced approaches to engagements and to provide reasonable, objective and supportable advice and products.

SERVICES

- **Critical Path Method (CPM) Scheduling**
  - Preparation/Production of Baseline Schedules
  - Performance & Cashflow Monitoring
  - Periodic Progress Updates
  - Impact & Recovery Schedules
  - Delayed/Accelerated Schedule Analysis
- **Owner's & Lender's Representative Services**
  - Feasibility & Due Diligence Analyses
  - Pro Forma Evaluations
  - Design Professional Procurement Assistance
  - Design Phase Management
  - Detailed Cost Evaluation
  - Regulatory Review Process Assistance
  - Contractor Procurement
  - Construction Administration, Quality Management & Cost Control
  - Project Close-Out & Facility Commissioning
- **Schedule & Cost Analyses**
  - As-Planned Schedule Validation & Revision
  - Daily Specific As-Built Schedule Preparation
  - Identification & Quantification of Critical Delay
  - Delay Causation & Responsibility Determinations
  - Time Impact & Accelerated Performance Analyses
  - Extended Performance Cost Analysis
  - Impacted & Accelerated Performance Cost Analysis
  - Requests For Equitable Adjustment
  - Claim Preparation or Review
- **Dispute Resolution & Litigation Support**
  - Consulting & Testifying Experts
  - Schedule & Cost Analyses
  - Document Organization, Preservation & Systemization
  - Demonstrative Evidence Preparation
  - Negotiation/ADR/Litigation Support

COURT HOUSE RESEARCH

Mohr Information Services

P.O. Box 3185
Winchester, VA 22604
Phone: (888) 525-4576
Fax: (888) 525-4479

See Criminal Records Research

COURT REPORTERS

Need an extra copy of the **Martindale-Hubbell Law Directory?** Or of a specific volume? Call Martindale-Hubbell Customer Relations at **1-800-526-4902.**

WASHINGTON (Continued)

Court Reporters (Continued)

Alderson Reporting
1-800-FOR-DEPO

1-800-For-Depo-Alderson Reporting
Since 1938

One*call*

1-800-FOR-DEPO(*sition*) 1-800-367-3376
www.1-800-FOR-DEPO.COM

any*where*
on the globe
on the internet
on the phone
US, Canada, Europe, Far East

any*time*
in real time
interactive (Depo on the Net)
manager on call 24/7
online scheduling/ordering

process servers
subpoena service
records retrieval
realtime court reporters
certified video reporters
tape/video transcribers
certified language interpreters
cleared personnel and facility
court room video playback technicians
temporary staff for exhibit marking
document production
state of the art conference rooms
internet broadcast conference room

written interrogatories
depositions
Patent and Trademark
arbitrations
trials
conventions
press conferences
pro bono services
Congressional hearings
living wills
day-in-the-life
technology presentations
mock depositions

any*format*
paper/video/audio

LiveNote and CaseView
ASCII, Summation, Amicus, MS Word, Word Perfect
Captioned
Imaged
Digitized to CD-ROM
Synchronized
Compressed
Indexed
Archived Online

E-transcript transfer, case-wide master word indexes, customized billing reports, document and transcript repositories, two cameras, S-VHS, VHS, Beta, Hi8, CD-ROM for video and text, video teleconferencing, trial presentations.

Serving important litigators and U.S. Senators since 1938 and the Justices of the Supreme Court of the United States since 1980.

1-800-FOR-DEPO
1-800-367-3376
1-800-367-3310 Fax
202-289-2260 (Washington, DC)
www.1-800-FOR-DEPO.com

SEE OUR AD ON PAGE DC10S

AA BETA REPORTING

Stenotype Reporters

When you absolutely must have it...
On Time...
Accurate and Reasonably Priced!

910 17th Street, N.W.
Suite 200
Washington, DC 20006

601 King Street
Suite 400
Alexandria, VA 22314

(202) 638-2400
(703) 684-BETA (2382)
1-800-522-BETA (2382)

Email: John@betareporting.com
www.betareporting.com

Worldwide Coverage

24 Hours A Day - 7 Days a Week

STENOTYPE REPORTERS

- Depositions & General Reporting
- Real-Time, Same-Day & Rush Transcripts
- Certified Livenote & Caseview
- Case-wide Master Word Index & Condensed Transcripts
- ASCII, Discovery ZX, WordPerfect, CAT-Links, etc.
- Video Tape Depositions - Broadcast Quality
- Deposition Suites
- Hearings, Arbitrations, etc.
- Personalized Rates & Services
- D.O.D. Security Clearance
- Litigation Management Services
- Case Management
- Data Base Design
- Full-Text Retrieval Software
- Archived Transcripts
- Audio & Video Tape Transcription Service

A Full Service Reporting Company

...There is No Substitute for Quality

SEE OUR AD ON PAGE DC6S

WASHINGTON (Continued)

Court Reporters (Continued)

ACE·FEDERAL

ACE-FEDERAL REPORTERS, INC.

Stenotype Reporters

Over 50 Years of Complete Reporting Service

1120 G Street, N.W., Suite 500 20005

800-336-6646

DEPOSITIONS, ARBITRATIONS & CONFERENCES

Notaries in D.C., VA & MD

REAL-TIME AND RUSH DELIVERY

CERTIFIED LEGAL VIDEOTAPE SPECIALISTS

CONDENSED TRANSCRIPTS & DISKETTES

DEPOSITION SUITES

WORLDWIDE COVERAGE

PROCESS SERVICE

AUTHORIZED DISCOVERY DEALER AND TRAINER

LITIGATION SUPPORT CONSULTATION

Specializing in project management, database design, and demonstrations and training of full-text retrieval software

24-Hour Switchboard

202-347-3700

Facsimile 202-737-3638

Call Toll Free 800-336-6646

SEE OUR AD ON PAGE DC9S

Alexander Gallo & Associates, Inc.

COURT REPORTING & VIDEO SERVICES

• TECHNOLOGICAL LEADERS IN LITIGATION SUPPORT •

Provided with Every Deposition:

- Full Sized and Condensed Transcript
- Word Index
- All Exhibits Scanned and Provided on CD-ROM (No scanning charge)
- Digitized Audio Recording of Deposition Provided on CD-ROM
- All Videotaped Depositions Provided on VHS Tapes as well as Digitized and Burned onto CD-ROM. (No digitizing charge)

* * *

- Specializing in complex litigation matters
- Full Case Management / Worldwide Deposition Scheduling
- Expedited transcripts available
- Specializing in Real-Time / LiveNote computers available
- Document Repository services available
- Complimentary conference rooms available
- Complimentary return car service to airport

Toll Free Phone: (877) 495-0777

Toll Free Fax: (866) 495-0766

www.GalloReporting.com

AMICUS REPORTING

DONNA L. LINTON, RMR
44164 Mossy Brook Square
Ashburn, Virginia 20147
Phone: (703)729-2536
Fax: (703)729-2536

E-mail: donnalinto@aol.com

BIOGRAPHY

President of **Amicus Reporting, Donna L. Linton**
Born in Queens, N.Y. attended Herkimer County Community College - Associates in Applied Science.
Performed reporting services in metropolitan New York; Tampa, Florida; D.C., Maryland and Virginia.
17 years in Business.

SERVICES AVAILABLE

- **DAILY/EXPEDITED COPY**
- **CONFERENCE ROOMS (can be made available)**
- **REFERENCES AVAILABLE UPON REQUEST**
- **NOTARY PUBLIC - Maryland, D.C. & Virginia**
- **ASCII DISKETTES AVAILABLE**
- **DEPOSITIONS ∗ ARBITRATIONS ∗ HEARINGS ∗ TRIALS**
- **COMPUTER-AIDED TRANSCRIPTION**
- **DISCOVERY ZX**
- **SUMMATION**
- **AMICUS**
- **VIDEOGRAPHY (arrangements can be made)**
- **TELECONFERENCING (arrangements can be made)**
- **MIN-U-SCRIPT / CONDENSED TRANSCRIPTS (Free of Charge)**
- **LITIGATION SUPPORT SERVICES**
- **REAL TIME TRANSCRIPTION**
- **KEYWORD INDEXING**
- **RUSH/SAME DAY SERVICE**
- **MEDICAL / TECHNICAL / ARCHITECTURAL**

MEMBERSHIPS

President of the Virginia Court Reporters Association
Member of the National Court Reporters Association
Registered Merit Reporters
USAA Security Clearance.

Notary in D.C., Maryland & Virginia

Art Miller & ASSOCIATES
COURT REPORTERS AND VIDEOGRAPHERS

ART MILLER & ASSOCIATES, LLC
Court Reporters & Videographers
Over 40 Years of Reporting Experience
NCRA Certificate of Merit Qualified

COMPLETE COVERAGE OF STATE OF MARYLAND AND WASHINGTON, D.C.
with branches in
BALTIMORE, COLUMBIA, TOWSON, and WASHINGTON, D.C.

COURT REPORTING/VIDEOGRAPHY SERVICES:

- REAL TIME WITH LIVENOTE©
- "IN-HOUSE" VIDEO SPECIALISTS
- WORD INDEXING
- CONDENSED TRANSCRIPTS
- ASCII DISKETTES
- AUDIO-TAPED BACKUPS FOR QUALITY CONTROL
- AUDIOTAPE AND VIDEOTAPE TRANSCRIPTION

LITIGATION SUPPORT SERVICES

- VIDEO TO TRANSCRIPT SYNCHRONIZATION
- COURTROOM POWER POINT PRESENTATIONS
- VHS to CD CONVERSION
- COPY SERVICES
- DOCUMENT IMAGING
- ARCHIVING

MEDICAL • TECHNICAL • RUSH COPY SPECIALISTS

CALL TOLL FREE 1-800-837-2285
OR
EMAIL: artmillerassoc@aol.com
Website: www.artmiller.com

CONFERENCE ROOMS PROVIDED AT THE LOCATION OF YOUR CHOICE!

Baltimore, MD Office:
111 S. Calvert Street
Suite 2700
Baltimore, MD 21202
Call Toll Free 1-800-837-2285
Fax: 410-367-3883

Washington, D.C. Office
1050 Connecticut Ave. N.W.
Suite 1000
Washington, D.C. 20036
Call Toll Free 1-800-837-2285
Fax: 202-234-8467

WASHINGTON (Continued)

Court Reporters (Continued)

SEE OUR AD ON PAGE DC22S

WASHINGTON (Continued)

Court Reporters (Continued)

Providing outstanding service to law firms and court reporting firms nationwide since 1983

Video Depositions

Certified Legal Video Specialists

Single Camera & Multi-Camera Depositions

Videotape Editing

Video Duplication

Video Conversion to CD Rom

Text-to-Video Synchronization

"Day In The Life Of" Video Production

Settlement Brochure Video Production

Professional Videotaping Services for:

Seminars

Client/Trial Preparation

Courtroom Playback Support

Professional Photographic Services

Film and Digital formats

CERTIFIED VIDEO SERVICES, INC.
13105 Pennerview Lane
Fairfax, VA 22033

Virginia (703) 631-1858
Washington, D.C. (202) 833-2442
Toll Free 1-877-631-1858
email info@certvid.com ❖ www.certvid.com

COURT REPORTERS, ETCetera, Inc.

"We'll Cover Your Job ANYWHERE in the Country!"
Toll Free: 1-800-947-DEPO (3376)
D.C.: 202-628-DEPO M.D.: 410-653-1115
Fax 410-653-9641

Call Anytime!

- Real-Time Reporters
- Videographers
- Interpreters
- Tape Transcriptionists
- Process Servers
- Depositions
- Court Hearings
- Arbitrations
- Conferences
- Video Conferencing

"We Specialize in RUSH DELIVERY!"

At Court Reporters Etcetera, we have developed a reputation for outstanding quality and excellence in the field of court reporting. We are committed to providing our clients with the highest quality of service. We have designed our web site to inform you about the many litigation support services we offer. We invite you to explore our site to learn more about our services. We promise quality, reliability and efficiency in all of the services we provide.

www.courtreportersetc.baweb.com
For questions, email us at CREDEPO@gte.net

SEE OUR AD ON PAGE DC23S

THE CUNNINGHAM GROUP, INC.

Specialists in Court Reporting and Litigation Management
111 Gillett Street
Hartford, CT 06105
Telephones: 860-521-3664
1-800-842-4486 - Nationwide
Fax: 860-524-5021
www.cunninghamreporting.com
cgroup@compuserve.com

Serving the legal and corporate communities since 1965.

Complete court reporting and litigation service including: Computer-aided transcription, instant-real-time, daily and expedited delivery, videography, and telecommunications. Diskettes in all standard formats: ASCII, Summation, Discovery, WordPerfect, Word Star, Zyindex, etc. Customized formats on request.

Registered Professional Reporters and Notaries; experienced in federal and state court depositions; patent, medical and public utilities; Environmental litigation a specialty.

Deposition rooms. Subpoena preparation and service.

Member National Court Reporters Association, Connecticut, Massachusetts, New Hampshire, New York, Texas, Ohio and California Court Reporters Associations, Reporters Cooperative, Inc., and American Arbitration Association.

Please have notice read: "Before Margherita R. Cunningham or other competent authority within and for the State of... "

References furnished on request.

Additional services include customized document databases, customized software for search and retrieval, document repository and distribution center, imaging, computer-generated document numbers, deposition exhibit databases, deposition digesting.

DEPOSITION SERVICES, INC.

1-800-333-1042

Maryland Office
6245 Executive Boulevard
Rockville, Maryland 20852
Telephone: 301-881-3344
Email: DepoServ@aol.com
Website: www.DepositionServices.com

D.C. Office
2300 M Street, N.W.
Suite 800
Washington, D.C. 20037
Telephone: 202-785-1239

FAX: 301-881-3338

COURT REPORTERS

Experienced in Legal, Medical and
Technical Terminology.

STANDARD DELIVERY IN FIVE WORKING DAYS

Expedited Delivery Available
High Quality Transcripts
Deposition Suites Available

VIDEO DIVISION

Video Depositions a Specialty
Certified Videography

LITIGATION SUPPORT

Min-U-Scripts & Disk
Complimentary with transcript order

TAPE TRANSCRIPTION

4-Track Cassette - Microcassette
8-Track Reel-to-Reel
Videotape & Digital Recordings

TRANSCRIPTION DIRECT FROM VIDEO CASSETTE

SECURITY CLEARANCE

Reporters and Transcribers with
Top Secret Security Clearance

MINUTES FROM CIRCUIT COURT

"ALWAYS ON TIME"

DIVERSIFIED REPORTING SERVICES, INC.

1025 Vermont Ave, N.W.
Suite 1250
Washington, D.C. 20005

202-296-2929
1-800-937-2929
FAX: 202-296-3468

www.diversifiedreporting.com

WE ARE DEDICATED TO EXCELLENCE AND SERVICE

- Convenient downtown location
- Deposition suite available
- Depositions and arbitrations
- Meetings and conferences
- Compressed format transcripts
- PC disks
- Videotaped testimony
- Computer-aided transcription
- DC, VA, and MD notaries
- 24-hour answering service
- Visa/Mastercard accepted

Professional Reporters Experienced In Medical and Technical Testimony

CALL US FOR ACCURATE TRANSCRIPTS DELIVERED ON TIME

WASHINGTON (Continued)

Court Reporters (Continued)

Doerner&Goldberg inc.
Deposition and Litigation Support Services

Serving Law Firms and their Clients Since 1971
A Full Service Court Reporting Firm
1-800-525-9915
www.doernergoldberg.com

Complimentary Limousine Service to and from Airport

Deposition Services
Realtime
CaseView
Instant Transcripts
Word Indexes
Daily, Expedited, Encrypted E-mail and ASCII deliveries
Condensed Transcripts

Expertise
Environmental
Civil Litigation
Patent /Commercial Litigation
Securities
Bankruptcy
Arbitrations
Medical Malpractice

Videotaping
Depositions
Video to CD-ROM
Courtroom Playback
Corporate Video
Video teleconferencing

Conference Room Facilities
Nationwide Locations
(call for details on specific locations)

Litigation Support
Summation
Discovery ZX
Case Archiving
Expert Witness Databases
OCR, Document Imaging and Coding
Trial Presentation

Additional Services
Translations
Interpreting
Software Training and Support
Disk Conversions
Encrypted Digital Certification

EVANS REPORTING
S E R V I C E, I N C.

2422 Southwest Road
Baltimore, Maryland 21234
410.882.0208

Registered Professional Reporters

1.800.256.8410

Serving all of Maryland, DC, Delaware and Virginia

Computer aided transcription
Video Depositions
Min-U-Script Condensed Transcripts
Daily Copy Specialists
ASCII and Discovery ZX
Realtime via LiveNote

410.882.0833 FAX

Visit our website @ www.evansreporting.com
devans@evansreporting.com

FOR THE RECORD, INC.

Stenotype Court Reporting and Litigation Support

Serving: Maryland, Washington, D.C., Northern Virginia

(800) 921-5555
FAX (301) 870-8333

www.ftrinc.net

State-of-the-Art Services, Including:

Computer-Aided Transcription
Free Condensed Transcripts with Concordance
NCRA-Certified Reporters/Notaries Public
Realtime Reporting (Meets ADA Requirements)
Case*View* Attorney Interactive Reporting
ASCII/WordPerfect/E-Transcript Diskettes
24-Hour Phone Availability
NCRA-Certified Videotaping
Conference Facilities

***Specialties, Including*:**

Medical, Construction, Technical Depositions
Health Claims Arbitration Hearings
Maryland State Hearings (current contract)
Arbitrations/Mediations
Conventions/Business Meetings

QUALITY, ON-TIME TRANSCRIPTS, REASONABLE RATES

HUDSON REPORTING & VIDEO, INC.

124 West 30th Street
Suite 214-216
NY, NY 10001
and
287 Wood Avenue
Edison, NJ 08820

TOLL FREE: 1-800-310-1769
NY Tel: 212-273-9911
Fax: 212-273-9915
NJ Fax 732-906-4139
Email: Hudsonrep@aol.com

Hudson Reporting & Video, Inc. is a company which provides court reporting and video services to attorneys and their firms. We provide those services to our clients at depositions, arbitrations, meetings and in the courtroom. The transcripts we produce are made available to our clients in various formats using the latest technology and software available.

SERVICES AVAILABLE:

Expedited, Daily Delivery
Video Services
ASCII Disk
Condensed Transcripts/with Keyword Index
Real Time
Rough ASCII
Interpreters
Audio/Video Transcriptions
E-Transcript
Conference Room In (NY)
Member of the National Court Reporters Association

We can cover depositions Nationwide

SEE OUR AD ON PAGE DC8S

HUTCHINGS
COURT REPORTERS, LLC
CSR 649

HUTCHINGS SINCE 1953

GLOBAL LEGAL SERVICES

FAMILY OWNED AND OPERATED
Local ★ National ★ International

EASY 24-HOUR CENTRALIZED SCHEDULING

800.697.3210
— OR —
www.hutchings.com
— OR —
fax 323.888.6333

- Court Reporters
- Interpreters
- Videographers

Page for Page Our Formatting Policies Result in Substantial Savings

✓ **CORPORATE and CARRIER COORDINATION PROGRAMS**
Centralized Billing
Regional Rate Uniformity
Custom Billing & Analysis Reports
Quality Control Assurance

✓ **CONFERENCE ROOMS**
Complimentary at all Hutchings Offices and Affiliate Facilities

✓ **TECHNOLOGICAL SERVICES & SUPPORT**
Realtime Transcription
Interactive Software & Remote Access
Internet and BBS File Transfer
Transcripts via e-mail

✓ **MULTIPARTY LITIGATION CASE MANAGEMENT**
Imaging to CD-ROM
Document Depositories
Master Calendar
Custom Indices

✓ **IN-HOUSE LEGAL VIDEO SERVICES**
Videoconferencing
Videotaped Depositions and Playbacks
Video Synchronization
Time-Stamping and Editing

Headquarters:
5701 S. Eastern Ave., Suite 530
Los Angeles, CA 90040-2831
800.697.3210
fax 323.888.6333
Email: hutchcal@hutchings.com
www.hutchings.com

A Tradition of Personal Service Since 1953

WASHINGTON (Continued)

Court Reporters (Continued)

Jane Rose
President and Managing Reporter

Jane Rose Reporting

Website: www.janerose.net
37 West 16th Street
New York, New York 10011
Telephone: 800-825-3341
Fax: 800-825-9055

Business Focus: Court reporting management of high-profile and complex litigation throughout the United States.

Services: Daily Copy; Realtime Reporting; Exhibit Scanning; Online Transcript Management; Litigation Support Services.

Reporting Experience: Commercial Business Litigation; Antitrust and Trade Regulation; Bankruptcy/Creditors' Rights; Class Actions; Environmental Insurance Coverage Litigation; Patent/Intellectual Property; Products Liability; Mass Tort; Securities and Corporate Governance; Tax Litigation.

Certifications: Certified Realtime Reporter, National Court Reporters Association (1994); Certified Shorthand Reporter, State of California (1992); Certified Shorthand Reporter, State of New Jersey (1994); Registered Professional Reporter, National Court Reporters Association (1990).

Website: www.janerose.net

LYON REPORTING, INC.
Certified Court Reporters

Suite 100, 5899 New Peachtree Road
Atlanta, GA 30340

1-800-767-2030

FAX 1-800-298-4277

www.lyonreporting.com

Mailing Address: P.O. Box 81124
Atlanta, GA 30366

"Sandi Lyon - Who's Who in Executives & Professionals"

DEPOSITIONS - GENERAL REPORTING:
— Fully Computerized
— Medical and Technical Expertise
— Near All Major Hospitals
— Mini/Condensed Transcripts
— Realtime, LiveNote, CaseView
— ASCII, Discovery ZX, CAT-Links
— Videotaping In-House
— Document Imaging
— Conference Rooms Available
— Airport Conference Room Available
— Nationwide Reporter Referral Service
— Visa and MasterCard Accepted

25 Years of Service

1-800-767-2030

1-888-767-2030

STATE CERTIFICATIONS:
— Georgia
— California
— Colorado
— Michigan
— Texas

NATIONAL ACCREDITATIONS:
— Certified Realtime Reporter
— Registered Diplomate Reporter
— Registered Merit Reporters
— Registered Professional Reporters

MEMBERSHIPS:
— National Court Reporters Association
— Georgia Shorthand Reporters Association
— Georgia Certified Court Reporters Association
— California Court Reporters Association
— Colorado Court Reporters Association
— Michigan Association of Professional Court Reporters
— Board of Court Reporting, State of Georgia, 1986-1990
— Member Set Depo Referral Service

1-800-767-2030

Serving the Legal Profession since 1974

SEE OUR LISTINGS IN ATLANTA, GA, LOS ANGELES, SAN FRANCISCO, CHICAGO & NEW YORK

WASHINGTON (Continued)

Court Reporters (Continued)

WASHINGTON (Continued)

CRIMINAL RECORDS RESEARCH

COURT RESEARCH AND DOCUMENT RETRIEVAL

MOHR INFORMATION SERVICES

A Full Service Information Provider

P.O. Box 3185
Winchester, VA 22604

1-888-525-4576
fax: 1-888-525-4479
info@mohrinformation.com
www.mohrinformation.com

Since 1993, Mohr Information Services has provided "hands on" court research and document retrieval services in and around the Nation's capital including DC, Virginia and Maryland.

- ⇨ The majority of our research is performed within 24 hours.
- ⇨ Rush orders available, including 2-3 hour turnaround.
- ⇨ All reports are computer printed in an easy to use format.
- ⇨ Our employees are thoroughly trained and tested to ensure the highest quality research.

Law firms, lending institutions and companies requiring public information have relied upon our team of experienced court researchers, title examiners and paralegals to provide them with accurate information within stringent deadlines.

We Specialize In:

Criminal Records
Civil Litigation
Federal, State Tax Liens and Judgements
Marriage and Divorce Records
Driving Records
Business Filings
Articles of Incorporation
Voter Registration
Property Ownership and Current Owner Property Searches
Traffic Records
Patent and Trademark Records
Professional Licenses
UCC/Financing Records
Library of Congress
Document Filing
Document Pick Up and Delivery Services
Point of Law and Statute Research (Law Libraries)
Honesty and Customer Service Testing

We strongly believe court research isn't a matter of apples versus apples. We offer a superior product and stand behind our work. We understand how important the bottom line is to our clients. We offer high volume clients substantial discounts. Even clients without high volumes are offered discounts if they use Mohr Information Services for the counties we service.

visit us on the web at www.mohrinformation.com

DOCUMENT IMAGING

Advanced Imaging Solutions, Inc., an award winning legal vendor, is a leading Value-Added Reseller of litigation support software and offers a full range of systems, consulting, training programs and quality outsourcing services (imaging, coding, OCRing) to assist in managing case critical information from discovery to trial.

We have the staff and the resources to meet the most demanding deadlines. Our staff is well known for their years of experience and knowledge of transcript and document management technology. We also coordinate & manage other needed services such as real-time court reporting, demonstrative evidence, video depositions and photocopying nationwide.

Our success is attributed to maximizing the partnership with our law firm, corporate legal and federal government agency clients. One advantage legal professionals who use Advanced Imaging Solutions have over the competition is that they are able to gain the benefits of technology without having to build and manage behind the scenes support systems over the course of the case.

AIS is your "one-stop-shop" for litigation support when it just has to be done right.

Advanced Imaging Solutions, Inc.

1600 K Street, NW, Suite 400, Washington, DC 20006
Tel. (202) 955-7944 fax: (202) 955-7946 visit www.aislegal.com

FAST ... EASY ... FLEXIBLE ...

The Martindale-Hubbell® Law Directory on CD-ROM™

Get instant access to information on nearly every legal professional in the U.S., Canada, and the international community with the **Martindale-Hubbell® Law Directory on CD-ROM.™** Easy-to-use menus, pop-up screens, and flexible search criteria help you zero in on any of over **1,000,000** lawyers and law firms.
The possibilities are endless!

For more information
call **1-800-323-3288.**

LexisNexis™ Martindale-Hubbell®

DOCUMENT RESEARCH, RETRIEVAL & FILING

An **A&E, Inc.** Company

Torri's Legal Services

Quality Legal Service

BASED ON CONFIDENCE, TRUST AND RESULTS

(800) 990-SERV
(800) 990-7378
Fax: (800) 845-2131
Internet: www.torrilegalservices.com
email: tlsnc@erols.com

We Service:

Maryland, Washington, D.C. & Northern Virginia

*24 Hour Service * 7 Days A Week * Weekends * Holidays*

WE SPECIALIZE IN:

- Document Retrieval
- Court Filings
- Computerized Searches
- Personal Services
- Nationwide Service of Process
- Summons, Complaints, Subpoenas
- Emergency Service
- Defendants And Witness
- International Service

Member:
National Association of Professional Process Servers

SEE OUR AD ON PAGE DC27S

ACCU-FAX

SERVICES

A Division Of CEO Corporate Security Group, Inc.

NATIONWIDE COVERAGE
ESTABLISHED 1986

1436D GRAVEL PIKE
POST OFFICE BOX 177
PERKIOMENVILLE, PA 18074-0177

1-800-336-1001
215-234-0700
FAX 215-234-0905

We Specialize in:

CRIMINAL HISTORY & STATEWIDE RESEARCH
COURTHOUSE RESEARCH
AUTHENTIC DOCUMENT RETRIEVAL
PRE-EMPLOYMENT SCREENING
EMPLOYMENT VERIFICATION

UNITED STATES DISTRICT COURT
UNITED STATES BANKRUPTCY COURT

ASSET RESEARCH
CIVIL LITIGATION FILINGS
JUDGEMENTS & TAX LIENS
DEPARTMENT OF STATE
DEPARTMENT OF MOTOR VEHICLES
CHANCERY COURT RESEARCH
UNIFORM COMMERCIAL CODE
REAL PROPERTY RESEARCH

Anywhere in America

Trust ACCU-FAX.
Our experience makes the difference

- Established Professional Reputation
- Highest legal & ethical standards
- Personalized Service
- Accurate, Hand Searches
- State-of-the-Art Computer Technology
- Comprehensive, Documented Reports
- Individually Tailored Screening Program
- Complies with FCRA, EEOC, ADA, CRA
- Rapid and Efficient Turnaround
- Competitive Pricing Nationwide
- Professional References Available

For More Information Visit Our Website At:
www.employmentscreening.com

AMERICAN LEGAL DOCUMENT COURIERS

10570 Main Street, Suite 123
Fairfax, Virginia 22030

Serving Northern Virginia, Maryland and Washington D.C.

(703) 934-6777
Call 800-747-0820

We believe that technology, paired with the right people, practices and vision, can provide an important competitive edge in today's ever-changing business world. Because we focus on understanding business goals in conjunction with a technological direction , we can manage projects from the planning phase to the production support phase.

We offer our clients a very different approach. We provide services to transform your entire enterprise-your strategy, processes, information technology, and people. In addition, we focus on the realization that changing business processes is necessary to achieve the promised returns from strategy and technology. This approach enables the delivery of very different-results clients can build on because we help make organizations more robust and adaptable to future shifts in the environment.

Our aim is to develop effective and mutually beneficial working partnerships by introducing an innovative yet practical approach towards solving your problems. Our staff succeeds by listening carefully to your needs and then providing world-class products, solutions, and expertise. **We will get the results you need.**

SERVICES PROVIDED

PUBLIC RECORDS RETRIEVAL
POST OFFICE CHECKS
DOCUMENT RETRIEVAL FILING & RESEARCH
DATABASE & REAL PROPERTY SEARCHES
DMV/UCC/CREDIT HEADER SEARCHES
SAME DAY & RUSH SERVICE AVAILABLE
UNDERCOVER/SURVEILLANCE, VIDEO
ATTORNEY SERVICES
LITIGATION SUPPORT
COUNTY, STATE & FEDERAL COURTS
SUBPOENAS BY FAX
CONTACTS/TRAVEL WORLDWIDE
WITNESS STATEMENTS TAKEN
SKIP TRACING, MISSING PERSONS
CHILD CUSTODY, FAMILY, SPOUSAL, MARITAL
PRE-EMPLOYMENT, BACKGROUND CHECKS
POLYGRAPH SERVICES AVAILABLE

MEMBERSHIPS

NAPPS
PISA

SEE OUR AD ON PAGE DC26S

The **Martindale-Hubbell Law Directory** is now available online...exclusively through the LEXIS®-NEXIS® services.

CAPITOL PROCESS SERVICES, INC.
CAPITOL INVESTIGATOR SERVICES

1827 18th Street, N.W.
Washington, DC 20009-5526
1-877-708-SERV
Local: (202) 667-1407
Fax (202) 667-2520
www.capitolinvestigators.com

Since 1981, we have provided dedicated service to the legal community, combining an understanding of our clients' needs with proven investigative and process service strategies. We pride ourselves on the efficiency and effectiveness of our investigative and process serving techniques and the presentation of meaningful and helpful information. As a current member of the National Association of Professional Process Servers, we are able to provide specialized services NATIONWIDE.

Providing the following services:

SERVICE OF PROCESS	INVESTIGATIVE SERVICES
Court Filing	Fraud Prevention & Investigations
Court Research	Surveillance – Domestic & Workman's Compensation
Document Retrieval	Background Investigation
Skip Tracing	Asset Searches
Domestic Relations	Employee Theft
Witness Statements	Industrial Security

LICENSED AND BONDED IN WASHINGTON, DC, VIRGINIA & MARYLAND

An **A&E, Inc.** Company

Torri's Legal Services

OFFICES NATIONWIDE
24 Hour Service
Weekends & Holidays
7 Days a Week

- **Nationwide Service of Process**
- **Summons, Complaints, Subpoenas**
- **Document Retrieval**
- **Rush Service**
- **Court Filings**
- **Hard to Locate and Serve Defendants and Witnesses**

Quality Legal Service
BASED ON CONFIDENCE, TRUST AND RESULTS

1-800-990-SERV

(or 1-800-990-7378) • Toll Free Fax: 1-800-845-2131
www.torrilegalservices.com • E-mail: tlsnc@erols.com

WASHINGTON (Continued)

Document Research, Retrieval & Filing (Continued)

Mohr Information Services
P.O. Box 3185
Winchester, VA 22604
Phone: (888) 525-4576
Fax: (888) 525-4479

See Criminal Records Research

E-BUSINESS

OPTIMUS
corporation

Computer and Communications Law Consultants
Division of OPTIMUS Corporation
8601 Georgia Avenue, Suite 700
Silver Spring, MD 20910
Phone: (888) 867-4332
Fax: (301) 585-7976
http://www.OptimusCorp.com
Email: Law@OptimusCorp.com

The Computer and Communications Law (CCL) Division of OPTIMUS Corporation is a professional consultancy comprised of engineers and analysts who have on average 15 years subject matter experience. In most cases our consultants hold law degrees with dual degrees in one or more of the following: Electrical/Electronic Engineering, Computer Science, Software Engineering, and Communication and Information Sciences. In addition, our consultants hold Government clearances up to Top Secret, and patents for innovations in software, communications, and satellite communications technologies.

Our consultants have extensive working experience in many complex computer and communication technologies. This experience is further augmented with legal training and courtroom experience. Thus, we are able to relieve our clients and the court of the burden of deciphering the most sophisticated aspects of technology.

CCL Division has a modern, in-house technical and law library equipped with computerized on-line search services. CCL provides expert witness testimony, research, code comparison, modeling and simulation, pre-trial strategy, and technical audits and analysis in support of the following key areas:

- Power/Utility Deregulation
- Wireless Communications with advocacy support before the Federal Communications Commission (FCC), Federal Trade Commission (FTC), and State Public Service Commissions (PSCs)
- Case Evaluation
- Computer Fraud and Abuse
- Cleanroom Software Development
- Electronic Commerce and Digital Signature
- Electronic Communication, Privacy, and Security-ECPA, European Union (EU) Data Privacy Directive, Digital Millennium Copyright Act (DMCA), and Child On-line Protection Act
- Intellectual Property in Cyberspace (including computer hardware/software and HTML)
- Intellectual Property (including copyright, patent and trade secret litigation support)
- ISP Liability (Defamation, Indecency, Intellectual Property Infringement)
- Global Positioning System (GPS technologies)
- Technology Innovator Support including Broadband Multimedia, PCS, Direct Broadcast Satellites, Digital Audio Broadcasting, Mobile Satellites, Cellular Radio, LEOS, MEOS, and Global Positioning System (GPS).

For more information or to obtain a consulting fee schedule call toll free at (888) 867-4332, extension 2240 or email your request to: Law@OptimusCorp.com

ECONOMIC AND STATISTICAL CONSULTING SERVICES

Analysis and Inference, Inc.
215 Haverford Ave
Swarthmore, PA 19081
Phone: (610) 543-0159
Fax: (610) 543-8952

See Statistics

Analysis Group/Economics
Suite 250
1747 Pennsylvania Ave., N.W.
Washington, DC 20006
Phone: (202) 785-6300
Fax: (202) 530-0436

See Expert Witness-Economics/Economists

WASHINGTON (Continued)

Economic and Statistical Consulting Services (Continued)

WASHINGTON (Continued)

Economic and Statistical Consulting Services (Continued)

Charles River Associates Incorporated

1201 F Street, NW, Ste 700
Washington, DC 20004-1204
Telephone (202) 662-3800 ♦ Fax (202) 662-3910 ♦ www.crai.com

Boston ♦ Berkeley/Oakland ♦ College Station ♦ London ♦ Los Angeles ♦ Melbourne ♦ Mexico City ♦ Palo Alto ♦ Salt Lake City ♦ Toronto ♦ Washington, DC ♦ Wellington

Charles River Associates is a leading economics and business consulting firm, serving industry, the legal profession, and government since 1965. CRA's *Competition* practice provides economic and financial analysis, expert testimony, and other support to clients engaged in legal or regulatory proceedings. The hallmark of CRA's work for lawyers is rigorous analysis combined with careful attention to detail. Our analysis enables clients to make the best possible presentation of the economic and financial issues relevant to their cases.

We provide expert assistance to attorneys on economic aspects of matters involving:

- Antitrust
- Bankruptcies
- Commodity futures
- Contract disputes
- Damages
- Environment
- Finance and valuation
- Intellectual property
- International trade
- Mergers and acquisitions
- Regulation
- Securities fraud
- Tax and transfer pricing issues

Selected services CRA performs for clients include identifying relevant economic issues; building models or analytic frameworks; analyzing and preparing documents for deposition, trial testimony, and cross-examination of expert witnesses; developing and testing hypotheses; collecting primary source data; designing and conducting innovative market research; providing testimony on economic issues before courts and regulatory agencies; and making presentations to enforcement agencies.

We also consult to business executives and government agencies. Our clients span many industries:

- Aerospace and defense
- Automotive
- Chemicals and polymers
- Commercial banking and financial services
- Consumer products
- Energy—electricity, natural gas, coal, petroleum
- Food manufacture and distribution
- Healthcare and pharmaceuticals
- Materials and manufacturing
- Minerals and metals
- Professional sports
- Telecommunications and cable
- Transportation
- Utilities
- Wholesale and retail distribution

Selected Senior Staff and Consultants: James Burrows, *President and CEO*; Jan Acton; Gregory Adams; Jagdish Agarwal; José Alberro-Semerena; Gregory Bell; Stanley Besen; Michael Black; Douglas Bohi; Richard Boltuck; Daniel Brand; Steven Brenner; William Burnett; Phil Cooper; Joseph Coote; Bradford Cornell; Hans van Doesburg; Christopher Doyle; Stephen Doyle; George Eads; Kenneth Elzinga; Franklin Fisher; Stephen George; Joen Greenwood; George Hay; Lance Hoch; William Hughes; Michael Hunter; Stephen Kalos; Seth Kaplan; Firoze Katrak; Michael Katz; Carl Kaysen; J.R. Kearl; Michael Kemp; S. P. Kothari; Robert Larner; Robert Laslett; Arnold Lowenstein; Paul Maleh; Frank Matheson; Christopher Maxwell; Paul Milgrom; Bradley Miller; Bridger Mitchell; Ian Moncrieff; David Montgomery; Rowland Moriarty; Jane Murdoch; Kevin Neels; Monica Noether; Patricia O'Brien; Paul O'Rourke; Thomas Overstreet; Brian Palmer; John Parsons; Timothy Partridge; Howard Pifer III; Jonathan Putnam; Gordon Rausser; Gary Roberts; Craig Romaine; Richard Ruback; Garth Saloner; Steven Salop; Margaret Sanderson; Carl Shapiro; Anne Smith; Julie Solomon; Robert Spann; Michael Thomas; Michael J. Trebilcock; Mike Walker; Steven Wiggins; Louis Wilde; Ralph Winter; John Woodbury; Deloris Wright.

SEE OUR AD ON PAGE DC29S

THE KARDON CORP.

Tel: (336) 766-5608 Fax: (336) 766-5608
E-mail: bkardonphd@aol.com Web: www.kardoncorp.com

Bruce Kardon, Ph.D., President (Left)
Randy Sease, CFE, Vice President (Right)
(*Former FBI Agent*)

The Kardon Corp. offers investigative and consulting services and expert witness testimony throughout the United States. We specialize in case development for *product liability, personal injury, insurance, healthcare, and antitrust issues and prepare timely, easily understood, and technically sound reports.* Our extensive network of professionals include former FBI and Secret Service agents, Ph.D.s, and accountants. Each principal has over 30 years of experience.

We have expertise in:

- **Fraud & Embezzlement**
- **Civil & Criminal Investigation**
- **Forensic Accounting**
- **Information & Computer Systems**
- **Statistical Sampling**
- **Opinion Surveys**
- **Damage Projections**
- **Business Evaluation**
- **Medicare Regulations**
- **Statistical Analysis**
- *and* **Security Control**

We perform:

- **Audits**
- **Investigations**
- **Surveys**
- **Projections**
- **Model Development**
- **Risk Management Studies**
- *and* **Forecasting**

Please contact us it we may be of assistance to you.

LECG

ECONOMICS
FINANCE

1725 Eye Street, NW, Suite 800
Washington, DC 20006

Telephone **888-858-LECG** • Email **experts@lecg.com** • **www.lecg.com**

Buenos Aires • Cambridge • College Station • Emeryville • Evanston
London • Los Angeles • New York • Palo Alto • Salt Lake City
San Francisco • Toronto • Washington, DC • Wellington

LECG, LLC is a global economic consulting services firm that provides sophisticated economic and financial analysis, expert testimony, and litigation support to the world's leading law firms, Fortune 500 companies, private and public sector industries, and government agencies. Our core areas of expertise include:

- Antitrust & Competition
- Mergers & Acquisitions
- Intellectual Property
- Finance & Damages
- Valuation
- Transfer Pricing
- Accounting
- Regulation
- Strategic Consulting
- Public Policy
- Auctions
- International Trade

LECG experts have testified in municipal, state, and federal courts, and before administrative, legislative, and regulatory agencies, in matters spanning a diverse array of industries. Some of our industries of specialization are:

- Environmental
- Financial Institutions
- High Technology
- Healthcare
- Electric Power
- Oil & Natural Gas
- Telecommunications
- Transportation

Our Directors and Principals are leading authorities in economics and finance, and include renowned academics, respected private industry leaders, and former senior-level government officials. Supported by a highly educated and experienced professional staff, our experts can provide you with a full-range of consulting services - expert testimony for complex litigation, regulatory design and testimony, financial valuation, and strategic consulting.

SEE OUR AD ON PAGE DC30S

NERA

Economic Consulting

50 Main Street, 14th Floor
White Plains, NY 10606
Tel. 914.448.4000
Fax. 914.448.4040

1255 23rd Street, NW, Suite 600
Washington, DC 20037
Tel. 202.466.3510
Fax. 202.466.3605

www.nera.com

NERA provides economic consulting, expert testimony, research and litigation support services in:

- Antitrust
- Commercial Damages
- Employment & Discrimination
- Energy and Environmental
- Health Care
- Intellectual Property
- Mass Torts
- Securities/Banking/Finance
- Privatization
- Regulation
- Sports Economics
- Telecommunications

Our senior staff has extensive experience testifying before courts, administrative agencies and legislative bodies.

Senior Officers: Sumanth Addanki, Andrew Carron, Gary Dorman, Fred Dunbar, Gregory Duncan, David Evans, Louis Guth, David Harrison, Jr., Andrew Joskow, Vinita Juneja, Howard Kitt, Robert Mackay, Jeff Makholm, Denise Martin, Marcia Kramer Mayer, Thomas McCarthy, Linda McLaughlin, Eugene Meehan, Todd Morrison, Richard Rapp, Michael Rosenzweig, Richard Rozek, David Salant, Steven Schwartz, Marion Stewart, William Taylor.

Special Consultants: Kent Anderson, David Babbel, Gary Biglaiser, David Blanchflower, James Brickley, Richard Duvall, Eugene Ericksen, Kenneth Froot, Stuart Gabriel, Victor Goldberg, Kenneth Gordon, Bruce Grundy, Robert Hahn, Jerome Hass, Sally Hunt, Jules Joskow, Alfred Kahn, Peter Max, Craig Merrill, Robert Porter, Michael Salinger, Richard Schmalensee, Bernard Shull, Jeremy Stein, Robert Stricker, David Sunding, Michael Tennican, Stephen Usher, W. Kip Viscusi, Anthony Yezer.

Representative Clients: Baker & McKenzie; Bryan Cave; Chadbourne & Parke; Cravath, Swaine & Moore; Covington & Burling; Dechert Price & Rhoads; Fulbright & Jaworski; Gibson Dunn & Crutcher; Heller Ehrman White & McAuliffe; Howrey, Simon, Arnold & White, Hunton & Williams: Kaye, Scholer, Fierman, Hays & Handler; Latham & Watkins; Mayer, Brown & Platt; Morgan & Finnegan; Morgan, Lewis & Bockius; Pillsbury Madison & Sutro; Schiff Hardin & Waite; Shearman & Sterling; Simpson Thacher & Bartlett; Sullivan & Cromwell; Vinson & Elkins; Weil, Gotshal & Manges; Williams & Connolly; Wilmer, Cutler & Pickering; Winston & Strawn.

Additional Offices: Brussels, Cambridge, Chicago, Ithaca, London, Los Angeles, Madrid, Philadelphia, San Francisco, Sydney.

An *MMC* Company

WASHINGTON (Continued)

Economic and Statistical Consulting Services (Continued)

PA Consulting Group

PA is a leading management, systems and technology consulting firm established in 1943, with over 4,000 staff operating worldwide from over 40 offices in 20 countries

PA has 25 groups organized around services and industries, including strategy, energy, IT, project management, life sciences, product and process engineering, government services, environment and telecoms

PA's Energy Economics group has focused expertise in emerging energy industry issues...

- electricity market activities and transactions
- electricity market rules and operations
- competition, trade practices and market power
- electricity and gas trading activities and practices
- market risk assessment and management
- spot market price assessments and projections
- merchant power plans and IPPs
- power contracts
- strategic asset and company translations
- transmissions system operation and property rights

... and general litigation consulting expertise

- damages analysis
- liability assessment
- state and federal regulation
- commercial disputes
- economic assessment of regulation
- case management in large, multiple-witness cases
- complex data- & analysis- intensive cases

For more information, call or send an e-mail to

Edward Kee, Energy Economics Practice

+1 202 442 2000

ed.kee@paconsulting.com

ELECTRONIC FILING

CourtLink®

Suite 100

13427 N.E. 16th St.

Bellevue, WA 98005

Phone: (866) 500-4955

See Online Public Records Service

EMPLOYMENT SCREENING

Accu-Fax Services, A Division of CEO Corporate Security Group, Inc.

1436D Gravel Pike, P.O. Box 177

Perkiomenville, PA 18074-0177

Phone: (800) 336-1001

Fax: (215) 234-0905

See Document Research, Retrieval & Filing

ENVIRONMENTAL & ECOLOGICAL SERVICES

ZymaX FORENSICS

71 Zaca Lane, San Luis Obispo, CA 93401-7300

Vox: 805-544-4696 Fax: 805-544-8226

Email: forensics@zymaxusa.com

Site: www.zymaxforensics.com

www.zymaxusa.com

Specialties: Environmental forensics and geochemistry consulting, litigation support and expert witness testimony.

Analytical: Petroleum hydrocarbon analysis, gas geochemistry, biomarkers, PNA's, PCB's, oxygenates, fuel ID, mixing ratios, age dating, metal analysis by ICP/MS, inorganic and wet chemistry, stable isotope analysis, hydrology, geothermal analytical.

We have developed or modified analyses that allow us to:

- identify the types of products released
- distinguish products from different sources
- estimate the mixing ratios of products
- estimate the age of the product
- assign probable responsibility for sources of the contamination
- give expert witness testimony
- represent either plaintiffs or defendants

Expert Witness: Dr. Isaac R. Kaplan, Senior Consultant, is Professor Emeritus of Geology and Geochemistry at UCLA (retired 1993). Expert Witness in numerous environmental litigation cases nationwide. Contracted to the USGS and the DOD. See full resume at web site.

Publications: Dr. Kaplan has published over 300 papers in books and international journals on environment, sedimentary and petroleum geochemistry and is associate and past editor of several professional journals. See full list at web site.

Professional Societies: Amer Geophysical Union, Amer Chemical Soc, Amer Assn of Petroleum Geologists, Geochemical Soc, Amer Assn for the Advancement of Science, Amer Inst of Chemists, Geological Soc of Amer Geochemical Soc & European Assn for Geochemistry.

Laboratory: 12,000 square foot modern laboratory facility.
Lab Staff: 57 personnel: 5 Ph D's, 5 MS's, 34 Bachelors.

ENVIRONMENTAL CONSULTANTS

ZymaX FORENSICS

71 Zaca Lane, San Luis Obispo, CA 93401-7300
Vox: 805-544-4696 Fax: 805-544-8226
Email: forensics@zymaxusa.com
Site: www.zymaxforensics.com
www.zymaxusa.com

Specialties: Environmental forensics and geochemistry consulting, litigation support and expert witness testimony.

Analytical: Petroleum hydrocarbon analysis, gas geochemistry, biomarkers, PNA's, PCB's, oxygenates, fuel ID, mixing ratios, age dating, metal analysis by ICP/MS, inorganic and wet chemistry, stable isotope analysis, hydrology, geothermal analytical.

We have developed or modified analyses that allow us to:

- identify the types of products released
- distinguish products from different sources
- estimate the mixing ratios of products
- estimate the age of the product
- assign probable responsibility for sources of the contamination
- give expert witness testimony
- represent either plaintiffs or defendants

Expert Witness: Dr. Isaac R. Kaplan, Senior Consultant, is Professor Emeritus of Geology and Geochemistry at UCLA (retired 1993). Expert Witness in numerous environmental litigation cases nationwide. Contracted to the USGS and the DOD. See full resume at web site.

Publications: Dr. Kaplan has published over 300 papers in books and international journals on environment, sedimentary and petroleum geochemistry and is associate and past editor of several professional journals. See full list at web site.

Professional Societies: Amer Geophysical Union, Amer Chemical Soc, Amer Assn of Petroleum Geologists, Geochemical Soc, Amer Assn for the Advancement of Science, Amer Inst of Chemists, Geological Soc of Amer Geochemical Soc & European Assn for Geochemistry.

Laboratory: 12, 000 square foot modern laboratory facility.
Lab Staff: 57 personnel: 5 Ph D's, 5 MS's, 34 Bachelors.

ENVIRONMENTAL INVESTIGATIONS

ZymaX FORENSICS

71 Zaca Lane, San Luis Obispo, CA 93401-7300
Vox: 805-544-4696 Fax: 805-544-8226
Email: forensics@zymaxusa.com
Site: www.zymaxforensics.com
www.zymaxusa.com

Specialties: Environmental forensics and geochemistry consulting, litigation support and expert witness testimony.

Analytical: Petroleum hydrocarbon analysis, gas geochemistry, biomarkers, PNA's, PCB's, oxygenates, fuel ID, mixing ratios, age dating, metal analysis by ICP/MS, inorganic and wet chemistry, stable isotope analysis, hydrology, geothermal analytical.

We have developed or modified analyses that allow us to:

- identify the types of products released
- distinguish products from different sources
- estimate the mixing ratios of products
- estimate the age of the product
- assign probable responsibility for sources of the contamination
- give expert witness testimony
- represent either plaintiffs or defendants

Expert Witness: Dr. Isaac R. Kaplan, Senior Consultant, is Professor Emeritus of Geology and Geochemistry at UCLA (retired 1993). Expert Witness in numerous environmental litigation cases nationwide. Contracted to the USGS and the DOD. See full resume at web site.

Publications: Dr. Kaplan has published over 300 papers in books and international journals on environment, sedimentary and petroleum geochemistry and is associate and past editor of several professional journals. See full list at web site.

Professional Societies: Amer Geophysical Union, Amer Chemical Soc, Amer Assn of Petroleum Geologists, Geochemical Soc, Amer Assn for the Advancement of Science, Amer Inst of Chemists, Geological Soc of Amer Geochemical Soc & European Assn for Geochemistry.

Laboratory: 12, 000 square foot modern laboratory facility.
Lab Staff: 57 personnel: 5 Ph D's, 5 MS's, 34 Bachelors.

WASHINGTON (Continued)

EXAMINERS OF QUESTIONED DOCUMENTS (HANDWRITING EXPERTS)

EXPERT WITNESS

ACCOUNTING

Lindquist Forensic Partners

Suite 800
2121 K St. NW
Washington, DC 20037
Phone: (202) 261-3548
Fax: (202) 261-3508

See Financial Investigation/Forensic Accounting

BANKING

Specializing in: Finance

Analysis Group/Economics
Suite 250
1747 Pennsylvania Ave., N.W.
Washington, DC 20006
Phone: (202) 785-6300
Fax: (202) 530-0436

See Expert Witness-Economics/Economists

CHEMICAL PROCESS

Specializing in: Safety

GRANBERRY & ASSOCIATES, INC.
EDWIN P. GRANBERRY, JR
2431 Aloma Avenue
Suite 276
Winter Park, Florida 32792
Telephone: 407-671-6050
Fax: 407-671-5399
Email: epgchem@mindspring.com
GRANBERRYCHEMISTRY.COM

SUMMARY OF PROFESSIONAL EXPERIENCE

Over 42 years employed in the Occupational Safety, Industrial Hygiene and Environmental Profession with direct, hands-on experience in the following areas of specialization:

- OSHA Compliance
- EPA Compliance
- Accident Investigation
- Marine Cargo Operations
- Safety Training Courses
- Disaster Preparedness/Planning
- Solid Propellant Rocket Motors
- Safety, Industrial Hygiene and Environmental Audits
- Hazardous Waste Management
- Chemical Process Safety
- Industrial Toxicology
- Explosives/Ordinance Safety
- Aviation Safety
- Indoor Air Quality
- Industrial Hygiene
- Aerospace/Missile Operations Safety

CERTIFICATIONS

Certified Professional Chemist (CPC)
Certified Occupational Health & Safety Technologist (COHST)
Certificate: Hazardous Waste Management- University of Florida
Certificate: Hazardous Materials Chemistry- University of Toledo
Certificate: Toxicology for Chemists- American Chemical Society
Certified Environmental Specialist (CES)
Diplomate - Board Certified Forensic Examiner-Chemistry/Materials Science (#3165)
Fellow - American College of Forensic Examiners (#398)
Fellow - American Institute of Chemists

EDUCATION

MBA: Aviation; Embry Riddle Aeronautical University, Daytona Beach, FL
B.S.: Chemistry; Rollins College, Winter Park, FL
Graduate School: Chemical Engineering/Chemistry; American University, Washington, DC, Wayne University, Detroit, MI

PROFESSIONAL MEMBERSHIPS

American Society of Safety Engineers (ASSE), since 1971
American Chemical Society, Member since 1951
American Board of Forensic Examiners - Diplomate
American Society of Testing Materials
National Fire Protection Association
American Institute of Chemists, Fellow 1984, Member 1961-

A complete Curriculum Vitae is Available Upon Request

COMMUNICATIONS

Computer and Communications Law Consultants
Suite 700
8601 Georgia Ave.
Silver Spring, MD 20910
Phone: (888) 867-4332
Fax: (301) 585-7976

See Expert Witness-Intellectual Property/Infringement Damages

Telecommunications Consulting Group, Inc.
Suite 800
1133 20th St., NW.
Washington, DC 20036
Phone: (202) 419-3357
Fax: (202) 955-5059

See Expert Witness-Telecommunications

COMPUTER & BUSINESS INFORMATION SYSTEMS

Computer and Communications Law Consultants
Suite 700
8601 Georgia Ave.
Silver Spring, MD 20910
Phone: (888) 867-4332
Fax: (301) 585-7976

See Expert Witness-Computer Science/Intellectual Property

The Kardon Corp.
P.O. Box 653
Clemmons, NC 27012
Phone: (336) 766-5608
Fax: (336) 766-5608

See Expert Witness-Accounting

WASHINGTON (Continued)

Expert Witness (Continued)

COMPUTER FORENSICS/DATA RECOVERY

FOUNDSTONE

Foundstone, Inc.

1776 I Street, 9th Floor
Washington, DC 20006
202.756.4866
fax: 202.756.1301

email: ir@foundstone.com
www.foundstone.com

Foundstone has assembled a highly trained and experienced team of computer network investigators. As a group, they have performed computer forensic analysis on over 200 different systems around the globe. The team has provided expert witness testimony in criminal and civil litigation in both the United States and overseas. This case experience is available to augment your staff in resolving internal or external computer related incidents. Further, the team's members are internationally recognized expert speakers and trainers on computer evidence and litigation.

Forensic Investigation and Litigation Support: This service is aimed at providing the highest level of court admissible evidence to support potential litigation or administrative action. Our team will use a court proven computer forensic toolkit and processes to identify, recover and extract computer based evidence. We provide the leverage necessary for successful litigation.

Program Development: Foundstone's senior consultants perform a review of your organization's existing policies and procedures to identify any gaps from existing best practices. Foundstone will help your legal and information technology teams develop polices that meet the regulatory and legal challenges unique to your industry.

Private Training: Our team has trained the Federal Bureau of Investigations, the Central Intelligence Agency, Royal Canadian Mounted Police, and other Government agencies. We have also developed custom training for a number of the Fortune 100 firms. Foundstone will develop a custom training curriculum that will teach the best practices in forensic and incident response while addressing the unique requirements of your business.

SEE OUR AD ON PAGE DC38S

Litigation Support

Electronic Evidence Discovery
Computer Forensics Examination
Expert Witness Testimony
Risk Management

Foundstone's litigation support experts have worked on over 200 cases involving electronic evidence, with skills honed at the highest corporate and government levels. We are the authors of the best-selling book "Incident Response: Investigating Computer Crime" and well-known speakers and instructors in Computer Forensics. Foundstone's experience and expertise are available today for all your litigation support needs.

FOUNDSTONE

1776 I Street, 9th Floor
Washington, DC 20006
202.756.4866 / fax 202.756.1301
ir@foundstone.com / www.foundstone.com

COMPUTER SCIENCE/INTELLECTUAL PROPERTY

OPTIMUS
corporation

Computer and Communications Law Consultants

Division of OPTIMUS Corporation
8601 Georgia Avenue, Suite 700
Silver Spring, MD 20910
Phone: (888) 867-4332
Fax: (301) 585-7976
http://www.OptimusCorp.com
Email: Law@OptimusCorp.com

The Computer and Communications Law (CCL) Division of OPTIMUS Corporation is a professional consultancy comprised of engineers and analysts who have on average 15 years subject matter experience. In most cases our consultants hold law degrees with dual degrees in one or more of the following: Electrical/Electronic Engineering, Computer Science, Software Engineering, and Communication and Information Sciences. In addition, our consultants hold Government clearances up to Top Secret, and patents for innovations in software, communications, and satellite communications technologies.

Our consultants have extensive working experience in many complex computer and communication technologies. This experience is further augmented with legal training and courtroom experience. Thus, we are able to relieve our clients and the court of the burden of deciphering the most sophisticated aspects of technology.

CCL Division has a modern, in-house technical and law library equipped with computerized on-line search services. CCL provides expert witness testimony, research, code comparison, modeling and simulation, pre-trial strategy, and technical audits and analysis in support of the following key areas:

- Power/Utility Deregulation
- Wireless Communications with advocacy support before the Federal Communications Commission (FCC), Federal Trade Commission (FTC), and State Public Service Commissions (PSCs)
- Case Evaluation
- Computer Fraud and Abuse
- Cleanroom Software Development
- Electronic Commerce and Digital Signature
- Electronic Communication, Privacy, and Security-ECPA, European Union (EU) Data Privacy Directive, Digital Millennium Copyright Act (DMCA), and Child On-line Protection Act
- Intellectual Property in Cyberspace (including computer hardware/software and HTML)
- Intellectual Property (including copyright, patent and trade secret litigation support)
- ISP Liability (Defamation, Indecency, Intellectual Property Infringement)
- Global Positioning System (GPS technologies)
- Technology Innovator Support including Broadband Multimedia, PCS, Direct Broadcast Satellites, Digital Audio Broadcasting, Mobile Satellites, Cellular Radio, LEOS, MEOS, and Global Positioning System (GPS).

For more information or to obtain a consulting fee schedule call toll free at (888) 867-4332, extension 2240 or email your request to: Law@OptimusCorp.com

CONSTRUCTION

RBS Consulting Group

8402 Boxwood Drive
Tampa, Florida 33615-4939

❑ Claims Specialists
❑ Expert Testimony
❑ Litigation Support
❑ Cost Analysis
❑ CPM Schedule Analysis

Telephone: (813) 886-6633
(800) 909-7692
Fax: (813) 886-6892
Email: RBSConsulting@aol.com
Web Page: Http://www.RBSConsulting.com

WASHINGTON (Continued)

Expert Witness - Construction (Continued)

URS

URS/O'Brien Kreitzberg
1101 17th Street NW, Suite 1000
Washington, DC 20036
(202) 293-4694 tel
(202) 293-9564 fax
www.urscorp.com

O'Brien Kreitzberg is now part of URS Corporation, the largest engineering and construction services firm (ENR 04/01) in the nation. We specialize in dispute resolution, litigation support and construction management, with the backing of more than 16,000 engineering and construction professionals operating nationwide. We offer the industry's finest professionals in program, project and construction management; architecture and engineering; scheduling and cost engineering; estimating; inspection; and information systems.

Our specialists understand construction disputes. Before construction begins, we review the contract documents and develop procedures aimed at avoiding disputes. We also analyze risk and recommend risk-mitigation measures. During construction, we provide technical support to resolve current issues and recommend measures to mitigate exposure to future claims. After construction, we focus on timely and cost-effective resolution of issues.

Our clients include legal counsels; federal, state and local agencies; communities, special districts and authorities; private owners; contractors; insurance companies; and design and construction professionals.

Services
Construction Claims Analysis
Alternative Dispute Resolution (ADR)
Expert Witness

Expertise
- Construction Management
  - Scheduling
  - Cost Estimating
  - Accounting
- Architecture
- Engineering
  - Civil
  - Dam
  - Electrical
  - Environmental
  - Geotechnical
  - Land Surveyor
  - Mechanical
  - Noise Control
  - Nuclear
  - Structural
- Science
  - Ecology
  - Environmental Toxicology
  - Geology
  - Geophysics
  - Ground Water
  - Soil

DAMAGE VALUATION

Analysis Group/Economics
Suite 250
1747 Pennsylvania Ave., N.W.
Washington, DC 20006
Phone: (202) 785-6300
Fax: (202) 530-0436

See Expert Witness-Economics/Economists

The Kardon Corp.
P.O. Box 653
Clemmons, NC 27012
Phone: (336) 766-5608
Fax: (336) 766-5608

See Expert Witness-Accounting

ECONOMICS/ECONOMISTS

ANALYSIS GROUP/*Economics*
An Analysis Group Company

1747 Pennsylvania Avenue NW, Suite 250
Washington, D.C. 20006

Telephone (202) 785-6300
Facsimile (202) 530-0436
AGWeb@analysisgroup.com
www.analysisgroup.com

Analysis Group/Economics provides economic and financial consulting services to assist law firms in all aspects of complex litigation, including pretrial discovery, damages estimation, expert reports and testimony, and critique of opposing expert analyses.

- Antitrust
- Commercial Litigation
- Employment
- Energy
- Entertainment & Sports
- Environmental Economics
- Financial Institutions
- Health Care Property
- Intellectual Property
- Real Estate
- Securities
- Telecommunications
- Valuation

Analysis Group/Economics' offices are located in Boston, Denver, Los Angeles, Menlo Park, Montreal, New York, San Francisco, and Washington, D.C.

Senior staff: Elizabeth Becker, Laura G. Boothman, Pierre Y. Cremieux, Bruce F. Deal, Mark H. Egland, John D. Finnerty, Rodney Frame, Paul E. Greenberg, John C. Jarosz, Edward P. Kahn, Jeffrey H. Kinrich, John H. Landon, R. Jeffrey Malinak, Atanu Saha, Martha S. Samuelson, Robert A. Sherwin, Bruce E. Stangle, Richard M. Starfield, Christopher A. Vellturo, Deloris R. Wright, Bruce J. Ambrose, Almudena Arcelus, Coleman Bazelon, Howard G. Birnbaum, David Campbell, Robert Comment, Elizabeth A. Evans, Peter H. Griffes, Steven Herscovici, Carla S. Mulhern, Stanley I. Ornstein, Michael J. Quinn. Laura O. Robinson, Ronald D. Rudkin, Chetan Sanghvi, Tamar Sisitsky, and Bruce A. Strombom and Robert L.Vigil.

Academic and industry experts: Dennis J. Aigner, Ray Ball, Arnold I. Barnett, Ernst R. Berndt, Marshall E. Blume, John Y. Campbell, Roger Craine, Dwight B. Crane, Ronald C. Curhan, Francis X. Diebold, Paul J. Feldstein, George Foster, Robert Goldscheider, Robert E. Hall, John R. Hauser, Thomas W. Hazlett, Donna L. Hoffman, Mitchell C. Jensen, John M. Lacey, Robert Litan, Burton G. Malkiel, Joseph P. Newhouse, Sharon M. Oster, Robert S. Pindyck, John A. Rizzo, Anthony M. Santomero, Eduardo S. Schwartz, G. William Schwert, Meir Statman, Robert Stavins, Roman L. Weil, Susan E. Woodward, Richard J. Zeckhauser, and Andrew Zimbalist.

Representative clients: Akin, Gump, Strauss, Hauer & Feld; Fish & Neave; Fulbright & Jaworski; Gibson, Dunn & Crutcher; Goodwin, Procter; Hale and Dorr; Hogan & Hartson; Jones, Day, Reavis and Pogue; Latham and Watkins; McDermott, Will & Emery; Mayer, Brown & Platt; Morrison & Foerster; Paul, Hastings, Janofsky & Walker; Pennie & Edmonds; Pillsbury,Winthrop; Shearman & Sterling; Sidley & Austin; Simpson, Thacher & Bartlett; Skadden, Arps, Slate, Meagher & Flom; Steptoe and Johnson; Sullivan and Cromwell; Weil, Gotshal & Manages; Winston & Strawn.

Charles River Associates Incorporated
Suite 700
1201 F St., NW
Washington, DC 20004-1204
Phone: (202) 662-3800
Fax: (202) 662-3910

See Economic and Statistical Consulting Services

LECG
ECONOMICS
FINANCE

1725 Eye Street, NW, Suite 800
Washington, DC 20006

Telephone **888-858-LECG** • Email **experts@lecg.com** • **www.lecg.com**

Buenos Aires • Cambridge • College Station • Emeryville • Evanston
London • Los Angeles • New York • Palo Alto • Salt Lake City
San Francisco • Toronto • Washington, DC • Wellington

LECG, LLC is a global economic consulting services firm that provides sophisticated economic and financial analysis, expert testimony, and litigation support to the world's leading law firms, Fortune 500 companies, private and public sector industries, and government agencies. Our core areas of expertise include:

- Antitrust & Competition
- Mergers & Acquisitions
- Intellectual Property
- Finance & Damages
- Valuation
- Transfer Pricing
- Accounting
- Regulation
- Strategic Consulting
- Public Policy
- Auctions
- International Trade

LECG experts have testified in municipal, state, and federal courts, and before administrative, legislative, and regulatory agencies, in matters spanning a diverse array of industries. Some of our industries of specialization are:

- Environmental
- Financial Institutions
- High Technology
- Healthcare
- Electric Power
- Oil & Natural Gas
- Telecommunications
- Transportation

Our Directors and Principals are leading authorities in economics and finance, and include renowned academics, respected private industry leaders, and former senior-level government officials. Supported by a highly educated and experienced professional staff, our experts can provide you with a full-range of consulting services - expert testimony for complex litigation, regulatory design and testimony, financial valuation, and strategic consulting.

ECONOMICS/ECONOMISTS

Specializing in: Financial Valuation

The Brattle Group
44 Brattle St.
Cambridge, MA 02138-3736
Phone: (617) 864-7900
Fax: (617) 864-1576

See Economic and Statistical Consulting Services

WASHINGTON (Continued)

Expert Witness - Economics/Economists - Financial Valuation (Continued)

RICHARD B. EDELMAN, Ph.D.

ECONOMIC ANALYSIS FOR LITIGATION SUPPORT

Visit at www.economic-analysis.com

The Business —

We provide economic analysis and economic damages/expert witness testimony in personal injury, wrongful death, wrongful termination, wrongful discharge, business valuation and divorce cases. Economic losses include lost income, diminished earnings capacity, lost fringe benefits, household services, medical expenses, life care expenses and lost profits. We also perform the valuation of investments such as pensions, stocks, bonds, small businesses and structured settlements for bankruptcies, divorce and churning cases. Work includes both the calculation of damages for plaintiff cases and the analysis of economic reports for defense cases. We can arrange supporting expert services in vocational rehabilitation, taxes, and forensic accounting/financial statement reconstruction.

Background —

Dr. Edelman has participated in numerous cases in various Federal and local jurisdictions. He holds a Doctor of Business Administration Degree from the University of Maryland (1975) with a concentration in Financial Economics and minor areas in statistical analysis and accounting theory. He also holds an M.B.A. (1970) and B.S. With High Honors (1968) in Finance from the University of Maryland. He is currently a Senior Professor of Finance at the American University in Washington, D.C., has served as the Director of Economic Analysis at COMSAT and Associate and Assistant Professor of Finance at the University of Hawaii. Dr. Edelman has published over sixty articles in the area of financial economics and presented over one hundred papers at professional conferences.

Philosophy —

Our philosophy is to present conservative and supportable economic analysis based on both the facts of the case and a reasonable evaluation of the present and anticipated economic climate.

It is recognized that the selection of an expert witness is critical to a case and we will be happy to answer any additional questions you might have and provide references, a vita, resume and a list of cases in which testimony has been presented.

8515 Whittier Boulevard
Bethesda, Maryland 20817

Call: 301-469-9575 or 1-800-257-8626
E-mail to: richard@economic-analysis.com

LECG, LLC

Suite 800
1725 Eye St., NW
Washington, DC 20006
Phone: (888) 858-5324

See Economic and Statistical Consulting Services

Specializing in: Statistics

Analysis and Inference, Inc.

215 Haverford Ave
Swarthmore, PA 19081
Phone: (610) 543-0159
Fax: (610) 543-8952

See Statistics

ECONOMICS/STATISTICS

The Kardon Corp.

P.O. Box 653
Clemmons, NC 27012
Phone: (336) 766-5608
Fax: (336) 766-5608

See Expert Witness-Accounting

EMPLOYMENT PRACTICES

Analysis Group/Economics

Suite 250
1747 Pennsylvania Ave., N.W.
Washington, DC 20006
Phone: (202) 785-6300
Fax: (202) 530-0436

See Expert Witness-Economics/Economists

ENERGY & UTILITIES

Analysis Group/Economics

Suite 250
1747 Pennsylvania Ave., N.W.
Washington, DC 20006
Phone: (202) 785-6300
Fax: (202) 530-0436

See Expert Witness-Economics/Economists

PA Consulting Group

PA is a leading management, systems and technology consulting firm established in 1943, with over 4,000 staff operating worldwide from over 40 offices in 20 countries

PA has 25 groups organized around services and industries, including strategy, energy, IT, project management, life sciences, product and process engineering, government services, environment and telecoms

PA's Energy Economics group has focused expertise in emerging energy industry issues...

- electricity market activities and transactions
- electricity market rules and operations
- competition, trade practices and market power
- electricity and gas trading activities and practices
- market risk assessment and management
- spot market price assessments and projections
- merchant power plans and IPPs
- power contracts
- strategic asset and company translations
- transmissions system operation and property rights

... and general litigation consulting expertise

- damages analysis
- liability assessment
- state and federal regulation
- commercial disputes
- economic assessment of regulation
- case management in large, multiple-witness cases
- complex data- & analysis- intensive cases

For more information, call or send an e-mail to

Edward Kee, Energy Economics Practice

+1 202 442 2000

ed.kee@paconsulting.com

ENVIRONMENTAL

The Brattle Group

44 Brattle St.
Cambridge, MA 02138-3736
Phone: (617) 864-7900
Fax: (617) 864-1576

See Economic and Statistical Consulting Services

ENVIRONMENTAL CONSULTANT

ZymaX FORENSICS

71 Zaca Lane, San Luis Obispo, CA 93401-7300
Vox: 805-544-4696 Fax: 805-544-8226
Email: forensics@zymaxusa.com
Site: www.zymaxforensics.com
www.zymaxusa.com

Specialties: Environmental forensics and geochemistry consulting, litigation support and expert witness testimony.

Analytical: Petroleum hydrocarbon analysis, gas geochemistry, biomarkers, PNA's, PCB's, oxygenates, fuel ID, mixing ratios, age dating, metal analysis by ICP/MS, inorganic and wet chemistry, stable isotope analysis, hydrology, geothermal analytical.

We have developed or modified analyses that allow us to:

- identify the types of products released
- distinguish products from different sources
- estimate the mixing ratios of products
- estimate the age of the product
- assign probable responsibility for sources of the contamination
- give expert witness testimony
- represent either plaintiffs or defendants

Expert Witness: Dr. Isaac R. Kaplan, Senior Consultant, is Professor Emeritus of Geology and Geochemistry at UCLA (retired 1993). Expert Witness in numerous environmental litigation cases nationwide. Contracted to the USGS and the DOD. See full resume at web site.

Publications: Dr. Kaplan has published over 300 papers in books and international journals on environment, sedimentary and petroleum geochemistry and is associate and past editor of several professional journals. See full list at web site.

Professional Societies: Amer Geophysical Union, Amer Chemical Soc, Amer Assn of Petroleum Geologists, Geochemical Soc, Amer Assn for the Advancement of Science, Amer Inst of Chemists, Geological Soc of Amer Geochemical Soc & European Assn for Geochemistry.

Laboratory: 12, 000 square foot modern laboratory facility.
Lab Staff: 57 personnel: 5 Ph D's, 5 MS's, 34 Bachelors.

ENVIRONMENTAL CONTAMINATION/SPILLS

ZymaX Forensics

71 Zaca Ln.
San Luis Obispo, CA 93401-7300
Phone: (805) 544-4696
Fax: (805) 544-8226

See Forensic Geochemistry

WASHINGTON (Continued)
Expert Witness (Continued)

ENVIRONMENTAL HEALTH & SAFETY

GRANBERRY & ASSOCIATES, INC.

EDWIN P. GRANBERRY, JR

2431 Aloma Avenue
Suite 276
Winter Park, Florida 32792

Telephone: 407-671-6050
Fax: 407-671-5399
Email: epgchem@mindspring.com
GRANBERRYCHEMISTRY.COM

SUMMARY OF PROFESSIONAL EXPERIENCE

Over 42 years employed in the Occupational Safety, Industrial Hygiene and Environmental Profession with direct, hands-on experience in the following areas of specialization:

- OSHA Compliance
- EPA Compliance
- Accident Investigation
- Marine Cargo Operations
- Safety Training Courses
- Disaster Preparedness/Planning
- Solid Propellant Rocket Motors
- Safety, Industrial Hygiene and Environmental Audits
- Hazardous Waste Management
- Chemical Process Safety
- Industrial Toxicology
- Explosives/Ordinance Safety
- Aviation Safety
- Indoor Air Quality
- Industrial Hygiene
- Aerospace/Missile Operations Safety

CERTIFICATIONS

Certified Professional Chemist (CPC)
Certified Occupational Health & Safety Technologist (COHST)
Certificate: Hazardous Waste Management- University of Florida
Certificate: Hazardous Materials Chemistry- University of Toledo
Certificate: Toxicology for Chemists- American Chemical Society
Certified Environmental Specialist (CES)
Diplomate - Board Certified Forensic Examiner-
Chemistry/Materials Science (#3165)
Fellow - American College of Forensic Examiners (#398)
Fellow - American Institute of Chemists

EDUCATION

MBA: Aviation; Embry Riddle Aeronautical University, Daytona Beach, FL
B.S.: Chemistry; Rollins College, Winter Park, FL
Graduate School: Chemical Engineering/Chemistry; American University, Washington, DC, Wayne University, Detroit, MI

PROFESSIONAL MEMBERSHIPS

American Society of Safety Engineers (ASSE), since 1971
American Chemical Society, Member since 1951
American Board of Forensic Examiners - Diplomate
American Society of Testing Materials
National Fire Protection Association
American Institute of Chemists, Fellow 1984, Member 1961-

A complete Curriculum Vitae is Available Upon Request

FORENSIC ACCOUNTING

The Kardon Corp.
P.O. Box 653
Clemmons, NC 27012
Phone: (336) 766-5608
Fax: (336) 766-5608

See Expert Witness-Accounting

FRAUD

The Kardon Corp.
P.O. Box 653
Clemmons, NC 27012
Phone: (336) 766-5608
Fax: (336) 766-5608

See Expert Witness-Accounting

Lindquist Forensic Partners
Suite 800
2121 K St. NW
Washington, DC 20037
Phone: (202) 261-3548
Fax: (202) 261-3508

See Financial Investigation/Forensic Accounting

GOVERNMENT CONTRACT CLAIMS

SHAW CONSULTING GROUP

Contract Compliance, Training and Business Development
4312 – 13th Place, N.E.
Washington, D.C. 20017

The Shaw Consulting Group is a management consulting and research firm. We provide your company with every possible advantage. It's about having an experienced and powerful consulting resource at your command. ***The Shaw Consulting Group*** sets stringent performance goals for each contract using the latest methods and technology, in conjunction, with sound management and quality assurance practices.

From the start, we strive to make doing business with us convenient. ***The Shaw Consulting Group*** directs its talents on delivery of exceptional services. That is why we offer an array of services to help you meet your goals and objectives. These highly specialized services are in the following areas:

- Litigation Consultant (Expert Witness)
- Contract Compliance/Oversight
- Project Management
- Technical Assistance
- Training
- Computer Management Services
- Business Development and Marketing
- Conference Planning/Logistics

Our highly skilled and qualified personnel have extensive experience and knowledge in the government, private sector and international markets. The combined expertise of more than 100 years of experience from our group of professionals creates a unique tapestry in today's highly competitive environment. ***The Shaw Consulting Group's*** philosophy is to make a difference. As such, we are capable of providing fresh ideas, innovative approaches and creative solutions for our clients. Our work is tailored to our clients' needs and we deliver inventive solutions on time, at the negotiated cost and a service in which customer satisfaction is guaranteed.

Client information is available upon request. Please call 202-529-3373.
Thank you!

HEALTH CARE PLANS

MANAGED LIABILITY ASSOCIATES

50 F Street, NW Suite 600 Washington, DC 20001
Tel: (202) 585-1811 Fax: (202) 628-9244
www.MLA-USA.com
E-mail: ErlingHansen@msn.com

Background

Managed Liability Associates ("MLA") is the nation's most experienced managed care litigation consulting group. We are a partnership of executives and consultants who have over 75 cumulative years of knowledge and experience with both medical care delivery as well as managed healthcare.

Areas of Expertise

EXPERT CASE REVIEW AND TESTIMONY ON:

- Industry standards
- Medical management and utilization review
- Hospital and physician provider contracting
- Malpractice liability
- Financial reimbursement models and capitation analysis
- Provider and member communications
- Grievance and appeal procedures including external review
- Subrogation and third party recovery
- Referral and certification issues

CONSULTATION AND EXPERTISE ON ISSUES OF:

- HMO and managed care law
- COBRA, EMTALA and HIPAA
- ERISA
- National accreditation guidelines
- Class action litigation
- Medicare, Medicaid and FEHBP

(This Listing Continued)

Managed Liability Associates (Continued)

RISK MANAGEMENT CONSULTATION

- Case specific liability review
- Organization-wide liability audits
- Coordinated team approach to corrective action recommendations

Principal Consultants

Robert Chabon: MD – Georgetown University (Pediatrics); JD – University of Maryland School of Law; MPH – University of Pittsburgh Graduate School of Public Health. Extensive experience as hospital VPMA and managed care CMO. Lecturer on managed care liability and reviewer of thousands of potential liability cases over 25 years.

Erling Hansen: JD – Syracuse University College of Law. Over 25 years of managed care experience including contract specialist with the FEHB Program, General Counsel of national HMO trade association, Director of Legal and Regulatory Affairs for federally-qualified, NCQA accredited HMO and private law practice with managed care clients. Named one of "Leading Lawyers of Managed Care" by *The National Law Journal.*

Brian Heller: PhD – University of Chicago. 30 years of experience establishing and operating managed care organizations including HMOs, PPOs and PHOs for commercial, Medicaid and Medicare markets. Expert Witness in numerous managed care lawsuits in many states.

INTELLECTUAL PROPERTY/INFRINGEMENT DAMAGES

Analysis Group/Economics

Suite 250
1747 Pennsylvania Ave., N.W.
Washington, DC 20006
Phone: (202) 785-6300
Fax: (202) 530-0436

See Expert Witness-Economics/Economists

The Brattle Group

44 Brattle St.
Cambridge, MA 02138-3736
Phone: (617) 864-7900
Fax: (617) 864-1576

See Economic and Statistical Consulting Services

Charles River Associates Incorporated

Suite 700
1201 F St., NW
Washington, DC 20004-1204
Phone: (202) 662-3800
Fax: (202) 662-3910

See Economic and Statistical Consulting Services

WASHINGTON (Continued)

Expert Witness - Intellectual Property/Infringement Damages (Continued)

OPTIMUS corporation

Computer and Communications Law Consultants

Division of OPTIMUS Corporation
8601 Georgia Avenue, Suite 700
Silver Spring, MD 20910
Phone: (888) 867-4332
Fax: (301) 585-7976
http://www.OptimusCorp.com
Email: Law@OptimusCorp.com

The Computer and Communications Law (CCL) Division of OPTIMUS Corporation is a professional consultancy comprised of engineers and analysts who have on average 15 years subject matter experience. In most cases our consultants hold law degrees with dual degrees in one or more of the following: Electrical/Electronic Engineering, Computer Science, Software Engineering, and Communication and Information Sciences. In addition, our consultants hold Government clearances up to Top Secret, and patents for innovations in software, communications, and satellite communications technologies.

Our consultants have extensive working experience in many complex computer and communication technologies. This experience is further augmented with legal training and courtroom experience. Thus, we are able to relieve our clients and the court of the burden of deciphering the most sophisticated aspects of technology.

CCL Division has a modern, in-house technical and law library equipped with computerized on-line search services. CCL provides expert witness testimony, research, code comparison, modeling and simulation, pre-trial strategy, and technical audits and analysis in support of the following key areas:

- Power/Utility Deregulation
- Wireless Communications with advocacy support before the Federal Communications Commission (FCC), Federal Trade Commission (FTC), and State Public Service Commissions (PSCs)
- Case Evaluation
- Computer Fraud and Abuse
- Cleanroom Software Development
- Electronic Commerce and Digital Signature
- Electronic Communication, Privacy, and Security-ECPA, European Union (EU) Data Privacy Directive, Digital Millennium Copyright Act (DMCA), and Child On-line Protection Act
- Intellectual Property in Cyberspace (including computer hardware/software and HTML)
- Intellectual Property (including copyright, patent and trade secret litigation support)
- ISP Liability (Defamation, Indecency, Intellectual Property Infringement)
- Global Positioning System (GPS technologies)
- Technology Innovator Support including Broadband Multimedia, PCS, Direct Broadcast Satellites, Digital Audio Broadcasting, Mobile Satellites, Cellular Radio, LEOS, MEOS, and Global Positioning System (GPS).

For more information or to obtain a consulting fee schedule call toll free at (888) 867-4332, extension 2240 or email your request to: Law@OptimusCorp.com

SEE OUR AD ON PAGE DC46S

LECG, LLC

Suite 800
1725 Eye St., NW
Washington, DC 20006
Phone: (888) 858-5324

See Economic and Statistical Consulting Services

OIL & GAS

ZymaX Forensics

71 Zaca Ln.
San Luis Obispo, CA 93401-7300
Phone: (805) 544-4696
Fax: (805) 544-8226

See Forensic Geochemistry

PETROLEUM SOURCE ID

ZymaX Forensics

71 Zaca Ln.
San Luis Obispo, CA 93401-7300
Phone: (805) 544-4696
Fax: (805) 544-8226

See Forensic Geochemistry

PREMISES SECURITY & LIABILITY

Secure Source Inc.

710 S. Kimball Ave.
Southlake, TX 76092
Phone: 011-525-611-1090

See Investigators

PRODUCT LIABILITY

David F. Goldsmith PhD

Dept. Environmental & Occupational Health
The George Washington University
2300 K Street, Suite 201
Washington, DC 20037
Phone: (202) 994-1734
Fax: (202) 994-0011
http://www.OccupationalEpi.com
Email: eohdfg@gwumc.edu

Specialties: Occupational/environmental epidemiology, including Daubert expertise; health hazards of silica, silicosis and cancer, pulmonary and autoimmune diseases; health effects of pesticides; California's Proposition 65; environmental risk assessment; asbestos; silicone products; air toxics.
Degrees/Lic: MSPH, PhD.
Formal Educ: BA, Sociology, Antioch College, 1972; MSPH, Epidemiology, University of North Carolina, 1977; PhD, Epidemiology, University of North Carolina, 1983.
Previous/Current Position: Associate Research Professor, The George Washington University, School of Public Health & Health Services, Washington DC, University of SF, University of CA, San Diego and Davis Schools of Medicine; Senior Scientist, Public Health Institute, Berkeley, CA; Special Assistant for Risk Assessment, U.S. EPA, San Francisco, CA; Epidemiologist, NIOSH, Morgantown, WV; Staff Scientist, National Academy of Sciences, Washington, DC; GRA Occupational Health Studies Group, University of North Carolina; Environmental Epidemiologist, Research Triangle Institute, Research Triangle Park, NC.
Honors/Awards: National Institute of Environmental Health Sciences Traineeship; Contributing Editor - - American Journal of Industrial Medicine.
Prof. Affil. Served as consultant or peer-reviewer for many health journals, for NIH study sections, CA Dept. Health Services, National Academy of Sciences, Office of the Surgeon General, International Agency for Research on Cancer, EPA, CDC-NIOSH; Society for Epidemiology Research; Society for Occupational and Environmental Epidemiology; International Epidemiology Association.
Publications: 50+ (International Agency for Research on Cancer Monograph on the Evaluation of the Carcinogenic Risk of Chemicals to Humans – Silica and Some Silicates. Volume 42. Lyon, France)
Prior Expert: 15+ years of consulting on cases in California, Texas, Ohio, North Carolina, New Jersey, Washington D.C., Oregon, Nevada, Florida, Maryland and New York on silica, asbestos, construction, silicone breast implants and other hazardous exposures. Numerous Depositions, Daubert and Proposition 65 hearings and trial appearances for both plaintiff and defense.

The Kardon Corp.

P.O. Box 653
Clemmons, NC 27012
Phone: (336) 766-5608
Fax: (336) 766-5608

See Expert Witness-Accounting

WASHINGTON (Continued)

Expert Witness (Continued)

RAPE/SEXUAL ASSAULT

PAGE VERLANDER R.N., MS, Ph.D.

Sexual Assault Specialist
13725 Brandycrest Drive
Chesterfield, VA 23832
Phone: (804) 739-9429

Dr. Page Verlander is a Sexual Assault / Forensic Toxicologist. She offers Expert Witness Testimony in cases related to sexual assault, rape, child abuse, and patterned physical evidence related to crimes. Dr. Verlander additionally specializes in toxicology.

Concurrently, Dr. Verlander is an Administrator responsible for emergency services in Central Virginia. Additionally, she works as a Medical Services Consultant whereby she handles process improvement with Emergency Services within various hospital facilities, and assists with the development of sexual assault forensic programs.

EDUCATION

Graduate Program Forensic Toxicology (2001 - Present)
University of Florida, Gainesville, FL

Doctorate Health Administration (1999 - 2001)
Kennedy Western University, Cheyenne, WY

Master of Science in Criminal Justice (1997 - 2001)
Virginia Commonwealth University, Quantico, VA
held at Federal Bureau of Investigation

Bachelor of Science in Nursing (1993 - 1997)
Medical College of Virginia, Richmond, VA

PROFESSIONAL ORGANIZATIONS

American College of Forensic Examiners
American Professional Society on the Abuse of Children
International Association of Forensic Nurses
Virginia Chapter of International Association of Forensic Nurses
Emergency Nurses Association
Virginia Nurses Association
American Society of Criminology
Academy of Criminal Justice Sciences
Virginia Nurses Association

SECURITIES LAW

WILLIAM A. COLLISON, JR., P.A.

800-407-4834

RENDERING PROFESSIONAL SERVICES IN:

- **Case Evaluation**
- **Litigation Support**
- **Expert Witness Testimony**
- **Forensic Accounting**
- **Damage Studies**
- **Mediation**

PROVIDING EXPERT WITNESSES FOR DISPUTES CONCERNING:

- **Unsuitable Investments**
- **Misrepresentation**
- **Unauthorized Trading**
- **Mismanagement**
- **Churning**
- **Mutual Fund Switching**
- **Breach of Fiduciary Responsibility**
- **U-5 Defamation**
- **Wrongful Termination**

THE FIRM OFFERS EXPERTISE IN THE FOLLOWING AREAS:

- **Stocks and Bonds**
- **Mutual Funds**
- **Limited Partnerships**
- **Index Trading**
- **Options**
- **Insurance Products**

Each of our Experts has at least 10 years of experience in their areas of expertise. We are capable of serving the needs of Attorneys who represent either the Claimant/Plaintiff or Respondent/Defendant.

Curriculum Vitae, References, Transcripts and Fee Schedules furnished upon request.

FOR MORE INFORMATION CONTACT:
WILLIAM A. COLLISON, JR., CFP, CMFC, President
1-800-407-4834 OR (252) 636-3580
FAX: (252) 636-0166
EMAIL: secexpwit@aol.com
WEBSITE: http://hometown.aol.com/secexpwit/secexpwit.html

SECURITIES/LITIGATION SUPPORT

Analysis Group/Economics

Suite 250
1747 Pennsylvania Ave., N.W.
Washington, DC 20006
Phone: (202) 785-6300
Fax: (202) 530-0436

See Expert Witness-Economics/Economists

Charles River Associates Incorporated
Suite 700
1201 F St., NW
Washington, DC 20004-1204
Phone: (202) 662-3800
Fax: (202) 662-3910

See Economic and Statistical Consulting Services

SECURITY CONSULTANTS

Secure Source Inc.
710 S. Kimball Ave.
Southlake, TX 76092
Phone: 011-525-611-1090

See Investigators

TELECOMMUNICATIONS

The Brattle Group
44 Brattle St.
Cambridge, MA 02138-3736
Phone: (617) 864-7900
Fax: (617) 864-1576

See Economic and Statistical Consulting Services

CPT ASSOCIATES, INC.
1700 Briar Ridge Road
McLean, Virginia 22101

Carlton P. Tolsdorf, Jr.
President & CEO

Telephone: (703) 532-7370
EFax: 800-784-7512 Fax: (703) 532-0547
e-mail: Tolsdorf@erols.com

CPT Associates, Inc. founded in 1992 by Carlton P. Tolsdorf, Jr. Has provided cost effective expertise to law firms & high technology fortune 500 companies worldwide. The company was founded in response to a growing need fro Expert technology and business process consulting.

The Firm's Mission

- To provide independent technical analysis & opinions concerning complex technology issues
- Turnkey solutions offering one stop shopping for expertise needed
- Cost effective winning solutions

Practice Areas

- Intellectual Property
- High Technology Disputes
- Government & Commercial Contracts
- Emerging Market Telecommunication Operating Company Development
- Information System Technologies

Areas of Expertise

- Patents
- Trade Secrets
- Contracts
- Telecommunication Network & Systems Design and Implementation Analyses
- Business case analyses
- Technology Expertise
  - -Telecommunications
  - -Information Systems Technology
  - -Underwater Acoustics
  - -Global Positioning
  - -Satellite Systems (GEO/LEO)

Referrals available upon request
Please call Carlton Tolsdorf @ (703) 532-7370

WASHINGTON (Continued)

Expert Witness - Telecommunications (Continued)

Telecommunications Consulting Group, Inc.

1133 20th Street NW
Suite 800
Washington DC 20036
Phone: 202-419-3357
Fax: 202-955-5059
E-mail: jgw@teleconsultinggroup.com
Website: www.teleconsultinggroup.com/expert1.htm

The Telecommunications Consulting Group was founded in 1981 and is located in Washington, DC. The firm provides consulting services to the telecommunications and information industries and to governmental agencies and ministries. The group combines expertise in business planning, economics, legislation, regulation and technology in order to assist carriers, service and equipment providers, investors, users, regulators and policymakers.

Dr. John G. Williams provides litigation support and expert witness services. He advises attorneys in cases involving telecommunications network engineering and related business planning matters. He has furnished assistance at various stages of actions, including: framing the problem from a technological perspective, formulating strategies, drafting interrogatories and testimony, and serving as an expert witness. His background includes a Ph.D. in Computer Science and positions at Bell Laboratories and the Federal Communications Commission.

For more information, please view our website at:
www.teleconsultinggroup.com/expert1.htm

TOXICOLOGY

Page Verlander R.N., MS, Ph.D.

13725 Brandycrest Dr.
Chesterfield, VA 23832
Phone: (804) 739-9429

See Expert Witness-Rape/Sexual Assault

TRANSPORTATION

National Trucking Safety Consultants

Roland B. Brown, *President*
2709 Winbrell Court
Waldorf, MD 20601-4905
Tel. No (301) 843-4987
Fax No. (301) 638-1634
Email address: alabama@erols.com

Specializing in trucking safety, DOT regulations, driver training and hiring practices and Top Management supervision

- Twenty years working experience in top management in trucking industry.
- Since 1984 worked with insurance companies, as a consultant, in underwriting, claims processing and accident prevention.
- Served as Expert Witness in litigation since 1981.
- Worked as consultant with plaintiff and defense attorneys in litigation preparation.
- Served as Expert Witness for approximately sixty cases.
- Testified in 15 - 20 State Courts and in Federal Courts in numerous Jurisdictions.
- Worked as independent Consultant to fleet operations ranging from 10-600 trucks.

Specializing in: Aviation

- FAA ENFORCEMENT ACTIONS -

JACOBY AND ASSOCIATES

Richard Jacoby Stuart, Esq.
Available "Of Counsel"
28112 Edelweiss Court
Laguna Niguel, CA 92677 USA
(949) 831-6980 (24hr message center and Fax)
yeochrie@hotmail.com

Experience with U.S. Department of Transportation, California State Legislature, Federal Aviation Administration, Boeing Aircraft Co., United, Northwest Orient, Aveaco Airlines, Thompson Express Travel, Air Line Pilots Association, Teamsters, E.E.O.C., Flight Crews International, Garden Grove City College. Expertise in air transportation litigation cases, dealing in pilot wrongful termination and in nearly all aspects of flight operations and related Federal Air Regulations. Expertise in B727, DC-8, DC-10, B 747 acquisition and F.A.A. compliance. Expertise in Department of Transportation legal filings for Domestic and International airline licenses, routes and landing rights.

Specializing in "Deposition Preparation Analysis", Dispute Resolution and F.A.A. Enforcement Actions.

BACKGROUND (38 years in Aviation- 28 years Air Carrier Experience)

Jacoby and Associates (since 1968) - Administrative Aviation Law
CNF/Emery Worldwide Airlines (since 1991) - DC-10 Captain (ALPA)
Alta Financial Corporation - Of Counsel/Real Estate
Evergreen International Airline - DC8; 747 Pilot
Northwest Orient Airline - 747 Pilot Training
US Air / Piedmont - 727 Flight Engineer (ALPA)
British American Airline - DC8 Captain. Founder
Flying Tiger Airline - DC8 Pilot Training
Golden West Airline (FAR 121) - SD-3 Captain (ALPA)
Van Nuys Aviation - General Manager, FAR 141, 135
Edwin G. Davies, Esq. and Associates - Of Counsel/Estate Planning

Education

LL.B - La Salle Law College, Chicago
Brokers License - California Department of Real Estate
Teaching Credential - University of California at Los Angeles
Ph.D. - Psychology of Religion & Oriental Languages - COS
M.A. - Comparative Religion - UCLA / College of Oriental Studies
B.A. - Philosophy/Theology - CAL State University
A.A. Orange Coast College

F.A.A. Certification

Airline Transport Pilot - ASMEL, SD-3, DC-3, DC-8; DC-10; B747 (Loft)
Flight Engineer - Turbojet 727
Certified Ground Instructor - Advanced and Instrument
Certified Flight Instructor - Airplane Single and Multi Engine Land
Certified Flight Instructor - Instrument

Professional Organizations

Corporate Lawyer Association, 1987
Air Line Pilots Association International - 17 years
American Bar Association - 13 years
"NTSB" Bar Association, Since 1997

EXPERT WITNESS REFERRAL SERVICES

EXPERT RESOURCES INC.®

Headquarters: 4700 North Prospect Road, Suite 1B
Peoria Heights, Illinois 61614-6451

Telephone: 800-383-4857
Telephone: 202-397-1177

Fax: 888-815-2778
www.expertresources.com

Since 1979

WASHINGTON, D.C. ATTORNEYS CALL EXPERT RESOURCES, INC.--

THE EXPERTS ON EXPERTS®

Regardless of your time constraints, a telephone call to our toll-free number puts you in touch with **ERI** staff who can assist you in:

- pinpointing the exact area of expertise you need
- promptly -- usually within 24 hours -- connecting you with experts so that you can make your decision regarding qualifications

ERI can call on experts and consultants in all fields for attorneys (plaintiff and defendant), insurance companies, government agencies, and corporations. **ERI** reviews your request with experts in the specialty you need before suggesting them to you. After this review, the expert allows **ERI** to release a copy of his/her résumé to you, along with the address and telephone number where the expert can be contacted.

ERI's suggestion of an expert to you does not obligate you in any way. We will quote all rates, terms and responsibilities you may incur if you use the suggested expert's services.

ERI encourages you to call suggested experts and discuss your case needs -- no obligation.

ERI will conduct a confidential search for the needed expert, **at no cost to you,** if our registered experts have a conflict of time or interest. Search and referral services are provided without charge. Our administrative charge is included in the expert's rate we will quote to you at the time we suggest the expert, or several experts, if you so request.

WHY SPEND VALUABLE HOURS TRYING TO LOCATE THE RIGHT EXPERT, IN THE RIGHT PLACE WITHOUT CONFLICT OF INTEREST OR TIME?

LEAVE THIS TO THE

EXPERTS ON EXPERTS®

Call today if you need an expert, or want to receive a Confidential Inquiry Form and Expertise Listing.

Telephone: 800-383-4857

WASHINGTON (Continued)

Expert Witness Referral Services (Continued)

Silicon Valley Expert Witness Group Inc.

S V E W G

800 W. El Camino Real, Suite 450
Mountain View, CA 94040
Telephone: 888-873-4420 Fax: 888-873-4421
E-mail: dmcdonald@svewg.com
Website: www.svewg.com

The Silicon Valley Expert Witness Group, Inc. (SVEWG) is a high technology legal consulting and intellectual property asset management firm that provides three distinct yet synergistic legal support services, including: expert witness, forensic engineering and intellectual property asset management services. We assist our client in recruiting the world-class expertise necessary to support critical legal matters. Our services support high technology litigation, insurance claim matters and technical, business, and marketing requirements. Our focus is on consulting requirements and litigation support that requires top-level expertise in the following areas of high technology.

- Computer Sciences and Technology
- Consumer Electronics
- Electronic and Electrical Engineering
- Internet and eCommerce
- Manufacturing Equipment
- Microelectronics
- Project Management
- Semiconductor
- Software
- Telecommunications

Our consultants are individuals with decades of hands-on experience, and high academic achievement. SVEWG offers exceptional consulting expertise to our clientele from a registry of distinguished subject matter experts. Our consultants are particularly skilled in the analysis of technology issues that are relevant to intellectual property matters, including copyright infringement; patent infringement; patent validity analysis, prior art research, and theft of trade secrets. From background research to testimonial witness you can demand and expect the best from the Silicon Valley Expert Witness Group.

Call, email, or visit our website today for additional information.

888-873-4420
dmcdonald@svewg.com
http://www.svewg.com

TASA

SINCE 1961

TECHNICAL ADVISORY SERVICE FOR ATTORNEYS
Headquarters: 1166 DeKalb Pike, Blue Bell, PA 19422-1853
U.S. and Canada: 800-523-2319 Fax: 800-329-8272
United Kingdom: 0800-89-1292
Email: experts@tasanet.com • Website: www.tasanet.com

THE BEST SOURCE FOR EXPERTS WORLDWIDE®

North America's Largest And Most Experienced Expert Referral Service® is the leading source of Consulting Experts, Testifying Experts, and ADR Specialists for attorneys and insurance firms.

TASA SAVES YOU TIME AND MONEY

- Thousands of independent experts
- Over 8,000 categories, including medical and ADR
- Over 200,000 clients • over 40 years' experience
- For cases of all kinds and sizes; plaintiff or defense
- Competitive fees • Unbeatable service

NO CHARGE FOR REFERRALS

A small sample of expertise available through TASA:

AGRICULTURE: chemicals, machinery, explosions, crops, feed, forestry.

AUTOMOTIVE/TRANSPORTATION: accident reconstruction, seat belts, vehicle/road design, trucks, railroads, aviation.

BUSINESS/FINANCE/ECONOMICS: banking, securities, insurance, economic valuation, appraisals, real estate, franchising.

COMPUTERS AND ELECTRONICS: year 2000; computer hardware, software, languages, security, networking, viruses, hacking, simulation; embedded systems; telecommunications; wiring, cable.

CONSTRUCTION/ARCHITECTURE: building design, maintenance, structural integrity, HVAC, plumbing; bridges, equipment.

CRIMINOLOGY/POLICE PROCEDURES: document examination, fingerprinting, ballistics, prisons, tape analysis, DNA testing.

ELEVATORS/LIFTS: cranes, controls, design and safety.

ENVIRONMENT: water, air & noise pollution; hazardous waste, asbestos, ecology.

FALLS: lighting, surfaces, ladders, scaffolding, weather.

FIRES: explosions, arson, flammable clothing, codes, alarms.

MACHINERY: design/safety; industrial, agricultural, appliances.

MARITIME: seamanship, cargo handling, ship/boat design, accident reconstruction, navigational aids.

MEDICAL/HEALTH CARE: issues relating to medical personnel, institutions, equipment, and procedures.

MATERIALS: metals, polymers, glass, wood; textiles.

INTELLECTUAL PROPERTY: patents/copyrights/trademarks.

PERSONNEL/LABOR: wages & hours, discrimination, workplace safety, ADA issues, sexual harassment.

PHARMACEUTICALS/TOXICOLOGY: drugs, food poisoning, labels & warnings, cosmetics, coatings.

SPORTS/RECREATION: equipment, supervision, facilities.

Call for TASA's free Directory of Expertise.

800-523-2319

FINANCIAL INVESTIGATION/FORENSIC ACCOUNTING

The Kardon Corp.
P.O. Box 653
Clemmons, NC 27012
Phone: (336) 766-5608
Fax: (336) 766-5608

See Economic and Statistical Consulting Services

LINDQUIST FORENSIC PARTNERS

2121 K. Street NW
Suite 800
Washington, D.C. 20037

Phone: 202-261-3548
Fax: 202-261-3508

E-mail: forensic@aol.com

For over three decades, Counsel has routinely entrusted Lindquist with highly sensitive and critical information on behalf of their clients. From Fortune 500 corporations to government leaders our clients have included a variety of international businesses, foreign and domestic governments and non-governmental entities.

The role of the forensic and investigative accountant today is extremely broad. Ours is a financial fact-finding specialty, in which Lindquist can manage all aspects of a financial investigation, providing Counsel with all relevant information from the financial world (positive and negative to their case). This information will relate directly to and at times beyond her or his client and the matters at hand. At all times, we set the standard of care and professionalism "suitable to a court of law".

Lindquist provides Counsel with the large case management experience of the "Big 5" firms, whether a domestic or international case, and we ensure that all times, no conflict of interest exists both before or during an investigation.

LINDQUIST...
ASSISTING LEADING COUNSEL
IN PURSUIT OF

Asset Tracing, Bankruptcy, Breach of Fiduciary Duty, Bribery, Business Crime, Business Intelligence, Commercial Disputes, Computer Forensics, Conflict of Interest, Construction Fraud, Corruption, Employee Fraud/Theft, Estate & Trust, Family Business Disputes, Fidelity Claims, Foreign Corrupt Practices Act, Fraud, Illegal Shipment of Assets, Insider Knowledge, Internal Investigations, Investor Fraud, Loan Fraud, Management Fraud/Theft, Manipulation of Financial Statements, Money Laundering Investigations, Planned Bankruptcy, Political Corruption, Procurement Fraud, Securities and Investment Fraud, Stock Market Manipulations, Surety Claims, Trust/Escrow Account Fraud/Theft, Tax Fraud, Who Has Criminal/Civil Knowledge

SEE OUR AD ON PAGE DC54S

FORENSIC FINANCIAL ANALYSIS

Lindquist Forensic Partners
Suite 800
2121 K St. NW
Washington, DC 20037
Phone: (202) 261-3548
Fax: (202) 261-3508

See Financial Investigation/Forensic Accounting

FORENSIC GEOCHEMISTRY

ZymaX FORENSICS

71 Zaca Lane, San Luis Obispo, CA 93401-7300
Vox: 805-544-4696 Fax: 805-544-8226
Email: forensics@zymaxusa.com
Site: www.zymaxforensics.com
www.zymaxusa.com

Specialties: Environmental forensics and geochemistry consulting, litigation support and expert witness testimony.

Analytical: Petroleum hydrocarbon analysis, gas geochemistry, biomarkers, PNA's, PCB's, oxygenates, fuel ID, mixing ratios, age dating, metal analysis by ICP/MS, inorganic and wet chemistry, stable isotope analysis, hydrology, geothermal analytical.

We have developed or modified analyses that allow us to:
- identify the types of products released
- distinguish products from different sources
- estimate the mixing ratios of products
- estimate the age of the product
- assign probable responsibility for sources of the contamination
- give expert witness testimony
- represent either plaintiffs or defendants

Expert Witness: Dr. Isaac R. Kaplan, Senior Consultant, is Professor Emeritus of Geology and Geochemistry at UCLA (retired 1993). Expert Witness in numerous environmental litigation cases nationwide. Contracted to the USGS and the DOD. See full resume at web site.

Publications: Dr. Kaplan has published over 300 papers in books and international journals on environment, sedimentary and petroleum geochemistry and is associate and past editor of several professional journals. See full list at web site.

Professional Societies: Amer Geophysical Union, Amer Chemical Soc, Amer Assn of Petroleum Geologists, Geochemical Soc, Amer Assn for the Advancement of Science, Amer Inst of Chemists, Geological Soc of Amer Geochemical Soc & European Assn for Geochemistry.

Laboratory: 12, 000 square foot modern laboratory facility.
Lab Staff: 57 personnel: 5 Ph D's, 5 MS's, 34 Bachelors.

GENEALOGICAL SERVICES

Hoerner Bank
Oststrasse 77
Heilbronn, DEU D-74072
Phone: (0) 7131/9322-255
Fax: (0) 7131/9322-299

See Heir Tracers

WASHINGTON (Continued)

HEIR TRACERS

SEIT 1849

HOERNER BANK

AKTIENGESELLSCHAFT

GENEALOGICAL RESEARCH

HOERNER BANK
A BANK LICENSED IN GERMANY

- THE OLDEST ESTABLISHED AND ONE OF THE LARGEST FIRMS SPECIALIZING IN GENEALOGICAL RESEARCH
- LOCATION OF MISSING HEIRS AND SEARCHES FOR PERSONS WHO ARE ENTITLED TO ASSETS OF ALL DESCRIPTIONS
- SERVICES RENDERED TO SURROGATE COURTS, PERSONAL REPRESENTATIVES OF ESTATES, HEIRS, BENEFICIARIES AND PERSONS ENTITLED TO ASSETS OF MISSING PERSONS
- SERVICES INCLUDE SEARCHES FOR UNKNOWN OR MISSING HEIRS, REQUIRED RESEARCH TO LOCATE AND COLLECT ASSETS WORLD-WIDE
- HIGHLY QUALIFIED RESEARCH STAFF CONSISTING OF LICENSED LAWYERS, ACCOUNTANTS AND SPECIALISTS IN GENEALOGICAL RESEARCH, ALL EXPERTS IN WORLD-WIDE RESEARCH
- TRANSLATIONS AND SERVICES WITH RESPECT TO ALL EUROPEAN LANGUAGES
- SUPERVISION, ADVICE AND FACILITATION OF REAL ESTATE SALES, COLLECTIONS, TRANSFER OF BANK ACCOUNTS AND SECURITIES
- PREPARATION OF LEGAL DOCUMENTS, INITIATING AND COMPLETING LEGAL PROCEEDINGS AFFECTING MISSING PERSONS WORLD-WIDE
- ALL OTHER TRADITIONAL BANKING BUSINESS
- CONTINGENT FEE OR FEES AS OTHERWISE AGREED TO BY PARTIES

CHALLENGE OUR EFFICIENCY

D-74072 HEILBRONN, OSTSTRASSE 77
GERMANY

TEL. (0) 7131 / 9322-255   FAX (0) 7131 / 9322-299

Email: reichert@hoernerbank.de

Website: http://www.heirsearcher.com

INTERPRETERS

LanguageWorks
Suite 201
1123 Broadway
New York, NY 10010
Phone: (800) 247-5020
Fax: (212) 447-6257

See Translation Services

The Legal Translators.com
45 Mount Auburn St.
Watertown, MA 02472
Phone: (800) 671-2034
Fax: (877) 290-0280

See Translation Services

INTERPRETERS & TRANSLATORS

Japan Communication Consultants, LLC

The Japanese Language Experts™

For over twenty years Japan Communication Consultants has served the legal community with a full range of Japanese language services. JCC's clients return to us consistently because we provide the highest quality Japanese legal translation and interpretation services available in North America.

Our services include:

- Expert translation of contracts, patents, transcripts, filings, pleadings, complaints, discovery materials, and legal documentation in any field. Evaluation and assessment of translations done by others.
- Highly experienced professional interpreters available around the world for trials, hearings, depositions, litigation preparation and support, conferences, meetings, and events.
- All Translations are proofread and edited before delivery by native speakers, and can be certified upon your request.
- We give you a realistic deadline for the completion of your project based on your needs, then comprehensively manage it to completion, and deliver it on time to your specifications. We have *never* missed a deadline at JCC.
- At JCC you always get the personal service and attention you deserve, combined with our commitment to maintaining the very highest quality standards in our field.

For more information about JCC please see our website at the address below. For a free estimate, or to discuss your Japanese language needs, please call or e-mail us (attach document or sample free for fastest service).

Japan Communication Consultants, LLC
www.japancc.com
236 East 47th Street, 28th Floor
New York, NY 10017
Tel: 212-759-2033
Fax: 212-759-2149
Email: jcc@japancc.com

LanguageWorks

Suite 201
1123 Broadway
New York, NY 10010
Phone: (800) 247-5020
Fax: (212) 447-6257

See Translation Services

The Legal Translators.com

45 Mount Auburn St.
Watertown, MA 02472
Phone: (800) 671-2034
Fax: (877) 290-0280

See Translation Services

INVESTIGATIVE CONSULTANTS

Capitol Process Services, Inc.,
Capitol Investigator Services

1827 18th St., N.W.
Washington, DC 20009-5526
Phone: (877) 708-7378
Fax: (202) 667-2520

See Process Servers & Document Delivery Services

INVESTIGATORS

Hickey, Miller & Bailey, Inc.

Investigative Services

Maryland - Washington, D.C. - Virginia

16064 Kings Mountain Road
Woodbridge, VA 22191
Tel: (703) 739-0458
Fax: (703) 739-6158

We're a group of retired Metropolitan police officers and investigative specialists from Washington, D.C. who provide attorneys with civil and criminal litigation support. We also handle affairs for private corporations, aid litigants in recovering monies won through civil judgements, and assist clients with environmental protection matters.

Our number-one priority is serving our clients as effectively, discreetly and cost-consciously as possible. We have built our reputation for thoroughness and efficiency one case at a time. With over one-hundred years of collective experience in investigative work, we have accumulated a high number of invaluable contacts in the field. We would be happy to assist with any questions you may have regarding services and fees.

Partners	Associate Partners
John J. Hickey, Jr.	*John S. Dabrowski*
Charles E. Miller	*Edward E. Curley*
Larry W. Bailey	*John T. Butler*
Reggie Guzman	*Gregory L. Peterson*
	Patrick J. Lennon

Investigator and Research Analyst
Dina-Maria Hack

John J. Hickey, Jr.
Mr. Hickey introduced and developed the Financial Investigation Unit of the Metropolitan Police Department. Mr. Hickey's work in a money-laundering investigation of a large drug organization was adopted as an instructive tool as part of agent training at the FBI Academy in Quantico, Virginia. He is highly experienced in the location and recovery of missing persons, and is a recognized expert in the field of financial investigations.

Contact Us By Email!
hmb-inv@att.net

Visit our Website!
www.hickeymillerbailey.com

Incorporated, bonded and insured in Maryland, Washington, D.C., and Virginia. Virginia license #11-1609

WASHINGTON (Continued)
Investigators (Continued)

The Kardon Corp.

P.O. Box 653
Clemmons, NC 27012
Phone: (336) 766-5608
Fax: (336) 766-5608

See Economic and Statistical Consulting Services

SECURE SOURCE INC.®

Consulting Services • Investigations • Executive Protection

Sometimes a job comes along that is too big to handle and you need to look to other *sources* for help. We can handle it. With our backgrounds in the Secret Service, the F.B.I., and investigative journalism, and having earned the trust of some of the largest privately and publicly held corporations in the world, we are capable. Our track record proves it.

Mailing Address:
710 South Kimball Avenue
Southlake, Texas 76092

Phone: 817-424-4444
Fax: 817-424-1111

E-mail: david@securesource.com
Website: www.securesource.com

David W. Nicastro, CPP, CFE, *President*
Charles N. Dickey, *Executive Vice President*

The Secure Source client benefits from decades of federal law enforcement and business experience. The firm maintains an extensive network of invaluable and trusted associates throughout the nation and around the world. A combination of time-tested investigative techniques, coupled with modern database research and analysis, has proven to be of significant value to Secure Source clients seeking the highest quality professional investigative support services.

Secure Source investigates and provides expert court testimony and security consulting in the following key areas:

- Forensic examination of evidence
- Handwriting analysis
- Retrieval of hidden computer data
- Location of hidden assets
- Witness interviews
- Due diligence inquiries
- Environmental and safety violations
- Financial fraud
- Extortion threats
- Audio-video enhancement & authenticity
- Polygraph examination
- Electronic "sweep" countermeasures
- Theft and embezzlement
- Litigation support
- Mergers and acquisitions
- "Undercover" and surveillance operations
- Industrial espionage
- Security consulting

JURY CONSULTANTS

On Trial Associates, Inc.
6406 Western Ave.
Chevy Chase, MD 20815
Phone: (301) 652-6228
Fax: (301) 652-9523

See Trial Consultants

LABORATORIES - GEOCHEMICAL/PETROLEUM/SOURCE ID

ZymaX Forensics
71 Zaca Ln.
San Luis Obispo, CA 93401-7300
Phone: (805) 544-4696
Fax: (805) 544-8226

See Forensic Geochemistry

LAW OFFICE AUTOMATION SERVICES

SAGE
Insightful Solutions in Technology Management

Technology Consultants to the Legal Profession

1020 19th St., NW
Suite 275
Washington, D.C. 20036
202-659-9390
Fax: 202-659-0024
www.sagesol.com

Contact: George W. Nicholson

Sage is a professional consulting organization focused exclusively on the management and use of technology in the practice and business of Law. Sage is comprised of a unique team of experienced legal technology and business professionals with backgrounds encompassing a wide range of experience including: law firm administration, internal law firm systems management, technology consulting, application development, large scale systems integration, website development and technical support. Sage consultants have extensive experience with technologies that law firms require, including: word processing, document management, electronic mail, Internet, Intranet, client accounting, litigation support, case management, database management and practice productivity tools. Sage offers a broad array of technology services in all aspects of law firm automation. Our services include:

* Technology and Organizational Audits
* Strategic, Acquisition and Contingency Planning
* Internet and Intranet Expertise
* Requirements Analysis
* System Design and Implementation
* Application Enhancement and Development
* Technical and End User Support

Sage is an independent consulting organization and does not resell hardware or software, thus ensuring the objectivity of any evaluation performed. Sage is also an active supporter of the various Bar Associations and of the Association of Legal Administrators. Sage conducts seminars and organizes technology events for both organizations. Additionally, Sage develops and conducts independent seminars on technology issues relevant to the legal community.

WASHINGTON (Continued)

LAWYER SEARCH & PLACEMENT CONSULTANTS

The Affiliates℠

1201 F Street NW
9th Floor
Washington, DC 20004
(202) 626-0260

Located in more than 30 major markets throughout the United States and Canada, including Washington, DC, *The Affiliates* is a premier provider of experienced project and full-time professionals for law officers and corporate legal departments. The firm places highly qualified candidates in a wide range of positions for the legal field, including attorney, paralegal, administrator, executive director, litigation support specialist, legal secretary, legal word processor and other legal support professionals.

Through its expertise, diligence and attention to meeting the needs of its clients, *The Affiliates* has earned a reputation for outstanding service and professionalism. Many of *The Affiliates'* account executives are attorneys and administrators who have experience working in law firms and legal departments. They possess an "insider knowledge" of our clients' needs, enabling them to serve as advisors on hiring and personnel management issues. On the candidate side, *The Affiliates* maintains an active referral network, an advanced e-cruiting program and an extensive database of highly qualified legal professionals currently available, all of which offer us access to a large talent pool for fulfilling the staffing needs of law practices and departments.

The Affiliates routinely assists law offices in identifying the appropriate personnel resources required for each particular case or project, and provides specialists whose specific training and experience make them ideal for the assignment, whether it is temporary or full-time.

The Affiliates also serves as a reliable information source on workplace trends and management issues within the legal community. We regularly conduct national surveys of attorneys and other legal professionals about topics ranging from new technologies and flexible work options to the fastest growing areas. In addition, *The Affiliates* has produced a number of informative pamphlets for management within law firms and corporate legal departments, complimentary copies of which may be requested by contacting *The Affiliates.*

For additional information, please visit *The Affiliates'* web site at www.affiliates.com.

HARBOR Consultants International, Inc.

2740 Chain Bridge Road
Vienna, Virginia 22181

703-352-1888
Email: harbor_resumes@attglobal.net

Harbor Consultants International, Inc. has been and is continually recognized for its abilities to attract the correct legal talent for law firms interested in expanding or replacing their legal practice areas. Harbor Consultant's placements include law firm partners, associates at all levels, practice groups, in-house lawyers as well as senior staff and administrators.

The majority of the assignments for Harbor Consultants are focused on the general legal practice areas such as corporate transactions, litigation, intellectual property, tax, trust and estates, employee benefits, and ERISA. With its presence in Washington D.C., Harbor Consultant's unique abilities to perform the due diligence on the candidates presented allows law firms to focus on the chemistry between potential candidates and existing staff to ensure a long-term working relationship beneficial for the firm and the candidate involved. Harbor Consultants has been recognized for its ability to understand the cultures and chemistry needed in order to make such relationships permanent.

On the candidate side, Harbor Consultants maintains an active referral network and an extensive database of highly qualified legal professionals to allow for the fulfilling of the staffing needs of law practices and departments. In most cases, Harbor Consultants has been called upon to help find the unique and high-level attorneys needed to fill the strategic openings within a law firm and its growth targets.

Harbor Consultants has routinely assisted law offices in identifying the appropriate personnel resources required for each particular case or project and is key in providing the legal resources for each particular case or project. In several cases, this has been done through the building of teams from disparate elements or in the transfer of an intact practice from one firm to another.

LegalLeaders, Inc.

1800G Diagonal Road
Alexandria, VA 22314
(703) 836-3222
Fax (703) 836-2255
www.legalleaders.com

In partnership with some of America's largest law firms with offices around the world, LegalLeaders seeks to identify that rare individual who is poised to lead an elite and *focused* legal practice. LegalLeaders engages exclusively in senior-level search assignments, thus narrowing the field of qualified candidates to the upper echelon of the legal profession.

In addition to their expertise in executive placement, the consultants at LegalLeaders provide unparalleled strategic planning services to firms that desire a larger share of their home market or plan to expand into new markets in the U.S. and abroad. Fundamental to their objective approach to mergers and acquisitions is the application of both quantitative and qualitative criteria to determine an ideal match of business models, profit potential, compensation structure, and firm culture.

LegalLeaders specializes in the acquisition of practice groups and boutique firms that are preeminent in their field and are expected to grow significantly within the next few years. From the traditional powerhouse practices of Securities and Litigation, to the burgeoning field of Intellectual Property, attorneys placed through LegalLeaders represent the industries that will shape the legal and business community of the 21st Century.

StaffWise Legal, Inc.

email us
jobs@staffwise.com

Please visit our website
www.staffwise.com

Attorneys • Paralegals • Support Staff • Techlawyers

Locations

Washington, DC 20036
1150 Connecticut Avenue, N.W., Suite 707
Telephone: 202-861-0100 Fax: 202-861-0349

Baltimore, MD 21201
36 South Charles Street, Suite 1908
(Voice) 410-783-1234 Fax: 410-528-9740

Chicago, IL 60602
77 West Washington Street, Suite 605
(Voice) 312-782-8800 Fax: 312-782-6600

New York, NY 10017
708 3rd Avenue, 29th Floor
Phone: 212-661-0220 Fax: 212-661-0234

Philadelphia, PA 19102
1760 Market Street, Suite 601
(Voice) 215-523-8600 Fax: 215-523-7567

St. Louis, MO 63105
7700 Bonhomme Ave., Suite 620
(Voice) 314-863-8900 Fax: 314-863-8969

WASHINGTON (Continued)

LEGAL PUBLICATIONS

BNA

The Bureau of National Affairs
1231 25TH St., N.W.
Washington, DC 20037
1-800-372-1033
www.bna.com

Founded in 1929, BNA is the recognized leader and publisher of legal information. BNA is the oldest wholly employee-owned company in the United States, with approximately 1,600 employees.

Today, BNA draws on the expertise of more than 600 editors, reporters, and domestic and international correspondents. Recognized for in-depth, unbiased reporting, BNA publishes more than 200 print and electronic products covering the gamut of legislative, government, international, and economic developments.

A SAMPLING OF BNA PRODUCTS
(Ask about Print, Web, Email formats)

Business and Financial Information
- Daily Report for Executives
- Daily Tax Report
- Securities Regulation & Law Report
- Antitrust & Trade Regulation Report
- Mergers & Acquisitions Law Report
- International Trade Reporter
- International Trade Daily

Corporate Law
- Corporate Practice Series
- Corporate Governance Report / Manual / Library on CD
- Corporate Counsel Weekly
- BNA/ACCA Compliance Manual: Prevention of Corporate Liability
- Corporate Law Daily

Environment and Safety
- Environment & Safety Library
- Food Safety Report
- Daily Environment Report

Health Care
- Medicare / Medicaid Program Library
- Health Law Reporter
- Health Care Fraud Report
- Health Care Program Compliance Guide
- Health Care Daily Report

Intellectual Property
- United States Patents Quarterly
- Patent, Trademark & Copyright Journal
- Intellectual Property Library
- Media Law Reporter
- Electronic Commerce & Law Report
- Computer Technology Law Report

Labor and Employment Law
- Daily Labor Report
- Employee Benefits Library
- Labor & Employment Library
- Labor Relations Reporter
- Employment Discrimination Report

(This Listing Continued)

The Bureau of National Affairs (Continued)

Litigation
- United States Law Week
- Bankruptcy Law Reporter
- Criminal Law Reporter
- Family Law Reporter
- Product Safety & Liability Reporter
- Toxics Law Reporter
- ABA/BNA Lawyers' Manual on Professional Conduct
- Class Action Litigation Report
- Toxics Law Daily
- Expert Evidence Report

Call 1-800-372-1033 today to begin a FREE TRIAL, or visit www.bna.com

CCH

Business & Finance Group
2700 Lake Cook Road
Riverwoods, IL 60015
www.business.cch.com
1-800-449-6435

CCH INCORPORATED

CCH INCORPORATED, headquartered in Riverwoods, Ill., was founded in 1913 and has served four generations of business professionals and their clients. The company produces more than 700 electronic and print products for the tax, legal, securities, human resources, financial services, health care and small business markets. CCH is a wholly owned subsidiary of Wolters Kluwer U.S.

A sample of CCH Business & Finance Group publications:

BUSINESS, UTILITIES & TRADE REGULATION
Trade Regulation Reports
Advertising Law Guide
Business Franchise Guide
Commercial Aircraft Transactions
Guide to Computer Law
Utilities Law Reports
Aviation Law Reports
Products Liability Reports
Consumer Product Safety Guide
Federal Energy Regulatory Commission Publications
Nuclear Regulation Reports
Federal Election Campaign Financing Guide
Multi-State Guide to Telecommunications Law
Copyright Law Reports
Federal Carriers Report
Business Strategies Guide
Sales Representative Law Guide
State Unfair Trade Practices Law
Product Distribution Law Guide
Master Franchising
Advertising 2000 Year in Review
RICO Business Disputes Guide
Congressional Index

GOVERNMENT CONTRACTING
Government Contracts Reporter
Contract Appeals Decisions
Cost Accounting Standards Guide
Federal Acquisition Regulations
Department of Defense FAR Supplement

SECURITIES
Derivatives Regulation Law Reporter
Federal Securities Law Reporter
SEC Accounting Rules
Blue Sky Law Reporter
Insurance Securities Law Reporter
Securities Transfer Guide
Various Exchange and Self-Regulatory Organization Guides
SEC Compliance Desktop Software:
- Section 16(a) Compliance
- Stock Options
- Employee Stock Purchase Plans

Corporate Secretary's Guide
Global Capital Market Internet Library

BANKING & FINANCE
Federal Banking Law Reporter
State Banking Law Reporter
Bank Compliance Guide
Financial Privacy Law Guide
Capital Changes
Consumer Credit Guide
Secured Transactions Guide
Personal Loan Compliance Guide
Mortgage Compliance Guide
Bank Insurance Sales Methods
Individual Retirement Plans Guide
Financial Institutions Advertising Law
2001 Bank Tax Guide
CCH Deposit Law Notes
Financial Institutions Security Library
How to Charter a Commercial Bank

The **Martindale-Hubbell Law Directory** is now available online...exclusively through the LEXIS®-NEXIS® services.

United States Government INFORMATION
PUBLICATIONS ★ PERIODICALS ★ ELECTRONIC PRODUCTS

U.S. Government Printing Office

Superintendent of Documents
Washington, DC 20402
http://bookstore.gpo.gov
Toll Free: (866) 512-1800
DC Area: (202) 512-1800

The United States Government Printing Office
Your prime source for purchasing U.S. Government information products

The U.S. Government Printing Office's Superintendent of Documents Sales Program is the legal and business community's easy-access route to the official versions of laws, regulations and guidelines, and much more. The Superintendent of Document Sales Program serves legal and business professionals who need the latest published information from federal agencies in all three branches of the U.S. Government.

A sample of GPO's collection of publications:

Federal Register
Code of Federal Regulations
- Regulations by Subject Area
- Full Set of CFR Titles
- CFR Index and Finding Aids

Congressional Documents
- United States Code on CD-ROM and Print
- Congressional Record
- Congressional Directory

Public Laws
- Bills, Resolutions, and Amendments
- Reports on Public Bills
- Deschler-Brown Precedents of the United States House of Representatives

Labor Relations and Federal Service
- Decisions and Orders of the National Labor Relations Board
- Weekly Summary of the National Labor Relations Board Cases
- FLRA Reports of Case Decisions, FSIP

Military Law
- Army Lawyer
- Military Law Review

Patents and Trademarks
- Manual of Patent Examining Procedure, 7th Edition
- Copyright Law of the United States of America
- Trademark Trial and Appeal Board Manual of Procedure

Taxation
- Internal Revenue Bulletin
- U.S. Tax Court Reports
- Rules of Practice and Procedure

United States Tax Court
- Study of Present-Law Taxpayer Confidentiality and Disclosure Provisions

Visit
http://bookstore.gpo.gov/regulatory/index.html
for our special collection of regulatory and business titles.

WASHINGTON (Continued)

LEGAL RESEARCH

CourtLink®
Suite 100
13427 N.E. 16th St.
Bellevue, WA 98005
Phone: (866) 500-4955

See Online Public Records Service

LEGAL SOFTWARE

CPi
Computer Packages Inc.
LEADERSHIP FOR THE BEST IDEAS IN THE WORLD

The CPi Systems are the most widely used Patent and Trademark Docketing Systems in the world. Why have over 1000 organizations selected CPi's Docketing Systems?

- The systems are very easy to use
- Unlimited on-site training and phone support for one full year included
- Over 50 full time employees dedicated to support
- Systems can be tailored to your exact needs
- Web-enabled solutions are available

In addition, the CPi Patent Annuity Payment Service is the largest Annuity Service in the United States, and the fastest growing Annuity Service in the world, because of the unique benefits we offer:

- Unlimited support - telephone, fax, email, and even on-site training of your personnel.
- Integrated services - use the CPi Patent Management System to exchange information with our Annuity Service reducing labor and increasing safety.
- Data Validation - only CPi checks your data reliability against public information in over 70 countries to ensure payment on the correct case.
- Very low fee, based on volume.
- No charge for input, updates, changes, deletions, budget reports, or special reports.

CPi has been able to save clients hundreds of thousands of dollars every year in outright savings and even more when your internal labor savings are factored in, and at the same time improve the accuracy and reliability of your patent records. We welcome the opportunity to meet with you to discuss how you can benefit from our services. Please contact us if we can be of assistance.

For more information, please call (301) 424-8890

Computer Packages Inc.
414 Hungerford Drive
Suite 300
Rockville, MD 20850
Telephone: (301) 424-8890
Fax: (301) 762-8663
Internet: www.computerpackages.com

Other Offices in: Breda, Netherlands • Chicago, IL • Houston, TX • San Francisco, CA

THE DEFINITIVE RESOURCE FOR INFORMATION ON LAWYERS AND LAW FIRMS ...

The Martindale-Hubbell® Law Directory

Since 1868, people who need current, authoritative, and accurate information on legal professionals have relied on the ***Martindale-Hubbell® Law Directory***. This is the only comprehensive resource that offers access to vital details on over 1,000,000 lawyers and law firms in the United States and Canada, and over 160 other countries worldwide. Thoroughly researched, it is the definitive reference work for both the legal profession and the general public.

For the first time, individual volumes of the ***Martindale-Hubbell Law Directory*** are available. Purchase only the volume which includes your state ... perhaps add the ones which contain neighboring states ... or get extra copies of the volumes you use more often.

For more information, call
1-800-526-4902

LexisNexis™ Martindale-Hubbell®

LEGAL SUPPORT PERSONNEL - TEMPORARY & PERMANENT

NRI Legal Resources

734 15th Street, N.W.
Suite #200
Washington, DC 20005

Phone: 202-628-3022
Fax: 202-628-2838

34 Years of Staffing Service Excellence

Legal Positions

Need one or more
temporary personnel
to get the work done?

NRI IS THE SOLUTION!

http://www.nri-staffing.com
nri-legal-dc@nri-staffing.com

ANNANDALE BALTIMORE RESTON ROCKVILLE WASHINGTON D.C.

NRI has served the Washington/Baltimore Metropolitan community for over thirty-three years. It is locally owned by the two senior executives of the company.

During that time we have strived to be on the cutting edge of the staffing services industry.

Our methodology of dedicated Recruiters and Account Managers is as unique - and to the advantage of our clients - as is our ability to fill orders with candidates in five different specialties and with equal competency for both permanent positions as well as "temp" assignments. To serve our clients in the most effective manner, we have blended our equally strong capabilities in permanent placement and temporary staffing into teams of Staffing Specialists whose mission is to serve our clients and provide solutions to staffing needs and situations.

NRI's Competitive Strength #1: The key to providing world-class staffing services is to be able to attract a large number of qualified candidates and temporary workers. It is the quality of our candidates upon which we have built our success in permanent placement for the past thirty-three years. Because of our strength as recruiters - and our reputation for permanent placement - we attract a great number of people that are seeking permanent positions (and some know they can work as temps for us as they await the right permanent position). As a result, one of our most effective recruitment resources is our base of placed candidates and satisfied temporary workers. Therefore...one of our unique competitive strengths is: We Have...or Can Find the People!!

NRI's Competitive Strength #2: Most staffing services have a primary competency in either permanent placement or temporary staffing. We were established as a search firm some 33 years ago - and the recruitment of people is one of our great strengths. This has resulted in a strong permanent placement firm, capable of attracting candidates without relying solely on classified advertising or the Internet. We added temporary help services to our service menu some 20 years ago. By being equally competent in both staffing arenas, we provide our clients with a single point of contact for their staffing needs. So another of our unique competitive strengths is: We Have Strong and Equal Competency in Both the Perm and Temp Arenas.

NRI's Competitive Strength #3: A measure of our quality is seen among the retention of our own associates. Our emphasis on staff training, certification through our national associations and company recognition programs makes NRI a company where our associates want to work. Many staff members have achieved tenure of 5, 10, or 15 years. Our clients work with an experienced team of professionals highly trained in the latest and best ways to serve you.

(This Listing Continued)

NRI Legal Resources (Continued)

Our Account Managers - the people who directly serve our clients - have a minimum of 15-18 months of experience as a NRI Recruiter before they ever fill an order... and many of our Account Managers have been in that position for three to five years, or longer. This means that another of our competitive strengths is: You will never have an inexperienced person filling your orders.

Today, NRI is a large regional staffing services company of almost 100 dedicated full-time associates.

NRI specializes in five disciplines, with twelve teams operating in six locations throughout metropolitan Washington and Baltimore. NRI's Account Managers and Recruiters specialize in one of these five areas and provide a full range of three different staffing services within each discipline. We call this our **"5 by 3 Service Matrix"**:

5 Disciplines:

Healthcare	NRI HealthCare (3 teams)
Office Support and Administrative	NRI Staffing Resources (5 teams)
Accounting & Finance	NRI Accounting Resources (2 teams)
Legal Support and Paralegals	NRI Legal Resources (1 team)
Technical, IT & E-Commerce	NRI Technology Solutions (1 team)

3 Staffing Services:

Permanent Placement
Temp-To-Hire Placement
Temporary Personnel Services & Contract Staffing

StaffWise Legal

Suite 707
1150 Connecticut Ave. NW
Washington, DC 20036
Phone: (202) 861-0100
Fax: (202) 861-0349

See Lawyer Search & Placement Consultants

LITIGATION SUPPORT SERVICES

CourtLink®

Suite 100
13427 N.E. 16th St.
Bellevue, WA 98005
Phone: (866) 500-4955

See Online Public Records Service

MANAGEMENT CONSULTANTS

The Kardon Corp.

P.O. Box 653
Clemmons, NC 27012
Phone: (336) 766-5608
Fax: (336) 766-5608

See Economic and Statistical Consulting Services

WASHINGTON (Continued)

Management Consultants (Continued)

MEDICAL EXPERT WITNESS

MANAGED CARE/HMO LITIGATION

Managed Liability Associates
Suite 600
50 F St., NW
Washington, DC 20001
Phone: (202) 585-1811
Fax: (202) 628-9244

See Expert Witness-Health Care Plans

NEWS/MEDIA SERVICES

U.S. Newswire
A Division of Medialink

U.S. NEWSWIRE

National Press Building
14th & F Streets, NW
12th Floor
Washington, DC 20045
Phone: 800-544-8995
e-mail: info@usnewswire.com
www.usnewswire.com

U.S. Newswire is the nation's leading media communications service, providing fast, professional and effective distribution of your legal news to the media, government, research and online communities.

Through USN's extensive wire service, broadcast fax, Internet and database distribution services, U.S. Newswire ensures your important news reaches the targeted media you need -- locally, nationally or worldwide.

Standard distribution includes:

NEWS MEDIA
- ♦ Top Daily Newspapers Nationwide
- ♦ Wire Service Bureaus (AP, Reuters, etc.)
- ♦ Broadcast Networks & Affiliates
- ♦ TV & Radio Stations in Top Markets

DATABASES
- ♦ Lexis/Nexis
- ♦ Data Times
- ♦ Dow Jones Interactive
- ♦ Bloomberg & dozens more...

GOVERNMENT NEWS SERVICES
- ♦ U.S. House & Senate News Systems
- ♦ White House Office of Media Affairs
- ♦ U.S. Department of Justice and other Cabinet Agency News Services

ONLINE/INTERNET NEWS SERVICES
- ♦ Yahoo!
- ♦ AOL
- ♦ Associated Press ALERT Services
- ♦ Pointcast, ExciteNews, Policy.com and more...
- ♦ MSNBC, CNN*Interactive* & others...

Call Brian Taylor at U.S. Newswire
for more information:
In Washington: (202) 347-2770
Nationwide: (800) 544-8995

WWW.USNEWSWIRE.COM

U.S. Newswire
News Releases Wired to
National Media and the Online World

ONLINE PUBLIC RECORDS SERVICE

CourtLink®
THE FUTURE OF LAW

CourtLink® Corp. is District of Columbia's online source for accessing and filing court records and documents. Join thousands of legal professionals from the nation's top 250 law firms who use CourtLink to *track and access vital court record information* and *electronically file documents with the courts.* With CourtLink:

Win More Cases -leverage knowledge of judge's rulings or opposing counsel's experience, or with access to motions already proven successful.

Save Time, Money and Energy - research across multiple courts at once, for the cases you want, when you want, based on your criteria.

Generate More Business - learn about a new case often before your client does, via-email notifications on new cases of interest.

Avoid Liability - receive e-mail alerts about new case developments in federal and state courts, especially those that impact your clients.

CourtLink eAccess

CourtLink delivers online access to over **200 million court records** and selected court documents from **over 850 federal, state and local courts,** including:

CONNECTICUT *Statewide*
- Superior Courts, Civil, Criminal Traffic & Family Divisions

MARYLAND
- Circuit Court, Montgomery County
- Circuit Court, Prince George's County

DELAWARE
- Delaware Court of Chancery

NEW JERSEY ***Statewide***
- Superior Courts, Civil Division

NEW YORK *content representing 70% of New York State's population*
- Supreme Court records from the following counties: Bronx, Dutches, Erie, Kings, Nassau, New York, Orange, Putnam, Queens, Richmond, Rockland, Suffolk, and Westchester
- New York County Clerk records
- New York Judgment Docket & Liens Books

CourtLink eFile

D.C., Maryland and Virginia attorneys are leading a national trend in transforming the American Courthouse. With CourtLink eFile, now you securely, easily and instantly file court documents, serve case parties and pay statutory fees online from your desktop in the following Northeast Corridor courts:

DISTRICT of COLUMBIA
- Superior Court
- Contract Appeals Board

MARYLAND
- Circuit Court for Baltimore City

www.CourtLink.com

1-866-500-4955

SEE OUR AD ON PAGE DC68S

WASHINGTON (Continued)

Online Public Records Service (Continued)

PARALEGAL SERVICES

Dawna Parker, Paralegal Services

8218 Cagle Road
Fort Washington, Maryland 20744
Phone: 301-686-1887
Fax: 301-686-1887

Email: Dawnaparalegal@aol.com

Donna K. Parker

Committed to provide quality legal service to our clients. We assist attorneys and government agencies in specialized legal services.

Professional Experience:

- ✓ **Draft Memorandums for Motion in Limine**
- ✓ **Prepare Pre-Trial Conference Memorandums**
- ✓ **Prepared Synthesis Memorandums**
- ✓ **Litigation**
- ✓ **Real Estate**
- ✓ **Domestic Relations/Family Law**
- ✓ **Personal Law**
- ✓ **Labor Relation Law**
- ✓ **Preformed legal research Lexis/Nexis & West Law**
- ✓ **Worked under direction of attorneys on statutory and case law**
- ✓ **Preformed legal research manually in a law library**
- ✓ **Proficient in Windows, Microsoft Office suite & WordPerfect Suite**
- ✓ **Newsletter writing**

Attorneys are able to concentrate on more complex legalwork.
Maximized cost, attorneys can save their clients money through the use of a paralegal service.

Member of the ABA, NALA, NFPA, NCAPA, & ATLA

NRI Legal Resources

Suite 200
734 15th St., N.W.
Washington, DC 20005
Phone: (202) 628-3022
Fax: (202) 628-2838

See Legal Support Personnel - Temporary & Permanent

StaffWise Legal

Suite 707
1150 Connecticut Ave. NW
Washington, DC 20036
Phone: (202) 861-0100
Fax: (202) 861-0349

See Lawyer Search & Placement Consultants

PATENT, TRADEMARK & COPYRIGHT SEARCH SERVICES

Computer Packages Inc.
Suite 300
414 Hungerford Dr.
Rockville, MD 20850
Phone: (301) 424-8890
Fax: (301) 762-8663

See Legal Software

THOMSON & THOMSON ™

Telephone 800-692-8833
www.thomson-thomson.com

Since 1922, Thomson & Thomson has provided intellectual property professionals with the information they need to make informed decisions on trademark and copyright matters. When your valuable trademark and copyright assets are at stake, trust Thomson & Thomson to provide you with the information you need to mitigate risk.

Check the availability of your proposed trademark, company name, logo or Internet domain name. Our experienced team of Search Analysts will work with you to conduct the most appropriate, comprehensive trademark search for your needs, using our proprietary database covering the U.S., Canada and over 200 other countries worldwide.

Protect your trademark against infringement. Our Watching services will alert you to potentially infringing or dilutive trademark applications as they are filed.

Conduct preliminary trademark research. With SAEGIS™, Thomson & Thomson's online trademark search tool, you have instant access to trademark and domain data. Use SAEGIS™ to search U.S. and international TRADEMARKSCAN® databases, to conduct SiteComber™ searches to uncover common law uses of proposed trademarks, and search for Internet domain names using the Domain Registrant Search.

Protect your entertainment production and merchandising against legal risks. Thomson & Thomson's Copyright and Title searches assist you in determining the copyright ownership of a selected work and the availability of a title, and in satisfying Errors & Omissions insurance requirements.

Obtain federal documents and file applications and forms. Thomson & Thomson's Document Services team makes it possible for you to file forms and applications, and to obtain certified document copies from the U.S. Patent and Trademark Office, the Copyright Office, and other Federal agencies, from anywhere in the U.S. or Canada.

To learn more about Thomson & Thomson's services, please call us at 800-692-8833 or visit our Web site at www.thomson-thomsom.com.

Thomson & Thomson
500 Victory Road, North Quincy, MA 02171
Tel 800-692-8833 Fax 617-786-8273

PETROLEUM SOURCE IDENTIFICATION

ZymaX Forensics
71 Zaca Ln.
San Luis Obispo, CA 93401-7300
Phone: (805) 544-4696
Fax: (805) 544-8226

See Forensic Geochemistry

PROCESS SERVERS & DOCUMENT DELIVERY SERVICES

An **A&E, Inc.** Company
Torri's Legal Services
Quality Legal Service
BASED ON CONFIDENCE, TRUST AND RESULTS

800-990-SERV
800-990-7378
Fax: 800-845-2131
Internet: www.torrilegalservices.com
email: tlsnc@erols.com

We Service

Maryland, Washington, D.C. & Northern Virginia

*24 Hour Service * 7 Days A Week * Weekends * Holidays*

WE SPECIALIZE IN:

- Nationwide Service of Process
- Summons, Complaints, Subpoenas
- Personal Services
- Document Retrieval
- Court Filings
- Emergency Service
- Defendants And Witness
- Computerized Searches
- International Service

Member:
National Association of Professional Process Servers

OFFICES NATIONWIDE

SEE OUR AD ON PAGE DC74S

ACCURATE LEGAL SERVICES

331 8th Street, NE
Washington, D.C. 20002
Telephone: (202) 547-5710
Telephone: (800) 236-9853
Fax: (202) 547-7836
E-mail: acculegal@aol.com

Serving:
District of Columbia • Northern Virginia
Maryland

Services Provided
Service of Process • Court Filing Service
Document Retrieval • Skip Tracing

Members of:
Founding Member of the
National Association of Professional Process Servers
California Association of Photocopiers and Process Servers
Florida Association of Professional Process Servers
Virginia Association of Professional Process Servers

AMERICAN LEGAL DOCUMENT COURIERS

10570 Main Street, Suite 123
Fairfax, Virginia 22030

Serving Northern Virginia, Maryland and Washington D.C.

(703) 934-6777
Call 800-747-0820

We believe that technology, paired with the right people, practices and vision, can provide an important competitive edge in today's ever-changing business world. Because we focus on understanding business goals in conjunction with a technological direction , we can manage projects from the planning phase to the production support phase.

We offer our clients a very different approach. We provide services to transform your entire enterprise-your strategy, processes, information technology, and people. In addition, we focus on the realization that changing business processes is necessary to achieve the promised returns from strategy and technology. This approach enables the delivery of very different-results clients can build on because we help make organizations more robust and adaptable to future shifts in the environment.

Our aim is to develop effective and mutually beneficial working partnerships by introducing an innovative yet practical approach towards solving your problems. Our staff succeeds by listening carefully to your needs and then providing world-class products, solutions, and expertise. **We will get the results you need.**

SERVICES PROVIDED

**PUBLIC RECORDS RETRIEVAL
POST OFFICE CHECKS
DOCUMENT RETRIEVAL FILING & RESEARCH
DATABASE & REAL PROPERTY SEARCHES
DMV/UCC/CREDIT HEADER SEARCHES
SAME DAY & RUSH SERVICE AVAILABLE
UNDERCOVER/SURVEILLANCE, VIDEO
ATTORNEY SERVICES
LITIGATION SUPPORT
COUNTY, STATE & FEDERAL COURTS
SUBPOENAS BY FAX
CONTACTS/TRAVEL WORLDWIDE
WITNESS STATEMENTS TAKEN
SKIP TRACING, MISSING PERSONS
CHILD CUSTODY, FAMILY, SPOUSAL, MARITAL
PRE-EMPLOYMENT, BACKGROUND CHECKS
POLYGRAPH SERVICES AVAILABLE**

MEMBERSHIPS

NAPPS
PISA

SEE OUR AD ON PAGE DC70S

WASHINGTON (Continued)

Process Servers & Document Delivery Services (Continued)

CAPITOL PROCESS SERVICES, INC.
CAPITOL INVESTIGATOR SERVICES

1827 18th Street, N.W.
Washington, DC 20009-5526
1-877-708-SERV
Local: (202) 667-1407
Fax (202) 667-2520
www.capitolinvestigators.com

Since 1981, we have provided dedicated service to the legal community, combining an understanding of our clients' needs with proven investigative and process service strategies. We pride ourselves on the efficiency and effectiveness of our investigative and process serving techniques and the presentation of meaningful and helpful information. As a current member of the National Association of Professional Process Servers, we are able to provide specialized services NATIONWIDE.

Providing the following services:

SERVICE OF PROCESS	INVESTIGATIVE SERVICES
Court Filing	Fraud Prevention & Investigations
Court Research	Surveillance – Domestic & Workman's Compensation
Document Retrieval	Background Investigation
Skip Tracing	Asset Searches
Domestic Relations	Employee Theft
Witness Statements	Industrial Security

LICENSED AND BONDED IN WASHINGTON, DC, VIRGINIA & MARYLAND

GUARANTEED SUBPOENA SERVICE, INC.

800-672-1952 • FAX: 800-236-2092
WE SERVE ANYTHING — ANYWHERE!

"If We Don't Serve It You Don't Pay Anything Anywhere in the Nation."

established 1965

800-672-1952 • FAX: 800-236-2092

E-mail: info@GuaranteedSubpoena.com
Website: www.guaranteedsubpoena.com

A full service company providing statewide and worldwide services of process. Normal turn-a-round time by third day, same day service available. reasonable rates with fixed cost. Success ratio is consistently over 96%. We serve anything, anywhere.

- Same day service when needed
- We serve any document anywhere: Summons, Complaints, Subpoena, Orders, Writs, Notices, and Warrants
- Document Retrieval
- Court Filings
- No charge for attempts
- Skip Tracing
- Licensed private investigators
- Flat Rate, No hidden fees or costs
- Status online
- 49.95 From State to same State.
  99.95 From State to any other State.
- Foreign Process Service Available
- WHY WOULD YOU USE ANYONE ELSE

All major credit cards accepted.

WASHINGTON (Continued)

Process Servers & Document Delivery Services (Continued)

SECRETARIAL SUPPORT

NRI Legal Resources
Suite 200
734 15th St., N.W.
Washington, DC 20005
Phone: (202) 628-3022
Fax: (202) 628-2838

See Legal Support Personnel - Temporary & Permanent

STATISTICS

Analysis and Inference, Inc.

Statistical Consulting and Research

William B. Fairley, Ph.D.
President and Senior Consultant
Ph.D., Harvard, Department of Statistics
B.A. Swarthmore (Economics)

P.O. Box 294
215 Haverford Avenue
Swarthmore, Pennsylvania 19081
Tel 610-543-0159 Fax 610-543-8952
wfairley@analysis-and-inference.com
www.analysis-and-inference.com

Analysis and Inference, Inc., led by William B. Fairley, provides compelling statistical analysis for law firms, corporations, and government agencies. Dr. Fairley, a widely published author in statistics, is skilled at presenting complex statistical ideas to non-experts. He has consulted and testified in negotiation, arbitration, and litigation in numerous state and national forums, helping legal counsel reach successful outcomes by clarifying factual aspects of disputes.

Project topic areas

Discrimination • Risk analysis • Audits, surveys, theft, and fraud
Liability and damages • Finance, regulation, and insurance
Public policy

Selected Clients
Law Offices

Ballard Spahr Andrews & Ingersoll
Covington & Burling
Foley Hoag & Eliot
Fried Frank Harris Schriver & Jacobson
Friedman Kaplan & Seiler
Kaye, Scholer, Fierman, Hays & Handler
Kramer, Levin, Naftalis & Frankel
Prince, Lobel & Tye
Thompson Coburn
Vedder Price Kaufman Kammholz & Day
Wilmer Cutler & Pickering
Bangser Klein Rocca & Blum
Kittredge Donley Elson Fullem & Embick
Kramer Levin Naftalis & Frankel
Menaker & Hermann
Shiff and Tisman
New York City Corporation Counsel
Massachusetts Attorney General
Maryland Attorney General
New York Attorney General
Pennsylvania Attorney General

Corporations, Government Agencies, Organizations

Departments of over 40 states
ATKearney
Blue Cross Blue Shield
The Boston Company
Digital Equipment Corporation
General Dynamics
General Motors
Glen-Gery
Johnson Matthey
Massachusetts Bay Transportation Authority
Massachusetts Port Authority
National Conf. for Uniform State Laws
National Assn. of Insurance Commissioners
National Council on Comp. Ins.
National Science Foundation
New York City Health & Hospitals Corporation
New York City Police Department
Olin Corporation
Packer Engineering
Primerica
Public Broadcasting Corporation
Sears Roebuck
Southern Calif. Rapid Transit District
Time Warner
Ultramar
Union of Concerned Scientists
U.S. Department of Labor
U.S. Department of Transportation
U.S. Nuclear Regulatory Commission
U.S. Senate Judiciary Committee

Publications

Harvard Law Review, Encyclopedia of the Statistical Sciences, Risk Analysis, Journal of the American Statistical Association, Bell Journal of Economics, University of Chicago Law Review, American Statistician, International

Encyclopedia of Statistics, Journal of Legal Studies, Journal of Risk and Insurance, Management Science, and many others.

SURVEYS & OPINION RESEARCH

The Kardon Corp.

P.O. Box 653
Clemmons, NC 27012
Phone: (336) 766-5608
Fax: (336) 766-5608

See Economic and Statistical Consulting Services

TRANSCRIPTION SERVICES

ACE-FEDERAL REPORTERS, INC.

Stenotype Reporters
Over 50 Years of Complete Reporting Service
1120 G Street, N.W., Suite 500 20005
800-336-6646

DEPOSITIONS, ARBITRATIONS & CONFERENCES
Notaries in D.C., VA & MD

REAL-TIME AND RUSH DELIVERY

CERTIFIED LEGAL VIDEOTAPE SPECIALISTS

CONDENSED TRANSCRIPTS & DISKETTES

DEPOSITION SUITES

WORLDWIDE COVERAGE

PROCESS SERVICE

AUTHORIZED DISCOVERY DEALER AND TRAINER

LITIGATION SUPPORT CONSULTATION
Specializing in project management, database design, and demonstrations and training of full-text retrieval software

24-Hour Switchboard
202-347-3700
Facsimile 202-737-3638
Call Toll Free 800-336-6646

TRANSLATION SERVICES

Japan Communication Consultants, LLC

236 E. 47th St., 28th Fl.
New York, NY 10017
Phone: (212) 759-2033
Fax: (212) 759-2149

See Interpreters & Translators

WASHINGTON (Continued)

Translation Services (Continued)

TRIAL CONSULTANTS

WASHINGTON (Continued)

VIDEO TAPE SERVICES

ACE-FEDERAL REPORTERS, INC.
Stenotype Reporters
Over 50 Years of Complete Reporting Service
1120 G Street, N.W., Suite 500 20005
800-336-6646
DEPOSITIONS, ARBITRATIONS & CONFERENCES
Notaries in D.C., VA & MD

REAL-TIME AND RUSH DELIVERY

CERTIFIED LEGAL VIDEOTAPE SPECIALISTS

CONDENSED TRANSCRIPTS & DISKETTES

DEPOSITION SUITES

WORLDWIDE COVERAGE

PROCESS SERVICE

AUTHORIZED DISCOVERY DEALER AND TRAINER

LITIGATION SUPPORT CONSULTATION
Specializing in project management, database design, and demonstrations and training of full-text retrieval software

24-Hour Switchboard
202-347-3700
Facsimile 202-737-3638
Call Toll Free 800-336-6646

Providing outstanding service to law firms and court reporting firms nationwide since 1983

Video Depositions

Certified Legal Video Specialists

Single Camera & Multi-Camera Depositions

Videotape Editing

Video Duplication

Video Conversion to CD Rom

Text-to-Video Synchronization

"Day In The Life Of" Video Production

Settlement Brochure Video Production

Professional Videotaping Services for:

Seminars

Client/Trial Preparation

Courtroom Playback Support

Professional Photographic Services

Film and Digital formats

CERTIFIED VIDEO SERVICES, INC.
13105 Pennerview Lane
Fairfax, VA 22033

Virginia (703) 631-1858
Washington, D.C. (202) 833-2442
Toll Free 1-877-631-1858
email info@certvid.com ❖ www.certvid.com